COLLINS COBUILD

COLLINS Birmingham University International Language Database

ENGLISH LANGUAGE DICTIONARY

COLLINS
PUBLISHERS

THE UNIVERSITY
OF BIRMINGHAM

COBUILD
is the Collins Birmingham University
International Language Database

This dictionary was developed and
compiled in the English Department
at the University of Birmingham as
part of a language research project
commissioned by Collins Publishers

COLLINS COBUILD

COLLINS Birmingham University International Language Database

ENGLISH LANGUAGE DICTIONARY

Collins
London and Glasgow

Collins ELT
8 Grafton Street
London W1X 3LA

COBUILD is a trademark of William Collins Sons & Co Ltd

First Published 1987

10 9 8 7 6 5 4 3 2 .

Cased edition ISBN 0 00 375021 3

Computer Typeset by C R Barber & Partners, Wrotham, England

Printed and bound in Great Britain by
William Collins Sons & Co Ltd, Glasgow

CIP - Kurztitelaufnahme der Deutschen Bibliothek

Collins COBUILD English language dictionary
[developed and comp. in the Engl. Dep. at the
Univ. of Birmingham]. Ed. in chief John Sinclair.
- London; Glasgow : Collins; Stuttgart : Klett 1987.
ISBN 3-12-517910-6 (Klett)
ISBN 0-00-370023-2 (Collins) Pb.
ISBN 0-00-375021-3 (Collins) cased ed.
NE: Sinclair, John [Hrsg.]

輸入 日本総代理店 (1987)
株式会社 秀文インターナショナル
東京都豊島区駒込 4 − 12 − 7

NOTE Entered words that we have reason to believe constitute trademarks have been designated as such. However, neither the presence nor absence of such designation should be regarded as affecting the legal status of any trademark.

EDITORIAL TEAM

EDITOR IN CHIEF
John Sinclair

MANAGING EDITOR
Patrick Hanks

EDITORS
Gwyneth Fox
Rosamund Moon
Penny Stock

SENIOR COMPILERS
Andrew Delahunty
Sheila Dignen
Ramesh Krishnamurthy
Elaine Pollard

COMPILERS
Stephen Bullon
Deborah Kirby
Helen Liebeck
Elizabeth Manning
John Todd

SENIOR COMPUTING OFFICER
Jeremy Clear

COMPUTING OFFICER
Eileen Fitzgerald

CLERICAL STAFF
Lynne Farrow
Janice Johnson
Brenda Nicholls
Pat Smith

COLLINS PUBLISHING DIRECTOR
Richard Thomas

Foreword

The Project Team

The final project team is set out above. Several other colleagues made a notable contribution in the early years, and continued to provide support throughout the life of the project. Antoinette Renouf, the original Project Co-ordinator led the team from 1980-83 and established the text corpus and maintained and developed corpus work. Dr Michael Hoey gave a great deal of help in administration and policy guidance in the early period and continued with strong academic guidance. From Collins, Beryl T Atkins played a formative role in the design of the project and in the general training; continuing in her capacity as General Editor she commented on draft dictionary texts throughout.

Some members of the team moved on before the work was completed. Wendy Morris and Clive Upton were two of the original editors. Nigel Turton, Martin Manser, Dieter Wachendorff, Judy Amanthis, Duncan Marshall, Emily Driver and Michael Rundell were compilers for substantial periods. Ian Sedwell helped with the computing. Heather Champion, Lorraine Dove, Cheryl Evans and Sue Smith were secretaries.

The project has also benefitted greatly from people who, while not regular members of the team, acted in a consultative capacity or provided a specialist service. In particular Marcel Lemmens, grammar consultant, must be mentioned, and Cathy Emmott who helped with the Extra Column.

Acknowledgments

I would like to thank many other people whose names do not appear on the team credits but who made a significant contribution to the compilation of the dictionary.

This project was part of the work of the English Department and its successful completion owes much to the support of the Head of the Department throughout, Professor J T Boulton. In various ways every one of the staff helped and encouraged the work and one or two must be singled out for specific contributions. Dr David Brazil devised the system of recording pronunciations, and transcribed most of them. Tim Lane ensured their transfer to electronic form and gave support on the computational side. Tim Johns encouraged the use of real examples and made experimental classes available. Chris Kennedy, Tony Dudley-Evans, Dr Mike McCarthy, Charles Owen, Phillip King and Martin Hewings all read drafts, picked holes in them and offered many suggestions for improvement.

Many colleagues in the University of Birmingham contributed notably to the project. Three Pro-Vice Chancellors in turn guided the project through various committees; Professor Harry Prime, Professor John Fage and Professor John Samuels. The Centre for Computing and Computer Sciences was deeply involved throughout and eased problems in the complex final editing.

I would also like to thank the past and present members of Collins staff who have helped in the project.

This dictionary is based on evidence and the evidence comes from hundreds of documents and conversations, kindly made available by the copyright holders. A full list is provided on page xxii.

Such a fundamental re-appraisal of a language requires a high degree of teamwork and large-scale co-ordination of resources. The success of this book and other books to come will owe a great deal to the people and groups mentioned above, and I am very grateful to them for their contributions.

John M Sinclair
Professor of Modern English Language
Editor in Chief

Guide to the Use of the Dictionary

This dictionary is written in ordinary, everyday English. There are only a few special symbols to understand and they are explained below. We also explain how to find things in a long entry. As far as possible each entry follows the same pattern. For instance, if you are looking for a note on the spelling, you will always find it near the beginning of the entry, but if you think you want to know about a phrase you should look near the end of the entry.
In the section that follows, on page xv, there is a short explanation of how this dictionary was designed and made, why it is new and different, and how you can make the best use of it.
The explanations given here refer only to the main text of the dictionary. By the side of the main text you will find an extra column of notes about the structures and meanings. To save space these notes are abbreviated and there is a key to the abbreviations on page xiii.

1 Entries

1.1 An entry in this dictionary is introduced by a word or group of words in large bold letters starting at the left-most side of the column.

> **agriculture** ... is the practice of farming and the methods that are used to raise and look after crops and animals.

1.2 The main factor in deciding whether or not to include a word as an entry in this dictionary was how often it occurred in our large corpus of texts. However, some words were left out, for example very technical words, the names of countries, cities and people, and some rare foreign words.

2 Order of Entries

2.1 All entries are given in strict alphabetical order, taking no notice of capital letters, hyphens, apostrophes or spaces between words.

> **aid**
> **aide**
> **aide-de-camp**
> **AIDS**
> **ail**
> **aileron**
> **ailing**
> **ailment**
> **aim**
> **aimless**
> **ain't**
> **air**
> **air base**
> **airbed**

2.2 Sometimes a word can be used either alone or followed by another word, and the addition of the extra word does not change the meaning. If there are no other entries between them in alphabetical order, the word and the combination are explained in the same entry.

> **wellington** ... **Wellingtons** or **wellington boots** are long rubber boots which you wear to keep your feet dry.

2.3 All the uses of a word are usually given together within the same entry. However, sometimes the same letters can form both a word and an abbreviation (no and No.), a set of initials called an acronym (salt and SALT), or a contracted form (shed and she'd). In these cases the word is explained first in all its uses and the abbreviations, acronyms and contractions are explained in separate entries immediately afterwards.

> **am**
> **Am.**
> **a.m.**
> **amalgam**

2.4 Special entries, each in a box □, also appear at their correct place in alphabetical order. Some of these explain how to read the extra column. Others show the ways in which you can express some important concepts such as age, measurement, number and time in English. For the full list of these special entries, see page xiii.

3 Pronunciation

3.1 The pronunciation is normally given only for the first form of the word at each entry and is placed immediately after that form.

> **cabin** /kæbɪn/, **cabins** ...

3.2 However, if the word is pronounced in different ways, for example when it is used as a noun and when it is used as a verb, these variations are explained after all the forms.

> **record, records, recording, recorded.**
> The verb is pronounced /rɪˈkɔːd/and the noun is pronounced /rɛkɔːd/.

3.3 Pronunciation is not given for the special entries in boxes, for abbreviations that are rarely used in spoken English, or for entries that consist of two or more words whose pronunciation is given at each of the separate words.

3.4 The system used for pronunciation is described on page xii.

4 Forms and Spellings

4.1 The spelling for each form of a word in the dictionary is given in large bold letters at the beginning of each entry.

4.2 The following forms are usually given, if they are commonly used:

4.2.1 - for nouns, the plural form.

> **aerosol** ... **aerosols** ...
> **bathing cap, bathing caps** ...

4.2.2 - for qualitative adjectives, the comparative and superlative forms.

> **happy** ... **happier, happiest** ...

Where no comparative or superlative forms are given for qualitative adjectives they are formed with 'more' and 'most'.

4.2.3 - for verbs, the third person form of the present tense (the -s form), the present participle (the -ing form), the past tense (the -ed form), and the past participle if it is not the same as the past tense.

> **place** ... **places, placing, placed** ...

> **take** ... **takes, taking, took, taken** ...

4.3 If a word can be used as a noun with a plural and as a verb, and the third person form of the present tense of the verb is the same as the plural form of the noun, the -s form is only given once.

alarm ... **alarms, alarming, alarmed** ...

4.4 If there are any special features about the use of the forms, for example if a particular form or set of forms is used only when a word is used with one particular meaning, these features are explained after the forms.

hang ... The forms **hang, hangs, hanging, hung** are used for the verb except in paragraph 6 where the forms are **hang, hangs, hanging, hanged**...

4.5 One of the forms of a word may also be explained in a separate entry if the form is very common or has a different meaning in some of its uses.

begin ... **begins, beginning, began, begun.** 1. If you **begin** to do ...

beginning ... **beginnings.** 1 The **beginning** of an event ...

5 Entry notes

5.1 Entry notes may be given after the first form, after the pronunciation, or after all the forms.

5.2 An entry note may show different spellings of the word.

polarize ... **polarizes, polarizing, polarized**; also spelled **polarise** ...

vapour ... **vapours**; also spelled **vapor** in American English ...

baby-sitter, baby-sitters; also spelled without a hyphen ...

5.3 An entry note may explain changes in pronunciation.

default /di'fɔ:lt/, **defaults, defaulting, defaulted**. The word **default** is also pronounced /di:fɔ:lt/ in paragraph 3.

5.4 An entry note may explain the particular form or forms used for a particular meaning of the words or when the word is used in American or British English.

burst ... **bursts, bursting**. The form **burst** is used in the present tense and is the past tense and past participle of the verb ...

anaesthesia ...; also spelled **anesthesia**, especially in American English.

analogue ... **analogues**; also spelled **analog**, especially for paragraph 3.

5.5 An entry note may refer to all the uses of a word.

assemblage ... **assemblages**; a formal word. 1 An **assemblage** is ... 2 **Assemblage** is ...

6 Explanations of meaning and use

6.1 The entry word is always explained by means of a complete sentence. This normally means that the user of the dictionary is shown the word in natural English.

appoint ... 1 If you **appoint** someone to a particular post or to do a particular job, you formally choose them for it or ask them to do it.

becalmed ... If a sailing ship is **becalmed**, it is unable to move because there is no wind.

brave ... 1 Someone who is **brave** shows in their behaviour that they have the courage to do something even though it is frightening, dangerous or difficult.

6.2 In the explanation, the entry word is printed in bold letters. This is done if it is the first word of the explanation or if it appears later on.

acumen ... is the ability to make good judgements and decisions in relation to a particular activity, especially business.

bareback ... If you ride **bareback** you ride a horse without a saddle.

6.3 A note about the way in which a word is used may be found after the explanation.

auspicious ... Something that is **auspicious** gives hope of success or evidence that success is likely; a fairly formal word.

6.4 If a word has several senses as a noun, verb, etc, in a particular pattern of use, the first part of the explanation is not repeated.

cistern ... A **cistern** is **1** a container which holds the water that is used to flush a toilet .. **2** a large tank in the roof of a house in which water is stored.

nod ... 1 If you **nod, 1.1** you move your head quickly up and down several times to show that you are answering 'yes' to a question, or to show agreement, understanding, or approval ... **1.2** you bend your head once to to indicate something or to give someone a signal to do something ... **1.3** you bend your head once when you meet or leave someone or when they leave you, as a way of saying hello or goodbye ... **1.4** you keep letting your head fall forward because you are falling asleep while sitting down ...

7 Ordering within an entry: paragraphs and sub-paragraphs:

7.1 If a word has only one common use, it is explained, sometimes with examples, within one paragraph and no numbers are used.

ostrich ... An **ostrich** is a large African bird that cannot fly. It has long legs, a long neck, a small head and large soft feathers.

7.2 If a word has several uses, the ordering within the entry has been decided by consideration of several criteria, including frequency, independence of meaning, and concreteness. For a fuller discussion of this point, see page xix.

7.3 If a word has several uses, but all the uses are as a noun, verb, etc, in a particular pattern, they are explained in one paragraph and each use is introduced by a whole number.

applause ... **Applause** is 1 an expression of enjoyment or appreciation by a group of people in which they all clap their hands ... **2** support or praise by a lot of people for something that has been done ...

7.4 If the uses of the word as a noun, or as a verb, etc, are very different from each other, each use may be given in a separate paragraph introduced by a whole number. These differences may be due to the following changes.

7.4.1 - changes in meaning:

clear ... **16** If your skin is **clear**, it is free from spots and rashes and looks healthy ...
17 If your conscience is **clear**, you do not feel guilty about anything ...
18 If you, your time, or your diary is **clear**, no appointments or arrangements have been made ...

join ... **2** If you **join** a queue, you go to stand at the end of it so that you are part of it ...
3 If you **join** a club, society or organization, you become a member of it or start work as an employee of it ...

7.4.2 - changes in grammar:

affront ... **1** If something is an **affront** to someone, it is a deliberate insult or challenge to their pride or dignity ...
2 If you are **affronted** by something, you feel insulted and your pride and dignity are hurt ...

7.5 Sub-paragraphs, introduced by numbers with a decimal point, may be used when there are more than two senses of a particular pattern.

dryer ... also spelled **drier**. **1** A **dryer** is **1.1** a machine for drying clothes. **1.2** a hairdryer.
2 **Dryer** and **drier** are the comparative forms of **dry**.

appointment ... **1** The **appointment** of someone to do a particular job is the act or process of choosing them to do it.
2 An **appointment** is **2.1** a job or position usually involving some responsibility ... **2.2** someone who has been chosen for a particular job or position ...

8 Examples

8.1 An example in this dictionary is a group of words that appear in italics within an entry. The examples have been selected to show typical contexts, collocations and grammatical structures. For a fuller discussion of the role of examples see page xv.

8.2 The first example in each entry, or in each paragraph or sub-paragraph, is always preceded by the letters EG in small capital letters.

waterhole ... A **waterhole** is a pond or pool in the desert or other dry area where animals and people can find water to drink. EG *We camped that evening by a waterhole.*

8.3 The examples will not always consist of complete sentences. When this is the case, they are introduced by three dots.

webbing ... is strong material which is woven in strips and used to make belts or straps, or used in seats to support the springs. EG *...A belt of green webbing... ...canvas webbing.*

8.4 Three dots are placed after an example to separate it from an example that follows.

8.5 Most of the examples in this dictionary are given exactly as they are found in our corpus, or with very minor changes which have been made in order to remove unnecessary distracting information.

9 The use of ▶

9.1 The symbol ▶ is used in this dictionary to introduce a slight change in the way a word is used. The particular change involved is explained immediately after the symbol.

9.2 It can introduce a slight change in meaning. For example, an adjective that usually describes people may also be used to describe their behaviour, or a noun that refers to a container may also refer to its contents.

bucket ... **1** A **bucket** is a container shaped like a cylinder and which has an open top and a handle. Buckets are often used for holding and carrying water. EG *The hotel cleaner entered carrying a bucket and a mop.* ▶ **Bucket** is also used to refer to the amount of liquid which a bucket contains. EG *... a bucket of warm water.*

9.3 It can introduce a change in the grammar of the word that has little or no effect on its meaning. For example, a word that is most commonly used as a verb may also be used as a noun referring to the action that the verb involves.

giggle ... If you **giggle**, you make soft and repeated laughing noises, especially because you are nervous or embarrassed. EG *The absurd sound made her giggle... 'Oh dear,' she giggled, 'I'd quite forgotten'... giggling helplessly at her own joke.* ▶ used as a noun. EG *...with a nervous giggle... We had a good giggle about that... ...stifling a giggle.*

9.4 The change may involve a count noun that can also be used as an uncount noun.

rope ... **1** A **rope** is a piece of very thick, strong string, usually made of hemp or nylon. EG *One of the characters in the play hangs herself with a rope... She picked up the end of the rope, and pulled with all her might.* ▶ used as an uncount noun. EG *...a piece of rope.* N COUNT ▶ N UNCOUNT

9.5 The change may involve the frequent use of a noun before another noun as if it were an adjective.

background ... **2** The **background** to an important event or situation consists of the facts that help to explain what caused it, why it happened in a particular way or at a particular time. EG *...the economic background to the present political crisis...* ▶ used as an adjective. EG *...background information.*

10 The use of ◇

10.1 Derived words can appear within an entry in small bold letters after the symbol ◇. They are words which are formed from the entry word by the addition of a suffix, according to rules that apply very generally in English. The words formed in this way are very similar in meaning to the entry word or to the particular meaning of the entry word in the paragraph or sub-paragraph in which they are placed. In such cases, there is no separate entry for the derived word.

touchy ... **1** A **touchy** person is easily upset, offended or irritated. EG *He thinks that all continental people are sensitive and touchy... They are touchy about criticism.*
◇ **touchiness**. EG *She was amused by his touchiness.*

10.2 Derived words include for example, adverbs that are formed from adjectives by adding -ly (eg. bravely from brave) or nouns and adjectives that are formed from verbs by adding -ing, -ness, -ity, -tion, etc. Grammatical information about all such words is given in the extra column.

adamant ... If you are **adamant** about something, you are determined not to change your mind about it. EG *The government remains adamant that it will not give yield to pressure* ... ◇ **adamantly**. EG *They are adamantly opposed to continued high U.S. interest rates.* — ADJ CLASSIF; ◇ADV WITH VB

10.3 However, where a derived word is very common or has a different meaning from the entry word from which it is formed, it is given as a separate entry at its correct place in the alphabetical list.

11 The use of ●

11.1 The symbol ● is used to introduce two different types of information: phrases or expressions and cross-references.

11.2 Phrases or expressions are groups of two or more words, including the entry word, that occur regularly in a particular combination which has a very different meaning from that of the entry word by itself. The main words of the phrase or expression are in bold letters.

11.3 They are usually placed at the end of a paragraph or sub-paragraph if they are very close in meaning to the meaning explained in that paragraph.

sailor ... A **sailor** is a person who works on a ship as a member of its crew. EG *He had been a sailor in the Italian navy.* ● If you are a **good sailor**, you are able to travel on a boat in rough weather without being seasick. EG *I thought you were a good sailor.*

11.4 If a phrase or expression is very frequently used, or is not very close in meaning to any other uses, it may be explained in a separate paragraph.

11.5 If there are many phrases or expressions at one entry, they are often grouped together in one paragraph at or near the end of the entry.

bag ... **8** The word **bag** is also used in the following expressions in informal English. **8.1** If you say that something is **in the bag**, you mean that you are certain that you will get it or achieve it. **8.2** If you **pack** your **bags**, you leave a place where you have been living. EG *I decided it was time to pack my bags.* **8.3** If you are thrown out of a place **bag and baggage**, you are made to leave and take all your belongings with you ... ● to **let the cat out of the bag**: see **cat**. ● a **mixed bag**: see **mix** ...

11.6 Cross-references indicate that more information about a word will be found at another entry, which is shown in bold letters immediately after the word 'See' or the words 'See also'.

attack ... **6** An **attack** of an illness is a short period in which you suffer badly from it and cannot control it. EG *I had an attack of giddiness... She had been left totally deaf by an attack of smallpox.* ● See also **heart attack**.

11.7 Cross-references may also indicate that a phrasal verb has a noun or adjective derived from it, which will be found as a separate entry.

break in ... **1** If someone **breaks in** or **breaks into** a building, they get into it by force ... ● See also **break-in**. — PHRASAL VB: V + ADV/PREP

break-in ... A **break-in** is the act of getting into a building by force... — N COUNT

11.8 If there are several cross-references from one entry to other entries in this dictionary, they are grouped together in one paragraph at the end of the entry, after the phrases or expressions and before the phrasal verbs (see 12).

land ... **16** If someone **lands** on their feet, they are lucky and successful after being in a difficult situation.
17 See also **landed, landing**. ● **the lie of the land**: See **lie**. ● to **see how the land lies**: see **lie**.
land up. if you **land up** in a place or situation, you ...

12 Phrasal verbs

12.1 Phrasal verbs are items which consist of a verb and a preposition or adverb and which have a separate meaning, often very different from the meaning of the verb by itself or with other prepositions and adverbs.

12.2 Phrasal verbs are placed at the end of a verb entry. Two or more phrasal verbs in the same entry are placed in alphabetical order within that entry.

12.3 A phrasal verb is printed in large bold letters like an entry, but is not placed at the left-most margin.

bring ... **1** When you **bring** someone or something ...
23 If something **brings** a particular price, it can be sold for that price ...
24 ● to **bring** something **into being**: see **being**.
bring about. To **bring** something about means to cause it to happen ...
bring along. If you **bring** someone or something **along**, you bring them with you when you come to a place ...
bring-and-buy-sale ...
brink ...

12.4 Only one form is given for a phrasal verb, because the other forms will always be the same as for the main word of the entry at which they occur.

12.5 Sometimes, if two phrasal verbs have the same meaning or meanings, they are explained in the same place. If the two phrasal verbs would normally be next to each other in the alphabetical order, the second one is not given a separate entry.

mess about ... **1** If you **mess about** or **mess around**, **1.1** you spend time doing things without any particular purpose or plan ... EG ... *talking, playing, messing about together... Some of the lads had been messing around when they should have been working... There was no messing about. When you got a job you had to get on with it.* **1.2** you interfere with things in a harmful way; used showing disapproval. EG *She didn't want you coming and messing about with things.* **1.3** you behave in a joking, teasing or silly way. EG *Stop messing about! I'm trying to tell you something important.*

2 if you **mess** someone **about** or you **mess** someone **around,** you treat them badly for example by not being honest with them, or by continually changing plans which affect them. EG *You've been messing me about all summer and I'm fed up with it.*

13 Extra column

13.1 The extra column in this dictionary is used to give two different types of information: grammar notes and semantic relationships.

13.2 **Grammar notes** are given in abbreviated form in capital letters with some symbols such as + and /. A full list of words used in the notes and an explanation of the symbols is given on page xiii.

abdominal ... is used to describe something that is situated in the abdomen or forms part of it. EG *They suffered abdominal pains.* — ADJ CLASSIF:USU ATTRIB

absorb ... 1 If something **absorbs** a liquid or gas, it soaks it up or draws it in ... — V + O

accomplice ... Someone's **accomplice** is a person who helps them to commit a crime or to do something wrong. EG *She was betrayed by her accomplice.* — N COUNT:USU POSS + N

13.3 Each grammar note is explained inside a box at its correct place in the alphabetical entry list of the dictionary.

ad infinitum ... If something happens or goes on **ad infinitum**, it is repeated again and again in the same way. EG *She then teaches it to her daughter, and so on ad infinitum.*

ADJ □ in this dictionary ADJ is used in the grammar notes beside entries to mean 'adjective'. For explanations of different kinds of adjective see □ at ADJ AFTER N, ADJ CLASSIF, ADJ COLOUR, and ADJ QUALIT. See also □ at ATTRIB and PRED.

adjacent ... if something is **adjacent** to something else...

13.4 Sequences of letters and symbols that occur frequently are also explained at their correct place in the alphabetical entry list of the dictionary, ignoring any symbols.

V-necked ...
V+O □ ...
V+O+A □ ...
VOC □ ...
V+O+C □ ...
vocabulary ...

13.5 Words that appear in italics in the grammar notes indicate that they are the words most commonly used with the entry word in a particular grammatical structure.

disadvantageous ... Something that is **disadvantageous** is harmful or likely to cause problems for you. EG *These factors made the 1976 agreement disadvantageous to the British.* — ADJ QUALIT IF + PREP THEN *to*

13.6 **Semantic relationships**: Words that appear in the extra column after the symbols ⇑ = and ≠ are semantic references. They offer users similar or opposite words for the word that is being explained.

13.7 The symbol ⇑ indicates that the following word has a more general meaning similar to the entry word or a particular use of the entry word. Such a word is called a superordinate.

automobile ... An **automobile** is a car, used especially in American English. — N COUNT ⇑ vehicle

13.8 The symbol = indicates that the following word is a synonym, and so is very similar in meaning to the entry word or use and can often be used instead of it.

assiduous ... Someone who is **assiduous** works hard or does things with care and dedication. EG ... *an assiduous student.* — ADJ QUALIT = diligent

13.9 The symbol ≠ indicates that the following word is an antonym, and so is often used with the opposite meaning to that of the entry word or use.

badly off ... 1 If you are **badly off** for something that you need or want, you do not have enough of it. EG *The school is really quite badly off for books.* — ADJ QUALIT PRED, USU + *for* ≠ well-off

amateur ... 1 An **amateur** is someone who does something such as acting or playing a sport as a hobby and not as a job. EG *It's a business for professionals not amateurs.* — N COUNT ≠ professional

14 **Usage**: In this dictionary we have employed a variety of strategies to indicate when a word is mainly used by a particular group of people or in a particular social context, or is used in order to convey an attitude or opinion of someone or something. This information has been placed at different points in the entries depending on its importance when using the word, although normally it comes after the explanation of meaning.

ostracism ... is the state of being ostracized or the act of ostracizing someone; a formal word.

bathroom ... 2 Some people say **bathroom** as a polite way of referring to the toilet; used especially in American English. EG *Can I go to the bathroom please?*

acquisitive ... Someone who is **acquisitive** is fond of getting new possessions; used showing disapproval. EG *He's a very acquisitive sort of person.*

after ... 21 Some British people refer to the pudding course of a meal as **afters**; an informal use. EG *What's for afters?*

bathe ... 2 In American English, to **bathe** means to have a bath. EG *After golf I would return to the flat to bathe and change for work.*

bathos ... is a sudden change in speech or writing from a serious or important subject to a ridiculous or very ordinary one; a technical term in literary criticism.

Pronunciation

In this dictionary a guide is given to the pronunciation of English words using the International Phonetic Alphabet. The accent represented is Received Pronunciation, or RP for short, which is a special type of Southern British English. There are several other accents of English, but RP is perhaps most widely used as a norm for teaching purposes.

Two kinds of information are needed if a word is to be properly pronounced: we need to know about each of the sounds that make up the word, and we need to know about stress. In each of the pronunciations shown in this dictionary, at least one vowel symbol is in heavier type and underlined. Sometimes more than one vowel is in heavier type:

res**u**lt /rɪz**ʌ**lt/
d**i**sapp**oi**nting /d**ɪ**səp**ɔɪ**ntɪŋ/

Heavy type and underlining signifies stress when the word is spoken in isolation. If two syllables are marked in this way, the second has primary stress while the first has secondary stress; if only one is marked, it has primary stress. A word spoken in isolation is called the citation form.

There is a more varied pattern of stress when the word is used in context. Quite commonly one of the stresses found in the citation form, or even both of the stresses, will be absent. The one-stress or two-stress patterns of English speech are associated not with individual words but with the information units that a speaker constructs:

The res**u**lt was disapp**oi**nting
/ðə rɪz**ʌ**lt wəz dɪsəp**ɔɪ**ntɪŋ/

A d**i**sappointing res**u**lt
/ə d**ɪ**səpɔɪntɪŋ rɪz**ʌ**lt/

V**e**ry disappointing ind**ee**d
/v**ɛ**ri^1 dɪsəpɔɪntɪŋ ɪnd**i:**d/

This information cannot be given in advance in a dictionary.

If a vowel is shown in heavy type, this indicates not only its role in being able to take stress, but also something about the way in which it is pronounced. Any vowel marked in heavy type and underlined is a protected vowel. This means that there is very little variation in the way in which a speaker pronounces it, whether or not it actually gets a stress in the information unit in which it occurs. In /s**ɪ**ti^1/ (city), the protected vowel /**ɪ**/ is unvariable within the chosen accent, but the unprotected vowel /i^1/ can vary between /ɪ/ and /i:/ in the usage of a single speaker.

In many cases, the amount of variation is negligible. Where it is not, where an unprotected vowel can range over several different sounds, there are small superscript numbers printed just above and beside the vowel symbol. The numbers indicate the range of likely variation. So, for example, /ə^1/ means variation between /ə/ and /ɪ/ as in /s**ɪ**nə^{1}mə/ (cinema); /ɪ^2/ means variation between /ɪ/ and /ɛ/ as in /j**u:**slɪ^{2}s/ (useless).

Some sounds, both vowels and consonants, are heard only in rather slow and careful speech. /j**u:**ʒʊəl (usual) and /k**ɒ**ləmnɪst/ (columnist) are often heard as /j**u:**ʒəl/ and /k**ɒ**ləmɪst/. In such cases, the superscript ^{0} indicates variation between full pronunciation of the sound and no pronunciation:

/j**u:**ʒʊ^{0}əl/, /k**ɒ**ləmn^{0}ɪst/

All superscripts and the variations that they stand for are given in the key below.

Pronunciation Key

Symbols Used

ɑ:	heart, start, calm.	b	bed	t	talk
æ	act, mass, lap.	d	done	v	van
aɪ	dive, cry, mind.	f	fit	w	win
aɪə	fire, tyre, buyer.	g	good	x	loch
aʊ	out, down, loud.	h	hat	z	zoo
aʊə	flour, tower, sour.	j	yellow	ʃ	ship
ɛ	met, lend, pen.	k	king	ʒ	measure
ɛɪ	say, main, weight.	l	lip	ŋ	sing
ɛə	fair, care, wear.	m	mat	tʃ	cheap
ɪ	fit, win, list.	n	nine	θ	thin
i:	feed, me, beat.	p	pay	ð	then
ɪə	near, beard, clear.	r	run	dʒ	joy
ɒ	lot, lost, spot.	s	soon		
əʊ	note, phone, coat.				
ɔ:	more, cord, claw.				
ɔɪ	boy, coin, joint.				
ʊ	could, stood, hood.				
u:	you, use, choose.				
ʊə	sure, poor, cure.				
ɜ:	turn, third, word.				
ʌ	but, fund, must.				
ə	the weak vowel in butter, about, forgotten.				

Superscripts

ə^0 (ə ⇔ 0)	ɪ^0 (ɪ ⇔ 0)
ə^1 (ə ⇔ ɪ)	ɪ^1 (ɪ ⇔ ə)
ə^2 (ə ⇔ ɛ)	ɪ^2 (ɪ ⇔ ɛ)
ə^3 (ə ⇔ æ)	ɪ^3 (ɪ ⇔ ɛɪ)
ə^4 (ə ⇔ ʊ)	ɪ^5 (ɪ ⇔ aɪ)
ə^5 (ə ⇔ aɪ)	i^1 (ɪ ⇔ i:)
ə^6 (ə ⇔ əʊ)	ɛ^1 (ɛ ⇔ ɪ)
ə^7 (ə ⇔ ɒ)	u^4 (u: ⇔ ʊ)
ə^8 (ə ⇔ ɔ:)	m^1(m ⇔ n)
ə^9 (ə ⇔ ʌ)	ŋ^1 (ŋ ⇔ n)

^{0} after a consonant symbol indicates probable omission; k^0, t^0, h^0, etc.

Special Entries

Below is a list of all the special entries contained in this dictionary. The special entries explain how to read the grammar notes in the extra column.
The following punctuation symbols are used in the grammar notes.

, A comma is used to show that two or more word classes are listed within the same grammar note, when all of them apply to the same paragraph or subparagraph. The comma separates the classes, and the last class is introduced by OR. For example, V, V+O, OR V+REPORT-CL means that the verb may be used in three ways: it may occur without an object, it may occur with an object, or it may occur with a report clause.

: A colon is used to introduce extra information after the basic word class has been stated. For example, ADJ CLASSIF: ATTRIB means that the classifying adjective is used in front of a noun.

/ A slash is used between two alternatives in the grammar notes. For example, N COUNT/UNCOUNT means that the noun can be used as either a count noun or an uncount noun. V+O: IF+PREP THEN *with/against* means that if there is a preposition after this verb structure, the preposition is normally *with* or *against*.

() Brackets are mainly used in the grammar notes beside verbs. They show that a particular sort of object or adjunct is used. For example, V+O(REFL) means that the object of the verb is a reflexive pronoun. V+O(NG/REFL) means that the object of the verb is either a noun group or a reflexive pronoun. V+A(*to*) means that the verb is followed by an adjunct that begins with the preposition *to*.

\+ A plus is used in two ways. With verbs, it is used to show that the verb occurs with an object (V+O) or an adjunct (V+A). With other words, it is used to show that the word is followed by a particular item. For example, ADV+ADJ/ADV means that the adverb is typically followed by an adjective or another adverb.

The following words are also used in the grammar notes.

USU means 'usually'. For example, a verb with the grammar note V+O: USU PASS is usually but not always used in the passive.

ONLY is used to report that we only have evidence showing that the word is used in this particular way. For example, V+O: ONLY PASS means that we have only found the verb used in the passive.

ALSO is used to mention an additional or alternative grammatical use. For example, N COUNT: ALSO IN TITLES means that a count noun can also be used as part of a title.

BEFORE and AFTER are used to show the normal order in which the grammatical items occur. For example N BEFORE N means that the noun is used in front of another noun; ADV AFTER VB means that the adverb is used following a verb.

WITH is used to say that a word normally occurs in company with a word from a particular class of words, which may occur before or after it. For example, ADV WITH VB means that the adverb normally occurs in company with a verb.

List of Special Entries

A
ADJ
ADJ AFTER N
ADJ CLASSIF
ADJ COLOUR
ADJ QUALIT
ADV
ADV AFTER VB
ADV BRD NEG
ADV SEN
ADV WITH VB
ADV+ADJ/ADV
AGE
ATTRIB
AUX
BE
BROAD NEG
C
COMB
COMPAR
CONJ COORD
CONJ SUBORD
CONT
CONVENTION
DARE
DATE
DET
DETPOSS
DO
EXCLAM
HAVE
IMPER
INF
-ING
MEASUREMENT
MOD
MODAL
MONEY
N
N BEFORE N
N COUNT
N MASS
N PART
N PLURAL
N PROPER
N SING
N UNCOUNT
N UNCOUNT/COUNT
NAME
NEED
NEG
NG
NUM
NUMBER
O
ORDINAL
PASS
PAST PART
PHR
PHRASAL VB
POSS
PRED
PREDET
PREFIX
PREP
PRON
PRON INDEF
PRONPOSS
PRON REFL
PRON REL
QUANTIF
QUOTE
RECIP
REFL
REPORT CL
S
SEMI MODAL
SUFFIX
SUPERL
SUPP
TIME
TITLE
to-INF
USED
USU
V
V-ERG
V+A
V+C
V+O
V+O+A
V+O+C
V+O+O
VB
VOC
WH

Introduction

The COBUILD Dictionary

This dictionary is for people who want to use modern English. It offers more, and more accurate, information on the way modern English is used than any previous dictionary. It is a useful guide to writing and speaking English as well as an aid to reading and understanding.

This dictionary looks rather like most others if you don't look too closely. Actually it is quite new and different. The techniques used to compile it are new and use advanced computer technology. For the user the kind of information is different, the quality of information is different, and the presentation of the information is different.

For the first time, a dictionary has been compiled by the thorough examination of a representative group of English texts, spoken and written, running to many millions of words. This means that in addition to all the tools of the conventional dictionary makers - wide reading and experience of English, other dictionaries and of course eyes and ears - this dictionary is based on hard, measurable evidence. No major uses are missed, and the number of times a use occurs has a strong influence on the way the entries are organized. Equally, the large group of texts, called the corpus, gives us reasonable grounds for omitting many uses and word-forms that do not occur in it. It is difficult for a conventional dictionary, in the absence of evidence, to decide what to leave out, and a lot of quite misleading information is thus preserved in the tradition of lexicography.

This dictionary makes a break with such traditions. We have gone back to basics and collected many millions of words, and put them into a very large computer. The dictionary team has had daily access to about 20 million words, with many more in specialized stores. The words came from books, magazines, newspapers, pamphlets, leaflets, conversations, radio and television broadcasts. The sources are gratefully acknowledged on page xxii. The aim was to provide a fair representation of contemporary English.

No set of texts, however large, can be fully relied on; all the time the information from the texts has been analysed and appraised by a team of lexicographers, whose professional knowledge has also been used wherever there is only a small amount of evidence of the usage of a word or phrase.

The quality of information in this dictionary is different from others. With our textual evidence it is possible to be precise about the shape of phrases and the extent of their variation; the relative importance of different senses of a word; and the typical environment in which a word or phrase is used. Even when statements like this are already familiar, they are made with a different kind of authority in this book.

Examples

Because of this opportunity to show the actual language to users of it, the examples in this dictionary have a new status and do a different job from examples in the conventional tradition. These examples are taken from actual texts wherever possible.

The use of 'citation' from actual texts is a noble tradition in lexicography. You will find cited examples in Dr Johnson's famous Dictionary of 1755 and in the Oxford English Dictionary begun by Murray in 1878. In the development of language teaching materials, however, in recent years it has become a habit to make up examples to illustrate a particular usage.

These examples have no authority apart from the thoughts of the person who creates them and they are very often quite unnatural. It is frequently difficult to imagine where they might be used in everyday speech and writing.

This language tradition has spilled over into the dictionaries that are specially written for language learners. However, in this dictionary we return to the well-established practice of selecting examples from actual instances.

Some of the examples are slightly adapted from the citation in our text files. In all cases we have attempted to preserve the common pattern of use, and have only changed or omitted words that seemed to us not to be affecting the use. The length of examples is critical in a dictionary that includes so many and, inevitably, some of them have been shortened. Occasionally also an example has been edited to make it easier to understand when it is removed from its context. Only on very rare occasions have we composed an example because there is no suitable one in the corpus.

The user can thus be confident that the examples display the language as it is used. Not only that, but the examples printed are typical of usage. A selection is normally made after a comparison of dozens of examples, and in the case of everyday words, hundreds or thousands.

We expect these examples to do a quite different job from invented examples; something more like the job done in Dr Johnson's dictionary and the OED. They are examples of good practice. They support the explanations and they illustrate usage. They provide a reliable guide for speaking and writing in the English of today.

In contrast, invented examples are really part of the explanations. They have no independent authority or reason for their existence, and they are constructed to refine the explanations and in many cases to clarify the explanations. They give no reliable guide to composition in English and would be very misleading if applied to that task. They do not say 'This is how the word is used', but rather 'This will help you to understand the sense'. We are so accustomed to invented examples that we often forget that they are only of value in helping to explain. Usage cannot be invented, it can only be recorded.

In this dictionary the examples show how the words are used, and in addition, of course, they give help in understanding the sense.

We expect that the user will find the examples interesting and sometimes unusual. They occasionally contain difficult words and phrases and they may sometimes illustrate uses and senses which seem slightly different from the explanations. This is because the examples in this dictionary give independent information about the language, sometimes extending what it is possible to write into the explanation. Extensive testing has convinced us that users appreciate examples of this kind, that they become accustomed to using them. In the first place examples from real usage are primary evidence and complement the secondary evidence of the explanation. In the second place, the open-ended nature of these examples, the way in which they are taken from the vast repertoire of English, give the student a feeling of genuine access to the language, including some of those more untidy and difficult aspects.

The examples are thus a major feature of this book and we hope that their richness and variety will be extensively used, and that their function will be fully understood and appreciated.

Style of Presentation

It is a principle of this dictionary that it should be easily understood by the learner for whom it is designed. Obviously, if the style of a dictionary is too difficult or too condensed for users, the work is useless.

This dictionary also breaks with a long-established tradition in the style in which the entries are written. Over the years, originally for reasons of space, dictionaries have established dozens of stylistic conventions, which require to be learned in addition to learning the everyday language before the dictionary can be fully understood. There are all sorts of uses of brackets and punctuation; of symbols and type faces, of abbreviations and special words. They make most dictionaries into texts which are obscure to most of their users, even native speakers.

For example, standard dictionaries will tell you that one meaning of *throw* is *to be subjected to (a fit)* or *to have (fit, tantrum, etc)*.

The compilers of this dictionary have considered each convention carefully, and rejected all but a few of them because of the trouble they cause. Those that are left represent what we believe to be the minimum consistent with economy and clarity. The dictionary is designed to read like ordinary English. Words appear in their normal full spelling forms and the explanations are written in real sentences.

The word being explained is normally mentioned in the explanation in such a way that you can see how it is typically used in English.

For example: **throw 18** If you **throw** a fit or tantrum, you suddenly lose control of yourself or your emotions.

In many cases, the explanation provides an illustration of the word in its typical grammatical context. This is thought to be more useful than an attempt to account for the meaning of the word in isolation.

The wording of each explanation shows the basic word class. So, the entry for an ordinary count noun like *door*, will begin, 'A **door** is ...'

An entry for a transitive verb like *conceal* will begin, 'If you **conceal** something, you ...' This suggests that the verb in this sense is typically used with a human subject and a wide range of direct objects, which are typically inanimate or abstract rather than human.

Variations of this style show variations in the typical range of grammatical subject and object. An explanation that begins, 'To **sink** a ship means to ..' implies that the range of typical subjects is very wide indeed - including both humans and inanimate objects - but that the range of direct objects for this sense is restricted to ships and things like ships.

In these explanations, the words 'if you say that...' very often signal metaphoric, figurative, and other non-literal meanings.

For example: **glue 4** If you say that someone's **eyes** are **glued** to something, you mean that they are watching it with all their attention.

Extra Column

The most noticeable departure from everyday English will be found in the extra notes at the side of each column. This is a new feature which has been added to increase the amount of systematic information given to the user.

The main entries are self-standing and it is never necessary to consult the Extra Column for everyday purposes. But this dictionary is designed for a wide range of users, including students and teachers who need quite a lot of technical information.

The main aim of the Extra Column is to provide the more advanced student with structural information, extending the statements of the main entry. It gives a word class, and indicates the range of syntactic uses. It points out typical syntactic patterns and choices available to the user of English, often going beyond what it is possible to give in examples.

One important reason for creating the Extra Column is to keep the main dictionary text simple and accessible. We did not want to keep interrupting the flow of entries with abbreviations and technical terms. Nor did we want to have hundreds of grammar codes, as some dictionaries have, which can only be understood by looking up another part of the book.

The terminology used here is fairly easy to understand and the statements give detailed information which would be too lengthy to include if it was written out fully. It is hoped that the conventions of the Extra Column will be quickly mastered by post-intermediate students, thus adding to the value of the dictionary. The terms used in the Extra Column are explained in the dictionary and you will find the entries in normal alphabetical order. For example, there is a full explanation of SUPP between *supine* and *supper*. It has a box drawn round it to make it easy to find.

In addition, there is a quick reference guide on page vii.

The Extra Column puts the words and phrases into categories. For example alongside sense 22 of *back* is the code N COUNT + SUPP. It is fairly easy to see that this means that *back* can be used as a count noun, and the noun group which it heads will normally have a supplement, and *a back* is not likely to appear on its own. If you are not sure what is meant by a count noun, then look up the special entry at N COUNT; if you want to know more about supplements, look up the special entry at SUPP. More examples are given in the special entry to tell you the range and variety of supplements and the typical nouns that take them.

So the Extra Column contains a large number of grammatical notes about individual words and senses. More than that, it draws attention to grammatical patterns which are common for that word in that sense. It is rare for grammar books to separate the patterns which actually occur from the ones which can in theory occur; it is also rare for grammars to be careful about relating the grammar to an individual sense of a word.

The Extra Column entries thus provide very substantial information which is otherwise difficult to record in a dictionary, but which is immensely useful for composing speech and writing in English. It is important, therefore to understand its function properly.

The Extra Column notes are written to apply only to the words alongside them. They are based on observation of the actual patterning of words and so they are intended to give guidance as to how the words can be used. The Extra Column does not constitute a grammar of English which can be separated from the rest of the dictionary because that would go well beyond the notes in a dictionary. It is a powerful aid and a support to the rest of the entry.

The main point to note is that a separate grammar would tell you what is, in principle, possible in the way of constructions. Such a grammar is not usually concerned with what actually occurs or is likely to occur. Grammars can produce structures which are quite correct, but which are not at all likely to be used. For example the verb *mightn't have been going to be tested* or the noun group *all seven of the very happy old brown grass-eating garden rodents*, are quite correct in grammar. But it is most unlikely that such complicated combinations would actually be used in a text.

The Extra Column of this dictionary contrasts very sharply with this sort of grammar. From all of the virtually endless combinations and permutations it picks out what is typical of the use of the word as found in the text collection. Hence the entries for apparently similar words or senses will only be identical if they are used in just the same way as each other. Apart from trivial variations in phrasing, which we have done our best to standardize, a marked difference in the Extra Column will probably indicate a difference of typical structure, of emphasis or frequency, or a noticeable tendency towards one pattern rather than another. Our policy is one of caution, so that the Extra Column entries should draw attention only to prominent features of the word in question.

As well as grammatical notes, we have included semantic information in the Extra Column wherever possible. Words of similar meaning (synonyms) and opposite meaning (antonyms) are noted, and more general words (superordinates) also. These allow meanings to be related to each other, so that the users can add to their vocabulary by making use of the dictionary.

Word and Environment

The most important result that has come from the work of preparing this dictionary concerns the way in which the patterns of words with each other are related to the meanings and uses of the words. However, it is difficult to show such patterns clearly in a dictionary. Every dictionary is based on an alphabetical list of words, and such an organization may lead people to believe that the senses of a word can be explained and illustrated without reference to other words. That is occasionally the case. Overwhelmingly, however, the sense of a word is bound up with a particular usage - a syntactic pattern perhaps, or a close association of words or a grouping of words into a set phrase. It is not really possible to talk about the meaning of the word in isolation - it only has a particular meaning when it is in a particular environment.

Some common words have very little independent meaning - the word *bet*, for example. The commonest use of *bet* is with *I* in front of it (often a modal verb between them), and it is used to add conviction to a statement a person is making: *I bet nobody's been here before*. If, however, the pronoun *you* appears in front of *bet* (without a modal and as a whole sentence) it is used as an enthusiastic response: '*Are you going to go?*' - '*You bet!*'

Several nouns are frequently qualified by the adjective *hard*. We talk of *hard luck, hard facts*, and *hard evidence*. We can also talk about *strong evidence* but are unlikely to use 'strong facts' or 'strong luck'; *tough luck* but not 'tough facts' or 'tough evidence'; *sad facts* but not 'sad luck' or 'sad evidence'. Of course, it is always possible to depart from the normal patterns of English, so it is not claimed that 'sad evidence' cannot occur - just that it's not worth following as a pattern.

Note that in the above examples of *hard*, there are two rather different meanings. In *hard luck, hard* means 'unfortunate', but in *hard facts* and *hard evidence* it means 'unlikely to be proved wrong'. Despite this, the patterns of collocation show that the near-synonym *strong* goes only with *evidence*. So the patterns of collocation are not governed by meaning.

The dictionary offers a lot of help in making this area clear. The style of explanation is equally capable of presenting single words or phrases, and can give alternatives. The examples pay careful attention to collocation and typical phrasing. The Extra Column is often useful for stating the limits of a usage, and its typical features; it may give a syntactic pattern that always, or nearly always, carries the usage; or it may point out that one preposition in particular is used, and no other, or that a usage is normally passive.

In addition to these features, the dictionary also uses cross references to help you find a usage that consists of more than one word.

Common Words

This dictionary makes a feature of the very common words of the language and pays them very close attention. Much more space is devoted to them than in any other dictionary of a similar size. Every dictionary has entries for the very common grammatical words of the language like *the, and, of*. However, we do not think that users find these entries very helpful. They are difficult to understand and they are attempts at arrangements by meaning rather than usage. It is clear from COBUILD research that the very common words in English have most of their usage in the sort of patterns just discussed in the previous section. The information needed to understand such words is largely found by studying their usage rather that their semantic content. Most dictionaries do not record usage in a way that brings this out.

This dictionary presents and explains the uses of these words in special ways. This makes them prominent and might cause some people to wonder why such an emphasis is put on words that are often called 'purely grammatical', 'empty', etc. There is an issue of principle here which we believe to be most important.

First of all, consider some basic facts about how often words occur in people's use of English. Studies of the way in which words occur in texts all come up with the same basic message: most actual usage is of frequent words. A relatively small number of words account for a very large percentage of what is written and spoken every day.

The following occur about once in every hundred thousand words: *secretly, jet, core, agony, preparation, privileged.*

The following are typical of words that occur about once in every ten thousand words: *speak, green, maybe, quickly, sorry.*

The following are typical of words that occur about once in every thousand words: *two, over, get, because, see, don't.*

Words like these occur about once in every hundred words: *in, that.*

A few words occur even more frequently, for example: *the, and, of.*

So in most texts that you will read, or in talks you will hear, or in conversations you will have, about three words in every four are the common ones.

These facts have been known for over fifty years, but their significance has been overlooked. Dictionaries have given a lot of space to the very rare and unusual words, which are interesting, no doubt, but not very useful, especially to someone who wants to write or speak good English.

The importance of very frequent words is not confined to the 50 or 100 commonest. The same features show in the top 2000-3000 words - those of great usefulness and complex usage, with a strong tendency to form patterns with words about them. They are the power-house of the language. Fluency in using these words is of much more value than knowing all sorts of peculiar words that are hardly ever used.

For many years scholars have searched for a 'basic English' that will make international communication easier. Up till now they did not have the facts with which to select and describe the core of the language, and they met serious problems. Whenever you restrict people who have a command of a language, they will rebel; whenever you distort their language, you will be ignored. In the treatment of common words in this book there is an invitation to devise your own basic English.

Non-native users of English have found it difficult to get access to the natural patterns of English, because the patterns presented to them are often not natural. They have resorted to building up a large vocabulary instead. Now they have a choice.

The Word List

Which words, then, should we put in a dictionary? The first answer, that most lexicographers will applaud, is 'as many as possible'. But there are still a number of different ways to organize the words. A dictionary for use in producing language and in communication in general, will pay attention to the statistics given above. The common words are very important. What is more, our research shows that the common words have many different patterns of use, and a subtle range of meanings. The simplest words for the lexicographer are the not very common ones with just one clear meaning, like *jabber, jackal, jackass, jackdaw* and *jacuzzi*.

This dictionary takes on the job of making a useful, readable and reliable description of the central core of the language. The book as a whole is big enough to ensure that, despite this, the less common vocabulary is not neglected, and there is information here on over forty thousand words. But do not look here for obsolete or dialectal or highly technical words. This dictionary is designed for everyday use.

It follows from this that if your English is already quite good, the information given in this book will often confirm what you already thought was likely. That is a most important function - just as important as informing you of something you had no idea about. How often do you turn to a dictionary to learn something utterly new? Anyone who can understand this Introduction or use the dictionary at all is already quite good at English. But for a number of reasons, you may seek reassurance that a word means what you think it means, or that a construction is made in one way rather than another. A language is capable of a great range of variation from the main patterns, but nevertheless has some underlying strict rules, and both the rules and the main variations can be got from these pages.

So this book is offered in part as a valuable way of bringing to your attention things that you were vaguely aware of anyway; of formulating them and clarifying areas of doubt concerning the limits of their use; of giving support and confidence in modern English usage. You will often find what you want by noticing an example that it close to your needs, or by skimming down the Extra Column for the sort of pattern you are interested in.

You may come across a sentence like *That is what we need so badly*, and you may feel sure that the usual meaning of *bad* is not appropriate. You get the strong impression that it is just being used to intensify the meaning of *need*, and the word *so* is often used in a meaning close to *very*. When you look up the dictionary, which says 'If you need or want something **badly**, you need or want it very much', you find you were correct, and the dictionary has helped you to make sure, and to give you more confidence in using it in your own speaking and writing.

Do not undervalue this function of the dictionary. Users of a language are not necessarily accurate reporters of usage, even their own. Most of our skill in using language is unconscious, and therefore difficult to recall, though easy to recognize. This is a surprising point, and very easy to test out in any language. Just take an ordinary piece of writing, and ask someone to read out any two consecutive words. Try to guess the next word. Usually you will not manage to guess it exactly, but when it is eventually read out it will usually fit in perfectly with the rest of the text.

Apart from the function of confirming our guesses, the dictionary offers a large amount of new information to any user. This will extend and improve usage and understanding, and help learners to use the language more skilfully.

Meaning and Function

Words and phrases *do* things. People apologize, invite, insult, mollify, persuade, and a hundred other things using words. Quite often a function of this kind is associated with a particular word or phrase, and in this dictionary we try to draw attention to such functions. They are just as important as the meanings.

In the case of phrases, it is sometimes difficult to record these in an alphabetical dictionary. Many groups of common words like *by the way, for one thing*, do not contain an obvious word for indexing purposes, and there is no terminology in common use. Nevertheless we have tried to present all the main phrases that have a function associated with them.

Those words which have a specialized function in conversation or writing are noted in the same way as meanings. So for example **better 8**, as in **'you'd better** make some notes' is said to be a polite way of telling, advising, warning or threatening people. Another example is *no kidding* which, in informal spoken English, is used to emphasize that what you are saying is true.

Many such functions have to do with organizing the discourse. For instance, there are markers of boundaries in conversation, like *right, now, okay*: *Right, I'm going to talk this afternoon about (fire hazards)...Okay, I think we'll stop there...Anyway, so much for modern art.*

If you want to make what you are saying sound less definite, forceful, or dogmatic, and therefore more acceptable to your audience you can use a phrase like *I don't know*, which you find at **know 20.2:** *I don't know* *about you, but (I didn't like it at all)... I don't really know how to put it, it's not really an arts subject.*

You could also use a fixed expression like *all things considered: He's okay, all things considered.*
There are lots of ways in which we emphasize the points that we make. Some common adverbs are used like *very* in: *they treated me very badly.*

Some fixed expressions are also used to emphasize what you are saying,like *here and now*, **here 11**: *I'll say here and now that I don't believe in ghosts.*

Another useful function is to draw the attention of the hearer or reader to what you are about to say. For example, **as 14** refers to phrases like *as for myself: As for myself, I had a glass of juice three times a day.*

Very general nouns such as *thing* or *aspect* are often used to indicate to the hearer that you are about to mention something more specific: *The other thing of course is that people never take him seriously... Far and away the most important aspect is the person's disposition.*

This dictionary pays particular attention to the functions of words and phrases, giving thousands of examples of the kinds of functions that have just been illustrated.

Organization of Entries

Dictionaries vary a lot in the way in which an entry is put together. This dictionary follows a simple principle of trying to make it easy for users to find what they want. So longer entries are divided up into sections and paragraphs, and phrases are gathered together at the end of a section. There are detailed notes on the organization on page viii.

To begin with, the entry contains information on the spelling, pronunciation and inflection of a word. All the different inflectional forms are listed. Then the first sense is given.

Wherever possible the first sense is a common one, and a fairly easy one - usually the sense that most people would expect. Unlike other dictionaries, this one is written in the knowledge of which are the common senses or usages, and this is taken into account. But because the commonest meaning is often not a clear and independent one, it is not always put first.

For example, about half the examples in the corpus of *bet* are of the sense numbered 3. There are not nearly as many examples of the senses 1 or 2, which are to do with risking money on a chance. But these senses are felt to be the ones to begin a description with. It is easy to identify the central, core meaning of a word. Most people who know the language well will agree that there usually is such a meaning and they will probably agree which it is - regardless of how frequent it is.

Another factor that we paid attention to is the contrast between abstract meanings and 'concrete' ones, denoting physical objects and events. Wherever it seemed reasonable, we gave preference to the concrete over the abstract because the concrete meaning is often easier to grasp, and abstract meanings can often be seen as variations on the concrete.

Some dictionaries put the earliest recorded meanings first, so that the present-day meanings are to be found much later in the entry. It should be said at once that this is not a historical dictionary; it is a description of what the language is like at the present time. The user is spared having to read through an account of earlier meanings and etymologies, and will not confuse old and new.

So in this dictionary the first sense is a common one and a central one; also an independent one and if possible it is concrete. The explanation shows what word class is typical of this sense. Then all the other usages of the same word class will normally follow. This organization avoids a lot of repetition because the same framework of explanation can be used again and again.

When the usage changes, so does the wording of the framework and there is a new paragraph. Again the usages are grouped. Examples follow each usage.

This organization means that where a word is used in the same sense but in different word classes, this sense will be given more than once. For example, **clot 1** is a noun, **clot 2** is a verb, and **clot 3** is another noun, quite different from **clot 1**.

Within each paragraph the different senses are grouped together as well as the word allows. Although the frequency of a sense is taken into account, the most important matter within a paragraph is the movement from one sense to another, giving as clear as possible a picture.

Words

A dictionary is organized by putting words in alphabetical order. In the main this is a simple task. There are, however, a number of problems affecting some unusual words and various combinations.

In general, we have stuck to strict alphabetical order of the written form of the word. When a word has more than one pronunciation, like *bow* or *absent*, this is noted at the beginning of the entry. Compounds, inflections or derived forms that merit a separate entry are given in their alphabetical place, and no account is taken of the hyphens or word spaces that are sometimes found in compounds. Phrases are recorded at the word we think the user will probably turn to first, but cross-referenced from other significant words. Technical terms about language, including the apparatus of the extra column, will all be found in alphabetical order, as will common abbreviations, weights and measures and many other items that sometimes appear separately in dictionaries.

What Kind of English?

Any dictionary in one volume, however large, has to make decisions about which words to include and which to exclude, which to mention briefly and which to concentrate on. It has already been pointed out (see Common Words, above) that this dictionary gives pride of place to the central core of the language. It is above all a guide to ordinary everyday English.

Technical Terminology

The texts from which this dictionary is derived are nearly all in ordinary everyday English, that any educated person might read or hear. The word list includes many hundreds of words which are technical in origin but which are regularly used in the central vocabulary - words like *hearsay, gynaecology, debug.* The meanings given are the meanings that are actually used in our ordinary texts and not necessarily what a specialist would say.

This is a tricky point; many words of technical origin in current use have highly specific meanings which are not really accessible to anyone who does not know the subject. They are explained, so to speak, within a scientific or humanistic discipline. If we just wrote out the 'official' explanation our users would hardly be helped at all. Most would have great difficulty in understanding the explanation; if they managed to understand it they might very well find that is was being used by a non-specialist in a much more general sense.

Hence we have explained the technical words according to the way we use them in ordinary English, and we have kept the explanations as simple as possible. If you need a lot of technical terms, you can find them in the many specialized dictionaries that are compiled by experts in each field. There are also dictionaries with a large number of headwords like Collins English Dictionary.

Social Variety

The texts in our collection come from as wide a range of sources as possible, within what we feel is 'ordinary English'. Each text has to be about something, and we have taken account of the subject matter in every instance. Where the sense or usage seems to be restricted to a particular subject area, this is mentioned in the text. For example, *chromosome* is called a technical word and *clarion call* is called a literary expression.

On some occasions you will find an explanation that is not followed by an example. This often tells you that it is not a very important word. But sometimes it indicates that we do not recommend you to use it without assistance. It is there to help you in reading and understanding but there are difficult features of its usage which make it unsafe to use without further information.

We have also made recommendations on matters of formality, politeness and rudeness in English. It is the job of a dictionary to record the way a language is used, and we have done this.

Formality differs between spoken and written English. An expression which is quite normal in conversation might look very informal if it was written down; so *formal* and *informal* are just general guides, and you can use more informal English in speech than in writing.

Anything said to be rude, offensive, obscene or insulting should be treated with great care. Unless you are absolutely sure of how to use such words and phrases, you should avoid them. Users of English today are quite open and straightforward in their language, and will use words which would have shocked people only a few years ago. However, it is an area of usage where great skill and judgment are required for effective use. Nowadays sex and religion are often joked about in most social groups, but racist talk is very offensive, and sexist talk irritates some people

Warnings are given whenever we feel thay are necessary, so please be very careful to avoid these words and phrases.

Geographical Variety

English is the most widely used language in the world. It is the native and often the only language of people in Britain, USA, Canada, Australia, New Zealand and many other territories. It is the main second language of many Commonwealth countries and is learned to a high level by millions more people who do not use it in their immediate society, but need it because of their international connections in trade, research, politics etc.

A single volume cannot hope to do justice to the immense variety that is found in modern English. There are now whole dictionaries of regional varieties, like the Macquarie Dictionary of Australian English. But this dictionary, originating in Britain, inevitably tends towards a British variety of English. It tries to avoid British usages which are not international. Equally, aspects of American, Canadian or Australian English which are distinctive to these regions have been left out, but those which are familiar to the international community have been recorded. So *automobile* is said to be used especially in American English, but there is no restriction on *automat*. The result of this is a description of a form of English which is widely used and usable throughout the world.

Within Britain, there is a bewildering variety of accents and dialects, and again we have had to work out an appropriate policy for this dictionary. The principle we have followed is that a user of this dictionary will expect to have a statement about a word which is as simple and clear as it can possibly be made. There should be as few ifs and buts as possible. Hence we do not record all the variety, and more space is made available for words that can be used anywhere. There is a good range of specialist texts on accents and dialects of British English, so someone with a particular query can probably find the answer to it in a good library. In this book we try to describe a norm of usage which will be accepted as normal by large numbers of people.

There is a separate statement on pronunciation on page xii. The long tradition of English teaching throughout the world has settled on a so-called 'variety' of English called Recieved Pronunciation or RP. This may be felt nowadays as a slightly dated variety arising from an elitist view of a language, but it is still the best documented variety and entirely serviceable as a model.

Correctness

With regard to usage, correctness and related matters of style in the wording of the dictionary entries we have adopted a slightly conservative position. Many of the newer features of contemporary English may have a short life, and should not be given a place in the language that implies permanence. Many established features are not much used by younger people but are still thought to be available to most competent speakers. These are our judgments. We hope that the the language presented in this book is above all reliable, not dated nor markedly avant-garde, nor unusual to the kind of person we think of as an average user.

Even this cautious reflection of modern usage will come as a surprise to many readers who are accustomed to following an older style of writing in English. For example, there is no attempt to avoid splitting infinitives. It is a regular feature of current speech and writing and we believe that it is now time to accept that the balance of usage is in favour of stylistic freedom in this instance. Also, we regularly refer to the indefinite pronouns such as *someone* by the words *they*, *them*, *their* because *he* and *she* are restricted to male and female referents respectively. We have abandoned the convention whereby *he* was held to refer to both men and women. This is done for several reasons; it is quite natural in speech; it is a very sensitive matter for those who have pointed out the built-in sexism of English; the 'singularity' of the indefinite pronouns is not as marked as the singularity of a common count noun.

These policies are representative of a number of small steps towards accepting some of the facts of everyday usage. We do not expect they will be welcomed by everyone, but would suggest that any who find them - as a whole - unacceptable are not really engaging with current English.

This brings up the question of usage and authority.

These concepts must support each other or no-one will respect either of them. If their close relationship breaks down, and authority is not backed up by usage, then no-one will respect it. It will be seen as unrealistic, arbitrary, old-fashioned and a barrier to free expression.

Similarly, no-one will respect usage if it is merely an unedited record of what people say and write. Unless they have the support of authority, people will be unable to distinguish between good and bad usage; it will not be possible to teach or use the language with any confidence. Those people - probably most of us - who get a general impression that the language is getting worse and worse as the years go by - will become quite upset if the whims and fashions of usage are not tempered by some yardstick or standard.

Any successful record of the language such as a dictionary is itself a contribution to authority. People tend to believe that dictionaries tell them what is or is not allowed in a language. Actually, the rules of a language are very flexible, but it is difficult to show all this in a dictionary. However much, in prefaces like this one, the editors may say they are only recording and following usage, there is no doubt whatsoever that they take thousands and thousands of decisions which contain an element of subjective judgment. And if they print new uses, the act of printing them in a dictionary seems to make them part of the language.

This dictionary has been compiled in the knowledge that it will be judged in the way just described. Hence the rather conservative stance. Sometimes in noting a usage we point out that a distinction has now been lost, or a rather pedantic convention has been abandoned. This is to help users who are expecting to find a usage which seems to have disappeared.

The Personality of a Dictionary

Much the same sort of remarks apply in general to the content of statements in this dictionary. Each dictionary presents a sort of corporate personality to the readership. Moral and political issues can be reduced to a minimum but cannot be entirely avoided. This is primarily a dictionary of the English language, and not a political document. Its position with reference to current English has been worked out with great thoroughness and a pooling of experience. Its position with reference to moral and political issues seeks always a neutral and fairly objective statement. It is certainly not intended to provoke.

We have tried at least to be consistent despite having a large team working for several years. We have tried to avoid extreme or sectarian positions, but we have taken note of the warnings in recent years that fairly ordinary use of language can be unconsciously sexist or racist or morally or politically offensive.

It is the hope of editors and publishers that this attempt to present senses in an uncontroversial fashion will be supported by readers writing in to point out places where they think it breaks down. In this way future editions can become more sensitive to public opinion.

Conclusion

So this is a very new and different dictionary, designed to be easy to use. The compilers have thousands of new things to say because of the unique view of English they have been able to get; at the same time they want to explain in simple and direct ways. We all hope that you, the user, will find it a genuinely helpful reference book.

John Sinclair
EDITOR IN CHIEF

Corpus Acknowledgements

We wish to thank the following, who have kindly given permission for the use of copyright material in the the Birmingham Collection of English Texts.

Associated Business Programmes Ltd for: *The Next 200 Years* by Herman Kahn with William Brown and Leon Martel first published in Great Britain by Associated Business Programmes Ltd 1977 © Hudson Institute 1976. David Attenborough and William Collins Sons & Co Ltd for: *Life on Earth* by David Attenborough first published by William Collins Sons & Co Ltd 1979 © David Attenborough Productions LTD 1979. James Baldwin for: *The Fire Next Time* by James Baldwin Published in Great Britain by Michael Joseph Ltd 1963 © James Baldwin 1963. B T Batsford Ltd for: *Witchcraft in England* by Christina Hole first published by B T Batsford Ltd 1945 © Christina Hole 1945. Michael Billington for: 'Lust at First Sight' by Michael Billington in the *Illustrated London News* July 1981 and 'Truffaut's Tolerance' by Michael Billington in the *Illustrated London News* August 1981. Birmingham International Council For Overseas Students' Aid for: BICOSA Information Leaflets 1981. Basil Blackwell Publishers Ltd for: *Breaking the Mould? The Birth and Prospects of the Social Democratic Party* by Ian Bradley first Published by Martin Robertson & Co Ltd 1981 © Ian Bradley 1981. *Seeing Green (The Politics of Ecology Explained)* by Jonathon Porritt first published by Basil Blackwell Publisher Ltd 1984 © Jonathon Porritt 1984. Blond & Briggs Ltd for: *Small is Beautiful* by E F Schumacher first published in Great Britain by Blond & Briggs Ltd 1973 © E F Schumacher 1973. The Bodley Head Ltd for: *The Americans (Letters from America 1969-1979)* by Alistair Cooke first published by Bodley Head Ltd 1979 © Alistair Cooke 1979. *Baby and Child Care* by Dr Benjamin Spock published in Great Britain by The Bodley Head Ltd 1955 © Benjamin Spock MD 1945, 1946, 1957, 1968, 1976, 1979. *What's Wrong With The Modern World?* by Michael Shanks first published by The Bodley Head Ltd 1978 © Michael Shanks 1978. *Future Shock* by Alvin Toffler first published in Great Britain by The Bodley Head Ltd 1970 © Alvin Toffler 1970. *Zen and the Art of Motorcycle Maintenance* by Robert M Pirsig first published in Great Britain by The Bodley Head Ltd 1974 © Robert M Pirsig 1974. *Marnie* by Winston Graham first published by the Bodley Head Ltd 1961 © Winston Graham 1961. *You Can Get There From Here* by Shirley MacLaine first published in Great Britain by The Bodley Head Ltd 1975 © Shirley MacLaine 1975. *It's An Odd Thing, But ...* by Paul Jennings first published by Max Reinhardt Ltd 1971 © Paul Jennings 1971. *King of the Castle (Choice and Responsibility in the Modern World)* by Gai Eaton first published by the Bodley Head Ltd 1977 © Gai Eaton 1977. *Revolutionaries in Modern Britain* by Peter Shipley first published by The Bodley Head Ltd 1976 © Peter Shipley 1976. *The Prerogative of the Harlot (Press Barons and Power)* by Hugh Cudlipp first published by The Bodley Head Ltd 1980 © Hugh Cudlipp 1980. *But What About The Children (A Working Parents' Guide to Child Care)* by Judith Hann first published by The Bodley Head Ltd 1976 © Judith Hann 1976. *Learning to Read* by Margaret Meek first published by The Bodley Head Ltd 1982 © Margaret Meek 1982. Bolt & Watson for: *Two is Lonely* by Lynne Reid Banks first published by Chatto & Windus 1974 © Lynne Reid Banks 1974. The British and Foreign Bible Society with William Collins Sons & Co Ltd for: *Good News Bible (with Deuterocanonical Books/Apocrypha)* first published by The British and Foreign Bible Society with William Collins Sons & Co Ltd 1979 © American Bible Society: Old Testament 1976, Deuterocanonical Books/Apocrypha 1979, New Testament 1966, 1971, 1976, © Maps, British and Foreign Bible Society 1976, 1979. The British Council for: *How to Live in Britain (The British Council's Guide for Overseas Students and Visitors)* first published for The British Council 1952 © The British Council 1984. Mrs R Bronowski for: *The Ascent of Man* by J Bronowski published by Book Club Associates by arrangement with The British Broadcasting Corporation 1977 © J Bronowski 1973. Alison Busby for: *The Death of Trees* by Nigel Dudley first published by Pluto Press Ltd 1985 © Nigel Dudley 1985. Tony Buzan for: *Make The Most of your Mind* by Tony Buzan first published by Colt Books Ltd 1977 © Tony Buzan 1977. Campbell Thomson & McLaughlin Ltd for: *Ring of Bright Water* by Gavin Maxwell first published by Longmans Green & Co 1960, published in Penguin Books Ltd 1976 © The Estate of Gavin Maxwell 1960. Jonathan Cape Ltd for: *Manwatching (A Field Guide to Human Behaviour)* by Desmond Morris first published in Great Britain by Jonathan Cape Ltd 1977 © Text, Desmond Morris 1977 © Compilation, Elsevier Publishing Projects SA, Lausanne, and Jonathan Cape Ltd, London 1977. *Tracks* by Robyn Davidson first published by Jonathan Cape Ltd 1980 © Robyn Davidson 1980. *In the Name of Love* by Jill Tweedie first published by Jonathan Cape Ltd 1979 © Jill Tweedie 1979. *The Use of Lateral Thinking* by Edward de Bono first published by Jonathan Cape 1967 © Edward de Bono 1967. *Trout Fishing in America* by Richard Brautigan first published in Great Britain by Jonathan Cape Ltd 1970 © Richard Brautigan 1967. *The Pendulum Years: Britain and the Sixties* by Bernard Levin first published by Jonathan Cape Ltd 1970 © Bernard Levin 1970. *The Summer Before The Dark* by Doris Lessing first published in Great Britain by Jonathan Cape Ltd 1973 © Doris Lessing 1973. *The Boston Strangler* by Gerold Frank first published in Great Britain by Jonathan Cape Ltd 1967 © Gerold Frank 1966. *I'm OK - You're OK* by Thomas A Harris MD first published in Great Britain as The Book of Choice by Jonathan Cape Ltd 1970 © Thomas A Harris MD, 1967, 1968, 1969. *The Vivisector* by Patrick White first published by Jonathan Cape Ltd 1970 © Patrick White 1970. *The Future of Socialism* by Anthony Crosland first published by Jonathan Cape Ltd 1956 © C A R Crosland 1963. *Funeral in Berlin* by Len Deighton first published by Jonathan Cape Ltd 1964 © Len Deighton 1964. *The Naked Civil Servant* by Quentin Crisp first published by Jonathan Cape Ltd 1968 © Quentin Crisp 1968. Chatto & Windus Ltd for: *A Postillion Struck by Lightning* by Dirk Bogarde first published by Chatto & Windus Ltd 1977 © Dirk Bogarde 1977. *Nuns and Soldiers* by Iris Murdoch published by Chatto & Windus Ltd 1980 © Iris Murdoch 1980. *Wounded Knee (An Indian History of the American West)* by Dee Brown published by Chatto & Windus Ltd 1978 © Dee Brown 1970. *The Virgin in the Garden* by A S Byatt published by Chatto & Windus Ltd 1978 © A S Byatt 1978. *A Story Like The Wind* by Laurens van der Post published by Clarke Irwin & Co Ltd in association with The Hogarth Press Ltd 1972 © Laurens van der Post 1972. *Brave New World* by Aldous Huxley published by Chatto & Windus Ltd 1932 © Aldous Huxley and Mrs Laura Huxley 1932, 1960. *The Reivers* By William Faulkner first published by Chatto & Windus Ltd 1962 © William Faulkner 1962. *Cider With Rosie* by Laurie Lee published by The Hogarth Press 1959 © Laurie Lee 1959 *The Tenants* by Bernard Malamud first published in Great Britain by Chatto & Windus Ltd 1972 © Bernard Malamud 1971. *Kinflicks* by Lisa Alther first published in Great Britain by Chatto & Windus Ltd 1976 © Lisa Alther 1975. William Collins Sons & Co Ltd for: *The Companion Guide to London* by David Piper published by William Collins Sons & Co Ltd 1964 © David Piper 1964. *The Bedside Guardian 29* edited by W L Webb published by William Collins & Sons Ltd 1980 © Guardian Newspapers Ltd 1980. *Bear Island* by Alistair MacLean first published by William Collins Sons Co Ltd 1971 © Alistair MacLean 1971. *Inequality in Britain: Freedom, Welfare and the State* By Frank Field first published by Fontana Paperbacks 1981 © Frank Field 1981. *Social Mobility* by Anthony Heath first published by Fontana Paperbacks 1981©Anthony Heath 1981. *Yours Faithfully* by Gerald Priestland first published by Fount Paperbacks 1979 © British Broadcasting Corporation 1977, 1978. *Power Without Responsibility: The Press and Broadcasting in Britain* by James Curran and Jean Seaton first published by Fontana Paperbacks 1981 © James Curran and Jean Seaton 1981. *The Times Cookery Book* by Katie Stewart first published by William Collins Sons & Co Ltd 1972 © Times Newspapers Ltd. *Friends from the Forest* by Joy Adamson by Collins and Harvill Press 1981 © Elsa Limited 1981. *The Media Mob* by Barry Fantoni and George Melly first published by William Collins Sons & Co Ltd 1980 © Text, George Melly 1980 © Illustrations, Barry Fantoni 1980. *Shalom (a collection of Australian and Jewish Stories)* compiled by Nancy Keesing first published by William Collins Publishers Pty Ltd 1978© William Collins Sons &Co Ltd 1978. *The Bedside Guardian 31* edited by W L Webb first published by William Collins Sons & Co Ltd 1982 © Guardian Newspapers Ltd 1982. *The Bedside Guardian 32* edited by W L Webb first published by William Collins Sons & Co Ltd 1983 © Guardian Newspapers Ltd 1983. *Design for the Real World* by Victor Papanek first published in Great Britain by Thames & Hudson Ltd 1972 © Victor Papanek 1971. *Food For Free* by Richard Mabey first published by William Collins Sons & Co Ltd 1972 © Richard Mabey 1972. *Unended Quest* by Karl Popper (first published as Autobiography of Karl Popper in The Philosophy of Karl Popper in The Library of Philosophers edited by Paul Arthur Schlipp by the Open Court Publishing Co 1974) published by Fontana Paperbacks 1976 © The Library of Living Philosophers Inc 1974 © Karl R Popper 1976. *My Mother My Self* by Nancy Friday first published in Great Britain by Fontana Paperbacks 1979 © Nancy Friday 1977. *The Captain's Diary* by Bob Willis first published by Willow Books/William Collins Sons & Co Ltd 1984 © Bob Willis and Alan Lee 1984 © New Zealand Scorecards, Bill Frindall 1984. *The Bodywork Book by Esme Newton-Dunn* first published in Great Britain by Willow Books/William Collins Sons & Co Ltd 1982 © TVS Ltd/Esme Newton-Dunn 1982. *Collins' Encyclopaedia of Fishing in The British Isles* edited by Michael Prichard first published by William Collins Sons & Co Ltd 1976 © William Collins Sons & Co Ltd 1976. *The AAA Runner's Guide* edited by Heather Thomas first published by William Collins Sons & Co Ltd 1983 © Sackville Design Group Ltd 1983. *Heroes and Contemporaries* by David Gower with Derek Hodgson first published by William Collins Sons & Co Ltd 1983 © David Gower Promotions Ltd 1983. *The Berlin Memorandum* by Adam Hall first published by William Collins Sons & Co Ltd 1965 © Jonquil Trevor 1965. *Arlott on Cricket: His Writings on the Game* edited by David Rayvern Allen first published by William Collins (Willow Books) 1984 © John Arlott 1984. *A Woman in Custody* by Audrey Peckham first published by Fontana Paperbacks 1985 © Audrey Peckham 1985. *Play Golf with Peter Alliss* by Peter Alliss published by the British Broadcasting Corporation 1977 © Peter Alliss and Renton Laidlaw 1977. Curtis Brown Ltd for: *The Pearl* by John Steinbeck first published by William Heinemann Ltd 1948 © John Steinbeck 1948. *An Unfinished History of the World* by Hugh Thomas first published in Great Britain by Hamish Hamilton Ltd 1979 © Hugh Thomas 1979, 1981. *The Winter of our Discontent* by John Steinbeck first published in Great Britain by William Heinemann Ltd 1961 © John Steinbeck 1961. *Burr* by Gore Vidal first published in Great Britain by William Heinemann Ltd 1974 © Gore Vidal 1974. *Doctor on the Job* by Richard Gordon first published by William Heinemann Ltd 1976 © Richard Gordon Ltd 1976. Andre Deutsch Ltd for: *How to be an Alien* by George Mikes first published by Andre Deutsch Ltd 1946 © George Mikes and Nicholas Bentley 1946. *Jaws* by Peter Benchley first published in Great Britain by Andre Deutsch Ltd 1974 © Peter Benchley 1974. *A Bend in the River* by V S Naipaul first published by Andre Deutsch Ltd 1979 © V S Naipaul 1979. *Couples* by John Updike first published by Andre Deutsch Ltd 1968 © John Updike 1968. *Games People Play* by Eric Berne published in Great Britain by Andre Deutsch Ltd 1966 © Eric Berne 1964. *The Age of Uncertainty* by John Kenneth Galbraith first published by The British Broadcasting Corporation and Andre Deutsche Ltd 1977 © John Kenneth Galbraith 1977. The Economist Newspaper Ltd for: *The Economist* (9-15 May 1981 and 22-28 August 1981) © published by The Economist Newspaper Ltd 1981. Faber And Faber Ltd for: *Lord of the Flies* by William Golding first published by Faber & Faber Ltd 1954 © William Golding 1954. *The Complete Book of Self-Sufficiency* by John Seymour first published in Great Britain by Faber & Faber Ltd 1976 © Text, John Seymour 1976, 1977 © Dorling Kindersley Ltd 1976, 1977. *Conversations with Igor Stravinsky* by Igor Stravinsky and Robert Craft first published by Faber & Faber Ltd 1959 © Igor Stravinsky 1958,1959. John Farquharson Ltd for: *The Moon's A Balloon* by David Niven published in Great Britain by Hamish Hamilton Ltd 1971 © David Niven 1971. John Gaselee for: 'Going it Alone' by John Gaselee in the *Illustrated London News* July 1981 and 'The Other Car's Fault' by John Gaselee in the *Illustrated London News* August 1981. Glidrose Publications Ltd for: *The Man with the Golden Gun* by Ian Fleming first published by Jonathan Cape Ltd © Glidrose Productions Ltd 1965. Victor Gollancz Ltd for: *The Next Horizon* by Chris Bonnington published by Victor Gollancz Ltd 1976 © Chris Bonnington 1973. *Summerhill: A Radical Approach to Education* by A S Neill first published by Victor Gollancz Ltd 1962 © A S Neill 1926 1932, 1937, 1953, 1961 (US permission by Hart Publishing Inc). *Lucky Jim* by Kingsley Amis first published by Victor Gollancz Ltd 1954 © Kingsley Amis 1953. *The Mighty Micro (The Impact of the*

Computer Revolution) by Christopher Evans first published by Victor Gollancz Ltd 1979 © Christopher Evans 1979. *The Longest Day* by Cornelius Ryan published by Victor Gollancz Ltd 1960 © Cornelius Ryan 1959. *Asking for Trouble (Autobiography of a Banned Journalist)* by Donald Woods published by Victor Gollancz Ltd 1980 © Donald Woods 1980. *The Turin Shroud* by Ian Wilson first published in Great Britain by Victor Gollancz Ltd 1978 © Ian Wilson 1978. *Murdo and Other Stories* by Iain Crichton Smith published by Victor Gollancz Ltd 1981 © Iain Crichton Smith 1981. *The Class Struggle in Parliament* by Eric S Heffer published by Victor Gollancz Ltd 1973 © Eric S Heffer 1973. *A Presumption of Innocence (The Amazing Case of Patrick Meehan)* by Lodovic Kennedy published by Victor Gollancz Ltd 1976 © Ludovic Kennedy 1976. *The Treasure of Sainte Foy* by MacDonald Harris published by Victor Gollancz Ltd 1980 © MacDonald Harris 1980. *A Long Way to Shiloh* by Lionel Davidson first published by Victor Gollancz Ltd 1966 © Lionel Davidson 1966. *Education After School* by Tyrrell Burgess first published by Victor Gollancz Ltd 1977 © Tyrrell Burgess 1977. *The View From Serendip* by Arthur C Clarke published by Victor Gollancz Ltd 1978 © Arthur C Clarke 1967, 1968, 1970, 1972, 1974, 1976, 1977. *On Wings of Song* by Thomas M Disch published by Victor Gollancz Ltd 1979 © Thomas M Disch 1979. *The World of Violence* by Colin Wilson published by Victor Gollancz Ltd 1963 © Colin Wilson 1963. *The Lightning Tree* by Joan Aiken published by Victor Gollancz Ltd 1980 © Joan Aiken Enterprises 1980. *Russia's Political Hospitals* by Sidney Bloch and Peter Reddaway published by Victor Gollancz Ltd 1977 © Sidney Bloch and Peter Reddaway 1977. *Unholy Loves* by Joyce Carol Oates first published in Great Britain by Victor Gollancz Ltd 1980 © Joyce Carol Oates 1979. *Consenting Adults (or The Duchess will be Furious)* by Peter De Vries published by Victor Gollancz Ltd 1981 © Peter De Vries 1980. *The Passion of New Eve* by Angela Carter published by Victor Gollancz Ltd 1977 © Angela Carter 1977. Gower Publishing Co Ltd for: *Solar Prospects (The Potential for Renewable Energy)* by Michael Flood first published in Great Britain by Wildwood House Ltd in association with Friends of the Earth Ltd 1983 © Michael Flood. *Voiceless Victims* by Rebecca Hall first published in Great Britain by Wildwood House Ltd 1984 © Rebecca Hall 1984. Graham Greene and Laurence Pollinger Ltd for: *The Human Factor* by Graham Greene first published by The Bodley Head Ltd 1978 © Graham Greene 1978. Syndication Manager, The Guardian, for: *The Guardian* (12 May 1981, 7 September 1981 and 15 September 1981) © published by Guardian Newspapers Ltd 1981. Hamlyn for: *How to Play Rugby* by David Norrie published by The Hamlyn Publishing Group Ltd 1981 © The Hamlyn Publishing Group Ltd 1981. *How to Play Badminton* by Pat Davies first published by The Hamlyn Publishing Group Ltd 1979 © The Hamlyn Publishing Group Ltd 1979. Margaret Hanbury for: *Crisis and Conservation: Conflict in the British Countryside* by Charlie Pye-Smith and Chris Rose first published by Pelican/Penguin Books Ltd 1984 © Charlie Pye-Smith and Chris Rose 1984. Paul Harrison for: *Inside the Third World* by Paul Harrison first published in Great Britain by The Harvester Press Ltd 1980 © Paul Harrison 1979.A M Heath & Co Ltd for: *Rembrandt's Hat* by Bernard Malamud published by Chatto & Windus Ltd 1982 © Bernard Malamud 1968, 1972, 1973. William Heinemann Ltd for: *It's an Old Country* by J B Priestley first published in Great Britain by William Heinemann Ltd 1967 © J B Priestley 1967. Heinemann Educational Books Ltd for: *The Environmental Crisis (A Handbook for all Friends of the Earth)* edited by Des Wilson first published by Heinemann Educational Books Ltd 1984 © Foreword, David Bellamy 1984 © Individual Chapters, the Author of the Chapter 1984 © In the selection and all other matter Des Wilson 1984. The Controller, Her Majesty's Stationery Office, for: Department of Health and Social Security leaflets published by Her Majesty's Stationery Office 1981 © The Crown. David Higham Associates Ltd for: 'Two Peruvian Projects' by E R Chamberlain in the *Illustrated London News* September 1981. *Akenfield: Portrait of an English Village* by Ronald Blythe first published by Allen Lane, Penguin Books Ltd 1969 © Ronald Blythe1969. *The Far Pavillions* by M M Kaye first published by Allen Lane/Penguin Books Ltd 1978 © M M Kaye 1978. *Staying On* by Paul Scott first published by William Heinemann Ltd 1977 © Paul Scott 1977. *Let Sleeping Vets Lie* by James Herriot first published by Michael Joseph Ltd 1973 © James Herriot 1973. *The Midwich Cuckoos* by John Wyndham first published in Great Britain by Michael Joseph Ltd 1957 © The Estate of John Wyndham 1957. DR K B Hindley for: 'Hot Spots of the Deep' by Dr K B Hindley in the *Illustrated London News July* 1981. Hodder and Stoughton Ltd for: *Supernature* by Lyall Watson first published by Hodder & Stoughton Ltd 1973 © Lyall Watson 1973. *Tinker Tailor Soldier Spy* by John Le Carre first published by Hodder & Stoughton Ltd 1974 © Le Carre Productions 1974. The Editor, Homes and Gardens, for: *Homes and Gardens* (October 1981) (Number 4 Volume 63) © published by IPC Magazines Ltd 1981. Hughes Massie Ltd for: *Elephants Can Remember* by Agatha Christie first published by William Collins Sons & Co Ltd 1972 © Agatha Christie Mallowan. Hutchinson Publishing Group Ltd for: *An Autobiography* by Angela Davis published in Great Britain by Hutchinson & Co Publishers Ltd by arrangement with Bantam Books Inc 1975 © Angela Davis 1974. *The Day of the Jackal* by Frederick Forsyth published in Great Britian by Hutchinson & Co Publishers Ltd 1971 © Frederick Forsyth 1971. *Roots* by Alex Haley first published in Great Britain by Hutchinson & Co Publishers Ltd 1977 © Alex Haley 1976. *The Climate of Treason* by Andrew Boyle first published by Hutchinson & Co Publishers Ltd 1979 © Andrew Boyle 1979. *The Collapsing Universe: The Story of Black Holes* by Isaac Asimov first published by Hutchinson & Co Publishers Ltd 1977 © Isaac Asimov. *XPD* by Len Deighton published by Book Club Associates by arrangement with Hutchinson & Co Publishers Ltd 1981 © Len Deighton 1981. *Show Jumping with Harvey Smith* by Harvey Smith first published by Stanley Paul & Co Ltd 1979 © Tyne-Tees Television Ltd, A Member of the Trident Group 1979. *2001: A Space Odyssey by* Arthur C Clarke first published by Hutchinson & Co Publishers Ltd 1968 © Arthur C Clarke and Polaris Productions Inc 1968 © Epilogue material, Serendip BV 1982, 1983. The Illustrated London News and Sketch Ltd for: *The Illustrated London News* (July 1981, August 1981 and September 1981) © published by the Illustrated London News and Sketch Ltd 1981. The Editor, International Herald Tribune, for: *International Herald Tribune* (25-26 July 1981) © published by International Herald Tribune with The New York Times and The Washington Post 1981. Michael Joseph Ltd for: *Chronicles of Fairacre: Village School* by Miss Read first published in Great Britain by Michael Joseph Ltd 1964 © Miss Read 1955, 1964. *Fire Fox* by Craig Thomas first published in Great Britain by Michael Joseph Ltd 1977 © Craig Thomas 1977. William Kimber & Co Ltd for: *Exodus* by Leon Uris originally published in Great Britain by Alan Wingate Ltd 1959 © Leon Uris 1958. Kogan Page Ltd for: *How to Save the World (Strategy for World Conservation)* by Robert Allen first published by Kogan Page Ltd 1980 © IUCN-UNEP-WWF 1980. Marketing Department, Lloyds Bank PLC, for: *Lloyds Bank Leaflets* (1981) © published by Lloyds Bank PLC 1981. Macmillan Publishers Ltd for: *Appropriate Technology: Technology with a Human Face* by P D Dunn first published by the Macmillan Press Ltd 1978 © P D Dunn 1978. John Murray Publishers Ltd for: *A Backward Place* by Ruth Prawer Jhabvala first published by John Murray Publishers Ltd 1965 © R Prawer Jhabvala 1965. *Food For All The Family* by Magnus Pyke first published by John Murray Publishers Ltd 1980 © Magnus Pyke 1980. *Simple Movement* by Laura Mitchell and Barbara Dale first published by John Murray Publishers Ltd 1980 © Laura Mitchell and Barbara Dale 1980. *Civilisation: A Personal View* by Kenneth Clark first published by the British Broadcasting Corporation and John Murray Publishers Ltd 1969 © Kenneth Clark 1969. The Editor, National Geographic, for: *National Geographic* January, February and March (1980) © published by The National Geographic Society 1979, 1980. The National Magazine Co Ltd for: *Cosmopolitan* (May 1981 and July 1981) © published by the National Magazine Co Ltd 1981. Neilson Leisure Group Ltd for: *NAT Holidays' 'Caravans and Tents in the Sun'* (Summer 1983) holiday brochure. Newsweek Inc for: *Newsweek* (11 May 1981, 27 July 1981 and August 1981) © published by Newsweek Inc 1981. The Associate Editor, Now!, for: *Now!* (14-20 November 1980) © published by Cavenham Communications Ltd 1980. Harold Ober Associates Inc for: *The Boys from Brazil* by Ira Levin first published by Michael Joseph Ltd 1976 © Ira Levin 1976. Edna O'Brien and A M Heath & Co Ltd for: *August is a Wicked Month* by Edna O'Brien first published by Jonathan Cape Ltd 1965 © Edna O'Brien 1965. Pan Books Ltd for: *Dispatches* by Michael Herr first published in Great Britain by Pan Books Ltd 1978 © Michael Herr 1968, 1968, 1970, 1977. *Health and Safety at Work* by Dave Eva and Ron Oswald first published by Pan Books Ltd 1981 © Dave Eva, Ron Oswald and the Workers' Educational Association 1981. *Democracy at Work* by Patrick Burns and Mel Doyle first published by Pan Books Ltd 1981 © Patrick Burns,Mel Doyle and the Workers' Educational Association 1981. *Diet for Life (A Cookbook for Arthritics)* by Mary Laver and Margaret Smith first published by Pan Books Ltd 1981 © Mary Laver and Margaret Smith 1981. Penguin Books Ltd for: *Inside the Company: CIA Diary* by Philip Agee first published in Allen Lane/Penguin Books Ltd 1975 © Philip Agee 1975. *The Girl in a Swing* by Richard Adams first published in Great Britain by Allen Lane in Penguin Books Ltd 1980 © Richard Adams 1980. Penguin Books Ltd and Spare Ribs Ltd for: *Spare Rib Reader* edited by Marsha Rowe first published in Penguin Books Ltd 1982 © Spare Ribs Ltd 1982. A D Peters & Co Ltd for: 'The Dark Side of Israel' by Norman Moss in Illustrated London News July 1981, 'Aftermath of Osirak' by Norman Moss in the *Illustrated London News* August 1981 and 'Turning Point for Poland' by Norman Moss in the *Illustrated London News* September 1981. 'Recent Fiction' by Sally Emerson in the *Illustrated London News* July 1981, August 1981 and September 1981. *The Complete Upmanship* by Stephen Potter first published in Great Britain by Rupert Hart-Davis Ltd 1970 © Stephen Potter. Elaine Pollard for: Personal Letters 1981 donated by Elaine Pollard. Laurence Pollinger Ltd for: *A Glastonbury Romance* by John Cowper Powys first published by MacDonald & Co Ltd 1933. Murray Pollinger for: *Kiss Kiss* by Roald Dahl published in Great Britain by Michael Joseph Ltd 1960 © Roald Dahl 1962. *Can You Avoid Cancer?* by Peter Goodwin first published by the British Broadcasting Corporation 1984 © Peter Goodwin 1984. Preston Travel Ltd for: Preston Sunroutes 'Camping and Self-Catering' (April to October 1983) holiday brochure. Punch Publications Ltd for: *Punch* (6 May 1981, 29 July 1981, 12 August 1981, 26 August 1981 and 9 September 1981) © published by Punch Publications Ltd 1981. The Rainbird Publishing Group Ltd for: *The Making of Mankind* by Richard E Leakey first published in Great Britain by Michael Joseph Ltd 1981 © Sherma BV 1981. Robson Books Ltd for: *The Punch Book of Short Stories 3* selected by Alan Coren first published in Great Britain by Robson Books Ltd in association with Punch Publications Ltd 1981 © Robson Books Ltd 1981.*The Best of Robert Morley* by Robert Morley first published in Great Britain by Robson Books Ltd 1981 © Robert Morley 1981. Deborah Rogers Ltd for: 'Picasso's Late Works' by Edward Lucie-Smith in the *Illustrated London News* July 1981, 'David Jones at the Tate' by Edward Lucie-Smith in the *Illustrated London News* August 1981 and 'Further Light on Spanish Painting' by Edward Lucie-Smith in the *Illustrated London News* September 1981. *The Godfather* by Mario Puzo first published in Great Britain by William Heinemann Ltd 1969 © Mario Puzo 1969. Routledge & Kegan Paul Ltd for: *How To Pass Examinations* by John Erasmus first published by Oriel Press Ltd 1967 © Oriel Press Ltd 1980. *Daisy, Daisy* by Christian Miller first published by Routledge & Kegan Paul Ltd 1980 © Christian Miller 1980. *The National Front* by Nigel Fielding first published by Routledge & Kegan Paul Ltd 1981 © Nigel Fielding 1981. *The Myth of Home Ownership* by Jim Kemeny first published by Routledge & Kegan Paul Ltd 1980 © J Kemeny 1981. *Absent With Cause (Lessons of Truancy)* by Roger White first published by Routledge & Kegan Paul Ltd 1980 © Roger White 1980. *The Powers of Evil (in Western Religion, Magic and Folk Belief)* by Richard Cavendish first published by Routledge & Kegan Paul Ltd 1975 © Richard Cavendish 1975. *Crime and Personality* by H J Eysenck first published by Routledge & Kegan Paul Ltd 1964 © H J Eysenck 1964, 1977. Martin Secker & Warburg Ltd for: *Changing Places* by David Lodge first published in England by Martin Secker & Warburg Ltd 1975 © David Lodge 1975. *The History Man* by Malcolm Bradbury first published by Martin Secker & Warburg 1975 © Malcolm Bradbury 1975. *Humboldt's Gift* by Saul Bellow first published in England by The Alison Press/Martin Secker & Warburg Ltd 1975 © Saul Bellow 1973, 1974, 1975. *Wilt* by Tom Sharpe first published in England by Martin Secker & Warburg Ltd 1976 © Tom Sharpe 1976. *The Last Days of America* by Paul E Erdman first published in England by Martin Secker & Warburg Ltd 1981 © Paul E Erdman

1981. *Autumn Manoeuvres* by Melvyn Bragg first published in England by Martin Secker & Warburg Ltd 1978 © Melvyn Bragg 1978. *The Act of Being* by Charles Marowitz first published in England by Martin Secker & Warburg Ltd 1978 © Charles Marowitz 1978. *As If By Magic* by Angus Wilson first published in England by Martin Secker & Warburg Ltd 1973 © Angus Wilson 1973. *All the President's Men* by Carl Bernstein and Bob Woodward first published in England by Martin Secker & Warburg Ltd 1974 © Carl Bernstein and Bob Woodward 1974. *The Myth of the Nation and the Vision of Revolution by J L Talmon* first published by Martin Secker & Warburg Ltd 1981 © J L Talmon 1980. *Animal Farm* by George Orwell first published by Martin Secker & Warburg 1945 © Eric Blair 1945. Anthony Sheil Associates Ltd for: *Daniel Martin* by John Fowles first published in Great Britain by Jonathan Cape Ltd 1977 © J R Fowles Ltd 1977. *Love Story* by Erich Segal published by Hodder & Stoughton Ltd 1970 © Erich Segal 1970. Sidgwick & Jackson Ltd for: *The Third World War* by General Sir John Hackett and others first published in Great Britain by Sidgwick & Jackson Ltd 1978 © General Sir John Hackett 1978. *Superwoman* by Shirley Conran first published by Sidgwick & Jackson Ltd 1975 © Shirley Conran 1975, 1977. *An Actor and His Time* by John Gielgud first published in Great Britain by Sidgwick & Jackson Ltd 1979 © John Gielgud, John Miller and John Powell 1979 © Biographical Notes, John Miller 1979. Simon & Schuster for: *Our Bodies Ourselves (A Health Book by and for Women)* by the Boston Women's Health Book Collective (British Edition by Angela Phillips and Jill Rakusen) published in Allen Lane and Penguin Books Ltd 1978 © The Boston Women's Health Collective Inc 1971, 1973, 1976 © Material for British Edition, Angela Phillips and Jill Rakusen 1978. Souvenir Press Ltd for: *The Bermuda Triangle* by Charles Berlitz (An Incredible Saga of Unexplained Disappearances) first published in Great Britain by Souvenir Press Ltd 1975 © Charles Berlitz 1974. Souvenir Press Ltd and Michael Joseph Ltd for: *Airport* by Arthur Hailey first published in Great Britain by Michael Joseph Ltd in association with Souvenir Press Ltd 1968 © Arthur Hailey Ltd 1968. Sunmed Holidays Ltd for: 'Go Greek' (Summer 1983) holiday brochure. Maurice Temple Smith Ltd for: *Friends of the Earth Pollution Guide* by Brian Price published by Maurice Temple Smith Ltd 1983 © Brian Price 1983. *Working the Land (A New Plan for a Healthy Agriculture)* by Charlie Pye-Smith and Richard North first published by Maurice Temple Smith Ltd 1984© Charlie Pye-Smith and Richard North 1984. Times Newspapers Ltd for: *The Sunday Times Magazine* (13 January 1980, 20 January 1980 and 11 May 1980) © published by Times Newspapers Ltd 1981. *The Times* (7 September 1981) © published by Times Newspapers Ltd 1981. Twenty's Holidays for: 'The Best 18-33 Holidays' (Winter 1982/83) holiday brochure. University of Birmingham for: Living in Birmingham (1984) © published by The University of Birmingham 1984. Birmingham University Overseas Student Guide © The University of Birmingham. Working with Industry and Commerce © published by The University of Birmingham 1984. University of Birmingham Prospectus (June 1985) © published by The University of Birmingham 1985. University of Birmingham Library Guide © published by The University of Birmingham. University of Birmingham Institute of Research and Development (1984) © published by the University of Birmingham 1984. Biological Sciences at The University of Birmingham (1985) © published by The University of Birmingham 1985. History at the University of Birmingham (1985) © published by the University of Birmingham 1985. Faculty of Arts Handbook (1984-85) © published by The University of Birmingham 1984. Virago Press Ltd for: *Benefits* by Zoe Fairbairns published by Virago Press Ltd 1979 © Zoe Fairbairns 1979. *Simple Steps to Public Life* by Pamela Anderson, Mary Stott and Fay Weldon published in Great Britain by Virago Press Ltd 1980 © Action Opportunities 1980. *Tell Me A Riddle* by Tillie Olsen published by Virago Press Ltd 1980 © this edition Tillie Olsen 1980. A P Watt (& Sons) Ltd for: *The Glittering Prizes* by Frederic Raphael first published in Great Britain by Penguin Books Ltd 1976 © Volatic Ltd 1976. *Then and Now* by W Somerset Maugham first published by William Heinemann Ltd 1946 © W Somerset Maugham 1946. *The Language of Clothes* by Alison Lurie published by William Heinemann Ltd 1981 © Alison Lurie 1981. 'Herschel Commemorative' by Patrick Moore in the *Illustrated London News* July 1981. 'The Outermost Giant' by Patrick Moore in the *Illustrated London News* August 1981. 'Cosmic Bombardment' by Patrick Moore in the *Illustrated London News* September 1981. Weidenfeld & Nicolson Ltd for: 'The Miraculous Toy' by Susan Briggs in the *Illustrated London News* August 1981. *The Needle's Eye* by Margaret Drabble first published by Weidenfeld & Nicolson Ltd 1972 © Margaret Drabble 1972. *Success Without Tears: A Woman's Guide to the Top* by Rachel Nelson first published in Great Britain by Weidenfeld & Nicolson Ltd 1979 © Rachel Nelson 1979. *Education in the Modern World* by John Vaizey published by Weidenfeld & Nicolson Ltd 1967 © John Vaizey 1967. *Rich Man, Poor Man* by Irwin Shaw first published in Great Britain by Weidenfield & Nicolson Ltd 1970 © Irwin Shaw 1969,1970. *Lolita* by Vladimir Nabokov first published in Great Britain by Weidenfeld & Nicolson Ltd 1959 © Vladimir Nabokov 1955, 1959, 1968, © G P Putnam's Sons 1963 © McGraw-Hill International Inc 1971. *The Third World* by Peter Worsley first published by Weidenfeld & Nicolson Ltd 1964 © Peter Worsley 1964, 1967. *Portrait of a Marriage* by Nigel Nicolson published by Weidenfeld & Nicolson Ltd 1973 © Nigel Nicolson 1973. *The Dogs Bark: Public People and Private Places* by Truman Capote first published in Great Britain by Weidenfeld & Nicolson Ltd 1974 © Truman Capote 1974. *Great Planning Disasters* by Peter Hall first published in Great Britain by George Weidenfeld & Nicolson Ltd 1980 © Peter Hall 1980. The Writers and Readers Publishing Co-operative Ltd for: *Working with Words, Literacy Beyond School* by Jane Mace published by The Writers and Readers Publishing Co-operative Ltd 1979 © Jane Mace 1979. *The Alienated: Growing Old Today* by Gladys Elder OAP published by The Writers and Readers Publishing Co-operative Ltd 1977 © Text, The Estate of Gladys Elder 1977 © Photographs, Mike Abrahams 1977. *Beyond the Crisis in Art* by Peter Fuller published by The Writers and Readers Publishing Co-operative Ltd 1980 © Peter Fuller 1980. *The War and Peace Book* by Dave Noble published by The Writers and Readers Publishing Co-Operative Ltd 1977 © Dave Noble 1977. *Tony Benn: A Political Biography* by Robert Jenkins first published by The Writers and Readers Publishing Co-operative Ltd 1980 © Robert Jenkins 1980. *Nuclear Power for Beginners* by Stephen Croall and Kaianders Sempler first published by The Writers and Readers Publishing Co-operative Ltd 1978 © Text, Stephen Croall 1978,1980 © Illustrations Kaianders Sempler 1978, 1980. Yale University Press for: *Life in the English Country House: A Social and Architectural History* by Mark Girouard published by Yale University Press Ltd, London 1978 © Yale University 1978. The British Broadcasting Corporation for transcripts of radio transmissions of 'Kaleidoscope', 'Any Questions', 'Money Box' and 'Arts and Africa' 1981 and 1982. The British Broadcasting Corporation and Mrs Shirley Williams for transcripts of television interviews with Mrs Shirley Williams 1979. Dr B L Smith, School of Mathematics and Physical Sciences, University of Sussex for programmes on Current Affairs, Science and The Arts originally broadcast on Radio Sussex 1979 and 1980 © B L Smith. The following people in the University of Birmingham: Professor J McH Sinclair, Department of English, for his tapes of informal conversation (personal collection). Mr R Wallace, formerly Department of Accounting and Finance, and Ms D Houghton, Department of English, for transcripts of his accountancy lectures. Dr B K Gazey, Department of Electrical Engineering and Mr T Johns, Department of English, for a transcript of Dr Gazey's lecture. Dr L W Poel, Department of Plant Biology, and Mr T Dudley-Evans, Department of English, for a transcript of Dr Poel's lecture. Professor J G Hawkes, formerly Department of Plant Biology, for recordings of his lectures. Dr M S Snaith, Department of Transportation for recordings of his lectures. Dr M P Hoey, Department of English, and Dr M Cooper, The British Council, for a recording of their discussion on discourse analysis. Ms A Renouf, Department of English, for recordings of job and academic interviews 1977. Mr R H Hubbard, formerly a B Phil (Ed) student, Faculty of Education, for his research recordings of expressions of uncertainty 1978-79. Mr A E Hare, formerly a B Phil (Ed) student, Faculty of Education, for his transcripts of telephone conversations 1978. Dr A Tsui, formerly Department of English, for her recordings of informal conversation. Mr J Couperthwaite, formerly Department of English, for a recording of informal conversation 1981. Ms C Emmott, M Litt student, Department of English, for a recording of informal conversation 1981. Mrs B T Atkins for the transcript of an account of a dream 1981. The British Council for 'Authentic Materials Numbers 1-28' 1981. Professor M Hammerton and Mr K Coghill, Department of Psychology, University of Newcastle-upon-Tyne, for tape recordings of their lectures 1981. Mr G P Graveson, formerly research student, University of Newcastle, for his recordings of teacher discussion 1977. Mr W R Jones, formerly research student, University of Southampton, for his recordings of classroom talk. Mr Ian Fisher, formerly BA student, Newcastle Polytechnic, for his transcripts of interviews on local history 1981. Dr N Coupland, formerly PhD student, Department of English, UWIST, for his transcripts of travel agency talk 1981. Professor D B Bromley, Department of Psychology, University of Liverpool, for his transcript of a research recording. Mr Brian Lawrence, formerly of Saffron Walden County High School, for a tape of his talk on 'The British Education System' 1979.

Every effort has been made to trace the copyright holders, but if any have been inadvertently overlooked the publishers will be pleased to make the necessary acknowledgments at the first opportunity.

We would also like to thank Mr S Strategakis and Mr S Georgiades of the Strategakis Schools of Languages in Northern Greece for cooperation in allowing research in their schools into the use of dictionaries by learners.

Aa

A, a /eɪ/, **A's, a's**. **1** A is the first letter of the English alphabet. N COUNT

2 From A to Z means including everything or including a very large number of things. EG *You have to have everything from A to Z.* PHR : USED AS AN A

3 From A to B means from one place to another. EG *I just want a car that takes me from A to B.* PHR : USED AS AN A

4 A, in music, is the sixth note in the scale of C major. N COUNT/UNCOUNT

5 If you get an **A** as a mark for a piece of work or in an exam, your work is considered to be extremely good. EG *She got three A's this week.* N COUNT/UNCOUNT

6 A or **a** is also an abbreviation for various words beginning with A or a, such as 'acceleration', 'ampere', 'answer', and 'at'.

> **A** □ In this dictionary A is used in the grammar notes beside entries to mean 'adjunct'. It is used in descriptions of verbs and descriptions of expressions. **1** It is used in descriptions of intransitive (V) and transitive (V+O) verbs that need to be followed by an adjunct. See □ at V+A and V+O+A. An example of a V+A is **behave**; an example of a V+O+A is **put**. EG *He behaved **in a very strange way**... They behaved **disgracefully**... I put the book **down**... He put the paper **in his pocket.*** **2** It is used in descriptions of expressions which function as an adjunct, see □ at PHR. Examples of PHR: USED AS AN A are **full blast** (see **blast 7.1**) and **of** your **own accord** (see **accord 2**). EG *A radio was going **full blast**... Mrs Taswell might tell you **of** her **own accord**... I left **of** my **own accord**.*

a, an. A or **an** is the indefinite article. It is used at the beginning of noun groups which refer to only one thing or person. The form **a** is usually pronounced /ə/, but it is pronounced /eɪ/ when you are emphasizing it. The form **an** is used in front of words that begin with vowel sounds. It is usually pronounced /ən/, but it is pronounced /æn/ when you are emphasizing it. **1** You use **a** or **an** at the beginning of noun groups for several reasons, for example when you are referring to someone or something by saying which particular class of people or things they belong to, when you do not want or need to say which particular person or thing you mean, or when you have not mentioned the person or thing before. Compare **the**. EG *The windows were open and Tom could see a hallway... The examination confirmed that the weapon was an airgun... She wanted to be an actress... You should be able to get a job in Europe... He put a foot up on the rim of the tub... ...a chap called Andrew.* DET+N COUNT IN SING

2 You can use **a** or **an** instead of the number 'one'. It is often used in front of the numbers 'hundred', 'thousand', 'million', and 'billion', and in front of fractions such as 'quarter' and 'half'. EG *...a million and a half dollars... ...a year or two ago... There were no officers on the patrol, just a corporal and six other guys.* DET+NUM, OR DET+N COUNT IN SING ▸ used after fractions such as 'half', 'quarter', 'third', etc, and in front of the noun to which the fraction refers. EG *...half a dozen... ...in less than one tenth of a second... ...three-quarters of a loaf of bread.* ▸ DET+N COUNT IN SING

3 When you express rates, ratios, prices, and measurements, you can use **a** or **an** to say how many units apply to each of the items being measured, charged, etc. EG *He charges 100 dollars an hour... ...once a year... ...five pounds a metre.* DET+N COUNT IN SING = per

4 You use **a** or **an** at the beginning of noun groups when you are saying something that applies to all members of the class, group, or type that is described by the noun group. Another way of making statements of this type is to use the plural, so that you can say 'a student has to work hard' or 'students have to work hard'. EG *An ostrich cannot fly... A cyclist has to pay when he goes over the ferry.* DET+N COUNT IN SING

5 You sometimes use **a** or **an** in spoken English in front of nouns without any adjective in order to indicate that something is fairly long, great, or good in amount, extent, or value. For example, 'It rained for a time' means that it rained for quite a long time, and 'That's an idea' means that you think that it is quite a good idea. DET+N COUNT IN SING = some

6 You can use **a** or **an** in front of uncount nouns when they are preceded by adjectives or followed by words that describe the uncount noun more fully. EG *...a tremendous earnestness... ...a happiness that he couldn't quite hide... ...a keen appreciation of the power of the media.* DET+N UNCOUNT +SUPP

7 You can use **a** or **an** in front of mass nouns when you are referring to one single portion, type, or brand of something. EG *Shall I pour you a coffee?... ...a fine red wine.* DET+N MASS IN SING

8 You use **a** or **an** in front of nouns that end with '-ing' and are formed from verbs when you refer to one instance of the activity described by the verb. EG *...a stamping of feet... A falling-off in business was expected.* DET+-ING

9 You use **a** or **an** in front of the names of days, dates, months, or festivals when you are referring to one particular instance of that day, date, month, or festival. EG *It's on a Friday, isn't it?... ...a Christmas that I shall never forget.* DET+N COUNT IN SING

10 You use **a** or **an** in front of the names of people **10.1** when you are referring to someone who you do not know personally or when you do not know anything about them except their name. EG *You don't know a Mrs Burton-Cox, do you?... A Mr Peter Walker agreed to buy the house from a Mrs Dorothy Boyle.* DET+N PROPER = a certain **10.2** when you want to refer to someone else who has the same character or qualities as the person named. EG *There is no way that an Iain Macleod or a Rab Butler would have agreed to such policies.* DET+N PROPER **10.3** when you refer to someone who belongs to the family with that surname. EG *She was a Robertson before she married.* DET+N PROPER

11 You use **a** or **an** in front of the names of painters, sculptors, or writers to refer to one individual painting, sculpture, or piece of writing by them. EG *She noticed a Renoir on the wall and two Matisses... There's a new David Lodge out this month.* DET+N PROPER

a- is added to adjectives to form other adjectives, which mean that someone or something does not have the feature or quality described by the original adjective. EG *...political→apolitical... ...moral→amoral... ...symmetrical→asymmetrical.* PREFIX = non-, un-

AA /eɪ eɪ/. **1** The **AA** is a British motoring organization that helps members when their cars break down; an abbreviation for 'Automobile Association'. N PROPER : *the*+N

2 AA is an organization that helps people who are suffering from alcoholism or who have given up alcoholic drinks for medical reasons; an abbreviation for 'Alcoholics Anonymous'. N PROPER

aback /əbæk/. See **take aback** at **take**.

abacus /æbəkəs/, **abacuses**. An **abacus** is a frame holding rods with sliding beads on them. It is used in some eastern countries for counting and in other countries for teaching children to count. N COUNT ⇑ calculator

abandon /əbændən/, **abandons, abandoning, abandoned**. **1** If you **abandon** something such as a place or object, you leave it permanently or for a long time, especially because you do not want to look after it any longer. EG *You're not supposed to abandon your car on the motorway.* V+O ≠ stay with

2 If you **abandon** someone, especially someone you have responsibility for, you leave them and never go back to them. EG *He then abandoned her and went off to live in Nigeria.* V+O = desert ≠ stay with

3 If you **abandon** something such as a piece of work, plan, or activity, you stop doing it before it is finished. EG *I had abandoned the search.* V+O = give up, quit ≠ continue

4 If you **abandon** an idea or way of thinking, you stop thinking in that way. EG *Reputable scholars have now abandoned the notion... I have abandoned the idea of consistency.* V+O = give up

5 If you **abandon ship**, you get off it because it is sinking. PHR : VB INFLECTS

6 If you **abandon** yourself to an emotion, you feel and think only about that emotion and nothing else. EG *She abandoned herself to grief.* V+O (REFL)+A (*to*) ⇑ release

7 If you do something with **abandon**, you behave in a wild, uncontrolled way and do not think or care N UNCOUNT : USU *with*+N about how you should behave. EG *The surplus food was consumed with joyous abandon.*

abandoned /əbændənd/. 1 An **abandoned** place or building is one that is no longer used or occupied. EG *...an abandoned factory.* — ADJ CLASSIF : USU ATTRIB = deserted, derelict

2 An **abandoned** way of behaving is one that is careless, wild, and unselfconscious. EG *Mr Reed gave an abandoned laugh.* — ADJ CLASSIF : USU ATTRIB = uninhibited

abandonment /əbændənmə[2]nt/. 1 The **abandonment** of a place, person, or thing is the act of leaving them permanently or for a long time. EG *...the abandonment of the farms.* — N UNCOUNT : USU +*of* = desertion

2 The **abandonment** of a piece of work, plan, or activity is the act of stopping doing it, especially before it is finished. EG *She disagreed with the abandonment of the project.* — N UNCOUNT : USU +*of* = shelving

abase /əbeɪs/, **abases, abasing, abased**. If you **abase** yourself, you behave in a way which shows that you accept that something or someone else is much more important than you are. EG *...the crowds in the square, abasing themselves in front of the gleaming glass statue.* — V+O (REFL) ⇑ lower = humble, belittle

abashed /əbæʃt/. If you are **abashed**, you feel embarrassed and ashamed. EG *Sam, abashed by his father's words, said nothing... The students looked guilty and abashed.* — ADJ QUALIT : PRED ≠ unashamed

abate /əbeɪt/, **abates, abating, abated**. When something **abates** or when someone **abates** it, it becomes much less strong or widespread; a fairly formal word. EG *My terror abated a little... The industry should use the best practicable methods to abate pollution.* — V-ERG ⇑ decrease = lessen ≠ increase

abatement /əbeɪtmə[2]nt/ means a reduction in the strength or power of something; a formal word. EG *...the Noise Abatement Society.* — N UNCOUNT

abattoir /æbətwɑː/, **abattoirs**. An **abattoir** is a place where animals are killed for meat. — N COUNT

abbess /æbɪ[2]s/, **abbesses**. An **abbess** is a nun who is in charge of the other nuns in a convent. EG *'When you leave here,' said the Abbess, 'you leave forever.'* — N COUNT : ALSO IN TITLES = mother superior

abbey /æbi[1]/, **abbeys**. An **abbey** is a church with buildings attached to it in which a community of monks or nuns live or used to live. EG *The town is dominated by its huge Benedictine abbey. ...Westminster Abbey.* — N COUNT : ALSO IN NAMES AFTER N ⇑ church = convent, monastery

abbot /æbət/, **abbots**. An **abbot** is a monk who is in charge of the other monks in a monastery or abbey. EG *The monks elected a new abbot.* — N COUNT : ALSO IN TITLES

abbr. or **abbrev.** are abbreviations for 'abbreviation' or 'abbreviated'.

abbreviate /ə[3]briːvieɪt/, **abbreviates, abbreviating, abbreviated**. 1 If you **abbreviate** something, you make it shorter. EG *Don't be afraid to abbreviate, to cut a paragraph here, to shorten one there.* ◊ **abbreviated**. EG *Her lecture was an abbreviated version of a talk she had given the previous year.* — V+O ⇑ shorten = reduce ≠ expand; ◊ ADJ CLASSIF ⇑ shortened = abridged

2 A word or phrase that **is abbreviated** has been made shorter by leaving out some of the letters or by using only the first letters of each word. EG *'Post Office' is often abbreviated to 'PO'.* — V+O ⇑ shorten ≠ lengthen

abbreviation /ə[3]briːvieɪʃə[0]n/, **abbreviations**. An **abbreviation** is a short form of a word or phrase, made by leaving out some of the letters or by using only the first letters of each word. EG *...British Broadcasting Corporation, or BBC to give it the usual abbreviation.* — N COUNT ⇑ shortening = contraction

ABC. 1 The **ABC** of a subject or activity is the parts of it that you have to learn and understand first because they are the most important and basic. EG *...good training grounds in which to learn the ABC of committee work.* — N SING : *the*+N+*of* ⇑ facts = basics

2 Children who have learned their **ABC** have learned to recognize, write, or say the alphabet. EG *She already knows her ABC.* — N SING : DETPOSS +N

abdicate /æbdɪkeɪt/, **abdicates, abdicating, abdicated**. 1 If a king or queen **abdicates**, he or she resigns. EG *...the day Edward VIII abdicated.* ◊ **abdication** /æbdɪkeɪʃə[0]n/, **abdications**. EG *...the abdication crisis of 1936.* — V OR V+O = step down; ◊ N UNCOUNT/COUNT

2 If you **abdicate** your responsibility for something, you refuse to accept the responsibility for it any longer. EG *...we would be abdicating our responsibility to the local community.* ◊ **abdication**. EG *...an abdication of political responsibility.* — V+O = shirk ≠ accept; ◊ N UNCOUNT/COUNT+SUPP

3 If you **abdicate** a right or some power that you have, you choose not to take advantage of it. EG *...abdicating her ability to control her environment.* — V+O

abdomen /æbdəmən, æbdəʊ-/, **abdomens**. The **abdomen** is the part of the body below the chest where the stomach and intestines are. EG *She was admitted to hospital with a pain in her abdomen.* — N COUNT

abdominal /ə[3]bdɒmɪnə[0]l/ is used to describe something that is situated in the abdomen or forms part of it. EG *They suffered abdominal pains.* — ADJ CLASSIF : USU ATTRIB

abduct /ə[3]bdʌkt/, **abducts, abducting, abducted**. If someone **abducts** another person, they take them away, using force. EG *He was afraid of being abducted by a rival gang.* ◊ **abduction** /ə[3]bdʌkʃə[0]n/. EG *...the recent abduction of his son.* — V+O ⇑ take away = kidnap; ◊ N UNCOUNT/COUNT

abed /əbed/. If you are **abed**, you are in bed; an old-fashioned word. — ADJ CLASSIF : PRED

aberrant /ə[3]berənt/ means unusual and not normal. EG *...aberrant behaviour... ...these aberrant ideas.* — ADJ QUALIT : USU ATTRIB

aberration /æbəreɪʃə[0]n/, **aberrations**. An **aberration** is an event, act, or way of behaving that is unusual and not normal. EG *This is a temporary aberration and will soon be put right.* — N COUNT/UNCOUNT ⇑ abnormality

abet /əbet/, **abets, abetting, abetted**. If you **abet** someone, you help or encourage them to do something wrong. EG *Some of them insisted we were aiding and abetting the enemy.* — V+O : NO IMPER ≠ hinder

abeyance /əbeɪəns/. If something is **in abeyance**, it is not operating or being used at the present time. EG *...in temporary abeyance... The title shall be deemed to be in abeyance.* — PHR : USED AS AN A ⇑ inactive

abhor /ə[3]bhɔː/, **abhors, abhorring, abhorred**. If you **abhor** something, you hate it very much, especially for moral reasons. EG *She abhors any form of cruelty.* — V+O : NO IMPER = loathe ≠ love

abhorrence /ə[3]bhɒrəns/. If you have an **abhorrence** of something, you hate it very much. EG *These new measures are regarded with suspicion and abhorrence by the majority of teachers... ...an abhorrence of war.* — N UNCOUNT ⇑ hatred = loathing ≠ love

abhorrent /ə[3]bhɒrənt/. If something is **abhorrent** to you, you consider it completely unacceptable, or you hate it very much. EG *...by methods which were abhorrent to them... ...a ruthless and utterly abhorrent system.* — ADJ QUALIT : USU PRED, IF+PREP THEN *to* ⇑ hateful = detestable

abide /əbaɪd/, **abides, abiding, abided**. 1 If you **can't abide** something, you dislike it very much. EG *Jane said she couldn't abide birds in cages... He likes you but he can't abide Dennis.* — PHR ⇑ hate = can't bear ≠ tolerate

2 If something **abides**, it continues to happen or exist for a long time. EG *We feel the need to lean on something that abides.* ◊ **abiding**. EG *Economic expansion has become the abiding interest of all modern societies.* — V = last, endure; ◊ ADJ CLASSIF : ATTRIB = lasting

3 If you **abide** somewhere, you live there; an old-fashioned word. EG *He would not return home, but would abide in the mountains.* — V+A = remain, bide

abide by. If you **abide by** something such as a law, agreement, or decision, you accept it and behave in accordance with it. EG *Germany and Russia agreed informally to abide by the agreement... Both parties must agree to abide by the court's decision.* — PHRASAL VB : V+PREP, HAS PASS = observe ≠ flout

ability /əbɪlə[1]ti[1]/, **abilities**. 1 Your **ability** to do something is the quality or skill that you have which makes it possible for you to do it. EG *...the ability to see... ...the ability of government to ensure social justice... Is that a fair summary of a computer's abilities?* — N COUNT/UNCOUNT : USU+*to*-INF
● If you do something **to the best of** your **ability** or **to the best of** your **abilities**, you do it as well as you possibly can. EG *You are just there to do your job to the best of your ability.* — ● PHR : USED AS AN A

2 Someone's **ability** is their general level of intelligence, or their level of skill in doing a particular thing. EG *Most schools catered for children of different abilities... I have great respect for his ability and integrity as a journalist... The acting abilities of both were well-known.* — N COUNT/UNCOUNT : WITH POSS

-ability is added in place of **-able** at the end of adjectives in order to form uncountable nouns. EG *...available→availability... ...capable→capability.* — SUFFIX : FORMS NOUNS

abject /æbdʒekt/. 1 **Abject** is used to emphasize how very shameful or depressing a situation, state, or quality is. EG *...abject poverty.* ◊ **abjectly**. EG *...abjectly poor agricultural labourers.* — ADJ CLASSIF : ATTRIB; ◊ ADV

2 Someone who is **abject** shows no self-respect, courage, or pride; used showing disapproval. EG *Even the most abject slaves joined in the revolt.* ▸ used of — ADJ QUALIT ⇑ humble = pathetic ≠ proud

people's actions or behaviour. EG ...*an abject letter of thanks.*

abjure /ə³bdʒʊə/, **abjures, abjuring, abjured.** If you **abjure** something such as a belief or way of life, you state publicly that you will give it up; a formal word. EG *The Government had abjured such a disreputable way of proceeding.* — V+O; ⇑ swear; = renounce, forswear

ablaze /əbleɪz/. **1** If something is **ablaze**, it is burning fiercely. EG *In a moment the tents were ablaze.* — ADJ CLASSIF : PRED; = on fire

2 If something is **ablaze** with lights or colours, it is very bright because of them. EG *The centre of the city was ablaze with lights.* — ADJ CLASSIF : PRED + *with*

3 If people's eyes or faces are **ablaze,** they are excited or angry. EG *His eyes were ablaze with anger.* — ADJ CLASSIF : PRED

able /eɪbə⁰l/, **abler, ablest. 1** If a person or thing is **able** to do something, **1.1** they can do it because they have the physical skill or the necessary knowledge to do it. EG *The frog is able to jump three metres... I wasn't able to do these quizzes.* — ADJ CLASSIF : PRED, USU + *to*-INF; ⇑ capable. **1.2** they can do it because they have enough freedom, time, or money to do it. EG *I just enjoy the freedom of the job-being able to organise my day as I want to... I really thought I wouldn't be able to visit you this week.* — ADJ CLASSIF : PRED, USU + *to*-INF

2 If someone has been **able** to do something, they have managed to do it, although it has been difficult or has caused a lot of problems. EG *I was able to buy a caravan after a long search... She put together the little information she had been able to acquire.* — ADJ CLASSIF : PRED + *to*-INF; ⇑ successful; ≠ unable

3 Someone who is **able** is very clever or is very good at doing something. EG *He was an unusually able detective... ...an able and ambitious industrial worker... There are some extremely able and intelligent children at Summerhill.* — ADJ QUALIT; = capable

-able 1 is added to verbs to form adjectives describing someone or something that can have the thing done to them which is described by the verb. EG ...*read→readable... ...recognize→recognizable... ...identify→identifiable.* — SUFFIX : FORMS ADJS

2 is added to uncountable nouns to form adjectives describing someone or something as being in a particular state or as having a particular quality. EG ...*comfort→comfortable... ...peace→peaceable... ...misery→miserable.* — SUFFIX : FORMS ADJS

able-bodied. An **able-bodied** person is physically strong and healthy. EG *In Central Java every able-bodied man spends several months of the year working away from home.* — ADJ CLASSIF : USU ATTRIB; ⇑ fit

ablutions /ə³bluːʃə⁰nz/ is a formal or humorous word for the activity of washing yourself. EG ...*watching his father's ablutions.* — N PLURAL

ably /eɪbli¹/ means skilfully and successfully. EG *They were ably supported by the Communist Party.* — ADV WITH VB; ⇑ well

abnegation /æbnɪ²geɪʃə⁰n/ means giving up something that you want, or not doing or taking it, even though you would like to; a formal word. — N UNCOUNT; ⇑ self-denial; ≠ selfishness

abnormal /æbnɔːmə⁰l/. Someone or something that is **abnormal** is unusual, especially in a way that is worrying or dangerous. EG *Maybe my child is abnormal... The circumstances were abnormal... They had an abnormal interest in food.* — ADJ CLASSIF; ≠ normal

abnormality /æbnə⁸mælɪti¹/, **abnormalities.** An **abnormality** in something, especially in a person's body or behaviour, is an unusual part or feature of it that may be worrying or dangerous. EG *It is caused by an abnormality in the blood... ...any listing of psychological abnormalities... I cannot express a view as to your normality or abnormality.* — N COUNT/UNCOUNT : USU + SUPP; ⇑ peculiarity

abnormally /æbnɔːmə⁰li¹/. **Abnormally** means **1** to a much greater extent than usual. EG *She had no mother, which meant abnormally close ties to her father... ...the abnormally warm day.* — ADV + ADJ/ADV; = exceptionally. **2** in an unusual, often worrying way. EG ...*police powers to detain citizens who are behaving abnormally.* — ADV; ⇑ unusually; = oddly

aboard /əbɔːd/. If you are **aboard** a ship or plane, or sometimes a train or bus, you are on or in it. EG *I'd felt sorry for him ever since he'd stepped aboard the Morning Rose.* — PREP; = on board. ▸ used as an adverb. EG *The plane crashed, killing all 271 aboard.* — ▸ ADV

abode /əbəʊd/, **abodes. 1** Someone's **abode** is the place where they live; an old-fashioned word. EG ...*the abode of a man of substance.* — N COUNT : USU WITH POSS; ⇑ home

2 If you have the right of **abode** in a particular country, you have a legal right to live there; a formal use. — N UNCOUNT : *of* + N

abolish /əbɒlɪʃ/, **abolishes, abolishing, abolished.** If you **abolish** something such as a system or practice, you formally put an end to it. EG *The death penalty is to be abolished before the end of this year... ...legislation to abolish fox hunting.* — V+O; ⇑ discontinue; = do away with; ≠ introduce

abolition /æbəlɪʃə⁰n/ is the formal ending of something such as a system or practice. EG ...*the abolition of slavery.* — N UNCOUNT + SUPP; = eradication

abolitionist /æbəlɪʃə⁰nɪst/, **abolitionists.** An **abolitionist** is someone who is in favour of abolishing a particular system or practice. — N COUNT; ⇑ reformer

A-bomb, A-bombs. An **A-bomb** is an atomic bomb. — N COUNT

abominable /əbɒmɪnəbə⁰l/. If something is **abominable**, it is very unpleasant, very bad, or very poor in quality; used showing strong disapproval. EG *They work six days a week in abominable conditions... Wages for servants before the First World War were abominable.* — ADJ QUALIT; = disgusting, awful. ◇ **abominably.** EG *She had been treated abominably.* — ◇ ADV; ⇑ badly

abominate /əbɒmɪneɪt/, **abominates, abominating, abominated.** If you **abominate** something, you dislike it very much. EG *She gave us swedes, which the children abominated, and no gravy.* — V+O; ⇑ hate; = detest, loathe

abomination /əbɒmɪneɪʃə⁰n/, **abominations. 1** An **abomination** is something bad that is completely unacceptable to you; an old-fashioned word. EG *The castration of male dogs is an abomination.* — N COUNT; ⇑ evil; = outrage

2 Abomination is great dislike and disgust. EG ...*their abomination of centralized power.* — N UNCOUNT; = abhorrence

aboriginal /æbərɪdʒɪ¹nə⁰l/. **1** An **Aboriginal** is an Australian Aborigine. — N COUNT

2 Aboriginal means belonging or relating to the Australian Aborigines. EG ...*an Aboriginal settlement.* — ADJ CLASSIF : USU ATTRIB

3 The **aboriginal** people or animals of a place are ones that have been there from the earliest known times or that were there before Europeans arrived. EG *They managed to wipe out the entire aboriginal population.* — ADJ CLASSIF : USU ATTRIB; ⇑ original; = indigenous, native

Aborigine /æbərɪdʒɪ¹ni¹/, **Aborigines.** An **Aborigine** is a member of one of the tribes which were living in Australia when Europeans arrived there. EG ...*pituri, a tobacco-like plant that Aborigines chew.* — N COUNT; ⇑ native; = Aboriginal

abort /əbɔːt/, **aborts, aborting, aborted. 1** If a pregnant woman **aborts**, if she **aborts** her unborn child, or if someone **aborts** her, her pregnancy is ended, and she loses the baby: compare **miscarry.** EG *Great numbers of women abort... Lynn knew she could not abort her baby.* — V-ERG OR V+O

2 If you **abort** a process, plan, or activity, or if it **aborts**, it stops before it has been completed. EG *Harris tried to abort the operation half-way through... ...without which all further plans must inevitably abort.* — V-ERG; ⇑ cancel

abortion /əbɔːʃə⁰n/, **abortions.** If a woman has an **abortion**, she ends her pregnancy and loses the baby, usually deliberately: compare **miscarriage.** EG *Abortions are offered to women who need them... ...the campaign for abortion on demand.* — N COUNT/UNCOUNT; = termination

abortionist /əbɔːʃə⁰nɪst/, **abortionists.** An **abortionist** is someone who performs abortions, usually illegally. — N COUNT

abortive /əbɔːtɪv/. An **abortive** attempt or action is unsuccessful. EG ...*after his abortive attempt to raise the subject... ...a year of demonstrations and abortive revolts.* — ADJ CLASSIF; = fruitless

abound /əbaʊnd/, **abounds, abounding, abounded. 1** If things **abound**, there are very large numbers of them. EG *Rumours abounded... ...the fish that abound on the reef.* — V : USU + A; ⇑ exist; ≠ be scarce

2 If something **abounds** with things, it contains very large numbers of them. EG *Its hills abound with streams and waterfalls.* — V + A (*with/in*); ⇑ have; = teem with

about /əbaʊt/. **1** If you talk or write **about** a particular thing, you talk or write on that subject. EG *They'll talk about anything, no matter who's there... This programme is all about nuclear power... She told Mrs Broadhurst all about it.* — PREP

2 About is used after some words to introduce the thing that someone's actions or feelings are related to. EG *He was in earnest about the desire to negotiate... I'll have to think about that... There is no doubt about it.* — PREP

3 If you do something **about** a particular problem or situation, you take action in order to solve it or to prevent it from happening. EG *They knew they had to* — PREP *do something about desegregating the schools... We couldn't do anything about it.*

4 When you mention the things that an activity or institution is **about**, you are saying what it involves and what its aims are. EG *Education is really about a search for meaning... This is what our job is all about.*
PREP

5 When you say that there is a particular quality or feature **about** someone or something, you are saying that this is a characteristic of theirs. EG *There's something peculiar about mankind... There is a strong feel about it of the West Coast of America... What I like about him is his sense of humour.*
PREP

6 About is used in front of numbers or amounts to show that they are approximate. EG *We went about forty miles... It must have been about 10 o'clock or later... We got married about a year ago.*
ADV+NUM = approximately ≠ exactly

7 If you put something **about** a person or thing, you put it around them. EG *I wanted to throw my arms about him... Her jacket was slung about her shoulders.*
PREP = round, around

8 If you move **about**, you move in a lot of different directions. EG *We saw them walking about... I'm waving my arms about.*
ADV AFTER VB = around

9 About is used in phrasal verbs such as 'lie about', 'sit about', and 'mess about' to show that someone is not achieving very much. More detailed information is given at the individual phrasal verbs. EG *What were you messing about in the dark for?... ...sitting about for hours.*
ADV AFTER VB

10 If someone or something is **about**, they are present in a particular place, or they are available. EG *There was no money about... When I went down to the house Abe was already about and he gave me coffee.* • **up and about**: see **up**.
ADJ CLASSIF : PRED = around

11 If you **are about to** do something, you are going to do it very soon. EG *Her father is about to retire... He was just about to go on stage again.*
PHR : VB INFLECTS

12 Expressions such as **while you're about it** and **while I'm about it** are used to suggest that someone could do a particular job while they are doing something else, because it is convenient. EG *Go and switch the kettle off, and while you're about it you can let the cat in.*
PHR : VB INFLECTS

13 You use expressions such as **that's about it** and **that's about all** when you think that you have reached the end of a conversation or an activity. EG *I think that's about it for the moment.*
CONVENTION = that's all

14 The word **about** is used in the following expressions, which are explained at other words in this dictionary. • **just about**: see **just**. • **how about**: see **how**. • **what about**: see **what**.

about-turn, about-turns. An **about-turn** or an **about-face** is a complete change of attitude or opinion. EG *The Conservatives performed a swift about-turn... Then she did a sudden about-face.*
N COUNT

above /əbʌv/. **1** If one thing is **above** another one, **1.1** it is higher than it and directly over it. EG *The children shouted, waving leafy branches above their heads... The whole sky above us was filled with huge brown birds... ...fifty miles above the surface of the earth.* ▸ used as an adverb. EG *Philip was reading his paper by the light of the gas lamp above.* **1.2** it is in a higher position than it and at one side of it. EG *...the hills above Barcelona... Two clergymen were standing above a hole in the ground.*
PREP ≠ beneath; ▸ ADV; PREP ⇑ over ≠ below

2 If you refer to something as being **above**, it is on the upper half of a wall, page, or other surface, or higher up on it than something else that is mentioned. EG *...a picture of a square with another square above.* ▸ used as a preposition. EG *There were only two other entries above his on the page.*
ADV ≠ below; ▸ PREP

3 Above a particular part of a body means slightly higher than it and very near to it. EG *Jane had been hit above her ear... ...high-heeled shoes, with straps above the ankle.*
PREP ≠ below

4 If you refer to a part of a building as **above**, it is upstairs or in a higher part of the building. EG *A lusty yelling noise was coming from the bedroom above.* ▸ used as a preposition. EG *He lived was on the first floor above a restaurant.*
ADV ≠ below; ▸ PREP

5 Above is used in writing to refer to something that has already been mentioned, discussed, or illustrated. EG *Nearly all the above items can be obtained from Selfridges... In addition to all of the above, he also received messages from Buckingham Palace.* ▸ used as an adverb. EG *The meanings of the terms used above are given in leaflet NI 12... ...in Chapter Four above.*
ADJ CLASSIF : ATTRIB, OR *the*+N = aforementioned ≠ below; ▸ ADV

6 If an amount, measurement, rate, or level is **above** a particular figure or level, it is greater than it. EG *...children above the age of 5 months... ...a fraction of a degree above absolute zero... She's selling you theatre tickets at 22% above box-office prices... I was a good student, above average, but not brilliant.* ▸ used as an adverb. EG *...aged 15 and above.*
PREP ≠ below; ▸ ADV

7 If you hear one sound **above** another one, it is louder or clearer than the second one. EG *I could barely hear the sound of my own voice above the noise of the wind.*
PREP = over ≠ below

8 If one sound is **above** another one, it is higher in pitch.
PREP

9 If someone is **above** someone else in a competition, contest, or class, they are more successful than the other person. EG *Margot Fonteyn comes out on top, above anybody else.*
PREP ⇑ better

10 If someone is **above** someone else, **10.1** they are in a position of authority over them. EG *He will certainly have an executive above him to whom he reports... ...orders from above.* **10.2** they are considered to be socially superior. EG *Paul's major contact with the social and cultural worlds above him was Clarissa... I had always thought Anthony priggishly above the rest of us.*
PREP/ADV ⇑ superior to ≠ below; PREP ≠ beneath

11 If you consider one thing or person **above** another, you consider that they are more important or valuable. EG *The warriors valued glory and honour above life itself... She admired Sister Catherine above all the teachers in the orphanage.*
PREP

12 If you are **above** a particular activity, you do not want to get involved in it, perhaps because you think that it is not suitable, important, or worthwhile enough. EG *It is well known that royalty is above politics... They consider themselves above such mercenary transactions... I was not above enjoying myself.*
PREP ≠ beneath

13 If someone or something is **above** criticism or suspicion, they cannot be criticized or suspected because of their good qualities or their position. EG *His successful pamphlet, Protest and Survive, is above intellectual reproach... The director of central intelligence ought to be above suspicion.*
PREP = beyond

14 If something is **above** you, it is too difficult for you to understand. EG *I'm afraid it was all rather above me.*
PREP = beyond

15 If you are getting **above** yourself, you are behaving as if you consider that you are better than everyone else.
PHR : USED AS AN A

16 The word **above** is used in the following expressions, which are explained at other words in this dictionary. • **cut above**: see **cut**. • **over and above**: see **over**. • See also **rise above**.

above board. If an arrangement or deal is **above board**, it is completely honest and open. EG *It was all above board.*
ADJ CLASSIF : PRED = legitimate

abracadabra /æbrəkədæbrə/ is a word that someone says when they are performing a magic trick in order to make the magic happen.
CONVENTION = hey presto

abrasion /əbreɪʒən/, **abrasions**. An **abrasion** is an area on a person's body where the skin has been broken or scraped. EG *The two doctors had noticed abrasions to the side of the neck.*
N COUNT ⇑ wound = graze

abrasive /əbreɪsɪv/, **abrasives**. **1** Someone who is **abrasive** is unkind, unpleasant, and rude in the way they talk to other people. EG *He could also be abrasive, self-destructive, and insensitive.* ▸ used of someone's behaviour or the things they say. EG *...an abrasive manner... ...abrasive criticism.*
ADJ QUALIT = harsh

2 An **abrasive** substance is rough and can be used to clean or polish hard surfaces by scratching or rubbing them. EG *...an abrasive cleaner.* ▸ used as a noun. EG *You're not supposed to use a harsh abrasive on enamel.*
ADJ CLASSIF; ▸ N COUNT ⇑ cleaner

abreast /əbrest/. **1** If people or things walk or move **abreast**, they are next to each other, side by side, and facing in the same direction. EG *...streets so narrow that two can barely walk abreast... ...ants scurrying along a dozen or so abreast.*
ADV WITH VB : USU NUM+ADV

2 If you are **abreast of** someone or something, you are level with them or in line with them. EG *They started shooting as the convoy came abreast of them.*
PREP

3 If you **keep abreast of** a subject or **are abreast of** it, you know all the most recent facts about it. EG *...to*
PHR : VB INFLECTS

keep abreast of the work being done at the University... They were of course well abreast of the war situation.

abridge /əbrɪdʒ/, **abridges, abridging, abridged**. If you **abridge** a book, play, article, or other piece of work, you make it shorter by removing some parts of it. EG *The play had been abridged for radio.* ◇ **abridged**. EG *...an abridged version of the novel.* V+O ⇑ shorten = cut ≠ expand ◇ ADJ QUALIT ⇑ shortened

abroad /əbrɔːd/. **1** If you go **abroad**, you go to a foreign country. EG *My friend has gone to live abroad... I just got back from abroad... ...a holiday abroad.* ADV ⇑ away = overseas

2 If something such as a story or feeling is **abroad**, people generally are aware of it and know about it or feel it. EG *There is clearly a new spirit abroad.* ADV = around

abrogate /æbrə⁶geɪt/, **abrogates, abrogating, abrogated**. If someone **abrogates** something such as a law, agreement, or practice, they put an end to it, usually in a formal way. EG *...if the unions were to abrogate their traditional role.* ◇ **abrogation** /æbrə⁶geɪʃə⁰n/. EG *...the abrogation of emergency laws.* V+O : NO IMPER = revoke, annul ◇ N UNCOUNT+*of*

abrupt /əbrʌpt/. **1** If an action, change, or ending is **abrupt**, it is sudden and perhaps surprising or unpleasant. EG *It came to an abrupt end... The change in George's circumstances was abrupt... ...with another abrupt movement.* ◇ **abruptly**. EG *I had to apply the brakes rather abruptly at a red light.* ◇ **abruptness**. EG *The train lurched forward with an abruptness that sent my tea flying.* ADJ QUALIT = sudden, unexpected ◇ ADV WITH VB = sharply ◇ N UNCOUNT

2 Someone who is **abrupt** is rather rude, unfriendly, or impolite. EG *...an abrupt young girl.* ▸ used of behaviour or words. EG *...David's abrupt and bullying manner.* ◇ **abruptly**. EG *I wouldn't have spoken so abruptly if I'd realized you were ill.* ◇ **abruptness**. EG *He hid his feelings behind a gruff abruptness.* ADJ QUALIT = brusque, curt ◇ ADV WITH VB ◇ N UNCOUNT

abscess /æbsɪ²s/, **abscesses**. An **abscess** is a painful swelling on the skin or in the body, containing thick yellowish-white liquid. N COUNT ⇑ infection = boil

abscond /ə³bskɒnd/, **absconds, absconding, absconded**. **1** If someone **absconds** with something, especially something they have stolen, they run away with it. EG *He absconded with everyone's wages.* V+A *(with)* ⇑ leave = run off

2 If someone **absconds** from somewhere such as a detention centre or a boarding school, they run away from it. V : IF+PREP THEN *from* ⇑ leave

abseil /æbseɪl/, **abseils, abseiling, abseiled**. If you **abseil** down a cliff or rock face, you go down it by sliding in a controlled way down a rope, with your feet against the cliff or rock. V : IF+PREP/ADV THEN *down* ⇑ slide

absence /æbsəns/, **absences**. **1** Someone's **absence** from a particular place or situation is the fact or state of them not being there. EG *In your parents' absence I am responsible for your welfare... They remained in their seats during my absence... ...frequent absences from school.* ● See also **leave of absence**. N UNCOUNT/COUNT : USU+SUPP ≠ presence

2 The **absence** of something from a particular place, thing, or situation is the fact that it is not there or is missing from it. EG *The absence of electricity made matters worse... The owner refused to accept his money in the absence of identification.* N SING WITH DET : USU+SUPP = lack ≠ presence

absent, absents, absenting, absented. The word **absent** is pronounced /æbsə²nt/ when it is an adjective, and /ə³bsent/ when it is a verb. **1** If someone is **absent** from a particular place, they are not there. EG *It would be less embarrassing to have a bath while Philip was absent... Seventy-five per cent of the able-bodied males might be absent from the villages at any one time.* ADJ CLASSIF : IF+PREP THEN *from* = away ≠ present

2 If something is **absent** from a particular thing or situation, it is not there or is missing from it. EG *In that province a conventional political system was absent... Something which is still absent from your work is any reference to class.* ADJ CLASSIF : PRED, IF+PREP THEN *from* = lacking ≠ present

3 If someone is **absent**, they are not paying attention to something because they are thinking about something else. EG *She was absent, pre-occupied.* ▸ used of behaviour or expressions. EG *...an absent stare.* ◇ **absently**. EG *'Did you?' Boylan said absently.* ADJ CLASSIF : PRED ⇑ inattentive ▸ ADJ CLASSIF : ATTRIB ◇ ADV WITH VB

4 If you **absent** yourself from a place or activity, you do not go there or do not take part in it. EG *He had absented himself for an entire day.* V+O (REFL)+A ≠ attend

absentee /æbsə²ntiː/, **absentees**. An **absentee** is a person who should be in a particular place but who is not there. EG *The only absentee was Lady Sackville.* N COUNT

absenteeism /æbsə²ntiːɪzə⁰m/ is the fact or habit of frequently being away from work or school, usually without a good reason. EG *...a high rate of absenteeism.* N UNCOUNT = truancy ≠ attendance

absentia /ə³bsentɪə/. If something is done to you **in absentia**, it is done to you when you are not present; a formal expression. EG *...if he or she wishes to have the degree conferred in absentia.* PHR : USED AS AN A

absent-minded. Someone who is **absent-minded** often forgets things and does not pay proper attention to what they are doing. EG *She is so absent-minded and careless.* ▸ used of behaviour or actions. EG *Tom went sightseeing in a rather absent-minded fashion.* ◇ **absent-mindedly**. EG *...if you absent-mindedly drop a diamond ring down the sink.* ADJ QUALIT ⇑ inattentive = forgetful, preoccupied ◇ ADV WITH VB

absolute /æbsə⁶luːt/, **absolutes**. **1** **Absolute** is used to emphasize what you are saying, especially when you are expressing an opinion. EG *He was an absolute dimwit... The script is an absolute mess.* ADJ CLASSIF : ATTRIB = complete

2 **Absolute** is used to describe a particular quality in order to emphasize that it is total or very strong. EG *...absolute loyalty and devotion... ...the necessity for absolute secrecy.* ADJ CLASSIF : USU ATTRIB = complete

3 An **absolute** ruler has complete power and authority over his or her country. EG *...an absolute monarch.* ▸ used of the power of such a ruler. EG *...absolute power.* ADJ CLASSIF : ATTRIB ▸ ADJ CLASSIF

4 **Absolute** is used to say that something is definite and will not change even if cirumstances change. EG *Such demands would in the present day include the absolute assurance of full employment... ...the absolute protection of free speech.* ● See also **decree absolute**. ADJ CLASSIF : USU ATTRIB

5 **Absolute** rules, principles, and beliefs do not change and are believed to be true, right, or relevant in all situations. EG *...absolute doctrines... ...an absolute rule.* ADJ CLASSIF : ATTRIB ⇑ universal

6 An **absolute** is a rule or principle that is believed to be true, right, or relevant in all situations. EG *One cannot proceed on the basis of rigid absolutes, such as 'divorce is always wrong'.* N COUNT

absolutely /æbsə⁶luːtli¹/. **1** **Absolutely** is used **1.1** to emphasize what you are saying, especially when you are expressing an opinion. EG *I absolutely agree... That's an absolutely fascinating piece of work... It's absolutely no business of hers... We were absolutely opposed to any Incomes Policy.* **1.2** in descriptions of situations or things in order to say that something is exactly and completely the case. EG *He forced himself to lie absolutely still... Choose a period at work or at home when you will be absolutely alone.* ADV = totally ADV+ADJ/ADV = quite

2 **Absolutely** is used in speech as an emphatic way of agreeing with someone or of saying yes. EG *'They are just silly.'–'Absolutely, I couldn't agree more.'... 'She's excellent though.'–'Absolutely.'* CONVENTION = certainly

3 **Absolutely not** is used in speech as an emphatic way of disagreeing with someone or denying something. EG *'Does this affect your attitude to your work, in any way?'–'Absolutely not.'* CONVENTION ⇑ no = certainly not

absolution /æbsə⁶luːʃə⁰n/. If someone is given **absolution**, they are forgiven for something wrong that they have done; a formal or religious word. EG *...a ritualistic absolution from my sins of the past.* N COUNT/UNCOUNT ⇑ forgiveness

absolutism /æbsə⁶luːtɪzə⁰m/ is a political system in which one ruler or leader has complete power and authority over a country. EG *...the fight against absolutism.* N UNCOUNT ⇑ despotism

absolve /ə³bzɒlv/, **absolves, absolving, absolved**. **1** If you **absolve** someone from something such as guilt, blame, or responsibility, you state publicly or formally that they are not guilty or are not to blame. EG *The captain is absolved from all blame and responsibility for the shipwreck... He cannot entirely absolve himself of the charge of having deserted.* V+O : IF+PREP THEN *from/of* ⇑ free = clear, exonerate

2 If you **absolve** someone of something wrong that they have done, you forgive them; a formal or religious use. EG *Before you die you're absolved of your sins.* V+O : IF+PREP THEN *of*

absorb /ə³bsɔːb, -zɔːb/, **absorbs, absorbing, absorbed**. **1** If something **absorbs** a liquid or gas, it soaks it up or draws it in. EG *Leather gloves are best because they absorb sweat... Frogs absorb water through their skins.* V+O = soak up

2 If something **absorbs** heat, light, or another form of energy, it takes it in rather than reflecting it. EG *The rocks absorb more energy than they reflect.* V+O ⇑ receive ≠ reflect

3 If something **absorbs** a force or shock, it reduces its effect. EG *Car bumpers are designed to absorb some of the impact.* V+O ⇑ prevent = deaden

4 If a person or group **is absorbed** into a larger group, they become part of the larger group and lose their identity or individuality. EG *Small businesses are absorbed by larger ones... The individual is completely absorbed into the crowd.* V+O : IF+PREP THEN *into* ⇑ be included = be assimilated

5 If something or someone **absorbs** changes or effects, they are able to deal with these changes or effects without being upset or too badly affected. EG *The societies of the Highlands were able to absorb these changes.* V+O ⇑ withstand

6 If something **absorbs** something such as money, space or time, it uses up a lot of it. EG *Salaries and so on will probably absorb all the profits... The role of administrator absorbed much of Benn's energy.* V+O ⇑ use up = take up, eat up

7 If you **absorb** something such as information or facts, you learn and understand it. EG *I had just about time to absorb this information.* V+O = digest, take in

8 If something **absorbs** someone, it interests them very much and takes up a lot of their time and energy. EG *An aeroplane over Whitelake Cottage completely absorbed everyone's attention.* V+O ⇑ interest = grip
◊ **absorbed**. EG *I was utterly absorbed in what I was doing.* ◊ ADJ QUALIT
◊ **absorbing**. EG *Council work is both absorbing and interesting.* ◊ ADJ QUALIT

absorbent /ə³bsɔːbənt, -zɔː-/. **Absorbent** material soaks up liquid easily. EG *Dry it inside and out with an absorbent cloth.* ADJ QUALIT ≠ water-repellent

absorber /ə³bsɔːbə, -zɔːbə/. See **shock absorber**.

absorption /ə³bsɔːpʃə⁰n, -zɔːp-/. **1** If you have an **absorption** in something, you are so interested in it that it takes up a lot of your time and energy. EG *...her growing absorption in the study of natural history... ...an absorption with politics.* N SING WITH DET + SUPP = fascination ≠ boredom

2 Absorption is the fact or activity of absorbing something. EG *...gastric absorption... ...the absorption of foreign minorities.* N UNCOUNT + SUPP

abstain /ə³bsteɪn/, **abstains, abstaining, abstained**. **1** If you **abstain** from doing something pleasant or enjoyable, you deliberately do not do it. EG *He abstained from eating for six days.* V : IF+PREP THEN *from* ⇑ hold back = refrain

2 If you **abstain** during a vote, you vote neither for nor against the proposal. EG *'I suppose you voted against.'–'I abstained, actually.'* V ⇑ refrain = opt out

abstemious /ə³bstiːmɪəs/. Someone who is **abstemious** is careful to avoid doing too much of something enjoyable such as eating or drinking. ADJ QUALIT ⇑ moderate = temperate

abstention /ə³bstenʃə⁰n/, **abstentions**. **1** An **abstention** is a formal act by someone of not voting either for or against a proposal. EG *There were 4 abstentions. We have the right of abstention on grounds of principle.* N COUNT/UNCOUNT

2 Abstention from something enjoyable is the practice of deliberately not doing it. EG *...total abstention from alcohol.* N UNCOUNT : IF+PREP THEN *from*

abstinence /æbstɪ¹nəns/is the practice of abstaining from something that you enjoy doing or that you would like to do. N UNCOUNT ⇑ refraining ≠ indulgence

abstract, abstracts, abstracting, abstracted. The word **abstract** is pronounced /æbstrækt/ when it is an adjective or a noun, and /ə³bstrækt/ when it is a verb. **1** An idea, argument, or way of thinking that is **abstract** is based on general ideas and principles rather than on particular things and events. EG *The arguments of contemporary science are so abstract that they are no longer intelligible... ...our capacity for abstract reasoning.* ADJ QUALIT = theoretical

2 An **abstract** quality or ideal is one that people believe in and talk about but that is not necessarily based on reality or everyday life. EG *...a passion for abstract good and abstract right.* ▸ used as a noun. EG *...always clinging to some big noble abstract.* ADJ CLASSIF : ATTRIB ≠ actual ▸ N COUNT

3 When you think or talk about something **in the abstract**, you think or talk about it as a type rather than as an individual or actual thing. EG *Think of a cat in the abstract, if that is possible.* PHR : USED AS AN A ⇑ in general

4 Abstract art is a style of art which uses shapes and patterns to represent things, people, and ideas, rather than showing people or things as they actually look. EG *...a large abstract painting... I don't understand abstract art.* ▸ used as a noun. EG *Several of her abstracts had been bought by the Tate.* ADJ CLASSIF : ATTRIB ≠ representational ▸ N COUNT ⇑ work

5 An **abstract** noun is a noun that describes something such as a quality, idea, or concept rather than something physical and real such as an object, person, or animal. ADJ CLASSIF : ATTRIB ≠ concrete

6 An **abstract** of an article or speech is a short piece of writing that summarizes the main points of it. EG *You are asked to submit an abstract of approximately 100 words.* N COUNT ⇑ summary

7 If you **abstract** information from an article, journal, or other piece of writing, you make a summary of the main points in it. V OR V+O ⇑ summarize

8 If you **abstract** yourself from an activity, you stop taking part in it; a formal use. EG *...a life from which he had voluntarily abstracted himself.* V+O (REFL)+A *(from)* = withdraw

9 If you **abstract** something from somewhere, you remove it; a formal or humorous use. EG *He could abstract any wallet from any pocket at ease.* V+O : IF+PREP THEN *from* = extract

abstracted /ə³bstræktɪ²d/. Someone whose behaviour is **abstracted** is thinking so deeply that they do not really notice what is happening around them. EG *She gave him a dreamy, abstracted stare.* ADJ CLASSIF ⇑ thoughtful = preoccupied, brooding
◊ **abstractedly**. EG *Her father listened abstractedly.* ◊ ADV

abstraction /ə³bstrækʃə⁰n/, **abstractions**. **1** An **abstraction** is a general idea rather than one relating to a particular object, person, or situation. EG *The seven-year-old reader exists only as a statistical abstraction.* N COUNT = notion

2 Abstraction is **2.1** the quality of being abstract and general rather than referring or relating to particular things or events. EG *They like concreteness, not abstraction.* N UNCOUNT **2.2** the state of being so deep in thought that you do not notice what is going on around you. N UNCOUNT
2.3 the activity of getting something out of something else, often as part of an industrial process. EG *...the abstraction of metal from ore.* N UNCOUNT = extraction

abstruse /ə³bstruːs/. Something that is **abstruse** is difficult to understand. EG *...abstruse scientific information.* ADJ QUALIT = obscure ≠ simple

absurd /ə³bsɜːd/. Something that is **absurd** is ridiculous because it is totally different from what you would normally expect. EG *It seemed absurd to try to carry a twenty-five-pound camera about... ...an absurd kind of hat.* ADJ QUALIT ⇑ improbable = crazy, preposterous
◊ **absurdity** /ə³bsɜːdɪti¹/, **absurdities**. EG *...the oddities and absurdities of the language... ...a feeling of absurdity.* ◊ N COUNT/UNCOUNT

absurdly /ə³bsɜːdli¹/. **1** If someone is behaving **absurdly**, their behaviour is ridiculous. EG *They were all laughing absurdly... Lionel was absurdly clumsy in his attempt to deflect attention.* ADV ⇑ senselessly = ridiculously

2 Absurdly is used to emphasize that a particular quality is present to an extent that seems ridiculous to you. EG *Please forgive this absurdly long letter... They paid an absurdly low rent for their cottage.* ADV+ADJ/ADV ⇑ extremely = ludicrously

abundance /əbʌndəns/. **1** An **abundance** of something is a large quantity of it. EG *...an abundance of evidence.* N PART : *an*+N = wealth

2 Abundance is the fact of being present in large quantities. EG *The various species differ mainly in size and abundance.* N UNCOUNT ⇑ quantity ≠ scarcity

3 If something is **in abundance**, there is a lot of it. EG *This is one resource which the third world has in abundance... There was grass in abundance.* PHR : USED AS AN A = in plenty

abundant /əbʌndə²nt/. Something that is **abundant** is present in large quantities. EG *...an abundant supply of food.* ADJ QUALIT ⇑ plentiful = generous

abundantly /əbʌndə²ntli¹/. **1 Abundantly** is used to emphasize an opinion, and to stress how true and obvious it is. EG *It has become abundantly clear that there is no time to lose... This point of view is abundantly justified by American Negro History.* ADV+ADJ/ADV ⇑ very = manifestly

2 Something that occurs **abundantly** is present or found in large quantities. EG *I came across the plant growing abundantly at the edges of a road... Raw materials are abundantly available in Britain.* ADV ⇑ plentifully = profusely

abuse, abuses, abusing, abused. The word **abuse** is pronounced /ə³bjuːs/ when it is a noun, and /ə³bjuːz/ when it is a verb. **1 Abuse** is rude, offensive, and unkind things that you say when you are angry. EG *The girls shrieked abuse at the prosecuting lawyers... ...a hail of abuse.* N UNCOUNT ⇑ discourtesy = insults

2 Abuse of someone is the cruel and violent treatment of them. EG *Her parents were found guilty of gross neglect and abuse.* N UNCOUNT : IF+PREP THEN *of*

3 Abuse of something is the use of it in a wrong way or for a bad purpose. EG *This book is about the uses and abuses of power... ...drug abuse... There is no freedom that is not open to abuse.* N UNCOUNT/COUNT : IF+PREP THEN *of* = misuse

4 If you **abuse** something, you use it in a wrong way or for a bad purpose. EG *It is important not to abuse your position as the boss's wife.*
V+O ⇑ use = misuse, take advantage of

5 If someone **abuses** you, **5.1** they say rude, offensive, or unkind things to you. EG *Most of the foremen abused the workmen in the foulest language... He did not like to hear Elaine abused or criticized in any way.*
V+O ⇑ attack = insult
5.2 they treat you cruelly and violently. EG *The patients were often physically abused or drugged.*
V+O = ill-treat

abusive /ə³bjuːsɪv/. Someone who is **abusive** says or writes rude, offensive, or unkind things. EG *Some of her friends had been positively abusive.* ▸ used of things that people say or write. EG *...abusive language.*
ADJ QUALIT = insulting ≠ polite

abut /əbʌt/, **abuts, abutting, abutted.** When land or a building **abuts** on something, it is next to it on one side; a fairly formal word. EG *...an enormous garden which abuts on to the graveyard.*
V+O, OR V+A (on) ⇑ touch = adjoin

abysmal /əbɪzmə⁰l/ is used to emphasize that something is unsuccessful, bad, or very poor in quality. EG *...the abysmal wages of rural labourers... ...the occasional abysmal failure.* ◊ **abysmally.** EG *He failed abysmally to hide his anxiety.*
ADJ QUALIT = appalling, dreadful; ◊ ADV

abyss /ə³bɪs/, **abysses**; a literary word. An **abyss** is **1** a very deep hole in the ground.
N COUNT
2 a very frightening or threatening situation. EG *The world was teetering on the edge of the abyss of World War III.*
N COUNT+SUPP : USU the+N
3 a very great difference between two people or groups. EG *God and man are divided by a fundamental abyss.*
N COUNT+SUPP ⇑ division = gulf, gap

AC /eɪ siː/ is used to refer to an electric current that continually changes direction as it flows; an abbreviation for 'alternating current'.
N UNCOUNT : USU BEFORE N

a/c is a written abbreviation for **account.**

acacia /ə³keɪʃə/, **acacias.** The plural can be either **acacias** or **acacia.** An **acacia** is a tree which grows in warm countries and which usually has small yellow or white flowers.
N COUNT

academic /ækədemɪk/, **academics. 1 Academic** is used **1.1** to describe work done in schools, colleges, and universities, especially work that involves studying and reasoning rather than practical or technical skills. EG *Academic standards were high... ...academic qualifications... The course is a combination of academic and practical work.* ◊ **academically.** EG *...people who are well qualified academically.*
ADJ CLASSIF : ATTRIB ⇑ intellectual; ◊ ADV
1.2 to describe things that relate to universities, colleges, or schools. EG *...when the new academic year came around in the autumn... The whole academic system is unfair.*
ADJ CLASSIF : ATTRIB

2 Children or people who are **academic** are good at studying or are interested in studying. EG *It's an exam for academic children.*
ADJ QUALIT ⇑ intellectual = studious

3 An **academic** is a member of a university or college who teaches or does research. EG *He was rather flattered that an English academic should be planning a book about him.*
N COUNT ⇑ worker = scholar

4 Academic is also used to indicate that the truth of a particular point is irrelevant and that it can have no real effect on what is happening or being discussed. EG *The matter was one of only academic interest... It was all academic, because there were never any profits to share out.*
ADJ QUALIT ⇑ unimportant = theoretical

academy /ə³kædə²mi¹/, **academies.** Some schools or colleges, especially ones that specialize in teaching a particular subject, are called **academies.** EG *...the Soviet Academy of Sciences... ...opening the doors of their military academies to young officers from overseas.*
N COUNT : USU+SUPP, ALSO IN NAMES ⇑ institution = college, institute

acc. is an abbreviation for **account.**

accede /ə³ksiːd/, **accedes, acceding, acceded.** If you **accede** to someone's request or opinion, you allow it or agree with it, usually rather unwillingly; a formal word. EG *He was upset by my refusal to accede to his request... To accede to such a contention would set a dangerous precedent.*
V : IF+PREP THEN to = give in, submit

accelerate /ə³kseləreɪt/, **accelerates, accelerating, accelerated. 1** When a process or the rate of something **accelerates** or when you **accelerate** it, it gets faster and faster. EG *Inflation rates began to accelerate... ...efforts to accelerate the process even further.*
V-ERG ⇑ speed = speed up

2 When moving vehicles, bicycles, or people **accelerate,** they go faster and faster. EG *This means you can accelerate rather more rapidly.*
V ⇑ speed = speed up

3 If you **accelerate** something, you make it happen sooner than it would have done otherwise. EG *His college gave him accelerated promotion to Associate Professor.*
V+O ⇑ speed

acceleration /ə³kseləreɪʃə⁰n/, **accelerations. Acceleration** is **1** the rate at which the speed of an object is increasing; a technical term in physics. EG *Force equals mass times acceleration.*
N UNCOUNT
2 the rate at which a car or other vehicle can increase its speed, often seen in terms of the time that it takes to reach a particular speed. EG *The acceleration and performance are very impressive... The car had not been built for high accelerations.*
N UNCOUNT/COUNT ⇑ power
3 the process of getting faster and faster. EG *...the acceleration of economic growth.*
N UNCOUNT = speeding up

accelerator /ə³kseləreɪtə/, **accelerators.** The **accelerator** in a vehicle is the pedal which you press with your foot in order to make the vehicle go faster.
N COUNT

accent, accents, accenting, accented. The word **accent** is pronounced /æksə²nt/ when it is a noun, and /æksent/ when it is a verb. **1** Someone who has an **accent** or who speaks with a particular **accent** pronounces the words of a language in a distinctive way which shows that they come from a different country or from a particular region or social class. EG *She spoke with an Irish accent... He had never lost his north-country accent.*
N COUNT+SUPP ⇑ pronunciation

2 An **accent** is also a short line or other mark which is written or printed above certain letters in some languages in order to show how those letters are pronounced. EG *He changed a word or two and put in an accent he had missed.*
N COUNT

3 If you say that the **accent** is on a particular feature of something, you mean that special importance is placed on it. EG *The accent is on presentation in this contest.*
N SING WITH DET ⇑ emphasis = stress

4 If you **accent** a word or a musical note, you emphasize it, for example by making it louder. EG *The choir claps and taps to accent the swing of the music.*
V+O = stress

accented /æksentɪ²d/. Language or speech that is **accented** is spoken with a particular accent. EG *'Don't let me disturb your lunch,' Liebermann said in his heavily accented English.*
ADJ QUALIT ⇑ pronounced

accentuate /ə³ksentʃueɪt/, **accentuates, accentuating, accentuated.** If someone or something **accentuates** a particular feature of a thing, this feature is emphasized or made more noticeable. EG *Laws such as these simply serve to accentuate inequality and exploitation.*
V+O ⇑ emphasize = heighten

accept /ə³ksept/, **accepts, accepting, accepted. 1** If you **accept** something that you have been offered, you say yes to it. EG *He readily accepted our invitation to speak about his case... I thanked him and accepted.*
V OR V+O ⇑ take ≠ refuse, turn down

2 If you **accept** something such as a document, plan, or piece of work, you agree to use or take it because it is of a high enough standard or is of the right sort. EG *Her article has already been accepted for publication... The Postmaster-General accepted the tender of the English Marconi Company.*
V+O = approve ≠ reject

3 If you **accept** someone's advice or suggestion, you agree to do what they say. EG *If she accepts the advice, she feels happier... I knew that they would accept my proposal.*
V+O/REPORT-CL ≠ reject

4 If you **accept** a story or statement, you say or show that you consider it to be true. EG *The panel accepted Carleson's version of the story... I don't accept that NATO is in disarray.*
V+O/REPORT-CL ⇑ believe ≠ reject

5 If you **accept** a particular situation that is difficult or unpleasant, **5.1** you get used to it and recognize that it cannot be changed. EG *He is unwilling to accept his past... I know he's dead but I just can't accept it... We must accept the fact that there is a great deal we cannot know.*
V+O/REPORT-CL = face up to
5.2 you do nothing to try to stop, resist, or change it. EG *...an increasing unwillingness to accept bad working conditions... Why was all this suffering accepted in silence?*
V+O ⇑ allow = put up with
5.3 you do nothing to avoid it, and perhaps take part in it willingly. EG *The astronaut accepts danger as being part of the job... ...ready and willing to accept the challenge of the unknown.*
V+O = take on ≠ avoid

6 If you **accept** the blame or responsibility for something, you admit or recognize that you are responsible for it.
V+O

7 When an institution or organization **accepts** someone who has applied for a job or for membership, they give them a job or allow them to join. EG *I was*
V+O ⇑ take ≠ turn down

accepted by the Open University... The Navy will be able to accept many more recruits.

8 If a group **accepts** someone, they begin to think of them as part of the group, treating them in the same way as other members of it. EG *The children gradually begin to accept her.* — V+O; ⇑ include; ≠ reject, ostracize

9 If a woman **accepts** a man or **accepts** his proposal of marriage, she agrees to marry him. — V+O; ≠ refuse

10 If a machine **accepts** a particular kind of thing, it is designed to take it and deal with it or process it. EG *...a new data system which can accept and process information from any source... The ticket machine won't accept 20p pieces.* — V+O

11 See also **accepted**.

acceptable /ə³ksɛptəbə⁰l/. **1** If something is **acceptable**, **1.1** people generally approve of it or allow it to happen. EG *In war killing is acceptable... At present no one language is acceptable as a national language for Nigeria... They have made revolutionary ideas more acceptable to Labour's membership.* — ADJ QUALIT; ⇑ admissible
◇ **acceptability** /ə³ksɛptəbɪlɪti¹/. EG *The proof of a doctrine is its acceptability to the man in the street.* — ◇ N UNCOUNT
◇ **acceptably**. EG *I simply did not know which subjects I could acceptably bring up... ...an acceptably low heat loss.* — ◇ ADV; = safely
1.2 it is considered to be good enough. EG *To my relief he found the article acceptable.* — ADJ CLASSIF; ⇑ adequate

2 If a gift is **acceptable**, it is suitable and will be liked by the person who receives it. EG *Fruit is very acceptable.* — ADJ QUALIT; = welcome

acceptance /ə³ksɛptəns/, **acceptances**. **1 Acceptance** of something that you have been offered is the act of taking it or of agreeing to use it. EG *...the acceptance of foreign aid... Within two days I had a letter of acceptance from one of the assistant editors.* — N UNCOUNT; ≠ refusal

2 If you receive an **acceptance** for a job or membership for which you have applied, you are offered the job or membership. EG *So far I've received two acceptances and four rejections.* — N UNCOUNT/COUNT; ≠ rejection

3 Acceptance of someone into a group is the act of beginning to think of them as part of the group, treating them in the same way as other members of it. EG *...his speedy acceptance into the San Diego community.* — N UNCOUNT/COUNT; ⇑ inclusion; = adoption

4 Acceptance of something such as an idea is a general belief or agreement that it is true or valid. EG *...their acceptance of his right to rule... There is still a widespread acceptance that the elderly have much to contribute.* — N UNCOUNT/COUNT

5 Acceptance of an unpleasant or difficult situation is the fact of getting used to it and recognizing that you cannot change or avoid it. EG *The agony of her loss had become numb acceptance of it... ...our ancestors' cheerful acceptance of their plight.* — N UNCOUNT; ⇑ recognition

accepted /ə³ksɛptɪ²d/. **Accepted** ideas are generally agreed to be correct or reasonable. EG *No precise and generally accepted definition of a prostitute exists... The doctor's reply ran counter to the accepted wisdom about old age.* — ADJ CLASSIF: ATTRIB; ≠ controversial

access /æksɛs/, **accesses, accessing, accessed**. **1** If you gain **access** to a building or other place, you succeed in getting into it. EG *They attempted to gain access through a side entrance... The entrance door gives access to a living room.* — N UNCOUNT: IF+PREP THEN *to*; = entry

2 Access is also **2.1** the opportunity or right to use or see something. EG *I demanded access to a telephone... By bribing her, I won access to some files.* — N UNCOUNT+*to*
2.2 the opportunity or right to see someone, for example in order to speak to them. EG *We all have right of access to the Prime Minister... Has Donald got access to the child?* — N UNCOUNT: IF+PREP THEN *to*

3 If you **access** information from a computer, you get it from the computer where it is stored. EG *The main problem was the time they took to access the information.* — V+O; ⇑ retrieve; ≠ store

accessible /ə³ksɛsə¹bə⁰l/. **1** If a place is **accessible** by a particular route or method of transport, you are able to reach it by this route or method. EG *The hidden room was accessible only through a secret back entrance.* — ADJ QUALIT; ⇑ attainable; = approachable
◇ **accessibility** /əksɛsə¹bɪlɪti¹/. EG *The site was picked because of its accessibility by rail.* — ◇ N UNCOUNT

2 If something is **accessible** to people, they are able to see it, use it, or buy it. EG *...computers cheap enough to be accessible to virtually everyone.* — ADJ QUALIT: PRED+*to*; = available
◇ **accessibility**. — ◇ N UNCOUNT

3 If a book, painting, etc is **accessible** to people, they are able to understand it and appreciate it. EG *...the most accessible opera by Wagner.* — ADJ QUALIT: USU PRED+*to*; ⇑ available

accession /ə³ksɛʃə⁰n/ is the act of taking up a position of authority, especially as the ruler of a country. EG *...Queen Victoria's accession in 1837.* — N UNCOUNT: IF+PREP THEN *to/of*

accessory /ə³ksɛsəri¹/, **accessories**. An **accessory** is **1** a part or device added to a machine, tool, or other object in order to make it more efficient or to enable it to perform an extra job. EG *Metallic finish is standard and accessories include a stereo radio.* — N COUNT; ⇑ addition

2 an article, such as a belt or handbag, which is worn or carried by someone, but which is not part of their main clothing. EG *Use new accessories to brighten up an old outfit.* — N COUNT: USU PL

3 someone who helps another person to commit a crime or to avoid arrest, although they are not present when the crime is committed; a legal use. — N COUNT: IF+PREP THEN *to*; = accomplice

accident /æksɪdə²nt/, **accidents**. **1** An **accident** is **1.1** an event which happens completely by chance. EG *They met through a series of accidents... I only came to Liverpool by accident.* — N COUNT, OR *by*+N
1.2 something unpleasant and unfortunate that happens and that often leads to injury or death. EG *The little boy had an accident when he was playing in his garden... I was busy filling out forms about the accident.* — N COUNT; ⇑ event; = mishap

2 An **accident** happens when a vehicle hits something such as another vehicle or knocks a person down. EG *Her son was killed in an accident last year... He lost both his legs in a train accident when he was a boy.* — N COUNT: USU MOD+N; ⇑ collision; = crash

accidental /æksɪdɛntə⁰l/. Something that is **accidental** happens by chance and without any deliberate intention. EG *More people die from accidental poisoning... Her death was completely accidental.* — ADJ CLASSIF; = inadvertent; ≠ deliberate
▸ used as a noun. EG *These statistics must contain a large element of the accidental.* — ▸ N SING: *the*+N
◇ **accidentally**. EG *It could easily happen accidentally... They met accidentally.* — ◇ ADV WITH VB; ≠ on purpose

accident-prone. Someone who is **accident-prone** keeps having accidents. EG *...an accident-prone policeman.* — ADJ QUALIT

acclaim /əkleɪm/, **acclaims, acclaiming, acclaimed**. **1** If you **acclaim** someone or something, you praise them or talk about them with great enthusiasm. EG *Everyone is acclaiming this play as the event of the new season... He has been widely acclaimed for his paintings.* — V+O; = applaud

2 Acclaim is praise for someone, or for something that they have done, written, or produced. EG *She has enjoyed modest critical acclaim... His book was published in 1919 and met with unusual acclaim.* — N UNCOUNT; ⇑ approval

acclamation /ækləmeɪʃə⁰n/ is a noisy or enthusiastic expression of approval for someone or something. EG *All her remarks were greeted with acclamation.* — N UNCOUNT: USU ADJ QUALIT+N; = applause

acclimatize /əklaɪmətaɪz/, **acclimatizes, acclimatizing, acclimatized**; also spelled **acclimatise**. When you **acclimatize** to something or **acclimatize** yourself to it, you become used to it. EG *Once you've acclimatized to the heat you won't feel so tired... They acclimatized themselves to the conditions before they went.* — V OR V+O (REFL): IF+PREP THEN *to*; = adapt, adjust

accolade /ækə⁶leɪd/, **accolades**. An **accolade** is praise, honour or an award that is given to someone who is greatly admired; a fairly formal word. EG *He well deserved the accolade of 'genius'... This was the highest accolade he could receive.* — N COUNT+SUPP: USU SING; = acclaim

accommodate /əkɒmədeɪt/, **accommodates, accommodating, accommodated**. **1** If you **accommodate** someone, you provide them with a place where they can stay, live, or work. EG *She can't accommodate guests at the moment... They have not given us proper financial support to accommodate these people properly.* — V+O: USU+A; ⇑ house; = put up

2 If a place or building can **accommodate** a number of people or things, it has enough room for them. EG *The cottage could comfortably accommodate up to five people... When fully developed this site could accommodate factories providing about two thousand jobs.* — V+O; ⇑ contain

3 To **accommodate** someone also means to be very helpful to them in your dealings with them. EG *The bank appears to be accommodating its customers more than it used to.* — V+O; ⇑ help; = oblige

4 If you **accommodate** to something new or **accommodate** yourself to it, you get used to it or adjust to it. — V+A (*to*), OR V+O (REFL)+A(*to*)

EG *It was less hard for us as teachers to accommodate to the idea of unpaid 'amateurs' in the classroom... It is usually very difficult for an industrialist to accommodate himself to the House of Commons.*

accommodating /əkɒmədeɪtɪŋ/. Someone who is **accommodating** is very willing to help you or to do something for you. EG *The warder was always accommodating in allowing visitors in.* ADJ QUALIT ⇑ helpful = obliging

accommodation /əkɒmədeɪʃəⁿn/, **accommodations**. **Accommodation** is 1 a room or building to stay or live in. EG *There is a shortage of accommodation... ...student accommodation.* N UNCOUNT/COUNT 2 a room, building, or space to work in. EG *...teaching accommodation... It provides accommodation for 5,360 civil servants.* N UNCOUNT+SUPP

accompaniment /əkʌmpəⁿnɪməⁿnt/, **accompaniments**. 1 The **accompaniment** to a song or to a tune being played on a musical instrument is the music that is played on another instrument or instruments at the same time and that forms a background to the song or tune. EG *The children sang to the accompaniment of a piano played by the teacher... ...a guitar accompaniment.* N UNCOUNT/COUNT: USU+SUPP ⇑ music

2 An **accompaniment** to something is something else that happens or exists at the same time and in the same place. EG *This was the necessary accompaniment of the other two developments... He entered to the accompaniment of loud cheers.* N COUNT: IF+PREP THEN *of/to*

accompanist /əkʌmpəⁿnɪst/, **accompanists**. An **accompanist** is a musician, especially a pianist, who plays one part of a piece of music while someone else sings or plays the main tune. N COUNT+SUPP

accompany /əkʌmpəⁿni¹/, **accompanies, accompanying, accompanied**. 1 If you **accompany** someone, you go somewhere with them as their companion. EG *She asked me to accompany her to the church... She came out of the house accompanied by Miss Jones.* V+O ⇑ go with = escort, attend

2 If something **accompanies** something else, 2.1 it happens or exists at the same time as it or as a result of it. EG *His words were accompanied by exclamations from the audience... A high fever often accompanies a mild infection.* V+O ⇑ happen = partner 2.2 the two things exist together. EG *The text that accompanied his picture explained who he was.* V+O = support

3 When you **accompany** a singer or a musician, you play one part of a piece of music while they sing or play the main tune. EG *Sarah sings and Bill accompanies her on the guitar.* V+O (NG/REFL)

accompli /ækɒmpli:/. See **fait accompli**.

accomplice /əkɒmplɪs, əkʌm-/, **accomplices**. Someone's **accomplice** is a person who helps them to commit a crime or to do something wrong. EG *She was betrayed by her accomplice.* N COUNT: USU POSS+N ⇑ helper = partner

accomplish /əkɒmplɪʃ, əkʌm-/, **accomplishes, accomplishing, accomplished**. If you **accomplish** something, you succeed in doing it or finishing it. EG *How were they able to accomplish so much so quickly?... I never seem to accomplish anything.* V+O: NO IMPER ⇑ complete = achieve

accomplished /əkɒmplɪʃt, əkʌm-/. If someone is **accomplished** at something, they are very good at it. EG *...an accomplished cook.* ADJ QUALIT ⇑ capable = expert

accomplishment /əkɒmplɪʃməⁿnt, əkʌm-/, **accomplishments**. 1 **Accomplishment** is 1.1 the state of having the knowledge or skill to be able to do something well. EG *Actors of similar experience and accomplishment were being interviewed for the job.* N UNCOUNT ⇑ capability = attainment 1.2 the achieving or finishing of something. EG *The accomplishment of this task filled him with great satisfaction.* N UNCOUNT+SUPP ⇑ completion

2 Your **accomplishments** are the things that you can do well. EG *One of her few accomplishments was the ability to do cartwheels.* N COUNT ⇑ skill = attainment

3 An **accomplishment** is something remarkable that has been done or achieved. EG *This is no small accomplishment... Children should learn about the great accomplishments of their nation.* N COUNT: USU+SUPP ⇑ deed = achievement

accord /əˀkɔːd/, **accords, according, accorded**. 1 If you **accord** someone a particular kind of treatment, you treat them in a particular way or show a particular feeling or attitude towards them. EG *Newsmen accorded her the kind of coverage normally reserved for film stars... Others are given more importance than we would accord to them if left to ourselves.* V+O+O, OR V+O+A *(to)* = grant ≠ deny

2 If an idea, policy, situation, etc **accords** with something else, it fits in with it and is in harmony with it; a fairly formal use. EG *I rewrote the article because it didn't accord with our policy.* V+A *(with)* ⇑ agree

3 **Accord** is agreement about what should be done or about the way to do it. EG *There are few issues on which the two are in perfect accord.* N UNCOUNT: *in*+N ≠ disagreement

4 An **accord** is a formal agreement or settlement between two or more groups of people. EG *...the Camp David accords... The government expected a final accord before the end of the year.* N COUNT

5 When you do something **of** your **own accord**, you do it freely and because you want to, without being asked, persuaded, or forced to do it. EG *He decided to let him alone until he stopped of his own accord... In the end she knew they would leave of their own accord.* PHR: USED AS AN A = willingly

6 If people do something **with one accord**, they do it because they are in agreement about when or how it should be done. EG *With one accord they began to creep as quietly as possible into the cottage.* PHR: USED AS AN A ⇑ together

accordance /əˀkɔːdəns/. If something is done **in accordance with** a particular principle, rule, or system, it is done in the way that the principle, rule, or system says that it should be done. EG *His case is being dealt with in accordance with Islamic law... Education is carried out in accordance with the principles of the school.* PREP ⇑ under = according to

accordingly /əˀkɔːdɪŋli¹/. 1 If you do something and then are treated **accordingly**, you are treated in a way that is appropriate to what you have done. EG *Sometimes the press went too far, and suffered accordingly... He wanted to be treated like any other star entertainer and be paid accordingly.* ADV ⇑ justly = appropriately ≠ unfairly

2 **Accordingly** is used when you are saying that something happened as the result of something else. EG *She complained of stiffness in her joints. Accordingly she was admitted to hospital for further tests... He had loved her and he had been, accordingly, good to her.* ADV SEN ⇑ so = consequently

according to. 1 **According to** is used in front of the name of a person, book, document, etc when you want to say that you have obtained some information from them. You can show by the tone of your voice whether or not you believe the information. EG *According to Dr Santos, the cause of death was drowning... The road was some forty miles long according to my map.* PREP

2 If something is done or arranged **according to** a particular principle or criterion, this principle or criterion is used as the basis for the way it has been done or arranged. EG *Each person was given tasks according to their skills... There are six classes organized according to age.* PREP ⇑ depending on ≠ irrespective of

3 If something happens or is done **according to** a particular plan or system, it happens or is done in the way that the plan or system says that it should be done. EG *Everything went according to plan.* PREP ⇑ by ≠ against

accordion /əˀkɔːdɪən/, **accordions**. An **accordion** is a fairly large box-shaped musical instrument which you hold in your hands and play by pressing keys or buttons on either side while moving the two sides together and apart. N COUNT = piano accordion

accost /əkɒst/, **accosts, accosting, accosted**. If you **accost** someone, especially a stranger, you stop them or go up to them and speak to them, especially in a way that they do not like. EG *In the hall he was accosted by two men.* V+O ⇑ encounter = confront, buttonhole

account /əkaʊnt/, **accounts, accounting, accounted**. 1 An **account** is a written or spoken report that gives you the details of something that has happened. EG *I believe you gave a very good account of what happened... There were accounts of the incident in the paper.* N COUNT: IF+PREP THEN *of*

2 **Accounts** are a detailed record of all the money that a person or business receives and spends. EG *He had to submit accounts of his expenditure.* N COUNT: USU PL

3 If you have an **account** with a bank or similar institution, you leave money with them and withdraw it when you need it. EG *I would like to open an account with you... What's the balance of my account, please?* ● See also **current account, deposit account**. N COUNT ⇑ facility

4 If you have an **account** with a shop, you can buy goods there and pay for them at a later date. EG *We have an account at Harrods.* ● If you buy something **on account**, you take it away with you and pay for it at a later date. EG *You can have this on account.* N COUNT+SUPP ● PHR: USED AS AN A = on credit

5 If you are **accounted** wise, **accounted** a genius, etc, V+O+C

you are thought to be wise, a genius, etc; a formal use. EG *She may be accounted a true virtuoso.*

6 The word **account** is also used in the following expressions. 6.1 If you say that something is the case **by all accounts** or **from all accounts**, you mean that everyone you talk to about it, or everyone who writes about it, says that it is so. EG *From all accounts she was a clever girl.* — PHR : USED AS AN A

6.2 If someone says that something happened in a particular way **by** or **according to** your **own account**, they mean that you said that it happened in that way. EG *By his own account the car was coming too fast round the bend.* — PHR : USED AS AN A

6.3 If you **take** something **into account** or **take account of** something, you include it in your consideration of a matter because you think that it is important. EG *We'll certainly take your feelings into account... Does it take account of the costs?* — PHR : VB INFLECTS ⇑ consider ≠ ignore

6.4 If you do something, or if something happens, **on account of** something else, you do it, or it happens, because of it. EG *'Auntie told me not to run,' he explained, 'on account of my asthma'... All our water was boiled on account of there being a danger of typhoid fever.* — PREP

6.5 If you do something **on** someone's **account**, you do it for their benefit. EG *Don't abstain from smoking on my account.* — PHR : USED AS AN A

6.6 If you say that someone did something **on this account** or **on that account**, you mean that they did it for the reason that you have just mentioned. EG *He decided on that account to leave the country.* — PHR : USED AS AN A

6.7 If you say that something should **on no account** be done, you mean that it should not be done under any circumstances. EG *On no account must strangers be let in.* — PHR : USED AS AN A ⇑ never

6.8 If you say that something is **of little account** or **of no account**, you mean that it does not matter very much, or that it does not matter at all. EG *It's of no account to me whether you go or stay.* — PHR : USED AS AN A ⇑ unimportant

6.9 If you say that something is **of some account**, you mean that it is important. EG *Their reactions were of some account to me.* — PHR : USED AS AN A

6.10 If you **turn** or **put** something **to good account**, you use it fully and profitably. EG *In this new job she can put her talents to good account.* — PHR : VB INFLECTS

6.11 If you **give a good account of** yourself in a particular situation, you act or behave in a way which brings you praise and respect from other people. EG *Your son gave a very good account of himself last night.* — PHR : VB INFLECTS

6.12 If you **bring** or **call** someone **to account** for something that they have done wrong, you ask them to explain why they did it and reproach them for it. EG *I was called to account for my conduct by the headmistress.* — PHR : VB INFLECTS

account for. 1 If you **account for** something that has happened or for something that you have done, you explain how it happened or why you did it. EG *How do you account for the dent in the car?... There are reports to be made and money to be accounted for.* — PHRASAL VB : V+PREP, HAS PASS

2 If something **accounts for** a particular part or proportion of something, it is what that part or proportion consists of. EG *Computer software accounts for some 70 per cent of our range of products.* — PHRASAL VB : V+PREP, HAS PASS

accountable /əkaʊntəbə[0]l/. If you are **accountable** for something that you do, you are completely responsible for it and must be prepared to justify your actions. EG *They cannot be held accountable for what they did... ...a public corporation fully accountable to Parliament.* — ADJ CLASSIF : PRED, IF+PREP THEN *for/to* = answerable

◇ **accountability**. EG *...the need for greater accountability of the police.* — ◇ N UNCOUNT

accountancy /əkaʊntənsi[1]/ is the theory and practice of keeping or inspecting accounts. EG *...a career in accountancy.* — N UNCOUNT

accountant /əkaʊntənt/, **accountants**. An **accountant** is a person whose job it is to inspect or keep accounts. EG *...the specialist advice of solicitors, accountants and tax advisers.* — N COUNT ⇑ official

accoutrements /əku:trə[1]mənts/ are all the things you have with you when you travel or when you take part in a particular activity; a formal or humorous word. — N PLURAL ⇑ objects = baggage

accredit /ə[3]kredɪt/, **accredits, accrediting, accredited.** 1 If someone **is accredited** in a particular position, for example as the representative of an organization, they are officially recognized and approved of as having that position. EG *...an accredited shop steward... He would check the tickets and let duly accredited passengers through.* — V+O : USU PASS ⇑ be approved = be authorized

◇ **accreditation** /ə[3]kredɪteɪʃə[0]n/. EG *...temporary accreditation papers.* — ◇ N UNCOUNT

2 If diplomats **are accredited** to a country, they are officially sent there and accepted as representatives of their own country. EG *Visiting ambassadors are accredited to the Court of St James.* — V+O+A *(to)* : USU PASS ⇑ be appointed

3 If an institution such as a school or college is **accredited**, it is officially declared to be of the required standard. EG *...a fully accredited college.* — V+O : USU PASS ⇑ be approved = be authorized

4 If you **accredit** a particular quality or action to someone, you are saying that they have that quality or have performed that action. EG *...the legitimacy accredited to traditional rulers... These saints are accredited with the blessed gift of healing.* — V+O+A *(to/with)* ⇑ ascribe = attribute, credit

accretion /ə[3]kri:ʃə[0]n/, **accretions.** 1 An **accretion** is a layer of material which gradually forms on top of something; a formal use. EG *...accretions of mud.* — N COUNT+SUPP ⇑ addition

2 **Accretion** is the process of new layers or parts being added to something so that it increases in size. EG *Coral is formed by a process of accretion.* — N UNCOUNT = addition

accrue /ə[3]kru:/, **accrues, accruing, accrued.** 1 If money or interest **accrues**, it gradually increases in amount over a period of time. EG *...£100,000 plus accrued interest at 8%... ...tax benefits accruing to owner-occupiers.* — V-ERG ⇑ collect = accumulate

2 If you **accrue** things or if they **accrue**, you collect them or allow them to accumulate over a period of time; a formal use. EG *We had accrued a fine collection of Chinese porcelain... Certain advantages accrue to a man or woman when they reach adult status.* — V-ERG

accumulate /ə[3]kju:mjə[4]leɪt/, **accumulates, accumulating, accumulated.** When you **accumulate** things or when they **accumulate**, you collect or gather them, or they increase in number or amount, over a period of time. EG *We packed up the things I had accumulated over the last four years... ...her accumulated resentment and bitterness.* — V-ERG = amass, build up

accumulation /ə[3]kju:mjə[4]leɪʃə[0]n/, **accumulations.** 1 An **accumulation** is a large group or amount of things which have been gathered together over a period of time. EG *...an accumulation of facts... ...large accumulations of capital.* — N COUNT+SUPP ⇑ collection = build up

2 **Accumulation** is the collecting together of things over a period of time. EG *...the accumulation of wealth.* — N UNCOUNT

accumulative /ə[3]kju:mjə[4]lətɪv/. 1 If something is **accumulative,** it becomes increasingly great in amount, number, or intensity over a period of time. EG *...the eventual accumulative effect of these substances.* — ADJ CLASSIF = cumulative

2 If someone is described as **accumulative**, they like to own and keep a lot of things; used showing disapproval. EG *We live in an accumulative society.* — ADJ QUALIT ⇑ greedy = acquisitive

accuracy /ækjə[4]rəsi[1]/. **Accuracy** is 1 the ability to perform a task without making a mistake or to reach a target precisely. EG *I admired the speed and accuracy with which she typed... ...the effectiveness and accuracy of their weapons.* — N UNCOUNT/N SING WITH DET = precision

2 the quality of being true or correct. EG *...the traditional reputation of The Times for accuracy.* — N UNCOUNT/N SING WITH DET ⇑ truth

accurate /ækjə[4]rə[1]t/. 1 An account or description that is **accurate** gives a true idea of what a situation, thing, person, etc is like. EG *His description had been reasonably accurate... ...an accurate picture of social history.* — ADJ QUALIT ⇑ correct = authentic

◇ **accurately**. EG *The story is accurately told in his account of the battle.* — ◇ ADV WITH VB = truthfully

2 A calculation, measurement, piece of work, etc, that is **accurate** is correct or precise. EG *The kitchen scales were accurate to half a gram... Their essays tend to be grammatically accurate.* ▸ used of people. EG *She is meticulously accurate in punctuation and spelling.* — ADJ QUALIT

◇ **accurately**. EG *I may not have drawn it accurately enough.* — ◇ ADV WITH VB = precisely

3 A person, device, or machine that is **accurate** is able to perform a task precisely and without making a mistake, or to reach a precise target. EG *Submarine-launched missiles are becoming more accurate...* ▸ used of an action, aim, or throw. EG *Her aim was devastatingly accurate.* — ADJ QUALIT ⇑ exact = precise

◇ **accurately**. EG *The weapons never fired accurately.* — ◇ ADV WITH VB

accursed /əkɜ:sɪd, əkɜ:st/; a formal word. 1 You can use **accursed** to describe an object, event, feeling, etc when you are very annoyed about it. EG *They begged and badgered me to take them to see that accursed film... ...this accursed pain.* — ADJ CLASSIF : ATTRIB ⇑ annoying = wretched

2 If a person is **accursed**, someone has put a curse on them. EG *...a being who was by God's own law accursed.* — ADJ CLASSIF = cursed ≠ blessed

accusation /ækjə⁴zeɪʃəⁿn/, **accusations**. 1 An **accusation** is 1.1 a statement, which may be either true or false, that someone has done something bad or wrong. EG *...accusations of cheating... The accusation against us was that we were biassed.* 1.2 a formal legal charge that someone has committed a crime. EG *The plaintiff makes one accusation after the other... Failure to do this is very likely to lead to accusation and prosecution for theft.* — N COUNT : IF + PREP THEN of/against, OR + REPORT-CL; N COUNT/UNCOUNT

2 **Accusation** is the act of showing by your voice, expression, or behaviour that you think that someone has done something wrong or bad. EG *Her eyes were full of accusation... She asked me with an air of accusation why I knew 'so much' about everything.* — N UNCOUNT ⇑ hostility

accusative /ə³kjuːzətɪv/. In the grammar of some languages, for example Latin, the **accusative** case is a case used for a noun when it is the direct object of a verb. It is also used with some prepositions. ▸ used as a noun. EG *It's in the accusative.* — ADJ CLASSIF; ▸ N SING : the+N

accusatory /ə³kjuːzə¹təⁿri¹/. An **accusatory** remark or tone of voice suggests blame or criticism. EG *Internal, accusatory dialogues are commonplace.* — ADJ CLASSIF = accusing

accuse /ə³kjuːz/, **accuses, accusing, accused**. 1 If you **accuse** someone of something, 1.1 you say that they have done something wrong or bad. EG *He was accused of incompetence... The French accuse us of being reserved.* 1.2 you formally say, especially in a court of law, that they have committed a particular crime. EG *He is accused of killing ten young women... ...the rights of accused criminals.* — V+O : IF+PREP THEN of ⇑ charge; V+O : IF+PREP THEN of = charge

2 If someone **stands accused** of something, 2.1 they are held responsible and blamed for doing something wrong or bad. EG *Their bankers stand accused of hindering economic recovery.* 2.2 they have been formally charged with a crime. EG *They stand accused of murder.* — PHR : VB INFLECTS; PHR : VB INFLECTS

accused /ə³kjuːzd/. **The accused** refers to the person or group of people being tried in a court for a crime. EG *Will the accused please stand... The accused are three men in their early twenties.* — N SING : the+N, VB CAN BE SING OR PL = defendant

accuser /ə³kjuːzə/, **accusers**. An **accuser** is a person who says that someone has done something wrong, especially that they have committed a crime. EG *I had to prepare to face my accusers.* — N COUNT

accusing /ə³kjuːzɪŋ/. If your expression or tone of voice is **accusing**, it shows that you think that someone has done something wrong or bad. EG *She gave him an accusing look... He smiled at her accusing face.* ◇ **accusingly**. EG *'You liked him,' he said accusingly.* — ADJ QUALIT ⇑ hostile; ◇ ADV WITH VB

accustom /ə³kʌstəm/, **accustoms, accustoming, accustomed**. If you **accustom** yourself or someone else to something different, you make yourself or them used to it. EG *He sat very still, trying to accustom himself to the darkness... I took her along, with some idea of accustoming her to travelling.* — V+O (NG/REFL) + A (TO) ⇑ train = adapt

accustomed /ə³kʌstəmd/. 1 If you are **accustomed** to something or to something happening, you are used to it or are familiar with it. EG *I am not accustomed to being interrupted... My eyes became accustomed to the dim lighting.* — ADJ QUALIT : PRED+to

2 **Accustomed** is used 2.1 to describe things which you do naturally and without a lot of thought, because you have done them many times before. EG *He drove with his accustomed, casual ease.* 2.2 to describe an object that is usually used by a particular person, or the way or method by which something usually happens or is done. EG *He was sitting in his accustomed chair... Things don't run in their accustomed channels.* — ADJ QUALIT : ATTRIB = practised; ADJ CLASSIF : ATTRIB ⇑ usual = customary

ace /eɪs/, **aces**. 1 An **ace** is a playing card which has a single symbol on it. EG *...the ace of spades.* — N COUNT

2 If you **have an ace up** your **sleeve**, you know something or are able to do something which you have kept secret so far, and which is likely to help you win or succeed. EG *He thinks he's won but I've got an ace up my sleeve.* — PHR : VB INFLECTS

3 If you **hold all the aces**, you have all the advantages in a contest. EG *It was a battle of wits, with Sandra holding all the aces.* — PHR : VB INFLECTS

4 If you **are** or **come within an ace of** something, you very nearly do or experience it. EG *He came within an ace of being run over.* — PHR : VB INFLECTS

5 A person who is **ace** at something is extremely good at it; an informal use. EG *...an ace marksman.* — ADJ CLASSIF = expert

6 If you say that something is **ace**, you mean that you think that it is very good; an informal use. EG *Their new record's really ace!* — ADJ QUALIT, OR EXCLAM = great

7 An **ace** is also a serve in tennis which is so good that the other player cannot reach the ball. — N COUNT

acerbity /ə³sɜːbɪti¹/ is sharpness or bitterness in a remark, or in your voice or manner; a formal word. — N UNCOUNT

acetate /æsi¹teɪt/ is a smooth man-made cloth, sometimes used for making clothes. — N UNCOUNT ⇑ fabric

acetic acid /əsiːtɪk æsɪd/ is a colourless acid. It is the main substance in vinegar. — N UNCOUNT

acetylene /əsetɪ⁰li¹n/ is a colourless gas which burns with a very hot bright flame. It is often used in lamps and for cutting and welding metal. — N UNCOUNT

ache /eɪk/, **aches, aching, ached**. 1 If you **ache** or if a part of your body **aches**, you feel a dull steady pain. EG *I was tired, aching, and miserable... His leg ached.* — V ⇑ hurt = be sore

2 If you **ache** to do something or for something, you want it very much. EG *I was aching to tell you all my news... She was aching for a cigarette.* — V : IF+PREP THEN for/with, OR V+to-INF

3 An **ache** is 3.1 a dull steady pain in a part of your body. EG *The dull ache in her side began... ...my usual aches and pains.* 3.2 a very strong feeling, usually of longing for something. EG *I felt a brief intense ache of happiness.* — N COUNT; N COUNT+SUPP

achieve /ə³tʃiːv/, **achieves, achieving, achieved**. 1 If you **achieve** something such as a particular aim or effect, you succeed in fulfilling it or in causing it to happen, usually after a lot of effort. EG *He will do anything in order to achieve his aim... Independence was achieved over a century ago... The riots achieved nothing.* — V+O ⇑ get

2 If you **achieve** in a particular area of work or activity, you are successful in it. EG *Women can achieve in areas where men traditionally have achieved.* — V : IF+PREP THEN in ⇑ succeed = get on

achievement /ə³tʃiːvmə²nt/, **achievements**. 1 An **achievement** is something which someone did or caused to happen, especially after a lot of effort. EG *It was an astonishing achievement... ...the achievements of the Labour Government.* — N COUNT : USU+SUPP ⇑ deed = accomplishment

2 **Achievement** is the process of achieving something or of something being achieved. EG *...the achievement of their political goals... This fact did not lessen her sense of achievement...* — N UNCOUNT ⇑ attainment = fulfilment

Achilles heel /əkɪliːz hiːl/, **Achilles heels**. Someone's **Achilles heel** is the weakest point in their character, where it is easiest for other people to attack or criticize them. EG *Status is the businessman's Achilles heel.* — N COUNT : USU POSS+N IN SING ⇑ weakness ≠ forte

Achilles tendon, Achilles tendons. Your **Achilles tendon** is the cord inside the back of your leg just above your heel. — N COUNT

acid /æsɪd/, **acids**. 1 An **acid** is a liquid with a pH value of less than 7, which is used in chemical processes and in some household substances. Strong acids can burn your skin and make holes in your clothes. EG *Dab it with a solution of weak acid.* — N COUNT/UNCOUNT ≠ alkali

2 An **acid** substance or liquid has a pH value of less than 7. EG *...an acid soil.* ◇ **acidity** /æsɪdɪti¹/. EG *It's a good idea to test the acidity of your wine.* — ADJ CLASSIF; ◇ N UNCOUNT

3 An **acid** fruit or drink has a sour or sharp taste. EG *These oranges are very acid.* ▸ used of a taste or smell. EG *The medicine had a sharp, acid taste.* — ADJ QUALIT = tart

4 An **acid** remark or **acid** humour is very unkind or critical. EG *...her trenchant, acid wit.* ◇ **acidly**. EG *'Nice of you to turn up,' she said acidly.* ◇ **acidity**. EG *I noticed a certain acidity in his comments.* — ADJ QUALIT; ◇ ADV WITH VB; ◇ N UNCOUNT

5 If you say that something is **an acid test**, you mean that it is a way of proving whether something is true or not, or of good quality or not. EG *This venture is seen as an acid test of the alliance.* — PHR : USED AS C

6 **Acid** is the same as **LSD**; an informal use. EG *One speaker was high on acid.* — N UNCOUNT

acidic /ə³sɪdɪk/. Something that is **acidic** contains acid or has a pH value of less than 7. EG *...an acidic soil.* — ADJ CLASSIF = acid ≠ alkaline

acid rain is rain polluted by acid which has been discharged into the atmosphere from factories and other industrial processes. The rain then destroys or damages plants, trees, and other parts of the environment. — N UNCOUNT ⇑ pollution

acknowledge /ə³knɒlɪdʒ/, **acknowledges, acknowledging, acknowledged**. 1 If you **acknowledge** a fact or a situation, you accept or admit that it is true or that it exists. EG *The state acknowl-* — V+O/REPORT-CL *edged the justice of their cause... Most people will now acknowledge that there is a crisis.*

2 If people or their status, qualities, or achievements **are acknowledged** by other people, they are widely known about and admired. EG *Edwin Lawrence Godkin was acknowledged as America's finest editorial writer... ...a woman of acknowledged charm and personality.* — V+O : IF+PREP THEN *as*, USU PASS ↑ be admired

3 If you **acknowledge** someone, for example with a nod or a smile, you show that you have seen and recognized them. EG *I took care not to acknowledge Janet with more than a nod... He never even bothered to acknowledge her presence.* — V+O : IF+PREP THEN *with*, OR V +REPORT-CL ↑ greet

4 If you **acknowledge** a message, letter, or parcel, you tell the person who sent it that you have received it. EG *The Colonel heard his Operations Officer acknowledge the message... You have to sign here and acknowledge receipt.* — V+O/REPORT-CL ↑ answer = confirm

5 If you **acknowledge** applause, compliments, or something which is done for you, you show your gratitude for it or your appreciation of it. EG *The president stood up to acknowledge the cheers of the crowd... I pushed a drink toward him; he acknowledged it, but continued talking.* — V+O ↑ appreciate

acknowledgement /ə[3]knɒlɪdʒmə[2]nt/, **acknowledgements**; also spelled **acknowledgment**. **1 Acknowledgement** is **1.1** accepting or admitting that something is true. EG *...his acknowledgement of his guilt... There was some acknowledgement that the parents had to be involved.* — N UNCOUNT/COUNT **1.2** showing that you have seen and recognized someone. EG *One of the uniformed men gravely raised an arm in acknowledgment.* — N UNCOUNT/COUNT **1.3** telling the sender of a message, letter, or parcel that you have received it. EG *...in acknowledgement of telephone orders.* — N UNCOUNT : IF+PREP THEN *of* **1.4** expressing your gratitude for or appreciation of something. — N UNCOUNT/COUNT

2 An **acknowledgement** is a letter or message telling the sender of a letter, message, or parcel that it has arrived. — N COUNT : IF+PREP THEN *of*

3 The **acknowledgements** at the beginning or end of a book or article are the short piece of writing in which the author thanks all the people who have assisted him or her. — N PLURAL : *the*+N

acme /ækmi[1]/. The **acme** of something is its highest point of achievement or excellence; a formal word. EG *...the acme of parental care.* — N SING : USU *the*+N = zenith

acne /ækni[1]/. If someone has **acne**, they have a lot of spots on their face, neck, and body. Acne is very common among teenagers. EG *...a youth with a stubborn case of acne.* — N UNCOUNT ↑ ailment

acolyte /ækəlaɪt/, **acolytes**. An **acolyte** is **1** someone who assists a priest in performing certain religious services. — N COUNT ↑ assistant **2** a follower or attendant of an important person; a literary use. — N COUNT = disciple

acorn /eɪkɔːn/, **acorns**. An **acorn** is a pale oval nut that grows in a cup-shaped case on an oak tree. — N COUNT

acoustic /əkuːstɪk/, **acoustics**. **1 Acoustic** means relating to sound or hearing. EG *Acoustic contact had been made.* — ADJ CLASSIF : ATTRIB

2 Acoustics is the scientific study of sound. — N UNCOUNT

3 The **acoustics** of a room are the structural features of it which determine how well you can hear music or speeches. EG *The theatre was large, with good acoustics.* — N PLURAL = audibility

4 An **acoustic** guitar or other musical instrument is one whose sound is not made louder by electrical apparatus. — ADJ CLASSIF : ATTRIB

acquaint /əkweɪnt/, **acquaints, acquainting, acquainted**. **1** If you **acquaint** someone with some information, you inform them about it or cause them to be aware of it; a fairly formal use. EG *I will acquaint you with the facts... I am acquainted with the names of at least eight such people.* — V+O (NG/REFL) +A (*with*) ↑ inform

2 If you **acquaint** someone with something, you cause them to become familiar with it or to know a lot about it. EG *They were well acquainted with modern farming methods... I had acquainted myself with their customs.* — V+O (NG/REFL) +A (*with*) ↑ teach

3 If you **are acquainted** with someone, you know them slightly but they are not a close friend. EG *Mrs Oliver is acquainted with my mother... The families were acquainted.* — V+C : IF+PREP THEN *with* : RECIP

4 If you **get** or **become acquainted** with someone, you get to know them. EG *Then we'll go back to your cabin and get acquainted.* — PHR : VB INFLECTS

acquaintance /əkweɪntəns/, **acquaintances**. **1** An **acquaintance** is someone whom you have met but do not know well. EG *My husband's cousin is an acquaintance of Lord Northcliffe... ... hundreds of friends and acquaintances.* — N COUNT : USU+SUPP

2 If you have **acquaintance** with someone, you know them slightly but not as a close friend. EG *He got the job through his acquaintance with the President.* — N UNCOUNT : IF+PREP THEN *with* ↑ friendship

3 If someone is **of** your **acquaintance**, you know them slightly, but not well. EG *...doctors of my acquaintance.* — PHR : NG+PHR

4 When you **make** someone's **acquaintance**, you meet them for the first time and get to know them a little. EG *That evening he made the acquaintance of a young actress.* — PHR : VB INFLECTS

5 On further or **closer acquaintance** with someone or something means after you have got to know them better. EG *On further acquaintance he seems quite pleasant.* — PHR : USED AS AN A

6 Your **acquaintance** with a subject is your knowledge or experience of it. EG *...her acquaintance with modern art.* — N SING WITH DET ≠ ignorance

7 If you have **a nodding** or **passing acquaintance** with a subject, you have some knowledge of it but not much. EG *At least a nodding acquaintance with physics was essential.* — PHR : USED AS O OR S

8 If you have **a nodding** or **passing acquaintance** with someone, you know them slightly but not very well. — PHR : USED AS O

acquiesce /ækwɪɛs/, **acquiesces, acquiescing, acquiesced**. If you **acquiesce** to something, you agree to do what someone wants or to accept what they do. EG *They acquiesced grudgingly... He acquiesced to the demand... The legislators acquiesced in the peace terms.* — V : IF+PREP THEN *to/in* = give in ≠ resist

acquiescence /ækwi[1]ɛsə[0]ns/ is agreement to do what someone wants or acceptance of what they do. EG *...passive acquiescence to the new arrangements... He didn't much care for her easy acquiescence in his treatment of the children.* — N UNCOUNT : IF+PREP THEN *to/in* ≠ resistance

acquiescent /ækwi[1]ɛsə[0]nt/. Someone who is **acquiescent** is ready to agree to do what someone wants or to accept what they do. EG *Like many acquiescent people she was over-decisive when angry.* — ADJ QUALIT ↑ submissive

acquire /ə[3]kwaɪə/, **acquires, acquiring, acquired**. **1** If you **acquire** something, you get or buy it for yourself, or you are given it. EG *...a company that Mr Wheeler acquired in 1978... I tried to acquire the information I needed.* — V+O ↑ obtain = get hold of ◇ **acquired**. EG *...a particular form of acquired wealth.* — ◇ ADJ CLASSIF

2 When you **acquire** a skill or habit, you learn it or develop it. EG *It is a habit well worth acquiring.* — V+O = adopt ◇ **acquired**. EG *...hereditary and acquired characteristics.* — ◇ ADJ CLASSIF

3 If something is **an acquired taste**, it is something that many people do not like at first but which they like after they have tried or experienced it a number of times. EG *Flying's a bit of an acquired taste.* — PHR : USED AS C

acquisition /ækwɪ[1]zɪʃə[0]n/, **acquisitions**. **1** An **acquisition** is something that you have obtained, especially as an addition to a collection of items which you already have. EG *He invited me to inspect his latest acquisition.* — N COUNT = find

2 Acquisition is **2.1** getting or being given something. EG *...the acquisition of land... The Government offered to provide 90% of the cost of acquisition.* — N UNCOUNT+SUPP **2.2** the process of learning a skill or of developing a habit. EG *...the acquisition of knowledge.* — N UNCOUNT+SUPP

acquisitive /əkwɪzɪtɪv/. Someone who is **acquisitive** is fond of getting new possessions; used showing disapproval. EG *He's a very acquisitive sort of person.* — ADJ QUALIT

acquit /əkwɪt/, **acquits, acquitting, acquitted**. **1** If you **acquit** someone of a crime in a court of law, you formally declare that they did not commit the crime. EG *The jury acquitted her of theft... John Campbell was acquitted on all charges.* — V+O : USU PASS ↑ exonerate = clear ≠ convict

2 If you **acquit** yourself in a particular way, other people feel that you behave in that way; a formal use. EG *She acquitted herself well in the meeting.* — V+O (REFL) = conduct

acquittal /əkwɪtə[0]l/, **acquittals**. **Acquittal** is a formal declaration in a court of law that someone who has been accused of a crime is innocent of it. EG *They were enraged at the acquittal of a policeman accused of murder.* — N UNCOUNT/COUNT ↑ exoneration ≠ conviction

acre /eɪkə/, **acres**. **1** An **acre** is an area of land measuring 4840 square yards or 4047 square metres. EG *...an acre of orchard... Ten pounds an acre has been paid for land.* — N PART ↑ measurement

2 If you say that there is **acres** of something, you — N PART : PLURAL mean that there is a large amount of it; an informal use. EG *Her wedding dress had acres of material in it.*

acreage /eɪkəʳrɪdʒ/. The **acreage** of a piece of land is its area measured in acres. EG *The financial value of its immense acreage was enormous.* N UNCOUNT ⇑ size

acrid /ækrɪd/. 1 An **acrid** smell or taste is strong and sharp, and usually unpleasant. EG *The room was filling with acrid smoke.* ADJ QUALIT = pungent

2 **Acrid** words or remarks are bitter and angry. EG *...an acrid attack on American capitalism.* ADJ QUALIT = caustic

acrimonious /ækrɪməʊnɪəs/. **Acrimonious** words or quarrels are bitter and angry; a fairly formal word. EG *An acrimonious dispute broke out.* ADJ QUALIT

acrimony /ækrɪməni¹/ is bitterness and anger about something; a fairly formal word. EG *...acrimony over the involvement of the police.* N UNCOUNT

acrobat /ækrə⁶bæt/, **acrobats**. An **acrobat** is an entertainer who performs difficult physical actions, such as running on his or her hands or walking along a rope or high wire. EG *...a team of Chinese acrobats.* N COUNT ⇑ performer = tumbler

acrobatic /ækrə⁶bætɪk/, **acrobatics**. 1 An **acrobatic** movement or display is graceful and clever, and involves swift turns, somersaults, or difficult balancing feats. EG *...an acrobatic dance... ...songs, comedy acts, and acrobatic numbers.* ▸ used of people. EG *My little daughter's really acrobatic.* ADJ QUALIT ⇑ athletic ▸ ⇑ skilful = agile

2 **Acrobatics** are acrobatic movements. EG *He can do the most amazing acrobatics.* N PLURAL

acronym /ækrə⁶nɪm/, **acronyms**. An **acronym** is a word composed of the initial letters of the name of something, especially an organization, or of the words in a phrase. Examples of acronyms are NATO, AIDS, and TEFL. N COUNT

across /əkrɒs/. 1 If you go **across** a country, area of land, room, etc, you go from one side of it to the other. EG *He wandered across Hyde Park... He blew a cloud of smoke across the table... ...the route across the Canadian border.* PREP

2 If something is written, drawn, etc **across** a flat surface, it is written, drawn, etc from one side of it to the other. EG *A straight line was ruled across the map... ...a rude word scrawled across the wall of the Post Office.* PREP

3 If something is situated or stretched **across** a gap, hole, valley, etc, it is situated or stretched from one side of it to the other so as to span it or to form a bridge over it. EG *...a banner stretched across the street... ...the bridge across the river.* PREP

4 If you go **across** something such as a bridge, you go along the length of it in order to cross a river or road. EG *We clattered across the bridge... ...a spectacular escape across a high wire.* PREP ⇑ over

5 If you go **across** to a particular place or person, you go through or over an area in order to reach them. EG *He went across to Madeleine... They've been coming across in aeroplanes.* ADV : IF+PREP THEN *to*

6 If you lean or stretch **across**, you lean or stretch in a particular direction, especially sideways or in front of someone or something. EG *The kettle boiled and Jane leant across and lifted it... He was leaning across my desk.* ADV AFTER VB, OR PREP = over

7 If you look or call **across** somewhere or **across** at someone or something, you look or call over an area towards them. EG *He turned his head and looked across at me... They'd shout across the room to one another.* PREP, OR ADV AFTER VB : ADV+ *at*

8 If something is situated **across** a street, river, etc, it is situated on the other side of it. EG *He stared at the houses across the street... She stared thoughtfully at the Englishman across the table.* ● If something is situated **across from** something else, it is situated opposite to it. EG *...the park across from the church... She sat across from him.* PREP ● PREP

9 If something happens or is broadcast **across** a particular country or continent, it happens or is broadcast everywhere in it. EG *He gave a series of interviews across Western Europe.* PREP = throughout

10 If something happens or is introduced **across** different groups of people or **across** different types of work or activity, it affects all of them. EG *This policy stretches across several different departments.* ● **across the board**: see **board**. PREP

11 If something goes or cuts **across** a social, religious, or political barrier, it is happening amongst more than one different group of people and often involves co-operation between them. EG *Issues tended to cut across party lines... The new arrangements cut across ethnic barriers.* PREP

12 If something is lying **across** an object or place, it is resting on it and partly covering it. EG *He had his gun across his knees... A shadow fell across the phone.* PREP

13 If a particular expression spreads **across** someone's face, their face shows that expression. EG *Smiles spread across every face.* PREP = over

14 **Across** is used before the name of a wide part of your body, for example your back, chest, or shoulders, especially when you are referring to its measurement, the clothes which cover it, or a pain which you have there. EG *He was experiencing severe pain across his chest... ...a white blouse that stretches tightly across her back.* PREP

15 If someone hits you **across** a part of your body, they hit you on that part. EG *The woman slapped the newspaper across his face.* PREP

16 **Across** is used in measurements to show the width of something. EG *That huge meteorite blasted a hole 200 kilometers across.* ADV : NUM+ADV = wide

acrostic /əkrɒstɪk/, **acrostics**. An **acrostic** is several lines of writing, usually a poem, in which the first, middle, or last letters of each line make a word or sentence. N COUNT ⇑ puzzle

acrylic /əkrɪlɪk/, **acrylics**. 1 **Acrylic** material, clothes, or blankets are made of cloth that is manufactured by a chemical process. EG *Acrylic blankets and shawls are both warm and washable.* ADJ CLASSIF : ATTRIB ⇑ synthetic

2 **Acrylic** paint is a type of paint used by artists. EG *He had painted on big wooden panels with bright acrylic paint.* ▸ used as a noun. EG *He painted in acrylics.* ADJ CLASSIF ▸ N PLURAL

act /ækt/, **acts, acting, acted**. 1 When you **act**, you do something for a particular purpose. EG *We have to act quickly... He acted alone in the shooting.* V : USU+A = work

2 If you **act** on advice, information, etc, you do what has been advised or suggested. EG *Why didn't you act on my warning?... They were content to provide information on which others could act.* V+A *(on/upon)*

3 When lawyers, estate agents, etc **act** for you or on your behalf, they are employed by you to deal with a particular matter. EG *...lawyers acting for Paul McCartney... ...independent financial advisers who act on behalf of their clients.* V+A *(for/on behalf of)* ⇑ do

4 If a force or a chemical substance **acts**, it has an effect. EG *Few, if any, drugs act sufficiently swiftly... There are forces acting on it.* V ⇑ work = operate

5 If you **act**, or **act** a part, in a play or film, you have a part in it. EG *I was acting in a play called The Return of the Prodigal... I acted Malvolio once at Sadler's Wells Theatre.* V OR V+O ⇑ perform

6 If someone **acts** in a particular way, they behave in that way. EG *He recalled how peculiarly she had acted towards him upon his return... We acted as if we had never set eyes on each other... You're acting like a lunatic.* ● to **act** your **age**: see **age**. ● **to act the fool**: see **fool**. ● **to act the goat**: see **goat**. V+A

7 If you **act** the way someone behaves in a particular situation, you deliberately behave in the way which is typical of that person. EG *At the table Smith acted the dutiful host... I wanted to be spoiled, to act the patient.* V+*the*+C ⇑ behave = play

8 If someone or something **acts** in a particular role or with a particular function, they have that role or function on a particular occasion. EG *Sometimes Chang was with me and acted as interpreter... The shark can twist its fins to act as brakes.* V+A *(as/like)*

9 If you **are acting**, you are behaving in a particular way in order to create a particular impression. EG *She's just acting that she's angry.* V OR V+O : USU CONT ⇑ pretend

10 An **act** is 10.1 a single thing, or a set of related things, done by someone. EG *He was accused of some 30 terrorist acts... ...an act of aggression... Sometimes just the act of writing down the problems straightens out your thinking.* N COUNT+SUPP ⇑ action 10.2 behaviour that is intended to create a particular impression but which does not express your real feelings or is not your normal behaviour. EG *Will you stop putting on this concerned parent act?... She appeared calm and confident but it was just an act.* N SING WITH DET ⇑ pretence = front, show

11 An **Act** is a law passed by the government. EG *...the 1944 Education Act... They were tried under the Suppression of Communism Act.* ● to **read the riot act**: see **riot**. N COUNT : ALSO IN NAMES AFTER N

12 An **act** in a play, opera, or ballet is one of the N COUNT

main parts into which the play, opera, or ballet is divided. EG *He sat with his back to the stage all through the first act... She was magnificent in Act One of 'Carmen'.*

13 An **act** in a show is a short performance which is one of several in the show. EG *...a spectacle consisting of songs, comedy acts and acrobatic numbers.* ▸ used of a person, group, or animal. EG *They're a brilliant comedy act.* — N COUNT ⇑ entertainment = number

14 **Act** is used in expressions such as 'disappearing act', 'balancing act', or 'juggling act' to refer to a clever piece of behaviour which helps you in a difficult situation. EG *He returned to England, repeating his disappearing act so he wouldn't have to discuss scripts... He kept up his balancing act between the two parties.* — N COUNT : MOD+N ⇑ behaviour = trick, stunt

15 **Act** is also used in the following expressions: 15.1 If you are **in the act of** doing something at a particular moment, you are doing it at that time. EG *He saw Jones in the act of snatching a gun.* — PHR : USED AS AN A
15.2 If you **catch** or **nab** someone **in the act**, you discover them doing something wrong or committing a crime. EG *We caught him in the act.* — PHR : VB INFLECTS
15.3 If you **get in on** or **muscle in on the act**, you take part in or take advantage of something that was started by someone else; an informal expression. EG *The studio assistants got in on the act five years later.* — PHR : VB INFLECTS ⇑ participate
15.4 When you **get** your **act together**, you organize your life or your affairs so that you are able to achieve what you want or to deal with something effectively; an informal expression. EG *The two countries will have to get their act together if they ever hope to achieve anything.* — PHR : VB INFLECTS

act out. 1 When you **act out** your feelings or ideas, you express them in your behaviour, especially as a means of relieving nervous tension or emotion. EG *...authoritarian adults acting out their preconceptions of how children should be brought up.* — PHRASAL VB : V+O+ADV ⇑ represent

2 If you **act out** an event which has happened, you copy the actions which took place and make them into a play. EG *The teacher gets the students to act out some historic event.* — PHRASAL VB : V+O+ADV ⇑ represent = depict

act up. 1 If something **is acting up**, it is not working properly; an informal expression. EG *Her washing machine was acting up again.* — PHRASAL VB : V+ADV = play up ≠ work

2 If someone, especially a child, **is acting up**, they are behaving badly; an informal expression. EG *I'm sorry he had to act up like this.* — PHRASAL VB : V+ADV ⇑ misbehave = play up

acting /æktɪŋ/. 1 **Acting** is 1.1 the profession of performing in plays or films. EG *It was not visions of film stardom that led McKellen into acting.* — N UNCOUNT
1.2 the art and skill with which a person plays a part in a play or film. EG *I have always been very impressed by his acting.* — N UNCOUNT ⇑ performing = artistry

2 **Acting** is used before the title of a job, usually one which involves some responsibility, to indicate that someone is doing that job temporarily and that it is not theirs permanently. EG *...Yassin Mohamed, acting Director of Adult Education.* — ADJ CLASSIF : ATTRIB ⇑ temporary

action /ækʃəⁿn/, **actions**. 1 **Action** is anything that you do in order to deal with or achieve something. EG *He had decided upon immediate action... It will restrict our freedom of action.* — N UNCOUNT ⇑ process
● If you **take action**, you do things in order to deal with or achieve something. EG *The government was already taking action to stop the strike. I had to take evasive action.* — ● PHR : VB INFLECTS, USU+to-INF/A = act
● See also **industrial action**.

2 An **action** is 2.1 something that you do, especially for a particular purpose. EG *He defended his original action in sacking Mr Rookes... He could not be held responsible for his actions.* — N COUNT ⇑ act = deed
2.2 a legal process in which you ask a court to order someone to stop doing something or to pay compensation for damage they have caused. EG *He brought an action against the union officials... ...a libel action.* — N COUNT ⇑ case = suit

3 An **action** is also a movement of part of your body. EG *Their every action and expression was recorded.* — N COUNT

4 A particular kind of **action** is a particular kind of movement, especially of part of your body. EG *...the sucking action of the baby's tongue... It needs a lot of wrist action.* — N UNCOUNT+SUPP ⇑ movement

5 The **action** of a device or machine is the way it moves when it operates. EG *It has a very smooth action.* — N SING WITH DET+SUPP

6 The **action** of a force or chemical substance is the way in which it operates or produces an effect. EG *Some washing powders break down proteins by chemical action.* — N UNCOUNT+SUPP

7 The **action** is 7.1 all the important, exciting, or up-to-date things that are happening or being done. EG *They felt they should be near the centre of the action.* — N SING : the+N ⇑ events
7.2 all the things that happen in a story or play. EG *All the action in The Ghost Train takes place at one station.* — N SING : the+N ⇑ events

8 **Action** is also fighting which takes place in a war. EG *...official reports of military action... ...a stubborn rearguard action.* — N UNCOUNT/COUNT
● If you **see action**, you take part in fighting in a war. EG *He'd seen a lot of action.* — ● PHR : VB INFLECTS

9 **in action**, or **into action**. 9.1 If a soldier is **in action**, or goes **into action**, he is fighting, or beginning to fight, in a war. EG *Henry's brother had been killed in action in Germany... They went into action against superior forces.* — PHR : USED AS AN A
9.2 If someone or something is **in action**, or goes **into action**, they are working, operating, or performing a particular function, or are beginning to do so. EG *He wanted to go there and see the system in action... Mum quickly went into action in the kitchen.* — PHR : USED AS AN A
● If you **put**, **bring**, or **call** an idea or policy **into action**, you begin to use it or cause it to operate. EG *He was capable not only of putting ideas forward, but also of putting them into action.* — ● PHR : VB INFLECTS = implement

10 If someone or something is **out of action**, especially due to injury or damage, they are not able to be used. EG *I was out of action with a sprained ankle... All three tanks were very quickly put out of action.* — PHR : USED AS AN A

actionable /ækʃəⁿnəbəⁿl/. If something that you do or say to someone is **actionable**, it gives them a valid reason for bringing a legal case against you. EG *That remark is actionable.* — ADJ CLASSIF : PRED

action replay, action replays. An **action replay** is a repeated showing of a film, often in slow motion, of an important part of an event, especially a sports match. EG *Let's just see an action replay of that incredible goal.* — N COUNT = instant replay

activate /æktɪˈveɪt/, **activates, activating, activated**. To **activate** something means to cause it to start working, to start doing something, or to start doing it more quickly. EG *It cannot produce enough heat to activate the electrons.* — V+O ≠ stop

active /æktɪv/. 1 If someone is **active** in a particular organization or cause, they are directly involved in it and work hard for it. EG *From the start, Benn was active in drawing public attention to African grievances... ...active members of Marxist organizations.* — ADJ QUALIT = energetic ≠ passive
▸ used of people's involvement in an organization or cause. EG *In less than eighteen months the group had lost the active support of more than 250 of its members.* — ▸ ADJ CLASSIF
◊ **actively**. EG *This provides them with a second parent who is able to be actively involved in their pre-school years.* — ◊ ADV WITH VB

2 When someone is **active** in a particular way, they work, move, or operate in that way. EG *Rebel forces were still active in the north... ...politically active.* — ADJ QUALIT : PRED+SUPP ⇑ operational

3 An **active** person or animal is energetic and always busy or moving about. — ADJ QUALIT = lively

4 **Active** is used to emphasize the strength or enthusiasm with which something is done. EG *The proposal is under active discussion in the UK, France and Belgium... ...the active encouragement of the government.* — ADJ CLASSIF : ATTRIB ⇑ emphatic = positive, keen
◊ **actively**. EG *It could be that the playing of games is actively discouraged by adults.* — ◊ ADV WITH VB

5 If a volcano is **active**, it has erupted quite recently or is expected to erupt quite soon. — ADJ CLASSIF ≠ extinct

6 If a substance or chemical is **active**, it is functioning or causing a reaction. — ADJ CLASSIF ⇑ effective

7 If an electronic device is **active**, it contains a source of power or is capable of sending out or amplifying signals; a technical use in physics. — ADJ CLASSIF : ATTRIB ≠ passive

8 In grammar, the **active** is the form of the verb in which the action is performed by the subject of the verb. — N UNCOUNT ≠ passive

active service. If you are on **active service**, you are fighting as a member of the armed forces in a war. EG *Another son was killed on active service... After active service in France, he had received a commission.* — N UNCOUNT ⇑ serving

activist /æktɪvɪst/, **activists**. An **activist** is a person who tries to bring about political or social change by campaigning in public or working for an organization. EG *...a vigorous civil rights activist.* — N COUNT = agitator

activity /æktɪvɪtiˈ/, **activities**. 1 **Activity** is 1.1 a situation in which a lot of things are happening. EG *There was a flurry of activity in the hall... ...periods* — N UNCOUNT ⇑ action *of high economic activity... ...the state of brain activity in young children.* **1.2** a situation in which a lot of things are being done, usually in order to achieve a particular purpose. EG *...officers engaged in anti-government activity... It was at the end of the 1950s that the first opportunities arose for activity rather than discussion.* N UNCOUNT ⇑ action

2 An **activity** is something you spend time doing for pleasure. EG *I still find tennis a very enjoyable activity... ...a council to organize joint cultural activities.* N COUNT ⇑ occupation

3 The **activities** of a particular group are the things that they do in order to achieve their aims, especially when these things seem highly organized, secret, or illegal. EG *We will bring in legislation to control the activities of trade unions... Many have ended up in prison for terrorist activities.* N PLURAL+SUPP ⇑ actions

act of God, acts of God. An **act of God** is an event that is beyond human control, especially one in which something is damaged or someone is hurt. EG *...some act of God - a typhoon, perhaps.* N COUNT = catastrophe

Act of Parliament, Acts of Parliament. An **Act of Parliament** is a law passed by the government. EG *...a profit-making industry licensed by Act of Parliament.* N COUNT, OR *by*+N

actor /æktə/, **actors**. **1** An **actor** is someone whose occupation is acting in plays or films. 'Actor' in the singular usually refers to a man. EG *He was an extremely fine actor... ...the eldest child of Ben and Sarah Terry, both actors.* N COUNT ⇑ performer **2** If you say that someone, especially a man, is a good or bad **actor**, you are talking about how good or bad they are at hiding their real feelings or thoughts. EG *She'll guess at once–I'm a terrible actor.* N COUNT : MOD+N

actress /æktrı²s/, **actresses**. **1** An **actress** is a woman whose occupation is acting in plays or films. EG *...a beautiful and talented actress.* N COUNT ⇑ performer **2** If you say a woman is a good or bad **actress**, you are talking about how good or bad she is at hiding her real feelings or thoughts. EG *It's difficult to tell just from appearance. Anyway, you may be an excellent actress.* N COUNT : MOD+N

actual /æktʃ⁰ʊəl/ is used **1** to emphasize that you are referring to a real place, object, person, etc, and not an imaginary one. EG *The predicted results and the actual results are diametrically opposed here... The interpretation bore no relation to the actual words spoken... Few Americans ever get to see an actual Marine.* ADJ CLASSIF : ATTRIB **2** to refer to the most important part of what you are discussing or describing. EG *The actual wedding procession starts at 10.55 a.m... It cost us £1,200 for the actual irrigation part of the scheme... The actual campaign runs for four or five months.* ADJ CLASSIF : ATTRIB
● **in actual fact**: see **fact**.

actuality /æktʃ⁰ʊælıti¹/ is the real existence of something or someone. EG *...the painful actuality of the factual world.* N UNCOUNT = reality ● **in actuality** is used to emphasize that what you are saying is true, especially when it contradicts what has just been said or what people expect you to say. EG *The party in actuality contains only a small minority of extremists.* ● PHR : USED AS AN A ⇑ in truth = really, actually

actually /æktʃ⁰ʊəli¹/. **1 Actually** is used when referring to the reality of a situation **1.1** to indicate that a situation or event happens or exists in real life and not in theory or in someone's imagination. EG *Can computers actually create language?... This load had actually been dispatched three months previously... No one actually saw this shark.* ADV ⇑ in truth = really ≠ theoretically **1.2** to indicate that you are giving exact details about a particular situation. EG *Large meteorites actually come from the asteroid belt... She's actually speaking for an hour and a half... He actually died in exile, didn't he?* ADV
1.3 to indicate that something is surprising or slightly shocking. EG *The real value of oil has actually been falling in the last two years... You may actually be doing the right thing by walking out... I was actually cruel sometimes.* ADV

2 Actually is often used in conversation simply to draw attention to what you are saying **2.1** when you are making a comment or giving a new piece of information. EG *I'm in the middle of writing an essay actually... Well they still haven't informed me officially, actually... That's what my father said actually.* ADV SEN = as it happens
2.2 to indicate that you are about to give extra information that contrasts with or corrects what you have already said. EG *It was nothing unusual after all. Just another divorce. Actually, it was more complicated than that... Actually, in the negotiations, our experience was quite different.* ADV SEN = as it happens **2.3** to indicate that you are about to introduce a totally new topic into the conversation. EG *Actually, Dan, before I forget, she asked me to give you this... Actually, I didn't come here just to help you with the party.* ADV SEN = by the way **2.4** when you are interrupting yourself to make a comment on what you are saying. EG *It's a woman, a friend of mine–actually I was at school with her–and she needs your help.* ADV SEN = in fact

3 Actually is often used in conversation as a way of expressing things more politely **3.1** when you are stating an opinion. EG *I'm not all that terribly surprised, actually... I think that's pretty cheap actually... You haven't been too satisfactory actually.* ADV SEN = really **3.2** when you are correcting or contradicting someone. EG *'Mr Hooper is a schoolteacher.'–'A University lecturer, actually,' said Hooper... 'I suppose you voted against.'–'I abstained, actually,' said Howard... I didn't mean it that way actually.* ADV SEN = as a matter of fact **3.3** when you feel nervous or embarrassed about what you are saying and when you think someone will be annoyed, disappointed, or upset by your words. EG *'Did you provide lunches?'–'Well actually I didn't do a really big lunch, no.'... 'Tell me, Oliver, have you heard from the Law School?'–'Actually, Father, I haven't definitely decided whether I want to study law or not.'* ADV SEN **3.4** when you are giving instructions or advice. EG *Actually it might be a good idea to stop the record player now... Actually, Sally, we normally all help wash up after the meal.* ADV SEN

actuary /æktʃ⁰ʊəri¹/, **actuaries**. An **actuary** is a person who is employed by insurance companies to calculate how much they should charge their clients for insurance. N COUNT

actuate /æktʃ⁰ʊeıt/, **actuates, actuating, actuated**. To **actuate** a mechanical device means to make it start to operate; a technical term. EG *The device was actuated by the transmitter.* V+O = activate, trigger

acuity /əkju:ıti¹/ is sharpness or quickness of vision, hearing, or thought; a formal word. EG *I prided myself on my mental acuity.* N UNCOUNT+SUPP

acumen /ækjʊmɛn, əkju:mən/ is the ability to make good judgements and decisions in relation to a particular activity, especially business. EG *...a man with big ideas and keen business acumen.* N UNCOUNT : USU MOD+N ⇑ judgement = sense

acupuncture /ækjʊpʌŋktʃə/ is the treatment of illnesses or pain by sticking the ends of needles into a person's body at particular places. EG *Some were undergoing acupuncture treatment for deafness.* N UNCOUNT

acute /ə³kju:t/. **1 Acute** is used to emphasize the severity or intensity of an unpleasant situation or feeling. EG *...acute staff shortages... With acute anxiety they awaited the result.* ADJ QUALIT ⇑ extreme ≠ slight

2 If a person is **acute** or if their mind is **acute**, they are quick to notice things and understand them clearly. EG *The more acute observers in the West had foreseen this.* ADJ QUALIT = perceptive ≠ obtuse

3 If your sight, hearing, or sense of smell is **acute**, it is sensitive and powerful. EG *The fish's sense of smell is most acute.* ADJ QUALIT = keen ≠ poor

4 An **acute** illness is one that quickly becomes severe and usually does not last long. EG *...acute appendicitis.* ADJ AFTER N

5 An **acute** angle is less than 90. ADJ CLASSIF

6 An **acute** accent is a symbol that is placed over vowels in some languages in order to indicate how the vowel is pronounced or over a letter of a word to indicate where it is stressed. ▸ used of a letter that has an acute accent. EG *It's spelled with e acute.* ADJ CLASSIF ▸ ADJ AFTER N

acutely /ə³kju:tli¹/. **Acutely** is used **1** in order to say that someone notices or feels a particular thing strongly. EG *They were acutely aware of the difficulties involved... Here the need for decisive longer-term vision is felt most acutely.* ADV ⇑ intensely = keenly

2 in order to emphasize the severity or intensity of a characteristic, feeling, or quality, especially one that is unpleasant. EG *It was acutely embarrassing... The cash position continues to be acutely difficult... Heissman looked acutely unhappy.* ADV ⇑ extremely = painfully

3 in order to say that someone shows a clear understanding of a situation. EG *...as Harris has acutely observed.* ADV = shrewdly

ad /æd/, **ads**. An **ad** is an advertisement; an informal word. EG *...a newspaper ad... ...the small ads.* N COUNT

AD /eı di:/ refers to the number of years or centuries which have passed since the time when Jesus N UNCOUNT : NUM+N

Christ is believed to have been born. EG *As early as AD 1200 there were massive iron smelters employing hundreds of people.... ... the year 2000 AD... ...the third century AD.*

adage /ædɪdʒ/, **adages**. An **adage** is something which people often say and which expresses a general truth about some aspect of life; an old-fashioned word. EG *She reminded me of the old adage: where there's love there's understanding.* N COUNT : MOD + N, OR N + REPORT-CL = maxim

Adam /ædəm/. If you say that you **don't know** someone **from Adam** or **wouldn't know** them **from Adam**, you mean that you do not know them or would not recognize them if you saw them; an informal expression. PHR : VB INFLECTS ≠ recognize

adamant /ædəmənt/. If you are **adamant** about something, you are determined not to change your mind about it. EG *The government remains adamant that it will not yield to pressure... They urged Jefferson to remain in office but he was adamant.* ADJ CLASSIF = resolute ≠ hesitant, pliable
◇ **adamantly**. EG *They are adamantly opposed to continued high U.S. interest rates.* ◇ ADV WITH VB

Adam's apple, Adam's apples. Your **Adam's apple** is the lump that sticks out of the front of your neck below your throat. N COUNT

adapt /ədæpt/, **adapts, adapting, adapted**. 1 If you **adapt** to a new situation or **adapt** yourself to it, you change in order to be able to deal with it successfully, especially by altering your ideas or habits. EG *This book is about change and how we adapt to it... He cannot adapt himself to being free... ...our capacity to adapt.* V OR V+O (REFL) : IF + PREP THEN *to* = adjust

2 If you **adapt** something, you change it in order to make it suitable for a new purpose or situation. EG *...the imagination necessary to adapt plans to changes in circumstances... Religious reformers attempted to adapt traditional religion.* V+O : IF + PREP THEN *to* = revise

3 If you **adapt** a book or play, you change it so that it can be presented in a different form, for example as a film or a television serial. EG *John Mortimer is adapting the Waugh novel for television... Her husband had adapted the play from Henry James' novel.* V+O

4 See also **adapted**.

adaptable /ədæptəbəl/. Someone who is **adaptable** can change their methods or attitudes in order to deal with new situations. EG *To succeed in this business, you have to be adaptable.* ◇ **adaptability** /ədæptəbɪlɪti/. ADJ QUALIT ⇑ flexible; ◇ N UNCOUNT ⇑ flexibility

adaptation /ædəpteɪʃən/, **adaptations**. 1 An **adaptation** is a play or film that was originally written in another form, for example as a novel. EG *...a new television adaptation of 'A Tale of Two Cities'.* N COUNT : IF + PREP THEN *of* = version

2 **Adaptation** is the changing of something so that it becomes suitable for a new purpose or situation. EG *...Sloan's adaptation of Duploye's method... ...a marked capacity for change and adaptation.* N UNCOUNT : IF + PREP THEN *of* ⇑ change = revision

adapted /ədæptɪd/. If something is **adapted** to or for a particular situation or purpose it is especially suitable for it. EG *The cleaner is particularly well adapted for use in the home and car... This method guaranteed seed precisely adapted to the area.* ADJ QUALIT : PRED + *for/to* ⇑ changed = suited

adaptor /ədæptə/, **adaptors**; also spelled **adapter**. An **adaptor** is 1 something which looks like a plug which you put into an electric socket. It enables you to plug several electrical devices into the socket, or to use a device with a plug that does not match the socket. N COUNT ⇑ device 2 a device for connecting two parts of a piece of equipment, especially two parts of different sizes. N COUNT

add /æd/, **adds, adding, added**. 1 If you **add** something to a particular thing or collection of things, you put it with the thing or collection. EG *She added a tree to the picture... Each party of boys added more wood and the pile grew.* V+O : IF + PREP THEN *to*

2 If you **add** numbers or amounts together, or if you **add** one number or amount to another, you calculate their total. EG *Add three and fourteen... I am very slow at adding and subtracting. The sums all add up now.* V, OR V+O (NUM) : USU + A

3 If one thing **adds** to something else or **adds** an amount to it, it makes the other thing greater in degree or amount. EG *He is given answers that only add to his confusion... This process can add £3 a barrel to the cost.* ◇ **added**. EG *There are added complications... ...the added financial burden of funding their children's education.* ● to **add insult to injury**: see **insult**. V + A (*to*), OR V + O : IF + PREP THEN *to* ≠ subtract; ◇ ADJ CLASSIF : ATTRIB = additional

4 To **add** a particular quality to something means to cause it to have that quality. EG *Stripes can add interest to a long narrow hall.* V+O : IF + PREP THEN *to* ⇑ give

5 To **add** a remark or point means to make another remark or point that supports or expands a previous one. EG *'I felt sorry for them,' he added... He added that the fee would be £100... I feel it is unnecessary for me to add any comment.* V+O/REPORT-CL/QUOTE ⇑ say

6 You can use the expressions **added to this, add to this**, and **if you add** to introduce a fact that proves, supports, or expands what you are saying. EG *Added to this, the birth rate is not so great as it was... ...add to this the terrible damage wreaked by heavy bombardment... ...if you add their total unsuitability for the job.* PHR : USED AS ADV SEN ⇑ also

add in. If you **add** something **in**, you include it as a part of something else. EG *We had to add in a couple of bits... If you add in his gains of last year he'd made no less than £20,000.* PHRASAL VB : V + O + ADV = bring in

add on. 1 If you **add** something **on**, you attach it to something else or make it part of something else. EG *We added on a bathroom last year.* PHRASAL VB : V + O + ADV = tack on

2 If you **add on** an extra item or amount to a list or total, you include it in the list or total. EG *They add on about nine per cent for service.* PHRASAL VB : V + O + ADV ⇑ attach

3 If you **add on to** something, you make it larger by including or attaching an extra part or thing. EG *They added on to the house and shop.* PHRASAL VB : V + ADV + PREP ⇑ enlarge

add up. 1 If you **add up** several numbers, you calculate their total. EG *We add all the marks up.* PHRASAL VB : V + O + ADV

2 If numbers or amounts **add up** to a particular total, they result in that total. EG *This adds up to 75,000 miles of new streets.* PHRASAL VB : V + ADV + *to* = amount

3 If things **add up** to something, they result in it or suggest it. EG *This adds up to a formidable list of qualifications.* PHRASAL VB : V + ADV + *to* = amount, constitute

4 If facts, events, or aspects of a situation **add up**, they cause you to realize or understand the true nature of the situation. EG *It all added up. I became aware that Halliday was the thief.* PHRASAL VB : V + ADV = fit, make sense

addendum /ədendəm/, **addenda**. An **addendum** is a section at the end of a book or document that contains extra information. N COUNT ⇑ addition = appendix

adder /ædə/, **adders**. An **adder** is a small poisonous snake which has a black zigzag pattern on its back. Adders are found in Europe and Asia. N COUNT = viper

addict /ædɪkt/, **addicts**. An **addict** is 1 someone who takes harmful drugs and cannot stop taking them. EG *...drug addicts... ...an 8-year-old heroin addict.* N COUNT ⇑ person 2 someone who is extremely fond of something or is extremely interested in it. EG *He was a confirmed radio addict: he kept a radio in his office!... ...addicts of garlic and wine cookery.* N COUNT : USU + SUPP ⇑ person = devotee

addicted /ədɪktɪd/. 1 If you are **addicted** to something, you like it so much that you do it, have it, or want it a lot. EG *He was addicted to chocolate.* ADJ QUALIT : IF + PREP THEN *to* = hooked on

2 Someone who is **addicted** to a harmful drug cannot stop taking it. EG *I am addicted to nicotine.* ADJ CLASSIF : IF + PREP THEN *to*

addiction /ədɪkʃən/, **addictions**. 1 **Addiction** is the condition of taking harmful drugs and being unable to stop taking them. EG *...drug addiction.* N UNCOUNT : IF + PREP THEN *to* ⇑ dependence

2 An **addiction** to something is a very strong desire or need for it. EG *...an addiction to food and strong drink.* N COUNT/UNCOUNT : IF + PREP THEN *to*

addictive /ədɪktɪv/. 1 If a drug is **addictive**, people who take it cannot stop taking it. EG *She believes that cocaine is not addictive.* ADJ QUALIT

2 Something that is **addictive** is so enjoyable that you want to have it or do it a lot. EG *...an addictive game.* ADJ QUALIT

addition /ədɪʃən/, **additions**. 1 **In addition** is used when you want to add an extra item to what you have already mentioned. EG *In addition, there were parallel meetings with trade unionists... They eat, in addition to leaves, a great deal of fruit.* PHR : USED AS AN A, IF + PREP THEN *to* ⇑ also

2 An **addition** to something is a thing which is added to it, for example as an extra part. EG *This will be an admirable addition to London's contemporary architecture... They can also award a weekly addition for extra heating.* N COUNT : USU + SUPP = supplement

3 The **addition** of something is the fact of it having been added as an extra. EG *These houses have been improved by the addition of bathrooms... He looked like Jefferson, with the addition of horn-rimmed glasses.* N UNCOUNT : IF + PREP THEN *to* ≠ removal

4 **Addition** is the skill or process of calculating the total of two or more numbers. EG *The children start by learning English and addition.* N UNCOUNT ⇑ arithmetic

additional /ə[3]dɪʃə[0]nəl, -ʃənə[0]l/ means extra or more than the ones mentioned or already there. EG *Additional troops were needed... This is an additional reason for not leaving. This problem is additional to their major financial anxieties.*
ADJ CLASSIF : IF + PREP THEN *to* ⇑ other = added, further

additionally /ə[3]dɪʃə[0]nəli[1], -ʃənə[0]li[1]/. 1 **Additionally** means to a greater extent than before. EG *There was no point in additionally burdening her with this painful news.*
ADV WITH VB = further

2 **Additionally** is used when you want to mention an extra point, fact, or reason. EG *They were quite unable to move them along the roads. Additionally, there were so many fires burning that any sort of orderly retreat was impossible.*
ADV SEN ⇑ also = moreover

additive /ædɪtɪv/, **additives**. An **additive** is a substance which is added in small amounts to something such as food or petrol in order to improve it, to make it easier to sell, or to make it last longer.
N COUNT

addle /ædə[0]l/, **addles, addling, addled**. If something **addles** someone's mind or brain, or if someone is **addled**, they are confused and unable to think properly. EG *...your addled little brain.*
V+O, OR V ⇑ mix up = befuddle

addled /ædə[0]ld/. An **addled** egg is one that has gone bad.
ADJ CLASSIF = rotten

address /ədres/, **addresses, addressing, addressed**. 1 Your **address** is the number of the house, the street, and the town where you live or work and where letters and parcels can be sent to you. EG *The address is 70 Brompton Road, London SW1... He took out his pen and wrote down his name and address.*
N COUNT : USU WITH POSS

2 If a letter, envelope, or parcel **is addressed** to someone, their name and address has been written on it so that it can be sent to them. EG *...a letter addressed to Dr Willoughby.*
V+O : USU PASS, IF + PREP THEN *to* ⇑ designated

3 An **address** is also a formal speech that someone makes to a group of people, often on a special occasion. EG *I gave an address to the American Psychological Association.*
N COUNT : IF + PREP THEN *to*

4 If you **address** a group of people, you make a speech to them. EG *He addressed a mass meeting.*
V+O ⇑ speak to

5 If you **address** a person, usually someone you do not know well, you talk to them, usually in a formal or careful way. EG *One of the newcomers boldly addressed John.*
V+O = accost

6 If you **address** a request or comments to someone, you ask them something or make comments to them. EG *Reece addressed some general remarks to the gathering.*
V+O+A *(to)* ⇑ direct

7 If you **address** someone as 'sir', 'darling', 'love', etc, you call them by that name or title when you are talking or writing to them. EG *She always addressed me as 'my daughter'.*
V+O+A *(as)*

8 If you **address** a problem or task, or if you **address** yourself to it, you give it your attention and try to understand it or deal with it. EG *...the only brand of economics which addresses itself to the problem of Britain's decline... He has not addressed the issue of the strike demands.*
V+O (REFL)+A *(to)*, OR V+O ≠ ignore

address book, address books; also spelled with a hyphen. An **address book** is a book in which you write people's names and addresses.
N COUNT

addressee /ædresi:/, **addressees**. The **addressee** of a letter or parcel is the person or company that it is addressed to.
N COUNT : *the*+N ≠ sender

adduce /ə[3]dju:s/, **adduces, adducing, adduced**. If you **adduce** something such as a fact or reason, you mention it in order to support an argument; a formal word. EG *Darwin adduced the fossil record as support for his theory.*
V+O = cite, give

adenoidal /ædɪ[1]nɔɪdə[0]l/. If someone is **adenoidal**, they speak in a nasal way because they have swollen adenoids.
ADJ CLASSIF

adenoids /ædɪ[1]nɔɪdz/ are soft lumps of flesh at the back and top of a person's throat that sometimes become swollen and have to be removed.
N PLURAL

adept, adepts. The word **adept** is pronounced /ə[3]dept/ when it is an adjective, and /ædept/when it is a noun. 1 Someone who is **adept** at something can do it skilfully. EG *They have become adept at reading and filling in forms.* ▸ used of a person's actions or behaviour. EG *...adept leadership.*
ADJ QUALIT : IF + PREP THEN *at/in* = expert, adroit

2 An **adept** is someone who is skilful at doing a particular thing.
N COUNT = expert

adequacy /ædɪ[1]kwəsi[1]/ is 1 the state of being great enough in amount. EG *The problem is not likely to be the adequacy of food resources.* 2 the quality of being good enough to be acceptable or usable. EG *...proof of the adequacy of the principles.*
N UNCOUNT; N UNCOUNT

adequate /ædɪ[1]kwə[1]t/. 1 If the amount of something is **adequate**, there is enough of it, but there is only just enough. EG *The pay was adequate... ...a country with adequate, steady rainfall.* ◇ **adequately**. EG *The children are not being adequately fed.*
ADJ CLASSIF = sufficient; ◇ ADV WITH VB = sufficiently

2 If something is **adequate**, it is good enough to be used or accepted. EG *She could not think of an adequate answer... Are transport systems adequate to deliver the food to remote areas?* ◇ **adequately**. EG *This has never been adequately explained.*
ADJ QUALIT ⇑ usable; ◇ ADV WITH VB = satisfactorily

adhere /ə[3]dhɪə/, **adheres, adhering, adhered**.

1 If something **adheres** to something else, it sticks firmly to it. EG *This helps the new plaster to adhere to the old.*
V OR V+A *(to)* ⇑ attach = stick

2 To **adhere** to a rule or agreement means to act in the way that it says you should. EG *The fire regulations have been adhered to.*
V+A *(to)* ⇑ obey = keep ≠ break

3 If you **adhere** to a particular opinion or belief, you support or hold it. EG *The government has firmly adhered to the view that this is a matter for individuals to decide.*
V+A *(to)* ⇑ believe

adherence /ə[3]dhɪərə[2]ns/ is 1 the fact of adhering to a particular rule or agreement. EG *...a question about this country's adherence to the treaty.* 2 the fact of supporting a particular belief or opinion. EG *...their adherence to democratic or totalitarian systems.*
N UNCOUNT + *to* ⇑ obedience; N UNCOUNT : IF + PREP THEN *to* ⇑ attachment

adherent /ə[3]dhɪərə[2]nt/, **adherents**. An **adherent** is someone who holds a particular belief or supports a particular person or group. EG *The cult gained adherents at an alarming rate.*
N COUNT ⇑ supporter = follower

adhesion /ə[3]dhi:ʒə[0]n/ is the state or fact of one thing sticking firmly to another.
N UNCOUNT

adhesive /ə[3]dhi:sɪv/, **adhesives**. 1 An **adhesive** is a substance such as glue which is used to make things stick firmly together.
N MASS

2 Something that is **adhesive** is able to stick firmly to something else. EG *...adhesive tape.*
ADJ CLASSIF = sticking

ad hoc /æd hɒk/. Something that is **ad hoc** or that is done on an **ad hoc** basis happens or is done only when the situation makes it necessary or desirable, rather than being arranged in advance or being part of a general plan. EG *The group met on an ad hoc basis, just as needs came up... ...an ad hoc committee.* ▸ used as an adverb. EG *Ministers were appointed ad hoc to their jobs.*
ADJ CLASSIF : ATTRIB ⇑ temporary = makeshift ≠ planned; ▸ ADV WITH VB

adieu /ə[3]dju:/, **adieux** or **adieus**. **Adieu** means the same as goodbye; a literary or old-fashioned word.
CONVENTION

ad infinitum /æd ɪnfɪnaɪtəm/. If something happens **ad infinitum**, it is repeated again and again in the same way. EG *She then teaches it to her daughter, and so on ad infinitum.*
PHR : USED AS AN A ⇑ for ever = endlessly

> **ADJ** □ In this dictionary ADJ is used in the grammar notes beside entries to mean 'adjective'. For explanations of different kinds of adjective, see □ at ADJ AFTER N, ADJ CLASSIF, ADJ COLOUR, and ADJ QUALIT. See also □ at ATTRIB and PRED.

adjacent /ə[3]dʒeɪsə[0]nt/. If something is **adjacent** to something else, or if two things are **adjacent**, they are next to each other. EG *The bench was adjacent to the court... He took me to the adjacent room.*
ADJ CLASSIF : IF + PREP THEN *to* = adjoining

> **ADJ AFTER N** □ In this dictionary ADJ AFTER N is used in the grammar notes beside entries to mean that an adjective can only be used after a noun. Examples are **elect 3** and **galore**. EG *The president **elect**... There are empty houses **galore**.* You do not say 'The president is elect' and you do not say 'There are galore empty houses'.

> **ADJ CLASSIF** □ In this dictionary ADJ CLASSIF is used in the grammar notes beside entries to mean that an adjective is a classifying adjective. ADJ CLASSIFS behave in the following ways: 1 They are adjectives that cannot have more or less of the particular quality that they describe, and so they cannot have adverbs like 'very', 'more', or 'rather' in front of them. Compare ADJ QUALIT. An example is **dead** . EG *...his **dead** wife... ...money inherited from a **dead** relative.. Tell him Antonio is **dead**.* You do not say 'His wife is more dead than she was yesterday'. 2 If a group of adjectives of different types are used together, an ADJ CLASSIF comes after a qualitative adjective (ADJ QUALIT) and a colour adjective (ADJ COLOUR). An example is **woollen** in *...a big red **woollen** scarf*, and **medieval** in *...a large **medieval** castle*. See also □ at ATTRIB and PRED.

ADJ COLOUR □ In this dictionary ADJ COLOUR is used in the grammar notes beside entries to mean that an adjective is a colour adjective such as *red* or *blue*. ADJ COLOURS behave in the following ways: 1 They can have another adjective before them which defines the colour more exactly, such as *pale, bright, clear,* and *light*. 2 If a group of adjectives of different types are used together, an ADJ COLOUR comes after a qualitative adjective (ADJ QUALIT) and before a classifying adjective (ADJ CLASSIF). An example is **red** in *...a big* ***red*** *woollen scarf.*

adjectival /ædʒə²ktaɪvə⁰l/ means consisting of or relating to adjectives. EG *...the structure of adjectival groups in English.* ADJ CLASSIF

adjective /ædʒəktɪv/, **adjectives**. An **adjective** is a word that gives more information about a noun or pronoun, by selecting or restricting its meaning. The abbreviation ADJ is used in the grammar notes beside the entries to mean 'adjective'. See □ at ADJ, ADJ AFTER N, ADJ CLASSIF, ADJ COLOUR, ADJ QUALIT, ATTRIB, and PRED. N COUNT

adjoin /ə³dʒɔɪn/, **adjoins, adjoining, adjoined**. If a room, place, or object **adjoins** another one, they are next to each other. EG *They had rooms adjoining mine.* ◊ **adjoining**. EG *People at adjoining tables looked at her in astonishment.* V+O; ◊ ADJ CLASSIF : USU ATTRIB

adjourn /ə³dʒɜːn/, **adjourns, adjourning, adjourned**. 1 If a meeting, conference, enquiry, or trial **adjourns**, or if someone **adjourns** it, it is stopped for a short time. EG *The conference adjourned... He announced that the trial would be adjourned until the next morning.* V-ERG ⇑ stop

2 If people **adjourn** to another room or place, they go there; used in fairly formal English. EG *Fanny suggested they should all adjourn to the garden.* V+A *(to)* = retire

adjournment /ə³dʒɜːnmə²nt/, **adjournments**. An **adjournment** is a temporary stopping of a trial, enquiry, or other meeting. N COUNT ⇑ break

ADJ QUALIT □ In this dictionary ADJ QUALIT is used in the grammar notes beside entries to mean a qualitative adjective. ADJ QUALITS behave in the following ways: 1 They are adjectives which can have more or less of the particular quality they describe, and so they can have adverbs like 'very', 'more', or 'rather' in front of them. Compare ADJ CLASSIF. Examples are **funny**, and **terrific 1**. EG *...a very* ***funny*** *film... I found it extremely* ***funny***... *It seemed rather* ***funny*** *at the time... ...a really* ***terrific*** *idea... You look absolutely* ***terrific*** *today.* 2 If a group of adjectives of different types are used together, an ADJ QUALIT comes before a colour adjective (ADJ COLOUR) and a classifying adjective (ADJ CLASSIF). An example is **big** in *...a* ***big*** *red woollen scarf.* See also □ at ATTRIB and PRED.

adjudge /ə³dʒʌdʒ/, **adjudges, adjudging, adjudged**. If someone is **adjudged** to be guilty, worthy, a criminal, etc, they are judged or considered to be that thing; a formal word. EG *I was adjudged an extremist.* V+O+C/*to*-INF

adjudicate /ə³dʒuːdɪkeɪt/, **adjudicates, adjudicating, adjudicated**. 1 If you **adjudicate** on an issue or **adjudicate** it, you make a formal or legal decision concerning it. EG *The boards have the right to adjudicate on the punishment of prisoners... ...to adjudicate disputes between unions and their members.* ◊ **adjudication** /ə³dʒuːdɪkeɪʃə⁰n/. EG *The matter is under adjudication.* V : IF+PREP THEN *on*, OR V+O ⇑ judge = decide; ◊ N UNCOUNT ⇑ judgement

2 If you **adjudicate** a competition, you officially decide who the winner is. ◊ **adjudication**. V OR V+O; ◊ N UNCOUNT

adjudicator /ə³dʒuːdɪkeɪtə/, **adjudicators**. An **adjudicator** is a person who adjudicates. N COUNT ⇑ judge

adjunct /ædʒʌŋkt/, **adjuncts**. 1 An **adjunct** is something that is linked or attached to something larger or more important. EG *He regarded it as an indispensable adjunct to the kind of life he wanted... Women want to be seen as independent forces, rather than adjuncts of men.* N COUNT : IF+PREP THEN *to/of* ⇑ addition = appendage

2 In grammar, an **adjunct** is one of the main elements of a clause. Adjuncts express time, place, manner, or condition. An adjunct can be a noun group, a prepositional group, or an adverbial group. In this dictionary the abbreviation A is used to mean 'adjunct' in the grammar notes beside entries. See □ at A, V+A, V+O+A, and PHR. N COUNT

adjure /ədʒʊə/, **adjures, adjuring, adjured**. If you **adjure** someone to do something, you ask or order them to do it; a formal word. EG *His lawyer had been adjuring him again not to answer questions.* V+O+*to*-INF, OR V+O+QUOTE

adjust /ə³dʒʌst/, **adjusts, adjusting, adjusted**. 1 If you **adjust** to a new situation or **adjust** yourself to it, you get used to it, especially by changing your behaviour or your ideas. EG *Couples do not give themselves time to adjust to marriage before a baby arrives... Some people never do adjust adequately.* • See also **adjusted**. V, OR V+O (REFL) : IF+PREP THEN *to* = adapt

2 If you **adjust** something, you change it so that it is more effective or appropriate. EG *We should adjust our approach.* V+O ⇑ alter = modify

3 If you **adjust** something such as a piece of clothing, a machine, or a device, you correct or alter its position or setting. EG *He spent several minutes adjusting his tie... I went to adjust the television set.* V+O

4 If something **adjusts**, it can be changed to different positions or settings. EG *It has a hinged head which adjusts to clean all sizes of window.* V = adapt

adjustable /ə³dʒʌstəbə⁰l/. If something is **adjustable**, it can be changed to different positions, settings, or levels. EG *...an adjustable spanner.* ADJ CLASSIF

adjusted /ə³dʒʌstɪ²d/. If you say someone is well **adjusted** or badly **adjusted**, you are talking about how balanced they are mentally and emotionally, and how well they can cope with the problems of life. EG *They grow up happy and well adjusted... ...a normally adjusted individual.* ADJ QUALIT ⇑ integrated

adjustment /ə³dʒʌstmə²nt/, **adjustments**. An **adjustment** is 1 an alteration or correction of something such as a machine or a way of doing something. EG *...this fine adjustment to an individual's pace of learning... Tappet adjustment has to be done with the engine cold.* 2 a change in a person's behaviour or thinking. EG *Thousands of young marines have quietly made the adjustment from combat... Those students have particular problems of adjustment to living in Britain.* N COUNT/UNCOUNT : IF+PREP THEN *to/in* ⇑ change = tuning; N COUNT/UNCOUNT : IF+PREP THEN *from/to*

adjutant /ædʒətənt/, **adjutants**. An **adjutant** is an officer in the army who deals with administrative work. N COUNT

ad-lib /ædlɪb/, **ad-libs, ad-libbing, ad-libbed**. 1 If you **ad-lib** something or if you **ad-lib** in a play, speech, piece of music, etc, you say or do something which is not part of the original text or music and which you have not planned or prepared beforehand. EG *It's all ad-libbed.* V OR V+O ⇑ improvise

2 An **ad-lib** is something which is said or done without having been planned or prepared beforehand. ▸ used as an adjective. EG *...ad-lib comments.* ▸ used as an adverb. EG *He spoke ad-lib.* N COUNT ⇑ improvisation; ▸ ADJ CLASSIF; ▸ ADV WITH VB

admin /ædmɪn/ means the same as administration; an informal word. EG *I help him do some of his admin... ...the new admin block.* N UNCOUNT

administer /ə³dmɪnɪstə/, **administers, administering, administered**. 1 To **administer** a country, company, institution, etc means to be responsible for managing and supervising it. EG *...a man who had a huge department to administer... The territory had been administered by South Africa.* V+O ⇑ control = run

2 If you **administer** something such as the law or justice or a punishment, test, oath, or plan, you organize or supervise it and make sure that it is put into practice properly. EG *Experts administer tests and quote the results... Who will administer the oath to the President?* V+O : IF+PREP THEN *to* = give

3 If you **administer** something such as a kick, blow, or shock to someone, you kick, hit, or shock them; used in fairly formal English. EG *...the calm clinical way in which the keepers administered the beating... The economic crisis administered a severe blow to their hopes.* V+O : IF+PREP THEN *to* ⇑ give = deal

4 If you **administer** something such as a drug to someone, you give it to them or supervise them taking it; a formal word. EG *...to administer a sedative.* V+O = dispense

administration /ə³dmɪnɪstreɪʃə⁰n/, **administrations**. 1 **Administration** is 1.1 the range of activities connected with organizing and supervising the way a company, institution, or other organization functions. EG *They need to spend less on administration.* 1.2 the action of administering something. EG *...the administration of justice.* N UNCOUNT = admin; N UNCOUNT : IF+PREP THEN *of*

2 The **administration** of a company, institution, or other organization is the group of people that manages and supervises it. EG *...negotiations between the University administration and the Student Union... ...the administration building.* N SING : *the*+N, USU+SUPP ⇑ management = admin

3 The **Administration** of a country, especially the N COUNT : USU

United States, is its government. EG *The Reagan Administration is planning a new war on drugs.*
the+MOD+N

administrative /ə3dmɪnɪstrətɪv/. **Administrative** work is the work of managing and supervising a company, institution, or other organization. EG *The council met to discuss purely administrative affairs.* ▸ used to describe people who do this work. EG *...the administrative head of the country's largest oil company.* ◊ **administratively**. EG *This is administratively impossible.*
ADJ CLASSIF ⇑ organizational = management ▸ ADJ CLASSIF : ATTRIB ◊ ADV SEN

administrator /ə3dmɪnɪstreɪtə/, **administrators**. An **administrator** is a person whose job involves helping to organize and supervise the way that a company, institution, or other organization functions.
N COUNT ⇑ organizer

admirable /ædmərəbə0l/. A quality, action, situation, etc that is **admirable** deserves to be praised and admired. EG *The trains ran with admirable precision... The author's management of all this is admirable.* ◊ **admirably**. EG *It fulfils its purpose admirably.*
ADJ QUALIT ⇑ good = excellent ◊ ADV = splendidly

admiral /ædmərəl/, **admirals**. An **admiral** is a very senior officer who commands a navy or fleet of ships. EG *...Admiral Fisher.*
N COUNT : ALSO IN TITLES

Admiralty /ædmə0rəlti1/. The **Admiralty** is the government department in Britain that is in charge of the navy. EG *There was a spy in the Admiralty.*
N PROPER : the+N

admiration /ædmə7reɪʃə0n/ is a feeling of liking, respect, and approval for a person or thing. EG *Benson had an enormous admiration for them all... He shook his head in admiration.*
N UNCOUNT : IF+PREP THEN for/of

admire /ə3dmaɪə/, **admires, admiring, admired**. If you **admire** someone or something, you 1 like, respect, and approve of them. EG *I admire cleverness–and courage too... They had been admired for their discipline.* 2 look with pleasure at them. EG *He went back along the lane admiring the autumn crocuses.*
V+O; V+O = appreciate

admirer /ə3dmaɪə0rə/, **admirers**. 1 A woman's **admirers** are the men who are attracted to her. EG *Of all her admirers the most permanent was Sir John.*
N COUNT ⇑ man = beau

2 An **admirer** is a person who likes, respects, and approves of another person. EG *There was a little cluster of admirers round the guest speaker.*
N COUNT : IF+PREP THEN of = fan

admiring /ə3dmaɪə0rɪŋ/. An **admiring** expression, look, etc shows pleasure and appreciation of someone or something. EG *She gave me one of her rare admiring looks.* ▸ used of people. EG *...an admiring housewife.* ◊ **admiringly**. EG *Ralph glanced at them admiringly.*
ADJ QUALIT = appreciative ◊ ADV WITH VB = appreciatively

admissible /ə3dmɪsə1bə0l/. Evidence or behaviour that is **admissible** is allowed in a particular situation. EG *The judge ruled the evidence admissible.*
ADJ CLASSIF = acceptable

admission /ə3dmɪʃə0n/, **admissions**. 1 **Admission** is 1.1 the act of allowing someone to go into a particular place or country. EG *...laws relating to the admission and exclusion of aliens... No admissions are permitted in the hour before closing.* 1.2 the act of allowing a person or a country to join an organization. EG *...the admission of China to the United Nations.*
N UNCOUNT/COUNT = admittance ≠ exclusion; N UNCOUNT : IF+PREP THEN of/to ⇑ inclusion ≠ exclusion

2 **Admission** or the **admission** fee is the amount of money that you pay to go into a place, for example a park or museum. EG *They would charge fifty cents admission.*
N UNCOUNT ⇑ fee = entry

3 An **admission** is an agreement or confession, often made unwillingly, that something is true or that you have done something wrong. EG *He submitted his resignation, together with an admission of his guilt... They made no admission that the newspaper had been fooling the public.*
N UNCOUNT/COUNT : IF+PREP THEN of, OR +REPORT-CL = acknowledgement

admit /ə3dmɪt/, **admits, admitting, admitted**. 1 If you **admit** something, you 1.1 agree, often reluctantly, that it is true. EG *I must admit I had my doubts... It is not, I admit, a good way of selling newspapers... 'I don't know,' he admitted.* 1.2 agree or confess that you have done something that you should not have done. EG *The Vice President admitted taking bribes.*
V+O/REPORT-CL/QUOTE = confess; V+A (to), V+-ING, OR V+to+NG/-ING ≠ deny

2 If you **admit defeat**, you accept that you cannot do something which you have started. EG *Her imagination failed her: she had to admit defeat.*
PHR : VB INFLECTS

3 To **admit** someone or something to a place means to allow them to enter it. EG *The Sovereign has never been admitted to the House of Commons... This ticket admits two... The door was opened, admitting a shaft of daylight.*
V+O : IF+PREP THEN to = let in ≠ shut out

4 If someone **is admitted** to hospital, they are taken there because they are ill and stay there for one or more nights. EG *He was admitted to hospital with an ulcerated leg.*
V+O : USU PASS, IF+PREP THEN to ⇑ be taken

5 If you **admit** someone to an organization or group, you allow them to join it or become part of it. EG *He was admitted to full membership of the academy... Soon afterwards he was admitted to British citizenship.*
V+O : IF+PREP THEN to/into ⇑ accept

6 If a room or building **admits** a particular number of people, it has room for that number; a formal use. EG *The new theatre will admit 400 people.*
V+O : NO CONT, NO IMPER = hold, accommodate

7 If an event or situation **admits** of something, it makes it possible for that thing to happen or be true; a formal use. EG *The relevant statute admitted of one interpretation only.*
V+A (of) ⇑ allow

admittance /ə3dmɪtə0ns/ is the act of entering a place or the right to enter it. EG *How was he to gain admittance?... Her admittance might be arranged.*
N UNCOUNT = admission

admittedly /ə3dmɪtɪ1dli1/ is used when you are giving some information which weakens the force of a statement or claim that you have just made. EG *My reputation was at stake. It was, admittedly, a slightly shaky reputation... Admittedly, economists often disagree among each other.*
ADV SEN = it's true

admonish /ə3dmɒnɪʃ/, **admonishes, admonishing, admonished**. If you **admonish** someone, you speak sternly to them or indicate in some other way that they have done something wrong; a formal word. EG *They are frequently admonished for their failure to act quickly.*
V+O/QUOTE, OR V+O+QUOTE : IF +PREP THEN for = rebuke

admonition /ædmə7nɪʃə0n/, **admonitions**. An **admonition** is a warning or rebuke about someone's behaviour; a formal word. EG *...with the admonition that you don't rush into marriage.*
N COUNT/UNCOUNT

ad nauseam /æd nɔːziæm, -sɪ-/. If someone does something **ad nauseam**, they do it repeatedly and over a long period of time, so that it becomes annoying or boring. EG *She went on ad nauseam about how well her children were doing at school.*
PHR : USED AS AN A = endlessly

ado /ədu:/. If you do something **without further ado** or **without more ado**, you do it at once, rather than discussing or delaying it any longer; a rather old-fashioned expression. EG *So, without more ado, let me introduce tonight's guests.*
PHR : USED AS AN A ⇑ immediately

adolescence /ædə7lesəns/ is the period of your life in which you develop from being a child into being an adult. EG *His adolescence was not a happy time for him.*
N UNCOUNT = teens

adolescent /ædə7lesə2nt/, **adolescents**. 1 An **adolescent** is a young person who is no longer a child but who has not yet become an adult.
N COUNT ⇑ youth = teenager

2 **Adolescent** girls and boys are developing from being children into being adults.
ADJ CLASSIF : ATTRIB

3 If you describe the behaviour or a remark of an adult as **adolescent**, you mean that it is immature and not at all sensible. EG *Her remarks about the Pentagon struck me as being adolescent and ill-judged.*
ADJ QUALIT = juvenile

adopt /ədɒpt/, **adopts, adopting, adopted**. 1 If you **adopt** someone else's child, you take it into your own family and make it legally your son or daughter: compare **foster**. EG *...people willing to adopt handicapped children.* ◊ **adopted**. EG *The parents of adopted children have special problems.* ◊ **adoption** /ədɒpʃə0n/, **adoptions**. EG *...the shortage of children available for adoption.*
V OR V+O ⇑ accept ◊ ADJ CLASSIF ◊ N UNCOUNT/COUNT

2 If you **adopt** a particular attitude, plan, or course of action, you begin to have it or to carry it out. EG *After the Revolution they adopted a more open policy towards the West... I had to adopt other methods of persuasion.* ◊ **adoption**. EG *That led to Labour's adoption of a radical foreign policy.*
V+O = take up ◊ N UNCOUNT+of

3 If you **adopt** a particular position, arrangement, posture, etc, you move yourself into it. EG *Green adopts a wide stance, his weight forward... As they advanced they barely bothered to adopt tactical formation.*
V+O = assume

4 If you **adopt** an accent, tone of voice, or gesture, you speak or behave differently from usual, especially in order to create an effect in a particular situation. EG *She spoke with a regional accent, which she had learned to adopt at will.*
V+O = assume, put on

5 If you **adopt** a country or name, you choose it to be
V+O

your own. ◊ **adopted**. EG *...Otto's devotion to his adopted country.* ◊ ADJ CLASSIF: ATTRIB

6 If a political party **adopts** someone as a candidate for an election, it officially chooses them to represent it. EG *The local constituency party adopted him as its candidate.* ◊ **adoption**. V+O+A *(as)* ⇑ select ≠ drop ◊ N UNCOUNT

adorable /ə^{3}dɔːrəbə^{0}l/. If you say that someone or something, especially a child or animal, is **adorable**, you think that they are very attractive and feel great affection for them. EG *...an adorable kitten... Isn't she adorable?* ADJ QUALIT = cute, sweet

adoration /ædə^{8}reɪʃə^{0}n/ is **1** a feeling of great admiration and love for someone or something. EG *He did not tell anyone of his adoration for her... ...the girl's adoration of her father... ...eyes wide with amazement and adoration.* N UNCOUNT: IF + PREP THEN *for/of* **2** the act or state of worshipping God or a god; an old-fashioned use. EG *...the statue before which they prostrated themselves in adoration.* N UNCOUNT

adore /ədɔː/, **adores, adoring, adored**. **1** If you **adore** someone, you feel great admiration and love for them. EG *She adored her sister.* ◊ **adoring**. EG *He had a wife at home, a simple, adoring woman.* V+O: NO CONT = idolize ◊ ADJ QUALIT: ATTRIB

2 If you **adore** something, you like it very much; used in informal English. EG *People will adore this film.* V+O: NO CONT = love

adorn /ədɔːn/, **adorns, adorning, adorned**; a literary word. **1** To **adorn** someone or something means to make them more beautiful by adding some kind of decoration or ornament to them. EG *Scarves and necklaces of many colours adorned their necks... ...a house adorned with statues.* V+O: IF + PREP THEN *with/by* ⇑ decorate = bedeck

2 If you say that someone **adorns** a place, event, or activity, you mean that they add quality and distinction to it by being there or taking part. EG *She felt her dining table adorned by the presence of the Minister... ...the profession you have adorned for so long.* V+O = grace

adornment /ədɔːnmə^{2}nt/, **adornments**. **1** An **adornment** is something that is intended to make someone or something more beautiful. EG *...adornments such as make-up and jewellery.* N COUNT = finery

2 **Adornment** is the act of making something more beautiful by adding something to it. EG *...styles of adornment over the centuries.* N UNCOUNT ⇑ decoration

adrenalin /ə^{3}drenəlɪn/; also spelled **adrenaline**. **Adrenalin** is a substance which is made inside your body when you are angry, nervous, or excited, and causes your heart beat faster and gives you more energy. EG *The dryness in my mouth vanished and I could feel the adrenalin flooding my body.* N UNCOUNT, OR N SING: *the*+N ⇑ hormone

adrift /ədrɪft/. **1** If a boat is **adrift**, it is floating on the water without being tied to anything or controlled by anyone. EG *They returned to find that someone had cut their boat adrift.* ADJ CLASSIF: PRED = loose ≠ controlled

2 If someone is or feels **adrift**, they have no clear purpose or idea of what to do. EG *Marsha felt frustrated, frightened, adrift.* ADJ QUALIT: PRED ⇑ purposeless

3 If something is or has gone **adrift**, it is no longer happening in the way that was intended. EG *It was obvious that something had gone adrift.* ADJ QUALIT: PRED ⇑ wrong

adroit /ə^{3}drɔɪt/. Someone who is **adroit** is quick and skilful in the way they think and behave. EG *Jamie was adroit at flattering others.* ◊ **adroitly**. EG *The young men picked the papers up adroitly.* ◊ **adroitness**. EG *...the adroitness with which he suggested that I should leave.* ADJ QUALIT = adept ◊ ADV AFTER VB ⇑ skilfully ◊ N UNCOUNT ≠ clumsiness

adulation /ædjə^{4}leɪʃə^{0}n/ is very great and uncritical admiration and praise. EG *She enjoyed a good deal of adulation.* N UNCOUNT = acclaim

adult /ædʌlt, ə^{3}dʌlt/, **adults**. **1** An **adult** is **1.1** a mature, fully developed person or animal. EG *A happy home is one in which children and adults have equal rights... I'd spent all my adult life in the army.* N COUNT = grown-up ≠ child

1.2 someone who has reached the age when they become legally responsible for their own decisions and actions and are no longer the responsibility of their parents. In Britain this happens when they reach the age of eighteen. EG *Children must be accompanied by an adult.* N COUNT ≠ minor

2 An **adult** person or animal is one that is fully developed and mature. EG *...adult insects.* ADJ CLASSIF: ATTRIB

3 Something that is **adult** is suitable for, or typical of, adult people. EG *She had very adult features... Children can assist in serious adult work at an early age.* ADJ QUALIT = grown-up

4 **Adult** films, shows, or books are about sex and are not considered suitable for children. EG *...an adult film.* ADJ CLASSIF: ATTRIB

adulterate /ə^{3}dʌltəreɪt/, **adulterates, adulterating, adulterated**. If you **adulterate** something, such as food or drink, you reduce its quality or make it weaker, for example by adding water to it. EG *The champagne had been adulterated.* ◊ **adulteration** /ə^{3}dʌltəreɪʃə^{0}n/. EG *...adulteration of milk and drugs.* V+O ⇑ debase = dilute ◊ N UNCOUNT

adulterer /ə^{3}dʌltə^{0}rə/, **adulterers**. An **adulterer** is someone who commits adultery. N COUNT ⇑ person

adulteress /ə^{3}dʌltrɪ^{2}s/, **adulteresses**. An **adulteress** is a woman who commits adultery. N COUNT

adultery /ə^{3}dʌltə^{0}ri^{1}/, **adulteries**. **Adultery** is the act of sexual intercourse when it involves someone who is married and a person that they are not married to. EG *Would he commit adultery?... Adultery was a ground for divorce.* N UNCOUNT/COUNT ⇑ misconduct

adulthood /ædʌlthʊd/ is the state or condition of being an adult, or the time of life during which someone is an adult. EG *There is no reason why she shouldn't survive into healthy adulthood.* N UNCOUNT = maturity ≠ childhood

ADV □ In this dictionary ADV is used in the grammar notes beside entries to mean 'adverb'. In general, adverbs are used before or after verbs (see □ at ADV AFTER VB, ADV WITH VB) or before some adjectives or other adverbs (see □ at ADV+ADJ/ADV). A few adverbs add a slightly negative quality to the clause they are in (see □ at ADV BRD NEG). There is also an important class of adverbs which are associated not with any other words, but with a clause or sentence as a whole. These are called ADV SEN in the grammar notes. In this dictionary the simple notation ADV is used in the following ways: **1** Adverbs which occur frequently both with verbs and with adjectives are called simply ADV in the grammar notes. Examples are **sufficiently** (see **sufficient**) and **classically** (see **classic 1**). EG *...people who care **sufficiently** about the city to secure its future... I had not been **sufficiently** alert to ask him... The initiatives have **classically** come from the colonels... He never looked such a **classically** good player as his brother.* Such adverbs can also be used with other adverbs, although this pattern is not common. An example is **sufficiently** in *I did not feel I knew her **sufficiently** well to ask her.* **2** ADV is also used for some other words which have specialized uses but which do not occur in any of the other ADV classes. An example is **above 4**. EG *...the room **above**... I prefer the picture **above**.* **3** ADV is also used in the grammar notes beside phrasal verbs to show that the second part of the phrasal verb is an adverb. See □ at PHRASAL VB.

ADV+ADJ/ADV □ In this dictionary ADV+ADJ/ADV is used in the grammar notes to mean that an adverb is not used with verbs but only in front of adjectives and other adverbs. It is not used in front of another adverb of the same type. This type of adverb is sometimes called an adverb of degree. Examples are **very**, **relatively**, and **wonderfully** (see **wonderful**). EG *It was **very** cold... I had known them for a **very** long time... The old lady came out **very** quietly... We were **relatively** unsuccessful... Natkin's work has sold **relatively** well... He told a **wonderfully** funny story... She was always **wonderfully** kind to me.*

ADV AFTER VB □ In this dictionary ADV AFTER VB is used in the grammar notes beside entries to mean that an adverb can only be used after a verb. If the verb is transitive (V+O) the adverb sometimes comes after both the verb and its object. See also ADV WITH VB. Examples are **down 1.2**, **aside 1**, and **indoors**. EG *She nodded and looked **down**... She had her head **down** and she didn't see him... Mr Casey stepped **aside**... She knocked his hand **aside**... She hurried **indoors**... Freda had taken Tom **indoors** for a bath.*

advance /ə^{3}dvɑːns/, **advances, advancing, advanced**. **1** To **advance** means **1.1** to move forward, especially in a threatening way or in order to attack someone. EG *The snake advances smoothly and silently... She advanced on him, shouting and waving her umbrella threateningly.* ◊ **advancing**. EG *I eyed the advancing figure carefully... ...the advancing enemy tanks.* V ⇑ approach ≠ retreat ◊ ADJ CLASSIF: ATTRIB **1.2** to make progress and become more sophisticated, especially in your knowledge or understanding of something. EG *We have greatly advanced in our understanding of the human body.* ● See also **advanced**. V = improve

2 When time **advances**, it passes by; a fairly formal use. EG *As the evening advanced we got more and more friendly.* V = wear on

3 If you **advance** a cause or interest, you support it and help it to be successful; a fairly formal use. EG *The government took every opportunity to advance the national interest.* V+O = further

4 To **advance** an event, or the time or date of an V+O event, means to bring it forward to an earlier time or date. EG *The date of the meeting was advanced by two weeks.*

5 If you **advance** a theory or idea, you put it forward for discussion; a fairly formal use. — V+O ⇑ suggest

6 If you **advance** a sum of money to someone, you lend it to them, or pay it to them before they are due to receive it. EG *The bank agreed to advance him £3000 to start his business... You may have to advance the builder some money for materials.* — V+O+O, OR V+O +A *(to)* ⇑ give

7 If you **advance** a tape, film, or clock, you turn or wind it forwards. EG *Close the camera and advance the film with the winder.* — V+O ⇑ reset

8 When prices or values **advance**, or when you **advance** them, they increase in amount; a formal use. — V-ERG = rise

9 An **advance** is **9.1** a forward movement of people or vehicles, especially of soldiers. EG *The enemy were planning a new advance on the capital... The convoy's speed of advance was twenty knots.* — N COUNT/UNCOUNT = approach ≠ retreat **9.2** money which is lent to someone or paid to them before they are due to receive it. EG *Authors are often given an advance on royalties.* — N COUNT **9.3** an increase in the price or value of something. EG *Is there any advance on five thousand?* — N COUNT = rise

10 If you make **advances** to someone, you try to persuade them to start a friendly or sexual relationship with you. EG *Her husband heard about the advances Simon had made to his wife... The unions seemed to respond favourably to the management's advances.* — N PLURAL ⇑ approaches = overtures

11 **Advance** in a particular field, subject, industry, etc is progress in understanding it or in developing new ideas and techniques. EG *The space programme has speeded up the rate of technological advance... Remarkable advances have been made recently in medicine.* — N COUNT/UNCOUNT = development

12 The **advance** of a future time or event is the gradual approach of it as time passes. EG *With the advance of old age he lost some of his enthusiasm for life.* — N UNCOUNT+SUPP = onset

13 An **advance** booking, warning, notice, etc is done or given before an event happens. EG *Advance booking is essential for very popular plays... We weren't given any advance warning of his visit.* — ADJ CLASSIF: ATTRIB = prior

14 An **advance** party or group is a small group of people who go on ahead of the main group, especially in order to make preparations or to find out what conditions are like. — ADJ CLASSIF: ATTRIB = reconnaissance

15 **in advance**. **15.1** If an idea or product is **in advance** of another one, it is more highly developed or more sophisticated. EG *Their training facilities are far in advance of anything we have.* — PHR+*of* = ahead ≠ behind **15.2** If you do something, or if something happens, **in advance**, you do it, or it happens, before the expected time. EG *He arrived half an hour in advance.* — PHR: USED AS AN A, IF+PREP THEN *of* = early **15.3** If you do something **in advance** of a date or event, you do it before that date or event. EG *We booked our seats well in advance of the date we wanted to travel... The landlady wanted three months' rent in advance.* — PHR: USED AS AN A, IF+PREP THEN *of* ⇑ ahead

advanced /ə3dvɑːnst/. **1** An **advanced** student has already learned the basic facts of a subject and is doing more difficult work. EG *...a dictionary for advanced learners.* — ADJ QUALIT ▸ used of a subject or course of study. EG *...advanced mathematics... ...an advanced course in the writing of plays for television.* — ▸ ADJ CLASSIF: ATTRIB ≠ elementary

2 A person or country that is **advanced** has reached a high level of development. EG *Japan is rapidly becoming the most advanced country technologically... Her youngest child is very advanced for his age.* — ADJ QUALIT ≠ backward

3 **Advanced** books or ideas are very modern and new, and are often considered unacceptable by ordinary people. EG *...a modern man with advanced ideas.* — ADJ QUALIT = avant-garde ≠ conventional

4 If someone is of **advanced** age or years, they are very old. EG *...a man of advanced years.* — ADJ QUALIT = mature

5 If you say that a day, year, etc is **advanced**, you mean that time has passed. EG *The day was not advanced enough for it to be really hot.* — ADJ QUALIT: PRED

advancement /ə3dvɑːnsmə2nt/ is **1** promotion in your job, or to a higher social class. EG *The new system leaves less opportunity for personal advancement.* — N UNCOUNT ⇑ progress **2** the process of helping something to happen or to succeed. EG *...the advancement of international peace.* — N UNCOUNT+SUPP = furtherance

advantage /ə3dvɑːntɪdʒ/, **advantages**. **1** An **advantage** is **1.1** something that puts you in a better position than other people. EG *Having a driving licence can be a big advantage... The voting system gives an advantage to the larger parties.* — N COUNT **1.2** a benefit or improvement that is likely to result from something. EG *What possible advantage could there be in changing your job now?... She explained the advantages of the new system over the old one.* — N COUNT ≠ drawback

2 **Advantage** is the state of being in a stronger or better position than others who are competing against you. EG *...a position of advantage... He had skilfully exploited the idea to electoral advantage.* — N UNCOUNT ⇑ supremacy

3 In tennis, **advantage** is used to refer to the first point scored after deuce in a game of tennis. EG *'Advantage McEnroe'.* — N UNCOUNT+N PROPER

4 **Advantage** is also used in the following expressions. **4.1** If a course of action **is to** your **advantage**, it will be useful for you to do it. EG *It might be to your advantage to learn Spanish.* — PHR: VB INFLECTS **4.2** If you **turn** a situation **to** your **advantage,** you act skilfully and manage to gain benefit from it, although it seemed at first to be unfavourable to you. — PHR: VB INFLECTS **4.3** If you **have the advantage over** someone, or something **gives** you **the advantage over** them, you are in a better position than they are. EG *His strength gives him the advantage over us.* — PHR: VB INFLECTS **4.4** If you **take advantage of** someone, you treat them unfairly or deceive them for your own benefit. — PHR: VB INFLECTS **4.5** If you **take advantage of** something, you make good use of it while you can. EG *We took advantage of the dry weather to paint the house.* — PHR: VB INFLECTS **4.6** If something is shown **to good advantage** or **to the best advantage**, it is shown in a way that emphasizes how attractive it is. EG *The plain walls show the paintings to good advantage.* — PHR: USED AS AN A ⇑ favourably = effectively

advantaged /ə3dvɑːntɪ2dʒd/. Someone who is **advantaged** is in a better social or financial position than other people. — ADJ QUALIT ⇑ favoured = privileged

advantageous /ædvə3nteɪdʒəs/. Something that is **advantageous** to you is likely to benefit you or improve your situation. EG *You're in a very advantageous position.* — ADJ QUALIT ⇑ helpful = favourable ◊ **advantageously**. — ◊ ADV

> **ADV BRD NEG** □ In this dictionary ADV BRD NEG is used in the grammar notes beside entries to refer to a small group of adverbs, which are sometimes called 'broad negatives'. They are **hardly, scarcely, barely, seldom** and one or two others. These adverbs have two main characteristics: **1** They add what appears to be a negative meaning to a clause, by denying the relevance of the positive statement they are making. An example is **hardly**. EG *I had **hardly** got into the house when the phone rang.* This means that although you had just got into the house, your attitude is that you have not really had enough time there for your being inside to be worth considering. Other examples are **scarcely** and **barely**. EG *I could **scarcely** believe what I heard... He **barely** listened to what his brother was saying.* **2** They feature in an unusual structure which emphasizes them. They are used as the first word in a clause, and are followed by an auxiliary or modal verb and then the subject. There is always another clause beginning with 'when' or 'than' or 'but' or a prepositional phrase beginning with 'without'. Examples are **hardly** and **seldom**. EG ***Hardly** had the car come to a standstill than she jumped out... **Seldom** did a week pass without a request for information.*

advent /ædvə2nt/. **1** The **advent** of something important is the fact of it starting or coming into existence; a rather formal use. EG *This sort of work would have been inconceivable before the advent of microprocessors.* — N SING: WITH POSS = appearance

2 The **advent** of a person at a place is their arrival there; a rather literary use. EG *Their eyes light up at Mr Roberts' advent.* — N SING: WITH POSS

adventitious /ædvɛ2ntɪʃəs/. An event or situation that is **adventitious** happens or exists by chance or unexpectedly; a formal word. EG *His knowledge of this particular bishop was somewhat adventitious.* — ADJ QUALIT ⇑ unexpected = accidental ≠ planned

adventure /ə3dvɛntʃə/, **adventures**. An **adventure** is something you do or a situation you become involved in that is unusual, exciting, and rather dangerous. EG *...my Arctic adventures... They were bored, and looking for adventure.* — N COUNT/UNCOUNT ⇑ experience

adventure playground, adventure playgrounds. An **adventure playground** is a rough area of land for children to play in, usually in cities. It has unusual wooden structures and equipment such as ropes, nets, and rubber tyres. — N COUNT

adventurer /ə3dvɛntʃərə/, **adventurers**. An **adventurer** is **1** a person, especially a man, who tries to become rich or powerful by using dishonest or — N COUNT = shark immoral methods; used showing disapproval. EG ...*rogues and adventurers from all over the world.* 2 a person who enjoys adventure. EG ...*an island race of adventurers.* **adventurous** /ə^{3}dvɛntʃərəs/. Someone who is **adventurous** is 1 willing to take risks and to try new methods. EG *I can't help wishing that Sinclair had been a bit more adventurous... They might perhaps be more adventurous in their repertoire.* ◊ **adventurously**. EG *We should be using the money more adventurously.* 2 eager to visit new places and have new experiences. EG *The romance of the east had appealed to his adventurous spirit.*

N COUNT
ADJ QUALIT ⇑ bold = daring ≠ cautious
◊ ADV WITH VB
ADJ QUALIT = bold, venturesome

adverb /ædvɜːb/, **adverbs**. An **adverb** is a word that adds information about the verb in a clause, or about a following adjective or adverb, or sometimes about a following prepositional group. Examples are *outside, extremely , physically* and *straight* in *They went outside... Progress was extremely slow... Judy seemed physically unwell... She went straight into the bathroom.* In this dictionary the abbreviation ADV is used in the grammar notes beside the entries to mean 'adverb'. See ADV, ADV+ADJ/ADV, ADV AFTER N, ADV AFTER VB, ADV BRD NEG, ADV SEN, ADV WITH VB.

N COUNT

adverbial group /ædvɜːbɪəl gruːp/, **adverbial groups**. In grammar, an **adverbial group** is a single adverb functioning on its own or a group of words of which the main word is an adverb.

N COUNT ⇑ adjunct

adversary /ædvəsə^{2}ri^{1}/, **adversaries**. Your **adversary** is the person or country that you are competing with, or arguing or fighting against. EG *His principal adversary was David Lloyd George... ...his political adversaries... Of the two potential adversaries, Britain was not yet ready to commit herself.*

N COUNT+SUPP = opponent ≠ ally

adverse /ædvɜːs/. **Adverse** decisions, conditions, or effects are unfavourable to you or the opposite of what you want or need. EG *Higher energy costs seem certain to have an adverse effect on the economy... ...adverse weather conditions.* ◊ **adversely**. EG *The majority of children are adversely affected.*

ADJ QUALIT : ATTRIB ⇑ bad ≠ favourable
◊ ADV WITH VB ⇑ badly

adversity /ə^{3}dvɜːsɪti^{1}/, **adversities**. **Adversity** is a situation in which you have many difficulties and problems and everything seems to be against you. EG *They continue to fight in the face of adversity.*

N UNCOUNT/COUNT ⇑ suffering = misfortune

advert /ædvɜːt/, **adverts**. An **advert** is an advertisement; an informal word.

N COUNT

advertise /ædvətaɪz/, **advertises, advertising, advertised**. 1 If you **advertise** a particular product or item for sale, you tell people about it in newspapers, on television, on posters, etc in order to persuade them to buy it. EG ...*a sign which advertised Calor gas... ...deodorants she had seen advertised on television.*

V+O : IF+PREP THEN *in/on* ⇑ publicize = promote

2 If you **advertise** a particular event, especially in a newspaper or on a poster, you announce that it is happening, so that people know about it and can go to it or take part in it. EG ...*a leaflet advertising a fishing competition.*

V+O : IF+PREP THEN *in/on* = publicize

3 If you **advertise** a particular job, or **advertise** for people to do a job, you have an announcement printed in a newspaper asking anyone interested to apply for it. EG ...*application forms for jobs advertised in the papers... The Council advertise from time to time for accountants and clerical staff.*

V+O : IF+PREP THEN *in/for* ⇑ request

4 If you **advertise** a particular quality or characteristic, you show it in your appearance, speech, or behaviour. EG *The crudeness of his features advertised his ruthless and brutish nature.*

V+O = proclaim ≠ conceal, hide

advertisement /ə^{3}dvɜːtɪsmə^{2}nt/, **advertisements**. 1 An **advertisement** is an announcement in a newspaper, on television, or on a poster about a product, event, job vacancy, etc. EG ...*an advertisement for Black and White whisky... ...all the applications we have received in answer to our advertisements.* 2 If someone or something is an **advertisement** for something, they show the advantages or benefits of it and are likely to convince other people that it is a good thing. EG *He wanted to make the Post Office an advertisement for public ownership.*

N COUNT ⇑ notice = advert, ad
N COUNT+*for* = advert

advertiser /ædvətaɪzə/, **advertisers**. An **advertiser** is a person or company that pays for a product, event, or job vacancy to be advertised on television, in a newspaper, etc. EG *We've had several phone calls already this morning from advertisers.*

N COUNT

advertising /ædvətaɪzɪŋ/ is the activity of telling people about products and making them seem attractive so that people want to buy them. EG ...*a job in advertising... ...an advertising agency... The tobacco industry spends 100 million pounds a year on advertising... ...the marketing and advertising of powdered milk.*

N UNCOUNT = promotion, publicity

advice /ə^{3}dvaɪs/. 1 If you give someone **advice**, you tell them what you think they should do in a particular situation. EG *She promised to follow his advice... They want advice on how to do it... One woman went to a psychiatrist for advice.* ● If you **take advice**, or **take legal advice**, you ask a lawyer about your position in law regarding a particular matter. EG *Taking legal advice is not something that any of us do lightly.*

N UNCOUNT : USU +SUPP ⇑ help = counsel
● PHR : VB INFLECTS

2 **Advice** is also an official, legal, or business document that states that something has been done or will be done, for example that the goods you have ordered from a firm have been sent. EG ...*an advice note... We received advice of delivery.*

N UNCOUNT + SUPP ⇑ notification

advisable /ə^{3}dvaɪzəbə^{0}l/. If a course of action is **advisable**, it is sensible, involves little risk, or is likely to achieve the result you want. EG *It's advisable to ring up first to make an appointment.* ◊ **advisability** /ə^{3}dvaɪzəbɪlɪti^{1}/. EG ...*the advisability of settling as near as possible to the centre of town... They pondered the advisability of another attempt.*

ADJ QUALIT = wise ≠ foolish, inadvisable
◊ N UNCOUNT : *the*+N+*of* ≠ folly

advise /ə^{3}dvaɪz/, **advises, advising, advised**. 1 If you **advise** someone to do something in a particular situation, you tell them that you think they should do it. EG *He advised me not to buy it... I would strongly advise you against it... It was his doctor who advised that he change his job.* ● See also **well-advised, ill-advised**.

V+O, V+O+*to*-INF/REPORT-CL, V+O+A (*on/against*), OR V+A (ON/AGAINST) ⇑ suggest = recommend

2 Someone who **advises** a particular person or organization regularly gives them suggestions about improving and developing their activities and methods. EG *The Advisory Council advises the BBC on Further Education problems.*

V OR V+O : IF+PREP THEN *on* ⇑ help = guide

3 If you **advise** someone of something, you inform them about it; a formal word. EG *The company spends a lot of time keeping its salesmen advised of new products.*

V+O : IF+PREP THEN *of* ⇑ tell

advisedly /ə^{3}dvaɪzɪ^{2}dli^{1}/. If you say that you are using a word or expression **advisedly**, you mean that you have deliberately chosen to use it, although it may sound odd or wrong, because it draws attention to what you are saying. EG ...*as requested. I use the phrase advisedly, because it depends who is doing the requesting.*

ADV = on purpose

adviser /ə^{3}dvaɪzə/, **advisers**; also spelled **advisor**. An **adviser** is someone who is asked to give suggestions to another person or to a group of people about what they should do. EG *I was Charlotte's friend and adviser... ...an independent legal adviser.*

N COUNT+SUPP ⇑ guide = counsellor

advisory /ə^{3}dvaɪzə^{0}ri^{1}/. An **advisory** group, or a group or person with an **advisory** role, regularly gives suggestions and help to people or organizations, especially about a particular subject or area of activity. EG ...*the National Women's Advisory Committee... His role is 'purely advisory'... Most of the advisory work is carried out over the phone.*

ADJ CLASSIF ⇑ guiding = consultative

advocacy /ædvə^{6}kəsi^{1}/. **Advocacy** of a particular action or plan is the act of supporting it publicly. EG ...*their advocacy of a strong state and a single party.*

N UNCOUNT : IF+PREP THEN *of* ⇑ support ≠ opposition to

advocate, advocates, advocating, advocated. The word **advocate** is pronounced /ædvə^{6}keɪt/ when it is a verb, and /ædvə^{6}kət/ when it is a noun. 1 If you **advocate** a particular action or plan, you support it publicly. EG *He advocated the creation of a permanent United Nations.*

V+O/REPORT-CL = recommend ≠ oppose

2 An **advocate** of a particular action or plan is someone who supports it publicly. EG ...*the advocates of women's rights... ...a leading advocate of free enterprise.* ● See also **devil's advocate**.

N COUNT WITH POSS ⇑ supporter

3 An **advocate** is a lawyer who speaks in favour of someone or defends them in a court of law.

N COUNT = barrister

ADV SEN □ In this dictionary ADV SEN is used in the grammar notes beside entries to show that an adverb or an expression with an adverbial function applies to a clause or a sentence as a whole. These adverbs are usually placed at the beginning of a clause followed by a comma or in the clause separated by commas. A few come at the end of the clause. 1 An ADV SEN may show the way in which sentences link together. An example of this is **however**. EG *I am not responsible for what my critics write.* ***However****, in this case, Fred is right... There is,* ***however****, an alternative approach... Most people think that David is really nice. Not me,* ***however****.* 2 An ADV SEN may make a comment on the main sentence. Examples are **unfortunately** and **of course** (see **course** 1). EG ***Unfortunately***, [illegible] *wasn't able to visit him... My own opinion,* ***unfortunately****, backs him up... 'Where shall we meet?'-'At the golf club,* ***of course****'.* **3** An ADV SEN may also be a signal in the spoken discourse which gives information to a hearer about, for example, a speaker's attitude or intention. An example of this is **anyway**. EG *We're all short of money-I am,* ***anyway****... And* ***anyway*** *I feel so mean bothering him about it... **Anyway**, what does it matter to you?*

ADV WITH VB □ In this dictionary ADV WITH VB is used in the grammar notes beside entries to mean that the adverb comments on a verb and is not used before an adjective or another adverb. An ADV WITH VB may come before or after the verb. If it comes after a transitive verb (V+O) it sometimes comes after both the verb and its object. Sometimes it is more usual for the adverb to come in one position in relation to the verb rather than the other and the examples in the entry will show this. See also □ at ADV AFTER VB. Examples are **busily**, **concisely**, and **voluntarily**. EG *Eddie was* ***busily*** *engaged in building a hut... Judy typed* ***busily****... She answered the vicar's questions calmly and* ***concisely****... No one could describe him as* ***concisely*** *as Cocteau has done in his caricature... He left* ***voluntarily****.*

adze /ædz/, **adzes**; also spelled **adz** in American English. An **adze** is a heavy tool used for cutting and shaping wood. It has a blade at right angles to its handle. N COUNT

-ae is added in place of -a at the end of some singular nouns to form the plural. Some of these nouns also have plural forms ending in -s that are used in less formal or less technical English. EG *...formula→formulae... vertebra→vertebrae... antenna→antennae.* SUFFIX: FORMS PLURALS

aegis /iːdʒɪs/. If you do something **under the aegis of** a person or organization, or you are **under** their **aegis**, you have their official support and backing; a formal expression. EG *The students spearhead a campaign under the aegis of Amnesty International.* PREP, OR PHR: USED AS AN A = under the auspices of

aeon /iː[7]n/, **aeons**; also spelled **eon** in American English. An **aeon** is an extremely long period of time. EG *...a dread that reaches back over the aeons to primitive man.* N COUNT: USU PL = age

aerate /ɛəreɪt/, **aerates, aerating, aerated**. If a substance in the form of a liquid **is aerated**, air or gas is passed through it in order to make it more fizzy or to make it less dense when it solidifies. EG *...some ghastly aerated chemical confection.* V+O: USU PASS

aerial /ɛərɪəl/, **aerials**. **1 Aerial** means fixed above the level of the ground, or moving through the air. EG *...its adaptation to an aerial existence... The remaining aerial walkway was removed.* ADJ CLASSIF: ATTRIB ≠ earth-bound, ground level

2 An **aerial** attack on a target is made from aeroplanes. EG *The British continued their aerial strikes... ...aerial warfare.* ADJ CLASSIF: ATTRIB

3 Aerial photographs are photographs of land, buildings, traffic, etc which are taken from an aeroplane. ADJ CLASSIF: ATTRIB

4 An **aerial** is a device made of metal rods or wire, which receives or sends out television or radio signals. Aerials are often attached to the outside of buildings, vehicles, radios, and television sets. EG *...an aerial among the chimney pots.* N COUNT = antenna

aero- is used at the beginning of words, especially nouns, that refer to things or activities connected with aeroplanes and air travel. PREFIX

aerobatics /ɛərə[6]bætɪks/ are skilful and difficult or dangerous movements made by someone flying an aeroplane. EG *They executed a series of aerobatics-criss-crossing, diving and soaring over our heads.* N PLURAL = stunts

aerobic /ɛərəʊbɪk/ means **1** using oxygen; a technical term in biochemistry. EG *During the aerobic or oxygen-consuming process, heat is given off.* ADJ CLASSIF: ATTRIB **2** relating to or involving aerobics. ADJ CLASSIF: ATTRIB

aerobics /ɛərəʊbɪks/ is a form of exercise which increases the amount of oxygen in your blood, and which strengthens your heart and lungs. N UNCOUNT

aerodrome /ɛərədrəʊm/, **aerodromes**. An **aerodrome** is a place or area where small aeroplanes can land and take off; used mainly in British English. EG *He circled over the aerodrome.* N COUNT = airfield

aerodynamic /ɛərə[6]daɪnæmɪk/, **aerodynamics**. **Aerodynamic** is an adjective, and **aerodynamics** is an uncount noun. **1 Aerodynamics** is the scientific study of the way objects move through air, and the way air and other gases move. N UNCOUNT

2 Aerodynamic means involving or relating to the principles of aerodynamics. EG *The wing outline of a bird conforms to the same aerodynamic principle as that of an aircraft.* ADJ CLASSIF: ATTRIB

3 Something such as a car that has an **aerodynamic** shape or design moves through the air easily and efficiently and goes faster and uses less fuel than other cars. ADJ QUALIT

aeronautical /ɛərə[6]nɔːtɪkə[0]l/ means involving or relating to the design and construction of aeroplanes. EG *...the Department of Aeronautical Engineering.* ADJ CLASSIF: USU ATTRIB

aeronautics /ɛərə[6]nɔːtɪks/ is the science of designing and constructing aeroplanes. EG *...his extensive knowledge of aeronautics.* N UNCOUNT ⇑ study

aeroplane /ɛərə[6]pleɪn/, **aeroplanes**. An **aeroplane** is a vehicle with wings and one or more engines that enable it to fly through the air; used mainly in British English. EG *It's a low-cost aeroplane and it doesn't use much energy.* N COUNT ⇑ aircraft = plane, airplane

aerosol /ɛərə[6]sɒl/, **aerosols**. An **aerosol** is a small metal container in which a substance such as paint, deodorant, or insecticide is kept under pressure. When you press a button the substance is forced out as a fine spray. N COUNT

aerospace /ɛərə[6]speɪs/. The **aerospace** industry and **aerospace** companies are involved in developing and making rockets, missiles, space vehicles, and equipment used in them. EG *...aerospace engineers.* ADJ CLASSIF: ATTRIB ⇑ space

Aertex /ɛəteks/ is a trademark for a loosely woven cotton material which is used for making shirts, underwear, and clothes worn while playing sports. EG *...an apple-green Aertex shirt.* N UNCOUNT ⇑ fabric

aesthete /iːsθiːt/, **aesthetes**; also spelled **esthete** in American English. An **aesthete** is someone who loves and appreciates works of art and beautiful things. N COUNT ⇑ person

aesthetic /iˈsθetɪk/, **aesthetics**; also spelled **esthetic** in American English. **Aesthetic** is an adjective, and **aesthetics** is an uncount noun. **1 Aesthetic** means relating to the appreciation of beauty or art. EG *...a purely aesthetic appeal... ...timeless aesthetic values.* ◊ **aesthetically**. EG *His best pieces seem aesthetically successful.* ADJ CLASSIF ◊ ADV

2 Aesthetics is a branch of philosophy concerned with the study of the concept of beauty. N UNCOUNT ⇑ theory

aether /iːθə/. See **ether**.

afar /əfɑː/; an old-fashioned or literary word. **1 From afar** means from a long way away. EG *He rode up and saw me from afar... She grinned at me from afar.* PHR: USED AS AN A

2 If you admire someone **from afar**, you admire them without having an opportunity to know or talk to them. EG *Bill's wife had worshipped him from afar.* PHR: USED AS AN A

affable /æfəbə[0]l/. Someone who is **affable** is pleasant and easy to talk to; a rather literary word. EG *The boy who brought it was very affable.* ▸ used of behaviour. EG *The interview was affable.* ◊ **affably**. EG *He received us affably.* ◊ **affability**/æfəbɪlɪti[1]/. EG *There was a pretence of affability.* ADJ QUALIT = genial ≠ disagreeable ◊ ADV WITH VB ◊ N UNCOUNT

affair /əfɛə/, **affairs**; also spelled **affaire** in paragraph 6. **1** You can refer to an event or a series of events as an **affair**, or as a particular kind of **affair** when you are summarizing all its features or aspects. EG *The Churchill affair was not a decisive factor... The wedding was a quiet affair... An enquiry will be conducted into the whole affair.* N COUNT+SUPP: USU SING = business, matter

2 You can refer to an object as a particular kind of **affair** when you want to summarize its features or your opinion of it; an informal use. EG *The house was an imposing, mock Georgian affair... Some wore quilted affairs like dressing gowns.* N COUNT+SUPP ⇑ thing = effort

3 Affairs relating to a particular subject, country, or organization are all the important information or events that are connected with it; a formal use. EG *...a specialist in Eastern European affairs... Participation in public affairs is encouraged... ...affairs of state.* ● See also **current affairs, state of affairs.** N PLURAL+SUPP = matters

4 Your **affairs** are all the things connected with your personal life and work which you consider to be private. EG *What had induced the absurd woman to meddle in his affairs?* N PLURAL: WITH POSS = concerns

5 Something that is your **affair** concerns you, and it is your right or duty to deal with it. EG *What went on behind that door was your own affair... It's no affair of mine.* N SING WITH DET: POSS+N = business

6 An **affair** or **affaire** is a temporary or secret sexual relationship between two people, especially when one or both of them are married to someone else. EG N COUNT

I had an affair with her before the war... ...an extramarital affair. ● See also **love affair**.

affect /ə[3]fɛkt/, **affects, affecting, affected.** 1 When something **affects** someone or something else, it influences them or causes them to change in some way. EG *...the ways in which computers can affect our lives... Insects are greatly affected by body temperature.*
V+O; = influence

2 When a disease **affects** someone or a part of their body, it causes them to become ill, or causes that part of their body to stop functioning properly. EG *The disease primarily affected Jane's lungs... Seven people were affected.*
V+O; ⇑ attack; = afflict

3 If someone or something **affects** a person, they cause that person to have strong feelings of sadness, pity, love, etc. EG *His letters affected her profoundly... The mother was badly affected. She broke down completely.* ● See also **affecting**.
V+O; ⇑ touch; = move, stir

4 If you **affect** a particular feeling or physical characteristic, you pretend to have it, usually in order to cause other people to react in a particular way; a rather formal use. EG *He affected to despise every Briton he met... She affected a lisp.* ● See also **affected**.
V+O, OR V+to-INF; = put on

5 If you **affect** a particular style or item of clothing, you like it and often wear it; used in formal English, sometimes showing disapproval. EG *...the polo-necked silk sweater which he habitually affected.*
V+O; ⇑ have; = adopt

affectation /æfɛkteɪʃə[0]n/, **affectations.** An **affectation** is an attitude, habit, or type of behaviour that is not genuine or natural, but which is intended to impress other people; used showing disapproval. EG *He was excited and his film star affectations had disappeared.*
N COUNT/UNCOUNT; = pose, airs

affected /ə[3]fɛktɪ[2]d/. Someone who is **affected** pretends to have habits, attitudes, or qualities which are not natural or genuine, in order to impress other people; used showing disapproval. EG *He thought that I was affected and conceited.* ▸ used of behaviour, attitudes, or qualities. EG *...a curious, almost affected, swagger.* ◇ **affectedly.** EG *She was singing it affectedly in a nasal tone.*
ADJ QUALIT; ⇑ unnatural; = pretentious; ≠ natural; ▸ = mannered; ◇ ADV WITH VB

affecting /ə[3]fɛktɪŋ/. Something that is **affecting** causes you to feel great emotion, especially sadness or pity; a rather literary word. EG *...a most affecting scene... It was writing which I found very, very affecting.*
ADJ QUALIT; ⇑ emotive; = moving, touching

affection /ə[3]fɛkʃə[0]n/, **affections. 1 Affection** is a feeling of fondness and caring, especially for another person. EG *She gazed with deep affection at his sleeping form... She had little affection for him and certainly didn't love him. ...a slight affection for the theatre.*
N UNCOUNT; ≠ dislike

2 Your **affections** are your feelings of sexual love for someone; a rather literary word. EG *The General transferred his affections to the other sister.*
N PLURAL : POSS+N; = attentions

affectionate /ə[3]fɛkʃənə[1]t/. Someone who is **affectionate** frequently behaves in a way that shows their love or fondness for another person. EG *They were an affectionate couple... His mother is a great deal more affectionate towards him.* ▸ used of thoughts or behaviour. EG *His tone was affectionate... ...affectionate memories.* ◇ **affectionately.** EG *'Poor boy' said Kim, affectionately.*
ADJ QUALIT; ⇑ loving; ▸ = tender; ◇ ADV WITH VB; = tenderly

affidavit /æfɪdeɪvɪt/, **affidavits.** An **affidavit** is a written statement which you swear is true and which may be used as evidence in a court of law. EG *The authors submit a dozen sworn affidavits.*
N COUNT

affiliate, affiliates, affiliating, affiliated; a formal word. **Affiliate** is pronounced /ə[3]fɪli[1]eɪt/ when it is a verb, and /ə[3]fɪli[1]ə[1]t/ when it is an adjective. 1 If an organization **affiliates** itself or is **affiliated** to another, larger organization, it forms a close association with it or becomes a branch or member of it. EG *Such a group had already affiliated itself to them... ...an experimental group affiliated with the Royal Shakespeare Company.* ◇ **affiliated.** EG *Questionnaires were sent to all affiliated trade unions.*
V, V+O (REFL), OR V+A (to/with); ⇑ join; = associate, ally; ◇ ADJ CLASSIF : ATTRIB

2 An **affiliate** is an organization which has a close association with, or is a member of, a larger organization. EG *The organization has exercised a decisive influence over its British affiliates.*
N COUNT; = associate

affiliation /ə[3]fɪli[1]eɪʃə[0]n/, **affiliations.** If one group has an **affiliation** with another group, it has a close connection with it, or is closely involved with it; a formal word. EG *Not having any religious affiliation, we can give an unbiased opinion.* ▸ used as an uncount noun. EG *They sought affiliation to the Labour Party... We have no affiliation with any particular insurance group.*
N COUNT : USU MOD+N; = attachment; ▸ N UNCOUNT : IF+PREP THEN to/with

affinity /əfɪnɪti[1]/, **affinities**; a formal word. 1 If you have an **affinity** with or for someone or something, you are attracted towards them and have a feeling of involvement with them. EG *They have found a natural affinity with immigrants in this country... I had this tremendous sense of affinity with the place.*
N COUNT/UNCOUNT : IF+PREP THEN with/for; ⇑ liking; = rapport

2 An **affinity** is a close similarity between two or more people or things. EG *In anatomical structure, Prehistoric Man has close affinities with modern humans.*
N COUNT/UNCOUNT; = resemblance

affirm /ə[3]fɜːm/, **affirms, affirming, affirmed**; a formal word. 1 When you **affirm** something, you state that it is true. EG *They affirmed that the girls did quite a bit of reading... 'Not yet, but it will,' he affirmed.*
V+O/REPORT/QUOTE; = assert; ≠ deny

2 If you **affirm** ideas, intentions, rights, or actions, you clearly indicate your belief in and support for them. EG *They affirm a policy of religious toleration... ...rejecting the power of the planters and affirming the rights of the people.*
V+O; = profess

3 If you **affirm** a belief or impression, you strengthen and renew it. EG *They rallied to his support, affirming the esteem in which he was held.*
V+O; = confirm

affirmation /æfəmeɪʃə[0]n/, **affirmations**; a formal word. 1 The **affirmation** of facts is the act of stating that they are true. EG *They required her affirmation of the fact.*
N UNCOUNT : IF+PREP THEN of

2 The **affirmation** of ideas, intentions, rights, or actions is a statement of your belief in and support for them. EG *...this denunciation of privilege and affirmation of equality.*
N UNCOUNT : IF+PREP THEN of

3 An **affirmation** is a solemn promise to tell the truth, which is made in a court of law by people who are not Christians and who do not swear on the Bible; a formal use.
N COUNT

affirmative /ə[3]fɜːmətɪv/, **affirmatives.** 1 An **affirmative** word or gesture is one which indicates that you agree with what someone has said or that the answer to a question is 'yes'. EG *...the affirmative nodding of my head.* ◇ **affirmatively.** EG *He replied affirmatively.* ● If you reply **in the affirmative**, you answer a question by saying 'yes' or by making a gesture that means 'yes'. EG *40 per cent replied in the affirmative.*
ADJ CLASSIF : ATTRIB; = positive; ≠ negative; ◇ ADV WITH VB; ● PHR : USED AS AN A

2 An **affirmative** is the word 'yes', or another word or expression which suggests your agreement. EG *This didn't seem to require even an affirmative, so I kept silent.*
N SING; ⇑ reply; ≠ negative

affix, affixes, affixing, affixed. The word **affix** is pronounced /ə[3]fɪks/ when it is a verb, and /æfɪks/ when it is a noun. 1 If you **affix** something somewhere, you stick, fasten, or attach it there; a fairly formal use. EG *A page of a magazine was affixed to the wall above the bed.*
V+O : IF+PREP THEN to; ⇑ fix

2 An **affix** is a letter or syllable which is added to the beginning or end of a word to make a different word, tense etc.
N COUNT; = prefix, suffix

afflict /ə[3]flɪkt/, **afflicts, afflicting, afflicted.** If something such as pain or sorrow **afflicts** someone, it causes them severe physical or mental suffering. EG *Only other sufferers know what it is like to be afflicted with this disease.*
V+O : IF PASS, THEN +by/with; ⇑ affect

affliction /ə[3]flɪkʃə[0]n/, **afflictions.** An **affliction** is something which causes someone physical or mental suffering. EG *Cal could not help his affliction... They suffer fewer of the usual afflictions.* ▸ used as an uncount noun. EG *It helped bring relief in affliction.*
N COUNT; = misfortune; ≠ blessing; ▸ N UNCOUNT

affluence /æfluəns/ is the state of having a lot of money or a high standard of living; a formal word. EG *...the relative affluence of the white world.*
N UNCOUNT; = prosperity; ≠ poverty

affluent /æfluənt/. Someone who is **affluent** has a lot of money or a high standard of living. EG *...affluent young professionals... ...an affluent society.* ▸ used also of places, conditions, etc. EG *They both come from relatively affluent backgrounds.*
ADJ QUALIT; = prosperous

afford /əfɔːd/, **affords, affording, afforded.** 1 If you can **afford** something, you have enough money to buy it or do it without causing yourself financial difficulty. EG *...families who can afford cars... I can't afford to rent this flat... If you can afford it, use specialists.*
V+O, OR V+to-INF : MODAL+V, NO IMPER OR CONT

2 If you can **afford** the time or energy to do
V+O : MODAL+V,

something, you have enough time or energy to spend on it without causing yourself inconvenience or tiredness. EG *I can't afford more than a day or so.* NO IMPER OR CONT = spare

3 If you say that you cannot **afford** to do something or to let something happen, you mean that it would be harmful or inconvenient if it did happen and so you must prevent it. EG *You can't afford to be careless in this job... We can't afford another scandal in the firm... They could afford to wait.* V+O, OR V+to-INF : MODAL+V, NO IMPER OR CONT = risk

4 If you **afford** support or protection to someone, you give it to them; a formal use. EG *...the protection afforded to the workers by the unions.* V+O, V+O+O, OR V+O+A (to) : NO IMPER

5 If something **affords** you a particular feeling, view, chance of doing something, etc, it gives you the opportunity of having it or doing it; a fairly formal use. EG *A door ajar to the right afforded a glimpse of the living room... These meetings with him always afforded me much pleasure.* V+O, V+O+O, OR V+O+A (to) : NO IMPER = offer

afforestation /əˈfɒrɪˈsteɪʃən/ is the process of planting large numbers of trees on bare land. EG *...the afforestation of the uplands.* N UNCOUNT ⇑ cultivation

affray /əfreɪ/, **affrays**. An **affray** is a noisy and violent fight, especially in a public place; a fairly formal word. EG *His success with her had resulted in the affray between him and John.* N COUNT = fracas

affront /əfrʌnt/, **affronts, affronting, affronted**. 1 If something is an **affront** to someone, it is a deliberate insult or a challenge to their pride or dignity. EG *Nell takes it as a personal affront... This is a serious affront to large numbers of citizens.* N COUNT : IF+PREP THEN to = slight

2 If you **are affronted** by something, you feel insulted and your pride and dignity are hurt. EG *They were deeply affronted by their abrupt dismissal.* V+O : USU PASS ⇑ insult = offend

Afghan /æfgən/, **Afghans**. 1 An **Afghan** is a person who comes from Afghanistan. N COUNT

2 **Afghan** means belonging or relating to Afghanistan, or to its people or language. EG *...the Afghan government.* ADJ CLASSIF

3 An **Afghan** is also 3.1 a tall, thin hunting dog which has long silky hair. N COUNT 3.2 a sheepskin coat, usually decorated with embroidery and trimmed with long fur. N COUNT

afield /əfiːld/. If someone comes from **far afield**, they come from a long way away. EG *Other groups, from as far afield as Scotland, have sent deputations... They go further afield for their holidays.* PHR : USED AS AN A = far away

afire /əfaɪə/; a rather literary word. 1 If something is **afire** or is set **afire**, it is on fire. EG *The farmers set afire the tall piles of weeds... ...ships sinking or afire.* ADJ CLASSIF : PRED, OR ADV = alight

2 If someone is **afire** with emotion, they are extremely enthusiastic and excited about something. EG *He was afire with missionary zeal... She was all afire.* ADJ CLASSIF : PRED, IF+PREP THEN with

aflame /əfleɪm/; a rather literary word. 1 If someone's face is **aflame**, it is bright red and feels hot because they are embarrassed or excited. EG *There she stood and blinked, cheeks aflame, hair awry... He was aflame with pride.* ADJ CLASSIF : PRED = aglow ≠ pale

2 If something is **aflame**, 2.1 it looks bright red or golden because the sun is shining on it. EG *The sun touched the horizon, set it aflame, and disappeared.* ADJ CLASSIF : PRED, OR ADV

2.2 it is on fire and burning. EG *Its wreckage was bent and the tyres aflame.* ADJ CLASSIF : PRED, OR ADV

afloat /əfləʊt/. 1 When someone or something is **afloat** in water, they remain partly above the surface of the water and do not sink. EG *By kicking constantly he could stay afloat without exhausting himself.* ADJ CLASSIF : PRED, OR ADV AFTER VB = floating ≠ sinking

2 When you are or spend time **afloat**, you are sailing on a boat. EG *In summer the hours spent afloat drift by.* ADJ CLASSIF : PRED, OR ADV AFTER VB

3 If you stay **afloat** or if you keep a business **afloat**, you have just enough money to pay your debts or to run your business. EG *They have kept the firm afloat during the recession... He had managed to keep himself afloat.* ADJ CLASSIF : PRED, OR ADV AFTER VB ⇑ solvent

4 If you **set** a business, scheme, etc **afloat**, you start it or put it into operation. EG *A rival company has set afloat a new credit scheme.* PHR : VB INFLECTS = launch

5 When something is **afloat** in the air, it moves, or appears to move, in the air without any support. EG *...the domes and walls of Delhi, afloat on the morning mist.* ADJ CLASSIF : PRED = floating

afoot /əfʊt/. When there is a project, scheme, or mischief **afoot**, there is something happening or being planned by other people which you do not know much about. EG *There was a campaign afoot to reinstate you... Something extraordinary was afoot.* ADJ CLASSIF : PRED

aforementioned /əfɔːmɛnʃənd/. The **aforementioned** person, matter, etc, is the person or matter which has just been referred to; a formal word. EG *...the works of all the aforementioned writers.* ADJ CLASSIF : ATTRIB, USU the+ADJ+N

aforesaid /əfɔːsɛd/ means the same as aforementioned. EG *The aforesaid arrangement seemed preposterous... ...the jewels and relics of the aforesaid church.* ADJ CLASSIF : ATTRIB, USU the+ADJ+N

afraid /əfreɪd/. 1 If you are **afraid** of someone or something or **afraid** to do something, you feel fear because you think that you will be hurt or that something horrible will happen to you. EG *They were afraid of you. They knew you had killed many men... He was afraid even to turn his head... She suddenly looked afraid.* ADJ QUALIT : PRED, IF+PREP THEN of/to-INF = frightened, scared

2 If you are **afraid** that an unpleasant or awkward situation or event will happen, you are worried about it and want to avoid it. EG *She was afraid that I might be embarrassed... She was terribly afraid of offending anyone... Don't be afraid to ask questions.* ADJ QUALIT : PRED+REPORT-CL/to-INF/of = scared

3 You use expressions such as **'I'm afraid'**, **'I'm afraid not'**, and **'I'm afraid to say'** in order to express politeness or regret, for example when you are apologizing or disagreeing with someone. EG *It's a bit stuffy in here, I'm afraid... I'm afraid I can't agree... 'Can you come round this evening?'-'I'm afraid not'... 'I hear that she's leaving. Is that right?'-'I'm afraid so'.* ADV SEN, OR CONVENTION ⇑ unfortunately

afresh /əfrɛʃ/. If you start **afresh** or you do something **afresh**, you start or do something again in a different way. EG *You're too old to start afresh somewhere you don't know... We are willing, in principle, to look afresh at the 1921 constitution.* ADV AFTER VB = anew

African /æfrɪkən/, **Africans**. 1 **African** means 1.1 belonging or relating to the continent of Africa, or to its countries or peoples. EG *...the flood plains of African rivers.* ADJ CLASSIF 1.2 belonging or relating to black people who come from Africa. EG *He impressed people by the way he presented the African case... ...African culture.* ADJ CLASSIF

2 An **African** is someone, especially a black person, who comes from Africa, or whose family originally came from Africa. EG *...a handsome African dressed in a Western business suit... ...a white man can be as good an African as a black man.* N COUNT ▸ used as an adjective. EG *...the African population of Johannesburg.* ▸ ADJ CLASSIF

Afrikaans /æfrɪkɑːns, -kɑːnz/. 1 **Afrikaans** is one of official languages of South Africa and is related to Dutch. EG *We ran articles in Afrikaans.* N UNCOUNT ⇑ language

2 **Afrikaans** means belonging or relating to the white people living in South Africa whose ancestors were Dutch. EG *An Afrikaans couple live in one of the houses opposite.* ADJ CLASSIF

Afrikaner /æfrɪkɑːnə/, **Afrikaners**. 1 An **Afrikaner** is a white person who lives in South Africa and whose ancestors were Dutch. EG *The Afrikaners are 60% of the white population.* N COUNT

2 **Afrikaner** means belonging or relating to the white people in South Africa whose ancestors were Dutch. EG *They had consolidated Afrikaner support.* ADJ CLASSIF : ATTRIB

Afro /æfrəʊ/, **Afros**. An **Afro** hairstyle is one in which your hair is cut and set in a short frizzy mass. EG *I went and had my hair cut in an Afro... ...Afro haircuts.* N COUNT

Afro- is added to the beginning of adjectives to form compound adjectives which describe something connected both with Africa and with another continent or country. EG *...Afro-American music.* PREFIX

aft /ɑːft/. If you go **aft** in a boat or plane, you go to the back of it. EG *I went aft to the saloon... ...100 feet aft of the passengers' cabins.* ADV WITH VB ≠ fore

after /ɑːftə/, **afters**. The form **afters** is only used in paragraph 21. 1 If something happens some time **after**, or happens **after** a particular date, event, etc, it happens during the period of time that follows the time or event mentioned. EG *Soon after, Faraday began his researches into electricity... She had arrived just after breakfast on her bicycle... ...after seven in the evening... The others began to be ill almost at once after eating.* PREP, ADV, OR CONJ SUBORD ≠ before

2 The day, year, etc **after** a particular date or event is the day or year that directly follows it. EG *'I could come the day after,' he said.* ADV AFTER N ⇑ following ≠ before

3 When you describe a particular state or condition **after** another state or condition which you have recently experienced, you are emphasizing the con- PREP

trast between them. EG *The interior was dark after the bright sunlight.*

4 If you talk about the reason why someone has behaved in a particular way **after** their previous experience or actions, or about the state of something now **after** a series of events, you are suggesting that their behaviour, or the present state of something, is unexpected or surprising. EG *People will ask why on earth you believe that after your experiences?... It's strange now, after everything that's happened, to recall how the project started.* PREP OR CONJ SUBORD ⇑ considering

5 When you describe your feelings, attitude, behaviour, etc **after** something which has been said or done, you are giving the reason for your feelings, attitude, or behaviour. EG *Well, after what you'd said in your last letter about Mr Smith I didn't particularly want to meet him.* PREP OR CONJ SUBORD = considering

6 If you go **after** someone who is already moving, you follow them. EG *She ran after him into the courtyard... I used to trail around after him like a small child.* PREP : USU V+PREP+PRON

7 If you say **after you** to someone, you are being polite and allowing them to go in front of you or through a doorway before you do. EG *'After you, my dear fellow.'–'No, after you.'* CONVENTION

8 If you call or gaze **after** someone, you call or look towards them when they are moving away from you. EG *'You're welcome, Mr Hunter!' she called after him... The circle of people stare after him.* PREP

9 If you close a door **after** someone, you close it when they have gone through it and left you. EG *I shut the door after her and sat down.* PREP = behind

10 If you are cleaning up, tidying up, etc **after** someone, you are cleaning up the mess which they have made. EG *It must be very depressing to spend your life cleaning up after people you never see.* PREP

11 If you are **after** something, especially something which someone else has, you are trying to get it for yourself. EG *Those youngsters are after my job.* PREP = angling for

12 If someone is **after** someone else, they are attracted by them and want to start a relationship with them. EG *I'm sure he's after her.* PREP

13 If you are, or go, **after** someone, you are chasing them or searching for them, especially in order to catch and punish them. EG *The Germans were after him... They were here after some man about social security.* PREP = looking for

14 If you tell someone that one place is a particular distance **after** another, you mean that it is situated beyond the other place and further away from you. EG *The garage is three hundred yards after the post office.* PREP = past ≠ before

15 If something is written **after** something else on a page, it is written next to it and following or underneath it. EG *I wrote my signature after Penny's at the bottom of the page... He's got lots of letters after his name.* PREP ⇑ beside

16 If someone or something is named **after** a person, they are given the same name as that person, usually as a sign of respect for them. EG *...a street named after my grandfather... I was named after my aunt Mary.* PREP

17 If a work of art is **after** a particular artist, writer, musician, etc, it is painted or written in a style which is similar to, or which imitates, theirs; a rather formal use. EG *...a painting after Leonardo da Vinci.* PREP

18 If you have a particular rank or position **after** someone else, you have a lower rank or position than they have. EG *I was appointed assistant editor, third in command after George Farr.* PREP ⇑ under

19 If you say that the time is a particular number of minutes **after** an hour, you mean that it is that number of minutes past the hour; used mainly in American English. EG *It was twenty after eight on July 12, 1974.* PREP

20 **After** is used in phrasal verbs such as 'take after' and 'look after'. For information about these, see the individual verb entries. ADV/PREP

21 Some British people refer to the pudding course of a meal as **afters**; an informal use. EG *What's for afters?* N UNCOUNT ⇑ dessert = pud

22 **After** is also used in the following expressions.

22.1 If you do several things, or if they happen, **one after the other**, you do them, or they happen, immediately following each other in time. EG *I went to Stratford to see the three historical plays one after the other.* PHR : USED AS AN A ⇑ consecutively

22.2 If you produce excuses, ideas, etc **one after another**, or you produce **one** excuse **after another**, or excuse **after** excuse, you produce many excuses, ideas, etc, following each other very quickly in time. EG *She found one excuse after another to postpone going to the doctor... He begins expertly opening bottles, one after another... Date after date for the maiden voyage was chosen and abandoned.* PHR : USED AS AN A/O, OR PREP

22.3 If something happens generation **after** generation, day **after** day, etc, it regularly happens in each generation or the period of time mentioned. EG *Some jokes go round school year after year after year... The pattern of child care tends to be repeated generation after generation.* PREP

23 • **after all**: see **all**. • **after** someone's **own heart**: see **heart**. • **after a fashion**: see **fashion**.

after- is added to the beginning of a noun to form an adjective which describes something taking place after the event or process referred to by the noun. EG *...after-lunch conversation... ...after-sales service.* PREFIX

afterbirth /ɑ:ftəbɜ:θ/. The **afterbirth** is the material that comes out of the womb of a woman or female animal soon after they have given birth. It consists of substances that protected or helped to feed the young baby or animal while it was in the womb. N SING : *the*+N

after-care; also spelled without a hyphen. **After-care** is the nursing and care of people who have been ill and treated in hospital, and who are now recovering. N UNCOUNT

after-effect, after-effects; also spelled without a hyphen. The **after-effects** of an activity or event are the feelings, illnesses, conditions, etc which are the result of it. EG *...the after-effects of radiation.* N COUNT : USU PL ⇑ consequence

afterlife /ɑ:ftəlaɪf/; also spelled with a hyphen. The **afterlife** is a life that some people believe begins when you die, for example a life in heaven or as another person or animal. EG *Do you think belief in an afterlife comes with old age?* N SING WITH DET = hereafter

aftermath /ɑ:ftəmɑ:θ, -mæθ/. The **aftermath** of an important event is the period of time that follows it and the situation that results from it. EG *In the immediate aftermath of the accident, no one was even sure how many people had been hurt.... ...the aftermath of war.* N SING : USU *the*+N+*of*

afternoon /ɑ:ftənu:n/, **afternoons**. 1 The **afternoon** is the part of each day which begins either at noon or at lunchtime, and which ends at about six o'clock, or, in winter, when it gets dark. EG *I'll do it this afternoon... They said you were out all afternoon... It's Saturday afternoon... ...the afternoon of 12 August.* ▸ used as an adjective. EG *...my afternoon walk.* N COUNT/UNCOUNT ▸ N BEFORE N

2 If it is a particular time **in the afternoon**, it is between noon and the start of the evening. EG *It was four in the afternoon when she arrived.* PHR : USED AS AN A = p.m.

afternoon tea, afternoon teas. Afternoon tea is a small meal in the afternoon that includes a drink of tea and, for example, bread and cakes; a fairly formal expression. EG *She was always inviting friends home for afternoon tea.* N UNCOUNT/COUNT

aftershave /ɑ:ftəʃeɪv/ is a liquid with a pleasant smell that men sometimes put on their faces after shaving. EG *He smelled of aftershave.* N UNCOUNT

aftertaste /ɑ:ftəteɪst/, **aftertastes**. An **aftertaste** is a taste that remains in your mouth after you have finished eating a piece of food. EG *It has a metallic or bitter aftertaste.* N COUNT : USU SING, ADJ+N ⇑ taste

afterthought /ɑ:ftəθɔ:t/, **afterthoughts**. An **afterthought** is something that you say, think, or do after something else and as an addition to it, but without careful thought or planning. EG *The pram was pushed into a corner of the yard almost as an afterthought.* N COUNT : USU SING, *an*+N

afterwards /ɑ:ftəwədz/. The form **afterward** is also used, mainly in American English. If you do something, or if something happens, **afterwards**, you do it, or it happens, after a particular event, date, time, etc. EG *Afterwards we all helped with the washing up... She died soon afterwards.* ADV SEN ⇑ after

again /əgen, əgeɪn/. 1 If you do something **again** or if something happens **again**, you do it or it happens one more time or on another occasion. EG *Try again in half an hour... Let's do it, I may never have the chance again.* • If you do something, or if something happens, **again and again** or **time and again**, you do it or it happens many times or on many occasions. EG ADV AFTER VB • PHR : USED AS AN A ⇑ often = repeatedly

He had asked her to marry him again and again... They said it time and again.

2 When something is in a particular state, condition, or place **again**, it has returned to the state, condition, or place that it used to be in. EG *At last the assembly was silent again... It was like being a child again... The head turns sharply to one side and back again.*
ADV = once more

3 You add **again** to the end of a question when you are asking someone to repeat something that they have already told you and which you have forgotten. EG *What's his name again?.. Where are we going again?*
ADV SEN

4 You can use **again** to indicate and emphasize a similarity between the situation, action, or subject that is happening or being discussed now and a previous one. EG *My last question is again a somewhat personal one... Again, that's very controversial... Once again there are striking parallels.*
ADV SEN = once more

5 If something is a particular amount **again**, it is that much more than the amount you have already referred to or which is known about. EG *This earthquake had a force one-third as great again as the 1906 San Francisco earthquake... I could eat at least as much again.*
ADV : NG+ADV

6 You can use **again**, especially in the expressions 'then again' and 'there again', to introduce a different point or opinion, often one which contradicts what has just been said. EG *I'm not sure. Again, on second thoughts... I don't think it should be an arts subject, no. But then again it's not really a science subject.*
ADV SEN ⇑ conversely = however, yet

7 now and again: see **now**.

against /əgenst, əgeɪnst/. **1** If someone leans **against** an object or surface, or something is placed **against** it, they are next to it and touching it. EG *Ralph leaned against a tree... She was pressing her nose against the window.*
PREP

2 If something moves or rubs **against** a surface or object, it moves on and across it, often making a harsh noise. EG *The train started, its wheels squealing against the metal tracks... She cleaned the edge of her knife against the plate.*
PREP

3 If something seems to have a particular colour or quality **against** something else, it seems to have that colour or quality because it contrasts with the thing it is next to or in front of. EG *The cat's grey coat was beautiful against the purple of the cushion.*
PREP

4 If something happens or is considered **against** a particular background of events, it happens or is considered in relation to those events. EG *The events stood out against a backcloth of industrial unrest.*
PREP

5 If you do something **against** someone or something, you do something that is intended to hurt, damage, or defeat them in some way. EG *They were not allowed to use arms against their enemies... They discriminated against women... ...the battle against inflation.*
PREP ≠ for

6 Evidence **against** a theory or person is evidence that suggests or proves that the theory is wrong or that the person is guilty of a mistake or crime. EG *There was no real evidence against Davis.*
PREP ≠ for

7 The person or team which is **against** you in a competition or sports match is the other person or team involved in the competition or match. EG *He played in the first Test against Australia... All western economies are competing against each other.*
PREP

8 If you are **against** or decide **against** an idea, policy, system, etc, you disagree with it or are opposed to it. EG *He was fanatically against American intervention in the war... Are you voting for or against?*
PREP, OR ADV AFTER VB = anti- ≠ for

9 If you are **against** someone, you dislike them or show hostility towards them. EG *People were prejudiced against her... My mother tried to put me against Celia.*
PREP
● If you **have** something **against** someone, you dislike them, often because you know something unpleasant about them or because they have done something unpleasant to you. EG *As far as I know she hadn't got anything against you.*
● PHR : VB INFLECTS

10 If an action is **against** your beliefs, principles, or wishes, you do not agree with it or are not willing to do it because of them. EG *People are being encouraged to join the services against their will... It's against my principles.*
PREP ⇑ contrary to = at odds with

11 If something is **against** the law, there is a law which says that you must not do it.
PREP ≠ within

12 If you advise **against** something or take action **against** something, you give advice or take action in order to try to prevent something from happening, or to protest about something that has happened. EG *...a mass demonstration against unemployment... We did warn them against buying that house... There was a majority of 294 for war, with only six voting against.*
ADV AFTER VB, OR PREP

13 If you rebel or react **against** something, you do not like or approve of it and try to avoid it or do the opposite. EG *My work had never been a reaction against Abstract Expressionism... ...a man who rebels suddenly against twenty-five years of routine.*
PREP ≠ towards

14 If you do something in order to protect yourself **against** something unpleasant or harmful, you do something which will make its effects on you less serious if it happens. EG *They had no insurance against an earthquake.*
PREP

15 If you take action **against** something happening, you try to prevent it from happening. EG *He has taken certain precautions against being killed by one of his customers.*
PREP

16 If something is measured or valued **against** something else, it is measured or valued by comparing it with the other thing. EG *The franc plunged to its lowest rate against the dollar in nearly ten years... Their crimes seemed trivial when you measured them against the crimes of the people in power.*
PREP
● If you discuss a particular set of facts or figures **as against** another set, you are comparing or contrasting the two sets of facts or figures. EG *The party emerged with 57 seats, as against 42 for the opposition... This is the distinguishing quality of the human as against the animal creature.*
● PREP ⇑ compared to = as opposed to

17 If one set of figures or data is plotted **against** another set on a graph, you are using the two sets of figures or data in order to calculate the relationship between them. EG *...if you plot response against distance.*
PREP ⇑ in relation to

18 If you are moving **against** the current, tide, flow, etc, you are moving in the opposite direction to it. EG *We had to row against the pull of the stream... I turned against the wind.*
PREP ≠ with

19 If you go **against** a fashion, trend, etc, you think or behave in a way which is different from the way most people are thinking or behaving at a particular time. EG *I suppose it is a bit against the current trend.*
PREP ≠ with

20 The chances or odds **against** something happening, or **against** a particular person or animal winning a race or competition, are the chances or odds that it will not happen or that they will not win. EG *The odds against another attack were astronomical... The more handicaps the gambler accepts, the higher the odds against.*
PREP, OR ADV AFTER N

21 up against: see **up**.

agape /əgeɪp/. If you are **agape** or if your mouth is **agape**, your mouth is open very wide, often because you are very surprised by something. EG *...people standing agape in the light of the flames... The shark swam up under the woman, jaws agape.*
ADJ AFTER N = gaping ≠ shut

agate /ægɪt/, **agates**. An **agate** is a very hard stone which is used for making jewellery.
N COUNT/ UNCOUNT

age /eɪdʒ/, **ages, ageing, aged**. The form **aging** is also used. **1** Someone's **age** is the number of years that they have lived. The **age** of a thing is the number of years since it was made. EG *Cathy would never let her age be known... He is eighty-two years of age... He committed suicide at the age of forty.*
N UNCOUNT/ COUNT

2 If you are at or are going through a particular **age**, you are at a particular period or stage in your life. EG *When I was your age I could only look forward... I reached undergraduate age... They go through a very vulnerable age.*
N SING : POSS+N OR N+SUPP

3 The word **age** is used in the following expressions:
3.1 If two people or things are **of an age**, they were born or made at approximately the same time; an old-fashioned expression. EG *We were of an age.*
PHR : USED AS AN A

3.2 If someone tells you to **be** your **age** or **act** your **age**, they are telling you to behave in a way that is suitable for someone as old or mature as you, rather than like a younger person or a child. EG *Be your age, Andrew, for goodness sake!... Why don't you act your age?*
PHR : VB INFLECTS = grow up ≠ be childish

3.3 If you **feel** your **age**, you are aware that you are getting older, because, for example, you feel tired more quickly than you used to. EG *I really feel my age this morning.*
PHR : VB INFLECTS

3.4 Someone who is **under age** is not legally old enough to do something, for example to buy an alcoholic drink or to become a soldier. EG *Boys are getting drinks under age... He had been*
PHR : USED AS AN A ≠ of age

under age when he joined the army. **3.5** Someone who is **over age** has become too old, according to law or to particular regulations, to do something. EG *His application was rejected because they said he was over age.* **3.6** Someone who is **of age** is legally an adult. In Britain this is when you are over 18 years old. EG *...the absence of identification proving him to be of age.* **3.7** When someone **comes of age**, they become legally an adult. EG *When he came of age he made a will.* **3.8** When something, such as a company, style of painting, etc **comes of age**, it reaches an important stage of maturity or development and is accepted and respected by a large number of people. • See also **coming-of-age**.
PHR : USED AS AN A ≠ under age; PHR : USED AS AN A ≠ under age; PHR : VB INFLECTS; PHR : VB INFLECTS ⇑ mature

4 Age is **4.1** the state of being old and no longer strong, healthy, or in good condition. EG *Your age and frailty are giving him cause for concern... ...an impression of age and decrepitude.* **4.2** the process of becoming physically or mentally older. EG *Age should have mellowed me... ...a shop full of medals, mostly stained with age.*
N UNCOUNT = old age ≠ youth; N UNCOUNT = time

5 When something **ages**, it becomes old or mature. EG *All university buildings are ageing.*
V = grow old

6 When someone **ages**, or when something **ages** them, they change in appearance or behaviour and seem much older, because, for example, they have suffered a lot. EG *She was dismayed to see how much he had aged... The strain of looking after her had considerably aged him.*
V-ERG

7 An **age** is a period in history. EG *We live in a permissive age... The great age of Greek sport... Woman's role has remained static throughout the ages.*
N COUNT : IF SING USU+SUPP = era

8 Ages or **an age** means a very long time; an informal use. EG *I've known him for ages... She took an age to dress... It's ages since we last wrote to each other.*
N COUNT : IF SING an+N, PL=SING = forever, years

9 • See also **dark age, golden age, ice age, Iron Age, middle age, Stone Age, aged, ageing**.

> **AGE** □ This entry shows some ways of referring to age. The following examples show ways of saying how old someone is. EG *She is twenty-five years old... ...if the child is over sixteen years of age... 'How old is she?'-'She must be nearly eighty.'... He was a man between fifty and sixty... ...a young woman of sixteen... She died in 1816 at the age of 83... ...their three children, Andrea, aged 17, Julie, aged 16, and Paul, aged 13.* If you say that someone is in their twenties, you mean that they are between twenty and thirty years old. If you say that someone is in their early fifties, you mean that they are over fifty, but less than fifty-five; if you say that someone is in their late fifties, you mean that they are over fifty-five, but less than sixty. The following examples show ways of referring to people who are a particular age. EG *...a forty-year-old female... ...a class of 4-year-olds... ...nursery schools for the fives and under.* The following examples show ways of referring to people and their birthdays. EG *My mother died just before my fourth birthday... She's eighteen... I was thirty-four last week.*

-age is **1** added to some verbs in order to form uncount nouns which refer to processes or to count nouns which refer to events. EG *...block→blockage... ...break→breakage.* **2** added to some nouns that refer to people or their occupations in order to form nouns referring to the building that they live in. EG *...vicar→vicarage.* **3** added to some nouns in order to form nouns that refer to the charges made for a particular service. EG *...post→postage.*
SUFFIX : FORMS NOUNS; SUFFIX : FORMS NOUNS; SUFFIX : FORMS NOUNS

aged. **Aged** is pronounced /eɪdʒd/ for paragraph 1 and /eɪdʒɪ²d/ for paragraph 2. **1** Someone who is **aged** 20, 42, 73, etc was born that number of years ago. EG *The typical migrant is aged between twenty-five and forty... ...Bill Ash, aged 62... ...women aged 60 and over.* • See also **middle aged**.
ADJ CLASSIF : PRED+NUM

2 Someone or something that is **aged** is very old. EG *...his aged aunt... He looked as aged as a turtle.* ▸ **The aged** is used to refer to people who are very old. EG *...the care of the aged.*
ADJ QUALIT; ▸ N PLURAL : the+N = the elderly

age group, age groups; also spelled with a hyphen. An **age group** is all the people in a place or organization who were born during a particular period of time, for example all the people aged between 18 and 25. EG *There is now more competition for jobs in this age group... Children spend more time with their own age group.*
N COUNT

ageing /eɪdʒɪŋ/; also spelled **aging**. **1** An **ageing** person, thing, system, etc is one that is becoming old, and usually less attractive or efficient than before. EG *...an ageing film star... They were committed to ageing and relatively inefficient technologies.*
ADJ CLASSIF

2 Ageing is the process of becoming old. EG *...the ageing and decay of things.*
N UNCOUNT

ageless /eɪdʒlɪ²s/. Someone or something that is **ageless 1** never seems to look any older. EG *You're looking absolutely marvellous, darling. Ageless.* **2** seems to be of no particular age or to have existed for ever. EG *His wealth of knowledge made him seem ageless... ...an ageless parish church.*
ADJ CLASSIF; ADJ CLASSIF ⇑ timeless

age limit, age limits; also spelled with a hyphen. An **age limit** is the oldest or youngest age at which you are allowed under particular regulations to do something. EG *They introduced an age limit... The age limit was 21.*
N COUNT

agency /eɪdʒənsi¹/, **agencies**. **1** An **agency** is **1.1** a business which provides particular services on behalf of another business. EG *We got him through an agency... I nearly joined an advertising agency.* **1.2** an administrative organization usually run by a government. EG *The agency initially approved the cuts in 1974... ...the Central Intelligence Agency.*
N COUNT; N COUNT

2 When something happens through or by the **agency** of someone or something, it happens with their help or influence. EG *He had found the job through the agency of another member of the firm.*
N SING : WITH POSS

agenda /ədʒɛndə/, **agendas**. An **agenda** is a list of items to be discussed at a meeting. EG *The main point on the agenda was the election of a new chairman.*
N COUNT

agent /eɪdʒə²nt/, **agents**. **1** An **agent** is **1.1** someone who you pay to do business or look after your affairs on your behalf. EG *I know you'll act as my agent... ...an election agent.* **1.2** someone who arranges work for actors, musicians, etc, in return for a fee. EG *'It's a good script,' said the agent.* **1.3** a person or company who represents a government, organization, or another company in a particular place. EG *He had been the company's agent at a Mogul trading centre upstream.* **1.4** someone who works for a country's secret service. EG *...a enemy agent who had been assassinated.* **1.5** a person, power, or force which has a particular effect or influence, or which is the means or cause of something happening. EG *...the agent of change... Censorship is a completely outside agent.* **1.6** a chemical or substance which causes a change in other chemicals or substances which it is in contact with. EG *Chemical agents were used in the attack... ...a drying agent.*
N COUNT : WITH POSS ⇑ representative; N COUNT; N COUNT : WITH POSS ⇑ representative; N COUNT = spy; N COUNT+SUPP ⇑ instrument; N COUNT+SUPP

2 See also **estate agent, travel agent**.

agent provocateur /æʒɑː prɒvɒkətɜː/, **agents provocateurs**. An **agent provocateur** is someone who is employed by the government or the police to encourage people who are causing trouble to break the law so that they can be arrested. EG *They were perhaps aided by agents provocateurs sent into our midst to disrupt the protest.*
N COUNT ⇑ instigator = trouble-maker

age of consent. The **age of consent** is the age at which a person can legally marry or have a sexual relationship with someone.
N SING : the+N

age-old. An **age-old** story, tradition, bond, etc has existed for longer than people can remember. EG *...the age-old ties between man and place.*
ADJ CLASSIF : USU ATTRIB = ancient, time-honoured

agglomeration /ə³glɒməreɪʃə⁰n/, **agglomerations**. An **agglomeration** is a lot of different things gathered together, often in no particular order or arrangement. EG *...an economic agglomeration created for the pursuit of profit... ...large agglomerations of capital.*
N COUNT+SUPP ⇑ collection = accumulation

aggrandizement /ə³grændɪzmə²nt/; also spelled **aggrandisement**. If you do something for **aggrandizement**, you do it in order to get power, wealth, and importance for yourself. EG *He may have sided with the masses for personal gain and aggrandizement.*
N UNCOUNT ⇑ growth

aggravate /ægrəveɪt/, **aggravates, aggravating, aggravated**. **1** If someone or something **aggravates** a situation, they make it worse. EG *America is aggravating Indian-Pakistani tensions... She aggravated an already difficult situation by her refusal to apologize.*
V+O ⇑ worsen = exacerbate ≠ improve

2 If someone or something **aggravates** you, they make you angry or annoyed. EG *It's the little things that aggravate you.* ◊ **aggravating**. EG *She knew exactly where I'd be when she wanted me, which was very aggravating.* ◊ **aggravation** /ægrəveɪʃə⁰n/. EG *I'm just trying to save you aggravation.*
V+O = irritate; ◊ ADJ QUALIT = irritating; ◊ N UNCOUNT/COUNT

aggregate /ægrɪ²geɪt/, **aggregates, aggregating, aggregated. 1** An **aggregate** is an amount that is made up of several smaller amounts. EG *He had spent an aggregate of fifteen years in various jails.* ▸ used as an adjective. EG *...newspapers with an aggregate circulation of over 6 million.*
N COUNT : IF + PREP THEN *of*
▸ ADJ CLASSIF : ATTRIB

2 An **aggregate** is also a number of people or things that are being considered as a group. EG *They're concerned with analysing the behaviour of aggregates of individuals.*
N COUNT : IF + PREP THEN *of*

3 In the aggregate or **in aggregate** means considered together as a group or total. EG *...reports that in aggregate might give the impression of a country in decline... ...a miscellany of objects as bizarre, in the aggregate, as anything I had ever seen.*
PHR : USED AS AN A
⇑ in total
= all told

4 If amounts or numbers **are aggregated**, they are added together to form a total. EG *The teams' points are aggregated over the five fixtures for final positions.*
V + O : USU PASS
⇑ be totalled

5 If things or people **are aggregated**, they are put into groups or are considered as a group. EG *Both sets of individuals can be aggregated into social categories.*
V + O : USU PASS, IF + PREP THEN *into*
⇑ grouped
= lumped

aggression /ə³grɛʃə⁰n/. **1** If someone has **aggression** in their character, they have a quality of anger and determination that makes them ready to attack people. EG *Every child has to have some aggression in order to force its way through life... Freud believed that aggression could not be eliminated.*
N UNCOUNT
≠ gentleness, passivity

2 If someone shows **aggression**, they deliberately make you feel frightened or threatened. EG *It was not an act of self-defence, but an act of aggression... Have you ever been frightened by sudden aggression from a stranger?*
N UNCOUNT
⇑ attack
= hostility

3 If a country or group shows **aggression** in its political or military activities, it constantly makes attacks on other people, especially people who seem innocent or peaceful. EG *The rallies and demonstrations were directed against police aggression in the capital.*
N UNCOUNT
⇑ attack
= hostility

aggressive /ə³grɛsɪv/. **1** A person or animal that is **aggressive** has a quality of anger and determination in their character that makes them ready to attack people. EG *Women are not supposed to be as aggressive as men... Domestic animals can become unusually aggressive because they are upset by a change... Mrs Zapp was in a highly aggressive mood.* ◊ **aggressively**. EG *I was aggressively ready to pounce on anyone who looked as if they were criticizing me.* ◊ **aggressiveness**. EG *Their aggressiveness stemmed from fear.*
ADJ QUALIT
⇑ hostile
= belligerent
≠ meek
◊ ADV
◊ N UNCOUNT
= belligerence

2 Someone who is **aggressive** in their work or other activities is eager to succeed and behaves in an insistent and forceful way without really caring about other people. EG *...aggressive salesmen and business men... U.S. business today finds itself challenged by aggressive overseas competitors.*
ADJ QUALIT
⇑ assertive
= ruthless
≠ timid

3 If a country or group is **aggressive** or if it acts in an **aggressive** way, it is likely to attack other people. EG *We will not allow a reunited Germany to become an aggressive force again.* ◊ **aggressively**. EG *The Red Army can still move quickly and aggressively when it has to.*
ADJ QUALIT
= offensive
≠ defensive
◊ ADV WITH VB

aggressor /ə³grɛsə/, **aggressors**. An **aggressor** is a person, group, or country that attacks other people, especially people who seem innocent or peaceful. EG *The guns were intended solely for use against aggressors.*
N COUNT
⇑ attacker

aggrieved /ə³griːvd/. Someone who is **aggrieved** is upset and angry because of the way they have been treated. EG *Many people have felt aggrieved, rightly or wrongly, at being refused permission.*
ADJ QUALIT
= resentful

aggro /ægrəʊ/ is used in informal spoken English to mean **1** aggressive or violent behaviour. EG *There wasn't a hint of aggro.* **2** the difficulties and problems that are involved in something. EG *I can't be bothered–it's too much aggro.*
N UNCOUNT
N UNCOUNT
⇑ difficulty
= hassle

aghast /əgɑːst/. Someone who is **aghast** is filled with horror and surprise. EG *What she had learned had left her aghast... She had been aghast at the idea.*
ADJ CLASSIF : IF + PREP THEN *at*
⇑ shocked

agile /ædʒaɪl/. **1** If a person or animal is **agile** or moves in an **agile** way, they can move and bend their body, arms, and legs quickly and easily. EG *He was quick and agile.* ◊ **agility** /ədʒɪlɪti¹/. EG *He leaped out of the car with surprising agility.*
ADJ QUALIT
⇑ mobile
= nimble
≠ clumsy
◊ N UNCOUNT

2 If someone has an **agile** mind, they think quickly and intelligently. EG *The middle-aged may have minds too agile for you.* ◊ **agility**. EG *...tests of mental agility.*
ADJ QUALIT
= alert
◊ N UNCOUNT
= liveliness

agin /əgɪn/. If you are **agin** something or take **agin** it, you disapprove of it; used especially in Scottish English. EG *She's agin comprehensive education.*
PREP
= against

aging /eɪdʒɪŋ/. See **ageing**.

agitate /ædʒɪteɪt/, **agitates, agitating, agitated. 1** If someone **agitates** for or against something, they talk and campaign energetically in public in an attempt to get it or to get rid of it. EG *...to agitate for better conditions for pensioners... ...a vigorous body of opinion agitating against the use of chemical fertilizers.* ◊ **agitation** /ædʒɪteɪʃə⁰n/. EG *...anti-imperialist agitation.*
V : IF + PREP THEN *for/against*
⇑ fight
= campaign
◊ N UNCOUNT

2 If someone or something **agitates** you, they worry you so much that you are unable to think clearly or calmly. EG *...difficulties which agitated her sisters... I don't want to agitate him unduly.* ◊ **agitation**. EG *I saw Peters glancing at his watch in some agitation.*
V + O
= trouble, upset
◊ N UNCOUNT
= anxiety

3 If you **agitate** something, you stir or shake it vigorously. EG *Ella pours in the chemicals and begins agitating the tank.*
V + O

agitated /ædʒɪteɪtɪ²d/. Someone who is **agitated** is so worried about something that they are unable to think clearly or act calmly. EG *He looked dishevelled and agitated... She heard his agitated voice calling after them... I sent agitated messages to Miss Gray.* ◊ **agitatedly**. EG *Alexander wondered agitatedly what he should do.*
ADJ QUALIT
= disturbed, nervous
◊ ADV WITH VB

agitator /ædʒɪteɪtə/, **agitators**. An **agitator** is someone who tries to bring about political or social change by talking and campaigning in public, often in a way that causes trouble. EG *...political agitators.*
N COUNT
⇑ activist

aglow /əgləʊ/. **1** If something is **aglow**, it is shining and bright with a soft, warm light; a literary word. EG *...long green grass, all aglow in the evening sunlight.*
ADJ CLASSIF : PRED, IF + PREP THEN *with*
= glowing

2 If someone is **aglow** or if their face or expression is **aglow**, they look excited. EG *...Daniel, still aglow with a sense of his victory.*
ADJ QUALIT : PRED, IF + PREP THEN *with*
= glowing

AGM /eɪ dʒiː ɛm/, **AGMs**. **AGM** is an abbreviation for 'Annual General Meeting': a meeting that a company or organization holds once a year in order to discuss the previous year's activities and accounts. EG *...elected at an AGM attended by no more than 500 members... ...AGM resolutions.*
N COUNT

agnostic /ægnɒstɪk/, **agnostics**. **1** An **agnostic** believes that it is not possible to say definitely whether or not there is a God: compare **atheist**.
N COUNT
⇑ unbeliever

2 Agnostic describes people who are agnostics or the beliefs of agnostics. EG *The agnostic attitude derives from a refusal to admit that anyone could be superior to man.*
ADJ CLASSIF
⇑ unbelieving

3 Someone who is **agnostic** about something has no definite opinion about it; a formal use. EG *He tends to be rather agnostic on this question.*
ADJ QUALIT
= sceptical

agnosticism /ægnɒstɪsɪzə⁰m/ is the belief that it is not possible to say definitely whether or not there is a God: compare **atheism**.
N UNCOUNT
⇑ doubt

ago /əgəʊ/. If something happened one year **ago**, it is one year since it happened. EG *Twenty-five years ago, I went to the tropics for the first time... I should have been there ten minutes ago... 'What time did you see them?'–'An hour ago.'... It was a very long time ago... How long ago was that?*
ADV : NG + ADV
⇑ back

agog /əgɒg/. If someone is **agog**, they are excited by an event, story, or piece of news, and are eager to see what happens next or to be told more. EG *Bill was all agog... She arrived, agog to discover what had prevented him being there.*
ADJ CLASSIF : PRED, IF + PREP THEN *with*
≠ indifferent

agonize /ægə⁷naɪz/, **agonizes, agonizing, agonized**; also spelled **agonise**. If you **agonize** over something, you feel very anxious about it, and spend a long time thinking about it or deciding whether or not to do it. EG *Patrick was known to agonize over questions of policy... Lucas prayed or agonised silently.*
V : IF + PREP THEN *over/about*
⇑ worry

agonized /ægə⁷naɪzd/; also spelled **agonised. Agonized** means showing by what you say or do that you are in great pain, either physically or mentally. EG *He could hear the prisoner's agonised moans... She spoke with agonized emphasis.*
ADJ CLASSIF
⇑ suffering
= tortured, anguished

agonizing /ægə⁷naɪzɪŋ/; also spelled **agonising. 1** Something that is **agonizing** causes you to feel great pain, either physically or mentally. EG *...a slow, agonizing death... I had agonizing feelings of shame and guilt.* ◊ **agonizingly**. EG *The sound was agonisingly painful.*
ADJ QUALIT
⇑ painful
= excruciating
◊ ADV

2 Agonizing decisions and choices are very difficult to make, so that you feel extremely worried or anxious. EG *The workers now face an agonising choice... The final decision to sell was an agonizing one.* ◊ **agonizingly**. EG *The choices are agonisingly difficult.*
ADJ QUALIT = painful; ◊ ADV = painfully

agony /ægəni/, **agonies**. If you are in **agony** or in **agonies**, you are suffering great physical or mental pain. EG *The blow made him scream in agony... In an agony of suspense and fear, I waited for the verdict... ...the agonies of losing children.* ● If someone **is piling on the agony**, they are exaggerating their sufferings and problems in order to get sympathy from other people; a very informal British expression.
N UNCOUNT/COUNT = anguish, torment; ● PHR : VB INFLECTS

agony aunt, agony aunts. An **agony aunt** is a person who writes in a newspaper and gives advice to readers about their personal problems; used in informal British English.
N COUNT ⇑ journalist

agony column, agony columns. An **agony column** in a newspaper or magazine is the part where letters from readers about their personal problems are printed and where advice about these problems is given.
N COUNT = problem page

agoraphobia /ægərəfəubɪə/ is the fear of open spaces or of going outside your home; a technical term.
N UNCOUNT

agoraphobic /ægərəfəubɪk/, **agoraphobics**. An **agoraphobic** is someone who suffers from agoraphobia.
N COUNT

agrarian /əgreərɪən/ means relating to the ownership and use of land, especially farmland, or relating to the part of a society or economy that is concerned with agriculture. EG *They established themselves as the party of radical agrarian reform... The system is rather well designed for an agrarian society.*
ADJ CLASSIF : USU ATTRIB = agricultural ≠ urban

agree /əgriː/, **agrees, agreeing, agreed**. **1** If one person **agrees** with another or if two or more people **agree**, they have the same opinion as each other. EG *Do you agree with him about this?... You agreed with me that we could rule out Watson... They may find it hard to agree... Few doctors agree on how you treat schizophrenia.*
V : IF + PREP THEN *with/on* = concur ≠ differ, disagree

2 If you **agree** that something is the case, you say or believe that it is so. EG *I agree that's what killed her... People agree that the law is behind the times... 'Oh, it will,' agreed Jenny.*
V + REPORT-CL/QUOTE : NO IMPER = allow, grant

3 If you **agree** to do something or **agree** to something, you say that you will do it or you allow someone else to do it. EG *She had agreed to let us use her flat while she was away... He had agreed to the use of force.*
V : IF + PREP THEN *to*, OR IF + VB THEN *to*-INF = consent ≠ refuse

4 If people **agree** on something or **agree** something, they reach a joint decision on it. EG *The government had still to agree on the provisions of the Bill... ...a 20% pay rise agreed with the coal board... 'Then all five of us sign it. Captain Imrie?'–'Agreed'.*
V : IF + PREP THEN *on/upon/with*, OR V + O ⇑ decide = settle

5 If people are **agreed** on something or if they are **agreed** that something is the case, they have reached a joint decision or a particular conclusion on it. EG *Are we agreed, gentlemen?... All the pro-Chinese groups are agreed on this point... We were agreed that business morals nowadays were very low.*
ADJ CLASSIF : PRED, IF + PREP THEN *on/upon* OR + REPORT-CL = agree ≠ disagree

6 If you **agree** with something such as an action or a proposal, you approve of it. EG *I agree with what they are doing.*
V + A *(with)* = hold with

7 If something **agrees** with you, it makes you feel healthy or contented. EG *The sea air really agrees with her.*
V + A *(with)* ⇑ benefit

8 If a particular food or drink does not **agree** with you, it gives you indigestion; an informal expression. EG *My milk doesn't seem to agree with the baby.*
V + BROAD NEG + A *(with)*

9 If two stories, accounts, totals, or other things **agree**, they are the same as each other or are so similar that both can be considered as being true or correct. EG *This bill doesn't agree with my calculations... My theories and his do not always agree.*
V : IF + PREP THEN *with/on* = correspond, match

agreeable /əgriːəbəl/. **1** If something is **agreeable**, it is pleasant and you enjoy it. EG *He had enjoyed the agreeable sensation... How agreeable it was to have her in the office.* ◊ **agreeably**. EG *As the evening drew on, Andrew and I got agreeably drunk.*
ADJ QUALIT ⇑ nice ≠ unpleasant; ◊ ADV = pleasantly

2 If someone is **agreeable**, they try to please other people in their behaviour towards them. EG *They were trying to be amiable and agreeable... She always made a particular point of being agreeable to them.*
ADJ QUALIT : IF + PREP THEN *to* ⇑ likeable = pleasant

3 If a person is **agreeable** to something or if it is **agreeable** to them, they are willing to do it or to allow it to be done. EG *Get your secretary to do it if she is agreeable... He was perfectly agreeable to being asked... Is that agreeable to you?*
ADJ QUALIT : PRED, IF + PREP THEN *to*

agreement /əgriːmənt/, **agreements**. **1** An **agreement** is a formal document which is signed by two or more people and which states in detail something that they have decided on. EG *Half of the land was given away under the same agreement... Agreements on nuclear weapons have not always worked.*
N COUNT ⇑ statement = contract

2 Agreement means **2.1** reaching a decision or conclusion about something that everyone involved finds acceptable. EG *We reached unanimous agreement... Agreement about these decisions is extremely difficult... There was no general agreement on the timing.* **2.2** saying or showing that you will accept something that has been proposed. EG *They nodded agreement... They kept on fighting, despite their agreement to a cease-fire.* **2.3** saying or showing that you believe that something is true. EG *There was general agreement that the fire was all important.*
N UNCOUNT : IF + PREP THEN *on/about* = concurrence ≠ disagreement; N UNCOUNT ⇑ acceptance = consent; N UNCOUNT + REPORT-CL ⇑ acceptance

3 If you are **in agreement** with someone, you have the same opinion as they have. EG *They were in complete agreement... I find myself in agreement with John.*
PHR : USED AS AN A = agree, be agreed ≠ disagree

agricultural /ægrɪkʌltʃərəl/. **1 Agricultural** means involving or relating to agriculture. EG *...the agricultural problems of Third World countries... ...modern agricultural methods.*
ADJ CLASSIF = farming, agrarian

2 An **agricultural** place or society is one in which agriculture is important or highly developed. EG *...a villager in an agricultural society.*
ADJ CLASSIF = agrarian, farming

agriculturalist /ægrɪkʌltʃərəlɪst/, **agriculturalists**. An **agriculturalist** is someone who is an expert on agriculture and who advises farmers.
N COUNT

agriculture /ægrɪkʌltʃə/ is the practice of farming and the methods that are used to raise and look after crops and animals. EG *...areas that are unsuitable for agriculture... The technical solutions exist to make African agriculture more productive.*
N UNCOUNT

aground /əgraund/. If a ship runs or goes **aground**, it touches ground in a shallow part of a river, lake, or the sea, and becomes stuck there. EG *The ship had simply run aground and broken up on the reef.*
ADV AFTER VB

ah /ɑː/. **'Ah'** is used in speech to express the following different responses and reactions: **1** to say that you agree with, accept, or understand what the previous speaker has said; sometimes also used to introduce a comment on or an objection to what has been said. EG *'We got the 12 o'clock train back.'–'Ah, yes.'... Ah well, we didn't come down that way... 'You're supposed to believe in souls.'–'Ah, but have you got a soul?'.* **2** to give emphasis, often as an introduction to a comment or piece of information. EG *There was a riot–and the police, ah there were thousands of police round the place.* **3** when hesitating in a conversation, for example when you are trying to remember something or to decide what to say next. EG *If you read a book or just want to get through it for, ah, entertainment, to pass the time.* **4** when showing sympathy, pleasure, pain, or some other feeling. EG *Ah, you poor fellow... Ah, it's beautiful.* **5** to say that you have just noticed something in the situation around you. EG *It isn't moving, not yet, ah now it's moved.* **6** to say that you have seen someone, before you ask them a question or ask them to do something. EG *Ah, Howard. Come on in.*
1 = yes; 2 = oh; 3 = er; 6 = yes

aha /ɑːhɑː/ is used in speech to express different sorts of responses and reactions, especially: **1** to say that you understand what the previous speaker has said. EG *'You have half board in most of the hotels.'–'Oh, I see, aha.'* **2** to express satisfaction that you have just found something or satisfaction at something that has just happened. EG *I had here somewhere a still more recent report. Aha, here we are.* **3** to express triumph about something that enables you to prove a point or to feel superior. EG *Aha, her nasty friends said, that's because of the money.* **4** as a response to a question when you want to suggest that there are a lot of interesting and relevant things you could say, but you are not willing to reveal them. EG *'How did it happen that you cut*
1 = ah, uh huh; 2 EXCLAM ⇑ ah; 3 EXCLAM = see; 4 EXCLAM = ah, well

yourself like that?'–'Aha,' says Henry, 'now there's a question.'

ahead /əhed/. **1 Ahead** means in front of you. EG *The road ahead is foggy... Up ahead I see the lights of a town... He could see it about half a mile ahead.*
ADV ⇑ before ≠ behind

2 If someone who is moving is **ahead** of you, they are in front of you and moving in the same direction. EG *Two people were ahead of us, and travelling fast.*
ADV : IF + PREP THEN *of* ⇑ before ≠ behind

3 If you look or stare **ahead**, you are looking directly in front of you. EG *A uniformed chauffeur stared straight ahead.*
ADV : IF + PREP THEN *of* ⇑ before

4 If a vehicle or person is moving **ahead**, they are moving forwards. EG *The train was speeding ahead... The boat lurched ahead.*
ADV AFTER VB

5 If someone or something is **ahead** of another person or thing in relation to their work or achievements, they are more advanced or have made more progress. EG *He is a good ten years ahead of the 'field'... We have made rapid strides ahead despite these initial handicaps.*
ADV : IF + PREP THEN *of* ⇑ in advance

6 If someone is **ahead** in a competition, contest, or something similar, they are winning or in a position of advantage over someone else. EG *Another Robson goal put United ahead... The Labour government was 2% ahead in the polls.*
ADJ QUALIT : PRED = in front

7 If someone goes **on ahead** or if something is sent **on ahead**, they leave for a particular place before other people or things and arrive there earlier. EG *Our parents had gone on ahead in our father's big car... I sent an expensive tape recorder on ahead.*
PHR : USED AS AN A = in front

8 If someone arrives **ahead** of someone else, they arrive before them. EG *Davis had for once arrived at the office ahead of him.*
ADV + *of*

9 If someone is **ahead** of someone else in a queue, they are in front of them and so will have less time to wait. EG *There were six other people ahead of him in the waiting-room.*
ADV + *of* ≠ behind

10 Ahead also means in the future, especially the immediate future. EG *...a forecast for a few days ahead... There are troubled times ahead... The Social Democrats are going to have some problems ahead of them.*
ADV : IF + PREP THEN *of* = in front ≠ behind

11 If you are thinking or planning **ahead**, you are thinking or planning about the future or events in the future. EG *I haven't had time to think that far ahead.*
ADV AFTER VB = in advance

12 If something happens **ahead** of a particular point in time, it happens before it. EG *Any further consultation with the guerrillas ahead of Thursday puts the plan into grave jeopardy... Well if you apply about a year ahead, you should get a grant.*
ADV : IF + PREP THEN *of* ⇑ before

13 If a plan or activity is moving or going **ahead**, it is happening or developing successfully in the way people have planned or expect. EG *Plans for the playing field are moving ahead... Our association is currently moving ahead fast and membership is growing.*
ADV AFTER VB

14 If someone goes **ahead** with a plan or activity or if it goes **ahead**, action is taken to start it or make it happen. EG *As I didn't want to worry you, I just went ahead and dealt with it... The ballot will go ahead immediately.*
ADV AFTER VB = on

ahoy /əhɔɪ/ is a shout that people in boats use in order to attract attention. EG *Ahoy there... Land ahoy!*
EXCLAM = hey

AI /eɪ aɪ/ is an abbreviation for **artificial intelligence** and 'artificial insemination'.

aid /eɪd/, **aids, aiding, aided. 1 Aid** is **1.1** money, equipment, or services that are provided for people in need. EG *...major programmes of overseas aid for the less developed countries... ...provision of food, clothing, shelter and medical aid... ...government aid to privately owned firms.*
N UNCOUNT + SUPP ⇑ help

1.2 advice, information, or support that is given to someone with a problem or a question. EG *He had sought the aid of the counter clerks.*
N UNCOUNT : USU WITH *the/POSS* ⇑ help = assistance

1.3 the help that is given to a person, for example when someone does some work for them. EG *The programmes had been prepared with the aid of exiled broadcasters from those countries... Detectives had enlisted the aid of their underworld friends.* • See also **legal aid, first aid.**
N UNCOUNT : WITH *the/POSS* = assistance

2 An **aid** is something that is useful or helpful because it makes things easier to do or understand. EG *For those disabled or using a wheelchair, aids and adaptations within the home make life much easier... Coins are an aid to dating a wreck.* • See also **hearing aid.**
N COUNT ⇑ help

3 To **aid** a country, organization, or person means to provide them with the money, equipment, or services that they need. EG *...the need to aid poorer countries... ...state intervention to aid private industry.*
V + O ⇑ help

4 To **aid** something means to make it easier or more likely to happen. EG *A healthy liver aids digestion and promotes well being... Inflation became an election issue, aiding a Conservative victory.*
V + O ⇑ help = promote, assist

5 If you **aid** someone, you help them with a job or a task by doing part of the work for them. EG *Scotland Yard, aided by the West Berlin police, managed to trace him.*
V + O = assist

6 Aid is also used in the following expressions: **6.1** An activity or event that is **in aid of** a particular cause raises money for that cause. EG *...a concert in aid of cancer relief.*
PREP

6.2 If you ask **what** something **is in aid of**, you are asking what the reason is for it; an informal expression. EG *What's all this noise in aid of?*
CONVENTION

6.3 If you do something with **the aid of** a particular thing, you use that thing in order to do it. EG *Eventually, with the aid of a little subterfuge, he got her to agree... To do this you will need the aid of a spanner or a wrench.*
PHR : USU *with* + PHR = the services of

6.4 If you **go to the aid of** someone or **come to** their **aid**, you try to help them when they are in danger or difficulty. EG *He was drowned when he went to the aid of a swimmer in difficulty... They had rushed to her aid.*
PHR : VB INFLECTS = rescue, assistance

aide /eɪd/, **aides**. An **aide** is a person who works as an assistant to someone with an important job, especially in government or the armed forces. EG *There we found General Washington and his aides.*
N COUNT

aide-de-camp /eɪd də kɒŋ/, **aides-de-camp**. An **aide-de-camp** is an officer in the armed forces who helps an officer of higher rank.
N COUNT

AIDS /eɪdz/ is an illness which completely destroys the natural system of protection that the body has against disease; an abbreviation for 'acquired immune deficiency syndrome'.
N UNCOUNT

ail /eɪl/, **ails, ailing, ailed. 1** If someone **ails**, or if something **ails** them, they are ill; an old-fashioned word. EG *I cannot decide what ails her: it's not a heat rash... He's ailed ever since he went up to the council house.*
V-ERG = sick ≠ recover

2 If something **ails** a group or area of activity, it is a problem or source of trouble for that group or activity. EG *It's all too easy to itemise what ails soccer off the field: hooliganism and violence.*
V + O

aileron /eɪlərɒn/, **ailerons**. An **aileron** is a flap on the back edge of the wing of an aeroplane that can be raised or lowered in order to control the plane's movement.
N COUNT

ailing /eɪlɪŋ/. **1** If someone is **ailing**, they are ill and are not getting any better. EG *...concern for his ailing wife... Peter had been ailing for some time.*
ADJ CLASSIF

2 If a group, organization, or area of activity is **ailing**, it is facing difficulties and is not succeeding or progressing as it should be. EG *...two ailing textile companies... ..an ailing economy... This might rejuvenate the ailing uplands... They would help revive ailing communities.*
ADJ CLASSIF ⇑ failing ≠ thriving

ailment /eɪlmə²nt/, **ailments**. An **ailment** is an illness, especially one that does not seem serious even though it might be unpleasant or painful and last a long time. EG *My uncles and aunts just talked about their ailments.*
N COUNT = affliction

aim /eɪm/, **aims, aiming, aimed. 1** If you **aim** at a person or thing, or if you **aim** a weapon or object at them, you judge the place where you want to hit them and point the weapon or object in their direction. EG *He aimed at the far wall and squeezed the trigger... Roger stopped, picked up a stone, aimed, and threw it at Henry.*
V OR V + O + A *(at)*

2 If you **aim** a kick or a punch at someone, you try to kick or punch them. EG *He aimed a slow punch at my jaw.*
V + O : IF + PREP THEN *at* = direct

3 If you **aim** at or for something, or **aim** to do something, you plan or hope to achieve it. EG *We are aiming at a higher production level... Professionalism is all about aiming for the best... What we aim to do is fairly advanced.*
V + A *(at/for)*, OR V + *to*-INF

4 If an action **is aimed** at doing something, it is intended or planned to achieve it. EG *A flood of propaganda was aimed at strengthening this sense of obligation.*
V + O + A *(at)* : ONLY PASS = be directed

5 If you **aim** an action or speech at a particular person or group, you intend that they should notice it and be influenced by it. EG *The judge's remarks were aimed at the journalists who were reporting the*
V + O + A *(at)* : USU PASS ⇑ direct = angle, gear towards

case... This anti-smoking campaign is mainly aimed at young teenagers.
6 An **aim** is the thing that a particular plan or course of action is intended to achieve. EG *Many of the basic aims of the committee remained constant... It is our aim to set up a workshop... The competition was started with the aim of encouraging new young writers.* — N COUNT : USU + SUPP ⇑ purpose = intention, ambition
7 Your **aim** is your skill or action in aiming a weapon or other object. EG *He leaned against a tree to steady his aim.* — N SING : *the/POSS* + N
8 If you **take aim** at something or someone, you point a weapon or object at them, ready to shoot or throw. EG *I took careful aim at his head and fired.* — PHR : VB INFLECTS

aimless /eɪmlɪ²s/. A person or activity that is **aimless** has no clear purpose or plan. EG *...an aimless youth of eighteen... ...aimless violence.* ◊ **aimlessly**. EG *She wandered aimlessly along the beach.* ◊ **aimlessness**. EG *He had been hanging around with apparent aimlessness at the camp.* — ADJ QUALIT ≠ purposeful; ◊ ADV; ◊ N UNCOUNT

ain't /eɪnt/ is used in nonstandard spoken English instead of 'am not', 'aren't', or 'isn't'.

air /ɛə/, **airs, airing, aired. 1 Air** is the mixture of gases which forms the earth's atmosphere and which we breathe. EG *She took a gulp of air... ...the chemical content of air... The air temperature was now well below freezing.* ▸ also used to refer to air when it is used to inflate things such as the tyres of cars and bicycles. EG *I let the air out of one of his tyres.* — N UNCOUNT ⇑ gas; ▸ ADJ CLASSIF : ATTRIB
2 The **air** is **2.1** the space around things above the ground. EG *My dog was lying on the floor with its feet in the air... She opened the door and the smell of cooking filled the air.* **2.2** the part of the sky which is attacked or defended by military organizations. EG *The allied forces did not expect heavy losses in the air.* ▸ used as an adjective. EG *...an air attack.* **2.3** the medium through which radio waves are transmitted. EG *The pop music that came over the air from France was a pleasant distraction.* ● If someone or something is **on the air**, they are broadcasting or being broadcast on radio or television. EG *The president went on the air to make a public statement.* If they are **off the air**, they are no longer broadcasting or being broadcast. EG *In Britain television usually goes off the air at about midnight.* — N SING : *the*+N; N SING : *the*+N; N SING : *the*+N; ● PHR : USED AS AN A; PHR : USED AS AN A
3 Air is used in expressions like 'by air' and 'air travel' to refer to travel in aircraft. EG *The fare by air from London to Luxembourg is £145 return... The worst part of air travel is the time you spend in airports.* — N UNCOUNT : *by* + N, OR BEFORE N ⇑ plane
4 If you say that someone or something has a particular **air**, **4.1** you mean that they produce some general feeling or impression. EG *Their house has a faintly old-fashioned, nostalgic air.* **4.2** you mean that they move, look, or behave in a particular way. EG *Her secretary came into the room with a slight air of apology.* — N SING WITH DET + SUPP; N SING WITH DET + SUPP
5 Airs are exaggerated, unnatural manners which people adopt in order to impress other people; used showing disapproval. EG *She didn't want him to think she was just putting on airs when she came to visit.* — N PLURAL
6 Someone who **gives** themselves **airs** behaves as if they are much more important than they really are. — PHR : VB INFLECTS
7 If you refer to someone's **airs and graces**, you are saying that they behave in a way that shows that they think that they are more important than other people. EG *I put up with her phoney airs and graces.* — PHR : USED AS O/S
8 An **air** is a simple tune which can be easily recognized and remembered. EG *I was humming an air from Mozart's 'Don Giovanni'.* — N COUNT + SUPP
9 If you **air** something such as your opinions, you make them known to other people. EG *He spoke on the radio, airing his views to the nation... They agreed to refrain from publicly airing their differences.* — V+O ⇑ disclose = reveal
10 If you **air** a room or building, you make it fresh or cool by allowing fresh air to circulate there. EG *The big windows had been opened to air the room.* — V+O ⇑ ventilate = freshen
11 If you **air** clothing or bedding, or if it **airs**, you put it somewhere warm and dry to make sure that it is completely dry. EG *She hung her clothes up to air before she put them away.* — V-ERG
12 in the air. 12.1 If something is **in the air** it is felt to be present, but it is not talked about. EG *The question hung in the air: how is he going to tell his father?... There is a feeling of conflict in the air.* **12.2** If a decision or matter is **up in the air** or **in the air**, it has not yet been fully planned or settled. EG *Where they were going was left up in the air, a kind of mystery.* — PHR : USED AS AN A = around; PHR : USED AS AN A ⇑ indefinite = uncertain ≠ decided
13 thin air. 13.1 If someone or something disappears **into thin air**, they disappear completely, leaving no trace behind. EG *He left the house and disappeared into thin air.* **13.2** If someone or something appears **out of thin air**, they appear suddenly and mysteriously. **13.3** If something is produced **out of thin air**, it is produced from nothing or from almost nothing, as if by magic. EG *I can't simply conjure up the money out of thin air.* — PHR : USED AS AN A; PHR : USED AS AN A; PHR : USED AS AN A
14 Air is also used in the following expressions: **14.1** If you have **a change of air**, you get away from home and work and have a short holiday or do something different for a time. EG *We decided to have a week or two at Brighton for a change of air.* **14.2** If you **take the air**, you go out for a walk; a old-fashioned expression. **14.3** If a bird or aircraft **takes to the air**, it starts to fly or travel through the air. EG *The birds took to the air... Many of us take to the air nowadays, even if only for a holiday abroad.* **14.4** If you are **walking on air** or **floating on air**, you are very happy about something. **14.5** If you do something to **clear the air**, you do it in order to get rid of any misunderstanding that there might be. EG *She feels relieved that she has cleared the air on the matter of the relationship between them... A little discussion would clear the air.* — PHR : USED AS O/S ⇑ break; PHR : VB INFLECTS; PHR : VB INFLECTS; PHR : VB INFLECTS; PHR : VB INFLECTS
15 See also **airing, hot air.**

air base, air bases. An **air base** is a centre where military aircraft take off or land and are serviced, and where many of the centre's staff live. — N COUNT

airbed /ɛəbɛd/, **airbeds**; also spelled with a hyphen. An **airbed** is a plastic or rubber mattress which can be folded or stored flat and which you fill with air before you use it. — N COUNT = lilo

airborne /ɛəbɔːn/. **1 Airborne** means carried through the air or by the wind. EG *They mounted airborne assaults on suitable targets, especially airfields.* — ADJ CLASSIF ⇑ aerial
2 If an aircraft is **airborne**, it is in the air and flying. EG *At last we were airborne.* — ADJ CLASSIF : PRED
3 Airborne soldiers are trained to fight on the ground after using parachutes to get into the enemy territory. — ADJ CLASSIF : ATTRIB

air brake, air brakes. An **air brake** is a brake which is used on heavy vehicles such as buses and trains and which is operated by means of compressed air. — N COUNT

airbrick /ɛəbrɪk/, **airbricks**; also spelled as two words. An **airbrick** is a brick with holes in it which is put into the wall of a building so that air can get in. — N COUNT ⇑ brick

airbus /ɛəbʌs/, **airbuses**; also spelled with a hyphen. An **airbus** is an aeroplane which is designed to carry a large number of passengers for fairly short distances. — N COUNT ⇑ aircraft

air-conditioned. If a building or room is **air-conditioned**, the air in it is kept cool and dry by means of an air-conditioner. — ADJ CLASSIF ⇑ ventilated

air-conditioner, air-conditioners; also spelled without a hyphen. An **air-conditioner** is a machine which keeps the air cool and dry in a building. — N COUNT

air-conditioning; also spelled without a hyphen. **Air-conditioning** is a method of providing buildings with cool dry air. — N UNCOUNT ⇑ ventilation

aircraft /ɛəkrɑːft/. **Aircraft** is both the singular and the plural form. An **aircraft** is a vehicle which can fly, for example an aeroplane, glider or helicopter. EG *The President and his wife emerged from their aircraft... ...aircraft accidents.* — N COUNT, OR *by*+N

aircraft carrier, aircraft carriers. An **aircraft carrier** is a warship with a long, flat deck where aircraft can take off and land. — N COUNT

aircrew /ɛəkruː/, **aircrews.** The **aircrew** on a plane are the pilot and other people who are responsible for flying it and for looking after the passengers. — N COUNT : IF SING, VB CAN BE SING OR PL ⇑ crew

airfield /ɛəfiːld/, **airfields.** An **airfield** is an area of ground where aircraft take off and land. It may have some permanent buildings but it is smaller than an airport. — N COUNT = aerodrome

air force, air forces; also spelled as one word. An **air force** is the part of a country's military organization which is concerned with attacks from the air — N COUNT/N PROPER ⇑ the military and fighting in the air. EG *The Royal Air Force still remained dangerously short of bombers.*

airgun /ɛəgʌn/, **airguns**; also spelled as two words. An **airgun** is a gun which is fired by means of air pressure. N COUNT ⇑ gun

air hostess, air hostesses; also spelled with a hyphen. An **air hostess** is a woman whose job is to look after the passengers in an aircraft. N COUNT = stewardess

airing /ɛərɪŋ/. **1** If you give a room an **airing**, you allow air into the room in order to freshen it or to remove unpleasant smells or cigarette smoke. EG *Give the room an airing by opening the window for a couple of minutes.* N SING : *an*+N

2 If you give bedding or clothing an **airing**, you put it somewhere warm or airy in order to make sure that it is completely dry. N SING WITH DET ⇑ drying

3 If you give your ideas or views an **airing**, you make them known to other people. EG *...the airing of anarchist ideas... Subjects like death and even loneliness regularly get an airing.* N SING WITH DET ⇑ disclosure

airing cupboard, airing cupboards. An **airing cupboard** is a warm cupboard where you put clothes and other things that have been washed and partly dried, to make sure they are completely dry. N COUNT

airlane /ɛəleɪn/, **airlanes**; also spelled as two words. An **airlane** is a route through the air which aircraft regularly use. N COUNT

airless /ɛəlɪ²s/. **1** An **airless** building or place has no fresh air circulating in it. EG *...a small airless theatre crammed with children.* ADJ QUALIT ⇑ stale = stuffy

2 If you describe weather or days, nights, etc as **airless**, you mean that there is no wind and it is stuffy. EG *...dry airless nights.* ADJ QUALIT ⇑ still ≠ windy

airletter /ɛəlɛtə/, **airletters**; also spelled as two words. An **airletter** is a letter which is sent by air, especially one written on a very thin sheet of paper that is then folded and does not need an envelope. EG *Many thanks for your airletter. We were glad to hear your news.* N COUNT

airlift /ɛəlɪft/, **airlifts, airlifting, airlifted**. **1** An **airlift** is an operation to move people, troops, or goods by air, especially in a war or when land routes are closed. EG *...the Berlin airlift back in the late nineteen forties.* N COUNT ⇑ transportation

2 To **airlift** people, troops, or goods means to carry them by air, especially in a war or when land routes are closed. EG *They were airlifted to Manchester.* V+O : USU+A *(to/into/from)* ⇑ transport

airline /ɛəlaɪn/, **airlines**. An **airline** is a company which provides aircraft services for passengers and goods. EG *There were no other airlines doing a direct flight to London.* N COUNT

airliner /ɛəlaɪnə/, **airliners**. An **airliner** is a large aeroplane that is used for carrying passengers. N COUNT ⇑ aircraft

airlock /ɛəlɒk/, **airlocks**; also spelled with a hyphen or as two words. An **airlock** is **1** a compartment between places which do not have the same air pressure, for example in a spacecraft or submarine. N COUNT

2 a blockage in a pipe which is caused by a bubble of air that prevents liquid from flowing through. N COUNT

airmail /ɛəmeɪl/ is the system of sending letters, parcels, or goods by air. EG *By airmail they notify the bank in Australia that £1,000 may be withdrawn... ...an airmail letter.* N UNCOUNT ⇑ mail

airman /ɛəmə³n/, **airmen**. An **airman** is a man who serves in his country's air force. N COUNT

air mattress, air mattresses. An **air mattress** is the same as an airbed. N COUNT

airplane /ɛəpleɪn/, **airplanes**. An **airplane** is a vehicle with wings and one or more engines that enable it to fly through the air; used in American English. EG *...his first flight in an airplane... ...an airplane crash.* N COUNT, OR *by*+N = plane, aeroplane

air pocket, air pockets. An **air pocket** is a downward flowing current of air which causes an aircraft to suddenly lose height when it flies into it. N COUNT

airport /ɛəpɔːt/, **airports**. An **airport** is a place, usually with a lot of buildings and facilities, where aircraft land and take off. EG *We landed at a small airport... ...an airport runway.* N COUNT

air raid, air raids; also spelled with a hyphen or as one word. An **air raid** is an attack by enemy aircraft, especially one in which they drop bombs. EG *There has been no air raid on the city for four months... ...air-raid shelters.* N COUNT = airstrike

air rifle, air rifles; also spelled with a hyphen. An **air rifle** is a rifle which is fired by means of air pressure. N COUNT

air-sea rescue is the use of helicopters, other aircraft, and boats to rescue people who are in danger of drowning in the sea. N UNCOUNT

airship /ɛəʃɪp/, **airships**. An **airship** is an aircraft that is supported in the air by a large structure like a balloon filled with gas. It is powered by an engine and passengers sit in a compartment underneath the balloon structure. N COUNT

airsick /ɛəsɪk/. Someone who is **airsick** feels or is sick because of the effects of flying in an aeroplane. EG *He felt cold, and more than a little airsick.* ADJ QUALIT : USU PRED

airspace /ɛəspeɪs/; also spelled as two words. A country's **airspace** is the part of the sky that is considered to belong to that country. EG *The plane crashed last Saturday just after entering British airspace.* N UNCOUNT : MOD/POSS+N ⇑ space

airspeed /ɛəspiːd/; also spelled as two words. An aircraft's **airspeed** is the speed at which it travels through the air. Compare **groundspeed**. N UNCOUNT/COUNT

airstrike /ɛəstraɪk/, **airstrikes**. An **airstrike** is the same as an air raid. EG *Airstrikes on civilians became a matter of routine.* N COUNT ⇑ attack

airstrip /ɛəstrɪp/, **airstrips**. An **airstrip** is a stretch of land which has been cleared so that aircraft can take off and land. EG *The plane landed on a grass airstrip.* N COUNT ⇑ airfield

air terminal, air terminals. An **air terminal** is a building in a town from which air passengers are taken by bus to the local airport. EG *He drove in from the airport to the London air terminal.* N COUNT

airtight /ɛətaɪt/; also spelled with a hyphen. **1** If a container is **airtight**, its lid fits so tightly that no air can get in or out. EG *Keep food in airtight tins.* ADJ CLASSIF ⇑ sealed = hermetic

2 If you say that an argument or idea is **airtight**, you mean that it has no errors in it or points that could be disputed. EG *This categorization is hardly airtight.* ADJ CLASSIF ⇑ conclusive = flawless

air time; also spelled as one word. **air time** is a period of time on radio or television during which a particular item is broadcast. EG *The BBC has said that it will consider applications from charities for air time.* N UNCOUNT

air-to-air describes things that are used or happen between aircraft when they are flying, such as missiles, attacks, etc. EG *The planes were armed with air-to-air missiles.* ADJ CLASSIF : ATTRIB

air-traffic control is **1** the activity of organizing the routes which aircraft are allowed to take through the sky and who keep in contact with pilots by radio about their routes. N UNCOUNT **2** the group of people who organize routes for aircraft. N UNCOUNT ⇑ organizers

airwaves /ɛəweɪvz/. **1 Airwaves** are the radio waves which are used in radio and television broadcasting. N PLURAL

2 Airwaves is used, especially in the expression 'on the airwaves', to refer to the activity of broadcasting on radio and television. EG *He was criticized for saying on the airwaves that he was in favour of capital punishment.* N PLURAL : USU *the*+N

airway /ɛəweɪ/, **airways**. **1** An **airway** is a route through the air which aircraft regularly use. EG *...the giant jets that increasingly dominate the world's airways.* N COUNT

2 The word **Airways** is used in the name of some airlines. EG *...British Airways.* N PLURAL : USED IN NAMES

airwoman /ɛəwʊ¹mə⁰n/, **airwomen**. An **airwoman** is a woman who serves in her country's air force. N COUNT

airworthy /ɛəwɜːði¹/. If an aircraft is **airworthy**, it is safe to fly. EG *They certified the plane as completely airworthy.* ◊ **airworthiness**. EG *All the helicopters received certificates of airworthiness.* ADJ CLASSIF ◊ N UNCOUNT ⇑ safety

airy /ɛəri¹/, **airier, airiest**. **1** If a place or building is **airy**, it has plenty of fresh air inside, usually because it is so spacious. EG *The church was airy and light inside.* ADJ QUALIT ⇑ large ≠ stuffy

2 You use the word **airy** to describe someone's behaviour or attitude when they are light-hearted and casual about things which should be taken seriously. EG *He applied in an airy way for the job of project manager.* ◊ **airily** EG *People's jobs matter, yet you're talking airily of closing our company.* ADJ QUALIT = offhand ≠ serious ◊ ADV WITH VB

3 Airy ideas or promises have little basis in fact or reality. EG *He's always full of airy promises.* ADJ QUALIT ⇑ imaginary

airy-fairy /ɛərɪfɛəri¹/ means vague and fanciful, with no basis in fact or common sense. EG *...airy-fairy nonsense.* ADJ QUALIT

aisle /aɪl/, **aisles**. 1 An **aisle** is a long narrow gap that separates rows of seats in a public building, for example in a church or theatre, or rows of shelves in a supermarket. EG *The ushers hurry up and down the aisle, beckoning people to their seats.* N COUNT: USU the+N = gangway

2 **The aisle** is used in expressions like 'walking down the aisle' or 'leading someone down the aisle' to refer to the activity of getting married. N SING: the+N

3 An **aisle** is also a long passage on the left or right side of a church that goes from the front to the back and is separated from the central part by pillars. EG *Aisles were added to the original Saxon building in the Norman period.* N COUNT

4 If the audience at a show is **rolling in the aisles**, people are laughing so much that they find it hard to stop or to control themselves; an informal expression. EG *It had us rolling in the aisles.* PHR: VB INFLECTS = in stitches

aitch /eɪtʃ/, **aitches**. 1 **Aitch** is the word used to represent the letter or sound H. EG *He couldn't even sound his aitches.* N COUNT

2 If someone **drops** their **aitches**, they speak with an accent in which they do not pronounce the sound H at the beginning of words or syllables. Some people consider that this accent is socially inferior. PHR: VB INFLECTS

ajar /əd͡ʒɑː/. If a door is **ajar**, it is slightly open. EG *She went out of the room, leaving the door ajar.* ADJ CLASSIF: PRED

akimbo /ə³kɪmbəʊ/. If you stand **with arms akimbo** or **arms akimbo** you stand with your hands on your hips and your elbows pointing outwards; an old-fashioned expression. EG *She stood, arms akimbo, looking round... Then she posed with arms akimbo.* PHR: USED AS AN A

akin /əkɪn/. If something is **akin** to something else, it is similar to it in some way, for example by having some qualities or features in common with it. EG *It was soul destroying work, akin to digging a hole and then filling it in again... She had answered with something akin to anger.* ADJ QUALIT: PRED, USU+to ⇑ related

alabaster /æləbɑːstə, -bæstə/ is a white stone that is used for making statues, vases, and other ornaments. N UNCOUNT ⇑ gypsum

à la carte /ɑː lə kɑːt/. If you eat **à la carte** in a restaurant, you choose from a range of individually priced dishes for each course on the menu, rather than paying a fixed price for a complete meal. EG *It's normally more expensive to eat à la carte.* ▸ used as an adjective. EG *...the à la carte menu.* ADV AFTER VB; ▸ ADJ CLASSIF: ATTRIB

alacrity /əlækrɪti¹/. If you do something with **alacrity**, you do it quickly and eagerly. EG *He accepted with alacrity.* N UNCOUNT: USU with+N ⇑ speed = haste

à la mode /ɑː lə məʊd/. If something, especially clothing or a style, is **à la mode**, it is the latest fashion; an old-fashioned or literary expression. EG *It became not only à la mode but required wear.* ▸ used as an adverb. EG *She knew just how far to go in dressing à la mode.* ADJ CLASSIF: PRED = chic, fashionable; ▸ ADV AFTER VB = fashionably

alarm /əlɑːm/, **alarms, alarming, alarmed**. 1 **Alarm** is a feeling of fear or anxiety that something unpleasant or dangerous might happen. EG *The locals view these road improvements with alarm... She looked round in alarm.* N UNCOUNT: USU with/in+N

2 An **alarm** is 2.1 an automatic device that warns you of something, for example by ringing a bell or flashing a light. EG *The alarm went off... He threw the switch of the alarm system...* N COUNT, OR N BEFORE N 2.2 the same as an alarm clock. N COUNT

3 If a person or animal **sounds the alarm** or **raises the alarm**, they warn other people or animals of danger. EG *The stallion is likely to sound the alarm with a braying danger call.* PHR: VB INFLECTS

4 If something or someone **alarms** you, they make you afraid or anxious that something unpleasant or dangerous might happen. EG *In some way I seemed to alarm him.* V+O ⇑ frighten = scare

5 See also **burglar alarm, false alarm, fire alarm**.

alarm clock, alarm clocks; also spelled with a hyphen. An **alarm clock** is a clock that you can set to wake you up by making a noise at a particular time. N COUNT

alarmed /əlɑːmd/. If someone is **alarmed**, they feel fear or anxiety that something unpleasant or dangerous might happen. EG *She looked alarmed... Don't be alarmed.* ADJ QUALIT: USU PRED, IF+PREP THEN by/at ⇑ afraid

alarming /əlɑːmɪŋ/. Something that is **alarming** causes people to be worried or concerned. EG *The world's forests are shrinking at an alarming rate... ...an alarming increase in racial hostility.* ADJ QUALIT ⇑ worrying = disquieting
◊ **alarmingly**. EG *McPherson's sight had begun to deteriorate alarmingly... More alarmingly, Sir George proceeded to upset Sir Kenneth.* ◊ ADV, OR ADV SEN

alarmist /əlɑːmɪst/, **alarmists**. Someone or something that is **alarmist** causes alarm unnecessarily in other people. EG *It is only too easy to be alarmist... The King took a less alarmist view.* ▸ used as a noun. EG *You're just an alarmist!* ADJ QUALIT; ▸ N COUNT

alas /ə³læs/ is 1 used to say that a particular situation seems sad, unfortunate, or regrettable to you; a rather formal or old-fashioned use. EG *There was, alas, no shortage of assassinations... Alas for good intents, no notice was taken of these things.* 2 an old-fashioned exclamation that expresses grief, regret, shame, or sympathy. EG *Alas, what ill luck has befallen us!* ADV SEN = sadly, unfortunately; EXCLAM

Albanian /ælbeɪnɪən/, **Albanians**. 1 An **Albanian** is someone who comes from Albania. N COUNT

2 **Albanian** is the language that is spoken by people who live in Albania. N UNCOUNT

3 **Albanian** means belonging or relating to Albania, or to its people or language. ADJ CLASSIF

albatross /ælbətrɒs/, **albatrosses**. 1 An **albatross** is a very large white seabird that lives in the Pacific and the South Atlantic. N COUNT

2 If you refer to something as an **albatross**, you are saying that it causes you great problems from which you cannot escape, or that it prevents you from doing what you want to do. EG *Nationalisation was an electoral albatross... She was an albatross around his neck.* N COUNT+SUPP: USU SING ⇑ handicap = millstone

albeit /ɔːlbiːɪt/. You use **albeit** to introduce a fact or comment which adds more detail to what you have just said and so reduces the effect or directness of it; a formal word. EG *It continues to publish, albeit irregularly, two journals... He is only an up-market interior decorator, albeit a rather good one.* CONJ SUBORD = although, though

albino /ælbiːnəʊ/, **albinos**. An **albino** is a person or animal that is born with a condition which causes them to have very white skin, white hair, and pink eyes. EG *It's almost like being an albino or a diabetic.* ▸ used as an adjective. EG *...an albino monkey.* N COUNT; ▸ ADJ CLASSIF

album /ælbəm/, **albums**. An **album** is 1 a record which usually has about 25 minutes of music, speech, etc on each side. EG *The album is called 'African Flight'... ...an album sleeve.* 2 a special book in which you collect something, for example photographs, stamps, or autographs. EG *...an album full of snapshots of Jackie and Dickie.* N COUNT = LP; N COUNT+SUPP

albumen /ælbjə⁴mɪ²n/, **albumens**. **Albumen** is the white or transparent part of the inside of an egg; a technical word. ● See also **albumin**. N UNCOUNT/COUNT ⇑ protein = egg white

albumin /ælbjə⁴mɪn/; also spelled **albumen**. **Albumin** is a protein that is found in blood plasma, egg white, and some other substances. N UNCOUNT

alchemist /ælkə²mɪst/, **alchemists**. An **alchemist** was a scientist in the Middle Ages who tried to discover how to change ordinary metals into gold. N COUNT

alchemy /ælkə²mi¹/. **Alchemy** is 1 the form of chemistry studied in the Middle Ages, which was especially concerned with trying to discover ways to change ordinary metals into gold. 2 the power to do something so well that it seems mysterious and magical; a literary use. EG *...the alchemy of his performance.* N UNCOUNT; N UNCOUNT: IF+PREP THEN of = magic

alcohol /ælkə⁶hɒl/. **Alcohol** is 1 drink such as beer, wine, and whisky that can make people drunk. EG *They were deeply under the influence of alcohol... I never touch alcohol in any form.* 2 a colourless liquid that is produced by fermenting sugars. It is found in drinks such as beer, wine, and whisky, and is also used as a solvent. N UNCOUNT = booze; N UNCOUNT

alcoholic /ælkə⁶hɒlɪk/, **alcoholics**. 1 If a drink is **alcoholic**, it contains alcohol and can intoxicate people. EG *...alcoholic beverages.* ADJ QUALIT ⇑ intoxicating

2 An **alcoholic** is a person who is addicted to alcoholic drink. EG *She claims she's not an alcoholic because she doesn't drink alone.* ▸ used as an adjective. EG *...my alcoholic relatives.* N COUNT ⇑ addict; ▸ ADJ CLASSIF ≠ teetotal

alcoholism /ælkə⁶hɒlɪzə⁰m/ is the condition of being addicted to alcohol. EG *He was treated a number of times for chronic alcoholism.* N UNCOUNT ⇑ addiction

alcove /ælkəʊv/, **alcoves**. An **alcove** is a small area in a room which is formed by one part of a wall being built further back than the rest of the wall. EG *His desk was in an alcove to one side of the chimney.* N COUNT ⇑ recess = niche

alder /ɔːldə/, **alders**. **Alder** can also be used as the plural form. An **alder** is a tree that grows in Northern temperate areas, often in damp places. It has cones and leaves with small points along the edges. N COUNT

alderman /ɔːldəmə³n/, **aldermen**. 1 An **alderman** in England and Wales until 1974 was a senior member of a local council who was elected by other councillors. N COUNT: ALSO IN TITLES ⇑ councillor

2 In the United States and Canada, an **alderman** is a member of the governing body of a city. N COUNT: ALSO IN TITLES

ale /eɪl/, **ales**. Ale is 1 beer that is made without hops. ● See also **ginger ale**. N MASS 2 any kind of beer; an old-fashioned or dialect use. N MASS ⇑ drink

alert /əlɜːt/, **alerts, alerting, alerted**. 1 If someone is **alert**, they are paying full attention and are ready or able to deal with anything that might happen. EG *...unnoticed except by the few people who were sufficiently alert to recognise them... He was hustled out by a couple of alert cops.* ADJ QUALIT = wide awake ≠ unprepared ◇ **alertly**. EG *We were all watching Dixon alertly.* ◇ ADV WITH VB ◇ **alertness**. EG *The job requires constant alertness and vigilance.* ◇ N UNCOUNT ⇑ readiness

2 If someone is **alert** to a fact or situation, they are fully aware of it. EG *They were both alert to the dangers in the grim business.* ADJ CLASSIF: PRED, USU+*to* = awake

3 An **alert** is 3.1 a situation in which military forces or the people in a place prepare themselves for something dangerous that might happen. EG *The city centre was on a nuclear alert... Events had been moving towards a general alert for some days.* N COUNT ≠ all clear 3.2 a warning of danger. EG *...147 false alerts.* N COUNT = alarm

4 If a person or animal is **on the alert**, they are paying full attention to a situation and are ready to deal with anything that might happen. EG *Prepare for action and be on the alert.* PHR: USED AS AN A = prepared

5 If you **alert** someone, you warn them of danger or trouble so that they are ready to act quickly and effectively. EG *He pressed the horn of the vehicle to alert the squadron.* V+O

6 If something or someone **alerts** you to a fact or situation, they make you fully aware of it. EG *The things they said alerted me, rather late, to the fact that this was a mistake.* V+O: USU+*to* ⇑ warn

A level, A levels. An **A level** is an educational qualification in a particular subject. A levels are awarded in England, Wales, and Northern Ireland. Schoolchildren take the examination for it after they have studied the subject to an advanced level. N COUNT

alfalfa /ælfælfə/ is a plant that is used for feeding farm animals. The shoots that develop from its seeds are sometimes eaten as a vegetable. N UNCOUNT = lucerne

alfresco /ælfreskəʊ/. An **alfresco** meal is one that is eaten in the open air. EG *...an alfresco lunch of prawns and brown bread.* ADJ CLASSIF: ATTRIB = outdoor ▸ used as an adverb. EG *They often dined alfresco in the warm summer evenings.* ▸ ADV AFTER VB = outside

algae /ældʒiː/ is a type of plant with no stems or leaves. Seaweed is a type of algae; other types grow on damp surfaces, and are green and slimy. N UNCOUNT = seaweed

algebra /ældʒɪ²brə/ is a branch of mathematics in which letters and other symbols are used to represent numbers. N UNCOUNT

algebraic /ældʒɪbreɪɪk/. **Algebraic** sums, questions, principles, or other things are based on or use algebra. EG *...algebraic equations.* ADJ CLASSIF: ATTRIB

Algerian /ældʒɪərɪən/, **Algerians**. 1 An **Algerian** is someone who comes from Algeria. N COUNT ⇑ person

2 **Algerian** means belonging or relating to Algeria or its people. EG *...an Algerian coffee shop.* ADJ CLASSIF

algorithm /ælgərɪðə⁰m/, **algorithms**. An **algorithm** is a special series of instructions that are carried out in a particular order, for example as part of a computer program. N COUNT ⇑ instruction

alia. See **inter alia**.

alias /eɪlɪəs/, **aliases**. 1 An **alias** is a false name, especially used by someone who is doing something criminal. N COUNT

2 **Alias** is used when stating someone's nickname or false name. EG *Peter Lewis, alias John Lord, was convicted of fraud.* PREP: N PROPER +PREP+N PROPER ⇑ named

alibi /ælɪbaɪ/, **alibis**. An **alibi** is 1 someone or something that proves that a person who has been accused of a crime was somewhere else when the crime was committed. EG *His alibi couldn't be shaken so the police were forced to release him... ...his alibi for the night of the murder.* N COUNT: IF+PREP THEN *for/of* ⇑ defence 2 an excuse for a failure or mistake; an informal use. EG *Interest rate policy was an alibi for overdue economy measures.* N COUNT: IF+PREP THEN *for/of*

alien /eɪljən, eɪlɪən/, **aliens**. 1 **Alien** means 1.1 belonging to a different country, race, or group. EG *...a social system which was determined by alien rulers.* ADJ CLASSIF: ATTRIB = foreign 1.2 strange and sometimes frightening, because of not being part of your normal experience. EG *...this totally alien and threatening environment.* ADJ QUALIT

2 If something is **alien** to your normal feelings, beliefs, or behaviour, it is not the way you would normally feel or behave. EG *Malice towards an enemy was completely alien to the man's nature.* ADJ CLASSIF: USU +*to* ⇑ strange = foreign

3 An **alien** is 3.1 someone who is not a legal citizen of the country in which they live; a legal term. EG *On arrival in the United Kingdom you must report to the Aliens Registration Office.* N COUNT = foreigner 3.2 someone who feels that they do not belong to the society in which they live. EG *They felt themselves to be rebels, aliens and exiles rather than heroes.* N COUNT ⇑ stranger = outsider 3.3 a creature from outer space, especially one that is considered to be threatening or hostile; used mainly in science fiction. N COUNT ▸ used as an adjective. EG *...an alien spacecraft.* ▸ ADJ CLASSIF

alienate /eɪljəneɪt, eɪlɪə-/, **alienates, alienating, alienated**. 1 If you **alienate** someone, you make them become unfriendly or unsympathetic to your point of view. EG *I managed to alienate Dennis too... The government had only succeeded in alienating public opinion.* V+O: NO IMPER ⇑ estranged = antagonize ◇ **alienation** /eɪljəneɪʃə⁰n, eɪlɪə-/. EG *...the problems of shop floor alienation which perturb management.* ◇ N UNCOUNT: IF+PREP THEN *of*

2 If someone is **alienated** from something with which they would normally be linked, they are emotionally or intellectually separated from it. EG *We live in an age in which people have been alienated from their roots... The leadership must never become alienated from the ordinary members.* V+O: USU PASS, IF+PREP THEN *from/of* ⇑ separate = estranged, isolate ≠ integrate ◇ **alienated**. EG *I felt alienated, angry and alone.* ◇ ADJ QUALIT ◇ **alienation**. EG *...the growing feeling of despair and alienation.* ◇ N UNCOUNT

3 To **alienate** land or property means to transfer the ownership of it to another person; a legal term. EG *She had no right to alienate so large a sum of money from her children.* V+O: IF+PREP THEN *from* ◇ **alienation**. EG *...large-scale alienation of village land.* ◇ N UNCOUNT

alight /əlaɪt/, **alights, alighting, alighted, alit**. 1 If something is **alight**, 1.1 it is burning. EG *On the tables there were candles alight... ...paraffin that has been poured on the ground and set alight.* ADJ CLASSIF: PRED 1.2 it is very bright in colour. EG *We walked through fields and over ditches, past bushes alight with glow-worms and fireflies.* ADJ CLASSIF: PRED, IF+PREP THEN *with* = ablaze

2 If you describe someone or their face or expression as **alight**, you mean that they are excited. EG *The Prime Minister had come alight... She was looking round at him, her eyes alight.* ADJ CLASSIF: PRED = alive

3 If a bird or insect **alights** somewhere, it lands there. EG *It flew across to the tree and alighted on a branch.* V: USU+A ⇑ land

4 If someone **alights** from a train, bus, or other vehicle, they get out of it after a journey. EG *Nobody met me at the station where I alighted... She greeted the first arrivals, as they alighted from their machine.* V: IF+PREP THEN *from* ⇑ leave ≠ board

align /əlaɪn/, **aligns, aligning, aligned**. 1 If you **align** yourself with a particular group or side in a quarrel or struggle, or if you **are aligned** with them, you support them politically. EG *The workers, in turn, can only benefit if they align themselves with pensioners.* V+O (REFL/NG) +A (*with/against*) = ally

2 If you **align** something, you place it in a certain position in relation to something else, usually along a particular line or parallel to it. EG *The Captain aligned the periscope on the bearing... ...three causeways of accurately aligned large stones.* V+O: IF+PREP THEN *with/on* = line up

alignment /əlaɪnmə²nt/, **alignments**. 1 An **alignment** is support for a particular group, especially in politics, or for a side in a quarrel or struggle. EG *This is the sign of a new alignment in British politics.* N COUNT ⇑ alliance

2 The **alignment** of something is its position in relation to something else or to its correct position. EG *...sensors which monitor tyre wear, brake power, steering alignment and so on... Something had slipped out of alignment.* N UNCOUNT

alike /əlaɪk/. 1 If two or more things are **alike**, they are similar in some way. EG *They all looked alike to me... The Vanbrugh sisters were remarkably alike in appearance.* ADJ QUALIT: PRED ≠ different

2 **Alike** means in a similar way. EG *The children are all treated alike... They did everything alike.* ADV AFTER VB ≠ differently

3 **Alike** is used after mentioning two or more people, groups, or things in order to emphasize that you are referring to both or all of them. EG *The strike is* ADV: NG+*and*+NG+ADV = equally

damaging to managers and workers alike... ...the southern and northern states alike.

alimentary /ælɪmentə⁰ri¹/ is used to refer to eating or digestion. EG *Alimentary regulations are not the same for all religions.* [ADJ CLASSIF : ATTRIB ⇑ digestive]

alimentary canal, alimentary canals. The **alimentary canal** in a person or animal is the passage in their body through which food passes from their mouth to their anus. [N COUNT]

alimony /ælɪməni¹/ is the money that a court of law orders someone to pay regularly to their wife or husband after they are separated or divorced. EG *...alimony payments.* [N UNCOUNT ⇑ maintenance]

alive /əlaɪv/. **1** If a person or animal is **alive**, they have life. EG *The doctors are working very hard to keep him alive... I think his father is still alive... More than forty people were burned alive.* [ADJ CLASSIF : PRED ⇑ living ≠ dead]

2 If a person seems or feels **alive**, they are very lively and enjoying everything that they do. EG *Young people are so alive and exciting... Her senses seemed alive and incredibly keen.* [ADJ QUALIT : PRED ⇑ active = vital]

3 If something such as an activity, organization, or situation is **alive**, it continues to exist or function, perhaps in spite of difficulties that have occurred. EG *Theatre outside London is very much alive... It was your way of keeping your marriage alive.* [ADJ QUALIT : PRED ⇑ existing ≠ extinct]

4 If a place is **alive** or **alive** with something, a lot of things are going on there and it seems busy or exciting. EG *The ditches beside the fields were alive with the croaking of frogs... London's alive. I feel free there.* [ADJ CLASSIF : PRED, IF+PREP THEN *with* = bustling]

5 If you are **alive** to a particular problem or situation, you are aware of it and realize how important it is. EG *They are alive to the limitations of the exam system... A music reviewer like Peter Hayworth is very alive to what is going on.* [ADJ QUALIT : PRED+*to* = sensitive]

6 If you **bring** a story or account **alive**, you make it more interesting or lively. EG *We used a lot of improvisation to bring the story alive.* [PHR : VB INFLECTS = animate]

7 come alive. 7.1 If someone or something in a novel, story, or description **comes alive**, they become interesting, lively, or realistic. EG *None of his characters actually comes alive... The best historical novels make the past come alive.* [PHR : VB INFLECTS = live] **7.2** If a person or place **comes alive**, they start to be active or lively again after a quiet or dull period. EG *The house had come alive and there was a great deal of bustling about.* [PHR : VB INFLECTS = wake up]

8 If someone or something is **alive and kicking**, they are not only still living or in existence, but are also very active and lively. EG *You wanted some assurance that I was alive and kicking and thinking of you.* [PHR : USED AS C = thriving]

9 If you say that someone or something, or a particular type of person or thing, is **alive and well**, you are emphasizing that they continue to survive. EG *The British eccentric is alive and well and living in Wimbledon.* [PHR : USED AS C ⇑ surviving]

alkali /ælkəlaɪ/, **alkalis.** An **alkali** is a substance or liquid with a pH value of more than 7. It forms a chemical salt if it is combined with an acid. [N MASS ≠ acid]

alkaline /ælkəlaɪn/. Something that is **alkaline** contains an alkali or has a pH value of more than 7. EG *...alkaline soils derived from chalk or limestone.* [ADJ QUALIT ≠ acidic]

all /ɔːl/. **1 All** is used **1.1** when you are referring to the whole of a particular group or thing. EG *All the girls think it's great... They lugged all the stuff into the hall... People who stay in one place all their lives.* [PREDET ≠ none] ▸ used as a pronoun. EG *All of the defendants were proved guilty... Some of them were sleeping, some knitting, some staring out of the windows, all unnaturally silent.* [▸ PRON : IF+PREP THEN *of* ≠ none] **1.2** when you are referring to everyone or everything of a particular kind. EG *Our aim should be that all children complete the primary course.* [PREDET OR QUANTIF+N UNCOUNT/N IN PLURAL] ▸ used as a pronoun. EG *It was the result of all that had happened previously.* [▸ PRON] **1.3** when you are referring to the whole of a particular period of time. EG *Elsa had cried all night... I waited in all the afternoon.* [PREDET/QUANTIF] **1.4** when you are referring to a situation or to life in general. EG *All was quiet in the jail... All seemed to be going happily.* [PRON+VB IN SING = everything]

2 All is used when you want to emphasize that a pronoun or noun refers to everyone or everything possible, or to the whole of something. EG *They all live together in the same house... These are all problems that he's concerned with... We would all be disappointed if you cancelled permission now... I enjoyed it all... ...the investment of time that we all of us make.* [PRON : IF+PREP THEN *of*]

3 All is also used **3.1** when you are mentioning a particular quality and want to emphasize that it is complete and total. For example, if you say something 'with all sincerity', you are showing that you are very sincere. EG *I say this in all seriousness.* [DET+N UNCOUNT = complete] **3.2** when you are referring to something and saying that it exists in very large quantities; used mainly in spoken English. EG *That's worse than all the violence you see in the movies... He didn't want to go through all that divorce hassle again.* [PREDET] **3.3** when you want to emphasize a preposition or adverb, especially 'over', 'along', 'round', 'around', 'through', or 'about'. EG *He spilled coffee all over himself... ...all along the front of the central region... I forgot all about him.* [ADV+PREP/ADV ⇑ completely] **3.4** when you want to emphasize an adjective or prepositional group. EG *I'm all alone now... He was living all by himself in an old house on the river... Those go-go girls have gotten you all excited.* [ADV+ADJ/PREP ⇑ completely] **3.5** when you are describing something or someone and want to say that a particular thing seems to be their chief or strongest characteristic. EG *The potatoes were wet and the sprouts were wet and the gravy was all water... He was all smiles... ...a beefy athlete, all bulging limbs.* [ADV : NG+ADV ⇑ chiefly]

4 All is used at the beginning of a clause or as a complement in structures where you are emphasizing the simple or basic facts about a situation. EG *All you do is add water... All I know is that a man's dying while we're talking... The meat was dry and flaky. All he could taste was mustard... It's all because of commercialism that this is so... Look, give me a chance. That's all I want.* [PRON : USU C]

5 All is used when you are stating the score in a game and both players or teams have the same score. EG *'What's the score?'–'Three all.'... They were thirty all in the last game when it started to rain.* [ADV : NUM+ADV ⇑ each]

6 All is used in structures like 'all the more' or 'all the better' to mean more or better than before or than would have happened otherwise. EG *You must work all the more quickly now... We can understand your feeling. All the more because we are Africans ourselves... If it's not there, then all the better.* [PREDET+*the*+ADV IN COMPAR = even]

7 Above all or **above all else** is used to emphasize that a particular thing, especially the last one in a list, is more important than other things. EG *The pressures–political, social and, above all, economic–are growing... Above all, there is a severe shortage of health visitors... Relax, and above all don't panic.* [PHR : USED AS ADV SEN]

8 After all is used **8.1** when you are stating a reason or opinion that relates to the previous statement. EG *They did not expect heavy losses in the air; after all, they had superb aircraft... It had to be recognized, after all, that I was still a schoolboy.* [PHR : USED AS ADV SEN] **8.2** when you are saying that something is or might be the case, in spite of things that have happened or that have been said or done. EG *The women began to think maybe she was not so mad after all... Could it be true, after all, that money did not bring happiness?* [PHR : USED AS ADV SEN = in fact]

9 All but. 9.1 All but a particular thing, person, way, etc means everything, everyone, or every way except for the one mentioned. EG *It was clear of all but the faintest trace of smoke... The paralysing effect of chemical warfare on all but those equipped to deal with it.* [PHR] **9.2 All but** is used to say that something is almost the case. EG *I had all but finished... She was all but stark naked.* [PHR = almost]

10 all in. 10.1 If you are **all in**, you are exhausted; an informal use. [PHR : USED AS C] **10.2** If something such as an activity is a particular price **all in**, that price includes everything that is offered; an informal use. EG *Evening on the river: dinner, dancing, wine–£30 all in.* [PHR : USED AS AN A = inclusive]

11 All in all is used to introduce a summary or generalization, or an opinion which is based on facts or reasons that have already been given. EG *All in all, consultations between the two groups lasted three weeks... All in all, I'm not in favour.* [PHR : USED AS ADV SEN]

12 All of followed by a number or amount is used in speech to say that a particular total is not less than this, and often to express surprise at how large or small it is. EG *There were all of six people there... It cost all of three hundred pounds.* [PHR+NUM]

13 All that is used in spoken English with negatives when you want to deny something without being too emphatic or definite. EG *He is not all that warm, just* [PHR : WITH BROAD NEG] *warm enough... I don't know him all that well, actually... It isn't as awful as all that.*

14 You use expressions like **all very well** and **all very fine** when you want to say that you consider a particular situation or thing unacceptable, although other people may think that there is nothing wrong with it; often used to express disagreement, scorn, dislike, annoyance, or envy. EG *I mean it's all very well to say that you dislike it, but what are you going to do about it?... It was all very fine for the birds, I supposed. However, I preferred a different sort of life... Look, Lynn, it's all very well, but he scared the life out of me....* PHR : USED AS C, IF + PREP/VB THEN *for/to*-INF

15 You can say **and all** 15.1 when you are referring vaguely to other things, qualities, actions, etc which are associated with the one or ones just mentioned. EG *The drawer was full of old love letters and holy medals and dirty pictures and all... He was getting drunk every night and having love affairs and all that sort of thing... They called for a doctor and all the rest of it.* PHR : USED AS AN A **15.2** when you want to emphasize that you are talking about the whole of a group or thing. EG *It would be embarrassing to everybody, foreign statesmen and all... It swallowed the bird whole, head and all.* PHR : USED AS AN A **15.3** in British English, to emphasize your agreement with what has just been said; an informal use. EG *'It's very good.'–'It is and all.'* PHR = too

16 **At all** is used to give emphasis in negative clauses, in clauses with words like 'any', 'anyone', or 'anything', in clauses with 'if' or 'whether', and in some kinds of questions. EG *We didn't go there at all... We've very little in those fields at all... I was ready to go anywhere at all... The meal would have been extremely late, if indeed it appeared at all... Haven't you got any at all?* PHR : USED AS AN A

17 If you say that a particular quality or thing **is all**, you are saying that it is very important. EG *Secrecy was all.* PHR : VB INFLECTS

18 **For all** is used **18.1** in opinions or statements in order to say that a particular fact does not affect or contradict them, although you are aware that it appears to do so. EG *It's pretty hard on such a sensitive girl, but for all her sensitivity, she's extremely tough.... For all their differences among themselves, they reached some kind of consensus, some common philosophy of life.* PHR : USED AS ADV SEN = despite **18.2** in expressions such as 'for all I know', 'for all we had heard', and 'for all he cares', when you want to emphasize that the possibility that you have just mentioned does not really matter. EG *It might have been tomato soup for all we knew... I might as well have been down in the blackest pit, chained to a post, for all the difference the seasons meant to me.* PHR : USED AS ADV SEN

19 If you **give** your **all**, you make the maximum effort possible. EG *He played fair, he gave his all.* PHR : VB INFLECTS

20 **In all** means in total. EG *There were twenty-two in all.* PHR : USED AS AN A

21 **Of all** is used to emphasize the words 'first' or 'last', or a superlative adjective or adverb. EG *This view is best of all towards the close of the day... I asked them first of all if they were Welsh.* PHR : SUPERL/ *first/last* + PHR

22 Expressions such as **of all things, of all people,** and **of all places** are used to suggest that a particular thing, person, or place seems surprising or unlikely. EG *Why should they, of all people, believe that this is the right thing to do?... They were arguing about the Emperor, of all things... She went to live in Naples of all places.* PHR : USED AS AN A, USU NG + PHR ⇑ surprisingly

23 Expressions such as **of all the cheek** or **of all the luck** are used to express anger, impatience, envy, etc at what someone else has said or done. EG *Of all the nerve!... Of all the dirty tricks!* CONVENTION

24 **One and all** means everyone present or everyone in a particular group. EG *Thank you, one and all.* PHR : USED AS S/O

25 You can say **that's all** at the end of a sentence when you are explaining, justifying, or correcting something and want to emphasize that nothing more happens or is the case. EG *'Why are you so worked up about it?'–'I'm not. I'm just excited, that's all...' The wind blew the door open. I had to close it, that's all.* PHR : USED AS ADV SEN

26 You use expressions such as **that's all I want** or **it was all I needed** in order to emphasize that you definitely did not want a particular thing to happen, and to express annoyance or impatience. EG *That's all I need!... A letter like that was all he wanted.* PHR : VBS INFLECT

27 The word **all** is used in the following expressions, which are explained at other places in this dictionary. ● **all along**: see **along**. ● **all the best**: see **best**. ● **all for**: see **for**. ● **on all fours**: see **four**. ● **free for all**: see **free**. ● **all go**: see **go**. ● **till all hours**: see **hour**. ● **all kinds**: see **kind**. ● **all manner of**: see **manner**. ● **not at all**: see **not**. ● **all or nothing**: see **nothing**. ● **all at once**: see **once**. ● **once and for all**: see **once**. ● **all over**: see **over**. ● **be someone all over**: see **over**. ● **be all over** someone: see **over**. ● **all over** somewhere: see **over**. ● **all the same**: see **same**. ● **have seen it all**: see **see**. ● **all sorts**: see **sort**. ● **all and sundry**: see **sundry**. ● **not all there**: see **there**. ● **in all things**: see **thing**. ● **at all times**: see **time**. ● **for all time**: see **time**. ● **of all time**: see **time**. ● **all told**: see **told**. ● **all too**: see **too**. ● **all the way**: see **way**. ● See also **be-all and end-all, overall.**

all- is 1 added to nouns or adjectives in order to form adjectives which describe something as consisting only of the thing mentioned or as having only the quality indicated. EG *...all wool jumpers... ...the all-white South African Cricket Association... ...new all-electronic digital exchanges.* COMB : FORMS ADJ CLASSIFS **2** added to present participles or adjectives in order to form adjectives which describe something as including or affecting everything or everyone. EG *...the belief that Christ was divine and all-knowing... ...his all-encompassing love and compassion... ...the all-pervading stench... ...an all-pervasive climate of gloom.* COMB : FORMS ADJ CLASSIFS **3** added to nouns in order to form adjectives which describe something as being suitable for or including all types of a particular thing. EG *...an all-weather football pitch... ...all-party support for the cause.* COMB : FORMS ADJ CLASSIFS

Allah /ælə/ is the name of God in Islam. N PROPER

allay /ə3leɪ/, **allays, allaying, allayed.** If someone or something **allays** an emotion, especially fear, they cause it to be felt less strongly. EG *His efforts to allay her fears met with little success.* V+O ⇑ reduce = calm

all clear. The **all clear** is 1 a signal or announcement that indicates that a dangerous situation has ended, for example an air raid or explosion. EG *The all clear sounded... 'All clear!'* N SING : *the*+N, ALSO CONVENTION **2** an indication that you have permission to proceed with a plan. EG *As soon as we've got the all clear, I'll order the trucks.* N SING : *the*+N = go-ahead

all-comers refers to people, especially people taking part in a contest, regardless of their age, qualifications, experience, etc. EG *The champion was relaxing after an afternoon beating all-comers.* N PLURAL

allegation /ælɪ2geɪʃə0n/, **allegations.** An **allegation** is a statement, which may or may not be true, that someone has done something wrong. EG *...allegations of improper business dealings... They quoted allegations that several children died after crops were sprayed with this chemical.* N COUNT = claim

allege /ə3lɛdʒ/, **alleges, alleging, alleged.** If you **allege** that something is true, you say it but do not prove it. EG *Nearly 1,000 public officials were alleged to be members of an illegal secret society... An informer alleged that Samuel was a spy.* V+O/REPORT-CL : IF + *to*-INF THEN PASS ⇑ state = claim, reckon

alleged /ə3lɛdʒd/. If you refer to a fact as an **alleged** fact, you mean that there is no proof that it is true, and people may therefore doubt whether it is really true. EG *...alleged police brutality.* ◊ **allegedly.** EG *...the crimes he had allegedly committed.* ADJ CLASSIF : ATTRIB = supposed ◊ ADV = supposedly

allegiance /ə3liːdʒəns/, **allegiances.** A person or group's **allegiance** is their support for and loyalty to a particular group, person, or belief. EG *How can we win the allegiance of the masses?... You owe absolute allegiance to him... ...their traditional allegiances.* N UNCOUNT/ COUNT : IF + PREP THEN *to*

allegorical /ælɪ2gɒrɪkə0l/. An **allegorical** story, painting, etc uses allegory. EG *...allegorical poetry.* ADJ CLASSIF ⇑ symbolic

allegory /ælɪ2gə0ri1/, **allegories.** An **allegory** is a story, poem, picture, etc in which the characters and events are symbols of something else. Allegories usually make some moral, religious, or political point. EG *It should be read as an allegory.* N COUNT/ UNCOUNT = parable

alleluia /ælɪluːjə/. See **hallelujah**.

all-embracing. Something that is **all-embracing** includes or affects everyone or everything. EG *Political control was equally all-embracing and bureaucratic.* ADJ CLASSIF

allergic /ə3lɜːdʒɪk/. If you are **allergic** to something, 1 you become ill or develop a rash when you eat it or come into contact with it. EG *Are you allergic to dogs?* ▸ used of the reaction or physical sign of it. EG *It's a slight allergic rash... ...an allergic reaction to many of the things we eat.* ADJ CLASSIF : PRED + *to* ▸ ADJ CLASSIF : ATTRIB **2** in informal English, you ADJ QUALIT :

dislike it very strongly and try to avoid it. EG *I happen to be allergic to Europe.* PRED+*to* = averse

allergy /ælədʒiˈ/, **allergies**. An **allergy** is 1 the condition of becoming ill when you eat or come into contact with a particular substance which does not normally make people ill. EG *He had an allergy to milk for many years... Wheat causes allergy more often than other cereals.* N COUNT/UNCOUNT : IF+PREP THEN *to* 2 in informal English, a strong dislike of something. EG *...an allergy to third-rate music.* N COUNT+*to* = aversion

alleviate /əˈliːvieɪt/, **alleviates, alleviating, alleviated**. When you **alleviate** pain, suffering, or an unpleasant condition, you make it less intense or severe. EG *...minorities whose suffering cannot be alleviated in the present social systems... We want to help alleviate the national food shortage.* V+O ⇑ reduce = ease ≠ aggravate
◇ **alleviation** /əˈliːvieɪʃəⁿn/. EG *The organization is applying itself to the alleviation of the symptoms of industrial decline.* ◇ N UNCOUNT : IF+PREP THEN *of*

alley /ælɪˈ/, **alleys**. An **alley** is 1 a narrow passage or street with buildings or walls on both sides. EG *Davies' house was down a long narrow alley.* N COUNT = alleyway 2 a path in a park or garden, especially a path with trees or shrubs on both sides. EG *...a wide alley sheltered by plane trees.* ● See also **blind alley, bowling alley.** N COUNT = walk

alley cat, alley cats. An **alley cat** is a cat that lives in the streets of a town, is rather fierce, and is usually one not owned by anyone. N COUNT = stray

alleyway /ælɪweɪ/, **alleyways**. An **alleyway** is a narrow passage or street with buildings or walls on both sides. N COUNT = alley

alliance /əlaɪəns/, **alliances**. 1 An **alliance** is 1.1 a group of countries or political parties who are formally united and working together because they have similar aims. EG *...the SDP Liberal Alliance... ...the alliance of Labour Marxists and Communists.* N COUNT
1.2 a relationship or connection between two or more people or things. EG *This pleasant alliance between Mrs Bixby and the Colonel continued.* N COUNT = friendship
2 If two or more countries, political parties, or groups of people have an **alliance**, or are in **alliance** with each other, they are working together for the same purposes. EG *He took us into alliance with the French Socialist Party... The students tried to forge an alliance between themselves and the workers.* N COUNT, OR *in/into*+N : IF+PREP THEN *with/between* ⇑ partnership

allied /ælaɪd/. 1 **Allied** countries, forces, political parties, etc are united by a political or military agreement. EG *Other allied leaders have not stated their views with equal force.* ▸ used of actions. EG *Allied artillery fire caused heavy losses.* ADJ CLASSIF : USU ATTRIB, IF+PRED THEN *to*
2 The **Allied** forces were the armed forces of the countries that fought against Germany and Japan in World War Two. ADJ CLASSIF : ATTRIB
3 **Allied** describes industries, skills, feelings, etc that are related to other industries, skills, or feelings because they have particular qualities or characteristics in common. EG *The aircraft and allied industries were nationalized.* ADJ CLASSIF : USU ATTRIB ⇑ like = connected
4 See also **ally**.

alligator /ælɪgeɪtə/, **alligators**. An **alligator** is a large animal similar to a crocodile but with shorter jaws. Alligators live in lakes and rivers in America and China. ▸ used of the animal's skin. EG *...an alligator handbag.* N COUNT ⇑ reptile ▸ N UNCOUNT ⇑ leather

alliteration /əlɪtəreɪʃən/ is the use in speech or writing of several words close together which all begin with the same letter or sound; a technical term. EG *His prose was full of alliteration.* N UNCOUNT

allocate /æləˈkeɪt/, **allocates, allocating, allocated**. If you **allocate** something to a particular person or for a particular purpose, you decide that it should be given to them or used for that purpose. EG *They have some influence on the way resources are allocated... Government doctors would be allocated to some villages.* V+O, V+O+O, OR V+O+A *(to)* = assign

allocation /æləˈkeɪʃəⁿn/, **allocations**. 1 An **allocation** is an amount of something, especially money, that will be given to a particular person or used for a particular purpose. EG *...the allocation for nursery education... They would have to do all this within the allocations made to them.* N COUNT
2 The **allocation** of something is the decision that it should be given to a particular person or saved for them. EG *...the allocation of responsibilities.* N UNCOUNT : IF+PREP THEN *of/to* = designation

allot /əˈlɒt/, **allots, allotting, allotted**. If you **allot** something to someone or for a particular purpose, you give it to them or save it for them, or keep it for that purpose. EG *She would be content to sleep in any corner allotted to her... All seats in the Public Gallery are allotted in advance.* ◇ **allotted**. EG *...at the end of the allotted span of their lives.* V+O, V+O+O, OR V+O+A *(to)* ⇑ decide = allocate ◇ ADJ CLASSIF : ATTRIB

allotment /əˈlɒtməˀnt/, **allotments**. 1 In Britain, an **allotment** is a small area of land in a town or city which a person rents to grow vegetables on. There are usually several allotments together on an area of land. EG *Start digging your allotment in early spring.* N COUNT = plot
2 An **allotment** of something is a share or amount of it that is given to someone or saved for them. EG *We have a limited allotment of free holidays.* N SING WITH DET +*of* = allocation

all-out. You use **all-out** to describe aggressive actions that are carried out in a very energetic and determined way, using all the resources available. EG *...an all-out attack on trade unions... ...all-out opposition to the invasion of Europe.* ADJ CLASSIF : ATTRIB ⇑ total

allow /əlaʊ/, **allows, allowing, allowed**. 1 If you **allow** someone to do something, especially someone you have authority over, you let them do it and do not try to stop them. EG *After some hesitation, he agreed to allow me to take the course... You're not allowed to use calculators in examinations... Henry doesn't allow smoking in his office.* V+O+*to*-INF, OR V+O/-ING = permit ≠ forbid
2 If you say **'allow me'**, you are politely offering to do something for someone, or are politely introducing something you want to say. EG *Mr Smith jumped up and said, 'Allow me'... Please allow me to introduce myself.* CONVENTION, OR PHR+*to*-INF = permit me
3 If you **allow** something to happen or if you **allow** yourself to be affected by something, especially something unpleasant or dangerous, you let it happen or you let yourself be affected by it, even though you could control or prevent it. EG *The further this process is allowed to go, the more difficult it will be to reverse it... He did not allow himself to be too upset by the news.* V+O (NG/REFL) +*to*-INF = permit ≠ prevent
4 If something **allows** you to do something or **allows** something to happen, it gives the ability or opportunity for you to do it or for it to happen. EG *The creatures had warm blood, which allowed them to be active at night... Roads and railways allowed the world market to extend.* V+O+*to*-INF ⇑ help = enable ≠ prevent
5 If you **allow** someone something, especially something special or important, you let them have or do it. EG *Sometimes, we were allowed a special treat... Mrs Pennington allowed herself small indulgences.* V+O (NG/REFL) +O ⇑ give = afford ≠ deny
6 If you **allow** someone a particular amount of something, you let them have that amount and no more. EG *You're allowed a small case as hand luggage... She allowed herself a brief moment of regret... The bus stopped in Washington, allowing time for sightseeing.* V+O (NG/REFL) +O ⇑ permit
7 If you **allow** a particular period of time or amount of something, you set aside that period of time or get that amount for a particular purpose. EG *How long did you allow yourself?... Allow 4 metres.* V+O, OR V+O (NG/REFL)+O ⇑ permit
8 If you **allow** someone to be a member of a particular organization or **allow** them to be in a particular place, you let them belong to it or go there or stay there. EG *The union would not allow women members... No one is allowed here after dark.* V+O : USU+A ⇑ permit ≠ bar, exclude
9 If you **allow** that something is true, you admit or agree that it is true. EG *He allowed that even world leaders could make mistakes.* V+REPORT-CL = acknowledge
allow for. If you **allow for** problems, delays, extra expenses, etc, you include some extra time or money in your planning so that you will be able to deal with the problems, expenses, etc when they occur. EG *If you are self-employed, allow for tax and national insurance.* PHRASAL VB : V+PREP ⇑ accommodate

allowable /əlaʊəbəˀl/. 1 Expenses, costs, etc that are **allowable** are deducted from your income before the amount of tax you must pay is calculated; a technical term in taxation. EG *Losses on shares are now allowable against personal income tax.* ADJ CLASSIF
2 If you decide that something is **allowable**, you let it exist or happen without trying to change it or stop it. EG *...allowable departures from the norms of behaviour.* ADJ CLASSIF = acceptable

allowance /əlaʊəns/, **allowances**. 1 A particular kind of **allowance** is money that is given regularly to someone, usually by the government, in order to help them pay for the things that they need in a particular situation. EG *...a maternity allowance... They were receiving a fuel allowance.* N COUNT+SUPP = grant
2 An **allowance** is money that is given regularly to N COUNT

someone, especially a child, for them to spend. EG *Some parents don't give their children a proper allowance.*

3 If you **make allowances** for someone, you let them behave in a way which you would not normally approve of, or deal with them less severely, because they have special problems or difficulties. EG *We must make allowances for her. Etta is an unhappy woman.* — PHR : VB INFLECTS ⇑ excuse

4 If you **make allowances** for something, you take it into account in your plans or actions. EG *They make no allowances for a child's age... ...a method of teaching that makes full allowance for individual differences.* — PHR : VB INFLECTS ⇑ accommodate = allow

alloy /ælɔɪ/, **alloys**. An **alloy** is a metal that is made by mixing two or more types of metal together. EG *...an alloy of copper and tin.* — N MASS : IF + PREP THEN *of*

all-powerful. 1 Someone who is **all-powerful** has control over everyone or everything in a particular place. EG *...an all-powerful king.* — ADJ CLASSIF ⇑ powerful = omnipotent

2 Someone or something that is **all-powerful** has more influence than anyone or anything else. EG *Money is considered to be all-powerful... The unions are all-powerful.* — ADJ CLASSIF ⇑ influential = omnipotent

all right; also spelled **alright**. 1 If you say a particular person, thing, situation, etc is **all right**, you are indicating that you find it satisfactory or acceptable. Depending on the tone of voice used, 'all right' can indicate quite a range of meaning from very satisfactory to a clear lack of interest or enthusiasm. EG *'Do you like the champagne?'- 'It's all right'... Is everything all right, sir?.. That's all right by me.* — ADJ CLASSIF : PRED = okay

2 If you say that something happened or went **all right**, you mean that it happened in a satisfactory or acceptable manner. EG *I got him up all right, but overbalanced in the process... He's getting on all right, or was at Christmas.* — ADV AFTER VB = okay

3 If you say that something is true **all right** or something will happen **all right**, you mean that there is absolutely no doubt that it is true or that it will happen. EG *You'll get the money back all right... While it was a promise all right, it was not a promise given on paper.* — PHR : USED AS ADV SEN ⇑ definitely = for sure

4 If someone or something is **all right**, they are well or safe. EG *Someone should see if she's all right... The boat will be alright overnight.* — ADJ CLASSIF : PRED = okay

5 You say **'all right'** to an arrangement that someone is suggesting to say that you agree to it. EG *'Can you help?'-'All right. What do you want me to do?'* — CONVENTION = okay

6 You say **'all right'** in the middle of an argument or discussion as a way of stopping people from disagreeing with you, especially by showing that you know what they are going to say or that you accept their point of view. EG *I'm talking about written work, but, all right, it could be oral work... 'What the hell would you know about it?'-'All right, all right, sorry I spoke.'* — PHR : USED AS ADV SEN ⇑ yes = okay

7 If you say **'all right?'** after you have given an instruction or an explanation to someone, you are checking that they have understood and accepted what you said. EG *If you begin to feel dizzy again put your head in your hands, all right?.* — PHR : USED AS ADV SEN = okay

8 If someone in a position of authority says **'all right'**, and suggests talking about or doing something else, they are marking the end of a particular activity or topic and indicating that it is time to start a new one. EG *Alright team, let's move on if we may to another question.* — PHR : USED AS ADV SEN = okay

9 You say **'all right'** before a statement or question to indicate that you are challenging or threatening someone. EG *All right, what's the joke?* — PHR : USED AS ADV SEN = okay, well

all-rounder, all-rounders. An **all-rounder** is someone who is good at a lot of different skills, academic subjects, sports, etc; a British expression. EG *He's the best all-rounder that we've had in years.* — N COUNT

allspice /ɔ:lspaɪs/ is a powder used as a spice in cooking, which is made from the berries of a tropical American tree. — N UNCOUNT = pimento

all-star. An **all-star** cast or performance is one which contains only famous or extremely good players or performers. — ADJ CLASSIF : ATTRIB = star-studded

all-time. If you say that something is the **all-time** best, at an **all-time** low, etc, you mean that it is the best, lowest, etc that there has ever been. EG *Prices are at an all-time high.* — ADV + ADJ, OR ADJ CLASSIF : ATTRIB

allude /ə³lj⁰u:d/, **alludes, alluding, alluded.** If you **allude** to something, you mention it in a very indirect way; a fairly formal word. EG *I've already alluded to the interest that has been shown.* — V + A *(to)* = refer

allure /ə³lj⁰ʊə/. The **allure** of a person, place, activity, etc is the pleasing or exciting quality of it that attracts people to it. EG *...the allure of foreign travel.* — N COUNT : USU SING, IF + PREP THEN *of* ⇑ attraction = fascination

alluring /ə³lj⁰ʊərɪŋ/. Someone or something that is **alluring** has a quality or appearance which makes them very attractive to people. EG *...an alluring, golden-haired, dark-eyed beauty.* — ADJ QUALIT

allusion /ə³lj⁰u:ʒə⁰n/, **allusions**. An **allusion** is a reference to a person, event, story, etc in which the person, event, story, etc is not mentioned specifically or in detail but is only indirectly referred to. EG *When there is any allusion to his size he becomes embarrassed... English literature is full of allusions to Latin and Greek authors.* — N UNCOUNT/COUNT : IF + PREP THEN *to*

alluvial /ə³lu:vɪəl/. **Alluvial** soils are soils which consist of earth and sand left behind on land which has been flooded or where a river once flowed. — ADJ CLASSIF ⇑ deposited

ally, allies, allying, allied. The word **ally** is pronounced /ælaɪ/ when it is a noun, and /ə³laɪ/ when it is a verb. 1 An **ally** is 1.1 a country that has a treaty or an agreement to help and support another country, especially during a war. EG *Some of the allies, notably France and Canada, were unhappy over this decision... ...our European allies.* — N COUNT = confederate ≠ enemy **1.2** a person who helps and supports you in what you are trying to do, especially when there are other people who oppose you. EG *She felt she wanted an ally so badly.* — N COUNT ⇑ helper = associate

2 If you **ally** yourself with another person, country, or organization, you support them and join with them, especially in order to oppose other people or countries. EG *...European countries who do not ally themselves with either of the super powers... She cannot be seen to ally herself with the children against the father.* — V + O (REFL) + A *(with)* = align, range

3 See also **allied**.

alma mater /ælmə mɑ:tə, meɪtə/. Your **alma mater** is the school or university which you went to; a formal expression. EG *She was wearing a sweat shirt emblazoned with the name of her alma mater.* — N SING : POSS + N ⇑ institution

almanac /ɔ:lmənæk/, **almanacs**. An **almanac** is 1 a book published every year which contains information about events connected with a particular subject or activity, and facts and figures about the activity; a rather old-fashioned word. EG *...Wisden's Almanac, the bible of cricket.* — N COUNT + SUPP = yearbook **2** a book that is published every year that contains information about the movements of the planets, the phases of the moon and the tides, and the dates of important anniversaries. — N COUNT = calendar

almighty /ɔ:lmaɪtɪ/. 1 If you describe God as **Almighty**, you are emphasizing that He has power over everything. EG *Almighty God appeared to Jacob in the land of Canaan.* ▸ used as a noun. EG *...the mercy of the Almighty.* — ADJ CLASSIF ⇑ powerful; ▸ N PROPER : *the* + N

2 **God Almighty** and **Christ Almighty** are sometimes used as swear words to express surprise, horror, or anger; an offensive use. — EXCLAM

3 An **almighty** row, problem, mistake, etc is a very great or serious one. EG *Make the most almighty fuss if there's an overdraft... It will be an almighty wrench when I leave.* — ADJ CLASSIF : ATTRIB = enormous

almond /ɑ:mənd/, **almonds**. An **almond** is a pale oval nut which you can eat or use in cooking. EG *...chocolate bars with almonds.* ▸ used also to refer to the tree on which these nuts grow. EG *The almonds were in bloom.* — N COUNT; ▸ ⇑ tree

almond paste is marzipan. — N UNCOUNT

almost /ɔ:lməʊst/ means very nearly, but not completely, totally, or exactly. **Almost** is used to qualify an adjective, adverb, noun group, verb, or conjunction. EG *I spent almost a month in China... In Oxford Street, you can buy almost anything... I had almost forgotten about the trip... Cats are in fact almost colour blind... The door opened almost before Brody had finished knocking... He's almost certainly been murdered.* — ADV = practically

alms /ɑ:mz/ are gifts of money, clothes, food, etc to poor people; an old-fashioned word. — N PLURAL = donation

almshouse /ɑ:mzhaʊs/, **almshouses**. An **almshouse** is a house which was built and run by a charity for poor or old people to live in who could not afford to pay rent. — N COUNT = poorhouse

aloft /əlɒft/ means up in the air or in a higher place or position. EG *He was suddenly jerked off his feet* — ADV AFTER VB/PREP *and borne aloft... He stood surveying his handiwork from aloft... She called aloft.*

alone /əlaʊn/. **1** When someone is **alone**, **1.1** they are not with any other people. EG *I wanted to be alone... Barbara spent most of her time alone in the flat... What are you doing out here all alone?* **1.2** they are not with a particular person or a friend, but are amongst people who they do not know. EG *She was going all alone to Paris to visit her daughter... I spent a few sessions alone in the library.* **1.3** they have no family or friends and they feel miserable. EG *I had never felt so alone and without hope in my life.*
ADJ CLASSIF : PRED = by yourself; ADJ CLASSIF : PRED ⇑ unaccompanied = by yourself; ADJ QUALIT : PRED ⇑ isolated = lonely, lost

2 If one person is **alone** with another person, or if two people are **alone**, they are together, without anyone else present. EG *I was alone with the attendant... We'd never spent such a long time alone together.*
ADJ CLASSIF : PRED = on your own

3 When someone does something **alone**, especially something which is difficult or against the law, they do it without help from other people. EG *I was left to bring up my two children alone... He acted alone in the shooting.* ● When someone **goes it alone**, they have opinions which differ from those of other people, or they do something without any help or support from other people; an informal expression. EG *He no longer aimed to 'go it alone' politically.*
ADV AFTER VB ⇑ unaided = by yourself; ● PHR : VB INFLECTS

4 If someone **alone** does or knows something, or if someone is **alone** in a particular situation, they are the only person who does or knows it, or who is in that situation. EG *Simon alone knew the truth... They are not alone in their belief.*
ADJ CLASSIF : PRED, OR ADV, NG + ADV

5 If someone or something **alone** is involved, or if something consists of one idea, feature, etc **alone**, no other people or things are involved. EG *Pride alone prevented her from giving up... Democracy does not consist in Parliament alone... We must have gained 100 members from this alone.*
ADJ AFTER N ⇑ only

6 If one fact or piece of evidence **alone** makes something clear, no further facts or evidence are necessary. EG *The headline alone made me know that she was involved.*
ADJ AFTER N ⇑ only = on its own

7 ● to **leave** someone or something **alone**: see **leave**. ● to **let** someone or something **alone**: see **let**. ● **let alone**: see **let**.

along /əlɒŋ/. **1** When someone or something moves or travels **along** something long and thin, for example a road or wire, they go forwards on it for some distance and follow where it leads. EG *He was driving his car along a lane in East Surrey... She led them along a carpeted corridor... The current passes along this wire here.*
PREP = down

2 Something that is situated or is happening **along** something long and thin, especially a road, river, or coastline, is situated or is happening continuously or at various places beside it from one end of it to the other. EG *There had been several patches of yellow marigolds along the path... ...the trees all along Bear Creek.*
PREP = down

3 When you look **along** something long and thin, you look down the length of it and towards one end. EG *They look along racks of bright clothes... She glanced along the corridor.*
PREP

4 A place, building, or room that is situated **along** a particular street or corridor is situated at some point on it or beside it. EG *...an old house along the Lanark Road... Room 64 was half way along on the right.*
PREP/ADV ⇑ on

5 If something is placed **along** a vertical surface, such as a wall, it is placed very close to it with the back or one of the longer sides next to it. EG *...a striped sofa along the wall.*
PREP ⇑ beside = against

6 When someone or something moves **along**, they move forward for a period of time, usually steadily and continuously. EG *I put my arm around him as we walked along... The soldiers trudged along behind the tanks.*
ADV AFTER VB

7 If something that is happening or being done is going **along** in a particular way, it is continuing to happen or progress in that way. EG *His divorce was dragging along, he said... It was going along nicely.*
ADV AFTER VB ⇑ on

8 If someone is a particular distance **along** in an activity or on a scale, they have progressed to that extent. EG *We're no further along in our research.*
ADV ⇑ on = forward

9 If someone or something is coming **along** or is sent **along**, they are coming or being sent to the place where you are. EG *Tell him to come along to Mr Gerran's room... I was originally sent along by an employment agency... The train won't be along for more than a half hour.*
ADV AFTER VB

10 If you take someone **along** when you go somewhere, you take them with you. EG *She always took her children along.*
ADV AFTER VB

11 If you have known something **all along** or if something has been happening **all along**, you have known it or it has been happening over a long period of time. EG *Perhaps they had been mistaken all along... ...a desire which has been there all along.*
PHR : USED AS AN A, WITH PAST PART = all the time

12 If you do something **along with** someone else or if something happens **along with** something else, you do it at the same time as them or the two things happen at the same time. EG *Along with thousands of others, he fled the country... The eggs were delivered from the farm along with the milk.*
PREP = together with

13 The word **along** is also used in the following expressions, which are explained at other places in this dictionary. ● **along the way**: see **way**. ● **along the lines of**: see **line**. ● **get along with you**: see **get along**. ● to **go along with** something: see **go along**.

alongside /əlɒŋsaɪd/. **1** If something is situated **alongside** something else or **alongside**, the two things are situated directly next to each other. EG *There was a butcher's shop alongside the theatre... A highway patrol car drew up alongside.*
PREP/ADV ⇑ beside

2 If several people, especially people doing different jobs, are working **alongside** other people or **alongside**, they are working in the same place and are cooperating with each other. EG *The idea is to get them working on simple things alongside other people.*
PREP/ADV = together with

3 When you talk about one system, attitude, philosophy, etc existing **alongside** another one, you are comparing or contrasting them, and considering whether they can exist together in harmony. EG *I cannot imagine two political systems less likely to live at peace alongside each other... 'Mariculture'–farming the ocean's food resources–will take its place alongside 'Agriculture.'*
PREP = beside

aloof /əluːf/. **1** Someone who is **aloof** likes to be alone and does not talk much to other people or take part in activities with them. EG *He was aloof, a loner... Guy became aloof and silent, gazing past Gertrude.* ◊ **aloofness**.
ADJ QUALIT ⇑ detached = distant; ◊ N UNCOUNT

2 If someone stays **aloof** from something, they do not become involved or concerned with it. EG *The Emperor kept aloof from all political parties.*
ADJ QUALIT : PRED, IF + PREP THEN *from* ⇑ distant

aloud /əlaʊd/. **1** When you say something **aloud** or read **aloud**, you speak so that other people can hear you, and do not just think the words in your mind. EG *She read aloud to us from the newspaper... In no previous war could men say aloud what was on their minds.*
ADV AFTER VB ⇑ audibly = out loud ≠ silently

2 When someone speaks or laughs **aloud**, they speak or laugh in a normal voice rather than quietly. EG *You must never speak aloud in theatres, I was told.*
ADV AFTER VB ≠ quietly

alpaca /ælpækə/ is a kind of wool which is used for making clothes. EG *...an alpaca cardigan.*
N UNCOUNT

alpha /ælfə/, **alphas**. **Alpha** is the first letter of the Greek alphabet, sometimes used as a mark or grade given for a student's work.
N COUNT/UNCOUNT

alphabet /ælfəbɛt/, **alphabets**. An **alphabet** is a set of letters arranged in a fixed order which are used for writing the words of a particular language or group of languages. EG *...a code in which we substituted z for a, y for b, and so on, throughout the alphabet.*
N COUNT : *the* + N IN SING

alphabetical /ælfəbɛtɪkəl/ means arranged according to the order of the letters in the alphabet. EG *...an alphabetical list... The names are not in alphabetical order.* ◊ **alphabetically**. EG *Books are catalogued alphabetically by author.*
ADJ CLASSIF : ATTRIB ⇑ ordered; ◊ ADV WITH VB ⇑ in order

alpine /ælpaɪn/, **alpines**. **1 Alpine** means existing in or relating to the high parts of mountains or mountainous regions. EG *...alpine meadows.*
ADJ CLASSIF : USU ATTRIB = mountain

2 An **alpine** is a flowering plant that grows high up on mountains and is sometimes grown in gardens. There are many types of alpine.
N COUNT

already /ɔːlrɛdi/. **1** If something has **already** happened or been done, **1.1** it has happened or been done earlier than was expected. EG *I'm half an hour behind already... By the time he got home, Julie was already in bed.* **1.2** it has happened or been done before the present time, so that it no longer needs to happen or be done. EG *I've already seen them... I've had tea already, thank you.*
ADV SEN; ADV SEN

2 When you say that a particular situation exists
ADV SEN

already, you mean that it exists now and you do not want it to become worse or greater in degree. EG *You've too many ideas in your head already... This thing is complicated enough already.*

alright /ɔːlraɪt/. See **all right**.

Alsatian /ælseɪʃəⁿn/, **Alsatians**. An **Alsatian** is a large, usually fierce dog that is often used to guard buildings or by the police to help them find criminals. N COUNT

also /ɔːlsəʊ/. 1 You use **also** when you are giving more information about a person or thing, or adding another fact which is relevant to what you have been talking about. EG *Tony Nuttall is Vice-Chancellor and also a Professor of English at Sussex... ...and we'll also be hearing about the work of Una Woodruff... ...also available in blue and green... They didn't only censor, they also helped out.* ADV ⇑ additionally

2 You often use **also** at the beginning of a sentence when you are about to say something else which supports the point you are making or is relevant. EG *I think it's also worth bearing in mind that he was under a lot of stress at the time... I thought it was the perfect answer. Also, Tony and I had never done an historical subject.* ADV SEN ⇑ additionally

3 You use **also** to say that the same quality, attitude, state, etc that applies to the person or thing you are talking about applies, or has applied, to someone or something else. EG *His first wife was also called Margaret... He was my favourite and, I suspected, John's also... If that light blows, then every other light on the circuit will also have gone.* ADV WITH VB, OR ADV : NG + ADV

4 You use **also** to link and contrast two different qualities, states, or actions when their association is unexpected. It is inserted before the second quality or action is mentioned. EG *She often made cheap jokes at their expense. Yet she could also be witty, very ladylike, and gracious... Knowledge, which is in many ways our blessing, is also our curse.* ADV WITH VB : USU AFTER CONJ *(but/yet)*

also-ran, also-rans. An **also-ran** is someone who has been or is likely to be unsuccessful in a contest because they do not have much skill or ability; an informal word. N COUNT ⇑ failure = loser ≠ winner

altar /ɒltə/, **altars**. 1 An **altar** is 1.1 a table in a Christian church on which the bread and wine used in the service of communion are blessed. EG *The vicar took a candlestick from the altar.* N COUNT : USU *the* + N, USU SING 1.2 a table in the temples of many religions on which gifts are offered to a god and on which religious sacrifices are made. EG *...the altar of Zeus.* N COUNT : USU *the* + N

2 If you sacrifice something, for example your pride or a plan, on a particular kind of **altar** you sacrifice it because of something which you think is much more important. EG *He had been prepared to sacrifice this company on the altar of his own political ambitions.* N SING WITH DET + SUPP

alter /ɒltə/, **alters, altering, altered**. When something **alters** or when you **alter** it, it changes in some way. EG *America must radically alter its traditional economic policy... This doesn't alter the fact that the problem has got to be dealt with... The weather could alter violently.* ◊ **altered**. EG *He's an altered man, particularly these last ten years.* V-ERG ⇑ change ◊ ADJ QUALIT ⇑ different = changed

alteration /ɒltəreɪʃəⁿn/, **alterations**. 1 An **alteration** is 1.1 a change in something. EG *It is not possible to make major alterations to existing arrangements... Did you see any alteration in his behaviour?* N COUNT : USU + SUPP

1.2 a change in the size or design of a building which already exists. EG *In a house as big as that, the alterations must have been a terrific price.* N COUNT

2 The **alteration** of something is the changing of it. EG *...the profound and long-term alteration of the earth's climate.* N UNCOUNT : USU + SUPP

altercation /ɒltəkeɪʃəⁿn/, **altercations**. An **altercation** is a noisy argument or disagreement; a formal word. EG *There was a slight altercation on the way up the stairs.* N COUNT ⇑ conflict = dispute

alter ego /ɒltər iːgəʊ/, **alter egos**. 1 Your **alter ego** is the other side of your personality from the one which people normally see. N COUNT : USU POSS + N

2 An **alter ego** is a very close and intimate friend. EG *I wanted a journalistic and political alter ego on the staff.* N COUNT = counterpart

alternate, alternates, alternating, alternated. The word **alternate** is pronounced /ɒltəneɪt/ when it is a verb, and /ɒ⁸ltɜːnət/ when it is an adjective.

1 When you **alternate** two things, **alternate** between two things, or when one thing **alternates** with another, you regularly do or use one thing and then the other, or two things regularly occur after each other. EG *The Third World suffers from an annual cycle of drought alternating with flood... They alternated between patronising us and totally ignoring us... I choose to alternate my fishing methods.* V OR V + A *(with)* : RECIP, OR V + A *(between)* ⇑ change ◊ **alternating**. EG *...alternating bands of white and dark hair.* ◊ ADJ CLASSIF ◊ **alternation** /ɒltəneɪʃəⁿn/. EG *...an alternation of right-wing and left-wing governments.* ◊ N UNCOUNT/COUNT : USU + SUPP

2 **Alternate** actions, processes, or states regularly occur after each other. EG *...the alternate contraction and relaxation of muscles.* ADJ CLASSIF : ATTRIB ◊ **alternately**. EG *Each piece of material has to be washed alternately in soft water and coconut oil.* ◊ ADV WITH VB = in turn

3 If something happens on, for example, **alternate** Mondays, it happens on one Monday, and then does not happen on the next one, and then happens on the one after it, and so on. Similarly, something can happen in **alternate** weeks, years, etc. EG *We saw each other on alternate Sunday nights.* ADJ CLASSIF : ATTRIB ⇑ second = every other

4 An **alternate** plan, action, position, etc is different from the one you already have, or from another one, and can be done or used instead. EG *For rainy days make sure you have alternate plans... He also had a watchman on half a dozen alternate routes.* ADJ CLASSIF : ATTRIB ⇑ other = alternative

alternating current. An **alternating current** is an electric current that continually changes direction as it flows. N UNCOUNT ⇑ current

alternative /ɒ⁸ltɜːnətɪv/, **alternatives**. 1 An **alternative** is something that you can choose to have or do instead of something else. EG *Are there alternatives to prison?... The ministry will have no alternative but to raise our rates.* N COUNT : IF + PREP THEN *to* ⇑ choice = option

2 An **alternative** plan, action, position, etc is different from the one you already have, or from another one, and can be done or used instead. EG *But still people try to find alternative explanations... He couldn't block the deal unless alternative buyers existed.* ADJ CLASSIF : ATTRIB = other

3 **Alternative** forms of energy, technologies, lifestyles, etc approach a situation or problem in a completely different way from usual, especially in a simpler, more natural, or cheaper way. EG *...sources of alternative energy... ...street theatres and alternative newspapers.* ADJ CLASSIF : ATTRIB ≠ conventional

alternatively /ɒ⁸ltɜːnətɪvli¹/. You use **alternatively** to introduce a statement in which you mention something different from what has just been mentioned. EG *Alternatively, you can use household bleach... We can arrange for a car to be delivered or, alternatively, you may book through our London office.* ADV SEN = otherwise

alternator /ɒltəneɪtə/, **alternators**. An **alternator** is a device, used especially in a car, that creates an electrical current that changes direction as it flows. N COUNT

although /ɔːlðəʊ/. **Although** is used to introduce subordinate clauses. It introduces 1 a clause which contains a statement or comment that makes the main clause of the sentence seem surprising or unexpected. EG *Although he was late he stopped to buy a sandwich... Gretchen kept her coat on, although it was warm in the room.* CONJ SUBORD = though 2 a clause which gives some information that is relevant to the main clause and which modifies it because the statement in it is too strong. EG *Although I advise the children about money, I never actually pay their debts... Although you don't grease it for quite the same reasons, you should care for your car as you do your face... It was not for myself that I wanted the old piano, although I could play a little.* CONJ SUBORD = though 3 a clause, which often contains 'not', that modifies the main clause and corrects a wrong idea or impression that someone might get from it. EG *I have a lot of my grandfather's features, although I'm not so tall as he was... Parents of children under 14 would no longer have been fined, although they might have been required to pay compensation.* CONJ SUBORD ⇑ but = though

altimeter /æltɪ¹miːtə/, **altimeters**. An **altimeter** is an instrument in an aircraft that shows the height above the ground. N COUNT

altitude /æltɪtjuːd/, **altitudes**. The **altitude** of a place or of a position in the sky is its height above sea level. EG *The valley lies at an altitude of about 8,000 ft... ...an airliner flying at high altitude... The noise diminishes as we reach lower altitudes.* N UNCOUNT/COUNT

alto /æltəʊ/, **altos**. 1 An **alto** is 1.1 a woman who has a singing voice in the lowest female range of musical notes. EG *They are looking for an extra alto... Are you soprano or alto?* 1.2 a man who has a singing voice in the highest male range of musical notes. N COUNT/UNCOUNT ⇑ singer = contralto; N COUNT ⇑ singer

2 **Alto**, or the **alto** part, is a part, for example in an oratorio, for a singer with an alto voice. EG *She's singing alto.* N UNCOUNT

3 An **alto** musical instrument has a range of musical notes of medium pitch. EG *...an alto sax.* ADJ CLASSIF : ATTRIB

altogether /ɔ:ltəgɛðə/. 1 **Altogether** is used 1.1 to emphasize that something has stopped or has been done or finished completely. EG *The noise had stopped altogether... He drank more and more, and abandoned his work altogether.* 1.2 to emphasize a quality in someone or something, especially a quality which is different from that in someone or something else. EG *...an altogether different kind of support... But Asia was another matter altogether.* 1.3 to summarize a situation, opinion, argument, etc. EG *Altogether, they got on very well... Yes, it's quite a pleasant place altogether.* ADV AFTER VB ⇑ entirely = completely; ADV+ADJ = completely; ADV SEN = all in all

2 If you say that you do **not altogether** trust someone, believe someone, etc, you mean that you have very little trust or belief in them. EG *'You don't believe him?'–'No. Not altogether.'* PHR : USED AS AN A ≠ completely

3 If you say that something is **not altogether** true, **not altogether** satisfactory, etc, you mean that it is not completely true, satisfactory, etc. EG *Such methods are not altogether satisfactory.* PHR+ADJ ≠ completely

4 If several numbers, amounts, etc add up to a particular number or amount **altogether**, that number or amount is the total of them. EG *You will get more than £340 a week altogether... Altogether, he played in 44 Test matches.* ADV SEN ⇑ together = in all

5 When someone is **in the altogether**, they are not wearing any clothes; an informal expression. PHR = naked

altruism /æltru:ɪzə⁰m/ is concern for the happiness and welfare of other people rather than for your own. N UNCOUNT = unselfishness

altruistic /æltru:ɪstɪk/. If your behaviour or motives are **altruistic**, you show concern for the happiness and welfare of other people rather than for your own. EG *My invitation was not completely altruistic... Less altruistic motives predominated.* ▸ used of people. EG *He was no more altruistic than the other Senators.* ADJ QUALIT = unselfish ≠ self-centred

aluminium /æljə⁴mɪnɪəm/; also spelled **aluminum** /əlu:mɪnəm/ in American English. **Aluminium** is a light, silver-coloured metal which is used especially for making cooking equipment and aircraft parts. EG *...an aluminium frying pan.* N UNCOUNT

alumna /ə³lʌmnə/, **alumnae** /ə³lʌmni¹/. A woman who is an **alumna** of a school, college, or university used to be a student there; used in American English. N COUNT ⇑ graduate = old girl

alumnus /ə³lʌmnəs/, **alumni** /ə³lʌmnaɪ/. A man who is an **alumnus** of a school, college, or university used to be a student there; used in American English. N COUNT ⇑ graduate = old boy

always /ɔ:lwɪ³z/. 1 If you **always** do a particular thing or if you **always** do things in a particular way, you act in that way all the time or on every possible occasion. EG *Always use a fireguard in front of a fire... She always arrives half an hour early... In the old days we always used goose grease.* ADV WITH VB ⇑ ever ≠ never

2 If something is **always** the case, or has **always** been the case, it is the case all the time, or has been the case for as long as you can remember. EG *Things do not always go right... I had always been poor.* ADV WITH VB ≠ never

3 If you say that you will do something **always**, you mean that you will do it for all of the time in the future. EG *I shall always love you... I shall treasure it always.* ADV WITH VB ⇑ forever ≠ never

4 If you say that someone is **always** doing something, or that something is **always** happening, especially something which annoys you, you mean that they do it, or it happens, often and repeatedly. EG *You're always looking for faults... It's always raining.* ADV WITH VB (-ING) = forever

5 If you say that someone **always** did prefer something, or **always** did have a particular characteristic or habit, you mean that the preference, characteristic, or habit is very typical of them and is part of their nature. EG *He always did prefer redheads... You always were an idealist.* ADV WITH VB ⇑ typically

6 If you say that someone can **always** take a particular course of action, you mean that they can take this action if all other courses of action prove to be unsuccessful or undesirable. EG *You could always ask to see a copy of your aunt's will... Oh well, I can always come back later... 'How shall I get there?'–'There's always the bus.'* ADV : USU MODAL +ADV+VB = of course

am /æm/ is the first person singular of the present tense of **be**. In speech, it is often shortened to **'m**.

Am. is an abbreviation for **American**.

a.m. is used to refer to a particular time in the morning, between midnight and noon. EG *...from 9.30 a.m. to 12 noon... About 85 students were still in the hall at 2 a.m.* ADV : NUM+ADV ⇑ morning

amalgam /ə³mælgəm/, **amalgams**. An **amalgam** of two or more things is a mixture of them. EG *...a simple amalgam of previous doctrines.* N COUNT

amalgamate /ə³mælgəmeɪt/, **amalgamates, amalgamating, amalgamated**. When two or more organizations **amalgamate** with each other, they join together and become one large organization. EG *...two unions which had amalgamated years before... ...the Variety Artistes Federation, which has since amalgamated with Equity.* ◇ **amalgamation** /ə³mælgəmeɪʃə⁰n/, **amalgamations**. EG *...the amalgamation of several large businesses... They have been rationalizing their structure through amalgamations.* V OR V+A (with) : RECIP; ◇ N UNCOUNT/COUNT = merging

amanuensis /ə³mænjuɛnsɪs/, **amanuenses** /ə³mænjuɛnsi:s/. An **amanuensis** is someone whose job is to write down what another person says, for example when that person is writing a book; a formal word. EG *They had to find him an amanuensis.* N COUNT ⇑ secretary

amass /əmæs/, **amasses, amassing, amassed**. When you **amass** something, especially wealth or information, you get more and more of it over a period of time until you have a lot of it. EG *As soon as they had amassed enough money they decided to travel round the world... He carefully amassed evidence to support his case.* V+O ⇑ collect = accumulate

amateur /æmətjʰʊ⁰ə, -tʃə/, **amateurs**. 1 An **amateur** is someone who does something such as acting or playing a sport as a hobby and not as a job. EG *It's a business for professionals not amateurs... ...a very good amateur viola player.* N COUNT ≠ professional

2 **Amateur** can also mean the same as amateurish. EG *It was a very amateur performance.* ADJ QUALIT

amateurish /æmətjʰʊ⁰ərɪʃ/. If you describe something as **amateurish**, you mean that it is not very skilfully made or done; used showing disapproval. EG *Their publications were amateurish and inadequately researched.* ADJ QUALIT ≠ professional

amateurism /æmətjʰʊ⁰ərɪzə⁰m/ is the belief that people should take part in sports and other activities as a hobby, for pleasure, rather than as a job, for money. EG *They still seem to believe in some form of British amateurism.* N UNCOUNT ≠ professionalism

amatory /æmətə⁰ri¹/. An **amatory** poem, gesture, intention, etc expresses romantic or sexual love; a literary word. ADJ CLASSIF ⇑ loving

amaze /əmeɪz/, **amazes, amazing, amazed**. If something **amazes** you, it surprises you so much that you find it almost impossible to believe it. EG *She was amazed that I was only twenty... I was amazed at the beauty of the people... He was amazed by the response... It amazed them to learn that things were so expensive.* ◇ **amazed**. EG *I saw her amazed look.* V+O ⇑ surprise = astound; ◇ ADJ QUALIT

amazement /əmeɪzmə²nt/ is what you feel when something surprises you so much that you find it almost impossible to believe it. EG *Her eyes were wide with amazement... Ralph stood up in amazement... To my amazement, he burst out laughing.* N UNCOUNT ⇑ surprise = astonishment

amazing /əmeɪzɪŋ/. If you describe something as **amazing**, you mean that it causes you to feel great surprise or wonder and admiration. EG *New York is an amazing city... It's amazing how useful they are... They do an amazing amount of work... Her general knowledge is amazing.* ◇ **amazingly**. EG *Our holiday was amazingly cheap.* ADJ QUALIT ⇑ wonderful = incredible; ◇ ADV+ADJ/ADV

ambassador /æmbæsədə/, **ambassadors**. An **ambassador** is an important official who is sent by his or her government to live in a foreign country and to represent his or her own country's interests there. EG *He was the British Ambassador to Turkey during the Second World War... ...our ambassador in Berlin.* N COUNT : ALSO IN TITLES ⇑ diplomat

ambassadorial /æmbæsədɔ:ri¹əl/. **Ambassadorial** means belonging or relating to an ambassador. EG *...the ambassadorial residence.* ADJ CLASSIF : ATTRIB ⇑ official

amber /æmbə/. 1 **Amber** is a hard yellowish-brown substance that is used for making jewellery. EG *...a necklace of silver, glass, and amber.* — N UNCOUNT ⇑ resin

2 Something that is **amber** is yellowish-brown or orange. EG *...abundant clusters of amber berries... She rolled her amber brown eyes at me.* ▸ used as a noun. EG *The lights constantly switch from red to amber, then green.* — ADJ COLOUR; ▸ N UNCOUNT

ambiance /æmbi¹əns/. See **ambience**.

ambidextrous /æmbɪdekstrəs/. Someone who is **ambidextrous** can use their right and left hand equally skilfully. EG *Some babies stay ambidextrous for the first year or so.* — ADJ CLASSIF

ambience /æmbi¹əns/; also spelled **ambiance**. The **ambience** of a place is a particular character or quality which it seems to have; a literary word. EG *It has a gentleness, an ambience, a wistful elegance... ...the 'liberal' ambience of the average university.* — N SING WITH DET ⇑ spirit = atmosphere

ambient /æmbi¹ə²nt/. The **ambient** temperature is the temperature of the air above the ground in a particular place; a technical word. EG *Caves maintain moderate ambient temperatures.* — ADJ CLASSIF

ambiguity /æmbɪgjuːɪti¹/ **ambiguities**. 1 **Ambiguity** is the state or condition of being unclear or confusing, or of being able to be understood in more than one way. EG *To remove any ambiguity we have to include other information.* — N UNCOUNT ⇑ uncertainty ≠ clarity

2 An **ambiguity** is a word or statement which is not clear and which can be understood in more than one way. EG *They were full of errors, ambiguities, and omissions.* — N COUNT

3 An **ambiguity** in a situation or in someone's character means that it contains several different qualities, attitudes, etc which do not fit well together. EG *...a region of moral ambiguity... ...the ambiguity inherent in the human condition... There were severe ambiguities and dark places in their relationship.* — N UNCOUNT/COUNT = contradiction

ambiguous /æmbɪgju⁴əs/. Something that is **ambiguous** 1 is unclear or confusing because it can be understood in more than one way. EG *She gave an ambiguous nod... There was nothing ambiguous in the message thumped out in his newspaper articles.* — ADJ QUALIT ⇑ vague ≠ obvious

◊ **ambiguously**. EG *The announcement that the strike was over was ambiguously worded.* — ◊ ADV

2 contains several different ideas, attitudes, etc which cause difficulty because they do not fit well together. EG *It was hard to live in this ambiguous social position.* — ADJ QUALIT ⇑ difficult = uncertain

ambit /æmbɪt/. The **ambit** of something is its range or extent; a formal word. EG *This point, however, hardly falls within the ambit of a book about nutrition... ...a form of status display that occurs right outside the ambit of ordinary social events.* — N SING : *the*+N+*of* = scope

ambition /æmbɪʃə⁰n/, **ambitions**. 1 If you have an **ambition** to be something or do something, you want very much to be it or do it. EG *Her lifelong ambition was to be a teacher... I think that of all my ambitions, the greatest is to make good wine.* — N COUNT ⇑ aim = dream

2 **Ambition** is the desire to be successful, powerful, rich, or famous; sometimes used showing disapproval. EG *...men of enterprise, energy, and ambition... Knowledge of inequality has stimulated envy, ambition and greed.* — N UNCOUNT

3 If someone has **ambitions** of a particular kind, they want to be successful or famous in a particular activity. EG *Senator Hearst's son was nursing political ambitions of his own.* — N PLURAL ⇑ desires = aspirations

ambitious /æmbɪʃəs/. 1 Someone who is **ambitious** has a strong desire to be successful, powerful, rich, or famous; sometimes used showing disapproval. EG *...a student who has always seemed ambitious and diligent... ...the Vice-President's ambitious wife.* — ADJ QUALIT ⇑ aspiring ≠ unambitious

◊ **ambitiously**. — ◊ ADV

2 An **ambitious** idea, programme, plan, etc is on a large scale and needs a lot of hard work and skill for it to be achieved or carried out successfully. EG *She then attempted something more ambitious, a novel of 120,000 words.* — ADJ QUALIT ⇑ difficult = adventurous

ambivalence /æmbɪvələ²ns/. 1 If you are in a state of **ambivalence** about something or if you show **ambivalence** towards it, you are not sure whether you want it or not, or whether you approve of it or not. EG *She was in a state of ambivalence about having children... ...showing ambivalence to traditional Christian ideas.* — N UNCOUNT ⇑ indecision = uncertainty

2 If there is **ambivalence** in a document, report, etc, it contains attitudes or ideas which seem to be opposite to each other and which do not fit well together. EG *...the ambivalence of its election programmes... The only possible explanation for this is ambivalence at the highest level.* — N UNCOUNT = ambiguity

ambivalent /æmbɪvələnt/. Someone who is **ambivalent** does not know or does not make it clear whether they want or do not want something, or whether they approve of it or do not approve of it. EG *Americans are ambivalent about the whole business of royalty.* ▸ used of a person's attitude or feelings. EG *I must have acquired an ambivalent attitude towards women from her.* — ADJ QUALIT ⇑ uncertain = undecided ≠ decided

amble /æmbə⁰l/, **ambles, ambling, ambled**. 1 When you **amble**, you walk slowly and in a relaxed manner. EG *'Why, sure,' he said, ambling off down the path... I just ambled home through the village.* — V : USU+A = stroll

2 An **amble** is a slow and relaxed pace and style of walking. EG *He slowed down to his usual steady amble.* — N SING WITH DET

ambulance /æmbjə⁴ləns/, **ambulances**. An **ambulance** is a special vehicle that is used for taking people to and from hospital. EG *She sent someone to ring for an ambulance.* — N COUNT

ambulanceman /æmbjə⁴lənsmə³n/, **ambulancemen**. An **ambulanceman** is someone whose job is to drive an ambulance or take care of sick people in an ambulance until they get to hospital. — N COUNT

ambush /æmbʊʃ/, **ambushes, ambushing, ambushed**. 1 If people, usually soldiers, **ambush** another group of people, they attack them after hiding and waiting for them. EG *Weyler's troops successfully ambushed a rebel force... An entire platoon was ambushed during a patrol and wiped out.* — V+O = waylay

2 An **ambush** is 2.1 an attack on someone from a place where you have been hiding and waiting for them. EG *A whole battalion got caught in an ambush sprung from behind.* — N COUNT = trap

2.2 a place where people are waiting and hiding in order to attack other people. EG *The convoy was no more than 800 metres from the ambush.* — N COUNT

3 **Ambush** is the act of hiding and waiting for someone and then attacking them. EG *They had been lying in ambush in the cowshed.* — N UNCOUNT

ameba /əmiːbə/. See **amoeba**.

ameliorate /əmiːljəreɪt/, **ameliorates, ameliorating, ameliorated**. When someone or something **ameliorates** a situation, they make it better or easier in some way; a formal word. EG *They advocated increased intervention in the economy to ameliorate the worse effects of capitalism.* — V+O = improve, alleviate

◊ **amelioration** /əmiːljəreɪʃən/. EG *...a further amelioration in her father's condition.* — ◊ N UNCOUNT+SUPP

amen /eɪmen, ɑːmen/. 1 **Amen** is said or sung at the end of a prayer by the person saying the prayer and by the people who are listening in order to express their approval and agreement. EG *This we ask in the name of Thy Son Jesus Christ, Amen.* — CONVENTION

2 If you say **amen** to something, you are showing your approval of or agreement with what someone else has said. EG *'There's an awful lot of unkindness around.'–'Amen to that!'* — PHR/CONVENTION = hear hear

amenable /ə³miːnəbə⁰l/. If you are **amenable** to something, you are willing to do it, for example because someone else has suggested it. EG *The peasants were, on the whole, much less amenable... He was amenable to some of the things that we were trying to do.* — ADJ QUALIT : IF+PREP, THEN *to* ⇑ reasonable

amend /ə³mend/, **amends, amending, amended**. 1 If you **amend** something, for example a law or a text, you change the wording of it in order to correct it or improve it. EG *...the Child-minders Act of 1948, amended in 1968... 'Well, no,' she said, amending her last statement... They all participate in amending or adding to the text.* — V+O = revise

2 If you **make amends** for a mistake or for something harmful that you have done, you do something to make things better, or behave in a way which shows that you are sorry. EG *It made him wish to make amends for his former unkindness to the boy.* — PHR : VB INFLECTS ⇑ apologize = atone

amendment /ə³mendmə³nt/, **amendments**. 1 An **amendment** is 1.1 a passage that is added to a law or rule in order to change and improve it. EG *The councillors have tabled an amendment to the main motion for debate... Her arrest violated the First Amendment to the Constitution.* — N COUNT ⇑ addition

1.2 an improvement — N COUNT

or correction of something, especially a piece of writing. EG *She made a few amendments to the letter before signing it.*

2 Amendment is the act or process of changing and improving something, for example a particular law or rule, or your behaviour. EG *...the promise of reform and amendment.* N UNCOUNT ⇑ change = improvement

amenity /əmiːnɪti¹/, **amenities**. An **amenity** is something such as a shopping centre, restaurant, or sports facility that has been provided for people's convenience, comfort, or enjoyment. EG *When you are young you want the amenities of the town... ...the Astoria and the Holiday Inn, both first class hotels with every amenity.* N COUNT ⇑ provision

American /əmerɪkən/, **Americans**. **1** An **American** person or thing is someone or something that belongs or relates to the United States of America. EG *Her voice had a faint American accent... ...the strength of the American economy.* • See also **Latin American**. ADJ CLASSIF

2 An **American** is a person who comes from the United States of America. EG *There were two Americans, three Canadians and a German boy.* N COUNT

Americanism /əmerɪkənɪzə⁰m/, **Americanisms**. An **Americanism** is an expression or custom which is characteristic of or used by people in the United States of America. EG *...newly acquired Americanisms.* N COUNT ⇑ habit

Americanize /əmerɪkənaɪz/, **Americanizes, Americanizing, Americanized**; also spelled **Americanise**. To **Americanize** something means to make it follow American customs and practice. EG *They say you are Americanizing the department in every possible way.* V+O

amethyst /æmə¹θɪst/, **amethysts**. **1** An **amethyst** is a purple stone which is used in making jewellery. N COUNT ⇑ gem

2 Something that is **amethyst** is purple or violet in colour. ADJ COLOUR

amiability /eɪmɪəbɪlɪti¹/ is the quality in people of being friendly and pleasant. EG *He strove to retain a degree of amiability.* N UNCOUNT ⇑ friendliness

amiable /eɪmɪəbə⁰l/. Someone who is **amiable** is friendly and pleasant to be with. EG *Hamilton was most amiable.* ▸ used of behaviour, relationships, etc. EG *...the bluff and amiable manner of the successful American man.* ◇ **amiably**. EG *He chatted amiably with Dorothy.* ADJ QUALIT ⇑ friendly ≠ curt ◇ ADV

amicable /æmɪkəbə⁰l/. An **amicable** relationship, situation, etc involves being pleasant and polite to other people, and trying to solve problems by agreement and without quarrelling. EG *Her marriage has come to an amicable end... ...to settle the dispute in an amicable way.* ▸ used of people's feelings towards other people. EG *...different ways to signal our amicable feelings towards our companions.* ◇ **amicably**. EG *They ought to part amicably and go their separate ways.* ADJ QUALIT = friendly ≠ hostile ◇ ADV = pleasantly

amid /əmɪd/; the form **amidst** is also used. **1** If something happens **amid** a lot of other things, it happens at the same time as them, often in an exciting, confused, or noisy situation. EG *...amid all the crying and shouting... The debate took place amid a mood of growing political hysteria.* PREP ⇑ in = throughout

2 If something is **amid** a group of other things, it is in the middle of them or surrounded by them. EG *Tombstones stood amid the swaying grass.* PREP ⇑ among = in the midst of

amidships /əmɪdʃɪps/ means halfway along the length of a ship. EG *Her steel bow rammed the ancient steamer amidships.* ADV AFTER VB

amidst /ə³mɪdst/. See **amid**.

amiss /əmɪs/. **1** If something is **amiss** in a particular situation, there is something wrong, or it is not as you expected. EG *Something was horribly amiss... There was nothing amiss that I could see.* ADJ QUALIT : PRED ≠ okay

2 If you do or say something **amiss**, you do or say something that annoys or upsets someone. EG *Have I said something amiss?* ADJ QUALIT : PRED

3 If someone **takes** something **amiss**, they are offended by it. EG *Now don't take this amiss.* PHR : VB INFLECTS

4 If you say that something would **not come amiss** or would **not go amiss**, you mean that it would be very welcome and useful. EG *A little calm and detachment wouldn't come amiss.* PHR : VB INFLECTS

amity /æmɪti¹/ is peaceful, friendly relations between people or countries; used in formal English. N UNCOUNT ⇑ friendship

ammo /æməʊ/ is ammunition for guns and other weapons; an informal word. EG *The Marines were always running out of things, even food, ammo and medicine.* N UNCOUNT

ammonia /əməʊnɪə, -njə/ is a colourless liquid or gas that has a very strong, sharp smell and is used in making household cleaning substances, explosives, and fertilizer. EG *...the strong smell of ammonia.* N UNCOUNT ⇑ chemical

ammunition /æmjə⁴nɪʃə⁰n/ is **1** bullets, rockets, or shells that are made to be fired from a gun or other weapon. EG *I went out and bought a .38 revolver and a lot of ammunition.* N UNCOUNT ⇑ projectiles **2** information that you can use against someone else. EG *They knew that the letters might be used as ammunition by reactionary groups.* N UNCOUNT ⇑ facts

amnesia /æmniːzɪə/ is the partial or total loss of a person's memory. EG *It could have happened when he was suffering from amnesia.* N UNCOUNT ⇑ condition

amnesty /æmnɪ²sti¹/, **amnesties**. An **amnesty** is **1** an official pardon granted by the state, especially to people being punished for political crimes. EG *They pressed for the release of all political prisoners and for a total amnesty.* N COUNT **2** a period of time in which people can confess to a crime or give up weapons without being punished. EG *When he wanted to hand in his gun at the amnesty, it had disappeared.* N COUNT ⇑ truce

amoeba /əmiːbə/, **amoebas, amoebae** /əmiːbi¹/; also spelled **ameba** in American English. The plural can be either **amoebas** or **amoebae**. An **amoeba** is the smallest kind of living creature. Amoebas consist of only one cell, and are found in water or soil. N COUNT

amok /əmʌk, əmɒk/; the form **amuck** is also used. A person or animal that **runs amok** behaves in a violent and uncontrolled way. EG *The elephants had a tendency to panic and run amok.* PHR : VB INFLECTS = go berserk ≠ keep calm

among /əmʌŋ/; the form **amongst** is also used. **1** When someone or something is **among** a group of people or things, they are in the middle of them and are surrounded by them. EG *We stood there among piles of wooden boxes smelling of fish... Thousands of injured people still lay amongst the rubble of their homes.* PREP ⇑ in = amidst

2 When something is **among** a group or collection of things, such as clothes or papers, it is in the middle of them and forms part of the group or collection. EG *I had found a little photograph of Charlotte among her effects... Among his baggage was a medicine chest.* PREP ⇑ in = amidst

3 If you are **among** a particular group of people, you are with them and in their company. EG *I was among friends... City life is strange, in a strange place, amongst strange people.* PREP

4 If you move **among** a crowd of people or group of things, you move about through them in no particular direction. EG *After James had circulated among his guests dinner was announced... I wandered amongst the ruins.* PREP = throughout

5 If something is considered to be **among** a particular group or class, it is considered to belong to that group or class. EG *It is among the most moving pieces that she ever wrote... There were no women among her close friends.* PREP

6 If you say something is one characteristic, example, situation, etc **among** others or **among** many, you are indicating that there are many other characteristics, examples, situations, etc which you could have mentioned instead. EG *It would be right to describe your father, among other things, as a very private person... Irving Bluestone, among other union leaders, argued that a strike would cause irreparable damage.* PREP = amidst

7 If a particular idea, opinion, or situation exists **among** a particular group of people, it exists in or affects that group in particular. EG *He has always been popular among Conservative MPs... Unemployment amongst married women reached a peak.* PREP = amidst

8 If something such as a noise happens **among** or comes from **among** a particular group of people, some or all of the people in that group are causing it. EG *A murmur rose among the boys.* PREP

9 If there is a particular attitude **among** a group of people, the members of that group have that attitude towards each other. EG *Very effective co-operation has taken place among scientists of different nationalities.* PREP

10 If something is divided **among** three or more people, it is divided between them, usually so that they all have an equal share. EG *Half a chicken among four won't go very far... The estate was divided among his brothers and sisters.* PREP = between

11 If people talk, argue, etc **among** themselves, they talk or argue together as a group, without anyone else being involved. EG *They talked quietly among themselves at the far end of the tent... We would discuss amongst ourselves the relevant issues.* PREP

12 If people **keep** something **among** themselves, they keep it secret. PHR : VB INFLECTS

amongst /əmʌnst/ means the same as among.

amoral /æmɒrəl, eɪ-/. Someone who is **amoral** does not care whether what they do is considered to be right or wrong; used showing disapproval. EG *From what little I had heard of him, I decided he must be totally amoral... ...clever, amoral politicians.* ADJ QUALIT = unprincipled ≠ moral
◊ **amorality** /æmɒrælɪti[1], eɪ-/. EG *She loathed his amorality.* ◊ N UNCOUNT

amorous /æmə[8]rəs/. **Amorous** feelings, behaviour, relationships, etc involve or express sexual love; a literary use. EG *He had disentangled himself from amorous affairs before... ...my amorous triumphs.* ADJ CLASSIF ⇑ passionate
▸ used of people. EG *He was always sweet and welcoming and amorous.* ▸ ⇑ loving

amorphous /əmɔːfəs/. Something that is **amorphous** has no clear shape, structure, or boundaries. EG *...an amorphous cloud... ...a large and amorphous department.* ADJ CLASSIF = shapeless

amount /əmaunt/, **amounts, amounting, amounted**. **1** An **amount** of something, especially of money or food, is how much there is of it that you can measure. EG *...the amount of potatoes and bread that people buy... ...three times the normal amount... We estimate, month by month, the amounts of cash that will be needed.* N COUNT : ALSO N +of+N IN PL/N UNCOUNT ⇑ quantity

2 An **amount** of a quality, feeling, effort, work, etc, is the extent or degree of it, especially when there is a lot of it. EG *I was horrified by the amount of work I had to do... ...people for whom I had a certain amount of respect... All tests contain a fair amount of unreliability.* N PART+N UNCOUNT = quantity

3 If something which has several different parts or which summarizes a large number of different things **amounts** to a particular total, all the parts of it add up to that particular total. EG *...very high fees which amount to £2,000... Dutch shipping in Indonesia only amounted to 24,000 tons.* V+A *(to)* = totals

4 If an idea, feeling, statement, action, etc **amounts** to something else, it is almost the same as or equivalent to it. EG *His attitude towards her amounted to loathing... In 1970 I had what amounted to a fresh start.* V+A *(to)* ⇑ adds up

5 If something **amounts** to little, to a great deal, etc, it has that particular worth or importance. EG *It is unlikely that the forthcoming talks will amount to very much... What do these rumours amount to?* V+A *(to)* = is worth

6 If there is **any amount** of something, or **any amount** of people or things, there is a lot of it, or a large number of them. EG *...retired army officers like myself–I know any amount of them... He could put up with any amount of boredom.* PHR+of

amour /ə[3]muə/, **amours**. An **amour** is a love affair, especially one which is kept secret; an old-fashioned or literary word. N COUNT

amp /æmp/, **amps**. An **amp** is **1** the unit used for measuring electric current; an abbreviation for 'ampère'. N COUNT : USU AFTER NUM **2** the same as an amplifier; an informal use. N COUNT

ampère /æmpɛə/, **ampères**. An **ampère** is a unit which is used for measuring electric current. Its abbreviation is 'amp'. N COUNT : USU AFTER NUM

amphetamine /æmfɛtəmi[1]n/, **amphetamines**. **Amphetamine** is a drug which increases people's energy, makes them excited, and reduces their appetite. EG *The abuse of amphetamine ('speed') leads to physical and emotional exhaustion.* N MASS

amphibian /æmfɪbɪən/, **amphibians**. An **amphibian** is an animal such as a frog that is able to live on land and in water. EG *The great majority of amphibians still mate in water.* N COUNT ▸ used as an adjective. EG *A few were better suited to amphibian existence.* ▸ ADJ CLASSIF

amphibious /æmfɪbɪəs/. **1** An animal that is **amphibious** can live on land and in water. EG *Its ancestors were true amphibious salamanders.* ADJ CLASSIF ⇑ adaptable

2 An **amphibious** military force is made up of both army and navy, in order to use ships or boats to attack a place from the sea. EG *They seemed most likely to be an amphibious landing group.* ADJ CLASSIF : ATTRIB

3 An **amphibious** vehicle is able to move on both land and water. EG *They had made the fullest possible use of amphibious tanks and armoured vehicles... ...an amphibious landing craft.* ADJ CLASSIF : ATTRIB

amphitheatre /æmfɪθɪətə/, **amphitheatres**; also spelled **amphitheater** in American English. An **amphitheatre** is **1** a large round or oval structure without a roof, containing many rows of seats each of which is higher than the row in front. Amphitheatres were built, especially in Greek and Roman times, for performances and entertainments. EG *They would have continued to fight each other in the amphitheatre of Arles.* N COUNT ⇑ arena **2** an area of land in the shape of an amphitheatre, which is surrounded on all sides by hills. EG *The fort is on the rim of an immense amphitheatre... ...a large natural amphitheatre, about a hundred yards across.* N COUNT

ample /æmpə[0]l/. **1** If there is an **ample** amount or supply of something, there is enough of it and usually some extra or spare. EG *This leaves her ample time to prepare three meals a day... ...ample supplies of civilian goods.* ADJ QUALIT ⇑ sufficient ≠ inadequate ◊ **amply**. EG *This has been amply demonstrated over the past few years.* ◊ ADV

2 Ample means large in quite a pleasant or attractive way. EG *His arms were folded across his ample stomach... ...an ample lawn.* ADJ QUALIT : ATTRIB ≠ meagre

amplifier /æmplɪfaɪə/, **amplifiers**. An **amplifier** is an electronic device used with a radio, stereo system, etc, which causes sounds or signals passing through it to become louder. EG *...surrounded by a mass of microphones, amplifiers, speakers, and other electronic equipment.* N COUNT

amplify /æmplɪfaɪ/, **amplifies, amplifying, amplified**. **1** If you **amplify** a sound, speech, music, etc, you make it louder, usually by using electronic equipment. EG *These signals are then amplified... Many frogs amplify the sound of their voices using special sacs in their throats.* V+O ◊ **amplification** /æmplɪfɪkeɪʃə[0]n/. EG *They need some amplification for this evening's lecture.* ◊ N UNCOUNT ◊ **amplified**. EG *...an amplified electric guitar.* ◊ ADJ QUALIT

2 If you **amplify** an idea, statement, or piece of writing, you explain it more fully or describe it in greater detail. EG *They were simply rough ideas. They need amplifying, of course... The photographs in this book did a lot to amplify the text.* V+O = add to, expand ≠ summarize
◊ **amplification, amplifications**. EG *His story needed confirmation and amplification... She listened attentively, interrupting now and then with a comment, an amplification.* ◊ N UNCOUNT/COUNT ≠ précis

3 If you **amplify** the power or strength of something, you increase its intensity, range, or importance. EG *It lies in our grasp to amplify computer power a thousandfold.* V+O = magnify ≠ diminish

ampoule /æmpj[0]uːl/, **ampoules**; also spelled **ampule** in American English. An **ampoule** is a small container, usually made of glass, that contains a drug which will be injected into someone. N COUNT ⇑ container = phial

amputate /æmpjə[4]teɪt/, **amputates, amputating, amputated**. When a surgeon **amputates** someone's arm or leg, they cut part or all of it off during an operation, usually because it is diseased. EG *They had to amputate his leg.* V OR V+O ⇑ remove ≠ transplant
◊ **amputation** /æmpjə[4]teɪʃə[0]n/, **amputations**. EG *Punishment for a thief was amputation of a hand.* ◊ N UNCOUNT/COUNT

amuck /əmʌk/. See **amok**.

amulet /æmjə[4]lə[2]t/, **amulets**. An **amulet** is a small object that you wear or carry because you think it will bring you good luck and protect you from evil or injury. EG *The men wore bead necklaces and amulets to protect them.* N COUNT = charm, talisman

amuse /ə[3]mjuːz/, **amuses, amusing, amused**. **1** If someone or something **amuses** you, they seem funny to you and make you laugh or smile. EG *The Corsican laughed as if the idea amused him... Playfulness and rowdiness suddenly cease to amuse, and become instead the cause of annoyance.* V OR V+O : USU V+O ⇑ entertains, delights ≠ depress

2 If you **amuse** yourself or if someone **amuses** you, you do something which helps you to pass the time pleasantly and not become bored. EG *Sam amused himself by throwing branches into the fire... We had to keep thinking of things to amuse her.* V+O (NG/REFL) = entertain ⇑ occupy

amused /ə[3]mjuːzd/. **1** Someone who is **amused** at or by something thinks that it is funny and usually smiles or laughs because of it. EG *I was highly amused by a comment Bernard Shaw made once... She smiled, amused.* ADJ QUALIT ⇑ delighted ▸ used of feelings, expressions, or behaviour. EG *...a shrug of amused distaste...* ▸ ADJ QUALIT : ATTRIB

Daniel gets a momentary amused stare.
◇ **amusedly**. EG *He looked at her amusedly.* ◇ ADV AFTER VB

2 If you **keep** yourself **amused**, you find things to do which stop you from being bored. EG *The children are able to keep themselves amused.* PHR : VB INFLECTS

amusement /ə³mju:zmə²nt/, **amusements**. 1 **Amusement** is 1.1 the feeling that you have when you think that something is funny. EG *I remember with particular amusement my attempts at riding a bike... She smiled in amusement... Slowly, with an air of amusement, he nodded.* 1.2 the process of getting pleasure and enjoyment from being entertained or from spending time doing something interesting. EG *Every kind of facility was laid on for their amusement... Their preparation can provide hours of amusement.* N UNCOUNT ⇑ enjoyment; N UNCOUNT ⇑ entertainment

2 An **amusement** is a way of passing the time pleasantly and without becoming bored. EG *What amusements have you found to keep a young boy out of mischief?* N COUNT ⇑ diversion = pastime

3 **Amusements** are electronic games and gambling machines, and rides on roundabouts and other machines, which you can enjoy at a fairground or holiday resort. EG *There were a dozen coin-in-the-slot amusements... ...seafront amusements.* N PLURAL

amusement arcade, amusement arcades. An **amusement arcade** is a large room in which you can play games on machines which work when you put money in them, such as fruit machines and electronic games. EG *Computer games are already common in amusement arcades and pubs.* N COUNT

amusement park, amusement parks. An amusement park is the same as a funfair. N COUNT

amusing /ə³mju:zɪŋ/. Someone or something that is **amusing** is funny and makes you laugh or smile. EG *Francis was such a witty chap, so amusing... There was an amusing story in the paper this morning.* ADJ QUALIT = entertaining
◇ **amusingly**. EG *He talked lightly and amusingly of kings and cardinals.* ◇ ADV

an is used instead of 'a', the indefinite article, in front of words that begin with vowel sounds: see **a**. It is usually pronounced /ən/, but it is pronounced /æn/ when you are emphasizing it. EG *...an exercise... ...an old friend... ...an understanding... ...an hour... ...an M.A.* ▸ Notice that **a**, not **an**, is used in front of a word that begins with 'u' when 'u' is not pronounced as a vowel. EG *...a university.* DET

-an is added 1 to the names of places in order to form nouns or adjectives that describe someone or something as being from that place. EG *...Mexican... ...Texan... ...European.* 2 to the names of famous people in order to form adjectives or nouns that describe something or someone as connected with or typical of that person's work or the time at which they lived. EG *...Dantean... ...Shakespearean... ...Elizabethan.* SUFFIX : FORMS NOUNS/ADJ CLASSIFS; SUFFIX : FORMS ADJ CLASSIFS/ NOUNS

anachronism /ə³nækrə⁷nɪzə⁰m/, **anachronisms**. An **anachronism** is 1 something or someone that seems very out of date or old-fashioned. EG *The English public schools are an anachronism.* 2 something in a book, play, film, etc that seems wrong because it could not have happened or existed at the historical period in which the book, play, or film is set. N COUNT ⇑ reversion; N COUNT ⇑ mistake

anachronistic /ə³nækrə⁷nɪstɪk/. Something that is **anachronistic** is 1 out of date or old-fashioned. EG *...a peculiarly anachronistic view of communism.* 2 wrong because it could not have happened or existed at the historical period stated. ADJ QUALIT; ADJ CLASSIF

anaemia /ə³ni:mɪə/; also spelled **anemia**, especially in American English. **Anaemia** is a medical condition in which you feel tired and look pale because of having too few red cells in your blood or too little hemoglobin in the red cells. EG *After a lengthy examination, she was found to be suffering from anaemia.* N UNCOUNT ⇑ complaint

anaemic /ə³ni:mɪk/; also spelled **anemic**, especially in American English. 1 Someone who is **anaemic** suffers from anaemia. EG *They had diagnosed him as anaemic.* ADJ CLASSIF ⇑ unhealthy

2 If you describe someone or something as **anaemic**, you mean 2.1 that they are very pale, often in a rather unpleasant or unhealthy way. EG *Her superb self-confidence made me feel quite timid and anaemic by contrast... ...the pale, anaemic flowers of the south.* 2.2 that they are not interesting or exciting. EG *Much of this so-called 'new writing' consists of anaemic re-hashes of old work.* ADJ QUALIT = colourless; ADJ QUALIT

anaesthesia /ænəsθi:zɪə/; also spelled **anesthesia**, especially in American English. **Anaesthesia** is 1 the use of anaesthetics in medicine and surgery. EG *This means the mother will want the least possible anaesthesia during childbirth.* 2 a state in which you are unable to feel anything in your body or a particular part of your body, for example because you have been injected with an anaesthetic drug. EG *The effect of this is a kind of anaesthesia.* N UNCOUNT; N UNCOUNT = numbness

anaesthetic /ænəsθetɪk/, **anaesthetics**; also spelled **anesthetic**, especially in American English. 1 An **anaesthetic** is a substance that stops you feeling pain, either in the whole of your body when you are unconscious, or in a particular part of your body when you are awake. EG *He was undergoing an operation, and was under the effect of an anaesthetic.* N COUNT

2 Something that is **anaesthetic** uses or involves anaesthesia. EG *...the anaesthetic influence of acupuncture.* ADJ CLASSIF = numbing

anaesthetist /ə³ni:sθətɪst/, **anaesthetists**; also spelled **anesthetist**, especially in American English. An **anaesthetist** is 1 in British English, a doctor who specializes in giving anaesthetics to patients. 2 in American English, a nurse or other person who gives anaesthetics to patients. N COUNT; N COUNT

anaesthetize /ə³ni:sθətaɪz/, **anaesthetizes, anaesthetizing, anaesthetized**; also spelled **anesthetise** or, especially in American English, **anesthetize**. To **anaesthetize** someone means to give them an anaesthetic so that they will feel no pain during a surgical operation. EG *The animals were anaesthetized for all or part of the experiment.* V+O

anagram /ænəgræm/, **anagrams**. An **anagram** is a word or phrase that is formed by changing the order of the letters in another word or phrase. EG *Triangle is an anagram of integral.* N COUNT ⇑ puzzle

anal /eɪnə⁰l/ is used referring to the anus of a person or animal. EG *...the anal sphincter.* ADJ CLASSIF : ATTRIB

analgesic /ænə⁰ldʒi:zɪk, -sɪk/, **analgesics**. An **analgesic** is a drug which lessens the effect of pain. EG *...experiencing labour pains and demanding analgesics.* ▸ used as an adjective. EG *This has very good analgesic properties and will help to reduce pain.* N COUNT = painkiller; ▸ ADJ CLASSIF : ATTRIB

analogous /ənælə⁷dʒəs/. If something is **analogous** to something else, the two things are similar to each other in some way. EG *We find in art a process exactly analogous to that now occurring in the verbal language.* ADJ CLASSIF : IF PREP THEN *to* = equivalent

analogue /ænəlɒg/, **analogues**; also spelled **analog**, especially for paragraph 3. 1 If something is an **analogue** of something else, the two things are similar to each other in some way. EG *The system would seek analogues, that is images and symbols from its previous experience... ...a right-wing analogue of Lukacs's 'proletarian consciousness'.* N COUNT ⇑ copy

2 An **analogue** watch or clock shows what it measures by means of a pointer that moves round a dial, rather than by displaying numbers: compare **digital**. EG *...a conventional analogue watch.* ADJ CLASSIF : ATTRIB

3 An **analogue** device measures information by using voltage or another physical quantity that is variable, not fixed. EG *...thousands of different operations which analogue circuits can perform.* ADJ CLASSIF : ATTRIB

analogue computer, analogue computers; also spelled **analog computer**. An **analogue** computer measures information by using a variable quantity such as voltage: compare **digital computer**. N COUNT

analogy /ənælə⁷dʒi¹/, **analogies**. An **analogy** is a comparison or similarity between two things that are alike in some way. EG *He drew an analogy between horticulture and God watching over the world... The whole process can be modelled using analogies from classical mechanical behaviour.* N COUNT = similarity ≠ difference

● **By analogy** means using or making a comparison between two things in order to explain or understand something. EG *The models are meant to show, by analogy, how matter is built up.* ● PHR : USED AS AN A

analyse /ænəlaɪz/, **analyses, analysing, analysed**; also spelled **analyze** in American English. 1 If you **analyse** something, 1.1 you consider it carefully and in detail in order to understand or explain it. EG *Specialists may be useful to analyse a situation and suggest solutions... ...certain paintings which I have described and analysed elsewhere.* 1.2 you find V+O; V+O

out what it consists of by testing it scientifically. EG *I had no facilities for analysing food.*
2 When a psychotherapist or psychiatrist **analyses** someone who is mentally ill or emotionally disturbed, he or she examines or treats them by asking them about their feelings and their past in order to discover hidden feelings or past experiences which may be causing their condition. EG *If things do not improve we might have Dr Cutler analyse her.* V+O = psychoanalyse

analysis /ənælɪ¹sɪs/, **analyses**. 1 **Analysis** or an **analysis** is 1.1 the process of considering something carefully and in detail in order to understand or explain it. EG *This could explain many things that otherwise defy rational analysis... ...linguistic analysis.* N UNCOUNT/COUNT ⇑ examination 1.2 a scientific examination of something in order to discover what it consists of. EG *...a chemical analysis of the poison.* N UNCOUNT/COUNT
2 An **analysis** is also an explanation or description that is the result of considering something carefully and in detail. EG *He offers a calm analysis of the political situation.* N COUNT
3 **Analysis** is also the process of analysing someone who is mentally ill or emotionally disturbed in order to cure them. EG *Many adults broke through their emotional hang-ups in analysis.* N UNCOUNT ⇑ treatment = psychoanalysis
4 **In the final analysis** or **in the last analysis** is used to indicate that a statement is about the basic nature or cause of something or the basic facts of a situation. EG *In the final analysis power rested in the hands of one man... They realized that in the last analysis their job was to tell the public the facts.* PHR : USED AS AN A ⇑ essentially = ultimately

analyst /ænəlɪst/, **analysts**. An **analyst** is 1 someone whose job involves analysing something and giving their opinion about it. EG *Some analysts view the recent slide in share prices as temporary... ...political analysts.* N COUNT = commentator 2 someone who treats people who are mentally ill or emotionally disturbed by analysing them. N COUNT ⇑ psychiatrist = psychoanalyst

analytic /ænəlɪtɪk/ or **analytical** /ænəlɪtɪkə⁰l/ refers to the use of logical reasoning about a subject or problem. EG *I want now to turn his analytic approach back upon itself... ...her acute analytical powers... Some, more analytical than others, saw the new development as a major change in policy.* ADJ QUALIT

analyze /ænəlaɪz/. See **analyse**.

anarchic /ænɑːkɪk/ means paying no attention to rules or laws that everyone else obeys and believes in; used showing disapproval. EG *This system is economically inefficient and politically anarchic.* ADJ CLASSIF ⇑ free = lawless ≠ conformist

anarchism /ænəkɪzə⁰m/ is a political belief that the laws and power of all governments and organizations should be replaced by people and groups working together freely. EG *...Marxism and anarchism with all their variations.* N UNCOUNT = anarchy

anarchist /ænəkɪst/, **anarchists**. An **anarchist** is 1 a person who believes in anarchism. EG *...the great pioneer socialist Jimmy Maxton and the anarchist Guy Aldred.* N COUNT ▸ used as an adjective. EG *...anarchist ideals... ...the history of the anarchist movement.* ▸ ADJ CLASSIF 2 someone who seems to pay no attention to rules or laws that everyone else obeys; used showing disapproval. EG *He's a complete anarchist... ...the ravings of an obsessed anarchist.* N COUNT ≠ conformist

anarchistic /ænəkɪstɪk/ means showing signs of or believing in anarchism. EG *...a period of anarchistic movements and terrorism.* ADJ QUALIT : ATTRIB = anarchist

anarchy /ænəki¹/ is 1 a situation where nobody seems to pay attention to any rules or laws; used showing disapproval. EG *...anarchy and economic chaos.* N UNCOUNT = disorder 2 belief in anarchism. EG *...the red flags of Marxism, the black flags of anarchy.* N UNCOUNT

anathema /ə³næθəmə/. If something or someone is **anathema** to you, you disapprove of it strongly or hate it. EG *Taxes were always anathema to the Yankee... For many Conservatives, state intervention was anathema.* N UNCOUNT : IF + PREP THEN *to* ⇑ hated

anatomical /ænətɒmɪkə⁰l/ is used referring to the structure of the bodies of people and animals. EG *...the number of anatomical features that certain animals have in common.* ADJ CLASSIF : ATTRIB ⇑ structural

anatomist /ə³nætə⁷mɪst/, **anatomists**. An **anatomist** is an expert in anatomy. EG *A very eminent anatomist analysed the structure of its skull.* N COUNT

anatomy /ə³nætə⁷mi¹/, **anatomies**. 1 **Anatomy** is the study of the structure of the bodies of people or animals. EG *Professor Day was teaching anatomy to his students.* N UNCOUNT ⇑ science
2 The **anatomy** of a particular animal is the structure of its body. EG *...the anatomy of a fish.* N COUNT : USU SING
3 Your **anatomy** is your body; often used humorously. EG *He had an uncanny ability to develop pains in various parts of his anatomy when there was hard work to be done.* N COUNT : USU POSS + N IN SING = frame
4 An **anatomy** of a particular subject or idea is an examination or investigation of it. EG *...a fascinating anatomy of the political system.* N COUNT + *of* : USU SING = analysis

ancestor /ænsɛstə/, **ancestors**. 1 Your **ancestors** are the people in former times from whom you are descended. EG *...an old family firm founded by their French ancestor Jacques Lequesne... ...the place where our ancestors had fought so passionately for freedom.* N COUNT = forebear ≠ descendant
2 An **ancestor** of something modern is something that existed in former times and from which the modern version has developed. EG *These creatures are the ancestors of modern man... This simple device is the ancestor of the modern computer.* N COUNT

ancestral /ænsɛstrəl/ means 1 relating to or obtained for your family in former times. EG *...Gladstone's ancestral home at Hawarden.* ADJ CLASSIF : ATTRIB 2 relating to something that existed in former times, and from which something modern developed. EG *...an ancestral form from which all the higher primates evolved.* ADJ CLASSIF : USU ATTRIB ⇑ early

ancestry /ænsɛstri¹/, **ancestries**. 1 Your **ancestry** is the family or racial group of people from whom you are descended. EG *...American citizens of Japanese ancestry... Her Slavonic ancestry was unmistakeable.* N COUNT : WITH POSS/SUPP ⇑ group = descent
2 The **ancestry** of something modern is the various things which existed in former times, from which the modern thing has developed. EG *The two main groups of whales have different ancestries.* N COUNT : WITH POSS/SUPP

anchor /æŋkə/, **anchors, anchoring, anchored**. 1 An **anchor** is a heavy hooked object that is dropped from a boat into the water at the end of a chain in order to prevent the boat from moving. EG *Go and check that the anchor is secure.* N COUNT ● If a boat is **at anchor**, it is floating in a particular place and prevented from moving by its anchor. EG *...vessels lying safely at anchor... ...bobbing gently at anchor.* ● PHR : USED AS AN A ⇑ still
● If you **drop anchor** or **cast anchor**, you drop a boat's anchor into the water in order to prevent the boat from moving. EG *They cast anchor in the River Hooghly.* ● PHR : VB INFLECTS ⇑ stop ● If you **weigh anchor** or **up anchor**, you raise the anchor of a boat so that you can sail away in it. EG *For the first time since we'd weighed anchor, Conrad spoke... It was agreed that we should up anchor and make a run for it.* ● PHR : VB INFLECTS ⇑ depart
2 When a boat **anchors** or when you **anchor** a boat, its anchor is dropped into the water so that it is prevented from moving. EG *We went out to where Ben's boat is anchored... A steam frigate arrived and anchored in the bay.* V-ERG ⇑ stop
3 If you **anchor** an object, you prevent it from moving by attaching it to something heavy or solid, or by placing something heavy on it or against it. EG *We should anchor his wheelchair to a huge stone.* V+O : USU + A *(to, with)* ⇑ attach
4 If something **is anchored**, it is linked firmly with something permanent, settled, or secure. EG *We need a fixed place, a permanently anchored home... They are anchored to a stable tradition.* V+O : USU PASS ⇑ fix = root
5 An **anchor** is also something important that you believe in and trust because it is permanent, settled, or secure. EG *...the anchor of marriage... Your material body is the anchor of consciousness.* N COUNT ⇑ stabilizer = mainstay

anchorage /æŋkə⁰rɪdʒ/, **anchorages**. An **anchorage** is a place where a boat can anchor. EG *There was a deep-water anchorage for ocean ships.* N COUNT

anchor man, anchor men; also spelled with a hyphen. An **anchor man** in broadcasting is a person in a central studio who acts as a link between different parts of a programme and maintains contact with people and reporters in other studios. N COUNT

anchovy /æntʃə⁶vi¹/, **anchovies**. An **anchovy** is a very small fish that you can eat. Anchovies have a strong, salty taste. EG *...anchovies on toast... ...anchovy paste.* N COUNT

ancient /eɪnʃənt/, **ancients**. 1 **Ancient** means 1.1 belonging to the distant past. In the history of European civilization, it refers to the time before the end of the Roman Empire. EG *...ancient Greece and Rome. ...ancient monuments.* ADJ QUALIT ⇑ old 1.2 having a very long history or having existed for a very long time. EG *He* ADJ QUALIT *came from an ancient Catholic family... The law of equity is ancient and complicated.* **1.3** looking or being very old. EG *...old men with ancient faces... ...an ancient looking woman.* ADJ QUALIT

2 The **ancients** are the people of an old civilization, especially that of classical Greece or Rome. N PLURAL : *the*+N

ancient history is the history of ancient civilizations, especially Greece and Rome. ● In informal English, if you describe something as **ancient history**, you mean that it happened in the past and is no longer relevant to the present. EG *'He wants to talk about the row you had in 1975.'–'But that's all such ancient history now.'* N UNCOUNT

ancillary /ænsɪləri[1]/. **1** The **ancillary** workers in an institution or organization are the workers such as cleaners, cooks, hospital porters, etc, whose work supports the main work of the organization. EG *...hospital ancillary workers... ...the unions involved with manual and ancillary staff.* ADJ CLASSIF : ATTRIB ⇑ secondary ≠ auxiliary

2 If something is described as **ancillary**, it is a small or additional part of something else. EG *Local resources were ancillary to a wider, national system of control... I had a small ancillary sleeping tent, shaped like a cone.* ADJ CLASSIF : IF+PREP THEN *to* ⇑ subsidiary

and /ə[3]nd/. **1 And** is used to link words in the following ways: **1.1** simply to link two or more words, groups, or clauses. EG *...my mother and father... ...banks, post offices, and police stations... It was lovely and warm outside... He was an elegant and articulate man... I came here in 1972 and I have lived here ever since.* CONJ COORD **1.2** to link two nouns or pronouns that refer to the same person or thing. EG *The television director and critic, Iain Johnstone, is here in the studio with me... Here's your friend and mine, John Peel.* CONJ COORD **1.3** to link two identical words or phrases in order to emphasize the degree of something or to suggest that something continues to happen or increase over a period of time. EG *Her marks are getting worse and worse... He became more and more annoyed... We talked for hours and hours... When Bill was happy, he laughed and laughed.* CONJ COORD **1.4** to indicate that two numbers are to be added together. EG *Two and two is four... What's six and eight?* CONJ COORD = plus **1.5** to link two statements about actions or events, when the second happened later in time than the first. EG *He opened the car door and got out... She finished her Coke and put the bottle down under the bench.* CONJ COORD = then **1.6** to link two statements that contrast with each other. EG *I meant to buy some tea yesterday and I forgot... It can be difficult when you do not think something is important and someone else does.* CONJ COORD = but **1.7** to link two clauses when the second clause is a result of the first clause. EG *Expect everything to go wrong and you won't feel quite so bad when it does... Do as you're told and you'll be all right.* CONJ COORD = then **1.8** in informal English, to link two verbs when the two actions are done at the same time. The first verb is a verb such as 'try', 'come', 'go', or 'wait,' and the second verb, which is stressed when spoken, describes an action. EG *We must try and understand... Stop and think about it... He went and kissed his mother.* CONJ COORD

2 And is used to introduce statements in spoken or informal English in the following ways: **2.1** at the beginning of a sentence in order to introduce something else that you want to say. EG *Get your hands off. And don't call me 'love'... I didn't mean to scare you. And I'm sorry I'm late.* CONJ COORD **2.2** to interrupt yourself in order to make a comment on what you are saying. EG *Finally- and I really ought to stop in a minute–I wish to make the following recommendations... Some people, and I make no criticisms at all, have not been around much lately.* CONJ COORD **2.3** to introduce a question which relates directly to what someone else has just said. EG *'I was born at our house in Norfolk.'–'And did you like it there?'... 'I'm Bill Whitman, from the New York Times.'–'And?'... 'I don't think he felt well.'–'And Fred Potter?'–'Same thing.'* CONJ COORD

3 And is used by broadcasters and people making announcements when they start talking about a topic they have just mentioned, or when they are telling you what is happening. EG *Football–and Manchester City are in the final of the European Cup... And now it's 8.30 and time for 'Any Questions'.* CONJ COORD

4 And is also used in saying numbers. **4.1** In saying numbers larger than one hundred, **and** is used before a number between 1 and 99. EG *...three hundred and fifty people... ...a thousand and one... ...sixteen thousand five hundred and thirty-one.* CONJ COORD : NUM+CONJ+NUM **4.2** In saying complex numbers, **and** is used before a fraction that comes after a whole number. EG *...two and a half years... ...eleven and three sixteenths.* CONJ COORD : NUM+CONJ+NUM

andante /ændænti[1]/, **andantes**. **Andante** is an instruction in a piece of music to say that it should be played fairly slowly. ▸ used as a noun. EG *I think he played the andante much too fast, don't you?* ▸ used as an adjective. EG *...a long andante section.* ADV WITH VB ▸ N SING : *the*+N ▸ ADJ CLASSIF : ATTRIB

androgynous /ændrɒdʒə[1]nəs/. An **androgynous** person, animal, or plant has both male and female characteristics; a formal or technical word. ADJ CLASSIF

anecdotal /ænɪ[2]kdəʊtə[0]l/. **Anecdotal** speech or writing is full of anecdotes or is based on anecdotes. EG *We do not have to dig deep into anecdotal material to find out about Mozart's private life... ...anecdotal evidence.* ADJ CLASSIF

anecdote /ænɪ[2]kdəʊt/, **anecdotes**. An **anecdote** is a short, entertaining account of something that has happened, usually to the person telling it. EG *She told him anecdotes about the hospital and the patients... He followed this up with a few horrifying anecdotes from his own past.* N COUNT ⇑ story

anemia /əniːmɪə/. See **anaemia**.

anemic /əniːmɪk/. See **anaemic**.

anemone /ə[3]nɛməni[1]/, **anemones**. An **anemone** is a plant that is grown in gardens. Some types grow from bulbs and have red, purple, or white flowers with black centres, and other types grow from a root and have white or pink flowers on long stems. N COUNT

anesthesia /ænəsθiːzɪə/. See **anaesthesia**.

anesthesiologist /ænəsθiːzɪɒlədʒɪst/, **anesthesiologists**; also spelled **anaesthesiologist**. An **anesthesiologist**, in American English, is a doctor who specializes in giving anaesthetics to patients. N COUNT = anaesthetist

anesthetic /ænəsθɛtɪk/, **anesthetics**. See **anaesthetic**.

anesthetist /əniːsθətɪst/, **anesthetists**. See **anaesthetist**.

anesthetize /ə[3]niːθətaɪz/, **anesthetizes, anesthetizing, anesthetized**. See **anaesthetize**.

anew /ə[3]njuː/. If you do something **anew**, you do it **1** again and in the same way as before; a rather literary word. EG *Joseph leant his head against the rough wood and wept anew... The process of conflict and destruction would begin anew.* ADV AFTER VB = afresh **2** again and in a different way. EG *...starting life anew in a fresh place.* ADV AFTER VB = afresh

angel /eɪndʒə[0]l/, **angels**. **1** An **angel** is one of the spiritual beings that some people believe live with God in heaven and act as God's servants and messengers. EG *...an angel of the Lord.* N COUNT ⇑ spirit ● If you say that someone **is on the side of the angels**, you believe that they are doing what is right. EG *Charles Conrad is on the side of the angels.* ● PHR : VB INFLECTS ● See also **guardian angel**.

2 If you call someone an **angel**, you are saying that they are very good, kind, considerate, or gentle. EG *I was hardly an angel before I went to boarding school at fourteen... Darling, you're an angel!.* N COUNT : ALSO VOC = saint ▸ used as a term of affection. EG *'My angels,' he heard Uncle Harold say as they went in.* ▸ = love

angelic /ændʒɛlɪk/. **1** Someone who is **angelic** is or seems to be very good, kind, considerate, or gentle. EG *Despite his reputation for bad temper, he was positively angelic this time.* ADJ QUALIT ⇑ perfect = saintly

2 Angelic also means like an angel or coming from heaven. EG *...a demon in angelic form.* ADJ CLASSIF : ATTRIB

anger /æŋgə/, **angers, angering, angered**. **1 Anger** is the strong emotion that you feel about an action or situation which you consider unacceptable, unfair, cruel, or insulting, and about the person responsible for it. EG *There was anger at the sufferings inflicted by the bombing... Yet I couldn't feel anger against him because I liked him too much... 'You're a spiteful fool.'–'Am I?' he said, red with anger.* N UNCOUNT ⇑ feeling = resentment, rage

2 If someone or something **angers** you, they make you feel angry. EG *...legislation that is bound to anger minorities even more... His hostile attitude angered her.* V+O = enrage

angina /ændʒaɪnə/ is severe pain in a person's chest and left arm, caused by heart disease. N UNCOUNT

angle /æŋgə[0]l/, **angles, angling, angled**. **1** An **angle** is **1.1** the space or distance between two lines or surfaces at the point where they join together. Angles are measured in degrees. EG *The base angles of an isosceles triangle are equal... Oxford Road joins* N COUNT

the High Street at an angle of ninety degrees. ● See also **right angle**. **1.2** the shape that is created where two lines or surfaces join together. EG *He lay in the boat with his head against the angle of its bow... ...the intricacies and angles of Gothic architecture.* **1.3** the position or direction from which you look at something or photograph it. EG *He held the vase close to his face, peering at it from all angles... They photograph people from the most surprising angles.*
N COUNT = corner; N COUNT

2 If something is **at an angle**, it is not straight, horizontal, or vertical. EG *He crossed the lawn at an angle... ...an old table leaning at a crazy angle.*
PHR : USED AS AN A

3 An **angle** on something is a special way of considering or dealing with a particular idea or subject, in which you emphasize some things and ignore other things. EG *David's play was amusing and its pacifist angle had a great appeal... They were afraid a member of the rival team might spot a story or news angle they hadn't thought of.*
N COUNT+SUPP ⇑ approach = slant

4 If you **angle** something or if it **angles** in a particular direction, it faces or points in that direction, especially one that is not horizontal or vertical. EG *On the balcony, a man stood playing a trombone, the horn angled up into the air... The submarine angled slightly upwards and levelled off.*
V-ERG : USU+A ⇑ point

5 If you **angle** for something, you try to make someone offer it to you without asking for it directly. EG *He got the invitation to Washington he had been angling for... I am quite sure she was not angling for a compliment.*
V+A *(for)* = fish

6 If you **angle** an activity, idea, or subject in a particular way, you consider or present it in that way. EG *The whole thing was angled towards flirtation and amusement.*
V+O : IF+PREP THEN *to/towards* ⇑ aim = slant

7 See also **angling**.

angler /æŋglə/, **anglers**. An **angler** is someone who fishes with a fishing rod, especially as a hobby.
N COUNT = fisherman

Anglican /æŋglɪkən/. An **Anglican** is a Christian who is a member of the Church of England. ▸ used as an adjective. EG *...an Anglican bishop.*
N COUNT; ▸ ADJ CLASSIF

Anglicanism /æŋglɪkənɪzə⁰m/ is the beliefs and practices of the Church of England.
N UNCOUNT ⇑ Christianity

anglicize /æŋglɪsaɪz/, **anglicizes, anglicizing, anglicized**; also spelled **anglicise**; often spelled with a capital letter. If a word, custom, person, idea, etc, **is anglicized,** it changes so that it resembles or becomes part of the English language or culture. EG *...the Italian composer Giuseppe Verdi's anglicized name, which is Joseph Green... ...the new class of Anglicized Indians, including lawyers and government officials.*
V+O : USU PASS

angling /æŋglɪŋ/ is the activity or sport of fishing with a fishing rod. EG *The most popular sport in this country is angling.*
N UNCOUNT

Anglo- is added to adjectives that describe nationalities in order to form other adjectives that describe something or someone as connected with England or Britain, or as connected with relations between the two countries. EG *...the 1921 Anglo-Irish treaty... ...Anglo-German friendship.*
PREFIX

Anglo-Saxon /æŋgləʊsæksə⁰n/, **Anglo-Saxons**. **1** **Anglo-Saxon** is used **1.1** to describe the history, language, culture, and people of England from the fifth century A.D. to the Norman Conquest in 1066. **1.2** to describe people who are members of or descended from the English race. **1.3** to describe societies, cultures, or ideas that are strongly influenced by English culture. EG *...this Anglo-Saxon view of things.*
ADJ CLASSIF; ADJ CLASSIF; ADJ CLASSIF

2 An **Anglo-Saxon** is **2.1** one of the people who lived in England between the fifth century A.D. and the Norman Conquest. **2.2** someone who is descended from the English race or people.
N COUNT; N COUNT

3 **Anglo-Saxon** is the language that was spoken in England between the fifth century A.D. and the Norman Conquest.
N UNCOUNT = Old English

Angolan /æŋgəʊlə⁰n/. **1** **Angolan** means belonging or relating to Angola or to its people. EG *...an escort of 20 Angolan soldiers.*
ADJ CLASSIF

2 An **Angolan** is a person who comes from Angola.
N COUNT

angora /æŋgɔːrə/. **1** An **angora** goat, rabbit, or cat is a particular breed that has long silky hair.
ADJ CLASSIF : ATTRIB

2 **Angora** cloth or clothing is made from the hair of the angora goat or rabbit. ▸ used as a noun to refer to cloth.
N BEFORE N; ▸ N UNCOUNT

angry /æŋgri¹/, **angrier, angriest**. **1** Someone who is **angry** feels or shows strong emotion about an action or situation which they consider unacceptable, unfair, cruel, or insulting, and about the person responsible for it. EG *Are you angry with me?... He was angry at Sally Gardner for accusing him... Pegler often got angry about many foolish things... This made him even angrier.* ▸ used of people's actions or words. EG *...sending angry letters to the newspapers.* ◇ **angrily**. EG *This was angrily denied by the dead man's family.*
ADJ QUALIT : USU PRED = cross, incensed; ▸ ADJ QUALIT : USU ATTRIB; ◇ ADV WITH VB = hotly

2 An **angry** wound or rash is hot, red, and painful.
ADJ CLASSIF

3 If you describe the sky or clouds or the sea as **angry**, you mean that they are dark and stormy; a rather literary word. EG *...great angry thunder clouds.*
ADJ QUALIT : USU ATTRIB = threatening

angst /æŋst/ is an anxious feeling that is caused by worrying about the state of the world; a literary word. EG *she was full of uncertainty and angst.*
N UNCOUNT = anxiety

anguish /æŋgwɪʃ/ is great pain and suffering, especially mental rather than physical pain. EG *...a quarrel which caused her intense unhappiness and anguish... She was doubled over, her whole face distorted in anguish.*
N UNCOUNT = agony

anguished /æŋgwɪʃt/ means suffering or showing great mental pain. EG *...the anguished cries, weeping, and prayers continued.*
ADJ QUALIT = tormented

angular /æŋgjəˈlə/. **1** **Angular** people or things have shapes that contain a lot of straight lines and sharp points. EG *Hooper listened, his angular face placid... ...women in angular hats and sensible shoes.*
ADJ CLASSIF = pointed ≠ rounded

2 **Angular** directions or movements are straight, but not horizontal or vertical. EG *...their apparent angular movement.*
ADJ CLASSIF

animal /ænɪmə⁰l/, **animals**. **1** An **animal** is **1.1** a living creature such as a dog, lion, monkey, or rabbit, rather than a bird, fish, reptile, insect, or human being. EG *They used to hunt wild animals for food... ...domestic animals such as dogs and cats... No birds or animals came near.* **1.2** any living thing that is not a plant, including people. EG *Man is a very weak animal... It is this that most clearly divides us from the rest of the animal kingdom.*
N COUNT = mammal; N COUNT ⇑ being

2 If you refer to someone as an **animal**, you mean that they behave in a rough and unacceptable way, usually because they are dirty or cruel. EG *Her husband was an animal.*
N COUNT : ALSO VOC = monster

3 If you refer to someone or something as a particular kind of **animal**, you mean that you are considering them in relation to a particular characteristic that thy have, especially when this seems unusual or interesting. EG *South American Trotskyism is a very different animal from its British or European counterpart... I had never been a political animal.*
N COUNT+SUPP

4 **Animal** qualities, feelings, or abilities relate to someone's physical nature and instincts rather than to their mind. EG *Animal instinct at once warned me to tread carefully... He had a kind of animal courage.*
ADJ CLASSIF : USU ATTRIB ⇑ instinctive

animate, animates, animating, animated; pronounced /ænɪmeɪt/ when it is a verb and /ænɪmət/ when it is an adjective. **1** To **animate** something means to make it lively and more cheerful. EG *An identical expression of amusement animated their faces.*
V+O = enliven, fire

2 Something that is **animate** has life, in contrast to things in the world like stones and machines which do not. EG *...man's exploitation of the natural world, both animate and inanimate.*
ADJ CLASSIF = living ≠ inanimate

animated /ænɪmeɪtɪ²d/. **1** Someone or something that is **animated** is lively and interesting. EG *The conversation that followed was animated... He had a mobile, expressive, animated face... ...an animated group in the centre of the room.* ◇ **animatedly**. EG *The other occupants of the car were talking animatedly.*
ADJ QUALIT = enthusiastic; ◇ ADV WITH VB = excitedly

2 An **animated** drawing or film has been filmed by means of animation. EG *...an animated cartoon.*
ADJ CLASSIF

animation /ænɪmeɪʃə⁰n/ is **1** a method of making films in which you photograph a series of drawings or a series of positions in which a puppet or model is placed. When the film is projected quickly, the drawings, puppet, or model appear to move. **2** liveliness and interest in the way you speak, look, or behave. EG *She seemed to talk with animation.*
N UNCOUNT ⇑ filming; N UNCOUNT = enthusiasm

animator /ænɪmeɪtə/, **animators**. An **animator** is a person who makes films by means of animation.
N COUNT

animosity /ænɪmɒsɪtɪ/, **animosities**. **Animosity** is a feeling of strong dislike and anger. EG *The two neighbours are caught in a circle of animosity and distrust... Local animosities were forgotten in the face of the greater threat to the whole community.*
N UNCOUNT/COUNT = hostility, enmity

animus /ænɪməs/ is a feeling of strong dislike for someone, especially when there is no good reason for it. EG *He may have some kind of animus against you.* N SING WITH DET

aniseed /ænɪsi:d/ is a substance made from the liquorice-flavoured seeds of a plant, which is used as a flavouring in sweets, drinks, and medicines. N UNCOUNT

ankle /æŋkə⁰l/, **ankles**. 1 Your **ankle** is the joint where your foot joins your leg. EG *Rosa fell and sprained her ankle.* N COUNT 2 **Ankle** socks and boots are short and reach a point on your leg just above your ankle. N BEFORE N

annals /ænə⁰lz/. You refer to the **annals** of a nation, society, activity, etc when you are referring to something that is recorded as part of its history. EG *...the two most improbable soldiers in the annals of military history.* N PLURAL: *the*+ N+SUPP = chronicles

annex /ænɛks/, **annexes, annexing, annexed**; also spelled **annexe**. 1 An **annex** is a building which is joined to or near the main building of a hotel, school, or institution, and which is used because the main building is too small. EG *...the annexe to the Town Hall.* N COUNT ⇑ extension

2 If a country **annexes** another country or an area of land, it seizes it, usually by force, and takes control of it. EG *The state was conquered and annexed in 1832.* V+O ⇑ conquer = take over

◊ **annexation** /ænɛkseɪʃə⁰n/. EG *...the annexation of Hawaii.* ◊ N UNCOUNT

3 If you **annex** something, you take possession of it without permission. EG *There were examples of people occupying public squares and annexing the pavement next to their lands.* V+O ⇑ seize = commandeer

annihilate /ənaɪəleɪt/, **annihilates, annihilating, annihilated**. 1 If bombs or other weapons **annihilate** a place or a group of people, they destroy it completely. EG *...if the human race should be annihilated.* V+O = wipe out, exterminate, obliterate ◊ **annihilation** /ənaɪəleɪʃə⁰n/. EG *...world leaders debating the possibility of global annihilation.* ◊ N UNCOUNT ⇑ destruction

2 If you **annihilate** something, you put an end to it or make it completely ineffective. EG *They annihilated all opposition within six weeks.* V+O ⇑ destroy = wipe out ◊ **annihilation**. EG *The result would be the annihilation of the Labour Party.* ◊ N UNCOUNT

3 If you **annihilate** someone in a contest, game, or argument, you defeat them completely. EG *The new party was annihilated at the polls in the 1931 election.* V+O = crush ◊ **annihilation**. ◊ N UNCOUNT

anniversary /ænə¹vɜ:sə⁰ri¹/, **anniversaries**. An **anniversary** is a date which is remembered or celebrated because a special event happened on that date in a previous year. EG *...the fiftieth anniversary of the Russian Revolution... It was his wedding anniversary.* N COUNT

Anno Domini /ænəʊ dɒmɪnaɪ, -ni:/ is the unabbreviated form of **AD**. It means 'in the Year of our Lord.' ADV

annotate /ænə⁶teɪt/, **annotates, annotating, annotated**. If you **annotate** a written work or diagram, you add notes to it, for example in order to explain it. EG *The pages were annotated and signed 'Paul Schmidt' in pencil... ...annotated sketches.* V+O: USU PASS

annotation /ænəʊteɪʃə⁰n/, **annotations**. 1 An **annotation** is a note that is added to a text or diagram, often in order to explain it. EG *...a cryptic pencil annotation.* N COUNT = footnote 2 **Annotation** is the activity of annotating something. N UNCOUNT

announce /ə³naʊns/, **announces, announcing, announced**. 1 If you **announce** something, 1.1 you tell people about it publicly or officially. EG *It was announced that the Prime Minister would speak on television that evening... A number of politicians announced that they were going to oppose the Bill... Mr Heath announced his decision... Their engagement was officially announced on 5th August... There had been a pay cut announced to them the previous week.* V+O/REPORT-CL/QUOTE: IF+PREP THEN *to* ⇑ say = reveal, declare 1.2 you say it in a deliberate and sometimes slightly aggressive way. EG *'I am Mrs Jones,' she announced... He announced to his wife that he was leaving.* V+O/REPORT-CL/QUOTE: IF+PREP THEN *to* = proclaim

2 If you **announce** something in a public place such as a railway station or an airport, you tell people about it by means of a loudspeaker or Tannoy system. EG *As soon as the train to Hong Kong was announced, people poured onto the platform.* V+O/REPORT-CL/QUOTE

3 When servants or masters of ceremonies **announce** people arriving at a formal party, they call out the names of these people as they enter the room. EG *'Mr Desmond Burton Cox,' announced George, showing the guest into the room... ...the sort of parties at which footmen announced duchesses.* V+O/QUOTE ⇑ introduce

4 If a notice, sign, or sound **announces** something, it informs people about it. EG *A sign by the road announces the name of the village... Meals were announced by the ringing of a bell.* V+O = signal

5 If something **announces** a particular event or state of affairs, it shows that it is happening or that it is the case; a rather literary word. EG *Crocuses and snowdrops announced the arrival of spring.* V+O = herald

announcement /ə³naʊnsmə³nt/, **announcements**. 1 An **announcement** is 1.1 a public statement which gives information about something that has happened or that will happen. EG *The government made a public announcement about the progress of the talks on nuclear disarmament... ...railway announcements.* N COUNT 1.2 a short advertisement telling people about something, for example in a newspaper or on the radio. EG *Its windows were filled with announcements about retirement bungalows... I learned of his death through an announcement in the newspaper.* N COUNT = notice

2 The **announcement** of something is the act of telling people about it. EG *...the events which follow the announcement of your threatened resignation.* N SING WITH DET: USU N+*of* = revelation

announcer /ə³naʊnsə/, **announcers**. An **announcer** is 1 someone who introduces programmes on radio or television. EG *'That's the end of broadcasting for today,' the announcer said. 'So goodbye until tomorrow.'* N COUNT 2 someone who makes announcements in a railway station, airport, etc. EG *The announcer called his bus, and he had to go.* N COUNT

annoy /ə³nɔɪ/, **annoys, annoying, annoyed**. 1 If someone **annoys** you, or if their behaviour **annoys** you, they make you feel fairly angry. EG *You're just saying that to annoy me... She didn't want to annoy him... He couldn't spell, which particularly annoyed her.* V+O ⇑ anger = irritate

2 If a man **annoys** a woman, he causes her trouble and distress by making sexual suggestions to her or about her, or by trying to touch her. EG *Is this man annoying you?* V+O = harass

annoyance /ə³nɔɪəns/, **annoyances**. 1 **Annoyance** is the feeling of anger and impatience that you get when someone says or does something that displeases you. EG *The Englishman showed no signs of his annoyance... 'Really,' said Mrs Oliver to herself with some annoyance, 'girls!'* N UNCOUNT = irritation

2 An **annoyance** is something that makes you feel angry and impatient. EG *The villagers had plenty of annoyances to put up with, like open drains and unlaid roads.* N COUNT = unpleasantness

annoyed /ə³nɔɪd/. If you are **annoyed**, you are fairly angry about something that has happened or that has been done. EG *I got really annoyed because my father started to talk in the middle of the film... She shook her head, annoyed with herself for forgetting his name.* ADJ QUALIT: PRED = upset

annoying /ə³nɔɪɪŋ/. An **annoying** person, action, or thing makes you feel fairly angry and impatient. EG *He was tapping an annoying rhythm on his glass with his fork... They're always doing annoying things.* ADJ QUALIT = maddening, irritating ◊ **annoyingly**. EG *She was annoyingly vague... Heissman, inconveniently and most annoyingly, was nowhere to be seen.* ◊ ADV OR ADV SEN = irritatingly

annual /ænjʊ⁰əl/, **annuals**. 1 **Annual** means 1.1 happening or done once a year or every year. EG *...the annual meeting of the Association... ...her annual holiday.* ADJ CLASSIF: ATTRIB = yearly ◊ **annually**. EG *Independence day is celebrated annually.* ◊ ADV WITH VB 1.2 happening or calculated over a period of one year. EG *...an annual income of roughly twelve thousand dollars... ...the average annual rate of increase.* ADJ CLASSIF: ATTRIB = yearly ◊ **annually**. EG *They imported 500 million tonnes of crude oil annually.* ◊ ADV WITH VB

2 An **annual** is 2.1 a book or magazine that is published once a year, especially one for children. N COUNT ⇑ periodical 2.2 a plant that grows, flowers, produces seed, and dies within one year or one season. N COUNT

annuity /ənju:ə¹ti¹/, **annuities**. An **annuity** is an investment or insurance policy that pays a fixed sum of money to someone each year. EG *...to ensure a guaranteed income by the purchase of an annuity.* N COUNT

annul /ənʌl/, **annuls, annulling, annulled**. If a contract or a marriage is **annulled**, it is declared invalid, so that legally it is considered never to have V+O ⇑ invalidate = dissolve existed. EG *The marriage had subsequently been annulled.*

annulment /ənʌlmə²nt/. **Annulment** of a contract or marriage is a declaration that it is invalid, so that legally it is considered never to have existed. EG *This applies whether your marriage has ended by death, divorce, or annulment.* [N UNCOUNT/COUNT]

annum /anəm/. See **per annum**.

Annunciation /ənʌnsɪeɪʃə⁰n/. In Christian belief, the **Annunciation** is the announcement described in the Bible when the archangel Gabriel tells Mary that she is going to give birth to the son of God. [N PROPER : *the*+N]

anode /ænəʊd/, **anodes**. An **anode** is the positive electrode in a cell such as a battery; a technical term in electronics. [N COUNT ≠ cathode]

anodyne /ænə⁶daɪn/, **anodynes**. 1 If you refer to something as an **anodyne**, you mean that it lessens or prevents the effects of distress or unhappiness. EG *He used to speak of work as 'the great anodyne'.* [N COUNT : USU SING = palliative]

2 Something that is **anodyne** is neutral, not dangerous or distressing. EG *We kept the talk on a safely anodyne level.* [ADJ CLASSIF ⇑ neutral = bland]

anoint /ənɔɪnt/, **anoints, anointing, anointed**. If you **anoint** someone or **anoint** a part of their body, you put oil or another liquid on a part of their body for religious or ceremonial reasons. EG *They saved their most precious oils to anoint his feet.* [V+O : IF+PREP THEN *with* ⇑ smear]

anomalous /ənɒmələs/. Something that is **anomalous** is different from what is normal or usual, and is therefore often considered unsatisfactory; a formal word. EG *...but these calculations have given anomalous results.* [ADJ CLASSIF ⇑ unusual ≠ ordinary]

anomaly /ənɒməli¹/, **anomalies**. An **anomaly** is a rule or practice that is different from what is normal or usual, and which is therefore unsatisfactory; a formal word. EG *We must correct these injustices and anomalies.* [N COUNT ⇑ oddity]

anomie /ænə⁷mi¹/ is lack of moral standards; a technical term in sociology. [N UNCOUNT]

anon /ə³nɒn/ means quite soon; an old-fashioned or informal word. EG *Well, see you anon.* [ADV AFTER VB ⇑ later]

Anon. is written after a poem, a saying, etc to show that nobody knows who its author is; an abbreviation for 'anonymous'.

anonymity /ænə⁷nɪmɪti¹/. 1 **Anonymity** is the state of not having your name or identity known, especially when you have done a particular thing. EG *...a benefactor who insisted on anonymity.* [N UNCOUNT ≠ publicity]

2 The **anonymity** of something is 2.1 the fact that it hides the identity of people connected with it or the person who created it. EG *...the anonymity of a typewritten letter... ...the anonymity of life in big cities.* [N UNCOUNT+SUPP] 2.2 its lack of unusual or interesting features which would distinguish it from other similar things. EG *...the anonymity of a hotel room.* [N UNCOUNT+SUPP ⇑ quality ≠ individuality]

anonymous /ə³nɒnɪməs/. 1 If someone remains **anonymous** when they do something or give something, their name is not revealed or announced because they do not wish it to be. EG *The donor prefers to remain anonymous... ...drab-suited anonymous officials.* ▸ used of actions or things. EG *...anonymous letters... ...an anonymous gift.* ◊ **anonymously**. EG *Anyone who wanted to make a complaint could do so anonymously.* [ADJ CLASSIF ⇑ unknown ≠ known, named] [◊ ADV WITH VB]

2 Something that is **anonymous** 2.1 does not reveal the identity of people connected with it. EG *A taxi is anonymous. Nobody knows who's inside.* [ADJ CLASSIF] 2.2 has no unusual or interesting features. EG *He's got an anonymous face... ...an anonymous little town.* [ADJ CLASSIF ⇑ ordinary ≠ memorable]

anorak /ænə⁸ræk/, **anoraks**. An **anorak** is a warm, waterproof jacket that usually has a hood. [N COUNT = windcheater]

anorexia /ænə⁷rɛksɪə/ is an illness in which a person has an overwhelming fear of becoming fat, and so refuses to eat properly and becomes thinner and thinner. [N UNCOUNT]

anorexic /ænə⁷rɛksɪk/ If someone is **anorexic**, they are suffering from anorexia and so are very thin. [ADJ CLASSIF]

another /ənʌðə/. 1 When you refer to **another** thing or person, you are referring to 1.1 an additional thing or person of a similar kind to the one that you have just been talking about. EG *She finished her cigarette, then lit another one immediately... When they had dealt with the fire another crisis arose.* ▸ used as a pronoun. EG *He made a drink for Meadows, then poured another for himself... ...a tin of pink paint and another of brown.* [DET+N COUNT IN SING = a further ≠ the same] [▸ PRON : SING] 1.2 a thing or person that is different from the one that you have just been talking about or from yourself. EG *They made it a crime to marry a person of another race... ...making physical contact with another person... It's all past history and it happened in another country... The argument can be put another way.* ▸ used as a pronoun. EG *He took his woollen scarf from one nail and his cap from another... ...a minor civil war–one tribe against another. It was not her own experience that she was describing but another's.* [DET+N COUNT IN SING] [▸ PRON : SING]

2 **Another** is also used before a word referring to a distance, length of time, or other amount, to indicate that this amount is in addition to a previous one or to one that has been previously mentioned. EG *We walked another hundred yards... I waited another week... I've got another three books to read.* [DET+NUM+N IN PLURAL, OR DET+N IN SING ⇑ additional]

3 You use **one another** to indicate that each member of a group does something to the others, or that there is a particular connection between each of the members of the group. EG *They didn't dare to look at one another... Members usually meet regularly in one another's homes.* [PHR : USED AS O = each other]

4 If you say that a person, place, or event is **another** Garbo, **another** Silicon Valley, **another** Vietnam, etc, you mean that they are just like Garbo, Silicon Valley, Vietnam, etc. [DET+N PROPER ⇑ second]

5 If you say that **one** thing **after another** happens or is done, you mean that the same sort of thing happens continuously or repeatedly, often for a long time. EG *She found one excuse after another to postpone it... He begins opening bottles, one after another.* [PHR : USED AS S/O]

6 The expression **or another** is used after 'one' or occasionally 'some' when you cannot or do not want to be precise about which of several alternatives or possibilities you are referring to. EG *...sport of one kind or another... We'll get there one way or another... One or another of them is given priority... ...protectionism in some form or another.* [PHR = other]

7 **one thing and another**: see **thing**.

answer /ɑːnsə/, **answers, answering, answered**. 1 When you **answer** someone who has asked you something or said something to you, you say something to them telling them what they want to know, saying yes or no, or showing that you have heard them. EG *'What's up?' said Sue. He didn't answer... I didn't know how to answer her... She asked many questions and I tried my best to answer them... He answered that the price would be £5,200... 'Did he win?'–'No,' I answered.* [V OR V+O/REPORT-CL/QUOTE = reply, respond]

2 An **answer** is something that you say when you answer someone who asks you a question or speaks to you. EG *The answer is no!... 'Is there anyone here?' I asked. There was no answer... She made a number of remarks that did not need an answer... This was a question to which she did not know the answer... John was perfectly frank with him in answer to this direct question.* [N COUNT, OR *in*+N : IF+PREP THEN *to* = reply, response]

3 To **answer** a letter or advertisement means to write to the person who wrote it. EG *You never answered my letters... She answered an advertisement for a fulltime mother's help.* ▸ used as a noun. EG *I got their answer to my letter telling them we were coming... He wrote off letters in answer to advertisements in professional journals.* [V OR V+O = reply to, respond to] [▸ N COUNT, OR *in*+N : IF+PREP THEN *to* = reply, response]

4 When you **answer** the telephone or the door, you pick up the telephone when it rings or go to the door when you hear a knock or the bell. EG *At 7.05 the doorbell rang and Brody answered it... I'm scared to answer the phone... When they answered, he asked to talk to Lord Halifax.* ▸ used as a noun. EG *I rang the doorbell, but there was no answer.* [V OR V+O] [▸ N COUNT]

5 An **answer** to a problem is a possible solution to it. EG *There is no easy answer to the problem of pollution... Mother's helps can be the answer for couples who cannot afford a nanny... Do you think that nuclear power is the answer?* [N COUNT : IF+PREP THEN *to*]

6 Something that **answers** a need or purpose satisfies it. EG *These discussion groups are obviously answering a need.* [V OR V+O ⇑ satisfy]

7 The **answer** to a question in a test or in a lesson is something that a student writes or says in an attempt to give the correct fact or to get the result that is asked for. EG *I think the answer to No. 5 is fourteen... You get full marks for getting the right answer... The answers are very easy to mark...* ▸ used as a verb. EG *You have to answer four questions.* [N COUNT : IF+PREP THEN *to*] [▸ V+O]

8 An **answer** to an action or event is something that someone does as a reaction or response to it. EG *They had no answer to napalm attacks, other than to retreat... 'Hello,' he said. She gave him a dreamy stare in answer.* ▸ used as a verb. EG *Sam answered her look with a grin... ...a major incursion which would be answered by massive retaliation.*
N COUNT, OR *in*+N : IF+PREP THEN *to* = reply
▸ V+O+A *(with)* = counter

9 Your **answer** to a criticism or accusation is what you say or write in your own defence against it. EG *What would your answer be to the accusation that you are old-fashioned?... In answer to your criticism, I would suggest that you have completely misunderstood the purpose of my work.* ▸ used as a verb. EG *How would you answer that charge?... There is certainly a case to answer.*
N SING : POSS+N, OR *in*+N = reply
▸ V+O

10 Someone or something that **answers** a particular description or **answers to** it, has the characteristics described. EG *A man answering his description has been seen in the Bedford area.*
V+O, OR V+A *(to)* ⇑ correspond = match

answer back. If someone, especially a child, **answers** you **back** or **answers back**, they speak rudely to you when you have told them to do something or said something critical to them; an informal expression. EG *I could never resist the temptation to answer teachers back.*
PHRASAL VB : V+ADV, OR V+O+ADV

answer for. 1 When someone **answers for** something bad that they have done, they are punished for it. EG *One of these days you will have to answer for your crimes.* ● If you say that someone **has a lot to answer for**, you mean that their actions have had a lot of bad results. EG *I think that motorists have a lot to answer for.*
PHRASAL VB : V+PREP, HAS PASS = pay
● PHR : AUX INFLECTS

2 If you say that you can or will **answer for** someone or for their qualities, you mean that you are sure that they they will do what is wanted or that they have the qualities referred to. EG *I can answer for his loyalty.*
PHRASAL VB : V+PREP, HAS PASS = vouch for

answerable /ɑːnsəʳrəbəʳl/. 1 If you are **answerable** to someone, you have to report and explain your actions to them because they have authority over you. EG *Area Health Authorities are answerable to their regional Health Authorities... I am answerable to no one.*
ADJ CLASSIF : PRED+*to* = accountable

2 If you are **answerable** for your actions or for someone else's actions, you are considered to have responsibility for them. EG *We are answerable for the actions of our children.*
ADJ CLASSIF : PRED+*for* = responsible

answering /ɑːnsəʳrɪŋ/. An **answering** action or remark is one that is done or said in response to something. EG *He looked around for answering smiles... 'Forward with the revolution' came the answering cry from 5000 people.*
ADJ CLASSIF : ATTRIB

answering machine, answering machines. An **answering machine** is a device which you connect to your telephone so that it records telephone calls while you are out.
N COUNT

ant /ænt/, **ants**. An **ant** is a small insect that lives in large groups. There are several kinds of ant.
N COUNT

antagonise /æntægənaɪz/. See **antagonize**.

antagonism /æntægənɪzəʳm/ is hatred or hostility. EG *...a mother who feels antagonism towards her children.*
N UNCOUNT : IF+PREP THEN *towards* ⇑ dislike

antagonist /æntægənɪst/, **antagonists**. Your **antagonist** is someone who you are having a contest, fight, or quarrel with. EG *Clinton was a formidable antagonist.*
N COUNT

antagonistic /æntægənɪstɪk/. Someone who is **antagonistic** to a person or thing feels or shows hatred or hostility towards them. EG *Many of them are equally antagonistic towards the President... He is openly antagonistic to the media, particularly newspapers... ...antagonistic feelings.*
ADJ QUALIT : IF+PREP THEN *towards/to* ⇑ opposed = hostile ≠ friendly

antagonize /æntægənaɪz/, **antagonizes, antagonizing, antagonized**; also spelled **antagonise**. If you **antagonize** someone, you make them feel angry or hostile towards you. EG *He had antagonized local tribesmen... ...a 'monarchal' style in office that has strongly antagonized many ordinary Frenchmen.*
V+O ⇑ anger = alienate

Antarctic /æntɑːkʳtɪk/. The **Antarctic** is the region around the South Pole. EG *...their final expedition to the Antarctic... ...the killing cold of the Antarctic nights.*
N PROPER : *the*+N ⇑ region

ante /ænti¹/. If you **up the ante** or **raise the ante**, 1 you increase the value of the stake in a gambling game; an informal expression. 2 you increase your demands when you are in dispute or fighting for something; an informal expression. EG *Environmentalists recently upped the ante; a decade ago they sought only 60,000 acres-Now they want over 100,000.*
PHR : VB INFLECTS
PHR : VB INFLECTS

ant-eater, ant-eaters. An **ant-eater** is an animal with a long snout that eats termites or ants. Ant-eaters live in warm countries.
N COUNT

antecedent /æntɪsiːdənt/, **antecedents**. 1 The **antecedent** of something such as an event, an organization, or a living creature is something else that happened or existed before it and that is related to it or similar to it in some way. EG *Its antecedents were the great campaigns of the Liberal Party... ...the prehistoric antecedents of the horse.*
N COUNT : IF+PREP THEN *of/to* = forerunner

2 Someone's **antecedents** are their ancestors or the family that they come from and its past history. EG *It is important to know a little at least about the antecedents of people.*
N PLURAL : POSS+N ⇑ origins = background

antechamber /æntɪtʃeɪmbə/, **antechambers**; also spelled with a hyphen. An **antechamber** is a small room leading into a larger room.
N COUNT = anteroom

antedate /ænti¹deɪt/, **antedates, antedating, antedated**. Something that **antedates** something else happened or existed before it; a formal word. EG *The Egyptians' written records antedated those of the Greeks by thousands of years.*
V+O ⇑ precede = predate

antediluvian /æntɪdɪ⁵luːvɪən/. Something that is **antediluvian** is extremely old or old-fashioned; a literary word often used humorously. EG *Old women with antediluvian ideas still ruled the roost.*
ADJ CLASSIF = antiquated

antelope /æntɪləʊp/, **antelopes**. The form **antelope** can also be used for the plural. An **antelope** is an animal with long legs and horns, which looks like a deer, can run ver fast, and eats grass or leaves. There are many kinds of antelope. Antelopes live in Africa and Asia. EG *...a herd of antelopes.*
N COUNT ⇑ herbivore

antenatal /ænti¹neɪtəʳl/, **antenatals**; also spelled with a hyphen. 1 **Antenatal** means relating to the medical care of women when they are expecting a baby. EG *Much of the ante-natal care is being undertaken in hospital... ...an antenatal clinic.*
ADJ CLASSIF : ATTRIB = prenatal ≠ post-natal

2 An **antenatal** is a medical examination of a pregnant woman. EG *I'm going for my antenatal this morning.*
N COUNT

antenna /æntenə/, **antennae, antennas**. The plural can be **antennae** or **antennas**. For paragraph 2 it is usually **antennas**. 1 The **antennae** of an insect or of an animal such as a prawn or lobster are the two long, thin parts that are attached to its head and that it uses to feel with. EG *These insects have a well-defined head with compound eyes and antennae.*
N COUNT : USU PL = feelers

2 The **antenna** of a piece of radio equipment is its aerial; used in American English. EG *...TV antennas... ...the ship's long-range antenna.*
N COUNT

anterior /æntɪərɪə/; a formal word. **Anterior** means 1 situated at or towards the front of something. EG *...the whale's anterior hump.* 2 happening or existing at an earlier time.
ADJ CLASSIF
ADJ CLASSIF

anteroom /ænti¹ru⁴m/, **anterooms**; also spelled with a hyphen. An **anteroom** is a small room in which people can wait before going into a larger room in which a formal event is taking place. EG *They were waiting in an anteroom for interrogation... The ante-room was full of posters and advertisements.*
N COUNT = antechamber

anthem /ænθəm/, **anthems**. An **anthem** is a kind of formal song or religious hymn written for a special occasion, such as a church service or a coronation. EG *We want to practise the anthem 'The valleys stand so thick with corn'.* ● See also **national anthem**.
N COUNT

ant hill, ant hills; also spelled with a hyphen. An **ant hill** is a mound of earth formed by ants when they are making a nest.
N COUNT

anthology /ænθɒlədʒi¹/, **anthologies**. An **anthology** is a collection of poems, plays, stories, songs, etc, by different writers, which are published together in one book. EG *...an anthology of English poetry.*
N COUNT : IF+PREP THEN *of*

anthracite /ænθrəsaɪt/ is a type of very hard coal which burns slowly, with a small flame and very little smoke, producing a lot of heat.
N UNCOUNT

anthrax /ænθræks/ is a disease of cattle and sheep, in which they get painful sores and a fever.
N UNCOUNT

anthropoid /ænθrəpɔɪd/, **anthropoids**. 1 An **anthropoid** creature is one that is very like a human being. EG *...nothing more than a terrestrial anthropoid ape.*
ADJ CLASSIF

2 Anthropoids are the apes that are most closely related to humans. EG *...man and the anthropoids.* — N COUNT

anthropology /ænθrəpɒlədʒi¹/ is the scientific study of people, society, and culture. EG *The relevance of biology and anthropology is evident enough.* ◊ **anthropologist, anthropologists.** EG *...an English anthropologist, Colin Turnbull.* ◊ **anthropological.** EG *...anthropological research.* — N UNCOUNT; ◊ N COUNT; ◊ ADJ CLASSIF

anthropomorphic /ænθrəpəmɔːfɪk/ means **1** involving or resulting from the belief that a god resembles a human being in appearance, feelings, or behaviour. EG *...our anthropomorphic image of God.* — ADJ CLASSIF
2 involving or resulting from the belief that an animal or object has feelings like those of a human being. EG *We are being anthropomorphic, attributing human feelings to animals.* — ADJ CLASSIF

anthropomorphism /ænθrəpəmɔːfɪzə⁰m/ is **1** the belief that a god resembles a human being in appearance, feelings, or behaviour. **2** the belief that an animal or object has feelings like those of a human being. — N UNCOUNT; N UNCOUNT

anti- is placed in front of a word, to form another word that means **1** opposed to a particular system or practice. EG *...apartheid→anti-apartheid... ...abortion→anti-abortion.* **2** opposed to a particular group of people or their policies, culture, or power. EG *...American→anti-American.* **3** intended to prevent something from happening or to destroy something harmful. EG *...poverty→anti-poverty... ...freeze→antifreeze... ...aircraft→anti-aircraft.* **4** intended to prevent something from having any harmful effects. EG *...an anti-roll bar.* **5** having the opposite effect or going in the opposite direction. EG *...clockwise→anticlockwise.* — PREFIX ≠ pro-; PREFIX ≠ pro-; PREFIX; PREFIX; PREFIX

anti-aircraft. An **anti-aircraft** weapon or system of defence is intended to destroy enemy aircraft. EG *...anti-aircraft missiles.* — ADJ CLASSIF: ATTRIB ⇑ defensive

antibiotic /ænti¹baɪɒtɪk/, **antibiotics.** An **antibiotic** is a chemical or drug that is used in medicine to kill bacteria and to cure infections. There are many different kinds of antibiotics. EG *She is still taking the antibiotics.* — N COUNT: USU PL

antibody /ænti¹bɒdi¹/, **antibodies.** An **antibody** is a substance which a person's or an animal's body produces in their blood in order to destroy substances which carry disease. — N COUNT ⇑ protein

anticipate /æntɪsɪpeɪt/, **anticipates, anticipating, anticipated. 1** If you **anticipate** an event or happening, you realize that it may happen before it actually does happen, so that you are prepared for it. EG *The Secretary had anticipated the question... Incomes rose faster than anticipated... Get some instruction even though you don't anticipate using it... It's impossible to anticipate when it will happen.* ◊ **anticipation** /æntɪsɪpeɪʃə⁰n/. EG *The financial markets had raised interest rates in anticipation of a squeeze.* — V+O/REPORT-CL ⇑ expect = foresee; ◊ N UNCOUNT = expectation
2 If you **anticipate** something that you know is going to happen or that you know you are going to receive, you act as though it had already happened or as though you had already received it. EG *They were anticipating the decision by several hours.* — V+O ≠ wait for
3 If you **anticipate** something pleasant or exciting that is going to happen, you look forward to it with pleasure. EG *She had often pleasurably anticipated the moment when she would be handing in her notice.* ◊ **anticipation.** EG *'Please!' the children would chorus, jumping up and down in anticipation.* — V+O ⇑ await; ◊ N UNCOUNT = eagerness
4 If you **anticipate** part of a story or account that you are telling, you tell people about something that happened later before you tell them about the things that happened earlier. EG *I am anticipating a little... Coherence and continuity make it desirable to anticipate here the course and outcome of the campaign.* — V OR V+O

anticipatory /æntɪsɪpeɪtə⁰ri¹/. An **anticipatory** feeling or action is one that you have or that you do because you are expecting something to happen soon; a formal word. EG *...anticipatory delight... ...anticipatory actions.* — ADJ CLASSIF: ATTRIB ⇑ expectant = eager

anticlimax /ænti¹klaɪmæks/, **anticlimaxes.** An **anticlimax** is a situation or event which disappoints you because it is not as exciting as you expected or because it happens after something which was very exciting. EG *Polling day was uneventful, a bit of an anticlimax... ...a sense of anticlimax.* — N COUNT/UNCOUNT = disappointment, let down

anticlockwise /ænti¹klɒkwaɪz/. If something is moving **anticlockwise**, it is moving in the opposite direction to the direction in which the hands of a clock move; used in British English. EG *He drove round the courtyard anticlockwise.* ▸ used as an adjective. EG *It was travelling in an anticlockwise direction.* — ADV AFTER VB; ▸ ADJ CLASSIF: ATTRIB

antics /æntɪks/. **Antics** are **1** funny and unusual ways of behaving or of moving around. EG *The jokes and the antics will continue until he is obliged to go back to school... I lay back, smiling with pleasure at the antics of red squirrels.* **2** actions which other people do which seem silly and ridiculous to you; used showing disapproval. EG *The press has pointed an accusing finger at the antics of the main political parties.* — N PLURAL = clowning; N PLURAL ⇑ activities

anticyclone /ænti¹saɪkləʊn/, **anticyclones.** An **anticyclone** is an area of high atmospheric pressure which causes settled weather conditions and, in summer, clear skies and high temperatures. — N COUNT

antidote /ænti¹dəʊt/, **antidotes.** An **antidote** is **1** a chemical substance that stops or controls the effect of a poison. EG *Poison and antidote are sometimes found in the same place.* **2** something that helps you to overcome or change a difficult or unpleasant situation. EG *Work is a wonderful antidote to misery... Economics did not provide any immediate antidote to inflation.* — N COUNT = remedy; N COUNT: IF+PREP THEN *to* ⇑ cure = remedy, answer

antifreeze /ænti¹friːz/ is a liquid which is added to water to stop it freezing, used in the radiator of a car in cold weather. — N UNCOUNT

antigen /æntɪdʒə²n/, **antigens**; a technical word. An **antigen** is a protein in the body of a person or animal which may cause them to develop an infection or allergy. Your blood normally produces another protein, an antibody, to fight against an antigen. — N COUNT

antihero /ænti¹hɪərəʊ/, **antiheroes.** An **antihero** is a main character in a novel, play, or film who behaves in a completely different way from the way that people expect a hero to behave. — N COUNT

antihistamine /ænti¹hɪstəmi¹n/, **antihistamines.** An **antihistamine** is a drug used to treat illnesses that are caused by allergies, for example hay fever. — N COUNT

antimacassar /ænti¹məkæsə/, **antimacassars.** An **antimacassar** is a decorative cloth that is put over the back of a chair to keep it clean. — N COUNT

antimatter /ænti¹mætə/ is, in scientific theory, a form of matter whose particles have characteristics and properties opposite to those of ordinary matter. — N UNCOUNT

antimony /æntɪməni¹/ is a silvery-white metal which is often used in alloys to strengthen other metals. — N UNCOUNT

antipathetic /æntɪpəθetɪk, æntɪpə-/. If you are **antipathetic** to someone or something, you have a strong feeling of dislike or hostility towards them. EG *He is completely antipathetic to the aims of our organisation.* — ADJ QUALIT: USU PRED, IF+PREP THEN *to* = hostile ≠ sympathetic

antipathy /æntɪpəθi¹/, **antipathies. Antipathy** to someone or something is a strong feeling of dislike or hostility towards them. EG *Both share a common antipathy to colonialism... There was a certain amount of antipathy between the two actors.* — N UNCOUNT: IF+PREP THEN *to/towards* = antagonism ≠ affection

Antipodes /æntɪpədiːz/. The **Antipodes** is used by people in the northern hemisphere to refer, often humorously, to Australia and New Zealand. — N PROPER: *the*+N

antiquarian /æntɪkweəriən/, **antiquarians. 1 Antiquarian** means concerned with old and rare objects that help to explain the past. EG *...antiquarian and archaeological research.* — ADJ CLASSIF: ATTRIB
2 An **antiquarian** bookseller or bookshop deals in old or second-hand books. EG *He always found time for an hour or two in the antiquarian bookshops.* — ADJ CLASSIF: ATTRIB
3 An **antiquarian** is the same as an antiquary. — N COUNT

antiquary /æntɪkwə²ri¹/, **antiquaries.** An **antiquary** is a person who studies the past, or who collects or buys and sells old and valuable objects. — N COUNT = antiquarian

antiquated /æntɪkweɪtɪ²d/. **1 Antiquated** practices, ideas, or objects are very old-fashioned and no longer appropriate or relevant, and need to be replaced. EG *...a real desire to modernise Britain and free it from antiquated tradition... ...the clatter of the antiquated air-conditioning machine.* — ADJ QUALIT: USU ATTRIB = outmoded ≠ modern
2 If you say someone is **antiquated**, in informal English, you mean that they seem to you to be very old, especially because they have ideas which you think are old-fashioned. EG *You're positively antiquated, Dad!* — ADJ QUALIT

antique /æntiːk/, **antiques**. An **antique** is an old object, for example a piece of china or furniture, which is valuable because of its beauty or rarity. EG *How do you clean the brass inlay on a polished antique?* ▸ used as an adjective. EG *...antique furniture.* — N COUNT; ▸ ADJ CLASSIF : ATTRIB

antique shop, antique shops. An **antique shop** is a shop where antiques are sold. — N COUNT

antiquity /æntɪkwɪti¹/, **antiquities**. 1 **Antiquity** is used to refer to the distant past, especially the time of the ancient Egyptians, Greeks, and Romans. EG *...the great lost paintings of antiquity... The origins of this practice are lost in antiquity.* — N UNCOUNT : USU *in/of*+N

2 An **antiquity** is a very old building or ruin, or a statue, painting, coin, etc which was made in ancient times and which has been preserved until the present day. EG *...the Cairo Museum of Antiquities.* — N COUNT : USU PL; ⇑ relic

3 The **antiquity** of something is its great age. EG *...a famous landmark of great antiquity... ...the antiquity of the custom.* — N UNCOUNT : USU + *of*

anti-Semite /ænti¹siːmaɪt/, **anti-Semites**. An **anti-Semite** is a person who strongly dislikes and is prejudiced against Jewish people. — N COUNT; ⇑ racist

anti-Semitic /æntɪ¹sə²mɪtɪk/. Someone or something that is **anti-Semitic** is hostile to and prejudiced against Jewish people. EG *Two anti-Semitic letters appeared in the paper.* — ADJ CLASSIF; ⇑ racist

anti-Semitism /ænti¹sə²mɪtɪzə⁰m/is intense dislike for and prejudice against Jewish people. EG *He declared that no anti-Semitism existed among the Board of Directors.* — N UNCOUNT; ⇑ racism

antiseptic /ænti¹septɪk/, **antiseptics**. 1 An **antiseptic** is a substance that kills germs and harmful bacteria. EG *I washed out the wound with antiseptic.* ▸ used as an adjective. EG *They tell us that marjoram has antiseptic qualities.* — N UNCOUNT/COUNT; ▸ ADJ CLASSIF; ⇑ cleansing

2 If you describe something as **antiseptic**, you mean that it lacks excitement or emotion; used showing disapproval. EG *...a dry antiseptic statement of policy... I remained completely unmoved in Anthony's antiseptic presence.* — ADJ QUALIT; = sterile, bland

anti-social. 1 Someone who is **anti-social** is unwilling to meet and be friendly with other people; used showing disapproval. EG *They both were proud and shy and anti-social.* — ADJ QUALIT; = unsociable; ≠ gregarious

2 An activity that is **anti-social** does not give you much opportunity to meet or be with other people. EG *Children nowadays find reading and writing are indoor, anti-social activities.* — ADJ QUALIT; ⇑ solitary; ≠ sociable

3 Behaviour that is **anti-social** is annoying or upsetting to other people; used showing disapproval. EG *Don't let your children develop an anti-social habit such as bullying... 'I don't like people phoning at this hour,' Davis complained. 'It's anti-social.'* — ADJ QUALIT; ⇑ inconsiderate

anti-tank. An **anti-tank** weapon is designed for destroying military tanks. EG *...an anti-tank rocket launcher.* — ADJ CLASSIF : ATTRIB

antithesis /æntɪθə¹sɪs/, **antitheses** /æntɪθə¹siːs/; a formal word. 1 The **antithesis** of something is the exact opposite of it. EG *He was a dry, poor speaker, a man of few words, the antithesis of a driving politician... ...one of the most direct antitheses between socialism and capitalism.* — N COUNT : USU SING, IF + PREP THEN *of*

2 **Antithesis** is the placing next to each other of two different statements, ideas, methods, etc, in order to emphasize a contrast between them and to give an effect of balance; a technical term in literary criticism. EG *...a skilful use of antithesis.* — N UNCOUNT; ⇑ juxtaposition

antithetical /æntɪθetɪkə⁰l/. Something that is **antithetical** to something else is opposite to it and unable to exist with it; a formal word. EG *This attitude is antithetical to my beliefs.* — ADJ CLASSIF : IF + PREP THEN *to*; = incompatible

antitoxin /ænti¹tɒksɪn/, **antitoxins**. An **antitoxin** is a substance which is produced by your body or taken as a medicine in order to control the effects of a poison. — N COUNT; ⇑ antibody

antitrust /ænti¹trʌst/. In America, **antitrust** laws are laws intended to stop large firms taking over their competitors, fixing prices with their competitors, or interfering with free competition in any other way. — ADJ CLASSIF : ATTRIB

antler /æntlə/, **antlers**. The **antlers** of a male deer are a pair of branched horns on its head. EG *In spring the stags drop their antlers.* — N COUNT : USU PL; ⇑ horn

antonym /æntə⁶nɪm/, **antonyms**. The **antonym** of a word is another word which means the opposite. EG *'Good' is the antonym of 'bad'.* — N COUNT; ≠ synonym

antonymous /æntɒnə¹məs/. Words that are **antonymous** are opposite in meaning. EG *'Good' and 'bad' are antonymous.* — ADJ CLASSIF; ≠ synonymous

anus /eɪnəs/, **anuses**. The **anus** of a person or animal is the hole between the buttocks, where faeces leave their body; a formal or medical term. — N COUNT; ⇑ opening

anvil /ænvɪl/, **anvils**. An **anvil** is a heavy iron block on which hot metals are beaten into a particular shape. EG *They had been working two pieces of metal together on the anvil.* — N COUNT

anxiety /æŋzaɪɪti¹/, **anxieties**. 1 **Anxiety** is a feeling of nervousness or worry about something, for example that something bad might happen. EG *'What do you think?' asked the Belgian with a touch of anxiety... This can lead to unnecessary anxiety over a child's quite normal behaviour.* — N UNCOUNT : IF + PREP THEN *about/over*; ⇑ fear; = concern

2 An **anxiety** is something which causes you to feel nervous or worried. EG *It should represent the views and anxieties of party members to the cabinet.* — N COUNT; ⇑ fear; = worry

3 An **anxiety** to do something is a strong wish to do it, often mixed with a feeling of worry that you might not be able to. EG *...the anxiety of people to receive treatment... ...their anxiety not to offend.* — N UNCOUNT + *to*-INF; ⇑ desire; = eagerness

anxious /æŋk⁰ʃəs/. 1 Someone who is **anxious** is nervous or worried about something, for example that something bad might happen. EG *It's time to be going home, your mother will be anxious... She was anxious about her job.* ▸ used of someone's expression or behaviour. EG *Karl was still peering round with sharp, anxious looks.* ◊ **anxiously**. EG *'I'm not boring you?' she said, anxiously.* ◊ **anxiousness**. EG *Symptoms are irritability, anxiousness, and restlessness.* — ADJ QUALIT : IF + PREP THEN *about*; ⇑ fearful; = concerned; ▸ ADJ QUALIT; ◊ ADV WITH VB; ◊ N UNCOUNT; = anxiety

2 An **anxious** time, situation, or question is one during which or because of which you feel nervous and worried. EG *You must have had an anxious day... It raised the anxious question as to whether enough had been done.* — ADJ QUALIT : ATTRIB; = worrying

3 If someone is **anxious** to do something or **anxious** that something should happen, they very much want to do it or very much want it to happen. EG *He was very anxious that we should have lunch one day soon... She's anxious to get abroad... ...civil servants anxious for promotion.* — ADJ QUALIT : PRED + *to*-INF/REPORT-CL OR PREP *(for)*; ⇑ desirous; = eager, keen

any /ɛni¹/. 1 You use **any** in negative statements, questions, and conditional clauses 1.1 when you want to mention something but when you do not want to say that it definitely exists. EG *I hadn't had any breakfast and I was getting hungry... She had hardly any money... It won't do any good... Were you in any danger?... It is unnecessary for me to add any comment... The customs man asked if I had any foreign newspapers.* ▸ used as a pronoun. EG *I don't like any of this... Did any of you see that play on television?... Discuss it with your female colleagues, if you are lucky enough to have any... Some students will know a lot of English; others will not have learnt any at all.* 1.2 when you are suggesting that something is so small or unimportant that it is not worth mentioning or considering. EG *It isn't any distance at all... Nothing else was of any account.* — DET; ▸ PRON OR QUANT : IF + PREP THEN *of*; DET + N COUNT IN SING; = much

2 You use **any** in positive statements when you are referring to something or someone without saying exactly what, who, or which kind you mean, often because being exact is not possible or does not matter. EG *Any big tin container will do... ...things that any man might do under pressure... ...at twilight or any other time... Cars can be rented at almost any U.S. airport... He did not make more than one purchase at any one shop.* ▸ used as a pronoun. EG *After that, any of the hunters could follow her more easily... The meeting was different from any that had gone before.* — DET; ≠ a specific; ▸ PRON OR QUANT : IF + PREP THEN *of*

3 **Not just any** means that the person or thing referred to is special in some way. EG *He is not just any footballer.* ● **any old**: see **old**. — DET

4 You can also use **any** to emphasize a comparative adjective or adverb in a negative statement. EG *I couldn't stand it any longer... He doesn't know any better... Nobody in the village will be any the wiser... He didn't want to express himself any more strongly than he had to.* — ADV + ADJ/ADV IN COMPAR, WITH NEG

5 In nonstandard American English, **any** can be used to emphasize a whole clause. EG *It didn't bother us any.* — ADV; = at all

6 The word **any** is also used in the following expressions, which are explained at other places in this

dictionary. • **in any case**: see **case**. • **by any chance**: see **chance**. • **in any event**: see **event**. • **by any means**: see **means**. • **at any rate**: see **rate**.

anybody /ɛnɪbɔ⁷di¹/. See **anyone**.

anyhow /ɛnɪhaʊ/. 1 **Anyhow** means the same as **anyway**.

2 **Anyhow** is also used to indicate that something has been done in a careless or untidy way or with an untidy result; an informal use. EG *They were all jumbled in anyhow... They did it just anyhow.* ▸ used as an adjective. EG *The room was all anyhow.* — ADV WITH VB; ▸ ADJ CLASSIF : PRED

anyone /ɛnɪwə⁹n/. The form **anybody** is also used. You use **anyone** and **anybody** when you are talking about people rather than things. Compare **anything**.

1 You use **anyone** or **anybody** in negative statements, questions, and conditional clauses, to mention a person when you do not want to say that they definitely exist. EG *There wasn't anyone there... Was there anyone behind you?... If anyone asks where you are I'll say you've just gone out... There really wasn't much room for anybody else anyway.* — PRON INDEF

2 You use **anyone** and **anybody** in positive statements to refer to a person or to people in general, when you cannot or do not want to say which particular person or people you are referring to. EG *Their laughter woke anyone who was not already up... Anyone can miss a plane... It could happen to anyone... He took longer than anybody else... 'Could I perhaps bring a friend with me?'–'Of course. Anyone.'* — PRON INDEF

3 You can also use **anyone** and **anybody** in expressions such as 'anyone who is anyone' to refer to people who are special, important, or influential. EG *Everybody who is anybody has one, because it is a status symbol.* — PRON INDEF

anything /ɛnɪθɪŋ/. You use **anything** when you are talking about possible things, events, or ideas, rather than people. 1 You use **anything** in negative statements, questions, and conditional clauses 1.1 to refer to an event, thing, or idea when you do not want to say that it definitely exists; EG *I did not say anything... He never seemed to do anything at all... If anything should happen, I can take care of myself... I've told her to come to you if she wants anything... Why do we have to show him anything?* ▸ used with an adjective. EG *They're surprised if anything good happens... They couldn't afford anything better... Hugel denied doing anything illegal or improper.* 1.2 when you are suggesting that something is so small or unimportant that it is not worth mentioning or considering. EG *When I was fifteen I went to my first school. I didn't know anything, so I had to catch up... That doesn't prove anything.* — PRON INDEF; ▸ PRON INDEF + ADJ; PRON INDEF

2 You can use **anything** in positive statements 2.1 to refer to a thing, an event, or an idea without saying exactly which one you mean, often because being exact is not possible or does not matter. EG *The situation was very tense; anything might happen... 'Do you like beer?'–'I like anything alcoholic'... To me, it's more important than anything else.* 2.2 to refer to an amount, number, time, quality, or thing within the range stated, when you do not want to be exact. EG *An average rate of anything between 25 and 60 per cent is usual... Grated lemon peel gives a fresh flavour to almost anything from soup to fruit.* — PRON INDEF : USU + ADJ; PRON INDEF

3 You use **anything** with a negative in expressions such as 'not anything like' for emphasis, when you are saying that something is not at all like something else. EG *It didn't taste anything like soup... The total wasn't anything near what we'd expected.* — ADV + *like/near* = remotely

4 **Anything** is also used in the following expressions:

4.1 If you say that someone or something is **anything but** funny, attractive, useful, etc, you mean that they are not at all funny, attractive, or useful. EG *The operation was anything but funny... He was anything but forceful.* 4.2 Expressions such as **as** fast **as anything** or **as** boring **as anything** are used in informal spoken English for emphasis, for example to say that someone or something is moving very fast, is very boring, etc. EG *It was as easy as anything... ...running as fast as anything down the road.* — PHR + ADJ : USED AS C = far from; PHR : USED AS AN A/C

4.3 You can say **like anything** in informal spoken English to indicate that an action is done with great force, energy, or enthusiasm. EG *She waved to us and we waved back like anything... The wheel was going round like anything.* 4.4 In informal spoken English, you can say that you **would not** do or be something **for anything** to emphasize that you definitely would not want to do something or to be a particular thing. EG *He told her he wouldn't miss it for anything... I wouldn't be a nurse for anything.* 4.5 You can say **not just anything** in informal English to refer to something special. EG *It isn't just anything; it's a very special occasion for me, and I want you to be there.* — PHR : USED AS AN A ⇑ a lot = like mad; PHR : USED AS AN A; PRON INDEF = nothing

4.6 You can add **or anything** to the end of a clause or sentence in informal spoken English in order to refer vaguely to other things that are or may be similar to what has just been mentioned. EG *Have you got any skis or anything?... I woke up. But not in a state of shock or anything, just having had a very vivid dream.* — PHR

5 The word **anything** is also used in the following expressions, which are explained at other places in this dictionary. • **anything goes**: see **go**. • **I'd give anything**: see **give**. • **if anything**: see **if**.

anyway /ɛnɪweɪ/. The form **anyhow** is also used. These words are used especially in spoken English. You use **anyway** or **anyhow** 1 to indicate that a statement explains or supports a previous point or makes that point seem less important. EG *We ought to spend less on the defence missiles, which I reckon are pretty useless anyway... I decided to postpone the idea of doing a course, and anyway I got accepted by the Council.* 2 to suggest that a statement is true or relevant in spite of other things that have been said. EG *'I can give you a lift if you wait.'–'No, I'll walk. Thanks, anyway.'... ...but we found a way to do it anyhow.* 3 to correct or modify an opinion or statement, for example to limit it to what you definitely know to be true. EG *'All of them?' I ask. 'Some, anyway.'... That's all it ever did. As far as we knew, anyhow.* 4 to indicate that you are asking what the real situation is or what the real reason for something is. EG *'What are you phoning for, anyway?'–'To see if you need a visa.'* 5 to change the topic or return to a previous topic. EG *She was on trial for his murder. It sounds like a squalid business. Anyway, Agate was in court when the woman was asked what was her first thought when she realized what had happened.* 6 to indicate that you are missing out some details in a story and passing on to the next main point or event. EG *I'd heard there was a flat available, so I went. Anyway I didn't get it.* 7 when you want to end the conversation. EG *Anyway, I've got to go. I'll see you tonight, then.* — ADV SEN = besides; ADV SEN; ADV SEN = at least; ADV SEN; ADV SEN = well; ADV SEN = well; ADV SEN = well

anywhere /ɛnɪwɛə/. 1 You can use **anywhere** in negative statements, questions, and conditional clauses 1.1 to refer to a place without saying exactly where you mean, for example because being exact is not possible or does not matter. EG *I changed my mind and decided not to go anywhere... There is not a sound anywhere... Is there an ashtray anywhere?... ...in Eastern Europe, or anywhere else for that matter... He came to see if there was a chaplain anywhere around.* 1.2 to refer to any part or aspect of a situation or area of life. EG *That had not happened anywhere in human history... There is no evidence anywhere that he ever thought of changing this policy.* 1.3 when you are suggesting that there are no places important enough to be worth mentioning or considering. EG *We haven't been anywhere this summer.* • If you say that a place or building is **miles from anywhere**, you mean that it is a very long way from any villages, towns, or other interesting places; an informal expression. EG *The cottage was miles from anywhere.* — ADV; ADV; ADV ⇑ somewhere; • PHR : USED AS AN A ⇑ isolated

2 You can also use **anywhere** in positive statements, 2.1 for emphasis with an expression that refers to a place or area. EG *They are the oldest dated rock paintings anywhere in North America... More of them lie in those waters than anywhere in the world... It is better to have it in the kitchen than anywhere else.* 2.2 to refer to a point within a stated range when you do not know what the point is. EG *I put the time scale on that anywhere from zero to fifteen years from now... I expected to find him in a mood anywhere between stiff outrage and cool disapproval.* **Not anywhere near**: see **near**. — ADV : USU + *else*/PREP; ADV + PREP *(from/between)*

3 If you say that someone or something **is not getting** or **going anywhere**, you mean that they are not making progress or achieving a satisfactory result. EG *This must be the first priority if the negotiation is to get anywhere... I'm not earning any money; I'm not going anywhere.* — PHR : VB INFLECTS

AOB /eɪ əʊ biː/ is an abbreviation for 'any other business', referring to an item on the agenda for a meeting, usually at the end, when anyone present can raise matters which have not been dealt with under any other item. N UNCOUNT ↑ item

aorta /eɪɔːtə/, **aortas**. Your **aorta** is the main artery through which blood leaves your heart before it flows through the rest of your body. N COUNT : USU SING ↑ tube

apace /əpeɪs/. If something is happening or growing **apace**, it happens or grows quickly; a literary word. EG *Darkness was coming on apace... Suspicion of learning grew apace.* ADV AFTER VB ↑ fast = rapidly

apart /əpɑːt/. 1 When someone or something is situated **apart** from another person or thing, there is a space or distance between them. EG *...a small shed set well apart from the main building... I was sitting somewhat apart from the rest... He stood with his legs planted apart... ...places as far apart as New York, Amsterdam, and Lagos.* ADV AFTER VB, ADJ CLASSIF PRED, + *from*

2 If two things are a particular distance **apart**, they are that distance away from each other. EG *Their faces were a couple of inches apart.* ADJ CLASSIF : PRED

3 If two things are moving **apart** or are being pulled **apart**, they are moving away from each other or are being separated. EG *They straightened and jumped apart... I rushed in and tried to pull the dogs apart.* ADV AFTER VB ≠ together

4 If two people are **apart**, they are not in each other's company and are living or spending time in different places. EG *They could not bear to be apart.* ADJ CLASSIF : PRED = separated ≠ together

5 If someone or something is considered to be **apart** from other people or things, they are considered to be different because they are unusual in some way. EG *Other religions think of God as being completely apart.* ADJ QUALIT : PRED, OR ADV, NG+ADV ≠ connected

6 If two people or groups of people grow **apart**, they develop different opinions, interests, or lifestyles, and do not have very much in common with each other. EG *As we travelled together, we started to grow apart... The communities generally got too far apart.* • **poles apart**: see **pole**. • **worlds apart**: see **world**. ADV AFTER VB = distant

7 If you take something **apart** or if something comes or falls **apart**, the various pieces that make up the whole separate from each other. EG *Houses built of fragile materials simply fall apart after a short time.* ADV AFTER VB = to bits

8 If something such as an organization, situation, or relationship falls **apart** or if it is pulled **apart**, it is seriously harmed. EG *I was tired of groups that fell apart when faced with the slightest difficulty... Their marriage began to fall apart.* ADV AFTER VB

9 If two events happen a week, month, year, etc **apart**, there is that amount of time between them. EG *The two women had their babies about four weeks apart.* ADV : NG+ADV

10 If you **can't tell** two people or things **apart**, thy both look exactly the same to you. EG *He couldn't tell the boys apart.* PHR : VB INFLECTS

11 **Apart** is used after a noun to indicate that you have finished talking about that subject or that you are excluding it from your discussion, and that you are now going to talk about something else. EG *Cooking apart, what a bride needs to know most about is money.* • **joking apart**: see **joke**. ADV : NG+ADV = aside

12 **apart from** is used 12.1 to refer to something, often something small or unimportant, which is an exception to the general situation or state of affairs. EG *Apart from Patrick, the car was empty... She had no money, apart from the five pounds that Christopher had given her... I'm away for about one week. But apart from that I'm around.* 12.2 to say that you want to ignore a particular subject or line of argument for the moment, so that you can mention another aspect of the situation which is less obvious or which has not yet been considered. EG *Apart from sport, my other interest outside class is music... But quite apart from the expense and the problem of the children, I don't think I would want to fly out anyway.* PREP ↑ excepting = aside from; PREP ↑ excluding = aside from

apartheid /əpɑːthaɪt, -heɪt/ is a political system used in South Africa in which people of different races are kept apart by law. EG *...the practical effects of apartheid on the daily lives of blacks.* N UNCOUNT

apartment /əpɑːtmə²nt/, **apartments**. An **apartment** is 1 a set of rooms for one family to live in, usually in a house or building which is divided into several such sets of rooms; used especially in American English. EG *They pay 2,000 dollars a month for their three-bedroomed apartment.* 2 a large room, usually with rich decorations and furnishings, which is used by an important person such as a king, queen, or president. EG *He moved into his main London palace, with splendid apartments of state.* N COUNT ↑ dwelling = flat; N COUNT

apartment house, **apartment houses**. An **apartment house** is a tall building which contains many different apartments on different floors; used in American English. EG *There are many thousands of apartment houses in this city.* N COUNT

apathetic /æpəθetɪk/. Someone who is **apathetic** is not interested in or enthusiastic about anything. EG *...bored, apathetic youngsters... Children lose hope and become apathetic.* ◊ **apathetically**. EG *The onlookers applauded apathetically.* ADJ QUALIT ↑ dull = listless ≠ enthusiastic ◊ ADV WITH VB

apathy /æpəθi¹/ is a state of mind in which you are not interested in or enthusiastic about anything. EG *...public apathy about politics.* N UNCOUNT ↑ boredom ≠ interest

ape /eɪp/, **apes, aping, aped.** 1 **Apes** are animals such as chimpanzees or gorillas. They are similar to monkeys, but are larger and do not have tails. EG *We watched two apes grooming each other.* N COUNT ↑ primate

2 If you call a man an **ape**, you mean that he is very stupid, clumsy, or ugly; used showing impatience or disapproval. EG *Show me your identity card instead of shooting at my foot, you ape.* N COUNT ↑ person

3 If you **ape** something, especially someone's speech or behaviour, you try to imitate it. EG *...behaviour that people lower down the social ladder would ape.* V+O ↑ copy = mimic

aperitif /ə³perɪti¹f/, **aperitifs**. An **aperitif** is an alcoholic drink that you have before a meal. EG *A couple of hours later, they were sipping aperitifs in Malaga.* N COUNT

aperture /æpətʃə/, **apertures**. 1 An **aperture** is a hole or gap, especially one that is small and narrow; a formal word. EG *Into this aperture a droplet of mercury was poured.* N COUNT ↑ opening

2 The **aperture** of a camera or telescope is the opening through which light passes into it. EG *I thought I would get a better picture using a larger aperture.* N COUNT ↑ size

apex /eɪpeks/, **apexes**. 1 The **apex** of something is the pointed end or top of it. EG *Bear Island is triangular in shape with its apex to the south.* N COUNT : IF+ PREP THEN *of* ↑ point

2 The **apex** of an organization or system is the highest and most important position in it. EG *The group was headed by an elite with a charismatic leader at its apex.* N COUNT : IF+ PREP THEN *of* ↑ top = head

APEX /eɪpeks/. An **APEX** ticket is a ticket for a journey by air which costs less than the standard ticket, but which you have to book a specified period in advance. EG *Fares range upwards from £220 for an Apex return in the low season.* N BEFORE N

aphid /eɪfɪd/, **aphids**. **Aphids** are very small insects which live on plants and suck their juices. They are common garden pests. N COUNT ↑ insect

aphorism /æfə⁸rɪzə⁰m/, **aphorisms**. An **aphorism** is a short and clever or witty sentence, which expresses a general truth. N COUNT ↑ saying

aphrodisiac /æfrə⁶dɪziæk/, **aphrodisiacs**. An **aphrodisiac** is a food, drink, or drug which makes people want to have sex. EG *...ginseng's reputation as a Chinese aphrodisiac.* ▸ used as an adjective. EG *Now there's something really aphrodisiac.* N COUNT ↑ stimulant ▸ ADJ QUALIT

apiece /əpiːs/. If items cost a particular amount **apiece**, or if two or more people have a particular number of items **apiece**, the items cost that amount each, or the people have that number each. EG *'How much are the birds?'-'Thirty-five cents apiece.'* ADV : NUM+N+ ADV

aplomb /əplɒm/. If you do something with **aplomb**, you do it with great confidence. EG *She went on with wonderful aplomb considering that no one seemed interested.* N UNCOUNT : USU *with*+N ↑ assurance = cool

apocalypse /əpɒkəlɪps/. 1 The **Apocalypse** is the total destruction and end of the world. EG *...a far from comforting vision of the Apocalypse.* N PROPER : *the*+ N

2 The **apocalypse** of something such as a civilization is its total destruction. EG *They were pulled together from the wreckage which had survived the apocalypse.* N SING WITH DET

apocalyptic /əpɒkəlɪptɪk/. **Apocalyptic** means 1 relating to the total destruction of something, especially of the world. EG *...an apocalyptic nuclear exchange... ...the apocalyptic confrontation between capitalism and socialism.* 2 relating to or involving prophecy about future disasters and the destruction of the world. EG *There is something apocalyptic* ADJ CLASSIF : ATTRIB ↑ catastrophic; ADJ CLASSIF ↑ prophetic *about the tone of his writings... ...a sudden apocalyptic vision.*

apocryphal /əpɒkrɪ¹fə⁰l/. An **apocryphal** story or joke is one that is not generally thought to be true or to have happened. EG *...the apocryphal story of Columbus and the egg.*
ADJ CLASSIF ⇑ untrue = dubious

apolitical /eɪpəlɪtɪkə⁰l/. Someone who is **apolitical** is not interested in or active in politics and does not support a particular political party. EG *The rally included many people who were normally quite apolitical.* ▸ used of behaviour. EG *Many of the organization's activities are apolitical and egocentric.*
ADJ QUALIT ⇑ neutral

apologetic /əpɒlədʒɛtɪk/. Someone who is **apologetic** shows by what they say or by the way they behave that they are sorry that they have hurt, upset, or caused trouble for someone else. EG *'Oh, I'm sorry,' said the girl, immediately apologetic... He had been apologetic about his behaviour at dinner.* ▸ used of speech and behaviour. EG *I had detected an apologetic note in his voice.* ◊ **apologetically**. EG *He smiled apologetically.*
ADJ QUALIT ▸ = penitent ◊ ADV WITH VB = ruefully

apologia /æpələʊdʒɪə/, **apologias**. An **apologia** is a statement in which you defend something that you strongly believe in, for example a way of life, an institution, or a philosophy; a formal word. EG *...a magnificent apologia for the House of Lords.*
N COUNT : USU SING+for ⇑ defence = apology

apologise /əpɒlədʒaɪz/. See **apologize**.

apologist /əpɒlədʒɪst/, **apologists**. An **apologist** for an idea, cause, or belief is a person who writes or speaks in defence of it; a formal word. EG *Late modernism and its apologists deny this.*
N COUNT : IF+ PREP THEN for/of ⇑ supporter = defender

apologize /əpɒlədʒaɪz/, **apologizes, apologizing, apologized**; also spelled **apologise**. When you **apologize** to someone, you say that you are sorry that you have hurt or upset them or caused trouble for them. EG *I apologise for my late arrival... I must apologize to you... 'Sorry I haven't called you yet,' Beynon apologized... She apologized for her behaviour.*
V : IF+PREP THEN for/to, OR V+QUOTE

apology /əpɒlədʒi¹/, **apologies**. **1 Apology** or an **apology** is something that you say or write in order to tell someone that you are sorry that you have hurt them, upset them, or caused trouble for them. EG *I have an apology to make to you, Lonnie... He sent a letter of apology to the publisher... He phoned after talking to Marsha and was full of apologies.*
N COUNT/ UNCOUNT : IF+ PREP THEN for/to

2 An **apology** for a particular thing is a very poor example of it; used showing disapproval. EG *They served up an apology for a meal.*
N COUNT : USU SING+for ⇑ substitute = excuse

3 An **apology** is also a statement in which you defend something that you strongly believe in; a formal use.
= apologia

apoplexy /æpəplɛksi¹/ is a stroke; an old-fashioned word. EG *He was so furious I thought he would have apoplexy.*
N UNCOUNT = stroke

apostasy /əpɒstəsi¹/. Someone's **apostasy** is the abandoning of their religious faith, political loyalties, or principles; a formal word. EG *...his only punishment for his apostasy.*
N UNCOUNT/ COUNT ⇑ desertion = rebellion

apostate /əpɒstɪ³t/, **apostates**. An **apostate** is someone who abandons their religious faith, political loyalties, or principles; a formal word. EG *...a family of apostates.* ▸ used as an adjective. EG *He was an apostate Catholic.*
N COUNT ⇑ deserter = renegade ≠ loyalist ▸ ADJ CLASSIF : ATTRIB

a posteriori /eɪpɒstɪərɪɔːraɪ/. **A posteriori** reasoning is based on observation or experience, so that you work out a general principle or theory from particular examples or evidence. The sentence: 'There is smoke coming from the chimney, therefore somebody must be at home' is an example of a posteriori reasoning: compare **a priori**.
ADJ CLASSIF : ATTRIB, OR ADV SEN = empirical ≠ a priori

apostle /əpɒsə⁰l/, **apostles**. **1** The **Apostles** were the followers of Jesus Christ who went from place to place telling people about him and trying to persuade them to become Christians. EG *...the preaching of the Apostles... ...the Apostle Paul.*
N COUNT ⇑ follower = disciple

2 An **apostle** of a particular philosophy, policy, cause, etc is someone who strongly believes in it and works hard to promote it. EG *...an apostle of change... ...the apostle of democracy.*
N COUNT ⇑ proponent = champion

apostolic /æpə⁷stɒlɪk/. **Apostolic** means **1** belonging or relating to a Christian religious leader, especially the Pope, who is considered to inherit authority from Christ's early followers. EG *...the apostolic succession... ...his apostolic blessing.* **2** belonging or relating to the early followers of Christ and to their teaching.
ADJ CLASSIF : ATTRIB; ADJ CLASSIF : ATTRIB ⇑ Christian

apostrophe /əpɒstrəfi¹/, **apostrophes**. An **apostrophe** is a mark written before or after a letter to indicate that one or more other letters have been omitted, as in, for example, 'can't' and 'he'll'. An apostrophe is also written before or after an 's' at the end of a word to indicate that what follows belongs or relates to the person or thing that the word refers to, as in, for example, 'the cat's whiskers' and 'the players' entrance'.
N COUNT

apothecary /əpɒθɪkəri¹/, **apothecaries**. An **apothecary** was a person who prepared medicines for people; an old-fashioned word.
N COUNT = chemist

apotheosis /əpɒθɪəʊsɪs/, **apotheoses**. **1** If a particular thing is the **apotheosis** of something, it is an ideal or perfect example of it; a formal word. EG *He seemed the apotheosis of generosity.*
N SING WITH DET +of = epitome

2 When a person's **apotheosis** happens, they become, or are declared to be, a god or a goddess. EG *This scene may represent the apotheosis of the dead princess.*
N COUNT : WITH POSS, USU SING ⇑ glorification = deification

appal /əpɔːl/, **appals, appalling, appalled**; also spelled **appall, appalls** in American English. If something **appals** you, it makes you feel disgust or dismay because it seems so bad or unpleasant. EG *People were appalled by the news... She hated the house–its very architecture appalled her.*
V+O : USU PASS = horrify

appalled /əpɔːld/. If you are **appalled** at something or **appalled** by it, you feel disgust or dismay because it seems so bad or unpleasant. EG *I was absolutely appalled at the quality of the reporting... She felt appalled and sick.* ▸ used of someone's expression or behaviour. EG *There was an appalled silence.*
ADJ QUALIT : USU +at/by/to-INF ⇑ shocked = horrified ▸ ADJ CLASSIF : ATTRIB

appalling /əpɔːlɪŋ/. **1** Something that is **appalling** is so bad or unpleasant that it makes you feel disgust or dismay. EG *Some of these people live in appalling conditions.* ◊ **appallingly**. EG *He had behaved appallingly.*
ADJ QUALIT = shocking, dreadful ◊ ADV WITH VB = dreadfully

2 Appalling is used to emphasize that something is extremely bad. EG *I had the most appalling depression.* ◊ **appallingly**. EG *We face an appallingly difficult period of transition... The situation has deteriorated appallingly since 1951.*
ADJ QUALIT : ATTRIB = awful ◊ ADV

apparatus /æpəreɪtəs/, **apparatuses**. **1 Apparatus** is the tools, machines, and other objects which are used for a particular purpose or which are needed to do a particular job or activity. EG *Hertz noticed a tiny spark on a piece of apparatus... ...large apparatus like slides and climbing frames.*
N UNCOUNT = equipment

2 An **apparatus** is a piece of equipment that is used for a particular purpose. EG *Wertheimer has constructed a similar apparatus.*
N COUNT+SUPP ⇑ appliance

3 The **apparatus** of an organization or system is its structure and method of operation; often used showing disapproval or impatience. EG *...the whole apparatus of the welfare state... ...a bureaucratic apparatus.*
N COUNT+SUPP = machine

apparel /əpærə⁰l/. Someone's **apparel** is the clothes that they are wearing, especially on an important occasion; a formal word. EG *...photographs of local brides in full wedding apparel.*
N UNCOUNT : POSS/MOD+N ⇑ clothing = attire

apparent /əpærənt/. **1** An **apparent** situation, quality, etc seems to exist, although you cannot be certain that it exists. EG *...the apparent success of these arranged marriages... The committee is investigating some apparent discrepancies.*
ADJ CLASSIF : ATTRIB = seeming

2 If something is **apparent** to you, it is clear and obvious to you. EG *It was becoming increasingly apparent to me that he disliked me... This attitude is apparent in some of the things they say... Everyone present ran out for no apparent reason.*
ADJ QUALIT : PRED, USU+to/in/REPORT-CL = evident

3 See **heir apparent**.

apparently /əpærəntli¹/. **Apparently** is **1** used to indicate that the information that you are giving is something that you have heard but you are not sure that it is true. EG *Apparently she's been living quite a while with them... 'I thought he owned the whole thing.'–'So did I. But apparently not.'* **2** used to refer to a situation that seems to exist although you are not sure that it exists. EG *She was standing by the window, apparently quite calm and relaxed.*
ADV SEN = it appears; ADV = seemingly

apparition /æpərɪʃə⁰n/, **apparitions**. An **apparition** is someone or something, especially a person who is dead, that you think that you see but that is not really there. EG *He is visited by an apparition, a girl mysteriously resembling his dead daughter.*
N COUNT ⇑ spirit = phantom

appeal /əpiːl/, **appeals, appealing, appealed**. **1** If you **appeal** for something that you need, espe-
V+A (for)/to-INF,

cially money, help, or sympathy, you make a serious and often urgent request for it. EG *He was appealing for funds to build a new school... 'Ladies,' the Chairman appealed. 'Could we possibly begin?'* OR V+QUOTE ⇑ ask

2 If you **appeal** to someone's sense of honour, reason, justice, etc, you suggest indirectly that if they want to seem honourable, reasonable, just, etc, they should do what you ask. EG *We went into the Professor's office confident we could appeal to his reason... They appeal to her sense of duty.* V+A *(to)* ⇑ invoke

3 If you **appeal** to someone in a position of authority against a decision that has been made, you formally ask them to change it. EG *He appealed to the Inland Revenue for a tax rebate... McEnroe appealed against the linesman's decision.* V+A *(to/against)* ⇑ apply

4 If you **appeal** to a court against a legal decision or sentence, you formally ask the court to change the decision or reduce the sentence. EG *He appealed against the five-year sentence he had been given.* V : IF+PREP THEN *to/against* ⇑ apply

5 An **appeal** is **5.1** a serious, often urgent, request for something, especially for money or help. EG *A radio appeal she made to ask for money for cancer research raised £75,000.* N COUNT : IF+PREP THEN *for* **5.2** a formal request to someone in a position of authority to change a decision that has been made. EG *His job is to hear our appeals against assessment for income tax.* N COUNT : IF+PREP THEN *against/to* **5.3** a formal request to a court of law for an earlier decision to be changed, or for a fine or sentence to be reduced. EG *The Supreme Court had just turned down our appeal... He had been given ten years in prison. On appeal it was reduced to five.* N COUNT/UNCOUNT ⇑ petition

6 An **appeal** to someone's sense of honour, reason, justice, etc is an indirect suggestion to them that if they have this quality they should do what you ask. EG *...an appeal to her maternal feelings.* N COUNT+*to* = call

7 If something **appeals** to you, you find it attractive or interesting. EG *These books are designed to appeal to children... The idea of becoming Lord Roseburn appealed to him.* V+A *(to)* ⇑ please

8 The **appeal** of a person, place, idea, etc is a quality or characteristic that they have which people find attractive. EG *What is the appeal of social democracy?... Theoretical subjects have lost their appeal for most students... ...a better car with greater driver appeal.* N UNCOUNT+SUPP ⇑ interest = attraction

appealing /əpiːlɪŋ/. **1** Someone or something that is **appealing** is pleasing and attractive. EG *...an appealing sense of humour... The idea of having enough money to retire at the age of 50 is very appealing.* ADJ QUALIT = engaging ◊ **appealingly**. EG *The old villa seemed appealingly rustic.* ◊ ADV+ADJ/ADV

2 An **appealing** expression, tone of voice, etc indicates to someone that you want help or advice. EG *From across the room she gave me an appealing look.* ADJ CLASSIF : ATTRIB = pleading ◊ **appealingly**. EG *'Could I stay with you, just for a short time,' she said appealingly, 'till I get fixed up?'* ◊ ADV WITH VB = beseechingly

appear /əpɪə/, **appears, appearing, appeared. 1** When something which you could not see before **appears**, it moves into a place or position where you can see it. You also say that something **appears** when you move into a place or position where you can see it. EG *A glow of light appeared over the sea... Two men suddenly appeared from nowhere... When we reached the top of the hill, a church tower appeared.* V : USU+A = materialize ≠ disappear

2 When something new or different **appears**, it begins to exist or reaches a stage of development where its existence can be noticed. EG *Apes first appeared in Africa twenty million years ago... The newest political party to appear in Britain is the SDP.* V : USU+A ⇑ develop = surface ≠ disappear

3 When a book or item **appears**, it is published or becomes available for people to buy. EG *His second novel appeared under the title 'Getting By'... It was several years ago that video recorders first appeared in the shops.* V : USU+A = come out

4 When a name, reference, number, etc, **appears** in a book or on a list, it is written there. EG *His name doesn't appear on the list.* V : USU+A *(in/on)* ⇑ occur = figure

5 When someone **appears** in a play or show, they take part in it in front of an audience. EG *He is currently appearing in the TV series 'Funny Man'.* V+A *(in)* ⇑ perform

6 When someone **appears** at or **appears** before a court of law or enquiry, they go there because they are formally required to do so, especially in order to answer charges made against them or as a witness to give information. EG *She appeared as a witness in the Kempton trial... He had to appear before the magistrate.* V : USU+A ⇑ attend

7 If someone or something **appears** to have a particular characteristic or to be in a particular condition, they seem to you to have that characteristic or to be in that condition. EG *As often as your baby appears hungry at this stage, feed it... The stranger appears confident.* V+C, OR V+*to*-INF = look

8 If you say that something **appears** to be the way that you describe it, you are reporting what you believe or what you have been told. EG *Their offer appears to be the most attractive... He had always seemed the perfect husband but it now appeared that he had frequently beaten his wife... I don't appear to have written down his name.* V+*to*-INF, OR *it*+V+REPORT-CL = seem

appearance /əpɪərəns/, **appearances. 1** The **appearance** of someone or something in a particular place is their arrival there, especially when it is sudden or unexpected. EG *The fight was soon stopped, thanks to the prompt appearance of the police.* N COUNT : USU *the*+N IN SING+*of*

2 The **appearance** of something new or different is its coming into existence or into use. EG *With the appearance of credit cards more people got into debt.* N SING : *the*+N+*of* = advent

3 When you make an **appearance** in a play or show, you take part in it in front of an audience. EG *She has made several television appearances recently.* N COUNT ⇑ performance

4 If you **put in an appearance** at an event, you go to it for a short time but do not stay. EG *I ought at least to put in an appearance at the party.* PHR : VB INFLECTS ⇑ attend

5 Someone's **appearance** in a court of law is their attendance there in order to answer charges made against them. EG *This was his first court appearance.* N COUNT : IF+PREP THEN *in*

6 Someone or something's **appearance** is also the way that they look to other people. EG *I had ceased to worry about my appearance... The two sisters were remarkably alike in appearance... The building has changed the character and appearance of the whole area.* N UNCOUNT : USU POSS+N, OR *in*+N ⇑ aspect = looks

7 When something **has the appearance of** something or **has all the appearances** of something, it has the qualities or characteristics which are typical of that thing. EG *It had all the appearances of being the body of a murdered woman... ...a vendetta that has all the appearances of personal spite.* PHR : VB INFLECTS

8 If something is true **to all appearances** or **by all appearances**, it seems from what you know about it that it is true, although it may not be. EG *To all appearances he doesn't work hard.* PHR : USED AS AN A

9 If something is true **contrary to all appearances** or **against all appearances**, it is true even though all the available evidence suggests that it is not true. EG *He would try and prove against all appearances that she was innocent.* PHR : USED AS AN A

10 Appearances is used in expressions such as 'to do something for the sake of **appearances**' and 'to judge by **appearances**' when you are referring to the impression that people give of themselves, especially through the way that they dress or behave. EG *I am personally not too worried about appearances.* N PLURAL ⇑ impressions ● If you try to **keep up appearances**, you continue to dress and behave in the way that people have come to expect of you, especially when you can no longer afford it but are too proud to admit it. EG *I have other things to do than worry about keeping up appearances.* ● PHR : VB INFLECTS ⇑ pretend

appease /əpiːz/, **appeases, appeasing, appeased. 1** If you try to **appease** someone, you try to prevent them harming you or being angry with you by giving them what they want. EG *Peasants still place small offerings of food there to appease the mighty rain gods.* V+O ⇑ soothe = placate

2 If you **appease** a feeling, for example hunger or guilt, you cause it to be felt less strongly; a formal or literary use. V+O = assuage

appeasement /əpiːzmənt/. **Appeasement** is the act or practice of trying to prevent someone from harsarm 1 ing you or being angry with you by giving them what they want. EG *...a policy of appeasement towards foreign dictatorships.* N UNCOUNT ⇑ pacification ≠ provocation

appellation /æpɪleɪʃən/, **appellations**. An **appellation** is a name or title; a formal word. EG *Few other bold experimenters would shudder at the appellation 'architect'.* N COUNT

append /əpend/, **appends, appending, appended.** When you **append** something to something V+O : IF+PREP THEN *to* else, especially a piece of writing, you add it or join it on to the end of it; a formal word. EG *He appends a brief note on this subject to his report.*

appendage /ə³pɛndɪdʒ/, **appendages**. An **appendage** is something that is joined to something larger or more important; a formal word. EG *...a pair of feathery appendages... The House of Commons must not be only an appendage of the Executive.*
N COUNT : IF + PREP THEN *to/of* ⇑ part

appendices /ə³pɛndɪsiːz/ is a plural of **appendix**.

appendicitis /əpɛndɪˈsaɪtɪ¹s/ is an illness in which your appendix is infected and painful. It is usually treated by removing the appendix. EG *He came down with appendicitis.*
N UNCOUNT

appendix /ə³pɛndɪks/, **appendices** or **appendixes**. 1 Your **appendix** is a small tube inside your body which is closed at one end and is joined to your digestive system at the other end. It has no particular function. EG *She had had her appendix removed.*
N COUNT : USU SING ⇑ organ

2 An **appendix** to a book is extra information or further discussion of a subject that is placed after the end of the main text. EG *A select list of hotels is given in the Appendix... We make some comment on this in Appendix 2.*
N COUNT, OR *in* + N + NUM ⇑ addition

appertain /æpətɛɪn/, **appertains, appertaining, appertained**. If something **appertains** to something else, it relates to it or belongs to it; a formal word. EG *...duties appertaining to Members of Parliament.*
V + A *(to)* ⇑ belong

appetite /æpəˈtaɪt/, **appetites**. 1 Your **appetite** is your desire to eat and your feeling about how much you want to eat. EG *The gin's killed my appetite... All that work on the cycle has given me an appetite... Sudden decrease in appetite is sometimes a sign of illness.*
N COUNT/ UNCOUNT

2 An **appetite** is a strong desire for something that you think you will enjoy. EG *...an unsuspected, long repressed appetite for sensual pleasure... A man must decide either to curb his appetites or surrender to them.* ● to **whet someone's appetite**: see **whet**.
N COUNT : IF + PREP THEN *for* = passion

appetizer /æpəˈtaɪzə/, **appetizers**; also spelled **appetiser**. An **appetizer** is a small amount of food or drink that you eat before a meal in order to give you an appetite.
N COUNT

appetizing /æpəˈtaɪzɪŋ/; also spelled **appetising**. Food that is **appetizing** looks attractive or smells delicious, and makes you want to eat it; used showing approval. EG *...a most appetizing breakfast dish.* ▸ used of the smell or appearance of food. EG *...an appetizing smell of grilled herring.* ◊ **appetizingly**. EG *The meal is appetizingly prepared and presented.*
ADJ QUALIT = tempting, tasty
◊ ADV = deliciously

applaud /əplɔːd/, **applauds, applauding, applauded**. 1 When a group of people **applaud**, they clap their hands, in order to show approval, for example when they have enjoyed a play or concert, or in order to welcome an important person. EG *The children applauded at the end of the song... The whole assembly applauded him.*
V OR V + O ⇑ approve

2 When an action, attitude, etc **is applauded**, people say that they approve of it and admire it. EG *These changes will be applauded... One might applaud his sense of duty.*
V + O = praise, support

applause /əplɔːz/. **Applause** is 1 an expression of enjoyment or appreciation by a group of people in which they clap their hands. EG *The delegates burst into loud applause.* 2 support or praise by a lot of people for something that has been done. EG *The applause given in 1974 to the government's decision was overwhelming.*
N UNCOUNT = clapping
N UNCOUNT ⇑ agreement

apple /æpə⁰l/, **apples**. 1 An **apple** is a round fruit which grows on a tree and which has a smooth red, yellow, or green skin and firm white flesh inside it. EG *Eat an apple a day... ...a big piece of apple pie... We sat under the apple tree.*
N COUNT/ UNCOUNT

2 If you say that someone is **the apple** of your **eye**, you mean that you are extremely fond of them or proud of them. EG *She had another son, who was the apple of her eye.*
PHR : USED AS C ⇑ favourite

3 See **crab apple, toffee apple**.

applecart /æpə⁰lkɑːt/. If you **upset the applecart** or **upset** someone's **applecart**, you do something which causes a plan, arrangement, or system to go wrong; an informal expression.
PHR : VB INFLECTS ⇑ disturb

apple-pie. If a room, desk, etc is **in apple-pie order**, it is tidy and everything is in its correct place; used showing approval. EG *Guy had left everything in apple-pie order.*
PHR : USED AS AN A = shipshape

appliance /əplaɪəns/, **appliances**. 1 An **appliance** is a device or machine that does a particular job in your home, especially one that works by electricity or gas. EG *Their gas appliances were serviced regularly... ...heating appliances.*
N COUNT

2 An **appliance** is also a fire engine; a technical use.
N COUNT

applicable /æplɪkəbə⁰l, əplɪkə-/. Something that is **applicable** to a particular situation is relevant or appropriate to it. EG *Include fuel costs, if applicable, and operator costs... ...principles applicable on a wider scale... ...a rule applicable to any case.*
ADJ QUALIT : USU PRED, IF + PREP THEN *to* ⇑ important

applicant /æplɪkənt/, **applicants**. An **applicant** is someone who formally asks to be given something, such as a job or a place at a college or university. EG *...a long waiting list of applicants for jobs.*
N COUNT : IF + PREP THEN *for* ⇑ person = candidate

application /æplɪkeɪʃə⁰n/, **applications**. 1 An **application** for a job or for a place at a college or university is a formal request in writing to be given the job or to be allowed to work or study at the college or university. EG *The school receives up to 3,300 applications each year... ...his application to do research in the British Museum.*
N COUNT

2 An **application** for permission to do something is a formal request to be allowed to do it. EG *We sent our application to the Council.*
N COUNT

3 The **application** of a rule, piece of knowledge, etc is the using of it in a particular situation. EG *Do the results have any practical application?... ...the application of systems techniques to urban problems.*
N UNCOUNT/ COUNT : IF + PREP THEN *of* ⇑ usage

4 **Application** is **4.1** the making of a formal written request for something. EG *Full details are obtainable on application... Early application is advised.* **4.2** hard work and concentration on what you are doing over a period of time. EG *...immense talent, boundless energy and unremitting application.*
N UNCOUNT
N UNCOUNT ⇑ effort = diligence

5 The **application** of something, for example a coat of paint or skin cream, is the act or process of putting it on to a surface. EG *The application of a cold wet cloth will stop the swelling.*
N UNCOUNT/ COUNT : IF + PREP THEN *of*

applied /ə³plaɪd/. An **applied** subject of study is one that has a practical use. EG *...applied science... ...applied art.*
ADJ CLASSIF : ATTRIB

apply /əplaɪ/, **applies, applying, applied**. 1 If you **apply** to have something or to do something, you fill in a form or write a letter asking formally to be allowed to have it or to do it. EG *I've applied for another job... I made up my mind to apply for a scholarship.*
V : IF + PREP THEN *for* ⇑ request = put in for

2 If you **apply** yourself or **apply** your mind or attention to something, you concentrate hard on doing something or on thinking about it. EG *I can't say he's applied himself very energetically to looking for a job... It is difficult to apply much creative thought to this question.*
V + O (REFL/NG) : IF + PREP THEN *to* = devote, address

3 If something **applies** to someone or if it **applies** in a particular situation, it concerns the person or is relevant in the situation. EG *The leaflet explains how the system will apply to you... This chart no longer applies.*
V : USU + A *(to)* ⇑ be relevant

4 If you **apply** a particular rule, system, etc, you use it in a particular situation. EG *...countries which have been the first to apply the death penalty.*
V + O = employ

5 If you **apply** a label or name to someone or something, you refer to them by that label or name. EG *The label 'cold-blooded', so often applied to reptiles, is a very misleading one.*
V + O : USU PASS, IF + PREP THEN *to* ⇑ give

6 If you **apply** an idea, process, skill, etc to a particular job or activity, you adapt it and use it in the job or activity. EG *...the capacity to develop and apply technology.*
V + O : IF + PREP THEN *to* ⇑ exploit = harness

7 When you **apply** something to a surface, you put it onto the surface or rub it into it. EG *Apply a little liquid wax polish... He examined the cut and applied a plaster.*
V + O : IF + PREP THEN *to*

8 If you **apply** something such as a device, you cause it to operate. EG *I had to apply the brakes rather abruptly.*
V + O ⇑ use

9 See also **applied**.

appoint /əpɔɪnt/, **appoints, appointing, appointed**. 1 If you **appoint** someone to a particular post or to do a particular job, you formally choose them for it or ask them to do it. EG *Ramsay MacDonald appointed him Secretary of State for India... He was appointed as Chief Justice... The President has appointed a committee to consider what action should be taken... She had been appointed to a most responsible teaching post.*
V + O : USU + A/ *to*-INF, OR V + O + C = assign

2 If you **appoint** something such as a time or place for something to happen, you decide when or where it will happen. ◇ **appointed**. EG *I arrived on his doorstep one minute after the appointed hour... The men worked hard to finish their own appointed tasks.* — V+O = allot; ◇ ADJ CLASSIF : ATTRIB = allotted

-appointed /əpɔɪntɪ²d/ combines with adverbs such as 'well', 'pleasantly', or 'badly' to form expressions describing a building or room. These expressions describe the building or room as having furniture or features of a particular quality or quantity; a fairly formal word. EG *...her exquisitely appointed drawing-room.* — COMB : FORMS ADJS ⇑ furnished

appointee /ə³pɔɪntiː/, **appointees**. An **appointee** is someone who has been chosen for a particular job or position. EG *...political appointees at the State Department.* — N COUNT ⇑ person = appointment

appointment /əpɔɪntmə²nt/, **appointments**. **1** The **appointment** of someone to do a particular job is the act or process of choosing them to do it. EG *Their duties include the appointment of all the staff... He congratulated me on my appointment as editor... ...Kitchener's appointment to the War Office.* — N UNCOUNT/COUNT : IF+PREP THEN *of* ⇑ choice

2 An **appointment** is **2.1** a job or position, usually one involving some responsibility. EG *She applied for and got the appointment... He asked Northcliffe to accept the appointment of Ambassador.* — N COUNT = post. **2.2** someone who has been chosen for a particular job or position. EG *...a sociologist from Howard's department, a new appointment.* — N COUNT ⇑ person = appointee

3 An **appointment** with someone or an **appointment** to see them is an arrangement to see them at a particular time, usually in connection with their job. EG *I had an appointment with the editor of the Arkansas Gazette... I'd like to make an appointment to see one of the doctors this morning... The appointment was for 11 am.* — N COUNT : IF+PREP THEN *with*, OR+*to*+INF ⇑ arrangement

4 If you cannot do something except **by appointment**, you have to arrange in advance to do it at a particular time. EG *They allow people to visit by appointment during the first weekend in every month.* — PHR : USED AS AN A

apportion /əpɔːʃə⁰n/, **apportions, apportioning, apportioned**. When you **apportion** something, especially praise or blame, you decide how much of it different people or groups deserve or should be given. EG *He tried to apportion blame for this very serious wastage of talent.* — V+O : IF+PREP THEN *between/among* ⇑ distribute

apposite /æpəzɪt/. Something that is **apposite** is very suitable or appropriate to what is happening or being discussed; a formal word. EG *...apposite questions... The image of the tomb seemed particularly apposite in this case.* — ADJ QUALIT = apt, relevant

apposition /æpəzɪʃə⁰n/. If a noun or group of words is **in apposition** to another, they refer to the same person or thing and are placed one after the other without being joined by a conjunction; a grammatical term. — PHR : USED AS AN A, IF+PREP THEN *to* ⇑ adjacent

appraisal /əpreɪzə⁰l/, **appraisals**. **1** An **appraisal** of a situation is a careful judgement about what is happening and why. EG *...my appraisal of the domestic and international situation... She was prevented from making a detailed appraisal.* — N COUNT/UNCOUNT : IF+PREP THEN *of* = assessment

2 An **appraisal** of a person is a careful judgement about their character or abilities. — N COUNT/UNCOUNT

appraise /əpreɪz/, **appraises, appraising, appraised**. When you **appraise** someone or something, you consider them carefully and form an opinion about their character, quality, worth, etc. EG *Harris stood back and appraised his work.* ◇ **appraising**. EG *She was looking at me with coolly appraising eyes.* — V+O ⇑ judge = assess, evaluate; ◇ ADJ CLASSIF

appreciable /əpriːʃɪ⁰əbə⁰l, -sɪ-/. An **appreciable** amount, distance, effect, etc is large enough to be important or clearly noticed. EG *...an appreciable percentage of the university's expenditure... There had been appreciable progress recently.* ◇ **appreciably**. EG *The weather had turned grey, and it was appreciably colder.* — ADJ CLASSIF : ATTRIB = considerable ≠ negligible; ◇ ADV+ADJ/ADV

appreciate /əpriːʃɪeɪt, -sɪ-/, **appreciates, appreciating, appreciated**. **1** If you **appreciate** something, for example a piece of music or good food, you recognize and understand the good qualities or features that it has and like or admire it because of them. EG *He appreciated beautiful things... They really appreciated the peace and quiet of rural Wales.* — V+O = value

2 If you **appreciate** a situation, problem, or difficulty, you understand it and know what it involves. EG *I appreciate the reasons for your anxiety... You appreciate, Mr Davis, that this expedition involves certain dangers.* — V+O/REPORT-CL ⇑ recognize

3 If you say that you **appreciate** something which someone has done for you or that you **appreciate** help or advice which someone has given you, you mean that you are pleased and grateful to them for it. EG *We would much appreciate guidance from an expert... Well, thanks, I really appreciated that.* — V+O ⇑ like = welcome

4 When something, for example a piece of jewellery or some shares, **appreciates** over a period of time, its value increases. EG *These diamonds should appreciate in value.* — V ⇑ increase = go up

appreciation /əpriːʃɪeɪʃə⁰n, -sɪ-/, **appreciations**. **1 Appreciation** of something is **1.1** recognition of its beauty or good qualities, and the pleasure or enjoyment that you get because of them. EG *'This trout is delicious,' he added, with appreciation... He had little appreciation of great plays.* — N UNCOUNT : IF+PREP THEN *of*. **1.2** gratitude for something which someone has done for you or for the help and advice which they have given you. EG *...their appreciation of his services... It's just a little something to show my appreciation.* — N UNCOUNT : IF+PREP THEN *for/of*

2 An **appreciation** of a situation, problem, difficulty, etc is an understanding of it or of what it involves. EG *...a full appreciation of the implications.* — N UNCOUNT = grasp

3 Appreciation in the value of something is the increase in its value over a period of time. EG *There has been an appreciation of 31.2 per cent in these shares.* — N UNCOUNT/COUNT ≠ depreciation

4 An **appreciation** of someone or an **appreciation** of a poem, work of art, etc is a discussion and evaluation of them. EG *...an appreciation of the life and work of Dame Flora Robson.* — N COUNT : IF+PREP THEN *of*

appreciative /əpriːʃɪ⁰ətɪv/. **1** An **appreciative** reaction, gesture, expression, etc shows the pleasure and enjoyment that you are getting from something. EG *There was a rumble of appreciative laughter... The reaction of the audience had been overwhelmingly appreciative.* ◇ **appreciatively**. EG *He tucked in appreciatively to his bacon and eggs.* — ADJ QUALIT ⇑ favourable; ◇ ADV WITH VB

2 Someone who is **appreciative** of something is pleased and grateful for it. EG *She won't be appreciative of his efforts.* ▸ used of someone's expression or behaviour. EG *'Thank you,' I said, flashing him an appreciative smile.* ◇ **appreciatively**. EG *'Want a lift?' Patroni nodded appreciatively. 'Thanks.'* — ADJ QUALIT; ▸ ADJ QUALIT : USU ATTRIB; ◇ ADV WITH VB ⇑ gratefully

apprehend /æprɪhend/, **apprehends, apprehending, apprehended**; a formal word. **1** If someone, especially a policeman, **apprehends** someone, they catch and arrest them. EG *The police are anxious to apprehend a middle-aged man believed to be armed with a shot gun.* — V+O = stop

2 If you **apprehend** something, you understand it fully. EG *We often fail to apprehend the real nature of change.* — V+O = grasp

apprehension /æprɪhenʃə⁰n/, **apprehensions**. **1 Apprehension** or **apprehensions** are feelings of worry or fear about the future, or that something unfortunate or terrible may happen. EG *His mother and father trembled with apprehension about his future... Berry clasped his hands in apprehension... The threat was a real one and gave rise to deep apprehensions.* — N UNCOUNT/COUNT = misgiving

2 Apprehension of something is full knowledge and understanding of it; a formal use. EG *...an apprehension of reality.* — N UNCOUNT : IF+PREP THEN *of*

3 The **apprehension** of someone who is thought to be a criminal is their capture or arrest; a formal use. EG *They will begin to co-operate in the apprehension of these gangsters.* — N UNCOUNT : IF+PREP THEN *of*

apprehensive /æprɪhensɪv/. Someone who is **apprehensive** is worried or afraid about the future, for example because they are afraid that something unpleasant or terrible may happen. EG *He was rather apprehensive of the consequences... I felt a bit apprehensive about the whole operation.* ▸ used of someone's expression or behaviour. EG *They exchanged apprehensive glances.* ◇ **apprehensively**. EG *The door opened. She looked up apprehensively.* — ADJ QUALIT : IF+PREP THEN *about* = fearful, doubtful; ▸ = uneasy; ◇ ADV WITH VB = fearfully

apprentice /ə³prentɪs/, **apprentices, apprenticing, apprenticed**. **1** An **apprentice** is a young person who works, often for a fixed period of time, with another person whose job involves a particular skill, in order that they can learn the skill. — N COUNT ⇑ learner

EG *I am now doing my final year as an apprentice... ...an apprentice instrument maker.*

2 If you **apprentice** someone to a person whose job involves a particular skill, you arrange for them to work, often for a fixed period of time, with the skilled person so that they can learn how to do the job; an old-fashioned use. EG *His father apprenticed him to a linen draper... Tate was apprenticed to a grocer at the age of thirteen.* V+O (NG/REFL): IF+PREP THEN *to*

apprenticeship /ə³prentɪsʃɪp/, **apprenticeships**. 1 Someone who has an **apprenticeship** works for a fixed period of time with a person who has a particular skill in order to learn the skill. EG *I am supposed to have served a five-year apprenticeship.* N COUNT/UNCOUNT ⇑ training

2 Someone's **apprenticeship** is also a period of time at the beginning of their career during which they gain experience in a particular area of activity or work which will be useful to them later. N SING WITH DET

apprise /əpraɪz/, **apprises, apprising, apprised**. When you **apprise** someone of something, you inform them about it; a formal word. EG *I apprised him of the political situation in Washington.* V+O+A *(of)* ⇑ tell

appro /æprəʊ/. If you get something **on appro**, you get it on approval; an informal expression in British English. PHR : USED AS AN A

approach /əprəʊtʃ/, **approaches, approaching, approached**. 1 When someone **approaches** you, they get nearer to you. EG *He opened the car door for her as she approached... Someone was approaching the village.* V OR V+O

2 If you **approach** someone about something, you speak to them about it for the first time, especially in order to ask them to do something or because you want to find out their opinion. EG *He was approached by the Head of the Security Service and offered a job.... They had approached us about working with their party.* V+O ⇑ talk to = buttonhole

3 When you **approach** a situation or problem in a particular way or from a particular point of view, you think about it or deal with it in that way or from that point of view. EG *Governments must approach the subject of disarmament in a new spirit... I'd approached it from the foreign language side.* V+O+A ⇑ consider

4 When a particular event **approaches**, or when you **approach** it, it gradually becomes nearer in time and will happen soon. EG *Exam week approached... We are fast approaching the day of reckoning... ...his own approaching death.* V-ERG

5 If something **approaches** a high level of quality or an extreme state or condition, it almost reaches that level, state, or condition. EG *By the 1960's rocket planes approached speeds of 4000 mph... The system was approaching collapse... She set a record which nobody else can remotely approach.* ◊ **approaching**. EG *We have bills of approaching a million pounds... It never had anything approaching the resources which would have been required.* V+O = come close to; ◊ PREP = verging on

6 The **approach** of someone or something is their gradually getting nearer to you. EG *We heard the rumble of tank engines and saw the approach of headlights... In the city dogs began to bark as if aware of our approach.* N COUNT+SUPP : USU SING = advance

7 An **approach** to a place is a road, path, etc that leads to it and that is an official means of reaching it. EG *The track was not intended as an approach to the palace... The troops secured the approaches to Belgrade.* N COUNT : IF+PREP THEN *to*

8 An **approach** from someone about something is an informal request that you do something for them, or an informal inquiry whether you would be interested in having something, especially a job. EG *Following approaches from the Department of Health, the drug was withdrawn... I had had an approach to join the staff of the Daily Mail.* N COUNT = proposal

9 An **approach** to a situation or problem is a way of thinking about it or of dealing with it. EG *We need a new approach to this problem... He was highly commercial in his approach.* N COUNT : IF+PREP THEN *to* = attitude

10 The **approach** of a particular event is the gradual passing of time before it happens and the changing circumstances during that time that suggest that it is getting near. EG *You could feel the approach of winter... ...the approach of saturation point.* N SING WITH DET +SUPP ⇑ coming = nearing

11 You also describe something as an **approach** to something else when it is similar to it in some way. EG *This office is probably the nearest approach to hell that there is!* N SING WITH DET : IF+PREP THEN *to* = thing

approachable /əprəʊtʃəbə⁰l/. 1 Someone who is **approachable** is friendly and easy to talk to. EG *He was very young, approachable, and jolly... ...a hotel with approachable staff and high standards.* ADJ QUALIT ≠ aloof

2 A place or building which is **approachable** by a particular route can be reached by that route. EG *The statue is approachable by steps inside the column.* ADJ CLASSIF : PRED+*by/from* = accessible

approbation /æprə⁶beɪʃə⁰n/ is approval of something or agreement to it; a formal word. EG *He surveyed the document with approbation.* N UNCOUNT

appropriate, appropriates, appropriating, appropriated. The word **appropriate** is pronounced /ə³prəʊprɪət/ when it is an adjective, and /ə³prəʊprɪeɪt/ when it is a verb. 1 Something that is **appropriate** is correct, suitable, or acceptable. EG *...the institutional structure appropriate to each country... ...a general test of English appropriate for that particular level... ...the appropriate leaflet... It seemed appropriate to end with a joke.* ◊ **appropriately**. EG *He reminded himself to thank Louis appropriately-after the job was done.* ADJ QUALIT : IF+PREP THEN *to/for* ⇑ right = relevant; ◊ ADV ⇑ suitably

2 If you **appropriate** something which does not belong to you, you take it for yourself without having the right to do so; a formal word. EG *The materials are exported in a raw state and other countries appropriate the profits.* V+O = purloin, steal

3 If a person or organization **appropriates** an amount of money for a particular purpose or project, they reserve it for that purpose or project. EG *The government was forced to appropriate extra funds for the new airport.* V+O : IF+PREP THEN *for* = earmark

appropriation /ə³prəʊprɪeɪʃə⁰n/, **appropriations**. **Appropriation** is a formal word. 1 **Appropriation** is the administrative process of reserving an amount of money for a particular purpose or project. EG *Any appropriation of funds will have to wait until next year.* N UNCOUNT ⇑ allocation

2 An **appropriation** is an amount of money that an organization is keeping for a particular purpose or project. EG *The proposed budget calls for cutting appropriations for most departments.* N COUNT = allocation

approval /ə³pruːvə⁰l/. 1 **Approval** is 1.1 agreement to or acceptance of an idea, plan, decision, etc. EG *The decision met with the committee's approval... The room soon filled with mutterings of approval.* N UNCOUNT : IF+PREP THEN *of/for* = approbation
1.2 a formal or official statement that something is acceptable. EG *These appliances have the British Gas seal of approval.* N UNCOUNT ⇑ acceptance 1.3 formal or official permission to do something. EG *He was still a boy and thus required his father's approval.* N UNCOUNT+SUPP 1.4 a feeling of liking and admiration for someone. EG *Mrs Oliver looked at Simon with approval... He enjoyed general theatrical and public approval.* N UNCOUNT = favour

2 If you buy something **on approval**, you have the right to return it to the person or shop that you bought it from, usually within a particular period of time, if you decide afterwards that you do not want it. EG *I got it on seven days approval, so if you don't like it we can change it.* PHR : USED AS AN A ⇑ provisionally = on appro

approve /ə³pruːv/, **approves, approving, approved**. 1 If you **approve** of an action, event, situation, etc, you are pleased that it has happened or that it is going to happen. EG *My grandfather did not approve of my father's marriage... His return to the office was widely approved of.* V : USU+*of* ⇑ agree ≠ condemn

2 If you **approve** of a person or a book, painting, etc, you like and admire the person, book, painting, etc. EG *His mother had not approved of Julie... He did not approve of my pictures.* V : USU+*of*, USU WITH BROAD NEG

3 If someone in a position of authority **approves** something such as a plan or arrangement, they formally or officially agree to it and say that it can happen or be put into effect. EG *The firm's directors quickly approved the new deal... Legislation has to be approved by parliament.* V+O = sanction

4 If someone in a position of authority **approves** something such as a product, building, institution, etc, they say formally or officially that it is of an acceptable or suitable standard or that it can be used for a particular purpose. EG *...premises which have been approved by the local authority... The agency initially approved the proposal in 1974.* V+O ⇑ accept = pass

approved /ə³pruːvd/. 1 An **approved** method, course of action, practice, etc is generally or officially accepted as appropriate or correct in a particular situation. EG *This is the surest and most approved* ADJ QUALIT = favoured *method of dealing with it... In Scandinavia this arrangement is officially approved.*

2 Someone who is **approved** in a particular role or position has been formally or officially accepted in that role or position by people in authority. EG *...lists of approved candidates... ...the closing of the frontiers to all but approved travellers.*
ADJ CLASSIF ⇑ permitted = authorized

approving /ə³pruːvɪŋ/. An **approving** reaction, gesture, expression, etc shows support or agreement for something, or satisfaction with it. EG *Cameron gave Scylla an approving nod... The play had an immediate and warmly approving reaction from its audience.* ▸ used of people. EG *The majority were most approving of the new building.* ◊ **approvingly**. EG *His wife watched approvingly.*
ADJ QUALIT = appreciative ≠ disapproving
◊ ADV WITH VB

approx. is an abbreviation for 'approximately'. EG *The cellar measures approx. 11ft x 9ft.*

approximate, approximates, approximating, approximated. The word **approximate** is pronounced /ə³prɒksə¹mət/ when it is an adjective, and /ə³prɒksə¹meɪt/ when it is a verb. 1 An **approximate** number, amount, time, position, etc is close to the correct number, amount, etc, but is probably slightly different from it because it has been calculated quickly rather than exactly. EG *She gave me some approximate figures... ...the approximate value of the property.* ◊ **approximately**. EG *We have approximately 40 pupils... The committee meets approximately once every two months.*
ADJ QUALIT ⇑ near = estimated, rough ≠ exact
◊ ADV = about, approx

2 An idea or description of something that is **approximate** provides some indication of what it is like but is not intended to be absolutely precise or accurate. EG *This will give you an approximate idea of the situation.* ◊ **approximately**. EG *St James's Park is approximately a long triangle... His story was at least approximately true.*
ADJ QUALIT = rough ≠ exact
◊ ADV = roughly

3 If something **approximates** to a particular number, amount, or size, it is close to it. EG *The cost of the project will approximate to £10,000... It approximated in size to the toffee bars already being produced.*
V+O, OR V+A *(to)* = come close to

4 If something **approximates** to something else, it is similar to it but does not have all its features or qualities. EG *There was nothing which even approximated to 'Art'... Worsening social conditions approximate to those of the early thirties.*
V+O OR V+A *(to)* = resemble

approximation /ə³prɒksɪ¹meɪʃə⁰n/, **approximations**. An **approximation** is 1 an object, description, situation, etc that is very like something else but which does not have all its features or qualities. EG *It should be possible to piece together some kind of approximation of what he was talking about... ...an approximation to the truth.* 2 a number, amount, calculation, etc that is close to the correct figure, but probably varies from it slightly. EG *The figure we have is only an approximation of the actual cost involved.*
N COUNT : IF+ PREP THEN *of/to* ⇑ estimation
N COUNT : IF+ PREP THEN *of/to* = estimation

appurtenances /ə³pɜːtə⁰nənsɪz/ are minor or additional features or possessions; a formal word. EG *...the appurtenances of modern civilisation.*
N PLURAL : IF+ PREP THEN *of* = accessories, trappings

Apr. is an abbreviation for April. EG *5 Apr. 1940.*

après-ski /æpreɪskiː/ is evening entertainment and social activities which take place in ski resorts. EG *Come just for the après-ski if you like.*
N SING WITH DET : USU *the*+N ⇑ socialising

apricot /eɪprɪkɒt/, **apricots**. 1 An **apricot** is a small, round fruit with yellowish-orange flesh, a soft furry skin, and a large stone inside. EG *...gleaming jars of yellow peaches, apricots, pears and mulberries.* ▸ used also of the tree that apricots grow on.
N COUNT
▸ ⇑ tree

April /eɪprə¹l/ is the fourth month of the year in the Western calendar. EG *He said he would be seventy-five next April... The Treaty was signed on 4 April 1949.* ● **April Fool's Day** is April 1st.
N UNCOUNT

a priori /eɪpraɪɔːraɪ/. **A priori** reasoning involves using a known or assumed cause or a general principle to work out facts or effects in a particular situation. The sentence: 'You've been rushing around all day, you must be tired,' is an example of a priori reasoning.
ADJ CLASSIF : ATTRIB, OR ADV SEN = deductive ≠ empirical

apron /eɪprən/, **aprons**. An **apron** is 1 a piece of clothing that you put on over the front of your normal clothes and tie round your waist, especially when you are cooking, in order to prevent your clothes from getting dirty. EG *Ida wiped her hands on her apron... ...a maid in a white apron over a short black dress.* 2 an area of concrete or tarmac at an airport where aircraft stand while they are not being used. EG *He insisted on driving straight to the apron where the helicopter was waiting.*
N COUNT
N COUNT

3 If a man, is **tied to his mother's** or **to his wife's apron strings**, he is controlled or influenced too much by her. EG *I couldn't possibly marry a man who is still tied to his mother's apron strings.*
PHR : USED AS C ⇑ dominated ≠ independent

apropos /æprə⁶pəʊ/. 1 Something which is **apropos**, or **apropos of**, a subject or event, is connected with or relevant to it. EG *And apropos of space medicine, I would like to mention a new development... ...apropos some doings at Cardiff.*
PREP ⇑ regarding

2 **Apropos** is used to introduce something that you are going to say which is related to the subject you have just been talking about; a formal use. EG *I was at school with his sister. Apropos, I have often wondered what became of my old schoolfriends.*
ADV SEN

3 Something that is **apropos** is very suitable in a particular situation; a formal use. EG *You look very apropos today in that suit!*
ADJ CLASSIF : PRED = appropriate

apt /æpt/. 1 If someone or something is **apt** to behave in a particular way, you know that they are likely to behave in that way because they usually do. EG *Babies who are small at birth are apt to grow faster... I was apt to fidget a good deal during a long performance.*
ADJ QUALIT : PRED+*to*-INF = prone

2 Someone who is **apt**, or who is **apt** at doing something, is intelligent or clever. EG *...a very apt student... He's very apt at making toys for the children.*
ADJ QUALIT : IF+ PREP THEN *at*

3 Something that is **apt** is especially suitable for a particular situation or purpose, often because it has been carefully chosen. EG *...an apt quotation from 'Jude the Obscure'... Eliade's phrase is particularly apt in relation to the events which have taken place.* ◊ **aptly**. EG *...as Dr Hochstadt so aptly remarked to his wife.*
ADJ QUALIT = appropriate, fitting
◊ ADV WITH VB

aptitude /æptɪtjuːd/, **aptitudes**. Someone's **aptitude** for a particular job or skill is their ability to learn it quickly and easily and to do it well. EG *He had an aptitude for journalism... ...people who share the same interests and aptitudes.*
N COUNT : IF+ PREP THEN *for* = talent

aptitude test, aptitude tests. An **aptitude test** is a test that is specially designed to find out how easily and how well you can do something. EG *They're handing out forms for an aptitude test.*
N COUNT

aqualung /ækwəlʌŋ/, **aqualungs**. An **aqualung** is a piece of equipment used by divers which consists of a large bottle containing air that is connected by means of tubes to a face mask. It is used so that the divers can breathe underwater.
N COUNT

aquamarine /ækwəməriːn/, **aquamarines**. 1 An **aquamarine** is a clear, greenish-blue stone used especially for making jewellery.
N COUNT/ UNCOUNT ⇑ gemstone

2 Something that is **aquamarine** is a greenish-blue colour.
ADJ COLOUR

aquarium /əkweəriəm/, **aquaria, aquariums**. The plural can be either **aquaria** or **aquariums**. An **aquarium** is 1 a glass tank filled with water, in which people keep fishes and small underwater animals. 2 a building, especially in a zoo, where fish and underwater animals are kept.
N COUNT
N COUNT

aquatic /əkwætɪk, əkwɒt-/. 1 An animal or plant that is **aquatic** lives or grows in water. EG *The caterpillar will feed on lily pads and other aquatic plants.*
ADJ CLASSIF : ATTRIB

2 **Aquatic** means involving, relating to, or occurring in water. EG *...an aquatic environment... ...systematic use of aquatic resources... ...instruction in aquatic sports of every kind.*
ADJ CLASSIF : ATTRIB

aqueduct /ækwɪ¹dʌkt/, **aqueducts**. An **aqueduct** is a long, high structure made of stone or brick, which looks like a bridge with many arches, and which carries a water supply or a canal over a valley.
N COUNT ≠ viaduct

aquiline /ækwɪlaɪn/. An **aquiline** nose curves round into a point like the beak of an eagle. EG *...a large, aquiline nose, and sharp, powerful eyes.* ▸ used also of someone's face or features. EG *His aquiline features held a mixture of reverence and contempt.*
ADJ CLASSIF = hooked
▸ ⇑ angular

Arab /ærəb/, **Arabs**. An **Arab** is a member of a people who originally lived in Arabia, and who now live throughout the Middle East and North Africa. EG *His writings are no doubt influenced by his early life among the Arabs.* ▸ used as an adjective. EG *The Ambassadors of several Arab countries were called to the Foreign Office.*
N COUNT ⇑ person
▸ ADJ CLASSIF

arabesque /ærəbe̲sk/, **arabesques**. An **arabesque** is a position in ballet dancing, in which the dancer stands on one leg with their other leg lifted and stretched out backwards. The dancer's arms are also outstretched. N COUNT ⇑ pose

Arabian /əre̲ɪbiən/ means belonging or relating to Arabia, especially to Saudi Arabia and other countries near it. EG *...the Arabian peninsula.* ADJ CLASSIF : ATTRIB

Arabic /æ̲rəbɪk/. 1 **Arabic** is a language that is spoken in the Middle East and in parts of North Africa. EG *The boys wrote their names in Arabic, as they had been taught.* N UNCOUNT

2 Something that is **Arabic** belongs or relates to the language, writing, or culture of the Arabs. EG *...Arabic books and manuscripts.* ADJ CLASSIF

3 An **Arabic** numeral is one of the written figures, such as 1,2,3,4, etc. ADJ CLASSIF : ATTRIB

arable /æ̲rəbə⁰l/. 1 **Arable** land is used, or is suitable, for growing crops. EG *...a hectare of arable land.* ▸ used as a noun. EG *Most was converted to conifers, the rest to arable.* ADJ CLASSIF : USU ATTRIB ▸ N UNCOUNT

2 An **arable** farm or farmer grows crops such as corn, rather than keeping animals. ▸ used of crops. EG *Arable crops are concentrated in the east.* ADJ CLASSIF : ATTRIB ⇑ crop

arbiter /ɑ̲:bɪtə/, **arbiters**. An **arbiter** is 1 someone who judges and settles a quarrel between two other people or groups; a formal use. EG *The Court was an arbiter between the States and the federal government.* N COUNT ⇑ judge = arbitrator 2 someone or something that has great control or influence over people's activities or fate. EG *His design is to establish newspapers as the final arbiter of human destiny.* N COUNT : IF+ PREP THEN *of* ⇑ controller

arbitrary /ɑ̲:bɪtrəri¹, ɑ̲:bɪtri¹/. Something that is **arbitrary** is 1 not done or decided according to any plan or system, or for any particular reason. EG *It is difficult to discern the motive of this seemingly arbitrary attack... ...pieces of arbitrary size and shape.* ADJ QUALIT = random ◊ **arbitrarily**. EG *Such names were quite arbitrarily given.* ◊ ADV 2 is done without consideration for the wishes of the people affected and cannot be prevented or changed; used showing disapproval. EG *...the brutal and arbitrary expulsion of immigrants.* ▸ used of power or authority. EG *...arbitrary management power.* ADJ QUALIT ⇑ inconsiderate = high-handed ◊ **arbitrarily**. EG *...laws that empowered them to close down any newspaper arbitrarily.* ◊ ADV WITH VB

arbitrate /ɑ̲:bɪtreɪt/, **arbitrates, arbitrating, arbitrated**. If you **arbitrate** a quarrel or dispute, or if you **arbitrate** between groups of people who are quarrelling, you consider all the facts and claims involved and decide who is right or whose claim is more justified. EG *They called on the European Economic Community to arbitrate the dispute... He acts as the referee: setting the rules and arbitrating between contending forces.* V OR V+O : IF+ PREP THEN *between* ⇑ judge

arbitration /ɑ̲:bɪtreɪʃə⁰n/ is the judging of a quarrel or dispute between people or groups by someone not involved in the dispute whose decision both sides agree to accept. EG *The government was prepared to submit the dispute to arbitration... Both sides in the dispute have agreed to go to arbitration.* N UNCOUNT ⇑ judgement

arbitrator /ɑ̲:bɪtreɪtə/, **arbitrators**. An **arbitrator** is someone who judges and settles a quarrel between other people or groups. EG *They would turn to the President as final arbitrator.* N COUNT ⇑ judge = arbiter

arboreal /ɑ:bɔ̲:rɪəl/. An animal that is **arboreal** lives mainly in the tops of trees. EG *All these species are arboreal and occur only in Africa.* ▸ used of the animal's life-style. EG *These apes are excellently adapted for the arboreal life.* ADJ CLASSIF

arbour /ɑ̲:bə/, **arbours**; also spelled **arbor** in American English. An **arbour** is a shelter in a garden, which is formed by leaves and stems of plants growing close together over a light framework. EG *The arbour was furnished only with a wooden seat.* N COUNT = bower

arc /ɑ̲:k/, **arcs, arcing, arced**. 1 An **arc** is 1.1 a smoothly curving shape or line of movement. EG *The ball rose in an unsteady arc and landed about 150 yards away... Within the irregular arc of coral the lagoon was still.* N COUNT ⇑ curve = sweep 1.2 a section of the line that forms the outside of a circle; a technical term in geometry. N COUNT ⇑ curve

2 If something **arcs** in a particular direction, it forms a smoothly curving line or path. EG *They are grown largely on the banks of Route 128 which arcs round Boston... Pretty rainbows would arc down to the earth.* V+A ⇑ curve

3 When an electric current **arcs**, it jumps across a gap between two contact points and produces a line of sparks. V

arcade /ɑ:ke̲ɪd/, **arcades**. An **arcade** is 1 a covered passageway, often between two streets, where there are shops or market stalls. EG *...the little specialist shops of Prince's Arcade.* N COUNT : ALSO IN NAMES AFTER N 2 a large covered area where there are many shops or stalls. EG *...a bus station on the ground floor, and a shopping arcade on the first floor.* N COUNT 3 a covered passage next to a building, which has pillars and arches along one side. EG *There was a long line of taxis waiting under the pillared arcade.* N COUNT ⇑ passageway

arcane /ɑ:ke̲ɪn/. Something that is **arcane** is very secret or mysterious; a formal word. EG *...arcane and unwanted emotions.* ▸ used as a noun. EG *She was fascinated by the forbidden, the arcane.* ADJ CLASSIF ▸ N SING : *the*+N

arch /ɑ̲:tʃ/, **arches, arching, arched**. 1 An **arch** is 1.1 a structure that has two pillars on either side of a space which support a curved roof, or which form part of a bridge carrying a road or railway. EG *We turned through the arch into the yard... ...an old warehouse beneath the railway arches.* N COUNT 1.2 a tall curved opening or doorway in a wall or building. EG *Almost immediately you are out again, through an arch and into a huge square.* N COUNT = archway 1.3 a smooth curved shape or line. EG *...the smooth arch of her hips.* N COUNT = curve

2 The **arch** of your foot is the curved section of bone at the top. EG *He was cursed with deformed arches.* N COUNT ⇑ curve

3 When something such as a part of your body **arches** or when you **arch** it, it forms a curved shape or line. EG *She looked at him and her thin eyebrows arched... He arched his back... The rockets arched into the night sky.* V-ERG ⇑ curve

4 An **arch** look or expression is mischievous or cunning. EG *She giggled and gave me an arch look.* ADJ QUALIT : ATTRIB ◊ **archly**. EG *She caught his eye and smiled archly.* ◊ ADV WITH VB

5 A tone of voice that is **arch** suggests that you think you are more important or clever than everyone else. EG *His tone of voice tends to be rather arch.* ADJ QUALIT = superior ≠ humble ◊ **archly**. EG *'The point is taken,' Lynn said archly.* ◊ ADV WITH VB

6 See also **arched**.

arch- is added to some nouns that refer to people in order to form other nouns. Nouns formed in this way refer to someone as having more of a particular quality than anyone else. EG *They're arch-enemies on the sports field.* PREFIX = deadly

archaeology /ɑ̲:ki¹ɒ̲lədʒi¹/; also spelled **archeology**, especially in American English. **Archaeology** is the study of the history and culture of ancient societies, by examining the remains of their buildings, tombs, tools, and other objects. EG *What does archaeology have to contribute to modern society?* N UNCOUNT ◊ **archaeologist, archaeologists**. EG *Archaeologists date the fragment between 4650 and 4500 BC.* ◊ N COUNT ◊ **archaeological**. EG *...the most dramatic archaeological discovery of this century.* ◊ ADJ CLASSIF

archaic /ɑ:ke̲ɪɪk/. 1 Things that are **archaic** are 1.1 old-fashioned or out-of-date, and need to be replaced; used humorously or showing disapproval. EG *...the archaic stove in the corner of the kitchen... The Shops Act is somewhat archaic in its approach.* ADJ QUALIT = outmoded ≠ modern 1.2 old and dating from an earlier period of history; a literary use. ADJ CLASSIF = primitive

2 Language that is **archaic** was once standard and used regularly, but is now usually found only in old literature. EG *They find the archaic language difficult to understand.* ADJ CLASSIF = antiquated

archangel /ɑ̲:keɪndʒə⁰l/, **archangels**. An **archangel** is an angel of the highest rank. EG *...the Archangel Gabriel.* N COUNT : ALSO IN TITLES ⇑ angel

archbishop /ɑ̲:tʃbɪʃəp/, **archbishops**. An **archbishop** is a bishop of the highest rank, especially in the Catholic, Anglican, and Orthodox branches of Christianity, who is in charge of all the churches in a particular area. EG *...the Archbishop of Canterbury... ...the Roman Catholic Archbishop of Westminster.* N COUNT : ALSO IN TITLES ⇑ bishop

archdeacon /ɑ̲:tʃdi̲:kə⁰n/, **archdeacons**. An **archdeacon** is a clergyman of high rank who works as an assistant to a bishop, especially in the Anglican church. N COUNT : ALSO IN TITLES

archdiocese /ɑ̲:tʃda̲ɪəsɪs/, **archdioceses**. An **archdiocese** is the area over which an archbishop has control. EG *...the Boston archdiocese.* N COUNT ⇑ diocese

arched /ɑ̲:tʃt/. 1 A roof, window, doorway, etc that is **arched** has a curved roof or top that is supported on either side by a pillar or wall. EG *...arched windows... ...the arched roof over the staircase.* ADJ CLASSIF ⇑ rounded

2 Something that is **arched** curves sharply upwards and then down again. EG *...his arched black eyebrows.* ADJ CLASSIF ↑ curved

archeology /ɑːkɪɒlədʒi¹/. See **archaeology**.

archer /ɑːtʃə/, **archers**. An **archer** is someone who shoots with a bow and arrow. EG *They went to Agincourt as archers.* N COUNT ↑ person

archery /ɑːtʃə⁰ri¹/ is a sport in which you shoot at a target with a bow and arrow. EG *...an archery contest.* N UNCOUNT ↑ shooting

archetypal /ɑːki¹taɪpə⁰l/. Someone or something that is **archetypal** has all the most important characteristics of a particular kind of person or thing and is a perfect example of them; a fairly formal word. EG *...the archetypal Romantic heroes.* ◊ **archetypally**. EG *Stratford is so archetypally English, isn't it?* ADJ CLASSIF : ATTRIB ↑ typical = classic ◊ ADV+ADJ = typically

archetype /ɑːkɪtaɪp/, **archetypes**. An **archetype** is something that is considered to be a perfect example of a particular kind of person, thing, system, etc, because it has all their most important characteristics. EG *Let us now consider the highly integrated society. The archetype is Guinea... ...the great original archetype of lawn tennis.* N COUNT : IF+ PREP THEN *of* ↑ concept = model

archipelago /ɑːkɪpelɪgəʊ/, **archipelagos**. An **archipelago** is 1 a group of small islands. EG *...the Philippine archipelago.* N COUNT 2 an area of sea where there are many small islands. N COUNT

architect /ɑːkɪtekt/, **architects**. 1 An **architect** is a person who designs buildings. N COUNT ↑ designer

2 The **architect** of an idea, system, event, etc is the person who is responsible for its invention or for it happening. EG *...the architect of the helicopter fiasco... He was the real architect of the country's independence.* N COUNT : IF+ PREP THEN *of* ↑ inventor

architectural /ɑːki¹tektʃərə⁰l/ means relating to the design and construction of buildings. EG *...the architectural style suitable for modern British government buildings... ...an architectural award.* ◊ **architecturally**. EG *It was probably not architecturally very striking.* ADJ CLASSIF : ATTRIB ↑ building ◊ ADV SEN

architecture /ɑːkɪtektʃə/. 1 A particular style of **architecture** is the style in which buildings were designed and constructed, especially at a particular time or place. EG *...the ghastly Late Victorian architecture of the Chapel... It's a very fine example of traditional architecture.* N UNCOUNT+ SUPP

2 The **architecture** of a particular building or group of buildings is their style and layout, and artistic or decorative features. EG *She hated the house–its very architecture appalled her.* N SING : USU WITH POSS ↑ design

3 **Architecture** is the art and science of planning, designing, and constructing buildings. N UNCOUNT

4 The **architecture** of something is its structure and design. EG *...the architecture of Polymer molecules.* N SING : *the*+N+ *of*

archive /ɑːkaɪv/, **archives**. 1 **Archives** are a collection of documents, records, photographs, etc that contain information about the history of a country, place, organization, art form, etc. EG *I went to the State Department to consult the archives... She spent several hours in the film archives... I've used a lot of archive material.* N PLURAL

2 An **archive** is a place where historical documents and records are stored. EG *It houses the national archive of wills.* N COUNT ↑ store

archivist /ɑːkɪvɪst/, **archivists**. An **archivist** is a person whose job is to collect, sort, and preserve historical documents and records. N COUNT ↑ historian

archway /ɑːtʃweɪ/, **archways**. An **archway** is a passage or entrance that has a curved roof and that leads between two walls, pillars, trees, etc. EG *A big archway leads through into a courtyard... ...an archway of huge trees.* N COUNT ↑ arch

arctic /ɑːk⁰tɪk/. 1 The **Arctic** is the area of the world around the North Pole, where it is extremely cold and where there is very little light in winter and very little darkness in summer. EG *This is the most isolated island in the Arctic... ...an Arctic explorer.* N PROPER : *the*+ N ≠ Antarctic

2 **Arctic** clothing or equipment is designed to be used in very cold conditions. EG *...an Arctic sleeping bag.* ADJ CLASSIF : ATTRIB ↑ warm

3 A room or building that is **arctic** feels extremely cold. EG *...the arctic chill of the bathroom.* ADJ QUALIT = bitter

Arctic Circle. The **Arctic Circle** is an imaginary line drawn around the northern part of the world at approximately 66 North. EG *We were based three hundred miles north of the Arctic Circle.* N PROPER : *the*+ N

ardent /ɑːdə⁰nt/. 1 Someone who is **ardent** about something is very keen and enthusiastic about it. EG *Even the most ardent revolutionaries never went that far... He was young, ardent, and appallingly long-winded... ...an ardent photographer.* ▸ used of someone's beliefs or behaviour. EG *...an ardent religious faith... Their ardent exchange was interrupted by a party of tourists.* ◊ **ardently**. EG *He has always been ardently pro-French.* ADJ QUALIT = dedicated ▸ ADJ QUALIT : ATTRIB = fervent ◊ ADV = avidly

2 If you are **ardent**, you have strong and passionate feelings for someone and you show these feelings in your behaviour. EG *Her admirers were fewer, and fatter, and less ardent.* ▸ used of feelings and behaviour. EG *...ardent love-making.* ◊ **ardently**. EG *He responded ardently to her advances.* ADJ QUALIT = amorous ◊ ADV WITH VB ↑ passionately

ardour /ɑːdə/; also spelled **ardor** in American English. **Ardour** is 1 an intense and passionate feeling, often inspired by something that you believe in very strongly. EG *He criticized them for lack of revolutionary ardour... His eyes were bright with ardour and indignation.* N UNCOUNT ↑ passion = fervour 2 an intense and passionate feeling of love for someone. EG *His ardour was stilled by the impact of her words.* N UNCOUNT ↑ passion 3 a great liking or enthusiasm for something. EG *Any honest lawyers will cool their clients' ardour for litigation.* N UNCOUNT+*for*

arduous /ɑːdjuːəs/. Something that is **arduous** is difficult, tiring, and involves a lot of effort. EG *..a long and arduous journey... The work was arduous and poorly paid.* ADJ QUALIT = strenuous

are /ɑː/ is the plural and the second person (singular and plural) of the present tense of the verb **be**. EG *Are these your children?... You aren't ill, are you?*

area /eərɪə/, **areas**. 1 An **area** is 1.1 a particular part or region of a city, country, the world, etc. EG *...a dry area that gets only a few months rain a year... ...all areas of Great Britain... ...the Brighton area... The University is the largest employer in the area.* N COUNT : USU+ SUPP ↑ place = district 1.2 a part of a surface that has a particular characteristic or appearance so that it looks different from its surroundings. EG *...an uncomfortable, pink area on the front of his thighs... He began chipping off the white paint from a small area on the top of the table.* N COUNT+SUPP = spot

2 A particular **area** of a room, building, or other place is a part of it that is used for a particular purpose or activity. EG *...an outdoor play area... ...a communal washing area.* N COUNT : USU+ SUPP

3 The **area** of something such as a piece of land is its total extent measured in square feet, square metres, hectares, etc. EG *The farm was about 50 or 60 square kilometres in area.* N COUNT, OR *in/by*+N ↑ size

4 An **area** of knowledge, interest, or activity is a particular subject or kind of activity or a range of related subjects or activities. EG *His special interest lies in the area of literature... ...the electronics area... Telecommunications is one of the main growth areas.* N COUNT+SUPP ↑ part = field

5 An **area** of life, experience, etc is a particular part of it. EG *It has opened up new areas of experience... ...an area for concern... ...all areas of society.* N COUNT+SUPP ↑ part

arena /əriːnə/, **arenas**. 1 An **arena** is an area of land or a large room where sports, entertainments, and other public events take place. EG *...the dance arena... Noise filled the arena.* N COUNT = stadium

2 A particular **arena** is the centre of activity or of attention in a particular situation or context, especially one where a lot of argument takes place. EG *Workers were being drawn into the arena of political protest... ...unfettered competition in the economic arena.* N COUNT+SUPP = forum

aren't /ɑːnt/ is 1 the usual spoken form of 'are not'. EG *We aren't ready... They are coming, aren't they?* 2 the form that is usually used instead of 'am' in negative questions in spoken English. EG *I'm hopeless at French, aren't I?*

Argentinian /ɑːdʒə²ntɪnɪən/, **Argentinians**. 1 An **Argentinian** is a person who comes from Argentina. N COUNT

2 Someone or something that is **Argentinian** belongs or relates to Argentina or to its people. EG *...the Argentinian Revolutionary Workers' Party.* ADJ CLASSIF

argot /ɑːgəʊ/, **argots**. An **argot** is a special vocabulary used by a particular group of people, which other people find difficult to understand; a formal word. EG *...modern street argot... ...the argot of the sixties.* N COUNT+SUPP : USU SING = slang

arguable /ɑːgjuəbə⁰l/. An idea, point, assumption, etc that is **arguable**, 1 is not obviously true or correct and should be questioned or doubted. EG *Whether he was right or not is arguable.* ADJ CLASSIF = debatable 2 can be ADJ CLASSIF

supported by good reasons or evidence, and is probably true or correct. EG *It is arguable that the real damage will only be evident in the years to come.*
⇑ plausible = possible

◊ **arguably**. EG *Deforestation is arguably the most serious environmental issue of our time.*
◊ ADV SEN

argue /ɑːgjuː/, **argues, arguing, argued**. 1 If you **argue** that something is the case, you state your opinion about it and give the reasons why you think it is true or correct. EG *There are those who argue that the existence of nuclear weapons has helped to maintain peace... Bureaucracy, he argues, is killing the spirit of spontaneity... The United States should, it was argued, attempt to remain aloof.*
V+REPORT-CL/QUOTE ⇑ explain = contend

2 If you **argue** for or **argue** against something, you give reasons why something should or should not happen and try to convince people that you are right. EG *Some politicians argued against giving women the vote.*
V+A *(for/against)* ⇑ explain

3 If you **argue** someone **out of** a particular course of action, you persuade them not to do it by talking to them. EG *He argued the man out of suicide.*
PHR : VB INFLECTS = dissuade

4 If two or more people **argue** a point or **argue** about an idea, plan, or situation, they discuss the good and bad features or aspects of it. EG *A gathering of women sat and argued these points... What we are arguing about is not survival but the quality of life. I argued about fishing rights with the manager.*
V+O/A *(about)* : IF+PREP THEN *with*, RECIP = debate

5 If you **argue** with someone about something, you say things which show that you disagree with them about it. EG *Don't argue with me, George, just do as you're told... She was too exhausted to argue... She was now arguing with Dad on race.*
V OR V+A *(with)* : RECIP, IF +PREP THEN *about/on* = bandy words

6 If two people **argue**, or if one person **argues** with another, they speak angrily to each other about something that they disagree about. EG *They were still arguing like mad at six in the evening... The children were arguing over which programme they should watch on television.*
V OR V+A *(with)* : RECIP

7 to **argue the toss**: see **toss**.

argue out. When you **argue** something **out**, you discuss in detail all the aspects and possible consequences of it in order to reach a decision. EG *Our proposals were argued out in meetings that seemed never to end.*
PHRASAL VB : V+O+ADV

argument /ɑːgjə⁴mə²nt/, **arguments**. 1 An **argument** is a set of statements in support of an opinion or proposed course of action. It is expressed in an orderly way, and is used to try to convince someone that the opinion or course of action is correct. EG *Do you accept this argument?... There are strong arguments against these measures... Perhaps more common is the argument that disarmament agreements cannot work.*
N COUNT : USU+ *for/against/* REPORT-CL ⇑ reasoning = contention

2 An **argument** is also a disagreement over a particular matter between two or more people, sometimes resulting in them shouting angrily at each other. EG *He and David had been drawn into a ferocious argument about their jointly owned car... I said no and we got into a big argument over it.*
N COUNT ⇑ disagreement = row

3 **Argument** is the act of disagreeing with something or questioning whether it is correct. EG *We accepted it without argument... This belief is open to argument.*
N UNCOUNT = dispute

argumentative /ɑːgjə⁴mentə¹tɪv/. Someone who is **argumentative** is always ready to disagree with you and to start quarrelling; used showing disapproval. EG *The girl was known for being irritable and argumentative.* ▸ used of someone's voice or behaviour. EG *'And what did you mean by that?' said young Spear, in an argumentative tone.*
ADJ QUALIT = quarrelsome

argy-bargy /ɑːdʒi¹bɑːdʒi¹/ is a lot of argument or fuss about something; an informal expression. EG *She just couldn't face all the argy-bargy at home.*
N UNCOUNT ⇑ arguing = squabbling

aria /ɑːrɪə/, **arias**. An **aria** is an elaborate song for one singer in an opera or choral work. EG *She knows every aria in 'The Magic Flute'.*
N COUNT ⇑ song

arid /ærɪd/. 1 Land that is **arid** is so dry that very few plants can grow on it. EG *...a harsh, arid landscape... Over half the continent is arid or semi-arid.*
ADJ QUALIT ≠ fertile

◊ **aridity** /ærɪdɪti¹/. EG *...a desert of unrelenting aridity.*
◊ N UNCOUNT

2 A subject or piece of writing that is **arid** is dull and uninteresting. EG *I was bored stiff by this arid stuff... Disarmament is no mere arid question of military organization.* ◊ **aridity**. EG *...the formal aridity of their education.*
ADJ QUALIT = dry; ◊ N UNCOUNT = dryness

3 A period of time in your life that is **arid** is a time during which you accomplish very little or very little happens, so that you are bored or unhappy. EG *After two arid years, it was good to come home.*
ADJ QUALIT

aright /əraɪt/; a rather old-fashioned word. 1 If you hear or understand something **aright**, you hear or understand it correctly, even though you find it difficult to believe. EG *Morris wondered if he had heard aright.*
ADV AFTER VB ⇑ correctly

2 If you **set** or **put** an affair or situation **aright**, you deal with any problems that have arisen and arrange things in a satisfactory manner. EG *Before he could set matters aright, Brown committed suicide.*
PHR : VB INFLECTS

arise /əraɪz/, **arises, arising, arose, arisen**. 1 If a situation, opportunity, problem, or question **arises**, it begins to exist or comes to your attention. EG *A serious problem has arisen... He promised to help Rufus if the occasion arose.*
V ⇑ occur = crop up

2 When something **arises** out of a particular situation or **arises** from it, it is created or caused by the situation. EG *Resentment against your work seems to arise from the fact that people don't understand it... Let me pick up a few points arising out of what you've just been saying.*
V+A *(from/out of)* ⇑ come = result

3 When something such as an organization or system **arises**, it begins to exist and gradually develops into something lasting or successful. EG *If we want to consider how life arose we have to look back a further thousand million years... A whole community now arose.*
V ⇑ appear = evolve

4 If a noise, smell, sound, etc **arises** from a particular place or from among a group of people, it comes from the place or from the people. EG *A kind of chorus arose from the table, saying 'Please, mum, please'.*
V : USU+A ⇑ come = rise

5 If people **arise**, especially as a group, to demand their rights, fair treatment, etc, they all co-operate and fight together in order to obtain what they want. EG *Women arise to demand their rightful place.*
V = rise up

6 When you **arise** in the morning, you get out of bed; a formal or old-fashioned use. EG *I arose at six.*
V : USU+A = get up

7 When you **arise** from a chair, you stand up; a formal or old-fashioned use. EG *He arose to greet her.*
V : USU+A = get up

8 If something **arises**, especially when you are travelling towards it, it becomes visible; a fairly formal use. EG *A huge wooden house arose in a circular clearing.*
V : USU+A ⇑ appear = loom

aristocracy /ærɪ¹stɒkrəsi¹/, **aristocracies**. The **aristocracy** is a class of people whose families have a high social rank and who hold special titles in some countries. EG *The English aristocracy have always been most eccentric... ...a landed aristocracy... ...in societies dominated by land-holding aristocracies.*
N COUNT : IF SING, USU *the*+N, VB CAN BE SING OR PL = nobility, gentry

aristocrat /ærɪstə⁶kræt/, **aristocrats**. An **aristocrat** is someone whose family has a high social rank, especially someone who holds a title. EG *...the Marquis de la Falaise, a penniless French aristocrat.*
N COUNT ⇑ person

aristocratic /ærɪstə⁶krætɪk/. 1 Someone who is **aristocratic** belongs to the aristocracy. EG *...an aristocratic family.*
ADJ CLASSIF = noble, patrician

2 Something that is **aristocratic** has characteristics which are considered to be typical of people of high social rank. EG *...his aristocratic features.*
ADJ QUALIT = noble ≠ common

arithmetic. **Arithmetic** is pronounced /ə³rɪθmə²tɪk/ when it is a noun, and /ærɪθmetɪk/ when it is an adjective. **Arithmetic** is 1 the part of mathematics that is concerned with the addition, subtraction, multiplication, and division of numbers. EG *I blame the school for not making him learn arithmetic.* ▸ used as an adjective. EG *...simple arithmetic problems... ...an arithmetic test.* 2 a numerical calculation or sum which is worked out from a particular set of figures. EG *I was busy correcting Eric's arithmetic at his desk... Similar arithmetic applies to the cooking oil business... ...the arithmetic of the election.* 3 the process or manner of working out the answer to a sum or calculation. EG *They struggled with their arithmetic... The waiter got his arithmetic wrong.*
N UNCOUNT; ▸ ADJ CLASSIF; N UNCOUNT; N SING WITH DET = sums

arithmetical /ærɪθmetɪkə⁰l/. **Arithmetical** problems, formulae, etc relate to or involve the addition, subtraction, multiplication, or division of numbers. EG *...arithmetical solutions to the problem.*
ADJ CLASSIF ⇑ mathematical

ark /ɑːk/. In the Bible, the **ark** was a large wooden boat which Noah built in order to save his family and two of every kind of animal from the Flood. ● If you say that something came **out of the ark**, you mean
N PROPER : *the*+N; ● PHR : USED AS AN A

that it is extremely old or old-fashioned; a humorous, informal expression. EG *This cash register must have come out of the ark.*

arm /ɑːm/, **arms, arming, armed.** 1 Your **arms** are the two long parts of your body that are attached to your shoulders and that have your hands at the other end. EG *She put her arm around his neck and kissed him... They took me by the arm... He tucked the shell under his arm... She was weeping in my arms.* N COUNT ↑ limb

2 The word **arm** is used in the following expressions.
2.1 If you hold or carry something **at arm's length**, you hold it at a distance from your body, for example because it is unpleasant or because you can see it more easily there. EG *Women were rushing about, carrying dresses at arm's length... He was holding the paper at arm's length.* PHR : USED AS AN A ≠ close 2.2 If you **keep** someone **at arm's length**, you avoid becoming too friendly or involved with them. EG *We all understood the necessity of keeping Michie at arm's length.* PHR : VB INFLECTS ≠ encourage 2.3 If you would **give** your **right arm for** something, you want it very much and would be willing to do almost anything to get it. EG *He would give his right arm for a job at the BBC.* PHR : VB INFLECTS 2.4 A list, document, etc that is **as long as** your **arm** is extremely long. EG *He filled up a form as long as your arm... ...a shopping list as long as my arm.* PHR : USED AS C 2.5 If you are walking **arm in arm** with someone, you are walking side by side with them with your arm bent at the elbow and linked through their arm. EG *I remember strolling arm in arm with you along the boulevards of Paris.* PHR : USED AS AN A 2.6 If you are pushed **into** someone's **arms**, you come under their influence or control. EG *We might be pushed into the arms of the liberals.* PHR : USED AS AN A

3 **with open arms.** 3.1 If you welcome someone **with open arms**, you hold your arms stretched out and apart, ready to take hold of them affectionately. EG *Claire went to him with open arms.* PHR : USED AS AN A 3.2 If you welcome something such as a situation, event, or change **with open arms**, you are very pleased about it and accept it gladly. EG *A teaching degree is welcomed with open arms.* PHR : USED AS AN A

4 The **arm** of a piece of clothing is the part of it that covers your arm. EG *The arm of his jacket was torn.* N COUNT = sleeve

5 The **arm** of a chair is the part of it on which you rest your arm when you are sitting down. EG *An ashtray was balanced on the arm of a chair... He sat with his legs slung over the arm of an easy chair.* N COUNT : IF+ PREP THEN *of*

6 The **arm** of something such as a piece of machinery is a long thin part of it, especially a part that sticks out or moves from side to side. EG *In the distance was a line of windmills, their great arms glittering in the sun as they turned... He stops the van in front of the arm and takes a ticket from the automatic machine.* N COUNT : IF+ PREP THEN *of*

7 An **arm** of water or land is a long thin area of it that is joined to a broader area. EG *Hamelin Pool is one small arm of this vast inlet.* N COUNT : USU+ *of*

8 An **arm** of an organization is a section or part of it that is usually responsible for one particular kind of activity or for the work of the organization in a particular region. EG *...the political arm of an established trade union movement.* N COUNT+SUPP = wing

9 **Arms** are weapons or devices that are used to hurt or kill people, especially in a war. EG *They were not allowed to use arms... ...a genuine and sincere effort at arms limitation... They established a trade monopoly on the spice islands by force of arms.* N PLURAL

10 The word **arms** is also used in the following expressions. 10.1 If a country has people **under arms**, it has people trained to use weapons and ready to fight a war. EG *At this time Britain had more forces under arms than ever before.* PHR : USED AS AN A 10.2 If you **take up arms** against someone, you prepare to attack them and fight against them. EG *They will surely take up arms against you in the not too distant future.* PHR : VB INFLECTS
10.3 If you **lay down** your **arms**, you stop fighting and surrender; a rather old-fashioned expression. EG *The exhausted soldiers laid down their arms.* PHR : VB INFLECTS 10.4 If someone is **up in arms** about something, they are very angry about it and are protesting strongly. EG *Feminists are now up in arms over the new laws.* PHR : USED AS AN A

11 If you **arm** someone with a weapon, especially a gun, you provide them with a weapon. EG *We must know how to arm ourselves... Sheriff O'Keene armed his men with shotguns.* V+O (NG/REFL)

12 If you **arm** someone with authority, information, evidence, etc, you provide them with something that will be necessary or useful in a particular situation. EG *This was a man destined later to be armed with awesome powers by the Nationalists.* V+O : USU PASS+ *with* = prime

13 The **arms** of a city or noble family are its coat of arms. N PLURAL

14 See also **armed.**

15 • **armed to the teeth**: see **tooth.** • **babe in arms**: see **babe.** • to **twist** someone's **arm**: see **twist.**

armada /ɑːmɑːdə/, **armadas.** An **armada** is a large fleet of warships. EG *The troops, together with a large naval armada and aerial support, are fighting a mock battle.* N COUNT

armadillo /ɑːmədɪləʊ/, **armadillos.** An **armadillo** is a small animal which has a body covered with large bony scales and which rolls itself into a ball when it is attacked. Armadillos live in South America. They eat insects and live in burrows. N COUNT ↑ mammal

armament /ɑːməməʔnt/, **armaments.** 1 **Armaments** are weapons and military equipment belonging to an army or country. EG *For several years the world has spent more on armaments than on education... ...high-profit armaments industries.* N PLURAL = arms

2 **Armament** is the process of increasing the number of weapons, and their quality and effectiveness, by a country, so that it is prepared for war. EG *More money is needed for purposes other than armament.* N UNCOUNT = defence

armband /ɑːmbænd/, **armbands.** An **armband** is a band of fabric that you wear round your arm at an event in order to show that you have an official position. Some people also wear a black armband to show that a friend or relation has died. EG *...stewards wearing official armbands.* N COUNT ↑ band

armchair /ɑːmtʃɛə/, **armchairs.** 1 An **armchair** is a comfortable chair which has a support on each side for your arms. EG *He was sitting quietly in his armchair, smoking a pipe and reading the morning paper.* N COUNT ↑ chair

2 An **armchair** sportsman, critic, traveller, etc knows about a particular subject from what he or she has read or heard about it rather than from practical experience; sometimes used showing disapproval. EG *...an armchair anthropologist... I'm afraid I'm only an armchair traveller.* N BEFORE N ↑ theoretical

armed /ɑːmd/. 1 Someone who is **armed** is carrying a weapon, especially a gun. EG *The police and military were armed and in many cases had to use force... ...two or three armed and masked men.* ADJ CLASSIF ≠ unarmed ▸ used of an attack, conflict, etc. EG *...armed action against British imperialism... We can expect more armed assaults on homes, stores, and warehouses.* ▸ ADJ CLASSIF : ATTRIB

2 Someone who is **armed** with something such as authority, information, or a particular skill has something that will be necessary or useful in a particular situation. EG *The management was armed with the report of an official enquiry... Armed with secretarial skills, a woman will easily find a job.* ADJ CLASSIF : PRED+*with* ↑ provided = equipped

-armed. Someone who is thin-**armed**, hairy-**armed**, etc has arms of the size, shape, or appearance mentioned. COMB : FORMS ADJS

armed forces. The **armed forces**, or the **armed services**, of a country are its military forces, usually the army, navy, and air force. EG *The conference called for the major powers to cut their armed forces by a third.* N PLURAL

armful /ɑːmfʊl/, **armfuls.** An **armful** of something is the amount of it that you can carry in one or both of your arms. EG *She came back with an armful of paperbacks... ...armfuls of rotten wood.* N COUNT ↑ quantity

armhole /ɑːmhəʊl/, **armholes.** An **armhole** is an opening in a shirt, coat, jacket, etc through which you put your arm, where the sleeve is attached if there is one. EG *Make sure that the armholes are not too tight for you.* N COUNT

armistice /ɑːmɪstɪs/, **armistices.** **Armistice** or an **armistice** is an agreement between countries who are at war with one another to stop fighting for a time and to discuss ways of making a peaceful settlement. EG *They dismissed our offer of an armistice... In his view a declaration of armistice would have provoked a revolution.* N COUNT/ UNCOUNT ↑ truce

armour /ɑːmə/; also spelled **armor** in American English. 1 **Armour** is 1.1 special metal clothing that soldiers used to wear for protection in battle. EG *...knights in armour.* N UNCOUNT 1.2 a group of armoured vehicles, especially tanks. EG *They spotted armour moving up the valley.* N UNCOUNT

2 The **armour** of something is the thick, hard outer covering that protects it against attack, for example the body of a tank or other military vehicle, or the shell of some animals. EG *...the steel armour of a tank... The animal has an armour of horny scales.* — N SING WITH DET +SUPP

3 Your **armour** consists of the attitudes and feelings you have which you use to protect yourself emotionally. EG *Their sense of justice gave them armour against the contempt of others.* — N UNCOUNT = defence

armoured /ɑːməd/; also spelled **armored** in American English. **1** An **armoured** vehicle is fitted with a hard metal covering in order to protect it from bullets and missiles. EG *The rebellion was widespread, and armoured cars, helicopters and armed forces were brought in.* ▸ used of a military force which has such vehicles, or actions in which they are used. EG *There were 8,200 men in armoured divisions.* — ADJ CLASSIF ⇑ protected; ▸ ADJ CLASSIF : ATTRIB

2 An animal that is **armoured** has spines or a hard outer covering of bone to protect it when it is attacked. — ADJ CLASSIF ⇑ covered

armourer /ɑːmərə/, **armourers**; also spelled **armorer** in American English. An **armourer** is someone who makes or supplies weapons. — N COUNT ⇑ person

armour-plated; also spelled **armor-plated** in American English. Something, especially a vehicle, that is **armour-plated** has a hard metal covering to protect it when it is attacked. EG *She arrived in an armour-plated car.* — ADJ CLASSIF ⇑ protected

armoury /ɑːməri[1]/, **armouries**; also spelled **armory** in American English. **1** An **armoury** is a place where weapons, bombs, and other military equipment are stored. EG *'Go into the armoury,' Boylan said, 'and hunt around for a few grenades.'* — N COUNT ⇑ storeroom

2 A country's **armoury** is all the military equipment and weapons that it has. EG *They did not want to use any of their considerable nuclear armoury.* — N COUNT : USU SING = arsenal

3 An **armoury** is also a collection of different things that you keep for a particular purpose. EG *...the housewife's armoury of medicines... This trick is one more part of her political armoury.* — N COUNT+SUPP = store

armpit /ɑːmpɪt/, **armpits**. Your **armpit** is the area of your body that is under your arm at the place where your arm joins your shoulder. EG *He was scratching under his armpit.* — N COUNT

arms race. The **arms race** is the attempt by powerful countries always to have more and better weapons than their rivals. EG *...the nuclear arms race.* — N SING : the+N ⇑ competition

army /ɑːmi[1]/, **armies**. **1** An **army** is a large organized group of people who are armed and trained to fight on land in a war. Most armies are organized and controlled by governments. EG *Their father became a general in the Army... Both armies suffered thousands of wounded or dead... ...the Army is in a high state of readiness... ...the army are clearing up quite a bit of the land.* — N COUNT : IF SING, USU the+N, VB CAN BE SING OR PL

2 An **army** of people, animals, or things is a large number of them, especially when they are regarded as a force of some kind. EG *...an army of statisticians... ...an army of ants... ...the growing army of the unemployed.* — N COUNT+of ⇑ group = host

aroma /ərəʊmə/, **aromas**. An **aroma** is a strong, pleasant smell, especially of food. EG *The whole house was filled with the aroma of coffee and garlic... ...the most delicious kitchen aromas.* — N COUNT+SUPP

aromatic /ærə[6]mætɪk/. A plant or food that is **aromatic** has a fairly strong, pleasant smell of spice or herbs. EG *The whole plant is highly aromatic... ...a refreshing, aromatic tea made from jasmine.* ▸ used of a smell or taste. EG *...sweet aromatic odours.* — ADJ QUALIT ⇑ fragrant

arose /ərəʊz/ is the past tense of **arise**.

around /əraʊnd/. **1 Around** is an alternative form of **round** when it is an adverb, preposition, or the second part of a phrasal verb. Examples of these uses of **around** are explained under **round**. — ADV AFTER VB, OR PREP

2 Around is also used in the following expressions: **2.1** If someone or something **is around**, they are present or available. EG *He went back down again to see who was around... It's a familiar old gadget which has been around for hundreds of years.* **2.2** If someone **has been around**, they have had a lot of experience of different people, places, life-styles, and situations; an informal expression. EG *I've been around and I know how to handle people like him.* — PHR : VB INFLECTS ⇑ is present = is about; PHR : VB INFLECTS ⇑ is experienced

arousal /əraʊzə[0]l/. **1 Arousal** is the state of being alert or excited, often in a sexual way. EG *...feelings of sexual arousal... ...the state of arousal produced by adrenalin.* — N UNCOUNT : USU +SUPP

2 The **arousal** of someone's feelings or interest is the process of causing such feelings or interest to develop. EG *The impulse to attack involves the immediate arousal of acute fear.* — N SING WITH DET +of = awakening

arouse /əraʊz/, **arouses, arousing, aroused**. **1** If someone or something **arouses** your interest or attention, it causes you to become interested in it or to notice it. EG *It may arouse his interest in a subject that has given me endless pleasure.* — V+O ⇑ cause = awaken, stir up

2 If something **arouses** a particular feeling in people, it makes them have that feeling. EG *Discontent was aroused by the various attempts to change the law... ...a move that would arouse opposition.* — V+O ⇑ cause = awaken, stir up

3 If something **arouses** a group of people, it makes them feel angry. EG *Something seems to have aroused the blacks.* — V+O ⇑ provoke = anger

4 If you **are aroused** by something, it makes you feel sexually excited. EG *Many men are aroused by the odours of women.* — V+O : USU PASS ⇑ excite = turn on

5 When people or things **arouse** you from sleep, they wake you up. EG *Diana had aroused them just before dawn.* — V+O = rouse

arr. is an abbreviation for 'arrives'. It is used on timetables for buses, trains, etc to indicate what time a bus or train will reach a place. EG *dep. Victoria 1927, arr. Ramsgate 2110.* — V+NAME+NUM ≠ dep.

arraign /ə[3]reɪn/, **arraigns, arraigning, arraigned**. If someone **is arraigned** on a particular charge, they are brought before a court of law to answer that charge; a formal word. EG *He had just been arraigned on a charge of murdering his wife.* — V+O : IF+PREP THEN *on*

arrange /ə[3]reɪndʒ/, **arranges, arranging, arranged**. **1** If you **arrange** an event, meeting, etc, you make plans and preparations for it to happen at a future time. EG *Could you come up here and I'll arrange a meeting?... Progressive Tours Ltd arrange holidays in Eastern Europe... I arranged everything with the management.* — V+O ⇑ plan = organize

2 If you **arrange** with someone else to do something, you make plans with them about what you are going to do, and about how, when, and where it will be done. EG *Don't worry if you've arranged with somebody else to go with them... It was suddenly arranged that Celia should come to Switzerland.* — V+A *(with)*/ REPORT-CL/ *to*-INF = fix up

3 If you **arrange** something for someone, you make it possible for them to have it or to do it. EG *We can arrange temporary loans or grants... I asked if it could be arranged for me to meet one of the national leaders... Will the shop you're buying the machine from arrange to have it installed?... Please arrange for a taxi to collect us after the performance.* — V+O : USU+*for*, V+*for*+NG+*to*-INF, OR V+*to*-INF ⇑ enable = fix, organize

4 If you **arrange** things, such as flowers in a vase or books on a shelf, you put them in a particular position or order, usually to make them look attractive or tidy. EG *...four wooden chairs arranged around the square oak table... He began arranging his things.* — V+O : USU+A = organize ≠ muddle

5 If someone **arranges** a piece of music or a dance, they change it or adapt it so that it is suitable for particular instruments or voices or for a particular performance. EG *...folk songs arranged by Luciano Berio.* — V+O : USU PASS

arranged /ə[3]reɪnʒd/. An **arranged** marriage is a marriage in which the parents choose the person who their son or daughter will marry. EG *They still have the system of arranged marriages.* — ADJ CLASSIF

arrangement /ə[3]reɪnʒmə[2]nt/, **arrangements**. **1 Arrangements** are plans and preparations which you make so that something will happen or be possible. EG *I know you've made all the arrangements for the conference... I made arrangements which enabled me to continue working.* — N PLURAL : IF+ PREP THEN *for*, OR *to*-INF ⇑ plan

2 An **arrangement** is **2.1** an agreement that you make with someone to do something or not to do something. EG *He made an arrangement to rent the property... By prior arrangement, I was not introduced as her fiancé.* **2.2** a plan or procedure for doing something. EG *What are the sleeping and eating arrangements?... It is the normal working arrangement with all my customers.* **2.3** a group of things, for example flowers or furniture, that have been set out in a particular position or order so that they look attractive or tidy. EG *There was an arrangement of books in the window... A room arrangement that suits one teacher may not suit another.* — N COUNT, OR *by*+N ⇑ plan; N COUNT; N COUNT+SUPP = layout

3 In music, an **arrangement** is a piece of music that has been changed or adapted so that it is suitable for particular instruments or voices or for a particular performance. EG *...a Mozart symphony in an arrangement for piano duet.* N COUNT ⇑ version = adaptation

arrant /ærənt/ is used to emphasize that someone or something is very bad in some way; used showing disapproval. EG *...an arrant coward... That was probably the most arrant piece of folly you have committed in your life.* ADJ QUALIT : ATTRIB ⇑ absolute = unmitigated

array /əreɪ/, **arrays, arraying, arrayed.** 1 An **array** of things or people is a large number of different things or people, especially when they are impressive or attractive. EG *...a vast array of new responsibilities... ...a distinguished array of world leaders and statesmen... They looked in the window, at the array of cakes and cookies.* N COUNT : USU SING+*of* ⇑ group = assortment

2 A military or battle **array** is a group of soldiers placed in positions ready for battle. EG *The soldiers were all in battle array.* N COUNT : MOD+N ⇑ order

3 If things **are arrayed** in a particular way, they are displayed carefully or attractively; a formal use. EG *Daggers and pistols were arrayed on the mouldy walls... Diverse innovations are arrayed before society.* V+O : USU PASS+A ⇑ arrange = display

4 If soldiers **are arrayed** in a particular position or order, they are placed in that order ready for battle; a formal use. EG *They trembled when they saw the troops arrayed against them.* V+O : USU PASS+A = range

5 If you **array** yourself or **are arrayed** in attractive or beautiful clothes, you dress yourself or are dressed in them; an old-fashioned or formal use. EG *The women array themselves in silk... Arrayed in his robes, Donald climbed into the pulpit.* V+O *(NG/REFL)* +A *(in)* ⇑ clothe = deck

arrears /ərɪəz/. 1 **Arrears** are amounts of money that you owe, especially amounts that should have been paid regularly over a period of time. EG *He vanished leaving massive arrears... The arrears payments were even more crippling.* N PLURAL ≠ credit

2 **in arrears. 2.1** If someone is **in arrears** with their payments, or if their payments are **in arrears**, they have not paid the amounts of money that they should have paid regularly. EG *The council complained that his rent was in arrears.* PHR : USED AS AN A ⇑ late **2.2** If you are paid **in arrears**, your wages are paid to you at the end of the period of time in which they were earned. EG *She was paid every four weeks in arrears.* PHR : USED AS AN A ≠ in advance

arrest /ərest/, **arrests, arresting, arrested.** 1 If the police **arrest** someone, they catch them and take them somewhere in order to decide whether they should be charged with an offence. EG *A friend had been arrested for possession of explosives.* V+O : IF+PREP THEN *for* = detain

2 When the police make an **arrest**, they arrest someone. EG *The riots led to the arrest of many union leaders... I have a warrant for your arrest... Several arrests had already been made... He fled the country to avoid arrest.* N COUNT/ UNCOUNT : IF+ PREP THEN *of* ⇑ capture ● If someone is **under arrest**, they have been caught by the police and are not allowed to go free. EG *He has been under arrest since March.* ● PHR : USED AS AN A ≠ free
● If someone is **under house arrest**, they are not allowed to leave their house or to go anywhere or meet anyone. EG *Mr Acher himself remains under house arrest.* ● PHR : USED AS AN A

3 If you **arrest** something or **arrest** its progress, you stop it happening or make it happen more slowly. EG *He tried to arrest the course of destruction... Pan Am has cut back in an effort to arrest losses that threaten its survival.* V+O = check

4 If something **arrests** your attention, it causes you to look at it or listen to it carefully, usually because it interests or surprises you. EG *Among entries that arrested my attention was one from a blind girl.* V+O ⇑ attract = catch
◊ **arresting.** EG *On page 13 was an arresting drawing of people turning into animals.* ◊ ADJ QUALIT

arrival /əraɪvəˈl/, **arrivals.** 1 Your **arrival** at a place is the act of arriving there. EG *British Airways announce the arrival of flight BA072 from New York... I apologize for my late arrival... Both were dead on arrival at the hospital.* N UNCOUNT : IF+ PREP THEN *of/ in/at* ≠ departure

2 The **arrival** of something new is its beginning to happen or to exist. EG *Industry has been revolutionized by the arrival of the computer.* N SING WITH DET = advent

3 The **arrival** of a new baby is the event of its being born. EG *We had a party to celebrate the arrival of our son.* N SING WITH DET = birth

4 An **arrival** is **4.1** someone who has just reached or come to a place. EG *One of the new arrivals at the college was an old friend of mine... We waited in the arrivals lounge.* N COUNT ⇑ newcomer **4.2** a baby that has just been born; a humorous use. EG *And how's the latest arrival, then?* N COUNT : USU SING, MOD+N

arrive /əraɪv/, **arrives, arriving, arrived.** 1 When you **arrive** at a place, **1.1** you reach it at the end of a journey. EG *I sent a telegram to my mother saying I had arrived safely... He arrived back at his hotel soon after midnight... It was raining when we arrived in Canton... ...recently arrived visitors from overseas.* V : USU+A ≠ depart **1.2** you come to it for the first time in order to stay there or live there. EG *Since arriving in England in 1979, she has established herself as a major writer... ...newly arrived students.* V : IF+PREP THEN *in/at* ≠ leave

2 When a letter, parcel, or message **arrives**, it is brought or delivered to you. EG *Thank you for your letter, which arrived on Monday... News arrived of an invasion in the south of the country.* V = come

3 If you **arrive** at a particular idea, conclusion, situation, etc, you reach that idea, conclusion, or situation after a lot of time, effort, or thought. EG *It took us several hours to arrive at a decision... We finally arrived at a situation where we were making a small profit.* V+A *(at)*

4 When something new **arrives**, it begins to exist, or is made or used for the first time. EG *People's social habits have changed since television arrived.* V : NO CONT = appear

5 When a baby **arrives**, it is born. EG *The baby arrived at six in the morning.* V : USU+A = is born

6 When a particular moment or event **arrives**, it happens, especially after you have been waiting for it for a long time. EG *Summer has arrived at last... The moment for action had arrived.* V = come

7 You say that someone **has arrived** when they have become successful or famous in their career; an informal expression. EG *Now that she has her own TV show, she has really arrived.* PHR : AUX INFLECTS

arrogance /ærəgəns/ is the quality of being arrogant; used showing disapproval. EG *He had a reputation for arrogance.* N UNCOUNT ⇑ attitude

arrogant /ærəgənt/. Someone who is **arrogant** behaves in a proud, unpleasant way towards other people because they believe that they are much better or cleverer or more important than others; used showing disapproval. EG *He was petulant, selfish, arrogant and occasionally callous... I think it would be arrogant if I tried to give any advice.* ADJ QUALIT = conceited
◊ **arrogantly.** EG *The group had rather arrogantly assumed themselves to be in command.* ◊ ADV WITH VB = haughtily

arrogate /ærəgeɪt/, **arrogates, arrogating, arrogated.** If you **arrogate** something such as a responsibility or privilege to yourself, you claim or take it even though you have no right to do so; a formal word, used showing disapproval. EG *The company has adopted a new role, arrogating to itself the right to change conditions without consultation.* V+O+*to*+O *(REFL)* ⇑ assume

arrow /ærəʊ/, **arrows.** 1 An **arrow** is a long thin weapon which is sharp and pointed at one end and which often has feathers at the other end. An arrow is shot from a bow. EG *He fired his second arrow... ...a long, curved bow and a quiver of arrows.* N COUNT

2 An **arrow** is also a written sign that consists of a straight line with another line bent at a sharp angle at one end. The arrow points in a particular direction, and shows you where something is. EG *The exit sign is marked with an arrow.* N COUNT

arrowhead /ærəʊhed/, **arrowheads**; also spelled with a hyphen. An **arrowhead** is the sharp, pointed end of an arrow. N COUNT ⇑ tip

arrowroot /ærəˢruːt/ is a starch obtained from a West Indian plant that is used in cooking, for example for thickening sauces or in making biscuits. N UNCOUNT

arse /ɑːs/, **arses, arsing, arsed.** Your **arse** is your bottom; an informal or rude word. N COUNT ● If someone tells you to **move your arse** or **shift your arse**, they are telling you very impolitely to make a space for them to sit down. ● PHR : VB INFLECTS = shift up ● If someone tells you to **get off your arse**, they are telling you very impolitely that you should hurry up and do something or get on with what you are supposed to be doing. ● PHR : VB INFLECTS ● **a pain in the arse**: see **pain**.

arse about. If you say that someone **is arsing about** or **arsing around**, you mean that they behaving in a silly and irritating way instead of getting something done; an informal or rude expression. PHRASAL VB : V+ADV = muck about

arsehole /ɑːshᵒəʊl/, **arseholes**; a very rude word.
1 A person's **arsehole** is their anus. N COUNT
2 People call someone an **arsehole** or refer to them N COUNT

as an **arsehole** when they dislike them very much or think that they are stupid.

arsenal /ɑːsənəl/, **arsenals**. 1 An **arsenal** is a building where weapons and pieces of military equipment are stored and made. EG *They raided a British arsenal and ambushed several convoys.* — N COUNT ↑ store = armoury

2 An **arsenal** of weapons, equipment, etc is all the weapons and military equipment which a country or group has. EG *The superpowers have a vast arsenal of nuclear weapons... Their arsenal totalled 36 pistols and a few rifles.* — N COUNT = store, supply

3 An **arsenal** of ideas or objects is a large number or collection of ideas or objects, especially when they can be used to hurt people. EG *...mankind's arsenal of horrors.* — N COUNT+SUPP = stock

arsenic /ɑːsənɪk/ is a very strong poison, often in the form of a white powder, which is sometimes used to kill insects and rats, and which can also kill people. EG *One group was virtually wiped out when arsenic was added to their food.* — N UNCOUNT ↑ poison

arson /ɑːsən/ is the crime of deliberately setting fire to something, especially a building. EG *Fighting, plundering and arson have erupted all over the city.* — N UNCOUNT ↑ crime

art /ɑːt/, **arts**. 1 **Art** is 1.1 the creation and production of drawings, paintings, sculpture, etc when these things are considered to be beautiful or to express in a unique way a particular idea or meaning. EG *Sandra doesn't know much about art... ...the study of contemporary art.* — N UNCOUNT **1.2** objects, such as paintings or pieces of sculpture, which are considered to be beautiful and which are part of a society's culture. EG *They hold regular sales of oriental art... ...an art collection.* — N UNCOUNT = works of art **1.3** the creation and production of literature, music, painting, sculpture, etc, when these things are considered to be beautiful and to be part of a society's culture. EG *There were explorations in poetry, dance, and art of various forms.* — N UNCOUNT **1.4** the activity or skill of drawing or painting. EG *I've never been any good at art.* — N UNCOUNT **1.5** paintings, drawings, models, etc made by children or by older people as a hobby. EG *...an exhibition of children's art.* — N UNCOUNT = works ▸ used as a plural noun, especially in the expression 'arts and crafts'. EG *There were also arts and crafts, dancing, and games.* — ▸ N PLURAL

2 A particular **art** is an activity such as drama, poetry, or sculpture in which people try to create something beautiful or to express a particular idea or meaning through their works. EG *The strongest 20th century art is film... ...the visual arts.* — N COUNT ↑ activity

3 **The arts** refers to the creation or performance of poetry, music, drama, painting, sculpture, etc, especially in a particular country or region. EG *It is very hard to make the arts self-supporting... How much will they spend on sport and recreation, how much on the arts?* — N PLURAL : the+N ↑ culture

4 **Arts** or the **arts** is also used to refer to subjects such as history or languages in contrast to scientific subjects. EG *The proportion of students in arts is fairly high... ...education in the arts and sciences... ...an arts degree.* • See also **Bachelor of Arts, Master of Arts.** — N PLURAL = humanities ≠ sciences

5 You describe an activity as an **art** when it requires a high level of skill which someone has naturally or which they develop through experience. EG *It was quite an art, talking to Janet... ...the art of survival... There is a special art in teaching handicapped children.* — N SING WITH DET • If you **get** something **down to a fine art**, you are able to do it in the best and most efficient way because you have had a lot of experience of doing it and have tried many different methods. — • PHR : VB INFLECTS

6 If someone uses **art** to do something, especially something which is considered wrong or mean, they use great skill and cleverness in order to do it. EG *They would use their whole art to twist the meeting... Getting the balance exactly right involves a lot of art.* — N UNCOUNT = cunning

artefact /ɑːtɪfækt/, **artefacts**; also spelled **artifact**. An **artefact** is an object that is made by a person, for example a tool or an ornament. EG *...gold and silver artefacts.* — N COUNT ↑ object

arterial /ɑːtɪərɪəl/. 1 **Arterial** means involving or relating to your arteries and the movement of blood through your body. EG *...arterial and heart disease.* — ADJ CLASSIF : ATTRIB

2 An **arterial** road or railway is a road or railway that is the main route from one place to another. EG *...an ambitious system of new arterial highways.* — ADJ CLASSIF : ATTRIB = trunk

artery /ɑːtəri/, **arteries**. An **artery** is 1 a tube in your body that carries blood from your heart to the rest of your body. EG *...changes in the blood pressure within the artery.* — N COUNT ≠ vein **2** an important road or railway. EG *...the place where the three main arteries of West London traffic met.* — N COUNT ↑ route

artesian well /ɑːtiːzɪən wel/, **artesian wells**. An **artesian well** is a well in which the water is continuously forced up out of the ground as a result of pressure from water flowing into the well from a higher level. — N COUNT

artful /ɑːtfʊl/. Someone who is **artful** 1 is clever and skilful, especially at achieving what they want by deceiving people. EG *...the artful schemer.* ▸ used of plans, actions, etc. EG *No one's ever come up with anything as artful as you have.* ◇ **artfully**. EG *Prices have been artfully raised.* — ADJ QUALIT = crafty; ◇ ADV WITH VB **2** uses great skill in expressing a particular idea or creating a particular impression. EG *He is the most artful of American sports writers.* ▸ used of someone's creative work. EG *Artful set changes in the play won admiration.* ◇ **artfully**. EG *The patio lighting was artfully arranged to flatter people's faces.* — ADJ QUALIT ↑ skilful = clever; ◇ ADV = cleverly

arthritic /ɑːθrɪtɪk/, **arthritics**. 1 Someone who is **arthritic** has stiff and painful joints in their body. EG *Mrs James is very arthritic.* ▸ used as a noun to refer to a person. EG *...a cookery book for arthritics.* — ADJ QUALIT ↑ diseased; ▸ N COUNT

2 An **arthritic** pain, condition, etc is the result of someone's joints being swollen. EG *His hands ached with arthritic pains.* — ADJ CLASSIF : ATTRIB ↑ crippling

arthritis /ɑːθraɪtɪs/ is a condition in which the joints in someone's body, especially in their hands, are swollen and painful. EG *I am half crippled with arthritis.* — N UNCOUNT

artichoke /ɑːtɪtʃəʊk/, **artichokes**. 1 An **artichoke** or **globe artichoke** is a round, green vegetable which has a cluster of fleshy leaves. The centre of the vegetable and the bottom part of each leaf can be eaten when the artichoke has been cooked. — N COUNT ↑ vegetable

2 An **artichoke** or **Jerusalem artichoke** is a small, yellowish-white vegetable that grows underground and that looks like a potato. — N COUNT ↑ vegetable

article /ɑːtɪkəl/, **articles**. 1 An **article** is 1.1 a piece of writing on a particular subject that has been written for publication in a newspaper or magazine. EG *...an article by J B Priestley in the New Statesman... Brody finished reading the article and set the paper on the desk.* — N COUNT **1.2** a particular object or item. EG *He was ordered to pay for or replace the articles he had stolen... Place the wet article on a towel and leave to dry... ...an article of furniture.* — N COUNT, OR N PART+N UNCOUNT

2 An **article** of a formal or official agreement or document is a section or paragraph of it which deals with a particular point or subject. EG *...an article of the constitution... The invasion contravened article 51 of the UN charter.* — N COUNT : DET+N, OR N+NUM = clause

3 A person's **articles** are an agreement by which they spend a period of time working and training with a firm in order to become qualified, for example as a lawyer or an accountant. — N PLURAL ↑ agreement

4 **Article** is the term used in grammar for the words 'a', 'an', and 'the'. 'A' and 'an' are called the 'indefinite articles', and 'the' is called the 'definite article'. In this dictionary these words are described as DET. See ☐ at DET. — N COUNT

articled /ɑːtɪkəld/. Someone who is **articled**, for example to a firm of lawyers or accountants, is employed by the firm and is training to become qualified. EG *I had been articled for three years... ...an articled clerk.* — ADJ CLASSIF ↑ apprenticed

article of faith, articles of faith. An **article of faith** is something that you feel very strongly about, and that affects the way you think and behave. EG *Nationalism was a deep-rooted article of faith.* — N COUNT ↑ belief = tenet

articulate, articulates, articulating, articulated. **Articulate** is pronounced /ɑːtɪkjələt/ when it is an adjective, and /ɑːtɪkjəleɪt/ when it is a verb. 1 If you are **articulate**, you are able to express yourself easily and well, especially when you are dealing with difficult ideas. EG *She was bright and articulate.* ▸ used of speech or writing. EG *This is a very articulate book.* ◇ **articulateness**. EG *His articulateness makes an interview a matter of keeping up with him.* — ADJ QUALIT ↑ clear = lucid; ▸ ↑ clear; ◇ N UNCOUNT = lucidity

2 When you **articulate** your ideas or feelings, you say in words what you think or how you feel; a formal use. EG *I could not define or articulate the dissatisfaction I felt.* — V+O = express

articulated /ɑːtɪkjə⁴leɪtɪ²d/. An **articulated** vehicle, especially a lorry, is made in two sections which are joined together by a metal bar, so that it can turn corners more easily. ADJ CLASSIF : ATTRIB ⇑ coupled

articulation /ɑːtɪkjə⁴leɪʃəⁿn/, **articulations**. 1 The **articulation** of an idea or feeling is the expression of it, especially in words; used in formal English. EG *...an articulation of the feelings I had when I first came here.* N UNCOUNT

2 The **articulation** of a sound or word is the way in which it is produced or spoken, especially when you are considering how clear it is. EG *...the articulation of the American word.* N UNCOUNT/COUNT ⇑ pronunciation

artifact /ɑːtɪfækt/. See **artefact**.

artifice /ɑːtɪfɪs/, **artifices**; a formal word. 1 An **artifice** is a clever trick or deception. EG *...small and subtle artifices... They saw through the artifice.* N COUNT

2 **Artifice** is the clever use of tricks and devices. EG *...the audience's awareness of the play's artifice.* N UNCOUNT

artificial /ɑːtɪfɪʃəl/. 1 An **artificial** state, situation, or attitude would not have existed naturally and exists or happens because people have created it. EG *These results appear only in very artificial conditions... The artificial scarcity of his product increases its value.* ◊ **artificially**. EG *The government keeps prices artificially high.* ◊ **artificiality** /ɑːtɪfɪʃi¹ælɪti¹/. EG *...the artificiality of a three hour written examination.* ADJ QUALIT = false, contrived ≠ natural; ◊ ADV; ◊ N UNCOUNT

2 **Artificial** objects or materials do not occur naturally and are created by people. EG *...artificial fibres... ...an artificial lake... ...artificial flowers.* ◊ **artificially**. EG *It might be possible to manufacture petrol artificially from coal or gas... She had artificially waved dark hair.* ADJ CLASSIF = man-made ≠ natural; ◊ ADV

3 An **artificial** arm, leg, or heart is one which is made of metal or plastic and is fitted to or placed in someone's body when their own arm, leg, or heart has been removed. ADJ CLASSIF : ATTRIB

4 Someone who is **artificial** pretends to have attitudes, feelings, manners, etc which other people realize are not natural; used showing disapproval. EG *A lot of Hollywood types are frightfully artificial...* ▸ used of someone's expression or behaviour. EG *...an artificial tone of voice... They jump at the suggestion with artificial enthusiasm.* ◊ **artificiality**. EG *...the unexpected artificiality of her behaviour.* ADJ QUALIT = false ≠ genuine; ◊ N UNCOUNT = insincerity

artificial intelligence is the study of how to make computers work in an intelligent way, to do things that humans do, especially in the areas of language, vision, and movement. N UNCOUNT = AI

artificial light is light that is created by gas, electricity, etc, rather than being produced by the sun. EG *...a room without windows, lit by artificial light.* N UNCOUNT ≠ sunlight

artificial respiration is the forcing of air into the lungs of someone who has stopped breathing, usually by blowing through their mouth or nose, in order to keep them alive and to help them to start breathing again. N UNCOUNT ⇑ resuscitation

artillery /ɑːtɪləri¹/. 1 **Artillery** is large, powerful guns which are transported on wheels and which are used by an army. EG *...heavy artillery, missiles and jets... Artillery fire caused heavy losses.* N UNCOUNT ⇑ weaponry

2 The **Artillery** is a section of the army in which soldiers are specially trained to use large, powerful guns. N PROPER : *the*+N

artisan /ɑːtɪzæn/, **artisans**. An **artisan** is a person who has a job which requires skill with their hands. EG *Industry has destroyed the livelihood of village artisans.* N COUNT ⇑ workman = craftsman

artist /ɑːtɪst/, **artists**. An **artist** is 1 someone who draws, paints, produces sculpture, etc as a job or as a hobby. EG *This abstract picture was painted by John Hoyland, an artist who emerged in the 1960's... ...a ceramic artist.* 2 someone who is very skilled at a particular activity. EG *He knew that he was good, that he was an artist... In my opinion she was no artist at all as regards dancing!* 3 someone such as a musician, actor, or dancer who is a performer or an entertainer. EG *She has acted with great artists like Edith Evans and Peggy Ashcroft.* N COUNT; N COUNT : USU USED AS C; N COUNT

artiste /ɑːtiːst/, **artistes**. An **artiste** is a professional entertainer, for example a singer, dancer, or a circus performer. EG *He's an artiste dedicated to the stage.* N COUNT

artistic /ɑːtɪstɪk/. 1 Someone who is **artistic** is able to create or appreciate good paintings, sculpture, etc. EG *I talked to many artistic people; writers, dancers, and film makers... She is very artistic.* ◊ **artistically**. EG *...artistically gifted, especially in dance.* ADJ QUALIT; ◊ ADV

2 Something that is **artistic** relates to art or to artists. EG *The preview was a social rather than an artistic occasion... ...artistic freedom.* ADJ CLASSIF

3 A design, arrangement, pattern, etc that is **artistic** is beautiful or attractive. EG *...a very artistic design.* ◊ **artistically**. EG *The flowers were artistically arranged.* ADJ QUALIT ⇑ pleasing; ◊ ADV

artistry /ɑːtɪstri¹/ is 1 the creative skill or understanding of an artist, writer, actor, musician, etc. EG *Many people overlooked the exquisite artistry in Ray's story of a rural Bengali family.* 2 skill and cleverness at doing or arranging something. EG *If the change was made with sufficient artistry it would be difficult to detect.* N UNCOUNT; N UNCOUNT

artless /ɑːtlɪ²s/. Someone who is **artless** is simple and honest, and does not think of deceiving other people. EG *Jonathan was innocent and artless.* ▸ used of speech and behaviour. EG *...Willie's artless simplicity.* ◊ **artlessly**. EG *Betty artlessly divulged where they had been.* ◊ **artlessness**. EG *The sincerity and artlessness with which she discussed the problem was disarming.* ADJ QUALIT = open; ◊ ADV WITH VB; ◊ N UNCOUNT

art nouveau /ɑːnuːvəʊ/ is a style of art that was common in the 1890s and that has flowing lines and patterns of flowers and leaves. EG *...art nouveau tiles.* N UNCOUNT ⇑ ornamentation

artwork /ɑːtwɜːk/; also spelled as two words. **Artwork** is drawings and photographs that are prepared in order to be included in a book or an advertisement. N UNCOUNT ⇑ illustrations

arty /ɑːti¹/. Someone who is **arty** seems to be very interested in painting, sculpture, etc; often used showing disapproval. EG *...arty types.* ▸ used of someone's appearance or behaviour. EG *The whole arty get-up seemed oddly at variance with the way she behaved.* ADJ QUALIT = creative

arty-crafty /ɑːti¹ krɑːfti¹/ means relating to or involving the creation or use of objects made by craftsmen and craftswomen; often used showing disapproval. EG *...members of an arty-crafty clique.* ADJ QUALIT

as /ə³z/. **As** has very little meaning in itself, but it forms an important part of many structures, which are shown in the following paragraphs. 1 You use **as** to introduce clauses that refer to time. 1.1 If something happens **as** something else happens, the two things are happening at the same time. EG *She wept bitterly as she told her story... Jot down notes on thoughts as they come... As men retire they are replaced on the board.* 1.2 You use **as** when you are mentioning the times when a particular action is necessary and the circumstances that cause it. EG *Reseal as required... Parts would be replaced as necessity dictated.* CONJ SUBORD = when, while; CONJ SUBORD

2 You use the structure **as...as** in comparisons and statements in the following ways: 2.1 when you are describing the degree or amount of something by saying that it is just like something else. EG *The meal was as awful as the conversation... I'm as good a cook as she is... Has everyone eaten as much as they want?* ▸ Sometimes the first 'as' is omitted in literary English. EG *Practice had made Jack silent as the shadows.* 2.2 when you are emphasizing an adjective or adverb by using a simile like 'as quiet as a mouse' or an expression like 'as soon as possible'. Many of these similes and expressions are explained in this dictionary as phrases at one of the other words. EG *...as white as a sheet... Sheila looked as bright as a button... Treat the patient as soon as possible... The living-room was as crowded as ever.* ▸ Sometimes the first 'as' is omitted. EG *There he sat, pleased as Punch.* 2.3 when you are expressing an amount, measurement, or degree by saying that it is the same as something else, or that it is a particular number of times more or less than it. The second part of the structure is omitted if you have already mentioned the thing to which you are comparing the amount, measurement, or degree. EG *She had taken five days to write. I thought I was entitled to take as many days thinking about my reply... This fish is twice as big... There are thought to be three times as many species of insect as of all other kinds of animal put together... This earthquake had a force one third as great again as the 1906 San Francisco earthquake.* ADV *(as)*+ADV/ADJ+PREP *(as)*; ▸ PREP; ADV *(as)*+ADJ/ADV+PREP *(as)*; ▸ PREP; ADV *(as)*+ADJ/ADV+PREP *(as)*

2.4 when you are emphasizing how surprising or ADV *(as)*+ADJ/

remarkable something is. EG *There were as many as five hundred baboons... They beat their wings as fast as 80 times a second... Opinion polls showed Giscard trailing Mitterrand by as much as 3 points.* ADV+PREP (as) ● **as far as**: see **far.** ● **as good as**: see **good.** ● **as long as**: see **long.** ● **not so much as**: see **much.**

3 You use the structures **as...as** and **so...as** with negative words like 'not', 'never', and 'nothing' when you express the difference in degree or amount between two things. EG *I don't think weddings are as pretty as they used to be... You've never been as late as this without telephoning... There is no one as dangerous as an idealist with a machine gun... I had seldom seen him looking so pleased with himself as he was now.* ADV (as/so)+ ADJ/ADV+PREP (as)

4 You use **as** **4.1** in order to introduce a word, expression, or clause which gives information about the subject or object of the sentence. EG *You regard the whole thing as a joke... He defended the arts as 'Man's expression of his joy in labour'... They met at Knole almost as strangers... The sudden change had come as a shock to Castle... I always thought of myself as a very understanding father... Do you see English teaching as being principally an education in values?... You have been quoted as saying that you believe in capital punishment.* PREP, OR PREP+ -ING **4.2** in order to introduce a clause which states more clearly the particular nature of something. EG *This is a picture of my great-grandfather, as photographed in about 1890... This report only discusses unemployment as measured by statisticians but not as experienced by actual people.* CONJ SUBORD

5 You use **as** when you are describing aspects, roles, and functions in the following ways: **5.1** when you are specifying the particular aspect of something that you are concerned with. EG *He established his reputation as a radical with his very first speech... How do you find out about universities as places?... ...its desirability as building land.* PREP **5.2** when you are stating the role, job, or function of a person or thing. EG *Over the summer she worked as a waitress... We all work together as a team... Keep an empty plastic shopping bag to use as a wastepaper basket.* PREP **5.3** when you are referring to someone's role, status, age, etc in relation to a particular time, activity, or opinion. EG *...a story she had heard many times as a girl... As a historian this kind of assertion always amuses me... I can only speak as a married man without children.* PREP = being

6 You use **as** when you are mentioning the way that something happens or is done. EG *I like the freedom to organise my day as I want to... ...an attempt to see oneself as others see one... They were people who spoke and thought as he did.* CONJ SUBORD ⇑ like

7 You use **as** in the following ways to introduce a clause which describes a similarity: **7.1** when you want to say that two events or situations are alike in some way. EG *She had pushed him, as she had pushed her son... As with the railways, so with coal.* ▸ When the first clause begins 'just as', the second clause usually begins 'so'. EG *Just as one gesture can have many different meanings, so many different gestures can have the same meaning.* CONJ SUBORD ⇑ like **7.2** when you refer back to what you have just said in order to say that it also applies to someone or something else. EG *He looked over his shoulder as Jack had done... Many elderly people are at last starting out, as I did, on the road towards further education... Napalm should be banned, as should the development, production, and stockpiling of all chemical weapons.* CONJ SUBORD = like **7.3** You also use **as** in structures after 'same': see **same.** EG *I found she was staying in the same small hotel as I was... 'What did he say?'–'The same as you'... Soon after, Lamb was asleep, the same as always.* PREP : same+ PREP

8 You use **as** to introduce an example or further instance of something in order to help you to explain a particular point or idea. EG *Keep shoes on plastic racks piled on top of each other, as in a shop... As with so much in the Sixties, it was Authority that was challenged... He stammers when he gets nervous, as, for example, when he has to speak to a large group of people.* CONJ SUBORD = like

9 You use **as** in the following ways to introduce a comment about what you are saying: **9.1** when you want to give extra information, often about how usual the situation is that you are describing. EG *As usual at the weekend, the club was almost empty... He was totally unprepared, as is the way with American he-men, for anything that could not be settled with a fist or a gun... Her pregnancy was not seven months along, as he had believed, but only five... ...Margaret, or Molly as she was called.* CONJ SUBORD **9.2** when you want to mention where it has been said before, to indicate that you are quoting, or to point out that it is already known by the person you are speaking to. EG *As I said a moment ago, we each want to write a best seller... As Peter Jenkins put it: 'The Party was rotting at the grass roots'... As you know, I have spent a lifetime commuting... As you can see we've got a problem with the engine.* CONJ SUBORD : USED IN ADV SEN **9.3** You use expressions like **as I see it** and **as I understand it** to indicate that you are giving your own opinion or stating what you believe to be true. EG *As I see it things are a bit like they were when I was a boy... As I understand it a Barbary duck is a cross between a wild duck and an ordinary duck.* PHR : VB INFLECTS, USED AS ADV SEN = in my view

10 You use **as** in the following ways when you are stating reasons: **10.1** when you are explaining why something is the case. EG *She bought herself an iron, as she felt she couldn't keep borrowing Anne's... He thinks he would like to teach, but as his subjects are Greek and Moral Philosophy he's not likely to find a job... As he had been up since 4 a.m. he was no doubt now very tired.* CONJ SUBORD = because, since **10.2** when you are explaining the circumstances behind a particular fact or feeling. EG *Loving New York as I do, it would be extremely difficult to leave.* CONJ SUBORD = like **10.3** when you are explaining the purpose behind a particular action. EG *As a special treat the doctor had brought her along.... She sought temporary work as a strategy for finding friends... Brave men were prepared to go to prison as a matter of principle.* PREP = by way of

11 You use **as** when you mention something which you accept is true but which nevertheless does not affect the main thing you are saying. EG *Flattered as I was by his attention, I somehow knew that he wasn't the man for me... As young as he was, Kunta was already familiar with most of these stories.* CONJ SUBORD = though

12 You use **as if** and **as though** **12.1** when you are giving a possible explanation for something, although it is probably not the correct one. EG *The furniture looked as though it had come out of somebody's attic... As if conscious of my gaze she opened her eyes... He looked at me as if I were mad.* CONJ SUBORD **12.2** when you want to emphasize strongly that something is not important, relevant, or reasonable. EG *He keeps worrying about what wine to buy. As if it mattered... The mother (as if she didn't have enough to do already!) has to remember to pay some attention to her husband.* CONJ SUBORD

13 You use expressions like **it isn't as if** and **it's not as though** in order to introduce a statement in which you say that a particular thing is not the case, although it might explain something puzzling if it was. EG *I can't understand why she likes him so much. It isn't as though he's good-looking at all... Why was James at the party? It was not as if he were a relative.* PHR

14 You use **as for** and **as to** at the beginning of a sentence in order to introduce a topic or point that is different from what has just been said although it is related to it. EG *Mary's diet required an unusually big effort on her part. As for myself, I had a glass of juice three times a day... That's the answer. As for the cause, how do I know?... As to your suggestion that I fly out to see you, I don't think this would be a good idea... As to what goes on inside the brain, that I must leave to the next chapter.* PREP = regarding

15 You also use **as to** to specify the particular subject or area that you are talking about; used in British English. EG *John had been given no directions as to what to write... I was asked my opinion as to why Charles Whitman climbed a tower at the University... We must have no illusions as to the road to working class power.* PREP = on

16 If you say that something will happen **as of** or **as from** a particular date or time, you mean that it will happen then or from that time. EG *As of next week I'll be working at home... I'll be retired as from the end of August.* PREP

17 You say **as it were** in order to make what you are saying sound less definite. EG *So far doctors have been using the drug to run it in, as it were... That was as it were part of the job.* PHR : USED AS ADV SEN = so to speak

18 You use expressions like **as it is, as it turns out,** and **as things stand** when you are stating what the actual situation really is, often in contrast to what might have been expected or planned. EG *To create a new market the magazine had to be brilliant. As it turned out, it wasn't... As things stand, the rural areas bear the cost of raising children to working age... My friend was knocked down and could have been killed. As it was, he suffered severe back injuries.* PHR : USED AS ADV SEN = in the event

19 You say **as you wish, as you like,** or **as you prefer** to someone who has made a request to you in order to indicate that you are willing to grant it. These responses are sometimes used simply to show politeness in a fairly formal way, but they are also used when you want to indicate that you do not fully agree with the request or approve of it. EG *'I want to see my client immediately.'-'Of course. As you wish.'* PHR : USED AS ADV SEN = whatever you say

20 The word **as** is also used in the following expressions, which are explained at other places in this dictionary. ● **as against**: see **against.** ● **as ever**: see **ever.** ● **as follows**: see **follow.** ● **as opposed to**: see **oppose.** ● **as regards**: see **regard.** ● **as such**: see **such.** ● **as well**: see **well.** ● **as yet**: see **yet.** ● **such as**: see **such.**

asbestos /æsbɛstɒs/ is a grey material which does not burn and which is used as a protection against fire or heat. Clothing and mats are sometimes made from it. EG *Always use an asbestos mat on an electric hob... ...asbestos tiled roofs.* N UNCOUNT ⇑ fireproofing

ascend /əsɛnd/, **ascends, ascending, ascended**; a literary or formal word. **1** If something **ascends**, it moves upwards. EG *I ascended in a creaky lift to the top floor... The sound must have ascended to the room above.* V : USU+A = go up ≠ descend

2 If you **ascend** a hill or a flight of steps, you go up it. EG *He ascended the flight of narrow stairs to his bedroom.* V+O = climb, scale

3 You say that something such as a flight of steps **ascends** to a higher position when it leads to that position. EG *...a Senate House with tiers of seats ascending to the roof... The stairs began to ascend more steeply.* V : IF+PREP THEN *to* ⇑ rise ≠ descend

4 When someone **ascends the throne**, they become king or queen. EG *Queen Victoria ascended the throne in 1837.* PHR : VB INFLECTS

5 See also **ascending.**

ascendancy /əsɛndənsi[1]/ is the state of being more powerful or having more influence than someone or something else; a formal word. EG *...Unionist ascendancy over the Catholic minority.* N UNCOUNT : IF+ PREP THEN *over* ⇑ power = dominance

ascendant /əsɛndənt/. **1** An **ascendant** group of people in society has more power or influence than any other group; a formal use. EG *...the use of racism as a tool of the economically ascendant class.* ADJ CLASSIF : ATTRIB ⇑ powerful = dominant

2 Someone or something that is **in the ascendant** has more power, influence, or popularity than other people or things, or is increasing in power, influence, or popularity. EG *His party is no longer in the ascendant.* PHR : USED AS AN A = rising

ascending /əsɛndɪŋ/. When a group of things is arranged in **ascending** order, each thing is higher in position or greater in amount or importance than the thing before it. EG *Arrange the four digits in ascending order... ...little houses built on ascending levels on the slopes of hills... She sang an ascending scale.* ADJ CLASSIF : ATTRIB ≠ descending

ascent /əsɛnt/, **ascents. 1** An **ascent** is **1.1** an act of travelling upwards, for example by climbing something. EG *The final ascent took only half an hour.* N COUNT : USU SING **1.2** an upward slope, especially one that you are walking up. EG *John toiled up the dusty ascent.* N COUNT : USU SING

2 A person's **ascent** is a process by which they become more important, successful, or advanced than they were before; a formal use. EG *Nick and he had both succeeded, though Nick's ascent had been more honourable.* N UNCOUNT+ SUPP ⇑ rise ≠ fall

ascertain /æsətɛɪn/, **ascertains, ascertaining, ascertained. 1** If you **ascertain** that something is the case, you find out that it is the case. If you **ascertain** what something is, you find out what it is; a formal word. EG *I ascertained that Lo was still sound asleep... We're unable to ascertain who the owners are.* V+O/REPORT-CL ⇑ find out = establish

ascetic /əsɛtɪk/, **ascetics**. People who are **ascetic** have a way of life that is simple and strict with no luxuries or physical pleasures, usually because of their religious beliefs. ▸ used of a person's behaviour or appearance. EG *He subjected himself to a strenuous ascetic discipline... Garroway was a thin man with a lean, ascetic face.* ▸ used as a noun. EG *...a religious ascetic.* ADJ QUALIT ⇑ austere = puritanical ≠ hedonistic

asceticism /əsɛtɪsɪzəm/ is a simple, strict way of life with no luxuries or physical pleasures, which people usually lead because of their religious beliefs. N UNCOUNT ⇑ self-denial

ascribe /ə[3]skraɪb/, **ascribes, ascribing, ascribed. 1** If you **ascribe** something to a particular situation or event, you consider that it is caused by that situation or event. EG *It is wrong to ascribe all that has happened simply to the war... This loss of human lives can be ascribed to three main causes... ...headaches which may be ascribed to stress.* V+O+A *(to)* = attribute, put down

2 If you **ascribe** a quality or characteristic to someone, you consider that they possess it. EG *Husbands are often mistaken in the virtues they ascribe to their wives.* V+O+A *(to)* = attribute

3 If you **ascribe** a work of art or an action or event to someone, you say that they created it or caused it to happen. EG *...a magnificent painted ceiling, doubtfully ascribed to Holbein... Common report ascribed his murder to Caesar.* V+O+A *(to)* = attribute

aseptic /ə[3]sɛptɪk/. Something such as a wound or a dressing that is **aseptic** is clean and free from germs; a technical term in medicine. ADJ CLASSIF

asexual /eɪsɛksjuʊ[0]əl/. **1** Something that is **asexual** has no sex or involves no sexual activity. EG *...two methods of reproduction, sexual and asexual.* ADJ CLASSIF ≠ sexual

2 Someone who is **asexual** is not sexually attracted to anyone. ADJ CLASSIF

ash /æʃ/, **ashes. 1 Ash** is the grey or black powdery substance that is left after a fire has been burning. EG *The town was covered with ash and falling rock from the volcano... ...cigarette ash.* ▸ used as a plural noun. EG *Ashes blew into Ralph's face from the dead fire.* N UNCOUNT ⇑ powder ▸ N PLURAL

2 A dead person's **ashes** are the ashes that are left after their body has been burnt in a funeral service. EG *She went to collect her mother's ashes from the Crematorium.* N PLURAL : USU WITH POSS ⇑ remains

3 An **ash** is a tree that has a smooth grey bark, small greenish flowers, and seeds in the shape of wings. ▸ **Ash** is also used to refer to the wood of this tree. N COUNT ▸ N UNCOUNT

ashamed /əʃeɪmd/. **1** Someone who is **ashamed** feels embarrassed or guilty because of something that they have done or something that has happened. EG *She was ashamed of her tears. Normally she never cried... These things happen to everyone, it's nothing to be ashamed of... You should be ashamed of yourself.* ADJ QUALIT : PRED, IF+PREP THEN *of* ≠ proud

2 Someone who is **ashamed** to do something does not want to do it because it is something that they feel embarrassed or uncomfortable about. EG *Your father was a drunkard. I was ashamed to say hello to him in the street... I'll bet that's exactly what happened, only you're ashamed to admit it... I'm ashamed to say I have been sitting at home doing absolutely nothing all weekend.* ADJ QUALIT : PRED+*to*-INF ≠ proud

3 If you are **ashamed** of someone, you disapprove of something that they have done and feel embarrassed to be connected with them. EG *He was bitterly ashamed of her for writing such lies.* ADJ QUALIT : PRED+*of* ≠ proud

ashcan /æʃkæn/, **ashcans**. An **ashcan** is the same as a dustbin; used in American English. N COUNT

ashen /æʃə[0]n/. Someone who is **ashen** looks very pale, especially because they are shocked or afraid. EG *Joan collapsed, pale and trembling, her face ashen.* ADJ QUALIT = white

ashore /əʃɔː/. Something that comes **ashore** comes from the sea onto the shore. EG *He managed to swim ashore... One was washed ashore in Norway.* ADV AFTER VB

ashtray /æʃtreɪ/, **ashtrays**. An **ashtray** is a small dish in which people who smoke put the ash from their cigarettes and cigars. EG *...an ashtray full of old cigarette stubs.* N COUNT

ashy /æʃi[1]/. Something that is **ashy** is covered in ash or has the colour of ash. EG *...the ashy grate... My face was an ashy grey.* ADJ QUALIT

Asian /eɪʃən, eɪʒən/, **Asians. 1** Someone or something that is **Asian** comes from Asia. EG *His philosophy is a mixture of both Western and Asian thought... ...Central Asian independence movements.* ADJ CLASSIF

2 An **Asian** is a person who comes from India, Pakistan, Bangladesh, Sri Lanka, or another part of Asia. EG *Large numbers of Asians now work as labourers in the Arab oil states.* N COUNT ▸ N COUNT

Asiatic /eɪʃɪˈætɪk, -zɪ-/ means the same as Asian. ADJ CLASSIF

aside /əˈsaɪd/, **asides**. 1 If you move something **aside**, you move it to a position to one side of you and not directly in front of you. EG *He threw the manuscript aside... She stood looking out through the window, holding aside the curtains.* ADV AFTER VB

2 If you **take** someone **aside**, you take them a little way away from a group of people in order to talk to them in private. EG *He took me aside and began to talk to me about his boyhood.* ● See also **put aside, set aside.** PHR : VB INFLECTS

3 If you move **aside**, you move to one side of someone or something, especially in order to get out of a person's way. EG *She stepped aside, holding the door wide open... He moved aside to watch.* ADV AFTER VB ⇑ sideways

4 If you brush a feeling or a suggestion **aside**, sweep it **aside**, etc, you reject it because you do not consider it to be important or worth thinking about. EG *The Chief waved his objection aside... She brushed his protests aside... The realities of the war swept those doubts aside.* ADV AFTER VB ⇑ away

5 **Aside from** means the same as apart from; used especially in American English. PREP

6 **Aside** is used to indicate that you have finished talking about something, or that you are leaving it out of your discussion, and that you are about to talk about something else. EG *The dazzle of high technology aside, New England's economy is still largely based on fishing.* ADV AFTER NG : USED AS ADV SEN = apart

7 An **aside** is 7.1 a comment that a character in a play or film makes to the audience, which the other characters in the play or film are supposed not to be able to hear. N COUNT 7.2 a comment that you make quietly but that you intend other people to hear. EG *She said, in a loud aside, 'Oh, I am so hungry!'* N COUNT 7.3 something that you say that is not directly connected with the subject you are talking about. EG *In an aside he said to his servant, 'See that man gets something to eat.'* N COUNT ⇑ digression

asinine /ˈæsɪnaɪn/. Someone or something that is **asinine** is very foolish; a formal or literary word. ADJ QUALIT

ask /ɑːsk/, **asks, asking, asked**. 1 If you **ask** someone something, you say something to them in the form of a question because you want to know the answer. EG *'How many languages can you speak?' he asked... A young man asked if we were students... I asked him what he wanted... He started asking Diana a lot of questions... He asked me my name... There is something I want to ask you about.* V+O/QUOTE/REPORT-CL, V+O+O/REPORT-CL, V+O+A *(about)*, OR V

2 If something is yours **for the asking**, you can have it simply by asking for it. PHR : USED AS AN A

3 If you **ask** someone to do something, you say to them that you want them to do it. EG *He fell in love with her and asked her to marry him... He asked me to tell him where I had been... The noise became so great that he was asked to leave.* V+O : USU+ *to*-INF ⇑ request

4 If you **ask** someone's opinion, permission, etc, you try to obtain it by by putting a question to them. EG *I was asked my opinion about the new car... I should have asked permission to leave.* V OR V+O ⇑ request

5 If you **ask** someone somewhere, you invite them to go there. EG *I asked her to the party... She asked me in and gave me a long talk... There are always people to ask me out.* V+O+A

6 You sometimes use the word **ask** when you want to be very polite, when it is obvious that you are asking something. It can also be used in a sarcastic way to emphasize that you are asking something which should not need to be asked. EG *I must ask you to be quiet. People are doing exams in there... How many people, may I ask, have you invited to my party?* V+O/REPORT-CL, OR V+O+ *to*-INF/O/REPORT-CL

7 You can say '**if you ask me**' to emphasize that you are stating your personal opinion about a situation. EG *The whole thing's stupid if you ask me.* PHR : USED AS ADV SEN

8 If you say '**I ask you!**', you are emphasizing how shocking you think something is; used in informal English. EG *'Children sticking knives in people's backs–I ask you!' she exclaimed.* PHR ⇑ really

ask after. If you **ask after** someone, you ask how they are. EG *She asked after my father.* PHRASAL VB : V+PREP

ask for. 1 If you **ask for** someone, you say that you would like to speak to them. EG *My mother said that Tom had called asking for me.* PHRASAL VB : V+PREP

2 If you **ask for** something, you say that you would like it. EG *She asked for a drink of water... My husband wrote asking for one of his books... I asked for help with my project.* ● Someone or something that is **as** good, kind, etc **as** you **could ask for** is the best, kindest, etc that you could possibly hope to have. EG *She is as kind a mother as I could ask for.* PHRASAL VB : V+PREP = request ● PHR : USED AS AN A

3 If you say that someone **is asking for** something, you mean that they are behaving in a way that makes it very likely that something unpleasant will happen to them; an informal expression. EG *You're really asking for trouble speaking to me like that.* PHRASAL VB : V+PREP, USU CONT ⇑ invite = look for

askance /əˈskæns/. If you **look askance** at someone, you look at them in a doubtful or suspicious way. PHR : VB INFLECTS

askew /əˈskjuː/. Something that is **askew** is not straight or level. EG *His hair was a mess and his tie was askew.* ▸ used as an adverb. EG *The dress hangs askew on the door.* ADJ QUALIT : PRED ▸ ADV AFTER VB

asking price, asking prices. The **asking price** of something is the price which the person selling it says that they want for it. N COUNT

asleep /əˈsliːp/. 1 Someone who is **asleep** is sleeping. EG *He was asleep before I left the room... He found her asleep in the chair.* ADJ CLASSIF : PRED ≠ awake

2 When you **fall asleep**, you start sleeping. EG *The minute my head touched the pillow I fell asleep.* PHR : VB INFLECTS

3 Someone who is **fast asleep** or **sound asleep** is sleeping deeply. EG *The baby was lying fast asleep on the sofa.* PHR : USED AS C ≠ wide awake

4 If a part of your body is **asleep**, it feels numb because you have stayed in one position for so long. EG *When I woke my left arm was asleep.* ADJ CLASSIF : PRED

5 If you are **asleep** or half **asleep**, you are not listening or paying attention because you are tired or daydreaming; an informal use. ADJ CLASSIF : PRED ⇑ inattentive

asparagus /əˈspærəgəs/ is a vegetable with straight pale green shoots, which are cooked and eaten when they are young and tender. N UNCOUNT

aspect /ˈæspɛkt/, **aspects**. 1 An **aspect** of something is one of the parts of its character or nature. EG *The most terrifying aspect of nuclear bombing is radiation... Economic affairs have got political and psychological aspects to them... ...a book about cinema in all its aspects... ...the great influence which America had on many aspects of British cultural life... Disarmament should be simply one aspect of a larger plan.* N COUNT ⇑ part = facet

2 A particular **aspect** is one way of considering something, when there are many possible ways. EG *There is also the legal aspect: I am the landlord and you are my tenant, don't forget... This aspect of the business had just occurred to him... We need an accountant to help from the accounts and tax aspect.* N COUNT+SUPP ⇑ view = side

3 An **aspect** is a position from which you can see a view; a formal use. N COUNT

4 The **aspect** of a building or a window is the direction in which it faces; a formal use. EG *...an office with a south-west aspect.* N COUNT : USU MOD+N

5 If something acquires a new or different **aspect**, it acquires a new or different appearance or quality, especially if this seems different at other times or in other circumstances. EG *The bank clerk stared ferociously through the grille (which took on the aspect, suddenly, of a restraining cage)... The whole scheme began to take on a more practical aspect... My periods of freedom assumed the aspect of holidays.* N COUNT+SUPP : USU SING = air

6 Someone's **aspect** is the expression on their face; a fairly formal use. EG *A young woman, of a sullen aspect, was sitting alone on the bench.* N COUNT+SUPP : USU SING

7 **Aspect** is the term used in grammar to describe the way a verb or verbal group shows whether an activity is continuing, is repeated, or is completed. Compare **tense**. N UNCOUNT

aspen /ˈæspən/, **aspens**. An **aspen** is a tall kind of poplar tree with leaves that rustle a lot in the wind. N COUNT

asperity /æˈspɛrɪti[1]/ is impatience and sternness that you express in your tone of voice; a formal word. EG *I said, with some asperity, that that was no concern of mine.* N UNCOUNT ⇑ severity = sharpness

aspersions /əˈspɜːʃəⁿnz/. If you **cast aspersions** on someone, you criticize them with comments that may damage their reputation; a formal expression. EG *I was not casting aspersions on the capacities of your hound.* PHR : VB INFLECTS, IF+PREP THEN *on*

asphalt /ˈæsfælt, -fɔːlt/, **asphalts, asphalting, asphalted**. 1 **Asphalt** is a hard black substance used to make roads and other surfaces. EG *The asphalt on the road became soft and sticky in the heat... ...the asphalt playground.* N UNCOUNT ⇑ surfacing = tarmac

2 To **asphalt** a surface such as a roof or a road means to cover it with asphalt. ◊ **asphalted**. EG *...buildings with asphalted yards.* V+O ◊ ADJ CLASSIF

asphyxia /æsfɪksɪə/ is death or loss of consciousness caused by not being able to breathe enough oxygen. N UNCOUNT = suffocation

asphyxiate /æsfɪksɪeɪt/, **asphyxiates, asphyxiating, asphyxiated.** If someone **is asphyxiated** by gas, smoke, or fumes, they are unable to get oxygen when they breathe, so that they choke or even die. EG *Most of the people who died in the fire had been asphyxiated by the fumes.* ◊ **asphyxiating.** EG *...a resolution banning use of asphyxiating gases in war.* ◊ **asphyxiation** /æ³sfɪksɪeɪʃə⁰n/. EG *There was a gas leak and the old woman died of asphyxiation.* V+O ⇑ kill = suffocate; ◊ ADJ CLASSIF ⇑ lethal; ◊ N UNCOUNT = suffocation

aspic /æspɪk/ is clear, shiny jelly made from meat juices and used in making cold savoury dishes. EG *...chicken in aspic.* N UNCOUNT

aspirant /æspə¹rənt, əspaɪərənt/, **aspirants.** Someone who is an **aspirant** to something such as a powerful or important position has a strong desire to achieve this position. EG *...aspirants to political power.* N COUNT : IF + PREP THEN *to* = candidate

aspirate, aspirates, aspirating, aspirated. The word **aspirate** is pronounced /æspə¹rɪ³t/ when it is a noun and /æspə¹reɪt/ when it is a verb. **1** An **aspirate** is the sound represented in English by the letter 'h'; a technical term in phonetics. N COUNT

2 To **aspirate** a letter in a word means to pronounce it with the sound of the letter 'h'. EG *The 'h' in honour isn't aspirated.* V+O

aspiration /æspə¹reɪʃə⁰n/, **aspirations. 1** A person's **aspirations** are their ambitions or desires to achieve something. EG *The book is a study of the political aspirations of the ordinary people at that time... The report shows that educational standards and aspirations have risen in recent years... ...aspirations to fame and greatness.* N COUNT/ UNCOUNT : IF + PREP THEN *to* ⇑ desire = ambition

2 Aspiration or the **aspiration** of a particular letter is the act of aspirating it; a technical term in phonetics. N UNCOUNT ⇑ pronunciation

aspire /əspaɪə/, **aspires, aspiring, aspired.** If you **aspire** to something, you have a strong ambition to achieve it. EG *Edward Heath has always aspired to leadership.* ◊ **aspiring.** EG *...an aspiring concert pianist... Aspiring writers were always sending scripts to him.* V+A *(to)*, OR V+ *to*-INF ⇑ aim; ◊ ADJ CLASSIF : ATTRIB = would-be

aspirin /æspɪ⁰rɪn/, **aspirins. Aspirin** is a common mild drug which reduces pain and fever. It is usually in the form of white tablets. You take aspirin, for example, when you have a headache. EG *...a bottle of aspirin.* ▸ An **aspirin** is one of these tablets. EG *I woke with a slight headache and took two aspirins.* N UNCOUNT ⇑ analgesic; ▸ N COUNT ⇑ tablet

ass /æs/, **asses. 1** An **ass** is **1.1** an animal related to a horse but smaller and with longer ears. **1.2** someone who says or does silly things; an informal use. EG *You are a silly ass, why on earth did you tell him that?... What an ass I am!* ● If someone **makes an ass of** themselves, they behave in such a silly way that people get a bad impression of them; an informal expression. EG *He made a bit of an ass of himself at the party.* N COUNT; N COUNT : ALSO VOC = clot; ● PHR : VB INFLECTS = embarrass

2 Your **ass** is your bottom; an informal American use. N COUNT

3 Ass is also used by men to refer to women when they are talking about them in a sexual way; an offensive use, used in American English. N UNCOUNT = skirt

assail /əseɪl/, **assails, assailing, assailed**; a literary word. **1** If you **assail** someone, **1.1** you attack them violently. **1.2** you criticize them strongly. EG *She was his most persistent adversary, assailing him at public meetings.* V+O; V+O = attack

2 Things that **assail** you arrive or happen in large numbers in an undesirable way. EG *All sorts of problems assailed us suddenly... We were assailed by reports, articles, and documentaries on the subject.* V+O : USU PASS ⇑ attack = beset

3 Fears, doubts, etc that **assail** you trouble and worry you greatly. EG *He was assailed by doubts.* V+O : USU PASS = beset

assailant /əseɪlənt/, **assailants.** A person's **assailant** is someone who physically attacks them; a formal word. EG *He dared not take his eyes off his assailant for a second.* N COUNT : USU POSS+N

assassin /əsæsɪn/, **assassins.** An **assassin** is a person who assassinates someone. EG *Stricter gun controls might deprive would-be assassins of weapons.* N COUNT ⇑ murderer

assassinate /əsæsɪneɪt/, **assassinates, assassinating, assassinated.** When an important person **is assassinated**, they are murdered for political reasons. EG *The president was assassinated as he left the building.* ◊ **assassination** /əsæsɪneɪʃə⁰n/, **assassinations.** EG *...assassinations of leaders... An assassination attempt can do a lot for a politician.* V+O ⇑ murder; ◊ N UNCOUNT/ COUNT ⇑ murder

assault /əsɔːlt/, **assaults, assaulting, assaulted. 1** An **assault** by an army is a strong attack made against the enemy, especially at an important place which the army wants to capture. EG *The enemy opened the assault on the Venlo position... They responded with assaults against the enemy's bases.* N COUNT : IF + PREP THEN *on/ upon/against*

2 An **assault** on a person is a physical attack on them which is considered to be a crime. EG *A series of racialist assaults have taken place over the past year... He was threatened with assault in the street.* ▸ used as a verb. EG *She was found guilty of assaulting a police officer... A man has sexually assaulted and then killed a child.* N COUNT/ UNCOUNT : IF + PREP THEN *on/ upon*; ▸ V+O

3 An **assault** on someone's beliefs or attitudes is a strong or angry criticism of them which is often an attempt to change them. EG *Liberals called for an all-out assault on racism.* N COUNT : USU + *on* = attack

assault and battery is the crime of threatening to attack someone physically and then actually attacking them; a legal term. EG *You're being charged with assault and battery.* N UNCOUNT

assault course, assault courses. An **assault course** is an area of land covered with obstacles such as walls or ditches, which soldiers run over as an exercise to improve their skills and strength. N COUNT

assay /ə³seɪ/, **assays, assaying, assayed.** To **assay** a metal or other substance means to test it, especially in order to find out how pure it is; a technical term. V+O

assemblage /ə³sɛmblɪdʒ/, **assemblages**; a formal word. **1** An **assemblage** is a collection of people, animals, or things. EG *The greatest assemblage of marsupials today live in Australia.* N COUNT+SUPP = group

2 Assemblage is the process of putting things together, for example in order to construct something. EG *...the assemblage of ideas.* ▸ An **assemblage** is something that has been constructed in this way. EG *...a bone assemblage.* N UNCOUNT : IF + PREP THEN *of*; ▸ N COUNT : USU +SUPP

assemble /ə³sɛmbə⁰l/, **assembles, assembling, assembled. 1** When people **assemble**, they gather together in a group, usually for a particular purpose. EG *The four leaders assembled in Paris for a summit meeting.* ◊ **assembled.** EG *Wait until all the guests are assembled... She announced to the assembled relatives that she intended to sell the house and move abroad.* V-ERG ⇑ collect; ◊ ADJ CLASSIF ⇑ gathered = congregated

2 To **assemble** something means to fit the parts of it together. EG *...equipment for assembling cars... When the rest of the rifle was assembled he laid it on the ground... I won't attempt to assemble the evidence here.* V+O ⇑ construct ≠ dismantle

assembly /ə³sɛmbli¹/, **assemblies. 1** An **assembly** is **1.1** a gathering of people or things. EG *He called to the White House a great assembly of senators and congressmen.* **1.2** a group of people who meet regularly to make laws for a region or country. N COUNT : USU SING; N COUNT ⇑ institution

2 Assembly is **2.1** the gathering together of people for a particular purpose, for example for a public meeting. EG *They are demanding rights of assembly and expression... Buildings such as schools, assembly halls and community centres, can be used.* **2.2** a gathering of all the teachers and pupils in a school at the beginning of each school day. EG *Assembly is at 9 o'clock.* N UNCOUNT ⇑ congregating; N UNCOUNT/ COUNT ⇑ meeting

3 The **assembly** of the parts of something such as a machine is the process of fitting them together. EG *I'll have to leave the gear sprockets for assembly later this week.* N UNCOUNT ⇑ construction

4 An **assembly** is also something which has been fitted together, especially a part of a machine. EG *This motor bike has a power assembly and a running assembly.* N COUNT ⇑ structure

assembly line, assembly lines; also spelled with a hyphen. An **assembly line** is an arrangement of workers and machines in a factory where each worker makes only one part of a product. The product passes from one worker to another, usually on a conveyor belt, until it is finished. EG *We have to accept the monotony of work on the assembly line... ...the ability to mass-produce on large-scale assembly lines.* N COUNT

assent /ə³sɛnt/, **assents, assenting, assented.**
1 If someone gives their **assent** to something that has been proposed, they agree to it. EG *There was a murmur of assent from the crowd... They all give their wholehearted assent to the plan... Haldane acted in these talks with the full assent of Grey and the Foreign Office.* ● If something such as a parliamentary bill **receives Royal Assent** or **is given Royal Assent**, the king or queen agrees to it and signs it so that it becomes law. EG *The act received Royal Assent on 30th April 1958.*
N UNCOUNT : IF + PREP THEN *from/to* ⇑ agreement = approval
● PHR : VB INFLECTS

2 If you **assent** to something that has been proposed, you agree to it. EG *They all assented to the proposition... 'Yes', assented Bishop Brain.*
V : IF + PREP THEN *to*, OR V + QUOTE

assert /ə³sɜːt/, **asserts, asserting, asserted.** 1 If someone **asserts** something such as a fact, belief, or opinion, they state it firmly and forcefully. EG *From the beginning, he asserts, the two communities worked happily together... 'The state is responsible,' asserted the feminists, 'for the breakdown of family life'... We encouraged him to assert his own view of the matter.* ◊ **assertion** /ə³sɜːʃə⁰n/, **assertions.** EG *I challenge the assertion that there is increasing women's liberation in Britain.*
V + O/REPORT-CL/QUOTE = declare
◊ N UNCOUNT/COUNT = declaration

2 If you **assert** your right or claim to something, you insist that you have the right to it. EG *The protesters asserted their right to be heard... In many countries minorities are now asserting their rights against the nation-state.* ◊ **assertion.** EG *The assertion of the right to freedom is very important to all peoples.*
V + O ⇑ insist on
◊ N UNCOUNT/COUNT

3 If you **assert** your authority, character, etc, you make it clear by your behaviour that you have that authority, character, etc. EG *He wished to assert his authority in his own house.* ◊ **assertion.** EG *Jack had meant to leave him in doubt, as an assertion of power.*
V + O ⇑ show = establish
◊ N UNCOUNT/COUNT

4 If you **assert** yourself, you speak and act in a forceful way so that people pay attention to you and your opinions. EG *People are beginning to assert themselves and to demand the opportunity to be involved in running the country... He wished to assert himself at work, but did not know how to do it.*
V + O (REFL) ⇑ express

assertive /ə³sɜːtɪv/. An **assertive** person speaks and acts in a forceful way so that people pay attention to them. EG *Her son was an energetic, assertive boy, always ready to argue.* ▸ used of a person's behaviour or actions. EG *Pointing directly at a listener is an assertive, authoritarian act.* ◊ **assertively.** EG *He spoke so assertively that we were sure he must be right.* ◊ **assertiveness.** EG *Her confidence and assertiveness were starting to be seen as arrogance.*
ADJ QUALIT = pushy ≠ timid
◊ ADV WITH VB
◊ N UNCOUNT

assess /ə³sɛs/, **assesses, assessing, assessed.**
1 When you **assess** a situation, problem, etc, you consider all the facts about it and decide what the position is and what is likely to happen. EG *They meet monthly to discuss policy and assess the current political situation... You will need time to settle in and assess your surroundings... Ellen tried to assess how she felt.*
V + O/REPORT-CL = gauge

2 When you **assess** someone or something, you consider and judge their quality or worth. EG *They say they can assess intelligence from these tests... ...methods of assessing students... In the programme this week, we assess the new National Savings Certificate.*
V + O = evaluate

3 When you **assess** the amount of money that something is worth or **assess** how much should be paid for something, you calculate or estimate it. EG *She looked over the house quickly and assessed its rough market value... Get your tax assessed separately from your husband's.*
V + O

assessment /ə³sɛsmə²nt/, **assessments.** 1 An **assessment** of a situation, problem, etc is a consideration of all the facts about it and a judgement or opinion of the position and of what is likely to happen. EG *There has to be a clear assessment of the country's social needs... Success in this game depends on making correct assessments of other players' intentions.*
N COUNT/UNCOUNT = evaluation

2 An **assessment** of someone or something is an estimate of their quality or worth, especially by using a test or examination. EG *...the assessment of his academic progress... ...assessment methods.*
N UNCOUNT/COUNT ⇑ judgement

3 An **assessment** of the amount of money that something is worth or of how much should be paid for something is a calculation or estimate of the amount. EG *...appeals against assessments made by the tax man... ...a shrewd assessment of his financial resources.*
N COUNT/UNCOUNT

assessor /ə³sɛsə/, **assessors.** An **assessor** is 1 a person who is employed to calculate the value of something or the amount of money that should be paid, for example in tax. 2 a person who is an expert in a subject and is asked to advise a court of law on that subject; a legal term.
N COUNT ⇑ valuer
N COUNT

asset /æsɛt/, **assets.** 1 An **asset** is someone or something that is considered useful or that helps a person or organization to be successful. EG *A large garden is an asset when you have young children... Her only asset was a gentle nature... With all his experience abroad he was a major asset to the company.*
N COUNT : IF + PREP THEN *to* ⇑ benefit ≠ liability

2 The **assets** of a company or an individual person are everything they own which could if necessary be sold to pay debts. EG *He had a lot of assets in the business... The company were forced to sell off some of their assets in order to reduce borrowing... Despite total assets of 3 million, the takeover bid valued at only 2.5 million was successful.*
N PLURAL ⇑ possessions ≠ liability

assiduous /əsɪdjuːəs/. Someone who is **assiduous** works hard or does things with care and dedication. EG *...an assiduous student... Some friends were particularly assiduous in the campaign for his release.* ▸ used of a person's behaviour or actions. EG *...assiduous research.* ◊ **assiduously.** EG *Throughout 1954 he assiduously studied law.*
ADJ QUALIT = diligent
▸ = diligent
◊ ADV = diligently

assign /əsaɪn/, **assigns, assigning, assigned.**
1 If you **assign** a piece of work to someone or **assign** someone to do a piece of work, you give them the work to do. EG *She kept calling him up to assign some new task to him... Boys are assigned chores in the garage... She had been assigned to work in the fields for six months... They had assigned someone to watch me twenty-four hours a day.*
V + O, V + O + O, V + O + *to*-INF, OR V + O + A *(to)* = delegate

2 To **assign** something to someone also means to give it to them to use for a particular length of time. EG *The bed assigned me in the tenth-floor dormitory was large enough, but uncomfortable... I was assigned a pleasant, cheery room to work in.*
V + O, V + O + O, OR V + O + A *(to)* = allocate

3 If someone **is assigned** to a particular place, they are sent there, especially in order to work there. EG *She had arranged to be assigned to the crowded men's wards.*
V + O : USU PASS + *to*

4 If someone **is assigned** to a group or person, they are made a part of the group or put under the authority of the person. EG *...British forces assigned to NATO and stationed in Germany.*
V + O : USU PASS + *to* ⇑ move = detail

5 If you **assign** a particular role, name, value, etc to someone or something, you give it to them or consider them to have it. EG *Mother and father play out the roles assigned to them... We should be able to assign values to each of these components.*
V + O, V + O + O, OR V + O + A *(to)* = allot

assignation /æsɪgneɪʃə⁰n/, **assignations.** An **assignation** is a secret meeting with someone, especially with a lover; a formal word. EG *He cancelled an assignation he had made with her for the following day.*
N COUNT

assignment /əsaɪnmə²nt/, **assignments.** 1 An **assignment** is 1.1 a particular task that you are officially given to do, especially as part of your job. EG *My first major assignment as a reporter was to cover a large-scale riot... This would be a challenging assignment.* 1.2 a piece of academic work given to students. EG *The course has heavy reading assignments but a flexible assessment system.*
N COUNT
N COUNT

2 The **assignment** of a person to do something or to go somewhere is the act of assigning them to it. EG *The original uproar about his assignment to the case has died down.*
N UNCOUNT : WITH POSS, IF + PREP THEN *to* = appointment

assimilate /əsɪmɪleɪt/, **assimilates, assimilating, assimilated.** 1 If you **assimilate** ideas, etc from other people, you learn them and make use of them. EG *He was bright, inventive, and quick to assimilate new ideas... ...a generation of people who have assimilated influences from many cultures.* ◊ **assimilation** /ə³sɪmɪleɪʃə⁰n/. EG *...the rapid assimilation of new techniques in industry.*
V + O ⇑ understand = absorb
◊ N UNCOUNT = absorption

2 When people such as immigrants **assimilate** or **are assimilated** into a group or community, they become an accepted part of the group or community. EG *Foreign worker populations should be assimilated into the local culture.* ◊ **assimilation.** EG *Assimilation for them was impossible.*
V-ERG : IF + PREP THEN *into* = integrate
◊ N UNCOUNT

assist /əsɪst/, **assists, assisting, assisted.** 1 If you **assist** someone with a job or task, you help them by doing part of the work for them. EG *Madeleine spent the day assisting Matron with her inventory... The police had been drafted to Rome to assist in keeping the hotel under constant surveillance... For a short period, I was assisting David Hicks, a highly respected veterinary surgeon.* — V OR V+O : IF+ PREP THEN *with/in*

2 If you **assist** someone who asks you for advice or information, you give them the advice or information. EG *It is the duty of the policeman to assist the aggrieved person.* — V+O = help

3 If something **assists** you with a job or task that you are doing, it makes it easier for you. EG *With these clues to assist us, we can begin to identify the parents... The machine contains pebbles to assist in the grinding process.* — V OR V+O : IF+ PREP THEN *with/in* = help, aid

4 If you **assist** a person who cannot move easily, for example because they are old or ill, you help them by giving them physical support. EG *He stepped forward to assist a shaken Madame de Gaulle to her feet... Bring the horse and assist him to mount.* — V+O

5 If you **assist** a person who needs money, you provide them with money or pay for something that they need. EG *They can no longer rely on financial help from the students' hardship fund to assist with the tuition fees.* — V OR V+O : IF+ PREP THEN *with/in* ⇑ help = aid

assistance /əsɪstəns/. 1 If you give someone **assistance**, 1.1 you help them with a job or task. EG *...a letter of thanks the Prime Minister wrote to me for my assistance during the Marconi case.* — N UNCOUNT : USU WITH POSS 1.2 you give them advice or information. EG *The Samaritans offer assistance to people who are very depressed.* — N UNCOUNT = help 1.3 you provide them with money that they need. EG *The department provides special assistance to those with large families... She persuaded the Cabinet to agree to 1.2 million pounds assistance for the industry.* — N UNCOUNT = help 1.4 you give them physical support so that they can move more easily. EG *They could not walk without assistance.* — N UNCOUNT

2 Someone or something that is **of assistance** to you is helpful or useful to you. EG *I would be of little assistance in the kind of work he was doing... The squirrel's tail is of considerable assistance in balancing.* — PHR : USED AS AN A = of use

assistant /əsɪstənt/, **assistants.** 1 An **assistant** director, **assistant** officer, etc is a person who is second in importance or authority to another person or to other people doing the same work. **Assistant** is often part of a person's job title. EG *...assistant editors... ...the Assistant Executive Director... ...Assistant Secretary of State.* — ADJ CLASSIF : ATTRIB, USED IN TITLES ⇑ status

2 A person's **assistant** is someone who is employed to help them in their work. EG *...a plumber's assistant... Dr Watson worked as Sherlock Holmes' assistant.* — N COUNT : POSS+ N ⇑ helper

3 An **assistant** or **shop assistant** is a person who works in a shop selling things to customers. — N COUNT ⇑ employee

assizes /əsaɪzɪz/ are court sessions which used to take place regularly in all English and Welsh counties; a legal term. — N PLURAL = county court

Assoc. is an abbreviation for 'association' or 'associated'.

associate, associates, associating, associated. The word **associate** is pronounced /ə³səʊsi¹eɪt/ when it is a verb and /əsəʊsi¹ət/ when it is a noun or an adjective. 1 If you **associate** someone or something with an idea, feeling, quality, etc, they make you think of that idea, quality, etc because you connect the two things in your mind. EG *Dignity is the quality which I associate mostly with her... Daintry didn't associate his daughter with child-like tenderness... The smoking of pipes is often associated with old-fashioned 'masculine' values.* — V+O+A *(with)*

2 If one thing **is associated** with another thing, the two things are connected with each other, especially because they always happen or exist together. EG *Zuse worked on engineering problems associated with aircraft design... ...the Executive and its associated committees and departments.* — V+O : USU PASS, IF+PREP THEN *with*

3 If you **are associated** with a particular organization, cause, point of view, etc, or if you **associate** yourself with it, you are connected with it in people's minds, especially because you have said that you agree with it. EG *He was associated with, although he never joined, the British environmentalists... Two of its most prominent members became closely associated with the International Socialists... She had associated herself with the left for years... He refused to associate himself with the decision.* — V+O (NG/REFL) +A *(with)* = linked

4 If you **associate** with a particular group of people, you spend a lot of time in their company; often used showing disapproval. EG *She spent her adolescence associating with criminals... She knew her father wouldn't dare to stop her associating with her friends.* — V+A *(with)* = mix

5 Your **associates** are the people who you are connected with, especially at work. EG *The series is directed by my old associate Jack Good... I've got a new job and a new set of work associates.* — N COUNT ⇑ person = colleague

6 **Associate** is used before a rank, title, position, etc to indicate a different rank, title, position, etc. For example, an associate member of an organization does not have all the privileges that a member has. EG *Non-professional people could only be Associate Members... ...Mr William F Thompson, Associate Dean of the Harvard Law School.* — ADJ CLASSIF : ATTRIB, ALSO USED IN TITLES ⇑ status

Associated /ə³səʊsi¹eɪtɪ²d/ is used in the name of a company to indicate that the company is made up of a number of smaller companies which have joined together. EG *...Associated Industrial Consultants... ...Associated Newspapers.* — ADJ CLASSIF : ATTRIB, USED IN NAMES

association /ə³səʊsi¹eɪʃə⁰n, -ʃi¹-/, **associations.** 1 An **association** is a group of people who have joined together because they have a common occupation, aim, or interest. EG *The President of the British Medical Association holds office for one year... The meeting was attended by representatives from the AUT, the Association of University Teachers... She has formed a housing association to build homes for single mothers.* — N COUNT : ALSO IN NAMES

2 Your **association** with a person, group, organization, etc is the connection that you have with them. EG *He joined the Labour Party, where he began his long association with Trotskyism... We shall help each other as far as we can while our business association lasts... I feel able at last to reveal the story of my brief association with the lady years ago.* — N UNCOUNT+ SUPP = involvement

● If a person or an organization does something or makes something **in association with** another person or organization, they do it or make it together. EG *The programme was made in association with Radio Brighton.* — ● PREP

3 If something has a particular **association** for you, you connect it in your mind with a particular memory, idea, feeling, etc. EG *A number of tunes have a really strong association for individuals... The name has many strange associations.* — N COUNT+SUPP ⇑ connection = link

assorted /ə³sɔːtɪ²d/. 1 A group of **assorted** things is a group of similar things that have different sizes, shapes, colours, etc. EG *...a small bunch of assorted wild flowers... She opened the top volume of the assorted books on the sofa.* — ADJ CLASSIF : ATTRIB ⇑ mixed = various

2 People who you see together and who are well **assorted**, oddly **assorted**, etc are well or oddly suited to each other in personality, tastes, etc. EG *During the meal this strangely assorted pair had their first opportunity to talk.* — ADJ QUALIT : ADV +ADJ = matched

assortment /əsɔːtmə²nt/, **assortments.** An **assortment** is a group of similar things that have different shapes, sizes, colours, etc. EG *...an assortment of plastic bags... ...a splendid assortment of rugs.* — N COUNT : IF+ PREP THEN *of* = variety

asst. is an abbreviation for 'assistant'.

assuage /ə³sweɪdʒ/, **assuages, assuaging, assuaged;** a literary word. 1 If you **assuage** an unpleasant feeling that someone has, you make them feel it less strongly. EG *He tried to calm the woman but could not assuage her terror.* — V+O ⇑ reduce = alleviate ≠ aggravate

2 If you **assuage** a need or desire for something, you satisfy it. EG *Her thirst for knowledge could never be assuaged.* — V+O

assume /ə³sjuːm/, **assumes, assuming, assumed.** 1 If you **assume** that something is true, you accept that it is true although you have had no real proof of it. EG *When you have a language degree people assume that you can speak the language fluently... I was mistakenly assumed to be a Welshman because of my surname... I assume you don't drive, Mr Sharpe?... I am assuming that the misunderstanding will be cleared up.* — V+REPORT-CL, OR V+O+*to*-INF ⇑ believe = presume ● **Let us assume** or **let's assume** is used when you want to suppose that something is true even though it might not be, so that you can think about what the consequences — ● PHR+REPORT-CL : USED AS AN ADV SEN would be. EG *They say he was in America. Let's assume that he was... But let's assume for the moment that everything goes according to plan.*

2 If someone **assumes** power, responsibility, or control of something, they take power, responsibility, or control of it, often without being asked to do so. EG *Hitler assumed power in 1933... He assumed command of the Eighth Army... I made a mistake and I will assume responsibility for it.* V+O

3 If something **assumes** a particular quality or appearance, it starts to have this quality or appearance. EG *Her eyes assumed a strange, weary, indifferent look... This factor assumes increasing importance.* V+O ⇑ acquire = take on

4 If you **assume** a particular expression or way of behaving, you look or behave in this way deliberately in order to give people a particular impression. EG *He would assume an expression of saintly resignation... Civil servants assume a certain military air.* V+O = put on

assumed name, assumed names. If you do something under an **assumed name**, you do it using a name that is not your real name. EG *He lived and worked there under an assumed name... She wrote an anti-Nazi novel under an assumed name.* N COUNT = pseudonym

assuming /ə³sjuːmɪŋ/ or **assuming that** is used when you are considering that something is true even though it might not be true, so that you can think about what the consequences would be or give an opinion about it. EG *But, assuming agreement can be reached on worker participation, what about the other shareholders?... Keep your money or goods (assuming that you have any) separate from those of your husband.* CONJ SUBORD ⇑ if

assumption /ə³sʌmpʃə⁰n/, **assumptions.** 1 If you make an **assumption**, you accept that something is true although you have had no real proof of it. EG *His suggestions are based on an assumption that the prison system is out of date and worthless... His arguments are full of false assumptions and errors of fact... The general assumption was that I was one of them.* N COUNT ⇑ belief = notion, idea

2 Someone's **assumption** of power, responsibility, or control is their taking of power, responsibility, or control of something, especially when they have not been asked to do so. EG *...the assumption of total responsibility... He is guilty of the secret assumption of a power that the Constitution denies him.* N UNCOUNT+*of* ≠ refusal

assurance /ə³ʃʊərəns/, **assurances.** 1 If you give someone an **assurance** that something is true, you say that it is definitely true, in order to make them feel less worried. EG *One must be content with assurances that progress is being made... The United States was respecting the President's assurances of neutrality... This agreement offers real progress and an assurance of future achievement... 'Do I have your assurance,' the colonel asked, 'that you won't contact the press?'... I'd hoped that the roses would have been some assurance that I was thinking of you.* N COUNT/UNCOUNT: SING=PL ⇑ declaration = assertion

2 **Assurance** is **2.1** a feeling of confidence and lack of doubt. EG *'She'll like that,' said Lally with assurance... They were simply waiting, patiently, and with assurance, for me to discover the truth for myself.* N UNCOUNT **2.2** insurance that provides for events that are certain rather than probable, for example death. EG *...an Assurance company.* ● See also **life assurance.** N UNCOUNT: ALSO IN NAMES

assure /ə³ʃʊə/, **assures, assuring, assured.** 1 If you **assure** someone that something is true, you tell them that it is definitely true, often in order to make them feel less worried about something. EG *Please assure Matthew that my house is not about to fall down... Kurt assured me that he was an excellent climber... Oh, yes, he assured her, he loved pizza.* V+O+REPORT-CL/QUOTE ⇑ persuade = reassure

2 If you **are assured** of something, you feel sure and confident about it. EG *One can always be assured of the best in Nellie's place... Once assured of his daughter's safety, he was casual and relaxed.* V+O+A *(of)*: USU PASS

3 If you **assure** yourself of something or if you **are assured** of it, it is certain that you will get it in the future. EG *He could resign if he wanted and assure himself of £156,000 a year in pension... Will you be assured of a career and adequate salary if you go there?... This film had assured him a place in movie history.* V+O+A(*of*), OR V+O+O ⇑ ensure = guarantee

4 You say **I can assure you** or **I assure you** when you want to emphasize how confident you are that what you are saying is true. EG *Food poisoning! Not from this kitchen, I can assure you. Never had a case in my life... I can assure you that this feeling of inadequacy will soon pass.* PHR+REPORT-CL: USED AS ADV SEN = believe me

5 You say **rest assured** when you want to reassure people about something that they are worried or doubtful about. EG *Rest assured that everything's under control... You can rest assured your son didn't die in vain.* PHR+REPORT-CL: USU IMPER = be certain

assured /ə³ʃʊəd/. 1 Someone who is **assured** is very confident. EG *He was completely at home, thoroughly assured in this atmosphere... He had the round, assured voice of a man who inspired confidence in people.* ADJ QUALIT

2 Something that is **assured** is certain to happen. EG *His promotion was assured.* ADJ CLASSIF: PRED

assuredly /ə³ʃʊərə¹dli¹/. If something is **assuredly** true, it is definitely true. EG *She would assuredly be back.* ADV OR ADV SEN ⇑ certainly

aster /æstə/, **asters.** An **aster** is a garden plant that has white, blue, purple, or pink daisy-like flowers. N COUNT

asterisk /æstə⁰rɪsk/, **asterisks, asterisking, asterisked.** 1 An **asterisk** is the sign *. It is used in writing and printing, especially to indicate that there is a comment at the bottom of the page. EG *Why have some of the names got an asterisk above them?* N COUNT ⇑ symbol = star

2 If a word or piece of writing **is asterisked**, it is marked with an asterisk. V+O: USU PASS = star

astern /əstɜːn/; a technical word. 1 Something that is **astern** is at the back of a ship or behind the back part. EG *The captain was astern, talking to one of the passengers... Just before nightfall, with Italy far astern, we spotted a sail on the horizon.* ADJ CLASSIF: PRED

2 A ship that is moving **astern** is moving backwards. EG *The steamer is capable of some forty knots retreating astern.* ADV AFTER VB

asteroid /æstə⁰rɔɪd/, **asteroids.** An **asteroid** is one of the very small planets that move around the sun between the orbits of Mars and Jupiter. N COUNT ⇑ planet

asthma /æsmə/ is a chest disease which makes breathing difficult. EG *'Auntie told me not to run,' he explained, 'on account of my asthma.'* N UNCOUNT

asthmatic /æsmætɪk/, **asthmatics.** 1 Someone who is **asthmatic** suffers from asthma. ▸ An **asthmatic** is a person who suffers from asthma. EG *Mr Smith is an asthmatic.* ADJ CLASSIF ▸ N COUNT

2 Something that is **asthmatic** is caused by asthma or relates to asthma. EG *...asthmatic breathing.* ADJ CLASSIF

astonish /ə³stɒnɪʃ/, **astonishes, astonishing, astonished.** If something or someone **astonishes** you, they surprise you very much. EG *We have found much to astonish and delight us... He used to astonish me with the clarity of his recollections.* V+O OR V = amaze

astonished /ə³stɒnɪʃt/. If you are **astonished**, you are very surprised about something. EG *She was astonished to hear him speak English... Mary was astonished by John's behaviour... They were astonished at the extraordinary beauty of the picture... We were confronted by groups of astonished customers.* ADJ QUALIT: USU PRED = amazed

astonishing /ə³stɒnɪʃɪŋ/. Something that is **astonishing** is very surprising. EG *The subtlety and variety of such actions is astonishing... The shape of their bodies changes with astonishing speed... It's astonishing what dogs can know.* ◊ **astonishingly.** EG *Birth rates there are astonishingly high... The play, astonishingly, celebrates its quarter century this year.* ADJ QUALIT = amazing; ◊ ADV OR ADV SEN ⇑ surprisingly = amazingly

astonishment /ə³stɒnɪʃmə²nt/ is a feeling of great surprise. EG *They looked at each other with astonishment... John stared at him in astonishment... To the astonishment of his friends, he took off his shoes.* N UNCOUNT = amazement

astound /ə³staʊnd/, **astounds, astounding, astounded.** If something or someone **astounds** you, you are shocked and amazed by it or by them. EG *This remark astounded me... What newspapers will do for a story never fails to astound me.* V+O OR V = astonish, amaze

astounded /ə³staʊndɪ²d/. If you are **astounded** by something, you are shocked or amazed that it could exist or happen. EG *Visitors to Sweden were astounded by its cleanliness... You'd be astounded at the amount of cheating that goes on.* ADJ QUALIT: USU PRED = astonished

astounding /ə³staʊndɪŋ/. If something is **astounding**, you are shocked or amazed that it could exist, happen, or be true. EG *The accuracy of his memory is astounding... It seemed an astounding decision.* ◊ **astoundingly.** EG *He had done astoundingly well... Astoundingly, they laughed.* ADJ QUALIT ⇑ amazing = incredible; ◊ ADV OR ADV SEN

astrakhan /æstrəkæn, -kɑːn/ is black or grey curly fur made from the skins of lambs. It is used for making coats and hats. EG *...a man in a grey astrakhan hat.* — N UNCOUNT : USU BEFORE N

astral /æstrə^{0}l/ means relating to the stars; a formal or technical word. EG *...astral bodies.* — ADJ CLASSIF ⇑ starry

astray /əstreɪ/. **1** If you **lead** someone **astray**, **1.1** you make them believe something that is not true. EG *Don't be led astray. He does not want your opinion... They have been led astray by the so-called 'experts'.* — PHR : VB INFLECTS ⇑ mislead

1.2 you make them behave in a foolish way, for example by getting them drunk or by making them spend all their money. EG *I was an innocent youth led astray... Don't worry, I won't lead you astray.* — PHR : VB INFLECTS = corrupt

2 If something **goes astray**, it gets lost while it is being taken or sent somewhere. EG *The letter had gone astray.* — PHR : VB INFLECTS = go missing

astride /əstraɪd/. If you sit or stand **astride** something, you sit or stand with one leg on each side of it. EG *Karen sat astride a large white horse... He woke to find Tom standing astride him.* — PREP ⇑ straddling

astringent /əstrɪndʒə^{7}nt/, **astringents**. **1** An **astringent** is a liquid or substance that you put on a wound in order to stop it bleeding or that you put on your skin to make it less greasy. EG *I examined the cut, put on astringent and applied a plaster.* ▸ used as an adjective. EG *...an application of an astringent lotion.* — N COUNT/UNCOUNT; ▸ ADJ CLASSIF

2 Astringent behaviour is behaviour in which you criticize someone or something severely. EG *His conversation was astringent and stimulating... They directed their most astringent attacks at me.* ▸ used of people. EG *...the funniest and most astringent TV critic to date.* — ADJ QUALIT ⇑ harsh = caustic

astrologer /ə^{3}strɒlədʒə/, **astrologers**. An **astrologer** is a person who uses astrology in order to tell you things about your character and your future. — N COUNT ⇑ forecaster

astrology /ə^{3}strɒlədʒi^1/ is the study of the movements of the planets, sun, moon, and stars in the belief that these movements can influence people's lives and show what will happen in the future. EG *Do you believe in astrology?* ◊ **astrological**. EG *...astrological literature.* — N UNCOUNT; ◊ ADJ CLASSIF

astronaut /æstrə^{7}nɔːt/, **astronauts**. An **astronaut** is a person who is trained to fly in a spacecraft. — N COUNT = spaceman

astronomer /ə^{3}strɒnəmə/, **astronomers**. An **astronomer** is a scientist who studies the stars, planets, and other natural objects in space. EG *Astronomers used to ask why only Saturn has rings.* — N COUNT

astronomical /æstrə^{7}nɒmɪkə^{0}l/. **1** A value, price, or amount that is **astronomical** is very large indeed. EG *The odds against another attack were astronomical... ...an astronomical price.* ◊ **astronomically**. EG *The wine is astronomically expensive.* — ADJ CLASSIF ⇑ high = enormous; ◊ ADV+ADJ/ADV

2 Astronomical also means relating to astronomy. EG *...The Royal Astronomical Society.* — ADJ CLASSIF ⇑ scientific

astronomy /ə^{3}strɒnəmi^1/ is the scientific study of the stars, planets, and other natural objects in space. EG *...the discoveries of astronomy... ...a professor of astronomy.* — N UNCOUNT ⇑ science

astrophysics /æstrəʊfɪzɪks/ is the study of the physical and chemical structure of the stars, planets, and other natural objects in space. — N UNCOUNT ⇑ physics

astute /ə^{3}stjuːt/. Someone who is **astute** is clever and skilful at understanding behaviour and situations and at using this knowledge for their own advantage. EG *He is an astute politician... ...one of the most astute of Hollywood agents.* ▸ used of behaviour. EG *With astute management the problem can be overcome.* ◊ **astutely**. EG *I had by now astutely concluded that we could not win.* — ADJ QUALIT = canny, shrewd; ◊ ADV WITH VB = shrewdly

astuteness /ə^{3}stjuːtnɪ^{2}s/ is astute behaviour. EG *Every move was made with an astuteness designed to outfox his opponents.* — N UNCOUNT = shrewdness

asunder /ə^{3}sʌndə/. If you tear or rend something **asunder**, you violently separate it into two or more parts or pieces; a literary word. EG *The Party would be torn asunder... They have sufficient destructive power to blow a battleship asunder.* — ADV AFTER VB ⇑ apart

asylum /ə^{3}saɪləm/, **asylums**. **1** An **asylum** is the same as a mental hospital. EG *They put him into an asylum.* — N COUNT

2 Asylum is protection that is given by a government to foreigners who leave their own country for political reasons. EG *The government gave asylum to some extremists from across the border.* — N UNCOUNT

asymmetric /æsɪmetrɪk, eɪ-/ means the same as asymmetrical. EG *...an asymmetric skull.* — ADJ CLASSIF

asymmetrical /eɪsɪmetrɪkə^{0}l/. Something that is **asymmetrical** has two sides or halves that are different in shape, size, or style. EG *...an elaborate, asymmetrical pattern... ...asymmetrical designs.* — ADJ CLASSIF ≠ symmetrical

asymmetry /æsɪmɪtri^1, eɪ-/ is the appearance that something has when its two sides or halves are different in shape, size, or style. EG *...the asymmetry of the view.* — N UNCOUNT ⇑ irregularity ≠ symmetry

at /ə^{3}t/. **1** If something happens or is situated **at** a place, that is the place where it happens or is situated. EG *The whole play takes place at a beach club... They sat at a table near the back... Only one hospital, at Angal, is functioning... We landed at a small airport... Tighten the screws at both ends... There was a knock at his door.* — PREP

2 If you are **at** a public event, you are there while it is taking place. EG *The whole village were out at a funeral... He made his remarks at a press conference... He had had a fight at a high school dance.* — PREP

3 If you are **at** a factory, office, school, etc, you are going there regularly to work or be educated. EG *I was 27 years at that office... They've been away from home at a boarding school.* — PREP

4 If you are **at** breakfast, lunch, etc, you are eating your breakfast, lunch, etc. EG *I was still home at lunch.* — PREP

5 If you are looking or gesturing **at** someone or something, you are looking or gesturing towards that person or thing. EG *They were staring at a garage roof... She waved down at him... He grinned at Gretchen.* — PREP

6 If you throw something **at** a person or object, you throw it towards that person or object with the intention of hitting them. EG *Supporters threw petals at his car.* — PREP

7 If something is **at** a distance from something else, or **at** an angle to something else, it is in that place or position in relation to it. EG *The cat got up and followed at a distance... Place it at right angles to the door.* — PREP

8 If something happens **at** a particular time, that is the time when it happens. EG *She leaves her house every day at 11 a.m... She had come in at dawn... I must stop this at once... You can re-enter the job market at a later stage... This is hard to accept at a time of high unemployment.* — PREP

9 If you do something **at** a particular age, you do it when you are that age. EG *He started work at sixteen... Earl Warren died at eighty-three.* — PREP

10 You say that something happens **at** a particular rate to say how quickly or regularly it is happening. EG *The high technology companies have grown at an astonishing rate... Planes were taking off at ninety-second intervals.* — PREP

11 If you buy or sell something **at** a particular price, you buy it or sell it for that amount of money. EG *The book is published by Paper Tiger at $7.95... The pipeline's cost is now put at 2.7 billion pounds.* — PREP

12 You say that something is moving **at** a particular speed to say how fast it is moving. EG *He hurtles through the air at 600 miles per hour.* — PREP

13 You say that music or a radio is playing **at** a particular volume to say how loud it is. EG *She had the radio playing at full volume.* — PREP

14 You say that something is **at** a point on a scale to say how high it is on the scale. EG *You could set a pass mark at 60 per cent... The increase worked out at one teacher for every extra 100 pupils.* — PREP

15 If you are working **at** something or aiming **at** something, you are trying to do it or achieve it. EG *It means working harder at your thesis... The cuts are aimed at bringing down the rate of inflation.* — PREP

16 If something is done **at** someone's command, invitation, etc, it is done as a result of their command, invitation, etc. EG *At the director's command, the thirty or forty people left... She went at the invitation of an unknown man.* — PREP

17 At is also used **17.1** to say that someone or something is in a particular state or condition. EG *He remains at liberty... Boylan looked debonair, at ease... Two nations are at war... The government is putting more jobs at risk.* — PREP **17.2** to say how something is being done. EG *He seemed to read at random... A line of guardsmen herded them back at gun point... I'm flying at their expense.* — PREP **17.3** to show that you are — PREP doing something in a tentative way. EG *Rudolph sipped at his drink... His mother just picked at her food.* **17.4** to say that someone or something has more of a particular quality than at any other time. EG *She is still at her best... ...science fiction at its most imaginative.* PREP

18 You say **at** a guess, **at** an estimate, etc to indicate that you are guessing or estimating something. EG *I'd say twenty, at a guess... At a rough estimate, it'll take three weeks.* PREP

19 If you are good **at** something, bad **at** something, etc, you do it well, badly, etc. EG *They seemed to be very good at reading... They are equally adept at concentrated study... Parking is something we're very bad at... She is an expert at it.* PREP : ADJ/N+PREP

20 If you are delighted **at** something, appalled **at** something, etc, you are delighted, appalled, etc because of it. EG *I was appalled at the quality of the reporting... He didn't know whether to feel glad or sorry at his dismissal.* PREP ⇑ about

21 In informal English, if you say that a place, activity, etc is **where it's at**, you mean that it is the most exciting place, activity, etc that there is. EG *This pub is where it's at... Jogging's where it's at.* PHR : USED AS C

22 At all: see **all**.

atavistic /ætəvɪstɪk/. If you describe your feelings or ways of behaving as **atavistic**, you are suggesting that they are like the feelings or behaviour of your primitive ancestors; a formal word. EG *Many of those present felt this atavistic fear.* ADJ CLASSIF ⇑ primitive

ate /eɪt/ is the past tense of **eat**.

atheism /eɪθi¹ɪzə⁰m/ is the belief that there is no God: compare **agnosticism**. EG *He was accused of impiety and atheism.* N UNCOUNT

atheist /eɪθi¹ɪst/, **atheists**. An **atheist** is a person who believes that there is no God: compare **agnostic**. EG *He is a convinced atheist.* N COUNT

atheistic /eɪθi¹ɪstɪk/. Something that is **atheistic** relates to or expresses the belief that there is no God. EG *...atheistic and radical utterances.* ▸ used of people and groups. EG *...an atheistic society.* ADJ CLASSIF ≠ religious

athlete /æθli:t/, **athletes**. An **athlete** is a person who is very good at sport and who takes part in sports competitions. EG *He was a great athlete and an outstanding coach.* N COUNT ⇑ sportsman

athletic /æθletɪk/, **athletics**. **Athletic** is an adjective and **athletics** is an uncount noun. **1 Athletics** consists of track and field sports such as running, the high jump, the javelin, etc. EG *...an athletics meeting... He has recently retired from active athletics... The athletics start tomorrow.* N UNCOUNT ⇑ sport

2 Athletic means relating to athletes and athletics. EG *...the athletic traditions of Harvard University.... All this has to do with athletic excellence.* ADJ CLASSIF : ATTRIB

3 An **athletic** person is a person with a strong healthy body who is good at sports and other physical activities. EG *...a couple of tall and athletic young men.* ▸ used of someone's body. EG *He had square shoulders and an athletic frame... ...his lean, athletic build.* ADJ QUALIT = able-bodied; ▸ = muscular

-ation, -ations. **-ation**, **-tion**, and **-ion** are added to some verbs in order to form nouns. Nouns formed in this way often refer to a state or process; for example, starvation is the process of starving, and victimization is the process of being victimized. Many nouns like these are not defined in this dictionary but are dealt with at the related verbs. EG *...confirm→confirmation... ...realize→realization... ...create→creation... ...produce→production... ...protect→protection... ...purify→purification.* SUFFIX : FORMS NOUNS

atishoo /ə³tɪʃu:/ is used, especially in writing, to represent the sound that you make when you sneeze.

atlas /ætləs/, **atlases**. An **atlas** is a book of maps. EG *Check where Louisiana is in your atlas.* N COUNT

atmosphere /ætməsfɪə/, **atmospheres**. **1** A planet's **atmosphere** is the layer of air or other gas around it. EG *...the composition of Jupiter's atmosphere.* ▸ The **atmosphere** is the earth's atmosphere. EG *...changes in the climate due to pollution of the atmosphere... ...the testing of nuclear weapons in the atmosphere.* N COUNT; ▸ N SING : *the*+N

2 The **atmosphere** of a place is **2.1** the air that you breathe there. EG *...the polluted atmosphere of towns and cities.* **2.2** the general impression that you get of the place. EG *It's got such a friendly atmosphere... ...an atmosphere of contentment.* N SING WITH DET; N SING WITH DET : USU+SUPP ⇑ feel

3 If a place has **atmosphere**, it feels special, interesting, or exciting to you; used showing approval. EG *The place has no character, no atmosphere... The log fire gave the room a bit of atmosphere.* N UNCOUNT

atmospheric /ætməsferɪk/ is used to describe something which relates to the earth's atmosphere. EG *...atmospheric pollution.* ADJ CLASSIF : ATTRIB ⇑ climatic

atoll /ætɒl, ə³tɒl/, **atolls**. An **atoll** is a ring of coral rock or a group of coral islands surrounding a lagoon. N COUNT ⇑ island

atom /ætə⁰m/, **atoms**. An **atom** is **1** the smallest amount of a substance that can take part in a chemical reaction; a technical use in science. EG *...the forces within the nucleus of an atom... A molecule of water has 2 atoms of hydrogen and one of oxygen.* **2** a tiny amount of something. EG *The slightest atom of dust can harm the workings... There's not one atom of romance in her.* N COUNT ⇑ particle; N PART ⇑ bit = hint

atom bomb, atom bombs; also called **atomic bomb**. An **atom bomb** is a bomb that causes an explosion by a sudden release of energy that results from splitting atoms. N COUNT ⇑ bomb

atomic /ə³tɒmɪk/ means **1** relating to power that is produced from the energy released by splitting atoms. EG *...atomic energy... ...atomic scientists... ...atomic weapons... ...an atomic explosion.* **2** relating to the atoms of substances. EG *...a heavy atomic nucleus such as uranium.* ADJ CLASSIF : USU ATTRIB = nuclear; ADJ CLASSIF : ATTRIB ⇑ particle

atomize /ætəmaɪz/, **atomizes, atomizing, atomized**; also spelled **atomise**. **1** If a structure or system such as a community **is atomized**, it is divided up into a lot of very small parts and so loses its unity; a fairly formal use. EG *In Latin America the pre-colonial society was totally atomized.* V+O : USU PASS ⇑ divide = fragment

2 If people or things **are atomized**, they are destroyed completely by nuclear weapons. EG *The skyscrapers would still be there long after the human race had been atomized.* V+O : USU PASS ⇑ destroy

atomizer /ætəmaɪzə/, **atomizers**; also spelled **atomiser**. An **atomizer** is a device which turns a liquid such as perfume into a very fine spray. N COUNT

atone /ətəʊn/, **atones, atoning, atoned**. If you **atone** for something that you have done, you show that you are sorry you did it and make amends; a formal word. EG *He has to atone for his sins... Lacey wishes to atone for his mistake in bringing you here.* V : IF+PREP THEN *for* ⇑ apologize = make amends

atonement /ətəʊnmə³nt/ is something that you do to show that you are sorry for having done something wrong; used in formal English. EG *They're still trying to make some sort of atonement and reparation.* N UNCOUNT : IF+PREP THEN *for* ⇑ apology

atop /ətɒp/. If something is **atop** something else, it is on top of it; used in American English. EG *They perched atop the sheds... She let her hands rest, one atop the other, on her stomach.* PREP

A to Z, A to Zs. An **A to Z** is a trademark for a map or book of maps showing every street or road in a particular city or area. N COUNT

atrocious /ətrəʊʃəs/. **1** Something that is **atrocious** is extremely bad in quality. EG *...speaking French with an atrocious accent.* ◊ **atrociously**. EG *They sang atrociously.* ADJ QUALIT = appalling; ◊ ADV WITH VB = dreadfully

2 An action or way of behaving that is **atrocious** is shocking because it is very rude or cruel. ◊ **atrociously**. EG *The farm animals are treated atrociously.* ADJ QUALIT = appalling; ◊ ADV WITH VB

atrocity /ətrɒsɪti¹/, **atrocities**. An **atrocity** is an action that is shocking because it is very cruel, often something that is done during a war. EG *They were guilty of the most barbarous and inhuman atrocities.* ▸ used as an uncount noun to refer to a person's behaviour. EG *...this saga of atrocity and historic tragedy.* N COUNT : USU PL = cruelty; ▸ N UNCOUNT ⇑ behaviour = savagery

atrophy /ætrə⁶fi¹/, **atrophies, atrophying, atrophied**; a formal word. **1** If a muscle or other part of the body **atrophies** or **is atrophied**, it decreases in size or strength, often as a result of an illness. EG *Muscles only weaken and atrophy when they are not used.* ▸ used as a noun. EG *...physical atrophy of the optic nerves.* V-ERG = wither; ▸ N UNCOUNT

2 If something **atrophies** or **is atrophied**, it decreases in size or strength. EG *If the economy is not to atrophy, immediate steps must be taken... Many rural communities have atrophied... His personality was increasingly more stunted and atrophied.* ▸ used as a noun. EG *Their society is in a state of atrophy.* V-ERG = degenerate; ▸ N UNCOUNT = degeneration

attach /ətætʃ/, **attaches, attaching, attached**. **1** To **attach** something to an object means to join it V+O : USU+*to* or fasten it to the object. EG *Eventually the caterpillar will attach itself to a plant and spin a cocoon... ...a big wooden table with benches attached to it... Attached to the letter to Lord Marton was a list of his employees.* ● **no strings attached**: see **string**.

2 If someone **is attached** to an organization or group of people, they are working with them or helping them, often for a short while. EG *I was attached to the expedition as a medical adviser... Hospital officers would in future be attached to hospitals later in their careers.* — V+O : USU PASS+ *to* ⇑ join

3 If one organization or institution **is attached** to a larger organization, it is part of the larger organization and is controlled and administered by it. EG *The Institute is attached to the University of Southern Maine.* — V+O : USU PASS+ *to*

4 If you **attach** importance or some other quality to someone or something, you consider that they have that quality. EG *It would be unwise to attach too much importance to what he said... He couldn't guess what significance she might attach to the event... ...a job which had some prestige attached to it.* — V+O+A *(to)* = assign

5 A particular quality or feature that **attaches** to someone or something is one that has become associated with them, especially as the result of something that they have done; a formal use. EG *Considerable guilt attaches to the person who breaks off such a relationship.* — V+A *(to)*

6 See also **attached**.

attaché /ætæʃeɪ/, **attachés**. An **attaché** is a member of staff in an embassy, especially someone who has special duties to perform. EG *He aspired to be Cultural Attaché in the Diplomatic Service.* — N COUNT ⇑ official

attaché case, attaché cases. An **attaché case** is a shallow rectangular briefcase that is used for carrying business documents and papers. — N COUNT

attached /ətætʃt/. If you are **attached** to someone or something, you are very fond of them. EG *He had become attached to a student called Hilary... The French are very attached to their national traditions.* — ADJ QUALIT : PRED+*to*

attachment /ətætʃmə²nt/, **attachments**. 1 An **attachment** to someone or something is a feeling of affection that you have for them. EG *She continued to feel a very strong attachment to General Ravenscroft.* — N COUNT : IF+ PREP THEN *to*

2 **Attachment** to a particular cause or ideal is a strong feeling of belief in it and loyalty to it. EG *Their attachment to Western ways and ideals was well-known.* — N UNCOUNT : IF+ PREP THEN *to*

3 An **attachment** is **3.1** something that fastens things to each other. EG *This bone serves as an attachment for the muscles which flap the wings.* — N COUNT ⇑ fastening **3.2** a device that can be fixed onto a machine in order to make it do different work. EG *The vacuum cleaner has special attachments for curtains and upholstery.* — N COUNT

4 Someone who is **on attachment** to a place where they do not normally work has been given a temporary job or temporary duties there. EG *Officers spend two weeks on attachment to a general hospital.* — PHR : USED AS AN A, IF+PREP THEN *to* ⇑ assigned

attack /ətæk/, **attacks, attacking, attacked**. 1 To **attack** someone means to use violence against them in order to hurt them, for example by hitting them or stabbing them. EG *The court decided that he was temporarily insane when he attacked and mutilated the women... She was attacked by a shark.* — V+O OR V = assault ▸ used as a noun. EG *...a worrying increase in attacks on old people.* — ▸ N COUNT : IF+ PREP THEN *on*

2 If a group of people such as an army **attacks** buildings, towns, or other armies, they start to use weapons violently against them in order to damage or destroy them, especially at the beginning of a war or battle. EG *We are attacking an enemy submarine... We attack at dawn.* — V OR V+O ⇑ fight ▸ used as a noun. EG *The planes began their attack on Beirut... Guerrilla attacks would be launched against the police... There were no defences against nuclear attack.* — ▸ N COUNT/ UNCOUNT : IF+ PREP THEN *on* = raid

3 If you **attack** someone or something such as a belief or idea, you criticize them strongly. EG *The senator also attacked the press for misleading the public.... It was racism that had to be attacked.* — V+O = condemn ▸ used as a noun. EG *Nearly all our editorials were attacks on various aspects of apartheid... Burt's work came under violent attack in October 1976.* — ▸ N COUNT/ UNCOUNT : IF+ PREP THEN *on* ⇑ criticism

4 If something such as a disease, a chemical, or an insect **attacks** something, it harms it or spoils it. EG *The venom attacks the nervous system... Nuclear radiation can attack the cells in living tissue... The ants were attacking the entire collection of stuffed birds.* — V+O

5 If you **attack** something such as a job or a problem, you start to deal with it with energy and enthusiasm. EG *He attacked his task with determination... The problem was handed over to Roger who attacked it with vigour.* — V+O = tackle

6 When players **attack** in a game of football, hockey, etc, they try to score goals. EG *After half time the team rallied and began to attack in earnest.* — V ≠ defend ▸ used as a noun. EG *The team was brilliant in attack.* — ▸ N UNCOUNT ≠ defence

7 An **attack** of an illness is a short period in which you suffer badly from it and cannot control it. EG *I had an attack of giddiness... She had been left totally deaf by an attack of smallpox.* ● See also **heart attack**. — N COUNT : IF+ PREP THEN *of*

attain /əteɪn/, **attains, attaining, attained**. 1 If you **attain** something that you are aiming for, you gain it or achieve it, often after a lot of effort. EG *She attained her ambition of becoming an M.P.... The country attained its independence in 1961.* — V+O = obtain

2 To **attain** a particular stage or condition means to reach it as a result of natural development. EG *He survived the war and attained a great age.* — V+O

attainable /əteɪnəbə⁰l/. Something that is **attainable** can be reached or achieved. — ADJ CLASSIF = realizable

attainment /əteɪnmə²nt/, **attainments**; a formal word. 1 The **attainment** of an aim is the act or process of achieving it. EG *...the attainment of independence.* — N UNCOUNT+ SUPP = achievement

2 An **attainment** is a special skill or ability that is gained by a lot of effort or over a long period. EG *...appreciation of your high talents and literary attainments.* — N COUNT = accomplishment

attempt /ə³tɛmpt/, **attempts, attempting, attempted**. 1 If you **attempt** something, or **attempt** to do something, you try to do it or achieve it, especially when it is something difficult. EG *Some of the crowd attempted to break through police cordons... A long time had elapsed since I had attempted any serious study.* — V+*to*-INF, OR V+O = endeavour

2 An **attempt** is an act of trying to do something, especially when this is unsuccessful. EG *Lloyd came into the office in a vain attempt to have the report suppressed... It was the only faint attempt at a joke... The young birds manage to fly several kilometres at their first attempt.* — N COUNT : IF+ PREP THEN *at/ to*-INF ⇑ try ▸ used to refer to an object produced as a result of such an act. EG *Have you got your attempt with you?* — ▸ N COUNT = effort

3 An **attempt on** someone's **life** is an attempt to kill them. EG *...the likelihood of some attempt being made on the President's life.* — PHR : USED AS S/ O/C ⇑ attack

attempted /ə³tɛmptɪ²d/. An **attempted** act is an unsuccessful effort to do something, often to commit a crime or to commit suicide. EG *He had been charged with attempted murder... ...the attempted assassination of President Reagan.* — ADJ CLASSIF : ATTRIB

attend /ə³tɛnd/, **attends, attending, attended**.

1 If you **attend** an event such as a meeting or a ceremony, you are present at it. EG *I stopped off in London to attend a conference... I had not attended a funeral for many years... The plays here are always well attended.* — V OR V+O

2 If you **attend** an institution such as a school, college, or church, you go to it regularly. EG *The school was attended almost entirely by local children.* — V OR V+O

3 If you **attend** to something such as a problem, you deal with it. EG *I had two items of business to attend to before I could relax... If we do not attend to the problem, it will certainly grow.* — V+A *(to)* = see to

4 If you **attend** someone, you look after them, for example when they are ill; a formal use. EG *Doctors were rare and only attended very sick patients.* — V+O

5 If someone working in a shop **attends** to a customer, they find out what the customer wants and serve him or her; a formal use. EG *Are you being attended to?* — V+A *(to)*

6 If you **attend** to something, you pay attention to it; a formal use. EG *She was still apparently attending closely to the music.* — V : IF+PREP THEN *to* ≠ ignore

7 Something that **attends** something else happens or exists at the same time as it, usually as a result of it; a formal use. EG *She hated all the publicity and gossip which attended her activities... He feared the consequences that might attend such experiments.* — V+O = accompany

attendance /ə³tendəns/, **attendances**. 1 The **attendance** at a meeting or gathering is the number of people who are present at it. EG *There have been heavy attendances at recent conferences... At Easter, attendances at churches rose.* — N COUNT/UNCOUNT : IF+PREP THEN *at*

2 **Attendance** at an event or an institution is the act of being present at the event or of going regularly to the institution. EG *He decided to improve himself by attendance at evening classes.* — N UNCOUNT : IF+PREP THEN *at*; ≠ absence

3 If you are **in attendance** in a place or with a person, you are present in that place or with that person; a formal expression. EG *Proposals were placed before the people in attendance.* — PHR : USED AS AN A; ≠ absent

4 **Attendance** on or of a person is the act of looking after them or serving them; a formal use. EG *There was no longer any reason to keep Gerald in attendance on him.* • to **dance attendance on** someone: see **dance**. — N UNCOUNT : IF+PREP THEN *on/upon/of*

attendant /ə³tendənt/, **attendants**. 1 An **attendant** is someone whose job is to serve people in a shop, museum, etc. EG *She stopped the car at a petrol station and told the attendant to fill it up... ...a museum attendant.* — N COUNT; ⇑ assistant

2 **Attendant** is used **2.1** to refer to someone who is accompanying another person in order to help or protect that person. EG *The doctor marched along the ward with retinues of attendant students and nurses.* **2.2** to refer to something that results from the situation or thing already mentioned or is connected to it in some way; a fairly formal use. EG *They were fighting against nuclear energy and its attendant dangers.* — 2.1 ADJ CLASSIF : ATTRIB; = accompanying. 2.2 ADJ CLASSIF : ATTRIB; = associated

attention /ə³tenʃə⁰n/, **attentions**. 1 If you give a subject or activity your **attention**, you look at it, listen to it, or think about it carefully. EG *When he felt he had their attention, he began... He was finding it a strain to hold his students' attention... He switched his attention back to the magazines... They were listening with close attention to the Chief of Staff.* — N UNCOUNT : USU WITH POSS; ⇑ thought; = concentration

2 If someone brings something important or interesting to your **attention** or if it comes to your **attention**, it is pointed out to you or you notice it as something that you need to think about carefully. EG *He drew attention to the rising unemployment among dockers... I feel it is my duty to bring to your attention the following facts... It had not, as he recalled, come to his attention... He directed the government's attention to the dangers of Hitler in 1933.* — N UNCOUNT : USU POSS+N

3 **Attention** is great interest that is shown in someone or something, often by the general public when they want to find out more about them. EG *The princess is getting all the attention at the moment... She was the centre of attention.* — N UNCOUNT; ≠ indifference

4 If something **attracts** your **attention** or **catches** your **attention**, you suddenly notice it and are interested by it. EG *A poster caught her attention... How can I attract the captain's attention?* — PHR : VB INFLECTS; ⇑ interest

5 **Attention** to something is the act of dealing with it or caring for it. EG *The engine bearing is wearing badly and needs immediate attention... They needed urgent medical attention.* — N UNCOUNT; ⇑ care; ≠ neglect

6 **pay attention**. If you **pay attention** to someone or something, **6.1** you watch them or listen to them carefully, especially in order to make sure that you do not miss something. **6.2** you show great interest in them and try to find out more about them. EG *There's far too much attention being paid to these hooligans.* — 6.1 PHR : VB INFLECTS. 6.2 PHR : VB INFLECTS

7 If you **pay no attention** or **pay little attention** to someone or something, you behave as if you are not aware of them or as if they do not matter. EG *Pay no attention to this fact... We didn't pay any attention to him... ...members who often pay little attention to their leaders' calls for equality.* — PHR : VB INFLECTS, IF+PREP THEN *to*; ⇑ ignore; ≠ notice

8 **Attentions** that you pay to someone are things that you do to help them and to show your affection for them. EG *She did all she could, by a thousand little attentions, to win favour.* — N PLURAL

9 When soldiers, policemen, etc **stand to** or **at attention**, they stand up straight with their feet together and their arms at their sides. EG *We were ordered to stand to attention... They sprang to attention... The soldiers were standing at attention.* — PHR : VB INFLECTS. ▸ The word **Attention!** is also used as a command to soldiers, policemen, etc to stand in this way. — ▸ CONVENTION

attentive /ə³tentɪv/. Someone who is **attentive** 1 pays close attention to the person or thing that they are listening to or looking at. EG *...an attentive audience.* ◊ **attentively**. EG *He was listening attentively to a senior colleague... I could see he was following the play attentively.* **2** is very helpful and polite to someone else, often because they like them very much. EG *He was unfailingly attentive... ...a habit of not being too attentive to women.* ◊ **attentively**. EG *They circled attentively with drinks and olives.* — 1 ADJ QUALIT; = intent; ≠ inattentive. ◊ ADV WITH VB; = carefully. 2 ADJ QUALIT; ⇑ caring; = solicitous; ≠ offhand. ◊ ADV WITH VB

attenuate /əteṉju:eɪt/, **attenuates, attenuating, attenuated**. To **attenuate** something means to reduce it or weaken it; a formal word. EG *The artillery could only attenuate somewhat the force of the attack.* — V+O; ≠ strengthen

attenuated /əteṉju:eɪtɪ²d/. An **attenuated** object is unusually thin and long; a formal word. EG *They have thin, attenuated bodies.* — ADJ CLASSIF; ≠ squat

attest /ə³teṉst/, **attests, attesting, attested**; a formal word. To **attest** something or to **attest** to something means **1** to show or prove that it is true. EG *The perfection of their design is attested by the fact that they survived for thousands of years... Historic documents and ancient tombstones all attest to this.* **2** to say that you believe it is definitely true, often formally in a law court. EG *I have never, as those of you who know me will attest, judged people by their appearance.* — 1 V+O, OR V+A (*to*); ⇑ certify; = testify. 2 V+A (*to*), OR V+REPORT-CL; ⇑ confirm

attestation /æ̱testeɪʃə⁰n/, **attestations**. An **attestation** is a statement which you make and declare to be true; a formal word. EG *We both signed the attestation.* — N COUNT

attic /æ̱tɪk/, **attics**. An **attic** is a room at the top of a house just below the roof. EG *Thomas climbed the narrow steps to the attic... ...an attic full of dusty, broken furniture.* — N COUNT; = loft

attire /ə³taɪə/. Your **attire** is the clothes that you wear on a particular occasion, especially when you are dressed formally or smartly; a formal word. EG *He obviously felt it was the correct attire for a Prime Minister.* — N UNCOUNT : USU POSS/ADJ+N; = apparel

attired /ə³taɪəd/. Someone who is **attired** in a particular way is dressed that way; a formal word. EG *He was elegantly attired in a cashmere coat.* — ADJ CLASSIF : IF+PREP THEN *in*; = clad

attitude /æ̱tɪtju:d/, **attitudes**. 1 Your **attitude** to something is the way that you think and feel about it. EG *Attitudes are beginning to change... They are adopting our attitude to life... ...our attitude of superiority towards the outside world... She took the attitude that acting was a sort of recreation.* — N COUNT; ⇑ view

2 Your **attitude** to someone is the way that you behave when you are dealing with them, especially when this shows how you feel about them. EG *McPherson's general attitude suggested that he regarded me as an upstart... I resented his attitude.* — N COUNT : USU WITH POSS; ⇑ behaviour; = manner

3 Your **attitude** is also the position in which you hold your body. EG *They sat around in easy attitudes... ...her arms flung out in an attitude of surrender.* — N COUNT : USU+SUPP; = posture

attorney /ə³tɜ̱:ni¹/, **attorneys**. An **attorney** is a person, especially a lawyer, who acts for someone else in a legal matter; used in American English. EG *He later became a prominent attorney... No one wanted the position of defense attorney.* • See also **district attorney**. — N COUNT; ⇑ representative

Attorney General, Attorneys General. A country's **Attorney General** is its chief law officer who advises its king, queen, or government. EG *...John Mitchell, the former U.S. Attorney General.* — N COUNT; ⇑ lawyer

attract /ə³træ̱kt/, **attracts, attracting, attracted**. 1 If something **attracts** people or animals, it has features that cause them to come to it. EG *The show attracted large crowds this year... Industries attract people to the towns... Moths seem to be attracted to lights.* — V+O : IF+PREP THEN *to*; = draw

2 If someone or something **attracts** you, they have particular qualities which cause you to like or admire them. EG *She didn't attract me physically... The picture attracted me.* — V+O; ⇑ interest

3 If a particular quality **attracts** you to a person or thing, it is the reason why you like them. EG *What really attracted me to Valeria was her sense of humour... Maybe it was the emptiness of the land that attracted them.* — V+O : IF+PREP THEN *to*; = draw; ≠ repel

4 If something **attracts** support, publicity, etc, it receives support, publicity, etc as a result of people's interest in it. EG *The women's movement has attracted a lot of publicity.* — V+O; ⇑ receive; = excite

5 If something **attracts** your attention, it makes you notice it. EG *We would have to arrange a meeting and* — V+O; ⇑ stimulate; = excite

this would attract attention... I tried desperately to attract his attention.
6 If something such as a magnet **attracts** an object, particle, etc, it causes the object, particle, etc to move towards it by a magnetic force. V+O OR V ⇑ draw ≠ repel
attracted /ətrækti²d/. If you are **attracted** to someone or something, you like them and are interested in them. EG *I was becoming attracted to a girl from the next office... They were attracted to each other sexually... I'm not attracted to sociology.* ADJ QUALIT: PRED+*to* = drawn ≠ repelled by
attraction /ə³trækʃə⁰n/, **attractions**. 1 **Attraction** is 1.1 a feeling of liking someone very much, of enjoying their company, and often of being sexually interested in them. EG *He couldn't explain his attraction to her... ...physical attraction between two people.* N UNCOUNT: IF+PREP THEN *to* 1.2 a quality that something has of being able to interest people or to offer them pleasure or enjoyment. EG *The success of the centre will depend on the extent of its attraction for young people... The attraction of the house lay in its simplicity.* N SING: WITH *the*/POSS, OR N UNCOUNT = appeal
2 An **attraction** is 2.1 a particular feature which makes something or someone interesting or desirable. EG *One of the main attractions of the city was its superb transport system... The scheme had one big attraction: it was cheap... ...an older woman, certain of her attractions.* N COUNT = attribute 2.2 something that people can go to for interest or enjoyment, for example a famous building, a beautiful piece of countryside, or a concert. EG *There is time to visit the tourist attractions.* N COUNT
attractive /ə³træktɪv/. 1 Something that is **attractive** 1.1 seems nice or interesting to you because it is likely to bring you advantages. EG *The company offers more time off and attractive pay... Do you have any ideas for making rail travel more attractive?* ADJ QUALIT = appealing ≠ unattractive ◇ **attractiveness**. EG *They plan to improve the attractiveness of their savings schemes.* ◇ N UNCOUNT 1.2 has a pleasant appearance or sound. EG *Illustrations for children's books should be attractive... ...an attractive name.* ADJ QUALIT ≠ ugly ◇ **attractively**. EG *Try to dress attractively.* ◇ ADV WITH VB ◇ **attractiveness**. EG *...the attractiveness of her voice.* ◇ N UNCOUNT
2 A person who is **attractive** is pretty or handsome. EG *That's a remarkably attractive girl with Mr Guitry, don't you think?... The photos made him look quite attractive.* ADJ QUALIT = good-looking ◇ **attractiveness**. EG *I have said nothing of her age or attractiveness.* ◇ N UNCOUNT

> **ATTRIB** □ In this dictionary ATTRIB is used in the grammar notes beside an adjective to mean that it comes in attributive position, i.e. before a noun. If an adjective always occurs before a noun it is described as ATTRIB. If it usually occurs before a noun, it is described as USU ATTRIB. An adjective described as ADJ QUALIT: ATTRIB is a qualitative adjective used before a noun, as in **happy** 6. EG *...a* ***happy*** *coincidence... This is a most* ***happy*** *circumstance.* You do not say 'The coincidence was happy'. An adjective described as ADJ CLASSIF: ATTRIB is a classifying adjective used before a noun, for example **classic** 1. EG *...a* ***classic*** *case of bureaucracy.* Compare □ at PRED.

attributable /ə³trɪbjə⁴təbə⁰l/. If something is **attributable** to an event or situation, it is likely that it was caused by the event or situation. EG *This is directly attributable to the problem of unemployment.* ADJ CLASSIF: PRED+*to*
attribute, attributes, attributing, attributed. The word **attribute** is pronounced /ə³trɪbju:t/ when it is a verb, and /ætrɪbju:t/ when it is a noun. 1 If you **attribute** something to an event or situation, you say or think that it was caused by that event or situation. EG *The President attributed the worsening situation to increased guerrilla activity.* V+O+A *(to)* = ascribe
2 If you **attribute** a remark, a piece of writing, or a work of art to someone, you say that they said it, wrote it, or created it. EG *...a remark that was later attributed to Haldane himself.* V+O+A *(to)* = accredit ◇ **attribution** /ætrɪbju:ʃə⁰n/. EG *He was once thought to be the author of a Portrait of a Lady but the attribution has since been changed.* ◇ N UNCOUNT
3 If you **attribute** a particular quality, feature, etc to someone or something, you say or think that they have got it. EG *I shrink from attributing mean motives to anyone.* V+O+A *(to)* = ascribe, assign ◇ **attribution**. EG *...an example of the attribution of human emotions and characteristics to animals.* ◇ N UNCOUNT: IF+PREP THEN *to*
4 An **attribute** is a quality or feature that someone or something has. EG *They appeared to possess all the attributes of a ruling class... Any incomes policy must embody the attributes of fairness and flexibility... ...her physical attributes.* N COUNT ⇑ characteristic
attributive /ə³trɪbjə⁴tɪv/. When an adjective is used in **attributive** position it comes before a noun; a grammatical term. Compare **predicative**. In this dictionary adjectives that are always attributive are given the label ATTRIB in the grammar notes beside the entry. See □ at ATTRIB. ADJ CLASSIF ◇ **attributively**. ◇ ADV WITH VB
attrition /ə³trɪʃə⁰n/ is a process in which you steadily reduce the strength of an enemy by continually attacking them; a formal word. EG *...attrition of the enemy forces... ...a war of attrition.* N UNCOUNT ⇑ weakening
attuned /ə³tju:nd/. 1 If you are **attuned** to something, you can understand and appreciate it. EG *The public is not quite attuned to this kind of art.* ADJ QUALIT: PRED+*to*
2 If your ears are **attuned** to something, you can hear it and recognize it quickly. EG *Her ears were sharply attuned to anything coming from the bedroom.* ADJ QUALIT: PRED+*to* ⇑ sensitive
atypical /eɪtɪpɪkə⁰l/. Something that is **atypical** is not a typical thing of its kind. EG *I soon tumbled to the fact that my weekends were atypical.* ADJ CLASSIF ⇑ unusual = odd ◇ **atypically**. EG *He was well-informed and atypically open to new information.* ◇ ADV ⇑ unusually
aubergine /əʊbəd⁰ʒi:n/, **aubergines**. An **aubergine** is a vegetable with a smooth, dark purple skin and soft, white flesh; used especially in British English. N COUNT = eggplant
auburn /ɔ:bə⁰n/. Hair that is **auburn** is a reddish brown colour. EG *...her auburn hair.* ADJ COLOUR
auction /ɔ:kʃə⁰n/, **auctions, auctioning, auctioned**. 1 An **auction** is a public sale of goods or property where people offer higher and higher prices until the goods are sold to the person who offers the highest price. EG *Renata was attending an auction... The Big House was sold by auction.* N COUNT, OR *at/for/by*+N
2 If you **auction** something, you sell it in an auction. EG *They are going to auction the pictures at the end of the month.* V+O
auction off. If you **auction off** a number of things, you get rid of them all by selling them at an auction. EG *The furniture was auctioned off.* PHRASAL VB: V+O+ADV ⇑ sell
auctioneer /ɔ:kʃənɪə/, **auctioneers**. An **auctioneer** is a person in charge of an auction who announces the items for sale, calls out the offers of prices, and makes sure that the buyer offering the highest price gets the object for sale. EG *The auctioneer opened the bidding.* N COUNT
audacious /ɔ:deɪʃəs/. **Audacious** behaviour is behaviour in which you take risks in order to achieve something; usually used showing approval. EG *...a series of audacious ventures... You may be called upon to take audacious decisions.* ▸ used of people and groups. EG *...an audacious chef.* ADJ QUALIT ⇑ brave = bold ≠ cowardly ◇ **audaciously**. EG *They will happily and audaciously carry the torch of progress.* ◇ ADV WITH VB
audacity /ɔ:dæsɪti¹/ is audacious behaviour. EG *It was remarkable what you could accomplish with audacity... He had the audacity to blame Baldwin for their failure... Judy was amazed at her own audacity.* N UNCOUNT = daring
audible /ɔ:dɪ¹bə⁰l/. Something that is **audible** is loud enough to be heard. EG *Her breathing was audible... I woke to hear a strange, barely audible sound from downstairs.* ADJ QUALIT ≠ inaudible ◇ **audibly**. EG *The clock ticked audibly.* ◇ ADV ◇ **audibility** /ɔ:dɪ¹bɪlɪti¹/. EG *...varying degrees of clarity and audibility.* ◇ N UNCOUNT
audience /ɔ:dɪəns/, **audiences**. 1 When **audience** is used in the singular with the following meanings, it can be used with either a singular or a plural verb. An **audience** is 1.1 the group of people who are watching or listening to a play, concert, show, film, or public speaker. EG *Someone in the audience began to laugh.... She spoke before an audience of schoolchildren... Cinema audiences are becoming more sophisticated.* N COUNT 1.2 all the people who watch television or listen to the radio. N COUNT 1.3 the people who look at the pictures of an artist, read the books of a writer, or hear about the ideas of a thinker. EG *An artist wants an audience... He had an audience of ten million readers... ...the need for intellectuals to communicate their ideas to a wider audience.* N COUNT = public 1.4 a group of people who are listening to you while you tell them something. EG *Give him a captive audience, and he can sell anything... He became aware that he had lost his audience.* N COUNT = listeners
2 If you have an **audience** with someone, usually N COUNT

someone important, you have a formal meeting with them. EG *His mother begged for an audience with the governor... He stood up to show that the audience was over... ...a private audience.*

audio /ɔːdɪəʊ/ equipment is equipment for recording and reproducing sound. EG *...a display of audio equipment... ...the use of audio and video tapes.* ADJ CLASSIF: ATTRIB

audio-typist, audio-typists; also spelled without a hyphen. An **audio-typist** is a typist who types letters, reports, etc that have been dictated into a tape-recorder. EG *We have a vacancy for an audio-typist.* N COUNT

audio-visual; also spelled without a hyphen. **Audio-visual** materials or equipment are materials or equipment that involve both recorded sound and pictures, which are often used for teaching purposes. EG *...the use of audio-visual materials... ...audio-visual aids for language teaching.* ADJ CLASSIF: ATTRIB

audit /ɔːdɪt/, **audits, auditing, audited**. 1 If someone **audits** an organization's accounts, they examine the accounts officially in order to make sure that they have been done correctly. EG *The accounts have to be audited by a firm of external auditors.* V+O

2 An **audit** is an official examination of an organization's accounts by an accountant. EG *The company hasn't had a proper audit for over a year.* N COUNT ⇑ inspection

audition /ɔːdɪʃəⁿn/, **auditions, auditioning, auditioned**. 1 An **audition** is a short performance that an actor, actress, or musician gives so that a director can decide if they are good enough to act in a play or film, become a member of an orchestra, or be given a place at a drama school or music college. EG *I was told to return that afternoon for an audition.* N COUNT ⇑ test

2 If you **audition** or if someone **auditions** you, you perform an audition. EG *She auditioned for a course in drama at Manchester... We have to go all over the world to audition likely acts.* V-ERG: IF+PREP THEN *for*

auditor /ɔːdɪtə/, **auditors**. An **auditor** is an accountant who officially examines the accounts of organizations in order to make sure that they have been done correctly. EG *Once a year an auditor came to audit the accounts.* N COUNT

auditorium /ɔːdɪtɔːrɪəm/, **auditoriums, auditoria**. The plural form can be either **auditoriums** or **auditoria**. An **auditorium** is 1 the part of a theatre or concert hall where the audience sits. EG *The theatre in King Street had an elegant auditorium.* N COUNT 2 a large building for public meetings, concerts, etc; used especially in American English. EG *...the domed auditorium next to the pier.* N COUNT

auditory /ɔːdɪtəⁿri¹/ means relating to hearing; a technical or formal word. EG *...conflict between visual and auditory information.* ADJ CLASSIF

au fait /əʊfeɪ/. If you are **au fait** with something, you are familiar with it and know about it. EG *I'm not exactly au fait with the rules of cricket.* ADJ QUALIT: PRED, IF+PREP THEN *with*

Aug. is an abbreviation for August.

augment /ɔːgment/, **augments, augmenting, augmented**. To **augment** something means to make it larger by adding something to it; a fairly formal word. EG *They mixed flour and water into noodles to augment the diet of the peasants... They hit upon another idea to augment their income... The crowds were augmented by refugees from smaller places.* V+O ⇑ increase = supplement

augur /ɔːgə/, **augurs, auguring, augured**. If something **augurs** well or badly for someone, it is a sign that things will go well or badly for them in the future; a fairly formal word. EG *This unexpected result might be thought to augur well for the Socialists... The start could not have augured better for success.* V+A: IF+PREP THEN *for*

augury /ɔːgjʊri¹/, **auguries**. An **augury** is a sign of what will happen in the future; a literary word. EG *Let us hope it is an augury.* N COUNT = omen

august. The word **august** is pronounced /ɔːgəst/ when it is a noun and /ɔːgʌst/ when it is an adjective. It is spelled with a capital letter for paragraph 1. 1 **August** is the eighth month of the year in the Western calendar. EG *I must be back by August the 22nd... War broke out on August 4th... ...the fourth of August, 1952... You start your new job in August.* N UNCOUNT

2 Someone or something that is **august** is dignified and impressive; a literary use. EG *He was probably the most august figure in the House of Lords... I'd never been in that august chamber before.* ADJ QUALIT = imposing

auk /ɔːk/, **auks**. An **auk** is a bird with a heavy body and short tail that dives into the sea for its food. There are several kinds of auk. N COUNT

aunt /ɑːnt/, **aunts**. Your **aunt** is the sister of your mother or father, or the wife of your uncle. EG *My aunt sat sewing by the fire... Aunt Alice is coming for the weekend.* ● See also **agony aunt**. N COUNT: ALSO IN NAMES BEFORE N ⇑ relative

auntie /ɑːnti¹/, **aunties**; also spelled **aunty**. Your **auntie** is your aunt; an informal and affectionate word. EG *I used to live with my auntie... ...Auntie Elsie.* N COUNT: ALSO IN NAMES BEFORE N ⇑ relative ≠ uncle

au pair /əʊpɛə/, **au pairs**. An **au pair** is a young foreigner, usually a young woman, who lives for a time with a family in order to learn the language. Au pairs usually look after the children of the family and do some of the housework, in return for a small wage. EG *She's now working as an au pair near Lyons... ...an au pair girl.* N COUNT ⇑ home help

aura /ɔːrə/, **auras**. An **aura** is a quality or feeling that is associated with a person or place and that seems to surround it or come from it. EG *...an aura of glamour and prestige... There had always been an aura of despair about the flat.* N COUNT: USU+ *of* = air

aural /ɔːrəl/. **Aural** means 1 related to the sense of hearing: compare **oral** and **acoustic**. EG *I have used written and aural material, backed by photographic evidence.* ADJ CLASSIF 2 related to a person's ability to understand a language when it is spoken. EG *...aural comprehension.* ADJ CLASSIF: ATTRIB

au revoir /ɔːrəvwɑː/ is a French expression for goodbye; used when you expect or hope to see the other person again. EG *Au revoir, Frieda dear.* CONVENTION

aurora borealis /əˢrɔːrə bɔːri¹eɪlɪs/. The **aurora borealis** consists of moving bands of coloured light sometimes seen in the sky in Arctic regions. N SING: *the*+N = Northern lights

auspices /ɔːspɪsɪz/. If something is done **under the auspices of** a particular person or organization, it is done with their support and approval. EG *The conference was held under the auspices of the United Nations.* PREP patronage, guidance

auspicious /ɔːspɪʃəs/. Something that is **auspicious** gives hope of success or evidence that success is likely; a fairly formal word. EG *It was an auspicious start to their election campaign.* ADJ QUALIT = promising, favourable

Aussie /ɒzi¹/. **Aussie** means Australian; an informal word. EG *...the stereotyped image of the Aussie male.* ADJ CLASSIF: ATTRIB

austere /ɒstɪə/. 1 Something that is **austere** is plain and not decorated. EG *The interior of the church, although sober and austere, is very fine... It is an austere statue.* ◊ **austerely**. EG *She dressed austerely rather than smartly.* ADJ QUALIT = stark ◊ ADV

2 An **austere** person is strict, serious, and does not seem to approve of enjoying life. EG *She was an austere religious woman of Spanish origins.* ▸ used of someone's behaviour. EG *He permitted himself an austere smile.* ADJ QUALIT = severe, stern

3 An **austere** way of life is one that is simple and without comfort or luxuries. EG *In these austere times, we are all having to cut back... His way of life is austere and controlled.* ADJ QUALIT = stark

austerity /ɒsterɪti¹/, **austerities**; a formal word. **Austerity** is 1 great simplicity in your way of life, for example by having very few comforts and luxuries. EG *...a man of dignity and austerity... ...the elegant austerity of these surroundings.* N UNCOUNT ≠ materialism 2 the hardship and lack of comforts that the people in a country suffer when the country's economy is not healthy; used especially to describe the time during or just after a war. EG *...the change from affluence to austerity... As always at times of austerity, cuts were made... After the austerities of the war years, people spent a lot of money on expensive goods.* N UNCOUNT OR N COUNT: ONLY PL

Australasian /ɒstrəleɪʒən/. Something that is **Australasian** belongs or relates to Australasia, or to its peoples. EG *...the Australasian countries.* ADJ CLASSIF

Australian /ɒstreɪlɪən/, **Australians**. 1 Something that is **Australian** belongs or relates to Australia, or to its people. EG *...Australian sheep-farming... ...the Australian novelist Patrick White.* ADJ CLASSIF

2 An **Australian** is someone who comes from Australia. N COUNT

3 **Australian** is the form of English which is spoken in Australia. N UNCOUNT

Austrian /ɒstrɪən/, **Austrians**. 1 Something that is **Austrian** belongs or relates to Austria, or to its people. EG *...the Austrian border.* ADJ CLASSIF

2 An **Austrian** is someone who comes from Austria. N COUNT

autarchy /ɔ:tɑ:ki[1]/, **autarchies**. **Autarchy** is government of a country by one person or group that has complete power; a rare and formal word. EG *We have suffered decades of foolish autarchy.* ▸ used to refer to a country with a government of this type. — N UNCOUNT = autocracy, dictatorship; ▸ N COUNT

authentic /ɔ:θentɪk/. **1** If something such as a painting or piece of writing is **authentic**, it is known to be genuine rather than being an imitation. EG *They inserted among the authentic documents several that had been forged... It is an authentic Air Force jacket.* ◊ **authentically**. EG *The room has been furnished as authentically as possible.* — ADJ CLASSIF = real, bona fide ≠ fake, false; ◊ ADV

2 If an account or information is **authentic**, it is reliable and accurate and so can be believed. EG *The book gives an authentic account of that awful war... Is it derived from authentic data, or is it just another theory?* — ADJ QUALIT ⇑ true

authenticate /ɔ:θentɪkeɪt/, **authenticates, authenticating, authenticated**; a formal word. If you **authenticate** something, **1** you state officially that it is genuine after examining it. EG *You need to get someone to authenticate the photograph... The letter has not yet been authenticated.* ◊ **authentication** /ɔ:θentɪkeɪʃə[0]n/. EG *We must wait for the authentication of the signature.* **2** you prove or confirm that it is true. EG *These stories seem to be well authenticated.* ◊ **authentication**. — V+O; ◊ N UNCOUNT; V+O; ◊ N UNCOUNT

authenticity /ɔ:θentɪsɪti[1]/. If you refer to something's **authenticity**, you mean **1** that it has truly been made, painted, or written by the person who is thought to have done it or at the time it is thought to have been done. EG *He challenged the authenticity of the letter... The painting is of doubtful authenticity.* **2** that it is reliable and accurate and able to be believed. EG *No historian has ever doubted the authenticity of Haldane's account.* — N UNCOUNT = genuineness; N UNCOUNT

author /ɔ:θə/, **authors, authoring, authored**. **1** The **author** of a piece of writing is the person who wrote it. EG *...Bill Davies, author of a new book on money in the 1980's.* ▸ used as a verb. EG *Steve had authored a pamphlet on the subject.* — N COUNT: *the*+N, USU+*of* = writer; ▸ V+O

2 An **author** is a person whose occupation is writing books. EG *...Simone de Beauvoir, the French author.* — N COUNT = writer

3 The **author** of a plan or scheme is the person who causes it to begin or come into existence; a fairly formal use. — N COUNT: WITH *the*/POSS

authoress /ɔ:θə[0]rɪ[2]s/, **authoresses**. An **authoress** is a woman whose occupation is writing books; an old-fashioned word. — N COUNT = writer

authorise /ɔ:θə[0]raɪz/. See **authorize**.

authoritarian /ɔ:θɒrə[1]teəri[1]ən/, **authoritarians**. Someone who is **authoritarian** wants to control and influence other people's thoughts and actions rather than letting them choose and decide things themselves; used showing disapproval. EG *He became more authoritarian... ...authoritarian parents... ...an authoritarian regime.* ▸ used of a person's behaviour and attitudes. EG *She had criticized David for his authoritarian and moralistic attitude.* ▸ used as a noun. EG *The old rulers were essentially authoritarians.* — ADJ QUALIT ⇑ dictatorial; ▸ N COUNT

authoritarianism /ɔ:θɒrə[1]teəri[1]ənɪzə[0]m/ is the belief that people with power, especially the State have the right to control other people's thoughts and actions; a formal word. EG *Authoritarianism in government repelled him.* — N UNCOUNT ⇑ dictatorship

authoritative /ɔ:θɒrə[1]tətɪv/. **1** Someone or something that is **authoritative** gives an impression of power and importance and is likely to be obeyed. EG *...a deep authoritative male voice... The name was written in large authoritative letters.* ◊ **authoritatively**. EG *'Don't do that,' he said authoritatively.* — ADJ QUALIT ⇑ dominating; ◊ ADV WITH VB

2 A person, book, etc that is **authoritative** has or shows a lot of knowledge or understanding of a particular subject. EG *This is the most authoritative study of the subject.* — ADJ QUALIT

authority /ɔ:θɒrə[1]ti[1]/, **authorities**. **1** The **authorities** are the people who have the power to make decisions, especially the government of a country. EG *I think that the authorities have got to clamp down on people like this... The union continued to seek dialogue with the authorities.* — N PLURAL: *the*+N

2 An **authority** is an official organization or government department that has the power to make decisions. EG *She sold the house to the local authority... ...Area Health Authorities.* — N COUNT: USU MOD+N

3 Authority is **3.1** the right to command and control other people. EG *Respect for the authority of the State is everywhere reduced.... He would be reported to those in authority... He had made efforts to reassert his authority over them.* **3.2** a quality or strength of personality that someone has that causes other people to obey them or take notice of what they say. EG *Her voice carried a note of authority... 'I'll make sure it's done,' he said, with great authority.* **3.3** official permission to do something. EG *They gave authority for Allied aircraft to cross the border... Have you been ordering taxis without signed authority?* — N UNCOUNT: IF+ PREP THEN *over* = power; N UNCOUNT ⇑ forcefulness; N UNCOUNT

4 An **authority** on a particular subject is someone who knows a lot about it. EG *She is the greatest authority on African fish... He has become one of the leading authorities on American accents.* — N COUNT: IF+ PREP THEN *on* = expert

5 If you **have it on good authority** that something is true, you are fairly certain that it is true because you trust the person who told you about it. EG *I have it on good authority that Frieda Maloney will be prosecuted.* — PHR: VB INFLECTS ⇑ are assured

authorization /ɔ:θəraɪzeɪʃə[0]n/, **authorizations**; also spelled **authorisation**. **Authorization** is official permission to do something, especially when it is written down. EG *You can't even send a cable without government authorization... Has the authorisation for my visa come through yet?* — N UNCOUNT/ COUNT

authorize /ɔ:θəraɪz/, **authorizes, authorizing, authorized**; also spelled **authorise**. **1** If someone in a position of authority **authorizes** something, they give their official permission for it to happen. EG *The president authorized the bombings... We're not supposed to authorize loans for that kind of thing.* — V+O ⇑ permit

2 If someone **is authorized** to do something, they have the official permission to do it. EG *I am not authorized to approve payments from the fund.* — V+O+*to*-INF ⇑ allow

authorship /ɔ:θəʃɪp/. **1** The **authorship** of a piece of writing is the identity of the person who wrote it. EG *The letter's authorship could not be kept secret... The Bible is a work of collective authorship.* — N UNCOUNT: USU WITH POSS ⇑ origin

2 Authorship is the activity or job of writing books or articles. EG *I depend upon authorship for my entire living.* — N UNCOUNT

autism /ɔ:tɪzə[0]m/ is a severe mental illness that affects children and makes them unable to respond to other people. Such children often do not learn to speak. — N UNCOUNT ⇑ handicap

autistic /ɔ:tɪstɪk/. Someone who is **autistic** suffers from autism. — ADJ CLASSIF ⇑ handicapped

auto /ɔ:təʊ/, **autos**. An **auto** is a car; used in informal American English. EG *...the auto industry... ...an auto accident.* — N COUNT: USU BEFORE N

autobahn /ɔ:tə[6]bɑ:n/, **autobahns**. An **autobahn** is a German motorway. — N COUNT ⇑ road

autobiographical /ɔ:tə[6]baɪəgræfɪkə[0]l/. A piece of writing that is **autobiographical** relates to events in the life of the person who has written or told it. EG *All his novels are autobiographical in some way.* — ADJ CLASSIF

autobiography /ɔ:tə[6]baɪɒgrəfi[1]/, **autobiographies**. **1** An **autobiography** is an account of your own life, which you write yourself. EG *She describes in her autobiography a visit to Russia in 1909.* — N COUNT: WITH POSS

2 Autobiography is the form of literature which consists of books and stories that people write about their own lives and experiences. EG *Autobiography is often less truthful than biography.* — N UNCOUNT

autocracy /ɔ:tɒkrəsi[1]/, **autocracies**. **Autocracy** is **1** government of a country by one person who has complete power. EG *...the principle of autocracy.* ▸ used to refer to a country with a government of this type. EG *It had been an autocracy for 20 years.* **2** a style of management in which the person in charge makes decisions and gives orders without having to ask anyone else's advice. EG *It is time to substitute power-sharing for managerial autocracy.* — N UNCOUNT = dictatorship; ▸ N COUNT; N UNCOUNT ⇑ authoritarianism

autocrat /ɔ:tə[6]kræt/, **autocrats**. An **autocrat** is **1** a ruler who has complete power. EG *He reigned like a medieval autocrat.* **2** a person who makes decisions and gives orders without asking anyone else's advice, for example when running a business. EG *She was a bit of an autocrat.* — N COUNT = dictator; N COUNT = authoritarian

autocratic /ɔ:tə[6]krætɪk/. **1 Autocratic** means relating to government by one ruler who has complete power. EG *...feudal states ruled by autocratic kings... The 1970's saw Spain and Portugal move from autocratic regimes to democratic ones.* — ADJ CLASSIF: USU ATTRIB = despotic

2 Someone who is **autocratic** makes decisions and gives orders without asking anyone else's advice. EG *Some chairmen were a bit autocratic... ...autocratic leadership.* — ADJ QUALIT = dictatorial ≠ democratic

autocue /ɔːtəʊkjuː/, **autocues**. An **autocue** is a device used by people speaking on television, which displays words for them to read so that they can look straight at the camera when they are speaking. EG *An ability to read the autocue is essential.* — N COUNT ⇑ prompter

autograph /ɔːtə⁶grɑːf/, **autographs, autographing, autographed**. 1 An **autograph** is the signature of someone famous; used especially when you have asked the person to write it for you. EG *Would you send me your autograph?... ...autograph hunters.* — N COUNT : USU WITH POSS

2 If you **autograph** something, you put your signature on it. EG *She bought a paperback copy of his book for him to autograph... We'll send him an autographed copy of our report.* — V+O

automat /ɔːtə⁶mæt/, **automats**. An **automat** is a vending machine from which you can get food; also used to refer to a restaurant where food is served from machines; used mainly in American English. — N COUNT

automate /ɔːtə⁶meɪt/, **automates, automating, automated**. To **automate** a factory, office, or industrial process means to install machines which can do the work instead of people. EG *What about those plans to automate the mills?... It ought to be possible to automate the control process.* — V+O ⇑ mechanise
◊ **automation** /ɔːtə⁶meɪʃə⁰n/. EG *This is an age of high technology and automation.* — ◊ N UNCOUNT

automatic /ɔːtə⁶mætɪk/, **automatics**. 1 An **automatic** machine is one which has controls that enable it to perform a task without needing to be operated by a person. EG *...automatic washing machines... This missile is fully automatic.* ▸ used of the work done by a machine like this. EG *...automatic data processing.* — ADJ CLASSIF ≠ manual
◊ **automatically**. EG *A computer automatically guided the plane to the target... The lights come on automatically when the light falls below a certain level.* — ◊ ADV = by itself

2 An **automatic** is 2.1 a gun that keeps reloading itself and firing shots until you stop pulling the trigger. — N COUNT 2.2 a car in which the gears change automatically as the car's speed increases so that the driver does not have to change gear using a gear lever. — N COUNT 2.3 a washing machine which washes and spins the washing in the same container when you have set the controls. — N COUNT

3 If something that you say or do is **automatic**, it is said or done by you without thinking about it, usually because you have done it many times before. EG *Most of our decisions in day-to-day life are automatic... ...an automatic gesture.* — ADJ QUALIT = mechanical ≠ conscious ◊ **automatically**. EG *Billy found himself automatically walking up to the house.* — ◊ ADV

4 If something such as a response, action, or punishment is **automatic**, it always happens as a natural or usual result of something else. EG *These offences carry automatic fines.* — ADJ CLASSIF = inevitable ◊ **automatically**. EG *Once people retire they automatically cease to be union members.* — ◊ ADV

automatic pilot, automatic pilots. 1 An **automatic pilot** is a device in an aircraft that automatically keeps it on a particular course. EG *The plane is now on automatic pilot.* — N COUNT, OR *on*+N

2 If you are **on automatic pilot**, you are acting without thinking about what you are doing, usually because you have done it many times before. EG *I had lost all interest in the game. I was on automatic pilot now.* — PHR : USED AS AN A

automaton /ɔːtɒmətɒn/, **automatons, automata**. The plural form can be either **automatons** or **automata**. An **automaton** is 1 a person who acts without thinking about what they are doing, for example because they are tired or bored. EG *Eventually you become an automaton, saying the same dull things over and over again.* — N COUNT = zombie 2 a small mechanical figure that can move automatically. — N COUNT ⇑ robot

automobile /ɔːtəmə⁶biːl/, **automobiles**. An **automobile** is a car; used especially in American English. EG *Expensive automobiles were parked in the driveway... ...the automobile industry.* — N COUNT ⇑ vehicle

autonomous /ɔːtɒnəməs/. 1 A country, organization, or group that is **autonomous** governs or controls itself rather than being controlled by another country, organization, or group. EG *...the autonomous republic of Byelorussia... This organization is independent and autonomous.* — ADJ QUALIT ⇑ separate = self-governing

2 Someone who is **autonomous** makes their own decisions about what to do rather than being influenced by someone else; a formal use. EG *...if these women can manage to become autonomous people.* — ADJ QUALIT ⇑ free = independent

autonomy /ɔːtɒnəmi¹/ is 1 the control or government of a country, organization, or group by itself rather than by others. EG *...a movement for real autonomy in the republics... The proposals include the ending of university autonomy.* — N UNCOUNT ⇑ state = independence 2 the ability to make your own decisions about what to do rather than being influenced by someone else or told what to do; a formal use. EG *These parents see autonomy in their youngsters as a threat.* — N UNCOUNT = independence

autopsy /ɔːtɒpsi¹, ɔːtə⁷p-/, **autopsies**. An **autopsy** is 1 an examination of a dead body by a doctor who cuts it open to try to discover the cause of death. EG *Since the family opposed an autopsy, the death was officially listed as drowning.* — N COUNT = post-mortem 2 a careful and detailed analysis of a subject; a formal use. — N COUNT

autumn /ɔːtəm/, **autumns**. **Autumn** is the season between summer and winter. In the autumn the weather becomes cooler and leaves change colour and fall from many trees and plants. EG *Summer was alright, but he much preferred the autumn... ...autumn leaves... The rain began in the late autumn... There will probably be a general election this autumn... The bracken was turning to the dusky gold of a fine autumn.* — N UNCOUNT/COUNT = fall

autumnal /ɔːtʌmnə⁰l/. Something that is **autumnal** has features that are characteristic of autumn. EG *The light was autumnal... ...autumnal browns and golds.* — ADJ CLASSIF ⇑ mellow

AUX □ AUX is used in the entries for 'be', 'do' and 'have' to show that they are used as auxiliaries. See □ at BE, DO, and HAVE.

auxiliary /ɔːgzɪljəri¹, -lə⁰ri¹/, **auxiliaries**. 1 An **auxiliary** is a person employed to help another more important person or group of people in their work, especially a medical worker or a member of the armed forces. EG *Nursing auxiliaries help nurses with their basic duties... ...naval auxiliaries.* — N COUNT ⇑ assistant ▸ used as an adjective. EG *...six auxiliary squadrons of the Royal Air Force Regiment.* — ▸ ADJ CLASSIF : ATTRIB = supporting

2 **Auxiliary** equipment such as a machine or tool is extra equipment that is used when necessary in addition to the main machine or tool. EG *...auxiliary scaffolding.* — ADJ CLASSIF : ATTRIB ⇑ additional = secondary

3 In grammar, an **auxiliary** or an **auxiliary verb** is one of a small class of verbs that are used before a main verb to show tense, voice, mood, etc. The words 'be', 'do', and 'have' can be used as auxiliaries and in this dictionary they have AUX in the grammar note beside the entries. See □ at AUX, BE, DO, and HAVE. Words like 'can', 'might', and 'will' are sometimes called 'modal auxiliaries'. In this dictionary they are described as MODAL. See □ at MODAL. — N COUNT

avail /əveɪl/, **avails, availing, availed**. 1 If something that you do is **of no avail, to little avail**, etc, you do not achieve any success from doing it. EG *They were fighting to no avail... Speeches and protests were of no avail.* — PHR : USED AS AN A ⇑ unsuccessful

2 If you **avail** yourself of an offer or an opportunity, you accept the offer or make use of the opportunity; a formal use. EG *I haven't felt inclined to avail myself of your kind offer.* — V+O (REFL)+A (*of*)

available /əveɪləbə⁰l/. 1 If something is **available**, 1.1 you are able to use it or obtain it, for example because it is not kept secret or because it is on sale in shops. EG *Television isn't yet available here... ...the amount of money available for spending... More information becomes available through the use of computers... Details were made available by the Americans.* — ADJ CLASSIF ≠ unavailable ◊ **availability** /əveɪləbɪlɪti¹/. EG *Laws still controlled the availability of contraceptives and abortion... ...a widespread reduction in the world availability of oil.* — ◊ N UNCOUNT : IF+PREP THEN *of/for* 1.2 it is not being used and is therefore free for you to use. EG *Will your accommodation be available next October?* — ADJ CLASSIF

2 Someone who is **available** 2.1 is not busy and is therefore free for you to talk to. EG *The MP was not available for comment yesterday.* — ADJ CLASSIF ≠ busy 2.2 is free or willing to begin a relationship with someone, for example because they do not already have a boy- — ADJ QUALIT = unattached

friend, lover, wife, etc. EG *So many girls were available and willing.*

3 **Available** time is time when someone is free. EG *I have very few days available at the moment.*
ADJ CLASSIF

avalanche /ævəlɑːntʃ/, **avalanches**. An **avalanche** is 1 a large mass of snow and ice that falls down the side of a mountain. EG *A group of skiers were buried by an avalanche last night.* 2 a very large quantity of things that all arrive or happen at the same time. EG *He had set off a terrible avalanche of events... ...an avalanche of tourists.*
N COUNT ⇑ landslip
N COUNT+SUPP ⇑ mass = flood

avant-garde /ævɒŋgɑːd/. 1 Something that is **avant-garde** belongs to a style of art, fashion, or writing whose methods and ideas are experimental or more modern than those generally accepted. EG *...avant-garde art... These productions were considered very avant-garde and appealed only to a limited audience.*
ADJ QUALIT = progressive ≠ traditional

2 The **avant-garde** are the artists, writers, musicians, etc who introduce new and very modern ideas. EG *...Eugene Ionesco, a leader in the avant-garde of French writers.*
N PLURAL : *the*+N ⇑ progressives

avarice /ævərɪs/ is extreme greed for money and possessions. EG *Driven by avarice, he ruthlessly exploited his workers.*
N UNCOUNT

avaricious /ævərɪʃəs/. Someone who is **avaricious** is very greedy for money and possessions; used showing disapproval. EG *These people are avaricious and will do anything for money.*
ADJ QUALIT

Ave. is an abbreviation for 'avenue', when it is part of the name of a road. EG *...184, Poplar Ave.*
N IN NAMES AFTER N

avenge /ə³vendʒ/, **avenges, avenging, avenged**. If you **avenge** a wrong or harmful act or if you **avenge** someone who has been wronged or harmed, you hurt or punish the person who has done the wrong or harm. EG *He was determined to avenge his father's death... Our brothers will avenge us... He wanted to avenge himself for his sufferings.*
V+O (NG/REFL) ≠ forgive

avenue /ævɪ¹njuː/, **avenues**. 1 The word **Avenue** is a name sometimes used for a street in a town. EG *Many London theatres are in Shaftesbury Avenue.*
N COUNT : ALSO IN NAMES AFTER N

2 An **avenue** is **2.1** a wide road with trees on either side, often leading to a large house. EG *...long open avenues lined by trees.* **2.2** a way of getting something done. EG *No sooner was one promising avenue closed than a hundred more opened... We must explore every avenue before admitting defeat.*
N COUNT
N COUNT = means

aver /ə³vɜː/, **avers, averring, averred**. If you **aver** something, you say very firmly that it is true; a formal word. EG *He averred his innocence... 'I know he didn't steal it,' she averred... Certain critics scoffed, averring that nobody would pay to see it.*
V+O/REPORT-CL/QUOTE = assert

average /ævə⁰rɪdʒ/, **averages, averaging, averaged**. 1 An **average** is **1.1** the result you get when you add two or more numbers together and divide the total by the number of numbers you added together. EG *These pupils took a total of 39 examinations, an average of 6.5 examinations for each pupil... The average of 11, 14 and 20 is 15... Income in New England is commonly 10% below the national average.* ▸ used as an adjective. EG *In 1959, the average age of teachers was thirty-nine years... ...the average national wage.* **1.2** the number or size of something that varies but is always approximately the same. EG *The queen bee lives for an average of four to six years.*
N COUNT ⇑ number = mean
▸ ADJ CLASSIF : ATTRIB
N SING : *an*+N+*of*

2 **Average** is used of a person or thing to indicate that they are of a standard or normal type. EG *Today the average American car owner drives 10,000 miles per year... An average thirteen-year-old child could understand it... Take a sheet of paper of average thickness.*
ADJ CLASSIF : ATTRIB ⇑ ordinary

3 An amount or quality that is the **average** is the normal amount or quality for a particular group or category of things or people. EG *They have long working hours-50 a week is about the average... Their language development and reading is below average.* ▸ used as an adjective. EG *...above average inflation.*
N SING : *the*+N = norm
▸ ADJ CLASSIF

4 Something that is **average** is neither very good nor very bad in quality. EG *It was an average piece of work.* ◊ **averagely**. EG *...an averagely attractive woman.*
ADJ QUALIT = fair
◊ ADV

5 To **average** a particular amount of things means to do, get, or produce that amount as an average over a period of time. EG *Their factories average ten times the output of European factories.*
V+C OR O

6 **On average** or **on an average** is used to indicate that a number you mention is the average of several numbers. EG *We can discover how many words, on average, a person reads in a minute... On an average they invested 8,000 pounds a year on each project.*
PHR : USED AS ADV SEN

7 If you say that something is true **on average**, you mean that it is generally true. EG *Babies on average have milder colds than older members of the family.*
PHR : USED AS ADV SEN ⇑ typically

8 You refer to **the law of averages** when you are arguing that something is bound to happen at some time, considering the number of times that it generally happens and the number of people it could happen to. EG *By the law of averages, you can safely assume that you will be burgled at some time.*
PHR : USED AS O/S

average out. When you **average out** a set of numbers or when it **averages out** at a particular figure, you work out the average or approximate figure. EG *If you average it out, it comes to one car stolen every three minutes... 'How many hours do you work?'–'I suppose it averages out at about 40 a week'.*
PHRASAL VB : V+ADV, OR V+O+ADV

averse /ə³vɜːs/. If you are **averse** to something, you feel strongly that you are not willing to do it or that you do not like it; often used with a negative to indicate something that you are willing or even keen to do. EG *They were not averse to making money on the Stock Exchange... He's not averse to a little fun during rehearsals... He was averse to reporters and the press.*
ADJ QUALIT : PRED+*to* ⇑ object

aversion /ə³vɜːʃə⁰n/, **aversions**. If you have an **aversion** to someone or something, you dislike them very much. EG *She had a great aversion to children... I can well understand your aversion to meeting all these people.* ▸ also used of the person or thing that you do not like. EG *...yogurt or stewed apple or whatever his current aversion may be... Smoking is my pet aversion.*
N COUNT : USU SING : IF+PREP THEN *to* ≠ liking
▸ N COUNT : USU WITH POSS

avert /ə³vɜːt/, **averts, averting, averted**. 1 If you **avert** something unpleasant, you prevent it from happening, often by behaving in a decisive way. EG *There must be immediate action if total chaos is to be averted... A war was averted by skilful negotiation.*
V+O ⇑ stop

2 If you **avert** your eyes, gaze, etc from someone or something, you turn your eyes away from them. EG *Brian could only avert his eyes; he had never seen a woman naked... She averted her eyes from the figure on the bed.*
V+O : IF+PREP THEN *from* = look away

aviary /eɪvjəri¹/, **aviaries**. An **aviary** is a large cage or covered area in which birds are kept.
N COUNT

aviation /eɪvɪeɪʃə⁰n/ is the operation and production of aircraft. EG *They were pilots in the early days of aviation.*
N UNCOUNT ⇑ flying

aviator /eɪvɪeɪtə/, **aviators**. An **aviator** is, in old-fashioned English, a pilot of a plane, especially in the early times of aviation.
N COUNT = flyer

avid /ævɪd/. 1 **Avid** is used to describe someone who is extremely interested in something so that they do it with great enthusiasm. EG *TV offers avid viewers the chance to watch all day long.* ◊ **avidly**. EG *Sheila reads avidly... They listened avidly as witnesses to the murder told what they had seen.*
ADJ QUALIT : ATTRIB = keen
◊ ADV WITH VB = eagerly

2 Someone who is **avid** for something is eager to get it. EG *The boy was avid for praise from his teacher.*
ADJ QUALIT : PRED+*for*

avocado /ævə⁶kɑːdəʊ/, **avocados**. An **avocado** or an **avocado pear** is a tropical fruit in the shape of a pear with a dark green skin and a large stone inside. It is often eaten as the first course of a meal.
N COUNT/UNCOUNT

avocet /ævəset/, **avocets**. An **avocet** is a black and white bird that has a long thin beak which curves up at the end. Avocets live on the shores of seas and lakes.
N COUNT

avoid /əvɔɪd/, **avoids, avoiding, avoided**. 1 If you **avoid** something, you take action in order to prevent it from happening or affecting you. EG *...a book on how to avoid a heart attack... ...techniques that will avoid mistakes.*
V+O = avert

2 If you **avoid** doing something, you make a deliberate effort not to do it. EG *Thomas turned his head, trying to avoid breathing in the vapour... You must avoid giving any unnecessary information.*
V+-ING ⇑ stop

3 If you **avoid** someone or something, you keep away from them. EG *Once they were on the boat, Joy tried to avoid her... They had driven through the towns to avoid the motorway... Judy glanced down into her lap to avoid Clarissa's stare.* ● to **avoid** someone or something **like the plague**: see **plague**.
V+O ≠ encounter

avoidable /ə³vɔɪdəbə⁰l/. Something that is **avoidable** can be prevented from happening. ADJ CLASSIF ≠ unavoidable

avoidance /əvɔɪdəns/. **Avoidance** of someone or something is the act of avoiding them. EG *There was a careful avoidance of the issue... ...the avoidance of future problems.* N UNCOUNT + SUPP

avow /əvaʊ/, **avows, avowing, avowed.** If you **avow** something, you admit it or declare it; a formal or literary word. EG *She was obliged to avow openly that she had been there.* V+O/REPORT-CL

avowal /əvaʊə⁰l/, **avowals**. An **avowal** of something such as an emotion is an admission or declaration of it; a formal or literary word. EG *He made a shy avowal of love.* N COUNT/UNCOUNT

avowed /əvaʊd/. If you are an **avowed** believer in something, you have declared that you support those beliefs and try to live according to them; a formal word. EG *She is an avowed feminist.* ▸ also used to describe the thing that a person has declared. EG *The avowed aim of revolutionaries is to disrupt modern society.* ADJ CLASSIF: ATTRIB = professed

avuncular /əvʌŋkjə⁴lə/. A man who is **avuncular** acts in a friendly, caring, and helpful way towards someone younger; an old-fashioned word. EG *The avuncular doctor smiled kindly at his patient.* ▸ used of a person's actions or behaviour. EG *In my best avuncular fashion I put my arm round her shoulder.* ADJ QUALIT = genial ▸ = fatherly

await /əweɪt/, **awaits, awaiting, awaited**; a fairly formal word. **1** If you **await** someone or something, you wait for them. EG *I retired to my study to await a call from Darley... I returned to the States to find the FBI awaiting me... The full story of the war must await a detailed analysis... Huey was awaiting trial for murder.* V+O ⇑ wait

2 An event or situation that **awaits** you is going to happen or come to you in the future. EG *...the adventures that awaited him... She thought of the life of ease and luxury that awaited her in Bombay.* V+O = lie ahead of

awake /əweɪk/, **awakes, awaking, awoke, awoken. 1** Someone who is **awake** is not sleeping. EG *He is still not really awake... He lay awake all night, thinking about his new job.* ● Someone who is **wide awake** is fully awake and not at all ready for sleep. EG *By six o'clock she was wide awake.* ADJ QUALIT: PRED ● PHR: USED AS C

2 Someone who is **awake** to a situation or problem is completely aware of it and understands its likely effects. EG *She was awake to the dangers of the situation.* ADJ QUALIT: PRED+*to* = alert

3 When you **awake** or when something **awakes** you, you wake up; a literary use. EG *In the morning I awoke from a deep sleep... The noise of the wind did not awake her.* V-ERG = awaken

awaken /əweɪkə⁰n/, **awakens, awakening, awakened**; a literary word. **1** To **awaken** an emotion in a person means to cause them to feel this emotion. EG *My first visit to a theatre awakened an interest which never left me... I can only hope to awaken some enthusiasm for my subject.* V+O = arouse, stir

2 When you **awaken** to a situation or when someone **awakens** you to it, you become aware of it. EG *People are at last awakening to their responsibilities... He attempted to awaken the country to a sense of its danger.* V-ERG+A *(to)*

3 When you **awaken** or when something **awakens** you, you wake up. EG *She was awakened by a loud bang.* V-ERG = awake

awakening /əweɪkə⁰nɪŋ/, **awakenings**; a formal word. **1** The **awakening** of a particular emotion or feeling in someone is the start of this feeling in them. EG *There has been a sudden awakening of public opinion to the dangers of nuclear power... ...the awakening of love for another person.* N COUNT: USU+SUPP ⇑ arousal

2 An **awakening** is the time when something such as an activity or an interest begins. EG *He was interested in the awakening of the Renaissance.* N COUNT: USU+SUPP ⇑ beginning

3 If you have a **rude awakening**, you suddenly realize that what you are doing or the situation you are in is not satisfactory. EG *The student who goes out every night is likely to have a rude awakening when he sits his exams.* PHR: USED AS O/S ⇑ shock

award /əwɔːd/, **awards, awarding, awarded.**
1 An **award** is **1.1** a prize or certificate that you are given by an organization for doing something well or doing it better than other people. EG *The new library has won an architectural award.* N COUNT ⇑ reward **1.2** a sum of money that the government or an organization gives you for special training or study. EG *You could apply for an award if you want to learn a new skill.* N COUNT = grant **1.3** a sum of money that a court of law decides should be given to someone. EG *He received an award of £10,000 in compensation for his injuries.* N COUNT = settlement

2 To **award** someone something such as a prize or a mark means to give it to them to show what standard they have achieved. EG *This year's board awarded the top prize to reporter Carol Clay... When do you award 10 out of 10 for a piece of work?* V+O, V+O+O, OR V+O+A *(to)*

3 When a government or an organization **awards** someone a sum of money, it gives it to them for special training or study. EG *The British Government awarded him a grant of £1500.* V+O, V+O+O, OR V+O+A *(to)* ⇑ give

4 If someone such as a judge or referee **awards** something to a person, they decide and declare that the person will be given it. EG *It was the biggest libel settlement awarded up to that time... After much discussion, she was awarded the point.* V+O, V+O+O, OR V+O+A *(to)* ⇑ give

aware /əwɛə/. **1** If you are **aware** that something such as an important problem or difficulty exists or if you are **aware** of it, you know about it, either because you have thought about it or because you have just noticed it. EG *He was aware that he had drunk too much whisky... If only you were aware of all the facts, you would immediately change your mind... I was quite aware of this before we married... As far as I am aware attention was first drawn to this by American researchers.* ◇ **awareness**. EG *...the present public awareness of the need for conservation.* ADJ QUALIT: PRED+*of*/REPORT-CL ≠ ignorant, unaware ◇ N UNCOUNT+*of*/REPORT-CL = realization

2 If you are **aware** of something or **aware** that something exists or is happening, you realize it because you hear it, see it, smell it, or feel it. EG *Ralph was aware of the heat for the first time that day... She became aware, out of the corner of one eye, of a sudden movement.* ADJ QUALIT: PRED+*of*/REPORT-CL = conscious ≠ unaware

3 Someone who is **aware** pays a lot of attention to the things that are happening around them and is interested in why they are happening. EG *Some people are more politically aware than others... Public opinion was aware and angry... Children should be creative and aware.* ◇ **awareness**. EG *He was surprised by the students' political awareness.* ADJ QUALIT: USU PRED ◇ N UNCOUNT ⇑ knowledge

awash /əwɒʃ/. **1** If the ground or a floor is **awash**, it is covered in water, often because of heavy rain or as the result of an accident. EG *In the monsoon the whole place is awash.* ADJ CLASSIF: PRED ⇑ wet = flooded

2 If a place or a period of time is **awash** with a particular type of thing or person, it contains a large number or amount of it, especially when this is considered to be too much. EG *During the mid-1960s the world became awash with dollars.* ADJ CLASSIF: PRED+*with* ⇑ full = flooded

away /əweɪ/. **1** If you move **away** from somewhere, you move so that you are further from that place. EG *He rose and walked slowly away... I kissed her goodbye and drove away... I want to get away from here.* ADV AFTER VB ⇑ off ≠ back, towards

2 If you look or turn **away** from someone or something, you move your head so that you are no longer looking at that person or thing. EG *He looks away... Castle turned away... 'Nonsense,' Etta said, turning her head away.* ADV AFTER VB ≠ towards

3 If something is situated **away** from a person or thing, it is at a distance from that person or thing. EG *He stood near the door, away from Uncle Harold... I tried to keep as far away from people as possible... ...a pleasant green picnic spot away from the city.* ADV+PREP: USU +*from* ⇑ distant

4 You say that a place is situated a particular distance **away** in order to indicate how far that place is from where you are or how long it takes you to travel there. EG *Jack was standing under a tree about ten yards away... It's miles away... She had offers of scholarships from colleges as far away as California... I was only four hours away from Oslo.* ADV = off

5 If a landscape stretches or extends **away**, it stretches or extends into the distance. EG *...lovely flat fields which rolled away for miles and miles to the sky.* ADV AFTER VB

6 If you put something **away** or hide it **away**, you put or hide it in a safe or secret place. EG *Tom put the book away... ...this impressive tomb, hidden away in the depths of the country... This work on Sachsenhausen is not yet ready to be filed away in the archives.* ADV AFTER VB

7 If you are **away**, you are not at home or in the place mentioned, but somewhere else, for example on holiday. EG *The Spanish consul in Cardiff was* ADV AFTER VB *away at the time... Is he at home or has he gone away?... They've been away from home at a boarding school.*

8 If an event is a particular period of time **away**, it will happen that amount of time in the future. EG *The debate on the Afghan crisis is only a fortnight away.*
ADV

9 If you give something **away** or if someone takes it **away** from you, it is given to someone else and so is no longer in your possession. EG *She gave a fortune away... She took you away from me, Alistair.*
ADV AFTER VB

10 If a team such as a football team or a hockey team is **away** or is playing **away**, it is playing a game on its opponents' ground, not on its own. EG *We're playing away on Saturday.* ▸ used as an adjective. EG *...an away match.*
ADV AFTER VB ≠ at home
▸ ADJ CLASSIF : ATTRIB ≠ home

11 Away is also used **11.1** to show that something slowly and gradually disappears or dies so that it no longer exists. EG *The snow had all melted away... The hut rotted away... A murmur rose among the boys and died away.* **11.2** to show that something is removed or destroyed. EG *The damaged wood will probably have to be cut away... Her fingernails were worn away... Children always hope that 'someone else' will clear the mess away.* **11.3** to show that there has been a change or development from one state or situation to another. EG *We must wrench the Parliamentary system away from its feudal origin... His people wanted to move away from the rigid conservative orthodoxy that had prevailed until now... ...the shift away from crimes of theft.* **11.4** to show that numbers, amounts, or rates are less than they were. EG *The student membership fell away substantially at the beginning of the 1970s... Official Trade Union support dropped away.*
ADV AFTER VB / ADV AFTER VB / ADV WITH VB ≠ towards / ADV AFTER VB ⇑ off

12 Away is also used after verbs to emphasize a continuous or repeated action. EG *Howard, forgetful of the time, was still working away in the university library... She was coughing away... He gazed for a few moments at his wife in front of him, stitching away.*
ADV AFTER VB

13 ● **far and away**: see **far**. ● **right away**: see **right**. ● See also **straightaway**.

awe /ɔ:/, **awes, awed. 1 Awe** is the feeling of respect and amazement that you have when you are faced with something wonderful, frightening, or completely unknown. EG *The child stared at him in silent awe... An expression of awe animated their faces... ...something to be treated with awe and wonder.*
N UNCOUNT ⇑ respect = wonderment

2 When you **are in awe of** someone or **stand in awe of** them, you have a lot of respect for them and are actually slightly afraid of them because they seem much more important than you are. EG *He seems slightly in awe of his own wife... She is in awe of his learning and of him... They rather stand in awe of Charles.*
PHR : VB INFLECTS

3 If something or someone **awes** you, they make you feel utterly amazed and often rather frightened; a literary use. EG *The silence awed them... They were awed by him and looked at each other in uneasy admiration.* ◇ **awed.** EG *The men looked at one another silently, awed... ...talking in an awed whisper.*
V+O : NO CONT ⇑ overwhelm = impress
◇ ADJ CLASSIF ⇑ overwhelmed

awe-inspiring. Someone or something that is **awe-inspiring** causes you to feel respect for them because they are slightly frightening or are very important. EG *I found her somewhat awe-inspiring and difficult to talk to... It was an awe-inspiring sight.*
ADJ QUALIT ⇑ overwhelming = awesome

awesome /ɔ:səm/. Something that is **awesome** has the power or quality to make people feel amazed and full of admiration or fear because of its size, difficulty, etc. EG *...the awesome complexity of the universe... ...an awesome responsibility... ...an awesome weapon of war.* ◇ **awesomely.** EG *The crowd, orderly, awesomely hushed, had filled the square.*
ADJ QUALIT ⇑ overwhelming
◇ ADV

awe-struck; also spelled as one word. Someone who is **awe-struck** or **awe-stricken** is suddenly faced with something that gives them a feeling of awe; a fairly formal word. EG *I am a little awestruck by what I heard... Celia's tone was awe-struck... ...watching with awestruck interest.*
ADJ QUALIT ⇑ overwhelmed

awful /ɔ:ful/. **1** If you say that something is **awful**, you mean that it is **1.1** not very good or not very nice. EG *Isn't the weather awful?... Gas smells awful... The road is awful; narrow and bumpy... What an awful thing to say... ...married to that awful man.* **1.2** very unpleasant or very bad, causing people to feel shock, fear, or sadness. EG *...an account of that awful war... My second husband had an awful death.*
ADJ QUALIT ⇑ nasty = dreadful ≠ wonderful / ADJ QUALIT = horrific

2 If someone looks or feels **awful**, they look or feel ill. EG *I felt awful last night... God, he looks awful... My neck felt awful.*
ADJ QUALIT = terrible ≠ well

3 Awful, especially in the expression **an awful lot**, is used to emphasize how good, bad, etc something is or how much of something is needed. EG *It must have taken an awful lot of courage... I don't know an awful lot about it... It takes an awful long while.* ◇ **awfully.** EG *She was awfully nice... It was awfully difficult trying to talk to her... He was an awfully good rugby player... I'm not awfully certain what they are... I'm awfully sorry, we haven't got any... It's awfully good of you to come with me.*
ADJ CLASSIF : ATTRIB ⇑ great = tremendous
◇ ADV+ADJ/ADV ⇑ very = terribly

4 Awful also means causing fear and awe; a literary use. EG *...an awful calm.*
ADJ CLASSIF : ATTRIB = awesome

awhile /əwaɪl/ means for a short time. EG *Can't you just wait awhile and not talk?... I don't want to get married yet awhile.* ● If you do something **for awhile**, you do it for a short time. EG *He watched, enjoying the spectacle for awhile.*
ADV
● PHR : USED AS AN A

awkward /ɔ:kwəd/. **1** A movement or a position that is **awkward** is uncomfortable and clumsy and not at all elegant. EG *...an awkward gesture... One of his arms hung in an awkward way that told Kunta it had been broken.* ◇ **awkwardly.** EG *He manoeuvred the boat awkwardly round... He fell and lay awkwardly, covered in mud.*
ADJ QUALIT ≠ graceful
◇ ADV WITH VB ≠ skilfully

2 Someone who is **awkward 2.1** feels embarrassed, shy, or nervous and behaves in a way that shows other people that this is how they feel. EG *I hated the big formal dances and felt very awkward and out of place.* ◇ **awkwardly.** EG *She had wept, and Sonia had patted her shoulder awkwardly.* ◇ **awkwardness.** EG *She and Diana were great friends and there was no awkwardness between them.* **2.2** is difficult to live or to deal with because you are never quite sure how they are going to react or because they make unreasonable demands. EG *Of course Julia is a very awkward girl to be with... He will have to leave early because his wife is so awkward.*
ADJ QUALIT = uncomfortable ≠ relaxed
◇ ADV WITH VB
◇ N UNCOUNT ⇑ unease
ADJ QUALIT

3 A tool, machine, or job that is **awkward** is difficult to handle, use, or do. EG *The machine was very awkward to use.*
ADJ QUALIT = tricky ≠ easy

4 A situation that is **awkward** is embarrassing and difficult to deal with. EG *It was going to be awkward keeping my news from Ted... The press conference came at an awkward time for me... You get some bloke who asks you a lot of awkward questions.* ◇ **awkwardness.** EG *They were great friends and there was no awkwardness between them.* ● If someone **makes things awkward** for you, they make them as difficult as possible, and cause you a lot of trouble and worry. EG *McPherson started making things awkward for him too.*
ADJ QUALIT = tricky ≠ easy
◇ N UNCOUNT
PHR : VB INFLECTS

awning /ɔ:nɪŋ/, **awnings.** An **awning** is a piece of canvas or thick material, attached to a caravan, building, etc, which shelters people or things from the rain or the sun. EG *The shop was freshly painted, with a large green awning to protect the plate glass window... ...vegetables standing outside under a leaky canvas awning.*
N COUNT ⇑ shelter = canopy

awoke /əwəʊk/ is the past tense of **awake**.

awoken /əwəʊkəⁿn/ is the past participle of **awake**.

awry /əraɪ/. **1** If something is **awry**, it is not in its normal or proper position, or it is not tidily arranged. EG *His tie was awry.*
ADJ QUALIT : PRED = askew

2 If something goes **awry**, it does not happen in the way it had been planned and it goes wrong. EG *A nuclear test went awry when they underestimated the power of the explosion... A strike threw all the schedules awry.*
ADJ QUALIT : PRED

axe /æks/, **axes, axing, axed. 1** An **axe** is a tool used for cutting wood, for example for cutting down trees or for chopping logs. It consists of a rectangular metal blade, sharpened on one side and attached at the other side to the end of a handle. EG *One of them chopped through the planks with her axe.*
N COUNT

2 If you **have an axe to grind**, you have a particular belief or a desire to make something happen, which you keep telling people about in order to persuade them that you are right or that something must be done. EG *The group claimed that it had no axe to grind... ...evidence of the members of the council, who have no axe to grind.*
PHR : VB INFLECTS

3 If the government, an organization, or a company
V+O

axes something, it suddenly ends it completely or reduces it drastically, usually because there is not enough money for it. EG *The new chairman decided to axe parts of the group, in an attempt to return to profitability... After six months the project was axed by the government.* ▸ used as a noun. EG *...the Government spending axe.* ▸ N COUNT : USU SING + SUPP

axes. Axes is pronounced /æksɪz/ in sense 1 and /æksi:z/ in sense 2. **Axes** is 1 the plural of **axe**. 2 the plural of **axis**.

axiom /æksɪəm/, **axioms**. An **axiom** is a statement of an idea which people accept as being true, although it is not necessarily so. EG *It is an old axiom that the more people know a secret, the less of a secret it is likely to be.* N COUNT ⇑ principle = saying

axiomatic /æksɪəmætɪk/. If something is **axiomatic**, it seems to be very obvious and therefore does not need to be proved; a formal word. EG *It has come to be regarded as axiomatic that good nutrition must always imply eating expensively.* ADJ CLASSIF : USU PRED ⇑ obvious

axis /æksɪs/, **axes**. 1 An **axis** is an imaginary line along which something can be divided equally, or around which it moves evenly. EG *The island was approximately twelve miles long on its north-south axis... The earth's axis is tilted at an angle of about 23½... ...the strategic importance of identifying the two main axes of attack.* N COUNT

2 An **axis** of a graph is one of the two sides of a graph, on which a particular quantity or quality is measured. The two axes are often referred to as the X axis and the Y axis. EG *Temperature is on the Y axis.* N COUNT ⇑ side

axle /æksəˀl/, **axles**. An **axle** is a rod connecting a pair of wheels on a car or other vehicle, on which the wheels turn. N COUNT

aye /aɪ/, **ayes**; also spelled **ay**. 1 **Aye** means yes; used in some dialects of British English, especially in Scotland. EG *'It was awful cold.'–'Aye, it was.'* CONVENTION = yes

2 If you vote **aye**, you vote in favour of something. ▸ used also to refer to a person who votes **aye**. EG *...37 ayes and 15 noes.* ADV ▸ N COUNT

azure /æʒʊˀə, eɪ-/. Something that is **azure** is bright blue, like the colour of the sky on a sunny day; a literary word. EG *...the azure sky... His eyes were azure.* ▸ used as a noun. EG *...the pure azure of the sky.* ADJ COLOUR ▸ N UNCOUNT

Bb

B, b /bi:/, **Bs, b's**. 1 **B** is the second letter of the English alphabet. N COUNT

2 **B**, in music, is the seventh note in the scale of C major. N COUNT/UNCOUNT

3 If you get a **B** as a mark for a piece of work or in an exam, your work is considered to be fairly good. N COUNT/UNCOUNT

4 **b.** is an abbreviation for 'born' which is written in front of dates, for example on memorials or in books. EG *Henry Smith, b. 1821.*

5 **B** or **b** is also an abbreviation for other words beginning with B or b, such as 'black', 'bay', 'bowled', and 'book'.

BA /bi: eɪ/, **BAs**. **BA** is an abbreviation for 'Bachelor of Arts'; a first degree awarded by universities or polytechnics to people who have studied arts or social science subjects. EG *She took a B.A. in French.* ▸ used, especially after a person's name, to refer to someone who holds a BA degree. EG *I found out that she is a BA... ...Jonathan Adams B.A.* N COUNT ▸ N COUNT : ALSO IN TITLES AFTER NAMES ⇑ graduate

babble /bæbəˀl/, **babbles, babbling, babbled**. 1 If you **babble**, you talk in a confused or excited way, so that other people find it difficult to understand what you are saying. EG *He babbled on and on about old enemies... 'I feel perhaps-Her great age, you know,' babbled the vicar.* V : IF + PREP THEN *on/away*, OR V + QUOTE = gabble

2 When babies **babble**, they make meaningless sounds because they have not yet learned to say words. EG *Little Emma had been babbling away all morning.* V : IF + ADV, THEN *away/on*

3 When a stream **babbles**, it makes a low, bubbling sound, for example because it is flowing quickly over stones; a literary use. EG *As I slipped into sleep, the stream babbled softly.* V : USU + A = burble

4 **Babble** is talk which is confused or excited, or which you cannot hear properly, and which therefore does not make much sense. EG *I could hear the distant babble of women's voices.* N SING WITH DET = hubbub

babe /beɪb/, **babes**. 1 A **babe** is a baby; a rather old-fashioned use. EG *'Such a pretty babe,' said Mrs Morrison.* N COUNT

2 Some people say **babe** as an affectionate way of addressing their wife, husband, lover, etc; used especially in informal American English. EG *Do you want a lift, babe?... Take it easy, babe.* N VOC ⇑ woman = baby

3 If you say that someone is **a babe in arms**, you mean that they do not have the right experience, knowledge, or attitude to do what needs to be done. EG *He was a babe in arms when it came to verbal quarrels.* PHR : USED AS C ⇑ infant

babel /beɪbəˀl/. If there is a **babel** of noise or of voices, you hear a lot of people talking at the same time, so that you cannot understand what they are saying. EG *The hall filled with a babel of voices demanding money.* N SING WITH DET : USU + *of* ⇑ sound = babble

baboon /bəbu:n/, **baboons**. A **baboon** is a type of monkey that has a pointed face, large teeth, and a long tail. Baboons live in Africa. N COUNT

baby /beɪbi¹/, **babies**. 1 A **baby** is a very young child, usually one that has not yet started to walk or talk. EG *More and more women want to have their babies by natural childbirth... Your mum could go with your baby sister.* N COUNT = infant

2 If you describe an older child or an adult as a **baby**, you mean that they behave in a childish way, for example crying a lot when they are hurt or upset; used showing disapproval. EG *Don't be such a baby; it didn't hurt.* N COUNT : USU SING = wimp, coward

3 Some people say **baby** as an affectionate way of addressing their wife, husband, lover, etc; used especially in informal American English. N VOC = darling

4 You can use **baby** to describe something that is very small compared with other things of the same kind. EG *It was described as a thunderstorm, but was in fact a baby hurricane.* N BEFORE N = miniature

5 If you say that a project or plan is your **baby**, you mean that you have a special interest in it or responsibility for it, often because you first thought of it; used in informal English. N SING : POSS + N

6 If you **are left holding the baby**, you are placed in a situation in which you are responsible for something or in charge of it, often in an unfair way because other people failed to do something or refused to do it; an informal expression. PHR : VB INFLECTS

7 If you **throw the baby out with the bathwater**, you lose the good things as well as the bad things in something because you reject it completely instead of just removing the bad parts; an informal expression. EG *They turned against all of their traditional cultural values, flinging the baby out with the bathwater.* PHR : VB INFLECTS

baby buggy, baby buggies. A **baby buggy** is a small chair with wheels and handles, in which a baby or child can sit and be pushed around; used especially in American English. N COUNT = pushchair

babyhood /beɪbi¹hʊd/. Your **babyhood** is the period of your life when you were a baby. N UNCOUNT = infancy

babyish /beɪbi¹ɪʃ/. Something that is **babyish** is suitable for a baby, or has some of the characteristics of a baby. EG *Don't think that a picture book is too babyish... Bob said, 'Thank you, ma'am' in his soft babyish voice.* ADJ QUALIT ⇑ infantile = young

baby-minder, baby-minders; also spelled without a hyphen. A **baby-minder** is a woman who takes babies into her own home and looks after them while their parents are working. N COUNT ⇑ person = childminder

baby-sit, baby-sits, baby-sitting, baby-sat; also spelled without a hyphen. If you **baby-sit** for someone, you look after their children while they are out. EG *Young students will occasionally baby-sit in the evenings.* ◊ **baby-sitting**. EG *Grandmother helps with washing, cleaning and baby-sitting.*
V
◊ N UNCOUNT

baby-sitter, baby-sitters; also spelled without a hyphen. A **baby-sitter** is a person who goes to someone else's home to look after their children while they go out. EG *Can't you find a baby-sitter and come over for dinner?*
N COUNT

baby talk; also spelled with a hyphen. **Baby talk** is the language used by babies when they are just learning to speak, or the way in which some adults speak when they are talking to babies. EG *The songs and the baby-talk had been a secret between Andy and his foster-mother.*
N UNCOUNT
= prattle

bacchanalian /bækəneɪlɪən/. A **bacchanalian** party is one at which people drink a lot of alcohol and behave in an extremely uncontrolled way, often involving sexual activity; a literary word. EG *...a night of bacchanalian revelry.*
ADJ QUALIT : ATTRIB
= riotous

bachelor /bætʃᵊlə/, **bachelors**. A **bachelor** is a man who has never been married. EG *A surprising number of men stay bachelors.*
N COUNT

Bachelor of Arts, Bachelors of Arts. A **Bachelor of Arts** is a person with a first degree from a university or polytechnic, usually in an arts or social science subject.
N COUNT
⇑ graduate
= BA

Bachelor of Science, Bachelors of Science. A **Bachelor of Science** is a person with a first degree from a university or polytechnic in a science subject.
N COUNT
⇑ graduate
= B.Sc.

bachelor's degree, bachelor's degrees. A **bachelor's degree** is a first degree, such as a BA or a BSc.
N COUNT

back /bæk/, **backs, backing, backed**. Paragraphs 1 to 15 explain **back** when it is used as an adverb, paragraphs 16 to 28 explain **back** when it is used as a noun or adjective, and paragraphs 29 to 36 explain **back** when it is used as a verb. **1** You can use **back** to describe the movement of someone or something **1.1** when they move in the opposite direction to the one they are facing or in which they were moving before. EG *She moved back a little towards the window... The child stepped back nervously... She pushed back her chair... Her head jerked back.* **1.2** when they return to or move towards a place that they have just come from or where they have been before. EG *I went back to the kitchen... ...when she came back into the room... Most of them will come back again... They'll be travelling to Mars and back... She turned and went back down the lane... ...driving back from Southampton. Helen is back... I'll be back in five minutes.*
1.1 ADV AFTER VB
= backwards
≠ forwards
1.2 ADV AFTER VB
⇑ here

2 You can use **back** to describe the position of someone or something **2.1** when someone or something is situated, kept, or stands at a distance away from a particular place, especially a place where something is happening. EG *Police struggled to keep the crowd back... Stand back from the edge of the platform... The house is set back from the road behind a green lawn.* **2.2** when something such as hair, clothing, or a curtain is tied or held so that it is not hanging loosely or is not covering something else. EG *She pushed the tangled hair back from her face.*
2.1 ADV AFTER VB
2.2 ADV AFTER VB

3 If you lie or sit **back**, you move into a relaxed position and lie with your face pointing upwards or sit with the upper part of your body leaning away from the direction you are facing. EG *I lay back in the grass and looked up at the sun... He sat back, sighed, and waited.*
ADV AFTER VB

4 If you look or shout **back** at something or someone, they are behind you and you turn round to look or shout at them. EG *Charlie kept glancing back.*
ADV AFTER VB

5 You can use **back** to indicate that someone or something is in a state or situation in which they were before, after not being in it for a while. EG *He went back to sleep without a murmur... All the politicians are back at work... I was hoping that things would soon get back to normal.*
ADV AFTER VB, OR BEFORE PREP

6 If you get, take, or have something **back**, you have it again after someone else had it for a while. If you put something **back**, you put it where it was before. EG *He asked for his deposit back... You'll get the money back with interest... She put it back on the shelf... I grabbed the glasses back... They wanted their children back.*
ADV AFTER VB : V +O+ADV

7 If something goes or stretches **back** to a particular time, it has existed from that time until the present. EG *...a legal doctrine that goes back to the fifteenth century... I have the family records back to the Civil War.*
ADV AFTER VB, OR BEFORE PREP

8 If something happened a year **back**, it happened a year before the present time. EG *...ten years back.*
ADV : USU NUM + ADV

9 If you say that something happened **back** in a particular period of time, you mean that it happened a long time ago or you are trying to make it seem a long time ago, for example because it was unpleasant or embarrassing. EG *I invested in the company way back in 1971... ...the anguish and depression he had gone through back in November.*
ADV + *in*

10 If you think or go **back** to something in the past, you remember it or try to remember it. EG *'What was the book called?' Mrs Oliver said, casting her mind back.*
ADV AFTER VB

11 You can use **back** in conversation or writing to introduce a situation or event that is happening at the same time as the one you were talking about previously, but is happening in another place. EG *Back in the Central Lobby, people were getting restless... Meanwhile back in London, Caro was working on a new sculpture.*
ADV BEFORE PREP
≠ here

12 If you go or come **back** to a particular subject or point in a conversation, you mention or discuss it again. EG *Let me go back for a moment to what you think are the main causes of the problem... I'd like to come back to this later.*
ADV AFTER VB : USU BEFORE PREP *(to)*

13 You can use **back** with words that describe writing, telephoning, speaking, or looking to indicate that someone replies or reacts to what someone else has done by performing a similar action. EG *I shall make some enquiries and call you back... The secretary wrote back and said, 'So sorry you didn't enjoy your meal.'... He looked at her with raised eyebrows, and the girl stared back.*
ADV AFTER VB

14 If you say that something is **back**, you mean that it is fashionable again after it has been unfashionable for a time. EG *Mini skirts are back... Hats are coming back into fashion.*
ADJ CLASSIF : PRED, OR ADV AFTER VB
⇑ in
≠ out

15 If someone or something moves **back and forth**, they move first in one direction and then in the opposite direction. EG *Someone was pacing back and forth behind the curtains... His eyes dart back and forth wildly... The sky becomes filled with birds wheeling back and forth.*
PHR : USED AS AN A
= to and fro

16 Your **back** is the part of your body from your neck to the top of your legs which is behind you and that you cannot easily see. EG *We lay on our backs under the ash tree... She tapped him on the back... I felt his eyes upon my back as I left the room.*
N COUNT : USU WITH POSS OR *the* +N IN SING
≠ front

17 The **back** of an animal or a fish is the part of its body which is on the top, opposite its legs or belly. EG *He placed the saddle gently over the horse's back... We could see some long fish with grey backs and white bellies.*
N COUNT : USU SING+SUPP

18 The **back** of an object is the side of it that people do not normally see or do not normally use. EG *She wiped her lips with the back of her hand... Pin your food list on the back of the larder door... Scrape it off with the back of a knife... He tucked the back of his shirt down into his trousers.*
N COUNT : USU *the*+N IN SING+ SUPP
≠ front

19 The **back** of a building, room, or container is **19.1** the inside part that is farthest from the main entrance or the front. EG *He went to the small counter at the back of the store... Keep some long-life milk at the back of your refrigerator.* **19.2** the outside part of it that is farthest from the front, or the area behind it. EG *They trooped down some steps at the back of the building to a side street.* ▸ used as an adjective. EG *The back door opens, and there is Myra... ...back gardens.* ● You can say **out the back** or **round the back** when you are talking about the area behind a house or other building; an informal expression. EG *...the dreadful view out the back over the canal... The dustbins are round the back.*
19.1 N COUNT : USU *the*+N IN SING+ SUPP
= rear
19.2 N COUNT : USU *the*+N IN SING+ SUPP
▸ ADJ CLASSIF : ATTRIB
● PHR : USED AS AN A

20 The **back** of a car, lorry, or other vehicle is the part behind the driver's seat, for example part of the inside with seats for passengers or a section for carrying luggage and goods, or part of the outside. EG *There was a woman at the wheel and about eight children in the back... We filled the back of the car with wood... She comes up to the van, and opens the back.* ▸ used as an
N COUNT : USU *the*+N IN SING+ SUPP
≠ front
▸ ADJ CLASSIF :

adjective. EG *...the back wheels... ...a suitcase on the back seat.* ATTRIB = rear ≠ front

21 The **back** of a piece of paper or of an envelope is the side that is less important, for example because it has no writing or pictures on it, or has information which begins on the other side. EG *Sign the declaration on the back of the prescription form... ...shopping lists written on the backs of envelopes.* N COUNT : USU *the*+N IN SING+SUPP ≠ front

22 The **back** of a chair is the part that you lean against when you are sitting on it. EG *She sat with an arm on the back of the couch... ...three chairs with higher backs.* N COUNT+SUPP

23 The **back** of a book is the part nearest the end. Reference books often have indexes or notes at the back. EG *She tore several sheets of paper out of the back of the book... Send in the blue page at the back of your order book.* ▸ used as an adjective. EG *...the back pages of the book.* N COUNT : USU *the*+N IN SING+SUPP ≠ beginning ▸ ADJ CLASSIF : ATTRIB

24 The **back** of a crowd or group of people means the people who are farthest away from where the action is taking place. EG *...the ones at the back of the crowd who were not seen at all.* N COUNT : USU *the*+N IN SING+SUPP

25 In football or hockey, a **back** is a player who is concerned mainly with preventing the other team from scoring goals, rather than with scoring goals for his or her own team. N COUNT : USU MOD+N = defender

26 A **back** road or street is small and quiet, with very little traffic. EG *...driving through back streets towards the outskirts of town... She lived near the main shopping district in a back lane.* ADJ CLASSIF : ATTRIB ≠ main

27 The **back** legs of an animal are the legs by its tail and farthest from its head. EG *The horse reared up on his back legs.* ADJ CLASSIF : ATTRIB = hind

28 The noun **back** is also used in the following expressions. **28.1** If you describe a place as **the back of beyond**, you mean that it is very lonely and isolated, and a long way from any towns or cities; an informal expression. EG *We found ourselves in the back of beyond.* PHR : USED AS O = the sticks **28.2** If you are wearing something **back to front**, you are wearing it incorrectly, with the back of it on the front of your body. EG *You've got your jumper on back to front.* PHR : USED AS C/A **28.3** If you do or say something **behind** someone's **back**, you do or say it without them knowing about it, often in a deceitful or nasty way. EG *People used to laugh at him–discreetly and behind his back.* PHR : USED AS AN A, N INFLECTS ≠ openly **28.4** If you **break** your **back** to do or get something, you work very hard to do it or get it. EG *...knowledge and possessions they have broken their backs to obtain.* PHR : VB AND N INFLECT **28.5** If you **have broken the back of** a job, you have done most of it, including the important or difficult parts. EG *We expect to have broken the back of the job by next July.* PHR : VB INFLECTS **28.6** If someone **gets off** your **back**, they stop criticizing, nagging, or putting pressure on you; an informal expression. EG *Just get off my back, will you?... I wish I could get him off my back.* PHR : VB AND N INFLECT **28.7** If you **have** your **back to the wall**, you have very great problems, which you may not be able to overcome. EG *They were fighting with their backs to the wall.* PHR : VB AND N INFLECT **28.8** If you are **living off the backs of** other people, you are exploiting them. EG *Developed countries, in effect, live off the backs of the Third World.* PHR : VB AND N INFLECT ⇑ exploit **28.9** If you are **on** your **back**, you are so ill, weak, or badly injured that you cannot get out of bed and move around on your own. EG *She was on her back for about three months after the accident.* PHR : USED AS AN A, N INFLECTS ⇑ bedridden **28.10** If you **put** your **back into** something, you work hard at it physically, using a lot of effort. PHR : VB AND N INFLECT **28.11** If you **put** someone's **back up**, you say or do something that makes them feel annoyed; an informal expression. PHR : VB AND N INFLECT **28.12** If you say that you will **scratch** someone's **back** if they scratch yours, you mean that you will do something to help them or as a favour for them, if they agree to do something to help you; an informal expression. PHR : VB AND N INFLECT **28.13** If you say that you will be pleased to **see the back of** someone, you mean that you want them to go away and leave you alone. EG *I'll be glad to see the back of him.* PHR : VB INFLECTS **28.14** If you **turn** your **back**, you turn round so that you are facing away from someone or something. EG *He turned his back and started rattling his pots.* PHR : VB AND N INFLECT ⇑ face **28.15** If you **turn** your **back on** someone or something, you ignore them or refuse to help or support them. EG *We have turned our backs on the very principles we were elected to uphold.* PHR : VB AND N INFLECT

29 If a building **backs** onto something, the back or rear of it faces in that direction. EG *The gardens and the houses backing onto them looked neat and cheerful.* V+A *(onto)* ≠ face

30 When a car **backs** or when you **back** a car, it moves backwards for a little way. EG *She backed out of the driveway, and drove to the university... As I backed into the space, somebody else nipped in behind me.* V-ERG : USU+A = reverse

31 If you **back** someone into a particular place or in a particular direction, you make them walk backwards in that direction. EG *He kissed her cheek, and backed her into the corner.* V+O+A ⇑ propel

32 If someone or something **is backed** by a person or organization, they are given support or help by them, especially financial help. EG *The organization is backed by the U.N. and the Soviet Union... A spokesman said last night that the union would be backing Mr Healey... The rulers of these countries were backed by powerful military support.* V+O

33 In gambling, if you **back** a particular person, team, or horse in a race or competition, you bet money on them, so that you win money if they win the race or competition. EG *I managed to back the winner for once.* V+O

34 If something **is backed** with a particular material, a layer of that material is put onto the back of it in order to strengthen or protect it. EG *This curtain lining is aluminium-backed.* V+O : USU PASS, IF+PREP THEN *with*

35 If rock or pop musicians or singers **back** a particular singer, they provide music or singing as an accompaniment for him or her. EG *He's always backed by the same group.* V+O ⇑ accompany

36 If the wind **backs**, the direction in which it is blowing changes in an anticlockwise manner, for example it blows from the east after blowing from the south; a nautical or technical term. V ≠ veer

37 See also **backing**.

back away. If you **back away** from someone or something, you walk slowly backwards and away from them, especially because you are nervous or frightened. EG *The waitress, having put the tray down, rose and backed away... Mrs Bixby put a hand up to her mouth and started backing away.* PHRASAL VB : V+ADV ⇑ retreat

back down. If you **back down** on a demand or claim that you made earlier, you withdraw it. EG *They refused to back down... Eventually he backed down on the question of seating.* PHRASAL VB : V+ADV ⇑ reconsider

back off. If you **back off** from someone or something, you move away from them and leave them alone. EG *Brody was ready for a fight, but he backed off.* PHRASAL VB : V+ADV = withdraw

back out. If you **back out** of something that you had previously agreed to do, you decide not to do it. EG *Everything was set up. Then, mysteriously, he backed out.* PHRASAL VB : V+ADV = pull out

back up. **1** If you **back up** a claim or story, you supply evidence to prove it is true. EG *This claim is backed up by the fact that every year more and more money is being spent on arms... He backed this up with a few horrifying anecdotes.* PHRASAL VB : V+O+ADV = support ≠ refute

2 To **back** someone **up** means **2.1** to give them help and support when they are in a difficult situation. EG *We need the economic resources to back up our social commitments.* PHRASAL VB : V+O+ADV **2.2** to confirm that what they are saying is true, sometimes even when you know that it is not. EG *He said he'd been with her all evening, and she backed him up.* PHRASAL VB : V+O+ADV = support ≠ contradict

3 If you **back up**, **3.1** the lorry, car, or other vehicle you are driving moves backwards a little way. EG *I backed up three hundred yards to the station entrance.* PHRASAL VB : V+ADV = reverse **3.2** you walk backwards a little way. EG *She backed up a few steps, then ran at the water.* PHRASAL VB : V+ADV = retreat

4 See also **back-up**.

backache /bækeɪk/ is a dull pain in your back. N UNCOUNT

backbench /bækbentʃ/, **backbenches**; also spelled with a hyphen. The **backbenches** refers to the Members of Parliament who are not ministers in the government and who do not hold an official position in an opposition party: compare **front bench**. EG *A rumble of discontent is spreading from the backbenches to the leadership of his party. The bill got the support of several Labour backbench MPs.* N COUNT : *the*+N, OR N BEFORE N ≠ front bench

backbencher /bækbentʃə/, **backbenchers**; also spelled with a hyphen. A **backbencher** is a Member of Parliament who is not a minister in the government and who does not hold an official position in an N COUNT ⇑ MP opposition party. EG *He has always been popular among Conservative backbenchers.*

backbiting /bækbaɪtɪŋ/; also spelled with a hyphen. **Backbiting** is the saying of unpleasant or unkind things about someone who is not present. N UNCOUNT ⇑ gossip

backbone /bækbəʊn/, **backbones**. **1** The **backbone** of a person or animal is the column of small linked bones along the middle of their back. N COUNT = spine

2 The **backbone** of something such as an organization or system is the part of it that gives it its main strength or unity. EG *Business people are the backbone of the nation... The novel has a single narrative as its backbone.* N SING WITH DET +SUPP

3 If someone has **backbone**, they have the courage to do things which involve danger or risks. EG *I don't have the backbone to do it.* N UNCOUNT : USU +BROAD NEG OR SUPP

back-breaking; also spelled as one word. **Back-breaking** work involves a lot of hard physical effort. EG *...the back-breaking work of painting these ceilings.* ADJ QUALIT ≠ easy

backchat /bæktʃæt/; also spelled with a hyphen. **Backchat** is a series of slightly rude or cheeky remarks that you make in reply to someone, especially someone in authority such as your teacher or employer; an informal word used in British English. N UNCOUNT = cheek, sauce

backcloth /bækklɒθ/, **backcloths**; also spelled with a hyphen. **1** A **backcloth** is a large piece of cloth, often with scenery or buildings painted on it, that is hung at the back of a stage while a play is being performed; used mainly in British English. N COUNT ⇑ cloth = backdrop

2 The **backcloth** to an event is the general situation in which it happens; used in British English. EG *The events stood out against a backcloth of industrial unrest in Britain.* N SING WITH DET +SUPP = backdrop

back-comb /bækkəʊm/, **back-combs, back-combing, back-combed**. If you **back-comb** your hair, you move a comb through your hair towards your scalp instead of away from it, so that your hair looks thicker. V+O ⇑ comb

back copy, back copies. A **back copy** of a magazine or newspaper is an edition of it that was published some time ago and is not the most recent one. N COUNT+SUPP = back number

backdate /bækdeɪt/, **backdates, backdating, backdated**. If an arrangement or document **is backdated**, it is considered to be valid from a date before the date when it is completed or signed. EG *The pay rise is 4 per cent, backdated to January.* V+O : USU PASS ⇑ date ≠ postdate

backdoor /bækdɔː/; also spelled with a hyphen. **Backdoor** is used to describe something that is done or achieved in a secret, indirect, or dishonest way; used showing disapproval. EG *...charges of backdoor nationalization... He was using backdoor methods.* ADJ CLASSIF : ATTRIB = underhand ≠ overt

backdrop /bækdrɒp/, **backdrops**. **1** A **backdrop** is a large piece of cloth, often with scenery or buildings painted on it, that is hung at the back of a stage while a play is being performed; used mainly in American English. N COUNT = backcloth

2 You can use **backdrop** to refer to something such as a row of hills or trees that is seen behind a place. EG *...the steep hills that form a backdrop to the city.* N SING WITH DET : USU+SUPP = background

-backed is added to nouns and adjectives to form adjectives that indicate the material that something such as a piece of furniture is covered with, or the shape of the part of it that you lean on. EG *...a velvet-backed couch... ...a high-backed chair.* COMB : FORMS ADJS

backer /bækə/, **backers**. A **backer** is someone who gives support and often financial help to a person or project. EG *...the party's chief financial backers.* N COUNT ⇑ supporter

backfire /bækfaɪə/, **backfires, backfiring, backfired**. **1** If something such as a plan or project **backfires**, it has the opposite effect or result to the one you had intended. V ⇑ go wrong

2 When a motor vehicle or its engine **backfires**, it produces a loud noise that sounds like an explosion in the exhaust pipe because of a fault in the engine. V

backgammon /bækgæmən/ is a game played by two people in which you throw dice and move round playing pieces around a board marked with long triangles. N UNCOUNT

background /bækgraʊnd/, **backgrounds**. **1** Your **background** is the kind of family you come from, for example rich or poor, the kind of education you have had, the things you have done, etc. EG *We looked pretty closely into her background... ...people from working-class backgrounds... ...Monty's family background.* N COUNT+SUPP ⇑ history = environment

2 The **background** to an important event or situation consists of the facts that help to explain what caused it, why it happened in a particular way or at a particular time, etc. EG *...the economic background to the present political crisis... ...against a background of poor housing conditions.* ▸ used as an adjective. EG *...background information.* N SING WITH DET +SUPP ⇑ setting ▸ N BEFORE N

3 You can use **background** to refer to **3.1** things or people that you can see behind the main things or people in a picture or scene. EG *In the background is a tall cypress tree... ...a group of people silhouetted against a background of leaping flames.* ● Someone who is **in the background** has an unimportant role or job and is not given much attention. EG *He does keep himself very much in the background.* **3.2** sounds, for example music, which you can hear but which you are not listening to with your full attention. EG *The TV set was blaring in the background... They made husky conversation against a background of violin music.* ▸ used as an adjective. EG *...background music.* N SING WITH DET ≠ foreground ● PHR : USED AS AN A N SING WITH DET ▸ N BEFORE N

4 The **background** of a design or picture is the colour or pattern onto which the design or picture is painted or printed. You can see the background between the parts of the design or picture. EG *...blue flowers on a grey background.* N COUNT : USU SING+SUPP

backhand /bækhænd/, **backhands**. **1** A **backhand** is a shot or stroke in tennis, squash, etc, that you make with your arm across your body and the back of your hand facing the direction in which you are hitting the ball. EG *...a backhand return... I can't do backhands.* N COUNT

2 In tennis, squash, etc, your **backhand** is your left side if you normally hold your racket in your right hand. EG *I served to her backhand.* N COUNT : POSS+ N IN SING

backhanded /bækhændɪ²d/; also spelled with a hyphen. **1** A **backhanded** shot or blow is one that you do with the back of your hand facing in the direction in which you are hitting. EG *...a backhanded slap.* ADJ CLASSIF : USU ATTRIB

2 A **backhanded** compliment or remark is one that seems to express admiration but that could also be an insult. ADJ QUALIT : USU ATTRIB ⇑ ambiguous

backhander /bækhændə/, **backhanders**; also spelled with a hyphen. A **backhander** is **1** a small bribe; used in informal English. EG *She had to pay the backhander which bank officials invariably demanded.* **2** a comment that is in fact an insult or criticism although it may appear not to be. N COUNT N COUNT ⇑ remark

backing /bækɪŋ/, **backings**. **1** If someone or something has the **backing** of an institution, group, or important person, **1.1** they receive approval, support, and help from them. EG *He had the whole-hearted backing of the armed forces... The bid has the backing of the directors... ...secret Government backing.* **1.2** they are given money by them in order to be able to achieve something. EG *They refused all financial backing... Watson produced the backing needed to build a Mark Two model.* N UNCOUNT+ SUPP = aid N UNCOUNT = funding

2 A **backing** is a layer of something, for example cloth, that is put onto the back of something in order to strengthen or protect it. N COUNT/ UNCOUNT

3 In a performance or recording of a popular song, the **backing** is the music which is sung or played to accompany the main tune. EG *His band produce a beautifully soothing backing... ...a backing group.* N SING WITH DET ⇑ accompaniment

back issue, back issues. A **back issue** of a magazine or newspaper is the same as a back number. N COUNT

backlash /bæklæʃ/. A **backlash** is a sudden strong reaction against a tendency or recent development in society or politics. EG *...a backlash against the Thatcher government... ...the backlash of intolerance.* N SING WITH DET = revolt

backless /bæklɪ²s/. A **backless** dress leaves most of a woman's back uncovered down to her waist. ADJ CLASSIF

backlog /bæklɒg/, **backlogs**. A **backlog** is a large amount of something or a large number of things that have accumulated over a period of time and must now be dealt with or looked at. EG *There is a large backlog of cases to hear... ...the backlog of demand for housing.* N COUNT : USU SING+PREP *(of)* ⇑ accumulation = build up

back number, back numbers. A **back number** of a magazine or newspaper is an edition of it that was published some time ago and is not the most recent one. EG *...back numbers of the American Bee Journal.* N COUNT = back copy, back issue

backpack /bækpæk/, **backpacks**; also spelled with a hyphen. A **backpack** is a container like a large bag that you carry on your back; used mainly in American English. N COUNT = rucksack

back passage, back passages. You can use **back passage** as a polite way of referring to your rectum. N COUNT

back pay is money which an employer owes an employee for work which he or she did in the past. EG *I should get two months' back pay this month.* N UNCOUNT

back-pedal /bækpɛdəºl/, **back-pedals, back-pedalling, back-pedalled**; also spelled **back-pedaling, back-pedaled** in American English. If you **back-pedal**, 1 you express a different or less forceful opinion about something from the one that you had previously expressed. V ↑ change = backtrack 2 you do something different from what you were going to do, or do it more slowly or reluctantly. V ↑ change = backtrack

backroom boy, backroom boys. The **backroom boys** in an organization or activity are the people in it who do important work but are often not seen or known about by the public, for example because the work is secret, is presented to the public by other people, or is done some time beforehand. N COUNT : USU PL ↑ worker

back-seat driver, back-seat drivers. A **back-seat driver** is a person, for example a passenger in a car, who repeatedly gives advice without being asked for it. N COUNT

backside /bæksaɪd/, **backsides**; an informal word. Your **backside** is the part of your body that you sit on. EG *He landed on his backside.* N COUNT : USU POSS+N ● If someone **sits on** their **backside**, they are lazy and try to avoid doing any work; used showing disapproval. EG *He was content to sit on his backside and do as little as possible.* ● PHR : VB INFLECTS ↑ idle = sit around

backsliding /bækslaɪdɪŋ/; also spelled with a hyphen. **Backsliding** means failing to do something that you agreed or promised to do, especially starting to do something bad again after you had stopped doing it. EG *She had, despite the occasional backsliding in training, successfully competed in the Championships... ...no backsliding into nationalist tendencies.* N UNCOUNT ↑ regression

backstage /bæksteɪdʒ/; also spelled with a hyphen and as two words. 1 In a theatre, **backstage** refers to the areas behind or beside the stage, and the dressing rooms and other areas used by the performers. EG *After the performance he went backstage to greet the great man.* N UNCOUNT, OR ADV AFTER VB ▸ used as an adjective. EG *...backstage bickering.* ▸ ADJ CLASSIF : ATTRIB

2 You can use **backstage** to indicate that something happens in private or in secret, although it may often be connected with other things that are happening in public. EG *Are there any developments backstage?* N UNCOUNT = behind the scenes ▸ used as an adjective. EG *...backstage negotiations.* ▸ ADJ CLASSIF : ATTRIB

back street, back streets. 1 The **back streets** of a town or city are the areas of smaller, poorer, and older streets with houses and small shops, rather than the main roads with grand buildings, shopping centres, large office blocks, etc. EG *...across the town, through back-streets of old, wooden dwellings... ...a little back-street store.* N COUNT : USU PL

2 **Back-street** activities are carried out unofficially, secretly, and often illegally, for example by people without professional qualifications. EG *Women relied on back-street abortions.* ADJ CLASSIF : ATTRIB ↑ illegal ▸ used of people involved in such activities. EG *...a back-street lawyer gave him some forged papers.*

backstroke /bækstrəʊk/ is a way of swimming in which you lie on your back, kick your legs, and move your arms back over your head. EG *I've never been able to do backstroke... She won the backstroke last year.* N UNCOUNT/N SING WITH DET

backtrack /bæktræk/, **backtracks, backtracking, backtracked**; also spelled with a hyphen. If you **backtrack**, 1 you go back along a path or route you have just used, for example to find something that you have lost. V ↑ return 2 you say that you did not really mean what you have just said. V = back-pedal

back-up; also spelled as one word. 1 **Back-up** is help or support from people or machines, without which you would not be able to achieve what you want. EG *...the tremendous computer back-up which each mission required... ...a vast back-up team.* N UNCOUNT ↑ support = reinforcement

2 If you have a second piece of equipment, set of plans, etc as **back-up**, you have arranged for them to be available for use in case the first one is unsuccessful or unsatisfactory in any way. EG *You can use a conventional heating system as back-up... ...back-up plans.* N UNCOUNT ↑ alternative = stand-by

backward /bækwəd/. 1 **Backward** movements are done with your back facing in the direction you are moving. EG *She took a backward step.* ADJ CLASSIF : ATTRIB ≠ forward

2 A **backward** gesture or look is made in the direction that is behind you and away from you. EG *Without a word or a backward glance, he walked away... ...a backward jerk of my head.* ● See also **backwards**. ADJ CLASSIF : ATTRIB ≠ forward

3 A country or society that is **backward** does not have a lot of modern industries and machines; often used showing disapproval. EG *...the backward nomadic hunting societies.* ADJ QUALIT = primitive ≠ developed ◊ **backwardness**. EG *Their inferior economic situation and backwardness were the result of centuries of misrule.* ◊ N UNCOUNT ≠ modernity

4 A child who is **backward** does not make normal progress in learning and mental development compared to other children of a similar age. EG *We are sorry to tell you that your son is backward.* ADJ QUALIT = retarded ◊ **backwardness**. EG *These symptoms lead to backwardness at school.* ◊ N UNCOUNT

backward-looking attitudes, ideas, or actions are based on old-fashioned opinions or methods; used showing disapproval. EG *...their traditional, backward-looking suspicion of gadgets. ...inefficiency, stupidity, backward-looking notions.* ADJ QUALIT ≠ forward-looking, progressive

backwards /bækwədz/. The form **backward** is also used in American English. 1 If you move **backwards**, you move with your back facing in the direction you are moving. EG *The hummingbird can fly backwards... Brody stepped backward.* ADV AFTER VB ≠ forward

2 You can use **backwards** 2.1 to indicate that something moves in the direction that is behind you and away from you. EG *I stretched my arm backwards.* ADV AFTER VB ≠ forward

2.2 to indicate that someone or something is looking or facing behind them, away from the front. EG *...glancing backward at the lady with the bags.* ADV AFTER VB ≠ forward 2.3 to indicate that something changes or develops in a way that is not an improvement, but is a return to old ideas or methods. EG *This is a step backwards technologically.* ADV AFTER VB/NG ↑ regression ≠ forwards

3 If you go or look **backwards** in time, you consider or become aware of situations or events that existed or happened in the past or before others. EG *Twenty-eight years? Looking backwards, that takes us to the end of World War Two.* ADV AFTER VB/NG = back

4 If something is done **backwards**, it is done in the opposite way to the usual or correct way. EG *Listen to the tape played backwards... But in fact of course you're always working backwards.* ADV AFTER VB = in reverse

5 **Backwards** is also used in the following expressions. 5.1 If someone or something moves **backwards and forwards**, they move repeatedly first in one direction and then in the opposite direction. EG *He ran backwards and forwards along the cliff... The wipers move backwards and forwards in front of them.* PHR : USED AS AN A = to and fro, back and forth 5.2 If you **know** something **backwards**, you know it very well. EG *They know the whole tale backwards... He knew their history backwards.* PHR : VB INFLECTS 5.3 to **bend over backwards**: see **bend**.

backwash /bækwɒʃ/; also spelled with a hyphen. 1 The **backwash** of a boat is the wave that spreads behind it on either side as it moves along. N SING : *the*+N = wake

2 The **backwash** of an event or situation is the situation, usually unpleasant, that exists after it and as a result of it. EG *...food shortages in the backwash of the war.* N SING WITH DET, USU+SUPP = aftermath

backwater /bækwɔːtə/, **backwaters**. A **backwater** is a place or an institution that is isolated from modern ideas or influences and from the main events that are happening in the world; often used showing disapproval. EG *...a cultural backwater.* N COUNT : USU SING

backwoods /bækwʊdz/. Someone who lives in the **backwoods** lives in a place in the countryside that is a long way from large towns and is isolated from modern life and modern ideas. EG *With television, even peasants in the backwoods could be in touch with world events... ...this tiny backwoods community.* N PLURAL : USU *in*+*the*+N, OR N BEFORE N

back yard, back yards; also spelled with a hyphen or as one word. A **back yard** is 1 in British English, a small area of ground behind a house or other building, usually with a concrete surface and with a wall round it. N COUNT ↑ yard 2 in American English, a N COUNT garden or small area of ground behind a house. EG *We all sat on the grass in the back yard.*

bacon /beɪkən/. 1 **Bacon** is meat which has been taken from the back or sides of a pig and salted and sometimes also smoked. EG *...bacon and eggs... ...a rasher of bacon.* N UNCOUNT

2 If someone or something **saves** your **bacon**, they get you out of a dangerous or difficult situation; used in informal British English. PHR : VB INFLECTS ⇑ rescue

3 **bring home the bacon.** 3.1 The person in a family who **brings home the bacon** provides the family with money, food, and other necessary things; used in informal English. EG *Who's going to bring home the bacon if you quit your job?* PHR : VB INFLECTS ⇑ provide 3.2 If you **bring home the bacon**, you achieve what you wanted to achieve; used in informal English. PHR : VB INFLECTS ⇑ succeed

bacteria /bæktɪərɪə/ are very small organisms which live in air, water, soil, plants, and animals. Some bacteria can cause disease. EG *Bacteria break up decaying vegetation.* N PLURAL

bacterial /bæktɪərɪəl/. Something that is **bacterial** relates to or is caused by bacteria. EG *...bacterial infection.* ADJ CLASSIF

bacteriology /bæktɪərɪɒlədʒi¹/ is the science and study of bacteria. ◇ **bacteriologist, bacteriologists**. ◇ **bacteriological**. EG *...bacteriological warfare.* N UNCOUNT ◇ N COUNT ◇ ADJ CLASSIF

bacterium /bæktɪərɪə⁴m/ is the singular of **bacteria**.

bad /bæd/, **worse, worst**. 1 Something that is **bad** is 1.1 unpleasant, harmful, undesirable, or likely to involve difficulties or problems. EG *I have some very bad news... He was a bad influence... Candy is bad for your teeth... 'It looks bad,' he said. 'The infection is spreading.'* ADJ QUALIT ≠ good 1.2 severe or unpleasant to a great amount or degree. EG *Is the pain bad?... The weather was bad... The traffic was bad in Watford.* ADJ QUALIT ≠ slight, mild ◇ **badly**. EG *The house was badly damaged.* ◇ ADV 1.3 of an unacceptably low standard or quality. EG *Her handwriting is bad... ...bad roads... His flat is in bad condition... ...bad management.* ADJ QUALIT = poor ≠ good ◇ **badly**. EG *It was badly organized... The party did badly in the election.* ◇ ADV WITH VB 1.4 lower in quantity or amount than is acceptable or suitable. EG *The light's bad... Many people were leaving because the pay was so bad.* ADJ QUALIT poor ◇ **badly**. EG *The room was so badly lit I couldn't see what I was doing.* ◇ ADV WITH VB

2 The **bad** is used to refer to things or people that are bad. EG *The bad or good that came out of it was at least human bad and good.* N SING : the+N

3 Someone who is **bad** is considered to be evil, wicked, or morally unacceptable. EG *There are always bad people around who will take advantage of other people's ignorance.* ▸ used of behaviour. EG *He gave up his bad ways.* ADJ QUALIT ≠ good

4 Someone who is **bad** at doing something 4.1 is not very skilful or successful at it. EG *I was bad at sports... ...a bad actor... I've always been terribly bad at language learning.* ADJ QUALIT = useless 4.2 fails to do it regularly or when they should do it. EG *Students are very bad at turning up for lectures.* ADJ QUALIT : PRED+*at*

5 A substance, especially food, that has gone **bad** is unsuitable to eat, drink, or use because it is too old and has started to decay. EG *The milk's gone bad.* ADJ CLASSIF = off, stale ≠ fresh

6 If you have a **bad** leg, heart, eye, etc, it is weak, painful, injured, or affected by disease. EG *The wooden bed was good for my bad back... You'd better not have one if your liver's bad.* ADJ CLASSIF

7 If you tell a child or animal that they are a **bad** boy, dog, etc, you mean that they are naughty and disobedient. EG *You are a bad girl!* ADJ QUALIT : ATTRIB

8 **Bad** language contains a lot of unacceptable and offensive words such as swear words. ADJ QUALIT = foul

9 You can describe someone's mood, temper, or behaviour as **bad** when you think that they are unreasonable or unacceptable. EG *She's in one of her bad moods... ...a final spasm of bad temper... The children were tired and bad-tempered... ...bad-mannered oafs... It is bad manners to point.* ADJ QUALIT ≠ good

10 You can use **bad** after a negative, especially 'not', to indicate, sometimes reluctantly or with surprise, that something is quite good, acceptable, or successful. EG *It was an awful job, but the money wasn't bad... He is selling them for £125; not a bad price at all... Not bad for a beginner.* ADJ CLASSIF : WITH BROAD NEG ◇ **badly**. EG *He certainly hadn't done badly on the deal... So far, things haven't gone too badly.* ◇ ADV WITH VB : WITH BROAD NEG

11 If you **feel bad** about something that you have done or that has happened, you feel rather sorry and sad about it. EG *When I look back on it all, it makes me feel bad... I really feel bad about having to say he can't go.* PHR : VB INFLECTS

12 You can say **too bad, it's too bad**, or **that's too bad**, in informal English, 12.1 to express regret when you are apologizing, or to express disappointment about something. EG *I'm sorry. It's too bad that it had to happen... 'We don't play that kind of music any more.'–'That's too bad. David said you were terrific.'* CONVENTION = it's a pity 12.2 to indicate rather harshly or impatiently that nothing can be done to change the situation or that someone cannot have what they want. CONVENTION = hard luck, tough

13 The word **bad** is also used in the following expressions in informal English. 13.1 If you describe someone as **a bad lot, sort, type,** etc, you consider their behaviour to be unacceptable or immoral. EG *You don't want to get involved with them, they're a bad lot.* PHR : USED AS C ⇑ person = trouble-maker 13.2 If you tell someone that they must **take the bad with the good**, you mean that they must learn to accept the unpleasant things as well as the nice things that happen in life. PHR : VB INFLECTS 13.3 If a situation **goes from bad to worse,** it becomes even more difficult and unpleasant. EG *Well, after that things just went from bad to worse.* PHR : VB INFLECTS ⇑ deteriorate ≠ improve

14 The word **bad** is also used in the following expressions which are explained at other places in this dictionary. ● **bad blood**: see **blood.** ● to **be in** someone's **bad books**: see **book**. ● to have **bad breath**: see **breath.** ● **a bad buy**: see **buy.** ● **bad feeling**: see **feeling.** ● **bad form**: see **form.** ● **with a bad grace**: see **grace.** ● to **give** someone **up as a bad job**: see **job.** ● to **make the best of a bad job**: see **job.** ● **bad luck**: see **luck.** ● **a bad name**: see **name.** ● **give a dog a bad name**: see **dog.** ● **bad news**: see **new.** ● to **have a bad night**: see **night.** ● to **turn up like a bad penny**: see **penny.** ● to **get a bad press**: see **press.** ● **bad taste**: see **taste.** ● to **make bad time**: see **time.** ● **a bad turn**: see **turn.** ● **in a bad way**: see **way.**

15 See also **worse, worst.**

bad cheque, bad cheques. A **bad cheque** is a bank cheque that will not be paid because there is a mistake on it or because there is not enough money in the account. N COUNT

bad debt, bad debts. A **bad debt** is a debt that is owed to you but is not likely to be paid. EG *I wrote off six thousand dollars worth of bad debts.* N COUNT

baddy /bædi¹/, **baddies**. A **baddy** is a person in a story, film, etc who is considered to be evil or wicked, or who is fighting on the wrong side; an informal word. EG *...the goodies and the baddies... You don't want him to win–he's a baddy!* N COUNT : USU PL = villain ≠ hero

bade /bæd, beɪd/ is a form of the past tense of **bid**.

badge /bædʒ/, **badges**. A **badge** is 1 a small piece of plastic, metal, cloth, etc with a design or message on it which you pin or sew onto your clothing to indicate that you have a particular rank, belong to a group or organization, support a particular cause, etc. EG *...a shirt with a company badge on the pocket.* N COUNT

2 any feature that someone or something has which is regarded as a sign that they have a particular quality, power, status, etc. EG *Wisdom is the badge of maturity... For some working people, voting Tory is a badge of respectability.* N COUNT : USU N +*of*+N UNCOUNT

badger /bædʒə/, **badgers, badgering, badgered**. 1 A **badger** is a wild animal which has grey fur and a white head with two wide black stripes on it. Badgers live underground and usually come up to feed at night. N COUNT

2 If you **badger** someone, you repeatedly tell them to do something or repeatedly ask them questions. EG *Brody badgered his mother until she bought him one... They used to badger him with questions.* V+O ⇑ trouble = pester

badinage /bædɪnɑːʒ/ is a series of remarks or a conversation that is humorous, not very serious, and often involves teasing someone; a formal or literary word. N UNCOUNT = banter

badly /bædli¹/. 1 If you need or want something **badly**, you need or want it very much. EG *We need the money badly... I want you so badly... I am badly in need of advice.* ADV ⇑ extremely 2 You can use **badly** with verbs such as 'reflect', 'come out of', and 'think of' when you mean that something happens in a way that is unfavourable to someone, something, or their reputation. EG *The story reflected badly on Amity and worse on Brody... I'm afraid we came out of the whole business rather badly... I don't think badly of him for what he did.* ADV AFTER VB ⇑ unfavourably = poorly ≠ well

3 Other meanings of **badly** can be found in the entry for **bad** in paragraphs 1 and 9.
4 badly done by: see **do.**

badly off, worse off, worst off. 1 If you are **badly off** for something that you need or want, you do not have enough of it. EG *The school is really quite badly off for books.* — ADJ QUALIT : PRED, USU+*for* ≠ well-off

2 If you are **badly off**, you do not have very much money. — ADJ QUALIT : PRED

badminton /bædmɪntən/ is a game in which the players use rackets to hit a small feathered object called a shuttlecock over a high net. — N UNCOUNT

baffle /bæfə⁰l/, **baffles, baffling, baffled.** If you **are baffled** by something, you cannot understand or explain it or think of a solution to it. EG *I was baffled by his refusal... Until very recently the medical profession was baffled... The TV reporters looked slightly baffled.* ◊ **baffling.** EG *...a baffling problem.* — V+O : USU PASS ⇑ confound = mystify, puzzle; ◊ ADJ QUALIT

bafflement /bæfə⁰lmə²nt/ is the state of being baffled. — N UNCOUNT

bag /bæg/, **bags, bagging, bagged.** 1 A **bag** is a container made of thin paper or plastic and used especially in shops to put things in that a customer has bought. EG *...a paper bag.* ▸ **Bag** is also used to refer to the things or the amount of things that a bag contains. EG *He ate a whole bag of sweets.* — N COUNT; ▸ N PART

2 A **bag** is also a strong container made of cloth, plastic, leather, etc with a handle or handles, in which you keep personal things that you will need during the day, or put shopping in, or put belongings in when you are travelling somewhere. EG *She opened her bag and took out a handkerchief... He was carrying a red shopping bag... He packed his bags and drove to the airport.* ● See also **shoulder-bag, sleeping bag.** — N COUNT

3 If you have **bags** under your eyes, you have puffy areas or folds of skin under your eyes, for example because you have not had enough sleep or you are old. — N PLURAL

4 If you say there is **bags of** something or there are **bags of** particular things, you mean that there is a large amount of it or a large number of them; used in informal British English. EG *There's bags of room... We've got bags of things to do before we leave.* — N PART : PLURAL = heaps of

5 If you **bag** something that a lot of people want, you get it for yourself before anyone else can get it; used in informal British English. EG *Can you bag the front seats for us?* — V+O, V+O+O, OR V+O+A *(for)* = reserve

6 If you **bag** an animal or bird, you shoot or catch it while hunting. — V+O

7 If you call a woman an old **bag** or a stupid **bag**, you are insulting her; a rude and offensive use. — N COUNT : ALSO VOC

8 The word **bag** is also used in the following expressions in informal English. **8.1** If you say that something is **in the bag**, you mean that you are certain that you will get it or achieve it. **8.2** If you **pack** your **bags**, you leave a place where you have been living. EG *I decided it was time to pack my bags.* **8.3** If you are thrown out of a place **bag and baggage**, you are made to leave and take all your belongings with you. — PHR : USED AS AN A; PHR : VB INFLECTS; PHR : USED AS AN A

9 The word **bag** is also used in the following expressions which are explained at other places in this dictionary. ● to **let the cat out of the bag**: see **cat.** ● a **mixed bag**: see **mix.** ● a **bag of bones**: see **bone.** ● a **bag of tricks**: see **tricks.**

bag up. If you **bag up** a quantity of something, you put it into bags. — PHRASAL VB : V+O+ADV

bagatelle /bægətel/, **bagatelles.** If you describe something as a **bagatelle**, you mean that you consider it unimportant or easy to achieve; a formal or literary word. — N COUNT : USU USED AS C = trifle, nothing

baggage /bægɪdʒ/ refers to all the suitcases and bags that you take with you when you travel; used especially in American English. EG *The porter helped her into a taxi with her baggage.* ● **bag and baggage**: see **bag.** — N UNCOUNT ⇑ belongings = luggage

baggy /bægi¹/, **baggier, baggiest.** If a piece of clothing is **baggy**, it hangs loosely on your body because it is too big for you or because it has stretched. EG *...a baggy suit.* — ADJ QUALIT ⇑ loose ≠ tight

bagpipes /bægpaɪps/ refers to a musical instrument played by blowing air into a leather bag and squeezing it out through pipes that have fixed notes and a pipe whose note can be varied by covering different holes in it. Bagpipes are especially popular in Scotland. — N PLURAL

bah /bɑ:, bæ/. Some people say **'Bah'** in order to express scorn, disappointment, or irritation; an old-fashioned word. — EXCLAM ⇑ huh = pah

Bahamian /bəhɜ:mɪən, -hɑ:-/, **Bahamians.** 1 Something that is **Bahamian** belongs or relates to the Bahamas or its people. — ADJ CLASSIF

2 A **Bahamian** is a person who comes from the Bahamas. — N COUNT

Bahraini /bɑ:reɪni¹/, **Bahrainis.** 1 Something that is **Bahraini** belongs or relates to Bahrain or to its people. — ADJ CLASSIF

2 A **Bahraini** is a person who comes from Bahrain. — N COUNT

bail /beɪl/, **bails, bailing, bailed**: also spelled **bale** in paragraph 5 and in **bail out**, senses 1.2 and 2.
1 **Bail** is **1.1** an amount of money that a judge or magistrate decides must be given to a law court before an arrested person can be released, as a way of making sure that they will return to court when it is time for their trial. EG *Bail was set at half a million dollars... She was released on $2,500 bail.* **1.2** permission for an arrested person to be released after bail has been paid. EG *The judge refused to grant bail.* — N UNCOUNT ⇑ guarantee = surety; N UNCOUNT ⇑ release

2 If you **stand bail** or **go bail** for someone, you provide the money that must be given as bail before they can be released. — PHR : VB INFLECTS

3 If a prisoner **jumps bail**, he or she does not come back for his or her trial after being released on bail. — PHR : VB INFLECTS

4 In cricket, the **bails** are the two small pieces of wood that are laid across the top of the stumps to form the wicket. — N COUNT : USU PL

5 If you **bail** water from a boat or **bail** it **out**, you remove it by using a container such as a bucket. EG *They began bailing with their helmets.* — V OR V+O : IF+ PREP THEN *out*

bail out. 1 If you **bail** someone **out**, **1.1** you pay bail on their behalf so that they can be released. EG *I had to borrow £1,000 to bail my friend out.* **1.2** you help them out of a difficult situation, for example by giving them money. EG *The government was forced to bail the company out... We assume that technology will always bale us out of our troubles.* — PHRASAL VB : V+O+ADV; PHRASAL VB : V+O+ADV = rescue

2 If you **bail out** of an aircraft, you jump out of it with a parachute because it is damaged and likely to crash. — PHRASAL VB : V+ADV : IF+PREP THEN *of*

bailiff /beɪlɪf/, **bailiffs.** A **bailiff** is 1 a law officer who makes sure that the decisions of a court are obeyed, especially by taking someone's personal property away if they do not pay their rent; used mainly in British English. EG *The bailiffs had arrived.* — N COUNT

2 a minor official in a court of law who carries messages or looks after prisoners; used mainly in American English. **3** a person who is employed to look after land or property for the owner; used mainly in British English. — N COUNT; N COUNT

bairn /beən/, **bairns.** A **bairn** is a child; used mainly in Scottish and Northern English. — N COUNT

bait /beɪt/, **baits, baiting, baited.** 1 **Bait** is a small amount of food which you put on a hook or in a trap in order to attract a fish or animal which you want to catch. EG *I took a slice of white bread to use for bait.* — N UNCOUNT ⇑ lure

2 When you **bait** a hook or trap you put bait on it or in it. EG *Bait the hook with a raisin.* — V+O : IF+PREP THEN *with*

3 A person or thing that is **bait** is intended to tempt or encourage someone to do something. EG *They said something awful about Lang having been bait... He's using my papers as a bait.* — N UNCOUNT, OR N SING : *the*/POSS+N ⇑ lure

4 If you **rise to the bait** or **take the bait** you react to something that someone says or does in exactly the way that they were trying to make you react. EG *I asked Carol if she'd had a nice time at the party but she didn't rise to the bait.* — PHR : VB INFLECTS

5 When you **bait** someone, you deliberately try to make them angry by teasing them. EG *Lucy seemed to take a positive delight in baiting him.* — V+O ⇑ tease = needle

6 If you **bait** an animal such as a bear or badger, you make dogs attack it as a sport or entertainment. EG *...badger baiting.* — V+O

baize /beɪz/ is a thick woollen material, usually green, which is often used for covering snooker tables and card tables. — N UNCOUNT ⇑ fabric

bake /beɪk/, **bakes, baking, baked.** 1 When you **bake** food or when it **bakes** it is cooked in an oven without using extra liquid or fat. EG *She said she would bake a cake to celebrate... I cleaned the kitchen while the bread was baking.* ◊ **baked.** EG *...baked potatoes.* — V OR V-ERG ⇑ cook; ◊ ADJ CLASSIF

2 When something that contains moisture, for exam- — V-ERG

ple earth or clay, is **baked** or **bakes**, it becomes dry and hard as a result of heat, for example from the sun. EG *The ground was baked hard.*

3 See also **baking**.

baked beans are haricot beans which have been cooked in tomato sauce, and are usually sold in tins. N PLURAL

Bakelite /beɪkəlaɪt/ is a trademark for a type of hard plastic that was used in the past for making toys, telephones, and other objects. N UNCOUNT

baker /beɪkə/, **bakers**. A **baker** is a person who bakes and sells bread, cakes, etc. ▸ The **baker** or the **baker's** is used to refer to a shop where bread and cakes are sold. EG *Are you going to the baker's.* N COUNT ▸ N SING : the+N ⇑ shop

baker's dozen. A **baker's dozen** is a group of thirteen things; an old-fashioned expression. N SING : a+N ⇑ amount

bakery /beɪkəʳri¹/, **bakeries**. A **bakery** is a building where bread, cakes, etc are baked and sometimes sold. N COUNT

baking /beɪkɪŋ/. 1 **Baking** is the activity of making bread, cakes, pastry, etc. EG *There were brick-lined ovens for baking... ...a baking tin.* N UNCOUNT ⇑ cooking

2 You can use **baking** to describe temperatures or places that are very hot indeed. EG *He stared out across the baking roofs of Rome... ...a baking hot day.* ADJ CLASSIF = sweltering

baksheesh /bækʃiːʃ/ is, in some countries in the Middle East and Asia, money that you give to a beggar or as a tip to someone who has done something for you. N UNCOUNT

balaclava /bæləklɑːvə/, **balaclavas**. A **balaclava** or a **balaclava helmet** is a close-fitting woollen hood that covers every part of your head except your face. N COUNT ⇑ headgear

balalaika /bæləlaɪkə/, **balalaikas**. A **balalaika** is a musical instrument with a triangular body and three strings, which is mainly used in Russia. N COUNT

balance /bæləns/, **balances, balancing, balanced**. 1 If a person or thing **balances**, or if a person **balances** something, the person or thing is steady and does not fall over, or the person places the thing in a stable position. EG *An ashtray was balanced on the arm of her chair... Balancing on one leg is an excellent exercise.* V OR V-ERG : IF+ PREP THEN on

2 **Balance** is 2.1 the steadiness that someone or something has when it is balanced on something. EG *She lost her balance... I found it difficult to keep my balance.* 2.2 a state or situation in which all the different parts or forces involved have the right amount of importance, influence, or strength, or the same amount of it. EG *It had damaged the ecological balance in the lake... ...a balance of power.* 2.3 the way in which the parts of something, for example a picture, are skilfully arranged or exist in the correct amounts. N UNCOUNT ⇑ equilibrium; N SING WITH DET +SUPP ⇑ stability = equilibrium ≠ imbalance; N UNCOUNT ⇑ harmony

3 If you are **off balance** you are 3.1 in an unsteady position and about to fall. EG *One wrestler pulled another off balance.* 3.2 surprised or confused. EG *This reception made me nervous and threw me off balance.* PHR : USED AS AN A; PHR : USED AS AN A

4 If you **balance** something with something else or if several things **balance** each other, each of the things has the same strength, weight, importance, etc. EG *Any escapism in the magazine is balanced by more practical items... Demand and supply could be balanced.* ◊ **balanced**. EG *The country had a delicately balanced economy.* V-ERG : ALSO V OR V+A (with) : RECIP; ◊ ADJ CLASSIF

5 If the **balance** swings or tips in someone's favour, they start winning in a contest or struggle of some kind. EG *Competition was keen, and the balance swung this way and that... His popularity is increasing and the balance may well tip in his favour.* N SING : the+N = scales

6 If you **hold the balance** of power in a situation, you do not have much power yourself but are very important, because the main people or groups involved have equal power, and the person or group that you decide to support will win. PHR : VB INFLECTS

7 If something is **in the balance** or lies or hangs **in the balance**, it is uncertain and unclear and may happen or be successful or may not. EG *Everything was still in the balance... The destiny of our race lies in the balance.* PHR : USED AS AN A ⇑ undecided

8 When you **balance** one thing or idea against another, you consider its importance in relation to the other one. EG *I constantly had to balance the need for training against the money it cost.* V+O+A (against)

9 You can say **on balance** to indicate that you are stating an opinion or making a decision only after considering all the relevant facts or arguments. EG *On balance, he felt he could leave it for at least a month.* PHR : USED AS ADV SEN

10 If someone **balances** their budget or a government **balances** the economy of a country, they make sure that the amount of money that they spend is not greater than the amount that they have been given. V+O ⇑ work out

11 If you **balance** your accounts or books or if your accounts or books **balance**, you have proved by calculation that the amount of money you have received is equal to the amount that you have spent, often as part of an official statement. V-ERG ⇑ work out

12 The **balance** of an amount of something, especially money, is the part that remains after some of it has been spent or used. EG *You will be given the balance as a cash payment.* N SING : the+N ⇑ residue = remainder

13 The **balance** in your bank account is the amount of money you have in it. EG *He demanded the amount of his current balance.* N COUNT : USU WITH the/POSS

14 A **balance** is a device used for weighing things. It consists of two dishes hanging from the ends of a horizontal bar which is supported at the middle. When the items in each dish weigh the same, the bar remains horizontal. N COUNT = scales

balance out. If two or more things **balance out**, they are equal in amount or value, for example after a period of time or when they have been added up. EG *The debits and credits should theoretically balance out over a few weeks.* PHRASAL VB : V+ ADV = even out

balanced /bælənst/. 1 An account or report that is **balanced** contains all the relevant information about something and presents it in a fair and reasonable way; used showing approval. EG *...a balanced summary of the debate.* 2 Something that is **balanced** is pleasing or beneficial because its parts are skilfully arranged or exist in the correct amounts; used showing approval. EG *...a beautifully balanced play... ...a balanced diet.* 3 Someone who is **balanced** remains calm and thinks clearly even in a difficult situation; used showing approval. ADJ QUALIT = objective; ADJ QUALIT : USU ADV+ADJ; ADJ QUALIT : USU ADV+ADJ

4 See also **balance**.

balance of payments, balances of payments. A country's **balance of payments** is the difference between the payment that is made for imports and the payment that is received from exports. EG *The economy continued to expand and the balance of payments improved.* N COUNT : USU SING

balance sheet, balance sheets. A **balance sheet** is a written statement of the amount of money and property a company has, the amount of money it is owed, and the amount of money it owes to other people. N COUNT

balancing act, balancing acts. If you do a **balancing act**, you try to please two or more people or groups who are in opposition to each other. EG *He kept up his balancing act by making promises to each side.* N COUNT : USU SING = juggling act

balcony /bælkəni¹/, **balconies**. 1 A **balcony** is a platform with a railing or wall around it which is attached to the outside wall of a building, usually above ground level, with a door leading out onto it. EG *The Queen appeared with her family on the balcony of Buckingham Palace.* N COUNT

2 The **balcony** in a theatre or cinema is the area of seats upstairs, especially the seats near the top of the building. N COUNT : USU SING ⇑ gallery

bald /bɔːld/, **balder, baldest**. 1 Someone who is **bald** or whose head is **bald** has little or no hair on the top of their head. EG *You're going bald... He has a large bald patch.* ◊ **baldness**. EG *I think you'll suffer from early baldness.* ADJ QUALIT ≠ hairy, hirsute; ◊ N UNCOUNT

2 Something that is **bald** does not have the natural covering which you might expect it to have, for example fur or grass. EG *...a bald granite outcrop.* ADJ QUALIT ⇑ denuded = bare

3 A tyre that is **bald** has become very smooth and is unsafe because it can slide over the road surface. ADJ QUALIT ⇑ worn

4 A **bald** statement, question, account, etc has no unnecessary words in it, and is made without any attempt to be polite or to conceal anything. EG *...a bald question.* ◊ **baldly**. EG *To put it baldly, I can't stand the man.* ADJ QUALIT : ATTRIB = blunt; ◊ ADV WITH VB

bald eagle, bald eagles. A **bald eagle** is a type of large white-headed eagle that lives in North America. N COUNT ⇑ bird

balderdash /bɔːldədæʃ/. If you say that something that has been said or written is **balderdash**, you mean that you think it is completely untrue or very stupid; an old-fashioned word. EXCLAM/N UNCOUNT = rubbish

balding /bɔːldɪŋ/. Someone who is **balding** is beginning to lose the hair on the top of their head. EG *...a trim, balding man in his early 60's.* ADJ CLASSIF

bale /beɪl/, **bales, baling, baled.** 1 A **bale** is a large quantity of something such as cloth, paper or hay which is tied into a tight bundle. EG *...bales of old newspaper.* N COUNT : ALSO N PART

2 When you **bale** something, especially hay or straw, you tie it into large bundles. V+O

3 See also **bail**.

baleful /beɪlful/. Something that is **baleful** has harmful effects or expresses someone's harmful intentions; a rather literary word. EG *He challenged the baleful influence of the paper's proprietor... We saw his baleful eye fixed on us.* ◊ **balefully.** EG *He glared at me balefully as I entered.* ADJ CLASSIF ⇑ unfriendly ≠ benign ◊ ADV WITH VB

balk /bɔːlᵒk/, **balks, balking, balked**; also spelled **baulk.** 1 If you **balk** at something you are very reluctant to do it or to let it happen, and you may even refuse to do it or try to prevent it. EG *I balked at cleaning the lavatory. The administration does not baulk at such a prospect.* V : IF+PREP THEN *at* ⇑ protest = jib, recoil

2 When a horse or other animal **balks** at something like a jump or a fence, it stops suddenly and unexpectedly or turns away from it. V

3 If someone **is balked**, they are prevented from doing or getting something they want; a rather literary word. EG *But I was in no mood to be balked by a man like him... She was balked of the chance to see Toby.* V+O : USU PASS = thwarted

ball /bɔːl/, **balls, balling, balled.** 1 A **ball** is 1.1 a round object that children often play with or that is hit, thrown, or kicked in games such as tennis, cricket and football. EG *...a golf ball.* 1.2 something or an amount of something that has a round shape. EG *...a ball of wool... He rolled the socks into a ball.* N COUNT ⇑ sphere; N COUNT : ALSO N PART

2 **Ball** is also used in the following expressions. 2.1 If you **start** or **set the ball rolling** or **keep the ball rolling**, you start an activity or event involving several people or make sure that it continues. EG *The banks set the ball rolling when they reduced their lending rates.* 2.2 If you **play ball**, you willingly do what someone wants you to do; an informal expression. 2.3 If you say that **the ball is in** a particular person's **court**, you mean that it is his or her responsibility to take the next action or decision in a particular situation. 2.4 If someone is **on the ball**, they understand things and react quickly, and know the most recent information about things. EG *A reputation for being on the ball depends on not making too many mistakes.* PHR : VB INFLECTS; PHR : VB INFLECTS; PHR : VB INFLECTS; PHR : USED AS AN A ⇑ alert ≠ dozy

3 When you refer to a good **ball**, a long **ball**, a difficult **ball**, etc, you are referring to the skill, intention, or effect with which a ball is hit, kicked, or thrown in a game. N COUNT : MOD+N ⇑ shot

4 The **ball** of your foot or the **ball** of your thumb is the rounded part where your toes join your foot or where your thumb joins your hand. N COUNT+*of*

5 When you **ball** something or when it **balls**, it becomes round and takes up less space. EG *She balled her fists.* V-ERG ⇑ roll up

6 A **ball** is also a large formal social event at which people dance. ● If you **have a ball**, you have a very enjoyable time; an informal expression. N COUNT ● PHR : VB INFLECTS

7 A man's **balls** are his testicles; a very rude and offensive use. N COUNT : USU PL

8 You can use **balls** to refer to the courage or fighting spirit of a person, usually a man; a very informal use, often considered rude. EG *...a bunch of tired old men who've lost their balls.* N PLURAL

9 You say **balls** when you think that something is stupid, wrong, or nonsense; a very rude and offensive use. EXCLAM, OR N UNCOUNT : USED AS C/O

10 See also **balls up**.

ballad /bæləd/, **ballads.** A **ballad** is 1 a long song or poem which tells a story in simple language and which often has lines which are repeated at the end of each verse. 2 a slow, romantic, popular song. N COUNT; N COUNT

ballast /bæləst/ consists of 1 a substance such as sand, iron, or water that is used in ships or balloons to make them heavier and more stable. 2 small pieces of rock that are spread over an area of ground as a foundation for railway lines or a road. N UNCOUNT ⇑ weight; N UNCOUNT ⇑ base

ball bearing, ball bearings; also spelled with a hyphen. A **ball bearing** is a small metal ball. Ball bearings are placed between moving parts of a machine in order to make them move smoothly and easily over each other. N COUNT

ballcock /bɔːlkɒk/, **ballcocks.** A **ballcock** is a device in a water tank consisting of a floating ball attached to a hinged rod. When you use water from the tank, the ball sinks and the rod opens a hole through which water enters to fill the tank up again. N COUNT

ballerina /bælərɪːnə/, **ballerinas.** A **ballerina** is a woman ballet dancer. N COUNT

ballet /bæleɪ, bæleɪ/, **ballets.** 1 **Ballet** is a type of dancing in which complicated and carefully planned movements are used to tell a story or to express an idea. EG *...the elegance of classical ballet... ...a ballet dancer.* N UNCOUNT ⇑ dance

2 A **ballet** is 2.1 an artistic work involving ballet dancing, the music written to accompany the dancing, or a performance of the work. EG *...a ballet by Michel Fokine.* 2.2 a professional group of ballet dancers. EG *...the Russian Ballet.* N COUNT; N COUNT : ALSO IN NAMES

ball game, ball games. 1 A **ball game** is a baseball match; used in American English. N COUNT

2 If you say that a situation is **a whole new ball game, a completely different ball game**, etc, you mean that it is completely different from the previous one or from any that you have ever experienced or dealt with before; an informal expression. PHR : USED AS C

ballistic /bəˈlɪstɪk/, **ballistics.** 1 **Ballistics** is the study of the movement of objects that are shot or thrown through the air, for example bullets fired from a gun. N UNCOUNT ⇑ science

2 **Ballistic** means relating to ballistics. ADJ CLASSIF

ballistic missile, ballistic missiles. A **ballistic missile** is one that is guided automatically in the first part of its flight, but which falls freely when it gets near its target. N COUNT

balloon /bəluːn/, **balloons, ballooning, ballooned.** 1 A **balloon** is 1.1 a small, thin, rubber bag with a narrow neck that you blow into until it is round and firm. Balloons are used as toys or as decorations at parties. EG *Each child was blowing up a balloon.* 1.2 a large, strong balloon filled with gas or hot air, which can carry passengers in a basket or compartment underneath. Some balloons also have engines. EG *...an air balloon.* 1.3 a rough circle that is drawn near the head of a character in a cartoon and in which words are written that tell you what he or she is saying or thinking. N COUNT ⇑ toy; N COUNT ⇑ airship; N COUNT ⇑ outline

2 When something **balloons**, 2.1 it quickly becomes bigger in size and rounder in shape because air is blowing into the inside of it. EG *She crossed the park, her skirt ballooning in the wind.* 2.2 it increases rapidly in amount. EG *Trade deficits have ballooned.* V ⇑ swell = billow; V = soar, rocket

3 If you say that **the balloon went up**, you mean that a situation or activity began, often an unpleasant situation caused when secret information or a mistake or crime is discovered. EG *The balloon went up and demands were made for a full inquiry.* PHR

ballot /bælət/, **ballots, balloting, balloted.** 1 A **ballot** is 1.1 a secret vote in which people mark a piece of paper to indicate the person they choose in an election, or what they think about some other subject. EG *80% of the workforce voted for a strike in a secret ballot... She may not win an overall majority on the first ballot... Committee members were picked by ballot.* 1.2 a piece of paper on which you indicate your choice or opinion in a ballot. N COUNT, OR *by*+N; N COUNT

2 If you **ballot** a group of people you find out what they think about a subject by organizing a secret vote. EG *We intend to ballot our members on this issue.* V+O ⇑ probe = poll

ballot box, ballot boxes; also spelled with a hyphen. 1 A **ballot box** is the box into which ballot papers are put after people have voted. 2 The **ballot box** is used to refer to the system of democratic elections. EG *Social change can be achieved through the ballot-box.* N COUNT; N SING : *the*+N

ballot paper, ballot papers. A **ballot paper** is a piece of paper on which you indicate your choice or opinion in a ballot. N COUNT

ballpoint /bɔːlpɔɪnt/, **ballpoints**; also spelled with a hyphen. A **ballpoint** or a **ballpoint pen** is a pen with a small metal ball at the end which transfers the ink onto the paper. N COUNT = Biro

ballroom /bɔːlruᵘm/, **ballrooms.** 1 A **ballroom** is a very large room, often in a hotel, palace, or other grand building, that is used mainly for dancing or for formal balls. N COUNT ⇑ room

2 **Ballroom** dancing refers to the social activity of dancing in which a man and a woman dance together, using fixed steps and movements, to music played in a fixed rhythm. ADJ CLASSIF : ATTRIB

balls up, ballses up, ballsing up, ballsed up; balls ups. **Ballses up** is the third person singular present tense of the verb. **Balls ups** is the plural of the noun. When this word is used as a noun, it is also spelled with a hyphen or as one word. If you **balls up** a task or activity, you do it very badly, making a lot of mistakes or doing it without any skill; a very informal expression. EG *How did he manage to balls up such a simple job?* PHRASAL VB : V+O+ADV = botch, mess up ▸ used as a noun. EG *You can rely on George to make a balls-up of everything.* ▸ N COUNT

ballyhoo /bæli'hu:/. A **ballyhoo** is an unnecessary and exaggerated fuss made about something and often intended to trick or deceive people; an informal and rather old-fashioned word. EG *I saw through all the ballyhoo.* N SING : USU DET +N = to-do

balm /bɑ:m/, **balms**. **Balm** is 1 a sweet-smelling oil that is obtained from some tropical trees and is used to make ointments that heal wounds or lessen pain. N UNCOUNT/COUNT ⇑ medicine
2 anything which is comforting or soothing. EG *Prayer had been balm to her spirit.* N UNCOUNT ⇑ consolation

balmy /bɑ:mi[1]/, **balmier, balmiest.** 1 When the weather is **balmy**, it is mild and pleasant. EG *The air was warm and balmy.* ADJ QUALIT
2 See **barmy**.

baloney /bələʊni[1]/ is nonsense; an informal word used especially in American English. EG *The plot of the film is pure baloney.* N UNCOUNT, OR EXCLAM

balsa /bɔ:lsə/ is a very light wood from a South American tree, which is used to make things such as rafts and model aeroplanes; also used to refer to the tree. N UNCOUNT

balustrade /bæləstreɪd/, **balustrades**. A **balustrade** is a railing or wall on a balcony, staircase, etc which is intended to stop people from falling off it. N COUNT ⇑ barrier = banister

bamboo /bæmbu:/, **bamboos**. **Bamboo** is 1 a tall tropical plant which has thick, hollow stems and edible shoots. N UNCOUNT/COUNT 2 the stems of this plant, which are used for making furniture and other things. EG *...bamboo poles... ...a bamboo fence.* N UNCOUNT : USU BEFORE N

bamboozle /bæmbu:zə[0]l/, **bamboozles, bamboozling, bamboozled.** If you **bamboozle** someone, you trick them or mislead them in order to gain some advantage; an informal word. EG *Their sermons were intended to bamboozle the workers into obedience.* V+O : IF+PREP THEN *into* = hoodwink

ban /bæn/, **bans, banning, banned.** 1 To **ban** something means to state officially that it must not be done, shown, used, etc. EG *The treaty bans all nuclear tests... McEwan's play was banned by the BBC.* V+O ⇑ prevent = forbid, bar ◊ **banning**. EG *...the banning of dogs from parks.* ◊ N UNCOUNT
2 To **ban** someone from doing something means to state officially that they are not allowed to do it. EG *I am banned from driving.* V+O : IF+PREP THEN *from*
3 A **ban** is an official statement that something must not be done, shown, used, etc. EG *...a nuclear test ban treaty... There was no ban on smoking cigarettes.* N COUNT : IF+PREP THEN *on*

banal /bə[3]nɑ:l/. A remark, idea, or situation that is **banal** is so ordinary and unoriginal that it is not at all effective or interesting. EG *I couldn't think of anything to say that wouldn't sound banal.* ADJ QUALIT = trite, hackneyed ◊ **banality** /bə[3]nælɪti[1]/, **banalities**. EG *He couldn't believe the banality of the question... Television, whatever its faults and banalities, is the new conscience of the world.* ◊ N UNCOUNT/COUNT

banana /bənɑ:nə/, **bananas**. 1 A **banana** is a long curved fruit with a bright, yellow skin and firm, cream-coloured flesh. EG *...a bunch of bananas.* N COUNT/UNCOUNT
2 If you say that someone is **bananas**, you mean that they are silly or mad; an informal expression. EG *You didn't save any of it? You must be bananas.* ADJ CLASSIF : PRED = daft
3 If people or animals **go bananas**, **3.1** they behave in a silly and excited way; an informal expression. EG *That dog goes bananas whenever you pick up its lead.* PHR : VB INFLECTS = flip **3.2** they become very angry; an informal expression. EG *He went bananas when I told him.* PHR : VB INFLECTS

banana republic, banana republics. If you refer to a country as a **banana republic**, you mean that it is poor, unimportant, and politically unstable; an offensive term. N COUNT

banana skin, banana skins. A **banana skin** is used to refer to a remark or incident involving a politician or other famous person which makes them look foolish and causes difficulties for them; an informal expression. N COUNT ⇑ mistake = gaffe

banana split, banana splits. A **banana split** is a dessert made of a banana cut in half along its middle, with ice cream, nuts, sauce, etc on top. N COUNT/UNCOUNT

band /bænd/, **bands, banding, banded.** 1 A **band** is **1.1** a group of musicians who play jazz, rock, or some other kind of popular music. EG *...a rock band... ...the original Dixieland Jazz Band.* N COUNT **1.2** a group of musicians who play brass or percussion instruments: compare **orchestra**. EG *...a brass band... He played the cornet in the school band.* N COUNT
1.3 a group of people who have joined together because they share something, such as an interest or belief. EG *...a small band of revolutionaries.* N COUNT : USU+SUPP = company
2 A **band** is also **2.1** a flat, narrow strip of cloth which is worn around the head or wrists or which forms part of a piece of clothing. EG *...a panama hat with a red band... ...a man with a black band around his arm.* N COUNT **2.2** a thin flat strip of metal, elastic, or other material, which is put around something to strengthen it or is used to hold several things together. N COUNT **2.3** a strip of colour, light, land, material, etc, which contrasts with the areas on either side of it. EG *The tea-pot was brown with yellow bands... ...a band of sunlight.* N COUNT+SUPP = stripe **2.4** a particular range of numbers or values within a system of measurement. EG *...a very wide band of radio frequencies... This disease seems only to occur within a very narrow age-band.* N COUNT+SUPP
3 If something **is banded** with something of another colour or material, it has a band or bands of that colour or material. EG *The house was in red brick banded with stone.* V+O+A *(with)* : ONLY PASS = be striped

band together. If people **band together,** they meet and act together as a group in order to try and achieve something. EG *Everywhere, small groups of women banded together to talk about liberation.* PHRASAL VB : V-ERG+ADV ⇑ unite

bandage /bændɪdʒ/, **bandages, bandaging, bandaged.** 1 A **bandage** is a long strip of cloth which is wrapped around a wound or a part of your body that you have injured to protect it while it heals. EG *She was wearing a bandage round her head... Claude will be in bandages for at least three more weeks.* N COUNT ⇑ dressing
2 If you **bandage** a wound or part of someone's body, you tie a bandage around it. V+O ◊ **bandaged**. EG *...a man with a bandaged arm.* ◊ ADJ CLASSIF ⇑ bound

bandage up. If you **bandage up** a wound or part of someone's body, you bandage it completely. EG *I bandaged him up with a rag.* PHRASAL VB : V+O+ADV ⇑ bind

Band-Aid, Band-Aids. Band-Aid is a trademark for a type of sticky plaster used to cover small cuts on your body. N COUNT/UNCOUNT

bandanna /bændænə/, **bandannas**; also spelled **bandana**. A **bandanna** is a large brightly-coloured handkerchief which is worn around a person's neck or head. N COUNT

b and b is an abbreviation for 'bed and breakfast'; used in British English, especially in newspaper advertisements and on signs outside houses. N UNCOUNT

-banded combines with colours, numbers, etc to indicate that something has a band or bands of a particular colour or a particular number of bands. EG *...the little three-banded armadillo.* COMB : FORMS ADJ CLASSIFS = striped

bandit /bændɪt/, **bandits**. A **bandit** is an armed robber, especially one who works with a gang and waits in isolated places to steal from travellers. ● See also **one-armed bandit**. N COUNT = brigand, marauder

bandsman /bændzmə[3]n/, **bandsmen**. A **bandsman** is a musician in a brass band or a military band. N COUNT

bandstand /bændstænd/, **bandstands**. A **bandstand** is a platform with a roof where a military band or a brass band can play in the open air. N COUNT

bandwagon /bændwægən/. If you say that someone has **jumped** or **climbed on the bandwagon** you mean that they have become involved in an activity or cause because it is suddenly fashionable to do so or because they think it is likely to be successful. PHR : VB INFLECTS ⇑ copy

bandy /bændi[1]/, **bandies, bandying, bandied.**
1 If you **bandy** ideas or arguments, you discuss them with other people in a casual way. EG *Many of the programmes started off as ideas just bandied to and fro between producer and writer.* V+O+A ⇑ exchange
2 If you **bandy words with** someone, you argue with them. EG *I'm not going to bandy words with Jimmy.* PHR : VB INFLECTS
3 **Bandy** also means the same as bandy-legged. ADJ QUALIT

bandy about. If you **bandy** a word, name, expres- PHRASAL VB :

sion, or remark **about**, you keep mentioning or using it often, usually because you want to impress people. EG *The words dedication and loyalty are bandied about regularly at our board meetings.* ORDER V+O+ADV

bandy-legged. Someone who is **bandy-legged** has legs which curve outwards at the knees. ADJ QUALIT

bane /beɪn/. 1 Someone or something that is the **bane** of a particular person or organization causes unhappiness or distress to that person or organization. EG *...a journalist regarded by some as the bane of Whitehall... ...a costly system of files and folders–the bane of hospital administration.* N SING : the+N+of ⇑ trial = scourge

2 Someone or something that is **the bane of** your **life** causes you constant unhappiness or distress. PHR : USED AS C

bang /bæŋ/, **bangs, banging, banged**. 1 If you **bang** something, you hit it or put it somewhere violently so that it makes a loud noise. EG *The boys used to bang on the doors with sticks... He banged the bowl down on the table.* V+A, OR V+O+A = drum

2 If something **bangs**, it makes a loud noise. EG *A shed door banged... The jeep rattled and banged.* V

3 If you **bang** a door, you close it violently so that it makes a loud noise. EG *Don't bang the door!* V+O = slam

4 If you **bang** something or part of your body against something else, you accidentally bump it. EG *I bang my head against that shelf every time I sit back.* V-ERG : USU+A ● If you complain that you **are banging** your **head against a brick wall,** you mean that you are wasting your efforts and not making any progress. ● PHR : AUX INFLECTS ⇑ getting nowhere

5 A **bang** is 5.1 a sudden, short, loud noise. EG *She slammed the drawer shut hard with a bang... They cover their ears and wait for the bang.* N COUNT : USU SING 5.2 a bump against something such as a part of your body or a vehicle when something hits it accidentally. EG *I got a nasty bang on the head.* N COUNT = knock

6 **Bang** is also used in the following expressions in informal English: 6.1 If something starts or goes **with a bang**, it is very successful and impressive and has a great effect. PHR : USED AS AN A 6.2 If you say **bang goes** something, you mean that it has suddenly become obvious that it cannot now succeed or be achieved. EG *Bang goes the Massachusetts vote!* PHR : VB INFLECTS 6.3 If something is **bang** in a particular position or moves **bang** into something else, it is in exactly that position or moves suddenly into it. EG *Emory University is bang in the middle of Atlanta, Georgia... I walked slap bang into a herd of forty camels.* ADV : VB+ADV+A = right

7 To **bang** a woman means to have sex with her; a very rude and offensive use. V+O

bang about. 1 To **bang** something or someone **about** means to treat them very roughly so that they become damaged or hurt; an informal expression. EG *Don't bang your vacuum cleaner about, it's a sensitive machine.* PHRASAL VB : ORDER V+O+ADV ⇑ ill-treat = bash about

2 If you **bang about** or **bang around**, you move around a room doing things noisily; an informal expression. EG *We listened to her singing while she banged about in the kitchen.* PHRASAL VB : V+ADV/PREP = clatter around

bang away. If someone is **banging away**, they are making a lot of banging noises, usually by hitting something. EG *He used the knocker vigorously. Nothing happened. He banged away even harder.* PHRASAL VB : V+ADV ⇑ knock

bang out. To **bang out** a tune on a musical instrument means to play it loudly and not very well; an informal expression. PHRASAL VB : V+O+ADV

banger /bæŋə/, **bangers**; used mainly in informal British English. A **banger** is 1 a sausage. EG *...bangers and mash.* N COUNT 2 an old car that is in bad condition. EG *...banger racing.* N COUNT 3 a small firework that makes a loud noise when you light it. N COUNT = squib

Bangladeshi /bæŋglədeʃi¹/, **Bangladeshis**. 1 Something that is **Bangladeshi** belongs or relates to Bangladesh or to its people. ADJ CLASSIF

2 A **Bangladeshi** is a person who comes from Bangladesh. N COUNT

bangle /bæŋgə⁰l/, **bangles**. A **bangle** is a band of stiff metal, glass, plastic, etc that is worn round a person's wrist or ankle as decoration. N COUNT ⇑ jewellery = bracelet

bang-on means absolutely correct or perfect; used in informal British English. ADJ CLASSIF : PRED

banish /bænɪʃ/, **banishes, banishing, banished**. 1 To **banish** someone means to send them away from the country where they live, and not allow them to return. EG *She was banished from the country for three years.* V+O : IF+PREP THEN from ⇑ expel = exile

2 If you **banish** something from your thoughts, you make an effort to stop thinking or worrying about it. EG *He tried to banish the thought.* V+O : IF+PREP THEN from = dismiss

banishment /bænɪʃmə²nt/ is the act of banishing someone or the state of being banished. EG *After his banishment Trotsky's supporters were soon also expelled.* N UNCOUNT : IF+PREP THEN of ⇑ expulsion

banister /bənɪstə/, **banisters**; also spelled **bannister**. A **banister** is a handrail which is supported by posts and fixed along the side of a staircase. N COUNT ⇑ barrier = balustrade

banjo /bændʒəʊ/, **banjos** or **banjoes**. A **banjo** is a musical instrument with a long neck, a hollow, circular body, and four or more strings which you pluck with your fingers. N COUNT

bank /bæŋk/, **banks, banking, banked**. 1 A **bank** is an institution where people or businesses can keep their money and which also offers services such as lending, exchanging, or transferring money. EG *You should ask your bank for a loan... Have you got any money in the bank?* ▸ used to refer to a building where a bank offers its services. EG *The bank opens at nine thirty.... Turn left at the bank.* N COUNT ▸ ⇑ building

2 If you **bank** with a particular bank, you have an account with that bank. V+A (with) ⇑ deal

3 If you **bank** money, you pay it into a bank. V+O

4 The **bank** in a gambling game is the money that belongs to the dealer or to the casino management. ● To **break the bank**: see **break**. N COUNT

5 A **bank** of something such as computer data or blood is a store of it that is kept ready for use when needed. EG *...access to huge banks of public data or library information.* N COUNT+SUPP ⇑ reserve = collection

6 A **bank** is also 6.1 the raised ground along the edge of a river or lake. EG *He followed the man along the river bank...* N COUNT 6.2 the sloping side of an area of raised ground. EG *We watched her scramble up the bank to the road.* N COUNT ⇑ slope 6.3 an area of raised ground with a flat top and one or two sloping sides. EG *The town is on high banks on either side of a river.* N COUNT ⇑ slope 6.4 a long high row or mass of something. EG *The rhododendrons were massed in great banks of pink and purple... Soon we were between banks of old snow... ....a bank of fog along the beach.* N COUNT+of = mound

7 A **bank** of switches, keys, etc on a machine is a row of switches or keys on it. N COUNT+OF ⇑ row

8 To **bank** something such as earth, snow, or sand means to heap or arrange it in such a way that it forms a slope or wall. EG *The storm had banked sand inside the lagoon.* V+O : USU+A ⇑ amass = pile up

9 If something **is banked** by something else, it is bordered by something that forms a slope or wall along its edge. EG *...the waters are banked by high, dark, red brick buildings.* V+O : USU PASS ⇑ be edged

10 When an aircraft **banks**, one of its wings rises higher than the other, usually when it is changing direction. EG *The aircraft turned, banking slightly.* V-ERG ⇑ tilt

bank on. If you **bank on** something happening, you expect it to happen and rely on it happening. EG *I was banking on your coming today.* PHRASAL VB : V+PREP, HAS PASS = count on

bank up. 1 To **bank up** earth, sand, etc means to pile it into a mound or against a wall. PHRASAL VB : V+O+ADV

2 If you **bank up** a fire, you put a large quantity of coal onto it so that it will keep burning for a long time. PHRASAL VB : V+O+ADV

bank account, bank accounts. A **bank account** is an arrangement with a bank which allows a customer to deposit money in the bank, to withdraw it when needed, and to have all the transactions recorded. EG *Arthur had enough money left in his bank account... ...a joint bank account.* N COUNT

bank balance, bank balances; also spelled with a hyphen. Someone's **bank balance** is the amount of money that they have in their bank account at a particular time. N COUNT : USU POSS+N

banker /bæŋkə/, **bankers**. A **banker** is 1 someone involved in banking at a senior level. EG *...industrialists and bankers.* N COUNT ⇑ person 2 a person who is in charge of the bank in a gambling game. N COUNT

banker's card, banker's cards. A **banker's card** is the same as a cheque card. N COUNT

banker's order, banker's orders. A **banker's order** is the same as a standing order. N COUNT

bank holiday, bank holidays. A **bank holiday** is, in England, Wales and Northern Ireland, a public holiday when banks are closed by law. EG *They came to see us on August Bank Holiday.* N COUNT

banking /bæŋkɪŋ/ is the business activity of banks or similar institutions. EG *...in banking and the manu-* N UNCOUNT *facturing trades... ...information on international banking.*

banking house, banking houses. A **banking house** is a bank; an old-fashioned or formal expression.
N COUNT = bank

bank loan, bank loans. A **bank loan** is a sum of money that a bank lends you for a period of time and that you have to pay back with interest. EG *We got a bank loan to buy a car.*
N COUNT

bank manager, bank managers. A **bank manager** is a person who is in charge of a branch of a bank.
N COUNT

banknote /bæŋknəʊt/, **banknotes**; also spelled with a hyphen or as two words. A **banknote** is a piece of paper money with a particular value. EG *...wads of bank notes stuffed carelessly in his pocket.*
N COUNT = bill

bank rate; also spelled with a hyphen. The **bank rate** is the rate of interest at which a bank lends money, especially the minimum rate of interest that banks are allowed to charge, which is decided from time to time by the country's central bank. EG *The bank-rate was increased to 8 per cent.*
N SING : USU *the*+N

bankroll /bæŋkrɒl/, **bankrolls, bankrolling, bankrolled.** 1 If you **bankroll** a person, organization, or project, you provide the financial resources that they need; an informal expression used especially in American English. EG *...money to furnish your hotel and bankroll your casino.*
V+O ⇑ help = finance

2 A **bankroll** is the financial resources used to back a person, project, or institution; used especially in American English.
N COUNT

bankrupt /bænkrəᵊpt/, **bankrupts, bankrupting, bankrupted.** 1 A person, business, or organization that is **bankrupt** or goes **bankrupt** does not have enough money to pay their debts. If this is officially declared in a court of law, they have to stop their business activities, and their property is sold by an official appointed by the court and the money is used to pay as many of these debts as possible. EG *The company has gone bankrupt.*
ADJ CLASSIF = bust

2 To **bankrupt** a person or organization means to make them go bankrupt. EG *...unprofitable contracts which would bankrupt the company.*
V+O = ruin

3 A **bankrupt** is a person who has been declared bankrupt by a court of law.
N COUNT

4 Something that is **bankrupt** is completely lacking in a particular quality or has completely lost it. EG *...a society which is morally bankrupt and politically unstable.*
ADJ CLASSIF = deficient

bankruptcy /bænkrəᵊptᵊsiˡ/, **bankruptcies.** 1 **Bankruptcy** is 1.1 the state of being bankrupt. EG *A really big strike will throw the firm into bankruptcy.*
N UNCOUNT = insolvency

1.2 the state of completely lacking a particular quality or of having completely lost it. EG *...moral bankruptcy.*
N UNCOUNT : USU +SUPP = vacuum

2 A **bankruptcy** is an instance of an organization or person going bankrupt. EG *...a frightening increase in business bankruptcies.*
N COUNT ⇑ failure = collapse

bank statement, bank statements. A **bank statement** is a list of all the money transactions into and out of a bank account. Bank statements are usually sent by the bank to the customer at regular intervals.
N COUNT ⇑ record

banner /bænə/, **banners.** 1 A **banner** is 1.1 a long strip of cloth that is stretched high above the ground, often across a street, and used for decoration or for advertising, giving information, etc.
N COUNT

1.2 a sign, usually consisting of a piece of cloth stretched between two poles, which is carried by someone marching in a demonstration or a procession. EG *...crowds filled the streets carrying banners proclaiming their support for the miners.*
N COUNT = placard

1.3 a word or phrase that is thought of as representing a cause, idea, or belief. EG *Those parts of the world that exist under the banner of capitalism.*
N COUNT : USU+SUPP ⇑ heading = name

banner headline, banner headlines. A **banner headline** is a large headline in a newspaper that stretches across the front page. EG *The paper proclaimed in big banner headlines: 'End of War in Europe'.*
N COUNT

bannister /bænɪstə/, **bannisters.** See **banister**.

banns /bænz/. When a vicar reads or publishes the **banns**, he makes a public announcement in church that two people are going to be married.
N PLURAL : *the*+N

banquet /bæŋkwɪt/, **banquets.** A **banquet** is a grand, formal dinner, usually consisting of many different courses and often followed by speeches. EG *The city is required to arrange a banquet for the new President.*
N COUNT

banshee /bænʃiː, bænʃiː/, **banshees.** A **banshee** is a female spirit in Irish folklore who warns you by her long, sad cry that someone in your family is going to die. EG *The kettle whistled like a banshee screaming.*
N COUNT

bantam /bæntəm/, **bantams.** A **bantam** is a small-sized breed of chicken.
N COUNT

banter /bæntə/, **banters, bantering, bantered.** 1 **Banter** is 1.1 teasing or joking talk that is amusing and friendly. EG *Other people at the bar begin some routine banter about wives.*
N UNCOUNT = repartee

2 To **banter** means to tease someone or to joke with them in an amusing, friendly way. EG *We just stood and bantered for half an hour.*
V : IF+PREP THEN *with/abou*

Bantu /bæntuː/ is used to describe 1 a group of black African tribes in central and southern Africa. EG *...the history of the Bantu peoples.*
ADJ CLASSIF

2 a group of languages spoken by black people in central and southern Africa. EG *She began to speak, not in a Bantu tongue but in broken English.*
ADJ CLASSIF

banyan /bænjəᵊn/, **banyans.** A **banyan** is an Indian fruit tree whose branches grow down into the ground to form additional trunks.
N COUNT

baptise /bæptaɪz/. See **baptize**.

baptism /bæptɪzəᵊm/, **baptisms.** A **baptism** is a Christian religious ceremony in which a person is sprinkled with water or goes under water as a sign that they have become spiritually pure and that they are now a Christian: compare **christening**. EG *The baptism took place a fortnight later... Many people brought their children for baptism.*
N COUNT/UNCOUNT

Baptist /bæptɪst/, **Baptists.** A **Baptist** is a Christian who believes that baptism is necessary for a Christian, and that it should happen only to someone who is old enough to understand what they are doing. EG *They are strict Baptists... ...the son of a Baptist minister.*
N COUNT

baptize /bæptaɪz/, **baptizes, baptizing, baptized**; also spelled **baptise**. When someone **is baptized**, water is sprinkled on them or they are immersed in water by a Christian minister as a sign that they have become a member of a Christian Church and that their sins have been washed away: compare **christen**.
V+O : USU PASS ⇑ initiate

bar /bɑː/, **bars, barring, barred.** 1 A **bar** is 1.1 in America, a place where you can buy and drink alcoholic drinks. EG *Leaving Rita in a bar, I made for the town library.*
N COUNT

1.2 in Britain, one of the rooms in a pub, usually one where prices are slightly lower and that contains a dart board and other pub games. EG *Where will you be, in the lounge or the bar?*
N COUNT : USU *the*+N = public bar

1.3 a room, for example in a hotel, where alcoholic drinks are served. EG *...the terrace bar of the Continental Hotel.*
N COUNT

1.4 a counter on which alcoholic drinks are served. EG *He put the glass back on the bar... Sally herself serves behind the bar.* ● See also **lounge bar, public bar, saloon bar, singles bar, wine bar**.
N COUNT : USU *the*+N

2 A sandwich **bar**, refreshment **bar**, or tea **bar** is a small shop or stall where you can buy food and drink.
N COUNT : AFTER N

3 A **bar** is also 3.1 a long, straight, rigid piece of metal. EG *...an iron bar.*
N COUNT

3.2 one of a set of strong, thin, vertical pieces of metal that are fixed in front of the windows in a prison or are made into a door or a cage in order to prevent people, animals, or birds from escaping. EG *We clasped our hands through the bars.* ● If someone is **behind bars**, they are in prison; an informal expression.
N COUNT : USU PL; ● PHR : USED AS AN A

3.3 a piece of something which has been made into a regular, often rectangular shape. EG *...a bar of chocolate... ...a bar of soap... ...gold bars.*
N COUNT+SUPP ⇑ slab

4 A **bar** of an electric fire is a piece of metal with wire coiled round it that glows and provides heat when the fire is switched on.
N COUNT = element

5 If you **bar** a door, you place something in front of it or a piece of wood or metal across it in order to prevent it from being opened.
V+O ⇑ block

6 If you **bar** someone's **way or path** , you prevent them from going somewhere by standing in front of them.
PHR : VB INFLECTS ⇑ obstruct

7 If you **bar** someone from a place or from doing something, you officially prevent them from going there or doing it. EG *Demands were made for the leader of the sect to be barred from Britain... If I were in charge, I would bar tourists.* ▸ used as a
V+O : IF+PREP THEN *from* = ban; ▸ N COUNT+

noun. EG *There should be a bar on people coming across... This was no bar to anyone who wanted to emigrate.* • See also **colour bar**. SUPP = ban

8 If someone in authority **bars** the use or the production of something or the performance of an act, they make it illegal for it to be used, made, or done. EG *...restrictions barring the use of US-supplied weapons.* V+O ⇑ forbid = ban ≠ allow

9 If you say that there are **no holds barred** when people are fighting or competing for something, you mean that they are no longer following or required to follow any rules in their efforts to win. EG *There were no holds barred now.* PHR

10 The **Bar** is used to refer to the profession of a barrister in England, or of any kind of lawyer in the United States. N PROPER : *the*+N

11 **Bar** also means the same as except; a fairly formal word. EG *Almost every woman, bar the very young, can produce tales of this sort... Nothing else–bar a pile of mail, which I wasn't going to face today.* • You use **bar none** to add emphasis to a statement that someone or something is the best of their kind. EG *He has established himself as the fastest sprinter in the world, bar none...* • **all over bar the shouting**: see **shouting**. PREP ⇑ excluding = save • PHR : NG+PHR = without exception

12 In music, a **bar** is one of the several short parts of the same length into which a piece of music is divided and which is used to establish the rhythm. EG *The orchestra played again the last twelve bars of the anthem.* N COUNT ⇑ part

barb /bɑːb/, **barbs**. A **barb** is **1** a sharp curved point on the end of an object such as an arrow or fish-hook which makes the object difficult to pull out. N COUNT

2 one of the pointed parts on barbed wire. **3** a remark which criticizes someone or something, often in an unpleasant, but cleverly humorous or sarcastic way. EG *That particular barb has been ascribed to many people.* N COUNT : USU+SUPP = dig, gibe

Barbadian /bɑːbeɪdɪən/. **1** Something that is **Barbadian** belongs or relates to Barbados or to its people. ADJ CLASSIF

2 A **Barbadian** is a person who comes from Barbados. N COUNT

barbarian /bɑːbeərɪən/, **barbarians**. A **barbarian** is **1** a person who belongs to an uncivilized tribe. EG *They were not rough barbarians like the Huns, the Goths, or the Vandals.* **2** someone who behaves in a rough and bad-mannered way, especially one who has no respect for art, literature, or education; used showing disapproval. EG *Anyone who dislikes Mozart must be a barbarian.* N COUNT = savage; N COUNT

barbaric /bɑːbærɪk/. If you describe a person or their behaviour as **barbaric**, you mean that they are **1** rough and uncivilized. EG *...a magnificent, barbaric gesture.* **2** extremely cruel. EG *How can you approve of the barbaric sport of hunting?* ADJ CLASSIF; ADJ QUALIT = brutal

barbarism /bɑːbərɪzəᵒm/ is **1** behaviour which is so rough, uncivilized, or cruel, that people are shocked by it. EG *War is barbarism; I am tired and sick of war.* N UNCOUNT = savagery

2 the behaviour or way of life of an uncivilized tribe. EG *The shift from barbarism to civilization.* N UNCOUNT

barbarity /bɑːbærɪtiˡ/, **barbarities**. **1** **Barbarity** is extremely cruel behaviour. EG *Both sides were guilty of barbarity... ...scenes of squalid barbarity.* N UNCOUNT ⇑ cruelty = brutality

2 A **barbarity** is an extremely cruel and shocking act. EG *Many barbarities were mentioned, including the shooting of six hundred children.* N COUNT ⇑ cruelty = atrocity

barbarous /bɑːbərəs/. Something that is **barbarous** is **1** so uncivilized or rough that people are shocked by it. EG *Everything looked primitive and barbarous, dirty, and odious.* **2** extremely cruel. EG *...the most barbarous and inhuman atrocities.* ADJ QUALIT = backward; ADJ QUALIT = brutal

barbecue /bɑːbɪkjuː/, **barbecues, barbecuing, barbecued**. **1** A **barbecue** is **1.1** a grill on which meat, fish, and other foods are cooked over hot charcoal, usually out of doors. EG *Instructions for assembly of an outdoor barbecue.* **1.2** a meal cooked on a barbecue. **1.3** a party that is held out of doors and where the guests eat food cooked on a barbecue. EG *I went to a barbecue on the beach last night.* N COUNT; N COUNT; N COUNT

2 If you **barbecue** food, especially meat, you cook it on a barbecue. EG *Barbecue the meat for five minutes.* V+O

barbecue sauce is a highly seasoned sauce used to flavour food, especially meat cooked on a barbecue. N UNCOUNT

barbed /bɑːbd/. **1** An arrow, a fish-hook, or other sharp pointed object that is **barbed** has one or more curved parts near its tip, which make it difficult to pull out. ADJ CLASSIF

2 A **barbed** remark or joke is one that may seem humorous or straightforward, but contains a cleverly hidden criticism. EG *A barbed compliment... His remarks were rather barbed, I thought.* ADJ QUALIT ⇑ ambiguous = loaded, snide

barbed wire is strong wire with sharp points sticking out of it, which is used to prevent people or animals getting into or out of a field or the grounds of a building. EG *All round the building are high barbed wire fences.* N UNCOUNT

barber /bɑːbə/, **barbers, barbering, barbered**. **1** A **barber** is a man who cuts men's hair. N COUNT
▸ The **barber's** is used to refer to the shop or place where a barber works. EG *He went to the barber's to please his mother.* ▸ N SING : *the*+N

2 To **barber** something means to cut or shape it neatly and carefully. V+O

barbershop /bɑːbəʃɒp/ is a type of singing in close harmony that is popular in the USA and is usually performed by four men. EG *...a barbershop quartet.* N UNCOUNT, OR N BEFORE N

barber's pole, barber's poles. A **barber's pole** is a red and white striped pole, which is the traditional sign outside a barber's shop in Britain. N COUNT

barbiturate /bɑːbɪtjəˡrɪ³t/, **barbiturates**. A **barbiturate** is a drug which people take to make them calm or to put them to sleep. EG *He's on barbiturates.* N COUNT : USU PL = tranquillizer

bard /bɑːd/, **bards**. A **bard** is a poet; an old-fashioned or literary word. N COUNT

bare /beə/, **barer, barest; bares, baring, bared**. **1** If a part of your body is **bare**, it is not covered by any clothing. EG *She worried about splinters in her bare feet... They were all bare from the waist up.* • If someone does something **with** their **bare hands**, they do it without using any weapons or tools. EG *He killed those two men with his bare hands.* ADJ CLASSIF ⇑ uncovered = naked • PHR : USED AS AN A

2 If a surface or something such as a floor or table is **bare**, it is not covered or decorated by anything. EG *He walked noisily across the bare floor... Bare wood should be painted as soon as possible.* ADJ CLASSIF : USU ATTRIB ⇑ uncovered

3 An area of ground that is **bare** has no plants growing on it. EG *...a hilly patch of bare red rock.* ◊ **bareness**. EG *No moss, no ivy, nothing cluttered the bareness of the place.* ADJ CLASSIF : USU ATTRIB; ◊ N UNCOUNT

4 If a tree or a branch is **bare**, it has no leaves on it. ADJ CLASSIF

5 A room, cupboard, or other place that is **bare** is empty or contains very few things. ADJ QUALIT : IF+PREP THEN *of*

6 If someone gives you the **bare** facts or the **barest** details of something, they tell you only the most basic and simple aspects of it with no extra details. EG *I had hardly begun telling you the barest details when you flew into a rage.* • **the bare bones**: see **bone**. ADJ CLASSIF : ATTRIB = plain ≠ detailed

7 If you talk about the **bare** minimum or the **barest** essentials, you mean only the most basic and important things that are absolutely necessary for something. EG *I had only the barest of essentials... She packed the barest minimum of clothing... Two hundred is the bare minimum.* ADJ QUALIT : ATTRIB = absolute

8 **Bare** is used in front of an amount to emphasize how surprisingly small it is. EG *A bare five per cent of the country is properly mapped... Last year the boys went for a bare fortnight, including the travelling.* ADJ CLASSIF : ATTRIB ⇑ only = mere

9 To **bare** something means to uncover or reveal it. EG *He bared his left arm... They waved their bared swords.* • If a man **bares** his **head**, he takes off his hat as a way of expressing respect, for example in a Christian church. V+O • PHR : VB INFLECTS

10 If you **bare** your **soul** you tell someone your most secret thoughts and feelings. PHR : VB INFLECTS

11 **lay bare**. If you **lay** something **bare**, **11.1** you uncover it completely and leave it without protection. EG *...the floor of what was once a Roman house laid bare.* **11.2** you reveal or expose something secret or sensitive. EG *In the book he lays bare his social relationships.* PHR : VB INFLECTS = expose; PHR : VB INFLECTS

bareback /beəbæk/. If you ride **bareback**, you ride a horse without a saddle. ▸ used as an adjective. EG *...a bareback rider.* ADV AFTER VB ▸ ADJ CLASSIF

barefaced /beəfeɪst/ means not caring about how wrongly you are behaving; used showing disapproval. EG *He's a barefaced liar... How she had the barefaced gall to do it, I don't know!* ADJ QUALIT : ATTRIB = brazen

barefoot /beəfʊt/. Someone who is **barefoot** or **barefooted** is not wearing anything on their feet. EG *A few people were barefoot, but most wore sandals.* ADJ CLASSIF

▸ used as an adverb. EG *She ran barefoot through the field.* ▸ ADV AFTER VB

bareheaded /bɛəhɛdɪ[2]d/. Someone who is **bareheaded** is not wearing a hat or any other covering on their head. ADJ CLASSIF

barely /bɛəli[1]/. 1 You can use **barely** to indicate that the thing you are talking about is only just true or is only just the case. EG *He was so drunk by midday that he could barely stand... This is barely possible... She looked barely thirty... It was barely two months old.* ADV BRD NEG = scarcely

2 If you say that one thing had **barely** happened when something else happened, you mean that the first event was followed immediately by the second. EG *I had barely said my name before he had led me to the interview room.* ADV: *barely...when* ↑ just = hardly

bargain /bɑːgɪn/, **bargains, bargaining, bargained.** 1 A **bargain** is an agreement between two people or groups, especially in business, in which they agree what each of them will do, pay, or receive. EG *You keep your part of the bargain, and I'll keep mine... We shook hands on the bargain... In many ways it was a bad bargain.* N COUNT = deal

2 When one person or group **strikes** or **makes** a **bargain** with another, they agree about what each of them will do, pay, or receive. PHR: VB INFLECTS

3 If you say that someone **drives a hard bargain**, you mean that they argue with determination to make an arrangement which is favourable to them. EG *You drive a hard bargain... They're going to drive a hard bargain with Britain over fishing limits.* PHR: VB INFLECTS

4 If one person or group **bargains** with another about something, they discuss what each of them will do, pay, or receive, in order to come to an agreement. EG *Trade unions bargain with employers for better conditions of pay and employment... He might bargain for immunity.* ◊ **bargaining.** EG *He can't understand the kind of bargaining that goes on in industry.* V: IF+PREP THEN *with/for* = negotiate; ◊ N UNCOUNT = negotiation

5 A **bargain** is also something which is sold at a low price and which you think is good value for the money. EG *He couldn't resist a bargain... They were a bargain!... ...bargain prices... ...bargain hunters.* N COUNT

6 You can say **into the bargain** when you are adding an extra piece of information which emphasizes the point you are making. EG *She was an exceptional mathematician and an unusually beautiful one into the bargain.* PHR: USED AS AN A ↑ also = to boot

bargain for. If you say that someone had not **bargained for** something, or got more than they **bargained for**, you mean that they did not expect it to happen or to happen to such an extent. EG *They had not bargained for such opposition... They went more slowly than Ralph had bargained for... She got more than she bargained for!* PHRASAL VB: V+PREP, HAS PASS = anticipate

barge /bɑːdʒ/, **barges, barging, barged.** As a verb, **barge** is a fairly informal word, used showing disapproval. 1 If you **barge** into a place or **barge** your way through, you push into a place or through a crowd in a rather rough and rude way. EG *How dare you barge your way through like that!... I got up from my seat and barged through the ladies to the door.* V+A *(through/into)*, OR V+O+A *(through/into)* = shove

2 If you **barge** into someone, you bump against them rather roughly and rudely while you are walking. EG *I hate shopping in town–people are always barging into you.* V+A *(into)* ↑ knock = jostle

3 A **barge** is a boat with a flat bottom which is used for carrying heavy loads, especially on canals. N COUNT

barge in. If someone **barges in** or **barges into** a conversation, they rudely interrupt what someone else is doing or saying. EG *I'm sorry to barge in on you like this... He just barged into the conversation.* PHRASAL VB: V+ADV/PREP

bargee /bɑːdʒiː/, **bargees.** A **bargee** is a person in charge of a barge. N COUNT ↑ boatman

barge pole. If you say that you **wouldn't touch** someone or something **with a barge pole,** you mean that you do not want to have anything to do with them, for example because you think that they are untrustworthy or unreliable; an informal expression used in British English. EG *I wouldn't touch him with a barge pole!... I wouldn't touch those cars with a barge pole–they're rubbish.* PHR: VB INFLECTS

baritone /bærɪtəʊn/, **baritones.** A **baritone** is a man with a fairly deep singing voice that is lower than that of a tenor but higher than that of a bass. EG *...one of the finest baritones in the country... He had a fine baritone voice.* N COUNT ↑ singer

barium /bɛərɪəm/ is a soft, silvery-white metal. N UNCOUNT

bark /bɑːk/, **barks, barking, barked.** 1 When a dog, fox, or other animal **barks,** it makes a sudden, loud, rough noise. EG *At the sound of the bell Buller began to bark.* ◊ **barking.** EG *...the ferocious barking of a neighbour's dog.* ● If you say that someone is **barking up the wrong tree,** you mean that they are trying to do something without realizing that they have no chance of success; an informal expression. EG *If Axel thought for a minute that he was going to borrow any money, he was barking up the wrong tree.* V ↑ cry; ◊ N UNCOUNT; ● PHR: VB INFLECTS

2 A **bark** is the sudden, loud, rough-sounding noise that dogs and some other animals make. EG *His dog waited, making happy little barks and wagging his tail.* ● If you say that someone's **bark is worse than** their **bite,** you mean that they seem much more unpleasant, rude, or violent than they really are; an informal expression. N COUNT; ● PHR: VB INFLECTS

3 If someone **barks** at someone else, they suddenly shout at them in a loud, rough voice. EG *...the teacher, who barks at his pupils, 'Sit up straight!'... He would bark an order and everyone would run to obey.* V, V+O, V+A *(at)*, OR V+REPORT-CL/QUOTE ↑ shout = snap

4 To **bark** means to suddenly make a loud, sharp, rough noise. EG *The guns barked flame and smoke.* ▸ used as a noun. EG *Above all the noise, I heard the bark of the public-address system.* V OR V+O = crackle; ▸ N COUNT+SUPP = blare

5 **Bark** is the tough material that covers the outside of a tree. EG *We gathered some dead sticks and bits of bark to start the fire.* N UNCOUNT

barley /bɑːli[1]/ is a tall, grass-like plant that has long, spiky hairs growing from the head at the top of each stalk. It is grown by farmers for food and the production of beer and whisky. **Barley** also refers to the grain produced by this plant. N UNCOUNT ↑ cereal

barley sugar; also spelled with a hyphen. **Barley sugar** is a hard sweet made from boiled sugar. N UNCOUNT

barley water is a non-alcoholic drink made from pearl barley. N UNCOUNT

barley wine is an alcoholic drink which is a kind of very strong, sweet beer. N UNCOUNT

barmaid /bɑːmeɪd/, **barmaids.** A **barmaid** is a woman who serves drinks in a bar or pub. N COUNT

barman /bɑːmə[3]n/, **barmen.** A **barman** is a man who serves drinks in a bar or pub. N COUNT = bartender

bar mitzvah /bɑː mɪtsvə/, **bar mitzvahs.** A **bar mitzvah** is a ceremony and celebration that takes place on the thirteenth birthday of a Jewish boy, after which he has the status, religious duties, and responsibilities of an adult man. N COUNT

barmy /bɑːmi[1]/, **barmier, barmiest**; an informal word used in British English. 1 Someone who is **barmy** is slightly mad or very foolish. EG *The old woman's very rich and quite barmy.* ADJ QUALIT = crazy

2 Something that is barmy is foolish and badly thought-out. EG *The whole scheme seems barmy to me.* ADJ QUALIT = stupid, silly

barn /bɑːn/, **barns.** A **barn** is a large building on a farm in which crops or animal food can be kept. N COUNT

barnacle /bɑːnəkə[0]l/, **barnacles.** A **barnacle** is a small shellfish that fixes itself tightly to rocks and the hulls of boats. Barnacles are usually found in large numbers together and are difficult to remove. N COUNT ↑ crustacean

barn dance, barn dances. A **barn dance** is an informal dance that people go to for country dancing. N COUNT

barnstorming /bɑːnstɔːmɪŋ/. **Barnstorming** is the act of travelling to a lot of small towns and villages in order to make speeches as part of a political campaign or to present a show; used mainly in American English. N UNCOUNT ↑ campaigning

barnyard /bɑːnjɑːd/, **barnyards.** A **barnyard** is a yard next to or near a barn. N COUNT ↑ yard

barometer /bərɒmə[1]tə/, **barometers.** 1 A **barometer** is an instrument that measures the air pressure and shows when the weather is going to change. N COUNT

2 A **barometer** of a situation is something that indicates how people feel about something or what they are doing or planning in secret. EG *The recent press statements have been the most telling barometer of the government's anxiety.* N COUNT+SUPP ↑ indicator = measure

baron /bærən/, **barons.** 1 A **baron** is a man who is a member of the peerage of the lowest rank. EG *...Diana Mitford, daughter of Baron Redesdale... ...if the visitor was a baron or above.* N COUNT: ALSO IN TITLES

2 the word **baron** is also used to refer to an extreme- N COUNT+SUPP:

ly powerful businessman, especially someone who owns and controls a large amount of a particular industry. EG *...the papers controlled by the press barons... ...the rich money of oil and wheat barons from Wall Street and Chicago.* USU PL = mogul

baroness /bærənɪ²s/, **baronesses**. A **baroness** is a female member of the nobility who is of the same rank as a baron or who is the wife of a baron. EG *...the Baroness von Hodenburg.* N COUNT: ALSO IN TITLES

baronet /bærənɪ²t/, **baronets**. A **baronet**, in Britain, is a man who holds the title of honour 'baronet', which is passed down from father to son. EG *...Sir Edwin Simcox, the sixth baronet.* N COUNT: ALSO IN TITLES

baronetcy /bærənɪ²tsi¹/, **baronetcies**. A **baronetcy** is the rank or position of a baronet. EG *Sir Arthur was the holder of a baronetcy dating back to Charles I.* N COUNT

baronial /bərəʊnɪəl/ means belonging or relating to a baron or barons. EG *...baronial wars.* ADJ CLASSIF: USU ATTRIB

barony /bærəni¹/, **baronies**. A **barony** is the rank or position of a baron. N COUNT

baroque /bə³rɒk, bə³rəʊk/. 1 **Baroque** architecture and art is a European style of the late sixteenth to the early eighteenth century. Baroque buildings, paintings, and other objects are typically very elaborate and heavily decorated. ▸ Used as a noun. EG *This is what historians call Classical rather than Baroque.* ADJ CLASSIF: ATTRIB ▸ N UNCOUNT

2 **Baroque** music is a style of European music that was used by composers such as Bach and Handel in the eighteenth century. ADJ CLASSIF: ATTRIB

3 Something that is **baroque** is extremely complicated, rich, and elaborate; used showing disapproval. EG *I find her horror novels altogether too baroque and alarming for my taste.* ADJ QUALIT

barque /bɑːk/, **barques**. A **barque** is a boat, especially a kind of sailing ship with three masts; an old-fashioned or poetic word. N COUNT

barrack /bærək/, **barracks, barracking, barracked**. 1 If you **barrack** someone, you shout loudly in order to interrupt them when they are making a speech, because you disagree with them. V OR V+O = heckle
◊ **barracking**. EG *He was constantly interrupted by organized barracking.* ◊ N UNCOUNT = heckling

2 A **barracks** is 2.1 a building or group of buildings where soldiers or other members of the armed forces live and work together. EG *There's a barracks near our house. ...Legionnaires from the nearby barracks... ...Waterloo Barracks... ...a barracks block... Barrack life is squalid, monotonous, and unpleasant.* N COUNT: IF SING, VB CAN BE SING OR PL ⇑ housing
2.2 a group of large ugly buildings which look the same as each other, often built as homes for poor people. EG *These cities are suitable barracks for workers.* N PLURAL ⇑ housing

barracuda /bærəkj⁰uːdə/, **barracudas**. A **barracuda** is a large tropical sea fish with a protruding lower jaw and sharp teeth, which attacks people. N COUNT

barrage /bærɑːʒ/, **barrages**. 1 A **barrage** of questions, complaints, criticisms, etc is a great number of them when people suddenly raise them in an angry or aggressive way. EG *His comments provoked a barrage of criticism... Rodin faced a barrage of queries and complaints.* N COUNT+SUPP: USU SING ⇑ attack = storm, hail

2 A **barrage** is 2.1 the firing of a large number of guns at the beginning of a battle over a wide area rather than at a single target, so that soldiers can move forward over that area; a military term. EG *Khe Sanh received the most brutal artillery barrage of the war.* N COUNT: USU SING
2.2 a construction that is built across a river to control the level of the water. EG *The Thames barrage had at last been completed.* N COUNT ⇑ dam

barrage balloon, barrage balloons. **Barrage balloons** are a group of large balloons flying high above a city or other place in wartime, which are tethered to the ground by strong steel cables. The cables are intended to destroy low-flying enemy aircraft. N COUNT: USU PL

barred /bɑːd/. 1 **Barred** is the past tense and past participle of **bar**.

2 A **barred** window or door has bars to prevent people from getting out of a room or into it. ADJ CLASSIF = grilled

barrel /bærə⁰l/, **barrels**. 1 A **barrel** is a round container for liquids that is wider in the middle than at the top and bottom. Barrels are usually made of wood and held together by metal strips. EG *...a wine barrel.* ▸ **Barrel** is also used to refer to the contents of a barrel. EG *I'll buy you a barrel of beer.* N COUNT ▸ N PART

2 In the oil industry, a **barrel** is a unit of measurement equivalent to 159 litres. EG *The Syrian pipeline has a capacity of 1.2 million barrels a day.* N COUNT: USU NUM+N ⇑ measure

3 The **barrel** of a gun is the long, cylindrical part through which the bullet travels when the gun is fired. EG *...a light weapon with a short barrel.* N COUNT ⇑ cylinder

4 The **barrel** of a lock is the part into which you put a key. N COUNT

5 If you **have** someone **over a barrel**, you have put them in a difficult situation where they have little choice but to do what you want them to do; used in informal English. EG *He's got us over a barrel, we'll have to accept his terms.* PHR: VB INFLECTS

6 If you say that you are **scraping the barrel** or the **bottom of the barrel**, you mean you are having to use people or things of the poorest quality because everything better has already been used or taken; an informal expression. PHR: VB INFLECTS

7 **lock, stock, and barrel**: see **lock**.

barrel organ, barrel organs; also spelled with a hyphen. A **barrel organ** is a large old-fashioned machine that plays music when you turn the handle on the side. They used to be played especially in the streets to entertain passers-by. N COUNT ⇑ instrument

barren /bærə⁰n/. 1 **Barren** land is 1.1 land which is very dry and bare. ADJ QUALIT
1.2 land which has soil of such poor quality that plants cannot grow on it. EG *The land still remained barren.* ADJ CLASSIF ≠ fertile

2 **Barren** means not producing any successful results; often used of a period of time during which you do not achieve anything of value. EG *His years in the political wilderness between 1960-63 had not been barren ones for him.* ADJ CLASSIF: ATTRIB ⇑ useless = unproductive ≠ fruitful

3 A **barren** woman or female animal is one who is unable to have babies; a technical or literary word. EG *Barren women are rejected by the tribesmen.* ADJ CLASSIF = infertile

4 A **barren** tree or other plant is one that produces no fruit. ADJ CLASSIF = infertile

barricade /bærɪkeɪd/, **barricades, barricading, barricaded**. 1 A **barricade** is a line of objects, vehicles, or people that is placed across a road or passage in order to stop people getting past. Barricades are often put up during street fighting. EG *They refused to man the barricades during the uprising.* ▸ used as a verb. EG *...barricaded roads.* N COUNT ⇑ barrier = road block ▸ V+O ⇑ block

2 If you **barricade** yourself inside a room or building, you put something heavy against the door or in the entrance, so that you cannot get out or so that other people cannot get in. EG *We rushed into the bedroom and barricaded ourselves in... They barricaded themselves behind concrete slabs.* V+O (NG/REFL) +A ⇑ shut

barrier /bærɪə/, **barriers**. 1 A **barrier** is 1.1 something that prevents two people or groups from agreeing or communicating with each other, for example their different social backgrounds, or their different languages. EG *These newcomers have helped to break down some of the old barriers between the two parties... ...the language barrier.* N COUNT ⇑ division
1.2 something such as a fence or wall, especially a temporary one, that prevents people or things from getting from one area to another. EG *They were on different sides of a high barrier... Show your ticket at the barrier.* ● See also **sound barrier**. N COUNT

2 A **barrier** to the happening or achievement of something is something that makes it difficult or impossible for it to happen or to be achieved. EG *...barriers to human understanding.* N COUNT: IF+ PREP THEN *to* ⇑ obstacle = block

barring /bɑːrɪŋ/. **Barring** is used to indicate that the person, thing, or event that you are mentioning is an exception to your general statement. EG *It is hard to imagine anyone, barring a lunatic, starting a war they couldn't win. Barring complications, the aircraft will be in operation next year.* PREP

barrister /bærɪstə/, **barristers**. In British English, a **barrister** is a lawyer who speaks in the higher courts of law on behalf of either the defence or the prosecution. N COUNT

bar-room, bar-room; also spelled without a hyphen. A **bar-room** is a room in which alcoholic drinks are served over a counter; used in American English. N COUNT = bar

barrow /bærəʊ/, **barrows**. A **barrow** is 1 a small cart with a wheel at the front and two handles at the back. Barrows are often used to collect rubbish in when you are gardening. N COUNT = wheelbarrow
2 a cart filled with goods, especially fresh food, to be sold in the street. N COUNT
3 a N COUNT

mound of earth which contains graves of prehistoric people.

bartender /bɑːtendə/, **bartenders**. A **bartender** is a person who sells drinks in a bar; used in American English. N COUNT = barman

barter /bɑːtə/, **barters, bartering, bartered.** If you **barter** goods, you exchange them for other goods rather than sell them for money. EG *They bring meat, grain, and vegetables to sell or barter.* ▸ used as a noun. EG *They are being offered for barter.* V OR V+O = trade ▸ N UNCOUNT

basalt /bæsɔːlt/ is a type of black rock that is produced by volcanoes. N UNCOUNT

base /beɪs/, **bases, basing, based; baser, basest.** 1 The **base** of something is 1.1 its lowest point, especially the point where it touches the ground. EG *The driver anxiously examined the chain around the base of the post... At the base of a long sandstone cliff.* 1.2 the point at which it grows from or is attached to something else. EG *Most birds have a large oil gland near the base of the tail.* N COUNT : USU the+N+of = bottom ≠ top; N COUNT : USU the+N+of

2 The **base** of a box, vase, or other object is the flat lower surface of it that touches or faces the ground. EG *Starch tends to leave a nasty brown mark on the base of the iron... The cup had 'Paris' written in blue on the base.* N COUNT : USU WITH POSS = underneath

3 The **base** of an object that has several sections and that rests on a surface is the lowest section of it. EG *...the switch on the lamp base.* N COUNT : USU WITH POSS ⇑ section

4 The **base** of a triangle or other geometrical figure is the lowest side of it. N COUNT : USU WITH POSS

5 If something is a **base** for something else, 5.1 it is the object or surface that is underneath it and supports it. EG *I turned over a cardboard box to use as a base for a rinsing bowl.* 5.2 it is a layer or a background on which other things lie, are placed, are drawn, etc. EG *...foundation that acts as a base for the rest of your make-up.* N COUNT : IF+ PREP THEN *for* = stand; N COUNT : IF+ PREP THEN *for*

6 If you **base** one thing on another, you develop its general form, subject, or nature from that other thing. EG *The new agreement is based on the original United Nations proposal... ...movies based on Britain and British life... ...the figures on which he based that calculation.* V+O+A *(on/ upon)*

7 A **base** for something such as a system of ideas or a subject of study is a central and very important part of it from which other ideas, more advanced studies, etc are developed. EG *This innovation was regarded as a sensible base for teaching and research... ...a broad base, a consensus of ideas.* • See also **database**. N COUNT : IF+ PREP THEN *for* = basis, foundation

8 If you have a **base**, you are in a position from which you can achieve power or success, especially in relation to politics or economics. EG *The League had no real power base on which it could build... ...a limited industrial base.* N COUNT : USU MOD+N ⇑ basis

9 If you **are based** at or in a particular place, you are positioned, stationed, or staying there. EG *I was based in London... ...if these missiles are based on British soil... We were suggesting that they base themselves at a hotel.* V+O (NG/REFL) : USU PASS+A ⇑ be

10 A military **base** is a place which has military buildings and installations and where part of an army, navy, or air force is stationed or positioned. EG *...a military base... ...the new air base at Buzaruto... The Tornados abandoned the chase and returned to base.* N COUNT/ UNCOUNT

11 Your **base** is the main place where you work, stay, or live, although you spend a lot of your time somewhere else or going out to different places. EG *The company made Luxembourg city their base... The best base for the visitor to London must be the West End.* N COUNT : USU POSS+N, OR N UNCOUNT

12 A **base** for an expedition or operation is a camp or other place where supplies are kept and from where the expedition, etc is controlled. EG *...base camps... The climbers returned to base.* N COUNT/ UNCOUNT ⇑ centre

13 The **base** of a substance such as paint or food is the main form or ingredient of it, to which other substances can be added in order to make different paints, foods, etc. EG *For the walls, she suggested a pink base with a touch of brown.* N COUNT = foundation

14 A **base** is also 14.1 a system of counting and expressing numbers. The decimal system uses base 10, and the binary system uses base 2. 14.2 a chemical compound that forms a salt and water when it combines with an acid; a technical term in chemistry. N COUNT : USU+ NUM; N COUNT

15 A **base** rate or amount is the form of something to which other ones can be related or compared. EG *...a unified base price... ...if you took 1960 as being a base year and gave that a figure of 100.* N COUNT : USU BEFORE N ⇑ guide

16 A **base** in baseball or rounders is one of the places at each corner of a square on the pitch that a batter must reach in order to score a run or rounder. N COUNT ⇑ position

17 **Base** behaviour is behaviour that is immoral or dishonourable; a literary word. EG *...base and unpatriotic motives.* ADJ QUALIT = ignoble ≠ honourable

baseball /beɪsbɔːl/ is a game played by two teams of nine players in which each player from one team hits a ball with a bat and then tries to run round all four bases before the other team can get the ball back. N UNCOUNT ⇑ sport

-based 1 combines with nouns referring to places to mean positioned, stationed, or existing mainly in the place mentioned, or operating or organized from that place. EG *...two London-based organizations... ...ground-based radar sensors.* 2 combines with nouns to mean having the thing mentioned as a central and very important part or feature. EG *...an export-based economy... ...computer-based teaching.* COMB : FORMS ADJ CLASSIFS; COMB : FORMS ADJ CLASSIFS

3 combines with adverbs to mean having a particular kind of basis. EG *...a very broadly based selection.* COMB : FORMS ADJ QUALITS

baseless /beɪslɪ²s/. Something such as a story or belief that is **baseless** is not based on facts. EG *...baseless gossip.* ADJ CLASSIF = unfounded

baseline /beɪslaɪn/, **baselines**; also spelled with a hyphen. 1 The **baseline** of a tennis or badminton court is one of the lines at each end of the court that mark the limits of play. N COUNT ⇑ line

2 A **baseline** is a value or starting point on an imaginary scale with which other values be compared. EG *It serves as a baseline from which you are able to improve.* N COUNT

basement /beɪsmə²nt/, **basements**. The **basement** of a building is a floor built partly or wholly below ground level. EG *There are rats in the basement. ...a small basement flat.* N COUNT

base metal, base metals. A **base metal** is a metal, such as copper, zinc, tin, or lead, that is not a precious metal. N COUNT

base rate, base rates. The **base rate** is the rate of interest that banks use as a basis when they are calculating the rates that they charge on loans. EG *They cut their base rate by 1%.* N COUNT

bases is 1 the plural of **base**, pronounced /beɪsɪz/. 2 the plural of **basis**, pronounced /beɪsiːz/.

bash /bæʃ/, **bashes, bashing, bashed**; an informal word. 1 If you **bash** someone or something or **bash** at them, you deliberately hit them hard. EG *She was bashing him over the head with a saucepan... I went on bashing and thumping at him.* V+O : USU+A, OR V+A *(at)* = beat

2 If you **bash** something or **bash** into it, you hit it or bump into it accidentally with quite a lot of force. EG *He bashed into a tree... The cradle swayed and bashed against the walls... I've bashed my elbow.* V+O, OR V+A *(into)* = bang

3 A **bash** is a hard blow. EG *...a bash on the nose.* N COUNT

4 If you **have a bash** at something or **give it a bash**, you try to do it, even though you are do not really think that you will succeed; an informal expression. EG *She was going to have a bash at swimming the Channel.* PHR : VB INFLECTS

5 If you **bash** a person or group, you criticize them severely and unfairly or do something which makes things difficult for them. EG *...the age-old policy of bashing the workers.* V+O = knock

bash on. If you **bash on** with a task you carry on doing it, often in a rather unenthusiastic way. EG *I'd better bash on with this report.* PHRASAL VB : V+ ADV, IF+PREP THEN *with*

bash up. If you **bash** people or things **up**, you attack them violently, so as to hurt or damage them. EG *Her son seemed to feel the need to bash up things and wreck things.* PHRASAL VB : V+ O+ADV

bashful /bæʃfʊl/. Someone who is **bashful** is shy and easily embarrassed. EG *Most new parents are bashful about asking questions.* ◊ **bashfully**. EG *He smiled bashfully.* ADJ QUALIT = diffident; ◊ ADV WITH VB = shyly

-bashing 1 combines with nouns referring to people or groups, to mean severely and unfairly criticizing the people mentioned. EG *...another round of union-bashing.* 2 combines with nouns referring to things, to mean energetically doing an activity connected with the thing mentioned. EG *...a bible-bashing preacher.* COMB : FORMS N UNCOUNTS; COMB : FORMS ADJ CLASSIFS

basic /beɪsɪk/, **basics**; **basic** is an adjective, **basics** is a plural noun. 1 **Basic** means that the thing mentioned is **1.1** the main feature or aspect of something else, when you are considering it generally. EG *The basic theme of these stories never varies... We never seem to be able to solve the basic economic problems... We have taken this basic arrangement and elaborated it.* ADJ CLASSIF : ATTRIB ⇑ general = fundamental **1.2** a very important part of a person's aims or beliefs, which affects the way he or she thinks about things. EG *In China, some of my most basic beliefs were shaken... What is your basic aim in life?* ADJ QUALIT : ATTRIB ⇑ main = fundamental **1.3** is necessary for the achievement or success of something else. EG *There are certain things that are absolutely basic to a good relationship...* ADJ QUALIT : PRED, IF+PREP THEN *to* = vital

2 Basic is also used to describe something that involves or relates to only the simplest and most important aspects of a subject or an activity, which you need to know in order to do it or understand it. EG *...basic mathematical skills... ...people with only a basic education.* ADJ QUALIT : USU ATTRIB ⇑ simple = elementary ≠ advanced

3 Basic is also used of things, for example food or equipment, that you need to use regularly in your ordinary life. EG *They also produce sugar and other basic foodstuffs... The basic necessities of life.* ADJ CLASSIF : ATTRIB ⇑ essential ≠ luxury

4 Something that is **basic** is very simple in style and has only the most important features and no luxuries. EG *People are having to move from luxury homes, to basic two-roomed flats... The facilities are terribly basic.* ADJ QUALIT = primitive ≠ luxurious

5 Basics or the **basics** are the most important principles, ideas, or facts of an issue, on which everything else is based. EG *Let's get down to basics.* N PLURAL ⇑ foundations = fundamentals

6 The **basics** of a subject or activity are the simplest and most important aspects of it, which you need to know in order to do it or understand it. EG *For a year I learnt the basics of journalism.* N PLURAL : USU *the*+N, IF+PREP THEN *of* = rudiments

7 The **basics** are also simple types of food, which you eat regularly as an important part of your diet. EG *During the war people were only allowed the basics–tea, sugar, flour, etc.* N PLURAL : *the*+N ≠ luxuries

BASIC /beɪsɪk/ is a simple code for computer programming in which English words are used; an abbreviation for Beginner's All-purpose Symbolic Instruction Code. N PROPER

basically /beɪsɪkə⁰li¹/ is used **1** when you are indicating what the most important feature of something is, when you are explaining something simply, or when you are giving a general description of something complicated. EG *This was basically a political row... My work is basically to train people to help other people... There are basically three types of vacuum cleaner... They're all basically the same.* ADV SEN = essentially

2 mainly in spoken English, to emphasize that what you are saying is the most important point that you want to mention. EG *Basically, I think Britain shouldn't have gone into the Common Market... To answer your question, I would say, basically, yes... This is basically where we differ.* ADV SEN ⇑ really

basil /bæzə⁰l/ is a strongly scented herb that is used to add flavour in cooking, especially with tomatoes. N UNCOUNT

basilica /bəzɪlɪkə/, **basilicas**. A **basilica** is a Roman building or a church which is rectangular in shape with a rounded end and two aisles. N COUNT

basin /beɪsə⁰n/, **basins**. **1** A **basin** is **1.1** an open round bowl-shaped container, used especially for mixing or storing food. EG *Cover the basin with a clean cloth.* N COUNT ▸ **Basin** is also used to refer to the substance inside it or the amount it contains. EG *...a basin of water.* ▸ N PART **1.2** any bowl-shaped container that is designed to hold water or other liquids. EG *She sat on the edge of the basin of one of the two big fountains.* N COUNT+SUPP

1.3 a large sheltered area of deep water where boats or ships can be moored. EG *...the canal basin.* N COUNT **1.4** a large bowl on a stand or fixed to the wall in a bathroom or bedroom, used by people when they wash themselves. N COUNT = wash-basin

2 The **basin** of a large river, lake, or sea is the area of land around it from which water and streams run down into it. EG *...the Amazon basin.* N COUNT : ALSO IN NAMES

basis /beɪsɪs/, **bases**. **1** The **basis** of or for something is the central and most important part of it, from which it has been or can be further developed. EG *Many of the old actors used a script merely as a basis for improvization... This was the basis of the final design... Such dreams are the basis on which you later structure your life. ...the modern Christian basis of Western civilisation.* N COUNT : IF+PREP THEN *for/of/on* = foundation

2 If you decide or do a particular thing **on the basis** of something, it gives you a reason for doing it. EG *I shall make up my own mind on the basis of the advice I've been given... The choice might have been made on the basis of convenience... Everything in the village is allocated by the chief on the basis of giving to each according to his need.* PHR+*of*/CONJ *(that)*

3 If something happens or is done **on a** particular **basis**, it happens or is done in that way or using that method. EG *The National Chairman is paid on a part-time basis... ...on a daily basis... We run the meals-on-wheels service on a voluntary basis.* PHR : USED AS AN A ⇑ system

4 The **basis** for something is the thing that provides a reason or means for it, and makes it possible. EG *There is no basis for this belief... ...arguments which had no logical basis.* N COUNT : USU SING, IF+PREP THEN *for* = grounds

bask /bɑːsk/, **basks, basking, basked**. **1** If you **bask** in the sunshine or some other pleasant source of heat means you lie there in a relaxed way, enjoying the warmth. EG *I want to spend the whole holiday basking in the sun... The flat countryside was already basking in the warm sunshine.* V, OR V+A *(in)*

2 If you **bask** in someone's approval or favour, you enjoy the amount of attention that you are getting. EG *...the journalist who liberated a country and basked in the gratitude of the new rulers.* V+A *(in)* = revel, glory

basket /bɑːskɪ²t/, **baskets**. **1** A **basket** is a container that has a fixed shape and is used for carrying things such as shopping or clothes. Baskets are usually made of thin strips of wood or cane woven together and have either one or two handles. EG *...the wife carrying a wicker shopping basket containing groceries... ...a log basket.* N COUNT : USU+SUPP ⇑ container ▸ **Basket** is also used to refer to the contents of a basket. EG *...heaped baskets waiting for ironing... She had a big basket of washing in her arms.* ▸ N COUNT : IF+PREP THEN *of* ⇑ amount See also **wastepaper basket**. ● to **put all your eggs in one basket**: see **egg**.

2 Basket is also used to refer to a group or collection of things. EG *...a basket of different currencies.* N COUNT+*of*

3 In basketball, the **basket** is a circular net hanging from a metal ring through which players try to throw the ball in order to score points. N COUNT : *the*+N

basketball /bɑːskɪ²tbɔːl/ is a game in which two teams of five players each try to score goals by throwing a large ball through a circular net fixed to a metal ring at each end of the court. The players bounce the ball while running, and pass it to each other often. N UNCOUNT ⇑ sport

basketry /bɑːskɪ²tri¹/ is **basketwork**. N UNCOUNT

basketweave /bɑːskɪ²twiːv/ is a weave of two or more threads in wool or linen cloth that gives a criss-cross effect to the cloth, so that it looks like a basket. N UNCOUNT

basketwork /bɑːskɪ²twɜːk/; also spelled with a hyphen. **Basketwork** is **1** baskets and other objects woven from wicker, cane, or raffia. N UNCOUNT **2** the skill and practice of making baskets. N UNCOUNT

bas-relief /bæsrɪliːf/, **bas-reliefs**. **1 Bas-relief** is a technique of sculpture in which shapes are carved so that they stand out from the background. N UNCOUNT

2 A **bas-relief** is a sculpture carved on a surface so that it stands out from the background. N COUNT

bass, basses. **Bass** is pronounced /beɪs/ for paragraphs 1, 2, 3, and 4, and /bæs/ for paragraph 5. **Basses** is the plural for paragraphs 1 and 3, and **bass** is the plural for paragraph 5. **1** A **bass** is **1.1** a man with a voice in the lowest range of musical notes. N COUNT **1.2** the lowest part in a piece of sung music with several parts. N COUNT

2 A **bass** drum, guitar, or other musical instrument is one that produces a deep sound in the lowest range of musical notes. ADJ CLASSIF : ATTRIB ⇑ low-pitched

3 In popular music, a **bass** means a bass guitar or a double bass. EG *...a new bass player... Who have they got on bass?* N COUNT : SING NEEDS NO DET ⇑ instrument

4 The **bass** on a hi-fi, radio, etc is its ability to reproduce the lower musical notes or the knob which controls this. N SING : *the*+N

5 A **bass** is also an edible fish that is found in rivers or the sea. There are several types of bass. N COUNT

bassoon /bəsuːn/, **bassoons**. A **bassoon** is a woodwind musical instrument which makes a very low, deep sound. A bassoon consists of a long wooden pipe with keys, and a metal mouthpiece curving away from the instrument. N COUNT

bastard /bɑ:stəd, bæs-/, **bastards**. 1 A **bastard** is someone who is the child of parents who are not married to each other. EG *Spare the child the slur of being a bastard... Mr Zoyland was the bastard son of the Marquis.* N COUNT
2 If someone calls someone else a **bastard**, 2.1 they are referring to them or addressing them in an insulting way; a very offensive use. N COUNT 2.2 they are referring to or addressing someone for whom they feel sympathy, envy, or even affection; a very informal use. N COUNT : ADJ+N
3 In very informal English, people sometimes call a problem or a thing a **bastard** when they find it extremely annoying or difficult to deal with. N COUNT

baste /beɪst/, **bastes, basting, basted**. 1 If you **baste** meat, you pour hot fat and the juices from the meat itself over it while it is cooking. V+O ⇑ moisten
2 If you **baste** pieces of material, you sew them together with big, loose stitches before sewing them properly. V OR V+O = tack

bastion /bæstɪən/, **bastions**. A **bastion** is 1 something that is regarded as being important and effective in defending a particular way of life or in protecting people from something unpleasant. EG *They regard the wealth-producing system as a bastion of capitalistic privilege... Love is a bastion against loneliness.* N COUNT : IF+ PREP THEN *of* ⇑ refuge = stronghold 2 part of the wall of a castle or fortress which sticks out from the main part of the wall. N COUNT ⇑ tower

bat /bæt/, **bats, batting, batted**. 1 A **bat** is a specially shaped piece of wood that is used for hitting the ball in cricket, baseball, rounders, or table-tennis. Its shape depends on the game being played. EG *...a cricket bat.* N COUNT
2 If you are **batting**, you are having a turn at hitting the ball with a bat in cricket, baseball, or rounders. EG *He went out to bat... Which team is batting at the moment?* V ⇑ play
3 A **bat** is also a small flying animal that looks like a mouse with leathery wings and that is active at night. EG *Hundreds of bats flitted about in the cave.* N COUNT
● **blind as a bat**: see **blind**.
4 If someone does something **off** their **own bat**, they do it without anyone else suggesting it or advising them to do it. PHR : USED AS AN A ≠ prompted
5 If you say that someone did **not bat an eyelid**, you mean that they showed no sign of surprise or concern. PHR : VB INFLECTS ≠ react
6 If you say that someone is **bats** you mean that they are foolish or slightly mad; an informal use. ADJ CLASSIF : PRED

batch /bætʃ/, **batches**. A **batch** of things or people is a group of things or people of the same kind, especially a group that is dealt with at the same time or that is sent to a particular place at the same time. EG *Another batch of letters came in... ...the next batch of trainees.* N COUNT : IF+ PREP THEN *of*

bated /beɪtɪ²d/. If you wait for something **with bated breath**, you are so anxious that you can hardly breathe. PHR : USED AS AN A ⇑ anxiously

bath /bɑ:θ/, **baths, bathing, bathed**. 1 A **bath** is a long, rectangular container which you fill with water and sit or lie in, while you wash your body. N COUNT : USU SING WITH DET
2 When you have or take a **bath** or when you are in the **bath**, you wash your body while sitting or lying in a bath filled with water. EG *I'm going to have a bath... Andy's in the bath.* N SING WITH DET : VB+a+N, OR *in*+*the*+N
3 If you give a baby or other person a **bath**, you wash them in a bath. N SING : a+N
4 If you **bath** a baby or other person, you wash them in a bath. V+O
5 When you **run a bath**, you turn on the taps and fill a bath with water. PHR : VB INFLECTS
6 A **baths** is the same as a **swimming bath**. EG *I take my older children to the baths once a week.* N PLURAL : USU *the*+N
7 A **bath** of a particular liquid such as a dye is a container of this liquid in which something is immersed, usually as part of a manufacturing or chemical process. N COUNT+SUPP
8 See also **bloodbath, bubble bath, Turkish bath**.

bathe /beɪð/, **bathes, bathing, bathed**. 1 If you **bathe** or go **bathing**, you swim or play in a sea, river, lake, or other large area of water. EG *It is dangerous to bathe in the sea here.* V, OR V+A *(in)* ▸ used as a noun. EG *I'll come when I've had a bathe and something to eat.* ▸ N SING : a+N ◊ **bathing**. EG *I know a place where we can go bathing... She said she would like to change into her bathing things.* ◊ N UNCOUNT ⇑ swimming
2 In American English, to **bathe** means to have a bath. EG *After golf I would return to the flat to bathe and change for work.* V
3 If you **bathe** a wound or part of someone's body when they have been injured, you wash it gently, using water or another liquid, often with an antiseptic solution in it. V+O ⇑ clean
4 If something such as an area **is bathed** in light, it is covered with light, especially a gentle, pleasant light. EG *The room was bathed in sunlight... A candle bathed them in a golden light.* V+O+A *(in/with)* : USU PASS
5 If someone or part of their body **is bathed** in sweat, they are sweating a great deal. V+O+A *(in)* : ONLY PASS
6 If someone or something **is bathed** in love or another emotion, they are affected completely by it. EG *She was bathed in the love and affection of the Heath family.* V+O+A *(in)* : USU PASS

bather /beɪðə/, **bathers**. A **bather** is a person who is swimming or playing in a sea, river, lake, etc. EG *A great white shark killed four bathers in New Jersey on one day.* N COUNT ⇑ swimmer

bathing cap, bathing caps; also spelled with a hyphen. A **bathing cap** is a rubber cap which fits tightly over your head to keep your hair dry when you go swimming. N COUNT

bathing costume, bathing costumes; also called a **bathing suit**. Both terms are also spelled with a hyphen. A **bathing costume** or **bathing suit** is a tight-fitting garment covering a person's trunk, which women wear when they go bathing; used in British English. N COUNT = swimming costume, swimsuit

bathing trunks; also spelled with a hyphen. A man's or boy's **bathing trunks** are the shorts that he wears when he goes bathing; used in British English. N PLURAL

bathmat /bɑ:θmæt/, **bathmats**; also spelled with a hyphen. A **bathmat** is a mat which you stand on while you dry yourself after getting out of the bath. N COUNT ⇑ mat

bath oil, bath oils; also spelled with a hyphen. **Bath oil** is thick, perfumed liquid that you can add to your bathwater to soften it and make it smell nice. N MASS

bathos /beɪθɒs/ is a sudden change in speech or writing from a serious or important subject to a ridiculous or very ordinary one; a technical term in literary criticism. N UNCOUNT ⇑ anti-climax

bathrobe /bɑ:θrəʊb/, **bathrobes**; also spelled with a hyphen. A **bathrobe** is 1 a piece of clothing made of towelling, which is like a loose-fitting coat which you can wear before or after you have a bath or a swim. N COUNT ⇑ garment
2 a dressing gown; used especially in American English. N COUNT

bathroom /bɑ:θru⁴m/, **bathrooms**. 1 A **bathroom** is a room in a house that contains a bath or shower, a wash-basin, and sometimes a toilet. EG *She went into the bathroom and took a shower.* N COUNT ⇑ room
2 Some people say **bathroom** as a polite way of referring to the toilet; used especially in American English. EG *Can I go to the bathroom, please?* N SING WITH DET : USU *the*+N

bath salts; also spelled with a hyphen. **Bath salts** are mineral salts that dissolve in water, which you can put in your bathwater to soften it and to make it smell nice. N PLURAL

bath-towel, bath-towels; also spelled without a hyphen. A **bath-towel** is a very large towel used for drying your body after you have had a bath. N COUNT

bathtub /bɑ:θtʌb/, **bathtubs**; also spelled with a hyphen. A **bathtub** is a large, long container which you fill with water and sit in while you wash your body; an old-fashioned word. N COUNT

bathwater /bɑ:θwɔ:tə/; also spelled with a hyphen or as two words. Your **bathwater** is the water in which you sit or lie when you have a bath. EG *'Ryan, are you using my bath water?' I asked, enraged.* N SING : *the*+N OR POSS+N ● to **throw out the baby with the bathwater**: see **baby**.

batik /bætɪk/, **batiks**. 1 **Batik** is a process in which designs are printed on cloth by putting wax onto the areas that are not going to be coloured before putting the cloth into the dye. EG *Four of us are doing batik... ...Java's batik industry.* N UNCOUNT ⇑ printing
2 A **batik** is a cloth which has been printed with a batik design. EG *Anne Bolsover was most impressed with the batiks.* N COUNT

batman /bætmə³n/, **batmen**. A **batman** is the personal servant of an officer in the army, navy, or air force; used in British English. N COUNT

baton /bætɒ⁰n/, **batons**. A **baton** is 1 a light, thin stick used by a conductor to direct an orchestra or a choir. N COUNT 2 a short metal or wooden stick that is passed N COUNT from one runner to another in a relay race. **3** a short heavy stick used as a weapon by a policeman. N COUNT = truncheon

baton charge, baton charges. A **baton charge** is an attacking forward movement made by a large group of policemen carrying batons. N COUNT

batsman /bætsmə³n/, **batsmen.** In cricket, a **batsman** is **1** a player whose turn it is to bat. N COUNT **2** a player who has a particular skill at batting. N COUNT

battalion /bətælɪ⁰jən/, **battalions.** A **battalion** is a large group of soldiers that consists of three or more companies. EG *Major Rodin commanded the battalion... The 1st Battalion of the 9th Marine Regiment.* N COUNT ⇑ unit

batten /bætə⁰n/, **battens, battening, battened.** A **batten** is a long strip of wood that is fixed to something to strengthen it or to hold it firm. EG *The lid of the crate was fixed down with battens.* N COUNT ⇑ board

batten down. If you **batten** something **down**, you make it secure by fixing battens across it or by closing it firmly. EG *The hatches were battened down as the storm grew fiercer.* PHRASAL VB : V+O+ADV

batten on. If someone **battens on** or **upon** another person, they live comfortably or become successful by using that person's money or position in society for their own benefit. PHRASAL VB : V+PREP, HAS PASS = sponge on

batter /bætə/, **batters, battering, battered. 1** To **batter** someone, especially a child or a woman, means to injure them by hitting them many times. EG *Such parents have been known to batter their children.* ◊ **battering.** EG *This may lead to baby battering.* V+O = beat ◊ N UNCOUNT

2 If you **batter** something or **batter** at or on something, you hit it many times, for example with your fists, in order to knock it down or to make a loud noise. EG *He was battering on the wall.* V+A, OR V+O = hammer

3 When the wind, rain, or sea **batters** something, it keeps striking it with great force. EG *The ship was being battered by the waves.* V+O ⇑ strike = buffet

4 Batter is a thick, liquid mixture of flour, eggs, and milk that you can use to make things such as pancakes or put on the outside of food before frying it. N UNCOUNT

5 In baseball, a **batter** is **5.1** a player whose turn it is to bat. N COUNT **5.2** a player who has a particular skill at batting. N COUNT

batter down. To **batter down** something such as a door means to hit it repeatedly and so hard that it breaks and falls down. PHRASAL VB : V+O+ADV = break down

battered /bætəd/. Something, for example a car or a hat, that is **battered** is old, worn, and damaged as a result of being used a lot or of being treated roughly. EG *...a battered old car... He took Rudolph's battered hat and laid it on the table... Buildings were old, grim, and battered.* ADJ QUALIT = dilapidated

battering /bætə⁰rɪŋ/, **batterings.** A **battering** is an experience in which someone suffers badly through being attacked or criticized. EG *The Eighth Army had taken the worst battering... ...the kind of ideological battering that they've taken.* N COUNT = hammering

battering ram, battering rams. A **battering ram** is a long heavy piece of wood that was used for breaking down the doors of fortified buildings. N COUNT

battery /bætə⁰ri¹/, **batteries. 1** A **battery** is a device that produces electricity, used to provide power for something such as a torch or radio. EG *The battery was dead... Does your battery need recharging?* N COUNT

2 A **battery** of large guns, missile launchers, etc is a group of such weapons operated together in one place. EG *...a battery of six guns... The missile batteries gave away their positions.* N COUNT : IF+PREP THEN *of*

3 A **battery** of things, people, or events is a large number of them that are together in one place or a large number of similar events happening within a short period of time. EG *Batteries of cameras were set to record every phase of the eclipse... We would both undergo a battery of tests.* N COUNT+*of* = barrage

4 A **battery** farm is one that uses a system of producing eggs in which many hens are kept in small cages to produce large numbers of eggs at the smallest cost to the farmer. EG *...battery hens.* ADJ CLASSIF : ATTRIB

5 See also **assault and battery.**

battle /bætə⁰l/, **battles, battling, battled. 1** A **battle** is **1.1** a fight between armies or between groups of ships or planes. EG *...the Battle of Balaclava... The general was killed in battle.* N COUNT/UNCOUNT **1.2** a process in which two people or two groups of people compete for power or try to achieve opposite things. EG *...the battle between the sexes... The government fought two decisive battles against the National Union of Mineworkers... ...the biggest takeover battle in American corporate history.* N COUNT+SUPP : USU+*against/between/for* ⇑ conflict **1.3** an attempt by a group of people to achieve something that is difficult and that can only be achieved slowly, for example an attempt to change people's attitudes about an important issue. EG *...the battle for women's liberation... ...the battle against inflation.* N COUNT : USU+*for/against* = struggle, fight

2 Battle is also used in the following phrases. **2.1** A **battle of wits** is a situation in which people who disagree or have opposite aims compete with each other using their intelligence and their ability to think quickly, rather than violence. PHR : USED AS C ⇑ contest **2.2** If you **do battle with** someone, you try in a determined way to achieve something that they want to prevent you from achieving. EG *He continues to do battle with the city council... His supporters are preparing to do battle over the composition of the electoral college.* PHR : VB INFLECTS ⇑ fight = cross swords

2.3 If you say that something is **half the battle** you mean that it is the most important step towards achieving something. EG *You've got to get a good piece of meat to start off with. That's half the battle.* PHR : USED AS C

2.4 If you are **fighting a losing battle**, you are trying to achieve something but are not going to be successful. PHR : VB INFLECTS

2 To **battle** means to fight. EG *The males settle their problems over females by battling between themselves... Dad was soon battling for his life.* V+A

battle-axe, battle-axes; also spelled without a hyphen. **1** A **battle-axe** is a large axe that used to be used as a weapon. N COUNT

2 If you call a middle-aged or older woman a **battle-axe**, you mean that she is very difficult and unpleasant because of her fierce and determined attitude. EG *She was a terrible old battle-axe.* N COUNT : USU ADJ+N = dragon

battle cry, battle cries. A **battle cry** is **1** a phrase that is used to urge people to take part in activities connected with a particular cause or campaign. EG *'One man, one vote' became our battle-cry.* N COUNT ⇑ slogan = rallying cry

2 a shout that soldiers utter as they go into battle.

battlefield /bætə⁰lfi:ld/, **battlefields.** A **battlefield** is the place where a battle is being fought or has been fought. EG *Small nuclear weapons, used on the battlefield, would reduce the risk of civilian losses... ...a tour of the First World War battlefields.* N COUNT = battleground

battleground /bætə⁰lgraʊnd/, **battlegrounds.** A **battleground** is **1** a **battlefield.** N COUNT **2** a subject over which people disagree or compete and try to achieve opposite things. EG *The theory of evolution is no longer a battleground.* N COUNT

battlements /bætə⁰lmə²nts/. The **battlements** of a castle or fortress consist of a wall built round the top of it with regular gaps through which guns or arrows could be fired. N PLURAL ⇑ parapet

battleship /bætə⁰lʃɪp/, **battleships.** A **battleship** is a very large, heavily armoured warship. N COUNT

batty /bæti¹/, **battier, battiest.** Someone who is **batty** is rather eccentric or slightly mad; an informal word. EG *She must be going batty.* ▸ used of someone's behaviour. EG *That was a batty thing to do!* ADJ QUALIT = dotty

bauble /bɔ:bə⁰l/, **baubles.** A **bauble** is a small, bright ornament or piece of jewellery, especially when it is cheap. EG *...Christmas tree baubles.* N COUNT = trinket

baulk /bɔ:⁰k/. See **balk.**

bauxite /bɔ:ksaɪt/ is a clay-like ore from which aluminium is obtained. N UNCOUNT

bawdy /bɔ:di¹/, **bawdier, bawdiest.** A story, joke, etc that is **bawdy** contains humorous references to sex. EG *...bawdy songs.* ADJ QUALIT ⇑ rude = lewd, dirty

bawl /bɔ:l/, **bawls, bawling, bawled. 1** If you **bawl**, you shout or sing something very loudly and rather harshly. EG *...an old man bawling, 'Prepare ye the way of the Lord!' They bawl down the telephone at me.* V, V+O/REPORT-CL/QUOTE, OR V+A = yell

2 If a child is **bawling**, it is crying loudly. EG *Josephine started bawling.* V = wail

bawl out. 1 If someone **bawls** you **out**, they tell you off angrily for doing something wrong; used in informal English. EG *I was used to being bawled out at school for not doing homework.* PHRASAL VB : V+O+ADV ⇑ reprimand = scold

2 If you **bawl** something **out**, you shout or sing it very loudly and rather harshly. EG *...hecklers bawling out, 'What about pensions?'* PHRASAL VB : V+O/REPORT-CL/QUOTE+ADV

bay /beɪ/, **bays, baying, bayed. 1** A **bay** is **1.1** a part of a coastline where the land curves inwards. EG *...a bay surrounded on three sides by vertical cliffs...* N COUNT : ALSO IN NAMES ⇑ area

...*Shark Bay... ...the Bay of Biscay.* **1.2** a space or area in a building or yard that is intended to be used for a particular purpose. EG ...*the corridor beyond the loading bay.* • See also **sick bay**. **1.3** an area of a room that is set back from the rest of the room, often one that juts out beyond the main walls of the building. N COUNT: USU+SUPP / N COUNT ↑ recess

2 At bay. 2.1 If you **keep** or **hold** something that frightens or upsets you **at bay**, you keep it at a safe distance or prevent it from happening. EG ...*lighting a fire to keep dangerous animals at bay... Only an orderly approach to our work will keep chaos at bay.* PHR: VB INFLECTS ↑ repel = ward off

2.2 If an animal or person is **at bay**, they have been forced into a place or situation where they cannot escape from the people who are attacking or pursuing them. EG ...*a stag at bay.* PHR: USED AS AN A ↑ trapped

3 When a dog or wolf **bays**, it makes a deep howling noise. EG ...*wolves baying at the moon.* V ↑ howl

4 A **bay** is also **4.1** a small evergreen tree. Its leaves are dried and used as a herb in cooking. EG ...*a bay leaf.* **4.2** a reddish-brown horse. N COUNT: USU BEFORE N / N COUNT

bayonet /beɪənɪ²t/, **bayonets, bayoneting, bayoneted. 1** A **bayonet** is a long, sharp blade that can be fixed to the end of a rifle and used as a weapon. N COUNT

2 To **bayonet** someone means to stab them with a bayonet. V+O

bay window, bay windows; also spelled with a hyphen. A **bay window** is a window that sticks out from the outside wall of a house, where there is an area set back from the rest of the room inside the house. N COUNT

bazaar /bəzɑː/, **bazaars**. A **bazaar** is **1** an area where there are many small shops and stalls, especially in the Middle East and India. **1.2** a sale, often of home-made things, to raise money for charity. N COUNT ↑ market / N COUNT = fete

bazooka /bəzuːkə/, **bazookas**. A **bazooka** is a long, tube-shaped gun that is held on the shoulder and fires rockets. N COUNT ↑ weapon

BBC. The **BBC** is a British organization which broadcasts programmes on radio and television; an abbreviation for 'British Broadcasting Corporation'. EG *How should the BBC be financed?* ▸ **BBC** is also used to refer to particular channels on television and radio. EG *It's on Monday evenings on BBC2.* N PROPER: *the*+N ↑ company / ▸ N UNCOUNT: *on*+N+NUM

B.C. is an abbreviation for 'before Christ'; used when referring to a particular year or century before the year in which Jesus Christ was born. EG *It was not until about 1600 B.C. that the chariot was invented.* N UNCOUNT: NUM+N

be /biː/, **am, are, is; was, were; being, been.** For explanations of the use of these forms, see the individual entries. **1 Be** is used as an auxiliary in the following ways to form many of the tenses of English verbs: **1.1** with a present participle to form the continuous tenses of verbs. EG ...*a problem which is getting worse and worse... I don't know where the people were all going... I've been coming here for almost twenty years now.* AUX+-ING: SEE □ BELOW

1.2 to form the passive voice, followed by a past participle. EG *More than 40,000 demonstrators were arrested... They were all seated at the table... Most of the world's energy is supplied from fossil fuels... You have been warned... New plans are now being made.* AUX+PAST PART: SEE □ BELOW AND AT PASS

1.3 with an infinitive to say that something is planned to happen, that it will definitely happen, or that it must happen. EG *After dinner they were to go to a movie... It is to be a peaceful, non-violent protest... He is to be honoured for it... You are to be home by 10 o'clock at the latest.* AUX+*to*-INF: SEE □ BELOW

1.4 with an infinitive to say or ask what should happen or be done in a particular situation, how it should happen, or who should do it. EG *What is to be done with the wastelands of old industry?... Who is to question him?... He is to be congratulated on his success.* AUX+*to*-INF: SEE □ BELOW

1.5 in the past tense, 'was' and 'were', to talk about something that happens later than the time you are discussing. EG *There was to be a general election... He was to change dramatically during his adolescence.* AUX (*was/were*) +*to*-INF: SEE □ BELOW

1.6 to say that something can be seen, heard, or found in a particular place or doing a particular thing. EG *It is now to be found in the Tate Gallery... He is to be seen every evening taking his dog for a walk.* AUX+*to be*+PAST PART+A/-ING: SEE □ BELOW

2 Be is used to express the relationship between the subject of a sentence and its complement or adjunct. It brings them together in one clause so that more information can be added about the subject. It is used in the following ways: **2.1** followed by a noun or a proper noun to name someone or something. EG *I'm Julian and this is my friend Sandy... It's a frog, isn't it?... Are you Colonel Argoud?... Her name is Melanie... The head of the corporation is Sir Paul Simpson.* V+C

2.2 with the impersonal pronoun 'it' to describe something or mention one of its qualities. EG *It was terribly hot and airless... It's a pity, but there's nothing we can do... It's a lovely day, isn't it?* V+C: *it*+V

2.3 to bring together complex subjects and complements in a wide variety of structural forms, some of which are shown here. EG *The problem is knowing when to stop... This attempt to influence the ballot is in breach of the rules... All you have to do is put another engine in... The prospect is not quite as black as the politicians suggest... Their aim was to arrive at exactly six o'clock.* SEE EXAMPLES

2.4 with a partly redundant subject to delay the final piece of information. It is possible to omit part of the subject and 'be' and yet still convey the same information. For example, 'It was John who bought the car' can be changed to 'John bought the car'. EG *What I'm talking about is the satellite that fell out of its orbit... What is needed is something more radical... It is love that makes the world go round.* V+C: *it/what*+V

2.5 to introduce a statement or question and indicate its general type, nature, or subject. EG *The rule is: if in doubt, dry clean... The trouble is, then it's too late... The interesting thing is how do people perceive it?* V+CLAUSE: NG+V

2.6 followed by a noun or a pronoun to give more information about the subject of the clause. EG *Marc was an extraordinarily bright lad... He was an old friend of mine... It isn't a very good drawing, is it?... The books were his.* V+C

2.7 followed by an adjective or a prepositional phrase to give more information about the subject, often by mentioning one of its qualities or features. EG *The house was big and old... 'Is he Jewish?' she asked... He was in the German army... Are you ready?* V+C (ADJ), OR V+A (PREP)

2.8 to give information about time, days, dates, etc. EG *It was about four o'clock in the afternoon... Morris thought it was a little early in the morning for whisky... This was in May 1973.* V+C, OR V+A: *this/that/it*+V

2.9 to give information about the age of a person or thing. EG *Rose Gibson is twenty-seven and works as a money dealer... The day centre itself is five years old in March.* V+C, OR V+A

2.10 followed by an adverb or a prepositional group of place to tell you where the subject is. EG *This time next week I'll be back in St Louis... Is she in Oxford?... His father was not in the house... The iron was in her left hand... I was at a reading of poems... They are downstairs.* V+A

2.11 after a modal, especially 'should', 'would', and 'could', to say what the best or most effective action, solution, etc. is. EG *The role of government should be to restrain demand... The best thing to do would be to write a letter.* V (*be*)+*to*-INF: MODAL+V

2.12 with the impersonal pronoun 'there' to say that something exists or happens. 'Be' cannot usually be used without a complement or adjunct, so this structure has the word 'there' as the subject, and the noun group that you want to refer to becomes the complement. EG *There is little evidence of a religious revival... There is no such thing as a happy marriage... They were frightened there would be another earthquake... There was a rustling of papers... There were a lot of books on shelves along the walls...* V+C: *there*+V

3 In formal English, the form 'be' is used occasionally instead of the normal forms of the present tense, especially after 'whether'. EG *If you see somebody stealing something, go to the nearest person in authority, whether it be a schoolmaster or a policeman.* V (*be*)+C

4 Be is used in the forms 'be' or 'don't be' when you are giving someone advice, asking them to behave in a particular way, or encouraging them to do something. EG *'Be careful,' she said... 'Pa,' Gretchen said, 'be serious.'... Don't be jealous of your children's affection for their teacher.* V+C: ONLY IMPER

5 If someone **is**, for example, a doctor, an engineer, or a farmer, they have the job mentioned. EG *He's a civil servant.* V+C

6 If someone or something intends or is going to **be** a particular type of person or thing, they intend or are going to become that person or thing. EG *He simply decided to be a prince... ...How to be a good gardener.* V (*to be*)+C

7 Something that **is** a particular amount of money costs that amount. EG *'How much was it?'–'£55'...* V+C, OR V+A = cost

Estimate what fuel and telephone bills will be by looking up last year's costs.

8 Something that **is** a particular substance or material or **is** of a particular substance or material is made of it. EG *The cups were real china... The blankets were of soft wool.* — V+C, OR V+A (of) = be made of

9 If someone **is** at a particular place in a particular amount of time or by a particular time, they get to or arrive at that place in that time or by that time. EG *We could be there in a couple of minutes... In two days' time we'll be in Rome.* — V+A+A

10 To **be** yourself means to behave in the way that you feel is right for you and for your personality. EG *She told him to be himself and not to be influenced by other people.* — V+C (REFL)

11 If something **is**, it exists; used especially in literary or philosophical language. EG *To be or not to be... God is.* — V = exist

12 If someone or something is, for example, **as** happy **as can be** or as silent **as could be**, they have that quality or feeling to the greatest extent possible. EG *It was as quiet as could be.* — PHR : USED AS A

13 You say **to be fair, to be frank, to be serious,** etc in order to introduce a statement and to indicate that you are now changing the tone or the mood of what you were saying, and that you are being fair, frank, or serious. EG *To be frank, I see them every morning.* — PHR : USED AS ADV SEN = actually

14 be that as it may. You say **'Be that as it may'** when you want to change the subject, without reaching a decision about whether what has just been said is right or wrong. — PHR : USED AS ADV SEN

be in for. If you **are in for** something, you are going to experience it or get it; an informal expression. EG *You'll only be in for a disappointment... We may be in for some student trouble here.* — PHRASAL VB : V+ADV+PREP

be on to. 1 Someone who **is on to** or **onto** something has discovered something that is likely to lead to success or to solve a problem; an informal expression. EG *Mr Haig is on to something.* — PHRASAL VB : V+ADV+PREP, OR V+PREP

2 If you **are on to** or **onto** someone, you have discovered what they are doing, even though they were trying to keep it secret; an informal expression. EG *I think they're on to us.* — PHRASAL VB : V+ADV+PREP, OR V+PREP = suspect

> **BE** □ **Be** can be used as a V+C or a V+A and as an auxiliary. The meanings of the auxiliary, described as AUX in the grammar notes, are given in paragraph 1 of the entry for **be**. BE used as an auxiliary behaves in the following ways: **1** It is followed by a present participle, a past participle, or a *to*-infinitive. **2** It inflects. **3** *Am, are, is, was,* and *were* are used before the subject in questions, as in ***Is** she going?...How **was** he feeling?* **4** *Am, are, is, was,* and *were* are used before the negative *not* , as in *I **am** not a doctor.* The word *not* has a shortened form *n't* which can be added to *is, are, was,* and *were* as in *They **aren't** very pleased... She **isn't** there.* **5** It can be used to stand for a previous verbal group in which 'be' is used as auxiliary, as in *'Was she at the same hotel?'–'No, she **wasn't**'... She wasn't enjoying it but the children **were**.* **6** It is used in tags, as in *She's Welsh, **isn't** she?... They weren't ready, **were** they?* **7** It can be used after another auxiliary or modal and before another form of 'be', as in *It **is** being built... I have **been** there before... She must **be** sleeping.*

be- is a prefix which is added to verbs, usually past participles, and to adjectives formed from a noun and an '-ed' suffix to indicate that a person or object is covered with something. EG *...jewel→bejewelled... ...smear→besmeared... ...deck→bedecked.* — PREFIX

beach /biːtʃ/, **beaches, beaching, beached. 1** A **beach** is an area of sand or pebbles beside the sea. EG *...a sandy beach... Tourists go there to walk on the beach.* — N COUNT ⇑ shore

2 If you **beach** a boat or if a boat, whale, or other large object **is beached**, it is pulled or forced out of the water and onto land. EG *Our boat was beached on a sandbank... The boats beached and men began to walk ashore.* — V-ERG

beach ball, beach balls. A **beach ball** is a large, light ball filled with air, which people play with, especially at the seaside. — N COUNT ⇑ toy

beachcomber /biːtʃkəʊmə/, **beachcombers**; also spelled with a hyphen. A **beachcomber** is someone who spends their time wandering along beaches looking for usable things, especially objects of value. — N COUNT

beachhead /biːtʃhɛd/, **beachheads**; also spelled with a hyphen. A **beachhead** is an area of land next to the sea or a river where an attacking army has taken control and can prepare to advance further inland. EG *The Allies established a firm beachhead in Normandy.* — N COUNT

beacon /biːkən/, **beacons.** A **beacon** is **1** a light or a fire on a hill or tower, which acts as a signal or a warning that something is happening. EG *...lighting the first beacon of a chain of 101 signals... Her influence for good shone from her like a beacon.* — N COUNT = torch **2** a hill where a light or fire used to be lit as a signal or a warning of enemy invasion. EG *We walked along the top to the Worcestershire Beacon.* — N COUNT : ALSO IN NAMES ● See also **Belisha beacon.**

bead /biːd/, **beads. 1 Beads** are small pieces of coloured glass, wood, plastic, etc, usually round in shape with a hole through the middle. Beads are often put together on a piece of string or wire to make necklaces, bracelets, etc. EG *...bead necklaces... ...strings of beads.* — N COUNT : USU PL ⇑ ball

2 A **bead** of moisture, for example sweat, is a small drop of it. EG *Silver beads of perspiration began to form on his brow.* — N PART+N UNCOUNT

beaded /biːdɪ²d/. **1** A **beaded** dress, cushion, or other object is decorated with beads. — ADJ CLASSIF : IF+PREP THEN *with*

2 If part of your body is **beaded** with sweat, it is covered in small drops of sweat. EG *His face was completely beaded with perspiration.* — ADJ CLASSIF : PRED+*with*

beading /biːdɪŋ/ is a narrow strip of wood that is used for decorating or edging furniture, doors, etc. — N UNCOUNT/COUNT

beady /biːdi¹/, **beadier, beadiest. Beady** eyes are eyes that are small, round, and bright. — ADJ QUALIT : USU ATTRIB

beagle /biːgə⁰l/, **beagles.** A **beagle** is a short-haired black and brown dog with long ears and short legs. It is kept as a pet or used for hunting hares. — N COUNT ⇑ hound

beak /biːk/, **beaks. 1** A **beak** is the hard curved or pointed part of a bird's mouth which it uses for picking up food. EG *The woodpecker uses its beak like a drill to excavate wood-boring beetles.* — N COUNT : USU WITH POSS = bill

2 In informal English, someone's nose is sometimes referred to as a **beak** if it is very large. EG *What a beak he's got.* — N COUNT : USU POSS+N

3 In rather old-fashioned British English, people sometimes use the **beak** to refer to a magistrate, judge, or headmaster in an informal and slightly disrespectful way. — N COUNT : *the*+N

beaker /biːkə/, **beakers.** A **beaker** is **1** a plastic cup used for drinking, usually with no handles. EG *...great beakers of iced water.* — N COUNT ⇑ cup **2** a glass or plastic jar which is used in chemistry. — N COUNT

be-all and end-all. If someone thinks that something is **the be-all and end-all** of their life or of a particular activity, they think that it is the only really important thing in life or the only good reason for doing something. EG *For some people, competing is the be-all and end-all of their running.* — PHR : USED AS C ⇑ reason

beam /biːm/, **beams, beaming, beamed. 1** If you **beam**, you smile broadly because you are happy or pleased about something. EG *He beamed at Ralph... 'You are wonderful,' beamed Bella... ...beaming faces... The vicar beamed his thanks.* — V : IF+PREP THEN *at*, OR V+O/QUOTE ▸ used as a noun. EG *...a beam of satisfaction.* — ▸ N COUNT

2 A **beam** of light is a line of light that shines from an object such as a torch or the sun. EG *I could see the beam of his flashlight waving around in the dark.* — N COUNT ⇑ ray

3 If a source of light **beams**, it sends light out. EG *The sun beamed down.* — V, OR V+A ⇑ shine

4 A **beam** of electric particles or electric waves is a line of particles or waves sent in a particular direction. EG *...an electron beam.* — N COUNT+SUPP

5 If you **beam** signals or information to a place some distance away, you send it by means of radio waves. EG *We were able to beam pictures of the riots out to Denmark.* — V+O+A

6 A **beam** is also a long thick bar of wood, metal, or concrete, especially one which is used to support the roof of a building. EG *...the low oak beams of the living-room.* — N COUNT

7 The **beam** is a piece of apparatus in women's gymnastics that consists of a horizontal wooden bar on which the gymnasts balance and perform movements. — N SING : *the*+N

8 If you say that someone is **off beam** or **off the beam**, you mean that they are wrong or mistaken; a fairly informal expression. — PHR : USED AS AN A

9 Someone who is **broad in the beam** has wide hips; an informal expression. — PHR : USED AS C

beam-ends. If someone is **on** their **beam-ends**, they have no money left to live on; an informal expression. — PHR : USED AS AN A ⇑ destitute

bean /biːn/, **beans**. 1 **Beans** are 1.1 the pods of a tall climbing plant, or the seeds which the pods contain, which are eaten as a fresh vegetable. There are many different kinds of beans. EG *...served with a choice of green beans, French beans, or broad beans.* ▸ used also to refer to the whole plant. EG *...a garden where they grow beans.* 1.2 the large dried seeds of a bean plant, which are eaten as a vegetable after being soaked in water and boiled or baked. EG *...a jar of beans... I had opened a can of baked beans.* N COUNT : USU PL ⇑ vegetable; N COUNT : USU PL ⇑ pulse

1.3 the seeds of various plants which are used for different purposes, for example to make drinks such as coffee or cocoa, or to produce oil. EG *...coffee beans.* N COUNT + SUPP ⇑ seed

2 **Bean** is used in the following informal expressions.

2.1 If you **haven't a bean**, you have no money at all. EG *They always seemed to be very happy, although they hadn't a bean in the world.* PHR : VB INFLECTS 2.2 If you say that something **isn't worth a bean**, you mean that it is worth very little or nothing. PHR : VB INFLECTS 2.3 If someone is **full of beans**, they are very lively and full of energy and enthusiasm. PHR : USED AS C 2.4 If you **spill the beans**, you tell someone something that people have been trying to keep secret. PHR : VB INFLECTS ⇑ reveal

bean feast, bean feasts. A **bean feast** is a party or jolly social event; an informal expression used in British English. N COUNT

beanpole /biːnpəʊl/, **beanpoles**. If you describe or refer to someone as a **beanpole**, you mean that they are very tall and thin; an informal word. N COUNT = rake

beansprout /biːnspraʊt/, **beansprouts**. **Beansprouts** or **beanshoots** are small shoots grown from beans. They are eaten raw or lightly cooked, especially in Chinese food. N COUNT : USU PL

bear /bɛə/, **bears, bearing, bore, borne**. 1 A **bear** is a large, strong wild animal with thick fur and sharp claws. There are several different kinds of bears, and they live in the cooler parts of the world. EG *The bear attacked me from behind.* ● See also **grizzly bear, polar bear, teddy bear**. N COUNT

2 If you say that someone is **like a bear with a sore head**, you mean that they are very bad-tempered and irritable; an informal expression. PHR : USED AS C

3 If there is a **bear** market on the Stock Exchange, a lot of people are selling shares with the intention of buying them back when the price has fallen, thus making a profit; a technical use. N BEFORE N ≠ bull

4 When people or animals **bear** something, especially something heavy or large, they carry it; a fairly formal use. EG *Camels and donkeys bear those goods inland... The old man arrived, bearing a large bundle on his head... He was borne in front of her on the stretcher.* V+O : USU+A

5 If you **bear** someone something such as a present or letter, you bring it to them; a fairly formal use. EG *We always visit friends who are ill, bearing a large bunch of grapes.* V+O+O, OR V+O, OR V+O+A *(to)* ⇑ carry

6 When the wind, air, or sea **bears** something somewhere, it moves it from one place to another; a fairly formal or literary use. EG *The wind steadied the kite and bore it round the sky... The sound of the children playing was borne across the garden to the house.* V+O+A ⇑ take = carry

7 If something **bears** the weight of something heavy, it supports the weight of that thing. EG *His ankle felt strong enough to bear his weight without too much pain... Four columns bear the magnificent roof.* V+O ⇑ hold = support

8 If something **bears** something such as a sign or mark or writing, it has it on its surface or attached to it where it can be seen. EG *Every piece of furniture bears a number and letter... ...a petition bearing nearly half a million signatures... ...a car bearing Irish licence plates.* V+O ⇑ have = carry

9 If someone or something **bears** signs of possessing a particular quality or of having had a particular experience, they behave in a way that shows that they have that quality or have had that experience. EG *He still bore the scars of his unhappy childhood... The scene bore all the marks of a country wedding.* V+O+A *(of)*

10 Someone or something that **bears** a particular name or title has that name or title; a fairly formal use. EG *This is my first son, who bears his grandfather's name... The law which bears his name was passed on 30th April 1946.* V+O ⇑ have

11 If you **bear** a difficult, unpleasant, or upsetting situation, you accept it bravely and are able to deal with it mentally. EG *It was painful of course but I bore it... This disaster was more than some of them could bear... Others cannot bear his burden for him.* ● to **grin and bear it**: see **grin**. V+O = endure

12 If you say that you **can't bear** something, you mean that you feel very upset or impatient about it. EG *I couldn't bear him to leave me for someone else... I can hardly bear to tell you about it, it was so sad... Stop keeping me in suspense! I can't bear it!* PHR : VB INFLECTS

13 If you say that you **can't bear** someone or something, you mean that you dislike them very much. EG *I couldn't bear staying in the same town as that man... I can't bear him!... I like dirt. I couldn't bear a job where I was clean all day.* PHR : VB INFLECTS = can't abide

14 If something can **bear** a particular strain or pressure, it is strong enough or well-made enough to be able to survive it. EG *Their policies are putting a greater strain on the economic system than it can bear.* V+O ⇑ take = sustain

15 If something does not **bear** examination or inspection, it will not be found to be good or accurate enough if it is examined critically. EG *The results just don't bear examination.* ● to **bear comparison**: see **comparison**. V+O ⇑ take = stand up to

16 If you **bear** the responsibility for something such as payment of money or someone's behaviour, you accept responsibility for it. EG *It would be unjust for him to bear personally the great expenses involved.* V+O = shoulder

17 If something **bears** no resemblance or no relationship to something else, it is not at all like it. EG *The interpretation bore no relation to the actual words spoken... The model must bear some resemblance to reality.* V+O ⇑ have

18 When a woman **bears** a child or **bears** her husband a child, she gives birth to it. EG *She bore three children in three years... She had borne him a daughter.* V+O, V+O+O, OR V+O+A *(to/for)* = have

19 When a plant or tree **bears** flowers, fruit, or leaves, it produces them. EG *Some plants only bear fruit once every twenty-five years... It bears cream-coloured flowers.* V+O ⇑ produce

20 If you **bear** left or right when you are driving or walking along, you turn slightly in that direction. EG *Bear right down the south side of the church.* V+A

21 If you **bear** yourself or your head or body in a particular way, you move, stand, or behave in the way mentioned; a rather literary use. EG *She bore her head high... She bore herself like a queen... He bore himself well at the funeral.* V+O (NG/REFL) +A = carry

22 If you **bear** someone a particular feeling such as love or hate, you feel that emotion towards them; a rather literary use. EG *He bore his children no illwill.* V+O+O = wish

23 If you **bring** pressure or influence **to bear** on someone, you use it to try and persuade them to do something. EG *The group's aim is to bring pressure to bear on Parliament to get the law changed.* PHR : VB INFLECTS

24 The verb **bear** is also used in the following expressions, which are explained at other places in this dictionary. ● to **bear the brunt of** something: see **brunt**. ● to **bear** something **in mind**: see **mind**. ● to **bear witness**: see **witness**.

bear down. 1 If something large **bears down** on someone or something, it moves quickly towards them in a threatening way. EG *We struggled to turn the boat as the wave bore down on us.* PHRASAL VB : V+ADV+A *(on/upon)* ⇑ approach

2 To **bear down** on something means to push or press downwards with quite a lot of steady pressure. EG *You have to bear down on the screw quite hard to get it to turn.* PHRASAL VB : V+ADV+A *(on)* = lean

bear on. If a fact or situation **bears on** or **upon** something, it is relevant to it or connected with it; a formal expression. EG *Certain facts bearing on the choice of time should be carefully considered.* PHRASAL VB : V+PREP, HAS PASS ⇑ affect

bear out. If someone or something **bears** someone **out** or **bears out** a claim they are making, they support what that person is saying or claiming. EG *The claims are not borne out by the evidence... ...and, Gill, perhaps you'll bear me out on this, we got very similar results to Hobson's.* PHRASAL VB : V+O+ADV = uphold, confirm

bear up. 1 If something does not **bear up**, it is not good enough or accurate enough to survive criticism or careful examination. EG *The results just don't bear up at all.* PHRASAL VB : V+ADV = stand up

2 If you **bear up** when experiencing difficulties or problems, you remain cheerful and show courage in spite of them. EG *You have to bear up under the strain.* PHRASAL VB : V+ADV = hold up

bear with. If you ask someone to **bear with** you, PHRASAL VB : V+

you are asking them to be patient, for example because although what you are saying may seem complicated or boring at first it will become easier to understand or more interesting later on. EG *I hope you'll bear with me as I explain... 'This course is awful!' 'Bear with it–it gets better.'* PREP, HAS PASS

bearable /bɛərəbəl/. Something that is **bearable** is of a type, amount, or intensity that you feel you can accept or deal with. EG *The heat was just bearable... He hoped for some news that would make life more bearable.* ADJ QUALIT ⇑ acceptable = tolerable

beard /bɪəd/, **beards**. 1 A man's **beard** is the hair that grows on his chin and cheeks. EG *He had a long grey beard... Henry Beamish had grown a beard.* N COUNT

2 A goat's **beard** is the long hair that grows under its chin. N COUNT

bearded /bɪədɪd/. A **bearded** man is a man who has a beard. EG *...a bearded thirty-five-year-old... ...his great bearded face.* ADJ CLASSIF : ATTRIB ≠ clean-shaven

bearer /bɛərə/, **bearers**. 1 A **bearer** is 1.1 a person who carries something, for example a stretcher or coffin. EG *The four bearers lifted the coffin slowly.* N COUNT = carrier 1.2 in India and elsewhere in former times, a native servant of a European. N COUNT

2 The **bearer** of something such as a letter or a piece of news is the person who brings it to someone. EG *...the bearer of the invitation.* N COUNT : IF+ PREP THEN *of* ⇑ carrier

3 The **bearer** of a document, for example a cheque or passport, is the person who has it in their possession and who has the authority or right to possess it; a formal or technical use. EG *The identification document contains the bearer's ethnic origin and fingerprints.* N COUNT : USU *the*+N ⇑ possessor = holder

4 The **bearer** of a particular name or title is the person who has that name or title. EG *He is the current bearer of the Sackville title.* N COUNT : IF+ PREP THEN *of*

bear hug, bear hugs. A **bear hug** is a rather rough, tight hug. N COUNT

bearing /bɛərɪŋ/, **bearings**. If something **has some bearing** or **a bearing on** a situation or event, it has some effect on it or some connection with it. EG *That is all in the past. It has no bearing on what is happening today... It was just coincidence and had no bearing on my choice.* PHR : VB INFLECTS ⇑ influence

2 Someone's **bearing** is the way in which they move or stand, especially when this shows their character. EG *Because of her bearing I realized that she was someone important... ...that tall, slightly stooped, and distinguished bearing.* N SING WITH DET : USU POSS+ N ⇑ stance = air

3 If something is **beyond** or **past all bearing** or distresses or worries you **beyond bearing**, it is so bad or upsetting that you cannot accept it and deal with it mentally. EG *Her state afflicted him beyond bearing.* PHR : USED AS AN A

4 If you take a **bearing** with a compass, you use it to work out the direction in which a particular place lies or in which something is moving. EG *Father took bearings off the lighthouse.* N COUNT

5 If you **get, find,** or **take** your **bearings**, you find out exactly where you are, what direction you should go in, or what you should do next. EG *They stopped to get their bearings... After a week in the job, she had got her bearings.* PHR : VB INFLECTS

6 If you **lose** your **bearings**, you do not know exactly where you are or what you should do next. EG *Young people can lose their bearings so easily.* PHR : VB INFLECTS

7 A **bearing** is a part of a machine that supports or holds another part which turns or moves and which is designed to reduce friction. EG *...the wheel bearings.* • See also **ball bearing**. N COUNT : USU PL

-bearing combines with nouns to indicate that one substance, for example rock, earth, or water, carries inside it small amounts of another substance, such as a mineral or gas. EG *...oil-bearing rock... ...oxygen-bearing water.* COMB : FORMS ADJ CLASSIFS

bearskin /bɛəskɪn/, **bearskins**. A **bearskin** is 1 a tall fur hat that is worn by some British soldiers on ceremonial occasions. N COUNT = busby 2 the skin and fur of a bear, used for example as a rug or a cover. N COUNT

beast /biːst/, **beasts**. 1 A **beast** is an animal, especially a large, dangerous wild animal; a fairly literary use. EG *...that most feared and dangerous of all beasts–a maddened buffalo... We were surrounded by birds and beasts and plants.* N COUNT

2 If you describe or refer to someone as a **beast**, you mean that they are nasty, annoying, unkind, or selfish; a fairly informal use. EG *The selfish little beast!* N COUNT = pig

3 If you describe or refer to a man as a **beast**, you mean that his behaviour, especially his sexual behaviour, is uncontrolled and cruel; a fairly literary use. EG *He is a raging beast.* N COUNT : USU SING

4 The **beast** in a person is the part of their nature which is considered to be like that of animals and consists of strong aggressive emotions such as rage, greed, lust, etc. EG *Her behaviour always brings out the beast in you, doesn't it?* N SING : *the*+N, USU+*in* ⇑ animal

5 If you say that something such as a task is a **beast**, you mean that it is difficult or unpleasant to do or to deal with; a fairly informal use. EG *It's a beast of a job.* N SING : *a*+N ⇑ problem

beastly /biːstli[1]/; an informal word. 1 Something that is **beastly** is very unpleasant. EG *...a beastly cut on the knee... It's so beastly there.* ADJ QUALIT = horrible

2 Someone who is **beastly** is unkind, mean, and spiteful. EG *He was so beastly, you've no idea.* ADJ QUALIT = horrid

3 **Beastly** is used to emphasize that something has a particular quality, usually an unpleasant quality, to a very great degree; a British English usage. EG *The nights up here get beastly cold.* ADV+ADJ = horribly

beast of burden, beasts of burden. A **beast of burden** is an animal such as an ox or a donkey that is used for carrying or pulling things. N COUNT

beast of prey, beasts of prey. A **beast of prey** is a wild animal which kills and eats other animals. N COUNT = predator

beat /biːt/, **beats, beating, beaten**. The form **beat** is used in the present tense and is the past tense of the verb. 1 If someone **beats** another person, they hit them many times so as to hurt or punish them, usually with something such as a stick. EG *His stepfather used to beat him with an iron bar... I have seen him nearly beat a man to death.* V+O

2 If someone or something **beats** on, at, or against something or **beats** something, they hit it hard, usually several times or continuously for a period of time. EG *We called out threats and beat on the bars of our cells... The rain beat against the window... He beat the water with his hands.* V+A, OR V+O = pound ▸ used as a noun. EG *The floor shook to the beat of the dancer's feet.* ▸ N SING : USU *the*+N+*of* ◊ **beating**. EG *We could hear only the beating of the rain on the tin roof of the shed.* ◊ N SING : USU *the*+N+*of*

3 When a bird or insect **beats** its wings or when its wings **beat**, they move up and down in a regular rhythm. EG *Some birds beat their wings as fast as 80 times a second.* V-ERG = flap ▸ used as a noun. EG *Flies are capable of moving their wings at speeds up to 1000 beats per second.* ▸ N COUNT ◊ **beating**. EG *...bats filling the air with the beating of their skinny wings.* ◊ N SING : *the*+ N+*of*

4 When your heart or pulse **beats** in a particular way or **is beating**, it continually makes movements up and down with a regular rhythm. EG *His heart beat faster... Philip felt his pulse beating.* V ⇑ move = pound ▸ used as a noun. EG *He could feel the beat of her heart.* ▸ N COUNT : USU +SUPP

5 If you **beat** a drum, tambourine, etc, you hit it in order to make a sound. V+O ▸ used as a noun. EG *They heard the beat of a tom-tom.* ▸ N SING : USU DET+N+*of*

6 The **beat** of a piece of music is the main rhythm that it has. EG *A funky dance beat... The various instruments were stopping and starting but keeping to the beat.* N SING : *the*+N

7 A **beat** in music is one of the stressed notes in a bar of music that gives the music its rhythm. N COUNT ⇑ stress

8 If you **beat time** to a piece of music, you move your hand or foot up and down in time with the rhythm. A conductor beats time with his baton in order to show the orchestra how fast the music should be played. PHR : VB INFLECTS

9 If you **beat** eggs, cream, butter, etc, you mix them thoroughly using a fork or whisk. EG *Beat two eggs and add them to the butter and sugar.* V+O ◊ **beaten**. EG *Add the beaten eggs to the mixture and stir well.* ◊ ADJ CLASSIF : ATTRIB

10 If someone **beats** a path or way through something such as a jungle or long grass, they make a path by pushing aside or treading on plants or grass. EG *...to beat a path through the bush.* V+O+A *(through)* = force

11 When people **beat** or when they **beat** an area of land, they move over the land hitting the bushes or heather in order to drive birds or animals into the open so that they can be shot, usually for sport. V OR V+O

12 If you **beat** someone in a game, race, competition, etc, you defeat them. EG *They were playing draughts and she beat him... Arsenal beat Oxford United five one... He's going to be a jolly tough candidate to beat when the election comes round.* V+O • If you **beat** • PHR : VB

someone **hollow** you defeat them very easily and by a great amount. EG *She admitted she wasn't much good at it and that you had beaten her hollow.* INFLECTS = thrash

13 If you **beat** something that you are fighting against, for example a social system or organization, you stop it doing something that you think is wrong, or you succeed in doing something that you think is right even though the system is trying to stop you. EG *They were trying to find ways to beat the bureaucracy... We've got to beat racism... ...beating the system.* V+O U ⇑ overcome

14 If you **beat** a record or previous achievement, you do better than that. EG *They all seem to be trying to beat the record... He beat his own previous best time of three minutes fifty-five seconds... ...and we got it all into 1700 pages. Beat that!* V+O ⇑ surpass

15 To **beat** an event or something that is going to happen means to do something that you want to do before the other event happens. EG *Everyone said how sensible we were to beat the Christmas rush... Buy your petrol now and beat the Budget!* V+O ⇑ precede ● If you intend to do something but someone **beats** you **to it,** they do it before you do. EG *The Italians beat them to it by about 36 hours.* ● PHR : VB INFLECTS ⇑ precede

16 If you say that something **beats** something else, you mean that it is better than that thing; a fairly informal use. EG *To my mind nothing beats a bowl of natural yogurt... What's wrong with being a shoe salesman? It sure beats making bombs.* V+O : NO CONT ⇑ surpass = top

17 If you say that you cannot **beat** a particular thing or group of people for a particular feature or quality, you mean that they are the best with regard to that feature or have most of that quality. EG *For autumn fruit and leaf colour, it is hard to beat the spindle trees... You can't beat Americans for friendliness.* V+O+A *(for)* : WITH BROAD NEG ⇑ surpass = outdo

18 **Beat** is used in expressions such as **'It beats me'**, and **'What beats me is'** to indicate that you cannot understand or explain something; a fairly informal use. EG *What beats me is where they get the money from... 'He wanted to know where you were.'–'What for?'–'Beats me.'* CONVENTION

19 You say **'Can you beat that?'** or **'Can you beat it?'** to indicate that you are very surprised and perhaps annoyed about something that has happened; an informal expression. CONVENTION

20 The **beat** of someone such as a policeman is the area in a town or in the country for which they are responsible in their job. EG *His ability to keep order was so unquestioned he could pound his beat unarmed... We listened to a newspaper editor talk about his beat, an area of 30 square miles.* N COUNT : USU POSS+N IN SING = patch ● A policeman **on the beat** is on duty, walking around the particular area for which he or she is responsible. EG *Like other policemen on the beat, Bob is armed only with a small, two-way radio.* ● PHR : USED AS AN A = on patrol

21 You tell someone to **beat it** when you want them to go away, for example because they are annoying you or because they should not be there; an informal expression. EG *'Beat it,' the man said. 'Go on. Get out.'* CONVENTION = hop it, scram

22 The word **beat** is also used in the following expressions, which are explained at other places in this dictionary. ● to **beat about the bush**: see **bush**. ● **two hearts that beat as one**: see **heart.** ● **to beat a retreat**: see **retreat.** ● See also **beaten, beating, dead beat**.

beat down. **1** When the sun **beats down**, it is very hot and bright. PHRASAL VB : V+ADV

2 When the rain **beats down**, it rains very hard. EG *...torrential rains that beat down on her like hailstones.* PHRASAL VB : V+ADV

3 When you **beat down** a person who is selling you something, you force them to accept a lower price for it than they had hoped to get. EG *I beat him down from £500 to £400.* PHRASAL VB : V+O+ADV ⇑ haggle

beat out. **1** If you **beat out** sounds on a drum, you make the sounds by beating the drum. EG *The drummers walked among them, beating out a rhythm to match their movements.* PHRASAL VB : V+O+ADV = bang

2 If you **beat out** a fire, you cause it to go out by hitting it, usually with an object such as a blanket or a brush. PHRASAL VB : V+O+ADV ⇑ extinguish

beat up. To **beat** someone **up** means to hit or kick them many times so that they are badly hurt. EG *He told us that he had been beaten up by the police.* PHRASAL VB : V+O+ADV

beaten /bi̲ːtəⁿn/. **1 Beaten** metal is metal that has been shaped or flattened by beating it. EG *The helmet was made of beaten gold.* ADJ CLASSIF : ATTRIB

2 off the beaten track: see **track**.

beaten-up. A **beaten-up** car or other object is old, battered, and in bad condition. EG *...a beaten-up yellow mini.* ADJ QUALIT = beat-up

beater /bi̲ːtə/, **beaters.** A **beater** is **1** a tool or part of a machine for beating eggs, cream, etc. EG *Use an egg beater to make the mixture stiff and frothy.* N COUNT = whisk **2** a person whose job is to beat an area of land in order to drive animals and birds into the open to be shot for sport. N COUNT

beatific /bi̲ːətɪ̲fɪk/. A **beatific** expression shows or expresses great happiness and calmness; a literary word. ADJ CLASSIF = blissful

beatify /biˈæ̲tɪfaɪ/, **beatifies, beatifying, beatified.** To **beatify** someone means to declare formally in a church ceremony that someone who is dead is a blessed person, usually as the first step in making them a saint. V+O ◇ **beatification** /biˈæ̲tɪfɪkeɪ̲ʃəⁿn/. ◇ N UNCOUNT

beating /bi̲ːtɪŋ/, **beatings. 1** If you are given a **beating** you are hit hard many times, especially with something such as a stick, often as a punishment. EG *She had left home after a savage beating... Her children always showed signs of recent beatings.* N COUNT = thrashing

2 If a team takes a **beating**, it is defeated by a large amount in a game or contest. EG *England's cricketers took a terrible beating in the West Indies last winter.* N SING : a+N ⇑ defeat = thrashing

3 If you say that something will **take some beating**, you mean that it is very good and it is unlikely that anything better will be done or made; an informal expression. EG *Woody Allen's last film will take some beating.* PHR : VB INFLECTS

beating up, beatings up. A **beating up** is an attack on someone in which they are hit and kicked so that they are very badly hurt. EG *They gave him an awful beating up.* N COUNT = thrashing

beatnik /bi̲ːtnɪk/, **beatniks.** A **beatnik** was a type of young person in the late 1950's who wore strange clothes and had unconventional beliefs rather than traditional ones; sometimes used showing disapproval. N COUNT ⇑ youth

beat-up. A **beat-up** car, piece of equipment, or other object is old and in bad condition; an informal word. EG *...my beat-up 1958 Buick.* ADJ CLASSIF : ATTRIB = battered

beau /bəʊ̲/, **beaux, beaus**; the plural can be either **beaux** or **beaus**. A woman's **beau** is her boyfriend or admirer; an old-fashioned word. EG *...Caro's rejected beau.* N COUNT ⇑ man

beaut /bju̲ːt/, **beauts.** You describe something as a **beaut** when you think it is very good; a very informal word. EG *That shot was a real beaut.* N COUNT : USU AS C

beauteous /bju̲ːtiˈəs/ means the same as beautiful; a literary word. ADJ QUALIT : USU ATTRIB ⇑ beautiful

beautician /bjuːtɪ̲ʃəⁿn/, **beauticians.** A **beautician** is a person whose job is giving people beauty treatments such as cutting and polishing their nails, treating their skin, etc. N COUNT

beautiful /bju̲ːtɪfʊl/. **1** Someone or something that is **beautiful** is very good and pleasing to look at. EG *You're beautiful... ...a very beautiful girl... ...a beautiful house... The table looked beautiful.* ◇ **beautifully.** EG *...beautifully dressed young men.* ADJ QUALIT ⇑ attractive = lovely ≠ ugly ◇ ADV = gorgeously

2 Something that is **beautiful** is very pleasant or pleasing. EG *...beautiful music... It's such a beautiful day... She had beautiful manners... Everything in life is beautiful.* ◇ **beautifully.** EG *She behaved beautifully today.* ADJ QUALIT ⇑ good = heavenly, exquisite ◇ ADV ⇑ well

3 A **beautiful** action is one that is done very skilfully. EG *That's a beautiful shot!* ▸ used of people who do a particular activity. EG *He's a beautiful tennis player, but he has an ugly temper.* ◇ **beautifully.** EG *Doesn't he play the piano beautifully?... It's a beautifully constructed book.* ADJ QUALIT ▸ ADJ QUALIT : ATTRIB ◇ ADV WITH VB = exquisitely

4 A **beautiful** experience or event is one that is very moving and makes you feel a deep happiness. EG *Falling in love is a beautiful experience.* ADJ QUALIT = wonderful

beautify /bju̲ːtɪfaɪ/, **beautifies, beautifying, beautified.** To **beautify** something means to cause it to look more beautiful. EG *Charlotte went on beautifying her home.* V+O ⇑ decorate

beauty /bju̲ːtiˈ/, **beauties. 1 Beauty** is the fact, quality, or condition of being beautiful. EG *Even a thoughtless person can appreciate beauty... Her beauty grew in her old age... The train was a thing of beauty... ...an evening of quite remarkable beauty.* N UNCOUNT = loveliness ≠ ugliness

2 A **beauty** is a woman who is considered to be very beautiful. EG *...famous beauties... No one had told me* N COUNT = belle

that Vita had turned into a beauty... My mother was no beauty.
3 You describe something as a **beauty** when you think it is very good; an informal use. EG *This bike's a real beauty.* — N COUNT: USU USED AS C
4 The **beauties** of something are its beautiful qualities or features. EG *I'm often stirred by the beauties of nature.* — N COUNT+SUPP: USU PL = glory
5 If you say that a particular feature is **the beauty** of something, you mean that it is what makes that thing so good or so much better than other similar things. EG *That's the beauty of the plan–it's so simple... The real beauty of democracy is that everyone has a say in how they are governed.* — PHR+of ⇑ advantage = attraction
6 **Beauty** is used of things and people that are involved in make-up and treatments that are considered to make people look beautiful. EG *His table was covered with beauty products... ...the magazine's beauty editor.* — N BEFORE N ⇑ cosmetic

beauty contest, beauty contests. A **beauty contest** is a competition in which young women parade in front of judges who decide which one is the most beautiful. — N COUNT

beauty parlour, beauty parlours. A **beauty parlour** is a place where women can go to have their skin treated, their nails manicured, and other treatment to make them look more beautiful. — N COUNT = beauty salon

beauty queen, beauty queens. A **beauty queen** is a woman who has won a beauty contest. — N COUNT

beauty salon, beauty salons. A **beauty salon** is the same as a beauty parlour. — N COUNT

beauty sleep. Your **beauty sleep** is sleep that you have after going to bed quite early, which is considered to help you stay looking young and beautiful; a rather humorous expression. EG *You've had your beauty sleep?* — N UNCOUNT

beauty spot, beauty spots. A **beauty spot** is **1** a place that is famous and popular because of its beautiful countryside or beautiful view. EG *Ashness Bridge is a popular beauty spot.* — N COUNT **2** a small black dot that women used to stick on their faces in the eighteenth century because people thought that this looked beautiful. — N COUNT ⇑ patch

beaver /biːvə/, **beavers. 1** A **beaver** is a furry animal which is rather like a large rat with a big flat tail. Beavers live partly on land and partly in streams, where they make ponds by building dams. — N COUNT
2 **Beaver** is the fur of a beaver, when it is used for making coats, hats, and other clothes. — N UNCOUNT: USU N+N
3 Someone who is described as an **eager beaver** is considered to be too enthusiastic about something or to work too hard; an informal expression. — N COUNT = busy bee

beaver away. If someone is **beavering away**, they are working very hard at a job. EG *...these billions of micro-organisms, beavering away to build up the fertile layer of soil.* — PHRASAL VB: V+ADV ⇑ work = slog away

becalmed /bɪkɑːmd/. If a sailing ship is **becalmed**, it is unable to move because there is no wind. — ADJ CLASSIF ⇑ still

became /bi¹keɪm/ is the past tense of **become.**

because /bi¹kəˀz/. **1 Because** is used **1.1** to introduce the reason for a statement or to introduce the answer to a 'why' question. EG *I couldn't see Helen's expression, because her head was turned... Don't use an abrasive cleaner on the bath, because it may scratch the surface... 'Why shouldn't I come?'–'Because you're too busy.'... Because these were the only films we'd ever seen of these people, we got the impression that they did nothing else but dance to classical music.* — CONJ SUBORD **1.2** to add a remark which gives your reason for stating a fact or an opinion, after you have stated it. EG *Fortunately someone was in the house, because I could hear music playing faintly... He was a modest man, because I found on checking that he had a war decoration, a fact which he had never mentioned to me... Look on the bright side, because there always is a bright side.* — CONJ SUBORD
2 Because of is used to state the reason for something. EG *He retired last month because of illness... It was largely because of this that 50,000 of them fled from the city.* — PREP
3 Just because is used, in informal spoken English, when you want to say that a particular situation should not necessarily make you come to a particular conclusion. EG *Just because you're better than me doesn't mean I'm lazy.* — PHR

beck /bɛk/, **becks. 1** A **beck** is, in Northern British English, a small stream. — N COUNT = brook
2 If you are **at** someone's **beck and call**, you have to be constantly available and ready to do what they ask. — PHR: USED AS AN A

beckon /bɛkəⁿn/, **beckons, beckoning, beckoned. 1** If you **beckon** to someone, you signal to them to come to you by moving your hand or finger repeatedly in a curving movement towards your body. EG *He beckoned and the girl came over... Claus beckoned to him excitedly. 'Come here, come here!'... He beckoned me to follow him... He beckoned me on.* — V: IF+PREP THEN to, OR V+0, ALSO+to-INF = motion
2 If something **beckons**, it is so interesting, attractive, or important to someone that they feel they must become involved in it or deal with it. EG *Vast countries beckon to young men in search of adventure... Fame beckoned.* — V: IF+PREP THEN to, OR V+0 ⇑ attract = call

become /bi¹kʌm/, **becomes, becoming, became.** The form **become** is used in the present tense and is also the past participle of the verb. **1** To **become** means to change or develop in the way that is mentioned, or to start being something different in the way that is stated. EG *The smell became stronger and stronger... One must expect this situation to become increasingly common... It became clear that the Conservatives were not going to win... We became good friends at once... It was not until 1845 that Texas became part of the USA... Day-dreams had become realities.* — V+C
2 If you wonder **what has** or **what will become of** someone or something, you wonder where they are and what has happened to them, or where they will be and what will happen to them. EG *What a terrific cheek he had, that chap Boon. I wonder what became of him... Whatever became of that gold watch you used to have?* — PHR
3 If something **becomes** someone, it is appropriate for them, for example by being the right kind of behaviour for them or the right kind of thing to make them look attractive; a slightly formal word. EG *Sarcasm doesn't become you.* — V+O: NO CONT = suit

becoming /bi¹kʌmɪŋ/; a formal, fairly old-fashioned use. **1** A piece of clothing, a colour, or a hairstyle that is **becoming** makes the person who is wearing it look attractive. EG *She was dressed in an extremely becoming trouser suit.* ◇ **becomingly.** EG *She was dressed becomingly in black.* — ADJ QUALIT = fetching; ◇ ADV WITH VB = fetchingly
2 Behaviour or language that is **becoming** is appropriate and proper in the circumstances. EG *Is such language becoming?* ◇ **becomingly.** EG *...becomingly modest.* — ADJ CLASSIF: USU PRED; ◇ ADV+ADJ = suitably

bed /bɛd/, **beds, bedding, bedded. 1** A **bed** is **1.1** a piece of furniture that you lie on when you sleep. EG *It was a small room, with a bed, a chair and a table... He sat down on the bed... He went to bed at ten... I have to put the kids to bed... I was in bed all day with a headache... I'm sorry, have I got you out of bed?* — N COUNT, OR PREP+N **1.2** a place to stay as a guest in a hotel or as a patient in hospital. EG *...much needed hospital beds... She tried to get a bed at the Hotel Kempinski.* — N COUNT
2 A **bed** in a garden or a park is an area of ground which is specially prepared so that plants can be grown in it. EG *Beds of golden marigolds... ...a flower bed... ...the rose bed.* ● **a bed of roses**: see **rose.** — N COUNT+SUPP = plot
3 A **bed** of shellfish or coral is an area of the sea where a particular type of shellfish can be caught in large quantities or where coral grows. EG *...oyster beds.* — N COUNT+SUPP
4 The **bed** of the sea or of a river or lake is the ground at the bottom of it. EG *...on the sea bed... ...a dried-up river bed.* — N COUNT+SUPP
5 A **bed** of rock is a layer of rock that is found within a larger area of rock. EG *...horizontal beds of sandstone.* — N COUNT+SUPP = stratum
6 A **bed** is also a specially prepared surface on which something is placed or built. EG *...a railway line, laid on a bed of gravel.* — N COUNT+SUPP ⇑ foundation
7 To **go to bed with** someone means to have sex with them. EG *I like you a lot, but I have no intention of going to bed with you.* — PHR: VB INFLECTS ● If you say that someone is **in bed** with someone else, you mean that they are having sex. EG *Guy came home and found his wife in bed with his best friend.* — ● PHR: USED AS AN A
8 To **bed** someone means to have sex with them; an informal use. — V+O
9 If you say that someone has **got out of bed on the wrong side**, you mean that they have been cross ever since they woke up that morning. — PHR: VB INFLECTS ⇑ be cross

10 When you **make the bed**, you arrange the sheets and covers neatly on the bed so that it is ready to sleep in. ● If you say to someone that they **have made** their **bed, and now** they **must lie in it**, you mean that since they have chosen to do a particular thing, they must now accept the unpleasant results of it. PHR : VB INFLECTS ● PHR : VBS INFLECT

11 See also **bedded, bedding**.

bed down. **1** If you **bed** someone **down**, you get them into bed and ready to go to sleep. EG *...after the kids were bedded down.* PHRASAL VB : V+O+ADV = settle

2 If you **bed down** somewhere, you sleep for the night in a particular place, usually somewhere that is not your own bed or that is not a bed at all, for example on the floor. PHRASAL VB : V+ADV+A = doss down

3 When something **beds down,** it becomes firmly pressed down so that further movement or use will not shake it loose. EG *...in order to allow the loose fibres to bed down.* PHRASAL VB : V+ADV ↑ settle

bed out. If you **bed out** small plants, you move them from the pot or seed tray where they have been growing, into a flower bed. PHRASAL VB : V+O+ADV ↑ plant = transplant

B.Ed. is an abbreviation for 'Bachelor of Education': a degree awarded to people who have studied to be a teacher. N COUNT : ALSO IN TITLES

bed and breakfast, in Britain, is a system of accommodation in a hotel or guest house in which you pay for a room for the night and breakfast the following morning. EG *...£15.50 a night for bed and breakfast. We stayed in a bed and breakfast place in Devon.* N UNCOUNT ↑ accommodation

bed-bath, bed-baths; also spelled without a hyphen. A **bed-bath** is a thorough wash given to someone who is ill in bed. N COUNT = blanket bath

bedbug /bedbʌg/, **bedbugs**. A **bedbug** is a small insect with a round body and no wings, which lives in dirty houses and feeds by biting people and sucking their blood when they are in bed. N COUNT ↑ parasite

bedchamber /bedtʃeɪmbə/, **bedchambers**; also spelled with a hyphen. A **bedchamber** is a bedroom; an old-fashioned, formal word. EG *...the royal bedchamber.* N COUNT ↑ room

bedclothes /bedkləʊðz/; also spelled with a hyphen. **Bedclothes** are the sheets and covers which you put over you when you get into bed. EG *Jamie pulled back the bedclothes and climbed into bed.* N PLURAL

-bedded combines with numbers and words such as 'twin' or 'double' to indicate how many beds, or what type of beds, a particular room contains. EG *...a twin-bedded room.* COMB : FORMS ADJ CLASSIFS

bedding /bedɪŋ/ is sheets, blankets, and covers that are used on beds. EG *She changed the bedding.* N UNCOUNT = bedclothes

bedding plant, bedding plants. A **bedding plant** is a plant which is put in a flower bed before it flowers, and then removed when it has finished flowering. N COUNT

bedeck /bɪˈdek/, **bedecks, bedecking, bedecked**. To **bedeck** something with flags, etc means to hang flags and other things all over it in order to decorate it. EG *Madison Square and Fifth Avenue were bedecked with flags.* V+O : IF+PREP THEN *with* = festoon

bedevil /bɪˈdevəˈl/, **bedevils, bedevilling, bedevilled**. If something **bedevils** someone or something, it constantly causes problems and difficulties for them. EG *They are besieged by complaints and bedevilled with problems.* V+O : USU PASS ↑ trouble = beset, plague

bedfellow /bedfeləʊ/, **bedfellows**; also spelled with a hyphen. You refer to two things or people as **bedfellows** when they have become associated or related in some way, or when they occur in the same situation or place. EG *The oddest of enemies might become bedfellows.* N COUNT ↑ companion

bedhead /bedhed/, **bedheads**; also spelled with a hyphen. The **bedhead** is a board which is fixed to the end of a bed behind your head. N COUNT

bedlam /bedləm/. If you say that a place or situation is **bedlam**, you mean that it is very noisy and disorderly. EG *It's bedlam in here!... ...a nightmarish bedlam of shrieking, weeping, praying and vomiting.* N UNCOUNT ↑ chaos = madhouse

bed linen; also spelled with a hyphen. **Bed linen** is sheets and pillowcases. EG *White bed linen always looks crispest.* N UNCOUNT

Bedouin /beduɪn/, **Bedouins**. **Bedouin** can also be used as the plural form. A **Bedouin** is a member of the nomadic Arab tribe of this name. EG *The Bedouin came with their dark muffled faces... ...the Bedouin tribes.* N COUNT = nomad

bedpan /bedpæn/, **bedpans**; also spelled with a hyphen. A **bedpan** is a shallow bowl shaped like a toilet seat, which is used instead of a toilet by people who are too ill to get out of bed. N COUNT

bedpost /bedpəʊst/, **bedposts**; also spelled with a hyphen. A **bedpost** is one of the four vertical supports at the corners of a bed with an old-fashioned wooden or iron frame. N COUNT ↑ post

bedraggled /bɪˈdrægəˈld/. Someone or something that is **bedraggled** is untidy and disorderly, because they have become wet or dirty. EG *She came in looking grubby and bedraggled... ...a bedraggled flower.* ADJ QUALIT = scruffy

bedridden /bedrɪdəˈn/; also spelled with a hyphen. Someone who is **bedridden** is so ill or disabled that they cannot get out of bed. ADJ CLASSIF

bedrock /bedrɒk/. The **bedrock** of something is the principles, ideas, or facts on which it is based and without which it could not continue to exist in the same form. EG *The Act reaffirmed family values as the moral bedrock of the nation.* N UNCOUNT : USU +SUPP ↑ foundation

bedroll /bedrəʊl/, **bedrolls**; also spelled with a hyphen. A **bedroll** is a rolled-up sleeping bag or other form of bedding, which you can carry with you. N COUNT

bedroom /beduˈm/, **bedrooms**. **1** A **bedroom** is a room which is used mainly for sleeping in. EG *A hotel bedroom... The bedroom door was closed... There are only one-bedroom flats in this block.* N COUNT ↑ room

2 Bedroom is used in expressions such as 'the bedroom scene' or 'bedroom rituals' to refer to people having sex. N BEFORE N ↑ sex

-bedroomed combines with numbers to indicate the number of bedrooms in a building. EG *...a four-bedroomed house.* COMB : FORMS ADJ CLASSIFS

bedside /bedsaɪd/. **1** Your **bedside** is the area beside your bed. EG *An excellent breakfast had been left on the tray by his bedside... ...a bedside light.* N SING WITH DET

2 The **bedside** of someone who is ill is the space around the bed in which they are lying. EG *He always visited the bedside of friends who were ill.* N SING WITH DET = sickbed

bedside manner. A doctor's **bedside manner** is the way in which he or she talks to a patient, and the extent to which this is friendly and reassuring. EG *She has a lovely bedside manner.* N SING WITH DET

bedsitter /bedsɪtə/, **bedsitters**; also spelled with a hyphen. A **bedsitter** or **bedsit** is a room you rent which you use for both living in and sleeping in; used in British English. Some bedsitters have cooking and washing facilities as well. EG *A lot of students live off campus in flats, houses, and bedsitters.* N COUNT ↑ accommodation

bedspread /bedspred/, **bedspreads**. A **bedspread** is a decorative cover which is put over a bed, on top of the sheets and blankets. N COUNT = coverlet

bedstead /bedsteˈd/, **bedsteads**. A **bedstead** is the metal or wooden frame of an old-fashioned bed. EG *...bits of old iron bedsteads.* N COUNT

bedtime /bedtaɪm/; also spelled with a hyphen. A child's or person's **bedtime** is the time when they usually go to bed. EG *It's long past bedtime... He always read to me at bedtime... ...a bedtime story.* N UNCOUNT ↑ time

bee /biː/, **bees**. **1** A **bee** is an insect that makes a buzzing noise in flight, that can sting, and usually has a yellow-and-black striped body. Bees make honey, and live in large groups with other bees. N COUNT

2 If you **have a bee in** your **bonnet** about something, you are so enthusiastic or worried about something over a period of time that you keep mentioning or thinking about it. PHR : VB INFLECTS

3 If you describe someone as a **busy bee**, you mean they are working especially hard or have a lot of work to do; an informal expression. PHR : USED AS C

4 Someone or something that is described as **the bee's knees** is excellent or superior in some way; an informal expression. EG *He thinks he's the bee's knees.* PHR : USED AS C = the cat's whiskers

beech /biːtʃ/, **beeches**. **1** A **beech** is a tree with a smooth grey trunk and branches that grow sideways rather than upwards from the trunk. EG *...under the shade of a huge beech... ...forests of ash, elm, and beech.* ● See also **copper beech**. N COUNT/UNCOUNT

2 Beech is the wood of a beech or beeches. N UNCOUNT

beef /biːf/, **beefs, beefing, beefed**. **1 Beef** is the meat of a cow, bull, or sometimes ox. EG *We had a joint of roast beef for lunch on Sunday... ...beef sandwiches.* ● See also **corned beef**. N UNCOUNT

2 If you **beef** about something, you keep on com- V : IF+PREP plaining about it; an informal use. EG *Every time there's a fare increase, the public starts beefing.* THEN about ⇑ complain = gripe

beef up. If you **beef** something **up**, you strengthen it or make it more interesting, significant, or important. EG *They had beefed up the early evening news programme.* PHRASAL VB : V+O+ADV ⇑ improve

beefburger /bi:fbɜ:gə/, **beefburgers**. A **beefburger** is a flat, round piece of minced beef mixed with flour and flavourings, which is grilled or fried and put in a bun to be eaten. N COUNT

beef cattle are cattle which are bred to provide meat. N UNCOUNT

Beefeater /bi:fi:tə/, **Beefeaters**. A **Beefeater** is a guard at the Tower of London, with a uniform in the style of the sixteenth century. N COUNT

beefsteak /bi:fsteɪk/ is the same as steak. N UNCOUNT

beef tea; also spelled with a hyphen. **Beef tea** is a drink made from boiling little pieces of beef, which is given to people who are ill. N UNCOUNT

beefy /bi:fi[1]/, **beefier, beefiest**. Someone, especially a man, who is **beefy** is strong and muscular; an informal word. ADJ QUALIT = brawny

beehive /bi:haɪv/, **beehives**; also spelled with a hyphen. A **beehive** is a structure in which bees are kept, which is designed so that the keeper can collect the honey that they produce. N COUNT = hive

beeline /bi:laɪn/. If you **make a beeline for** something or a particular place, you go or move there as quickly and directly as possible; an informal word. EG *Three of them made a beeline for the pub.* PHR : VB INFLECTS

been /bi:n, bɪn/. **1 Been** is the past participle of **be**. EG *He'd been sick for years... 'How long have you been married?'*

2 Been is also used after the auxiliaries 'has' and 'have' in the following ways: **2.1** If you **have been** somewhere, you have gone there or visited there. EG *She has not been to church for almost twenty years... I haven't been to Birmingham.* V : AUX *(has/have)*+V (PAST PART)+A*(to)* ⇑ go **2.2** If someone such as a postman or milkman **has been**, they have called at your house. EG *Will the milkman have been yet?* V : AUX *(has/have)*+V (PAST PART) = call

3 If you say that someone has **been and** done something, you are expressing surprise or horror at something that they have done; an informal expression. EG *That dog of yours has been and dug up all my daffodils!... You've been and done it now, you really have!* V : AUX *(has/have)*+V (PAST PART)+*and* VB = gone

beep /bi:p/, **beeps, beeping, beeped**. A **beep** is a fairly short, harsh sound like that made by a car horn or the engaged tone of a telephone. ▸ used as a verb. N COUNT ▸ V, OR V+O

beer /bɪə/, **beers**. **Beer** is a bitter alcoholic drink made from grain. There are a lot of different kinds of beer. EG *She had drunk a few pints of beer... ...a bottle of beer.* ● See also **ginger beer**. N MASS

2 A **beer** is a glass, bottle, or can that is full of beer. EG *Buy me a beer, Howard.* N COUNT ⇑ amount

beer belly, beer bellies. A **beer belly** or **beer gut** is a big fat stomach which is caused by drinking too much beer; an informal expression. N COUNT = paunch

beeswax /bi:zwæks/ is wax that is made by bees and used especially for making candles and furniture polish. EG *...beeswax candles.* N UNCOUNT

beet /bi:t/ is a root vegetable used as food for animals, especially cows. EG *They talked endlessly about beet and cattle feed.* ● See also **sugar beet**. N UNCOUNT ⇑ vegetable

beetle /bi:tə[0]l/, **beetles, beetling, beetled**. **1** A **beetle** is an insect with a hard, usually black covering to its body. N COUNT

2 If you **beetle** somewhere, you move there hurriedly; an informal use. EG *Before I could stop him he had beetled off.* V+A = scuttle

beetle-browed. Someone who is **beetle-browed** has very bushy or overhanging eyebrows. ADJ CLASSIF

beetroot /bi:tru:t/, **beetroots**. **1 Beetroot** is a dark red root vegetable which can be cooked, eaten in salads, or pickled. N UNCOUNT/COUNT

2 If you say that someone has gone **beetroot**, you mean that their face has become reddish in colour, for example because they are very embarrassed or angry. EG *If you said anything to one of the boys, they went beetroot.* ADJ CLASSIF

befall /bi[1]fɔ:l/, **befalls, befalling, befell, befallen**. If something bad or unfortunate **befalls** someone, it happens to them; a formal or literary word. EG *She knew no harm would ever befall her... A similar fate befell Io in Greek myth.* V+O ⇑ happen = overtake

befit /bi[1]fɪt/, **befits, befitting, befitted**. When you say it **befits** someone or something to do something, you mean that the thing mentioned is appropriate or proper for them; a formal use. EG *It ill befits somebody who represents a political party to behave in such an immoral fashion... The food, as befits a four-star hotel, was excellent.* V+O ⇑ suit = become, fit

befitting /bi[1]fɪtɪŋ/. Something that is **befitting** is appropriate or proper for someone or something. EG *You live very nicely, in the manner befitting salesmen for large German firms... The office was furnished in streamlined stainless steel and glass, as befitting the director's image.* PREP, OR ADJ QUALIT ⇑ appropriate for = suited to

before /bi[1]fɔ:/. **1** If something happens **before** a particular date, event, etc, it happens earlier than this date or event, or during the period of time that precedes it. EG *Can I see you before you go, Helen?... It is just before two o'clock when Howard gets back to his room... It was just before Christmas... Brody arrived at police headquarters before Meadows and Hooper.* CONJ SUBORD, OR PREP ≠ after

2 If a situation existed, or a series of events happened **before** a particular event, time, etc, this situation existed or the events happened continuously over a long time previous to this particular event or time. EG *Before the First World War, the farmers used to use horses instead of tractors.* CONJ SUBORD, OR PREP = until

3 If you say that something happened the day **before,** the weekend **before,** etc, you mean that it happened during the period of time directly preceding the period of time mentioned. EG *The two had met in Bonn the weekend before... It had rained the night before.* ADJ AFTER N ⇑ earlier ≠ after

4 If someone has done something **before or if something has happened before**, they have done it, or it has happened, in the past. EG *Have you been to Greece before?... She had never been drunk before in her life.* ADV

5 If there is a period of time or if several things are done **before** something happens, it takes that amount of time or effort for this thing to happen. EG *It was almost an hour before the ambulance arrived... A dozen ideas were considered and rejected before he finally hit on the plan.* CONJ SUBORD = until

6 If a particular situation has to happen or exist **before** something else happens, this situation must happen or exist in order for the other thing to happen. EG *You have to pay out fifty dollars in cash before they'll give it to you.* CONJ SUBORD

7 If **before** you are able to do a particular thing, something else happens, you are prevented from doing this particular thing by being stopped in some way. EG *Before he could get any further, the telephone rang... The next moment, before he had time to realize what was happening, he was hit over the head.* CONJ SUBORD

8 If you say that **before** doing a particular thing, something else should be done, you are indicating that you wish to delay this particular activity for a short while. EG *But before we examine this new militancy among the young, I'd like to think briefly about the problems of multicultural education... And before we do anything else, let me tell you the latest news from the pop world.* CONJ SUBORD

9 If you tell someone that **before** forming or expressing an opinion they should think about another aspect of the situation, you are politely warning them that their opinion may not be correct. EG *But before laughing and jeering too much, one ought to weigh up the issues raised by this statement.* CONJ SUBORD

10 If someone or something stands or is put **before** a person or thing, they are in a position in front of the person or thing mentioned a fairly formal use. EG *He stood before the panelled door leading to the cellar... ...the tea had been set before him.* PREP

11 When you say that a place is a particular distance **before** another place, you mean that the first place is that distance in front of the second place when you are travelling towards it. EG *The garage is some two hundred yards before the cross-roads.* PREP ≠ after

12 When a case, problem or person is **before** a judge, committee, etc, the case, problem or person is being dealt with or considered by the judge or committee. EG *The matter finally came before the Council... He will stay in jail until the following morning, then appear before the magistrate... We have decided to* PREP *lay our grievance before the European Court of Human Rights.*

13 If something happens **before** a particular person or large numbers of people, it is seen by or happens in the presence of this person or these people. EG *One contributor to this magazine had his wedding televised before seven hundred million viewers.* PREP = in front of

14 **Before** is used to indicate someone's reaction, especially fear, when they are attacked or confronted by something that is considered to be an enemy. EG *The Prime Minister must be quailing before the onslaught of the radical press... Traditional rural culture is fast disappearing before the onward march of urbanization.* PREP

15 When you have a job, task, or difficult situation **before** you, you have to deal with that job or task or face a difficult situation in the near future. EG *I have a difficult job before me... These are the bleak alternatives before him.* PREP+PRON = ahead of

16 When you say that you have the afternoon, the whole day, etc **before** you, you are referring to a period of time that starts immediately and that you can use as you want. PREP+PRON = ahead of

17 **Before** is also used to indicate that one person or thing is considered to be more important or valuable than another person or thing else; a slightly formal use. EG *He loved his wife before anyone else... Should we place the needs of Europe's working classes before the needs of the masses of Africa and Asia?* PREP = above

18 • **before** your **very eyes**: see **eye.** • **before** your **time**: see **time.** • **before long**: see **long.**

beforehand /bɪˈfɔːhænd/. If something was done **beforehand**, it was done earlier than a particular time, event, etc. EG *I'd rung up beforehand to book a table... Kathleen Wild got married without telling anyone beforehand.* ADV

befriend /bɪˈfrɛnd/, **befriends, befriending, befriended.** If you **befriend** someone, you make friends with them or behave in a friendly way towards them, especially when they are weaker or less fortunate than yourself. EG *In Liverpool he was befriended by a passing student.* V+O

befuddle /bɪˈfʌdəˡl/, **befuddles, befuddling, befuddled.** If something **befuddles** you, for example alcohol, it confuses or muddles your mind or thoughts. EG *They never thought that senility could ever befuddle their senses.* ◊ **befuddled.** EG *Captain Imrie's words had penetrated his befuddled mind.* V+O ⇑ confuse = muddle, disorient ◊ ADJ QUALIT ⇑ confused

beg /bɛg/, **begs, begging, begged.** 1 If someone **begs** food or money or **begs** for it, they ask people, especially people they do not know, to give it to them, because they are very poor. EG *...children begging in the subways... ...emaciated kids begging milk from the callous Governor... ...females begging for food around the station.* V OR V+O : USU+A (*for/from*)

2 If you **beg** someone to do something or **beg** for something, you ask them very seriously for it, usually because you are extremely unhappy. EG *She begged the doctor not to tell her husband how ill he was... 'Don't be unhappy,' Karen begged. 'I hate to see you looking so miserable.'... I've come to beg a favour... You must say you are sorry and beg for forgiveness... 'Don't, I beg you.'* V+O/REPORT-CL/QUOTE, OR V+A : ALSO +*to*-INF = beseech

3.1 If something **is going begging**, it is available because no one else wants it. EG *I'll eat that last biscuit if it's going begging.* PHR : AUX INFLECTS

3.2 If you say you **beg to differ**, you are politely disagreeing with someone but in a determined way. PHR : FIRST VB INFLECTS = disagree

4 When a dog **begs** it sits up with its forelegs raised. V

5 • to **beg** someone's **pardon**: see **pardon.** • to **beg the question**: see **question.**

beg off. If someone **begs off,** they say apologetically that they are unable to do something that they had agreed to do. PHRASAL VB : V+ADV ⇑ cancel = cry off

began /bɪˈgæn/ is the past tense of **begin.**

beget /bɪˈgɛt/, **begets, begetting, begot, begotten.** 1 To **beget** something means to cause it to happen or be created; a formal or old-fashioned word. EG *Before long, repetition begets boredom... The Polish food shortage begot significant political change.* V+O = generate, create

2 When a man **begets** a child, he becomes the father of the child; an old-fashioned or literary use. V+O = sire

beggar /bɛgə/, **beggars, beggaring, beggared.** 1 A **beggar** is someone who lives by asking people to give him or her money or food. EG *...beggars with skinny bodies and dusty skin.* N COUNT ⇑ person

2 If something **beggars** a person, organization, country, etc, it makes them very poor; a formal use. V+O ⇑ impoverish

3 If you call someone a **beggar**, you are referring to them in a friendly but usually slightly critical or envious way; an informal use. EG *Your daughter's a cheeky little beggar, isn't she?... Fancy winning £10,000. Lucky beggar!* N COUNT : ADJ+N = so-and-so

4 If you say that something **beggars description**, you mean that it is impossible to describe. EG *The cold rain slanting in from the sea seems to beggar description.* PHR : VB INFLECTS

beggarly /bɛgəliˡ/. A sum of money that is **beggarly** is very small and not at all generous. EG *He only received a miserly, beggarly, begrudging pittance.* ADJ QUALIT : USU ATTRIB = stingy

begin /bɛgɪn/, **begins, beginning, began, begun.** 1 If you **begin** to do or feel something, you start doing or feeling it from a particular time. EG *The actors began to rehearse a few scenes... I was beginning to feel better... We began chattering and laughing together.* V+*to*-INF, OR V+-ING ≠ stop

2 When something **begins** or when you **begin** something, it takes place from a particular time onwards. EG *The concerts begin at 8 pm... My career as a journalist was about to begin... Mr Carter was about to begin his term as President.* V OR V-ERG = commence, start ≠ end

3 If someone **begins** with something, or **begins** by doing something, they start an activity, process, etc by doing the thing mentioned as the first part of it. EG *We decided that we would begin with something familiar... The broadcast began with close-up film of babies crying... The Abbot began his Maundy ceremonies by washing the feet of thirteen aged men.* V+A (*by/with*), OR V+O+A = commence, open ≠ conclude

4 You use the expression **to begin with** 4.1 to say that something happens at the very first stage of an event, process, etc. EG *To begin with, the ratio between attackers and defenders was roughly the same... All went well for him to begin with.* **4.2** to say that something was in a particular state or condition before an event or process took place. EG *I didn't do it; it was like that to begin with.* **4.3** to introduce the first of a number of things that you want to say, especially when you want to correct something that someone else has just said. EG *'How did you fare with Sir Hugo Foster?'–'To begin with his name wasn't Foster.'... To begin with, the invitation for eight really means eight-thirty to nine.* PHR : USED AS AN A = initially, at first; PHR : USED AS AN A; PHR : USED AS AN A = firstly

5 If you **begin** by saying something, you say that thing first. EG *He began by saying that he would make the province ungovernable... 'This is intolerable,' began Haze... I don't know how to begin.* V, OR V+QUOTE ≠ conclude

6 If one thing **began** as another, it first existed in that form. EG *The newspaper had begun as a duplicated broadsheet... These clubs began as coffee-houses in the seventeenth century.* V+A (*as*), OR V+O+A (*as*) = start out

7 Someone who **began** their career as something worked for the first time by doing the job mentioned. EG *She began as an actress... He began his Civil Service career as a boy clerk at twelve shillings a week.* V OR V+O : IF+PREP THEN *as* = start out

8 If you say that you cannot **begin** to explain, understand or imagine something, you are emphasizing that it is very difficult or impossible to explain, understand, or imagine. EG *That did not begin to explain why she had married him... There were certain aspects of the case that he did not begin to understand.* V : MODAL+BROAD NEG+V+*to*-INF

9 Where a region, place, type of countryside, etc **begins** is where its boundary starts. EG *There is no one place where the Central Plains end and the Great Plains begin... Still farther out the true ocean depths begin.* V, OR V+A ≠ end

10 If something that is printed or written **begins** with a particular letter, word, sentence, etc, this word, letter, etc is its first part. EG *...the quotation that begins this book... Think of all the names beginning with D.* V+O, OR V+A (*with*) ≠ end

beginner /bɪˈgɪnə/, **beginners.** A **beginner** is someone who is doing something for the first time and is not skilful at the activity. EG *This is the sort of thing that beginners write... The ski run had been closed to beginners... ...not bad for a beginner.* N COUNT ⇑ learner = novice

beginning /bɪˈgɪnɪŋ/, **beginnings.** 1 The **beginning** of an event or process is the first part or parts of it. EG *This is just the beginning... That was quite a promising beginning... The war's end was as dramatic and sudden as its beginning... The sixteenth and seventeenth century beginnings of British Art.* N COUNT : USU *the*+N, IF+PREP THEN *of* = start ≠ end

2 The **beginning** of something, especially a period of time, is the time at which it starts. EG *I came back at the beginning of the term... The number had increased to thirty-eight by the beginning of the following year.* — N SING : the+N, IF+PREP THEN of = start ≠ end

3 The **beginning** of something that is printed or written is the first words or sentences of it. EG *...the beginning of this chapter... ...the word list at the beginning of the chapter.* — N COUNT : IF+PREP THEN of ≠ end

begot /bi'gɒt/ is the past tense of **beget**.

begotten /bi'gɒtə⁰n/ is the past participle of **beget**.

begrudge /bɪgrʌdʒ/ **begrudges, begrudging, begrudged**. 1 If you **begrudge** someone something, you feel that they do not deserve the pleasant thing that they have got or been given and you feel resentful or envious about it. EG *I do not begrudge her that happiness.* — V+O+O = grudge

2 If you **begrudge** something that you have to give to someone, you feel unwilling to give it. EG *She begrudged the money.* — V+O = grudge

beguile /bi'gaɪl/, **beguiles, beguiling, beguiled**. If someone or something **beguiles** you, they trick you into doing something stupid, especially by making it seem attractive. EG *He used his newspapers to beguile the readers into buying shares in his company.* — V+O+A (with/into) ⇑ trick = entice

beguiling /bi'gaɪlɪŋ/. Something that is **beguiling** is charming and attractive, sometimes in a rather false way. EG *The voice was low but beguiling.* — ADJ QUALIT = enticing

begun /bi'gʌn/ is the past participle of **begin**.

behalf /bi'hɑːf/. If you do something **on behalf of** someone else or **on** their **behalf**, you do it for that person as their representative. EG *A number of scientists are campaigning on our behalf... W A Wilkins spoke at the meeting, on behalf of the Labour Party.* — PHR+NG : USED AS AN A

behave /bi'heɪv/, **behaves, behaving, behaved**. 1 If you **behave** in a particular way, you act in this way, especially because of the situation you are in or the people you are with. EG *She wanted to tell him why she was behaving this way... He was very foolish to behave like that... She was still angry with herself for behaving badly in the hospital.* — V+A

2 If you tell someone to **behave** or to **behave** themselves, you are telling them that they should act in a way that people think is correct and proper. EG *'Behave yourself!' said Mrs Jane... The others prefer to persuade him to behave rather than complain to the teacher... He's old enough to behave himself.* — V OR V+O (REFL) ≠ misbehave, play up

3 If an object, substance, etc **behaves** in a particular way, it functions in a way that follows the laws of science. EG *...the way matter behaves at the very lowest temperatures... ...a circuit which behaves in exactly the same way as a transistor.* — V+A ⇑ act = function

behaviour /bi'heɪvjə/; also spelled **behavior** in American English. 1 A person's **behaviour** is the way they act in general, especially in relation to the situation they are in or the people they are with. EG *As always with human behaviour, there are exceptions to this general rule... ...patterns of behaviour... ...a doctor who has studied the behaviour of hundreds of babies.* — N UNCOUNT : IF+PREP THEN of ⇑ action

2 Animal **behaviour** is the way in which a type of animal acts. — N UNCOUNT : USU +SUPP

3 The **behaviour** of something is the typical way in which it functions, according to the laws of science. EG *The laws that govern the behaviour of light are universal... Fleming noted the behaviour of penicillin on human infections.* — N UNCOUNT : IF+PREP THEN of ⇑ action = functioning

behaviourism /bi'heɪvjərɪsə⁰m/; also spelled **behaviorism** in American English. **Behaviourism** is the belief held by some psychologists that the only valid method of studying the psychology of people or animals is to observe how they behave. — N UNCOUNT ⇑ theory

behead /bi'hed/, **beheads, beheading, beheaded**. To **behead** someone means to cut off their head. — V+O : USU PASS ⇑ kill = decapitate

beheld /bi'held/ is the past tense of **behold**.

behest /bi'hest/, **behests**. If something is done at someone's **behest** it is done because they have ordered or requested it; a formal word. EG *It was done at the behest of Queen Victoria.* — N COUNT : USU at +the+N+of ⇑ request = bidding, command

behind /bi'haɪnd/, **behinds.** 1 If something or someone is **behind** something, they are on the other side of it or at the side that is considered to be the back, often with the result that they are hidden from view. EG *They parked the motorcycle behind some bushes... She sat down behind the hedge... Just behind the cottage was a sort of shed... I saw it slinking behind the trees... The sun went behind a cloud... In one corner behind a partition was a lavatory... Sandy stared at me, his eyes widening behind his rimless glasses.* — PREP/ADV ≠ in front of

2 If something is **behind** someone it is situated in the direction that their back is facing, so that they cannot see it unless they turn round. EG *There were two boys sitting behind me on the bus... Behind Chloe is a large mirror... A sound behind him made him turn... Her neck also was uncommonly fine when seen from behind.* — PREP/ADV = ahead of, in front of

3 If you are walking or travelling **behind** someone or something you are following them. EG *I hate being behind middle-aged drivers... He walked back to the village behind his brother.* — PREP/ADV

4 When you refer to the person **behind** the desk, counter, bar, etc you are referring to the person who is working on the other side of the desk, shop counter, etc that you see when you walk into a shop, office, or pub. EG *He was given a form to fill in by the woman behind the desk... She serves behind the bar.* — PREP ⇑ at

5 If someone or something is **behind** bars, glass, etc they are in a place enclosed by bars or glass so that they cannot escape or be taken away or stolen. EG *...the strain of seeing her daughter locked behind bars... ...racks of shotguns and hunting rifles locked in behind glass.* — PREP

6 Something that is, or that happens **behind** something that is considered to be a barrier or boundary is on the other side of it; used especially when it is thought that something interesting or secret is happening there. EG *Sales of his novels were most brisk behind the Iron Curtain... ...large, comfortable houses behind green lawns.* — PREP

7 When you tell someone that a particular place is **behind** a well-known or easily recognizable place you mean that it is at the side that is considered to be the back, or in a smaller or less important street that is at the back of the well-known place. EG *Now she lived with her Polish mother somewhere behind Marble Arch... ...just behind Selfridges... ...an extension of the main shopping area, behind Lord Street.* — PREP

8 **Behind** is used when talking about scenery that can be seen in the distance beyond a particular place. EG *The bare hills behind Agadir in the west are built of blue limestone.* — PREP

9 If you say that someone shuts or locks the door, gate, etc **behind** them you are indicating that the door has been deliberately closed after a they have left a room, building, etc. EG *He left the studio quietly, locking the outer door behind him... Mrs Oliver shut the door firmly behind her.* — PREP+PRON

10 If something happens or follows **close behind,** or **not far behind**, it happens very quickly after something else. EG *Assassination was not far behind... Famine and disease follow close behind.* — PHR : USED AS AN A

10 The events, reasons, etc **behind** a situation or event are the causes of it or the background to it. EG *Precisely such irresponsibility lay behind the city's school crises... These were the unspoken reasons behind Macleod's statement that legislation was necessary.* — PREP ⇑ causing

11 The person **behind** a particular idea, project, event, etc is the person who is responsible for creating or developing it. EG *The man behind the modernizing of the station was Mr Brown... There must have been a master mind behind it all.* — PREP

12 If someone or a group of people is **behind** a particular idea, person, etc they are in agreement with and support that idea or person. EG *The country was behind the President.* — PREP ⇑ supporting

13 **Behind** is also used when talking about qualities, thoughts, beliefs, etc, that someone has but that are not revealed to other people. EG *She would find out that behind his lofty manner he was inexperienced.* — PREP = beneath

14 When someone is **behind** they are delayed in their work or making less progress than they or other people think they should. EG *I just got slowly more and more behind... I'm half an hour behind already... The defence programme had been allowed to fall behind.* — ADV, PREP, OR ADJ CLASSIF : PRED = behindhand ≠ ahead

15 If someone or something is **behind** another person or thing, for example in a competition or scale of success, they are not as successful or important as this person or thing. EG *Both Watson and Trevino lag* — PREP

well behind Nicklaus in major championship victories.

16 If an experience is **behind** you it happened in the past and will not happen or be experienced again, or no longer affects you. EG *We must leave adolescence behind and grow up... The fantasies of the night were safely behind her.* ADV OR PREP

17 If someone has a particular experience **behind** them they have had this experience in their past; used especially when other people consider these things to be important, valuable, or significant. EG *The man who did the design job had ten years' training behind him... I certainly had experience and a life of wide reading behind me.* PREP+PRON

18 If you stay or linger **behind,** you remain in a particular place after other people have gone. EG *He will linger behind occasionally to chat... Afterwards Vorster asked me to stay behind.* ADV AFTER VB

19 If you leave something **behind** you do not take it with you when you leave; used especially when this is done accidentally. EG *Millie had left her cloak behind.* ADV AFTER VB

20 Your **behind** is the part of your body that you sit on. EG *He slapped her on her behind with his racket.* N COUNT = backside, bottom

21 • to do something **behind** someone's **back**: see **back.** • **behind the scenes:** see **scene.** • **behind the times:** see **time.**

behindhand /bi'haɪndhænd/. If someone is **behindhand**, for example with their work, they are delayed in their work or making less progress than they or other people think they should. EG *I'm a bit behindhand with my work.* ADV = behind

behold /bi'həʊld/, **beholds, beholding, beheld**; an old-fashioned or literary word. **1** If you **behold** someone or something, you see them or notice them when they come into view. EG *Indeed, she was a terrible sight to behold... His eyes had never beheld such opulence.* V+O : USU *to*+-INF = set eyes on

2 You say **behold** to draw attention to something important or surprising that you are about to mention or show; sometimes used humorously. EG *'Behold, I show you a mystery,' the Vicar read... And, behold, the Pentagon gave in.* • **lo and behold**: see **lo.** CONVENTION ⇑ look = lo

beholden /bi'həʊldəⁿn/. If you are **beholden** to someone, you feel that you have a duty to them because they have helped you. EG *I am beholden to you, John, for looking after us.* ADJ QUALIT : PRED ⇑ grateful = indebted

beholder /bɪhəʊldə/, **beholders.** The **beholder** of something is someone who watches or sees it. EG *Beauty's in the eye of the beholder.* N COUNT ⇑ onlooker

behove /bi'həʊv/, **behoves, behoving, behoved**; also spelled **behoove** in American English. If it **behoves** you to do something, it is right, necessary, or advantageous for you to do it; a formal and old-fashioned word. EG *It behoves us to be cautious about imposing our ideas on them.* V+O+*to*+-INF ⇑ benefit

beige /beɪʒ/. Something that is **beige** is a very pale creamy brown colour. EG *...his pale beige summer coat.* ▸ used as a noun. EG *The walls have been done in beige.* ADJ COLOUR ▸ N UNCOUNT

being /bi:ɪŋ/. **1 Being** is the present participle of **be.** EG *Julie, you're being unreasonable... Nothing was going to stop Sandy from being a writer.*

2 Being is also used to explain why a statement has been made, instead of using 'because' followed by a finite clause. EG *The council has the right to sell this house, being the owners... I had to search for my purse which was well-hidden, this being late at night... ...promotion prospects being what they are at Rummidge.* V : V *(CONT)*+ NG/REPORT-CL ⇑ as

3 A **being** is **3.1** a person. EG *In every other way this man is a practical and rational being... ...a human being.* **3.2** something that is alive, but which it is difficult to put into any particular category of creature. EG *...beings from outer space.* N COUNT ⇑ creature; N COUNT

4 Being is also life itself; used especially in philosophy. EG *Can you explain to me the purpose of being?* N UNCOUNT = existence

5 Something that is **in being** already exists. EG *It violated laws already in being.* PHR : USED AS AN A

6 If something comes **into being or is called or brought into being**, it has been formed or brought into existence. EG *Senator Erwin called his committee into being because he suspected fraud... The group came into being against firm opposition.* PHR : USED AS AN A

7 • **other things being equal**: see **equal.** • **for the time being**: see **time.**

bejewelled /bi'dʒu:əⁿld/: also spelled **bejeweled** in American English. A **bejewelled** person or object is wearing a lot of jewellery or decorated with jewels. EG *...bejewelled women.* ADJ CLASSIF ⇑ adorned

belabour /bi'leɪbə/, **belabours, belabouring, belaboured**; also spelled **belabor** in American English. **1** If you **belabour** someone or something, you hit them hard and repeatedly; an old-fashioned word. EG *Marie was about to belabour her with the walking stick.* V+O ⇑ beat

2 If you **belabour** a point in a discussion or explanation, you keep talking about it or emphasizing it in a boring way. EG *There's no need to belabour the point.* V+O ⇑ exaggerate = labour

belated /bi'leɪtɪᵈd/. Something that is **belated** happens or comes later than it should have done. EG *Guppy gave Etta a belated welcome... The Government is making a belated attempt to stop profiteering.* ◊ **belatedly.** EG *You called me here because you have belatedly come to the conclusion that you need me.* ADJ QUALIT ⇑ late = delayed; ◊ ADV+VB

belch /beltʃ/, **belches, belching, belched. 1** If someone **belches**, they make a noise when air from their stomach is suddenly forced up through their throat. EG *The baby drank his milk and belched.* ▸ used as a noun. EG *Brody stifled a belch.* V = burp; ▸ N COUNT

2 If something **belches** out smoke, steam, fire, or a loud sound, it gives out that thing in large amounts; a literary word. EG *A truck stalled and belched black smoke... ...belching out clouds of grey ash... The church organ belched and roared.* V OR V+O ⇑ emit = spew

beleaguered /bi'li:gəd/. **1** A **beleaguered** person, organization or project is one that is having a lot of difficulties or is being opposed or criticized by many people; a fairly formal word. EG *The word processor is a godsend to beleaguered secretaries... ...the beleaguered space programme.* ADJ CLASSIF : ATTRIB ⇑ harassed = busy

2 A **beleaguered** place or group of people is one that has been surrounded by enemies and is being besieged; a fairly formal word. EG *...a beleaguered city.* ADJ CLASSIF : ATTRIB

belfry /belfri¹/, **belfries.** The **belfry** of a church is the part of the tower or steeple where the bells are hung. N COUNT

Belgian /beldʒən/, **Belgians. 1** A **Belgian** is someone who comes from Belgium. N COUNT

2 Belgian means belonging or relating to Belgium or to its people. ADJ CLASSIF

belie /bi'laɪ/, **belies, belying, belied**; a formal word. If one thing **belies** another, **1** it makes it seem less interesting or extreme than it really is. EG *These simple words belie the ambitious nature of Johnson's task... His unlined face belied his fifty-five years.* **2** it indicates it is not true, real, or genuine. EG *Their lives belie the popular image of the swashbuckling rock musician... The promises in this manifesto were belied as rapidly as his other promises.* V+O ⇑ obscure ≠ reveal; V+O ⇑ invalidate = disprove

belief /bi'li:f/, **beliefs. 1 Belief** is **1.1** a feeling of certainty that something exists or is good. EG *...belief in one universal god... ...a belief in the goodness of human nature... ...his belief in the fundamental value of parliamentary democracy.* **1.2** an opinion that you feel sure about. EG *It is my firm belief that more women should stand for Parliament... She could not accept the religious beliefs of her parents.* N COUNT/ UNCOUNT : IF+ PREP THEN *in* = faith; N COUNT = conviction

2 The word **belief** is also used in the following expressions. **2.1** If you do something **in the belief that** a particular thing is true or will happen, you do it because you think this. EG *They had elected Thompson in the belief that he would be better at getting government support.* **2.2** You use the expression **contrary to popular belief** to introduce a statement that is the opposite of what is thought to be true by most ordinary people. EG *Contrary to popular belief, science does not offer us certainties.* **2.3** You use **beyond belief** to emphasize that something exists or has happened to a very great degree. EG *I was embarrassed beyond belief... His stupidity is beyond belief.* **2.4** You use **to the best of my belief** to indicate that what you are saying is only your opinion but that it is true according to all the information you have. EG *...the town of Kasbeam, where, to the best of my belief, the red fiend had been scheduled to appear.* CONJ SUBORD; PHR : USED AS ADV SEN; PHR : USED AS AN A; PHR : USED AS AN A

believable /bi'li:vəbəⁿl/. A **believable** thing or character is one that you think is likely or seems real. EG *...a believable explanation... Do you think he handles his other characters well? Are they believable people?* ADJ CLASSIF ⇑ realistic = plausible

believe /bi'li:v/, **believes, believing, believed.** 1 If you **believe** that something is true, you have the opinion that it is true, even when it cannot be proved. EG *Most scientists believe the atmosphere of Jupiter is too unstable for life... It is believed that two of the prisoners have already died... We believed him dead... I secretly believed him to be right.* V+REPORT-CL, V+O+ADJ, V+O+to-INF : NO CONT ⇑ consider = think

2 You say **I believe** 2.1 to indicate that you are not completely sure that what you are saying is true or accurate. EG *I believe I once tried looking it up in the directory... He's very well known, I believe, in Germany.* PHR = I think 2.2 to make a statement sound factual or businesslike rather than emotional. EG *I believe I still owe you seven hundred pounds.* PHR+REPORT-CL

3 If you **believe** someone or what they are saying, you accept that they are telling the truth. EG *Don't believe a word he says... He knew I didn't believe him.* V+O : NO CONT ⇑ trust ≠ disbelieve ● You say **believe me** or **believe you me** to emphasize that what you are saying is true. EG *I don't like to buttonhole you this way, but believe me, it's important.* ● CONVENTION = honestly

4 The word **believe** is also used in the following expressions. 4.1 If you use an expression such as 'I don't believe it' and 'Would you believe it', you are expressing extreme surprise. EG *I don't believe it! He's a magistrate!... There he was, looking none the worse for it, would you believe it?... I couldn't believe my luck... Edward, I do believe you're jealous!* V+O/REPORT-CL : MODAL+V 4.2 If you say that someone could **not believe** their **eyes** or **ears**, you are emphasizing that they were very surprised at something they saw or heard. EG *The Dean could not believe his ears. 'Did I hear you right, Mr Barrett?'... Pete could scarcely believe his eyes when he saw tough old Jimmy dancing and laughing.* PHR : MODAL+PHR ⇑ be astonished = be dumbfounded 4.3 You say **believe it or not** when you think that someone is going to be surprised at what you are saying. EG *Believe it or not, I'm feeling quite homesick.* PHR : USED AS ADV SEN ⇑ surprisingly

5 If you **believe** or **believe** in God or a god, you are sure of the existence of God or that god. V : IF+PREP THEN *in*

6 If you **believe** in fairies, life after death, miracles, etc, you are sure that they exist or happen. EG *I don't believe in ghosts... I believe in reincarnation.* V+A *(in)*

7 If you **believe** in an idea or policy, you are in favour of it because you think it is good, right, or will have the desired result. EG *...all those who believe in democracy... Do you believe in public expenditure cuts?... You believed in giving everybody access to all the information.* V+A *(in)* ⇑ support

8 If you **believe** in someone or in something that they are doing, you have confidence in that person and think that they will be successful. EG *No one would believe in us or what we were doing.* V+A *(in)* = trust

believer /bi'li:və/, **believers.** 1 A **believer** in a particular idea or activity thinks that it is good, right, or beneficial. EG *I am an unrepentant believer in free enterprise... Bob is a great believer in jogging... ...a passionate believer in their right to existence.* N COUNT+*in* ⇑ supporter ≠ opponent

2 A **believer** is someone who is sure of the truth of a particular religion or the existence of God. EG *None of my friends were Christian believers... This gave the believer a feeling of superiority over the heathen.* N COUNT ⇑ follower ≠ pagan

Belisha beacon /bəli:ʃə/, **Belisha beacons.** A **Belisha beacon** is a post with a round orange light on top which flashes on and off. Belisha beacons are used next to zebra crossings in order to warn motorists that people are crossing the road at this point. N COUNT

belittle /bi'lɪtəᵒl/, **belittles, belittling, belittled.** If you **belittle** someone or something, you make them seem not very important, great, or good by what you say or do. EG *The press gave the by-election no publicity and belittled its significance... Don't belittle yourself.* V+O (NG/REFL) ⇑ minimize = trivialize ≠ emphasize

bell /bel/, **bells.** 1 A **bell** is 1.1 a device that makes a ringing sound and is used to give a signal or attract people's attention. EG *He approached the front door and rang the bell... The door bell rang, and Brody answered it... Ring the bell if you want the bus to stop... The bell rang to end class.* N COUNT 1.2 the sound of a bell ringing. EG *There's the bell,–it's time to go home.* N COUNT : USU SING 1.3 a hollow metal object shaped like a cup which has a loose piece inside it that hits the sides and makes a sound. EG *In the distance a church bell was ringing.* N COUNT ⇑ instrument

2 The word **bell** is also used in the following informal expressions. 2.1 If you **give** someone **a bell**, you telephone them. EG *Give me a bell some time before the weekend, will you?* PHR : VB INFLECTS 2.2 If you say that something **rings a bell**, you mean that it reminds you of something else, but you cannot remember exactly what it is. EG *The name rings a bell.* PHR : VB INFLECTS ⇑ remind

belladonna /beləd**ɒ**nə/ is a drug obtained from the leaves and roots of the deadly nightshade. N UNCOUNT

bell-bottomed trousers are very wide at the bottom of the leg, near your feet. ADJ CLASSIF ⇑ flared

bellboy /belbɔɪ/, **bellboys.** A **bellboy** is a man or boy who works in a hotel, carrying bags or bringing things to the guests' rooms. N COUNT ⇑ porter = bellhop

belle /bel/, **belles.** A **belle** is a beautiful woman, especially the most beautiful woman at a party or in a group; a rather old-fashioned word. EG *She has become the reigning belle.* N COUNT = beauty

bellhop /belhɒp/, **bellhops.** A **bellhop** is a bellboy; used in American English. N COUNT

bellicose /belɪkəus, -kəuz/. Someone who is **bellicose** is aggressive and likely to start an argument or a fight; a rather literary word. EG *...bellicose governments.* ▸ used of people's behaviour or speech. EG *...bellicose pronouncements by public men.* ADJ QUALIT = belligerent

-bellied combines with adjectives to indicate that a person or animal has a belly of a particular size, shape, or colour. EG *...big-bellied dukes.* ● See also **pot-bellied.** COMB : FORMS ADJS

belligerence /bɪ'lɪdʒəᵒrəns/ is the quality of being hostile and aggressive. EG *They watched him, their eyes heavy with belligerence.* N UNCOUNT = hostility

belligerent /bɪ'lɪdʒəᵒrənt/, **belligerents.** 1 Someone who is **belligerent** is hostile and aggressive. EG *He had a belligerent and deeply suspicious look on his face.* ▸ used of actions, attitudes, etc. EG *...his belligerent attitude toward me.* ADJ QUALIT ⇑ quarrelsome = pugnacious ≠ peaceable

2 A **belligerent** country is one that is fighting a war; a technical use. EG *No support could come by sea to the belligerent countries.* ADJ CLASSIF : ATTRIB = warring

3 A **belligerent** is a person or country that is fighting in a war; a technical term. N COUNT

bellow /beləu/, **bellows, bellowing, bellowed.** 1 If someone **bellows**, they shout in a loud, deep voice. EG *'Sir,' Stanley bellowed above the din... They bellowed at us through loudhailers... The president enjoyed this and bellowed with laughter.* ▸ used as a noun. EG *...shouts and bellows of laughter.* V, V+O, OR V+QUOTE/REPORT-CL = roar ▸ N COUNT

2 When a bull or other large animal **bellows** it makes a loud, deep sound. ▸ used as a noun. EG *...a prolonged, mournful bellow from the doomed elephant.* V ▸ N COUNT

3 **Bellows** are 3.1 a device used for blowing air into a fire to make it burn more fiercely. Bellows consist of a soft leather bag fixed between two wooden boards with handles that you pull apart and press together repeatedly. EG *...a bellows made out of a goat skin... ...a pair of bellows.* N COUNT : VB CAN BE SING OR PL 3.2 a device that is part of a musical instrument such as an accordion and blows air into it in order to produce sound. EG *...a new set of bellows for the organ.* N COUNT : VB CAN BE SING OR PL

bell push, bell pushes; also spelled with a hyphen. A **bell push** is a button that you press in order to cause a bell to ring, usually outside the front door of a building. N COUNT : OFT HYPHEN

bell-ringing is the activity of ringing church bells. N UNCOUNT

belly /beli¹/, **bellies, bellying, bellied.** 1 Your **belly** is 1.1 the part of your body, especially your stomach, that holds and digests food; in British English, an informal word. EG *Their bellies were now filled with nourishing food.* N COUNT 1.2 the part of the front of your body below your chest. EG *Uncle John was rather jolly with a big belly and a pipe.* ● See also **pot belly.** N COUNT = paunch

2 The **belly** of an animal is the lower or underneath part of its body. EG *Lions and panthers were creeping on their bellies through the high grass.* N COUNT ⇑ underside

3 The **belly** of an object is a part of it that is round and curved, or that is in a similar position to the belly of a person or animal. EG *...the belly of a ship.* N COUNT+SUPP : USU SING

belly out. When a large piece of fabric, for example the sail of a ship, **bellies out**, it becomes rounded because the wind is filling it. EG *The sheets bellied out in the wind.* PHRASAL VB : V+ADV ⇑ swell = billow

bellyache /beli¹eɪk/, **bellyaches, bellyaching, bellyached**; used mainly in informal English. 1 A **bellyache** is a pain inside your abdomen, especially in your stomach. N COUNT/UNCOUNT

2 If you say that someone is **bellyaching**, you mean they are complaining loudly and frequently about something, often in an unreasonable or unfair way. EG *If only mother would stop bellyaching!* V ⇑ complain = moan

belly button, belly buttons. Your **belly button** is your navel; used mainly by children. N COUNT

belly dance, belly dances; also spelled with a hyphen. A **belly dance** is a Middle Eastern dance performed by women, in which the dancer moves her hips and abdomen vigorously. N COUNT

belly dancer, belly dancers; also spelled with a hyphen. A **belly dancer** is a woman who performs a belly dance. N COUNT

belly flop, belly flops. A **belly flop** is an unskilful dive in which the whole of the front of your body hits the water at the same time. N COUNT

bellyful /be̲li¹ful/. If you say that you have **had a bellyful of** something, you mean that you have had too much of it and don't want any more; an informal expression. EG *Their only function is killing and I've had a bellyful of that.* PHR : VB INFLECTS

belly laugh, belly laughs; also spelled with a hyphen. A **belly laugh** is a very loud, deep laugh. N COUNT

belong /bi¹lɒ̲ŋ/, **belongs, belonging, belonged.** 1 If something **belongs** to someone, 1.1 it is owned by them. EG *The land belongs to a big family... He had taken some valuables belonging to another person.* 1.2 it is done, made, or produced by them. EG *That handwriting belongs to my sister... The voice belonged to a human being.* V+A *(to)* V+A *(to)*

2 If a particular thing **belongs** to someone or something, 2.1 it is a part of them. EG *You can see that this skull belonged to a child.* 2.2 they have the right to have, do, use, or deal with it, or it is certain and inevitable that they will. EG *The last word belonged to the chairwoman... Space belongs to the astronaut... The future belonged to automation.* 2.3 it is associated with them, for example because they have it or use it. EG *...a myth belonging to some tribe in Western Australia... Absolute freedom is a quality that belongs to God alone.* V+A *(to)* V+A *(to)* V+A *(to)*

3 If someone **belongs** to a particular organization, they are a member of it. EG *The majority of the nation did not belong to trade unions... She belongs to the Labour Party.* V+A *(to)*

4 If someone or something **belongs** to a particular category, type, or group, they are of that type or in that category or group. EG *...several million bats, belonging to eight different species... Henry and I belong to very different generations.* V+A *(to/in)*

5 If something **belongs** to a particular place or time, it comes from, began in, or existed in that place or time. EG *His wife belongs to the village... ...behaviour belonging to an earlier phase of human evolution.* V+A *(to)* ⇑ come from

6 If one object **belongs** to another object, it matches or fits it. EG *I can't find the keys that belong to this cupboard.* V+A *(to)* ⇑ match = fit

7 When you say that a baby or child **belongs** to a particular adult, you mean that that adult is the child's parent or the person who is looking after it. EG *The baby seemed to belong to the youngest of the women.* V+A *(to)*

8 When lovers say that they **belong** to each other they are expressing their closeness and commitment to each other. V+A *(to)*

9 If you **belong** in a particular place, it is the right place for you, for example because it is where you were born. EG *You shouldn't be in this country. You don't belong here... Go back home where you belong... Monsters like him belong in jail.* V+A ⇑ fit

10 If something **belongs** in a particular place, that is where it is kept or where it should be put. EG *The plates don't belong in that cupboard... This diagram doesn't belong on this side of the page.* V+A ⇑ fit = go

11 If you **belong** in a particular community or group of people, you feel happy, comfortable, and accepted among them. EG *For a lot of my life I've never felt that I belonged... I don't belong here, mother, I am not like you... They have a strong sense of belonging.* V OR V+A = fit in

belongings /bi¹lɒ̲ŋɪŋz/. Your **belongings** are things you own that are small enough to be carried. EG *While tidying up her belongings, he came across an envelope... We packed the few belongings we had and began to walk.* N PLURAL : USU POSS+N ⇑ possessions = effects

beloved /bi¹lʌ̲vɪ²d/. When the adjective is used after a verb such as 'be', it can also be pronounced /bi¹lʌ̲vd/. 1 A **beloved** person, thing, or place is one for which you feel great affection. EG *He was pleased to be in Austria, close to his beloved wife... ...our beloved Queen... He withdrew to his beloved Kent in 1966... ...Marilyn Monroe, beloved of men in their millions.* ADJ CLASSIF : ATTRIB, OR PRED +*of* ⇑ loved = cherished

2 Your **beloved** is the person that you love; an old-fashioned use. EG *Each lover is now alone with his beloved.* N SING : USU POSS +N = sweetheart

below /bi¹ləʊ̲/. 1 If something is **below** a particular thing, it is in a lower position than that thing; used especially when you are looking down from a higher position. EG *You can see the town spread out below... Down below in the valley the first chimneys were smoking... The high canopy of tree crowns shades the ground below... This time the fish attacked from below... ...a mile below the surface of the Pacific Ocean.* ● If something is situated or happens **below ground** or **below the ground** it is situated or happens in the ground. EG *They spend their lives below ground sucking sap from roots... The only permanent water supply was below the ground.* ADV OR PREP ⇑ underneath ≠ above ● PHR : USED AS AN A ⇑ underground

2 If something is **below** something else on a mountain or slope it is further down the slope than that thing. EG *One summer noon, just below the tree line, I saw a grizzly bear... ...just below the summit.* PREP ⇑ under = beneath ≠ above

3 If something is **below** something else it is directly under it and touching it. PREP = beneath

4 If something is **below** a particular thing on a tall vertical surface, for example a wall, or on something that is considered to have a top and a bottom, such as a page, it is lower than that thing. EG *His name plate was screwed into the door frame immediately below the bell... The title was written in large letters, with the names of the authors below.* ADV OR PREP ⇑ under = underneath = above

5 If something is **below** a particular part of the body it is slightly lower than that part and very near to it. EG *The muscles below Peter's knees were beginning to ache a little... She straightened her skirt and pulled it down below her knees.* PREP OR ADV ≠ above

6 A part of a river or a place by a river that is **below** a particular place is further down the river than that place, in the direction that the water is flowing. EG *Below Wapping the river widens.* PREP = downstream of ≠ above

7 Someone or something that is **below** in a building is downstairs, or in a lower part of the building. EG *She heard two men talking below... ...the floor below... There's a young man below who wants to see you immediately... The room below this is my study.* ADV : NG+ADV, OR PREP ≠ above

8 Someone or something that is **below** in a ship or boat is in the lower part of the ship or boat. EG *Why don't you go below to your cabin?... It's far too cold. You should be below.* ADV

9 **Below** is used in writing to refer to something that will be mentioned, discussed, or illustrated later in the book, chapter, etc. EG *The two documents mentioned below are top secret... This information is summarized below... This reduces the number of qualifying years you need (see below).* ADV ≠ above

10 If something is **below** a particular amount, rate, or level it is less than that amount, rate, or level. EG *This algae is active at temperatures even below freezing... Our circulation of 21,000 had slumped to below 18,000... Their language development and reading is below average... Inflation will not fall below its present level... She will be living below the poverty line.* PREP ≠ above

11 If a temperature is **below** zero or freezing, or a particular number of degrees **below,** it is lower than freezing point. EG *It had been fourteen below zero when they woke up... The air temperature was now well below freezing... It was twenty below.* PREP OR ADV : NG+ADV ⇑ under ≠ above

12 If a note or frequency is **below** another note or frequency it is lower in pitch. EG *Most sopranos can't get below middle C comfortably.* PREP ⇑ under ≠ above

13 **Below** is also used to refer to someone's feelings, or to aspects of the character or nature of someone or something, which are not shown to other people or are not obvious. EG *The old man was obsessed by confused memories, and deep below these by the vague stirring of an obscure desire... Below his grave and practical words there had been amusement.* PREP = beneath, underneath

14 You use **below** when talking about people who are lower in rank than others, and who have less power and authority. EG *Below him are 14 Regional Health Authorities... Decisions occur at the departmental level or below.* ADV OR PREP ≠ above

15 **Below** is also an old-fashioned way of referring to ADV

Hell. EG *His dreams were populated by slimy, savage things that rose from below.*

belt /belt/, **belts, belting, belted.** 1 A **belt** is a strip of leather, cloth, etc that you tie or buckle round your waist. EG *From his belt there dangled a large ring of keys... He undid the clasp of his belt.* ● See also **safety belt, seat-belt, suspender belt.** N COUNT

2 The word **belt** is also used in the following expressions. 2.1 If you have an object, for example a weapon, **at your belt**, it is hanging from or attached to your belt. EG *A security man wandered over with a gun at his belt.* PHR : USED AS AN A 2.2 If in boxing or in a fight you hit someone **below the belt**, you hit them in the groin. PHR : USED AS AN A

2.3 If you say something that is **below the belt** or if you **hit** someone **below the belt**, you criticize them rather cruelly; a fairly informal expression. EG *That comment was a bit below the belt.* PHR : USED AS AN A, OR PHR : VB INFLECTS ⇑ unfair 2.4 If you have something **under** your **belt**, you have already achieved or done that thing, and perhaps are intending to achieve or do more. EG *I'm glad I've got that essay under my belt.* PHR : USED AS AN A = completed 2.5 When you **tighten** your **belt**, you spend less or use less because you cannot afford to spend or use as much as before. EG *We've all got to tighten our belts, you know.* PHR : VB INFLECTS ⇑ economize

3 When you **belt** your coat, trousers, etc, you fasten them with a belt. EG *...two men in belted raincoats.* V+O

4 When you **belt** something such as a weapon to your waist, you put on a belt that it is kept in or attached to. EG *...wearing two revolvers belted to his waist.* V+O+A *(to/on)* ⇑ attach

5 A **belt** is also a circular strip, usually of rubber, that is used in a machine to drive moving parts or to move objects along. EG *A belt snapped in the vacuum cleaner today... She works all day at a moving belt.* ● See also **conveyor belt, fan belt.** N COUNT

6 A **belt** of land, sea, air, or space is a long narrow strip of it that contains or is characterized by a particular thing. EG *This part of America is known as the corn belt... Third world cities have vast belts of poverty... The spaceship travelled into the asteroid belt.* ● See also **green belt.** N COUNT+SUPP ⇑ area = zone

7 If someone **belts** you, they hit you very hard so that it hurts; an informal use. EG *Her Dad belted her when she got home late... He belted her one.* ▸ used as a noun. ◊ **belting.** EG *I'll give him a right belting if I catch him.* V+O = thump ▸ N COUNT ◊ N COUNT = walloping

8 If you **belt** somewhere, you move or travel there very fast; an informal use. EG *She belted down the garden path... We were belting along the motorway at 80 miles per hour.* V+A = speed

9 If someone is or has a **belt** of a particular colour in judo or karate they have reached the standard that that colour represents. ● See also **black belt.** N COUNT : USU ADJ COLOUR+N ⇑ grade

belt out. If you **belt out** a song, you sing or play it very loudly; an informal expression. EG *She was belting out 'My Way' at the top of her voice.* PHRASAL VB : V+O+ADV

belt up. If you tell someone to **belt up**, you are telling them to stop talking; a very informal and impolite expression. PHRASAL VB : V+ADV ⇑ be quiet = shut up

bemoan /bɪ¹məʊn/, **bemoans, bemoaning, bemoaned.** If you **bemoan** something, you express sorrow and dissatisfaction about it; a formal word. EG *The farmer bemoaned his loss.* V+O = mourn

bemused /bɪ¹mjuːzd/. Someone who is **bemused** is rather puzzled or confused. EG *She was faintly bemused by his questions.* ADJ QUALIT = bewildered

bench /bentʃ/, **benches.** 1 A **bench** is a long seat, usually made of wood or metal and sometimes without a back, which has room for two or more people. EG *Two old men were sitting on a park bench and talking.* N COUNT

2 The government **benches,** the Labour **benches, etc** are the seats in Parliament which are used by Members of Parliament who belong to the political party indicated; used in British English. EG *...loud cheers from the government benches.* ● See also **backbenches, front bench.** N PLURAL ⇑ section

3 The **bench** in a court of law is the desk where the judge or magistrate sits. EG *...something that would shake the judges from their benches.* ▸ The **bench** is also used to refer to the judge or magistrates in a court of law. EG *Would the witness please address his remarks to the bench.* N COUNT : USU SING, the+N ▸ N SING : the+N

4 If someone **serves** or **sits on the bench** they work as a judge or magistrate. EG *...before a new JP is let loose to sit on the Bench.* PHR : VB INFLECTS

5 A **bench** is also a long table or worktop, for example in a workshop or laboratory. N COUNT = work bench

benchmark /bentʃmaːk/, **benchmarks.** A **benchmark** is 1 a mark on a fixed object such as a stone post, stating the height above sea level, which is used as a reference point in surveying. N COUNT 2 something whose quality, quantity, or capability is known and which can therefore be used as a standard with which other things can be compared. EG *...having used economic criteria as the sole benchmark for establishing success, value, or achievement.* N COUNT : USU SING

bend /bend/, **bends, bending, bent.** 1 When you **bend** you move the top part of your body downwards and forwards; also used of other tall upright things, such as plants, which can move in this way. EG *He bent down and undid the laces... He was having a wash, bending over the basin and splashing his face... He found it difficult to bend these days... ...making the flowers bend and nod like people agreeing.* ◊ **bent.** EG *At one end of the room, Dan is bent over the fireplace.* V : USU+A *(over/down)* ◊ ADJ CLASSIF : PRED

2 When you **bend** your head you move your head forwards and downwards. EG *Her hands were folded modestly before her and her head was bent... She bent her brown curls over the desk.* V-ERG = bow

3 When you **bend** your arm, leg, finger, etc or when it **bends** it moves from a straight position so that the joint forms an angle. EG *Bend the arm at the elbow.* ▸ used as a noun. EG *...knee bends and arm stretching sessions for everyone.* ◊ **bent.** EG *Get down with your knees bent and your back straight.* V-ERG ⇑ move ≠ straighten ▸ N COUNT ◊ ADJ CLASSIF, OR ADJ AFTER N

4 When you **bend** something long and thin, or flat, you make a curved or angular shape in it by applying force to it. EG *...pliers for bending wire... It's obviously not going to bend.* ◊ **bent.** EG *...two bent pipe-cleaners.* V-ERG ≠ straighten ◊ ADJ CLASSIF ≠ straight

5 When or where something **bends** it changes in direction or shape to form a curve or angle. EG *...the way that light bends as it passes from water to air... It measures how sharply the curve bends around.* V-ERG ⇑ turn

6 A **bend** in something such as a road, river, or pipe is a curved part of it. EG *When I was out of sight around the first bend I ran as fast as I could... ...towards the bend in the Rhine near Frankfurt.* ● See also **hairpin bend.** N COUNT ⇑ curve

7 If you say that someone **is bending over backwards** to do something, you are emphasizing that they are trying as hard as they can to do it, even if it causes them problems or extra work. EG *We should bend over backwards to keep young people out of prison.* PHR : VB INFLECTS

8 **round the bend.** 8.1 If someone or something **drives** or **sends** you **round the bend,** or you are **going round the bend** because of them, they annoy, irritate, or frustrate you very much. EG *That job drove me round the bend... I would have gone round the bend if I'd stayed there any longer.* PHR : VB INFLECTS ⇑ annoy 8.2 If you say that someone is **round the bend,** you mean that they do foolish or silly things. PHR : USED AS AN A = mad ≠ sensible

9 When you **bend** someone or their opinions, or when someone **bends** to some sort of persuasion, they believe or do something different because they have been persuaded, especially by unpleasant, unacceptable, or forceful methods. EG *...calculated to bend the readers' opinions in favour of capital punishment... ...the extraordinary way in which the BBC bent to Russian pressure.* V-ERG : IF V THEN +A *(to)* ⇑ change

10 If you **bend the rules,** you interpret particular rules in a way that suits your purpose so that you can do something that the rules usually prevent you from doing. EG *He has never tried to bend the rules of the parliamentary game.* PHR : VB INFLECTS

11 The **bends** are a painful condition, suffered especially by deep sea-divers, in which you have bubbles of gas in your blood because you have come too quickly from a place where the pressure is high to one where it is low. N PLURAL : the+N, VB CAN BE SING OR PL

12 ● **bent double**: see **double.** ● See also **bent.**

bended /bendɪ²d/. **On bended knee** means kneeling; a formal expression. EG *On bended knee, he asked her to marry him.* PHR : USED AS AN A

bender /bendə/, **benders**; an informal word. When someone goes on a **bender,** they drink a very large amount of alcohol. EG *I'm going to go on a bender when the exams finish.* N COUNT = binge

bendy /bendi¹/, **bendier, bendiest.** Something that is **bendy** 1 has many curves and angles. EG *...a very bendy road.* ADJ QUALIT 2 bends easily into a curved or angular shape. ADJ QUALIT = flexible

beneath /bɪ'niːθ/. 1 If a particular thing is **beneath** someone or something, it is 1.1 directly under them but some distance away from them; a slightly literary or formal word. EG *Wood dust beneath a piece of furniture is a sure sign of woodworm... ...the sleeping figure beneath the mosquito net.* PREP ≠ above
1.2 directly under them and touching them. EG *She concealed the bottle beneath her mattress... The car was buried beneath tons of rubble.* PREP = underneath
1.3 lower than and slightly to one side of them. EG *On the step beneath her stood Judy... The slightly higher land that lay beneath the mountain was good pasture... Far beneath them, the trees of the forest sighed in the breeze.* PREP OR ADV = below ≠ above

2 If something is **beneath** a particular thing on a tall vertical surface, for example a wall, or on something that is considered to have a top and a bottom, such as a page, it is lower than that thing. EG *At the top of the picture there are angels, and beneath them the Christ figure... She was sitting directly beneath the painting.* PREP ⇑ under = below

3 When you say that someone's legs or knees buckle, shake, give, etc **beneath** them you mean that their legs feel very weak or that they are falling over. EG *Stephen's knees began to buckle beneath him.* PREP+PRON = under

4 If something is **beneath** a particular part of the body it is lower than that part and near to it. EG *There were dark rings of fatigue or pain beneath the eyes... Why beneath her bony knees should her legs be like a pair of matchsticks?* PREP ⇑ under = below

5 **Beneath** is used when describing the face of a person who is wearing a hat. EG *Beneath his turned-up Stetson his face is ruddy.* PREP = under

6 **Beneath** is used of the ground that you are walking or standing on. EG *The ground was slippery beneath her... ...the soft ground beneath his feet... The surface would crunch beneath our steps.* PREP

7 If a particular thing is **beneath** a piece of clothing, blanket, etc, it is covered by it. EG *A little cold trickle of sweat ran down his spine, beneath the loose cotton shirt... We snuggled beneath the blankets.* PREP ⇑ under

8 **Beneath** is also used to refer to someone's feelings, or to aspects of the character or nature of someone or something, which are not shown to other people or are not obvious. EG *Beneath Stryker's tissue-thin veneer of civilisation, he was a very vulgar man... But beneath the icy exteriors there beat hearts of passion... Things rapidly became calm, though beneath the surface the argument rumbled on.* PREP = under

8 If you think that someone is **beneath** you, you consider them to be socially inferior to yourself. EG *The people she would have liked to befriend would consider her beneath them... The Duke married beneath him, some thought.* PREP+PRON

9 Something, especially behaviour, that is **beneath** you is something that you consider you should not do or have because of your good character, intelligence, social position, etc. EG *Don't do anything that is beneath you... He regarded the Prime Ministership itself as beneath his dignity.* ● **beneath contempt**: see **contempt**. PREP

Benedictine /bɛnɪ'dɪktiːn/, **Benedictines**. 1 A **Benedictine** is a monk or nun who is a member of a Christian religious community that follows the rule of St Benedict. EG *...a huge Benedictine Abbey.* N COUNT ⇑ Christian

2 **Benedictine** is a yellow liqueur. N UNCOUNT

benediction /bɛnɪ'dɪkʃən/, **benedictions**; a formal or technical word. 1 A **benediction** is a prayer asking God to bless someone. N COUNT = blessing

2 **Benediction** is the act of blessing someone. EG *I raised my hand in benediction.* N UNCOUNT

benefactor /bɛnɪ'fæktə/, **benefactors**. A **benefactor** is someone who helps a person or an institution, especially by giving them money. EG *He went to Long Beach to thank his benefactor... ...a public benefactor.* N COUNT ⇑ helper

benefactress /bɛnɪ'fæktrɪs/, **benefactresses**. A **benefactress** is a woman who is a benefactor. N COUNT

beneficent /bɪ'nɛfɪsənt/. Someone or something that is **beneficent** helps people or results in something good; a fairly formal word. EG *...the most beneficent regime in history.* ADJ QUALIT ⇑ helpful = liberal

beneficial /bɛnɪ'fɪʃəl/. Something that is **beneficial** does people good or helps them. EG *Most of the effects of science are really quite beneficial to people... Such influences can be beneficial.* ADJ QUALIT: USU PRED, IF+PREP THEN *to* ⇑ useful

beneficiary /bɛnɪ'fɪʃəri/, **beneficiaries**. 1 The **beneficiary** of something such as a system or change in a system is the person who is helped by it. EG *The middle classes emerged as the main beneficiaries of these revolutionary changes.* N COUNT = recipient

2 A **beneficiary** is someone who is left money or property by someone else in their will. EG *He wrote a will naming his wife and children as beneficiaries.* N COUNT = heir

benefit /bɛnɪfɪt/, **benefits, benefiting, benefited**. 1 A **benefit** is a good result of something that makes life better for you. EG *The industrial age has brought innumerable benefits... So only a few reap the benefits of agricultural advance.* ● See also **fringe benefits**. N COUNT = advantage, profit

2 If something is done for your **benefit** or is of **benefit** to you, it helps you and makes you better off in some way. EG *The parents co-operate for the benefit of the child... This will be of benefit to the country as a whole... He spends less time at work, to the benefit of the whole family.* N UNCOUNT: WITH POSS, OR N +*to* = advantage ● If you do something **for the benefit of** someone, you do it specially for that person because they need it or because you want them to see or hear it. EG *For the benefit of those who weren't here last week, I'll go over what I said... He smiled for the benefit of the assembled reporters.* ● PHR: USED AS AN A

3 If something **benefits** you or if you **benefit** from it, it helps you or makes you better off in some way. EG *The firm benefited from his ingenuity... Neither of them benefited by what happened... ...a medical service which will benefit rich and poor.* V-ERG: IF V THEN +A *(from/by)* ⇑ improve = profit

4 If you have the **benefit** of something, you are able to use it so that you can achieve something else. EG *...every great nation which has sought to humble others without the benefit of sea power... With the benefit of hindsight we can see that this was a mistake... I happen to have had the benefit of a privileged education.* N SING: *the*+N+*of* ⇑ asset = advantage

5 If you **give** someone **the benefit of the doubt**, you treat them as if they were telling the truth or as if they have done what they should have done, even though you are not sure that this is the case. EG *They decided to give the President the benefit of the doubt.* PHR: VB INFLECTS ⇑ believe

6 **Benefit** is a payment or series of payments, usually made by the government, to someone who is entitled to receive it, for example because they are unemployed or ill. EG *You are entitled to child benefit for them... He is unemployed and receiving benefit.* ● See also **supplementary benefit, unemployment benefit**. N UNCOUNT/COUNT: USU MOD +N ⇑ allowance

7 A **benefit** or a **benefit** concert, performance, sports match, etc is one which is held in order to raise money to give to a particular charity or person. EG *...a benefit concert for Belgian refugees.* N OR N BEFORE N

benevolence /bɪ'nɛvələns/ is the quality of being kind, helpful, and tolerant. EG *Grandma was looking on with amused benevolence.* N UNCOUNT ⇑ kindness

benevolent /bɪ'nɛvələnt/. 1 Someone who is **benevolent** is kind, helpful, and tolerant. EG *...a benevolent uncle... We are fortunate enough to live under a benevolent government.* ▸ used of actions, facial expressions, etc. ◊ **benevolently**. EG *He smiled benevolently.* ADJ QUALIT = benign, liberal; ◊ ADV WITH VB = benignly

2 A **benevolent** organization is one that gives money and help free to people in need. EG *He lived off contributions from some benevolent society for theatre people.* ADJ CLASSIF: ATTRIB = charitable

benevolent fund, benevolent funds. A **benevolent fund** is an amount of money that used to help members of a particular group of people when they are in need. N COUNT

Bengali /bɛŋgɔːli/, **Bengalis**. 1 A **Bengali** is a person who comes from West Bengal or Bangladesh. N COUNT

2 **Bengali** means belonging or relating to West Bengal or Bangladesh, or to their people. ADJ CLASSIF

3 **Bengali** is the language which is spoken by people who live in Bangladesh and by many people in West Bengal. EG *The company published newspapers in Urdu and Bengali.* N UNCOUNT

benighted /bɪ'naɪtɪd/ describes someone whom you consider to be unfortunate or ignorant; used in literary English. EG *...the poor, benighted sons of bitches.* ADJ CLASSIF: ATTRIB = unenlightened

benign /bɪ'naɪn/. 1 Someone who is **benign** is kind, gentle, and harmless. EG *...a benign creature from space.* ▸ used of actions, facial expressions, etc. EG *...the plump, benign features of Mr Potts.* ◊ **benignly**. EG *He smiled benignly at his guest.* ADJ QUALIT = friendly; ▸ = genial; ◊ ADV WITH VB

2 A **benign** tumour is one that will not cause death or serious illness. EG *Tests showed the lump to be benign.* ADJ CLASSIF ⇑ harmless

3 A **benign** climate, environment, system, etc is one that it is easy or pleasant to live in or with. ADJ QUALIT = temperate

bent /bent/. **1** If an old person or thing is **bent**, they or their limbs are curled up and difficult to move, or at an unusual angle, instead of being straight and supple. EG *...old Mr Halliday, bent and white-haired... The trees are so bent.* ADJ QUALIT = hunched ≠ supple, upright

2 An object, especially a metal object, that is **bent** contains a lot of dents and is damaged and misshapen. EG *...tottering piles of bent saucepans... Metal dustbins make a noise and get bent.* ADJ QUALIT = dented

3 If you are **bent** on doing something, you are determined to do it. EG *There is always a proportion of the crowd bent on harrying the speakers.* ● See also **hell-bent**. ADJ QUALIT: PRED+*on/upon* = set

4 If you have a **bent** for a particular subject or area of activity, you have a natural interest and ability in it. EG *...a boy with a mechanical bent who later on becomes a good engineer.* N SING+SUPP: *a* +N = flair

5 A person in a responsible position who is **bent** is dishonest or corrupt; an informal use. EG *...a bent copper.* ADJ QUALIT

6 Someone who is **bent** is homosexual; a rude and offensive use. ADJ CLASSIF

7 Bent is also the past participle and past tense of **bend**.

bequeath /bɪˈkwiːð/, **bequeaths, bequeathing, bequeathed**. **1** If you **bequeath** your money or property to someone, you write an instruction in your will saying that they should receive it when you die. EG *The forty million dollars he bequeathed Phoebe enabled his son to continue his studies.* V+O+O, OR V+O +A *(to)* ⇑ give = leave

2 If you **bequeath** a particular state of affairs, system, set of beliefs, etc to your successor or to the next generation, you leave it for them to have, to deal with, or to enjoy when you go away or when you die. EG *Look at the run-down country your generation has bequeathed us.* V+O+O, OR V+O +A *(to)* = hand down

bequest /bɪˈkwest/, **bequests**. A **bequest** is money or property which a person leaves to someone else in their will. EG *With the exception of a few small bequests to relatives, he left all his property to charity.* N COUNT ⇑ gift = legacy

berate /bɪˈreɪt/, **berates, berating, berated**. If you **berate** someone, you scold them angrily; a formal word. EG *He continued to scream and berate me when I did something wrong.* V+O ⇑ criticize = revile

bereaved /bɪˈriːvd/. A **bereaved** person or a person who has been **bereaved** is one with a close relative or friend who has recently died. EG *...the tactful respect due to someone recently bereaved.* ▸ The **bereaved** is used to refer to bereaved people. EG *We provide a counselling service for the newly bereaved.* ADJ CLASSIF, OR ADJ AFTER N; ▸ N PLURAL: *the* +N

bereavement /bɪˈriːvməʼnt/, **bereavements**. **Bereavement** is the experience or state of having had a close relative or friend die. EG *She did not seem to be getting over her bereavement.* N UNCOUNT/COUNT ⇑ death = loss

bereft /bɪreft/; a formal word. **1** If someone or something is **bereft** of a particular quality, ability, or thing, they do not have it, often when they previously had it. EG *Her cheeks were bereft of colour... The room was bereft of pictures.* ADJ CLASSIF: PRED+*of* ⇑ without = devoid

2 Someone feels **bereft** when a close friend or relative has left or when they no longer have something that was important to them. EG *He had imagined her as utterly bereft and friendless.* ADJ CLASSIF: PRED = cut off

beret /bereɪ/, **berets**. A **beret** is a round flat hat with no brim, which is made of a soft fabric. N COUNT

berk /bɜːk/, **berks**. If you call someone a **berk**, you are saying that you think they are stupid or irritating; a very informal and offensive word in British English. N COUNT/VOC ⇑ fool

berry /beriˈ/, **berries**. A **berry** is a small, round, soft fruit that grows on a bush or a tree. Some berries are edible. EG *This tree bears clusters of amber berries.* N COUNT: USU PL

berserk /bəzɜːk, -sɜːk/. If someone goes **berserk**, they lose control of themselves and become very violent. EG *The crowd went berserk and stoned his home.* ADJ CLASSIF: USU *go*+ADJ ⇑ mad = crazy

berth /bɜːθ/, **berths, berthing, berthed**. **1** If you **give** something **a wide berth**, you avoid going near it because it is unpleasant or dangerous. EG *The milkman has obviously given this place a wide berth.* PHR: VB INFLECTS

2 A **berth** in a harbour is a space by the quay where a ship can stay for a period of time. N COUNT = mooring

3 When a ship **berths** or when someone **berths** a ship, the ship sails into a harbour and stops at the quay. EG *The ship berthed at noon.* V-ERG = dock

4 A **berth** is a bed on a boat, train, or caravan. EG *Miss Ryan was curled up in her berth.* N COUNT = bunk

beseech /bɪˈsiːtʃ/, **beseeches, beseeching, beseeched, besought**. The past tense and past participle can be either **beseeched** or **besought**. If you **beseech** someone to do something, you ask them in an intense and desperate way to do it because you very much want them to and you are afraid that they will not; used in literary English. EG *He heard men crying out, beseeching Allah to save them.... I beseech you to tell me.* V, V+O, V+O+ *to*-INF, OR V+O+ QUOTE ⇑ beg = implore

beseeching /bɪˈsiːtʃɪŋ/. A **beseeching** expression, gesture, or tone of voice suggests that the person who has or makes it very much wants someone to do something. EG *She was staring at me with great beseeching eyes... Mary Stuart put a beseeching hand on my arm.* ◊ **beseechingly**. EG *Larsen looked beseechingly at Rudolph.* ADJ CLASSIF: USU ATTRIB ⇑ begging = imploring; ◊ ADV WITH VB = imploringly

beset /bɪˈset/, **besets, besetting**. The form **beset** is used in the present tense and is also the past tense and past participle of the verb. **1** If you are **beset** with difficulties, problems, fears, etc, there are so many of them or they are so great that they are difficult for you to deal with. EG *The problems which beset us and threaten to destroy us... The maintenance of an effective incomes policy is beset with problems.* V+O: USU PASS+ *with/by* ⇑ afflicted

2 If you are **beset** by a group of people, they are attacking you or bothering you. EG *The frantic beast was beset by a mob wielding sticks.* V+O: USU PASS+ *with/by* ⇑ attacked = harassed

beside /bɪˈsaɪd/. **1** If someone or something is **beside** something, it is at the side of it or next to it. EG *I sat down beside my wife... An apple pie stood beside a joint of roast beef... There right beside the road is a large grey house.* PREP/ADV ⇑ near = by

2 When one person or group works or fights **beside** another person or group, they work or fight together in co-operation in order to achieve something. EG *The nation will not regard them as respectable allies beside whom American troops should fight.* PREP ⇑ with = alongside

3 If you stay **beside** someone else, you stay with them, keeping them company or supporting them; used in formal English. EG *He was delighted at this unexpected opportunity to keep his favourite daughter beside him at Knole.* PREP

4 If you are **beside** yourself with a particular feeling or emotion, you are so deeply affected by it that you have very little control over what you say or do. EG *Christopher was understandably beside himself with rage... She was quite beside herself with enthusiasm.* PHR+REFL+ *with*: USED AS C

5 If you say that something has a particular quality or value **beside** something else, you are comparing the quality or value of the two things. EG *...the eternal and infinite Brahman, beside which there exist only dreams and shadows.* PREP ⇑ compared to = alongside

6 See also **besides**. ● **beside the point**: see **point**.

besides /bɪˈsaɪdz/: also **beside** in paragraph 1. **1 Besides** or **beside** means in addition to the object, situation, activity, etc that is mentioned. EG *What languages do you know besides Arabic and English?... Thomas was the only blond in the family, beside the mother... He's guilty of six killings, and more besides.* PREP OR ADV = apart from

2 Besides is used to emphasize an additional point that you are making, especially one that you consider to be important or that is the reason for a particular situation or action. EG *The driver couldn't see either. Besides, the roads are nearly impassable... Besides, by their nature such businesses take risks, and these have been the key to New England's recent development.* ADV SEN ⇑ anyway

besiege /bɪˈsiːdʒ/, **besieges, besieging, besieged**. **1** If a group of people, especially soldiers, **besiege** a town or other place, they surround it in an attempt to capture it. EG *They were besieged for six months but refused to surrender... ...a besieged town.* V+O: USU PASS

2 If a person or organization **is besieged** by a number of people, those people are continually making demands on them or bothering them. EG *All surviving hospitals were still being besieged by* V+O: USU PASS+ *by/with* ⇑ pressurize = pestered, inundated *crowds of casualties needing treatment... She was besieged with requests for her autograph.*

besmirch /bi'smɜːtʃ/, **besmirches, besmirching, besmirched.** If you **besmirch** someone or their reputation, you say that they are a bad person or that they have done something wrong, usually when this is not true; used in literary English. EG *...his readiness to discredit and besmirch those who stood in his way.*
V+O ⇑ discredit = tarnish

besotted /bi'sɒtɪ^{2}d/. If you are **besotted** with someone or something, you like it so much that you seem foolish or silly. EG *He was besotted with me... ...an age besotted with the concept of the unattainable.*
ADJ QUALIT = infatuated, smitten

besought /bi'sɔːt/ is a past tense of **beseech.**

bespeak /bi'spiːk/, **bespeaks, bespeaking, bespoke, bespoken.** If someone's action or behaviour **bespeaks** a particular quality or feeling, it indicates that they have that quality or feeling; used in formal or old-fashioned English. EG *...action which bespeaks readiness to engage in combat.* ● See also **bespoke.**
V+O ⇑ express = denote

bespectacled /bi'spektəkə^{0}ld/. Someone who is **bespectacled** is wearing spectacles; a formal word. EG *...a sallow, bespectacled young man.*
ADJ CLASSIF

bespoke /bi'spəʊk/. A **bespoke** tailor makes or sells clothes that are specially made to fit the customer who ordered them. ▸ also used to describe clothes specially made to fit a particular customer. EG *...a bespoke suit.*
ADJ CLASSIF : ATTRIB; ▸ = made-to-measure

best /best/. **1 Best** is the superlative of **good** and **well.**

2 Best means of the highest standard or quality. EG *That was one of the best films I've seen... Of the three Jemima books it is the best.* ▸ used as an adverb. EG *...the best preserved mediaeval township in the world.* ▸ The **best** is used to refer to things or treatment of the highest quality or standard. EG *I want her to have the very best. Private room. Special nurses. Everything.*
ADJ QUALIT : SUPERL; ▸ ADV : SUPERL; ▸ N SING : *the*+N

3 Best also means **3.1** most successful or skilful. EG *...some of our best English actors have gone to live in Hollywood.* ▸ used as an adverb. EG *Whatever works best is what she should adopt.* **3.2** most suitable, appropriate, or satisfactory. EG *...the best way to do it... This was the best place to study... Is this strategy the best?* ▸ used as an adverb. EG *Work out where and how these forces would best be used.* **3.3** greatest in degree or extent; used of something that is considered to be desirable or beneficial. EG *...the best chance of success... ...my best friend.* ▸ used as an adverb. EG *Which did you like best–the Vivaldi or the Schumann?... I think mine would suit her best... Who did he love the best?* **3.4** of most benefit or advantage to someone or something. EG *I'm doing what is best for you.* ▸ used as an adverb. EG *I felt I could best serve the Association by representing it.* **3.5** most pleasant or enjoyable. EG *It was the best holiday they'd ever had... There were real hills and trees and, best of all, a lake full of lilies.*
ADJ QUALIT : SUPERL; ▸ ADV : SUPERL; ADJ QUALIT : SUPERL; ▸ ADV : SUPERL; ADJ QUALIT : SUPERL; ▸ ADV : SUPERL, ALSO *the*+ADV; ADJ QUALIT : SUPERL; ▸ ADV : SUPERL; ADJ QUALIT : SUPERL = nicest

4 The **best** or someone's **best** is the greatest and most effective effort, or the highest standard of achievement, which a particular person or thing is capable of. EG *The secret of getting the best out of a diesel is to drive it with sympathy... Hyenas are even slower than lions. The best they can manage is about 65 kph... You're not really at your best... They are trying their best to discourage them.* ● to **do** your **best**: see **do.**
N SING : *the/*POSS +N

5 If you say that something is the **best** that can be said or hoped for, you mean that it is the most pleasant, beneficial, or advantageous thing that can be said or hoped for. EG *The best you could hope for was that it didn't happen too often... The best that can be said of him is that he tries hard.*
N SING : *the*+N+ REL-CL

6 You say that it would be **best** to do a particular thing when you are giving advice or expressing an opinion about what should be done. EG *It's best to wear your wellies... It's best if carpets and rugs are cleaned before storage... White House officials thought it best not to respond.*
ADJ CLASSIF : PRED+*to*-INF/ REPORT-CL = wisest

7 If you say that someone **had best** do something, you mean that they ought to do it. Some people consider this to be nonstandard.
PHR+INF = had better

8 Your **best** is a set of clothing that is of good quality and that you wear only on special occasions. EG *The villagers, dressed in their best, lined the streets.*
N SING : POSS+N

9 The word **best** is also used in the following expressions. **9.1** You use **at best** to indicate that the word you are using to describe something of low standard is the most favourable word you can use. EG *The accommodation was makeshift at best... At best the proposal was a lame compromise...* **9.2** You also use **at best** to say that something is quite bad even in the most favourable circumstances or conditions. EG *The house is always chilly. At the very best it is always November in here.* **9.3** If you **make the best of** a bad or unsatisfactory situation, you accept it and try to be cheerful about it. EG *There is nowhere else to go, so make the best of it.* ● to **make the best of a bad job**: see **job. 9.4** Something that is done or said **for the best** is intended to help or benefit someone. EG *She meant it all for the best... ...decent people who only wanted to act for the best.* **9.5** If someone does something **as best** they **can,** they try as hard as they can to succeed in doing it. EG *I kept out of trouble as best I could... However, he smothered, as best he was able, these feelings.* **9.6** You say **all the best** when you are saying goodbye to someone, or at the end of a letter, to indicate that you hope everything goes well for them. EG *I'll see you next week; all the best.* **9.7** If someone, usually a schoolchild, is given **six of the best,** they are hit six times with a cane or with someone's hand as a punishment.
PHR : USED AS AN A; PHR : USED AS AN A; PHR : VB INFLECTS; PHR : USED AS AN A; PHR : USED AS AN A; CONVENTION; PHR : USED AS O

10 The word **best** is also used in the following expressions, which are explained at other places in this dictionary. ● **to the best of** your **ability**: see **ability.** ● **to the best of** someone's **belief**: see **belief.** ● to **be the best thing since sliced bread**: see **bread.** ● to **hope for the best**: see **hope.** ● to **know best**: see **know.** ● **to the best of** your **knowledge**: see **knowledge.** ● **best of luck**: see **luck.** ● **the best part of** something: see **part.** ● **at the best of times**: see **time.** ● **the best of both worlds**: see **world.** ● See also **second-best.**

11 Best is also used to form the superlative of compound adjectives formed with 'good' and 'well'. EG *I think the best-known Irishman in Britain is Dave Allen... ...the best-looking women and the best-dressed men.*
ADV : SUPERL

bestial /bestɪəl/. If you say that someone is **bestial,** you mean that they are behaving in a revolting or disgusting way; a rather formal or literary word. ▸ used of behaviour and actions. EG *She began to look upon the act of love as bestial and repulsive.*
ADJ CLASSIF ⇑ animal = brutish, gross

bestiality /besti'ælɪti^1/ is **1** revolting or disgusting behaviour; a formal or literary word. EG *...the depths of bestiality to which Man could sink.* **2** sexual activity in which a person has sex with an animal; a legal term.
N UNCOUNT = depravity; N UNCOUNT

bestir /bi'stɜː/, **bestirs, bestirring, bestirred.** If you **bestir** yourself, you become active and move after you have been resting a formal word.
V+O (REFL) = rouse

best man. The **best man** at a wedding is the man who acts as an attendant to the bridegroom. EG *She remembered the speech the best man had made at their wedding.*
N SING : USU *the* +N, NEEDS NO DET

bestow /bi'stəʊ/, **bestows, bestowing, bestowed.** If you **bestow** a gift, honour, or praise on someone, you give them a gift, or praise or honour them; a formal word. EG *She received every honour that the scientific world could bestow... The same unstinting praise could not be bestowed on all its aircraft and equipment.*
V+O : IF+PREP THEN *on* = confer

bestowal /bi'stəʊə^{0}l/. The **bestowal** of something is the giving of it as a special gift, an honour, or praise to someone or something; a formal word.
N SING : *the*+N+ *of*

best seller, best sellers. A **best seller** is a book of which a great number of copies has been sold.
N COUNT

bet /bet/, **bets, betting.** The form **bet** is used in the present tense and is also the past tense and past participle of the verb. **1** If you **bet** on a future event such as a horse race or **bet** someone an amount of money, you agree with someone an amount of money that they will give to you if the event happens in the way you have predicted, or that you will give to them if it doesn't. People sometimes bet on the result of a horse race or a sports match. EG *I told him on which horse and how much to bet... He bet me a hundred I won't get through.* ◊ **betting.** EG *Horse racing is the nation's most popular betting sport.*
V+O, V+O+O, OR V+O+A *(on)* ⇑ gamble = wager; ◊ N UNCOUNT ⇑ gambling

2 A **bet** is an agreement that you make with someone when you bet on something. EG *I didn't put a bet on... We'll take bets on it.*
N COUNT : IF+ PREP THEN *on*

3 You use **bet** in informal expressions such as 'I bet',
PHR : USU+

'I'll bet', 'I am willing to bet', and 'my bet is', to say that you are certain that what you are saying is true or will definitely happen. EG *I bet nobody's been here before... My bet is he'll bounce right back.*
REPORT-CL ⇑ I expect

4 You say **'You bet'** as an emphatic way of saying yes or a way of emphasizing a statement. EG *'Are you going to go?'–'You bet!'... You bet I'm getting out... They're all drawing benefit too, you bet your life.*
CONVENTION

5 I bet. 5.1 You use **I bet** in reply to a statement that someone has made, to show that you agree with the statement or that you expected it to be true; an informal expression. EG *'He's laughing all over his face.'–'I bet he is.'* **5.2** You use **I bet** or **I'll bet** in reply to a statement that someone has made, to show in a sarcastic way that you don't believe the statement; an informal expression. EG *'Maybe I will do something.'–'I bet,' Thomas said.*
CONVENTION; CONVENTION = my eye

6 If you say **don't bet on** something or **I wouldn't bet on** something, you are saying that you do not think it is very likely to happen or to be true. EG *Do you think it'll be sunny tomorrow?–I wouldn't bet on it... 'Just don't bet on old Arnold gaining a lot of ground.'*
PHR : USU IMPER

7 If you reply to someone **'do you want a bet?'** or **'do you want to bet?'**, you are saying that you are certain that what they have said is wrong. EG *'You'll wind up in hospital,' Claude said.–'D'you want a bet?'*
CONVENTION

8 If you advise someone that something is **a good bet**, or that it is their **best bet**, you are suggesting that it is the thing or course of action that is most likely to be successful. EG *For high rate taxpayers this method is a good bet... The Job Release Scheme may be a better bet... Your best bet is to go to Thomas Cook in High Street.*
PHR : USU USED AS C

9 If you say that it is **a good bet,** or **a safe bet** that something will happen or is true, you are saying that it is extremely likely to happen or to be true. EG *It's a good bet that Wheelock will soon be killed.*
PHR OR PHR + REPORT-CL : USED AS C

10 When someone **hedges** their **bets** they follow two courses of action or avoid making a decision between two things for a while because they are not sure which one is right. EG *French money men were hedging their bets... I'm deliberately hedging my bets here.*
PHR : VB INFLECTS = play safe

11 See also **betting**.

beta /biːtə/, **betas**. **Beta** is the second letter of the Greek alphabet, and is sometimes used as a mark given for a student's work.
N COUNT/ UNCOUNT

betel /biːtəˡl/ is a plant that grows in Southeast Asia, where some people chew its leaves and red nuts as a type of drug.
N UNCOUNT : USU BEFORE N

bête noire /betnwɑː/, **bêtes noires**. A person, thing, or situation that you describe as your **bête noire** is one that you especially hate or that annoys you a great deal. EG *Smokers are my bête noire.*
N COUNT : POSS + N, USED AS C = pet hate

betide /biˈtaɪd/. If you say **woe betide** someone who does a particular thing, you mean that something unpleasant will happen to them if they do it; a formal expression. EG *Woe betide the player who scores an own goal!... Woe betide us if we're not ready on time.*
PHR + N + REPORT-CL = heaven help

betoken /biˈtəʊkən/, **betokens, betokening, betokened.** If something **betokens** something else, it is a sign of this thing; an old-fashioned or formal word. EG *...an expression which clearly betokened how deeply his feelings had been hurt.*
V + O/REPORT-CL ⇑ show = indicate

betray /biˈtreɪ/, **betrays, betraying, betrayed. 1** If you **betray** someone who thinks they have your support and love, you are disloyal to them, for example by telling their enemies where they are or what they have done. EG *His best friend betrayed him... Daintry felt betrayed.*
V + O = sell out, double-cross

2 If you **betray** someone's trust, confidence, etc or you **betray** your principles, you fail to act in the good and morally correct way that was expected of you. EG *You betrayed a position of trust.*
V + O ⇑ use = abuse, violate

3 If you **betray** a secret, a plan, etc you tell people things that you have been asked to keep secret. EG *He never betrayed the secret to a soul.*
V + O/REPORT-CL = disclose

4 To **betray** a feeling or a quality means to show it without wanting to or intending to. EG *His face betrayed his grief... Such optimism betrays a singular ignorance of human nature.*
V + O ≠ conceal

5 If you **betray** your husband, wife, or lover, you have sex with someone else. EG *I will never betray you.*
V + O = be unfaithful to

betrayal /biˈtreɪəˡl/, **betrayals. 1** A **betrayal** is an action that betrays someone or something. EG *It's such a betrayal for her to come and talk to you.*
N COUNT : IF + PREP THEN *of* = sell-out

2 Betrayal is **2.1** the act of betraying someone or something. **2.2** the fact of being betrayed. EG *...a sense of betrayal.*
N UNCOUNT; N UNCOUNT = letdown

betrothal /biˈtrəʊðəˡl/, **betrothals.** A **betrothal** is an engagement to be married; an old-fashioned word. EG *...the betrothal of Catherine of Aragon to Prince Arthur.*
N COUNT : USU SING, IF + PREP THEN *of/to*

betrothed /biˈtrəʊðd/; an old-fashioned word. If you are **betrothed** to someone, you are engaged to be married to them. EG *I am betrothed to the mistress Smethurst.* ▸ The **betrothed** is used to refer to people who are betrothed. EG *The betrothed lined up to enter the wedding tent.*
ADJ CLASSIF : PRED, IF + PREP THEN *to*; ▸ N PLURAL : *the* + N

better /betə/, **betters, bettering, bettered. 1 Better** is the comparative form of **good** and **well**.

2 Something that is **better** than something else is of a higher standard or quality. EG *Your French is probably better than mine... The results were much better than might have been expected... That's quite a good photograph, oh, that's a better one of me.* ▸ used as an adverb. EG *People are better housed than ever before, and better educated... I think Japanese cars are a bit better finished.*
ADJ QUALIT : COMPAR ⇑ superior ≠ inferior, worse; ▸ ADV : COMPAR ≠ worse

3 Someone who is **better** at something or who does it **better** is more successful or skilful. EG *His price is higher, but he is of course a much better dentist... Some people can ski better than others... I was better at mathematics than other subjects... He will manage better on his own.*
ADJ QUALIT : COMPAR, IF + PREP THEN *at*, OR ADV : COMPAR ≠ worse

4 Something that is, looks, tastes, or feels **better** is more pleasant or enjoyable. EG *The result tastes better... How much better he looked without his glasses... The tour is going okay. My last tour was better though.*
ADJ QUALIT : COMPAR, OR ADV : COMPAR = nicer ≠ worse

5 Better also means **5.1** greater in degree or extent; used of something that is considered to be desirable or beneficial. EG *You get a better understanding of the way they think... The pilot dipped to 1,500 feet to give the tourists a better view... He moved aside into better light.* ▸ used as an adverb. EG *The next day I left better prepared... Armed with this information, parents will be better able to cater for their children's needs... You'll be paid better for the same job... I like your books better.* **5.2** more suitable, appropriate, or satisfactory. EG *It would have been better if you had drawn that section there... Ireland had to be persuaded that there was a better way forward by closer cooperation... It wasn't great but it was better than nothing... Who better to describe the British position than Dr Abraham?... You will please go into the other room, or better still, go home.* ▸ used as an adverb. EG *They are much better described as amphibians.*
ADJ QUALIT : COMPAR ⇑ improved; ▸ ADV : COMPAR = more; ADJ QUALIT : COMPAR; ▸ ADV : COMPAR

6 You use **better** or **it is better** when you are giving advice or expressing an opinion about what should happen. EG *He's asleep. Better not wake him... It's better if I don't see her... It would have been better to have waited until the spring... Better no canal than an unfortified canal... I think you're far better having a small wine list.* ▸ used as an adverb. EG *You'll do better washing them in lukewarm water gently by hand.*
ADJ QALIT : COMPAR; ▸ ADV : COMPAR

7 If a particular thing is **better** for someone or something or if it is **better** to do something, it is of more benefit or advantage to them. EG *Orange juice is much better for you than fizzy lemonade... The trout figured it was better to stay where they were.*
ADJ QUALIT : COMPAR, IF + PREP/VB THEN *for/to*-INF

8 If you say that someone **had better** do something, you mean that they ought to do it. It is often used as a polite way of telling, advising, warning, or threatening people. EG *I'd better go... I had better introduce myself... Better put it over there... You better be careful you don't overdo it, Edward... You'd better make some notes... 'Will she be happy there?'–'She'd better'... 'The case will be dropped.'–'It better be.'*
PHR + *INF*

9 You say **that's better** in order to praise or encourage someone. EG *Go on, close your eyes. That's right. That's better. Good girl.*
CONVENTION

10 Better is used in expressions like **the sooner the better, the more the better,** to say that something will be more advantageous, beneficial, or satisfactory if it is done sooner or more often. EG *The sooner they change the better... The less he knows the better... He can come at any time, the sooner the better.*
CONVENTION

11 better off. 11.1 If someone **is better off** in a particular place or doing a particular thing, it is a
PHR : VB INFLECTS

more beneficial, advantageous, or satisfactory situation or position for them. EG *She will be better off in the hospital... She would have been better off simply to say, 'No'.* **11.2** If you are **better off** than you were or than someone else, you have more money. EG *You could pay it back afterwards when you are better off.* PHR : VB INFLECTS

12 If you say **so much the better** or **all the better** about a particular situation, you mean that the situation is or would be an advantage or benefit. EG *Try to shop just once a week and if you can do all your shopping at one supermarket so much the better... If it's not really there then all the better.* PHR : USED AS C OR AN A

13 If something will **be all the better for** something, it will be improved by or will benefit from the thing mentioned. EG *It'll be all the better for a coat of paint.* PHR : VB INFLECTS

14 If something changes **for the better,** it improves. EG *The weather hadn't changed for the better.* PHR : USED AS AN A

15 If you say that something has happened **for better or worse,** you mean that you are not sure what the consequences will be, but they will have to be accepted because the action has been taken. EG *For better or for worse I boarded the train for New York... Then for better or worse they fall in love.* PHR : USED AS AN A

16 If someone does something **the better** to do something else, the first thing is done in order to do the second thing more effectively. EG *She supported her sketch-book on it the better to admire her drawing.* PHR + *to*-INF

17 If something **gets the better of** someone or something, it defeats and takes control of them, or influences their behaviour. EG *My curiosity got the better of me.* PHR : VB INFLECTS = overcome

18 If you are feeling **better** after an illness or injury, you are improved or stronger in health. EG *'Feeling a bit better?'–'Lots, Doctor. Lots better.'... 'You were tired when you arrived.'–'I feel better now.'* ADJ QUALIT : PRED

19 When you are **better** after an illness or injury, you are completely recovered. EG *Her cold was better... Medicine is about getting people better.* ADJ CLASSIF : PRED, OR ADV : COMPAR = cured

20 If someone is a **better** person, they are behaving in a morally more acceptable or correct way. EG *All people long to be better, more spiritual... He was a much better man than I took him for.* ADJ QUALIT : COMPAR = finer, worthier

21 If you **better** yourself or your status, position, or situation, you improve it. EG *...the idea of people bettering themselves by bettering their accents... ...bettering the lot of the lower paid.* V+O (NG/REFL) ↑ benefit

22 To **better** something means to achieve a higher standard or a more successful result than a previous one achieved by yourself or someone else. EG *We couldn't have bettered last year's figures.* V+O ↑ improve = top, beat

23 Your **betters** are people who are of higher status or rank than yourself. N PLURAL : POSS +N

24 **Better** is also the comparative of compound nouns and adjectives that are formed with 'good' and 'well.' EG *She's pretty well known in this country, but much better known in Europe... Patients on the whole are better informed... My husband was better looking than that.* ADJ/ADV : COMP

25 The word **better** is also used in the following expressions, which are explained at other places in this dictionary. • **better the devil you know**: see **devil.** • **discretion is the better part of valour**: see **discretion.** • **better half**: see **half.** • to **know better**: see **know.** • **better nature**: see **nature.** • **the better part of**: see **part.** • to **think better of** something: see **think.**

betterment /betəmənt/. The **betterment** of something is the act or process of improving its standard or status; a fairly formal word. EG *We are working for the betterment of society.* N UNCOUNT ↑ improvement

betting /betɪŋ/. The **betting** is used in expressions like 'what's the betting' and 'the betting is' to suggest that something is very likely to happen or to be true. EG *What's the betting they'll be asleep when we get back?* N SING : *the*+N ↑ chance = odds

betting shop, betting shops; also spelled with a hyphen. A **betting shop** is a place where people can go to bet on something such as a horse race. N COUNT = bookies

between /bɪ'twiːn/. **1** If something is **between** or **in between** two things, **1.1** it has one of the two things on either side of it. EG *We can build it just here, between the bathing pool and the platform... The revolver lay between the two bodies... Myra and Barbara sat in the back, the baby between them... The island of Santa Catarina is roughly midway between Sao Paolo and Porto Alegre.* PREP **1.2** it is held by or is touching the two things on either side of it. EG *She put the cigarette between her lips and lit it... His wife continued to twist her handkerchief between her hands.* PREP **1.3** it is considered to be a barrier or division that separates the two things. EG *...as though a curtain had been drawn between it and the roadway.* PREP ↑ dividing

2 If someone or something is or moves **between** or **in between** a number of things, they are positioned or are moving in the spaces separating the things. EG *He walked drearily between the trunks, his face empty of expression... The shadows and the spaces in between the trees were turning from grey to black. ...Penn Close, Court Road and all the little side streets in between.* PREP OR ADV : NG+ADV

3 If someone or something moves **between** one place and another, they go from the first place to the other. EG *I have spent a lifetime commuting between Britain and the United States... ...trade between China and Indonesia... Moves between departments occasionally occur.* PREP

4 **Between** is used to refer to a person or organization that links two other people or organizations. EG *The Count was an arbiter between the States and the federal government.* PREP

5 **Between** is also used in the following ways to express relationships or interaction between people or things. It indicates **5.1** the people who are involved in a particular relationship with each other. EG *...a certain uneasy partnership between a number of countries... ...marriages between Dutch men and African women.* PREP ↑ involving **5.2** the two people or organizations who have a particular attitude towards or feeling about each other. EG *He saw the tension between East and West steadily grow... ...the abnormally chill relations between Charlotte and her daughter... She sensed that things weren't right between us.* PREP **5.3** the people or groups of people who are involved in a discussion, conversation, or arrangement with each other. EG *There had been talk between Jenny and myself of driving back overland... ...negotiations between Britain and Germany... It's always been a taboo subject between us... Concorde? Now that's a specific venture between two countries.* PREP **5.4** the people, organizations, etc, who are involved in a fight or disagreement with each other. EG *In some ways the book charts a running battle between architects and planners... ...a clash between the two gangs... ...the growing confrontation between East and West.* PREP **5.5** social or cultural divisions or barriers that separate people. EG *The gulf between cultures was too great to be easily bridged... There need be no real barrier between arts and science... ...the division between white-collar and blue-collar workers.* PREP ↑ dividing **5.6** something that is considered to be a barrier because it prevents you from doing or having something that you want. EG *These men stand between you and the top jobs.* PREP

6 If you say that something is, happens, or is done **between** the upper and lower limits of a stated scale or range of things, it happens or is done at some point on this scale or range; used especially when you are estimating something. EG *The house was built between 1840 and 1852... You'll have to go between 9 and 10 tomorrow morning... All mammals keep their bodies at temperatures between 36 and 39°C... ...a loss of between 16,000 and 20,000 jobs... ...a man aged between 20 and 25.* PREP+NUM+*and*+NUM • The expression **in between** is used as an adverb in the same sense. EG *Everyone seemed either seventy or thirty. No one was in between.* • PHR : USED AS AN A

7 If something happens **between** or **in between** two other things or events, it happens in the interval after one thing has finished and before another similar thing happens or begins. EG *Having an hour between planes we took a cab to town.... Between conference sessions I spent my time with my husband... They might have to wait an hour or two between each customer... Elsa had cried all night, in between bouts of telling him that she was leaving him... He left the zoo with her, but what happened in between?* PREP/ADV

8 If something happens or is done **between** one date and another, it happens over the period of time from one date to another date. EG *The whole action of the book takes place between August and December in* PREP+N+*and*+N *one year... These slides were taken by my family mainly between 1890 and 1902.*

9 When there is an amount of time **between** or **in between** one event and another, this is how long the interval is from one event to another. EG *There are nine months between conception and biological birth... There was a gulf of ten years between him and the youngest sister.* PREP

10 Between is also used in the following ways when you are comparing things: **10.1** with words like 'difference' or 'similarity' when you are considering two things together in order to compare them. EG *I asked him whether there was much difference between British and European law... Do other countries have the same distinction between amateur and professional that we do?... The choice is between defeat or survival.* PREP **10.2** to show that something is neither one thing nor another, but a mixture of both. EG *I was eating nothing but Quark (something between yoghurt and cottage cheese)... ...a cross between a limousine and a charabanc.* PREP+N+*and*+N

11 If two or more people have an amount of something **between** them, they have this amount together, when the amounts that all the individuals have are added together. EG *Ford and Chrysler lost more than £700 million between them... They have both been married once before and have five children between them.* PREP+PRON

12 When something is divided or shared **between** two or more people, they share it, usually equally. EG *The land was divided equally between them.* PREP = among

13 When you introduce a statement by saying **between you and me** or **between ourselves**, you are showing that you do not want anyone else to know what you are saying, especially because it may not be true or may only be a rumour. EG *It was what I would call, between you and me, a bribe.* PHR : USED AS AN A

bevelled /bɛvəºld/. A **bevelled** edge is a sloping edge of a piece of wood, metal, etc, for example on a picture frame. ADJ CLASSIF

beverage /bɛvəºrɪdʒ/, **beverages**. A **beverage** is a drink, for example, tea, alcohol, or fruit juice; a slightly formal word. N COUNT

bevy /bɛviˡ/, **bevies**. A **bevy** of people or things is a group of people or things that are similar in some way; often used showing disapproval. EG *...a bevy of village girls flanked by two stout matrons... ...a bevy of eager experts... The researches of Booth and Rowntree were followed by a bevy of similar studies.* N PART+N IN PLURAL ⇑ collection = flock, convoy

bewail /biˡweɪl/, **bewails, bewailing, bewailed**. If you **bewail** something, you express great sorrow about it. EG *Frequently they bewail the ingratitude of their children.* V+O = lament

beware /biˡwɛə/. If you tell someone to **beware of** someone or something, you are warning them to be careful of, or to be on their guard against, someone or something that might be dangerous, cause them difficulties, or deceive them. EG *Beware the man who speaks softly of love and marriage... Beware of cheap imitations... We have to beware that missionary zeal doesn't blind us to the realities here... Beware of the dog!* V : USU IMPER, IF +PREP THEN *of*

bewhiskered /biˡwɪskəd/. A man who is **bewhiskered** has a long beard or sideboards; a literary or humorous usage. ADJ CLASSIF ≠ clean-shaven

bewilder /biˡwɪldə/, **bewilders, bewildering, bewildered**. If something **bewilders** you, it is so confusing or difficult that you cannot understand it. EG *A confession of this nature would bewilder and perhaps anger some of my Indian friends... You bewilder me.* V+O ⇑ confuse = baffle, mystify

bewildered /biˡwɪldəd/. If you are **bewildered**, you are completely confused and are unable to make a decision about something or to understand it. EG *His wife watched him, bewildered... She looked distressed and bewildered... We were all bewildered by the play... He approached various authorities, bewildered and angry at his loss.* ADJ CLASSIF : IF+ PREP THEN *by/at/about* = bemused, stunned

bewildering /biˡwɪldəºrɪŋ/. Something that is **bewildering** is very confusing and difficult to understand. EG *The variety at first seems bewildering... Going to church was at the same time a bewildering and exciting experience... All this was a bit bewildering to Aunt Emily.* ADJ QUALIT = overwhelming

bewilderment /biˡwɪldəməˀnt/. **Bewilderment** is the feeling of being bewildered. EG *'But I don't follow you,' Morris protested in bewilderment... To my complete bewilderment, she rang Kurt the next day.* N UNCOUNT

bewitch /biˡwɪtʃ/, **bewitches, bewitching, bewitched**. **1** To **bewitch** someone or something means to cast a spell or seem to cast a spell on them. EG *The devil himself has bewitched us... Maybe the sea has bewitched us both.* V+O = enchant ◊ **bewitched**. EG *...bewitched travellers.* ◊ ADJ CLASSIF = spellbound

2 If someone or something **bewitches** you, you are so excited and attracted by them that you cannot pay attention to anything else. EG *...bewitching the audience with her singing... ...a certain kind of man that controlled and bewitched her.* V+O ⇑ attract = captivate, enthral ◊ **bewitching**. EG *...a bewitching smile.* ◊ ADJ QUALIT = captivating

beyond /biˡjɒnd/. **1** Something that is **beyond** a place or boundary is on the other side of it or outside it. EG *She had been born near a farm out beyond Barnham... He indicated the room, the windows, the street beyond... The room beyond proved to be a mirror image of the first room.* ADV : USU N+ ADV, OR PREP

2 Something that happens or exists **beyond** a stated area of work, organization, etc happens more generally or widely than just in that particular organization or area of work. EG *Do your duties as a priest extend beyond the university?... My responsibilities at the Department of Industry go beyond computers and their technology.* PREP ⇑ outside

3 If you say that someone or something is **beyond** understanding, control, or repair, you are emphasizing that they are impossible to understand, control, or repair. EG *The social situation has changed beyond recognition... Love is beyond all human control... The task involved is almost beyond comprehension.* PREP+N UNCOUNT ⇑ past

4 Beyond is used to mention a fairly unimportant exception to what you have said. EG *They had no money beyond Sir Arthur's salary... Parents and children have little in common beyond the biological link... He decided not to comment beyond saying that it was jolly hard luck on me.* PREP, OR CONJ SUBORD = apart from

5 Beyond is also used before a particular measurement, rate, or level to mean more than that measurement, rate, or level. EG *Few children remain in the School beyond the age of 16.* PREP OR ADV = above, over

6 If you refer to something happening **beyond** a particular date, you mean later than that date. EG *It might be unwise to delay it beyond 1987... This will be argued about in the seventies and beyond.* ADV OR PREP ⇑ after

7 If something or someone has grown or developed **beyond** a particular state, they have become something that is greater or more important than this earlier state. EG *Local politics has not proceeded beyond the ideals of early Victorian radicalism... She had been there for twenty-five years without progressing one inch beyond her secretarial status.* PREP

8 If you say that something is **beyond** you, you mean that you find it too difficult to understand. EG *The economy's beyond me... How he managed to find us is beyond me.* PREP : USU+ PRON = above

9 If a task or job is **beyond** someone, it is too difficult for them to do. EG *This technique does not demand skills and know-how which are beyond them... This type or work is far beyond the capacity of many children.* PREP : USU+ PRON

10 The word **beyond** is also used in the following expressions, which are explained at other places in this dictionary. • **the back of beyond**: see **back**. • **beyond the pale**: see **pale**. • **beyond** someone's **means**: see **mean**. • **beyond** your **wildest dreams**: see **dream**. • **beyond a joke**: see **joke**.

BFPO is used with a number or name as part of an address, to give the location of British armed forces living abroad when sending letters or parcels by post; an abbreviation for 'British Forces Post Office'. N COUNT+NUM/ NAME

bi- is **1** used at the beginning of nouns and adjectives that have two as part of their meaning. EG *biped... ...biplane... ...bilingual... ...bisexual.* PREFIX **2** added to the beginning of adjectives that describe something as happening once a year, once a month, etc, in order to form adjectives describing something as happening twice a year, twice a month, etc. EG *...annual→biannual... ...monthly→bi-monthly... ...weekly→bi-weekly.* PREFIX

biannual /baɪænjuºəl/. A **biannual** event happens or is done twice a year. EG *...a biannual check-up.* ADJ CLASSIF : USU ATTRIB

bias /baɪəs/, **biases, biasing, biased**; also spelled **biasses, biassing, biassed**. **1** A **bias** is **1.1** a tendency to show prejudice against one group and N UNCOUNT/ COUNT : USU SING favourtism towards another, or to be influenced so much by something that you do not judge things fairly. EG *There's an intense bias against women candidates... You're accusing me of political bias in my marking... ...a bias towards a certain type of personality.* [+SUPP] 1.2 a tendency for something to happen in one way rather than another or to be associated with one group more than another. EG *...a chronic bias towards inflation... The results show a bias in favour of women.* [N COUNT/UNCOUNT : USU SING+SUPP] 1.3 a feature, talent, or quality of a particular kind that is dominant in someone or something or characteristic of them. EG *I didn't really have the artistic and creative bias that you needed... Their policies have little or no educational bias.* [N COUNT/UNCOUNT : USU SING, MOD+N ⇑ tendency = inclination]

2 If something or someone **biases** you or your choice or opinion, they influence your decision or action in favour of a particular choice. EG *Genes only bias cultural choices... I therefore decided to bias my eating habits towards the diet.* [V+O]

biased /baɪəst/; also spelled **biassed**. Someone or something that is **biased** 1 shows prejudice against one group and favouritism towards another, or is influenced so much by something that they do not judge things fairly. EG *They were biased against the British... In her husband's biased eyes she is the most beautiful creature on earth.* [ADJ QUALIT = prejudiced ≠ impartial] 2 concentrates more on one kind of thing than another. EG *The university is biased towards the sciences.* [ADJ CLASSIF : USU PRED+*towards* = weighted]

bib /bɪb/, **bibs**. A **bib** is 1 a piece of cloth or plastic which is tied under the chins of very young children when they are eating to protect their clothes from spilt food. [N COUNT] 2 a patch of feathers on the front of a bird, or fur on the front of an animal, which is different in colour from the feathers or fur surrounding it. [N COUNT ⇑ marking] 3 the part of an apron or pair of dungarees that covers a person's chest. [N COUNT]

bible /baɪbəl/, **bibles**. 1 The **Bible** is the sacred book which the Christian religion is based on. EG *...a new translation of the Bible.* [N SING : *the*+N = scriptures]

2 A **bible** is a copy of the Bible. EG *I sat next to a Marine who took a bible from his pack and began reading.* [N COUNT ⇑ book]

3 The **bible** of a particular subject is the book which is considered to be the best and most useful or important one for that subject. EG *...the airmen's bible... This book was adopted at the Paris meeting and has remained the bible of Trotskyism since then.* [N COUNT+SUPP = manual]

biblical /bɪblɪkəl/ means contained in, or relating to the Bible. EG *...the Biblical account of creation... The Jordan used to be called Judaea and Samaria in Biblical times.* [ADJ CLASSIF : ATTRIB]

bibliography /bɪbliɒgrəfi/, **bibliographies**. A **bibliography** is 1 a list of books on a particular subject. EG *I had decided to ask him to help me draw up a bibliography on basic works in philosophy.* [N COUNT] 2 a list of the books, articles, etc that have been used in producing a book, or that are referred to in the book. [N COUNT]

bicarb /baɪkɑːb/ is bicarbonate of soda; an informal word. [N UNCOUNT]

bicarbonate of soda /baɪkɑːbənɪt əv səʊdə/ is a white powder which is used in baking to make cakes rise, and also as a medicine to help your stomach if you have indigestion. [N UNCOUNT ⇑ soda = bicarb]

bicentenary /baɪsentiːnəri/, **bicentenaries**. A **bicentenary** is the year in which you celebrate something important that happened exactly two hundred years earlier. EG *...bicentenary celebrations.* [N COUNT : USU WITH *the*POSS ⇑ centenary]

bicentennial /baɪsentenɪəl/. **Bicentennial** celebrations are held to celebrate a bicentenary. EG *...during the American bicentennial year.* [ADJ CLASSIF : ATTRIB] ▸ used as a noun. EG *...it is scheduled to open for the bicentennial in 1976.* [▸ N COUNT : USU WITH *the*POSS ⇑ centennial]

biceps /baɪseps/. **Biceps** is both the singular and the plural form. Your **biceps** is the large muscle in the front of your upper arm. [N COUNT]

bicker /bɪkə/, **bickers, bickering, bickered**. If you **bicker** with someone, you quarrel with them, usually about something unimportant. EG *Parents in London are more likely to quarrel and bicker than in country districts... ...a herdsman bickering over the price of three strands of rope.* [V OR V+A (*with*) : USU RECIP = squabble, wrangle] ◇ **bickering**. EG *...constant bickering over interest rates.* [◇ N UNCOUNT ⇑ quarrelling]

bicycle /baɪsɪkəl/, **bicycles, bicycling, bicycled**. 1 A **bicycle** is a vehicle that has two wheels and that you move by turning pedals around with your feet. You steer it by turning a bar that is connected to the front wheel. EG *...learning to ride a bicycle... I think it would be quicker to go by bicycle... ...a bicycle pump.* [N COUNT = bike, cycle]

2 If you **bicycle** somewhere, you cycle there; a rather old-fashioned or formal use. EG *Tim had bicycled into the village with Gertrude.* [V : USU+A = cycle]

bid /bɪd/. The forms for the verb in paragraph 1 are **bid, bids, bidding**; the form **bid** is both the present tense and the past tense and past participle. The forms for the verb in paragraphs 3 and 4 are **bids, bidding, bade, bidden**. In paragraph 2, the form **bids** is the plural of the noun. 1 If you **bid** for something that is being sold, for example in an auction, you offer to pay a particular amount of money for it. EG *I can't afford to bid more than £150 for the table... 'What am I bid for this beautiful vase? Who'll give me £10?'... Are you planning to bid?* [V OR V+O : IF+ PREP THEN *for*] ◇ **bidding**. EG *The bidding went against me, I'm afraid.* [◇ N SING : *the*+N]

2 A **bid** is 2.1 an offer to pay a particular amount of money for something, for example at an auction. EG *I believe a bid was made–something like 200,000 pounds.* [N COUNT : IF+ PREP THEN *for*] 2.2 an attempt to do something or to obtain something. EG *A militant group who made a bid to gain control of the movement in 1969... ...if he makes a bid for power.* [N COUNT : IF+ PREP THEN *for/to-INF* = try]

3 If you **bid** someone good morning, farewell, etc, you say hello or goodbye to them; a formal use. EG *Ladies and gentlemen, I bid you good morning... We bade her farewell.* [V+O+O/QUOTE, OR V+O+A (*to*) ⇑ say = wish]

4 If you **bid** someone do something, you ask or invite them to do something; a formal use. EG *The holy man blessed them and bade them rise from their knees... They sent letters to her, bidding her improve her mind with good books... As bidden, Mrs Oliver sat in a chair.* [V+O+INF ⇑ ask]

5 See also **bidding**.

bidden /bɪdən/ is a past participle of **bid**.

bidder /bɪdə/, **bidders**. 1 A **bidder** is a person or organization that bids for something. [N COUNT]

2 If you say that you will sell or offer something to the **highest bidder**, you mean that you will sell it to the person who offers more for it than anyone else. [N COUNT : *the*+N]

bidding /bɪdɪŋ/; a formal word. 1 If you do something **at** someone's **bidding**, you do it because they have asked you to do it. EG *At his mother's bidding, Mr Jones wrote a letter to our father.* [PHR : USED AS AN A]

2 If you **do** someone's **bidding**, you do what they have asked you to do. EG *He assumes she is only there to do his bidding.* [PHR : VB INFLECTS]

bide /baɪd/, **bides, biding, bided**. 1 If you **bide** somewhere, you stay or wait there; used in old-fashioned English. EG *On days like this it's hard for young men to bide quiet at home.* [V+A]

2 If you **bide** your **time**, you wait for something to happen or for a good opportunity before doing something. EG *She hadn't quit. She was just biding her time.* [PHR : VB INFLECTS]

bidet /biːdeɪ/, **bidets**. A **bidet** is a low basin found in some bathrooms which you can fill with water and sit on to wash your bottom. [N COUNT]

biennial /baɪenɪəl/. 1 A **biennial** event happens or is done once every two years. EG *Every union has its own annual or biennial conference.* [ADJ CLASSIF : USU ATTRIB]

2 A **biennial** is a plant that lives for two years. It flowers, produces seed, and dies in its second year. [N COUNT ⇑ flower]

bier /bɪə/, **biers**. A **bier** is movable stand or frame on which a corpse or coffin is placed or carried at a funeral. [N COUNT]

biff /bɪf/, **biffs, biffing, biffed**. If you **biff** someone, you hit them with your fist; an informal word. EG *Then I biffed him on the chin.* [V+O : USU+A (*on*)] ▸ used as a noun. EG *I'll give you a biff on the nose if you don't shut up!* [▸ N COUNT : IF+ PREP THEN *on*]

bifocal /baɪfəʊkəl/, **bifocals**. **Bifocals** are glasses with lenses made in two halves. The top part is for looking at things some distance away, and the bottom part is for reading and looking at things nearby. [N PLURAL : ALSO *a pair of*+N] ▸ used as an adjective. EG *...the first pair of bifocal spectacles.* [▸ ADJ CLASSIF]

big /bɪg/, **bigger, biggest**. 1 Something that is **big** 1.1 is large in size. EG *She was holding a big black umbrella... She liked big cars... ...a house big enough for family weekends... She took a big bite out of her bread and butter.* [ADJ QUALIT = sizeable] ◇ **biggish**. EG *...a biggish white enamel bowl... He's a biggish man with very dark black hair.* [◇ ADJ QUALIT : USU ATTRIB] 1.2 contains or consists of many people or things. EG *a big crowd had gathered... He got a big majority... There was a big wave of strikes.* [ADJ QUALIT : ATTRIB ⇑ large] ◇ **biggish**. EG *...a biggish rent.* [◇ ADJ QUALIT]

2 Someone who is **big** has a large or tall body. EG *Ronald was big, beefy and aggressive... She was a big woman in her early forties... I'm sure nobody shot Big Jack on purpose.* ADJ QUALIT

3 Something that is **big** is also important, and significant or serious or complex. EG *I have noticed a big change in Sue... The biggest problem at the moment is unemployment... I think we're onto something big.* ADJ QUALIT

4 A **big** institution or person is important and has a lot of influence or authority. EG *He's big in publishing.* ADJ QUALIT : ATTRIB

5 **Big** is also used to emphasize the importance of something and to express your attitude towards it. EG *It really makes a big difference, you know... 'You're making a big mistake,' he said... Somewhere out there in the big wide world.* ADJ QUALIT : ATTRIB = great, huge

6 If someone does something **in a big way**, they do it in a very grand or successful way, especially on a large scale with a great deal of determination. EG *We're going into the arms business in a big way... They entertained in a very big way, with concerts and enormous parties.* PHR : USED AS AN A

7 If someone has **big** ideas, they are confident and proud of themselves and what they can do; often used showing disapproval. EG *He's got big ideas about buying a sports car.* ADJ QUALIT ⇑ conceited = grandiose

8 If someone **talks big**, they are boasting about what they can do and saying things which are not true in order to impress other people; an informal expression. PHR : VB INFLECTS ⇑ boast = brag

9 If you tell someone to **think big**, you are saying that their plans should be on a large scale or should involve a lot of money, time, and effort. EG *Think big! This is the secret of success!* PHR : VB INFLECTS

10 If you say that someone has **made it big**, you mean that they have become successful and famous; used in informal English. EG *She could have made it big as a singer.* PHR : VB INFLECTS ⇑ succeed

11 If you call someone a **big** cheat, a **big** bully, etc you are emphasizing your dislike of them with respect to the quality mentioned. EG *He's a big cheat.* ADJ QUALIT : ATTRIB = great

12 A **big** girl, boy, your **big** sister, etc is a child who is older, and therefore often larger in size; used in informal English. EG *Sometimes the big boys would dash off suddenly, jeering back at the little ones... Chris admired his big brother.* ADJ CLASSIF : ATTRIB ⇑ old

13 **Big** letters, or a **big** letter A, B, etc is an informal way of referring to a capital letter. EG *When I write words I write them in big letters.* ADJ CLASSIF : ATTRIB

14 A **big** word is one which is long or rare and has a meaning which is difficult to understand. EG *What's that big word mean–dulcet?* ADJ QUALIT : ATTRIB

15 If you say that someone has a **big** heart, you mean that they are generous to other people, and willing to help them even if this causes problems or difficulties for themselves. EG *He had been an idiot, his heart was too big.* ADJ QUALIT ⇑ kind

16 If you say to someone 'that's **big of** you', you are being sarcastic and suggesting that they have not been at all generous or helpful; used in informal English. PHR + PRON : USED AS C

17 A woman who is pregnant is sometimes described as being **big** when she is near the end of her pregnancy. EG *She became big with child.* ADJ CLASSIF = heavy

18 • **big deal**: see **deal**. • **too big for** your **boots**: see **boot**.

bigamist /bɪgəmɪst/, **bigamists**. A **bigamist** is a person who commits the crime of marrying someone when they are already legally married to someone else. N COUNT ⇑ criminal

bigamous /bɪgəməs/. A **bigamous** marriage is one in which one of the partners is already married to someone else. ADJ CLASSIF ⇑ illegal

bigamy /bɪgəmi¹/ is the crime of marrying a person when you are already legally married to someone else. N UNCOUNT

big bang theory. The **big bang theory** is a theory in astronomy that suggests that the universe was created as a result of a massive explosion. N SING : the+N

big brother, big brothers. If you describe a government, ruler, or person in authority as a **big brother**, you consider that they have too much power and control over you, and limit your freedom and range of activities. EG *...a one-party tyranny or a single-minded big brother overseeing every act and thought.* N SING NEEDS NO DET

big business. 1 **Big business** is business or commerce which involves very large companies and very large sums of money. EG *...the great male-dominated world of industry and big business.* N UNCOUNT : USED AS C

2 Something that is **big business** is something which people spend a lot of money on, and which has become an important commercial activity. EG *English private coaching schools have become big business in Turkish cities... Elections are now big business.* N UNCOUNT

big cat, big cats. A **big cat** is a large animal which belongs to the cat family, for example a lion or a tiger. N COUNT

big city. The **big city** is used to refer to a large city which seems attractive to you because there are many exciting things to do there, and many opportunities to earn a lot of money. EG *They may be following some vague dream of the big city.* N SING : the+N

big dipper, big dippers. 1 A **big dipper** is a narrow railway track at a fairground which goes over steep hills and round sharp bends, and on which people can ride for enjoyment and excitement. N COUNT = roller coaster

2 The **Big Dipper** is an American word for 'The Plough'. N SING : the+N

big end, big ends. A car's **big end** is the end of a long rod in its engine where it joins the crank. N COUNT ⇑ part

big fish. **Big fish** is both the singular and the plural form. Someone who is a **big fish** is powerful or important; used in informal English. EG *...a big fish in a little pond.* N COUNT ⇑ person ≠ small fry

big game. Large, dangerous wild animals such as lions or elephants are referred to as **big game**, especially when they are being hunted. N UNCOUNT

biggish /bɪgɪʃ/. See **big**.

big hand, big hands. The **big hand** on a clock is the hand that points to the minutes; used mainly by children. N COUNT : USU the+N

big head, big heads. A **big head** is a person who thinks that they are very clever and know everything about a subject; an informal expression used showing disapproval. N COUNT : USU a +N, ALSO VOC = know-all

big-headed. Someone who is **big-headed** thinks that they are very clever and know everything about a subject; used showing disapproval. ADJ QUALIT ⇑ confident = cocksure

big-hearted. Someone who is **big-hearted** is kind and generous to other people, and always willing to help them. ADJ QUALIT ≠ mean

big money is an amount of money which seems to you to be large in the situation you are discussing. EG *You have to travel abroad to make big money.* N UNCOUNT

big mouth, big mouths. If you say that someone is a **big mouth** or that they have a **big mouth,** you mean that they tell other people things that should have been kept secret; an informal expression used showing disapproval. EG *Shut up, big mouth... Once again that boy's big mouth was going to get them all punished... Shut your big mouth!* N COUNT : ALSO VOC = blabbermouth

big name, big names. A **big name** is a person who is successful and famous because of their work. EG *He had become a big name, a real pop hero.* N COUNT = success

big noise. Someone who is a **big noise** has an important position in a group or organization; an informal expression. N SING : USU a+N ⇑ person = big shot

bigot /bɪgət/, **bigots**. A **bigot** is a bigoted person; used showing disapproval. N COUNT

bigoted /bɪgətɪ²d/. Someone who is **bigoted** has very strong, often unreasonable, attitudes and opinions and believes that anyone who has a different opinion must be wrong; used showing disapproval. EG *He is biased, bigoted, boring and, above all, brutal.* ADJ QUALIT ⇑ biased = prejudiced ≠ tolerant

bigotry /bɪgətri¹/ is the having or expression of very strong, often unreasonable, attitudes and opinions; used showing disapproval. EG *A certain hostility to religious bigotry is not altogether surprising.* N UNCOUNT ⇑ bias = prejudice ≠ tolerance

big shot, big shots. A **big shot** is an important and powerful person in an organization; used in informal English. EG *He is an Englishman, once a big shot in the BBC.* N COUNT = big noise

big time. The **big time** is used in informal English to refer to the highest level of an activity or career where you achieve the greatest amount of success, fame, or importance. EG *We've made the big time now... I became involved in 'big time' politics.* N SING : the+N

big toe, big toes. Your **big toe** is the largest toe on your foot. N COUNT

big top. A **big top** is a large round tent that a circus uses for its performances. N SING : the+N ⇑ marquee

bigwig /bɪgwɪg/, **bigwigs**. A **bigwig** is an important person; used in informal English. EG *We could* N COUNT = VIP *vote for Richardson, or, even worse, for the local bigwig who was a member of everything!*

bijou /bi:ʒu:/ is used to describe a place or building that is very fashionable and usually rather snobbish. EG *...a bijou St John's Wood residence... ...bijou boutiques.* ADJ CLASSIF : ATTRIB = chic

bike /baɪk/, **bikes**. 1 A **bike** is a bicycle or a motorcycle; an informal word. N COUNT ⇑ vehicle

2 You say **'On your bike!'** to someone when you want to tell them angrily to go away; an informal expression used in British English. CONVENTION = get lost

bikini /bɪki:ni¹/, **bikinis**. A **bikini** is a two-piece swimming costume worn by women. N COUNT

bikini pants are small, tight-fitting underpants for women. N PLURAL ⇑ briefs

bilateral /baɪlætə⁰rəl/. **Bilateral** negotiations, meetings, agreements, etc involve an exchange between two groups or people. EG *The two countries have signed several bilateral agreements.* ADJ CLASSIF

bilberry /bɪlbə⁰ri¹/, **bilberries**. A **bilberry** is a small bush which produces small edible blue or blackish berries. ▸ **Bilberry** is also used to refer to the fruit of this plant. EG *...that American national dish, bilberry pie.* N COUNT

bile /baɪl/ is 1 a bitter liquid that is produced by your liver and passes into your bowels, where it helps you to digest fat. N UNCOUNT ⇑ secretion 2 the bad-smelling liquid that comes out of your mouth when you vomit with no food in your stomach. EG *He felt bile rise in his throat.* N UNCOUNT

bilge /bɪldʒ/. If you refer to something as **bilge** or **bilge water**, you mean that it is absolute nonsense; used in informal English. EG *You're talking a load of utter bilge... Don't hand me any bilge water about it being too late!* N UNCOUNT ⇑ nonsense = rot

bilingual /baɪlɪŋgwəl/. 1 **Bilingual** means involving or using two languages. EG *He searched the bilingual dictionaries for a suitable translation.* ADJ CLASSIF

2 Someone who is **bilingual** is able to speak two languages fluently. ADJ CLASSIF

bilious /bɪlɪəs/. 1 **Bilious** is used to describe something that is unpleasant and rather disgusting and perhaps causes you to feel sick. EG *...a rather bilious green.* ADJ CLASSIF = sickly

2 If you feel **bilious**, you feel sick and have a headache. ADJ CLASSIF = queasy

3 Someone who is **bilious** is bad-tempered. ADJ QUALIT

bill /bɪl/, **bills, billing, billed**. 1 A **bill** is a written statement of money that you owe for goods or services that you have received. EG *I received an enormous electricity bill... The bill for dinner was over twelve dollars.* N COUNT : USU DET+N+SUPP

2 A **bill** in parliament or government is a formal statement of a proposed new law that is discussed and then voted on. EG *Lloyd George introduced his first National Insurance Bill in 1911... The Bill was defeated by 238 votes to 145... The American Congress passed a special bill forbidding the army to waste any more money.* ● See also **Private Member's Bill.** N COUNT : USU SING+SUPP ⇑ proposal

3 A **bill** is also 3.1 a piece of paper money; used in American English. EG *Ethel gave him a dollar bill.* N COUNT : USU MOD+N 3.2 a poster advertising an event, especially a small poster that is stuck on an outside wall. EG *The official sign on the wall read, 'Stick no bills'.* N COUNT : USU+SUPP = ad

4 The **bill** of a show, concert, etc is 4.1 the people who are going to appear in it. EG *There were some famous names on the bill.* N SING : *the*+N 4.2 the items of entertainment that the show, concert, etc consists of. EG *The movie was accompanied by a full bill of cartoons, shorts and feature films... The Vienna Chamber Opera is offering a double bill of Mozart and Haydn.* N SING WITH DET ⇑ programme

5 If someone **is billed** to appear at a particular show or entertainment, it has been advertised that they are going to be in it. EG *They were billed to appear together at the same pop festival.* V+O : USU PASS, USU+*to*-INF ◇ **billing**. EG *She was booked for two or three weeks at the Coliseum with top billing.* ◇ N UNCOUNT

6 If you **bill** a person or an event as a particular thing, you advertise that person or event as having particular qualities or abilities. EG *It was billed as an 'extraordinary' congress... The Kansas border town of Elgin was billing itself the 'Greatest Cattle Shipping Point of the U.S.A'.* V+O+A ⇑ describe

7 When you **bill** someone for an amount of money, you give or send them a bill stating how much they owe you. EG *I bill my company for all expenses incurred on the job... Bill me at my London address, please.* V+O : NO CONT ⇑ charge

8 A bird's **bill** is its beak. EG *The humming-bird has a long curving bill for extracting nectar from blossoms.* N COUNT

9 Lovers who are **billing and cooing** are kissing and cuddling each other and talking together in an intimate way. EG *The park was full of lovers billing and cooing under the trees.* PHR : VBS INFLECT = smooch

10 If you say that something or someone **fits** or **fills the bill**, you mean that they are suitable for the purpose that you have in mind. ● to **foot the bill**: see **foot**. PHR : VB INFLECTS ⇑ be suitable

billboard /bɪlbɔ:d/, **billboards**. A **billboard** is a very large board outdoors on which posters are displayed. EG *They plan to increase cigarette advertising on billboards.* N COUNT : USU PL ⇑ board = hoarding

-billed combines with adjectives to indicate that a bird has a beak of a particular kind or appearance. EG *...yellow-billed ducks.* COMB : FORMS ADJS

billet /bɪlɪt/, **billets, billeting, billeted**. 1 If members of the armed forces **are billeted** in a particular place, that place is provided for them to stay in for a period of time. EG *...the soldiers that were billeted in private houses in Sutton.* V+O : USU PASS+ *in* ⇑ lodge

2 A **billet** is a house or lodging where a member of the armed forces has been billeted. N COUNT

billet-doux /bɪlɪdu:/, **billets-doux**. Both the singular and the plural are pronounced in the same way. A **billet-doux** is a love letter; a humorous or literary word. N COUNT

billfold /bɪlfəʊld/, **billfolds**. A **billfold** is a wallet; used in American English. N COUNT

bill-hook, bill-hooks. A **bill-hook** is a tool consisting of a very wide knife blade fixed into a wooden handle. It is used, for example, for pruning trees. N COUNT

billiards /bɪli¹ədz/ is a game played by two people on a large cloth-covered table, in which you use a long stick to hit small heavy balls against each other or into pockets around the sides of the table. N UNCOUNT

billion /bɪljən/, **billions**. A **billion** is a number representing a thousand million, or a million million in rather old-fashioned British English: see ☐ at NUMBER. EG *The solar system formed 4.5 billion years ago... You're talking about the days before sport was a billion dollar industry... Two Spanish firms have won a £1 billion contract from Indonesia's state-owned oil business.* NUM : USU *a*/NUM +*billion* ▸ A **billion** and **billions** are also used to mean an extremely large amount. EG *...billions of tons of ice. They rolled the papers off by the billion.* ▸ NUM WITH PL : USED AS N PART ⇑ many

bill of fare, bills of fare. The **bill of fare** at a restaurant is a list of the food for a meal from which you may choose what you want to eat; a rather old-fashioned expression. N COUNT = menu

bill of health. If you are given a clean **bill of health** after a medical examination, you are told that you are fit and that there is nothing wrong with you. N SING WITH DET : USU *a*+N

Bill of Rights. A **Bill of Rights** is a written list of citizens' rights, usually part of the constitution of a country. N SING WITH DET ⇑ charter

billow /bɪləʊ/, **billows, billowing, billowed**. 1 When something made of cloth, for example a sail, **billows**, it swells out and flaps slowly because it is being blown by the wind or a stream of air. EG *Hundreds of scarlet flags billowed in the breeze.* V ⇑ swell = flutter

2 When something such as smoke or cloud **billows**, it rolls slowly upwards or along in large quantities. EG *Clouds of white dust billowed out as the first passengers alighted... Smoke billowed up from burning hedgerows.* V : USU+A ⇑ roll = swirl

3 A **billow** of smoke, steam, etc is a billowing mass of it. EG *The flames illuminated billows of smoke.* N COUNT = swirl

bill poster, bill posters; also spelled with a hyphen. A **bill poster** or a **bill sticker** is a person who sticks notices or posters onto walls, often illegally. EG *Bill posters will be prosecuted.* N COUNT ⇑ worker

billy /bɪli¹/, **billies**. A **billy** or a **billy can** is a metal can or pot used for cooking over a camp fire or stove. N COUNT ⇑ container

billy goat, billy goats. A **billy goat** is a male goat. N COUNT

billy-o; also spelled **billy-oh**. If you say that something is being done or is happening **like billy-o**, you mean that it is being done or is happening with great excitement, speed, or force; an informal expression used in British English. EG *It's raining like billy-o.* PHR : USED AS AN A = like mad

bimonthly /baɪmʌnθli¹/. A **bimonthly** event, magazine, etc, or something that happens or appears **bimonthly** 1 happens or appears every two months. EG *We review our progress bimonthly, and produce a bimonthly report.* 2 happens or appears twice per month. ADJ CLASSIF, OR ADV / ADJ CLASSIF, OR ADV

bin /bɪn/, **bins**. A **bin** is 1 a container, usually with a lid, used for putting rubbish in. EG *She threw both letters in the bin... ...a litter bin.* N COUNT : USU the+N 2 a container, usually with a lid, used for keeping or storing things in. EG *There were several rolls of tape in the computer storage bin... He took out a book from the bin and went over to the counter.* ● See also **bread-bin, dustbin, pedal bin.** N COUNT : USU+SUPP

binary /baɪnə⁰ri¹/. 1 The **binary** system is a system of expressing numbers in which you use only the two digits 0 and 1. It is used especially in computing. EG *...binary numbers.* ADJ CLASSIF : USU ATTRIB ⇑ numerical

2 **Binary** describes something that has two different parts. EG *...a binary star... ...a binary policy.* ADJ CLASSIF : ATTRIB

bind /baɪnd/, **binds, binding, bound.** 1 If you **bind** someone or something, you tie a piece of string, rope, cloth, etc tightly round them so that they are held in place or held firmly together. EG *His hands were bound behind the post... Bundles of five-pound notes were bound in lots of twenty.* V+O : USU+A = truss

2 If you **bind** an object or piece of cloth, you put a strip of fabric round the edge of it, or stitch over the edge of it, in order to prevent it fraying, to make it stronger, or to decorate it. EG *Bind the edges with tape to prevent fraying... ...a high black hat bound round with a shiny ribbon.* V+O : IF+PREP THEN *with*

3 If something **binds** people, it unites them or makes them feel a connection with it by creating a strong feeling of love, respect, responsibility, etc. EG *We were bound together, since the death of my mother, by our common grief... They have bound themselves by marriage... Was it not Freud who said: 'Love and work bind people to sanity'?* V+O : USU+A ⇑ join = bond

4 If two or more things **are bound** to each other, they are considered as being closely related and having an effect on each other. EG *Air power and oil were still inextricably bound together.* V+O : USU PASS ⇑ join = mix ≠ separate

5 If you **bind** a mixture of food, you make the ingredients in it stick together; a term used especially in cookery. EG *Add a beaten egg to bind the mixture.* V+O ⇑ bond

6 If something such as duty or a legal order **binds** you to a course of action, it forces you to do this. EG *You have to swear before a magistrate, which binds you to secrecy... Duty bound him.* V+O : USU+A ⇑ force = constrain

7 When a book **is bound**, the pages are joined together and the cover is put on. EG *...beautifully bound books.* V+O : USU PASS ⇑ covered

8 If you say that something is a **bind,** you mean that you find it unpleasant and troublesome to do; an informal use. EG *I think it's a terrible bind to have to cook your own meals... Life is an unbearable bind.* N SING : a+N ⇑ nuisance = pain, drag

9 See also **binding, bound.**

bind over. If someone **is bound over** by a court or a judge, they are given an order and are legally obliged to do as the order says for a particular period of time. EG *The magistrate bound him over to keep the peace.* PHRASAL VB : V+O+ADV

binder /baɪndə/, **binders**. A **binder** is 1 something such as string or twine that is used to fasten things together. EG *Cut and tie the crop with a tight binder if you have one... ...binder twine.* N COUNT ⇑ fastener 2 a hard cover with metal rings attached inside, used to hold loose pieces of paper or magazines. N COUNT

binding /baɪndɪŋ/, **bindings**. 1 A promise, agreement, etc that is **binding** is one which must be obeyed or carried out. EG *They had a contract equally as binding as a marriage contract... ...a Spanish law that is still binding in California.* ADJ CLASSIF ⇑ obligatory

2 A **binding** is 2.1 the cover of a book. EG *I identified the book's binding and gilt lettering right away... ...durable leather binding.* N COUNT/UNCOUNT 2.2 a strip of material that you put round the edge of a piece of cloth or an object, in order to strengthen it or decorate it. N COUNT/UNCOUNT

bindweed /baɪndwi:d/ is a plant that has large, white, trumpet-shaped flowers and that climbs and twists round other plants as it grows. N UNCOUNT

binge /bɪndʒ/, **binges**; an informal word. 1 When someone goes on a **binge,** they drink a great deal of alcohol. EG *Barber had gone on a monumental binge the night before and was still drunk at midday.* N COUNT ⇑ bout = bender

2 A **binge** is a fairly short period of time in which a particular activity is done very much or very intensely. EG *...a shopping binge.* N SING WITH DET +SUPP = spree

bingo /bɪŋgəʊ/. 1 **Bingo** is a game played for money or prizes, in which numbers are read out to the players who have special cards with numbers printed on them. You win when you can show that all the numbers on your card have been read out. EG *Mum has gone to bingo.* N UNCOUNT

2 You can say **bingo!** to indicate that something pleasant or something that you hoped for has happened, especially in a surprising, unexpected or sudden way; an informal use. EG *I pulled the lever a second time and, bingo, the door swung open... I started to study biology to satisfy my science requirement, and–bingo!–I was hooked.* CONVENTION ⇑ suddenly

binoculars /bɪ⁵nɒkjə⁴ləz/ are a device consisting of two small telescopes joined together side by side, which you look through to help you to see things that are a long way away. EG *He studied the house through his binoculars.* N PLURAL : ALSO *a pair of*+N

bio- is used at the beginning of nouns and adjectives that refer to life or to the study of living things. EG *...biography... ...biology... ...biophysicist... ...biomedical.* PREFIX

biochemist /baɪə⁶kemɪst/, **biochemists**. A **biochemist** is a scientist or student who studies biochemistry. N COUNT ⇑ chemist

biochemistry /baɪə⁶kemɪstri¹/. **Biochemistry** is a science which involves studying the chemical processes that happen in living things, such as plants, animals, or organs in your body. N UNCOUNT ⇑ chemistry

biodegradable /baɪə⁶dɪ²greɪdəbə⁰l/. Something that is **biodegradable** breaks down or decomposes naturally without any special scientific treatment, and can therefore be thrown away without causing pollution. EG *All British detergents were made biodegradable in 1964.* ADJ CLASSIF ⇑ disposable

biographer /baɪɒgrəfə/, **biographers**. A **biographer** is a person who writes an account of someone's life. N COUNT ⇑ writer

biographical /baɪə⁶græfɪkə⁰l/. **Biographical** information, work, etc is concerned with information about someone's life. EG *Maddeningly, they give us no biographical detail... Voting papers give a short biographical note on each candidate.* ADJ CLASSIF ⇑ historical

biography /baɪɒgrəfi¹/, **biographies**. 1 A **biography** is an account of someone's life that has been written by someone else. EG *I have been asked to write a biography of Dylan Thomas.* N COUNT

2 **Biography** is the branch of literature which deals with accounts of people's lives. N UNCOUNT

biol. is an abbreviation for 'biology' or 'biological'.

biological /baɪəlɒdʒɪkə⁰l/. 1 A **biological** process, system, product, etc is connected with or produced by natural processes in plants, animals, and other living things. EG *The natural light-dark cycle is tied to human biological rhythms... Computers could have electronic components modelled on biological components in the real brain.* ◊ **biologically.** EG *Apes are biologically different from humans.* ADJ CLASSIF = physical / ◊ ADV+ADJ/ADV

2 A **biological** study, science, etc is connected with or produced by study or research in biology. EG *The biological sciences are developing rapidly... Our research has made several biological breakthroughs.* ◊ **biologically.** EG *Their curriculum is very biologically biased towards the natural sciences.* ADJ CLASSIF : USU ATTRIB ⇑ scientific / ◊ ADV+ADJ/ADV

3 A child's **biological** parent is its natural parent who is related by blood rather than by adoption. EG *An adopted child may want to find out about its biological parents.* ADJ CLASSIF : ATTRIB

4 **Biological** weapons, warfare, etc involve the use of chemicals or living organisms which damage people, animals, and plants. EG *The superpowers are stockpiling bacteriological and biological weapons.* ADJ CLASSIF : USU ATTRIB ⇑ chemical = toxic

5 **Biological** washing powder contains enzymes which digest natural stains such as those made by blood or grass. EG *One person in five is allergic to biological washing powder.* ADJ CLASSIF : USU ATTRIB ⇑ organic

biology /baɪɒlədʒi/. 1 **Biology** is 1.1 a science which explains how living things work and describes and classifies plants, animals, and other forms of life. N UNCOUNT ◊ **biologist** /baɪɒlədʒɪst/, **biologists**. EG *This thinking was ridiculed by another group of biologists.* ◊ N COUNT 1.2 the science of biology studied as a subject at school or university. N UNCOUNT

2 The **biology** of a living thing is the way that it works. EG *I'd like to learn about the biology of genes.* — N SING WITH DET; ⇑ mechanics

bionic /baɪɒnɪk/. If you describe someone as **bionic**, you mean that they seem to have superhuman powers, such as being incredibly strong or having exceptionally good sight, as if parts of their body had been replaced by machinery; an informal word. EG *...the bionic woman.* — ADJ CLASSIF : USU ATTRIB

biophysics /baɪəᵘfɪzɪks/ is a science which explains biology by using the laws of physics. ◇ **biophysicist** /baɪəᵘfɪzɪsɪst/, **biophysicists**. — N UNCOUNT; ◇ N COUNT

biosphere /baɪəsfɪə/. The **biosphere** is the part of the earth's surface and atmosphere which is inhabited by living things; a technical term. EG *We are poisoning the biosphere with industrial pollution.* — N SING : *the*+N; ⇑ world

biotechnology /baɪəᵘtɛknɒlədʒiʲ/ is the use of living parts such as cells or bacteria for benefit in industry and technology; a technical term. EG *They will be using robotics and biotechnology to aid industrial research.* — N UNCOUNT

bipartisan /baɪpɑːtɪzæn, baɪpɑːtɪzəᵊn/ means concerning or involving two different political parties or groups. EG *The Labour Party rejected Churchill's offer of a bipartisan reform.* — ADJ CLASSIF : USU ATTRIB; ⇑ partisan

biped /baɪpɛd/, **bipeds**. A **biped** is a creature with two feet; a technical term in biology. — N COUNT

biplane /baɪpleɪn/, **biplanes**. A **biplane** is a rather old-fashioned type of aeroplane with two pairs of wings, one above the other. — N COUNT; ⇑ plane

birch /bɜːtʃ/, **birches**. **1** A **birch** is a tall tree that has thin peeling bark. There are different kinds of birch trees. EG *...forests of pine, birch, beech, and larch.* ● See also **silver birch**. — N COUNT/UNCOUNT

2 The **birch** is a cane or bunch of twigs made of birch wood, which is used to hit people with as a punishment. EG *A criminal might receive twelve strokes of the birch.* ▸ used to refer to the punishment of hitting someone with the birch. EG *Some MPs think we should bring back the birch.* — N SING : *the*+N; = rod

bird /bɜːd/, **birds**. **1** A **bird** is a creature with feathers, two legs, and two wings, which lays eggs. Most birds can fly. EG *All birds lay eggs... I could hear birds singing in the trees.* — N COUNT

2 The explanation of sex and sexual reproduction is sometimes referred to as **the birds and the bees**; used especially in a humorous way. — PHR : USED AS O OR S

3 If you say that **a bird in the hand is worth two in the bush**, you mean that something that you have already got or achieved is worth far more than something that you might try to get or achieve which would involve risking the loss of what you already have. — PHR

4 If you say that a particular action will **kill two birds with one stone**, you mean that this one action will have two beneficial effects. — PHR : VB INFLECTS

5 If, when you are chasing someone or looking for them, you say that **the bird has flown,** you mean that they have escaped. — PHR : AUX INFLECTS

6 A **bird** is also, in informal English, **6.1** a word used by men to refer to a young woman; women often find this use slightly insulting. EG *There were some smashing birds there.* — N COUNT; ⇑ girl = chick **6.2** a person of a particular quality or kind mentioned. EG *He's a rare bird.* — N COUNT : USU ADJ+N

bird-brained. Someone who is **bird-brained** is stupid and always concerned with unimportant things; an informal word showing disapproval. — ADJ CLASSIF; ⇑ silly = frivolous

birdcage /bɜːdkeɪdʒ/, **birdcages**; also spelled with a hyphen or as two words. A **birdcage** is a cage, usually made of wire, in which a bird is kept. — N COUNT

birdie /bɜːdiʲ/, **birdies**. **1** A **birdie** is a bird; used especially by children or by adults who are talking to children. — N COUNT

2 If you get a **birdie** in golf, you get the golf ball into a hole in one stroke fewer than the number that it is thought a good golfer should take. — N COUNT

bird-like; also spelled as one word. Someone who is **bird-like** resembles a bird in their appearance or behaviour. EG *She was a small, bird-like woman... Her darting birdlike eyes peeped round the door.* — ADJ CLASSIF

bird of paradise, birds of paradise. A **bird of paradise** is a songbird which is found mainly in New Guinea. The male birds have very brightly coloured feathers. — N COUNT

bird of prey, birds of prey. A **bird of prey** is a bird, such as an eagle or a hawk, that kills and eats other birds and animals. — N COUNT; ⇑ predator

bird-seed is seed for feeding birds. — N UNCOUNT

bird's eye view, bird's eye views. A **bird's eye view** is **1** a view that you see from far above, so that things look very small. EG *From this tower you get a bird's eye view of the city, including the racecourse and the airport.* — N COUNT : USU SING, IF+PREP THEN *of* **2** a general or overall impression of something. EG *...then we'll have a bird's eye view of what we've done so far.* — N COUNT : USU SING, IF+PREP THEN *of*; ⇑ overview

bird watcher, bird watchers; also spelled with a hyphen. A **bird watcher** is someone whose hobby is watching and studying wild birds in their natural surroundings. EG *There are over 2 million serious bird watchers in the United States.* — N COUNT; ⇑ person = ornithologist

Biro /baɪrəʊ/, **Biros**. **Biro** is a trademark for a pen with a small metal ball on one end which transfers the ink onto the paper. — N COUNT; = ballpoint

birth /bɜːθ/, **births**. **1** The **birth** of a baby is the time when it comes out of its mother's body. EG *The birth of her first child was a difficult time... The average baby's weight is a little over 7 pounds at birth... ...premature babies and problem births... ...a girl deaf from birth... ...my son's birth certificate.* — N UNCOUNT/COUNT; ⇑ emergence ≠ death

● See also **date of birth**. ● When a mother **gives birth**, she goes through the natural process of producing a baby from her body. EG *She had been granted a year's maternity leave after giving birth... The females congregate every spring to give birth to their young.* — ● PHR : VB INFLECTS, IF+PREP THEN *to*; ⇑ produce

2 If someone has a particular nationality **by birth,** they have that nationality because their parents have it, or because they were born in the country referred to. EG *They both had something of the Latin in them, she by birth, he by long residence in France... Dr Cort's father is a Russian by birth but left the Soviet Union in 1975.* — PHR : USED AS AN A

3 The country, town, village, etc **of** your **birth** is the place where you were born. EG *...begging him to save the people of the village of his birth.* — PHR : USED AS AN A; ⇑ origin

4 You use **birth** to refer to the fact of someone having been born into a family of a particular social position, especially of a high social position. EG *...respect for the qualities of position and birth, education and social grace... He certainly could not count upon his birth to launch him on a career... ...young men of noble birth.* — N UNCOUNT

5 The **birth** of something is the beginning or origin of it. EG *...Susan Briggs's admirable account of the birth, youth, and maturity of radio and early television.* — N SING : USU *the* +N+*of*; = start

● Something that **gives birth to** something else is the cause of its beginning or origin. EG *This horror did not give birth to his extremism.* — ● PHR : VB INFLECTS

birth control; also spelled with a hyphen. **Birth control** is the same as contraception. — N UNCOUNT

birthday /bɜːθdeɪ/, **birthdays**. Your **birthday** is the anniversary of the date on which you were born. People usually celebrate their birthday each year. EG *For her birthday I bought her a bicycle... Happy birthday!... ...a birthday party.* — N COUNT

birthmark /bɜːθmɑːk/, **birthmarks**. A **birthmark** is a mark on someone's skin that has been there since they were born. — N COUNT; ⇑ mark

birthplace /bɜːθpleɪs/, **birthplaces**. **1** Someone's **birthplace** is the place where they were born; used especially in connection with someone famous. EG *...Schubert's birthplace... We walked up from Gelatao, birthplace of Benito Juarez.* — N COUNT : WITH POSS; ⇑ place

2 The **birthplace** of a particular important event or organization is the place where it began or originated. EG *Angevin is often credited as being the birthplace of romantic love.* — N COUNT : IF+PREP THEN *of*; ⇑ place

birth rate, birth rates; also spelled with a hyphen. The **birth rate** is the number of babies born for every 1000 people in a specified area over a particular period of time. EG *A boom in the birth-rate might be expected... ...the country's falling birth rate.* — N COUNT; ⇑ statistic

birthright /bɜːθraɪt/, **birthrights**. Something that is your **birthright** is something that you feel you have a basic right to have, simply because you are a human being. EG *He felt that a decent standard of education and health care was his birthright.* — N UNCOUNT/COUNT : USU POSS +N; ⇑ right

biscuit /bɪskɪt/, **biscuits**. **1** A **biscuit** is **1.1** in British English, a small flat piece of baked cake mixture that is crisp and usually sweet. There are many different kinds of biscuit. EG *...a chocolate biscuit... ...a biscuit tin.* — N COUNT; = cookie **1.2** in American English, a small dry cake that sometimes has dried fruit in it and is eaten with butter and jam. — N COUNT; = scone

2 You might say that someone or something **takes** — PHR : VB the **biscuit** when someone has done something very annoying, disappointing, or surprising; an informal expression. INFLECTS

bisect /baɪsekt/, **bisects, bisecting, bisected.**
1 If something long and thin **bisects** an area or line, the part of the area or line on one side of it is the same size as the part on the other side. EG *The main north-south road bisects the town.* V+O ↑ divide
2 If you **bisect** something, especially an angle, you draw a line that divides it into two equal parts; a technical term in geometry. V+O ↑ divide = halve

bisexual /baɪseksjuᵒəl/, **bisexuals.** Someone who is **bisexual** is sexually attracted to both men and women. ▸ used as a noun. EG *He is a bisexual.* ADJ CLASSIF ▸ N COUNT

bishop /bɪʃəp/, **bishops.** 1 A **bishop** is a clergyman of high rank, especially in the Roman Catholic, Anglican, and Orthodox branches of Christianity, who is in charge of all the clergymen of lower rank in a particular area. EG *...the Bishop of Exeter... ...Bishop Fisher.* N COUNT: ALSO IN TITLES
2 In chess, a **bishop** is a piece that can be moved diagonally across the board on squares that are the same colour. N COUNT

bishopric /bɪʃəprɪk/, **bishoprics.** A **bishopric** is the area for which a bishop is responsible or the rank or office of being a bishop. N COUNT

bison /baɪsəᵒn/, **bisons. Bison** can also be used as the plural form. A **bison** is a large hairy animal of the cattle family which has a large head and shoulders and which used to be very common in North America and Europe. N COUNT ↑ ox = buffalo

bistro /biːstrəʊ/, **bistros.** A **bistro** is a small restaurant or bar. N COUNT

bit /bɪt/, **bits.** 1 A **bit** of something is a small amount of it; an informal use. EG *There'll be a bit of sunshine... I was in the West End doing a bit of shopping.* N PART: SING = spot
2 **a bit**; used in informal English. 2.1 **A bit** means to a small extent or degree. EG *He was a bit deaf... Percival's a bit like me... My sister's boots were a bit too small... It's a bit more expensive.* PHR+ADJ/PREP: USED AS C = slightly 2.2 **A bit** also means to quite a large extent or degree; used to emphasize something or to make a particular statement sound less extreme. EG *That sounds a bit complicated for me... You're a bit late, aren't you?* PHR+ADJ: USED AS C
2.3 You describe someone or something as **a bit of a** particular thing to make your statement less extreme than it would be if you described them as that thing directly. EG *Our room was a bit of a mess... Tony's a bit of a bore... This has all come as a bit of a shock.* PHR+NG: USED AS C ↑ quite 2.4 **Quite a bit** or **a bit** means quite a lot. EG *I've spent quite a bit of time studying for these exams... ...a rich Irishman who's made quite a bit of money.* PHR+*of* 2.5 If you say that something is **a bit much, a bit steep, a bit strong**, etc, you mean that it is too extreme or excessive in some way; used especially when you want to criticize something without seeming aggressive. EG *He kills the villains, and he gets the rich girl, and it's all a bit much, like most of the plot... It's asking a bit much to expect a lift.* PHR: USED AS C 2.6 If you do something **for a bit**, you do it for a short period of time. EG *Why can't we stay here for a bit?... She ought to go into hospital for a bit... We argued a bit, and then I said I'd go.* PHR: USED AS AN A 2.7 If you do something **for quite a bit**, you do it for quite a long time. EG *Mr Heissman was away for quite a bit.* PHR: USED AS AN A 2.8 You use **not a bit** when you want to make a strong negative statement. EG *It was all very clean and tidy, not a bit like his back garden... You haven't changed a bit... 'Are you frightened of me?'-'Not a bit.'* PHR ↑ not ≠ very 2.9 You say **not a bit of it** to indicate that something that you might expect to be the case is not the case. EG *You'd expect it to come out looking home-made; but not a bit of it.* PHR
3 You say that someone or something is **every bit as** good, important, annoying, etc as someone or something else to indicate emphatically that they are just as good, important, annoying, etc. EG *She wanted to prove to them that she was every bit as clever as they were.* PHR+ADJ: USED AS C
4 In fairly informal English, you can refer to 4.1 a particular part of something or a small area of it as a particular **bit** of it. EG *The heart of a lettuce is the pale, yellowish-white bit... ...the crowded bits of Spain... We've got to find out who owns this bit of land.* N PART ↑ part 4.2 a particular part of a book, story, film, etc as a particular **bit** of it. EG *I really enjoyed your letter, especially the bits about Dr O'Shea... 'Where was I?'-'You were at the bit where you and Christopher were on the bus.'* N COUNT+SUPP ↑ part
5 In informal English, a **bit** of something is also 5.1 a small piece of it. EG *She stepped from the mat to the bit of newspaper... ...a loaf of bread and a little bit of cheese... He washed off every bit of dirt.* N PART+N UNCOUNT = scrap 5.2 a particular item or one of a set or group of things. EG *How much you charge for every bit of work is laid down in the rules... Another bit of jargon that's often used is 'time-sharing'... Never bring any bit of furniture into your home without checking it first.* N PART+N UNCOUNT ↑ piece
6 **to bits.** 6.1 If something is smashed or taken **to bits** or falls **to bits**, it is broken or comes apart so that it is in several pieces. EG *The dog was pulling the Christmas tree to bits.* PHR: USED AS AN A 6.2 You use **to bits** to indicate that someone feels a particular emotion, especially pleasure or fear, very strongly; an informal use. EG *She was thrilled to bits... It would frighten her to bits, I bet.* PHR: USED AS AN A ↑ extremely
7 **Bits and pieces** is used in the following expressions in informal English. 7.1 **Bits and pieces** are a lot of small objects which are all different. EG *We shovelled all the bits and pieces back into the tin box.* PHR: USED AS O OR S 7.2 Your **bits and pieces** are all the small objects that belong to you or that you have with you. EG *I saw her gathering up her bits and pieces for the move to the cabin.* PHR+POSS: USED AS S OR O ↑ possessions = things 7.3 **Bits and pieces** are also parts of something that have been taken or copied from other things. EG *...prophets who have borrowed bits and pieces from every religion under the sun.* PHR: USED AS O OR S
8 If you do something **bit by bit**, you do it slowly or in stages. EG *He moved his hand bit by bit over the mirror... We eased the lid off, bit by bit.* PHR: USED AS AN A = gradually
9 If you **do** your **bit**, you do something that, to a small or limited extent, helps to make a large organization or system successful or helps to achieve something. EG *...having done his bit for King and Country... Everyone was expected to do his bit to make sure that Amity remained a desirable resort.* PHR: VB INFLECTS ↑ assist
10 The word **bit** is used in expressions such as 'the motherly bit' and 'the whole marriage bit' to refer to everything that is involved in a particular idea, way of life, type of behaviour, etc; used in informal English. EG *It is important not to overdo the motherly bit... ...Bi-Proteen, Nutrament, the whole diet supplement bit.* N SING: *the*+MOD+N = scene, thing
11 You describe someone or something as **a bit of all right** when you think they are very attractive, pleasant, or good; a very informal expression. EG *Wonderful, he thought, rubbing his hands. This is a bit of all right... He's a bit of all right.* PHR: USED AS C = OK
12 In computing, a **bit** is the smallest unit of information that is held in a computer's memory. It is either 1 or 0. Several bits form a byte. N COUNT = binary digit
13 A **bit** is also a piece of metal that is held in a horse's mouth by the reins and is used to control the horse when you are riding. ● When you **get** or **take the bit between** your **teeth**, you become very enthusiastic about a particular job that you have to do. N COUNT ● PHR: VB INFLECTS
14 **Bit** is also the past tense of **bite**.

bitch /bɪtʃ/, **bitches, bitching, bitched.** 1 If you call a woman a **bitch**, you mean that she behaves in an unpleasant and nasty way to other people; a rude and offensive use. N COUNT/VOC = cow
2 A **bitch** is a female dog. N COUNT
3 If someone **bitches**, they complain about someone or something in a nasty way; an informal use showing disapproval. EG *You haven't done a thing except bitch ever since we got here... Ben always bitches about all the chatter that goes on between them.* V: IF+PREP THEN *about* = nag
4 If you have a **bitch** about someone who is not present, you say nasty things about them; an informal use. N SING: *a*+N = moan

bitchy /bɪtʃiˈ/, **bitchier, bitchiest.** Someone who is **bitchy** says nasty things about other people. EG *Being bitchy was one of Cindy's failings.* ▸ used of people's actions and behaviour. EG *...a bitchy remark.* ADJ QUALIT = catty ▸ = snide

bite /baɪt/, **bites, biting, bit, bitten.** 1 When a person or animal **bites** something or **bites** into it, through it, etc, they use their teeth to cut through it or cut a piece off it, or to hold it tightly. EG *My sister's dog bit me... She bit into her rock cake... The lion bit off a piece of meat... I have a nervous habit of biting my nails... He fought like a wild-cat, biting and clawing.* V OR V+O: USU+A
2 When a person or animal takes a **bite** or gives someone a **bite**, they bite someone or something. EG N COUNT

Madeleine took a bite. 'Yes, it is delicious.'... It gives each of its victims a quick bite to immobilize them... The rat paused between bites.

3 A **bite** is an injury which is the result of being bitten by an animal. EG *I'm allergic to dog bites.* — N COUNT

4 A **bite** of food is a piece of food that you have bitten off with your teeth. EG *Brody was in the midst of swallowing a bite of egg sandwich... She took a big bite out of her bread and butter.* — N COUNT : IF + PREP THEN *of/out of* = mouthful

5 A **bite** to eat or a **bite** of something is a small meal or a snack; an informal expression. EG *We'll have a bite to eat before we go to the theatre.* — N SING : a+N

6 When an insect or a snake **bites** you, it pierces your skin with its mouth or teeth and often causes an area of your skin to be itchy or painful. EG *A mosquito had bitten her on the wrist.* ▸ used as a noun. EG *My face and hands are covered with mosquito bites.* — V+O ⇑ wound; ▸ N COUNT ⇑ wound

7 If you **are bitten** by an interest in something or a desire to do something, you become extremely interested in it or want to do it very much indeed. EG *He had been bitten by the bug of photography... By 1634 the Dutch were bitten by this new craze.* — V+O : ONLY PASS ⇑ be attracted = be smitten

8 If you get a **bite** when you are fishing, a fish takes the hook at the end of your fishing line in its mouth. ▸ used as a verb. EG *Are the fish biting today?* — N COUNT = catch; ▸ V

9 If an object or surface **bites**, it grips another object or surface rather than slipping on it or against it. EG *Let the clutch in slowly until it begins to bite.* — V ⇑ grip = catch

10 When some action, law, or policy begins to **bite**, it begins to have an effect, usually one that the people affected find unpleasant. EG *The sanctions are beginning to bite.* — V ⇑ take effect = pinch

11 If a type of food or drink has **bite**, it tastes pleasantly sharp or strong. EG *I like a sauce with a bit of bite to it.* — N UNCOUNT = edge

12 If the air or the wind has a **bite**, it feels very cold. EG *The bite of the cold air seemed to give him energy.* — N SING WITH DET = nip

13 The word **bite** is also used in the following expressions. **13.1** You say to someone that a particular person or thing **won't bite** or **won't bite** them as a way of telling them not to be frightened of approaching that person or handling that thing. — PHR : AUX INFLECTS **13.2** If you **bite off more than** you **can chew**, you try to do something that is too difficult for you or that there is not enough time to do. — PHR : FIRST VB INFLECTS, AUX INFLECTS **13.3 Once bitten, twice shy** is an expression used to say that someone who has done something which resulted in an unpleasant experience for them will not wish to do it again. — PHR **13.4** The word **bite** is also used in the following expressions, which are explained at other places in this dictionary. • someone's **bark is worse than** their **bite**: see **bark**. • to **bite the dust**: see **dust**. • to **bite the hand that feeds** you: see **hand**. • to **bite** someone's **head off**: see **head**.

bite back. If you **bite back** something that you were going to say, you stop yourself from saying it. EG *The word 'Sorry' rises to Morris's lips, but he bites it back.* — PHRASAL VB : V+O+ADV ⇑ suppress

bite into. If an object **bites into** something firm, it cuts or presses into its surface. EG *The rope bit into his wrists.* — PHRASAL VB : V+PREP, HAS PASS

biting /baɪtɪŋ/. 1 A **biting** wind or **biting** cold is extremely cold. EG *...a biting east wind... ...the biting chill of the water.* — ADJ QUALIT : USU ATTRIB = bitter

2 **Biting** is used to describe speech or writing that is sharp and clever in a way that makes other people feel uncomfortable. EG *...a writer with a biting wit... ...biting retorts.* — ADJ QUALIT = caustic

bit part, **bit parts**. A **bit part** is a small and unimportant part for an actor in a film or play. — N COUNT

bitten /bɪtə⁰n/ is the past participle of **bite**.

bitter /bɪtə/, **bitterest; bitters**. 1 Someone who is **bitter** feels angry and resentful as a result of a disappointment or because they believe that they have been treated unfairly. EG *He was a jealous, slightly bitter man... The manufacturers felt bitter about the increase in tax.* ▸ used of people's actions and behaviour. EG *...a bitter sneer.* ◊ **bitterly**. EG *'I'm glad somebody's happy,' he said bitterly.* ◊ **bitterness.** EG *He remembers with bitterness how his father was cheated.* — ADJ QUALIT = embittered; ◊ ADV = resentfully; ◊ N UNCOUNT = resentment

2 A **bitter** disappointment or experience causes you to have deep feelings of anger or unhappiness. EG *I have had long and bitter experience of dealing with that sort of person... ...the great expectations of 1964 and the bitter disappointments that followed... It was the bitterest blow for the new party.* • If you continue doing something difficult or unpleasant **to the bitter end**, you continue doing it until it is completely finished although it is not enjoyable to do it. EG *We have pursued everything to the bitter end.* — ADJ QUALIT : ATTRIB ⇑ unpleasant; • PHR : USED AS AN A

3 A **bitter** argument, war, or struggle is one in which the people involved hate each other and argue or fight fiercely and angrily. EG *The argument became more bitter... ...two years of bitter and ferocious fighting... ...the bitter Presidential campaign of 1932.* — ADJ QUALIT ⇑ angry = acrimonious, vicious

4 A **bitter** wind or **bitter** weather is very cold and unpleasant. EG *...a bitter easterly wind... They stood for four hours in the bitter cold.* — ADJ QUALIT = biting

5 Something that is **bitter** has a sharp, unpleasant taste. EG *It tasted faintly of bitter almonds.* — ADJ QUALIT

6 **Bitter** is a British beer that is made with more hops than most beers and has a slightly bitter taste. EG *...two pints of bitter.* — N MASS

7 **Bitters** is a strong alcoholic drink that contains products from plants and is usually drunk mixed with another alcoholic drink. — N UNCOUNT ⇑ spirit

bitter lemon, bitter lemons. **Bitter lemon** is a fizzy drink that is made partly from the juice of lemons and is drunk on its own or mixed with other drinks. — N MASS

bitterly /bɪtəli¹/. 1 **Bitterly** means strongly and intensely; used to refer to strong emotions such as anger, hatred, shame, or misery. EG *No man could have hated the old order more bitterly... He was bitterly ashamed... I was bitterly disappointed... She sat in her room and wept bitterly.* — ADV = desperately

2 If the weather is **bitterly cold** or if you are **bitterly cold,** it is extremely cold or you are extremely cold. EG *...on a bitterly cold New Year's Day.* — ADV+ADJ = freezing

bitter-sweet. 1 Something that tastes or smells **bitter-sweet** seems both bitter and sweet at the same time. EG *...the bitter-sweet scent of blackcurrant leaves.* — ADJ QUALIT

2 An experience or a memory that is **bitter-sweet** has both happy and sad qualities or features. EG *...the bitter-sweet memory of their first meeting.* — ADJ QUALIT

bitty /bɪti¹/, **bittier, bittiest**. Something that is **bitty** seems to be formed from a lot of different parts which do not fit together or go together well; an informal word. EG *The play was very bitty in the second act.* — ADJ QUALIT ⇑ inconsistent = patchy

bitumen /bɪtjə⁴mən/ is a black sticky substance which is obtained from tar or petrol and is used in making roads. — N UNCOUNT

bivouac /bɪvuæk/, **bivouacs, bivouacking, bivouacked**. 1 A **bivouac** is a temporary camp made by soldiers or mountaineers. — N COUNT

2 If you **bivouac** in a particular place, you stop and stay in a bivouac there. EG *...regiments that had bivouacked at places like Valley Forge.* — V+A ⇑ camp

bizarre /bi¹zɑː/. Something that is **bizarre** is very odd and strange. EG *He had some bizarre conversations with his landlady... ...steam-powered mousetraps and other bizarre gadgets.* — ADJ QUALIT = weird ≠ ordinary

blab /blæb/, **blabs, blabbing, blabbed**. If you **blab**, you reveal a secret; an informal word. EG *I wonder who blabbed... He's been blabbing to the Press.* — V : IF+PREP THEN *to/about* = talk

blabber /blæbə/, **blabbers, blabbering, blabbered**. If you **blabber**, you talk about something in a way that is considered boring, irritating, or foolish; an informal word. EG *...blabbering on about human rights.* — V : USU+A = babble

blabbermouth /blæbəmauθ/, **blabbermouths**. A **blabbermouth** is a person who tells other people things that you did not want them to know; an informal word. — N COUNT : ALSO VOC = big mouth

black /blæk/, **blacker, blackest; blacks, blacking, blacked**. 1 Something that is **black** is of the darkest colour that there is, the colour of the sky at night when there is no light at all. EG *...a black leather coat... ...a girl with long black hair.* ▸ used as a noun. EG *...a woman dressed in black.* ◊ **blackness**. EG *We were walking through deserted streets in the blackness... ...the river's glistening blackness.* — ADJ COLOUR ⇑ dark; ▸ N UNCOUNT; ◊ N UNCOUNT

2 Someone who is **black** belongs to a race of people with dark skins, especially a race from Africa. EG *...black musicians.* ▸ used as a noun. EG *He was the first black to be elected to the Congress.* ◊ **blackness**. — ADJ CLASSIF; ▸ N COUNT; ◊ N UNCOUNT

3 **Black** is used of things relating to black people. EG *...the black area of the city.* ADJ CLASSIF : ATTRIB

4 Coffee or tea that is **black** has no milk or cream added to it. EG *Do you want your coffee black?* ADJ CLASSIF ≠ milky

5 If your bank account is **in the black**, you have money in the account and are not overdrawn. PHR : USED AS AN A = in credit

6 If you **black** someone's eye, you hit them in the eye and bruise the area round it. V+O ⇑ injure

7 If you **black** boots or shoes, or metal objects such as stoves, you polish them with black polish. ● See also **blacking**. V+O

8 If you describe a situation as **black**, you mean that it is bad and is not likely to improve. EG *I don't think the future is as black as that... You paint a rather black picture of the situation.* ADJ QUALIT = dismal ≠ hopeful

9 If you are in a **black** mood or feel **black** despair, hatred, etc, you feel very unhappy and depressed or very hostile and angry. EG *She killed herself in a fit of black despair.* ADJ QUALIT : USU ATTRIB ⇑ extreme = desperate

10 A **black** look or expression expresses great anger, annoyance, or hatred. EG *She gave him a black look.* ADJ QUALIT : USU ATTRIB
● Someone who looks **as black as thunder** looks very angry indeed. EG *He came in with a face as black as thunder.* ● PHR : USED AS AN A

11 **Black** is also used to describe things that are very evil and wicked; a literary use. EG *This was one of the blackest crimes ever committed... His black heart rejoiced at their sufferings.* ● If you say that someone is **not as black as** they **are painted**, you mean that they are not as unpleasant or bad as they are often said to be. ADJ QUALIT ⇑ evil = dastardly ● PHR : VB INFLECTS

12 **Black** magic is magic that is intended to harm people or that involves communicating with evil spirits. EG *...the black arts.* ADJ CLASSIF : ATTRIB

13 **Black** humour involves jokes about things that are very sad or unpleasant. EG *...a black comedy.* ADJ QUALIT : ATTRIB

14 When a group of people, for example a trade union, **black** particular goods or particular people, they refuse to handle these goods or have dealings with these people. EG *They blacked all coal from mines that had continued working during the strike.* V+O = boycott

black out. 1 If you **black out**, you lose consciousness for a short time. PHRASAL VB : V+ADV

2 If someone **blacks out** a place, they make it completely dark by switching off all the lights or covering the windows. PHRASAL VB : V+O+ADV ⇑ darken

3 If people **black out** a television or radio programme, they prevent it being broadcast, usually in protest against something. PHRASAL VB : V+O+ADV ⇑ stop

4 If you **black out** something that has been written or drawn, you hide it by covering it with paint or ink. PHRASAL VB : V+O+ADV ⇑ conceal

5 See also **blackout**.

black Africa is the part of Africa to the south of the Sahara Desert. N PROPER

black and blue. Someone who is **black and blue** is badly bruised, usually because they have been hit by someone. EG *He used to beat me black and blue.* ADJ CLASSIF : PRED

black and white. 1 A photograph, film, or picture that is **black and white** or in **black and white** contains only black, white, and grey. EG *...a black-and-white film... I saw it in black and white.* ADJ CLASSIF ⇑ monochrome ≠ colour

2 A **black-and-white** television set, camera, reel of film, etc shows or produces a black-and-white picture. ADJ CLASSIF ≠ colour

3 If something is **in black and white,** it is in writing or in print. EG *I want to see that agreement down on paper, in black and white.* PHR : USED AS AN A

4 A **black-and-white** issue, problem, or situation, or one that is seen in **black and white**, is one which is considered to involve issues that are simple and straightforward and therefore easy to decide about. EG *This is not a black-and-white issue... She sees everything in very black-and-white terms.* ADJ QUALIT = clear-cut

blackball /blækbɔːl/, **blackballs, blackballing, blackballed.** If you **blackball** someone, you prevent them from joining a club or other group by voting against their joining. V+O ⇑ exclude = bar

black belt, black belts. A **black belt** is worn by someone who has reached a high standard in judo or karate. EG *He's got a black belt in karate.* ▸ **Black belt** is also used to refer to someone who has a black belt. EG *She's a black belt now at judo.* N COUNT ⇑ grade

blackberry /blækbəri[1]/, **blackberries.** A **blackberry** is a small, soft, black or dark purple fruit that is made up of lots of round sections and grows on bushes that often grow wild in Europe; used also of the bush that it grows on. N COUNT = bramble

blackberrying /blækberi[1]ɪŋ/. If you go **blackberrying**, you go out and pick wild blackberries. N UNCOUNT ⇑ gathering

blackbird /blækbɜːd/, **blackbirds.** A **blackbird** is a common, fairly small European bird. The male has black feathers and a yellow beak, and the female has brown feathers. N COUNT ⇑ bird

blackboard /blækbɔːd/, **blackboards.** A **blackboard** is a board which is usually black or another dark colour, and on which people, especially teachers in a classroom, write or draw with chalk. N COUNT = board

black box, black boxes. A **black box** is 1 an electronic device which is fitted in an aircraft and which collects and stores information about the aircraft during its flight. It is used especially to provide evidence about accidents. 2 a part in an electronic or computer system which you can understand how to use without knowing exactly what parts it is made up of. N COUNT = flight recorder N COUNT

blackcurrant /blækkʌrənt/, **blackcurrants.** A **blackcurrant** is a very small dark purple fruit that grows in bunches on a bush and is usually cooked before being eaten; used also of the bush that it grows on. N COUNT ⇑ currant

black economy, black economies. The **black economy** of a country is the earning of money that goes on without the government being informed, in order to avoid paying tax on it. N COUNT : USU SING

blacken /blækən/, **blackens, blackening, blackened.** 1 When someone or something **blackens** something else, they make it black or very dark in colour. EG *His face was blackened with charcoal.* V+O ⇑ darken

2 If you **blacken** someone's reputation, you damage it by saying that they are bad or that they have done something wrong, usually when this is not true. EG *...a smear campaign to blacken the Labour Party... French spokesmen took pains not to blacken the image of their country.* V+O = discredit

black eye, black eyes. If you have a **black eye,** you have a dark-coloured bruise around your eye as a result of being hit. N COUNT ⇑ injury

blackguard /blægɑːd, -gəd/, **blackguards.** If you describe someone as a **blackguard**, you mean that they are wicked and dishonourable; an old-fashioned word. EG *Now don't lie to me, you young blackguard!* N COUNT : ALSO VOC = scoundrel

blackhead /blækhɛd/, **blackheads.** A **blackhead** is a very small black spot on the skin that is caused by a pore in the skin being blocked by dirt. N COUNT

black hole, black holes. A **black hole** is an area in space that is believed to exist, where gravity is so strong that nothing, not even light, can move away from it. N COUNT

black ice is a thin, transparent layer of ice on a road or path that is very difficult to see. N UNCOUNT

blacking /blækɪŋ/ is a type of polish that was used in former times to make shoes or metal objects such as stoves blacker. N UNCOUNT

blackish /blækɪʃ/. Something that is **blackish** is dark in colour and contains black tones. EG *...blackish clouds.* ADJ COLOUR

blackjack /blækdʒæk/, **blackjacks.** 1 **Blackjack** is the same as pontoon.

2 A **blackjack** is a short, thick weapon used for hitting people, with one end made of lead and covered with leather; used in American English. N COUNT ⇑ cosh

blackleg /blækleg/, **blacklegs.** A **blackleg** is someone who continues to work when the people that they work with are on strike, or who works instead of people who are on strike; used in British English, usually showing disapproval. N COUNT = scab

blacklist /blæklɪst/, **blacklists, blacklisting, blacklisted.** 1 A **blacklist** is a list which is made by a government, organization, or important person and which contains the names of people or organizations who they think cannot be trusted or who have done something wrong. EG *Many of the teachers had been placed on a blacklist.* N COUNT ⇑ list

2 If someone **blacklists** a person or organization, they put them on a blacklist. V+O ⇑ list

blackmail /blækmaɪl/, **blackmails, blackmailing, blackmailed. Blackmail** is the action of threatening to do something unpleasant to someone, for example to reveal a secret about them or to harm them, unless they give you money or behave in the way you want them to. EG *This amounted to blackmail... ...emotional blackmail.* ▸ used as a verb. EG *He tried to blackmail me... The group could blackmail the government into meeting its demands.* N UNCOUNT ⇑ extortion ▸ V+O ⇑ threaten

blackmailer /blækmaɪlə/, **blackmailers**. A **blackmailer** is someone who blackmails someone else, usually in order to get money from them. N COUNT

black Maria /blæk mərɑɪə/, **black Marias**. A **black Maria** is a black van that the police use to transport prisoners in. N COUNT ⇑ vehicle

black mark, black marks. If something is a **black mark** against someone, it is something bad that they have done or a bad quality that they have which affects the way people think about them. EG *My refusal to go would be a black mark against me.* N COUNT : IF + PREP THEN *against* ≠ plus

black market, black markets. The **black market** is a system of buying and selling goods, or changing money, which is not in accordance with the laws of a country or part of its usual trading system. EG *He was arrested while trying to sell jeans on the black market.* N COUNT : USU SING ⇑ trade

black marketeer /blæk mɑːkətɪə/, **black marketeers**. A **black marketeer** is someone who trades on the black market. N COUNT ⇑ trader

blackout /blækaʊt/, **blackouts**. A **blackout** is 1 a period of time, especially in wartime, when a place is deliberately made completely dark by switching all the lights off or covering the windows of buildings where there are lights on. EG *We couldn't get home before the blackout.* N COUNT 2 a period of time when the electricity supply to a place stops completely. EG *Faults in the power lines have led to occasional blackouts lasting a few hours each.* N COUNT = power cut 3 the prevention of the broadcasting of a television or radio programme. N COUNT : USU + SUPP 4 the prevention of the reporting of news about a particular event. EG *I want a news blackout.* N COUNT : USU + SUPP
5 a temporary loss of consciousness. EG *I must have had a blackout: I can't remember a thing.* N COUNT

black pepper is pepper which is dark in colour and has been made from the dried fruits of the pepper plant, including their black outer cases. N UNCOUNT

black pudding, black puddings. **Black pudding** is a thick sausage which has a black skin and is made from pork fat and pig's blood. It is eaten mainly in northern parts of Britain. N UNCOUNT/COUNT

black sheep. **Black sheep** is both the singular and the plural form. A **black sheep** is someone who is considered bad or worthless by members of their family or another group that they belong to. EG *He's always been regarded as the black sheep of the family.* N COUNT : USU SING ⇑ reprobate

blacksmith /blæksmɪθ/, **blacksmiths**. A **blacksmith** is someone whose job is making things out of metal, for example horseshoes or farm tools. N COUNT = smithy

black spot, black spots. A **black spot** is 1 a place on a road where accidents often happen. N COUNT 2 an area of a country or place where a particular situation is especially bad. EG *Government money should be diverted to unemployment black spots.* N COUNT

black tie. A **black tie** event is a formal event such as a party at which the men wear formal clothes, including dinner jackets and bow ties. ADJ CLASSIF

bladder /blædə/, **bladders**. 1 Your **bladder** is an organ in your body, shaped like a hollow bag, where urine is held until it leaves your body. EG *He had a weak bladder.* • See also **gall bladder**. N COUNT
2 A **bladder** is also a hollow bag of skin, leather, plastic, etc which may be filled with air or liquid so that it becomes round. EG *...the rubber inner bladders of footballs.* N COUNT + SUPP

blade /bleɪd/, **blades**. 1 The **blade** of a knife or other tool used for cutting things is the thin, flat piece of metal with a sharp edge which is the part of it that cuts. EG *...a knife blade... Tractors equipped with special blades levelled more than 1,000 acres of forest.* N COUNT
2 A **blade** is also a long, flat piece of metal, wood, etc which is part of something such as a propeller, electric fan, or oar and which pushes against or is pushed by the air or water. EG *...the whirling horizontal blades of a helicopter... He balanced the blades of the oars above the water.* N COUNT + SUPP
3 A **blade** of grass is a flat, narrow piece of grass. N COUNT
4 See also **razor blade, shoulder blade**.

blah /blɑː/. You use **blah, blah, blah** to refer to something that is said or written without giving the actual words, because you think that they are boring or unimportant; used in informal English. EG *He said they were marvellous, couldn't have been more helpful, blah, blah, blah.* = etc.

blame /bleɪm/, **blames, blaming, blamed**. 1 If you **blame** someone or something for something bad that has happened, or if you **blame** it on them, you think or say that they are responsible for it or that they caused it. EG *I was blamed for the theft... Delinquency is often blamed on the fact that more mothers are working... Don't blame me.* ▸ used as a noun. EG *You haven't said a word of blame.* V + O : IF + PREP THEN *for* ⇑ accuse ▸ N UNCOUNT ⇑ accusation
2 If someone or something **is to blame** for something bad that has happened, they are responsible for it or they caused it. EG *I was partly to blame... The severe housing shortage is largely to blame for the inflated rents.* PHR : IF + PREP THEN *for*, VB INFLECTS ⇑ be responsible
3 The **blame** for something bad that has happened is the responsibility for causing it or letting it happen. EG *He had to take the blame for everything... So far, women have been able to lay most of the blame on men... No political party is free from serious blame.* N UNCOUNT ≠ credit
4 If you say that you cannot or do not **blame** someone for doing something, you mean that you do not think that it is wrong or unreasonable for them to do it. EG *I can't really blame him for wanting to make me suffer... You could hardly blame them.* V + O : WITH BROAD NEG, IF + PREP THEN *for* ⇑ criticize

blameless /bleɪmlɪ²s/. Someone who is **blameless** has not done anything bad or wrong. EG *On that score, he was blameless.* ▸ used of people's actions and behaviour. EG *He has always lived a blameless life.* ADJ QUALIT

blameworthy /bleɪmwɜːði¹/. Someone who is **blameworthy** has done something bad or wrong. EG *I hardly feel I am blameworthy.* ADJ QUALIT = at fault

blanch /blɑːntʃ/, **blanches, blanching, blanched**. 1 If you **blanch**, you become very pale because you are shocked, frightened, cold, or ill. EG *Her normally rosy cheeks had been blanched by the wind...* ◇ **blanched**. EG *The men returned, their faces blanched.* V-ERG ⇑ whiten ◇ ADJ QUALIT
2 If you **blanch** vegetables, fruit, or nuts, you put them into boiling water for a short time, for example in order to remove their skins or to kill germs on them before freezing them. V + O ⇑ boil
3 If you **blanch** vegetables such as celery or leeks, you pile earth round their stems while they are growing in order to keep the lower part white. V + O

blancmange /bləmɒnʒ/, **blancmanges**. **Blancmange** is a cold, jelly-like pudding made from milk, sugar, cornflour, and flavouring. N UNCOUNT/COUNT ⇑ dessert

bland /blænd/, **blander, blandest**. 1 Someone who is **bland** is calm and unexcited, and perhaps quietly polite. EG *...bland, evasive, middle-of-the-road men.* ▸ used of people's attitudes and behaviour. EG *...bland optimism.* ◇ **blandly**. EG *Mr Jones blandly dismissed their arguments as irrelevant.* ADJ QUALIT = insipid ≠ lively ◇ ADV
2 Food that is **bland** has very little flavour; usually used showing disapproval. ADJ QUALIT ⇑ tasteless
3 Something such as music that is **bland** is rather dull and uninteresting; used showing disapproval. EG *The album had a bland, uneventful sort of sound.* ADJ QUALIT

blandishments /blændɪʃmə²nts/ are pleasant things that someone says or offers to another person in order to persuade the person to do something; a formal word. EG *He remained impervious to all Nell's sulks and blandishments.* N PLURAL ⇑ inducements

blank /blæŋk/, **blanker, blankest; blanks**. 1 A **blank** piece of paper has no writing or other marks on it. EG *The landlord made him sign a blank sheet of paper.* ADJ CLASSIF ⇑ unmarked
2 A **blank** is a space which is left in a piece of writing or on a printed form for you to fill in particular information. N COUNT
3 Something that is **blank** is plain or empty and has nothing on it; used especially of something that is all one colour with no decoration or variety. EG *...a blank wall... They gazed at the blank blue sky.* • See also **point-blank**. ADJ QUALIT
4 If you look **blank** or if your face is **blank**, your face shows no feeling, understanding, or interest. EG *Her face went blank... She looked blank.* ◇ **blankly**. EG *I sat quietly, staring blankly ahead.* ADJ QUALIT = vacant ◇ ADV WITH VB
5 If your mind or your memory of something is a **blank**, you cannot think of anything or remember what happened. EG *My mind's a blank... All I can remember is hitting the ground–the rest is a blank.* N SING : a + N ⇑ void
• If you **go blank** or your mind **goes blank**, you suddenly cannot think of anything appropriate to say, for example in reply to a question. EG *I keep* • PHR : VB INFLECTS ⇑ forget

thinking I know all the answers and then going blank.

6 If you **draw a blank** when you are looking for someone or something, you fail to find them; a fairly informal expression. [PHR : VB INFLECTS = get nowhere]

7 A **blank** is also a cartridge for a gun which contains explosive but does not contain a bullet, so that nothing comes out when you fire the gun. [N COUNT = dummy]

blank cheque, blank cheques. A **blank cheque** is a cheque that you sign and give to someone for them to write in the amount of money that they want you to pay them. ● If you **give** someone **a blank cheque**, you give them the authority to do what they think is best in a particular situation or to spend as much money as they think is necessary. [N COUNT] [● PHR : VB INFLECTS ⇑ authorise]

blanket /blæŋkɪ²t/, **blankets, blanketing, blanketed.** 1 A **blanket** is a large square or rectangle of warm cloth, especially one which covers you when you are in bed. EG *He got back into bed and pulled the blankets up around him.* ● See also **electric blanket, wet blanket.** [N COUNT ⇑ cover]

2 If a quantity of something **blankets** an area, it covers the area in a continuous layer. EG *Beech, oak, and larch blanket 70 percent of the island... The snow came in, blanketing the mountains.* [V+O ⇑ cover]

3 A **blanket** of something such as cloud or fog is a continuous layer of it which hides what is below or beyond it. [N PART]

4 A **blanket** of an unpleasant emotion or a bad quality is an amount of it which is so great that it makes you unable to feel or notice anything else. EG *...a suffocating blanket of despair.* [N PART = excess]

5 **Blanket** is used to describe something such as a statement or law which affects or refers to the whole of a particular group or thing, and does not mention or allow any exceptions. EG *...our blanket acceptance of everything they say... ...the blanket indictment of a whole country.* [ADJ CLASSIF : ATTRIB = wholesale ≠ qualified]

blanket stitch is a type of stitch which is used along the edges of blankets or other thick material to prevent fraying. [N UNCOUNT ⇑ sewing]

blank verse is poetry that does not rhyme. In English Literature it usually consists of lines with five stressed syllables. [N UNCOUNT]

blare /blɛə/, **blares, blaring, blared.** When a horn, siren, radio, etc **blares,** it makes loud harsh sounds which are unpleasant to hear. EG *...blaring horns... The TV set was blaring in the background...* ▸ used as a noun. EG *The note became a strident blare... ...a note of warning wavers in the blare of conversation.* [V] [▸ N SING WITH DET : IF+PREP THEN *of*]

blare out. When a radio, record player, etc **blares out** music or noise, or when music or noise **blares out,** unpleasantly loud music or noise is produced from it. EG *A radio was blaring out the news... Indian music had been blaring out all evening.* [PHRASAL VB : V-ERG+ADV ⇑ emit]

blarney /blɑːni¹/ consists of a lot of pleasant but perhaps untrue things that someone says to you, especially in order to make you like them or to persuade you to do something. [N UNCOUNT = smooth talk]

blasé /blɑːzeɪ/. Someone who is **blasé** shows no excitement, interest, or pleasure in things that other people consider exciting or interesting, usually because they have experienced them before. EG *I was trying to sound blasé and experienced.* ▸ used of people's attitudes and behaviour. EG *...her petulant, blasé air.* [ADJ QUALIT = unmoved, cool ≠ bubbling]

blaspheme /blæsfiːm/, **blasphemes, blaspheming, blasphemed.** If someone **blasphemes,** they say rude or disrespectful things about God or religious matters, or use God's name as a swear word. EG *He felt no longer afraid of blaspheming against any God... Do not blaspheme.* [V : IF+PREP THEN *against*, OR V+QUOTE ⇑ offend]

blasphemous /blæsfə¹məs/. Someone who is **blasphemous** says or does things that show disrespect for God and that are considered shocking. EG *She was foul-mouthed and blasphemous.* ▸ used of words and behaviour. EG *...a blasphemous poem... To them the very idea is blasphemous.* [ADJ QUALIT = irreverent, profane]

blasphemy /blæsfə¹mi¹/, **blasphemies. Blasphemy** is the saying or doing of something that shows disrespect for God and is considered shocking. EG *Any attempt to violate or degrade that image is blasphemy... You have just heard his blasphemy!... It would be regarded as a blasphemy.* [N UNCOUNT/COUNT = sacrilege ≠ piety, reverence]

blast /blɑːst/, **blasts, blasting, blasted.** 1 A **blast** is a big explosion, especially one caused by a bomb. EG *Nobody had been hurt in the blast.* [N COUNT]

2 If people or things **blast** something, they destroy or damage it with an explosion, bomb, or other force. EG *America and Russia now have enough nuclear weapons to blast each other apart ten times over... That huge meteorite blasted a hole 200 kilometres across... ...areas blasted by lightning.* [V OR V+O]

3 If you **blast** your way somewhere, you get there by shooting at people or causing an explosion. EG *...assassins blasting their way through the windows of the embassy.* [V+O+A ⇑ force]

4 When people **blast** rock, **blast** a tunnel or hole, etc they make a hole in a mass of rock using an explosive such as dynamite. EG *Tunnels have been blasted through bedrock beneath the city.* ◊ **blasting.** EG *...the lieutenant who had been supervising the blasting.* [V+O] [◊ N UNCOUNT]

5 A **blast** is also 5.1 a sudden strong rush of air, for example caused by a strong wind. EG *...icy blasts... ...blasts of air.* 5.2 a short loud sound made by blowing a whistle or a musical wind instrument. EG *Ralph blew a series of short blasts.* [N COUNT : USU+SUPP] [N COUNT]

6 When something such as a radio or a horn **blasts** music or noise, or when music or noise **blasts** from it, it produces a very loud noise. EG *...with his little radio blasting in his ear.* [V-ERG = blare]

7 **at full blast.** 7.1 If a radio, record player, etc is on **at full blast** or **full blast,** it produces sound at the loudest possible volume. EG *She insists on having the radio on at full blast.* 7.2 If someone or something is moving or working **at full blast** or **full blast,** they are moving or working as quickly or as much as they can. EG *The cement plant was going full blast.* [PHR : USED AS AN A ⇑ loud] [PHR : USED AS AN A]

8 You say **blast** or **blast** it, them, etc to express irritation or annoyance about something or someone; a mild swear word. ● See also **blasted.** [EXCLAM = damn, drat]

blast away. 1 If someone **blasts away** with a gun or if a gun **blasts away,** the gun is fired continuously for a period of time. EG *...blasting away with a gun in each hand.* [PHRASAL VB : V+ADV ⇑ fire]

2 When something such as a radio or a music band is **blasting away,** it is producing a very loud noise. EG *The marching bands were still blasting away.* [PHRASAL VB : V+ADV ⇑ sounding]

blast off. When a space rocket **blasts off,** it leaves the ground at the start of its journey. ● See also **blast-off.** [PHRASAL VB : V+ADV, USU+A]

blast out. When something such as a radio or a music band **blasts out** music or noise, or when music or noise is **blasting out,** very loud music or noise is produced. EG *The band blasts out its unique version of 'Amazing Grace'.* [PHRASAL VB : V-ERG+ADV = belt out]

blasted /blɑːstɪ²d/. You refer to someone or something as a **blasted** person or thing when you are annoyed or irritated; a mild swear word. [ADJ CLASSIF : ATTRIB = damned, ruddy]

blast furnace, blast furnaces. A **blast furnace** is a furnace in which iron ore is heated under pressure so that it melts and the pure iron metal separates out and can be collected. [N COUNT ⇑ equipment]

blast-off is the moment when a rocket leaves the ground and rises into the air to begin a journey into space. [N UNCOUNT = lift-off]

blatant /bleɪtəᵒnt/ is used to describe an action or thing, usually a bad one, that is very obvious and not concealed in any way. EG *...blatant propaganda... ...blatant discrimination... ...blatant clues.* ▸ used of people. EG *I wasn't quite as blatant as that.* ◊ **blatantly.** EG *They blatantly ignored the truce agreement... Its faults are blatantly obvious.* [ADJ QUALIT = overt ≠ discreet] [◊ ADV = glaringly]

blaze /bleɪz/, **blazes, blazing, blazed.** 1 When a fire or something that is on fire **blazes,** it burns strongly and brightly. EG *The fire was still blazing, lighting up the sky... Our ships are blazing hulks.* [V ⇑ burn]

2 A **blaze** is a large fire in which things are damaged or destroyed; used especially in journalistic English. EG *...the blaze at the night club.* [N COUNT]

3 If a light **blazes** or if something **blazes** with light or colour, the light or colour that it sends out is extremely bright. EG *Cars went by with headlights blazing... The flower beds blazed with colour.* [V : IF+PREP THEN *with* ⇑ shine]

4 A **blaze** of light or colour is an extremely great or bright amount of it. EG *...a blaze of sunlight... The flower beds were a blaze of colour.* [N COUNT+SUPP ⇑ burst]

5 If you say that someone's eyes are **blazing,** you mean that they look very bright because the person is angry or excited; a literary use. EG *She turned and* [V : IF+PREP THEN *with* ⇑ shine = burn]

faced him, her eyes blazing... Her eyes were at once blazing and bewildered.

6 If someone **blazes** with a particular feeling, they behave in a way that shows that they feel it very strongly and intensely; a literary use. EG *...a very young man blazing with devotion to the American cause.* V : IF+PREP THEN *with* = burn

7 A **blaze** of something is a large and intense or exciting quantity of it. EG *...a blaze of publicity... He left office in a blaze of glory.* N SING WITH DET +*of* ↑ display

8 If a piece of news **is blazed** across a newspaper or poster, it is written in big letters because it is exciting or important. ● If a piece of news **is blazed abroad**, it is told to many people; an old-fashioned expression. V+O : USU PASS+A ● PHR : VB INFLECTS ↑ spread

9 If guns **blaze** or **blaze away**, or if someone **blazes away** with a gun, the gun is fired continuously, making a lot of noise. EG *The armoured infantry-carriers followed, guns blazing... The police burst into the building blazing away with their guns.* V OR V+ADV ↑ fire

10 **Blazes** is used in the following informal expressions. 10.1 If someone or something does something **like blazes**, they do it very fast or intensely. EG *You stand there and you wave like blazes to make sure they've seen you.* 10.2 You use **the blazes**, usually in questions, when you feel strongly about something, especially when you are angry or cannot explain something. EG *How the blazes did he do it?... Who the blazes does he think he is?* 10.3 You tell someone to **go to blazes** when you are angry with them and want them to leave you alone; a rude expression. PHR : USED AS AN A = like mad; PHR : WH+PHR = the dickens, the devil; PHR : ONLY IMPER = go to hell

11 If someone **blazes a trail**, they discover or explore something new and exciting. EG *They're currently blazing a trail in the biotechnology field.* PHR : VB INFLECTS = pioneer

blaze away. If a fire or something that is on fire **blazes away**, it burns very strongly and brightly. PHRASAL VB : V+ADV

blaze up. If a fire **blazes up**, it suddenly burns strongly and brightly after it has been burning weakly. PHRASAL VB : V+ADV ↑ burn

blazer /bleɪzə/, **blazers**. A **blazer** is a jacket, often one which is a special colour and has a badge on it, worn by members of a particular group or institution such as a sports team or a school. EG *...dressed in his school blazer.* N COUNT

blazing /bleɪzɪŋ/. 1 **Blazing** is used to describe the weather or a place in order to indicate that it is very hot, dry, and sunny. EG *We moved out into the blazing sun... ...along the blazing beach... ...the blazing heat of the plain.* ▸ used as an adverb. EG *Already the square was blazing hot.* ADJ CLASSIF : ATTRIB ↑ baking; ▸ ADV+ADJ/*hot* = boiling

2 A **blazing** red, orange, etc is a very bright one. EG *...a blazing red dress.* ADJ CLASSIF : ATTRIB

3 **Blazing** is also used to describe a situation, especially an argument, in which people behave in a very noisy and excited way because they feel very strongly about something. EG *We had a blazing row.* ADJ CLASSIF : ATTRIB = violent, flaming

blazon /bleɪzə⁰n/, **blazons, blazoning, blazoned**. If particular words **are blazoned** on something, or if something **is blazoned** with particular words, those words are written on it and can be seen clearly; a formal word. EG *The boat had the name Lolly May blazoned on her bow.* V+O : USU PASS ↑ display

bleach /bliːtʃ/, **bleaches, bleaching, bleached**. 1 When a person or the sun **bleaches** material or someone's hair, or when the material or hair **bleaches**, it is made white or pale in colour, either with a chemical or by the sunlight. EG *He bleaches his hair... I left the cloth in the sun to bleach.* V-ERG ↑ whiten

2 **Bleach** is a chemical that is used to make clothes, sheets, etc white, or to clean things thoroughly and kill germs. EG *...a strong household bleach.* N UNCOUNT

bleak /bliːk/, **bleaker, bleakest**. 1 A situation that is **bleak** is unpleasant or bad, and unlikely to improve. EG *The future looked bleak... It's a bleak prospect... ...the bleak truth.* ◊ **bleakness**. EG *...the bleakness of the post war years.* ADJ QUALIT = dismal, gloomy ≠ bright; ◊ N UNCOUNT

2 A place that is **bleak** looks cold, bare, and unwelcoming. EG *...the bleak coastline... ...a bleak bedroom.* ◊ **bleakness**. ADJ QUALIT ↑ dreary; ◊ N UNCOUNT

3 When the weather is **bleak**, it is cold, dull, and unpleasant. EG *...the bleak winters.* ADJ QUALIT

4 If someone feels, looks, or sounds **bleak**, they feel, look, or sound depressed, hopeless, or unfriendly. EG *I felt a bit bleak, landing alone... ...a bleak face.* ▸ used of people's actions and behaviour. EG *His book has received a bleak reception.* ◊ **bleakly**. EG *He stared bleakly ahead.* ADJ QUALIT ↑ dismal ≠ cheerful; ◊ ADV

bleary /blɪəri¹/, **blearier, bleariest**. If your eyes are **bleary**, they are red and watery, for example because you have not had enough sleep. EG *Through bleary eyes I looked back at them.* ◊ **blearily**. EG *He looked up blearily at Tom.* ADJ QUALIT ↑ tired; ◊ ADV

bleat /bliːt/, **bleats, bleating, bleated**. 1 When a sheep or goat **bleats**, it makes the sound that sheep and goats usually make. EG *She heard a lamb bleating in the distance.* ▸ used as a noun. EG *...the bleat of a goat.* V ↑ cry; ▸ N COUNT ↑ cry

2 If someone **bleats**, they speak in a weak, high, complaining voice, usually because they are unhappy or nervous about something. EG *They bleat about how miserable they are... 'Now?' Dixon bleated.* ▸ used as a noun. EG *...the bleats of frightened children.* V OR V+QUOTE/REPORT-CL ↑ moan = whimper; ▸ N COUNT

bled /blɛd/ is the past tense and past participle of **bleed**.

bleed /bliːd/, **bleeds, bleeding, bled**. 1 When you or a part of your body **bleeds**, you lose blood as a result of injury or illness. EG *His feet had begun to bleed... He could cut himself and bleed to death... He was bleeding heavily.* ● See also **bleeding, nosebleed**. V

2 If you **bleed** someone, you remove blood from their body. In the past, doctors used to bleed people in order to cure them. ● If you **bleed** a person or organization **dry** or **bleed** them **white**, you take all their money from them over a period of time. V+O ↑ treat; ● PHR : VB INFLECTS = drain

3 When someone **bleeds** something such as a radiator or brake system that is usually kept sealed, they let out a small amount of liquid or gas from it. V+O ↑ empty

4 If a coloured piece of cloth **bleeds** when it is washed, it loses some of the dye or colour in it. V ↑ runs

bleeder /bliːdə/, **bleeders**. **Bleeder** is a fairly rude word used in very informal English to refer to a particular person, usually a man, especially one you dislike or feel sorry for. EG *They didn't give the poor bleeder a chance.* N COUNT : USU MOD+N = blighter

bleeding /bliːdɪŋ/. 1 **Bleeding** is the state of losing blood from your body as a result of injury or illness. EG *Had the bleeding stopped?* N UNCOUNT

2 **Bleeding** is also a swear word used to emphasize what you are saying, especially when you feel strongly about something or dislike something. ADJ CLASSIF : ATTRIB, OR ADV WITH VB = blooming

bleep /bliːp/, **bleeps, bleeping, bleeped**. A **bleep** is a short, high-pitched sound, usually one of a series, that is made by an electrical device. EG *If you hear long bleeps, the phone is engaged.* ▸ used as a verb. EG *The alarm was bleeping.* N COUNT ↑ signal; ▸ V

2 If you **bleep** someone, for example a doctor, you inform them that they are wanted by making an electrical device bleep. V+O ↑ call

bleeper /bliːpə/, **bleepers**. A **bleeper** is an electrical device which someone, for example a doctor, carries around with them and which bleeps to tell them that they are needed. N COUNT

blemish /blɛmɪʃ/, **blemishes, blemishing, blemished**. 1 A **blemish** is a mark that spoils the appearance of something, especially a mark or small injury on a person's skin or on a fruit. EG *There wasn't a blemish on his body.* N COUNT = flaw

2 If something, especially someone's skin or a fruit, **is blemished**, its appearance or nature is spoiled by a mark, small injury, or some other ugly or unpleasant feature. ◊ **blemished**. EG *The peaches were cheap because their skins were blemished.* V+O : USU PASS = mar, flaw; ◊ ADJ CLASSIF

3 If someone or something **blemishes** someone's reputation, they spoil it, when previously it had been very good. EG *The scandal has blemished her shining reputation.* V+O = tarnish

blench /blɛntʃ/, **blenches, blenching, blenched**. If you **blench** at something, you are very frightened of it, sometimes so frightened that you move away in fear. EG *Even strong men blench at the thought of walking into their boss's office.* V OR V+A *(at)* ↑ recoil = quail

blend /blɛnd/, **blends, blending, blended**. 1 When you **blend** two or more substances together, you mix them together so that they become one very smooth substance, for example by using a blender. EG *Blend the butter and sugar together... Next, blend the tomatoes, garlic, and cream to form a paste.* V, OR V+O : IF+PREP THEN *with/into*

2 If a product such as tea, coffee, or whisky **is blended**, different types of the product are mixed together in order to get a particular flavour. ◊ **blended**. EG *...a blended whisky.* V+O : USU PASS ↑ mix; ◊ ADJ CLASSIF

3 A particular **blend** of tea, coffee, whisky, etc is one that has been produced by mixing different types of the product together. EG *He will arrange for your preferred blend of coffee to be made in your office... We'll mix them–They're all blends anyway.* — N COUNT : IF + PREP THEN *of* ↑ type

4 If someone or something shows a **blend** of qualities or feelings, these qualities or feelings are combined together in such a way that they produce a new effect, especially an effect that is admired. EG *She showed a brisk blend of tact and independence... ...the company's American-style blend of modern and classical dance.* ▸ used as a verb. EG *We must learn to blend our concern for people with our respect for them... Fear and guilt and fury blended in a thrust of excruciating pain.* — N SING WITH DET + *of* ↑ combination = mixture; ▸ V-ERG : IF + PREP THEN *with* ↑ combine

5 When colours, sounds, or things **blend**, they come together or are combined in a pleasing way. EG *...their voices blending marvellously as they sing in harmony... ...the colour of the vegetables blending with the wine and the table cloth.* ▸ used as a noun. EG *...a lovingly designed blend of flowers and shrubs and trees.* — V : IF + PREP THEN *with* ↑ combine = harmonize; ▸ N COUNT ↑ combination

blend in. If something **blends in** or **blends into** something in the background, it is so similar to the background in appearance or sound that it is difficult to see or hear separately. EG *The music carried through the open window and blended into the roar of passing traffic... Tree snakes are bright green, but they blend so well into foliage.* — PHRASAL VB : V + ADV, OR V + PREP = merge into

blender /blɛndə/, **blenders**. A **blender** is a machine used in the kitchen for mixing liquids and soft foods together at high speed to form a smooth liquid substance. — N COUNT = liquidizer

bless /blɛs/, **blesses, blessing, blessed, blest**. The forms **blessed** and **blest** are both used as the past tense and past participle. 1 When someone such as a priest **blesses** someone or something, they ask for or give God's favour and protection for that person or thing. EG *...the historic occasion when the Pope of Rome blessed the President of the United States... ...bringing baskets of food to the church to be blessed.* — V + O

2 If someone is **blessed with** a particular quality or skill, they have this quality or skill which is admired or which is an advantage to them. EG *She is blessed with immense talent and boundless energy.* — PHR + NG : USED AS C = endowed with

3 If something such as a plan or project **is blessed** by someone, they support it and agree to it. EG *...the unit, blessed by the law, the state, and the priests.* — V + O : USU PASS ↑ agreed = approved

4 If you **bless** someone for something, you thank them for it. EG *Then how you will bless me day and night for taking you there.* — V + O : IF + PREP THEN *for*

5 If you say **God bless, God bless you**, or **bless you** to someone, you are expressing your affection, thanks, or good wishes to them. EG *God bless you, it's terribly good of you to come... He wants more than I can give him, bless him... So until I hear from you, God bless.* — CONVENTION

6 You say **bless you** to someone who has just sneezed. — CONVENTION

7 **Bless my soul** is an expression of surprise; used in rather old-fashioned English. — CONVENTION = goodness me

blessed. The word **blessed** is pronounced /blɛsɪ²d/ when it is used before the noun it describes and /blɛst/ when it is used after the noun. You use **blessed** 1 to describe something that you think is wonderful, and that you are thankful for or relieved about. EG *All things could be said on this blessed afternoon... ...blessed freedom.* ◇ **blessedly**. EG *We walked through the blessedly cool oasis of the airport.* 2 as a mild swear word or exclamation. EG *I'm blessed if I know!... It happens every blessed morning.* — ADJ CLASSIF : ATTRIB = glorious; ◇ ADV = gloriously; ADJ CLASSIF = dashed

blessing /blɛsɪŋ/, **blessings**. 1 Something that is a **blessing** is a good thing that happens or something good that you have. EG *Health is a blessing that money cannot buy... It would be a blessing if this building burnt down.* — N COUNT ↑ gift = godsend

2 If something is done with someone's **blessing**, or if it has their **blessing**, they approve of it and support it. EG *She did it with the full blessing of her parents... The project had been denied even this superficial official blessing.* — N COUNT + SUPP ↑ agreement = approval

3 Something that is **a blessing in disguise** is something that seems to cause problems and difficulties at first but which is seen later to be an advantage. EG *A crisis can be a blessing in disguise.* — PHR : USED AS C ↑ deceptive

4 If you tell someone to **count** their **blessings**, you are saying that they should think about how lucky they are and about what they have that is good instead of complaining. — PHR : VB INFLECTS = be grateful

5 A situation that is described as a **mixed blessing** is one that has both advantages and disadvantages. — PHR : USED AS C

6 The **blessing** is the prayer usually said at the end of a Christian church service asking God to bless or look kindly upon the people who are present. — N SING : *the* + N = benediction

blether /blɛðə/, **blethers, blethering, blethered**. If you say that someone is **blethering**, you mean that they are talking stupidly and not making sense; an informal word. EG *What are you blethering about?* — V : IF + PREP THEN *about* = jabber

blew /bluː/ is the past tense of **blow**.

blight /blaɪt/, **blights, blighting, blighted**. 1 **Blight** is a disease which makes plants wither. There are several types of blight. EG *...potato blight.* — N UNCOUNT

2 Something that is referred to as a **blight** is something that causes great difficulties and unpleasantness and that damages or spoils something. EG *A learning difficulty can be a perpetual blight on their lives... We think of pollution as a modern blight, but it is not.* ▸ used as a verb. EG *...the vast conurbations that have blighted so much of the world... Her career has been blighted by some long-standing clashes with the authorities.* — N COUNT + SUPP : USU SING ↑ affliction = curse; ▸ V + O : USU PASS ↑ damage

blighter /blaɪtə/, **blighters**. Someone who you refer to as a **blighter** is someone you do not like, or who you feel has done something wrong. It is also sometimes used to express sympathy or mild envy; an informal word. EG *Let's make these blighters pay... Gosh, do you poor blighters have to put up with this?... You lucky blighter!* — N COUNT ↑ person = devil

blimey /blaɪmi¹/. You say **'Blimey'** or **'Cor blimey'** to indicate how surprised you are or how strongly you feel about something; used in informal British English. EG *'Blimey, you were asking for trouble.'... Caron listened in silence. 'Blimey!' he said at last.* — EXCLAM = crikey, gosh

blind /blaɪnd/, **blinds, blinding, blinded**. 1 Someone who is **blind** is unable to see because their eyes are damaged. EG *The accident had left him almost totally blind... He was blind in one eye... We went to the blind school.* ▸ used as a verb. EG *The acid went on her face and blinded her.* ◇ **blindness**. EG *Eye damage can result in temporary or permanent blindness.* ▸ The **blind** is used to refer to people who are blind. EG *What do you think of the help that's given to the blind?* — ADJ CLASSIF ↑ disabled; ▸ V + O; ◇ N UNCOUNT; ▸ N PLURAL : *the* + N ↑ disabled ≠ sighted

2 If something such as light **blinds** you, you are unable to see for a short period of time because of its effect. EG *My eyes were momentarily blinded by flash bulbs... The dust from the roads in the summertime was enough to blind you.* ▸ used as an adjective. EG *She had trodden on the broken bottle, blind as she was with tears and rage.* — V + O; ▸ ADJ CLASSIF : IF + PREP THEN *with*

3 A **blind** is a wide roll of cloth, paper, or strips of plastic, which you can pull over a window in order to keep out the light or prevent people from looking in. EG *She slammed the window down and pulled the blind.* — N COUNT ↑ fixture = shade

4 Someone who is **blind** to something is unable to understand it, to make sensible judgements, or to be reasonable about it. EG *I realized how blind the series had made me.* ▸ used of people's actions or behaviour. EG *Mrs Haze never ceases to amaze me with her blind faith in the wisdom of her Church... She had driven him into a blind rage.* ◇ **blindness**. EG *I marvelled at whatever blindness it had been that allowed me to stay in that hopeless relationship.* — ADJ QUALIT : IF + PREP THEN *to* ↑ unthinking = irrational, unreasoning; ◇ N UNCOUNT : IF + PREP THEN *to*

5 If something **blinds** you to the real situation, it prevents you from noticing or being aware of its reality. EG *We have to beware that missionary zeal doesn't blind us to the realities here.* — V + O (NG/REFL) + A (TO) ↑ prevent = deaden

6 If someone is **blind** to something that is the truth or reality, they are unaware of it, sometimes deliberately. EG *The girls were completely blind to the consequences of their actions... They were not blind to the defects of Western society.* ◇ **blindness**. EG *Their blindness to the problem was astonishing.* — ADJ QUALIT : PRED + *to* = impervious ≠ sensitive; ◇ N UNCOUNT

7 If you **blind** someone with science, facts, etc, you make them confused, especially by tricking them with clever words that they do not understand. — V + O : IF + PREP THEN *with* ↑ confuse = dazzle

8 If someone **turns a blind eye** to something that someone else is doing, they pretend not to notice what is happening, even though they would normally criticize or punish such behaviour. EG *He had often turned a blind eye to Barber's drinking sessions.* — PHR : VB INFLECTS ↑ ignore ≠ acknowledge

9 If you say that someone is **as blind as a bat**, you either mean that they have very bad eyesight, or you are teasing them for not being able to find or see something that is very obvious. PHR : USED AS C

10 If you say that something is a case of **the blind leading the blind**, you mean that it is a situation where someone completely ignorant is getting help, advice, or guidance from someone who is almost equally ignorant. PHR : USED AS C

11 **Love is blind** is an expression used to say that when you love someone, especially if you have just fallen in love with them, you cannot judge their qualities properly and you certainly do not notice any of their faults. PHR

12 If you do something such as fly an aeroplane or drive a vehicle **blind**, you do not judge distances or directions by looking outside the aeroplane or vehicle, but instead you measure your position and progress by using instruments that are inside it. EG *The outward part of this first mission had been flown blind.* ADV AFTER VB

13 Something, for example a window, that is **blind** is impossible to see through. EG *The room facing the lake presented blind and shuttered windows to the evening guests.* ADJ CLASSIF = impenetrable

14 A **blind** wall or building is one which has no windows or doors. EG *The big block proves on approach to be blind, with all the windows boarded up.* ADJ CLASSIF ↑ blank

15 A **blind** is also a trick, pretence, or false excuse that you use in order to prevent someone from realizing the truth; an informal use. EG *Renshaw probably saw through the blind, but listened calmly to it all.* N COUNT : USU SING

16 If someone says that they **swear blind** that something happened or is true, they are emphasizing their certainty that it really did happen or is true; an informal expression. EG *I would have sworn blind it was water... Jean swore blind that she had seen me the week before.* PHR + REPORT-CL : VB INFLECTS = insist, vow

17 If you say that someone is **not taking a blind bit of notice** of someone or something, you are emphasizing that they are taking absolutely no notice; an informal expression, used especially when you are annoyed at someone for not paying attention. EG *'You're not taking a blind bit of notice of what I'm saying, are you?'* PHR : VB INFLECTS ↑ ignoring ≠ attending

18 See also **blinding, blindly, colour blind.**

blind alley, blind alleys. If a method of working or thinking is leading you up a **blind alley** or down a **blind alley**, it is turning out to be useless or not leading to good results. N COUNT = dead end

blind date, blind dates. A **blind date** is an arrangement made by one of your friends for you to go out on a date with someone who you have never met before. EG *I first met my wife on a blind date.* N COUNT

blind drunk. Someone who is **blind drunk** is very drunk indeed. ADJ CLASSIF : PRED

blindfold /blaɪndfəʊld/, **blindfolds, blindfolding, blindfolded.** 1 A **blindfold** is a strip of cloth that can be tied round someone's head so that it covers their eyes and prevents them from being able to see. N COUNT

2 If you **blindfold** someone, you tie a blindfold over their eyes. ◊ **blindfolded.** EG *He was shoved down into a canoe, still blindfolded.* V + O ◊ ADJ CLASSIF

3 If someone does something **blindfold**, they do it while wearing a blindfold, or as if they were wearing one. EG *Editing a newspaper in that country was like walking blindfold across a minefield... I guarantee I could read that script blindfold, I've been through it so many times.* ADV AFTER VB ↑ blind

blinding /blaɪndɪŋ/. 1 A **blinding** light is one that is so bright that you cannot see properly. EG *Hiroshima vanished in a flash of blinding light.* ADJ CLASSIF : USU ATTRIB = dazzling

2 **Blinding** is used to emphasize that something is very striking, remarkable, or shocking. EG *The other dancers fly past them at blinding speed... All of them voted for the government, with the blinding exception of Mr Heath.* ◊ **blindingly.** EG *Isn't it blindingly obvious?* ADJ CLASSIF : USU ATTRIB ↑ extreme = remarkable ◊ ADV + ADJ/ADV

blindly /blaɪndli¹/. If you do something **blindly**, 1 you do it in a way that shows that you are unable to see properly. EG *A few men were shooting blindly into the flames... His arm was on fire and he ran blindly across the clearing, screaming.* ADV WITH VB = unseeingly 2 you do it without having much information or understanding, or without thinking about it. EG *With the information we have now, we can only speculate blindly... Of course it is wrong for young people to accept blindly existing standards.* ADV

blind man's buff is a children's game in which one person has a piece of cloth tied over their eyes so that they cannot see, and then has to catch the other children. N UNCOUNT

blind spot, blind spots. 1 If you have a **blind spot** about one small aspect of a subject, you are unable to understand this aspect, although you find the rest of the subject easy to understand. EG *Ford always had a terrible blind spot about these things.* N COUNT : USU SING : a + N ↑ flaw = weak spot

2 A **blind spot** is one part of something that you cannot see properly, especially a part of the road that you cannot see when you are driving a car. N COUNT : USU SING ↑ area

blink /blɪŋk/, **blinks, blinking, blinked.** 1 When someone **blinks**, when they **blink** their eyes, or when their eyes **blink**, they shut their eyes and very quickly open them again, sometimes several times. EG *He took off his glasses and blinked at them... They looked at each other without blinking... The girl blinked her eyes several times.* ▸ used as a noun. EG *It was his guilty blink that always gave us away.* V OR V-ERG ▸ N COUNT ↑ movement

2 When a light **blinks**, it flashes on and off. EG *Dots and dashes blinked out from a signal light.* ▸ used as a noun. EG *There was a blink of bright light beyond the forest.* V ▸ N COUNT + SUPP ↑ flash

3 If you refer to a period of time as **a blink of an eye** or **a blink of an eyelid**, you are emphasizing that it is a very short period of time. EG *A million years is just a blink of an eye geologically.* PHR : USED AS C ↑ moment = second

4 If a machine goes **on the blink**, it stops working properly; an informal expression. EG *The Hoover is on the blink again.* PHR : USED AS A ↑ broken

5 See also **blinking.**

blinkered /blɪŋkəd/; used mainly in British English. 1 A **blinkered** view, attitude, approach, etc is one that considers only a narrow point of view and does not take into account other people's opinions or the important aspects of a situation; used showing disapproval. EG *The attitude on both sides of the Atlantic amounts to blinkered self-interest.* ADJ CLASSIF ↑ limited = narrow-minded

2 A horse that is **blinkered** is wearing blinkers. ADJ CLASSIF

blinkers /blɪŋkəz/; used mainly in British English. 1 **Blinkers** are two pieces of leather which are attached to a horse's bridle at the side of each eye so that the horse can only see straight ahead and is not distracted. N PLURAL : ALSO *a pair of* + N ↑ screens

2 If you describe someone as wearing **blinkers**, you suggest that they are not considering or do not know about all the important aspects or different opinions of a situation. EG *...this sense of having blinkers put on you.* N PLURAL : ALSO *a pair of* + N

blinking /blɪŋkɪŋ/ is used as a mild swear word to describe someone or something which irritates or annoys you. ADJ CLASSIF : ATTRIB ↑ annoying = blasted

blip /blɪp/, **blips.** 1 A **blip** is a small spot of light, sometimes occurring with a short, high-pitched sound, which flashes on and off regularly on a piece of equipment such as a radar screen. N COUNT

2 A **blip** in a straight line , for example on a computer screen, is a point at which the line makes a sudden, sharp, V-shaped bend before continuing. N COUNT ↑ irregularity = pulse

bliss /blɪs/ is a situation or feeling that gives you a great deal of pleasure and makes you very happy. EG *For a couple of months weekends were bliss.* N UNCOUNT ↑ happiness

blissful /blɪsfʊl/. 1 An experience or period of time that is **blissful** is extremely happy and peaceful. EG *After those blissful two years, I began to hate school... They sat there together in blissful silence.* ◊ **blissfully.** EG *His eyes shut blissfully and he smiled.* ADJ QUALIT = heavenly ◊ ADV WITH VB

2 If someone is in **blissful** ignorance, they are carefree and unaware of something unpleasant or serious that exists. ◊ **blissfully.** EG *Most people remain blissfully unaware of the problem... Mr Swallow himself is blissfully ignorant of his responsibility.* ADJ CLASSIF : ATTRIB ◊ ADV + ADJ

blister /blɪstə/, **blisters, blistering, blistered.** 1 A **blister** is a painful swelling on the surface of a person's skin which contains clear liquid and can be caused by burning or by something rubbing constantly against the skin. EG *His boots had given him blisters on his heels.* N COUNT

2 When part of your body **blisters** or when something **blisters** it, a painful swelling appears on the surface of the skin as a result of burning or rubbing. V-ERG ↑ swell

EG *Blistering can be prevented by using foot powder.* ◊ **blistered.** EG *My feet were blistered and aching.* [◊ ADJ QUALIT]

3 When paint, rubber, etc **blisters** or when something **blisters** it, small bumps appear on its surface as a result of something such as heat which swells the material. [V-ERG = bubble]

4 A **blister** is also a bump in the surface of paint, rubber, etc where the material has swollen. [N COUNT = bubble]

blistering /blɪstəʳrɪŋ/. 1 When the weather or the sun is **blistering**, it is so hot that it is uncomfortable. EG *...the blistering days of midsummer... ...blistering heat.* [ADJ QUALIT = scorching, sweltering]

2 A **blistering** remark or reply expresses great anger or sarcasm, and is intended to attack or hurt someone. [ADJ CLASSIF = scathing]

blithe /blaɪð/. 1 **Blithe** is used to indicate that something is done without serious or careful thought. EG *I made a blithe comment about the fine weather... Planners, for the most part, proceed in blithe ignorance of the Arrow theorem.* ◊ **blithely.** EG *...blithely violating the Constitution in the process... ...the blessing of good health which I blithely take for granted.* [ADJ QUALIT = cheerful; ◊ ADV WITH VB = gaily]

2 Someone who is **blithe** is carefree and cheerful; an old-fashioned use. EG *I was feeling unusually blithe and dauntless.* ◊ **blithely.** EG *Mollie strolled blithely into the yard.* [ADJ QUALIT; ◊ ADV WITH VB = gaily]

blithering /blɪðəʳrɪŋ/. If you call someone a **blithering** idiot, you are emphasizing how stupid you think they are; an informal word. [ADJ CLASSIF : ATTRIB]

blitz /blɪts/, **blitzes, blitzing, blitzed.** 1 When a city or building **is blitzed** during a war, it is attacked by bombs dropped by enemy aircraft. ◊ **blitzing.** EG *...the blitzing of Queen's Hall in Portland Place.* [V+O : USU PASS = bombard; ◊ N UNCOUNT]

2 The **Blitz** was the heavy bombing of British cities by German aircraft from 1940-41. EG *She was killed in the Blitz.* [N PROPER : *the*+N ⇑ attack]

3 When you have a **blitz** on something, you make a big effort to get it done; an informal use. EG *We're going to have a blitz on the house and get it all decorated by Christmas.* [N COUNT : IF+ PREP THEN *on* ⇑ onslaught]

blitzkrieg /blɪtskri:g/, **blitzkriegs.** A **blitzkrieg** is a fast military attack that takes the enemy by surprise and is intended to achieve a very quick victory. [N COUNT ⇑ offensive = lightning attack]

blizzard /blɪzəd/, **blizzards.** A **blizzard** is a very bad snow storm with strong winds. [N COUNT]

bloated /bləʊtɪ²d/. 1 Something that is **bloated** is much larger than normal because it has too much liquid, gas, etc inside it. [ADJ QUALIT ⇑ inflated = swollen]

2 If you are **bloated** after eating a meal, you feel very full and uncomfortable because you have eaten so much. EG *You should aim to feel satisfied but not bloated after a meal.* [ADJ QUALIT ⇑ full]

bloater /bləʊtə/, **bloaters.** A **bloater** is a herring that has been salted in brine and smoked. [N COUNT ⇑ fish]

blob /blɒb/, **blobs.** 1 A **blob** of thick or sticky liquid is a small amount of it. EG *...a blob of glue.* [N PART+N UNCOUNT]

2 Something that cannot be seen clearly, for example because it is in the distance, is sometimes described as a **blob.** EG *He saw the white blob of Fanucci crossing the street... You see a blob of grey in the distance.* [N COUNT = dot]

bloc /blɒk/, **blocs.** A **bloc** is a group of countries or people in power that have similar political aims and interests and that act together over some issues. EG *This would upset the balance of the East-West blocs... African deputies had formed a parliamentary bloc of their own... ...an Eastern bloc country.* [N COUNT : MOD+N = alliance]

2 If several people or things do something **en bloc** or are considered **en bloc,** they do it or are considered as a group. EG *...a system which teaches the young, en bloc, a number of beliefs.* [PHR : USED AS AN A = en masse]

block /blɒk/, **blocks, blocking, blocked.** 1 A **block** of flats or offices is a large building, especially a tall one, containing flats or offices. EG *...a large office block... His flat is on the fourth floor of this five-storey block... ...the school physics block.* [N COUNT : IF+ PREP THEN *of*]

2 A **block** in a town or city is an area of land with buildings on it and with streets on all its sides. EG *I went around the block again... The store was three blocks away.* [N COUNT]

3 A **block** of stone, wood, etc is a large piece of it which is rectangular in shape. EG *...rough-hewn blocks of grey stone... ...a block of ice... ...a cement block.* [N PART = slab]

4 If you threaten to **knock** someone's **block off,** you are so angry with them that you are threatening to hit them on the head with your fist; an informal expression. [PHR : VB INFLECTS]

5 If someone **lays** or **puts** their **head on the block,** they are risking their reputation or position by taking a particular course of action or stating their opinion. [PHR : VB INFLECTS = stick your neck out]

6 If someone or something **blocks** a road, channel, pipe, etc, they place something across it or in it so that nothing can get through it. EG *The Turks had blocked the land routes.* ◊ **blocked.** EG *The road was completely blocked... ...what to do when your sink gets blocked.* [V+O ⇑ obstruct = seal, clog; ◊ ADJ CLASSIF]

7 If someone or something **blocks** your view, they prevent you from seeing something, either by being between you and the thing you are trying to see or by putting something between you and the thing. EG *He parks directly in front of the shop, blocking the view of the street.* [V+O = obstruct]

8 If you **block** someone's way or path, you prevent them from going somewhere by standing in their way. EG *He was preparing to block my way.* [V+O ⇑ obstruct = bar]

9 A **block** is also something that is blocking a pipe, tube, tunnel, etc and preventing things from moving along it. [N COUNT ⇑ obstruction = blockage]

10 If you **block** something that is being arranged or agreed such as a deal, a payment, etc, you prevent it from being done or completed. EG *He couldn't block the deal... Agreement had been blocked by certain governments.* [V+O = halt]

11 A **block** of tickets, shares, etc is a large quantity of them, especially when they are of the same type and in a sequence or order. [N PART+N IN PLURAL ⇑ lot = stack]

12 If you have a **block** or a mental **block,** you have a short period during which you are unable to do something that you can normally do which involves using your brain or memory. EG *...just a mental block... I've had what they call writer's block. The words won't come.* [N COUNT : USU MOD+N ⇑ seizure ≠ inspiration]

13 See also **breeze-block, building block, roadblock, stumbling block, tower block.** ● **a chip off the old block:** see **chip.**

block in. 1 If you **block** someone **in,** you park your car so close to their car that they cannot drive away. [PHRASAL VB : V+O+ADV]

2 If you **block in** a figure that is drawn only with an outline, you fill it in by covering the area inside the figure with pencil, ink, etc. [PHRASAL VB : V+O+ADV = shade in]

block off. When you **block off** a door, window, passage, etc, you put something across it and cover it completely so that nothing can pass through it. [PHRASAL VB : V+O+ADV = seal off]

block out. 1 If someone **blocks out** something such as news, information, or something that they are thinking, they prevent it from being known or considered. EG *Governments can try to block out unwelcome ideas from abroad... He struggled to block out all thoughts of his coming trial.* [PHRASAL VB : V+O+ADV ⇑ keep out = exclude]

2 Something that **blocks out** light prevents it from reaching a place. EG *...curtains blocking out the sunlight.* [PHRASAL VB : V+O+ADV = blot out, shut out]

block up. If you **block** something **up** or if it **blocks up,** it becomes completely blocked. EG *Never block up ventilators... The sink keeps blocking up.* [PHRASAL VB : V+ADV, OR V+O+ADV = clog up]

blockade /blɒkeɪd/, **blockades, blockading, blockaded.** A **blockade** is action that is taken, usually by a government or a naval force, to prevent goods from reaching a particular country or place. EG *Both superpowers are to enforce a blockade of arms-carrying ships.* ▸ used as a verb. EG *The Atlantic Squadron promptly blockaded Santiago.* [N COUNT = siege; ▸ V+O ⇑ besiege]

blockage /blɒkɪdʒ/, **blockages.** 1 A **blockage** in a pipe, tube, tunnel, etc is something that is blocking it and preventing things from moving along it. [N COUNT = obstruction]

2 **Blockage** is the prevention of liquid or a fine substance from getting through a pipe or tube by something inside the pipe or tube. [N UNCOUNT ⇑ obstruction]

block and tackle. A **block and tackle** is a device for lifting heavy things, consisting of a rope or chain that is passed around a pair of blocks containing pulleys. [N SING WITH DET]

blockbuster /blɒkbʌstə/, **blockbusters.** A new film, book, etc that is described as a **blockbuster** is one that will be very popular and successful because of the exciting or sensational events shown or described in it. [N COUNT = sensation, best seller]

block capitals are simple capital letters that are not decorated in any way. EG *Please write in block capitals.* [N PLURAL : USU *in*+N = block letters]

blockhead /blɒkhɛd/, **blockheads**. If you call someone a **blockhead**, you mean that they are stupid; an informal word. N COUNT = dummy

block letters are simple capital letters that are not decorated in any way. EG *A poster instructed us, in block letters, to 'Work Hard for the Continuing Revolution'.* N PLURAL : USU in+N = block capitals

block vote, block votes. A **block vote** is a large number of votes that are all cast in the same way by one person on behalf of a group of people. N COUNT

bloke /bləʊk/, **blokes**. A **bloke** is a man; an informal word used in British English. EG *...the bloke next door... He's a good bloke... ...my bloke.* N COUNT = chap

blonde /blɒnd/, **blondes**; also spelled **blond**, especially when referring to a man's hair. **1** A **blonde** person has pale yellow-coloured hair. EG *...a beautiful blonde woman... ...a tall, blond Englishman.* ▸ also used of a person's hair of this colour. EG *...snowflakes melting in her long blonde hair... ...the light, blonde fuzz on his cheeks.* ADJ QUALIT ⇑ man ▸ ADJ COLOUR ⇑ fair

2 A **blonde** is a person, especially a woman, who has blonde hair. EG *She was a plump blonde of about thirty.* N COUNT ≠ redhead, brunette

blood /blʌd/, **bloods**. **1 Blood** is the red liquid that flows around your body. EG *...the circulation of the blood... Her right hand was covered with blood.* N UNCOUNT

● When you **give** or **donate blood**, you allow some of your blood to be taken from your body and stored so that it can be used in an operation or a blood transfusion. ● PHR : VB INFLECTS

2 If someone **has** a person's **blood on** their **hands**, they are responsible for that person's death. PHR : VB INFLECTS

3 If you **are after** someone's **blood**, you are very angry with them and are intending to have an argument with them. PHR : VB INFLECTS

4 If your **blood is up**, you are very angry about something and want to take strong or violent action. PHR : VB INFLECTS

5 If someone or something **makes** your **blood boil**, they make you very angry. PHR : VB INFLECTS

6 Bad blood is used to refer to feelings of hate and anger. EG *He said that the rebels hoped to create bad blood and ultimately war between Spain and the United States.* PHR : USED AS O OR S ⇑ ill will

7 If something violent and cruel, especially a murder, is done **in cold blood**, it is done deliberately and in an unemotional way. EG *People were being murdered in cold blood.* PHR : USED AS AN A ⇑ cruelly

8 If something **makes** your **blood freeze** or **makes** your **blood run cold**, it makes you feel very frightened. PHR : VB INFLECTS

9 If you **sweat blood** for something, you work very hard to achieve it. EG *...the qualifications he had sweated blood for.* PHR : VB INFLECTS = slog

10 If you say that trying to achieve something is like trying to **get blood from a stone**, you mean that it is almost impossible to achieve. EG *Getting information out of Darley is like getting blood from a stone.* PHR : VB INFLECTS

12 Blood is used to refer to the race or social class that someone's family came from, and the way that this is shown in their appearance or character. EG *There was eastern blood on her mother's side... ...a young man of aristocratic blood.* N UNCOUNT : USU MOD+N ⇑ breeding

13 If a particular quality or talent **is in** someone's **blood**, it is part of their nature and one which they share with other members of their family. PHR : VB INFLECTS = it's in your nature

14 New people who are introduced into an organization and whose fresh ideas are likely to improve it and make it stronger, better, or more efficient, are referred to as **new**, **fresh**, or **young blood**. EG *What this company needs is an injection of new blood.* PHR : USED AS O OR S ⇑ innovation

blood bank, blood banks. A **blood bank** is a place where blood is stored until it is needed for blood transfusions. N COUNT

bloodbath /blʌdbɑːθ/, **bloodbaths**; also spelled as two words or with a hyphen. A **bloodbath** is a fight or other event in which a lot of people or animals are killed very violently. N COUNT ⇑ killing = massacre

blood brother, blood brothers; also spelled with a hyphen. A man's **blood brother** is a man whom he has sworn to treat as a brother, often in a ceremony in which their blood is mingled. N COUNT ⇑ friend

blood cell, blood cells. A **blood cell** is one of the small red or white cells which are found in your blood. N COUNT

blood count, blood counts. A **blood count** is a check on the number of red and white blood cells in someone's blood, to see how healthy they are. N COUNT ⇑ examination

bloodcurdling /blʌdkɜːdlɪŋ/; also spelled with a hyphen. A **bloodcurdling** sound or story is one that is very frightening and horrible. EG *...dancers who were making bloodcurdling noises as they sprang high into the air.* ADJ CLASSIF : ATTRIB = chilling

blood donor, blood donors; also spelled with a hyphen. A **blood donor** is someone who allows some of their blood to be taken from their body so that it can be used for transfusions or operations. N COUNT ⇑ volunteer

blood group, blood groups. A **blood group** is one of the different types of blood that is found in different people. EG *What blood group are you?* N COUNT = blood type

bloodhound /blʌdhaʊnd/, **bloodhounds**. A **bloodhound** is a large dog with a very good sense of smell, which is sometimes used to follow people or to find them if they are lost. N COUNT

bloodless /blʌdlɪ²s/. **1** If you describe someone's face or skin as **bloodless**, you mean that it is very pale in colour. EG *...flat dark hair and bloodless cheeks.* ADJ CLASSIF = anaemic

2 A **bloodless** coup, battle, etc is one in which events are not as violent as expected, or in which nobody is killed. ADJ CLASSIF ≠ bloody

blood-letting is violence or killing of particular people for a particular reason, especially between rival gangs or families. N UNCOUNT = bloodshed

blood lust; also spelled as one word. **Blood lust** is a strong desire for violence as a way of getting excitement. EG *...a spectacle designed to satisfy the blood lust of the spectators.* N UNCOUNT

blood money is money that you are paid either for information which is used to harm or kill someone or for keeping this information secret. N UNCOUNT

blood poisoning; also spelled with a hyphen. **Blood poisoning** is is serious illness resulting from an infection in your blood. EG *She had blood poisoning which had carried the infection to her knee.* N UNCOUNT

blood pressure; also spelled with a hyphen. Your **blood pressure** is a measure of the amount of force with which your blood flows around your body. EG *I have high blood pressure and heart trouble.* N UNCOUNT

blood-red. Something that is **blood-red** is bright red in colour. ADJ COLOUR = crimson

blood relation, blood relations. A **blood relation** is a relative who is part of your family by birth rather than by marriage. N COUNT = kinsman

bloodshed /blʌdʃɛd/ is violence in which people are killed or wounded. EG *There was no evidence of bloodshed or attack.* N UNCOUNT = slaughter

bloodshot /blʌdʃɒt/. If your eyes are **bloodshot**, the parts that are usually white seem red or pink instead. ADJ QUALIT = inflamed

blood sport, blood sports; also spelled with a hyphen or as one word. A **blood sport** is a sport such as hunting in which animals are killed. EG *...campaigning for the abolition of bloodsports.* N COUNT

bloodstained /blʌdsteɪnd/; also spelled with a hyphen. Something that is **bloodstained** is stained with blood. EG *...bloodstained clothing.* ADJ CLASSIF = bloodied

bloodstock /blʌdstɒk/. Thoroughbred horses that have been specially bred for a particular purpose such as racing are referred to as **bloodstock.** EG *...bloodstock sales.* N UNCOUNT ⇑ breed

bloodstream /blʌdstriːm/, **bloodstreams**. Your **bloodstream** is your blood as it flows around your body. EG *...a drug that dissolves in the bloodstream quite slowly.* N COUNT : USU the/POSS+N IN SING ⇑ circulation

bloodthirsty /blʌdθɜːrsti¹/ **bloodthirstier, bloodthirstiest**. Someone who is **bloodthirsty** is eager to be violent or to see other people being violent; used showing disapproval. EG *I could hear the bloodthirsty fans chanting.* ADJ QUALIT = sanguinary ≠ squeamish

blood type, blood types. A **blood type** is one of the different types of blood that is found in different people. N COUNT = blood group

blood vessel, blood vessels; also spelled with a hyphen. A **blood vessel** is a narrow tube through which blood flows in your body. N COUNT = capillary

bloody /blʌdi¹/, **bloodies, bloodying, bloodied; bloodier, bloodiest**. **1 Bloody** is a swear word used to emphasize something you are saying, especially something you dislike or feel strongly about; used mainly in British English. ADJ CLASSIF : ATTRIB, OR ADV + ADJ

2 A situation or event that is **bloody** is one in which there is a lot of violence and a lot of people are killed. EG *The effects will be violent, disruptive, and probably bloody... The battles grew into the bloodiest* ADJ QUALIT ⇑ violent *of the spring.* ◇ **bloodily.** EG *Helen was most horribly, most bloodily, killed.* ◇ **bloodiness.** EG *...the bloodiness of war.* ◇ ADV WITH VB ◇ N UNCOUNT

3 Something that is **bloody** has a lot of blood on it. EG *...hands that were black and bloody.* ◇ **bloodily.** EG *Ten minutes into the film someone is messily and bloodily blown up.* ADJ CLASSIF ◇ ADV WITH VB = violently

4 If something **is bloodied**, blood is spilt on it. EG *Jack stood up as he said this, the bloodied knife in his hand.* V+O : USU PASS ↑ stain

5 If someone comes out of a situation **bloodied but unbowed**, they have suffered a lot in trying to achieve it, and have probably failed, but they are still proud of what they have done. PHR : USED AS C ↑ defiant, unabashed, unrepentant

6 A situation or action that is described as **bloody** is one that is unpleasant; an old-fashioned use. EG *I've been perfectly bloody to him.* ADJ QUALIT ↑ awful = dreadful

bloody mary, bloody marys. A **bloody mary** is a drink that is made from vodka and tomato juice. N COUNT ↑ cocktail

bloody-minded. If someone is being **bloody-minded**, they are deliberately making difficulties for someone else instead of helping them; used showing disapproval. EG *...not so much inefficient as downright bloody-minded.* ◇ **bloody-mindedness.** EG *It's sheer bloody-mindedness on their part.* ADJ QUALIT ↑ awkward = cussed, perverse ◇ N UNCOUNT

bloom /blu:m/, **blooms, blooming, bloomed. 1** A **bloom** is the flower on a plant; a literary or technical use. EG *The air was heavy with the fragrance of lush wild blooms.* ● A plant or tree that is **in bloom** or **in full bloom** has flowers on it. EG *The lilies were in bloom.* N COUNT : USU PL ● PHR : USED AS AN A = in flower

2 When a plant or tree **blooms**, it produces flowers. EG *This variety of rose blooms late into the autumn.* V : USU+A = blossom

3 When a flower **blooms**, the flower bud opens. EG *It has a beautiful orange flower which blooms in May.* V : USU+A = blossom

4 If someone or something **blooms**, they develop very good, attractive, or successful qualities. EG *Instead of blooming into further beauty, she became pale and sad... He was possessed of a rare talent that had never bloomed.* V = blossom

5 A **bloom** is also a healthy or fresh appearance, especially that of a person's face. EG *She had a round face from which all the bloom of youth had long departed.* N SING WITH DET ↑ freshness = glow

6 See also **blooming**.

bloomer /blu:mə/, **bloomers. 1 Bloomers** are an old-fashioned kind of women's underwear which consists of wide, loose trousers gathered at the knees. N PLURAL : ALSO *a pair of*+N

2 A **bloomer** is a mistake; a rather old-fashioned use. EG *I made a bit of a bloomer.* N COUNT = blunder

blooming /blu:mɪŋ/. **1 Blooming** is a mild swear word used to emphasize what you are saying, especially when you are annoyed or irritated; used in British English. EG *It's a blooming nuisance.* ADJ CLASSIF : ATTRIB = flipping

2 Someone who is **blooming** looks attractively healthy and full of energy. EG *Martha appeared, blooming and pretty... She was blooming with health.* ADJ QUALIT = glowing

blossom /blɒsəm/, **blossoms, blossoming, blossomed. 1 Blossom** refers to the flowers of a tree that appear before the fruit appears. EG *The trees along the road were heavy with yellow blossoms... ...the white and pink blossom of apple trees.* ● A tree that is **in blossom** or **in full blossom** has blossom on it. N UNCOUNT/COUNT ● PHR : USED AS AN A = in bloom

2 When a tree **blossoms**, it produces flowers. V

3 When a flower **blossoms**, the flower bud opens. EG *...the petals of a blossoming flower.* V = bloom

4 If someone or something **blossoms**, they develop very good, attractive, or successful qualities. EG *Harold had suddenly blossomed at university... She had blossomed into a real beauty... Their friendship blossomed.* V : IF+PREP THEN *into* = bloom

blot /blɒt/, **blots, blotting, blotted. 1** A **blot** is a drop of liquid, especially ink, that is spilled onto a surface. EG *...ink blots on the paper.* N COUNT ↑ spot

2 If something is a **blot** on the reputation of a person, family, country, etc, it spoils their reputation, which was previously good. EG *...this blot on our civilization.* ● to **blot** your **copybook**: see **copybook**. N SING WITH DET +*on* = blemish, stain

3 If something is a **blot** on the landscape or on a place, it is ugly and spoils the appearance of the place. N SING WITH DET +*on* = eyesore

4 If you **blot** a surface, you remove liquid from it by pressing a piece of soft paper or cloth onto it. EG *She signed the agreement and blotted it carefully... Blot the skin dry with a soft towel.* V+O ↑ dry

blot out. 1 If one thing **blots out** another thing, it is in front of the other thing and prevents it from being seen. EG *The resulting dust cloud could have blotted out the sun.* PHRASAL VB : V+O+ADV ↑ hide = obliterate

2 If a particular idea, experience, or feeling that you have **blots out** all other ones, it becomes the only one that you can think about. EG *It was as though the money had blotted out everything else.* PHRASAL VB : V+O+ADV = obscure

3 If you try to **blot out** a memory or thought, you try not to think of it. PHRASAL VB : V+O+ADV

blot up. If you **blot up** a liquid, you remove it from a surface by pressing a piece of soft paper or cloth on to it. PHRASAL VB : V+O+ADV = absorb

blotch /blɒtʃ/, **blotches.** A **blotch** is a small area of colour with an irregular shape, for example on someone's skin. EG *There were purple blotches around her eyes.* N COUNT : USU PL ↑ mark = patch

blotched /blɒtʃt/. Something that is **blotched** with areas of a particular colour has them on its surface. EG *...clothes blotched with dark brown stains.* ADJ CLASSIF ↑ marked = mottled

blotchy /blɒtʃi[1]/, **blotchier, blotchiest.** Something that is **blotchy** has a lot of blotches on it, often ones that spoil its appearance. EG *His skin was blotchy.* ADJ QUALIT ↑ marked

blotter /blɒtə/, **blotters.** A **blotter** is a large sheet of blotting paper with a firm piece of cardboard on the back. After writing in ink on a piece of paper, you press it on the blotter to dry the ink. N COUNT

blotting paper; also spelled with a hyphen. **Blotting paper** is thick soft paper that you use for soaking up and drying the ink on a piece of paper, when you have just written something on it with a pen. N UNCOUNT

blotto /blɒtəʊ/. Someone who is **blotto** is extremely drunk; an informal word. ADJ CLASSIF : PRED

blouse /blaʊz/, **blouses.** A **blouse** is a kind of shirt worn by a girl or woman. EG *...a white blouse.* N COUNT ↑ garment

blow /bləʊ/, **blows, blowing, blew, blown. 1** When a wind, breeze, or draught **blows**, the air moves. EG *There seemed to be a gale blowing all the time... The winds had been steadily blowing from the west.* V, OR V+A ↑ move

2 When the wind **blows** something somewhere or when something **blows** somewhere, the thing is moved by the wind. EG *A gust of wind blew snow in her face... The wind blew his papers away... The dust blew all over the decks... The washing was blowing in the wind.* V-ERG : USU+A ↑ move = waft

3 If you **blow**, you send out a stream of air from your mouth. EG *Eric put his lips close to the hole and blew softly... The device made a noise when you blew through it... He lit his cigarette and blew a cloud of smoke across the table.* V OR V+O : USU+A ↑ exhale = puff

4 If you **blow** something somewhere, you move it by blowing at it. EG *She blew the dust off it.* V+O+A

5 If you **blow** bubbles, smoke rings, etc, you make them by blowing air out of your mouth through liquid or smoke. V+O

6 When you **blow** a musical instrument, or when it **blows**, it makes a sound because you blow into it or send air into it. EG *The guard blew his whistle... The children were blowing flutes, ringing bells, and rattling tin cans... A horn blew outside the garage.* V-ERG

7 When you **blow** your nose, you force air out through your nose in order to clear it. ▸ used as a noun. EG *Have a good blow!* V+O ▸ N COUNT : USU SING

8 A **blow** is **8.1** a hard hit that you give someone with your fist or with a weapon. EG *He knocked Thomas unconscious with one blow of his fist... One constable's hand was severed by a sword blow... ...a blow on the back of the neck.* ● If two people or groups **come to blows**, they start fighting, especially by hitting each other with their fists. **8.2** something that happens unexpectedly or that you suddenly hear about and that makes you very disappointed or unhappy. EG *It must have been a fearful blow to him... ...a further blow to Vatican hopes of reconciliation.* ● If someone or something **softens** or **cushions the blow** for you, they help to make you able to accept an unpleasant experience or piece of news without being too upset or shocked. EG *They had alcohol to soften the blow.* N COUNT : USU+SUPP ↑ stroke ● PHR : VB INFLECTS N COUNT : IF+PREP THEN *to* = disappointment ● PHR : VB INFLECTS

9 A **blow** for or against a particular cause, belief, or ideal is an important action that helps it to succeed or gain support. EG *He struck a blow for liberty... ...a blow against the bomb.* N COUNT+*for/against*

10 If someone or something **blows** something off, out, V+O+A

etc, they violently remove it or destroy it with an explosion. EG *He would have blown his hand off if he'd fired the gun... Everything around him was blown to pieces... It blew a hole in the roof.*
11 If you **blow** a tyre or if a tyre **blows,** it suddenly gets a hole in it and loses the air inside it. V-ERG ↑ burst
12 When a fuse **blows** or when you **blow** a fuse, it burns and is destroyed because too much electricity has been sent through it. V-ERG ↑ burn
13 If you **blow** a large amount of money, you spend it quickly, especially on something that you do not really need; an informal use. EG *We blew twenty-three bucks on a lobster dinner.* V+O : IF+PREP THEN *on* = squander
14 If you **blow** an attempt or opportunity to do something, you are not successful because you do not take full advantage of it; an informal use. EG *He blew it!... Trust me to go and blow a chance like that.* V+O = muff
15 If a secret **is blown**, other people become aware of its existence or nature; an informal use. EG *Had the whole operation been blown?* V+O : USU PASS ↑ reveal = expose
16 If something such as an idea or a book **blows** your **mind**, it is very unusual and exciting, and perhaps makes you think about life or something else important in a completely new way; an informal expression. PHR : VB INFLECTS ↑ excite = overwhelm
17 The word **blow** is also used in the following expressions in informal English. 17.1 If you say **'Blow** him', **'Blow** the expense', etc, you mean that you do not care about what someone else wants or thinks, or how much something costs, etc. EG *Make the most of today and blow what happens tomorrow.* V+O ↑ forget = hang 17.2 If you say **'Blow me'**, **'Blow me down'**, or **'I'll be blowed'**, you are expressing surprise at something; an old-fashioned expression. EXCLAM 17.3 If you say 'I'm **blowed if** I'll do something' or 'I'll **be blowed if** I'll do it', you are emphasizing that you are determined not to do it. EG *I'm blowed if I'm going to apologize.* PHR 17.4 If you say **blow** you are expressing annoyance at something. EG *Blow! I've left my bag behind.* EXCLAM = bother
18 The word **blow** is also used in the following expressions, which are explained at other places in this dictionary. • to **blow the cobwebs away**: see **cobweb**. • to **blow hot and cold**: see **hot**. • to **blow** your **top**: see **top**. • to **blow** your **own trumpet**: see **trumpet**. • to **blow the whistle on** something: see **whistle**.

blow out. 1 When a person or a wind **blows out** a flame or fire, or when the flame or fire **blows out,** it stops burning completely because of the sudden movement of air over it. EG *Rudolph blew out the candles.* PHRASAL VB : V-ERG+ADV ↑ extinguish
2 If a storm **blows** itself **out,** it comes to an end. PHRASAL VB : V+O (REFL)+ADV
3 See also **blow-out**.

blow over. 1 If something such as an argument or some trouble **blows over,** it comes to an end and perhaps is forgotten about. EG *The row has blown over.* PHRASAL VB : V+ADV ↑ finish = die down
2 When a storm **blows over,** it becomes less fierce and ends. PHRASAL VB : V+ADV

blow up. 1 If you **blow** something **up** or if it **blows up,** it is destroyed by an explosion. EG *He was going to blow the place up... One of the submarines blew up and sank.* • to **blow up in** someone's **face**: see **face**. PHRASAL VB : V+ADV, OR V+O+ADV ↑ destroy = explode
2 If you **blow up**, you lose your temper and become very angry; an informal use. PHRASAL VB : V+ADV
3 If you **blow up** something such as a balloon or a tyre, you fill it with air. PHRASAL VB : V+O+ADV
4 If you **blow up** a photograph or picture, you print a larger copy of it. • See also **blow-up**. PHRASAL VB : V+O+ADV
5 If a storm **blows up**, the weather becomes stormy. EG *We were warned of a storm blowing up off the East coast.* PHRASAL VB : V+ADV

blow-by-blow. A **blow-by-blow** account, description, etc mentions or describes every stage of an event or series of events. ADJ CLASSIF : ATTRIB ↑ thorough = detailed

blow-dry, blow-dries, blow-drying, blow-dried. A **blow-dry** is a way of drying someone's hair and giving it a particular style by blowing warm air on to it with a hairdryer. EG *He is having a cut and blow-dry.* N SING WITH DET ▸ used as a verb. EG *I told her I wanted it blow-dried.* ▸ V+O

blower /bləʊə/, **blowers**. The **blower** is used in informal British English to refer to the telephone. EG *Miss Callaghan was on the blower to Atkinson.* N SING : *the*+N

blowlamp /bləʊlæmp/, **blowlamps**. A **blowlamp** is a device which produces a hot flame. You hold the blowlamp in your hand and aim it either at a piece of metal to heat it or at a wooden or metal surface to remove old paint. N COUNT ↑ burner = blowtorch

blown /bləʊn/ is the past participle of **blow**. • See also **full-blown**.

blow-out, blow-outs. A **blow-out** is 1 a meal that is larger than you normally have; an informal use. EG *Have a blow-out on your birthday.* N COUNT = binge 2 a sudden loss of air from a tyre because the tyre has burst. EG *My car had a blow-out.* N COUNT ↑ puncture 3 a sudden uncontrolled rush of oil or gas from a well. N COUNT

blowpipe /bləʊpaɪp/, **blowpipes**. A **blowpipe** is a long tube from which weapons such as arrows can be blown. N COUNT

blowsy /blaʊzi[1]/, **blowsier, blowsiest**; also spelled **blowzy**. A **blowsy** woman is rather fat, untidy in appearance, and often red-faced. ADJ QUALIT = sloppy

blowtorch /bləʊtɔːtʃ/, **blowtorches**. A **blowtorch** is the same as a blowlamp. N COUNT ↑ burner

blow-up, blow-ups. A **blow-up** is an enlargement of a photograph or picture. N COUNT

blowy /bləʊi[1]/. If the weather is **blowy,** it is windy; an informal word. ADJ QUALIT = blustery

blowzy /blaʊzi[1]/. See **blowsy**.

blubber /blʌbə/, **blubbers, blubbering, blubbered**. 1 **Blubber** is the fat of whales, seals, and similar sea animals. N UNCOUNT
2 If you **blubber**, you cry noisily and in an unattractive way. EG *I was blubbering helplessly.* V, OR V+QUOTE/REPORT-CL

bludgeon /blʌdʒəⁿn/, **bludgeons, bludgeoning, bludgeoned**. 1 A **bludgeon** is a heavy stick which is thicker at one end and which is used for hitting people. N COUNT = club
2 If you **bludgeon** someone, you hit them with a heavy object to hurt them badly. EG *Ed had bludgeoned his wife and put her into a car.* V+O ↑ beat = batter
3 If you **bludgeon** someone into doing something, you make them do it by bullying them or threatening them. V+O+A *(into)* ↑ force = bulldoze

blue /bluː/, **bluer, bluest; blues, blueing, blued**. 1 Something that is **blue** is the colour of the sky on a sunny day. EG *She had bright blue eyes and a friendly smile... ...a clear blue sky.* ADJ COLOUR ▸ used as a noun. EG *He was dressed in blue.* ▸ N MASS
2 If your skin is **blue**, it is a slightly purple colour, often because you are very cold. EG *She was turning blue with cold, poor thing.* ADJ COLOUR : USU PRED • If you say that someone can shout, call, etc **till** they **are blue in the face**, you mean that however much they shout or call for something to happen, it will not happen; an informal expression. EG *You can shout till you're blue in the face, I'm not going to change my mind.* • PHR : USED AS AN A, VB INFLECTS
3 Something that happens **out of the blue** happens suddenly and is completely unexpected. EG *They would suddenly, out of the blue, for no reason at all, start shouting and screaming.* PHR : USED AS AN A ↑ unexpectedly
4 Someone who feels **blue** feels sad and depressed, perhaps when there is no particular reason for this feeling; an informal, old-fashioned use, mainly in American English. ADJ QUALIT : USU PRED ↑ unhappy = down
5 If you have got the **blues,** you feel sad and depressed; an informal use. N PLURAL : *the*+N
6 **Blues** refers to a type of music which is like jazz, but is always slow and sounds sad. EG *...a blues singer.* N UNCOUNT : USU *the*+N
7 Something such as a film, joke, etc that is **blue** shows sexual acts or mentions sex in a way that offends many people. ADJ QUALIT = obscene
8 A **blue** or someone who has got a **blue** is a person who has played for Oxford or Cambridge University in a particular sport. EG *...a rugby blue.* N COUNT ↑ sportsman
9 If you **blue** a lot of money on something, you spend it all at once, especially on something that you do not really need; an old-fashioned, informal use in British English. V+O : IF+PREP THEN *on* = blow
10 **a bolt from the blue**: see **bolt**. • **once in a blue moon**: see **moon**. • to **scream blue murder**: see **murder**.

bluebell /bluːbɛl/, **bluebells**. A **bluebell** is a small European plant that often grows in woods and has a long stem and blue, bell-shaped flowers in early summer. N COUNT ↑ flower

blueberry /bluːbəⁿri[1]/, **blueberries**. A **blueberry** is a very small North American fruit that is very dark blue and that is usually cooked before being eaten; also used to refer to the bush that it grows on. N COUNT

bluebird /bluːbɜːd/, **bluebirds**. A **bluebird** is a small, North American bird that has blue feathers and can sing. There are several kinds of bluebird. N COUNT ↑ bird

blue-black. Something that is **blue-black** is 1 very dark blue in colour. EG *...large blue-black eyes.* 2 black in colour, but looks blue when the light shines on it. EG *The bird was busy preening his glossy blue-black feathers.* ADJ COLOUR / ADJ COLOUR

blue-blooded. A **blue-blooded** person belongs to a royal or noble family. ADJ CLASSIF

bluebottle /blu:bɒtə°l/, **bluebottles**. A **bluebottle** is a large fly with a shiny dark blue body, which makes a buzzing noise when it flies. N COUNT

blue chip, blue chips. A **blue chip**, or a **blue-chip** investment, company, etc is an investment or a company in which it is considered to be profitable and safe to invest. N COUNT : USU BEFORE N

blue-collar workers do manual work as opposed to office work. EG *Many women whose husbands were blue-collar workers had white-collar jobs themselves.* ADJ CLASSIF ≠ white-collar

blue-eyed boy, blue-eyed boys. Someone's **blue-eyed boy** is the boy or man that they like more than anyone else and therefore treat especially well; used in informal British English. N COUNT : POSS+N = pet, favourite

blueish /blu:ɪʃ/. See **bluish**.

blue pencil, blue pencils. If you go over a piece of writing with a **blue pencil**, you delete or alter parts of it in order to improve it. EG *...a potentially good scene that needs the blue pencil and a rewrite.* N COUNT

blueprint /blu:prɪnt/, **blueprints**. 1 A **blueprint** of a plan or idea is the original description that explains the basic facts of how it is expected to work. EG *...a blueprint for a better world.* N COUNT : IF+PREP THEN *for/of* = scheme

2 A **blueprint** of an architect's plan for a building, town, etc is a photographic print of it consisting of white lines on a blue background. N COUNT : IF+PREP THEN *for/of* = design

blue riband /blu: rɪbənd/, **blue ribands**; also spelled **ribband**. A **blue riband** or **blue ribbon** is a prize in the form of a blue ribbon that is awarded to the person who comes first in certain sporting contests. N COUNT ⇑ prize

bluestocking /blu:stɒkɪŋ/, **bluestockings**. A **bluestocking** is a clever, highly educated woman who is more interested in academic ideas than in behaving in a traditionally feminine way; a rather old-fashioned word used showing disapproval. N COUNT ⇑ highbrow

blue tit, blue tits. A **blue tit** is a small European bird which is blue on the top of its head, wings, and tail, and has a yellow front. N COUNT

bluff /blʌf/, **bluffs, bluffing, bluffed**. 1 A **bluff** is an attempt to deceive someone by making them believe that you will do something when in fact you have no intention of doing it. EG *The soldiers thought it was a bluff.* ▸ used as an uncount noun. EG *His threats are merely bluff.* ● If you **call** someone's **bluff** when they have been threatening to do something, you tell them to go ahead and do it, usually in order to prove that they will not really do it. EG *It is time to call their bluff.* N COUNT ⇑ deception = blind ▸ N UNCOUNT ● PHR : VB INFLECTS ⇑ challenge

2 If you **are bluffing** or if you **bluff** someone, you deceive them by making them believe that you will do something when in fact you have no intention of doing it. EG *Her only chance was to use her wits to bluff and outsmart the enemy.* V OR V+O

3 A **bluff** is also a steep cliff or bank, especially by a river or the sea. N COUNT

bluish /blu:ɪʃ/; also spelled **blueish**. Something that is **bluish** is slightly blue in colour. EG *...bluish-grey water.* ADJ COLOUR

blunder /blʌndə/, **blunders, blundering, blundered**. 1 A **blunder** is a big mistake, especially one which seems to be the result of carelessness or stupidity. EG *Signing the agreement was a major blunder on the Prime Minister's part.* N COUNT = gaffe

2 If you **blunder**, you make a big mistake, especially a careless or stupid mistake. EG *Clearly, Sir Alec had blundered badly.* V = bungle

3 If you **blunder** along, into something, etc, you move in a clumsy and uncertain way, without taking care about where you are going. EG *...silken threads that tell the spider when a victim has blundered into the web.* V+A

blundering /blʌndə°rɪŋ/ is used to emphasize that someone, or an attempt at something, is very clumsy and careless. EG *...a record of blundering miscalculations and miseries... You blundering idiot!* ADJ CLASSIF : ATTRIB

blunt /blʌnt/, **blunts, blunting, blunted**. 1 When someone is being **blunt**, they are speaking directly and simply without making any effort to be polite or to avoid upsetting people. EG *Let me ask a blunt question... To be blunt, I am afraid that sooner or later you will no longer be needed here.* ◊ **bluntly**. EG *He told them bluntly what was acceptable and what was not.* ◊ **bluntness**. EG *Other leaders have stated their views with equal bluntness.* ADJ QUALIT = frank ≠ subtle, tactful ◊ ADV WITH VB ◊ N UNCOUNT

2 A long, thin object that is **blunt** has a rounded or flat end rather than a pointed end. EG *Remove the blockage with a wooden spoon or similar blunt instrument... My pencil's blunt.* ADJ QUALIT ≠ pointed

3 A knife that is **blunt** has an edge that does not cut well. ADJ QUALIT ≠ sharp

4 If someone or something **blunts** a knife, tool, pair of scissors, etc, they make it less sharp or less pointed. EG *You'll blunt the scissors if you use them to cut card... The sharp tip of the bullet had been slightly blunted.* V+O ⇑ damage

5 If something **blunts** an emotion, sense, feeling, etc, it weakens its effect. EG *...blurred and blunted senses... This side of his personality has been blunted and crushed by toil.* V+O ⇑ weaken

blur /blɜ:/, **blurs, blurring, blurred**. 1 A **blur** is a shape or area which you cannot see clearly because it has no distinct outline or because it is moving very fast. EG *Everything becomes a blur when you travel beyond a certain speed.* N COUNT : USU SING ⇑ smudge = fuzz

2 When a thing **blurs** or when something **blurs** it, you cannot see it clearly because its edges are not distinct. EG *Tears blurred my vision.* ◊ **blurred**. EG *...a blurred snapshot... ...a landscape of blurred outlines.* V-ERG = smear ◊ ADJ QUALIT = fuzzy

3 If a memory or idea **blurs** or if something **blurs** it, the effect of it is weakened in people's minds. EG *...a determination to blur the line between art and reality.* ◊ **blurred**. EG *The distinction between reform and revolution had become blurred in Benn's mind.* V-ERG ⇑ weaken ◊ ADJ QUALIT = unclear

4 A memory, time, place, etc that is described as a **blur** is one that you cannot remember clearly. EG *I visited many other places that seem a blur to me now.* N SING : *a*+N = haze

blurb /blɜ:b/. The **blurb** about a book, exhibition, etc is information about it that is written in order to attract people's interest. EG *'Murder Mystery', as the blurb makes haste to assure us, contains no explicit violence... I noticed his name in the blurb that you let me have.* N SING : *the*+N ⇑ publicity

blurry /blɜ:ri¹/, **blurrier, blurriest**. A **blurry** shape is one that has an unclear outline. EG *The trees and hedges were just blurry shapes.* ADJ QUALIT = fuzzy ≠ distinct

blurt /blɜ:t/, **blurts, blurting, blurted**. 1 If you **blurt out** something that you have been afraid to say before, you suddenly say it. EG *He burst into tears, blurting out his guilt before his horrified parents... She suddenly blurted out, 'I'm not going.'* V+O/REPORT-CL/QUOTE+A *(out)*, OR V+QUOTE ≠ bottle up

2 If you **blurt** something **out**, you say it without thinking first about the consequences, often with the result that you regret it afterwards. EG *He blurted it out before I had time to stop him.* V+O/REPORT-CL/QUOTE+A *(out)*

blush /blʌʃ/, **blushes, blushing, blushed**. 1 When you **blush**, you become red in the face because you suddenly feel a strong emotion, especially shame or embarrassment. EG *Philip blushed and laughed uneasily... I felt myself blushing.* V = redden

2 A **blush** is the red colour on your face that results from blushing. EG *The freckles on Jack's face disappeared under a blush of embarrassment.* N COUNT : USU SING

3 If you **spare** someone's **blushes**, you avoid saying or doing things that might make them embarrassed or ashamed. EG *He didn't spare my blushes. He gave the whole story with all its sordid details.* PHR : VB INFLECTS = be tactful

bluster /blʌstə/, **blusters, blustering, blustered**. 1 If you **bluster**, you speak or behave noisily and aggressively because you are angry or offended. EG *They blustered and swore that the pictures were fakes.* V

2 **Bluster** is a noisy, aggressive way of talking that shows that you are angry or offended. EG *She simply ignored his bluster as empty rhetoric.* N UNCOUNT ⇑ talk

blustery /blʌstə°ri¹/ weather is very rough and windy. ADJ QUALIT = wild

bn is an abbreviation for 'billion'. N COUNT

B.O. is an abbreviation for 'body odour'; an unpleasant smell caused by stale sweat on a person's body. EG *He's got B.O.* N UNCOUNT

boa /bəʊə/, **boas**. A **boa** is a large, strong snake that kills animals and birds by wrapping itself round their bodies and squeezing them to death. Boas are found N COUNT mainly in South and Central America. • See also **feather boa**.

boar /bɔː/, **boars**. **Boar** can also be used as the plural form. A **boar** is **1** a male pig, especially one that is kept for breeding purposes. N COUNT **2** a wild pig. N COUNT

board /bɔːd/, **boards, boarding, boarded**. **1** A **board** is a flat, thin, rectangular piece of wood, cardboard, plastic or similar material. Boards are made in a wide variety of sizes and can be used for many purposes; for example, a board can be **1.1** a surface, especially one made of wood, on which something can be put, spread out, or cut. EG *When the dough has risen, turn it onto a floured board and knead it.* N COUNT **1.2** a square piece of wood or stiff cardboard with a pattern on it, used for playing games such as chess or ludo. EG *If you have a good player on the other side of the board it increases the fun... ...a chess board.* N COUNT ↑ game **1.3** a large piece of wood on which a message or advertisement is written, and which is held by someone or put where people can see it. EG *The television director held a board up in front of the studio audience... ...house agents' boards.* N COUNT : USU+SUPP ↑ notice **1.4** a long rectangular piece of wood which is used to make a flat surface, for example a floor, wall, or shelf. EG *...little huts patched together out of mud and old boards and pieces of sacking... He gazed at the cracks between the creaking boards of his ceiling.* N COUNT ↑ plank

2 You also use **board** to refer to something which has 'board' as part of its name, when the thing has already been mentioned or when you are using it; for example 'diving board', 'chopping board', 'notice board', 'blackboard'. EG *I can't dive off the top board yet... I'll write the sum up on the board.* • See also **ironing board**. COUNT : USU *the* +MOD+N

3 The **board** of a company or organization is the group of people who control it and direct it. EG *The board is likely to meet tomorrow... All the investment decisions are taken by boards of directors... ...board meetings... ...the British Railways Board.* N COUNT : USU+SUPP, OR *the*+N IN SING ↑ management

4 If you **board** a train, ship, or aircraft, you get on to it in order to travel somewhere; a fairly formal use. EG *Flo and I decided to board a train for Geneva... We joined the passengers waiting to board.* V OR V+O

5 on board. **5.1** When you are **on board**, you are on or in a train, ship, or aircraft. EG *We almost felt we were on board the spacecraft.* PHR : USED AS AN A **5.2** If you **take** a task or job **on board**, you accept responsibility for doing or arranging it. PHR : VB INFLECTS **5.3** If you **take on board** an idea, problem, etc, you understand or accept it; an informal expression. EG *...technological knowledge that he would have to take on board before he was capable of tackling the problem.* PHR : VB INFLECTS

6 If you **board** with someone, you live in their home for a period of time, usually in return for payment. EG *He boarded with an Italian family.* • See also **boarding school**. V+A *(with)*

7 Your **board** is food which is provided when you stay somewhere, for example in a hotel. EG *...the low price that my hostess was asking for board and bed.* • See also **full board**, **board and lodging**. N SING : POSS+N, OR N UNCOUNT

8 If you say that something such as an arrangement or deal is **above board,** you mean that it is being done honestly in the correct or official way and that there is nothing hidden or deceitful about it. EG *That house deal was all above board.* PHR : USED AS AN A = honest ≠ shady

9 If a policy or a situation applies **across the board**, it affects everything or everybody in a particular group, place, or situation. EG *We're aiming for a 20% reduction across the board.* PHR : USED AS AN A = throughout

10 If an arrangement or plan **goes by the board**, it fails completely and is not used or has to be cancelled. PHR : VB INFLECTS ↑ fail

11 If someone **sweeps the board** in a competition or election, they are so successful that they win everything or nearly everything. PHR : VB INFLECTS ↑ conquer

12 The stage in a theatre is sometimes referred to in an old-fashioned way as the **boards**. EG *Many actresses spend more time on the dole than on the boards... ...treading the boards.* N PLURAL : *the*+N

board out. If you **board out** someone who is in your care, you send them to stay with someone else for a period of time. EG *Almost half of all children in care were boarded out with foster parents.* PHRASAL VB : V+O+ADV = foster

board up. If you **board up** a door or window, you fasten boards over it so that it is covered up. EG *Shopkeepers were boarding up their windows.* PHRASAL VB : V+O+ADV ↑ cover

board and lodging is food and a place to sleep, usually provided in a boarding house or sometimes offered as part of the conditions of a job. EG *The staff are paid £8 a month with board and lodging.* PHR : USED AS O OR S ↑ accommodation

boarder /bɔːdə/, **boarders**. A **boarder** is a pupil who lives at school during term time. N COUNT

board game, board games; also spelled with a hyphen. A **board game** is a game such as chess or snakes and ladders, which people play by moving small objects around on a board. N COUNT

boarding /bɔːdɪŋ/, **boardings**. **1 Boarding** is a collection of wooden boards which can be made into a structure with a solid surface, for example a floor or a fence. N UNCOUNT ↑ wood

2 Boarding is used to refer to the system in which children live at school during the term. EG *Annual day fees stood at £1038, and average boarding fees at £2289.* ADJ CLASSIF : ATTRIB

3 Boarding is also used to refer to the system of looking after people's pets in kennels for a short period of time. EG *League Kennels offer short term boarding facilities to all dog owners... ...boarding kennels.* ADJ CLASSIF : ATTRIB

boarding card, boarding cards. A **boarding card** is a card which a passenger must have when boarding an aeroplane or a boat before a journey. N COUNT ↑ pass

boarding house, boarding houses; also spelled with a hyphen. A **boarding house** is a house which has rooms which people pay to stay in for a short time. N COUNT ↑ hostel

boarding school, boarding schools; also spelled with a hyphen. A **boarding school** is a school where some or all of the pupils live at the school during term time. N COUNT

boardroom /bɔːdruːm, -rum/, **boardrooms**; also spelled as two words. The **boardroom** is a room where the board of a company meets. EG *I got a summons to the boardroom up on the top floor.* N COUNT ↑ room ▸ The **boardroom** is also used to refer to the people at the highest level of management in a company. EG *...a clear demand for the devolution of power from the boardroom to the shop floor... ...the long social path to the boardroom and the executive suite.* ▸ N SING : *the*+N = management

boardwalk /bɔːdwɔːk/, **boardwalks**. A **boardwalk** is a footpath which is made of wooden boards, usually next to the sea; used in American English. N COUNT ↑ path

boast /bəʊst/, **boasts, boasting, boasted**. **1** If you **boast**, you talk about something that you have done or something that you own in a way that shows you are proud or pleased about it, usually excessively proud or pleased. EG *Williams boasted of his influence over the Prime Minister... He boasted that it was the most expensive film ever made... He boasted to newsmen: 'I am a long distance runner'... British Rail can boast about their safety record as well... 'He listened to mine,' boasted Millie.* V, OR V+REPORT-CL/QUOTE

2 A **boast** is a statement that someone makes which shows that they are proud of something, usually excessively proud. EG *It is his boast that on one such occasion he read Paradise Lost in a single evening.* N COUNT = brag

3 If something or someone **boasts** something such as an achievement or possession, they have done or possess the thing mentioned. EG *The village boasted only one small general store... The company can boast an array of gifted directors.* V+O ↑ exhibit

boastful /bəʊstful/. Someone who is **boastful** talks too proudly about something that they possess or have done; used showing disapproval. EG *I think I can say this without being boastful-I have never failed an examination.* ▸ used of actions and behaviour. EG *It was a wild, boastful military display.* ADJ QUALIT = bragging ≠ humble ◇ **boastfully**. EG *'I've got a better bicycle than yours,' she said boastfully.* ◇ ADV WITH VB ◇ **boastfulness**. EG *I am well aware of his defects but boastfulness is not one of them.* ◇ N UNCOUNT ↑ pride

boat /bəʊt/, **boats**. **1** A **boat** is **1.1** a small vessel for travelling on water, especially one which only carries a few people. There are many different kinds of boats. EG *John took me down the river in the old boat... We are going by boat... ...a fishing boat.* N COUNT, OR *by*+N **1.2** a ship, especially one which carries passengers; a fairly informal use. EG *She was getting off in Hamburg to take the boat to Stockholm.* N COUNT

2 The word **boat** is used in the following expressions in informal English. **2.1** If someone **rocks the boat**, they upset a calm situation and cause trouble for other people. PHR : VB INFLECTS **2.2** If you **miss the boat**, you lose the chance of doing or having something because you do PHR : VB INFLECTS not act quickly enough. **2.3** If two or more people are **in the same boat**, they are in the same unpleasant situation; often used to give comfort to someone who is worrying about something. EG *We are all in the same boat.* **2.4** If you **push the boat out**, you spend a great deal of money on something, especially on a party or a special meal. **2.5** If you **burn** your **boats**, you act very firmly in a way that will not allow you the opportunity to change your mind later. — PHR : USED AS AN A; PHR : VB INFLECTS; PHR : VB INFLECTS = burn your bridges

3 See also **gravy boat, sauce-boat.**

boater /bəʊtə/, **boaters**. A **boater** is a hard straw hat with a flat top and a brim. — N COUNT

boat-hook, boat-hooks; also spelled without a hyphen. A **boat-hook** is a long pole with a hook at the end, which is used to pull a boat in to the bank or to push it away from other boats. — N COUNT

boathouse /bəʊthaʊs/, **boathouses**. A **boathouse** is a small building at the edge of a river or lake, in which boats are kept. — N COUNT ↑ store

boating /bəʊtɪŋ/ is travelling on a lake or river in a small boat for pleasure. EG *Uncle Jack once took me out boating... ...a number of boating accidents.* — N UNCOUNT ↑ activity

boatman /bəʊtməⁿn/, **boatmen**. A **boatman** is a man who is paid by people to take them across an area of water in a small boat, or who hires boats out to them for a short time. — N COUNT ↑ worker

boatswain /bəʊsəⁿn/, **boatswains**. The **boatswain** on a ship is the officer whose job it is to look after the maintenance of the ship and its equipment. — N COUNT = bosun

boat train, boat trains; also spelled with a hyphen. A **boat train** is a train that takes you to or from a port. EG *We went straight from the boat train to Paddington.* — N COUNT

bob /bɒb/, **bobs, bobbing, bobbed**. **Bob** is both the singular and the plural form of the noun in paragraph 5. **1** If something **bobs**, it moves up and down, like something does when it is floating on water. EG *The float bobbed gently on the ripples... Everything around me seemed to be bobbing up and down... He disappeared into a mass of bobbing heads.* — V+A ↑ jump

2 If you **bob** up, down, or in some other direction, you move suddenly in that direction, especially into or out of view. EG *Suddenly an object bobbed up from below the surface... She bobbed down behind the hedge... The receptionist bobbed back into the rear office.* — V+A ↑ jump

3 When you **bob** your head, you move it quickly up and down once, for example in greeting. EG *He bobbed his head at the audience.* ▸ used as a noun. EG *...with a bob of her head.* — V+O = nod; ▸ N COUNT

4 If you **bob** a curtsey or if you **bob**, you make a little curtsey or bow. EG *I bobbed him a curtsey.* ▸ used as a noun. EG *She did her bob to the altar.* — V+O, OR V; ▸ N COUNT

5 A **bob** is a shilling, in informal old-fashioned English. EG *They used to get four bob an hour.* — N COUNT : a+N, OR NUM+N

6 A **bob** is also a hair style in which the hair is cut to about chin length all round the head, except for the fringe. EG *...a stout lady with a raven-black bob.* — N COUNT ↑ haircut

7 If you **bob** someone's hair, you cut it in a bob. ◊ **bobbed**. EG *...a girl with blonde bobbed hair.* — V+O; ◊ ADJ CLASSIF

8 Bits and bobs are small objects or parts of something; an informal expression. EG *We'll work out where all the other bits and bobs go later.* — PHR : USED AS O OR S = odds and ends

9 You can say **Bob's your uncle** after describing an action, to indicate that the result comes easily and quickly; an informal expression. EG *You just run it through the computer, and Bob's your uncle!* — CONVENTION = hey presto

bobbin /bɒbɪn/, **bobbins**. A **bobbin** is a small round object on which thread or wool is wound in order to hold it, often one which is put in a sewing machine. — N COUNT = spool

bobble /bɒbəⁿl/, **bobbles**. A **bobble** is a small ball of material, usually made of wool, which is used for decorating clothes, lampshades, etc. EG *...a cap with a bobble on top.* — N COUNT

bobby /bɒbi¹/, **bobbies**. A **bobby** is a policeman; an informal word used in British English. EG *...the village bobby.* — N COUNT ↑ cop

bobsled /bɒbslɛd/, **bobsleds**. A **bobsled** is the same as a bobsleigh. — N COUNT

bobsleigh /bɒbsleɪ/, **bobsleighs**. A **bobsleigh** is a vehicle with long thin strips of metal fixed to the bottom, which is used for racing downhill on ice. — N COUNT ↑ sledge

bod /bɒd/, **bods**. A **bod** is a person; an informal word used in British English. EG *He's a nice bod.* — N COUNT = chap

bode /bəʊd/, **bodes, boding, boded**. If something **bodes well**, or **bodes ill** or **no good**, it suggests that something good, or something bad, is likely to happen. EG *This does not bode well for his chances against the champion... Her expression boded ill for somebody.* — PHR : VB INFLECTS, USU+for

bodge /bɒdʒ/, **bodges, bodging, bodged**. If you **bodge** something, you make it or mend it in a way that is not as good as it should be; an informal word used in British English. EG *We'll have to bodge it.* ▸ used as a noun. EG *...a kind of bodge good carpenters strive to avoid.* — V+O = botch; ▸ N COUNT

bodice /bɒdɪs/, **bodices**. The **bodice** of a dress is the upper part of it above the waist. EG *...a nice grey dress with a fitted bodice and flared skirt.* — N COUNT ↑ top

bodily /bɒdɪli¹/. **1 Bodily** is used **1.1** to describe something that relates to someone's body. EG *They have no interests beyond their bodily needs... ...a general slowing up of the bodily functions.* **1.2** to refer to an action that involves the whole of someone's body. EG *He carried her bodily past the rows of empty seats... He hurled himself bodily at the Prince.* — ADJ CLASSIF : ATTRIB = physical ≠ spiritual; ADV WITH VB ↑ physically

2 If a large object is moved **bodily** somewhere, the whole of it is moved, perhaps without being taken to pieces. EG *A brick cellar was moved bodily 40 feet to one side.* — ADV WITH VB = intact

bodkin /bɒdkɪn/, **bodkins**. A **bodkin** is a thick needle with a blunt end. — N COUNT

body /bɒdi¹/, **bodies**. **1** A person's or animal's **body** is **1.1** all their physical parts, including their head, limbs, flesh, and organs. EG *He lay with his whole body feeling as if it were on fire... ...death through loss of body heat... Her mind was floating somewhere apart from her body.* **1.2** the main part of their body, not including their head, neck, or limbs. EG *They respond with slow movements of their arms, legs, and bodies... Its body is about the size of that of an otter.* ● to **keep body and soul together**: see **soul**. — N COUNT : USU POSS+N ≠ mind, soul, spirit; N COUNT : USU POSS+N = torso, trunk

2 A **body** is the dead body of a person. EG *We've just found a body in the water... The undertakers came to collect the body... His body has not been found.* ● **over my dead body**: see **dead**. — N COUNT = corpse

3 A **body** is also an organized group of people who are in charge of something or who work together. EG *...a unique body called the Inner London Education Authority... ...local voluntary bodies.* — N COUNT : USU+SUPP ↑ organization ≠ individual

4 A **body** of people is a group of people who are together or who are connected with each other in some way. EG *...a body of people who feel that they are a nation.* ● If people do something **in a body**, they do it together in a group. EG *The students went in a body to the Assembly Hall.* — N COUNT : N+of +N IN PL ↑ mass; ● PHR : USED AS AN A

5 The **body** of something, for example a large building or document, is the main or largest part of it. EG *...the main body of the church... ...the metal cover which fits over the body of the tap.* — N SING : the+N+of = bulk

6 The **body** of a car or aeroplane is the main structure of it, not including the engine, wheels, or wings. EG *Halfway home the body of the car literally fell to pieces.* — N COUNT+SUPP = shell

7 A large **body** of information is a large amount of it. EG *There is a growing body of evidence pointing to these effects... ...a vast body of data.* — N PART+N UNCOUNT = quantity

8 A **body** of water is an area of water, for example a lake; a formal use. — N PART+N UNCOUNT

9 In physics, a **body** is an object that is physically separate from all other objects. EG *Voyager I proved Amalthea to be a dark red, rocky, cigar-shaped body.* ● See also **foreign body, heavenly body.** — N COUNT

10 If you say that a particular wine, brandy, or whisky has **body**, you mean that it is full and strong. EG *'Grain' whisky has a lighter flavour and less body.* — N UNCOUNT = fullness

body blow, body blows; also spelled with a hyphen. A **body blow** is something that causes great disappointment and difficulty to someone who is trying to achieve something. EG *The news of his resignation was yet another body blow.* — N COUNT = setback ≠ boost

body-building is the activity of doing special exercises regularly in order to make your muscles grow bigger. ◊ **body-builder, body-builders.** EG *...weight-lifters and body-builders, whose arms seem to dangle in space.* — N UNCOUNT; ◊ N COUNT

bodyguard /bɒdi¹gɑːd/, **bodyguards**. A **bodyguard** is a person or a group of people employed to protect someone who is in danger of being attacked. EG *He has an army of bodyguards... ...one of the Rajah's personal bodyguard.* — N COUNT ↑ guard

body language; also spelled with a hyphen. **Body language** is the way in which you show your feelings — N UNCOUNT ↑ communication or thoughts to other people by means of the position or movements of your body rather than with words. EG *...displays of impatient body language.*

body odour is the smell of a person's body; usually used to describe the unpleasant smell caused by someone sweating. EG *They had no body odour... Is their personal body odour attractive to you?* N UNCOUNT = B.O.

body politic. The **body politic** is all the people of a nation; a formal word. EG *It was not in the interests of the body politic at the present moment.* N SING WITH DET = state

body stocking, body stockings; also spelled with a hyphen. A **body stocking** is a piece of clothing that covers the whole of someone's body and fits tightly. Dancers often wear body stockings when they are performing. N COUNT ⇑ covering

bodywork /bɒdi¹wɜːk/. The **bodywork** of a motor vehicle is the main part of it; usually used to refer to the painted outside of the main part. EG *A second hand car dealer will always look at the bodywork rather than the engine.* N UNCOUNT ⇑ shell

Boer /bəʊə, bɔː/, **Boers**. A **Boer** is a descendant of the Dutch people who went to live in South Africa. N PROPER ⇑ person

boffin /bɒfɪn/, **boffins**. A **boffin** is a scientist; an informal word used in British English. EG *...mad boffins.* N COUNT

bog /bɒg/, **bogs, bogged**. 1 A **bog** is 1.1 an area of land which is very wet and muddy. N COUNT 1.2 a toilet; an informal use in British English. N COUNT = loo

2 **bogged down**. 2.1 If you are **bogged down** in a particular thing, it prevents you from making progress or getting something done. EG *Don't get bogged down in details... We had been bogged down in bureaucratic red tape.* PHR : USED AS AN A = immersed 2.2 If a vehicle is **bogged down** in mud or snow, it is stuck in it and cannot move. PHR : USED AS AN A

bogey /bəʊgi¹/, **bogeys**; also spelled **bogie** or **bogy**. 1 A **bogey** is 1.1 something that people are worried about, perhaps without cause or reason. EG *We must put to rest the old bogey that military expenditure is vital for national security.* N COUNT ⇑ worry 1.2 a piece of dried mucus that comes from inside your nose; an informal use. N COUNT

2 A **bogey** or a **bogeyman** is an imaginary frightening evil spirit. EG *They see bogeys in every bush... You should never threaten her with bogeymen.* N COUNT ⇑ monster

boggle /bɒgəᵒl/, **boggles, boggling, boggled**. 1 If your mind **boggles** at something or if something **boggles** your mind, you find it difficult to imagine it or understand it fully and are therefore very confused by it. EG *The mind boggles... My imagination boggled at the thought of her reaction... The questions raised by the new biology simply boggle the mind.* V-ERG : IF+PREP THEN *at* ⇑ gawp

2 If you **boggle** at something, you are unwilling to do it or accept it. EG *There is no reason why we should boggle at a capital gains tax.* V : IF+PREP THEN *at* ⇑ hesitate

boggy /bɒgi¹/, **boggier, boggiest**. Land that is **boggy** is very wet and muddy. ADJ QUALIT = marshy

bogie /bəʊgi¹/. See **bogey**.

bogus /bəʊgəs/. Something that is **bogus** is false, or is not done according to the proper laws or rules; used especially of something that someone is pretending is real, genuine, or valid. EG *...bogus names... ...bogus scientific arguments... She was speaking with a terrible bogus accent.* ADJ CLASSIF = phoney ≠ genuine

bogy /bəʊgi¹/. See **bogey**.

bohemian /bəʊhiːmɪən/, **bohemians**. A **bohemian** is someone who lives in a very casual way that is different from the way most people in their society live, especially someone who is interested in art, music, literature, etc; sometimes used showing disapproval. EG *...radical bohemians.* N COUNT ⇑ nonconformist ▸ used as an adjective. EG *My parents were slightly disapproving of the bohemian life that Ellen led.* ▸ ADJ QUALIT

boil /bɔɪl/, **boils, boiling, boiled**. 1 When a hot liquid **boils**, bubbles appear in it and it starts to change into steam or vapour. EG *When the water has boiled let it cool.* V ⇑ bubble ◇ **boiling**. EG *Fill the teapot with boiling water.* ◇ ADJ CLASSIF : ATTRIB ● See also **boiling**.

2 You use **the boil** in expressions such as 'bring something to the boil', 'come to the boil', and 'on the boil' to refer to the temperature at which a liquid starts to boil when it is heated, when talking about how much the liquid should be heated. EG *Bring to the boil and simmer gently... I'll keep the kettle on the boil until you come in.* N SING : *the*+N = boiling point

3 When you **boil** a liquid or a container with liquid inside, or when it **boils**, it is heated until the liquid boils. EG *He boiled the kettle and made the tea... Get everything else ready while the water boils... The kettle's boiling.* V-ERG

4 When you **boil** food or when it **boils**, it is cooked by being heated in a pan that contains boiling water. EG *She didn't know how to boil an egg... Leave the cabbage to boil for about 5 minutes.* V-ERG ⇑ cook ◇ **boiled**. EG *...boiled potatoes.* ◇ ADJ CLASSIF ● If food or water that is being boiled in a pan **boils dry**, there is no water left in the pan because it has all turned to steam. EG *The sprouts have boiled dry.* ● PHR : VB INFLECTS

5 When you **boil** clothes or linen, you wash them by leaving them to boil in a pan of water. V+O

6 If you are **boiling** with a strong emotion such as anger, you feel very angry or hostile. EG *I was boiling with anger... ...boiling emotions.* V : USU+A *(with)*, USU CONT = seething ● to **make** someone's **blood boil**: see **blood**.

7 If a place or area of activity is **boiling** with activity or emotion, it is full of people doing things or feeling strong emotion. EG *The art market is boiling with an activity never known before.* V : USU+A *(with)*, USU CONT = bustling, bubbling

8 A **boil** is a red, painful swelling on the skin, which contains a thick yellow liquid called pus. N COUNT ⇑ sore

boil away. When a liquid that is being heated **boils away**, all of it changes into steam or vapour. PHRASAL VB : V+ADV

boil down. 1 When you **boil down** a liquid, you boil it until there is less of it because some of the water in it has changed into steam or vapour. EG *Boil the sauce down to half its original volume.* PHRASAL VB : V-ERG+ADV

2 If you **boil down** an amount of information, you keep only the most important parts and details. EG *...sorting through data and boiling it down.* PHRASAL VB : V+O+ADV = condense

boil down to. If you say that a situation, issue, or question **boils down to** a particular thing, you mean that this is the most important thing in the situation, issue, or question. EG *What it all seemed to boil down to was money... The question boils down to one of social priorities.* PHRASAL VB : V+ADV+PREP ⇑ be = amount to

boil over. 1 When a liquid that is being heated in a container **boils over**, it rises and flows over the edge of the container. EG *The milk's boiling over.* PHRASAL VB : V+ADV ⇑ overflow

2 If a situation in which people are very angry or excited **boils over**, they become so angry or excited that the situation gets out of control. EG *The simmering quarrel between the opposing parties boiled over.* PHRASAL VB : V+ADV = explode, erupt

boil up. When you **boil** something **up**, usually a liquid, you heat it until it boils. EG *If the insides of aluminium pans discolour, boil up some water in them with a squeezed lemon.* PHRASAL VB : V+O+ADV

boiler /bɔɪlə/, **boilers**. A **boiler** is 1 a large device which burns gas, oil, or other fuel in order to provide hot water, especially for central heating in a house. EG *Oil and gas-fired boilers use electric pumps or fans.* N COUNT 2 a container used for boiling water in. EG *Wash handkerchiefs in a boiler or an old saucepan.* N COUNT

boiler suit, boiler suits; also spelled with a hyphen. A **boiler suit** is a piece of clothing consisting of trousers and a top that are joined together in one piece, which people wear when they are working in order to keep their ordinary clothes clean; used in British English. EG *...an oil-stained denim boiler suit.* N COUNT ⇑ garment = overalls

boiling /bɔɪlɪŋ/. 1 Something that is **boiling** or **boiling hot** is very hot. EG *It's boiling in here!... She was running boiling hot water into the tub.* ADJ CLASSIF

2 If you say that you are **boiling**, you mean that you feel very hot, usually unpleasantly hot. EG *Mind if I open the window? I'm boiling.* ADJ CLASSIF : PRED = sweltering

boiling point, boiling points. 1 The **boiling point** of a liquid is the temperature at which it starts to change into steam or vapour by heating. EG *The boiling point of water is 100C... After the pan has reached boiling point, turn gas as low as possible.* N COUNT/UNCOUNT

2 If a situation reaches **boiling point**, the people involved have become so agitated or angry that they can no longer remain calm and in control of themselves. EG *Emotions are reaching boiling point.* N UNCOUNT

boisterous /bɔɪstə¹rəs/. Someone who is **boisterous** is noisy, lively, and full of energy. EG *Will came clattering in, boisterous, burly, and jovial.* ADJ QUALIT ≠ docile ▸ used of people's behaviour. EG *The fat man received him with his usual boisterous cordiality.*

bold /bəʊld/, **bolder, boldest**. 1 Someone who is **bold** is 1.1 not afraid to do things which involve risk or danger. EG *...the most ambitious, bold, and imaginative of Europe's citizens.* ADJ QUALIT ⇑ brave = daring ≠ cautious ▸ used of actions. EG *It was a bold move... ...bold conjectures.* ◇ **boldly**. EG

...boldly going where no man had gone before. ◇ **boldness.** EG *For any success, boldness is required.* ◇ N UNCOUNT

1.2 not shy about looking at or talking to people, and perhaps does not show enough respect. ▸ used of people's appearance and behaviour. EG *She had bold brown eyes.* ◇ **boldly.** EG *He returned her gaze boldly.* ◇ **boldness.** ADJ QUALIT = forward ≠ shy, modest ◇ ADV

● You describe someone as being **as bold as brass** to emphasize how bold they are; an informal expression. EG *He came into my office, as bold as brass, and told me he was leaving.* ● PHR : USED AS AN A = fearless

● You say **'if I may be so bold'** when asking someone a question, in order to indicate that you hope you are not offending them by asking it; a very polite, formal expression. EG *If I may be so bold, how long do you intend to stay?* ● PHR : USED AS ADV SEN

2 Bold lines or designs are painted or drawn in a clear, strong, and decisive way. EG *...bold loopy handwriting... She began to paint her lips with bold, defiant strokes.* ADJ QUALIT ↑ strong

3 A **bold** colour or pattern is very bright or dark and very noticeable. EG *...a building of bold red brick... ...his bold black-and-white striped shirt.* ADJ QUALIT = vivid

4 If printed letters are in **bold** print or typeface, they are thicker and look blacker than ordinary printed letters. **This sentence is in bold type.** ADJ CLASSIF : ATTRIB ↑ heavy

bole /bəʊl/, **boles.** The **bole** of a tree is its trunk. N COUNT+SUPP

bolero /bəˈlɛərəʊ/, **boleros.** A **bolero** is **1** a short jacket that does not quite reach to the waist, worn especially by women. N COUNT **2** a traditional Spanish dance. N COUNT

Bolivian /bəˈlɪvɪən/, **Bolivians.** **1** Something that is **Bolivian** belongs or relates to Bolivia or its people. ADJ CLASSIF

2 A **Bolivian** is a person who comes from Bolivia. N COUNT

bollard /bɒlɑːd, bɒləd/, **bollards.** A **bollard** is **1** a strong thick post, usually made of concrete and used to mark the boundary of an area of ground and stop cars from passing through. N COUNT **2** a thick post, often with a light inside, which is placed in the middle of a road to mark junctions so that motorists can see them more clearly and people can cross the road more easily. N COUNT

bollocks /bɒləks/; used in British English. **1 Bollocks** is a rude swear word which is used in very informal English to express disagreement, dislike, or defiance. EXCLAM

2 If you say that something someone has said, written, or done is **bollocks**, you are saying in a rude and offensive way that you think that it is completely wrong or foolish. EXCLAM, OR N UNCOUNT = bullshit

3 A man's **bollocks** are his testicles; a very rude and offensive use. N PLURAL

Bolshevik /bɒlʃəˈvɪk/, **Bolsheviks.** **1 Bolshevik** is used to describe the political system and ideas that Lenin and his supporters argued for and introduced in Russia after the Russian Revolution in 1917. EG *The Bolshevik Revolution of 1917... International Socialists maintain the old Bolshevik slogans of arming the workers.* ADJ CLASSIF : ATTRIB ↑ Communist

2 A **Bolshevik** was a person who supported Lenin and his political ideas. N COUNT ↑ Communist

Bolshevism /bɒlʃəˈvɪsm/ is the political system and ideas that Lenin and his supporters argued for and introduced in Russia. N UNCOUNT ↑ Communism

bolshy /bɒlʃiː/; also spelled **bolshie.** Someone who is **bolshy** behaves in a bad-tempered or difficult and rebellious way; an informal word used in British English. ADJ QUALIT = stroppy

bolster /bəʊlstə/, **bolsters, bolstering, bolstered.** **1** If you **bolster** someone's confidence, you give them encouragement or support so that they feel stronger or more confident. EG *They bolstered their egos by telling each other how much they were needed... This has the virtue of bolstering their sense of security.* V+O = buck up ≠ undermine

2 A **bolster** is a firm pillow shaped like a long tube, which is often put right across a bed underneath the ordinary pillows. N COUNT

bolster up. If you **bolster** something **up**, you give it support and help in order to improve it. EG *The associated industries provided the work that bolstered up the system... To bolster up their case, they quoted a speech by Ray Gun.* PHR : VB INFLECTS = back-up

bolt /bəʊlt/, **bolts, bolting, bolted.** **1** A **bolt** is a long round metal object that looks like a screw with a flat end. It screws into a nut and is used to fasten two things together. EG *The bolts are all tight enough.* ● **nuts and bolts:** see **nut.** N COUNT

2 When you **bolt** one thing to another, you fasten them firmly together, using a bolt. EG *He was held prisoner in chains that were bolted to the walls... The only furnishing was an iron cot bolted to the floor.* V-ERG : USU+A (to/on/onto)

3 A **bolt** on a door or window is a metal bar attached to it that you can slide across in order to fasten the door or window. N COUNT ↑ fastening

4 When you **bolt** a door or window, you slide the bolt across to fasten it. V+O ↑ lock

5 If a person or animal **bolts, 5.1** they suddenly start to run very fast, often as a result of being frightened. EG *He bolted blindly towards his father's fallen goat... I was terrified that the horse would bolt and I would not know how to stop it.* V : USU+A = scarper **5.2** they escape from someone or somewhere. EG *He's been warned not to try and bolt.* ● to **shut the stable door after the horse has bolted**: see **stable.** V, OR V+A

6 If someone **makes a bolt for** somewhere or **makes a bolt for it,** they make a sudden escape. EG *He panicked and tried to make a bolt for it.* PHR : VB INFLECTS = dash

7 If someone is sitting or standing **bolt upright,** they are sitting or standing very straight. PHR : USED AS AN A

8 A **bolt** of lightning is a flash of lightning that is seen as a white line in the sky, especially one that hits something on the ground. EG *Lightning bolts came crashing down all around us.* N COUNT+SUPP

9 If a piece of news comes like **a bolt from the blue,** it is completely unexpected and very surprising. PHR : USED AS AN A

10 If you say that someone has **shot** their **bolt,** you mean that they have made their last effort to achieve something, but they have failed and can now do nothing else. EG *The government had, by this time, shot its bolt: it had led the country into economic disaster.* PHR : VB INFLECTS

11 A **bolt** of cloth is a long piece of it that is wound into a roll round a piece of cardboard. N PART+N UNCOUNT

12 When vegetables such as lettuce or onions **bolt,** they grow too quickly and produce flowers and seeds, and therefore become less good to eat. V

13 If you **bolt** your food or **bolt** it **down,** you eat it so quickly that you hardly chew it or taste it. V+O ≠ peck at

bolt-hole, bolt-holes. If you have a **bolt-hole,** you have a place you can go to in order to get away from other people; used in British English. EG *He used the garden shed as a bolt hole for when the children got too noisy.* N COUNT ↑ refuge

bomb /bɒm/, **bombs, bombing, bombed.** **1** A **bomb** is a weapon which explodes and damages or destroys a large area. Some types of bomb are left in the place where they are intended to explode, and other types are dropped from an aircraft. EG *A bomb was dropped into the Thames... The building was being checked out for a bomb allegedly planted during the night.* ● See also **atom bomb, hydrogen bomb, letter-bomb, neutron bomb, stink bomb, time bomb.** N COUNT

2 People talk about **the bomb** to refer to the atom bomb when considering the possession of nuclear weapons as a political issue. N SING : *the*+N ↑ defence

3 If people **bomb** a place, they attack it by dropping bombs on it from an aircraft. EG *On 29 October they attacked Egypt, bombing Alexandria and Port Said... Walker's premises were bombed in the Second World War.* ◇ **bombing, bombings.** EG *A lot of the bombing nearby had done heavy damage... The current wave of bombings, protests, and street clashes is claiming many innocent lives.* V+O ◇ N UNCOUNT/COUNT

4 If something costs a **bomb,** it costs a great deal of money; an informal use in British English. EG *It would cost us a bomb in petrol... I made a bomb on the horses.* N SING : *a*+N ↑ lot = fortune

5 If a car, bike, etc **goes like a bomb,** it goes very fast indeed; an informal expression. EG *That car of his goes like a bomb.* PHR : VB INFLECTS = zoom

6 If an event **goes like a bomb** or **goes down a bomb,** it is extremely successful; an informal expression in British English. EG *The concert went like a bomb.* PHR : VB INFLECTS ↑ succeed

7 If you **bomb** along, you move very quickly, usually in a vehicle; an informal expression. EG *We went bombing along the motorway at 90 mph.* V+A *(along)* = speed ≠ crawl

bomb out. If a building **is bombed out** or if people in a building **are bombed out,** the building is completely destroyed by a bomb. EG *Their factories were bombed out... These were people bombed out by the Allies.* PHRASAL VB : V+O+ADV : ONLY PASS ↑ devastate

bombard /bɒmbɑːd/, **bombards, bombarding, bombarded.** **1** If people **bombard** a building or area of land, they attack it with continuous heavy V+O gunfire or bombs. EG *They bombarded the port of Juniyah.*

2 If one thing **bombards** another, it attacks this thing continuously and with a lot of force, for example by hitting it with something. EG *Electrical storms raged in the clouds, bombarding the land and the sea with lightning.* V+O : IF+PREP THEN *with* ⇑ attack

3 If you **bombard** someone with questions, criticism, etc, you keep asking them aggressive questions or saying aggressive things to them. V+O : IF+PREP THEN *with* ⇑ overwhelm

bombardment /bɒmbɒːdmə²nt/, **bombardments**. 1 A **bombardment** is a strong and continuous attack of gunfire or bombing. EG *Terrible damage was caused by heavy bombardment of guerrilla-controlled areas.* N UNCOUNT/COUNT : USU+SUPP

2 A **bombardment** of questions, criticism, etc is constant aggressive questioning or complaining from people. EG *The daily bombardment of messages and complaints is very wearing... ...the bombardment of the mass media.* N UNCOUNT/COUNT : IF+PREP THEN *of* = onslaught

bombastic /bɒmbæstɪk/. Language that is **bombastic** contains long and important sounding words, chosen in order to impress other people rather than to express meaning clearly. ADJ QUALIT = pompous

bomb disposal squad, bomb disposal squads. A **bomb disposal squad** is a group of people whose job is to deal with unexploded bombs that have been found by defusing them or blowing them up in a controlled explosion. N COUNT : IF SING VB CAN BE SING OR PL ⇑ technicians

bomber /bɒmə/, **bombers**. A **bomber** is an aircraft which drops bombs during flight from the air onto the land below. N COUNT ⇑ plane

bomber jacket, bomber jackets. A **bomber jacket** is a short jacket which is gathered into a band at the waist or hips. N COUNT

bombshell /bɒmʃɛl/, **bombshells**. A **bombshell** is a sudden piece of news which is shocking and unpleasant. EG *My sacking was a real bombshell... Then she dropped her bombshell. 'I'm pregnant.'* N COUNT : USU SING

bombsite /bɒmsaɪt/, **bombsites**. A **bombsite** is an empty area where a bomb has destroyed all the buildings. EG *The place looks like a first world war bombsite.* N COUNT ⇑ zone

bona fide /bəʊnəfaɪdi¹/, **bona fides**. **Bona fide** is an adjective, and **bona fides** is a noun. 1 Something that is **bona fide** is genuine or real. EG *All bona fide cases of hardship will receive help... There was not one bona fide trade union that agreed with its proposals.* ADJ CLASSIF ≠ bogus

2 A person's good or sincere intentions are referred to in legal language as their **bona fides**. EG *He wanted to check on my bona fides... They may have difficulty in establishing their political bona fides.* N PLURAL ⇑ sincerity

bonanza /bənænzə/, **bonanzas**. A **bonanza** is a period of very good fortune, often one during which a person suddenly becomes rich. EG *Bargain hunters enjoyed a real bonanza today... ...the bonanza mining period.* N COUNT = boom

bond /bɒnd/, **bonds, bonding, bonded**. 1 A **bond** between two or more people is 1.1 a strong feeling of friendship, love, or shared beliefs that unites them. EG *...the bond between mother and child... ...bonds of friendship.* N COUNT : IF+PREP THEN *between/of* ⇑ link 1.2 a close connection that they have with each other when they have a special agreement or are joined in a particular way. EG *Many see the ideal of marriage as a permanent bond... ...a country where family bonds are particularly strong.* N COUNT : IF+PREP THEN *between/of* = union

2 A **bond** is an investment certificate issued by a government or company which shows that you have lent them an amount of money and that they promise to pay you a fixed rate of interest. EG *Investors would refuse to buy the bonds at the low interest rate offered... The city council proposed a £75 million bond issue to finance the tax rebate.* ● See also **premium bond**. N COUNT

3 **Bonds** are 3.1 chains, ropes, etc that are used to tie down a prisoner; a rather literary use. N PLURAL 3.2 a feeling, duty, or custom that forces you to behave in a particular way. EG *Loosening the bonds of party discipline... They are only helping to tighten the bonds put upon them by an earlier generation.* N PLURAL : USU+SUPP ⇑ tie

4 If someone says that their **word is** their **bond**, they mean that they will definitely do what they have promised. PHR : VB INFLECTS

5 When two things **bond** or when you **bond** them, the two things are stuck together using adhesive. V-ERG ⇑ stick

bondage /bɒndɪdʒ/. **Bondage** is 1 the condition of belonging to someone else as their slave. EG *From birth onwards, they were kept in bondage to their masters.* N UNCOUNT = slavery 2 the practice of being tied up in order to gain sexual pleasure. N UNCOUNT

bone /bəʊn/, **bones, boning, boned**. 1 A person's or animal's **bones** are the hard parts inside their body which together form the skeleton. EG *...shoulder and hip bones... Mary broke a bone in her back... The shark's teeth sliced through the flesh and bones of its prey... Its eye sockets are completely encircled by bone... They will have to dig up the dead man's bones.* N COUNT/UNCOUNT ▸ **Bone** is also used to refer to the bone in a joint of meat or piece of fish. EG *Don't eat the bones... There wasn't much meat left on the bone by the time he had had his third helping.* ▸ N COUNT

2 If you **bone** a piece of meat or fish, you remove the bones from it before cooking it. EG *My butcher sells completely boned sirloins of Scotch beef.* V+O ⇑ prepare = fillet

3 Something that is **bone** is made of bone; used especially of tools or ornaments. EG *They fished with carefully carved bone harpoons... Keep bone or wooden handles out of water.* ADJ CLASSIF

4 If someone is **a bag of bones** or is all **skin and bone**, they are very thin; used showing disapproval in informal English. PHR : USED AS C = skinny

5 If you **work** your **fingers to the bone**, you work very hard indeed. EG *I'm working my fingers to the bone while you're out enjoying yourself.* PHR : VB INFLECTS = slave away

6 If you **feel** or **know** something **in** your **bones**, you are certain that this feeling or knowledge is right, although you cannot explain why. EG *He felt in his bones he could do it... James knew in his bones that she was the right girl for him.* PHR : VB INFLECTS ⇑ believe

7 The **bare bones** of something are the most important basic details of it. EG *You'll have to cut it down to the bare bones.* PHR : USED AS O/C

8 If you **make no bones** about doing something, especially something unpleasant or difficult, you do not hesitate or have any doubts about doing it. EG *I made no bones about criticizing the book... They made no bones about acknowledging their debt to his genius.* PHR : VB INFLECTS ≠ hesitate

9 If you say that you **have a bone to pick with** someone, you mean that you are cross with them about something and intend to discuss it with them; a fairly informal expression. PHR : VB INFLECTS

10 If you say that something that someone has said is **close to the bone**, you mean that although they are teasing you, their criticism or comment is so close to the truth that you feel hurt by it. PHR : USED AS AN A = risqué

bone china is very fine porcelain that contains powdered bone. EG *She sat sipping gin from a bone china cup.* N UNCOUNT

bone dry; also spelled with a hyphen. Something that is **bone dry** is very dry indeed. EG *A tumble drier gets things bone dry.* ADJ CLASSIF : PRED

bone meal is a substance made from dried and ground animal bones which is used as a fertilizer. N UNCOUNT

bone of contention, bones of contention. If a particular matter or issue is a **bone of contention**, people are arguing about it. N COUNT

boneshaker /bəʊnʃeɪkə/, **boneshakers**. A **boneshaker** is an old, shaky, uncomfortable vehicle; an old-fashioned word. N COUNT ⇑ wreck

bonfire /bɒnfaɪə/, **bonfires**. A **bonfire** is a fire that is made outdoors, especially in order to burn rubbish from a garden. N COUNT ⇑ fire

bonfire night, bonfire nights. **Bonfire night** is the night of November 5 when many people in Britain have bonfire parties and let off fireworks. N UNCOUNT, OR N COUNT : USU SING

bong /bɒŋ/, **bongs**. A **bong** is a long, deep sound such as the sound made by a big bell. N COUNT ⇑ crash

bongo /bɒŋgəʊ/, **bongos**. A **bongo** is a small drum that you play with your hands. N COUNT

bonhomie /bɒnəmi¹/ is warm, jolly friendliness that a person shows. EG *Their eyes were full of friendliness and bonhomie... I'm sick of her blustering bonhomie.* N UNCOUNT = camaraderie

bonkers /bɒŋkəz/. If you say that someone is **bonkers**, you mean that they are silly or mad; an informal word. EG *You must be flaming bonkers!* ADJ QUALIT : PRED = crackers

bonnet /bɒnɪt/, **bonnets**. 1 The **bonnet** of a car is the metal cover over the engine at the front of the car; used in British English. EG *I unlocked the boot and laid the tools on the bonnet.* N COUNT ⇑ covering

2 A **bonnet** is a hat that is tied under the chin; used N COUNT

especially of a pretty cap worn by a baby, or a hard hat with a big brim surrounding the face which women used to wear. • to **have a bee in** your **bonnet**: see **bee**.

bonny /bɒni¹/, **bonnier, bonniest**. Someone or something that is **bonny** is attractive and nice to look at; used especially in Scottish, Northern, or old-fashioned English. EG *She had a big bonny boy with fair hair... There's a bonny bay beyond it.* — ADJ QUALIT = lovely, attractive ≠ ugly

bonsai /bɒnsaɪ/, **bonsais**. **Bonsai** can also be used as the plural form. A **bonsai** is a tree or shrub that has been kept very small by growing it in a little pot. EG *The room was decorated with trimmed dwarf Japanese bonsai trees.* — N COUNT : USU N BEFORE N

bonus /bəʊnəs/, **bonuses**. A **bonus** is 1 an amount of money that you get as well as your usual pay or income, either as a gift or as a reward for a particular piece of work that you have done. EG *The farmer gave his men a five pound bonus each for getting the harvest in... Did you get your Christmas bonus?* — N COUNT : USU SING ⇑ payment = extra 2 something good that you do not expect to get in addition to something else, although you are very glad if you do get it. EG *If it also works, that is an added bonus.* — N COUNT = plus

bon voyage /bɒnvɔɪɑːʒ/. You say **bon voyage** to someone who is going on a journey, as a way of saying goodbye and wishing them good luck. EG *Have a nice trip! Bon voyage!* — CONVENTION

bony /bəʊni¹/, **bonier, boniest**. 1 A person or part of their body that is **bony** is very thin, with very little flesh covering the bones. EG *He was tall, thin, and bony... He sat in a high armchair, his long bony fingers clasping the arms.* — ADJ QUALIT = skinny ≠ fat

2 A **bony** part of an animal's body is made mainly of bone. EG *The animal possessed bony jaws lined with teeth.* — ADJ CLASSIF : ATTRIB

3 If a fish that you eat is **bony**, it has a lot of bones in it. EG *I wish kippers weren't so bony.* — ADJ QUALIT ≠ filleted

boo /buː/, **boos, booing, booed**. 1 If you **boo** someone who is giving a performance or a speech, you shout 'boo' or make other loud sounds to indicate that you do not like them or their performance, or that you disagree with what they are saying. EG *By now most of the audience was booing... When he tried to speak he was loudly booed... The children hiss and boo at the baddy... He was booed off the stage.* — V OR V+O = hoot ≠ cheer ▸ used as a noun. EG *They were greeted with loud boos.* — ▸ N COUNT = hooray

2 You say **boo** loudly and suddenly when you want to surprise someone who does not know that you are near them. — EXCLAM • If you say that someone **wouldn't** or **couldn't say boo to a goose**, you mean that they are very timid and shy; an informal expression. — • PHR : VB INFLECTS ⇑ be timid

boob /buːb/, **boobs, boobing, boobed**; an informal word. 1 A **boob** is a stupid mistake; used in British English. EG *Inviting her mother was a bit of a boob, wasn't it?* — N COUNT = blunder ▸ used as a verb. EG *I've boobed again!* — ▸ V = blunder

2 A woman's **boobs** are her breasts; a rude and offensive use. — N COUNT : USU PL

3 A **boob** or a **booby** is a person who is silly or stupid; an old-fashioned use. EG *...a gangling young booby in steel spectacles.* — N COUNT : ALSO VOC ⇑ fool = twit

booby prize, booby prizes. A **booby prize** is a prize that is given to the person who comes last in a competition. EG *Looks like you get the booby prize.* — N COUNT

booby-trap, booby-traps, booby-trapping, booby-trapped; as a noun, also spelled without a hyphen. 1 A **booby-trap** is 1.1 a bomb which is hidden or disguised and which explodes when it is touched, so that it catches people who don't know that it is there. EG *They searched the ground for booby traps... Two policemen were seriously injured by a booby-trap bomb.* — N COUNT = mine 1.2 something that someone arranges in order to surprise another person and perhaps hurt them slightly, for example a bucket of water that is balanced over a door and falls on them when they open the door. — N COUNT = joke

2 If something **is booby-trapped**, a booby-trap is placed in it or on it. EG *How do you know it's not booby-trapped?* — V+O : USU PASS

boogie /buːgi¹/, **boogies, boogieing, boogied**. When you **boogie**, you dance to fast pop music; an informal word. EG *We all boogied, either as couples or singly.* — V

boohoo /buːhuː/, **boohoos, boohooing, boohooed**. 1 If someone **boohoos**, they cry noisily like a child; used especially when the crying is not serious or not necessary. EG *Don't just sit there boohooing like a baby.* — V

2 **Boohoo** is used in written English to represent the sound of noisy, childish crying. EG *'I ain't.'–'You are.'–'Boohoo.'* — = sob sob

book /bʊk/, **books, booking, booked**. 1 A **book** is 1.1 a number of pieces of paper, either blank or with words printed on, which have been fastened together along one edge and fixed inside a cover of stronger paper or cardboard. EG *She opened the book and put the envelope between the pages... ...a little brown book... Just sign your name in the book each time you use the machine... She put the phone on the table, found the number in the book and dialled it.* — N COUNT ⇑ object 1.2 the story, the ideas, or the information written in a book. EG *I'm reading a really good book at the moment... I brought him a copy of a book by John Fisher about Emily Hobhouse... ...a book on hypnotism... ...Penelope Leach in her book, 'Babyhood', says... ...a cookery book... ...a splendid book which examines the realities of marriage.* — N COUNT ⇑ work 1.3 one of the large sections into which a very long written work such as the Bible is divided. EG *...the book of Isaiah... ...the first two books of Gulliver's Travels.* — N COUNT : IF+PREP THEN *of* = volume • See also **cheque book, exercise book, log book, paying-in book, pension book, phone book, phrase book, statute book**.

2 A **book** of stamps, matches, tickets, etc is a small number of these objects that have been fastened together between covers in order to make them convenient to use and carry. EG *A book of first-class stamps, please.* — N COUNT+*of* ⇑ group

3 When you **book** a hotel room, a ticket, an entertainer, etc, you arrange with someone to have or use the thing or the person's services at a particular time in the future; used in British English. EG *I'd like to book a table for four for tomorrow night... Go to the Youth Hostel and book yourself a place for the night... He booked a ticket to Washington... He had booked Madison Square Park for another firework display... Before leaving the airport he booked himself on the next afternoon's flight... Book early to avoid disappointment.* • See also **booking**. — V, V+O, OR V+O (NG/REFL)+O ≠ cancel

4 **booked up, fully booked up, fully booked**. 4.1 If a hotel, restaurant, or theatre is **booked up**, **fully booked up**, or **fully booked**, it has no rooms, tables, or tickets available for a particular time or date because they are all booked. EG *We couldn't get a room at the first hotel; they were fully booked... Are they booked up?* — PHR : USED AS C = full ≠ empty 4.2 If someone is **booked up, fully booked up**, or **fully booked**, they have made so many arrangements to do something such as entertain or speak in public that they are unable to accept any more bookings. EG *We can't do any more concerts this year, we are fully booked up.* — PHR : USED AS C ⇑ busy ≠ available 4.3 If someone is **booked up** at a particular time, they have arranged to do something else at that time. EG *I'm booked up all next week.* — PHR : USED AS C, USU+A = busy ≠ free

5 When a police officer **books** someone, he or she officially records their name and the offence that they may be charged with; an informal use. EG *I was booked for speeding yesterday.* — V+O : IF+PREP THEN *for* = charge, do

6 When a football referee **books** a player who has seriously broken the rules of the game, he or she officially records the player's name. If players are booked twice during a game, they are sent off the field. EG *He was booked for punching another player.* — V+O : IF+PREP THEN *for* ⇑ record

7 A company's or organization's **books** are its written records of money that has been spent and earned or of the names of people who belong to it. EG *He's going to help me go over my books. He has a better head for figures than I have... His name is no longer on our books.* — N PLURAL : *the*/POSS+N

8 **Book** is used in the following expressions referring to betting. 8.1 If you **open** or **start a book** on something, you start taking bets on it. EG *They've opened a book on the date of the next General Election.* — PHR : VB INFLECTS ⇑ take bets 8.2 If you **keep a book** on something, you are willing to accept bets on it. EG *They're keeping a book on whether it will be a white Christmas.* — PHR : VB INFLECTS = take bets

9 The word **book** is also used in the following expressions. 9.1 If you **throw the book at** someone, you accuse them of every offence that is possible in a particular situation, or give them the greatest punishment that you are allowed to. EG *It'll serve him right if they throw the book at him.* — PHR : VB INFLECTS 9.2 If a — PHR : VB

particular subject **is a closed book to** you, you do not know anything about it. EG *It's no good talking to me about physics, it's a closed book to me.* **9.3** If you **bring** someone **to book,** you punish them for an offence or make them explain their behaviour officially, especially when it has taken a long time to catch them or to prove that they committed the offence. EG *He was eventually brought to book for his treachery.* **9.4** If you are **in** someone's **bad books** or **black books,** they are annoyed with you. If you are **in** their **good books,** they are pleased with you. EG *I'm in his bad books at the moment.* **9.5 In my book** means in my opinion and according to my beliefs and standards. EG *He likes football and in my book that makes him OK.* • **to take a leaf out of** someone's **book**: see **leaf**. INFLECTS / PHR : VB INFLECTS : IF + PREP THEN *for* = call to account / PHR : USU POSS + N / PHR : USED AS AN A = to me

book in; used in British English. 1 When you **book in,** or when you **book into** a hotel, you officially announce your arrival and your acceptance of accommodation, usually by signing your name in a register. EG *It was too late to go shopping, so he booked in at the Hotel d'Angleterre.* PHRASAL VB : V + ADV = check in, register at

2 When you **book** someone **in** at a hotel or **book** them **into** a hotel, you arrange for a room to be reserved for them there on a particular date. EG *I had booked us in at a hotel in Torquay... I have taken the liberty of booking you into adjoining rooms.* PHRASAL VB : V + O + ADV

bookable /bʊkəbəºl/. A **bookable** theatre seat, plane ticket, etc can be booked in advance. ADJ CLASSIF

bookbinding /bʊkbaɪndɪŋ/; also spelled with a hyphen. **Bookbinding** is the work of fastening books together and putting covers on them. N UNCOUNT = binding

bookcase /bʊkkeɪs/, **bookcases**. A **bookcase** is a piece of furniture containing shelves on which books are kept. N COUNT = bookshelf, bookshelves

book club, book clubs. A **book club** is an organization that offers books at reduced prices to its members. N COUNT

bookend /bʊkɛnd/, **bookends**; also spelled with a hyphen. **Bookends** are a pair of supports which are used to hold a row of books in an upright position by placing one at each end of the row. N COUNT : USU PL ⇑ support

bookie /bʊki¹/, **bookies**. A **bookie** is a bookmaker; an informal word used in British English. N COUNT

booking /bʊkɪŋ/, **bookings**. A **booking** is the arrangement that you make when you book something such as a theatre seat, a hotel room, or an entertainer. EG *The manager came in to find out who had made the booking... If you can just sign the booking form there for me please... We've got a booking on 19th May to dance at Knowle village fair.* N COUNT : USU + SUPP = reservation

booking office, booking offices. A **booking office** is a room where tickets are sold and booked, especially in a theatre or a railway station. N COUNT = box office

bookish /bʊkɪʃ/. Someone who is **bookish** enjoys studying and reading serious books; often used showing disapproval. EG *He was bookish, bespectacled, nonathletic, and not her type at all.* ADJ QUALIT = studious

bookkeeping /bʊkki:pɪŋ/; also spelled with a hyphen. **Bookkeeping** is the job or activity of keeping an accurate record of the sums of money that are spent and received by a business or other organization. EG *...evening classes in bookkeeping.* N UNCOUNT ⇑ accounting
◊ **bookkeeper, bookkeepers**. ◊ N COUNT

book learning ; also spelled with a hyphen. **Book learning** is learning by studying books rather than by experiencing things; a fairly informal expression. EG *He failed in his university exams because he hated book learning.* N UNCOUNT ⇑ study

booklet /bʊkle¹t/, **booklets**. A **booklet** is a book that has a small number of pages and a paper cover and gives information about something. N COUNT = pamphlet

bookmaker /bʊkmeɪkə/, **bookmakers**. A **bookmaker** is a person whose job involves taking people's money when they bet, for example on whether a horse will win a race, and paying money out if they win the bet. N COUNT = turf accountant

bookmark /bʊkmɑ:k/, **bookmarks**; also spelled with a hyphen. A **bookmark** is a narrow piece of card, leather, or plastic that you put between the pages of a book so that you can find a particular page again easily. N COUNT ⇑ marker

book plate, book plates; also spelled with a hyphen. A **book plate** is a piece of decorated paper which is stuck in the front of a book and on which the owner's name is printed or written. N COUNT ⇑ label

bookseller /bʊksɛlə/, **booksellers**. A **bookseller** is a person who sells books. N COUNT ⇑ shopkeeper

bookshelf /bʊkʃɛlf/, **bookshelves**. 1 A **bookshelf** is a shelf on which you keep books. N COUNT
2 Some people use **bookshelf** or **bookshelves** to refer to a bookcase. N COUNT

bookshop /bʊkʃɒp/, **bookshops**. A **bookshop** is a shop where books are sold; used especially in British English. N COUNT ⇑ shop

bookstall /bʊkstɔ:l/, **bookstalls**. A **bookstall** is a very small shop with an open front, or sometimes just a table, for example at a railway station, where books and magazines are sold. N COUNT ⇑ stall

bookstore /bʊkstɔ:/, **bookstores**. A **bookstore** is a bookshop; used especially in American English. N COUNT

book token, book tokens. A **book token** is a small piece of paper or card that you can buy and then use instead of money to buy books. EG *I've won a £10 book token!* N COUNT

bookworm /bʊkwɜ:m/, **bookworms**. A **bookworm** is 1 a person who is very fond of reading. 2 an insect that damages books by eating the binding and the paste that holds them together. N COUNT / N COUNT

boom /bu:m/, **booms, booming, boomed**. 1 A **boom** is a fast increase or development in something, often in the popularity or success of something, especially one that results in a lot of money being made. EG *We must take advantage of the boom in world shipping... ...the population boom... Computing is a boom industry... Britain prospered in the boom days of the late fifties and early sixties.* N COUNT : USU SING, IF + PREP THEN *in* = growth ≠ slump
▸ used as a verb. EG *The gardening industry is booming... Angling will continue to boom as a sport.* ▸ V ⇑ flourish

2 When something such as a big drum, a cannon, or someone's voice **booms**, it makes a loud, deep, echoing sound. EG *The cannon boomed again... 'Nonsense!' boomed Mrs Pringle.* ◊ **booming**. EG *He had a booming voice and the build of a rugby player.* V OR V + O/QUOTE / ◊ ADJ CLASSIF : USU ATTRIB
▸ used as a noun. EG *The boom of the cannon echoed along the street... 'Boom!' went the drum.* • See also **sonic boom**. ▸ N COUNT ⇑ noise

3 The **boom** of a boat is a long pole that is attached to the mast at one end and is also attached to the bottom of the main sail. N COUNT : USU *the* + N = beam

4 A **boom** is also a long pole which has something, usually a microphone, on the end and which can be moved around. N COUNT

boom out. When someone **booms out** something or when their voice **booms out,** they speak in a very loud, deep voice. EG *He boomed out: 'Good evening ladies and gentlemen!'... Hogan's voice boomed out of the telephone receiver.* PHRASAL VB : V + ADV, USU + O/QUOTE/A = blast out

boomerang /bu:məræŋ/, **boomerangs, boomeranging, boomeranged**. 1 A **boomerang** is a curved piece of wood which, when thrown in the right way, can be made to return to the person who throws it. Boomerangs were first used by Australian natives as weapons. N COUNT

2 If a plan **boomerangs,** its result is not the one that was intended and is harmful to the person who made the plan. EG *If one of these children dies this whole thing's liable to boomerang on us.* V = backfire

boom town, boom towns; also spelled with a hyphen. A **boom town** is a town which has become very rich and full of people, usually because industry or business has developed there. EG *This used to be a boom town until they closed down all the car factories.* N COUNT

boon /bu:n/, **boons**. Something that is a **boon** makes life better or easier for you. EG *The bus service is a great boon to old people.* N COUNT : USU SING, IF + PREP THEN *to* = blessing

boon companion, boon companions. Someone's **boon companion** is their close friend, especially one who they drink and have a good time with; a literary expression. N COUNT = best mate

boor /bʊə/, **boors**. A **boor** is someone who behaves in a rough, impolite, clumsy way; an old-fashioned word. N COUNT = brute

boorish /bʊərɪʃ/. Someone who is **boorish** behaves in a rough, impolite, clumsy way. EG *They were so boorish, so insensitive.* ADJ QUALIT = coarse ≠ genteel

boost /bu:st/, **boosts, boosting, boosted**. 1 If one thing **boosts** another, it causes it to increase and improve by a large amount. EG *This new technology will boost food production... ...an auxiliary motor capable of boosting our speed to fifteen knots.* V + O ⇑ raise
▸ used as a noun. EG *This will be a great boost to the* ▸ N COUNT : USU SING

economy... The Government released figures showing a sharp 8.5 per cent boost in exports.

2 If someone or something **boosts** your confidence, morale, etc, they improve your confidence or morale, for example by encouraging you. EG *There is nothing like winning to boost the morale of players.* ▸ used as a noun. EG *...another boost to your confidence.* V+O = bolster ▸ N COUNT : USU SING

3 If you **boost** someone or something that they have done, you praise them or publicize them in order to make them more popular. EG *Her books have been boosted in the Sunday Observer recently.* ▸ used as a noun. EG *His play was given a boost in last week's TV review.* V+O ⇑ promote = plug, push ▸ N COUNT : USU SING = plug

booster /buːstə/, **boosters**. A **booster** is a small injection that you have some time after a larger one, in order to make sure that the first injection will remain effective. N COUNT = jab

boot /buːt/, **boots, booting, booted**. 1 A **boot** is 1.1 a shoe that covers your whole foot and the lower part of your leg. EG *I put on my fur coat and boots.* 1.2 a strong, heavy shoe which covers your ankle and has a thick sole, worn for example by climbers and walkers. EG *I haven't got any climbing boots... ...hobnail boots.* ● **wellington boot**: see **wellington**. N COUNT : USU PL / N COUNT : USU PL

2 If you **boot** something, you kick it hard; an informal use. EG *She booted the ball back onto the pitch.* ▸ used as a noun. EG *What he needs is a good boot up the backside!* V+O : USU+A ▸ N SING : a+N+SUPP

3 The **boot** of a car is the space at the back or front of the car, covered by a lid, in which you carry things such as luggage, shopping, or tools; used in British English. EG *Is the boot open?* N COUNT : USU the+N IN SING = trunk

4 If you say that someone is **licking** a person's **boots**, you mean that they are constantly trying to please and flatter the person; used showing disapproval. PHR : VB INFLECTS

5 If you say that someone is **getting too big for** their **boots**, you are criticizing them for becoming too proud and too pleased with themselves; an informal expression. PHR : VB INFLECTS = conceited

6 If you say that **the boot is on the other foot**, you mean that someone now has power over a person who used to be more powerful than they were. PHR : VB INFLECTS

7 If someone **gets the boot** or if they **are given the boot**, they are dismissed from their job; an informal expression. PHR : VB INFLECTS

8 If someone **puts the boot in**, 8.1 they say something cruel to a person who is already feeling weak or upset; an informal expression. EG *You didn't have to put the boot in like that, did you?* 8.2 they kick a person repeatedly and viciously, especially when the person is already lying on the ground; an informal expression. PHR : VB INFLECTS ⇑ attack / PHR : VB INFLECTS

9 You say **to boot** when you have just added a further comment to something that you have said; an old-fashioned or literary expression. EG *She was brilliant, rich, and beautiful to boot.* PHR : USED AS AN A ⇑ also = too

boot out. If someone **is booted out** of a job, an organization, or a place, they are expelled from it; an informal expression. EG *The member who made that speech was booted out by Conservative Party leaders.* PHRASAL VB : V+O+ADV ⇑ expel = kick out

bootee /buːtiː/, **bootees**. A **bootee** is a baby's soft boot that covers the ankle and is usually made out of wool. N COUNT ⇑ boot

booth /buːð/, **booths**. A **booth** is 1 a small area that has been separated from a larger public area by screens or narrow walls where, for example, people can make a telephone call or vote in private. EG *He went into the booth and dialled the number.* 2 a small tent or stall, usually at a fair, which offers some form of entertainment or goods for sale. N COUNT ⇑ enclosure = box / N COUNT

bootlace /buːtleɪs/, **bootlaces**. A **bootlace** is a long narrow cord that is used to fasten a boot. N COUNT

bootleg /buːtlɛg/. **Bootleg** alcohol, fuel, etc is made or transported illegally. EG *...a sixteen year old carrying a hip flask of bootleg liquor.* ADJ CLASSIF : USU ATTRIB ⇑ illegal

bootlegger /buːtlɛgə/, **bootleggers**. A **bootlegger** is someone who makes or transports things illegally, especially alcohol. EG *...a group of Italian bootleggers who smuggled alcohol and whiskey in from the States.* N COUNT = trafficker

bootstraps /buːtstræps/. If you **pull** yourself **up by** your **bootstraps**, you achieve something with very little help or support from anyone else. PHR : VB INFLECTS ⇑ succeed

booty /buːti¹/. **Booty** is a collection of valuable things, especially the things that soldiers take away from their enemies after they have won a battle. EG *The victorious Mandinka forces were laden with enemy booty.* N UNCOUNT ⇑ goods

booze /buːz/, **boozes, boozing, boozed**; an informal word. 1 **Booze** is alcoholic drink, especially drink that is not of a high quality. EG *You could smell the booze on his breath a mile off.* N UNCOUNT = alcohol

2 When people **booze**, they drink a lot of alcohol. EG *All these lads do is loll about and booze.* V

3 If someone is **on the booze**, they are drinking a lot of alcohol. PHR : USED AS AN A

boozer /buːzə/, **boozers**; an informal word. 1 The **boozer** is a pub, especially one near to where you live or work; used in British English. EG *We're off to the boozer. Coming?* N COUNT

2 A **boozer** is a person who drinks a lot of alcohol. EG *He was a notorious boozer.* N COUNT ⇑ drinker

booze-up, booze-ups. A **booze-up** is a party or similar occasion in which people drink a lot of alcohol, usually in order to get very drunk together; an informal word. N COUNT ⇑ session = bender

boozy /buːzi¹/. A **boozy** person drinks a lot of alcoholic drink; an informal word. EG *He doesn't want Gertrude to meet his boozy drinking companions.* ▸ used of people's behaviour. EG *...the men's thick boozy singing.* ADJ CLASSIF : USU ATTRIB ▸ ⇑ drunken

bop /bɒp/, **bops, bopping, bopped**; an informal word. 1 A **bop** is a dance. EG *Shall we go and have a bop?* ▸ used as a verb. EG *There we were, bopping away till the small hours.* N COUNT ▸ V : USU+A

2 If someone **bops** you, they hit you. EG *This man got bopped in the face.* ▸ used as a noun. EG *...a bop on the nose.* V+O ▸ N COUNT : USU +SUPP

borax /bɔːrə³ks/ is a white powder used, for example, in the making of glass and as a cleaning chemical. N UNCOUNT ⇑ mineral

bordello /bɔːdɛləʊ/, **bordellos**. A **bordello** is a brothel; a literary word. N COUNT

border /bɔːdə/, **borders, bordering, bordered**. 1 The **border** between two countries or other political regions is the dividing line between them, and also sometimes the land close to this line. EG *He lives in the French Alps near the Swiss border... They crossed the border into Mexico... ...a tiny principality near the northern borders of the Punjab.* ▸ The **Border** is sometimes used to refer to a particular border, for example the border between England and Scotland, or between Northern and Southern Ireland. EG *This is true for people north of the Border.* N COUNT : USU+SUPP ⇑ boundary = frontier ▸ N SING : the+N

2 A country that **borders** another country or **borders on** it is next to that country and shares a border with it. EG *Soviet territory facing the West borders on Poland, Czechoslovakia, and Hungary.* V+O OR V+A (on) ⇑ neighbour

3 A **border** is also 3.1 a strip or band around or along the edge of something, often put there for decoration. EG *It's painted in white with a gold border.* 3.2 a narrow strip of ground that is planted with plants and flowers, usually along the edge of a lawn. EG *...unkempt flower borders.* N COUNT ⇑ edging / N COUNT ⇑ edging = bed

4 The **border** of something such as a field, lake, or area of land is the outer edge or part of it. EG *...a flower found typically in field borders and the edges of woods.* N COUNT : WITH POSS

5 If something **borders** something else, it forms a border along the edge of it. EG *Huge elm trees bordered the road... ...the properties bordering the river. ...a path bordered with flowers.* V+O = flank

border on. When you say that something **borders on** a particular state or condition, you mean that it is almost in that state or condition. EG *I was in a state of excitement bordering on insanity... Their rough treatment of each other bordered on brutality.* PHRASAL VB : V+PREP = verge on, approach

borderland /bɔːdəlænd/. The **borderland** between two things is an area which contains features from both of these things so that it is not possible to say that it belongs to one or the other. EG *...that perplexing borderland between working-class anarchism and middle-class conformity.* N SING WITH DET : IF+PREP THEN *between*

borderline /bɔːdəlaɪn/. 1 Something that is **borderline** is very nearly unacceptable as a member of a class or group because it is doubtful whether it has the features or qualities necessary to be included in that group. EG *He is a borderline candidate for a special school. ...borderline cases.* ADJ CLASSIF

2 The **borderline** between two conditions, qualities, etc is the division between them. EG *...this narrow* N SING WITH DET : IF+PREP

borderline between laughter and tears... He is close to the borderline of consciousness.
THEN between/of

bore /bɔ:/, **bores, boring, bored.** 1 If someone or something **bores** you, they make you lose interest and feel tired and often impatient because you find them dull and uninteresting. EG *Most of the book had bored him, with the exception of one chapter... I won't bore you with the details... To tell you the truth, birds bore me too.*
V+O : IF+PREP THEN with ⇑ tire

● If something **bores** you **to tears, bores** you **to death,** or **bores** you **stiff,** it bores you very much indeed; an informal expression. EG *I like acting but the film world bores me to tears... The subject bores them stiff.*
● PHR : VB INFLECTS ⇑ bore

2 You describe someone as a **bore** when you think that they talk in a very uninteresting way and often too much. EG *Steve is the most frightful bore.*
N COUNT ⇑ person

3 You describe a situation as a **bore** when you find it annoying or a nuisance. EG *I say, what a bore. I was just getting the hang of it and it's time to stop!*
N SING : a+N = drag

4 If you **bore** a hole in something, you make a deep round hole in it using a special tool such as a drill. EG *They were shown how to bore rivet holes in the sides of ships... The engineer's job was to bore deep concrete-lined wells through to the water... There was no water so we had to bore.*
V, OR V+O : USU +A ⇑ cut = drill

5 If someone's eyes **bore** into you, they are staring intensely at you. EG *Vorster's eyes bored into me. He said 'We are at war. You cannot afford to refuse.'*
V+A (into) ⇑ stare = burn

6 A **bore** is also a very large wave that moves quickly up certain river estuaries from the sea at particular times of the year as a result of unusual tides. EG *...the Severn bore.*
N COUNT : USU MOD+N

7 **Bore** is also the past tense of **bear**.

8 See also **bored, boring**.

-bore combines with a number to indicate the diameter of the barrel of a gun. EG *...a twelve-bore shotgun.*
COMB : FORMS ADJ CLASSIFS ⇑ size

bored /bɔ:d/. When you are **bored**, you feel tired and often impatient because you have lost interest in something or because you have nothing to do. EG *I'm bored. I don't have anything to do... The syllabus is enormously varied, there is no chance of getting bored... ...the bored gaze of the successful film star.*
ADJ QUALIT : IF+ PREP THEN with = fed up ≠ enthusiastic

boredom /bɔ:dəᵊm/ is 1 the state that someone has of being bored. EG *Many of the audience walked out through sheer boredom.* 2 the quality that something has of being boring. EG *She seems so depressed by the monotony and boredom of her city life.*
N UNCOUNT : IF+ PREP THEN with; N UNCOUNT

borehole /bɔ:həʊl/, **boreholes**. A **borehole** is a deep round hole made by a special tool or machine, especially one that is made in the ground when searching for oil or water.
N COUNT ⇑ hole

boring /bɔ:rᵊɪŋ/. Something that is **boring** 1 is so dull and uninteresting that it makes people feel tired and often impatient. EG *Was it a boring journey?... ...all those boring evenings with people I never wanted to see... Are all your meetings this boring?* 2 has been made in an uninteresting and unimaginative way. EG *The gardens were a bit boring, rather municipal... ...faded towels and boring bedspreads... Their houses were so boring they were glad to get to the pub.*
ADJ QUALIT = tedious ≠ interesting; ADJ QUALIT ⇑ plain = pedestrian ≠ appealing

born /bɔ:n/. 1 When a baby **is born**, it comes out of its mother's body at the beginning of its life; also used of birds and other animals when they come out of their eggs. EG *Morris had been born and brought up in New York... Many husbands participate actively in the delivery and see the baby being born... Willie was born in 1863... ...a ten-week-old puppy that was born on April twenty-sixth... They had been born into a world of blows and rows and partings.*
V+O : ONLY PASS, NO IMPER

2 If you say that a child **is born to** someone, you are referring in a rather formal way to the birth of the child and indicating who its parents are. EG *She adopted a child that had been born to Miss Kathleen Fenn... A baby has been born to them.*
PHR : AUX INFLECTS

3 If you say that a child **is born of** a particular person, you are saying in a formal way that that person is one of the child's parents. EG *He was born in Cuba, of an American father and a Cuban mother... Some of the children were born of slave mothers.*
PHR : AUX INFLECTS

4 If you say that a child **is born of** particular circumstances, you mean that the child is born as a result of these circumstances. EG *Most of these children were born of adultery or of prostitution.*
PHR : AUX INFLECTS

5 If you say that you **wish** you **had never been born,** you are emphasizing how very unhappy and perhaps ashamed or sorry you are.
PHR : FIRST VB INFLECTS

6 If someone **is born** with a particular characteristic, illness, or handicap, for example if they **are born** blind or handicapped, they have that characteristic, illness, or handicap from the time that they are born. EG *It is a tragedy when a baby is born abnormal... He was born a fighting handful–cheeky and self-centred... Different children are born with quite different temperaments... Their son was born with spina bifida.*
V+O+A (with), OR V+O+C : ONLY PASS, NO CONT

7 Someone who **is born** illegitimate, an aristocrat, etc has the position or social status mentioned from birth because of the position or status of their parents. EG *...adopted girls who were born illegitimate... Sita was born an Italian countess... You have to be born into the right family to be successful.*
V+O+C : ONLY PASS, NO CONT

8 If you **were born**, for example, Margaret Eadie Holmes, this is the name that you were given at birth. EG *She wasn't born Madge Henrietta.*
V+O+C (N PROPER) : ONLY PASS, NO CONT

9 If you are, for example, a **born** swimmer or a **born** musician, or if you were **born** to do a particular activity, you are so good at this activity and find it so natural and easy to do that it seems as if your ability to do it was already present when you were born. EG *You're a born lecturer... He was a born cook.*
ADJ CLASSIF : USU ATTRIB, OR IF PRED + to-INF ⇑ successful = instinctive

10 When an idea, organization, etc **is born**, it comes into existence. EG *At that moment the concept of the computer was born... In Sicily the Mafia was born.*
V+O : ONLY PASS ⇑ start

11 If something **is born of** a particular activity or emotion, it exists as a result of this activity or emotion. EG *He did the job with the speed and expertise born of a lifetime of practice... Brody was growing angry–an anger born of frustration and humiliation.*
PHR

12 If you say to someone **'I wasn't born yesterday'**, you mean that you have not been deceived by something and that you are not as stupid as they may have suggested; a fairly informal expression. EG *I know what's going on, Jane, I wasn't born yesterday!*
PHR

13 See also **first-born**. ● **born with a silver spoon in** your **mouth**: see **spoon**.

-born combines with the name of a place to indicate that a person was born in that place. EG *They have appointed South African-born Gus Calderwood to captain the British team.*
COMB : FORMS ADJ CLASSIFS

borne /bɔ:n/. 1 **Borne** is the past participle of **bear**.

2 If it **is borne in upon** or **on** someone that something is the case, they are made to realise it; a formal expression. EG *It is borne in upon him that he is being entrusted with a great responsibility.*
PHR : VB INFLECTS

-borne combines with nouns to form adjectives that describe the method or means by which something is moved or transported. EG *...sea-borne trade and supplies.*
COMB : FORMS ADJ CLASSIFS ⇑ carried

borough /bʌrə/, **boroughs**. A **borough** is a town, or a district within a large town, which has its own council. EG *She is the leader of the council in the London Borough of Lewisham... ...families from all over the borough... ...a borough councillor.*
N COUNT : ALSO IN NAMES AFTER N

borrow /bɒrəʊ/, **borrows, borrowing, borrowed.** 1 If you **borrow** something that belongs to someone else, they allow you to have it or use it for a period of time. EG *Could I borrow your car?... Could I borrow this off you for a while?*
V+O : IF+PREP THEN from/off

2 If you **borrow** money from someone or from a bank, they give it to you and you agree to pay it back at some time in the future. EG *He always borrows money from his friends and never pays it back... I need to borrow five thousand pounds.*
V OR V+O : IF+ PREP THEN from/off ⇑ take

3 If you **borrow** a book from a library, you take it away with you for a fixed period of time.
V+O = take out

4 If you **borrow** something such as an idea or a word from another person, their work, or another language, you take it and use it in your own work or language. EG *Most of her ideas were borrowed from other sources... Lots of these words are borrowed from other languages.*
V+O+A (from) = pirate

5 Someone who is **living** or **existing on borrowed time** has continued to live or do something for longer than expected, and is likely to die or be stopped from doing it very soon.
PHR : VB INFLECTS

borrower /bɒrəʊə/, **borrowers**. A **borrower** is a person or institution that borrows money. EG *They increased the surcharge for big borrowers.*
N COUNT

borrowing /bɒrəuɪŋ/, **borrowings.** 1 **Borrowing** is the action of borrowing money. EG *There's a need to keep down public borrowing... Lowering interest rates will make borrowing cheaper.* N UNCOUNT

2 A **borrowing** is an idea or word that you take from another person, their work, or another language, and use in your own work or language. EG *There are considerable borrowings from other languages.* N COUNT

borstal /bɔːstəˀl/, **borstals.** A **borstal** is a prison in Britain for young criminals, usually teenagers, who are not old enough to be sent to ordinary prisons. EG *Most of the boys in borstals are from bad backgrounds... He was sent to borstal.* N COUNT, OR PREP+N

bosh /bɒʃ/. If you say that something someone has said is **bosh**, you mean that you think that it is foolish or untrue; an informal old-fashioned word. EG *'I won't risk spoiling our relationship.'–'Oh bosh.'* EXCLAM ⇑ nonsense = rot

bosom /bʊzəˀm/, **bosoms**; a formal, old-fashioned, or literary word. 1 A woman's **bosom** or **bosoms** are her breasts. EG *She had a very large bosom... ...bare bosoms.* N COUNT

2 A person's **bosom**, especially a woman's, is the top front part of their body. EG *...hugging the cat to her bosom.* N COUNT : POSS+N ⇑ chest

3 The **bosom** of a dress, blouse, etc is the part of it that covers a woman's bosom. EG *She drew the bosom of the dress together.* N SING : *the*+N+*of* = front

4 If someone is in the **bosom** of their family or of a community, institution, etc, they are among people who love, accept, and protect them. EG *...an American torn from the bosom of his own family... ...acceptance into the bosom of the Establishment.* N SING : *the*+N+*of* ⇑ centre = heart ● If you **take** someone **to** your **bosom,** you start to treat them with affection. ● PHR : VB INFLECTS

5 You refer to someone's **bosom** when you are referring to their emotions and thoughts. EG *...some dark, sinful passion you're nursing in your bosom... These philosophies found no place in the bosom of the Peruvian.* N COUNT : WITH POSS = soul, heart

6 A **bosom** friend is a very close and dear friend. EG *...the son of her bosom friend Klara.* N BEFORE N

bosomy /bʊzəmiˡ/. A **bosomy** woman has large breasts. ADJ QUALIT = busty

boss /bɒs/, **bosses, bossing, bossed.** 1 Your **boss** is the person who is in charge of the organization or department where you work and who tells you what work to do. EG *I met his boss at a dinner party... The crisis occurred while the boss was away... The workers here can elect and control their bosses.* N COUNT ⇑ superior ● If you **are** your **own boss,** you work for yourself or make your own decisions and do not have to ask other people for work or for permission to do something. EG *I'm my own boss now, thank God.* ● PHR : VB INFLECTS

2 If you are the **boss** in a group or relationship, you are the person who makes all the decisions and gives orders to the other person or people in the group or relationship; an informal use. EG *You're not the boss around here.* N COUNT : USU *the*+N ⇑ leader = head

3 If someone **bosses** you, **bosses** you **around,** or **bosses** you **about,** they keep telling you what to do as if they had authority over you; used showing disapproval. EG *They've bossed us around enough... Some people like to be bossed and bullied.* V+O : IF+ADV, THEN *around/ about* = order around

4 A **boss** is also a round, ornamental raised section on something such as the ceiling of an old building or a shield. EG *...decorative bosses.* N COUNT ⇑ decoration = knob

boss-eyed. If someone is **boss-eyed**, they have eyes that look inward towards each other; an informal word. ADJ QUALIT = cross-eyed

bossy /bɒsiˡ/, **bossier, bossiest**. Someone who is **bossy** enjoys telling other people what to do, especially when they do not want or need to be told what to do. EG *She was really quite bossy.* ◊ **bossiness**. EG *His bossiness as a husband didn't worry her unduly.* ADJ QUALIT ⇑ dominating = overbearing ◊ N UNCOUNT

bosun /bəʊsəˀn/, **bosuns**; also spelled **bo's'n** and **bo'sun.** The **bosun** on a ship is the officer whose job it is to look after the maintenance of the ship and its equipment. N COUNT

botanic /bəˀtænɪk/ means the same as botanical.

botanical /bəˀtænɪkəˀl/ is used to describe things relating to the scientific study of plants. EG *...Victorian botanical drawings... Have you seen the exhibition at the botanical gardens?* ADJ CLASSIF : ATTRIB

botanist /bɒtənɪst/, **botanists**. A **botanist** is a student or scientist who studies plants. EG *...a flower so rare that few living botanists had ever seen it.* N COUNT

botany /bɒtəniˡ/ is the scientific study of plants. EG *I think we should spend a little while on the botany of grasses.* N UNCOUNT ⇑ science

botch /bɒtʃ/, **botches, botching, botched**; an informal word. 1 If you **botch** a piece of work, you do it very badly or clumsily. EG *I hope I don't do something stupid and botch it... ...her botched attempt at suicide... ...a botched job.* ▸ used as a noun. EG *His gloved hand made a botch of turning over the page.* V+O = bungle ▸ N COUNT

2 A **botch** or a **botch-up** is a piece of work that has been botched. EG *The first attempt is always a botch... We wanted a proper shed, not some botch-up.* N COUNT ⇑ mess

botch up. If you **botch up** a piece of work, you do it very badly or clumsily. EG *He really botched it up.* PHRASAL VB : V+O+ADV

both /bəʊθ/. 1 **Both** is used to refer to two things, people, situations, etc, when you are making a statement that is true about each of them. EG *Both her parents were dead... Both policies make good sense.* ▸ used as a pronoun. EG *Most of them speak either good English or good German or both... He got angry with both of them... He's fond of you both... She and Edith both agreed to come... We were both young.* PREDET OR QUANTIF+N IN PLURAL ▸ PRON : IF+ PREP THEN *of*

2 The structure **both...and** is used when you are giving two facts, things, or alternatives, and you are emphasizing that each of them is true, possible, or likely to happen. EG *These are dangers that threaten both men and women... I am looking for opportunities both in this country and abroad... The prospects both excited and worried me.*

bother /bɒðə/, **bothers, bothering, bothered.** 1 If you do not **bother** to do something, or do not **bother** with something, you do not do it or deal with it because you think it is unnecessary or involves too much effort; usually used in negative statements or questions. EG *I never bother to iron my shirts... Why bother learning all those facts?... She didn't even bother to hide her anger... Don't bother with the washing-up... Don't bother about the rug.* V WITH BROAD NEG : IF+PREP THEN *with/ about,* OR V+-ING/*to*-INF+ BROAD NEG = trouble ● If you say that you **can't be bothered** to do something, you are emphasizing that you are not going to do it because you think it is unnecessary or involves too much effort. EG *Oh, I can't be bothered!... I can't be bothered to cook for myself.* ● PHR : VB INFLECTS

2 **Bother** is trouble, fuss, or difficulty. EG *We found the address without any bother... He never causes me any bother... It's just too much bother.* N UNCOUNT

3 If you say **'It's no bother'** after offering to do something for someone, you are emphasizing that you really want to do it and that it will take little effort. EG *'It's very kind of you. Are you sure?'–'Oh, it's no bother.'* PHR

4 If you **go to the bother** of doing something or **go to all the bother** of doing it, you do it although it involves quite a lot of effort or difficulty. EG *I didn't want to go to the bother of hiring a car just for one day.* PHR : VB INFLECTS : USU+ *of*+-ING

5 If a task or a person is a **bother,** they are boring or irritating to deal with; a fairly informal word. EG *It's a bit of a bother, I know... Sorry to be a bother, but could you sign this for me?* N SING : *a*+N = nuisance

6 If something **bothers** you or if you **bother** about it, you are worried, concerned, or upset about it. EG *Is something bothering you?... What bothers me is that it won't be legal... The only question bothering me is: how?... I didn't bother about what I looked like... She's not worth bothering about, honestly.* V+O, OR V+A *(about)* ⇑ trouble = worry ◊ **bothered**. EG *She was bothered about Olive.* ◊ ADJ QUALIT : USU PRED ● **hot and bothered**: see **hot**.

7 If someone tells you not to **bother** yourself or not to **bother** your **head** about something, they mean that you need not think or worry about it, for example because they are dealing with it themselves or do not think you are capable of dealing with it; an informal expression. EG *Don't you bother yourself about it at all... You really shouldn't bother yourself on my account... Don't bother your pretty little head about a thing.* PHR : VB INFLECTS : USU WITH BROAD NEG ⇑ trouble

8 If you say that something does not **bother** you or that you do not **bother** about it, you mean that you do not mind what someone else does in a particular situation. EG *You can come along too, if you like–it doesn't bother me... Do they bother about things like long hair?* V+O, OR V+A *(about)* : USU WITH BROAD NEG ◊ **bothered.** EG *'Shall I open the window?'–'I'm not bothered.'* ◊ ADJ QUALIT : PRED

9 If you **bother** someone, you talk to them when they want to be left alone, or interrupt them when they are busy. EG *We wanted her to go home to London and stop bothering us... Don't bother me with little things like that... I'm sorry to bother you, but do you know where the toilets are?... I didn't want to bother him while he was working.*
V+O : IF+PREP THEN *about/with* ⇑ trouble = pester, disturb

10 You can use **bother** to refer to serious trouble, often involving quarrelling or fighting, especially when you want to make it seem less serious than is the case; an informal use. EG *We had a bit of bother with the police.*
N UNCOUNT

11 Some people say **bother** or **bother it** when they are annoyed about something; used in rather old-fashioned British English. EG *'Bother!'–'What?'–'My watch has stopped.'*
EXCLAM = drat

12 You can say **bother** something or someone to indicate that you do not care about them or do not consider them important in a particular situation; used in informal British English. EG *You'll just have to come home, and bother the money.*
V+O : ONLY IMPER = blow

botheration /bɒðəreɪʃən/. Some people say **botheration** when they are rather annoyed; used in old-fashioned British English.
EXCLAM = drat

bothersome /bɒðəsəm/. Someone or something that is **bothersome** is annoying or irritating; an old-fashioned, informal word. EG *Aircraft noise is particularly bothersome here since we're close to Heathrow Airport.*
ADJ QUALIT = troublesome

bottle /bɒtəl/, **bottles, bottling, bottled. 1** A **bottle** is a container used for keeping liquids in. Bottles are usually made of glass or plastic and shaped like a cylinder with a narrow top, and are closed with a cap, top, or cork. EG *Boris took out a bottle and a glass... I threw a gin bottle at him... She was screwing the top back on to her scent bottle.*
N COUNT

▸ **Bottle** is also used to refer to the liquid inside a bottle or the amount of liquid it contains. EG *She drank at least half a bottle of whisky a day.*
▸ N PART

2 If you **bottle** wine or beer, you put it into bottles after it has been made. EG *When was this wine bottled?*
V+O

3 The **bottle** is used in informal English to refer to the frequent drinking of a lot of alcohol. EG *Hope is the only thing that keeps me from the bottle.*
N SING : *the*+N = drink

● If someone **hits the bottle,** they drink a lot of alcohol. EG *I started hitting the bottle every evening.*
● PHR : VB INFLECTS

● If someone **takes to the bottle,** they start drinking a lot of alcohol regularly. EG *...an ageing film star who had taken to the bottle.*
● PHR : VB INFLECTS

4 A **bottle** is also a drinking container used by babies which has a special rubber part at the top through which they can suck their drink. EG *The baby went on sucking the bottle.*
N COUNT

▸ **Bottle** is also used to refer to the liquid inside a bottle. EG *Has she finished her bottle?*
▸ ⇑ drink

5 The **bottle** or a **bottle** is used to refer to a method of feeding babies in which they drink cow's milk or a liquid like milk from a bottle rather than sucking milk from their mother's breasts. EG *The baby may prefer the bottle and reject the breast altogether... ...a baby who is on a bottle... She plans to wean her baby from breast to bottle soon.*
N SING WITH DET, OR N UNCOUNT

6 When you **bottle** fruit, you put fresh fruit into jars with special lids and heat the jars slowly in an oven. EG *When bottling fruit, pack the jars as tightly as you can.*
V+O

7 Bottle is courage or boldness; used in informal British English. EG *Skiing? He hasn't got the bottle!... I didn't want them to think I'd lost my bottle.*
N SING WITH DET = nerve

bottle out. If you **bottle out** just before doing something difficult or frightening, you lose your courage at the last moment, and do not do it; used in informal British English. EG *She'll bottle out when she sees the other competitors.*
PHRASAL VB : V+ADV, IF+PREP THEN *of* = chicken out

bottle up. If you **bottle up** a strong emotion that you feel, you do not express it for a long time and often become very upset or suddenly express it in an extreme way. EG *Express your emotions–don't bottle them up... All the rage that had been bottled up in him for so long flooded out in a torrent of abuse.*
PHRASAL VB : V+O+ADV ⇑ repress = contain, imprison

bottled /bɒtəld/. **1 Bottled** beer, water, or other drinks are sold in bottles rather than being taken from a barrel or tank or being sold in cans. EG *There is much more bottled beer sold than draught beer.*
ADJ CLASSIF

2 Bottled gas is gas that is kept under pressure in special metal cylinders which can be moved from one place to another. Different types of gases are stored in this way and used for cooking or for medical or industrial purposes.
ADJ CLASSIF : ATTRIB

bottle-feed, bottle-feeds, bottle-feeding, bottle-fed. A baby who **is bottle-fed** is given milk or a liquid like milk in a bottle rather than sucking milk from its mother's breasts. EG *Bottle-fed babies fuss as much as breast-fed babies if their feed is late.*
V+O, OR V ⇑ feed

bottle-green means dark green in colour; used mainly in British English. EG *...a bottle-green jumper.*
ADJ COLOUR

bottleneck /bɒtəlnɛk/, **bottlenecks.** A **bottleneck** is **1** a place where a road becomes narrow or where there is an important junction, and where the traffic often has to slow down or stop. EG *The bottlenecks at the bridges create tremendous traffic jams.*
N COUNT

2 a situation that stops a process or activity from progressing. EG *The shortage of skilled labour is often a serious industrial bottleneck.*
N COUNT ⇑ problem = hold-up

bottle-opener, bottle-openers. A **bottle-opener** is a metal device for removing lids from bottles.
N COUNT

bottom /bɒtəm/, **bottoms, bottoming, bottomed. 1** The **bottom** of something is the lowest part of it. EG *I stood there at the bottom of the steps... ...at the bottom of the hill... The cliff plunged in a vertical drop to the bottom... His new purchases went into the bottom of one of his suitcases.*
N COUNT : USU *the*+N IN SING, IF +PREP THEN *of* ≠ top

2 The **bottom** thing or layer in a series of things or layers is the lowest one. EG *...the bottom button of my waistcoat. ...the bottom layer is a mixture of sand and clay.*
ADJ CLASSIF : ATTRIB

3 The **bottom** of a place such as a valley or ditch is the lowest or deepest part of it; also used to refer to the ground underneath the sea, a river, or a lake. EG *It sank to the bottom of the lake... ...the sea bottom... The bottom of the trench was muddy and very slippery.*
N COUNT : USU *the*+N IN SING, IF +PREP THEN *of* ⇑ surface

4 The **bottom** of a box or other hollow object is **4.1** the flat outside surface of it that touches or faces the ground. EG *...the top, bottom, and sides of a box... She turned a tea-cup upside down and looked at the marks on the bottom.*
N COUNT : USU *the*+N IN SING, IF +PREP THEN *of* = underneath

4.2 the flat surface at the lowest point inside it. EG *Some rice had stuck to the bottom of the pan.*
N COUNT : USU *the*+N IN SING, IF +PREP THEN *of*

5 The **bottom** of a street, garden, field, etc is the end of it that is furthest away from you or from the entrance. EG *...right down at the bottom of the meadow... I walked down the long garden path to the sheds at the bottom... ...the bottom of Drummond Street.*
N COUNT : USU *the*+N IN SING, IF +PREP THEN *of* ⇑ point

6 The **bottom** of a page, piece of paper, list, or piece of writing is the lowest point on it, or the last item on it. EG *...at the bottom of page 40... She looked at the small print at the bottom of the section.*
N COUNT : USU *the*+N IN SING, IF +PREP THEN *of* = foot

7 The **bottom** of an organization or social system, or of a scale, is the least successful, powerful, or important level in it, or the lowest point on it. EG *I'm at the bottom of my class in maths... Officials at the top make the decisions; men at the bottom carry them out... What is the salary for someone on the bottom rung of the pay scale?... More and more families are joining the bottom of the heap in our society.*
N SING : *the*+N, IF+PREP THEN *of* ≠ top

▸ used as an adjective to describe someone who is at the bottom, especially at school or in a competition. EG *He was always bottom of the class.*
▸ ADJ CLASSIF : PRED ≠ top

8 The word **bottom** is also used in the following expressions. **8.1** When you talk about **getting to the bottom of this** or **it,** you are talking about discovering the real truth about a situation or the real cause of a problem. EG *I'm going to get to the bottom of this, once and for all.*
PHR : VB INFLECTS ⇑ understand = fathom, unravel

8.2 The thing that **lies** or **is at the bottom of** a situation or attitude, especially an undesirable one, is the real cause of it or the real reason for it. EG *Greed lies at the bottom of our ecological predicament... ...influences from the remote past that are at the bottom of his troubles.*
PHR : VB INFLECTS = be behind

8.3 You can say **at bottom** to emphasize that you are stating what you think is the real nature of something or the real truth about a situation. EG *At bottom, U.S. policy reflects a belief that India will accept the deal... English reserve is, at bottom, really fear.*
PHR : USED AS ADV SEN ⇑ really = basically

8.4 You can say that you believe something **at the bottom of** your **heart**, or wish something, apologize, etc **from the bottom of** your **heart**, to emphasize how sincerely or truly you believe or mean it. EG *I'd always at the bottom of my heart believed that... I wish you every possible happiness from the bottom of my heart.*
PHR : USED AS ADV SEN

8.5 If the bottom drops or **falls out** of a
PHR : VB

particular market or industry, people stop buying the products involved. EG *The bottom fell out of the grain market.* INFLECTS **8.6** Some people say **bottoms up** to each other just before they drink an alcoholic drink; used mainly in informal British English. EG *'Bottoms up,' I said and poured the whisky down my throat.* CONVENTION = cheers

9 Your **bottom** is the part of your body between your back and your legs that you sit on. EG *Her bottom was pressed firmly against the wall.* N COUNT : USU POSS+N = behind

10 You can refer to the lower part of a bikini as a bikini **bottom**, and the trousers of a track-suit or of a pair of pyjamas as track-suit **bottoms** or pyjama **bottoms**. EG *He was wearing pyjama bottoms and a vest.* N COUNT : USU MOD+N ⇑ garment ≠ top

bottom out. When something that has been getting worse, or getting lower in amount or value, **bottoms out,** it stops getting worse or lower and remains at a particular rate, amount, or value. EG *Even if the recession has bottomed out, it will not help the unemployed.* PHRASAL VB : V+ADV = level out

bottom drawer, bottom drawers. If a woman buys or gets something for her **bottom drawer**, she keeps it to use when she is married; used mainly in old-fashioned British English. N COUNT : USU POSS+N ⇑ store

bottomless /bɒtəmlɪ^{2}s/. Something that is **bottomless** is **1** very large or contains a very large amount of something, especially money, and seems never to end or run out. EG *The company offered to meet the entire cost from its bottomless funds... ...American millionaires with bottomless purses.* ADJ CLASSIF = inexhaustible, unlimited **2** very deep and seems to have no bottom. EG *...a bottomless pit.* ADJ CLASSIF = fathomless

botulism /bɒtjə^{4}lɪzə^{0}m/ is a serious form of food poisoning caused by eating preserved food which has gone bad; a medical term. N UNCOUNT

boudoir /buːdwɑː, -dwɔː/, **boudoirs**. A **boudoir** is a woman's bedroom or private sitting room; an old-fashioned word. N COUNT ⇑ room

bouffant /buːfɔːŋ/, **bouffants**. A **bouffant** is a hairstyle in which your hair is raised away from your head by combing it backwards and upwards. N COUNT ⇑ domed

bougainvillaea /buːgənvɪlɪə/, **bougainvillaeas**. **Bougainvillaea** is a climbing plant that has thin, red or purple flowers and grows mainly in hot countries. N UNCOUNT/COUNT

bough /baʊ/, **boughs**. A **bough** is a large branch of a tree; a rather literary word. EG *We lay on the soft moss under a roof of leafy boughs.* N COUNT

bought /bɔːt/ is the past tense and past participle of **buy.**

bouillabaisse /buːjəbɛs/ is a rich stew or soup of fish and vegetables. N UNCOUNT

bouillon /buːjɒŋ/, **bouillons**. **Bouillon** is a liquid made by boiling meat and bones or vegetables in water and used to make soups and sauces. EG *...beef bouillon.* N COUNT/UNCOUNT ⇑ broth = stock

boulder /bəʊldə/, **boulders**. A **boulder** is a big rounded rock. EG *We heard the sounds of the river rushing past boulders below.* N COUNT

boulevard /buːlə^{0}vɑːd^{0}/, **boulevards**. A **boulevard** is a wide street in a city, usually with trees along the sides of it. EG *...strolling arm in arm along the boulevards of Paris.* N COUNT : ALSO IN NAMES AFTER N = avenue

bounce /baʊns/, **bounces, bouncing, bounced**. **1** When something such as a ball **bounces**, it springs upwards or away immediately after hitting the ground or another surface. EG *The grenade bounced twice and exploded... The ball bounced five yards to my right... Enormous hailstones hit the roofs and bounced off the pavements.* V OR V+A ⇑ spring = rebound ▸ used as a noun. EG *She had not reached the ball before its second bounce... The van turned off the road, and after two or three big bounces, rode up a grassy slope.* ▸ N COUNT ⇑ spring = rebound

2 When you **bounce** something such as a ball, you throw it hard against the ground or another surface so that it immediately springs upwards or away. EG *She bounced the ball once or twice before serving.* V+O, OR V+O+A

3 If something such as sound or light **bounces** off a surface, it reaches the surface and travels or is reflected back. EG *Bats can tell the nature of the object by the intensity of the sound bouncing back... Its flickering light bounced off the walls... A mirror will increase light, as it bounces it back into a room.* V OR V+O : USU+A *(off/back)* ⇑ reflect

4 If something **bounces**, it swings or wobbles up and down. EG *The white curls on her head bounced as she trotted along... The rucksack bounced and jingled on my shoulders... The cables bounced and swayed as he inched his way along.* V ⇑ shake = bob

5 If you **bounce** on something, you jump up and down on it repeatedly. EG *They were all bouncing on the mattress to demonstrate its resilience.... ...bouncing on a trampoline.* V+A = bound

6 When you **bounce** a child on your knee, you lift them up and down quickly and repeatedly for fun. V+O, OR V+O+A

7 A **bounce** is also a quick lively jump or leap from one place to another; used in informal English. EG *She reached the front door in a single bounce.* N COUNT = bound

8 If someone **bounces** along a road, into a place, etc, they move or behave with a great deal of lively energy, especially because they are feeling happy; used in informal English. EG *He came bouncing in, grinning with glee.* V+A ⇑ go = bound ▸ used as a noun. EG *Her lively bounce contrasted curiously with her husband's dull lethargy.* ▸ N UNCOUNT ⇑ liveliness = exuberance

9 If people **bounce** from one activity, place, or idea to another, they move quickly from one to the other, spending only a short time on each one. EG *We bounce from film to film with very little assessment of our work... Poor people bounce from job to job.* V : IF+PREP THEN *from* = skip ≠ stay

10 If something such as a carpet or someone's hair has **bounce**, it is very springy and will not flatten easily when it is pressed down. N UNCOUNT = spring

11 When a cheque **bounces** or when the bank **bounces** a cheque, the bank refuses to accept the cheque and pay out the money, because there is not enough money in the account. EG *Your bank can't bounce any cheques which have your cheque card number on the back.* V-ERG ⇑ fail = reject

bounce back. When you **bounce back** after a disappointing or unpleasant experience, you return successfully or with enthusiasm to your normal activities again, especially after only a short period of time. EG *You'll bounce back, don't worry... My bet is he'll bounce right back.* PHRASAL VB : V+ADV ⇑ recover

bouncer /baʊnsə/, **bouncers**. A **bouncer** is a strong person who is employed to stand at the door of a club, dance, etc, in order to prevent unwanted people from coming in and to throw people out if they get too drunk or start fighting; an informal word. N COUNT ⇑ doorman

bouncing /baʊnsɪŋ/. If you say that someone is **bouncing** with health, or if you refer to a child as a **bouncing** baby you mean that they are looking very healthy. ADJ CLASSIF : IF+PREP THEN *with*

bouncy /baʊnsi^{1}/, **bouncier, bounciest**. **1** A person or animal that is **bouncy** has lots of energy and is very lively and enthusiastic. EG *Rick arrived the next day, all bouncy and enthusiastic and full of energy... The puppy looked in good condition, fit and bouncy.* ADJ QUALIT = buoyant ≠ lethargic

2 Something that is **bouncy** is **2.1** able to bounce very well, like a ball. EG *Tennis balls are bouncier than cricket balls.* ADJ QUALIT **2.2** very springy and will not flatten easily when it is pressed down. EG *...her reddish hair all bouncy round her face.* ADJ QUALIT ≠ flat

bound /baʊnd/, **bounds, bounding, bounded. 1** If you say that something **is bound to** happen or that someone **is bound to** do something, you are saying that it is certain to happen or be done. EG *Sooner or later, it was bound to happen... You're almost bound to make a mistake.* PHR : VB INFLECTS = sure to

2 You can say **I'll be bound** after a statement to indicate that you think it is very likely to be true, especially when this is something that you disapprove of; a rather old-fashioned expression. EG *They'll be up to no good, I'll be bound.* PHR : USED AS ADV SEN = I bet

3 If you are **bound** by something such as an agreement or law, you have a duty or responsibility to do what the agreement says, or to obey the law. EG *They were bound to the treaty by international law... They are bound by legal but not moral obligations... The government declares that it is not bound by the agreement.* ADJ CLASSIF : PRED, IF+PREP THEN *by/to* = tied ≠ free

4 If you **feel bound** to do something, you feel a moral duty or responsibility to do it. EG *An agent, whatever he suspected, would feel bound to pass it on... Others felt bound to follow suit.* PHR : VB INFLECTS

5 You say **'I am bound to say'** or **'I am bound to admit'** to emphasize something that you feel you must say, and often to suggest that you feel rather ashamed about it. EG *I am bound to say that it is the British who are mostly to blame... Sometimes, I'm bound to say, they are a hopeless muddle.* PHR : USED AS ADV SEN

6 If something is **bound up with** a particular problem, situation, activity, etc, it is closely connected PHR : USED AS C ⇑ concerned with the problem, situation, or activity. EG *The evolution of the Labour Party is very closely bound up with the evolution of parliamentary democracy... All this was bound up with what was happening in Egypt... Dominant and submissive behaviour is closely bound up with childhood experiences.*

7 If someone or a vehicle is **bound** for a particular place, they are travelling or intending to travel there. EG *He put her aboard the steamer bound for New York.* — ADJ CLASSIF: PRED+*for* ⇑ directed = destined

8 To **bound** means to run or move suddenly and quickly, and with large leaps and jumps. EG *He would see the kids bounding towards him after school... Goats were bounding off in all directions... Boulders slid and bounded down.* — V: USU+A ⇑ rush = leap

9 A **bound** is a long or high jump. EG *...leaping spectacularly into the air with soaring bounds three metres high.* — N COUNT = leap

10 If something changes **by leaps and bounds**, it changes very quickly, suddenly, and by large amounts. EG *These cars have been gaining popularity by leaps and bounds.* — PHR: USED AS AN A

11 The **bounds** of something are the limits which restrict what you can do, how you can behave, or what is possible in a particular situation. EG *Artists strove to escape from the bounds set by traditional culture... They live their everyday lives within these bounds... It is not outside the bounds of possibility.* — N PLURAL: IF+ PREP THEN *of* = boundaries

12 If someone's emotion, success, etc **knows no bounds**, it is so strong or intense that you cannot imagine a maximum limit to it. EG *Her anger and rage knew no bounds.* — PHR: VB INFLECTS ⇑ be intense

13 If a place is **out of bounds,** it is an area where people are forbidden to go. EG *'I will be in trouble. Already we are out of bounds.'* — PHR: USED AS AN A

14 If something **bounds** an area of land, it marks or is situated around the boundary of it. EG *The weeds bounded and identified each woman's plot... On every side they were bounded by other villages.* — V+O ⇑ surround = border

15 Papers that are **bound** have been made into a book with a front and back cover. EG *My uncle showed me his bound volumes of Bruce Feather's cartoons... ...a pocket diary bound in black imitation leather.* — ADJ CLASSIF ⇑ covered

16 **Bound** is also the past tense and past participle of **bind**.

boundary /baʊndəºri¹/, **boundaries**. 1 The **boundary** of an area of land is the line which marks the outer edge of it and which separates it from the land adjoining it. EG *...the boundary of the Snowdonia National Park... ...territorial boundaries... You have to stay within your county boundary.* — N COUNT: USU+ SUPP = border

2 The **boundary** of an area of thought, a problem, a condition, etc, is the limit or extent of it, and the line which distinguishes it from others of a similar kind. EG *...the boundaries of the problem... They have never attained the boundary line where word becomes deed... The old boundaries between specialities are collapsing.* — N COUNT+SUPP

bounder /baʊndə/, **bounders**. A **bounder** is a man who behaves in an unkind, deceitful, or selfish way; an old-fashioned word. — N COUNT/VOC = cad ≠ gentleman

boundless /baʊndlı²s/. When you say that something is **boundless**, you mean that there is so much of it that there seems to be no limit to it. EG *She decided to employ her boundless energies by returning to the stage... They were boundless in their gratitude.* — ADJ CLASSIF ⇑ vast ≠ limited

bounteous /baʊntıəs/ means the same as bountiful; a literary word.

bountiful /baʊntıfʊl/. Something that is **bountiful** is provided very generously or in large amounts, either naturally or because someone has given it; a rather literary word. EG *...a bountiful supply of Madame's favourite cigarettes... Life was good and bountiful.* — ADJ QUALIT ⇑ generous = bounteous

bounty /baʊnti¹/, **bounties**. 1 Someone's **bounty** is their generosity in giving something freely; a literary use. EG *'I think we should drink to the bounty of nature'... They must accept the colonel's bounty.* — N SING: WITH POSS = munificent

2 **Bounty** is something that is provided or given generously and in large quantities; a literary use. EG *When heaven sends bounty, it too often sends monotony. ...potatoes and peas, ducks and turkeys, all the bounty of the freezer.* — N UNCOUNT/ COUNT ⇑ plenty

3 A **bounty** is money that is given as a gift or a reward. EG *...this take-over alone providing bounties of more than $30 million... They made the custom popular by offering bounty money for the scalps of their enemies.* — N COUNT

bouquet /bəʊkeı, bu:-/, **bouquets**. 1 A **bouquet** is a bunch of flowers which is beautifully arranged and given as a present. EG *He hugged her and handed her a bouquet of winter roses... The flowers came. Two enormous bouquets.* — N COUNT: IF+ PREP THEN *of*

2 The **bouquet** of something, especially wine or flowers, is the pleasant smell that it has. EG *It was flat, stale, strangely lacking in bouquet... Herbs were used to give an especially aromatic bouquet to the wine.* — N SING: USU POSS +N = fragrance

bourbon /bʊəbəºn/, **bourbons**. **Bourbon** is a type of whisky that is made mainly in America. EG *When he saw the bourbon, his eyes lit up... Scotch or Bourbon?... Two bourbons, please.* — N MASS

bourgeois /bʊəʒwa:/. **Bourgeois** is both the singular and the plural form of the noun in paragraph 2. 1 **Bourgeois** is 1.1 used to refer to the lifestyle, attitudes, and beliefs that are considered to be typical of quite rich middle-class people in towns; used showing disapproval. EG *I found their ideas insufferably bourgeois... They're the most conventional, dull, bourgeois people you've ever met... Cocktails? Romance? I have no time for such bourgeois concerns.* — ADJ QUALIT = banal

1.2 used to describe or refer to the capitalist system according to Marxist theory, and the social class in such a system who own most of the wealth. EG *...a new phase in the evolution of bourgeois capitalism... She condemns modern bourgeois society.* — ADJ CLASSIF ⇑ middle class

2 A **bourgeois** is a person who belongs to the bourgeoisie, according to Marxist theory. EG *You have the spirit of a bourgeois.* — N COUNT

bourgeoisie /bʊəʒwa:zi:/. The **bourgeoisie** are the people belonging to a social class which, according to Marxist theory, includes the middle class people who own most of the wealth in a capitalist system. EG *...a radical distinction between the proletariat and the bourgeoisie... The bourgeoisie are the same the world over... ...the coming into being of an industrial bourgeoisie... Traders and artisans do not constitute a bourgeoisie in the strict sense.* — N SING WITH DET: VB CAN BE SING OR PL ⇑ middle classes

bout /baʊt/, **bouts**. 1 A **bout** of an illness or feeling is a short period when you are severely affected by it. EG *Following a bout of malaria, he was transferred to Java... ...that sudden bout of self-pity the previous night.* — N COUNT: IF+ PREP THEN *of* ⇑ attack = spell

2 A **bout** of activity is a short time when you put all your effort and energy into doing something. EG *...frenzied bouts of writing... ...this bout of ugly violence.* — N COUNT: IF+ PREP THEN *of* = burst

3 A **bout** is also a boxing or wrestling match. EG *He had seen the fight and was offering them a bout in London in six weeks.* — N COUNT ⇑ fight

4 Some people use **bout** in written English to represent the word **about** when it is pronounced in an informal way. — PREP OR ADV

boutique /bu:ti:k/, **boutiques**. A **boutique** is a small shop that sells fashionable clothes, jewellery, etc. EG *French boutiques sell the latest Parisian fashions.* — N COUNT

bovine /bəʊvaın/. 1 **Bovine** means relating to cattle; a technical term. EG *...bovine tuberculosis.* — ADJ CLASSIF: ATTRIB

2 If you say that someone's behaviour or appearance is **bovine**, you mean that they are slow-moving, stupid, or ugly. EG *...the typical media woman's bovine leer... ...the bovine apathy of members.* — ADJ QUALIT ⇑ brutish

bovver /bɒvə/ is aggressive behaviour or violence; used in informal British English. — N UNCOUNT = aggro

bow, bows, bowing, bowed. The word **bow** is pronounced /baʊ/ for paragraphs 1 to 4 and for the phrasal verbs, and /bəʊ/ for paragraphs 5 and 6. 1 When you **bow**, you briefly bend your body forward while you are standing in front of someone or walking past them as a formal way of greeting them or of showing respect. EG *His daughter bowed... 'Goodbye, Miss Drew,' he said, bowing to her.* — V: IF+PREP THEN *to*
▸ used as a noun. EG *He made her a little bow... The usher opened the door with a bow.* — ▸ N COUNT
● When an actor or entertainer **takes a bow** he or she shows appreciation of an audience's applause by bowing to them. — ● PHR: VB INFLECTS

2 If you **bow** your head, you bend it downwards so that you are looking towards the ground in order to pray, to show respect for someone who has died, or to show that you are ashamed about something. EG *She bowed her head... The children bowed their heads.* — V+O = lower ≠ raise
◊ **bowed**. EG *Their shaved heads were bowed.* — ◊ ADJ CLASSIF

3 If you **bow** to someone's wishes, to pressure, to the inevitable, etc, you accept completely what someone wants you to do, or what happens to you, without making any great effort to alter the situation. EG *They are inclined to bow to all her wishes regardless of their own... The Department of the Environment seems to be bowing to pressure from industry to ignore the recommendations.* — V+A (to) ⇑ submit = bend, yield

4 The **bow** or **bows** of a ship or boat is the front part of it. EG *A massive wave caught the trawler on her port bow... Little waves were beginning to creep around the bows of the Morning Rose.* — N COUNT : USU+SUPP = prow

5 A **bow** is **5.1** a knot with two loops and two loose ends that is used especially in tying shoelaces and hair-ribbons. It is easily untied by pulling the loose ends. EG *...girls with bows in their hair... Tie it in a bow.* — N COUNT **5.2** a weapon for shooting arrows, consisting of a long piece of wood bent into a curve by a string attached to both its ends. EG *He owned not much more than his bow and arrows.* — N COUNT

6 The **bow** of a violin or other stringed instrument is a long thin piece of wood with horsehair stretched along it, which you move across the strings of the instrument in order to play it. EG *He told me I was holding my bow too tightly.* — N COUNT ⇑ rod

bow down. If you **bow down**, you bow very low in order to show great respect. EG *The angels were commanded to bow down.* — PHRASAL VB : V+ADV, IF+PREP THEN *to*

bow out. If you **bow out** of something, you stop doing it or taking part in it, often in order to allow someone else to take your place. EG *We may do one more performance before we bow out.* — PHRASAL VB : V+ADV, IF+PREP THEN *of*

bowed. The word **bowed** is pronounced /bəʊd/ for paragraph 1, and /baʊd/ for paragraphs 2 and 3. **1** Something that is **bowed** is bent into a curve, or shaped like one. EG *He had slightly bowed legs.* — ADJ QUALIT = curved ≠ straight

2 If a person's body is **bowed**, it is bent forward. EG *An elderly woman walked by, her back and shoulders bowed under the bundle she was carrying.* — ADJ QUALIT = stooped ≠ erect

3 Another meaning of **bowed** can be found in the entry for **bow** in paragraph 2.

bowel /baʊəˡl/, **bowels. 1** Your **bowels** are the tubes in your body that pass unwanted substances from your stomach to your anus. The bowels, like the heart, are traditionally considered to be the source of strong emotions. EG *Changes of water may upset the baby's bowels... ...minor disorders of the bowels... He stood on the cliff edge his heart thumping and his bowels melting.* — N PLURAL ⇑ guts ▸ The **bowel** is used in more formal or technical English. EG *...digestion of fats in the bowel... ...cancer of the bowel.* — ▸ N SING : *the*+N ● If you talk about **moving, relieving,** or **emptying** your **bowels**, you are referring in a polite way to the act of excreting faeces from your body. EG *The doctor will be sure to ask them how recently they have moved their bowels... He went behind a bush to relieve his bowels.* — ● PHR : VB INFLECTS = defecate

2 Bowel is used to describe something relating to the bowels. EG *...bowel cancer... ...bowel movements.* — N BEFORE N

3 The **bowels** of something are the parts deep inside it, which are often considered to be the most important, central, or secret parts of it. EG *They say that there are giants living deep in the bowels of the earth... The message had sprung from the bowels of a computer.* — N PLURAL : *the*+N+*of* = depths, heart

bower /baʊə/, **bowers.** A **bower** is a shady, leafy shelter in a garden or wood; a literary word. — N COUNT = arbour

bowl /bəʊl/, **bowls, bowling, bowled. 1** A **bowl** is a container that is open at the top, fairly shallow, and usually circular. Bowls are used, for example, for serving food, mixing ingredients when cooking, keeping fruit in, or washing-up. EG *...a bowl of cornflakes with sugar and cream... She shook some sugar lumps into a china bowl... Heap up the flour round the sides of the bowl and put the yeast in the middle... ...salad bowls.* ● See also **finger bowl.** — N COUNT ⇑ dish ▸ **Bowl** is also used to refer to the contents of a bowl. EG *She lived on one bowl of milk a day.* — ▸ N PART

2 The **bowl** of something, for example a lavatory, a pipe, or a spoon, is the part of it that is shaped like a bowl. EG *He lit his pipe, crushing the tobacco in the bowl with precision... Do not throw waste material of any kind into the toilet bowl.* — N COUNT : USU+SUPP ⇑ container

3 In cricket, to **bowl** a ball means to throw the ball down the pitch towards the batsman by moving your arm round in a large circular movement behind your shoulder and over your head. EG *He bowled well enough in the first innings... I bowled two more overs after tea.* — V OR V+O

4 In cricket, to **bowl** the batsman means to get him out by bowling a ball that hits the wicket behind him. EG *Botham bowled him for a very fine 83.* — V+O ⇑ dismiss

5 If something or someone **bowls** along, **bowls** down the street, etc, or if something **bowls** them along, they move or roll along at a great speed. EG *The leaves were bowling about all over the place... We were in Jerusalem, bowling down the Jaffa road to King David Street.* — V-ERG+A

6 Bowls is a game that is usually played outdoors on a very smooth area of grass. The players roll large wooden balls towards a small ball and try to bring them as near to it as possible. — N UNCOUNT

7 A **bowl** is also **7.1** one of the large wooden balls used in the game of bowls. — N COUNT **7.2** a large heavy ball that is used in tenpin bowling. It has holes into which you place two fingers and a thumb of one hand in order to grip it. — N COUNT

8 When you **bowl** in the games of bowls or bowling, you have a turn at rolling the ball. — V OR V+O ⇑ roll

9 If you **bowl** a particular number of points, you score that number of points in the games of bowls or bowling. — V+O

10 To **bowl** a hoop means to roll it along the ground by pushing the top of it with your hand or with a stick. Children used to bowl hoops as a game. — V+O

11 A **bowl** is also a large bowl-shaped area where entertainments are held, for example a sports stadium or an open-air concert area. EG *The orchestra will play at the Crystal Palace concert bowl.* — N COUNT : MOD+N = arena

12 See **bowling.**

bowl out. 1 To **bowl out** a team in cricket means to get them all out. EG *We were bowled out for 220.* — PHRASAL VB : V+O+ADV

2 When a batsman is **bowled out** in cricket, the bowler hits the wicket with the ball and the batsman is out. EG *He was bowled out for 32.* — PHRASAL VB : V+O+ADV = dismissed

bowl over. 1 If you **bowl** someone **over**, you knock them down by colliding with them when you are moving very quickly. EG *They leapt aside to avoid being bowled over by three boys as they raced past.* — PHRASAL VB : V+O+ADV

2 If you **are bowled over** by someone or something, you are very deeply affected by them because they are so surprising, different, or exciting. EG *I was bowled over by the beauty of Malawi... The sight of her just bowled him over.* — PHRASAL VB : V+O+ADV, USU PASS = overwhelm

bow-legged /bəʊ lɛgɪˡd/. Someone who is **bow-legged** has legs that curve outwards at the knees. — ADJ CLASSIF

bowler /bəʊlə/, **bowlers.** A **bowler** is **1** the person who is bowling the ball in a game of cricket. EG *He is the finest fast bowler I have ever seen.* — N COUNT **2** the same as a bowler hat. — N COUNT

bowler hat, bowler hats. A **bowler hat** or **bowler** is a round, hard, black hat with a narrow curved brim, worn especially by some British businessmen. — N COUNT = derby

bowling /bəʊlɪŋ/ is **1** a game in which you roll a heavy ball down a long narrow track towards a group of wooden objects in order to knock down as many of them as possible. — N UNCOUNT **2** the action or activity of bowling the ball in cricket. EG *His bowling has steadily declined in quality since 1981... The bowling was generally better than the batting.* — N UNCOUNT

bowling alley, bowling alleys. A **bowling alley** is **1** a building which contains several tracks for tenpin bowling. — N COUNT **2** the track down which you roll the ball in tenpin bowling. — N COUNT

bowling green, bowling greens. A **bowling green** is an area of very smooth, short grass on which the game of bowls is played. — N COUNT

bow tie, bow ties; also spelled with a hyphen. A **bow tie** is a man's tie in the form of a bow, worn especially for formal occasions. — N COUNT

bow window, bow windows; also spelled with a hyphen. A **bow window** is a curved window that sticks out further than the surface of the wall. EG *The bow window on the ground floor.* — N COUNT

bow-wow /baʊ waʊ/, **bow-wows.** Small children often use **bow-wow 1** to refer to a dog. — N COUNT **2** as a way of representing the noise of a dog barking. — = woof

box /bɒks/, **boxes, boxing, boxed. 1** A **box** is a square or rectangular container which is made, for example, from cardboard or wood and which sometimes has a lid. EG *...a cardboard box... ...boxes filled with old clothes... ...a box of matches... Please put your contribution in the donations box by the main door.* — N COUNT : IF+PREP THEN *of*

2 If you refer to a house or flat as a **box**, you mean that it is small and uninteresting and that it is very similar to a lot of other houses or flats. EG *I refuse to buy a grotty little box on some estate.* N COUNT ⇑ dwelling = hole

3 A **box** on a form that you fill in is a square or rectangular space in which you have to write something. EG *If you agree, put a tick in the box marked 'yes'.* N COUNT

4 A **box** on a sports pitch or on a road is a square or rectangular area marked by lines which indicate that the area is used for a particular purpose. EG *Do not enter the box until your exit is clear.* N COUNT

5 A **box** in a theatre is an area like a little room where a small number of people can sit to watch the performance away from the rest of the seats. EG *Is it very expensive to get a box at the Kings Theatre?* N COUNT ⇑ enclosure

6 You can use **box** to refer to something such as a letter-box or telephone box that has 'box' as the second part of its name, when the thing has already been mentioned or has been indicated by another word; an informal use. EG *I wanted to phone you but I couldn't find a box... 'Where can I post this letter?'-'There's a box just up the road.'* N COUNT

7 You can say the **box** when you are referring to the television; used mainly in informal British English. EG *What's on the box tonight?* N SING WITH DET : USU *the*+N = telly, TV

8 **Box** is used, followed by a number, as a postal address by organizations that receive a lot of mail. Letters sent to an organization are kept together under their box number and are then collected or delivered together. EG *Smithfield and West, Box 26, Orpington.* N COUNT : USU+NUM

9 A **box** is also a specially shaped piece of hard plastic which is worn by sportsmen to protect their genitals. N COUNT ⇑ shield

10 If you **box**, **box** against someone, or **box** them, you fight them according to the rules of the sport of boxing. EG *He used to box, run and swim for his school.* V : IF+PREP THEN *against*, OR V+O ● If someone **boxes** a child's **ears**, they hit the child's head and ears because they are angry or as a punishment. EG *He irritated her so much that she could have boxed his ears... Mother did no more than box my ears.* ● PHR : VB INFLECTS

11 **Box** is a small evergreen tree with dark leaves which is often used to form hedges. EG *...a box hedge.* N UNCOUNT

12 See **boxed**, **boxing**.

13 ● See also **black box**, **fuse box**, **horse-box**, **letterbox**, **money-box**, **penalty box**, **pillar box**, **post-box**, **royal box**, **signal box**, **telephone box**, **window box**, **witness box**.

box in. If you are **boxed in**, you are unable to move from a particular place or position because you are surrounded by other people or because your car has other vehicles parked just in front of it and just behind it. EG *Unless you go ahead early on in the race there's a danger you'll get boxed in... Some fool parked his car too close to mine and boxed me in.* PHRASAL VB : V+O+ADV = hem in

box off. To **box off** an area means to make a small enclosed area within a larger area by building walls around it. EG *You could box off the area under the stairs to make a cupboard.* PHRASAL VB : V+O+ADV ⇑ partition

box camera, box cameras. A **box camera** is a simple type of camera, shaped like a box. N COUNT

boxcar /bɒkskɑː/, **boxcars**. A **boxcar** is a railway wagon with high sides and a roof in which goods are carried; used in American English. N COUNT

boxed /bɒkst/. Something that is **boxed** is sold in a box. EG *...a boxed set of Beethoven's symphonies... ...boxed cereals.* ADJ CLASSIF ⇑ packaged ≠ loose

boxer /bɒksə/, **boxers**. A **boxer** is 1 a sportsman whose sport is boxing. N COUNT 2 a dog with short light-brown hair and a rather flat face and nose. N COUNT

box girder, box girders. A **box girder** is a hollow girder which is square or rectangular in shape. N COUNT

boxing /bɒksɪŋ/ is a sport in which two men fight according to special rules, by punching each other with their fists, wearing large padded gloves. EG *...a boxing match... ...the heavyweight boxing championship.* N UNCOUNT ⇑ fighting

Boxing Day is the twenty-sixth of December, the day after Christmas Day. Officially, if the twenty-sixth is a Sunday, the twenty-seventh is called Boxing Day. N UNCOUNT

boxing glove, boxing gloves; also spelled with a hyphen. **Boxing gloves** are big padded gloves worn for boxing. N COUNT

box junction, box junctions. In Great Britain, a **box junction** is a road junction with yellow lines painted on the road in the central section. If the road beyond the junction is blocked you must not drive onto the marked area. N COUNT ⇑ cross-roads

box kite, box kites. A **box kite** is a kite which is shaped like a box but open at both ends. N COUNT

box number, box numbers. A **box number** is a number used as an address, especially one given by a newspaper for replies to a private advertisement. EG *The advert didn't give the address, just a box number.* N COUNT ⇑ location

box office, box offices; also spelled with a hyphen. 1 A **box office** is the place in a theatre, cinema, or concert hall where the tickets are sold. N COUNT ⇑ shop

2 The **box office** is also used to refer to the degree of success that films, plays, actors, etc achieve in terms of the number of people who go to watch them. EG *She was a very hot box office attraction indeed... Mozart would not last a week at the box office.* N SING : *the*+N, OR N BEFORE N

box pleat, box pleats. A **box pleat** is a type of pleat used especially in skirts, which consists of two large pleats that are folded away from each other. N COUNT ⇑ fold

boxroom /bɒksru[4]m/, **boxrooms**. A **boxroom** is a small room in a house where you keep things which you do not use very often. You can also use a boxroom as a bedroom. N COUNT

boxwood /bɒkswʊd/ is a type of hard wood which is obtained from a box tree: see **box 11**. N UNCOUNT

boy /bɔɪ/, **boys**. 1 A **boy** is a male child. EG *There were hundreds of boys and girls on the lawn... The eldest child was a boy of five... You are a silly little boy... He was no longer a boy.* N COUNT = lad

2 If you say **boys will be boys**, you mean that people shouldn't be surprised when boys are rough, naughty, and noisy, because this is considered to be normal and natural male behaviour. CONVENTION

3 Someone's son, whether they are a child or a man, can be referred to as their **boy**; an informal use. EG *The Jones boys were perfectly at ease... I have three beautiful boys.* N COUNT : USU+POSS

4 A man can be referred to as a **boy**, especially by someone who is in a position of authority, power, or superiority over them; an informal use. EG *I could see them thinking, 'that's our boy', and I got the job... O'Neill regards the Treasury chief as a local boy made good... Nixon is a small-town boy.* N COUNT : USU+SUPP

5 Some people say **my boy**, **my dear boy**, and **boys** when addressing a man or a group of men; an old-fashioned use. EG *That's fine by me, my boy... And that, my dear boy, is the whole point of the exercise... Take him away, boys.* N VOC = lad

6 A group of men who are involved in a particular activity or who have particular skills are sometimes referred to as the **boys** in relation to their activity or skill. EG *We may need the help of the science boys... ...some of the big business boys.* N PLURAL+SUPP : *the*+N = experts

7 **The boys** and **our boys** are affectionate or patriotic ways of referring to the men in your country's armed forces, especially during a war. EG *...when the boys come marching home... I'm thinking of our boys out at the front.* N PLURAL : *the*/POSS+N ⇑ soldiers = lads

8 The **boys in blue** are the police; used in old-fashioned, informal British English, humorously or showing approval. PHR : USED AS S OR O = cops

9 A man is described as **one of the boys** when he is accepted within a group of male friends who do things that are thought of as typically masculine. PHR : USED AS C

10 **Boy** is used to address a male animal such as a dog or horse. EG *Whoa there, Captain. Easy, boy, easy... Down, boy!* N VOC = lad

11 Some people say **'Boy'** or **'Oh boy'** in order to express strong feelings such as excitement or admiration. EG *Boy, I really enjoyed that... Boy oh boy, was that some party!... Oh boy, wait until you see this film!* EXCLAM = wow, gosh

12 See also **bully boy**, **old boy**, **teddy boy**, **whipping boy**, **wide boy**.

boycott /bɔɪkɒt/, **boycotts, boycotting, boycotted**. A **boycott** is a refusal to be involved with something that you strongly disapprove of, for example a refusal to go to a particular meeting or buy food from a particular country. EG *...an Olympic boycott... The boycott of British goods began in 1906.* N COUNT : IF+PREP THEN *of/on/against* ⇑ rejection ≠ endorsement ▸ used as a verb. EG *He urged all citizens to boycott the polls... ...a cinema which refused to boycott the film.* ▸ V+O ≠ support

boyfriend /bɔɪfrɛnd/, **boyfriends**. Someone's **boyfriend** is a man or boy with whom they are having a romantic or sexual relationship. EG *This is my boyfriend Oliver... I had lots of boyfriends.* — N COUNT: USU a/POSS+N ↑ lover

boyhood /bɔɪhʊd/ is the time during which a male person is or was a boy. EG *He began to talk to me about his boyhood in London.* — N UNCOUNT/N SING WITH DET ↑ childhood

boyish /bɔɪɪʃ/. 1 If you say that a man is **boyish**, you mean that he is very youthful in appearance or behaviour; used showing approval. EG *...a boyish smile... This incident was not a boyish prank... He still seemed boyish.* ◊ **boyishly**. EG *He grinned boyishly.* — ADJ QUALIT ↑ youthful; ◊ ADV

2 If you say that a girl or woman is **boyish**, you mean that she looks or behaves like a boy, for example because she has short hair and a small bust. EG *She was very thin and boyish... ...her boyish clothes.* ◊ **boyishly**. EG *Mrs Curry had boyishly cut brown hair.* — ADJ QUALIT ↑ masculine ≠ girlish; ◊ ADV

Br is an abbreviation for 'British'.

bra /brɑː/, **bras**. A **bra** is a piece of underwear that women wear to support their breasts. EG *She fastened her bra.* — N COUNT

brace /breɪs/, **braces, bracing, braced**. **Brace** is both the singular and plural form of the noun in paragraph 7. 1 If you **brace** yourself, you prepare yourself for something unpleasant. EG *She had braced herself to read the letter... She braced herself for her forthcoming ordeal.* — V+O (REFL): USU+to-INF/for

2 If you **brace** yourself or a part of your body against something, you press against it in order to steady your body, avoid falling, or stand up. EG *He braced a hand against the door... I grasped the edge of a table to brace myself.* — V+O (NG/REFL)

3 If you **brace** your shoulders, legs, or arms, you keep them in a stiff, steady, and tense position. EG *He stood to attention, his shoulders braced... Brace your knees.* — V+O

4 To **brace** something means to strengthen or support it with something else. EG *His knees are braced and bandaged before every game.* — V+O

5 A **brace** is 5.1 a metal device that is sometimes fastened to a child's teeth in order to help them grow straight and in the right place. 5.2 a device attached to a part of a person's body, for example to a weak leg, in order to strengthen or support it. EG *Barnett has begun to learn to walk with the use of braces.* — N COUNT; N COUNT

6 In British English, **braces** are a pair of straps that you use instead of a belt to prevent your trousers from falling down. The straps pass over your shoulders and are fastened to your trousers at the front and at the back. EG *He wore scarlet braces.* — N PLURAL: ALSO a pair of+N = suspenders

7 You can refer to two things of the same kind as a **brace**, especially two wild birds or animals that have been killed for sport or for food. EG *He had a brace of pheasants on his desk... There's six brace of them for you, Charlie.* — N PART = pair, couple

brace and bit, braces and bits. A **brace and bit** is a tool that is used for boring holes in wood and that is worked by hand. — N COUNT

bracelet /breɪslɪ²t/, **bracelets**. A **bracelet** is a chain or band, usually made of metal, which you wear around your wrist or arm as jewellery. EG *She used to wear huge bracelets on her wrists.* — N COUNT

bracing /breɪsɪŋ/. If you describe something such as a place, its climate, or an activity as **bracing**, you mean that it causes you to feel fit and energetic. EG *The air was like mountain air, bracing and heady.* — ADJ QUALIT ↑ healthy = invigorating

bracken /brækə⁰n/ is a plant like a large fern that grows, for example, on hills and in woods. EG *There was a rustle in the bracken.* — N UNCOUNT ↑ undergrowth

bracket /brækɪ²t/, **brackets, bracketing, bracketed**. 1 **Brackets** are 1.1 a pair of marks that are placed around a word, sentence, etc in a piece of writing to indicate that the rest of the piece of writing can be read and understood without this word or sentence. EG *The comments in brackets are the author's.* 1.2 a pair of marks that are placed around a series of symbols in a mathematical expression to indicate that this series functions as a separate group within the expression. EG *Put brackets round '2a+b'... The constant doesn't go inside the bracket.* — N COUNT: USU PL = parenthesis; N COUNT: USU PL ↑ symbol

2 If you **bracket** a word, sentence, section, number, etc, you put brackets round it. EG *...a bracketed question mark.* — V+O ↑ enclose

3 If a person or thing is in a particular **bracket**, they are within a particular range of amounts, for example a particular range of income, age, or price. EG *...a professional in a high income bracket... A significant majority were in the 14-16 age bracket... Their incomes are brought into a higher bracket.* — N COUNT+SUPP

4 If you **bracket** one word, number, or other item on a written list with another, you put a curly bracket next to them to indicate that they belong together or should be considered together. EG *Why are these names bracketed together?* — V+O+A (with/together) ↑ link

5 When you **bracket** two or more things or people together, you consider them as being similar or related in some way. EG *He brackets government and many of the advanced technology companies together... Should current affairs be bracketed with documentary?* — V+O+A (with/together) = classify, group

6 A **bracket** is also a piece of metal, wood, or plastic, often L-shaped, that is fastened to a wall to support something, for example a shelf. EG *If you're screwing shelf brackets to the wall always used screws and plugs.* — N COUNT

brackish /brækɪʃ/ water is slightly salty. EG *These reeds grow best in brackish water.* — ADJ QUALIT ≠ fresh

brag /bræg/, **brags, bragging, bragged**. If you **brag**, you you say in a very proud way that you have done or will do a particular thing or that you possess a particular thing. EG *I didn't brag about the salary... He bragged to two nurses that he had killed a man... I bragged of my connections with the aristocracy... We were aware that she was not bragging.* — V: IF+PREP THEN to/about/of, OR V+REPORT-CL = boast

braggart /brægət/, **braggarts**. A **braggart** is a person, usually a man, who brags about what he has done or will do or what he possesses; an old-fashioned word used showing disapproval. EG *The force of events will reveal him for the braggart that he is.* — N COUNT = show off

Brahmin /brɑːmɪn/, **Brahmins**; also spelled **Brahman**. A **Brahmin** is a Hindu of the highest caste. EG *...an elegant young Brahmin.* — N COUNT

braid /breɪd/, **braids, braiding, braided**. 1 **Braid** is a narrow piece of decorated cloth or a band made of twisted threads, which is used to decorate clothes, curtains, etc. EG *...a cap with gold braid all over it.* — N UNCOUNT ↑ trimming

2 If you **braid** hair or a group of threads, you plait it; used in American English and old-fashioned British English. EG *They wore their hair braided in long pigtails.* — V+O

3 A **braid** is a length of someone's hair which has been twisted together and tied; used in American or old-fashioned English. EG *Carole was plump, with long wavy braids and a sweet face.* — N COUNT = plait

braided /breɪdɪ²d/. Something, especially a piece of clothing, that is **braided** is decorated with braid. EG *...a braided maroon uniform jacket.* — ADJ CLASSIF: IF+PREP THEN with

Braille /breɪl/ is a system of printing for blind people in which the letters are printed as groups of raised dots that they can feel with their fingers. — N UNCOUNT

brain /breɪn/, **brains, braining, brained**. 1 Your **brain** is 1.1 the organ inside your head which enables you to think and to feel things such as heat and pain. EG *We've got only a very minor understanding of how the brain works... When the heart stops, the brain is deprived of fresh blood and oxygen... These drugs can cause permanent brain damage.* 1.2 your mind and the way you think. EG *He had one clear and strong wish in his confused brain... Our job is to fill their brains with facts.* ● If someone **has** something **on the brain**, they keep thinking about it or remembering it; an informal expression, often used showing disapproval. EG *You've got food on the brain... I've got that tune on the brain.* — N COUNT = cerebrum; N COUNT: USU POSS+N = head; ● PHR: VB INFLECTS ↑ be preoccupied

2 **Brains** refers to the greyish matter which the brain of a person or animal consists of. EG *The top of her head was a mess of bone, brains, hair, and blood.* — N PLURAL
● If you **blow** someone's **brains out**, you shoot them in the head and kill them; an informal expression. — ● PHR: VB INFLECTS
● If you **beat** someone's **brains out**, you hit their head very hard and kill them; an informal expression. — ● PHR: VB INFLECTS

3 If you say that someone has **brains** or a particular type of **brain**, you mean that they have the ability to learn and understand things quickly, solve problems, and make good decisions. EG *He had his mother's brains and his father's good looks... He'd got brains but wouldn't use them... She has a very capable business brain... How I envied his brain.* — N COUNT ↑ intelligence ≠ stupidity

4 If you **pick** someone's **brains**, you ask them to help you with a problem because they know a lot about the subject involved; an informal expression. EG *I've come to pick your brains.* • to **rack** your **brains**: see **rack**. PHR : VB INFLECTS ⇑ consult

5 A **brain** is a very intelligent person, especially one who spends a lot of time thinking and studying; an informal use. EG *Not even the great brains of Cambridge can solve his problem.* N COUNT ⇑ genius

6 If you refer to the **brains** of an organization or business, you mean the person who thinks about, plans, and decides its activities, as opposed to the people who do the actual work; an informal use. EG *She was the brains of the organization... Who's the brains behind the project?.* N PLURAL : the+N, IF+PREP THEN *of/behind* ⇑ manager

7 If you **brain** someone, you hit them very hard on the head; an informal use. EG *I'll brain him when I get hold of him.* V+O = crown

brainchild /breɪntʃaɪld/. Someone's **brainchild** is an idea, plan, or invention that they have thought up or created. EG *The project was the brainchild of Max Nicholson.* N SING : WITH POSS

brain death. **Brain death** occurs when someone's brain stops functioning, even though their heart may be kept beating using a machine. N UNCOUNT

brain drain; also spelled with a hyphen. If you talk about a **brain drain**, you are referring to the movement of a large number of scientists, engineers, academics, etc away from their own country to other countries where the conditions and salaries are better. EG *We risk a major loss of talent to overseas jobs via a brain drain.* N SING WITH DET ⇑ emigration

brainless /breɪnlɪ[2]s/. Someone who is **brainless** is stupid and silly. EG *The generals were singularly brainless men.* ▸ used of actions and behaviour. EG *She was in no mood for their brainless gabble this afternoon.* ADJ CLASSIF

brainstorm /breɪnstɔːm/, **brainstorms**. **1** If you have a **brainstorm**, you suddenly become unable to think clearly and sensibly; used in British English. EG *I can't imagine why I bought it. I must have had a brainstorm.* N COUNT = mental aberration

2 A **brainstorm** is a clever idea that you suddenly think of; used in American English. N COUNT = brainwave

brainstorming /breɪnstɔːmɪŋ/. A **brainstorming** session is a meeting of people in order to develop ideas together. N UNCOUNT

brain teaser, brain teasers. A **brain teaser** is a question or problem that is difficult to answer or solve, but is not serious or important. N COUNT ⇑ game

brainwash /breɪnwɒʃ/, **brainwashes, brainwashing, brainwashed**. If you **brainwash** someone, you force them to believe something, usually something false, by continually telling them or showing them evidence that it is true, and preventing them from thinking about it properly or considering other evidence; used showing disapproval. EG *They tried to brainwash me... The public continues to be brainwashed into believing that a nuclear war could be survived... ...political or religious brainwashing.* V+O : IF+PREP THEN *into* ⇑ influence

brainwave /breɪnweɪv/, **brainwaves**. A **brainwave** is a clever idea that you suddenly think of. EG *Then he had a brainwave. He could ask the librarian who the girl was.* N COUNT

brainy /breɪni[1]/, **brainier, brainiest**. Someone who is **brainy** is clever and good at learning things; an informal word. EG *She's really brainy.* ADJ QUALIT = intelligent

braise /breɪz/, **braises, braising, braised**. When you **braise** meat or a vegetable, you fry it quickly and then cook it slowly in a covered dish with a small amount of liquid. EG *...braised beef.* V+O

brake /breɪk/, **brakes, braking, braked**. **1** A **brake** is a device in or on a vehicle that is used to make it go slower or stop. EG *Put the brake on... There was a sudden screech of brakes... I had to apply the brakes rather abruptly at a red light.* N COUNT

2 When a vehicle or its driver **brakes**, the driver tries to make the vehicle slow down or stop by using the brakes. EG *As he braked a tyre burst... Try to avoid sudden braking.* V

3 A **brake** is also something that has the effect of slowing down or stopping action or progress. EG *Restrictive practices were putting a savage brake on enterprise... The 1972 White Paper on Education took the brakes off nursery education.* N COUNT : IF+PREP THEN *on/upon/off* ⇑ restriction

4 Something that **brakes** action or progress causes it to slow down or stop. EG *Traditional forms of land tenure brake technological progress.* V+O

brake light, brake lights; also spelled with a hyphen. The **brake lights** of a motor vehicle are the red lights at the back which light up when the driver uses the brakes. N COUNT : USU PL

bramble /bræmbə[0]l/, **brambles**. A **bramble** is a wild bush covered with thorns that produces blackberries. EG *...a large house, all overgrown with briars and brambles... ...a bramble patch.* N COUNT : USU PL

bran /bræn/ refers to the small brown flakes that are left when wheat grains have been used to make white flour. EG *...breakfast cereals containing bran.* N UNCOUNT

branch /brɑːntʃ/, **branches, branching, branched**. **1** A **branch** is a part of a tree which grows out from the trunk and has leaves, flowers, or fruit growing on it. EG *A bird flew across to the tree and alighted on a branch... The trees were leafless except for the topmost branches.* N COUNT = bough

2 A **branch** of an organization such as a business, a trade union, or a political party is one of the offices, shops, or local groups which belong to it. A branch of a business serves customers in a particular town or area. EG *...the Ipswich branch of Marks and Spencer... Report to the Branch Manager as soon as you've settled in... All the organizations in this list have local branches.* N COUNT = sub division

3 A **branch** of an organization such as a government is a part of it that is responsible for doing one particular aspect of the work of that organization. EG *...the executive branch of government... In the Second World War the OSS, the secret operations branch of United States Intelligence, was set up... We have got what we call a fire prevention branch.* N COUNT+SUPP = division, section, wing

4 A **branch** of an academic subject or of an artistic or industrial skill or activity is a particular subject, skill, or activity that forms part of it. EG *...specialists in particular branches of medicine... An effective cooling system is important in many branches of technology.* N COUNT+SUPP = field

5 A **branch** of a family is a group of its members who are all descended from one particular person. EG *The Foster-Smith branch of the family emigrated to Australia.* N COUNT+SUPP ⇑ line

6 When something, usually something long and narrow, **branches**, it divides at a particular point into two parts and develops in different directions, like the top part of a Y. EG *These creatures sprout five arms which, in some species, branch repeatedly.* V ⇑ split

branch off. **1** A road or path that **branches off** starts from another, larger one and goes in a slightly different direction. EG *The road to Oxford branches off here.* PHRASAL VB : V+ADV/PREP

2 If someone who is speaking **branches off**, they stop talking about one thing and start talking about something slightly different. EG *Do you not think then, to branch off that subject a little, that their upbringing is important too?* PHRASAL VB : V+ADV/PREP = digress from, wander off

branch out. If you **branch out**, you do something different from your normal activities or work, especially something unusual or risky. EG *I can't think why we didn't move years ago when we felt the urge to branch out... She decided to branch out alone and launch a concerted campaign.* PHRASAL VB : V+ADV ⇑ develop

branch line, branch lines; also spelled with a hyphen. A **branch line** is a railway line that goes to small towns rather than one that goes between large cities. N COUNT

brand /brænd/, **brands, branding, branded**. **1** A particular **brand** of a product is the version of that product made by one particular manufacturer. EG *What brand of soap powder do you use?... These are rather more expensive than the usual supermarket brands.* N COUNT : IF+PREP THEN *of* ⇑ variety = make

2 A **brand** of something such as a way of thinking or behaving is a particular kind or variety of it. EG *They brought their particular brand of politics to this country... ...a new brand of humour.* N COUNT+*of* = strain

3 If someone is **branded** as being something unacceptable or disgraceful, they are generally believed to be like that. EG *Anyone who favours a measure of redistribution is branded as a dangerous revolutionary... His political supporters had also been branded traitors.* V+O+C, OR V+O+A *(as)* ⇑ characterize = label

4 When you **brand** an animal, especially a farm animal, you put a permanent mark on its skin, V+O : IF+PREP THEN *with*

usually by burning it on, in order to indicate whose property it is.

5 A **brand** is also **5.1** a permanent mark, usually burnt onto the skin of an animal, which indicates who the owner is. N COUNT **5.2** a piece of burning wood used as a torch; a literary use. N COUNT

6 See also **brand-new**.

branded /brændɪ^{2}d/. A **branded** product is one which is made by a well-known manufacturer and has the manufacturer's label on it. ADJ CLASSIF : ATTRIB

branding iron, branding irons. A **branding iron** is a long piece of metal with a design at one end which is used to brand animals. N COUNT ⇑ implement

brandish /brændɪʃ/, **brandishes, brandishing, brandished**. If you **brandish** something, especially a weapon, you hold it and wave it vigorously in the air as a sign of aggression or triumph. EG *They sprang high into the air brandishing their spears... She was at the door brandishing tickets.* V+O ⇑ display

brand name, brand names. A **brand name** is the name by which a product made by a particular manufacturer is sold. N COUNT

brand-new; also spelled without a hyphen. Something that is **brand-new** is completely new and has not been used before. EG *There's no reason why it shouldn't start. It's a brand-new machine.* ADJ CLASSIF ≠ old

brandy /brændi^{1}/, **brandies**. **Brandy** is a strong alcoholic drink, usually made from wine. EG *He ordered coffee and brandy.* N MASS ⇑ liqueur

brandy butter is a thick paste made from butter, sugar and brandy, eaten especially at Christmas with pudding or mince pies. N UNCOUNT

brandy snap, brandy snaps; also spelled with a hyphen. A **brandy snap** is a very thin, crisp biscuit in the shape of a hollow cylinder, flavoured with ginger. N COUNT

brash /bræʃ/, **brasher, brashest**. If someone's behaviour is **brash**, they are speaking too loudly or being too confident and aggressive; used showing disapproval. EG *He seemed designed for TV with his brash authority and handsome features... Jenny was alarmed by these brash and brilliant children.* ADJ QUALIT = flashy, loud-mouthed
◊ **brashness**. EG *...looking back with distaste to the brashness of my late adolescence.* ◊ N UNCOUNT = cockiness

brass /brɑːs/, **brasses**. 1 **Brass** is a yellow-coloured metal that is made from copper and zinc, and used especially for making ornaments and some musical instruments. EG *I like working in brass... ...shining brass jugs filled with flowers and leaves... ...brass buttons.* N UNCOUNT

2 A **brass** is a block of brass with writing or a picture cut into it and that is found especially in churches, set into the floor or a wall as a memorial to a good or famous person. EG *This church has some of the best memorial brasses in London.* • See also **brass rubbing**. N COUNT

3 The **brass** in an orchestra is the group of musical wind instruments that are made out of brass, including the trumpet, the tuba, and the trombone. N SING : *the*+N, OR N BEFORE N

4 Some people, especially in Northern England, use **brass** to refer to money; an informal use. N UNCOUNT

5 If you say that someone has the **brass** nerve, cheek, etc to do something, you mean that they dare to do it, without worry or shame about the results of their actions; an informal use. EG *Do you have the brass cheek to choose between them?... It's quite exciting; all you need is a deep breath and a brass nerve.* • **as bold as brass**: see **bold**. ADJ CLASSIF : ATTRIB = bold

6 See also **top brass**.

brassed off. If you are **brassed off**, you are tired and annoyed; used in very informal British English. EG *I'm really brassed off... I'm brassed off with this stupid essay.* ADJ QUALIT : PRED, IF+PREP THEN *with*

brasserie /bræsəri^{1}/, **brasseries**. A **brasserie** is a small and usually cheap restaurant or bar. N COUNT

brass hat, brass hats; also spelled with a hyphen. A **brass hat** is a military officer of very high rank; used in informal English. N COUNT

brassiere /bræsɪə, bræz-/, **brassieres**. A **brassiere** is a bra; a formal or old-fashioned word. N COUNT

brass knuckles means the same as **knuckle-duster**; used in American English. N PLURAL

brass-monkey weather is very cold weather indeed; used in very informal British English. ADJ CLASSIF : ATTRIB

brass rubbing, brass rubbings. A **brass rubbing** is a picture made by placing a piece of paper over a block of brass that has writing or a picture on it, and rubbing it with a wax crayon to copy it onto the paper. N COUNT

brass tacks. If you get down to **brass tacks**, you discuss the basic and most important facts, truths, or realities of a situation. EG *Now, let's get down to brass tacks: how much did we actually lose last year?* N PLURAL

brasswork /brɑːswɜːk/ is the craft of making things from brass and decorating them. N UNCOUNT

brassy /brɑːsi^{1}/, **brassier, brassiest**. 1 If you describe something as **brassy**, you mean that it has a yellowish and metallic colour, especially when you think it should not. EG *Your hair's looking a bit brassy–what have you been doing to it?* ADJ QUALIT ⇑ yellow

2 A sound that is **brassy** is unpleasantly harsh and loud. EG *The music played incessantly; now soft and slow, now brassy and loud... Joanna gave a brassy laugh.* ADJ QUALIT

3 If you describe a person's appearance or their behaviour as **brassy**, you mean that they do not have good taste, and dress or behave in a way that is too bright, daring, harsh, or lively; used showing disapproval. ADJ QUALIT = flashy ≠ refined

brat /bræt/, **brats**. A **brat** is a person, especially a child, who is behaving badly or annoying you; an informal word used showing disapproval. EG *He's a spoilt brat... If he was going to have to keep her and her brat she could damn well clean the place up.* N COUNT : ALSO VOC

bravado /brəvɑːdəʊ/ is an outward appearance of courage or confidence that someone does not really feel, but that they put on in order to impress others. EG *Some mad, defiant act of bravado... It was more with bravado than conviction that I told him.* N UNCOUNT : IF+ PREP THEN *of* = daring

brave /breɪv/, **braver, bravest; braves, braving, braved**. 1 Someone who is **brave** shows in their behaviour that they have the courage to do something even though it is frightening, dangerous, or difficult; used showing approval. EG *I think you were brave to defy convention... He made a brave attempt to prevent the hijack.* ADJ QUALIT = courageous ≠ cowardly
◊ **bravely**. EG *Kunta bravely bit his lip to avoid crying out.* ◊ ADV WITH VB = valiantly

2 If you say that someone is **putting a brave face on** a difficult situation, you mean that they are pretending in a brave way that they are happy or that they can deal with the problem easily, even though it is something very difficult or awful. PHR : VB INFLECTS

3 If you **brave** a difficult, painful, dangerous, or frightening situation, you deliberately experience it, in order to get or achieve something. EG *Farmers braved wintry conditions to rescue the sheep.* V+O ⇑ endure = face ≠ shun

4 **Brave** also means fine or glorious; a literary use. EG *The whole brave American dream seemed to be crumbling around our ears.* ADJ CLASSIF : ATTRIB = proud

5 A **brave** is a young man, especially a warrior, who belongs to a North American Indian tribe. N COUNT

brave out. If you **brave** something **out**, you face something that is frightening or upsetting and deal with it in a brave way. PHRASAL VB : V+O+ADV ⇑ endure

Brave New World. The **Brave New World** is used to refer to an ideal new society or government which is based on the principles of progress, justice, and freedom. EG *...a benevolent government in the 'Brave New World' pattern.* N SING : USU *the*/*a*+N = utopia

bravery /breɪvə^{ə}ri^{1}/ is the quality of being able to do something even though it is frightening, dangerous, or difficult; used showing approval. EG *Being a nurse requires infinite patience and bravery... ...an act of bravery.* N UNCOUNT = courage ≠ cowardice

bravo /brɑːvəʊ/ is used to express appreciation when someone has done something well; an old-fashioned or formal word. EG *Kate applauded with the rest and shouted out 'Bravo!'* EXCLAM = well done

bravura /brəvj^{ə}ʊərə/ is a way of doing something in which you add unnecessary extra actions that emphasize your skill or importance; a literary word. EG *There is no bravura, no show; everything is very precisely done... ...in between flashing smiles and bravura flourishes of the gold pen.* N UNCOUNT ⇑ show = flash

brawl /brɔːl/, **brawls, brawling, brawled**. A **brawl** is a rough fight or struggle, especially one in which people use their fists to hit each other. EG *His two front teeth were knocked out in a brawl.* N COUNT = punch-up
▸ used as a verb. EG *Usually you could see them, playing or brawling in the street.* ▸ V = scrap

brawn /brɔːn/ is 1 physical strength. EG *Too little bone and brawn had isolated Bernard from his fellow men.* N UNCOUNT = muscle 2 food made from pieces of pork and N UNCOUNT jelly pressed together so that it is solid and can be sliced.

brawny /brɔ:ni[1]/. Someone, especially a man, who is **brawny** is strong and muscular. EG *...young brawny chaps.* ADJ QUALIT = beefy

bray /breɪ/, **brays, braying, brayed.** 1 When a donkey **brays**, it utters a loud, harsh sound. ▸ used as a noun. EG *...the querulous bray of a waking donkey.* V ▸ N COUNT : IF+ PREP THEN *of* ⇕ sound

2 To **bray** means to make a loud harsh sound or talk in a loud harsh way; used showing disapproval. EG *Her dreadful, braying, laughter... With a braying flourish of trumpets, the music started up.* V = blare

brazen /breɪzə[0]n/. Someone who is **brazen** is very bold and does not care if other people think that they are behaving wrongly. EG *...a brazen whore.* ▸ used also of things people say or do in this way. EG *...a brazen accusation... I could not do anything so brazen as that.* ◇ **brazenly.** EG *No industry is more brazenly orientated towards quick, easy profits.* ADJ QUALIT = shameless ◇ ADV WITH VB ⇑ boldly

brazen out. If you **brazen out** a difficult or embarrassing situation, you behave confidently and without appearing to be ashamed, although you may be guilty of doing something wrong and may feel bad about it. EG *He'll brazen it out.* PHRASAL VB : V+O+ADV

brazier /breɪzɪə/, **braziers.** A **brazier** is a large metal container in which coal or charcoal is burned, especially to keep people warm when they have to stay outside in cold weather, for example because of their work. EG *There was a coke brazier outside their canvas hut.* N COUNT ⇑ heater

Brazilian /brə[3]zɪlɪən/, **Brazilians.** 1 A **Brazilian** thing or person belongs or relates to Brazil or to its people. EG *...the Brazilian jungle... ...the Brazilian government.* ADJ CLASSIF

2 A **Brazilian** is a person who comes from Brazil. EG *The Brazilians will supply £350 million worth of soya beans.* N COUNT

breach /bri:tʃ/, **breaches, breaching, breached.** 1 A **breach** of an agreement, law, promise, etc is the act of breaking it. EG *Does refusal to work on rest days constitute a breach of contract?... This attempt to influence the ballot is in breach of Trade Union rules... ...a breach of security... ...prisoners charged with serious breaches of discipline.* N COUNT/ UNCOUNT : IF+ PREP THEN *of* = violation

2 If you **breach** an agreement, law, promise, etc, you break it. EG *...the ethical questions involved in breaching the confidentiality of patients.* V+O

3 A **breach** in a friendship, relationship, etc is a serious disagreement between the people involved, often resulting in the friendship or relationship ending for a period of time. EG *Perhaps the most profound breach in our marriage has been over the question of the children's education... ...the deep political breach between his father and uncle.* N COUNT = rupture, rift

4 If someone **steps into the breach**, they do a job or task which another person was supposed to do, because that person is suddenly unable to do it, for example because of illness. EG *...Alfred Cooper, who had loyally stepped into the breach as official Tory candidate.* PHR : VB INFLECTS

5 A **breach** in something such as a wall or fence is a gap or crack in it, especially one caused suddenly and deliberately by someone or something damaging it. EG *They rush to defend any breach in the walls.* N COUNT : IF+ PREP THEN *in*

6 To **breach** something, for example a wall or fence, means to deliberately make a gap in it by damaging it, especially in order to let someone or something through. EG *He scrambled up the mined headlands where he breached the enemy barbed wire... It must have some weak spot by which its defences can be breached.* V+O

breach of the peace, breaches of the peace. A **breach of the peace** is noisy or violent behaviour in a public place which is illegal because it disturbs other people; a technical term in law. EG *They were arrested for causing a breach of the peace.* N COUNT : USU SING ⇑ disturbance

bread /bred/, **breads.** 1 **Bread** is a very common food made from flour, water, and often yeast. The mixture is made into a soft dough and baked in an oven. Bread is often cut into slices and eaten with, for example, butter, jam, or cheese. EG *...some bread and cheese from yesterday's lunch... ...a loaf of bread... ...three large slices of bread.* ● See also **breaded.** N MASS

2 If you say that someone **knows which side their bread is buttered on**, you mean that they know what to do or who to please in order to remain in a good situation or to avoid a bad one, and will not do anything risky or unexpected; an informal expression. PHR : VB INFLECTS

3 If you say that something is **the best thing since sliced bread**, you are emphasizing how good you think it is; an informal expression. EG *He thinks their new album is the best thing since sliced bread.* PHR : USED AS C ⇑ superior

4 **Bread** is also used to refer to the food that people need to stay alive; a rather formal use. EG *Peace had not given bread to the masses.* N UNCOUNT = sustenance

5 Some people say **bread** as a way of referring to money; an informal use. EG *I'm paying out a lot of bread for the house... I desperately need the bread.* N UNCOUNT

bread and butter. 1 The **bread and butter** of a person or organization is the activity or work that provides their main source of income. EG *It's their living, it's their bread and butter... Comedies and pantomimes are the bread and butter of the local theatre... This was just bread-and-butter work for which he couldn't spare creative energy.* N UNCOUNT : USU WITH POSS = subsistence

2 The **bread and butter** issues, questions, etc are those that are the most basic and important in relation to a particular subject. EG *People vote only on immediate, bread-and-butter issues.* ADJ CLASSIF : ATTRIB

bread-bin, bread-bins. A **bread-bin** is a container for keeping bread in. N COUNT

bread-board, bread-boards; also spelled without a hyphen. A **bread-board** is a wooden board for cutting bread on. N COUNT

breadcrumb /bredkrʌm/, **breadcrumbs. Breadcrumbs** are lots of tiny pieces of bread, used especially in cooking. EG *Mix together the onions, mushrooms, breadcrumbs, herbs, and lentils... Spread the fish with the breadcrumb mixture.* N COUNT : USU PL ⇑ crumbs

breaded /bredɪ[2]d/. Food that is **breaded** has been covered in breadcrumbs before it is cooked. EG *...breaded veal cutlets.* ADJ CLASSIF ⇑ coated

breadfruit /bredfru:t/, **breadfruits.** A **breadfruit** is a large, round fruit that grows on trees in the Pacific Islands and tropical parts of America. When it is baked, it looks and feels like bread. N COUNT/ UNCOUNT ⇑ fruit

breadline /bredlaɪn/. Someone who is on or near the **breadline** is very poor indeed. EG *One family in four was on the breadline or just above it... Some of us are very near the breadline.* N SING : *the*+N

breadth /bredθ/. 1 The **breadth** of something, or its measurement in **breadth**, is the distance between its two sides. EG *They were tall in relation to their breadth... The wheat is six or seven swathes in breadth and some fifty yards long.* ● the **length and breadth** of somewhere: see **length.** ● See also **hair's breadth.** N UNCOUNT : USU +*of* = width

2 The **breadth** of something is its quality of consisting of, or involving, many different things. EG *The very breadth of the subject gives it an added interest... The modern world sadly misses this kind of breadth of vision.* N UNCOUNT + SUPP ⇑ scope = range

breadwinner /bredwɪnə/, **breadwinners**; also spelled with a hyphen or as two words. The **breadwinner** in a family is the person in it who earns the money or most of the money that the family needs. EG *He could no longer fulfil his function as breadwinner for the family.* N COUNT ⇑ worker

break /breɪk/, **breaks, breaking, broke, broken.** 1 When an object **breaks** or when you **break** it, it splits into pieces as a result of an accident, for example because you have dropped it or hit it too hard. EG *He has broken a window with a ball... She stepped backwards onto a coffee cup and saucer, which broke into several pieces... There was a smash of breaking china.* V-ERG ⇑ damage = smash

2 When something long and narrow **breaks** or when you **break** it, it snaps into two pieces because it has too much pressure put on it, for example because you are pulling or pushing it at one end. EG *The string broke... Branches break under their weight.* V-ERG ⇑ split = snap

3 When you **break** a bone in your body, you damage it in an accident so that it cracks or splits. EG *She's broken her ankle... If he breaks a leg he needs support for it while the bone sets.* ▸ used as a noun. EG *That looks like a nasty break.* V+O = fracture ▸ N COUNT = fracture

4 To **break** something that is covering or sealing something means to split it open. EG *I can't see any skin broken... The seals of the packet had been broken.* V+O

5 When a tool or piece of machinery **breaks** or when V-ERG

you **break** it, it is damaged and no longer works. EG *...a broken television set.*

6 If you **break** a law, rule, promise, or agreement, you do something that disobeys it. EG *We're not breaking the law... He didn't like to break the rules... They tried to break the promises made in negotiations.* V+O ⇑ disobey ≠ keep, abide by

7 If someone **breaks free**, **breaks loose**, **breaks** someone's **hold**, etc, **7.1** they free themselves by force, for example when someone is holding them firmly, or when they have been tied up to prevent them from escaping. EG *Thrashing to break free, he was jabbed savagely with sharp sticks... He had my hands behind my back in a hold that was impossible to break... Kunta lunged back and forth trying to break his bonds.* PHR: VB INFLECTS ⇑ free **7.2** they change their situation or alter their plans in order to have more freedom in their actions or decisions. EG *Your life begins to take off when you break free from the family chains... Maybe I can break loose at two o'clock.* PHR: VB INFLECTS ⇑ escape = break away

8 When something such as an emotion or state of affairs **breaks loose**, it begins or develops very suddenly and violently so that people are unable to control it. EG *Precisely at the moment when all panic should have broken loose inside me, I felt calmer... If we had been broadcasting all this a year ago, all hell would have broken loose.* PHR: VB INFLECTS ⇑ develop = erupt, break out

9 When someone **makes a break** from prison or captivity, they escape. EG *Fugitives made a sensational prison break from Dartmoor in 1979.* PHR: VB INFLECTS

10 To **break** a connection, contact, or relationship means to destroy or end it. EG *Radio contact was broken... The policy would have broken the link we have with the government... I had just recently been forced to break my close ties with the Panthers.* V+O = sever

11 A **break** with a group, person, or something else that you have a connection with, is the act of separating from them, often because of a disagreement. EG *...their break with the Labour Party in 1968... ...our break with the past... What an enormous relief you will feel for having made the break at last.* N COUNT: USU SING ⇑ separation = split

12 To **break** something such as a system or a situation in which no progress can be made means to destroy or put an end to this system or situation. EG *They are out to break the system... Everything you've tried has failed to break the deadlock.* V+O ⇑ weaken

13 When a person **breaks** a strike, they go to work even though their trade union has told them to strike. EG *The hungriest of them can always be tempted to break strikes.* V+O ⇑ defy

14 To **break** a habit, idea, feeling, etc that someone has, or to **break** them of it, means to put an end to it by causing them to believe, feel, or do something else. EG *They cannot break the habit... ...the risk of breaking public trust in the television news... ...breaking a child of its bad habits.* V+O, OR V+O+A (of) ⇑ stop = curb, kick

15 To **break** someone or their patience, will, resolve, etc means to strain or upset them so much that they cannot tolerate any more. EG *Would they continue to try to break her will?... The criticisms finally broke her... He had tried her patience to breaking point.* V+O = destroy, crush
● to **break** someone's **heart**: see **heart**.

16 To **break** someone also means to destroy their success, career, hopes, etc. EG *This committee can save him or break him... ...a prestigious competition which could make or break his career.* V+O ⇑ weaken = crush

17 To **break** the silence, monotony, etc in a situation means to do or say something to end it or change it, for example making a noise or doing something unusual. EG *At last Maurice broke the silence... The stillness was broken by the ferocious barking of a dog... It breaks the monotony.* V+O = interrupt ● If you **break** your **silence**, you tell a secret that you have been refusing to reveal for a long time. EG *She had broken her silence.* ● PHR: VB INFLECTS

18 A **break** in a line, sound, process, etc is a gap or interruption in its continuity. EG *Each marriage and each death represented a break in the normal time process... We cannot hear a break between sounds of less than one tenth of a second.* N COUNT ▸ used as a verb. EG *The taut blue horizon encircled them, broken only by the mountain-top.* ▸ V+O ⇑ interrupt

19 When you **break** your **step** or **pace**, you change the way that you are walking so that the rhythm of your step is interrupted. EG *Bending quickly without breaking pace, Kunta picked up a small stone.* PHR: VB INFLECTS

20 A **break** is also **20.1** a short period of time when you stop what you are doing in order to have a rest before you begin again. EG *I'm taking a break... We all met in the pub during the lunch break.... The doctors had worked without a break.* N COUNT ▸ used as a verb. EG *We broke for tea for an hour... I suggest we break for lunch now rather than going straight on to the second part.* ▸ V: IF+PREP THEN for **20.2** a holiday, or a period of time when you do something different from the job or activity that you are involved with, in order to have a rest from it. EG *You need a break, a change... To give himself a well-deserved break, Morris decided to take a trip to London.* N COUNT

21 In British schools, **break** is a period of time between lessons when children can play or talk. EG *'What time's break?'–'Twenty-five to twelve.'* N UNCOUNT = playtime

22 To **break** the force of something such as a blow or fall means to weaken its effect. EG *...his fists meeting and breaking the force of the descending club... Fortunately, the tree broke her fall.* V+O = check

23 When someone **breaks** a piece of news or when a piece of news **breaks**, the news is told to people. EG *It was Ted who broke the news to me... The news broke in Paris that Kennedy had been shot... You're not very good at breaking bad news, are you?* V-ERG ⇑ tell

24 You can use **break** to refer to a lucky opportunity that someone gets to become successful, especially in their career; an informal use. EG *He has been running for 12 years, but his main break came last spring in Australia.* N COUNT

25 If you **break** a record, especially in a sports event, you beat the previous record for a particular performance or achievement. EG *Oliver Barrett was out to break his New York-Boston speed record... He was the first man to break the four minute mile.* V+O

26 When a storm **breaks**, it starts suddenly. V

27 When the weather **breaks**, it suddenly changes after it has been the same for some time, for example it rains after several days of sunshine. V

28 When day **breaks**, it starts to grow light after the night has ended. EG *The day was about to break when I finally left the hotel.* V = dawn

29 Something that happens **at the break of day** happens at the time when it begins to grow light after the night; a literary expression. PHR: USED AS AN A = at dawn, at daybreak

30 When a wave **breaks**, the water at the top of it falls down, for example when it reaches the shore. EG *I could see the line of white foam where the waves broke on the beach.* V ⇑ crash

31 When a company or person running a business **breaks even**, they make neither a profit nor a loss. EG *Even without profit we could still make our way by breaking even... With assistance the company would break even by 1971.* PHR: VB INFLECTS ≠ profit, lose

32 break the bank. **32.1** If you **break the bank** when you are gambling or playing cards, you win all the money that belongs to the dealer or to the casino management. PHR: VB INFLECTS = clean up **32.2** If you say that the cost of something won't **break the bank**, you mean that it is not a very large sum of money; an informal expression. EG *'It costs 50p to get in.'–'Well, that won't break the bank will it?'* PHR: VB INFLECTS

33 If you **break** a secret code, you work out how to read it. EG *...a signal in an easy code which we had broken long ago.* V+O ⇑ solve = crack, decipher

34 When a boy's voice **breaks**, usually at about the age of fourteen, it becomes deeper and sounds more like a man's voice. V ⇑ change = deepen

35 To **break** a safe, door, etc, or to **break** it open means to open it by force, often by using explosives. EG *Thieves broke the safe open with dynamite.* V+O: USU+A = force open

36 In tennis, a **break** or a **break** of serve is an advantage that you gain by winning a game in which your opponent was serving. EG *McEnroe still has one break of serve.* N COUNT+SUPP

37 If you **break** someone's serve or service in tennis, you win a game in which your opponent was serving. V+O

38 In snooker and billiards, a **break** is the number of points that a player scores during one turn in a game. EG *Steve Davis went into the lead with a break of 71.* N COUNT+SUPP ⇑ score

39 The word **break** is also used in the following expressions which are explained at other places in this dictionary. ● to **break fresh ground**: see **ground**. ● to **break wind**: see **wind**. ● to **break cover**: see **cover**. ● to **break ranks**: see **rank**. ● to **break camp**: see **camp**. ● to **break the ice**: see **ice**. ● **when the waters break**: see **water**.

40 See also **broke** and **broken**.

break away. 1 When you **break away** from a group, you stop being part of it, for example because of a disagreement. EG *Two United Party senators broke away to form the Federal Party.* PHRASAL VB: V+ADV, IF+PREP THEN *from*

2 To **break away** from someone or something means to move away from them. EG *I broke away from her and raced for the door... The land mass of Australia, after it had broken away from Antarctica, continued to drift.* PHRASAL VB: V+ADV, IF+PREP THEN *from* = cut loose

3 See also **breakaway**.

break down. 1 When a machine **breaks down**, it stops working, for example because it is damaged. EG *Garages never seemed to be open when the car broke down... Mum's TV has broken down.* PHRASAL VB: V+ADV = pack up, go

2 When a system, plan, discussion, etc **breaks down**, it fails because of a problem or disagreement. EG *This efficient communication system started to break down... The talks broke down over differences on doctrine.* PHRASAL VB: V+ADV ⇑ fail = founder

3 To **break down** something such as an idea or statement means to separate it into its parts in order to make it easier to understand or deal with. EG *Learn to break down large tasks into manageable units... Complicated instructions can always be broken down into a collection of simple steps.* PHRASAL VB: V+O+ADV ⇑ reduce = analyse

4 When a substance **breaks down** or when something **breaks** it **down**, it changes into a different form because of a chemical or biological process. EG *Enzymes break down proteins by chemical action.* PHRASAL VB: V-ERG+ADV = decompose

5 To **break down** something such as a fixed idea or a difficult situation means to change people's attitudes so that the idea or situation no longer exists. EG *This would help break down the barriers between young and old... Newcomers have broken down many of the old community ideas.* PHRASAL VB: V+O+ADV ⇑ alter = remove

6 If someone **breaks down**, 6.1 they lose control of themselves, especially by crying because of extreme sadness. EG *He had broken down and cried... I have seen Virginia break down at rehearsals... They adlibbed so much and broke down in chuckles so often.* PHRASAL VB: V+ADV ⇑ collapse

6.2 they become ill, especially mentally ill, because they are not able to cope with their problems. EG *She broke down completely and had to go into hospital... Nearly fifty per cent of the students broke down physically or psychologically.* PHRASAL VB: V+ADV ⇑ collapse = crack up

7 To **break down** something such as a door means to hit it so hard that it is broken and falls to the ground, for example when entering a building or room by force. PHRASAL VB: V+O+ADV = demolish

8 See also **breakdown**.

break in. 1 If someone **breaks in** or **breaks into** a building, they get into it by force. EG *He broke into a shop one night and killed the proprietor... Offices and professors' rooms were broken into and files removed... They had broken in through a gardener's gate.* • See also **break-in**. PHRASAL VB: V+ADV/PREP ⇑ enter

2 If you **break in** on someone's conversation or activity, you interrupt them, especially by talking to them. EG *'Crow –' began Spear excitedly, but his wife broke in... 'Don't look at me,' Etta broke in brusquely... 'Sorry to break in on you like this, Dr Marlowe.'* PHRASAL VB: V+ADV, IF+PREP THEN *on/upon*

3 To **break** someone **in** means to cause them to experience gradually a situation or activity that they have not experienced before. EG *Chief Brody liked to break in his young men slowly... Five years constituted little more than a breaking-in period for a family moved to a new community.* PHRASAL VB: V+O+ADV ⇑ accustom

4 When you **break in** something such as a new pair of shoes or boots, you use them for short periods of time until they are comfortable and suitable for normal use. EG *I broke in a new pair of very stiff leather shoes.* PHRASAL VB: V+O+ADV

5 If you **break in** a wild or young horse, you train it to become obedient and unafraid of humans. PHRASAL VB: V+O+ADV

break into. 1 If you **break into** a run, a song, laughter, etc, you suddenly begin to do the thing mentioned. EG *When Rudolph saw her, he broke into a run... Piggy broke into noisy laughter... The boys broke into applause.* PHRASAL VB: V+PREP ⇑ start

2 If you **break into** an activity or process that is going on, you interrupt it. EG *He became so pensive that she did not like to break into his thought... This was not only tiring them but breaking into their favourite feeding times.* PHRASAL VB: V+PREP, HAS PASS

3 If you **break into** a new area of activity, especially an area of business, you become involved in it, or gain power or influence in it. EG *...women wanting to break into the labour market.* PHRASAL VB: V+PREP, HAS PASS

4 If you **break into** a sum of money that you have been saving, you start to spend it. EG *She was so desperate that she broke into the holiday money.* PHRASAL VB: V+PREP, HAS PASS

5 When you **break** something **into** smaller parts, you divide it into smaller parts. EG *...breaking words into syllables.* PHRASAL VB: V+O+PREP, HAS PASS

break off. 1 When part of something **breaks off** or when you **break it off**, this part of the main object is removed by being broken. EG *Garroway broke off another piece of bread and chewed at it... I broke a branch off and stabbed at the ground with it... A little bit has broken off the left hand corner.* PHRASAL VB: V-ERG+ADV ⇑ detach

2 If you **break off** when you are doing or saying something, you suddenly stop doing or saying it. EG *He would break off the rehearsal... 'I thought –' he broke off, then smiled. 'Sorry, not my business.'* PHRASAL VB: V+ADV, OR V+O+ADV

3 If you **break off** a relationship or agreement with someone, you end it. EG *Men seem to be more skilled at breaking off relationships than women... I've broken off my engagement.* PHRASAL VB: V+O+ADV

break out. 1 If something such as a fight, argument, or disease **breaks out**, it begins suddenly, often in a violent way. EG *Fierce fighting broke out between rival groups... War broke out in Europe on 4 August... Disease broke out during the journey.* PHRASAL VB: V+ADV, USU+A ⇑ begin

2 If someone **breaks out** from a place where they have been held in captivity, they escape from it. EG *He broke out one spring night in 1946 and hitched south.* PHRASAL VB: V+ADV

3 If you **break out** in spots, sweat, rashes, etc, or if they **break out** on your body, they start to appear on the surface of your skin. EG *She broke out in a rash... She felt the sweat break out on her forehead.* PHRASAL VB: V+ADV, USU+A *(in)* ⇑ come out

4 If you **break out** of an undesirable or dull situation or way of behaving, you manage to change what you do or the way you behave. EG *We've got to break out of this vicious circle... She has managed to break out of the mould and achieve something individual... My dear father broke out of his normal reticence and asked me to tell him frankly what I wished to do.* PHRASAL VB: V+ADV+PREP *(of)* ⇑ get away from

break through. 1 If you **break through** something such as a barrier, you succeed in forcing your way through it. EG *I struggled up the side of the gully and broke through the nettles and elder bushes... Some of the crowd attempted to break through police cordons.* PHRASAL VB: V+PREP ⇑ get through = penetrate

2 If you **break through** something that is preventing you from achieving something, you deal successfully with it so that it no longer causes you difficulties. EG *She could not break through such a barrier of indifference... I want to try to break through conventional situations... They gradually and tactfully broke through my reserve.* PHRASAL VB: V+PREP ⇑ deal with = overcome

3 When something **breaks through**, it appears in a place where it was previously hidden or unseen. EG *Sometimes the instinctual impulses break through in your work... The sun managed to break through for a while this afternoon.* PHRASAL VB: V+ADV/PREP ⇑ appear

4 See also **breakthrough**.

break up. 1 When something **breaks up** or when you **break it up**, it is divided into several smaller parts. EG *The great southern land-mass eventually began to break up... Most birds still have a need to break up their food... The wood was so rotten that, when they pulled, it broke up into a shower of fragments.* PHRASAL VB: V-ERG+ADV ⇑ divide = split up

2 If you **break up** with your boyfriend, girlfriend, etc, your relationship with that person ends. EG *Today, many couples break up... Tim and I broke up... Their marriage is breaking up... Have you broken up with a boyfriend recently?* PHRASAL VB: V+ADV, OR V+ADV +A *(with)*, RECIP = finish, split up

3 If a group of people or an organization **breaks up**, the people who belong to it separate from each other. EG *His Committee broke up into rival groups... The crowd broke up in panic... Families broke up in the move from country to town.* PHRASAL VB: V+ADV = split up

4 If an activity **breaks up** or you **break it up**, it is brought to an end, especially suddenly and violently. EG *The policemen broke the fight up... Disruptive tactics of breaking up meetings... The long drunken party had just broken up.* PHRASAL VB: V-ERG+ADV

5 To **break up** a continuous activity or process means to do something different at intervals during this activity or process, usually in order to make it PHRASAL VB: V+O+ADV ⇑ interrupt

less boring. EG *It breaks up the day... These games could be used to break up the monotony.*

6 When schools or the pupils in them **break up**, the school term ends and the pupils start their holidays; used mainly in informal British English. EG *We're lucky, we break up quite early.* PHRASAL VB : V+ ADV

7 See also **break-up**.

break with. 1 If you **break with** a group or person that you have been connected with, you separate from them, usually because of a disagreement. EG *In 1929 he broke with the Liberal Party over Lloyd George's Programme... The Chinese church broke with Rome in 1957... He broke with Shaw altogether.* PHRASAL VB : V+ PREP = break away

2 If you **break with** tradition or a belief, you do or believe something that is very different. EG *We have broken irretrievably with the past... On 7 February 1951, he broke with precedent by making his maiden speech on a controversial subject.* PHRASAL VB : V+ PREP, HAS PASS = depart from

breakable /breɪkəbəᵊl/. An object that is **breakable** is easy to break by accident. EG *My wife let her play with breakable ornaments.* ADJ CLASSIF ⇑ delicate = fragile

breakage /breɪkɪdʒ/, **breakages.** 1 A **breakage** is something that has been broken, or the value of the objects broken. EG *The breakages were appalling... All breakages have to be paid for.* N COUNT

2 **Breakage** is the act of breaking something; a formal or legal term. EG *Accidental breakage of your household glass will be covered by the policy.* N UNCOUNT ⇑ damage

breakaway /breɪkəweɪ/. 1 A **breakaway** group is a group of people who separate from a larger group, for example because of a disagreement. EG *A breakaway organization rapidly appeared... ...the African National Congress and its breakaway youth wing.* ADJ CLASSIF : ATTRIB = splinter group

2 A **breakaway** is an act of breaking away from a group. EG *Two new opposition parties were formed in a breakaway from the United Party.* N COUNT : USU SING = split

breakdown /breɪkdaʊn/, **breakdowns.** 1 The **breakdown** of a system, plan, discussion, etc is the failure of it because of a problem or difficulty. EG *There was a serious breakdown of communications... There were periods of civil war, unrest or breakdown of law and order... They blame the police for the breakdown in community relations.* N COUNT+SUPP : USU SING = collapse

2 If you have a **breakdown** in your car, it stops working, usually when you are in the middle of a journey. EG *Spark plugs in bad condition make you very prone to breakdowns... We had a breakdown on the motorway.* N COUNT ⇑ failure

3 A **breakdown** of something is a description of it in a more simple form in terms of its separate parts. EG *I forget what the breakdown of hours is.* N COUNT : IF+ PREP THEN *of* = analysis

4 The **breakdown** of a state of affairs, idea, tradition, etc is the ending of it. EG *There had been a breakdown of class in England.* N COUNT+SUPP : USU SING

5 A **breakdown** is also the same as a **nervous breakdown**. EG *I shall probably have another breakdown if I stay any longer in this house.* N COUNT ⇑ illness

breaker /breɪkə/, **breakers.** 1 A **breaker** is a big sea wave, especially at the point when it reaches the shore. EG *The long, grinding roar of the breakers on the reef.* N COUNT : USU PL

2 See also **circuit breaker**.

breakfast /brekfəst/, **breakfasts, breakfasting, breakfasted.** 1 **Breakfast** is the first meal of the day, which most people eat early in the morning. EG *I would get up early and eat my breakfast and go... I hadn't had any breakfast and I was getting quite hungry... They had hard-boiled eggs for breakfast... I open the mail immediately after breakfast... ...breakfast cereal.* • See also **bed and breakfast.** N COUNT/ UNCOUNT

2 When you **breakfast**, you have breakfast; a literary or old-fashioned use. EG *She dressed early, and breakfasted, and Joy didn't see her for the rest of the day.* V ⇑ eat

breakfast table. The **breakfast table** is a table which is being used or which is going to be used for breakfast. EG *They were still sitting at the breakfast table.* N SING : *the*+N

breakfast television refers to television programmes which are broadcast in the morning at the time when most people are having breakfast. EG *I never watch breakfast television.* N UNCOUNT

break-in, break-ins. A **break-in** is the act of getting into a building by force. EG *He said he knew nothing of the break-in.* N COUNT ⇑ entry

breakneck /breɪknek/. Something that happens or travels at **breakneck** speed is happening or travelling very fast indeed. EG *The construction of other hotels proceeded at breakneck speed... ...the breakneck pace of change.* ADJ CLASSIF : ATTRIB

breakthrough /breɪkθruː/, **breakthroughs.** A **breakthrough** is a new and successful development or achievement. EG *Scientists are hovering on the brink of a major breakthrough... Perry's breakthrough in international trade... This innovation was considered by many to be a breakthrough in government-industry relations.* N COUNT ⇑ success

break-up, break-ups. 1 The **break-up** of a group, organization, or system is the act of it coming to an end because its members or parts separate from one another, especially as a result of difficulty or disagreement. EG *This caused the break-up of the coalition... We are on the brink of a break-up of the two-party system... ...the break-up of western empires in Asia.* N COUNT/ UNCOUNT : USU+ *of* ⇑ destruction

2 The **break-up** of a marriage, relationship, etc is the act of it coming to an end because the partners decide that it is not working successfully. EG *...the break-up of a marriage... All marriage break-ups are traumatic.* N COUNT = split

3 The **break-up** of an activity is the act of it finishing. EG *I'd like a word with you before the break-up of this happy occasion.* N SING WITH DET : USU+*of* ⇑ end

4 The **break-up** of something such as a ship is the act of it breaking gradually into several pieces. EG *...the dramatic break-up of oil tankers.* N COUNT+SUPP ⇑ demolition

breakwater /breɪkwɔːtə/, **breakwaters.** A **breakwater** is a very large wall of stone that extends from the shore into the sea and is built in order to protect a harbour or beach from the force of the waves. N COUNT = mole

breast /brest/, **breasts, breasting, breasted.**

1 A woman's **breasts** are the two soft, round pieces of flesh on a woman's chest that can produce milk to feed a baby. EG *...a statue of a beggar girl with a baby at her breast... ...women with small breasts.* N COUNT = bosom

2 A man's **breast** is the upper part of his chest. EG *The bullet pierced Joel's breast.* N COUNT

3 The **breast** is considered to be the part of your body where your emotions and feelings are; a literary use. EG *...the creation of national pride in the breasts of Frenchmen.* N COUNT : WITH *the*/POSS ⇑ heart

4 A bird's **breast** is the front part of its body. EG *There was blood on the breast feathers.* N COUNT = chest

5 The **breast** of a shirt, jacket, coat, etc is the part which covers the top part of the chest. EG *...a red shirt with an alligator on the breast.* N SING : *the*+N ⇑ front

6 If you **breast** something, you push your way through it, touching it with your chest; a literary use. EG *...walking out into the sea, breasting the waves.* V+O = plough through

7 A piece of **breast** is a piece of meat that is cut from the front part of a bird or lamb. EG *Two chicken breasts, please... ...breast of lamb.* N COUNT/ UNCOUNT+SUPP

8 If you **make a clean breast of** something, you tell someone the truth about yourself or about something wrong that you have done. EG *Wouldn't it be better to make a clean breast of it?* PHR : VB INFLECTS ⇑ confess = own up

9 See also **chimney breast**.

breastbone /brestbəʊn/, **breastbones.** Your **breastbone** is the long, flat, vertical bone in the centre of your chest. N COUNT ⇑ bone = sternum

breast-feed, breast-feeds, breast-feeding, breast-fed. If a woman **breast-feeds** a baby, she feeds it with milk from her breast, rather than from a bottle. EG *A good percentage of mothers are eager to breast-feed... ...mothers who choose not to breast-feed their babies.* ◇ **breast-feeding.** EG *A big advantage of breast-feeding is that the milk is always pure.* ◇ **breast-fed.** EG *There is less thumb-sucking among breast-fed babies.* V OR V+O ⇑ feed ≠ bottle-feed ◇ N UNCOUNT ⇑ feeding ◇ ADJ CLASSIF ≠ bottle-fed

breastplate /brestpleɪt/, **breastplates**; also spelled with a hyphen. A **breastplate** is a piece of armour that covers and protects the chest. N COUNT

breast pocket; also spelled with a hyphen. The **breast pocket** of a man's coat or jacket is a pocket, usually on the inside, next to his chest. EG *He reached into his breast pocket.* N COUNT : DET+ N

breaststroke /breststrəʊk/ is a swimming stroke which you do lying on your front in the water, moving your arms in a horizontal, circular movement below the surface of the water, and kicking like a frog. N UNCOUNT

breath /breθ/, **breaths.** 1 Your **breath** is the air which you take into and let out of your lungs when N COUNT : *the*/ POSS+N : USU you breathe. EG *Piggy let out his breath with a gasp... You could smell the whisky on his breath.* SING

2 You can use **breath** to refer to the air in your lungs and the act of breathing it in, especially when considering how much air you need or use in order to do a particular activity. EG *He had little breath left for running... Jenny paused for breath.* N UNCOUNT

3 When you take a **breath**, you breathe in. EG *He took a deep breath and blew into the bag.* N COUNT

4 When you **draw breath**, you stop in the middle of an energetic activity or rest after it, in order to allow your breathing to return to normal. EG *She can swim for four minutes without drawing breath.* PHR : VB INFLECTS

5 When you are **out of breath**, you breathe very quickly and with difficulty because you have been doing something energetic. EG *We were still out of breath from the climb.* PHR : USED AS AN A = breathless, puffed

6 When someone is **short of breath**, they find it difficult to breathe properly, for example because they are ill. PHR : USED AS C

7 When you **get** your **breath** back, you start breathing easily again and at the normal rate after doing something energetic. PHR : VB INFLECTS = recover

8 When you **hold** your **breath**, you stop breathing for a short while. EG *We all held our breaths till the bomb burst.* ● **with bated breath**: see **bated**. PHR : VB INFLECTS

9 **catch** your **breath**. 9.1 If you **catch** your **breath** when you are doing something energetic, you stop in order to breathe more easily. EG *I had to pause halfway to catch my breath.* PHR : VB INFLECTS = recover 9.2 Something that makes you **catch** your **breath** is so beautiful, exciting, or shocking that it makes you take a sudden deep breath. EG *A sharp pain in her ankle made her catch her breath... He caught his breath at her beauty.* PHR : VB INFLECTS = gasp

10 Something that **takes** your **breath away** is so beautiful, amazing, or exciting that you can hardly breathe or speak. EG *It was so beautiful it took her breath away.* PHR : VB INFLECTS ⇑ overwhelm

11 If you say something **under** your **breath**, you say it in a very quiet voice, often because you do not want other people to hear what you are saying. EG *She was counting under her breath.* PHR : USED AS AN A ⇑ quietly

12 If you tell someone to **save** their **breath** or tell them that they are **wasting** their **breath**, you mean that they should not bother to say what they planned to say to another person, because that person will not take any notice. EG *I don't know why I speak to my daughter. I might as well save my breath.* PHR : VB INFLECTS

13 If someone says something, and **in the same breath** says something else, they say two things which contradict each other or are very different from one another. EG *He says he is never going to see her again, and in the same breath he asks when he can phone her.* PHR : USED AS AN A = simultaneously

14 Someone who does something with their **last breath** or their **dying breath** does it just before they die. EG *She begged him with her dying breath to look after the children.* PHR

15 If you say that something is **the breath of life** to someone, you mean that they enjoy it or need it very much. EG *The theatre was the breath of life to Sybil.* PHR : USED AS C ⇑ essential

16 Someone who has **bad breath** has breath that smells unpleasant, often because of germs in their mouth. PHR

17 If you go outside for **a breath of air**, you go outside because you feel that it is too stuffy indoors, or sometimes because you want to be away from a difficult situation for a short while. PHR : USED AS O

18 A **breath** of air, wind, etc is a very slight movement of air. EG *Not a breath of wind stirred the trees.* N SING : *the/a*+N +*of*

19 A **breath** of something is a very small amount or sign of it; a formal or literary use. EG *There was hardly a breath of dissension at the meeting... ...the breath of spring.* N PART = murmur

breathable /bri̲ːðəbəᵊl/. Air that is **breathable** is fresh and able to support life. ADJ CLASSIF

breathalyze /bre̲θəlaɪz/, **breathalyzes, breathalyzing, breathalyzed**; also spelled **breathalyse**. If the police **breathalyze** you when you have been driving a car, they ask you to breathe into a special bag containing chemicals. The chemicals indicate whether you have drunk more alcohol than you are legally allowed to when you are driving; used mainly in British English. V+O ⇑ test

Breathalyzer /bre̲θəlaɪzə/, **Breathalyzers**; also spelled **Breathalyser**. **Breathalyzer** is a trademark in Britain for a device used to measure the amount of alcohol that someone has in their breath. N COUNT

breathe /bri̲ːð/, **breathes, breathing, breathed.** 1 When people or animals **breathe**, they take air into their lungs and let it out again. EG *I stood by the window and breathed deeply... 'Please open the window. I can't breathe'... Let's get out and breathe a little country air.* V OR V+O ⇑ respire

2 When someone **breathes again** or **breathes** more **easily** after a frightening or worrying experience, they relax again because the danger or difficulty has passed. EG *As the pages passed from hand to hand, I breathed again. The case was proven... He breathed easier; he had made it.* PHR : VB INFLECTS ⇑ be relieved

3 If you say that someone is **breathing down** your **neck**, you mean that they are paying such careful attention to everything you do that you feel uncomfortable and unable to act freely or make your own decisions; used showing disapproval. EG *They will not have the shareholders breathing down their necks all the time.* PHR : VB INFLECTS ⇑ watch

4 If someone **breathes** their **last**, they die; a literary expression. EG *He gave a loud cry and breathed his last.* PHR : VB INFLECTS

5 If you **breathe** smoke or fumes over someone, you cause smoke or fumes to come out of your mouth as you breathe out. EG *...breathing whisky fumes all over my face... ...the dealers with velvet voices breathing cigar smoke.* V+O ⇑ exhale = blow

6 If someone **breathes** something, they say it so quietly that it can hardly be heard. EG *'Frank.' she breathed. 'Help me, please.'* V+O/QUOTE ⇑ whisper

7 Someone who **breathes** life, confidence, or excitement into something gives this quality to it. EG *A teacher should try to breathe life into her subject.* V+O : IF+PREP THEN *into* = instil

8 When you let wine **breathe**, you open the bottle to allow air to get to it for a short while before you drink it. V

breathe in. When you **breathe in**, you take a breath of air into your lungs. EG *Don't pant, breathe in slowly... We lifted our heads to breathe in the fresh, clear air.* PHRASAL VB : V+ADV, OR V+O+ADV = inhale

breathe out. When you **breathe out**, you make air come out of your lungs through your nose or mouth. EG *She breathed out through parted lips to try and cool the hot liquid.* PHRASAL VB : V+ADV, OR V+O+ADV = exhale

breather /bri̲ːðə/, **breathers.** If you take or have a **breather**, you stop what you are doing for a short time and have a rest; used in informal English. EG *I stopped and had another breather and considered... He was taking a breather.* N COUNT = break

breathing /bri̲ːðɪŋ/ is the action of taking air into your lungs and letting it out again, and the sound that this makes. EG *Her breathing became loud and strenuous... All I could hear was heavy breathing down the telephone.* N UNCOUNT ⇑ respiration

breathing space, breathing spaces; also spelled with a hyphen. A **breathing space** is a short period of time between two activities in which you can recover from the first activity and prepare for the second one. EG *This would buy a further breathing space before the German problem once more needed attention.* N COUNT ⇑ pause = respite

breathless /bre̲θlɪ²s/. If you are **breathless**, 1 you have difficulty in breathing properly, for example because you have been running or because you are ill. EG *She opened the door of the apartment, a little breathless from climbing the stairs.* ◇ **breathlessly.** EG *We walked breathlessly up the hill to the house.* ◇ **breathlessness.** EG *Obesity causes breathlessness.* ADJ QUALIT = puffed, out of breath ◇ ADV WITH VB

2 you are hardly able to breathe because you are so excited or afraid. EG *They followed the match with breathless interest.* ADJ CLASSIF = feverish

breathtaking /bre̲θteɪkɪŋ/. Something that is **breathtaking** is so exciting or wonderful that you feel you can hardly breathe. EG *We were travelling at breathtaking speed down the motorway.... ...breathtaking scenery.* ◇ **breathtakingly.** EG *Fashion magazines display breathtakingly beautiful gowns.* ADJ QUALIT = overwhelming, unbelievable ◇ ADV+ADJ/ADV = stunningly

bred /bre̲d/ is the past tense and past participle of **breed**.

breech /bri̲ːtʃ/, **breeches.** In paragraph 1 the form **breeches** is pronounced /brɪtʃɪz/ and in paragraph 2 it is pronounced /bri̲ːtʃɪz/. 1 **Breeches** are trousers which reach as far as your knees. EG *...riding breeches.* N PLURAL

2 The **breech** of a gun is the part of the barrel at the back into which you load the bullets.
N COUNT : USU SING

breed /briːd/, **breeds, breeding, bred.** 1 A **breed** of an animal is a particular type of that animal, for example a terrier is a breed of dog. You use **breed** especially when talking about domestic and farm animals rather than wild animals. EG *...the very finest breeds of hunting dogs... They are a new breed.*
N COUNT = species

2 If you **breed** animals or plants, you keep them for the purpose of producing more animals or plants with particular qualities in a controlled way, for example by choosing which animal should mate with another. EG *Princess Anne and her husband breed horses at Gatcombe Park... Successive strains of the plant have been bred that resist more diseases.* ◊ **breeding.** EG *We retain a small proportion of bulls for breeding purposes.*
V+O = rear
◊ N UNCOUNT = mating

3 When animals **breed**, they mate and produce offspring. EG *They become sexually mature and breed.* ◊ **breeding.** EG *The breeding season is a very long one.*
V = reproduce
◊ N UNCOUNT

4 To **breed** a particular situation, feeling, or quality means to cause it to develop. EG *Success breeds success, failure breeds failure... The rumours bred hope and doubt.*
V+O ⇑ cause = generate

5 If someone **is bred** for a particular activity or situation, they are trained or taught as they grow up to have particular beliefs or to behave in a particular way. EG *Danny was bred for the sea... ...a post-nuclear generation bred to fear the radioactive world.*
V+O : USU PASS, IF+PREP/VB THEN *for/to*-INF = be brought up

6 Someone who was **born and bred** in a particular place was born there and spent their childhood and youth there. EG *I was born and bred in Edinburgh... He is Lagos born and bred.* ● See also **breeding**.
PHR : USED AS A/C ⇑ brought up

7 A **breed** of person is a particular type of person with special characteristics or skills. EG *This required a special skill and a whole new breed of actors.*
N COUNT+SUPP = strain

breeder /briːdə/, **breeders.** 1 A **breeder** is a person who breeds animals in order to sell them.
N COUNT ⇑ owner

2 See also **fast breeder reactor**.

breeding /briːdɪŋ/. 1 Someone who has **breeding** has been taught how to behave correctly and with good manners, especially in upper class society. EG *...good breeding... She certainly lacked breeding.*
N UNCOUNT ⇑ upbringing

2 Other meanings of **breeding** can be found in the entry for **breed** in paragraphs **2** and **3**.

breeding ground, breeding grounds; also spelled with a hyphen. 1 A place that is a **breeding ground** for a particular situation, activity, or type of behaviour is an area where it is very likely to develop. EG *...breeding grounds for passport and ticket forgery... The public schools of England are the breeding ground of snobbery.*
N COUNT+SUPP = source

2 A **breeding ground** of a particular type of animal is a place where those animals go to produce their offspring. EG *Those cliffs are the finest bird breeding grounds in the Northern Hemisphere.*
N COUNT

breeze /briːz/, **breezes, breezing, breezed.** 1 A **breeze** is a wind that blows very gently. EG *There was a gentle breeze... A sudden breeze shook the fringe of palm trees.*
N COUNT : USU SING

2 If you **breeze** in or **breeze** into a place, you enter it briskly and in a very casual or carefree manner. EG *I just breezed into her room, flinging the door wide.*
V+A ⇑ go = sail

breeze-block, breeze-blocks; also spelled without a hyphen. A **breeze-block** is a large, grey-coloured kind of brick made from ashes and cement and used for building houses, factories, etc. EG *...unpainted breeze-block walls.*
N COUNT/ UNCOUNT

breezy /briːzi¹/, **breezier, breeziest.** 1 Someone who behaves in a **breezy** way behaves in a brisk, casual, cheerful, and confident manner. EG *Remind him in a friendly, firm, and breezy tone that he has just had a drink... The auctioneer handed over to a breezy young colleague.*
ADJ QUALIT = cheery

2 When the weather is **breezy**, there is a quite strong but pleasant wind blowing, often in short bursts. EG *...breezy summer afternoons.*
ADJ QUALIT ⇑ windy

brethren /brɛðrɪ²n/ is used to refer to the members of a particular organization or association, especially a religious group; an old-fashioned word. EG *Why should only select brethren have been allowed to see it?*
N PLURAL

brevity /brɛvɪti¹/. **Brevity** is 1 the fact of lasting only a short time. EG *...the brevity and frailty of human existence.* 2 the quality of saying or writing something using very few words. EG *Daniel delivered his message with telegraphic brevity.*
N UNCOUNT
N UNCOUNT

brew /bruː/, **brews, brewing, brewed.** 1 When you let tea or coffee **brew**, you leave it for a few minutes so that the flavour has a chance to develop properly. EG *Pour out the tea, Lucy. It's brewed.*
V ⇑ prepare

2 When you **brew** beer, you make it. EG *The best beer will be the stuff you brew from the malt you have made yourself... ...strong beer specially brewed at Burton-on-Trent.*
V+O

3 When you **brew** a hot drink, you make it by pouring hot water onto, for example, tea or coffee. EG *He brewed cups of thick Turkish coffee.*
V+O

4 A **brew** is a drink made by mixing something such as tea or coffee or substances with hot water. EG *She dosed Ash with herbal brews of her own concoction.*
N COUNT = infusion

5 A **brew** is also a beer that is produced in a particular place or during a particular year; an informal use. EG *...a potent brew from South West Africa... ...last year's brew.* ● See also **home brew**.
N MASS

6 When a difficult or unpleasant situation **is brewing**, it is starting to develop. EG *A crisis was brewing... There is a storm brewing here against the Prime Minister.*
V : USU CONT ⇑ form = hatch

brew up. 1 If you **brew up**, you make a pot of tea; used in informal British English. EG *I'll be brewing up about ten... ...brewing up their morning cuppa.*
PHRASAL VB : V+ADV, OR ORDER V+ADV+O

2 When a difficult or unpleasant situation **is brewing up**, or when someone **brews** it **up**, it starts to develop. EG *It was obvious that a big storm was brewing up.*
PHRASAL VB : V+ADV, OR ORDER V+ADV+O ⇑ form = cook

brewer /bruːə/, **brewers.** A **brewer** is a person who makes beer or who owns a place where beer is made.
N COUNT ⇑ manufacturer

brewery /bruəri¹/, **breweries.** A **brewery** is a company which makes beer or a place where beer is made. EG *...an old-established family brewery.*
N COUNT ⇑ factory

briar /braɪə/, **briars**; also spelled **brier**. A **briar** is a wild rose with long, thorny stems. EG *...a large house, all overgrown with briars and brambles.*
N COUNT ⇑ shrub

bribe /braɪb/, **bribes, bribing, bribed.** 1 If you **bribe** someone, you offer them money or something valuable, in order to persuade them to do something for you. EG *The attempt to bribe the clerk had failed.*
V+O = buy off

2 A **bribe** is a sum of money or something valuable that you offer to someone in order to persuade them to do something for you. EG *The Vice President admitted taking bribes.*
N COUNT ⇑ inducement

bribery /braɪbəᵒri¹/ is the act of offering money or something valuable to someone in order to persuade them to do something for you. EG *A Federal jury found Williams guilty of bribery and conspiracy.*
N UNCOUNT = corruption

bric-a-brac /brɪkəbræk/ consists of small, ornamental objects of no great value. EG *Julia spent hers all on dresses and bric-a-brac.*
N UNCOUNT = knick-knacks

brick /brɪk/, **bricks, bricking, bricked.** 1 A **brick** is a rectangular block used for building walls, houses, etc. Bricks are usually reddish brown or yellow in colour.
N COUNT

2 You use **brick** to refer to bricks regarded as a building material. EG *...a massive old building of crumbling red brick... ...a brick wall... The brick-red industrial landscape of eastern Massachusetts.*
N UNCOUNT

3 If you **come down on** someone **like a ton of bricks**, you show them that you are extremely angry with them because of something that they have done wrong; an informal expression. EG *The judges will come down on the police like a ton of bricks.*
PHR : VB INFLECTS ⇑ are severe

4 A **brick** of ice cream is a rectangular block of ice cream.
N COUNT+SUPP

5 If you say that someone is a **brick**, you mean that they have been very helpful to you when you were in a difficult situation; an old-fashioned word. EG *You can be such a brick.*
N COUNT : IF SING a+N ⇑ friend = pal

brick in. If you **brick** something **in**, you build a wall of bricks to enclose it or to fill it.
PHRASAL VB : V+O+ADV

brick off. If you **brick off** an area, you build a wall of bricks that separates this area from another. EG *The lift was long dead, and the shaft bricked off.*
PHRASAL VB : V+O+ADV ⇑ separate

brick up. If you **brick up** a hole or space, you build a wall of bricks to enclose it or to fill it. EG *If you want to stop burglars you have to board or brick the windows up.*
PHRASAL VB : V+O+ADV = brick in

bricklayer /brɪkleɪə/, **bricklayers.** A **bricklayer** is a person whose job is to build walls or buildings using layers of bricks.
N COUNT ⇑ worker

brickwork /brɪkwɜːk/ refers to bricks and the way that they have been used to make a wall or building. EG *...the old brickwork of St James's Palace... ...cracks in brickwork or cement.* N UNCOUNT ⇑ masonry

bridal /braɪdəºl/ is used to describe something that belongs or relates to a bride, or to both a bride and her bridegroom. EG *...her bridal trousseau... ...the bridal suite.* ADJ CLASSIF: ATTRIB = wedding

bride /braɪd/, **brides**. A **bride** is a woman who has just got married or who is just about to get married; used especially of a woman on her wedding day. EG *George took his bride to the city.* N COUNT

bridegroom /braɪdgru⁴m/, **bridegrooms**. A **bridegroom** is a man who has just got married or who is just about to get married; used especially of a man on his wedding day. EG *The bridegroom was dressed in a grey suit.* N COUNT = groom

bridesmaid /braɪdzmeɪd/, **bridesmaids**. A **bridesmaid** is a woman or a young girl who is a bride's attendant on the day that the bride gets married. EG *I was one of her bridesmaids.* N COUNT = maid of honour

bride-to-be, brides-to-be. A **bride-to-be** is a woman who is soon going to be married. EG *He glanced lovingly at his bride-to-be.* N COUNT = intended

bridge /brɪdʒ/, **bridges, bridging, bridged**. 1 A **bridge** is a structure that is built over a river, railway, road, etc so that people or vehicles can cross from one side to the other. EG *We walked across the railway bridge... ...the little bridge over the stream.* ● **water under the bridge**: see **water**. N COUNT: ALSO IN NAMES AFTER N

2 To **bridge** a river, valley, etc means to build a bridge across it. EG *The problem was how to bridge the river.* V+O ⇑ join = span

3 If you say that you will **cross that bridge when** you **come to it,** you mean that you will deal with the problem that has just been mentioned when it happens and do not intend to think about it until then. EG *Never mind that, we shall cross that bridge when we come to it.* PHR: VB INFLECTS

4 If you **burn** your **bridges,** you do something that prevents you from stopping a course of action or from avoiding doing something. EG *I decided to burn my bridges and sell the company.* PHR: VB INFLECTS

5 A **bridge** between two places is something that joins or connects them. EG *...a land bridge that once connected Tunisia and Italy.* N COUNT ⇑ link

6 Something that **bridges** the gap between two people or groups makes it easier for them to communicate with, understand, or be friends with each other. EG *The Citizens Advice Bureaux were set up to bridge the gap between the people and the bureaucrats... The gulf between their cultures was too great to be easily bridged... In his writing, he can bridge the distance between himself and his readers.* ▸ used as a noun. EG *We need to build a bridge between East and West.* V+O ⇑ overcome ▸ N COUNT: USU SING ⇑ link = connection

7 Someone or something that **bridges** the gap between two things or between a person and a thing makes it easier for the difference between them to be made smaller or to be overcome. EG *...bridging the gap between what society needs and what the government can provide... ...an attempt to bridge the knowledge gap... There is a gap to be bridged between the lax amateur world and the cool professional world.* ▸ used as a noun. EG *These revelations serve as bridges to true knowledge.* V+O ⇑ reduce = fill ▸ N COUNT

8 If someone's life, period of work, etc **bridged** two or more periods of time, it took place within both or all of them. EG *...militants whose careers bridged the pre- and post-war eras... ...a dog whose companionship had bridged widely different phases in their lives.* V+O = span

9 The **bridge** of a ship is the raised part from which the ship is steered and where the captain stands. EG *There's nobody in charge on the bridge, nobody steering!* N COUNT: USU SING ⇑ platform

10 The **bridge** of your nose is the thin top part of your nose, between your eyes. EG *His horn-rimmed spectacles rested on the bridge of his nose.* N COUNT: USU SING

11 The **bridge** of a pair of spectacles is the part that rests on your nose. N COUNT: USU SING

12 The **bridge** of a violin, guitar, etc is the little piece of wood under the strings that holds them up. N COUNT

13 A **bridge** is also a piece of metal that holds false teeth in your mouth by connecting them to your natural teeth. N COUNT ⇑ dentures

14 **Bridge** is a card game for four players which is similar to whist and involves bidding to determine which suit will be trumps. EG *Mrs Aydie has bridge parties every Thursday.* N UNCOUNT

bridgehead /brɪdʒhɛd/, **bridgeheads**. A **bridgehead** is a good position which an army has taken in the enemy's territory and from which it can advance or attack. EG *Two brigades seized bridgeheads on the far side of the river.* N COUNT

bridging loan, bridging loans. A **bridging loan** is money that a bank or other company lends you for a short time to cover the period until you get money from somewhere else, for example so that you can buy another house before you have sold the one you already own; used mainly in British English. N COUNT

bridle /braɪdəºl/, **bridles, bridling, bridled**. 1 A **bridle** is a set of straps that is put around a horse's head and mouth. It is attached to the reins so that the person riding or driving the horse can control the horse. N COUNT ⇑ harness

2 If you **bridle** a horse, you put a bridle on it. EG *Her horse was already saddled and bridled.* V+O

3 If you **bridle**, you show that you are angry or displeased, especially by moving your head and body upwards in proud way. EG *Mrs Pringle bridled. 'I've never been so insulted in my life!'... Smith bridled at anonymous criticism in the press.* V: IF+PREP THEN *at/with*, OR V+QUOTE ⇑ react = bristle

bridle path, bridle paths; also spelled as one word. A **bridle path** is a path which is intended to be used by people riding horses. N COUNT = bridleway

bridleway /braɪdəºlweɪ/, **bridleways**. A **bridleway** is the same as a bridle path. N COUNT

brief /briːf/, **briefer, briefest; briefs, briefing, briefed**. 1 Something that is **brief** lasts for only a short time. EG *There was a brief scuffle... This brief period of tolerance did not last long... As they talk, they exchange only the briefest of glances.* ● See also **briefly**. ADJ QUALIT ≠ lengthy

2 **Brief** is used of a period of time when you want to emphasize that it is a relatively short time. EG *We've managed within a few brief decades to change all that... For a brief year I was free of suffering.* ADJ CLASSIF: ATTRIB ≠ long

3 A piece of writing or speech that is **brief** does not contain too many words or details. EG *They started with a brief description of their work... Mrs Oliver made a brief note on the telephone pad... For an academic work it is commendably brief.* ▸ used of people. EG *I shall have to be moderately brief.* ADJ QUALIT ⇑ short = concise ▸ = succinct

4 **In brief**. 4.1 You say **in brief** to indicate that you are about to say something in as few words as possible or summarize what you have just said. EG *In brief then, do you two agree to join me?* 4.2 **In brief** also means in a shortened form, with few details. EG *And now for the news in brief.* PHR: USED AS ADV SEN = in short; PHR: USED AS AN A ≠ in full

5 Someone who is **brief** when talking to another person does not say very much because they do not really want to speak to that person or discuss that subject. EG *He was a bit brief this morning when I asked him how it had gone.* ▸ used of remarks. EG *'Not yet.' This brief riposte indicated that she considered the subject closed.* ADJ QUALIT ⇑ short = abrupt ▸ ⇑ short = brusque

6 A **brief** skirt, pair of shorts, etc is very short. EG *She was wearing the briefest of miniskirts.* ADJ QUALIT = skimpy

7 **Briefs** are pants or knickers. EG *She was wearing white cotton briefs.* N PLURAL: ALSO *a pair of*+N

8 When you **brief** someone, you give them information that they need or give them instructions before they do or deal with something. EG *A meeting is held in order to brief the new volunteer... They had been well briefed about the political situation.* V+O ⇑ inform = fill in, prepare

9 If someone is given a **brief**, they are officially given instructions to do something or deal with something; a fairly formal use. EG *Some advocates never got important briefs... I was appointed and given the brief of developing local history research... These claims are outside the Ombudsman's brief.* N COUNT

10 If you **hold no brief for** a particular cause, idea, practice, or group of people, you are not a strong supporter of it or them; a formal expression. EG *He held no particular brief for monetarism.* PHR: VB INFLECTS ≠ support

briefcase /briːfkeɪs/, **briefcases**. A **briefcase** is a firm rectangular case, often made of leather, which has a small handle at the top. You use a briefcase to carry files, papers, books, etc. EG *Davis was carrying a briefcase... Muller opened his briefcase and took out a sheet of paper.* N COUNT ⇑ case

briefing /briːfɪŋ/, **briefings**. A **briefing** is 1 a meeting at which information or instructions are N COUNT/UNCOUNT given to people, especially just before they do or deal with something. EG *The colonel introduced the general and the briefing began.* 2 the information or instructions that you get at a meeting. N COUNT

briefly /briːfli¹/. 1 Something that happens or is done **briefly** happens or is done for a very short period of time. EG *He smiled briefly... 'Good morning, Tommy,' he said, looking up briefly.* ADV AFTER VB ⇑ quickly = fleetingly

2 If you say something **briefly**, you use very few words or give very few details. EG *She told them briefly what had happened... Robertson answered briefly and without interest... Put briefly, his argument was this.* ADV AFTER VB ≠ at length

3 You can say **briefly** to indicate that you are about to say something in as few words as possible, rather than giving a full description or explanation or to indicate that you are about to summarize what you have just been talking about. EG *The facts, briefly, are these... For reasons beyond my control (briefly, money) I once moved five times in eighteen months.* ADV SEN = basically

brier /braɪə/, **briers**. See **briar**.

brig /brɪg/, **brigs**. A **brig** is a type of ship with two masts and square sails. N COUNT

Brig. is an abbreviation for **Brigadier**. EG *...Brig. Gerald Haywood.* N IN TITLES

brigade /brɪgeɪd/, **brigades**. 1 A **brigade** is one of the groups into which an army is divided and which make up a division. EG *The colonel commanded a brigade of the 4th Infantry Division... They had a small army: a mere five brigades.* N COUNT: IF SING, VB CAN BE SING OR PL

2 You can also use **brigade** humorously and disapprovingly in expressions which refer to a particular group of people who believe very strongly in a particular thing. EG *The anti-nuclear brigade protested, of course... ...the hanging-and-flogging brigade.* N COUNT: USU the+MOD+N IN SING: IF SING, VB CAN BE SING OR PL = lot

brigadier /brɪgədɪə/, **brigadiers**. A **brigadier** is an officer in the British army who is in charge of a brigade and has the rank above colonel. EG *...a retired British brigadier... Brigadier Tomlinson wants to see you, sir.* N COUNT: ALSO IN TITLES

brigand /brɪgənd/, **brigands**. A **brigand** is someone who attacks people and steals their property, especially in mountainous areas or forests; a literary word. N COUNT ⇑ criminal = bandit

bright /braɪt/, **brighter, brightest**. 1 A **bright** colour is strong, intense, and noticeable, and not dark. EG *Her eyes were bright blue.* ▸ used of coloured things. EG *Bright birds flash through the air.* ◇ **brightly**. EG *...brightly coloured silk blouses.* ◇ **brightness**. ADJ QUALIT+COLOUR ▸ ADJ QUALIT: USU ATTRIB ◇ ADV WITH VB ◇ N UNCOUNT

2 A light that is **bright** is shining strongly. EG *I was woken by a bright light shining in my face... The sun was bright and hot.* ◇ **brightly**. EG *The sun shone brightly.* ◇ **brightness**. EG *Already the stars were losing their brightness.* ADJ QUALIT = dazzling ◇ ADV WITH VB ◇ N UNCOUNT = radiance

3 A place or day that is **bright** has a lot of light or sunshine. EG *We sat in a bright, sunlit room... ...a clear, cold, bright day.* ◇ **brightly**. EG *...the brightly lit forecourt.* ADJ QUALIT ≠ dark ◇ ADV WITH VB = brilliantly

4 Something such as metal or water that is **bright** is shiny and reflects the light. EG *...bright new kettles and pans.... ...big bright eyes.* ◇ **brightly**. EG *It sparkles so brightly.* ADJ QUALIT = sparkling ◇ ADV WITH VB = brilliantly

5 Someone who is **bright** is quick at learning or noticing things. EG *They were the brightest girls in the school... I wanted to go to medical school, but my teachers said I wasn't bright enough.* ADJ QUALIT ⇑ clever = brainy

6 A **bright** idea is one that is good, clever, and original. EG *Then he had the bright idea of putting the engine at the back... She's full of bright ideas.* ADJ CLASSIF: ATTRIB = brilliant

7 If someone or their expression is **bright**, they are happy and cheerful. EG *He was bright and cheerful.* ◇ **brightly**. EG *'That's all right,' Billy answered brightly.* ADJ QUALIT = lively ◇ ADV WITH VB

8 If the future is or seems **bright**, it is likely to be pleasant and successful. EG *Those under 35 might have bright futures... The economic outlook is bright.* ADJ QUALIT = promising

9 If you **look on the bright side**, you try to be cheerful about a bad situation by thinking of some aspect of it that is advantageous or not as bad as it could have been. EG *Look on the bright side: at least you've still got your job.* PHR: VB INFLECTS

10 If you do something **bright and early**, you do it very early in the morning. EG *I was up bright and early, eager to be off.* PHR: USED AS AN A

brighten /braɪtəⁿn/, **brightens, brightening, brightened**. 1 If someone or their face **brightens** or **brightens up**, they suddenly look or feel happy or happier than they did before. EG *She seemed to brighten up a bit at this... Her face brightened. 'Oh, hi! It's you.'* V, OR PHRASAL VB: V+ADV ⇑ change = perk up

2 When someone's eyes **brighten**, they begin to look interested, excited, or hopeful. EG *Their eyes brighten, as they always do when such news comes.* V = light up

3 If you **brighten up** a place, or **brighten** it, you make it more colourful and attractive. EG *These flowers will brighten up your garden.* V+O, OR PHRASAL VB: V+O+ADV = liven up

4 Someone or something that **brightens** or **brightens up** a period of time or a situation for someone, causes it to become more pleasant and enjoyable for them. EG *The music brightened things up a little... You girls brighten our Sundays.* V+O, OR PHRASAL VB: V+O+ADV ⇑ improve = liven up

5 If a situation **is brightening up** or **brightening**, it is becoming better and more likely to bring success. EG *The prospects are brightening.* V, OR PHRASAL VB: V+ADV = look up

6 If the weather **brightens up** or **brightens**, it becomes clearer and sunnier. EG *It should brighten up in the afternoon.* V, OR PHRASAL VB: V+ADV ⇑ improve

7 When a light **brightens** a place or when a place **brightens**, it becomes brighter, lighter, or sunnier. EG *Stars brighten the night sky.* V-ERG = lighten

8 When a light **brightens**, it shines more strongly. EG *They stood on the dock in the brightening light.* V = grow

9 If you **brighten up** something such as metal, or **brighten** it, you clean it so that it looks shinier and reflects the light more brightly. V+O, OR PHRASAL VB: V+O+ADV = polish

bright lights. If someone talks about the **bright lights**, they are referring to a big city where you can do a lot of enjoyable and interesting things and be successful. EG *...heading for the bright lights of Elysium, Ohio.* N PLURAL: USU the+N = high life

bright spark, bright sparks. In informal English, a **bright spark** is someone who is intelligent and lively; often used sarcastically of someone who has done something stupid. EG *Some bright spark at the university has lost my application.* N COUNT = genius

brill /brɪl/. If someone says **brill!** or that something is **brill**, they are very pleased about it or think that it is very good; an informal word used in British English. EG *Oh brill, you remembered to bring the camera.* EXCLAM, OR ADJ QUALIT = great

brilliance /brɪljəns/. 1 **Brilliance** is very great cleverness or skill; used to refer to someone's ability or the quality of their work. EG *Dorothy Sayers was a writer of tremendous brilliance... ...an opening chapter of quite stunning brilliance.* N UNCOUNT = virtuosity

2 The **brilliance** of a colour, light, or coloured or shiny thing is its great brightness. EG *The painting has been restored to its former brilliance... ...the brilliance of the lagoon under the burning sun.* N UNCOUNT = vividness

brilliant /brɪljənt/. 1 Someone who is **brilliant** is extremely clever or skilful. EG *...a brilliant young engineer... I was a good student, above average, but not brilliant...* ▸ used of work, achievements, or ideas. EG *It was a brilliant idea, and it worked... ...a brilliant parody.* ◇ **brilliantly**. EG *He acted brilliantly in a wide range of parts.* ADJ QUALIT = outstanding ▸ = masterly ◇ ADV WITH VB = superbly

2 You say **brilliant!** or that something is **brilliant** when you are very pleased about it or think that it is very good; used in informal British English. EG *'Did you enjoy your holiday?'-'Yes, it was brilliant!'* EXCLAM, OR ADJ QUALIT = great

3 A **brilliant** career, future, success, etc is splendid or very successful. EG *He predicted a brilliant future for the child.* ◇ **brilliantly**. EG *In England, he had succeeded brilliantly in county cricket... Sotheby's publicity stunt came off brilliantly.* ADJ CLASSIF: ATTRIB ◇ ADV WITH VB ⇑ well = splendidly

4 A **brilliant** colour is extremely bright. EG *The early-morning skies were a clean, brilliant blue.* ◇ **brilliantly**. EG *Many are brilliantly coloured.* ADJ QUALIT: ATTRIB ◇ ADV WITH VB

5 You describe light, or something that reflects light, as **brilliant** when it shines very brightly. EG *The sea sparkled in the brilliant sunlight.* ◇ **brilliantly**. EG *A downstairs window was brilliantly illuminated by a streetlamp.* ADJ QUALIT = dazzling ◇ ADV WITH VB

6 A **brilliant** smile is a big smile that shows that you are extremely happy. EG *She stood there with a brilliant smile on her face.* ◇ **brilliantly**. EG *'Good evening, sir,' said the Indian, smiling brilliantly.* ADJ QUALIT: ATTRIB ◇ ADV WITH VB = radiantly

Brillo pad /brɪləʊ pæd/, **Brillo pads**. **Brillo pad** is a trademark for a type of pad used to clean metal pots and pans. Brillo pads are made of metal threads N COUNT ⇑ scourer and soap in a solid rectangular shape. EG *Clean the base of the iron with a damp Brillo pad.*

brim /brɪm/, **brims, brimming, brimmed.** 1 The **brim** of a hat is the bottom part of it that sticks outwards. EG *She wore a hat with a huge brim.* N COUNT ↑ rim

2 If a container is filled **to the brim** with something, usually a liquid, it is filled right up to the top. EG *She filled her glass to the brim... The swimming pool was full to the brim with brown, smelly water.* PHR : USED AS AN A

3 Something that **brims** with what it has inside it, usually a liquid, is full right up to the edge or top. EG *Her eyes brimmed with tears.* ◊ **brimming.** EG *...the flooded ditches and brimming ponds.* V : IF+PREP THEN *with* ◊ ADJ CLASSIF : IF+PREP THEN *with*

4 If someone or something **brims** with things of a particular kind, they have or contain a very large number of them. ◊ **brimming.** EG *...a group of youngsters, all brimming with ideas... ...August gardens brimming with bumblebees.* V : IF+PREP THEN *with* ◊ ADJ CLASSIF : IF+PREP THEN *with*

brim over. 1 When a container or what is inside it **brims over**, its contents spill out. EG *He had splashed wine into Daniel's glass until it had brimmed over onto the tablecloth.* PHRASAL VB : V+ADV/PREP = spill over

2 Someone or something that **brims over** with something else is full of it. EG *She rushed to her mother, brimming over with joy and pride... She's always brimming over with questions.* PHRASAL VB : V+ADV+*with* = burst

brimful /brɪmfʊl/. 1 A container that is **brimful** of something is full right up to the top. EG *He was holding a bottle brimful of milk.* ADJ CLASSIF : PRED+*of* ↑ full up

2 Someone or something that is **brimful** of something else has or contains a lot of it. EG *He joined up at once, brimful of patriotism... The letter is brimful of slangy, vivid expressions.* ADJ CLASSIF : PRED+*of* ↑ full

brimstone /brɪmstə[6]n/, **brimstones.** 1 **Brimstone** is the same as sulphur; an old-fashioned use. N UNCOUNT

2 People use **fire and brimstone** as a way of referring to hell and of emphasizing how people are punished there after death; a literary expression. EG *The preacher warned us of the fire and brimstone that awaits sinners.* PHR : USED AS O

3 A **brimstone** is a type of yellow butterfly. N COUNT

brine /braɪn/ water which contains salt, especially salty water which is used for preserving food. EG *I bought a tin of mushrooms in brine.* N UNCOUNT ↑ liquid

bring /brɪŋ/, **brings, bringing, brought.** 1 When you **bring** someone or something with you when you come to a place, they come with you or you have them with you, for example in a bag or a pocket. EG *He would have to bring Judy with him... The children could bring comics... Please bring your calculator to every lesson.* V+O : USU+A ↑ take

2 If you **bring** something somewhere, you deliberately move it into a different place or position. EG *Sheldon brought his right hand to his head... He brought the whip down on the horse's back... He opened the glove case and brought out a pair of dark glasses.* V+O+A

3 If you **bring** something to someone, you fetch it for them or carry it to them. EG *Bring me a glass of Dubonnet... A servant would bring out a chair for him.* V+O+O, OR V+O+A

4 If something, for example the wind or an explosion, **brings** something else down or into a particular position, it causes it to fall down or be moved into that position. EG *The wind had brought several trees down... The blast brought a large part of the wall crashing to the ground... He hooks a foot round the door to bring it slamming to as he leaves.* V+O+A ↑ push

5 If something **brings** someone to a particular place, it causes them to come there or is their reason for coming. EG *A message would quickly bring him to Juffure any time... The drum brought the men rushing back to the village... The festival brings a great many people to Glastonbury... What brings you here?* V+O+A ↑ fetch

6 If a path, road, or route **brings** you to a particular place, you arrive at that place when you follow it. EG *The path brings you to the lake... Belgrave Road will bring you down into St George's Square.* V+O+A = lead, take

7 If you **bring** something such as a new product or a new fashion to a particular place, you cause it to be introduced into that place. EG *It will be some time before we bring technology to central China... They were responsible for bringing jazz to Europe... ...the unexpected outcome of bringing computers into schools.* V+O+A = introduce

8 To **bring** someone or something into a particular state, condition, or situation means to cause them to be in that state, condition, or situation. EG *These ideas had brought him into conflict with Stalin... Ida's voice brought me back to the present... There is no extra land to bring into cultivation.* V+O+A ↑ put

9 To **bring** something to an end, halt, stop etc means to cause it to finish or to stop moving along. EG *The Executive tried to bring the sit-in to an end... He brought the car to a stop.* V+O+A *(to)*

10 To **bring** something such as a price up or down means to cause it to become higher or lower. EG *...the fight to bring down inflation... Printing brought the cost of books down... The Equal Pay Act has failed to bring women's earnings up to the same level.* V+O+A *(up/down)* = push, pull

11 If a thing or event **brings** a particular quality, feeling, or achievement, it causes it to be experienced or acquired by people. EG *Could it be true that money did not bring happiness?... Each change brings with it a need for new learning... The war had brought prosperity to Port Philip... All the Acts of Parliament in the world will not bring equality for women.* V+O : IF+PREP THEN *to/for* ↑ create

12 If you **bring** shame, hatred, etc on a group of people that you belong to, or you **bring** honour to them, you cause them to experience that feeling or to be thought of in that way because of what you have done. EG *Don't bring shame on the family... He brings credit to the family.* V+O+A *(on/to)* = fetch

13 If you have **brought** trouble or unhappiness on yourself, it is your fault that you are experiencing it, often because you have done something foolish. EG *He brought it all on himself.* V+O+A *(on/upon)* = fetch

14 When something that you do or say **brings** something such as applause or criticism from someone, it gets that reaction from them. EG *This generosity brought applause from the boys... His performance brought more jeers than cheers... This news brought a rebuke from Sir Kenneth.* V+O : IF+PREP THEN *from* = draw, provoke

15 To **bring** a thing or quality to something means to cause that thing or quality to appear in it or on it. EG *The wine brought pink spots to her cheeks... The biting wind brought tears to their eyes.* V+O+A *(to)* ↑ fetch

16 If a period of time **brings** a particular thing, it happens during that time. EG *Winter brought the fogs... You wonder what the next two years are going to bring for him.* V+O = fetch

17 If you cannot **bring** yourself to do something, you cannot make yourself do it. EG *I could not bring myself to touch him... She could hardly bring herself to go... One wonders how they ever brought themselves to commit this grotesque act.* V+BROAD NEG+O (REFL)+*to*-INF = force

18 If you **bring** a particular quality or ability to a task or to the work of a group of people, you have it and use it or show it in that task or work. EG *They bring to their studies a sharpness and a shrewdness which you do not expect in an 18 year old.* V+O+A *(to)* = fetch

19 You say in a talk or discussion that something **brings** you to something else to indicate that you are about to mention a new subject or point connected with the one that you have just been talking about. EG *This brings me to the work of the day centre... Man will find a way of making use of them; which brings us to the question of just what that use could be.* V+O+A *(to)* = lead, take

20 To **bring** a television or radio programme to people means to make and broadcast it so that people can watch or listen to it. EG *This programme will be brought to you live by satellite from New York... In these programmes we've been bringing to you something of the activities that take place at the university.* V+O+O, OR V+O+A *(to)* = present

21 If you **bring** a legal action or a charge against someone, you officially accuse them of committing a crime or of doing something unlawful. EG *He brought an action against the union officials... ...a list of criminal charges brought against him by the government.* V+O : IF+PREP THEN *against* = institute

22 If you **bring** evidence against someone, especially in a court of law, you officially produce it. EG *There is no definite evidence which could be brought against her.* V+O : IF+PREP THEN *against* = submit

23 If something **brings** a particular price, it can be sold for that price. EG *Today Remington's pictures bring incredible prices.* V+O = fetch

24 ● to **bring** something **into being**: see **being.** ● to **bring the house down**: see **house.**

bring about. To **bring** something **about** means to cause it to happen. EG *The Administration helped* PHRASAL VB : V+O+ADV *bring about a peaceful settlement... Wrong ways of thinking and living bring about intolerable situations.*

bring along. If you **bring** someone or something **along**, you bring them with you when you come to a place. EG *Bring your friends along.* PHRASAL VB : V+O+ADV = fetch

bring back. 1 Something in the present that **brings back** something that happened to you a long time ago makes you think about it. EG *Losing a lover can bring back memories of childhood loss... It brings it all back.* PHRASAL VB : V+O+ADV ↑ evoke

2 When people **bring back** a thing, practice, or method that existed or was used at an earlier time, they introduce it again. EG *They are trying to bring back the crew cut... He was all for bringing back the cane as a punishment in schools.* PHRASAL VB : V+O+ADV = revive

bring down. 1 When people or events **bring down** a government or ruler, they cause them to lose power. EG *A national strike would bring the government down.* PHRASAL VB : V+O+ADV = topple

2 When someone **brings down** a person, animal, bird, or aeroplane, they shoot them so that they fall to the ground. EG *I brought down two of their men.* PHRASAL VB : V+O+ADV

bring forth. 1 To **bring** something **forth** means to produce it or cause it to happen or be experienced; a formal expression. EG *This brought forth a distinct shudder of revulsion... ...a new way to live which, in time, will bring forth new results and new happiness.* PHRASAL VB : V+O+ADV = create, result in

2 When a woman **brings forth** or **brings forth** a child, she has a baby; an old-fashioned or literary expression. EG *...the old idea that women should bring forth children in anguish.* PHRASAL VB : V+ADV, OR V+O+ADV = bear

bring forward. 1 If you **bring forward** a meeting, lecture, etc, you arrange for it to be at an earlier time or date than it was previously arranged for. EG *The meeting has been brought forward to Tuesday.* PHRASAL VB : V+O+ADV, IF+PREP THEN *to*

2 When the sum of the figures on a page or in a column **is brought forward,** it is written at the top of the next page or column so that it can be added to the figures on that page or in that column. PHRASAL VB : V+O+ADV, USU PASS ↑ transfer

3 If you **bring forward** something such as an argument or proposal, you mention it in order that people can consider it and discuss it. EG *He brought forward some very cogent arguments.* PHRASAL VB : V+O+ADV = advance, produce

bring in. 1 When a government, company, etc **brings in** something such as a new law or system, they introduce it. EG *Both Labour and Conservative administrations intend to bring in legislation to control their activities... I'd like to see a compulsory day release scheme brought in.* PHRASAL VB : V+O+ADV

2 Someone or something that **brings in** money, makes or earns it. EG *Tourism is a big industry, bringing in £7 billion a year... Children are sent out to clean shoes to bring in extra money.* PHRASAL VB : V+O+ADV = produce, make

3 If you **bring in** someone or **bring** them **into** something, you invite them to take part in an activity EG *It would be fatal to bring in an outsider... Jordan has got to be brought into this... He planned to bring Northcliffe into the government.* PHRASAL VB : V+O+ADV/PREP = introduce

4 If you **bring in** a particular point or subject or **bring** it **into** a discussion or talk, you include it or mention it. EG *I try to bring in the moral points as well.* PHRASAL VB : V+O+ADV/PREP

5 When a jury **bring in** a particular verdict, they officially give it as their verdict; a legal term. PHRASAL VB : V+O+ADV

bring off. If someone **brings off** something difficult, they do it successfully; an informal expression. EG *The most brilliant manoeuvre was brought off by Japan... The Ghost is the hardest thing to bring off in 'Hamlet'.* PHRASAL VB : V+O+ADV = pull off ≠ bungle

bring on. 1 Something that **brings on** an illness or pain, especially one that the person affected gets quite often, causes it to occur. EG *It'll bring on his cough again.* PHRASAL VB : V+O+ADV = induce

2 To **bring** someone **on** means to improve their ability to do something; a rather old-fashioned word. EG *I want to learn to be a coach so that I can help to bring on young cricketers.* PHRASAL VB : V+O+ADV = coach

bring out. 1 When a person or company **brings out** a new product, especially a new book or record, they make or produce it and sell it. EG *I've just brought out a little book on Dostoevski... Colin Bradbury has now brought out a second album.* PHRASAL VB : V+O+ADV

2 Something that **brings out** a particular kind of behaviour or feeling in someone causes them to have it although they do not normally have it or show it. EG *These dreadful circumstances bring out the worst in absolutely everybody... He brings out the animal in me.* PHRASAL VB : V+O+ADV = draw out

3 If someone such as an actor or musician **brings out** a particular quality or feature in a work that they are performing, they make people aware that that quality or feature exists in the work. EG *The effect is to bring out all sorts of things in the poetry... In both works, Giulini brings out a sort of serenity.* PHRASAL VB : V+O+ADV = draw out, reveal

4 To **bring** someone **out** means to encourage or cause them to be less shy or quiet. EG *He talks to them and brings them out... It's really brought him out, and it's done him the world of good.* PHRASAL VB : V+O+ADV

5 If something, for example food, **brings** you **out** in a rash or in spots, it causes you to have them on your skin. EG *Strawberries bring me out in blotches.* PHRASAL VB : V+O+ADV+*in* ↑ cover

6 If someone **brings out** some words, they say them with difficulty or with an effort. EG *They even brought out a few English words... 'It's so typical,' Etta at last brought out.* PHRASAL VB : V+O/QUOTE+ADV

bring round. 1 If someone or something **brings round** a person who is unconscious, they cause him or her to become conscious again. EG *Nobody was making any attempt to bring her round.* PHRASAL VB : V+O+ADV = resuscitate

2 If you **bring** someone **round,** you cause them to change their opinion about something so that they have the same opinion as you have. EG *We did our best to bring him round to our point of view.* PHRASAL VB : V+O+ADV, USU+*to* = win over

bring to. If you **bring** someone **to,** you cause them to become conscious again after being unconscious. PHRASAL VB : V+O+ADV

bring up. 1 When you **bring up** a child, you look after it until it is grown up and you try to give it particular beliefs and attitudes. EG *I brought up two children alone... Tony was brought up strictly... Women are brought up to be suspicious of each other.* ● You describe someone young as **well brought up, badly brought up,** etc when you think that their behaviour shows that they were, or were not, taught how to behave properly when they were a child. EG *She was a good, properly brought up young woman.* PHRASAL VB : V+O+ADV = raise, rear ● PHR : USED AS C

2 When you **bring up** a particular subject, you mention it or introduce it into a discussion or conversation. EG *I advised her to bring the matter up at the next meeting.* PHRASAL VB : V+O+ADV = broach, raise

3 When you **bring up** food, you vomit; an informal use. EG *The child is bringing up his breakfast!* PHRASAL VB : V+O+ADV

bring-and-buy sale, bring-and-buy sales. In British English, a **bring-and-buy sale** is an informal sale to raise money for a charity or other organization. People who come to the sale bring things to be sold and buy things that other people have brought. N COUNT

brink /brɪŋk/. 1 If you are on the **brink** of something, usually something important, terrible, or exciting, you are just about to do or experience it. EG *The country was on the brink of civil war... I was on the brink of losing my cool... They managed to pull the company back from the brink of disaster.* N SING : *the*+N, IF+PREP THEN *of* ↑ edge = verge

2 The **brink** of a cliff or deep hole is the edge of it; a literary use. EG *He stepped back from the brink of the gorge.* N SING : *the*+N

brinkmanship /brɪŋkmənʃɪp/ is a method of behaviour, especially in politics, in which you deliberately get into dangerous situations which could result in disaster but which could also bring success. EG *They have a tradition of political brinkmanship.* N UNCOUNT = risk-taking

briny /braɪni[1]/. Something that is **briny**, for example sea water or a smell, is salty; a literary word. EG *The seaweed swayed in the briny water.* ADJ CLASSIF

briquette /brɪket/, **briquettes.** A **briquette** is a small block which is made from coal dust and which is used as fuel for a fire. N COUNT

brisk /brɪsk/, **brisker, briskest.** 1 Someone who is **brisk** behaves in a busy, confident, lively way that shows that they want to get things done quickly. EG *...a brisk, well-organized, and self-possessed woman... Lynn's tone was brisk.* ◊ **briskly.** EG *'We've been into that,' said Posy briskly.* ◊ **briskness.** EG *She adopted her usual briskness with him.* ADJ QUALIT ↑ practical = businesslike, no-nonsense ◊ ADV WITH VB ◊ N UNCOUNT

2 A **brisk** action is one that is done quickly and in an energetic way. EG *I went for a brisk swim... You need to keep the story moving at a brisk pace.* ◊ **briskly.** EG *He walked briskly down the street.* ◊ **briskness.** EG *He was walking with unusual briskness.* ADJ QUALIT : ATTRIB ◊ ADV WITH VB ◊ N UNCOUNT

3 If trade or business is **brisk**, things are being sold very quickly and a lot of money is being made. EG *They are doing a brisk trade in used cardboard...* ADJ QUALIT ↑ good = roaring

They stopped at the refreshment tent where trade was gratifyingly brisk.

4 If weather is described as **brisk**, it is fresh and cold and refreshing. EG *It all happened one brisk April morning... The light breezes became brisk winds.* ADJ CLASSIF = bracing

brisket /brɪskɪt/ is beef that comes from the breast of the cow. EG *The butcher gave us a lump of brisket.* N UNCOUNT ⇑ meat

bristle /brɪsəᵊl/, **bristles, bristling, bristled.** 1 You use **bristles** or **bristle** to refer to **1.1** thick, strong, animal hairs that feel hard and rough. Bristles are sometimes used to make brushes. EG *It has a short stumpy tail covered with bristles... This toothbrush is real bristle.* N COUNT: USU PL, OR N UNCOUNT ⇑ hair **1.2** the short, thick hairs that grow on part of your body after you have shaved it. EG *His chin was covered with bristles.* N COUNT: USU PL, OR N UNCOUNT

2 The **bristles** of a brush are the thick hairs or the fairly long, thin pieces of plastic which are attached to the main part of it. EG *Never stand a paintbrush on its bristles.* N PLURAL ⇑ hair

3 If the hair on an animal's or person's body **bristles**, it rises away from their skin because they are cold, frightened, angry, etc. EG *I felt the hairs bristle ever so slightly along the back of my neck... The cat's back bristled at the sudden sound.* V ⇑ rise

4 If you **bristle** at something, you react to it angrily or indignantly, and show this in the expression on your face or the way you move. EG *Mrs Pringle bristled at the memory... 'He's a jerk,' said Bob. Eva bristled.* V: IF+PREP THEN *at* = bridle

bristle with. 1 Something that **bristles with** things that are long, thin, and sharp has a large number of them sticking out of it. EG *The creature had a long nose bristling with whiskers... The circle of soldiers bristled with spears.* PHRASAL VB: V+PREP

2 Something that **bristles with** something else, has or contains a large amount of it; used mainly in informal British English. EG *The hotel was bristling with policemen at every entrance... Some people are absolutely bristling with life.* PHRASAL VB: V+PREP = burst with

bristling /brɪslɪŋ/ is used to describe moustaches, eyebrows, etc that are thick, hairy, and rough. EG *...an old man with a bristling moustache.* ADJ CLASSIF: ATTRIB

bristly /brɪsliⁱ/, **bristlier, bristliest.** 1 Hair that is **bristly** is rough, coarse, and thick. EG *He had short, bristly brown hair.* ADJ QUALIT = spiky

2 If someone's skin, especially on their chin, is **bristly**, it is covered with bristles because it has not been shaved for a day or more. EG *He ran a hand over his bristly chin.* ADJ QUALIT ⇑ rough

Brit /brɪt/, **Brits.** A **Brit** is a person who comes from Great Britain or who is a citizen of the United Kingdom; an informal word. EG *What do the Brits want out of it?... He did his duty like a True Brit.* N COUNT

Brit. is an abbreviation for **British.** ADJ CLASSIF

British /brɪtɪʃ/. 1 Someone or something that is **British** **1.1** belongs or is related to the United Kingdom of Great Britain and Northern Ireland, or to its people or languages. EG *...British citizenship... ...my British friends.* ADJ CLASSIF **1.2** has characteristics that are considered to be typical of someone or something that comes from the United Kingdom. EG *Vita at that age was British through and through.* ADJ QUALIT

2 The **British** are the people who come from the United Kingdom; used especially to refer to the whole nation. EG *But all you British are arrogant... They will be increasingly dependent on the support of the British, French, or Dutch.* N PLURAL: USU *the*+N

Britisher /brɪtɪʃə/, **Britishers.** A **Britisher** is a person who comes from Great Britain or who is a citizen of the United Kingdom; an informal word not used by British people. N COUNT

Briton /brɪtəᵊn/, **Britons.** A **Briton** is a person who comes from Great Britain or who is a citizen of the United Kingdom. EG *The youth, a 17-year-old Briton, was searched and arrested.* N COUNT

brittle /brɪtəᵊl/, **brittler, brittlest.** 1 An object or substance that is **brittle** is hard but delicate and easily broken. EG *The letter was brittle and yellowed with age... ...dry sticks as brittle as candy.* ADJ QUALIT ⇑ breakable

2 If you describe something such as a relationship, system, or way of life, as **brittle**, you mean that it is not firmly based and therefore easy to damage or destroy. EG *It was an extraordinarily brittle empire.* ADJ QUALIT = fragile ≠ deep-rooted

3 Someone who is **brittle** appears to be very confident and often uncaring and insensitive. EG *'Why not?' she said, wanting to be as bright and brittle as all the other people.* ADJ QUALIT

4 A sound that is **brittle** is short, loud, and sharp. EG *There was a sharp, brittle tinkling.* ADJ QUALIT

broach /brəʊtʃ/, **broaches, broaching, broached.** 1 When you **broach** a difficult or awkward subject, you mention it in order to start a discussion on it. EG *She had never yet managed to broach the subject with him... She first broached the idea of a partnership in 1985.* V+O ⇑ introduce = bring up

2 If you **broach** a bottle or barrel, you open it so that you can drink its contents; a formal or humorous use. V+O

broad /brɔːd/, **broader, broadest; broads.** 1 Something such as a road or river that is **broad** is very wide. EG *The streets of this town are broad... ...a broad ditch full of water... He was tall, with broad shoulders... ...a broad, hefty Irish nurse.* ADJ QUALIT ≠ narrow

2 A rectangular object that is a particular distance **broad** measures that distance between its two longer sides. EG *...a flat case about two feet long by eighteen inches broad.* ADJ AFTER N = wide

3 If you describe something flat as **broad**, you mean that it is very large. EG *North of the Serpentine lie broad fields... ...seated behind a desk which showed a broad expanse of polished wood.* ADJ QUALIT: ATTRIB = substantial

4 A **broad** smile is one in which your mouth is stretched very wide because you are very pleased or amused. EG *...a broad grin.* ADJ QUALIT: ATTRIB ≠ faint, tight

5 **Broad** is used to describe something such as a range of things or a survey that consists of, deals with, or is concerned with a large number of different things. EG *She had a broader range of interests than Jane... This syllabus is a broad one.* ADJ QUALIT ⇑ wide = extensive ≠ limited

6 A **broad** word or expression refers to or describes a wide range of different things. EG *...a broad term like 'traditionalism'... ...'cultural' in the broadest sense of the word.* ADJ QUALIT: ATTRIB = general ≠ strict

7 A **broad** group of people consists of people with a very wide range of views or interests. EG *...a broad coalition of community groups in the area.* ADJ QUALIT: ATTRIB ≠ insular

8 **Broad** is also used to refer to something that is **8.1** experienced by many people, or by people of many different kinds. EG *...a broad feeling that the West lacks direction... ...a youth organization with a broader appeal... This take-over bid has broader implications.* ADJ QUALIT ⇑ general = widespread ≠ specific **8.2** defined or described in a general way or that includes many different things. EG *He distinguished three broad possibilities... Agreement on broad policy objectives has been obtained... He gave us a very broad introduction to linguistics.* ADJ QUALIT: ATTRIB ≠ precise

9 You can use **broad** to describe something such as sarcasm or a hint, to indicate that its meaning is very obvious. EG *Broad hints were aired that the paper should be closed down... 'Oh yeah,' said Jenny with broad sarcasm.* ADJ QUALIT: ATTRIB ≠ subtle

10 A **broad** accent is a strong and noticeable regional or foreign accent. EG *She spoke in a broad Wiltshire accent.* ADJ QUALIT = pronounced

11 Something such as a crime that is done **in broad daylight**, is done during the day, rather than at dusk or at night when you might expect it to be done. EG *Mugging in the streets, even in broad daylight, was common.* PHR: USED AS AN A ⇑ openly

12 A **broad** is a woman; an offensive use in very informal American English. N COUNT

13 See also **broadly.**

broad bean, broad beans. In British English, **broad beans** are large, flat, light-green beans that you can eat; used also to refer to the plant that they grow on. EG *We were served steak with broad beans.* N COUNT: USU PL ⇑ bean

broadcast /brɔːdkɑːst/, **broadcasts, broadcasting, broadcasted.** The form **broadcast** is used in the present tense and also as the past tense and past participle of the verb. The form **broadcasted** is sometimes used as the past tense and past participle. 1 A **broadcast** is something that is heard on the radio or seen on television, for example a speech or a concert. EG *At the end of December he gave a Party Political Broadcast... He was criticized for making these broadcasts.* N COUNT ⇑ transmission = programme

2 To **broadcast** a programme means to send it out by radio waves, so that it can be heard on the radio or seen on television. EG *Episode One was broadcast last night... ...an illegal radio station which broadcast from a different place each week.* V OR V+O ⇑ transmit = relay

3 To **broadcast** a speech or talk means to give it on radio or television. EG *Ten days after I broadcast this talk, I had a letter from London.* V OR V+O

4 If you **broadcast** a piece of news, you tell it to V+O

everyone that you meet; an old-fashioned or informal use. EG *Don't broadcast it, but I'm looking for another job.*

broadcaster /brɔːdkɑːstə/, **broadcasters**. A **broadcaster** is someone who gives talks or takes part in interviews and discussions on radio or television programmes. EG *He had managed to earn a living as a broadcaster... ...Anthony Howard, the journalist and broadcaster.* N COUNT

broadcasting /brɔːdkɑːstɪŋ/ is the making and sending out of television and radio programmes. EG *...the scope and purpose of educational broadcasting... ...the Australian Broadcasting Commission.* N UNCOUNT ⇑ transmitting

broadcast /brɔːdəⁿ/, **broadens, broadening, broadened**. 1 When something **broadens**, it becomes wider. EG *As the stream descends it broadens... Her smile broadened a little.* V = widen ≠ narrow

2 When you **broaden** something or when it **broadens**, 2.1 it consists of, includes, or is concerned with a larger number of things or people. EG *Some members wished to broaden the scope of the campaign... For some it is a way to broaden their circle of social contacts... It would do me good to broaden my outlook... The middle years of their lives are a time of broadening horizons.* V-ERG ⇑ enlarge = widen, extend 2.2 it is experienced by or affects more people. EG *He made another attempt to broaden his appeal.* V-ERG = extend

3 If an experience **broadens** your **mind**, it makes you more willing to accept or tolerate other people's beliefs and ways of doing things. EG *Travel broadens the mind... Meeting people was very good for you because it broadened your mind.* PHR : VB INFLECTS ⇑ educate

broaden out. 1 When something such as a road or river **broadens out**, it becomes wider. PHRASAL VB : V+ADV

2 When you **broaden** something **out** or when it **broadens out**, it consists of, includes, or is concerned with a larger number of things or people. EG *It was part of a broadening out of our political awareness.* PHRASAL VB : V-ERG+ADV

broadly /brɔːdliˡ/. 1 You can say **broadly** or **broadly speaking** to mean that although there may be a few exceptions to what you are saying, it is true in almost all cases. EG *Broadly, if you keep to your left, you will go through the rooms where the Oriental art is displayed... You can see that, broadly speaking, it is really quite straightforward.* ADV SEN ⇑ generally = roughly speaking

2 **Broadly** is used to say that something happens to a large extent and in all the ways or matters that are important. EG *I was broadly in favour of it... Units were mostly organized broadly on US models... It was to be done broadly as planned.* ADV+PREP = largely, roughly

3 If someone smiles **broadly** their mouth is stretched very wide because they are very pleased or amused. ADV WITH VB ≠ faintly

broadly-based. Something that is **broadly-based** consists of or involves many different kinds of things or people. EG *He wants it to be a broadly-based movement.* ADJ QUALIT = broad

broadminded /brɔːdmaɪndɪˡd/. Someone who is **broadminded** is very tolerant and does not disapprove of actions or attitudes that other people disapprove of. EG *She assured me that her parents were broadminded.* ADJ QUALIT = liberal ≠ narrow-minded

> **BROAD NEG** □ In this dictionary BROAD NEG is used in the grammar notes beside entries to indicate that a word or phrase is used in a broadly negative environment. It is used with a negative word such as **not** or **never**, with an ADV BRD NEG like **barely** or **scarcely**, or in question forms without a negative word. Examples of words which usually occur in a broadly negative environment are **bother 1**, **necessarily 1**, and **ever**. EG *I never **bothered** to check his accounts... People do not **necessarily** need to live near their workplaces... I don't think I've **ever** been so surprised... They were scarcely **ever** apart.*

broadsheet /brɔːdʃiːt/, **broadsheets**. In British English, a **broadsheet** is a newspaper or advertisement that is printed on one large sheet of paper. N COUNT = leaflet, handout

broadside /brɔːdsaɪd/, **broadsides**. 1 If a ship is **broadside** to something, it has its longest side facing in the direction of that thing; a technical term. EG *As the ship came close and turned broadside, we saw that there was only one man on it.* ADV AFTER VB = sideways

2 A **broadside** is 2.1 the firing of all the guns on one side of a warship at the same time; an old-fashioned use. N COUNT 2.2 a strong written or spoken attack on someone. EG *The broadside which landed the newspaper in trouble was the accusation that the Minister had deliberately lied.* N COUNT = tirade

brocade /brəˡkeɪd/ is a thick, heavy, expensive material, often of silk, that has a raised pattern on it. EG *She wore a kimono of beige and white brocade.* N UNCOUNT ⇑ fabric

broccoli /brɒkəliˡ/ is a vegetable with green stalks and green or purple flower buds. N UNCOUNT

brochure /brəʊʃjˡʊˡə/, **brochures**. A **brochure** is a booklet with pictures that gives you information about a product or company or that advertises something. EG *...travel brochures... ...a brochure about retirement homes.* N COUNT = pamphlet

brogue /brəʊg/, **brogues**. 1 If someone has a **brogue**, they speak English with a strong accent, especially Irish or Scots. EG *Mrs Joyce spoke in a thick Galway brogue.* N SING WITH DET +SUPP

2 **Brogues** are thick leather shoes for walking in. N COUNT : USU PL

broil /brɔɪl/, **broils, broiling, broiled**. If you **broil** food, you grill it. EG *...trout broiled over charcoal.* V+O ⇑ cook

broiler /brɔɪlə/, **broilers**. A **broiler** is a young chicken that is suitable for roasting or grilling. N COUNT

broiling /brɔɪlɪŋ/. If the weather is **broiling**, it is very hot; an informal word used especially in American English. EG *...a broiling August night.* ADJ CLASSIF = sweltering

broke /brəʊk/. 1 **Broke** is the past tense of **break**.

2 If you are **broke**, you have no money; an informal use. EG *He'd taken the job because he was broke.* ADJ QUALIT : PRED

3 If a company **goes broke**, it loses money and is unable to continue in business; an informal expression. EG *The paper was going broke and would cease publication.* PHR : VB INFLECTS = go bust

4 If you **go for broke**, you take the most extreme or risky of the possible courses of action in order to try to achieve a great success; an informal expression. EG *She can go for broke by sacking her accountant.* PHR : VB INFLECTS ⇑ risk ≠ play safe

broken /brəʊkəⁿn/. 1 **Broken** is the past participle of **break**.

2 An object that is **broken** has split into pieces, for example because it has been hit or dropped. EG *He sweeps away the broken glass under the window... ...broken branches.* ADJ CLASSIF = fragmented

3 A bone in your body that is **broken** has cracked or split as a result of an accident or a blow. EG *Barnett was rushed to the hospital with a broken back after a 40-foot fall.* ADJ CLASSIF ⇑ damaged

4 Something such as a tool or a piece of machinery that is **broken** is damaged and no longer works. EG *The telephone box on the corner is broken... The hinge on the door has been broken for two years.* ADJ CLASSIF = bust

5 A line, sound, process, etc that is **broken** is interrupted or disturbed rather than continuous. EG *...a broken curve... John Crow replied in broken phrases... ...angry crying with broken, irregular screaming.* ADJ CLASSIF = disjointed

6 **Broken** ground or water is rough rather than smooth and level. ADJ CLASSIF : USU ATTRIB

7 Someone who is **broken** is extremely weak, either physically or mentally, because of what they have suffered. EG *He is a broken man... Today he is thin and weak, stooped and broken by years of cruelly hard labour.* ADJ CLASSIF = crushed

8 If you describe a promise or contract as **broken**, it has not been kept or obeyed. ADJ CLASSIF = violated

9 A **broken** relationship, for example a marriage, has been ended. EG *There was certainly more stress and more broken marriages.* ADJ CLASSIF : ATTRIB ⇑ destroyed

10 If someone talks in **broken** English, **broken** French, etc, they speak slowly and make a lot of mistakes because they do not know it very well. EG *Fania's broken English was extremely difficult to make out.* ADJ QUALIT : ATTRIB ≠ perfect, fluent

broken-down. 1 If a vehicle or machine is **broken-down**, it no longer works because it has something wrong with it. EG *...two men pushing a broken-down car.* ADJ CLASSIF ⇑ damaged

2 If a building is **broken-down**, it is in very bad condition or has partly fallen down. EG *...broken-down hovels.* ADJ CLASSIF = tumbledown

broken-hearted. Someone who is **broken-hearted** is very sad and emotionally upset. ADJ CLASSIF

broken home, broken homes. A **broken home** is a family which does not live together, because the mother and father are separated or divorced. EG *He comes from a broken home.* N COUNT

broker /brəʊkə/, **brokers**. A **broker** is a person whose job is to buy and sell shares, foreign money, or goods for other people. EG *...an insurance broker.* N COUNT : USU MOD+N ⇑ agent

brolly /brɒli¹/, **brollies**. A **brolly** is an umbrella; an informal word used in British English. N COUNT

bromide /brəʊmaɪd/, **bromides**. A **bromide** is 1 a drug which you take to calm you down quickly when you are unhappy or worried. EG *Pregnant women should not take bromides.* 2 a comment which is intended to calm someone down when they are angry, but which has been expressed so often that it has become boring and meaningless; a formal use. EG *She came out with the same old bromides.* N COUNT; N COUNT ⇑ cliché = platitude ≠ novelty

bronchial /brɒŋkɪəl/. **Bronchial** means 1 affecting or concerned with the bronchial tubes; a medical term. EG *...a bronchial infection.* 2 caused by or reminding you of bronchitis; an informal use. EG *'I'll never see ninety-one,' he croaked, coughing his most bronchial cough... There was a chugging sound like a bronchial road drill.* ADJ CLASSIF: ATTRIB; ADJ QUALIT: ATTRIB ⇑ ill

bronchial tube, bronchial tubes. Your **bronchial tubes** are the two tubes which connect your windpipe to your lungs; a medical term. N COUNT ⇑ tube

bronchitis /brɒŋkaɪtɪ¹s/ is an illness like a very bad cold in the chest, in which your bronchial tubes become sore and infected. EG *She suffered from bronchitis as a child.* N UNCOUNT ⇑ coughing

bronco /brɒŋkəʊ/, **broncos**. A **bronco** is a wild horse that cowboys ride in order to try to tame it; used especially in films and books about the American Wild West. N COUNT

brontosaurus /brɒntəsɔːrəs/, **brontosauruses, brontosauri**. The plural can be either **brontosauruses** or **brontosauri**. A **brontosaurus** was a dinosaur with four feet, a small head, and a long neck and tail, which ate plants rather than animals. N COUNT

bronze /brɒnz/, **bronzes**. 1 **Bronze** is a yellowish brown metal which is made of a mixture of copper and tin. EG *The urn appeared to be made of some sort of bronze... ...a large bronze statue of a tigress.* N UNCOUNT
▸ used of a statue or sculpture made of bronze. EG *The best bronze in London is outside the National Gallery; it's of James II.* ▸ N COUNT ⇑ sculpture
2 **Bronze** is also a yellowish-brown colour, the colour of the metal bronze. EG *...the beautiful bronze and green in the landscape.* ▸ used as an adjective. EG *...shoulder-length, brilliant bronze hair.* N UNCOUNT ⇑ colour; ▸ ADJ COLOUR

bronzed /brɒnzd/. Someone who is **bronzed** is suntanned and looks fit and healthy; used showing approval. EG *...bikini-clad girls and their bronzed admirers.* ADJ QUALIT ⇑ brown

bronze medal, bronze medals. If you win a **bronze medal**, you come third in a competition, especially a sports contest, and you are awarded a small circular piece of bronze as your prize. N COUNT = third place

brooch /brəʊtʃ/, **brooches**. A **brooch** is a small piece of jewellery that has a pin on the back of it. Women often wear a brooch as a decoration on a dress or blouse. EG *Her earrings matched the brooch... ...diamond brooches.* N COUNT

brood /bruːd/, **broods, brooding, brooded**. 1 A **brood** is a group of baby birds that were all born at the same time to the same mother. EG *They were trying to find food for their brood.* N COUNT: IF SING, VB CAN BE SING OR PL ⇑ family
2 If you talk about someone's **brood**, you are referring humorously to their young children, especially when there are a lot of them and they are lively and noisy. EG *...a squabbling brood of children.* N COUNT: IF SING, VB CAN BE SING OR PL
3 If something **broods**, it hangs or stands above people without any sound or movement; a formal use. EG *Over this vista broods a terrace of tall houses.* V = loom
4 If someone **broods** about something, they think about it deeply, silently, and privately, often with strong feelings of bitterness, resentment, or revenge. EG *I slunk away to my room, to brood in front of the mirror... Recently he had caught himself brooding about the meaning of life.* V: IF+PREP THEN *about* ⇑ think = ponder

brood on. If you **brood on** or **brood over** something unpleasant, you keep on and on thinking about it. EG *He took to his bed for two days and brooded on his failure... He'd been brooding over how furious he was with my father.* PHRASAL VB: V+PREP, HAS PASS = dwell on ≠ dismiss

brooding /bruːdɪŋ/, **broodings**. 1 Something that is **brooding** causes you to feel threatened and afraid. EG *The silent, brooding presence of the woman made him uncomfortable... Her films show a dark, brooding sense of fear.* ADJ CLASSIF ⇑ disturbing
2 If you refer to **broodings** or **brooding**, you mean someone's deep, silent, and private thoughts, which are usually about something unpleasant; an informal use. EG *Remembering their broodings about what had happened before, I decided not to confide in them this time... He has plainly done a painful amount of brooding and self-analysis.* N PLURAL OR N UNCOUNT ⇑ pondering

broody /bruːdi¹/. 1 Someone who is **broody** thinks deeply, silently, and privately about things, often in a rather negative way. EG *She will become broody and resentful if you don't treat her right.* ADJ QUALIT = gloomy ≠ carefree
2 A **broody** hen, duck, or goose is one that is ready to lay or sit on eggs. ADJ CLASSIF ⇑ motherly
3 If you describe a young woman as **broody**, you mean, in informal English, that she is rather restless because she wants to have a baby; used mainly in British English. EG *I was feeling broody.* ADJ QUALIT ⇑ motherly

brook /brʊk/, **brooks, brooking, brooked**. 1 A **brook** is a small stream with quickly flowing water. EG *...the waters of a mountain brook.* N COUNT
2 If you do not **brook** something, for example argument or delay, you do not allow or accept it; a formal use. EG *...an unmistakably domineering female who will brook no nonsense... She doesn't brook any argument.* V+O: WITH BROAD NEG = tolerate

broom /bru⁴m/, **brooms**. 1 A **broom** is a kind of brush with a long handle. You use a broom for sweeping the floor. EG *Joseph stopped sweeping and rested on his broom.* N COUNT ⇑ brush
2 **Broom** is a wild bush with a lot of thorns and tiny yellow flowers which grows on waste ground or sandy ground. EG *We clambered through broom and briar right to the top of the hill.* N UNCOUNT

broomstick /bru⁴mstɪk/, **broomsticks**. A **broomstick** is the long handle of a broom which has a bundle of twigs rather than neat bristles at the end. It is most frequently used when referring to the traditional idea that witches fly on broomsticks. EG *I've seen her flying about on her broomstick many a winter's night.* N COUNT ⇑ broom

bros. or **Bros.** is an abbreviation for 'brothers'; used especially in the name of a company. EG *...the glossy windows of Moss Bros.* N PLURAL: ALSO IN NAMES AFTER N

broth /brɒθ/, **broths**. 1 **Broth** is soup, usually with vegetables or rice in it. EG *The trout lay in a deep copper dish, in a kind of broth... ...Scotch broth.* N UNCOUNT = consommé
2 A **broth** is a specially made substance on which biologists grow small organisms, such as fungus. N COUNT: USU SING

brothel /brɒθəᵒl/, **brothels**. A **brothel** is a building where men visit prostitutes and pay to have sex with them. EG *He was reputed to frequent a Mayfair brothel.* N COUNT = whore house

brother /brʌðə/, **brothers, brethren**. **Brothers** is the usual plural of **brother**, but **brethren**, which is old-fashioned, is still used as one of the plurals for the meaning defined in paragraph 5. 1 Your **brother** is a boy or a man who has the same parents as you have. EG *I have two brothers and one sister... She went to New York for the wedding of her youngest brother... Northcliffe received a letter from his brother Harold.* • See also **big brother, half-brother**, and **stepbrother**. N COUNT ⇑ sibling ≠ sister
2 You might describe as your **brother** a man who belongs to the same race, religion, profession, or trade union as you, or who has ideas or attitudes that are similar to yours. EG *All men are our brothers... Both he and his brother judges had been considerably amused... Then, Brothers and Sisters, I asked him to withdraw his accusation.* N COUNT: USU PL
3 One man might very informally address another man as **brother**, especially if they do not know each other. EG *No way, brother... Hey, brother, who owns this field?* N COUNT: ALSO VOC = mate
4 If you describe one thing as being a **brother** to something else, you mean that they have a lot of features in common. EG *It is slightly superior in intelligence, but is a brother to the chimpanzee and gorilla.* N COUNT: IF+PREP THEN *to/of* ⇑ relation
5 **Brother** is a title given to a man who belongs to a religious institution such as a monastery, but who is not a clergyman. EG *...Brother Michael, one of the Anglican Chaplains... The schools were staffed by Christian Brothers who were invariably Irish... ...the Brethren of the Trinity.* N COUNT: ALSO IN TITLES
6 You might exclaim **brother**! when you want to express amazement, disappointment, or annoyance; an old-fashioned use. EG *Oh brother, what a mess!* EXCLAM = oh boy, cor

brotherhood /brʌðəhʊd/, **brotherhoods**. 1 **Brotherhood** is the affection and loyalty you feel for people with whom you have something in common. N UNCOUNT: IF+PREP THEN *of* = companionship

EG ...*a deepening sense of brotherhood... ...the ideas of socialist brotherhood and equality... ...the brotherhood of man.*

2 A **brotherhood** is 2.1 an organization whose members have the same political aims and beliefs or who have the same job or profession. EG *The brotherhood was financed by the Party.* 2.2 a group of men, especially monks, who live together in order to lead a religious life. N COUNT: IF+PREP THEN *of* / N COUNT: IF+PREP THEN *of*

brother-in-law, brothers-in-law. Your **brother-in-law** is the brother of your husband or your wife, or the man who is married to your sister or to your wife's or your husband's sister. EG *He went with his brother-in-law to book a holiday.* N COUNT ⇑ relative

brotherly /brʌðəli[1]/ means showing the feelings of love and loyalty which you expect a brother to show. EG ...*brotherly love.* ADJ CLASSIF: ATTRIB ⇑ loyal

brougham /bruːəm/, **broughams.** A **brougham** is a type of light carriage pulled by one horse, used in Europe and America in the 19th century. N COUNT

brought /brɔːt/ is the past tense and past participle of **bring.**

brow /brau/, **brows.** 1 Your **brow** is your forehead; used especially when you are describing emotions that cause you to wrinkle your forehead or physical effort that causes your face to sweat. EG *She sat there staring at him, her brow wrinkled, her mouth slightly open... He mopped his sweating brow.* • To **knit** your **brow**: see **knit.** N SING WITH DET: USU *the/* POSS+N

2 A **brow** is the same as an eyebrow; used in old-fashioned English. EG *I've got a scar on my eye here, just below the brow.* N COUNT

3 The **brow** of a hill or a slope is the top part of it. EG *A tank appeared over the brow of a hill.* N COUNT: USU SING+*of*

browbeat /braubiːt/, **browbeats, browbeating, browbeaten.** The form **browbeat** is used in the present tense and the past tense. If you **browbeat** someone, you bully them and try to force them to do what you want. EG *How dare you suggest that I would try and browbeat Aunt Elizabeth!* V+O bludgeon

browbeaten /braubiːtən/. Someone who is **browbeaten** has been bullied so much that they have become quiet, obedient, and depressed. EG *Cora is quite simply a browbeaten wife.* ADJ CLASSIF = ground down, oppressed

brown /braun/, **browner, brownest; browns, browning, browned.** 1 Something that is **brown** is the colour of earth or of wood. EG *His brown eyes twinkled at them... ...her long brown hair loose about her shoulders.* ▸ used as a noun. EG *I never wear brown.* ADJ COLOUR ▸ N MASS

2 Someone who is **brown** 2.1 has darker skin than usual because they have been in the sun. EG *His body was golden brown... ...her long brown legs.* ▸ used as a noun. EG *Her legs were of a deep golden brown.* • If you say that someone is **as brown as a berry**, you mean that they have been in the sun for a long time and are very brown indeed; used mainly in British English. 2.2 belongs to a race of people who have brown-coloured skins, for example an Indian race. EG *Ordinary people, black and white, yellow and brown, rich and poor, joined together to protest.* ADJ COLOUR = tanned ▸ N MASS ● PHR: USED AS C = very tanned ADJ CLASSIF

3 When something **browns** or when you **brown** it, it becomes browner in colour, either from the heat of the sun or from cooking. EG *Grass browned and trees drooped that summer... Uncover the chicken for the last fifteen minutes to brown nicely.* V-ERG

browned off. If you are **browned off** with something, you no longer feel any enthusiasm for it, and might even be slightly angry about it; used in informal British English. EG *He was a bit browned off with the job.* ADJ QUALIT: PRED, IF+PREP THEN *with* = fed up

brownie /brauni[1]/, **brownies.** 1 A **Brownie** or a **Brownie Guide** is a junior member of the Guides. Brownies are usually between seven and ten years old. N COUNT ⇑ child

2 If you earn yourself **brownie points**, you do something and you get credit for doing it; used in informal English. PHR: USED AS O

3 A **brownie** is also a small flat chocolate cake with nuts in it; used in American English. N COUNT

brownish /brauniʃ/ means slightly brown in colour. EG *The grass was a brownish yellow on that winter day.* ADJ COLOUR

brown rice is rice which has not had its outer covering removed. N UNCOUNT

brownstone /braunstəun/, **brownstones.** 1 **Brownstone** is a kind of stone that is reddish brown in colour. It is used for building. N UNCOUNT ⇑ sandstone

2 A **brownstone** is, in America, a house that has its front built from brownstone. N COUNT

browse /brauz/, **browses, browsing, browsed.** 1 If you **browse,** 1.1 you look through a book or magazine in a casual way, reading little bits of it that you find interesting. EG *He spent half an hour browsing through sections he had already read.* V: IF+PREP THEN *through* ⇑ flick

1.2 you look at several things, for example at books in a bookshop or at objects in an antique shop, in a casual, unhurried way, in the hope that you might find something interesting. EG *She browses a while, then picks up a glossy magazine.* ▸ used as a noun. EG ...*a browse around in the children's picture book section.* V: USU+A = look around ▸ N COUNT+SUPP

2 When animals such as deer **browse,** they feed on plants, especially on their young twigs or leaves, in an unhurried way. EG ...*the first mammals that browsed in the forests of fifty million years ago... A cow browsed amid a profusion of mountain flowers.* V: USU+A = graze, nibble

bruise /bruːz/, **bruises, bruising, bruised.** 1 A **bruise** is an injury, usually produced when a part of the body is hit by something and the skin is not broken but is coloured by a purple or brown mark. EG *It's going to be a huge ugly bruise... I'm okay; just a few cuts and bruises.* N COUNT

2 When a part of your body **bruises** or when you **bruise** it, you damage it, especially by hitting it, without breaking the skin but producing a purple or brown mark on the skin. EG *I bruise easily... He was severely bruised.* ◊ **bruised.** EG *He had a cut forehead and a bruised cheek.* ◊ **bruising.** EG *The bruising will be painful for a week or so.* V-ERG ⇑ injure ◊ ADJ QUALIT ◊ N UNCOUNT

3 A **bruise** on a piece of fruit is a dark mark caused by pressure on the fruit which has not broken its skin but has spoilt its appearance. EG ...*a tomato with a bruise on it.* N COUNT

4 When a piece of fruit **bruises** or when you **bruise** it, it gets a dark mark on its skin caused by something pressing on it and so its appearance and taste are spoilt. ◊ **bruised.** EG ...*a bag of bruised peaches.* V-ERG ⇑ marks ◊ ADJ QUALIT

5 If someone **is bruised** by something that happens, they are hurt mentally or emotionally. EG *I feel a little bruised by recent events.* ◊ **bruising.** EG ...*a bruising experience.* V+O: USU PASS ⇑ wound ◊ ADJ QUALIT

bruiser /bruːzə/, **bruisers.** A **bruiser** is a big strong man, especially one who enjoys fighting; used in informal English. EG *That son of yours will be an incredible bruiser.* N COUNT = bully, tough

brunch /brʌntʃ/, **brunches. Brunch** is a meal that you eat in the late morning. It is a combination of breakfast and lunch. EG *Sunday brunches are served at the Trade Winds restaurant.* N UNCOUNT/COUNT ⇑ meal

brunette /bruːnet/, **brunettes.** A **brunette** is a white woman or girl with dark hair. EG ...*a pretty brunette.* N COUNT

brunt /brʌnt/. If someone **bears the brunt** or **takes the brunt** of something unpleasant, they take the main part or force of it. EG *Let her take the brunt of your anger in private... Indian troops bore the brunt of the Burma campaigns.* PHR: VB INFLECTS ⇑ suffer

brush /brʌʃ/, **brushes, brushing, brushed.** 1 A **brush** is an object made of wood, plastic, or metal, which has a large number of bristles attached to it. There are many different sizes and shapes of brushes, which are used for different purposes, such as cleaning your teeth, tidying your hair, or sweeping the floor. EG ...*dustpans and brushes with wooden handles... The brushes and paints had been set out in the art room... ...a new thin paint-brush... ...a wide flat brush.* N COUNT ⇑ tool

2 If you **brush** something, 2.1 you clean, sweep, or tidy it using a brush. EG *I'm going to brush my teeth... An elderly servant slowly brushed the carpet... She began vigorously to brush her hair before the mirror.* ▸ used as a noun. EG *If you give the carpet a hard brush, maybe that'll help.* 2.2 you remove something by using quick light brushing movements, especially with your hands. EG *She brushed back the hair from her eyes... Tears welled up in his eyes and he brushed them aside with his sleeve... She brushed out the wrinkles in her dress nervously.* V+O ▸ N SING: *a*+N V+O+A

3 To **brush** or to **brush** something means to touch it lightly but not on purpose, especially while passing V OR V+O: RECIP

it. EG *Something brushed against the back of the shelter... The girl's hair brushed his cheek.*

4 If you have a **brush** with someone or something, you come very close to having something very unpleasant happen to you, but you manage to escape safely. EG *A near miss brush with death had left her shaken... His attitude has led to some brushes with authority.* N COUNT + *with* ⇑ encounter = skirmish

5 **Brush** is, **5.1** in American English, small bushes and trees that grow all over rough open land; used also to refer to the land itself. EG *...a wide grazing area of low brush and grass... Some ranchers control brush with herbicides.* N UNCOUNT ⇑ scrub **5.2** small dead branches and twigs that have broken off from trees and bushes. EG *They were picking up light brush and small fallen branches for firewood.* N UNCOUNT ⇑ wood = brushwood

6 The **brush** of a fox is its tail. N COUNT

brush aside. If you **brush aside** something such as an idea, thought, or feeling or if you **brush** it **away**, you refuse to consider it or to accept it because you think it is not necessary or important. EG *She brushed his protests aside, politely... She brushed the thought away.* PHRASAL VB : V+O+ADV ⇑ ignore

brush by. If you **brush by** someone, you go quickly past them, often nearly touching them, usually in order to avoid having to talk to them. EG *I brushed by him, opened the door and stopped.* PHRASAL VB : V+PREP ⇑ hurry past = brush past

brush down. If you **brush down** your trousers, skirt, etc, you remove dirt or creases from them with quick movements of your hands or a brush. EG *She crawled out and brushed down her skirt.* PHRASAL VB : V+O+ADV = dust down

brush off. 1 If you **brush** someone **off**, you refuse to talk to them or be pleasant to them, especially by ignoring them or by saying something rude. EG *He tried to start a conversation but she brushed him off.* PHRASAL VB : V+O+ADV

2 See also **brushoff**.

brush past. If you **brush past** someone, you go quickly past them, often nearly touching them, usually in order to avoid having to talk to them. EG *She laughed, and brushed past me out of the room... A marine brushed past us.* PHRASAL VB : V+PREP ⇑ hurry pass

brush up. If you **brush up** or **brush up on** a particular subject, you already know something about it but you revise or improve your knowledge of it by studying it carefully. EG *I would like to brush up my zoology... I really need to brush up on my French.* PHRASAL VB : V+O+ADV, OR V+ADV+PREP

brushed /brʌʃt/. **Brushed** fabrics have been treated in a special way so that they feel soft and furry. EG *Sheets are often made of cotton or brushed nylon.* ADJ CLASSIF : ATTRIB

brushoff /brʌʃɒf/. If you **give** someone **the brush-off**, you refuse to talk to them or be pleasant to them, especially by ignoring them or by saying something rude; an informal expression. PHR : VB INFLECTS

brushwood /brʌʃwʊd/. **Brushwood** is 1 a collection of small dead branches and twigs that have broken off from trees and bushes. EG *...a pile of brushwood and dead leaves.* N UNCOUNT ⇑ wood 2 an assortment of small bushes and trees that grow all over rough open land; also used to refer to the land itself. EG *His horse broke through the brushwood.* N UNCOUNT = brush

brushwork /brʌʃwɜːk/ is the particular technique that an artist has of using his or her brush to put paint on a canvas and the effect that this has in the picture. EG *...the individualistic brushwork employed by Leonardo.* N UNCOUNT

brusque /bruːsk, -usk/. Someone who is **brusque** spends as little time as possible in saying or doing something and does not show much consideration for other people. EG *He was sometimes brusque with me.* ADJ QUALIT = sharp, abrupt ▸ used of a person's speech or behaviour. EG *I made a brusque apology and left... She has quite a brusque manner.* ▸ = abrupt ◇ **brusquely.** EG *'Sorry–no time to waste,' she said brusquely... Billy kissed her brusquely.* ◇ ADV WITH VB = abruptly ◇ **brusqueness.** EG *His brusqueness is really rather off-putting.* ◇ N UNCOUNT = gruffness

brussels sprout, brussels sprouts; also spelled **brussel sprout**. A **brussels sprout** is a vegetable like a very small cabbage which you cook and eat. N COUNT

brutal /bruːtəᵒl/. 1 Someone who is **brutal** behaves in a cruel and violent way towards other people. EG *The captain was a brutal man.* ADJ QUALIT = savage, vicious ▸ used of actions and behaviour. EG *...the government's brutal treatment of political prisoners... ...a brutal killing.* ▸ = savage ◇ **brutally.** EG *Richard II was brutally murdered.* ◇ ADV WITH VB = savagely

2 Honesty or frankness is described as **brutal** if it expresses something in an unpleasantly clear and accurate way. EG *...the brutal and detailed candour of Holbein's portrait... He spoke with brutal frankness.* ADJ QUALIT ⇑ extreme ◇ **brutally.** EG *The photograph was brutally honest.* ◇ ADV+ADJ

3 **Brutal** is used to emphasize that an unpleasant quality is not reduced in any way. EG *There have been bitter protests about the brutal nature of the commercials.* ADJ CLASSIF : ATTRIB = unmitigated ◇ **brutally.** EG *We must ensure Britain's economic recovery in a brutally competitive world.* ◇ ADV = ruthlessly

4 If you say that the weather or climate is **brutal**, you mean that it is harsh and difficult to bear. EG *The winters must have been brutal... ...the brutal afternoon sun.* ADJ QUALIT = cruel ◇ **brutally.** EG *...the brutally dry countryside.* ◇ ADV+ADJ = cruelly

brutalise /bruːtəᵒlaɪz/. See **brutalize**.

brutality /bruːtæləˈtiˈ/, **brutalities.** 1 **Brutality** is cruel and violent treatment or behaviour. EG *In Jon's seventeen years he had seen more brutality than most people can expect to see in a lifetime... There is so much brutality on the screen.* N UNCOUNT ⇑ cruelty = violence

2 A **brutality** is an instance of cruel and violent treatment or behaviour. EG *...the brutalities of the totalitarian.* N COUNT = atrocity

brutalize /bruːtəᵒlaɪz/, **brutalizes, brutalizing, brutalized**; also spelled **brutalise**. If suffering or some other unpleasant experience **brutalizes** someone, it makes them cruel, violent, or lacking in normal human feeling. EG *Her childhood was so awful it's a wonder she was not brutalized by it.* V+O ⇑ harden = desensitize

brute /bruːt/, **brutes.** 1 A **brute** is **1.1** a rough and insensitive man, especially one who has a tendency to behave violently. EG *Go ahead and hit me, you big brute... He's an ugly brute.* N COUNT : ALSO VOC = beast **1.2** an animal, especially one that you feel sorry for. EG *The lions I am talking about are the poor half-starved brutes reserved for tourists.* N COUNT = beast

2 **Brute** strength or force is completely physical and instinctive, like that of an animal. EG *We will never yield to brute force.* ADJ CLASSIF : ATTRIB

3 **Brute** is used to describe something which lacks human intelligence. EG *He was a symbol of brute stupidity... He looked upon animals simply as brute beasts provided for our pleasure.* ADJ CLASSIF : ATTRIB = mindless

brutish /bruːtɪʃ/. If you describe human life or behaviour as **brutish**, you mean that it seems to be like an animal's and shows little evidence of human intelligence or feelings. EG *Man's life is nasty, brutish and short... His expression was brutish and mocking.* ADJ QUALIT = coarse, bestial

BS is an abbreviation for 'British Standard'; a standard that something must reach in a test to prove that it is satisfactory or safe. Each standard has a number for reference. EG *Manufactured to BS 96504.* N UNCOUNT + NUM

B.Sc., B.Scs. B.Sc. is an abbreviation for 'Bachelor of Science'; a first degree awarded by universities and polytechnics to people who have studied scientific subjects. EG *...B.Sc. students... He's got a B.Sc.* N COUNT ▸ used, especially after a person's name, to refer to someone who holds a B.Sc. degree. EG *Thomas Grantham B.Sc.* ▸ N COUNT : ALSO IN TITLES AFTER NAME ⇑ graduate

BST is an abbreviation for 'British Summer Time'; the time used in Great Britain from late March to late October, when clocks are set one hour ahead of Greenwich Mean Time. N UNCOUNT

bubble /bʌbəᵒl/, **bubbles, bubbling, bubbled.** 1 A **bubble** is **1.1** a ball of air that appears in liquids, for example when a liquid is boiling or when air gets trapped under it and rises to the surface. EG *A bubble of air escaped from the drowned woman's mouth... Hundreds and hundreds of tiny bubbles were rising up from the dissolving tablets...* N COUNT : IF + PREP THEN *of* = globule **1.2** a hollow, delicate ball of soap or a liquid. EG *Her elbows were covered in bubbles... She knows how to blow bubbles with washing-up liquid... She was busy sucking the last bubbles of her milk shake up the straw.* N COUNT : IF + PREP THEN *of* **1.3** a transparent ball or dome made of glass or plastic. EG *The ornament was encased in the most delicate bubble of Venetian glass.* N COUNT : USU + *of*

2 When a liquid **bubbles**, **2.1** it forms bubbles, because it is boiling, is fizzy, or is moving quickly. EG *Cook the mixture until it bubbles... The champagne bubbled in her glass.* V ⇑ move = froth **2.2** it flows in the form of bubbles. EG *Pools of soapy water bubbled across the floor.* V+A ⇑ move

3 If something **bubbles**, it makes a sound like water boiling or air bubbles rising to the surface of a liquid. EG *The spring bubbled out of the hillside.* V = gurgle ▸ used as a ▸ N COUNT

noun. EG *The roar of the geyser suddenly diminished to a quiet bubble.*
4 If a feeling, influence, etc **bubbles**, it becomes more and more active. EG *All the anger that I felt towards the man was bubbling away deep down inside me... Beneath the surface of the Sixties, strange things bubbled and seethed.* V = ferment, boil
5 If you are **bubbling** with a good feeling, you are full of it and very lively. EG *She was bubbling with confidence... At the end of the day I was bubbling with excitement.* V : USU -ING + *with* = brimming
6 **Bubble** is used in expressions like 'the bubble burst' when you are talking about a feeling, scheme, success, etc which seems perfect and wonderful at first but which disappears or is ruined suddenly and without warning. EG *One day she may wake up to find that all this happiness has burst like a bubble.* N COUNT
bubble over. If you are **bubbling over** with joy, happiness, etc, you are so full of this good feeling that you keep expressing it to everyone around you. EG *He was bubbling over with excitement... Mrs Morgan bubbled over with suggestions.* PHRASAL VB : V + ADV, USU + *with* ⇑ react
bubble up. If a liquid **bubbles up**, it rises to the top of the pan, glass, etc in the form of bubbles. EG *Champagne bubbled up over the edge of the glass.* PHRASAL VB : V + ADV ⇑ boil
bubble and squeak is a food made by mixing together cold cooked cabbage and potato, sometimes with meat, and then grilling or frying the mixture; used in British English. N UNCOUNT
bubble bath, bubble baths. 1 **Bubble bath** is a special soap that makes a lot of foam and smells nice in the bath. N MASS ⇑ toiletries
2 A **bubble bath** is a bath of water with bubble bath in it. EG *I'm having a nice relaxing bubble bath when I get back home tonight.* N COUNT
bubble gum; also spelled with a hyphen or as one word. **Bubble gum** is chewing gum that you can blow out of your mouth in the shape of a bubble. N UNCOUNT
bubbly /bʌbli[1]/, **bubblier, bubbliest**. 1 Someone who is **bubbly** is full of liveliness and cheerfulness; an informal use. EG *She's such a bubbly little girl.* ADJ QUALIT ⇑ lively = bouncy
2 A liquid that is **bubbly** is full of bubbles. EG *I like my mineral water bubbly rather than still.* ADJ QUALIT = fizzy
3 **Bubbly** is champagne; an informal use. EG *...a bottle of bubbly.* N UNCOUNT
buccaneer /bʌkənɪə/, **buccaneers**. A **buccaneer** is 1 a pirate, especially one who attacked and stole from Spanish ships in the 17th and 18th centuries. N COUNT 2 a person who is clever and successful, especially in business, but who you do not completely trust. EG *Selling cars is big business in which the buccaneers make huge profits.* N COUNT = entrepreneur
buccaneering /bʌkənɪərɪŋ/. Someone who is **buccaneering** is eager to be involved in risky or dishonest activities, especially in order to make money. ADJ QUALIT ⇑ adventurous
buck /bʌk/, **bucks, bucking, bucked**. 1 A **buck** is a US or Australian dollar; used in informal American English. EG *It cost me four bucks.* N COUNT : USU NUM + N ● In informal English, to **make a fast buck** or **a quick buck** means to earn a lot of money quickly, especially by doing something dishonest. EG *Eminent politicians were making a fast buck at the expense of their innocent supporters.* ● PHR : VB INFLECTS ⇑ profit
2 A **buck** is also 2.1 the male of various animals, including the deer and rabbit. EG *The female deer attracts the buck with high-pitched sounds.* N COUNT 2.2 a South African antelope, whether it is male or female. EG *The eland is a type of big buck.* N COUNT ⇑ deer
3 If an animal such as a horse **bucks**, it jumps into the air wildly with all four feet off the ground. EG *I fell off every time she bucked... ...a bucking pony.* V ⇑ jump = kick
4 If you **buck** a problem or an issue, you avoid it; an informal use. EG *I don't want to buck the question.* V + O
5 If you **pass the buck**, you refuse to accept responsibility for something and behave as if you expect someone else to deal with it; an informal expression. EG *You're passing the buck, professor! It was up to you to check!* PHR : VB INFLECTS
6 You say **'the buck stops here'** to say that it is your responsibility to deal with a particular problem; used when other people who are more junior than you are have refused to accept the responsibility. CONVENTION
7 **Buck** teeth are upper front teeth which stick forwards out of your mouth. EG *She laughed, and her buck teeth showed.* ADJ CLASSIF : ATTRIB = goofy
buck up. 1 To **buck** someone **up** or to **buck up** their spirits, morale, etc means, in informal English, to encourage them to be more cheerful. EG *I need something to buck my spirits up today... He has bucked up the morale of the nation with his optimistic policies for social change.* PHRASAL VB : V + O + ADV
2 In informal English, if you **buck up**, 2.1 you become more cheerful. EG *Come on, Charlie, buck up! It's not the end of the world, is it?* PHRASAL VB : V + ADV 2.2 you hurry up. EG *Buck up, we haven't got all day!* PHRASAL VB : V + ADV
3 If you tell someone to **buck** their **ideas up**, you mean that they should start behaving in a much more positive and efficient way. PHR : VB INFLECTS ⇑ improve
bucked /bʌkt/. If you are **bucked**, you feel pleased because you have been praised or something has gone well; an informal use. EG *I was pretty bucked by her approval, I must admit.* ADJ QUALIT : PRED ⇑ cheered = chuffed
bucket /bʌkɪt/, **buckets, bucketing, bucketed**. 1 A **bucket** is a container which is shaped like a cylinder and which has an open top and a handle. Buckets are often used for holding and carrying water. EG *The hotel cleaner entered carrying a bucket and a mop.* N COUNT = pail ▸ **Bucket** is also used to refer to the amount of liquid which a bucket contains. EG *...a bucket of warm water.* ▸ N PART ⇑ amount = bucketful
2 A **bucket** is also something that has a similar shape to a bucket, for example part of a machine. N COUNT
3 To **kick the bucket** means to die; an informal expression. EG *As soon as D.H. Lawrence kicked the bucket he started to become famous.* PHR : VB INFLECTS = snuff it
4 You can use **buckets** to refer to a large amount of rain or tears; an informal use. EG *We're going to get buckets of rain... She cried buckets.* N PART : PLURAL
5 If rain **buckets**, or **buckets down**, it falls very heavily; used in informal English. EG *It was really bucketing outside... It started to bucket down.* V, OR PHRASAL VB : V + ADV = pelt
bucketful /bʌkɪ[2]tfʊl/, **bucketfuls**. A **bucketful** is the amount contained in a bucket. EG *Pour a bucketful of cold water on top of the fire.* N PART = bucket
bucket seat, bucket seats. A **bucket seat** is a seat for one person in a car, aeroplane, etc which has rounded sides that partly enclose and support the body. N COUNT
bucket shop, bucket shops. A **bucket shop** is a travel agency that sells airline tickets cheaply in order to fill seats which would otherwise be empty; used in British English. N COUNT
buckle /bʌkə[0]l/, **buckles, buckling, buckled**. 1 A **buckle** is a piece of metal or plastic attached to one end of a belt or strap and used to fasten the belt or strap. EG *...a wide belt with a heavy brass buckle.* N COUNT ⇑ fastening
2 If you **buckle** a belt, shoe, or something else which has a buckle, you fasten it. EG *The cuffs of the raincoat are tightly buckled.* V + O ≠ unbuckle
3 If an object **buckles**, or if something **buckles** it, it becomes bent as a result of very severe heat or force. EG *If you put a hot frying pan into water it will hiss and perhaps buckle... The building buckled in upon itself... The hidden forces within the earth have buckled the strata.* V-ERG ⇑ distort
4 If your knees, legs, or arms **buckle**, they bend because they have become very weak or tired. EG *Cassidy's knees buckled, and he sank to the ground... His legs began trembling and buckling under him.* V = give way
buckle down. If you **buckle down** or **buckle down** to something, you start working seriously at it. EG *I'm going to buckle down to the training course.* PHRASAL VB : V + ADV, IF + PREP THEN *to*
buckle in. If you **buckle** someone **in** or **buckle** them **into** something, you fasten them there with a buckle. EG *She was buckling her son into his harness.* PHRASAL VB : V + O (NG/REFL) + ADV/PREP
buckle on. If you **buckle** something **on**, you attach it by means of buckles. EG *He buckled on his revolver.* PHRASAL VB : V + O + ADV ⇑ put on
buckled /bʌkə[0]ld/. **Buckled** shoes have buckles on them, either as a fastening or as a decoration. ADJ CLASSIF
buckshot /bʌkʃɒt/ consists of large pellets of lead shot used for hunting animals. N UNCOUNT
buckskin /bʌkskɪn/, **buckskins**. 1 **Buckskin** is soft, strong leather made from the skin of a deer or a goat. EG *He had white buckskin shoes with rubber soles.* N UNCOUNT
2 **Buckskins** are trousers made of buckskin. EG *They were dressed in buckskins and moccasins.* N PLURAL : ALSO *a pair of* + N
buck-toothed. Someone who is **buck-toothed** has teeth that stick forwards out of their mouth. ADJ CLASSIF = goofy
buckwheat /bʌkwi:t/ is a type of small black grain used for feeding animals and making flour; also used to refer to the flour itself. N UNCOUNT

bucolic /bjuːkɒlɪk/ means relating to the countryside; a literary word. EG *There was a charming bucolic print above the fireplace.* — ADJ CLASSIF ↑ rural = rustic

bud /bʌd/, **buds, budding, budded.** 1 A **bud** is a small pointed lump that appears on a branch or stem of a plant and develops into a leaf or flower. EG *The trees had already put out their leaves and there were buds everywhere.* — N COUNT ↑ shoot ● When a tree, plant, etc is **in bud**, it has buds on it. EG *The cherry trees were in bud.* — ● PHR : USED AS AN A

2 When a tree, plant, etc **buds**, it begins to develop new buds which will become leaves or flowers. EG *The trees began to bud... Upon a twisted branch a few leaves were budding.* — V : USU CONT ↑ grow = develop

3 To **nip** something **in the bud** means to put an end to it at an early stage in its development. EG *This incident very nearly nipped his political career in the bud.* — PHR : VB INFLECTS

4 Men sometimes use **bud** as a form of address to other men; used in informal American English. EG *Listen, bud, I don't like guys who answer me back.* — VOC = mate

5 A cotton **bud** is a small stick with a ball of cotton wool on the end which is used, for example, for cleaning your ears. — N COUNT

6 See also **taste bud**.

7 See also **budding**.

Buddha /bʊdə/, **Buddhas.** 1 **Buddha** or the **Buddha** is the title given to Gautama Siddhartha, who was a religious teacher and the founder of Buddhism. — N PROPER

2 A **Buddha** is a statue or picture of the Buddha. EG *...a low table with a Buddha and lighted incense on it.* — N COUNT

Buddhism /bʊdɪzə[0]m/ is the religion that teaches that the way to end suffering is by overcoming your desires. Buddhism is practised especially in eastern and central Asia. — N UNCOUNT

Buddhist /bʊdɪst/, **Buddhists.** 1 **Buddhist** means belonging to or relating to Buddhism. EG *...a Buddhist monk... ...Buddhist philosophy.* — ADJ CLASSIF ↑ religious

2 A **Buddhist** is a person who believes in Buddhism and follows its teachings. EG *I am a true Buddhist.* — N COUNT ↑ believer

budding /bʌdɪŋ/. A **budding** poet, artist, etc is one who is just beginning to develop and be successful. EG *She's a budding genius... By the time he was twenty our budding capitalist had his own grocery business.* — ADJ CLASSIF : ATTRIB ↑ developing

buddy /bʌdi[1]/, **buddies.** 1 A **buddy** is a close friend, especially a male friend of a man; used in informal English. EG *The two of them have become great buddies.* — N COUNT = pal

2 Men sometimes use **buddy** as a form of address to other men; used in informal American English. EG *You dialled the wrong number, buddy.* — VOC = mate

budge /bʌdʒ/, **budges, budging, budged.** 1 If someone will not **budge** on a matter, they refuse to change their mind or to compromise. EG *She has not budged on any issue she considers important... John refuses to budge.* — V : IF+PREP THEN *on/from* ↑ give way = yield

2 If something or someone will not **budge** or if you cannot **budge** them, they will not move at all from a particular place or position. EG *The screw just will not budge... He refuses to budge off that stool... She could not budge the wheel.* — V-ERG : USU WITH BROAD NEG = shift

budge up. If you **budge up**, you move along a seat in order to make space for someone else to sit down; an informal expression. EG *Budge up, will you.* — PHRASAL VB : V+ADV = move up

budgerigar /bʌdʒə[0]rɪgɑː/, **budgerigars.** A **budgerigar** is the same as a budgie. — N COUNT

budget /bʌdʒɪ[2]t/, **budgets, budgeting, budgeted.** 1 A **budget** is a financial plan which a person, institution, or government has, and which shows in detail how much money there is available and how it is to be spent. EG *It is sensible to work out a weekly budget... They were on a tight budget... Education and NHS budgets have been cut by 10 per cent.* — N COUNT : USU+SUPP

2 To **budget** or to **budget** for something means to plan your expenditure carefully so that you know how much money you can spend on something. EG *He could count on a regular salary and thus budget for the future... Budgeted expenditure for 1983-84 came to £253 million.* — V : IF+PREP THEN *for* ◇ **budgeting.** EG *Through careful budgeting they had equipped the entire school.* — ◇ N UNCOUNT ↑ planning

3 If you **budget** your **time**, you plan your activities carefully by deciding how much time can be spent on each one. — PHR : VB INFLECTS

4 The **Budget** is the financial plan announced by a government, which states how much money they intend to get through taxation and how they intend to spend it. EG *Many people try to beat the Budget by buying things they fear will increase in price.* — N COUNT : USU *the*+N IN SING

5 **Budget** is used in advertising to suggest that the price of something is low. EG *...budget prices... ...budget travel.* — ADJ CLASSIF : ATTRIB = cheap, economy

budget for. If you **budget for** something, you take account of it in your budget. EG *The Chancellor budgeted for an unemployment rate of 8.5 per cent... These bills have all been budgeted for.* — PHRASAL VB : V+PREP, HAS PASS = allow for

budget account, budget accounts. A **budget account** is an account with a large shop or a bank into which you make regular payments either to pay for things that you buy at the shop or to pay household bills. — N COUNT

budgetary /bʌdʒɪ[2]tə[0]ri[1]/. A **budgetary** matter, question, policy, etc is one that is concerned with the amount of money that is available and how it is to be spent. EG *...disagreements over budgetary policies.* — ADJ CLASSIF : ATTRIB ↑ financial

budgie /bʌdʒi[1]/, **budgies.** A **budgie** is a brightly coloured bird, like a small parrot. Budgies are often kept as pets. EG *She was not allowed to keep budgies.* — N COUNT = budgerigar

buff /bʌf/, **buffs, buffing, buffed.** 1 Something that is **buff** is a dull pale-brown colour. EG *Rolland flicked open the buff file lying on his desk... She was wearing a buff uniform.* — ADJ COLOUR

2 If you **buff** your shoes, fingernails, etc, you rub them with a piece of soft material in order to make them shine. EG *Give the shoes a coat of polish and buff them well... His fiancée buffed her nails.* — V+O = polish

3 A **buff** is someone who knows a lot about a subject and who likes to talk about it; an informal use. EG *Huggins was an movie buff... His twelve-year-old boy is a Civil War buff.* — N COUNT : MOD+N ↑ expert = enthusiast

4 If you are **in the buff**, you are naked; an old-fashioned, humorous expression. EG *I caught him in the buff... They were stripping down to the buff.* — PHR : USED AS AN A

5 See also **blind man's buff**.

buffalo /bʌfələʊ/, **buffaloes.** The plural can be either **buffalo** or **buffaloes**. A **buffalo** is a wild animal like a large cow with long curved horns. There are several different kinds of buffalo and they live in Asia, Africa, and America. EG *We passed a herd of buffaloes... On the plain were more buffalo than they had ever seen.* — N COUNT = bison

buffer /bʌfə/, **buffers, buffering, buffered.** A **buffer** is 1 something that prevents something else from causing serious harm. EG *The world lacks the buffer of large international grain reserves... It acts as a buffer against harmful environmental change.* — N COUNT ↑ shield = safeguard ▸ used as a verb. EG *When the fish bites, hold the rod high to buffer any sudden shocks.* — ▸ V+O 2 one of a pair of metal discs on springs at the front or back of a railway train or at the end of a railway line. The buffers on the train reduce the shock when the train hits something. The buffers at the end of the line are intended to prevent trains from crashing off the end; used mainly in British English. EG *The train ran into the buffers.* — N COUNT : USU PL ↑ disc 3 a rather foolish old person, especially a man; an old-fashioned use. EG *That's what swayed the old buffers on the panel.* — N COUNT : *old*+N

buffet, buffets, buffeting, buffeted. The word **buffet** is pronounced /bʊfeɪ/ for paragraph 1, and /bʌfət/ for paragraphs 2 and 3. 1 A **buffet** is 1.1 a café in a railway station, coach station, etc. EG *They went across to the station buffet.* — N COUNT = snack bar 1.2 a carriage on a passenger train where you can buy sandwiches, tea, beer, etc. EG *...a train with a buffet.* — N COUNT 1.3 a meal of cold food at a party or public occasion. Guests usually help themselves to the food and eat it standing up. EG *We found a huge buffet laid out... I met her at a buffet lunch.* — N COUNT ↑ meal

2 If a wind or the sea **buffets** something, it pushes against it suddenly and violently. EG *The vessel was buffeted by huge waves... ...a sharp, buffeting wind.* — V+O ↑ knock ◇ **buffeting.** EG *Ships have to be built to withstand the buffeting of the sea.* — ◇ N UNCOUNT = pounding

3 If you **are buffeted** by something, it gives you a lot of shocks or unpleasant experiences; a formal use. EG *He is severely buffeted by events and forces beyond his control.* — V+O : USU PASS ▸ used as a noun. EG *All life's buffets should be met with dignity and good sense.* — ▸ N COUNT ↑ blow = knock

buffet car /bʊfeɪ kɑː/, **buffet cars.** A **buffet car** is the carriage on a passenger train where you can buy sandwiches, tea, beer, etc. EG *The buffet car is situated in the centre of the train.* — N COUNT ↑ carriage

buffoon /bʌfu:n/, **buffoons**. A **buffoon** is a person who does silly things that make you laugh; an old-fashioned word. EG *We tend to see him as a buffoon.* — N COUNT = clown

buffoonery /bʌfu:nəºriˈ/ is silly behaviour that makes you laugh; an old-fashioned word. EG *There was a lot of buffoonery and playing around.* — N UNCOUNT ⇑ behaviour = clowning

bug /bʌg/, **bugs, bugging, bugged**. 1 A **bug** is 1.1 a tiny insect, especially one that causes damage or that people find unpleasant. EG *The bugs looked like little black beetles... You have to keep the millet free of bugs.* — N COUNT : USU PL ⇑ insect
1.2 a minor illness such as a cold that people catch very quickly from each other. EG *There must be a bug going around.* — N COUNT = germ
1.3 a small fault or mistake in a computer program. — N COUNT
1.4 a tiny hidden microphone which secretly records what people are saying. EG *I'll be able to plant the bug in a day or two.* — N COUNT ⇑ microphone

2 To **bug** a place means to hide tiny microphones there in order to secretly record what people are saying. EG *Don't speak in the bedrooms; they are bugged... ...electronic bugging devices.* — V+O ⇑ monitor

3 If something or someone **bugs** you, they annoy or upset you; an informal use. EG *That's what bugs me about the whole business... Why do you let him bug you like this?* — V+O ⇑ irritate = needle

4 If you **are bitten by** a **bug**, you become suddenly enthusiastic about something; an informal expression. EG *How long will it be before they get bitten by the skiing bug?* — PHR : AUX INFLECTS = be hooked

bugbear /bʌgbɛə/, **bugbears**. A **bugbear** is something that worries or upsets people. EG *Noise from engines is a current bugbear... Wage costs are much the biggest bugbear.* — N COUNT ⇑ nuisance

bugger /bʌgə/, **buggers, buggering, buggered**. **Bugger** is a rude, offensive, swear word in British English. It is mainly used to express anger, annoyance, or contempt. 1 People call someone a **bugger** or describe them as a **bugger** 1.1 when they are angry with them. EG *You bugger! You had no right to tell him he could come. It's not your party!* — N COUNT : USU ADJ+N, ALSO VOC
1.2 when they are pretending to be rude to them as a joke, although they are actually fond of them or friendly with them. — N COUNT : USU ADJ+N, ALSO VOC
1.3 in order to show contempt for them when they have done something foolish. — N COUNT : ALSO VOC = twit

2 People refer to someone as a **poor bugger** when they are sorry for them. — PHR : N INFLECTS, ALSO VOC

3 People say that a task or a job is a **bugger** when it is very difficult to do. — N SING : a+N ⇑ problem

4 People say **bugger** or **bugger it** when they are angry because something has gone wrong. — EXCLAM = blast

5 People say **bugger me** when they are very surprised about something. — EXCLAM = bless me

6 **Bugger all** means very little or nothing at all. People use this expression when they are angry or annoyed about something. — PHR : USED AS O ⇑ nothing

7 People use **bugger** before a word or phrase in order to say that they do not care about the person or thing that the word or phrase refers to. — V+O = blow

8 When people say that they **do not give a bugger**, **do not mind a bugger**, etc about something, they mean that they are not concerned about it. — PHR : AUX INFLECTS

9 To **bugger** someone means to have anal intercourse with them. — V+O

bugger about. 1 If you **bugger about** or **bugger around**, you waste time doing unnecessary things. — PHRASAL VB : V+ADV

2 If you **bugger** someone **about** or **bugger** them **around**, you cause them problems. EG *They really buggered me about when I tried to get my money back.* — PHRASAL VB : ORDER V+O+ADV

bugger off. If someone **buggers off**, they go away quickly or suddenly. — PHRASAL VB : V+ADV

bugger up. To **bugger** something **up** means to ruin it or spoil it. — PHRASAL VB : V+O+ADV

buggered /bʌgəd/ is a swear word used in British English. 1 If someone says that they will be **buggered** if they will do something, they mean that they will definitely not do it. — ADJ CLASSIF : PRED+*if*

2 If someone says that they are **buggered**, they mean that they are exhausted. — ADJ QUALIT : PRED

3 If someone says that something is **buggered**, they mean that it is completely ruined or broken. — ADJ CLASSIF : PRED

4 People say **I'll be buggered** in order to express amazement. — EXCLAM

5 People use **be buggered** after a word or phrase in order to suggest that they do not care about the thing or person referred to by the word or phrase. — PHR : N+PHR

buggery /bʌgəriˈ/ means anal intercourse. — N UNCOUNT

buggy /bʌgiˈ/, **buggies**. 1 A **buggy** is 1.1 a small lightweight carriage pulled by one horse. EG *I got back in the buggy.* — N COUNT
1.2 a lightweight, folding pram. — N COUNT
2 See also **baby buggy**.

bugle /bju:gəºl/, **bugles**. A **bugle** is a simple brass musical instrument that looks like a small trumpet. — N COUNT

build /bɪld/, **builds, building, built**. 1 To **build** something means to make it by joining things together, for example to make a house by joining bricks and other materials together. EG *John had built a house facing the river... They were building a bridge... Eddie would build us a temporary windbreak.* — V+O, V+O+O, OR V+O+A *(for)* = construct
◊ **built**. EG *Their nests are roughly built platforms of twigs.* — ◊ ADJ CLASSIF : ADV/ADJ+ADJ

2 To **build** something such as an organization or a society means to gradually form it. EG *They began to build an independent organization... They struggled to build a more democratic society... We aim to build a new social order.* — V+O = construct, develop

3 Your **build** is the shape that your bones and muscles give to your body. EG *She was in her early thirties, with a lean, athletic build... He had a booming voice and the build of a rugby player.* — N SING WITH DET, OR N UNCOUNT = physique

4 See also **built**.

build into. 1 To **build** something **into** a wall, rock, etc means to make it in such a way that all or part of it is inside the wall, rock, etc. EG *There was a cupboard built into the whitewashed wall... ...the massive fortress built into the rock.* — PHRASAL VB : V+O+PREP, HAS PASS ⇑ incorporate

2 To **build** something **into** a policy, system, etc means to make it a part of the policy, system, etc. EG *It is possible to build into an incomes policy special differentials... ...the inequalities built into our system of financing... The company does not deliberately build obsolescence into its product.* ● See also **built-in**. — PHRASAL VB : V+O+PREP, HAS PASS ⇑ incorporate

build on. 1 To **build** an organization, system, etc **on** something or **upon** something means to make the thing determine what form the organization, system, etc will have. EG *...the principles on which these organizations are built... ...an economy built upon manufacturing industry.* — PHRASAL VB : V+O+PREP, HAS PASS = base on

2 If you **build on** or **upon** the success of something, you take advantage of this success in order to make further progress. EG *We must try to build on the success of these growth industries.* — PHRASAL VB : V+PREP, HAS PASS ⇑ exploit

build up. 1 If something **builds up** or if you **build** it **up**, it gradually gets bigger or higher as a result of something being added to it. EG *Mud builds up in the lake... The pressure builds up... We're trying to build up a collection of herbs and spices.* ● See also **build-up**. — PHRASAL VB : V-ERG+ADV = accumulate

2 If you **build up** someone's trust, confidence, etc, you gradually make them more trusting, more confident, etc. EG *Being a bobby means building up trust with the people on the streets... I found myself trying to reassure Ron, trying to build up his morale.* — PHRASAL VB : V+O+ADV ⇑ develop

3 If you **build up** a person or thing, you tell people that the person or thing is very special or important. EG *He does not need to build me up.* ● See also **build-up**. — PHRASAL VB : V+O+ADV ⇑ recommend = plug

4 To **build** someone **up** also means to cause them to be their normal weight again after they have been ill. EG *The patient badly needs building up.* — PHRASAL VB : V+O+ADV ⇑ strengthen

5 When a piece of land **is built up**, a lot of houses are built on it. EG *It has been like this since the area was built up several years ago.* ● See also **built-up**. — PHRASAL VB : V+O+ADV, USU PASS

build upon. See **build on**.

builder /bɪldə/, **builders**. A **builder** is a person who builds houses and other buildings as a job. EG *Her father was a builder and decorator in Birmingham.* — N COUNT ⇑ worker

building /bɪldɪŋ/, **buildings**. A **building** is a structure with a roof and walls, for example a house, a hotel, or a factory. EG *...a small farm building about fifty yards off the road... There were still people trapped inside fallen buildings.* — N COUNT

building block, building blocks. A **building block** is one of the separate parts that combine to make something. EG *The basic building blocks of the computer have become smaller.* — N COUNT : USU PL ⇑ constituent = component

building society, building societies. In Britain, a **building society** is a business which will lend you money when you want to buy a house. You can also invest money in a building society, where it will earn interest. EG *He had bought his house with the help of a building society.* — N COUNT

build-up, build-ups. A **build-up** is 1 a gradual increase in something. EG *Over the island the build-up of clouds continued... ...a massive build-up of nuclear weapons.* 2 a description of a person or thing in which you tell people that the person or thing is very special or important. EG *She was getting a fair amount of publicity build-up.* N COUNT : USU SING = accumulation; N COUNT/UNCOUNT : USU SING

built /bɪlt/. 1 **Built** is the past tense and past participle of **build**.

2 If you say that someone is heavily **built**, slightly **built**, etc, you mean that they have that particular kind of body. EG *Johnny was well built with fair hair... I've never seen anyone so heavily built move quite so fast... She didn't look as if she was built for this kind of work.* ADJ CLASSIF : USU ADV+ADJ = made

built-in. 1 A **built-in** device is a device which is made as part of a larger device or machine. EG *...missiles equipped with built-in homing devices... ...a dishwasher with a built-in waste disposal unit.* ADJ CLASSIF : ATTRIB ⇑ incorporated = inbuilt

2 **Built-in** features are included in something as an essential part of it. EG *I refer to the built-in safeguards in this system.* ADJ CLASSIF : ATTRIB = inbuilt

built-up. 1 A **built-up** area is an area such as a town or city, which has many buildings on it. EG *We were now driving through built-up areas... The land to the west is nearly all built-up.* ADJ CLASSIF : USU ATTRIB = urbanized

2 **Built-up** shoes are shoes with very thick soles and heels that people wear in order to appear taller than they really are. EG *I noticed that he was wearing built-up boots.* ADJ CLASSIF : ATTRIB

bulb /bʌlb/, **bulbs**. A **bulb** is 1 the part of an electric lamp which is made of glass and which gives out light when electricity passes through it. EG *Only a few of the bulbs were working... The veranda was lit by a dim bulb.* 2 a root that is shaped like an onion and that grows into a flower or plant. EG *Below the windows some bulbs were growing... Plant lily bulbs in the autumn.* 3 something that has a round shape like a flower bulb. EG *...the bulb of the thermometer.* N COUNT = light bulb; N COUNT; N COUNT ⇑ sphere

bulbous /bʌlbəs/. Something that is **bulbous** is round and fat in a rather ugly way. EG *...people with great bulbous noses... ...the bulbous legs of a Jacobean table.* ADJ CLASSIF ⇑ swollen = bulging

Bulgarian /bəˈlgɛərɪən/, **Bulgarians**. 1 Someone or something that is **Bulgarian** belongs or relates to Bulgaria, to its people, or to its language. EG *...the Bulgarian Government.* ADJ CLASSIF

2 **Bulgarian** is the main language spoken by people who live in Bulgaria. N UNCOUNT

3 A **Bulgarian** is a person who comes from Bulgaria. N COUNT

bulge /bʌldʒ/, **bulges, bulging, bulged**. 1 If something **bulges**, 1.1 it sticks out from a surface. EG *Her eyes bulged from their sockets... Guns bulged on their hips... His tunic bulged over a premature paunch.* ◊ **bulging**. EG *The lifeguard had bulging muscles... The curtains hung in bulging folds against his shoulder.* 1.2 it is very full of things or people; an informal use. EG *Official files bulged with medical evidence... The shelves were bulging with knick-knacks.* ◊ **bulging**. EG *He arrived in the office with a bulging briefcase and a determined look on his face.* V ⇑ protrude; ◊ ADJ CLASSIF : ATTRIB; V : IF+PREP THEN *with* = burst; ◊ ADJ CLASSIF : ATTRIB

2 A **bulge** is 2.1 a lump on a surface that is normally flat. EG *'What's under there?' I asked, seeing the bulge at his waistline... He could see the bulge of the body against the side of the tent.* 2.2 a sudden large increase in something which later returns to a normal level. EG *...the population bulge of the nineteen fifties.* N COUNT = bump; N COUNT : USU SING

bulk /bʌlk/, **bulks, bulking, bulked**. 1 A **bulk** is a large mass of something. EG *Willie looked with loathing at the dark bulk of the building.* N COUNT : USU SING, IF+PREP THEN *of*

2 A large or fat person's **bulk** is their body. EG *Flora swung her big bulk off the bed... Behind her was the unmistakable bulk of Harry Meadows.* ▸ also used to refer to a person's weight or size. EG *For a man of his vast bulk, Gerald had a surprisingly high voice.* N COUNT : USU SING; ▸ N UNCOUNT ⇑ size = proportions

3 The **bulk** of something is most of it. EG *The bulk of his days are spent quietly... They constitute the overwhelming bulk of the population.* N PART : SING = majority

4 If you buy or sell something **in bulk**, you buy or sell it in large quantities, instead of buying or selling it when it has been divided into smaller quantities. EG *They buy food in bulk... Goods can be made very much cheaper if they're sold in bulk.* PHR : USED AS AN A ⇑ in quantity

5 **Bulk** goods are bought and sold in large quantities. EG *She has a useful list of bulk food suppliers.* ADJ CLASSIF : ATTRIB

6 If something **bulks large**, it seems very large when you look at it; a literary expression. EG *The Senate House bulked large to the west.* PHR : VB INFLECTS

bulk buy, bulk buys, bulk buying, bulk bought. If you **bulk buy** goods, you buy them in large quantities in order to save time and money. EG *We live in the city and don't often bulk buy.* V OR V+O

bulkhead /bʌlkhɛd/, **bulkheads**. A **bulkhead** is a wall which divides the inside of a ship or aeroplane into separate sections; a technical term. N COUNT = partition

bulky /bʌlkiˈ/, **bulkier, bulkiest**. 1 Something that is **bulky** is large, heavy, and usually difficult to move. EG *The equipment was so bulky that it had to be wheeled around on a large trolley... ...a bulky sweater.* ADJ QUALIT = cumbersome

2 A person or animal that is **bulky** looks large, strong, and powerful. EG *The males are bulkier than the females.* ADJ QUALIT ⇑ big = chunky

bull /bʊl/, **bulls**. 1 A **bull** is 1.1 a male animal of the cow family. EG *...two great bulls facing each other in a head-on challenge.* 1.2 the male of some animals such as the elephant or the whale. EG *...a bull elephant.* 1.3 a man who is big, clumsy, and often aggressive, and who has little consideration for other people's feelings. EG *Through the door burst a dark bull of a man.* 1.4 the small circular area at the centre of a target or dartboard. EG *He aimed for the bull.* 1.5 an official statement, document, or letter that is issued by the Pope and that deals with a particular subject; a technical term. 1.6 an investor on the stock market who buys shares in expectation of a price rise, in order to make a profit by reselling the shares quickly. N COUNT; N COUNT; N COUNT; N COUNT = bull's-eye; N COUNT = decree; N COUNT ⇑ speculator

2 If you say that something is **bull**, you mean that it is complete nonsense or absolutely untrue; used in very informal English, especially American English. EG *What a load of bull!* N UNCOUNT = rubbish

3 If you say that someone is **like a bull in a china shop**, you mean that they are extremely clumsy. PHR : USED AS AN A

4 • to **take the bull by the horns**: see **horn**.

bulldog /bʊldɒg/, **bulldogs**. A **bulldog** is a dog that is small but strong and often fierce, with a large, square head and short hair. N COUNT ⇑ dog

bulldog clip, bulldog clips. In British English, a **bulldog clip** is a large metal clip with a spring lever that opens and closes two flat pieces of metal. It is used for holding bunches of paper together. N COUNT

bulldoze /bʊldəʊz/, **bulldozes, bulldozing, bulldozed**. 1 If you **bulldoze** something such as a building, you knock it down and destroy it using a bulldozer. EG *Settlements have been bulldozed out of the way... ...bulldozed ruins.* V+O = flatten

2 If you **bulldoze** earth, stone, or other heavy material, you move it using a bulldozer, usually in order to make land level. V+O

3 If you **bulldoze** someone into doing something, you persuade them to do it in an unpleasantly forceful way. EG *Why did you bulldoze me into buying you coffee?* V+O : IF+PREP THEN *into* = push

bulldozer /bʊldəʊzə/, **bulldozers**. A **bulldozer** is a large, powerful tractor with a broad metal blade at the front, which is used for knocking down buildings, moving large amounts of earth or stone, and flattening areas of ground. EG *The old house was being demolished by bulldozers.* N COUNT

bullet /bʊlɪˈt/, **bullets**. A **bullet** is a small piece of metal or rubber with a pointed or rounded end, which is fired out of a gun. EG *A bullet shot through the window... The car was covered with bullet holes.* N COUNT ⇑ missile

bulletin /bʊlɪˈtɪn/, **bulletins**. A **bulletin** is 1 a short news report on the radio or television. EG *I listened to the radio news bulletin.* 2 a short official announcement that is made publicly to inform people about an important matter. 3 a regular newspaper or leaflet that is produced by an organization or group such as a school or church. EG *The Institute publishes a fortnightly bulletin... ...the school bulletin.* N COUNT; N COUNT; N COUNT

bulletin board, bulletin boards. A **bulletin board** is the same as a noticeboard; used in American English. N COUNT

bullet-proof. Something that is **bullet-proof** can stop bullets passing through it. EG *...security guards wearing bullet-proof vests.* ADJ CLASSIF ⇑ protective

bullfight /bʊlfaɪt/, **bullfights**. A **bullfight** is a public entertainment in which a man makes a bull angry by sticking short spears in it before killing it with a sword. Bullfights are especially popular in Spain. N COUNT

bullfighter /bʊlfaɪtə/, **bullfighters**. A **bullfighter** is a man who takes part in a bullfight. N COUNT ⇑ performer

bullfighting /bʊlfaɪtɪŋ/. The public entertainment involving bullfights is called **bullfighting**. EG *Bullfighting in Spain is becoming less and less profitable.* N UNCOUNT ⇑ entertainment

bullfinch /bʊlfɪntʃ/, **bullfinches**. A **bullfinch** is a small bird with a pinkish breast and a black head, usually found in woodlands or gardens. N COUNT

bullfrog /bʊlfrɒg/, **bullfrogs**. A **bullfrog** is a large American type of frog that makes a loud croaking noise. N COUNT ⇑ frog

bullion /bʊlɪ⁰jən/ is gold or silver in the form of lumps or bars. Bullion is often turned into coins or jewellery. N UNCOUNT = ingots

bull market, bull markets. A **bull market** is a situation on the stock market when the price of shares is likely to rise, allowing people to make a profit by buying at a low price and selling again when the price has risen. N COUNT

bullock /bʊlək/, **bullocks**. A **bullock** is a young bull that has been castrated. N COUNT ⇑ bull

bullring /bʊlrɪŋ/, **bullrings**. A **bullring** is a circular area of ground surrounded by rows of seats where bullfights take place. N COUNT ⇑ arena

bull's-eye, bull's-eyes. A **bull's-eye** is 1 the small circular area at the centre of a target or a dartboard. EG *He hit the bull's-eye and won the prize.* ▸ also used to refer to a shot or throw of a dart that hits this centre area. 2 a large, round, hard sweet, usually with black and white stripes, which has the flavour of mint. N COUNT : USU the+N IN SING ▸ N COUNT ⇑ shot N COUNT

bullshit /bʊlʃɪt/, **bullshits, bullshitting, bullshitted**; a very rude or swear word. 1 If you say **'bullshit!'**, you are telling someone that you think what they have just said is complete nonsense or absolutely untrue. EXCLAM/N UNCOUNT = rot, rubbish

2 If someone **bullshits** you, they tell you something that is complete nonsense or absolutely untrue. EG *Don't bullshit me... Probably he thinks I'm bullshitting him.* V OR V+O : USU V +O ⇑ trick = con

bull terrier, bull terriers. A **bull terrier** is a strong dog with a short, whitish-coloured coat and a long nose. N COUNT

bully /bʊli¹/, **bullies, bullying, bullied**. 1 A **bully** is someone who uses their strength or power to hurt or frighten other people; used showing disapproval. EG *He was a violent bully, destructive and full of hate... There was a high proportion of sadists and bullies among the camp guards.* N COUNT

2 If you **bully** someone, you treat them in a very unpleasant way by using your strength or power to hurt or frighten them. EG *For the first month or two at my new school I was bullied constantly.* ◇ **bullying**. EG *All cases of bullying will be severely dealt with.* V OR V+O : USU V +O = terrorize ◇ N UNCOUNT

3 If you **bully** someone into doing something, you persuade them to do it in an unpleasantly forceful way so that they feel that they have to do what you want. EG *He was a total stranger who had been bullied unmercifully into driving her home.* V+O : IF+PREP THEN *into* = bulldoze

4 If you say **'bully for you'**, **'bully for him'**, etc, you mean that you do not think that what someone has done is a great achievement or very exciting; an informal expression. EG *'I've run round the garden fifteen times this morning.'–'Bully for you!'* PHR = so what

bully boy, bully boys; also spelled with a hyphen. A **bully boy** is a rough, aggressive man, especially one who has been paid to injure another person. EG *...thugs and bully boys.* N COUNT = heavy

bulrush /bʊlrʌʃ/, **bulrushes**. **Bulrushes** are tall, stiff reeds that grow on the edges of rivers. N COUNT : USU PL

bulwark /bʊlwək/, **bulwarks**. A **bulwark** is something strong that protects you against unpleasant or dangerous situations. EG *The fund is a bulwark against your benefits being cut.* N COUNT : IF+ PREP THEN *against/of* ⇑ protection

bum /bʌm/, **bums, bumming, bummed**; a very informal word. 1 A **bum** is 1.1 a person who lives like a tramp; used showing disapproval. EG *Why don't you stop behaving like a bum and get this place cleaned up?* 1.2 a worthless or irresponsible person. EG *'What an illiterate lot of bums you are!'... If he doesn't leave his wife and kids provided for, he's a bum.* 1.3 a person who is not at all good at doing a particular job. EG *He's a real bum of an artist.* N COUNT N COUNT = lout N COUNT : USU USED AS C

2 Your **bum** is the part of your body between your back and your legs, which you sit on; used in informal British English. EG *He sat down on his big fat bum.* N COUNT : USU POSS+N

3 People sometimes use **bum** to refer to something that is very bad in quality or not working properly. EG *He gave me some bum advice... ...a bum looking bloke.* ADJ QUALIT : ATTRIB ⇑ poor = useless

4 If you **bum** something off someone, you get it from them by asking them to give it to you. EG *Can I bum a cigarette off you?* V+O : IF+PREP THEN *off* = scrounge

bum around. If you **bum around** or **bum about**, 1 you travel casually for pleasure from one place to another with very little money. EG *I just bummed around northern Europe for a few months.* 2 you live lazily without using your time for any particular purpose. EG *He's been bumming around since he left college... Are you going to bum about all summer?* PHRASAL VB : V+ ADV/PREP = drift PHRASAL VB : V+ ADV = laze around

bumble /bʌmbə⁰l/, **bumbles, bumbling, bumbled**. If you **bumble**, 1 you speak in a confused way so that people cannot understand what you are saying. EG *What on earth are you bumbling about?* 2 you move in a clumsy and awkward way. EG *She came bumbling in with a saucepan of water.* V : IF+PREP THEN *about* V+A = lumber

bumblebee /bʌmbə⁰lbiː/, **bumblebees**. A **bumblebee** is a large hairy bee. N COUNT ⇑ bee

bumbling /bʌmblɪŋ/. A **bumbling** person behaves in a very confused, disorganized way and often makes mistakes. EG *Michael Hordern plays the bumbling Englishman yet again... ...Jimmy, the old bumbling fool.* ▸ used of a person's behaviour or actions. EG *...his bumbling ineptitude.* ADJ CLASSIF : ATTRIB = bungling, inept ▸ = awkward

bumf /bʌmf/; also spelled **bumph**. **Bumf** consists of documents and written information which you have to read or deal with but which you think are extremely boring; an informal word, used in British English. EG *I've had some bumf through the post from the trade department... I've just got as far as the educational bumph at the beginning.* N UNCOUNT = stuff

bummer /bʌmə/, **bummers**. If you say that something is a **bummer**, you mean that you find it very unpleasant or troublesome; a very informal word. EG *The job was a real bummer from start to finish.* N COUNT : IF SING a+N ⇑ nuisance = pain

bump /bʌmp/, **bumps, bumping, bumped**. 1 If you **bump** into something, you hit it or knock it while you are moving. EG *He turned on the lamp so that he could find his way without bumping into anything... The big ship slid slowly into her place, bumping gently against the high stone walls... I've bumped my head on that shelf again!* V+A, OR V+O ⇑ collide = bang

2 If you **bump** over a surface, usually in a vehicle, you travel in a rough, bouncing, and uncomfortable way because the surface is very uneven. EG *The jeep was approaching the crest, bumping over stumpy ground... ...bumping down an enormous staircase.* V : USU+A ⇑ move

3 A **bump** is 3.1 an accident in which a moving object hits something. EG *It is fortunately not a bad bump, and Henry is only slightly grazed... Her car got three severe bumps while parked in London.* 3.2 a fairly gentle sound of something falling to the ground or colliding with something else. EG *It slipped from his fingers and fell with a bump. What was that bump I heard just now?* 3.3 a small, raised, swollen shape that appears on part of the surface of your body as a result of a blow. EG *You've got a bump on your forehead like an egg.* 3.4 a raised, uneven part on a surface such as a road. EG *If the motor cycle goes over a bump, the engine misfires... Only the worst bumps disturbed the passengers.* N COUNT ⇑ collision = knock N COUNT = thump N COUNT ⇑ swelling = lump N COUNT ⇑ lump

bump into. If you **bump into** someone you know, you meet them by chance, for example in the street or a public place. EG *I bumped into Mary an hour ago... We happened to bump into one another in town.* PHRASAL VB : V+ PREP = run into

bump off. To **bump** someone **off** means to kill them; an informal expression. EG *In the story he bumps off his wife and goes to live in Australia.* PHRASAL VB : V+ O+ADV = murder

bump up. To **bump up** the amount of something means to increase it suddenly by a large amount; an informal expression. EG *She was going to charge £140, but the extra work bumped up the price to £200.* PHRASAL VB : V+ O+ADV = boost

bump up against. If you **bump up against** someone, you meet them and get to know them by chance rather than by making any effort. EG *He rarely bumped up against anyone who approved of what he was doing.* PHRASAL VB : V+ ADV+PREP

bumper /bʌmpə/, **bumpers**. 1 A **bumper** is a bar along the lower part of a car, lorry, or van at the N COUNT front and back, which provides extra protection if the vehicle bumps into something in an accident.

2 If traffic is **bumper to bumper**, the vehicles are so close to one another that they are almost touching and are moving very slowly. EG *It was bumper to bumper, like going down Prince's Street in the rush hour.* PHR : USED AS AN A OR C = nose to tail

3 A **bumper** crop, harvest, etc is one that is larger than usual. EG *We had a bumper crop of apples last year.* ADJ CLASSIF : ATTRIB

4 A **bumper** is also the same as a railway buffer; used in American English. N COUNT = buffer

bumph /bʌmf/. See **bumf**.

bumpkin /bʌmpkɪn/, **bumpkins**. A **bumpkin** is a person who comes from a country area and is often considered to be stupid or ignorant; an informal word. EG *...narrow-minded country bumpkins.* N COUNT = yokel

bumptious /bʌmpʃəs/. Someone who is **bumptious** is constantly expressing their own opinions and ideas in a self-important way; used showing disapproval. EG *...the big-headed, loud-mouthed, bumptious youngster.* ADJ QUALIT ⇑ egotistic = conceited

bumpy /bʌmpi[1]/, **bumpier, bumpiest**. **1** Something such as a road that is **bumpy** has a rough, uneven surface. EG *The track got bumpier and muddier the further we went... ...bumpy whitewashed walls.* ADJ QUALIT ≠ smooth

2 If a journey in a vehicle is **bumpy**, it is uncomfortable, bouncy, and rough, usually because you are travelling over an uneven surface. EG *The ride may be a bit bumpy but at least you'll get there.* ADJ QUALIT ≠ comfortable

bun /bʌn/, **buns**. **1** A **bun** is **1.1** a small cake or bread roll, often containing currants or spices. N COUNT **1.2** a woman's hairstyle in which her long hair is fastened into a round shape at the back of her head. EG *She wore her hair in a tight bun.* N COUNT

2 If you say that a woman **has got a bun in the oven**, you mean that she is pregnant; a very informal and offensive expression in British English. PHR : VB INFLECTS

bunch /bʌntʃ/, **bunches, bunching, bunched**.

1 A **bunch** of people is a group who are alike in some way, or who you are talking about as a group. EG *They're a bunch of tired old men who've lost their nerve... They were acting like a bunch of spoiled children... A fine bunch they are, full of spirit and originality... Ranchers are an independent bunch.* N PART : USU+N IN PLURAL = lot

2 A **bunch** of flowers is a group of flowers on their stalks that you have picked or that have been tied together to be sold. EG *We picked quite a big bunch of poppies.* N PART : USU+N IN PLURAL = posy

3 A **bunch** of fruit is a group of fruit growing on the same stem. Fruit such as bananas and grapes grow in bunches. EG *I bought a bunch of bananas.* N PART : USU+N IN PLURAL ⇑ cluster

4 A **bunch** of similar things is a group of them that are situated, held, or fastened closely together. EG *He had a big bunch of keys in his hands... You'll see a bunch of our trucks parked on the road... 'What's in the sauce?'-'Ginger, soy sauce, a whole bunch of things.'* N PART : USU+N IN PLURAL ⇑ lot = mass

5 The pick of the bunch or **the best of the bunch** is the best person or thing among a group. PHR : USED AS C

6 The best of a bad bunch is the person or thing that you think is not as bad as the others among a group that you have already judged to be unsuitable or of poor quality. PHR : USED AS C

7 If a girl wears her hair in **bunches**, her hair is parted down the middle of her head and tied on each side of her head above her ears. EG *She had her hair tied in bunches.* N PLURAL : USU in+N

8 If people **bunch** together or **bunch** up, they stay close together in a group. EG *'Don't bunch together. Spread out!'* V : IF+ADV THEN together/up ⇑ cluster

9 If you **bunch** things together or **bunch** them up, you gather them together to make a tight bundle. EG *She was holding her skirts bunched up over one arm.* V+O, V+A (together/up), OR V+O+A (together/up)

bundle /bʌndə[0]l/, **bundles, bundling, bundled**.

1 A **bundle** is **1.1** a number of things that have been tied together so that they can be carried or stored. EG *I sorted the socks, rolling them into neat little bundles... ...a bundle of five-pound notes... He tied the wood into a bundle.* N PART ⇑ bunch **1.2** a number of things wrapped up in a cloth or sheet so that they can be carried. EG *She carried a white bundle... He had his bundle of personal belongings under his arm.* N COUNT ⇑ package = parcel

2 You can refer to a person, especially a baby, as a **bundle**; an informal use. EG *...that screaming bundle of waving arms and legs... Joseph, a tiny bundle, would lie propped on the bed.* N COUNT = heap

3 If you say that someone is a **bundle** of fun, joy, etc, you mean that they are full of fun, joy, etc. EG *Sheila's a bundle of fun.* N SING WITH DET +of

4 If you say that someone is a **bundle of nerves**, you mean that they are very nervous. EG *I'm a bundle of nerves today.* PHR : USED AS C

5 In informal English, if you say that you don't **go a bundle on** something, you mean that you do not like it very much. EG *I really don't go a bundle on this kind of music.* PHR : VB INFLECTS = love

6 If you **bundle** someone or something somewhere, you push them there in a rough and hurried way. EG *Williams was bundled into a car... He led her to the window and bundled her out... Len bundled the knives and forks into a drawer.* V+O (NG/REFL) +A = shove

bundle off. If you **bundle** someone **off** somewhere, you send them there in a hurry. EG *Jack was bundled off to Ely to stay with friends.* PHRASAL VB : V+O+ADV, IF+PREP THEN *to* = pack off

bundle up. **1** If you **bundle up** a mass of things, you make a bundle by gathering or tying them together. EG *My mother bundled up all my comics and threw them out... She bundled up her knitting and put it away.* PHRASAL VB : V+O+ADV ⇑ gather

2 If you **bundle up**, you dress in a lot of warm clothes because the weather is very cold. EG *We bundled up tightly against the cold... I bundled the kids up in sweaters and anoraks before letting them out.* PHRASAL VB : V+ADV, OR V+O (NG/REFL)+ADV = wrap up

bung /bʌŋ/, **bungs, bunging, bunged**. **1** A **bung** is a round piece of wood, cork, rubber, etc which you use to close the hole in something such as a barrel or flask. EG *Take the bung out.* N COUNT = stopper

2 If you **bung** something somewhere, you put it or send it there in a quick and careless way; an informal British English use. EG *Just bung it in the oven... We're just going to bung the car into the garage and let them deal with it.* V+O+A = shove

bungalow /bʌŋgələʊ/, **bungalows**. A **bungalow** is a house which has only one storey. EG *Anyone was free to apply for a new flat or bungalow.* N COUNT

bunged up. In informal English, if something such as a hole is **bunged up**, it is blocked. EG *The sink's bunged up again... Your eyes got bunged up... My nose is all bunged up.* PHR : USED AS C

bungle /bʌŋgə[0]l/, **bungles, bungling, bungled**. If you **bungle** something, you fail to do it properly, because you make mistakes or are clumsy. EG *They bungled the whole operation... You can't do a thing without bungling it.* ◊ **bungled**. EG *...the bungled murder of Bernard Lustig.* ◊ **bungling**. EG *...this bungling administration.* V OR V+O = botch ◊ ADJ CLASSIF ◊ ADJ CLASSIF : ATTRIB

bungler /bʌŋglə/, **bunglers**. A **bungler** is a person who often fails to do things properly because they make mistakes or are clumsy. N COUNT, ALSO VOC = incompetent

bunion /bʌnjən/, **bunions**. A **bunion** is a large painful lump on the first joint of your big toe. N COUNT

bunk /bʌŋk/, **bunks**. **1** A **bunk** is a bed fixed to a wall, especially in a ship or caravan. EG *I ran to my cabin and threw myself on the bunk... Thomas was lying in the lower bunk.* N COUNT

2 In informal English, if you describe something that someone has said or written as **bunk**, you mean that it is foolish or untrue. EG *That's all bunk-there can't be equality... History that omits economics is sheer bunk.* N UNCOUNT = nonsense

3 In informal English, if you **do a bunk**, you suddenly leave a place without telling anyone. EG *The next thing I knew, the whole family had done a bunk.* PHR : VB INFLECTS = bolt

bunk bed, bunk beds. A **bunk bed** consists of two beds, one above the other, held in a frame. EG *There were bunk beds for the children to sleep in.* N COUNT ⇑ bed

bunker /bʌŋkə/, **bunkers**. **1** A **bunker** is **1.1** a place, usually underground, that has been built with strong walls to protect it against heavy gunfire and bombing. EG *There had been heavy airstrikes against the bunkers that night.* N COUNT ⇑ shelter **1.2** a container for coal or other fuel. EG *...a coal bunker.* N COUNT

2 On a golf course, a **bunker** is a large hole filled with sand. Bunkers often make it more difficult to hit the ball directly at the hole. EG *If the bunker has no lip, you might be able to putt the ball out.* N COUNT ⇑ obstacle

bunny /bʌni[1]/, **bunnies**. A **bunny** or a **bunny rabbit** is a rabbit; a word used by children. EG *Bunnies love to eat lettuce.* N COUNT

bunny girl, bunny girls. A **bunny girl** is a young woman who serves drinks in a nightclub and who N COUNT ⇑ hostess wears a costume that includes a pair of rabbit's ears and a rabbit's tail.

bunsen burner /bʌnsəⁿn bɜːnə/, **bunsen burners**. A **bunsen burner** is a small gas burner used for heating things in laboratories. N COUNT

bunting /bʌntɪŋ/ consists of rows of small coloured flags that are used to decorate streets and buildings on special occasions. EG *The street was decorated with red, white and blue bunting.* N UNCOUNT

buoy /bɔɪ/, **buoys, buoying, buoyed**. A **buoy** is a brightly-coloured floating object attached by a long chain or rope to the seabed. Buoys show ships and boats where they can go, and warn them of danger. EG *It took the vessel only twenty minutes to reach the buoy.* N COUNT ⇑ float = marker

buoy up. If you **buoy** someone **up**, you keep them cheerful in a situation in which they might feel depressed. EG *He did his best to buoy her up.* PHRASAL VB : V+O+ADV = hearten

buoyancy /bɔɪənsiⁱ/ is 1 the ability that something has to float on a liquid or in the air. EG *New chambers were added to provide buoyancy... Each of the balloons has its own buoyancy and lift.* N UNCOUNT 2 a person's ability to remain cheerful, even in sad or unpleasant situations. EG *His personal buoyancy and vigour were a tonic... We will miss her buoyancy and charm.* N UNCOUNT = bounce 3 a feeling of cheerfulness. EG *...a sensation of buoyancy and freedom.* N UNCOUNT

buoyant /bɔɪənt/. 1 If you are **buoyant**, you feel cheerful and behave in a lively way. EG *He suddenly smiled, feeling buoyant and at ease... His mood became buoyant.* ADJ QUALIT = carefree ◇ **buoyantly**. EG *'I hope she will,' said Pratt buoyantly.* ◇ ADV WITH VB = cheerfully

2 Something that is **buoyant** floats or is able to float on a liquid or in the air. EG *...a row of buoyant cylinders.... The birds become less buoyant and can dive in pursuit of fish.* ADJ QUALIT ◇ **buoyantly**. EG *Little elegant ship models ride buoyantly in mid-air.* ◇ ADV WITH VB = lightly

3 A **buoyant** economy is a successful economy in which there is a lot of trade and economic activity. EG *...a generally more buoyant economy... The most buoyant sector is the arms business.* ADJ QUALIT = healthy

burble /bɜːbəⁿl/, **burbles, burbling, burbled**. 1 If something or someone **burbles**, they make a low continuous bubbling sound. EG *Hot mud burbled down from a side valley... Lucy was making burbling noises.* V = gurgle

2 If someone **burbles** about something, they talk about it in a confused way; used showing disapproval. EG *He burbled about the restoration of democracy.* V+A OR V+O/REPORT-CL/QUOTE = babble

burden /bɜːdəⁿn/, **burdens, burdening, burdened**; a fairly formal word. 1 A **burden** is 1.1 something that causes you a lot of worry or hard work. EG *He was weighed down by the burden of state secrets he carried with him... This would relieve the initial burden on hospital staff* N COUNT = pressure, strain 1.2 a heavy load that is difficult to carry. EG *Men and women came bearing heavy burdens of provisions.* N COUNT
● See also **beast of burden**.

2 The **burden** of something that someone says or writes is what they are trying to express. EG *The burden of his message did not strike me as being very original... What do you think was actually the burden of this play?* N SING : *the*+N+*of* ⇑ theme = gist

3 The **burden of proof** is the task of proving that you are correct, for example when you have accused someone of a crime. EG *The burden of proof lies with the accuser.* PHR : USED AS S OR O

4 If someone **burdens** you with something such as a problem or difficult decision, they tell you about it. EG *I felt it was unfair to burden them with my decision.* V+O+A *(with)* ⇑ trouble = worry

burdened /bɜːdəⁿnd/; a fairly formal word. 1 If you are **burdened** with something, it causes you a lot of worry or hard work. EG *He was burdened with endless paperwork... Even the rich feel burdened by the lack of an ideal.* ADJ QUALIT : PRED+*with/by* ⇑ troubled = saddled

2 If you are **burdened** with a heavy load, you are holding or carrying it with difficulty. EG *They stood around in groups, burdened with sleeping bags and blankets.* ADJ CLASSIF : PRED : IF+PREP THEN *with/by* = loaded

burdensome /bɜːdəⁿnsəⁿm/. Something that is **burdensome** is worrying or tiring; a formal word. EG *...a burdensome responsibility.* ADJ QUALIT = onerous

bureau /bjʊərəʊ/, **bureaux, bureaus**. The plural can be either **bureaux** or **bureaus**. 1 In the United States, a **bureau** is 1.1 an office, organization, or government department that collects and distributes information. EG *The weather bureau promised a sunny weekend... ...the United States Children's Bureau.* N COUNT : ALSO IN NAMES AFTER N 1.2 an office of a company or organization which has its headquarters in another town or country. EG *...the Washington bureau of a Midwestern newspaper.* N COUNT = branch

2 A **bureau** is also 2.1 a chest of drawers; used in American English. N COUNT 2.2 a writing desk with shelves and drawers and a lid that opens to form the writing surface; used in British English. EG *He was going through the drawers of the bureau... ...a compartment in the back of the bureau.* N COUNT

bureaucracy /bjʊərɒkrəsiⁱ/, **bureaucracies**. 1 A **bureaucracy** is an administrative system operated by a large number of officials following rules and procedures. EG *A just, ordered society without a bureaucracy has yet to be established... A top-heavy and inefficient bureaucracy often slows simple decisions for months.* N COUNT ▸ used of the officials who work in a bureaucracy. EG *My lawyers pressured the jail bureaucracy to let me have regular visits.* ▸ N SING : *the*+N

2 **Bureaucracy** is all the rules and procedures followed by government departments and similar organizations; often used showing disapproval. EG *...the bureaucracy of immigration procedures... One of the problems is the bureaucracy the claimant has to face.* N UNCOUNT = red tape, officialdom

bureaucrat /bjʊərəᵉkræt/, **bureaucrats**. A **bureaucrat** is an official who works in a bureaucracy, especially one who you think follows rules and procedures too strictly; often used showing disapproval. EG *Brussels bureaucrats hope to negotiate a similar deal... ...endless paper-work dished out by bureaucrats.* N COUNT

bureaucratic /bjʊərəᵉkrætɪk/. 1 **Bureaucratic** rules and procedures are complicated ones which can cause long delays; used showing disapproval. EG *...a nightmare of bureaucratic procedures... Rose had to fight lengthy bureaucratic battles with her local council.* ADJ QUALIT = administrative

2 **Bureaucratic** also means related to a system of bureaucracy. EG *It will be a long time before the last bureaucratic hierarchy is obliterated.* ADJ CLASSIF : USU ATTRIB

bureaux /bjʊərəʊz/ is a plural form of **bureau**.

burgeon /bɜːdʒəⁿn/, **burgeons, burgeoning, burgeoned**. If something **burgeons**, it develops or grows rapidly; a literary word. EG *The spring came and the leaves burgeoned... Life in the sea burgeoned into many forms.* V ⇑ develop = blossom ◇ **burgeoning**. EG *...a burgeoning manufacturing industry. ...the country's burgeoning pacifist movement.* ◇ ADJ CLASSIF : ATTRIB = growing, thriving

burgher /bɜːgə/, **burghers**. A **burgher** is a person who lives in a city, especially a member of the city's middle class; an old-fashioned or literary word. EG *...the burghers of New York.* N COUNT : USU PL ⇑ resident = citizen

burglar /bɜːglə/, **burglars**. A **burglar** is a thief who breaks into a house and steals things. EG *I felt like a burglar breaking and entering.* N COUNT ⇑ criminal

burglar alarm, burglar alarms; also spelled with a hyphen. A **burglar alarm** is an electric device that makes a bell ring loudly if someone tries to break into a building. EG *A burglar alarm was ringing somewhere.* N COUNT

burglarize /bɜːgləraɪz/, **burglarizes, burglarizing, burglarized**. If someone **burglarizes** a building, they burgle it; used in American English. V+O

burglary /bɜːgləriⁱ/, **burglaries**. 1 **Burglary** is the crime of breaking into a building and stealing things. EG *He was found guilty of burglary.* N UNCOUNT = theft

2 If someone carries out a **burglary**, they break into a building and steal things. EG *Contact the police as soon as possible after a burglary.* N COUNT ⇑ robbery

burgle /bɜːgəⁿl/, **burgles, burgling, burgled**. If someone **burgles** a building, they break into it and steal things. EG *She thought that they might be criminals come to burgle the house... ...the man whose house he had burgled and ransacked.* V+O = burglarize

Burgomaster /bɜːgəmɑːstə/, **Burgomasters**. A **Burgomaster** is a mayor of a town in Germany, the Netherlands, and some other European countries. EG *...the last liberal Burgomaster of Vienna.* N COUNT : ALSO IN TITLES ⇑ official

burial /beriⁱəl/, **burials**. A **burial** is 1 the ceremony that takes place when a dead body is put into a grave in the ground. EG *The bodies are brought home for burial... He read swiftly through the burial service.* N COUNT/UNCOUNT = interment 2 the ceremony that takes place when a dead N COUNT body is put into the sea from a ship after someone has died at sea. EG *...burials at sea.*

burial ground, burial grounds. A **burial ground** is a place where bodies are buried, especially an ancient site, or a site used to bury large numbers of soldiers killed in a battle. N COUNT ⇑ graveyard

burlesque /bɜːle̱sk/, **burlesques.** 1 A **burlesque** is a piece of writing which makes fun of a particular style by copying it in a humorous and exaggerated way. EG *The poem is really a burlesque... They make fun of them through ridicule, satire, or burlesque.* N COUNT/UNCOUNT = caricature, parody

2 **Burlesque** was a type of comedy show which was popular in America in the late 19th and early 20th centuries. EG *We could have joined any burlesque show in the country.* N UNCOUNT/COUNT ⇑ entertainment

burly /bɜ̱ːli[1]/, **burlier, burliest.** A **burly** man has a broad body and strong muscles. EG *...a burly red-faced man... ...two burly Irish workers.* ▸ also used of a man's body. EG *...his tall, burly frame... ...his burly form.* ADJ QUALIT = brawny ▸ = stocky

Burmese /bɜːmi̱ːz/. **Burmese** is both the singular and the plural form. 1 Someone or something that is **Burmese** belongs or relates to Burma, to its people, or to its language. ADJ CLASSIF

2 **Burmese** is the main language spoken by the people who live in Burma. N UNCOUNT

3 A **Burmese** is a person who comes from Burma. N COUNT

burn /bɜ̱ːn/, **burns, burning, burned, burnt.** The past tense and past participle can be either **burned** or **burnt**. The form **burned** can be pronounced either /bɜ̱ːnd/ or /bɜ̱ːnt/. 1 If something **burns**, it is on fire. EG *She had seen Bristol burn one night in the war... The stubble was burning in the fields... I rescued her from a burning house.* V
◇ **burning.** EG *There was an ugly smell of burning.* ◇ N UNCOUNT
◇ **burnt.** EG *...a charred bit of burnt wood... ...the smell of burnt wool.* ◇ ADJ CLASSIF : ATTRIB

2 If you **burn** something, you destroy it by fire. EG *We couldn't burn the rubbish because it was raining... He burnt all papers connected with the incident.* V+O = incinerate
◇ **burning.** EG *...the burning of the Embassy during the riots.* ◇ N UNCOUNT
● If something **burns to the ground** or if it **is burned to the ground**, it is completely destroyed by fire. EG *In 1872, Chicago was burned to the ground.* ● PHR : VB INFLECTS ⇑ destroy

3 If you **burn** something that you are cooking, or if it **burns**, you spoil it by cooking it for too long or by using too great a heat. EG *The pan may be ruined if food has been burnt in it... His dinner burned while he was answering the phone.* V-ERG

4 If you **burn** a fuel or if it **burns**, it is used in order to produce heat, light, or energy. EG *...the combustion system in which the fuel burns... ...the energy derived from burning coal.* V-ERG

5 If you **burn** a part of your body or if you **burn** yourself, you are injured by fire or by friction. EG *'What's the matter with your hand?'-'I burned it on my cigar.'.. The filler cap was so hot it burned my fingers... I was afraid the man would burn himself... Claude lay moaning, holding his burnt arm.* ▸ used as a noun. EG *...third degree burns.* V+O (NG/REFL) ⇑ injure ▸ N COUNT ⇑ injury

6 To **burn** someone means to kill them by means of fire. EG *They nearly all got burned at the stake.* ● If someone **is burned alive** or **is burned to death**, they are killed by fire, for example in a burning building. EG *More than forty people were burned alive... They were burned to death.* V+O ● PHR : VB INFLECTS ⇑ die

7 If your face or your cheeks **are burning**, they are red because you are embarrassed or upset. EG *My cheeks would begin burning like mad.* V : USU CONT = flame

8 If you **are burning** with anger, humiliation, etc, you are very angry, very humiliated, etc. EG *He had to sit there, burning with humiliation.* V+*with* : USU CONT = seethe

9 If you **are burning** to do something, you want to do it very much. EG *She was burning to point at the man dining opposite.* V : USU CONT+*to*-INF = itch, long

10 If something such as a light is **burning**, it is producing or reflecting light. EG *There was a light burning in the garage... Her topaz ring burned in the sun.* V = blaze

11 If a fire **is burning**, it is alight. EG *The first thing he saw was a fire burning in the hearth.* V : USU CONT

12 If the sun **burns** you or **burns** your skin, it makes your skin become a darker colour, sometimes painfully. EG *Simon was burned by the sun to a deep tan... ...skin that usually burns in the sun.* V-ERG = fry

13 You also say that something **burns** when it gives you a painful hot feeling. EG *The whiskey he had drunk burned in his chest... The blister throbbed and burned.* V ⇑ hurt ◇ **burning.** EG *They cooled their burning throats... Some people experienced a burning sensation.* ◇ ADJ CLASSIF : ATTRIB

14 In Scotland, a **burn** is a stream or brook. EG *We used to go to the tank at the burn side for water.* N COUNT

15 See also **burning.** ● to **burn the candle at both ends**: see **candle.** ● to **burn the midnight oil**: see **midnight.**

burn down. If a building **burns down** or if someone **burns** it **down**, it is completely destroyed by fire. EG *The mansion burned down four years ago... His school had been burned down in the riots.* PHRASAL VB : V-ERG+ADV

burn out. 1 If a fire **burns out** or **burns** itself **out**, it stops burning because there is nothing left to burn. EG *We let the fire burn out... All the fires had now burned themselves out.* PHRASAL VB : V+ADV, OR V+O (REFL)+ADV ⇑ stop = die down

2 If a piece of machinery **burns out** or if you **burn** it **out**, it stops working because it has been used too much or worked too hard. EG *If his points or plugs burn out, he's done for.* PHRASAL VB : V+O+ADV OR S+V+ADV = wear out

3 If you **burn** yourself **out**, you make yourself exhausted or ill by working too hard; an informal use. PHRASAL VB : V+O (REFL)+ADV = exhaust

4 see also **burnt out.**

burn up. 1 If something **burns up**, it is completely destroyed by fire or strong heat. EG *The satellite had burned up on re-entering the atmosphere.* PHRASAL VB : V+ADV

2 If you say that an engine **burns up** fuel, you mean that it uses a lot of fuel. PHRASAL VB : V+O+ADV

burned out. See **burnt out.**

burner /bɜ̱ːnə/, **burners.** 1 A **burner** is a device which produces heat or a flame, especially as part of a cooker or a heater. N COUNT = jet

2 If you **put** a particular problem or matter **on the back burner**, you do not deal with it immediately but leave it for later because you do not think it is urgent or important; an informal expression. EG *This is simply putting the issue on the back burner.* PHR : VB INFLECTS ⇑ postpone

burning /bɜ̱ːnɪŋ/. 1 You use **burning** or **burning hot** to describe something that is extremely hot. EG *...burning deserts... ...burning hot irons.* ADJ CLASSIF : ATTRIB

2 A **burning** colour such as red or orange, or a **burning** light, is extremely bright. EG *Her body was a burning red.* ADJ CLASSIF : ATTRIB

3 If you have a **burning** interest, enthusiasm, or desire, you are extremely interested or excited about something or want to do something very much. EG *They all share a burning interest in independence.* ADJ QUALIT : ATTRIB = passionate

4 A **burning** issue or question is a very important or urgent one that people feel very strongly about. EG *...campaigns on housing, race, burning local issues.* ADJ QUALIT : ATTRIB = vital

burnish /bɜ̱ːnɪʃ/, **burnishes, burnishing, burnished.** When you **burnish** metal, you polish it so that it shines; a literary word. V+O = polish

burnished /bɜ̱ːnɪʃt/. Something that is **burnished** is bright or smooth; a literary word. EG *...burnished leaves... ...her burnished skin.* ADJ CLASSIF = shiny

burnt /bɜ̱ːnt/ is a past tense and past participle of **burn.**

burnt offering, burnt offerings. A **burnt offering** is 1 an animal that is burned as a sacrifice to a god or goddess. 2 a meal that has accidentally been burnt; a humorous use. N COUNT / N COUNT ⇑ food

burnt-out or **burned-out**; also spelled without a hyphen. 1 Someone who is **burnt-out** is unable to do things because they have made themselves too tired, weak, or ill; an informal use. EG *She is furiously busy one moment, burnt out and inert the next... ...a burned-out layabout.* ADJ CLASSIF ⇑ finished = wasted, weakened

2 Something such as a vehicle or building that is **burnt out** or **burned out** has been very badly damaged by fire. EG *They barricaded the streets with burnt-out cars.* ADJ QUALIT : USU ATTRIB = gutted

burp /bɜ̱ːp/, **burps, burping, burped.** 1 If someone **burps**, they make a noise when air from their stomach is suddenly forced up through their throat. EG *She burped into the sleeve of her new dressing gown.* ▸ used as a noun. EG *She said 'Excuse me' whenever a slight burp interrupted her flowing speech.* V = belch ▸ N COUNT = belch

2 If you **burp** a baby, you pat it on the back and cause it to burp after it has had a drink. V+O = wind

burr /bɜː/, **burrs, burring, burred**; also spelled **bur** for the meaning in paragraph 1. 1 A **burr** is the part of some plants which contains seeds and which N COUNT has little hooks on the outside so that it sticks to clothes or fur. EG *...removing burrs from a dog's coat.*

2 If someone has a **burr**, they speak English with a regional accent in which 'r' sounds are pronounced more noticeably than in the standard way of speaking. EG *He had a slight Irish burr.* — N COUNT: USU SING

3 A **burr** is also a whirring or humming sound. EG *He could hear the burr of a car in the distance.* ▸ used as a verb. EG *The telephone burred.* — N SING WITH DET; ▸ V

burrow /bʌrəʊ⁰/, **burrows, burrowing, burrowed.** 1 A **burrow** is a tunnel or hole in the ground that an animal such as a rabbit digs, especially in order to live in it. EG *The rabbit is resting in its burrow.* — N COUNT = dwelling

2 When an animal **burrows**, it digs a tunnel or hole in the ground. EG *As the pools shrink, the fish burrows into the mud at the bottom... ...earthworms burrowing their way through the soil... ...worm trails that have been burrowed through the mud.* — V OR V+O: USU+A ⇑ dig

3 You **burrow** in a container or a pile of things when you are searching for something which is hidden in it underneath other things. EG *She began burrowing underneath the tissue paper... You may have to dive in and burrow for whatever frozen packet you want.* — V+A ⇑ search = rummage

4 When you **burrow** into something, you move underneath it or press against it, especially in order to feel warmer or safer. EG *We would shudder and burrow deeper into the blankets... His face burrowed closer to my damp shoulder.* — V+A = snuggle

bursar /bɜːsə/, **bursars**. The **bursar** of a school or college is the person who is in charge of its finance or general administration. — N COUNT ⇑ treasurer

bursary /bɜːsə⁰ri¹/, **bursaries**. A **bursary** is a sum of money which is given to someone to allow them to study in a college or university, or to do work such as painting or writing. — N COUNT: USU+SUPP ⇑ grant = scholarship

burst /bɜːst/, **bursts, bursting**. The form **burst** is used in the present tense and is the past tense and past participle of the verb. 1 When something **bursts** or when you **burst** it, it suddenly breaks open or splits open, especially because there is too much pressure inside it, and the air or other substance inside it comes out. EG *As he braked a tyre burst... She burst the balloon... ...a burst water pipe... The abscess burst.* ▸ used as a noun. EG *I've got to phone the plumber. I've got a burst.* — V-ERG ⇑ break = puncture; ▸ N COUNT ⇑ break

2 When something **bursts** apart or when you **burst** it, it breaks apart, especially because it has been hit with great force. EG *The port wing burst apart... The boar burst the advancing line of hunters.* — V-ERG: IF+ADV THEN *apart* ⇑ break

3 When a door or lid **bursts open,** it opens very suddenly and violently because someone pushes it or because there is great pressure behind it. EG *I was sure the door was going to burst open any minute.* — PHRASAL VB: V+A OR V+O+A = fly open

4 If you **burst** into or through something, you suddenly go into it or through it with a lot of energy because you are in a great hurry. EG *O'Shea burst in through the opposite door... A woman burst her way through the guests at the buffet... The others burst from their tents.* — V+A, OR V+O+A = rush

5 If something **bursts** out, it suddenly becomes significant in a particular situation and has a great effect on it, especially after being hidden or not known about. EG *An election will allow pent-up political forces to burst out... Let me describe some of the developments waiting to burst from our laboratories and factories... The computer burst upon the scene around 1950.* — V+A = spring

6 You say that someone is about to **burst** with a particular emotion in order to emphasize that they feel it very strongly. EG *I could have burst with pride... I thought my heart was going to burst.* — V: IF+PREP THEN *with* = brim over

7 When a bomb or firework **bursts** in the air, it explodes. EG *We all held our breaths till the bomb burst somewhere on the other side of London.* — V = explode

8 A **burst** of activity or effort is a sudden short increase in the effort or the speed with which something is done or in the amount of what is done. EG *Bursts of growth were punctuated with periodic setbacks... ...frightened bursts of speed... The kangaroo, in bursts, can reach speeds of 60 kph.* — N COUNT: IF+PREP THEN *of* = spurt

9 A **burst** of something is a short and sudden period of it. EG *There was a burst of automatic rifle fire... ...a highly excitable man given to ungovernable bursts of rage... ...a burst of ultraviolet radiation.* — N COUNT+*of* ⇑ outbreak

burst in on. If you **burst in on** someone, you suddenly and quickly enter the room that they are in. — PHRASAL VB: V+ADV+PREP ⇑ intrude

burst into. 1 If you **burst into** tears, laughter, etc, you suddenly begin to cry, to laugh, etc. EG *I keep bursting into tears... The whole room burst into laughter... Uncle Tony burst into song.* ● to **burst into flames**: see **flame**. — PHRASAL VB: V+PREP = break

2 When plants **burst into** leaf, blossom, flower, etc, their leaves or flowers suddenly open. — PHRASAL VB: V+PREP

burst out. 1 If you **burst out** laughing, crying, etc, you suddenly begin laughing, crying, etc, usually loudly. — PHRASAL VB: V+ADV+-ING ⇑ break out

2 You use **burst out** when you are reporting what someone said to indicate that they said it suddenly and loudly. EG *Then he burst out, 'Get into the car, Phil, can't you?'* — PHRASAL VB: V+ADV+QUOTE ⇑ exclaim

bursting /bɜːstɪŋ/. 1 A place or container that is **bursting** is very full or crowded. EG *Parks, once bursting with flowers, were being torn up.* — ADJ CLASSIF: PRED, IF+PREP THEN *with*

2 If a place is **bursting at the seams**, it is very full or crowded; an informal expression. EG *The psychiatric wards are bursting at the seams.* — PHR: USED AS C = be packed

3 Someone who is **bursting** with a particular feeling or quality is full of it. EG *Claud was triumphant, bursting with pride and excitement... Jamie is bursting with energy.* — ADJ CLASSIF: PRED+*with*

4 Someone who is **bursting** to do something, is very eager to do it; an informal word. EG *I was bursting to tell someone... All the children were bursting to take part.* — ADJ QUALIT: PRED+*to*-INF

5 If you say you are **bursting**, you mean you need to urinate very soon; an informal use. — ADJ CLASSIF: PRED = desperate

burton /bɜːtə⁰n/; an old-fashioned British English word. 1 If something **goes for a burton**, it is lost or damaged, or made useless. EG *Well, that's our pay rise gone for a burton.* — PHR: VB INFLECTS = go down the drain

2 If someone **goes for a burton**, they fall off something. — PHR: VB INFLECTS

bury /beri¹/, **buries, burying, buried**. 1 When you **bury** someone who is dead, you put their body into a grave and cover it, usually with earth. EG *She will be buried here in the church... ...buried corpses.* — V+O: USU+A = inter

2 When you say that you **have buried** a particular relative, you mean that that relative has died. EG *I won't have it! I have buried enough children!... He buried his wife last week.* — V+O ⇑ inter

3 When a person or animal **buries** something, they put it into a hole in the ground and cover it up. EG *Reptiles bury their eggs in holes or under stones... ...buried treasure.* ● to **bury the hatchet**: see **hatchet**. — V+O: USU+A ⇑ hide

4 When you **bury** something in a substance or under a large quantity of things, you put it there, often in order to hide it. EG *Then they buried the meat in salt... She buried the gun under a pile of leaves.* — V+O+A ⇑ place

5 If someone or something **is buried** under something that falls on top of them, for example rocks or a building, they are completely covered and often cannot get out or be reached. EG *People who had been indoors were now buried beneath mountains of rubble... Many people remained buried alive.* — V+O: USU PASS+A ⇑ cover

6 If something **is buried** somewhere, it is beneath or behind other things where it cannot be seen and is difficult to find. EG *She found some coffee buried in the depths of her store cupboard.* — V+O: USU PASS+A ⇑ hide

7 When you **bury** your face or head in something soft, especially in another part of your body or someone else's body, you press it against that thing so that it is hidden or partly hidden. EG *She buried her face in her hands... She stood for a moment with her head buried against his neck... She turned further away, burying her face in the pillow.* — V+O+A ⇑ hide

8 When something **buries** itself somewhere or when someone **buries** it there, it is pushed very deeply in there. EG *The bullet had buried itself in the tree... You could bury your two hands in the bran.* — V+O (REFL)+A ⇑ stick

9 If you **bury** a particular feeling or memory of something, you try not to have or show that feeling or try to forget that thing. EG *The anger which had been buried inside me rose to the surface... ...buried memories... They agreed to bury their differences.* — V+O ⇑ suppress

10 If you **bury** yourself in a particular place, away from other people or important events, you go and spend some time there, usually alone. EG *He would voluntarily bury himself in these desert regions... ...a child who is continuously burying herself in a corner with a book.* — V+O (REFL)+A ⇑ occupy = ensconce

11 If you **bury** yourself or your head or face in — V+O (NG/REFL)

something, especially something that you are reading, you concentrate hard on it. EG *Their faces were buried in their evening newspapers... He buried himself deep in the wine list... He buried himself in his work.* +A (in) = immerse

bury away. If something **is buried away** somewhere, it is in a place where it is difficult to find or reach. EG *Buried away inside the paper, in a tiny paragraph, was an account of his visit... Here I am, buried away in the Orient.* PHRASAL VB : V+O+ADV, USU PASS = hide away, tuck away

burying /beri¹ɪŋ/. A **burying** place or **burying** ground is the same as a burial ground. ADJ CLASSIF : ATTRIB

bus /bʌs/, **buses; busses, bussing, bussed**. **Buses** is the plural of the noun. **Busses** is the 3rd person singular, present tense, of the verb. The verb is also spelled **buses, busing, bused** in American English. **1** A **bus** is a large vehicle which carries passengers from one place to another. A bus is driven along a particular route and you have to pay to travel on it. EG *I'm waiting for the bus back to town... I could go by bus... Jenny must've missed the last bus again... ...a bus driver.* N COUNT, OR by+N

2 When someone **busses** to a particular place or when they **are bussed** there, they travel there on a bus. EG *One has the option of walking one way and boating or bussing back... Supporters were bussed in to take part in the march.* V-ERG : USU+A ⇑ transport

3 In the United States, if children **are bussed** to school, they are transported by bus to a school in a different area in order that children of different social classes or races can be educated together. V+O ⇑ transport

busby /bʌzbi¹/, **busbies**. A **busby** is a tall fur hat that is worn by some British soldiers on ceremonial occasions. N COUNT ⇑ headgear

bus conductor, bus conductors. A **bus conductor** is an official on a bus who collects money from the passengers and checks their tickets. N COUNT

bush /bʊʃ/, **bushes**. **1** A **bush** is a large plant which is smaller than a tree and has a lot of woody branches. EG *...a gorse bush... I peered through the bushes.* N COUNT = shrub

2 The **bush** is the wild, uncultivated area of Australia, New Zealand, Africa, and other hot countries. EG *I went for a walk in the bush... ...the Mozambique bush... ...a bush fire.* N SING : the+N, OR N BEFORE N ⇑ wilderness = scrubland

3 If you say that someone has a **bush** of hair, you mean that they have a large amount of it. EG *Her spectacles were nestling in her grey bush of hair.* N COUNT+of ⇑ mass = shock

4 If you do not **beat about the bush**, you say what you want to say or answer a question immediately and directly rather than trying to avoid doing so. EG *Don't beat about the bush no matter how embarrassed you are.* PHR : VB INFLECTS

bushbaby /bʊʃbeɪbi¹/, **bushbabies**; also spelled as two words. A **bushbaby** is a small furry African animal that has very large eyes and a long tail and lives in trees. N COUNT

bushed /bʊʃt/. If you say that you are **bushed**, you mean that you are very tired; an informal word. EG *I'm pretty bushed after last night.* ADJ QUALIT : PRED = beat

bushel /bʊʃə⁰l/, **bushels**. **1** A **bushel** is a unit of volume that is equal to eight gallons or about 36.4 litres. EG *...five bushels of oats.* N PART : USU+N UNCOUNT

2 If you **hide** your **light under a bushel** or **hide** your talents, abilities, etc **under a bushel**, you keep your abilities or good qualities hidden from other people. EG *There were many lights hidden under his bushel... He was not a man much given to hiding his own brilliance under a bushel.* PHR : VB INFLECTS ≠ blow your own trumpet

Bushman /bʊʃmə³n/, **Bushmen**. A **Bushman** is a member of one of the tribes of people in southern Africa. N COUNT ⇑ tribesman

bushy /bʊʃi¹/, **bushier, bushiest**. Hair or fur that is **bushy** grows very thickly. EG *...bushy eyebrows... ...a bushy tail.* ADJ QUALIT ⇑ thick = shaggy

busily /bɪzili¹/. If you do something **busily**, you do it in a very active way, or with a lot of concentration. EG *Some children were busily catching crabs... I went on writing busily.* ADV WITH VB

business /bɪznɪs/, **businesses**. **1** **Business** is **1.1** work relating to the production, buying, and selling of goods or services. EG *He had made a lot of money in business... ...a leading industrialist with business interests in Germany... Phone during business hours.* N UNCOUNT, OR N BEFORE N

1.2 the activity of buying, selling, or exchanging goods in deals with people or companies. EG *Firms that do business with Britain... You should deal fairly in business.* N UNCOUNT ⇑ dealing

2 If **business** is good for a particular shop or company, it is selling a lot of goods or services, and if **business** is bad, it is not selling a lot of goods or services. EG *Business was awful... 'How's business?'-'Quiet.'* N UNCOUNT = custom, trade

3 A **business** is an organization which produces and sells goods or which provides a service. EG *He set up a small travel business... ...the company directors who actually run the business... The new business grew and grew.* N COUNT = company, firm

4 **Business** is also work or some other activity that you do as part of your job as opposed to activities that you do for pleasure. EG *Are you in San Francisco for business or pleasure?... He had a business appointment... When travelling on business I take my tiny travel sewing kit.* N UNCOUNT, OR N BEFORE N

5 The particular **business** that you are in is the area of activity in which you work in order to earn your living. EG *What business are you in?... There are good profits to be made in the hotel business.* • See also **show business**. N SING WITH DET : USU the+N ⇑ trade

6 Your **business** is **6.1** something that you are doing or concerning yourself with at the moment. EG *He wanted to be left alone to go about his business... She got on with the business of clearing up.* N SING WITH DET : USU WITH POSS ⇑ concern **6.2** something that concerns you personally and that other people have no right to ask you about or get involved in, or something that you have a right to know about or be involved in. EG *Let me worry about my business... That's her business... It's no business of mine what you choose to read... He made it his business to find out... It is not our business to enquire why he did it.* N SING : WITH POSS ⇑ concern = affair

7 **Business** is also important matters that you have to discuss or deal with. EG *I've some important business to discuss... Let's talk business... Let's get down to business now.* N UNCOUNT ⇑ matter

8 You can refer to an event, activity, or situation as, for example, 'a dreadful **business**' or 'this assassination **business**' rather than referring to it in a more exact or detailed way. EG *The whole business affected him profoundly... It's a dreadful business... This assassination business has gone far enough... Clearing the forest is a laborious business.* N SING WITH DET +SUPP ⇑ matter = affair, thing

9 You can also use **business** to refer to behaviour or activity of a particular kind when you are being unclear and not giving details about it. EG *...secret business... They run the universities and all that kind of business.* N UNCOUNT

10 You describe a task as a **business** when you find it difficult or boring and annoying. EG *It's a real business filling in this form.* N SING WITH DET ⇑ nuisance = bother

11 If you say that a dog or other animal **is doing its business**, you mean that it is defecating; an informal expression. PHR : VB INFLECTS ⇑ defecate

12 If you say that someone **has no business** to do something, you mean that they have no right to do it. EG *She had no business to publish his letters to her.* PHR : VB INFLECTS+to-INF

13 In informal English, if someone says they **are in business**, they mean that they have got or arranged everything they need in order to do something and can now start it. EG *Now we're really in business.* PHR : VB INFLECTS = all set

14 A person, shop, or company that is **in business** is currently operating and trading. EG *50% of these stores were not in business five years ago.* PHR : USED AS AN A

15 If you say that someone is doing something **like nobody's business** or that something is happening **like nobody's business**, you mean that they are doing it or it is happening very quickly and actively; a rather old-fashioned, informal expression. EG *They're working away like nobody's business.* PHR : USED AS AN A = like anything

16 If someone **means business**, they are serious about what they are doing, especially if it is something that will harm or upset other people, and they are determined to do it; an informal expression. PHR : VB INFLECTS

17 If you say to someone **'mind your own business'**, you are telling them not to ask about or get involved in something that does not concern them; an informal and rude expression. PHR : VB INFLECTS = nothing to do with you

18 If you say that something is **none of** someone's **business**, you mean that it is something that does not concern them and that they have no right to know about. EG *That's none of your business.* PHR : USED AS C

19 People, shops, or companies go **out of business** when they do not make enough money to continue PHR : USED AS AN A trading. EG *Umbrella sellers went out of business... They could put us out of business.*

business end, business ends. The **business end** of a tool or weapon is the part of it which does the work or causes damage, for example the sharp end of a knife rather than the handle; used in informal English. N COUNT : USU SING

businesslike /bɪznɪslaɪk/. Someone who is **businesslike** deals with things in an efficient way without wasting time. EG *How businesslike you are!* ▸ used of actions or behaviour. EG *The visit to Copenhagen was brisk and businesslike.* ADJ QUALIT ⇑ practical

businessman /bɪznɪsmə³n/, **businessmen.** 1 A **businessman** is a man who works in business, for example a man who runs a commercial or industrial firm. EG *My father was a businessman in the city.* N COUNT ⇑ trader

2 If you describe a man as a good **businessman**, a shrewd **businessman**, etc you mean that he knows how to deal with money and make good deals. N COUNT : MOD+N ⇑ entrepreneur

businesswoman /bɪznɪswʊ¹mə⁰n/, **businesswomen.** 1 A **businesswoman** is a woman who works in business, for example a woman who runs a commercial or industrial firm. N COUNT ⇑ trader

2 If you describe a woman as a good **businesswoman**, a shrewd **businesswoman**, etc you mean that she knows how to deal with money and make good deals. N COUNT : MOD+N ⇑ entrepreneur

busk /bʌsk/, **busks, busking, busked.** Someone who **is busking** is playing music or singing for money in a busy city street or station; used in British English. V : USU CONT ⇑ entertain

busker /bʌskə/, **buskers.** A **busker** is a person who plays music or sings for money in busy city streets or stations; used in British English. EG *There were always buskers at places like Earl's Court Station.* N COUNT ⇑ musician

busman's holiday /bʌsmənz hɒlɪdeɪ/. If you have a holiday or a day off from work and spend it doing something similar to your usual work instead of resting or doing something different, you can refer to it as a **busman's holiday.** PHR : USED AS O OR C

bus-shelter, bus-shelters. A **bus-shelter** is a bus stop that has a roof and at least one open side, which protects you from the rain when you are waiting for a bus. N COUNT

bus stop, bus stops; also spelled with a hyphen. A **bus stop** is a particular place along a road, usually marked by a pole or a shelter with a sign on it, where a bus stops to let passengers on and off. EG *There were long queues at all the bus stops.* N COUNT

bust /bʌst/, **busts, busting, busted.** The form **bust** can be used as the past tense and past participle of the verb as well as the present tense. 1 When you **bust** something, you break or damage it so badly that it cannot be used; an informal use. EG *She found out about Jack busting the double bass and was very annoyed.* V+O

2 If something is **bust**, it is broken or very badly damaged; used in informal English. EG *That clock's been bust for weeks.* ADJ CLASSIF : PRED

3 If a company **goes bust**, it loses so much money that it is forced to close down; used in informal English. EG *It is a bad situation for some cities whose railroad link has gone bust.* PHR : VB INFLECTS

4 When the police **bust** someone, they arrest them; used in informal English. EG *I've never been busted before. It was a memorable experience.* V+O

5 When the police **bust** a place, they raid it in order to arrest people who are doing illegal things; used in informal English. V+O

6 A **bust** is a statue of the head and shoulders of a person. EG *At the top of the steps was a bust of Shakespeare on a pedestal.* N COUNT : IF+ PREP THEN *of*

7 A woman's **bust** is 7.1 her breasts; used especially when referring to their size. EG *She has a very large bust.* N COUNT ⇑ chest 7.2 the measurement around the top part of her body at the level of her breasts. EG *'Bust 34' means that the garment is a size 12.* N UNCOUNT+ NUM ⇑ size

bust out. If you **bust out** of a place, you escape from it using force; an informal expression. EG *He bust out of jail.* PHRASAL VB : V+ ADV = break out

bust up. 1 If you **bust up** an event, meeting, etc, you stop it from continuing by causing a disturbance or fight; used in informal English. EG *They busted up the Miss America competition last November.* PHRASAL VB : V+ O+ADV ⇑ interrupt

2 If you **bust up** with someone such as your boyfriend or girlfriend, you have a quarrel with them which ends your relationship. EG *She's been staying here since she bust up with Toby.* PHRASAL VB : V+ ADV, OR V+ADV +A (*with*) : RECIP = finish

3 See also **bust-up.**

buster /bʌstə/ is used in very informal English to address a man in a way that suggests that you do not like or respect him. EG *'That's enough, buster!'* N SING : ONLY VOC = mate

bustle /bʌsə⁰l/, **bustles, bustling, bustled.** 1 When someone **bustles** about, they move around hurriedly, working quickly because they are very busy. EG *She bustled about, all smiles.... He was bustling around the kitchen cooking up a huge pot of stew.* V : IF+ADV THEN (*about/around/round*) ⇑ hurry

2 When someone **bustles** somewhere, they move there in a hurried and determined way. EG *James bustled in... I sat watching housewives bustle in and out of a supermarket.* V+A ⇑ hurry

3 **Bustle** is busy, noisy activity. EG *Everything was bustle and talk... ...the bustle of the airport.* N UNCOUNT

4 A **bustle** is a cushion or frame that was worn by women in the late 19th century to hold out their dress below the waist at the back. N COUNT

bustling /bʌslɪŋ/. 1 A **bustling** place is full of people and very busy and lively. EG *Grimsby is a bustling fishing town... Around him the airport was bustling with activity.* ADJ CLASSIF : IF+ PREP THEN *with* = hectic

2 A **bustling** person always seems to be very busy and moves quickly from one job to another. EG *...the bustling curator of the quaint Museum of the Holy Shrine.* ADJ CLASSIF ⇑ energetic

bust-up, bust-ups; an informal word. A **bust-up** is 1 a serious quarrel, especially one which ends a relationship. EG *They've had another bust-up.* N COUNT 2 a fight. EG *There was a bust-up down at the pub last night.* N COUNT

busty /bʌsti¹/, **bustier, bustiest.** A woman who is **busty** has very large breasts; an informal word. ADJ QUALIT

busy /bɪzi¹/, **busier, busiest; busies, busying, busied.** 1 When you are **busy**, you are working hard or concentrating on a task, so that you are not available to do anything else. EG *He was busy on the telephone... He had been busier than usual for several days before the meeting... 'Not now, Barry, I'm busy.'* ADJ QUALIT = tied up

2 A **busy** person has so many things arranged to do that they do not have any spare time. EG *She's going to be busy till about Friday... They're busy people, with active social lives.* ADJ QUALIT ⇑ active ≠ idle

3 A **busy** time, day, evening, etc is a period of time during which you have a great deal to do and not very much spare time. EG *I've had a busy day... It had been a busy summer.* ADJ QUALIT = hectic ≠ languid

4 When you say that someone is **busy** doing something, you mean that what they are doing is taking all their attention. EG *People like you and me are too busy chasing after money to care about such things... Her assistant was busy putting the instruments away.* ADJ QUALIT : PRED+-ING ⇑ occupied

5 A place that is **busy** is full of people who are doing things or moving about. EG *...a busy office... Curzon Street is usually very busy.* ADJ QUALIT ⇑ active ≠ quiet

6 When a telephone line is **busy**, you cannot talk to the person you are trying to phone because that person is already using the line to talk to someone else. EG *He dialled her number. The line was busy.* ADJ CLASSIF = engaged ≠ free

7 When you **busy** yourself with something, you deal with it using a lot of energy or effort. EG *I decided to busy myself with our untidy lawn... She turned up the next morning, busying herself about the kitchen as if nothing had happened.* V+O (REFL) : USU+A = occupy ≠ relax

8 A **busy** painting, sculpture, pattern, etc is one which consists of a lot of different parts put together in a complicated way. EG *...a busy, vigorous group in bronze.* ADJ QUALIT ≠ quiet

busybody /bɪzi¹bɒdi¹/, **busybodies.** If you refer to someone as a **busybody**, you mean that they interfere in other people's affairs; an informal word, used showing disapproval. EG *...a detective whom some busybody had hired to see what I was up to.* N COUNT : ALSO VOC ⇑ nosy-parker

but /bʌt, bət/, **buts.** 1 You use **but** after you have made a negative statement to introduce a statement about what is in fact the case. EG *This is not the result of unemployment but the result of sheer vandalism... The family doesn't see it as a chore but a sensible necessity... They don't need to know all the answers but they need to know how to find out the answers.* CONJ COORD : AFTER BROAD NEG

2 You can also use **but** to introduce a statement which contradicts or makes a contrast with what has just been said, or which indicates that the previous CONJ COORD = yet

statement is not significant in relation to what you are about to say. EG *The chapel was just an ordinary, crumbling box, but inside was the most magnificent marble altar... ...a cheap but incredibly effective carpet cleaner... We'll have a meeting. But not today... It was a long walk but it was worth it... He has promised reform but failed to deliver it... This vital exuberance might make one think the soil is very fertile. But it isn't... In 1950 oil supplied only about 10% of our total energy consumption; but now it is up to about 40% and still rising.*

3 You can also use **but** when you are about to add something further in a discussion, for example when you think that a particular point has not been adequately discussed. EG *'I think Brooks has actually looked towards British humour as a guiding light in this respect.'–'But another thing that he brings in is the comedy of being Jewish.'* CONJ COORD

4 You can also use **but** after 'yes' or 'no' to add a comment which, although it does not contradict your answer, indicates that your 'yes' or 'no' does not fully express what you think and that something else needs to be said. EG *'Nobody can understand James Joyce.'–'Ah yes, but that's the beauty of him you know.'... 'It was Montefiori,' one of them said. 'No, but it started with an M.'... 'I thought you'd make your home with me.'–'Yes, but–'–'There's no yes but.'* CONJ COORD: *yes/no*+CONJ = though

5 You can also use **but** to indicate that you are about to change the topic of what you are saying. EG *Later we'll be discussing the films of Alfred Hitchcock, but first, this week's new releases... But let's start at the beginning.* CONJ COORD = though

6 You can also use **but** to introduce a reply to someone when you want to indicate reluctance, disbelief, refusal, or protest. EG *That's very kind of you. But I'm terribly busy on Saturdays... 'Somebody wants you on the telephone.'–'But no one knows I'm here.'* CONJ COORD

7 You can also use **but** after you have said that two things are alike when you give the feature which makes one different from the other. EG *Wolfe. Like the animal. But with an e... The bear was about my height when it stood up, but round and large and powerful.* CONJ COORD = except, only

8 You can also use **but** after you have made an apology for what you are just about to say. EG *I'm sorry, but she's not in at the moment... Excuse me, but I think you're wrong there... Forgive my ignorance, but just what is Arista?* CONJ COORD

9 You can also use **but** to introduce a view or a statement which you have already criticized or tried to excuse, because you still feel that it is important enough to mention. EG *I may be old-fashioned, but why don't they write nice songs any more?... Call it a national vice, but most Englishmen dote on authoritarian women.* CONJ COORD

10 You can also use **but** to emphasize your surprise, admiration, shock, etc at a particular situation. EG *It's bad enough to come home and find one daughter pregnant. But both of them!... I thought I might get a couple of replies. But this is astonishing!... It was mink. But what a glorious colour!* CONJ COORD

11 You can also use **but** to emphasize the word you have just used by introducing a repetition of the word. EG *It had everything but everything, even an indoor waterfall.* CONJ SUBORD = yes

12 You use **but then** 12.1 to introduce a remark that suggests that what you have just said may not be right, or a piece of information that slightly contradicts what you have just said. EG *Iron would do the job better. But then you can't bend iron so easily... I always thought that. But then I'm probably wrong... You're the first person who's ever accused me of being irresponsible. But then it depends what you mean by responsible.* PHR: USED AS ADV SEN = still **12.2** to add a remark which suggests that what you have just said should not be regarded as surprising. EG *They're very close. But then, they've known each other for years and years... He's been a bit off-colour for the past few days. But then, who hasn't?* PHR: USED AS ADV SEN = still

13 **But** also means **13.1** except. EG *She couldn't eat anything but cucumbers... It hurt nobody but himself... It could do everything but stop... Who but a madman would administer a deadly poison... All but one of the thieves were caught.* PREP = apart from **13.2** only. EG *Low cost and high speed are but two of the advantages of electronic data handling... When I first met her she had but recently divorced... 'Will you be able to do it?'–'I can but try.'* ADV = just, only

14 You use **but for** to introduce the only factor that causes a particular thing not to happen or not to be completely true. EG *But for the sense of something watching them, Ralph would have shouted at him... But for you, I would be dead now... But for his ice-blue eyes, he looked like a bearded, wiry Moor.* CONJ SUBORD

15 You use **cannot but** and **could not but** when you want to emphasize that you believe something must be true and that there is no possibility of anything else being the case; used in formal English. EG *This phenomenal rate cannot but have some effect on the children... One cannot but admire him... We couldn't help but admire it.* CONJ SUBORD: MODAL *(can/could)*+CONJ ↑ must

16 The word **but** is also used in expressions like 'no buts', 'ifs and buts' to refer to a reason that someone gives for not doing something, especially when the speaker does not think that it is a good reason. EG *We are going–and no buts!... I'm tired of all your ifs and buts.* N PLURAL = excuses, objections

17 • **anything but**: see **anything**. • **last but one**: see **last**. • **not only ... but also**: see **only**.

butane /bju:teɪn, bju:teɪn/ is a gas that is obtained from petroleum and is used as a fuel. N UNCOUNT

butch /bʊtʃ/. **1** If people describe a woman as **butch**, they mean that she behaves or dresses in a masculine way and that they think she is a lesbian; an offensive use. ADJ QUALIT

2 If people describe a man as **butch**, they mean that he behaves in an exaggeratedly masculine way; sometimes used showing approval. EG *He's interesting, he's exciting, he's butch.* ADJ QUALIT = macho ≠ effeminate

butcher /bʊtʃə/, **butchers, butchering, butchered**. **1** A **butcher** is a shopkeeper who sells meat. Usually butchers sell the meat of animals that other people have killed, but some butchers kill the animals themselves. EG *He became a cattle-dealer and butcher... My father was a butcher by trade.* N COUNT

▸ The **butcher** or the **butcher's** is used to refer to a shop where meat is sold. EG *There's a family butcher at the end of our road.* ▸ N SING: *the*+N ↑ shop

2 If you call a man a **butcher**, you mean that he has committed a lot of cruel murders. EG *These summary executions earned him the title of Butcher.* N COUNT = murderer

3 If someone **butchers** an animal, they kill it for meat. EG *The pig was butchered at Christmas.* V+O = slaughter

4 If someone **butchers** people, they kill them cruelly. EG *He butchered tens of thousands of people.* V+O = slaughter

butchery /bʊtʃəri[1]/, **butcheries**. **1 Butchery** is **1.1** the cruel killing of a lot of people. EG *...the butchery of two hundred innocent citizens.* N UNCOUNT = massacre **1.2** the work that a butcher does in preparing meat for sale. EG *Cleanliness is essential in all butchery operations.* N UNCOUNT

2 A **butchery** is a butcher's shop; an old-fashioned use. EG *It was an old and flourishing High Class Butchery.* N COUNT

butler /bʌtlə/, **butlers**. A **butler** is the most important male servant in a house. EG *I used to have a butler, a cook, and a gardener.* N COUNT

butt /bʌt/, **butts, butting, butted**. **1** The **butt** of something such as a pistol or rifle is the thick end of its handle. EG *...the padded butt of the rifle... ...the butt end of a spear.* N COUNT: IF+ PREP THEN *of* ↑ tip

2 The **butt** of a cigarette or cigar is the small part of it that is left when you have finished smoking it. EG *Cigarette butts and beer cans were strewn everywhere.* N COUNT = dog end, stub

3 A **butt** is a large barrel used for collecting or storing liquid. EG *...wooden rain butts.* N COUNT = cask

4 If you are the **butt** of teasing, criticism, etc, people tease you, criticize you, etc a great deal. EG *I would have become the butt for teasing and ridicule... They made him the butt of endless practical jokes.* N SING: *the*+N = target

5 If a person or an animal **butts** something, they give it a hard blow, using their head or their horns. EG *He lowered his head and butted Stuart in the chest... Nearly half of them were butted or kicked to death.* V OR V+O ↑ knock

6 If you **butt your way** somewhere, you move forward pushing your body through something that is obstructing you such as a crowd of people. EG *The boar shunted and butted its way through the forest... He butted his way against the bitter east wind.* PHR: VB INFLECTS = shove

7 In informal American English, your **butt** is your bottom. EG *It's time you were getting off your butt and doing something.* N COUNT = backside

butt in. If you **butt in**, you rudely join in a private PHRASAL VB: V+

conversation or activity without being asked to; used showing disapproval. EG *You can't just butt in on someone else's discussion... I was always butting in and saying the wrong thing.* ADV ⇑ interrupt

butter /bʌtə/, **butters, buttering, buttered. 1 Butter** is 1.1 a yellowish fat made from cream which you spread on bread or use in cooking. EG *He refused to eat any more bread and butter... ...big blocks of butter... ...a shelf where the butter and cheese were kept.* • See also **bread and butter.** N UNCOUNT ⇑ food **1.2** a thick creamy substance made from a plant or vegetable. EG *...cocoa butter.* N UNCOUNT+SUPP

2 When you **butter** bread, toast, etc, you spread butter on it. EG *She buttered herself a piece of bread... Rosamund went on buttering her potato pancake.* V+O, V+O (NG/REFL)+O, OR V+O+A (for)
• to **know which side your bread is buttered on**: see **bread.**

3 When you **butter** vegetables, you put a piece of butter on top of them when they have been cooked, so that the butter melts and spreads over them. V+O ⇑ garnish
◊ **buttered.** EG *...a heaped bowl of buttered peas... ...buttered potatoes.* ◊ ADJ CLASSIF

4 If you say that **butter wouldn't melt in** someone's **mouth**, you mean that they look very innocent and not capable of doing anything wrong but that you know that they have done something wrong or are intending to. EG *She looked as though butter wouldn't melt in her mouth... He looked at me through his long lashes. Butter wouldn't melt in his mouth.* PHR : VB INFLECTS

butter up. If you **butter** someone **up**, you praise or try to please them, because you want to ask them a favour. EG *I'm buttering him up for a pay rise.* PHRASAL VB : V+O+ADV ⇑ flatter

buttercup /bʌtəkʌp/, **buttercups.** A **buttercup** is a small plant with bright yellow flowers, which grows in grassy places. N COUNT ⇑ plant

butterfingers /bʌtəfɪŋgəz/. You say **'butter-fingers'** when someone drops something, or when they fail to catch something that you have thrown to them; a humorous word. EG *The coin rolled into the grass at my feet. 'Butterfingers!' called Mr Ben.* EXCLAM, ALSO VOC ⇑ clumsy

butterfly /bʌtəflaɪ/, **butterflies. 1** A **butterfly** is an insect with large colourful wings and a thin body. There are many kinds of butterfly. EG *The large blue butterfly became extinct in 1979... ...one of Britain's most attractive butterflies.* N COUNT

2 If you have **butterflies** or **butterflies in** your **stomach**, you are very nervous about something; an informal expression. EG *I always get butterflies before an exam... I could feel the butterflies in my stomach.* PHR : USED AS O = nerves

3 The **butterfly** or the **butterfly stroke** is a way of swimming in which you lie on your stomach, kick your legs, and lift your arms out of the water together, bringing them down into the water in front of you. EG *I could never do the butterfly.* N SING : *the*+N

buttermilk /bʌtəmɪlk/ is the liquid that remains when fat has been removed from cream in order to make butter. You can drink buttermilk or use it for making bread or cheesecake. N UNCOUNT ⇑ food

butterscotch /bʌtəskɒtʃ/, **butterscotches. Butterscotch** is a hard yellowish-brown sweet substance made from butter and sugar boiled together. N UNCOUNT/COUNT

buttery /bʌtəʳri¹/, **butteries. 1** Something that is **buttery** tastes of butter or contains a lot of butter. EG *...a buttery cake.* ADJ QUALIT ⇑ creamy

2 A **buttery** is a room where you can obtain meals and drinks, especially in a university. EG *You could purchase tea and buns at the buttery.* N COUNT ⇑ tea shop

buttock /bʌtəᵒk/, **buttocks.** Your **buttocks** are the part of your body between your back and your legs, which you sit on. N COUNT : USU PL

button /bʌtəᵒn/, **buttons, buttoning, buttoned.**
1 A **button** is **1.1** a small hard object sewn on to shirts, coats, etc. You fasten the shirt, coat, etc by pushing its buttons through holes called buttonholes. EG *She opened the top two buttons of her dress... I was sewing buttons on one of my shirts.* N COUNT ⇑ fastener **1.2** a small object that you press in order to operate a machine or electrical device. EG *I couldn't remember which button turns it off... The gate slid open at the push of a button.* • See also **push-button.** N COUNT **1.3** a small badge that you wear in order to show that you support a particular organization, movement, etc; used in American English. EG *A student held out a button for him to wear on his lapel... Tom handed out 'Vote for Reagan' buttons.* N COUNT = badge

2 If you **button** a shirt, coat, etc or **button it up**, you fasten it by pushing its buttons through buttonholes. EG *Sam stands up, buttoning his jacket... He began to gather his papers and button up his coat.* V+O, OR PHRASAL VB : V+O+ADV

button-down. A **button-down** shirt or a shirt with a **button-down** collar is a shirt which has a button under each end of the collar which you can fasten. ADJ CLASSIF

buttonhole /bʌtəᵒnhəʊl/, **buttonholes, buttonholing, buttonholed. 1** A **buttonhole** is **1.1** a hole that you push a button through in order to fasten a shirt, coat, etc. N COUNT **1.2** a flower that you wear in the buttonhole of your jacket or coat lapel; used in British English. EG *...a white flower for my wedding buttonhole.* N COUNT

2 If you **buttonhole** someone, you make them listen to you. EG *I was just on my way out and he buttonholed me.* V+O = corner

buttress /bʌtrɪs/, **buttresses, buttressing, buttressed. 1** A **buttress** is a support, usually made of stone or brick, that supports a wall of a building. EG *...Gothic cathedrals with spectacular buttresses.* N COUNT

2 To **buttress** a wall means to support it with a buttress. V+O

3 To **buttress** an argument, system, etc means to give support and strength to it. EG *The present system serves to buttress the social structure in Britain... Such attitudes buttress economic misconceptions.* V+O ⇑ strengthen = reinforce ≠ undermine

buxom /bʌksəᵒm/. If you describe a woman as **buxom**, you mean that she looks healthy and attractive and has big breasts. EG *...the buxom ladies in Rubens' paintings.* ADJ QUALIT = voluptuous

buy /baɪ/, **buys, buying, bought. 1** If you **buy** something, you obtain it by paying money for it. EG *She could not afford to buy it... Many people have their cars bought for them by the firm they work for... Let me buy you a drink... Why don't you buy yourself a new dress?... They bought back the cottage at the original price.* V+O, V+O (NG/REFL)+O, OR V+O+A (for) = purchase

2 The amount that a certain sum of money **buys** is its value in terms of the quantity of goods or currency that can be obtained with it. EG *The value of the pension declines in relation to the things that it buys.* V+O = purchase

3 If you **buy** freedom, time, etc, you offer something in return for your freedom, more time, etc. EG *They tried to buy time by saying that it would be ready next week.* V+O = gain

4 If someone **buys** someone else, they get their help or services by bribing or corrupting them. EG *I won't be bought that easily!* V+O ⇑ bribe

5 If you say 'I'll **buy** that', you mean that you accept or believe what somebody has told you; an informal use. EG *Okay, I'll buy that... You've got no chance. He'll never buy it!* V+O : MODAL+VB+*it/that*

6 If you say that something is a good **buy**, a bad **buy**, etc, you mean that it has the quality mentioned, especially in relation to its price, how long it will last, or how good it is. EG *Other good buys include cameras and toys... These shoes were an excellent buy.* N COUNT : MOD+N = purchase

buy in. If you **buy in** something such as food, you buy large amounts of it for a future occasion, or for a time when it might not be available. EG *We bought in plenty of coal before the strike started.* PHRASAL VB : V+O+ADV = stockpile

buy into. When someone **buys into** a business or organization, they buy part of it, for example in order to gain some control over it. EG *He's been trying for years to buy into the printing industry.* PHRASAL VB : V+PREP, OR V+O (NG/REFL)+PREP

buy off. If you **buy** someone **off**, you pay them money so that they do not act against you. EG *They tried to buy off the witnesses.* PHRASAL VB : V+O+ADV

buy out. 1 If you **buy** someone **out** you buy their share of some property or a business that you have previously owned together. EG *He borrowed a large sum of money in order to buy out his partner.* PHRASAL VB : V+O+ADV

2 If you **buy** yourself **out** of one of the armed forces, you pay a sum of money so that you can leave before the end of the period you had agreed to stay for. PHRASAL VB : V+O (NG/REFL)+ADV, USU+*of*

buy over To **buy** someone **over** means the same as to buy them off. PHRASAL VB : V+O+ADV = buy off

buy up. If someone **buys up** land, property, etc, they buy large quantities of it, or all that is available. EG *They were trying to buy up every acre in sight... The company has quietly bought up nearly $3 million worth of stock.* PHRASAL VB : V+O+ADV ⇑ buy = amass

buyer /baɪə/, **buyers**. 1 A **buyer** is a person who is buying something or who intends to buy it. EG *I have a buyer for the house.* — N COUNT ⇑ customer

2 A **buyer** who works in a large store decides what goods will be bought from manufacturers to be sold in the store. EG *She is the chief fashion buyer for Sparks & Fraser.* — N COUNT ⇑ agent

3 A **buyer** who works for an industrial firm selects and buys the raw materials that the firm's factories will process. — N COUNT

buyer's market, buyer's markets. When there is a **buyer's market** for a particular product, there are more goods for sale than there are people wanting to buy them, and therefore buyers can influence prices. — N COUNT

buzz /bʌz/, **buzzes, buzzing, buzzed**. 1 A **buzz** is a continuous /z/ sound, like the sound of a bee when it is flying. EG *'Ms' sounds like the buzz of an insect.* — N COUNT = buzzing

2 Something that **buzzes** makes a continuous /z/ sound. EG *Bees buzzed outside... She could hear the phone buzzing in the other room.* ◇ **buzzing**. EG *...the buzzing of flies. ...a buzzing noise.* — V = hum; ◇ N UNCOUNT = droning

3 If something such as a fly or plane **buzzes** around, it moves along making a buzzing sound. EG *...those light planes I had seen buzzing around all day... ...a fly buzzing round her head... There was a wasp buzzing about her ear and she wanted to kill it.* — V+A *(around/round/about)* ⇑ move

4 If someone or something **buzzes** around, they move around a place very quickly and busily. EG *The rickshaw drivers buzz around... The girls all buzzed around, expecting May Noble.* — V+A *(around/round)* = race

5 If thoughts **are buzzing** round your head, or if your head **is buzzing** with thoughts, you are thinking about a lot of things, especially in a confused or worried way. EG *Anne's head buzzed with angry, crazy thoughts... ...with so many problems buzzing around my head.* — V+A = hum, race

6 If your ears **are buzzing**, they are filled with an unpleasant humming sound which makes it difficult for you to hear properly. EG *My ears were still buzzing when I stepped off the plane.* — V : USU CONT = ring

7 If a place is **buzzing** with conversation, questions, etc, it is filled with the sound of a lot of people talking excitedly. EG *The foyer was buzzing with speculation before the curtain went up... The room buzzed with excited questions.* — V : IF+PREP THEN *with* = hum, throb

8 A **buzz** of conversation is the sound of a lot of people talking excitedly. EG *The buzz of conversation around her was mostly about the election.* — N SING WITH DET : IF+PREP THEN *of*

9 A place that has a **buzz** has an atmosphere of activity and excitement; an informal use. EG *I like Newcastle. There's a real buzz there.* — N SING WITH DET

10 The **buzz** is the latest news or rumour about something; an informal use. EG *What's the buzz?* — N SING : *the*+N

11 When you **buzz** someone in the same building as you, you call them using an internal telephone line or a buzzer; an informal use. EG *I'll buzz you when I need you.* — V+O

12 If you tell someone that you will **give** them **a buzz**, you mean that you will telephone them; an informal expression. EG *I'll give you a buzz later in the week.* — PHR : VB INFLECTS = phone

13 If an aircraft **buzzes** people, buildings, or other planes, it flies low over them in a threatening way. EG *Choppers would fly low along the beach, buzzing the Marines.* — V+O ⇑ menace

buzz off. If someone **buzzes off**, they go away; used in informal English, often as a rude way of telling someone to go away. EG *'Now buzz off,' shouted Mrs Coggs with exasperation... We'll buzz off at midday.* — PHRASAL VB : V+ADV, USU IMPER = beat it

buzzard /bʌzəd/, **buzzards**. A **buzzard** is a large bird of prey belonging to the hawk family. — N COUNT

buzzer /bʌzə/, **buzzers**. A **buzzer** is an electronic device that makes a buzzing sound and that is used in alarm clocks, office telephones, etc. EG *Press the buzzer... The intercom buzzer sounded.* — N COUNT

buzz word, buzz words. A **buzz word** is a word or expression that has a special significance in a particular field, and that becomes fashionable because it is used a great deal on television or in the newspapers; used in informal English. EG *'Community policing' is a buzz word at the moment.* — N COUNT

by /baɪ/. 1 You use **by** 1.1 with verbs that are in the passive form to indicate the person or thing that performs the action of the verb, or the thing that is the cause of the action of the verb. EG *He was brought up by an aunt... ...new legislation to be announced by the government... The cemetery was surrounded by a chain fence... He had been poisoned by a mushroom... I was startled by his anger.* — PREP : O+VB IN PASS+PREP+S

1.2 after nouns referring to actions, to indicate the person or thing that performs the action. EG *...the refusal by the government to recognize the new party... ...a long debate about the use of pocket calculators by schoolchildren... Other remarks by Mr Schmidt were equally critical.* — PREP : N+PREP+N

1.3 with the present participle of a verb to indicate that someone performs a particular action and to state that something happens as a result of this action. EG *By bribing a nurse I was able to see some files... They were making a meagre living by selling souvenirs to the tourists... He then tries to solve his problems by accusing me of being corrupt.* — PREP+-ING

1.4 to indicate the means that are used in order to achieve something. EG *The money will be paid each quarter by cheque... We have heard from them by phone a couple of times... The contest was settled by a practical test... She was reading a book by candlelight.* — PREP+NG ⇑ via

1.5 to indicate the circumstances which lead to something happening and which can be intentional or unintentional. EG *They had met by chance... I was not now homeless by choice... I ended up here by accident.* — PREP : USU+N UNCOUNT = through

1.6 when you are referring to what you or someone else has said, and when you are asking about or explaining the meaning of what has been said. EG *What did you understand by his remarks?... What do you mean by that?... By 'John' I assumed he meant John Fletcher.* — PREP+NG/QUOTE

2 If you say that a book, play, piece of music, painting, etc is **by** a particular person, you mean that that person has written, created, or made it. EG *...three books by a great Australian writer... ...a collection of pieces by Mozart.* — PREP+NG/N PROPER

3 When you go somewhere **by** bus, train, bike, etc, you use this form of transport to go there. EG *I always go home by bus... We were trying to decide whether to risk going to Oxford by car or to take a train... There will be a lift to go up and down by.* — PREP+N ⇑ in

4 If you enter or leave a room or building **by** a particular door, window, etc, you use this entrance or exit. EG *He came in by the back door.* — PREP+NG = through

5 Someone or something that is **by** something else is beside it and close to it. EG *She lingered by the door... I sat by her bed... There were lines of parked cars by each kerb.* — PREP+NG ⇑ near

6 When someone or something walks, drives, rushes, etc **by** you or **by** somewhere, they move past without stopping. EG *People rushed by us... We stood at the side of the road and watched the cars whizz by.* — PREP, OR ADV AFTER VB

7 If something happens **by** a particular time, it happens at or before the time that is mentioned. EG *I arrived a mile outside the town by mid-afternoon... He can wash, change, cook the tea and be out by seven o'clock... By 1940 the number had grown to 185 millions... There should be some advance publicity for the book by now... By the time I went to bed, I was absolutely exhausted.* — PREP+ADV/A

8 **By** law, **by** a particular rule, **by** certain standards, etc means according to that law, rule, or standard. EG *Each year in November, by law, state pensions must be reviewed... By Inland Revenue rules this is income... He would be classified as rich by Chinese standards.* — PREP+NG

9 If you are **by** yourself or **all by** yourself, you are alone. EG *What are you going to do all weekend by yourself in Brighton?... He was standing by himself in a corner of the room.* — PREP+PRON REFL

10 If you do something **by** yourself or **all by** yourself, you succeed in doing it alone without anyone to help you. EG *Did you put those shelves up all by yourself?... She did not think she could manage by herself.* — PREP+PRON REFL

11 In arithmetic, you use **by** before the second number in a multiplication or division sum. EG *Twelve divided by three is four... Multiply it by three.* — PREP+NUM

12 When you are giving the measurements of something, you use **by** after you have given one measurement of it and before you give the next measurement. EG *The lounge is twenty feet by fourteen.* — PREP : NUM+PREP+NUM

13 Things that are made, sold, dealt with, etc **by** the million, thousand, dozen, etc are made, sold, or dealt with in the quantity mentioned; often used to emphasize the great quantities involved. EG *Robots are now manufactured by the million... Computer books can be mailed by the dozen in small envelopes.* — PREP+*the*+NUM

14 You can also use **by** in expressions like 'one by — PREP : N/NUM+

one', 'bit by bit', 'year by year', etc to indicate the rate or speed at which something happens. EG *The children had one by one fallen asleep... Radiation is actually eroding the planet's surface atom by atom... Their irritation slipped off them bit by bit... The university gets bigger year by year.* PREP+N/NUM ↑ after

15 You can also use **by** 15.1 to indicate the amount of increase or decrease that occurs in something. EG *Its grant is to be cut by more than 40 per cent... My salary went up by half when I moved South.* PREP: USU+ NUM/*more than/ at least* 15.2 to indicate the part of something or the part of someone's body that you are holding. EG *She took him by the hand... Hold it by the handle!* PREP+*the*+N

16 You can also use **by** with certain nouns, to indicate that something is your job or that something is part of your character. EG *By trade he was a dealer in antique furniture... She was by nature a long range planner... By temperament he was an artist... He belongs by birth to the elite.* PREP+N ↑ according to

17 If you do something **by** day or **by** night, you do it during the day or during the night. EG *By day he was a bricklayer, but his reputation as a singer was growing fast... By night, the huge electric signs light up the whole street.* PREP+N, USED AS AN A

18 **By and by** is a rather old-fashioned expression meaning a little later in time. EG *By and by, they came to a bridge over the river.* PHR: USED AS AN A ↑ later

19 • **by and large**: see **large**. • **by all means**: see **mean**. • **side by side**: see **side**.

bye /baɪ/. **Bye** and **bye-bye** are informal ways of saying goodbye. CONVENTION

bye-byes. If you tell a child to **go to bye-byes**, you are telling them to go to sleep or to go to bed; an informal use. PHR: VB INFLECTS

byelaw /baɪlɔː/, **byelaws**. See **by-law**.

by-election, by-elections. A **by-election** is an election that is held to choose a member of parliament to replace a previous member who has resigned suddenly or died. By-elections are held at a different time from a general election. EG *...the Warrington by-election.* N COUNT

bygone /baɪgɒn/, **bygones**. 1 **Bygone** means happening or existing a very long time ago. EG *...a home built to the standards of a bygone age... ...empires established in bygone centuries.* ADJ CLASSIF: ATTRIB = past ≠ future

2 If you say to someone **'let bygones be bygones'**, you are suggesting that you should both forget about unpleasant things that have happened between you in the past. EG *Let's concentrate on what's to be done next and let bygones be bygones.* PHR: VB INFLECTS

by-law, by-laws; also spelled **byelaw**. A **by-law** is a law which is made by a local authority or council and which applies only in their particular area. EG *...cars parked in violation of local by-laws.* N COUNT

by-line, by-lines. A **by-line** is a line at the top of an article in a newspaper or magazine giving the author's name; a technical term. EG *It appeared in the San Francisco Examiner under the by-line of Ed Montgomery.* N COUNT

bypass /baɪpɑːs/, **bypasses, bypassing, bypassed**; also spelled with a hyphen. 1 If you **bypass** someone in authority, you avoid asking their permission to do something, especially so that you can do it more quickly. EG *This is what happens when the worker by-passes his foreman.* V+O = side-step

2 If you **bypass** a difficulty, you avoid discussing it or getting involved in it. EG *It's no good trying to bypass the issue... It completely by-passes the whole question of ethics.* V+O = skirt

3 A **bypass** is a main road which is built to take traffic round the edge of a town rather than through the middle of it. EG *...the construction of a new bypass around the ancient town of Sandwich... ...the Oxford bypass.* N COUNT: ALSO IN NAMES AFTER N

4 To **bypass** a town, city, etc means to build a bypass round it. EG *35 million pounds is to be spent on bypassing Holywell.* V+O ↑ loop

5 If you **bypass** a town or city, you travel round it rather than through it. EG *We should be able to bypass Oxford.* V+O ↑ avoid

6 A **bypass** operation is a surgical operation in which the flow of blood is redirected, especially so that it does not flow through a part of the heart which is diseased or blocked. EG *...by-pass surgery.* N BEFORE N ↑ redirect ▸ used as a verb. EG *He suffered a heart attack while undergoing surgery to bypass three arteries.* ▸ V+O ↑ avoid

by-play is something that is happening at the same time as something else, but that is not as important, especially in a play on the stage. N UNCOUNT ↑ action

by-product, by-products. 1 A **by-product** is something which is made during the manufacture or processing of another product. Some by-products are very useful in industry. EG *They are looking into possible uses for the by-products of the extraction process.* N COUNT: IF+ PREP THEN *of* ↑ derivative = spin-off

2 A **by-product** of an event or situation is something that happens as a result of it, especially something that was not expected or planned. EG *Another punishment that was a by-product of being banned was considerable loss of income... Their empires arose almost as a by-product of the individual pursuit of wealth.* N COUNT: IF+ PREP THEN *of* = side-effect

byre /baɪə/, **byres**. A **byre** is a cowshed; an old-fashioned or literary word. N COUNT

bystander /baɪstændə/, **bystanders**. A **bystander** is a person who is at the place where something happens and who watches it but does not take part in it. EG *She spoke to the nearest bystander, which happened to be me... ...an innocent bystander.* N COUNT = onlooker

byte /baɪt/, **bytes**. A **byte** is a unit of storage in a computer. The amount of space that the computer has in its memory, or that it takes to do a particular task, is measured in bytes. EG *For this task the text translator needs only 3,000 bytes of memory.* N COUNT: USU NUM+N

byway /baɪweɪ/, **byways**. A **byway** is a small road which is not used by many cars or people. EG *He took to the little byways and one-way streets.* N COUNT: USU PL

byword /baɪwɜːd/, **bywords**. 1 Someone or something that is a **byword** for a particular quality is well known for having that quality. EG *The department had become a byword for ignorance, obstinacy and brutality.* N COUNT+*for* ↑ symbol

2 A **byword** is a word or phrase which is used very often and by a lot of people. EG *'Caring' became a byword among politicians during the election.* N COUNT

Cc

C, c /siː/, **C's, c's**. 1 **C** is the third letter of the English alphabet. N COUNT

2 **C**, in music, is the first note in the scale of C major. N COUNT/ UNCOUNT

3 If you get a **C** as a mark for a piece of work or in an exam, your work is considered to be average. N COUNT/ UNCOUNT

4 **C** is an abbreviation for 'century' or 'centuries'. You put 'C' in front of or after a number which refers to a particular century. EG *...living in the C14... ...the 14th C.*

5 **c.** is written in front of a date or number to indicate that it is approximate. It is an abbreviation for the Latin word 'circa'. EG *He was born c. 834 A.D.*

6 **C** or **c** is also an abbreviation for other words beginning with C or c, such as 'cold', 'cent', 'centigrade', or 'Celsius'.

7 **C** is the Roman numeral for 100.

C □ In this dictionary c is used in the grammar notes beside entries to mean 'complement'. The complement provides additional information about either the subject or the object of the verb. 1 It is used in descriptions of verbs which have a complement. See □ at V+C and V+O+C. Examples of V+C are **be 2.1, 2.2** and **seem 1**. EG *It was **terribly hot and airless**... The book that won is **'Midnight's Children'** by Salman Rushdie... The sun seemed **a little cooler**.* Examples of V+O+C are **call 2** and **make 11**. EG *I used to call him **babe** when he was young... The women made her **welcome**.* 2 It is used in descriptions of phrases which function as a complement.

See □ at PHR. Examples of PHR: USED AS C are **a blessing in disguise** (see **disguise 6**) and **done in** (see **do 20.12**). EG *A crisis can sometimes be **a blessing in disguise**... Honestly I feel completely **done in**.*

cab /kæb/, **cabs**. 1 A **cab** is a taxi. EG *Morris hurried off eagerly to get a cab.* — N COUNT, OR by+N

2 The **cab** of a lorry, bus, or train is the front part in which the driver sits when he or she is driving. EG *...the mangled cabs of overturned army lorries.* — N COUNT

C.A.B. /si eɪ biː/, **C.A.B.s**. The **C.A.B.** is a voluntary organization in Britain which gives people free advice on legal problems; an abbreviation for 'Citizens' Advice Bureau'. — N COUNT/PROPER: the+N

cabal /kəˈbæl/, **cabals**. A **cabal** is a small group of people who meet secretly, especially for political purposes. EG *...a secret cabal of powerful 'insiders'.* — N COUNT: IF SING, VB CAN BE SING OR PL = clique

cabaret /kæbəreɪ/. 1 **Cabaret** is entertainment consisting of dancing, singing, or comedy acts, which is performed in the evenings in restaurants or nightclubs. EG *London has good nightclubs with cabaret... ...a cabaret artiste.* — N UNCOUNT = floor show

2 A **cabaret** is 2.1 a show that is performed in a restaurant or nightclub. 2.2 a restaurant or nightclub which provides such entertainment. — N COUNT; N COUNT

cabbage /kæbɪdʒ/, **cabbages**. 1 A **cabbage** is a vegetable which looks like a large ball of leaves. There are several different kinds of cabbage, with leaves that are green, white, or purple. — N COUNT/UNCOUNT

2 If you say that someone is a **cabbage**, you mean that they show no awareness of things or that they are not interested in anything, often because they have suffered brain injuries; an informal use, sometimes showing disapproval. EG *I would rather be awake and in pain than just remain a cabbage and learn nothing.* — N COUNT ⇑ person = vegetable

cabbie /kæbi¹/, **cabbies**; also spelled **cabby**. A **cabbie** is a person who drives a taxi; used mainly in old-fashioned British English. — N COUNT

cabin /kæbɪn/, **cabins**. A **cabin** is 1 a small room in a ship or boat in which people live or sleep. EG *When we got to the cabin she was sitting on the edge of a bunk holding her coat.* 2 one of the areas inside a plane for people to use, either one in which the passengers sit or one in which the captain, pilot, and navigator work. EG *...the curtains that conceal the First Class cabin.* 3 a small house, especially one made of wood in an area of forests or mountains. EG *Our cabin stood on the crest of a hill.* — N COUNT; N COUNT ⇑ compartment; N COUNT = chalet

cabin cruiser, cabin cruisers; also spelled with a hyphen. A **cabin cruiser** is a motor boat which has a cabin for people to live or sleep in. — N COUNT

cabinet /kæbɪ¹nɪ²t/, **cabinets**. 1 A **cabinet** is a cupboard used for storing particular types of things, for example medicine or alcoholic drinks, or for displaying attractive or interesting objects. EG *...a cocktail cabinet... ...a glass cabinet with Chinese things in it.* ● See also **filing cabinet**. — N COUNT: USU MOD+N

2 The **Cabinet** is a group of the most senior and powerful ministers in a government, or advisers to a president, who meet regularly to discuss and decide policies. EG *Harold Lever was in the cabinet as Paymaster-General... ...the first man to be appointed to the Kennedy cabinet... ...a former cabinet minister.* ● **In cabinet** means at a meeting of the cabinet. EG *In cabinet, Benn was criticized for undermining the Government.* — N COUNT: USU the+N IF SING, VB CAN BE SING OR PL ⇑ executive; ● PHR: USED AS AN A

cabinet-maker /kæbɪ¹nɪ²tmeɪkə/, **cabinet-makers**; also spelled without a hyphen. A **cabinetmaker** is a person who makes high-quality wooden furniture. — N COUNT ⇑ craftsman

cable /keɪbəᵒl/, **cables, cabling, cabled**. 1 A **cable** is 1.1 a very strong, thick rope made of wires twisted together. EG *...the suspension cables of the bridge.* 1.2 a bundle of wires inside a rubber or plastic covering, along which electricity flows or electronic signals are passed. EG *...ten metres of electrical cable.* 1.3 a message that is sent by means of electricity along a wire over a long distance, often to another country, and then is printed out at the other end: compare **telegram**. EG *I sent a cable to Cairo saying I was on my way... ...the cable and telegraph services.* — N COUNT; N COUNT ⇑ wire; N COUNT, OR by+N ⇑ communication

2 If you **cable** a message to someone, you send it to them by cable. EG *The editor cabled, 'What happened? Where is the series?'... I cabled him from Amsterdam.* — V+O, V+QUOTE, V+O+O

3 If you **cable** money to someone, you get it to them by sending an instruction by cable to a bank. EG *He had already cabled a thousand dollars to Mrs Ruiz.* — V+O, V+O+O, OR V+O+A (to) ⇑ send

cable car, cable cars. A **cable car** is a vehicle which is pulled by a moving cable. It is used to take passengers up mountains or steep hills. EG *They take you up in cable cars to the Monte Del Rosa.* — N COUNT, OR by+N

cable railway, cable railways. A **cable railway** is a railway on which the wagons are pulled up a steep slope by a moving cable. — N COUNT, OR by+N

cable television is a television system in which signals are sent along wires to people's television sets after they have been transmitted to a central receiver. — N UNCOUNT

cache /kæʃ/, **caches**. A **cache** is a quantity of things, for example weapons or drugs, that have been hidden. EG *One of the patrols had discovered an arms cache... ...an unoccupied fort containing caches of food and water.* — N COUNT ⇑ store = hoard

cachet /kæʃeɪ/. If someone or something has a certain **cachet**, they have a quality which makes people admire them or approve of them; a formal or literary word. EG *The visit to Hollywood had given me a certain cachet in her parents' eyes.* — N SING WITH DET+SUPP ⇑ attraction = status

cackle /kækəᵒl/, **cackles, cackling, cackled**. 1 If you **cackle**, you laugh in a loud unpleasant way, making short hard sounds, often because you are pleased about something unpleasant that has happened to someone else. EG *She cackled with delight... 'Fools!' she cackled.* ▸ used as a noun. EG *He gave a malicious cackle.* — V OR V+QUOTE = screech; ▸ N SING+SUPP a+N

2 When hens make a noise after laying an egg, they **cackle**. — V = cluck

3 If you say **cut the cackle** to someone, you are telling them to stop chattering; an informal use. EG *Cut the cackle, please, and get us another drink.* — CONVENTION ⇑ be quiet = shut up

cacophony /kəkɒfəni¹/. A **cacophony** is a very loud, unpleasant noise, especially one that consists of a lot of different sounds together; a formal word. EG *...a cacophony of squeaks and rattles... ...children with their cacophony of laughter.* — N SING WITH DET = din, row

cactus /kæktəs/, **cactuses, cacti** /kæktaɪ/. The plural can be **cactuses, cacti**, or **cactus**. A **cactus** is a thick fleshy plant that has no leaves, is covered in spikes, and grows in deserts. EG *I could see nothing but jackals and cacti... ...the stones and cactus of the Mexican desert.* — N COUNT ⇑ succulent

cad /kæd/, **cads**. If you say that a man is a **cad**, you mean that he deceives other people, especially women, or treats them badly or unfairly; an old-fashioned, informal word. EG *I thought I could trust you not to behave like a cad.* — N COUNT: ALSO VOC ⇑ villain = scoundrel ≠ gentleman

cadaver /kədeɪvə, -dæv-/, **cadavers**. A **cadaver** is a corpse; a formal or medical word, used especially in American English. — N COUNT

cadaverous /kədævəᵒrəs/. Someone who is **cadaverous** is very thin and pale, and looks unhealthy; a formal word. EG *He was tall and spare, with a cadaverous face.* — ADJ QUALIT = gaunt

caddie /kædi¹/, **caddies, caddying, caddied**; also spelled **caddy**. A **caddie** is a person who carries golf clubs and other equipment for a person playing golf. ▸ used as a verb. EG *He was a member of the golf club and we used to caddy for him.* ● See also **tea caddy**. — N COUNT ⇑ attendant; ▸ V

cadence /keɪdəᵒns/, **cadences**. A **cadence** is 1 the way your voice gets higher and lower as you speak. EG *His voice had an unfamiliar cadence; Fanny recollected that he was Welsh.* 2 the close of a musical phrase or sequence. EG *There was a pause at the end of each cadence.* — N COUNT ⇑ intonation = lilt; N COUNT

cadenza /kədenzə/, **cadenzas**. A **cadenza** is a complex solo in a piece of classical music written for an orchestra and a soloist. EG *This virtuosity shows up particularly in the cadenza.* — N COUNT

cadet /kədet/, **cadets**. A **cadet** is a young man or woman who is being trained in the army, navy, air force, or police. EG *...the cadets from the nearby Air Force training school.* — N COUNT ⇑ trainee

cadge /kædʒ/, **cadges, cadging, cadged**. If you **cadge** something from someone or if you **cadge** off them, you ask them for something such as food, money, or help and succeed in getting it; used showing disapproval in informal British English. EG *He would never come here, unless it was to cadge free drinks... ...living by cadging off relatives and doing odd jobs.* — V OR V+O: IF+PREP THEN off/from ⇑ beg = bum, scrounge

cadger /kædʒə/, **cadgers**. A **cadger** is a person who is always asking for things from other people; used showing disapproval in informal British English. N COUNT ⇑ beggar = scrounger

cadre /kɑ:də/, **cadres**. A **cadre** is a small group of people who have been specially chosen, trained, and organized for a particular purpose, especially by a political organization. EG *...the creation of revolutionary cadres in universities and colleges.* N COUNT : IF SING, VB CAN BE SING OR PL

Caesarean /si'seəriən/, **Caesareans**. A **Caesarean** or a **Caesarean section** is an operation that is performed on a woman who has difficulty giving birth. The baby is lifted out of her womb through an opening cut in her abdomen. N COUNT, OR *by*+N

café /kæfeɪ/, **cafés**. A **café** is a place where you can buy drinks and light meals or snacks. In Britain cafés do not serve alcoholic drinks. N COUNT = snack bar

cafeteria /kæfɪ'tɪərɪə/, **cafeterias**. A **cafeteria** is a restaurant where you choose your own food from a counter and carry it to your table yourself. N COUNT

caffeine /kæfi:n/; also spelled **caffein**. **Caffeine** is a chemical substance found in coffee, tea, and cocoa which makes your brain and body more active. N UNCOUNT ⇑ stimulant

caftan /kæftæn, -tɑ:n/, **caftans**; also spelled **kaftan**. A **caftan** is a long loose garment with long sleeves, worn by men in Arab countries, and by women in America and Europe. EG *...society women in their silk caftans.* N COUNT

cage /keɪdʒ/, **cages**. A **cage** is a structure of wire or metal bars in which birds or animals are kept. EG *In one corner he spotted a large parrot in a cage... There was a tiger looking at him through the bars of its cage.* N COUNT ⇑ enclosure

caged /keɪdʒd/. A **caged** bird or animal is one that is kept in a cage. ADJ CLASSIF ≠ free

cagey /keɪdʒi'/. When people are being **cagey**, they are being careful not to give a firm opinion about something or are reluctant to agree to do something; an informal word. EG *He was biting his finger-nails, as was his habit when he was being cagey.* ◊ **cagily**. EG *He cagily stayed clear of the subject.* ◊ **caginess**. EG *...their caginess about the existence and nature of the alleged offences.* ADJ QUALIT ⇑ cautious = chary ◊ ADV WITH V ◊ N UNCOUNT

cagoule /kəgu:l/, **cagoules**. A **cagoule** is a lightweight waterproof jacket that you wear over other clothes to prevent them getting wet. N COUNT ⇑ anorak

cahoots /kəhu:ts/. If you are **in cahoots with** someone, you are working in close co-operation with them, especially when you are planning something that will harm someone else. EG *Evidently Halliday was in cahoots with the person who was so handy with poison.* PHR+NG : USED AS AN A

cairn /kɛən/, **cairns**. A **cairn** is a pile of stones which marks a boundary, a route across rough ground, or the top of a mountain, or one which has been built in memory of someone. N COUNT ⇑ mound

cajole /kədʒəʊl/, **cajoles, cajoling, cajoled**. If you **cajole** someone into doing something, you eventually manage to persuade them to do it by flattering them, praising them, or by saying other things that they want to hear. EG *McKinley and Sherman were cajoled into coming with us.* V+O : USU+A = coax

cake /keɪk/, **cakes, caking, caked**. **1** A **cake** is **1.1** a sweet food made by baking a mixture of flour, eggs, sugar, fat, etc in an oven. Cakes may be large and cut into slices, or they may be small and intended for one person only. EG *She said she would bake a cake for my birthday... She cut the cake and gave me a piece.* ▸ used as an uncount noun. EG *...a slice of cake... I enjoyed sitting down with friends over coffee and cake when the day's work was over.* N COUNT ▸ N UNCOUNT

1.2 food that has been formed into a flat, round shape, usually before it is baked or fried. EG *...fish cakes... ...cakes of pounded rice.* N COUNT+SUPP

2 A **cake** of something such as soap or wax is a small block of it. EG *He was given a pink cake of soap, which smelled of disinfectant.* N COUNT : ALSO N +*of*+N UNCOUNT = bar

3 If something has **caked**, it has changed from a thick liquid into a dry layer or lump. EG *He sat slumped forward, with dried blood caked in his hair.* V : IF+PREP THEN *on/in* ⇑ solidify

4 If a surface is **caked** with something, it is covered with something thick and liquid such as mud or plaster, which dries and forms a hard layer. EG *His shoes were caked with mud.* V+O : USU PASS+*with* ⇑ cover = encrust

5 The word **cake** is used in several informal expressions. **5.1** If you say that something is **a piece of cake**, you mean that it is very easy to do. EG *'How did you manage to get into the house?'–'It was a piece of cake; the bedroom window was open.'* **5.2** If things are **selling like hot cakes**, they are selling well, and people are very eager to buy them. **5.3** If someone says that **you can't have your cake and eat it**, they are criticizing you for wanting to have the advantages of choosing both available alternatives, although it is fair or reasonable to choose only one. **5.4 the icing on the cake**: see **icing**. PHR : USED AS C; PHR ⇑ successful; PHR

cake mix, cake mixes; also spelled with a hyphen. **Cake mix** is a powder that you can buy which contains all the dry ingredients you need to make a cake. N UNCOUNT/N COUNT

cake tin, cake tins; also spelled with a hyphen. A **cake tin** is **1** a metal container with a lid, which you put a cake into in order to keep it fresh. **2** a metal container which you bake a cake in. N COUNT; N COUNT ⇑ tin

cal, cals. **cal** is an abbreviation for **calorie**; often used on packets of food. EG *Marvel contains 355 cals (approx) per 100g.*

calamitous /kəlæmɪ'təs/. Something that is **calamitous** is very unfortunate indeed, usually because it involves a disaster of some kind; sometimes used in a slightly humorous way. EG *...calamitous floods... I'm always expecting something calamitous to happen.* ADJ CLASSIF ⇑ bad = disastrous, catastrophic

calamity /kəlæmɪ'ti'/, **calamities**. A **calamity** is an event that causes a great deal of damage, destruction, or personal sadness and distress. EG *...the calamity of the dole queues... ...the glee with which the media report scientific calamities.* N COUNT/UNCOUNT = catastrophe

calcium /kælsɪəm/ is a soft white element which is the basis of many chemical compounds. It is found in bones and teeth, and also in limestone, chalk, and marble. N UNCOUNT

calculate /kælkjə'leɪt/, **calculates, calculating, calculated**. **1** If you **calculate** something, **1.1** you work out a number or amount from information that you have, usually by doing some arithmetic. EG *The number of votes cast in each section will then be calculated... He paused and calculated for a moment. 'We'll have one hundred and seventy-three pounds profit.'* **1.2** you think about something such as a problem and arrive at your view or opinion of it after you have considered all the relevant factors. EG *...actions whose consequences can in no way be calculated.* V OR V+O/REPORT-CL ⇑ find = count; V+O/REPORT-CL ⇑ estimate = determine

2 If something is **calculated** to do something, it is specially done or arranged in order to have a particular effect. EG *I adopted a cool dignified attitude that was calculated to discourage familiarity... ...newspaper articles which were calculated to sway the reader's opinions.* ● If something **is scarcely calculated** to do something, it is very unlikely to do it. EG *...an offer scarcely calculated to attract shareholders.* V+O+*to*-INF : ONLY PASS ⇑ meant = designed; ● PHR : VB INFLECTS+*to*-INF

calculated /kælkjə'leɪtɪ'd/. **1** Bad or violent behaviour that is **calculated** is very carefully planned or arranged. EG *...the deliberate, calculated use of violence to achieve their objectives... ...a calculated act of political irresponsibility.* **2** A **calculated** risk is one where you are aware of the possible bad consequences but think that the risk is worth taking because of what you will gain if you are successful. EG *'Suppose someone gets killed.'–'It's a calculated risk, but I think it's worth it.'* ADJ QUALIT ⇑ deliberate = premeditated; ADJ CLASSIF : ATTRIB ⇑ considered

calculating /kælkjə'leɪtɪŋ/. A **calculating** person is one who arranges situations and controls people in order to get what he or she wants, without caring about anyone else; used showing disapproval. EG *...the most calculating and selfish men in the community... ...a cold, calculating criminal.* ADJ QUALIT ⇑ deliberate = scheming

calculation /kælkjə'leɪʃə'n/, **calculations**. **1** A **calculation** is **1.1** something that you think about and work out mathematically, or one that you do on a machine such as a calculator. EG *'How long will it take me?' I did a rapid calculation. 'About ten years,' I said... ...the figures on which he based his calculation... Peter's calculations were correct.* **1.2** something that you think about and arrive at a view or opinion on, after having considered all the relevant factors. N COUNT/UNCOUNT = sum; N COUNT ⇑ estimate

2 Calculation characterizes someone's behaviour when they are thinking only of themselves and any benefit that they will get from their actions rather than of the way their actions will affect other people; N UNCOUNT = contrivance used showing disapproval. EG *His behaviour seems free of all calculation.*

calculator /kælkjə⁴leɪtə/, **calculators**. A **calculator** is a small electronic device that you use for doing mathematical calculations. EG *...a pocket calculator.* N COUNT

calculus /kælkjə⁴ləs/ is a branch of advanced mathematics which deals with variable quantities. EG *...competence in areas such as statistics and calculus.* N UNCOUNT

caldron /kɔːldrən/. See **cauldron**.

calendar /kælɪ¹ndə/, **calendars**. A **calendar** is 1 a chart or set of charts which shows a particular year divided up into months, weeks, and days, and shows what the date of each day is in that year. EG *He glanced up at the wall calendar–Today was Thursday.* N COUNT ● A **calendar** month is one of the twelve named periods of time that a year is divided into. EG *It costs one hundred dollars per calendar month.* ● ADJ CLASSIF: ATTRIB ● A **calendar** year is a period of 365 days, or 366 days in a leap year. ● ADJ CLASSIF: ATTRIB

2 A **calendar** is also 2.1 a system for dividing up time, which establishes year zero, numbers the years, and arranges the days into months and years. EG *...the Muslim calendar.* N COUNT: USU SING+SUPP 2.2 a list of dates within a given year that are important for a particular organization or kind of activity. EG *...the British Professional Athletics calendar... ...a major event in the theatrical calendar.* N COUNT: USU SING+SUPP ⇑ schedule

calf /kɑːf/, **calves**. 1 A **calf** is 1.1 a young cow. EG *...a one-year-old calf.* N COUNT 1.2 a young elephant, giraffe, buffalo, whale, or seal. N COUNT

2 **Calf** or **calfskin** is leather made from the skin of a calf. N UNCOUNT

3 Your **calf** is the thick part at the back of your leg between your ankle and your knee. N COUNT

caliber /kælɪbə/. See **calibre**.

calibrate /kælɪbreɪt/, **calibrates, calibrating, calibrated**; a technical term. If you **calibrate** an instrument or tool, 1 you mark it so that you can use it to measure something accurately. V+O ◊ **calibrated**. EG *...a calibrated glass beaker.* ◊ ADJ CLASSIF 2 you correct or adjust it so that it measures accurately. V+O ⇑ measure

calibre /kælɪbə/, **calibres**; also spelled **caliber** in American English. 1 The **calibre** of a person is their ability and intelligence, especially when these are of a high standard. EG *...worker directors of the right calibre... ...a quite exceptional calibre of headmaster... ...high calibre people on its staff.* N UNCOUNT+SUPP ▸ also used of organizations and activities. EG *This appears again to be merely a matter of the calibre of management... The care of the aged generally is of a high calibre.*

2 The **calibre** of a gun is the width of the inside of its barrel; used also to refer to the size of the bullets and shells that it can fire. EG *By 1990 all troops should have the same calibre guns and rifles, using the same ammunition.* N COUNT+SUPP = bore

calico /kælɪkəʊ/ is plain white fabric made from cotton. N UNCOUNT

caliper /kælɪpə/. See **calliper**.

caliph /keɪlɪf/, **caliphs**; also spelled **calif**. A **Caliph** was a moslem ruler. EG *...Omar, the second Caliph, third after Muhammad the Prophet.* N COUNT: ALSO IN TITLES ⇑ ruler

calisthenics /kælɪsθenɪks/. See **callisthenics**.

call /kɔːl/, **calls, calling, called**. 1 If someone or something is **called** a particular thing, it is their name or title. EG *She had a boyfriend called David... My friends call me Bing... She wrote a novel called 'Memoirs of a Survivor'... My students usually call me by my Christian name.* V+O+C (N PROPER), OR V+O+A (by)

2 If you **call** someone or something a name, you give them the name that they will be known by. EG *We called our son Iain... They are going to call the new town Skelmersdale.* V+O (NG/REFL) +C (N PROPER) = christen

3 If something **is called** a particular name, it is properly known by it. EG *This tiny screw is called a grub screw... ...an automatic device called an autocue... We often call things by the wrong names.* V+O+C (NG): USU PASS ⇑ describe = term

4 If you **call** people or situations something, you use a particular word or phrase to describe them, especially one which makes it obvious what you think about them. EG *President Nixon called his opponents traitors... 'Was it a good play?'–'Well, I wouldn't call it awful, but it wasn't very well written.'... There have been some developments towards what could be called a West European foreign policy.* V+O+C = label ● If you **call** someone **names**, you insult them by using offensive words such as 'stupid', 'idiot', etc. ● PHR: VB INFLECTS ● Something that you can **call** your **own** is something that belongs to you. EG *He had nothing he could call his own.* ● PHR: VB INFLECTS

5 If you **call** yourself something, you claim that this is what you are, although it might not be true. EG *He is an autocratic type who calls himself a revolutionary... Although it calls itself a 'School', it is becoming less and less involved with teaching and concentrates more on research.* V+O (REFL)+C = style

6 If you **call** something, you say it in a loud voice, usually because you are trying to attract someone's attention. EG *'Edward!' she called. 'Edward! Lunch is ready!'... I could hear a voice calling my name.* V+O/QUOTE, OR V+A (for/to/from) = shout ▸ used as a noun. EG *We heard a call for help from the pond.* ▸ N COUNT = cry ● See also **call out**.

7 If you **call** a name or a number, you read it aloud from a list to see whether everyone is present. EG *Please come to the front when I call your name.* V+O = announce

8 If you **call** someone, 8.1 you telephone them. EG *'I want to speak to Mr Landy, please.'–'Who is calling?'... Call me when you get home.* V OR V+O = phone, ring 8.2 you ask them to come to you, usually by shouting to them or by telephoning them. EG *Supper's ready, call the kids... The editor called me to his office to tell me the news... The police were called, but the burglars had gone... When Margaret collapsed, I called the doctor, who arrived almost immediately.* V+O ⇑ summon = send for

9 A **call** is 9.1 a communication that you receive or make by telephone. EG *There have been two telephone calls for you... I made a long-distance call to Aberdeen.* N COUNT 9.2 a request from someone asking you to go to them. EG *The firemen in our town receive about twelve hundred calls a year... The doctor was soon on his way to answer the next call.* N COUNT ● If someone such as a doctor is **on call**, they are ready to go out to work when someone asks them to, especially when there is an emergency. EG *The nurse had been on call for twenty-four hours... The army were always on call for situations where force was thought necessary.* ● PHR: USED AS AN A

10 If the person in charge of a meeting **calls** someone **to order**, he or she asks them to behave according to the rules of the meeting; a formal expression. EG *He called the speaker to order.* PHR: VB INFLECTS

11 If you **call** something such as a meeting or a rehearsal, you arrange for it to take place at a particular time. EG *He called a press conference to explain his proposals... The Prime Minister called a general election for June 9th... Whenever the union called a strike, the management agreed to negotiate.* V+O ⇑ organize = announce

12 If someone **is called** before a court of law or some other judicial committee, they are ordered to appear there, usually to give evidence. EG *Mrs Flanagan had been called as a witness in her son's divorce case.* V+O, OR V+O+A (as): USU PASS ⇑ summon

13 If you **feel called** to do something or **are called** to do something, you feel certain that God wants you to do it. EG *He believed that he had been called to become a monk. He felt called to work in the developing countries.* PHR: VB INFLECTS ⇑ be destined

14 If you **call** on someone, you make a short visit to see them or to deliver something. EG *'Goodnight. Do call again.'... The postman calls about 7 o'clock every morning.* V: IF+PREP THEN on/at ▸ used as a noun. EG *We went to pay a call on some people I used to know...* ▸ N COUNT

15 When a bus, train, or ship **calls** at a particular place, it stops there for a short time to allow people to get on or off. EG *The 9 o'clock train calls at every station between Glasgow and Edinburgh.* V+A ⇑ stop

16 In games and sports, if you **call**, you say that a coin will land with either the heads or the tails side upwards. You usually do this in order to decide who will do something such as serve first in tennis or bat first in cricket. EG *Gower called heads unsuccessfully for the third successive time.* V OR V+O (heads/tails) ⇑ guess

17 If you use **call** in such expressions as 'Let's call it £5' and 'Shall we call it a pound?', you are suggesting to the person you are talking to that they should agree to the amount mentioned. EG *'I owe you some money. We'll call it £10, shall we?'–'That sounds about right.'* V+O (it)+C

18 A **call** for something is a demand or desire for it to be done or to be provided. EG *Labour MPs renewed their call for the abolition of the House of Lords... There is little call for his services.* N COUNT: IF+PREP THEN for ⇑ request

19 If you say that **there is no call for** someone to behave in a particular way, you are indicating that PHR: VB INFLECTS

you disapprove of their behaviour and think that there is no good reason for it. EG *There is no call for you to be so rude.*

20 If you **have first call on** someone's time, help, etc, you know that if you ask them to do something they will do it before they do anything else because you are very important to them. EG *He has first call on his daughter's time.* PHR : VB INFLECTS

21 The **call** of something such as a place is the attraction or fascination that it has for you. EG *All his life he felt the call of the sea.* N SING : *the*+N, IF+PREP THEN *of* = lure

22 If you have or feel a **call**, you believe that there is something that God wants you to do. EG *He decided that he must answer the call and become a priest.* N SING WITH DET ⇑ vocation

23 A **call** is also **23.1** the sound or cry made by a bird or an animal. EG *Each type of animal produces its own characteristic call... The boys spent the whole of one afternoon practising bird calls.* N COUNT **23.2** a decision made by referee, umpire, or linesman in a sports match as to whether a ball is in or out of play. EG *McEnroe disagreed with the linesman's call.* N COUNT

24 The word **call** is also used in the following expressions, which are explained at other places in this dictionary. ● to **call** someone's **bluff**: see **bluff**. ● to **call it a day**: see **day**. ● to **call a halt**: see **halt**. ● to **call** something **to mind**: see **mind**. ● **a call of nature**: see **nature**. ● to **call** something **into question**: see **question**. ● to **call it quits**: see **quit**. ● to **call a spade a spade**: see **spade**. ● to **call the tune**: see **tune**. ● See also **curtain call**.

call back. If you **call** someone **back**, **1** you telephone them again or in return for a telephone call that they have made to you. EG *I told him I would call him back when I had some news... 'I'm sorry, Mr Smith is out.'–'Would you ask him to call me back as soon as possible.'* PHRASAL VB : V+ADV, OR V+O+ADV ⇑ contact = ring back **2** you ask them to return. EG *I was just leaving when my friend called me back.* PHRASAL VB : V+O+ADV

call down. If you **call down** something unpleasant on someone, you pray that it will happen to them. EG *She called down God's anger on her husband.* PHRASAL VB : V+O+ADV, IF+PREP THEN *on*

call for. **1** If you **call for** someone, you go to their house to collect them because you are going out somewhere together. EG *I'll call for you about eight.* PHRASAL VB : V+PREP, HAS PASS = pick up

2 If you **call for** something, **2.1** you go somewhere to collect it. EG *The parcel was kept at the Post Office until someone called for it.* PHRASAL VB : V+PREP **2.2** you demand that it should happen. EG *They passed a resolution attacking the government and calling for financial aid for the miners... The declaration called for an immediate cease-fire.* PHRASAL VB : V+PREP, HAS PASS ⇑ request

3 Something that **calls for** a particular action or quality needs it in order to be successful. EG *Controlling a class calls for all your skill as a teacher.* PHRASAL VB : V+PREP, HAS PASS = require

call forth. To **call** something **forth** means to make it exist; used in formal English. EG *He is not capable of calling forth much emotion in his readers.* PHRASAL VB : V+O+ADV = inspire

call in. **1** If you **call** someone **in**, you ask them to come to see you or to take action of some kind, often because you need help. EG *I was called in by my boss and given the good news... We called in the police and accused the boys of stealing.* PHRASAL VB : V+O+ADV = send for

2 If you **call in**, you make a telephone call, often to the place where you work, to report where you are or what you are doing. EG *He called in to say he was feeling ill.* PHRASAL VB : V+ADV = phone

3 If someone **calls** something **in**, they ask for it to be returned, for example because it might be dangerous or because it is needed. EG *Ford called in some Escorts to check their brakes... The university called in all library books for stocktaking.* PHRASAL VB : V+O+ADV = recall

call off. **1** If you **call off** something that has been planned, you cancel it. EG *They hoped that the strike would be called off... I shall feel myself free to call off.* PHRASAL VB : V+ADV, OR V+O+ADV

2 If you **call** a dog or a person **off**, you order them to stop attacking something or someone else. EG *He called his dog off when he saw that mine was frightened of it.* PHRASAL VB : V+O+ADV

call on. **1** If you **call on** or **upon** someone to do something, you appeal to them to do it. EG *The Opposition called on the Prime Minister to stop the arms deal.* PHRASAL VB : V+PREP, USU+*to*-INF, HAS PASS ⇑ ask

2 If you **call on** or **upon** something such as your strength, you summon it up and use it. EG *She had to call on all her courage to accept her child's death.* PHRASAL VB : V+PREP, USU+*to*-INF = summon up

call out. **1** If you **call** something **out**, you shout it in a loud voice because you want someone to hear you. EG *Karen called out and told us to be quiet... The driver didn't stop or even call out thank you... She turned into the yard, calling out to the porter that she'd arrived.* PHRASAL VB : V+ADV OR V+ADV+O/REPORT-CL/QUOTE = cry out

2 To **call** someone **out** means **1.1** to order them to come to help, especially in an emergency. EG *The government called out the army to help put out the fires... The National Guard has been called out by Governor Duck.* PHRASAL VB : V+O+ADV **1.2** to order them to go on strike. EG *They were called out for half a day.* PHRASAL VB : V+O+ADV

3 If one thing **calls out for** another, there is a very strong need for it to happen. EG *Even the smallest act of oppression calls out for universal condemnation.* PHRASAL VB : V+ADV+PREP = cry out for

call up. **1** If you **call up** or **call** someone **up**, you telephone them; an informal use. EG *The radio station had an open line on which listeners could call up to discuss various issues... Many of my friends called me up to congratulate me on my success.* PHRASAL VB : V+ADV, OR V+O+ADV ⇑ contact = phone up

2 To **call** someone **up** means to order them to join the army, navy, or air force. EG *I was extremely lucky not to be called up to fight in the last war.* PHRASAL VB : V+O+ADV = draft ▸ also used to ask people to be prepared to play in a sports match. EG *The manager of Aston Villa has called up his latest recruit as reserve for Saturday.* ● See also **call-up**.

3 If something **calls up** a memory of some person or event, it causes you to remember them. EG *The museum called up memories of my childhood.* PHRASAL VB : V+O+ADV = evoke

4 If you **call up** information that a computer holds, you instruct the computer to present it to you. EG *He was able to call up the information he needed direct from the resource catalogue.* PHRASAL VB : V+O+ADV ⇑ summon = access

call box, call boxes; also spelled with a hyphen. A **call box** is the same as a telephone box. N COUNT

caller /kɔ:lə/, **callers**. A **caller** is **1** a person who comes to see you for a short visit. EG *I had a lot of callers when I came home from hospital.* N COUNT ⇑ visitor **2** a person who is making a telephone call. EG *The telephone rang and the caller asked to speak to my mother.* N COUNT

call girl, call girls. A **call girl** is a prostitute who arranges meetings with her clients by telephone. N COUNT

calligraphy /kəlɪgrəfi[1]/ is **1** the art of producing beautiful handwriting using a brush or a special pen. N UNCOUNT **2** beautiful and artistic handwriting. EG *...an exhibition of Arabic calligraphy.* N UNCOUNT ⇑ writing

calling /kɔ:lɪŋ/. A **calling** is **1** a profession or career, especially one which involves helping other people. EG *Teaching is said to be a worthwhile calling.* N SING WITH DET = occupation **2** a strong feeling that you must do a particular job which involves helping people, especially as a priest. N SING WITH DET = vocation

calliper /kælɪpə/, **callipers**; also spelled **caliper**. **Callipers** are **1** instruments that are used to measure the size of things. They consist of two long thin pieces of metal joined together at one end by a hinge. N COUNT : USU PL ⇑ device **2** devices for supporting a person's leg when they cannot walk properly. They consist of metal rods that are held together by straps. N COUNT : USU PL ⇑ support

callisthenics /kælɪsθenɪks/; also spelled **calisthenics**. **Callisthenics** are simple exercises that you do to keep fit and healthy. EG *After a few days of doing calisthenics together, we added some simple karate exercises.* N PLURAL

callous /kæləs/. Someone who is **callous** is severe and cruel, and shows no concern for other people's feelings; also used to describe a person's behaviour. EG *She was selfish, arrogant and often callous... ...a shocking act of callous irresponsibility.* ADJ QUALIT ⇑ insensitive = unfeeling, heartless ≠ caring ◊ **callousness**. EG *It always distressed her, the callousness with which people were made to suffer.* ◊ N UNCOUNT

calloused /kæləst/. A foot or hand that is **calloused** is covered in calluses. EG *My feet became blackened, tough, split and calloused.* ADJ CLASSIF ⇑ roughened

callow /kæləʊ/. A young person who is **callow** has very little experience or knowledge of the way they should behave as an adult. EG *...a very callow youth.* ADJ QUALIT

call sign, call signs; also spelled with a hyphen. A **call sign** is the letters and numbers which identify a person, vehicle, or organization that is broadcasting on the radio or sending messages by radio. N COUNT ⇑ identification

call-up, call-ups. **1** If a person gets their **call-up** papers, they receive an official order to join the army, navy, or air force; used in British English. N BEFORE N = draft

2 A **call-up** is the number of people who are ordered to report for service in the armed forces. N COUNT = draft

callus /kæləs/, **calluses**. A **callus** is an area of unwanted, unnaturally thick skin, usually on the N COUNT ⇑ growth palms of your hands or the soles of your feet, which has been caused by rubbing.

calm /kɑːm/, **calmer, calmest; calms, calming, calmed.** 1 Someone who is **calm** does not show any worry or excitement. EG *Gary was a calm and reasonable man... 'Sit down and keep calm'... Her voice was calm, just loud enough to make itself heard over the crowd... I felt calmer and more composed.* ◊ **calmly.** EG *It was a wonder that she could sit there so calmly... She calmly wiped the blood away with her hand.* ◊ **calmness.** EG *A great sense of calmness began to settle upon her.* — ADJ QUALIT ⇑ unemotional = quiet, steady; ◊ ADV WITH VB = coolly; ◊ N UNCOUNT

2 **Calm** is a state of quietness and peacefulness, when there is no loud noise or hurried movement from things such as traffic and crowds of people. EG *...the peace of the countryside, the calm of the vicarage... There is a wonderful calm in the park... Calm descended once again on the village as the last coach left.* — N UNCOUNT ⇑ quiet = peace ≠ bustle

3 A sea or lake that is **calm** does not have any big waves because there is no strong wind. EG *He was not afraid, for the water was calm, and he wasn't very far from shore... ..a clear, blue sky and calm sea.* — ADJ QUALIT ⇑ still ≠ rough

4 Weather that is **calm** is very still without any wind. EG *It was a calm, sunny evening.* ▸ used as a noun. EG *The calm was almost oppressive.* — ADJ QUALIT; ▸ N COUNT ⇑ stillness

5 When the weather or the sea **calms** or when something **calms** it, it becomes quiet and still. — V-ERG

6 If you **calm** someone or **calm** their fears, you do something to make them less upset, worried, or excited. EG *She began to weep in gasping, choking sobs, and Meadows tried to calm her... He was starting to shake with excitement, and to calm himself he walked over to the window... The chairman tried to calm their fears.* — V+O (NG/REFL) = quieten ≠ excite

calm down. If you **calm down** or if someone **calms** you **down**, you become less upset, excited, or lively. EG *'Please, Mrs Kinter,' said Brody. 'Calm down. Let me explain'... An officer tried to calm them down but had no success.* — PHRASAL VB : V-ERG+ADV = cool down

Calor gas /kælə gæs/is a trademark in Britain for gas that is sold in portable metal containers. People use it for cooking and heating when they are camping or living in a place where there is no gas supply. EG *...a little Calor gas stove.* — N UNCOUNT

calorie /kæləri¹/, **calories.** A **calorie** is 1 a unit of measurement for the energy value of food. EG *He was put on a diet of only 1,700 calories a day to lose weight... A nursing mother needs extra calories for the baby's milk.* 2 the amount of heat needed to raise the temperature of one gram of water by 1C; a technical term in physics. — N COUNT : USU PL; N COUNT : USU PL

calorific /kælərɪfɪk/ means relating to calories or heat; a technical term. — ADJ CLASSIF : ATTRIB

calumny /kælə°mni¹/, **calumnies. Calumny** or a **calumny** is an untrue statement made about someone in order to reduce other people's respect and admiration for them; a formal word. EG *The Lord Chancellor became the target for further calumny.* — N UNCOUNT/ COUNT ⇑ falsehood = slander

calve /kɑːv/, **calves, calving, calved.** When cows or some other animals **calve**, they give birth to calves. EG *The whales stay near Hawaii for several months, calving, mating and singing.* ◊ **calving.** EG *We got eight out of ten heifers during the calving.* — V; ◊ N UNCOUNT

calves /kɑːvz/ is the plural of **calf.**

calypso /kəlɪpsəu/, **calypsos.** A **calypso** is a song about something topical or interesting, sung in a style which comes from the West Indies. — N COUNT

cam /kæm/, **cams.** A **cam** is a part of an engine which is designed to change circular motion into motion up and down or from side to side; a technical term. — N COUNT ⇑ device

camaraderie /kæmərɑːdəri¹/ is a feeling of trust and friendship that exists among a group of people who have known each other or worked together for a long time. EG *There was a camaraderie between the girls.* — N UNCOUNT = comradeship

camber /kæmbə/, **cambers.** A **camber** is a gradual downward slope from the centre of a road to each side of it. EG *The road-builders dug out earth for the camber.* — N COUNT

cambric /kæɪmbrɪk/ is thin, white cloth made of linen or cotton. — N UNCOUNT

came /keɪm/ is the past tense of **come.**

camel /kæmə°l/, **camels.** A **camel** is a large animal that lives in desert areas and is used for carrying goods and people. Camels have long necks and one or two humps on their backs, depending on the species they belong to. — N COUNT

camel hair is soft, thick woollen cloth, usually creamy brown in colour, which is used especially for making coats. — N UNCOUNT : USU BEFORE N

camellia /kəmiːlɪə/, **camellias.** A **camellia** is a tall plant that has shiny leaves and large white, pink, or red flowers similar to a rose. — N COUNT

cameo /kæmɪəu/, **cameos.** A **cameo** is 1 a short description or piece of acting which expresses cleverly and neatly the nature of a particular situation, event, or person's character. EG *She has starred in several small but delightful cameo parts. He gave cameos of debates with exquisite touches of irony.* 2 a piece of jewellery, usually oval in shape, consisting of a raised stone figure or design fixed on to a flat stone of another colour. — N COUNT ⇑ representation; N COUNT

camera /kæmə°rə/, **cameras.** 1 A **camera** is 1.1 a piece of equipment that is used for taking photographs or films. EG *I took a camera and photographed some of the flora... ...the film's superb camera work... Is it acceptable to make such a film, to point the camera so relentlessly at a dying man?* 1.2 a piece of equipment that focuses on something to be broadcast on television and that turns the image into electrical signals. EG *The press and television cameras were gathered... Television pictures were transmitted from a camera in the plane.* ● If people are **on camera**, they are being televised. — N COUNT; N COUNT; ● PHR : USED AS A C

2 If a trial or a hearing is held **in camera**, the public or press is not allowed to attend; a legal term. — PHR : USED AS AN A

cameraman /kæmə°rəmə³n/, **cameramen.** A **cameraman** is a person who operates a camera for television or film making. EG *The film was shot by cameraman Chris Menges.* — N COUNT ⇑ operator

camera-shy. Someone who is **camera-shy** is nervous and uncomfortable about being filmed or about having their photograph taken. — ADJ QUALIT

camomile /kæməmaɪl/; also spelled **chamomile. Camomile** is a scented plant with daisy-like flowers. It is often used to make herbal tea. — N UNCOUNT

camouflage /kæməflɑːʒ/, **camouflages, camouflaging, camouflaged.** 1 **Camouflage** consists of things such as leaves, branches, or brown and green paint, which are used to hide military forces and equipment from the enemy. EG *The soldiers dived into the camouflage as 'Target seen!' was bellowed.* ▸ used as a verb. EG *The Royal Artillery were well camouflaged.* — N UNCOUNT ⇑ cover; ▸ V+O ⇑ conceal

2 **Camouflage** is a way in which animals avoid being seen and caught by being coloured and shaped to blend in with their natural surroundings. EG *The snake's skin has the colours and patterns necessary for perfect camouflage.* — N UNCOUNT ⇑ concealment

3 To **camouflage** something such as a situation or a fact means to hide it or make it appear to be something different. EG *I could sense already a camouflaged violence in this town.* ▸ used as a noun. EG *...the enrichment of privilege behind the camouflage of hereditary pageantry.* — V+O ⇑ conceal = disguise; ▸ N UNCOUNT = disguise, screen

camp /kæmp/, **camps, camping, camped.** 1 A **camp** is a place where people live in tents or stay in tents on holiday. EG *The camp had a beautiful view of the mountains... He's going off to scout camp on Friday.* — N COUNT, OR PREP+N UNCOUNT

2 If you **make camp**, you put up your tent in a place where you are going to stay. EG *Let's make camp for the night here.* — PHR : VB INFLECTS

3 If you **break camp**, you put away your tent and leave the place where you have been staying. EG *When we broke camp in the morning, we found animal tracks all around us.* — PHR : VB INFLECTS

4 If you **camp**, you stay or live somewhere for a short time in a tent or a caravan. EG *That night I camped in the hills... Are we going to go camping? ...camping equipment.* — V

5 A **camp** is also 5.1 a collection of huts and other buildings that is specially built by the army for soldiers so that they can live and work there while they are in the army. EG *The road between the camp and the hospital compound was guarded day and night... When we got to camp, he put in his report, 'One killed in action.'* 5.2 a number of buildings that has been specially built for particular people to live in, especially prisoners who are sent there and guarded. EG *The general moved George and his fellow prisoners to a camp nearer the capital... ...the* — N COUNT, OR PREP+N UNCOUNT; N COUNT : USU+ MOD

extermination camp... Three fifths of the refugees in the camp were starving.

6 You can also use **a camp** to refer to a group of people who all support a particular idea, person, or belief. EG *The dilemma is serious for conservatives in the Western camp... The realignment produced two clear-cut camps, reformists and reactionaries.* — N COUNT+SUPP = faction

7 Something that is **camp** is designed or made in an exaggerated or vulgar style that makes it interesting and amusing; an informal use. EG *...the Albert Room, brightly lit by electricity and done out in camp Victorian detail.* ▸ used as a noun. EG *...the cheap theatre, a world of high camp and low life.* — ADJ QUALIT ⇑ excessive ≠ subtle, tasteful; ▸ N UNCOUNT

8 A man who is **camp** behaves or dresses in an exaggerated or affected way that many people consider to be typical of homosexuals; an informal use, often showing disapproval. — ADJ QUALIT ⇑ effeminate

9 If you **camp it up**, you deliberately act in an exaggerated or affected way; an informal expression, used mainly in British English. — PHR : VB INFLECTS

camp out. If you **camp out**, you sleep outdoors in a tent. — PHRASAL VB : V+ADV

campaign /kæmpeɪn/, **campaigns, campaigning, campaigned**. A **campaign** is 1 a planned set of activities that people deliberately carry out over a period of time in order to produce a particular result, especially in order to achieve social or political change. EG *She was asked to help plan Labour's election campaign... The black response to these laws was a campaign of violence... ...the campaign against world hunger.* ▸ used as a verb. EG *He campaigned for political reform... They successfully campaigned to get their scheme accepted... The reforms follow six years of campaigning by pressure groups.* 2 a series of planned movements or activities carried out by the armed forces in order to achieve a particular result during a war. EG *...the enormous catastrophe of the Dardanelles campaign in the First World War... ...the right to conduct bombing campaigns against military targets in Britain.* — N COUNT = crusade; ▸ V ⇑ work = battle; N COUNT = expedition

campaigner /kæmpeɪnə/, **campaigners**. A **campaigner** is a person who campaigns for social or political change. EG *Boaks is an energetic campaigner in the cause of road safety... ...anti-apartheid campaigners.* ● If you describe someone as an **old campaigner**, you mean that they have had a lot of experience in a particular activity. — N COUNT = crusader; ● PHR

camp bed, camp beds; also spelled with a hyphen. A **camp bed** is a bed that you can fold up and take with you when you go camping, or use as a spare bed in your home. — N COUNT

camper /kæmpə/, **campers**. A **camper** is 1 a person who goes camping or who stays in a holiday camp. EG *...the makers of equipment for hunters, campers and fishermen.* 2 a van that has been specially designed so that you can live, cook, and sleep in it. EG *People are parking their cars and campers all over the hillside... ...a camper van equipped with an oven.* — N COUNT; N COUNT

camp fire, camp fires; also spelled with a hyphen. A **camp fire** is a fire that you light out of doors when you are camping. EG *...a circle of boys round a camp fire.* — N COUNT

camp follower, camp followers; also spelled with a hyphen. A **camp follower** is 1 someone who does not officially belong to a particular group or organization but who is interested in it and supports it, often because it makes them feel important. EG *She wanted to be more than a hanger-on, a camp follower: she wanted to be a full member.* 2 a person who obtains money by travelling with a group of people such as an army and doing jobs for them. — N COUNT ⇑ follower = minion; N COUNT ⇑ follower

campground /kæmpgraʊnd/, **campgrounds**. A **campground** is a campsite; used mainly in American English. EG *The campgrounds he stopped at were filled with people.* — N COUNT

camping site, camping sites. A **camping site** is the same as a campsite. — N COUNT

campion /kæmpɪən/, **campions**. A **campion** is a plant that grows wild in Europe and has red, pink, or white flowers. — N COUNT

campsite /kæmpsaɪt/, **campsites**; also spelled with a hyphen or as two words. A **campsite** is a place where people who are on holiday can put up their tents and stay, or can stay in tents that are provided for them. — N COUNT

campus /kæmpəs/, **campuses**. A **campus** is the area of land that contains the main buildings of a university such as the lecture rooms, administration offices, sports facilities, and some living accommodation for students. EG *The new concert hall will be built on the university campus... How many students live on campus at the moment?* — N COUNT, OR PREP+N UNCOUNT = grounds, site

camshaft /kæmʃɑːft/, **camshafts**. A **camshaft** is a part of an engine consisting of a rod with one or more cams attached to it; a technical term. — N COUNT

can, could; cans, canning, canned. In paragraphs 1 to 4.3, the word **can** is pronounced /kæn/ or /kən/; in paragraphs 5 to 9.2 it is pronounced /kæn/. The form **could** is used in paragraphs 1 to 4.3, and the forms **cans, canning, canned** are used in paragraphs 5 and 6. The modal verb **could** is normally used in reported speech where the words that were said included 'can', and so in that sense it acts as a past tense of the modal verb **can**. It is also used as the past tense of **can** in paragraph 3. Otherwise, the relationship between **can** and **could** is that **could** is used for events that are less likely or less definite. **1 Can** is used **1.1** to indicate that it is possible for someone to do something or for something to happen. EG *Anybody can become a qualified teacher... I know a place where you can hire boots... Many elderly people cannot afford telephones... 'Will you stay for lunch?'–'I can't,' the colonel said... They complained that they couldn't sleep.* **1.2** with verbs expressing belief or opinion to indicate that you find something reasonable or acceptable or that you are prepared to do something. EG *We can see what he meant... I cannot accept this view... You can understand their feelings... I don't think you can draw a distinction between them... There can be no doubt about this.* **1.3** with 'I' and 'we' to indicate that an action is possible and that the person speaking is considering doing it. EG *I can pop in and see you tomorrow... We can plant a few trees in the garden.* — MODAL; MODAL; MODAL ⇑ will

2 Can is used to express possibility in place of a range of other modals. It is used **2.1** to say that someone is allowed to do something. Some speakers of English think that it is incorrect to use 'can' instead of 'may' with this meaning, but in fact most speakers use both 'can' and 'may'. EG *In a Moslem marriage, the man can have as many wives as he wants... You can borrow that pen if you want to... There are rather detailed rules of when you can and can't appeal.* **2.2** in questions when you are asking for something, asking for permission to do something, or asking whether you can help. EG *Can I speak to Nicky please?... Can I light the fire? I'm cold... Can we have something to wipe our hands on please... Can I help you?... What can I do for you?* **2.3** in questions when you are asking someone to do something for you. EG *Can you tell me the time?... Can you do me a favour?... If you can just sign the booking form there for me please!* **2.4** in speech as a polite way of interrupting someone or of introducing what you are going to say next. These are polite requests which are not normally refused. EG *That sounds, if I can interrupt you, that sounds a very complicated argument... Can I just intervene for one moment?... Can I ask a question here now?* — MODAL; MODAL : USU+*I/we* = could, may; MODAL : USU+*you* = could; MODAL : USU+*I* = could

3 Can is also used to indicate that you have a particular skill or ability and are therefore able to do the thing mentioned. EG *Some people can ski better than others... He cannot dance... My wife can't sew... A lot of them couldn't read or write... I enjoyed teaching and I could actually do it.* — MODAL

4 Can is also used in the following ways with a negative. **Cannot** or **can't** is used **4.1** to indicate that you think that it is very important or necessary that something should not happen or that someone should not do something. EG *We can't stop now. We've got to keep on struggling... 'I'm going to post a letter.'–'You can't!' said Phyllis. 'Suppose you're seen...' We can hardly blame her for ignorance.* **4.2** in questions when you are urging someone to do something, especially when there is some difficulty or when they do not want to do it. EG *Can't you find a baby-sitter and come over for dinner?... Can't we talk about it?... For goodness sake! Can't you keep your voice down?* **4.3** to indicate that you feel sure that something is not true or that something will not happen. EG *This cannot be the whole story... The repression can't last... Top secret, he said–but that* — MODAL WITH BROAD NEG = mustn't; MODAL+*not*; MODAL WITH BROAD NEG *can't apply to you, can it?... The two conflicting messages cannot possibly both be true.* • **Can't have** is used to indicate that you are sure that what you are saying is true, or that you are right to deny something, although you have no proof and do not know for certain. EG *He can't have said that. He just can't... Twenty francs can't have been nearly enough to pay for all the food.* — MODAL WITH BROAD NEG

5 A **can** is a metal container in which something such as food, drink, paint, etc is put. The container is usually sealed so that the contents remain fresh for a long time. EG *...cans of beans... ...a tray of beer cans... ...a can of petrol.* — N COUNT = tin

6 If you **can** food or drink, you put it into a metal container and seal it so that no air can get in and it will remain fresh for a long time. EG *They discovered how to can food.* ◇ **canned.** EG *Fruits and vegetables may be fresh, canned, frozen, or dried... ...canned beer.* ◇ **canning.** EG *...a canning factory.* • See also **canned.** — V+O ↑ preserve; ◇ ADJ CLASSIF = tinned; ◇ N UNCOUNT, OR N BEFORE N

7 If you have to **carry the can**, you have to take all the blame for something that has happened; an informal expression in British English. — PHR : VB INFLECTS

8 If you say that something such as a job that you are doing is **in the can**, you mean that it is completely finished; an informal expression. — PHR : USED AS AN A ↑ completed

9 In informal American English, the **can** is **9.1** prison. EG *He spent two years in the can for armed robbery.* — N SING : *the*+N
9.2 the toilet. — N SING : *the*+N

Canadian /kəneɪdɪən/, **Canadians. 1** Someone or something that is **Canadian** belongs or relates to Canada or to its people. — ADJ CLASSIF

2 A **Canadian** is a person who comes from Canada. — N COUNT

canal /kənæl/, **canals.** A **canal** is **1** a long, narrow stretch of water that has been made for boats to travel along or to bring water to a particular area. EG *...the canals of Venice... ...the Suez Canal... ...irrigation canals.* **2** a narrow tube inside your body for carrying food, air, or other substances. EG *...the alimentary canal.* — N COUNT ↑ waterway; N COUNT

canalize /kænəlaɪz/, **canalizes, canalizing, canalized**; also spelled **canalise.** To **canalize** feelings or activities means to direct them into something in order to try to achieve a particular result; a formal word. EG *Their discontent could be canalized into political revolution.* — V+O ↑ direct = channel

canapé /kænəpeɪ/, **canapés.** A **canapé** is a small piece of biscuit, toast, etc with meat, cheese, or other savoury food on top. Canapés are often served with drinks at parties. — N COUNT

canard /kænɑːd/, **canards.** A **canard** is an idea or a piece of information that is false. Canards are often made up and spread deliberately, sometimes in order to discredit someone or their work. EG *This might risk perpetuating the canard that blacks are the cause of racial tension.* — N COUNT ↑ rumour = myth

canary /kəneəri[1]/, **canaries.** A **canary** is a small yellow bird which sings beautifully. People sometimes keep canaries in cages as pets. — N COUNT

can-can, can-cans. The **can-can** is a dance in which women kick their legs in the air and shake their skirts to fast music. — N COUNT : USU *the*+N IN SING

cancel /kænsəl/, **cancels, cancelling, cancelled**; also spelled **canceling** and **canceled** in American English. **1** If you **cancel** something that had been arranged, you stop it from happening. EG *The performances were cancelled because the leading man was ill... British Airways are temporarily cancelling flights to Poland and Turkey.* ◇ **cancellation** /kænsə'leɪʃə⁰n/, **cancellations.** EG *...the cancellation of the tour.* — V+O = call off; ◇ N UNCOUNT/ COUNT

2 If you **cancel** something that you have reserved, for example a hotel room or a seat at a theatre, you tell the management that you no longer want it. EG *I'll cancel those seats at the theatre.* ◇ **cancellation, cancellations.** EG *I've had two cancellations already this morning.* — V+O ↑ give up; ◇ N COUNT

3 If you **cancel** something such as a cheque or a business contract, you cause it to be no longer valid. EG *He said he would cancel the debt if he could marry his daughter.* — V+O ↑ invalidate = erase

4 If you **cancel** a piece of writing, you cross it out by putting a line through it. — V+O = delete

cancel out. If one thing **cancels** another thing **out** or if two things **cancel** each other **out**, the two things have opposite effects so that when they are combined no real effect is produced. EG *The one effect tends to cancel the other out... These political factions cancelled each other out.* — PHRASAL VB : V+ ADV OR V+O+ ADV : RECIP = neutralize

cancer /kænsə/, **cancers. 1 Cancer** or a **cancer** is a serious disease in which cells in a part of a person's body increase in number rapidly in an uncontrolled way, producing abnormal growths. EG *He had cancer of the throat... Nicholas was dying of lung cancer... These rays falling on unprotected fair skin can produce a cancer... ...an attempt to prevent cancer cells spreading.* — N UNCOUNT/ COUNT

2 A **cancer** is a situation which you consider to be evil and unpleasant and which is becoming rapidly more common and widespread; a formal use. EG *What was happening was a sickness, a cancer in society that could not be helped.* — N COUNT = blight

cancerous /kænsərəs/. Something that is **cancerous** is connected with the disease cancer. EG *...cancerous cells in the blood.* — ADJ CLASSIF ↑ diseased

candelabra /kændə²lɑːbrə/, **candelabrum, candelabras.** The singular can be either **candelabra** or **candelabrum** and the plural can be either **candelabra** or **candelabras.** A **candelabra** is an ornamental holder for two or more candles. EG *...a splendid great brass candelabra... ...a heavy bronze candelabrum... ...two giant candelabra.* — N COUNT

candid /kændɪd/. When you are **candid** with someone, you speak honestly to them and do not try to hide anything. EG *We should aim to be as candid as possible about our disappointments... I take it that you've been quite candid with me, and that you are no longer involved.* — ADJ QUALIT ↑ truthful = frank, open ≠ guarded

candidacy /kændɪdəsi[1]/ is the position of being a candidate in an election. EG *He had already formally announced his candidacy... ...the party which has been supporting Mr Benn's candidacy.* — N UNCOUNT : USU POSS+N = candidature

candidate /kændɪdɛ⁰ɪt/, **candidates.** A **candidate** is **1** a person who is being considered for a position, for example one of the people who stand in an election or one of the people who apply for a job. EG *If no candidate gets 50 per cent or more, a second ballot must be held... She was adopted as Labour candidate for Stoke-on-Trent... We're prepared to take candidates from any academic discipline.* **2** a person who is taking an examination. EG *Sixty per cent of the candidates failed their examinations.* **3** a person or thing that is regarded as being suitable for a particular purpose or as being likely to be affected by something. EG *Sea urchins and corals are promising candidates for preservation... Middle-size oil companies are likely candidates for take-over.* — N COUNT ↑ applicant; N COUNT; N COUNT ↑ possibility

candidature /kændɪtətʃə/. Someone's **candidature** is their candidacy; a formal British word. EG *...the controversial tactics of people supporting his candidature.* — N UNCOUNT/ COUNT

candidly /kændɪdli[1]/. **1** If you speak **candidly** to someone, you speak honestly and do not try to hide anything. EG *She answered his questions fully and candidly.* — ADV = frankly

2 You sometimes use **candidly** when you want your hearers to realize that you are expressing your honest opinion, and perhaps saying something slightly indiscreet which you do not want them to repeat to other people. EG *Candidly, Daniel, I hoped I might manage to avoid going to her party this time.* — ADV SEN = frankly

candied /kændi[1]d/. **Candied** fruit or other food has a covering of sugar or has been cooked in sugar syrup in order to preserve it. EG *...currants and candied peel.* — ADJ CLASSIF : USU ATTRIB ↑ sugared

candle /kændə⁰l/, **candles. 1** A **candle** is a stick or block of hard wax with a piece of string through the middle which you light in order to give a flame that provides light. EG *I blew out my candle and went to sleep... The little scullery was lit by one wavering candle.* — N COUNT

2 The word **candle** is also used in the following informal expressions. **2.1** If you **burn the candle at both ends**, you try to do too many things and so you have to stay up very late at night and get up very early in the morning in order to get them all done. EG *It can be done within the time allowed if I burn the candle at both ends.* **2.2** Someone or something that **can't hold a candle to** someone or something else is of a much lower standard, quality, or value in comparison. EG *This production can't hold a candle to Jonathan Miller's.* **2.3** If you say that **the game is not worth the candle**, you mean that something is not worth the effort or trouble that is needed to achieve — PHR : VB INFLECTS; PHR : AUX INFLECTS ↑ be inferior to; PHR : VB INFLECTS or obtain it. EG *We began to wonder whether the game was worth the candle.*

candlelight /kændəᵒllaɪt/ is the light that a candle produces. EG *His eyes were shining in the candlelight... She was reading a book by candlelight.* N UNCOUNT

candlelit /kændəᵒllɪt/. A room, table, etc that is **candlelit** is lit by the light of candles. EG *...a little candlelit restaurant.* ADJ CLASSIF: USU ATTRIB

candlestick /kændəᵒlstɪk/, **candlesticks**. A **candlestick** is a narrow object with a hole or a spike at the top which holds a candle. N COUNT ⇑ holder

candour /kændə/; also spelled **candor** in American English. **Candour** is the quality of speaking honestly and openly and not hiding any facts. EG *They were talking of personal matters with unusual candour.* N UNCOUNT = frankness

candy /kændi¹/, **candies**. A **candy** is a sweet, and **candy** is sweets in general; used especially in American English. EG *You eat too much candy. It's bad for your teeth... ...cookies and candies.* N UNCOUNT/COUNT ⇑ food = sweet

candy floss is a large soft mass of pink or white sugar threads which is put on a stick and eaten, usually out of doors; used in British English. N UNCOUNT = cotton candy

candy-striped. **Candy-striped** cloth has narrow alternate white and coloured stripes, especially white and pink. ADJ CLASSIF ⇑ striped

cane /keɪn/, **canes, caning, caned**. **1** **Cane** is **1.1** the long hollow stems of a plant such as bamboo. EG *...sugar cane.* N UNCOUNT **1.2** strips of the stems of plants that are used for weaving things such as baskets or the seats of chairs. EG *It was made entirely of cane... ...cane chairs.* N UNCOUNT ⇑ material

2 A **cane** is **2.1** a tall narrow stick, usually made of bamboo, which is used for supporting plants in gardens. N COUNT **2.2** a long thin flexible stick used to hit people as a punishment, especially at school. N COUNT **2.3** a long specially-shaped stick that people lean on to help them walk. Canes like this used to be carried as a fashion. The white sticks carried by blind people are also sometimes referred to as 'canes'. EG *...elderly American ladies leaning on their canes... ...a young man with eye-glass and cane.* N COUNT ⇑ support

3 At school, if a child is given the **cane**, he or she is punished by being hit with a cane. EG *I got the cane for smoking.* N SING: *the*+N

4 If you **cane** someone, you hit them with a cane as a punishment. EG *If you even said 'Dash', you got caned.* V+O ⇑ punish = beat

canine /keɪnaɪn, kæn-/, **canines**. **1** **Canine** means relating to dogs or resembling a dog. ADJ CLASSIF: ATTRIB

2 **Canines** or **canine teeth** are pointed teeth near the front of the mouths of humans and some animals. Humans have four canines. EG *She was getting a crown put on a left upper canine.* N COUNT: USU PL ⇑ tooth

canister /kænɪstə/, **canisters**. A **canister** is **1** a container with a lid which is used for storing foods such as sugar or flour. EG *He opened the lid of a canister of tea.* N COUNT = caddy **2** a sealed can containing a substance which is forced out when you press a button. EG *...a canister of shaving cream.* N COUNT **3** a strong metal container which is used for holding gases or chemical substances. EG *...canisters of nerve gas.* ⇑ container N COUNT

canker /kæŋkə/, **cankers**. **1** A **canker** is something evil that spreads and affects things or people; a formal word. EG *There is no time to lose in cutting out the Nazi canker... Hypocrisy is the canker in the soul of these people.* N COUNT = cancer, scourge

2 **Canker** is **2.1** a disease which affects the mouth and ears of animals and people, spreading quickly and making the skin sore. N UNCOUNT **2.2** a disease which affects the wood of shrubs and trees, making the outer layer peel away to expose the inside of the stem. N UNCOUNT

cannabis /kænəbɪs/ is a drug made from the hemp plant which some people smoke like a cigarette to make them feel relaxed. Cannabis is illegal in many countries. EG *He was imprisoned for three years for dealing in cannabis.* ▸ **Cannabis** is also used to refer to the plant from which the drug is made. N UNCOUNT = marijuana, pot

canned /kænd/. **1** **Canned** music, laughter, or applause has been recorded beforehand rather than being produced at the time that you hear it; used showing disapproval. EG *Sometimes one gets tired of canned music.* ADJ CLASSIF: USU ATTRIB = instant ≠ live

2 Someone who is **canned** is drunk; an informal use. EG *We get canned every Saturday night.* • See also **can**. ADJ QUALIT: PRED

cannery /kænəri¹/, **canneries**. A **cannery** is a factory where food is canned. N COUNT

cannibal /kænɪbəᵒl/, **cannibals**. A **cannibal** is **1** a person who eats the flesh of other human beings. N COUNT **2** an animal which eats other animals of its own type. EG *...cannibal fish.* N COUNT

cannibalism /kænɪ¹bəlɪzəᵒm/. People or animals who practise **cannibalism** eat the flesh of living things of the same type as themselves. N UNCOUNT

cannibalize /kænɪ¹bəlaɪz/, **cannibalizes, cannibalizing, cannibalized**; also spelled **cannibalise**. If you **cannibalize** a machine or vehicle, you take parts from it in order to repair another machine or vehicle. V+O

cannon /kænən/, **cannons, cannoning, cannoned**. The plural of the noun can be either **cannon** or **cannons**. A **cannon** is **1** a large gun, usually on wheels, which used to be used in battles to fire heavy metal balls at the enemy. EG *They entered battle with just 600 men, seventeen horses and ten cannon.* N COUNT **2** a heavy automatic gun that is fired from an aircraft. N COUNT

cannon into. To **cannon into** people or things means to collide with them with great force. EG *Running round the corner, she cannoned into the headmistress.* PHRASAL VB: V+PREP ⇑ bump into

cannonade /kænəneɪd/, **cannonades**. A **cannonade** is an intense and continuous attack on something using guns. EG *There was a sudden cannonade of artillery.* N COUNT = barrage

cannon ball, cannon balls. A **cannon ball** is a heavy metal ball that is fired from a cannon. N COUNT ⇑ ammunition

cannon fodder. Soldiers who were expected to fight in battles in which large numbers of people would be killed were sometimes referred to as **cannon fodder**, especially in the First World War. EG *These people are cannon fodder in rivalries with bordering states.* N UNCOUNT = pawn

cannot /kænɒt, kænɒt/ is the negative form of **can**.

canny /kæni¹/, **cannier, canniest**. Someone who is **canny** is **1** clever and quick-witted. EG *...a canny lad.* ADJ QUALIT ▸ used of a person's behaviour. EG *...a canny smile.* ▸ ADJ QUALIT ◊ **cannily**. EG *I've watched you looking at people cannily.* ◊ ADV **2** careful and clever, especially when dealing with money. EG *...a canny Scots housekeeper.* ADJ QUALIT = shrewd ▸ used of a person's actions. EG *Tim made a cannier bargain this time.*

canoe /kənu:/, **canoes**. A **canoe** is a small light boat, often pointed at each end, that you row using a paddle. N COUNT

canoeing /kənu:ɪŋ/ is the sport of racing and performing tests of skill in canoes. EG *The centre provides facilities for rock climbing, sailing, and canoeing.* N UNCOUNT

canon /kænən/, **canons**. A **canon** is **1** a member of the clergy who is on the staff of and so is attached to a cathedral. EG *John Drury was until last year canon of Norwich Cathedral... Canon Barnett was evidently a powerful speaker.* N COUNT: ALSO IN TITLES ⇑ clergyman **2** one of the rules or principles on which something is based; a formal use. EG *Internationalism was a fundamental canon of Trotskyism... ...the traditional canons of literary and artistic judgement.* N COUNT+SUPP ⇑ principle = rule **3** all the writings by a particular author which are known to be genuine; a technical use in literature. EG *He was planning a book on Jane Austen which would work through the whole canon, one novel at a time.* N COUNT: USU SING ⇑ works

canonical /kənɒnɪkəᵒl/ means allowed by canon law. ADJ CLASSIF: ATTRIB

canonize /kænənaɪz/, **canonizes, canonizing, canonized**; also spelled **canonise**. If a dead person **is canonized**, it is officially announced that he or she is a saint and should be honoured by the rest of the church; used especially in the Catholic Church. EG *Two years after his death the bishop was canonised.* V+O: USU PASS ⇑ glorify = beatify

canon law is the law of the Christian church. It has authority only for that church and its members. EG *Canon law decreed that adultery was as reprehensible for a husband as for a wife.* N UNCOUNT

canoodle /kənu:dəᵒl/, **canoodles, canoodling, canoodled**. If two people are **canoodling**, they are kissing and cuddling each other a lot; an informal word in British English. EG *Over in the corner a couple sat canoodling.* V ⇑ cuddle

canopied /kænəpi¹d/. A building or piece of furniture that is **canopied** is covered with a roof or piece of material supported by poles. EG *The houses all had bright windows and canopied balconies.* ADJ CLASSIF

canopy /kænəpi¹/, **canopies**. A **canopy** is 1 a cover such as a roof or piece of material which is placed over something in order to provide shelter or as a decoration. EG *There was a large bed with a silk canopy over it.* 2 something else that spreads out and covers an area, such as the branches and leaves that spread out at the top of trees in a forest. EG *He climbed a tree and parted the canopy... The leaves created a dense canopy that cut out much of the light.* N COUNT = awning; N COUNT : USU SING ↑ cover = screen

cant /kænt/. Moral or religious statements are referred to as **cant** when they are made by someone who does not really believe what they are saying. EG *There has been a good deal of hypocritical cant.* N UNCOUNT ↑ insincerity = humbug ≠ honesty

can't /kɑ:nt/ is the usual spoken form of 'cannot'.

cantankerous /kə³ntæŋkə⁰rəs/. A **cantankerous** person is always finding things to argue or complain about. EG *Their boredom made them quarrelsome and cantankerous.* ADJ QUALIT

cantata /kæntɑ:tə/, **cantatas**. A **cantata** is a fairly short musical work for singers and instruments. EG *He sang arias from Bach cantatas.* N COUNT ↑ music

canteen /kænti:n/, **canteens**. A **canteen** is 1 a part of a factory or other place of work where workers go to eat. EG *...the works canteen... I had a cup of tea in the canteen.* 2 a temporary kitchen that is set up, often in a caravan, to provide food for people such as soldiers or policemen when they are working outside. EG *...a police mobile canteen.* 3 a special box containing a set of cutlery. EG *...a canteen of cutlery.* N COUNT = cafeteria; N COUNT; N COUNT

canter /kæntə/, **canters, cantering, cantered**. When a horse **canters**, it moves at a speed which is slower than a gallop but faster than a trot. EG *She heard the sound of his horse cantering up the sandy path.* ▸ used as a noun. EG *It broke into an easy canter.* V ↑ move; ▸ N COUNT : USU a+N IN SING

canticle /kæntɪkə⁰l/, **canticles**. A **canticle** is a short religious song, especially one that uses words taken from the Bible. N COUNT

cantilever /kæntɪli:və/, **cantilevers**. A **cantilever** is a long piece of metal, wood, etc that is fastened to something at one end, and the other end is used to support a structure such as an arch or bridge. N COUNT

cantilever bridge, cantilever bridges. A **cantilever bridge** is a bridge made of or supported by two cantilevers which meet in the middle. N COUNT

canto /kæntəʊ/, **cantos**. A **canto** is one of the main sections of a long poem. N COUNT

canton /kæntɒn/, **cantons**. A **canton** is a political or administrative region in some countries, for example Switzerland. EG *Which canton is Zurich in?* N COUNT = district

cantonment /kəntu:nmə²nt/, **cantonments**. A **cantonment** is a group of buildings or a camp where soldiers live. N COUNT = quarters

canvas /kænvəs/, **canvases**. 1 **Canvas** is strong, heavy cloth usually made of cotton or linen. It is used for making things such as tents, sails, and bags. EG *...a shelter of canvas slung over bamboo poles... I saw him looking at my name painted on the canvas of my kit bag... ...seats with striped canvas awnings.* N UNCOUNT

2 If you are living and sleeping **under canvas,** you are living and sleeping in a tent. PHR : USED AS AN A

3 A **canvas** is a piece of canvas or similar material on which a painting can be done, usually using oil paints. EG *... oil paintings on canvas.* ▸ also used of the painting itself. EG *...the canvases of Hieronymus Bosch.* N COUNT/UNCOUNT; ▸ N COUNT

canvass /kænvəs/, **canvasses, canvassing, canvassed**. 1 If you **canvass** or **canvass** people or a place, you go round a particular area trying to persuade people to vote for a particular candidate or political party in an election. EG *I was canvassing in Fairbourne Road... He had canvassed for Mr Foot in the leadership election.* ◇ **canvassing**. EG *...house-to-house canvassing.* V+O, OR V : USU +A; ◇ N UNCOUNT

2 A **canvass** is the activity of going round asking people to support a particular party or candidate in an election. EG *It was the fullest canvass I've ever managed to do.* N COUNT = campaign

3 If you **canvass** opinion, you find out how people feel about a particular subject by asking them. EG *They decided to canvass opinion before making a final decision.* V+O ↑ investigate

canyon /kænjən/, **canyons**. A **canyon** is a narrow valley with very steep sides, often with a river at the bottom. EG *The cold wind sweeps down the canyon... ...the Grand Canyon.* N COUNT : ALSO IN NAMES AFTER N = ravine

cap /kæp/, **caps, capping, capped**. 1 A **cap** is 1.1 a soft flat hat which is usually worn by men or boys. EG *On his head he wore a brown cloth cap... ...a big man in a workman's cap.* 1.2 a special hat, usually flat, which is worn as part of a uniform. EG *Matron stood in the doorway, her starched cap on her head... ...my school cap.* 1.3 a special hat given as a sign of honour to sports players, especially when they are chosen to play for their country. EG *He won his England cap.* ▸ used as a verb. EG *She was capped twenty times.* 1.4 a small flat lid on a bottle or container. EG *Brody grabbed the bottle, twisted off the cap, and sniffed.* 1.5 a contraceptive device used by women; an informal word. N COUNT; N COUNT; N COUNT ↑ award; ▸ V+O; N COUNT = top; N COUNT : USU SING

2 If you go to someone **cap in hand,** you go to them very humbly, usually because you are asking them for something or because you are apologizing for something that you have done. EG *It's bad enough having to go cap in hand to ask for a rise.* PHR : USED AS AN A = meekly

3 You say **'If the cap fits'** to someone when you mean that they can take a remark as applying to them if they feel that it is appropriate. PHR

4 If you **cap** one thing with another, you put the other thing on top of it. EG *...sweets coated with chocolate and capped with a cherry.* V+O+A *(with)* = crown

5 If you **cap** something such as a story or a joke, you tell a story or joke that is better than the ones that have been told earlier. EG *He capped his performance by telling the funniest joke I have ever heard.* V+O ↑ improve = crown

6 A **cap** is also a small amount of explosive that is wrapped in paper and causes a small explosion when it is fired. Caps are often used in toy guns. N COUNT

capability /keɪpəbɪlə¹ti¹/, **capabilities**. 1 If you have the **capability** or the **capabilities** to do something, you have the ability or the qualities that are necessary to do it. EG *Some jobs still are beyond their capabilities... ...her capabilities as a parent... ...questions about the capability of society to meet those needs.* N UNCOUNT/COUNT : USU N IN PL+SUPP ↑ ability = competence

2 A country's **capability** is the ability that it has to take a particular kind of military action. EG *The French nuclear capability was never used, however.* N UNCOUNT/COUNT : +SUPP ↑ ability

capable /keɪpəbə⁰l/. 1 If a person or thing is **capable** of doing something, they are able to do it, and perhaps are likely to do it. EG *We sought a man capable of killing the President... The poison was capable of causing death within a few minutes... A calculator that is capable of being programmed to perform any mathematical function... Moths are capable of speeds of 50 kph.* ADJ CLASSIF : PRED+*of* ↑ able ≠ incapable

2 A **capable** person has the skill or qualities necessary to do a particular thing well or is able to do most things well. EG *Basil proved a capable cricketer... I have seen a child as young as 14 who was extremely capable and dependable.* ◇ **capably**. EG *...a capably performed dance.* ADJ QUALIT ↑ able = competent ≠ inept; ◇ ADV

capacious /kəpeɪʃəs/. Something that is **capacious** has a lot of room or space to put things in. EG *She put her knitting into one of the capacious pockets of her apron.* ADJ QUALIT ↑ large = voluminous

capacity /kəpæsə¹ti¹/, **capacities**. 1 The **capacity** of something is 1.1 the largest amount that it can hold, produce, or carry. EG *The pipeline has a capacity of some 1.2m barrels a day... The theatre was full, crowded even beyond its two thousand seat capacity.* N UNCOUNT ↑ limit

● If something is filled **to capacity,** it is as full as it can possibly be. EG *The ship set sail in 1740 with her hold filled to capacity with rich goods.* ● PHR : USED AS AN A

2 A **capacity** crowd or audience fills a theatre, sports ground, etc completely, so that there is no room for any more people. EG *People packed the hall from floor to ceiling, a capacity audience.* N BEFORE N ↑ maximum

3 The **capacity** of a person, society, or system is 3.1 the power or ability that they have to do a particular thing. EG *We are living in a society which demands of everyone the capacity to read and write... ...industrial systems with the capacity for sustaining growth... Research and development capacities are extremely limited.* 3.2 the ability that they have to do a particular thing well or to keep on doing it. EG *There was a job to be done; it was clear, simple and within her capacity... People have different capacities for learning.* N COUNT+SUPP ↑ potential = facility; N COUNT ↑ power = capability

4 Someone's **capacity** is the amount that they can eat or drink. EG *...Farquharson, a reporter with a* N UNCOUNT : POSS +N

prodigious capacity for beer... His capacity for brandy was phenomenal.

5 If you say that a person does something **in a** particular **capacity** or **in** their **capacity as** something, you mean that they do it as part of the duties of the particular job or position that they have. EG *I was involved in an advisory capacity with a parliamentary committee last year... Classified information was given to them in their capacities as Commanders-in-Chief.* PHR : USED AS AN A

6 **Capacity** in a factory or industry is the level of production in it and the quantity of things that are produced; a technical term in economics. EG *We need to raise productivity and expand capacity if we want to be competitive... ...the unused capacity thrown up by the recession.* N UNCOUNT

7 **Capacity** is used to measure the size and power of engines. EG *Volkswagen currently make the best-selling small car... What capacity is your car?–Two litres.* N UNCOUNT/COUNT

cape /keɪp/, **capes**. A **cape** is 1 a large piece of land that sticks out into the sea from the coast. EG *...Soya, the northern cape of Japan... Magellan rounded Cape Horn and came north again up the coast of Chile.* 2 a short cloak. EG *Waving a red cape, Delgado provoked the bull to charge.* N COUNT : ALSO IN NAMES = promontory; N COUNT

caper /keɪpə/, **capers, capering, capered**. 1 **Capers** are the flower buds of a type of Mediterranean bush, which are pickled and used to season food. EG *...wild duck in caper sauce.* N COUNT : USU PL ⇑ seasoning

2 If you **caper**, you dance or leap about energetically in a light-hearted, happy way. EG *The little girl then capered towards Bill.* V : USU+A ⇑ jump = scamper

3 A **caper** is also 3.1 a light-hearted practical joke or trick; an old-fashioned word. 3.2 a crime or illegal activity; an informal word. EG *The affair is now familiarly called 'the Watergate caper'.* N COUNT; N COUNT

5 If you use the expression **and all that caper**, you are talking about something that you consider to be unnecessary or foolish. EG *I never bother to work out my financial position and all that caper.* PHR ⇑ nonsense = rot

capillary /kəpɪləri[1]/, **capillaries**. 1 A **capillary** is a very thin hair-like blood vessel in the body of a person or animal. N COUNT ⇑ tube

2 **Capillary** tubes are very thin tubes, especially ones that are used in medical and scientific equipment. EG *...the capillary tube in the thermometer.* ADJ CLASSIF : ATTRIB ⇑ tube

capital /kæpɪtə[0]l/, **capitals**. 1 **Capital** is 1.1 a large sum of money which you use to start or expand a business, or which you invest in order to make more money. EG *How can it attract capital from the stock exchanges and banks?... He gained overall control by putting up most of the capital.* 1.2 a sum of money which you do not spend but which you save in a bank or invest in a business in order to receive regular payments of interest from it. EG *She had an allowance of 2,500 pounds a year, of which the capital was to become hers on her mother's death.* N UNCOUNT = funds; N SING WITH DET = principal

2 **Capital** investment or expenditure is money which is spent on buildings, machinery, etc which are necessary in order to produce goods or make a business more efficient, but which do not make money directly. EG *...substantial increases in capital expenditure on automated exchanges and telephones... It will make it much harder for them to finance further capital investment.* N BEFORE N ⇑ investment

3 **Capital** is also the knowledge or skill which a person has in a particular subject or for a particular job; a formal word. EG *It's a misuse of human capital... By the time that happens he will have invested his academic capital elsewhere.* N UNCOUNT+SUPP ⇑ resources = assets

4 If you **make capital of** or **out of** a situation, you use it in such a way that you gain some advantage for yourself from it. EG *At the time much political capital was made of the intention to increase top people's salaries.* PHR : VB INFLECTS ⇑ exploit

5 The **capital** of a country is its main city or town and is usually where the government of the country meets. EG *In the Danish capital it was far too late to go shopping.* N COUNT

6 The **capital** of a particular industry, product, or activity is a place which is famous for it. EG *...the peach capital of America... Rome was, I suppose, the capital of the art world.* N COUNT+SUPP = centre

7 A **capital** or a **capital** letter is a letter which is used especially at the beginning of a sentence or a name. 'T', 'B', and 'F' are capital letters. EG *Her writing was curious–small sharp little letters with no capitals... On its menus was embossed a pair of capital 'R's'.* N COUNT, OR ADJ CLASSIF ATTRIB

8 If something is written **in capitals** or **in capital letters**, it emphasizes how important or urgent it is. EG *Then he left a note which declared his love in capital letters... The item that headed the list, in painfully neat capitals, was to find himself a room.* PHR : USED AS AN A

9 If you say 'Life **with a capital** L', etc, you are emphasizing that the word has a particular significance in the situation you are talking about; an informal expression. EG *It was not 'Art' (with a capital 'A').* PHR : USED AS AN A

10 A **capital** crime is one for which the punishment of death is allowed by law. EG *Members of the TV crew were accused of the capital offence of the murder of a policeman... They will be tried on a capital charge of instigating the riots and murdering three police officers.* ADJ CLASSIF : ATTRIB ⇑ serious

11 **Capital** is also used to express approval or admiration of something; an old-fashioned informal word. EG *It will be a capital joke, remembered till their last days.* ADJ CLASSIF ⇑ good = marvellous

12 A **capital** is also the top part of a stone column, which is sometimes decorated with stone leaves or other patterns; a technical term in architecture. EG *The capitals of the lower arches are severe and clean-cut.* N COUNT ≠ base

capital gains are the profits that you make when you buy something and then sell it again. N PLURAL ⇑ profit

capitalise /kæpɪtəlaɪz/. See **capitalize**.

capitalism /kæpɪtəlɪzm/ is an economic and political system in which property, business and industry are owned by private individuals and not by the state, and in which companies are run in competition with each other in order to make a profit. EG *They will have to make a revolutionary change, end capitalism and build a socialist society... What is occurring now is not a crisis of capitalism, but of industrial society itself.* N UNCOUNT = private enterprise

capitalist /kæpɪtəlɪst/, **capitalists**. 1 A **capitalist** country or society is one which supports capitalism. EG *He recognized the enormous strength and influence of capitalist America... This is one of the most powerful economic motivations in capitalist societies.* ADJ CLASSIF

2 A **capitalist** system or economy is based on the principles of capitalism. EG *Japan successfully built up a modern capitalist economy... Many countries operate variants of the free enterprise capitalist system... ...capitalist foreign policy.* ADJ CLASSIF

3 A **capitalist** is 3.1 someone who believes in and supports the principles of capitalism. EG *The Government does not allow former capitalists and their supporters to vote.* 3.2 someone who owns a business which they run in order to make a profit for themselves. EG *The social climate has to be such that capitalists are encouraged to put their wealth into new industries... By the time he was twenty, the budding capitalist had his own grocery business.* N COUNT; N COUNT ⇑ businessman = entrepreneur

4 **Capitalist** is used to describe groups consisting of capitalists or activities considered typical of capitalists; often used showing disapproval. EG *The primary objective was to take power out of the hands of the capitalist class... Anyone who had indulged in such a capitalist activity as golf would have been laughed at.* ADJ CLASSIF : ATTRIB = bourgeois

capitalistic /kæpɪtəlɪstɪk/ means supporting or based on the principles of capitalism; often used showing disapproval. EG *...the economic crisis in the capitalistic world... ...a bastion of capitalistic privilege.* ADJ CLASSIF

capitalize /kæpɪtəlaɪz/, **capitalizes, capitalizing, capitalized**; also spelled **capitalise**. 1 If you **capitalize** on a situation, you use it in order to gain some advantage for yourself. EG *Mr Healey has been capitalising on the anxiety expressed throughout the House... Party workers in the industrial cities did their utmost to capitalise upon this situation.* V : IF+PREP, THEN *on/upon* ⇑ exploit = profit

2 If you **capitalize** a word, you use a capital letter at the beginning of it, or for the whole of it. EG *To distinguish this use from their usual meanings, Parent, Adult, and Child will be capitalized throughout the book.* V+O ⇑ write

3 If you **capitalize** something that belongs to you, V+O

you sell it in order to raise money. EG *They'll have to capitalize their assets.*

capital punishment is punishment which involves the legal killing of a person who has committed a serious crime such as murder. EG *He's well-known for having liberal views, like being opposed to capital punishment.* — N UNCOUNT = the death penalty

capitulate /kəpɪtjə¹leɪt/, **capitulates, capitulating, capitulated.** If you **capitulate**, you stop fighting or resisting another person, organization, or country, and do what they want you to do. EG *Economic pressures finally forced the Government to capitulate to our demands... He threatened her, but she never capitulated.* — V : IF+PREP THEN *to* ⇑ surrender = submit, yield
◊ **capitulation**/kəpɪtjə¹leɪʃə⁰n/. EG *The Prime Minister's capitulation to his right wing on the issue didn't help matters.... A capitulation agreement was forced upon the enemy.* — ◊ N UNCOUNT : IF+PREP THEN *to* ⇑ surrender

capon /keɪpə⁷n/, **capons.** A **capon** is a male chicken that has had its sex organs removed and has been specially fattened up to be eaten. EG *...plump, tender capons raised by a local farmer.* — N COUNT

caprice /kə³priːs/, **caprices. 1** A **caprice** is an unexpected change of mind or action without any strong reason or purpose. EG *Newspapers became subject to the whims and caprices of their owners. We cannot control the caprices of Mother Nature.* — N COUNT : USU PL ⇑ impulse = vagary, quirk
▸ used of a person's behaviour. EG *He alternated between being gloomy and being comical according to caprice.* — ▸ N UNCOUNT = humour

capricious /kə³prɪʃəs/. **1** Someone who is **capricious** often changes their mind or their behaviour unexpectedly. EG *Authoritarian rulers are typically capricious... ...lovely, capricious, and merciless women.* — ADJ QUALIT ⇑ unpredictable = wayward
▸ used of a person's behaviour. EG *...capricious fluctuations of support.* — ▸ = fickle
◊ **capriciously.** EG *The children had capriciously decided to despise Alexander.* — ◊ ADV
2 Something that is **capricious** often changes unexpectedly and cannot be relied on. EG *...a capricious postal system... ...a capricious summer breeze.* — ADJ QUALIT ⇑ unpredictable

caps is an abbreviation for capital letters: see **capital.** EG *Write the title in caps.*

capsicum /kæpsɪkəm/, **capsicums.** A **capsicum** is a vegetable that is a type of pepper. — N COUNT/ UNCOUNT

capsize /kæpsaɪz/, **capsizes, capsizing, capsized.** When you **capsize** a boat or when it **capsizes**, it turns upside down in the water. EG *Ships capsize when struck by these waves... ...a capsized boat.* — V OR V-ERG ⇑ overturn

capsule /kæpsjuːl/, **capsules. 1** A **capsule** is **1.1** a very small, rounded container with medicine in the form of a powder inside, which you swallow. EG *He produced a packet of violet-blue capsules.* — N COUNT **1.2** a small strong container used for storing or carrying things. EG *The plastic capsule was transparent all the way round.* — N COUNT **1.3** a structure in a plant or animal which does not open unless it is split, for example the seed case of a poppy. EG *The stamens are packed inside a sealed capsule of petals.* — N COUNT ⇑ container = sheath **1.4** the part of a spacecraft in which people travel in space and in which they return to earth. — N COUNT = space capsule
2 A **capsule** description of an event or situation describes it in very few words. — ADJ CLASSIF : ATTRIB ⇑ short = concise

Capt. is a written abbreviation for 'Captain'; often used as part of a person's military title. EG *...Capt. Paul Eckel, the group's head.*

captain /kæptɪn/, **captains, captaining, captained. 1** A **captain** is **1.1** the person in charge of a ship or boat, especially an officer in the navy. EG *...the captain of a battleship... Captain Cook sailed to Australia.* — N COUNT : ALSO IN TITLES **1.2** an officer of middle rank in the army or the United States Air Force. EG *...a captain of artillery named Robert Ponard.* — N COUNT : ALSO IN TITLES **1.3** the pilot in charge of an aeroplane which is carrying passengers. — N COUNT : ALSO IN TITLES **1.4** a leader of a group or team of people. EG *Fred is captain of the hockey team... I was the captain of the debating team at school.* — N COUNT+SUPP = head
2 If you **captain** a group or team of people, you are their leader. EG *Willis is probably the best player to have captained England.* — V+O ⇑ lead

caption /kæpʃə⁰n/, **captions, captioning, captioned. 1** A **caption** is all the words printed underneath a picture or cartoon in a book or a newspaper which explain what the picture is about. EG *Underneath the picture was a caption that said: 'The greatest power on this earth'... The man was identified in the caption as Kenneth H. Dahlberg.* — N COUNT ⇑ title = inscription, legend
2 If you **caption** a picture or photograph, you print words underneath it to explain what it is about. EG *You can caption it 'Heroism'.* — V+O, OR V+O+C

captivate /kæptə¹veɪt/, **captivates, captivating, captivated.** If someone or something **captivates** you, they fascinate or attract you so much that you find it difficult to think of anything else. EG *At eighteen he had been captivated by a charming brunette named Sybil...* — V+O
◊ **captivating** EG *Roosevelt was a captivating speaker.* — ◊ ADJ QUALIT = enthral

captive /kæptɪv/, **captives. 1** A **captive** is a prisoner, especially one who is captured in a war. EG *The soldiers marched on, driving thousands of captives before them.* — N COUNT = hostage
2 A person or animal that is **captive** is being kept imprisoned or enclosed. EG *...the shocking degree of confinement endured by captive animals.* — ADJ CLASSIF ⇑ restricted ≠ free
3 If you **take** someone **captive** or **hold** them **captive**, you take them or keep them as a prisoner. EG *Nine Indians were taken captive... They were holding George captive.* — PHR : VB INFLECTS
4 If you have a **captive audience**, you have a group of people who are there and who cannot leave and so have to watch or listen to you. EG *Give him a captive audience, and he can sell anything.* — PHR

captivity /kæptɪvɪti¹/ is the state of being kept as a captive. EG *...wild birds raised in captivity.* — N UNCOUNT ≠ freedom

captor /kæptə/, **captors.** A **captor** is someone who has captured a person or animal. — N COUNT : USU POSS+N

capture /kæptʃə/, **captures, capturing, captured. 1** If you **capture** someone, you take them prisoner, especially in a war or after a struggle. EG *They had been captured and thrown in chains... ...a captured German officer.* — V+O = seize
▸ used as a noun. EG *He hadn't eaten anything since the night before his capture.* — ▸ N UNCOUNT : USU POSS+N = seizure
2 When military forces **capture** a town or a country, they take control of it by force. EG *The city took 24 days to capture.* — V+O = conquer
▸ used as a noun. EG *...the capture of the city.* — ▸ N SING : *the*+N +*of*
3 If you **capture** an animal, you catch it or trap it. EG *How are they going to capture all the animals?* — V+O
4 To **capture** something means to gain control of it. EG *In August, overseas firms captured almost 41 per cent of the market... The Labour Party must capture the imagination of youth.* — V+O ⇑ take = win
5 To **capture** something such as an atmosphere or quality means to represent it successfully in pictures, music, or words, especially when this is difficult to do. EG *With his camera he tried to capture changes as they took place before his eyes... The disturbing mood of the time is captured perfectly in a letter sent to William Charles... ...local heroes all captured here in penetrating sketches.* — V+O = depict, record

car /kɑː/, **cars.** A **car** is **1** a road vehicle that usually has four wheels and is powered by an engine. Cars need a driver and usually have room for three or four passengers. EG *He parked the car about a hundred yards from the gates... The car drove off, and Mrs Foster was left alone... ...Britain's troubled car industry.* — N COUNT, OR *by*+N = motor **2** a carriage on a train that is used for a particular purpose, for example for sleeping in or for eating in; used mainly in British English. EG *...passengers in the dining car... ...the sleeping car.* — N COUNT : USU MOD+N **3** a railway carriage; used mainly in American English. EG *Snippets of railway car conversation still buzzed around in my head.* — N COUNT : MOD+N • See also **cable car.**

carafe /kəræf, -rɑːf/, **carafes.** A **carafe** is a glass container in which you serve water or wine. — N COUNT
▸ **Carafe** is also used to refer to the liquid inside it or to the amount of liquid that it contains. EG *We drank a carafe of house-wine.*

caramel /kærəmə⁰l, -mɛl/, **caramels. 1** A **caramel** is a chewy sweet made from sugar, butter, and milk. — N COUNT
2 Caramel is burnt sugar used for colouring and flavouring food. — N UNCOUNT

carat /kærət/, **carats;** also spelled **karat** in American English. A **carat** is **1** a unit for measuring the weight of diamonds and other precious stones that is equal to 0.2 grams. EG *It weighs 530 carats and is the biggest cut diamond ever.* — N COUNT : NUM+N **2** a unit for measuring the purity of gold. The purest gold is 24-carat gold. — N COUNT : NUM+N, USU BEFORE N

caravan /kærəvæn/, **caravans.** A **caravan** is **1** a vehicle with beds and other equipment inside, in which people live or spend their holidays. Caravans are usually pulled by a car; used especially in British English. EG *The community adviser gave us a cara-* — N COUNT *van to live in... He went on a caravan holiday.* **2** a group of people and animals who travel together for safety in places such as deserts. EG *Once we were part of a caravan of twelve thousand camels.* N COUNT = party

caravanning is the activity of having a holiday in a caravan. EG *We went caravanning in North Wales.* N UNCOUNT ⇑ touring

caravanserai /kærəvænsəraɪ, -reɪ/, **caravanserais.** A **caravanserai** is **1** a large number of people or things that seem busy or complicated. EG *Nobody seems to pay any attention to the caravanserai of detectives and journalists.* **2** a large inn in Eastern countries where caravans stop. EG *You may find yourself in some ancient caravanserai where traders rested their animals.* N COUNT : ALSO N +*of*+N IN PL ⇑ group = gaggle; N COUNT

caraway /kærəweɪ/ is a plant with seeds that are used in cooking. N UNCOUNT

carbine /kɑːbaɪn/, **carbines.** A **carbine** is a light automatic rifle. EG *The carbines offered an advantage over existing weapons.* N COUNT

carbohydrate /kɑːbəʊhaɪdreɪt/, **carbohydrates. Carbohydrate** is a substance found in food such as sugar and bread, that gives you energy. EG *You have too much carbohydrate in your diet.* N UNCOUNT, OR COUNT : USU PL ⇑ nutrient

▸ **Carbohydrate** is also used to refer to food that contains a lot of carbohydrates. EG *...refined carbohydrates such as white flour and white sugar.* ▸ N COUNT

carbolic acid /kɑːbɒlɪk æsɪd/ is a liquid that is used as a disinfectant and antiseptic. N UNCOUNT ⇑ acid

carbon /kɑːbəⁿn/, **carbons. 1 Carbon** is a chemical element that diamonds, graphite, and coal are made of and that all organic substances contain. N UNCOUNT

2 A **carbon** is **2.1** a copy of a piece of writing that is made using carbon paper. **2.2** a sheet of carbon paper. N COUNT; N COUNT

carbonated /kɑːbəneɪtɪᵈd/. **Carbonated** drinks are fizzy drinks that contain small bubbles of carbon dioxide; a fairly formal word. ADJ CLASSIF : USU ATTRIB

carbon copy, carbon copies. A **carbon copy** is **1** a copy of a piece of writing that is made using carbon paper. EG *I kept a carbon copy of my letter.* **2** a person or thing that is identical or very similar to another person or thing. EG *It is possible that man will be able to make biological carbon copies of himself.* N COUNT; N COUNT, IF+ PREP THEN *of* ⇑ copy = clone, replica

carbon dating is the system of calculating the age of a very old object, such as a fossil, by measuring the amount of radioactive carbon it contains. N UNCOUNT = radiocarbon dating

carbon dioxide /kɑːbən daɪɒksaɪd/ is the gas that animals and humans breathe out, and is also formed as the result of some chemical reactions. Carbon dioxide is used for example in making fizzy drinks and in fire extinguishers. EG *Carbon dioxide is expelled from the tissues and oxygen is absorbed.* N UNCOUNT

carbon monoxide /kɑːbən məⁿnɒksaɪd/ is a poisonous gas formed when carbon is burnt in a very small amount of air. EG *Carbon monoxide comes from motor vehicles.* N UNCOUNT

carbon paper is a piece of thin paper with a dark substance coating one side. You can put it between two pieces of paper so that when you write or type on the top piece the writing also appears on the bottom piece. N UNCOUNT = carbon

carbuncle /kɑːbʌŋkəᵒl/, **carbuncles.** A **carbuncle** is a large swelling under the skin like a boil. N COUNT

carburettor /kɑːbəᵒretə/, **carburettors**; also spelled **carburetor** in American English. A **carburettor** is the part of an engine, usually in a car, in which air and petrol are mixed together. N COUNT ⇑ device

carcass /kɑːkəs/, **carcasses**; also spelled **carcase. 1** A **carcass** is the body of a dead animal. EG *We came across the carcass of a lion... Use a raw chicken carcass to make chicken soup.* N COUNT

2 You can refer to someone's body in a very informal way as their **carcass**, for example when you are telling them rather rudely to move. EG *Shift your great carcass!* N COUNT+POSS

carcinogen /kɑːsɪnədʒən, kɑːsɪnədʒen/, **carcinogens.** A **carcinogen** is a substance which can cause cancer; a medical term. N COUNT

carcinogenic /kɑːsɪnəᵒdʒenɪk/. Something that is **carcinogenic** is likely to cause cancer; a medical term. ADJ CLASSIF

card /kɑːd/, **cards. 1** A **card** is **1.1** a piece of stiff paper or thin cardboard that has information written on it. EG *...report cards... She pulled out a blank card and asked him his name, age, and address.* **1.2** a piece of cardboard, paper, or plastic with information on it that shows your identity or proves that you have the right to do or have a particular thing. EG *...a medical card... You will then receive your club membership card... ...a Diners Club card.* ● See also **cheque card, credit card, identity card. 1.3** a piece of stiff paper folded in half with a picture and often a message printed on it, which you sign and send to someone, for example on their birthday or at Christmas. EG *...a birthday card... The two children used to send me a card at Christmas time.* **1.4** the same as a postcard. EG *We wrote him a card that said, 'Having a wonderful time, wish you were here.'* **1.5** a small piece of thin cardboard that has your name, address, occupation, and telephone number printed on it and that you give to other people, especially for business purposes. EG *Here's my card if you need any help.* **1.6** a rectangular piece of thin cardboard with a number or picture printed on it, which is part of a set of 52 that you use to play games. EG *He shuffled the cards and dealt them.* N COUNT; N COUNT+SUPP; N COUNT; N COUNT; N COUNT : POSS+ N ⇑ identification; N COUNT : USU PL = playing card

2 If you play **cards** or play a game of **cards**, you play a game using cards. EG *He came round to talk and play cards.* N PLURAL : VB CAN BE SING OR PL

3 Card is strong stiff paper or thin cardboard. EG *Make a second copy on card or paper.* N UNCOUNT

4 If you say that someone is a **card**, you mean that they behave in an odd or amusing way; a rather old-fashioned use. EG *He was funny, engaging and a real card in many ways.* N COUNT : USU AS C ⇑ eccentric = character

5 You can also refer to something that gives you an advantage in a particular situation as a **card.** EG *He possessed one card which trumped everyone–he was a close friend of Mr Darley... Agrarian reform placed all the cards in the hands of the landowners.* ● **trump card**: see **trump.** N COUNT ⇑ advantage

6 The word **card** is also used in the following expressions. **6.1** If you **play** your **cards right**, you are skilful in the way that you handle a situation and make use of all your advantages. EG *He should get in at the General Election if he plays his cards right.* PHR : VB INFLECTS

6.2 If you say that something is **on the cards**, you mean that it is very likely to happen. EG *It is on the cards that it will happen, somewhere, soon.* **6.3** If you **lay** your **cards on the table** or **put** your **cards on the table**, you tell people about your feelings, plans, or ideas, especially when you have been keeping them secret. EG *He's actually laid his cards on the table at last.* PHR : VB INFLECTS; PHR : VB INFLECTS ⇑ reveal = come clean

cardamom /kɑːdəməm/ is a spice that comes from the seeds of a plant that grows in Asia. N UNCOUNT

cardamon /kɑːdəmən/ is the same as cardamom. N UNCOUNT

cardboard /kɑːdbɔːd/. **1 Cardboard** is very thick, stiff paper that is used to make boxes and other objects. EG *...newspaper and cardboard... ...a large cardboard box.* N UNCOUNT

2 Cardboard people, emotions, or ideas seem unreal or boring, especially because they are not very complex; used showing disapproval. EG *...a play full of cardboard characters... She adored and idolised him, but it was stupid, cardboard love.* ADJ CLASSIF : USU ATTRIB ⇑ unreal = artificial

card-carrying. A person who is a **card-carrying** member of a political organization is an official, fully committed member. EG *All of these people are card-carrying party members.* ADJ CLASSIF : ATTRIB ⇑ practising

cardiac /kɑːdiæk/ means relating to the heart; a medical term. EG *Death is caused by cardiac failure... ...the nursing officer in charge of the cardiac unit.* ADJ CLASSIF : ATTRIB

cardiac arrest, cardiac arrests. A **cardiac arrest** is a heart attack; a medical term. N COUNT/ UNCOUNT

cardigan /kɑːdɪgən/, **cardigans.** A **cardigan** is a knitted jacket that is fastened up the front with buttons or a zip. N COUNT ⇑ sweater

cardinal /kɑːdɪnəᵒl/, **cardinals. 1** A **cardinal** is one of the members of the clergy of high rank in the Catholic church who elect the Pope and advise him. EG *...Cardinal Hume.* N COUNT : ALSO IN TITLES ⇑ clergyman

2 A **cardinal** principle, idea, etc or something of **cardinal** importance is extremely important because other things are based on it or depend on it; a formal use. EG *An emphasis on the community is a cardinal feature of our society... The speaker emphasized the cardinal importance of building a party to lead the country.* ADJ QUALIT : ATTRIB = paramount, vital

3 A **cardinal** is the same as a cardinal number. N COUNT

cardinal number, cardinal numbers. A **cardinal number** is a number that tells you how many things there are in a group but not what order they N COUNT are in, for example one, two, three, etc: compare **ordinal number**.

cardinal point, cardinal points. A **cardinal point** is one of the four main points of the compass, either north, south, east, or west. N COUNT

cardinal sin, cardinal sins. A **cardinal sin** is a particular action or way of behaving that is strongly disapproved of; sometimes used in a humorous way. EG *I had committed the cardinal sin of not shutting the door behind me.* N COUNT ⇑ misdemeanour = crime

card index, card indexes; also spelled with a hyphen. A **card index** is a number of cards with information written on them, which are arranged in a particular order, usually alphabetical. EG *She flipped through the card index... ...a card-index system.* N COUNT

card sharp, card sharps. A **card sharp** or **card sharper** is a professional card player who cheats in order to win and so make money. N COUNT ⇑ cheat

card table, card tables; also spelled with a hyphen. A **card table** is a small light table which can be folded up and which is sometimes used for playing games of cards on. N COUNT

card vote, card votes. A **card vote** is a method of voting, used especially at Trade Union Conferences, in which the vote of each delegate represents all the votes of the members of his or her particular organization or trade union. N COUNT

care /kɛə/, **cares, caring, cared**. 1 If you **care** about something, you feel that it is very important or interesting and are concerned about it. EG *...people who care about the environment and political issues... We teased him because all he cared about was birds... I'm too old to care what I look like... The average individual knows little and cares less about technology.* V : USU+A

2 If you do not **care** what you do or what happens, it does not matter to you at all. EG *I don't care what we do or where we go... He was so sick and weak that he no longer cared if he lived or died... I don't care a damn about the job.* V WITH BROAD NEG : USU+REPORT-CL = mind

3 If you **care** for someone or **care** about them, you like them a great deal and feel a lot of affection for them. EG *'Do you think she still cares for him?'–'I don't think so.'* V : IF+PREP THEN *for/about*

4 If someone **cares** to do something, they choose to do it. EG *We have power if we only cared to exercise it... We just had to wait for whenever he cared to appear... It's wrong whichever way you care to look at it.* V+to-INF = choose

5 If you would not **care** to do or have something, you would not like to do it or have it. EG *It was a memorable experience but I shouldn't care to repeat it... That happened rather more years ago than I care to remember... I wonder if you would care to join me in a drink?... Would you care for a cup of tea?* V+to-INF, OR V+*for* : USU WITH BROAD NEG = like, fancy

6 A **care** is a feeling of concern, anxiety, or worry about something. EG *She sat there singing happily as if she had no cares at all... You could be walking about in the sun without a care in the world.* N COUNT/UNCOUNT = trouble

7 **Care** is the act of constantly providing what a person or thing needs to keep them in good condition or to make them well, and of making sure that they do not come to any harm. EG *More training in the care of mentally disordered patients is needed... The disease affected Jane's lungs and she needed a lot of care at home... She is having treatment under the care of one of the specialists from St Andrews Hospital... She has a duty to protect the children in her care.* N UNCOUNT ⇑ attention ≠ neglect

8 If you do something with **care**, you do it fairly slowly and with great attention because you want to do it properly and not make any mistakes or damage anything. EG *He chose every word with care... The records are kept with meticulous care... There was a label on the crate saying 'Glass. Handle with care.'* N UNCOUNT = precision

9 **take care**. 9.1 If you **take care of** something or someone, you provide them with everything they need to keep them in good condition or to make them well, and make sure that they come to no harm. EG *It certainly is normal for a mother to want to take care of her own baby... He takes good care of my goats... Tooth decay could be much reduced if greater care were taken of the teeth in childhood.* PHR : VB INFLECTS ⇑ attend to = look after

9.2 You say **'take care'** or **'take care of yourself'** when you are saying goodbye to someone informally, or at the end of an informal letter. EG *'Night night, Mr Beamish,' called Chloe. 'Take care.'... Cheerio, with love from us both. Take care. Dad.'* CONVENTION

9.3 If you are able to **take care of** yourself, you can protect yourself in a dangerous situation or when someone is trying to harm you. EG *Don't worry. If anything should happen, I can take care of myself.* PHR+PRON REFL : VB INFLECTS = look after

9.4 If you **take care** to do something, you make absolutely certain that you do it or that it happens. EG *He was very discreet and took care never to offend the visitors... Take great care not to spill the mixture... I took good care that they got their money.* PHR+to-INF/REPORT-CL : VB INFLECTS = take pains

9.5 If you **take care of** a problem or something that needs attention, you deal with it. EG *There was business to be taken care of... However, this was taken care of in the amendment to the Bill... If you'd prefer, they can take care of their own breakfast.* PHR : VB INFLECTS ⇑ do = attend to

10 Children who are **in care** or who have been taken **into care** are living in a home that is owned and run by the state because their parents are dead or are unable to look after them properly. EG *Why is the baby in care?... Children are put into care as a last resort when family life breaks down.* PHR : USED AS AN A

11 If you send a letter or parcel to someone **care of** a particular person or place, you send it to that person or place, and it is then passed on to the person it is intended for. PHR : USED AS AN A

12 The word **care** is also used in the following informal expressions. 12.1 If you say that someone **couldn't care less** about something, you are saying in an emphatic way that it does not matter to them at all. EG *She couldn't care less what they thought of her.* PHR OR PHR+REPORT-CL

12.2 If you say **'for all I care'**, you are indicating in an emphatic way that it does not matter to you at all what someone does. EG *'Do you mind if I put this flag up?'–'You can fly the Jolly Roger for all I care.'* PHR : USED AS ADV SEN

12.3 You say **'who cares?'** to show that something does not matter to you at all. EG *'You're breaking the rules!' shouted Robert. 'Who cares?' she yelled back... Who cares where she is?* CONVENTION

care for. 1 If you **care for** someone or something, you provide them with all the things that they need to keep them well and make sure that they do not come to any harm. EG *You can't really find out how to care for children from books... Only £65 million was given to help care for the mentally retarded... Who would care for the farm when they were away?* PHRASAL VB : V+PREP, HAS PASS ⇑ attend = look after

2 If you do not **care for** something, you do not like it or enjoy it. EG *He didn't drink, he didn't care for the taste of it... I did not care for the play... I didn't much care for the way he looked at me either.* PHRASAL VB : V+PREP, WITH BROAD NEG = be keen on

career /kərɪə/, **careers, careering, careered**. 1 Someone's **career** is the series of jobs that they have in their life, especially in the same area of work, in which they usually progress so that they have more money and responsibility. EG *Maths is no longer a prime requirement for a career in accountancy... ...the political career of David Lloyd George... My career as a journalist was about to begin.* N COUNT ⇑ work

2 **Career** politicians, soldiers, nannies, etc work in the same area of work for all or most of their working lives, and usually progress in it. ADJ CLASSIF : ATTRIB ⇑ professional

3 **Careers** advisers, offices, etc give you information about jobs and professions. EG *...careers teachers.* N BEFORE N

4 A **career** in a particular occupation or type of work is the time that you spend doing it. EG *Many of us have had a school career punctuated with exams and tests.* N COUNT : USU SING, USU+SUPP = life

5 If someone or something **careers** along, they move very quickly and as if they are not in control of themselves. EG *The green car came careering back across the highway, only inches ahead of him.* V+A ⇑ rush = bolt

career girl, career girls. A **career girl** is the same as a career woman. N COUNT

careerist /kərɪərɪst/, **careerists**. A **careerist** is a person who thinks that their career is more important than anything else, and who will do anything to succeed in it. N COUNT

career woman, career women. A **career woman** is a woman who has a career and wishes to work and progress in her job until she retires. EG *...the middle-class career women of the United States.* N COUNT ⇑ careerist = career girl

carefree /kɛəfri:/. A person who is **carefree** has no worries, troubles, or responsibilities. EG *...carefree millionaires.* ▸ used of someone's feelings, behaviour, or life. EG *He was aware of a glorious carefree feeling of joy.* ADJ QUALIT = untroubled ≠ troubled

careful /kɛəful/. 1 If you tell someone to **be careful**, or if you say **'careful!'** to them, you are telling them to behave sensibly and think about what they are doing, so that they do not have an accident, do any damage to anything, or make a mistake. EG *Be careful of the floor. I've just polished it... 'Be careful with that,' Paul warned her... You be careful, you'll get yourself arrested if you don't watch out!... Careful! You'll break it!* CONVENTION ⇑ beware = watch out

2 If you are **careful**, 2.1 you behave sensibly and think about what you are doing, so that you do not have an accident, do any damage to anything, make a mistake, or do something you will regret later. EG *The new legislation will presumably encourage more careful driving... We must be careful not to say anything libellous... ...the careful phrasing of his statement.* ADJ QUALIT ⇑ cautious ≠ reckless ◊ **carefully**. EG *Drive carefully... He walked carefully around the broken glass... ...choosing her words carefully.* ◊ ADV WITH VB = cautiously ◊ **carefulness**. EG *It is not easy to draw the line between realistic carefulness and anxiety.* ◊ N UNCOUNT = prudence 2.2 you make sure that you do not omit or miss any details and that everything is accurate and correct. EG *He made a careful copy of the notes... The doctor gave him a careful examination... ...careful preparation.* ADJ QUALIT = thorough, detailed ◊ **carefully**. EG *The policeman wrote down the details carefully... Now listen carefully everybody.* ◊ ADV WITH VB 2.3 you do not spend money unnecessarily. EG *They had to be very careful about money... He has the reputation for being a little careful with his money.* ADJ QUALIT = canny

careless /kɛəlɪ²s/. 1 If you are **careless**, 1.1 you do not pay enough attention to what you are doing with the result that you are clumsy, you lose things, you make mistakes, or accidents happen. EG *I had been careless and let him wander off on his own... It has been left by some careless person... She's careless about her hair and her skin and her clothes.* ADJ QUALIT = thoughtless, negligent ≠ careful ◊ **carelessly**. EG *He gathered up the bills and stuffed them carelessly into his pocket.* ◊ ADV ◊ **carelessness**. EG *There seems to have been some carelessness recently at the office.* ◊ N UNCOUNT = negligence 1.2 you do not think sensibly about how you can best use something such as your money or time. EG *I'm very careless with money.* ADJ QUALIT = irresponsible ≠ thrifty ◊ **carelessly**. EG *Never use your time carelessly.* ◊ ADV

2 You do something in a **careless** way 2.1 when you are relaxed, untroubled, and unconcerned. EG *...her simplicity and careless grace... She was bending over the bowl, careless of her hair.* ADJ CLASSIF ≠ concerned, bothered ◊ **carelessly**. EG *He watched as Boylan carelessly dropped some ice into the glasses... ...a shirt carelessly open at the neck.* ◊ ADV = casually ◊ **carelessness**. EG *She handled his body with the carelessness of an expert.* ◊ N UNCOUNT 2.2 when you are trying to give the impression that you are relaxed and that something is not important to you. EG *She put a careless hand to her hair... ...a careless laugh.* ADJ CLASSIF: ATTRIB = casual ◊ **carelessly**. EG *'No reason,' Rudolph said carelessly.* ◊ ADV

carer /kɛərə/, **carers**. A **carer** is someone who looks after a person who is ill or old, especially someone who looks after a relative at home. N COUNT

caress /kərɛs/, **caresses, caressing, caressed**. If you **caress** a person or sometimes a thing, you stroke them gently, especially to express affection. EG *I gently caressed her hair and we kissed.* V+O = stroke ▸ used as a count noun. EG *...a loving caress.* ▸ N COUNT

caretaker /kɛəteɪkə/, **caretakers**. 1 A **caretaker** is a person who looks after a large building such as a school and deals with small repairs to it. EG *The children can help clear up after a school event if the caretaker is ill.* N COUNT = janitor

2 A **caretaker** president, head teacher, etc is a person who does an important job for a short period of time while the person who usually does it is unable to do it, or until a new person is appointed. ADJ CLASSIF: ATTRIB ⇑ temporary = acting ≠ permanent

careworn /kɛəwɔ:n/. A person who looks **careworn** looks worried, tired, and unhappy. EG *She detected in his face a careworn, grief-stricken expression... He looked careworn and refused to talk.* ADJ QUALIT ⇑ troubled

cargo /kɑ:gəu/, **cargoes**. You refer to the goods that a ship, plane, or large vehicle is carrying as its **cargo**. EG *...a cargo of wool... The main bulk of her cargo comprised Indian textiles... ...a cargo plane.* N COUNT/UNCOUNT ⇑ load = consignment

caribou /kærɪbu:/, **caribous**. **Caribou** can also be used as the plural form. A **caribou** is a large North American deer. N COUNT

caricature /kærɪkətjuə/, **caricatures, caricaturing, caricatured**. 1 A **caricature** is 1.1 a drawing or description of someone that exaggerates parts of their face or personality so much that they appear rather ridiculous. Caricatures are usually done for amusement or satire. EG *His profile was like a caricature of a Roman Emperor... ...a man who by caricature exposed the pretensions of the nobility... ...a complaint that the schoolmaster and his wife were caricatures.* N COUNT/UNCOUNT ⇑ exaggeration = mockery 1.2 an incomplete and inaccurate imitation of something, especially one that emphasizes particular features and ignores others. EG *...an outrageous caricature of the truth.* N COUNT: IF + PREP THEN *of* = travesty

2 If you **caricature** someone, you portray them in a way that exaggerates their features or their personality, often in order to make people laugh. EG *The royal family is now being caricatured as savagely as it has ever been.* V+O ⇑ depict = send up, satirize ◊ **caricatured**. EG *...the caricatured social image given to feminism.* ADJ CLASSIF: ATTRIB = grotesque

caricaturist, **caricaturists**. A **caricaturist** is a person who portrays other people in drawings or writing and exaggerates their features or personalities so that they seem rather ridiculous. N COUNT ⇑ parodist

caries /kɛərɪi:z/ is decay in teeth; a technical term in dentistry. EG *...the appallingly high incidence of dental caries.* N UNCOUNT

carillon /kərɪljən/, **carillons**. A **carillon** is a set of bells hung in a tower, or a tune played on these bells. N COUNT ⇑ instrument

caring /kɛərɪŋ/. 1 A **caring** person is one who shows affection for other people, provides them with the things that they need to keep them well, and is helpful and sympathetic when they are in trouble. EG *This type of society creates less competitive, more caring beings... Phyllis was a soft, caring person.* ADJ QUALIT ⇑ thoughtful = compassionate ▸ used of a country or society. EG *We need a more caring society.*

2 The work of **caring** organizations and the **caring** professions involves looking after people who are ill or who need help in coping with their lives. EG *...health centres and other caring agencies.* ADJ CLASSIF: ATTRIB

3 **Caring** is 3.1 loving or affectionate behaviour, or affectionate feelings. EG *...emotions like loving and caring.* N UNCOUNT ⇑ loving 3.2 helpful, sympathetic behaviour which shows concern for other people, especially when they are in trouble. EG *...if there was just more caring and sharing in the neighbourhood.* N UNCOUNT = warmth

carmine /kɑ:maɪn/ is a deep bright red colour. EG *The flowers may be anything from light carmine to crimson in colour.* ADJ COLOUR

carnage /kɑ:nɪdʒ/ is the violent killing of large numbers of people, especially in war. EG *Refugees crossed the border to escape the carnage in their homeland.* N UNCOUNT = slaughter

carnal /kɑ:nəºl/. **Carnal** desires and feelings are sexual and sensual ones, as opposed to spiritual ones; a literary or formal word. EG *He had forced her to submit to his carnal desires.* ADJ CLASSIF: ATTRIB

carnal knowledge is sexual intercourse; a formal or legal expression. N UNCOUNT

carnation /kɑ:neɪʃəºn/, **carnations**. A **carnation** is a plant which has narrow greyish-green leaves and a white, pink, or red flower. Carnations are often used in bouquets and are sometimes worn by men in the buttonholes of their jackets. EG *He had a white carnation in his buttonhole.* N COUNT

carnival /kɑ:nɪvəºl/, **carnivals**. A **carnival** is a special occasion or period of time that involves public entertainment, often with processions and dancing in the street. EG *When are we going to start organizing next year's carnival?* N COUNT ⇑ festival

carnivore /kɑ:nɪvɔ:/, **carnivores**. A **carnivore** is an animal that mainly eats meat. EG *...carnivores like the lion and the cheetah.* N COUNT ≠ herbivore

carnivorous /kɑ:nɪvəºrəs/. An animal that is **carnivorous** mainly eats meat. EG *...large carnivorous birds.* ADJ CLASSIF ▸ also used of plants that eat insects. EG *...carnivorous plants such as the Venus Fly Trap.*

carob /kærəb/, **carobs**. 1 A **carob** is an evergreen Mediterranean tree that has dark brown edible pods. N COUNT

2 You also use **carob** to refer to the pods of the carob tree which are powdered and often used instead of cocoa in health foods. EG *...'diet' bars of chocolate made from carob powder.* N UNCOUNT

carol /kærəl/, **carols, carolling, carolled**; also spelled **caroling** and **caroled** in American English. 1 A **carol** is a religious song that people sing at Christmas time. EG *That evening we sang carols... ...beautiful carol music.* N COUNT

2 When people or birds **carol**, they sing joyfully; a rather old-fashioned word. EG *The choir was carolling* V

away with Miss Gray at the piano. • When a group of people **go carolling**, they go from house to house at Christmas time singing carols, especially in order to collect money for charity. • PHR : VB INFLECTS ⇑ sing

carotid artery /kərɒtɪd ɑ:təri¹/, carotid arteries. A **carotid artery** is one of the two arteries in the neck that supply the head with blood; a medical term. N COUNT ⇑ artery

carouse /kəraʊz/, **carouses, carousing, caroused**. If you **carouse**, you enjoy yourself drinking a lot of alcohol and making a lot of noise with a group of people. EG *...drunken soldiers carousing in the streets.* V ⇑ drink = make merry

carousel /kærəsel, -zel/, **carousels**. A **carousel** is 1 a large rotating mechanical device that has plastic or wooden animals, cars, etc on it which children can sit on; used mainly in American English. N COUNT 2 at an airport, a belt that moves round from which passengers can collect their luggage; used especially in American English. N COUNT

carp /kɑ:p/, **carps, carping, carped**. **Carp** is both the singular and the plural form of the noun. 1 A **carp** is a large fish that lives in lakes and rivers. N COUNT

2 If you **carp**, you keep complaining about things that are not important. EG *All this carping and criticizing won't get us anywhere.* V : IF+PREP THEN *at/about* ⇑ complain

car park, car parks; also spelled with a hyphen. A **car park** is an open area of ground or a building with several storeys where people can leave their cars, usually if they pay a small amount of money; used mainly in British English. EG *...the entrance to the multi-storey car park.* N COUNT = parking lot

carpenter /kɑ:pɪntə/, **carpenters**. A **carpenter** is a person whose job is making and repairing wooden things, especially parts of buildings. N COUNT ⇑ craftsman

carpentry /kɑ:pɪntri¹/ is the skill or the work of a carpenter. N UNCOUNT

carpet /kɑ:pɪt/, **carpets, carpeting, carpeted**.
1 A **carpet** is a thick, heavy covering, usually made from a material like wool, which is put on floors and stairs so that they are warm and comfortable to walk on. EG *...pale-coloured walls with matching curtains, fitted carpets and mirrors... He asked what the marks were on the stair carpet.* N COUNT

2 If you **carpet** a room or other area of a building, you lay a carpet on the floor. EG *We hadn't got enough money to carpet the whole house.* V+O ⇑ cover
◇ **carpeted**. EG *She led them along a carpeted corridor.* ◇ ADJ CLASSIF ⇑ covered

3 A **carpet** of things is a quantity of them which are so close together that they form a layer which completely covers the ground or some other surface. EG *Its surface was covered by a glistening carpet of cockroaches... The forest is an endless woven carpet of dense, dark green.* N COUNT+SUPP ▸ used as a verb. EG *The ground was carpeted with flowers.* ▸ V+O ⇑ cover

4 If you are **on the carpet**, you are in trouble with someone who is angry with you because of what you have done; an informal expression. PHR : USED AS AN A

5 to **sweep** something **under the carpet**: see **sweep**.

carpetbagger /kɑ:pɪtbægə/, **carpetbaggers**. A **carpetbagger** is someone who tries to become a politician in an area which is not their home, simply because they think they are more likely to succeed there; used in American English showing disapproval. N COUNT ⇑ opportunist

carpeting /kɑ:pɪtɪŋ/. You use **carpeting** to refer to the carpets that are fitted in a room or building, or the type of material that is used for carpets. EG *...wall-to-wall carpeting... ...a shabby house with worn carpeting on the stairs.* N UNCOUNT

carpet slipper, carpet slippers. **Carpet slippers** are comfortable, fairly plain, slippers. N COUNT : USU PL ⇑ slipper

carpet sweeper, carpet sweepers. A **carpet sweeper** is a device with a long handle and a brush fixed to a roller on the bottom of it which turns and picks up dirt when you push it over a carpet. N COUNT ⇑ cleaner

car port, car ports. A **car port** is a shelter for one or two cars which is attached to a house and consists of a flat roof supported on pillars. N COUNT

carriage /kærɪdʒ/, **carriages**. 1 A **carriage** is 1.1 in British English, one of the separate sections of a train that carries passengers. EG *The man left his seat by the window and crossed the carriage to where I was sitting.* N COUNT ⇑ vehicle = coach 1.2 an old-fashioned four-wheeled vehicle for passengers which is pulled by one or more horses. EG *...a horse and carriage... The couple go by carriage to the Palace.* N COUNT, OR *by*+N = coach 1.3 a movable part of a machine that supports another part. EG *...a typewriter carriage.* N COUNT

2 A person's **carriage** is the way they hold their head and body when they are walking, standing, or sitting. EG *Her carriage and diction were always faultless.* N UNCOUNT = deportment

3 **Carriage** is the cost of delivering or transporting something. EG *It costs only £49, with carriage included.* N UNCOUNT

carriageway /kærɪdʒweɪ/, **carriageways**. A **carriageway** is one of the two sides of a motorway or dual carriageway, where traffic travels in one direction only, in two or three lanes; used mainly in British English. EG *...the southbound carriageway of the M1.* N COUNT

carrier /kærɪə/, **carriers**. A **carrier** is 1 a vehicle or device that is used for carrying things or people. EG *...an oxygen carrier... ...a potential nuclear weapons carrier... ...an infant carrier.* N COUNT : USU+SUPP = transporter 2 the same as an aircraft carrier. N COUNT 3 a person, animal, or thing that is infected with a germ or a disease which they can give to other people or animals and make them ill. EG *Both she and Derek must have been carriers... Bottled milk, improperly handled, is a lethal carrier of bacteria.* N COUNT

carrier bag, carrier bags; also spelled with a hyphen. A **carrier bag** is a bag made of paper or plastic that is used especially for carrying shopping in; used in British English. N COUNT

carrier pigeon, carrier pigeons; also spelled with a hyphen. A **carrier pigeon** is a pigeon that has been trained to fly from one place to another, and is used to send small written messages which are attached to its body. N COUNT ⇑ homing pigeon

carrion /kærɪən/ is the decaying flesh of dead animals. EG *These birds live by scavenging carrion.* N UNCOUNT

carrot /kærət/, **carrots**. A **carrot** is 1 a long, thin, orange-coloured vegetable that grows under the ground. EG *She served us sliced beef with carrots and potatoes.* N COUNT/UNCOUNT 2 something that is offered to someone in order to persuade them to do something. The word 'stick' is used to refer generally to the harsher methods of persuasion. EG *Higher education grants are a carrot with which to entice students... The president's policy so far is all sticks and no carrots.* N COUNT = incentive

carroty /kærəti¹/. If someone's hair is **carroty**, it is bright reddish-orange in colour. ADJ COLOUR

carry /kæri¹/, **carries, carrying, carried**. 1 If you **carry** something, you hold it or support it so that it does not touch the ground, and take it with you as you go somewhere. EG *He picked up his suitcase and carried it into the bedroom... Two of them carried off the whimpering dog... My father carried us on his shoulders.* V+O = bear

2 If something such as a river or a wind **carries** something somewhere, it moves it there by its force. EG *A gentle current carried him slowly downstream... The ship was carried along by the prevailing tides... The waste is carried hundreds of miles by the wind.* V+O+A ⇑ take = bear, sweep

3 When a vehicle **carries** people, they travel inside it from one place to another. EG *The bus will have carried 36,000 passengers... It's an aeroplane that carries lots of people relatively cheaply... The second car carries Mrs Travers and Mrs Patel.* V+O ⇑ take = transport, convey

4 If you **carry** something with you, you have it with you wherever you go, for example by keeping it in your pocket or in your handbag. EG *I wasn't allowed to carry a gun... Not enough people were carrying kidney donor cards.* V+O

5 If a person, animal, or thing **carries** a germ or a disease, they are infected with it and are capable of giving it to someone and making them ill. EG *Rats carry very nasty diseases... He carries the virus with him.* V+O+A = convey

6 If someone **carries** something such as a new idea or a message from one place to another, they spread it or take it there. EG *They are ready to carry English culture to the far side of the globe... She could run errands and carry messages.* V+O+A

7 If a situation, action, or idea **carries** a particular quality or meaning, it has that quality or meaning as a clearly recognizable or necessary feature. EG *What he is saying carries more conviction than the rival theories... Any job carries with it daily stretches of boredom... It carries a lot of risk.* V+O : NO PASS, NO CONT ⇑ include

8 If you **carry** something such as an idea or a method to a particular point or extent, you develop it to that extent. EG *Georg Simmel carried this idea one* V+O+A = take

step further... Industrial democracy has been carried to its logical conclusion... The emphasis on the mechanics of picture-making has been carried far enough.

9 If a newspaper or poster **carries** a picture or a piece of writing, it contains it or displays it. EG *The Wall Street Journal carried a long report on the growth of vigilante groups... A poster carried a portrait of Churchill... The placards will carry the words: PROTECT THE BRITISH PRESS.* V+O ⇑ contain = have

10 In a formal meeting or debate, if a proposal or motion **is carried**, a majority of people vote in favour of it. EG *My proposal was not carried... The Government's motion was carried by 259 votes to 162.* V+O : USU PASS = approve, pass ≠ defeat, reject

11 If an action such as breaking a law **carries** a particular punishment, anyone doing it will receive that punishment. EG *Adultery in most cultures carried the death penalty... Violations of rules carry automatic fines.* V+O : NO CONT = incur

12 If a sound **carries**, it can be heard a long way away. EG *Sound seems to carry better in the still evening air... He spoke in a faint voice which carried no farther than the front three rows.* V = travel

13 If something **carries** you through a particular period of time, it makes it possible for you to survive or endure something unpleasant during that time. EG *They had enough grain to carry them through a few weeks... She had signed up for a series of philosophy lectures to carry her through the autumn evenings.* V+O+A *(through)* ⇑ help = see

14 If you **carry** people who are lazy or inefficient, you support them, for example by doing some of their work for them. EG *She carries the entire office... You can no longer afford to carry shirkers of any kind.* V+O

15 If someone **carries** a state or area, they win the majority of votes in that area in an election. EG *He carried only two States in the election.* V+O : NO PASS = take ≠ lose

16 If someone such as an actor or politician **carries** people with them, they make people sympathize with them, believe in them, or support them. EG *He carries his audience with him... You have got to carry the people of the country with you.* V+O+A *(with)* = take

17 If you **carry** yourself in a particular way, especially in a proud or graceful way, you move around in that way. EG *From their manner of carrying themselves I could tell how proud they were.* V+O (REFL)

18 If a woman or a female animal **is carrying** a child, she is pregnant; a rather old-fashioned word. EG *While I was carrying Mary her father left me.* V+O = expect

19 The word **carry** is also used in the following expressions. **19.1** If you **carry a load** or **carry a burden**, you have a serious problem or responsibility, or a lot of work. EG *This is a case of a very heavy load carried by a social worker... ...the heavy burden of insurance carried by two marine insurance firms.* PHR : VB INFLECTS

19.2 If a person or their opinion **carries weight**, **carries a lot of weight**, etc, they are respected by people and have the ability to influence them. EG *What you and I think doesn't carry much weight around here... He carries little weight in the party.* PHR : VB INFLECTS

19.3 If you **carry** information of some kind **in** your **head** or **in** your **mind**, you are able to remember it without needing to write it down or be reminded of it by other people. EG *...the list which he carried in his head.* PHR : VB INFLECTS = retain **19.4** If you **carry the day**, you are the winner in a battle, debate, competition, etc. EG *The orator was trying to carry the day by an emotional appeal.* PHR : VB INFLECTS ⇑ win ≠ lose

19.5 If a person or a method that they use **carries everything before** them, **carries all before** them, etc, they easily succeed in achieving something. EG *As usual she carried everything before her... His approach carried all before it.* PHR : VB INFLECTS **19.6** • to **carry the can**: see **can**. • to **carry coals to Newcastle**: see **coal**.

carry away. If you **are carried away** or **get carried away**, you are so eager or enthusiastic about something that you behave in a hasty or foolish way. EG *It is worth looking in at a sale, but do not get carried away... 'Did I say you could kiss me?'-'Sorry. I was carried away.'* PHR : VB INFLECTS = lose control ≠ keep control

carry off. **1** If you **carry** something **off**, you succeed in doing it. EG *She would have carried everything off beautifully.* PHRASAL VB : V+O+ADV ⇑ perform = bring off

2 If you **carry off** a prize or an award, you win it. EG *Vita carried off all the prizes... Liane Aukin carried off the Best Play Adaptation.* PHRASAL VB : V+O+ADV = take

carry on. **1** If you **carry on** doing something, you continue to do it. EG *I carried on with my Open University studies... She was not in the least disturbed, and carried on reading... I could never have carried on without their support... 'I'm not boring you am I?'-'No, no. Carry on.'... ...carrying on the family tradition.* PHRASAL VB : V+ADV, OR ORDER V+ADV+O = keep on ≠ stop, finish

2 If you **carry on**, you make a fuss about something, often by talking in a noisy or excited way; an informal use. EG *The child was screaming and carrying on... Anyone would think you owned the whole hill the way you carry on.* PHRASAL VB : V+ADV = go on

3 If you **carry on** a particular kind of work, a conversation, or a love affair, you do it or take part in it. EG *Our work is carried on in a completely informal atmosphere... It was the worst possible place to carry on his research. She could not carry on a sensible conversation.* PHRASAL VB : V+O+ADV = conduct

4 If you **carry on** with someone, you have a love affair with them; a rather old-fashioned, informal word used showing disapproval. EG *Helen was carrying on with Hogan.* PHRASAL VB : V+ADV, OR V+ADV+A *(with)*, RECIP

5 See also **carry-on**.

carry out. **1** If you **carry** something **out**, you begin doing it and continue until it is finished. EG *They have to carry out many administrative duties... 'Woman' magazine has just carried out a survey into women in wedlock... The first experiments were carried out by Dr Preston McLendon.* PHRASAL VB : V+O+ADV ⇑ perform = undertake, conduct

2 If you **carry out** an order or an instruction, you do what you are told to do. EG *He explained that he was simply carrying out instructions... The policies proposed at congress are being carried out without dissent.* PHRASAL VB : V+O+ADV = implement

carry over. If you **carry over** something from one situation or state to another, you make it continue to exist in the new situation or state. EG *Obedience becomes institutionalized and is carried over from the war into the peace... Small children live a life of fantasy and they carry this fantasy over into action.* PHRASAL VB : V+O+ADV ⇑ transfer = bring over

carry through. If you **carry** something **through**, you finish doing it, often when it is difficult to do. EG *...the task of carrying through the necessary reforms... We are united on these policies and determined to carry them through.* PHRASAL VB : V+O+ADV ⇑ achieve = see through

carrycot /kæri¹kɒt/, **carrycots**. A **carrycot** is an object for a baby to sleep in which is shaped like a box and has handles so that it can be carried; used especially in British English. N COUNT

carry-on. A **carry-on** is behaviour that you think is annoying and unnecessary, for example fussing about something; an informal word used in British English showing disapproval. EG *Well, what a carry-on.* N SING WITH DET = fuss

carsick /kɑ:sɪk/. If you are **carsick**, you feel ill while travelling in a car. EG *They had to stop twice because Billy got carsick.* ADJ QUALIT : USU PRED ⇑ sick

cart /kɑ:t/, **carts, carting, carted**. **1** A **cart** is **1.1** a heavy wooden vehicle with two wheels that is pulled by horses or cattle and is used on farms or to transport heavy goods. EG *...a cart loaded with hay... Huge carts lumber along, pulled by bullocks.* N COUNT ⇑ vehicle = wagon **1.2** a small light wooden vehicle for passengers that has two wheels and is pulled by a horse. EG *...a little pony cart.* N COUNT **1.3** a small wooden vehicle with two or four wheels that is pushed or pulled along by hand and used for transporting goods. EG *People pulled carts of fruits and vegetables along the streets.* N COUNT = barrow, handcart

2 If you **put the cart before the horse**, you do things in the wrong order. PHR : VB INFLECTS

3 To **cart** something means to transport it in a cart. EG *I want the hay carted.* V+O : USU+A

4 If you **cart** things or people somewhere, you carry them or transport them there, especially with some difficulty or effort; an informal use. EG *I don't have to worry about carting belongings all over the world.* V+O+A = lug

cart off. If you **cart** someone **off**, you take them somewhere, especially when they are unwilling to go there or have not been asked whether they want to go there. EG *His father was carted off to jail.* PHRASAL VB : V+O+ADV, USU+A

carte blanche /kɑ:t blɑ:nt⁰ʃ/. If you have **carte blanche**, you have complete power to do exactly as you wish, which is given to you by someone who has authority over you. EG *They gave him carte blanche to publish his proposals.* N UNCOUNT : USU +*to*-INF

cartel /kɑ:tel/, **cartels**. A **cartel** is an association of similar companies or businesses that have N COUNT grouped together in order to prevent competition and to control prices. EG *...the setting up of an international cartel like the oil producers' OPEC.*

carthorse /kɑːthɔːs/, **carthorses**. A **carthorse** is a big powerful horse that is used to pull carts, wagons, carriages, etc. N COUNT ⇑ horse

cartilage /kɑːtɪ⁰lɪdʒ/, **cartilages**. **Cartilage** is a strong, flexible substance inside the body, for example in your nose and around your joints. The skeletons of young animals and some fish are also made of cartilage. ▸ also used of a piece of this substance in one part of the body, especially in the knee. EG *He's torn a cartilage.* N UNCOUNT ⇑ tissue ▸ N COUNT

cartographer /kɑtɒgrəfə/, **cartographers**. A **cartographer** is a person whose job is drawing maps. N COUNT

cartography /kɑːtɒgrəfi¹/ is the art of drawing maps. N UNCOUNT

carton /kɑːtə⁰n/, **cartons**. A **carton** is 1 a strong cardboard box which is closed by flaps at the top and in which you pack goods for storage and transport. EG *...a cardboard carton full of photographic equipment.* 2 a container made of cardboard or plastic in which goods are sold, especially food and drink. EG *...a cereal carton... ...a plastic carton filled with fried potatoes.* ▸ also used to refer to the things inside a carton. EG *He drank a carton of milk.* N COUNT ⇑ container; N COUNT; ▸ N PART

cartoon /kɑːtuːn/, **cartoons**. A **cartoon** is 1 a drawing, usually in a newspaper or magazine and often with a comment underneath it, which is funny or makes a political point or criticism. EG *Cartoons portrayed emaciated kids begging milk from the callous Governor.* 2 in British English, a series of drawn pictures, especially in a newspaper or magazine, that show an amusing story or an adventure in the life of a particular character. 3 a film in which the characters and scenes are drawn rather than being real people and objects. EG *We watched a Tom and Jerry cartoon.* 4 a large, detailed drawing that is made in preparation for a painting, tapestry, etc, so that the painting or tapestry can be copied from it. EG *...Holbein's tremendous cartoon of Henry VII.* N COUNT; N COUNT = comic strip; N COUNT = animated cartoon; N COUNT+SUPP

cartoonist /kɑːtuːnɪst/, **cartoonists**. A **cartoonist** is a person who draws cartoons, especially as a job for newspapers and magazines. N COUNT ⇑ artist

cartridge /kɑːtrɪdʒ/, **cartridges**. A **cartridge** is 1 a metal or cardboard tube that is put in a gun and contains a bullet and a substance that will explode and send the bullet out when the gun is fired. 2 the part of the arm of a record player that holds the needle and that can be taken off. 3 a thin plastic tube containing ink that can be fitted into a special kind of pen. N COUNT ⇑ container; N COUNT; N COUNT

cartridge paper is a strong type of paper that is suitable for drawing on. N UNCOUNT

cartwheel /kɑːtwiːl/, **cartwheels**, **cartwheeling**, **cartwheeled**. A **cartwheel** is 1 a fast acrobatic movement in which someone throws themselves sideways onto one hand, then puts the other hand down, and then ends up back on their feet, so that they look like a wheel spinning along. EG *She kicked off her shoes and turned three perfect cartwheels across the grass.* ▸ used as a verb. EG *...progressing by cartwheeling and rolling.* 2 a wheel with large wooden spokes and a metal tyre, which is attached to a cart. N COUNT; ▸ V; N COUNT

carve /kɑːv/, **carves**, **carving**, **carved**. 1 If you **carve** an object, you make it by cutting it out of a substance such as stone or wood. EG *The statue was carved by John Gibson... ...candles carved in the shape of Buddhas.* V+O : USU+A = sculpt

2 If you **carve** a design or a letter on an object, especially one made of wood, you cut it into the surface of the object. EG *He begins to carve his initials on the beech tree... ...an intricately carved door.* V OR V+O : USU+A

3 If you **carve** a cooked bird or piece of meat, you cut slices from it, especially when serving it at a meal. EG *She carved me a piece of roast pork... Will you carve, John?* V, V+O, OR V+O+O

4 If a river, wind, etc **carves** a particular shape in land, it changes the appearance of the landscape over a long period of time by wearing away rock or carrying away soil. EG *It must have taken the Colorado River a century or so to carve this canyon out of red clay soil.* V+O : USU+A ⇑ cut

5 See also **carving**.

carve out. 1 If people **carve out** something such as a particular place, they create it in a larger area, often with difficulty. EG *A small airport had been carved out of an endless pine forest on a plateau.* PHRASAL VB : V+O+ADV, IF+PREP THEN *of*

2 If someone **carves out** a career or a good position, they get it by hard work and effort; an informal use. EG *She's carved out a successful career for herself in the Foreign Office.* PHRASAL VB : V+O+ADV ⇑ create = make

carve up. 1 If you **carve** something **up**, you divide it into smaller areas or pieces. EG *When the old man died the estate was carved up and sold.* PHRASAL VB : V+O+ADV

2 If you **carve** someone **up**, you wound them badly with a knife; an informal use. PHRASAL VB : V+O+ADV

carvery /kɑːvə⁰ri¹/, **carveries**. A **carvery** is a restaurant where you can eat roast meat that is carved for you at a special counter in the same room. N COUNT

carving /kɑːvɪŋ/, **carvings**. 1 A **carving** is 1.1 a small statue or decorative object that has been cut out of stone, wood, etc. EG *Small valuable items, such as miniature carvings, should be packed in cotton wool.* 1.2 a pattern or design that has been cut into a piece of furniture, a ceiling, etc. EG *It's an interesting piece of furniture. Some nice carving on it too.* N COUNT; N COUNT/UNCOUNT

2 **Carving** is the art of carving objects, patterns, or designs. EG *Here you can see English carving at its best.* N UNCOUNT

carving knife, **carving knives**. A **carving knife** is a large knife that is used to cut cooked meat. N COUNT

cascade /kæskeɪd/, **cascades**, **cascading**, **cascaded**. 1 A **cascade** is 1.1 a small waterfall or group of waterfalls flowing down a rocky hillside. EG *From there the river fell in a series of cascades down towards the Hudson.* 1.2 an amount of cloth, hair, etc that falls or hangs in folds over something; a literary use. EG *Her dark hair was down, falling in a cascade over her shoulders.* N COUNT; N COUNT

2 When water **cascades**, it flows fast down a hillside or over rocks. EG *The water cascaded over the rocks.* V+A = gush

3 If cloth or hair **cascades** over something, it falls or hangs in folds over it; a literary use. EG *He had long white hair that cascaded in uncombed disarray over his thin shoulders.* V+A ⇑ fall

case /keɪs/, **cases**, **casing**, **cased**. 1 A **case** is 1.1 a particular situation that you are considering on its own or on an individual basis, especially when you are using it as an example of something, or when you are comparing it with something else. EG *These plants are staffed by migrant workers (in Fiat's case, from Sicily, Sardinia and Calabria)... Parts of the fleet were running short of food and (in the case of the submarines) fuel... These tribes are a classic case of people living in harmony with their environment.* 1.2 a particular incident that you are describing or explaining. EG *Over and over again we hear of cases where machinery like this has been bought... All cases of bullying will be severely dealt with.* N COUNT : USU SING, USU+SUPP; N COUNT+SUPP = instance, occurrence

2 **In any case** is used 2.1 when you state a fact or opinion that gives an additional reason or piece of information that supports a point made previously. EG *I couldn't shelter behind him all the time, and in any case he wasn't always with me... The precise function of this organ is not certain. It probably varies in any case from species to species.* 2.2 when you are returning to a topic, for example after giving an opinion or some extra details. EG *That was when the trouble started. I don't know what he did. Perhaps he did nothing. In any case, there was a brief scuffle.* 2.3 to show that you are limiting an opinion or statement you have made to what is definitely known to be true. EG *The influence of economists, or in any case the influence of economics, is far-reaching.* PHR : USED AS ADV SEN = anyway, besides; PHR : USED AS ADV SEN = anyway; PHR : USED AS AN A = at any rate, at least

3 **In case** is used 3.1 to introduce something that may possibly happen, which is the reason why something else is done. EG *I ran away down the hill in case she tried to follow... I've got the key in case we want to go inside... I wanted to be sure in case of a sudden emergency that we gave the right advice.* 3.2 to refer vaguely to the possibility of something happening, which you do not actually specify, and which is the reason why you do something or suggest something. EG *Do you want me to hold one of them just in case?... She ought to be there in case.* 3.3 when you are giving a piece of information in order to introduce the reason why you are giving it. EG *Little Melanie, in case you've forgotten, hasn't forgiven* CONJ SUBORD, OR PREP+*of* ⇑ if; PHR : USED AS AN A, USU *just*+PHR; CONJ SUBORD ⇑ if

you... In case you didn't know, there are three basic wines: red, white, and rosé.

4 The word **case** is also used in the following expressions. **4.1** When you say that something happens **in** many **cases, in** a number of **cases**, etc, you are stating how often it happens in a particular way, especially in relation to the total number of times that it happens. EG *We manufacture a vast range of materials which rival, and in many cases surpass, traditional materials... This causes problems in some cases... This system works well in at least nine out of ten cases.* PHR : USED AS AN A

4.2 When you say that a situation **is a case of** something, you are stating the way that the situation actually is, sometimes when you are contrasting it with the way that other people think it is. EG *It was a case of not knowing what else to do.* PHR : VB INFLECTS

4.3 If you say that something **is a case in point**, you mean that it is an interesting or important example of something that you have just mentioned. EG *Observing recent events there, one comes to the conclusion that the system can only be changed by force. The election is a case in point.* PHR : VB INFLECTS

4.4 You say **in that case, in which case**, etc, before giving an opinion, suggestion, or conclusion that is a consequence of something said previously. EG *'The bar is closed,' the waiter said. 'In that case,' McFee said, 'allow me to invite you back to my flat for a drink...' I greatly enjoy these meetings unless I have to make a speech, in which case I'm in a state of dreadful anxiety.* PHR : USED AS ADV SEN = therefore

4.5 When you say that something **is the case**, you mean that the situation that is being discussed or described is true. EG *The majority, led by Pablo, argued that this was the case.... That was not the case with the American women in our delegation..., ...a regime under which abortion and divorce are constitutionally prohibited (as is the case in the Irish Republic.)* PHR : VB INFLECTS ⇑ be = be so

4.6 You say **as the case may be, whatever the case may be**, etc when it is not clear which of the two or more alternatives you have stated is most likely to happen. EG *The union is sitting things out until Labour is returned to office in a couple of years. Or not, as the case may be.* PHR

5 A **case** is also **5.1** a person or a problem that someone such as a doctor, solicitor, or social worker is dealing with. EG *They discussed her case fully... Doctor Chevington will take over the case... She is clearly a case for treatment.* N COUNT

5.2 a person with a particular illness or medical problem. EG *...road accident cases... She was definitely a mental case.* N COUNT : MOD+N ⇑ patient

5.3 a crime or mystery that the police or detectives are investigating. EG *...one of Sherlock Holmes's cases.* N COUNT

6 If you say that someone is a sad **case**, a hopeless **case**, etc, you mean that they are in a sad situation, hopeless situation, etc. EG *Bill seemed a hopeless case.* N COUNT : ADJ+N, USU USED AS C ⇑ person

7 If you say that someone is **a case**, you mean that they behave in a very silly way; used in informal English, often humorously. N SING : a+N ⇑ person = nutter, nutcase

8 The **case** for or against a particular plan or idea is the arguments that you use, together with the facts and reasons that support them. EG *There was a very good case indeed for introducing a degree in the subject... Those opposed to gambling continued to argue the case against it on moral and social grounds... He stated his case.* N COUNT : USU SING, IF+PREP THEN *for/against* ⇑ argument

9 make a case. 9.1 If you **make a case** or **make out** a **case**, you state strong arguments for or against a particular thing. EG *They made out a case for more arms control.* PHR : VB INFLECTS, IF+PREP THEN *for/against*

9.2 If you **make** your **case** or **make the case** for something, you prove it by means of arguments, reasons, and facts. EG *Today the relative failures of the state make the case for more individual freedom... I suggest that any one of these arguments is enough to make my case.* PHR : VB INFLECTS, IF+PREP THEN *for/against*

10 A **case** in law is **10.1** a trial or other legal inquiry to settle a lawsuit or decide whether a person is guilty or not. EG *...cases about equal pay... That's the way it seemed until a recent case came up in court... He had lost the case.* • See also **test case.** N COUNT ⇑ process

10.2 the evidence that is presented for or against a particular person or issue in a court of law; sometimes used to refer to the way the evidence is presented, or how strong the evidence is. EG *...the case for the defence... There is no case against the suspected official.* N COUNT : USU SING, IF+PREP THEN *for/against*

11 A **case** is also **11.1** a box or other container that is specially designed to hold or protect something, often so that it can be carried easily or safely. EG *...scissors in a leather case.* • See also **attaché case, briefcase, pillowcase, vanity case.** N COUNT

11.2 a suitcase. EG *They unload their trunks and cases.* N COUNT

11.3 a container, usually made of glass and wood, in which objects can be displayed, for example in a museum or a shop. EG *The sword was mounted in a mahogany case... ...a glass case.* • See also **bookcase, showcase.** N COUNT : USU MOD+N

11.4 a box containing twelve bottles of wine, sherry, or other alcoholic drink, which is sold as a single unit. ▸ also used to refer to the number of bottles inside a case. EG *I bought a couple of cases of sweet wine.* N COUNT ⇑ container ▸ N PART

11.5 an outer covering that contains the seed of a plant, a developing insect, etc. EG *The insect jerks itself free and hangs on the empty pupa case... ...seed cases.* N COUNT

12 In grammar, the **case** of a noun, pronoun, or other word is the form of it which shows its relationship to other words in the sentence. For example, in English, the words 'we' and 'us' have different cases. N COUNT : USU MOD+N ⇑ category

13 See also **lower case, upper case.**

14 A thing that **is cased** in something is covered or surrounded by it. EG *His feet were cased in black mud.* ◊ **cased.** EG *The park stretched out cased in thick white fog.* V+O+A *(in)*: ONLY PASS ◊ ADJ CLASSIF : PRED+*in*

15 If someone, usually someone who is intending to commit a crime, **cases** a place, they have a look at it to see how they can enter it or to see what it is like; an informal use. V+O

casebook /keɪsbʊk/, **casebooks.** A **casebook** is a written record of the cases dealt with by a doctor, social worker, police officer, etc. N COUNT

case history, case histories; also spelled with a hyphen. A **case history** is the history and background of someone or something, and the problems affecting them. Doctors and social workers study the case histories of their patients or clients. EG *They seem to have had no case history of illness... The episode has some interest as a case history in this study of the uses and abuses of Press power.* N COUNT

case law is law established by following decisions that have been made by judges in earlier cases; a technical term in law. N UNCOUNT ≠ statute law

casement /keɪsmə²nt/, **casements.** A **casement** is a window that opens by means of hinges, usually at the side. EG *I threw open the casement windows.* N COUNT

case study, case studies; also spelled with a hyphen. A **case study** is an account that gives detailed information about a person, group, or thing and their development over a period of time. EG *...case studies of particular pieces of legislation.* N COUNT

casework /keɪswɜːk/ is social work that involves actually dealing or working with people who need help. N UNCOUNT

cash /kæʃ/, **cashes, cashing, cashed. 1 Cash** is **1.1** money in the form of notes and coins rather than cheques. EG *How much cash do you have?... ...four million pounds in cash... You're paying in cash, are you?... ...a weekly cash payment.* • See also **hard cash, petty cash.** N UNCOUNT

1.2 in informal English, money. EG *We've run out of cash.* N UNCOUNT

2 If you **cash** a cheque, you exchange it at a bank for the amount of money that it is worth. EG *A giro cheque must be cashed within 3 months of the date shown on it.* V+O

cash in. If you **cash in** on a situation, you take advantage of it, especially by doing something slightly unfair or dishonest. EG *People were nervous, and the military establishments, backed by arms industries, cashed in... They use the American dream of freedom to cash in on other people's inequality.* PHRASAL VB : V+ADV, IF+PREP THEN *on* ⇑ exploit

cash-and-carry, cash-and-carries. A **cash-and-carry** is a large shop where you can buy goods in large quantities if you work for a business or organization, and where the goods are usually cheaper than in ordinary shops. N COUNT = wholesale shop

cash book, cash books; also spelled with a hyphen and as one word. A **cash book** is a book in which a record is kept of payments made and money received by an organization or a person. N COUNT

cash box, cash boxes; also spelled with a hyphen. A **cash box** is a strong box, usually made of metal, with a lock on it, in which money is kept. N COUNT

cash crop, cash crops. A **cash crop** is a crop that is grown in order to be sold. EG *Bananas and citrus fruits are the only cash crops grown in the area.* N COUNT

cash-desk, cash-desks; also spelled without a hyphen. A **cash-desk** is the place in a large shop where you pay for the things that you want to buy. N COUNT ↑ counter = checkout

cash dispenser, cash dispensers. A **cash dispenser** is the same as a cashpoint. N COUNT

cashew /kæʃu:, kæʃu:/, **cashews**. A **cashew** or a **cashew nut** is a curved nut that you can eat. N COUNT

cash flow The **cash flow** of a firm or business is the movement of money into and out of it. EG *Work out a projected cash flow for your first 12 months trading... ...cash flow problems.* N SING

cashier /kəˈʃɪə/, **cashiers, cashiering, cashiered**. 1 A **cashier** is the person that customers pay money to or get money from in a shop, bank, garage, etc. N COUNT ↑ employee

2 To **cashier** someone means to officially force them to leave the army, navy, or air force because they have done something wrong. EG *Stevens was cashiered in 1938.* V+O ↑ discharge = drum out

cashmere /kæʃmɪə/ is a very fine soft wool. EG *...her cream-coloured cashmere shawl.* N UNCOUNT : USU BEFORE N

cashpoint /kæʃpɔɪnt/, **cashpoints**. A **cashpoint** is a machine on the outside of some banks where you can take out money at any time by using a special card and typing your code number. EG *...drawing money from the cashpoint... ...a cashpoint card.* N COUNT = cash dispenser

cash register, cash registers; also spelled with a hyphen. A **cash register** is a machine in a shop, pub, or restaurant that is used to add up and record how much money people pay, and in which the money is kept. N COUNT = till

casing /keɪsɪŋ/, **casings**. A **casing** is something that covers or surrounds something else, usually in order to protect it. EG *...a bomb casing.* N COUNT ↑ covering

casino /kəsi:nəʊ/, **casinos**. A **casino** is a building or room where people play gambling games such as roulette. N COUNT ↑ place

cask /kɑ:sk/, **casks**. A **cask** is a wooden barrel that is used for storing alcoholic drink. EG *The wood of the brandy cask smelt of alcohol.* ▸ also used to refer to the drink inside a cask. EG *...a cask of beer.* N COUNT ↑ container ▸ N PART ↑ amount

casket /kɑ:skɪt/, **caskets**. A **casket** is 1 a small box, often beautifully decorated, in which you keep jewellery or other valuable items. EG *Her exquisite jewel casket was painted by Rossetti.* 2 in American English, a coffin. N COUNT ↑ container; N COUNT

cassava /kəsɑ:və/ is 1 a South American plant with thick roots that is grown for food. 2 flour that is obtained from the roots of the cassava plant. N UNCOUNT; N UNCOUNT

casserole /kæsərəʊl/, **casseroles, casseroling, casseroled**. 1 A **casserole** is 1.1 a dish that is made by cooking meat or fish with vegetables in liquid at a low temperature in an oven. EG *...a casserole of fresh leeks and wild rabbit.* 1.2 a large, deep container with a lid, often made of pottery, in which food can be cooked in an oven and then served. N COUNT; N COUNT ↑ dish

2 When you **casserole** meat, vegetables, etc, you cook them in liquid slowly in an oven. V+O

cassette /kəˈset/, **cassettes**. A **cassette** is 1 a small, flat, rectangular plastic container which holds a tape that is used for recording or playing sound. 2 a cassette player or a cassette recorder. EG *I decided to listen to some music and put Eric Satie into the cassette.* N COUNT; N COUNT

cassette player, cassette players. A **cassette player** is a machine that is used for playing cassettes and sometimes also recording them. N COUNT

cassette recorder, cassette recorders. A **cassette recorder** is a machine that is used for recording and playing cassettes. N COUNT ↑ tape recorder

cassock /kæsək/, **cassocks**. A **cassock** is a long robe, often black, that is worn by members of the clergy in some churches. EG *He was wearing a black cassock and a dog collar.* N COUNT

cast /kɑ:st/, **casts, casting**. **Cast** is used in the present tense and as the past tense and past participle of the verb. 1 The **cast** of a play or a film consists of all the people who act in it. EG *Even my friends in the cast had doubts about accepting me to direct the play... We had a splendid cast.* N COUNT : IF SING, VB CAN BE SING OR PL = dramatis personae

2 To **cast** an actor or a part means to choose a particular actor to play a character in a play or film. EG *I was cast as the husband, a man of about fifty... Caliban is always a difficult part to cast in The Tempest.* V+O, OR V+O+A (as)

3 If you **cast** someone in a particular way, you describe them in that way because you think it explains their character or attitude. EG *What does your party have to gain by casting the unemployed as work-shy?... They still had the American reluctance to be cast in the role of scorners of the law.* V+O (NG/REFL) +A (as/in) ↑ classify = brand, label

4 If you **cast** looks in a particular direction or **cast** your eyes in a particular direction, you look in a particular direction or at a particular person. EG *He kept casting worried glances over his shoulder... The three prefects cast looks of despair at Madeleine... Her eyes were cast downward.* V+O+A

5 If you **cast** your **mind back** to a time in the past, you think about it and remember what happened. EG *Casting her mind back to youthful days, she remembered many pleasant walks by this river... He cast his mind back over the day.* PHR : VB INFLECTS

6 If something **casts** light or shadow onto a place or thing, it causes light or shadow to appear there; a fairly literary use. EG *The smoky fires cast dancing shadows over the wide circle of faces.* V+O+A = throw

7 When you **cast** a vote, you vote. EG *I couldn't decide how to cast my vote.* V+O ↑ give

8 If you **cast** doubt or suspicion on something, you cause other people to be unsure about it. EG *The Minister had cast subtle doubt on some of the traditional beliefs of his party.* V+O : IF+PREP THEN on/upon = throw

9 When someone such as a witch **casts** a spell on someone or something, they do some magic that affects that person or thing. ● If a person **casts** their **spell** on you or if a place or thing **casts** its **spell** on you, you are fascinated or charmed by them or it. EG *She cast her spell on the whole audience.* V+O : IF+PREP THEN on; ● PHR : VB INFLECTS, IF+PREP THEN on

10 If you **cast** someone somewhere, you force them into an unpleasant place or situation; a literary use. EG *He was cast into prison without trial.* V+O+A ↑ put = throw

11 If you **cast** a thought or feeling from your mind, you deliberately no longer think it or feel it at all; a fairly formal use. EG *Cast all thoughts of freedom from your mind... Ultimately, no doubt, love casts out fear.* V+O+A ↑ remove = banish

12 If you **cast** something, you throw it; an old-fashioned or formal use. EG *He was casting stones into the water.* ▸ used as a noun. EG *I had a good hit on my third cast but missed it.* V+O : USU+A; ▸ N COUNT ↑ attempt

13 When someone **casts** a fishing line, they throw one end of it into water. EG *I was casting a line out into the river.* ▸ used as a noun. EG *You sometimes have to make a hundred false casts before you place the fly.* V OR V+O; ▸ N COUNT

14 When an animal such as a snake **casts** its skin, it loses the top layer. V+O = shed

15 When someone **casts** a large object, they make it by pouring hot liquid metal or glass into a specially shaped container and leaving it there until it has hardened into the required shape. EG *This statue of Achilles, cast in bronze, is a tribute to his skill as a sculptor.* V+O

16 A **cast** is 16.1 an object that has been made by pouring a liquid substance such as plaster or heated metal into a hollow container so that when it hardens it has the same shape as the container. EG *Casts taken from the inside of their skulls have provided much information about their evolution.* 16.2 a container into which you pour a liquid substance such as heated metal so that the substance will have a particular shape when it hardens. 16.3 the same as a plaster cast. EG *She came in on crutches that morning, her foot still in a cast.* N COUNT ↑ copy = mould; N COUNT = mould; N COUNT

17 The **cast** of someone's character or mind is the quality and nature of it; a formal use. EG *The man he's going to have to work with is not of the same cast of mind as himself.* N COUNT+of : USU SING = type

18 A **cast** is also an eye defect which causes you to look to one side all the time and never straight ahead. EG *He looked an odd character with his bad teeth and the cast in his eye.* N COUNT : USU SING = squint

19 The word **cast** is also used in the following expressions, which are explained at other places in this dictionary. ● to **cast anchor**: see **anchor**. ● **the die is cast**: see **die**. ● to **cast** your **eye over** something: see **eye**. ● to **cast lots**: see **lot**. ● to **be cast in the same mould, be cast in** someone's **mould**, etc: see **mould**. ● to **cast** your **net wider**: see **net**. ● to **cast pearls before swine**: see **pearl**.

20 See also **casting**.

cast about. If you **cast about** or **cast around**, you look for something; a formal expression. EG *Jack cast* PHRASAL VB : V+ADV, IF+PREP *about for something he could use to get the box open.* THEN *for* = look around

cast aside. If you **cast** someone or something **aside**, you get rid of them because you no longer like them or approve of them. EG *The figure who is an honour to his country is cast aside and disgraced... ...a notion which has been cast aside in anger and indignation.* PHRASAL VB : V+O+ADV = reject

cast away. If you **cast** something **away**, you get rid of it completely; a literary expression. EG *He says he finds his life of little account and is proud to cast it away.* ● See also **castaway**. PHRASAL VB : V+O+ADV = discard, throw away ≠ keep

cast down. To **cast** someone **down** means to cause them to lose their social status; a formal expression. EG *Men of high status were cast down.* PHRASAL VB : V+O+ADV, USU PASS = relegate ≠ raise up

cast off. 1 If you **cast** something **off**, you get rid of it because you no longer want it or because it is preventing you from making progress. EG *Organizations must cast off those bureaucratic practices... They fail to cast off the old and embrace new technologies.* ● See also **cast-off**. PHRASAL VB : V+O+ADV = reject ≠ adopt

2 If you **cast off**, you remove or untie the rope fastening a boat to a harbour wall so that the boat can move away. EG *Hendricks cast off the bow line and walked to the stern.* PHRASAL VB : V+ADV, OR V+O+ADV = undo, unfasten

3 In knitting, to **cast off** stitches means to get rid of them, especially in order to finish a piece of knitting. EG *Cast off in rib.* PHRASAL VB : V+ADV, OR V+ADV+O ≠ cast on

cast on. In knitting, to **cast on** stitches means to make them on a needle in order to begin a piece of knitting. EG *Using 4mm needles cast on 53 stitches.* PHRASAL VB : V+ADV, OR V+ADV+O ≠ cast off

cast out. If you **cast** someone **out**, you get rid of them because you no longer like them or no longer want to be responsible for them; a literary expression. EG *She had abandoned him, she had cast him out... What will such vulnerable creatures do when they are cast out into the open like pet animals left to fend for themselves?* PHRASAL VB : V+O+ADV ⇑ reject = throw out ≠ take in

cast up. If the sea or tide **casts** something **up**, it leaves it on the beach at high tide. EG *His body was cast up onto the shore.* PHRASAL VB : V+O+ADV = wash up

castanet /kæstənet/, **castanets**. **Castanets** are a Spanish musical instrument which consists of two small round pieces of wood or plastic connected by a cord. You hold the castanets in your hand and knock the pieces together to make a noise. N COUNT : USU PL, ALSO *a pair of*+PL

castaway /kɑːstəweɪ/, **castaways**. A **castaway** is a person who has managed to swim or float to a lonely island or shore after their boat has been shipwrecked. EG *...castaways marooned on a desert island.* N COUNT

caste /kɑːst/, **castes**. 1 A **caste** is 1.1 one of the four hereditary classes into which Hindu society is traditionally divided. EG *Sushma came from a lower caste... ...the Brahmin caste.* ▸ also used of the Hindu system of society that is based on dividing people into these classes. EG *...the caste system... Caste was the final barrier to industrialization.* 1.2 a social class or system in any country that is based on dividing people into groups according to their family, rank, wealth, profession, etc. EG *You also have a caste system in England.* N COUNT ⇑ class; ▸ N UNCOUNT; N COUNT/UNCOUNT

2 If you **lose caste**, you lose your social position and the respect of other people. PHR : VB INFLECTS

castellated /kæstə[1]leɪtɪ[2]d/. A **castellated** wall or building has turrets and battlements like a castle; a technical term in architecture. ADJ CLASSIF : USU ATTRIB ⇑ fortified

caster /kɑːstə/. See **castor**.

caster sugar; also spelled **castor sugar**. **Caster sugar** is finely ground white sugar that is often used in cooking. N UNCOUNT

castigate /kæstɪgeɪt/, **castigates, castigating, castigated**. If you **castigate** someone or something, you scold them or criticize them severely; a formal word. EG *He watched me closely and castigated me for mistakes... They castigated the government's report.* ◊ **castigation** /kæstɪgeɪʃə[0]n/, **castigations**. V+O = chastise; ◊ N UNCOUNT/COUNT

casting /kɑːstɪŋ/, **castings**. A **casting** is a metal object or piece of equipment which has been made by pouring liquid metal into a container so that it hardens into the required shape. EG *Overhead a creaking conveyor carried red hot castings.* N COUNT = cast

casting vote, casting votes. A **casting vote** is the vote that the chairperson of a committee gives when an equal number of votes have been given for and against a proposal. This vote decides whether or not the proposal will be passed. EG *R A Butler used his casting vote as chairman to defeat the motion by 6 votes to 5.* N COUNT : USU SING

cast iron; as an adjective, usually spelled with a hyphen. 1 **Cast iron** is iron which contains a small amount of carbon. It is hard but breaks easily and so it has to be made into objects by casting. EG *...sturdy pillars of cast iron... In the house is the studio with its cast-iron stove.* N UNCOUNT : USU N BEFORE N

2 A **cast-iron** alibi, excuse, or guarantee is one that is absolutely certain to be effective and will not fail you. ADJ CLASSIF : ATTRIB = watertight

castle /kɑːsə[0]l/, **castles**. 1 A **castle** is 1.1 a large building or group of buildings which was made secure against attack. Castles were lived in by rulers and powerful people, and some are still lived in today. EG *...Windsor Castle... ...a ruined castle... ...the castle courtyard.* ● See also **sand castle**. 1.2 one of the two chess pieces which stand in the corner of the board at the beginning of a game. N COUNT : ALSO IN NAMES; N COUNT = rook

2 If you are building **castles in the air**, you are making plans that you know are very unlikely to succeed or happen. EG *He's only building castles in the air.* PHR : USED AS O ⇑ dream

cast-off, cast-offs. 1 **Cast-off** clothes are clothes which you do no longer wear, because they do not fit you or you do not like them, and which you give to someone else. EG *She might be put in the embarrassing position of wearing cast-off shoes or sports jackets.* ▸ used as a noun. EG *She was sick of wearing her elder sister's cast-offs.* ADJ CLASSIF : ATTRIB ⇑ old; ▸ N COUNT

2 **Cast-off** is also used to describe something which has been got rid of because it is no longer wanted or it has become a nuisance. EG *...the dwelling places of the cast-off old.* ADJ CLASSIF : ATTRIB = rejected, unwanted

castor /kɑːstə/, **castors**; also spelled **caster**. A **castor** is a small plastic or metal wheel that is fitted to the legs of chairs, beds, etc, so that they can be moved more easily. N COUNT

castor oil is thick yellow oil that is obtained from the seeds of the castor oil plant. It is used to make someone vomit or defecate. N UNCOUNT

castor sugar. See **caster sugar**.

castrate /kæstreɪt/, **castrates, castrating, castrated**. To **castrate** a man or a male animal means to remove their testicles so that they no longer produce sperm. EG *The two bulls had to be castrated.* ◊ **castration** /kæstreɪʃə[0]n/. V+O ⇑ neuter; ◊ N UNCOUNT

casual /kæʒjʊ[0]əl/, **casuals**. 1 Something that is **casual** 1.1 happens or is done by chance or without planning. EG *Her casual remark caused a political storm... ...a casual meeting.* ◊ **casually**. EG *...a casually acquired object.* 1.2 is rather careless and done without much interest. EG *I had a casual glance at the papers... ...a casual friendship.* ◊ **casually**. ADJ CLASSIF ⇑ accidental; ◊ ADV WITH VB; ADJ CLASSIF = superficial; ◊ ADV WITH VB

2 If you are **casual**, you are, or you pretend to be, calm and not very interested in what is happening or what you are doing. EG *He tried to appear casual as he asked her to dance... ...a casual wave.* ◊ **casually**. EG *I walked casually into his room.* ◊ **casualness**. EG *With studied casualness he mentioned it to Hilary.* ADJ QUALIT = nonchalant, unconcerned; ◊ ADV WITH VB; ◊ N UNCOUNT

3 **Casual** clothes are clothes that are suitable for when you are at home or doing things other than working, but are not suitable for work or formal occasions. EG *...a casual shirt.* ▸ used as a plural noun. EG *...smart casuals.* ◊ **casually**. EG *He was dressed casually.* ADJ CLASSIF : ATTRIB ⇑ informal; ▸ N PLURAL; ◊ ADV WITH VB

4 **Casual** work is done for only a short time, and not on a permanent or regular basis. EG *They employ casual workers to pick the fruit... ...a casual job.* ADJ CLASSIF : ATTRIB = temporary

casualty /kæʒjʊ[0]əlti[1]/, **casualties**. 1 A **casualty** is 1.1 a case of death or serious injury to a person in a war, accident, or disaster. EG *The battle cost each side a quarter of a million casualties... There were heavy casualties on both sides.* 1.2 a person who has been killed or injured in a war, accident, or disaster. EG *The casualties were taken to the nearest hospital.* N COUNT : USU PL; N COUNT = victim

1.3 a person or a thing that has suffered badly as a result of a particular event or situation. EG *Truth was an early casualty of the newspaper campaign.* N COUNT : USU+*of* ⇑ loser = victim

2 **Casualty** is the part of a hospital where people who have been hurt in accidents are taken for emergency treatment. EG *The young doctor in Casualty had shown an unprofessional lack of control... ...the casualty ward.* N UNCOUNT ⇑ department

casuistry /kæzjuɪstri¹/ is reasoning that is extremely subtle and designed to mislead other people; a formal word. N UNCOUNT = sophistry

cat /kæt/, **cats**. 1 A cat is 1.1 a small furry animal with a tail, whiskers, and sharp claws that kills smaller animals such as mice and birds. Cats are often kept as pets. EG *She put out a hand and stroked the cat softly... ...domestic animals such as dogs and cats.* N COUNT = moggy, puss 1.2 any animal belonging to the family that includes lions and tigers. EG *Lions will hunt as a team and they are the only cats to do so... ...members of the cat family.* • See also **big cat**. N COUNT

2 The word **cat** is also used in the following expressions. 2.1 If you talk about a **game of cat and mouse**, you are talking about a situation in which one person is more powerful than another and uses this advantage in an unfair or cruel way. EG *There followed a game of cat and mouse with my tormentor... He was forced to play a tense cat-and-mouse game with the snipers.* PHR : USED AS O/ S/C 2.2 If you **let the cat out of the bag**, you make known something that was being kept secret. PHR : VB INFLECTS 2.3 If people are fighting **like cat and dog**, they are fighting or disagreeing violently. PHR : USED AS AN 2.4 If you say that someone **looks like something the cat brought in** or **dragged in**, you mean that they look very untidy or dirty. PHR : VBS INFLECT 2.5 You say **'look what the cat's brought in!'** when you are surprised and pleased to see someone. CONVENTION 2.6 If you say **'there are more ways than one to skin a cat'**, you mean that there are many different ways of doing a particular thing, although people might consider some of them to be unusual or wrong. PHR 2.7 If you say **'there's not enough room to swing a cat'**, you mean that the place you are talking about is very small or crowded. PHR : *be* INFLECTS 2.8 If you say **'while the cat's away, the mice will play'**, you mean that people behave differently when the person in charge of them is not there, for example by enjoying themselves more or behaving badly. PHR 2.9 • **to set the cat among the pigeons**: see **pigeon**. • **to rain cats and dogs**: see **rain**. • **has the cat got your tongue**: see **tongue**.

cataclysm /kætəklɪsəᵒm/, **cataclysms**; a fairly literary word. A **cataclysm** is 1 a great disaster such as a flood or an earthquake. EG *...the cataclysm that would bring the world to an end.* N COUNT = catastrophe 2 a very important or violent social, military, or political event, especially one that fundamentally changes life or society. N COUNT = upheaval

cataclysmic /kætəklɪzmɪk/; a fairly literary word. A **cataclysmic** event is one that changes a situation or society very greatly, especially in an unpleasant way. EG *...a cataclysmic economic crash... ...a sudden cataclysmic crisis.* ADJ QUALIT = catastrophic, disastrous

catacomb /kætəkəʊm, -ku:m/, **catacombs**. **Catacombs** are a series of underground passages and rooms where bodies used to be buried, especially in ancient Rome. EG *...a painting from the catacombs.* N COUNT : USU PL

Catalan /kætələˀn/ is a language which is spoken in parts of Spain and which is quite similar to Spanish. N UNCOUNT

catalogue /kætəlɒg/, **catalogues, cataloguing, catalogued**; also spelled **catalog** in American English. 1 A **catalogue** is 1.1 a book containing a list of goods that you can buy in a shop or through the post, together with prices and illustrations. EG *I got a catalogue from Debenhams.* N COUNT 1.2 a book containing a list of all the objects in an exhibition, museum, or art gallery, usually with extra information and illustrations. EG *I read in the catalogue that this picture was bought for £500,000...* N COUNT 1.3 a list in a library of the books and journals that the library has, usually organized alphabetically by, for example, author or title. EG *...a periodicals catalogue...* N COUNT

2 If you **catalogue** a collection of things or pieces of information, you classify them and list them in a catalogue, for example in a museum or library. EG *I am cataloguing the Old Masters.* V+O

3 A **catalogue** of events, ideas, qualities, etc is a list or number of them that are connected in some way and are being considered together. EG *He was given a heavy jail sentence for a whole catalogue of serious crimes... Mrs Zapp recited a catalogue of her husband's sins to me.* N COUNT+*of*

4 If you **catalogue** a series of similar events, qualities, etc, you list them. EG *As a last resort the sceptic may fall back on cataloguing Man's supposedly unique abilities.* V+O

catalysis /kətælɪsɪs/ is the speeding up of a chemical reaction by adding a catalyst to it. N UNCOUNT

catalyst /kætəlɪst/, **catalysts**. A **catalyst** is 1 a substance that speeds up the rate of a chemical reaction without itself changing or being affected in any way; a technical term in chemistry. N COUNT ⇑ accelerator 2 something that causes a change or event to happen, especially an important one. EG *The military action of 15 August can now be seen as a catalyst... It acted as a catalyst to set off new trains of thought.* N COUNT : USU SING

catamaran /kætəmərən/, **catamarans**. A **catamaran** is a sailing boat with two parallel hulls that are held in place by a single deck. N COUNT

catapult /kætəpʌlt/, **catapults, catapulting, catapulted**. 1 A **catapult** is 1.1 in British English, a device for shooting small stones. It is made of a Y-shaped stick with a piece of elastic tied between the two top parts. N COUNT 1.2 a device that is used to launch aircraft from an aircraft carrier. N COUNT

2 When something **catapults** or **is catapulted** through the air, it moves very suddenly, quickly, and violently through the air. EG *...the risk of a back-seat passenger being catapulted into the windscreen.* V-ERG ⇑ pitch

3 If something **catapults** you into a particular state or situation, you are suddenly and unexpectedly caused to be in that state or situation. EG *He was catapulted to prominence by his first speech in Parliament.* V+O+A ⇑ throw

cataract /kætərækt/, **cataracts**. A **cataract** is 1 an area of the lens of a person's eye that has become whitish instead of clear, so that the person cannot see properly. EG *He had a cataract removed... ...an elderly gentleman who had had a cataract operation.* N COUNT 2 a large waterfall. EG *The way is blocked by the tall cataract, eighty feet of foaming white water.* N COUNT

catarrh /kətɑ:/ is a condition in which a lot of mucus is produced in your nose and throat, for example when you have a cold. EG *Someone with catarrh was sniffing loudly behind her.* N UNCOUNT

catastrophe /kətæstrəfi¹/, **catastrophes**. A **catastrophe** is 1 an extremely bad thing that happens to you, which you can do nothing to avoid. EG *For each man who loses his job unemployment is a personal catastrophe... She was for ever predicting disaster and catastrophe.* N COUNT/ UNCOUNT ⇑ event = disaster 2 a sudden and terrible disaster in which a lot of people die. EG *...regions devastated by natural catastrophes.* N COUNT = cataclysm

catastrophic /kætəstrɒfɪk/. 1 If something bad that happens to you is **catastrophic**, it has an extremely serious effect on you and you can do nothing to avoid it. EG *The impact on Belgium has already been catastrophic... ...catastrophic mistakes.* ADJ QUALIT = disastrous 2 Something that is **catastrophic** 2.1 involves or causes a sudden terrible disaster in which many people die. EG *...a single, catastrophic nuclear exchange.* ADJ CLASSIF ⇑ disastrous 2.2 is unsuccessful and very bad; an informal use. EG *...catastrophic exam results.* ADJ CLASSIF ⇑ poor = diabolical

catcall /kætkɔ:l/, **catcalls**; also spelled with a hyphen. A **catcall** is a loud noise that someone makes to show that they disapprove of something, for example at a football match or a public meeting. EG *There were catcalls as he took his seat in the theatre.* N COUNT = jeer ≠ cheer

catch /kætʃ/, **catches, catching, caught**. 1 To **catch** an animal, fish, bird, etc means to capture it and stop it from moving freely, usually after chasing it or after using a trap or other weapon. EG *Have you ever caught a shark?... A wounded leopard, unable to catch its normal prey, may be driven to hunting people... ...a wild otter caught in a trap.* V+O ≠ release

2 If you **catch** a ball or some other object which has been thrown towards you or is moving towards you through the air, you take hold of it when it comes near you. EG *She threw the ball up in the air towards me. I couldn't catch it because I was carrying my shoes... 'Catch,' said Howard. He threw the book over to her.* V+O ≠ drop ▸ used as a noun. EG *Botham took a magnificent catch.* ▸ N COUNT

3 If the police **catch** someone, they stop them from committing any more crimes or from running away after they have committed a crime, sometimes by arresting them. EG *The main culprits were caught and heavily sentenced... Do you realize we can get six months in prison if they catch us?* V+O ⇑ apprehend

4 If you **catch** someone, you succeed in finding them before they leave, usually because you want to talk to them. EG *'Can I speak to you, Howard?' she said, 'I've been trying to catch you for ages.'... I suppose it's too late to catch the doctor now.* V+O = get hold of ≠ miss

5 If you **catch** someone doing something, you find them doing that they should not be doing. EG *A gardener was immediately sacked if he was caught smoking... He caught them in bed together.* V+O+-ING, OR V+O: USU+A ⇑ discover

6 If you **catch** someone looking at you, you notice them looking at you, especially when you are rather surprised by this. EG *I caught her looking at me once or twice... She caught him staring at her.* V+O+-ING = see

7 If you **catch** yourself doing something, you suddenly become aware that you are doing it. EG *Recently he had caught himself brooding about the meaning of his life.* V+O (REFL)+-ING ⇑ notice = find

8 If you **catch** yourself, you stop yourself from doing something, usually because you feel it may be unwise or stupid to do it. EG *Mrs Bixby was about to say yes to this, but caught herself just in time.* V+O (REFL)

9 If you **catch** someone or their arm, you quickly grasp or take hold of them. EG *He rushed up to her and caught her in his arms... She caught my arm with both hands.* V+O

10 If something **catches** something else, it hits it with a lot of force. EG *That massive wave had caught the trawler on her port bow... His foot lashed up and caught the man in the belly... I was balancing well, but someone turned and caught my tray with their elbow.* V+O: USU+A ⇑ hit

11 If something **catches** on material, fur, etc, it sticks to it or becomes attached to it. EG *There was a bit of rabbit's fur caught on a clump of thistles.* V+O, OR V+A ⇑ stick

12 If you **catch** your finger, sleeve, etc or if it **catches**, you get it trapped between two objects. EG *I knew a baby once who caught his fingers in the spokes of the pram wheel.* V-ERG ⇑ trap

13 If you **catch** a bus, train, or other vehicle, you get on it in order to travel on it. EG *I caught a train to Newton Abbott... She caught the 3.15 plane to Brussels... Castle was usually able to catch the six thirty-five train from Euston.* V+O = take ≠ miss

14 If you **catch** a television programme, concert, film, etc, you manage to see it or hear it; a fairly informal use. EG *'Did you see him last night on Question Time?'–'Yes I caught the last minute of it.'... I try to catch The Sound of Music wherever it is being shown.* V+O ≠ miss

15 If you **catch** something that someone has said, you manage to hear it. EG *Evans caught the words 'personal ambition'... She whispered to him something he could not catch... I don't think I caught the name.* V+O ≠ miss

16 If you **catch** a look, a smell, or an emotion, you notice it. EG *I catch a fleeting look of relief from Sylvia... Now and again, he caught a whiff of a peculiar smell... Brody caught the tone of incipient hysteria in her voice.* V+O ⇑ notice

17 If something **catches** your attention, imagination, or interest, you notice it, are interested in it, or think about it a lot. EG *A poster caught her attention... The campaign caught the public imagination... It's up to the school somehow to work it out, to catch their interest.* V+O

18 If you **catch sight** of something or someone or **catch a glimpse** of them, you suddenly notice them. EG *I walked slowly, casually, hoping she would catch sight of me... Out of the corner of my eye I caught a glimpse of two men in guard's uniforms.* PHR+*of*: VB INFLECTS ⇑ see

19 If you **catch** an idea, a suggestion, or a hint, you understand the implications of what someone is saying. EG *Those who did cast their eyes over his drawings and caught the power of his ideas were also clever enough to see his potential... You have to know Shakespeare pretty well in order to catch all those innuendoes.* V+O

20 If you **catch** someone else's feeling or emotion, you are so strongly influenced by it that you begin to feel the same way. EG *He began to catch her fear.* V+O

21 If you **catch the post**, you manage to put a letter or parcel in a post-box just before it is emptied. EG *I shall be going to catch the post shortly.* PHR: VB INFLECTS

22 If you say something like **'you wouldn't catch me** doing that', you mean that it is very unlikely that you would ever do it; an informal use. EG *You won't catch me doing dull arithmetic and things!... You wouldn't catch him giving money to charity.* PHR+O+-ING

23 If a fire **catches**, it starts burning. EG *The fire took a long time to catch.* V = light

24 If you **are caught** in the rain, a storm, or some other unpleasant situation, you are in it and find it difficult to get out of it. EG *Perhaps she doesn't want to be caught in the rain, Gordon... They were caught in an earthquake.* V+O+A *(in)*: ONLY PASS

25 If you **are caught** in a particular kind of life, you are forced to live that kind of life and cannot escape from it. EG *It is a society caught in the agony of revolutionary change... My aunt was caught in that dreadful English middle-class trap of snobbishness.* V+O+A *(in)*: ONLY PASS = trapped

26 If you **are caught** without something, you do not have it when you need it. EG *She was never going to be caught without any savings... She always catches me without any sugar in the house.* V+O+A *(without)*: USU PASS

27 If you **catch** a cold, a chill, or a disease, you get it or become infected with it. EG *Philip caught a cold which lasted for approximately a year... Around Christmas she caught a bad chill.* V+O = contract

28 To **catch** a liquid means to collect it in a container. EG *Pots and bowls sat everywhere catching waterdrops that fell from the ceiling.* V+O: USU+A

29 If the light **catches** something, it makes it look bright or shiny. EG *The sunlight caught each tiny separate hair and made it shine... The grass is sparkling where the sunlight catches small drops from the rain.* V+O

30 If something **catches the light** or **catches the sunlight**, it reflects the light and looks bright or shiny. EG *His fine-featured face and crinkly brown hair caught the light.* PHR: VB INFLECTS

31 If something or someone **catches** a mood, an atmosphere, a personality, etc, they successfully represent it in pictures, music, or words, even though it is normally considered difficult or impossible to represent. EG *The wonderful camera work perfectly catches the Californian atmosphere... This pamphlet seems to have caught the conscience of the times.* V+O = capture

32 If the wind or water **catches** something, it carries or pushes it along. EG *The wind caught her hat... The rubber raft was caught by the current and drifted out to sea.* V+O = take

33 A **Catch-22** situation is one in which you cannot do one thing until you do another thing, but you cannot do the second thing until you do the first thing. It is therefore impossible for you to do anything. EG *You can't get a job if you haven't got experience, and you can't get experience if you haven't got a job–it's Catch-22.* N UNCOUNT: USU BEFORE N

34 If you say to someone **'You'll catch it'**, you mean that they will get into trouble if anyone finds out what they have done; an informal, rather old-fashioned expression. CONVENTION

35 A **catch** is **35.1** the total number of fish that someone has caught. EG *Their total catch was one minnow... They won't be able to land their catches at the home port.* N COUNT ⇑ haul **35.2** a device, such as a hook, that fastens or locks a door, window, lid, etc. EG *He put his hand through the hole in the glass and released the catch.* N COUNT: USU SING **35.3** a hidden problem, difficulty, or obstacle in a plan or course of action, especially one that you suspect exists but are not sure about. EG *'There's a catch in this.'–'There's no catch, Gordon. I swear it.'* N SING WITH DET

36 A **catch** in your voice is a short quick pause in your breathing while you are talking. It is caused by sadness, fear, or some other strong emotion. EG *There was still the catch of a dying sob in her voice.* N SING WITH DET ⇑ break

37 Catch is **37.1** a game in which two or more people catch a ball that they throw to each other. N UNCOUNT **37.2** a game in which one person chases other people and tries to touch or catch one of them. N UNCOUNT = tag

38 The word **catch** is also used in the following expressions, which are explained at other places in this dictionary. • to **catch** your **breath**: see **breath**. • to **catch** someone's **eye**: see **eye**. • to **catch fire**: see **fire**. • to **catch hold of** something: see **hold**. • to be **caught short**: see **short**. • to **catch the sun**: see **sun**.

catch at. If you **catch at** something, you quickly take hold of it or try to take hold of it. EG *The children caught at my skirts and tugged me back.* PHRASAL VB: V+PREP, HAS PASS = grasp at

catch on. 1 If someone **catches on** to something, they understand and learn it. EG *He'll catch on eventually... He hasn't really caught on to the system.* PHRASAL VB: V+ADV, IF+PREP THEN *to*

2 If something **catches on**, it becomes popular. EG *The idea is catching on... Short haircuts became the rule, ballroom dancing caught on.* PHRASAL VB: V+ADV

catch out. 1 If you **catch** someone **out**, you make PHRASAL VB: V+

them make a mistake, often by an unfair trick. EG *Why are you trying to catch me out?* O+ADV

2 If you **are caught out** by something that happens, you find yourself in an unfortunate situation or a weak position. EG *He had also been caught out by the nationalization of Britain's oil industry.* PHRASAL VB : V+O+ADV, ONLY PASS

catch up. 1 If you **catch up** with someone who is in front of you, you reach them by walking faster than they are doing. EG *He is dawdling behind, not wanting to catch up... Simon tried to catch up with the others... She stood still, allowing him to catch her up.* PHRASAL VB : V+ADV, IF+PREP THEN with, OR V+PRON+ADV

2 If you **catch up** with someone, you reach the same standard or level as they are. EG *Most leaders were obsessed with catching up with the West.* PHRASAL VB : V+ADV, IF+PREP THEN with

3 To **catch up** on or with something means to spend time or effort doing something that you have not had time to do properly until now. EG *They would be going straight to the office to catch up on correspondence... I was just catching up on my sleep, that's all.* PHRASAL VB : V+ADV, IF+PREP THEN on/with

4 If you **are caught up** in something, you are involved in it, usually unwillingly. EG *...a society caught up in complex, high-speed change... He was determined not to get caught up in any sort of publicity nonsense.* PHRASAL VB : V+O+ADV+PREP, ONLY PASS

catch up with. 1 To **catch up with** someone who has committed a crime or done something wrong means to succeed in finding them, especially in order to arrest or punish them. EG *When Birmingham authorities finally caught up with her, she had spent all the money.* PHRASAL VB : V+ADV+PREP ⇑ find

2 If something **catches up with** you, you find yourself in an unpleasant situation which you have been able to avoid until now but which you are now forced to deal with or accept responsibility for. EG *I am sure that the truth will catch up with him... Poverty may catch up with the apparently most secure.* PHRASAL VB : V+ADV+PREP

catching /kæ̲tʃɪŋ/. 1 If an illness or a disease is **catching**, it is easily passed on or given to someone else. EG *Measles is very catching.* ADJ QUALIT : PRED = infectious

2 If a feeling or emotion is **catching**, it has a strong influence on other people and spreads quickly, for example through a crowd. EG *Panic is catching.* ADJ QUALIT : PRED

catchment area /kæ̲tʃmənt ɛ̲ərɪə/, **catchment areas**. The **catchment area** of a school, hospital, etc is the area that it serves. N COUNT

catch-phrase, catch-phrases; also spelled without a hyphen. A **catch-phrase** is a short sentence or an expression which is well-known because it is often used by a particular well-known person, especially an entertainer who appears on television. N COUNT

catchy /kæ̲tʃi¹/, **catchier, catchiest**. If something such as a title or tune is **catchy**, it attracts your interest or attention and is easily remembered. EG *The songs are irresistibly catchy.* ADJ QUALIT ⇑ pleasant

catechism /kæ̲tɪkɪzə⁰m/, **catechisms**. A **catechism** is a series of questions and answers about the religious beliefs of a particular church, which is learned by people before they become full members of that church. N COUNT : USU SING

categorical /kætə¹gɒ̲rɪkə⁰l/. If you are **categorical** about something, you are completely certain about it. EG *On this point we can be clear and categorical.* ADJ CLASSIF ⇑ definite = positive

◇ **categorically.** EG *The government have stated quite categorically that we're going to see a change in priorities.* ◇ ADV WITH VB ⇑ definitely = positively

categorize /kæ̲tə¹gəraɪz/, **categorizes, categorizing, categorized**; also spelled **categorise**. If you **categorize** people or things, you divide them into sets of people or things which have characteristics in common, or say which set they belong to. EG *Animals can be categorised according to the kind of food they eat... He was categorized as a schizophrenic.* V+O, OR V+O+A (as) ⇑ sort = classify

◇ **categorization** /kætɪgə⁰raɪze̲ɪʃə⁰n/, **categorizations.** EG *We don't think it's necessary to have such rigid categorization.* ◇ N UNCOUNT/COUNT ⇑ grouping

category /kæ̲tə¹gəri⁰/, **categories**. A **category** is a set of people, actions, objects, etc which all have a particular characteristic or quality in common. EG *Gestures fall into six main categories... Five of these are unique to category 1... ...the broad category of engineering.* N COUNT ⇑ group = class

cater /ke̲ɪtə/, **caters, catering, catered.** 1 To **cater** for a person or group means to provide all the things that they need or want in a particular situation. EG *We can cater for all age groups in our summer schools... In a consumer society no effort is made to cater for the needs of the elderly... Fred Terry catered to the public taste for sentimental plays.* V+A (for/to)

2 To **cater** for an occasion such as a wedding or a party means to provide food and drink for the large number of people there. EG *'The Upper Crust' is one of many new agencies providing cooks to cater for boardroom meetings.* V+A (for)

caterer /ke̲ɪtərə/, **caterers**. A **caterer** is a person or a company that is paid to provide food and drink for large numbers of people at parties, weddings, etc. N COUNT

catering /ke̲ɪtə⁰rɪŋ/ is the provision of food and drink for a large number of people at a wedding, party, etc. EG *Who did the catering?* N UNCOUNT ⇑ supplying

caterpillar /kæ̲təpɪlə/, **caterpillars**. A **caterpillar** is a small worm-like animal that feeds on plants and develops into a butterfly or moth. N COUNT ⇑ larva

caterpillar tracks. The **caterpillar tracks** of a heavy vehicle such as a tank or a bulldozer are the ridged belts it has round its wheels on each side, which enable it to grip soft ground. N PLURAL

caterwaul /kæ̲təwɔːl/, **caterwauls, caterwauling, caterwauled.** If an animal or a person **caterwauls**, they make an unpleasant noise by wailing or howling loudly. ▸ used as a noun. EG *We were woken by a high, snarling caterwaul, a sort of screaming wail.* V ⇑ wail ▸ N SING WITH DET ⇑ wail

catfish /kæ̲tfɪʃ/. **Catfish** is both the singular and the plural form. A **catfish** is a fish with long thin spines that look like whiskers around its mouth. N COUNT ⇑ fish

catharsis /kə³θɑ̲ːsɪs/ is a way of getting rid of strong emotions, fears, tension, or unhappy memories that you have, especially by talking about them openly or expressing them in some way; a formal word. EG *The writing of this diary was for her much more than an act of catharsis.* N UNCOUNT = purge

cathartic /kə³θɑ̲ːtɪk/. Something that is **cathartic** has the effect of catharsis; a formal word. EG *I felt the cathartic power of his speech.* ADJ QUALIT ⇑ purgative

cathedral /kəθi̲ːdrə⁰l/, **cathedrals**. A **cathedral** is a large and important church which has a bishop in charge of it. The area which a bishop administers has one cathedral and many smaller churches. EG *...the cloisters of Salisbury Cathedral... ...the cathedral city of Gloucester.* N COUNT : ALSO IN NAMES AFTER N

catherine wheel /kæ̲θərɪn wiːl/, **catherine wheels**. A **catherine wheel** is a firework in the shape of a circle which spins round and round. N COUNT

cathode /kæ̲θəʊd/, **cathodes**. A **cathode** is the negative electrode in a cell such as a battery; a technical term in electronics. N COUNT

cathode-ray tube, cathode-ray tubes. A **cathode-ray tube** is a device used for example in televisions and computers, in which an image is produced by sending a beam of electrons onto a photosensitive screen. N COUNT

Catholic /kæ̲θə⁰lɪk/, **Catholics**. The adjective in paragraph 2 is not spelled with a capital letter. 1 A **Catholic** is a person who belongs to the branch of the Christian church which accepts the Pope as leader of the church and which is based in the Vatican in Rome. EG *She was a devout Catholic... There are forty-eight million Catholics in America.* ▸ used as an adjective. EG *His book was banned by the Catholic Church until 1835... He came from an old Catholic family.* N COUNT = Roman Catholic ▸ ADJ CLASSIF

2 If someone has a **catholic** range of tastes or interests, they like or are interested in a wide range of things; a fairly formal use. ADJ QUALIT ≠ narrow

Catholicism /kəθɒ̲lɪsɪzə⁰m/ is the set of Christian beliefs that are held by Catholics and by their church. EG *My brother, sister, and I inherited our Catholicism from my mother.* N UNCOUNT ⇑ belief = Roman Catholicism

catkin /kæ̲tkɪn/, **catkins**. A **catkin** is a long thin soft flower that hangs on some trees, for example birch trees and hazel trees. N COUNT

catnap /kæ̲tnæp/, **catnaps, catnapping, catnapped**; also spelled with a hyphen. A **catnap** is a short sleep; an informal word. EG *...six hours' sleep plus a few daytime catnaps.* ▸ used as a verb. EG *He cat-napped in his seat.* N COUNT = doze ▸ V = doze

cat's cradle, cat's cradles; also spelled with a hyphen. 1 **Cat's cradle** is a game in which you make shapes from a loop of string that you hold and twist between your fingers. N UNCOUNT

2 A **cat's cradle** is a shape made by playing with string by looping it over your fingers. N COUNT

cat's-eye, cat's-eyes; also spelled without a hyphen. **Cat's-eyes** are small pieces of glass that are put along the middle of a road or at the side of a road and that reflect vehicle's lights, so that drivers can see the road at night. N COUNT ⇑ reflector

cat's paw, cat's paws; also spelled with a hyphen. A **cat's paw** is a person who is used by someone else to do something that is unpleasant, difficult, or dangerous; a rather old-fashioned expression. N COUNT = dupe

cat suit, cat suits; also spelled with a hyphen. A **cat suit** is a piece of clothing, usually worn by women, that is made in one piece and fits closely over the body and legs. N COUNT

catsup /kætsəp/ is a thick cold sauce, usually made from tomatoes; used in American English. EG *They poured catsup on their hamburgers.* N UNCOUNT = ketchup

cattle /kætə^{0}l/ are cows and bulls that are kept for farming or for carrying loads. EG *Cattle were sold for next to nothing.* N PLURAL ⇑ livestock

cattle-grid, cattle-grids; also spelled without a hyphen. A **cattle-grid** is a grid of metal bars which is set into the surface of a road so that cattle and sheep cannot cross but people and vehicles can. N COUNT

cattleman /kætə^{0}lmə^{3}n/, **cattlemen**. A **cattleman** is a man who looks after or owns cattle, especially in America or Australia. N COUNT

cattle market, cattle markets; also spelled with a hyphen. A **cattle market** is 1 a market where cattle are bought and sold. N COUNT 2 an event such as a beauty contest where women are being considered only for their sexual attractiveness; used showing disapproval. EG *The Miss World contest is nothing more than a cattle market.* N COUNT

catty /kæti^1/, **cattier, cattiest**. Someone who is **catty** is unpleasant and spiteful; used showing disapproval, especially of women. EG *Certain girls are catty and difficult to live with.* ADJ QUALIT ⇑ nasty = bitchy ◊ **cattiness**. EG *In the cafe there was a lot of cattiness.* ◊ N UNCOUNT ⇑ nastiness

catwalk /kætwɔːk/, **catwalks**. A **catwalk** is 1 a narrow bridge high in the air between two parts of a tall building or on the outside of a large structure. EG *...tiptoeing on the catwalk of a skyscraper in a high wind.* N COUNT = walkway 2 a narrow platform that models walk along to display clothes in a fashion show. EG *The new spring season's clothes were being paraded on the catwalk.* N COUNT : IF SING USU the+N

caucus /kɔːkəs/, **caucuses**. A **caucus** is 1 a small group of people within a political party or other organization who meet to discuss important matters and who have a lot of influence within the organization. EG *...the continued support and goodwill of the Labour caucus on the council... He was bound by his party's caucus resolutions.* N COUNT : USU MOD+N 2 a meeting of a group of people within an organization. EG *There were midnight meetings and caucuses at dawn.* N COUNT

caught /kɔːt/ is the past tense and past participle of **catch**.

cauldron /kɔːldrən/, **cauldrons**; also spelled **caldron**. A **cauldron** is a large round metal pot which is used for boiling liquids or cooking food over a fire. EG *There was a great smoking cauldron of water.* N COUNT

cauliflower /kɒlɪflauə/, **cauliflowers**. A **cauliflower** is a vegetable with green leaves around a large white ball of flower buds. N COUNT/ UNCOUNT

causal /kɔːzə^{0}l/. **Causal** is used to describe the relationship between two or more events, when one event causes another event to happen. EG *There is a causal chain involved in all technological developments... It is hard to see how such a causal relationship could be proved.* ADJ CLASSIF : ATTRIB ◊ **causally**. EG *They are causally related.* ◊ ADV WITH VB

causality /kɔːzælɪti^1/ means the same as causation. N UNCOUNT

causation /kɔːzeɪʃə^{0}n/ is the relationship of cause and effect; a formal word. EG *From what sense data is our knowledge of causation received?* N UNCOUNT = causality

cause /kɔːz/, **causes, causing, caused**. 1 A **cause** is 1.1 something that makes something else happen. EG *Nobody knew the cause of the explosion... Too many governments have chosen to remove the symptoms rather than the cause... Death was due to natural causes.* N COUNT ≠ effect, result 1.2 an aim or principle which a particular group of people supports or is fighting for. EG *He is sympathetic to our cause... ...the cause of world peace... ...a plan to revive the socialist cause.* N COUNT : USU+ SUPP

2 If you say that something is **in a good cause** or for **a good cause**, you mean that it is worth doing or contributing to because it will help other people, for example by raising money for charity. EG *It's all in a good cause, so please be generous.* ● See also **lost cause**. PHR : USED AS AN A

3 If you have **cause** for a particular feeling or action, you have a reason for feeling it or doing it. EG *Do you see any cause for hope for a real lasting settlement?... Your age and frailty are giving him cause for concern... I have no cause to go back... Give her as little cause as possible to dislike you.* N UNCOUNT+ for/to-INF = grounds

4 To **cause** something means to make it happen or to make a person do it. EG *We have a good idea what causes an earthquake... Does smoking cause cancer?... That's going to cause me a lot of trouble... The sound of approaching hooves caused her to step aside.* V+O, V+O+O, OR V+O+to-INF = bring about, result in

cause célèbre /kɔːzsɛlɛbrə^0/, **causes célèbres**. Both the singular and the plural are pronounced in the same way. A **cause célèbre** is a controversial issue, person, or criminal trial that attracts a lot of public attention. EG *The strike has now exploded into a national cause célèbre... ...the boy scout leader from Bristol who became a cause célèbre of the Left.* N COUNT : USU SING

causeway /kɔːzweɪ/, **causeways**. A **causeway** is a raised path or road that crosses water or marshland. N COUNT

caustic /kɔːstɪk/. 1 A chemical substance that is **caustic** is a powerful one that can eat into materials and damage them. EG *You're not supposed to use a caustic cleaner on enamel areas.* ADJ CLASSIF = corrosive

2 A **caustic** remark or comment is very unpleasant, sarcastic, or bitter. EG *Some caustic things have been written about media stars.* ADJ QUALIT : USU ATTRIB = biting, acid

caustic soda is a powerful chemical substance used to make strong soaps and drain cleaners. N UNCOUNT

cauterize /kɔːtəraɪz/, **cauterizes, cauterizing, cauterized**; also spelled **cauterise**. If you **cauterize** a wound, you burn it with heat or with a chemical in order to close it up and prevent it from becoming infected. EG *He cauterized the wound and the bleeding stopped.* V+O

caution /kɔːʃə^{0}n/, **cautions, cautioning, cautioned**. 1 **Caution** is great care which you take in order to avoid possible danger. EG *You must proceed with extreme caution... The employers prepared, with all due caution, for a conference with the Trade Unions.* N UNCOUNT = prudence ≠ carelessness

2 If someone **cautions** you, they warn you of possible problems or danger. EG *My tutor solemnly cautioned me that I might not pass my exams.* V+O/REPORT-CL/ QUOTE ▸ used as a noun. EG *A word of caution is important here!... Caution! All fires are dangerous.* ▸ N UNCOUNT/ COUNT ⇑ warning

3 A **caution** is a formal warning of possible legal proceedings. EG *The demonstrators who were arrested have been released with a caution.* N COUNT

cautionary /kɔːʃənə^{0}ri^1/. A **cautionary** story or piece of advice is one that is intended to give a warning to people. EG *Bill's mother told him the cautionary tale of the little boy who wouldn't eat his food.* ADJ CLASSIF : ATTRIB

cautious /kɔːʃəs/. Someone who is **cautious** acts very carefully in order to avoid possible danger. EG *Her husband is reserved and cautious, never making a swift decision about anything... My mother was a very cautious driver.* ADJ QUALIT ⇑ careful = circumspect, wary ≠ foolhardy ▸ used of a person's behaviour or actions. EG *Lindley urged a more cautious approach.* ◊ **cautiously**. EG *We moved cautiously forward.* ◊ ADV WITH VB

cavalcade /kævəlkeɪd/, **cavalcades**. A **cavalcade** is a procession of people on horses or in cars or carriages. EG *A great cavalcade swept dramatically into the castle courtyard.* N COUNT

cavalier /kævəlɪə/. Someone who behaves in a **cavalier** way behaves arrogantly without considering the feelings of other people or the seriousness of a situation. EG *He treated women in a cavalier fashion... Farmers were adopting a very cavalier attitude to what were very dangerous substances.* ADJ QUALIT ⇑ arrogant = uncaring

cavalry /kævəlri^1/. The **cavalry** is 1 the part of an army that uses fast armoured vehicles for fighting. EG *When the war came he was sent at once to join the cavalry at Curragh Camp in Ireland.* N SING : the+N, OR N UNCOUNT ≠ infantry 2 the group of soldiers in an army who fight or parade on horses. EG *...the Household Cavalry.* N SING : the+N ≠ infantry

cave /keɪv/, **caves, caving, caved**. A **cave** is a large hole in the side of a cliff or hill, or under the ground. EG *The cliffs are riddled with caves.* N COUNT = cavern

cave in. 1 When something such as a roof or a ceiling **caves in** or when something **caves** it **in**, it PHRASAL VB : V-ERG+ADV collapses inwards, for example into the room or building below. EG *In order to prevent the sides caving in it is usually lined with bricks... The blow caved in his skull.* ● See also **cave-in**.

2 If you **cave in**, you give in or surrender to someone or something, especially when you are under pressure. EG *I more or less caved in, though I still defended my explanation... The spies had given the invaders a few days to cave in.* PHRASAL VB : V+ADV = capitulate

caveat /keɪviæt, kæv-/, **caveats**. A **caveat** is 1 a warning that you have to take something into account before you act or carry out plans; a formal use. EG *We will mark six of the areas most ripe for change, with the caveat that these are not necessarily the most sensible ones to start with.* N COUNT = caution 2 a formal notice in a law court that a particular action should not be taken without telling the person who is giving this notice; a technical term in law. N COUNT

cave-in, cave-ins. A **cave-in** is the sudden collapse of a roof, ceiling, etc into a building, room, or cave below it. N COUNT

caveman /keɪvmæn/, **cavemen**. A **caveman** is one of the people who were alive in prehistoric times and who are believed to have lived mainly in caves. N COUNT

cavern /kævəⁿn/, **caverns**. A **cavern** is a large deep cave. N COUNT

cavernous /kævənəs/. Something that is **cavernous** is large, deep, and hollow, so that it reminds you of a cave; used especially of buildings. EG *The engine noise boomed in the cavernous building... The car park is a low, cavernous place, devoid of people.* ADJ CLASSIF

caviar /kævɪɑː, kævɪɑː/; also spelled **caviare**. **Caviar** is the salted eggs of a fish called the sturgeon, eaten as a delicacy especially at the beginning of a meal. N UNCOUNT ⇑ food

cavil /kævəˡl/, **cavils, cavilling, cavilled**; also spelled **caviling** and **caviled** in American English. If someone **cavils**, they complain about things that are not important. EG *Captain Paget could find nothing to cavil at.* ▸ used as a noun. EG *A cavil followed, causing the loss of valuable time.* V : IF+PREP THEN *at* = quibble ▸ N COUNT = quibble

cavity /kævəˡtiˡ/, **cavities**. A **cavity** is 1 a small hole or gap in something solid, for example in a person's body. EG *...the nasal cavity... Water is sucked in at one end of the cavity and expelled at the other.* N COUNT

2 a hole or soft area in a tooth, which is caused when part of the tooth decays. N COUNT

cavity wall, cavity walls. A **cavity wall** is a wall that consists of two separate walls with a space between them. Cavity walls help to keep out noise and cold. N COUNT

cavort /kəˢvɔːt/, **cavorts, cavorting, cavorted**. When people **cavort**, they leap about in a noisy and excited way, especially because they are playing energetic games. EG *...children cavorting in an adventure playground.* V ⇑ prance = caper, romp

caw /kɔː/, **caws, cawing, cawed**. When a bird such as a crow or a rook **caws**, it makes a loud harsh sound. EG *Rooks cawed in the great beeches all around.* ▸ used as a noun. EG *The crane let out a raucous caw.* V ⇑ call ▸ N COUNT

cayenne pepper /keɪen pepə/is a hot-tasting red powder made from dried peppers that is used to flavour food. N UNCOUNT ⇑ spice

CB is an abbreviation for 'citizens' band'; the range of radio waves which the general public is allowed to use in order to send messages to one another. CB is used especially by lorry drivers and other motorists who use radio sets in their vehicles to communicate with each other. EG *...CB radio equipment... ...his new CB rig.* N UNCOUNT/COUNT

CBE is an abbreviation for 'Commander of the Order of the British Empire'; an honour granted to a person by the King or Queen for an outstanding service or achievement. The letters are used after the name of the person who has been awarded the honour. EG *...Major-General David Mostyn CBE.* N IN TITLES : AFTER NAME

CBI is an abbreviation for 'Confederation of British Industry'; an organization which a large number of companies belong to and which is concerned with all aspects of business and industry. It also represents the interests of businessmen in discussions with the government or trade unions. EG *The CBI will be pressing for a limit on business rates.* N PROPER : *the*+N

cc. In written English, **cc** is both the singular and the plural form for the sense in paragraph 1. **1 cc** is an abbreviation for 'cubic centimetre'; used to measure the volume or capacity of something. EG *...500cc motorbikes.* N COUNT : NUM+N ⇑ unit

2 cc is used at the end of a business letter to indicate that a copy is being sent to another person. EG *...cc J. Chater, S. Cooper.*

CCTV, CCTVs. **CCTV** is an abbreviation for 'closed circuit television'. N COUNT

CD, CDs. **CD** is an abbreviation for 'compact disc'. EG *...a CD player.*

cease /siːs/, **ceases, ceasing, ceased**. 1 If something **ceases**, it stops happening or existing; a fairly formal word. EG *Hostilities must cease at once... Towards midnight the rain ceased and the clouds drifted away.* V = stop, end ≠ start, commence

2 If you **cease** to do something or **cease** doing it, you stop doing it; a fairly formal word. EG *Once people retire they automatically cease to be union members... He forced the vicar to cease making such remarks.* V+*to*-INF/-ING ≠ start

3 If you **cease** something, you bring it to an end. EG *Just two weeks later the magazine ceased publication... They threatened to cease financial support to the university.* V+O ⇑ stop ≠ begin

ceasefire /siːsfaɪə/, **ceasefires**; also spelled with a hyphen. A **ceasefire** is an arrangement in which people or countries who are fighting each other agree to stop fighting, usually in order to meet and discuss their disagreement. EG *...the ceasefire between the Allies and Germany... Mr Habib would not disclose any details of the cease-fire agreement.* N COUNT = truce

ceaseless /siːslɪˢs/ means going on for a very long time without stopping or changing; a fairly formal word. EG *...his ceaseless rebellion against discipline... ...the ceaseless traffic of the day.* ◊ **ceaselessly**. EG *Clarissa was talking ceaselessly.* ADJ CLASSIF : ATTRIB = continual ◊ ADV WITH VB

cedar /siːdə/, **cedars**. A **cedar** is a large evergreen tree that has wide branches and small needle-shaped leaves. EG *...beeches and cedars... ...a great cedar tree.* ▸ also used of the sweet-smelling wood that is obtained from it. EG *...cedar wood.* N COUNT ▸ N UNCOUNT ⇑ wood

cede /siːd/, **cedes, ceding, ceded**. If you **cede** or **cede** something to someone, you let someone else do or have something, often unwillingly and because you have been forced to. EG *The Social Democrats have had to cede the leadership of the current coalition to the Republicans... The Louisiana colony was ceded to Spain in 1762.* V OR V+O : IF+PREP THEN *to* ⇑ yield = concede ≠ take over

cedilla /sɪˢdɪlə/, **cedillas**. A **cedilla** is a symbol that is written under a letter 'c' in French, Portuguese, and some other languages to show that you pronounce it like a letter 's' rather than like a letter 'k'. It is written ç. N COUNT

ceilidh /keɪliˡ/, **ceilidhs**. A **ceilidh** is an informal entertainment in Scotland or Ireland, at which there is folk music, singing, and dancing. N COUNT ⇑ event

ceiling /siːlɪŋ/, **ceilings**. A **ceiling** is 1 the surface that forms the top part or roof inside a room. EG *...a large room with a high ceiling... She opened her eyes and stared at the ceiling.* N COUNT ≠ floor 2 the greatest height at which a particular type of aeroplane can fly safely; a technical use. N COUNT : USU+SUPP 3 an official upper limit on things such as prices, wages, etc that is decided by the government or other organization, and above which they are not supposed to increase. EG *The CBI will be pressing for a ceiling on business rate increases.* N COUNT : IF+PREP THEN *on*

5 ● to **hit the ceiling**: see **hit**.

celebrant /seləˡbrənt/, **celebrants**. A **celebrant** is a person who performs or takes part in a religious ceremony. N COUNT

celebrate /seləˡbreɪt/, **celebrates, celebrating, celebrated**. 1 If you **celebrate** or **celebrate** something, you do something enjoyable such as having a party in order to show that an event or occasion is special or to honour someone's success or victory. EG *We ought to celebrate; let's have a bottle of champagne... Independence Day is celebrated annually... His victory was celebrated with music and dancing... People gathered to celebrate the formation of the new party.* V OR V+O

2 If a company, organization, country, etc is **celebrating** a period of time, it has existed for that time, and often does something as a special event. EG *The company was celebrating its fiftieth birthday... The country is celebrating one hundred years of freedom.* V+O = commemorate

3 If you **celebrate** someone or something, you praise V+O, OR V+O+A

them for their good qualities; a fairly formal use. EG *People were celebrating him as a bright alternative to Nixon.* (as/for) = extol

4 When a priest **celebrates** Mass, he officially performs the actions and ceremonies that are involved in the Mass. V+O

celebrated /sɛləˈbreɪtɪ²d/. Someone or something that is **celebrated** for a particular quality or achievement is famous for it. EG *Her mother was a celebrated actress... ...Churchill's celebrated remark.* ADJ QUALIT : IF + PREP THEN *for* = renowned

celebration /sɛləˈbreɪʃəⁿn/, **celebrations.** 1 A **celebration** is a special event that people organize to enjoy themselves because something pleasant has happened or because it is someone's birthday or anniversary. EG *We ought to have a little celebration of our own... ...a great national celebration... The celebrations marking the 300th anniversary have been cancelled. It was a time of celebration.* N COUNT/UNCOUNT

2 The **celebration** of someone or something is praise and appreciation which is given to them; a formal use. N UNCOUNT + SUPP

celebratory /sɛləˈbrətri¹/ means organized or happening in order to celebrate a birthday, anniversary, or something pleasant or exciting; a formal word. EG *...traditional celebratory dinners on special occasions.* ADJ CLASSIF : ATTRIB

celebrity /səˈlɛbrɪti¹/, **celebrities.** A **celebrity** is someone who has become famous for something, especially for something connected with acting or show business. EG *Lots of celebrities have stayed here... Mr Geard had become a local celebrity.* N COUNT ⇑ person = star, personality ≠ nonentity, unknown

celerity /sɪ²ˈlɛrɪti¹/ is exceptional speed; a formal word. EG *He will have to get away with celerity.* N UNCOUNT = rapidity

celery /sɛləri¹/ is a vegetable with long pale green stalks that you can eat; used also to refer to the whole plant. N UNCOUNT

celestial /sɪ²ˈlɛstɪəl/. Something that is **celestial** is 1 concerned with the sky or with heaven; a formal use. EG *Our destinies depend on celestial bodies.* 2 very beautiful or perfect; a literary use. EG *She believed, with a kind of celestial trust, that nothing would change.* ADJ CLASSIF : USU ATTRIB; ADJ CLASSIF : USU ATTRIB = divine

celibacy /sɛləˈbəsi¹/. If you are in a state of **celibacy**, 1 you have not had sex with anyone for a long time or during a particular period of your life. EG *...one month of enforced celibacy.* 2 you have stayed unmarried, usually because of your religious beliefs. EG *We still take vows of poverty and celibacy and obedience.* N UNCOUNT = chastity; N UNCOUNT = chastity ≠ marriage

celibate /sɛlɪbəˈt/, **celibates.** A **celibate** is 1 someone who does not marry or have sex because of their religious beliefs. ▸ used as an adjective. EG *...the celibate life.* 2 someone who does not have sex with anyone over a long time or during a particular period of their life. ▸ used as an adjective. EG *It wasn't my choice to remain celibate.* N COUNT; ▸ ADJ CLASSIF; N COUNT; ▸ ADJ CLASSIF = chaste

cell /sɛl/, **cells.** A **cell** is 1 the smallest part of an animal or plant that is able to exist by itself. EG *...the chemical processes inside the cell... ...cancer cells... ...the cell walls of plants.* 2 a small room in which a prisoner is locked in a prison or a police station. EG *There were four bunks in the cell... The cell doors were unlocked.* 3 a small room in which a monk or nun lives in a monastery or a convent. 4 a small space that has been specially made or built by an insect or other small creature and which it lives in or uses for a particular purpose. EG *The queen lays eggs in the cells that have been built by the workers.* N COUNT; N COUNT; N COUNT; N COUNT

5 a small group of people who have been specially trained and organized to work together as part of a larger organization. EG *...a Trotskyist cell within the Labour organisation.* 6 a device that uses energy from chemicals, heat, or light to produce electricity. EG *They wanted cells to generate electricity on satellites.* N COUNT : USU MOD + N; N COUNT

cellar /sɛlə/, **cellars.** A **cellar** is 1 a room in the ground underneath a house or other building, that is often used to store things in. EG *She had gone down into the cellar... ...the cellar steps.* 2 a place where wine is stored; used also to refer to the range of wines that is stored there. EG *He orders the wine from the firm's cellars each week... They had a good cellar.* N COUNT ≠ attic, loft; N COUNT = wine cellar

cellist /tʃɛlɪst/, **cellists.** A **cellist** is a person who plays a cello. N COUNT ⇑ musician

cello /tʃɛləʊ/, **cellos.** A **cello** is a musical instrument that looks like a large violin. You hold it upright and play it with a bow while you are sitting down. N COUNT

cellophane /sɛlə⁶feɪn/ is a thin, strong, transparent material that is used to cover or wrap things such as food in order to protect them. EG *...cheese and biscuits wrapped in cellophane... ...a cellophane bag.* N UNCOUNT

cellular /sɛljə⁴lə/. 1 **Cellular** means consisting of or involving the cells of animals or plants. EG *Vitamin deficiency results in a defect in cellular function... ...basic cellular structures.* ADJ CLASSIF : ATTRIB

2 **Cellular** blankets, clothes, or fabrics are very loosely woven and keep you very warm. ADJ CLASSIF : ATTRIB

celluloid /sɛljə⁴lɔɪd/. 1 **Celluloid** is a type of plastic that is now used especially for making children's toys but was formerly used for making photographic film. EG *Jenny was playing with her celluloid ducks and ships... He wore a celluloid collar and lace-up boots.* N UNCOUNT

2 **Celluloid** is used to refer to films and the cinema in general; a literary use. EG *Her genius is there on celluloid for future generations to see... ...the celluloid world of Hollywood.* N UNCOUNT : USU *on* + N

cellulose /sɛljə⁴ləʊz, -ləʊs/ is a substance that exists in the cell walls of plants and is used to make paper, plastic, and various textiles and fibres. EG *Carbohydrates may be used as cellulose to form the structure of the plant... ...cellulose paint.* N UNCOUNT

Celsius /sɛlsɪəs/ is a scale for measuring temperature, in which water freezes at 0 degrees and boils at 100 degrees. It is represented by the symbol C. EG *...about 30 degrees Celsius.* N UNCOUNT : USU AFTER NG = centigrade ≠ Fahrenheit

Celt /kɛlt, sɛlt/, **Celts.** If you describe someone as a **Celt**, you mean that they come from Scotland, Wales, Ireland, or some other areas such as Brittany. N COUNT ⇑ person

Celtic /kɛltɪk, sɛl-/. 1 If you describe something as **Celtic**, you mean that it is connected with the people and the culture of Scotland, Wales, Ireland, and some other areas such as Brittany. EG *...the Celtic legends... Their faces are Celtic.* ADJ CLASSIF

2 **Celtic** is used to refer to a group of related languages that are or were once spoken in Scotland, Wales, Ireland, and some other areas such as Brittany. N UNCOUNT, OR ADJ CLASSIF ⇑ language

cement /sɪmɛnt/, **cements, cementing, cemented.** 1 **Cement** is 1.1 a grey powder made from limestone and clay which is mixed with sand and water in order to make concrete or mortar. EG *...a sack of cement... He mixed in a little more sand than usual with the cement.* 1.2 concrete or mortar. EG *...slabs of cement... ...bits of stone joined together with cement... ...a little cement courtyard.* 1.3 a type of glue made for sticking particular substances together. EG *...a tube of balsa-wood cement.* N UNCOUNT; N UNCOUNT ⇑ material; N UNCOUNT

2 If you **cement** something, you 2.1 cover or fill a place or area with concrete or mortar. EG *The floor has been cemented over.* 2.2 stick or glue it to something else. EG *The lice lay little white eggs and cement them to the base of a hair.* V+O; V+O

3 The **cement** of a group or organization is the thing that unites the people in it and makes them support and help each other. EG *...the effort to find a new cement for the alliance... Families should be the cement of the nation.* N COUNT + SUPP

4 If you **cement** a relationship or agreement, you do something that makes it stronger or more official. EG *We would really do the company some good by cementing relationships with business contracts.* V+O ⇑ confirm = seal

cement mixer, cement mixers. A **cement mixer** is 1 a machine with a large revolving container into which you put cement, sand, and water in order to make concrete. 2 a special lorry that is used to transport liquid cement. N COUNT; N COUNT

cemetery /sɛməˈtri¹/, **cemeteries.** A **cemetery** is a place or area where dead people are buried, especially one that is not immediately next to a church. EG *We climbed a hill and arrived at the cemetery... ...the Jewish cemetery.* N COUNT

cenotaph /sɛnətɑːf/, **cenotaphs.** A **cenotaph** is a monument that is built in honour of soldiers who died in a war. EG *All men used to raise their hats when passing the Cenotaph.* N COUNT = memorial

censor /sɛnsə/, **censors, censoring, censored.** 1 If someone **censors** a book, a play, or a film, they officially examine it and cut out or ban any parts of it that are considered to be immoral, usually according to the instructions of their government. EG V+O

...*the abolition of the Lord Chancellor's power to censor plays.*
2 If someone **censors** letters written by soldiers or articles written by journalists, they officially examine them according to the instructions of a government or military commander, and cut out any parts that reveal military secrets or are considered to damage the country's reputation. EG *Believe it or not they censor your letters here... ...a heavily censored despatch.* V+O
3 A **censor** is a person who has been officially appointed by a government to examine plays, films, books, etc and to cut out or ban any parts of them that are considered to be immoral. EG *A film critic was complaining that the censor was being too tolerant.* N COUNT ⇑ official

censorious /sensɔ:rɪəs/. Someone who is **censorious** disapproves strongly of someone else's actions or behaviour and criticizes them. EG *He wasn't smiling but he wasn't being censorious either... This time they were much more censorious of the Prime Minister.* ADJ QUALIT : IF + PREP THEN *of* = critical ≠ approving

censorship /sensəʃɪp/ is the practice or policy of censoring books, plays, films, reports, etc, especially by government officials. EG *Government censorship is relaxing a bit to allow kissing on screen... ...the censorship of bad news in wartime.* N UNCOUNT : IF + PREP THEN *of*

censure /senʃə/, **censures, censuring, censured**. 1 **Censure** is strong disapproval and condemnation of something that has been done, or of the way it was done. EG *Labour brought a motion of censure on the Government's handling of the issue... She had won for her family a position immune to censure.* N UNCOUNT ⇑ criticism
2 If you **censure** someone, you tell them that you strongly disapprove of them or of their actions. EG *He was something of a trouble-maker but was never censured for it.* V+O ⇑ criticize = condemn

census /sensəs/, **censuses**. A **census** is an official survey of the population of a country that is carried out by the government in order to get details of the number of people living in the country, their ages and occupations, where they live, etc. EG *The 1890 census was completed in record time... Do you think that the information in these census returns was fairly accurate?* N COUNT

cent /sent/, **cents**. 1 A **cent** is a small unit of money which is worth one hundredth of the main unit of money in many countries, for example in the United States, Australia, and Singapore. EG *She never paid more than ninety-five cents for a meal.* N COUNT
2 See also **per cent**.

cent- /sent/. **Cent-** or **centi-** is 1 sometimes used at the beginning of nouns or adjectives that have 'one hundred' as part of their meaning. EG *...century... ...centipede... ...centennial.* PREFIX 2 used at the beginning of nouns referring to measurements or units of money that are one-hundredth of other measurements or units of money. EG *...centimetre... ...centilitre.* PREFIX

cent. is used as an abbreviation for words beginning with 'cent', such as 'centigrade', 'century', or 'central'.

centaur /sentɔ:/, **centaurs**. A **centaur** is a creature in classical mythology which has the head, arms, and top half of a man and the body and legs of a horse. N COUNT

centenarian /sentə¹neərɪən/, **centenarians**. A **centenarian** is a person who is a hundred years old or older. N COUNT

centenary /senti:nə⁰ri¹/, **centenaries**. A **centenary** is the year in which you celebrate something important that happened exactly one hundred years earlier. EG *The year 1928 was the centenary of Ibsen's birth... ...an exhibition of Picasso in the centenary year of his birth... ...the centenary celebrations.* N COUNT ⇑ anniversary

centennial /sentenɪəl/, **centennials**. A **centennial** is a the same as a centenary; a formal word. N COUNT ⇑ anniversary

center /sentə/. See **centre**.

centi- /senti¹/. See **cent-**.

centigrade /sentɪgreɪd/ is a scale for measuring temperature, in which water freezes at 0 degrees and boils at 100 degrees. It is represented by the symbol C. EG *The temperature was still 23 degrees centigrade.* N UNCOUNT : USU AFTER NG = Celsius ≠ Fahrenheit

centilitre /sentɪli:tə/, **centilitres**. A **centilitre** is one hundredth of a litre. N COUNT

centimetre /sentɪmi:tə/, **centimetres**; also spelled **centimeter** in American English. A **centimetre** is a unit of length in the metric system equal to ten millimetres or one-hundredth of a metre. EG *...a low wall about 10 centimetres high... They are thirty centimetres or so in length.* N COUNT

centipede /sentɪpi:d/, **centipedes**. A **centipede** is a small, thin creature that looks rather like a worm but has a lot of very short legs. N COUNT

central /sentrəl/. 1 Something that is **central** is positioned in the middle of an object or an area. EG *The monster had two eyes and a single central nostril... The houses are arranged around a central courtyard... He walked down the central corridor.* ADJ CLASSIF
◊ **centrally**. EG *The pin is centrally positioned on the circle.* ◊ ADV WITH VB
2 **Central** is often used as part of the description or the name of a region that is in the middle of a particular town, country, or continent. EG *She made a film about central Poland... She was on the way from Heathrow to Central London... ...the peoples of Central and Southern Europe.* ADJ CLASSIF : ATTRIB = inner, inland
3 A place that is **central** is easy to reach because it is in the centre of a city where there are good transport services. EG *The cafe was on Tottenham Court Road near Oxford Street, very central for her.* ADJ QUALIT : USU ATTRIB ≠ far out
◊ **centrally**. EG *...a centrally located flat.* ◊ ADV WITH VB
4 A **central** group or organization is one which makes all the important decisions and plans the policies that must be followed throughout a country or a larger organization. EG *Their activities are strictly controlled by a central committee... She is a former employee of the government's Central Intelligence Agency.* ADJ CLASSIF : ATTRIB ⇑ main ◊ **centrally**. EG *France has a centrally organized system.* ◊ ADV WITH VB ≠ locally
5 A person, idea, aim, etc that is **central** is the most important or essential part of something. EG *The central character in the film was played by William Hurt... Ceremonies are of central importance in traditional societies... The case of the civil servant is central to this issue.* ADJ CLASSIF : IF + PREP THEN *to* = main ◊ **centrally**. EG *He's been centrally concerned with the subject of unhappiness.* ◊ ADV WITH VB = primarily

central government, central governments. A **central government** is the government of a whole country, when this is in contrast to smaller organizations which govern local areas. EG *Special machinery was created to link local and central government... We'd like to run education without any control at all from the central government.* N UNCOUNT/COUNT : USU SING ≠ local government

central heating is a system of heating a building. Air or water is heated in one main tank and travels round the building through pipes and radiators. EG *...a luxurious flat with fitted carpets and central heating... Have you thought of installing your own central heating system?* N UNCOUNT

centralise /sentrəlaɪz/. See **centralize**.

centralism /sentrəlɪzə⁰m/ is a way of governing a country or organizing something such as industry, education, or politics, by having one central group of people who give instructions to all the other regional groups. EG *The opposition attacked its rigid centralism.* N UNCOUNT ≠ regionalism

centrality /sentrælə¹ti¹/ is the quality of being central; a formal word. EG *Fine Art tradition was given cultural centrality.* N UNCOUNT + SUPP ⇑ importance

centralize /sentrəlaɪz/, **centralizes, centralizing, centralized**; also spelled **centralise**. To **centralize** a country, state, etc means to create a system of government or organization by which one central group of people gives out instructions to all the other regional groups. EG *They show little reluctance to centralize.* V, OR V+O : USU PASS ⇑ organize ◊ **centralized**. EG *We believe in a strong centralized state.* ◊ ADJ CLASSIF
◊ **centralization** /sentrəlaɪzeɪʃə⁰n/. EG *Large-scale technology brings centralization.* ◊ N UNCOUNT

centrally heated. A building that is **centrally heated** has central heating. EG *It's a centrally heated house.* ADJ CLASSIF ⇑ heated

centre /sentə/, **centres, centring, centred**; also spelled **center, centers, centering** and **centered** in American English. 1 The **centre** of something is the middle of it. EG *The sun reached the centre of the sky... He moved the table over to the centre of the room.* N COUNT : USU SING, IF + PREP THEN *of* ▸ used as an adjective. EG *...a black wig with a centre parting... I sat in the centre stalls.* ▸ ADJ CLASSIF : ATTRIB
2 A **centre** is a building where people have meetings or where they go to get particular help, treatment, N COUNT : ALSO IN NAMES AFTER N

or training, or to take part in a particular activity. EG *They're starting up a new arts centre there... ...a child-care centre... Treatment should be available from the university's health centre... Orange Street Chapel is a centre of worship for the Protestants... ...the Careers Advisory Centre.*

3 The **centre** of a town or city is the part where there are the most shops, cinemas, and other facilities. EG *They had organized a Christmas procession through the centre of town... The M5 and M6 motorways encircle the centre of Birmingham.* N COUNT : USU the+N SING+of ≠ outskirts, suburbs

4 If somewhere is a **centre** for a particular industry or activity, that industry or activity is particularly important there. EG *The region began as a centre for sheep-raising... Industry has been concentrated in a few large urban centres in each country.* N COUNT+SUPP : USU SING ⇑ place = region

5 The **centre** of something such as a situation, event, or belief is the person, place, idea, etc that is considered to be the most important, basic part from which everything else develops. EG *The Workers' movement was at the centre of the 1972 strike... Swallow was right in the centre of the action... Economics has moved into the very centre of public concern... There is a series of political flaws at the centre of the play which make it less convincing as a whole.* N COUNT+SUPP : IF SING, USU the+N+of ⇑ middle = heart

6 If someone or something is the **centre** of attention or interest, they attract a lot of attention or interest. EG *The television screen remained the centre of attention... She was the centre of public admiration... Recently the Circus has been the centre of a violent controversy.* N COUNT+SUPP : IF SING, USU the+N+of = focus

7 The **centre** in politics is the political party, group, or set of political beliefs that is seen as being halfway between two political extremes and is therefore often considered reasonable and balanced. EG *The House of Lords commanded the support of the centre of British politics... We are in a time of profound re-thinking in the centre, the left, and the far left.* ▸ used as an adjective. EG *The SDP is not a centre party. It is a socialist party.* N SING : the+N ≠ extreme, right, left ▸ ADJ CLASSIF : ATTRIB

8 The **centre** of sweet, chocolate, or other object is the inside or inner part of it. EG *This toffee has a soft centre.* N COUNT = core

9 The **centre** of a line or shape is the point that is the same distance from each end of the line or from all sides of the shape; a technical term in geometry. N COUNT : USU SING ⇑ middle

10 A **centre** in a sports team is a player who plays most of the time in the middle area of the playing field. N COUNT

11 If you **centre** something, you move it so that it is exactly balanced or is at the exact centre of something else. EG *The telescopic sight did not appear to be quite centred... He centred himself so that the raft lay flat.* V+O (NG/REFL) ⇑ adjust = balance

centre around. If something **centres around** a person or thing or if you **centre** it **around** them, they are the main feature or subject of attention; usually used when you are generalizing rather than describing specific details of a subject. EG *The workers' demands centred around pay and conditions... Psychiatric treatment of the family centred around separating the children from their parents... Tonight's programme was centred around the life of a Liverpool comedian.* PHRASAL VB : V-ERG+PREP ⇑ concentrate on

centre on. If something **centres on** a person or thing or if you **centre** it **on** them, they are the main feature or subject of attention; usually used when you are describing specific details of a subject rather than generalizing. EG *In promising them money, she was inevitably forced to centre on the exact sum offered... Attention was for the moment centred on Michael Striker.* PHRASAL VB : V-ERG+PREP ⇑ concentrate on = focus on

centre round. To **centre round** means the same as to centre around. EG *Our holidays centred very much round horse-racing.* PHRASAL VB : V-ERG+PREP

centred /sentəd/. Someone or something that is **centred** in a particular place has that place as a base. EG *I'm more in favour of community centred action... Cuban affairs are centred in a special branch.* ADJ CLASSIF+SUPP : IF+PREP THEN in = based

centre of gravity, centres of gravity. The **centre of gravity** of an object is the point on the object at which it balances perfectly. EG *In a canoe, the centre of gravity is below the surface of the water.* N COUNT : USU SING

centrepiece /sentəpi:s/, **centrepieces**. **1** The **centrepiece** of a set of things that is greatly admired is something that you show as the best example of the set. EG *The centrepiece of the modern navy is the nuclear submarine... This Bill is the centrepiece of Labour's legislative programme.* N SING : the+N+of = pride

2 A **centrepiece** is an ornament which you put in the middle of something, especially displayed on a table. EG *...a beautiful vase of orchids as a centrepiece.* N COUNT

centrifugal force is the force that makes objects move outwards when they are spinning around something or travelling in a curve; a technical term in physics. EG *You can't hold the bike up because of centrifugal force.* N UNCOUNT ≠ centripetal force

centrifuge /sentrɪfju:dʒ/, **centrifuges**. A **centrifuge** is a machine that spins mixtures of different substances around very quickly so that they separate by centrifugal force. N COUNT

centripetal force /sentrɪpi:tə⁰l fɔ:s, sentrɪpə¹tə⁰l/ is the force that makes objects move inwards when they are spinning around something or travelling in a curve; a technical term in physics. N UNCOUNT ≠ centrifugal force

centrist /sentrɪst/, **centrists**. A **centrist** is a person or group whose political views are moderate rather than extreme. EG *...a minority government of Centrists and Liberals.* ▸ used as an adjective. EG *...centrist policies.* N COUNT ≠ extremist ▸ ADJ CLASSIF : USU ATTRIB

centurion /sentjʊərɪən/, **centurions**. A **centurion** was an officer in the Roman army. N COUNT ⇑ soldier

century /sentʃəri¹/, **centuries**. **1** A **century** is **1.1** a period of a hundred years that is used when stating a date. The 20th century, for example, began in 1900. EG *...Italian paintings of the fifteenth and sixteenth centuries... 'Middlemarch' is a marvellous 19th century novel... Francis Bacon is one of the finest British painters of the century.* • **the turn of the century**: see **turn**. **1.2** a period of a hundred years; often used when discussing events during that period. EG *...a century of progress in science and technology... ...the journey to socialism, stretching over half a century... ...a book written centuries ago.* N COUNT / N COUNT

2 In cricket, a **century** is a total of one hundred runs scored by a batsman. EG *He scored the most fantastic century I have ever witnessed.* N COUNT ⇑ score

ceramic /sɪ¹ræmɪk/, **ceramics**. **1 Ceramic** is a hard substance that is made by heating clay to a very high temperature. EG *Various metals and ceramics are used in making these components.* ▸ used as an adjective. EG *...ceramic tiles.* N MASS = pottery ▸ ADJ CLASSIF : USU ATTRIB

2 A **ceramic** is a work of art made of ceramic, for example a pot or a statue. EG *...Chinese ceramics.* N COUNT : USU PL ⇑ artwork

3 Ceramics is the art of making artistic objects out of clay. N UNCOUNT = pottery

cereal /sɪərɪəl/, **cereals**. A **cereal** is **1** a plant such as wheat, maize, or rice that produces edible grain, especially one that is grown as food; also used of the grain itself. EG *Wheat may have been the first cereal to be cultivated... ...cereal crops.* **2** a food made from grain and often other things such as sugar or fruit, which is usually mixed with milk and eaten for breakfast. EG *...a new breakfast cereal... ...a box of cereal.* N COUNT/UNCOUNT ⇑ grass / N COUNT/UNCOUNT

cerebral /serə¹brəl/. Something that is **cerebral 1** relates to rational and intellectual thought rather than to feelings; a formal use. EG *Telemann's style is warmer, lighter and less cerebral than Bach's... ...the cerebral challenge of police work.* **2** relates to the brain; a technical term in anatomy. EG *Val died of a cerebral hemorrhage... ...the cerebral cortex.* ADJ QUALIT = intellectual, mental / ADJ CLASSIF : ATTRIB

cerebral palsy /serəbrəl pɔ:lzi¹/ is an illness caused by damage to a baby's brain before it is born, which makes its limbs and muscles permanently weak. N UNCOUNT

cerebrum /serɪbrəm/, **cerebrums, cerebra**. The plural can be either **cerebrums** or **cerebra**. The **cerebrum** is the front part of the brain which is concerned with thought and perception; a technical term in anatomy. N COUNT

ceremonial /serə¹məʊnɪəl/, **ceremonials**. **1** You use **ceremonial** to describe something that is used in a ceremony or relates to a ceremony. EG *...a brilliant ceremonial robe from Africa... She passionately desired to see the ceremonial dances.* ◊ **ceremonially**. EG *The bride is veiled at first and then ceremonially shown to the crowd.* ADJ CLASSIF ◊ ADV WITH VB

2 The **ceremonial** of a formal occasion such as a religious ceremony consists of all the traditional N UNCOUNT, OR N COUNT+SUPP rules about what you say, do, or wear on the occasion. EG ...*the ceremonial of the Roman Catholic church... ...the highly-coloured ceremonial of the Houses of Parliament.*

ceremonious /serə'məʊnɪəs/. Someone whose behaviour or actions are **ceremonious** behaves in a excessively polite and formal way. EG *Mussorgsky's manners were always ceremonious... He bid her an unusually ceremonious farewell.* ◊ **ceremoniously**. EG *He filled all their glasses ceremoniously... He ceremoniously rose to shake hands with her.* — ADJ QUALIT; ◊ ADV ⇑ respectfully

ceremony /serə'məni[1]/, **ceremonies**. 1 A **ceremony** is 1.1 a set of formal and traditional actions and words that are performed or spoken at a special occasion such as a wedding or an important public event. EG *I watched the entire ceremony on television... ...a coronation ceremony.* ● See also **master of ceremonies**. 1.2 an action that is done in a very formal and polite way. EG *The waiter gave them fresh glasses and there was the ceremony of tasting the wine once more... ...the ceremony of exchanging gifts at Christmas.* — N COUNT ⇑ ritual = rite; N COUNT : USU SING = ritual

2 **Ceremony** consists of 2.1 all the special actions, words, etc, that are required or performed on a special occasion. EG *All the pomp and ceremony was quite magnificent.* 2.2 very formal and polite behaviour towards someone, especially on a special occasion. EG *At the BBC she was received with respectful ceremony.* — N UNCOUNT ⇑ ritual; N UNCOUNT

3 If you do something **without ceremony**, you do it quickly, in a casual way. EG *He had his head cut off without much ceremony... He produced the book, without further ceremony, from under his bed.* — PHR : USED AS AN A ⇑ casually

4 If you say that someone **stands on ceremony**, you mean that they are too formal in the way they behave. EG *There's no need to stand on ceremony.* — PHR : VB INFLECTS, USU WITH BROAD NEG

cert /sɜːt/, **certs**. If you say that something is a dead **cert**, you mean that you are certain it will happen or succeed; used in informal British English. EG *Are you going to bet on it?–Of course! It's a dead cert!* — N COUNT : USU SING = certainty

cert. is a written abbreviation for **certificate**. — N COUNT

certain /sɜːtə[0]n/. 1 If you are **certain** about something, you have no doubt in your mind about it. EG *He felt certain that she would disapprove... I'm absolutely certain of that... We're not quite certain how much there is.* ● If you know something **for certain**, you have no doubt at all about it. EG *It is not known for certain where they are now.* — ADJ QUALIT : PRED, USU + REPORT-CL ⇑ confident = sure; ● PHR : USED AS AN A = definitely

2 If you say that something such as an event or situation is **certain** or **certain** to happen, you mean that it is generally accepted that it will definitely happen. EG *The growth in demand is certain to drive up the price... It is almost certain that he will be elected... No treatment more certain of arousing American sympathy could have been devised... Such a vote would mean the certain defeat of the government.* — ADJ QUALIT : PRED + to-INF/of, OR ADJ CLASSIF : ATTRIB ⇑ likely = assured

3 Something that is **certain** is known to be true, correct, or accurate. EG *It is important to know what is hearsay and what is certain knowledge.* — ADJ CLASSIF

4 **make certain**. 4.1 When you **make certain** of something or someone, you check that it is true or that it has a particular quality by testing it, asking questions, etc. EG *Parents who take on an au pair without making certain of her interest in children are asking for trouble.* 4.2 When you **make certain** that something happens or is done, you take action to ensure that it happens. EG *We need to make certain that governments adhere to disarmament agreements.* — PHR : VB INFLECTS, IF + PREP THEN of = make sure; PHR : VB INFLECTS, USU + REPORT-CL

5 You use **certain** 5.1 to indicate that you are referring to one particular thing, person, or group that can be specified. EG *She arranged to meet him at three o'clock on a certain afternoon... The impresario wanted very badly to get a certain singer from Vienna... Certain areas in Sussex are better than others for keeping bees... There would be, in certain circumstances, a tax liability.* ● If you say that something is true **to a certain extent** or **to a certain degree**, you mean that it is true but only to a limited extent. EG *That takes care of my anxieties to a certain extent.* 5.2 before the name of a person you are mentioning in order to indicate in a rather formal way that they are not well-known and you do not know them personally. EG ...*a certain Monsieur Bronchevil, a French national... A recent case concerned a certain Mrs Wendy Smith who worked for a large company in Leeds.* 5.3 to suggest that a quality or condition is noticeable or worthy of attention. EG *He wore a tweed overcoat which gave him a certain distinction... There's a certain confusion of technology there.* — ADJ CLASSIF : ATTRIB; ● PHR : USED AS AN A = to some degree; ADJ CLASSIF : a + ADJ + N PROPER = one; ADJ CLASSIF : ATTRIB, a + ADJ + N UNCOUNT = kind of

6 When you refer to **certain** of a group of things or people, you are referring to some particular members of that group. EG *Certain of our judges have claimed that this is the case... Will you all write a short story bearing in mind certain of the salient points of what we've talked about?* — PRON + of

certainly /sɜːtə[0]nli[1]/. 1 Something that is **certainly** true is true without any doubt at all. EG *Ellie was certainly a student at the university but I'm not sure about her brother... If nothing is done there will certainly be an economic crisis... Your answer is almost certainly right.* — ADV = undoubtedly

2 You use **certainly** 2.1 to emphasize that you feel strongly about what you are saying. EG *It certainly looks wonderful doesn't it?... I'm fascinated by hang-gliding; I would certainly like to try it... This isn't a very high temperature. Certainly not in my opinion.* 2.2 to emphasize that you agree with a particular statement, idea, or theory that has just been stated or discussed. EG *'Would you agree that it is still a difficult world for women to live in?'–'Oh certainly.'... Certainly, yes, I think that this is one of the major problems.* 2.3 to say enthusiastically that you will do something you have been asked to do. EG *'Do you think you could possibly give me a lift?'–'Certainly. Where are you going?'* — ADV WITH VB = definitely; ADV SEN = for sure; ADV SEN, OR CONVENTION ⇑ yes = of course

3 You say **certainly not** when you want to say 'no' in a strong way, usually in answer to a question and often showing that you are rather annoyed by the question. EG *'Had you forgotten?'–'Certainly not.'... 'Oh leave me alone, please do.'–'Certainly not. You agreed to finish it and we are relying on you.'* — CONVENTION = absolutely not

certainty /sɜːtə[0]nti[1]/, **certainties**. 1 **Certainty** is 1.1 the state of having no doubts at all about something. EG *Answers to such questions would never be known with certainty... There was a lack of certainty about what to do next... Young people can no longer look forward with any certainty to a career or even a job.* 1.2 the state of something being certain to happen. EG *Quite ordinary men have faced certainty of death in battle.* — N UNCOUNT = assurance; N UNCOUNT : IF + PREP THEN of = inevitability

2 A **certainty** is something that is not doubted or questioned. EG *It's by no means a certainty that we'll win... The result of the election was a certainty.* — N COUNT = foregone conclusion

certifiable /sɜːtɪfaɪəbə[0]l/. Someone who is **certifiable** can be declared insane. EG ...*people who are certifiable under the Mental Health Act.* — ADJ CLASSIF

certificate /sətɪfɪ[1]kət/, **certificates**. A **certificate** is 1 an official document which states that the facts written on it are true, for example giving proof of someone's birth or death. EG *When you apply for a passport, you have to send your birth certificate with the form and the fee... Absence from work of more than three days requires a doctor's certificate.* 2 an official document that someone receives when they have successfully completed a course of study or training. ▸ also used of the actual course of study or training. EG *After university he took a Certificate in the Teaching of English as a Foreign Language.* — N COUNT : USU + SUPP; N COUNT ⇑ diploma; ▸ N COUNT + SUPP

certify /sɜːtɪfaɪ/, **certifies, certifying, certified**. 1 When you **certify** something, you declare formally that it is true or that it has happened. EG *I certify that the facts written here are the truth... He received a piece of paper certifying the payment of his taxes.* — V+O/REPORT-CL

2 To **certify** someone means 2.1 to give them a certificate which states that they have successfully completed a course of training for a particular profession. EG *The pilots are certified by the navy.* ◊ **certified**. EG *After four years' hard work she is now a certified teacher.* 2.2 to officially declare that they are legally insane. EG *Her father was certified insane and spent the rest of his life in a mental hospital.* — V+O, OR V+O+C = qualify; ◊ ADJ CLASSIF; V+O+C, OR V+O + A (as)

certitude /sɜːtɪtjuːd/ is the same as certainty; a formal word. — N UNCOUNT

cervical /sɜːvɪkə[0]l, səvaɪ-/ means 1 relating to the cervix; a technical term in anatomy. EG ...*cervical cancer.* 2 relating to the neck; a technical term in anatomy. EG *It severed the spinal column just above the first cervical vertebra.* — ADJ CLASSIF : ATTRIB; ADJ CLASSIF : ATTRIB

cervix /sɜːvɪks/, **cervixes, cervices.** The plural can be either **cervixes** or **cervices.** The **cervix** is the entrance to the womb; a technical term in anatomy. EG *She has cancer of the cervix.* N COUNT ⇑ part of the body

cessation /sɛseɪʃəⁿn/. The **cessation** of something is the stopping of it; a formal word. EG *Both sides wanted a cessation of hostilities.* N UNCOUNT+*of*: USU DET+N+*of*

cesspit /sɛspɪt/, **cesspits.** A **cesspit** is a hole or tank in the ground into which waste water and sewage flow. N COUNT

cf. is used in writing to introduce something that should be considered in connection with the subject you are discussing. EG *Juniper-tree; cf. the Biblical story of Elijah.* ⇑ consider = compare

ch. is a written abbreviation for 'chapter' or 'church'. N UNCOUNT

cha-cha /tʃɑ tʃɑ/, **cha-chas.** A **cha-cha** is a Latin American dance with small fast steps; also used of music for this dance. N COUNT: USU *the*+N

chafe /tʃeɪf/, **chafes, chafing, chafed.** 1 When your skin **chafes** or when something such as a piece of clothing **chafes** it, it becomes sore as a result of the clothing rubbing against it. EG *Baby powder helps to avoid chafing.* V OR V-ERG ⇑ rub

2 If you **chafe** at something, you feel irritated at not being able or allowed to do something. EG *They chafe at the imprisonment... ...the rising bourgeoisie chafing under the restrictions imposed on it.* V+A *(at/under)*

chaff /tʃɑːf/. 1 **Chaff** is the outer parts of grain such as wheat that are removed by beating before the grain is used as food. EG *The girls brushed away the husks and chaff.* N UNCOUNT ⇑ covering = husks

2 When you **separate the wheat from the chaff, sift the wheat from the chaff,** etc, you decide which things or people in a group are good or important and which are bad or unimportant. EG *I expect the actors to sift the wheat from the chaff and to know when I suggest good ideas.* PHR: VB INFLECTS ⇑ evaluate

chaffinch /tʃæfɪntʃ/, **chaffinches.** A **chaffinch** is a small European songbird. Male chaffinches have reddish-brown fronts and grey heads. N COUNT ⇑ finch

chagrin /ʃægrɪn/, **chagrins, chagrining, chagrined;** a formal word. 1 **Chagrin** is a feeling of annoyance or disappointment. EG *Thomas discovered to his great chagrin that he was broke.* N UNCOUNT

2 If you **are chagrined,** you feel annoyed or disappointed about something. EG *I was particularly chagrined at their failure to hear about my activities.* V+O: USU PASS, IF+PREP THEN *at* ⇑ be annoyed

chain /tʃeɪn/, **chains, chaining, chained.** 1 A **chain** consists of rings of metal or some other substance that are connected together in a line. Chains are used for example as jewellery or for fastening things together. EG *...a girl with a silver cross hanging on a chain around her neck... ...bicycle chains... ...paper chains... ...a length of chain.* N COUNT/ UNCOUNT

2 **Chains** are thick rings of metal that are connected together and fixed round the ankles or wrists of prisoners to prevent them from escaping. Chains were used mainly in former times. EG *Captured criminals were paraded in chains through the crowded streets.* N PLURAL ⇑ bonds = shackles

3 When you **chain** a person or thing to something, you fasten them to it with a chain. EG *They chained themselves to the fence.* V+O: USU+A

4 A **chain** is also something such as a feeling or duty that limits your freedom because it prevents you from doing what you want. EG *New opportunities present themselves when you break free from the family chains... They have nothing to lose but their chains.* N COUNT ⇑ bond = fetter

5 If you **are chained** to a place, situation, or way of life, you are forced to remain in it and you find that it is very difficult or impossible for you to get free of it. EG *I'm chained to my desk in London... We were chained to a vicious circle of violence.* V+O: USU PASS, IF+PREP THEN *to* ⇑ confine = tie

6 A **chain** is also 6.1 a number of things joined to each other or arranged in a line. EG *...the island chains of the Pacific.* N COUNT+SUPP = string 6.2 a large number of similar shops or hotels in different towns, that are owned by the same person or company. EG *He now owns a chain of 970 food stores.* N COUNT+SUPP 6.3 a number of things that happen or are done one after another. EG *He set up a chain of interviews with major networks.* N COUNT+*of* = series 6.4 a series or system of things or events in which each one is affected by the one before it. EG *I was personally involved in the brief chain of events that led up to her death... ...a nuclear chain reaction... ...a chain of command running from the boss down to the office junior.* ● See also **food chain.** N COUNT+SUPP

chain up. If you **chain up** someone or something, you fasten them to something using a chain. EG *He keeps his dog chained up all day.* PHRASAL VB: V+O+ADV ⇑ tie up

chain letter, chain letters. A **chain letter** is a letter asking for something or promising something such as money, which is sent to several people who are asked to send copies of it to a number of other people. N COUNT

chain mail; also spelled with a hyphen. **Chain mail** is armour made from small metal rings joined together so that they are like a piece of cloth. N UNCOUNT

chain saw, chain saws; also spelled with a hyphen. A **chain saw** is a big saw with teeth fixed in a chain that is driven round by a motor. N COUNT

chain-smoke, chain-smokes, chain-smoking, chain-smoked. Someone who **chain-smokes** smokes cigarettes or cigars continuously. EG *She had taken to chain-smoking when she worked.* V OR V+O

chain-smoker, chain-smokers; also spelled without a hyphen. A **chain-smoker** is a person who chain-smokes. N COUNT

chain store, chain stores. A **chain store** is a department store or supermarket that is part of a chain of shops or stores. EG *...your local, good quality chain store.* N COUNT ⇑ shop

chair /tʃɛə/, **chairs, chairing, chaired.** 1 A **chair** is 1.1 a piece of furniture for one person to sit on, with a seat raised above the ground and a support for the back. EG *He pulled up a kitchen chair and sat down on it... I sat in low chair by the fire, reading... Tom took off his jacket and put it neatly over the back of the chair.* ● See also **easy chair, musical chairs.** N COUNT 1.2 a professor's post in a university. EG *He was still in his thirties when he got his chair at Leeds.* N COUNT = professorship

2 The **chair** is 2.1 a method of execution in which the person being executed is strapped to a special chair and a powerful electric current is passed through him or her; used especially in informal English. N SING: *the*+N = electric chair 2.2 the role of chairman at a meeting or debate. ▸ also used of the person who has this role. EG *You should address your remarks to the chair.* N SING: *the*+N ● Someone who is **in the chair** at a meeting or debate is the chairman of the meeting. EG *Alderman Harry Hennessy was in the chair.* ● PHR: USED AS AN A = chairing

3 If you **chair** a meeting or debate, you are the chairman at it. EG *I'd like you to chair the weekly meeting.* V+O ⇑ officiate = preside over

chairlift /tʃɛəlɪft/, **chairlifts.** A **chairlift** is a line of chairs that hang from a moving cable and carry people up or down a mountain or other steep slope. N COUNT ⇑ cable car

chairman /tʃɛəmə³n/, **chairmen.** 1 The **chairman** of an official meeting or debate is the person who is in charge and who decides when each person is allowed to speak. A chairman can be either a man or a woman, but some people prefer the neutral words 'chairperson' or 'chair'. EG *She likes being called Madam Chairman.* N COUNT, ALSO VOC

2 The **chairman** of a committee or organization is the head of it. EG *The thirty-eight members chose a committee including chairman, secretary, and treasurer... ...Chairman Mao.* N COUNT: IF+ PREP THEN *of*, ALSO USED IN TITLES

3 The **chairman** of a company is the head of it; used in British English. EG *If there is a new chairman or managing director we can expect a change in company policy... ...the chairman of the board.* N COUNT: IF+ PREP THEN *of* = president

chairmanship /tʃɛəmə³nʃɪp/. Someone's **chairmanship** is the fact that they are chairman, or the period during which they are chairman. EG *...the efforts of the Spartacus League, under the chairmanship of Peter Gowan.* N SING: WITH POSS ⇑ leadership

chairperson /tʃɛəpɜːsəⁿn/, **chairpersons.** The **chairperson** of a meeting or debate is the person who is in charge; used especially when you want to avoid stating whether the person is male or female. N COUNT ⇑ official

chairwoman /tʃɛəwʊ¹məⁿn/, **chairwomen.** The **chairwoman** of a committee or organization is the woman who is in charge of it. EG *Margaret Downes is this year's chairwoman of the Irish Institute.* N COUNT: IF+ PREP THEN *of* ⇑ head

chaise longue /ʃeɪz lɒŋ/, **chaises longues;** also spelled with a hyphen. The singular and the plural are both pronounced in the same way. A **chaise longue** is a couch with only one arm and usually a back along half its length. N COUNT

chalet /ʃæleɪ/, **chalets**. A **chalet** is a small wooden house with a sloping, pointed roof. Chalets are often built in mountain regions, or in groups on a holiday camp. EG *...a mountain chalet.*
N COUNT = cabin

chalice /tʃælɪs/, **chalices**. A **chalice** is a large gold or silver cup with a thin stem, used for example to hold the wine in the Christian service of Holy Communion.
N COUNT = goblet

chalk /tʃɔːk/, **chalks, chalking, chalked**. 1 **Chalk** is 1.1 a soft white rock. EG *...the chalk uplands of Wiltshire.* ▸ used of soil containing a lot of this rock. EG *This plant is easy to grow in all soils, including chalk.*
N UNCOUNT
1.2 small rods of white or coloured chalk used for writing or drawing with, especially on a blackboard. EG *...a piece of chalk... They were drawing patterns on the board in coloured chalks.*
N COUNT/UNCOUNT ⇑ writing tool

2 If you say that two people or things are as different as **chalk and cheese**, you mean that they are completely different from each other. EG *We appeared on the surface as different as chalk and cheese... The two were chalk and cheese, and resentment smouldered on for weeks.*
PHR : USED AS AN A = poles apart

3 If you say that something is not true **by a long chalk**, you are emphasizing that it is far from the truth. EG *Not every farm-worker belongs to the union by a long chalk.*
PHR : USED AS AN A, WITH BROAD NEG = by any means

4 When you **chalk** something on a surface, you draw or write it with a piece of chalk. EG *A line was chalked round the body... ...a young man chalking on the blackboard.*
V+A, OR V+O

chalk up. 1 If you **chalk up** something such as a success or a victory, you achieve it, especially as one of a series of successes or victories. EG *The Campaign for Economic Democracy began to chalk up successes in city elections.*
PHRASAL VB : V+O+ADV

2 If you **chalk up** a number of contests or points in a game, you win them; used especially when it is a large number. EG *She's chalked up four wins already this season.*
PHRASAL VB : V+O+ADV = notched up

chalky /tʃɔːki¹/, **chalkier, chalkiest**. Something that is **chalky** contains chalk or is covered with chalk. EG *...the white, chalky road... Dolly put her inky, chalky hand under the desk.*
ADJ QUALIT

challenge /tʃælɪ²ndʒ/, **challenges, challenging, challenged**. 1 A **challenge** is 1.1 something new and exciting or difficult which you have the opportunity of doing and which requires great effort and determination if you are going to succeed. EG *She was willing to accept the challenge of the unknown... Mount Everest presented a challenge to Hillary... Nowadays people face a greater challenge.*
N COUNT/UNCOUNT ⇑ difficulty
1.2 an invitation or suggestion from someone that you should compete with them in some way. EG *They soon recognized the nature of the Conservative challenge... Her smile held a tiny hint of a challenge.*
N COUNT = dare
1.3 a questioning of the truth, necessity, or usefulness of something, or of a person's right to do or have something. EG *The challenge to authority is accompanied by a much more serious consideration... These ideas are open to challenge.*
N COUNT/UNCOUNT ≠ acceptance

2 If you **challenge** someone, 2.1 you invite or cause them to fight you or compete with you in some way. EG *They had challenged and beaten the best teams in the world... U.S. business today is challenged by aggressive overseas competitors.*
V+O, OR V+O+*to*-INF = dare
2.2 you question whether they have the right to do or have something, or whether what they are saying is true. EG *The idea has never been challenged... The general strike is a means of challenging the total authority of the government... 'Since when have you been so keen on him?' Etta challenged Clarissa.*
V+O, OR V+O+QUOTE ≠ accept
2.3 you order them to stop and tell you who they are or why they are there. EG *The party was challenged by the sentry: 'Halt! Who comes there?'*
V+O
2.4 you officially state that you do not want them to be part of a jury. EG *His lawyer challenged three of the jury.*
V+O = object to

challenger /tʃælɪ²ndʒə/, **challengers**. A **challenger** is a person who competes with you for something that you already have, for example for the leadership of a political party or for a sports championship. EG *He was once a challenger to Mitterrand's leadership... ...a contest between champion Larry Holmes and Gerry Cooney, a white challenger.*
N COUNT : IF+PREP THEN *to* = competitor, rival

challenging /tʃælɪ²ndʒɪŋ/. 1 A **challenging** task or job requires great effort and determination if you are going to succeed at it. EG *She performed the most challenging task without a mistake... Life as a housewife does not seem very challenging to the highly educated girl.* ◇ **challengingly**. EG *He has a challengingly difficult part in the new play.*
ADJ QUALIT = demanding ≠ easy
◇ ADV

2 Someone who does something in a **challenging** way seems to be inviting people to compete against them or to tell them that what they are doing is wrong. EG *She narrowed her eyes and gave Etta a suspicious challenging look... ...Clarissa's challenging stare... She had a challenging attitude.* ◇ **challengingly**. EG *He looked challengingly at the Doctor.*
ADJ QUALIT = defiant
◇ ADV = defiantly

chamber /tʃeɪmbə/, **chambers**. 1 A **chamber** is 1.1 a large room that is used for formal meetings, for example of Parliament or of city councils. EG *...the Council Chamber... Labour MPs left the Chamber in protest.*
N COUNT = hall
1.2 a room that is designed and equipped for a particular purpose, often for example for punishing, hurting, or killing people. EG *...gas chambers... ...the torture chamber.*
N COUNT+SUPP ⇑ room
1.3 a bedroom or other private room; an old-fashioned use.
N COUNT

2 **Chamber** is used to refer to a group of people who are elected or appointed to form a parliament, or part of a parliament, in order to make laws and govern the country. In many countries, the parliament has two chambers, one of which is more powerful than the other. EG *...the need to maintain an efficient second chamber... ...the Chamber of Deputies.*
N COUNT ⇑ assembly = house

3 A **Chamber** of Commerce or **Chamber** of Trade is a group of business people who work together to improve business in their town or area. EG *...the local Chamber of Commerce.*
N COUNT+*of* = consortium

4 **Chambers** are 4.1 a set of offices, especially ones used by a group of barristers. EG *All the barristers in the relevant Chambers seemed to be out.*
N PLURAL
4.2 a room where a judge deals with a case that does not need to be dealt with in an ordinary court. EG *We entered chambers for the preliminary hearing.*
N PLURAL ≠ open court

5 A **chamber** is also 5.1 a hollow place inside a gun in which the bullet is put.
N COUNT
5.2 a hollow place inside the body of a person or animal, or inside a plant. EG *The rumen is a chamber of the stomach.*
N COUNT : +SUPP ⇑ cavity
5.3 a hollow sealed container that is used in scientific experiments.
N COUNT

chamber concert, chamber concerts. A **chamber concert** is a concert of chamber music.
N COUNT

chamberlain /tʃeɪmbəlɪn/, **chamberlains**. A **chamberlain** is the person who is in charge of the household affairs of a king, queen, or noble.
N COUNT ⇑ steward

chambermaid /tʃeɪmbəmeɪd/, **chambermaids**. A **chambermaid** is a woman who works in a hotel cleaning and tidying the bedrooms.
N COUNT = maid

chamber music is classical music that is written for a small number of instruments.
N UNCOUNT

chamber orchestra, chamber orchestras. A **chamber orchestra** is a small orchestra which plays classical music.
N COUNT

chamber pot, chamber pots; also spelled with a hyphen. A **chamber pot** is a round container shaped like a very large cup. Chamber pots used to be kept in bedrooms so that people could urinate in them during the night.
N COUNT = potty

chameleon /kəmiːlɪən/, **chameleons**. A **chameleon** is a lizard whose skin changes colour to match the colour of its surroundings.
N COUNT

chammy /ʃæmi¹/, **chammies**. A **chammy** is a chamois leather; an informal word.
N COUNT

chamois /ʃæmwɑː/. **Chamois** is both the singular and the plural form. A **chamois** is 1 a small goat-like antelope that lives in the mountains of Europe and SW Asia.
N COUNT
2 a chamois leather.
N COUNT

chamois leather, chamois leathers. A **chamois leather** is a soft, leather cloth made from the skin of chamois, sheep, goats, or deer. It is used for cleaning and polishing.
N COUNT = chammy

chamomile /kæməmaɪl/; also spelled **camomile**. **Chamomile** is a scented European plant with daisy-like flowers. The flowers are used to make herbal tea.
N UNCOUNT ⇑ herb

champ /tʃæmp/, **champs, champing, champed**. 1 If a person or an animal **champs** or **champs** something, they eat it noisily and with enjoyment. EG *They lived on the sea floor, champing their way through mud... A small boy stood champing gum.*
V+A, OR V+O = munch

2 If you are **champing** or **champing at the bit**, you
V+A

are very impatient to do something, but you are prevented from doing it, usually by circumstances which you have no control over. EG *The press was champing under the restraint of not being able to tell the full story.*

3 A **champ** is a champion; an informal use. EG *He's a real champ.* N COUNT ⇑ winner

champagne /ʃæmpeɪn/ is an expensive French white wine that has lots of bubbles in it. EG *Willie poured himself another glass of champagne.* N UNCOUNT

champers /ʃæmpəz/ is champagne; an old-fashioned informal word. EG *Come and have some more champers.* N UNCOUNT ⇑ wine = bubbly

champion /tʃæmpɪən/, **champions, championing, championed.** 1 A **champion** is 1.1 someone who has won the first prize in a competition, or who has beaten everyone else in a contest, fight, etc. EG *...the school tennis champion... I think he was the world champion last year...* N COUNT ⇑ winner **1.2** an animal, flower, vegetable, etc that has won the first prize in a competition. N COUNT ⇑ winner **1.3** someone who supports or defends a particular person, cause, or principle. EG *...a champion of liberty... Is the Labour Party the great champion of the working man?... Western Europe might soon be clamouring for such a champion.* N COUNT : IF+ PREP THEN *of* = defender, supporter

2 If you **champion** a person, cause, or principle, you support or defend them. EG *Greenberg was the first of the critics to champion Pollock... He went on to champion the rights of accused criminals to have access to their lawyers.* V+O

championship /tʃæmpɪənʃɪp/, **championships.** 1 A **championship** is 1.1 a competition or contest which is held to find the best player or players of a particular sport. EG *...the American national golf championship... ...the World Snooker championships... ...championship golf.* N COUNT ⇑ game **1.2** the title, rank, or status of someone who is the winner of a sports championship. EG *He's in training for the heavyweight championship of the world.* N COUNT : USU+ SUPP

2 **Championship** is the act of supporting or defending a particular person, cause, or principle. EG *They had dropped their championship of Jones, who had given up hope of getting justice.* N UNCOUNT+ SUPP ⇑ support

chance /tʃɑːns/, **chances, chancing, chanced.** 1 A **chance** is the extent to which something is possible or likely to happen, especially something that is pleasant or desirable. EG *I think we've got a good chance of winning... Is there any chance of you having a holiday this year?... There's little chance that the situation will improve... What are her chances of getting the job?* N COUNT/N UNCOUNT+SUPP/ REPORT-CL ⇑ probability = possibility, likelihood ● If you say that someone doesn't **stand a chance** or doesn't **stand much chance** of doing something, you mean that you think they are very unlikely to do it. EG *She didn't stand a chance of winning against Navratilova.* ● PHR : VB INFLECTS, WITH BROAD NEG

2 A **chance** to do something is an opportunity to do it. EG *She put the phone down before I had a chance to reply... The extra day's holiday gave us a chance to paint the house.* N COUNT : USU+ *to*-INF/*of* ● If you **take** your **chances**, you make the most of all the opportunities that come along. ● PHR : VB INFLECTS

3 A **chance** is also a possibility that something dangerous or unpleasant will happen. EG *We may lose a lot of support, but that's a chance we'll have to take... If you want to make money you've got to take chances.* N COUNT = risk

4 If you **chance** something, you take a risk that something bad may happen. EG *There's a risk that I'll be caught, but I'm going to chance it.* V+O

5 **Chance** is the way that things happen without seeming to have any cause or plan. EG *It was pure chance that led to this discovery... ...a chance meeting.* N UNCOUNT ⇑ accident ● If something happens **by chance, by pure chance**, or **by sheer chance**, it happens without anyone planning it or doing anything to make it happen. EG *Almost by chance I found myself involved in trying to talk to him.* ● PHR : USED AS AN A ⇑ accidentally = luck

6 You use **by any chance** in questions in order to find out whether something that you think might be true is actually true. EG *Are you by any chance the new teacher?* PHR : USED AS ADV SEN ⇑ possibly = perhaps

7 If you **chance** to do something, it happens without you planning it or doing anything to make it happen. EG *I chanced to overhear them talking about your work. ...to reduce the risk of detection if either chanced to look up.* V+*to*-INF ⇑ happen

chance on. If you **chance on** or **upon** someone or something, you meet or discover them unexpectedly. EG *I chanced on an old school-friend in the street yesterday... Castle began to regret that he had chanced on that poem.* PHRASAL VB : V+ PREP, HAS PASS = stumble on

chancel /tʃɑːnsəᵒl/, **chancels.** A **chancel** is the part of a church containing the altar, where the clergy and the choir usually sit. N COUNT

chancellor /tʃɑːnsəᵒlə/, **chancellors.** 1 The **Chancellor** is 1.1 the head of government in several European countries. EG *...Chancellor Helmut Schmidt of West Germany.* N COUNT : ALSO IN TITLES **1.2** the Chancellor of the Exchequer. EG *Harold Wilson chose Jim Callaghan as his Chancellor... The Chancellor bowed to City advice.* N COUNT : ALSO IN TITLES ⇑ minister **1.3** the official head of a British university. This is an honorary position, so the Chancellor does not actually run the university. EG *I think he's the Chancellor of the Open University now.* N COUNT : USU SING ALSO IN TITLES

2 See also **vice-chancellor.**

Chancellor of the Exchequer, Chancellors of the Exchequer. The **Chancellor of the Exchequer** is the minister in the British government who makes decisions about finance and taxes. N COUNT : ALSO IN TITLES

chancy /tʃɑːnsiˡ/, **chancier, chanciest.** Something that is **chancy** involves a lot of risk or uncertainty; an informal word. EG *Taking a case to the High Court is a chancy matter... Many teachers think this is too chancy and they make lists to remind them.* ADJ QUALIT ⇑ uncertain = rickety, dicey

chandelier /ʃændəˡlɪə/, **chandeliers.** A **chandelier** is a circular frame with branches to hold light bulbs or candles. It hangs from the ceiling and is often decorated with lots of hanging pieces of glass. EG *...a huge crystal chandelier.* N COUNT ⇑ light fitting

change /tʃeɪndᵒʒ/, **changes, changing, changed.** 1 If there is a **change** in something, it becomes different in some way. EG *...a radical change in attitudes... ...a change of pace... He was shaken by the changes that had taken place since he had left China... Minor changes have been made to the steering wheel and pedals... I disliked change of any kind... There had been little change.* N COUNT/ UNCOUNT ⇑ difference = alteration ● If you make a **change of direction**, you go in a different direction or you change your mind about something and do it differently. ● PHR : VB INFLECTS = alter

2 If you say that something is a **change**, you mean that it is different, often in a pleasant or interesting way. EG *Quite a change from university, isn't it?... You need a break, a change... It is a refreshing change for her to meet a woman executive.* N SING : *a*+N ⇑ difference ● If you say that something **makes a change**, you mean that it is different and more pleasant or enjoyable than the thing you were previously doing. EG *Being out in the country made a refreshing change.* ● PHR : VB INFLECTS ⇑ improvement

3 If you say that something is happening **for a change**, you mean that it is better or more enjoyable than the thing that usually happens. EG *They were more than glad to leave their cars parked and walk for a change... It's nice to see you with your books for a change.* PHR : USED AS AN A = for once ≠ as usual

4 When something **changes** or when you **change** something, **4.1** it becomes different. EG *Her disdain changed to surprised respect... They can be used to change uranium into plutonium... Little has changed since then... You can't change human nature.* V-ERG ⇑ become = alter ◊ **changed.** EG *He returned to parliament a changed man... I had been in the desert for almost a year now and I was a changed woman.* ◊ ADJ QUALIT : ATTRIB ◊ **changing.** EG *They are anachronisms in a changing world.* ◊ ADJ CLASSIF **4.2** it starts following a slightly different plan or course of action. EG *...one of the architects who have dramatically changed course... ...ideas that change the course of history.* V-ERG = alter **4.3** it turns so that it is moving in a different direction. EG *A bird changes direction by dipping one wing and lifting the other.* V-ERG ⇑ turn = alter

5 To **change** something also means **5.1** to replace it or to use, have, or get something of a similar kind instead of the thing you previously used or had. EG *I changed the bulb... It was his doctor who advised that he change his job... I took the saucepan back and changed it for a non-stick one.* V+O : IF+PREP THEN *for* **5.2** to move it to a different position. EG *It's all right if you just change the furniture around... She changed the kitten from one shoulder to the other.* V+O+A

6 If there is a **change** of something, it is replaced, or something else of a similar kind is used or got instead of the one previously used. EG *...a change of government... That motorcycle needs a change of* N COUNT+SUPP : USU+*of* ⇑ replacement

oil... *Perhaps, after all, he would profit from a change of scene... ...job changes.*

7 When you **change** or **change** your clothes, you take off some or all of your clothes and put on different ones. EG *I went to my dressing room to change... She changed into the working clothes she had brought with her... I want to change my socks.* — V OR V+O : IF V+PREP THEN *into/out of*

8 A **change** of clothes is another set of clothes, especially one that you take with you when you are going to stay somewhere else; also used when you put on different clothes. EG *I packed two changes of underwear... I've spent 3 days without a bath or a shave or a change of clothes.* — N COUNT+*of*

9 When you **change** a baby or **change** its nappy, you take off its dirty or wet nappy and put on a clean one. EG *She fed the baby some milk and changed its nappies... On this mat the baby can be dried, dressed, and changed.* — V+O ⇑ replace

10 When you **change** a bed, you take off the dirty sheets and put on clean ones. EG *She and another volunteer changed the bedding of the elderly patients... I've got to change the bed today.* — V+O ⇑ replace

11 If you **change** or if you **change** buses or trains, you get off one bus or train and on to another in order to continue your journey. EG *Change at Crewe... In Albany you'll change for Ohio... You could change buses at Polegate crossroads... Do I have to change?* — V OR V+O ⇑ transfer = switch, connect

▸ used as a noun. EG *He had come from London on the slow afternoon train, with a change at Swindon on the way... He lived ten miles and three expensive changes of bus away from his job.* — ▸ N COUNT ⇑ transfer

● The announcement **'All change!'** is sometimes heard at a railway, tube, or bus station to tell everyone on a train, tube, or bus to get off because it is not going any further. — ● CONVENTION

12 When a signal **changes**, it indicates something by changing colour or by moving to a different position. EG *The traffic light changed and Renshaw crossed the street... The lights changed to green.* — V : IF+PREP THEN *to* = alter

13 When you **change** gear or **change** into or out of gear, you move the gear lever on a car, bus, bicycle, etc in order to use a different gear. EG *He changed into fourth... She had to change from third to second gear... I find changing gear is awkward in this car.* — V+O, OR V+A ⇑ alter

▸ used as a noun. EG *You still need to work on your gear changes.* — ▸ N COUNT = selection

14 When the wind **changes**, it starts blowing from a different direction. EG *The wind had changed, the dust was clearing.* — V ⇑ alter = turn

15 You use **change** when you want to describe the gradual way a series of things, especially the seasons, follow one another. EG *...watching the seasons change... Summer changed to autumn.* — V : IF+PREP THEN *to* ⇑ give way = turn

16 Change is **16.1** the money that you receive when you pay for something with more money than it costs because you do not have exactly the right amount of money. EG *As he took the change, Rudolph had an impulse to buy another ticket... Morris handed Hooper his change.* — N UNCOUNT **16.2** smaller coins or notes which you give to someone in exchange for the same amount of money in larger coins or notes. EG *Have you got change for a fiver?... I'm sorry, we haven't got change for a twenty pound note–have you got anything smaller?* — N UNCOUNT+*for* **16.3** coins rather than notes. EG *We only had 80p in change... ...a bag for carrying loose change.* — N UNCOUNT ⇑ money ≠ notes

17 When you **change** money, **17.1** you give someone an amount of money in smaller coins or notes in exchange for the same amount of money in larger coins or notes. EG *Can anyone change a ten pound note?* — V+O **17.2** you give or are given an amount of one country's money in exchange for an equivalent amount of another country's money. EG *The bank could only change roubles into hard currency, and not vice versa... Do you change foreign currency?* — V+O : IF+PREP THEN *into*

18 If you say that you will **get no change out of** or **from** someone, you mean that you will get no help or cooperation from them; an informal expression. — PHR : VB INFLECTS, WITH BROAD NEG

19 ● **change hands**: see **hand**. ● **change one's mind**: see **mind**. ● **ring the changes**: see **ring**. ● **change the subject**: see **subject**. ● **change tack**: see **tack**. ● **change one's tune**: see **tune**.

change down. When you **change down**, you move the gear lever on a car, bus, bicycle, etc in order to use a lower gear. EG *You'll have to change down into second to get round the corner.* — PHRASAL VB : V+ADV

change over. **1** To **change over** from one thing to another means to stop doing, using, or having one thing and start doing, using, or having something else. EG *The brandy market began just at this time to change over to whisky... The school changed over from having a system of streaming to having mixed ability classes... They had been Liberal till several years ago, then they changed over to Conservative.* — PHRASAL VB : V+ADV, USU+A (*from/to*) = switch

2 You say that two people **change over** when each of them does what the other person was previously doing or when each of them goes to where the other person was. EG *They gave each other little friendly pats on the shoulder as they changed over... Let's change over–you paint the wall and I'll paint the door.* — PHRASAL VB : V+ADV = swap

3 See also **changeover**.

change up. When you **change up**, you move the gear lever on a car, bus, bicycle, etc in order to use a higher gear. EG *She changed up into fourth.* — PHRASAL VB : V+ADV

changeable /tʃeɪndʒəbəl/. If you describe someone or something as **changeable**, you mean that they are likely to vary greatly at different times, so that it is difficult to predict what they will be like at any one time. EG *He was as changeable as the weather... ...a changeable sky... She knew how impulsive and changeable Sophie could be.* — ADJ QUALIT ⇑ variable ≠ unreliable

changeless /tʃeɪndʒlɪs/. Something that is **changeless** never seems to change in its nature or its qualities. EG *...a changeless image... ...the changeless nature of women.* — ADJ CLASSIF ⇑ constant = everlasting

changeling /tʃeɪndʒlɪŋ/, **changelings**. A **changeling** is a child who was substituted for another child when they were both very young babies. In stories changelings were often taken or left by fairies. — N COUNT

change of life. The **change of life** is the menopause. — N SING : *the*+N

changeover /tʃeɪndʒəʊvə/, **changeovers**; also spelled with a hyphen. A **changeover** is a change from one activity, system, or way of working to another one, especially one which you hope will be better than the first. EG *This changeover has been completed in most of India... The changeover had taken place in the Easter vacation.* — N COUNT : IF+PREP THEN *to* = switch

channel /tʃænəl/, **channels, channelling, channelled**; also spelled **channeling** and **channeled** in American English. **1** A **channel** is **1.1** a specific wavelength which is used to receive the television or radio programmes that are broadcast by a particular company; used also to refer to the actual company that broadcasts the programmes. EG *He switched to the other channel... ...a new season of foreign films on Channel Four.* — N COUNT = station **1.2** a specific wavelength on which you can receive and send messages by radio. EG *There was interference with communications on all channels... I picked him up on Channel 19.* — N COUNT = band **1.3** a system or method that is used as a way of achieving something that you want to do or to get. EG *...diplomatic channels... Stevens promptly notified the German authorities through the normal channels... The Minister's statement closed this channel of protest.* — N COUNT : USU+SUPP ⇑ means

2 If you **channel** something such as money or resources, you control and direct it so that it is used in a particular way or for a particular purpose. EG *...the need to channel North Sea oil revenues into industry... Funds channelled through this project are now being spent on library books.* — V+O : USU+A

3 A **channel** is also **3.1** a passage along which water or some other liquid flows or is carried. EG *...irrigation channels.* — N COUNT = canal **3.2** a long, deep, narrow space that runs along a surface or between two high sides. EG *...a plastic channel into which the double glazing slides... ...the deep channel between the outer and inner walls.* — N COUNT = groove **3.3** a route that is used by boats to cross a particular area of water. EG *The main channels had been closed by enemy submarines.* — N COUNT

4 The **Channel** or the **English Channel** is the narrow area of water between England and France that joins the North Sea to the Atlantic Ocean. EG *...the other side of the Channel... ...the French Channel ports... ...the Channel Ferry.* — N PROPER : *the*+N

chant /tʃɑːnt/, **chants, chanting, chanted**. **1** A **chant** is **1.1** a word or group of words that is repeated over and over again, usually by more than one person. EG *The assembly broke into a chant. 'What's your name? What's your name?'* — N COUNT ⇑ utterance **1.2** a religious prayer or song that is spoken or sung on — N COUNT = incantation

only a very few notes so that there is not much variation in it.

2 If you **chant** something or you **chant**, 2.1 you repeat a word or group of words over and over again. EG *A thousand demonstrators chanted: 'Kevin, Kevin'... From my office I could hear the chanting of the pickets outside.* 2.2 you sing or say a religious song or prayer. EG *'And God is powerful,' the preacher was chanting.* V OR V+O/QUOTE = intone; V OR V+O/QUOTE

chaos /keɪɒs/ is a state of complete disorder and confusion. EG *Chaos began to develop on the roads... ...economic chaos... In the midst of the chaos which followed the shooting, the gunman escaped.* N UNCOUNT

chaotic /keɪɒtɪk/. Something that is **chaotic** is in a state of complete disorder and confusion. EG *The scene was chaotic... ...a chaotic jumble of motor vehicles of every description.* ADJ QUALIT ⇑ disordered

chap /tʃæp/, **chaps**; an informal word. 1 You can use **chap** to refer to a man or boy. EG *The chap she danced with was a very good friend of mine... You're a good chap, Castle... What do you think of this chap Kroop then?* N COUNT = bloke, guy

2 People sometimes use **chap** 2.1 when they are talking in a rather patronizing way to or about another man or boy; used especially by men. EG *Pour me another whisky, would you, Percival, there's a good chap... You chaps are doing a splendid job... The new chaps in power in Mozambique seem an interesting bunch.* 2.2 when they are talking in an affectionate and friendly way to or about their friends. EG *Come on, chaps, we're late!... Are you chaps giving me dinner or not?* N COUNT = fellow; N COUNT : ALSO VOC, USU PL = lads

3 See also **chapped**.

chap. is an abbreviation for 'chapter'; used especially in references and bibliographies. EG *...the South Kensington Museums (see Chap. 12).* N HAS PL : USU+NUM

chapel /tʃæpəˀl/, **chapels**. 1 A **chapel** is 1.1 a place in a church or cathedral which has its own altar and is used for private prayer and for some religious services. EG *St George's Chapel is dedicated to the dead of 1914-18... ...the Chapel of St Peter... The chapels on the other side of the cathedral are all medieval.* 1.2 a room or small church that is attached to a school, hospital, prison, etc, and is used for Christian worship. EG *...the candlelit chapel at King's College, Cambridge.* 1.3 a building which is used for religious worship by Christians who do not belong to the Anglican or Roman Catholic churches. EG *...a Methodist chapel... There was no music in the village then except at the chapel or the church.* N COUNT : ALSO IN NAMES; N COUNT : ALSO IN NAMES; N COUNT, OR *at/to*+N ⇑ church

2 If you describe someone as **chapel**, you mean that they worship at a Protestant Nonconformist church, rather than at an Anglican or Roman Catholic church. EG *They were Chapel families, with high ethical standards.* ADJ CLASSIF ⇑ nonconformist ≠ church

chaperone /ʃæpərəʊn/, **chaperones, chaperoning, chaperoned**; also spelled **chaperon**. A **chaperone** is 1 an older or married woman who used to accompany a young unmarried woman on social occasions, especially when there were men present. EG *She went to Italy with her old governess as a chaperone.* ▸ used as a verb. EG *She had been far too strictly chaperoned to allow him to have any speech with her.* 2 someone who accompanies a group of young people or children, especially in order to make sure that they behave properly. ▸ used as a verb. EG *...with one of the mistresses to chaperone us.* N COUNT ⇑ escort; ▸ V+O ⇑ escort; N COUNT ⇑ guardian; ▸ V+O

chaplain /tʃæplɪn/, **chaplains**. A **chaplain** is a member of the Christian clergy who does religious work in an institution such as a hospital, school, prison, etc, or who works for an important person, for example a bishop or a king. EG *When I was first ordained, I served as a hospital chaplain... ...a naval chaplain... Andreas Capellanus was chaplain to Philip II.* N COUNT : IF+PREP THEN *of/to*

chaplaincy /tʃæplɪnsiˡ/, **chaplaincies**. 1 A **chaplaincy** is the building or office in which a chaplain works. EG *There's a barbecue at the Catholic Chaplaincy on Friday night.* N COUNT : USU SING

2 **Chaplaincy** is the position or work of a chaplain. EG *What is chaplaincy work like in a modern university?* N UNCOUNT

chapped /tʃæpt/. Skin that is **chapped** is dry, cracked, and sore, usually caused by cold weather or wind. EG *His lips were all chapped and rough.* ADJ QUALIT ⇑ damaged

chapter /tʃæptə/, **chapters**. 1 A **chapter** is 1.1 one of the parts that a book is divided into. Chapters usually have a number and sometimes a title. EG *This will be discussed in more detail in chapter 8... ...a chapter on how to introduce people to one another.* 1.2 a period of time in someone's life or in history during which a major event or series of related events takes place. EG *A new and more responsible chapter of my career as a journalist was about to commence... ...a new chapter in the history of international relations.* N COUNT, OR N HAS PL : USU+NUM ⇑ part; N COUNT+SUPP = era

2 If you give someone **chapter and verse**, you tell them precisely the source or authority for what you are saying. EG *I don't want chapter and verse, just give me a rough idea.* PHR : USED AS O

3 If you describe something as **a chapter of accidents**, you mean that a whole series of unpleasant events has happened quickly, one after the other. EG *'Rather a chapter of accidents for me, I'm afraid,' says Henry.* PHR : USU USED AS C

4 A **chapter** is also 4.1 the group of Christian clergy who work in or who are connected with a cathedral. EG *The Dean called a meeting of the chapter.* 4.2 a branch of a society or club, especially a secret one. N COUNT : IF SING VB CAN BE SING OR PL; N COUNT

chapter house, chapter houses; also spelled with a hyphen. A **chapter house** is the building or set of rooms in the grounds of a cathedral where the members of the clergy hold their meetings. N COUNT

char /tʃɑː/, **chars, charring, charred**. 1 **Char** is tea; an informal and old-fashioned use. N UNCOUNT

2 A **char** is the same as a charwoman; an old-fashioned use. N COUNT ⇑ cleaner

3 If a woman is **charring**, she is working as a cleaner in an office or private house; an old-fashioned word. V = clean

4 See also **charred**.

charabanc /ʃærəbæŋ/, **charabancs**. A **charabanc** is a large old-fashioned motor coach with many rows of seats. It was used especially for taking people sightseeing or on holiday. EG *Outside in the yard the charabanc waited.* N COUNT : OR *by*+N

character /kærəˀktə/, **characters**. 1 The **character** of a person, group of people, place, etc consists of all the qualities they have that combine to form their personality or atmosphere. EG *There was another side to his character... People were affected by the character of New York.* N COUNT : USU WITH POSS = nature

2 If you say that someone is behaving **in character**, you mean they are behaving in the way you would expect them to behave, knowing how they usually react to things. EG *Such a gesture would be in character with Smithy's behaviour.* ● If you say that someone is behaving **out of character**, you mean that they are behaving in a way which you would not expect, knowing how they usually behave or react to things. EG *Her reading glasses had bright green frames, which seemed out of character.* PHR : USED AS AN A = in keeping; ● PHR : USED AS AN A

3 If something has a particular **character**, it has that particular quality. EG *We need to emphasize the radical character of our demands... Concessions are not always purely negative in character... He lit several candles, giving the meeting a clandestine character.* N UNCOUNT : USU +SUPP ⇑ identity = nature

4 When you talk about **the English character, the Irish character,** etc, you are thinking of the qualities that people from a particular country or race are believed to have. EG *...the independence of the Spanish character... Acting is not in the English character.* PHR = make up, psyche

5 If you describe someone as being of high **character**, good **character**, etc, you are emphasizing how much they are respected by other people. EG *All complaints were withdrawn, acknowledging McKinley's irreproachable character... ...beautiful women of high character.* N UNCOUNT : ADJ +N ⇑ reputation = good name

6 Your **character** is your personality, considered especially in relation to how honest and reliable you are. EG *...a confidential assessment of Mr Charles Boon's character... He was asked to write a character reference for Mr Stevens.* N COUNT : USU POSS+N

7 If someone has **character**, they have the ability to deal effectively with difficult, unpleasant, or dangerous situations; used showing approval. EG *It takes considerable character not to just give up and go home... I think Jenny has great strength of character.* N UNCOUNT ⇑ strength

8 If you say that a place has **character**, you mean that it has a special, interesting, and unusual quality that makes you notice or like it; used showing N UNCOUNT = atmosphere

approval. EG *'I like this place,' she declared. 'It's got character.'... ...an old house of great character.*

9 The **characters** in a film, book, or play are the people that the film, book, or play is about. EG *...the tensions that develop between the two main characters.* N COUNT: USU PL ⇑ person

10 A **character** is **10.1** a person, especially when you are mentioning a particular quality that he or she has. EG *He's a strange character, my friend Evans... ...a seedy character with a cigarette butt jammed behind his ear.* N COUNT: USU ADJ+N ⇑ person **10.2** a very interesting, unusual, or amusing person. EG *Dooley was a local character... She was a real character.* N COUNT: USU ADJ+N ⇑ personality = eccentric

11 A **character** is also a letter, number, or other symbol that you write or print. EG *...the twenty-six characters of the English alphabet.* N COUNT

character actor, character actors. A **character actor** is an actor who specializes in playing unusual or eccentric people. N COUNT ⇑ actor

character assassination is the deliberate attempt to destroy someone's reputation, especially by criticizing them in an unfair and dishonest way when they are not there, so that everyone doubts their good qualities. EG *Allegations of an immoral relationship were described as 'a character assassination'... ...hypocrisy, double-dealing, innuendo and character assassination.* N UNCOUNT = hatchet job

characteristic /kæ̱rə³ktərɪ̱stɪk/, **characteristics. 1** A **characteristic** is a quality that is typical of a particular person, place, or thing, and that makes them easy to recognize or notice. EG *Ambition is a characteristic of all successful businessmen... ...a family characteristic... ...all the characteristics that distinguish birds from other animals.* N COUNT: IF+ PREP THEN *of* = feature, trait

2 Something that is **characteristic** of something or someone is typical of that person or thing and makes them easy to recognize. EG *...those large curved brick tiles so characteristic of East Anglia... Each whale has its own characteristic song.* ADJ QUALIT: IF+ PREP THEN *of* = unique
◊ **characteristically.** EG *He proposed a characteristically brilliant solution.* ◊ ADV

characterize /kæ̱rə³ktəraɪz/, **characterizes, characterizing, characterized;** also spelled **characterise. 1** If one thing **characterizes** another, it is very typical of it. EG *...the incessant demand for change that characterizes our time... ...the broad strokes and graceful curves that characterize this type of lettering.* V+O = typify

2 To **characterize** something as being a particular thing means to give it the quality by which it can most easily be recognized or described. EG *The revolutionaries characterize the seventies as an era of attack... His essays characterized decency as a British peculiarity.* V+O, OR V+O+A *(as)* ⇑ render

3 If you **characterize** someone or something, you say what their characteristics are. EG *How would you characterize a shanty town from that picture?* V+O, OR V+O (NG/REFL)+A *(as)*

characterless /kæ̱rə³ktəlɪ²s/. Something or someone that is **characterless** is dull and uninteresting. EG *The small room was characterless now.* ADJ CLASSIF

charade /ʃərɑ̱:d/, **charades. 1** A **charade** is a piece of absurd and unnecessary pretence which is so obvious that nobody is deceived by it. EG *They had been carrying out a charade of negotiations with the government... They reduce the very process of consultation to a charade.* N COUNT: IF+ PREP THEN *of*

2 Charades is a game in which the players are divided into teams, with one team acting a word or phrase, syllable by syllable, for the other players to guess the whole word or phrase. EG *He is brilliant at charades.* N UNCOUNT

3 A **charade** is also a word that is being acted in a game of charades, or the actual playing of the game. EG *We acted out our charade with lots of giggling and whispering.* N COUNT

charcoal /tʃɑ:kəʊl/ is **1** a black substance like coal that is obtained by burning wood without much air. Charcoal can be used as a fuel. EG *By them lay a stick of charcoal brought down from the fire... ...glowing charcoal fires.* N UNCOUNT ⇑ carbon **2** small sticks of this black substance which are used for drawing with. EG *The artist sketches the pattern in charcoal on the cloth... ...a charcoal drawing.* N UNCOUNT

charge /tʃɑ̱:dʒ/, **charges, charging, charged.**
1 If you **charge** someone an amount of money, you ask them to pay that amount for something that they have bought or received. EG *'How much do you charge?'–'6 pounds a night.'... The bank charges me 25% interest on the loan... They charged fifty cents admission.* V, V+O, OR V+O +O ⇑ demand

2 If something is **charged to** your **account**, the amount of money that you have to pay for it is recorded on your account at a particular shop. At some time in the future you will be sent a bill telling you how much you owe. EG *Please charge the bill to my account.* PHR: VB INFLECTS

3 A **charge** is the price that you have to pay for a service or for something you buy. EG *...increases in postal and telephone charges... No charge is made for repairs.* N COUNT ● If something is **free of charge**, it does not cost anything. EG *They're happy to give their services free of charge.* ● PHR: USED AS AN A OR C = free

4 A **charge** is also a formal accusation, made by an authority such as the police, that someone is guilty of a crime and has to stand trial in a court of law. EG *The police arrested her on a charge of conspiracy to murder... ...a murder charge... Most of the charges were dropped.* N COUNT: IF+ PREP THEN *against* ⇑ indictment

5 To **charge** someone means to accuse them formally of having done something illegal. EG *He was arrested and charged with a variety of offences... He denied the crimes with which he was charged.* V+O, OR V+O+A *(with)* = indict

6 If you have **charge** of something or someone, you are the person in control and have responsibility for them. EG *She intended to take charge of the boy herself... My first concern is for people under my charge.* N UNCOUNT+ SUPP ● If you are **in charge** of someone or something, you are the person in control and are responsible for them. EG *Who's in charge here?... ...a nurse in charge of several babies... He was minister in charge of government business.* ● PHR: USED AS AN A, IF+PREP THEN *of*

7 If someone is your **charge**, they have been given to you to look after and you are responsible for them; a formal use. EG *He wanted to ensure that Michelle did not become a public charge... He spoke to his two charges.* N COUNT: USU POSS+N ⇑ responsibility

8 If you **charge** towards someone or something, you move quickly and deliberately towards them, especially in order to attack them. EG *Suddenly the lion charged at me... A car door slammed, and Len Hendricks charged into the station house... She charged off to the bedroom.* V: USU+A ▸ used as a noun. EG *The troops mounted one charge after the other... He ducked to evade the beast's desperate charge.* ▸ N COUNT/ UNCOUNT

9 When you **charge** something such as a battery or **charge** it **up**, you pass an electrical current through it in order to make it store the electricity. EG *It requires electricity to charge up its batteries.* V+O
◊ **charged.** EG *Simply exchange a dead battery pack for a fully charged one.* ◊ ADJ CLASSIF: ATTRIB

10 An electrical **charge** is the amount of electricity that is obtained or carried by something; a technical term in physics. N COUNT

11 If you **charge** someone to do something, you order them to do it; a formal use. EG *I have no option but to charge you strictly to say nothing about it.* V+O+*to*-INF

12 The **charge** in a cartridge or shell is the explosive in it; also used of the cartridge or shell itself. N COUNT

13 See also **charged.**

chargeable /tʃɑ̱:dʒəbə⁰l/. **1** If something is **chargeable, 1.1** you have to pay tax on it. EG *...the disposal of a chargeable asset... It is chargeable with duty of sixpence only.* ADJ CLASSIF: IF+ PREP THEN *with* **1.2** you have to pay a sum of money for it. EG *A late entry fee of $20 is chargeable.* ADJ CLASSIF **1.3** you are allowed to claim back the money you have spent, usually from your employer or from the tax office. EG *...chargeable expenses.* ADJ CLASSIF

2 If a crime is **chargeable**, it is serious enough for you to be formally accused of having committed it. EG *Some minor offences should not be chargeable.* ADJ CLASSIF

charged /tʃɑ̱:dʒd/. Something that is **charged** is filled with emotion and so creates an atmosphere of tension or excitement. EG *He interrupted what had become a highly charged silence... ...his voice was charged with suppressed merriment... ...a morally charged thriller about politics.* ADJ QUALIT: IF+ PREP THEN *with* ⇑ fill

chargé d'affaires /ʃɑ̱:ʒeɪdæfe̱ə/, **chargés d'affaires.** Both the singular and the plural form are pronounced in the same way. A **chargé d'affaires** is **1** a person appointed to act as the head of a diplomatic mission in a foreign country while the ambassador is away. N COUNT ⇑ diplomat **2** the head of a small or not very important diplomatic mission in a foreign country. N COUNT ⇑ diplomat

charge hand, charge hands. A **charge hand** is a workman who is slightly less important than a foreman. N COUNT

charge nurse, charge nurses. A **charge nurse** is a nurse who is in charge of a hospital ward. N COUNT

charger /tʃɑːdʒə/, **chargers**. A **charger** is 1 a device used for charging or recharging batteries. EG *...battery chargers.* 2 a strong horse that a knight in the Middle Ages used to ride in battle. EG *...a knight on a white charger.* N COUNT; N COUNT = war horse

charge sheet, charge sheets. A **charge sheet** is the official form which is used by the police when they write down legal charges against a person. N COUNT ⇑ document

chariot /tʃærɪət/, **chariots**. A **chariot** is a vehicle with two wheels that was used in ancient times. It was pulled by horses and used for racing and fighting. N COUNT

charioteer /tʃærɪətɪə/, **charioteers**. A **charioteer** was, in ancient times, a chariot driver. N COUNT

charisma /kərɪzmə/ is the ability to attract, influence, and inspire people by your personal qualities. EG *He possessed the qualities of a leader, charisma, energy and eloquence.* N UNCOUNT = magnetism

charismatic /kærɪzmætɪk/. 1 Someone who is **charismatic** is able to attract, influence, and inspire people by their personal qualities. EG *...a charismatic leader of people.* ADJ CLASSIF = magnetic

2 The **charismatic** church is the part of the Christian Church that believes that people can obtain special supernatural gifts from God, for example prophecy, healing, and speaking in tongues. EG *...the charismatic movement in the Church.* ADJ CLASSIF : USU ATTRIB

charitable /tʃærɪtəbəºl/. 1 Someone who is **charitable** has a kind or tolerant attitude towards someone. EG *She was being unusually charitable to me today.* ▸ used of a person's behaviour or actions. EG *...a charitable remark.* ◊ **charitably**. EG *He charitably chose to ignore her impertinence.* ADJ QUALIT ⇑ kindly; ▸ ⇑ kindly; ◊ ADV WITH VB ⇑ generously

2 A **charitable** organization, activity, etc is concerned with helping and supporting people or animals in need. EG *...a charitable home for 'distressed people in London'... This wing of the hospital was financed entirely by charitable donations.* ADJ CLASSIF : ATTRIB ⇑ benevolent

charity /tʃærɪti¹/, **charities**. 1 **Charity** is 1.1 a kind and sympathetic attitude which you show towards other people by being tolerant, helpful, or generous to them. EG *She found the charity in her heart to forgive them for this wrong.* 1.2 money or gifts which are given to people because they are poor. EG *He's far too proud to accept charity.* N UNCOUNT ⇑ virtue; N UNCOUNT ⇑ gift = alms

2 If you say that **charity begins at home**, you mean that people should care for the welfare of their own family or people near to them before they think about the needs of others. EG *With so much money given away in foreign aid the government ought to be reminded that charity begins at home.* PHR

3 A **charity** is an organization which raises money for a particular cause, for example to help people in need or to provide medical facilities. EG *The proceeds will go to local charities... ...a donation to an African charity... ...charity workers.* N COUNT

charlady /tʃɑːleɪdi¹/, **charladies**. A **charlady** is the same as a charwoman. N COUNT ⇑ cleaner

charlatan /ʃɑːlətəºn/, **charlatans**. A **charlatan** is someone who deceives other people by pretending to have special skills or knowledge that they do not really possess; used showing disapproval. EG *The doctor was either a charlatan or a shrewd old rogue.* N COUNT ⇑ impostor

charleston /tʃɑːlstəºn/, **charlestons**. The **charleston** is a lively dance that was popular in the 1920s. N COUNT : USU the+N IN SING

charm /tʃɑːm/, **charms, charming, charmed**. 1 **Charm** is the attractive and pleasant quality that a person, place, or thing has. EG *The narrow streets of the old town are full of charm... Her great personal charm makes her a very popular member of the staff... I had to use all my charms to persuade them to come.* N UNCOUNT/COUNT = appeal, attraction

2 If you **charm** someone, you use your charm to please them. EG *I was flattered by his interest in me and charmed by his courtesy.* V+O = delight

3 A **charm** is 3.1 a small ornament, usually made of silver or gold, that is fixed to a bracelet or necklace, often with several others. 3.2 an act, saying, or object that is believed to have magic powers or to bring good luck. EG *Charms and spells are still common in Ceylon.* N COUNT = trinket; N COUNT = spell, talisman

4 If you say that someone **leads a charmed life** or **has a charmed life**, you mean that they are always lucky. PHR : VB INFLECTS ⇑ be lucky

charmer /tʃɑːmə/, **charmers**. A **charmer** is a charming person, often someone who uses his or her charm to influence people. EG *They're both tremendous charmers in their different ways.* • See also **snake charmer**. N COUNT : USU AS C = flatterer

charming /tʃɑːmɪŋ/. Someone or something that is **charming** is very pleasant and has great charm; a slightly old-fashioned word. EG *Celia is a charming girl... He lived in a charming house.* ◊ **charmingly**. EG *I thought her script was charmingly written.* ADJ QUALIT ⇑ nice = delightful; ◊ ADV

charred /tʃɑːd/. Something that is **charred** is partly burnt and made black by fire. ADJ QUALIT

chart /tʃɑːt/, **charts, charting, charted**. 1 A **chart** is 1.1 a diagram, illustration, or table which shows information in a visual form. EG *Look at the chart to see which benefits you can get if you are unemployed... On three walls are pinned large charts illustrating world poverty.* 1.2 a map of the sea or of the stars. EG *...charts of the Indian Ocean and the China Sea.* N COUNT = diagram, graph; N COUNT

2 The **charts** are the official lists that show which pop and rock records have sold the most copies each week. EG *They've got a hit single in the charts.* N PLURAL : the+N = hit parade

3 If you **chart** the development or progress of something, you observe it and record it carefully. EG *The child's health progress was charted in detail... We charted their movements.* V+O

4 If you **chart** a course of action, you plan it. EG *Party workers had little time to chart a detailed way out of their troubles.* V+O = plot

5 If you **chart** an area of land or water, you draw it or show it on a map. EG *On this map we have charted the course of the Helford River.* V+O

charter /tʃɑːtə/, **charters, chartering, chartered**. 1 A **charter** is 1.1 a document which describes the rights of a particular group of people or which demands rights for them. EG *...the Working Women's Charter... ...a new charter for the mentally ill.* 1.2 a formal document issued by the government or ruler of a country which allows an organization or institution to be founded and lists its rights and functions. EG *...the charter of the University... Campbell obtained a charter and the new Swedish Company was formed.* 1.3 a list of the aims and principles of an organization. EG *It contravened article 51 of the UN charter.* N COUNT : USU+SUPP; N COUNT; N COUNT = constitution

2 To **charter** an organization or institution means to issue a charter for it to be founded. V+O

3 A **charter** plane or boat is one which is hired for use by a particular person or group and which is not part of a regular service. EG *He is travelling on a charter flight.* N COUNT : USU BEFORE N

4 If you **charter** transport such as a plane or boat, you hire it for your private use. EG *They had chartered a plane to find a lost ship... We plan to charter a special train for London.* V+O

chartered /tʃɑːtəd/. Someone who is a **chartered** accountant or a **chartered** surveyor has passed all the examinations necessary in order to be fully qualified in their profession. ADJ CLASSIF : ATTRIB

charwoman /tʃɑːwʊ¹məºn/, **charwomen**. A **charwoman** is a woman who is employed to clean houses or offices; an old-fashioned word. N COUNT ⇑ cleaner = daily

chary /tʃeəri¹/. Someone who is **chary** is careful and cautious about what they do or say. EG *Enterprises are becoming increasingly chary of taking on new workers... She started a chary descent of the stairs.* ADJ QUALIT : USU PRED+of = wary

chase /tʃeɪs/, **chases, chasing, chased**. 1 If you **chase** a person or an animal, you run after them or follow them quickly in order to catch them. EG *Youngsters chase one another up trees and play tag... As a child, I loved to chase the chickens barefoot round the yard... I couldn't chase after them–they were running too fast.* ▸ used as a noun. EG *They abandoned the chase and returned home... ...a car chase.* V+O, OR V+A (after) ⇑ pursue; ▸ N COUNT ⇑ pursuit

2 If you **chase** a person or animal from a place, you force them to leave the place by threatening or attacking them or running after them. EG *They were chased from the village... On my sheet was yet another snake, dozing. I chased it off.* V+O+A = drive

3 To **chase** somewhere means to run or rush there. EG *The dog went chasing up the beach... I spent the summer chasing around Europe.* V+A

4 If you **chase** something that you want such as work or money, you spend a lot of time and effort trying to get it. EG *Many men become workaholic, chasing success and often neglecting their children... Joe was away in Bombay, chasing after some film job.* — V+O, OR V+A (after) ⇑ pursue

5 If you **chase** someone, you make an effort to be with them and talk to them because you want to have a closer relationship with them, for example a sexual relationship. EG *Some men chase other men's wives.* — V+O = run after

chase up. 1 If you **chase** someone **up**, you remind them or urge them to do something that you want. EG *I'll chase her up for those reports.* — PHRASAL VB: V+O+ADV = badger, chivvy

2 If you **chase** something **up**, you try to find it because it is needed. EG *Can you chase up those statistics for me?* — PHRASAL VB: V+O+ADV ⇑ FIND

chaser /tʃeɪsə/, **chasers.** A **chaser** is 1 a milder drink such as beer that you have after a strong alcoholic drink such as whisky; also used to refer to a strong drink that you have after a weak drink. — N COUNT 2 a person who is chasing someone or something. — N COUNT = pursuer

chasm /kæzəᵒm/, **chasms.** A **chasm** is 1 a very deep crack in rock, earth, or ice. EG *The range itself was a series of mountains, chasms, canyons and valleys.* — N COUNT = abyss, ravine 2 a very large difference between two things, groups of people, ideas, etc, especially one that you think will never change. EG *There's a chasm between rich and poor in that society.* — N COUNT: IF+PREP THEN between/in = gulf, rift

chassis /ʃæsiˡ/. The plural form is **chassis** /ʃæsiˡz/. A **chassis** is the framework that a vehicle is built on. — N COUNT

chaste /tʃeɪst/. 1 Someone who is **chaste** does not have sex with anyone, or only has sex with their husband or wife; an old-fashioned use, used showing approval. EG *She was a holy woman, innocent and chaste.* — ADJ CLASSIF ⇑ pure ≠ promiscuous ▸ used of people's behaviour. EG *We had a beautiful chaste relationship for over a year.* — ▸ ADJ CLASSIF

2 Something that is **chaste** is very simple in style, without much decoration. EG *...chaste houses built in 1732.* — ADJ QUALIT

chasten /tʃeɪsəᵒn/, **chastens, chastening, chastened.** If you **chasten** someone, you make them realize that they have been wrong or naughty and that they should improve their behaviour; an old-fashioned use. EG *They slunk out of the study like two schoolboys chastened by the headmaster.* — V+O = reprimand

chastise /tʃæstaɪz/, **chastises, chastising, chastised.** If you **chastise** someone, 1 you scold them for something that they have done. EG *He chastised the members at the Conference for not taking things seriously enough.* — V+O 2 you punish them severely for doing something wrong, especially by beating them; a rather old-fashioned use. EG *Dr O'Shea chastised his son with the end of his belt.* — V+O

chastisement /tʃæstaɪzmə²nt/ is the same as punishment; an old-fashioned word. — N UNCOUNT

chastity /tʃæstɪtiˡ/ is the state of not having sex with anyone, or of only having sex with your husband or wife; an old-fashioned word or a religious term. EG *A monk makes vows of poverty, chastity and obedience.* — N UNCOUNT ⇑ purity

chat /tʃæt/, **chats, chatting, chatted.** 1 When people **chat**, they talk in an informal, friendly way, usually about things which are not very serious or important. EG *We sat by the fire and chatted all evening... My sister discussed politics at the party, but I chatted about books.* — V: IF+PREP THEN about/to/with = natter ▸ used as a noun. EG *Chat at the party was mainly about his new film... He enjoys chat for its own sake.* — ▸ N UNCOUNT ⇑ conversation

2 A **chat** is an informal, friendly conversation, usually about things which are not serious or important. EG *We had a nice long chat about our schooldays... My friends often come in for coffee and a chat.* — N COUNT = natter

chat up. If you **chat up** someone, you talk to them in a friendly way, often in a flirting way because you are attracted to them and want to have a closer relationship with them; an informal expression, used mainly in British English. EG *Hughie queued up for coffee and chatted up the women serving it.* — PHRASAL VB: V+O+ADV

château /ʃætəʊ/, **châteaux.** A **château** is a large country house or castle in France. EG *...a château built by a French marquess in the seventeenth century... ...the châteaux of the Loire.* — N COUNT

chat show, chat shows. A **chat show** is a television or radio show in which an interviewer and his or her guests talk in a friendly, informal way about different topics; used mainly in British English. — N COUNT ⇑ programme = talk show

chattel /tʃætəᵒl/, **chattels.** A **chattel** is something that belongs to you; an old-fashioned word. EG *He left all his worldly goods and chattels to his daughter.* — N COUNT: USU PLURAL ⇑ possession = belonging

chatter /tʃætə/, **chatters, chattering, chattered.** 1 If you **chatter**, you talk quickly and continuously, usually about things which are not important. EG *Joy thought Sheila chattered too much... Off we set, with Bill chattering away all the time.* — V: IF+PREP THEN about = babble ▸ used as a noun. EG *The actors could hardly be heard above the chatter of the audience... At teatime there was much excited chatter.* — ▸ N UNCOUNT = hubbub

2 When birds and certain animals **chatter**, they make quick, short, high-pitched noises. EG *The monkeys chattered in the trees.* — V ⇑ noise ▸ used as a noun. EG *I was woken by the loud chatter of the birds.* — ▸ N UNCOUNT+SUPP

3 When something **chatters**, it makes quick rattling or clicking sounds repeatedly. EG *I felt my body shivering and heard my teeth chattering with the cold... Teleprinters chatter away all day in his office.* — V = rattle ▸ used as a noun. EG *...the constant chatter of the machines.* — ▸ N UNCOUNT+of

chatterbox /tʃætəbɒks/, **chatterboxes.** A **chatterbox** is a person, especially a child, who talks a great deal, usually about things which are not important; used in informal English. EG *Mary's such a chatterbox!* — N COUNT: USU USED AS C = chatterer

chatterer /tʃætərə/, **chatterers.** A **chatterer** is the same as a chatterbox. — N COUNT

chatty /tʃætiˡ/, **chattier, chattiest.** Someone who is **chatty** is fond of talking in a friendly, informal way. EG *The taxi driver was chatty and merry.* — ADJ QUALIT ⇑ talkative ▸ used of someone's style of writing or talking. EG *She wrote a nice, chatty letter, full of news and gossip.* — ▸ ADJ QUALIT

chauffeur /ʃəʊfə, ʃəʊfɜː/, **chauffeurs, chauffeuring, chauffeured.** 1 A **chauffeur** is a person who is employed to drive a car for someone else. Chauffeurs usually wear a uniform. EG *She even sent her car and chauffeur to collect her guests.* — N COUNT ⇑ driver

2 If you **chauffeur** someone, you drive them somewhere in a car, usually as part of your job. EG *The Prime Minister and his colleagues come and go in chauffeured limousines.* — V+O

chauvinism /ʃəʊvɪnɪzəᵒm/ is a strong and unreasonable belief that your own country or race is more important and morally better than other people's; used showing disapproval. EG *They showed increased national chauvinism and distrust or envy of foreign nations.* — N UNCOUNT ⇑ bigotry = jingoism ◇ **chauvinist.** EG *...chauvinist pride.* — ◇ N COUNT, OR ADJ CLASSIF: ATTRIB ● See also **male chauvinism.**

chauvinistic /ʃəʊvɪnɪstɪk/. Someone who is **chauvinistic** 1 has a strong and unreasonable belief that their own country or race is more important and morally better than other people's; used showing disapproval. EG *...chauvinistic nationalism and ethnic prejudice.* — ADJ QUALIT = jingoistic 2 has an unreasonable belief that their own social, religious, or political values are more important or morally better than other people's; used showing disapproval. EG *...the chauvinistic male world's idea of what a woman should be.* — ADJ QUALIT = prejudiced

cheap /tʃiːp/, **cheaper, cheapest.** 1 Something that is **cheap** costs very little money or costs less than is usual or expected. EG *...cheap plastic bowls and buckets... A solid fuel cooker is cheap to run.* — ADJ QUALIT ⇑ inexpensive ≠ dear ◇ **cheaply.** EG *...an opportunity to buy oil cheaply.* — ◇ ADV WITH V

2 **Cheap** goods cost less money than average because they are less good in quality. EG *...cheap red wine... ...cheap cuts of meat... Clothing manufacturers took ideas from Paris and made cheap copies.* — ADJ CLASSIF: ATTRIB ⇑ inferior = economy

3 A **cheap** ticket costs less than the normal price because it is intended to be used by a particular group of people such as children or old people, or used at a time when fewer people use the transport or service. EG *You get a cheap rate, but you've got to produce your travel pass... ...the issue of cheap tickets on production of a pension book.* — ADJ CLASSIF: ATTRIB = budget, economy

4 Something that is **cheap and nasty** costs very little money and is very bad in quality; used showing disapproval. EG *Plastics used to be considered cheap and nasty.* — PHR: USED AS = shoddy, tacky

5 You say that facilities or services are **cheap** or that the people who provide them are **cheap** when you pay only a small amount of money for the facilities or services. EG *...a cheap cafe... ...a cheap electrician... The buses are very cheap in Sheffield.* — ADJ QUALIT ⇑ reasonab ◇ **cheaply.** EG *Fletcher and Co. decorated my home quickly, cheaply, and efficiently.* — ◇ ADV WITH ⇑ reasonat

6 A **cheap** service is also one which people pay less for than they ought to, because they are taking unfair advantage of a situation; often used showing disapproval. EG *...the developing country's vast supply of cheap labour... ...the use of volunteers as a cheap way of providing tuition.* — ADJ QUALIT ⇑ exploited

7 If you do something or buy something **on the cheap**, you spend less money on it than you should, and it is not done properly or fairly because of this; an informal expression, used showing disapproval. EG *He was simply being employed on the cheap so they could film a story based on a rotten novel... It was a bad idea in the first place, done on the cheap.* — PHR : USED AS AN A = cheaply

8 If someone says that a person's life is **cheap**, they mean that it is unimportant and that it does not matter what happens to the person. EG *Of course, human life out there is cheap.* — ADJ QUALIT : PRED ⇑ worthless

9 You say that a person's behaviour or remarks are **cheap** when they are being unkind or unfair in a way that is very obvious and unnecessary; used showing disapproval. EG *He could not resist being unkind to people, making cheap jokes at their expense... That's so cheap I'm not going to answer it... ...a piece of cheap opportunism.* — ADJ QUALIT ⇑ low = shabby

cheapen /tʃi:pəⁿn/, **cheapens, cheapening, cheapened.** 1 If something **cheapens** you, it lowers your reputation or dignity; used showing disapproval. EG *I would not cheapen myself by doing such a thing.* — V+O (NG/REFL)

2 If you **cheapen** something, you reduce its price in order to sell it more easily. — V+O

cheat /tʃi:t/, **cheats, cheating, cheated**; used showing disapproval. 1 When someone **cheats**, they lie or behave dishonestly in order to get what they want. EG *We all used to cheat in exams.* ◊ **cheating**. EG *...accusations of cheating.* — V ⇑ deceive; ◊ N UNCOUNT ⇑ fraud

2 If someone **cheats** you of something or **cheats** you out of it, they get it from you by behaving dishonestly or unfairly. EG *He still remembers how his father was cheated of his land twelve years ago... She cheated her little sister out of some money.* — V+O : IF+PREP THEN *of/out of* ⇑ take = trick

3 If you **feel cheated**, you feel that you have been treated wrongly or unfairly because you have not got what you want. EG *He will compare your life-style with his own and feel cheated.* — PHR : VB INFLECTS

4 A **cheat** is 4.1 something dishonest or unfair that someone does in order to make people believe that something is true when it is not. EG *We would film in England, so it would be a bit of a cheat because it would appear to be Iceland.* — N COUNT ⇑ deceit. 4.2 a person who lies or behaves dishonestly in order to get what they want. EG *He's just a big cheat.* — N COUNT : IF SING, USU *a*+N = fraud

cheat on; an informal expression. 1 If you **cheat on** someone when you are having a relationship with them, especially a sexual relationship, you behave dishonestly towards them by secretly having another relationship with someone else. EG *A private detective has been assigned to find out whether she's cheating on her husband.* — PHRASAL VB : V+PREP, HAS PASS = be unfaithful to

2 To **cheat on** someone also means to lie or behave dishonestly towards them in order to get what you want. — PHRASAL VB : V+PREP = trick

check /tʃek/, **checks, checking, checked.** 1 If you **check** something or someone or **check on** them, you make sure that they are correct, safe, making progress, etc. EG *I changed the bulb and checked the fuse... Check where Louisiana is in your atlas... He needed a chance to check with Hooper to see if his theory was plausible... All through the night, he would wake up to check on me... Tony came in from time to time, to check on my progress.* — V, V+O/REPORT-CL, OR V+A *(on/with)* ⇑ examine. ● If you **double check** something, you check it a second time in order to be absolutely sure about it. EG *We've checked it and double checked it and we still can't find anything wrong.* — ● V OR V+O

2 A **check** is an examination or inspection to make sure that everything is correct or safe. EG *...security checks... Police checks on banks at night were increased.* — N COUNT : IF+PREP THEN *on*

3 To **check** something also means to stop it from continuing or spreading. EG *...a campaign to check the influence of the unions... The destruction of the bridge checked the enemy's advance.* — V+O = curb

4 If someone **checks** you or if you **check** yourself, you suddenly stop what you are doing or saying. EG *He began to saunter off, then checked himself and turned back... Sudhir held up his hand to check him. 'Can't you see this lady is telling me something?'* — V+O (NG/REFL)

5 If you **check** a feeling, you control it and prevent it from showing in your behaviour or speech. EG *Mrs Hochstadt, who hated to see litter, had to check an impulse to run after it and pick it up.* — V+O = repress

6 If you **keep** something or someone **in check** or **hold** them **in check**, you control them and prevent them from becoming stronger or more powerful. EG *He had not conquered inflation but he had held it in check... Their troops are being held in check.* — PHR : VB INFLECTS = keep at bay

7 If one piece of information **checks** with another piece of information or if both pieces **check**, they agree with each other. EG *Yeah-that all checks with our data here.* — V : USU+A *(with)*

8 In a restaurant, your **check** is your bill; used in American English and in some British dialects. EG *He waved to a waiter and got the check.* — N COUNT = bill

9 In a game of chess, you say **check** when you are attacking your opponent's king. EG *Bishop to King's knight five, check.* ● If you are **in check**, your own king is being attacked. — CONVENTION; ● PHR : USED AS AN A

10 **Check** is a pattern that consists of squares, usually of two colours. EG *...their fondness for plaids and checks.* ▸ used as an adjective. EG *...a tall blond man in a check suit... ...pink and white check cloth.* — N UNCOUNT/COUNT; ▸ ADJ CLASSIF

11 **Checks** are a check pattern, especially on cloth. EG *...a green jacket with sky-blue checks.* — N PLURAL

12 See **cheque**.

check in. 1 When you **check in** or when someone **checks** you **in** at a hotel, you arrive at the hotel and make arrangements to stay there. EG *I checked in at the Gordon Hotel... He arrived back in Austria and checked into a small boarding house... He worked at the desk, checking in the guests.* — PHRASAL VB : V-ERG+ADV/PREP = register

2 When you **check in** at an airport or other port, you show your ticket and hand in your luggage before you begin a journey by plane or ship. EG *You have to check in by 12.30.* ● See also **check-in**. — PHRASAL VB : V+ADV, IF+PREP THEN *at* = register

check off. When you **check** a number of things **off**, you examine them or count them by looking at a list to make sure that everything is right. EG *We waited while Mr Wilde checked off the things on the list.* — PHRASAL VB : V+O+ADV = tick off

check out. 1 When you **check out** of a hotel, you give back your key and arrange to leave. EG *The following morning he checked out.* — PHRASAL VB : V+ADV

2 If you **check** something **out**, you discuss it or examine it carefully because you want to make sure that everything is correct or safe. EG *It might be difficult to transfer your money, so check it out with the manager... The building was being checked out for a bomb.* — PHRASAL VB : V+O+ADV

3 To **check** someone **out** means to obtain information about them, often in order to find out if they are suitable for something; an informal use. EG *We'd better check him out before we let him join the group... He turned back to the title page to check out the author.* — PHRASAL VB : V+O+ADV ⇑ investigate

4 See also **checkout**.

check up. If you **check up** on someone or something, you obtain information about them, often secretly, in order to find out if they are suitable for something. EG *The council had checked up on her and decided that she was unsuitable for employment... He had been aware that they would be checking up on him... They think there is a security leak and are trying to check up.* ● See also **check-up**. — PHRASAL VB : V+ADV, IF+PREP THEN *on* ⇑ investigate

checked /tʃekt/. Something that is **checked** has a check pattern. EG *...a checked blouse.* — ADJ CLASSIF = check

checker /tʃekə/, **checkers.** 1 **Checkers** is the game of draughts; used in American English. EG *The men played checkers and listened to records.* — N UNCOUNT

2 A **checker** is a person whose job is to check something. — N COUNT ⇑ examiner

checkered /tʃekəd/. See **chequered**.

check-in, check-ins. A **check-in** is the place in an airport or port where you check in. EG *...a thousand passengers arriving all at once at a check-in counter.* — N COUNT ⇑ counter

checkmate /tʃekmeɪt/, **checkmates, checkmating, checkmated**; also spelled with a hyphen. **Checkmate** is 1 a winning position in a game of chess in which your opponent's king cannot move away from your direct attack. — N UNCOUNT = mate. 2 a situation in which all progress of a plan has been stopped. EG *It was checkmate, with both countries refusing to negotiate.* ▸ used as a verb. EG *The United Nations decision was checkmating the United States.* — N UNCOUNT; ▸ V+O

checkout /tʃekaʊt/, **checkouts**; also spelled with a hyphen. A **checkout** is the place in a supermarket — N COUNT : USU SING where the price of your goods is added up and you pay for them. EG *...queueing at the checkout counter.*

checkpoint /tʃɛkpɔɪnt/, **checkpoints**. A **checkpoint** is a place where people and vehicles have to be examined or identified, for example at a frontier between two countries. EG *...a roadside checkpoint manned by four soldiers.* — N COUNT

check-up, check-ups. A **check-up** is a medical examination that a doctor or dentist gives you to check that your health is all right. EG *See the doctor for a blood test and check-up.* — N COUNT

cheddar /tʃɛdə/, **cheddars**. **Cheddar** is a type of hard cheese. EG *...English cheddar.* — N MASS

cheek /tʃiːk/, **cheeks, cheeking, cheeked**. 1 Your **cheeks** are the soft parts of your face on each side of your nose and mouth. EG *She kissed him on both cheeks and went out.* — N COUNT ● **tongue in cheek**: see **tongue**. ● **cheek by jowl**: see **jowl**. ● If you **turn the other cheek**, you decide not to get angry or violent when people treat you badly. EG *I always try to turn the other cheek.* — ● PHR : VB INFLECTS ⇑ ignore

2 Your **cheeks** are also your buttocks; an informal use. — N COUNT : USU PL

3 A person who has **cheek** is not afraid or embarrassed to do or say things that shock or annoy people. EG *I never thought he'd have the cheek to ask to borrow my car again after crashing it last time.* — N UNCOUNT : ALSO *the*+N+ *to-INF* = nerve

4 **Cheek** is also words or behaviour that show a lack of respect, for example towards a parent or teacher. EG *I've had enough of your cheek–get out of my class!* — N UNCOUNT = insolence

5 To **cheek** someone means to be rude or disrespectful to them. EG *Charlie cheeked his dad today.* — V+O

cheekbone /tʃiːkbəʊn/, **cheekbones**. Your **cheekbones** are the two bones at the top of your cheeks just below your eyes. — N COUNT : USU PL ⇑ bone

-cheeked combines with words referring to colours or shapes to describe the appearance or quality of a person's cheeks. EG *...their healthy, rosy-cheeked faces.* — COMB : FORMS ADJ CLASSIFS

cheeky /tʃiːki¹/, **cheekier, cheekiest**. Someone who is **cheeky** is rude or disrespectful. EG *...that cheeky nephew of yours.* ▸ used of a person's behaviour or actions. EG *Don't be so cheeky... I found his cheeky self-confidence unbearable.* ◇ **cheekily**. EG *'Bet you can't,' retorted Tom cheekily.* — ADJ QUALIT ⇑ impertinent = saucy; ◇ ADV WITH VB

cheer /tʃɪə/, **cheers, cheering, cheered**. 1 When you **cheer**, you shout loudly and joyfully to show your approval of something or to encourage someone, for example a football team. EG *When they saw the food they would laugh and cheer... His speech was cheered by the crowds... There was a confused sound of music and cheering.* ▸ used as a noun. EG *I heard a great cheer go up.* — V OR V+O ≠ boo; ▸ N COUNT ≠ boo

2 If you **are cheered** by something, it makes you feel more cheerful when you have been unhappy or worried. EG *I was cheered by my solicitor telling me how difficult he had found it to get a mortgage himself.* ◇ **cheering**. EG *It is so cheering to find that other people are just as untidy as you are.* — V+O = hearten; ◇ ADJ QUALIT = heartening

3 **Cheer** is a feeling of cheerfulness; a rather old-fashioned use. — N UNCOUNT ⇑ happiness

4 **'Cheers'** is **4.1** something that people say to each other just before they drink an alcoholic drink. **4.2** an informal way of saying 'thank you'; used in British English. EG *'Here's that book you wanted.'–'Oh, cheers.'* **4.3** an informal way of saying 'goodbye'; used in British English. EG *See you at six, then. Cheers!* — CONVENTION; CONVENTION = ta; CONVENTION ⇑ good bye = bye

cheer on. If you **cheer** someone **on**, you cheer loudly in order to encourage them in what they are doing. EG *Some students stood on the roof, cheering the rioters on.* — PHRASAL VB : V+O+ADV

cheer up. When you **cheer up** or when someone or something **cheers** you **up**, you stop feeling depressed and become more cheerful. EG *She cheered up a little as Miss Livingstone went out... Her friends tried to cheer her up, telling her she wasn't missing much... Oh Peter, cheer up–it's not the end of the world, you know.* — PHRASAL VB : V-ERG+ADV = buck up

cheerful /tʃɪəful/. 1 Someone who is **cheerful** is happy and joyful and shows this in their behaviour. EG *She had remained cheerful and energetic throughout the trip... She had a naturally cheerful and serene expression.* ▸ used of a person's behaviour or manner. EG *She was in a cheerful mood.* ◇ **cheerfully**. EG *He smiled cheerfully at everybody.* ◇ **cheerfulness**. EG *They worked with great energy and cheerfulness.* — ADJ QUALIT = bright, merry; ◇ ADV WITH VB; ◇ N UNCOUNT ⇑ happiness

2 Something that is **cheerful** is pleasant to look at or experience and makes you feel happy. EG *I've been looking for literature of a more cheerful nature... It was a good hospital with a cheerful atmosphere.* — ADJ QUALIT = jolly

3 **Cheerful** behaviour is also willing and enthusiastic behaviour. EG *She showed a cheerful commitment and dedication to her work.* ◇ **cheerfully**. EG *Every morning, she would go off cheerfully to work.* — ADJ QUALIT : ATTRIB; ◇ ADV WITH VB

4 You also say that someone is **cheerful** about something when they are not worried about it, although you think that they should be worried. EG *...the cheerful conviction that sensible people will never start a nuclear war.* ◇ **cheerfully**. EG *He has lung cancer, yet he cheerfully smokes twenty cigarettes a day.* — ADJ QUALIT : ATTRIB ⇑ happy = blithe; ◇ ADV WITH VB ⇑ happily = blithely

cheerio /tʃɪəriəʊ/ is an informal way of saying 'goodbye'; used especially in British English. — CONVENTION = bye

cheerleader /tʃɪəliːdə/, **cheerleaders**. A **cheerleader** is one of the people who leads the crowd in cheering at a large public event, especially a sports event. — N COUNT ⇑ leader

cheerless /tʃɪəlɪ²s/. Something that is **cheerless** is gloomy and depressing. EG *It was a cold, cheerless, grey sort of morning.* — ADJ QUALIT

cheery /tʃɪəri¹/, **cheerier, cheeriest**. People who are **cheery** are cheerful, bright, and happy. EG *Mr Phillips was a cheery man.* ▸ used of behaviour. EG *On the way out I saw Jack McFall, who gave his usual cheery wave... I wrote cheery letters home, telling everyone how I was progressing.* ◇ **cheerily**. EG *'Hello!' I shouted cheerily.* — ADJ QUALIT; ◇ ADV WITH VB

cheese /tʃiːz/, **cheeses**. 1 **Cheese** is a food made from milk. It is usually white or yellow in colour. There are many different kinds of cheese, for example ones that are soft and do not have much taste, and ones that are hard and have a strong taste. EG *...cheddar cheese... I made a nice cheese soufflé... You can't live on bread and cheese.* — N MASS

2 A **cheese** is a solid block of cheese before it has been cut up for selling or eating. EG *...a big Stilton cheese.* — N COUNT

3 **'Say cheese'** is something that you say to make someone smile when you want to take a photograph of them. — CONVENTION = smile please

4 **chalk and cheese**: see **chalk**.

cheeseboard /tʃiːzbɔːd/, **cheeseboards**. A **cheeseboard** is a board on which you put several kinds of cheese so that people can choose the ones that they want to eat. ▸ The **cheeseboard** is the course at the end of a meal when cheese is served on a cheeseboard. EG *Would you like a sweet, sir, or the cheeseboard?* — N COUNT ⇑ board; ▸ N SING : *the*+N ⇑ course

cheesecake /tʃiːzkeɪk/, **cheesecakes**. 1 **Cheesecake** is a dessert which has a layer of biscuit covered with a soft mixture that contains cream cheese. EG *She made a delicious cheesecake... ...a portion of strawberry cheesecake.* — N COUNT/ UNCOUNT

2 **Cheesecake** is also used to refer to photographs of naked or half-dressed women, for example in pornographic magazines; an informal and offensive use. — N UNCOUNT

cheesecloth /tʃiːzklɒθ/ is cotton cloth that is very light and loosely woven. EG *...a cheesecloth shirt.* — N UNCOUNT ⇑ fabric

cheesed off. If you are **cheesed off**, you are annoyed, bored, or disappointed; an informal expression in British English. EG *I was really cheesed off when he didn't turn up.* — ADJ QUALIT : PRED ⇑ annoyed

cheese-paring is behaviour in which you are extremely careful with your money and spend as little as possible; used showing disapproval. EG *He thought about industrial accidents and the cheese-paring of employers when it came to safety precautions.* ▸ used as an adjective. EG *This calls for a much more generous, less cheese-paring attitude.* — N UNCOUNT = stinginess; ▸ ADJ QUALIT : USU ATTRIB = stingy

cheetah /tʃiːtə/, **cheetahs**. A **cheetah** is a large, wild, cat-like animal with black spots, which can run very fast. Cheetahs are found mainly in Africa. — N COUNT

chef /ʃɛf/, **chefs**. A **chef** is a cook in a restaurant or hotel, especially the head cook. — N COUNT

chef-d'oeuvre /ʃɛdɜːvrə⁰/, **chefs-d'oeuvre**. Both the singular and the plural are pronounced in the same way. Someone's **chef-d'oeuvre** is their masterpiece; a formal or literary expression. — N COUNT : USU+POSS

chemical /kɛmɪkə⁰l/, **chemicals**. 1 **Chemical** means concerned with chemistry or made by a process in chemistry. EG *...a change in the chemical composition of the atmosphere... ...chemical fertilizers... Warmth speeds up chemical reactions.* — ADJ CLASSIF : ATTRIB

◊ **chemically**. EG *Chemically, this substance is similar to cellulose.* ◊ ADV, OR ADV SEN

2 A **chemical** is a substance such as a liquid, powder, or gas that is used in a chemical process or that is made by a chemical process. EG *...synthetic chemicals such as pesticides... ...chemicals ranging from hormones to vaccines.* N COUNT

3 **Chemical** warfare is warfare in which poisonous chemicals are used as weapons. EG *They are using chemical warfare... There were frequent outcries about the use of chemical weapons.* ADJ CLASSIF ATTRIB

chemist /kɛmɪst/, **chemists**. 1 The **chemist** or the **chemist's** is a shop where you can buy medicine that has been prescribed by your doctor and also other medicines, cosmetics, etc; used in British English. EG *He bought the perfume at the chemist in St James's Arcade... I found her buying bottles of vitamin tablets at the chemist's.* N SING : *the*+N = drugstore, pharmacy

2 A **chemist** is also 2.1 a person who is qualified to give people medicines that are prescribed by a doctor; used in British English. EG *...a dispensing chemist.* N COUNT = pharmacist 2.2 a person who studies chemistry or who does chemical research or work. EG *Any nation that has one physicist, one chemist, and one metallurgist can produce a nuclear bomb... ...a research chemist.* N COUNT ↑ scientist

chemistry /kɛmɪstri¹/. 1 **Chemistry** is the scientific study of the characteristics and composition of substances and the way that they react with other substances. EG *She did a degree in chemistry... ...a new chemistry lab.* N UNCOUNT ↑ science

2 The **chemistry** of a particular substance is its characteristics and composition and the way that it reacts with other substances. EG *He is studying the chemistry of medicinally important compounds.* N UNCOUNT+*of*

3 **Chemistry** is also used to refer to the way in which two people react to each other, for example when their work needs them to have a close relationship or when they are having a sexual relationship; an informal use. EG *For them, the chemistry was right: they had hit it off from the start.* N UNCOUNT : USU +SUPP ↑ reaction

chemotherapy /ki:məʊθɛrəpi¹/ is the treatment of disease using chemicals. Chemotherapy is often used in treating cancer. N UNCOUNT

chenille /ʃə³ni:l/ is thick furry cord that is used for decorating cloth. ▸ **Chenille** is also used to refer to cloth made from this cord. EG *...a pink chenille bedspread.* N UNCOUNT

cheque /tʃɛk/, **cheques**; also spelled **check** in American English. A **cheque** is a piece of paper that you can use instead of money to pay for things. You sign it and write on it the name of the person you are paying and the amount of money that you are paying them. The person will then be paid the money from your bank account. EG *Ellen gave the landlady a cheque for 80 pounds... Did you pay by cheque?... Who do I make the cheque payable to?* ● See also **blank cheque, pay cheque, traveller's cheque**. N COUNT, OR *by*+N ≠ cash

chequebook /tʃɛkbʊk/, **chequebooks**; also spelled with a hyphen and as two words; also spelled **checkbook** in American English. A **chequebook** is a book of cheques with your bank's name and your name printed on them, which you are given by your bank to use to pay for things. N COUNT

cheque card, cheque cards. A **cheque card** is a small plastic card which your bank gives you and which you have to show when you are paying for something by cheque or when you are cashing a cheque at another bank; used in British English. EG *We only accept cheques if you have a cheque card.* N COUNT = banker's card

chequered /tʃɛkəd/; also spelled **checkered** in American English. 1 If a person, organization, etc has had a **chequered** career or history, they have had a varied past with periods of difficulty or failure as well as times when they have been successful or popular. EG *The Journal was a paper with a lurid and chequered history.* ADJ QUALIT : ATTRIB

2 Something that is **chequered** has a pattern with squares of two or more different colours. EG *...a long chequered dress of black and white velvet.* ADJ CLASSIF ↑ patterned = check

cherish /tʃɛrɪʃ/, **cherishes, cherishing, cherished**. 1 If you **cherish** something such as a hope or a memory, you keep it in your mind so that it gives you happy feelings. EG *I cherish a hope that one day the family will be reunited... It'll be an experience you'll cherish all your life.* V+O = treasure ◊ **cherished**. EG *...cherished memories.* ◊ ADJ QUALIT = treasured

2 If you **cherish** someone or something, you care for them lovingly and tenderly. EG *Comfort and cherish those you love... The hand-carved cart had lain cherished in their garage for years.* V+O

3 If you **cherish** something such as a right or a privilege, you regard it as so important and valuable that it must be carefully maintained. EG *There were no freedoms here of the variety we cherished... Can he preserve the positive values he cherishes in his own culture?* V+O = value ◊ **cherished**. EG *One of its cherished privileges is the right of free speech.* ◊ ADJ QUALIT = valued

cheroot /ʃəru:t/, **cheroots**. A **cheroot** is a cigar with both ends cut flat. N COUNT

cherry /tʃɛri¹/, **cherries**. 1 A **cherry** is a small, round, soft fruit with a red or black skin and a hard round stone in the centre. EG *...an ice cream with a cherry on top.* ▸ also used of the tree that the fruit grow on. EG *...a cherry orchard.* N COUNT

2 If you have **another bite at the cherry** or **a second bite at the cherry**, you have another chance to do something, especially after you have failed the first time; an informal expression. PHR : USED AS O

3 Something that is **cherry** or **cherry red** is bright red in colour. EG *...her cherry lips... ...a cherry-red vinyl binder.* ADJ COLOUR

cherub /tʃɛrəb/, **cherubs**. A **cherub** is 1 an angel that is represented in art as a plump, naked child with wings. EG *High on its façade you can see a naked cherub.* N COUNT 2 a sweet, pretty child or young person; used showing approval. EG *...the white-jacketed trainee waiters, smiling cherubs the lot of them.* N COUNT

cherubic /tʃəru:bɪk/. If you say that someone looks **cherubic**, you mean that they look sweet and innocent like a cherub; a rather literary word. EG *...a cherubic child.* ▸ used of someone's face or expression. EG *The child had a round, cherubic face.* ADJ QUALIT

chervil /tʃɜ:vɪl/ is a herb that tastes of aniseed. N UNCOUNT

chess /tʃɛs/ is a game for two players who each start with sixteen playing pieces of various kinds to move on a chessboard. The aim is to move your pieces so that your opponent's king cannot escape being taken. EG *Do you play chess?... ...a good game of chess.* N UNCOUNT ↑ board game

chessboard /tʃɛsbɔ:d/, **chessboards**. A **chessboard** is a square board that you play chess on. It is divided into sixty-four squares of two alternating colours, usually black and white. N COUNT ↑ board

chessman /tʃɛsmə³n/, **chessmen**. A **chessman** is a playing piece used in chess, usually coloured black or white. Each player has sixteen chessmen at the start of the game. N COUNT

chest /tʃɛst/, **chests**. 1 Your **chest** is the top part of the front of your body, between your neck and your waist, where your ribs, lungs, and heart are. EG *He folded his arms on his chest... She has severe pains in her chest... ...a chest X-ray.* N COUNT

2 A **chest** is a large, heavy box, usually made of wood, which is used for storing things or for moving personal possessions from one place to another. EG *...an oak chest... Among his baggage was a medicine chest stuffed with drugs.* N COUNT = trunk ▸ **Chest** is also used to refer to the things inside a chest. EG *...chests of valuables.* ▸ N COUNT+*of*

3 If you **get** something **off** your **chest**, you tell people what you have been thinking or worrying about and this is a relief because you have not talked about it before; an informal expression. EG *At least I've got it off my chest now.* PHR : VB INFLECTS, N INFLECTS ≠ bottle up

chestnut /tʃɛsnʌt/, **chestnuts**. 1 A **chestnut** is 1.1 a shiny reddish-brown nut that grows inside a prickly green outer covering. You can eat chestnuts. EG *...chestnut puree.* N COUNT 1.2 a tree on which chestnuts grow. It is tall and has broad leaves, each with five pointed ends. EG *I stood waiting under the chestnut tree... ...chestnut leaves.* ● See also **horse chestnut**. N COUNT

2 Something that is **chestnut** or **chestnut-brown** is dark reddish-brown in colour; used especially of people's hair and of horses. EG *...a little boy with chestnut-brown hair... He was riding a chestnut mare.* ADJ COLOUR

3 An **old chestnut** is a joke or story which is so well known that it is no longer funny; an informal expression, used showing disapproval. EG *Not that old chestnut again, Andrew!* PHR : N INFLECTS = tale

chest of drawers, chests of drawers. A **chest of drawers** is a piece of furniture with drawers which you keep clothes or other things in. N COUNT = cabinet

chesty /tʃɛsti¹/. If you have a **chesty** cough, you have a lot of catarrh in your lungs. ADJ QUALIT ≠ dry

chevron /ʃɛvrən/, **chevrons**. A **chevron** is 1 a V shape. EG *A road sign of black and white chevrons indicates a sharp bend.* 2 one of a number of V shapes worn on the sleeve by a person in the armed forces or by someone in the police force. It shows his or her rank. EG *His action had got him the officer's chevrons he had longed for.* — N COUNT; N COUNT = stripe

chew /tʃuː/, **chews, chewing, chewed**. 1 When you **chew** food, you bite it several times with your teeth while it is inside your mouth, so that it becomes softer and easier to swallow. EG *He had started to chew a piece of meat... He was still chewing on his cake... He broke off another piece of bread and chewed at it.* ▸ used as a noun. EG *Have a good chew before you swallow.* ● to **chew the cud**: see **cud**. — V OR V+O : IF+PREP THEN *at/on* = masticate; ▸ N COUNT

2 If you **chew** something, you keep biting it with your teeth, especially in order to taste the flavour of it without eating it, or because you are nervous about something. EG *He chews gum... He sat and chewed his fingernails... He stood there, chewing at his moustache.* — V OR V+O : IF+PREP THEN *at/on* ⇑ bite = nibble

3 To **chew** a hole in something means to make the hole by biting it several times with your teeth. EG *A beetle pauses over the hole she has just chewed in a lily leaf... The fish must have chewed right through it.* — V+A, OR V+O+A ⇑ bite

4 A **chew** is a small hard sweet that becomes softer when you chew it inside your mouth. — N COUNT

5 If you **chew** on or **chew** over something such as a problem, you think carefully about it; used in informal English. EG *His mind chewed on this new complication... In discussion we chew over problems and work out possible solutions.* — V+A *(on)*, OR V+O+A *(over)* ⇑ consider = mull over

6 If you **bite off more than** you **can chew**, you try to do too many different things, or to do something which is too difficult for you, so that you are not likely to be successful; an informal expression. — PHR : FIRST VB AND AUX INFLECT = overdo it

chew up. If you **chew** food **up**, you chew it until it is completely crushed or softened. EG *Lally put it into her mouth and chewed it up happily.* — PHRASAL VB : V+O+ADV = munch

chewing gum; also spelled with a hyphen. **Chewing gum** is a kind of sweet which you can chew for a long time but which you do not swallow. — N UNCOUNT = gum

chewy /tʃuːi[1]/, **chewier, chewiest**. Food that is **chewy** needs to be chewed a lot before you can swallow it; an informal word. EG *Oatmeal makes very chewy bread.* — ADJ QUALIT = firm

chic /ʃiːk, ʃɪk/. Something that is **chic** is fashionable and sophisticated. EG *She was in chic khaki and Cartier bangles... ...a very chic Art College.* ▸ used as a noun to refer to this quality. EG *Vermont and New Hampshire have acquired a rural chic... Over the years he had developed an air of understated chic.* — ADJ QUALIT; ▸ N UNCOUNT

chicanery /ʃɪkeɪnə[0]ri[1]/, **chicaneries**. **Chicanery** is the same as trickery; a formal word. EG *The government was guilty of flagrant injustices, chicanery and corruption.* — N UNCOUNT/COUNT = trickery

chick /tʃɪk/, **chicks**. A **chick** is a baby bird. EG *The mother birds stay together while they're feeding the chicks.* — N COUNT = fledgling

chicken /tʃɪkɪn/, **chickens, chickening, chickened**. 1 A **chicken** is a bird which is kept on a farm for its eggs and for its meat. Chickens are usually brown, black, or white, or a mixture of these colours. EG *She loved to chase the chickens.* ▸ used of the meat of a chicken which is cooked and eaten. EG *There was fried chicken and mashed potatoes for dinner.* — N COUNT ⇑ fowl; ▸ N UNCOUNT ⇑ poultry

2 If you say to someone **'Don't count your chickens'**, or **'Don't count your chickens before they're hatched'**, you are warning them not to make plans according to what they expect to happen before it has actually happened; an informal expression. EG *I hope he's not counting his chickens.* — PHR : VB INFLECTS ⇑ anticipate

3 If you say that something is **a chicken and egg situation**, you mean that it is a situation where it is impossible to decide which of two things caused the other one; an informal expression. — PHR : USED AS C

4 You describe someone as a **chicken** when they are too afraid to do something; an informal use. EG *I was too much of a chicken to fight.* ▸ used as an adjective. EG *Don't be so chicken!* — N COUNT : IF SING a+N = coward; ▸ ADJ QUALIT : PRED

chicken out. If you **chicken out** of something, you decide not to do it because you are too afraid; an informal expression, used showing disapproval. EG *I chickened out at the last moment.* — PHRASAL VB : V+ADV, IF+PREP THEN *of* ⇑ opt out

chickenfeed /tʃɪkɪnfiːd/ is an amount of money which is so small that it is hardly worth having or considering; an informal word. EG *He's earning chickenfeed compared to what you get.* — N UNCOUNT = peanuts

chickenpox /tʃɪkɪnpɒks/; also spelled as two words and with a hyphen. **Chickenpox** is a disease caught especially by children, in which they have a high temperature and red spots that itch. EG *She got chicken pox just before her exam.* — N UNCOUNT

chickpea /tʃɪkpiː/, **chickpeas**. **Chickpeas** are hard, round seeds that look like pale brown peas. They can be cooked and eaten. — N COUNT : USU PL ⇑ pulse

chickweed /tʃɪkwiːd/ is a plant with small leaves and white flowers which grows close to the ground and is regarded as a weed. — N UNCOUNT

chicory /tʃɪkəri[1]/ is a plant with crunchy, sharp-tasting leaves which are used in salads. ▸ **Chicory** is also used to refer to the roots of the plant when they are roasted and used in making coffee. — N UNCOUNT

chide /tʃaɪd/, **chides, chiding, chided**. If you **chide** someone, you scold them because they have behaved badly or foolishly; a rather old-fashioned word. EG *Maurice chided him for his carelessness... 'Fusspot,' chided Clarissa.* — V+QUOTE, OR V-O : IF+PREP THEN *for* = rebuke

chief /tʃiːf/, **chiefs**. 1 A **chief** is 1.1 a person who has authority over a group or an organization, for example in the police or the government. EG *...Jean Ducret, chief of the Presidential Security Corps.... ...the current CIA chief... Defence chiefs urged mobilization at once.* 1.2 the head of a tribe. EG *...Chief Matansima of the Transkei... Land in the village is allocated by the chief.* — N COUNT+SUPP ⇑ leader; N COUNT : ALSO IN TITLES = headman

2 The **chief** cause, part, member, etc of something is the most important or significant one. EG *The 1902 Education Act was the chief cause of the Progressives' downfall... His country is one of the chief sources of cocaine... I was his chief opponent.* — ADJ CLASSIF : ATTRIB = main, major

3 The **chief** worker in a group, firm, etc is the highest in rank; often used in the titles of jobs. EG *Mr Zuckermann summoned his chief cashier... ...the unit's chief electrician.* — ADJ CLASSIF : ATTRIB = head

4 Your **chief** is the person who has authority over you in your job; an informal use. EG *The chief wants to see you in his office... OK, chief.* — N COUNT, ALSO VOC = boss

5 If you say **'Too many chiefs and not enough Indians'** or **'All chiefs and no Indians'**, you are suggesting that work is being done inefficiently because there are too many people saying what should be done and not enough people actually carrying out the work; an informal expression. EG *That's the trouble with the Civil Service nowadays–too many chiefs and not enough Indians.* — PHR

Chief Constable, Chief Constables. A **Chief Constable** is an officer who is in charge of the police force in a particular county or area in Britain. EG *...Greater Manchester's Chief Constable.* — N COUNT : ALSO IN TITLES ⇑ police officer

Chief Justice, Chief Justices. A **Chief Justice** is the head judge of a court, especially a supreme court. EG *...Chief Justice Warren.* — N COUNT : ALSO IN TITLES

chiefly /tʃiːfli[1]/. 1 You use **chiefly** to indicate that a particular reason, situation, feature, etc is the most important or significant one. EG *Those who find fault with it do so chiefly on the grounds that it is not all it might be... The experiment was not a success, chiefly because the machine tools were of poor quality.* — ADV, OR ADV SEN ⇑ basically = mainly

2 If something is done **chiefly** in a particular way, in a particular place, etc, it is done mostly or mainly in that way, in that place, etc. EG *The quality of care was often poor, with heating chiefly by oil stoves... The film was made in Scotland, chiefly in Glasgow.* — ADV

Chief of Staff, Chiefs of Staff. The **Chiefs of Staff** are the highest-ranking officers of each service of the armed forces. — N COUNT

chieftain /tʃiːftə[1]n/, **chieftains**. A **chieftain** is the head of a tribe. EG *...a great warrior chieftain.* — N COUNT = headman

chiffon /ʃɪfɒn, ʃɪfɒn/ is a very thin silk or nylon cloth that you can see through. EG *...a green chiffon scarf.* — N UNCOUNT ⇑ fabric

chihuahua /tʃɪwɑːwɑː, -wə/, **chihuahuas**. A **chihuahua** is a very small short-haired dog. — N COUNT

chilblain /tʃɪlbleɪn/, **chilblains**. A **chilblain** is a painful or itchy red swelling which you get on your fingers or toes when they get too cold. EG *I get terrible chilblains in winter.* — N COUNT

child /tʃaɪld/, **children**. 1 A **child** is 1.1 a person from the time of birth to the time when they become an adult. EG *I had my first seaside holiday when I was* — N COUNT ⇑ human being ≠ adult *a child of fourteen or fifteen... The men sat round one fire and the women and children round another... ...a family with young children.* **1.2** a newly born or unborn baby. EG *Think of the unborn child.* **1.3** a son or daughter of any age. EG *He has a wife and four children... ...a father and his two teenage children... Their children are all married.* **1.4** an immature or childish person; used showing disapproval. EG *Don't be such a child.* — N COUNT; N COUNT = offspring; N COUNT : USU USED AS C

2 If you say that someone is a **child** of a particular time or place or of particular circumstances, you mean that they are so strongly influenced by that time or place or by those circumstances; a formal use. EG *He's a true child of the 1960's.* — N COUNT + *of*

3 If a woman is **with child**, she is pregnant; an old-fashioned expression. — PHR : USED AS AN A

childbearing /tʃaɪldbɛərɪŋ/. **1 Childbearing** is the process of giving birth to babies. EG *She had stretch marks from childbearing.* — N UNCOUNT

2 A woman of **childbearing** age is of an age when women are normally able to give birth to children. — ADJ CLASSIF : ATTRIB

childbirth /tʃaɪldbɜːθ/ is the act of giving birth to a child. EG *His mother died in childbirth.* — N UNCOUNT = labour

childhood /tʃaɪldhʊd/, **childhoods**. **1** A person's **childhood** is the time of life during which they are a child. EG *Her early childhood had been very happy... ...memories of childhood... ...childhood games.* — N UNCOUNT/COUNT ⇑ infancy

2 If you say that someone is **in** their **second childhood**, you mean that they are so old that they are behaving like a child again. — PHR : USED AS AN A = senile

childish /tʃaɪldɪʃ/. **1** You describe a person as **childish** when you think that they behave in an immature way; used showing disapproval. EG *I thought her nice but rather childish.* ▸ used of a person's behaviour or actions. EG *...childish manners.* ◊ **childishly**. EG *'It's too hot here,' he complained childishly.* ◊ **childishness**. EG *I was annoyed at the childishness of her remark.* — ADJ QUALIT = puerile; ◊ ADV; ◊ N UNCOUNT

2 Something that is **childish** is typical of a child or relates to a child. EG *She had a childish face... Love is a childish emotion.* — ADJ QUALIT ⇑ young = childlike

childless /tʃaɪldlɪ²s/. Someone who is **childless** has no children. EG *...childless couples.* — ADJ CLASSIF

childlike /tʃaɪldlaɪk/. Someone who is **childlike** is like a child in appearance, character, or behaviour. EG *She looked at me with her big, childlike eyes... ...a young woman with a childlike figure.* — ADJ QUALIT ⇑ young

childminder /tʃaɪldmaɪndə/, **childminders**; also spelled with a hyphen. A **childminder** is a person who is qualified to look after children outside their home. EG *Mrs Evans is a registered childminder.* — N COUNT

childminding /tʃaɪldmaɪndɪŋ/; also spelled with a hyphen. **Childminding** is the supervision and care given to children by a childminder or by a local government authority. — N UNCOUNT = child care

child prodigy, child prodigies. A **child prodigy** is a child with a very great talent. EG *...a child prodigy like Mozart.* — N COUNT ⇑ genius

childproof /tʃaɪldpruːf/. Something that is **childproof** is designed in a way which ensures that children cannot harm it or be harmed by it. EG *Medicines should be kept in childproof containers.* — ADJ CLASSIF ⇑ safe

children /tʃɪldrən/ is the plural of **child**.

children's home, children's homes. A **children's home** is a place where children are sent to live if their parents cannot look after them properly, for example if their parents have treated them badly or are very ill. — N COUNT

child's play. If you say that something is **child's play**, you mean that it can be done very easily; an informal expression. EG *The test was real child's play.* — N UNCOUNT : USU USED AS C

chili /tʃɪli¹/. See **chilli**.

chill /tʃɪl/, **chills, chilling, chilled**. **1** When you **chill** something or when it **chills**, you lower its temperature so that it becomes colder but does not freeze. EG *White wine should be slightly chilled... Glass can break because of too rapid heating or chilling.* — V-ERG ⇑ cool ≠ heat

2 If you **are chilled**, you feel really cold. EG *I'm chilled to the marrow.* ◊ **chilling**. EG *...a chilling wind... ...a chilling London winter morning.* — V+O : USU PASS; ◊ ADJ QUALIT = freezing

3 If something **chills** you, it causes you to feel suddenly frightened by making you realize how serious or dangerous something is; a rather literary use. EG *A thin wail out of the darkness chilled them.* ◊ **chilling**. EG *Their report on the plans for nuclear war is a chilling document.* ◊ **chillingly**. EG *The following excerpts are chillingly familiar to us.* — V+O ⇑ frighten = terrify; ◊ ADJ QUALIT; ◊ ADV

4 A **chill** is **4.1** a mild illness which can give you a slight fever and headache and make you sneeze. EG *She caught a bad chill.* **4.2** a sudden feeling of anxiety that makes you physically cold for a second or two, which is caused by fear or by something that someone says. EG *The sound sent a chill down my spine.* ▸ used as an adjective. EG *The headline was a chill reminder of the danger to life on our planet.* — N COUNT; N COUNT = shiver; ▸ ADJ CLASSIF : ATTRIB

5 Chill is used to describe the weather when it is cold and unpleasant. EG *It was a chill autumn day when I left London... The falling seeds glinted in the chill November sun.* ▸ used as a noun. EG *...the chill of the early night... She turned on the fire to take the chill from the air.* — ADJ QUALIT = raw; ▸ N COUNT : USU SING = nip

chilli /tʃɪli¹/, **chillies**; also spelled **chili**. A **chilli** is a small red or green seed pod of a plant belonging to the pepper family. Chillies have a very hot, spicy taste and are used for flavouring meat, vegetables, and sauces. — N COUNT/UNCOUNT ⇑ capsicum

chilli powder is dark red powder made from dried chillies. It is used for flavouring food. — N UNCOUNT ⇑ spice

chilly /tʃɪli¹/, **chillier, chilliest**. **1** Something that is **chilly** is rather cold and unpleasant. EG *It was not as cold as in winter, but rather chilly... A draught of chilly air entered the room.* — ADJ QUALIT

2 If you feel **chilly**, you do not feel quite warm enough to be comfortable. EG *Light the fire if you feel chilly.* — ADJ QUALIT : PRED ⇑ cold

3 If a relationship between people or a response to something you have done is **chilly**, it is not very friendly, welcoming, or enthusiastic. EG *The Third World response to the offer of limited aid was chilly... She had given him a very chilly look.* — ADJ QUALIT ⇑ hostile = cool

chime /tʃaɪm/, **chimes, chiming, chimed**. **1** When bells **chime**, they make clear, resonant, ringing sounds. EG *The cathedral bells were chiming through the night.* — V ⇑ ring

2 When a clock **chimes** a particular number of times, it tells you what time it is. EG *The church bell chimed five.* ◊ **chiming**. EG *...the faint chiming of the town hall clock.* — V+O; ◊ N SING WITH DET : USU + *of*

3 A **chime** is the musical sound made by a bell or a clock. EG *...the silvery chime of the old stable clock... ...the chimes of Big Ben.* — N COUNT

4 Chimes are a set of small objects which make musical or ringing sounds. EG *...door chimes.* — N PLURAL : USU MOD+N

chime in. If someone **chimes in**, they say something just after someone else has spoken, usually to agree with them or to support their argument. EG *Bill Henderson chimed in with 'This is an emergency situation.'* — PHRASAL VB : V+ADV+QUOTE, IF +PREP THEN *with*

chime in with. If one thing **chimes in with** another thing, the two things are consistent with each other and can be understood together. EG *What you tell me chimes in with what I've been hearing from other people.* — PHRASAL VB : V+ADV+PREP ⇑ agree

chimera /kɪ⁵mɪərə/, **chimeras**. A **chimera** is **1** a hope that is very unlikely to be fulfilled, or an unrealistic idea that you have about something; a formal or literary word. EG *I let myself be dazzled by the gilt chimeras of the career of writing.* **2** a mythological monster with the head of a lion, the body of a goat, and the tail of a serpent. — N COUNT ⇑ fantasy = illusion, dream; N COUNT

chimney /tʃɪmni¹/, **chimneys**. A **chimney** is **1** a pipe which goes up from a fireplace or factory furnace to above the level of the roof, so that smoke escapes into the air and not into the building. EG *I sat in front of the fire, watching the sparks fly up the chimney... Factory chimneys and church spires were silhouetted against the evening sky.* **2** a long, narrow, vertical gap in the rock on a mountain or cliff face, or in a cave; a technical use. EG *After wriggling down narrow winding chimneys, you come at last to two low galleries.* — N COUNT ⇑ duct; N COUNT ⇑ crack = fissure

chimney breast, chimney breasts; also spelled with a hyphen. A **chimney breast** is the part of a wall in a room which is built out round a chimney; used in British English. — N COUNT

chimney pot, chimney pots; also spelled with a hyphen and as one word. A **chimney pot** is a short pipe, often made of earthenware, which is fixed to the top of a chimney. — N COUNT

chimney stack, chimney stacks; also spelled with a hyphen and as one word. A **chimney stack** is — N COUNT the part of a chimney that is above the roof of a building; used in British English.

chimney sweep, chimney sweeps; also spelled with a hyphen and as one word. A **chimney sweep** is a person whose job is to clean the soot out of the insides of chimneys. N COUNT ⇑ cleaner

chimp /tʃɪmp/, **chimps**. A **chimp** is a chimpanzee; an informal word. EG *The mother chimp sat hugging her baby.* N COUNT

chimpanzee /tʃɪmpə³nzi:/, **chimpanzees**. A **chimpanzee** is a small African ape which has black or brown fur, large ears, and is very intelligent. EG *Chimpanzees are adept climbers, sleeping and feeding in trees.* N COUNT ⇑ animal = chimp

chin /tʃɪn/, **chins**. 1 Your **chin** is the part of your face that sticks out below your mouth and above your neck. EG *His chin and his upper lip were clean-shaven... He had his overcoat buttoned under his chin.* N COUNT 2 If you say that someone **took it on the chin**, you mean that they accepted an unpleasant or difficult situation bravely and without making a lot of fuss about it; an informal expression. PHR : VB INFLECTS ⇑ accept

china /tʃaɪnə/ is 1 very thin clay from which cups, saucers, plates, etc are made. EG *...tea served in real china cups and saucers... He treated her with great gentleness, as though she were made of china.* N UNCOUNT ⇑ ceramic 2 cups, saucers, plates, dishes, etc made of china. EG *She laid out a small tray with the best china and a little lace cloth.* N SING : the/POSS +N ⇑ tableware 3 objects made of china or porcelain, especially ornaments and vases. EG *...an old house crammed with beautiful furniture, glass and china...* N UNCOUNT ● **a bull in a china shop**: see **bull**.

China tea is tea made from large dark green or reddish-brown tea leaves. It is usually drunk without milk or sugar. EG *There was sweet and sour pork, rice and China tea.* N UNCOUNT ⇑ drink

Chinese /tʃaɪni:z/. **Chinese** is both the singular and the plural noun form. 1 Something that is **Chinese** is concerned with or belongs to the country of China, its language, or its people. EG *...a team of Chinese acrobats... Workers come into Chinese schools to teach industrial production.* ADJ CLASSIF

2 A **Chinese** is a person who comes from China. EG *A young Chinese lent me his bicycle... The Chinese issued their own proposal.* N COUNT

3 **Chinese** is one of the languages spoken by people who live in China. EG *When they saw us they rushed forward, chanting in Chinese.* N PROPER ⇑ language

4 A **Chinese** is also a meal eaten in a Chinese restaurant in Britain, or a meal which you buy in a Chinese restaurant and take home to eat; an informal use in British English. EG *At 9 o'clock I woke up and went for a Chinese.* N COUNT

Chinese puzzle, Chinese puzzles. A **Chinese puzzle** is a puzzle consisting of several different boxes which you try to fit inside one another. EG *It was like the last piece in a Chinese puzzle.* N COUNT

chink /tʃɪŋk/, **chinks, chinking, chinked**. 1 A **chink** is 1.1 a very small narrow opening. EG *Through a chink she could see a bit of blue sky... ...a chink of light.* N COUNT : IF + PREP THEN of 1.2 a short, light, ringing sound made by objects such as glasses or coins when they touch each other. EG *...the chink of ice cubes in frosted glasses... ...the chink of money.* N COUNT : USU SING + of = clink ▸ used as a verb. EG *Empty bottles chinked as the milkman put them into his crate.* ▸ V = clink

2 If someone has **a chink in** their **armour**, they have a small but dangerous weakness that makes it easy for people to attack or hurt them, especially emotionally. EG *In his first question he found a chink in Carmichael's armour.* PHR = Achilles heel

chinless /tʃɪnlɪ²s/. If you describe someone as **chinless**, you mean that they are weak and rather cowardly. ADJ QUALIT = spineless

chintz /tʃɪnts/ is cotton fabric with bright patterns on it. It is used for making curtains or for covering chairs and cushions. EG *They sat on the chintz sofa hand in hand.* N UNCOUNT

chintzy /tʃɪntsi¹/. Something that is **chintzy** is decorated or covered with chintz. EG *...a chintzy bedroom.* ADJ QUALIT

chinwag /tʃɪnwæg/. A **chinwag** is a long enjoyable conversation between friends; an informal word. EG *I had a good chinwag with my sister yesterday.* N SING : a+N = natter

chip /tʃɪp/, **chips, chipping, chipped**. 1 In British English, **chips** are long thin pieces of potato fried in oil or fat. EG *He went off to the staff restaurant for steak pie and chips... ...fish and chips.* N COUNT : USU PL = French fry

2 In American English, **chips** or **potato chips** are very thin slices of potato that have been fried until they are hard, dry, and crunchy. EG *The children could not even afford to buy a bag of potato chips for lunch.* N COUNT : USU PL = crisp

3 A **chip** is a very small piece of silicon inside a computer. It has electronic circuits on it and can hold large quantities of information or perform mathematical or logical operations; a technical use. EG *The entire contents of a book will be located on a single silicon chip... America and Japan are working on chips which will hold a million words.* N COUNT = micro chip

4 The **chip** or the **silicon chip** is used to mean modern computer technology in general. EG *The universal power of the chip affects every aspect of our society... ...the silicon chip society.* N SING : the+N

5 When you **chip** something or when it **chips**, you accidentally damage it by breaking a small piece off it. EG *He put down his glass of whisky so hard that he chipped the glass... Plastics aren't magic and can scratch, burn, and chip.* V-ERG ◊ **chipped**. EG *She was sipping tea from a chipped mug.* ◊ ADJ QUALIT

6 A **chip** is also 6.1 a piece which has been broken or cut off a larger object. EG *It's made of granite chips joined together with cement... Their job is to hammer the rough blocks into smaller chips.* N COUNT : ALSO N PART+N UNCOUNT 6.2 the mark left on a plate, cup, dish, etc, when a small piece has been broken off; an informal use. EG *It's the only mug we've got that hasn't got a chip in it.* N COUNT = crack

7 **Chips** are also plastic counters used in gambling to represent a certain amount of money. EG *...poker chips... They're playing with hundred-dollar chips.* N COUNT : USU PL ⇑ token

8 The words **chip** and **chips** are also used in the following informal expressions: 8.1 If you say that someone is **a chip off the old block**, you mean that they are like one of their parents in character or behaviour; a rather old-fashioned expression. PHR : USED AS C 8.2 You use the expression **when the chips are down** to refer to a very serious situation in which people become aware of the true value of something or someone. EG *It's difficult to tell who is 'average' and who is not until the chips are down.* PHR : USED AS AN A 8.3 If you say that someone has **a chip on** their **shoulder**, you mean that they behave rudely and aggressively because they feel inferior or because they think that they have been treated unfairly. PHR : USED AS O ⇑ grievance 8.4 If you say that someone **has had** their **chips**, you mean that they have had their last chance and you are not prepared to give them another one. PHR : VB INFLECTS

chip in; an informal expression. 1 When a number of people **chip in**, each person gives some money so that they can pay for something together. EG *If anyone was ill, they all chipped in to pay the doctor's bill.* PHRASAL VB : V+ADV = contribute

2 If someone **chips in** during a conversation, they interrupt it in order to add something to it. EG *'Do you know,' said Mrs Oliver, chipping in again, 'whether Celia was there or not?'* PHRASAL VB : V+ADV, OR V+ADV +QUOTE ⇑ speak

chip off. If you **chip off** a coating of paint, rust, etc, you remove it in small pieces using something such as a knife. EG *With extreme care, he began chipping off the white paint.* PHRASAL VB : V+O+ADV ⇑ remove

chipboard /tʃɪpbɔ:d/ is a hard material made out of wood chips, which have been pressed together. It is often used instead of wood for making doors and furniture because it is cheaper. N UNCOUNT ⇑ board

chipmunk /tʃɪpmʌŋk/, **chipmunks**. A **chipmunk** is a small animal which looks rather like a squirrel but which has a striped back. N COUNT ⇑ rodent

chip shop, chip shops. In Britain, a **chip shop** is a shop which sells fish and chips, pieces of chicken, meat pies, etc. The food is cooked in the shop and people take it away to eat at home or in the street. N COUNT ⇑ take away

chiropodist /kɪrɒpədɪst/, **chiropodists**. A **chiropodist** is a person whose job is to treat and care for people's feet. N COUNT

chiropody /kɪrɒpədi¹/ is the professional treatment and care of people's feet. N UNCOUNT

chirp /tʃɜ:p/, **chirps, chirping, chirped**. 1 When a bird or insect **chirps**, it makes short high-pitched sounds. EG *Birds had begun to chirp and twitter among the trees... Grasshoppers chirped and chattered.* V = chirrup ▸ used as a noun. EG *She heard nothing but the chirps and whirrs of insects.* ▸ N COUNT = chirrup

2 You say that a person **chirps** when they speak in a cheerful high-pitched voice. EG *She always chirped 'good morning' to the people at the bus stop.* V, OR V+O/ QUOTE/REPORT-CL = pipe

chirpy /tʃɛpi¹/, **chirpier, chirpiest**. Someone who is **chirpy** is very cheerful and lively; a fairly informal word. EG *It was good to see her looking so bright and well and chirpy... ...his quick wit and chirpy humour.* ADJ QUALIT

chirrup /tʃɪrəp/, **chirrups, chirruping, chirruped**. When a bird or insect **chirrups**, it makes short high-pitched sounds. EG *A cricket chirruped tirelessly.* ▸ used as a noun. EG *With a frightened chirrup, the bird flew away.* V = chirp ▸ N COUNT = chirp

chisel /tʃɪzə⁰l/, **chisels, chiselling, chiselled**; also spelled **chiseling, chiseled** in American English.
1 A **chisel** is a tool that has a long metal blade with a sharp edge at the end. It is used for cutting and shaping wood, metal, and stone. EG *...a hammer and chisel.* N COUNT
2 If you **chisel** something such as wood, metal, or stone, you use a chisel to cut and shape it. EG *I couldn't possibly chisel the whole thing out intact.* V+O = carve

chit /tʃɪt/, **chits**. 1 A **chit** is a short official note, such as a receipt, an order, or a memo, usually signed by someone in authority. EG *This chit is signed Percival... A mother must have a chit from a health worker to get skimmed milk for her baby.* N COUNT ⇑ document = chitty
2 People refer to a girl as a **chit** when they think that she behaves in a wild, silly, or childish way; an old-fashioned use. EG *He's thrown it all away on some silly chit... ...a spoilt, curly-haired chit called Elaine Somers.* N COUNT

chit-chat is informal talk about things that are not very important. EG *I felt unequal to any cosy chit-chat about the new publication.* N UNCOUNT ⇑ conversation = chat

chitter /tʃɪtə/, **chitters, chittering, chittered**. When a bird or an insect **chitters**, it makes short high-pitched sounds. EG *A mongoose chittered angrily among the shadows.* V = chatter

chitty /tʃɪti¹/, **chitties**. A **chitty** is a short official note, such as a receipt, order, or memo, usually signed by someone in authority; an informal word. N COUNT = chit

chivalrous /ʃɪvəlrəs/. A man who is **chivalrous** is polite, honourable, kind, and unselfish, especially towards women. EG *He knew the truth of her manoeuvres but he was too chivalrous to mention it... They were treated with chivalrous consideration.* ADJ QUALIT = courteous
◇ **chivalrously**. EG *'A pleasure' said Colonel Cameron chivalrously.* ◇ ADV = gallantly

chivalry /ʃɪvəlri¹/. 1 **Chivalry** is behaviour that is polite, kind, and helpful, especially by men towards women. EG *He had a sort of instinctive chivalry in him.* N UNCOUNT ⇑ quality = gallantry
2 The system of **chivalry** was the one that was believed in and followed by medieval knights. It had strict religious, moral, and social ideals, for example courtesy, loyalty, and service to women. EG *This ceremony is a serious and moving memory of chivalry... ...knightly chivalry and romance.* N UNCOUNT

chives /tʃaɪvz/ is a plant with long thin hollow leaves that you cut into small pieces and add to food to give it a flavour similar to onions. ▸ used of the leaves. EG *Snip the chives and mix these in with the potatoes.* N UNCOUNT ▸ N PLURAL ⇑ herb

chivvy /tʃɪvi¹/, **chivvies, chivvying, chivvied**: also spelled **chivy**, especially in American English. If you **chivvy** someone, you keep urging them to do something that they do not want to do. EG *I chivvied everyone up to make the place tidy... Gifford needed to chivvy us into our fielding practice this morning.* V+O : USU+A = nag

chloride /klɔːraɪd/, **chlorides**. A **chloride** is a chemical compound of chlorine and another substance; a technical term. EG *...sodium chloride.* N COUNT/ UNCOUNT : USU MOD+N

chlorinate /klɔːrɪneɪt/, **chlorinates, chlorinating, chlorinated**. To **chlorinate** water, for example in a swimming pool, means to disinfect it by putting chlorine into it. ◇ **chlorinated**. EG *...swimming up and down the chlorinated Cowley baths.* V+O ◇ ADJ CLASSIF

chlorine /klɔːriːn/ is a greenish-yellow poisonous gas with a strong unpleasant smell, used especially to disinfect water and to make cleaning products. EG *There's too much chlorine in that swimming-pool water... ...chlorine bleach.* N UNCOUNT ⇑ chemical

chloroform /klɒːrəfɔːm/, **chloroforms, chloroforming, chloroformed**. 1 **Chloroform** is a colourless liquid with a strong sweet smell, which makes you unconscious if you breathe its vapour. N UNCOUNT ⇑ chemical
2 To **chloroform** a person or an animal means to use chloroform in order to make them unconscious or kill them. EG *The victim had been chloroformed and then strangled.* V+O ⇑ anaesthetize

chlorophyll /klɒːrəfɪl/ is a green substance in plants which enables them to use the energy from sunlight in order to grow. N UNCOUNT = pigment

choc-ice /tʃɒkaɪs/, **choc-ices**; also spelled without a hyphen. A **choc-ice** is a small block of ice cream covered with chocolate. N COUNT

chock-a-block. A place that is **chock-a-block** is very full of people, things, or vehicles; an informal word. EG *The house was chock-a-block... London is chock-a-block with tourists at the moment.* ADJ CLASSIF : PRED, IF+PREP THEN *with* = packed

chock-full. Something that is **chock-full** is completely full; an informal word. EG *The garden was chock-full of weeds.* ADJ CLASSIF : PRED, IF+PREP THEN *of*

chocolate /tʃɒkə⁰lɪ²t/, **chocolates**. 1 **Chocolate** is 1.1 a sweet, hard, brown food made from cocoa beans, which is eaten as a sweet or used in making cakes, biscuits, puddings, etc. EG *...a bar of chocolate... ...chocolate cake.* 1.2 a hot drink made with milk and a powder containing chocolate. EG *Hercule Poirot drank his morning chocolate.* N UNCOUNT ⇑ confectionery N UNCOUNT
2 A **chocolate** is a sweet or nut covered with a layer of chocolate. EG *...a box of chocolates... ...delicious chocolates with cream fillings.* N COUNT
3 Something that is **chocolate** is dark brown in colour. ADJ COLOUR

chocolate-box. **Chocolate-box** scenery, pictures, etc are very pretty, but often in a boring or conventional way. EG *We drove through chocolate-box countryside.* ADJ QUALIT : ATTRIB

choice /tʃɔɪs/, **choices; choicer, choicest**. 1 A **choice** is 1.1 the range of different things that exist or are available in a particular situation, from which you are able to choose one particular thing; used especially to talk about their quantity or quality. EG *There's a choice of eleven sports... The choice was very limited... ...the choice between peace and war.* N COUNT : USU SING = selection
1.2 one of the individual things in a range from which you are able to choose in a particular situation. EG *Each applicant has five choices.* 1.3 someone or something that you choose. EG *Choices have to be made... Mr Lefever is President Reagan's choice as assistant secretary of state... He congratulated the chef on his choice of dishes.* N COUNT = option N COUNT ⇑ decision = preference
2 If you **have no choice** but to do something, it is the only thing that you can do in a particular situation. EG *The President had no choice but to agree... You have no other choice, you must go on!* PHR : VB INFLECTS
3 If you say to someone **'It's your choice'**, you mean that they are responsible for their own actions, and that you do not want to influence them or make a decision for them. PHR
4 Something or someone **of** your **choice** is a thing or person that you choose yourself, rather than one that is chosen for you by someone else. EG *She could not be prevented from marrying the man of her choice.* PHR : N+PHR
5 **Choice** things are of specially high quality. EG *...choice cuts of meat... I had put a vase of my choicest roses on the table.* ADJ QUALIT : ATTRIB = fine, select

choir /kwaɪə/, **choirs**. 1 A **choir** is a group of people who sing together, for example in a church or a school. EG *We visited the church where Schubert sang in the choir... The Edinburgh Bach Choir do the B Minor Mass every year.* N COUNT : ALSO IN NAMES AFTER N
2 In a church building, the **choir** is the area in front of the altar where the choir sits. N COUNT : USU SING

choirboy /kwaɪəbɔɪ/, **choirboys**. A **choirboy** is a boy who sings in a church choir. N COUNT ⇑ chorister

choirmaster /kwaɪəmaːstə/, **choirmasters**. A **choirmaster** is a person whose job is to train a choir. N COUNT

choke /tʃəʊk/, **chokes, choking, choked**. 1 When you **choke** or when something **chokes** you, you are unable to breathe properly because you cannot get enough air into your lungs. EG *Jack began to choke and cough... Philip choked on his drink... The pungent smell of sulphur choked him.* ◇ **choking**. EG *She began to weep in gasping, choking sobs... ...a cloud of choking, blinding dust.* ▸ used as a noun. EG *...their suppressed chokes and snorts of amusement.* V-ERG : IF+PREP THEN *on* ⇑ asphyxiate = splutter ◇ ADJ QUALIT ▸ N COUNT ⇑ gasp
2 If someone **chokes** you, they squeeze your neck, usually because they are very angry with you or because they want to kill you by stopping you breathing. EG *An old woman was found choked to death.* V+O (NG/REFL) = strangle
3 If things **choke** a place, they fill it and prevent any V+O : USU PASS+

movement in it. EG *Leaves were choking the brook... The centre of the city was choked with cars.* A (with) ⇑ full = clog, jam

4 Plants that **choke** other plants grow close to them and prevent them from growing properly. EG *Weeds would outgrow and choke the rice crop.* V+O ⇑ kill = overrun

5 The **choke** in the engine of a car, lorry, etc is a device that reduces the amount of air going into the engine and makes it easier to start. N COUNT ⇑ control

6 **Choke** is the reduction in the amount of air going into an engine when the choke is being used. EG *It's right on full choke and it still won't start.* N UNCOUNT ⇑ block

choke back. If you **choke back** a strong emotion that you feel, you force yourself not to show it. EG *I choked back my anger... She choked back her sobs.* PHRASAL VB: V+O+ADV ⇑ control = suppress

choked /tʃəʊkt/. 1 If you say something in a **choked** voice or let out a **choked** cry, your voice does not have its full sound, for example because you are upset or afraid. EG *'Poor Miss Musson,' said Scylla in a choked voice... He let out a choked scream.* ADJ QUALIT ⇑ suppressed = strangled

2 If you are **choked** about something, you are so angry, upset, or disappointed that you cannot speak. EG *He was too choked to say anything more.* ADJ QUALIT = overcome

choker /tʃəʊkə/, **chokers.** A **choker** is a necklace that fits very closely round a woman's neck. EG *She wore a choker of jet beads.* N COUNT: IF+ PREP THEN *of*

cholera /kɒlərə/ is a serious and often fatal disease that affects your digestive organs. It is caused by drinking infected water or eating infected food. EG *His parents died of cholera.* N UNCOUNT

choleric /kɒlərɪk/. Someone who is **choleric** is very angry; a formal word. EG *The captain was choleric with rage.* ADJ QUALIT

cholesterol /kəlestərɒl/ is a substance that exists in the fat, tissues, and blood of all animals. Too much cholesterol in your blood can cause heart disease. EG *The fat from meat tends to raise the cholesterol level in the blood.* N UNCOUNT

chomp /tʃɒmp/, **chomps, chomping, chomped.** If a person or animal **chomps** their food, they chew it noisily; an informal word. V OR V+O = munch

choose /tʃuːz/, **chooses, choosing, chose, chosen.** 1 If you **choose** something or someone, you decide which one you want from a range of things or people. EG *Churchill's nanny chose his books, his food and his friends... They were choosing sweets from one of the stalls... Harold Wilson chose Jim Callaghan as his Chancellor.* ◊ **chosen.** EG *They undergo training in their chosen professions.* ● to **pick and choose**: see **pick**. V, V+O, V+O+A (as), OR V+O+to-INF. = pick, select ◊ ADJ CLASSIF: ATTRIB = preferred

2 If you **choose** to do something or to act in a particular way, you decide to do it because you want to or because you feel that it is right. EG *He chose to ignore her impertinence... I can go anywhere I choose... They could fire employees whenever they chose.* V: USU+to-INF ⇑ please

3 If there is **little to choose between** things, **not much to choose between** them, etc, the things are so similar that it is difficult to decide which is better, more suitable, etc. EG *There's nothing to choose between the two wretched countries.* PHR: USED AS C ≠ a world of difference

4 When people talk about the chosen few, they are referring to a particular group of people who are special or important in some way. EG *The chosen few do not bother to make a secret of their vast wealth.* PHR: *a/the*+PHR ⇑ elite

choosy /tʃuːzi¹/, **choosier, choosiest.** People who are **choosy** are difficult to please because they will only accept something if it is exactly what they want, or only if it is of very high quality. EG *I'm very choosy about my whisky.* ADJ QUALIT ⇑ fussy

chop /tʃɒp/, **chops, chopping, chopped.** 1 If you **chop** something, you cut it with energetic movements, usually with a sharp tool such as an axe. EG *I don't like chopping wood... Wouldn't it be simpler to chop that tree down?... Many famous people had their heads chopped off in the Tower of London.* ▸ used as a noun. EG *The trunk started to tilt after the first chop.* V OR V+O: USU+A ▸ N COUNT

2 If you **chop** food, you cut it roughly into smaller pieces. EG *Peel, slice, and chop the apple... Add chopped garlic and some vinegar.* V+O = dice

3 If you **chop** with your hand, you make a sharp downward movement with it, for example when you are fighting. EG *He chopped down with his free hand, just once.* ▸ used as a noun. EG *...the forehand chop with the edge of the palm.* V+A, OR V+O ⇑ move = strike ▸ N COUNT = strike

4 If you **chop** something connected with money, you make it smaller; an informal use. EG *You can save energy and chop your fuel bills... We've chopped more than £1,000 off the budget.* V+O ⇑ reduce

5 A **chop** is a small piece of meat on a bone, usually cut from the ribs of a sheep or pig. EG *...lamb chops.* N COUNT

6 The word **chop** is also used in the following informal expressions: 6.1 If you get **the chop** or are given **the chop**, you lose your job; used in British English. N SING: *the*+N = boot, push 6.2 If something is **for the chop**, it is going to be stopped or closed down; used in British English. EG *The small theatres will be first for the chop.* PHR: USED AS AN A 6.3 When people **chop and change**, they keep changing their minds about what to do or how to act. EG *All this chopping and changing is very confusing.* PHR: VBS INFLECT ⇑ vacillate

chopper /tʃɒpə/, **choppers.** A **chopper** is a helicopter. N COUNT

chopping board, chopping boards. A **chopping board** is a board that you cut meat and vegetables on. N COUNT

choppy /tʃɒpi¹/, **choppier, choppiest.** When the sea, a river, or a lake is **choppy**, there are a lot of small waves on it because it is windy. EG *The sea suddenly turned from smooth to choppy.* ADJ QUALIT

chopstick /tʃɒpstɪk/, **chopsticks. Chopsticks** are a pair of thin sticks which you use to eat food with, especially in China and the Far East. EG *We ate with chopsticks.* N COUNT ⇑ utensil

chop suey /tʃɒpsuːi¹/ is a Chinese-style meal made with chopped meat, bean sprouts, and other vegetables in a sauce. N UNCOUNT

choral /kɔːrəl/. Something that is **choral** involves singing by a choir. EG *His new work combines symphonic, choral, and operatic elements... ...the pleasures of choral singing.* ADJ CLASSIF: USU ATTRIB ⇑ vocal

chord /kɔːd/, **chords.** 1 A **chord** is 1.1 a number of musical notes played or sung at the same time with a pleasing or satisfying effect. EG *He played some random chords... There were three distinctive organ chords and then a silence.* N COUNT ⇑ group 1.2 a straight line connecting two points on the circumference of a circle; a technical term in geometry. N COUNT

2 If something **strikes a chord** or **touches a chord**, it makes you feel a particular emotion, usually of sympathy or enthusiasm. EG *It certainly struck a responsive chord because it's been voted Musical of the Year... These pronouncements touched a chord in the American people.* PHR: VB INFLECTS ⇑ affect

chore /tʃɔː/, **chores.** A **chore** is a task that must be done and that you find unpleasant or boring. EG *Does your husband do his fair share of the household chores?... Writing essays should be an intellectual challenge rather than a chore.* N COUNT: USU PL = task

choreograph /kɒrɪəgræf/, **choreographs, choreographing, choreographed.** 1 When someone **choreographs** a ballet or other dance, they invent the steps and movements that will be used in it and tell the dancers how to perform them. EG *This is the first time he has choreographed a full-length ballet.* V OR V+O ⇑ compose

2 You say that an activity involving several people **is choreographed** when it is arranged but is intended to appear natural. EG *The scene had a choreographed air about it... They were subjected to a series of choreographed indignities.* V+O: USU PASS = stage

choreography /kɒrɪɒgrəfi¹/ is the art of inventing the steps and movements of ballets or other dances. EG *Our studies include choreography.* ▸ **Choreography** is also used to refer to the steps and movements themselves. EG *The choreography was superb.* ◊ **choreographer.** EG *He joined the company as a choreographer in 1975.* N UNCOUNT ◊ N COUNT ⇑ dancer

chorister /kɒrɪstə/, **choristers.** A **chorister** is a singer in a church choir. N COUNT

chortle /tʃɔːtəºl/, **chortles, chortling, chortled.** When someone **chortles**, they laugh with pleasure or amusement. EG *She chortled to herself with delight.* ▸ used as a noun. EG *He gave a chortle.* V OR V+QUOTE = chuckle ▸ N COUNT

chorus /kɔːrəs/, **choruses.** 1 A **chorus** is 1.1 a large group of people who sing together. EG *I arranged this huge chorus of 120 in groups.* N COUNT = choir 1.2 a piece of music which is written to be sung by a large group of people. EG *They continued with the Soldiers' Chorus from Faust.* N COUNT 1.3 a part of a song which is repeated after each verse. N COUNT 1.4 a group of singers or dancers who perform together in a show, in contrast to the soloists. EG *She began her professional career in the chorus line of Oklahoma.* N COUNT ⇑ performers

2 A **chorus** is also something expressed by a lot of N COUNT: USU+

people at the same time. EG *In recent weeks the chorus of complaining has been growing... His statement was made to a chorus of groans.* — of ⇑ group

3 When a group of people **chorus** something, they say it or sing it together at the same time. EG *'Shall I tell you a story?'–'Please!' the children would chorus.* — V+O/QUOTE

4 When people sing or speak **in chorus**, they sing or speak the same thing at the same time. EG *They all replied in chorus, 'Yes please!'* — PHR : USED AS AN A = in unison

5 When a number of birds or small animals make a noise together, this noise is sometimes referred to as a **chorus**. EG *The evening chorus of birds' song was deafening... They had been kept awake by the chorus of frogs.* — N COUNT : USU+ of

chorus girl, chorus girls. A **chorus girl** is a young woman who sings and dances in the chorus of a show or film. — N COUNT

chose /tʃəʊz/ is the past tense of **choose**.

chosen /tʃəʊzəⁿn/ is the past participle of **choose**.

chow /tʃaʊ/, **chows. 1** A **chow** is a dog with a thick coat and a curled tail, originally from China. — N COUNT

2 Chow is food; an informal word. EG *The chow is awful.* — N UNCOUNT = grub

chowder /tʃaʊdə/ is a thick soup containing pieces of fish or shellfish. — N UNCOUNT

chow mein /tʃaʊ meɪn/ is a Chinese-style meal of fried noodles with cooked meat or vegetables. EG *...chicken chow mein.* — N UNCOUNT ⇑ food

Christ /kraɪst/. **1 Christ** is one of the names of Jesus, whom Christians believe to be the son of God and whose teachings are the basis of Christianity. EG *...the teachings of Christ... ...a believer in God and a follower of Christ.* — N PROPER

2 Christ is also a swear word that some people use to express surprise, shock, annoyance, etc, or to emphasize what they are saying. — EXCLAM

christen /krɪsəⁿn/, **christens, christening, christened. 1** When a clergyman **christens** a baby, he gives the baby a name during the Christian ceremony of baptism, as a sign that the baby is now a member of the Christian Church. EG *She was christened Victoria Mary, but was known as Rosie... Charles II was christened in this church.* — V+O, OR V+O+C : USU PASS ⇑ baptize

2 To **christen** something also means **2.1** to give it a name, especially when other people call it by this name afterwards. EG *The crew christened the hot geysers the 'black smokers'... I was wondering why Olmsted should have christened the proposed park 'Central' Park.* — V+O+C **2.2** to use it for the first time; an informal use of 'christen'. EG *The new dance hall was christened with a fancy dress ball... Let's christen our new wine glasses!* — V+O

Christendom /krɪsəⁿndəm/ is all the Christian people and countries in the world; a rather old-fashioned word. EG *At the height of its power Christendom was mighty and unified.* — N PROPER

christening /krɪsəⁿnɪŋ/, **christenings.** A **christening** is a Christian ceremony in which a baby is made a member of the Christian church by being given a name by a clergyman: compare **baptism**. — N COUNT

Christian /krɪstʃən/, **Christians. 1** A **Christian** is a person who believes in Jesus Christ and who follows his teachings. EG *Is he a Christian?... He had preached about the need for true Christians to fight all forms of injustice.* — N COUNT ▸ used as an adjective. EG *...a Christian missionary called Percy Ibbotson.* — ▸ ADJ CLASSIF

2 Something that is **Christian** is based on Christianity. EG *Charity is the greatest of Christian virtues... ...the Christian basis of his philosophy.* — ADJ CLASSIF

3 People are also sometimes described as **Christian** when they show goodness, kindness, and other good qualities associated with Christ and Christianity; used showing approval. EG *She was a really Christian woman.* ▸ used of a person's behaviour or actions. EG *I wouldn't call that a very Christian attitude.* — ADJ QUALIT : ATTRIB ⇑ good

Christianity /krɪstiænɪti¹/ is a religion that is based on the teachings of Jesus Christ and the belief that he was the son of God. EG *How can people reconcile astrology with Christianity?... He learnt Hebrew and Greek in order to pursue his researches in Christianity.* — N UNCOUNT

Christian name, Christian names. A **Christian name** is a name that is given to someone when they are born or when they are christened. EG *Do all your students call you by your Christian name?* — N COUNT = first name, forename ≠ surname

Christmas /krɪsməs/, **Christmases. Christmas** is the Christian festival when the birth of Jesus Christ is celebrated, on the twenty-fifth of December. At Christmas special food is eaten and people give each other cards and presents. EG *Merry Christmas and a Happy New Year!... ...Christmas cards... We plan to stay in Edinburgh over Christmas... At school they did a little play at Christmas... ...the Christmas holidays.* — N UNCOUNT = Xmas ▸ used as a count noun. EG *The past few Christmases had been very quiet.* — ▸ N COUNT

Christmas Day is the twenty-fifth of December, when Christmas is celebrated. EG *On Christmas Day, we had goose for dinner.* — N UNCOUNT

Christmas Eve is the twenty-fourth of December, the day before Christmas Day. EG *On Christmas Eve they went to a party.* — N UNCOUNT

Christmas pudding, Christmas puddings. A **Christmas pudding** is a special pudding that is eaten at Christmas. It is made from dried fruit, spices, and suet. EG *The Christmas pudding was set on the table.* — N COUNT/UNCOUNT = plum pudding

Christmas tree, Christmas trees. A **Christmas tree** is a fir tree, or an artificial tree that looks like a fir tree, which people put in their houses at Christmas and decorate with coloured lights and balls. — N COUNT

chrome /krəʊm/ is a hard, shiny, silver-coloured metal that is used in covering metal objects to prevent them from rusting. It is also mixed with other substances to make paints and dyes. EG *Clean chrome bath taps with a cloth and soapy water.* — N UNCOUNT = chromium

chromium /krəʊmiəm/ is the same as chrome. — N UNCOUNT

chromosome /krəʊməsəʊm/, **chromosomes.** A **chromosome** is a rod-shaped part of a cell in an animal or plant. It contains genes which determine what characteristics the animal or plant will have. Each cell contains a number of chromosomes; a technical word. EG *Every human being possesses 23 pairs of chromosomes.* — N COUNT

chronic /krɒnɪk/. **1** A **chronic** illness lasts for a very long time. EG *...chronic asthma... In spite of chronic ill health, she wrote ten books.* — ADJ CLASSIF : USU ATTRIB = recurring, severe ◇ **chronically.** EG *...pensions for the injured and chronically sick.* — ◇ ADV+ADJ

2 You describe someone's bad habits or behaviour as **chronic** when they have behaved like that for a long time and do not seem to be able to stop themselves. EG *...chronic drunkenness.* ▸ used of people. EG *Marijuana could be detrimental to some chronic users.* — ADJ CLASSIF : ATTRIB ⇑ habitual

3 A **chronic** situation or problem is very severe and unpleasant. EG *...chronic food shortages... The airline's problems are chronic.* — ADJ CLASSIF : USU ATTRIB ◇ **chronically.** EG *...an adult education service that is chronically short of finance.* — ◇ ADV+ADJ/ADV = severely

chronicle /krɒnɪkəⁿl/, **chronicles, chronicling, chronicled. 1** When someone **chronicles** a series of events, they describe or record them in the order in which they happened; a formal use. EG *Xenophon chronicled the Persian Wars... The Chinese chronicled how 'the stars fell like rain' in 687 BC.* — V+O/REPORT-CL

2 A **chronicle** is a formal account or record of a series of events, described in the order in which they happened. EG *Kaiser believes this chronicle to have been written in AD 115.* — N COUNT

3 The word **Chronicle** is sometimes used as part of the name of a newspaper. EG *...an article published in the San Francisco Chronicle.* — N COUNT : USED IN NAMES AFTER N

chronological /krɒnəlɒdʒɪkəⁿl, krəʊ-/. **1 Chronological** means relating to the order in which a series of things actually happened. EG *The chairman liked to have the events in strict chronological order.* — ADJ CLASSIF ⇑ sequential ◇ **chronologically.** EG *The collection is arranged chronologically.* — ◇ ADV ⇑ sequentially

2 A person's **chronological** age is their actual age, rather than the stage that they have reached in their mental or physical development. EG *His chronological age is ten but he has a mental age of four.* — ADJ CLASSIF : ATTRIB ≠ mental, physical ◇ **chronologically.** EG *Ricky Gallant was only eleven years old chronologically, but he suffered from an ageing disease.* — ◇ ADV

chronology /krənɒlədʒi¹/. The **chronology** of a series of past events is the times at which they happened in the order in which they happened. EG *The chronology of subsequent events was as follows... My memories are sharp, but have no chronology.* — N UNCOUNT : IF+ PREP THEN of ⇑ sequence

chrysalis /krɪsəlɪs/, **chrysalises.** A **chrysalis** is a butterfly or moth in the stage of development between a larva and a fully grown adult, when it has a — N COUNT ⇑ pupa hard protective covering and does not move. ▸ used also of the hard protective covering that the insect has. EG *...a butterfly that won't come out of its chrysalis.*

chrysanthemum /krɪsænθəməm/, **chrysanthemums**. A **chrysanthemum** is a flower with a lot of long, thin petals that are dark pink, yellow, or orange in colour. Chrysanthemums are often grown in gardens. EG *...a bunch of chrysanthemums.* — N COUNT

chubby /tʃʌbi[1]/, **chubbier, chubbiest**. Someone who is **chubby** is rather fat and round; often used when you are describing children. EG *Her brother was chubby and cheerful... ...chubby little fingers.* — ADJ QUALIT = plump, podgy

chuck /tʃʌk/, **chucks, chucking, chucked**; an informal word. 1 When you **chuck** something somewhere, you throw it there in a casual or careless way. EG *I feel like chucking the bottle through the windscreen... Chuck my tights across, please.* — V+O+A

2 If you **chuck** someone out of a place, you force them to leave. EG *He was chucked off the bus for swearing at the conductor... We were chucked out of the meeting.* — V+O+A ⇑ eject = throw

3 If you **chuck** your job or some other activity or if you **chuck** it up, you stop doing it. EG *That night he decided to chuck his job.* — V+O, OR V+O+A (up) = jack in

4 If you **chuck** your boyfriend or girlfriend, you end your relationship with them because you do not want it to continue; used in British English. EG *He's fed up because his girlfriend's just chucked him.* — V+O = finish with

chuck away. If you **chuck** something **away** or **chuck** it **out**, you throw it away, because you do not need it or cannot use it. EG *It has to be chucked away because it hasn't worked.* — PHRASAL VB : V+O+ADV

chuckle /tʃʌkə[0]l/, **chuckles, chuckling, chuckled**. When you **chuckle**, you laugh quietly to yourself. EG *They were chuckling over the photographs... 'Yeah,' Arnold chuckled.* ▸ used as a noun. EG *He shook his head with a soft chuckle.* — V, OR V+QUOTE = chortle; ▸ N COUNT : USU SING

chuck steak is meat from the neck or shoulder of a cow. — N UNCOUNT ⇑ steak

chuffed /tʃʌft/. If you are **chuffed** about something, you are very pleased about it; an informal word in British English. — ADJ QUALIT : PRED, IF+PREP THEN *about*

chug /tʃʌg/, **chugs, chugging, chugged**. 1 When a vehicle or engine **chugs**, it makes short thudding sounds. EG *The engine chugged quietly... The boat lurched ahead, chugging.* ▸ used as a noun. EG *I could hear the chug of its ancient engine.* — V; ▸ N COUNT : USU SING

2 When a vehicle **chugs** in a particular direction, it moves along quite slowly with the engine making short thudding sounds. EG *The bus chugged along... A small fishing boat comes chugging towards them.* — V+A ⇑ move

chum /tʃʌm/, **chums, chumming, chummed**; a rather old-fashioned informal word. 1 Your **chum** is your friend, especially one whom you have known for a long time. EG *He's an old school chum.* — N COUNT = pal, buddy

2 Men sometimes address each other as **chum**, usually in a slightly aggressive or unfriendly way. EG *You've had it, chum.* — N VOC = mate

chum up. If you **chum up** with someone, you make friends with them. EG *He'd go and chum up with the chaps over the bar... We chummed up together when we were in Egypt.* — PHRASAL VB : V+ADV, IF+PREP THEN *with*

chummy /tʃʌmi[1]/, **chummier, chummiest**. **Chummy** means the same as friendly; a rather old-fashioned informal word. EG *She always wanted to be chummy.* — ADJ QUALIT

chump /tʃʌmp/, **chumps**. You call someone a **chump** when you want to tell them in a friendly way that they have done something silly; an informal word. EG *'You chump,' she said, smiling at me.* — N COUNT : USU USED AS C ⇑ idiot = clot

chunk /tʃʌŋk/, **chunks**. 1 A **chunk** of something solid is a piece of it. EG *...a great chunk of meat... They spent their time chopping chunks out of stone tablets.* — N COUNT : ALSO N PART+N UNCOUNT = lump

2 A **chunk** is also a large amount or part of something; a slightly informal use. EG *He owns a chunk of Texas... Research and development now gobble up a sizeable chunk of the military budget.* — N COUNT : ALSO N +*of*+N UNCOUNT

chunky /tʃʌŋki[1]/, **chunkier, chunkiest**. 1 You describe people as **chunky** when they are broad and heavy. EG *Some babies are born to be big-boned and square and chunky.* — ADJ QUALIT

2 A **chunky** object is large and thick. EG *...great chunky cardigans... ...chunky pieces of meat.* — ADJ QUALIT = bulky

church /tʃɜːtʃ/, **churches**. 1 A **church** is a building in which Christians worship. EG *There were no services that day, and the church was empty... ...St Mary's Church.* ▸ **Church** is also used to refer to the religious services that are held in a church. EG *His parents go to church now and then.* — N COUNT : ALSO IN NAMES AFTER N; ▸ N UNCOUNT

2 A **Church** is one of the groups of people within the Christian religion, for example the Catholics or the Methodists, who have their own beliefs, clergy, and forms of worship. EG *...the teachings of the Catholic Church... A number of authoritative voices in his own Church disagreed with him... ...the British Council of Churches.* — N COUNT+SUPP ⇑ denomination

3 The **Church** or the **church** refers to **3.1** the people who belong to a particular Church, considered as a group. EG *Jane had been officially received into the Church a month previously.* **3.2** the people who have authority in a Church and who decide what that Church's doctrines are. EG *Should the Church now relax her teaching on contraception?... The Christian church taught obedience to the established order.* — N SING : *the*+N ⇑ congregation; N SING : *the*+N

churchgoer /tʃɜːtʃgəʊə/, **churchgoers**. A **churchgoer** is a person who goes to church regularly. — N COUNT

churchman /tʃɜːtʃmə[3]n/, **churchmen**. A **churchman** is the same as a clergyman. EG *Several leading churchmen attended the debate.* — N COUNT : USU PL = clergyman

Church of England. The **Church of England** is the main church in England, which has the Queen as its head and which does not recognize the authority of the Pope. EG *On this issue he found himself in opposition to most of the Church of England... She had brought her children up in the Church of England.* — N PROPER : *the*+N ⇑ Anglican church

churchwarden /tʃɜːtʃwɔːdə[0]n/, **churchwardens**. A **churchwarden** is a person who is chosen by a congregation to help the vicar of a parish with administration and other duties. — N COUNT

churchyard /tʃɜːtʃjɑːd/, **churchyards**. A **churchyard** is an area of land around a church where people who have belonged to that church can be buried. — N COUNT ⇑ graveyard

churlish /tʃɜːlɪʃ/. **Churlish** behaviour is unfriendly, bad-tempered, or impolite. EG *I wanted to be on my own but it seemed churlish to send him away.* ▸ used of people. EG *At home he was churlish, parsimonious, and cruel to his daughters.* — ADJ QUALIT ⇑ rude = uncivil

churn /tʃɜːn/, **churns, churning, churned**. 1 A **churn** is a container which is used for making milk or cream into butter. — N COUNT

2 If you **churn** milk or cream, you stir it vigorously in order to turn it into butter. — V+O

3 If something **churns** mud or water or **churns** it **up**, or if it **churns**, it moves about violently. EG *The water was thrashing and churning about under the propellers... She could see the bulldozers churning the mud... The wind howled and churned up the water into a swirling foam.* — V-ERG ⇑ agitate

4 When your stomach **churns**, you feel movements inside it which make you feel sick, usually because you are nervous or affected by a strong emotion; an informal use. EG *My stomach churned when I saw them together.* ◊ **churning**. EG *He felt a churning in his stomach.* — V ⇑ turn = heave; ◊ N UNCOUNT = butterflies

churn out. If you **churn** things **out**, you produce them in large numbers very quickly; sometimes used showing disapproval. EG *His campaign organization began churning out tracts and posters... The heavy industries linked with national governments continue to churn out weapons.* — PHRASAL VB : V+O+ADV = turn out, pump out

churn up. When something **churns** you **up**, it makes you feel worried, frightened, or angry; an informal expression. EG *Something seemed to be churning her up inside... She had been all churned up and not really responsible for what she did.* — PHRASAL VB : V+O+ADV ⇑ upset = cut up

chute /ʃuːt/, **chutes**. A **chute** is 1 a steep, narrow slope down which things such as coal or parcels can be slid so that they do not have to be carried. 2 a parachute; an informal use. — N COUNT ⇑ tube; N COUNT

chutney /tʃʌtni[1]/, **chutneys**. **Chutney** is a strong-tasting mixture of fruit, vinegar, sugar, and spices which is eaten with savoury food such as meat or cheese. EG *...mango chutney.* — N MASS ⇑ sauce = pickle

CIA /siː aɪ eɪ/ is an abbreviation for 'Central Intelligence Agency'; a United States agency that tries to obtain secret information about the political and military activities of individuals or governments in other countries. — N PROPER : *the*+N ⇑ organization

cicada /sɪkɑːdə/, **cicadas**. A **cicada** is a large insect that lives in hot countries and makes a loud high-pitched noise. N COUNT

CID /siː aɪ diː/ The **CID** is a branch of the police force in Britain which is concerned with finding out who has committed crimes. EG *...Chief Superintendent Meadows of the CID.* N PROPER : USU *the*+N

cider /saɪdə/, **ciders**. **Cider** is an alcoholic drink made from apples. N MASS

cigar /sɪgɑː/, **cigars**. **Cigars** are rolls of dried tobacco leaves which people smoke. EG *Cigar smoke hung in the room.* N COUNT

cigarette /sɪgəᵒret/, **cigarettes**. **Cigarettes** are small tubes of paper containing finely cut tobacco which people smoke. EG *Boylan lit a cigarette.* N COUNT

cigarette end, cigarette ends. A **cigarette end** is the part of a cigarette that you put in your mouth and that you throw away when you have finished smoking. EG *...ashtrays full of cigarette ends.* N COUNT ↑ remnant = stub, butt

cigarette holder, cigarette holders; also spelled with a hyphen. A **cigarette holder** is a narrow tube that you can put a cigarette into in order to hold it while you smoke it. N COUNT

cigarette lighter, cigarette lighters. A **cigarette lighter** is a device which produces a small flame when you flick a switch and which you use to light a cigarette or cigar. N COUNT = lighter

cigarette paper, cigarette papers. A **cigarette paper** is a small thin piece of paper which you put tobacco on and roll into a tube in order to make a cigarette. N COUNT

cinch /sɪntʃ/. If you say that something **is a cinch**, you mean that it is very easy to do or to achieve. EG *Beating Rangers should be a cinch.* PHR : VB INFLECTS = doddle

cinder /sɪndə/, **cinders**. **1 Cinders** are pieces of the material that is left after something such as wood or coal has burned. EG *The grey cinders glowed again as the air blew through.* N COUNT : USU PL = ember

2 If you burn something **to a cinder**, you burn it until it is completely black. PHR : USED AS AN A

cinder track, cinder tracks. A **cinder track** is a running track that is covered with fine cinders; used in British English. N COUNT

cine camera /sɪni¹ kæməᵒrə/, **cine cameras**; also spelled with a hyphen. A **cine camera** is a camera that takes a moving film rather than photographs. N COUNT = movie camera

cinema /sɪnə¹mə/, **cinemas**. **1** A **cinema** is a place where people go to watch films for entertainment. EG *...films made for the cinema and for television.* N COUNT, OR N SING : *the*+N = flicks

2 Cinema is the business and art of making films. EG *...one of the classic works of Hollywood cinema... ...the cinema industry.* N UNCOUNT = film

cinematic /sɪnə¹mætɪk/ means relating to films for the cinema. EG *...scenes containing painstaking cinematic detail.* ADJ CLASSIF : USU ATTRIB

cinematography /sɪnə¹mətɒgrəfi¹/ is the technique of making films for the cinema. N UNCOUNT

cinnamon /sɪnəmən/ is a spice in the form of a light brown powder or small sticks, which comes from the bark of a tree. Cinnamon is used especially in flavouring sweet food such as fruit or cakes. N UNCOUNT

cipher /saɪfə/, **ciphers**; also spelled **cypher**. **1** A **cipher** is a secret system of writing that you use to send messages so that nobody can understand them unless they know the system. EG *They had been corresponding with one another in cipher.* ▸ used to refer to the message that you have written. EG *...a cipher concealed among the lines of his letter.* N COUNT, OR *in*+N = code ▸ N COUNT ↑ message

2 If you refer to someone as a **cipher**, you mean that they have no power and are used by other people to achieve a particular purpose; used showing disapproval. EG *He's no more than a cipher in the organization.* N COUNT ↑ person = nobody

ciphered /saɪfəd/. A **ciphered** message is written or spoken in a secret code; a formal or technical word. EG *I read Wilkinson's version of my ciphered letter.* ADJ CLASSIF = coded

circa /sɜːkə/ is used in front of a particular year to say that this is the approximate date when something happened; a formal word. EG *...an old British newspaper, circa 1785.* PREP = around ≠ exactly

circle /sɜːkəᵒl/, **circles, circling, circled**. **1** A **circle** is **1.1** a flat regular shape consisting of a curved line completely surrounding an area. Every part of the line is the same distance from the centre of the area. EG *...an orange tie decorated with black circles.* **1.2** an object or area in the shape of a circle. EG *Stand your paint tin on a circle of aluminium foil... The fires were now alight across a circle with a radius of approximately fifteen kilometres.* **1.3** a group of people or things arranged in the shape of a ring or a circle. EG *He looked round the circle of eager faces... The students sit in a circle on the floor... They ran round in little circles.* N COUNT = ring; N COUNT : IF+ PREP THEN *of*; N COUNT : IF+ PREP THEN *of*

2 If a bird, aircraft, etc **circles**, it moves round in a circle in the air. EG *Hawks circled overhead looking for prey... The pilot circled and came down very fast.* V ↑ move = wheel

3 If someone or something **circles** something, **3.1** they move round it. EG *Galileo saw four moons circling Jupiter in 1610... ...animals circling each other.* **3.2** they are arranged in a circle around it. EG *By now, the trench circled the camp almost completely.* V+O ↑ go round; V+O ↑ surround = encircle

4 If you **circle** something on a piece of paper, you draw a circle round it. EG *One village on the map had been circled in red.* V+O = ring

5 A **circle** of people, friends, etc is a group of people who meet each other regularly because they are friends or because they belong to the same profession or share a particular interest. EG *I have widened my circle of acquaintances... ...Miss Spencer, the President of the Music Circle... This proposal caused an uproar in parliamentary circles.* N COUNT+SUPP

6 The **circle** in a theatre or cinema is an area of seats on the upper floor. N SING : *the*+N ↑ section

7 The word **circle** is also used in the following expressions: **7.1** If you say that someone who is trying to achieve something is **going round in circles**, you mean that they are not achieving anything because they keep coming back to the same point or problem; an informal expression. EG *It's no use–we're just going round and round in circles.* **7.2** If you say that someone is **running round in circles**, you mean that they are very busy doing a lot of things or going to a lot of places in order to achieve something, often without success; an informal expression. EG *Alan Dutton had me running round in circles trying to find a journal.* **7.3** If you say that something has **come full circle**, you mean that after a long series of events or changes the same situation exists as at the beginning. EG *I felt I had come full circle... It sometimes takes the wheel of fashion a long time to come full circle.* **7.4** See also **vicious circle**. PHR : VB INFLECTS ≠ progress; PHR : VB INFLECTS = rush around; PHR : VB INFLECTS

circlet /sɜːklɪ²t/, **circlets**. A **circlet** is a decorated band of precious metal worn round a person's head, especially in former times. EG *...a circlet of pearls.* N COUNT : USU+ *of* ↑ crown

circuit /sɜːkɪt/, **circuits**. An electrical **circuit** is a complete route which an electric current can flow around. EG *...the current flowing through the circuit.* ● See also **closed circuit**. N COUNT

2 A **circuit** is also **2.1** a series of places or events that are all visited or attended regularly in a particular order by a person or group of people. EG *...the three-month Highland Games circuit... ...the American college lecture circuit... ...the judicial circuit.* **2.2** a journey all the way around a particular place or area. EG *One cannot make a complete circuit of the grounds by horse.* N COUNT : MOD+ N; N COUNT : USU+ *of* ↑ tour = round

3 A racing **circuit** is a track on which races for cars, motorbikes, or cycles take place. EG *...a selected number of drivers driving round a circuit.* ▸ **Circuit** is also used to refer to the distance round a track. EG *Lauda has now completed twenty-two circuits.* N COUNT = course ▸ = lap

circuit breaker, circuit breakers; also spelled with a hyphen. A **circuit breaker** is a device which can stop the flow of electricity around a circuit by switching itself off if anything goes wrong. EG *You can have your house fitted with circuit breakers in place of fuses.* N COUNT

circuitous /sə⁵kjuːɪtəs/. A **circuitous** route or journey is long, slow, and complicated rather than simple and direct; a formal or literary word. EG *The taxi moved in zigzags and circuitous routes... ...a long and circuitous journey by train and boat.* ADJ QUALIT : USU ATTRIB ↑ indirect = roundabout

circuitry /sɜːkɪtri¹/ is a system of electric circuits. EG *Now he could see the electronic circuitry of the unit.* N UNCOUNT

circular /sɜːkjə⁴lə/, **circulars**. **1** Something that is **circular** is in the shape of a circle. EG *...plates with circular holes in them... ...a circular pond... ...circular motions.* ADJ CLASSIF : USU ATTRIB = round

2 A **circular** journey, route, etc is one in which you go to a place and return by a different route. ADJ CLASSIF

3 A **circular** argument or theory is one which is not valid because it uses a statement to prove the conclusion and the conclusion to prove the statement. ◊ **circularity** /sɜ:kjə^{4}lærɪ^{1}ti^1/. EG *My argument suffered from circularity.*
ADJ CLASSIF : USU ATTRIB ⇑ illogical ◊ N UNCOUNT

4 A **circular** is an official letter or advertisement that is sent to a large number of people at the same time. EG *...a circular from a radical publisher, announcing new publications.* ▸ used as an adjective. EG *...a circular letter.*
N COUNT ▸ ADJ CLASSIF : ATTRIB

circulate /sɜ:kjə^{4}leɪt/, **circulates, circulating, circulated. 1** When you **circulate** something such as a letter, report, or book or when it **circulates**, the information or copies of the writing are spread among all the people in a particular group. EG *The report was eventually circulated to all the members... A union newspaper was circulating at the congress.* ◊ **circulation.** EG *...the circulation of illegal books.*
V-ERG = pass round ◊ N UNCOUNT = distribution

2 When something **circulates** or when you **circulate** it, it moves easily and freely within a closed place or system. EG *We are governed by the hormones that circulate around our bodies... A fan gently circulated air through the compartment.* ◊ **circulation.** EG *...the circulation of air.*
V-ERG : USU+A ⇑ move ◊ N UNCOUNT ⇑ movement

3 When traffic **circulates** in a town or city, it moves without difficulty through the streets. EG *The traffic circulates freely.* ◊ **circulation.** EG *A new roundabout was built to improve the traffic circulation.*
V = flow ◊ N UNCOUNT = flow

4 If you **circulate** at a party or other social occasion, you move among the guests and talk to many different people. EG *After John had circulated amongst his guests, dinner was announced.*
V = mingle

5 When you **circulate** food or drink at a party or other social occasion, or when it **circulates**, it is passed round and offered to all the guests. EG *John Hargreaves circulated the sherry.*
V-ERG ⇑ pass = hand round

6 If a story, joke, rumour, etc **circulates** or if you **circulate** it, it is talked about and spread among a group of people. EG *Stories about him circulated at his club.*
V-ERG

circulation /sɜ:kjə^{4}leɪʃə^{0}n/. **1** The **circulation** of a newspaper or magazine is the number of copies that are sold each time it is produced. EG *They were disappointed by the circulation figures of the morning journal... The local paper had a circulation of only six thousand.*
N COUNT+SUPP : USU SING = sales

2 Your **circulation** is the movement of blood through your body. EG *My circulation deteriorated and I was always cold... He jumped up and down to get the circulation going.*
N SING : WITH *the/*POSS ⇑ flow

3 Money that is in **circulation** is being used by the public. EG *The government tried to restrain demand by taking money out of circulation... A new coin was put into circulation... The £ note might be withdrawn from circulation.*
N UNCOUNT : PREP+N ⇑ distribution

4 If you are **in circulation again** or **back in circulation**, you have returned to your normal routine and are meeting people again, for example after a period of illness.
PHR : USED AS AN A

circulatory /sɜ:kjə^{4}lətə^{0}ri^1, -leɪtə^{0}ri^1/ means relating to the circulation of blood in the body; a formal or medical term. EG *...the circulatory system.*
ADJ CLASSIF : ATTRIB

circumcise /sɜ:kəmsaɪz/, **circumcises, circumcising, circumcised.** To **circumcise** a person means to cut off the loose skin at the end of a male's penis or to slit the skin covering a female's clitoris, especially in a religious ceremony. ◊ **circumcision** /sɜ:kəmsɪʒə^{0}n/.
V+O ◊ N UNCOUNT/COUNT

circumference /səkʌmfə^{0}rəns/, **circumferences.** The **circumference** of a circle, place, or round object is **1** its edge. EG *He went jogging around the circumference of the reservoir every morning.* **2** the distance around its edge. EG *...an iron dome, over seven hundred feet in circumference.*
N COUNT+SUPP; N COUNT : IF+ REP THEN *of*, OR *in*+N

circumflex /sɜ:kəmflɛks/, **circumflexes.** A **circumflex** or a **circumflex** accent is a symbol written over a vowel in French and other languages, usually to indicate that it should be pronounced longer than usual. It is used for example in the word 'rôle'.
N COUNT, OR ADJ CLASSIF : ATTRIB

circumlocution /sɜ:kəmləkju:ʃə^{0}n/, **circumlocutions.** A **circumlocution** is a way of saying or writing something using more words than necessary instead of being clear and direct; a formal word. EG *...the use of circumlocutions like 'concerted action'.*
N COUNT/UNCOUNT

circumscribe /sɜ:kəmskraɪb/, **circumscribes, circumscribing, circumscribed. 1** If something such as a person's freedom **is circumscribed**, it is limited or restricted; a formal use. EG *His authority was circumscribed... The individual's freedom is circumscribed by his responsibility to his colleagues.*
V+O : USU PASS

2 If you **circumscribe** a geometrical figure, you draw a circle round it that touches all the figure's points or corners; a technical term in geometry.
V+O

circumspect /sɜ:kəmspɛkt/. Someone who is **circumspect** is cautious and avoids taking risks; a fairly formal word. EG *Physicians are now a good deal more circumspect about making recommendations for its use.* ▸ used of a person's behaviour or actions. EG *If he'd gone through my belongings, he'd done it in a very circumspect way.* ◊ **circumspectly.** EG *He would have to behave circumspectly.*
ADJ QUALIT = careful ≠ reckless ▸ = discreet ◊ ADV WITH VB = prudently

circumspection /sɜ:kəmspɛkʃə^{0}n/ is cautious behaviour; a formal word. EG *They behaved with considerable sense and circumspection.*
N UNCOUNT = caution

circumstance /sɜ:kəmstə^{3}ns/, **circumstances. 1** Particular **circumstances** are the particular conditions of a situation which have an effect on what is done or on the way something is done. EG *In normal circumstances I would have resigned immediately... Even under the most favourable circumstances this is not easy... ...the political and economic circumstances that exist in Ireland.*
N PLURAL+SUPP

2 If you say **in the circumstances** or **under the circumstances** before or after a statement, you are indicating that you are making the statement as a result of considering the conditions affecting a particular situation. EG *In the circumstances it was not surprising that there was trouble... Under the circumstances Dolores had better stay away.*
PHR : USED AS AN A

3 If you say that something must happen **under no circumstances**, you are emphasizing that it must not happen or will not happen. EG *Never, under any circumstances, block up ventilators... Under no circumstances whatsoever will I support Mr Baldwin.*
PHR : USED AS AN A ⇑ never

4 The **circumstances** of an event are the way it happened or the way it was caused. EG *She died without ever learning the circumstances of her grandfather's death... We inquired about the precise circumstances surrounding the arrest... He disappeared under mysterious circumstances.*
N PLURAL+SUPP ⇑ facts

5 Someone's **circumstances** are the conditions of their life such as the amount of money that they have and the sort of home that they live in. EG *The change in George's circumstances was abrupt... ...the financial circumstances of the parents... ...intolerable home circumstances.*
N PLURAL : USU+SUPP = fortunes

6 Circumstance is events and situations which have not been planned and cannot be controlled; a formal or literary use. EG *...a victim of circumstance... Ambitions are thwarted by circumstance.*
N UNCOUNT = fate

circumstantial /sɜ:kəmstænʃə^{0}l/; a formal word. **1 Circumstantial** evidence is evidence which makes it seem likely that something happened, but which does not clearly prove it. EG *I can't prove it-yet. But the circumstantial evidence is overwhelming... We need hard evidence. What we have got is purely circumstantial.*
ADJ CLASSIF ⇑ indirect

2 An account or description that is **circumstantial** is very detailed. EG *I gave her a much more circumstantial account than I had originally meant to.*
ADJ QUALIT = full

circumvent /sɜ:kəmvɛnt/, **circumvents, circumventing, circumvented. 1** If someone **circumvents** a rule or restriction, they avoid being prevented from doing something by the rule or restriction in a clever and perhaps dishonest way; a formal word. EG *Although charging interest is contrary to their law, the landlords circumvent this by accepting a compulsory 'gift'.*
V+O = bypass, get round

2 If you **circumvent** someone, you cleverly prevent them from achieving something, especially when they are trying to harm you; a formal word. EG *We all know what they are trying to do and we must try to circumvent them.*
V+O = outwit

circus /sɜ:kəs/, **circuses. 1** A **circus** is a group that consists of people such as clowns, acrobats, and jugglers and specially trained animals, which travels around to different places to give performances of their entertainment. EG *...the trainers from a nearby circus... ...circus elephants.* ▸ The **circus** is the show that is presented by these people. EG *We were going to take the children to the circus.*
N COUNT ▸ N SING : *the*+N

2 Circus is used to describe situations in which
ADJ CLASSIF :

everyone seems happy and excited. EG *There was a circus atmosphere about the whole occasion.* ATTRIB ⇑ exciting = carnival

cirrhosis /sɪrəʊsɪs/ is a disease, often caused by drinking too much alcohol, which destroys a person's liver and can kill them; a technical term. N UNCOUNT

cirrus /sɪrəs/ is a type of thin cloud that occurs very high in the sky; a technical term. EG *...a high blanket of cirrus... ...cirrus clouds.* N UNCOUNT

cissy /sɪsi¹/, **cissies**. See **sissy**.

cistern /sɪstən/, **cisterns**. A **cistern** is 1 a container which holds the water that is used to flush a toilet. EG *...the water supply to the cistern was turned off.* 2 a large tank in the roof of a house in which water is stored. EG *...the cold water storage cistern.* N COUNT; N COUNT

citadel /sɪtədə²l/, **citadels**. A **citadel** is 1 a castle or strong building in or near a city, in which people in former times could shelter for safety, for example during a battle. EG *...the fighting along the canals southwest of the citadel.* 2 a powerful system, organization, or belief that is very strongly defended by the people involved in it, often in a way that makes other people unable to become involved and unable to change it; a rather literary use. EG *At last I had a lucky break into the great citadel of publishing... Something ultimate has been challenged, some last citadel of certainty stormed... His London flat became a place of solitude, a citadel of loneliness.* N COUNT = fortress, stronghold; N COUNT+SUPP = bastion

citation /saɪteɪʃə⁰n/, **citations**; a rather formal word. A **citation** is 1 an official document or speech which praises a person for having done something brave or special. EG *The three policemen subsequently received citations for their action... He was named Radio Sports Personality of the Year, with a citation which read 'a genuinely funny man'... ...a citation for distinguished services.* 2 a summons to appear before a court of law; a legal term. 3 a quotation from a book or other piece of writing. N COUNT ⇑ commendation; N COUNT; N COUNT

cite /saɪt/, **cites, citing, cited**; a rather formal word. 1 If you **cite** something, 1.1 you mention it, especially as an example or as proof of what you are saying. EG *The most commonly cited example of a primitive device is the abacus... ...traits that Freud cited as proof of failure.* 1.2 you quote from a written work, especially as an example or as proof of what you are saying. EG *The passages which had been marked exactly corresponded to those cited by the reviewer.* V+O : IF+PREP THEN *as* ⇑ refer to; V+O

2 To **cite** someone or something in a legal action means to officially mention or name them. EG *...the woman who was cited in his divorce action... Neither side had cited adultery.* V+O ⇑ mention

3 To **cite** someone means 3.1 to officially summon them to appear before a court of law. EG *Two judges had cited him for dubious financial dealings.* 3.1 to officially praise them in a report or other document because they have done something brave or special. EG *She was cited by the Greek government for doing an outstanding piece of work.* V+O : IF+PREP THEN *for*; V+O : IF+PREP THEN *for* = commend

citizen /sɪtɪzən/, **citizens**; a rather formal word. A **citizen** is 1 a person who lives in a particular country, state, or city; used especially when referring to their rights or duties. EG *...the citizens of Massachusetts... Price rises had made it a rare delicacy for ordinary citizens... ...the involvement of every citizen in the aims and activities of their society.* 2 a person who has a particular nationality; used especially when they are in another country or change their nationality. EG *...Dr Joseph Court, an American citizen living in Britain... He became a British citizen... Those of us who were not citizens had to be especially careful.* N COUNT = inhabitant; N COUNT+SUPP = national

citizenry /sɪtɪzənri¹/. The **citizenry** refers to the people living in a country, state, or city; a literary word. EG *These issues were explained and debated by the citizenry... ...teeming markets and busy citizenry.* N UNCOUNT : IF SING, VB CAN BE SING OR PL = inhabitants

Citizens' Band is the range of radio waves which the general public is allowed to use in order to send messages to one another; used especially by lorry drivers and other motorists who use radio sets in their vehicles. EG *...Citizens' Band Radio... I'm not a citizens' band freak by any manner of means.* N PROPER : USU BEFORE N

citizenship /sɪtɪzənʃɪp/ is 1 the particular nationality that you have and the official status, rights, and duties that you have because of it. EG *...before you obtain British citizenship.* 2 the fact of belonging to a community because you live in it, and the things you are expected to do and the way you are expected to behave by the other people in it. EG *...the responsibilities of citizenship.* N UNCOUNT+SUPP; N UNCOUNT

citric acid /sɪtrɪk æsɪd/ is a weak acid found in many kinds of fruit, especially citrus fruits such as oranges and lemons. N UNCOUNT

citrus fruit /sɪtrəs fruːt/, **citrus fruits**. A **citrus fruit** is a juicy, sharp-tasting fruit such as an orange, lemon, or grapefruit. Citrus fruits grow in warm or hot countries. EG *Bananas and citrus fruits are its only cash crops.* N COUNT/UNCOUNT

city /sɪti¹/, **cities**. 1 A **city** is a large town where there are many houses, offices, factories, shops, theatres, etc, and where many people live and work. EG *High blocks of flats seem inevitable in overcrowded cities... ...the industrial cities of Europe... ...the city's traffic problems... ...New York City... ...a modern city centre... ...the city of Cambridge.* ▸ The **city** is also used to refer to the people who live there. EG *The whole city turned out to cheer the Pope.* ● See also **inner city**. N COUNT : ALSO IN NAMES AFTER N, AND *the*+N+*of*+N PROPER = conurbation; ▸ N SING : *the*+N ⇑ population

2 The **City** is the part of London where many important financial institutions, for example the Bank of England and the Stock Exchange, have their main offices. EG *He has a new office in the City at Angel Court... He's something in the City... She has no regrets at having become a City banker.* ▸ used also to refer to the financial institutions themselves and the people who work there. EG *Members come from both sides of industry and from the City... ...her colleagues in the City.* N PROPER : *the*+N; ▸ N SING : *the*+N

city hall, city halls. The **city hall** is the building which a city council uses as its main offices. EG *There is a proposal that we march to City Hall to lodge our demands.* N UNCOUNT/COUNT ⇑ office

civic /sɪvɪk/ is used to describe 1 people or things that have an official or important status in a particular town or city. EG *...the civic centre... ...a civic leader from the local Pakistani community.* 2 duties, rights, feelings, etc that people have because they are members of a particular community. EG *She was determined to carry out her civic responsibilities... ...civic pride.* ADJ CLASSIF : ATTRIB = municipal; ADJ CLASSIF : ATTRIB = communal

civics /sɪvɪks/ is the study of the way in which local government works and of the rights and duties of the citizens of a city or district. N UNCOUNT

civies /sɪvɪz/. See **civvies**.

civil /sɪvə⁰l/. 1 **Civil** is used to describe 1.1 things that exist or occur within a country and involve the relationship between the different groups of people in it. EG *...a society in which wars or civil disturbances can never happen... ...civil and racial equality.* 1.2 people or things in a country that are not connected with its armed forces. EG *They decided to attack civil and military communications centres... ...a supersonic civil airliner named the Concorde.* ADJ CLASSIF : USU ATTRIB = public; ADJ CLASSIF : USU ATTRIB ≠ military = civilian

2 If you say that someone is **civil** in their attitude or behaviour, you mean that they are polite but perhaps not very friendly. EG *He'd been careful to be civil to everyone... For a few months there was a civil exchange of letters.* ◇ **civilly**. EG *He was somewhat upset but he answered civilly enough... I made my farewells as civilly as I could under such provocation.* ADJ QUALIT = courteous ≠ rude; ◇ ADV = politely

civil defence, civil defences. 1 **Civil defence** is the organization and training of the ordinary people in a country so that they can help the armed forces, medical services, police force, etc, for example when the country is attacked by an enemy. EG *His job is to establish a centre of civil defence in every village.* N UNCOUNT ⇑ security

2 A country's **civil defences** are the preparations that it makes to protect its people and buildings and to make sure that the government and police, medical and other essential services can continue to function, for example when an enemy attacks the country. EG *...the UK's civil defences against air attack... ...civil defence measures... ...the civil defence corps.* N PL ⇑ security

civil disobedience is the refusal by ordinary people in a country to obey laws, pay taxes, etc, usually in order to protest about something and to try to persuade the government to change its policies or the law. EG *They achieved their ends through non-violent demonstrations and civil disobedience.* N UNCOUNT

civil divorce, civil divorces. A **civil divorce** is one which is recognized by the state but not by the church. N COUNT/UNCOUNT

civil engineer, civil engineers. A **civil engineer** is a person whose job is concerned with planning, designing, and constructing roads, bridges, harbours, and public buildings. N COUNT ⇑ specialist

civil engineering is the planning, design, and construction of roads, bridges, harbours, and public buildings. EG *The Incas were capable of great feats of civil engineering... ...a four year course in civil engineering.* N UNCOUNT ⇑ technology

civilian /sɪvɪljən/, **civilians.** A **civilian** is a person who is not a member of the armed forces. EG *They tried to avoid bombing civilians... Civilian casualties were high.* N COUNT

civilise /sɪvə'laɪz/. See **civilize.**

civility /sɪvɪlɪti'/, **civilities. 1 Civility** is behaviour which is polite but not friendly. EG *I told him to have the civility next time to ask permission before walking through my garden... ...to abandon all pretence of civility.* N UNCOUNT ⇑ politeness ≠ rudeness

2 Civilities are polite words or actions, which often have very little warmth or friendliness in them. EG *Even the civilities that you would give a passing acquaintance are forbidden... Here controversies were smothered by soft-spoken civilities.* N COUNT : USU PL = courtesies ≠ insults

civilization /sɪvə'laɪzeɪʃə"n/, **civilizations**; also spelled **civilisation. 1** A **civilization** is a human society which has its own highly developed social organization, culture, and way of life which makes it distinct from other societies. EG *...the entire history of Western civilisation... ...the earliest great civilizations: Egypt, Sumer, Assyria.* N COUNT/ UNCOUNT

2 You can use **civilization** to refer to all the societies in the world as a whole. EG *The survival of civilisation as we know it is under threat.* N UNCOUNT ⇑ humanity

3 Civilization is **3.1** the state of having a high level of social organization, culture, and a comfortable way of life. EG *The Romans brought civilization to many of the lands they conquered.* N UNCOUNT ≠ barbarism, savagery **3.2** a place where you can enjoy the comforts that you consider to be necessary; used in a humorous way. EG *The first thing I did after my return to civilization was to have a bath.* N UNCOUNT ⇑ sophistication

4 You can also use **civilization** to refer to the quality of being well-educated, polite, and cultured that a person or group of people has. EG *Beneath the veneer of civilisation lay something very crude indeed.* N UNCOUNT = refinement

civilize /sɪvɪlaɪz/, **civilizes, civilizing, civilized**; also spelled **civilise. 1** To **civilize** a person or society means to educate them so that they can improve their social organization, culture, or way of life. EG *Their mission of civilizing and modernizing that society had to be abandoned... He treated them as savages to be tamed and civilised.* ◊ **civilizing.** EG *...the early civilizing process.* V+O; ◊ ADJ CLASSIF : ATTRIB

2 If you **civilize** a place, you make it more pleasant or comfortable, or more acceptable to other people. EG *The new shopping centre has helped to civilize that part of town.* ◊ **civilizing.** EG *A park is a civilizing influence.* V+O ⇑ improve = refine; ◊ ADJ CLASSIF : ATTRIB

civilized /sɪvɪlaɪzd/; also spelled **civilised. 1** A society that is **civilized** has a highly developed culture, technology, and system of government, and a comfortable way of life for most of its inhabitants. EG *He did not believe that a civilized country would kill chickens unless they needed to. ...the amenities of civilized life... Their aim is to create an orderly, just and civilised society.* ADJ CLASSIF ≠ primitive, barbaric

2 If you describe a person as **civilized**, you mean that they are polite and reasonable in their attitudes and behaviour towards other people. EG *He was, above all a civilized man.* ADJ QUALIT = refined

4 If you describe a place or thing as **civilized**, you mean that it is attractive or comfortable and indicates that its owner or designer has good taste. EG *The floor is discreetly civilised, a simple pattern in black and white marble... The car we drove was a decidedly civilized sedan.* ADJ QUALIT = tasteful

civil law is the part of a country's set of laws which is concerned with the private affairs of citizens, for example marriage, business contracts, property ownership, etc, rather than with crime. EG *These debts, unlike all others, were not recoverable at civil law.* N UNCOUNT ≠ criminal law

civil liberty, civil liberties. A person's **civil liberties** are the rights they have to say, think, and do what they want as long as they respect other people's rights. EG *Here too there has been a similar attack on civil liberties.* N COUNT : USU PL, OR N UNCOUNT

civil marriage, civil marriages. A **civil marriage** is a marriage ceremony which is performed by a government official and not by an official representative of a religion such as a priest. N COUNT/ UNCOUNT

civil rights are the rights that people have in a society to equal treatment and equal opportunities, whatever their race, sex, or religion may be. EG *The American battle for civil rights helped the battle for women's liberation... ...the civil rights movement.* N PLURAL ⇑ equality

civil servant, civil servants. A **civil servant** is a person who works in the Civil Service. EG *The ministers make the decisions on the data provided by the civil servants.* N COUNT ⇑ administrator

Civil Service. The **Civil Service** consists of all the government departments that administer the affairs of a country and all the people who work in them. It does not include members of the armed forces, members of Parliament, or law officers. EG *The civil service was strongly opposed to the new system... ...the Indian Civil Service.* N SING : the+N, VB CAN BE SING OR PL ⇑ administration

civil war, civil wars. A **civil war** is a war which is fought between different groups of people who live in the same country. EG *His brother was killed in the Spanish Civil War... There might be civil war again in this area.* N COUNT/ UNCOUNT ⇑ fighting

civvies /sɪvi'z/; also spelled **civies. Civvies** are ordinary clothes that are not part of a uniform; an informal word. EG *The tall fair-haired man in civvies is my husband.* N PLURAL ≠ uniform

civvy street /sɪvi' striːt/ refers to ordinary life and work which is not connected with the armed forces; used in informal British English. EG *You've got a secure job in the army, whereas in civvy street you can get thrown out any time.* N UNCOUNT

cl is an abbreviation for 'centilitre'.

clack /klæk/, **clacks, clacking, clacked. 1** A **clack** is a short loud noise made by two hard objects hitting against each other, for example objects made of wood. EG *...the clack of ball on bat... ...the clack of high heels as she crosses the yard.* N COUNT : USU SING, IF+PREP THEN *of* ⇑ sound

2 If you **clack** something or if it **clacks**, it makes a short loud noise. EG *I picked up the shears and began to clack them menacingly in mid-air.* V-ERG

clad /klæd/. If you are **clad** in particular clothes, you are wearing them; a rather old-fashioned or literary word. EG *On the morning of 29 October 1618, clad in black velvet, he addressed the crowd... She was clad in jeans... She liked to see people sensibly clad.* ADJ CLASSIF : USU PRED+SUPP, IF+PREP THEN *in* = dressed

cladding /klædɪŋ/ is a covering of tiles, wooden boards, or other material that is fixed to the outside of a building to protect it against bad weather or to make it look more attractive. EG *The roof cladding and kitchen shutters were made from corrugated iron.* N UNCOUNT = facing

claim /kleɪm/, **claims, claiming, claimed. 1** If someone **claims** something, they say that it is true or is a fact, although they might not be able to prove it and other people might not believe them. EG *He claimed that he found the money in the forest... He claimed to be a Scot but had a powerful Liverpool accent... They claimed to have shot down twenty two planes... The marines were invited, it is claimed, by the government.* V+O/QUOTE/ REPORT-CL, OR V+to-INF = assert, maintain

2 If someone **claims** innocence or **claims** responsibility or credit for an action or achievement, they say that they are innocent or say that they were responsible or deserve the credit for the action or achievement, even though they might not be able to prove it and other people might not believe them. EG *The freedom fighters claimed responsibility for the bombing... A theatre audience can claim some credit for the success of a play... She claims total innocence of any involvement in the tragic events.* V+O ⇑ assert

3 If someone **claims** something of value such as property, money, land, a title, etc, they say that it legally belongs to them, for example when it was lost for a time, or someone else has it, or its ownership was uncertain. EG *...claiming back land lost by his father... European claims were often based upon ancient treaties.* V+O

4 If you **claim** money from the government, your employers, an insurance company, or other organization, **4.1** you officially apply to them for it, because you think you are entitled to it according to their V+O, OR V+A (for/on/to)

rules. EG *People with low incomes can claim free medicine... Voluntary workers in some instances can claim travelling expenses... Don't forget to claim for a first-class rail ticket to London.* **4.2** you demand it from them because you think you deserve or need it. EG *Ford manual workers are claiming a pay rise of about £20 a week.* — V+O

5 If someone or something **claims** your attention, they need or require you to spend your time and effort on them. EG *She resented her children claiming all her attention.* — V+O

6 If violent events such as war or rioting **claim** someone's life, the person is killed in the course of these events. EG *The wave of bombings, protests and street clashes is claiming new lives every day... There has been a resurgence of the fanaticism which claimed so many political victims in the past.* — V+O ↑ take

7 A **claim** is **7.1** a statement that something is true or is a fact, although other people might dispute it and not believe it. EG *Forecasts do not support the government's claim that the economy is picking up... Having made such bold claims, she finds it hard to admit that she was wrong.* — N COUNT: ALSO N + *to*-INF/REPORT-CL = assertion **7.2** a demand that people should recognize your good qualities or status, or your right to something such as land or a title. EG *The American claim to leadership imposes a special responsibility on that country... Was the winning novel attractive enough for the five judges to ignore the claims of the other six authors?... Watson's victory in England further emphasized his claim to be the world's greatest golfer.* — N COUNT+SUPP **7.3** the right to have or to get something. EG *They denied her rightful claim to the property... Henry Cooper's chief claim to fame is that he knocked down Mohammed Ali... Most people in Parliament have no hereditary claims to power or status.* — N COUNT: USU+ *to*/*to*-INF **7.4** the right that you feel you have to demand that someone does things for you. EG *She realized that she had no claims on the man.* — N COUNT+*on*/*upon* **7.5** something that you say is yours, especially an area of land which you believe contains gold or other minerals. EG *Kimberley was once a collection of prospectors' claims.* — N COUNT ↑ demand **7.6** money which you officially apply for because you think you are entitled to it. EG *After the crash the airline faced millions of dollars in claims... When the Social Security office gets your claim form they will arrange for you to see them.* — N COUNT: IF+ PREP THEN *for* ↑ application **7.7** a demand for something that you want, for example money or better working conditions. EG *Steel workers put in a pay claim for £6 a week... They decided to strike, in support of their claim for a shorter working day.* — N COUNT: IF+ PREP THEN *for*

8 If someone **lays claim to** something, they say that it is theirs and expect that other people will agree with them; a formal expression. EG *Both Ethiopia and Somalia laid claim to the territory.* — PHR: VB INFLECTS ↑ demand ● to **stake a claim**: see **stake**.

claimant /kleɪmənt/, **claimants**. A **claimant** is **1** a person who asks to be given something, especially money, which they think they are entitled to. EG *It is not always clear whether a claimant is entitled to benefit... The disabled claimant may be eligible for an invalid care allowance.* — N COUNT ↑ applicant **2** a person who says that they have a right to something, especially a title or land. EG *...a newly arrived claimant to the throne of whom nobody had heard.* — N COUNT ↑ applicant

clairvoyance /kleəvɔɪəns/ is the special ability that some people claim to have which enables them, for example, to know about future events or to communicate with dead people. EG *...the power of magic and clairvoyance.* — N UNCOUNT = second sight

clairvoyant /kleəvɔɪənt/, **clairvoyants**. If you described someone as **clairvoyant**, you believe that they are able, for example, to know about future events or to communicate with dead people. — ADJ CLASSIF = psychic ▸ used as a noun. EG *I'm like a clairvoyant, a spirit medium receiving messages.* — ▸ N COUNT = psychic

clam /klæm/, **clams, clamming, clammed**. A **clam** is an animal that lives in sand or mud under the sea. It has a soft body that you can eat and a shell in two parts that can close together very tightly. — N COUNT ↑ mollusc ● If someone **shuts up like a clam**, they suddenly stop talking, or refuse to talk about a particular subject; an informal expression. EG *Everybody shuts up like a clam as soon as you mention it.* — ● PHR: VB AND N INFLECT

clam up. If someone **clams up**, they stop talking, often because they are nervous or shy; used in informal English. EG *He was impressive on paper, but he completely clammed up in the interview.* — PHRASAL VB: V+ ADV

clamber /klæmbə/, **clambers, clambering, clambered**. If you **clamber** somewhere, you climb there with difficulty, usually using your hands and feet. EG *Every Friday afternoon 1000 Turkish workers clamber aboard a train leading north... We clambered up the hill... She came clambering over the pile of old junk.* — V+A = scramble ▸ used as a noun. EG *Angelica was exhausted from the clamber up the hill.* — ▸ N COUNT

clammy /klæmi¹/, **clammier, clammiest**. Something that is **clammy** is damp and sticky, usually in an unpleasant way. EG *His handshake is cold and clammy... ...clammy river weeds.* — ADJ QUALIT ↑ moist = slimy

clamorous /klæmərəs/; a rather formal or literary word. **1** If you say that people or their voices are **clamorous**, you mean they are shouting noisily. EG *He was deafened by the clamorous voices.* — ADJ CLASSIF ↑ noisy

2 People or things that are **clamorous** express strong feelings in a forceful way in order to make other people pay attention. EG *...a clamorous campaign of denunciation against the regime... ...a pile of clamorous public relations handouts.* — ADJ QUALIT = strident ≠ moderate

clamour /klæmə/, **clamours, clamouring, clamoured**; also spelled **clamor** in American English; a rather formal or literary word. **1** If people **clamour** for something, they demand it noisily or angrily. EG *All Western Europe might soon be clamouring for such a leader... ...changes in the law for which people are clamouring.* — V+A *(for)* = howl

2 Clamour is great anger or strong feeling that is expressed by a lot of people. EG *The war happened because of popular clamour encouraged by the newspapers.* — N UNCOUNT: IF+ PREP THEN *for*

3 When large groups of people **clamour**, they all talk and shout together loudly. EG *Old women clamoured over tanned hides in the market... The clamouring crowd was spreading.* — V OR V+QUOTE/ REPORT-CL ▸ used as a noun. EG *...the clamour of voices from the living-room.* — ▸ N UNCOUNT/ COUNT

clamp /klæmp/, **clamps, clamping, clamped**. **1** A **clamp** is a device, usually made of metal or wood, that holds two things firmly together. EG *...plywood containers which are sealed with metal clamps... ...a dozen bottles held in place by spring clamps.* — N COUNT

2 When you **clamp** one thing to another, you fasten the two things together with a clamp. EG *...special trays that were clamped to the arm of a chair.* — V+O: USU+A ≠ release

3 To **clamp** something in a particular place means to put it or hold it there firmly and tightly. EG *They clamped handcuffs around my wrists... Flaggerty had his large hand clamped round Sandy's neck.* — V+O+A ≠ remove

4 If you **clamp** your teeth or eyelids together, you press them together very tightly. EG *Kunta had clamped his jaws shut... His eyes were clamped shut.* — V+O: USU+A

clamp down. To **clamp down** on someone or something means to take strong official action to stop or control an activity or the people who are doing it. EG *The authorities have got to clamp down on these trouble-makers.* — PHRASAL VB: V+ ADV, IF+PREP THEN *on* ↑ restrain ≠ ease up

clampdown /klæmpdaʊn/, **clampdowns**. A **clampdown** is a sudden restriction on a particular activity by a government or other authority. EG *...a clampdown on wasteful spending.* — N COUNT: USU+ *on* ↑ ban ≠ easing up

clan /klæn/, **clans**. A **clan** is **1** a group of families, especially in Scotland, that are related to each other because they are all descended from the same ancestor. EG *He's from the Campbell clan... ...a power struggle between two Somali clans.* — N COUNT: IF SING, VB CAN BE SING OR PL ↑ family **2** a group of people who all have a particular quality or characteristic; used in a humorous way. EG *He had married into a clan of music experts... ...the riding clan from Mayfair.* — N COUNT: USU+ SUPP = crowd, set

clandestine /klændestɪ⁵n/; a rather formal or literary word. Something that is **clandestine** is hidden, kept secret, or done secretly, often because it is illegal. EG *...a clandestine radio station called 'Freedom Radio'... I hated this furtive, clandestine existence.* — ADJ CLASSIF = surreptitious ≠ blatant, open

clang /klæŋ/, **clangs, clanging, clanged**. When something made of heavy metal **clangs** or when you **clang** it, it makes a loud, deep noise. EG *...the sound of the bells clanging... She was methodically clanging the brass bell.* — V-ERG ↑ peal ▸ used as a noun. EG *The door opened with a heavy clang.* — ▸ N COUNT: USU SING

clanger /klæŋə/, **clangers**. If you **drop a clanger**, you do or say something embarrassing which you — PHR: VB AND N INFLECT regret afterwards; an informal expression in British English. EG *He dropped a bit of a clanger the other day.*

clangour /klæŋə/; also spelled **clangor** in American English. **Clangour** is a continuous loud clanging noise; a fairly formal word.
N UNCOUNT ⇑ peals

clank /klæŋk/, **clanks, clanking, clanked.** If something **clanks**, it makes a loud noise because solid metal objects are crashing together or against something hard. EG *The train creaked and clanked... All about him he heard chains clanking.* ▸ used as a noun. EG *...the clank of metal upon stone.*
V-ERG ⇑ bang
▸ N SING WITH DET : USU+*of*

clap /klæp/, **claps, clapping, clapped.** 1 When you **clap**, you make a noise by hitting your hands together several times, usually in order to express appreciation or excitement. EG *The audience clapped enthusiastically and called for more... They clapped their hands in time to the music.* ▸ used as a noun. EG *Spontaneously they began a clap and presently the platform was loud with applause.*
V OR V+O = applaud
▸ N COUNT : IF+ PREP THEN *of*

2 If you **clap** an object or your hand onto something else, you put it there quickly and firmly. EG *He claps his hands to his head... He went out clapping his workman's cap firmly on his head.*
V+O+A = smack

3 If you **clap** someone on the back or on the shoulder, you hit their back or shoulder with your hand in a friendly way, for example to congratulate them or to express your pleasure or excitement. EG *He clapped her on the back and laughed.* ▸ used as a noun. EG *The claps on the back and the smiles are heartier than before.*
V+O+A = slap
▸ N COUNT+ PREP

4 If you **clap hands** on someone, you catch them doing something that they should not be doing; used in informal British English. EG *The principal had clapped hands on a student drinking in a pub after hours.* • to **clap eyes on someone**: see **eye**.
PHR : VB INFLECTS = surprise

5 To **clap** someone in prison or in chains means to put them in prison or put chains round their body; an informal use.
V+O+A = slam

6 A **clap** of thunder is a sudden loud noise of thunder. EG *A clap of thunder reverberated through the house.*
N COUNT+*of* = crack

7 The **clap** is a disease that you can catch by having sexual intercourse with someone who has it; used in very informal English. EG *Hope he didn't give you the clap.*
N SING : *the*+N, OR N UNCOUNT

clapboard /klæpbɔˢd/, **clapboards.** A **clapboard** is a long, narrow piece of wood. Clapboards are used to make houses or are fixed onto the outside walls of a house in order to protect it from the weather; used in American English. EG *...a clapboard house.*
N COUNT

clapped-out. Something such as a machine that is **clapped-out** is old and no longer working properly; used in informal British English. EG *The last car was a clapped-out old Ford.*
ADJ QUALIT = worn out

clapper /klæpə/, **clappers.** 1 If you move **like the clappers**, you move extremely fast; used in informal British English. EG *She ran like the clappers down the hill.*
PHR : USED AS AN A = like the wind

2 A **clapper** is a small piece of metal that hangs inside a bell and makes the bell sound by striking its side.
N COUNT ⇑ hammer

clapperboard /klæpəbɔ:d/, **clapperboards.** A **clapperboard** is a device used by people making films which helps them to match the pictures and sound. It consists of two pieces of wood which are connected by a hinge and have the scene number written on them. Just before filming a scene, the clapperboard is held in front of the camera and the boards are banged together loudly.
N COUNT

claptrap /klæptræp/ is talk which you think is foolish and should not be believed; an informal word. EG *The claptrap that is often talked about the 'dignity of man' is unbelievable.*
N UNCOUNT = nonsense, rubbish

claret /klærət/, **clarets. Claret** is a type of red wine, made especially near Bordeaux in France.
N MASS

clarify /klærɪfaɪ/, **clarifies, clarifying, clarified.** 1 To **clarify** something or to **clarify** someone's mind on something means to make it easier to understand and remove any doubts or confusion, for example by giving more details or a simpler explanation; a rather formal word. EG *If you don't understand, ask the speaker to clarify the point... My mind was clarified and changed on this issue.*
V+O ⇑ enlighten ≠ confuse
◊ **clarification** /klærɪfɪkeɪʃəⁿn/, **clarifications.** EG *We need clarification of the legal position.*
◊ N UNCOUNT/ COUNT

2 To **clarify** butter or some other substance means to remove the water or impurities from it by heating it; a technical use. ◊ **clarified.** EG *...clarified butter.*
V+O
◊ ADJ CLASSIF

clarinet /klærɪnet/, **clarinets.** A **clarinet** is a woodwind instrument with a straight tube and a single reed in its mouthpiece. ▸ used of a person who plays this instrument in an orchestra or a band. EG *...Colin Bradbury, principal clarinet of the BBC Symphony Orchestra.*
N COUNT
▸ ⇑ player

clarinettist /klærɪnetɪst/, **clarinettists.** A **clarinettist** is a person who plays the clarinet.
N COUNT ⇑ musician

clarion call, clarion calls. A **clarion call** is a strong encouragement to do something, which is presented to people in an emotional and direct way, for example in a newspaper article; a literary expression. EG *And then came the clarion call: 'Let us build a new nation together!'... ...a clarion call to support the American President.*
N COUNT+SUPP ⇑ exhortation = cry

clarity /klærɪti¹/ is 1 the quality of being well explained and easy to understand. EG *...the clarity of her explanation.* 2 the ability to think clearly. EG *She was forcing me to think with more clarity about what I had seen... ...clarity of mind.* 3 the quality of being clear in outline or in sound. EG *I was impressed by the clarity of the pictures... ...the clarity of the singer's voice.*
N UNCOUNT : IF+ PREP THEN *of*
N UNCOUNT+ SUPP = lucidity
N UNCOUNT+ SUPP

clash /klæʃ/, **clashes, clashing, clashed.** 1 If someone **clashes** with someone else or if two people **clash**, they fight, argue, or disagree with each other because they have different ideas or beliefs. EG *Youths clashed with police in the streets around the ground... Richard Ingrams clashed frequently with Goldsmith.*
V OR V+A (*with*) : RECIP ⇑ confront

2 A **clash** is a fight, argument, or disagreement between people who have different ideas or beliefs from each other. EG *...demonstrations which ended in violent clashes with the police... ...the first public clash between the two party leaders.*
N COUNT : IF+ PREP THEN *between/of/ over/with* ⇑ confrontation

3 Beliefs, ideas, or qualities that **clash** with each other are opposed to each other because they are so different. EG *This belief clashes with all that we now know about human psychology... People's perspectives vary and even clash in many ways.* ▸ used as a noun. EG *...a clash of cultures... ...a personality clash.*
V OR V+A (*with*) : RECIP ⇑ conflict ≠ agree
▸ N COUNT

4 If two events or appointments **clash**, they happen at the same time so that you cannot attend them both. EG *A religious convention had clashed with a flower show.* ▸ used as a noun. EG *I've got a clash in my timetable.*
V OR V+A (*with*) : RECIP
▸ N COUNT

5 When two or more colours or styles **clash**, they look ugly or incorrect together. EG *She was wearing a pink jacket which clashed violently with the colour of her hair... The fittings clash with the architecture.* ▸ used as a noun. EG *...a colour clash.*
V OR V+A (*with*) : RECIP ≠ match
▸ N COUNT

6 When metal objects **clash** or when you **clash** them, they make a lot of noise by being hit together. EG *...the pots clashing in the sink.* ▸ used as a noun. EG *...a clash of cymbals.*
V-ERG ⇑ bang
▸ N COUNT

clasp /klɑ:sp/, **clasps, clasping, clasped.** 1 If you **clasp** someone or something, you hold them tightly in your hands or arms. EG *The woman was standing in the doorway clasping the sleeping baby in her arms... 'Oh dear,' Mr Boggis said, clasping her hands... Jack drew up his legs, clasped his knees, and frowned.* ▸ used as a noun. EG *Darley stopped him with a light clasp on the arm.*
V+O ⇑ hug = grasp
▸ N COUNT : USU SING

2 A **clasp** is a small device that fastens something or holds it shut. EG *...a black velvet bag with a silver clasp.*
N COUNT ⇑ fastening

3 To **clasp** something means to fasten it or hold it shut. EG *...the brooch that clasped her bodice.*
V+O ≠ open

class /klɑ:s/, **classes, classing, classed.** 1 A **class** is one of the groups of people into which a society can be divided, by considering their different social or economic status within it. EG *The party had hoped to win mass support among the working class... The middle classes all thought that the working class was inferior. ... English society is still a class society... He comes from an upper-class background.*
N COUNT+SUPP : ALSO SING = PL, OR N UNCOUNT ⇑ stratum

2 A **class** of people or things is a number of people or things that are considered in a group together because they have similar characteristics. EG *We can identify several classes of fern... ...a class of solvents.*
N COUNT+SUPP ⇑ category = type, set

3 A **class** is also 3.1 a group of pupils or students who are taught together. EG *If classes were smaller, children would learn more.* 3.2 a short period of teaching in a particular subject, usually given regu-
N COUNT = form
N COUNT/ UNCOUNT

larly. EG *Peggy took evening classes in French... He's a good teacher and his classes are very popular.* 3.3 a classification which indicates the standard of achievement that someone has reached in their university degree; used in British English. EG *She left university with a first class honours degree in French.* N UNCOUNT : USU MOD+N ⇑ grade

4 A particular **class** of a service or a product is one of the official standards or qualities that it is divided into. EG *He always travelled first class... He sat in a second class carriage reading a newspaper... These eggs are all class A.* N UNCOUNT/ COUNT+SUPP ⇑ standard

5 If you say that someone or something has **class**, you mean they have a quality of elegance and sophistication which impresses people. EG *She's got real class.* N UNCOUNT = style

6 To **class** someone or something in a particular way means to consider them as belonging to a particular group or grade. EG *At nineteen you're still classed as a teenager.* V+O+A (among/as/ with) = categorize

7 The word **class** is also used in the following expressions. 7.1 If you say that someone is **in a class of** their **own** or that something is **in a class by** itself, you mean that their quality or skill is so excellent that they cannot be compared with any other person or thing. EG *As a player he is really in a class of his own.* PHR : USED AS AN A ⇑ incomparable 7.2 If you say that one person or thing is not **in the same class** as another, you mean that you don't think they are as good in quality or standard of achievement as the other. EG *I don't think Cavalli is in the same class as Monteverdi.* PHR WITH BROAD NEG : USED AS AN A, USU+as a patch on

class-conscious. Someone who is **class-conscious** believes in and is very aware of the differences between the various classes of people in society, and often has a strong feeling of belonging to a particular class. EG *...class-conscious, highly organized industrial workers.* ◊ **class-consciousness**. EG *A new and more strident class-consciousness was emerging.* ADJ QUALIT ⇑ hierarchical ◊ N UNCOUNT

classic /klæsɪk/, **classics**. 1 A **classic** example of a thing or situation has all the features or characteristics which you expect to find. EG *London is the classic example of the scattered city... This statement was a classic illustration of British politeness.* ◊ **classically**. EG *He had at first sight seemed a classically undesirable son-in-law.* ADJ CLASSIF : USU ATTRIB = archetypal, standard ◊ ADV

2 A **classic** piece of writing, film, etc is one that is thought to be of very high quality and has become a standard against which other similar things are judged. EG *...Brenan's classic analysis of Spanish history... ...one of the classic works of the Hollywood cinema.* ADJ CLASSIF : ATTRIB = definitive

3 A **classic** style, movement, etc is attractive by being simple in form. EG *The classic style is straightforward, unadorned, unemotional.* ADJ CLASSIF : ATTRIB ⇑ harmonious

4 A **classic** is 4.1 something which is a very good example of a particular style, action, or situation. EG *The cross-examination by F. E. Smith is one of the classics of English legal history... The meat hall is a classic of London art nouveau.* N COUNT+SUPP = masterpiece 4.2 a book which is well-known and thought to be of a very high literary standard. EG *We had all the standard English classics at home... Take a paperback copy of War and Peace, or any other classic.* N COUNT = masterpiece

5 **Classics** is the study of the ancient Greek and Roman civilizations, especially their languages, literature, and philosophy. EG *She obtained a first class degree in Classics.* N UNCOUNT ⇑ subject

classical /klæsɪkə°l/. 1 **Classical** means 1.1 traditional in form, style, or content; used of styles that have been used or developed over a long period of time. EG *We offer tuition in classical ballet, modern ballet, and ballroom dancing... The Keynesian system, like the earlier classical economic system, relied on certain disciplines... ...the classical Hindu scheme of values.* ADJ QUALIT : USU ATTRIB ≠ modern, new 1.2 attractive by being simple in style. EG *We all admire the spangled acrobat with classical grace.* ◊ **classically**. EG *She was tall, slender, with wonderful hair and classically beautiful.* ADJ CLASSIF : ATTRIB ◊ ADV

2 **Classical** music is music that is considered to be serious and of lasting value, as opposed to pop, jazz, folk, etc. EG *He was a lover of classical music... ...classical pianists.* ADJ CLASSIF : USU ATTRIB

3 Something that is **classical** belongs or relates to ancient Greek or Roman civilization. EG *...plays set in classical or heroic times.* ADJ CLASSIF

4 A **classical** language is a form of a language that was used in ancient times and is now no longer used or only used in formal writing. EG *...studying classical Arabic.* ADJ CLASSIF : ATTRIB

classicism /klæsɪsɪzə°m/ is a style of art that has simple, regular forms and in which the artist does not attempt to express strong emotions. It is associated especially with the 18th century in Europe. N UNCOUNT ≠ romanticism

classicist /klæsɪsɪst/, **classicists**. A **classicist** is a person who studies the ancient Greek and Roman civilizations, especially their languages, literature, and philosophy. N COUNT ⇑ scholar

classification /klæsɪfɪkeɪʃə°n/, **classifications**. 1 **Classification** of things is the activity or process of classifying them into different types. EG *The cataloguing and classification of all the plants on the island took many months.* N UNCOUNT ⇑ description

2 A **classification** is a division or category in a classifying system. EG *Your insurance group classification changes when you buy a bigger or more powerful car.* N COUNT ⇑ description

classified /klæsɪfaɪd/. Something that is **classified** is officially stated to be secret, for example by a government or government department, and only a few important people are allowed to know about it. EG *What I have to say is classified... This document contains some classified information.* ADJ CLASSIF ⇑ restricted

classify /klæsɪfaɪ/, **classifies, classifying, classified**. To **classify** things such as animals, plants, or books means to divide them into groups that have similar characteristics. EG *She disapproved of a library that actually classified books under light romance... Books are classified according to subject area.* V+O, OR V+O+A (as) : USU PASS ⇑ allocate = categorize

classless /klɑːslɪ²s/. A **classless** society is one in which all people are given the same social and economic status, and cannot be grouped into different social classes. ADJ CLASSIF : USU ATTRIB = egalitarian

classmate /klɑːsmeɪt/, **classmates**. A **classmate** is a pupil who is in the same class as you at school, or sometimes at college. N COUNT

classroom /klɑːsru⁴m/, **classrooms**. A **classroom** is a room in a school where lessons take place. N COUNT

classy /klɑːsi¹/, **classier, classiest**. If you say that someone or something is **classy**, you mean they are stylish and sophisticated; an informal word. EG *Her flat looks very classy.* ADJ QUALIT

clatter /klætə/, **clatters, clattering, clattered**. 1 A **clatter** is a continuous series of short, loud sounds that are made by hard things hitting each other. EG *...the clatter of her typewriter... ...the clatter of dishes being washed... She put her coffee cup down with an angry little clatter.* N SING WITH DET, OR N UNCOUNT : IF+PREP THEN of ⇑ noise = rattle

2 When someone or something **clatters** or when someone **clatters** something, they make a continuous series of short loud sounds, because they are doing something which involves hard objects hitting each other. EG *...a secretary who used to clatter away at her typewriter... Mr Evans began clattering with his fire-irons among the cold ashes... My sister was clattering the forks back into the drawer... ...the clattering and whining elevator.* V-ERG : USU+A ⇑ bang = rattle

clause /klɔːz/, **clauses**. 1 A **clause** is a particular section of a legal document such as a contract or a law passed by Parliament. EG *He included a clause in the contract that allowed him to buy the house back at the original price... ...clause 4 of the Party's constitution... He spoke against having any exclusion clauses in the Merchant Shipping Bill.* • See also **penalty clause**. N COUNT 2 A **clause** is, in grammar, a structure which has one or more of the following elements: subject, verbal group, object, complement, adjunct. Two types of clause are mentioned in this dictionary, subordinate clauses and main clauses. A main clause can be used on its own as a sentence; a subordinate clause can only be used with a main clause and is often introduced by a subordinating conjunction (see □ at CONJ SUBORD) or a sentence adverb (see □ at ADV SEN). N COUNT

claustrophobia /klɒstrə⁴fəʊbɪə, klɔːs-/ is 1 a fear that some people have which makes them avoid small, narrow, or enclosed places; a technical term. N UNCOUNT ⇑ phobia

2 the strong feeling of discomfort some people have when they are in small, narrow, or enclosed places. EG *Being in lifts gives me claustrophobia.* N UNCOUNT

claustrophobic /klɒstrə⁴fəʊbɪk, klɔ-/. 1 If you are **claustrophobic**, you have a fear of being in small, narrow, or enclosed places; a technical term. EG *She* ADJ CLASSIF ⇑ phobic *was thankful she wasn't claustrophobic, like poor Mrs Jenkins.*

2 If you feel **claustrophobic**, you feel very uncomfortable when you are in a small, narrow, or enclosed space. EG *I began to feel claustrophobic... Leave the door open, because I get very claustrophobic.* ADJ QUALIT

3 A place or a situation that is **claustrophobic** makes you feel uncomfortable and unhappy because you are enclosed or restricted. EG *...a claustrophobic passage... ...life can seem claustrophobic... ...a small claustrophobic restaurant.* ADJ QUALIT

clavichord /klævɪkɔːd/, **clavichords**. A **clavichord** is a musical instrument rather like a piano, in which wires are hit by pieces of metal when the keys are pressed. Clavichords were especially popular in the eighteenth century. EG *Haydn's clavichord is on display here.* N COUNT

claw /klɔː/, **claws, clawing, clawed**. 1 The **claws** of a bird or animal are the thin, hard, curved nails at the end of its feet. EG *That cat is always sharpening its claws on the chairs... ....a beast with claws that scratched... The owl swooped and picked up the mouse in its claws.* N COUNT = nail, talon

2 The **claws** of a lobster, scorpion, and some other creatures are two pointed parts at the end of a leg which can move apart and back together, and are used for grasping things, especially food. N COUNT ↑ limb = pincer

3 If an animal **claws** something, it digs its claws into it in order to hold it tightly or to wound it. EG *....a large bronze statue of a tigress clawing the back of a water buffalo.* V+O

4 If you say that someone **clawed** their **way** up or **clawed** their **way** through life, you mean that they achieved success only after overcoming great difficulties, and often by hurting other people. EG *He clawed his way through life... He clawed his way up from the back streets of Glasgow.* PHR+A : VB INFLECTS

claw at. If a person or animal **claws at** something, they try to get hold of it or damage it by using their nails or claws. EG *...shaking her head and clawing at my trousers... The buck is prancing madly up and down clawing at the wire.* PHRASAL VB : V+PREP, HAS PASS

claw back. When a government **claws back** money, it finds a way of taking money back from people that they were given in another way; used mainly in British English. EG *The Government intended to claw back the extra supplementary benefit.* PHRASAL VB : V+O+ADV ↑ recover

clay /kleɪ/. 1 **Clay** is a substance found in soil that is soft when it is wet and hard when it is dry. Clay is used to make things such as pots by shaping wet clay and then baking it to make it hard. EG *...glazed clay pots... ...modelling in clay.* N UNCOUNT

2 **Clay** is also used to describe soil that contains a lot of clay. EG *...trenches dug in the heavy red clay during the first German war.* N UNCOUNT

clean /kliːn/, **cleaner, cleanest; cleans, cleaning, cleaned**. 1 Something that is **clean** is free from dirt, stains, and other unwanted substances or marks. EG *...Japanese men dressed in business suits, ties, and clean white shirts... Carbon steel knives should be wiped clean after use... The room was spotlessly clean.* ▸ also used to describe people or animals who keep themselves or their surroundings clean. EG *She is so clean and tidy, a model daughter... Cats are such clean animals.* ADJ QUALIT ≠ dirty ▸ ≠ dirty

2 If you **clean** something, you make it free from dirt, stains, and other unwanted substances or marks, for example by washing or wiping it. EG *Clean the bathroom and lavatory thoroughly... She was cleaning her teeth... ...the industrial fluid used to clean grease from the hands.* ▸ used as a noun. EG *The windows could do with a clean.* ● See also **dry-clean, spring-clean**. V+O ≠ dirty ▸ N SING : a+N

3 When you **clean**, you make the inside of a house or other building and the furniture in it free from dirt and dust. EG *Her mother cooked and cleaned all day... I'd scribble a note for Martha to find when she came in to clean.* V

4 If a nuclear process, power station, or weapon is **clean**, it produces very few harmful radioactive particles; a technical use. EG *The tactical bomb is reasonably clean.* ▸ also used to describe an area, person, or object that is free from radioactive particles. EG *The Geiger counter indicated that the area was clean.* ADJ QUALIT ≠ dirty ▸ ADJ CLASSIF ≠ contaminated

5 In some religions such as Judaism, if an animal is **clean**, a person of that religion can lawfully eat the meat from it; a technical use. ADJ CLASSIF

6 Paper that is **clean** has no writing or drawing on it. EG *You'd better start a clean piece of paper.* ADJ CLASSIF = blank

7 A **clean** piece of writing or printed matter has had the mistakes in it corrected and does not have any notes or marks on it. EG *Let me have a clean copy of your report.* ADJ CLASSIF : ATTRIB ≠ rough

8 If you describe humour or the way someone behaves as **clean**, you mean that nothing that is said or done is considered morally unacceptable or offensive. EG *It's all good clean fun... You'll be all right if you lead a good clean life... ...clean jokes.* ADJ CLASSIF : USU ATTRIB ↑ decent

9 If a game or a fight is **clean**, it is played fairly and according to the rules. EG *When we played other schools the games were always clean... It was a remarkably clean fight.* ADJ QUALIT ↑ fair ≠ dirty

10 If someone's reputation or record is **clean**, they have never committed a crime or done anything dishonest or immoral. EG *They wanted to maintain a clean international reputation... Applicants must have a clean driving licence.* ADJ CLASSIF = spotless

11 In very informal English, if you say that a person is **clean**, you mean **11.1** that they have not committed a crime. EG *They can't touch me–I'm clean.* **11.2** that they are not in possession of anything stolen or illegal. EG *Dump the goods and run off, so if they do catch you, you are clean.* ADJ CLASSIF / ADJ CLASSIF : PRED

12 If you **come clean** about something that you have been keeping secret, you admit it or tell people about it; an informal expression. EG *She decided to come clean... You might as well come clean about that blonde you've been seeing.* PHR : VB INFLECTS, IF+PREP THEN about ↑ confess ≠ cover up

13 If you describe a smell, a taste, or the air as **clean**, you mean that it is fresh or is not mixed with other smells or tastes. EG *...the clean smell of the leather store.* ADJ QUALIT

14 A sound that is **clean** is pure, constant, or correct in pitch or tone. ADJ QUALIT

15 A surface that is **clean** is smooth, and has no rough edges or parts that stick out. EG *The grass stems had clean edges to them as though they had been cut... He was impressed by the boat's clean curves.* ADJ QUALIT ≠ jagged, rough

16 A **clean** movement such as a throw is skilful and accurate. ADJ QUALIT

17 In informal English, you can use **clean** to emphasize that an action or event takes place **17.1** smoothly and immediately. EG *The ninth shot went clean through the forehead... He lost all his toes. It cut them clean off.* **17.2** completely or thoroughly. EG *The thief got clean away... I'd clean forgotten to switch the oven on.* ADV+PREP/ADV = right / ADV+PREP/ADV

18 A **clean** action is one that happens or is done quickly and with as little disorder, damage, or distress as possible; used showing approval. EG *No mess. No fuss. Just a nice clean simple exit.* ADJ QUALIT ↑ painless ≠ messy

19 A **clean** break is a complete and usually sudden end to a relationship. EG *It's better to make a clean break.* ADJ CLASSIF : USU ATTRIB

20 If you **clean** a bird, fish, chicken, etc, you prepare it for cooking by removing the parts of it that you do not want to eat. EG *They'd been busy cleaning and plucking the birds.* V+O ↑ prepare

21 ● to **make a clean sweep**: see **sweep**. ● See also **cleaning**.

clean down. If you **clean down** a house, room, etc you clean it thoroughly. EG *First, clean down the walls.* PHRASAL VB : V+O+ADV

clean out. 1 If you **clean out** a cupboard, room, house, etc, you take everything out of it, often before cleaning it. EG *I was cleaning out my desk at the office on my last day there... Regularly clean out food cupboards.* PHRASAL VB : V+O+ADV ↑ clear out

2 If you **clean out** a person or a place, you take or steal all the money they have or everything of value that is in it; an informal use. EG *I've got no more money–they cleaned me out... Thomas thought idly of cleaning out the cash register.* PHRASAL VB : V+O+ADV

clean up. 1 If you **clean up** something or someone, you clean them fairly thoroughly, usually soon after they have become dirty or had something spilled on them. EG *Clean up food spills at once... I cleaned up Allen as best I could.* PHRASAL VB : V+O+ADV, OR V+ADV

2 If you **clean up** a place, you make it tidy by putting or throwing things away and often by cleaning things. EG *Any child would gladly stay behind to help* PHRASAL VB : V+ADV, OR V+O+ADV = clear up

me clean up the classroom... Leave everything, I'll clean up later.

3 If the police or the authorities **clean up** a place, they make it free from crime or other unacceptable activities. EG *Then they can begin to clean up the cities.* PHRASAL VB : V+O+ADV ⇑ improve

4 If people **clean up**, they make a large profit from a business deal; an informal use. EG *People who buy shares now will clean up when the price rises.* PHRASAL VB : V+ADV = make a killing

5 See also **clean-up**.

clean up after. If you **clean up after** a person or event, you clean or tidy a place that has been made dirty or untidy by them. EG *It must be very depressing to spend your life cleaning up after people you never see.* PHRASAL VB : V+ADV+PREP

clean-cut. 1 If someone is **clean-cut**, they are neat and have well-defined features. EG *The news editor was a clean-cut, pleasant-faced man.* ADJ QUALIT

2 If something is **clean-cut**, 2.1 it has a sharp well-defined edge or outline. EG *The capitals of the lower arches are severe and clean-cut.* ADJ QUALIT 2.2 it is clear, definite, and easy to understand. EG *James Bond lives in a clean-cut world: the goodies versus the baddies.* ADJ QUALIT = clear-cut ≠ muddled

cleaner /kliːnə/, **cleaners**. 1 A **cleaner** is 1.1 a person who is employed to clean the inside of a building, for example an office, and the furniture in it. EG *Don't leave it in a rubbish bin for the cleaner to find.* N COUNT ⇑ worker 1.2 a person whose job is to clean a particular type of thing. EG *Our regular window cleaner went off to Canada last year... Get a professional carpet cleaner to estimate for your carpets.* N COUNT : AFTER N ⇑ worker 1.3 a substance used for cleaning things. EG *...a spray oven cleaner... How much cleaner have we got left?* N COUNT/UNCOUNT : MOD+N 1.4 a machine or device used for cleaning something; used especially to refer to a vacuum cleaner. EG *Have you got an upright cleaner or one of those cylinder ones?* N COUNT 1.5 a person who runs a shop where clothes, curtains, etc can be taken to be dry cleaned. N COUNT : USU *the*+N ▸ The words **cleaner** and **cleaner's** are used to refer to the shop itself. EG *She collected the curtains from the cleaner's... He then went into the cleaner's for Willie's suit.* ▸ = dry cleaner ● See also **dry cleaner**.

2 If you say that someone is being **taken to the cleaner's**, you mean that they are losing a lot of money, for example in a business deal, a legal action, or in gambling, often in an unfair or dishonest way; an informal expression. EG *It has been alleged that we are taking companies to the cleaner's.* PHR : VB INFLECTS = fleece

cleaning /kliːnɪŋ/ is the activity or work of cleaning the inside of a house or other building and the furniture in it. EG *Her mother was always busy with the cleaning and dusting... The Job Centre has things like cleaning jobs... It won't take me more than an hour to do the cleaning.* N UNCOUNT

cleaning lady, cleaning ladies. A **cleaning lady** or **cleaning woman** is a woman who is employed to clean the inside of a building, for example an office or house, and the furniture in it. N COUNT ⇑ cleaner

cleanliness /klenlɪnəˀs/ is the practice or habit of keeping yourself and your surroundings clean. EG *We were brought up to have strict habits of cleanliness.* N UNCOUNT

cleanly /kliːnli¹/. If something is done **cleanly**, it is done smoothly, easily, and completely, without making a mess. EG *He pulled one cork cleanly, but the other crumbled... The paint flaked away cleanly from the old hard varnish... With the long knife, he lopped off its head cleanly at the shoulders.* ADV WITH VB ≠ messily

cleanse /klenz/, **cleanses, cleansing, cleansed**. 1 To **cleanse** a place or a person means to make them free from something dirty, unpleasant, or evil; a rather formal use. EG *They are to be applauded for their attempt to cleanse society of this iniquity... There were certain filthy images I could not cleanse from my mind after I had read it.* V+O : IF+PREP THEN *from/of* ⇑ purify

2 To **cleanse** your skin or a wound means to clean it, especially by using a special substance such as disinfectant. EG *She rolled up the sleeve of my shirt and cleansed the skin... Cleanse your face and then apply moisturizer.* V+O ⇑ clean

cleanser /klenzə/, **cleansers**. A **cleanser** is a liquid that you use for cleaning something, usually your skin. EG *Use a gentle cleanser.* N COUNT/UNCOUNT ⇑ substance

clean-shaven. If a man is **clean-shaven**, he does not have a beard or a moustache. ADJ CLASSIF

clean-up; also spelled as one word. A **clean-up** is a good, thorough clean. EG *This room could do with a good clean-up... ...a Europe-wide sulphur dioxide clean-up.* N SING : *a*+N ⇑ clean

clear /klɪə/, **clearer, clearest; clears, clearing, cleared**. 1 Something that is **clear** is 1.1 easy to understand and free from confusion, with all the details well explained in a sensible order. EG *I gave a clear, frank account of the incident... Mark could not see why Jane could not understand. It seemed clear enough to him... The discussions enabled them to have a clearer idea of the nature of the problem.* ADJ QUALIT = lucid ≠ confusing, unclear ◊ **clearly**. EG *That sets out the position clearly. It makes sense of something that I used to find very confusing... They've got to clearly define their policies.* ◊ ADV 1.2 definite and leaves no doubt about its existence or nature. EG *The letter contained a clear commitment to reopen disarmament talks... They are faced with clear alternatives.* ADJ QUALIT = clear-cut ≠ ambiguous ◊ **clearly**. EG *Canvassing and bartering are clearly forbidden under rule 7.* ◊ ADV ⇑ definitely 1.3 easy to see or hear. EG *He had clear, childish handwriting... The line of its footprints is still clear along one side of the river... We shouted out loud and clear the names and ranks of the officers.* ADJ QUALIT, OR ADV = distinct ≠ unclear ◊ **clearly**. EG *He was speaking loudly enough for most of the audience to hear him quite clearly... I couldn't see him clearly... Make sure that all your luggage is clearly labelled.* ◊ ADV ⇑ easily = distinctly

2 If you are **clear** about something, you understand it completely. EG *If you are not clear about anything in this chapter, ask me... I'm not clear from what you said whether you support the idea or not.* ADJ QUALIT : PRED ≠ confused, muddled

3 If you **get** something **clear**, you understand it properly. EG *I think I've got it pretty clear... Now let's get this clear. No way are we going to accept any redundancies.* PHR : VB INFLECTS

4 If you **make** yourself **clear** or you **make it clear**, you explain or state something in a way that is easy to understand so that there can be no doubt about your meaning, wishes, or intentions. EG *It is important to make clear your wishes about the funeral... You should make clear exactly what you want to know... He seemed to be unable to make himself clear... All of them made it clear they would support my decision... Do I make myself clear?* PHR : VB INFLECTS

5 You say **'Is that clear?'** after you have told someone to do something in order to make sure that they do it, and to emphasize your authority. EG *The report must be on my desk tomorrow morning. Is that clear, Sergeant?* CONVENTION

6 If your mind or your way of thinking is **clear**, you are able to think sensibly, reasonably, and logically and are not upset or confused. EG *Your grandfather's mind was never clearer than during the time he made this will... You need clear thought and action... Their aim is to promote clearer thinking on social policy issues.* ADJ QUALIT = lucid ≠ muddled ◊ **clearly**. EG *I hadn't really ever thought clearly about this division... Wait until you can think more clearly.* ◊ ADV

7 If a conclusion that you come to is **clear** after seeing, reading, or hearing something, it is obvious and evident. EG *It was clear from his letter that he was not interested... Each day it was becoming clearer to me that our chances of success were very low... It's far from clear that they will benefit from it.* ADJ QUALIT : USU PRED ≠ unclear ◊ **clearly**. EG *Whoever owned the house was clearly not expecting us... Some of the sheds were clearly in bad repair... Clearly, it is very important for a solution to be found quickly... ...a very pleasant man, educated and clearly intelligent.* ◊ ADV OR ADV SEN

8 If a substance is **clear**, you can see through it. EG *...clear plastic bags... ...a clear all-purpose glue... ...clear honey.* ADJ CLASSIF = transparent ≠ opaque

9 Water or air that is **clear**, is clean, fresh, and free from unpleasant substances that make it dirty or difficult to see through. EG *The water was so clear that you could see the oysters on the sea bed... The morning air was still clear and fresh... Sponge the stain immediately with plenty of clear cold water.* ADJ QUALIT ≠ dirty

10 A voice or a sound that is **clear** has a pure quality that contains no rough, harsh, or unpleasant notes. EG *The principal singer's voice remained pure and clear throughout the evening... Irene had a very distinctive voice, extremely clear and ringing... A clear tone cut the silence.* ADJ QUALIT ≠ harsh, rough

11 A colour or a light that is **clear** is bright and strong. EG *...the clear white morning light... All colours were clearer, the river below her was brilliant blue.* ADJ QUALIT ≠ dull

12 If someone's eyes are **clear**, they express calmness, innocence, and honesty. EG *Her eyes behind the huge spectacles are clear and untroubled... ...clear brown eyes.* ADJ QUALIT ⇑ calm ≠ shifty

13 A surface or a place that is **clear** is empty or is free from things that might cause an obstruction, a blockage, problems, or difficulties. EG *No other cars were involved; the road was clear and in good condition... A patch of floor that has been swept clear... The lines of approach for infantry units were still clear.* ADJ CLASSIF : USU PRED

14 If your view of something is **clear**, it is not blocked or obstructed in any way. EG *It was impossible to get a clear look at the princess... I had a clear view of the procession from my bedroom window.* ADJ QUALIT : ATTRIB ⇑ good

15 If the weather is **clear**, it is free from cloud, mist, or rain. EG *On a clear day you can see the Welsh hills... During the monsoons the afternoons were warm and clear... For the next few days the weather became clear and unusually calm.* ADJ QUALIT

16 If your skin is **clear**, it is healthy and free from spots or rashes. EG *...a shortish man of clear complexion.* ADJ QUALIT ≠ blemished, spotty

17 If your conscience is **clear**, you do not feel guilty about anything. EG *Now that I've told her everything, I can leave with a clear conscience.* ADJ CLASSIF ⇑ free ≠ guilty

18 If you, your time, or your diary is **clear**, you have no appointments or arrangements to deal with which prevent you from doing other things. EG *The whole of Tuesday and Thursday afternoon is clear... My diary is clear all next week.* ADJ CLASSIF : PRED ⇑ empty = free

19 If you have a **clear** day, a **clear** week, etc to do something in, you have a whole day, week, etc to do it in. EG *That gives us four clear days to finish the job.* ADJ CLASSIF : ATTRIB ⇑ complete

20 You can use **clear** as a way of indicating the sum of money that a person actually receives after taxes, expenses, and other deductions have been paid. EG *He gets £150 a week clear... I should think I'll get a clear hundred from the deal.* ADJ CLASSIF : ALSO AFTER N

21 If something or someone is **clear** of something else, they are not touching it. EG *Mr Cater was dead by the time he was pulled clear of the water... Raise the jack until the wheel is clear of the ground.* ADJ CLASSIF : PRED, IF+PREP THEN *of* = away from

22 If you **stay** or **steer clear** of a person or place, you do not go near them. EG *He took special care to stay clear of any place where Sally might be.* PHR : VB INFLECTS, IF+PREP THEN *of*

23 If someone is **in the clear**, they are free from blame, suspicion, guilt, or danger; an informal expression. EG *The tests proved negative so we're in the clear at last!* PHR : USED AS AN A = safe

24 To **clear** a surface or a place means to remove things from it in order to make it empty or free from things that you no longer want there. EG *In 1975 Brazil's forests were being cleared at the rate of 62,500 square miles a year... The children were helping me clear weeds from the pond... Will you clear the table when you've finished eating?... I helped to clear the ground of heather and birch trees... He cleared some magazines off a chair onto the floor.* V OR V-ERG : IF+PREP THEN *from/of/off*

25 To **clear** something such as a pipe, a road, or a passage means to remove whatever is blocking it so that things can move easily along it again. EG *Poke a stick down the pipe to clear it... The princess's aides had to advance before her to clear a passage... The treatment clears the sinuses... They attempted to clear their way through the rubble.* V+O ⇑ free ≠ block

26 To **clear** your mind or your head means to free it from confused thoughts, dullness, or the effects of drugs such as alcohol. EG *Why don't you go for a walk to clear your head?* V+O ≠ cloud

27 If you **clear** something such as work or a problem, you finish dealing with it successfully. EG *We've got to clear all this work before Friday.* V+O ⇑ do

28 If someone **clears** a particular sum of money, they earn it or get it as profit after all the expenses, taxes, etc have been deducted. EG *She's doing all right: she must be clearing £10,000 a year.* V+O ⇑ make

29 To **clear** a fence, a hedge, a jump, etc means to succeed in getting over it without touching it, for example in athletics or horse racing. EG *It was a spectacular jump and she nearly cleared it.* V+O

30 When a liquid **clears** or when you **clear** it, it becomes free from substances which make it dirty or difficult to see through. EG *Rinse the jumper until the water clears... Don't bottle the wine until it has cleared.* V-ERG

31 When you **clear** your **throat**, you make a short, quick sound like a cough in order to make it easier to speak or in order to attract someone's attention. EG *He cleared his throat and spoke in a queer, tight voice... They became restive and began to clear their throats.* PHR : VB INFLECTS

32 When something unpleasant **clears** or when you **clear** it, it gradually becomes less in degree or severity and finally disappears or stops altogether. EG *Outside the fog had cleared a little... We're expecting this weather to clear any moment... The fresh breeze cleared his headache.* V OR V-ERG ⇑ reduce = improve

33 When a cheque **clears** or when you **clear** it, it passes through the banking system and is accepted for payment; a technical use. EG *Your cheque will take three days to clear.* V-ERG

34 When your skin **clears**, it becomes free from spots or rashes and looks healthy again. EG *Your skin has cleared since you have been using that soap.* V OR V-ERG ⇑ improve

35 When your face **clears**, it returns to a normal expression after showing an unpleasant emotion such as worry or anger. EG *Bill's face cleared and he spoke out joyously... His brow cleared.* V ⇑ change ≠ cloud, darken

36 If someone in authority **clears** a plan or a course of action, they officially approve it before it is put into effect. EG *The proposals haven't been cleared by the local authority yet.* V+O ≠ reject

37 If an aircraft, ship, or person **is cleared**, they are given official permission to enter or leave an airport, a harbour, or a country, for example after their official documents or passports have been checked. EG *The plane was cleared for take off at 10.05h... I would have the threat of deportation hanging over me unless I cleared myself the next day with the immigration authorities.* V+O (NG/REFL) ⇑ authorize

38 If someone is **cleared** after an official investigation, **38.1** they have been checked and it has been decided that they can be trusted and given secret or important work. EG *Hugel was cleared by the CIA's office of security in just one week.* V+O = vet **38.2** they have been proved not guilty of a crime or mistake and are freed from blame or suspicion. EG *The tribunal finally reported, clearing all the people who had been accused... I returned to clear myself through the courts.* V+O (NG/REFL) ⇑ free

39 • **to clear the air**: see **air**. • **the coast is clear**: see **coast**. • **to clear the decks**: see **deck**. • See also **clearing**.

clear away. When you **clear away**, you put away the things that you have been using, for example while eating a meal or doing some work. EG *After dinner, when we had cleared away and washed up, we went for a walk.* PHRASAL VB : V+ADV, OR V+O+A ⇑ tidy up

clear off. If you say to someone **'clear off'**, you are telling them in a rude way to go away and leave you alone; used mainly in very informal British English. EG *Now you clear off and leave me alone.* PHRASAL VB : V+ADV = buzz off

clear out. **1** If you **clear out** of a place, you leave it, usually taking all your possessions with you; an informal use. EG *I've got to clear out of my place by next week.* PHRASAL VB : V+ADV, IF+PREP THEN *of*

2 If you say to someone **'clear out'**, you are telling them in a rude way to go away and not come back; used mainly in very informal British English. EG *Just clear out and leave me in peace!* PHRASAL VB : V+ADV = buzz off

3 If you **clear** things **out**, you collect them together and throw them away because you no longer want them. EG *All these old cans and jars should have been cleared out months ago.* PHRASAL VB : V+O+ADV ⇑ throw out

4 If you **clear out** a cupboard, a room, a house, etc, you tidy it and clean it and throw away the things in it that you no longer want. EG *It's time I cleared out the kitchen cupboards.* PHRASAL VB : V+O+ADV

5 See also **clear-out**.

clear up. **1** If you **clear up** or **clear** something **up**, you tidy things and put them away in their correct places. EG *I was too exhausted to clear up properly... Go and clear up your room... After lunch we can clear up the old tins and throw them away.* PHRASAL VB : V+ADV, OR V+O+ADV ◊ **clearing up**. EG *Don't do the washing on a Monday when you have all the clearing up from the weekend.* ◊ N UNCOUNT

2 If you **clear up** a problem, disagreement, or misunderstanding, you settle it or resolve it by explaining and discussing it. EG *I'm assuming that the misunderstanding will be cleared up soon... I went to* PHRASAL VB : V+O+ADV ≠ aggravate *clear the matter up with him... You will clear up the other point too?*

3 If someone's illness **clears up**, they no longer suffer from it and their health improves. EG *I was very lucky, it was only a minor infection and it all cleared up in a week.* PHRASAL VB : V+ADV ⇑ improve

4 When bad weather **clears up**, it stops raining or being cloudy and the sun begins to shine. EG *Look, it's cleared up now, we could go for our walk.* PHRASAL VB : V+ADV ⇑ improve

clearance /klɪərəns/, **clearances**. 1 **Clearance** is the removal of old buildings, trees, or other things that are not wanted or needed from an area. EG *He was responsible for slum clearance and rehousing programmes... Thirteen million pounds was spent on land clearance and street improvements.* N UNCOUNT/COUNT

2 If you get **clearance** for something that you want to do or have, you get official approval or permission to do or have it. EG *We should get clearance by next Monday, if we're lucky.* N UNCOUNT

3 If an aeroplane, a ship, or a person is given **clearance**, they are given official permission to enter or leave an airport, harbour, or country. N UNCOUNT ⇑ permission

clearance sale, clearance sales. A **clearance sale** is a sale in which the goods in a shop are sold at reduced prices, because the shopkeeper wants to get rid of them quickly or because the shop is closing down. N COUNT

clear-cut; also spelled without a hyphen. Something that is **clear-cut** is easy to understand and quite distinct from other things of the same type. EG *There are differences, but I think they're not as clear-cut as some people would say... The issues are clear-cut... There is no longer any clear-cut division between one social group and another.* ADJ QUALIT = obvious ≠ fuzzy

clear-headed, clearer-headed, clearest-headed. If you describe someone as **clear-headed**, you mean that they are sensible and think clearly, especially in a difficult or dangerous situation. EG *He was too clear-headed to deceive himself... ...clear-headed ruthlessness... ...Barbara Steiner, who was the clearest-headed of the lot of them.* ADJ QUALIT ≠ muddle-headed

clearing /klɪərɪŋ/, **clearings**. 1 A **clearing** is a small area of grass or bare ground which is surrounded by a much larger area of trees and other large plants. EG *They are alone in a clearing in the forest.* N COUNT

2 **Clearing** is the act of tidying up and getting rid of things that you no longer want. EG *...the clearing of desks at the end of term.* N UNCOUNT

clearing bank, clearing banks. A **clearing bank** is, in Britain, a bank that uses the central clearing house in London to deal with all its transactions with other banks. EG *The other three major clearing banks followed suit and raised their interest rates.* N COUNT

clearing house, clearing houses; also spelled with a hyphen. A **clearing house** is 1 an organization which collects, sorts, and distributes information. EG *Their national service committee, an information clearing house and resource centre... The less he knows the better. Let him be simply a clearing house for information.* N COUNT 2 a central bank which deals with all the transactions between the banks that use its services. N COUNT

clear-out. A **clear-out** is the activity of collecting together all the things that you do not want and throwing them away, and of tidying and cleaning the things that remain; an informal word used in British English. EG *This room is in a real mess! We'll have to have a good clear-out soon.* N SING WITH DET : USU *a*+N = tidy out

clear-sighted; also spelled without a hyphen. Someone who is **clear-sighted** is able to understand situations and people well and make good, sensible judgements and decisions about them. EG *He was too clear-sighted not to see what problems would follow... Chaos could be prevented only by a clear-sighted and absolutely united minority taking power.* ADJ QUALIT ⇑ clever

◇ **clear-sightedness**. EG *He lacked the courage and the clearsightedness to sever the relationship.* ◇ N UNCOUNT

clearway /klɪəweɪ/, **clearways**. A **clearway** is, in Britain, a road on which you are not allowed to stop unless your vehicle breaks down or develops a fault. N COUNT

cleavage /kliːvɪdʒ/, **cleavages**. 1 A woman's **cleavage** is the space between her breasts, especially the part you can see when she is wearing a dress that does not cover the upper surface of them. N COUNT : POSS+N, OR N UNCOUNT ⇑ chest

2 A **cleavage** between two people or things is a division or disagreement between them; a formal use. EG *There is no distinct cleavage between the classes... Increasingly deep cleavages separate one age group from another.* N COUNT : IF+PREP THEN *between* ⇑ split

cleave /kliːv/, **cleaves, cleaving**; a formal or literary word. The past tense can be either **cleaved** or **clove**, and the past participle can be **cleaved, cloven**, or **cleft**. 1 When you **cleave** something or when it **cleaves** in two, it is split or divided into two separate parts, often violently. EG *His spade cleaved the firm sand with a satisfying crunch... ...a child's head cloven in half... The front of the palace is cleft by the grand flight of steps.* V-ERG : IF V THEN +A *(in)*

2 When one thing **cleaves** to another or when you **cleave** one thing to another, you cannot move them apart because they seem to be stuck together. EG *Without this weight their feet no longer cleave to the ground... My tongue clove to the roof of my mouth.* V-ERG+A *(to)* ⇑ attach = stick

3 If someone **cleaves** to a particular way of thinking or behaving, they keep thinking or behaving in that way and refuse to change; sometimes used showing disapproval. EG *The Left had continued to cleave to that line of tradition.* V+A *(to)* = adhere, cling

cleaver /kliːvə/, **cleavers**. A **cleaver** is a knife with a large square blade, used for chopping meat or vegetables. N COUNT

clef /klɛf/, **clefs**. A **clef** is a symbol at the beginning of a line of a written piece of music that indicates what musical key it is in. N COUNT

cleft /klɛft/, **clefts**. 1 A **cleft** in a rock or in the ground is a narrow opening in it; a rather literary use. EG *He could see the valley through a cleft in the rocks.* N COUNT : IF+PREP THEN *in/between*

2 If you are **in a cleft stick**, you are in a difficult situation that will give you problems or harm you whatever you decide to do; used mainly in informal British English. PHR : USED AS AN A = in a hole

3 **Cleft** is a form of the past participle of **cleave**.

cleft palate, cleft palates. If someone has a **cleft palate**, they were born with a narrow opening along the roof of their mouth which makes it difficult for them to speak properly. N COUNT/UNCOUNT ⇑ deformity

clematis /klɛmətɪs/ is a climbing plant that has large colourful flowers. N UNCOUNT

clemency /klɛmənsi[1]/ is kind treatment that a person receives, especially from someone who has authority to punish them; a formal word. EG *...appeals for clemency by the lawyers of the condemned men.* N UNCOUNT = leniency ≠ harshness

clench /klɛntʃ/, **clenches, clenching, clenched**. 1 When you **clench** your fist, you curl your fingers up tightly, usually because you are very angry. EG *Ralph clenched his fist and went very red.* V+O ⇑ squeeze ≠ relax

2 When you **clench** your teeth, you squeeze them together firmly, usually because you are angry or upset. EG *She hissed through clenched teeth, 'You get out of here.'* V+O = press together

3 If you **clench** something in your hand or in your teeth, you hold it tightly with your hand or your teeth. EG *...a long pipe clenched in his teeth... Carol clenches her mother's hand.* V+O, OR V+O+A = clasp ≠ release

clergy /klɜːdʒi[1]/. The **clergy** are the officially appointed leaders of the religious activities of a particular church or temple. EG *...a church fund to provide pensions for retired clergy and their widows.* N PLURAL ⇑ churchmen

clergyman /klɜːdʒɪmə[3]n/, **clergymen**. A **clergyman** is a male member of the clergy. N COUNT = minister

cleric /klɛrɪk/, **clerics**. A **cleric** is a member of the clergy. N COUNT = clergyman

clerical /klɛrɪkə[0]l/. 1 **Clerical** jobs, skills, workers, etc involve or are concerned with routine jobs that are done in an office, for example filing papers and keeping records of daily activities. EG *...clerical skills.* ADJ CLASSIF

2 **Clerical** also means relating to the clergy. EG *...the clerical opposition to the reforms... ...a priest in a clerical grey suit with a dog collar.* ADJ CLASSIF ⇑ religious ≠ secular

clerk /klɑːk/, **clerks**. A **clerk** is 1 a person who works in an office, bank, or law court and whose job is to look after the records, accounts, etc. EG *We have a staff of three photographers and a clerk who keeps all the records straight... ...office clerks.* N COUNT ⇑ employee 2 a receptionist; used mainly in American English. N COUNT

clever /klɛvə/, **cleverer, cleverest**. 1 Someone who is **clever** 1.1 is intelligent and able to learn and understand things easily. EG *My sister was very clever and passed all her exams at school... He was one of the cleverest scientists in German industry.* ADJ QUALIT = brainy, bright ≠ stupid

▸ used of a person's face or expression that shows ▸ ADJ QUALIT this. EG *She has a clever face.* ◇ **cleverness.** EG *Her cleverness was seen at any early age.* **1.2** is skilful at a particular job or activity. EG *He was not very clever with his fingers.* ◇ **cleverly.** EG *He played the role of a simple man very cleverly.* **1.3** is good at planning things and dealing with situations and people, sometimes in a dishonest way, in order to gain an advantage or avoid any unpleasant results for themselves. EG *They are clever enough to make sure that no one will associate them with the act... He's a clever rogue.* ▸ used of a person's behaviour or actions. EG *...a clever plan.* ◇ **cleverly.** EG *How cleverly you work at winning these gentlemen over.*

◇ N UNCOUNT / ADJ QUALIT ≠ clumsy / ◇ ADV WITH VB / ADJ QUALIT = cunning, smart / ▸ = crafty / ◇ ADV WITH VB

2 If you say that someone is **too clever by half**, you mean that they are always planning things, often in a dishonest way, in order to get what they want from situations and are likely to get into trouble as a result; used in informal British English showing disapproval.

PHR : USED AS C

3 Something such as an idea, book, or invention that is **clever** is effective and shows the skill of the people involved. EG *This is a very clever way of running a college... It's such a clever gadget.* ◇ **cleverness.** EG *We all admired the cleverness of the device.*

ADJ QUALIT = ingenious / ◇ N UNCOUNT = ingenuity

cliché /kliːʃeɪ/, **clichés**; also spelled **cliche**. A **cliché** is an idea, expression, or way of behaving which has been used so much that it is no longer original or effective; used showing disapproval. EG *...sentimental clichés about 'peace' and 'the open air'... How true is the old cliché that trouble shows us who our friends really are?... I wanted to get right away from the usual clichés of historical films.*

N COUNT ⇑ platitude

clichéd /kliːʃeɪd/. Something that is **clichéd** has become a cliché; used showing disapproval. EG *...a clichéd character... It sounds rather clichéd.*

ADJ QUALIT = trite, hackneyed

click /klɪk/, **clicks, clicking, clicked.** **1** When you **click** something or when it **clicks**, it makes a short, sharp sound. EG *He clicked his fingers and the dog immediately sat down... His camera was clicking away... ...a loud clicking noise.* ▸ used as a noun. EG *The lock opened with a click... ...the click of a typewriter.* ● To **click** your **heels**: see **heel**.

V-ERG ⇑ snap / ▸ N COUNT/UNCOUNT

2 If something such as an idea that you have found difficult **clicks**, you suddenly understand it or find it obvious; an informal use. EG *The last detail had clicked into place... It finally clicked and he started to laugh.*

V

3 If two people **click** when they meet for the first time, they immediately like each other; an informal use. EG *We seemed to click as soon as we met.*

V ⇑ get on = hit it off

client /klaɪənt/, **clients.** A **client** of a professional person or organization is a person or company that receives advice or a service from them, usually in return for payment. EG *...a solicitor and his client... He has been a valued client of our bank for many years.*

N COUNT : USU+SUPP ⇑ customer

clientele /kliːɒntel/. The **clientele** of a particular place or organization refers to the people who are its customers or clients, especially its regular customers or clients. EG *...a restaurant with a predominantly upper-class clientele... The firm's clientele includes many royal patrons.*

N SING WITH DET : VB CAN BE SING OR PL

cliff /klɪf/, **cliffs.** A **cliff** is a high area of land with a very steep side, especially next to the sea. EG *...a cliff of red earth and rock... ...black cliffs that rose out of the water.*

N COUNT

cliff-hanger, cliff-hangers; also spelled without a hyphen. A **cliff-hanger** is a situation that is very exciting or frightening, because you are left for a long time not knowing what will happen next; an informal word. EG *There's a real cliff-hanger in the final scene.*

N COUNT ⇑ drama ≠ bore

climactic /klaɪmæktɪk/. A **climactic** moment or point in a situation is one in which a very exciting or important event occurs or one which represents the most exciting or important stage in the development of something. EG *He keeps it secret from her until a climactic point in the story... ...a time when industrialism was beginning its climactic forward surge.*

ADJ CLASSIF ⇑ ultimate

climate /klaɪmɪt/, **climates.** **1** The **climate** of a particular place refers to the general weather conditions that are typical of it. EG *It's a bit like the English climate... ...changes in climate due to pollution of the atmosphere.* ▸ **Climate** is also used to refer to the place that has those weather conditions. EG *In cold climates, cows may have to be kept indoors all winter.*

N COUNT/UNCOUNT ⇑ environment / ▸ N COUNT+SUPP

2 You can use **climate** to refer to people's attitudes or opinions at a particular time or concerning a particular situation. EG *In the present economic climate more progress may be made than previously... We want a climate favourable to large companies... ...thoughts and prejudices reflecting the current climate of opinion.*

N COUNT+SUPP

climatic /klaɪmætɪk/. **Climatic** conditions, changes, effects, etc are those that relate to the general weather conditions of a place. EG *...climatic changes... ...favourable climatic conditions.*

ADJ CLASSIF : ATTRIB ⇑ environmental

climax /klaɪmæks/, **climaxes, climaxing, climaxed.** **1** The **climax** of a process or sequence of events is the most exciting or important moment in it, which usually occurs at the end of it or causes the end of it. EG *This proved to be the climax of his political career... The battle approached a climax.*

N COUNT : IF+PREP THEN *of/in* ⇑ peak = culmination ≠ anticlimax

2 The **climax** of a book, play, piece of music, etc is the point at which the most exciting actions or most intense emotions occur, usually near the end. EG *The climax of the book happens in Egypt.*

N COUNT : IF+PREP THEN *of/in* ⇑ peak = denouement

3 A **climax** is also an orgasm.

4 When something **climaxes** a sequence of events or when the sequence **climaxes**, it ends with a dramatic and important event; a formal word. EG *The bombing climaxed an increasingly deadly series of attacks... ...economic deflation and political disillusionment, climaxed by the Government's defeat at the General Election.*

V-ERG ⇑ end = culminate

climb /klaɪm/, **climbs, climbing, climbed.** **1** If you **climb** or if you **climb** something tall such as a tree, mountain, or ladder, you move or travel towards the top of it, often with some effort or difficulty. EG *We started to climb the hill... He climbed the stairs to his bedroom... I climbed up the ladder.* ▸ used as a noun. EG *We were still out of breath from the climb.*

V OR V+O : IF+PREP THEN *up/to* = ascend ≠ descend / ▸ N COUNT ⇑ act

2 If you **climb** somewhere, you move there slowly, carefully, and often rather awkwardly, for example because you are moving into a small space or trying to avoid falling. EG *She walked across the street and climbed into her car... Four more men climbed down through the hatch... We climbed over the gate and sat down behind the hedge.*

V+A, OR V+O = clamber

3 A **climb** is a thing or place such as a steep hill that you climb up. EG *We reached the top of the climb and stopped for a rest.*

N COUNT

4 When something **climbs**, **4.1** it moves gradually upwards to a higher position. EG *As the day wears on, the sun climbs higher and higher... The plane climbed steeply and banked.* **4.2** it increases in value or amount. EG *The project's estimated cost has climbed to a staggering £35 billion... Conoco shares climbed 3.6 points on Thursday.*

V : USU+A ⇑ travel = ascend / V : USU+A = increase ≠ fall

5 If someone **climbs** in their job or social life, they become more successful and achieve a higher status. EG *There are many jobs in which a man may only climb if he is respectably married... ...the glittering heroes who have climbed up out of poverty.* ▸ used as a noun. EG *Describing his climb to fame, Graffman is modest... ...a climb up the class ladder.*

V, V+O, OR V+A ⇑ advance = rise ≠ fall / ▸ N COUNT : USU +A

6 to **climb on the bandwagon**: see **bandwagon**.

climb down. If you **climb down** in an argument or dispute, you admit that you are wrong or agree to reduce the demands or conditions that you were previously insisting on. EG *Even after these facts were published, he was unwilling to climb down.*

PHRASAL VB : V+ADV ⇑ give in = back down

climb-down, climb-downs. A **climb-down** in an argument or dispute is the act of admitting that you are wrong or of agreeing to reduce the demands or conditions that you were previously insisting on. EG *A much higher proportion of strikes may culminate in a climb-down on the part of management.*

N COUNT ⇑ withdrawal = retraction

climber /klaɪmə/, **climbers.** A **climber** is **1** a person or animal that climbs, especially with skill. EG *Kurt assured me that he was an excellent climber and could reach the nest... Chimpanzees are adept climbers.* **2** someone who climbs rocks or mountains as a sport or hobby. EG *Equipment is, for modern climbers, the greatest single expense.* **3** a plant that grows upwards by attaching itself to other plants or objects.

N COUNT ⇑ mammal / N COUNT = mountaineer / N COUNT

climbing /klaɪmɪŋ/ is the activity of climbing rocks or mountains as a sport or hobby. EG *Climbing is*

N UNCOUNT, OR N BEFORE N

popular, and more and more students are becoming interested in it... ...a pair of climbing boots.

climbing frame, climbing frames; also spelled with a hyphen. A **climbing frame** is a structure that is made for children to climb and play on. It consists of metal or wooden bars that are joined together. N COUNT

clime /klaɪm/, **climes**. A warm **clime**, wet **clime**, etc is a place with a climate of the type mentioned; a literary or old-fashioned word. EG *He retreats to sunny climes, leaving the winter behind.* N COUNT : MOD+N, USU PL

clinch /klɪntʃ/, **clinches, clinching, clinched**. If you **clinch** something such as an agreement or an argument, you settle it in a definite way. EG *The salesman was in Columbia trying to clinch a deal for his employer... Agreements between Mr Benn and the union would clinch it once and for all.* V+O = agree, finalize
◊ **clinching**. EG *This was the clinching argument.* ◊ ADJ CLASSIF

clincher /klɪntʃə/, **clinchers**. A **clincher** is something that you use as a way of finally settling an agreement or argument, for example because it proves that you are right or is such a generous offer that the other person cannot refuse it. EG *As a clincher, he made particular reference to previously negotiated agreements.* N COUNT

cling /klɪŋ/, **clings, clinging, clung**. 1 If you **cling** to someone or something, you hold onto them tightly with your arms. EG *The human baby is too weak to cling to its mother for hours on end... I clung to the door to support myself... He held me in his arms like a child and we clung desperately together.* V : IF+PREP THEN *to* = hang on

2 Something that **clings** to you is or seems to be closely attached to you. EG *...small beads of perspiration clinging all over his moustache like dew... The dress clung tight to Etta's waist and over her hips... ...the powerful odour of horse manure that clung about her.* V ⇑ stick

3 If you **cling** to someone you are fond of, you stay so close to them or spend so much time with them that they do not have enough freedom or independence; used showing disapproval. EG *A working woman is not so likely to cling to her children when it's their turn to leave.* V+A *(to)* = hang on

4 If you **cling** to an idea or way of behaving, you continue to believe in its value or importance, even though it may no longer be valid or useful. EG *They cling to all the old, inefficient methods of doing things... The adults cling to old emotional values.* V+A *(to)* = hang on, retain

clinging /klɪŋɪŋ/. Someone who is **clinging** becomes very attached to people and too dependent on them; used showing disapproval. EG *...something weak and clinging in his nature.* ADJ QUALIT

2 Clothing that is **clinging** fits tightly round your body. ADJ QUALIT ⇑ tight

clinic /klɪnɪk/, **clinics**. 1 A **clinic** is a building where people go to receive advice or treatment, especially a part of a hospital where doctors or other medical experts deal with particular aspects of people's health. EG *This should be checked by your own doctor or at the Child Health Clinic... ...dental clinics... ...the family planning clinic.* ▸ **Clinic** is also used to refer to the doctors or experts who work there. EG *Psychiatric clinics often recommend jobs for disturbed patients.* N COUNT : USU+SUPP

2 You can also use **clinic** to refer to a particular period of time during which someone such as a doctor or an expert in a particular subject gives help or advice to people. EG *His clinic is on Thursdays at 4.30.* N COUNT : USU POSS+N = surgery

clinical /klɪnɪkə⁰l/. 1 **Clinical** work, teaching, etc relates to the direct medical observation and treatment of patients rather than to theoretical research. EG *Doctors are hoping to start clinical tests next month... ...theories based on clinical observations... ...clinical psychologists.* ◊ **clinically**. EG *It is necessary to observe the patient clinically over a period of several days.* ADJ CLASSIF : USU ATTRIB ⇑ experimental ≠ theoretical ◊ ADV

2 **Clinical** treatment, buildings, etc relate to medical clinics, for example in hospitals. EG *...the first comprehensive clinical structure for treating children developed in the 1920's.* ADJ CLASSIF : ATTRIB

3 A **clinical** way of thinking or behaving is one in which you consider things only in a factual or logical way and without showing any emotion or personal involvement; used showing disapproval. EG *She adopted an icy, impersonal, clinical attitude... The most repellent feature of the process was the calm, clinical way in which the keepers administered the rules.* ▸ used of people. EG *He is far too cool, too detached, too clinical.* ◊ **clinically**. EG *She told me clinically, almost indifferently, what the situation was.* ADJ QUALIT = cold, detached ≠ emotional ▸ = cold ◊ ADV WITH VB = coldly

4 A room or building that is **clinical** is designed to look very plain, or is kept very neat and clean, with the result that people do not enjoy being in it or near it. EG *...tiny offices painted clinical white.* ADJ QUALIT = stark ≠ homely

clinical thermometer, clinical thermometers. A **clinical thermometer** is a thermometer that is used for measuring the temperature of the body of a person or animal. N COUNT ⇑ instrument

clink /klɪŋk/, **clinks, clinking, clinked**. 1 When objects made of glass, pottery, or metal **clink** or when you **clink** them, they touch each other and make a short, light sound. EG *She made a toast, clinking her glass against Rudolph's.* ▸ used as a noun. EG *I could hear the clink of cutlery.* V-ERG ▸ N COUNT/UNCOUNT

2 The **clink** means the same as prison; a very informal use in British English. EG *We could get six months in the clink if they catch us.* N SING : *the*+N = nick

clinker /klɪŋkə/ is a hard substance which forms in lumps as a result of burning coal at high temperatures in a furnace or stove. N UNCOUNT = cinders

clip /klɪp/, **clips, clipping, clipped**. 1 A **clip** is a small device, usually made of metal or plastic, that is specially shaped for holding things together. EG *He wore three pencils held by metal clips in his top pocket... ...hair clips.* ● See also **bulldog clip, paper clip.** N COUNT = grip

2 When something **clips** to something else or when you **clip** it there, it fastens to it by means of one or more clips. EG *It clips to the bed frame... Keep the list clipped to that notebook.* V-ERG+A ⇑ fasten

3 If you **clip** something, you cut small pieces from it, especially in order to shape it. EG *Mr Willet had come to clip the hedges... Roll the sheep over to clip the wool near the tail.* ▸ used as a noun. EG *One bad clip would ruin the pheasant's tail.* V+O ▸ N COUNT = snip

4 If you **clip** something out of a newspaper or magazine, you cut it out. EG *He had clipped an article from the 'Reader's Digest'.* V+O+A *(from/out of)*

5 When a ticket inspector **clips** your ticket, for example on a train, he punches a small hole in it to indicate that it has been used. V+O = punch

6 If you **clip** a small amount off something, you reduce it by that amount. EG *We could probably clip a few seconds off the current record.* V+O+A *(off)* = cut

7 If you **clip** someone or something, you hit them with a short, light blow. EG *I clipped him one... I just clipped the wall with the bumper as I was turning into the drive.* ▸ used as a noun. EG *You'll get a clip on the ear if you don't shut up!* V+O, OR V+O+O ▸ N COUNT

8 If someone or something **clips** a person's **wings**, they restrict that person's freedom to do what he or she wants. PHR : VB INFLECTS

9 A **clip** of a film or television programme is a short piece of it that is shown separately. EG *Medical students were shown film clips depicting murders and fights.* N COUNT : USU MOD+N = excerpt

10 If something moves or happens **at a clip, at a fast clip**, etc, it moves or happens quickly; an informal use. EG *They came marching towards us at an incredible clip... Visitors stream through at a steady and rapid clip.* PHR : USED AS AN A

11 See also **clipping, clipped.**

clipboard /klɪpbɔːd/, **clipboards**. A **clipboard** is a board with a clip at the top that holds together a number of pieces of paper that you need to carry around, especially to provide a firm base so that you can write on them while you are standing. N COUNT ⇑ board

clip clop is used to represent the sound of a horse's hooves as it walks or trots. EG *We could hear the clip clop of the horses' hooves.* N SING WITH DET

clip joint, clip joints. A **clip joint** is a nightclub in which customers are regularly charged very high prices for very poor drink or entertainment; used in informal English. N COUNT ⇑ night club

clip-on. A **clip-on** object is designed to be fastened to something by means of a clip. EG *...a plastic clip-on badge... ...a clip-on bow-tie.* ADJ CLASSIF : ATTRIB

clipped /klɪpt/. 1 Hair that is **clipped** is neatly trimmed. EG *...a handsome man with a clipped moustache.* ADJ CLASSIF

2 If you have a **clipped** way of speaking, you speak with quick, short sounds that are not joined together. EG *He talked with a clipped, upper-class accent.* ADJ QUALIT

3 A **clipped** style of language expresses things quickly and clearly, using as few words as possible. EG *Fraser gave him clipped and precise instructions... His plays are written in a very clipped, staccato style.* — ADJ QUALIT ⇑ abrupt

clipper /klɪpə/, **clippers**. **1** You use **clippers** to refer to a tool used for cutting small amounts from something, especially from someone's hair or nails, or from a hedge. EG *...a pair of nail clippers.* — N PLURAL : ALSO *a pair of*+N ⇑ shears ⇑ scissors

2 A **clipper** is a fast sailing ship that was used in former times. — N COUNT

clipping /klɪpɪŋ/, **clippings**. A **clipping** is **1** an article, picture, or advertisement that has been cut from a newspaper or magazine. EG *Dawlish read the newspaper clipping I gave him.* — N COUNT ⇑ paper = cutting **2** a small piece of something that has been cut or trimmed from a larger piece. EG *...grass clippings... ...fingernail clippings.* — N COUNT : USU PL, USU MOD+N

clique /kli:k, klɪk/, **cliques**. A **clique** is a small group of people who often spend their time only with other members of the group and seem unfriendly towards other people; used showing disapproval. EG *They had made a small, superior, isolated clique... There's always a little clique of older members who are jealous of the young.* — N COUNT : IF+PREP THEN *of*, IF SING VB CAN BE SING OR PL = elite

cliquey /klɪki[1], kli:ki[1]/. A group of people who are **cliquey** often spend their time only with other members of the group and seem unfriendly towards other people who are not in the group; used showing disapproval. EG *I'm not keen on the club, I find it a bit cliquey.* — ADJ QUALIT = exclusive

clitoris /klɪtərɪs, klaɪ-/, **clitorises**. A woman's **clitoris** is the small sensitive lump above her vagina which, when touched, causes pleasant sexual feelings that can lead to an orgasm. — N COUNT : USU SING

Cllr is a written abbreviation for 'Councillor'. — N IN TITLES

cloak /kləʊk/, **cloaks, cloaking, cloaked**. **1** A **cloak** is **1.1** a wide, loose coat that fastens at the neck and does not have sleeves. — N COUNT **1.2** something that completely covers the surface of something else. EG *It is covered by a soft furry cloak of skin.* — N COUNT : IF+PREP THEN *of* **1.3** a description, explanation, or activity that is intended to hide the truth. EG *He could be using the story as a cloak for more sinister activities... The cloak of secrecy had to be torn aside.* — N COUNT = cover

2 To **cloak** something means to cover it or hide it. EG *The countryside was cloaked in an early morning mist... ...continuing to fascinate, cloaked in its mystery.* — V+O : USU PASS, IF+PREP THEN *in* = shroud

cloak-and-dagger. A **cloak-and-dagger** situation or activity is one that involves mystery and secrecy. — ADJ CLASSIF : ATTRIB

cloakroom /kləʊkru[4]m/, **cloakrooms**. A **cloakroom** is **1** a place where you can leave your coat and hat, especially in a public building or place of entertainment; used mainly in British English. — N COUNT : USU *the*+N **2** a room containing toilets and washbasins, especially in a public building. — N COUNT : USU *the*+N

clobber /klɒbə/, **clobbers, clobbering, clobbered**; an informal word. **1** If you talk about someone's **clobber**, you mean the things that belong to them, especially coats, bags, and other things that they carry around with them. EG *Have you got all your clobber?* — N UNCOUNT ⇑ belongings = stuff

2 If you **clobber** someone, **2.1** you hit them. EG *If that kid bites me I'll clobber it.* — V+O **2.2** you defeat them easily or greatly reduce their strength. EG *We clobbered the opposition... We've been clobbered by the government's new tax laws.* — V+O

cloche /klɒʃ/, **cloches**. A **cloche** is a long, low cover made of glass or clear plastic that is put over young plants to protect them from the cold. — N COUNT

clock /klɒk/, **clocks, clocking, clocked**. **1** A **clock** is an instrument that measures time and shows you what time of day it is. The time may be indicated by the position of two pointers on a circular or rectangular area that has the numbers from 1 to 12 marked on its edges, or may be shown as a series of numbers. Clocks may stand on a shelf in a room, be fixed to a wall in a room or outside a building, etc. If the instrument is designed to be worn by people, it is called a watch. EG *...the ticking of the clock... The church clock struck eleven... Downstairs, a clock chimed softly. Ten o'clock.* ● See also **alarm clock, grandfather clock**. — N COUNT ⇑ timepiece

2 The **twenty-four hour clock** is a system of referring to time that is used especially in timetables. Each of the hours of the day is given a number between 0 and 23, starting at midnight, and the minutes are given as numbers after the hours. For example, half past seven in the evening is 19.30h. EG *Most airlines use the twenty-four hour clock.* — PHR

3 A time **clock** on a machine or system is a device that causes things to happen automatically and regularly at particular times. EG *Set the time clock on your central heating system to give heat only when it is needed.* — N COUNT ⇑ control = timer

4 A time **clock** in a factory or office is a device that is used to record the hours that people work. Each worker puts a special card into the device when they arrive or leave, and the times are printed on the card. EG *They do not have to punch a time clock at work.* — N COUNT

5 The **clock** in a car is an instrument that measures and shows the number of miles or kilometres it has travelled or its speed at a particular moment. EG *...a Mini with over 5,000 miles on the clock.* — N COUNT : USU SING, *the*+N

6 The word **clock** is also used in the following expressions. **6.1** If you work **round the clock**, you work all day and all night without stopping. EG *They're working round the clock to keep the runways clear.* — PHR : USED AS AN A = day and night **6.2** If you **keep** your **eyes on the clock, watch the clock**, etc, while you work, you keep looking to see what the time is, especially because you are bored by your work and want it to end as soon as possible; an informal expression. EG *Of those who worked, most had their eyes on the clock.* — PHR : VB INFLECTS **6.3** If you do something **by the clock** or **according to the clock**, you pay a lot of attention to what the time is, so that you are not late or do not spend too long on it. EG *They're people who just hate to do anything by the clock.* — PHR : USED AS AN A ⇑ timed **6.4** If you do something **against the clock**, you do it in a great hurry because there is very little time. EG *We're all working against the clock here.* — PHR : USED AS AN A **6.5** If you **put the clock forward, set the clock back**, etc, you change the time that the clock indicates, for example because it is no longer correct. — PHR : VB INFLECTS ⇑ adjust **6.6** To **turn the clocks back, put the clock forward**, etc to a particular time in the past or the future means to remember or imagine the situation at that time. EG *Tonight we're turning the clocks back to the nineteenth century with a new play by Pam Gems... To answer this we have to turn the clock back hundreds of years.* — PHR : VB INFLECTS **6.7** To **put the clock back, turn the clock back**, etc means to return to ideas or situations that existed a long time ago and to ignore the fact that things have changed a lot since then; used showing disapproval. EG *This government seems to want to see the clock put back.* — PHR : VB INFLECTS ⇑ regress

clock in. **1** When workers **clock in** at a factory or office, they record the time that they arrive by putting a special card into a device. EG *When they are late clocking in for factory work they may lose pay.* — PHRASAL VB : V+ADV = clock on ≠ clock off, clock out

2 If someone or something **clocks in** at a particular weight, amount, time, etc, they register that amount after being weighed, measured, or timed. EG *The truck clocked in at about two thousand pounds.* — PHRASAL VB : V+ADV, IF+PREP THEN *at*

clock off. When workers **clock off** in a factory or office, they record the time that they leave by putting a special card into a device. EG *It's time to clock off.* — PHRASAL VB : V+ADV

clock on. When workers **clock on** at a factory or office, they clock in. — PHRASAL VB : V+ADV

clock out. When workers **clock out** at a factory or office, they clock off. — PHRASAL VB : V+ADV

clock up. To **clock up** a particular number or total means to reach that total, especially when it is a large amount. EG *He reckons that he has clocked up more than 171,750 miles in a lifetime of cycling.* — PHRASAL VB : ORDER V+ADV+O ⇑ amass = chalk up

clockwise /klɒkwaɪz/. When something moves in a **clockwise** direction, it moves in a circle and in the same direction as the hands on a clock. EG *He pushed the bolt back in and twisted it clockwise.* — ADV WITH VB, OR ADJ CLASSIF : ATTRIB

clockwork /klɒkwɜ:k/. **1** If something happens with **clockwork** efficiency, precision, regularity, etc, or if it happens **like clockwork**, it happens without any problems or delays. EG *The place ran like clockwork... Everything went like clockwork.* — ADJ CLASSIF : ATTRIB; PHR : USED AS AN A ⇑ smoothly

2 Clockwork is the machinery in some types of toys or models that makes them move when they are wound up with a key. EG *This model moved by clockwork... ...clockwork toys.* — N UNCOUNT ⇑ mechanism

clod /klɒd/, **clods**. **1** A **clod** is a large lump of earth; a rather old-fashioned or literary use. EG *Two boys* — N COUNT = sod *were accused of throwing clods at other boys... ...clods of earth.*

2 If you call someone a **clod**, you mean that they have done something stupid; used in very informal English. EG *What a clod he must think I am.* N COUNT : USU USED AS C, ALSO VOC = idiot

clodhopper /klɒdhɒpə/, **clodhoppers**. A **clodhopper** is a clumsy person; used in informal English. EG *You great clodhopper–look what you've done!* N COUNT/VOC = oaf

clog /klɒg/, **clogs, clogging, clogged**. 1 When you **clog** something or **clog** it **up**, or when it **clogs up**, it becomes blocked and no longer works properly or no longer allows things to move freely in it or on it. EG *Many people are trying to leave the area, clogging the roads with their vehicles... If the cooling unit gets clogged up with ice it can't do its job efficiently... The vents clog up easily.* ◊ **clogged**. EG *My nose and throat felt clogged... His rifle was clogged with sand.* V+O OR PHRASAL VB : V-ERG+ADV, IF+PREP THEN *with* = jam ◊ ADJ CLASSIF

2 **Clogs** are 2.1 leather shoes with thick wooden soles. 2.2 shoes made entirely of wood that people wear as part of their traditional costume in some countries, especially in Holland. N COUNT : USU PL N COUNT : USU PL

cloister /klɔɪstə/, **cloisters, cloistering, cloistered**. 1 A **cloister** is a paved area round a square, especially in a monastery or a cathedral, that is covered with a roof and has one open side facing towards the square and supported by pillars. N COUNT

2 If you **cloister** yourself somewhere, you shut yourself away from the normal life of the world around you; a formal or literary use, often showing disapproval. EG *He cloistered himself in a small corner office.* V+O *(REFL)*+A

cloistered /klɔɪstəd/. If you have a **cloistered** way of life, you live quietly and are not involved in the normal busy life of the world around you. EG *...a young woman who burst into the cloistered life of Paul and Primula Gossett.* ADJ QUALIT : USU ATTRIB = sheltered

clone /kləʊn/, **clones, cloning, cloned**; a technical term. 1 A **clone** is an animal or plant that has been produced artificially, for example in a laboratory, from the cells of another animal or plant with the result that it is identical to the original. N COUNT ⇑ reproduction

2 To **clone** an animal or plant means to produce it as a clone. ◊ **cloning**. EG *Should there be laws to regulate cloning?* V+O ◊ N UNCOUNT

clonk /klɒŋk/, **clonks, clonking, clonked**. When a heavy, solid object **clonks** or when you **clonk** it, it makes a fairly loud, dull sound, for example by hitting something; an informal word. EG *The merry-go-round clonked up and down... I clonked the two buckets gently on to the kitchen floor.* ▸ used as a noun. EG *She put the pan down on the stove with a clonk.* V-ERG : USU+A ⇑ thud = clank ▸ N COUNT ⇑ thud = clank

clop /klɒp/, **clops, clopping, clopped**. When a horse **clops**, its hooves make a noise on the ground as it walks or trots. EG *The horse came clopping along the street.* ● See also **clip clop**. V : USU+A ⇑ plod

close, closes, closing, closed; closer, closest. The word **close** is pronounced /kləʊz/ whenever it is used as a verb and also when it is used as a noun in paragraph 12. It is pronounced /kləʊs/ whenever it is used as an adjective or adverb and also when it is used as a noun in paragraph 27. 1 When something such as a door or the lid of a box **closes** or when you **close** it, it moves so that it covers or fills a hole or a gap. EG *He opened the door and closed it behind him... It took a bit of pressure to make the lid close.* ◊ **closed**. EG *I fell asleep with my window closed tight... He was sitting in his wheelchair with closed eyes.* V-ERG = shut ≠ open ◊ ADJ CLASSIF = shut ≠ open

2 To **close** something such as a road, a border, or an airport means to block it in order to prevent people from using it. EG *The border with Hong Kong was closed just as my wife and daughters reached there.* V+O = shut ≠ open

3 When something such as a shop or a public building **closes** or when you **close** it, work or business stops there for a short period, for example at lunchtime, or until the next working day. EG *Many libraries close on Saturdays at 1 p.m.* ◊ **closed**. EG *It was Sunday and the garage was closed... The shop had a sign saying 'Closed'.* V-ERG = shut ≠ open ◊ ADJ CLASSIF ≠ open

4 If someone **closes** a factory, business, or public building or if it **closes**, all work or activity stops there, usually for ever. EG *The furnaces at Shotton Steelworks were closed with the loss of nearly 8,000 jobs... They had to decide whether or not they should close more railway stations.* V-ERG ⇑ discontinue = shut ≠ open

5 To **close** a subject, conversation, etc means to bring it to an end. EG *He spoke as though he wanted to close the conversation... The case is closed... 'Never,' she said, so firmly that it closed the subject.* ◊ **closing**. EG *...the closing stages of the election campaign... This was the situation during the closing weeks of 1967... He referred to her in his closing speech.* V+O ◊ ADJ CLASSIF : ATTRIB = final

6 If you **close** your account at a bank or a building society, you take all your money out and say that you will not be using the account any more. V+O ⇑ end

7 To **close a deal** with someone means to come to a successful business agreement with them. EG *He was trying to close a deal with the Argus Company.* PHR : VB INFLECTS ⇑ negotiate

8 If a group of people **closes** round you, they come very near to you and surround you. EG *She and her friends closed round me talking loudly.* V+A ⇑ gather = crowd

9 To **close** on someone or something means to get nearer and nearer to them, usually by travelling faster than they are. EG *The man closed on the woman and hurtled past... The second boat was about 200 yards away from us but closing fast.* V : IF+PREP THEN *on* ⇑ approach = gain

10 When a wound **closes** or when something **closes** it, the edges come together and help it to heal. EG *The gash in his leg eventually closed.* V-ERG ⇑ join

11 ● to **close the door on** something: see **door**. ● to **close** your **eyes** to something: see **eye**. ● to **close ranks**: see **rank**. ● See also **closed**.

12 The **close** of a period of time or an activity is the end of it; a rather formal use. EG *The view is best of all towards the close of the day... He vanished mysteriously after the close of business on Saturday night... At the close of the nineteenth century Britain was a wealthy country.* ● If you **bring** something **to a close** or if it **comes to a close** or **draws to a close**, it ends, usually gradually. EG *The war in Europe drew to a close... This dialogue would shortly come to a close.* N SING : *the*+N, IF+PREP THEN *of* ≠ beginning ● PHR : VB INFLECTS ⇑ end

13 Something that is **close** to something else is near to it, often so that the things are almost touching each other. EG *Their two heads were close together... I got close enough to see what the trouble was.* ▸ used as an adverb. EG *She sat close to him and did not speak... The children followed close behind them... He moved a bit closer.* ◊ **closely**. EG *The crowd moved in more closely around him.* ADJ QUALIT : PRED, IF+PREP THEN *to* ≠ far ▸ ADV WITH VB ◊ ADV = tightly

14 The word **close** is also used in the following expressions when you are talking about something being near to you. **14.1** Something that is **close by**, **close at hand**, or **close to hand** is near to you. EG *There was a small lamp on the table close by... A man sitting close by looked up at her... The wood he fetched was close at hand.* **14.2** If you look at something **close up** or **close to**, you look at it when you are very near to it. EG *The butterfly I had spotted proved spectacular close up... On the runways jumbo jets look very big. Therefore close up they should look even bigger... It was my first glimpse of him close to.* **14.3** If you do something **at close range** or **at close quarters**, you do it from a point which is very near to the person or thing that you mention. EG *He shot the President twice at close range... It was a privilege to observe her at such close quarters.* PHR : USED AS AN A = nearby PHR : USED AS AN A PHR : USED AS AN A

15 People who are **close** to each other like each other very much and have similar attitudes and emotions. EG *Father and I are very close... I felt very close to him... Not even my closest friends had any idea that something was wrong.* ▸ used of relationships between people. EG *Their friendship was as close as it had ever been.* ◊ **closeness**. EG *They felt a new closeness in relationships with their friends.* ADJ QUALIT : IF+PREP THEN *to* = intimate, near ◊ N UNCOUNT = intimacy

16 A **close** relative is one who is near to you in family relationships, for example your mother or your sister. EG *She had no very close relatives.* ADJ QUALIT : ATTRIB

17 If you keep **close** contact or a **close** connection with someone, you see them, speak to them, or write to them often, so that you know what is happening to them. EG *It's often difficult for divorced parents to keep in close contact with their children... My sons have maintained extremely close ties with a college friend.* ◊ **closely**. EG *I've always been fond of the theatre, because my family was so closely connected with it.* ADJ QUALIT : ATTRIB ⇑ continuous ◊ ADV WITH VB = strongly

18 People who are **close** partners, advisers, etc work together and are greatly involved in each other's activities. EG *He accepted the suggestions given to him by his closest advisers.* ▸ used of people's behaviour or actions. EG *There was a better way* ADJ QUALIT : ATTRIB = personal, confidential

forward by closer cooperation. ◊ **closely.** EG *Every doctor works closely with the Child Health Service... He was closely involved in monitoring daily progress.* ◊ ADV WITH VB

19 Close inspection or observation of something is careful, thorough, and often very detailed. EG *The plane could not hope to escape the close attention of the our air force... She crossed over to have a closer look at the car... The role the disaster played in the events deserves closer examination.* ◊ **closely.** EG *He studied the photographs very closely... He questioned me closely about the seriousness of our bid.* ADJ QUALIT : ATTRIB; ◊ ADV WITH VB ⇑ carefully = searchingly

20 Something such as a competition or election that is **close** is only won by a small amount. EG *The vote was close... It is close but we are going to win.* ADJ QUALIT

21 If you are **close** to something happening or if it is **close**, it is almost certain to happen soon. EG *We came very close to success... An agreement between the union seems close... She was close to tears.* ADJ QUALIT : PRED, IF+PREP THEN *to* = near

22 Something such as an opinion, emotion, or style that is **close** to something else is almost the same as it. EG *She regarded Lomax with something that was close to fear... My speech is now closer to a Midlands accent than it used to be.* ◊ **closely.** EG *Her dream house has become something much more closely resembling a nightmare.* ● Someone or something that is **the closest thing** to something else mentioned is the person or thing that is most similar to it. EG *Pat Branson was the closest thing to a manual worker among us.* ADJ QUALIT : PRED+*to* ⇑ similar = like; ◊ ADV WITH VB = strongly; ● PHR : USED AS C, USU+TO

23 If the atmosphere is **close**, it is uncomfortable with not enough air; used mainly in British English. EG *The room was hot and close and full of smoke... ...close, tormenting heat.* ◊ **closeness.** EG *She refused to take off the thick sweater she wore despite the closeness of the room.* ADJ QUALIT = stuffy; ◊ N UNCOUNT+SUPP

24 Someone who is **close** about something is silent about it because they want to keep it a secret. EG *Although they all knew the girl was there, the villagers kept close.* ADJ QUALIT = mum

25 Writing that is **close** has very little space between the lines or words. EG *I find it difficult to read such close print.* ◊ **closely.** EG *He used to read these things from closely typewritten scripts.* ADJ QUALIT = dense; ◊ ADV

26 If something is **close to** or **close on** a particular amount, it is slightly less than that amount. EG *The average baby gains close to two pounds a month... The Thompsons face a bill of close to £8,000 for a new roof... In 1983 there were close on three million unemployed in Britain.* PREP+NUM ⇑ about = nearly

27 Close is used in the names of streets to suggest a quiet road of private houses, often a cul-de-sac. EG *They lived at 7 Winchester Close.* N COUNT : ALSO IN NAMES AFTER N

28 Close is also used in the following expressions:
28.1 If you keep **a close eye** or **a close watch** on someone or something, you watch them carefully in order to make sure they are progressing as you want or not causing any trouble. EG *She was able to keep a close eye on her nephews as they grew up.* PHR : USED AS O+*on* ⇑ observe **28.2** If something is **a close shave**, **a close thing**, or a **close call**, it is very near to being an accident or disaster but you just manage to avoid this; used in informal English. EG *It was a very close shave. The car only just missed me.* PHR : USED AS O = narrow escape **28.3** ● **close to the bone**: see **bone**. ● to **bring** something **closer to home**: see **home**.

close down. 1 When a television or radio channel **closes down**, it stops broadcasting for the day. EG *Channel 4 closes down at about midnight most evenings.* ● See also **closedown**. PHRASAL VB : V+ADV = shut down

2 If someone **closes down** a factory, business, or public building, all work or activity stops there, usually for ever. EG *The mines had been closed down following a geological survey.* PHRASAL VB : V-ERG+ADV = shut ≠ open

close in. 1 To **close in** on someone or something means to come nearer and nearer to them and gradually surround them. EG *They closed in on the struggling pig... As the enemy closed in, the resistance of the villagers shrank to nothing.* PHRASAL VB : V+ADV : IF+PREP THEN *on/upon* ⇑ approach = converge

2 When the days **close in**, there are gradually fewer hours of daylight as winter gets nearer. EG *The days seem to be closing in very quickly this year.* PHRASAL VB : V+ADV ⇑ shorten

close off. To **close** something **off** means to separate it or isolate it from other things or people so that nobody can use it or get into it. EG *They lived in a castle in which most of the rooms were permanently closed off... The damage would cause the road to be closed off for hours.* PHRASAL VB : V+O+ADV = shut off

close up. 1 When you **close up** something such as a building or a business or when it **closes up**, you close it completely and securely, often because you are going away for some time. EG *The big house was closed up for the holidays.* PHRASAL VB : V-ERG+ADV = shut up

2 If people **close up**, they move nearer to each other. EG *She told the children to close up to allow everyone into the hall.* PHRASAL VB : V+ADV = move up

close-cropped. Hair or grass that is **close-cropped** is cut very short. EG *One of them had long hair and one was close-cropped with curls... ...a close-cropped golf green.* ADJ QUALIT

closed /kləʊzd/. 1 A **closed** group of people is one that is restricted to only a few people who are chosen or who have special qualifications. EG *He had a fairly closed circle of friends... Britain dearly loves its little closed societies.* ADJ QUALIT : ATTRIB = exclusive

2 If people do something **behind closed doors**, they do it in secret and do not admit other people. EG *On the whole these debates take place behind closed doors.* PHR : USED AS AN A = secretly

3 Something that is **a closed book** is something which you know nothing at all about. EG *Mathematics was a closed book to me all through school.* ● **to have a closed mind**: see **mind**. PHR : USED AS C = mystery

4 Other meanings of **closed** can be found in the entry for **close** in paragraphs **1** and **3**.

closed circuit, closed circuits. A **closed circuit** is an electrical circuit that is complete, so that electricity can flow round it; a technical term. N COUNT

closed-circuit television, closed-circuit televisions. A **closed-circuit television** is a television system that is used within a limited area such as a building, for example one that films customers in a shop so that the owner can identify shoplifters. N COUNT/UNCOUNT

closedown /kləʊzdaʊn/ is the end of broadcasting for the day on the television or radio. N UNCOUNT/COUNT

closed shop, closed shops. A **closed shop** is a factory, shop, or other business in which employees must be members of a particular trade union. EG *Last year's Employment Act laid down that new closed shops might be set up only if 80% of the workforce agreed... ...closed shop agreements with Labour councils.* N COUNT ⇑ monopoly

close-fitting. Clothes that are **close-fitting** fit tightly and show the shape of your body. ADJ QUALIT = tight

close-knit. A group of people who are **close-knit** are closely linked because they share similar social, political, or religious beliefs and activities. EG *In this village you all get to know each other and it's a very close-knit community.* ADJ QUALIT

close season. In Britain, the **close season** in hunting, fishing, and shooting is the time in the year when you are not allowed to kill particular birds, animals, or fish. N COUNT : *the*+N ≠ open season

close-set. Eyes that are **close-set** are very near to each other. EG *Henry squinted his close-set eyes at him.* ADJ QUALIT

closet /klɒzɪt/, **closets, closeting, closeted.** 1 A **closet** is 1.1 a cupboard; used in American English. EG *He took our coats and hung them in the closet.* N COUNT **1.2** a small, private room, for example a bedroom; a rather old-fashioned use. EG *...a closet for private study or prayer.* N COUNT **1.3** a kind of toilet in which you cover the faeces with earth or sand. EG *In a shady corner there was an earth closet.* N COUNT

2 To **closet** yourself in a private place means to spend time there because you want to be alone or you want to talk privately to someone. EG *I closeted myself in my study and read alone for hours.* ◊ **closeted.** EG *Judith is still closeted with those two lawyers... He's closeted away in Bletchley.* V+O (REFL)+A ⇑ confine = shut away, cloister; ◊ ADJ CLASSIF : PRED+A

3 Someone's **closet** beliefs, habits, or feelings are ones which they keep private and secret, often because they are embarrassed about them. EG *...closet fears.* ▸ used of people. EG *...closet alcoholics.* ADJ CLASSIF : ATTRIB

5 If you **come out of the closet**, you reveal that you have a particular belief or habit that you have previously kept secret, often because you are ashamed or embarrassed about it. PHR : VB INFLECTS

close-up, close-ups. A **close-up** is a photograph or a film that is taken very near to the subject so that it shows a lot of detail. EG *The space team anxiously awaited close-ups of the moon... There were some particularly vivid pictures, many of them in close up... The broadcast began with close-up film of babies crying.* N COUNT, OR *in*+N

closing time is the time when a shop, library, pub, etc closes and people have to leave. EG *No admissions are permitted in the hour before closing time... The streets were full of people, for it was closing time in the pubs.* N UNCOUNT/COUNT

closure /kləʊʒə/, **closures**. 1 The **closure** of a business, factory, etc is the permanent shutting of it, usually because it is no longer making a profit. EG *The plan involved the closure of half the national network of railway lines... The merger of the companies resulted in the closures of less profitable factories... Life in the newspaper industry is very bad just now, with papers threatened with closure.* N COUNT/UNCOUNT : USU+SUPP = shutdown ≠ opening

2 The **closure** of a road, border, canal, etc is the blocking of it in order to prevent people from using it. EG *...the closure of the Suez Canal.* N UNCOUNT+SUPP ⇑ blockage

3 A **closure** is something such as a piece of wire or a seal which is used for closing bags, bottles, etc in order to prevent the air from getting inside. EG *She didn't fasten the closure properly and the bread was stale the next morning... For date of manufacture see bag closure or label.* N COUNT ⇑ seal, tag

clot /klɒt/, **clots, clotting, clotted**. 1 A **clot** is a sticky lump that forms as a result of a liquid, especially blood, drying up and becoming thicker. EG *The blood will continue to ooze for some time before a clot forms... ...a blood clot.* N COUNT

2 When blood or another liquid **clots**, it becomes thick and forms into a lump. EG *...a mixture of clotted blood and thick, greyish-yellow slime.* V-ERG = congeal, coagulate

3 You call someone a **clot** when you think they have done or said something stupid or silly; used as a mild but friendly rebuke in informal British English. EG *That's what it's supposed to look like, you clot.* N COUNT/VOC = idiot, fool

cloth /klɒθ/, **cloths**. 1 **Cloth** is fabric which is made from cotton, wool, silk, nylon, etc by weaving, knitting, or other similar process. Cloth is used especially for making clothes. EG *Their women were makers of pots and weavers of cloth... ...strips of cotton cloth.* N MASS = material

2 A **cloth** is a piece of cloth which you use for a particular purpose, such as cleaning something or covering it. EG *Clean with a soft cloth dipped in warm soapy water... ...a table covered with a fine lace cloth.* • See also **dishcloth, face cloth, loincloth, tablecloth**. N COUNT

3 The **cloth** is used to refer to Christian priests and ministers, regarded as a group; a formal or literary use. EG *He has no respect for the cloth... ...a man of the cloth.* N SING : *the*+N = clergy ≠ laity

4 **to cut one's coat according to one's cloth**: see **coat**.

cloth cap, cloth caps. A **cloth cap** is a flat cap with a stiff brim at the front, worn by men. N COUNT ⇑ hat

clothe /kləʊð/, **clothes, clothing, clothed**; a rather formal or literary word. 1 If you are **clothed** in something, you are dressed in it. EG *They were already clothed and breakfasting... Mrs Travers and Mrs Patel followed, both clothed in green.* ADJ CLASSIF : USU PRED, IF+PREP THEN *in* = dress

2 To **clothe** someone means to provide them with clothes to wear. EG *Are we not better fed, better clothed, and better housed than ever before?* V+O (NG/REFL) : USU PASS ⇑ provide for

3 To **clothe** something means to cover it completely. EG *Warm yellow stone now clothes the building.* V+O : IF+PREP THEN *in* = envelop

4 See also **clothes, clothing**.

clothes /kləʊðz/ are the things that people wear, such as shirts, coats, trousers, and dresses. EG *I took off my shoes and all my clothes... They hadn't got any clothes on.* N PLURAL : DET+N, OR *in/with*+N = garments

clothes basket, clothes baskets; also spelled with a hyphen. A **clothes basket** is a basket in which you put dirty clothes before they are washed, or clean, wet clothes before they are dried and ironed. N COUNT = linen basket

clothes horse, clothes horses; also spelled with a hyphen. 1 A **clothes horse** is a folding framework used inside the house to hang wet washing on while it dries. N COUNT

2 You might call someone, especially a woman, a **clothes horse** when you consider that they think too much about their clothes; used showing disapproval. N COUNT

clothes line, clothes lines; also spelled with a hyphen. A **clothes line** is a rope or wire stretched across a garden or sometimes across a room on which wet washing is hung to dry. N COUNT = washing line

clothes peg, clothes pegs; also spelled with a hyphen. A **clothes peg** is, in British English, a small wooden or plastic device which you use to fasten clothes to a clothes line. N COUNT

clothes pin, clothes pins; also spelled with a hyphen. A **clothes pin** is a clothes peg; used in American English. N COUNT

clothing /kləʊðɪŋ/. 1 **Clothing** consists of the things people wear. If you use the word 'clothing' instead of the word 'clothes', you are thinking especially of all the clothes a person has or is wearing or of a particular type of clothes. EG *He'll have waterproof clothing... The big concern has been with food, clothing, and shelter for everyone.* N UNCOUNT = garments

2 **Clothing** is used to describe something which is concerned with the business of designing, manufacturing, or selling clothes. EG *...a clothing factory... ...the clothing industry.* ADJ CLASSIF : ATTRIB

clotted cream is very thick cream made by heating milk gently and taking the cream from the top. It is made and eaten mainly in the south west of England. N UNCOUNT ⇑ food

cloud /klaʊd/, **clouds, clouding, clouded**. 1 A **cloud** is a mass of water vapour that floats in the sky. Clouds are usually white or grey in colour. EG *The air was warm and there were little white clouds high in the blue sky... There is nothing to see from the plane except cloud, stretching to the horizon.* N COUNT/UNCOUNT

2 A **cloud** of smoke, dust, or something similar is a mass of it, floating or moving in the air. EG *Way off in the distance she sees a cloud of smoke.* N COUNT+SUPP ⇑ patch

3 A **cloud** of insects or birds is a very large number of them flying through the air together. EG *Clouds of birds rose from the tree-tops... The mosquitoes were coming up in clouds.* N COUNT+SUPP ⇑ flock

4 If something **clouds** or if you **cloud** it, it becomes less easy to see through. EG *Her cold breath clouded the mirror... My glasses kept clouding up.* V-ERG ⇑ mist up

5 If one things **clouds** another, 5.1 it confuses things so that you cannot understand or judge the situation properly. EG *His explanations clouded the issue.* V+O ≠ clarify **5.2** it affects things so that a situation becomes sadder or more unpleasant than it should be. EG *Insanity clouded the last years of his life.* V+O ⇑ spoil = blight, taint

6 If you are **on cloud nine**, you are very happy, and rather excited; an informal expression. PHR : USED AS AN A

7 If you are **under a cloud**, you are in disgrace and people have a poor opinion of you; an informal expression. EG *I was already under a cloud at the office.* PHR : USED AS AN A

8 If someone **has their head in the clouds**, they are not sufficiently aware of the real situation or its problems, because they are too concerned with their own theories, hopes, or ideals; used in informal English showing disapproval. PHR : VB INFLECTS

cloud over. 1 If it **clouds over** or if the sky **clouds over**, the sky becomes covered with clouds. EG *The sky had clouded over completely... It was clouding over and we thought it was going to rain.* PHRASAL VB : V+ADV ≠ clear

2 If a person's face or eyes **cloud over**, he or she suddenly looks sad or angry. PHRASAL VB : V+ADV

cloudburst /klaʊdbɜːst/, **cloudbursts**. A **cloudburst** is a sudden, very heavy fall of rain. N COUNT ⇑ downpour

cloud-cuckoo-land. If you say that someone is living in **cloud-cuckoo-land**, you mean that they are no longer paying any attention to what life is really like but think that everything is marvellous and will happen exactly as they want it to; used in informal English showing disapproval. N UNCOUNT ⇑ utopia ≠ reality

cloudless /klaʊdlɪ²s/. If the sky is **cloudless**, there are no clouds in it. ADJ CLASSIF ⇑ clear

cloudy /klaʊdi¹/. 1 If it is **cloudy**, there are a lot of clouds in the sky. EG *Tomorrow it will be cold, cloudy and foggy.* ADJ QUALIT ⇑ dull = overcast

2 If something such as a liquid is **cloudy**, it is less clear than it should be. EG *The water there is a cloudy blue.* ADJ QUALIT = murky

3 If ideas, opinions, etc are **cloudy**, they are confused or uncertain. EG *Their policies on this subject seem fairly cloudy.* ADJ QUALIT = unclear

clout /klaʊt/, **clouts, clouting, clouted**; an informal word. 1 To **clout** someone or something means to hit them. EG *I got clouted on the shin by a whirling block of wood... If you don't throw them out, I'm going to clout them.* V+O, OR V+O+A = belt, clobber

2 A **clout** is a fairly hard blow. EG *...a severe reprimand and a few resounding clouts.* N COUNT

3 If someone has **clout**, they have the influence and power to get things done. EG *The committee which meets on Friday has more clout... Ammunition companies grew in wealth and industrial clout.* N UNCOUNT

clove /kləʊv/, **cloves**. 1 A **clove** is a small, dried flower bud which looks like a little brown stick with a round top and is used as a spice in cooking. EG *...one teaspoon of ground cloves.* — N COUNT: USU PLURAL

2 A **clove** of garlic is a small part of a garlic bulb used for flavouring food. EG *Add a crushed clove of garlic.* — N COUNT+SUPP

3 **Clove** is the past tense of **cleave.**

cloven /kləʊvəⁿn/ is the past participle of **cleave.**

cloven hoof /kləʊvəⁿn hu:f/, **cloven hooves**. A **cloven hoof** or a **cloven foot** is the foot of an animal such as a cow, sheep or goat, which is divided into two parts. — N COUNT

clover /kləʊvə/. 1 **Clover** is a small plant with pink or white flowers in the form of a clustered head and three leaves together at the end of each stem. — N UNCOUNT/COUNT

2 If you are **in clover**, you are living a luxurious, comfortable life. — PHR: USED AS AN A

clown /klaʊn/, **clowns, clowning, clowned**. 1 A **clown** is 1.1 a performer in a circus, who dresses in strange clothes, has a brightly painted face, and who does funny or silly things in order to make people laugh. EG *There were performing monkeys, dancers, clowns, and acrobats.* — N COUNT ⇑ comic 1.2 someone who is always telling jokes or doing silly things in order to make people laugh. EG *He enjoys life. He can be rather a clown actually.* — N COUNT: ALSO VOC = joker

2 If you **clown** or **clown around**, you do silly things in order to make people laugh. EG *I clown to please her and the more I clown the less she likes me... They were clowning around when the teacher came in.* — V = lark about, play the fool

3 If you **make a clown of** yourself, you do something very silly which makes you appear foolish. EG *This meeting led Rothermere to make a clown of himself and also of his newspaper.* — PHR: VB INFLECTS ⇑ disgrace

4 You describe someone as a **clown** when you do not have very much respect for them. EG *Any clown with a PhD should be able to teach English.* — N COUNT: ALSO VOC = joker, fool

clownish /klaʊnɪʃ/. People who are **clownish** behave in a rather silly way, so that other people often believe they are foolish. EG *In spite of this rather clownish quality of his, Mr Boggis was not a fool... ...clownish good humour.* — ADJ QUALIT

cloying /klɔɪ:ɪŋ/. Something that is **cloying** is rather unpleasant because it is too sweet or sickly, or because there is too much of it. EG *The drinks of long ago were not so cloying as now... ...cloying sentimentality... ...the cloying scent of flowers.* ◊ **cloyingly**. EG *...cloyingly polite.* — ADJ QUALIT = nauseating; ◊ ADV

club /klʌb/, **clubs, clubbing, clubbed**. 1 A **club** is 1.1 an organization made up of people who are all interested in a particular activity, for example politics, films, or a type of sport. EG *Are you a member of the golf club?... ...the local Liberal club... ...a youth club... ...club members.* — N COUNT: USU+SUPP = association, society 1.2 a place where the members of a club meet. EG *I'll see you at the club.* — N COUNT: USU the/POSS+N ⇑ building

● See also **nightclub**.

2 A **club** is also a thick heavy stick that can be used as a weapon. EG *A heavy blow with a club knocked him senseless... The crowd was dispersed by policemen armed with clubs.* — N COUNT

3 If you **club** someone, you hit them with a thick heavy stick or with anything blunt and heavy. EG *We were going to club him to death.* — V+O

4 A **club** or a **golf club** is a long thin stick with a curved end that is used for hitting the ball in golf. There are several different types of golf club. — N COUNT: USU+SUPP

5 **Clubs** is one of the four suits in a pack of playing cards. Each card in the suit is marked with one or more black symbols in the shape of a leaf with three rounded parts. — N UNCOUNT/COUNT ⇑ suit

club together. If you **club together** for something or to do something, you all give money in order to share the cost of it; a British expression. EG *We all clubbed together to buy her a present when she retired.* — PHRASAL VB: V+ADV, USU+*for/to*-INF ⇑ join in

clubhouse /klʌbhaʊs/, **clubhouses**; also spelled with a hyphen and as two words. A **clubhouse** is the place where the members of a sports club meet. EG *We had a drink in the clubhouse.* — N COUNT ⇑ building

cluck /klʌk/, **clucks, clucking, clucked**. 1 When a hen makes a noise, it **clucks**. EG *From the hen run they could hear the birds clucking over their eggs... The children squatted in the straw like so many clucking hens.* — V ⇑ tut

2 If you **cluck** or **cluck over** someone or something, 2.1 you talk in a way that shows that you disapprove of them or of something that has been done or said. EG *The women clucked disapprovingly over the shortness of her curly hair.* ▸ used as a noun. EG *...a faint cluck of disapproval.* — V OR PHRASAL VB: V+PREP = tut, tut over; ▸ N COUNT 2.2 you talk in a way that shows that you like them or want to make a lot of fuss of them. EG *Elsa clucked over him and kept giving him glasses of orange juice... 'Such a pretty babe,' clucked Mrs Morrison.* ▸ used as a noun. EG *...a cluck of pleasure.* — V, V+QUOTE, OR PHRASAL VB: V+PREP = fuss over; ▸ N COUNT+SUPP

clue /klu:/, **clues**. 1 A **clue** is 1.1 something that provides information about or suggests the answer to a problem that you are trying to solve. EG *The clue to solving our energy problem lies in conservation... The sculpture offers a clue as to how Picasso's last phase must be interpreted... Ralph was puzzled and searched Simon's face for a clue.* — N COUNT: IF+PREP THEN *to* ⇑ sign 1.2 an object or a piece of information that helps the police or a detective discover who committed a crime. EG *The police searched all the houses but found no clues.* — N COUNT: IF+PREP THEN *to* = pointer, lead 1.3 a short piece of writing in a crossword, puzzle, or game which gives the information from which you have to work out the answer. EG *Read out a couple of clues.* — N COUNT ⇑ question

2 If you **haven't a clue** about something, you know nothing about it and have no ideas or suggestions about how it could be done or what the answer to it might be. EG *I hadn't got a clue how to spell it... The whole class haven't a clue what they're doing... 'Where's Nether Wallop?'–'I haven't a clue.'* — PHR: VB INFLECTS = have no idea, haven't the foggiest

clued-up. If someone is **clued-up**, they have a lot of detailed knowledge and information about something; an informal word used showing approval. EG *You really need to have good leaders all clued-up... ...advice that really is clued-up about the technical aspects.* — ADJ QUALIT = on the ball, well-informed

clueless /klu:lɪ²s/. If you describe someone as **clueless**, you mean that you think they are stupid and incapable of doing anything properly. — ADJ QUALIT = gormless

clump /klʌmp/, **clumps, clumping, clumped**. 1 A **clump** is 1.1 a small group of plants, people, buildings, or other things growing or standing together. EG *...a clump of thistles... ...primroses growing underneath in little clumps... ...a little clump of buildings.* — N COUNT+SUPP: IF SING, VB CAN BE SING OR PL = cluster 1.2 a large lump of earth. EG *We didn't break the clumps up until later in the year.* — N COUNT ⇑ piece

2 If people or things **clump** together, they gather together or are found near each other and so form a small group. EG *...mud houses clumped together on the hill.* — V ⇑ cluster

3 If someone **clumps** about or around, they walk with heavy, rather clumsy footsteps. EG *My sister came clumping back in her wellingtons... Stop clumping around.* — V+A = stomp

4 If something **clumps** down or on to something else, or someone **clumps** it down, it drops down with a thudding sound. EG *Something clumped heavily onto the deck.* — V-ERG+A ⇑ falls = thuds

clumsy /klʌmzi¹/, **clumsier, clumsiest**. 1 Someone who is **clumsy** moves or handles things in a careless, awkward way, often with the result that things are knocked over or broken. EG *He's careless and clumsy and uncoordinated... My fingers were too clumsy to handle it properly... Oh how clumsy of me!* ◊ **clumsily**. EG *She stumbled clumsily, as though drunk, and sat down.* ◊ **clumsiness**. EG *My natural clumsiness defied the delicate ballet steps.* — ADJ QUALIT ≠ careful; ◊ ADV; ◊ N UNCOUNT

2 Something that is **clumsy** is not neat in design, appearance, or construction, and is often difficult and awkward to use. EG *The weapon felt clumsy in my hand... Mechanical switches, he had found, were too clumsy and unreliable... Her knees showed pink above her clumsy wellingtons.* ◊ **clumsily**. EG *The furniture was clumsily designed... ...clumsily controlled heat.* — ADJ QUALIT = gauche ≠ elegant, neat; ◊ ADV

3 If something is done or said in a way that is **clumsy**, it is dealt with or expressed carelessly, tactlessly, or with little thought for how it could best be done. EG *Haldane's efforts at rehabilitation were clumsy and naive... The document was an example of clumsy diplomacy.* ◊ **clumsily**. EG *...a clumsily phrased apology... The treaty was clumsily drawn and to our disadvantage.* ◊ **clumsiness**. EG *Clumsiness or bullying on the part of the therapist will certainly cause the patient distress... He blamed Felix's legal clumsiness for the plan going awry.* — ADJ QUALIT = insensitive ≠ subtle; ◊ ADV; ◊ N UNCOUNT

clung /klʌŋ/ is the past tense and past participle of **cling**.

clunk /klʌŋk/, **clunks, clunking, clunked.** A **clunk** is a sound made by heavy wood, metal, or stone objects hitting against each other. EG *There was a metallic clunk as the gun struck the ground.* [N COUNT : USU SING ↑ clang]

cluster /klʌstə/, **clusters, clustering, clustered.** 1 A **cluster** is 1.1 a number of things gathered close together in a small group, especially around a central point. EG *There was a little cluster of admirers round the guest speaker... ...a cluster of cottages.* [N COUNT+SUPP = bunch] 1.2 a number of things of the same type growing close together. EG *I'm surprised I didn't find a cluster of mushrooms growing under there... ...the cluster of short hair at the back of her head.* [N COUNT+SUPP ↑ group = bunch]

2 If things **cluster** together, they gather or are found together in a small group, especially around a central point. EG *Passengers in the dining car were clustered round a radio... ...a hill where the white buildings clustered together.* [V : USU+A]

clutch /klʌtʃ/, **clutches, clutching, clutched.** 1 If you **clutch** something or **clutch** at something, you hold it tightly with your hand, usually because you are afraid or anxious. EG *The boy's mother was sitting in front of the desk, clutching a handkerchief... ... desperately clutching at her arm... ...with the baby clutched tightly in her arms... The bird managed to escape his clutching hands.* [V+O, OR V+A = grasp, grip] ▸ used as a noun. EG *...the small, cold clutch of his son... His fingers grasped John's flesh with a convulsive clutch.* [▸ N COUNT]

2 If a person or group has someone or something in their **clutches**, they have tremendous power, control, or influence over them; used showing disapproval. EG *Smith still has the press in his clutches... He escaped the clutches of the welfare service and the law.* [N PLURAL = grasp, grip]

3 The **clutch** in a car or other vehicle is the mechanism which allows the power from the engine to be disconnected from the wheels when you change gear; also used for the pedal which you press to make this happen. EG *He started his car and let out the clutch far too quickly.* [N COUNT]

4 A **clutch** is 4.1 a group of eggs laid by a bird. EG *They only lay a relatively small number of eggs in a clutch.* [N COUNT ↑ batch] 4.2 a small group of things. EG *I did a clutch of films in succession... ...her best hat, with a great clutch of bright red cherries pinned on its side.* [N COUNT = stack, bunch]

clutch at. If you **clutch** at something, you desperately attempt to use it for a particular reason, especially as an excuse or in order to solve a problem. EG *People clutch at the remnants of their self esteem... She would have clutched at any excuse to miss school for the day.* • **to clutch at straws**: see **straw.** [PHRASAL VB : V+PREP, HAS PASS = grasp at, hold on to ≠ let go of]

clutch bag, clutch bags; also spelled with a hyphen. A **clutch bag** is a handbag without a handle which a woman carries under her arm or in her hand. [N COUNT]

clutter /klʌtə/, **clutters, cluttering, cluttered.** 1 **Clutter** is a lot of things in an untidy state, especially things that are not useful or necessary. EG *The rooms were full of clutter... Brody eyed the clutter of pots and packages.* [N UNCOUNT]

2 If you **clutter** something such as a room or you **clutter** it **up**, you fill it untidily with a lot of unnecessary things. EG *I don't have much time for girls who overdose and clutter up the wards... He didn't want to clutter his mind with information.* [V+O, OR PHRASAL VB : V+O+ADV, IF+PREP THEN with ↑ fill up] ◊ **cluttered.** EG *He glanced around the small, cluttered room... The drive was cluttered with half a dozen cars.* [◊ ADJ QUALIT]

cm is an abbreviation for 'centimetre'. EG *...two rolls of sterile bandage 5 cm wide.*

CND is a British organization which opposes the development and use of nuclear weapons; an abbreviation for 'Campaign for Nuclear Disarmament'. EG *He was also a member of CND... Don't forget to wear your CND badge.* [N PROPER : ALSO the+N]

c/o. You write **c/o** before an address on an envelope or parcel when you want to send it to someone who works at that address or who is a guest or lodger at someone else's house; an abbreviation for 'care of'. EG *Mr A D Bright, c/o Sherman Ltd, 62 Burton Road, Bristol 8.* [PREP+N PROPER/NAME]

co- is added 1 to some verbs or nouns, in order to form other verbs or nouns that refer to people sharing things or doing things together. EG *...ownership→co-ownership... ...operate→co-operate... ...exist→coexist.* [PREFIX] 2 to nouns that refer to people who do a job or task, in order to form other nouns that refer to people who share a job or task with someone else. EG *...author→co-author... ...director→co-director... ...driver→co-driver.* [PREFIX]

Co. 1 **Co.** is an abbreviation for 'company', when it is part of the name of an organization. EG *...Seagram Co. Ltd... ...Morris, Marshall, Faulkner & Co.* [N SING : USED IN NAMES AFTER N]

2 **'and co.'** is also used to refer to a group of people associated with a particular person; usually used showing disapproval. EG *The time may be coming for Mrs Thatcher and co. to redeem themselves over the Budget Day gaffe.* [PHR : N PROPER +PHR]

3 **Co.** is also a written abbreviation for 'county'. It is used before the names of some counties, especially in Ireland. EG *...Co. Donegal.* [N BEFORE N = County]

C.O. is an abbreviation for 'commanding officer'. EG *The C.O. sent out patrols three times... He was viewed with suspicion by Alec's C.O.*

coach /kəʊtʃ/, **coaches, coaching, coached.** 1 A **coach** is 1.1 a large motor vehicle which carries passengers on long journeys by road; used in British English. EG *They travelled into London on the same coach... We usually go by coach... ...a coach trip.* [N COUNT, OR by+N = bus] 1.2 a vehicle carrying passengers that is part of a train; used in British English. EG *He conducted his electioneering tour in a private railway coach... Troops piled into the coaches.* [N COUNT = carriage] 1.3 an enclosed vehicle on four wheels pulled by horses in which passengers used to travel. Coaches are still used for ceremonial events. EG *Whitehall comes to life when the state coaches ride down it towards Parliament.* [N COUNT, OR by+N = carriage]

2 If you **coach** someone, 2.1 you train them in a particular sport. EG *She had been coached by a former Wimbledon champion.* [V OR V+O ↑ instruct] 2.2 you give them special teaching, especially in order to prepare them for an examination. EG *I used to coach in French... ...an actor coached for his part.* [V OR V+O ↑ teach = tutor]

3 A **coach** is also 3.1 someone who trains a person or a team of people in a particular sport. EG *He became their fulltime professional coach... ...a famous football coach.* [N COUNT ↑ instructor = trainer] 3.2 someone who gives people special teaching, especially in order to prepare them for examinations. [N COUNT = tutor]

coach-and-four, coach-and-fours. A **coach-and-four** was a coach pulled by four horses. EG *In 1825 a Mr Hunt drove a coach-and-four across the frozen Serpentine.* [N COUNT ↑ transport]

coachload /kəʊtʃləʊd/, **coachloads**; also spelled with a hyphen. A **coachload** is a large group of people who travel somewhere in a motor coach. EG *A whole coachload of football fans descended on our little cafe.* [N COUNT : ALSO N PART]

coachman /kəʊtʃmə^{3}n/, **coachmen.** A **coachman** was a man who drove a horse-drawn coach. EG *...a liveried coachman and groom.* [N COUNT ↑ driver]

coach park, coach parks; also spelled with a hyphen. A **coach park** is a place where coaches and buses are allowed to park; used in British English. [N COUNT]

coach station, coach stations. A **coach station** is a building where coaches leave from or arrive at on regular journeys; used in British English. [N COUNT = terminal]

coagulate /kəʊægjə^{4}leɪt/, **coagulates, coagulating, coagulated.** When a liquid such as paint or blood **coagulates**, or when something **coagulates** it, it becomes very thick. [V-ERG ↑ thicken = congeal, clot] ◊ **coagulation** /kəʊægjə^{4}leɪʃə^{0}n/. EG *They checked his arteries and lungs and timed his coagulation rate.* [◊ N UNCOUNT = clotting]

coal /kəʊl/, **coals.** 1 **Coal** is a hard black substance that is taken from under the earth and burned as a fuel. EG *They extract 10,000,000 tons of coal each year... ...the coal mining industry... Put another lump of coal on the fire... ...coal fires.* [N UNCOUNT ↑ mineral]

2 **Coals** are pieces of coal, especially when they are burning. EG *There were red coals in the grate... ...fat antelope haunches roasting over glowing coals.* [N COUNT : USU PL]

3 If you **take** or **carry coals to Newcastle**, you supply something to someone although they already have plenty of it. EG *Selling ice cream to the Italians? That's taking coals to Newcastle, isn't it?* [PHR : VB INFLECTS]

4 If a person in authority **hauls** or **drags** someone **over the coals**, he or she speaks to them severely about something wrong or foolish that they have done; an informal expression. EG *His editor hauled him over the coals for missing the story.* [PHR : VB INFLECTS ↑ reprimand]

coal black; also spelled with a hyphen. Something that is **coal black** is really black and not just dark grey or dark brown. [ADJ COLOUR]

coalesce /kəʊəlɛs/, **coalesces, coalescing, coalesced.** If two or more things **coalesce**, they come together and form a larger group or system; a formal word. EG *There is a tendency for both political and industrial systems to coalesce into large units.* — V; ↑ unite; = fuse

coalescence /kəʊəlɛsəns/is a process in which separate things come together and form a larger group or system; a formal word. — N UNCOUNT; ↑ union

coalface /kəʊlfeɪs/, **coalfaces**; also spelled with a hyphen and as two words. In a coal mine, the **coalface** is the part where the coal is being cut out of the surrounding rock. EG *The aim is to concentrate coal-mining in fewer coalfaces, with a higher output from each.* — N COUNT

coalfield /kəʊlfiːld/, **coalfields**. A **coalfield** is a region where there is coal under the ground. EG *...the South Yorkshire coalfield.* — N COUNT

coal gas is gas produced from coal. It is used especially for heating and cooking in people's homes: compare **natural gas**. EG *We used coal gas before natural gas came in... It might be necessary to convert the whole country back to coal gas.* — N UNCOUNT

coalition /kəʊəlɪʃəⁿn/, **coalitions**. A **coalition** is 1 a government consisting of people from two or more political parties who have decided to work together in order to govern. EG *Do you think the coalition can survive?... ...the fall of Asquith's Coalition Government... The Free Democrats have served as coalition partners with both the CDU and the SPD.* — N COUNT; ↑ alliance **2** a group or organization consisting of people from different political or social groups who are cooperating to achieve a particular aim. EG *...a broad coalition of community groups in the area.* — N COUNT; = amalgamation

coalman /kəʊlməⁿn/, **coalmen**. A **coalman** is a man who delivers coal to people's houses. EG *Ellen was standing at the front door, talking to the coalman.* — N COUNT

coalminer /kəʊlmaɪnə/, **coalminers**; also spelled with a hyphen. A **coalminer** is a man whose job is getting coal from under the ground. — N COUNT; ↑ worker; = miner

coal scuttle, coal scuttles; also spelled with a hyphen. A **coal scuttle** is a bucket for keeping coal in. It is specially shaped so that you can tip coal from it onto a fire more easily. — N COUNT

coal tar is a thick black liquid made from coal which is used for making drugs and chemical products. — N UNCOUNT; ↑ substance

coarse /kɔːs/, **coarser, coarsest**. **1** Something that is **coarse 1.1** has a rough texture. EG *...coarse white cloth... ...the coarse pink skin of her neck.* — ADJ QUALIT **1.2** consists of large particles or thick strands. EG *...coarse salt... ...his long coarse hair... The bank was covered with coarse grass.* — ADJ QUALIT; ≠ fine

2 Someone who is **coarse** talks and behaves in a rather rude and offensive way. EG *...a big, coarse man from somewhere in the north of England.* — ADJ QUALIT; = vulgar ▸ also used to describe things that people say. EG *He objected to her coarse and offensive remarks.* — ▸ = crude ◊ **coarsely**. EG *She speaks rather coarsely.* — ◊ ADV WITH VB ◊ **coarseness**. EG *With deliberate coarseness, he wiped his mouth with the back of his hand.* — ◊ N UNCOUNT; ≠ fastidiousness

3 Something such as food or wine that is **coarse** is ordinary and not very enjoyable. EG *She survived on coarse food... ...the coarse red wine.* — ADJ QUALIT; = plain

coarse fishing is the sport of catching fish that live in lakes or rivers and that are not trout or salmon; used in British English: compare **fly-fishing**. — N UNCOUNT; ↑ angling

coarsen /kɔːsəⁿn/, **coarsens, coarsening, coarsened.** If something or someone **coarsens** or **is coarsened**, they become less polite; used especially of people's behaviour and speech. EG *Manners in social life have been coarsened... She had coarsened since she married Charlie.* — V-ERG; ↑ deteriorate; = roughen

coast /kəʊst/, **coasts, coasting, coasted**. **1** A **coast** is **1.1** the edge of an area of land where the land meets the sea. EG *He landed on the coast of South Carolina... ...the rugged coast of Maine...* — N COUNT : IF SING USU the+N **1.2** the part of a country that is next to a sea. EG *We had made up our minds to stay on the East Coast... ...a promoter of women's tennis on the West Coast... ...the industrial cities of the coast.* — N COUNT : USU the+N IN SING; ↑ area

2 If something is **off** the **coast**, it is in the sea and near to the coast. EG *...a trawler fishing off the coast of Portugal.* — PHR : USED AS AN A, USU+of

3 If something happens or exists **from coast to coast**, it happens or exists in every part of a large country which has two or more coasts. EG *From coast to coast this newspaper has been attacked.* — PHR : USED AS AN A

4 If you say that **the coast is clear**, you mean that a particular danger is no longer there, and you can now move about safely. EG *Another twenty minutes and the coast would be clear... See if the coast is clear.* — PHR : VB INFLECTS

5 If a vehicle is **coasting**, it is continuing to move without being driven by its motor, or without being pushed or pedalled, usually down a slope. EG *I put in the clutch and let the car coast for a second or two.* — V

6 If you are **coasting** or **coasting along**, you are doing something without difficulty, worry, or effort; used in informal English. EG *We were coasting along quite nicely until he started interfering.* — V OR PHRASAL VB : V+ADV/PREP : USU CONT; ↑ progress; = sail

coastal /kəʊstəⁿl/ means in the sea or on the land near a coast. EG *Sea lions inhabit the coastal waters... ...the big coastal cities of the USA...* — ADJ CLASSIF : ATTRIB

coaster /kəʊstə/, **coasters**. A **coaster** is **1** a ship that sails along a coast taking goods to ports on the coast. — N COUNT **2** a small mat that you put underneath a glass or a bottle in order to protect the surface of a table. EG *The waitress put a paper coaster down.* — N COUNT ● See also **roller-coaster**.

coastguard /kəʊstgɑːd/, **coastguards**. A **coastguard** is an official who watches the sea near a coast, in order to get help for swimmers, sailors, and ships when they need it, and to prevent smuggling. — N COUNT ▸ The **coastguard** refers to the organization to which coastguards belong, or the service which they provide. EG *He called the Coastguard Station at Montauk.* — ▸ N SING : the+N

coastline /kəʊstlaɪn/, **coastlines**. A **coastline** is the outline of a coast, especially as it appears when you see it from the sea or from an aeroplane. EG *He looked back from the deck of the ship at the faint coastline of his country... ...a rocky and treacherous coastline.* — N COUNT : USU SING

coat /kəʊt/, **coats, coating, coated**. **1** A **coat** is **1.1** a piece of clothing with long sleeves that you wear over other clothes, especially in order to keep you warm or to protect you from bad weather. EG *She was wearing a heavy tweed coat... Get your coats on... She took out a book from her coat pocket.* — N COUNT; ↑ garment; = overcoat **1.2** the same as a jacket. — N COUNT

2 An animal's **coat** is the layer of fur or hair on its body that keeps it warm and protects it. EG *...a coat of dark bristly hair... It has developed a long and shaggy coat to protect it from the cold.* — N COUNT : USU+SUPP; ↑ covering

3 To **coat** something with something else means to cover it with a thin layer of a substance. EG *The sweets are then coated with chocolate... My face was coated with a fine layer of dust.* — V+O : USU PASS+with ▸ used as a noun. EG *Give it a coat of polish ... ...two coats of white paint.* — ▸ N COUNT : IF+PREP THEN of

4 If you **cut** your **coat according to** your **cloth**, you do not try to do more than you have the money, power, or ability to do. EG *We've just got to cut our coat according to our cloth.* — PHR : VB INFLECTS

-coated combines with nouns to form adjectives that describe something as being covered with a thin layer of a particular substance. EG *...slime-coated masonry.* — COMB : FORMS ADJ CLASSIFS

coat hanger, coat hangers; often spelled with a hyphen. A **coat hanger** is a curved piece of wood, metal, or plastic that you hang clothes on. Coat hangers have a hook in the middle which you can attach to something such as a rail. EG *I never seem to have enough coat hangers.* — N COUNT; ↑ bar

coating /kəʊtɪŋ/, **coatings**. A **coating** is a thin layer of something spread over a surface. EG *...a coating of dust.* — N COUNT+SUPP : USU SING; = film

coat of arms, coats of arms. A **coat of arms** is a design in the form of a shield with special patterns on it that is used as an emblem by a town, noble family, or other organization. EG *...the family coat of arms.* — N COUNT; ↑ device

coat of mail, coats of mail. A **coat of mail** is a piece of armour made of small metal rings linked together, which medieval soldiers wore over the top part of their bodies for protection. — N COUNT

coat-tails ; also spelled as one word. A man's **coat-tails** are two long pieces of material that hang down at the back of his dress coat. EG *My father once got his coat-tails stuck in a lift door.* — N PLURAL

2 If you **ride on** someone or something's **coat-tails**, you take advantage of something that they have done, without making any real effort yourself; an informal expression. EG *The Europeans could ride on* — PHR : VB INFLECTS; ↑ exploit *the coat-tails of US technology... He made his fortune riding on the coat-tails of a successful gimmick.*

co-author, co-authors. The **co-authors** of a book, play, etc are two or more people who have written it together. EG *...Robert Stobaugh, co-author of 'Energy Future'.* — N COUNT ↑ writer

coax /kəʊks/, **coaxes, coaxing, coaxed.** 1 If you **coax** someone to do something, you try to persuade them to do it by speaking in a gentle and pleasant way to them. EG *You just coax them into doing it... 'It won't hurt you,' Marsha coaxed.* ◊ **coaxing.** EG *...a coaxing and obsequious voice.* — V, V+QUOTE, V+O+to-INF, OR V+O : USU+A (into/out of) = cajole; ◊ ADJ QUALIT = wheedling

2 If you **coax** something such as information out of someone, you obtain it from them by behaving in a gentle and pleasant way towards them. EG *He coaxed out of me what I really felt about the film.* — V+O+A (out of) ↑ get = wheedle

3 If you **coax** a machine or device into doing something, you make it work by operating it very slowly, gently, or carefully. EG *He really enjoys himself attempting to coax his machines off the ground.* ◊ **coaxing.** EG *...door-handles that did not work without coaxing.* — V+O+A ↑ persuade = ease; ◊ N UNCOUNT

cob /kɒb/, **cobs.** A **cob** is a round loaf of bread; a British word. — N COUNT

cobalt /kəʊbɒlt, -bɔ:lt/ is 1 a hard silvery-white metal which is used in hardening steel and for producing a blue colouring substance. — N UNCOUNT 2 a deep greenish-blue colour. EG *The river below her was cobalt... ...that infinite dome of cobalt blue.* — ADJ COLOUR

cobber /kɒbə/ is an informal term that Australian men use to address each other by. — VOC = mate

cobble /kɒbəᵒl/, **cobbles, cobbling, cobbled.** **Cobbles** are cobblestones laid down as a road surface. EG *...across the expanse of cobbles and into the Boulevard de Montparnasse.* — N COUNT : USU PL = cobblestone

cobble together. If you **cobble** something **together**, you make or produce it roughly or quickly, especially by using things that you can easily find or get hold of; an informal expression, used showing disapproval. EG *Its author has cobbled together a guide to the islands... They tried to cobble together a compromise.* — PHRASAL VB : V+O+ADV

cobbled /kɒbəᵒld/. A street, square, etc that is **cobbled** has a surface made of cobblestones. EG *...a cobbled yard.* — ADJ CLASSIF ↑ paved

cobbler /kɒblə/, **cobblers.** 1 A **cobbler** is a person who mends or makes shoes for a living; a rather old-fashioned word. EG *Joyce was the daughter of the village cobbler.* — N COUNT ↑ craftsman = shoemaker

2 If you describe something that someone has just said as **cobblers**, you mean that it is nonsense; used in informal British English. EG *Cobblers!... What a lot of cobblers!* — EXCLAM = rubbish

cobblestone /kɒbəᵒlstəʊn/, **cobblestones.** A **cobblestone** is a hard rectangular stone with a rounded upper surface which was once used for making roads. EG *...the cold cobblestones of the market place... ...the old cobblestone courtyard.* — N COUNT ↑ stone = cobble

cob-nut, cob-nuts. A **cob-nut** is the same as a hazel nut; a fairly old-fashioned word. — N COUNT

cobra /kəʊbrə/, **cobras.** A **cobra** is a large, poisonous snake which can make the skin at the back of its head into a large hood. — N COUNT

cobweb /kɒbwεb/, **cobwebs.** 1 A **cobweb** is the net which a spider makes for catching insects. EG *Drops of moisture hung in the hedges and cobwebs... In the corners were pockets of dust enriched with cobweb.* — N COUNT/UNCOUNT

2 If something **blows the cobwebs away** or **clears away the cobwebs**, it makes you feel more mentally alert and lively when you had previously been feeling tired. EG *A walk in the fresh air might help to blow some of the cobwebs away.* — PHR : VB INFLECTS

cobwebbed /kɒbwεbd/. Something that is **cobwebbed** is covered with cobwebs. EG *...the dusty cobwebbed bulb.* — ADJ CLASSIF

Coca-Cola /kəʊkəkəʊlə/; a trademark. **Coca-Cola** is a non-alcoholic fizzy brown drink. EG *Do you want a Coca-Cola?* — N MASS = Coke

cocaine /kəᵋkeɪn/ is a drug which people take for pleasure but which they can then become addicted to. Cocaine is sometimes used by doctors as an anaesthetic. — N UNCOUNT

coccyx /kɒksɪks/, **coccyxes.** The **coccyx** is the small triangular bone at the lower end of the spine in human beings and some apes. — N COUNT

cochineal /kɒtʃɪni:l/ is a red substance that is used for colouring food and is obtained from an insect. — N UNCOUNT ↑ dye

cock /kɒk/, **cocks, cocking, cocked.** 1 A **cock** is an adult male chicken. EG *Cocks began to crow.* — N COUNT = cockerel

2 **Cock** is the term for a male bird of any kind, when you want to distinguish it from the female. EG *Not knowing at first that he was a cock bird, we called him Polly... ...a cock pheasant.* — N COUNT : USU BEFORE N

3 If you describe a man as **the cock of the walk** you mean that he behaves as if he is superior to other people in a group; used showing disapproval. — PHR : USED AS C = big head

4 A man's **cock** is his penis; a very rude word. — N COUNT

5 If you describe something that someone has said as **cock**, you mean that you think it is nonsense or rubbish; a rude and offensive word used in very informal British English. — N UNCOUNT

6 **Cock** is also a term of address used by men to one another when they are talking in an informal and friendly way. EG *Hello, cock, how are you?* — VOC = mate

7 If you **cock** a part of your body in a particular direction, you lift and turn it in that direction. EG *He cocked a thumb back... Then he stepped back, his head cocked to one side, to admire his work... A stray dog cocked his leg against a lamp-post.* — V+O : USU+A ↑ raise

8 If you **keep** your **ears** or **eyes cocked**, you are listening or watching very carefully for something. EG *She kept her ears cocked for any mention of her name... We try to keep half an eye cocked.* — PHR : VB AND N INFLECT ↑ be alert ● If you **cock an ear** in a particular direction, you are listening carefully for any sound from that direction. EG *He cocked an ear towards the stairs.* — ● PHR : VB INFLECTS, USU+A ↑ listen

9 To **cock** a gun means to set the hammer so that the gun is ready to fire. EG *I heard the sentry cock his sub-machine gun... The gun was loaded and cocked.* — V+O

10 A **cock** is also a tap or knob that controls the flow of liquid or gas through a pipe. — N COUNT = stopcock

cock up. If you **cock** something **up**, you do it so badly that you completely ruin or spoil it. EG *We don't want to cock the whole thing up.* ● See also **cock-up.** — PHRASAL VB : V+O+ADV = foul up

cock-a-hoop. If you are **cock-a-hoop**, you are extremely pleased about something you have done; an informal expression. — ADJ CLASSIF : PRED, IF+PREP THEN *about* = exultant

cock-and-bull story, cock-and-bull stories. A **cock-and-bull story** is an improbable or unbelievable story, especially one that is given as an excuse; an informal expression. EG *He gave me some cock-and-bull story about his brother being a film star.* — N COUNT = tall tale

cockatoo /kɒkətu:, kɒkətu:/, **cockatoos.** A **cockatoo** is a parrot from Australia and New Guinea which has a crest on its head. — N COUNT

cockcrow /kɒkkrəʊ/ is the dawn; a literary word. EG *We had to be up at cockcrow.* — N UNCOUNT : USU at+N

cocked hat, cocked hats. A **cocked hat** is a hat with three corners that used to be worn with some uniforms. — N COUNT ● If you say that one thing **knocks** or **beats** something else **into a cocked hat**, you mean that it is much better or much more successful than the other thing. EG *This certainly knocks knitting into a cocked hat.* — ● PHR : VB INFLECTS ↑ outdo = beat

cockerel /kɒkəᵒrəl/, **cockerels.** A **cockerel** is a young cock. — N COUNT = cock

cocker spaniel, cocker spaniels. A **cocker spaniel** is a small dog with silky hair and long ears. — N COUNT

cockeyed /kɒkaɪd/. 1 If something is **cockeyed**, it is not straight but twisted to one side. EG *It did not sink immediately, but floated at a cockeyed angle, bobbing on the surface.* — ADJ QUALIT = lopsided ≠ straight

2 If an idea, scheme, etc is **cockeyed**, it is stupid and very unlikely to succeed. EG *That sounds a cockeyed way of going about things.* — ADJ QUALIT ↑ foolish = crazy

cockfight /kɒkfaɪt/, **cockfights.** A **cockfight** is a fight between two cocks which have sharp pieces of metal fixed to their claws, that people watch for entertainment and to bet on. — N COUNT ↑ fight

cockle /kɒkəᵒl/, **cockles.** 1 A **cockle** is an edible shellfish. EG *...trays of freshwater cockles.* — N COUNT : USU PL

2 If something **warms the cockles of** your **heart**, it makes you feel pleased. EG *It warms the cockles of my heart to hear you talk like that.* — PHR : VB AND *heart* INFLECT

cockleshell /kɒkəᵒlʃεl/, **cockleshells.** A **cockleshell** is 1 the shell of a cockle. — N COUNT 2 a small light boat. — N COUNT

cockney /kɒkniᴵ/, **cockneys.** 1 A **cockney** is a person who was born in the East End of London. EG *The cockneys don't pronounce their h's... ...Cockney taxi drivers.* — N COUNT

2 **Cockney** is the dialect and accent of the East End — N UNCOUNT

of London. EG *We heard him speak to her in real Cockney... ...a cockney accent.*

cockpit /kɒkpɪt/, **cockpits.** 1 A **cockpit** is 1.1 the area of a small plane where the pilot sits to control the aircraft. 1.2 the driver's compartment in a racing car. — N COUNT: IF SING USU *the*+N; N COUNT: IF SING USU *the*+N

2 A **cockpit** is also an area where a battle or contest takes place. EG *Iran is now the cockpit between the China-Japan and EEC spheres of influence.* — N COUNT = arena

cockroach /kɒkrəʊtʃ/, **cockroaches.** A **cockroach** is a large brown insect that is especially found in dirty rooms and places where food is kept. — N COUNT

cockscomb /kɒkskəʊm/, **cockscombs.** A **cockscomb** is the red growth that a cock has on its head. — N COUNT

cocksure /kɒkʃʊə, -ʃɔː/. If someone is **cocksure**, they are too confident and sure of their own abilities; used showing disapproval. EG *He was a plump, cocksure man... He oughtn't to be too cocksure about that.* ▸ used of behaviour and attitude. EG *...her cocksure attitude.* — ADJ QUALIT ≠ timid, uncertain; ▸ = arrogant

cocktail /kɒkteɪl/, **cocktails.** 1 A **cocktail** is 1.1 an alcoholic drink which contains several ingredients including one or more spirits. EG *...a champagne cocktail... I'd just come from cocktails at the Hogans'... ...a cocktail party.* 1.2 a small portion of shellfish, grapefruit, or some other food, which is eaten at the beginning of a meal. EG *The waitress brought Ellen's shrimp cocktail.* • See also **fruit cocktail.** 1.3 something which is made by combining a number of different things, especially if these things are not usually combined in this way. EG *I never use a single worm on the hook, preferring a cocktail of worm and maggot.* • See also **Molotov cocktail.** — N COUNT; N COUNT: MOD+N ⇑ starter; N COUNT+SUPP ⇑ combination = mixture

2 A **cocktail** dress or other piece of clothing is one that is suitable for formal occasions. — N BEFORE N

cock-up /kɒkʌp/, **cock-ups.** A **cock-up** is something that is done very badly because of mistakes or stupidity; a rude word used in very informal English. EG *There has been a series of cock-ups.* — N COUNT ⇑ mistake

cocky /kɒki[1]/, **cockier, cockiest.** If you are **cocky**, you are very sure of yourself and perhaps rather cheeky. EG *Don't be too cocky... ...this cocky young woman.* ◇ **cockily.** EG *'I know what I'm doing', said the old man cockily.* ◇ **cockiness.** — ADJ = conceited; ◇ ADV; ◇ N UNCOUNT

cocoa /kəʊkəʊ/ is 1 a brown powder which is made from the crushed seeds of the cacao tree, and which is used in making chocolate. 2 a hot drink made from cocoa powder and milk or water. EG *...a cup of cocoa.* ▸ also used to refer to a cup of cocoa. EG *Do you want a cocoa?* 3 a medium brown colour. — N UNCOUNT; N UNCOUNT; ▸ N COUNT; ADJ COLOUR

coconut /kəʊkənʌt/, **coconuts.** 1 A **coconut** is a large fruit which has a hard hairy shell and inside contains milky juice and white flesh which you can eat. — N COUNT

2 **Coconut** is the white flesh of the coconut, especially when it is chopped into tiny pieces and used to flavour cakes and other food. — N UNCOUNT ⇑ food

coconut matting is a coarse, straw-coloured mat that is used for covering the floor and is made from the fibre from the outer shell of coconuts. — N UNCOUNT ⇑ matting

coconut palm, coconut palms. A **coconut palm** is a tree on which coconuts grow. — N COUNT

coconut shy, coconut shies. A **coconut shy** is a stall at a fair where you throw balls to try and hit coconuts off stands in order to win a prize. — N COUNT

cocoon /kəkuːn/, **cocoons, cocooning, cocooned.** 1 A **cocoon** is 1.1 a covering of silky threads that the larvae of moths and other insects make for themselves before they grow into adults: compare **chrysalis.** EG *The larva will attach itself to a plant and spin a cocoon.* 1.2 something that wraps you up like a cocoon. EG *I had wound myself in a cocoon of bedclothes.* 1.3 something that makes you feel protected and safe. EG *I lived in a cocoon of love and warmth.* — N COUNT ⇑ case; N COUNT: IF+PREP THEN *of*; N COUNT: IF+PREP THEN *of*

2 To **cocoon** something means to wrap it up completely, especially in order to protect it. EG *He picked up the child and cocooned her in a large shawl.* — V+O+A *(in)* = envelop

cocooned /kəkuːnd/. If you say that someone is **cocooned**, you mean that they are isolated and protected from everyday life and problems. EG *A historian cocooned in Oxford can easily lose touch with the real world.* — ADJ CLASSIF ⇑ sheltered = cloistered

cod /kɒd/. **Cod** is both the singular and the plural form. A **cod** is a large, edible sea fish found especially in the North Atlantic. EG *Cod is expensive at the moment.* — N COUNT/UNCOUNT

c.o.d. is the abbreviation for 'cash on delivery'; an arrangement under which you pay for goods that you are buying when they are delivered to you. EG *They'll send it c.o.d.* — ADV AFTER VB

coda /kəʊdə/, **codas.** A **coda** is 1 a piece of music added at the end of a longer piece of music in order to finish it off properly; a technical term. 2 a separate passage at the end of a book or speech that finishes it off properly. EG *The book's coda is a wry conclusion quoted from Shakespeare.* — N COUNT ⇑ ending; N COUNT ⇑ ending

coddle /kɒdəl/, **coddles, coddling, coddled.** 1 If you **coddle** someone, you treat them too kindly or generously and with too much protection. EG *Teachers shouldn't coddle their pupils.* — V+O = mollycoddle

2 When you **coddle** eggs, you cook them slowly in water that is just below boiling point. — V+O

code /kəʊd/, **codes, coding, coded.** 1 A **code** is 1.1 a set of ideas by a group of people about the proper way to behave. EG *Their code was based on generosity and sharing... ...a code of personal behaviour.* 1.2 a set of written rules which state how people should behave in a particular country, society, or business. EG *...the code of advertising standards and practice... ...the French civil code.* • See also **Highway Code.** 1.3 a system of changing a message by replacing all the letters or symbols in the message with other letters or symbols, so that the meaning of the message is a secret until it is decoded. EG *It is a code that even I can crack... The messages were typed in code.* — N COUNT: USU+SUPP ⇑ principle; N COUNT: USU+SUPP; N COUNT, OR *in*+N = cipher

2 If you **code** something, such as a message, 2.1 you change it by replacing all the letters or symbols in it with other letters or symbols, so that the meaning of the message is a secret to anyone who doesn't know the rules. ◇ **coded.** EG *Coded messages had been going out by telephone.* 2.2 you express your opinions or plans in a rather indirect way, usually because it would be dangerous or embarrassing to express yourself more plainly. ◇ **coded.** EG *It was a speech full of coded criticism of the government.* — V+O ⇑ translate = encode; ◇ ADJ CLASSIF; V+O ⇑ conceal; ◇ ADJ CLASSIF: USU ATTRIB

3 A **code** is also 3.1 a short group of numbers or letters which is used to identify something, such as an educational course or a postal address. EG *My university course code is E5L21.* • See also **post code, zip code.** 3.2 any system of signs or symbols that has a meaning, for example language, gestures, or social behaviour. EG *We invented a code of telephone rings.* • See also **morse code, machine code.** — N COUNT ⇑ identification; N COUNT

4 To **code** something means to identify it by a short group of numbers or letters. — V+O

5 A **code** is also the same as a dialling code. EG *The code is 010-974.* — N COUNT

code book, code books; also spelled with a hyphen. A **code book** is a book with codes in it, which you use to write a message in code or to help you understand one. — N COUNT

codeine /kəʊdiːn/ is a drug which is used to relieve pain, especially headaches, and cold symptoms. — N UNCOUNT

code name, code names; often spelled with a hyphen. A **code name** is a name used for someone or something such as a spy or police operation in order to keep their identity or activities secret. EG *He is still listed in the files by his code-name, the Jackal.* — N COUNT

code-named. If a police or military operation, etc is **code-named** something, that is the special name by which it is known only to the people involved in it. EG *It was code-named Operation Pegasus.* — ADJ CLASSIF: PRED+NAME

code of practice, codes of practice. A **code of practice** is a set of written rules which explains how people working in a particular profession should behave. — N COUNT ⇑ regulations

code word, code words; also spelled with a hyphen. A **code word** is a word or phrase that has a special meaning, different from its normal meaning, for the people who have agreed to use it in this way. — N COUNT ⇑ password

codex /kəʊdeks/, **codices.** A **codex** is an ancient book which was written by hand, not printed. — N COUNT ⇑ manuscript

codger /kɒdʒə/, **codgers.** If you refer to a man as an **old codger**, you are referring to him in an affectionate but sometimes slightly disapproving way. EG *I looked at this marvellous old codger laughing his head off.* — N COUNT: USU ADJ+N

codices /kəʊdɪsiːz, kɒdɪ-/ is the plural of **codex.**

codicil /kɒdɪsɪl/, **codicils**. A **codicil** is an instruction that is added to a will after the main part of it has been written; a technical term in law. N COUNT ↑ addition

codify /kəʊdɪfaɪ, kɒ-/, **codifies, codifying, codified**. If you **codify** something, you arrange it according to a system, so that all the rules and procedures are clearly stated. EG *When were the rules of snooker codified?... ...a codified system of law.* V+O ↑ organize

cod-liver oil is a thick yellow oil which is given as a medicine, especially to children, because it is full of vitamins A and D. N UNCOUNT ↑ tonic

codpiece /kɒdpi:s/, **codpieces**. A **codpiece** was a piece of material worn by men in the 15th and 16th centuries to cover their genitals. It was often brightly coloured or highly decorated. N COUNT ↑ covering

codswallop /kɒdzwɒləp/ is used to say that something that someone has said is nonsense; an informal word in British English. EG *Quintin Hogg dismissed his ideas as 'a load of old codswallop'.* N UNCOUNT

co-ed /kəʊɛd/. A **co-ed** school is a school which is attended by both boys and girls. ADJ CLASSIF : ATTRIB

co-educational /kəʊɛdjə⁴keɪʃə⁰nəl, -ʃənə⁰l/. Something that is **co-educational** involves or is concerned with the education of males and females together. EG *Schools should be co-educational because life is co-educational.* ADJ CLASSIF ↑ mixed

coefficient /kəʊɪfɪʃənt/, **coefficients**. A **coefficient** is a number that expresses a measurement of a particular quality of a substance or object under specified conditions; a technical term in science. EG *...a coefficient figure of 0.38.* N COUNT+SUPP

coelacanth /si:ləkænθ/, **coelacanths**. A **coelacanth** is a primitive sea fish. Coelacanths were thought to be extinct until a live one was discovered in 1938. N COUNT

coerce /kəʊɜ:s/, **coerces, coercing, coerced**. If you **coerce** someone into doing something, you persuade them forcefully to do something that they did not want to do. EG *We were not going to dictate or coerce... They tried to coerce me into changing my appearance.* V+O : IF+PREP THEN *into* ↑ force = pressurize

coercion /kəʊɜ:ʃə⁰n/ is the act or process of persuading someone forcefully to do something that they did not want to do. EG *No one was using coercion.* N UNCOUNT ↑ force = pressure

coercive /kəʊɜ:sɪv/. Something that is **coercive** is used to persuade people forcefully to do something that they did not want to do. EG *...the superior coercive power of the State.* ADJ CLASSIF ↑ forceful

coexist /kəʊɪ²gzɪst/, **coexists, coexisting, coexisted**. If two or more things **coexist**, they exist together at the same time or in the same place. EG *Large numbers of species coexist... The forest peoples can coexist with the forest.* V OR V+A *(with)* : RECIP ↑ exist

coexistence /kəʊɪ²gzɪstəns/ is the state of existing together, usually peacefully. EG *She changed her foreign policy from one of force to one of coexistence and cooperation.* N UNCOUNT ↑ existence

C of E is an abbreviation for 'Church of England'.

coffee /kɒfi¹/, **coffees**. **1 Coffee** is **1.1** a hot dark brown drink that you make by pouring boiling water onto coffee beans that have been ground up or onto instant coffee powder. EG *... a cup of coffee... Over coffee, he began to calm down a little.* ▸ also used to refer to a cup of coffee. EG *Do you want a coffee?* **1.2** the roasted beans or powder from which the drink coffee is made. EG *If you're going out, would you mind buying some coffee?* **1.3** the trees on which coffee beans grow. EG *The best land is reserved for coffee... ...coffee plantations.* N MASS ▸ N COUNT N UNCOUNT N UNCOUNT

2 Coffee also means medium to dark brown in colour. ADJ COLOUR

coffee bar, coffee bars; often spelled with a hyphen. A **coffee bar** is a small café where drinks and snacks are sold. N COUNT = snack bar

coffee bean, coffee beans. **Coffee beans** are the dark brown bean-like seeds of a tropical tree, which are roasted and ground up in order to make the drink coffee by pouring hot water over them. N COUNT ↑ seed

coffee break, coffee breaks; often spelled with a hyphen. A **coffee break** is a short time, usually in the morning and afternoon, when you stop working and have a cup of coffee. N COUNT ↑ pause = tea break

coffee cup, coffee cups; often spelled with a hyphen. A **coffee cup** is a cup in which coffee is served. Coffee cups are usually smaller than tea cups. N COUNT

coffee house, coffee houses; often spelled with a hyphen. A **coffee house** was a kind of club where coffee was served, especially in 18th century London. N COUNT ↑ restaurant

coffee mill, coffee mills; also spelled with a hyphen. A **coffee mill** is a machine for grinding coffee beans. N COUNT ↑ grinder

coffee morning, coffee mornings; also spelled with a hyphen. A **coffee morning** is an organized social event that takes place in the morning in someone's house, and is usually intended to raise money for charity. N COUNT ↑ gathering

coffee pot, coffee pots; often spelled with a hyphen and as one word. A **coffee pot** is a tall narrow pot with a spout and a lid, in which coffee is made or served. N COUNT

coffee shop, coffee shops; often spelled with a hyphen. A **coffee shop** is **1** a restaurant that sells coffee, tea, and light meals and snacks. **2** a shop which sells different types of coffee beans, ground coffee, and often tea. N COUNT N COUNT

coffee table, coffee tables; often spelled with a hyphen. A **coffee table** is a small, low table on which coffee is served, magazines and newspapers are arranged, etc. N COUNT

coffee-table book, coffee-table books. A **coffee-table book** is a large, expensive book with a lot of pictures, which is usually placed where people can see it easily and is designed to be looked at rather than to be read properly. N COUNT

coffer /kɒfə/, **coffers**. **1** A **coffer** is a large strong chest used for storing valuable objects such as money or gold and silver. N COUNT ↑ container

2 The **coffers** of an organization consist of the money that it has to spend, imagined as being collected together in one place. EG *The coffers are empty.* N PLURAL : USU+SUPP ↑ funds

coffin /kɒfɪn/, **coffins**. **1** A **coffin** is a box in which a dead body is buried or cremated. EG *...coffins draped with American flags.* N COUNT ↑ container

2 If you describe something as a **nail in** something or someone's **coffin**, you mean that it has helped or will help to lead to the failure or destruction of something, or to a person's downfall or dishonour. EG *Debit cards are the first nails in the coffin of traditional financial methods.* PHR : USED AS C OR O

cog /kɒg/, **cogs**. **1** A **cog** is **1.1** a wheel with square or triangular teeth around the edge, which is used in a machine to turn another wheel or part. **1.2** one of the teeth around the edge of a cog. N COUNT N COUNT ↑ projection

2 If you say that someone is **a cog in the machine** or **wheel**, you mean that they have no importance or power and are simply a small part of a large organization or group. EG *Workers on the production line feel that they are small cogs in the industrial machine.* PHR : USED AS C = pawn

cogency /kəʊdʒənsi¹/ is the power that a good reason, argument, or example has to make you believe or accept something; a formal word. EG *She justified it with cogency and conviction... Such arguments for atheism may not have much logic or cogency.* N UNCOUNT = force

cogent /kəʊdʒənt/. A reason, argument, or example that is **cogent** has the power to make you believe or accept something; a formal word. EG *He brought forward some very cogent arguments.* ◇ **cogently**. EG *His opinions were always cogently expressed.* ADJ QUALIT ↑ good = convincing ◇ ADV WITH VB

cogitate /kɒdʒɪteɪt/, **cogitates, cogitating, cogitated**. If you are **cogitating**, you are thinking deeply about something; a formal word. EG *He sat cogitating by the window.* ◇ **cogitation** /kɒdʒɪteɪʃə⁰n/. EG *I felt as if I'd interrupted a mood of cogitation.* V : IF+PREP THEN *about* ↑ think = ruminate ◇ N UNCOUNT = meditation

cognac /kɒnjæk/, **cognacs**. **Cognac** is a type of brandy made in south western France. N MASS

cognate /kɒgneɪt/. Words or languages that are **cognate** have the same source or origin. ADJ CLASSIF ↑ related

cognisance /kɒg⁰nɪzəns/. See **cognizance**.

cognisant /kɒg⁰nɪzənt/. See **cognizant**.

cognition /kɒgnɪʃə⁰n/ is the mental process of knowing, learning, and understanding things; a formal or technical word. EG *We have little evidence about how the brain functions in cognition.* N UNCOUNT

cognitive /kɒgnɪtɪv/ means relating to the process of learning, understanding, and representing knowl- ADJ CLASSIF : USU ATTRIB edge; a formal or technical word. EG ...*a study of the cognitive functions in learning to read.*

cognizance /kɒgənɪzəns/; also spelled **cognisance**; a formal word. 1 **Cognizance** is knowledge or understanding. EG *They were introduced to a world of which they had no cognizance.* N UNCOUNT : IF + PREP THEN *of* = comprehension

2 If you **take cognizance of** something, you notice it or are aware of it. EG *The strategies you use to teach a child to read must take cognisance of the child's starting point.* PHR : VB INFLECTS = acknowledge

cognizant /kɒgənɪzənt/; also spelled **cognisant**. If someone is **cognizant** of something, they are aware of it or understand it; a formal word. EG *I just want you to be cognizant of the possible political repercussions.* ADJ CLASSIF : PRED + *of* = conscious

cognoscenti /kɒnjəʊʃenti¹, kɒgnə-/. The **cognoscenti** are a group of people who know a lot about a particular subject; a formal word. EG *As a secretary yourself you are one of the cognoscenti who can spot the make of typewriter.* N PLURAL : *the* + N ↑ knowledgeable = connoisseurs

cohabit /kəʊhæbɪt/, **cohabits, cohabiting, cohabited**. If a man and woman are **cohabiting**, they are living together and have a sexual relationship, but are not married; a formal word. V OR V+A *(with)* : RECIP = live together ◊ **cohabitation**. EG *We were thinking of marriage, or at least cohabitation.* ◊ N UNCOUNT : IF + PREP THEN *with*

cohere /kəʊhɪə/, **coheres, cohering, cohered**; a formal word. 1 If an argument or set of ideas **coheres**, it leads to a satisfactory conclusion and all the steps fit together logically. V = hang together

2 If two or more objects **cohere**, they stick together firmly. V : USU + A

coherence /kəʊhɪərəns/ is 1 the quality that something has when it makes sense or is pleasing because all the parts or steps fit together well and logically. EG *The theory possesses a certain intellectual coherence and consistency... The stage sets were brilliant and they gave coherence to a piece which was bitty in the second half.* N UNCOUNT = unity, meaning 2 a state or situation in which all the parts or ideas fit together well so that they form a united whole. EG *His arrival threatens the coherence of the group.* N UNCOUNT = cohesion

coherent /kəʊhɪərənt/. 1 If something is **coherent**, 1.1 its parts fit together well so that it is clear and easy to understand. EG *They can offer no coherent answer... ...a coherent theory.* ADJ QUALIT ◊ **coherently**. EG *Businessmen should be told clearly and coherently what society expects of them.* ◊ ADV WITH VB 1.2 its parts fit together well so that it is a complete and pleasing whole. EG *It is a beautiful and remarkably coherent church.* ADJ QUALIT = harmonious

2 If someone is **coherent**, they are talking in a clear and calm way. EG *She was more coherent than she had been before.* ADJ QUALIT = lucid ◊ **coherently**. EG *Is she able to talk coherently now?* ◊ ADV WITH VB

3 A group of things is **coherent** when there is a clear connection between all the things in the group. ADJ QUALIT = unified

cohesion /kəʊhiːʒən/ is a state or situation in which all the parts or ideas fit together well so that they form a united whole. EG *We lack a sense of national purpose and social cohesion... There was no cohesion in our performance.* N UNCOUNT = cohesiveness

cohesive /kəʊhiːsɪv/. Something that is **cohesive** consists of parts that fit well together or that relate well to each other so that they form a united whole. EG *The poor do not see themselves as a cohesive group.* ADJ QUALIT ◊ **cohesiveness**. EG ...*a reduction in group cohesiveness.* ◊ N UNCOUNT = cohesion

cohort /kəʊhɔːt/, **cohorts**. A **cohort** is a group of people who support a particular person or belief. EG *Fortunately, my cohort of attorneys was willing to defend him... ...the Prime Minister and her cohorts.* N COUNT : IF + PREP THEN *of* = legion

coiffure /kwɑːfjʊə/, **coiffures**. A **coiffure** is a woman's hairstyle; a formal word. EG ...*her immaculate coiffure.* N COUNT

coil /kɔɪl/, **coils, coiling, coiled**. 1 A **coil** is 1.1 a continuous series of loops into which rope, wire, etc has been wound. EG *A couple of coils of rope still lay on the dock... ...a small coil of barbed wire.* N COUNT : IF + PREP THEN *of* 1.2 a single loop that is one of a series into which something has been wound. EG *Pythons kill by tightening their coils so that their victim cannot breathe.* N COUNT 1.3 a long shape which curves or twists like a spiral. EG ...*a coil of hair... ...blue coils of smoke.* N COUNT : IF + PREP THEN *of* = curl

2 A **coil** is also 2.1 a thick spiral of wire through which an electric current is passed, for example in order to create a magnetic field. N COUNT = induction coil 2.2 the part of a petrol engine that sends electricity to the spark plugs. N COUNT 2.3 a contraceptive device that is placed inside a woman's womb. N COUNT = IUD

3 If you **coil** something or if it **coils**, it curves into a continuous series of loops or into the shape of a ring. EG *Pythons coil themselves around their prey and kill it... The cat coiled round his legs.* V-ERG : IF + PREP THEN *around/round* ↑ wind

4 To **coil** also means to move or travel in a series of circles or loops. EG *Thick smoke coiled up over the fields... A huge procession of supporters coiled its way through the streets.* V+A = snake

coil up. If you **coil** something **up**, you wind it into a continuous series of loops. EG *He coiled up the garden hose.* PHRASAL VB : V+O+ADV

coiled /kɔɪld/. Something that is **coiled** is wound into a series of loops. EG ...*a coiled whip... ...coiled springs.* ADJ CLASSIF : USU ATTRIB

coin /kɔɪn/, **coins, coining, coined**. 1 A **coin** is a small piece of metal such as copper or silver, which is used as money. EG *I threw her a coin... ...a 10p coin.* N COUNT

2 **Coin** is used to describe money which consists of coins rather than bank notes or cheques. EG *The disadvantages of coin and paper money are obvious.* ADJ CLASSIF

3 If you are **coining** money or **coining it**, you are earning a lot of money quickly; used in informal English. EG *He's really coining it now.* V+O ↑ earn = rake in

4 If you **coin** a word or a phrase, you invent it or use it for the first time. EG *It was Asa Briggs who coined the phrase 're-drawing the map of learning'.* V+O ● You say **'to coin a phrase'** when you realize that you have just used a cliché or some other expression which is not new or meaningful; used humorously. EG *'What are you doing in a joint like that?' he said, 'to coin a phrase.'* ● PHR : USED AS ADV SEN

5 The word **coin** is also used in the following expressions. 5.1 If you say that two things are **two sides of the same coin**, you mean that they are two different ways of looking at the same situation. EG *Inflation and unemployment are two sides of the same coin.* PHR : USED AS C 5.2 If you say that something is **the other side of the coin**, you mean that it is the opposite way of looking at the situation you have been discussing. EG *Let us look at the other side of the coin.* PHR : USED AS O 5.3 If you **pay** someone **back in** their **own coin**, you treat them in the same way that they have treated you; used especially when they have treated you badly. PHR : VB INFLECTS ↑ retaliate

coinage /kɔɪnɪdʒ/, **coinages**. 1 **Coinage** is 1.1 the coins which are used in a country. EG *Upstairs is a display of British coinage.* N UNCOUNT ↑ money 1.2 the system of money used in a country. EG *Britain now uses decimal coinage.* N UNCOUNT/COUNT + SUPP = currency

2 A **coinage** is a word or phrase which has been invented. EG *'Privatization' is a recent coinage.* N COUNT ↑ invention

3 **Coinage** is also the invention of new words and phrases. EG *This cumbersome phrase was of Jefferson's coinage.* N UNCOUNT

coin box, coin boxes. A **coin box** is a public telephone in Britain where you have to put money into a slot in order to make a call. N COUNT = telephone box

coincide /kəʊɪnsaɪd/, **coincides, coinciding, coincided**. 1 If two or more events **coincide**, they happen at or around the same time. EG *I'm afraid our holidays don't coincide this year... Macmillan's departure coincided with Benn's return.* V OR V+A *(with)* : RECIP

2 If the opinions or ideas of two or more people **coincide**, they are the same or agree with one another. EG *On the whole their views coincided... This coincided with my own private opinion.* V OR V+A *(with)* : RECIP = tally

3 If two or more objects or places **coincide**, they are in exactly the same position or place. EG *The boundary of the L.E.A. coincides with a county boundary.* V OR V+A *(with)* : RECIP = coexist

coincidence /kəʊɪnsə¹dəns/, **coincidences**. 1 A **coincidence** is what happens when two or more things occur at the same time by chance in a way that is surprising. EG *It was quite a coincidence that my sister was on the same train... Is it coincidence that so many of these complaints are made by teachers?... By coincidence, that's who I want to see, too.* N COUNT/UNCOUNT = accident, fluke

2 The **coincidence** of two or more things is the fact that they are identical; used in formal English. EG *I was struck by the coincidence of the title with the name of my dentist.* N SING : *the* + N + *of*

coincident /kəʊɪnsɪdənt/. If two or more things are **coincident**, they are identical in their nature; a formal word. EG *Your views are roughly coincident with mine.* ADJ CLASSIF : IF + PREP THEN *with*

coincidental /kəʊɪnsɪdentəºl/. 1 Something that is **coincidental** is the result of a coincidence and has not been deliberately arranged. EG *Any similarity to real people is purely coincidental... It was coincidental that they were all women.* ADJ QUALIT = accidental

2 **Coincidental** also means the same as coincident; a formal use. ADJ CLASSIF : IF+ PREP THEN with

coincidentally /kəʊɪnsɪdentəºli¹/. You use **coincidentally** when you want to draw attention to a coincidence. EG *Quite coincidentally, this happened to be my favourite song, too... These players, coincidentally, are all left-handed.* ADV SEN = accidentally

coir /kɔɪə/ is a rough material made from coconut shells which is used to make ropes and mats. N UNCOUNT

coitus /kəʊɪtəs/ is sexual intercourse; a formal word. N UNCOUNT

coke /kəʊk/, **cokes**. The word **coke** is spelled with a capital letter for paragraph 2. 1 **Coke** is 1.1 a solid black material that is produced from coal and that is burned as a fuel. EG *The two stoves were reeking of coke.* 1.2 the same as cocaine, in informal English. N UNCOUNT; N UNCOUNT

2 **Coke** is also the same as Coca-Cola; a trademark. N MASS

col., **cols.** The abbreviation **col.** is spelled with a capital letter for paragraph 2. 1 **col.** is a written abbreviation for 'column' and 'colour'.

2 **Col.** is a written abbreviation for 'Colonel', used especially as part of a name. EG *Col. E. W. Harding.* N IN TITLES : BEFORE NAME

cola /kəʊlə/, **colas**. **Cola** is a sweet brown non-alcoholic fizzy drink. • See also **Coca-Cola.** N MASS = coke

colander /kɒləndə, kʌl-/, **colanders**. A **colander** is a bowl-shaped container with holes in it which you wash or drain food in. N COUNT

cold /kəʊld/, **colder**, **coldest**; **colds**. 1 Something that is **cold** has a very low temperature. EG *Wash delicate fabrics in cold water... The concrete floor is freezing cold.* ◇ **coldness**. EG *The coldness of the water helped to clear his head.* ADJ QUALIT ≠ hot, warm; ◇ N UNCOUNT ≠ heat

2 **Cold** is used to describe the weather, or the air in a room or building when the temperature is very low. EG *It's bitterly cold... The building was cold and draughty... It was cold in the room... ...cold winters.* ADJ QUALIT ≠ hot, warm

3 The **cold** is cold weather or a low temperature. EG *Why don't you come in out of the cold?... My fingers are so stiff from the cold... ...extremes of cold and heat.* N UNCOUNT : USU the+N ≠ heat

4 If you are **cold**, your body is at an unpleasantly low temperature. EG *Can I light the fire? I'm cold.* ADJ QUALIT : PRED

5 **With cold** means as a result of being cold. EG *She was turning blue with cold.* PHR : USED AS AN A

6 Something that is **cold** is at a lower temperature than is normal or acceptable. EG *Your food is getting cold... Use the choke to start the car when the engine is cold.* ADJ QUALIT ≠ hot

7 **Cold** food is not intended to be eaten hot, for example meat that has been cooked and cooled, or a salad. EG *She gave me some cold lamb for the sandwiches... ...a cold supper.* ADJ CLASSIF : ATTRIB

8 Someone who is **cold** does not show much emotion, especially affection; used showing disapproval. EG *The baby who doesn't get any loving will grow up cold and unresponsive.* ▸ used of the way someone looks, speaks, or behaves. EG *His voice was cold and decisive... ...cold blue eyes.* ◇ **coldly**. EG *'It's yours,' I said, politely, but coldly.* ◇ **coldness**. EG *Kay was a little stunned by the coldness in his voice.* ADJ QUALIT ⇑ unemotional = unfeeling ≠ warm ▸ = icy; ◇ ADV; ◇ N UNCOUNT = iciness

9 A **cold** colour or light is one that gives the impression of being cold. EG *Blues and greens are cold colours... The stars shone with a cold inner light.* ADJ CLASSIF : ATTRIB ≠ warm

10 A **cold** scent or trail is one that is old and therefore difficult to follow. EG *It's difficult to pick up a cold scent... Their trail seemed to go cold.* ADJ CLASSIF ⇑ faint ≠ fresh

11 If you say that someone is **cold** when they are trying to guess the correct answer to a question or puzzle, you mean that they are a long way away from the answer rather than getting close to it. EG *'Is he a sportsman?'–'No, you're getting colder.'* ADJ QUALIT : PRED ≠ close, warm

12 If you do something **cold**, you do it without preparation. EG *He believes he gets more insight into a character if he comes to it cold without reading up the background of the play.* ADV AFTER VB ⇑ unprepared

13 If something **leaves** you **cold**, it fails to excite or interest you. EG *Her performance left me cold.* PHR : VB INFLECTS

14 If you **have** or **get cold feet** about doing something, you are nervous or frightened of doing it, especially because you think you are going to fail. PHR : VB INFLECTS

15 If you are **left out in the cold**, or if you **find** yourself **out in the cold**, you are ignored by a group of people rather than being invited to take part in some activity with them. EG *She may find herself out in the cold.* PHR : VB INFLECTS

16 If someone is **out cold**, they are unconscious, especially as a result of being hit. EG *He knocked the man out cold with one blow... You'd be out cold if I promise you that.* PHR : USED AS AN A

17 A **cold** is a mild, very common illness which makes you sneeze a lot and gives you a sore throat or a cough. EG *Her cold was better.* • If you **catch cold**, you become ill with a cold. EG *Put on your dressing-gown. You'll catch cold... She'll catch her death of cold.* N COUNT = chill; • PHR : VB INFLECTS

18 The word **cold** is also used in the following expressions, which are explained at other places in this dictionary. • to **throw** or **pour cold water on** something: see **water**. • **in cold blood**: see **blood**. • to **make** your **blood run cold**: see **blood**. • to **blow hot and cold**: see **hot**.

cold-blooded. 1 Something or someone that is **cold-blooded** does not have or show much emotion or pity. EG *Seldom have I read a more graphic, cold-blooded description of a killing... That's what it is. Just cold-blooded malicious cruelty.* ◇ **cold-bloodedly**. EG *She was cold-bloodedly murdered.* ADJ QUALIT ⇑ unemotional = callous; ◇ ADV WITH VB = ruthlessly

2 An animal that is **cold-blooded** has a body temperature that changes according to the surrounding temperature. Reptiles, for example, are cold-blooded; a technical use. ADJ CLASSIF

cold chisel, **cold chisels**. A **cold chisel** is a narrow chisel made of steel and used for cutting stone, bricks, metal, etc. N COUNT

cold cream is a cream that is used for softening and cleaning the skin, used especially by women to keep the skin on their faces soft. N UNCOUNT

cold cuts are thin slices of cooked meat which are served cold; an American expression. N PLURAL

cold fish. If you say that someone is a **cold fish**, you mean that they are unfriendly and unemotional; used showing disapproval. N SING WITH DET : USU USED AS C

cold frame, **cold frames**. A **cold frame** is a wooden frame with a glass top in which you grow small plants to protect them from cold weather. N COUNT ⇑ construction

cold front, **cold fronts**. A **cold front** is the weather condition that occurs when the front part of a mass of cold air pushes into a mass of warm air; a technical term in meteorology. N COUNT

cold-shoulder, **cold-shoulders**, **cold-shouldering**, **cold-shouldered**. If you **cold-shoulder** someone, you behave towards them in an unfriendly way, to show them that you do not care about them or that you want them to go away. EG *At first we cold-shouldered him.* V+O ⇑ ignore = rebuff, snub

cold snap, **cold snaps**. A **cold snap** is a short period of cold and frosty weather. EG *...the effects of a sudden cold snap.* N COUNT

cold sore, **cold sores**. **Cold sores** are a group of small, sore spots that appear on or near someone's lips and nose when they have a cold. N COUNT

cold storage. 1 If something such as food is put in **cold storage**, it is kept in an artificially cooled place in order to preserve it. EG *The bananas are put in cold storage while they are waiting to be shipped.* N UNCOUNT

2 If you **put** an idea or plan **into cold storage**, you postpone it for a while rather than putting it into action as you originally planned. PHR : VB INFLECTS ⇑ delay = shelve

cold store, **cold stores**. A **cold store** is a building or room which is artificially cooled and where food is kept in order to preserve it. N COUNT

cold sweat. A **cold sweat** is the reaction of your body to fear and nervousness which makes you feel cold and makes you sweat. EG *He awoke trembling and in a cold sweat.* N SING WITH DET : USU a+N = panic

cold turkey is the unpleasant physical reaction that someone experiences when they suddenly stop taking a drug that they have become addicted to; an informal American expression. EG *I knew I would have to go through cold turkey.* N UNCOUNT = withdrawal

cold war is a state of extreme political unfriendliness between two or more countries although they do not actually fight each other. EG *He was opposed to the spread of the cold war... We argued for detente and peaceful coexistence rather than cold war... The 1950's were the 'Cold War' era.* N SING WITH DET, OR N UNCOUNT ⇑ hostility

coleslaw /kəʊlslɔː/; also spelled with a hyphen. **Coleslaw** is a salad made from chopped cabbage, N UNCOUNT carrots, onions, etc, which are all mixed together in mayonnaise.

coley /kəʊli[1], kɒli[1]/ is an edible fish with white or grey flesh. N UNCOUNT

colic /kɒlɪk/ is a painful illness in the stomach and bowels. Babies especially suffer from colic. EG *She has been miserable with colic.* N UNCOUNT

colicky /kɒlɪki[1]/. Someone who is **colicky**, especially a baby, is suffering from colic. ADJ QUALIT ↑ ill

colitis /kə[7]laɪtɪs/ is an illness in which your colon becomes inflamed. N UNCOUNT

collaborate /kəlæbəreɪt/, **collaborates, collaborating, collaborated**. 1 If two or more people **collaborate**, they work together to produce a piece of work, especially a book or some research. EG *Antony and I are collaborating on a paper for the conference... The film was directed by Carl Jones, who collaborated with Rudy de Luca in writing it.* V OR V+A (*with*) : RECIP, IF +PREP THEN *in/on* = team up

2 If someone **collaborates** with an enemy army or government which has taken control of their country by force, they give help to the enemy, for example by giving information. EG *I believe he collaborated with the Nazis... We are not willing to collaborate.* V OR V+A (*with*) : RECIP ↑ comply = co-operate

collaboration /kəlæbəreɪʃə[0]n/ is the act of working together to produce a piece of work, especially a book or some research. EG *...a good example of collaboration between industrialists and businessmen.* N UNCOUNT ↑ alliance = teamwork ● If you do something **in collaboration** with someone else, you share the work between you. EG *The work I did in collaboration interested me very much... Photographs published by Collins in collaboration with the Imperial War Museum.* ● PHR : USED AS AN A, USU+*with* ↑ together

collaborative /kəlæbə[0]rətɪv/. A **collaborative** piece of work is one that is done by two or more people working together. EG *The project is a collaborative one... ...a collaborative effort.* ADJ CLASSIF : ATTRIB ↑ joint = combined ◇ **collaboratively**. EG *This part of the work is being done collaboratively with ICI.* ◇ ADV WITH VB ↑ jointly

collaborator /kəlæbəreɪtə/, **collaborators**. A **collaborator** is 1 someone that you work with to produce a piece of work, especially a book or some research. EG *This production is by Charles Marowitz and collaborators.* N COUNT ↑ colleague = partner 2 someone who helps an enemy army or government which has taken control of their country by force, for example by giving information; used showing disapproval. N COUNT = traitor

collage /kə[7]lɑːʒ/, **collages**. 1 **Collage** is a method of making pictures by sticking together pieces of paper, cloth, photographs, etc. N UNCOUNT

2 A **collage** is 2.1 a picture that has been made by sticking together pieces of paper, cloth, photographs, etc. N COUNT 2.2 something that has been made by combining a number of very different things. EG *The book is an extraordinary collage of science fiction and the Old Testament.* N COUNT : IF+ PREP THEN *of* ↑ mixture = patchwork

collapse /kəlæps/, **collapses, collapsing, collapsed**. 1 If a building or some other structure **collapses**, it suddenly falls down. EG *These flimsy houses are liable to collapse in a heavy storm... The main gate had collapsed.* V ↑ fall = crumble ▸ used as a noun. EG *The collapse of buildings trapped thousands of people.* ▸ N UNCOUNT ↑ destruction

2 If something **collapses**, it falls inwards and become smaller in size or flatter in shape. EG *Suddenly the parachute collapsed... One of my lungs had collapsed.* V ↑ fall = cave in

3 If a system, institution, idea, etc **collapses**, it fails completely and suddenly. EG *Their marriage had collapsed... My hopes collapsed.* V = fall apart ▸ used as a noun. EG *...a company on the verge of collapse... ...the collapse of Asquith's Liberal Government.* ▸ N UNCOUNT/ COUNT = disintegration

4 If you **collapse**, 4.1 you suddenly fall down because you feel tired, weak, or ill, or because you become unconscious. EG *I carried on working until I thought I would collapse... Nearly collapsing under the pain, I stumbled forward.* V = faint ▸ used as a noun. EG *Upon her collapse she was rushed to hospital and had an emergency operation.* ▸ N UNCOUNT/ COUNT 4.2 you sit down very suddenly, for example because you feel tired or very upset. EG *The music stopped and they collapsed onto cushions.* V : USU+A = sink 4.3 you have no energy left and need a rest. EG *I seem to collapse around 6.30.* V ▸ used as a noun. EG *I was in a state of total collapse.* ▸ N UNCOUNT = exhaustion

5 If an object **collapses**, it is designed to be folded into a smaller size or a flatter shape when not being used. EG *When the cinema reopened, the seats did not collapse any more.* V ↑ fold

6 If you **collapse** something, you fold it into a smaller size or a flatter shape when it is not being used. EG *The guard jumped aboard, and collapsed the steps.* V+O

7 If you **collapse** a message or piece of writing, you make it much shorter. EG *Any message must be collapsed into a very brief communiqué.* V+O : IF+PREP THEN *into* = compress

collapsible /kəlæpsə[1]bə[0]l/. A **collapsible** object is designed to be folded into a smaller size or a flatter shape when it is not being used. EG *...a collapsible bed... ...collapsible handlebars.* ADJ CLASSIF ↑ temporary = folding

collar /kɒlə/, **collars, collaring, collared**. 1 The **collar** of a shirt, blouse, jacket, etc is the part which fits round the neck and is usually folded over. N COUNT

2 A **collar** for a dog, cat, or other animal is a leather band or a chain which is put round its neck. N COUNT

3 A **collar** of fur or feathers is a band of fur or feathers on the neck of an animal or bird. N COUNT+SUPP

4 **Collar** is also used to refer to a joint of meat which is cut from the neck of an animal. EG *...collar of bacon.* N UNCOUNT : IF+ PREP THEN *of*

5 If someone **collars** you, 5.1 they catch you and hold you, so that you cannot get away. EG *I was collared by the police.* V+O = seize 5.2 they catch you in order to speak to you. EG *The boss collared me this morning just as I was going out.* V+O ↑ detain = buttonhole

6 If someone **gets hot under the collar** about something, they get angry and indignant about it; an informal expression. EG *She gets very hot under the collar about fox hunting.* PHR : VB INFLECTS, IF+ PREP THEN *about* = get steamed up

7 See also **blue-collar, white-collar**.

collarbone /kɒləbəʊn/, **collarbones**. Your **collarbone** is one of the two long bones which run from the base of your neck to your shoulder at the front of your body. N COUNT ↑ bone

collate /kə[7]leɪt/, **collates, collating, collated**. When you **collate** pieces of information, you gather them all together, examine them carefully, and identify any differences between them. EG *It took an hour to collate all the findings... All the new evidence had been collated in a fresh dossier on the case.* V+O ↑ collect

collateral /kə[6]lætərəl/; a formal word. 1 **Collateral** is money or property which is used as a guarantee that someone will repay a loan. EG *They have nothing to offer as collateral... I had put up collateral.* N UNCOUNT = security

2 **Collateral** is used to describe people who are descended from the same person but who are not very closely related. EG *Collateral branches of the family can be found in Australia and Canada.* ADJ CLASSIF : ATTRIB ↑ distant

collation /kə[7]leɪʃə[0]n/, **collations**. 1 A **collation** is a light uncooked meal; a formal use. EG *We had a large cold collation at a lakeside restaurant.* N COUNT

2 **Collation** is the act or process of collating something. EG *The figures are ready for tabulation and collation.* N UNCOUNT/ COUNT

colleague /kɒliːg/, **colleagues**. A **colleague** is someone who you work with, especially in a professional job. EG *I talked to a colleague of yours recently... ...his Parliamentary colleagues.* N COUNT = associate

collect, collects, collecting, collected. The word **collect** is pronounced /kəlekt/ when it is a verb, adjective, or adverb, and /kɒlɪ[2]kt/ when it is a noun. 1 If you **collect** things, you bring together from several places a group of things or an amount of something. EG *She used to go for long walks collecting birds' eggs... They're collecting wood for the fire.* V+O ↑ gather

2 If you **collect** stamps, coins, or something else, you spend time getting a large number of different kinds, because you are interested in them. EG *Do you collect antiques yourself?* V+O ↑ accumulate

3 If you **collect** something or someone from somewhere, you get them from the place where they have been left or where they have spent some time. EG *I went to the jeweller's to collect my wristwatch... I have to collect the children from school.* V+O = pick up

4 When something **collects** in a place, it gathers there over a period of time. EG *There are certain places where a lot of dust collects... Damp leaves collect in gutters.* V+A ↑ gather = accumulate

5 If something **collects** dust, dirt, or some other substance, it becomes covered with it over a period of time. EG *My books are collecting dust.* V+O = gather

6 If something **collects** energy, heat, or light, it attracts it. EG *The plant has large leaves with which to collect as much light as possible.* V+O ↑ attract

7 If you **collect** for something, you ask people to give you money for a particular purpose, for example for a charity or a present for someone. EG *I'm collecting* V OR V+O : IF+ PREP THEN *for* ↑ take

for a leaving present for Mary... How much have you collected so far?

8 If you **collect** money from someone who owes it, you get it from them. EG *He collects his pension at the post office every fortnight... The main part of his work was collecting debts.* — V+O

10 If you **collect** yourself or **collect** your thoughts, wits, strength, etc, you make an effort to calm or prepare yourself in order to do or deal with something. EG *I had five minutes in which to collect my thoughts before the interview started... He collected himself enough to tell his friends about the accident.* — V+O (REFL/NG) = compose

11 A **collect** call is a phone call that is paid for by the person who you are ringing up; used in American English. ▸ used as an adverb. EG *You can call me collect.* — ADJ CLASSIF: ATTRIB; ▸ ADV AFTER VB

12 A **collect** is a short prayer said during some Christian church services. — N COUNT

collect up. If you **collect** something **up**, you collect it all together. EG *They collected up their gear.* — PHRASAL VB: V+O+ADV

collected /kəlɛktɪ²d/. **1** Someone's **collected** works, speeches, letters, etc are all their works, speeches, letters, etc published as one book or set of books. EG *The collected works of Proust.* — ADJ CLASSIF+N IN PL = complete

2 If someone is **collected**, they are calm and self-controlled; a fairly formal use. — ADJ QUALIT = composed

collecting /kəlɛktɪŋ/. **1 Collecting** is the hobby of collecting a particular type of thing such as stamps. EG *She was very fond of stamp collecting.* — N UNCOUNT: USU MOD+N

2 A **collecting** tin or box is one that is used to collect money for charity. EG *The collecting box grew heavier.* — ADJ CLASSIF: ATTRIB

collection /kəlɛkʃəⁿn/, **collections**. **1** A **collection** of things is **1.1** a group of things you have acquired over a period of time or brought together. EG *Davis had a large collection of pop records.... ...my video tape collection.* — N COUNT **1.2** a group of interesting or valuable objects such as works of art that have been acquired over a period of time and are perhaps shown to the public. EG *...a collection of early English portraits... ...the world-famous Holford Collection.* — N COUNT: ALSO IN NAMES AFTER N **1.3** a number of stories, poems, articles, etc published in one book or a number of pieces of music on one record. EG *...'The Price was High', a collection of Scott Fitzgerald's short stories.* — N COUNT ⇑ group = anthology **1.4** a group of things or people. EG *She was waiting with a collection of other girls... ...a collection of old ruins by the railway.* — N COUNT: ALSO N PART+N IN PLURAL = cluster

2 Collection is **2.1** the act of getting something or someone from where they were left or where you arranged to get them from. EG *Your curtains are ready for collection... They are able to make both deliveries and collections in the same call.* — N UNCOUNT/COUNT = pick-up

3 A postal **collection** is the time when a post box is emptied by a postman. EG *The next collection is at 9.30 am... There is no Sunday collection.* — N COUNT ⇑ unloading

4 A **collection** is also **4.1** the organized collecting of money from people who want to give it for a special purpose, for example charity. EG *They organized dances, football matches, and collections which raised £450.* — N COUNT/UNCOUNT ⇑ taking **4.2** money that is collected from the people in the church during some Christian services. EG *The priest took a special collection... ...the collection plate.* — N COUNT

collective /kəlɛktɪv/. **1 Collective** means shared by or involving every member of a group of people. EG *It was a collective decision.* ◊ **collectively**. EG *They were collectively responsible.* — ADJ CLASSIF: ATTRIB; ◊ ADV = jointly

2 A **collective** is a group of people who equally share the running, and often the ownership, of a farm, business, etc. EG *Control of the magazine fell to a collective in north London.* ▸ used to refer to the business or farm itself. — N COUNT: IF SING, VB CAN BE SING OR PL = co-operative

3 A **collective** farm, business, etc is one that is run by a collective. — ADJ CLASSIF: ATTRIB

4 A **collective** noun refers to a group of people or things; a grammatical term. EG *'Swarm' is the collective noun for bees.* — ADJ CLASSIF: ATTRIB

collective bargaining consists of talks that a trade union has with an employer which are intended to settle what the workers' pay or conditions should be. EG *The unions should concentrate on securing their demands through collective bargaining.* — N UNCOUNT ⇑ negotiation

collectively /kəlɛktɪvli¹/ is used when a group of things or people is being referred to or considered as a whole. EG *It is one of a small group of marsupials called, collectively, rat-kangaroos.* — ADV ⇑ together

collectivise /kəlɛktɪvaɪz/. See **collectivize**.

collectivism /kəlɛktɪvɪzəⁿm/ is a political system in which factories, farms, offices, etc are owned and controlled by the state or all the people in a country. — N UNCOUNT ⇑ socialism

collectivist /kəlɛktɪvɪst/ means relating to collectivism. — ADJ CLASSIF: USU ATTRIB

collectivize /kəlɛktɪvaɪz/, **collectivizes, collectivizing, collectivized**; also spelled **collectivise**. If farms or factories are **collectivized**, they are brought under state ownership and control, usually by combining a number of small farms or factories into one large one. EG *After 1929, farms were collectivized.* ◊ **collectivization** /kəlɛktɪvaɪzeɪʃəⁿn/. EG *...the collectivization of agriculture.* ◊ **collectivized**. EG *...a collectivized housing system.* — V+O: USU PASS ⇑ nationalize; ◊ N UNCOUNT; ◊ ADJ CLASSIF ⇑ nationalized

collector /kəlɛktə/, **collectors**. **1** A ticket **collector**, rent **collector**, etc is a person who collects tickets, rent, debts, etc, from other people, usually as a job. — N COUNT: USU MOD+N ⇑ taker

2 A **collector** of something is a person who collects things of a particular type because they are interesting, valuable, or beautiful. EG *...a butterfly collector.* — N COUNT

collector's item, collector's items. A **collector's item** is an object which is highly valued by collectors because it is so rare or beautiful. EG *I had a stack of Scrooge comic books, which were collector's items by now.* — N COUNT = showpiece

colleen /kɒli:n, kɒli:n/, **colleens**. A **colleen** is a girl; an Irish word. — N COUNT

college /kɒlɪdʒ/, **colleges**. **1** A **college** is **1.1** an institution where students study for qualifications or do training courses after they have left school. EG *Computer Studies is one of the many courses at the local technical college... The Royal College of Music... What do you plan to do after college?* — N COUNT/UNCOUNT: ALSO IN NAMES **1.2** in British English, one of the separate institutions which a university, for example Oxford, Cambridge, or London, is divided into. EG *Jesus College, Cambridge.* — N COUNT: ALSO IN NAMES AFTER N ⇑ institution

2 College is used in the titles of some secondary schools which charge fees. EG *Milton Ladies' College.* — N IN NAMES AFTER N

3 A **college** is also an organized group of people who have special duties and powers; a formal use. EG *Members of the House of Lords could be elected by a college of peers... ...the Royal College of Physicians.* — N COUNT+*of* ⇑ organization

collegiate /kə⁷li:dʒɪət/. **1** A **collegiate** university is one that is divided into several colleges. EG *Some new universities have attempted to adopt a collegiate system.* — ADJ CLASSIF: ATTRIB

2 Collegiate means belonging or relating to a college. EG *I enjoy collegiate life.* — ADJ CLASSIF: ATTRIB

collide /kəlaɪd/, **collides, colliding, collided**. **1** If two or more people or objects **collide**, they hit one another violently after one or both of them have been moving very quickly. EG *The two vehicles collided... He was so close behind me that he almost collided with me when I stopped.* — V OR V+A (*with*): RECIP

2 If two people or groups **collide**, they come together and have a big argument about something. EG *We were about to collide head-on in the defence debate.* — V OR V+A (*with*): RECIP = clash

collie /kɒli¹/, **collies**. A **collie** or **collie dog** is a dog used by farmers for controlling sheep. — N COUNT

colliery /kɒljəri¹/, **collieries**. A **colliery** is a coal mine and all the buildings and equipment which are connected with it; a British word. EG *...Chopwell Colliery... ...a colliery owner.* — N COUNT = pit

collision /kəlɪʒəⁿn/, **collisions**. A **collision** between two things is **1** when a moving object hits something else violently. EG *This car is safer in a collision... What is the possibility of a mid-air collision?... Henry and a window came into chance collision.* — N COUNT/UNCOUNT, IF+PREP THEN *between/with* = crash **2** when very different or opposing ideas meet, which leads to difficulty or a big argument. EG *His next film led to another collision with the censors... ...the collision of private and public interests.* — N COUNT/UNCOUNT, IF+PREP THEN *between/with* ⇑ confrontation = clash

collision course, collision courses. If two or more people or things are on a **collision course**, **1** there is likely to be a sudden and violent disagreement between them. EG *Conservation and agriculture are set on an eventual collision course... The Government has turned aside from its collision course with the unions.* — N COUNT: USU SING WITH DET, IF+PREP THEN *with* = confrontation **2** they are likely to meet and hit each other violently. EG *A meteor is on a collision course with the Earth.* — N SING WITH DET: IF+PREP THEN *with*

collocate, collocates, collocating, collocated; a technical term in linguistics. The word **collocate** is pronounced /kɒlə⁷kət/ when it is a noun, and /kɒlə⁷keɪt/ when it is a verb. **1** A **collocate** of a particular word is another word which often occurs with that word. N COUNT

2 If two or more words **collocate**, they often occur together. V OR V+A (*with*): RECIP

collocation /kɒlə⁷keɪʃəⁿn/ is the way that some words occur regularly whenever another word is used; a technical word in linguistics. N UNCOUNT ⇑ occurrence

colloquial /kələʊkwɪəl/. **Colloquial** is used to describe words, expressions, or language that are informal, and especially used in conversation rather than formal writing. In this dictionary, such words are described as 'informal'. EG *These stories are told in colloquial and everyday language.* ◇ **colloquially**. EG *This game is colloquially known as 'Buzz off, Buster'.* ADJ QUALIT = familiar; ◇ ADV = familiarly

colloquialism /kələʊkwɪəlɪzəⁿm/, **colloquialisms**. A **colloquialism** is a colloquial word or phrase. N COUNT

colloquium /kələʊkwɪəm/, **colloquia**. A **colloquium** is a large academic seminar; a formal word. N COUNT

colloquy /kɒləkwɪ/, **colloquies**. A **colloquy** is a conversation or meeting; a formal word. N COUNT

collude /kə⁷lu:d/, **colludes, colluding, colluded**. If you **collude** with someone, you cooperate with them secretly or illegally. EG *Some groups have colluded with the unions in avoiding holding a ballot.* V OR V+A (*with*): RECIP = collaborate

collusion /kə⁷lu:ʒəⁿn/is secret or illegal cooperation, especially between countries or organizations; a formal word used showing disapproval. EG *...the council's collusion with the strikers... They act in collusion to control the market.* N UNCOUNT: IF+ PREP THEN *of/ with* = collaboration

collywobbles /kɒlɪwɒbəⁿlz/. If you have **the collywobbles**, you are very nervous and worried; an informal word. EG *All this must have given the President the collywobbles.* N PLURAL: USU *the*+N

cologne /kələʊn/ is a mild perfume. EG *She powdered herself and dabbed cologne behind her ears.* N UNCOUNT

colon /kəʊlə⁷n/, **colons**. **1** A **colon** is a punctuation mark (:), which you can use in several ways. For example, you can put it before a list of things, before reported speech, or between two parts of a sentence, when each part has the grammatical structure of a sentence. N COUNT

2 Your **colon** is the part of your intestine above your rectum. EG *He had cancer of the colon.* N COUNT

colonel /kɜ:nəⁿl/, **colonels**. A **colonel** is a senior officer in an army or air force. EG *...the youngest colonel in the French army... ...Colonel Mitchell.* N COUNT: ALSO IN TITLES BEFORE NAME

colonial /kələʊnɪəl/, **colonials**. **1** Something that is **colonial** relates to a colony or colonies. EG *...a colonial economy.* ADJ CLASSIF: ATTRIB

2 A **colonial** is someone who comes from a colony; an old-fashioned use. EG *...their disdain for foreigners and colonials.* N COUNT ⇑ person

3 A building or piece of furniture that is **Colonial** was built or made in a style that was popular in North America over two hundred years ago. EG *...a Colonial church in New England.* ADJ CLASSIF

4 **Colonial** is used to describe animals and insects that live together in a large group, for example ants; a technical use. EG *...a colonial jellyfish... ...the colonial life of termites.* ADJ CLASSIF: USU ATTRIB ⇑ social

colonialism /kələʊnɪəlɪzəⁿm/is the practice by which a powerful country controls less powerful countries and uses their resources in order to increase its own power and wealth. EG *...the legacy of colonialism... ...European colonialism.* N UNCOUNT ⇑ exploitation

colonialist /kələʊnɪəlɪst/, **colonialists**. **1** Someone who is a **colonialist** believes in colonialism or helps their country to get colonies. EG *...the efforts of colonialists to build an African elite.* N COUNT = imperialist

2 Something that is **colonialist** is related to colonialism. EG *...colonialist ideology.* ADJ CLASSIF = imperialist

colonist /kɒlə⁷nɪst/, **colonists**. A **colonist** is someone who starts a colony or who is one of the first people to live in it. EG *...the Australian colonists.* N COUNT ⇑ person = settler

colonize /kɒlə⁷naɪz/, **colonizes, colonizing, colonized**; also spelled **colonise**. **1** To **colonize** a place, area, or country means to make it into a colony. EG *...the Europeans who colonized North America... ...nations that were never colonized.* ◇ **colonized**. EG *...nationalism in the colonized countries.* ◇ **colonizing**. EG *...the political traditions of the colonizing power.* ◇ **colonization** /kɒlə⁷naɪzeɪʃəⁿn/. EG *...British colonization in India.* V OR V+O ⇑ settle; ◇ ADJ CLASSIF; ◇ ADJ CLASSIF; ◇ N UNCOUNT

2 When animals **colonize** a place, they move into it and make it their home. EG *The insects colonized the land before the vertebrates.* ◇ **colonized**. EG *...a newly colonized patch of territory.* V OR V+O ⇑ occupy; ◇ ADJ CLASSIF: ATTRIB

colonnade /kɒlə⁷neɪd/, **colonnades**. A **colonnade** is a row of evenly spaced columns. EG *...Regency colonnades.* N COUNT

colony /kɒlə⁷ni¹/, **colonies**. **1** A **colony** is **1.1** a country controlled by a more powerful country, which uses the colony's resources in order to increase its own power or wealth. EG *...colonies like Kenya, Nyasaland and Rhodesia... ...the formation of the Gold Coast as a colony.* **1.2** a place or part of a town where a particular group of people lives. EG *...a leper colony... ...a large colony of tin shacks.* ▸ used to refer to the people who live there. EG *...the original colony of social drop-outs.* N COUNT ⇑ dominion; N COUNT+SUPP = settlement

2 In old-fashioned British English, **the colonies** means all the countries that used to be British colonies. EG *I wanted to go out to the colonies and start a new life.* N PLURAL: *the*+N = empire

3 A **colony** is also a group of insects or animals that live together. EG *In a fully formed colony there must be fifty or sixty thousand bees... ...a colony of termites.* N COUNT/PART

color /kʌlə/. See **colour**. N COUNT

coloration /kʌləreɪʃəⁿn/. The **coloration** of something, for example of an animal or a plant, is the colours that you can see on it, and the way that these colours are arranged in a pattern. EG *They are called butterfly fish because of the beauty of their coloration.* N UNCOUNT = colouring

coloratura /kɒlərətʊərə/; a technical word in music. **1** **Coloratura** is very ornamental and complicated music for a solo singer, for example in an opera or oratorio. N UNCOUNT ⇑ music

2 A **coloratura** is a singer, especially a woman, who is skilled at singing coloratura. N COUNT

color line. The **color line** is a system in which black people are not allowed to take part in particular activities with white people or go into particular places; an American expression. N SING WITH DET = colour bar

colossal /kəlɒsəⁿl/. Something that is **colossal** is very large. EG *...colossal sums of money... The problems would be colossal.* ◇ **colossally**. EG *She's improved colossally over the period of the course... ...colossally powerful teaching computers.* ADJ QUALIT ⇑ huge; ◇ ADV = immensely

colossus /kəlɒsəs/, **colossuses**. A **colossus** is **1** a very important person in a particular organization or profession; an informal use. EG *...the colossus of the Bombay film world.* **2** a very large statue. EG *...the stone colossus of the rain god.* N COUNT = giant; N COUNT

colour /kʌlə/, **colours, colouring, coloured**; also spelled **color** in American English. **1** The **colour** of something is the appearance that it has as a result of reflecting light. Red, blue, and green are colours. Sometimes black and white are thought to be colours. EG *What colour was the bird?-It was blue, with a yellow front... Her face was the colour of chalk... I don't like the colour of that carpet... All the rooms were painted different colours.* N COUNT, OR *in*+N

2 **Colour** is the pleasing effect of many bright colours all together. EG *The forest flared with colour... The cock bird throws his plumes up in a shimmering fountain of colour.* N UNCOUNT

3 A **colour** is a substance, for example a dye, that you add to something in order to give it a particular colour. EG *The colours were still wet... If you wash the dress in cold water, the colour won't run.* ● See also **water-colour**. N COUNT

4 Someone's **colour** is **4.1** the normal colour of their skin, for example brown. EG *They were made to feel ashamed of their colour... You must stop being so sensitive about your colour... It was illegal to discriminate on the grounds of colour.* **4.2** a reddish-pink colour in their face that shows that their health is good. EG *He'd lost a little colour from his cheeks... Colour was coming back into his face.* ● If someone **has a high colour**, their face is redder than usual in an unhealthy way. ● See also **off-colour**. N COUNT: USU POSS+N ⇑ complexion; N UNCOUNT ⇑ rosy; ● PHR: VB INFLECTS

5 When someone **colours** or **colours up**, their face becomes red because they are angry or embarrassed. V OR PHRASAL VB: V+ADV = blush

6 When something **colours** or when you **colour** it, it changes its colour. EG *Their small leaves colour* V-ERG *brilliantly... ...french polish that has been cunningly coloured.*

7 If you **colour** a drawing, picture, etc or you **colour** it **in**, you give it different colours using paints or crayons. EG *His little girl was busy colouring in her picture.* — V+O, OR PHRASAL VB : V+O+A *(in)* = crayon

8 If something **colours** your mind or judgement, it affects the way that you think about something. EG *Anger had coloured her judgement... His mind is coloured by his unremitting study of German literature.* — V+O ⇑ affect

9 A **colour** television, picture, photograph, etc is one that shows things in all their colours, and not just in black, white, and grey. EG *He rented a colour TV... ...marvellous colour illustrations.* — ADJ CLASSIF : ATTRIB ≠ black and white

10 A book, magazine, film, etc that is **in colour** or **in full colour** has been produced in all colours, and not just in black, white, and grey. EG *Look–it's all in colour... ...that marvellous sequence in colour towards the end... ...an expensively produced book in full colour.* — PHR : USED AS AN A

11 **Colour** is also a quality that makes something especially interesting or exciting. EG *The audiences liked the romance and colour of 'The Lady's Not for Burning'.* • See also **local colour**. — N UNCOUNT ⇑ interest = spice

12 **Colours** are a special badge given to people who represent their school or university in a particular sport. EG *Just before Christmas the various sports colours are awarded... In my final year I got my first team colours for tennis and cricket.* — N PLURAL : USU the/POSS+N ⇑ emblem

13 The **colours** of a country or regiment are the special flag of that country or regiment. — N PLURAL : USU the/POSS+N

14 If you achieve something **with flying colours**, you achieve it in an especially successful way. EG *The last stage had been accomplished with flying colours.* — PHR : USED AS AN A = brilliantly

15 If you **see** someone **in** their **true colours** or they **show** their **true colours**, you realize what they are really like, especially if they are not as nice as you thought they were. EG *We now saw our countrymen in their true colours.* — PHR : VB INFLECTS

16 If you **nail** your **colours to the mast**, you make your opinions clear about something, especially when you do not intend to change your mind. EG *Schlesinger has unfortunately nailed his colours to the mast.* — PHR : VB INFLECTS ⇑ decide

17 See also **coloured, colouring**.

colour bar; also spelled with a hyphen. A **colour bar** is a social system in which black people are not allowed to mix freely with white people. EG *They broke all the social taboos of their time in reaching across the colour bar.* — N SING WITH DET ⇑ segregation = color line

colour blind; often spelled with a hyphen. Someone who is **colour blind** has something wrong with their eyes, so that they find it difficult to distinguish between colours, especially red and green. — ADJ CLASSIF

colour blindness; often spelled with a hyphen. **Colour blindness** is the inability to distinguish easily between colours, especially red and green, because you have something wrong with your eyes. — N UNCOUNT ⇑ defect

colour-coded. Things that are colour-coded have different colours on them to indicate differences in what they contain. EG *On arrival, each member receives a colour-coded badge.* — ADJ CLASSIF

coloured /kʌləd/, **coloureds**; also spelled **colored** in American English. 1 Something that is **coloured** 1.1 has a particular colour, or a particular type of colour. EG *The sky was mauve-coloured... The centre section was coloured pink... The cage was full of vividly coloured birds.* — ADJ CLASSIF : WITH ADJ COLOUR/ADV 1.2 consists of colours such as red, blue, green, etc, rather than just white or black. EG *He drew patterns on the floor in coloured chalks... ...the coloured pages in your order book.* — ADJ CLASSIF

2 A person who is **coloured** belongs to a race of people who do not have white or pale skins. EG *There were about three hundred coloured voters in the constituency... ...the integration of coloured immigrants.* ▸ sometimes used offensively as a noun. — ADJ CLASSIF; ▸ N COUNT

3 In South Africa, a person who is **coloured** has some ancestors who were white and some who were black. EG *An old coloured passenger muttered something in Afrikaans.* ▸ used as a noun. EG *...the question of voting rights for Cape coloureds.* — ADJ CLASSIF; ▸ N COUNT : USU PL

colour fast. A fabric that is **colour fast** has a colour that does not change when the fabric is washed or worn. EG *Never soak fabrics which are not colour fast.* — ADJ CLASSIF

colourful /kʌləful/; also spelled **colorful** in American English. 1 Something that is **colourful** has bright colours or a lot of different colours, which make it appear cheerful and attractive. EG *...colourful posters of Paris and Venice.* ◊ **colourfully**. EG *She took off her colourfully dyed scarf.* — ADJ QUALIT = multicoloured ≠ dull; ◊ ADV = brightly

2 A **colourful** story is full of interesting or exciting details. EG *Many colourful stories were told about him.* — ADJ CLASSIF = picturesque ≠ boring

3 Someone who is described as **colourful** has an attractive personality, because they behave in an interesting, amusing, and often eccentric way. EG *He is one of the most colourful Parliamentary figures of his age.* — ADJ QUALIT = striking

colouring /kʌlərɪŋ/; also spelled **coloring** in American English. 1 The **colouring** of something is the particular colours that it has. EG *In spite of its quite vivid colouring, it tends not to be seen as a frog.* — N UNCOUNT = coloration

2 Someone's **colouring** is the colour of their hair, skin, and eyes. — N SING : POSS+N ⇑ appearance

3 **Colouring** is a substance that is added to food to make it a particular colour. — N MASS ⇑ dye

colourless /kʌləlɪ²s/; also spelled **colorless** in American English. Something that is **colourless** 1 is dull and uninteresting. EG *He spoke in the same colourless, plodding voice... Their children are meek and colourless.* — ADJ QUALIT = lacklustre 2 has no colour at all. EG *...a colourless and tasteless liquid.* — ADJ CLASSIF = clear

colour scheme, colour schemes. A **colour scheme** is an arrangement of colours that you choose, for example for the walls, curtains, and carpet in a room. EG *At a later date you may want to change your kitchen colour scheme.* — N COUNT

colour supplement, colour supplements. A **colour supplement** is a magazine that you get free, usually once a week, when you buy a particular newspaper; used in British English. EG *She was reading the travel stuff in the colour supplement.* — N COUNT

colt /kɒlt/, **colts**. A **colt** is a young male horse. — N COUNT

coltish /kɒltɪʃ/. A young person or animal that is **coltish** is full of energy but clumsy or awkward, because they lack physical skill or control. — ADJ QUALIT ⇑ lively = frisky

columbine /kɒləmbaɪn/, **columbines**. A **columbine** is a garden plant that has brightly coloured flowers with five petals. — N COUNT ⇑ flower

column /kɒləm/, **columns**. 1 A **column** is 1.1 a tall narrow structure shaped like a solid cylinder, usually made of stone and with a decorated top. It can support or decorate part of a building or stand by itself as a monument. EG *The house had two white columns framing the entrance... ...Nelson's Column.* — N COUNT = pillar 1.2 something that has a tall narrow shape. EG *I could see columns of smoke coming up here and there... I've been adding up columns of figures all day.* — N COUNT+SUPP : USU+*of* 1.3 a group of people or animals which moves in a long well-ordered line. EG *Behind the brass band came a column of workers.* — N COUNT ⇑ formation 1.4 a vertical section of print on the page of a newspaper, magazine, etc. EG *The headline ran across all six columns.* — N COUNT 1.5 a piece of writing in a newspaper or magazine which is always written by the same person or is always about the same topic. EG *Bill used to write a column for the Bristol Evening News... ...a sports column.* — N COUNT ⇑ article = feature

2 See also **agony column, gossip column, personal column, spinal column.**

columnist /kɒləmnᵒɪst/, **columnists**. A **columnist** is a journalist who writes a regular article in a newspaper or magazine. EG *...the chief columnist of the New York Times... ...a columnist friend of mine.* — N COUNT ⇑ writer

coma /kəʊmə/, **comas**. A **coma** is a state of deep unconsciousness, usually caused by a serious head injury or by drugs. EG *Sands had slipped into a coma at the weekend... She half closed her eyes and went into a kind of coma.* — N COUNT

comatose /kəʊmətəʊs, -təʊz/. A person who is **comatose** is 1 in a coma; a technical use. EG *Patients who are comatose or mentally deranged need careful nursing.* — ADJ CLASSIF ⇑ unconscious 2 in a deep sleep because they are tired or have had too much to drink; an informal use. EG *Wilks was still comatose on the sofa at lunch time.* — ADJ CLASSIF ⇑ asleep = insensible

comb /kəʊm/, **combs, combing, combed**. 1 A **comb** is a flat piece of plastic, metal, or bone with narrow pointed teeth along one edge, which you use to tidy your hair. Some women wear curved combs in their hair as an ornament. EG *Mary opened her bag and took out her comb.* — N COUNT ⇑ device

2 When you **comb** your hair, you tidy it using a comb. — V+O

EG *He doesn't bother to comb his hair.* ▸ used as a noun. EG *Your hair could do with a comb.* ▸ N SING : a+N

3 If you **comb** a place or a particular area of land, you search everywhere in it in order to find someone or something. EG *We'll comb the countryside till we find him.* V+O : IF+PREP THEN for = scour

comb out. If you **comb** something **out** of your hair, you remove it using a comb. EG *Head lice attach their eggs to the base of your hair, and you can't comb them out.* PHRASAL VB : V+O+ADV

> **COMB** □ In this dictionary COMB is used in the grammar notes beside entries to mean a combining word. This is a use of a word which only occurs in combinations with other words, like **-legged** in **bandy-legged** and **bow-legged**.

combat /kɒmbæt/, **combats, combating, combated.** 1 **Combat** is fighting that takes place in a war. EG *He was awarded the Military Cross for gallantry in combat... ...combat aircraft.* N UNCOUNT ⇑ conflict

2 A **combat** is a battle, or a fight between two people. EG *...the mighty combats between the West and the East.* N COUNT

3 If a person in authority or an organization **combats** something, they try to stop it happening. EG *The schools were fighting endlessly to combat truancy... We have to promote interest and combat apathy.* V+O ⇑ oppose = fight

combatant /kɒmbətəᵊnt, kʌm-/, **combatants.** A **combatant** is someone who takes part in the fighting in a war. EG *A small ship sailed from Florida to land arms and combatants... ...every combatant member of the officer corps.* N COUNT ⇑ fighter

combative /kɒmbətɪv, kʌm-/. A person who is **combative** is aggressive and eager to fight or argue. EG *...a severely agitated, combative child.* ADJ QUALIT = antagonistic

combination /kɒmbɪneɪʃəᵊn/, **combinations.** 1 A **combination** is 1.1 the mixture that you get when a number of things are combined together. EG *Communication between mother and child is a subtle combination of words, expressions and movements... ...a good colour combination... Perhaps it was a combination of all these reasons.* N COUNT : ALSO in +N, IF+PREP THEN with 1.2 a series of things in a particular order, for example the series of letters or numbers that you need to know in order to open a combination lock. EG *I can't remember the combination.* N COUNT ⇑ pattern 1.3 a motorcycle and sidecar. N COUNT

2 **Combinations** are an old-fashioned undergarment that covers your body and that has long arms and legs. N PLURAL ⇑ underwear

combination lock, combination locks. A **combination lock** is a lock which can only be opened by turning a series of dials using a special sequence of letters or numbers. N COUNT

combine, combines, combining, combined. The word **combine** is pronounced /kəˀmbaɪn/ when it is a verb, and /kɒmbaɪn/ when it is a noun. 1 If you **combine** two or more things or if they **combine,** 1.1 you cause them to exist together. EG *We would all prefer to combine liberty with order... Morality and national pride combine in his public statements.* V-ERG : ALSO V OR V+A (with) : RECIP ⇑ mix 1.2 they join together to make a single thing. EG *...methane, in which carbon combines directly with hydrogen.* V-ERG : ALSO V OR V+A (with) : RECIP

2 If two or more groups or organizations **combine** or if someone **combines** them, they form a single group or organization. EG *In April 1964 the groups combined to hold a conference... Later the two teams were combined.* V-ERG : ALSO V OR V+A (with) : RECIP ⇑ unite = merge

3 A **combine** is a group of people or organizations acting together for a particular purpose. EG *...a newspaper combine... ...a production expert from the tobacco combines.* N COUNT

4 If someone or something **combines** two or more qualities or features, they have those qualities or features at the same time. EG *...the man who combines knowledge with understanding... Carbon fibre combines flexibility with immense strength.* V+O, OR V+O+A (with) : RECIP

5 If someone **combines** two or more activities, they do them at the same time. EG *One person combines the work of both District Nurse and Health Visitor... It's difficult to combine family life with a career... He succeeded in combining business with pleasure.* V+O, OR V+O+A (with) : RECIP

combined /kəˀmbaɪnd/. 1 If you say that one quality or feature is **combined with** another, or that a person or thing has two qualities or features **combined,** you mean that that person or thing has both qualities or features at the same time. EG *...a perfect example of professional expertise combined with unforgettable personal charm... Experience is fine when it's combined with the right personality... Her eyes were wide with amazement and adoration combined.* ADJ CLASSIF : PRED+ with, OR AFTER N ⇑ mixed

2 A **combined** effort, operation, etc is one that is made by two or more groups of people. EG *The combined efforts of police and military were at last successful... The attack was met by the combined strength of two US divisions.* ADJ CLASSIF : ATTRIB = joint

combine harvester, combine harvesters. A **combine harvester** is a large machine which cuts, sorts, and cleans the grain in a field when you drive it through the field. N COUNT

combo /kɒmbəʊ/, **combos.** A **combo** is a small group of jazz musicians. EG *...the night spot where John played guitar with his all-black combo.* N COUNT

combustible /kəmbʌstəbəᵊl/. Something that is **combustible** catches fire and burns easily; a formal word. EG *...combustible material... Everything combustible was destroyed.* ADJ CLASSIF = inflammable

combustion /kəmbʌstʃəᵊn/ is the act of burning something or the process by which it burns. EG *...the combustion of fossil fuels... The paper was heated to combustion point.* • See also **internal combustion engine.** N UNCOUNT

come /kʌm/, **comes, coming, came.** The form **come** is used in the present tense and is the past participle of the verb. 1 To **come** means 1.1 to move from one place to another place. You usually use 'come' when you are thinking of someone or something moving towards the place where you are. EG *She looked up when they came into the room... I will come to see you on my way home... Come and look... The children came along the beach towards me.* V : USU+A, OR V +to-INF 1.2 to arrive at a particular place, especially the place where you are sitting, standing, or waiting. EG *The waiter came to take the order... He thought he'd have another drink before the train came.* V : USU+A, OR V +to-INF ≠ leave 1.3 to go somewhere with someone when they have said they are going or have asked you to go too. EG *Will you come with me to the hospital?... Can I come too?* V : IF+PREP THEN with 1.4 to reach the particular point, height, time, etc that is mentioned. EG *Her hair came right down to her waist... Mum doesn't even come up to my shoulder.* V+A 1.5 to reach the particular state that is mentioned, especially gradually. EG *I had little hope of my wish coming true... Ordinary sellotape comes unstuck.* V+C (ADJ) ⇑ become

2 If you **come** to a place, you reach it. EG *She eventually came to the town of Peconic.* V+A (to) ≠ leave

3 If you **come** to an event such as a party, meal, conference, etc, you travel to it and spend time there. EG *Can you and Myra come to a party next Saturday?... I've got some people coming for a meal this evening.* V : IF+PREP THEN to

4 If someone or something **comes** to a particular state, position, or situation, they are in it or get into it. EG *They had come to power ten years earlier... The elevator came to a stop... He had come to the conclusion that he was not a skier.* V+A (to) ⇑ reach

5 If someone or something **comes** into being, view, sight, etc, they begin to be in the state or condition that is mentioned. EG *Christianity came into being in a hostile environment... Some people stared at me when I came into sight.* V+A (into) = emerge

6 You can also use **come** 6.1 to emphasize the continuous nature of the movement or activity that is mentioned, indicating that the movement is towards you, your home, or the place where you are. EG *Hundreds of little warm waves came washing in under me... Other presents came tumbling in... She came clambering over a pile of old junk.* V+-ING 6.2 in front of an infinitive, to indicate that something happens gradually over a fairly long period of time. EG *I have come to like him quite a lot... The more useful a thing appears, the more it comes to be used.* V+to-INF

7 If you talk about a particular time **coming,** you are referring to it approaching or arriving in the normal course of events. EG *The time has come for a full campaign against the government's spending cuts... There will come a point in the future when computers will be able to make these decisions for us... Spring came late that year to the mountains.* V : USU+A = arrive ▸ used with the subject following the verb, to mean 'when the time or event that is mentioned happens'. EG *Come tomorrow you'll feel better about things... You'll have done enough revision come the exams.* ▸ V+S = by

● If you say that you will do something **come what may**, you mean that you will do it whatever happens. EG *I'll support you, come what may.* ● Time or an event **to come** is used to refer to a future period or to an event that will happen in the future. EG *He hoped to play a significant role in the Parliamentary battle to come... Your pocket money is going to be strictly limited for some time to come.*
● PHR : AFTER NG

8 If a state or achievement **comes** in a particular way , it develops in that way before it is completely achieved. EG *I fell in love. It came slowly... His success came with unbelievable speed.*
V+A ⇑ occur

9 If you **come** to do something, you do it by accident rather than on purpose. EG *How on earth did you come to lose your hockey stick?*
V+*to*-INF = happen

10 You say **'How come?'** when you are asking how something happened or what the reason for something is. EG *I can see your child is hurt. How come?... How come you're up so early?*
PHR

1 If something such as a memory or answer **comes** to you, you remember or realize it, often suddenly or when you are not thinking about it. EG *A memory comes to me of snowfields in June... The answer came to him just before noon... It came to me suddenly that what was wrong was that I was tired.*
V+A *(to)* = occur

12 The word **come** is used in expressions such as **'Come to think of it'** or **'When you come to think of it'** to indicate that you have suddenly realized something, often something obvious, which you feel you should have realized earlier. EG *Come to think of it, why should I apologize?... Twelve times a year is not much when you come to think of it.*
PHR : USED AS ADV SEN

13 If something **comes** to a particular number, price, or amount, it adds up to it. EG *My income now comes to £65 a week.*
V+A *(to)*

14 If you **come** to a subject, you start studying it or become interested in it. EG *Some students coming to Shakespeare nowadays know nothing about English history.*
V+A *(to)*

15 If money, property, etc **comes** to you, it is received by you, usually after the previous owner has died and left it to you in his or her will. EG *He could not prevent certain trust funds coming to her on her 21st birthday.*
V+A *(to)* = fall

16 If something **comes** from or out of a particular place, it has that place as its source or starting point. EG *There was music coming from the drawing-room.*
V+A *(from/out of)* = originate

17 To **come** from something means **17.1** to be obtained or derived from it. EG *Did you know the word 'idea' comes from Greek?... These rules come from the children themselves... Where is the money to come from?* **17.2** to be a part taken from something else. EG *This extract comes from a conversation I had... It comes from the radio feature 'From Wigan to Rome.'*
V+A *(from)*
V+A *(from)*

18 To **come** from something or to **come** of something also means to be the result of it. EG *Depression often comes from bad eating... I'll let you know what comes of the meeting... You're always reading. No good will come of it, you'll see!*
V+A *(from/of)*

19 If a person **comes** of a particular family or group of ancestors, he or she is descended from them. EG *She comes of royal blood.*
V+A *(of)*

20 If someone or something **comes** first, next, last, etc, **20.1** they occur at that point in the series or order. EG *What comes next then?... He pointed out that first things must come first.* **20.2** they finish a race, competition, etc in that place. EG *I was never in any race in which I didn't come last.*
V+A
V+A

21 If people or cases **come** before a court of law or some other official place, they are present or are presented there in order that a legal or other issue can be dealt with. EG *His case came before a tribunal... The major came before the Armed Services Committee.*
V+A *(before)*

22 If a product **comes** in a particular style, colour, etc or with particular features, it is available for you to get or buy in the way described. EG *The van came in two colours, medium brown or medium grey... Each copy of the book comes with its own magnifying glass.*
V : USU+*in*

23 To **come** can also mean to exist or be found in a particular form. EG *People come in all shapes and sizes.*
V+A, OR V+C ⇑ exist

24 When something such as news or an announcement or decision **comes**, it is announced or made in public, so that other people can hear or learn about it. EG *Mr Healey's accusation came on ITV's 'Weekend World' programme... The President's final decision came about 36 hours later.*
V : USU+A ⇑ happen

25 The word **come** is also used in expressions such as 'It came as a surprise' when you want to mention a person's reaction to something. EG *It comes as no surprise to discover that Americans usually love Britain... These events came as a traumatic shock.*
V : NG/*it*+V+A *(as)* ⇑ be

26 **Come** can also be used to indicate that you are about to start talking about a new topic or a new aspect of a topic. EG *Now we come to the most important thing... Coming to the secret bombing of Cambodia, the Senate were never consulted.*
V+A *(to)* = turn

27 The expression **'When it comes to'** is used to introduce a particular subject that you want to talk about. EG *I realized how inadequate words could be when it came to defining a very large idea.*
PHR+NG : VB INFLECTS

28 You can say **'Come again?'** in informal English to ask someone to repeat what they have just said, because you did not hear it or you are surprised by it.
CONVENTION = what?

29 **'If it comes to that'** is used when you are making an accusation or criticism in reply to one that has been made against you. EG *Well, you owe me a fiver, if it comes to that.*
PHR : USED AS AN A = for that matter

30 **'What is it all coming to?'** is an expression that people use when they feel that everything is getting worse and that they cannot see when it will start to improve. EG *I don't know what it's all coming to... He made his workers a slave. That was what it was coming to.*
PHR : VB INFLECTS

31 You can say **'Come'** to reassure someone or to encourage them to do something that they do not want to do. EG *Come, love, don't be afraid.*
CONVENTION

32 You say **'Come, come!'** to indicate that you disapprove of or disagree with something that has just been said. EG *Oh, come, come! No, I can't possibly agree with that.*
CONVENTION ≠ hear, hear

33 When you **come of age**, you reach the age at which you are legally considered to be an adult by the society you live in. In Britain people come of age when they are 18 years old. ● See also **coming-of-age**.
PHR : VB INFLECTS

34 If you say that someone is **as** stupid, pretty, miserable, etc **as they come**, you mean that they are extremely stupid, pretty, miserable, etc; an informal expression. EG *The girls were as daft as they come.*
PHR : USED AS C = as can be

35 If someone says that you **have it coming to** you, they mean that you deserve everything unpleasant that is going to happen to you, because you have behaved badly or done something wrong; an informal expression. EG *He had it coming to him.* ● If you **get what is coming to** you, you are punished or suffer an unpleasant experience because you have behaved badly or done something wrong; an informal expression.
PHR : VB *(have)* INFLECTS
● PHR : VB *(get)* +AUX INFLECT

36 If you say that things **come and go**, you mean that they change regularly. EG *Fashions come and go at a dizzying pace.*
PHR : VBS INFLECT

37 If you **do not know whether** you **are coming or going**, you are so busy that you are totally confused. EG *I've got so much to do I don't know whether I'm coming or going.* ● **Comings and goings**: see **coming**.
PHR : AUXS *(do/are)* INFLECT

38 If you say that you will have your tea, coffee, etc **as it comes**, you mean that you do not mind how strong or weak it is. EG *'How do you like your tea?'-'As it comes.'*
PHR : USED AS AN A

24 In informal English, if a person **comes** when having sex, he or she has an orgasm.
V

39 The word **come** is also used in the following expressions, which are explained at other places in this dictionary. ● to **come to the fore**: see **fore**. ● to **come to grips with**: see **grip**. ● to **come to a head**: see **head**. ● to **come to life**: see **life**. ● to **come to light**: see **light**. ● to **come into line**: see **line**. ● to **come to mind**: see **mind**. ● to **come to pass**: see **pass**. ● to **come into play**: see **play**. ● to **come up to scratch**: see **scratch**. ● to **come to terms with**: see **term**. ● to **come your way**: see **way**.

37 ● See also **coming**.

come about. If something **comes about**, it happens or takes place. EG *The discovery of adrenalin came about through a mistake... How did the invitation come about?*
PHRASAL VB : V+ADV ⇑ happen

come across. **1** If you **come across** someone or something, you meet or find them unexpectedly and by chance. EG *I came across a letter from Brunel the*
PHRASAL VB : V+PREP ⇑ encounter

other day... Everyone has come across the sort of problem which seems impossible to solve.

2 If an idea or meaning **comes across**, it is effectively communicated to the reader, audience, listener, etc. EG *Do you think this idea comes across in the play?* PHRASAL VB : V+ ADV ⇑ communicate

3 If a person or thing **comes across** in a particular way, they give people the impression of having a particular character or characteristic. EG *He wasn't coming across as the idiot I had expected him to be... It comes across as a play which could be effective if only it had a better cast.* PHRASAL VB : V+ ADV+PREP *(as)*

come along. 1 You say **'come along'** to someone 1.1 when you are encouraging them to do something they do not really want to do. EG *Come along, now, drink this.* PHR 1.2 when you are encouraging them to hurry up, especially if you are slightly irritated with them for being so slow. EG *Come along now, little ones, off to bed... Please come along! We're going to be terribly late.* PHR

2 When something **comes along**, it arrives or happens unexpectedly and by chance. EG *A really good 'Midsummer Night's Dream' seems to come along once in every ten years... A new generation of planners came along who were much more scientifically based.* PHRASAL VB : V+ ADV = arrive

3 If something **is coming along**, it is making progress or developing; used in informal English. EG *There are even cookers which tell you how the meat is coming along... Your son is really coming along.* PHRASAL VB : V+ ADV : ONLY CONT

come apart. If something **comes apart**, it breaks into two or more pieces. EG *I'm sorry, it just came apart in my hands.* PHRASAL VB : V+ ADV ⇑ break

come around. 1 If you **come around**, you call at someone's house to see them for a short time; used in informal English. PHRASAL VB : V+ ADV = come over

2 To **come around** also means the same as to come round. PHRASAL VB : V+ ADV

come at. 1 To **come at** someone means to move towards them in a threatening way and to attack them. EG *The bear came at me... Who knew what sharp implement might be coming at my shoulder blades?* PHRASAL VB : V+ PREP

2 If questions, facts, images, etc **come at** you, they all come together in a threatening or confusing way. EG *Questions came at me from all sides.* PHRASAL VB : V+ PREP = bombard

come away. 1 If you **come away** from a place, you leave it. EG *We came away with the uncomfortable feeling that we had not been welcome.* PHRASAL VB : V+ ADV = depart ≠ arrive

2 If something **comes away** from something else, it becomes separated or detached from it very easily, so that you do not have to pull it or force it at all. EG *The book's cover had come away from the spine.* PHRASAL VB : V+ ADV, IF+PREP THEN *from*

come back. 1 To **come back** somewhere means to return to that place. EG *He came back from the war... Are you ever coming back home?... Colour was coming back into his face.* PHRASAL VB : V+ ADV

2 To **come back** to a topic, question, idea, etc means to return to it, often because it is the explanation for something. EG *He always came back to this point... It comes back to what I said earlier... We'll come back to that question a little later.* PHRASAL VB : V+ ADV+*to*

3 If you **come back** with a new point or idea, you add it to what you have already said after someone has answered your first point. EG *She came back with an explanation of her original statement.* PHRASAL VB : V+ ADV ⇑ reply

4 If a scene, event, name, etc that you had forgotten **comes back** to you, you remember it, often quite suddenly. EG *Against his will, the whole episode came back to him... It was all coming back to him. She was the girl from the sweet shop.* PHRASAL VB : V+ ADV, USU+*to*

5 When something **comes back**, it becomes fashionable again, after being unfashionable for a time. EG *Ostrich feathers never really came back... At last reliability and efficiency seem to be coming back into fashion.* PHRASAL VB : V+ ADV ⇑ return ≠ go out

6 See also **comeback**.

come between. If something **comes between** two people, it causes trouble between them and so spoils their friendship. EG *I had come between him and his girlfriend... Legal action threatened to come between Tynan and Trevor-Roper.* PHRASAL VB : V+ PREP = divide ≠ unite

come by. To **come by** something means to find or obtain it, usually unexpectedly or by chance. EG *Jobs were hard to come by... He had not come by these things through his own labour.* PHRASAL VB : V+ PREP, HAS PASS ≠ lose

come down. 1 If the cost, level, or amount of something **comes down**, it becomes cheaper or less than it was before. EG *Inflation is starting to come down... Local government expenditure has come down by 20% since 1975.* PHRASAL VB : V+ ADV ⇑ diminish ≠ go up

2 If you **come down** to a place, you visit it; used when the place is farther south than the place you are coming from or is in the country. EG *Harold will be coming down next Sunday... I am coming down to London next week.* PHRASAL VB : V+ ADV, USU+A

3 If something such as a tradition, belief, or land **comes down** to a person or group of people, it is passed from one generation to another. EG *The religious doctrines which have come down to us are not always relevant to the present day... The house came down to him from his aunt.* PHRASAL VB : V+ ADV, IF+PREP THEN *to/from*

4 If something **comes down**, it falls to the ground. EG *He tripped over a branch and came down with a crash... In the storm a tree came down.* PHRASAL VB : V+ ADV = fall

5 If rain or snow **comes down**, it falls heavily; sometimes also used of thick fog. EG *It came down in sheets... Five inches of snow had fallen and more was coming down...* PHRASAL VB : V+ ADV = fall

6 When a university student **comes down**, he or she leaves university, especially at the end of a degree course; used in British English. EG *He came down from Oxford in 1958.* PHRASAL VB : V+ ADV ≠ go up

7 If someone has **come down in the world**, they are less wealthy or important than they used to be. EG *He has moved house and has certainly come down in the world.* PHR : VB INFLECTS

8 See also **come-down**.

come down on. If you **come down on** someone, you blame them for something, and criticize them severely for allowing it to happen. EG *Social workers like me come down harder on parents than on their children.* PHRASAL VB : V+ ADV+PREP ≠ praise

come down to. If a problem, decision, question, etc **comes down to** a particular consideration, it can be reduced to that basic consideration. EG *Your final choice of kitchen may well come down to cost... It all comes down to the mathematics taught in schools.* PHRASAL VB : V+ ADV+PREP ⇑ reduce

come down with. If you **come down with** an illness or disease, you catch it. EG *She came down with pneumonia.* PHRASAL VB : V+ ADV+PREP ⇑ contract

come for. 1 If someone **comes for** you, they move towards you quickly in a threatening way, in order to attack you. EG *Jake was coming for me with a knife.* PHRASAL VB : V+ PREP = come at

2 If you **come for** something or someone, you come to get it and take it away, usually because you have a right to do so or because it is your job to do so. EG *I had said I would come for Dolly in the afternoon... The dustmen came for the rubbish every Wednesday.* PHRASAL VB : V+ PREP ⇑ COLLECT

come forward. 1 If someone **comes forward** to do something, they offer to do what is required. EG *More coloured men are now coming forward to join the police... People won't come forward with evidence in court.* PHRASAL VB : V+ ADV = volunteer

2 If you **come forward** with a suggestion, proposal, solution, etc, you offer it. EG *I'll wait until he comes forward with some new proposals.* PHRASAL VB : V+ ADV+*with*

come from. To **come from** somewhere means to be born in a particular place, or into a particular family, or to have a particular background. EG *'Where do you come from?'–'India'... I don't come from the right background or the right school.* PHRASAL VB : V+ PREP ⇑ originate

come in. 1 If you **come in** or **come into** a room, house, etc, you enter it. EG *Come in, Celia, don't stand in the rain... Boylan came silently into the room.* PHRASAL VB : V+ ADV/PREP ≠ leave

2 When a train, plane, ship, etc **comes in**, it arrives. EG *Her train came in on time.* PHRASAL VB : V+ ADV

3 If something such as information or a report **comes in**, it is received. EG *Reports are coming in from Mexico of a major earthquake.* PHRASAL VB : V+ ADV = arrive

4 If you have money **coming in**, you earn it or receive it as your normal income. EG *The taxman is entitled to details of the money you have coming in.* PHRASAL VB : V+ ADV ≠ go out

5 If something such as a seasonal product or a fashion **is coming in**, it is becoming available or fashionable at a particular time. EG *Strawberries are just coming in... An absurd habit is coming in of calling a chairman or chairwoman a 'chair'.* PHRASAL VB : V+ ADV ≠ go out

6 If someone **comes in** on a discussion, they join in, sometimes interrupting someone who is already speaking. EG *Let me just come in on this, because Clive is not giving the whole story... Could I come in here?* PHRASAL VB : V+ ADV, USU+A ⇑ interrupt

7 If someone **comes in** on an arrangement, they join a group of other people and take part in what they are planning to do. EG *He should come in on the deal... You can come in for half-a-million.* PHRASAL VB : V+ ADV, USU+A = participate

8 When a government **comes in**, it wins an election and starts governing the country. EG *Labour governments come in promising to expand public expenditure.* PHRASAL VB : V+ ADV ≠ go out

9 If you ask where something or someone **comes in**, you are asking how they are involved in a situation. EG *Where does your husband come in?... This is where legislation comes in.* PHRASAL VB : V+ ADV

10 If you say, **'This is where we came in'**, you mean that the situation has returned to the same stage as it had reached when you first became involved with it. PHR : VBS INFLECT

11 If something **comes in useful** or **comes in handy**, it is a useful thing to have. EG *A toothbrush would come in handy... His medical degree will come in very useful in the future.* PHR : VB INFLECTS ⇑ serve

12 When the tide **comes in**, it rises, so that the water reaches higher up the shore. PHRASAL VB : V+ ADV

come in for. If someone or something **comes in for** criticism, blame, abuse, etc, they receive it, usually a lot of it. EG *British industry does come in for a great deal of criticism.* PHRASAL VB : V+ ADV+PREP = suffer

come into. **1** If someone **comes into** something, they inherit it. EG *She was going to come into some more money on her mother's death... He had come into the title the previous year.* PHRASAL VB : V+ PREP

2 If someone **comes into** their **own**, they begin to perform or work really well because the circumstances are just right. EG *Brooke came into his own when he was appointed Home Secretary.* PHR : VB INFLECTS = blossom ≠ fade

3 If you say that something **comes into it**, you mean that it is an important aspect of the situation you are talking about. EG *Prestige comes into it as much as other factors... Facts don't come into it a great deal as far as faith is concerned.* PHR : VB INFLECTS = feature

come off. **1** If something **comes off**, **1.1** it becomes unfastened, unstuck, or detached from something else.. EG *All the wall paper's coming off... He tugged at the metal handle and it came off in his hand.* PHRASAL VB : V+ ADV/PREP ⇑ detach **1.2** it is successful or effective. EG *The interaction between them came off brilliantly in their second film together.* PHRASAL VB : V+ ADV, USU+ADV **1.3** it takes place as planned. EG *How will you feel if the marriage comes off?* PHRASAL VB : V+ ADV

2 If you **come off** well or badly, you are in a good or bad position at the end of a process as a result of it. EG *Many academics are convinced that the universities came off so badly because the government did not understand their needs... He didn't really deserve to come off the winner.* PHRASAL VB : V+ ADV+ADV/C

3 When a play or film **comes off**, it stops being performed or shown in a particular theatre, cinema, etc. EG *The production had to come off because the theatre was already booked for a pantomime.* PHRASAL VB : V+ ADV = close

4 If someone **comes off** something such as a drug, medicine, or alcohol, they stop taking it. EG *I'd come off the pill if I were you... It's about time you came off the booze.* PHRASAL VB : V+ PREP = give up ≠ go on

5 You say **'come off it'** to someone to show them that you think what they are saying is stupid; an informal expression. EG *'He's absolutely right.'-'Oh, come off it. He doesn't know what he's talking about.'* CONVENTION

come on. **1** You say **'Come on' 1.1** when you want to encourage someone to do or say something they are reluctant to do or say. EG *Come on, Wendy, you say something.* PHR **1.2** when you want to encourage someone to hurry up. EG *Come on, or you'll miss your boat.* PHR **1.3** when you are very annoyed with someone and think that what they are doing or saying is silly or unreasonable. EG *Oh Jane, come on, for goodness sake.* PHR

2 When an actor or actress **comes on**, he or she appears on a stage or in a scene of a film. EG *Olivier dominated the play from the moment he came on the stage.* PHRASAL VB : V+ ADV/PREP

3 If you **come on** something or someone, you find or meet them, usually unexpectedly and by chance. EG *I came on the idea by pure chance... It was half an hour before he came on the note in his tray.* PHRASAL VB : V+ PREP

4 If a cold, headache, or some other medical condition **is coming on**, it is just starting. EG *I felt a cold coming on.* PHRASAL VB : V+ ADV ⇑ start

5 If something **is coming on**, it is making progress or developing. EG *My new book is coming on quite well now.* PHRASAL VB : V+ ADV, USU+A ⇑ develop

6 When electricity, gas, water, etc **comes on**, it starts working or functioning. EG *The lights came on... What time does the central heating come on?* PHRASAL VB : V+ ADV ≠ go off

7 See also **come-on**.

come on to. If you **come on to** a particular topic or idea, you start discussing it. EG *I want to come on to the question of disease in a minute.* PHRASAL VB : V+ ADV+PREP = turn to

come out. **1** When information **comes out**, it is revealed or made public; used especially of information that has deliberately been kept secret. EG *All the facts came out after Seery's death... It came out that the more money you make the less tax you are likely to pay.* PHRASAL VB : V+ ADV ⇑ emerge

2 If a fact **comes out**, it becomes known to people, for example after an inquiry. EG *Something that comes out very clearly in interviews is how predictable people's answers are... It was in those times that the best and the worst in people came out.* PHRASAL VB : V+ ADV ⇑ emerge

3 When something such as a book **comes out**, it is published or becomes available to the public. EG *Over the summer his book had come out... He asked me to send him any new stamps which might come out.* PHRASAL VB : V+ ADV, USU+A = appear

4 To **come out** in a particular position or in a particular way means to be in that position or way at the end of a contest, process, etc. EG *Who do you think will come out on top?... The press was coming out of the affair very badly... Her clothes always came out looking faintly home made... The numbers came out exactly right.* PHRASAL VB : V+ ADV, USU+A/C ⇑ finish

5 If what you say **comes out** in a particular way, it is said in that way. EG *The words came out more harshly than she had intended.* PHRASAL VB : V+ ADV+A ⇑ seem

6 In British English, to **come out** means to go on strike. EG *The whole work force promptly came out.* PHRASAL VB : V+ ADV

7 If someone **comes out**, they admit something about themselves openly and publicly that they were ashamed of or keeping secret, for example that they are homosexual. PHRASAL VB : V+ ADV

8 If you **come out** for or against something, you declare that you do or do not support it. EG *They all came out against abortion... He came out in support of the claim.* PHRASAL VB : V+ ADV+A

9 When the sun, moon, or stars **come out**, they appear in the sky. EG *It was cold and the sun never came out once.* PHRASAL VB : V+ ADV ≠ go in

10 If colours, stains, or marks **come out**, they fade or disappear. EG *Be careful when you're washing that towel or the colour will come out... That grass stain just won't come out.* PHRASAL VB : V+ ADV

11 If a photograph or something that has been photographed **comes out**, it is successful as a photograph, and all the details can be seen. EG *Did those photos come out that you took at Hilda's party?... Annabel did not come out well.* PHRASAL VB : V+ ADV

come out in. If you or your body **comes out in** spots, pimples, a rash, etc, you become covered with it. PHRASAL VB : V+ ADV+PREP = break out in

come out of. **1** If one thing **comes out of something else, the first thing** results from the second thing. EG *Expert systems have come out of artificial intelligence research.* PHRASAL VB : V+ ADV+PREP

2 If something **comes out of** a particular place or source, it originates or is produced there. EG *Information coming out of the country was unreliable... This was the first story of general interest to come out of Canada's Northwest for many years.* PHRASAL VB : V+ ADV+PREP

3 If you **come out of** yourself or **come out of** your **shell**, you force yourself to be less shy and reserved and more friendly to other people. PHR : VB INFLECTS = perk up

come out with. If someone **comes out with** something, they say it, often unexpectedly. EG *Occasionally they come out with fascinating snippets of gossip... One evening John came out with an unusual proposal.* PHRASAL VB : V+ ADV+PREP = announce

come over. **1** If something strange **comes over** you, it affects you and makes you behave in an uncharacteristic way. EG *She wondered what could have come over him all of a sudden... I don't know what came over me... A mysterious change came over my senses.* PHRASAL VB : V+ PREP ⇑ influence = affect

2 If you **come over** dizzy, shy, etc, you start feeling that way; an informal expression. EG *She comes over all shy when she has to meet new people.* PHRASAL VB : V+ ADV+ADJ

3 If you **come over**, **3.1** you come to the country which you are talking about from another country. EG *He'd come over on leave from Northern Ireland... He'd met her on the plane coming over.* PHRASAL VB : V+ ADV, USU+A **3.2** you call PHRASAL VB : V+

at someone's house to see them for a short time. EG *You can come over tomorrow at four... May I come over?* ADV ⇑ visit

4 If an idea or meaning **comes over**, it is effectively communicated to the reader, audience, listener, etc. EG *I don't think that the larger symbolic purpose really comes over in this particular painting.* PHRASAL VB : V+ADV = come across

6 If a person or thing **comes over** in a particular way, they give people the impression of having a particular character or characteristic. EG *It came over as a very half-hearted attempt.* PHRASAL VB : V+ADV+A = come across

come round. 1 If you **come round** to something that someone else believes or has suggested, you change your mind about it so that you now agree with it. EG *He knew I would have to come round to his way of thinking in the end.* PHRASAL VB : V+ADV, USU+*to* = come around

2 If you **come round** to someone that you disliked, you change your mind about them and begin to respect, like, or even love them. EG *At first I thought he was a bully; but I came round to him in the end.* PHRASAL VB : V+ADV, USU+*to* = warm

3 If something **comes round**, it happens as a regular or predictable event. EG *Don't wait for April to come round before planning your vegetable garden... She'll be a jolly tough candidate to beat when the election comes round.* PHRASAL VB : V+ADV ⇑ occur

4 If a person **comes round**, they recover consciousness. PHRASAL VB : V+ADV

5 If you **come round**, you call at someone's house to see them for a short time. EG *Is Nell coming round?... I could come round this evening if you like.* PHRASAL VB : V+ADV = come over

come through. 1 To **come through** a dangerous or difficult situation means to survive it and usually recover completely from it. EG *Most of the troops came through the fighting unharmed... When a couple comes through a crisis like this together, their relationship should be stronger than ever.* PHRASAL VB : V+ADV/PREP

2 If something **comes through**, it **2.1** is shown by what is said or done, and is communicated to the reader, audience, or listener. EG *I think the teacher's own personality has got to come through... What came through most forcibly was a sense of excitement.* PHRASAL VB : V+ADV = come across **2.2** arrives, especially after some procedure has been carried out. EG *Has my visa has come through yet?* PHRASAL VB : V+ADV ⇑ arrive

3 If you **come through** or **come through** with something, you produce or do something that is expected of you. EG *He finally came through with the documents.* PHRASAL VB : V+ADV, IF+PREP THEN *with*

come to. If a person **comes to**, they recover consciousness. EG *That's about all I remember, until I came to in a life-raft.* PHRASAL VB : V+ADV ⇑ wake = come round

come under. 1 If something **comes under** a particular authority or control, it is managed or controlled by it. EG *Day Nurseries come under the Department of Health and Social Security.* PHRASAL VB : V+PREP

2 If you **come under** criticism, attack, etc, you receive it, especially a lot of it. EG *The premier came under severe criticism... British produce came under pressure from foreign competition.* PHRASAL VB : V+PREP = suffer

3 If one thing **comes under** something else, it is in that class or category, or is filed in that place. EG *Records and tapes come under published material.* PHRASAL VB : V+PREP

come up. 1 If you **come up** or **come up** to someone, you approach them until you are standing next to them. EG *An old man came up and spoke to him... Bill came up to Ralph.* PHRASAL VB : V+ADV, IF+PREP THEN *to*

2 If something **comes up** in a conversation or meeting, it is mentioned or discussed. EG *His name came up at a buffet lunch... Egyptian art came up as a topic.* PHRASAL VB : V+ADV = crop up

3 If something **is coming up**, it is about to happen or take place. EG *There's a royal wedding coming up... The SDP are fighting any election that comes up anywhere.* PHRASAL VB : V+ADV

4 If an event or situation that is a problem **comes up**, it happens unexpectedly. EG *I can't see you tonight. Something's come up.* PHRASAL VB : V+ADV ⇑ occur = crop up

5 If someone **comes up**, they become a member of a higher social class than they were born into, or they become a respected member of their profession. EG *Boulton was a Birmingham craftsman who came up the hard way.* PHRASAL VB : V+ADV, USU+A ⇑ rise ● If you say that someone has **come up in the world**, you mean that they are in a higher social class or more successful than they used to be. ● PHR : VB INFLECTS

6 If someone or something **comes up**, they are put forward for discussion, or as a candidate in an election, etc. EG *A third of my colleagues will come up for election next May... The pension scheme has come up for review.* PHRASAL VB : V+ADV, IF+PREP THEN *for*

7 If a job **comes up**, it becomes available. EG *When I applied here, I didn't know this post in Oxford would come up.* PHRASAL VB : V+ADV

8 When the sun or moon **comes up**, it rises. EG *The sun comes up in the East.* PHRASAL VB : V+ADV

9 If a wind, sound, light, etc **comes up**, it grows stronger, louder, or brighter. EG *There's a wind coming up... The lights came up.* PHRASAL VB : V+ADV ⇑ intensify

10 If a case **comes up**, it is heard in a court of law. EG *A case on Corporate fraud came up in the Chancery Courts recently.* PHRASAL VB : V+ADV

11 When a seed, bulb, etc **comes up**, it grows and pushes through the soil. EG *It doesn't look as if any carrots are going to come up this year.* PHRASAL VB : V+ADV ⇑ grow

come up against. If you **come up against** a problem or difficulty, you are faced with it and have to deal with it. EG *Everyone comes up against discrimination sooner or later.* PHRASAL VB : V+ADV+PREP ⇑ meet

come upon. 1 If you **come upon** someone or something, you meet or find them unexpectedly and by chance. EG *They rounded a turn and came upon a family of lions.* PHRASAL VB : V+PREP ⇑ encounter = come across

2 If an idea or feeling **comes upon** you, it appears without you really being aware of it. EG *His new outlook on life had come upon him gradually.* PHRASAL VB : V+PREP = occur to

come up to. 1 If something **comes up to** something else, it is as good as the other thing or as good as people expected it to be. EG *His later books never really came up to expectations.* PHRASAL VB : V+ADV+PREP, USU WITH BROAD NEG = live up to

2 To **be coming up to** a time or state means to be getting near to it. EG *Some of them are coming up to retirement... It was just coming up to ten o'clock.* PHRASAL VB : V+ADV+PREP = approach

come up with. 1 If you **come up with** something such as a plan, idea, or solution, you think of it and suggest it. EG *I hope to come up with some of the answers... It didn't take her long to come up with a very convincing example.* PHRASAL VB : V+ADV+PREP ⇑ propose

2 If you **come up with** a sum of money, you produce it when it is especially needed. EG *You have no choice but to come up with the £120,000.* PHRASAL VB : V+ADV+PREP

comeback /kʌmbæk/, **comebacks. 1** If an activity, type of clothing, etc makes a **comeback**, it becomes fashionable again. EG *Body painting made a brief comeback in the 1960s.* N COUNT = reappearance

2 If a person makes or stages a **comeback**, they are successful again at something that they used to be successful at before. EG *I tried to make a comeback before I was thirty.* N COUNT

comedian /kəmiːdiən/, **comedians.** A **comedian** is **1** a person, usually a man, whose job is to make people laugh, especially by telling them jokes or funny stories. EG *...professional singers and comedians.* N COUNT ⇑ entertainer = comic **2** an actor who acts especially in comedy; an old-fashioned word. EG *He won a best-actor award as a comedian in The Alchemist.* N COUNT ≠ tragedian

comedienne /kəmiːdiɛn/, **comediennes.** A **comedienne** is a woman who is employed to make people laugh, especially by telling them jokes or funny stories. N COUNT ⇑ entertainer

come-down; also spelled as one word. You say that something is a **come-down** if you think that it is not as good as something else that you have just done or had. EG *Professionally it is considered a come-down to work in portrait classes... The Polytechnic seemed a bit of a come-down after Oxford... What a come-down!* N SING : *a*+N ⇑ disappointment = let down

comedy /kɒmɪ²di¹/, **comedies. 1** A **comedy** is a play or film that has a happy ending and that deals with real-life situations in a light-hearted way: compare **farce.** EG *...a country house comedy... ...a revival of Maugham's comedy Caroline... Comedy is about the fact that life goes on.* ● See also **musical comedy.** N COUNT/UNCOUNT ⇑ entertainment

2 Comedy is something that makes people laugh or amuses them in literature or in real life. EG *The play had plenty of melodrama and excitement as well as comedy... ...her rare gift for comedy on the stage... This provided some good comedy.* N UNCOUNT = humour

comely /kʌmli¹/, **comelier, comeliest.** A person, especially a woman, who is **comely** has an attractive appearance; an old-fashioned word. EG *...a comely girl.* ADJ QUALIT = good-looking ◊ **comeliness.** EG *...a desirable comeliness.* ◊ N UNCOUNT

come-on, come-ons. A **come-on** is something that is intended to make you want to do something, buy something, etc; used showing disapproval. EG *Re-* N COUNT ⇑ invitation *marks like this are a tease, a come-on... ...the come-on bargains at the chain stores.*

comer /kʌmə/, **comers**. 1 **All comers** refers to everyone who challenges or who might challenge someone, usually a champion, to a fight or contest. EG *The champion was relaxing after an afternoon beating all comers... He looked hearty enough to take on all comers.* PHR: USED AS O/S = challenger

2 **Comers** are people who arrive at a particular place. EG *The gates were firmly closed to all comers... The towel holds germs, then passes them on to the next comer.* N COUNT+SUPP: USU PL

comet /kɒmɪ²t/, **comets**. A **comet** is an object that travels around the sun leaving a bright trail behind it. EG *...Halley's comet.* N COUNT

come-uppance /kʌmʌpəns/. When someone gets their **come-uppance**, they are justly punished for something that they have done. EG *It is difficult not to be pleased at his come-uppance... They are at last getting their come-uppance for ignoring our needs.* N SING: DETPOSS +N ⇑ punishment

comfort /kʌmfət/, **comforts, comforting, comforted**. 1 **Comfort** is 1.1 the state of being physically relaxed that you get, for example, when you are warm and in an armchair or in bed. EG *She longed to stretch out in comfort... It was a hard narrow chair and not made for comfort.* N UNCOUNT ≠ discomfort 1.2 a style of life that is pleasant and in which you have enough money to live on without financial problems. EG *She wanted a life of reasonable comfort... ...a world of material comfort.* N UNCOUNT = luxury 1.3 a feeling of relief from worries, unhappiness, or disappointment. EG *I found comfort in his words... Your visits may give some comfort to the patient... Neither of the main parties can take much comfort from recent trends.* N UNCOUNT = consolation ▸ A **comfort** is someone or something that gives you this feeling. EG *It will be a comfort to him to know that you are standing by.* ▸ N COUNT ⇑ help

2 If you say that something is **too** close, thin, etc **for comfort**, you mean that the fact that it is close, thin, etc makes you worried and unhappy. EG *The exams were getting too close for comfort... Her comments were a little too revealing for comfort.* PHR: USED AS C

3 **Comforts** are things which are not necessary but which make your life easier and more pleasant, especially in your home. EG *I longed for the comforts of home... She did not earn sufficient to provide for the comforts she needed.* N COUNT: USU PL

4 To **comfort** someone means to make them feel less worried or unhappy. EG *Jeannie came to comfort him... The Red Cross had been sent to comfort the survivors... The familiar sound comforted her.* V+O ⇑ help = console ◇ **comforting**. EG *...a comforting thought.* ◇ ADJ QUALIT

comfortable /kʌmfə⁰təbə⁰l/. 1 Something that is **comfortable** makes you feel physically relaxed when you are using it, for example because of its shape, the things that it contains, or its appearance. EG *That chair is quite comfortable... The hotel was large and comfortable... ...comfortable suburban houses.* ADJ QUALIT = snug ≠ uncomfortable

2 If you are **comfortable**, 2.1 you are physically relaxed, because of the place or position that you are sitting or lying in. EG *Sit down and make yourself comfortable... Sam felt comfortable and even luxurious.* ADJ QUALIT = at ease ≠ uncomfortable ◇ **comfortably**. EG *They were too cold to sleep comfortably... I put my pillow on the saddle so I could ride comfortably.* ◇ ADV 2.2 you have enough money to be able to live without financial problems. EG *She was comfortable, even wealthy by old standards... ...comfortable middle-class women from America.* ADJ QUALIT = well-to-do ◇ **comfortably**. EG *She has been living quite comfortably since her husband died.* ◇ ADV 2.3 you feel confident and are not worried, afraid, or embarrassed. EG *He did not feel comfortable with strangers... Would you feel comfortable criticizing the state?* ADJ QUALIT: USU PRED = easy ≠ uncomfortable

3 When a person who has had an accident or who has fallen ill is **comfortable**, they are in a stable physical condition. EG *The two survivors are in hospital, where they are said to be comfortable.* ADJ QUALIT: PRED = satisfactory

4 A **comfortable** person is a person who is easy to talk to and relaxing to be with; used showing approval. EG *She was a comfortable grandmotherly woman.* ADJ QUALIT = cosy

5 A **comfortable** job, task, etc is one which is quite easy to do and which does not cause you many problems or worries. EG *They wanted to get their boys into nice comfortable jobs.* ADJ QUALIT = cushy ◇ **comfortably**. EG *I can manage the work comfortably.* ◇ ADV = easily

6 A **comfortable** opinion, belief, etc is one that is easy to accept because it helps you to forget about the difficult or unpleasant aspects of something; used showing disapproval. EG *...the comfortable belief that nothing is likely to go wrong.* ADJ QUALIT

comforter /kʌmfətə/, **comforters**. A **comforter** is 1 a person or thing that comforts you. EG *He rang up another comforter, seeking the same reassurances... The baby's bottle becomes a precious comforter at bedtime.* N COUNT 2 In American English, a baby's dummy. N COUNT 3 a scarf that you wear in order to keep you warm. EG *They spent their time knitting comforters.* N COUNT

comfrey /kʌmfri¹/ is a herb that is used to make drinks and medicines. N UNCOUNT

comfy /kʌmfi¹/, **comfier, comfiest**. **Comfy** means the same as comfortable; an informal word. EG *The first three women to arrive had the comfy chairs... 'Comfy?' he enquired.* ADJ QUALIT

comic /kɒmɪk/, **comics**. 1 Something that is **comic** amuses you and makes you want to laugh. EG *He likes wearing comic hats... ...a story rich in comic and dramatic detail.* ADJ QUALIT ⇑ amusing = funny

2 A **comic** is a person who tells jokes in order to make people laugh. EG *When the comic comes on they'll all laugh.* N COUNT = comedian

3 In British English, a **comic** is also a magazine, usually for children, that contains stories told in pictures. EG *He saw me reading a comic... ...a science fiction comic.* N COUNT = comic book

comical /kɒmɪkə⁰l/. A person, situation, etc that is **comical** amuses you and makes you want to laugh. EG *There is something slightly comical about him... He widened his eyes in a comical look of surprised seriousness.* ADJ QUALIT ⇑ amusing = droll, whimsical ◇ **comically**. EG *David looked comically astonished... He added comically, 'I think I'm one of the safest people around.'* ◇ ADV = absurdly

comic book, comic books. A **comic book** is a magazine, usually for children, that contains stories told in pictures; used in American English. EG *He seemed to read a lot of comic books.* N COUNT = comic

comic opera, comic operas. A **comic opera** is an opera which has an amusing story and in which there is speech as well as singing. N COUNT

comic strip, comic strips; also spelled with a hyphen. A **comic strip** is a series of drawings or cartoons that tell a story. EG *Later he became the inspiration for the American comic strip the Katzenjammer Kids.* N COUNT = cartoon

coming /kʌmɪŋ/, **comings**. 1 A **coming** event or time is an event or time that will happen soon. EG *He had decided to support the Labour Party at the coming election... The real struggle will take place in the coming weeks.* ADJ CLASSIF: ATTRIB ⇑ future = approaching

2 **Comings and goings** are the arrivals and departures of people at a particular place. EG *She it was who supervised their comings and goings... Their task was to keep tabs on the comings and goings of the guests.* PHR+SUPP: USED AS O/S = movements

comma /kɒmə/, **commas**. A **comma** is the punctuation mark (,) which is used to separate parts of a sentence or items in a list. In some countries it is also used in numbers instead of a decimal point. EG *Sometimes you miss out a comma because you're writing too quickly.* N COUNT

command /kəmɑːnd/, **commands, commanding, commanded**. 1 If you **command** someone to do something, you order them to do it. EG *'Stay here!' he commanded... She commanded me to lie down and relax... She will do whatever he commands.* V+O/QUOTE, V+O+*to*-INF/QUOTE, OR V = instruct ▸ used as a noun. EG *They waited for their master's command... ...the final word of command.* ▸ N COUNT/UNCOUNT = instruction

2 To **command** something means 2.1 to order that it shall happen or that it shall be brought to you. EG *The king had commanded his presence at court... Jocasta commanded another drink and leaned back.* V+O ⇑ demand 2.2 to obtain it as a result of being popular or important. EG *She was no longer in a position to command obedience or admiration... The campaign commanded support from all parties... ...a shirt that could command a good price in Boston or Manhattan.* V+O ⇑ get 2.3 to be in total control of it, especially as a result of being very powerful. EG *Once the Royal Navy had commanded the seas... ...the tiny country commanding the Bab al Mandab straits.* V+O = rule ▸ used as a noun. EG *Our forces improved their command of the air... Labour won almost total command of local government.* ▸ N UNCOUNT+*of*

3 An officer who **commands** part of an army, navy, or air force is the officer responsible for controlling V OR V+O: USU V+O

and organizing it. EG *He commanded a regiment of cavalry in Algiers.* ▸ used as a noun. EG *Monty took command of the Eighth Army on August 13... ...the British Forces under his command... He had been in command of HMS Churchill for nearly a year.* ▸ N UNCOUNT ⇑ control = charge

4 A **command** is also **4.1** a group of officers who are responsible for organizing and controlling part of an army. EG *The advance was halted once the enemy command realized what was going on... We wanted to infiltrate the German Army command.* N COUNT+SUPP : USU SING : IF SING, VB CAN BE SING OR PL **4.2** a group of soldiers that a particular officer is in charge of. EG *One mistake and half his command would get wiped out... His command looked in reasonable shape.* N COUNT+SUPP : USU SING : IF SING, VB CAN BE SING OR PL **4.3** a part of an army or an air force with a particular function. EG *...RAF Strike Command... ...North American Air Defence Command.* N COUNT : IN NAMES AFTER N **4.4** an instruction given to a computer; a technical term. EG *...a simple set of programs or command mechanisms.* N COUNT

5 Someone who is **second in command, third in command**, etc of an organization or group is the second, third, etc most important person in charge of the organization or group. EG *Williams was appointed assistant editor, third in command after George Farr... You'll have to refer that to my second in command.* PHR : USED AS S/O/C

6 **Command** is also control over a particular situation achieved by using your power or authority. EG *Lady Sackville, as usual, took command... The editorial policy of the Daily Mail was under his total command... He was looking more relaxed and in command than ever before.* N UNCOUNT = charge ● If you are **in command** of yourself, **in command** of your faculties, etc, you are able to react and behave the way that you want to in a particular situation. EG *She felt happy and in command of herself... She was in full command of all her faculties.* ● PHR : USED AS AN A, IF+PREP THEN *of* = in control of

7 Your **command** of something is your knowledge of it and your ability to use this knowledge. EG *...a good command of spoken English... ...his supreme command of revolutionary theory.* N UNCOUNT+*of* : USU DET+N = grasp ● If you have a particular skill or ability **at** your **command**, you have it and can use it fully in your work or in a particular task. EG *He was manoeuvring now with all the craft and skill at his command... ...a writer who has both elegance and passion at his command.* ● PHR : USED AS AN A

8 To **command** a view of a place means to be able to see all of it very clearly. EG *The Duke commanded a good view of the courtyard from his windows.* V+O = enjoy ▸ used as a noun. EG *...the Tower Gardens, with huge trees and an excellent command of the river.* ▸ N SING WITH DET

commandant /kɒməndænt/, **commandants**. A **commandant** is an army officer who is in charge of a particular place or group of people. EG *...the commandant of a concentration camp... ...Commandant Chapman.* N COUNT : ALSO IN TITLES

commandeer /kɒməndɪə/, **commandeers, commandeering, commandeered**. To **commandeer** something means **1** to officially take it from someone so that it can be used by the army, air force, navy, or police. EG *Lodge arrived in Saigon and commandeered the villa of the CIA chief... ...the thought of the federal government commandeering their land.* V+O = requisition **2** to take something from a less powerful person when you have no right to take it; used showing disapproval. EG *...a tiny office that he has commandeered from a secretary.* V+O = usurp

commander /kəmɑːndə/, **commanders**. A **commander** is **1** an officer in an army, navy, or air force who is in charge of a particular military operation or organization. EG *Montgomery was a cautious commander who never took risks.* N COUNT **2** an officer with a particular rank in the Royal Navy. EG *My father's a commander in the Navy... ...Commander Peter Keene.* N COUNT : ALSO IN TITLES

commander-in-chief, commanders-in-chief. A **commander-in-chief** is an officer who is in charge of all the forces fighting in a particular area or taking part in a particular operation. EG *That year Haig replaced French as Commander-in-chief of the western front.* N COUNT : ALSO IN TITLES

commanding /kəmɑːndɪŋ/. **1** If you are in a **commanding** position, situation, etc, you are in a position, situation, etc where you are able to control people and events. EG *Britain had lost her once commanding position in the world.* ADJ QUALIT : ATTRIB ⇑ powerful = dominant ≠ subordinate

2 A **commanding** voice, manner, etc is one that makes people respect you because they think that you are powerful or important. EG *He gave orders in a commanding voice.* ADJ QUALIT : USU ATTRIB = authoritative ◊ **commandingly**. EG *He speaks confidently and commandingly of his views and experiences.* ◊ ADV

3 A building that has a **commanding** position has good views of the surrounding area because it has been built in a high place. EG *The University stands in a commanding position overlooking Belfast Loch.* ADJ QUALIT : ATTRIB

commanding officer, commanding officers. A **commanding officer** is an officer who is in charge of a military unit. EG *The Colonel was a good commanding officer who stuck by his men.* N COUNT

commandment /kəmɑːndmə[ə]nt/, **commandments**. A **commandment** is one of the ten rules of behaviour which, according to the Old Testament of the Bible, God says that we should obey. EG *You must obey the Ten Commandments... 'Muriel,' she said, 'Read me the Fourth Commandment.'* N COUNT ⇑ law

commando /kəmɑːndəʊ/, **commandos**. A **commando** is a small group of soldiers that is specially trained to attack important targets that are difficult or dangerous to reach. EG *...the side road where the second commando of OAS men waited.* N COUNT : ALSO N +*of*+N IN PL ▸ **Commando** is used also of a member of the group. EG *The commandos headed across the bridges.* ▸ N COUNT ⇑ soldier

command post, command posts. A **command post** is a place from which a commander in the army controls and organizes his forces. EG *...a divisional command post.* N COUNT

commemorate /kəmeməreɪt/, **commemorates, commemorating, commemorated**. **1** An object that **commemorates** a person or an event has been made or built in order to make people remember the person or event. EG *...a monument commemorating a great administrator.* V+O = immortalize

2 If you **commemorate** an event, you do something special to show that you remember it, especially on an anniversary of the event. EG *Today we commemorate the end of the Second World War.* V+O = celebrate ◊ **commemoration** /kəmeməreɪʃə[0]n/, **commemorations**. EG *...the commemoration of the fiftieth anniversary of the revolution... ...a wreathlaying ceremony in commemoration of the death of a student killed during the uprising.* ◊ N UNCOUNT/COUNT : IF+PREP THEN *of* ⇑ remembrance

commemorative /kəmemə[0]rətɪv/. A **commemorative** stamp, medal, etc is a stamp, medal, etc that commemorates a particular event or person. EG *...the issue of commemorative stamps... ...a commemorative plaque.* ADJ CLASSIF : ATTRIB ⇑ special = memorial

commence /kəmens/, **commences, commencing, commenced**. **1** When something **commences**, it begins; a rather formal word. EG *The bidding commenced... ...a series of conversations, all of which commence with 'How've you been?'* V = begin, start

2 If you **commence** doing something, you begin doing it; a rather formal word. EG *I commenced a round of visits... He let his oars sink into the water and commenced pulling with long strokes.* V+O (NG/-ING) = start

commencement /kəmensmə[ə]nt/, **commencements**. **1** The **commencement** of something is its beginning; a formal word. EG *...the commencement of the flight... ...the commencement of the present century.* N UNCOUNT : USU *the*+N+*of*

2 In the United States, **Commencement** is a ceremony at a university in which graduates formally receive their degrees. EG *Seventeen thousand people jam into Harvard Yard on Commencement morning.* N UNCOUNT = graduation

commend /kəmend/, **commends, commending, commended**. **1** If you **commend** someone or **commend** something that they do, you praise them in a formal way. EG *I was commended by Richards for my reports... I especially want to commend the efforts of Dr Fitzgerald.* V+O : IF+PREP THEN *for/to* = applaud ≠ condemn ◊ **commendation** /kɒmendeɪʃə[0]n/. EG *His action earned the personal commendation of the prime minister.* ◊ N UNCOUNT/COUNT = acclaim

2 If you **commend** something to someone, you tell them that it is very good or important. EG *He commended the scheme warmly... Rothermere commended Baldwin to his readers as a great man.* V+O (NG/REFL) : IF+PREP THEN *to/as* ⇑ represent = recommend

3 If something **commends** itself to you, you approve of it. EG *Leninism obviously commends itself to a militant labour leader.* V+O (REFL)+A (*to*)

commendable /kəmendəbə[0]l/. Behaviour that is **commendable** is behaviour that you think should be admired and praised. EG *...a commendable sense of* ADJ QUALIT ⇑ good = admirable *purpose... It is commendable that a fifteen-year-old girl should be so responsible.*

commensurate /kəmɛnsərə¹t, -ʃə-/. If an amount is **commensurate** with another amount, it is in proportion to the other amount; a formal word. EG *The house brings in a return commensurate with its current market value.* ADJ CLASSIF: USU PRED+*with* = in line with

comment /kɒmɛnt/, **comments, commenting, commented. 1** If you **comment** on something, you say something that gives your opinion about it or an explanation for it. EG *Both of the girls commented on Chris's size... The minister refused to comment publicly on these claims... 'It needs washing,' she commented.* V: USU+A (*on/upon*), OR V+REPORT-CL/QUOTE ⇑ remark

2 A **comment** is a statement of opinion about something. EG *People in the town started making rude comments... He thanked me for it, but made no comment... He was not available for comment yesterday.* ● People say **no comment** as a way of refusing to answer a question during an interview or a press conference. EG *'Do you intend to keep them in prison?'-'No comment.'.* N COUNT/UNCOUNT: IF+PREP THEN *on/upon*, OR+REPORT-CL ● CONVENTION

3 A **comment** is also an event or situation that shows something good or bad about a particular society or state of affairs. EG *I think this is a very sad comment on what is happening to our country.* N COUNT: IF+PREP THEN *on/upon* = reflection

4 Comment is also criticism or discussion about a particular thing or idea. EG *Few organisations excite so much comment as the Prices and Incomes Board.* N UNCOUNT ⇑ reaction

commentary /kɒmɒntə⁰ri¹/, **commentaries.** A **commentary** is **1** a description of an event that you can listen to on the radio or on television while the event is taking place. EG *We were clustered round a radio to hear the commentary... ...a commentary on the Cheltenham Gold Cup.* **2** a book or article which has been written as a way of explaining or discussing something and making it easier to understand. EG *...a series of political commentaries in New Society... ...magazines carrying news as well as commentary.* N COUNT: IF+PREP THEN *on* N COUNT/UNCOUNT ⇑ writing

commentate /kɒmənteɪt/, **commentates, commentating, commentated.** To **commentate** means to give a radio or television commentary on an event. V: IF+PREP THEN *on* ⇑ describe

commentator /kɒmənteɪtə/, **commentators.** A **commentator** is **1** a broadcaster who gives a radio or television commentary on an event. EG *...the commentators for the World Cup in Mexico.* **1.2** an expert on a particular subject who often writes or broadcasts about it. EG *...Peter Jenkins, an experienced commentator on political affairs.* N COUNT N COUNT: IF+PREP THEN *on* = pundit

commerce /kɒmɜːs/ is **1** the activities and procedures involved in buying and selling things. EG *...the world of industry and commerce... Seacombe had always been a centre of commerce.* **2** relations between people or groups of people, especially when this involves the exchange of ideas, opinions, etc; an old-fashioned literary word. EG *...a flowering of commerce between heaven and earth... Friendship is a disinterested commerce between equals.* N UNCOUNT ⇑ business = trade N UNCOUNT

commercial /kəmɜːʃə⁰l/, **commercials. 1 Commercial** means involving or relating to commerce and business. EG *...commercial and industrial organisations... ...a course in commercial French.* ADJ CLASSIF: USU ATTRIB

2 Something is a **commercial** success, failure, etc if it succeeds or fails to make money. EG *People knew that Concorde would never be a commercial success... ...the commercial future of nuclear power.* ◇ **commercially.** EG *...a commercially competitive nuclear reactor.* ADJ CLASSIF: USU ATTRIB ⇑ financial ◇ ADV ⇑ financially

3 A **commercial** activity is an activity in which goods are produced in very large quantities in a highly organized way. EG *...commercial agriculture... ...a big commercial bakery... ...the commercial cinema.* ◇ **commercially.** EG *After the mid-nineteenth century, slate was quarried commercially.* ADJ CLASSIF: USU ATTRIB ⇑ industrial ◇ ADV

4 A **commercial** product is made to be sold to the public. EG *...a commercial rust remover... The first commercial versions of this computer may be on sale next year.* ◇ **commercially.** EG *A long time elapsed before typewriters became commercially available.* ADJ CLASSIF: USU ATTRIB ◇ ADV ⇑ publicly

5 Commercial television and radio are television and radio that are paid for by the broadcasting of advertisements between programmes. EG *...the case for commercial broadcasting.* ADJ CLASSIF: USU ATTRIB ⇑ sponsored

6 A **commercial** is an advertisement that is broadcast on television or radio. EG *...a Cinzano commercial.* N COUNT

commercial art is the activities, processes, and skills involved in producing advertisements and in designing the way that products look. N UNCOUNT ≠ fine art

commercial artist, commercial artists. A **commercial artist** is a person whose job involves producing advertisements and designing the way that products look. N COUNT

commercial bank, commercial banks. A **commercial bank** is a bank which makes short-term loans using money from current accounts; a technical term. N COUNT ≠ merchant bank

commercialism /kəmɜːʃəlɪzə⁰m/ is the practice of making a lot of money from things, without caring about their quality; used showing disapproval. EG *...the shoddy culture of mass commercialism.* N UNCOUNT

commercialization /kəmɜːʃəlaɪzeɪʃə⁰n/; also spelled **commercialisation. Commercialization** is the process by which something becomes commercialized. EG *...the commercialization of sport.* N UNCOUNT ⇑ exploitation

commercialized /kəmɜːʃəlaɪzd/; also spelled **commercialised.** Something that is **commercialized** is organized in a way that is mainly concerned with making money; used showing disapproval. EG *One always thinks of Majorca as being very commercialised... The ceremonies have degenerated into vulgar, commercialized spectacles.* ADJ QUALIT

commercial traveller, commercial travellers; also spelled **commercial traveler** in American English. A **commercial traveller** is a salesman or saleswoman who travels to different places and meets people in order to sell goods or take orders. N COUNT = travelling salesman

commercial vehicle, commercial vehicles. A **commercial vehicle** is a vehicle used for carrying goods or passengers along roads. EG *...the declining commercial vehicle market.* N COUNT

commie /kɒmi¹/, **commies.** A **commie** is someone who believes in communism; an informal and offensive word. N COUNT = communist

commiserate /kəmɪzəreɪt/, **commiserates, commiserating, commiserated.** If you **commiserate** with someone, you show them that you feel pity or sympathy for them when they are unhappy or when something unpleasant has happened to them. EG *I commiserated with him over the recent news.* V: IF+PREP THEN *with* ⇑ sympathize

commiseration /kəmɪzəreɪʃə⁰n/, **commiserations. Commiseration** is pity or sympathy for someone who has recently had an unhappy or unfortunate experience. EG *She gave him a look of commiseration.* ▸ You say **'commiserations'** to someone in order to express your sympathy for them. EG *Congratulations to the winners, and commiserations to the losers.* N UNCOUNT ▸ N PLURAL: ALSO USED AS CONVENTION

commissariat /kɒmɪseəriət/, **commissariats.** A **commissariat** is a military department that is in charge of food supplies. N COUNT: IF SING VB CAN BE SING OR PL

commissary /kɒmɪsə⁰ri¹/, **commissaries.** A **commissary** is a shop that provides food and equipment in a place such as a military camp or a prison; used in American English. EG *The only available source of real milk was the commissiary.* N COUNT

commission /kəmɪʃə⁰n/, **commissions, commissioning, commissioned. 1** If you **commission** something or **commission** someone to do something you formally arrange with someone to pay them to do a piece of work for you. EG *The Times commissioned a Public Opinion Poll... These pieces were commissioned by Queen Victoria... Brook commissioned a couple of dramatists to write a play for him.* V+O, OR V+O+*to*-INF ⇑ order = request, authorize

2 A **commission** is **2.1** a particular piece of work that an artist, designer, or other person or organization is asked to do and is paid for. EG *Red House was Webb's first independent commission as an architect... He was very good at getting commissions.* **2.2** in formal English, a job, duty, or task that has been given to someone. N COUNT ⇑ job N COUNT = mission

3 Commission or a **commission** is a sum of money paid to a salesman for every sale that he or she makes. EG *They get commission on top of their basic salary.* ● If you are **on commission** or paid **by commission,** you are paid by a system in which the amount that you receive depends on how much you sell. EG *You will be paid by commission... These jobs are all on commission only.* N UNCOUNT/COUNT ● PHR: USED AS AN A

4 A **commission** is also a group of people who have been appointed to find out about something or to control something. EG *A commission was appointed to investigate the assassination... The court accepted the commission's conclusions... ...the European Commission on Human Rights.* ● See also **High Commission**.
N COUNT: ALSO IN NAMES, IF SING, VB CAN BE SING OR PL

5 **Commission** of a crime or piece of wrongdoing is the act of doing it; a formal word. EG *They must satisfy the court that they have not contributed to the commission of the offence.*
N UNCOUNT

6 The **commission** of an officer in the army, navy, or air force is the authority given to him or her by his or her country to serve in the armed services and to give military orders. EG *Colonel Mitchell resigned his commission in 1959... In the 19th century, commissions in the British Army could be purchased.*
N COUNT

7 When an officer **is commissioned**, he or she receives a commission in the army, navy, or air force. EG *He was commissioned as an RAF pilot on 10 March 1945.*
V+O: USU PASS ⇑ appoint

8 If something is **out of commission**, it is broken or not working. EG *If this system is put out of commission, the economy loses the ability to react to sudden change.*
PHR: USED AS AN A = out of order

commissionaire /kəmɪʃənɛə/, **commissionaires**. A **commissionaire** is a man in a uniform who is employed to stand in the entrance of a hotel, theatre, cinema, etc to open doors and help customers or patrons.
N COUNT = doorman

commissioned officer, commissioned officers. A **commissioned officer** is an officer in the army, navy, or air force who has a commission, usually one who has been recruited and specially trained as an officer, rather than being promoted through a series of lower ranks.
N COUNT

commissioner /kəmɪʃəⁿnə/, **commissioners**. A **commissioner** is an important official in a government department or some other organization. EG *...a police commissioner... ...the Church Commissioners.* ● See also **High Commissioner**.
N COUNT: ALSO IN TITLES, USU MOD+N

commit /kəmɪt/, **commits, committing, committed**. 1 If someone **commits** a crime or something else which is wrong, they do it. EG *About 17% of all crime in 1938 was committed by people under 21... He has committed a criminal offence.* ● If someone **commits suicide**, they kill themselves.
V+O ⇑ perform; ● PHR: VB INFLECTS

2 If you **commit** money, resources, etc to something, you decide to use them for a particular purpose, and not for anything else. EG *Rolls Royce must commit its entire resources to the project... He commits an hour to reading the newspapers every morning.*
V+O: IF+PREP THEN *to* = allot, allocate

3 If you **commit** yourself to a course of action, you decide that you will do it and you let people know about your decision. EG *One of the strengths of a church wedding is that it commits two whole families to the support of the marriage... They want to experiment with computers without committing themselves to any capital expenditure.* ◊ **committed**. EG *He was a committed Marxist.*
V+O (REFL): IF +PREP THEN *to* = bind, pledge; ◊ ADJ QUALIT

4 If you do not want to **commit** yourself, you do not want to say clearly what you think about something or what you are going to do. EG *I really wouldn't like to commit myself... They didn't commit themselves on that.*
V+O (REFL): USU+BROAD NEG ⇑ express

5 If someone **is committed** to a hospital, prison, or some other institution means they are sent there officially for a time, either because they are ill or because they have done something wrong. EG *She was committed to a nursing home... He was committed to jail.*
V+O: USU PASS, IF+PREP THEN *to* = confine

6 If you **commit** something **to memory**, you memorize it. EG *You'll need these figures so often that you must commit them to memory.*
PHR: VB INFLECTS

7 If you **commit** something **to paper**, you write it down. EG *He held his tongue and committed his thoughts to paper only.*
PHR: VB INFLECTS = write down

8 See also **committed**.

commitment /kəmɪtmə²nt/, **commitments**. 1 **Commitment** is a strong belief in an idea or system, especially when it is shown by your actions and behaviour. EG *There is no doubting his enthusiasm or his commitment... ...your long commitment to feminism.*
N UNCOUNT = loyalty

2 A **commitment** is 2.1 something which takes up some of your time, because of agreements that you have made or responsibilities that you have. EG *She's got family commitments... My husband, because of his own professional commitments, is in Cambridge every week.*
N COUNT: USU PL ⇑ involvement = responsibility

2.2 a firm promise or agreement. EG *To become a disciple of his is to make a lifetime commitment... He gave a clear commitment to reopen disarmament talks.*
N COUNT = undertaking

committal /kəmɪtəⁿl/ is the process of officially sending someone to prison or to hospital. EG *A maximum of 110 days may elapse between committal and trial. ...a committal order.*
N UNCOUNT

committee /kəmɪti¹/, **committees**. A **committee** is a group of people who represent a larger group or organization and who make decisions or plans for it. EG *A special committee has been set up... The whole Committee are very grateful to you... ...the National Executive Committee... Coordination is difficult to achieve by committee.*
N COUNT: VB CAN BE SING OR PL, OR *by*+N

commode /kəməʊd/, **commodes**. A **commode** is a movable piece of furniture shaped like a chair or a stool, which has a large pot below or inside it. It is used as a toilet, especially by people who are too ill to be able to walk to the toilet easily.
N COUNT

commodious /kəməʊdɪəs/. A room or house that is **commodious** is large and has plenty of space. EG *...a commodious building suitable for conversion.*
ADJ QUALIT = spacious

commodity /kəmɒdɪti¹/, **commodities**. A **commodity** is something that is sold for money, such as food, clothing, or machinery. EG *The best land is reserved for such commodities as coffee, cotton and bananas... Labour is bought and sold like any other commodity.*
N COUNT ⇑ merchandise = product

commodore /kɒmədɔː/, **commodores**. A **commodore** is an officer of senior rank in the navy or air force.
N COUNT: ALSO IN TITLES

common /kɒmən/, **commoner, commonest; commons**. 1 If something is **common**, 1.1 it occurs or is found in large numbers or happens often. EG *Durand is a common name there... The rhesus is one of the commonest monkeys in India... I found out that it was quite common for dogs to be poisoned this way.* ◊ **commonly**. EG *The most commonly used argument is that clients do not like long delays.*
ADJ QUALIT ≠ rare, unique, unusual; ◊ ADV

1.2 it is possessed, done, or used by two or more people. EG *We shared a common language... It suppressed the desire for freedom common to all people.... Your country and mine have a common frontier.*
ADJ CLASSIF: IF+ PREP THEN *to* ⇑ shared

2 If two or more things have something **in common**, they have the same characteristic or feature. EG *What have these names in common?... They share two crucial features in common with the new countries of Afro-Asia... In common with many other companies, we advertise in the local press.* ● If two or more people have something **in common**, they share the same interests or experiences, which makes it easier for them to have a friendly relationship with one another. EG *I never thought I would ever have anything in common with George... You two have got a lot in common.*
PHR: USED AS AN A, IF+PREP THEN *with* ⇑ alike; ● PHR: USED AS AN A, IF+PREP THEN *with*

3 **Common** is also used 3.1 in the names of species of animals, plants, etc of which there are more than there are of other related species. EG *...the common European toad.*
ADJ CLASSIF: ATTRIB

3.2 to mention that something is ordinary and not special in any way. EG *Sodium chloride is better known as common salt... The common people in those days suffered a lot.*
ADJ CLASSIF: ATTRIB

3.3 to mention something, such as a way of behaving, which people expect other people in general to share. EG *The President cannot sacrifice common courtesy to some purely regional prejudice... ...common decency... They appealed to a sense of fair play and common justice.*
ADJ CLASSIF: ATTRIB = standard

4 **Common** knowledge, understanding, etc, is known or understood by people in general. EG *It was common knowledge that he lived alone in the mansion... He was by common agreement the best War Minister since Cardwell.* ◊ **commonly**. EG *Chauffeurs, it is commonly agreed, know more about what is going on than their employers think.*
ADJ CLASSIF: ATTRIB = popular; ◊ ADV WITH VB = generally, popularly

5 A person who is **common** behaves in a way that is socially unacceptable and that shows lack of taste, education, or good manners; used showing disapproval. EG *She was often ill-behaved, sometimes even common and rude.*
ADJ QUALIT = ill-bred ≠ refined

6 A **common** is an area of grassy land in or near a village where the public is allowed to go. EG *He met them on the common.*
N COUNT: ALSO IN NAMES AFTER N

7 The **Commons** is the more powerful of the two
N PROPER: *the*+

parts of parliament in Britain or Canada, to which members are elected by the adult population of the country. EG *The election was announced in the Commons by Bonar Law on 14 November 1918.* N = House of Commons

8 The word **common** is also used in the following expressions. 8.1 **Common or garden** is used to describe something which is ordinary and not special in any way. EG *These are common or garden transistors.* PHR : USED AS MOD/C 8.2 If something is done **for the common good** it is done for the benefit or advantage of everyone in the community. EG *... learn to cooperate efficiently for the common good.* PHR : USED AS AN A 8.3 **Common ground** is something which two or more people or groups agree about; used especially when they do not agree about other things. EG *There is no common ground upon which dialogue can be based... That the present system is unsatisfactory is common ground among a number of writers.* PHR : USED AS C/O 8.4 **The common touch** is a person's natural ability to have a good relationship with ordinary people and be popular with them. EG *Even his enemies had to admit he had the common touch... He despised his fellow MPs for affecting the common touch.* PHR : USED AS O ⇑ sociability

common cold, common colds. The **common cold** is a mild illness. If you have it, your nose is blocked, you sneeze a lot, and you have a sore throat or a cough. EG *A common cold could kill her.* N COUNT

common denominator, common denominators. A **common denominator** is 1 a number which can be divided exactly by all the denominators in a group of fractions; a technical term in mathematics. N COUNT
2 a characteristic or attitude that is shared by all members of a group of people. EG *Employer groups tend to reflect the lowest common denominator among their members.* N COUNT

commoner /kɒmənə/, **commoners**. A **commoner** is a person who is not a member of the nobility and so does not have a title. EG *Legislation was passed allowing the sons of peers to remain commoners.* N COUNT

common land is land which everyone is allowed to go on. N UNCOUNT

common law is the system of law, especially in England, which is based on judges' decisions and on custom rather than on written laws. EG *Our legal system is based on common law.* N UNCOUNT

common-law is used to describe a relationship that is regarded as a marriage because it has lasted a long time, although no official marriage contract has been signed. EG *...common-law marriage... ...his common-law wife.* ADJ CLASSIF : ATTRIB

Common Market. The **Common Market** is an organization of West European countries, including the UK, who make decisions together about their trade, agriculture, and other policies. N PROPER : *the*+N = EEC

commonplace /kɒmənpleɪs/, **commonplaces**. 1 Something that is **commonplace** occurs often or is seen often, and so is not surprising or worth remarking on. EG *Even in France, disposable cigarette lighters are commonplace... Air travel has now become commonplace... The most commonplace things excited her interest.* ADJ QUALIT ⇑ common = ordinary ≠ rare, unusual ▸ used as a noun. EG *In earlier centuries the death of children was a commonplace.* ▸ N COUNT : USU SING
2 A **commonplace** is a remark or opinion that is often expressed and so is perhaps not very interesting. EG *It is a commonplace that it always rains in Manchester.* N COUNT = platitude

common room, common rooms; also spelled with a hyphen. A **common room** is a room in an institution, especially a university or school, where people can sit, talk, and relax. EG *...the junior common-room.* N COUNT

common sense; also spelled with a hyphen and as one word. **Common sense** is a person's natural ability to make good judgements and to behave in a practical and sensible way. EG *Use your common sense... This precaution is simply common sense... It was a victory for commonsense.* N UNCOUNT ⇑ practicality ▸ used as an adjective. EG *...the commonsense view... Take a few common-sense steps to help the situation.* ▸ ADJ CLASSIF : ATTRIB

commonwealth /kɒmənwɛlθ/, **commonwealths**. 1 The **Commonwealth** is an association of countries that were once part of the British Empire and that still have political and other links with each other. EG *Previously, something like 45 percent of British trade was with the Commonwealth... ...the Commonwealth Games.* N PROPER : *the*+N 2 In old-fashioned or very formal English, a **commonwealth** is a nation, a state, or a federation regarded as a unit composed of people who have similar political interests for many purposes. N COUNT

commotion /kəməʊʃəⁿn/. A **commotion** is a lot of noise, confusion, and excitement. EG *There was a commotion at the other end of the bar... During all the commotion I had hardly noticed my little brother.* N SING WITH DET, OR N UNCOUNT

communal /kɒmjəⁱnəⁱl/. 1 Something that is **communal** is used by or belongs to a group of people rather than an individual. EG *...a communal dining-room... The fields are communal property and no one really owns them.* ADJ CLASSIF ⇑ shared = public ≠ private ◇ **communally**. EG *The mills are owned communally.* ◇ ADV WITH VB = jointly
2 **Communal** is used to describe a way of life in which a group of people all live and do things together. EG *...a communal style of life... ...a society that was communal.* ADJ CLASSIF ⇑ shared = collective ≠ individual ◇ **communally**. EG *...the problems of living communally.* ◇ ADV WITH VB

commune, communes, communing, communed. The word **commune** is pronounced /kɒmju:n/ when it is a noun, and /kəmju:n/ when it is a verb. 1 A **commune** is a group of people or families who all live together and share everything. EG *She went to live in a women's commune.* N COUNT : IF SING, VB CAN BE SING OR PL
2 If you **commune** with nature or some other power or spirit, you feel that you have a very close relationship with it, especially when you are on your own. EG *...a beautiful spot where one communed with God and Nature... I spent far too much time communing with the dead.* V+A *(with)* ⇑ communicate

communicant /kəmju:nɪkənt/, **communicants**. A **communicant** is a person in the Christian church who receives communion. EG *The bell was to summon communicants.* N COUNT ⇑ Christian

communicate /kəmju:nɪkeɪt/, **communicates, communicating, communicated**. 1 If you **communicate** with another person, place, living thing, etc, 1.1 you use signals, such as speech, radio signals, or body movements, to give them information. EG *He communicates with Miami by radio... Through signs she communicated that she wanted a drink... Bees have several ways of communicating.* V OR V+A *(with)* : RECIP
1.2 you contact them by writing a letter to them or calling them on the telephone; a fairly formal word. EG *Anthony and I hadn't communicated for years.* V OR V+A *(with)* : RECIP
2 If you **communicate** an idea or feeling to someone, you make them aware of it, often so that they then have that idea or feeling too. EG *...the failure of intellectuals to communicate their ideas to a wider audience... The restlessness communicated itself to all levels of society.* V+O (NG/REFL) +A *(to)* ⇑ convey = impart, transmit
3 If two people **communicate**, they feel that they can understand each other's feelings or attitudes. EG *Cliff talked to me a few times but we couldn't really communicate.* V OR V+A *(with)* : RECIP ⇑ relate

communicating /kəmju:nɪkeɪtɪŋ/ is used to refer to two rooms or apartments that are next to each other with a door between them, so that you can go from one into the other. EG *...a partition dividing the room into two communicating love nests... The two rooms were en suite, with a communicating door.* ADJ CLASSIF : ATTRIB ⇑ connecting

communication /kəmju:nɪkeɪʃəⁿn/, **communications**. 1 **Communication** is the activity or process of giving information to other people or to other living things, using signals such as speech, body movements, or radio signals. EG *Insects such as ants have a highly effective system of communication... ...electronic technology, with its wonders of communication... ...the level of communication between mother and child.* N UNCOUNT
2 **Communications** are the systems and processes that are used to communicate or to broadcast information, especially those that use electricity or radio waves. EG *...the current revolution in communications... ...to put large numbers of communications satellites into space... the relationship between the natural communications systems of other species and those of human beings.* N PLURAL ⇑ process
3 A **communication** is a letter, telephone call, or some other message; a formal use. EG *...a secret communication from the Foreign Minister... They had had no communications from Mr Starke.* N COUNT

communication cord, communication cords. In British English, the **communication cord** N COUNT is a rope or chain on a train that passengers can pull to stop the train in an emergency.

communicative /kəmjuːnɪkətɪv/. 1 Someone who is **communicative** is able and willing to talk to other people or be friendly. EG *She's not being very communicative.* — ADJ QUALIT = talkative

2 **Communicative** means relating to the ability to communicate. EG *No such communicative ability exists between other animals.* — ADJ CLASSIF

communion /kəmjuːnjən/, **communions**. 1 **Communion** is 1.1 the sharing of thoughts or feelings with a person, spirit, force, etc. EG *Society has lost all communion with the elementary sources of life.* 1.2 the religious ceremony during a Christian church service at which people eat bread and drink wine as a symbol of Christ's death and sacrifice. EG *He started going to Communion... ...a communion cup.* — N UNCOUNT; N UNCOUNT

2 A **communion** is a group of people who share the same religious beliefs. EG *...a communion of free and independent believers.* — N COUNT : IF + PREP THEN *of* = fellowship

communiqué /kəmjuːnɪkeɪ/, **communiqués**. A **communiqué** is an official statement or announcement to the public or to journalists. EG *In the communiqué published after the meeting, it was stated that there had been a frank exchange of views.* — N COUNT ⇑ report = bulletin

communism /kɒmjə⁴nɪzə⁰m/; often spelled with a capital letter. **Communism** is 1 the political belief that the state should own and control the means of producing everything, so that all levels of society can be made equal because everyone will do as much as they can and get as much as they need. EG *...unskilled and semi-skilled workers, drawn to communism by their low economic status... ...the belief that Communism is bad.* 2 the political and social system of the Soviet Union, Eastern Europe, and some other countries. — N UNCOUNT; N UNCOUNT

communist /kɒmjə⁴nɪst/, **communists**; often spelled with a capital letter. 1 A **communist** is 1.1 someone who believes in communism. EG *...a young communist from Cleveland, Ohio.* — N COUNT

2 **Communist** is used to refer to 2.1 people and groups who believe in communism. EG *I know you had some Communist friends... The communist government went on ruling the country.* 2.2 the ideas of communism. EG *This did not necessarily imply rejection of a communist future.* 2.3 the political and social system of the Soviet Union, the countries of Eastern Europe, and some other countries. EG *He was born in a Communist country.* — ADJ CLASSIF; ADJ CLASSIF; ADJ CLASSIF

community /kəmjuːnɪti¹/, **communities**. 1 The **community** is all the people who live in a particular area or place. EG *Members are drawn from all sections of the local community... What is best for the community?... ...community affairs.* — N SING : USU *the* +N ⇑ society

2 A **community** is 2.1 a particular group of people or part of society who are all alike in some way. EG *...the local Pakistani community... ...the business community.* 2.2 a particular group of countries who have all agreed to work together or help each other. EG *...the European Community.* 2.3 a particular group of animals or plants that all live or grow together. EG *...the whale community in Hawaii.* — N COUNT : IF SING, VB CAN BE SING OR PL = sector; N SING : *the*+N = pact; N COUNT+SUPP

3 **Community** is friendship that is created and maintained between people or groups who are different in some way. EG *I was anxious to strengthen this sense of community... The Indians tend to avoid contact and community with the Spaniards.* — N UNCOUNT = association

community centre, **community centres**. A **community centre** is a place that is specially provided for the people, groups, and organizations in a particular area, where they can go in order to meet one another and do things. — N COUNT ⇑ amenity

community policing is a system in which policemen work only in one particular area of the community, so that everyone knows them. — N UNCOUNT ⇑ policing

community service is organized work that is done in order to help other people. It is sometimes given instead of punishment as a sentence to minor criminals. — N UNCOUNT

commute /kəmjuːt/, **commutes, commuting, commuted**. 1 If you **commute**, you travel a long distance regularly between your home and your place of work. EG *Many inhabitants of Greater London commute by British Rail.* — V : USU+A

2 If a judge or minister **commutes** the death penalty, a prison sentence, or some other punishment, he or she changes it to one that is less severe. EG *Bethwell's sentence was commuted to life imprisonment.* — V+O : IF+PREP THEN *to/for*

3 To **commute** a pension, or some other kind of money payment, means to exchange it for another kind of money payment, usually a lump sum. — V+O

commuter /kəmjuːtə/, **commuters**. A **commuter** is a person who commutes to work, especially by train. — N COUNT ⇑ traveller

compact, compacts, compacting, compacted. The word **compact is pronounced** /kə⁷mpækt/ when it is an adjective or a verb, and /kɒmpækt/hen it is a noun. 1 Something that is **compact** takes up little space or no more space than is necessary. EG *The kitchen was small, compact, and immaculately clean... ...smaller, more compact computers.* ◇ **compactly**. EG *...liquid food compactly stored in a pressurized tank.* ◇ **compactness**. EG *We chose them for their compactness and ease of maintenance.* — ADJ QUALIT; ◇ ADV; ◇ N UNCOUNT

2 To **compact** something means to press it so that it becomes more dense; a fairly formal word. EG *Animals' hooves compact the soil.* — V+O = compress

3 A **compact** is a small flat round case for keeping in a woman's handbag, containing face-powder, a piece of soft material to put the powder on with, and usually a mirror. EG *She took her powder compact out of her bag.* — N COUNT

compact disc, compact discs. A **compact disc** is a round flat object, smaller than a gramophone record, on which sound, especially music, is recorded. You play a compact disc on a special player in which there is a laser. — N COUNT

companion /kə⁷mpænjən/, **companions**. A **companion** is 1 someone who you spend time with, either because they are your friend or because you are travelling with them. EG *He saw Vita as the companion of a lifetime... She was a somewhat gruff companion on our expeditions.* 2 a young woman who is employed to live or travel with an older woman. EG *She was acting as a companion to the old lady.* — N COUNT; N COUNT ⇑ employee

companionable /kəmpænjənəbə⁰l/. A person who is **companionable** is friendly and pleasant to be with. EG *He was companionable, active, intelligent, and well-read.* — ADJ QUALIT ≠ hostile

companionship /kəmpænjənʃɪp/ is the state of having a friend or a companion, rather than being on your own. EG *He longed for companionship... She missed her mother's companionship and love.* — N UNCOUNT ⇑ friendship = company

companionway /kəmpænjənweɪ/, **companionways**. A **companionway** is a stairway or ladder that leads from one deck to another on a ship. — N COUNT

company /kʌmpəni¹/, **companies**. 1 When **company** is used in the singular with the following meanings, it can be used with a singular or a plural verb. A **company** is 1.1 a business organization that exists in order to make money by selling goods or services. EG *He is a geologist employed by a big oil company... ...The Brooke Bond Tea Company... ...a company car.* 1.2 a group of actors, opera singers, or dancers who work together. EG *Flora Robson and James Mason were in the company... ...the Royal Shakespeare Company... It's the first time a French company has put on 'Peter Grimes'.* 1.3 a group of soldiers that is usually part of a battalion or regiment, and that is divided into two or more platoons. EG *...a captain commanding a regular Marine company... ...a company of infantry... ...the men of Company C.* — N COUNT : ALSO IN NAMES AFTER N = firm; N COUNT : ALSO IN NAMES AFTER N = troupe; N COUNT

2 **Company** is the state of having another person or other people or a pet with you, especially when this is pleasant or stops you feeling lonely. EG *I wanted company... You've left the door open. Are you expecting company?... She preferred his company to that of most people... Northcliffe had been seen in Lloyd George's company... I enjoy the company of animals better than people.* — N UNCOUNT = companionship

3 The **company** can also mean a group of guests or people who are together in one place for social purposes. EG *He entertained the company with an account of the personal habits of great opera singers.* — N UNCOUNT : *the* +N ⇑ people

4 The word **company** is used in a number of expressions referring to people being together. 4.1 If you **keep** someone **company**, you spend time with them and stop them feeling lonely or bored. EG *He kept his mother company in the late afternoons.* 4.2 If you do something **in company**, you do it when you are with a group of people, especially people with whom you — PHR : VB INFLECTS ⇑ be with; PHR : USED AS AN A ≠ in private

are expected to behave in a particular way. EG *This was not the sort of language to be employed in company.* **4.3** If you **keep company** of a particular kind, you spend a lot of time with a person or people of a particular kind. EG *You are judged by the company you keep... He's been keeping bad company recently.* **4.4** If you say **two's company** or **two's company, three's a crowd**, you mean that two people should be allowed to spend time together, without other people being there. PHR : VB INFLECTS / PHR

5 If you **part company** with someone, **5.1** you go in different directions after you have been going in the same direction together. EG *We parted company at the bottom of the street.* **5.2** you disagree with them about something, often when you agree about other things. EG *Even those who generally agree with the headmaster would part company with him there... In this matter, believer and unbeliever part company.* PHR : VB INFLECTS, IF + PREP THEN *with* / PHR : VB INFLECTS, IF + PREP THEN *with* ≠ go along with

6 If something **parts company** with something else, the two things come apart, often so that they go in different directions; a humorous expression. EG *The sole finally parted company with the rest of his shoe... There are going to be times when you and the horse part company.* PHR : VB INFLECTS, IF + PREP THEN *with* ⇑ separate

7 If you believe or know something **in company with** someone else, you both believe or know it. EG *In company with many other people, she had heard of his activities in Germany.* PREP = along with

8 If you say that someone who has a particular opinion, or who has taken a particular action, is **in good company**, you mean that they should not feel ashamed of their opinion or action, because some important or respected people have the same opinion or have done the same thing. EG *They are, if it is any consolation, in good company.* PHR : USED AS AN A ≠ out on a limb

9 In informal English, you can add **and company** after mentioning a person's name, to refer also to people who are associated with that person; used especially when you are showing disapproval. EG *They set out to expose the pro-capitalist role of Wilson and company to their supporters.* PHR

> **COMPAR** □ In this dictionary COMPAR is used in the grammar notes beside entires to describe an adjective in its comparative form. (SUPERL is used to describe an adjective in its superlative form.) The comparative form is usually made by adding **-er**, for example *faster*, *happier*, or by putting ***more*** before the adjective, for example ***more** difficult*, ***more** interesting*. COMPAR is used beside the comparative form of an adjective which is entered in the dictionary as an irregular form, for example **better**, or which is entered because the meaning or use of the comparative form is different from the simple form of the adjective, for example **earlier**. A few adverbs also have a comparative form. The grammar notes beside individual entries will tell you which these adverbs are. COMPAR is also used beside meanings of words which are used with a comparative adjective or adverb before or after them. Examples of words which are used with comparative structures are **ever 1.2** and **by far** (see **far 13**). EG *Information must flow faster than **ever** before... He was more handsome than Mr Chesterfield **by far**... **By far** the greater proportion of boys were of English extraction.*

comparable /kɒmpərəbə⁰l/. Something that is **comparable** to something else is **1** as good, as big, as important, etc as the other thing. EG *At that moment there seemed nothing in the world comparable to sleep... ...an example of capitalist injustice comparable to the case of the Tolpuddle Martyrs... The sums of money involved were not, of course, comparable.* ◇ **comparably**. EG *There is no other mammal of comparably indiscriminate ferocity... They asked for salaries in line with comparably qualified professions.* **2** similar to the other thing, and therefore able to be compared with it in order to show the differences or similarities between them. EG *They have 30 to 50 per cent better fuel consumption than comparable petrol-engined cars... The comparable figures for Digital Equipment were 16, 23, and 42.* ◇ **comparability** /kɒmpərəbɪlɪti¹/. EG *There are problems over the comparability of data.* ADJ QUALIT : IF + PREP THEN *to/with* ⇑ similar = equal / ◇ ADV + ADJ/ADV / ADJ CLASSIF : IF + PREP THEN *to/with* = equivalent / ◇ N UNCOUNT = equivalence

comparative /kə⁷mpærə¹tɪv/, **comparatives**. **1** **Comparative** peace, silence, etc is a state which is peaceful, silent, etc when you compare it to a previous state or to a state somewhere else. EG *This comparative peace continued for thousands of years... He was listened to in comparative silence.* ADJ CLASSIF : ATTRIB = relative ≠ absolute

2 A **comparative** stranger is someone who is less well known to you than the other people you know. EG *She behaved like this even in the presence of comparative strangers.* ADJ CLASSIF : ATTRIB = relative

3 A **comparative** study of something is a study that involves the comparison of two or more things of the same kind. EG *...a serious comparative study of Indian and Western spiritual achievements... ...comparative linguistics.* ▸ **Comparative** is also used of people who make these studies. EG *...a distinguished comparative mythologist.* ADJ CLASSIF : ATTRIB ⇑ relative

4 The **comparative** form or the **comparative** of an adjective or adverb is the form that shows an increase in quality, size, amount, etc when compared with something else. It is usually formed by adding *-er*, for example *faster, happier*, or by putting *more* before the adjective or adverb, for example *more difficult, more interesting*. It can be followed by *than* when it is used after a verb. When the comparative form of an adjective is mentioned in the grammar notes beside an entry, it is described as COMPAR. See □ at COMPAR. ADJ CLASSIF, OR N COUNT ≠ positive, superlative

comparatively /kə⁷mpærə¹tɪvli¹/. **Comparatively** few, little, etc means fewer, less, etc than usual or than you expect. EG *They lay comparatively few eggs... There was comparatively little pressure for change.* ADV + ADJ/ADV = relatively

compare /kə⁷mpɛə/, **compares, comparing, compared**. **1** To **compare** two or more things means to consider or look at them and discover or point out the differences or similarities between them. EG *It's interesting to compare the two university prospectuses... ...studies comparing Russian children with those in Britain... I haven't got anything to compare it to.* ● to **compare notes**: see **note**. V+O, OR V+O+A (WITH/TO) : RECIP ⇑ contrast

2 If you **compare** someone or something to someone or something else, you say that they are like the other person or thing. EG *As an essayist he is compared frequently to Paine and Hazlitt... A dominant idea can be compared to a river that has cut deep into the landscape.* V+O+A *(to)* = liken

3 If something **compares** favourably or unfavourably with something else, it is better or worse than the other thing. EG *The freedom and influence accorded to writers in his country compared favourably with that achieved by writers elsewhere... The managements compared unfavourably with the pre-war coal-owners... How do your courses compare with business study courses at other colleges?* V+A *(with)* : USU +ADV

4 You say that something is large, small, etc **compared to** or **compared with** something else, **4.1** when you want to say that it is larger, smaller, etc than the other thing, although you might not normally consider it to be large, small, etc. EG *My eyes under the goggles feel cool compared to the rest of my face... The fee is low, compared with that at many other independent schools.* **4.2** when you are introducing a fact, especially a statistic, which you want to contrast with one that you have just mentioned. EG *New cars today weigh 3,570 pounds on average, compared with 4,460 pounds seven years ago... Ninety-eight per cent of them were without a father, compared to only seventeen per cent without a mother.* PREP = in comparison with / PREP = as opposed to

5 If you say that something **does not compare** with something else, you mean that it is greatly inferior to it. EG *His intelligence doesn't compare with that of the average Londoner.* PHR : AUX INFLECTS, IF + PREP THEN *with*

6 If you say that something is **beyond compare**, you mean that it is greater or better than anything else of the same kind; a literary expression. EG *...happiness beyond compare.* PHR : NG + PHR = beyond measure

comparison /kə⁷mpærɪsən/, **comparisons**. **1** When you make a **comparison**, you **1.1** consider or look at two or more things and discover or point out the differences between them. EG *...a comparison of children exposed to nuclear radiation with normal children... Here, for comparison, is the French version... We have to find out more before we can make a proper comparison.* **1.2** say that something or someone is like something or someone else. EG *The comparison is not entirely fanciful... ...the comparison of the party conference to a circus.* N COUNT/UNCOUNT ⇑ consideration / N COUNT/UNCOUNT

2 If you say that something is large, small, etc **in comparison with** or **in comparison to** something else, you mean it is larger, smaller, etc than the other thing, although you might not normally consider it to be large, small, etc. EG *This is trifling in comparison with the devastations caused by war...* PREP = compared to, compared with

Their possessions were embarrassingly few in comparison to those of older men.

3 Something that is large, small, etc **in comparison** or **by comparison** is large, small, etc when it is compared to something that has just been mentioned. EG *He made me look, in comparison, a good, calm, reasonable person... The vast majority of social encounters are, by comparison, mild and muted affairs.* ADV SEN = by contrast

4 If something or someone **stands comparison** or **bears comparison** with something or someone else, they are as good as, or nearly as good as, the other thing or person. EG *...a truly popular work of art that stands comparison with 'Gone With the Wind.'... There are one or two really good novelists who bear comparison with past writers.* PHR : VB INFLECTS, IF + PREP THEN *with* = compare

5 If, when you are comparing two things, you say **there's no comparison**, you mean one of the things is very much better than the other one. EG *'Which do you think is the best?'–'Well, there's no comparison, really, is there?'* PHR

compartment /kə'mpɑːtmə'nt/, **compartments**. A **compartment** is 1 one of the separate enclosed spaces into which a passenger vehicle, especially a railway carriage, is divided. EG *I could hear the ticket collector in the next compartment... I had a first-class compartment to myself.* N COUNT ⇑ section 2 one of the separate parts of an object used for keeping things in, for example a wallet, a piece of furniture, or a refrigerator. EG *He tucked the ticket into the inner compartment of his wallet. ...a compartment in the back of the desk... ...a frozen food compartment.* N COUNT ⇑ holder ● See also **glove compartment**.

compartmentalize /kɒmpɑːtmɛntəlaɪz/, **compartmentalizes, compartmentalizing, compartmentalized**; also spelled **compartmentalise**. To **compartmentalize** something means to divide it into separate sections, so that every part of it belongs to a particular section. EG *I have found it best to compartmentalize my contracts.* V+O ◇ **compartmentalized**. EG *Most sciences and technologies have become woefully compartmentalized and specialized... ...their dangerously compartmentalized view of life.* ◇ ADJ QUALIT = divided

compass /kʌmpəs/, **compasses**. 1 A **compass** is an instrument that you use for finding directions. It has a fixed dial and a movable magnetic needle that always points to the north. EG *I set off clutching my map and compass... I set a compass course for the Rock.* N COUNT

2 A **compass** or **compasses** is a hinged V-shaped instrument that you use for drawing circles, measuring distances on maps, etc. N COUNT : USU SING = PL, ALSO *a pair of* + N IN PL

3 The **compass** of something is the range over which it can operate. EG *...reality beyond the mind's normal compass... ...the global compass of politics... The clarinet has a compass of three-and-a-half octaves.* N COUNT + SUPP : USU SING

compassion /kə'mpæʃəⁿn/ is a feeling of pity and sympathy for someone who is suffering and a desire to help them. EG *The suffering of the Cubans aroused their compassion.* N UNCOUNT

compassionate /kə'mpæʃənət/. Someone who is **compassionate** feels or shows pity and sympathy for other people when they are suffering, and wants to help them. EG *She was tender and compassionate... She was among the most compassionate of women.* ADJ QUALIT = sympathetic ▸ also used of feelings and behaviour. EG *This news aroused in Scylla more compassionate and tender feelings.* ▸ = sympathetic ◇ **compassionately**. EG *Liz looked at her compassionately.* ◇ ADV+VB

compassionate leave is time away from your work that your employer allows you for personal reasons, especially when a member of your family dies or is seriously ill. N UNCOUNT ⇑ leave

compass point, compass points. A **compass point** is one of the 32 marks on the dial of a compass that show direction, for example north, south, east, and west. N COUNT

compatible /kə'mpætəbəⁿl/. 1 People who are **compatible** are able to live or work together in a friendly and peaceful way. EG *We weren't really compatible... We now had a compatible board of directors.* ADJ QUALIT : IF + PREP THEN *with* ≠ incompatible ◇ **compatibility** /kə'mpætəbɪlɪti¹/. EG *Since no two people are exactly alike, the idea of perfect compatibility is illusory.* ◇ N UNCOUNT : IF + PREP THEN *between/of/with*

2 Two things, systems of belief, ideas, etc, that are **compatible** can exist in the same place and at the same time without harming each other. EG *A transfusion of human blood can only be given to a patient if it is compatible with his own blood type... The aims of the two groups are just not compatible.* ADJ QUALIT : IF + PREP THEN *with* ◇ **compatibility**. EG *They failed to achieve any compatibility of planning aims... ...an attempt to prove the fundamental compatibility between Islam and Christianity.* ◇ N UNCOUNT : IF + PREP THEN *between/of/with*

compatriot /kə'mpætrɪət/, **compatriots**. Someone who is your **compatriot** is from your own country. EG *They set out to improve the situation of their compatriots... He conferred with compatriots in Los Angeles.* N COUNT = countryman

compel /kə'mpɛl/, **compels, compelling, compelled**. 1 If someone or something **compels** you to do something, they force you to do it. EG *Indians were compelled to work in the mines... Such harsh dilemmas compel us to face facts and make a choice... He felt compelled to intervene in the dispute.* V+O+*to*-INF = oblige

2 To **compel** an attitude, feeling, or action means to make people have it or do it. EG *His appearance was so outlandish that it compelled attention... No one can compel love... ...the pressures which compel participation in the scheme.* V+O ⇑ cause = demand

compelling /kə'mpɛlɪŋ/. 1 An argument or reason that is **compelling** makes you believe that something is true or that something should be done. EG *...a compelling argument... The case for greater nationalization is compelling... I had ended a man's life for no compelling reason.* ADJ QUALIT ⇑ powerful = convincing

2 A poem, painting, etc that is **compelling** makes you want to keep reading it or looking at it, because it is attractive or interesting. EG *...the poet John Clare's compelling account of countryside change... ...a compelling sculpture at the Museum of Modern Art.* ADJ QUALIT ≠ boring

compensate /kɒmpə'nseɪt/, **compensates, compensating, compensated**. 1 To **compensate** someone for something means to pay them money or do something for them as a way of helping them to replace something that has been lost, damaged, or destroyed. EG *Rather than compensate people for unemployment should we not rebuild the economy?... This is one way a company can compensate a man for not paying him a higher salary.* V OR V+O : IF + PREP THEN *for* ⇑ repay

2 To **compensate** for something that has a bad effect means to do something that cancels out this effect. EG *Fish can compensate for the tiniest variation of current by moving their fins.* V : IF + PREP THEN *for* = make up

3 If you **compensate** for something that is wrong or missing in your life, you do something that removes or reduces the harmful effects it has for you. EG *They spend the rest of their lives trying to compensate for their inability to have children... She used her good looks to compensate for her lack of intelligence.* V+A *(for)* = make up

compensation /kɒmpə'nseɪʃəⁿn/. 1 **Compensation** is payment that you claim from a person or organization that is responsible for something unpleasant that has happened to you. EG *If you were killed, your dependants could get compensation... Workers who have been unfairly dismissed may claim compensation from employers.* N UNCOUNT = damages

2 A **compensation** is 2.1 an action or adjustment that cancels out another action, usually one that has a bad or destructive effect. EG *Look for some of the compensations your body has to make... There is a kind of balance, a law of compensation, inherent in the nature of things.* N COUNT/UNCOUNT ⇑ adaptation 2.2 an event or fact that makes you feel better in spite of something bad that has happened to you. EG *Letters that began to arrive from Nell were some compensation... In youth everything has its compensations.* N UNCOUNT/COUNT ⇑ reward

compensatory /kɒmpə'nseɪtəⁿri¹/. Something that is **compensatory** 1 involves or relates to the payment of compensation. EG *There must be compensatory payments to the farmers.* ADJ CLASSIF : USU ATTRIB 2 is designed to help people who have special problems or disabilities. EG *...compensatory education... ...compensatory language programmes.* ADJ CLASSIF : ATTRIB

compere /kɒmpɛə/, **comperes, compering, compered**. 1 A **compere** is the person on a radio or television show who introduces the show, chats and jokes with guests, asks the questions in a quiz, etc. EG *Your compere tonight is Jimmy Tarbuck.* N COUNT ⇑ presenter

2 If someone **comperes** a television or radio show, they act as its compere. EG *Esther Rantzen agreed to compere the Miss World contest.* V OR V+O ⇑ present

compete /kə⁷mpi:t/, **competes, competing, competed.** 1 When one firm **competes** with another firm, it tries to get people to buy the goods that it makes or sells, in preference to the other firm's goods. EG *This would enable British shipbuilders to compete on equal terms with foreign yards... ...a computer firm large enough to compete at home and abroad.* — V OR V+A (against/with): RECIP ⇑ trade

2 If you **compete** with someone for something which both of you want but only one of you can have, you try to get it for yourself. EG *Senior members of staff competed eagerly for the honour of representing the company... They find themselves heavily handicapped when they have to compete against other children... Other people feel obliged to compete.* — V OR V+A (against/ with?2RECIP ⇑ strive = vie

3 If you **compete** in a contest or a game, you take part in it and try to win it. EG *Dave Moorcroft has now competed in two Olympics... ...a television show on which women were competing for trips to Bermuda.* — V+A

4 If two explanations, claims, etc **compete**, they cannot both be right, or cannot both be accepted. ◊ **competing.** EG *The School suggests three competing explanations of the emergence of Fascism... ...the competing claims of journalism and art.* — V OR V+A (with): RECIP; ◊ ADJ CLASSIF: ATTRIB = conflicting

5 When something such as a sound or a smell **competes** with another sound or smell, it is as noticeable as the other sound or smell. EG *Bicycle bells competed with the shifting of gears... The smell of cooking competed with turpentine and tobacco.* — V OR V+A (with): RECIP = clash

competence /kɒmpə¹təns/ is the ability to do something well or effectively. EG *He showed great professional competence... Piero carried out his commission with his usual competence... He will be expected to show competence in the relevant methods of research.* — N UNCOUNT = capability ≠ incompetence

competent /kɒmpə¹tənt/. Someone who is **competent** has the ability, knowledge, and skill to do something in an efficient and effective way. EG *He was a competent amateur pilot... She was very competent at her work... A democracy should be ruled by the men most competent to rule it.* ▸ also used to describe things that people do. EG *It was a highly competent piece of work... Henry was attended to in a competent manner.* ◊ **competently.** EG *He carved the bird roughly, but competently.* — ADJ QUALIT = capable ≠ incompetent; ◊ ADV = capably

competition /kɒmpə¹tɪʃə⁰n/, **competitions.** 1 **Competition** is a situation in which two or more people or groups are trying to get something which only one person or group can have. EG *Competition for admission to the college is keen... The two parties were not in competition with each other... They offered no threat or competition.* ▸ The **competition** is used to refer to the people or people who you are competing with. EG *See what the competition is doing.* — N UNCOUNT ≠ cooperation; ▸ N SING WITH DET: USU the+N = opposition

2 **Competition** is also an activity involving two or more firms, in which each firm tries to get people to buy its goods in preference to the other firms' goods. EG *Part of the reason for the drop in sales is competition from overseas suppliers... The action was exposing the industry to fierce international competition.* ▸ The **competition** is used to refer to the goods that a rival organization is selling. EG *The new model is certainly roomier than the foreign competition.* — N UNCOUNT ≠ collaboration; ▸ N SING WITH DET: USU the+N = rival

3 A **competition** is an event in which many people take part in order to find out who is best at a particular activity. The winner of the competition usually gets a prize. EG *I entered one or two competitions and won prizes... ...the Segovia International Guitar Competition.* — N COUNT = contest

competitive /kə⁷mpetɪtɪv/. 1 Something that is **competitive** involves people or firms competing with each other. EG *Until recently schools tended to be so competitive... ...a highly competitive society... ...competitive tennis.* — ADJ QUALIT

2 A person who is **competitive** is eager to be more successful than other people. EG *I realize how awfully competitive I am... A woman is said to be less competitive, more dependent on the approval of others.* ▸ **Competitive** is used also of people's behaviour and abilities. EG *...an attempt to strengthen our competitive ability.* ◊ **competitively.** EG *They don't garden competitively like suburban men.* ◊ **competitiveness.** EG *Why should we put such an emphasis on individualism and competitiveness?* — ADJ QUALIT ⇑ keen = ambitious; ◊ ADV = ambitiously; ◊ N UNCOUNT = ambition

3 Goods that are **competitive** are likely to be bought, because they are good value when you compare them to other goods of the same kind. EG *General Motors has definitely succeeded in designing a competitive car for the 1980s.* ◊ **competitively.** EG *The banks would be allowed to pay competitively high rates.* — ADJ QUALIT = economical; ◊ ADV

competitor /kə⁷mpetɪtə/, **competitors.** 1 Someone who is your **competitor** is trying to sell goods or services to the same people as you are. EG *Mobil and Conoco are not really direct competitors in any significant markets... ...Austin-Rover's challenge to its foreign competitors.* — N COUNT = rival ≠ partner

2 A **competitor** is also a person who takes part in a competition or contest such as a sport. EG *Most of the competitors in the games had already arrived... She was glad she was a judge and not a competitor.* — N COUNT ⇑ participant = contestant

compilation /kɒmpɪleɪʃə⁰n/, **compilations.** 1 A **compilation** is a document, book, record, or programme that contains many different pieces of information or parts that have been gathered together. EG *...'The Great All-Time Baseball Record Book', a compilation of unconventional records.* — N COUNT ⇑ collection

2 **Compilation** is the act of compiling something. EG *One of the first steps taken was the compilation of a report.* — N UNCOUNT = assembling

compile /kəmpaɪl/, **compiles, compiling, compiled.** When you **compile** something, you write or produce it by collecting and putting together many pieces of information, writing, or film. EG *The department will compile a report... The programme was compiled and presented by Dr Brian Smith.* — V+O ⇑ gather = assemble

complacency /kə⁷mpleɪsənsi¹/ is the state of being complacent about a situation; often used showing disapproval. EG *No one has any cause for complacency... There is far too much political complacency in this country.* — N UNCOUNT = smugness ≠ concern

complacent /kə⁷mpleɪsənt/. If you are **complacent**, you are very pleased with yourself and do not think that there is any reason for you to worry or do anything about a situation; used showing disapproval. EG *You are being a bit complacent... We cannot afford to be complacent about the energy problem.* ◊ **complacently.** EG *Politicians squint at us complacently from the screens.* — ADJ QUALIT: IF+ PREP THEN about = smug ≠ concerned; ◊ ADV

complain /kə⁷mpleɪn/, **complains, complaining, complained.** If you **complain**, 1 you tell someone about a situation affecting you that you think is wrong or unsatisfactory and should be dealt with. EG *They complained to me about the noise.... He's always complaining... Women complain of pressure on them to get jobs... He complained that the office was not 'businesslike'.* 2 you say that you are feeling pain or feeling ill. EG *He complained of pain in the chest.* 3 you make a formal protest to someone. EG *The neighbours complained to the police about the noise.* — 1: V OR V+REPORT-CL/QUOTE: IF+ PREP THEN to/ about/of ⇑ protest = grumble, moan; 2: V+A (of), OR V+ REPORT-CL; 3: V: IF+PREP THEN to/about/ of

complainant /kə⁷mpleɪnənt/, **complainants.** A **complainant** is a person who starts a court case in a court of law; a legal term. — N COUNT = plaintiff

complaint /kə⁷mpleɪnt/, **complaints.** A **complaint** is 1 a statement in which you say that you find a situation wrong or unsatisfactory and that it should be dealt with. EG *Complaints about my lack of judgement... It is a common complaint that children lack discipline.... There were the usual complaints of violence... They have no real grounds for complaint.* — N COUNT/ UNCOUNT ⇑ objection = criticism

2 a reason for complaining. EG *Our main complaint is the lack of child-care facilities.* 3 a formal protest. EG *She wrote a letter of complaint to the manufacturer... He intends to make a complaint against the police.* 4 an illness, often one which is not very serious. EG *It turned out to be a minor urinary complaint.* — 2: N COUNT; 3: N COUNT/ UNCOUNT; 4: N COUNT = ailment

complaisance /kə⁷mpleɪzəns/ is willingness to accept what other people are doing without complaining; an old-fashioned literary word. — N UNCOUNT

complaisant /kə⁷mpleɪzənt/. If you are **complaisant**, you are willing to accept what other people are doing without complaining; an old-fashioned literary word. EG *It would be better to close our eyes like a complaisant husband whose wife has taken a lover.* — ADJ QUALIT = obliging

complement /kɒmplə¹mə²nt/, **complements, complementing, complemented.** 1 If one person or thing **complements** another, 1.1 they add desirable qualities to each other or help to reduce the weaknesses in each other, so that the combina- — V+O ⇑ enhance tion is more effective than they are separately. EG *Current advances in hardware development nicely complement British software skills... Tribal medicine and Western medicine can complement each other very successfully... We complemented one another.* ▸ used as a noun. EG *She was a perfect contrast and complement to Sally... The exercises are an ideal complement to my usual rehearsal methods.* ▸ N COUNT : IF + PREP THEN *to* **1.2** they emphasize the good qualities that the other thing has. EG *The tanned, slim young men perfectly complemented the long-legged girls... Crisp pastry complements the juicy fruit of an apple pie.* V+O = set off

2 A **complement** is a group of people who work together, for example the officers and crew of a ship. EG *44 of the original complement of 150 were dead... Over the next few years the staff complement changed.* N COUNT : ALSO N + *of* + N IN PL

3 The **full complement** of a group, set, or amount is every item or person that it normally includes or can include, without anything or anyone being missing. EG *...a full complement of one thousand passengers and crew... He lacks a full complement of teeth.* PHR : IF + PREP THEN *of* ⇑ whole = full quota

4 In grammar, a **complement** is an adjectival group or noun group that comes after a verb such as *be* and which adds information about the subject or object of the verb. In this dictionary, when a complement is mentioned in the grammar notes beside an entry, it is described as C. See □ at C, V+C, and V+O+C. N COUNT

complementary /kɒmplə[1]mentə[0]ri[1]/. If two or more things are **complementary**, they are different but together form a complete or better whole. EG *These two approaches are complementary... The roles of the sexes are complementary to one another.* ADJ CLASSIF : IF + PREP THEN *to*

complete /kə[7]mpliːt/, **completes, completing, completed.** **1 Complete** is used **1.1** to emphasize that something is as great in extent, degree, or amount as is possible. EG *You need a complete change of diet... They were in complete agreement... She was a complete bitch.* ◊ **completely.** EG *Her whole personality had suddenly changed completely... He was completely bald.* ADJ QUALIT : USU ATTRIB = total, absolute ≠ partial; ◊ ADV = totally **1.2** to suggest that someone is skilled at all aspects of a particular activity and is therefore the best example of that kind of person; used showing approval. EG *Ray is the complete film-maker.* ADJ CLASSIF : ATTRIB ⇑ perfect **1.3** to emphasize that you are talking about the whole of something and not just a part of it. EG *We were invited to design a complete city from scratch... The owner had to put a complete new roof on.* ADJ CLASSIF : ATTRIB = entire

2 If something is **complete**, **2.1** it has been finished. EG *The harvesting of groundnuts was complete... ...blocks of luxury flats, complete but half-empty.* ADJ CLASSIF : PRED **2.2** it contains all the parts that it should contain or that it previously had. EG *This is not a complete list... Now our little group is complete again... ...an almost complete skeleton of a dinosaur.* ◊ **completeness.** ADJ QUALIT ⇑ whole ≠ incomplete; ◊ N UNCOUNT

3 If you **complete** something, **3.1** you finish doing, making, or producing it. EG *The cathedral was begun in 1240 and completed forty years later.* V+O ≠ begin **3.2** you do all of it. EG *A teacher training course takes three years to complete... Give yourself plenty of time to complete a job.* V+O = finish

4 If someone or something **completes** a group or set, they are the last person or item that is needed to make it a full group or set. EG *A black silk knitted tie completed the outfit... The team organizer and one or two of the voluntary workers complete the Committee.* V+O

5 If you **complete** a form or questionnaire, you write down the answers to the questions on it. EG *He had been fined five pounds for failing to complete a national census form.* V+O = fill in

6 Something that is **complete with** something else has the second thing as an extra or additional part. EG *He arrived for the interview wearing full army uniform complete with badges and medals... He bought a lovely Beverly Hills mansion, complete with swimming pool.* PREP ⇑ with

completion /kə[7]mpliːʃə[0]n/ is the situation or state of affairs in which a particular piece of work is finished. EG *His work was still far from completion... ...a lengthy delay in completion of the pipeline... The house was due for completion in 1983.* N UNCOUNT

complex /kɒmpleks/, **complexes.** **1** Something that is **complex** **1.1** has or involves many different parts or things that are connected or related to each other. EG *...complex molecules... ...complex lace patterns... ...a complex and highly developed industrial society.* ADJ QUALIT **1.2** is difficult to understand or deal with because it involves so many parts or details. EG *It is a complex problem... ...complex decisions... He was a complex man.* ADJ QUALIT = complicated ≠ easy, simple

2 A **complex** is **2.1** a group or system of things that are very close to each other or are connected with each other in a way that is very difficult to describe. EG *...a complex of little roads... We are dealing with a whole complex of thoughts and prejudices.* N COUNT + SUPP **2.2** a group of buildings or a large building divided into several areas, all of which are used for one particular purpose. EG *...a splendid new sports and leisure complex... ...an industrial complex.* N COUNT + SUPP ⇑ building = development

3 If someone has a **complex**, they have a mental or emotional problem because they have had an unpleasant experience which continues to influence their feelings and the way that they behave. EG *Telling the child that he has a complex will not help... I am developing a guilt complex about it.* ● See also **inferiority complex.** N COUNT : IF + PREP THEN *about*

complexion /kə[7]mplekʃə[0]n/, **complexions.** **1** A person's **complexion** is the skin on his or her face, especially when you are talking about its colour or how rough, smooth, or healthy it is. EG *People with dark complexions... He said I had a good complexion.* N COUNT

2 The **complexion** of something is its general nature or character; a formal word. EG *This should be the aim of any government, of whatever complexion... The complexion of the problem had changed... That puts a different complexion on things.* N UNCOUNT + SUPP

complexity /kə[7]mpleksɪti[1]/, **complexities.** **1 complexity** is the state of having many different parts, which are connected or related to each other in a way that may be difficult to understand or to deal with. EG *There has been a dramatic reduction in the size and complexity of electronic components... ...to solve problems of varying complexity.* N UNCOUNT = intricacy ≠ simplicity

2 The **complexities** of something are its many connected parts, which make it difficult to understand or deal with. EG *We are unaware of the subtle complexities of many of our gestures and expressions... He worked hard to master the complexities of tax law.* N PLURAL : USU *the* + N + *of* ⇑ nature = intricacies

compliance /kə[7]mplaɪəns/ is willingness to do what you have been asked to do; a formal word. EG *There are ways of ensuring compliance... I was surprised by Melanie's compliance with these terms.* N UNCOUNT : IF + PREP THEN *with* ⇑ obedience = agreement

compliant /kə[7]mplaɪənt/. Someone who is **compliant** willingly does what they are asked to do; a formal word. EG *He is eager, willing, and compliant to the demands of others.* ADJ QUALIT : IF + PREP THEN *to* ⇑ obedient

complicate /kɒmplɪkeɪt/, **complicates, complicating, complicated.** To **complicate** a situation or explanation means to make it more difficult to understand or deal with by adding a problem to it or by adding too many details. EG *And just to complicate matters, I have to be back by the end of the month.... The situation was further complicated by uncertainty about the future leadership.* V+O = aggravate, confuse

complicated /kɒmplɪkeɪtɪ[2]d/. Something that is **complicated** has many parts or aspects which are connected to one another in a way that makes it difficult to understand or deal with. EG *I find the British legal system extremely complicated... The situation is much more complicated than that... The body is a very complicated machine.* ADJ QUALIT = complex, intricate

complication /kɒmplɪkeɪʃə[0]n/, **complications.** A **complication** is **1** a problem or detail that makes a situation harder to deal with. EG *Finally, there is the complication that wages help to determine the level of inflation... There's one further complication.* N COUNT ⇑ difficulty = snag **2** an additional medical problem which makes the treatment of the original illness more difficult; a technical term. EG *If the doctor foresees complications, he will advise going to hospital... She's got measles. Oh, nothing to worry about. No complications.* N COUNT : USU PL

complicity /kə[7]mplɪsɪti[1]/ is involvement with other people in an activity or plan that is illegal or wrong; a formal word. EG *She suspected him of complicity in Ashok's escape.* N UNCOUNT

compliment /kɒmplə[1]mə[2]nt/, **compliments, complimenting, complimented.** **1** A **compliment** is something that you do or say to someone in order to show your admiration or respect for them. EG *He knew that he had just been paid a great* N COUNT ⇑ honour ≠ insult *compliment... She took his acceptance as a great compliment... Thanks for the compliment.*

2 If you **return the compliment** to someone, you do the same thing to them that they did to you; often used when the thing that was done is unpleasant. PHR : VB INFLECTS ⇑ reciprocate

3 If you **compliment** someone, you praise them or tell them how much you like something that they own or that they have done. EG *He complimented Morris on his new car... She is to be complimented for handling the situation so well.* V+O : IF+PREP THEN *on/for* = congratulate

4 Compliments is used in expressions such as 'to send your compliments' and 'with my compliments' when you want to express good wishes or respect; used in a formal situation. EG *The Secretary of State presents his compliments and regrets that he is unable to attend... My compliments to the chef.* N PLURAL : USU POSS+N ⇑ greetings = respects ● If you send something to someone **with** your **compliments,** you mean that you are giving it to them free. EG *Send him a copy of the dictionary with our compliments.* ● PHR : USED AS AN A

complimentary /kɒmplәˈmentәºriˈ/. **1** Someone who is **complimentary** expresses admiration or respect for something or someone. EG *Everyone had been most complimentary about the costumes.* ▸ used of something that you say or do. EG *He made several complimentary references to the programme... In Russia a rhythmic slow hand-clap can be most complimentary.* ADJ QUALIT ⇑ approving = flattering

2 A **complimentary** seat, ticket, copy of a book, etc is one that is given to you free, for example for public-relations purposes. EG *Mrs Volkov has given me a couple of complimentary tickets for the concert on Wednesday.* ADJ CLASSIF : ATTRIB

comply /kәˀmplaɪ/, **complies, complying, complied.** If you **comply** with a request, order, or set of rules, you do what you are required or expected to do. EG *If you want to run a playgroup you must comply with the conditions laid down by the authorities... The tribunal ordered that Jones should be reinstated, but the employers refused to comply... New vehicles must comply with certain standards.* V : IF+PREP THEN *with* = conform

component /kәˀmpəʊnәnt/, **components.** A **component** is one of the parts or features from which something is created, made, or produced. EG *...electronic components... People, organizations and ideas are the basic components of all situations... What is the practical component of the course?* N COUNT ⇑ part ▸ used as an adjective. EG *The noise has to be broken down into its component parts for analysis... ...the membership totals of their component branches.* ▸ ADJ CLASSIF : ATTRIB, USU+N IN PL = constituent

comport /kәˀmpɔːt/, **comports, comporting, comported.** If you **comport** yourself in a particular way, you behave in that way; a formal word. EG *The Colonel gave me advice on how to comport myself in the White House.* V+O (REFL)+A = conduct

compose /kәˀmpəʊz/, **composes, composing, composed.** **1** If something **is composed** of particular things or people, it has those things or people as its parts or members. EG *The chair is composed of a series of hollow aluminium tubes... The committee was evenly composed of men and women.* V+O+A *(of)* : ONLY PASS

2 If a number of people or things **compose** something, they are the parts or members that form it. EG *He sees the whole, not the various lines which compose it... ...the elements which compose his individuality.* V+O = constitute

3 If you **compose** a piece of music, you write it. EG *Mozart composed his first symphony in 1764... He conducts and composes.* V+O, OR V

4 If you **compose** a short piece of writing such as a poem or a speech, you write it; used especially when this requires skill or effort. EG *She composed satirical poems for the New Statesman... It can't be too difficult to compose a nice little negative reply.* V+O = make up

5 If you **compose** a painting, a garden, or a piece of architecture, you arrange its different parts in a deliberate and usually attractive or artistic way; a formal or technical word. EG *Look at the way Hoyland composes his pictures... ...the formally composed semi-circle of the Victoria Memorial.* V+O

6 If you **compose** yourself, your thoughts, or your features, you make an effort to stop being angry, excited, or upset and become or appear calmer. EG *She lay on her bed and cried and then she composed herself... She composed her features.* V+O (REFL/NG) ⇑ calm = control

composed /kәˀmpəʊzd/. Someone who is **composed** is calm, unworried, and self-controlled. EG *She is a small, beautiful and composed blonde... I felt calmer and more composed than I had in a long time.* ADJ QUALIT = serene

composer /kәˀmpəʊzә/, **composers.** A **composer** is a person whose occupation is writing music, especially classical music. EG *...the Russian composer Shostakovich.* N COUNT

composite /kɒmpәzɪt/, **composites. Composite** is used to describe something that is made up of several different things, parts, or substances. EG *...the composite annual fee... Paul in the novel is a man made up of many men, a composite lover.* ADJ CLASSIF : ATTRIB ⇑ collective ▸ used as a noun. EG *His style is a composite of elements drawn from several different traditions.* ▸ N COUNT : IF+ PREP THEN *of* ⇑ mixture = synthesis

composition /kɒmpәzɪʃәºn/, **compositions. 1** The **composition** of something is the way in which its different parts, members, or substances are arranged, especially how much of each part there is. EG *...the chemical composition of the atmosphere... ...the ethnic composition of the voters of New York... This organization is mainly working class in composition.* N UNCOUNT : USU WITH POSS = make-up

2 A **composition** is **2.1** a piece of music written by a composer. EG *Another of his finer compositions–the B minor Sonata... He played many of his compositions for me.* N COUNT **2.2** a piece of written work, especially one that you write at school to show your skill and imagination. EG *The composition had to be at least three pages long.* N COUNT ⇑ writing = essay **2.3** a painting, photograph, or sculpture, especially when it is considered from the point of view of the way the parts fit together rather than what it represents. EG *...a vast and amorphous composition entitled 'Australian Diary'.* N COUNT ⇑ artwork = creation

3 Composition is also **3.1** the act of composing something such as a piece of music or a poem. EG *Do we know the period of composition of the Symphony? He began by reading a poem of his own composition.* N UNCOUNT ⇑ creation **3.2** the technique or skill involved in creating a work of art. EG *...19th-century architectural drawings, superb in composition or draftsmanship.* N UNCOUNT ⇑ arrangement = layout

compositor /kәˀmpɒzɪtә/, **compositors.** A **compositor** is a person whose occupation is setting up the text and illustrations of a book, magazine, or newspaper before it is printed. N COUNT

compos mentis /kɒmpәˀs mentɪs/. If you are **compos mentis**, you are able to think clearly and understand what you are doing because you are mentally normal and well. EG *By the time I was fully compos mentis again the worst was over.* ADJ QUALIT : PRED ⇑ sane ≠ mad

compost /kɒmpɒst/, **composts, composting, composted. 1 Compost** is **1.1** a mixture of decaying plants and animal dung, which you add to the soil because the mixture contains the chemicals that plants need in order to grow well. EG *Soil containing peat, leafmould or good compost... ...a compost heap.* N UNCOUNT ⇑ fertilizer **1.2** specially treated soil or peat mixed with fertilizer that you buy and use to grow seeds and plants in pots. N MASS

2 To **compost** something such as bits of plants or animal dung means to make it into compost. EG *Careful composting of vegetables is necessary... Old newspapers can be composted.* V+O

composure /kәˀmpəʊʒә/ is the quality or state of being calm, unworried, and unemotional; a rather formal word. EG *She had recovered her composure once again... She looked out over the auditorium with grave composure.* N UNCOUNT ⇑ calmness = equanimity

compote /kɒmpɒʊt/ is fruit stewed with sugar or in syrup. EG *...compote of oranges with candied peel.* N UNCOUNT/ COUNT

compound, compounds, compounding, compounded. The word **compound** is pronounced /kɒmpaʊnd/ when it is a noun, and /kәˀmpaʊnd/ when it is a verb. **1** A **compound** is **1.1** an area of land that is surrounded by fences, walls, or barbed wire and is used for a particular purpose, especially an area containing buildings and where the entry and exit of people is controlled. EG *He led the men into the prison compound... Inside the perimeter fence, the compound was subdivided into living areas.* N COUNT ⇑ enclosure **1.2** a combination of two or more features, qualities, or parts. EG *The new threat was a compound of nationalism and social revolution.* N COUNT ⇑ mixture

2 In chemistry, a **compound** is a substance that consists of two or more different substances or chemical elements. EG *The bacteria fed initially on various carbon compounds.* N COUNT

3 In linguistics, a **compound** is a word or expression N COUNT, OR ADJ that has a single meaning but is made up of two or more words. Most compounds in English are nouns. CLASSIF : ATTRIB

4 Compound is used to describe something which consists of two or more parts. EG *Butterflies have excellent compound eyes.* ADJ CLASSIF : ATTRIB

5 If you **compound** something, you put together different things or parts to make a whole. EG *Our scientists have learned to compound substances unknown to nature.* V+O ⇑ mix = combine

6 If something **is compounded** of or from several different things, it is made by adding or mixing them together. EG *They specialize in local dishes compounded of fresh fish and vegetables... His acting is compounded from theories of different kinds.* V+O : ONLY PASS, IF + PREP THEN *of/from* = be concocted

7 If someone or something **compounds** a problem, difficulty, or mistake, they make it worse by adding to it or increasing it. EG *Her uncertainty was now compounded by fear... Later, Sergeant Inglis compounded his error.* V+O ⇑ worsen

compound fracture, compound fractures. A **compound fracture** is a broken bone which has cut through the flesh or skin near it. N COUNT

compound interest is interest that is calculated not only on the original amount of money that has been invested, but also on the interest that is earned, which is added to the original amount: compare **simple interest**. N UNCOUNT

comprehend /kɒmprɪhend/, **comprehends, comprehending, comprehended.** If you cannot **comprehend** something, you cannot fully understand what it means. EG *She looked as if she did not comprehend... They did not comprehend how hard he had struggled.* V OR V+O/ REPORT-CL : USU WITH BROAD NEG = grasp

comprehensible /kɒmprɪhensəbəl/. Something that is **comprehensible** can be easily understood. EG *The object is to make our research readable and comprehensible.* ◊ **comprehensibly.** EG *Give your answers accurately and comprehensibly.* ◊ **comprehensibility** /kɒmprɪhensəbɪlɪti/. EG *What these explanations lack in accuracy, they gain in comprehensibility.* ADJ QUALIT ≠ incomprehensible; ◊ ADV WITH VB; ◊ N UNCOUNT

comprehension /kɒmprɪhenʃən/, **comprehensions. 1 Comprehension** is **1.1** the ability to understand something fully. EG *How anyone can write such rubbish is beyond my comprehension.* **1.2** full awareness and knowledge of the meaning of something. EG *She looked at him first in amazement, then dawning comprehension.* N UNCOUNT; N UNCOUNT = understanding ≠ incomprehension

2 A **comprehension** is an exercise in language teaching to find out how well you understand a piece of spoken or written language. EG *Now we are going to do a listening comprehension.* N COUNT

comprehensive /kɒmprɪhensɪv/, **comprehensives. 1** Something that is **comprehensive** includes everything that is essential or necessary. EG *Linda received comprehensive training after joining the firm... Here is a comprehensive list of all the items in stock.* ADJ CLASSIF ⇑ full ≠ partial

2 A **comprehensive** school or educational system is one in which children of all abilities and social backgrounds are taught together; used in British English. ▸ used as a noun. EG *Schools before comprehensives had different problems... ...Holland Park Comprehensive.* ADJ CLASSIF; ▸ N COUNT : ALSO IN NAMES

compress, compresses, compressing, compressed. The word **compress** is pronounced /kəmpres/ when it is a verb and /kɒmpres/ when it is a noun. **1** When you **compress** something or when it **compresses,** it is pressed or squeezed, so that it takes up less space. EG *A gas trapped by a piston in a cylinder is compressed to .9 of its original volume... ...compressed air... I could feel my lips compress into a white line.* ◊ **compression** /kəmpreʃən/. EG *...the compression of air by the piston.* V-ERG ⇑ press = compact; ◊ N UNCOUNT

2 If you **compress** a piece of writing, you make it take up less space by making it smaller or shorter. EG *I soon finished a paper, which I compressed to minimum length.* ◊ **compression.** EG *There will be even more compression of information... Alexander Pope was a master of compression.* V+O ⇑ reduce = condense; ◊ N UNCOUNT ⇑ reduction

3 If a development or the time that it takes **is compressed,** it takes less time to happen or be done than normal or than previously. EG *In contemporary Africa, similar phases have been compressed into a few years... Thirty years are compressed into a dozen sentences.* ◊ **compression.** V+O : USU PASS ⇑ reduce; ◊ N UNCOUNT

4 A **compress** is a pad of wet or dry cloth pressed on part of a patient's body to reduce fever, relieve pain, etc. EG *I made hot compresses but did not know what else I could do.* N COUNT

compressor /kəmpresə/, **compressors.** A **compressor** is a machine or part of a machine that squeezes gas or air and makes it take up less space. N COUNT

comprise /kəmpraɪz/, **comprises, comprising, comprised. 1** If something **comprises** particular things or people or **is comprised of** them, it has them as its parts or members. EG *The Privy Council comprised 283 members... The fountain was comprised of three stone basins.* V+O : IF PASS THEN + *of* ⇑ contain = consist of

2 If a number of things or people **comprise** something, they are the parts or members that form it. EG *Farmers comprise just 1.2 per cent of the country's population... A series of residential blocks which would comprise something like a complete township.* V+O = constitute

compromise /kɒmprəmaɪz/, **compromises, compromising, compromised. 1** A **compromise** is a situation in which people accept something slightly different from what they really want, because of circumstances or because they are considering the wishes of other people. EG *Delegates predict that some compromise will be reached... It was necessary for members to make compromises to ensure party unity... ...a historic compromise between the party leaders and the trade unions.* ▸ used as an uncount noun. EG *I'm a man of compromise... They have a genius for compromise.* N COUNT; ▸ N UNCOUNT

2 A **compromise** between two different things or ideas is something that is midway between the two of them. EG *...the compromises between idealism and reality... The English weather is a fair compromise between rain and fog.* N COUNT + *between*

3 If you **compromise** with someone about something, you reach an agreement with another person or group in which you both accept something less than or different from what you originally wanted. EG *The best thing to do is to compromise... Don't compromise: don't settle for second best.* V ⇑ agree ≠ stand firm

4 If you **compromise** your beliefs or principles or **compromise** yourself, you do something which causes people to doubt how sincere, moral, or honest you are. EG *The Government had compromised its principles... He vowed not to be lured into any associations that might compromise him.* ◊ **compromising.** EG *...a compromising situation.* V+O (NG/REFL); ◊ ADJ QUALIT

compulsion /kəmpʌlʃən/, **compulsions. 1** A **compulsion** is a strong desire to do something, especially a desire that you find difficult to control. EG *She feels a compulsion to tidy up all the time... He seemed driven by some mad compulsion.* N COUNT

2 Compulsion is the use of strong influence, threats, or violence to make people do something that they do not want to do. EG *There was no compulsion on employers to take part in the scheme... Pressed into rugby under compulsion, I began to enjoy the game.* N UNCOUNT ⇑ pressure

compulsive /kəmpʌlsɪv/. **1 Compulsive** is used to describe someone's behaviour when they have a strong desire to do something or develop a habit of doing it, and find it difficult to control their behaviour. EG *...a compulsive liar... ...a compulsive gambler.* ◊ **compulsively.** EG *He steals compulsively.* ADJ CLASSIF; ◊ ADV WITH VB

2 A book, television programme, etc which is **compulsive** is one that you find extremely difficult to stop reading or watching. EG *I found the book compulsive to read... It's compulsive viewing.* ◊ **compulsively.** EG *The book is compulsively readable.* ADJ QUALIT ⇑ absorbing = irresistible ≠ boring; ◊ ADV + ADJ

compulsory /kəmpʌlsəri/ is used to describe something that you have to do or accept because it is a rule or law or because someone in authority insists on it. EG *In most schools, sports are compulsory... They fear that there will be compulsory redundancies next month.* ADJ CLASSIF = obligatory ≠ voluntary

compunction /kəmpʌŋkʃən/ is a feeling of shame or guilt for something wrong that you have done; a formal word. EG *I could have shot him without any compunction... They had no compunction about taking the furniture.* N UNCOUNT : USU WITH BROAD NEG

computation /kɒmpjʊteɪʃən/, **computations. Computation** is mathematical calculation, especially when it is done using a machine. EG *Estimating the number of individual insects in the world seems beyond any computation... Here is the result of my computations.* N UNCOUNT/ COUNT

compute /kə⁷mpju:t/, **computes, computing, computed.** 1 To **compute** a value means to calculate it, especially by using a computer or calculator. EG *It is difficult to compute the loss in revenue... We shall soon have speedometers which compute your average speed.* — V+O = work out
2 See also **computing.**

computer /kə⁷mpju:tə/, **computers.** A **computer** is an electronic machine that can quickly make calculations, store, rearrange, and retrieve information, or control another machine. EG *Portable computers can be plugged into TV sets... ...computer games... The entire operation is done by computer.* — N COUNT, OR *by*+N

computerize /kə⁷mpju:təraɪz/, **computerizes, computerizing, computerized**; also spelled **computerise.** 1 To **computerize** a system, process, or type of work means to arrange for a lot of the work to be done by computers. EG *They're going to computerise all their overseas mail order operations... We are currently computerizing the Inland Revenue.* ◊ **computerization** /kə⁷mpju:təraɪzeɪʃə⁰n/. EG *...the economic benefits of computerization.* — V+O ⇑ automate; ◊ N UNCOUNT ⇑ automation
2 To **computerize** information means to store or process it in a computer. — V+O

computerized /kə⁷mpju:təraɪzd/. You say that an office or other organization is **computerized** when it uses computers for its work. EG *The Department of Linguistics is now fully computerized.* — ADJ CLASSIF: USU ATTRIB ⇑ automated

computing /kə⁷mpju:tɪŋ/ is 1 the use of computers, especially as a job, or in business, industry, or administration. EG *The impact of computing on routine office work... He's in computing.* 2 the activity of using a computer and writing programs for it. EG *I have never actually done any computing... The machine can be used both for serious computing and playing computer games.* — N UNCOUNT; N UNCOUNT

comrade /kɒmrɪ³d/, **comrades.** A **comrade** is 1 a person who belongs to the same political group or organization as yourself; used especially by people in socialist and communist groups. EG *This is what I propose, Comrades.* 2 a friend or companion, especially one who works with you or who experiences the same difficulties and dangers as you; a rather old-fashioned word. EG *Margaret was my only link to my comrades, my friends.* — N COUNT/VOC: ALSO IN TITLES BEFORE NAMES; N COUNT

comrade in arms, comrades in arms. A **comrade in arms** is someone who has worked for the same cause or purpose as you and has shared the same difficulties and dangers. — N COUNT: USU PL

comradely /kɒmrɪ³dli¹/. If you do something in a **comradely** way, you are being pleasant and friendly to other people. EG *We had a comradely chat... The debate was conducted in a comradely and constructive spirit.* — ADJ QUALIT

comradeship /kɒmrɪ³dʃɪp/ is friendship between a number of people who are doing the same work or who share the same difficulties or dangers. EG *..the close comradeship of war... There was a spirit of comradeship.* — N UNCOUNT = camaraderie

con /kɒn/, **cons, conning, conned**; used mainly in informal English. 1 If someone **cons** you, 1.1 they persuade you to do or to believe something by telling you things that are not true. EG *A lot of people are conned into thinking that they can't fight back.... Don't try to con the doctor into prescribing a tranquilliser... Lynn felt women had been conned.* — V+O: IF+PREP THEN *into* ⇑ deceive
1.2 they persuade you to give them your money or property, by telling you something that is not true. EG *I think she's been conned... He goes around conning people out of their money... They conned me into giving them £100 and then vanished.* — V+O: IF+PREP THEN *into/out of* ⇑ deceive = cheat
2 A **con** is 2.1 a trick in which someone deceives you by telling you something that is not true. EG *The whole thing was a big con, an elaborate put-down on a massive scale.* 2.2 a crime in which someone persuades you to give them money or property, by telling you something that is not true. EG *This man has already perpetrated cons all over the north of England.* — N COUNT; N COUNT = confidence trick
3 A **con** is the same as a convict; an informal use. — N COUNT
4 See also **mod cons.** ● **pros and cons**: see **pro.**

Con. is an abbreviation for 'constable'; used in Britain as part of a policeman's title. EG *Det. Con. Tucker.* — N IN TITLES

concatenation /kə⁷nkætə¹neɪʃə⁰n/ is the occurrence of a number of things or events one after another, because they are linked together; a formal word. EG *Which of these approaches is adopted depends on the concatenation of a number of factors.* — N UNCOUNT+*of*

concave /kɒnkeɪv, kɒnkeɪv/. A surface that is **concave** curves inwards in the middle. EG *He had tight-skinned, concave cheeks... ...a concave mirror.* — ADJ QUALIT = hollow ≠ convex

conceal /kə⁷nsi:l/, **conceals, concealing, concealed.** 1 If you **conceal** something, you cover it or hide it carefully, so that it cannot be seen. EG *The scarf concealed a revolver... The whole scene was recorded by concealed cameras.* — V+O ≠ reveal
2 If you **conceal** something such as your feelings or some information, you are careful not to let other people know about it. EG *She concealed her surprise... The duke might be concealing a secret from me.* — V+O: IF+PREP THEN *from* = disguise, hide ≠ reveal

concealment /kə⁷nsi:lmə²nt/ is 1 the state of being hidden or the act of hiding. EG *The trees offered concealment and protection for them. ...places of concealment.* 2 the state or act of keeping information or your feelings secret. EG *...the concealment of truth.* — N UNCOUNT ≠ discovery; N UNCOUNT

concede /kə⁷nsi:d/, **concedes, conceding, conceded**; used mainly in formal English. 1 If you **concede** something, 1.1 you admit, often unwillingly, that it is true or correct. EG *The company conceded that an error had been made... 'Maybe there's some truth in that,' conceded Stein... Each of them conceded the point that the present system was unfair... I'll concede you that.* 1.2 you give it to the person who has been trying to get it from you. EG *Neither their territory nor their rights would be conceded without fierce resistance.* — V+O/REPORT-CL/QUOTE, OR V+O+O ⇑ accept; V+O = relinquish
2 In sport, if you **concede** goals, points, etc, you are unable to prevent your opponents from scoring them. EG *We have conceded a lot of goals.* — V+O
3 If you **concede** or **concede** a game, contest, or argument, you end it by admitting that you can no longer win. EG *He refused to concede the match... Another strike will force the government to concede.* — V OR V+O = give up
4 If you **concede defeat**, you formally state that you accept that you have lost. EG *The government was forced to concede defeat.* — PHR: VB INFLECTS
5 If you **concede** something to someone, you give it to them as a right or privilege. EG *The government is prepared to concede substantial liberties to the individual.* — V+O, OR V+O+O: IF+PREP THEN *to*

conceit /kə⁷nsi:t/, **conceits.** 1 **Conceit** is excessive pride in your abilities or achievements. EG *His recent movies have shown signs of arrogance and conceit.* — N UNCOUNT ⇑ vanity = arrogance ≠ modesty
2 A **conceit** is a clever or unusual metaphor or comparison; a technical term. EG *The conceit amused him.* — N COUNT

conceited /kə⁷nsi:tɪ²d/. Someone who is **conceited** is excessively proud of their abilities or achievements. EG *...a conceited old fool... I am not conceited about my achievement.* — ADJ QUALIT: IF+PREP THEN *about* ⇑ vain

conceivable /kə⁷nsi:vəbə⁰l/ is used to describe something that you are able to imagine and that you think might happen or might be possible. EG *There is no conceivable reason why there should be any difficulty... Three or four sets of every conceivable document are required... It is conceivable that he drowned.* ◊ **conceivably.** EG *I might conceivably get somewhere better in Birmingham.* — ADJ QUALIT = imaginable ≠ unthinkable; ◊ ADV SEN = possibly

conceive /kə⁷nsi:v/, **conceives, conceiving, conceived.** 1 If you can **conceive** of something, you can imagine that it might happen or might be possible. EG *He could never conceive of such a thing happening to himself... I can conceive of no circumstances in which we would give in.* — V+A (*of*), OR V+REPORT-CL, OR V+O: USU WITH MODAL O
2 If you **conceive** something as something else, you consider it in that way. EG *A politician conceives the world as being a variety of conflicting values... Time can be conceived as the intervals during which events occur... We must do what we conceive to be the right thing.* — V+O: USU+*of/as*, OR *to*-INF ⇑ believe = see
3 If you **conceive** a plan or idea, you think of it and work out how it can be done or put into practice. EG *A Prices and Incomes policy was boldly conceived... It was the first building within London to be conceived and carried out in the classic Italian style.* — V+O ⇑ form = devise
4 If a woman **conceives** or **conceives** a child, she becomes pregnant. EG *My wife has not been able to conceive... The boy had been conceived on their honeymoon in Spain.* — V OR V+O

concentrate /kɒnsə²ntreɪt/, **concentrates, concentrating, concentrated.** 1 If you concen- — V: IF+PREP

trate, you give all your attention to something that you are listening to, reading, or trying to do. EG *Jenny, please, stop interrupting, I'm trying to concentrate... Concentrate on your driving.*
THEN *on*

2 If something **concentrates the mind**, it causes you to think very clearly and carefully. EG *The prospect of death concentrates the mind wonderfully.*
PHR : VB INFLECTS

3 If you **concentrate** on something, or **concentrate** your attention, energies, etc on something, you spend a lot of time and effort dealing with it or discussing it. EG *He believed governments should concentrate more on education... I concentrated on attacking my opponents... In the next chapter he concentrates his attention on the question of technology.*
V OR V+O : IF+ PREP THEN *on*
= focus on

4 When something **concentrates** or you **concentrate** it, a large amount of it or large numbers of it gather into a small area or space, or become the possession of a very few people.. EG *Modern industry has been concentrated in a few large urban centres... The jets concentrate the water into a steady stream... Power is concentrated in the hands of a few.*
V-ERG
≠ disperse

5 A **concentrate** is a liquid or substance from which unnecessary substances such as water have been removed in order to increase its strength and power or to decrease its bulk and make it easier to transport; a technical use. EG *...a gallon can of disinfectant concentrate which you can dilute.*
N MASS

concentrated /kɒnsə²ntreɪtɪ²d/. 1 A liquid or substance that is **concentrated** has been increased in strength, usually by the removal of unnecessary substances such as water. EG *...concentrated orange juice.*
ADJ CLASSIF
⇑ strong
≠ diluted

2 A **concentrated** activity is one that is directed with great intensity in one place. EG *...a heavily concentrated attack.*
ADJ QUALIT
= concerted
≠ half-hearted

concentration /kɒnsə²ntreɪʃə⁰n/, **concentrations**. 1 **Concentration** is giving all your attention to what you are doing or to what someone is saying. EG *It requires considerable concentration to maintain a false breathing rate.*
N UNCOUNT

2 **Concentration** on something is spending most of your time or effort dealing with it or discussing it. EG *His concentration on civil rights has improved his popularity.*
N UNCOUNT+*on*

3 A **concentration** of something is a large amount of it or large numbers of it in a small space or area. EG *...the densest concentrations of people in the Third World... Large concentrations of capital were in the hands of merchants... ...the concentration of power in the hands of a single group.*
N COUNT/ UNCOUNT
⇑ quantity
= accumulation

4 The **concentration** of a substance is the proportion of essential ingredients or substances in it; a technical or formal use. EG *Rocks of that age contain high concentrations of the element iridium... We can calculate the different concentrations of wine and water.*
N COUNT+*of* : USU PL

concentration camp, concentration camps. A **concentration camp** is a prison in which a large number of prisoners are kept in very bad conditions, especially during a war.
N COUNT

concentric /kə⁷nsentrɪk/. **Concentric** circles, rings, etc have the same centre. EG *In the field are mysterious concentric circles of stones... ...patterns of concentric ripples.*
ADJ CLASSIF : ATTRIB

concept /kɒnsept/, **concepts**. A **concept** is an idea or abstract principle which relates to a particular subject or to a particular view of that subject. EG *Monetarism is an extremely simple concept in principle... ...the concept of trade unionism... People will be familiar with the concept that all substances are made up of molecules.*
N COUNT : USU+ *of*/REPORT-CL
= notion

conception /kə⁷nsepʃə⁰n/, **conceptions**. 1 A **conception** is a general idea that you have in your mind when you think about something. EG *He had a definite conception of how he wanted things arranged... The eternal imposition on children of adult conceptions and values is a great sin.*
N COUNT : USU+ *of*/REPORT-CL
= concept, notion

2 **Conception** is 2.1 the forming of an idea for something in your mind. EG *The plan was very imaginative in conception.*
N UNCOUNT
⇑ formulation

2.2 the ability to imagine that something might happen or might be possible. EG *I have no conception of how your plan could work.*
N UNCOUNT : USU WITH BROAD NEG
⇑ understanding

2.3 the process in which an egg in a woman is fertilized by a male sperm so that she becomes pregnant. EG *The development of new methods of preventing conception... ...the nine months between conception and biological birth.*
N UNCOUNT
⇑ fertilization

conceptual /kə⁷nseptʃʊ⁰əl/ means related to the idea of concepts formed in the mind. EG *Most people have very little conceptual understanding of computers... During the first two years of life a child does not have conceptual 'thinking' tools–words.*
ADJ CLASSIF : ATTRIB
⇑ mental

conceptualize /kə⁷nseptʃəlaɪz/, **conceptualizes, conceptualizing, conceptualized**; also spelled **conceptualise**. If you **conceptualize** something, you form an idea of it in your mind. EG *In early childhood these notions are difficult to conceptualize.*
V+O
⇑ imagine

concern /kə⁷nsɜːn/, **concerns, concerning, concerned**. 1 **Concern** is worry that people have about a situation. EG *He insists there is no cause for concern.... Concern about germ warfare has been widespread... ...the growing public concern over Britain's poor economic performance... The shortage of airfields gave particular concern.*
N UNCOUNT : IF+ PREP THEN *about/over/at*
= anxiety

2 If something is **of concern**, it is worrying and unsatisfactory. EG *The potential mass exodus of people was of great concern to the government... ...a matter of serious concern.*
PHR : USED AS AN A, OR NG+PHR

3 If something is **of concern** to a group of people, it is interesting and important to them. EG *...issues and events of current interest and concern... This was of no concern to businessmen.*
PHR : USED AS AN A, OR NG+PHR

4 If something **concerns** you, it worries you and makes you upset. EG *One of the things that concerns me is the rise in vandalism.* ◇ **concerned**. EG *He was concerned about the level of unemployment in Scotland... There were letters from concerned parents.*
V+O
= disturb
◇ ADJ QUALIT
= worried
≠ unconcerned

5 A **concern** is 5.1 a fact or situation that worries you. EG *The main concern is the size of the Government's budget deficit... My concern is that many of these cases are going unnoticed.*
N COUNT
= worry

5.2 something that is important to you and that you think about a lot. EG *John never understood his parents' concern with tidiness... What are the concerns of ordinary people?*
N COUNT/ UNCOUNT : USU WITH POSS
⇑ thought

6 If you are **concerned** with something, or if you **concern** yourself with it, you are involved with it because it interests you or because you think that it is important. EG *We are more concerned with efficiency than expansion... I'd dearly love to see more women concerning themselves with such vital issues.*
V+O (NG/REFL) : IF+PREP THEN *with*

7 A person's **concern for** someone else is a feeling that they want them to be happy, safe, and well. EG *She shows a true concern for others... I didn't doubt Mum and Dad's love and concern.*
N SING WITH DET/ N UNCOUNT
= care
≠ indifference

8 If you **concern** yourself about someone, you care about what happens to them and want them to be happy, safe, and well. EG *It's interesting you should concern yourself so much about Dave.* ◇ **concerned**. EG *You've got a Mum who's really concerned about you... I'm concerned for him.*
V+O (REFL)+A *(about)*
◇ ADJ QUALIT
= caring

9 If a situation, event, or activity **concerns** you, it affects or involves you. EG *These are matters which some of my colleagues would think do not concern them.*
V+O
⇑ involve

10 If a situation or problem is your **concern**, it is something that you have a duty or responsibility to be involved with. EG *Education in the 12 Inner London Boroughs is the concern of the ILEA... That's your concern, I'm afraid.*
N SING : WITH POSS, USED AS C
= affair, business

11 If you say that something is **none of** your **concern**, you mean that there is no need for you to get involved with it. EG *It would be stupid to fight in a cause that was none of their concern... This quarrel is no concern of ours.*
PHR : USED AS C
= none of someone's business

12 You say **as far as** something **is concerned** and **where** something **is concerned** to indicate the subject that you are talking about. EG *We have rather a poor record as far as regional studies are concerned... She is such a difficult girl to please where men are concerned.*
PHR : USED AS AN A
= with regard to

13 **Concern** is used in expressions like 'as far as I'm concerned' to indicate that you are giving your own opinion. EG *This is all rubbish as far as I'm concerned... As far as we were concerned, they were foreigners.*
PHR : USED AS ADV SEN

14 If a book, speech, or piece of information **concerns** a particular subject or **is concerned with** it, it is about that subject. EG *The next extract concerned Nora, the writer's wife... This chapter is concerned*
V+O : IF PASS THEN+ *with*
⇑ be about

with changes that are likely to take place in the near future.

15 A **concern** is also a company or business. EG *...the giant West German chemical concern, Hoechst.* ● If a company is a **going concern**, it is one that is actually doing business rather than just being planned. N COUNT ● PHR : USED AS C

concerned /kə'nsɜːnd/. 1 The people **concerned** are the people who took part in something or were affected by it. EG *It was a perfect arrangement for all concerned... We've spoken to the lecturers concerned.* ADV AFTER N = involved

2 See also **concern**.

concerning /kə'nsɜːnɪŋ/ is used to indicate what you are talking or writing about. EG *He refused to answer questions concerning his private life... I will now, once and for all, destroy some myths concerning these animals... I wrote to the head of the firm concerning Robert.* PREP ⇑ relating to = re

concert /kɒnsət/, **concerts**. 1 A **concert** is a performance of music given by one or more musicians, usually in a large hall or theatre. EG *She had gone to the concert that evening... ...pop concerts... ...a concert hall.* N COUNT

2 **In concert** is used after the name of a musician or pop group to indicate that they are giving a live concert; used especially in advertisements or on records. EG *See 'The Who' in concert at the Palladium, Friday night.* PHR : USED AS AN A ⇑ playing

3 If a number of people do something **in concert**, they do it together and with a lot of cooperation with one another; a formal expression. EG *Sanctions will be more effective if they are undertaken in concert by a group of countries.* PHR : USED AS AN A

4 If someone is **at concert pitch**, they are fully prepared and ready for action. EG *All our athletes are at concert pitch* PHR : USED AS AN A

concerted /kə'nsɜːtɪ'd/ means 1 done or planned by several people or organizations acting together in order to achieve a particular result. EG *The committee decided to press for concerted action for higher wages.* 2 very serious, strong and sincere. EG *He's made a concerted effort to improve his behaviour.* ADJ CLASSIF : ATTRIB = concentrated ≠ half-hearted; ADJ CLASSIF : ATTRIB

concert-goer, concert-goers. A **concert-goer** is a person who goes to concerts regularly. N COUNT

concertina /kɒnsətiːnə/, **concertinas, concertinaing, concertinaed**. 1 A **concertina** is a musical instrument consisting of two flat end pieces made of wood or other hard material, with stiff paper or cloth that folds up between them. You play a concertina by pressing the end pieces towards each other and then pulling them apart in order to force air through it. You select the notes by pressing buttons on each end. N COUNT

2 To **concertina** means to get smaller by folding up like a concertina. EG *In a head-on crash the front of the car concertinas to absorb the impact.* V ⇑ fold up = telescope

concertmaster /kɒnsətmɑːstə/, **concertmasters**. A **concertmaster** is the leader of an orchestra; used in American English. N COUNT

concerto /kə'ntʃɜətəʊ/, **concertos**. A **concerto** is a long piece of music written for one or more solo instruments and an orchestra. EG *...Beethoven's Violin Concerto.* N COUNT ⇑ composition

concession /kə'nseʃə⁰n/, **concessions**. 1 A **concession** is 1.1 something that you agree to do or let someone else do or have, especially in order to end an argument or conflict. EG *The Prime Minister had been urged to make a concession by the Irish government... Ending the dispute was worth almost any concession.* 1.2 a special right or privilege that is given to someone. EG *Foreign oil companies were granted concessions.* N COUNT = compromise; N COUNT : USU PL

2 In very formal English, **concession** is the act of giving something to someone. N UNCOUNT ⇑ yielding

conch /kɒntʃ, kɒŋk/, **conches**. A **conch** is a shellfish with a large shell rather like a snail's; also used to refer to the shell. N COUNT

concierge /kɒnsɪeəʒ/, **concierges**. A **concierge** is a person, especially in France, who looks after a block of flats and checks people entering and leaving the building. EG *The concierge sat in her doorway and knitted.* N COUNT ⇑ caretaker

conciliate /kə'nsɪlɪeɪt/, **conciliates, conciliating, conciliated**. If you **conciliate**, you try to end a disagreement with someone by saying something to please them or by slightly changing your attitude or demands. EG *We are always ready to conciliate... He would not waste any more time trying to conciliate her.* ◊ **conciliation** /kə'nsɪlɪeɪʃə⁰n/. EG *Did you make any efforts at conciliation?* V OR V+O ⇑ calm = appease ≠ antagonize, provoke; ◊ N UNCOUNT

conciliatory /kə'nsɪljətri¹/. When you are **conciliatory** you are willing to end a disagreement with someone by saying something to please them or by slightly changing your attitudes or demands. EG *They were ruthless where they should have been conciliatory.* ▸ used of actions and behaviour. EG *She spoke in a conciliatory tone... ...a conciliatory visit.* ADJ QUALIT = placatory, amenable ≠ provocative, antagonistic

concise /kə'nsaɪs/. 1 Something that is **concise** says everything that is necessary without using any unnecessary words; used showing approval. EG *...a concise, comprehensive survey of English literature.* ◊ **concisely**. EG *Write clearly and concisely.* ◊ **conciseness**. ADJ QUALIT = succinct ≠ verbose; ◊ ADV WITH VB; ◊ N UNCOUNT

2 **Concise** is used in the title of an edition of a book which is shorter than the original edition. EG *...The Concise Oxford Dictionary.* ADJ CLASSIF : ATTRIB = abridged, compact

conclave /kɒŋ¹kleɪv/, **conclaves**. A **conclave** is a meeting at which people keep what happens secret; used especially of the meeting of cardinals held to elect a new Pope. EG *Had their conclave been overheard?... The cardinals were in secret conclave.* N COUNT, OR *in*+N ⇑ discussion

conclude /kə'nkluːd/, **concludes, concluding, concluded**. 1 If you **conclude** that something is true, you decide that it is true because you know that other things are true. EG *Darwin concluded that men were descended from apes... After listening at Eddie's door and concluding that he was out, I opened it... What do you conclude from all that?.* V+REPORT-CL : IF+PREP THEN *from* = deduce, infer, surmise

2 When you **conclude**, you say the last thing that you are going to say; a slightly formal word. EG *'That,' he concluded, 'is why we're so poor.'... Perhaps I ought to conclude with a slightly more light-hearted question.* ◊ **concluding**. EG *His concluding remark was prophetic.* V+QUOTE : IF+PREP THEN *with* = finish ≠ begin; ◊ ADJ CLASSIF : ATTRIB

3 When you **conclude** something that you are doing, you finish it; a slightly formal word. EG *The trawler had concluded its fishing trip.* V+O ≠ begin

4 When something **concludes** or when you **conclude** it, it ends in the way or at the time that you mention; a slightly formal use. EG *The matter concluded without too much fuss... The season concludes on April 7... I will conclude this chapter with a quotation from Orwell.* V-ERG : IF V THEN +A = close, end ≠ open

5 To **conclude** a treaty or business deal means to arrange or settle it finally. EG *Alexander III was compelled to conclude an alliance with Republican France... Attlee was able to conclude an historic compromise between the party leaders.* V+O = clinch

conclusion /kə'nkluːʒə⁰n/, **conclusions**. 1 A **conclusion** is something that you decide is true as a result of knowing that other things are true. EG *I came to the conclusion that I didn't really fancy civil engineering... Only one conclusion can be drawn from that.* ● If you **jump to a conclusion** or **jump to conclusions**, you decide too quickly that something is true, when you do not know all the facts. EG *Some people jumped rashly to the conclusion that something must be wrong... I don't want you or anyone else jumping to conclusions.* N COUNT, OR N COUNT+REPORT-CL ⇑ opinion; ● PHR : VB INFLECTS, ALSO+REPORT-CL ⇑ assume

2 The **conclusion** of something that has been taking place is its ending. EG *We tried an experiment which had an interesting conclusion... At the conclusion of the opening session, cheers were raised for Queen Victoria.* ● If something in the future is a **foregone conclusion**, it seems certain that it will happen in a particular way. EG *The result should be a foregone conclusion.* N SING WITH DET : USU+SUPP = end ≠ opening; ● PHR : DET+N = certainty ≠ impossibility

3 **In conclusion** is used to indicate that you are just about to say the last thing that you want to say. EG *In conclusion, let me suggest a number of practical applications.* PHR : USED AS ADV SEN = finally ≠ firstly

4 The **conclusion** of a treaty or a business deal is its final settlement. EG *...the conclusion of peace with Britain.* N SING WITH DET : IF+PREP THEN *of* ⇑ making

conclusive /kə'nkluːsɪv/. Facts, evidence, arguments, etc that are **conclusive** show with certainty that something is true. EG *The evidence is not conclusive... ...conclusive proof.* ◊ **conclusively**. EG *It has been difficult to prove conclusively that such treatment is beneficial.* ADJ QUALIT = indisputable; ◊ ADV WITH VB

concoct /kə'nkɒkt/, **concocts, concocting, concocted**. 1 If you **concoct** an excuse, explana- V+O tion, or account, you invent one that is false or misleading. EG *He had to hastily concoct an excuse.*

2 If you **concoct** something, especially something unusual, you make it by adding together several different things. EG *Nancy had concocted a red wine sauce to go with the pheasants.* [V+O ⇑ mix, create]

concoction /kəˀnkɒkʃəⁿn/, **concoctions**. 1 A **concoction** is food, medicine, or a drink made out of several ingredients mixed together; used especially when the mixture is an unusual one. EG *How does that concoction taste?... Chutney is a concoction of almost any fruit or vegetable you like... He gave me a pill of his own concoction.* ▸ used of any unusual mixture of things. EG *Even their uniforms are a concoction.* [N COUNT/UNCOUNT]

concomitant /kəˀnkɒmɪtənt/, **concomitants**. 1 One thing is described as **concomitant** with another thing when it happens at the same time and is connected with the other thing; a formal word. EG *This scheme will involve an excessive growth of bureaucracy, with its concomitant dangers of petty tyranny and corruption... I was aware of the high moral standards concomitant with the name I bore.* [ADJ CLASSIF: IF+PREP THEN *with* = attendant]

2 The **concomitant** of something is another thing that happens at the same time and is connected with it; a formal word. EG *Moodiness is a common concomitant of growing up.* [N COUNT: IF+PREP THEN *of*]

concord /kɒŋkɔːd/. 1 **Concord** is the state of living or working together in peaceful agreement; a formal word. EG *New York is the paragon of racial concord... One day we shall all live in peace, concord and union.* [N UNCOUNT = harmony ≠ discord, friction]

2 In grammar, **concord** is the relationship between words which determines whether they should be singular or plural, or masculine or feminine, and what the form of the verbal group should be. [N UNCOUNT ⇑ agreement]

concordance /kəˀnkɔːdəns/, **concordances**. 1 **Concordance** is the state of being similar to or consistent with something else; used especially of ideas and actions; a formal use. EG *There is a marvellous concordance between our two proposals.* [N UNCOUNT = similarity, concord]

● If something is **in concordance with** another thing, it is similar to or consistent with the other thing; used especially of ideas or actions. EG *This move would not be in concordance with our original plan.* [● PREP = compatible with]

2 A **concordance** is an alphabetical list of the words in a book or a set of books which also says where each word can be found and often how it is used. EG *...a concordance of Shakespeare. ...the analysis of concordance data.* [N COUNT ⇑ listing, index]

concourse /kɒŋ¹kɔːs/, **concourses**. A **concourse** is 1 a wide hall in a building, where people walk about or gather together. [N COUNT] 2 a large group of people gathered together; a formal use. EG *...an immense concourse of bishops and priests.* [N COUNT: USU SING, ALSO N+*of*+N IN PL ⇑ gathering]

concrete /kɒŋ¹kriːt/, **concretes, concreting, concreted**. 1 **Concrete** is a building material which is made by mixing together cement, sand, small stones, and water, and which hardens when it dries. EG *...a modern tower made of concrete and steel... ...a concrete floor.* [N UNCOUNT, OR N BEFORE N ⇑ substance]

2 When you **concrete** something such as a path, you cover it with concrete. [V+O]

3 Something that is **concrete** is 3.1 particular and definite rather than general or vague. EG *There were no specific, concrete proposals placed before the people... ...concrete evidence... They now realized that they could begin to do something concrete to fight racism.* [ADJ QUALIT ≠ vague] 3.2 real and able to be experienced by the senses rather than being abstract. EG *There were many concrete reminders of his existence.* [ADJ CLASSIF = substantial ≠ abstract]

concubine /kɒŋ¹kjəⁱbaɪn/, **concubines**. A **concubine** is a woman in former times who had a sexual relationship with a man who was not married to her and who may also have had a wife. The man usually gave the woman financial support and had some authority over her. EG *The palace housed the emperors with their many wives and concubines.* [N COUNT ⇑ mistress]

concur /kəˀŋ¹kɜː/, **concurs, concurring, concurred**. When you **concur**, you agree with someone about a particular statement or opinion; a formal word. EG *The judge concurred with earlier findings... Lord Dunnem concurred... Baghdad residents all concur that food shortages are acute.* [V: IF+PREP THEN *with*, OR V+QUOTE/REPORT-CL = reject]

concurrence /kəˀŋ¹kʌrəns/. **Concurrence** is 1 agreement; a formal use. EG *The French President gave his instant concurrence... The child was adopted by Jo and his wife, with the concurrence of Julie.* [N SING WITH DET: USU WITH POSS = consent] 2 the fact of two or more things happening at the same time. EG *...a bizarre concurrence of events.* [N UNCOUNT/COUNT = coincidence]

concurrent /kəˀŋ¹kʌrənt/. If two or more things are **concurrent**, they happen at the same time as one another. EG *His story makes poignant reading when one knows the concurrent drama of his private life... The two events were concurrent.* [ADJ CLASSIF: IF+PREP THEN *with* = simultaneous] ◊ **concurrently**. EG *Two subjects will be studied concurrently.* [◊ ADV WITH VB: ALSO ADV+*with*]

concuss /kəˀŋ¹kʌs/, **concusses, concussing, concussed**. When a blow or fall **concusses** someone, it causes their brain to be damaged, usually temporarily, so that they lose consciousness or feel sick or confused. EG *She hit her forehead on the kerb, concussing herself... He's not even concussed.* [V+O (NG/REFL) ⇑ stun]

concussion /kəˀŋ¹kʌʃəⁿn/ is damage to someone's brain caused by a blow or fall and which makes them lose consciousness or feel sick or confused. EG *She was in Newcastle Infirmary with concussion.* [N UNCOUNT]

condemn /kəˀndem/, **condemns, condemning, condemned**. 1 If you **condemn** something, you say that it is very bad and unacceptable. EG *Mr Wilson condemned the invasion... He condemned the report as partial and inadequate... I did not condemn him for what he had done.* [V+O (NG/REFL): IF+PREP THEN *for/as* = denounce ≠ endorse, praise]

2 To **condemn** someone to a particular punishment, especially death or hard labour, means to formally say in a court of law that this is how they will be punished. EG *Susan was condemned to death... So you'd condemn me to be shot at dawn?* [V+O+A (*to*), OR V+O+*to*-INF = sentence]

3 If circumstances **condemn** someone to an unpleasant situation, those circumstances make it certain that they will suffer in a particular way. EG *Lack of education condemns them to extreme poverty... Most of the applicants are condemned to spend all morning waiting to be seen.* [V+O+A (*to*), OR V+O+*to*-INF ⇑ compel = doom]

4 To **condemn** a building means to officially decide that it is not safe enough to be lived in or used. EG *Why do you think the fire department hasn't condemned the place?* [V+O]

5 If your face, words, or behaviour **condemn** you, they indicate that you are guilty of doing something wrong. EG *He was condemned by his own actions.* [V+O = gives away ≠ absolve]

condemnation /kɒndemneɪʃəⁿn/, **condemnations**. 1 **Condemnation** is the act of saying that something or someone is very bad and unacceptable. EG *This blatant act of oppression calls out for universal condemnation... ...their strong condemnation of her conduct.* [N UNCOUNT/COUNT: IF+PREP THEN *of* ⇑ criticism ≠ praise]

2 A **condemnation** of something or someone is a fact or situation that suggests how bad they are. EG *It's a great condemnation of the church that it's got caught up in all this.* [N SING WITH DET: IF+PREP THEN *of* = indictment]

condemnatory /kɒndemneɪtəⁱri¹, kəˀndemnətəⁱri¹/. Something that is **condemnatory** expresses strong disapproval. EG *His tone was condemnatory.* [ADJ CLASSIF ≠ approving]

condemned /kəˀndemd/. Someone who is **condemned** is going to be executed. EG *The condemned men were forced to dig their own graves.* [ADJ CLASSIF ⇑ doomed]

condemned cell, condemned cells. A **condemned cell** is a prison cell for someone who is going to be executed. [N COUNT]

condensation /kɒndenseɪʃəⁿn/. 1 **Condensation** consists of small drops of water which form when warm water vapour or steam touches a cold surface such as a window. EG *Check the walls for condensation.* [N UNCOUNT ⇑ moisture]

2 See also **condense**.

condense /kəˀndens/, **condenses, condensing, condensed**. 1 To **condense** something means to make it shorter or make it last for a shorter period of time, usually by including only the most important parts. EG *I tried to condense every report into as few words as possible.* [V+O: IF+PREP THEN *into/to* ⇑ shorten = summarize, edit] ◊ **condensation** /kɒndenseɪʃəⁿn/. EG *...the condensation of three thousand million years of history into one television series.* [◊ N UNCOUNT]

2 When a gas or vapour **condenses**, it changes into a liquid, usually because it has become cooler. EG *During cold nights, dew condenses on the leaves.* [V-ERG ≠ evaporate]

condensed milk is milk that has been thickened by removing some of the water in it and that has sugar added to it. [N UNCOUNT]

condescend /kɒndɪsend/, **condescends, condescending, condescended**. 1 If you **condescend** to people, you behave in a way which shows [V: IF+PREP THEN *to*] them that you think that you are superior to them. EG *He never condescended, never spoke down to me.*

2 If you **condescend** to do something, you agree to do it, but in a way that shows that you think that you are doing people a favour; used showing disapproval. EG *She did not condescend to have dinner with him... Anne condescended to acknowledge her family once or twice a year.*
V+*to*-INF = deign

condescending /kɒndɪse̲ndɪŋ/ Someone who is **condescending** talks or behaves in a way that shows that they think that they are superior to other people. EG *They were so condescending.* ▸ used of the way people talk or behave. EG *She addressed him with the same condescending tone.*
ADJ QUALIT = patronizing

condescension /kɒndɪse̲nʃəⁿn/ is the quality or act of being condescending. EG *He spoke to the labourers with kindness and understanding, with no condescension.*
N UNCOUNT

condiment /kɒndɪməⁿnt/, **condiments**. A **condiment** is a substance such as salt, pepper, or mustard that you add to food when you eat it in order to increase the flavour.
N COUNT = seasoning

condition /kəˀndɪʃəⁿn/, **conditions, conditioning, conditioned**. **1** The **condition** of a person or thing is the particular state that it is in. EG *Congress is to consider the unfavourable financial condition of the nation... You can't go home in that condition... They are in a permanent condition of intense emotion when they are together.*
N SING WITH DET +SUPP

● If someone is **in no condition to** do something, they are so ill or upset that it would be dangerous or unreasonable for them to do it. EG *He would probably be in no condition to drive.*
● PHR : USED AS AN A ⇑ unable = unfit

2 The **conditions** in which or under which something is done are all the factors and circumstances which directly affect it. EG *These experiments were carried out under almost unimaginable conditions... The failure of the crop was due to adverse weather conditions.*
N PLURAL+SUPP = circumstances

3 The **conditions** in which you live or work are all the factors such as heating, hygiene, safety, etc which affect the quality of your life or job. EG *We saw some appalling living conditions... Miners work in unenviable conditions underground... He wrote to protest against the conditions in Port Elizabeth jail.*
N PLURAL+SUPP ⇑ standards, environment

4 The **condition** of a group of people is their situation in life, especially regarding the difficulties or hardship they have; a formal use. EG *Plato maintained that slaves deserved their condition... ...the human condition... They were curious about the condition of black people in the United States.*
N SING WITH DET +SUPP = state

5 A **condition** is **5.1** something which must happen, be true, or be done first before it is possible for something else to happen. EG *What is the condition that you have to satisfy?... The right of our nation to independence is a condition for world peace.*
N COUNT : IF+ PREP THEN *for* = requirement

5.2 part of a contract or a law which must be agreed to or obeyed in order for something else to be allowed. EG *You have to live there as a condition of your job... Find out what the conditions of the contract are... That's the condition Mr Chase made.*
N COUNT : IF+ PREP THEN *of* ⇑ requirement = stipulation

6 When you agree to do something **on condition that** something else happens, you mean that you will only do it if this other thing happens or is agreed to first. EG *He has agreed to come on condition that there won't be any press or publicity... They could use the land for a year and half on condition they handed it back cleared of weeds.*
CONJ SUBORD = providing, as long as

7 The **condition** of something is its physical quality, which depends on its age and how well it has been looked after. EG *All the books were in a very poor condition... You're supposed to keep your car exterior in good condition by cleaning it.*
N UNCOUNT, OR N SING WITH DET+ SUPP ⇑ state

8 The **condition** of a person or animal is their state of health. EG *He was in a serious condition after a coronary attack... Mr Sandrucci was in good physical condition... Families had only intervened when the condition of hunger strikers became critical.*
N UNCOUNT, OR N SING WITH DET+ SUPP

● Someone who is **out of condition** is unhealthy and unable to do a lot of physical activity without getting tired. EG *The men are exhausted and badly out of condition.*
● PHR : USED AS AN A = unfit

9 A **condition** is also an illness or other medical problem that a person has. EG *He has a heart condition... Hypothermia is an extremely complex condition.*
N COUNT : USU SING, USU MOD+ N = complaint

10 To **condition** someone means to influence them over a period of time so that their character or attitudes develop in a particular way. EG *I had been conditioned by the world in which I grew up... Nell had conditioned her to see me as an enemy.*
V+O, OR V+O+ *to*-INF : USU PASS ⇑ mould

◊ **conditioning**. EG *It is very difficult to overcome your early conditioning.*
◊ N UNCOUNT

11 To **condition** hair, skin, etc means to keep it healthy by putting something on it.
V+O ⇑ treat

12 To **be conditioned by** something means to be under its control; a formal use. EG *The pub is conditioned by the licensing laws of the realm.*
V+O : USU PASS ⇑ influenced

conditional /kəˀndɪʃəⁿnəl, -ʃənəⁿl/. **1** If a situation or agreement is **conditional** on something, it is not definite and will only happen or be accepted if this thing happens. EG *Weapons sales have been made conditional upon provision of territory for bases... We have conditional acceptance, depending on our good behaviour... Workers Fight lent conditional support to the Unified Secretariat.*
ADJ CLASSIF : IF+ PREP THEN *on/upon* ⇑ dependent

◊ **conditionally**. EG *She said yes, conditionally.*
◊ ADV SEN

2 In grammar, a **conditional** sentence is a sentence in which the subordinate clause, usually beginning with 'if', gives a condition that must be fulfilled before what the main clause says can be true, possible, or done.
ADJ CLASSIF

conditioner /kəˀndɪʃənə/, **conditioners**. A **conditioner** is **1** a thick liquid which you can put on your hair after washing it in order to make your hair softer.
N COUNT/ UNCOUNT

2 a thick liquid which you can use when you wash clothes, towels, etc in order to make them feel softer.
N COUNT/ UNCOUNT

condole /kəˀnd<u>əu</u>l/, **condoles, condoling, condoled**. If you **condole** with someone, you express your sympathy for something that has happened to them, especially the death of a friend or relative; a formal word.
V : IF+PREP THEN *with* ⇑ sympathize

condolence /kəˀnd<u>əu</u>ləns/, **condolences**. **1 Condolence** is sympathy for something that has happened to someone, especially the death of a friend or relative. EG *...letters of condolence.*
N UNCOUNT

2 Your **condolences** are the expression of your sympathy to someone because a friend or relative of theirs has died recently. EG *She wished to offer her condolences.*
N PLURAL

condom /kɒndəⁿm/, **condoms**. A **condom** is a covering made of thin rubber which a man wears on his penis during sexual intercourse as a contraceptive.
N COUNT = sheath

condominium /kɒndəⁿmɪnɪəm/, **condominiums**. In the United States, a **condominium** is a block of flats in which each flat is owned by the person who lives there; also used to refer to one of the flats.
N COUNT

condone /kəˀnd<u>əu</u>n/, **condones, condoning, condoned**. If someone **condones** behaviour that is morally wrong, they accept it or allow it to happen. EG *We cannot condone anarchy... You sound as though you condone the terrorists.*
V+O ≠ condemn

condor /kɒndɔː/, **condors**. A **condor** is a large South American bird that eats the meat of dead animals.
N COUNT

conducive /kəˀndjuːsɪv/. If one thing is **conducive** to another thing, it has qualities that make this other thing likely to happen or be able to be done. EG *I was certain that Frankfurt was far more conducive to philosophical studies than any other place... Competition is not conducive to human happiness.*
ADJ QUALIT : PRED+*to* ⇑ favourable ≠ detrimental

conduct, conducts, conducting, conducted. The word **conduct** is pronounced /kəˀndʌkt/ when it is a verb, and /kɒndʌkt/ when it is a noun. **1** When you **conduct** an activity or task, you organize it and carry it out. EG *We have been conducting a survey of the region... We conducted a number of campaigns in the paper... ...the manner in which he conducted his public life.*
V+O ⇑ do = run

2 The **conduct** of an activity is the process of organizing it and carrying it out. EG *...an inquiry into the conduct of the Government's economic policy... Secrets are essential to the conduct of a war.*
N SING : WITH *the*/POSS+*of* ⇑ control = running

3 Someone's **conduct** is the way they behave in particular situations, especially with regard to morality. EG *A child learns to adapt to the rules of conduct of the society in which it lives... The minister had several good reasons for his conduct.*
N UNCOUNT : USU WITH POSS ⇑ action = behaviour

4 If you **conduct** yourself in a particular way, you behave or act in that way. EG *He instructed them*
V+O (REFL)+A = comport

thoroughly in how to conduct themselves inside the mosque.

5 When someone **conducts** an orchestra or choir, they stand in front of the orchestra or choir and direct their performance. EG *We saw Seija Ozawa conducting the Boston Symphony Orchestra... I remember when I first conducted in London.* V OR V+O

6 If you **conduct** someone to a place, you go there with them in order to show them the way. EG *I conducted him as far as the steps... The waiter conducts them to their table.* V+O+A ⇑ lead = escort

7 If something **conducts** heat or electricity, it allows the heat or electricity to pass through or along it. EG *Copper conducts electricity.* V OR V+O ⇑ transmit

conducted tour, conducted tours. A **conducted tour** is a visit around a building, town, or area during which someone goes with you and explains everything to you. EG *Moumouni took me on a conducted tour of his fields.* N COUNT ⇑ excursion = guided tour

conduction /kəˀndʌkʃəⁿn/ is the process by which heat or electricity passes through or along something; a technical term in science. EG *...the conduction of electricity through gases.* N UNCOUNT: IF+PREP THEN *of* ⇑ transfer = passage

conductor /kəˀndʌktə/, **conductors.** A **conductor** is 1 a person who sells tickets on a bus or sometimes a train. N COUNT 2 a person who stands in front of an orchestra or choir and conducts them. EG *...Martin Davidson, conductor of the Bach Society orchestra.* N COUNT 3 a substance that heat or electricity can pass through or along. EG *This material is not such a good conductor as metal, but better than wood.* ● See also **lightning conductor.** N COUNT

conductress /kəˀndʌktrɪˡs/, **conductresses.** A **conductress** is a woman who sells tickets on buses. N COUNT ⇑ employee

conduit /kɒndɪt, -djuɪt/, **conduits.** A **conduit** is a small tunnel, pipe, or channel through which water or electrical wires go. N COUNT

cone /kəʊn/, **cones, coning, coned.** A **cone** is 1 a geometrical shape with a circular or oval base and smooth curved sides ending in a point above the base. EG *...a cone-shaped hill.* N COUNT 2 anything shaped like a cone. EG *...the steep volcanic cones of central Japan... ...a cone of light.* N COUNT ⇑ object 3 a large plastic cone-shaped object, usually orange and white, that is placed with others to prevent people driving or parking on part of a road, especially where there are road-works. N COUNT ⇑ obstacle 4 the fruit of a tree such as a pine or fir which consists of a cluster of woody scales containing seeds. N COUNT 5 an ice cream cornet. EG *Do you want a cone or a chocolate ice?* N COUNT

cone off. To **cone off** a road or an area of ground means to place a line of large plastic cones there to prevent people driving on part of it. EG *One lane of the M25 has been coned off.* PHRASAL VB: V+O+ADV ⇑ close off

confection /kəˀnfɛkʃəⁿn/, **confections.** A **confection** is 1 an elaborately decorated cake or some other sweet food. EG *Cake-shops occasionally offer confections covered in blue icing.* N COUNT 2 something such as a piece of clothing that is elaborately made. EG *Her hat was a charming confection of net and feathers.* N COUNT ⇑ object = creation

confectioner /kəˀnfɛkʃəⁿnə/, **confectioners.** A **confectioner** is a person whose job is making or selling sweets and chocolates. N COUNT ⇑ cook

confectionery /kəˀnfɛkʃənəⁿriˡ/. **Confectionery** is 1 sweet food such as sweets and chocolates. EG *Confectionery sales are holding up well.* N UNCOUNT 2 the business of making or selling confectionery. N UNCOUNT

confederacy /kəˀnfɛdəⁿrəsiˡ/, **confederacies.** A **confederacy** is a union of states or people who are trying to achieve the same thing. N COUNT ⇑ alliance

confederate /kəˀnfɛdəⁿrɪt/, **confederates.** A **confederate** is someone you are working with in some secret activity. EG *He is one of her most trusted confederates.* N COUNT ⇑ ally = accomplice

confederation /kəˀnfɛdəreɪʃəⁿn/, **confederations.** A **confederation** is an organization or alliance consisting of smaller groups or states, especially for political or business purposes. EG *We are in favour of a loose confederation of states... ...the Confederation of British Industry.* N COUNT: ALSO IN NAMES

confer /kəˀnfɜː/, **confers, conferring, conferred.** 1 When people **confer** with each other, they discuss something together, exchanging ideas and opinions, usually in order to make a decision. EG *The jury conferred for only twelve minutes... He went home to confer with his wife, and then accepted the appointment.* V OR V+A *(with)*: RECIP = consult

2 To **confer** something such as an honour, a gift, or status on someone means to give it to them; a formal use. EG *Degrees are conferred in July and December... Certain cars have always tended to confer status... ...the superiority that is conferred on the rich by their wealth.* V+O: IF+PREP THEN *on/upon* = bestow

conference /kɒnfəⁿrəns/, **conferences.** A **conference** is 1 a meeting at which formal discussions take place. EG *The Managing Director has daily conferences with the other staff members... He was in conference for three hours... ...the conference table.* N COUNT, OR *in*+N 2 a meeting, often lasting a few days, which is organized on a particular subject or to bring together people who have a common interest. EG *He attended a conference on nuclear disarmament in London... ...a Linguistics Conference.* ● See also **press conference.** N COUNT = convention

confess /kəˀnfɛs/, **confesses, confessing, confessed.** 1 If you **confess** something or **confess** to something, you admit that you have done something that you feel ashamed of or embarrassed about. EG *Perhaps I shouldn't confess this, but I did on one occasion forge Tony's signature... I confess to a certain weakness for puddings... 'I worry about money,' she confessed... He once confessed to Vita that he really hated parties... She confessed herself completely ignorant of modern art.* V+O/REPORT-CL/QUOTE, V+A *(to)*, V+O (REFL)+C ⇑ reveal ≠ deny

2 **Confess** is used in expressions like 'I confess' and 'I must confess' to apologize slightly for admitting something that you are rather ashamed of or that you think might offend or annoy someone else. EG *I must confess that I find him a bore... I confess your letter was a blow to me.* PHR: USED AS AN ADV SEN ⇑ declare = admit

3 If you **confess** or if you **confess** to a crime, you admit that you have committed a crime. EG *They shot him before he confessed... Bianchi had confessed to five of the murders... Ted had openly confessed his guilt to me.* V: IF+PREP THEN *to*, OR V+O ≠ deny

4 If you **confess** or you **confess** your sins, you tell God or a priest about your sins so that you can be forgiven. EG *You must go back to the chapel and confess to God.* V OR V+O ⇑ communicate

confessed /kəˀnfɛst/ is used to say that a person admits quite openly that they have a particular fault or weakness. EG *He was self-indulgent and cynical, a confessed failure.* ADJ CLASSIF: ATTRIB ⇑ acknowledged = avowed

confession /kəˀnfɛʃəⁿn/, **confessions.** 1 A **confession** is 1.1 something that you confess. EG *I have a confession to make.* N COUNT 1.2 a formal statement by someone that they committed a particular crime. EG *The moment you sign a confession, you can have all the sleep you want... We need some evidence, or a confession.* N COUNT ⇑ statement 1.3 a formal or public announcement of your religious beliefs. EG *We will now make a confession of faith.* N COUNT = profession

2 **'Confessions'** is used in the titles of some books, films, and stories which claim to tell you sensational things about a particular lifestyle or job. EG *...Confessions of a Taxi Driver.* N PLURAL ⇑ revelations

3 **Confession** is 3.1 the act of confessing something. EG *...a torrent of confession.* N UNCOUNT 3.2 the formal process by which you tell God or a priest about your sins and ask for forgiveness. EG *He had gone to confession.* N UNCOUNT/COUNT

confessional /kəˀnfɛʃəⁿnəl, -ʃənəˡl/, **confessionals.** 1 A **confessional** is the small room in a church where Christians, especially Roman Catholics, go to confess their sins. EG *...the secrets of the confessional... ...the confessional box.* N COUNT ⇑ place

2 A **confessional** speech or letter is one in which you confess something. ADJ CLASSIF

confessor /kəˀnfɛsə/, **confessors.** A **confessor** is a priest who hears a person's confession. N COUNT ⇑ priest

confetti /kəˀnfɛtiˡ/. 1 **Confetti** is small pieces of coloured paper that are thrown in large quantities over the bride and groom at a wedding. N UNCOUNT

2 The word **confetti** is used in such phrases as 'like confetti' to suggest that a lot of things or pieces are spread or scattered over an area. EG *Newspapers were littering the streets like confetti.* N UNCOUNT

confidant /kɒnfɪdænt/, **confidants.** Someone's **confidant** is a man who they are able to discuss their private problems and other secret matters with; a formal word. EG *Colonel House was a friend and confidant of President Wilson.* N COUNT ⇑ friend = intimate

confidante /kɒnfɪdænt/, **confidantes**. Someone's **confidante** is a woman who they are able to discuss their private problems and other secret matters with; a formal word. N COUNT ⇑ friend

confide /kə⁷nfaɪd/, **confides, confiding, confided**. 1 If you **confide** a secret to someone, you tell them about it and trust them not to tell anyone else. EG *I never confided my fear to anyone... He had confided to me that he wasn't an Irishman at all... She confided that the subject did not interest her much.* V+O/REPORT-CL/QUOTE : IF+PREP THEN *to* = confess, disclose

2 If you **confide** something to someone, you give it to them so that they can look after it for you; a formal use. EG *...the part of creation which is confided to us by God.* V+O+A *(to)* = entrust

3 See also **confiding**.

confide in. If you **confide in** someone, you tell them about a private problem or some other secret matter because you trust them not to tell anyone else about it. EG *His father probably doesn't confide in him a great deal... May I confide in you?* PHRASAL VB : V+PREP, HAS PASS

confidence /kɒnfɪdəns/, **confidences**. 1 **Confidence** in a person or thing is the feeling that you can trust them to do what they are supposed to do and that they will not disappoint you or fail. EG *I have a lot of confidence in him... There has been a national effort to restore confidence in the pound... Wilson turned the strike into an issue of confidence.* ● See also **vote of confidence** and **vote of no confidence**. N UNCOUNT = faith

2 **Confidence** is 2.1 the belief that you can deal with situations successfully using your own abilities and qualities. EG *I was full of confidence... I've lost my confidence... Working in a group gives you a bit more confidence.* N UNCOUNT = self-assurance 2.2 a feeling of certainty that what you are saying is correct. EG *I can say with complete confidence that it would have been desirable not to have informed the public.* N UNCOUNT : USU *with*+N = authority 2.3 a situation in which you tell someone a secret or some other information that is not widely known, because you trust them not to tell anyone else. EG *I'm telling you this in the strictest confidence... ...a breach of confidence.* N UNCOUNT

3 If you **take** someone **into** your **confidence**, you tell them a secret or some other information that is not widely known, because you trust them. EG *Take her into your confidence as much as possible.* PHR : VB INFLECTS = confide in

4 A **confidence** is a secret or special piece of information that you tell someone. EG *Edith was used to receiving confidences.* N COUNT

confidence man, confidence men. A **confidence man** is the same as a con man; a formal expression. N COUNT

confidence trick, confidence tricks. A **confidence trick** is the same as a con trick; a formal expression. N COUNT

confident /kɒnfɪdənt/. 1 If you are **confident** about something, you are certain that it will happen in the way you want it to. EG *He said he was very confident that the scheme would be successful... He was confident of what he was doing... I feel confident about the future of British music.* ◊ **confidently**. EG *One could confidently rely on him not to make any kind of mistake.* ADJ QUALIT : USU PRED ⇑ sure ≠ sceptical ◊ ADV WITH VB = safely

2 People who are **confident** feel that they are able to deal with a situation successfully and so do not worry about it too much. EG *...a witty, young and confident lawyer... His manner is more confident these days.* ◊ **confidently**. EG *I strode confidently up the hall.* ADJ QUALIT = assured ◊ ADV WITH VB

3 If you are **confident** about something that you are saying, you are very sure that it is true. EG *You seem confident that there are only a few problems left.* ▸ used of something that you say. EG *...a confident reply.* ◊ **confidently**. EG *A swift victory would have been confidently predicted only a few years ago.* ADJ QUALIT : PRED, USU+REPORT-CL ⇑ certain = positive ◊ ADV WITH VB

confidential /kɒnfɪdɛnʃəˈl/. 1 Something that is **confidential** is meant to be kept secret or private and should not be discussed with other people. EG *...confidential information... This arrangement is to be kept strictly confidential... Your problems will obviously be treated as confidential.* ◊ **confidentially**. EG *I wrote to you confidentially in September concerning the forthcoming election.* ADJ QUALIT ≠ public ◊ ADV WITH VB = privately

2 A **confidential** whisper or way of speaking is one that shows that you want to talk about something private or secret to a particular person without anyone else hearing what you are saying. EG *Bill's voice dropped to a lower, more confidential pitch.* ▸ used of people. EG *He became very confidential.* ◊ **confidentially**. EG *She leaned forward and whispered to him confidentially.* ADJ QUALIT ⇑ intimate = private ≠ indiscreet ◊ ADV WITH VB = confidingly

3 A **confidential** clerk or secretary is one who can be trusted with private or secret information. ADJ CLASSIF : ATTRIB

confidentiality /kɒnfɪdɛnʃiˈæləˈtiˈ/. **Confidentiality** is 1 the state or condition of being secret or private. EG *Please respect the confidentiality of this information.* N UNCOUNT ⇑ secrecy 2 the ability to keep information secret or private when this is necessary. EG *Your discretion and confidentiality are being questioned.* N UNCOUNT ≠ indiscretion

confidentially /kɒnfɪdɛnʃəˈliˈ/. 1 **Confidentially** is used to say that what you are telling someone is a secret and should not be discussed with anyone else. EG *Confidentially, I don't like him at all.* ADV SEN = between ourselves

2 Other meanings of **confidentially** can be found in the entry for **confidential**.

confiding /kə⁷nfaɪdɪŋ/. Someone who is **confiding** is willing to talk to you about personal matters. EG *At first she was suspicious, then she became confiding.* ◊ **confidingly**. EG *Frau Doring leaned forward confidingly.* ADJ CLASSIF = trusting ◊ ADV

configuration /kə⁷nfɪgjəˈreɪʃəˈn/, **configurations**. A **configuration** is an arrangement of a group of things or parts; a formal word. EG *The blades collapse into an arrow-head configuration.* N COUNT

confine, confines, confining, confined. The word **confine** is pronounced /kə⁷nfaɪn/ when it is a verb, and /kɒnfaɪnz/ when it is a noun. 1 If something is **confined** to only one place, situation, person, or group, it only exists there or only affects that person or group. EG *The problem of underdevelopment appears to be confined to the tropics... This appears to be a male attitude not confined to judges.* V+O : USU PASS+A *(to)* = limited, restricted

2 If you **confine** yourself to something or you **confine** what you are doing to something, you do or are involved with only that thing and nothing else. EG *They confine themselves to discussing the weather... Confine your messages to official business... The report does not confine itself to married women.* V+O (NG/REFL) +A *(to)* = limit, restrict

3 To **confine** someone means to keep them in prison or some other place which they cannot leave. EG *William was confined to an institution for some years... A number of those previously confined to bed have become mobile.* V+O : USU+A

4 To **confine** something to a particular place or area means to stop it from spreading beyond that place or area. EG *It is very difficult to confine the disease to the farm where it has broken out... He had to confine his steps to the carpeted areas.* V+O+A *(to)* ⇑ limit

5 The **confines** of an area are the boundaries enclosing the area; also used of the enclosed area itself. EG *Our aim is to set up a workshop within the confines of the Gallery... A lock of hair had escaped from the confines of her hat.* N PLURAL : USU+*of*

6 The **confines** of a situation, system, or activity are the limitations or restrictions which it involves. EG *We haven't the resources to deal with these children within the confines of normal schooling.* N PLURAL : USU+*of* ⇑ limits = constraints

confined /kə⁷nfaɪnd/. A **confined** space or area is one that is small and completely enclosed by walls or boundaries. EG *I hate being in a confined space.* ADJ CLASSIF ≠ open

confinement /kə⁷nfaɪnməˈnt/, **confinements**. 1 **Confinement** is the state of being forced to stay inside somewhere, for example prison, for a period of time. EG *...his many years in confinement.* N UNCOUNT = detention

2 A **confinement** is the period of time just before and during which a woman gives birth to a child; a medical term. EG *Her previous confinements have been difficult.* N COUNT/UNCOUNT = labour

confirm /kə⁷nfɜːm/, **confirms, confirming, confirmed**. 1 If something **confirms** what you believe, suspect, or fear, it shows that what you believe, suspect, or fear is definitely true. EG *My suspicions were confirmed... He glanced round to confirm that he was alone... The letter confirmed everything.* ◊ **confirmation** /kɒnfɜːmeɪʃəˈn/. EG *For a long time there was neither confirmation nor refutation of these theories.* V+O/REPORT-CL ⇑ prove = substantiate ◊ N UNCOUNT ⇑ proof = verification

2 If you **confirm** something that has been stated or suggested, you say that it is true because you know about it. EG *She asked me if it was my car and I confirmed that it was... I neither confirmed nor denied the rumours.* ◊ **confirmation**. EG *'I'm good,' she said and looked at me for confirmation.* V+O/REPORT-CL ⇑ assert = corroborate ◊ N UNCOUNT ⇑ agreement

3 If you **confirm** an arrangement, appointment, etc, you say, usually in a letter or on the telephone, that the suggested arrangement or appointment is now V+O/REPORT-CL ⇑ finalize

definite. EG *I want to confirm my booking on this evening's ferry.* ◊ **confirmation.** EG *All timings are approximate and subject to confirmation when booking... Have we received the confirmation for this booking yet?* — ◊ N UNCOUNT/COUNT

4 When someone **is confirmed**, they are formally accepted as a member of a Christian church at a ceremony during which they say they believe what that church teaches. EG *They were confirmed in Westminster Abbey.* — V+O : USU PASS

5 If something **confirms** you in your belief, opinion, intention, etc, it makes your belief, opinion, intention, etc stronger. EG *Everything you have just told us confirms us in the view that nobody can be trusted.* — V+O+A *(in)* = strengthen

6 If something **confirms** its position, role, power, etc, it does something to make this position, role, power, etc, stronger or more definite. EG *Throughout the war the party confirmed its position of national dominance.* — V+O = strengthen

confirmation /kɒnfəmeɪʃəⁿn/, **confirmations.** **1** A **confirmation** of something that was believed, suspected, or feared is something that shows that it is definitely true. EG *This discovery was a well-timed confirmation of Darwin's proposition.* — N COUNT : IF + PREP THEN *of* = proof

2 Confirmation is the act or ceremony of being formally accepted as a member of a Christian church. EG *I went to my sister's confirmation last week.* — N UNCOUNT/COUNT

3 Other meanings of **confirmation** can be found in the entry for **confirm**.

confirmed /kə⁷nfɜːmd/ is used to describe someone who has a particular habit, attitude, or belief that they are very unlikely to change. EG *I am a confirmed non-smoker.* — ADJ CLASSIF : ATTRIB = inveterate

confiscate /kɒnfɪskeɪt/, **confiscates, confiscating, confiscated.** If you **confiscate** something from someone, you take it away from them, often as a punishment, when you have the authority or legal right to do this. EG *The yo-yo had been confiscated from one of his pupils... We had special instructions to confiscate all cameras.* ◊ **confiscation** /kɒnfɪskeɪʃəⁿn/. EG *I faced two years' jail plus the confiscation of the tapes and the vehicle.* — V+O = impound, seize; ◊ N UNCOUNT

conflagration /kɒnfləgreɪʃəⁿn/, **conflagrations.** A **conflagration** is a large fire which burns over a wide area and destroys property; a formal word. — N COUNT : USU SING = inferno

conflate /kə⁷nfleɪt/, **conflates, conflating, conflated.** If you **conflate** two or more accounts, ideas, or pieces of writing, you combine them in order to produce a single one; a formal word. EG *Four of Shakespeare's history plays were conflated by John Barton.* ◊ **conflation** /kɒnfleɪʃəⁿn/. — V+O : IF PASS THEN + *with*; ◊ N UNCOUNT/N COUNT + *of*

conflict, conflicts, conflicting, conflicted. The word **conflict** is pronounced /kɒnflɪkt/ when it is a noun, and /kə⁷nflɪkt/ when it is a verb. **1 Conflict** is **1.1** serious disagreement and argument about something important. EG *This is an area of major political conflict... ...the familiar conflict between government and opposition... There have been a number of conflicts in the engineering industry.* **1.2** a state of mind in which you find it impossible to make a decision or choice. EG *Frequently he is in a state of conflict or indecision.* — N UNCOUNT/COUNT = dispute ≠ agreement; N UNCOUNT = turmoil, agitation

2 If you **come into conflict** with someone, you disagree seriously and argue with them. EG *Whites came more and more often into conflict with the islanders..... We have often come into conflict.* — PHR, OR PHR + A *(with)* : RECIP, VB INFLECTS

3 If something **brings** you **into conflict** with someone, it causes you to have a disagreement or argument with them. EG *He expressed sentiments which would later bring him into conflict with the Party leadership... The two men were brought into conflict by their jobs* — PHR, OR PHR + A *(with)* : RECIP, VB INFLECTS = put at odds

4 If you are **in conflict with** someone, you have disagreed seriously with them about something and have not yet reached agreement about your differences. EG *Rothermere, in conflict with his chief of staff, resigned... Andrews and Westheath are in conflict over this.* — PHR, OR PHR + A *(with)* : RECIP, USED AS A = at odds ≠ in agreement

5 A **conflict** is **5.1** a serious difference between two or more beliefs, ideas, or interests, which cannot be reconciled. EG *Conflicts of loyalty arose... ...the conflict between principle and privilege... The men were permitted to do this whenever there was no conflict with their duties.* **5.2** fighting between two or more countries or groups of people. EG *...a conventional conflict might escalate to a nuclear confrontation... Europe was encircled by conflict.* — N COUNT/UNCOUNT ⇑ opposition = clash ≠ harmony; N COUNT/UNCOUNT

6 If two or more things are **in conflict**, they are very different and it seems impossible for each of them to be true or for each of them to be believed by the same person. EG *Full employment and economic viability are in conflict.* — PHR : USED AS AN A = opposed ≠ in accord

7 If two or more ideas, interests, accounts, etc **conflict**, they are very different and it seems impossible for them to exist together or for each of them to be true. EG *Part of his account conflicted with what he had told me two weeks ago... There is some research that conflicts with this view... These criteria might undoubtedly conflict.* ◊ **conflicting.** EG *There are too many conflicting interests... The evidence seems to be conflicting.* — V OR V+A *(with)* : RECIP = clash ≠ harmonize; ◊ ADJ QUALIT/VB = opposing ≠ compatible

confluence /kɒnfluəns/, **confluences.** **1** The **confluence** of two rivers is the place where they join and become one larger river. EG *...the confluence of the rivers Darwen and Ribble.* — N COUNT : IF + PREP THEN *of* ⇑ junction

2 A **confluence** is the point at which two or more things join together; a formal use. EG *...a confluence of social, economic, and intellectual change... I stared out at the grey confluence of sky and sea.* — N SING WITH DET : IF + PREP THEN *of* = meeting

conform /kə⁷nfɔːm/, **conforms, conforming, conformed.** **1** If you **conform**, you behave in the way that you are expected to behave or in the way that everyone else behaves. EG *You must be prepared to conform... Eventually even the United States conformed.* — V = comply ≠ rebel

2 If you **conform to** or **conform with** an ideal or fashion, you behave, think, or dress in a way that is decided by the ideal or fashion rather than by your own choice. EG *She is a woman who conforms to the current ideal... You're only conforming to type.* — V+A *(to/with)* = correspond to ≠ conflict with

3 If something **conforms to** or **conforms with** a law, regulation, wish, etc, it is of the type or quality that is required or desired. EG *Every home should have a fire extinguisher which conforms with British Standards... Such a change would not conform to the present wishes of the great majority of people.* — V+A *(to/with)* ⇑ be = comply

conformist /kə⁷nfɔːmɪst/, **conformists.** A **conformist** is someone who behaves or thinks like everyone else rather than doing things that are original or difficult; often used showing disapproval. EG *You're a strict conformist.* ▸ used as an adjective. EG *The general tendency is to expect girls to be conformist and helpful... The school had grown more conformist.* — N COUNT ≠ rebel; ▸ ADJ QUALIT

conformity /kə⁷nfɔːmɪtiˡ/ is behaviour, thought, or appearance that is the same as that of most other people and that is decided by a desire to be the same as other people rather than to be original or different. EG *All that seems to be required of us is conformity... Psychiatry already plays its part in encouraging conformity.* ● To be **in conformity with** or **to** something means to do or be what is expected or required. EG *This arrangement had every chance of being in conformity with the needs of human nature.* — N UNCOUNT ⇑ complicity ≠ eccentricity, rebellion; ● PHR : USED AS AN A

confound /kə⁷nfaʊnd/, **confounds, confounding, confounded.** **1** If something **confounds** you, it causes you to be confused, surprised, and unsure how to deal with the situation. EG *Nice people always confound me... The children love speaking French to confound their friends.* — V+O ⇑ puzzle

2 Confound is also used as a mild swear word, especially in the expression **confound it**, to express annoyance or irritation. EG *'Confound it,' he said, 'I must've left the key behind.'* — V+O : USED AS EXCLAM = blast, damn

confounded /kə⁷nfaʊndɪ²d/ is used to express your annoyance or irritation with something or someone. EG *...those confounded breakfast cereal packets... She is a confounded nuisance.* — ADJ CLASSIF : ATTRIB = wretched, damned

confront /kə⁷nfrʌnt/, **confronts, confronting, confronted.** **1** If a problem, task, or difficulty **confronts** you, or you are **confronted** with it, it is something that you cannot avoid and must deal with. EG *Can you think of some typical problems that confront Germans learning English?... I was confronted with the task of designing and building the new system.* — V+O : IF + PREP THEN *with* = face

2 If you **confront** a difficult situation, you accept the fact that it exists and try to deal with it. EG *I don't understand your refusal to confront reality... We will soon have to confront a fundamental question.* — V+O = face

3 If you are **confronted** by something, especially — V+O : IF PASS something unpleasant or difficult, it is there in front of you and you cannot get away from it. EG *When I am confronted by a microphone, my mind goes completely blank... As I write this I am confronted with rows of shelves loaded with books I haven't read.* THEN + *with/by* = face

4 If you **confront** someone, you meet them face to face, especially in a situation in which you are going to fight, argue, or compete with them. EG *'Hello,' she said, confronting them... They were confronted by a line of guardsmen... The two men confronted each other... I had to confront the reporters.* V+O = approach

5 If you **confront** a person with something, you present facts or evidence to them in order to accuse them of something or to criticize them. EG *I decided to confront her with the charges of racism... He did not feel it proper to confront her with things that had happened fifty years ago.* V+O+A *(with)*

confrontation /kɒnfrənteɪʃən/, **confrontations**. A **confrontation** is **1** a serious dispute between two groups of people, often as a result of them having opposing ideas or policies. EG *...the readiness of government to face a confrontation with the unions... ...a time of confrontation.* N COUNT/UNCOUNT ⇑ disagreement **2** a fight, battle, or war. EG *Every now and then there is a confrontation at the gate between the pickets and police... A conventional conflict might escalate to a nuclear confrontation.* N COUNT/UNCOUNT **3** an attempt to accept the realities of a difficult or unpleasant situation and to deal with them. EG *He tended to avoid direct confrontation with unpleasant truths.*

confuse /kə'nfjuːz/, **confuses, confusing, confused**. **1** If you **confuse** two things, you mix them up by mistake. EG *You seem to confuse the words 'satire' and 'satyr' in your paper... You must be confusing me with someone else.* V+O : IF+PREP THEN *with* = muddle

2 To **confuse** someone means to make it difficult for them to think clearly or to know exactly what is intended or what they should do. EG *Introducing a new set of road signs would simply tend to confuse the public... You're trying to confuse me... It's not surprising, really, that he should have been so confused by his mother's ambitions for him.* V+O = bewilder, muddle

3 To **confuse** a situation or problem means to make it seem complicated or difficult to understand. EG *You're just trying to confuse the issue... To confuse matters further, her sister is married to her husband's uncle.* V+O ⇑ complicate ≠ clarify

confused /kə'nfjuːzd/. **1** Something that is **confused** does not have any order or pattern and is difficult to understand because of this. EG *...a confused dream about the end of the world... There was a confused sound of music and cheering... My thoughts were confused.* ADJ QUALIT = muddled ≠ clear, lucid

2 If you are **confused**, **2.1** you do not understand what is happening or what is being said, often because it seems to mean two different things. EG *She was bewildered and confused.* ◊ **confusedly**. ADJ QUALIT = bewildered, bemused **2.2** you do not know what you should say or do because you are embarrassed. EG *I was shy and confused with the friends of my parents... He looked away, confused and sweating.* ADJ QUALIT ⇑ tongue-tied

confusing /kə'nfjuːzɪŋ/. Something that is **confusing** makes it difficult for people to know exactly what is happening or what is meant, and might even make them think the opposite of what they should think. EG *The plot is fairly confusing... They blamed him for sending confusing signals to Syria.* ADJ QUALIT ⇑ unclear
◊ **confusingly**. ◊ ADV

confusion /kə'nfjuːʒən/, **confusions**. **Confusion** is **1** making a mistake about someone or something and thinking that they are someone or something else. EG *There is danger of confusion between them... In order to avoid confusion, the bottom is labelled too.* N UNCOUNT ⇑ mix-up **2** a situation where it is not clear what is happening or what is intended, often because people say or believe different things or because something is misunderstood. EG *There were five Lady Harmsworths, causing confusion in the accounts department of Harrods... There's a good deal of confusion about what this notion involves.* N UNCOUNT = misunderstanding **3** a situation in which everything is in disorder, especially because there are a lot of different things happening at the same time. EG *There was confusion for 10 or 15 minutes... In all the confusion, both men managed to grab me.* N UNCOUNT = chaos **4** a state of mind where you do not know what to believe or what you should do, often because there seem to be at least two very different possibilities. EG *Her answers to his questions have only added to his confusion.* N UNCOUNT ⇑ indecisiveness **5** a feeling of embarrassment which makes you not know what to say or do. EG *She saw to her confusion that he was going to kiss her.* N UNCOUNT

congeal /kə'ndʒiːl/, **congeals, congealing, congealed**. When a liquid **congeals**, it becomes very thick and sticky and almost solid. EG *The blood had already congealed in the cold.* V-ERG ⇑ thicken

congenial /kə'ndʒiːnjəl, -nɪəl/. **1** A place, job, etc that is **congenial** is pleasant and suits your character very well. EG *A pub would be more congenial than a boarding house... It is difficult to find congenial work.* ADJ QUALIT ⇑ agreeable

2 Someone who you find **congenial** has similar interests and attitudes to you and so it is enjoyable to spend time with them. EG *They found each other congenial... She moved to the French Riviera to be in more congenial company.* ADJ QUALIT ⇑ agreeable, pleasant

congenital /kə'ndʒenɪtəl/. **1** A **congenital** disease or medical condition is one that a person has had from birth, but not one that is inherited; a medical term. EG *The brain damage was congenital.* ADJ CLASSIF
◊ **congenitally**. EG *She is congenitally disabled.* ◊ ADV

2 Congenital is used of a characteristic or feature that is so strong in a person that you cannot imagine it ever changing, although there may be no apparent reason for it. EG *He had a congenital dislike of France... We are congenital wheat-eaters.* ADJ CLASSIF ⇑ lifelong
◊ **congenitally**. EG *I'm congenitally unfaithful to women.* ◊ ADV

congested /kə'ndʒestɪd/. A road, area, etc that is **congested** is so crowded with traffic or people that normal movement there is impossible. EG *...heavily congested roads.* ADJ QUALIT = blocked ≠ deserted

congestion /kə'ndʒestʃən/. **Congestion** is **1** the condition of being so crowded with traffic or people that normal movement in the area is impossible. EG *He deplored the extent of traffic congestion in urban areas.* N UNCOUNT ⇑ overcrowding **2** a medical condition in which a blood vessel or an organ of the body becomes blocked with liquid or some other substance. EG *There were no signs of congestion in the lungs... ...nasal congestion.* N UNCOUNT + SUPP ⇑ blockage

conglomerate /kə'nglɒmərət/, **conglomerates**; a formal word. A **conglomerate** is **1** a large business firm consisting of several different companies that have joined together, especially companies that deal in different types of product. EG *The company was bought in 1978 by the national conglomerate Chesebrough Ponds.* N COUNT ⇑ organization **2** something that consists of several different things, often of different types, that have been joined together, so that the whole thing has become too large or is too disorderly; a formal word. EG *It should be run as a united department and not as a conglomerate of its component parts.* N COUNT + SUPP : USU SING ⇑ mixture

conglomeration /kə'nglɒməreɪʃən/, **conglomerations**. A **conglomeration** is a group of many different things, especially things that you would not expect to find together or things that have been put together in a disorderly way. EG *The gathering was an unlikely conglomeration of Marxist theoreticians, philosophers and sociologists... ...a conglomeration of white buildings.* N COUNT + SUPP : USU SING ⇑ mixture, gathering

congrats /kəngræts/ is a very informal word for congratulations. CONVENTION

congratulate /kəngrætjəleɪt/, **congratulates, congratulating, congratulated**. **1** If you **congratulate** someone, **1.1** you say something to them which indicates that you are pleased that something special and nice has happened to them. EG *Friends and relatives came to congratulate the parents and to see the baby.* V+O : IF+PREP THEN *on* = wish well to
◊ **congratulation** /kə'ngrætjəleɪʃən/. EG *...a letter of congratulation.* ◊ N UNCOUNT
1.2 you praise them for something difficult, skilful, or admirable that they have done. EG *I congratulate you, it's a beautiful piece of work... He was warmly congratulated for appearing on the same platform as his opponent... I congratulate the bosses on their foresight.* V+O : IF+PREP THEN *on/for* = compliment
◊ **congratulation**. ◊ N UNCOUNT

2 If you **congratulate** yourself, you are proud of having done something or of possessing a particular quality, or you are pleased about something that has happened to you. EG *We have very little reason to congratulate ourselves... I congratulated myself on not looking my age.* V+O (REFL) : IF + PREP THEN *on/for* ⇑ be proud of

congratulations /kə'ngrætjəleɪʃənz/. **1** You say **congratulations** to someone in order to congratulate CONVENTION = well done them on something nice that has happened to them or something admirable they have done. EG *'Congratulations,' the doctor said. 'You have a son.'... Let me offer you my congratulations on your success... Congratulations to all three winners.*

2 If you offer someone your **congratulations**, you congratulate them on something nice that has happened to them or on something admirable that they have done. EG *I offered him my heartiest congratulations... She received their congratulations with pleasure... ...a telegram of congratulations.* — N PLURAL

congratulatory /kəⁿngrætjə⁴lətri¹/. Something that is **congratulatory** expresses congratulations. EG *New fiancées receive congratulatory cards from the company... He patted Breslow's arm in a congratulatory manner.* — ADJ CLASSIF

congregate /kɒŋgrɪ²geɪt/, **congregates, congregating, congregated**. If a number of people or animals **congregate**, they gather together and form a group. EG *The crowds congregated around the pavilion... This is a place where swans congregate.* — V: USU+A = assemble ≠ disperse

congregation /kɒŋgrɪ²geɪʃəⁿn/, **congregations**. A **congregation** consists of the people who are attending or who regularly attend a church service. EG *There were only ten in the congregation... The congregation continued to grow.* — N COUNT: IF SING, VB CAN BE SING OR PL ↑ group, assembled

congress /kɒŋgrɛs/, **congresses**. A **congress** is a large meeting, usually of representatives belonging to a national or international organization, that is held to discuss issues, ideas, and policies. EG *Union leaders will meet the week after Congress to consider their attitude... ...the second Congress of Negro Writers and Artists.* — N COUNT/UNCOUNT = conference

Congress /kɒŋgrɛs/ is 1 the elected group of politicians that is responsible for making the law in the USA. It consists of two parts: the House of Representatives and the Senate. EG *The involvement of big business has raised squawks of protest in Congress... That might affect the constitutional power of the Congress.* — N PROPER, ALSO *the*+N ↑ legislature
2 a major political party in India. — N PROPER

congressional /kəⁿŋ¹grɛʃəⁿnəl, -ʃənəⁿl/ means belonging or relating to the U.S. Congress. EG *...a leading congressional Republican... Mr Reagan won congressional approval for his tax cuts.* — ADJ CLASSIF: ATTRIB ↑ political

congressman /kɒŋgrɛsmə³n/, **congressmen**. A **congressman** is a male member of the U.S. Congress, especially of the House of Representatives. — N COUNT ↑ politician

congresswoman /kɒŋgresswu¹məⁿn/, **congresswomen**. A **congresswoman** is a female member of the U.S. Congress, especially of the House of Representatives. — N COUNT ↑ politician

congruence /kɒŋgruəns/ is the quality of similarity or correspondence between two things; a formal word. EG *There are areas of powerful congruence between socialists and ecologists.* — N UNCOUNT: IF+ PREP THEN *between*

congruent /kɒŋgruənt/. If two things are **congruent**, there is a similarity or correspondence between them; a formal word. EG *The sentence was scarcely congruent with his crime.* — ADJ CLASSIF: IF+ PREP THEN *with* ↑ similar

conical /kɒnɪkəⁿl/. Something that is **conical** is shaped like a cone. EG *...a small conical shell.* — ADJ CLASSIF

conifer /kəunɪfə, kɒn-/, **conifers**. A **conifer** is a tall tree that has needle-like leaves, produces brown cones, and grows in cooler areas of the world. — N COUNT

coniferous /kə⁷nɪfəⁿrəs/. A forest or woodland that is **coniferous** is made up of conifers. EG *...coniferous woodland...* ▸ used to describe a tree that is a conifer. EG *...Sequoia, the coniferous redwood.* — ADJ CLASSIF: USU ATTRIB; ▸ ADJ CLASSIF

> **CONJ COORD** □ In this dictionary CONJ COORD is used in the grammar notes beside entries to refer to a small group of coordinating conjunctions, **and, but, yet, or**, and **nor**, and some other expressions beginning with one of these words, such as **or else**. A coordinating conjunction behaves in the following ways: **1** It joins words, expressions, or clauses of the same grammatical type, for example **and** and **but** in *Jack **and** Jill... The weather will be mainly sunny **but** showers will develop in the late afternoon.* **2** It comes between the two structures that it joins. **3** The structures which are joined by a coordinating conjunction often share one or more parts, for example the same subject or the same verb. The shared part does not need to be repeated. Examples are **and** and **but**. EG *The real pressure is much more subtle, **and** comes from women themselves... He found O'Shea asleep **and** Bernadette looking bored... Close up they should look even bigger–**but** in fact they don't.* **4** Except for **but**, CONJ COORDS can link several clauses or groups. **But**, on the other hand, can link only two clauses or groups, which usually have contrasting meanings.

conjectural /kə⁷ndʒɛktʃəⁿrəl/. A statement or conclusion that is **conjectural** is based on incomplete or doubtful information. EG *These estimates are so conjectural as to be almost worthless.* — ADJ QUALIT = hypothetical, uncertain

conjecture /kə⁷ndʒɛktʃə/, **conjectures, conjecturing, conjectured**. **1 Conjecture** is the formation of ideas or opinions from incomplete or doubtful information. EG *The exact figure is a matter for conjecture... That's largely conjecture.* ▸ used to refer to an idea or opinion that has been formed in this way. EG *They filled their columns with personal conjectures.* — N UNCOUNT = speculation; ▸ N COUNT
2 When you **conjecture**, you form an opinion or suggest that something is the case on the basis of incomplete or doubtful information. EG *He could only conjecture... Her mysterious friends were, Tim conjectured, probably women.. We may conjecture that he was there at the time.* — V OR V+REPORT-CL = speculate, surmise

> **CONJ SUBORD** □ In this dictionary CONJ SUBORD is used in the grammar notes beside entries to mean 'subordinating conjunction'. A subordinating conjunction behaves in the following ways: **1** It joins a subordinate clause to a main clause. A subordinate clause is a clause which cannot normally be a complete sentence on its own. Examples are **though** and **unless**. EG *They have been married for twelve years, **though** you wouldn't think it... Nothing gets started **unless** somebody starts it.* **2** It is usually the first word of the subordinate clause, although an adverb like *even* or *especially* can sometimes go before it. Examples are **because** and **though**. EG *I like the Americans **because** they are healthy and optimistic... **Because** it is less rewarding, there are fewer advantages for the rest of the family... He liked the college, especially **because** he found the course material interesting... **Though** he hadn't stopped working all day, he wasn't tired... I used to love listening to her, even **though** I could only understand about half of what she was saying.*

conjugal /kɒndʒə⁴gəⁿl/ means relating to marriage and the relationship between a husband and wife, especially their sexual relationship; a formal word. EG *Her husband has very conventional ideas about conjugal relationships... ...conjugal rights... ...conjugal happiness.* — ADJ CLASSIF: ATTRIB marital

conjunction /kə⁷ndʒʌŋkⁿʃəⁿn/, **conjunctions**. **1** A **conjunction** is a combination of things, characteristics, or features. EG *The cause of suicide is a nasty conjunction of personal and social factors.* — N COUNT: IF+ PREP THEN *of*
2 If two or more things are done **in conjunction**, they are done together rather than separately. EG *These regulations should be read in conjunction with the ordinary PhD regulations... We can work either separately or in conjunction.* — PHR: USED AS AN A, USU+*with* = jointly, in association
3 In grammar, a **conjunction** is a word or a group of words that join together words, groups, or clauses. In English there are two types of conjunction, coordinating conjunctions (EG *and* and *but*) and subordinating conjunctions (*although* and *if*). Words which are coordinating conjunctions have CONJ COORD in the grammar note beside the entry. Words which are subordinating conjunctions have CONJ SUBORD. See □ at CONJ COORD, CONJ SUBORD. — N COUNT ↑ word class

conjunctivitis /kə⁷ndʒʌŋktɪvaɪtɪs/ is a painful eye disease which causes the thin skin that covers the eyeball to become inflamed. — N UNCOUNT ↑ infection

conjure /kʌndʒə/, **conjures, conjuring, conjured**. **1** When you **conjure** something or **conjure** it **up**, **1.1** you make it appear by magic, or by a trick that makes it seem that magic has been used. EG *The rabbit appeared from nowhere, conjured out of thin air... He claimed that he was able to conjure up evil spirits.* — V+O: USU+A *(up)*
1.2 you get it or find it in a surprisingly short period of time or with a surprising lack of difficulty. EG *He appeared with a small bucket he'd apparently conjured from nowhere... He expects me to conjure up skilled and experienced men at a moment's notice!* — V+O: USU+A *(up)* ↑ produce
2 When you say that a particular name is **a name to conjure with**, you mean that it is a very important and influential name in the particular field you are discussing. EG *McLuhan is a name to conjure with.* — PHR: USED AS C

conjure up. **1** If you **conjure** something **up**, you create a memory, a picture, or an impression in your mind. EG *To many people, the name Kalahari conjures up images of a desert of unrelenting aridity...* — PHRASAL VB: V+O+ADV

They listened in astonishment while James conjured up pictures of fantastic machines.

conjurer /kʌndʒəʳrə/, **conjurers; also spelled conjuror.** A **conjurer** is a person who entertains people by doing tricks in which things are made to appear and disappear as if by magic. N COUNT ⇑ magician

conjuring trick, conjuring tricks. A **conjuring trick** is a trick in which something is made to appear or disappear as if by magic. N COUNT

conk /kɒŋk/, **conks, conking, conked**; an informal word in British English. Your **conk** is your nose. N COUNT

conk out. If something, such as a machine or vehicle, **conks out**, it stops working or breaks down. EG *The washing machine has finally conked out.* PHRASAL VB : V+ADV

conker /kɒŋkə/, **conkers.** 1 A **conker** is a large, round brown nut-like seed which comes from the horse chestnut tree. N COUNT

2 **Conkers** is a children's game in which you tie your conker to a piece of string and try to break your opponent's conker by hitting it as hard as you can with your own. N UNCOUNT

con man, con men. A **con man** is a man who persuades people to give him their money or property by lying to them. EG *They are experienced con men.* N COUNT ⇑ criminal = trickster

connect /kəˀnɛkt/, **connects, connecting, connected.** 1 When you **connect** a pipe, wire, etc to something, you join the end of it to the end of the other thing. EG *Connect the hose pipe to the tap... We'll have to connect these wires to make the radio work.* V+O : IF+PREP THEN *to* ⇑ attach ≠ disconnect

2 When you **connect** a machine, telephone, or house or you **connect** it **up**, you join it to an electricity or gas supply, or to a water supply. EG *The house is not connected to the mains water supply.* V+O : IF+PREP THEN *to* ≠ disconnect

3 If a telephone operator **connects** you, they enable you to speak to another person by telephone. EG *I'm trying to connect you, sir.* V+O ≠ cut off

4 If something **connects** two things or places, it joins them together and makes it possible to go from one to the other. EG *The Eustachian tube connects the ear with the throat... We're putting in another flight to connect Brussels directly with Manchester.* V+O, OR V+O+A *(with/to)* : RECIP

◇ **connecting.** EG *The rooms had connecting doors between them.* ◇ ADJ CLASSIF : ATTRIB

5 If a train, plane, or bus **connects** with another form of transport, it arrives at a time which allows passengers to change to that form of transport in order to continue their journey. EG *This train connects with a bus service to Worcester.* V : IF+PREP THEN *with* = link up

6 If you **connect** a person or thing with something, you realize that there is a relationship or link between them and the other thing. EG *I did not connect her with the theatre... There is no evidence to connect Griffiths with the murder... Do you connect the two events?* V+O, OR V+O+A *(with/to)* : RECIP = associate

connected /kəˀnɛktɪᵈd/. 1 If one thing is **connected** with another, it is related or linked with it in some way. EG *Good health is connected with diet... I have been connected with the opening of a new school... There are serious questions connected with radioactive waste disposal.* ADJ CLASSIF : USU PRED+ *with* = associated

2 If you are **connected** with or **connected** to someone, you are related by birth or marriage to them. EG *She was distantly connected with the Wedgwood family.* • See also **well-connected.** ADJ CLASSIF : USU PRED+ *with/to*

connecting rod, connecting rods. A **connecting rod** is a rod that joins two parts of a machine together. EG *The piston is connected to a crank shaft by a connecting rod.* N COUNT

connection /kəˀnɛkʃəⁿn/, **connections;** also spelled **connexion.** 1 A **connection** is a relationship between two things, for example the fact that one thing causes another thing to happen, or something that two or more people or things have in common. EG *I think his illness must have had some connection with his diet... I do not think there is any logical connection between the two halves of the question.* N COUNT : IF+PREP THEN *between/to/with* ⇑ link = association

2 If you talk or write to someone **in connection with** something, that is the thing that you want to talk or write to them about. EG *The police wanted to interview him in connection with the murder... My question is in connection with our discussion yesterday.* PREP = about, concerning

3 You say **in this connection** or **in that connection** to indicate that what you are talking about is related to what you have just mentioned. EG *They wanted to see him in this connection.* PHR : USED AS ADV SEN

4 A **connection** is also 4.1 the joint where two wires, pipes, etc are joined together. EG *There must be a loose connection.* 4.2 something that is put between two things in order to link them. EG *There are rail connections between London and all the major cities.* N COUNT ⇑ link; N COUNT

5 A train, bus, or plane **connection** is one which leaves at a convenient time for people to catch it and continue a journey which they have already started. EG *I missed my connection.* N COUNT ⇑ transport

6 Your **connections** are 6.1 the people who you know in the business or social world, especially when they are in a position to help you. EG *He's one of her husband's business connections.* 6.2 the people who you are related to. EG *We've got lots of Dundee connections.* N COUNT : USU PL ⇑ associate; N COUNT : USU PL = relation

connivance /kəˀnaɪvəns/ is a willingness to allow something to happen which you know is wrong and which you ought to prevent or report to someone. Sometimes you even actually help it to happen; usually used showing disapproval. EG *He kept out of jail with the connivance of corrupt police and government officials.* N UNCOUNT : USU +SUPP ⇑ consent = collusion

connive /kənaɪv/, **connives, conniving, connived.** 1 If you **connive** at something, you allow it to happen even though you know that it is wrong and should try to prevent it. Sometimes you deliberately do things that will allow it to happen. EG *He was assisted by his mother who connived at his laziness.* V+A *(at)* ⇑ ignore = abet ≠ deter

2 If you **connive**, you secretly try to achieve something or to cause something to happen which is to your advantage; used showing disapproval. EG *He was ready to connive with the Tammany bosses... They connived together to do the deed.* ◇ **conniving.** EG *She's a conniving bastard.* V OR V+A *(with)* : RECIP = scheme, plot; ◇ ADJ QUALIT = scheming

connoisseur /kɒnɪsɜː/, **connoisseurs.** A **connoisseur** is a person who knows a lot about the arts, food, drink, or some other subject, and can therefore recognize and appreciate something of good quality. *All the connoisseurs end up drinking claret... The Count was a renowned connoisseur of everything from blondes to smoked salmon.* N COUNT : IF+PREP THEN *of* ⇑ expert

connotation /kɒnəˢteɪʃəⁿn/, **connotations.** The **connotation** of a particular word or name are the ideas, qualities, places, etc which it makes you think of. EG *'Intermediate' has connotations of the inferior and the second rate.* N COUNT+SUPP : USU PL = association, undertone

connote /kəˀnəʊt/, **connotes, connoting, connoted.** If a word or name **connotes** something, it makes you think of a particular idea, quality, place, etc; a formal word. EG *For me, the word 'Galway' connotes peace and solitude.* V+O = suggest, imply

connubial /kəˀnjuːbɪəl/ means relating to marriage; a formal word. EG *We were well into our second spring of connubial delights.* ADJ CLASSIF : ATTRIB = conjugal, marital

conquer /kɒŋkə/, **conquers, conquering, conquered.** 1 If one country or group of people **conquers** another country or group of people, they take complete control of them or their land by defeating them in war. EG *Britain was conquered by the Romans in A.D. 43.* V OR V+O = take over

2 If a person or group of people **conquers** a place, they succeed in winning the admiration of the people there. EG *The band has still to conquer America.* V+O = win over

3 If you **conquer** something difficult or dangerous, you succeed in getting control of it, usually through great effort and determination. EG *She tried to conquer her feelings of nervousness... There has been a tremendous international effort to conquer cancer.* V+O ⇑ overcome = master

conqueror /kɒŋkərə/, **conquerors.** A **conqueror** is a person who conquers a country or group of people. EG *...the European conquerors of Mexico.* N COUNT ⇑ winner

conquest /kɒŋˈwɛst/, **conquests.** 1 **Conquest** is the act of conquering a country or group of people. EG *Negotiations are preferable to conquest... ...families whose ancestors came to Britain at the time of the Norman Conquest.* N UNCOUNT ≠ defeat

2 A **conquest** is 2.1 land that has been conquered in war. 2.2 an act of winning the love, admiration, or approval of someone. EG *He loved telling stories of his conquests of bored housewives.* N COUNT; N COUNT : IF+PREP THEN *of* = success with

3 The **conquest** of something difficult or dangerous is success in getting control of it, usually through great effort and determination. EG *...the conquest of space.* N SING : *the*+N+*of* = mastery

conscience /kɒnʃəns/, **consciences.** 1 Your **conscience** is the part of your mind that tells you N COUNT : USU WITH POSS whether what you are doing is right or wrong. EG *My conscience told me to vote against the others... Their consciences were troubled by stories of famine and war... ...disclosures which have shocked the moral conscience of the nation.*

2 If you get or have **a bad** or **guilty conscience**, you feel guilty because you know that you have done something that is wrong. EG *Not many children get a guilty conscience about not doing enough homework... When I got your letter it revived my guilty conscience.* PHR : USED AS O = guilt

3 If you have something **on** your **conscience**, you feel guilty about it because you know that what you have done is wrong. EG *I can't accept it, I'd have all those poor people on my conscience... ...a matter which has been on my conscience for a long time.* PHR : USED AS AN A ↑ worry

4 If you cannot **in all conscience** or **in good conscience** do something, you cannot do it because you believe that it is wrong. EG *In all conscience, I couldn't make things even more difficult for her... He realized that he could not in good conscience take office in the present Government.* PHR : USED AS ADV SEN = justifiably

5 **Conscience** is 5.1 doing what you believe is right even though it might be unpopular, difficult, or dangerous. EG *They take a position of conscience, and say that this is a bad law... ...a vote of conscience.* N UNCOUNT ↑ behaviour 5.2 a feeling of guilt because you know you have done something that is wrong. EG *They had no problems of conscience, no feelings of guilt... One event during the campaign gave me a slight twinge of conscience.* N UNCOUNT ≠ relief

conscience-stricken. Someone who is **conscience-stricken** feels very guilty about something wrong that they have done. EG *She looked conscience-stricken.* ADJ QUALIT

conscientious /kɒnʃɪenʃəs/. Someone who is **conscientious** is very careful to do their work properly; used showing approval. EG *He was a very conscientious minister.* ADJ QUALIT = painstaking, thorough ◊ **conscientiously**. EG *He'd been doing his job conscientiously for many years.* ◊ ADV WITH VB ◊ **conscientiousness**. EG *With her usual conscientiousness, she set about her latest task.* ◊ N UNCOUNT

conscientious objector, conscientious objectors. A **conscientious objector** is a person who refuses to join the armed forces because they think that it is morally wrong to do so. N COUNT ↑ pacifist

conscious /kɒnʃəs/. 1 If you are **conscious** of something, 1.1 you notice or realize what is happening. EG *She became conscious of Rudolph looking at her... I was conscious that he had changed his tactics.* ADJ QUALIT : PRED+*of*/REPORT-CL ◊ **consciousness**. EG *People have to wake up to the consciousness that they have a responsibility to others.* ◊ N UNCOUNT 1.2 you think about it more than other people do, because of the unusual or special way in which it affects you. EG *He is conscious of his limited achievements... Tony was very conscious of his ancestry.* ADJ QUALIT : PRED+*of*/REPORT-CL = sensitive ≠ ignorant

2 **Conscious** is used in expressions such as 'socially conscious' and 'politically conscious' to describe someone who believes that a particular aspect of life is important, especially when other people do not seem to notice it or be interested in it. EG *Hundreds of women had become politically conscious.* ADJ QUALIT : ADV + ADJ = alert, aware ≠ ignorant

3 Something that you do that is **conscious** is done deliberately and with you giving your full attention to it. EG *He made a conscious effort to look as though he was enjoying himself... There is still prejudice, even if it is not always conscious.* ADJ CLASSIF ↑ deliberate ≠ spontaneous ◊ **consciously**. EG *She couldn't believe that Mr Foster would ever consciously torment her.* ◊ ADV

4 Someone who is **conscious** is awake rather than asleep or unconscious. EG *The patient was fully conscious during the operation... Allen was now quite conscious, so I got him to his feet.* ADJ CLASSIF ↑ aware ≠ unconscious

5 **Conscious** is also used to describe thoughts, memories, etc that come into your mind and that you are aware of, in contrast to those that you are not aware of. EG *I can only tell you the things that are in my conscious memory.* ADJ CLASSIF ≠ subconscious

6 Your **conscious** is the part of your mind that you think with while you are awake. EG *...Freud's view of the conscious and unconscious.* N SING : *the*/POSS +N

-conscious combines with words such as 'safety', 'energy', or 'status' to indicate that a person thinks that a particular aspect of a situation is important, especially in the way it affects them. EG *We live in an energy-conscious world... The less important an executive is, the more status-conscious he is likely to be.* COMB : FORMS ADJS ↑ aware = oriented

consciousness /kɒnʃəsnɪ²s/, **consciousnesses**. 1 Your **consciousness** is your mind and your thoughts. EG *Doubts were starting to enter into my consciousness.* N COUNT : USU POSS+N IN SING = awareness

2 The **consciousness** of a group of people consists of all the ideas, attitudes, and beliefs shared by the group. EG *This is a novel that has become imprinted on the English consciousness.* N UNCOUNT + SUPP = mentality

3 **Consciousness** is an interest in and knowledge of a particular subject or idea. EG *...the awakening political consciousness of Africans.* N UNCOUNT = awareness

4 If you lose **consciousness**, you are unconscious rather than awake. If you have regained **consciousness**, you are awake again rather than unconscious. N UNCOUNT

conscript, conscripts, conscripting, conscripted. The word **conscript** is pronounced /kə⁷nskrɪpt/ when it is a verb and /kɒnskrɪpt/ when it is a noun. 1 If someone **is conscripted**, 1.1 they are officially made to join the armed forces of a particular country. EG *Nine countries decided to let women be conscripted on the same terms as men.* V+O : USU PASS ↑ enrol = draft ≠ enlist, volunteer ◊ **conscripted**. EG *...the conscripted element in the army.* ◊ ADJ CLASSIF 1.2 they are officially forced to work for a particular country or group of people. EG *Workers were conscripted into forced labour gangs to build the railways.* V+O : USU PASS ↑ force = draft ≠ volunteer ◊ **conscripted**. EG *...conscripted labourers from Indo-China.* ◊ ADJ CLASSIF

2 A **conscript** is a person who has been made to join the armed forces of a country. EG *There are 120,000 conscripts in an army of 218,000... ...a conscript army.* N COUNT

conscription /kə⁷nskrɪpʃə⁰n/ is officially making people in a particular country join the army, navy, or air force. EG *It is proposed that conscription be limited to a maximum of six months.* N UNCOUNT ≠ enlistment

consecrate /kɒnsɪ²kreɪt/, **consecrates, consecrating, consecrated**. 1 When a building, place, or object is **consecrated**, it is officially declared to be holy and able to be used for religious ceremonies and services. EG *King Edward consecrated the original church here in 1065.* V+O ↑ sanctify ◊ **consecrated**. EG *He was refused burial in consecrated ground.* ◊ ADJ CLASSIF = hallowed ◊ **consecration** /kɒnsɪ²kreɪʃə⁰n/. EG *...the consecration service.* ◊ N UNCOUNT ↑ sanctifying

2 When someone **consecrates** a religious minister, they officially declare in a religious ceremony that this person is now a bishop, priest, etc. EG *China's Catholic Church consecrated five new bishops last Friday.* V+O = ordain ◊ **consecration**. EG *...the first consecration involving more than one bishop.* ◊ N UNCOUNT = ordination

3 If the day on which something such as an event happened is **consecrated**, it is officially said to be special or important so that people will remember and think about the event for many years to come. EG *...a day that was consecrated to the memory of these brave young men.* V+O : IF+PREP THEN *to* ↑ set apart = dedicate

consecutive /kə⁷nsekjə⁴tɪv/. Periods of time or events that are **consecutive** happen one after the other and are not interrupted by a gap or by something different. EG *It was his seventeenth consecutive month in the country... ...three consecutive victories.* ADJ CLASSIF = successive ◊ **consecutively**. EG *For three years consecutively, workers had accepted these lower wages.* ◊ ADV = successively

consensus /kə⁷nsensəs/ is general agreement amongst a group of people about a subject or about how something should be done. EG *There was some consensus of opinion... I don't know if there is a medical consensus about jogging.* N UNCOUNT ≠ divergence

consent /kə⁷nsent/, **consents, consenting, consented**. 1 **Consent** is 1.1 permission given to someone to do something by a person who has authority over them. EG *She had threatened to marry without her parents' consent... It is a splendid idea, Dorothy. I give my consent.* N UNCOUNT : USU WITH POSS = approval 1.2 agreement about something between two or more people or groups. EG *By common consent they stopped... There was a basis for consent between the two parties.* N UNCOUNT ● See also **age of consent**.

2 If you **consent** to something, you agree to do it or to allow it to be done. EG *Would you consent to work for us?... He consented to the removal of the flags.* V : USU+*to*/*to*-INF

consenting /kə⁷nsentɪŋ/. A **consenting** adult is a person who is considered to be responsible or old enough to make their own decisions about what they do, especially about who they have sex with. ADJ CLASSIF : ATTRIB

consequence /kɒnsɪkwəns/, **consequences.** 1 A **consequence** of a situation or event is a result or effect of it. EG *...the dilemma that parents find themselves in today as a consequence of changes in society... ...the economic consequences of the computer revolution... I decided I would kill Liebermann regardless of the consequences.*
N COUNT ≠ cause

2 If something happens **in consequence** of something else, it happens as a result of it. EG *The fastest these animals can run is about 65 kph and in consequence their hunting methods have to be very efficient indeed.*
PHR : USED AS AN A, IF+PREP THEN *of* ⇑ therefore = hence, so

3 If you tell someone that they must **take the consequences** or **suffer the consequences**, you warn them that something unpleasant will happen to them if they do not stop behaving in a particular way. EG *'You apologize for what you did,' Tom said, 'or you take the consequences.'... Editors were warned to express the Government's point of view or suffer the consequences.*
PHR : VB INFLECTS

4 Someone or something that is of **consequence** is important or valuable. EG *...a very ordinary woman of little consequence... These are developments of such consequence that they deserve further investigation.*
N UNCOUNT : *of*+N ⇑ value = significance

consequent /kɒnsɪkwənt/ means happening as a direct result of a particular event or situation; a fairly formal word. EG *...the non-publication of the report and the consequent absence of public discussion.* ◇ **consequently.** EG *Absolute secrecy is essential. Consequently, the fewer who are aware of the plan the better.*
ADJ CLASSIF : ATTRIB ⇑ resulting = subsequent
◇ ADV SEN ⇑ therefore = so

consequential /kɒnsɪkwenʃə[0]l/. 1 Something that is **consequential** is important or significant; a formal word. EG *The school one attended became increasingly consequential for success in getting into university.*
ADJ QUALIT

2 **Consequential** means happening as a direct result of a particular event or situation; a fairly formal word. EG *...overcrowding and the consequential lack of privacy... ...the nature of their psychological situation, and the consequential nature of their marriage.*
ADJ CLASSIF : ATTRIB = consequent

conservation /kɒnsəveɪʃə[0]n/. 1 **Conservation** is 1.1 the preservation and protection of the environment and the natural things in it. EG *...the present public awareness of the need for conservation... ...a conservation area.*
N UNCOUNT ≠ pollution
1.2 the preservation and protection of historical objects or works of art such as paintings, sculptures, or buildings. EG *These pieces have responded well to cleaning and conservation by the museum.*
N UNCOUNT ⇑ preservation

2 The word **conservation** is used in the names of several principles of physics which say that, in any single system, the total quantity of the particular thing referred to can never vary; a technical term. EG *...the conservation of mass.*
N UNCOUNT+SUPP

3 • See also **conserve.**

conservationist /kɒnsəveɪʃənɪst/, **conservationists.** A **conservationist** is someone who cares greatly about the conservation of the environment and who works and campaigns actively to try to protect it. EG *Conservationists have won the battle to establish the area as a nature reserve.*
N COUNT = environmentalist

conservatism /kə[7]nsɜːvətɪzə[0]m/. In sense 1 **Conservatism** is always spelled with a capital letter. **Conservatism** is 1 the political philosophy of the Conservative Party in a country.
N UNCOUNT
2 political ideas and attitudes that are traditionally associated with the Conservative Party in a country, especially a cautious attitude towards change. EG *...the conservatism of President Reagan.*
N UNCOUNT = traditionalism
3 a general unwillingness to accept changes and new ideas. EG *He has been much criticized for his aesthetic conservatism... ...the conservatism of older teachers.*
N UNCOUNT = orthodoxy

conservative /kə[7]nsɜːvətɪv/, **conservatives.** In paragraphs 1 and 2 **Conservative** is usually spelled with a capital letter. 1 Someone who is **Conservative** is a member of the Conservative Party in a country or has political ideas and attitudes that are traditionally associated with the Conservative Party, in particular a belief in free enterprise and capitalism. EG *...a Conservative Member of Parliament... The industry had been denationalized by the Conservative government.* ▸ also used of policies, beliefs, etc. EG *...Conservative policies... We've always voted Conservative.*
ADJ CLASSIF = Tory

2 A **Conservative** is a person who supports or belongs to the Conservative Party in a country. EG *It was one of the things which helped the Conservatives win the last election.*
N COUNT = Tory

3 Someone who is **conservative** is 3.1 unwilling to accept changes and new ideas. EG *Publishers in Britain are more conservative, perhaps, than their continental counterparts.* ▸ used of a person's beliefs or behaviour. EG *...a conservative attitude to life.* ◇ **conservatively.** EG *...conservatively minded people.*
ADJ QUALIT = hidebound ≠ revolutionary ▸ = traditional
◇ ADV
3.2 is conventional in style and appearance rather than wearing unusual or daringly fashionable clothes. EG *He was very conservative with the colours he chose to wear.* ◇ **conservatively.** EG *...a man in his fifties who dressed conservatively.*
ADJ QUALIT ⇑ quiet ≠ daring
◇ ADV = conventionally

4 A **conservative** is someone who is not very willing to accept changes, either in ideas or fashions. EG *I know he won't like it–he's very conservative, you know.*
N COUNT

5 A **conservative** estimate or guess is one in which you are cautious and guess a low amount which is probably less than the real amount. EG *How long will it last? Three hundred years at a fairly conservative estimate.*
ADJ QUALIT = safe

Conservative Party. The **Conservative Party** is the political party, especially in Britain and Australia, which believes particularly in the importance of a capitalist economy with private ownership rather than state control.
N PROPER : *the*+N

conservatory /kə[7]nsɜːvətri[1]/, **conservatories.** A **conservatory** is 1 a room with glass walls and a glass roof that is usually attached to a house. Plants are often grown in a conservatory.
N COUNT ⇑ glasshouse
2 an institution where musicians are trained.
N COUNT : ALSO IN NAMES AFTER N

conserve /kə[7]nsɜːv/, **conserves, conserving, conserved.** 1 If you **conserve** a supply of something, you are very careful in the way that you use it so that it lasts as long as possible. EG *We turned the bicycle lights off to conserve the batteries... They made themselves wait quietly, conserving their strength.* ◇ **conservation** /kə[7]nsɜːveɪʃə[0]n/. EG *...energy conservation.*
V+O ⇑ save ≠ waste
◇ N UNCOUNT ⇑ saving

2 If someone or something **conserves** something, they keep it in its original form and protect it from harm, loss, or change. EG *Such laws exist only to conserve the privilege of this selfish minority.* ◇ **conservation.** EG *...the conservation of tradition.*
V+O = preserve
◇ N UNCOUNT

2 **Conserve** is jam containing a large proportion of fruit, usually in whole pieces. EG *...strawberry conserve.*
N MASS

consider /kə[7]nsɪdə/, **considers, considering, considered.** 1 If you **consider** a person or thing to be something, you have the opinion that this is what they are. EG *Some British generals considered the attack a mistake... They consider themselves to be very lucky... They do not consider a child as important... I considered it wiser not to criticize the report... I consider that one is enough... Charles Babbage is generally considered to have invented the first computer.*
V+O (NG/REFL) +C/*to*-INF/A (*as*), OR V+REPORT-CL ⇑ believe = think, deem

2 If you **consider** something, you think about it carefully. EG *He had no time to consider the matter.*
V OR V+O = study

3 If you are **considering** an offer, suggestion, or possibility, you are interested in it and are thinking about accepting it or carrying it out. EG *I had already begun to consider the possibility of joining a new company... You might consider moving to a smaller house.*
V+O, OR V+-ING = contemplate

4 When you say that someone should **consider** a particular fact or detail, you mean that they should think about it because it is important or relevant to a decision, plan, etc. EG *Other points to consider are size and weight.*
V+O/REPORT-CL ⇑ remember = bear in mind

5 You use **all things considered** to introduce or comment on a judgement that you make after taking all the facts into account. EG *Not a bad night, John thought, all things considered... He's okay, all things considered.*
PHR : USED AS ADV SEN = all in all

6 If you **consider** a person's needs, wishes, or feelings, you pay attention to them, especially because it is your duty. EG *You have to consider other people... I've got a family to consider.*
V+O ⇑ care about

7 If a group of people **considers** something such as a report or a case, they discuss it in order to come to a conclusion or decision about it. EG *They are having a meeting to consider the report... The case has been considered by the committee.*
V+O = debate

8 If someone **considers** something, they examine it
V+O

by looking at it carefully. EG *He considered its construction with the eye of an expert.*

9 See also **consideration, considered, considering**.

considerable /kə7nsɪdə0rəbə0l/. Something that is **considerable** is large in amount or degree. EG *The building suffered considerable damage as a result of the fire.* ◊ **considerably**. EG *His work had improved considerably... Large windows make the car feel considerably bigger.*
ADJ QUALIT = substantial, extensive
◊ ADV = significantly

considerate /kə7nsɪdə0rɪt/. Someone who is **considerate** pays attention to the needs, wishes, or feelings of another person and is kind to them. EG *My own friends were considerate enough to leave us alone... It was very considerate of you to remember her birthday.* ◊ **considerately**. EG *She considerately left the door open for me.*
ADJ QUALIT = thoughtful
◊ ADV = thoughtfully

consideration /kə7nsɪdəreɪʃə0n/, **considerations**. 1 **Consideration** of something is thinking carefully about it, and often discussing or examining it. EG *After careful consideration, her parents gave her permission... The whole thing needs to be given further consideration... Time limited us to the consideration of just two groups.*
N UNCOUNT ⇑ thought = deliberation

2 A **consideration** is something that should be thought about, especially when you are planning or deciding something. EG *An important consideration is the amount of time it will take.*
N COUNT ⇑ factor

3 **Consideration** is also attention that you pay to the needs, wishes, or feelings of another person. EG *Is it too much to expect reasonable politeness and consideration?... He showed no consideration for his daughters.*
N UNCOUNT = thoughtfulness

4 If you **take** something **into consideration**, you think about it because it is important or relevant to something that you are doing. EG *The first thing one has to take into consideration is the cost.*
PHR : VB INFLECTS ⇑ remember = consider

5 Something that is **under consideration** is being discussed. EG *The case was still under consideration.*
PHR : USED AS AN A

6 Something that is of **no consideration**, of **little consideration**, etc is not at all important. EG *Cost was no consideration.*
PHR : USED AS AN A = immaterial

considered /kə7nsɪdəd/. 1 A **considered** opinion or way of behaving is one that you have as a result of careful thought. EG *It's not something I have a considered opinion about... For once we found her behaving in a rational and considered manner.*
ADJ CLASSIF : ATTRIB = deliberate

2 Someone or something that is highly **considered** is greatly approved of and respected. EG *Her work is highly considered in some circles.*
ADJ QUALIT : ADV + ADJ = regarded

considering /kə7nsɪdə0rɪŋ/. **Considering** is used 1 before a statement of a fact to say that you are taking this fact into account in making another statement. EG *Considering that he received no help, his results are very good... Considering her dislike of Martin, it was surprising that she invited him.* 2 after a statement about a situation to suggest that it is surprisingly good since there have been difficult circumstances; an informal use. EG *She's quite well considering.*
CONJ SUBORD, OR PREP ⇑ remembering
ADV SEN : AT END OF SENTENCE

consign /kə7nsaɪn/, **consigns, consigning, consigned**; a formal word. 1 If you **consign** something you do not want to a particular place, you get rid of it by putting it where you cannot see it or where it will be destroyed. EG *I discovered some wheels that had been consigned to the loft as useless lumber.*
V+O+A (to) ⇑ put = relegate, banish

2 If something or someone is **consigned** to a particular situation or position, they are out in that situation or position. EG *Such a policy would consign the poor to indefinite poverty... Belinda had been consigned to Lizzie's care... Duty was a conception which she had consigned to the past.*
V+O+A (to) ⇑ put = commit

3 To **consign** goods to a person who is buying them means to send them to that person.
V+O : IF+PREP THEN to

consignment /kə7nsaɪnmə2nt/, **consignments**. A **consignment** of goods is a load that is being delivered to the person who is buying them. EG *The shop announced the arrival of a new consignment of dress materials.*
N COUNT : IF+ PREP THEN of = batch

consist /kə7nsɪst/, **consists, consisting, consisted**. 1 Something that **consists** of particular things or people is made up of or is formed from them. EG *The committee consists of scientists and engineers... Each convoy consisted of twelve ships... The remainder of the island consists largely of swamps.*
V+A (of) ⇑ be = comprise

2 Something that **consists** in something else has it as its main part or its only part. EG *Nineteenth-century trade consisted principally in luxuries such as silk, spices and ivory... A game of tennis is competitive and consists in beating your opponent.*
V+A (in)

consistency /kə7nsɪstənsi1/, **consistencies**. 1 **Consistency** is the condition of being consistent. EG *...consistency and continuity in government policy... They show a lack of consistency.*
N UNCOUNT ⇑ coherence

2 The **consistency** of a substance is its degree of thickness, smoothness, etc. EG *...a porridge-like consistency... The paint was thinned down in consistency before it was used...* ▸ used as a count noun. EG *...yoghurts of varying consistencies.*
N UNCOUNT ⇑ texture
▸ N COUNT ⇑ texture

consistent /kə7nsɪstənt/. 1 Someone who is **consistent** behaves in the same way all the time and never changes their behaviour or attitudes towards people or things. EG *Brook was Baldwin's most dangerous and consistent adversary... ...the consistent, unswerving loyalty and support of his colleagues.* ◊ **consistently**. EG *He consistently got marks of over 90%... Hearst consistently opposed Roosevelt's policies.*
ADJ QUALIT ⇑ continual = steadfast, constant
◊ ADV = constantly

2 Something such as an idea or an argument that is **consistent** is organized or presented so that each part of it agrees with all the other parts. EG *...a set of ideas that is consistent... ...the fastest rate of growth consistent with economic stability.*
ADJ QUALIT : IF+ PREP THEN with ⇑ harmonious = coherent ≠ contradictory

consolation prize, consolation prizes. A **consolation prize** is 1 a small prize which is given to a person who fails to win a competition. 2 something that happens or is given to a person to cheer them up when they have failed to achieve something better; often used in a humorous way. EG *...Dr Beeching (later, as a consolation prize, to become Lord Beeching).*
N COUNT
N COUNT ⇑ comforter

console, consoles, consoling, consoled. The word **console** is pronounced /kə7nsəʊl/ when it is a verb and /kɒnsəʊl/ when it is a noun. 1 If you **console** someone who is unhappy about something, you try to make them feel more cheerful and hopeful. EG *She tried to console me by saying that I'd probably be happier in a new job... She consoled herself with the thought that he was near.* ◊ **consoling**. EG *It is a consoling thought, in the circumstances, to know that somebody cares.* ◊ **consolation** /kɒnsəleɪʃə0n/. EG *A few words of consolation might have helped... My only consolation is that nobody knows yet.*
V+O (NG/REFL) : IF+PREP THEN by/with ⇑ encourage = comfort
◊ ADJ QUALIT = cheering
◊ N UNCOUNT/ COUNT = comfort

2 A **console** is 2.1 a panel with a number of switches or knobs that you use to operate a machine. EG *He moved to the control console and pushed a handle forward.* 2.2 a special cupboard in which a television, hi-fi system, or computer is fitted.
N COUNT = panel
N COUNT = cabinet

consolidate /kə7nsɒlɪdeɪt/, **consolidates, consolidating, consolidated**. 1 If you **consolidate** something that you have, for example power or a plan, you strengthen it so that it becomes more effective or secure; a formal use. EG *The new middle class consolidated its wealth and power... The party consolidated itself in a remote rural area.* ◊ **consolidation** /kə7nsɒlɪdeɪʃə0n/. EG *...the long-term consolidation of party power.*
V OR V+O (NG/ REFL) ⇑ establish = reinforce
◊ N UNCOUNT

2 If someone or something **consolidates** several small groups or firms, they are made into a larger organization. EG *British rule consolidated the states of the north into a unified Northern Region.* ◊ **consolidated**. EG *...Consolidated Gold Fields Ltd.* ◊ **consolidation**. EG *This is just the start of a dangerous trend toward consolidation that could destroy small businesses.*
V-ERG : ALSO V OR V+A (with) : RECIP = incorporate, combine
◊ ADJ CLASSIF
◊ N UNCOUNT = amalgamation

consommé /kɒnsɒmeɪ/, **consommés**. **Consommé** is a thin, clear soup, usually made from meat juices.
N MASS

consonant /kɒnsənənt/, **consonants**. 1 A **consonant** is a sound which you pronounce by stopping the air flowing freely through your mouth. Most words are pronounced with a combination of consonants and vowels: compare **vowel**. EG *He spoke precisely, sharply enunciating each vowel and consonant.*
N COUNT

2 Something that is **consonant** with something else fits or agrees with it; a formal use. EG *He tried as far as was consonant with his duties.*
ADJ QUALIT : PRED+with = in accordance

consort, consorts, consorting, consorted. The word **consort** is pronounced /kə7nsɔːt/ when it is a verb and /kɒnsɔːt/ when it is a noun. 1 If someone **consorts** with a particular person or group, they spend a lot of time with them; often used showing
V+A (with/ together) = associate, fraternize

disapproval. EG *Daddy would never approve of her consorting with drug addicts... They were not prepared to consort with the enemy.*

2 A **consort** is the wife or husband of the ruling monarch. EG *...dedicated by Queen Victoria to her beloved consort.* N COUNT

consortium /kə⁷nsɔːtɪəm/, **consortia, consortiums**. The plural can be either **consortiums** or **consortia**. A **consortium** is a group of people or firms involved in a similar kind of trade or business who have agreed to work in cooperation with each other. EG *...a newly formed consortium of Rummidge businessmen... The minister considered that competition between the UK consortia was wasteful.* N COUNT : IF SING, VB CAN BE SING OR PL ⇑ association

conspicuous /kə⁷nspɪkjuəs/. 1 Someone or something that is **conspicuous** is 1.1 more noticeable and more likely to be looked at than the other people or things around, usually because of their size, colour, or position. EG *Her freckles were more conspicuous than usual... She felt conspicuous.* ◊ **conspicuously**. EG *His chin was conspicuously covered in thick bristle.* 1.2 remarkable in some way, and therefore easily noticed by people. EG *The film was a conspicuous failure... He was awarded the Military Cross for conspicuous gallantry in combat.* ◊ **conspicuously**. EG *He had been conspicuously successful.* ADJ QUALIT ⇑ visible ≠ hidden; ◊ ADV ⇑ visibly; ADJ QUALIT ⇑ obvious = noticeable; ◊ ADV

2 If you say that someone or something **is conspicuous by** their **absence**, you are drawing attention to the fact that they are not in a particular place or situation where you think they should be. EG *Women are conspicuous by their absence in politics.* PHR : VB INFLECTS ⇑ absent

conspiracy /kə⁷nspɪrəsi¹/, **conspiracies**. 1 **Conspiracy** is the planning by a small group of people in secret to do something illegal, usually for political reasons. EG *Later police arrested her on a charge of conspiracy to murder... Very few people knew the details of the conspiracy.* N UNCOUNT/COUNT ⇑ plan = plot

2 A **conspiracy** is an agreement by one group of people which other people think is wrong or likely to be harmful. EG *This is all part of a conspiracy to make me look ridiculous... There is a world conspiracy of men against women.* ● A **conspiracy of silence** is an agreement by people not to talk publicly about something. EG *Is there a conspiracy of silence about the Royal wedding dress?* N COUNT ⇑ plot; ● PHR

conspirator /kə⁷nspɪrətə/, **conspirators**. A **conspirator** is a person who joins a conspiracy. EG *The coup was planned by a handful of conspirators.* N COUNT ⇑ criminal = plotter

conspiratorial /kə⁷nspɪrətɔːrɪəl/. 1 If you are being **conspiratorial**, you are behaving as if you are sharing a secret with someone. EG *What are you two being so conspiratorial about?... He spoke in a conspiratorial whisper.* ◊ **conspiratorially**. EG *They smiled at each other conspiratorially.* ADJ QUALIT ⇑ secretive ≠ open; ◊ ADV WITH VB ⇑ secretively

2 Something that is **conspiratorial** is secret and illegal, often with a political purpose. EG *...a conspiratorial group... ...conspiratorial revolution.* ADJ CLASSIF

conspire /kə⁷nspaɪə/, **conspires, conspiring, conspired**. 1 If you **conspire**, you join a group of people and make a secret agreement to do something illegal or harmful to people, often for political reasons. EG *Anarchists were conspiring to kill one by one the rulers of Europe... My enemies are conspiring against me... I disliked the feeling of conspiring with her father behind Hilary's back.* V OR V+A (*with*) : RECIP, USU+*to*-INF/*against* ⇑ plan = plot

2 If events **conspire** to lead to a particular result, everything that happens seems to work together to lead to this result. EG *Everything had conspired to make him happy... Three factors conspired against us.* V ⇑ happen = combine

constable /kʌnstəbə⁰l/, **constables**. A **constable** is the lowest rank of policeman in Britain and some other countries. ● See also **chief constable** and **police constable**. N COUNT : ALSO IN TITLES

constabulary /kənstæbjə⁴ləri¹/, **constabularies**. A **constabulary** is the police force of a particular place or area in Britain. EG *...the Wiltshire Constabulary.* N COUNT : ALSO IN NAMES AFTER N

constancy /kɒnstənsi¹/ is 1 the quality of staying the same even though other things change; used showing approval. EG *...the constancy of family life... He had a constancy of will that impressed me.* 2 faithfulness and loyalty to a particular person or belief even when you are in difficulty or danger; used showing approval. EG *I might have known not to expect constancy from someone like you.* N UNCOUNT : IF+PREP THEN *of* ⇑ permanence ≠ change; N UNCOUNT ≠ fickleness

constant /kɒnstənt/, **constants**. 1 Something that is **constant** happens all the time or is always there. EG *He was in constant pain... He is my constant companion... We should make constant use of the van.* ◊ **constantly**. EG *The world around us is constantly changing... I was bullied constantly.* ADJ CLASSIF : USU ATTRIB ⇑ continuous; ◊ ADV = continually

2 An amount or level that is **constant** stays the same over a particular period of time. EG *...a constant voltage... The blood pressure must remain constant at all times.* ADJ QUALIT ⇑ fixed

3 If you are **constant**, you are always faithful to a particular person or organization, or always believe in a particular thing. ADJ CLASSIF ⇑ true ≠ fickle

4 A **constant** is 4.1 a quantity or value that stays the same all the time, for example the speed of light. 4.2 a letter which is used to represent a number or amount that remains the same in a particular series of calculations or equations. 4.3 a thing or quality that stays the same even though other things in a particular situation or process change. EG *The family has been one of the constants in human existence.* N COUNT; N COUNT ⇑ symbol ≠ variable; N COUNT ≠ variable

constellation /kɒnstɪ²leɪʃə⁰n/, **constellations**. A **constellation** is 1 a group of stars in the sky which seem to form a pattern and which have a name. 2 a group of similar things or qualities; used in formal English. EG *I was reluctant to do this, for a whole constellation of reasons.* N COUNT; N COUNT+SUPP : USU+*of* ⇑ collection = multitude

consternation /kɒnstəneɪʃə⁰n/ is a feeling of astonishment and worry. EG *We looked at each other in consternation... To my utter consternation, he burst into tears.* N UNCOUNT = dismay

constipated /kɒnstɪpeɪtɪ²d/. Someone who is **constipated** is unable to defecate. EG *Sometimes babies who are getting hungry will become constipated.* ADJ QUALIT : USU PRED

constipation /kɒnstɪpeɪʃə⁰n/ is a medical condition which makes people unable to defecate. N UNCOUNT

constituency /kə⁷nstɪtjuənsi¹/, **constituencies**. A **constituency** is a town or area which is officially allowed to elect someone to represent them in parliament. EG *There were about 14,000 voters in the constituency.* ▸ used of the people who vote in a constituency. EG *On 5 May he told his constituency that he would resign.* N COUNT; ▸ N COUNT : IF SING, VB CAN BE SING OR PL ⇑ electorate

constituent /kə⁷nstɪtjuənt/, **constituents**. 1 A **constituent** is 1.1 someone who lives in a particular constituency, especially someone who is able to vote in an election. EG *An MP is the servant of his constituents.* 1.2 one of the things that a mixture, substance, or system is made from. EG *Nitrogen is one of the essential constituents of living matter.* N COUNT ⇑ person = voter; N COUNT ⇑ part = ingredient

2 **Constituent** is used to describe the various things that a mixture, substance, or system is made from. EG *What are the constituent parts of an atom?* ADJ CLASSIF : ATTRIB = component

constitute /kɒnstɪtjuːt/, **constitutes, constituting, constituted**. 1 If something **constitutes** a particular thing, it can be regarded as being that thing. EG *These questions constitute a challenge to established attitudes... There is considerable speculation as to whether these sounds constitute a language... What constitutes an emergency?* V+C : NO CONT = represent

2 If something **constitutes** something else, it is a particular part or fraction of that thing. EG *Conifers constitute about a third of the world's forests... These 75,000 men constituted the whole strength of the Dutch Army.* V+C : NO CONT ⇑ be = account for, make up

3 To **constitute** something means to form it from a number of parts or elements; a formal use. EG *...the way in which the modern artist constitutes his images... The recently constituted board may do something to change the status quo.* V+O ⇑ create = put together

constitution /kɒnstɪtjuːʃə⁰n/, **constitutions**. 1 The **constitution** of a country or organization is the system of laws and rules which formally states people's rights and duties. EG *...the US constitution... ...Clause IV of the Party's constitution.* ▸ used to refer to the constitution of the United States of America. EG *...the twenty-fifth Amendment to the Constitution.* N COUNT; ▸ N PROPER : *the*+N = American constitution

2 Your **constitution** is your health, especially with regard to how much you are affected when you are ill, injured, or tired. EG *He has a strong constitution.* N COUNT : USU SING

3 The **constitution** of something is what it is made of, and how its parts are arranged. EG *Questions were asked concerning the constitution and scope of the proposed commission.* N SING : *the*+N+*of* = make-up

constitutional /kɒnstɪtjuːʃə⁰nəl, -ʃənə⁰l/. 1 **Constitutional** means 1.1 involving or related to the constitution of a particular country or organization. EG ADJ CLASSIF ⇑ legal

Their right of free choice is of tremendous constitutional importance... ...a major constitutional change. ◊ **constitutionally**. **1.2** officially allowed by the constitution of a particular country or organization. EG *In Britain, the constitutional head of state is the Queen... ...constitutional privileges.* **1.3** forming a natural part of the character or health of a person or thing; a formal use. EG *Perhaps the idea conflicts with our constitutional optimism.* ◊ **constitutionally**. EG *Perhaps he was constitutionally frailer than any of us knew.*

ADJ CLASSIF : USU ATTRIB ⇑ official
ADJ CLASSIF = inbuilt, inherent
◊ ADV ⇑ naturally = inherently

2 A **constitutional** is a walk that you regularly have in order to improve your health; an old-fashioned word, sometimes used humorously. EG *At 7.30, rain or shine, he went off for his constitutional in the woods.* N COUNT

constitutionalism /kɒnstɪtju:ʃə⁰nəlɪzə⁰m/ is the practice of governing or organizing a particular country or organization according to a constitution; used also to refer to a belief in this. N UNCOUNT

constrain /kə⁷nstreɪn/, **constrains, constraining, constrained**. **1** To **constrain** someone means to force them to act in a particular way and to prevent them from doing what they want to. EG *Papa had told her that he would not constrain her in any way... A painful duty constrains me... I am constrained to point out the disadvantages of the scheme.* V+O OR V+O+to-INF = compel

2 To **constrain** something means to prevent it from developing freely. EG *The housing regulations constrain variety and diversity... Why should love be constrained all the time?* V+O = inhibit

constrained /kə⁷nstreɪnd/. **1** If you feel **constrained** to do something, you feel that you are forced to act in a particular way, even though you would prefer not to act like that. EG *He felt constrained to apologize... A lot of men feel very constrained by society's image of masculinity.* ADJ QUALIT : PRED, USU+to-INF/by

2 If someone's smile, voice, or behaviour is **constrained**, it is awkward and not at all natural. EG *A constrained silence fell between us.* ADJ CLASSIF : USU ATTRIB

constraint /kə⁷nstreɪnt/, **constraints**. **1** A **constraint** is something that limits or controls the way you behave or what you can do in a situation. EG *The constraint on most doctors is lack of time... In the public sector they were no longer subject to the constraints of the market economy.* N COUNT : IF+PREP THEN *of/on* ⇑ limitation

2 **Constraint** is control over the way you behave which prevents you from doing what you would prefer to do. EG *The list of instructions and guidelines brings with it a flavour of constraint.* N UNCOUNT

constrict /kə⁷nstrɪkt/, **constricts, constricting, constricted**. **1** To **constrict** something, such as a part of the body, means to squeeze it tightly, sometimes so that it becomes narrower. EG *He rubbed his ankles where the bindings had constricted him... Cold water applied to the head constricts the blood vessels.* ◊ **constricting**. EG *Her dress was too constricting.* V+O; ◊ ADJ QUALIT

2 To **constrict** someone means to limit their actions so that they cannot do what they want to do. EG *This frees him from many of the rules that constricted his predecessor.* ◊ **constricted**. EG *When modern man feels socially constricted his first impulse is to move.* ◊ **constricting**. EG *...a constricting ideology.* V+O; ◊ ADJ QUALIT = limited; ◊ ADJ QUALIT

constriction /kə⁷nstrɪkʃə⁰n/, **constrictions**. **1** A **constriction** is **1.1** a fact or situation that limits what you can do and prevents you from doing what you want to do. EG *Eventually, unable to bear the constrictions of family life, he left home.* **1.2** a feeling of tightness, especially in your chest or throat. EG *There was a certain constriction in his throat.*

N COUNT : USU PL = restriction
N SING WITH DET

2 **Constriction** is **2.1** the act of tightly squeezing something. EG *The more advanced snakes kill, not by constriction, but by poison.* **2.2** the limitation of someone's actions so that they cannot do what they want to do. EG *The feeling of constriction was terrible.*

N UNCOUNT
N UNCOUNT

construct, constructs, constructing, constructed. The word **construct** is pronounced /kə⁷nstrʌkt/ when it is a verb, and /kɒnstrʌkt/ when it is a noun. **1** To **construct** a building, vehicle, road, machine, etc means to build or make it. EG *We constructed a raft... Tree ants in South-East Asia construct nests by sewing leaves together... ...a building constructed of brick.* V+O = build

2 If you **construct** an idea, piece of writing, or system, you create it by putting different parts together. EG *Before the scientist can construct his theories, he must make certain assumptions... It's a beautifully constructed book.* V+O = formulate

3 A **construct** is **3.1** a complex idea formed by combining simpler ideas in your mind. EG *...theoretical constructs.* **3.2** something that is built, made, or created; a formal use. EG *These machines are vast constructs of cogs, screws, and wheels.*

N COUNT ⇑ concept
N COUNT ⇑ creation

construction /kə⁷nstrʌkʃə⁰n/, **constructions**. **1** **Construction** is **1.1** the building of buildings, roads, bridges, etc. EG *...the construction of the Panama Canal... A wall collapsed while the building was under construction... ...the construction industry.* **1.2** the building or making of a machine or other object by joining parts or pieces together. EG *...a century of progress in machine design and construction... Many boys are given toy cars and construction sets.* **1.3** the creating of something such as an idea, piece of writing, or system. EG *...the careful construction of a theory by logical means.*

N UNCOUNT ≠ demolition
N UNCOUNT ≠ destruction
N UNCOUNT : USU +*of* ⇑ creation

2 A **construction** is an object such as a building that has been made or built out of a number of parts or pieces. EG *Ants have produced the greatest animal constructions the world has seen... These wigs are complicated constructions of real and false hair.* N COUNT = structure

3 If something is **of simple construction, of solid construction**, etc, it is built in the way and with the strength that is mentioned. EG *The main walls of the building are of solid brick construction.* PHR : USED AS AN A, OR AFTER N

4 A **construction** is also the way in which people can interpret something that is written, said, or done; a formal use. EG *The MPs were unaware of the construction that might be put upon this clause.* N COUNT ⇑ interpretation

5 In grammar, a **construction** is the way in which words are arranged in a sentence, clause, or phrase. N COUNT ⇑ structure

constructive /kə⁷nstrʌktɪv/. Something such as a suggestion that is **constructive** is useful and helpful because it enables you to see how another thing could be improved or achieved. EG *He admitted that even world leaders needed constructive criticism now and then... I did not have anything constructive to say.* ◊ **constructively**. EG *You must channel your anger constructively.* ADJ QUALIT = positive ≠ destructive; ◊ ADV ⇑ usefully

construe /kə⁷nstru:/, **construes, construing, construed**. If you **construe** a situation, event, or statement in a particular way, you interpret its meaning in that way. EG *Any show of emotion would be construed as a weakness. These phrases are capable of being construed differently.* V+O+A : USU A *(as)*, USU PASS ⇑ understand

consul /kɒnsə⁰l/, **consuls**. A **consul** is an official who is sent by his or her government to live in a foreign city in order to look after and protect all the people and businesses there that belong to his or her own country. EG *...the British Consul.* N COUNT : ALSO IN TITLES

consular /kɒnsjə⁴lə/ means involving or relating to a consul or to the work of a consul. ADJ CLASSIF : ATTRIB

consulate /kɒnsjə⁴lə¹t/, **consulates**. A **consulate** is the place where a consul works. EG *...the Spanish consulate in Cardiff.* N COUNT

consult /kə⁷nsʌlt/, **consults, consulting, consulted**. **1** If you **consult** someone, you ask them for their opinion and advice. EG *If your baby is losing weight, you should consult your doctor promptly.* V+O

2 If two or more people **consult**, they talk and exchange ideas and opinions with one another. EG *We needed to consult each other nearly every day... The Americans would have to consult with their allies about any military action in Europe.* V OR V+A *(with)* : RECIP

3 If you **consult** something such as a book or a map, you refer to it for information which you need. EG *He pretended to consult the papers on his desk... He consulted his watch and stood up to go.* V+O = look at

consultancy /kə⁷nsʌltənsi¹/, **consultancies**. A **consultancy** is **1** a person or group of people who set up a company to give expert, professional advice on a particular subject or subjects. EG *You can start your own consultancy.* ▸ used to refer to the advice that is given. EG *We supply research and design consultancy to industry.* **2** the job of a hospital consultant. EG *He has been appointed to a consultancy in gynaecology.*

N COUNT
▸ N UNCOUNT
N COUNT

consultant /kə⁷nsʌltə²nt/, **consultants**. A **consultant** is **1** an experienced doctor who specializes in one area of medicine, especially one who has a senior position in a hospital. EG *I was the first woman consultant on the staff of Charing Cross Hospital.* **2** a person who gives expert advice to people who need

N COUNT
N COUNT ⇑ worker

professional help. EG *He got a job with a firm of public relations consultants.*

consultation /kɒnsəˈlteɪʃən/, **consultations**. 1 A **consultation** is a meeting which is held to discuss something and to decide what should be done about it. EG *After many consultations with architects and builders, I decided to demolish the house.* N COUNT: IF + PREP THEN about/with

2 **Consultation** is 2.1 discussion between people, especially when advice is being given. EG *He was called in for consultation... This is a matter for the Prime Minister to decide in consultation with the Ministry of Defence.* N UNCOUNT: IF + PREP THEN about/with 2.2 reference to a book or some other source of information. EG *I keep my car handbook near me for frequent consultation.* N UNCOUNT

consultative /kəˈnsʌltətɪv/. A committee, document, etc is described as **consultative** if it is formed or written in order to give advice or to make suggestions about something. EG *Some local authorities have set up air pollution consultative committees.* ADJ CLASSIF: USU ATTRIB = advisory

consulting room, consulting rooms; also spelled with a hyphen. A **consulting room** is a room in which a doctor sees his or her patients. N COUNT

consume /kəˈnsjuːm/, **consumes, consuming, consumed**. 1 If you **consume** something, you eat or drink it. EG *The bird consumes vast numbers of worms each day... They spend their evenings consuming vodka.* V+O

2 To **consume** an amount of fuel, energy, time, etc means to use it up. EG *The ship consumed a great deal of fuel... Whole days were consumed by exhausting discussions.* • See also **time-consuming**. V+O = use up

3 If a fire **consumes** something, it destroys it. EG *The fire consumed the whole city.* V+O ⇑ destroy

4 If a feeling or desire **consumes** you, it affects you so strongly that you are unable to think of anything else. EG *His hatred of them consumed him.* V+O ⇑ overwhelm

consumer /kəˈnsjuːmə/, **consumers**. A **consumer** is 1 a person who buys things or uses services. EG *The consumer is entitled to products that give value for money... ...consumer advice.* N COUNT = purchaser 2 a person or company that buys a particular thing or uses a particular service. EG *These changes affect all gas consumers, including industry.* N COUNT+SUPP ⇑ purchaser 3 something or someone that uses up a supply or amount of something. EG *These machines were enormous consumers of electricity... He was a massive consumer of food.* N COUNT+SUPP ⇑ user

consumerism /kəˈnsjuːmərɪzəm/ is the protection of the rights and interests of consumers. N UNCOUNT

consuming /kəˈnsjuːmɪŋ/. A **consuming** passion or interest is one that is more important to you than anything else. EG *Politics is the consuming passion of half the town... He had two consuming interests: rowing and polo.* ADJ CLASSIF: ATTRIB = overwhelming

consummate, consummates, consummating, consummated. The word **consummate** is pronounced /kɒnsjəmeɪt/ when it is a verb, and /kɒnsjəmət/ when it is an adjective. 1 If two people **consummate** a marriage or relationship, they make it complete by having sex; used in formal English. EG *In a clearing in the forest they were able finally to consummate their love.* V+O
◇ **consummation** /kɒnsjəmeɪʃən/. ◇ N UNCOUNT

2 To **consummate** something means do something which makes it complete; a formal word. EG *We need to consummate what we have so far achieved.* V+O ⇑ finish ≠ abandon
◇ **consummation**. EG *This expedition was the consummation of what he regarded as his life's work.* ◇ N UNCOUNT ⇑ completion

3 **Consummate** is used to describe someone who is extremely skilful; a formal word. EG *Stael and Bomberg were consummate draughtsmen... He was a fighter of consummate skill.* ADJ CLASSIF: ATTRIB

4 **Consummate** is also used to emphasize that something is a perfect or extreme example of a particular thing; a formal word. EG *We were both consummate snobs.* ADJ CLASSIF: ATTRIB ⇑ extreme = total, utter

consumption /kəˈnsʌmpʃən/. 1 The **consumption** of fuel, energy, etc is 1.1 the amount of it that is used up. EG *Oil used to make up 10% of our total energy consumption.* N UNCOUNT+SUPP 1.2 the act of using it up. EG *...our consumption of energy.* N UNCOUNT+SUPP

2 **Consumption** is 2.1 the act of eating or drinking something. EG *She regarded the consumption of animal flesh as unhealthy... The water was unfit for consumption.* N UNCOUNT ⇑ intake 2.2 the act of buying and using things. EG *...new patterns of consumption.* N UNCOUNT

3 If you say that a piece of information, a remark, etc is **for** a particular person's or group's **consumption**, you mean that it is intended for or allowed to be seen or heard by that particular person or group. EG *That prim declaration was strictly for George's consumption... We wrote little about these things for foreign consumption.* PHR: USED AS AN A

4 **Consumption** is also the same as tuberculosis; used in old-fashioned English. N UNCOUNT ⇑ illness

consumptive /kəˈnsʌmptɪv/, **consumptives**. Someone who is **consumptive** suffers from tuberculosis; used in old-fashioned English. ▸ used as a noun. EG *Watteau was a consumptive.* ADJ CLASSIF ⇑ sick ▸ N COUNT

> **CONT** □ In this dictionary CONT is used in the grammar notes beside entries to describe the continuous form of verbs, which is made up of the auxiliary 'be' and the present participle of a verb. An example of a verb used in continuous form is ***are doing*** in *What **are** you **doing** tonight?* CONT is used to comment on the typical use of the continuous, for example when a verb is not normally used in the continuous (NO CONT) or when it is only used in the continuous (ONLY CONT). An example of a verb that is not normally used in the continuous is **know**. You can say *We had been there before so we **knew** what to expect... I **know** from personal experience that you won't find it easy... I don't know what you mean.* You do not say 'I am not knowing what you mean'.

cont. is an abbreviation for 'continued'; used at the bottom of a page to indicate that a letter or story continues on another page. EG *...cont. p. 16... ...cont. overleaf.*

contact /kɒntækt/, **contacts, contacting, contacted**. 1 **Contact** with someone or something is 1.1 the state of communicating or spending time with them. EG *I'm in contact with a number of schools in Sussex... I feel uneasy when I come into contact with people who have had a good education... There is little contact between governors and parents... We have many contacts with local people.* N UNCOUNT/COUNT: IF + PREP THEN with/between ⇑ communication 1.2 the state of touching them. EG *We avoid physical contact with strangers... My hand came into contact with a small lump... One foot must always be in contact with the ground.* N UNCOUNT/COUNT: IF + PREP THEN with/between

2 If there is eye **contact** between people, they are looking straight at one another. EG *...the importance of eye contact in the classroom.* N UNCOUNT/COUNT

3 If you **make contact** with someone who you have been trying to find or speak to, you manage to speak to them or write to them. EG *I finally made contact with my friend.* PHR OR PHR + A (with): RECIP, VB INFLECTS

4 If you have **contact** with someone you are able to send messages to them, especially by radio. EG *Radio contact was broken... At that point we lost contact with the spacecraft.* N UNCOUNT: IF + PREP THEN with/between = communication

5 If you **lose contact** with someone who you have been friendly with, you no longer see them or hear from them. PHR OR PHR + A (with): RECIP, VB INFLECTS

6 If you **contact** someone, you telephone or write to them in order to tell or ask them something. EG *As soon as we find out anything, we'll contact you... Dr Soga could not be contacted.* V+O ⇑ communicate

7 A **contact** is a person who you know and who is able to give you special help or information relating to your job or to a particular subject. EG *He had contacts in America and Britain... Without contacts you can't succeed.* N COUNT = connection

8 A **contact** in an electrical circuit is the part of it which, when it is made to touch another part, completes the circuit. EG *The wheel moves a lever and closes the contacts.* N COUNT

contact lens, contact lenses. A **contact lens** is a small plastic lens that you put onto the surface of your eye so that you can see properly without needing to wear glasses. N COUNT

contagion /kəˈnteɪdʒən/, **contagions**. 1 **Contagion** is the spreading of disease, caused by someone touching another person who is already affected by the disease; a formal or medical term. EG *The doctor says there is no chance of contagion.* ▸ used of a disease that can spread in this way. EG *Thousands fled the contagion.* N UNCOUNT = contamination, infection ▸ N COUNT

2 **Contagion** is also the spreading of bad or unacceptable ideas, attitudes, feelings, etc among a group of people; a formal use. EG *Another problem is the swift contagion of uncertainty and fear... I took Harry away quickly, to save him from further contagion.* N UNCOUNT: USU + of ⇑ spread = transference

contagious /kə⁷nteɪdʒəs/. **1** A **contagious** disease is one that you catch by touching someone or something that is already affected by the disease. ADJ QUALIT

2 Someone who is **contagious** has a disease that can be transmitted to other people. EG *She is no longer contagious.* ADJ CLASSIF = infectious

3 An idea, attitude, feeling, etc that is **contagious** spreads quickly among a group of people. EG *His energy and enthusiasm became contagious as the campaign progressed... ...a contagious sense of humour.* ADJ QUALIT = catching, infectious

contain /kə⁷nteɪn/, **contains, containing, contained.** **1** If something such as a box, bag, room, or place **contains** a particular thing, it has that thing inside it. EG *She carried a shopping basket containing groceries... The room contained a couch, a glass cabinet, and a desk... At present the urban areas contain some 970 million people.* V+O : NO CONT = hold

2 If something **contains** something else, it has the other thing among its parts or ingredients. EG *Each pill contains 75 milligrams of aspirin... Does it contain sugar?... Organisms can be classified into groups containing tens of thousands of different species.* V+O ⇑ have

3 If a piece of writing, speech, or painting **contains** a statement, idea, or image, it has that statement, idea, or image in it. EG *He was expecting an important letter containing further details of the contract... This chapter contains brief descriptions of three political systems.* V+O ⇑ have

4 If an account, idea, system, etc **contains** a particular quality or character, it has this quality or character. EG *The story contained some truth... The single-party system of some of the new states contains dangers for democracy.* V+O ⇑ have

5 To **contain** something means **5.1** to prevent it from spreading or becoming more serious. EG *...the difficult task of containing their revolutionary activities... Measures to contain population growth have met with little success.* V+O ⇑ limit = control, curb **5.2** to keep it within a particular area or boundary. EG *The water rose above defensive banks built to contain it.* V+O = hold back **5.3** to enclose or form the boundary of an area; a formal use. EG *...a long thin square contained by tall terrace houses.* V+O : USU PASS

6 If you **contain** a feeling such as excitement or anger, or if you **contain** yourself, you prevent yourself from showing your feelings. EG *He could hardly contain his eagerness to leave... The news was so exciting that Philip could hardly contain himself.* V+O (NG/REFL) = control, restrain ≠ let go

contained /kə⁷nteɪnd/. Someone who is **contained** has their feelings under control and does not show their feelings to other people. EG *He's a very contained man.* ADJ QUALIT = calm, controlled

container /kə⁷nteɪnə/, **containers.** A **container** is **1** an object such as a box or bottle that is used to hold, carry, or store things in. EG *The seeds are stored in plastic containers... ...a soap container.* N COUNT = receptacle **2** a very large metal or wooden box used for transporting goods so that they can be loaded onto and off lorries, ships, or trains quickly and easily. EG *...44-foot shipping containers.* N COUNT

container ship, container ships. A **container ship** is a ship that is designed for carrying goods that are packed in large metal or wooden boxes. N COUNT

containment /kə⁷nteɪnmə²nt/. **1** **Containment** is the action or policy of keeping another country's power or area of control within acceptable limits or boundaries. EG *It was a policy of containment which had led to the treaty.* N UNCOUNT

2 The **containment** of something is the act or process or method of keeping it within a particular area or place. EG *Molten fuel burns through the pressure vessel and containment dome.* N UNCOUNT

contaminant /kə⁷ntæmɪnənt/, **contaminants.** A **contaminant** is something that contaminates water, food, or some other substance; a formal word. EG *Keep all contaminants out of your wine.* N COUNT = impurity

contaminate /kə⁷ntæmɪneɪt/, **contaminates, contaminating, contaminated.** **1** If a substance **contaminates** water, food, etc, or if someone **contaminates** water, food, etc with a substance, the substance is added to the water or food and makes it impure. EG *These chemicals contaminate water and poison animals... Particles of food had become contaminated by mould.* V+O ⇑ pollute ≠ purify ◇ **contaminated.** EG *Many had died from drinking contaminated water.* ◇ ADJ QUALIT ⇑ polluted ◇ **contamination** /kə⁷ntæmɪneɪʃə⁰n/. EG *These infections were caused by the contamination of milk.* ◇ N UNCOUNT

2 If radioactivity **contaminates** a place or person, the person or place is affected by being exposed to radiation. EG *...a nuclear device which seriously contaminated over 7000 square miles.* V+O = irradiate ◇ **contaminated.** EG *Bulldozers scooped up contaminated sand.* ◇ ADJ QUALIT = radioactive ◇ **contamination.** EG *...contamination of beaches and marine life... Missile attacks produced a high level of contamination.* ◇ N UNCOUNT

contd is a written abbreviation for 'continued'; used at the bottom of a page to indicate that a letter or story continues on another page. = cont.

contemplate /kɒntə²mpleɪt/, **contemplates, contemplating, contemplated.** **1** If you **contemplate** something or if you **contemplate**, you think about something in a deep and careful way and for a long time. EG *It is exciting to contemplate how many new ideas are lying dormant in people's minds... He sat there and contemplated.* V OR V+O/REPORT-CL = consider ◇ **contemplation** /kɒntə²mpleɪʃə⁰n/, **contemplations.** EG *Sunday should be a day of contemplation and rest... ...religious contemplation... It was at this point in his contemplations that he was interrupted.* ◇ N UNCOUNT/COUNT ⇑ thinking

2 If you **contemplate** something, **2.1** you think that you might do it. EG *Are you contemplating marriage?... He had never at any time contemplated selling the business... It is just too dangerous to contemplate.* V OR V+O/-ING = consider, think about **2.2** you look at it in a quiet and very thoughtful way. EG *She lay back on the grass to contemplate the high, blue sky.* V+O ◇ **contemplation.** EG *She looked at him sharply, then returned to the contemplation of the sunset.* ◇ N UNCOUNT

contemplative /kə⁷ntɛmplətɪv/. Someone who is **contemplative** is deeply thoughtful in a serious and quiet way. EG *I prefer the contemplative side of Sibelius.* ADJ CLASSIF ◇ **contemplatively.** EG *He gazed contemplatively down the table.* ◇ ADV WITH VB = thoughtfully

contemporaneous /kə⁷ntɛmpəreɪnɪəs/. If two events, situations, etc are **contemporaneous**, they happen or exist during the same period of time; a formal word. EG *The theories were more or less contemporaneous.* ADJ CLASSIF : IF + PREP THEN *with* ≠ separate

contemporary /kə⁷ntɛmprəri¹/, **contemporaries.** **1** **Contemporary** means existing or happening now, rather than in the past. EG *...life in contemporary America... My studies were devoted almost entirely to contemporary literature.* ADJ CLASSIF : USU ATTRIB ⇑ modern = present-day

2 **Contemporary** is used to describe people, events, accounts, etc which existed or happened during the same period of time in the past. EG *Here is a contemporary account of the execution of Charles I.* ADJ CLASSIF : ATTRIB

3 Someone who is your **contemporary** is a person who lives at the same time as you. EG *Darwin's contemporary, Sir James Simpson... I was better read than most of my contemporaries.* N COUNT : USU WITH POSS

contempt /kə⁷ntɛmpt/. **1** If you have **contempt** for someone or something, you do not like them and think that they are unimportant or of no value. EG *They would often look at us with unmistakeable contempt... Her contempt for foreigners was obvious... I shall treat that remark with the contempt it deserves... ...his contempt for the truth.* N UNCOUNT : IF + PREP THEN USU *for* = scorn ≠ respect

2 If you say that someone or something is **beneath contempt** or **beneath** your **contempt**, you mean that you think that they are so ridiculous or unimportant that they are not even worth feeling contempt for. EG *The poor were beneath her contempt.* PHR : USED AS AN A

3 If you **hold** someone or something **in contempt**, you feel contempt for them. EG *Such children hold their parents in contempt.* PHR : VB INFLECTS ⇑ despise

4 **Contempt** or **contempt of court** is the criminal act of disobeying an instruction from a judge or a court of law; a legal term. EG *He was warned that if he attempted to contact me he'd be jailed for contempt of court... Cliff was held to be in contempt of court.* N UNCOUNT ⇑ disobedience

contemptible /kə⁷ntɛmptəbə⁰l/. If you feel that someone or something is **contemptible**, you feel strong dislike and disrespect for them. EG *You are showing a contemptible lack of courage.* ADJ QUALIT = despicable ≠ admirable

contemptuous /kə⁷ntɛmptjuəs/. If you are **contemptuous** of someone or something, you do not like or respect that person or thing at all; a formal word. EG *His lack of success had made him contemptuous of the way the London theatre was run.* ADJ QUALIT : IF + PREP THEN *of* = disdainful, scornful ▸ used of a person's behaviour and attitude. EG *...contemptuous remarks... ...a contemptuous look.* ▸ ADJ QUALIT

◊ **contemptuously**. EG *He tossed the paper contemptuously on to the table.* — *◊ ADV WITH VB = scornfully*

contend /kəˈntɛnd/, **contends, contending, contended.** 1 If you have to **contend** with a problem or difficulty, you have to deal with it or overcome it. EG *I had to contend with deep-rooted prejudice... There were also the occasional police visits to contend with.* — *V+A (with/against) = face*

2 If you **contend** that something is true, you state or argue that it is true; a formal word. EG *I contend that the roof is of a later date than the rest of the church... 'Therefore,' he contends, 'the net effect is to increase, not decrease, the number of people entitled to the payment.'* — *V+REPORT-CL/QUOTE = assert, claim*

3 If you **contend** with someone for something, you compete with them in order to win or achieve it. EG *Three parties are contending for power.* — *V OR V+A (with): RECIP*

◊ **contending**. EG *A great deal of time has been spent in bargaining between the two contending parties... ...contending views.* — *◊ ADJ CLASSIF: ATTRIB ⇑ competing*

contender /kəˈntɛndə/, **contenders**. A **contender** in a competition or election is someone who competes with other people to win something. EG *He no longer saw himself as a contender in the Presidential election... Who are the main contenders for the title?* — *N COUNT*

content, contents, contenting, contented. The word **content** is pronounced /kɒntɛnt/ for paragraphs 1 to 5, and /kəˈntɛnt/ for paragraphs 6 to 8. 1 The **contents** of something such as a bottle, bag, or room are everything that is contained in it. EG *He swallowed half the contents of his glass in one gulp... She uncorked the bottled and poured out the contents... He allowed them to share his house and its superb contents.* — *N PLURAL*

2 The **contents** of a book, letter, etc are everything that it says or shows. EG *He knew by heart the contents of the note... I opened the letter and read its contents.* — *N PLURAL*

3 The list of **contents** in a book or magazine is the list at the beginning which gives the title of every section or article and the page it starts on. — *N PLURAL*

4 The **content** of a piece of writing, speech, television programme, etc is its subject matter and the ideas that are in it, in contrast to things such as its form or style. EG *She set about changing the content of the newspaper columns... His novels are all form and no content.* — *N UNCOUNT ⇑ meaning*

5 **Content** is used to refer to the part of something which consists of a particular substance, ingredient, etc. EG *No other food has so high an iron content.* — *N COUNT: USU MOD+N IN SING ⇑ amount*

6 If you are **content** to do something or you are **content** with something, you are willing to do, have, or accept it. EG *A few were content to pay the fines... It seems that he would have been content to continue for a long time... She is not content with these explanations.* — *ADJ QUALIT+to-INF/with*

7 If you are **content**, you are fairly happy and do not want anything else or any change in your life or situation. EG *However hard up they were, they stayed content.* — *ADJ QUALIT: PRED = contented*

8 If you **content** yourself with something, are happy or satisfied with that thing alone and do not bother with other things. EG *She hadn't said much but had contented herself with smoking cigarettes and smiling... I contented myself with the use of words.* — *V+O (REFL)+A (with)*

9 If something **contents** someone, it satisfies them because it is good enough and does not make them feel that they want something else. EG *Her answer seemed to content him... Perhaps I'm too easily contented.* — *V+O = satisfy*

8 **Content** is also the same as contentment; a slightly literary use. EG *Her mouth was fixed in a smile of pure content.* ● **to your heart's content**: see **heart**. — *N UNCOUNT ⇑ happiness ≠ discontent*

contented /kəˈntɛntɪd/. If you are **contented**, you are satisfied and quite happy and do not want anything else or any change in your life or situation. EG *My father was the most contented man I ever met... They smoked for a while, contented and at rest.* — *ADJ QUALIT = content ≠ discontented*

◊ **contentedly**. EG *He puffed contentedly on his cigar.* — *◊ ADV*

contention /kəˈntɛnʃən/, **contentions**; a formal word. 1 Someone's **contention** is the idea or opinion that they are expressing in an argument or discussion. EG *It is my contention that demand will exceed supply within the next five years... My main contention is that the project would be too expensive.* — *N COUNT = belief*

2 **Contention** is disagreement or argument about something. EG *This is an issue of great contention at the moment... There was very little political contention about the need for swift action.* ● See also **bone of contention**. — *N UNCOUNT ≠ agreement*

3 If someone is **in contention** for something or **in contention** to win something, they are competing with others to win it. EG *Three players are in contention to win the title.* — *PHR: USED AS AN A*

contentious /kəˈntɛnʃəs/; a formal word. 1 An issue, question, subject, etc that is **contentious** causes a lot of disagreement or arguments. EG *He is well known for his contentious views on mental illness.* — *ADJ QUALIT = controversial*

2 People who are **contentious** are always quarrelling. EG *You appear to belong to a contentious family.* — *ADJ QUALIT*

contentment /kəˈntɛntmənt/ is a feeling of quiet happiness and satisfaction. EG *I sighed with contentment... They seemed to radiate inner contentment.* — *N UNCOUNT = content ≠ discontent*

contest, contests, contesting, contested. The word **contest** is pronounced /kɒntɛst/ when it is a noun and /kəˈntɛst/ when it is a verb. 1 A **contest** is 1.1 a competition or game in which people try to do something better than others in order to win a prize. EG *We entered a fishing contest... ...a beauty contest.* — *N COUNT*

1.2 a struggle to win power or control. EG *He won the contest for the deputy leadership... There is always a contest between the management and the unions.* — *N COUNT ⇑ competition*

2 If someone **contests** an election, competition, tournament, etc, they take part in it in order to try to win it. EG *There was a by-election contested by six candidates... She contested eight of the eleven titles... ...a keenly contested football match.* — *V+O*

3 If you **contest** something such as a statement, claim, or decision, you object to it formally because you think it is wrong or unreasonable. EG *We would hotly contest this idea... I am going to contest the will.* — *V+O = challenge, dispute ≠ accept*

contestant /kəˈntɛstənt/, **contestants**. 1 A **contestant** in a competition, quiz, etc is a person who takes part in it in order to try to win. — *N COUNT = competitor*

2 A **contestant** for a job or position is one of the people who competes with others for it. EG *They may both be future contestants for the Labour leadership.* — *N COUNT = candidate*

context /kɒntɛkst/, **contexts**. 1 The **context** of something consists of the ideas, situation, events, or information that relate to it and make it possible to understand it fully. EG *We need to place present events in some kind of historical context... We must examine these ideas in the context of recent events... He always provides a context that makes his characters believable.* — *N COUNT*

2 The **context** of a word, sentence, or text consists of the words, sentences, or text that come before and after it and help to make its meaning clear. EG *Try and guess what it means from the context... Context is so important when you are translating.* — *N COUNT/UNCOUNT ⇑ setting*

3 If something is seen **in context** or if it is put **into context**, it is considered with all the factors that are related to it rather than just being considered on its own, so that it can be properly understood. EG *I think one has to see the oil issue in context.* — *PHR: USED AS AN A ≠ in isolation*

4 If a remark, statement, etc is taken or quoted **out of context**, it is only considered on its own and the circumstances in which it was said are ignored. It therefore seems to mean something different from the meaning that was intended. EG *This remark was taken completely out of context.* — *PHR: USED AS AN A = in isolation ≠ in context*

contextual /kəˈntɛkstjuəl/. Something that is **contextual** relates to a particular context. — *ADJ CLASSIF ⇑ relative*

contiguous /kəˈntɪgjuəs/. Things that are **contiguous** are next to each other or touch each other; a very formal word. EG *There may be as many as seven houses contiguous with the property... ...large contiguous areas of the globe.* — *ADJ CLASSIF: IF+PREP THEN to/with = adjacent, adjoining*

continence /kɒntɪnəns/ is control of your emotions and desires, especially your desire for sex; a formal word. EG *...sexual continence.* — *N UNCOUNT ⇑ restraint = abstinence*

continent /kɒntɪnənt/, **continents**. 1 In Britain, when people talk about the **Continent**, they mean the mainland of Europe, especially central and southern Europe. EG *On the Continent the tradition has been quite different... Sea traffic between the United Kingdom and the Continent was halted.* — *N PROPER: the+N ⇑ abroad*

2 A **continent** is a large area of land that is surrounded or almost surrounded by sea, and that usually — *N COUNT ⇑ land mass*

consists of several countries. Africa and Asia are continents. EG *...the South American continent.*

3 Someone who is **continent** is **3.1** able to control their bladder and bowels; a formal or medical term. ADJ CLASSIF

3.2 able to control their emotions and desires, especially their desire for sex; a formal use. ADJ CLASSIF

continental /kɒntɪnentəºl/, **continentals**. **1** In British English, **continental** means situated on or belonging to to the mainland of Europe, especially central and southern Europe. EG *...scientific co-operation between Britain and continental Europe... ...our continental neighbours.* ▸ used to describe something that is thought of as being typical of central and southern Europe. EG *Everything was so elegant, so continental, in such taste.* ADJ CLASSIF: ATTRIB ⇑ European ▸ ADJ QUALIT

2 In informal British English, a **continental** is someone who comes from the mainland of Europe, especially central or southern Europe. N COUNT: USU PL ⇑ European

3 Continental is also used to refer to something that belongs to or relates to a continent. EG *Birds and reptiles from continental South America had reached the Galapagos. ...the continental shelf.* ADJ CLASSIF: ATTRIB

continental breakfast, continental breakfasts. A **continental breakfast** is a light breakfast that usually consists of bread, butter, jam, and a hot drink, without any cooked food: compare **English breakfast**; used especially in British English. N COUNT/UNCOUNT ≠ English breakfast

contingency /kə⁷ntɪndʒənsi¹/, **contingencies**; a formal word. A **contingency** is something that might happen in the future. EG *...contingency plans for nuclear attack.* N COUNT ⇑ possibility

contingent /kə⁷ntɪndʒənt/, **contingents**; a formal word. **1** A **contingent** is **1.1** a group of people representing a country or an organization at a meeting or a conference. EG *...a contingent of European scientists... ...a powerful feminist contingent.* N COUNT: USU+SUPP ⇑ lobby

1.2 a group of armed soldiers, military vehicles, etc. EG *The force includes a contingent of the Foreign Legion... There was still one British contingent on station.* N COUNT: USU+SUPP

2 If something is **contingent** on something else, it depends on it in order to happen, to exist, or to have a particular form. EG *The raid was contingent on the weather... The role they play is contingent on their political ability and zeal.* ADJ CLASSIF: PRED+*on* ⇑ conditional = dependent

continual /kə⁷ntɪnjuºəl/. Something that is **continual** **1** continues to happen or exist without stopping. EG *It was sad to see her the victim of continual pain... Life is a continual struggle.* ◇ **continually**. EG *...the continually evolving political world.* **2** happens or is done again and again. EG *He still smoked, despite the continual warnings of his nurse.* ◇ **continually** EG *He complained continually that there was no money left.* ADJ CLASSIF: USU ATTRIB ◇ ADV ADJ CLASSIF: USU ATTRIB ◇ ADV WITH VB

continuance /kə⁷ntɪnjuəns/ means the same as continuation. EG *Our survival depends on the continuance of the existing system.* N UNCOUNT+SUPP: USU+*of*

continuation /kə⁷ntɪnjuːeɪʃəºn/, **continuations**. **1** The **continuation** of something is the fact that it continues to happen or exist. EG *...the continuation of full employment.* N UNCOUNT: USU +SUPP

2 If something is a **continuation** of something else, it follows it and seems like an extra part of it. EG *We saw the trip as a natural continuation of the tour... This idea is really a continuation of your earlier one.* N COUNT: USU SING, USU+*of* = extension, development

continue /kə⁷ntɪnjuː/, **continues, continuing, continued**. **1** If you **continue** to do something, you keep doing it and do not stop. EG *I continued to support the party in elections... The orchestra continued to play... One continues to learn things in life... He continued talking.* V+*to*-INF/-ING = carry on, go on ≠ cease, stop

2 If something **continues** or if you **continue** something, **2.1** it does not stop happening or existing. EG *If the strike continues, then violence is inevitable... They want to continue their education... ...the continuing conflict in Ireland.* **2.2** it lasts over a period of time without stopping. EG *The battle continued for an hour... ...women who had continued their careers throughout marriage.* **2.3** it starts again after stopping for a period of time. EG *The next day the performance continued... He arrived in Norway, where he continued his campaign.* V OR V-ERG = carry on ≠ end, stop V-ERG+A = goes on V OR V-ERG = resumes

3 If you **continue** with something, you keep doing it, using it, or being involved with it. EG *They'll have to continue with direct rule for the time being... Meanwhile she continues with the antibiotics.* V+A *(with)* = keep up ≠ give up

4 If you **continue**, **4.1** you begin speaking again after you have stopped or after someone has interrupted you. EG *'I'm leaving,' Owen Evans answered, 'and what's more,' he continued, 'I'm not coming back.'... 'May I continue?'–'Go on.'... She continued as though there had been no interruption.* **4.2** you keep walking or travelling in a particular direction. EG *We crossed the bridge and continued towards Villacoublay... She left the village and continued on her way.* V OR V+QUOTE V+A = carry on, proceed ≠ stay, stop

5 If a road, path, etc **continues**, it goes beyond a particular place. EG *The road continues to the harbour.* V: USU+A = carry on

6 If it says in a newspaper or a magazine that an article is **continued on** a particular page, it means that the next part of the article begins on that page. EG *Continued on page 16.* PHR+N *(p/page)* +NUM

continuity /kɒntɪnjuːɪti¹/, **continuities**. **Continuity** is **1** the smooth development and continuation of a system, way of life, etc over a period of time. EG *There is a high degree of political stability and continuity in the country. ...the great cosmic and social continuities.* **2** the smooth arrangement of scenes in a film or television programme, so that they follow each other without breaks or interruptions; a technical term in films and television. EG *...the make-up and continuity departments.* N UNCOUNT/COUNT ≠ discontinuity N UNCOUNT ⇑ organization

continuous /kə⁷ntɪnjuːəs/. **1** Something that is **continuous** **1.1** continues to happen or exist without stopping. EG *Time does not appear to him as a continuous, uninterrupted process... ...the steady and continuous increase in their military capacity.* ◇ **continuously**. EG *The volcano had been erupting continuously since March.* **1.2** exists without stopping throughout a period of time. EG *He has never experienced a continuous loving relationship.* ADJ CLASSIF: USU ATTRIB = unbroken ≠ spasmodic ◇ ADV ADJ CLASSIF: USU ATTRIB

2 A **continuous** line, surface, etc has no gaps or holes in it. ADJ CLASSIF: USU ATTRIB

3 In grammar, the **continuous** or the **continuous** form of verbs is formed by the auxiliary 'be' and the present participle of a verb. When a verb typically occurs in the continuous or when it is rarely used in the continuous, this is mentioned in the grammar notes beside the entry, using the form CONT. See ☐ at CONT. ADJ CLASSIF = progressive

continuum /kə⁷ntɪnjuəm/. A **continuum** is a long series of things in a particular order. Each thing is closely related to the thing that is next to it in the order, but the things at the beginning and end of the order are very different from each other; a formal or technical word. EG *Good and evil are two ends of the same continuum... ...the left-right political continuum.* N SING WITH DET ⇑ scale

contort /kə⁷ntɔːt/, **contorts, contorting, contorted**. When something **contorts** or when you **contort** it, it becomes twisted until it no longer has its natural shape or position and often looks unattractive. EG *My face contorted with anguish... I contorted my body until it refused to respond any more.* ◇ **contorted**. EG *Her mouth was contorted in pain... ...his mad contorted smile.* V-ERG ⇑ misshapen = twist, screw up ◇ ADJ CLASSIF

contortion /kə⁷ntɔːʃəºn/, **contortions**. A **contortion** is an act of twisting something, especially your body, into an unusual shape or position. EG *Their bodily contortions are an inseparable part of their art.* N COUNT/UNCOUNT ⇑ acrobatic

contortionist /kə⁷ntɔːʃənɪst/, **contortionists**. A **contortionist** is someone who twists their body into strange and unnatural shapes and positions in order to entertain other people, for example in a circus. EG *A contortionist did her act on top of a piano.* N COUNT ⇑ acrobat

contour /kɒntʊə/, **contours**. **1** The **contour** of something is its outer shape or outline. EG *...the contour of her brow... ...the contours of the hillside.* N COUNT: SING=PL, IF+PREP THEN *of*

2 A **contour** is one of the lines on a map that join together points of equal height and show you where hills and valleys are. EG *...the 300ft contour line... ...contour maps of the earth's surface.* N COUNT: USU BEFORE N ⇑ level

contraband /kɒntrəbænd/ refers to goods that are taken in or out of a country secretly and illegally, especially in order to avoid paying tax on them. EG *...valuable pieces of contraband.* ▸ used as an adjective. EG *He was engaged in running contraband goods.* N UNCOUNT ⇑ smuggled goods ▸ ADJ CLASSIF: ATTRIB

contraception /kɒntrəsepʃəºn/ is the use of contraceptives to prevent a woman from becoming pregnant during sexual intercourse. EG *...safe, easy methods of contraception.* N UNCOUNT = birth control

contraceptive /kɒntrəsɛptɪv/, **contraceptives**. 1 A **contraceptive** is a device that is used, or a pill that is taken, in order to prevent a woman from becoming pregnant during sexual intercourse. EG *There are clinics where women can be fitted with contraceptives.*
N COUNT = birth control

2 A **contraceptive** method or technique is a method or technique that prevents a woman from becoming pregnant during sexual intercourse. EG *...a long-term study of contraceptive methods.*
ADJ CLASSIF : ATTRIB = family planning

contraceptive pill, contraceptive pills. A **contraceptive pill** is a pill that is taken regularly by a woman to prevent her from becoming pregnant during sexual intercourse. EG *...the introduction of the contraceptive pill.*
N COUNT ⇑ birth control

contract, contracts, contracting, contracted. The word **contract** is pronounced /kɒntrækt/ when it is a noun, and /kə⁷ntrækt/ when it is a verb. 1 A **contract** is a formal written agreement between two organizations, two people, etc, which says that one of them will supply goods or do work in an agreed way and for an agreed sum of money. EG *The company won a contract to build fifty-eight planes... I made sure that I did not sign a contract with them.*
N COUNT ⇑ undertaking

● If a company **puts** work **out to contract**, it employs another company to do it rather than doing it itself.
● PHR : VB INFLECTS

● If you are **under contract** to someone, you have signed a contract agreeing to work for them, and for no one else, during a fixed period of time. EG *I was then under contract to a finance company... They have under contract many of the leading British artists.*
● PHR : USED AS AN A, IF+PREP THEN *to* ⇑ obliged

2 If you **contract** with someone to do something, you make a contract with them to do it; a formal use. EG *A general practitioner contracts with the state to provide a medical service... They contracted to supply Italy with 180,000 horses annually.*
V+A *(with)*+ to-INF, OR V+ to-INF ⇑ undertake

3 When something **contracts**, it becomes smaller. EG *Metals expand with heat and contract with cold... The empire's economic power had contracted over the years.* ◊ **contraction**. EG *We should promote expansion rather than contraction of the coal industry.*
V = shrink ≠ expand; ◊ N UNCOUNT

4 When your muscles **contract** or when you **contract** them, they tighten and become smaller. EG *The muscle contracts between these two points... He unbuttoned his shirt and contracted his stomach muscles.* ◊ **contraction, contractions**. EG *...the contraction of the heart muscle... You can feel strong contractions in both sets of muscles.*
V-ERG = tense ≠ relax; ◊ N COUNT/ UNCOUNT

5 If you **contract** an illness, you become ill with it; a formal use. EG *At the age of four she contracted pneumonia.*
V+O = develop, catch

6 If you **contract** a marriage, alliance, or other relationship with someone, you agree and arrange to have that relationship with them; a formal use. EG *She later became a German citizen by contracting a marriage with Ulrich... She had contracted an alliance with a wealthy man of rank.*
V+O+A *(with)* = enter into

contract in. If you **contract in** to a scheme or system, you formally say that you want to take part in it; a legal or formal expression. EG *You have to contract in if you want to participate in the scheme.*
PHRASAL VB : V+ ADV, IF+PREP THEN *to*

contract out. 1 If you **contract out** of a scheme or system, you formally say that you do not want to take part in it; a legal or formal expression. EG *You can apply to the Pensions Board to contract out.*
PHRASAL VB : V+ ADV, IF+PREP THEN *of*

2 If a company **contracts out** work, it employs another company to do it, rather than doing it itself. EG *...a move towards contracting out more work to private firms.*
PHRASAL VB : V+ O+ADV, IF+ PREP THEN *to*

contraction /kə⁷ntrækʃə⁰n/, **contractions**. 1 A **contraction** is a shortened form of a word or words. EG *She used the surname Terson (a contraction of Terry and Neilson).*
N COUNT ⇑ abbreviation

2 See also **contract**.

contractor /kɒntræktə, kəntræk-/, **contractors**. A **contractor** is a person who does particular jobs for people, especially jobs connected with building or with moving goods. EG *I had a talk with the contractor who built this place... ...heating contractors.*
N COUNT ⇑ worker

contractual /kə⁷ntræktjʊ⁰əl/. A **contractual** agreement or obligation is an agreement or obligation which is in the form of a contract or which is included in one; a formal word. EG *The union had a contractual agreement with the company... ...the contractual obligation of employees to work overtime.* ◊ **contractually**. EG *He asked if the agreements were contractually binding.*
ADJ CLASSIF : ATTRIB ⇑ legal, binding; ◊ ADV

contradict /kɒntrədɪkt/, **contradicts, contradicting, contradicted**. 1 If you **contradict** someone or something, you say the opposite of what someone has just said, so that you are telling them that they have been incorrect. EG *She knew Etta didn't like to be contradicted... She contradicts everything I say.*
V OR V+O (NG/ REFL) ⇑ challenge = dispute ≠ endorse

2 If two things **contradict** each other, they cannot both be true. EG *There is a mass of research evidence which contradicts this idea... All our briefings contradict each other.*
V+O (NG/REFL) ⇑ challenge ≠ reinforce, support

contradiction /kɒntrədɪkʃə⁰n/, **contradictions**. 1 A **contradiction** is a difference between two statements, proposals, or beliefs, in which, for example, both statements cannot be true, or both beliefs cannot logically be held at the same time by the same person. EG *There are a number of contradictions in their foreign policy... ...the contradiction between private ownership and social production.*
N COUNT/ UNCOUNT = inconsistency ≠ similarity

2 If you say that an expression is a **contradiction in terms**, you mean that it is meaningless, because it describes something as having properties that cannot be held at the same time by the same thing. EG *There has never been a rational religion before. It's almost a contradiction in terms.*
PHR : USED AS C ⇑ paradox

contradictory /kɒntrədɪktə⁰ri¹/. If two statements, beliefs, or proposals are **contradictory**, they cannot both be true. EG *Their answers were mutually contradictory... ...contradictory ideas about love... The government had made two contradictory promises.*
ADJ QUALIT ⇑ opposing ≠ compatible, identical

contralto /kə⁷ntræltəʊ, -trɑːl-/, **contraltos**. A **contralto** is 1 a woman's speaking voice which is fairly deep. EG *Her voice was low and velvety, a soft contralto.* ▸ used as an adjective. EG *...the contralto voice of Mrs Haze.* 2 a woman singer who sings with a range of notes that is fairly low. EG *I limit myself to music that's for contralto, mezzo, or lyric soprano.*
N SING WITH DET; ▸ ADJ CLASSIF : ATTRIB; N COUNT, OR *for* +N = alto

contraption /kə⁷ntræpʃə⁰n/, **contraptions**. You refer to a device, piece of machinery, etc as a **contraption** when you think that it has been made badly or that it is rather strange. EG *Over his door was a fretwork contraption with a sliding shutter... ...a strange-looking contraption of cast iron, nuts, and bolts.*
N COUNT : USU+ SUPP = gadget

contrapuntal /kɒntrəpʌntə⁰l/ is used to describe music in which two or more tunes are played at the same time; a technical term. EG *The composer makes use of contrapuntal devices.*
ADJ CLASSIF : ATTRIB = polyphony

contrary. The word **contrary** is pronounced /kɒntrəri¹/, except in sense 4, when it is pronounced /kə⁷ntreəri¹/. 1 You say **on the contrary** 1.1 when you have just said that something is not true and are going to explain how the opposite is true. EG *I have never been an enemy of monarchy; on the contrary, I consider monarchies essential for the wellbeing of new nations... There was nothing dowdy or ugly about her dress: on the contrary, she had a certain private elegance.*
PHR : USED AS ADV SEN = quite the reverse

1.2 when you want to contradict something that someone else has just said and to explain that the opposite is true. EG *'You'll get tired of it.'–'On the contrary. I shall enjoy it.'*
PHR : USED AS ADV SEN ⇑ no = not at all

1.3 when you are contrasting someone or something with another person or thing that you have just mentioned. EG *People used to say that a Broadway musical was written for musical slobs. Mr Sondheim, on the contrary, assumes that you have heard some Ravel and Debussy.*
PHR : USED AS ADV SEN = however, by contrast

2 **Contrary** ideas, opinions, or attitudes are completely different from each other in a way that makes it impossible for one person to accept more than one of them at the same time. EG *It is still a useful exercise to set such contrary ideas side by side... They happily tolerated the existence of opinions contrary to their own.*
ADJ CLASSIF : IF+ PRED THEN *to* ⇑ different = opposite

● If you say that something is true **contrary to** a particular belief or opinion, you mean that it is true in spite of that belief or opinion, which you think is wrong or mistaken. EG *Contrary to popular belief, the desert can produce crops... Contrary to what is generally assumed, the adjustment to this kind of work is relatively easily made.*
● PREP ⇑ despite

3 **To the contrary** is used to indicate that one thing, especially a statement, contradicts another thing. EG *This method, despite thousands of published statements to the contrary, has no damaging effects whatsoever.*
PHR : USED AS AN A

4 Someone who is **contrary** behaves in an unreasonable way that is annoying for other people; used showing disapproval. EG *Human beings have a way of behaving like a contrary child.* ◊ **contrariness** . EG *This place seemed to bring out all her contrariness.* ADJ QUALIT ↑ difficult = perverse ◊ N UNCOUNT

contrast, contrasts, contrasting, contrasted. The word **contrast** is pronounced /kɒntrɑːst/ when it is a noun, and /kəˀntrɑːst/ when it is a verb.

1 A **contrast** is a difference, especially a great difference, between two or more things, which is very clear when you compare them with each other. EG *...the contrast between their order of priorities and ours... There is a marked contrast between the group's actions and its professed principles... Let's have the two together to show the contrast.* N COUNT/UNCOUNT : IF+PREP THEN *between/with* = disparity ≠ similarity

2 You say **by contrast** or **in contrast** when you want to indicate how different one thing or person is from another thing or person that you mentioned earlier. EG *Their movement, in contrast, reached a membership of 100,000 in two years... By contrast, our use of oil has increased enormously... Chris, in contrast to them, seems to be back to his normal self.* PHR : USED AS ADV SEN, IF+PREP THEN *to/with* ≠ similarly

3 If you say that something is **in contrast** to something else, you mean that it is very different from it. EG *This is in stark contrast to the boom in private car sales... In contrast is the steady rise of the middle classes.* PHR : USED AS AN A, IF+PREP THEN *to/with* ≠ similar

4 If you say that something is a **contrast** to or with something else, you mean that it is very different from it. EG *The atmosphere of the Second War in London was a complete contrast to that of the First... He began the dispiriting life of a salesman–a complete contrast to the glamour of the debating tour.* N COUNT : IF+PREP THEN *to/with* ↑ difference = opposite

5 To **contrast** two or more things means to compare them and to notice or show the differences between them. EG *The book contrasts child-rearing methods in America and Russia... I cannot help contrasting her attitude with that of her friends.* V+O : IF+PREP THEN *with/to*

6 If one thing **contrasts** with another, it is very different from it. EG *His accent contrasted curiously with the earthiness of his language... These first two types of gesture contrast sharply with the third.* ◊ **contrasting.** EG *The issue evokes strong and contrasting reactions from different people... ...contrasting colours.* V OR V+A : RECIP = conflict ◊ ADJ CLASSIF : ATTRIB ≠ similar

6 **Contrast** is the degree of difference between the darker and lighter parts of a photograph or television picture. EG *The photographs are very good–nice strong contrast.* N UNCOUNT

contravene /kɒntrəviːn/, **contravenes, contravening, contravened.** If you **contravene** a law or regulation, you do something that is forbidden by that law or regulation; a formal word. EG *They contravened the apartheid laws regularly... He was threatened with imprisonment if he contravened the Act.* ▸ used of actions. EG *The invasion contravened article 51 of the UN charter... This form of selective aid contravenes the Commission's principles.* ◊ **contravention** /kɒntrəvenʃəⁿn/, **contraventions.** EG *...a minor contravention of the Act... Such a conversation was in contravention of parade rules.* V+O ↑ disobey = break, violate ≠ abide by ▸ = infringe ◊ N UNCOUNT/COUNT : USU+*of* = infringement

contretemps /kɒntrətɑːn/. **Contretemps** is both the singular and the plural form. A **contretemps** is a small disagreement that is rather embarrassing; a formal or literary word. EG *He felt obliged to smooth over the awkwardness of this contretemps with Smith.* N COUNT = clash

contribute /kəˀntrɪbjuːt/, **contributes, contributing, contributed.** 1 If you **contribute** money to something, you give money in order to help someone to pay for something. EG *Pat persuaded her friends to contribute £5000 to launch a public appeal... George was already contributing to Democratic Party Funds.* V OR V+O : IF+PREP THEN *to* ↑ give = donate

2 To **contribute** also means to do or say things that help to make something successful. EG *The elderly have much to contribute to the community... The children enthusiastically contributed ideas... We were all encouraged to contribute and have our say.* V OR V+O : IF+PREP THEN *to/towards* ↑ give

3 If something **contributes** to an event or situation, it is one of the causes of it. EG *Soaring land prices contribute to the high cost of housing... Advanced technology has directly contributed to the excessive growth of cities.* ◊ **contributing.** EG *Escalating levels of youth unemployment are a major contributing factor to this problem.* V+A *(to/towards)* ↑ influence ◊ ADJ CLASSIF : ATTRIB = contributory

4 If you **contribute** to a magazine, book, etc, you write articles, poems, etc that are published in it. EG *Mother contributed to magazines and wrote endless letters... ...distinguished writers who had contributed to cheap periodicals.* V OR V+O : IF+PREP THEN *to*

contribution /kɒntrɪbjuːʃəⁿn/, **contributions.** 1 A **contribution** is 1.1 something that you give, do, or say in order to help to make something successful. EG *The United Kingdom had to make a contribution of £1,000 million to the EEC budget... ...appeals for contributions to cancer research... ...the British contribution to the defence of Europe.* N COUNT : IF+PREP THEN *to* ↑ gift = donation 1.2 a part of your wages that you pay to the government or to the company that you work for and that you receive back as social security payments or as a pension; used mainly in British English. EG *...national insurance contribution rates.* N COUNT ↑ payment 1.3 an article, poem, story, etc that you write that is published in a book or magazine. EG *...a terrific output of books, magazines and pamphlets with contributions from well-known trade unionists.* N COUNT = material

2 The **contribution** of something is the act of contributing it. EG *The contribution of a sum of money was originally the Chairman's suggestion.* N UNCOUNT : IF+PREP THEN *of* = donation

contributor /kəˀntrɪbjəˀtə/, **contributors.** A **contributor** is 1 someone who contributes money, help, etc to something. EG *...contributors to a fund to save the house.* N COUNT : IF+PREP THEN *to* 2 someone who writes something that is published in a book, magazine, or newspaper. EG *...a contributor of short stories to a national weekly... Lenin was a regular contributor.* N COUNT : IF+PREP THEN *to* ↑ writer 3 one of the causes of an event or situation. EG *Drinking alcohol is another possible contributor to liver cancer.* N COUNT : IF+PREP THEN *to* ↑ cause

contributory /kəntrɪbjəˀtəⁿriˀ/. A **contributory** cause, factor, etc is one of a number of things that causes something to happen. EG *Hunger itself can be a contributory cause to poor nutrition... The lack of vegetables in a diet is often a contributory factor... ...a contributory reason for his action.* ADJ CLASSIF : USU ATTRIB, IF+PREP THEN *to* = contributing

contrite /kəˀntraɪt, kɒntraɪt/. If you are **contrite**, you are sorry and apologetic because you have done something wrong. EG *For the first and only time in our relationship Kurt was contrite... I tried to look contrite.* ◊ **contritely.** EG *'I'm sorry,' said Miss Clare contritely.* ◊ **contrition** /kəˀntrɪʃəⁿn/. EG *A look of contrition came on his face.* ADJ QUALIT : USU PRED = remorseful ◊ ADV ◊ N UNCOUNT = remorse

contrivance /kəˀntraɪvəns/, **contrivances.** 1 A **contrivance** is 1.1 a device or machine, especially a strange and unusual one or one that you make quickly for a particular purpose. EG *The villagers became suspicious about the weird contrivance... I set about improvising some makeshift contrivances.* N COUNT = contraption 1.2 a plan or scheme for getting an advantage for yourself; used showing disapproval. EG *...a deliberate contrivance to squeeze the peasant dry... ...a contrivance to raise prices.* N COUNT = ploy

2 **Contrivance** is the making of plans and schemes; a formal use. EG *Persuasion and contrivance swept aside many obstacles.* N UNCOUNT = manoeuvring

contrive /kəˀntraɪv/, **contrives, contriving, contrived.** 1 If you **contrive** an event or situation, you succeed in making it happen, often by deceiving or tricking people in some way. EG *She had contrived a match between her father and Frank's mother... ...a moving little drama that we could never have contrived deliberately.* V+O ↑ bring about = engineer, wangle

2 If you **contrive** a device, machine, etc, you invent and construct it in a clever or unusual way. EG *It had a balancing mechanism contrived from two arching tubes... ...glass jewels contrived by premier craftsmen.* V+O ↑ make = engineer

3 If you **contrive** to do something difficult, you succeed in doing it. EG *Ralph Richardson contrived to combine both these qualities to perfection.* V+to-INF ↑ manage

4 People also say that they **have contrived** to do something when they have done something foolish; a formal or humorous use. EG *We had contrived to lose six wickets for 44... Somehow we contrived to make a mess of it again.* V+to-INF = manage

contrived /kəˀntraɪvd/. 1 Something that is **contrived** is deliberate and planned, rather than natural and spontaneous; used showing disapproval. EG *The incident was obviously contrived.* ADJ QUALIT ↑ artificial ≠ genuine, natural

2 If you say that the plot of a play, novel, etc is **contrived**, you mean that it is artificial and unconvincing; used showing disapproval. EG *I thought the ending was a bit contrived.* ADJ QUALIT ↑ unnatural = implausible

control /kə⁷ntrəʊl/, **controls, controlling, controlled.** 1 **Control** of a country or an organization is the power to make all the important decisions about the way that it is run. EG *The Party had been able to gain control of a nation of over 100 million people... Political control over colonies also proved useful... They bought control of a building company and a glass factory... Earlier this year the bank took control of a Toledo television station.* N UNCOUNT : IF+PREP THEN *of/over*

2 **Control** is also 2.1 the ability to make something behave exactly as you want it to behave. EG *You should have control of your vehicle at all times... I was asserting control over my life.* ● See also **birth control, remote control.** N UNCOUNT : IF+PREP THEN *of/over* ⇑ domination = mastery 2.2 the ability to prevent yourself behaving in an excited or emotional way. EG *Miss Lenant gained control of herself with a visible effort... Indignation took away Ralph's control... He told himself that he mustn't lose control if he wanted to save his strength.* ● See also **self-control.** N UNCOUNT : IF+PREP THEN *of* ⇑ restraint = command

3 The word **control** is also used in the following expressions. 3.1 If you are **in control** of something, you have the power to make it do what you want it to do. EG *Man was not yet in control of his environment... Those who begin the revolution rarely stay in control to complete the process... She was in control of herself completely.* PHR : USED AS AN A, IF+PREP THEN *of* = in command 3.2 If something harmful is **under control**, it is being dealt with successfully, and no longer likely to cause any serious harm. EG *Everything is under control... The fever was brought under control.* PHR : USED AS AN A 3.3 If something is **under** your **control**, you have the power to decide what it will do or what will happen to it. EG *The money supply in those days was not under the control of governments... How can you decide when a village is under enemy control?* PHR : USED AS AN A 3.4 If something is **beyond** your **control** or **outside** your **control**, you do not have any power to decide or influence what will happen to it. EG *That's something beyond our control... The subsidy is being withdrawn for reasons outside anyone's control.* PHR : USED AS AN A 3.5 If something is **out of control**, nobody has any power over it. EG *Inflation got out of control... There was only one way to stop the fire getting out of control.* PHR : USED AS AN A = out of hand

4 To **control** something such as a country or an organization means to have the power to take all the important decisions about the way that it is run. EG *The Australian administration at that time controlled the island... His family had controlled The Times for more than a century... The capitalized sector of the economy was controlled by foreigners.* V+O = govern ◇ **controlling.** EG *The family bought a controlling interest in the firm.* ◇ ADJ CLASSIF : ATTRIB

5 To **control** a machine, process, system, etc means to make it work in the way that it is intended to work. EG *...the skill needed to control the machine... ...computer systems which control the lighting, heating and security of your home.* V+O = regulate ◇ **controlled.** EG *...the controlled release of water from reservoirs.* ◇ ADJ QUALIT = regulated

6 When a government **controls** something such as wages, prices, or the activities of a group or organization, it uses its power in order to restrict these things. EG *...a law to control incomes... ...the failure to control inflation... ...legislation to control the activities of trade unions.* V+O ⇑ limit = check, curb

7 To **control** the way that something is done in an organization means to make sure that it is done correctly. EG *Her responsibility is to control the final accounts.* V+O ⇑ check = verify ▸ used as a noun. EG *The task of quality control would be indescribably difficult... ...stock control.* ▸ N UNCOUNT : MOD+N ⇑ checking

8 If you **control** yourself, you make yourself behave calmly when you are feeling angry, excited, or upset. EG *Control yourself!... He was pleading with her to control herself until he could explain.* V+O (REFL) = restrain

9 If you **control** your voice, expression, gestures, etc, you make them appear normal in order to hide your real feelings. EG *He could barely control the smirk on his handsome face... I turned and walked on, trying to control my trembling chin and the tears that threatened to erupt.* V+O ⇑ restrain = master

10 To **control** something dangerous, such as a disease, means to prevent it from becoming worse or from spreading. EG *He had discovered a way of controlling cancer of the prostate.* V+O ⇑ restrict

11 A **control** is a device such as a switch or lever which you use in order to operate a machine. EG *Just turn the volume control up... ...a simple control lever... She explained the controls of the communal washing machine.* N COUNT ● If someone is **at the controls** of a vehicle or a machine, they are driving it or operating it. EG *The helicopter landed with Prince Charles at the controls.* ● PHR : USED AS AN A

12 **Controls** are the methods that a government or other official group uses in order to restrict increases in prices, wages, rents, etc. EG *The government argues that removing controls at the top of the market will stimulate trade... ...government price controls... ...the rent control board.* N UNCOUNT/COUNT+SUPP ⇑ limitation

13 **Controls** or **control** also refers to the parts of an airport, sea terminal, etc where your documents and luggage are officially checked to make sure that they are in order. EG *...passport and customs controls... We got off the plane and went through passport control together.* N UNCOUNT/COUNT : MOD+N ⇑ inspection

controllable /kə⁷ntrəʊləbə⁰l/. If something is **controllable**, you are able to control or influence it. EG *He tried to persuade himself that his situation was controllable.* ADJ QUALIT ≠ uncontrollable

controller /kə⁷ntrəʊlə/, **controllers.** A **controller** is 1 someone who has responsibility for everything that happens in a particular section of an organization. EG *...the Controller of Radio 4.* N COUNT = boss, head 2 someone who is in charge of the accounts of a business or government department. EG *...a former accountant and Controller of Humberside... ...the financial controller.* N COUNT ⇑ accountant

control tower, control towers. A **control tower** is a building at an airport from which people give instructions to aircraft when they are taking off or landing. N COUNT

controversial /kɒntrəvɜːʃə⁰l/. 1 Something that is **controversial** causes a lot of discussion and argument. EG *Many of the new taxes are controversial... ...this controversial aspect of computer research.* ADJ QUALIT = debatable 2 Someone who is described as **controversial** says or does things that many people do not approve of. EG *He is an astute if controversial politician... ...a controversial figure.* ADJ QUALIT = provocative

controversy /kɒntrəvɜːsi¹, kə⁷ntrɒvəsi¹/, **controversies. Controversy** is discussion and argument about an action or proposal that many people do not approve of. EG *The government tried to avoid controversy... ...a violent controversy over a commercial treaty... The figure aroused greater controversy than any piece of sculpture before.* N UNCOUNT/COUNT = dispute

contusion /kə⁷ntjuːʒə⁰n/, **contusions.** A **contusion** is a bruise; a formal or medical word. EG *...a large contusion to the left knee.* N COUNT/UNCOUNT

conundrum /kənʌndrəm/, **conundrums**; a formal or old-fashioned word. A **conundrum** is 1 a difficult or confusing problem. EG *The belief in reincarnation poses some conundrums.* N COUNT = riddle 2 a riddle or joke, especially one that involves a pun. N COUNT

conurbation /kɒnə⁵beɪʃə⁰n/, **conurbations.** A **conurbation** is a large urban area which has been formed by several towns or cities growing and spreading into each other; a formal word. EG *The bridge lies beyond the docks, to the west of the conurbation.* N COUNT

convalesce /kɒnvəlɛs/, **convalesces, convalescing, convalesced.** When you **convalesce**, you recover after being ill or after having an operation, especially by having a lot of rest. EG *She needed several weeks to convalesce.* V : IF+PREP THEN *from* = recuperate

convalescence /kɒnvəlɛsəns/ is the period of time during which you recover after being ill, or the process of recovering. EG *...a painful convalescence.* N UNCOUNT = recovery

convalescent /kɒnvəlɛsənt/, **convalescents.** 1 **Convalescent** means involving or relating to convalescence. EG *He was sent on convalescent leave to Marseilles... ...a convalescent home.* ADJ CLASSIF : ATTRIB 2 A **convalescent** is someone who is convalescing. EG *They found themselves classified as permanent convalescents.* N COUNT ⇑ patient

convection /kə⁷nvɛkʃə⁰n/ is the process by which heat travels through air, water, and other gases and liquids; a formal or technical term in science. EG *The vacuum eliminates conduction and convection losses... ...convection currents.* N UNCOUNT

convector /kə⁷nvɛktə/, **convectors.** A **convector** or a **convector heater** is a heater that heats a room by means of hot air. EG *I have a convector in the spare room.* N COUNT

convene /kə⁷nviːn/, **convenes, convening, convened**; a formal word. 1 If you **convene** a V+O

meeting or conference, you arrange it. EG *Roland convened a small meeting to discuss the issue... A special conference was convened.*
2 If an official group of people **convene**, they come together for a meeting. EG *The grand jury did not convene until February.* V ⇑ meet

convener /kə'nvi:nə/, **conveners**. See **convenor**. N COUNT

convenience /kə'nvi:nɪəns/, **conveniences**. 1 **Convenience** is the state or quality of being convenient. EG *New regulations will give customers the convenience of dealing with a local institution... When I'm doing the cooking we use all frozen stuff for convenience... The bicycle is a form of transport whose convenience we take for granted.* N UNCOUNT ≠ hassle, inconvenience
2 Your **convenience** is whatever is convenient for you. EG *The entire event had been arranged for their convenience... The government have considered only the convenience of the suppliers.* N UNCOUNT : WITH POSS ⇑ benefit
3 If something is arranged to happen **at your convenience**, it happens at a time that is most convenient for you. EG *I left the blankets outside my room for my landlady to remove at her convenience.* PHR : USED AS AN A
4 If you ask someone to do something **at their earliest convenience**, you are asking them to do it as soon as possible; a polite and very formal expression. EG *He was asked to make an appointment at his earliest convenience.* PHR : USED AS AN A
5 If you describe something as a **convenience**, you mean that it is very useful. EG *The system had many advantages and conveniences... A folding bath-tub is a convenience if you can afford it... ...a modern housewife with every modern convenience in her home.* N COUNT ⇑ help
6 A **convenience** is a toilet that is provided in a public place for anyone to use; a formal use used in British English. EG *...gentlemen's conveniences.* N COUNT : ALSO SING=PL

convenience food, convenience foods. A **convenience food** is food that is frozen, dried, or tinned, so that you can cook it quickly whenever you want. N UNCOUNT/COUNT = fast food

convenient /kə'nvi:nɪənt/. Something that is **convenient** is 1 suitable and arranged to fit in well with someone's particular plan or purpose. EG *May I come and talk with you whenever it's convenient?... ...a convenient time to visit the hospital.* ADJ QUALIT
◊ **conveniently**. EG *The report conveniently fails to remember our earlier criticisms.* ◊ ADV
2 useful because it saves you time and trouble. EG *The train is convenient–the service to London is fairly quick... We decided that it would be a rather convenient place to live... A quart measure marked in ounces is very convenient.* ADJ QUALIT = handy ≠ inconvenient
◊ **conveniently**. EG *The amount of fuel is displayed conveniently on a gauge.* ◊ ADV
3 near to you at a particular time, so that you can use it. EG *He sat in the shade on a convenient tree trunk.* ADJ CLASSIF : ATTRIB = handy

convenor /kə'nvi:nə/, **convenors**; also spelled **convener**. A convenor is 1 a trade union official who organizes the shop stewards at a particular factory; used in British English. EG *...an engineering shop stewards' convenor.* N COUNT
2 someone who convenes a meeting. N COUNT ⇑ organizer

convent /kɒnvə'nt/, **convents**. A **convent** is 1 a building or group of buildings in which a community of nuns live together. EG *...the Convent of St Joseph in Paris.* N COUNT : ALSO IN NAMES = nunnery
2 a school which is attached to a convent and in which many of the teachers are nuns. EG *My first boarding school was the Holy Cross Convent in Umtata... ...a convent school.* N COUNT : ALSO IN NAMES

convention /kə'nvenʃə'n/, **conventions**. 1 **Convention** is the ways of thinking and behaving that are believed to be normal and right by most people in a particular society. EG *You were very courageous to defy convention. A lot of the usual conventions are ignored when you go on holiday.* N UNCOUNT/COUNT ⇑ practice = custom
2 A **convention** is 2.1 a common way of doing something in art, the theatre, or literature. EG *...the convention of not naming the main character... He made use of 19th century fine art conventions.* N COUNT ⇑ practice
2.2 a list of rules of behaviour that is agreed between groups or countries. EG *...a convention on human rights for Africa... ...the Geneva Convention.* N COUNT ⇑ contract = agreement
2.3 a large gathering of people who meet to discuss the business of their organization or political group. EG *...the annual convention of the Union.* N COUNT = assembly

CONVENTION □ In this dictionary CONVENTION is used in the grammar notes beside entries to describe words and phrases which are standard expressions, such as 'how do you do', 'amen', or 'pardon?' A CONVENTION is an abbreviation for a conventional contribution to a discourse. It is an expression which has an established form and meaning, and which can be used by itself as a single utterance. The individual entries explain in what contexts such words or phrases are used. Examples are **no comment** (see **comment 1.2**), and **I know** (see **know 19.1**). EG *'Were the negotiations a success?'–'No comment'... 'She's coming at 6.'–'I know.'*

conventional /kə'nvenʃə'nəl, -ʃənə'l/. 1 Opinions and behaviour that are **conventional** are accepted as normal and right by most people in a particular society. EG *She had strayed from the path of conventional behaviour.* ▸ used of people and groups. EG *He longed to be normal, conventional and correct... ...the conventional and conservative Judge Parker.* ADJ QUALIT ⇑ standard ≠ unconventional ▸ = orthodox
◊ **conventionally**. EG *They went back to more conventionally acceptable ways of life.* ◊ ADV = traditionally
◊ **conventionality** /kə'nvenʃə'nælɪti'/. EG *He stands for the strictest conventionality.* ◊ N UNCOUNT
2 A **conventional** method, product, etc is accepted as normal because it has been used or produced for a long time. EG *There is a need to overcome the limitations of conventional politics... He has difficulty coping with a conventional exam paper.* ADJ CLASSIF : ATTRIB = traditional ≠ new
◊ **conventionally**. EG *This style of teaching was designed to shock conventionally educated students.* ◊ ADV = traditionally
3 The **conventional wisdom** about a particular matter is the generally accepted view of that matter among a group of people; a formal expression. EG *...the conventional wisdom about the need to conserve energy.* PHR : USED AS S/O/C = received view
4 **Conventional** wars and weapons are non-nuclear wars and weapons. EG *We have the ability to fight with conventional as well as nuclear weapons.* ADJ CLASSIF : ATTRIB ≠ nuclear

convent school, convent schools. A **convent school** is a school, especially one for girls, which is attached to a convent and in which many of the teachers are nuns. EG *She learned to cook at a convent school in Newbury.* N COUNT

converge /kə'nvɜ:dʒ/, **converges, converging, converged**. 1 When roads, paths, etc **converge**, they meet or join at a particular place. EG *The paths converge under the trees.* V : USU+A = merge ≠ separate
2 When groups of people, vehicles, etc **converge**, they meet in a particular place after arriving there from different directions. EG *Groups from throughout the country converged in Oakland, California.* V : USU+A *(in/on/upon)* = gather
3 When societies, tendencies, etc **converge**, they stop being separate or different and become the same. EG *Two radically different types of society were converging... In the mid-seventies, four tendencies began to converge.* V ⇑ join = merge ≠ diverge

convergence /kə'nvɜ:dʒəns/, **convergences**. The **convergence** of societies, tendencies, etc is the process by which they stop being separate or different and become the same; a formal word. EG *...the predicted convergence of the industrialized societies... We live in a unique period of convergence.* N UNCOUNT/COUNT : IF+PREP THEN *of/between* = fusion

conversant /kə'nvɜ:sə'nt/. If you are **conversant** with something, you are familiar with it, and therefore able to deal with it; a formal word. EG *You will need to be fully conversant with the running of the household.* ADJ QUALIT : PRED+*with* = at home

conversation /kɒnvəseɪʃə'n/, **conversations**. 1 If you have a **conversation** with someone, you talk with them in an informal situation. EG *Roger and I had a conversation about fishing... I had a long telephone conversation with my father... He spent some hours in conversation with me... She made no attempt to get into conversation with her neighbour.* N COUNT, OR *in/into*+N
2 If you **make conversation**, you have a conversation with someone in order to be polite, rather than because you really want to talk to them. EG *He didn't like having to make conversation...* EG *She had had years of having to make conversation with her husband's colleagues.* PHR : VB INFLECTS
3 **Conversation** is also 3.1 the things that you talk about in a conversation. EG *You quickly run out of conversation.* N UNCOUNT ⇑ subject
3.2 the act of having conversations. EG *...the art of conversation.* N UNCOUNT

conversational /kɒnvəseɪʃə'nəl, -ʃənə'l/. **Conversational** is used to describe something that is related to conversation. EG *His family fascinated me with their brilliant conversational powers.* ADJ CLASSIF : ATTRIB

conversationalist /kɒnvəseɪʃə'nəlɪst/, **conversationalists**. A good **conversationalist** is someone who talks about interesting things when they have N COUNT+SUPP ⇑ speaker = talker conversations. EG *It's always interesting to meet such a good conversationalist... I'm a poor conversationalist, I'm afraid.*

converse, converses, conversing, conversed. The word **converse** is pronounced /kəˀnvɜːs/ when it is a verb and /kɒnvɜːs/ when it a noun or an adjective; a formal word. **1** If you **converse** with someone, you have a conversation with them. EG *It was a pleasure to converse with her... I consider it a privilege to have met and conversed with you.* — V OR V+A (with): RECIP = speak

2 The **converse** of a statement is its opposite. EG *I actually believe that the converse of your last statement is true.* — N SING: the+N, IF+PREP THEN of = reverse

3 A **converse** opinion or statement is one that is opposite to the one that has just been stated. EG *I hold the converse opinion.* — ADJ CLASSIF: ATTRIB

conversely /kəˀnvɜːsliˡ/. You can say **conversely** to introduce a statement about a situation that is the opposite to the situation that you have just described. EG *You can use beer yeast for your bread making. Conversely, you can use bread yeast in your beer.* — ADV SEN

conversion /kəˀnvɜːʃəᵒn/, **conversions.** **1** A **conversion** is **1.1** the act or process of changing something into a different form. EG *...the conversion of chemical energy into electricity.* — N COUNT/UNCOUNT **1.2** a calculation in which you work out a weight, distance, etc in a different system of measurement. EG *He did a quick conversion in his head.* — N COUNT/UNCOUNT **1.3** a process in which someone changes their religious or political beliefs. EG *...religious and political conversions... ...conversion to a faith.* — N COUNT/UNCOUNT: IF+PREP THEN from/to

2 In rugby football, a **conversion** is a score made after a try by kicking the ball over the crossbar; a technical term. — N COUNT/UNCOUNT

convert, converts, converting, converted. The word **convert** is pronounced /kəˀnvɜːt/ when it is a verb, and /kɒnvɜːt/ when it is a noun. **1** When something **converts** into something else or when you **convert** it, it changes into a different form. EG *A solar cell takes radiation from the sun and converts it into electricity... Energy is converted from one form to another... ...a stool which converts to a stepladder.* — V-ERG: IF+PREP THEN from/into/to ⇑ change = transform

2 To **convert** a building, vehicle, ship, etc means to alter it so that it can be used for a different purpose. EG *Some 50-100 mills in New England have been converted into apartments... ...a French passenger ship converted to carry seaplanes.* ◇ **converted.** EG *They lived in an old whitewashed converted farmhouse.* — V+O OR V+O+to-INF: IF+PREP THEN into/to = adapt; ◇ ADJ CLASSIF: ATTRIB

3 If you **convert** a quantity from one system of measurement to another system, you calculate what the quantity is in the second system. EG *He knew the formula for converting kilometres to miles.* — V+O+A (into/to)

4 If you **convert** a machine or a system to a different fuel, you change it so that it can use the different fuel for its power. EG *It might be necessary to convert the entire country back to coal gas.* — V+O: IF+PREP THEN from/to = adapt

5 If you **convert** someone, **5.1** you make them change their opinion about something. EG *Not surprisingly, he failed to convert her.* — V+O: IF+PREP THEN from/to **5.2** you persuade them to become a follower of your religion. EG *She was converted by the Salvation Army... He thought he was converting a Methodist to the true doctrine.* — V+O: IF+PREP THEN to

6 A **convert** is someone who has been converted to a particular religious or political belief. EG *The missionary schools sought to produce converts to Christianity... ...a Catholic convert... ...new converts to Trotskyism.* — N COUNT: IF+PREP THEN to ⇑ supporter

7 In rugby football, if you **convert** a try or if you **convert**, you score a conversion; a technical term. EG *Williams scored a try but failed to convert it.* — V OR V+O

converter /kəˀnvɜːtə/, **converters**; also spelled **convertor**. A **converter** is a device that changes something into a different form. EG *...the master program converter... ...an AC to DC convertor.* — N COUNT: USU MOD+N

convertible /kəˀnvɜːtəbəᵒl/, **convertibles.** **1** A **convertible** is a car with a soft roof that can be folded down or removed. EG *The red convertible was following us.* — N COUNT

2 Money that is **convertible** can easily be exchanged for the money of another country. EG *...convertible currency.* — ADJ CLASSIF

3 A device that is **convertible** has been specially designed so that you can change it into something else. EG *...a convertible pram-cum-pushchair.* — ADJ CLASSIF ⇑ adaptable

convertor /kəˀnvɜːtə/, **convertors.** See **converter.**

convex /kɒnvɛks, kɒnvɛks/. Something that is **convex** curves outwards in the centre; a formal or technical word. EG *...the oval, convex base of the bottle... ...a convex lens.* — ADJ QUALIT ⇑ curved

convey /kəˀnveɪ/, **conveys, conveying, conveyed.** **1** To **convey** information, ideas, feelings, etc means to cause them to be known or understood by someone. EG *That was the message Haig seemed to convey to the conference... Other newspapers convey the impression that the war is nearing its end... 'Really?' I said, trying to convey that it did not really matter.* — V+O/REPORT-CL: IF+PREP THEN to ⇑ express = put across

2 To **convey** someone or something to a place means to carry or transport them there; a rather formal use. EG *The bearers conveyed the wounded man towards the ambulance... The space launches would convey cargo and personnel.* — V+O: USU+A ⇑ take

3 To **convey** the ownership of a property means to legally transfer it from one person to another; a legal term. — V+O IF+PREP THEN to

conveyance /kəˀnveɪəns/, **conveyances.** A **conveyance** is **1** a vehicle; an old-fashioned use. EG *I had never travelled on any public conveyance.* — N COUNT **2** a legal document transferring the ownership of a property from one person to another; a legal term. — N COUNT

conveyancing /kəˀnveɪənsɪŋ/ is the process of transferring the legal ownership of property; a legal term used in British English. EG *People might like to have a go at doing their own conveyancing.* — N UNCOUNT

conveyor belt, conveyor belts. A **conveyor belt** or a **conveyor** is a device that is used in factories for moving objects along from one place to another. It consists of a long continuous moving band of cloth, rubber, or metal or a series of metal rollers. EG *Slabs of toffee pass along a conveyor belt... Overhead a creaking conveyor carried red hot castings.* — N COUNT, OR by+N ⇑ device

convict, convicts, convicting, convicted. The word **convict** is pronounced /kəˀnvɪkt/ when it is a verb, and /kɒnvɪkt/ when it is a noun. **1** To **convict** someone of a crime means to find them guilty of it in a court of law. EG *We needed more information on which to convict him... He was convicted of spying.* ◇ **convicted.** EG *...convicted criminals.* — V+O: IF+PREP THEN of/for = find guilty ≠ acquit; ◇ ADJ CLASSIF: ATTRIB

2 A **convict** is a person who is serving a prison sentence. EG *...an escaped convict.* — N COUNT ⇑ prisoner

conviction /kəˀnvɪkʃəᵒn/, **convictions.** **1** A **conviction** is a strong belief or opinion. EG *Nothing would budge him from his conviction that he could run a newspaper successfully... ...the clarity and strength of Ernest's convictions.* — N COUNT: USU+REPORT-CL

2 If someone has **conviction**, they have strong beliefs or opinions or they have one particular strong belief. EG *He was full of energy and conviction... 'Yes,' I said without much conviction.* — N UNCOUNT ⇑ certainty = fervour ● If something **carries conviction**, it is likely to be true or likely to be believed. EG *This explanation carries more conviction than the rival theories... The threat of a general strike carries little conviction.* — ● PHR: VB INFLECTS = be plausible

3 A **conviction** is also the decision that is taken when someone is found guilty in a court of law. EG *...the trial and conviction of Stephen Ward... He had a long record of previous convictions.* — N COUNT/UNCOUNT: IF+PREP THEN of/for

convince /kəˀnvɪns/, **convinces, convincing, convinced.** If someone or something **convinces** you, **1** they make you believe that something is true or that something should be done. EG *It took me a day or two to convince her that I wasn't going to harm her... These experiences served to convince me of the drug's harmful effects.* — V+O+REPORT-CL, OR V+O: IF+PREP THEN about/of = assure **2** they persuade you to do something. EG *Powerful advertising can convince people to buy almost anything... ...a massive attempt to convince Filipinos to boycott the polls.* — V+O+to-INF = prevail upon

convinced /kəˀnvɪnst/. **1** If you are **convinced** of something, you are sure that it is true or correct. EG *She was convinced that her mother had been innocent... Brody was convinced he was right... I understand your criticism, but I'm not totally convinced of it.* — ADJ QUALIT: PRED, USU+REPORT-CL/of = certain ≠ doubtful

2 A **convinced** Hindu, Christian, etc is a Hindu, Christian, etc who believes completely in his or her religion. — ADJ CLASSIF: ATTRIB = devout

convincing /kəˀnvɪnsɪŋ/. **1** Something that is **convincing** has qualities which make you believe that it is true, correct, or real. EG *The argument is compel-* — ADJ QUALIT ⇑ good = persuasive *ling but not convincing... The whole effect is so convincing that everyone is taken in.*

2 A person who is **convincing** is able to make you believe that something is true. EG *To be a successful nurse one must be a convincing liar.* ◊ **convincingly**. EG *They were able to pretend convincingly that it had never happened.*
ADJ QUALIT ↑ plausible
◊ ADV = plausibly

convivial /kəˀnvɪvɪəl/. 1 A social event that is **convivial** is enjoyable and friendly; a rather formal use. EG *...a convivial club dinner.*
ADJ QUALIT = sociable

2 **Convivial** behaviour is behaviour in which you are friendly in a cheerful way. EG *Their hospitality is welcoming and convivial.* ▸ used of people and groups. EG *They are a happy and convivial group.* ◊ **conviviality** /kəˀnvɪvɪæ̲lɪti¹/. EG *...a sense of shared commitment and conviviality.*
ADJ QUALIT ↑ sociable
▸ = jovial
◊ N UNCOUNT = geniality

convocation /kɒ̲nvəkeɪ̲ʃəⁿn/, **convocations**. The **convocation** of a large assembly is the act of arranging for it to be held; a formal word. EG *...the convocation of a constituent assembly.* ▸ A **convocation** is a large assembly. EG *It seemed a rather subdued convocation.*
N SING WITH DET : USU+*of* ↑ gathering = summoning
▸ N COUNT

convoluted /kɒ̲nvəluːtɪ²d/; a formal word. 1 Something that is **convoluted** has many twists or bends. EG *...a convoluted glass apparatus... ...a long and convoluted road.*
ADJ QUALIT ↑ curving ≠ straight

2 A **convoluted** sentence, argument, etc is complicated in structure and therefore difficult to understand. EG *...convoluted sentences... ...convoluted reasoning.*
ADJ QUALIT ↑ complex = tortuous

convolution /kɒ̲nvəluː̲ʃəⁿn/, **convolutions**. A **convolution** is one of the curves in an object or design that has many curves; a formal word. EG *The facade was startling in its baroque convolutions... ...the convolutions of the cortex.*
N COUNT : USU PL ↑ curve

convoy /kɒ̲nvɔɪ/, **convoys**. A **convoy** is a group of vehicles or ships travelling together. EG *The convoy of seven vehicles halted.... Three ships of the troop convoy were hit... ...one of eight trucks moving in convoy.*
N COUNT, OR *in*+N

convulse /kəˀnvʌ̲ls/, **convulses, convulsing, convulsed**; a formal word. 1 If a part of your body **convulses**, it moves suddenly or violently in a way that you cannot control. EG *His lungs convulsed from the sharpness and coldness of the air.* ◊ **convulsed**. EG *Her face was troubled, but no longer convulsed with anger... ...the convulsed twitching of her cheeks.*
V : IF+PREP THEN *from/with* = twitch
◊ ADJ CLASSIF : ATTRIB = contorted

2 If someone **convulses**, they have convulsions. EG *She was on her side convulsing.*
V

3 If you **convulse** someone, you greatly amuse them and make them laugh a lot. EG *...the man who convulsed many thousands with 'Blazing Saddles'.*
V+O : IF+PREP THEN *with*

convulsion /kəˀnvʌ̲lʃəⁿn/, **convulsions**. If someone has a **convulsion** or **convulsions**, they suffer violent and uncontrollable movements of their muscles. EG *A convulsion is a frightening thing to see in a child... The person loses consciousness completely and has convulsions.*
N COUNT/UNCOUNT : SING=PL ↑ movement = fit

convulsive /kəˀnvʌ̲lsɪv/. 1 A **convulsive** movement is a movement which is sudden and violent and which you cannot control. EG *Her hands clutched the blanket, then released it, in a convulsive movement... The man's fingers clutched John with a convulsive grasp.* ◊ **convulsively**. EG *He was crying, his thin shoulders shaking convulsively.*
ADJ CLASSIF = spasmodic
◊ ADV WITH VB = jerkily

2 A **convulsive** illness is an illness which causes you to suffer convulsions. EG *Many have convulsive disorders... ...convulsive asthma.*
ADJ CLASSIF

coo /kuː̲/, **coos, cooing, cooed**. 1 When a dove or pigeon makes a soft sound, it **coos**. EG *A pigeon was cooing in one of the elms.* ◊ **cooing**. EG *...the cooing of doves.*
V ↑ call
◊ N UNCOUNT

2 When someone **coos**, they speak in a very soft, quiet voice. EG *She rocked back and forth cooing endearments to her child... He lifted his blue eyes and cooed, 'I am Mr Hearst.'* ◊ **cooing**. EG *From the corridor came the cooing voices of the maids at work.*
V OR V+O/QUOTE = croon
◊ ADJ CLASSIF : ATTRIB

3 People sometimes say **coo** when they are surprised or impressed by something; used mainly in British English. EG *'Coo, hark at her,' said Derek.*
EXCLAM = cor

cook /kʊ̲k/, **cooks, cooking, cooked**. 1 When you **cook** food, you prepare it for eating by heating it in a particular way, for example by baking, boiling, or frying it. EG *We cooked the pie in the brick oven... The meat was beautifully cooked... Let the stew cook for an hour... Come on downstairs and cook us a bit of supper... I can't be bothered to cook for myself.* ◊ **cooked**. EG *You can get a wide range of cooked, frozen and fresh poultry.*
V-ERG OR V : ALSO V+O+O, OR V+O +A *(for)*
◊ ADJ CLASSIF ↑ prepared

2 A **cook** is a person who cooks and prepares food, often as his or her job. EG *Are you a good cook?... Margaret employed a daily cook and cleaner.* ● If you say **too many cooks** or **too many cooks spoil the broth**, you mean something is being done badly because there are too many people doing it.
N COUNT = chef
● PHR

3 If you say that something **is cooking**, you mean that something is being planned but you are not sure what it is; an informal use. EG *I was sure something was cooking.*
V : ONLY CONT ↑ happen = brew

4 If someone **cooks** something such as figures or a written record, they change it in order to deceive people; an informal use. EG *He's quite capable of cooking the evidence.*
V+O = doctor

5 If someone **cooks the books**, they change figures or a written record in order to deceive people; an informal expression used showing disapproval. EG *I reckon they've cooked the books.*
PHR : VB INFLECTS

6 See also **cooking**.

cook up. If someone **cooks up** a plan or a scheme, they invent a plan or scheme that is rather dishonest; an informal expression. EG *They tend to cook up all sorts of little deals.*
PHRASAL VB : V+O+ADV = concoct, devise

cookbook /kʊ̲kbʊk/, **cookbooks**. A **cookbook** is the same as a cookery book. EG *...The Working Wives' Cookbook.*
N COUNT

cooker /kʊ̲kə/, **cookers**. 1 A **cooker** is 1.1 a large metal box-shaped object in a kitchen, that you use for cooking food by gas or electricity. EG *The food was warming in a saucepan on the cooker... Mum has just won a microwave cooker.* 1.2 an apple that is suitable for cooking but not for eating raw; an informal use used mainly in British English. EG *Are those apples eaters or cookers?*
N COUNT ↑ appliance
N COUNT : USU PL

2 See also **pressure cooker**.

cookery /kʊ̲kəⁿri¹/ is the activity of cooking and preparing food. EG *Both boys and girls need aprons for cookery... She had never learnt French cookery.*
N UNCOUNT

cookery book, cookery books. A **cookery book** is a book that contains recipes for preparing food. EG *He could make a new dish without referring to any cookery book... ...the first vegetarian cookery book.*
N COUNT = cookbook

cookie /kʊ̲ki¹/, **cookies**. 1 A **cookie** is the same as a biscuit; used in American English. EG *She made a batch of her special oatmeal cookies.*
N COUNT

2 If something happens and you say **'that's the way the cookie crumbles'**, you mean that is what often happens in situations like this and we cannot do anything to change it; an informal expression.
CONVENTION = that's life

cooking /kʊ̲kɪŋ/. 1 **Cooking** is 1.1 the activity of preparing and cooking food. EG *Boys are just as keen on cooking as girls are.* 1.2 food that has been cooked and prepared for eating. EG *I like Portuguese cooking... You know how she loves your cooking.*
N UNCOUNT = cookery
N UNCOUNT+SUPP

2 **Cooking** oil, sherry, etc is oil, sherry, etc that is used for cooking. EG *...a rag moistened in cooking oil... You can use cheap cooking sherry in a trifle.*
ADJ CLASSIF : ATTRIB

cool /kuː̲l/, **cooler, coolest; cools, cooling, cooled**. 1 Something that is **cool** has a temperature that is low but not cold. EG *The room was cool and sweet-smelling... It was cool and dark inside the wood... ...a cool breeze... ...a long cool drink.* ▸ used as a noun. EG *...the relative cool of the rivers and beaches.* ◊ **coolness**. EG *...the sweet coolness of the night air.*
ADJ QUALIT = fresh ≠ hot, warm
▸ N SING : *the*+N
◊ N UNCOUNT = cool

2 A piece of clothing or a bed cover that is **cool** is made of material that keeps you cool in hot weather. EG *She sat down, her cool skirt ballooning in the breeze... Cellular blankets are cool in summer, warm in winter.*
ADJ CLASSIF ≠ warm

3 A colour that is **cool** gives you an impression of coolness. Greens and blues are sometimes thought to be cool. EG *...a cool green.*
ADJ CLASSIF : ATTRIB = fresh ≠ warm

4 When something **cools** or when you **cool** it, it becomes cooler. EG *Cover the bowl and allow the liquid to cool... He cooled his burning feet in the stream.* ◊ **cooling**. EG *...the rate of cooling... Let me fetch you a nice cooling glass of fruit cup.*
V-ERG
◊ N UNCOUNT, OR ADJ QUALIT

5 Behaviour that is **cool** is 5.1 calm and unemotional, rather than angry or excited. EG *The police drew praise for their cool handling of the riots... ...the cool proficiency of the professional.* ▸ used of people and groups. EG *...a tough, cool Virginian who had earlier served in Cuba.* ◊ **coolly**. EG *Eventually he answered coolly and collectedly.* ◊ **coolness**. EG *Her coolness*
ADJ QUALIT = relaxed
◊ ADV
◊ N UNCOUNT

and authority had completely conquered the audience. **5.2** unfriendly behaviour that is not welcoming or enthusiastic. EG *Should she be cool and withdrawn, or warm and welcoming?... Relations were cool and polite.* ▸ used of people and groups. EG *She was a silent girl, cool and remote.* ◇ **coolness.** EG *This second marriage caused a temporary coolness in the family... ...the Administration's coolness towards the idea of aid.* ADJ QUALIT = frigid ≠ welcoming ▸ = distant ◇ N UNCOUNT ≠ enthusiasm

6 When a feeling or an emotion **cools** or when you **cool** it, it becomes less powerful. EG *Her passion for Harold had begun to cool... She hoped that by Monday their tempers would have cooled.* V-ERG ⇑ reduce = abate

7 In informal English, you use **cool 7.1** in order to emphasize how good or marvellous you think something is. EG *Hey, that's really cool. Can I look?* **7.2** in order to emphasize that a sum of money is very large, especially when it has been acquired relatively easily. EG *She earned a cool £25,000 from that deal.* ADJ QUALIT = great ADJ CLASSIF: ATTRIB

8 The word **cool** is also used in the following informal expressions. **8.1** If, in a particular situation, you **play it cool**, you deliberately behave in a calm and unemotional way. EG *They agreed that they would play it cool if they saw the boys again.* **8.2** If you **keep** your **cool**, you control your temper and behave in a calm way. EG *For goodness sake, keep your cool!* **8.3** If you **lose** your **cool**, you become angry and behave in an excited way. EG *I was on the brink of losing my cool.* **8.4** If you tell someone to **cool it**, you want them to stop being angry and aggressive and to behave more calmly. EG *Just cool it and let them do the talking.* PHR : VB INFLECTS PHR : VB INFLECTS = keep calm PHR : VB INFLECTS CONVENTION = calm down

9 • to **cool** your **heels**: see **heel**.

cool down. 1 If something **cools down** or if you **cool** it **down**, it becomes cooler until it reaches the temperature that you want it to be. EG *The engine will take half an hour to cool down.* PHRASAL VB : V-ERG+ADV

2 If someone **cools down** or if you **cool** them **down**, they become less angry. EG *Tom had cooled down considerably... I had the greatest difficulty in cooling him down.* PHRASAL VB : V-ERG+ADV = calm down

cool off. If something or someone **cools off**, they become cooler until they reach their normal temperature. EG *We cooled off from the heat with a refreshing swim.* • See also **cooling-off period.** PHRASAL VB : V+ADV

coolant /ku:lənt/, **coolants.** A **coolant** is a liquid used to keep a machine cool while it is operating. EG *The accident happened when the coolant failed.* N COUNT/UNCOUNT

cooler /ku:lə/, **coolers.** A **cooler** is a container for keeping something cool, especially drinks. EG *He went below and took three cans from a cooler... ...a beer cooler.* N COUNT ⇑ device

coolie /ku:li¹/, **coolies. Coolies** were unskilled workers in China, India, and other parts of Asia; an old-fashioned and offensive word. N COUNT

cooling-off period, cooling-off periods. A **cooling-off period** is an agreed period of time during which unions and management will try to resolve a dispute before taking any serious action. EG *Our union is opposed to any cooling-off period.* N COUNT ⇑ pause

cooling tower, cooling towers. A **cooling tower** is a very large, round, high building in which the water used in a factory is cooled. EG *...giant cooling towers.* N COUNT

coop /ku:p/, **coops, cooping, cooped.** A **coop** is a cage where you keep small animals or birds such as chickens, rabbits, etc. EG *The boys had made some really fine coops and runs... ...chicken coops.* N COUNT

coop up. If you **coop up** a person or an animal, you keep them in a building, room, cage, etc that is too small for them. EG *There's no need to coop ourselves up any longer... ...a prisoner cooped up in a cell... How would you like to be cooped up in a cage like that?* PHRASAL VB : V+O+ADV, USU PASS +A ⇑ confine = shut up

co-op /kəuɒp/, **co-ops.** A **co-op** is **1** a business such as a factory, shop, or farm which is jointly owned by the people who run it; an abbreviation for 'co-operative'. EG *They formed a co-op.* **2** a commercial organization with several shops in a particular district. Customers can join this organization and get a share of its profits; an abbreviation for 'co-operative society'. EG *She served at the Co-op... ...the Co-op bread van.* N COUNT N COUNT

co-operate /kəuɒpəreɪt/, **co-operates, co-operating, co-operated**; also spelled as one word. **1** If people **co-operate**, they work or act together for a purpose. EG *Japan is likely to co-operate with Australia... The entire work force co-operated with the management and the police... The editors agreed to co-operate.* ◇ **co-operation** /kəuɒpəreɪʃə⁰n/. EG *There is an urgent need for more co-operation between the sellers... ...talks on economic cooperation.* V, OR V+A (with) : RECIP ◇ N UNCOUNT = collaboration

2 If you **co-operate**, you help someone willingly when they ask you for your help. EG *I wish you'd cooperate instead of sitting there sulking!... I couldn't get the RAF to cooperate.* ◇ **co-operation.** EG *He asked for police cooperation... Thank you for your co-operation.* V ◇ N UNCOUNT = assistance

co-operative /kəuɒpə⁰rətɪv/, **co-operatives**; also spelled as one word. **1** A **co-operative** is a business such as a factory, shop, or farm which is jointly owned by the people who run it. EG *The greatest period of expansion for co-operatives was in the 1960s... ...a workers' cooperative.* N COUNT

2 A **co-operative** activity is an activity done by people working together. EG *We involve them in co-operative exercises... ...proposals for cooperative enterprises.* ◇ **cooperatively.** EG *The work is carried on co-operatively.* ADJ CLASSIF ⇑ shared = joint ◇ ADV WITH VB = jointly

3 Behaviour which is **co-operative** is behaviour in which someone helps you willingly when you ask them for their help. EG *The Swiss authorities had been very cooperative... Most co-operative of you, Doctor!* ▸ used of people and groups. EG *Parents hope to raise children who are considerate and co-operative.* ◇ **co-operatively.** EG *The nurse pushed me, and I rolled over cooperatively.* ADJ QUALIT ⇑ helpful = accommodating ≠ uncooperative ◇ ADV WITH VB = obligingly

co-operative society, co-operative societies. In Britain, a **co-operative society** is a commercial organization with several shops in a particular district. Customers can join this organization and get a share of its profits. EG *He was on the side of the little trader and against the co-operative society... ...The Royal Arsenal Co-operative Society.* N COUNT = co-op

co-opt /kəuɒpt/, **co-opts, co-opting, co-opted.** If the members of a committee or other organization **co-opt** you, they vote to make you a member of their committee or organization; a formal word. EG *Committees can always co-opt members... I suggest that you be co-opted as one of our directors.* ◇ **co-option** /kəuɒpʃə⁰n/. EG *I was a natural for co-option into the team.* V+O : IF+PREP THEN *as/into/onto* ◇ N UNCOUNT

co-ordinate, co-ordinates, co-ordinating, co-ordinated; also spelled as one word. The word **co-ordinate** is pronounced /kəuɔ:dɪneɪt/ when it is a verb, and /kəuɔ:dɪnət/ when it is a noun. **1** If you **co-ordinate** a project or activity, you organize the people taking part in it and to make sure that they work together properly. EG *She was able to co-ordinate the activities of all the emergency services... They were asked to help coordinate and plan Labour's election campaign.* ◇ **co-ordinated.** EG *...a co-ordinated missile onslaught.* ◇ **co-ordination** /kəuɔ:dɪneɪʃə⁰n/. EG *There should be greater co-ordination between doctors and biologists.* V+O ⇑ control ◇ ADJ QUALIT ◇ N UNCOUNT : IF+PREP THEN *between*

2 To **co-ordinate** the movements of parts of your body means to make the parts work together in order to perform particular actions. EG *The children could not co-ordinate their movements... This part of the brain co-ordinates the muscles of the mouth.* ◇ **co-ordination.** EG *Your child is very advanced in her bodily strength and co-ordination... Claudia was losing her coordination, stumbling over her equipment.* V+O ⇑ control = regulate ◇ N UNCOUNT ⇑ control

3 A **co-ordinate** is one of a pair of numbers or letters that indicate a particular point on a map or a graph; a technical term in mathematics. EG *The flight coordinates were altered at the last moment.* N COUNT : USU PL ⇑ reference

coordinating conjunction /kəuɔ:dɪneɪtɪŋ kəndʒʌŋkʃə⁰n/, **coordinating conjunctions.** A **coordinating conjunction** is, in grammar, a word which joins two words, groups, or clauses of the same quality or type, for example EG *and* in *Jack and Jill* and *but* in *The weather will be mainly sunny but showers will develop in the late afternoon.* Words which are coordinating conjunctions have CONJ COORD in the grammar note beside the entry. See CONJ COORD. N COUNT ⇑ conjunction

co-ordinator /kəuɔ:dɪneɪtə/, **co-ordinators.** The **co-ordinator** of a project or activity is a person who organizes the people taking part in the project or activity and makes sure that they work together properly. EG *...the co-ordinator of a project in Cornwall.* N COUNT : IF+PREP THEN *of* ⇑ organizer

coot /kuːt/, **coots**. A **coot** is **1** a water bird with black feathers and a white patch on its forehead. **2** a foolish person; used in old-fashioned British English. EG *...you silly old coot.* — N COUNT; N COUNT : USU MOD+N, ALSO VOC

cop /kɒp/, **cops, copping, copped**; an informal word. **1** A **cop** is a policeman or policewoman. — N COUNT

2 If you ask someone to **cop hold** of something, you want them to take hold of it; used in British English. EG *Cop hold of the other end.* — PHR : VB INFLECTS, USU+ of = grab hold

3 If you **cop** something unpleasant, it happens to you. — V+O

4 If you **cop it**, you are punished or scolded by someone for doing something wrong. EG *You'll cop it if your mum finds out.* — PHR : VB INFLECTS = catch it

5 If you say that something is **not much cop**, you mean that it is poor or disappointing; used in British English. EG *This is not much cop–what's on the other channels?.* — PHR : USED AS C = lousy

cop out. If you **cop out** of something that you ought to do, you avoid doing it because you are afraid or because it would be difficult or embarrassing; used showing disapproval. EG *He copped out of it at the last minute.* ● See also **cop-out**. — PHRASAL VB : V+ ADV, IF+PREP THEN of = duck out

cope /kəʊp/, **copes, coping, coped**. **1** If you **cope** with a task or a difficulty, you deal with it successfully. EG *...my inability to cope adequately with broadcasts or lectures... She had enough difficulties without having to cope with financial ones... They can no longer cope.* — V : USU+with = manage

2 If you **cope** with an unpleasant situation, you accept it or endure it. EG *We must try to cope with our own failure... Poor families have to cope with a lot of strain.* — V : USU+with = contend

3 If a machine or a system can **cope** with something, it is large enough or complex enough to deal with it satisfactorily. EG *...a computer capable of coping with domestic requirements... School systems have to cope with changing numbers of pupils.* — V : USU+with

4 A **cope** is a long cloak worn by some Christian priests on special occasions. — N COUNT

5 See also **coping**.

copier /kɒpɪə/, **copiers**. A **copier** is a machine which makes exact copies of writing or pictures on paper, usually by a photographic process. EG *We've got a small xerox copier.* — N COUNT

co-pilot, co-pilots; also spelled as one word. The **co-pilot** of an aeroplane is a pilot who assists the chief pilot and who sometimes flies the aeroplane. EG *Kontarsky sat behind the pilot and co-pilot.* — N COUNT

coping /kəʊpɪŋ/, **copings**. A **coping** is a layer of sloping or rounded bricks on the top of a wall. — N COUNT/ UNCOUNT

copious /kəʊpɪəs/. Something that is **copious** exists or is produced in large amounts or numbers. EG *Plants need good soil and copious sunshine... She took copious notes.* ◊ **copiously**. EG *Picasso was producing paintings copiously even when he was an old man... He cried copiously.* — ADJ QUALIT ⇑ plentiful = abundant ≠ sparse; ◊ ADV WITH VB ⇑ plentifully

cop-out, cop-outs. If you describe something as a **cop-out**, you mean that you think it is a way for someone to avoid doing something that they ought to do; an informal word used showing disapproval. EG *Such international co-operation is often merely a cop-out.* — N COUNT : USU a +N IN SING, USED AS C ⇑ evasion

copper /kɒpə/, **coppers**. **1 Copper** is a soft, reddish brown metal. EG *...a ship loaded with copper... ...a piece of copper wire.* ▸ **Copper** also means the colour of copper. EG *...her glossy copper hair.* — N UNCOUNT; ▸ ADJ COLOUR

2 A **copper** is **2.1** a brown metal coin of low value. EG *He fumbled in his pocket and brought out some coppers.* **2.2** a policeman or policewoman; used in informal British English. EG *You'd better wait till the coppers turn up.* **2.3** a large metal container in which you boil water. — N COUNT : USU PL; N COUNT = cop; N COUNT

copper beech, copper beeches. A **copper beech** is a tree with reddish-brown leaves. — N COUNT

copperplate /kɒpəpleɪt/; also spelled with a hyphen. **Copperplate** is a very neat and regular style of handwriting, in which letters are formed with a lot of loops. EG *It was written in her beautiful flowing copper-plate hand.* — N UNCOUNT

coppice /kɒpɪs/, **coppices**. A **coppice** is a small group of trees growing very close to each other. EG *...a neglected coppice... ...coppices of alders, aspens and birches.* — N COUNT = copse

cops and robbers is a children's game in which one group pretends to be thieves and another group pretends to be policemen trying to catch them. EG *...children playing at cops and robbers.* — N UNCOUNT

copse /kɒps/, **copses**. A **copse** is a small group of trees growing very close to each other. EG *The road was flanked with fields and copses.* — N COUNT = coppice

Coptic /kɒptɪk/ means belonging or relating to the Coptic Church. EG *The Coptic Pope is chosen by his own Church.* — ADJ CLASSIF : ATTRIB ⇑ Christian

Coptic Church. The **Coptic Church** is a part of the Christian Church which was founded in Egypt. — N PROPER : the+N

copula /kɒpjə⁴lə/, **copulas**. **Copula** is a term used in grammar for verbs which take a complement. The main copula is the verb 'be'. In this dictionary verbs that take complements are described as V+C. See □ at V+C. — N COUNT ⇑ verb

copulate /kɒpjə⁴leɪt/, **copulates, copulating, copulated**. If you **copulate** with someone, you have sex with them. Copulate is a technical term when you use it about animals, and usually a literary or formal word when you use it about people. EG *They copulate and the male fertilizes the female's eggs.* ◊ **copulation** /kɒpjə⁴leɪʃəⁿn/. EG *...the act of copulation.* — V OR V+A (with) : RECIP = couple; ◊ N UNCOUNT = sex

copy /kɒpi¹/, **copies, copying, copied**. **1** A **copy** is something that is made to look exactly the same as something else. EG *I will send you a copy of the letter... ...send a copy of the driving licence.* ● See also **carbon copy**. — N COUNT ⇑ reproduction = duplicate

2 If you **copy** something that someone has written or **copy** it **down** or **copy** it **out**, you write it down exactly as it was written before. EG *Barbara had written a comment she had copied from one of his notes... I shouldn't bother to copy these equations down... I remember copying out the whole play.* — V+O, OR PHRASAL VB : V+ O+ADV ⇑ write down = transcribe

3 If you **copy** something that someone has written, you cheat by looking at it during a test or an examination, and by writing it down yourself. EG *Please Miss, he's copying... The desks are spaced out so that they can't copy each other's work.* — V OR V+O

4 To **copy** something also means to make a copy of it, for example using a machine. EG *I copied this report on the photocopier.* — V+O = duplicate

5 If you **copy** someone or something, you do what they do or try to be like them, for example by moving, behaving, or dressing in the same way. EG *She danced and made me copy her... He tried to copy their style in his own clothes... Our scheme has since been copied by other universities.* — V+O = imitate

6 A **copy** is also one book, magazine, record, etc of which there are many others exactly the same. EG *Buy a copy of Do It Yourself Magazine... Most public libraries will have a copy... Sixty thousand copies of the record were sold.* ● See also **back copy**. — N COUNT

7 Copy is **7.1** written material that is ready to be printed. EG *I started setting more complicated copy... To my relief she found the copy acceptable.* **7.2** news or information that you can use as an article in a newspaper. EG *That story will make good copy.* **7.3** written material used in advertisements. EG *...a copy supervisor.* — N UNCOUNT; N UNCOUNT; N UNCOUNT

copybook /kɒpibʊk/. **1 Copybook** means done perfectly according to established rules. EG *The pilot made a copybook landing.* — ADJ CLASSIF : ATTRIB ⇑ perfect

2 If you **blot** your **copybook**, you spoil your good reputation by making a bad mistake or by doing something wrong. EG *I'd blotted my copybook by marrying without my father's approval... I can't have you blotting your copybook having punch-ups with students.* — PHR : VB INFLECTS

copycat /kɒpi¹kæt/, **copycats**. If you call someone a **copycat**, you are accusing them of copying your behaviour, dress, etc; an informal word, usually used humorously. — N COUNT : ALSO VOC ⇑ imitator

copyright /kɒpi¹raɪt/, **copyrights**. The **copyright** on a book, piece of music, etc is the legal right of its author, composer, or publisher to be the only person who is allowed to reproduce it. EG *The publishers have the copyright on the book... Copyright, W.R. Hearst.* — N UNCOUNT/ COUNT ⇑ right

copywriter /kɒpi¹raɪtə/, **copywriters**. A **copywriter** is a person who writes the words for advertisements. — N COUNT ⇑ writer

coquetry /kəʊki²tri¹, kɒk-/. **Coquetry** is coquettish behaviour; a formal or literary word. — N UNCOUNT = flirtatious

coquette /kəʊket, kɒket/, **coquettes**. A **coquette** is a woman who behaves in a coquettish way. EG *She's a bit of a coquette.* — N COUNT = flirt

coquettish /kəketɪʃ/. **Coquettish** behaviour is behaviour in which a woman acts in a playful way that — ADJ QUALIT = coy

is intended to make men find her attractive; a formal or literary word. EG *She gave a coquettish smile.* ▸ used also of women themselves. EG *Whenever she talked to Peter, she became very coquettish and feminine.* ◇ **coquettishly**. EG *She looked at him coquettishly.*
▸ = flirtatious
◇ ADV WITH VB = teasingly

cor /kɔ:/. You say **cor** when you are surprised or impressed; used mainly in British English. ● **cor blimey** is a rather old-fashioned expression that people used in order to express surprise.
EXCLAM
● EXCLAM = good heavens

coracle /kɒrəkə⁰l/, **coracles**. A **coracle** is a simple round rowing boat made of woven sticks covered with animal skins.
N COUNT

coral /kɒrə⁰l/, **corals**. 1 **Coral** is a hard substance that forms in the sea from the skeletons of very small animals. It is used to make jewellery. EG *The trigger fish feeds on coral... ...a coral necklace.*
N UNCOUNT

2 A **coral** is one of the very small sea animals whose skeletons form coral. EG *Each species of coral has its own pattern of growth... ...primitive creatures like jellyfish and corals.*
N COUNT ⇑ animal

3 Something that is **coral** in colour is a dark orangey pink. EG *...Charlotte's coral lips.*
ADJ COLOUR

coral reef, coral reefs. A **coral reef** is a ridge of coral and other substances, the top of which is usually just above or just below the surface of the sea. EG *...the butterfly fish that live on the coral reef.*
N COUNT

cor anglais /kɔ:r⁰ ɑ:ŋgleɪ/, **cors anglais**. A **cor anglais** is a woodwind instrument with a double reed. It is slightly lower in pitch than an oboe; used in British English.
N COUNT = English horn

corbel /kɔ:bə⁰l/, **corbels**. A **corbel** is a piece of stone or wood sticking out of a wall and supporting an arch, pillar, or beam. EG *There were grotesque corbel heads at the base of the arches.*
N COUNT ⇑ bracket = truss

cord /kɔ:d/, **cords**. 1 A **cord** is 1.1 a thick strong string. EG *She tied a cord around her box... Use picture wire or nylon cord to hang pictures.* 1.2 a wire covered in protective material and attached to electrical equipment in order to connect the equipment to the electricity supply. EG *...a small electric heater on a long cord.*
N COUNT/UNCOUNT
N COUNT ⇑ cable = flex

2 **Cords** are trousers made of corduroy. EG *She wore her beige cords.*
N PLURAL: ALSO *a pair of*+N

3 **Cord** means made of corduroy or of a material that looks like corduroy. EG *...a cord carpet.*
ADJ CLASSIF: ATTRIB ⇑ cloth

4 See also **spinal cord, umbilical cord, vocal cords, sash cord.**

cordial /kɔ:dɪəl/, **cordials**. 1 Behaviour that is **cordial** is warm and friendly. EG *They seemed to be on cordial terms... Mr Paget's tone did not sound particularly cordial.* ◇ **cordially**. EG *She shook hands very cordially with Charley Penfold.* ◇ **cordiality** /kɔ:dɪælɪti¹/. EG *My hostess greeted me with unexpected cordiality.*
ADJ QUALIT = affable
◇ ADV WITH VB
◇ N UNCOUNT = warmth

2 **Cordial** dislike or hatred is strong dislike or hatred; a formal use. EG *I developed a cordial dislike for the place.* ◇ **cordially** EG *We all cordially detest the management... She is cordially hated by most farmers in the UK.*
ADJ CLASSIF: ATTRIB
◇ ADV WITH VB = heartily

3 A **cordial** is a sweet non-alcoholic drink partly made from fruit juice; used in British English. EG *How about a cordial?*
N COUNT/UNCOUNT

cordite /kɔ:daɪt/ is an explosive substance used in guns and bombs. EG *...the acrid smell of cordite.*
N UNCOUNT

cordon /kɔ:də⁰n/, **cordons, cordoning, cordoned**. A **cordon** is a line or ring of police, soldiers, or vehicles preventing people from entering an area. EG *The crowd attempted to break through the police cordons.*
N COUNT ⇑ barrier

cordon off. If the police or soldiers **cordon off** an area, they prevent people from entering it by putting a cordon round it or in front of it. EG *They cordoned off the entire block... The area round the office had been cordoned off.*
PHRASAL VB: V+O+ADV ⇑ separate = close off

cordon bleu /kɔ:dɒn blɜ:/ is used to describe cookery or cooks of the highest standard. EG *...a cordon bleu cook.*
ADJ CLASSIF: ATTRIB

corduroy /kɔ:də⁰rɔɪ/, **corduroys**. 1 Corduroy is a thick cotton cloth with parallel raised lines on one side. EG *We can supply anything you like in crepe, satin, or corduroy... ...a black corduroy waistcoat.*
N UNCOUNT

2 **Corduroys** are trousers made of corduroy or needlecord; used in old-fashioned English.
N PLURAL: ALSO *a pair of*+N

core /kɔ:/, **cores, coring, cored**. 1 The **core** of a fruit is its hard central part which contains seeds or pips. EG *Take the core out with a small knife... She finished her apple and threw the core away.*
N COUNT ⇑ centre

2 When you **core** a fruit, you remove its core. EG *Wash and core four large cooking apples.*
V+O

3 The **core** of an object or a place is its central part. EG *The planet probably has a molten core... ...the core of Boston between Beacon Hill and the waterfront.*
N COUNT: USU+SUPP ⇑ centre = heart

4 A **core** is also a group of people or things that is always part of something, although the other parts may change. EG *...a student body led by a core of theoreticians and academics... Each child studies four core subjects.*
N SING WITH DET: ALSO N+*of*+N IN PL

5 The **core** of something such as a problem or a proposal is its most essential part; a formal use. EG *...the core of industry's problems in the Third World... They could not approve a programme so flawed at its core.*
N SING WITH DET: USU+SUPP ⇑ essence = heart

6 If you are conservative, socialist, etc **to the core**, you are thoroughly conservative, socialist, etc, in your views and judgements and are never likely to be anything else; a formal expression. EG *...a socialist to the core.*
PHR: C+PHR = through and through

7 If something affects you **to the core**, it affects you very strongly; a formal expression. EG *I was shaken to the core.*
PHR: USED AS AN A

coriander /kɒrɪændə/ is a plant with seeds that are used as a spice and leaves that are used as a herb. EG *Coriander grows wild in a few scattered places.* ▸ used also of the spice and the herb. EG *...a dessertspoonful of ground coriander.*
N UNCOUNT

cork /kɔ:k/, **corks, corking, corked**. 1 **Cork** is a very light, sponge-like substance that is the bark of a Mediterranean tree. It is used for making many things, especially mats and stoppers for bottles. EG *...cork table mats.*
N UNCOUNT

2 A **cork** is a piece of cork or plastic that is used for blocking the open end of a bottle. EG *He took the cork out of the bottle... ...champagne corks.*
N COUNT ⇑ stopper

3 To **cork** a bottle or to **cork** it **up** means to seal it by putting a cork in it. EG *Let Miss Drew have what she wants; then cork up the bottle.*
V+O, OR PHRASAL VB: V+O+ADV ⇑ close

corkscrew /kɔ:kskru:/, **corkscrews**. A **corkscrew** is a device used for pulling corks out of bottles. It has a twisted metal rod with a point that you push into the cork and a handle which you pull to remove the cork. EG *Tony pulled out a bottle of wine and a corkscrew from his bag.*
N COUNT ⇑ opener

cormorant /kɔ:mərənt/, **cormorants**. A **cormorant** is a dark-coloured bird with a long neck. Cormorants catch fish by diving into the sea. EG *...a Byzantine mosaic depicting cormorants and herons.*
N COUNT = shag

corn /kɔ:n/, **corns**. 1 In British English, **corn** refers to 1.1 crops such as wheat and barley that are grown in fields so that their seeds can be used for food. EG *We used to graze sheep on the fields where the corn is now... A mouse was peeping out from behind a sheaf of corn.* 1.2 the seeds from plants such as wheat and barley. They are used to feed animals, and are eaten by people, especially after they have been made into flour and bread. EG *A brown hen was pecking around for grains of corn... ...the effort to open overseas corn markets.*
N UNCOUNT
N UNCOUNT = grain

2 In American English, **corn** also means the same as maize. EG *...corn bread.*
N UNCOUNT

3 A **corn** is a piece of hard skin which forms on part of your foot, especially near your toes, and which can be painful. EG *He had a bad corn on his left foot.*
N COUNT ⇑ growth

cornea /kɔ:nɪə/, **corneas**. The **cornea** is the curved transparent skin that covers the outside of your eye.
N COUNT ⇑ covering

corned beef is beef which has been cooked and preserved in salt or salt water.
N UNCOUNT ⇑ meat

corner /kɔ:nə/, **corners, cornering, cornered**. 1 A **corner** of something is a point or an area where two or more of its edges, sides, or surfaces join. EG *He signed his name on the lower right-hand corner of the drawing... Melanie raised the corner of the table cloth... Our sand castle had a tower at each corner.*
N COUNT ⇑ angle

2 The **corner** of a room, box, etc is the area or space inside it near the place where two or three surfaces or edges meet. EG *There was a television set in the corner of the room... Brody tossed his shoes into a corner... ...a corner seat.* ▸ also used to refer to the corner of a boxing ring where a boxer sits between rounds.
N COUNT: IF+PREP THEN *of* ⇑ angle
▸ N COUNT

3 The **corner** of your mouth or eye is the side of it. EG *'Of course,' said the man out of the corner of his mouth... Out of the corner of my eye I caught a glimpse of two men in uniform.* N COUNT+*of*

4 A **corner** is also 4.1 a place where two streets join, especially one where there is a building. EG *There's a telephone box on the corner... ...the police station at the corner of the High Street... ...a corner house.* N COUNT : IF+ PREP THEN *of* 4.2 a sharp bend in a road or a bend that you cannot see round. EG *The lorry took the corner too fast... Suddenly Terry appeared around the corner.* N COUNT : IF+ PREP THEN *of*

5 A **corner** of the world or of a country is a place that is far away or difficult to get to. EG *You have carried Britain's fame to the remotest corners of the earth... Reporters swarmed into the city from almost every corner of the world.* N COUNT+SUPP : USU PL+*of*

6 In football or hockey, a **corner** is a free kick or shot, taken from the corner of the field. N COUNT

7 **Corner** is also used in expressions such as 'to force someone into a corner' and 'to be in a tight corner'. They refer to a situation that is difficult to escape from or deal with. EG *The unions have forced him into a corner... She didn't interrupt, happy for Laing to talk himself into a corner... I've been in some pretty tight corners in my time.* N COUNT : IF SING a+N, USED AFTER *in/into* = predicament

8 If you **corner** a person or animal, you get them into a place or situation which they cannot easily escape from. EG *The police pursued and cornered the wrong car... Josie cornered Mildred later on in the washroom.* ◊ **cornered**. EG *...a cornered animal... She had me cornered between the front porch and her car.* V+O = trap ◊ ADJ CLASSIF = trapped

9 If a car **corners** in a particular way, it goes round bends in the road in this way. EG *It's not a powerful car but it corners well.* V+A ⇑ go

10 If you **corner** a market or some other area of activity, you gain control over it so that no one else can have any success in that area. EG *He had a crazy scheme to corner the champagne market... The Japanese have cornered a third of all the contracts so far.* V+O = monopolize

11 If you **make a corner in** a particular commodity, you get control of the supply of that commodity. EG *She made a corner in millionaires.* PHR : VB INFLECTS

12 If you **cut the corner** of an area of land, you go diagonally across the corner rather than going along its edges, in order to save time. EG *They always cut the corner instead of using the path.* PHR : VB AND N INFLECT

13 If you **cut corners**, you do or make something quickly and simply by not following the proper procedure or rules. EG *You can't cut corners if you want your wine to be of the best quality.* PHR : VB INFLECTS

14 If something is **just around the corner**, it is 14.1 very nearby. EG *Diana and Nick lived just round the corner.* PHR : USED AS AN A 14.2 about to happen or be experienced very soon; a fairly informal use. EG *Hoover was saying that prosperity was just around the corner.* PHR : USED AS AN A ⇑ imminent

15 If you **turn the corner**, you begin to make a recovery from a serious illness or a difficult time. PHR : VB INFLECTS

corner shop, corner shops. A **corner shop** is a small shop, usually on the corner of a street, that sells mainly food and household goods. N COUNT

cornerstone /kɔːnəstəun/, **cornerstones**. 1 The **cornerstone** of something is the part or thing which its existence, success, or truth depends on. EG *Mathematics is the cornerstone of scientific certainty... The family and stable relationships will still be the cornerstones of our society.* N COUNT+SUPP : USU+*of* ⇑ basis = keystone

2 A **cornerstone** is a stone at one of the bottom corners of a building, especially one which is put in position in an official ceremony. N COUNT ⇑ stone

cornet /kɔːnɪ²t/, **cornets**. A **cornet** is 1 a small trumpet. EG *He played the cornet in the school band.* N COUNT ⇑ instrument 2 an ice cream in a soft thin biscuit shaped like a cone. N COUNT

cornfield /kɔːnfiːld/, **cornfields**. A **cornfield** is a field in which corn is being grown. N COUNT ⇑ field

cornflake /kɔːnfleɪk/, **cornflakes**. **Cornflakes** are a breakfast cereal of flakes made from maize, eaten with milk and sometimes sugar. EG *... a bowl of cornflakes... ...cornflakes packets.* N COUNT : USU PL

cornflour /kɔːnflauə/ is a fine white flour made from maize and used in cooking to thicken soups, gravy and sauces. N UNCOUNT

cornflower /kɔːnflauə/, **cornflowers**. A **cornflower** is a small plant with bright flowers, usually blue in colour. N COUNT

cornice /kɔːnɪs/, **cornices**. A **cornice** is a strip of plaster, wood, or stone which goes along the top of a wall or building. N COUNT

Cornish /kɔːnɪʃ/. Something that is **Cornish** comes from or is connected with the county of Cornwall. EG *...the Cornish countryside.* ADJ CLASSIF

Cornish pasty, Cornish pasties. A **Cornish pasty** is a flat semicircular pie with meat and vegetables inside it. N COUNT

corn on the cob, corn on the cobs. **Corn on the cob** is the long round part of the maize plant which has sweet corn on it and is eaten as a vegetable. N UNCOUNT/ COUNT

cornucopia /kɔːnjukəupɪə/. A **cornucopia** of good things is a large number of them which are available for you; a formal word, sometimes used humorously. EG *There was a positive cornucopia of fish fingers on my plate.* N SING WITH DET +*of* = abundance

corny /kɔːni¹/, **cornier, corniest**. Something that is **corny** is very obvious or sentimental and not at all subtle or original; used showing disapproval. EG *A red rose! How corny can you get?... Ben loves corny old jokes.* ADJ QUALIT

corollary /kərɒləri¹/, **corollaries**. A **corollary** of something is an idea, argument, or fact which is the direct result of it; a formal word. EG *Yet this change is the inevitable corollary of the social revolution I have just described.* N COUNT : IF+ PREP THEN *of/to* = consequence

corona /kərəunə/, **coronas**. A **corona** is 1 the circle of light that you can sometimes see around the moon at night, or around the sun during an eclipse; a technical term. N COUNT 2 a long cigar with flat ends. N COUNT

coronary /kɒrənə⁰ri¹/, **coronaries**. A **coronary** or a **coronary attack** is a sudden and sometimes fatal illness in which the flow of blood to your heart is blocked by a large blood clot. EG *He died of a massive coronary... He was in a serious condition after a coronary attack.* N COUNT = heart attack

coronary thrombosis, coronary thromboses. A **coronary thrombosis** is the same as a coronary; a medical term. EG *...the increased incidence of coronary thrombosis.* N UNCOUNT/ COUNT

coronation /kɒrəneɪʃə⁰n/, **coronations**. A **coronation** is the ceremony at which a king or queen is crowned. EG *...the coronation of Queen Elizabeth.* N COUNT = crowning

coroner /kɒrənə/, **coroners**. A **coroner** is an official who is responsible for investigating the deaths of people who have died in a sudden, violent, or unusual way. EG *The death has been reported to the coroner.* N COUNT : USU SING, *the*+N

coronet /kɒrənɪ²t/, **coronets**. A **coronet** is a small crown, especially one worn by princes or peers on formal occasions. N COUNT

Corp. is a written abbreviation for 'corporation' and 'corporal', in names and titles.

corpora /kɔːpərə/ is the plural of **corpus**.

corporal /kɔːpə⁰rəl/, **corporals**. A **corporal** is a non-commissioned officer in the army, with the rank immediately below that of sergeant. N COUNT : ALSO IN TITLES BEFORE NAME

corporal punishment is the practice of punishing people by beating or caning them. EG *She condemns any form of corporal punishment.* N UNCOUNT ⇑ punishment

corporate /kɔːpə⁰rɪt/. 1 **Corporate** means 1 relating to business corporations. EG *Take-over fever is gripping corporate America again. ...corporate bosses.* ADJ CLASSIF : ATTRIB 2 shared by all the members of a group or organization, rather than being done or possessed individually. EG *We tend to think of industries as if they had a corporate existence... ...a corporate identity.* ADJ CLASSIF : ATTRIB = collective ◊ **corporately**. EG *Let me explain how mankind, individually and corporately, should live.* ◊ ADV = collectively

corporation /kɔːpəreɪʃə⁰n/, **corporations**. A **corporation** is 1 a large business or company, or a group of companies that are all controlled and run together as a single organization. EG *...the British Aircraft Corporation... She worked for a large corporation.* N COUNT : ALSO IN NAMES AFTER N 2 in British English, the organization that is responsible for running a particular town or city and looking after the people who live there. EG *A petition was sent from the mayor and corporation... ...an Ipswich Corporation bus conductor.* N COUNT : IF SING, VB CAN BE SING OR PL = council

corporation tax is a tax that companies have to pay on the profits they make. N UNCOUNT

corporeal /kɔːpɔːrɪəl/ means involving or relating to the physical world rather than the spiritual world; a formal word. EG *...corporeal existence.* ADJ CLASSIF : USU ATTRIB ≠ spiritual

corps /kɔː/. **Corps** is both the singular and the plural form. A **corps** is 1 a part of the army which has N COUNT

special duties. EG ...*the Royal Army Ordnance Corps.*
2 a small group of people who have been specially organized or trained for a particular purpose. EG ...*the White House press corps... ...the diplomatic corps.* ● See also **esprit de corps**. — N COUNT+SUPP: USU SING

corpse /kɔ:ps/, **corpses**. A **corpse** is a dead body, especially the body of a human being. — N COUNT = body

corpulence /kɔ:pjə⁴ləns/ is the condition of being fat; a formal word. EG *Corpulence is often associated with high blood pressure.* — N UNCOUNT = obesity

corpulent /kɔ:pjə⁴lənt/. Someone who is **corpulent** is fat or plump; a formal word. EG *He had grown corpulent... ...his corpulent figure.* — ADJ QUALIT

corpus /kɔ:pəs/, **corpora, corpuses**. The plural can be either **corpora** or **corpuses**. **1** A **corpus** is a large number of articles, books, magazines, etc that have been deliberately collected together for some purpose; a formal or technical word. EG *We have been trying to collect a corpus of listening comprehension materials... ...that classic corpus of law, the Code Napoleon.* — N COUNT ⇑ collection = body
2 See also **habeas corpus**.

corpuscle /kɔ:pʌsə⁰l/, **corpuscles**. A **corpuscle** is a red or white blood cell; a technical term. — N COUNT

corral /kə⁷rɑ:l/, **corrals, corralling, corralled**. **1** A **corral** is a space surrounded by a fence where cattle or horses are kept, for example on a ranch or farm, in the United States. — N COUNT ⇑ enclosure
2 To **corral** cattle or horses means to drive them into a corral and keep them there. EG *Three thousand ponies were coralled along the stream.* — V+O ⇑ enclose

correct /kərekt/, **corrects, correcting, corrected**. **1** Something that is **correct** is accurate, in accordance with the facts, and without any mistakes. EG *That's the correct answer... I think your suspicions are entirely correct... 'You're referring to the President?'-'That's correct'.* ◊ **correctly**. EG *I hope I pronounced his name correctly... You correctly predicted the result.* ◊ **correctness**. EG *This confirmed the correctness of my decision.* — ADJ CLASSIF ≠ incorrect, wrong; ◊ ADV WITH VB = accurately; ◊ N UNCOUNT
2 If you are **correct**, you have said or thought something that is in accordance with the facts. EG *Jenkins is correct. We've got to change our strategy.* — ADJ CLASSIF: PRED ≠ wrong
3 The **correct** thing is the one that is required or most suitable in a particular situation. EG *Make sure you ask for the correct fuse... They have adopted the correct course of action.* ◊ **correctly**. EG *Rice, correctly cooked and prepared, is delicious.* — ADJ CLASSIF: ATTRIB = right, appropriate; ◊ ADV WITH VB = properly
4 If you **correct** something such as a mistake, you do or say something which puts it right. EG *I wish to correct a false impression which may have been created... He had asked her to correct his English.* — V+O = put right
5 If you **correct** someone, you say something which you think is more accurate or appropriate than what they have just said. EG *'How do you do, sir?'-'Phil,' he corrected me... 'I did not say we were not allowed to act,' corrected Frey... 'I'm a fighter like your dad is-or was,' Mr Cupples corrected himself.* — V+O (NG/REFL), V+QUOTE, OR V+O (NG/REFL)+QUOTE ● You say **'correct me if I'm wrong'** to indicate that you are not sure if what you are going to say is true. EG *I suspect-though correct me if I'm wrong-that things are beginning to change.* — ● PHR: USED AS ADV SEN ● You say **'I stand corrected'** to show that you accept that what you have just said was a mistake, when someone has informed you of this; a formal expression. EG *'Actually it was Churchill who said that.'-'I stand corrected.'* — ● PHR
6 When someone **corrects** a piece of writing, especially school work, they look at it and mark the mistakes in it. EG *Miss Lennox was seated at her desk correcting papers... She spent the day correcting proofs at the publishers.* — V+O ⇑ check
7 To **correct** a medical condition or some other problem or fault means to do something which cures it or gets rid of it. EG *Your new glasses will correct your eyesight... They are studying ways of correcting the imbalance between the rich and poor countries.* — V+O ⇑ change = rectify
8 **Correct** behaviour is behaviour that is in accordance with accepted standards of behaviour. EG *Charter's dealings with him have been wholly correct... He holds what no doubt are the correct advanced views.* ▸ used of people. EG *Our mother was very strict and correct.* ◊ **correctly**. EG *We tried to behave correctly.* ◊ **correctness**. EG *Such a person should be treated with polite correctness.* — ADJ QUALIT ⇑ acceptable = proper; ▸ = proper; ◊ ADV WITH VB; ◊ N UNCOUNT = civility

correcting fluid. is an opaque, usually white, liquid which you paint on errors in written or typed work in order to cover them. — N UNCOUNT

correction /kərekʃə⁰n/, **corrections**. **1** A **correction** is **1.1** something which puts right something that has been done, said, written, or believed wrongly. EG *We'll make the necessary corrections and send you another estimate... Thank you for the correction... A couple of mistakes need correction.* **1.2** an indication of a mistake in a piece of writing, especially school work. EG *My homework was covered in corrections.* — N COUNT/UNCOUNT ⇑ alteration; N COUNT ⇑ alteration
2 You can say **'correction'** when you realize that what you have just said is not accurate or appropriate, before saying something which expresses better what you mean; a formal use. EG *Gaskell went to his room. Correction. Cabin.* — CONVENTION ⇑ no
3 **Correction** is **3.1** the changing of something so that it is no longer faulty or unsatisfactory. EG *Deaf children need speech correction... He radioed a course correction to an Eastern 727.* **3.2** the improvement, perhaps by punishment, of the standard of behaviour of a person who has done something wrong, especially a young person; an old-fashioned word. EG ... *a place of correction.* — N UNCOUNT/COUNT; N UNCOUNT

corrective /kərektɪv/, **correctives**. **1** **Corrective** is used to describe something that is intended to put right something that is wrong. EG ...*corrective surgery... We'll have to take corrective action.* — ADJ CLASSIF: USU ATTRIB = remedial
2 If something is a **corrective** to a particular view, account, or quality, it gives you a more accurate, more varied, or fairer idea about the situation than you would have had without it. EG *This analysis provides an important corrective to the traditional view.* — N COUNT: IF+PREP THEN *to* = adjustment

correlate /kɒrə¹leɪt/, **correlates, correlating, correlated**. If two things **correlate** or if they **are correlated**, they always exist or happen together and have an effect on one another. EG *Age often correlates with conservatism... In Britain, class and region are strongly correlated.* ◊ **correlation** /kɒrə¹leɪʃə⁰n/. EG *There's no correlation between mental ability and physical strength... Success in life has little correlation with merit.* — V-ERG: ALSO V OR V+A *(with)*: RECIP = connect; ◊ N UNCOUNT = correspondence

correlative /kɒrelətɪv/ is used to describe something which always exists or happens together with something else; a formal word. EG ...*correlative ideas.* — ADJ CLASSIF = interdependent

correspond /kɒrɪspɒnd/, **corresponds, corresponding, corresponded**. **1** If one thing **corresponds** with or to another thing, it is similar to it because it looks similar or is used in a similar way. EG *His job in Moscow corresponds to your father's position here... This view corresponds less and less with reality.* — V OR V+A *(with/to)*: RECIP ⇑ resemble = equate
2 If two numbers, positions, or amounts **correspond**, they are the same, or are closely related. EG *Check the telephone numbers in case they don't correspond... The date of her birth, 1862, corresponded with the date of her father's affair in Paris.* — V OR V+A *(with/to)*: RECIP ⇑ match = tally
3 If two people **correspond**, they write letters to each other. EG *Elisabeth Irmin and I corresponded regularly... I've been corresponding with Tim Johns for months.* — V OR V+A *(with)*: RECIP
4 See also **corresponding**.

correspondence /kɒrɪspɒndəns/, **correspondences**. **1** **Correspondence** is **1.1** the act or process of writing letters to someone. EG *The judges' decision is final and no correspondence will be entered into.* **1.2** the letters that someone receives. EG *The letter had been among his correspondence that morning.* — N UNCOUNT: IF+PREP THEN *with*; N UNCOUNT = mail
2 A **correspondence** between two things is a close relationship or similarity between them. EG *In African languages there is a close correspondence between sounds and letters.* — N UNCOUNT/COUNT: IF+PREP THEN *between/with*

correspondence course, correspondence courses. A **correspondence course** is a course in which you study at home, receiving your work by post and sending it back by post. — N COUNT

correspondent /kɒrɪspɒndənt/, **correspondents**. A **correspondent** is **1** a reporter, especially one who reports from a particular place or about a particular subject. EG ...*the Economics correspondent of the Guardian.* **2** someone who writes letters. EG *I'm a poor correspondent.* — N COUNT ⇑ journalist; N COUNT ⇑ writer

corresponding /kɒrɪspɒndɪŋ/. **Corresponding** is **1** used to describe a change which is the result of a change in something else. EG *Any increase in complexity brings with it a corresponding probability of error... ...wage increases corresponding to the rise in the rate of inflation.* ◊ **correspondingly**. EG *The new edition is bigger and correspondingly more expen-* — ADJ CLASSIF ⇑ similar = equivalent; ◊ ADV SEN sive. 2 used to describe something which is similar to or has the same function as something you have just mentioned. EG *This figure is 16 per cent up on the corresponding month last year... ...a professional qualification corresponding to a first degree.* ADJ CLASSIF = equivalent

corridor /kɒrɪdɔ[8]/, **corridors**. A **corridor** is 1 a long passage in a building or train, which has doors and rooms or compartments on one or both sides, or which joins two or more parts of the building. EG *I walked down the corridor.* N COUNT 2 a long strip of land going through a foreign country that connects a country with the sea or with another area that belongs to that country. N COUNT ↑ passage

corridors of power. The **corridors of power** are the places where the most important decisions in government are made. EG *So much official money has been washing through the corridors of power that accusations of corruption can no longer be suppressed.* N PLURAL : the+N

corroborate /kərɒbəreɪt/, **corroborates, corroborating, corroborated**. If someone or something **corroborates** an idea, account, or argument, they provide evidence or information that supports it. EG *Abrams and Rose corroborated this view in their influential study of the subject... The Scotts entered the witness box one by one to corroborate these charges.* V+O = confirm ≠ deny, disprove

corroboration /kərɒbəreɪʃə[0]n/ is evidence or information that supports an idea, account, or argument. EG *Evangelina's story was later published without corroboration.* N UNCOUNT = proof, support

corroborative /kərɒbə[0]rətɪv/. A **corroborative** fact, statement, or witness supports an idea, account, or argument. EG *The distribution of many animals and plants adds corroborative evidence to the survey.* ADJ CLASSIF ↑ supportive ≠ negative

corrode /kərəʊd/, **corrodes, corroding, corroded**. 1 When a substance, especially metal, **corrodes** or when something else **corrodes** it, it is gradually destroyed by a chemical such as a strong acid or by rust. EG *This metal does not corrode easily... If fluid seeps out at the top of the battery it may corrode the case.* V-ERG ↑ decay = eat away ◊ **corroded**. EG *The generator was badly corroded.* ◊ ADJ QUALIT

2 If something, especially a bitter feeling, **corrodes** a person, relationship, society, etc, it gradually destroys or worsens them or it; a literary use. V+O = consume ◊ **corroding**. EG *...a corroding sense of futility.* ◊ ADJ CLASSIF

corrosion /kərəʊʒə[0]n/ is 1 the process by which something is corroded. EG *Paint could help preserve the metal from corrosion.* N UNCOUNT ↑ decay 2 the physical damage caused when something has corroded. EG *Check that the terminals of the battery are free from dirt and corrosion.* N UNCOUNT ↑ decay

corrosive /kərəʊsɪv/. 1 A substance such as acid that is **corrosive** is able to destroy solid materials by a chemical reaction. EG *...a corrosive poison... The effect of the sea-water becomes very corrosive after a few months.* ADJ QUALIT ↑ destructive

2 Something that is **corrosive** has a harmful effect over a period of time. EG *...the corrosive effects of inflation.* ADJ QUALIT = damaging ≠ beneficial

corrugated /kɒrə[4]geɪtɪ[2]d/ is used to describe flat materials that have been folded or pressed into a series of small parallel folds in order to make them stronger. EG *...corrugated iron... ...corrugated cardboard... ...a corrugated roof.* ADJ CLASSIF : USU ATTRIB ≠ flat

corrupt /kərʌpt/, **corrupts, corrupting, corrupted**. 1 Someone who is **corrupt** 1.1 is ready to do dishonest or illegal things in return for money or for something else they want; used of people in positions of authority or power. EG *It's pitiful what those corrupt politicians are doing to us.* ▸ used of the things that corrupt people do. EG *...corrupt practices.* ADJ QUALIT ≠ fair, honest, trusty

1.2 behaves in a way that is considered morally wrong, especially involving sexual activities. EG *...an all-night orgy involving a large number of corrupt young people.* ADJ QUALIT = depraved ≠ virtuous

2 To **corrupt** or to **corrupt** someone means 2.1 to cause them to become dishonest, unfair, and unable to be trusted. EG *Power and wealth corrupted him.* V OR V+O

2.2 to stop them from believing in or caring about the harmful effects of wrong behaviour. EG *I doubt that any film ever corrupted anyone... It is claimed that television corrupts.* V OR V+O = deprave

3 **Corrupt** is used, especially in the expression 'to corrupt a person's morals', to refer to the committing of some sexual offences, especially those which involve people who are too young to have sex legally; a legal term. EG *She has corrupted the morals of a minor.* V+O ↑ ruin

4 To **corrupt** something means to have a harmful effect on it by making it less pure. EG *In the last two hundred years Europe has destroyed or corrupted a great number of ancient cultures.* V+O ↑ ruin

5 If something such as data, a text, or a language is **corrupt**, it has been changed or has acquired mistakes so that it is no longer in its pure, original state. ADJ QUALIT ↑ unreliable

6 If something **corrupts**, it rots or becomes damaged or destroyed by decay. EG *The body corrupted quite quickly.* V ↑ deteriorate

corruption /kərʌpʃə[0]n/. 1 **Corruption** is 1.1 dishonesty and illegal behaviour by people in positions of authority or power. EG *He fought for reform in cities riddled with corruption... ...police corruption.* N UNCOUNT ↑ self-interest ≠ fairness 1.2 the act or process of rotting or decaying; a formal or technical use. EG *The organism generates heat to mimic the warmth produced by corruption.* N UNCOUNT = putrefaction

2 The **corruption** of someone is the process of making them behave in a way that is considered morally or sexually wrong. EG *His whole life seemed dedicated to the corruption of the young.* N UNCOUNT ↑ ruin

3 **Corruption** is used, especially in the expression 'the corruption of minors', to refer to the offence of having sex with someone who is too young to have sex legally; a legal term. N UNCOUNT

corsage /kɔːsɑːʒ/, **corsages**. A **corsage** is a very small bunch of flowers which is fastened to the front of a woman's dress below the shoulder. EG *...a corsage of orchids.* N COUNT : IF+PREP THEN *of*

corset /kɔːsɪ[2]t/, **corsets**. A **corset** is 1 a stiffened piece of underwear worn by some women that fits tightly around their hips and waist and makes them appear slimmer. N COUNT : ALSO SING=PL 2 a garment made of cloth and metal which someone wears around their hips in order to support their back after injuring it. N COUNT ↑ girdle

cortege /kɔːteɪʒ/, **corteges**. A **cortege** is a procession of people who are walking or riding in cars to a funeral. N COUNT : IF SING, VB CAN BE SING OR PL

cortex /kɔːteks/, **cortices** /kɔːtəsiːz/. The **cortex** of the brain or of another organ is its outer layer; a medical term. EG *...the cerebral cortex.* N COUNT : USU SING ↑ covering

cortisone /kɔːtɪsəʊn, -zəʊn/ is a hormone used in the treatment of arthritis, allergies, and some skin diseases. N UNCOUNT

cos /kɒs/. **Cos** is both the singular and the plural form. 1 **Cos** or **'cos** is a very informal way of saying 'because'. EG *'You'd better make a note of that, cos I haven't.'* CONJ SUBORD = because

2 A **cos** or a **cos lettuce** is a lettuce with long narrow crisp leaves. N COUNT/UNCOUNT

3 **Cos** is also an abbreviation for 'cosine'.

cosh /kɒʃ/, **coshes, coshing, coshed**. 1 A **cosh** is a heavy piece of rubber or metal which is used as a weapon. N COUNT = bludgeon

2 To **cosh** someone means to hit them hard on the head with a cosh or some other blunt weapon. EG *The driver was dragged out of his van and coshed.* V+O = cudgel

cosine /kəʊsaɪn/, **cosines**. A **cosine** is the ratio of the length of the adjacent side of a right-angled triangle to that of the hypotenuse; a technical term in trigonometry. N COUNT ↑ function

cosmetic /kɒzmetɪk/, **cosmetics**. 1 A **cosmetic** is a substance, such as lipstick or powder, which people, especially women, put on their face or body to make themselves look more attractive. EG *Many more millions are spent on dress and cosmetics than are spent on books and schools.* N COUNT : USU PL = make-up

2 Something that is **cosmetic** improves the outward appearance of something but does not change its basic character. EG *It was a purely cosmetic measure... This shift represented no more than a cosmetic change.* ADJ CLASSIF = surface, superficial

cosmetic surgery is surgery which is performed in order to make someone look more attractive and not because it is necessary for their health. N UNCOUNT ↑ plastic surgery

cosmic /kɒzmɪk/. **Cosmic** means 1 belonging or relating to the whole of the universe. EG *The other great cosmic reality is time... I believed in a cosmic spirit.* ADJ CLASSIF : USU ATTRIB 2 occurring in, or coming from, the part of space that lies outside earth and its atmosphere. EG *Perhaps the planet was destroyed in some cosmic catastrophe.* ADJ CLASSIF : USU ATTRIB 3 relevant to or affecting everyone in the world rather than just a few people. EG *This* ADJ CLASSIF *decision is cosmic in its significance... We need to change our personal view to a cosmic one.*

cosmic ray, cosmic rays. **Cosmic rays** are rays that reach earth from outer space and consist of atomic nuclei. N COUNT : USU PL ⇑ radiation

cosmology /kɒzmɒlədʒi¹/, **cosmologies.** 1 A **cosmology** is a theory about the origin and nature of the universe. EG *Trying to describe Aboriginal cosmology briefly is just about impossible.* N COUNT/ UNCOUNT

2 **Cosmology** is the study of the origin and nature of the universe. N UNCOUNT

cosmonaut /kɒzmə⁶nɔːt/, **cosmonauts.** A **cosmonaut** is a Soviet astronaut. N COUNT

cosmopolitan /kɒzmə⁶pɒlɪtə⁰n/, **cosmopolitans.** 1 A place that is **cosmopolitan** is full of people or things from many different countries and cultures. EG *I was very much struck by London–the fact that it's so cosmopolitan... It remains a cosmopolitan street.* ADJ QUALIT = international ≠ insular

2 A **cosmopolitan** person has travelled or lived in many different countries. EG *Oxford is considered by many cosmopolitan experts to be one of the most agreeable university towns in Europe.* ADJ CLASSIF ≠ insular

3 A **cosmopolitan** is someone who has travelled or lived in many different countries and who perhaps does not feel or show any strong connection with their own country. N COUNT ≠ nationalist

cosmos /kɒzmɒs/. You can refer to the universe as the **cosmos**, especially when considering it as having an order and pattern. EG *...the creation of the cosmos.* N SING : *the*+N

cosset /kɒsɪt/, **cossets, cosseting, cosseted.** If you **cosset** someone, you do everything possible for them and protect them from anything unpleasant, because you are fond of them. EG *We all yearn to be cosseted.* ◇ **cosseted.** EG *He slowly became the most cosseted member of the family.* V+O ⇑ indulge = pamper, mollycoddle ◇ ADJ QUALIT

cost /kɒst/, **costs, costing, costed.** The form **cost** is used in the present tense and is the past tense and past participle of the verb in paragraphs 2, 3, and 8. 1 The **cost** of something is the amount of money that is needed in order to buy, do, or make it. EG *The total cost of the holiday came to £300... The building was recently restored at a cost of £500,000... The car was repaired at no cost to the owner... You may have to bear the cost of any damage.* N COUNT : ALSO SING=PL ⇑ price, total

2 If something **costs** a particular amount of money, it is able to be bought, done, or made for that amount. EG *Those four books cost £2.95 each... A freezer doesn't cost much to run... Lodgings and food cost us around five thousand dollars.* ● If you say that something **costs money**, you mean that it has to be paid for and perhaps cannot be afforded. EG *He had known it was going to cost money and he'd panicked.* V+O, OR V+O+O = is priced at ● PHR : VB INFLECTS ≠ is free

3 If something will **cost** you, it will cost you a lot more money than you would usually expect to pay; an informal use. EG *Sure, we can do it, but it'll cost you.* V+O : USU *will*+V ⇑ set you back

4 If you **cost** something, you calculate how much money is needed to do or make it. EG *Drake passed the months in studying the map and costing an expedition that never sailed.* V+O ⇑ budget, estimate

5 Your **costs** are the total amount of money that you must spend on running your home or business. EG *She decided she needed to cut her costs by half... Moulton's have had to raise their prices still higher to cover increased costs.* N PLURAL ⇑ expenses

6 **Cost** also means the same as cost price. EG *I'll let you have them at cost.* N COUNT, OR *at*+N

7 The **cost** of something is also the loss, damage, or injury that is involved in trying to achieve it. EG *The battle was won, but the cost in human life had been enormous... No matter by what means, no matter what the cost to herself, she is determined to succeed.* N SING WITH DET ⇑ penalty = price ≠ reward

8 If an event or mistake **costs** you something, it causes that thing to be lost or ruined. EG *A single error here could cost you your life... It was a really spectacular mistake, costing the company several million pounds.* V+O, OR V+O+O

9 If something must be done **at all cost** or **at all costs**, it must be done regardless of how much time, money, effort, or sacrifice is needed. EG *We must keep him alive at all costs... Direct contact with the patient must be avoided at all cost.* PHR : USED AS AN A = whatever

10 If something must not be done **at any cost**, it must not be done regardless of how much time, money, effort, or sacrifice is needed. EG *Contact with other prisoners must not be allowed at any cost.* PHR WITH BROAD NEG : USED AS AN A = at all

11 If you **count the cost** of doing something, you consider all the risks that are involved in doing it before you do it. PHR : VB INFLECTS, IF+ PREP THEN *of*

12 If you know about something **to your cost**, you know about it because of an unpleasant experience that you have had. EG *Diving can be a very dangerous business, as I found to my cost.* PHR : USED AS AN A

cost accountant, cost accountants. A **cost accountant** is an accountant who records and analyses the various costs involved in running a business. N COUNT

cost accounting is the recording and analysis of all the various costs of running a business. N UNCOUNT

co-star, co-stars, co-starring, co-starred. 1 An actor or actress who **co-stars** in a particular film has one of the most important parts in it. EG *He co-starred with Joan Fontaine.* V OR V+A *(with)* : RECIP ⇑ appear with

2 If a film **co-stars** particular actors, they have the most important parts in it. V+O

3 A **co-star** is an actor or actress who has one of the most important parts in a film. EG *His co-star was Elizabeth Taylor.* N COUNT

cost-effective. Something that is **cost-effective** saves or makes a considerable amount of money in comparison with the costs involved. EG *We urgently need more cost-effective methods of production.* ADJ QUALIT = economical

costing /kɒstɪŋ/, **costings.** A **costing** is the estimation of all the costs involved in something, for example a project or business venture. EG *You'll find it's very expensive when you do a proper accountant's costing of it.* N COUNT/ UNCOUNT ⇑ budget, forecast

costly /kɒstli¹/, **costlier, costliest.** 1 Something that is **costly** 1 costs you a lot of money, especially over a period of time. EG *It proved a costly, and time-consuming mistake... Air conditioners are costly.* 2 uses up a lot of a time, effort, etc. EG *That route will be too costly in time.* ADJ QUALIT ⇑ expensive ADJ QUALIT : IF+ PREP THEN *in*

cost of living. The **cost of living** is the average amount of money that food, housing, clothing, etc, cost each person in the country over a period of time. EG *The cost of living will be higher than ever.* N SING : *the*+N ⇑ expenditure, expense

cost-plus. A **cost-plus** basis for a contract about work to be done is one in which the buyer agrees to pay the seller or contractor all the cost plus a profit. EG *Until 1968, the contracts were placed on a cost-plus basis.* ADJ CLASSIF

cost price, cost prices. The **cost price** of a product is its price when it is sold without any profit but only for what it cost the manufacturer to produce it or the seller to buy it. EG *Even if we sell at cost price we might not clear the stock.* N COUNT, OR *at*+N

costume /kɒstjuːm/, **costumes.** 1 A **costume** is a set of clothes worn by an actor or performer or by someone at a fancy dress party. EG *The cast makes its own costumes... ...an Elizabethan costume of padded breeches, square shoes and a ruff.* N COUNT ⇑ clothing = outfit

2 **Costume** is 2.1 the clothes worn by people at a particular time in history or in a particular country. EG *...a museum of costume... ...portraits of people dressed in 17th-century costume.* 2.2 the work involved in making the clothes worn by actors or performers; also used of the clothes themselves. EG *Scenery and costume were far more important to me than the acting.* N UNCOUNT = dress N UNCOUNT ⇑ clothing

3 A **costume** play or drama is one which is set in a period in the past and in which the actors wear the type of clothes worn in that period. ADJ CLASSIF : ATTRIB ≠ modern dress

4 See also **bathing costume, swimming costume.**

costume jewellery is jewellery that is not made from expensive materials, although it might look as if it is. N UNCOUNT = paste

costumier /kɒstjuːmɪə/, **costumiers.** A **costumier** is a person or firm that makes or supplies theatrical or fancy dress costumes. N COUNT ⇑ outfitter, tailor

cosy /kəʊzi¹/, **cosier, cosiest; cosies;** also spelled **cozy** in American English. 1 A house or room that is **cosy** is comfortable and warm, and usually not too large. EG *The room was wonderfully warm and cosy... They were beginning to miss the cosy flat in St John's Wood.* ◇ **cosily.** EG *...a cosily furnished house.* ADJ QUALIT = homely, snug, comfy ◇ ADV = comfy

2 If you are **cosy**, you are comfortable and warm. EG *A hot water bottle will make you feel cosier.* ◇ **cosily.** ADJ QUALIT = comfy, snug ◇ ADV

3 You also use **cosy** to describe a chat or other situation which is pleasant and friendly, and involves ADJ QUALIT = intimate

a close relationship between people. EG *We had quite a few cosy evenings together... ...a cosy chat.* ◊ **cosily**. EG *We spent the evening cosily gossiping.* ◊ ADV

4 A **cosy** is a soft cover which you put over something such as a teapot to keep it warm. EG *...a tea cosy... ...an egg cosy.* N COUNT+SUPP

cot /kɒt/, **cots**. A **cot** is 1 a bed for a baby or very young child, with bars or panels round it so that the child cannot fall out; used mainly in British English. N COUNT = crib

2 a narrow bed, usually made of a piece of canvas fitted over a frame which can be folded up; used mainly in American English. N COUNT = camp bed

cot death, cot deaths. **Cot death** is the sudden death of a baby while it is asleep, although the baby had not previously been ill. N UNCOUNT/COUNT

coterie /kəʊtəri[1]/, **coteries**. A **coterie** is a small group of people who are close friends or have a common interest, and who do not want other people to join them; a formal word. EG *The name is known to only a small coterie of concert-goers.* N COUNT: IF SING, VB CAN BE SING OR PL = circle, set, clique

cottage /kɒtɪdʒ/, **cottages**. A **cottage** is a small house, usually in the country. EG *They had lived in a cottage on the edge of the moors.* N COUNT ⇑ building

cottage cheese is a soft white lumpy cheese made out of sour milk. N UNCOUNT

cottage industry, cottage industries. A **cottage industry** is a small business that is run from someone's home, especially one that involves a craft such as knitting or pottery. N COUNT

cottage loaf, cottage loaves. A **cottage loaf** is a loaf of bread which has a smaller round part on top of a larger round part; used in British English. N COUNT

cottage pie, cottage pies. **Cottage pie** is a dish which consists of minced meat in gravy with mashed potato on top; used in British English. N UNCOUNT/COUNT

cottager /kɒtɪdʒə/, **cottagers**. A **cottager** is a person who lives in a cottage. N COUNT

cotton /kɒtə[ə]n/, **cottons, cottoning, cottoned**. **Cotton** is 1 a natural cloth made from the soft fibres that are produced by the cotton plant. EG *...a cotton dress.* ▸ used of clothes that are made of cotton. EG *Use very hot water for white cottons.* 2 a tall plant that is grown in warm countries and that has soft fine hairs surrounding its seeds which are used to produce cotton. EG *Was cotton always grown in Texas?... ...cotton fields.* 3 thread that is used for sewing, especially thread that is made from cotton; used in British English. EG *Then you get a needle and cotton and very carefully sew up the slit... ...reels of cotton.* N UNCOUNT ▸ N PLURAL N UNCOUNT N MASS

cotton on. If you **cotton on** to something, you understand it or realize it, especially without people telling you about it; an informal expression. EG *At long last he has cottoned on to the fact that I'm not interested in him!... The other man cottoned on and came running.* PHRASAL VB: V+ADV, IF+PREP THEN *to* ⇑ recognize

cotton candy is a large soft mass of pink or white sugar threads which is put on a stick and eaten, usually out of doors; used in American English. N UNCOUNT = candy floss

cotton wool; also spelled with a hyphen and as one word. **Cotton wool** is soft, fluffy cotton, used especially for applying liquids or creams to your skin, or for putting antiseptic onto a wound. N UNCOUNT ⇑ material

couch /kaʊtʃ/, **couches, couching, couched**. 1 A **couch** is 1.1 a long piece of furniture which more than one person can sit on. EG *I'll sleep on the couch.* N COUNT = sofa, settee

1.2 a bed in a doctor's or psychiatrist's consulting room, which patients lie on while they are being examined or treated. EG *Please lie on the couch.* ▸ used in informal English to refer to treatment by a psychiatrist or psychoanalyst. EG *It's doubtful whether the couch could cure him.* N COUNT ▸ N SING: *the*+N ⇑ treatment

2 If you **couch** a statement in a particular style of language, you express it in that style of language; a formal use. EG *Here was a resolution couched in forthright terms... The booklet was couched in legal jargon.* V+O: USU PASS+*in* = phrase

3 If an animal **couches**, it crouches or lies on its belly, especially when it is preparing to jump forward; a literary use. V: USU+A ⇑ crouch

couchette /kuːʃet/, **couchettes**. A **couchette** is a bed in a railway carriage or ferry boat, which is either folded against the wall or used as an ordinary seat during the day. N COUNT ⇑ folding bed

couch grass /kuːtʃ grɑːs/ is a type of grass that has long roots that make it spread quickly. N UNCOUNT

cougar /kuːgə/, **cougars**. A **cougar** is a wild animal that is a member of the cat family. Cougars have brownish-grey fur and live in mountain regions of North and South America. N COUNT = puma

cough /kɒf/, **coughs, coughing, coughed**. 1 When you **cough**, you force air out of your throat with a sudden, harsh noise. You cough when your throat is irritated or sometimes when you are embarrassed or want to attract someone's attention. EG *There was so much smoke that my sister started coughing... He stood at the door and coughed, and when this brought no result, he called softly.* ◊ **coughing**. EG *They suffered abdominal pains and intense coughing.* V ◊ N UNCOUNT

2 If you **cough** something such as blood or phlegm, you get rid of it from inside your throat by forcing it out of your mouth with a sudden, harsh noise. EG *He started coughing blood.* V+O ⇑ bring up

3 A **cough** is 3.1 a sudden, harsh noise made by someone forcing air out of their throat. EG *There was a muffled cough outside the study door.* 3.2 an illness in which you cough often and your chest or throat hurts. EG *I had a racking cough every winter.* ● See also **whooping cough**. N COUNT N COUNT

4 If an engine or other machine **coughs**, it makes a sudden, harsh noise. EG *Then the engine started missing, coughing and popping and spluttering.* V = hiccup

cough up. 1 If you **cough up** or if you **cough up** an amount of money, you give someone money that they need or that you owe them; an informal use. EG *They'll cough up the hundred million... Come on, cough up.* PHRASAL VB: V+ADV, OR V+O+ADV = pay up

2 If you **cough up** something such as blood or phlegm, you get rid of it from inside your throat by forcing it out of your mouth with a sudden, harsh noise. EG *She coughed up phlegm... He was coughing his insides up.* PHRASAL VB: V+O+ADV ⇑ bring up

could /kʊd, kəd/. 1 You use **could** as the past tense of 'can' in reported speech, and of 'can' in the sense of being able to do something: see **can**. EG *They complained that they couldn't sleep because it had gone so quiet... When I was young you could buy a packet for 2 shillings... It was difficult to find a house that he could afford... We just could not understand why he'd failed... She couldn't decide.* MODAL = were able

2 You use **could** 2.1 to indicate that you think it is possible that something will happen. EG *The river could easily overflow couldn't it?... It could be disastrous... As a matter of fact it could arrive tomorrow.* MODAL ⇑ might

2.2 to say that something is able to be done in theory even if it is not done in practice. EG *A lot of fires could be prevented... We could do a great deal more in this country to educate people... We could go on for a long time discussing this... I couldn't kill an animal myself, but I don't mind other people doing it.* MODAL ⇑ should

2.3 to indicate that you think that something is possibly true or is a possible explanation for something. EG *It could be a symbol, couldn't it?... That could be one reason... I won't say we are in an arms race, but I think we could be at the beginning of one.* MODAL: USU+*be* = might possibly

3 You also use **could** 3.1 with 'I' and 'we' to indicate that something is possible and that you are considering doing it. EG *I could ask her, I suppose... We could go on Friday.* 3.2 with 'I' and 'we' to indicate that you would like to do the thing mentioned, because you are feeling a strong emotion. EG *I could strangle him!... I could scream.* 3.3 to suggest to someone a possible course of action or a possible solution to a problem that they have. EG *You could phone her... You could always ask to see a copy of your Aunt's will... Couldn't you just build more factories?... I think the Company Officer could arrange this.* 3.4 as a polite way of asking someone to do something. EG *Could you just switch the projector on behind you?... Could you give me a few examples?... Perhaps you could expand on this a little bit.* 3.5 as a polite way of asking someone for permission to do something. EG *Could we put this fire on?... Could I speak to Sue, please?... I did want to ask you, if I could, about the problems of people in your area.* 3.6 as a polite way of interrupting someone or introducing what you are going to say next. EG *Could I just mention one statistic which I think is very important... Could I interrupt a moment?* 3.7 to say that someone ought to do the thing mentioned; used especially when you are feeling angry with someone. EG *You could give* MODAL: WITH *I/we* ⇑ be able to MODAL: WITH *I/we* MODAL: NOT WITH *I*, USU WITH *you* MODAL: USU WITH *you* ⇑ please will MODAL: USU WITH *I/we* = please may MODAL: USU WITH *I* ⇑ can MODAL = might

me some idea of when you're going to be home... He could at least tell me where he's going.

4 You use **could** after 'if' when you are talking about a situation which is possible or which you are imagining, in order to consider what the likely consequences might be. EG *If I could follow it, it might be okay... If one could measure this sort of thing, one might understand it better.* MODAL : *if*+S+ MODAL = were able to

5 You use **could have 5.1** to say that something was possible in the past, although it did not actually happen. EG *You were lucky. It could have been awful... I could've made myself more clear... I reckon you could have got a job last year.* MODAL+*have*+ PAST PART ⇑ might have **5.2** to indicate that you think something was possibly true or is a possible explanation for something that has happened. EG *This music sounds as though it could have come from the soundtrack of a film... It could have been an axe.* MODAL+*have*+ PAST PART ⇑ might have **5.3** to indicate that you would have liked to do something, or you think that it would have been appropriate in the circumstances, but that you did not actually do it. EG *I could have easily spent the whole year on it... I could have screamed.* MODAL+*have*+ PAST PART ⇑ might **5.4** to say that someone should have done a particular thing; used especially when you are very angry with someone. EG *You could have been a little bit tidier... You could have told me!* MODAL+*have*+ PAST PART ⇑ might have

6 You use **could** with the negative 'not' **6.1** to indicate that you think something is impossible and cannot be true. EG *It couldn't possibly be poison.* MODAL+*not* = can't **6.2** when you want to emphasize how much you feel something or how good, lovely, horrible, etc something is or seems. EG *I couldn't agree more... The setting couldn't have been lovelier... He couldn't have looked more shocked.* MODAL+*not* **6.3** to indicate that something such as a way of behaving seems unreasonable or unacceptable to you. EG *I couldn't let you do it on your own... How could you have done such a thing?* MODAL+*not* ⇑ wouldn't

7 You say **'I couldn't'** as a polite way of refusing an offer of more food or drink. EG *'Have another slice of cake.'–'I really couldn't.'* CONVENTION ⇑ no thanks

8 You use **couldn't have** to say that it is not possible that something happened or was true. EG *He didn't carry a dinghy, so he couldn't have rowed away... It couldn't possibly have been wrong.* MODAL+*not*+ *have*+PAST PART = can't have

9 could do with: see **do**.

couldn't /kʌdəⁿt/ is the usual spoken form of 'could not'.

could've /kʌdəᵊv/ is the usual spoken form of 'could have', especially when 'have' is an auxiliary verb.

council /kaʊnsəˡl/, **councils**. **1** A **council** is **1.1** in British English, a group of people who are elected to run a particular town, borough, city, or county. The council is responsible for looking after the roads, schools, buses, public buildings, and other services provided for the people living in the area. EG *...Wiltshire County Council... The council said it would close the flats and pull them down. I served seventeen years on my local council... ...council meetings.* N COUNT : IF SING, VB CAN BE SING OR PL, ALSO USED IN NAMES AFTER N = local authority **1.2** a group of people who are elected or appointed to make decisions or give advice about a particular subject, to represent a particular group of people, or to run a particular organization. EG *...the National Economic Development Council... ...the Arts Council... ...the British Council of Churches.* N COUNT : IF SING, VB CAN BE SING OR PL, ALSO USED IN NAMES AFTER N ⇑ body

2 A **council** house, flat, etc is one that is owned by the local council, and which you pay rent to live in. EG *...a small council flat... ...council estates... ...a council tenant.* ADJ CLASSIF : ATTRIB ≠ private ⇑ local authority

3 A **council** is also a specially organized meeting that is attended by a particular group of people. EG *That afternoon a council of ministers and generals was held at No. 10.* N COUNT : IF+ PREP THEN *of/for/on* ⇑ conference

councillor /kaʊnsəˡlə/, **councillors**. A **councillor** is a member of a local council. EG *...Councillor Bert Peglar... The party secured the election of 24 councillors in 1964.* N COUNT : ALSO IN TITLES BEFORE NAME ⇑ official

council of war, councils of war. A **council of war** is a meeting that is held in order to decide how a particular threat or emergency should be dealt with; a formal expression. N COUNT : USU SING ⇑ conference

counsel /kaʊnsəl/, **counsels, counselling, counselled**; also spelled **counseling** and **counseled** in American English. **1 Counsel** is advice to someone which is based on a lot of experience or serious thought; a formal use. EG *Her children would not listen to their mother's good counsel... He was a statesman whose voice had been heard before, giving counsel in times of stress.* N UNCOUNT

2 If people **take counsel** or **take counsel together**, they ask each other what they think they should do; a formal expression. PHR : VB INFLECTS

3 If you **keep** your **own counsel**, you keep your own opinions and intentions secret; a formal expression. PHR : VB INFLECTS

4 If you **counsel** someone to do something, you advise them to do it; a formal use. EG *I counselled them to avoid rash actions... I would strongly counsel the new administration against complacency... 'Ignore them,' Mrs Jones counselled.* V+O+*to*-INF/A *(against/on)*, OR V+QUOTE ⇑ advise, suggest

5 If you **counsel** a particular course of action, you recommend it; a formal use. EG *Some wanted to fight. Others counselled caution.* V+O

6 If you **counsel** someone, you give them advice, especially about a problem, as part of your job. EG *Part of her work is to counsel families when problems arise.* V+O, OR V+A *(about/on)*

7 A **counsel** is a lawyer or a group of lawyers that gives someone advice on a legal case and fights the case in court; a technical term. EG *...the prosecuting counsel... ...counsel for the defence... You should take the advice of counsel.* N COUNT/ UNCOUNT ⇑ barrister

counselling /kaʊnsəᵊlɪŋ/; also spelled **counseling** in American English. **Counselling** is the activity of giving people advice as part of your job. EG *Do you see chaplaincy work as essentially counselling?... He had a period of psychiatric counselling.* N UNCOUNT ⇑ aid

counsellor /kaʊnsəᵊlə/, **counsellors**; also spelled **counselor** in American English. A **counsellor** is a person whose job is to give advice to people who need it. EG *The hospital has trained counsellors who are used to dealing with depressed patients.* N COUNT = adviser

count /kaʊnt/, **counts, counting, counted. 1** When you **count**, you say all the numbers one after another up to a particular number. EG *He began to count out loud on his fingers... After counting sixty the rest set off in pursuit... She went into the lounge and counted to twenty... I'm going to count up to three.* V : USU+A *(to/up to)*, OR V+O (NUM) = enumerate

2 If you **count** all the things in a group or **count** them **up**, you add them up in order to find how many there are. EG *He withdrew to his office to count the money... You could count thirty mowers in the same field... I counted up my years of teaching experience.* V+O, OR PHRASAL VB : V+ O+ADV *(up)* = add up

3 A **count** is **3.1** a number that you get by counting a particular set of things. EG *The official government count has now risen to eight million.* • See also **head-count**. N COUNT : USU SING ⇑ figure **3.2** the counting up to a maximum of ten by the referee when a boxer is knocked down in a boxing match. If the boxer does not get up before the referee counts ten, the other boxer is the winner of the match. EG *Doyle went down for a count of seven in the third round.* N COUNT : IF+ PREP THEN *of* **3.3** a scientific measurement of the amount of a substance in something, for example in your body. EG *...a high cholesterol count.* N COUNT : MOD+ N, USU SING ⇑ level

4 If you **keep count** of a number of things or of the number of times that something happens, you keep a record in which you add one to the total each time one occurs. If you **lose count** of a number of things or of the number of times that something happens, you cannot remember how many have occurred while you have been trying to keep a record of them. EG *There is a turnstile, to keep count of consumers... Keep count of the unforeseen difficulties you encounter... I've lost count of the number of boyfriends she's had since she's been here.* PHR : VB INFLECTS, IF+ PREP THEN *of*

5 The thing that **counts** in a particular situation or activity is the thing that is most important in that situation or activity. EG *What counts is how you feel about yourself... In sport what really counts is not the winning but the playing.* V = matter

6 Someone who **counts** is someone who you regard as important. EG *When they see somebody who counts, they try to make a favourable impression... ...the doctrine that all individuals count.* V = matters

7 If you say that a particular thing **counts** for something, you mean that it is valuable or important. EG *I felt that all my years there counted for nothing... We all want to count for something.* V+A *(for)* = stand for

8 If something or someone **counts** as something of a particular kind, they can be regarded, or are regarded, as something of that kind. EG *These benefits do not count as income for tax purposes... There are very few British anthropologists. Leakey doesn't count; he is a Kenyan citizen.* V, V+A *(as)*, OR V +O+A *(as)* = qualify

9 If someone **is counted** a particular thing, they are considered to be that thing. EG *She was counted a success... He was counted a good parish man... Many husbands count themselves lords of the household.* V+O (NG/REFL) +C = regard

10 If you **count** something, you include it with something else, for example in a calculation. EG *I get ten pounds a week during the term; if I count the holidays I get six pounds a week.* V+O : IF+PREP THEN with • **Not counting** means not including. EG *...36,600,000 Americans (not counting children less than one year old).* • PREP = excluding ≠ including

11 You can refer to one of a series of points in a discussion or argument as a particular **count**. one of a series of points in a discussion or argument. EG *The use of these tests is criticized on two counts... They are right on the first count but wrong on the second.* N COUNT : AFTER on, USU PL = particular

12 In law, a **count** is one of a number of charges brought against someone in a law court. EG *He pleaded guilty to seven counts of attempted murder.* N COUNT = charge

13 A **count** is also a European nobleman with the same rank as an English earl. EG *His father-in-law was a count, and exceedingly wealthy... ...Count Lanfranco Rasponi.* N COUNT : ALSO IN TITLES BEFORE NAME

14 If someone is **out for the count**, they are unconscious and are not likely to become conscious again for several minutes; an informal expression. PHR : USED AS AN A = out cold

count against. If an action or characteristic **counts against** you, it may help to cause you to be punished, rejected, defeated, etc. EG *It would count heavily against me if I got the Director into trouble.* PHRASAL VB : V+PREP

count in. If you **count** someone **in**, you include them in a particular activity. PHRASAL VB : V+O+ADV

count on. 1 If you **count on** something, you expect it to happen and include it in your plans. EG *Doctors could now count on a regular salary... The campaign can count on the public support of a few Labour MPs.* PHRASAL VB : V+PREP, USU MODAL+V = rely on, bank on

2 If you **count on** someone, you rely on them to support you or help you. EG *You can count on me... We had over two hundred workers whom we could count on.* PHRASAL VB : V+PREP, USU MODAL+V = depend on

count out. 1 If you **count out** coins, banknotes, etc, you count them as you move them one by one from one pile to another or as you give them to someone else, until you reach a particular sum of money. EG *She counted out the money... He counted out five wads of twenty notes each.* PHRASAL VB : V+O+ADV ↑ check

2 If you **count** someone **out**, you exclude them from a particular activity. EG *If you're going to gossip, you can count me out.* PHRASAL VB : V+O+ADV = leave out ≠ count in

3 When a referee **counts out** a boxer who has been knocked down, he counts to ten before the boxer can get up, so that the boxer loses the match. PHRASAL VB : V+O+ADV

count towards. If something **counts towards** something that you want, it is regarded as being among the things that gives you the right to have it. EG *Any contributions you have paid will count towards your pension.* PHRASAL VB : V+PREP

count upon. If you **count upon** someone, you count on them. PHRASAL VB : V+PREP, HAS PASS

countable noun /kaʊntə[1]bə[0]l naʊn/, countable nouns. A **countable noun** is the same as a count noun. N COUNT

countdown /kaʊntdaʊn/, **countdowns**. A **countdown** is the counting aloud of numbers in reverse order before something happens, especially before a spacecraft is launched, to let people know exactly when it is going to happen. EG *The countdown was well under way.* N COUNT ↑ enumeration

countenance /kaʊntɪ[2]nəns/, **countenances, countenancing, countenanced**. 1 Your **countenance** is your face; a literary use. EG *He saw the boyish countenance of Tom Barter before him.* N COUNT : USU SING, OR N UNCOUNT = expression

2 If you **countenance** something, you allow it to happen and find it acceptable; a formal use. EG *He is unlikely to countenance the use of nuclear weapons... Surely Lord Egremont could not countenance such a miscarriage of justice?* V+O = tolerate, sanction

counter /kaʊntə/, **counters, countering, countered**. 1 A **counter** is a long narrow table or flat surface in a shop or cafe, where goods are displayed or sold. EG *...a small counter where postcards and stamps were sold... There was a long queue at the medicine counter.* N COUNT • If you buy goods **under the counter**, you buy them secretly and illegally. EG *Everybody gets bits and pieces under the counter these days.* • PHR : USED AS AN A, OR BEFORE N

2 If something has just been said and you **counter** it by saying something else, you say something that shows that what was said is wrong, or that makes it seem less important. EG *I countered by enquiring whether she actually knew this man... Mr Wedgwood Benn countered with a speech defining socialist policies.* V OR V+O/QUOTE/REPORT-CL : IF+PREP THEN by/with ↑ retaliate

3 If you **counter** something that is being done, you act in a way that makes it less effective. EG *He argued that Labour should counter this propaganda with a series of press statements... To counter this the police will equip themselves with riot shields and tear gas.* V+O : IF+PREP THEN by/with = counteract

4 If something **runs counter to** something else, it is in direct contrast with it. EG *The ideology of modern nationalism often runs counter to older nationalist ideology... She has taken up causes which run counter to the dictates of the leadership.* PHR : VB INFLECTS = oppose, act against

5 A **counter** is also a small flat round object used in board games. N COUNT ↑ disc

counter- is added to words to form other words which refer to actions or activities that are intended to prevent other actions or activities or that respond to them. EG *...attack→counter-attack... ...espionage→counter-espionage... ...act→counteract... ...revolutionary→counter-revolutionary.* PREFIX ↑ anti-

counteract /kaʊntərækt/, **counteracts, counteracting, counteracted**. To **counteract** something means to reduce its effect by doing something that produces an opposite effect. EG *We added malt flavouring to counteract the bitterness of the taste... No amount of freedom at school can completely counteract the influence of a bad home.* V+O ↑ cancel

counter-attack, counter-attacks, counter-attacking, counter-attacked. If you **counter-attack**, you attack someone who has attacked you. EG *We hadn't expected them to counter-attack so soon.* V OR V+O : USU V ↑ retaliate ▸ used as a noun. EG *...counter-attacks against enemy civilians.* ▸ N COUNT/UNCOUNT

counterbalance /kaʊntəbæle[0]ns/, counterbalances, counterbalancing, counterbalanced; also spelled with a hyphen. 1 To **counterbalance** something means to balance it or correct it with an equal effect, force, or amount. EG *...a condition caused by a lack of sufficient salt in the diet to counterbalance the amount of salt lost in sweat... Thus political power counterbalances the other influences in society.* V+O

2 A **counterbalance** is a weight, force, attitude, etc that balances another one. EG *The tail is held out stiffly so that it acts as a counterbalance.* N COUNT

counterclockwise /kaʊntəklɒkwaɪz/;also spelled with a hyphen. **Counterclockwise** means the same as anticlockwise; used in American English. ADV AFTER VB, OR ADJ CLASSIF : ATTRIB

counter-espionage consists of the measures that a country takes in order to find out whether another country is spying on it and to prevent it from doing so. N UNCOUNT

counterfeit /kaʊntəfi[1]t/, **counterfeits, counterfeiting, counterfeited**. 1 Something that is **counterfeit** is made so that it looks exactly like something else, in order to deceive people. EG *...a counterfeit coin.* ADJ CLASSIF = forged

2 If someone **counterfeits** something, they make it so that it looks exactly like something else, in order to deceive people. V+O = forge

counterfoil /kaʊntəfɔɪl/, **counterfoils**. A **counterfoil** is the part of a cheque, postal order, or receipt that you keep as a record of the money you have paid for something. N COUNT = stub

countermand /kaʊntəmɑːnd/, **countermands, countermanding, countermanded**. If you **countermand** an order, you cancel it, especially by giving a different order. V+O

counter-measure, counter-measures; also spelled as one word. A **counter-measure** is an action that you take in order to weaken the effect of another action or a situation, or to make it harmless. EG *Unless specific counter-measures are taken, unemployment will continue to rise.* N COUNT ↑ ploy

counterpane /kaʊntəpeɪn/, **counterpanes**. A **counterpane** is a decorative cover which is put over a bed, on top of the sheets and blankets; a fairly formal word. N COUNT

counterpart /kaʊntəpɑːt/, **counterparts**. The **counterpart** of a person or thing is a person or thing that has a similar function or position in another place or organization. EG *The Foreign Minister, Mr* N COUNT+SUPP = equivalent, opposite number

Genscher, met his Angolan counterpart, Mr Paulo Jorge, last week... ...the English merchant bank and its American counterpart, the Wall Street investment bank.

counterpoint /kaʊntəpɔɪnt/ is a technique in music in which two different tunes are played together at the same time in order to produce a particular effect. [N UNCOUNT]

counter-productive. Something that is **counter-productive** achieves the opposite result from the one that you want to achieve. [ADJ CLASSIF; ⇑ ineffective]

counter-revolution, counter-revolutions. A **counter-revolution** is a revolution that is intended to reverse the effects of a previous revolution. [N COUNT]

counter-revolutionary, counter-revolutionaries. A **counter-revolutionary** is a person who is trying to reverse the effects of a previous revolution. EG *They planned to overawe all counter-revolutionaries through sheer mass and armed might.* ▸ used of actions, groups, etc. EG *...illicit counter-revolutionary activity.* [N COUNT; ▸ ADJ CLASSIF]

countersign /kaʊntəsaɪn/, **countersigns, countersigning, countersigned**. If you **countersign** a document, you sign it after someone else has signed it, in order to confirm that their signature is genuine. [V+O; = witness]

countertenor /kaʊntətenə/, **countertenors**. A **countertenor** is a man who sings with a high voice that is similar in range and quality to a low female singing voice. [N COUNT; ⇑ alto]

countess /kaʊntɪ²s/, **countesses**. A **countess** is a woman who has the same rank as a count or earl, or who is married to a count or earl. EG *...the Countess of Derby.* [N COUNT: ALSO IN TITLES]

countless /kaʊntlɪ²s/ means very many. EG *He sent countless letters to the newspapers... Countless fishing villages dot the coasts.* [ADJ CLASSIF: ATTRIB; = innumerable]

count noun, count nouns. A **count noun** is a noun that has a singular and a plural form and is used always after a determiner in the singular. Count nouns often refer to objects, such as 'table', 'pen' and 'apple'. In this dictionary count nouns have N COUNT in the grammar note beside the entry. See ☐ at N COUNT. [N COUNT]

country /kʌntri¹/, **countries**. **1** A **country** is **1.1** one of the political and economic units of the world which has its own government, people, language, and culture. EG *...the gap between rich and poor countries... The level of unemployment in this country is too high... He loved his country.* [N COUNT; = nation] **1.2** the area of land with definite boundaries which is occupied by a particular country. EG *Forests cover about one third of the country... I've lived all my life in this country... I travelled all over the country.* [N COUNT; ⇑ territory]

2 The **country** means the people who live in a particular country. EG *The country was stunned... The President has well over sixty per cent of the country believing he is doing a good job.* [N SING: the+N; = population]

3 The **country** is also land which is away from towns and cities, including land used for farming. EG *We live in the country... ...schools in country areas.* [N SING: the+N; = countryside] ● If you go **across country**, you do not keep to roads, but go across fields and through woods. EG *We'll have to cut across country.* [● PHR: USED AS AN A]

4 Country means from the country, and therefore rough or simple. EG *I'm just a country boy.* [ADJ CLASSIF: ATTRIB]

5 A particular kind of **country** is **5.1** an area of land which has particular characteristics or which is suitable for a particular purpose. EG *We were in mountain country... This isn't the best camping country.* [N UNCOUNT: MOD+N; = terrain] **5.2** an area of land which is connected with a particular person, for example with a writer. EG *This is Max Ernst country.* [N UNCOUNT: N PROPER+N; = territory]

6 Country music is the same as country and western music. EG *...a country singer.* [ADJ CLASSIF: ATTRIB]

7 In Britain, when the Prime Minister **goes to the country**, he or she holds a general election. [PHR: VB INFLECTS]

8 If something is your **line of country**, it is something that you know quite a lot about; a fairly informal expression. EG *Not my line of country, to be honest.* [PHR: USED AS C, POSS+PHR; = field]

country and western is popular music in the style of white people's folk music of the southern United States. EG *A radio blasted country and western music.* [N UNCOUNT]

country club, country clubs. A **country club** is a club in the country where you can play sports and attend social events. [N COUNT]

country dancing. In the British Isles, **country dancing** is traditional dancing in which people dance in rows or circles. EG *They'd like to learn Scottish country dancing.* [N UNCOUNT]

country house, country houses. A **country house** is a large and beautiful house in the country, especially one that is owned by a rich or noble family, or used to be. [N COUNT]

countryman /kʌntrɪmə³n/, **countrymen**. **1** Someone who is your **countryman** is from your own country. EG *I hope this doesn't shock my fellow countrymen... He has been more appreciated in Germany than by his own countrymen.* [N COUNT: USU POSS+N; = compatriot]

2 A **countryman** is also a person who lives in the country rather than in a city or a town. EG *I'm a countryman born and bred.* [N COUNT]

country seat, country seats. A **country seat** is a large house and estate in the country, which is owned by someone who also owns a house in a town. [N COUNT; ≠ town house]

countryside /kʌntrɪsaɪd/. The **countryside** is land which is away from towns and cities, including land used for farming. EG *We longed for the English countryside... It's very nice countryside around there.* [N UNCOUNT; = country; ≠ town]

countrywoman /kʌntri¹wʊ¹mə⁰n/, **countrywomen**. A **countrywoman** is a woman who lives in the country rather than in a city or a town. [N COUNT]

county /kaʊnti¹/, **counties**. **1** A **county** is a region of Britain, Ireland, or the U.S.A. which has its own local government. EG *I was a long way from home, on the other side of the county... ...Issaquena County, Mississippi.* ▸ used of the local government. EG *Some school governors are appointed by the county.* [N COUNT: ALSO IN NAMES; ▸ = County Council]

2 Someone who is **county** talks and behaves in a way that is typical of upper class people living in the country; used in informal British English. [ADJ QUALIT]

county council, county councils. A **county council** an organization which administers local government in a county in Britain. EG *...Kent County Council... The county council's move to appoint the ten new teachers was heavily criticized.* [N COUNT: ALSO IN NAMES AFTER N; ⇑ administration]

county town, county towns. A **county town** is the most important town in a county, from which the county is administered; used in British English. [N COUNT]

coup /kuː/, **coups**. A **coup** is **1** an attempt by a group of people, often army officers, to get rid of the president or government of a country and to seize power for themselves. EG *His Action Service men had carried out the coup... A coup displaced the regime that had imprisoned him.* [N COUNT; ⇑ revolution; = coup d'état] **2** an achievement which is thought to be especially brilliant because it was very difficult. EG *Brooke went on to bigger things, his next notable coup being the case of Robert Scott.* [N COUNT; = masterstroke]

coup de grace /kuː də grɑːs/. A **coup de grace** is an action or event which finally destroys something, for example an institution, which has been gradually growing weaker; a formal expression. EG *This trouble finally gave the coup de grace to the crumbling edifice of empire.* [N SING WITH DET; = deathblow]

coup d'état /kuː deɪtɑː/, **coups d'état**. The plural form is pronounced the same as the singular form. A **coup d'état** is a coup intended to get rid of the president or government of a country. EG *Here governments are generally replaced by coups d'état.* [N COUNT/UNCOUNT]

coupé /kuːpeɪ/, **coupés**. A **coupé** is a car with a fixed roof, a sloping back, two doors, and seats for four people. [N COUNT]

couple /kʌpə⁰l/, **couples, coupling, coupled**. **1** A **couple** is **1.1** two people who are married, living together, or having a sexual relationship. EG *The young couple decided to start their tour immediately... This would raise pensions for married couples considerably.* [N COUNT: IF SING VB CAN BE SING OR PL] **1.2** two people who you see together on a particular occasion, for example two people who are dancing together. EG *They made a curious couple, Marsha skinny and penitent, Posy blustering and bold... He watched a couple revolving on the dance floor.* [N COUNT: IF SING VB CAN BE SING OR PL; = pair]

2 A **couple** of people or things means two people or things; an informal expression. EG *They've been helped by a couple of Washington newspaper reporters.* [N PART]

3 A **couple** of things or quantities means approximately two things or quantities. You use this informal expression when you are not sure of the exact number of things or quantities you are referring to [N PART+N IN PLURAL; ⇑ some; = a few] and the number is not important. EG *He met her a couple of years ago... ...a couple of hundred village boys... We had a couple more whiskies.*

4 If you **couple** something with something else, you do or deal with both things together. EG *I wonder if that ought not to be coupled with a re-examination of what kids actually want... Strong protests were made, coupled with demands for an international inquiry.*
V+O+A *(with)*: USU PASS = combine

5 If you **couple** two vehicles together, you join them together, so that one vehicle pulls the other. EG *...coupled coal trucks.*
V+O: USU+A *(to/together)*

6 To **couple** means to have sex; a literary word. EG *Adolescents regularly coupled in parked cars behind the school.* ◇ **coupling, couplings.** EG *...casual couplings and friendships.*
V OR V+A *(with)*: RECIP; ◇ N UNCOUNT/COUNT

couplet /kʌplɪˀt/, **couplets.** A **couplet** is two lines of poetry together, especially two lines that rhyme with each other and are the same length.
N COUNT ⇑ verse

coupon /kuːpɒn/, **coupons.** A **coupon** is 1 a piece of printed paper which gives you the right to pay less than usual for something or to get something without paying for it. EG *This coupon is worth five pounds.* 2 a small form which you write your name and address on and send to a company or organization so that they can send you back information about their product, service, etc. EG *The current brochure had a detachable coupon.* 3 a form which you fill in in order to enter a competition or to gamble on the football pools. EG *Every Thursday they fill in pools coupons.*
N COUNT = voucher; N COUNT; N COUNT

courage /kʌrɪdʒ/. 1 **Courage** is the quality shown by someone who decides to do something dangerous or something which may be disapproved of because they think they should do it, or who does not show fear in a dangerous situation; used showing approval. EG *She would never have had the courage to defy his will... He admired the British troops for their courage and endurance... He was awarded a medal for courage in the face of the enemy.*
N UNCOUNT = bravery, guts

2 The word **courage** is also used in the following expressions. 2.1 If you **have the courage of** your **convictions**, you have the confidence and strength of mind to do or say what you believe is right, even though other people may not agree or approve. 2.2 If you **take courage**, you begin to feel hopeful and confident about something. EG *Take courage and embark... I take courage from J Robert Oppenheimer's vision.* 2.3 If you **take** your **courage in both hands**, you decide to do something which you are afraid to do. EG *She took her courage in both hands and walked into the house.* 2.4 ● to **pluck up courage**: see **pluck**. ● to **screw up your courage**: see **screw**. ● See also **Dutch courage**.
PHR: VB INFLECTS; PHR: VB INFLECTS = take heart; PHR: VB INFLECTS = steel yourself

courageous /kəreɪdʒəs/. Someone who is **courageous** shows courage. EG *He had been courageous in battle... ...the most honest, courageous and talented of modern British politicians.* ▸ used of actions, statements, etc. EG *...his courageous attempt to get the facts published.* ◇ **courageously.** EG *She fought courageously for her principles.*
ADJ QUALIT = bold ≠ cowardly, timorous; ◇ ADV WITH VB = bravely

courgette /kʊəʒet/, **courgettes.** A **courgette** is a type of small vegetable marrow.
N COUNT

courier /kʊərɪə/, **couriers.** A **courier** is 1 a person employed by a travel company to look after people while they are on holiday. 2 a person who is paid to take a special letter or parcel from one place to another. EG *He was called to Palermo by an urgent message delivered by a courier.*
N COUNT = rep; N COUNT ⇑ carrier = messenger

course /kɔːs/, **courses, coursing, coursed.** 1 You say **of course** 1.1 when you are briefly mentioning something that you expect other people already realize or understand, or when you want to indicate that you think they should realize or understand it. EG *There is of course an element of truth in this argument... People might say how much better off we would be if there were no news. But of course that's not possible.* 1.2 when you are talking about an event or situation that does not surprise you. EG *I never did find out what happened. He never writes, of course... He said he had never read the text of Hamlet. Nobody believed him of course.* 1.3 as a polite way of saying yes, of giving permission, or of agreeing with someone. EG *'Dan, you remember Margaret?'–'Of course'... 'If I could make a telephone call,' he said. 'Of course,' Boylan said... 'I hope it's understood I'm just having a drink with you?'–'Of course. What else?'* 1.4 in order to emphasize a statement that you are making, especially when you are agreeing or disagreeing with someone. EG *'Do you love him, Dolly?'–'Of course I do. He's wonderful'... 'I'm only here to help you. You do trust me?'–'Of course I trust you, Boris.'... Everyone agreed that if a woman had to work then, of course, good child-care should be provided.*
PHR: USED AS ADV SEN = obviously, naturally; PHR: USED AS ADV SEN ≠ surprisingly; CONVENTION = sure, certainly; CONVENTION, OR PHR: USED AS ADV SEN = certainly

2 **Of course not** is an emphatic way of saying no. EG *'I hope I've not spoiled things.'–'Of course not, Myra.'... 'Do you want me to resign?'–'Of course not, my dear chap.'... 'Do you think he was killed?'–'No, no, of course not.'*
CONVENTION

3 A **course** is 3.1 a series of lessons or lectures on a particular subject. A course usually includes reading and written work that a student has to do. EG *I thought it might be useful to do a course like this... They have computer-science courses at 'O' level and 'A' level... The people on the course are really nice.... ...a course in novel writing.* ● See also **correspondence course, foundation course, refresher course, sandwich course.** 3.2 a series of things that you have regularly over a period of time, especially as medical treatment. EG *Another course of injections was prescribed.* 3.3 the route taken by a vehicle, especially a ship or aircraft. EG *Hilda was on the bridge, trying to keep a course... He was at the wheel again, with the Morning Rose back on course... We must be off course.* 3.4 the path or channel along which a river moves. EG *...the course of the Ganges.* 3.5 a piece of land where a particular sport is played or where races are held. EG *...a comfortable ranch-style house overlooking a golf course.* ● See also **racecourse, assault course.** 3.6 a part of a meal that is eaten separately from other parts of the meal. EG *The first course was soup with delicious crusty rolls... She had eaten course after course.* 3.7 a horizontal layer of building material, such as bricks or tiles; a technical term in building. ● See also **damp course.**
N COUNT; N COUNT+*of*; N COUNT, OR *off/on*+N; N COUNT+SUPP; N COUNT: USU MOD+N ⇑ site; N COUNT; N COUNT

4 A **course** or a **course of action** is one of the things that you can do in a particular situation. EG *The company has a choice of three courses of action... To take the first course would offend against the principle of fairness; to take the second course would be economically disadvantageous.*
PHR: N INFLECTS ⇑ plan = approach

5 The **course** of history, nature, etc is the way that it happens or develops. EG *It was one of those ideas that change the course of history... What effect might this have had on the course of the war?... In the normal course of events, he would have glanced at his reports over coffee.*
N SING: *the*+N+*of* ⇑ development = progress

6 If something happens **in the course of** a particular period of time, it happens during that period of time. EG *I hope that in the course of the next two or three weeks they'll make up their minds.* ● **in due course**: see **due.**
PREP

7 If something changes or becomes true **in the course of time**, it changes or becomes true over a long period of time. EG *...a row of saplings that, in the course of time, will turn into an avenue of trees.*
PHR: USED AS AN A = eventually

8 If you do something **as a matter of course**, you do it as part of your normal work or way of life. EG *They learn to take responsibility for others as a matter of course... Harry now flies overseas as a matter of course.*
PHR: USED AS AN A

9 If something **runs its course** or **takes its course**, it develops naturally and comes to a natural end. EG *The illness ran its course and she eventually recovered.*
PHR: VB INFLECTS ⇑ develop

10 If you **stay the course** or **stick the course**, you finish something that you have started, even though it has become very difficult or you have become discouraged. EG *They like to interview you to make sure you're likely to stick the course.*
PHR: VB INFLECTS = see something through

11 **Course** is also an informal, spoken form of the expression 'of course', when it is used as a way of saying 'yes' or to emphasize a statement.
ADV SEN = of course

12 If a liquid **courses** somewhere, it flows quickly; a literary use. EG *Tears coursed down my face.*
V: USU+A = stream

coursing /kɔːsɪŋ/ is a sport in which rabbits or hares are hunted with dogs.
N UNCOUNT

court /kɔːt/, **courts, courting, courted.** 1 A **court** is a place where legal matters are decided by a judge and jury or by a magistrate. EG *...evidence for possible use in court... The court case was being heard in London... ...divorce courts.* ▸ The **court** is
N COUNT, OR *in*+N; ▸ N COUNT: *the*

used to refer to the people in a court, especially the judge, jury, or magistrates. EG *The court dismissed the charges... The whole business should be left to the courts.* • See also **crown court**, **high court**, **kangaroo court**, **Supreme Court**.

2 If you **go to court** or **take** someone **to court**, you take legal action against them, with the result that they are tried in a court of law. EG *Higgs was forced to go to court... I told them I could take them to court.* PHR : VB INFLECTS = sue

3 If a legal matter is decided **out of court**, it is decided without legal action being taken in a court of law. EG *Isaacs was offering to settle out of court for 10,000 pounds... ...an out of court settlement.* PHR : USED AS AN A, OR BEFORE N

4 A **court** is also 4.1 the area in which you play a game such as tennis, badminton, or squash. EG *...an indoor court... Off court as well as on, Billie Jean has taken risks.* N COUNT, OR *off/on/out of*+N ⇑ place 4.2 a courtyard. EG *...four circular huts around a broad central court.* N COUNT

5 The **court** of a king or queen is the place where he or she lives and carries out ceremonial or administrative duties with the help of officials and advisers. EG *The king had commanded his presence at court... ...a court painter.* N COUNT, OR *at*+N ▸ used of the people at a royal court. EG *...the court of Louis XIV.* ▸ N COUNT

6 **Court** is also used in the names of large houses and blocks of flats. EG *...Chestnut Court.* N SING : USED IN NAMES AFTER N

7 If a man **courts** a woman, he pays a lot of attention to her because he wants to marry her; a rather old-fashioned use. EG *...Dr Cooper, who that summer courted my aunt.* V+O = woo

8 If a man and a woman **are courting**, they are spending a lot of time together, because they are intending to marry each other; a rather old-fashioned use. EG *We used to go there when we were courting... ...courting couples.* V OR V+O = be going out ◊ **courting**. EG *They began their courting more or less in secret.* ◊ N UNCOUNT

9 To **court** death, disaster, punishment, etc means to behave in a way that makes it likely to happen to you; a formal use. EG *Thousands courted arrest by deliberately defying the new law... Walston appears to be courting disaster.* V+O ⇑ invite = risk

10 To **court** something that you want means to try to persuade someone to give it to you; a literary use. EG *He brazenly courted favour from all the visiting nobility.* V+O ⇑ invite

11 If someone **holds court**, they are surrounded by people who pay a lot of attention to them, because they think that the person is important, interesting, etc. EG *He held court at one end of the bar.* PHR : VB INFLECTS

12 If you **laugh** someone or their opinions **out of court**, you say that their opinions are so ridiculous that they are not worth considering at all. EG *I was laughed out of court for my views.* PHR : VB INFLECTS ⇑ ridicule

courteous /kɜ̲:tɪəs/. Someone who is **courteous** is polite, respectful, and considerate. EG *He was quietly courteous to the staff... ...a grave, courteous man in late middle age.* ADJ QUALIT : IF+ PREP THEN *to* ▸ used of behaviour. EG *Our customers should always receive courteous treatment.* ◊ **courteously**. EG *The jailer received me courteously.* ◊ ADV WITH VB

courtesan /kɔ̲:tɪzæ̲n/, **courtesans**. A **courtesan** is a woman who, in former times, was looked after by the rich and important men that she had sexual relationships with. N COUNT ⇑ mistress

courtesy /kɜ̲:tɪsi[1]/, **courtesies**. 1 **Courtesy** is behaviour that is polite, respectful, and considerate. EG *He replied with promptness and courtesy... Common courtesy dictates that a guest should receive a welcome.* N UNCOUNT ⇑ politeness

2 **Courtesies** are polite remarks that you make, for example when you have just met someone. EG *There was a brief exchange of courtesies with Elizabeth.* N PLURAL = civilities

3 If something is done **by courtesy of** someone or **courtesy of** someone, it is done because they have given their permission for it to be done; often used when you are formally thanking someone. EG *We MPs do not sit here by courtesy of the Lords... And now here are some new pictures of Venus, courtesy of NASA.* PREP = thanks to

4 If something happens **by courtesy of** a situation or circumstance, it happens because the situation or circumstance makes it possible for it to happen; a formal expression. EG *We could see it purely by courtesy of the fact that we were on the bridge... He was Prime Minister by courtesy of an uneasy alliance with the Liberals.* PREP = because of

courtesy title, courtesy titles. A **courtesy title** is a title that the son or daughter of a lord sometimes has, although it is not a legal title. N COUNT

courthouse /kɔ̲:thaʊs/, **courthouses**. A **courthouse** is a building in which a court of law meets; used in American English. N COUNT

courtier /kɔ̲:tɪə/, **courtiers**. A **courtier** was a person who spent a lot of time at the court of a king, queen, or other ruler, or who had an official position there. EG *...Queen Elizabeth and her courtiers.* N COUNT ⇑ attendant

courtly /kɔ̲:tli[1]/, **courtlier, courtliest**. Someone who is **courtly** is polite, dignified, and well educated. EG *...a courtly old gentleman named John Jameson.* ADJ QUALIT = gracious

court-martial, court-martials, court-martialling, court-martialled. The noun is usually spelled without a hyphen. The technical plural is **courts martial**. 1 A **court martial** is the trial in a military court of a member of the armed forces who is charged with breaking a military law. EG *They arrested General Lee for disobedience, and ordered a court-martial.* N COUNT, OR *by*+N

2 To **court-martial** a member of the armed forces means to cause him or her to be tried in a court martial. EG *The colonel threatened to court-martial him.* V+O ⇑ try

court of appeal, courts of appeal. A **court of appeal** is a court in Britain and some other countries which deals with appeals against legal judgements. EG *The Lords are the final court of appeal for all other courts.* N COUNT

court of inquiry, courts of inquiry. A **court of inquiry** is a group of people who are officially appointed to investigate a serious accident or incident. EG *A court of inquiry sharply criticized the local authority.* ▸ also used to refer to the investigation. EG *...a court of inquiry into what happened.* N COUNT

court of law, courts of law. When you refer to a **court of law**, you are referring to a legal court, especially when talking about the evidence that might be given in a trial. EG *...evidence which would stand up in a court of law.* N COUNT

courtroom /kɔ̲:tru[4]:m/, **courtrooms**. A **courtroom** is a room in which a legal court meets. N COUNT = court

courtship /kɔ̲:tʃɪp/ is the activity of courting, or the period of time during which a man is courting a woman, or a man and a woman are courting. EG *Marriage can be an anti-climax after the romance of courtship.* ▸ also used of birds and animals. EG *Courtship will include displays in which the male fluffs up his feathers.* N UNCOUNT

courtyard /kɔ̲:tjɑ:d/, **courtyards**. A **courtyard** is a flat open area of ground that is surrounded by buildings or walls. It is often paved. EG *He went out through the courtyard and into the street... ...the courtyard gates.* N COUNT ⇑ yard

cousin /kʌzə[0]n/, **cousins**. 1 Your **cousin** is the child of your uncle or aunt. EG *Have you met my pretty cousin Corinne?... I have cousins in the village.* N COUNT ⇑ relative

2 You refer to people as your **cousins** when you are referring to people in a different place who are similar to you or who have the same opinions or interests. EG *We have many things in common with our American cousins.* N COUNT : USU POSS+N IN PL = comrade

3 • See also **first cousin, second cousin**. • **first cousin once removed**: see **removed**.

couture /ku:tʊ̲ə/ is high fashion designing and dressmaking. EG *Rome couture would be nowhere without Valentino... ...the big couture establishments.* N UNCOUNT

couturier /ku:tʊ̲ərɪeɪ/, **couturiers**. A **couturier** is a person who designs, makes, and sells fashion clothes for women. N COUNT = designer

cove /kəʊ̲v/, **coves**. A **cove** is a small bay on the coast. EG *...a window looking over a small cove... ...Fisherman's Cove.* N COUNT : ALSO IN NAMES AFTER N

covenant /kʌ̲və[0]nənt/, **covenants**. A **covenant** is 1 a formal, written promise to pay a sum of money each year for a fixed period, especially to a charity. N COUNT

2 a formal, written agreement between two people or groups of people which is recognized in law. N COUNT

Coventry /kɒ̲vəntri[1]/. If you **send** someone **to Coventry**, you avoid speaking to them whenever you meet them, as a punishment for something that they have done. EG *They punished me by sending me to Coventry for the rest of the summer holiday.* PHR : VB INFLECTS ⇑ punish = ostracize

cover /kʌ̲və/, **covers, covering, covered**. 1 If you **cover** something, you place or spread something else over it in order to protect it or hide it. EG *She* V+O (NG/REFL), OR PHRASAL VB : V+O+ADV *covered her face with her hands... She laid the child gently down on its bed. Then she covered it with a sheet... The tray was covered with a starched white cloth.*

2 If something **covers** something else, it forms a layer all over it. EG *Feathers covered its whole body, except for the legs... Indian rugs cover the downstairs floors... Her hand was covered with blood... The entire land was covered in snow.* V+O ⇑ coat

3 If something **covers** a particular area of land, it takes up that area of land or is everywhere in it. EG *The settlement may have covered as much as 14 acres... Three-quarters of the world's surface is covered by water.* V+O = occupy

4 If you **cover** a particular distance, you travel that distance. EG *I decided to cover approximately twenty miles a day.* V+C = cross

5 To **cover** soldiers, ships, etc means to protect them from enemy attack while they are carrying out a particular operation. EG *Iceland-based F-15s would cover the operations.* V+O

6 If you **cover** someone, you keep a gun pointed in the direction of people who may attack them, so that you are ready to shoot if necessary. EG *Cover me... We've got you covered.* V+O ⇑ guard

7 An insurance policy that **covers** someone or something guarantees that money will be paid by the insurance company if there is illness, damage, etc. EG *40 per cent of the people are covered by private health insurance... Will the goods be covered for loss or damage through fire?* V+O : IF+PREP THEN *for* ⇑ insure

8 If something such as a law **covers** a particular set of people, things, activities, etc, it applies to them. EG *Workers in factories are already covered by the Factories Act.* V+O ⇑ include

9 If you **cover** a particular topic, you discuss it in a lecture, course, etc. EG *We've covered a wide range of subjects today.* V+O ⇑ include = deal with

10 If a reporter, newspaper, television company, etc **covers** an event, they report on it. EG *My editor asked me to go over to England to cover a British general election.* V+O ⇑ describe

11 If a sum of money **covers** something, it is enough to pay for it. EG *Her husband's earnings don't cover the family needs.* V+O

12 If you **are covered** with or in a particular feeling, you feel it very strongly. EG *I was covered with confusion. I didn't know what to do... He stands there, covered in shame.* ADJ CLASSIF : PRED+*in/with* ⇑ be overcome

13 A **cover** is **13.1** something which is put over or which fits over something else, for example in order to protect it or keep it clean. EG *She put the cover on her typewriter... The metal cover fits over the body of the tap.* N COUNT **13.2** something that seems respectable or normal, but that is intended to hide secret or illegal activities. EG *It would be shocking if it were to become a cover for murder... ...a cover name.* N COUNT ⇑ screen = front

14 The **covers** on a bed are the sheet, blankets, quilt, etc that you have on top of you in order to keep yourself warm. EG *She was lying under the covers, with her hair spread on the pillow.* N PLURAL : *the*+N ⇑ bedding = bedclothes

15 The **cover** of a book or a magazine is the outside part of it. The cover of a book is thicker than its pages. EG *On the front cover was a picture of a woman... She read the book from cover to cover.* N COUNT

16 Cover is **16.1** trees, rocks, or other places where you shelter from the weather or hide from someone. EG *They crossed to the other side of the stream in search of cover.* N UNCOUNT = concealment **16.2** protection from enemy attack that is provided for soldiers, ships, etc while they are carrying out a particular operation. EG *The ships would no longer have air cover from large fleet carriers.* N UNCOUNT **16.3** a guarantee from an insurance company that money will be paid by them if there is illness, damage, etc. EG *This policy gives unlimited cover for hospital charges and specialist fees.* N UNCOUNT : IF+PREP THEN *for*

17 The word **cover** is also used in the following expressions. **17.1** If you **break cover**, you come out of a place where you have been hiding. EG *They broke cover into the sunlight.* PHR : VB INFLECTS **17.2** If you **take cover**, you shelter from the weather or from gunfire. PHR **17.3** If a person or thing is **under cover**, they are under something that protects them from the weather, for example a roof. EG *I've got to put the car under cover.* PHR : USED AS AN A ⇑ sheltered **17.4** If you do something **under cover of** something such as darkness or a disturbance, you do it using the darkness or disturbance to prevent you from being noticed. EG *The attack usually takes place under cover of darkness.* PREP **17.5** If you receive something from a firm **under plain cover**, you receive it in a plain envelope, with only your name and address on it. PHR : USED AS AN A **17.6** If something is sent to you **under separate cover**, it is sent in a separate envelope or package. EG *We acknowledge your order, and advise you that the goods will be despatched under separate cover.* PHR : USED AS AN A ⇑ separately

18 See also **covered, covering, loose covers.**

cover up. 1 If you **cover** something **up**, you place or spread something else over it in order to protect it or hide it. EG *Cover yourself up with this sheet.* PHRASAL VB : V+O+ADV

2 If you **cover up** something that you do not want people to know about, you hide it from them. EG *There is a great deal to cover up in this case... He had known all along, he had covered up, he had lied steadily... She tried to cover up for Willie.* ● See also **cover-up.** PHRASAL VB : V+ADV, OR V+O+ADV, IF+PREP THEN *for*

coverage /kʌvəʳrɪdʒ/ is the reporting in a newspaper or magazine, or on television or radio, of a particular activity or subject. EG *They put an immediate ban on all television coverage of their operations.* N UNCOUNT ⇑ description = reportage

cover charge, cover charges. A **cover charge** is a sum of money that you must pay in some restaurants and nightclubs in addition to the money that you pay there for your food and drink. N COUNT ⇑ payment

covered /kʌvəd/ is used to describe something that has a lid or a roof. EG *...covered boxes... ...a narrow covered alleyway.* ADJ CLASSIF : ATTRIB

cover girl, cover girls. A **cover girl** is an attractive woman whose photograph appears on the front of a magazine. N COUNT ⇑ model

covering /kʌvəʳrɪŋ/, **coverings.** A **covering** is a layer of something that exists or is placed over something else. EG *There are three separate coverings around the brain itself... Kitchen floor covering should be non-slip... You will need a couple of blankets for extra covering.* N COUNT/UNCOUNT

covering letter, covering letters. A **covering letter** is a letter that you send with a parcel or with another letter in order to give extra information or an explanation. N COUNT

coverlet /kʌvəlɪ²t/, **coverlets.** A **coverlet** is a decorative cover which is put over a bed, on top of the sheets and blankets; a fairly formal word. N COUNT

covert /kʌvət/, **coverts. 1** If something is **covert**, it is secret or hidden, and not done or shown openly; a formal use. EG *He searched through his mind for some clue she had given him, some covert signal.* ADJ QUALIT = clandestine ≠ overt ◊ **covertly.** EG *I would see them eyeing me covertly across the room.* ◊ ADV WITH VB

2 A **covert** is a group of small trees or bushes very close to each other where small animals or game birds can hide. EG *They surrounded the covert.* N COUNT ⇑ thicket

cover-up, cover-ups. A **cover-up** is an attempt to hide the truth so that people do not realize that there has been a crime or mistake. EG *He denied that he took any part in the cover-up.* N COUNT ⇑ concealment = whitewash

covet /kʌvɪt/, **covets, coveting, coveted.** If you **covet** something, you strongly want to have it for yourself; a fairly formal word. EG *It was an honour he had long coveted... She had succeeded in winning one of the coveted vacancies in the Foreign Office.* V+O = desire

covetous /kʌvɪtəs/. **Covetous** feelings and actions involve a strong desire to possess something, especially something that someone else has; a formal word. EG *The United States Steel Corporation was casting covetous eyes at his company.* ADJ QUALIT ◊ **covetously.** EG *She was beginning to eye the brooch covetously.* ◊ ADV WITH VB ◊ **covetousness.** EG *In her fine black eyes he saw ambition, cunning and covetousness.* ◊ N UNCOUNT = greed

cow /kaʊ/, **cows, cowing, cowed. 1** A **cow** is **1.1** a large female animal that is kept on farms for its milk. EG *Better management may enable one man to milk more cows.* N COUNT **1.2** any animal of this species, either male or female; not a technical use. You can refer to a number of these animals as 'cattle'. EG *...a herd of cows.* ● See also **sacred cow.** N COUNT : USU PL **1.3** the female of some mammals, especially elephants, whales, and seals; a technical term in zoology. EG *...a small group of whales-three cows and two calves... ...a cow elephant.* N COUNT

2 If you describe a woman as a **cow**, you mean that she is very unpleasant; an offensive use in very informal English. N COUNT : ALSO VOC = bitch

3 If someone **is cowed**, they are made afraid, or made to behave in a particular way because they have been frightened or oppressed. EG *The peasantry cannot be annihilated or even cowed by bombs... People shouldn't allow themselves to be cowed into this.* ◊ **cowed**. EG *...his tragically cowed and battered wife.* — V+O : USU PASS ⇑ frighten = scare, subdue ◊ ADJ QUALIT = terrorized

4 If you say that you could do something **till the cows come home**, you mean that you could keep doing it without getting bored or tired, because you enjoy doing it; an informal expression. EG *We could keep on talking till the cows come home.* — PHR : USED AS AN A ⇑ forever

coward /kaʊəd/, **cowards**. A **coward** is someone who is easily frightened and who avoids dangerous and unpleasant situations; used showing disapproval. EG *I was basically a dreadful coward... Fool! Coward!* — N COUNT : ALSO VOC = chicken

cowardice /kaʊədɪs/ is cowardly behaviour; used showing disapproval. EG *They would certainly have been accused of cowardice if they had let this opportunity pass... He despised them for their cowardice and ignorance.* — N UNCOUNT = faint-hearted ≠ courage

cowardly /kaʊədli[1]/. **Cowardly** behaviour is behaviour in which someone avoids doing something dangerous or unpleasant because they are afraid; used showing disapproval. EG *...a cowardly and perverse refusal to face reality.* ▸ used of people and groups. EG *Management was feeble and cowardly... ...corrupt and cowardly generals.* — ADJ QUALIT ⇑ weak = spineless ≠ courageous

cowboy /kaʊbɔɪ/, **cowboys**. A **cowboy** is 1 a man employed to look after cattle in America, especially in former times. EG *...cowboys driving herds of cattle.* — N COUNT ⇑ worker = cowman

2 a male character in a Western; used in informal English. EG *...cowboy films.* — N COUNT 3 a worker, for example a builder, who is not experienced, skilful, or careful, and whose business is often not run honestly; used in informal British English. EG *There are too many cowboys in the business these days... ...cowboy contractors.* — N COUNT ≠ professional

Cowboys and Indians is a children's game in which one group pretends to be cowboys and another group pretends to be Red Indians and the two groups pretend to fight each other. — N UNCOUNT

cower /kaʊə/, **cowers, cowering, cowered**. If you **cower**, you bend forward and downwards or move back because you are very frightened of someone or something. EG *Bernadette cowered in her seat.* — V : USU+A ⇑ crouch = cringe

cowhide /kaʊhaɪd/ is leather made from the skin of a cow. — N UNCOUNT

cowl /kaʊl/, **cowls**. A **cowl** is 1 a large loose hood covering a person's head or their head and shoulders. Cowls are especially worn by monks. — N COUNT 2 a metal cover that is put on top of a chimney in order to help the smoke come out and to prevent the wind coming down the chimney. — N COUNT

cowman /kaʊmə[3]n/, **cowmen**. A **cowman** is a person employed to look after cattle. — N COUNT = cattleman

cowpat /kaʊpæt/, **cowpats**. A **cowpat** is a pool of dung from a cow, especially in a field. — N COUNT ⇑ dropping

cowrie /kaʊri[1]/, **cowries**. A **cowrie** is a shellfish which has an oval shell with a long narrow opening. ▸ also used to refer to the cowrie's shell. — N COUNT ▸ ⇑ shell

cowshed /kaʊʃɛd/, **cowsheds**. A **cowshed** is a building where cows are kept or milked. — N COUNT = byre

cowslip /kaʊslɪp/, **cowslips**. A **cowslip** is a small wild plant with yellow, sweet-smelling flowers. — N COUNT

coy /kɔɪ/. 1 If a person or their behaviour is **coy**, 1.1 they pretend to be shy and modest; used especially of women. EG *...a coy little smile.* ◊ **coyly**. EG *They were looking at us coyly through their elegant lashes.* ◊ **coyness**. EG *There is no false modesty or coyness about her.* — ADJ QUALIT = demure ◊ ADV ◊ N UNCOUNT

1.2 they are unwilling to say exactly what they mean or to give information about something, in a way that people find slightly irritating. EG *Let us not be coy about the identity of this great man... They maintained a coy refusal to disclose his name.* ◊ **coyly**. EG *She began to ask me questions, which I answered coyly, guardedly.* — ADJ QUALIT = evasive ◊ ADV WITH VB = evasively

2 Something that is **coy** is pretty or sentimental in an exaggerated or inappropriate way. EG *...a coy little cut-out of a girl in a crinoline.* ◊ **coyly**. — ADJ QUALIT = twee ◊ ADV WITH VB

coyote /kɔɪəʊt, kɔɪəʊt, kɔɪəʊti[1]/, **coyotes**. A **coyote** is a small wolf which lives in the plains of North America. — N COUNT

cozy /kəʊzi[1]/. See **cosy**.

crab /kræb/, **crabs**. A **crab** is a sea creature that has a flat roundish body covered by a shell, and five pairs of legs with large claws on the front pair. Crabs usually move sideways. EG *The fish and crabs scavenge for decaying tissue.* ▸ **Crab** is used to refer to the flesh of crabs eaten as meat. EG *Crab is one of the specialities of this place.* — N COUNT ⇑ crustacean ▸ N MASS ⇑ seafood

crab apple, crab apples; also spelled with a hyphen. A **crab apple** is a tree like an apple tree that produces small sour fruit. EG *Crab apples have pink and white blossom.* ▸ also used to refer to the fruit. EG *He was lectured as a child on the dangers of eating crab apples.* — N COUNT ▸ N COUNT/UNCOUNT

crabbed /kræbɪ[0]d/. 1 **Crabbed** handwriting is handwriting that is squashed together and hard to read. EG *...the name of Duggan, written in a crabbed hand.* — ADJ QUALIT = cramped ≠ bold

2 **Crabbed** means the same as crabby; an old-fashioned use. EG *He met a crabbed, cantankerous director.* — ADJ QUALIT

crabby /kræbi[1]/. Someone who is **crabby** is bad-tempered and unpleasant to people. EG *Why are you so crabby today?* — ADJ QUALIT = irritable, sour

crabwise /kræbwaɪz/. If you move **crabwise**, you move sideways. EG *I edged my way crabwise along the row to my allotted place.* — ADV AFTER VB

crack /kræk/, **cracks, cracking, cracked**. 1 When something **cracks** or when you **crack** it, 1.1 it becomes slightly damaged, with a line or many lines appearing on its surface. EG *If you hold a glass under the hot tap, it may crack... Heat can crack the polish... Their feet skid out from under them and they can crack their pelvises.* — V-ERG ⇑ break = split

1.2 it makes a sharp sound like the sound of a gun or a whip or the sound of a piece of wood breaking. EG *The whips began to crack over their heads... The branches snapped with a dry cracking noise.* — V-ERG = snap

2 If you **crack** your head, knee, etc, you hurt it by accidentally hitting it hard against something. EG *He fell, cracking his head on the edge of the table.* — V+O = smash, bang

3 When you **crack** something such as an egg or nut, you break its shell in order to get out the yolk or kernel. EG *The cook was cracking eggs over a grill.* — V+O ⇑ open

4 If someone **cracks** a safe, they open it by means of force, for example to steal what is inside. — V+O

5 If you **crack** a problem, you solve it, especially after a lot of mental effort. EG *He has cracked one of the crucial problems... They were eager to crack the codes.* — V+O

6 If you **crack** a joke, you tell it. EG *I was cracking jokes in the kitchen.* — V+O

7 If someone **cracks** or **cracks up**, they lose control of themselves and become mentally ill. EG *I thought I might crack if I didn't get away soon... I'd crack up if there wasn't someone I could talk to.* ● See also **crack-up**. — V OR PHRASAL VB : V+ADV = break down

8 If your nerve **cracks**, you become worried or afraid, and lose confidence in yourself. — V ⇑ fail

9 If, when you are speaking or singing, your voice **cracks**, it makes high-pitched noises which you are cannot control, because you are feeling a strong emotion. EG *'You were supposed to meet me at one,' she said, her voice cracking.* — V ⇑ squeaks, fails

10 If a system, organization, relationship, etc **cracks**, it show signs that the people involved in it are no longer satisfied with it and do not want to continue with it. EG *The empire starts to crack under its own pressure... Marriages begin to crack from the strain.* — V = break down, fall apart

11 A **crack** is 11.1 a very narrow gap between two objects or surfaces. EG *...the cracks between the boards of the ceiling... I opened the door a crack.* — N COUNT : IF+PREP THEN *between/in* = slit

11.2 a line that appears on the surface of something when it is slightly damaged. EG *She found a crack in one of the tea-cups.* — N COUNT : IF+PREP THEN *in*

11.3 a sharp sound like the sound that a gun or a whip makes or the sound of a piece of wood breaking. EG *His voice was like the crack of a whip... He heard the sharp crack of a twig.* — N COUNT : USU SING

11.4 a humorous comment that is often slightly rude or cruel. EG *There were the routine cracks about the Prime Minister... One more crack and you're out.* — N COUNT ⇑ joke

12 A **crack** at something means an opportunity to succeed at it; an informal use. EG *He's hoping for a crack at the championship.* — N COUNT : IF+PREP THEN *at* = shot

13 A **crack** regiment, football team, etc is a regiment, football team, etc which is highly trained and very efficient. EG *...a crack British regiment... ...crack players.* ● Someone who is a **crack shot** is an expert at firing a pistol or a rifle. EG *By now they were crack shots with their new weapons.* — ADJ CLASSIF : ATTRIB = first-rate ≠ mediocre ● PHR : USED AS C ⇑ marksman

14 If you do something **at the crack of dawn**, you do — PHR : USED AS AN

it very early in the morning; a rather old-fashioned expression. EG *He always got up at the crack of dawn.* A = at daybreak

15 If you get **a fair crack of the whip**, you are allowed a reasonable opportunity to show how good you are at doing something. EG *They are not giving us a fair crack of the whip.* PHR : USED AS O, USU WITH BROAD NEG ⇑ chance

16 If you **have a crack at** something, you try to succeed at it; an informal expression. EG *Let's have a crack at it.* PHR : VB INFLECTS = have a shot

17 If you **paste over the cracks** or **paper over the cracks**, you try to hide all the things that are wrong with something. PHR : VB INFLECTS = cover up

18 If you say that someone or something is **not everything** or **not all** they **are cracked up to be**, you mean that they are not as interesting, impressive, etc as other people have said that they are; an informal expression. EG *The life of the married is not all it's cracked up to be.* PHR : USED AS C ⇑ disappointing

19 See also **cracked, cracking**.

crack down. To **crack down** on a group of people means to become stricter in making them obey rules or laws and in punishing those who do not obey the rules. EG *Her first reaction to the riots was to crack down hard... The police cracked down on vandals and drug offenders.* • See also **crackdown**. PHRASAL VB : V+ADV, IF+PREP THEN *in* ⇑ suppress = clamp down ≠ ease up

crackdown /krækdaʊn/, **crackdowns**. A **crackdown** is strong official action taken to punish people who break laws or rules in order to make sure that the laws or rules are obeyed in future. EG *We were expecting an even more severe crackdown... ...a crackdown on criminals.* N COUNT : IF+PREP THEN *on* ⇑ restriction = clampdown ≠ let-up

cracked /krækt/. **1** An object that is **cracked**, has a line or many lines on its surface because it has been damaged. EG *The rubber nozzle is all cracked... ...the big, cracked mirror.* ADJ QUALIT

2 A voice or musical instrument that is **cracked** sounds rough and unsteady because of emotion or age. EG *...a high, cracked voice... ...the cracked tones of that old piano.* ADJ QUALIT

3 Someone who is **cracked** is slightly mad; an informal use. EG *He's cracked, if you ask me.* ADJ QUALIT = potty

cracker /krækə/, **crackers**. **1** A **cracker** is **1.1** a thin, crisp biscuit which is often slightly salty and is often eaten with cheese. N COUNT **1.2** a hollow cardboard tube covered with coloured paper and usually containing a small toy and a paper hat. Crackers make a sharp sound when you pull them apart. They are given to people at parties and meals, especially at Christmas. N COUNT **1.3** a small firework which makes a loud noise when you light it. N COUNT **1.4** something or someone that you admire, for example a shot at goal in a football match, or a pretty girl; used in informal British English. EG *...a cracker of a shot... She's a cracker.* N COUNT = beauty

2 If you say that someone is **crackers**, you mean that they are mad, or behaving as if they are mad; used in informal British English. EG *She must think we're crackers.* ADJ CLASSIF : PRED = crazy, potty

cracking /krækɪŋ/. **Cracking** is used in the following informal ways. **1** If you tell someone to **get cracking**, you are telling them to start doing something immediately. EG *Get cracking or we'll never finish in time.* PHR : VB INFLECTS = get moving

2 If you walk somewhere at **a cracking pace**, you walk there very quickly. EG *Busby maintained a cracking pace.* PHR

3 If you say that something is **cracking**, you mean that it is very good. EG *He was a cracking leader.* ADJ CLASSIF = first-rate

crackle /krækəl/, **crackles, crackling, crackled**. To **crackle** means to make a rapid series of short, harsh noises. EG *A bonfire crackled in one of the gardens... The loudspeaker crackled.* V
▸ used as a noun. EG *The only sound was the crackle of the fire.* ▸ N COUNT/UNCOUNT

crackling /kræklɪŋ/ is **1** a rapid series of short, harsh noises. EG *...the crackling of Mr Willet's bonfire... The crackling became louder and louder.* N UNCOUNT ⇑ noise **2** the crisp, brown skin of pork when it has been roasted. EG *Do you like crackling?* N UNCOUNT ⇑ meat

crackpot /krækpɒt/, **crackpots**. A **crackpot** is a person with absurd ideas who is fond of expressing them; an informal word. EG *Every crackpot in the world writes to him.* N COUNT = crank, nutter ▸ **Crackpot** is also used to describe the things that the person does or says. EG *...a crackpot letter... ...crackpot warnings.* ▸ ADJ CLASSIF = daft, barmy

crack-up, crack-ups. If someone has a **crack-up**, they lose control of themselves and become mentally ill; an informal word. EG *People gossiped about his crack-up.* N COUNT = breakdown

cradle /kreɪdəl/, **cradles, cradling, cradled**. **1** A **cradle** is **1.1** a small bed for a baby. It is shaped like a long box and often has a curved base so that you can rock it from side to side. EG *Albert walked over to the cradle where the baby was lying.* N COUNT = crib • If something happens to you **from the cradle to the grave**, it happens throughout your life. EG *Their lives were conditioned from the cradle to the grave by patterns of belief.* • PHR : USED AS AN A = all your life **1.2** a platform or open box with a strong floor, which is pulled up and down the outside of a building or ship so that workmen can do repairs or painting or clean the windows. EG *...a painter's cradle... The cradle swayed and bashed against the wall.* N COUNT ⇑ hoist **1.3** the part of a telephone on which the receiver rests when the telephone is not being used. EG *He replaced the receiver on its cradle.* N COUNT = rest

2 The **cradle** of something that is historically important is the place where it began. EG *New England saw itself as the cradle of American technology and progress... ...South Lancashire, the cradle of the industrial revolution.* N COUNT : USU SING, *the*+N+*of* = birthplace

3 If you **cradle** something, you hold it carefully in a hollow formed by your arms or your hands. EG *She cradled a child in her arms... He was holding out his hands, cradling the kitten.* V+O

cradle-snatcher, cradle-snatchers. A **cradle-snatcher** is a person who marries someone much younger than themselves, or who has a sexual relationship with them; used mainly in informal British English showing disapproval. N COUNT

craft /krɑːft/, **crafts, crafting, crafted**. **1** A **craft** is **1.1** an activity such as weaving, carving, or pottery that involves making things skilfully by hand, often in a traditional way. EG *I am teaching the craft to my brother's son... ...an international craft festival.* N COUNT ⇑ skill, art **1.2** an activity or job that involves making or doing something skilfully. EG *He was still learning his journalistic craft... He is a master of the craft, particularly in the use of sound editing.* N COUNT = trade, skill

2 **Craft** is **2.1** the ability to do something skilfully and well. EG *He manoeuvred the boat with all the craft and skill at his command... She has learned to trust her craft and professionalism.* N UNCOUNT = skill **2.2** cunning or crafty behaviour; an old-fashioned word. EG *With quick feminine craft she concealed her surprise.* N UNCOUNT ≠ openness

3 A **craft** is also **3.1** a vehicle such as a boat, hovercraft, or submarine that carries people or things on or under water. EG *There were eight destroyers and fifty smaller craft... My little boat was too frail a craft to weather these storms.* • See also **landing craft**. N COUNT = vessel **3.2** a spacecraft. EG *...a superb craft, designed to function in orbit for long periods.* N COUNT **3.3** an aeroplane. N COUNT

4 If something **is crafted**, it is made or done skilfully. EG *The head and hands were crafted after the rest of the carving was complete... ...highly crafted poems by a mature poet.* V+O : USU PASS ⇑ produce

craftsman /krɑːftsmən/, **craftsmen**. A **craftsman** is **1** a man who makes beautiful things such as pottery or carved wooden objects by hand. EG *I wanted to create something useful and beautiful the way a craftsman does.* N COUNT ⇑ artist **2** a man who does a skilled job, usually a job that involves using his hands to make something. EG *The equipment could be manufactured cheaply by local craftsmen... No matter how many times a young craftsman did his work wrong his boss could not sack him.* N COUNT ⇑ worker = artisan **3** a man who you consider to be very good at doing something. EG *...that great craftsman Gary Player, whose golf never fails to impress.* N COUNT+SUPP = maestro

craftsmanship /krɑːftsmənʃɪp/ is the skill that someone uses when they make something beautiful with their hands. EG *...Bernini's great craftsmanship.* N UNCOUNT ⇑ workmanship, artistry ▸ **Craftsmanship** is also used to refer to quality of the things that they have made. EG *I bent down to examine the exquisite craftsmanship.*

craftswoman /krɑːftswʌmən/, **craftswomen**. A **craftswoman** is a woman who does something skilfully, especially one who makes beautiful things by hand. EG *The room was packed with talented craftswomen.* N COUNT ⇑ artist

crafty /krɑːfti/, **craftier, craftiest**. If a person or their behaviour is **crafty**, they obtain or achieve something by deceiving people in a clever way. EG *...the crafty tactics of journalists... He's a crafty old* ADJ QUALIT = cunning, sly sneaky *thing... ...the craftiest of all politicians.* ◇ **craftily**. EG *'I won't tell anyone' Lynn said craftily.* ◇ **craftiness**. EG *He shows the same craftiness as his brother.* ◇ ADV WITH VB ◇ N UNCOUNT = deviousness

crag /kræg/, **crags**. A **crag** is a steep rocky cliff or part of a mountain. EG *...a 200 foot high crag.* N COUNT

craggy /krægi¹/. **1** A mountain, cliff, etc that is **craggy** is steep and rocky. EG *...the craggy mountains of Scotland... Below craggy cliffs is a cave known as 'Hell's Mouth'.* ADJ QUALIT = rugged

2 A **craggy** face is a face with large features and deep lines. EG *He had a craggy face with grey hair tumbling over it.* ADJ QUALIT = rugged ≠ smooth

cram /kræm/, **crams, cramming, crammed**. **1** To **cram** people or things into a place means to put or push more of them into the place than there is room for. EG *Thirty of us were crammed into a small dark room... He crammed the bank notes into his pockets and ran off.* V+O+A = pack, stuff ≠ empty

2 If you **cram** for an examination, you learn as much as possible in a short time just before you take the examination. EG *He was cramming for his finals.* V : IF+PREP THEN *for* = swot

crammed /kræmd/. If something is **crammed** with or **crammed** full of things or people, it is very full of things or people, so that there is hardly room for anything or anyone else. EG *They lived in a big house crammed with beautiful furniture... The other rooms were crammed with congressmen... ...a concrete bunker crammed full of delicate radio equipment.* ADJ QUALIT : PRED+ *with/full of* = bursting with, chock-full of

cramp /kræmp/, **cramps, cramping, cramped**. **1** If you have **cramp** or **cramps**, **1.1** you feel a strong pain caused by a muscle suddenly contracting. If you get cramp in your arm or leg, you often cannot move the arm or leg. EG *I had the most excruciating cramp in my leg.* ● See also **writer's cramp**. **1.2** you feel a strong pain in your stomach. EG *She had severe stomach cramps.* N UNCOUNT OR N PLURAL / N UNCOUNT OR N PLURAL

2 If a part of your body **cramps**, it gets cramp. EG *He rubbed his legs to keep the muscles from cramping.* V = seize up

3 To **cramp** a feeling or a person's ability to do something means to stop it developing. EG *Keeping a baby in a pen may cramp the desire to explore.* ● If you **cramp** someone's **style**, you behave in their company in a way that prevents them from achieving something, especially from impressing other people; an informal expression. EG *He was always saying the wrong thing and cramping her style in the presence of other people.* V+O = restrict ● PHR : VB INFLECTS ⇑ restrain

cramped /kræmpt/. **1** A **cramped** room or building is a room or building which is not big enough for the people or things that are in it. EG *...parents bringing up children in cramped high-rise flats... He cooked for himself in the cramped kitchenette.* ADJ QUALIT = confined ≠ spacious

2 Cramped handwriting is handwriting in which the letters and words are squashed together. EG *...a fat document, written in very cramped, close handwriting.* ADJ QUALIT ≠ bold

cranberry /krænbəᵒri¹/, **cranberries**. A **cranberry** is a red berry with a sour taste, often used to make a sauce or jelly that you eat with poultry. EG *...turkey and cranberry sauce.* ▸ also used of the bush that these berries grow on. EG *This little shrub is a close relative of the cranberry.* N COUNT ⇑ berry ▸ ⇑ shrub

crane /kreɪn/, **cranes, craning, craned**. **1** A **crane** is **1.1** a machine with a long movable arm that moves heavy things by lifting them in the air. EG *...the cranes on the building sites... They will have to be moved by crane.* **1.2** a large bird with a long neck and long legs that eats fish. EG *A grey crane flew into the tree opposite.* N COUNT, OR *by*+N / N COUNT

2 If you **crane**, or if you **crane** your neck or your head, you stretch your head in a particular direction in order to see or hear something better. EG *She craned to watch... He craned his neck out of the window... He paused again, craning his head forward.* V OR V+O : USU+A

cranefly /kreɪnflaɪ/, **craneflies**; also spelled with a hyphen and as two words. A **cranefly** is a harmless flying insect with long legs. N COUNT = daddy-longlegs

cranial /kreɪnɪəl/ means relating to your cranium; a technical term in biology. EG *...the cranial cavity.* ADJ CLASSIF : ATTRIB

cranium /kreɪnɪəm/, **crania** or **craniums**. Your **cranium** is the round part of your skull that contains your brain; a technical term in biology. EG *The bottom part of the cranium is delicate and breaks easily.* N COUNT

crank /kræŋk/, **cranks, cranking, cranked**. **1** A **crank** is **1.1** a person who has peculiar ideas and who behaves in a strange way as a result of them; used showing disapproval. EG *I didn't want to be thought a crank... Any religious crank can read his own meanings into the Bible.* **1.2** a device that enables you to move something in a particular direction by turning a handle. EG *Brody began to turn the crank to reel in the fish.* **1.3** a handle that you turn in order to start an engine, especially the engine of a motor vehicle. EG *He went to the front and jerked the crank.* N COUNT / N COUNT / N COUNT

2 To **crank** something means to cause it to move in a particular direction by turning a handle. EG *She cranked down the window on her side.* V+O : USU+A = wind

3 If you **crank** an engine or **crank** it **up**, you make it start by turning a handle. EG *Willie's father cranked the engine and got back in... The owner cranked it up and drove away.* V+O, OR PHRASAL VB : V+O+ADV

crankshaft /kræŋkʃɑːft/, **crankshafts**. A **crankshaft** is the main shaft of an internal combustion engine; a technical term. EG *...diesel engine crankshafts.* N COUNT ⇑ shaft

cranky /kræŋki¹/, **crankier, crankiest**. **Cranky** behaviour is strange behaviour which results from someone having unusual ideas; used showing disapproval. EG *...a bachelor of cranky habits.* ▸ used of people and groups. EG *...a cranky old woman.* ADJ QUALIT ⇑ odd = quirky, eccentric

cranny /kræni¹/, **crannies**. A **cranny** is a very narrow opening in a wall or rock. EG *The fish have underwater crannies where they hide... ...the crannies of the rocks beside the road.* ● **every nook and cranny**: see **nook**. N COUNT ⇑ gap = crevice

crap /kræp/, **craps, crapping, crapped**; a rude word used in very informal English, except in paragraph 5. **1** You describe something that someone says or writes as **crap** when you think that it is wrong or foolish; an offensive use. N UNCOUNT : IF+PREP THEN *about* ⇑ nonsense

2 You refer to objects as **crap** if they are unimportant, useless, or in your way. N UNCOUNT = junk

3 Crap also means the same as faeces. N UNCOUNT

4 When you **crap**, you get rid of faeces from your body. ▸ used as a noun to refer to this process. V ▸ N SING : *a*+N

5 Craps or **crap** is a gambling game, played mainly in the United States, in which you throw two dice and bet on the total score. EG *The boys gathered there to play in the mild game of craps... He stopped for a moment to watch the crap game.* N UNCOUNT

crape /kreɪp/. See **crepe**.

crappy /kræpi¹/, **crappier, crappiest**. You describe something as **crappy** when you think that it is of very poor quality; a rude word used in very informal English. EG *They watch those crappy old films on TV.* ADJ QUALIT = trashy ≠ good

crash /kræʃ/, **crashes, crashing, crashed**. **1** A **crash** is an accident in which a moving vehicle runs into something and is badly damaged or destroyed. EG *Her mother was killed in a car crash... ...a plane crash.* ▸ used as a verb. EG *The plane crashed within seconds of taking off... He crashed his car into the bar.* N COUNT : USU MOD+N = smash ▸ V OR V-ERG

2 To **crash** means **2.1** to hit something violently, making a loud noise. EG *The door crashed open... The heavy club crashed against his temple.* **2.2** to fall to the ground or the floor breaking into pieces and making a loud noise. EG *A glass spins from a hand and crashes to the floor... The brick walls crashed down.* **2.3** to move through something making a series of loud noises. EG *Morris was crashing through the thistles... The pig went crashing away through the forest.* V : USU+A = thunder / V+A = hurtle / V+A *(through)*

3 A **crash** is also **3.1** a sudden, violent, loud noise. EG *...a terrific crash of thunder.* ▸ used as a verb. EG *Applause began to crash all round me... The opening chords crashed out.* **3.2** a serious failure of a business or financial institution. EG *...one of the most spectacular financial crashes of the decade.* ▸ used as a verb. EG *Another travel agency has crashed leaving hundreds of tourists stranded.* N COUNT ▸ V : IF+ADV THEN *out* / N COUNT : USU+SUPP = collapse ▸ V

4 If you **crash** a party or other event, you go to it although you have not been invited; an informal use. EG *They have crashed the party to get free drinks.* V+O = gatecrash

5 If you **crash** somewhere, you sleep there for the night; used in informal American English. EG *Mind if I crash in your place tonight?* V+A

6 See also **crashing**.

crash barrier, crash barriers. A **crash barrier** is a strong low fence built along the side of a road at a dangerous corner or between the two halves of a N COUNT motorway in order to prevent accidents; used mainly in British English. EG *The lorry hit the crash barrier and overturned.*

crash course, crash courses. A **crash course** is a short course in which you are taught the most important things you need to know about something, for example before you start a new job. EG *Crash courses in Arabic were arranged.* N COUNT: IF+ PREP THEN *in*

crash helmet, crash helmets; also spelled with a hyphen. A **crash helmet** is a helmet that motorcyclists wear in order to protect their heads if they have an accident. EG *...a young man in a white crash helmet.* N COUNT

crashing /kræʃɪŋ/ is used to emphasize the great extent or degree of something; an old-fashioned, informal word, usually showing disapproval. EG *I find him a crashing bore... She's just had a crashing row with a friend.* ◊ **crashingly**. EG *His parents are crashingly orthodox.* ADJ CLASSIF: ATTRIB = almighty ◊ ADV+ADJ/ ADV

crash-landing, crash-landings. A **crash-landing** is an emergency landing made by an aircraft in an abnormal and dangerous way, for example when it has developed a fault and cannot land normally. N COUNT

crass /kræs/, **crasser, crassest.** **Crass** behaviour is behaviour that is stupid and lacking in taste or sensitivity. EG *Running a big business is sordid and crass... ...well-informed but crass comment.* ▸ used of people and groups. EG *...some crass bespectacled fool surrounded by telephones.* ◊ **crassly**. EG *She would never behave so crassly and rudely.* ◊ **crassness**. EG *He behaved with unbelievable crassness.* ADJ QUALIT = gross ▸ = asinine ◊ ADV WITH VB ◊ N UNCOUNT = tactlessness

crate /kreɪt/, **crates, crating, crated.** 1 A **crate** is 1.1 a large box made of pieces of wood which is used for transporting or storing things. EG *We broke open the crate with a blow from the chopper.* ▸ also used to refer to the contents of the crate. EG *The bus had crates of chickens strapped to the back... ...a crate of oranges.* 1.2 a plastic, wire, or wooden tray divided into sections and used for carrying bottles of milk, beer, etc. EG *The bottles chinked as the milkman put them into his wire crate.* ▸ also used to refer to the contents of the crate. EG *He went down to the cellar to fetch another crate of beer.* 1.3 an old car or aeroplane that is in bad condition; used in informal English. N COUNT ↑ container ▸ N PART ↑ amount N COUNT ▸ N PART N COUNT = crock

2 To **crate** something or to **crate it up** means to put it into a crate so that it can be stored or taken somewhere. EG *The airlines won't carry that machine unless it's crated... We decided to keep the painting, rather than crate it up with everything else.* V+O, OR PHRASAL VB: V+ O+ADV ↑ pack = box

crater /kreɪtə/, **craters.** A **crater** is a very large hole in the ground or in the surface of the moon, a planet, etc caused by something hitting it or by an explosion. EG *We'd have to go on foot into the crater... ...bomb craters... ...a crater 10-15 miles in diameter.* N COUNT

cravat /krəvæt/, **cravats.** A **cravat** is a piece of cloth that a man wears wrapped around his neck and tucked inside the collar of his shirt. EG *The high white cravat suited the elegance of the hall... ...his beautiful lemon chiffon cravat.* N COUNT ↑ scarf

crave /kreɪv/, **craves, craving, craved.** If you **crave** something, you want to have it very much. EG *She craved luxury... ...the absolute security for which he had always craved... Baker was craving for a smoke.* V+O, OR V+A *(for)* ↑ desire = hanker after

craven /kreɪvə⁰n/ behaviour is behaviour in which you do not do something because you are afraid; an old-fashioned word, used showing disapproval. ▸ used of people and groups. EG *I had no doubt that the craven fellow would be only too pleased to back out.* ◊ **cravenly**. EG *With any luck, I thought cravenly, the dispute will be forgotten by then.* ADJ QUALIT = fearful ▸ = cowardly ◊ ADV WITH VB = weakly

craving /kreɪvɪŋ/, **cravings.** A **craving** is a very strong desire for something. EG *She had a craving for sympathy... I get sudden cravings for sweets.* N COUNT: IF+ PREP THEN *for/ to-INF* = longing

crawl /krɔːl/, **crawls, crawling, crawled.** 1 If you **crawl**, you move forward on your hands and knees, for example in order to get through a small space. EG *I doubled up my large body in order to crawl in... Her baby is crawling about and upsetting things... The cameraman crawls under people's feet.* V: USU+A

2 When an insect **crawls**, it moves slowly across a surface. EG *The horrid little creatures would crawl up my trouser leg.* ◊ **crawling**. EG *...cockroaches and other crawling insects.* V: USU+A = creep ◊ ADJ CLASSIF: ATTRIB

3 When a vehicle **crawls**, it moves forwards very slowly. EG *The car barely crawled along the last fifty miles... The train crawled deeper into Russia.* ▸ used as a noun. EG *His car slowed to a crawl... Traffic was moving at a crawl.* ● See also **pub crawl**. V: USU+A = advance ▸ N SING: *a*+N

4 If something **makes** your **skin crawl**, it makes you feel horrified or revolted; an informal expression. EG *I heard a noise that made my skin crawl.* PHR: VB INFLECTS

5 If you **crawl** to someone, you try to please them and to make them like you in order to gain some advantage for yourself; used in informal English showing disapproval. EG *Let's see who comes crawling to whom.* V: IF+PREP THEN *to* = grovel

6 The **crawl** is a way of swimming in which you lie on your stomach, kick your legs, and swing one arm forward over your head and then the other. EG *Can you do the crawl?* N SING: *the*+N ↑ stroke = front crawl

7 See also **crawling**.

crawler /krɔːlə/, **crawlers.** A **crawler** is a person who tries hard to please someone in order to gain some advantage; used showing disapproval. EG *He's a real crawler.* N COUNT ↑ flatterer = toady

crawling /krɔːlɪŋ/. If you say that a place is **crawling** with people or things of a particular kind, you mean that it is full of people or things of a kind that you do not like; an informal word. EG *Below was the forecourt crawling with security men... The organization is crawling with agents.* ADJ CLASSIF: PRED+*with* = swarming

crayfish /kreɪfɪʃ/, **crayfishes.** The form **crayfish** can also be used for the plural. A **crayfish** is a small shellfish with five pairs of legs which lives in rivers and ponds. It has strong pincers on its front legs which it uses for catching food. N COUNT

crayon /kreɪə⁷n/, **crayons, crayoning, crayoned.** 1 A **crayon** is a pencil containing coloured wax or clay which is used for drawing, especially by children. EG *He tried to take the crayon away from her... ...a box of crayons... They wanted to add their own comments in crayon.* N COUNT/ UNCOUNT

2 When you **crayon**, you draw something with crayons. EG *The children had chosen to crayon Christmas cards instead... In the infants' room a crayoning lesson was in progress.* V OR V+O

craze /kreɪz/, **crazes.** A **craze** is an activity, style of clothes, etc that many people show a strong interest in but only for a short time; used also of the interest that is shown. EG *...the latest dance craze imported from America... Flower-arranging has become a great craze in Suffolk.* N COUNT: USU+ SUPP, IF+PREP THEN *for* = fad, trend

crazed /kreɪzd/. 1 **Crazed** behaviour is wild and uncontrolled behaviour by someone who is unable to think sensibly. EG *He made a crazed effort to regain the safety of the house... She fought with crazed ferocity.* ▸ used of people and groups. EG *We saw those crazed mobs pouring into our sector... She knew that others would see her as a crazed woman.* ADJ QUALIT: ATTRIB = crazy, lunatic ▸ ADJ QUALIT: IF +PREP THEN *with* = demented

2 A ceramic surface that is **crazed** is covered with fine cracks or lines. EG *It was brown and slightly crazed like an old earthenware pot.* ADJ QUALIT ↑ cracked

crazy /kreɪzi¹/, **crazier, craziest; crazies**; an informal word. 1 **Crazy** behaviour or talk is behaviour or talk which appears very strange or foolish to other people. EG *It's crazy to have a picnic in October... I realized that it was a crazy idea... I don't want to hear any more of this crazy talk.* ▸ used of people and groups. EG *My fellow students thought I was crazy... The village thought we had gone crazy... There is a crazy American who looks like George Orwell.* ◊ **crazily**. EG *A man rushed past him shouting crazily... I never thought she would be so crazily jealous.* ◊ **craziness**. ADJ QUALIT = daft ≠ sensible ◊ ADV = insanely ◊ N UNCOUNT

2 A **crazy** is a person who behaves in a way which seems very strange or foolish to other people; used mainly in American English. EG *They're taking advantage of a group of crazies.* N COUNT: USU PL = loony

3 If you are **crazy** about something, you are extremely interested in it and enthusiastic about it. EG *They are crazy about football... Everyone was jazz crazy.* ADJ QUALIT: PRED+*about* OR AFTER N = mad

4 If something makes you **crazy**, it makes you feel extremely annoyed or upset. EG *The tourists were beginning to drive me crazy... I'll tell you why I'm smiling, but it will make you crazy.* ADJ QUALIT: PRED ↑ angry = mad

5 **Crazy** also means insane. EG *He was a little bit–well, not crazy, but not normal either.* ADJ QUALIT = insane

crazy paving consists of irregular pieces of flat stone that have been fitted together on the ground in N UNCOUNT ↑ paving order to make a path or terrace; used mainly in British English.

creak /kri:k/, **creaks, creaking, creaked**. If something **creaks**, it makes a harsh unpleasant sound when it moves or when you stand on it, sit on it, etc. EG *The door creaked and Castle turned quickly... The lift creaks its way up the central tower... ...rotten, creaking, uneven floorboards.* V: ALSO V+O+A = groan
▸ used as a noun. EG *The creak of the mattress did not wake her... Eventually I got used to the creaks and the groans.* ▸ N COUNT = squeak ◊ **creaking**. EG *There was silence except for the creaking of the carriage.* ◊ N UNCOUNT/COUNT

creaky /kri:ki¹/, **creakier, creakiest**. Something that is **creaky** makes a harsh unpleasant sound when it moves or when you stand on it, sit on it, etc. EG *He was careful on the creaky stairs.* ADJ QUALIT ⇑ noisy

cream /kri:m/, **creams, creaming, creamed**. 1 **Cream** is 1.1 a thick, fatty, yellowish-white liquid that is taken from milk and is used in cooking or poured on fruit or puddings. EG *...strawberries and cream... I had rhubarb tart with a lot of cream.* N UNCOUNT ⇑ food 1.2 an artificial substance that looks and tastes like cream and is used as a filling in cakes and chocolates. EG *...delicious chocolates with cream fillings.* N UNCOUNT ⇑ food
1.3 a pudding containing cream. EG *...orange cream.* N UNCOUNT
1.4 a substance that you rub into your skin in order to make it soft. EG *She wiped the cream off her face... ...the cream she put on to soothe her sunburn.* N MASS: USU+SUPP ⇑ cosmetic
2 A **cream** is 2.1 a smooth thick liquid formed by mixing a substance and a liquid together. EG *Blend the cornflour to a smooth cream with the cold milk.* N SING: a+N
2.2 a sweet made of a soft flavoured substance and often covered with chocolate. EG *...chocolate creams.* N COUNT: MOD+N
2.3 a sweet biscuit containing a layer of a creamy substance. EG *...custard creams.* N COUNT: MOD+N
3 See also **clotted cream, sour cream, ice cream**.
4 If you **cream** potatoes or other root vegetables, you mash them thoroughly and mix them with milk or cream and butter; a technical term in cookery. EG *Cream the potatoes and place on top of the fish... ...creamed swedes.* V+O: IF+PREP THEN *with*
5 If you **cream** two or more substances, you mix them together in order to form a smooth mixture, for example when you are making a cake or a sauce; a technical term in cookery. EG *Cream the yeast with 2 tablespoons of warm water... Add egg whites and flour to the creamed mixture.* V+O: IF+PREP THEN *with*
6 **Cream** is also a yellowish-white colour. EG *The shell was deep cream touched here and there with pink.* N UNCOUNT
▸ used as an adjective. EG *...large pale pink and cream flowers.* ▸ ADJ COLOUR
7 If you refer to the **cream** of a group of people or things, you mean the best people or things in that group. EG *They were the smartest young people in Germany, the cream of their generation... Its crew were the cream of the navy.* N SING: *the*+N, IF+PREP THEN *of* = elite, pick

cream off. To **cream off** part of a group of people means to take them away and treat them in a special way, because you think that they are better than the rest of the group. EG *The best pupils would be creamed off and given a superior training.* PHRASAL VB: V+O+ADV ⇑ separate = select

cream cheese is a very rich, soft, white cheese. N UNCOUNT

cream cracker, cream crackers. A **cream cracker** is a crisp unsweetened biscuit which is often eaten with cheese. N COUNT

cream tea, cream teas. A **cream tea** is, in Britain, an afternoon meal consisting of tea to drink and scones with jam and clotted cream to eat. It can also include sandwiches and cakes. N COUNT

creamy /kri:mi¹/, **creamier, creamiest**. Something that is **creamy** 1 has a yellowish-white colour. EG *...a house made of creamy limestone... ...bushes with their creamy blossoms.* ADJ COLOUR = cream 2 contains a lot of cream. EG *...five buckets of frothing creamy milk... We'd like a nice cup of creamy coffee... ...rich creamy pastries.* ADJ QUALIT

crease /kri:s/, **creases, creasing, creased**. 1 **Creases** are irregular lines that appear on cloth, paper, etc when it has been crushed. EG *She smoothed down the creases in her dress... ...crease-resistant material.* N PLURAL
2 A **crease** is a straight line in something that has been pressed or folded neatly, especially on the front and back of the legs of a pair of trousers. EG *He was dressed immaculately, the creases in his trousers perfect.* N COUNT
3 In cricket, the **crease** is a line on the pitch near the wicket. It marks the place where the batsman stands and the point which he has to reach when making a run. EG *Botham arrived at the crease.* N COUNT: USU *the*+N IN SING
4 If you **crease** something such as cloth or paper or if it **creases**, it gets lines in it because it has been crushed. EG *Don't screw it up like that-you'll crease it! It's made of material that doesn't crease.* V-ERG = crumple ≠ smooth
◊ **creased**. EG *His suit had become creased.* ◊ ADJ QUALIT
5 If your brow or forehead **creases** or something **creases** it, it gets lines on it because you are frowning. EG *A wrinkle of doubt creased his forehead.* V-ERG ⇑ line = wrinkle
6 If someone or something **creases** you or **creases** you **up**, they make you laugh a lot; an informal use. EG *That really creases me... She creased me up!* V+O, OR PHRASAL VB: V+O+ADV

create /kri:eɪt/, **creates, creating, created**. 1 To **create** something means 1.1 to cause it to happen or come into existence. EG *His work created enormous interest in England... Killing you would create more problems than it would solve... A bomb striking the centre of a large city would create a crater over 300 feet deep... This reaction creates hydrogen gas.* V+O ⇑ make = produce ≠ destroy
1.2 to increase something that already exists. EG *...the failure of successive governments to create employment in rural areas.* V+O = generate 1.3 to invent, design, or manufacture it, especially when it is something new, interesting, or useful. EG *Present day technology could not create a robot which could solve this problem... The industry responded by creating a new textile... Gill created the statue in front of Broadcasting House... ...his urge to create... Can computers actually create language?* V+O, OR V = develop 1.4 to produce a series of thoughts or images in your mind. EG *I convinced myself that my imagination had created this feeling of danger... Your words create the most beautiful images.* V+O ⇑ imagine = conjure up
2 If you say that someone **creates**, they express great annoyance, often by shouting; used mainly in informal British English. EG *I never eat breakfast, although my dad creates like anything.* V: USU+A ⇑ fuss

creation /kri:eɪʃə⁰n/, **creations**. 1 **Creation** is 1.1 the act of bringing something new into existence or making something happen. EG *They proposed the creation of Welsh and Scottish parliaments... ...the creation of new jobs... ...a job creation scheme... ...the creation of visual images.* N UNCOUNT: IF+PREP THEN *of* 1.2 the making of the universe, earth and creatures by God as described in the Bible. N UNCOUNT: USU *the*+N 1.3 the whole universe, including the world and all the things in it. EG *They seem to look upon everything in creation as material for exploitation... ...our own small corner of creation.* N UNCOUNT
2 A **creation** is 2.1 something, especially a work of art, that has been made as the result of imagination, skill, and invention. EG *He makes furniture as well as his ceramic creations... London was a creation of the Romans.* N COUNT: USU+SUPP 2.2 a thought or image that is produced in your mind and not based on fact. EG *...the creations of a frightened imagination.* N COUNT 2.3 an elaborate hairstyle or piece of clothing. EG *The latest creations from Paris will be unveiled at the spring fashion show next week.* N COUNT ⇑ style 2.4 an unusual and elaborate food, especially one that involves a lot of complicated preparation; often used humorously. EG *Hardly a day went by without some new delectable creation being set upon the table.* N COUNT ⇑ dish

creative /kri:eɪtɪv/. 1 Someone who is **creative** has the ability to invent and develop new and original ideas, especially in an artistic way. EG *A youngster has more time to be creative... These achievements establish Northcliffe as a major creative force of the early twentieth century.* ADJ QUALIT ⇑ imaginative ▸ used of things that people do. EG *I'd like to get involved in something creative... ...creative writing.* ▸ = artistic ◊ **creatively**. EG *I'd like to write creatively.* ◊ ADV WITH VB
2 **Creative** can also describe the use of something in a new and imaginative way to produce interesting and unusual results. EG *...the creative use of language.* ADJ CLASSIF ⇑ inventive ≠ conventional
◊ **creatively**. EG *...the desire to use mathematics creatively.* ◊ ADV WITH VB

creativity /kri:eɪtɪvɪti¹/ is the ability to invent and develop new and original ideas, especially in an artistic way. EG *Is creativity an exclusive attribute of man?... This is a major inspiration for their creativity in architecture.* N UNCOUNT

creator /kri:eɪtə/, **creators**. 1 The **creator** of something is the person who made or invented it. EG *The police were known as Peelers in honour of their* N COUNT: USU WITH POSS ⇑ maker

creator, Sir Robert Peel... ...Kit Williams, the creator of the book 'Masquerade'.
2 The **Creator** means the same as God. EG *...a song of praise to the Creator.* — N PROPER : *the*+N

creature /kri:tʃə/, **creatures**. **1** A **creature** is **1.1** any living thing that can move about, such as an animal, bird, insect, etc. EG *The opossum is a large rat-like creature... Worms are very simple creatures.* — N COUNT ⇑ organism
1.2 a strange or frightening animal or being of a type that you have never seen or heard of before, often an imaginary one. EG *...a creature from outer space.* — N COUNT
2 If you refer to someone as a particular kind of **creature**, you are emphasizing a particular quality that they have, usually in a way that expresses disrespect or contempt; a rather literary use. EG *She was a weak and spineless creature... ...a voluptuous creature with blonde bobbed hair... ...a creature of habit.* — N COUNT+SUPP = thing
3 If you describe someone as someone else's **creature**, you mean that they are controlled by and dependent on a more powerful person or organization; a formal or literary use. EG *Too often the grand jury becomes the creature of the prosecutor.* — N COUNT : USU WITH POSS ⇑ slave = tool

creature comforts are the things that you need to feel comfortable in your life, such as good food, nice clothes, etc. — N PLURAL ⇑ luxuries

crèche/krɛʃ/, **crèches**. A **crèche** is a place where small children can be left and looked after while a parent is working, shopping, etc. — N COUNT

credence /kri:dəºns/ is believing that something is true, or the quality that something has which makes people believe it is true; a formal word. EG *He did not give much credence to the story... Her denials of this charge served merely to lend it credence.* — N UNCOUNT = credibility

credentials /krɪ²dɛnʃəºlz/. Your **credentials** are **1** your previous achievements, training, and general background, which indicate that you are qualified to do something or to have a particular role. EG *He was a botanist with splendid credentials... I think he has established his credentials to take over... His credentials as a journalist were beyond dispute.* — N PLURAL : USU+SUPP ⇑ reputation **2** a letter or certificate that proves a person's identity or their qualifications. EG *Didn't you ask for his credentials?* — N PLURAL ⇑ reference

credibility /krɛdɪbɪlɪti¹/. **1** If someone or something has **credibility**, people believe in them and trust them. EG *He felt that he had lost credibility... ...doubts about the credibility of the nuclear deterrent.* — N UNCOUNT ⇑ quality
2 **Credibility** is the quality of being believable. EG *Her greed was beyond credibility.* — N UNCOUNT

credibility gap. A **credibility gap** is the difference between what a person says or promises and what they actually think or do. EG *There's rather a large credibility gap between their election pledges and the policies that they actually implemented.* — N SING WITH DET = inconsistency

credible /krɛdɪbəºl/. **1** Someone who is **credible** is able to convince you that what they are saying is true and that they can be trusted. EG *No politicians seem credible these days.* — ADJ QUALIT ⇑ trustworthy ◊ **credibly**. EG *The argument was put very credibly, but I still had my doubts.* — ◊ ADV WITH VB
2 Something that is **credible** can be believed. EG *Is it credible, is life really like that?... His latest statements are hardly credible.* — ADJ QUALIT = convincing ≠ incredible, unbelievable

credit /krɛdɪt/, **credits, crediting, credited**. **1** **Credit** is a period of time that someone is allowed before they have to pay for goods or services that they have bought or before they have to pay back money that they have borrowed. EG *In stores where once he had been able to obtain credit he was now forced to pay cash... The availability of cheap long-term credit would help small businesses.* — N UNCOUNT ⇑ loan ● If something is bought or sold **on credit**, it is not paid for at the time when it is taken or used but is expected to be paid for later. EG *They sold grain on credit during times of famine.* — ● PHR : USED AS AN A = on tick
2 Your **credit** is the belief or trust that other people, especially business people, have that you will pay them money that you owe them, which makes them prepared to let you take goods without paying for them at the time. EG *Keeping your credit good is important.* — N UNCOUNT : POSS +N ⇑ trustworthy
3 A **credit** is **3.1** a sum of money which is paid into an account, for example a bank account. EG *A credit of £40 was paid into your account on 15th May... The ledger shows £300 on the debit side and £50 on the credit side.* — N COUNT ≠ debit **3.2** a document similar to a cheque or bank note which promises that a particular amount of money will be paid. — N COUNT
4 To **credit** a sum of money to an account or to **credit** an account with a sum of money means to add the sum of money to the total that is already in the account. EG *£15 was credited to her account... Credit the customer's account with £15.* — V+O+A *(to/with)* ≠ debit
5 To **credit** someone with an amount or to **credit** an amount to someone means to state in the official records of a financial system that this amount has been paid by them or that they qualify for such an amount according to the rules of the system. EG *You can be credited with contributions for those periods when you were unemployed... The employer's contributions will be credited to you.* — V+O+A *(with/to)*
6 If you are **in credit** or if your bank account is **in credit**, your bank account still has some money in it, and you are not overdrawn. — PHR : USED AS AN A ≠ in the red
7 A **credit** balance or account indicates that there is still some money in the account after all debts or expenses have been paid. — ADJ CLASSIF : ATTRIB ≠ debit
8 **Credit** for something is the respect or praise that people give to someone who has behaved well or honourably or who has achieved something good. EG *We can't claim much credit for her tennis proficiency... He wanted to bring credit to his family... Some of the credit should go to Nick... We can really take credit for the team's success.* — N UNCOUNT : IF+PREP THEN *for* = honour ≠ discredit, shame, blame
9 The word **credit** is used in the following expressions with the general meaning of respect or praise.
9.1 If you say that something **does** someone **credit**, you mean that it causes other people to respect or admire them. EG *Your concern for us all does you the greatest credit... Your son does you credit, Mrs Forrest.* — PHR : VB INFLECTS **9.2** If you say that someone is **a credit to** their parents, family, or school, you mean that they deserve praise for a quality that suggests that their parents, family, or school have brought them up or educated them well. EG *He is a credit to the family.* — PHR+NG : USED AS C ≠ disgrace
9.3 If you say that an action or point of view is **to** someone's **credit**, you mean that they deserve praise for it; often used when the same person is being criticized for other things. EG *It is to their credit that the delay was imposed... Price, to his credit, denounced in private the brutalities of the regime.* — PHR : USED AS AN A ≠ to someone's shame **9.4** ● If you have one or more achievements **to** your **credit**, you have already achieved them. EG *She already had several London successes to her credit.* — ● PHR : USED AS AN A = under your belt
9.5 You say **on the credit side** in order to introduce one or more of the good things about a situation, thing, or person, usually when you have already mentioned the bad things or intend to mention them later. EG *On the credit side he could reasonably bank on his colleague's honesty.* — PHR : USED AS ADV SEN = on the plus side
10 If you **are credited** with an achievement or if it **is credited** to you, people generally believe that you were responsible for it, although they are not certain. EG *...the woman who is often credited with originating the movement... ...a hunting scene credited to a 15th century Dutch artist.* — V+O : USU PASS+ *with/to*
11 If you **credit** someone with a particular good quality or ability, you believe or say that they have it. EG *I used to credit you with a bit of common sense... The world credits us with being experts.* — V+O+A *(with)*
12 If you **give** someone **credit for** a particular good quality, you believe or say that they have it. EG *The public are more tolerant than they are often given credit for being.* — PHR : VB INFLECTS
13 A **credit** is also the successful completion of a part of a higher education course. At some universities and colleges you need a particular number of credits in order to be awarded a degree. EG *She had acquired four of the six credits needed for her degree at the Open University.* — N COUNT = unit
14 The **credits** on something such as a film, a record, or a television programme refers to the list of people who helped to make it, which is usually shown on the record cover or at the end of the film or programme. EG *It was such a bad film that the audience had left long before the credits appeared on the screen.* — N COUNT : USU PL ⇑ acknowledgement
15 If you cannot **credit** something, you cannot believe that it is true. EG *There must be many of you who find this case hard to credit... Would you credit it!* — V+O : NO CONT ≠ disbelieve
16 **Credit** is also the belief that something is true. EG *This theory is now gaining credit.* — N UNCOUNT = credence

creditable /krɛ̲dɪtəbə⁰l/. 1 Something that is **creditable** is of a reasonably high standard. EG *He polled a creditable 44.8 per cent.* ◇ **creditably**. EG *She mimicked my tone very creditably.* — ADJ QUALIT ⇑ good; ◇ ADV WITH VB ⇑ well

2 **Creditable** behaviour is behaviour that you can be proud of and that people should respect you for. EG *He began to suppress some of the less creditable features of his past... That, I think, was creditable on his part.* ◇ **creditably**. EG *We came out of the whole business rather creditably.* — ADJ QUALIT = respectable, honourable; ◇ ADV WITH VB

credit account, credit accounts. A **credit account** is an account that you have with a shop which allows you to buy its goods on credit, especially by using a credit card which they give you; used mainly in British English. — N COUNT = charge account

credit card, credit cards. A **credit card** is a plastic card that a shop or company gives to a customer which allows him or her to buy goods on credit in the shop or to borrow money from the company. EG *More people are using credit cards for the majority of their purchases.* — N COUNT

credit note, credit notes. A **credit note** is a piece of paper that a shop gives you when you return goods that you have bought from them, for example because they are faulty. It states that you are entitled to take goods of the same value without paying for them. — N COUNT

creditor /krɛ̲dɪtə/, **creditors**. A **creditor** of a person or company is a person or company that they owe money to. EG *He fled the country when his creditors started demanding money.* — N COUNT ⇑ lender ≠ debtor

credit transfer, credit transfers. A **credit transfer** is a direct payment of money from one bank account to another. EG *We get paid monthly by credit transfer.* — N COUNT/UNCOUNT = bank giro

creditworthy /krɛ̲dɪtwɜːði¹/; also spelled with a hyphen. If someone is **creditworthy**, you can safely lend them money or allow them to have goods on credit, for example because in the past they have always paid back what they owe. ◇ **creditworthiness**. EG *...the debt problem and the need to prove creditworthiness.* — ADJ QUALIT ⇑ trustworthy; ◇ N UNCOUNT

credo /kri̲ːdəʊ, kre̲ɪ-/, **credos**. A **credo** is a set of beliefs, principles, or opinions that strongly influence the way people live or work; a formal word. — N COUNT : USU SING = creed

credulity /krɪ²dju̲ːlɪti¹/ is a willingness to believe that something is real or true, even when you suspect that it is not. EG *Don't stretch my credulity too far.* — N UNCOUNT ⇑ belief ≠ incredulity

credulous /krɛ̲djə⁴ləs/. If you are **credulous**, you are always ready to believe what people tell you, and are easily deceived. EG *...the kind and credulous Farlows... This gimmick will convince none but the most credulous.* — ADJ QUALIT ⇑ naive = gullible

creed /kri̲ːd/, **creeds**. 1 A **creed** is a set of beliefs, principles, or opinions that strongly influence the way people live or work. EG *The destruction of public monopolies was an indispensable part of his creed... ...political creeds.* — N COUNT = credo

2 A **creed** also means the same as a religion; a formal use. EG *The superiority of any human being or race or class or creed is a myth.* — N COUNT

3 The **Creed** is a short ritual statement of Christian religious beliefs which is said during some Church services; a technical use. — N SING : *the*+N

creek /kri̲ːk/, **creeks**. 1 A **creek** is 1.1 a narrow inlet where the sea comes a long way into the land. EG *They went past the lighthouse down towards the creek... ...the muddy creeks of my home coast.* 1.2 a small, narrow stream or river; used mainly in American English. EG *By early summer the creek was almost dry... ...Paradise Creek.* — N COUNT : ALSO IN NAMES AFTER N; N COUNT : ALSO IN NAMES AFTER N

2 If you say that someone is **up the creek**, you mean they are in a very difficult situation; an informal expression. EG *If you get there and find you've left the keys behind, then you're really up the creek.* — PHR : USED AS AN A = in trouble ≠ laughing

creel /kri̲ːl/, **creels**. A **creel** is a basket in which you put fish that you have just caught. EG *He laid the fish with the others in the creel.* — N COUNT

creep /kri̲ːp/, **creeps, creeping, crept**. 1 When people or animals **creep**, they move quietly and slowly, usually in order to get to a place without being noticed. EG *They watched the boy hunch down and creep towards the bush... I heard my landlady creeping stealthily up to my door.* — V+A = sneak

2 If something **creeps**, it moves very slowly, so that you hardly notice that it is moving; a literary use. EG *Big clouds crept up... Here and there, little breezes crept over the water... The statues cast long creeping shadows.* — V : USU+A ⇑ move

3 If something **creeps** into your mind, heart, etc, it slowly becomes a part of the way that you think or feel; a literary use. EG *The shadow of doubt began to creep into her mind... A sense of disillusionment and fear began to creep slowly into their hearts.* — V+A *(into)* = sneak

4 If someone **gives** you **the creeps**, you feel a strong dislike or contempt for them; an informal expression. EG *My wife adores him, but he really gives me the creeps.* — PHR : VB INFLECTS

5 If something **gives** you **the creeps**, it gives you a feeling of horror or fear; an informal expression. EG *The thought gives me the creeps... That perishing clock gives me the creeps every time I hear it.* — PHR : VB INFLECTS ⇑ frighten

6 If something **makes** your **flesh creep**, it gives you a very strong feeling of horror or fear; an informal expression. EG *The sight made my flesh creep.* — PHR : VB INFLECTS

7 If you say that someone is a **creep**, you mean that you dislike them strongly, usually because they try to flatter people and impress them; an informal use. EG *He's such a creep. I hate him... Leave me alone, you little creep.* — N COUNT = crawler

8 See also **creeping**.

creep in. If something such as a custom **creeps in**, it gradually becomes used by people in a particular group. EG *New gestures do occasionally manage to creep in and establish themselves... The word 'intelligence' is beginning to creep back in... Elements of military uniform creep in.* — PHRASAL VB : V+ADV ⇑ come in = slip in

creep up on. 1 If you **creep up on** someone, you move slowly closer to them without being seen by them. EG *One child stands facing a wall while all the others creep up on him... He was aware of something dangerous creeping up on them under cover of the bush.* — PHRASAL VB : V+ADV+PREP ⇑ approach = sneak up on

2 If a feeling or state **creeps up on** you, you begin to experience it very slowly. EG *She paused, fighting the dizziness that was creeping up on her... A sense of unreality was beginning to creep up on me.* — PHRASAL VB : V+ADV+PREP

creeper /kri̲ːpə/, **creepers**. A **creeper** is a plant with long stems that wind themselves around objects or other plants. EG *On their left was an impenetrable tangle of creepers and trees... The whole place had been taken over by giant creepers.* — N COUNT

creeping /kri̲ːpɪŋ/. 1 A **creeping** plant is a plant that grows and spreads along the ground. EG *...a low creeping plant, with hairy runners and stalks... ...this little creeping shrub.* — ADJ CLASSIF : ATTRIB

2 A **creeping** process is one that happens very gradually, especially one that you do not approve of. EG *...creeping political decay... ...creeping nationalization.* — ADJ CLASSIF : ATTRIB

creepy /kri̲ːpi¹/, **creepier, creepiest**. Something that is **creepy** gives you a strange unpleasant feeling of fear; an informal word used especially by children. EG *It was very creepy in the woods... We've found a creepy caravan where a witch lives.* — ADJ QUALIT ⇑ frightening = scary, spooky

creepy-crawly, creepy-crawlies. A **creepy-crawly** is a small insect which gives you a feeling of fear or disgust; an informal word used especially by children. EG *Mummy, Mummy, there's a creepy-crawly on my bed!* — N COUNT

cremate /krɪ¹me̲ɪt/, **cremates, cremating, cremated**. If you **cremate** someone, you burn their dead body, usually as part of a funeral service. EG *Her husband will be cremated... It is intended to cremate the body.* — V+O

cremation /kri¹me̲ɪʃə⁰n/, **cremations**. A **cremation** is a funeral service during which a dead body is cremated. EG *Gertrude attended the cremation.* — N COUNT ⇑ ceremony

crematorium /krɛ̲mətɔ̲ːrɪəm/, **crematoria** or **crematoriums**. A **crematorium** is a building in which the bodies of dead people are burned as part of a funeral service. EG *Arrangements have been made for the placing of a memorial plaque at the crematorium.* — N COUNT

crème de la crème /krɛ̲ːm də lə³ krɛ̲ːm/. When you talk about the **crème de la crème**, you mean the very best things or people of their kind; a formal or literary term. EG *These trees are the crème de la crème in Britain's landscape.* — N SING : *the*+N = pick

creole /kri̲ːəʊl/, **creoles**. A **creole** is 1 a language that has developed from a mixture of different languages and has become the main language in a particular place: compare **pidgin**. EG *They speak* — N UNCOUNT/COUNT

English-based Creole. **2** a person descended from the Europeans who first colonized the West Indies or the southern United States of America. EG *The new states became the property of the rich Creole elites.* **3** a person of mixed African and European race, who lives in the West Indies and speaks a creole language. N COUNT N COUNT

creosote /krɪəsəʊt/, **creosotes, creosoting, creosoted.** 1 **Creosote** is a thick dark liquid made from coal tar, used especially for preventing wood from rotting. EG *...wood impregnated with creosote.* N UNCOUNT ↑ preservative

2 If you **creosote** something such as a wooden fence, you spread creosote over it in order to prevent it from rotting. EG *It will last a long time if you creosote it every now and then.* V+O

crepe /kreɪp/; also spelled **crape. Crepe** is **1** a thin fabric made of cotton, silk, or wool with an uneven, ridged surface. It is used for making blouses and dresses. EG *...a pink crepe evening gown.* **2** a type of rubber with a rough surface. It is used for making the soles of shoes. EG *Her father tiptoed down on crepe soles.* N UNCOUNT N UNCOUNT

crepe paper is a kind of paper with an uneven, ridged surface. It is used for making decorations. EG *We put white and blue crepe paper round them so they looked rather pretty.* N UNCOUNT

crept is the past tense and past participle of **creep.**

crescendo /krɪ²ʃendəʊ/, **crescendos** or **crescendi.** A **crescendo** is **1** a noise that gets louder and louder. EG *The ovation rose in a new crescendo... 'Meaning?' queried Mrs Pringle, in a menacing crescendo.* **2** a passage in a piece of music that gradually gets louder and louder; a technical term in music. **3** the point in time when a noise is at its loudest. EG *The noises reached a positive crescendo... The drummer had now worked up to his crescendo.* N COUNT : USU SING N COUNT : USU SING N SING WITH DET = climax

4 the time during which you are most aware of something; a formal or literary use. EG *The clamour in the press was reaching a crescendo.* N COUNT : USU SING = climax

crescent /kresə⁰nt, -zə⁰nt/, **crescents. 1** A **crescent** is a street, especially one that is curved. EG *We left Grosvenor Crescent at about five minutes to ten... ...23 Chestnut Crescent.* N COUNT : ALSO IN NAMES AFTER N

2 A **crescent** is also **2.1** a continuous row of houses built in a curve. EG *...John Wood's masterpiece, the earliest of English crescents.* **2.2** a curved shape that is wider in the middle than at its ends, like the shape of the moon during its first and last quarters. EG *The planet appeared as a dazzling silver crescent... There was a scar on her right arm, a jagged crescent of white.* N COUNT : ALSO IN NAMES AFTER N N COUNT

cress /kres/ is a plant with small, strong-tasting green leaves that are used in salads or as a garnish for food. There are several kinds of cress. • See also **watercress.** N UNCOUNT

crest /krest/, **crests.** A **crest** is **1** the highest part of a hill or a wave. EG *We had reached the crest of the hill... ...the crests of gigantic waves.* **2** a tuft of feathers on the top of a bird's head. EG *The birds' feather crests are raised.* **3** a line of scales or spikes along a reptile's back. EG *...large lizards with a crest of scales along their backs.* **4** a small picture or design that is the sign of a noble family, a town, or an organization and that you sometimes see on buildings, furniture, etc. EG *...a casket emblazoned with the family crest.* N COUNT : USU WITH POSS N COUNT N COUNT N COUNT = coat of arms

crested /krestɪ²d/. A **crested** bird is a bird that has a tuft of feathers on its head. EG *...the crested tit.* ADJ CLASSIF : ATTRIB

crestfallen /krestfɔːlən/. Someone who is **crestfallen** is rather sad and disappointed about something. EG *Elaine looked crestfallen.* ADJ QUALIT : USU PRED = downcast

cretin /kretɪn/, **cretins.** If you call someone a **cretin,** you mean that they are very stupid; an offensive word. N COUNT : ALSO VOC = idiot, moron

cretinous /kretɪ³nəs/. A **cretinous** person is very stupid; an offensive word. EG *...some cretinous peasant girl.* ADJ QUALIT = idiotic

crevasse /krɪvæs/, **crevasses.** A **crevasse** is a deep crack in thick ice, for example in a glacier. EG *...a little wooden bridge over one of the deeper crevasses.* N COUNT = fissure

crevice /krevɪs/, **crevices.** A **crevice** is a narrow crack or gap in rock or between large stones. EG *Most of the year the insects are hidden in rock crevices... The dog was having a wonderful time, sniffing beneath stones and into crevices.* N COUNT = chink

crew /kruː/, **crews. 1** A **crew** consists of **1.1** the people who work on and operate a ship, an aeroplane, or a spaceship. EG *The Captain ordered his crew to prepare for action... The 'Maine' carried a crew of three hundred and fifty... I was watching some crew members who had just come on to the deck.* **1.2** a group of people, especially people with special technical skills, who work together on a particular task or project, for example the making of a film. EG *The TV crews couldn't film at night... There were fifteen of us in all, ten members of the production crew and five of the cast... The maintenance supervisor would dispatch a crew to repair the damage.* N COUNT : IF SING, VB CAN BE SING OR PL ↑ personnel N COUNT : IF SING, VB CAN BE SING OR PL = team

2 In informal English, you can use **crew** to refer to any group of people that have some connection with each other; often used showing disapproval. EG *The President and his crew seem to find it remarkably easy to issue statements about world peace... ...a motley crew of punks and skinheads.* N SING WITH DET : VB CAN BE SING OR PL = crowd, gang

crew cut, crew cuts; also spelled with a hyphen and as one word. A **crew cut** is a hairstyle in which a person's hair, usually a man's, is cut very short. EG *...an ex-colonel with a bushy moustache and a crew cut.* N COUNT ↑ haircut

crewman /kruːmə³n/, **crewmen.** A **crewman** is someone who works as part of a crew. EG *One crewman scrambled out of the space capsule... Journalists and TV crewmen surrounded me.* N COUNT ↑ worker

crib /krɪb/, **cribs, cribbing, cribbed. 1** If you **crib,** you copy something that someone else has written, for example in an examination, and pretend that it is your own work; used showing disapproval. EG *The teacher thought we'd cribbed off each other... It is unlikely that the story was cribbed.* V OR V+O : IF+ PREP THEN *off/ from* = plagiarize

2 A **crib** is **2.1** something that you have cribbed from someone else's work. EG *His essay was full of cribs from the text-book.* **2.2** written information that someone uses, often dishonestly, to help them in an examination or to give the impression that they know more than they really do. EG *I could name all the chemical elements without a crib.* N COUNT : IF+ PREP THEN *from* N COUNT ↑ aid

3 A **crib** is also a baby's cot; used in American English and old-fashioned British English. EG *She used to throw her toys out of her crib.* N COUNT ↑ bed = cradle

4 Crib means the same as **cribbage**; used in informal English. N UNCOUNT ↑ game

cribbage /krɪbɪdʒ/ is a card game for two, three, or four players in which you record the score by putting pegs in a wooden board. EG *Fancy a game of cribbage?* N UNCOUNT = crib

crick /krɪk/, **cricks, cricking, cricked. 1** A **crick** is a feeling of pain and stiffness in your neck or your back caused by the muscles there becoming stiff. EG *My neck had a crick in it from glancing back at the animals.* N COUNT : USU SING, IF+PREP THEN *in*

2 If you **crick** your neck or back, you injure it so that it hurts and becomes stiff. EG *He cricked his neck while diving into the swimming pool.* V+O ↑ hurt

cricket /krɪkɪt/, **crickets. 1 Cricket** is an outdoor game played between two teams of eleven players. A player from one team stands in front of a wicket and uses a wooden bat to try and hit a hard ball and score points called runs. The players of the other team try to get the batsman out by bowling the ball and hitting the wicket, by catching the ball after it has been hit, etc. When the batting team are all out, the team that was bowling start to bat and try to score more runs than their opponents. EG *I spent the afternoon watching cricket... They play football in the winter and cricket in the summer... ...a cricket bat... ...England's cricket team.* • If you say that someone's behaviour is **not cricket,** you mean that they have not behaved in a fair or honourable way; an old-fashioned expression. EG *It's just not cricket.* N UNCOUNT • PHR : USED AS C = unfair, dishonest

2 A **cricket** is a small jumping insect that produces a sharp sound by rubbing its wings together. EG *We lay in our tent listening to the crickets.* N COUNT

cricketer /krɪkɪtə/, **cricketers.** A **cricketer** is a person who plays cricket. N COUNT ↑ player

crier /kraɪə/, **criers.** A **crier** is the same as a **town crier**; an old-fashioned word. EG *He took a group of boys to hear the Crier proclaim the accession on the Town Hall steps.* N COUNT : USU *the*+N IN SING ↑ official

crikey /kraɪki¹/. Some people say **crikey** in order to express surprise, or to add emphasis to an opinion EXCLAM = blimey

they are giving; used in informal and old-fashioned British English. EG *'Crikey, you were quick!'*

crime /kraɪm/, **crimes**. A **crime** is 1 an illegal action for which a person can be punished by law. EG *A crime has been committed... She is wanted for the crime of murder... ...a life of petty crime... The crime rate continued to increase.* 2 an action which is morally wrong but not illegal. EG *To waste good food is a crime against nature... There is no justification for so black a crime against humanity.* — N COUNT/UNCOUNT = offence; N COUNT : IF+PREP THEN against = sin

criminal /krɪmɪnə⁰l/, **criminals**. 1 A **criminal** is a person who has committed an illegal action. EG *He is one of the country's ten most wanted criminals... He has a lot of criminal contacts.* — N COUNT = offender

2 Something that is **criminal** is 2.1 connected with crime or with the punishment of crime. EG *He had done nothing criminal... It is a criminal offence... Scotland has its own criminal law.* ◇ **criminally**. EG *...the care of the criminally insane... They decided that he was not criminally responsible for what had happened.* 2.2 morally wrong, but not illegal. EG *To refuse medical aid would be criminal.* ◇ **criminally**. EG *The pay was criminally poor... His staff were criminally underpaid.* — ADJ CLASSIF; ◇ ADV+ADJ/ADV; ADJ QUALIT; ◇ ADV+ADJ/ADV

criminality /krɪmɪnælɪti¹/ is the committing of crimes. EG *Problems of overcrowding, poor accommodation and criminality are all prominent in revolutionary propaganda... ...violence and general criminality.* — N UNCOUNT

criminology /krɪmɪnɒləd3i¹/ is the scientific study of crime and criminals. EG *He is interested in the issues of crime and criminology.* ◇ **criminologist**, **criminologists**. EG *Death was caused by what the criminologists call a solid object.* — N UNCOUNT ↑ science; ◇ N COUNT ↑ specialist

crimp /krɪmp/, **crimps, crimping, crimped**. 1 If you **crimp** a piece of fabric or pastry, you make small folds along its edges. EG *She had crimped the edges with an iron.* ◇ **crimped**. EG *The hills on either side of the river were crimped like a pie crust.* — V+O ↑ fold; ◇ ADJ CLASSIF

2 If you **crimp** your hair, you style it into tight curls or waves, usually by using heated tongs. ◇ **crimped**. EG *She patted her crimped grey bun.* — V+O; ◇ ADJ CLASSIF

crimson /krɪmzə⁰n/, **crimsons**. 1 If something is **crimson**, it has a dark, purplish-red colour. EG *She was wearing a crimson dress... A crimson sun set over the plain.* ▸ used as a noun. EG *...the glowing, velvety crimson of the rose.* — ADJ COLOUR; ▸ N MASS

2 If a person is **crimson**, their face is red because they are very angry or embarrassed. EG *Ralph went crimson... Bradshaw turned crimson under the insults.* — ADJ COLOUR

cringe /krɪnd3/, **cringes, cringing, cringed**. If you **cringe**, 1 you move away from someone or something because you are afraid of them. EG *Terrified, they cried and cringed... She cringed against the wall.* 2 you are very embarrassed about something. EG *I used to cringe with embarrassment whenever my name was read out... Cringing under the stares of passers-by, I tried to read my newspaper.* — V : USU+A = cower, shrink; V : USU+A = wince

crinkle /krɪŋkə⁰l/, **crinkles, crinkling, crinkled**. 1 When something **crinkles** or when you **crinkle** it, it becomes slightly creased or folded. EG *The leaf was beginning to crinkle at the edges... His face crinkled into a smile.* ◇ **crinkled**. EG *...brown crinkled leaves.* — V-ERG ↑ crease; ◇ ADJ QUALIT

2 **Crinkles** are small creases or folds on a surface, for example on your skin. EG *There were crinkles at the outer corners of his eyes.* — N COUNT : USU PL = wrinkle

crinkly /krɪŋkli¹/. Something that is **crinkly** has many small folds, creases, or twists and is not flat, smooth, or straight. EG *He had crinkly brown hair... Her bodice was made of crinkly material.* — ADJ QUALIT

crinoline /krɪnə⁰lɪn/, **crinolines**. A **crinoline** is a very stiff petticoat which was worn by women in the nineteenth century in order to make their skirts stand out away from their legs. — N COUNT

cripple /krɪpə⁰l/, **cripples, crippling, crippled**. 1 A **cripple** is 1.1 someone who is very lame, or who cannot move their body properly because their spine is weak, injured, or affected by a disease. EG *My father was a cripple, my mother in poor health.* 1.2 someone who has a particular mental or social problem which prevents them from living a successful life. EG *The adult illiterate has been characterised as a social cripple, needing remedial care... I worried about whether you were going to be a mental cripple for life or not.* — N COUNT ↑ person; N COUNT : MOD+N ↑ person

2 If something **cripples** someone, it seriously injures them so that they can never move properly again. EG *...several painful falls that crippled him but did not deter him from working.* — V+O ↑ injure

3 If someone or something **cripples** an organization or system, they prevent it from working properly, especially by damaging it in some way; a formal or literary use. EG *The government had done much to cripple national enterprise.* — V+O ↑ damage

crippled /krɪpə⁰ld/. 1 Someone who is **crippled** is very lame, or is unable to move their body properly because their spine is weak, injured, or affected by a disease. EG *...his crippled mother... If they survive such burns, they will be badly scarred or crippled for life.* ▸ The **crippled** is used to refer to people who are crippled. EG *The installation of telephones for the crippled or bed-ridden should be a priority.* — ADJ CLASSIF ↑ handicapped; ▸ N PLURAL : the+N ↑ disabled

2 An organization or a system that is **crippled** is very badly damaged and is prevented from working or operating properly; a formal or literary use. EG *...this crippled society.* — ADJ QUALIT

crippling /krɪplɪŋ/. 1 A **crippling** illness or disability severely damages your health or your body. EG *In addition there is the dread of crippling disablement, of becoming housebound.* — ADJ QUALIT : ATTRIB ↑ severe

2 **Crippling** prices, taxes, etc have a serious or damaging effect on a person's or country's financial situation. EG *...its ailing economy, its national debts, its crippling taxes.* — ADJ QUALIT = swingeing

crisis /kraɪsɪs/, **crises** /kraɪsi:z/. 1 A **crisis** is 1.1 a situation where conflict, especially political conflict, has become so threatening or dangerous that people are afraid that there will be fighting or war. EG *The arrests caused a crisis... I was in Munich during the 1938 crisis... Even in crisis, military power should be accountable to Parliament.* 1.2 a situation where resources or goods have become very hard to get. EG *We hear a lot about the so-called energy crisis these days, but how real a problem is it?... They've still got an economic crisis on their hands... The need for jobs and job skills was at a crisis level in Black communities.* 1.3 the moment when a conflict or problem in your life becomes so great that you cannot deal with it any more. EG *Her first act was always to smoke a cigarette at any serious crisis in her life... The anxiety of this personal crisis turned his hair white... He had an emotional crisis and called his mother for advice.* — N COUNT/UNCOUNT = emergency; N COUNT/UNCOUNT : USU+SUPP = emergency ≠ boom; N COUNT = trauma

2 **Crisis** is a feeling of extreme conflict or suffering, so great that you cannot think of anything else. EG *She dealt with the accident in a calm, deliberate manner, without any sense of urgency or crisis... Who can you turn to in time of crisis?* — N UNCOUNT/COUNT = trauma ≠ calm

3 A **crisis** is also a situation where something, such as your confidence in someone or something, is so heavily attacked or questioned that there is serious doubt whether it will continue to exist. EG *The crisis of confidence which greeted Labour's victory was considerable... The crisis of capitalism is worsening.* — N COUNT+SUPP

crisp /krɪsp/, **crisper, crispest; crisps**. 1 Fruit and vegetables that are **crisp** are fresh and have a firm texture, so that when you bite them they are hard and crunchy; used showing approval. EG *...a salad of crisp lettuce and tomatoes... ...Beauty of Bath apples, crisp and sweet.* — ADJ QUALIT ≠ soft

2 Cooked food that is **crisp** has been fried or toasted until it is hard, dry, and crunchy; used showing approval. EG *...sausages rolled in crisp bacon... ...hot crisp rolls.* — ADJ QUALIT = crispy ≠ soggy

3 **Crisps** are potatoes that have been sliced very thin and then fried until they are hard, dry, and crunchy; used mainly in British English. EG *I'll have a packet of cheese and onion crisps.* — N COUNT : USU PL

4 If you say, in informal English, that something is burnt **to a crisp**, you mean that it is very burnt indeed; sometimes used humorously to describe someone who has got very sunburnt. EG *On the very first day of my holiday I was burnt to a crisp.* — PHR : USED AS AN A = frazzled

5 Paper or clothes that are **crisp** are stiff and fresh with no creases in them; used showing approval. EG *She was dressed in grey flannel slacks and a crisp linen jacket... I lay down on the freshly made bed with its crisp white sheets... ...crisp new bank notes.* — ADJ QUALIT ≠ crumpled

6 **Crisp** is also used to describe the feeling of fresh snow, frost, etc as it crunches under your feet; used showing approval. EG *Each step I take I can feel the* — ADJ QUALIT ≠ soggy

crisp frosty grass crunching softly underfoot... The sand felt crisp and dry.

7 When the air or the weather is **crisp**, it is fresh, cold, dry, and sharp; used showing approval. EG *...on a crisp October morning... We breathed the crisp blue Australian air.* ◊ **crispness**. EG *There was a crispness to the air that night.* ADJ QUALIT = chill, clear ≠ muggy ◊ N UNCOUNT ≠ heaviness

8 Writing and speech that is **crisp** does not waste any effort or space on unnecessary details; used showing approval. EG *He sent off two crisp telegrams... Obviously a crisper definition of creativity is required.* ◊ **crisply**. EG *She spoke crisply and with great precision... The book is crisply analytical.* ◊ **crispness**. EG *It has great crispness of style.* ADJ QUALIT = succinct ≠ wordy ◊ ADV ◊ N UNCOUNT

9 A building or a design that is **crisp** has sharp, clear outlines; used showing approval. EG *It's a lovely façade, with its columns and crisp sculptured decoration.* ADJ QUALIT = neat ≠ blurred

10 Behaviour that is **crisp** is cool, sharp, and unfriendly, and does not consider other people's feelings; used showing disapproval. EG *She spoke to me in a cool, crisp tone... They employed a crisp rudeness to overcome whatever guilt they felt.* ◊ **crisply**. EG *'What did she want?' Etta said crisply. 'Money?'* ADJ QUALIT = brusque ≠ warm ◊ ADV WITH VB ⇑ sharply

crispy /krɪspi¹/, **crispier, crispiest**. **Crispy** is used to describe food which has been fried or toasted until it becomes hard and crunchy; used showing approval. EG *...crispy fried bacon.* ADJ QUALIT = crisp ≠ soggy

criss-cross /krɪskrɒs/, **criss-crosses, criss-crossing, criss-crossed**. 1 If things **criss-cross** or **criss-cross** a place, they exist or move in such a way that they create a pattern of crossed lines. EG *Dozens of searchlights criss-crossed to pick out possible targets for the bombing... ...the freeways that criss-cross the whole of Los Angeles.* V OR V+O

2 A **criss-cross** pattern or design is one that has lines crossing over each other. EG *...a criss-cross diamond pattern... ...light brown boots with criss-cross laces all the way up the front.* ▸ used as a noun. EG *...a criss-cross of walls.* ADJ CLASSIF : ATTRIB ▸ N COUNT

criterion /kraɪtɪərɪən/, **criteria**. A **criterion** is a standard by which you judge or evaluate something. EG *Profitability is the sole criterion for our policy... The Commission did not apply the same criteria to advertising... ...Freud's criteria of mental health... My own criterion of success is the ability to work joyfully.* N COUNT : IF+ PREP THEN *for/ of*

critic /krɪtɪk/, **critics**. A **critic** is 1 someone who writes reviews and expresses opinions about artistic works such as books, plays, films, and music. EG *What did the New York critics have to say about the production?... ...the novelist and critic... ...sniping comments by a couple of television critics... ...art critics.* 2 someone who expresses criticism of a person or thing; often used of people who disapprove of a political leader or system. EG *The Prime Minister returned to London to face his parliamentary critics... Critics often claim the system has failed... ...critics of the Trade Union Movement.* N COUNT ⇑ judge = reviewer; N COUNT : USU PL = opponent ≠ supporter

critical /krɪtɪkə⁰l/. 1 A situation or time that is **critical** is 1.1 extremely important. EG *This was a critical moment in his career... ...changes of critical importance... The problem of food supplies is bound to be critical... The twelve weeks of summer were critical to most of the restaurants and pubs.* ◊ **critically**. EG *The army was facing a critically dangerous position.* 1.2 very serious and often dangerous. EG *The shortage of airfields was critical during the war... ...the critical state of the national economy... Her illness had reached a critical stage.* ◊ **critically**. EG *She knew her mother was sick but not critically... He was critically wounded.* ADJ QUALIT : IF+ PREP THEN *to* = crucial; ◊ ADV +ADJ; ADJ CLASSIF ⇑ severe = perilous; ◊ ADV WITH VB = dangerously

2 Someone who is **critical** 2.1 expresses severe judgements and criticisms of people or things. EG *She became critical and dogmatic... He had long been critical of Conservative policy.* ▸ used also of attitudes and behaviour. EG *He made critical speeches against the plan... Whole groups of nations adopted a more critical attitude towards apartheid.* ◊ **critically**. EG *He spoke critically of their beliefs.* 2.2 is able to examine and judge things carefully; used showing approval. EG *Each player regarding the other with critical interest. ... He submitted the plans to critical examination... A critical reader will notice many mistakes.* ◊ **critically**. EG *She studied herself critically.* ADJ QUALIT : IF+ PREP THEN *of* = censorious, disparaging; ADJ QUALIT : ATTRIB ⇑ careful = analytical; ◊ ADV WITH VB

3 **Critical** means relating to the work of a person who is a critic. EG *I was planning a serious critical study of Shakespeare... I enjoyed his critical essays on Dante.* ADJ CLASSIF : ATTRIB

criticise /krɪtɪsaɪz/. See **criticize**.

criticism /krɪtɪsɪzə⁰m/, **criticisms**. 1 **Criticism** is 1.1 the expression of disapproval of someone or something, by stating an opinion on their faults, weaknesses, or disadvantages in speech or writing. EG *The Government came in for severe criticism... Some fierce public criticism of the plan had been voiced.* 1.2 a serious examination and judgement of something, especially of a book, play, or other work of art. EG *She would write him vivid and constructive criticism as soon as she got home... She wrote a paper on linguistics and literary criticism.* N UNCOUNT ≠ praise; N UNCOUNT = analysis, critique

2 A **criticism** is 2.1 a comment which expresses disapproval of something or someone. EG *One of the main criticisms against him is that he is lazy... I don't mean this as a criticism... There have been criticisms that standards of care are low.* 2.2 a comment, often written, which expresses an opinion or judgement of a book, play, work of art, etc. EG *His criticisms of the exhibition were interesting.* N COUNT ⇑ judgement; N COUNT

criticize /krɪtɪsaɪz/, **criticizes, criticizing, criticized**; also spelled **criticise**. If you **criticize** someone or something, 1 you express your disapproval of them by saying or writing the things that you think are wrong with them. EG *Please don't get angry if I criticize you... I criticized the path the government was taking... He was criticized for pursuing a policy of conciliation... He criticised the things she wore.* 2 you make judgements about them after thinking about them carefully and deeply. EG *We read and criticise each other's poems.* V+O : IF+PREP THEN *for* ⇑ judge = censure ≠ praise; V+O = analyse, evaluate

critique /krɪtiːk/, **critiques**. A **critique** is a piece of writing that has been produced by careful, thoughtful examination and judgement of a situation or of a person's work or ideas. EG *His critique of Soviet Communism was published last year... ...an intelligent and incisive critique of our society.* N COUNT = analysis, evaluation, review

croak /krəʊk/, **croaks, croaking, croaked**. 1 When animals or birds **croak**, especially frogs and crows, they utter harsh, low sounds. EG *A bullfrog was croaking in the distance. ...the howling of the hyenas, and the croaking of the frogs.* ▸ used as a noun. V ▸ N COUNT

2 When someone **croaks**, 2.1 they speak in a hoarse, rough voice, for example because they have a sore throat or are very weak, thirsty, or upset. EG *'Brandy,' he croaked... He croaked her name: 'Melanie?'* ▸ used as a noun. EG *'Tea and toast?' His voice was a weak croak.* 2.2 they die; a very informal use. EG *I thought I was going to croak right there.* V, OR V+O/ QUOTE ▸ N COUNT; V = die

crochet /krəʊʃi³/, **crochets, crocheting, crocheted**. **Crochet** is a way of making clothes, shawls, etc out of wool, by using your fingers and a needle which has a small hook at the end: compare **knitting**. EG *...a black crochet shawl.* ▸ used as a verb. EG *She used to patiently crochet complex patterns... ...a crocheted beret.* N UNCOUNT ⇑ craft ▸ V OR V+O

crock /krɒk/, **crocks**. 1 A **crock** is a pot or jar made of earthenware; a rather old-fashioned or literary use. EG *...a big earthenware crock... ...two large crocks containing salted runner beans.* N COUNT : IF+ PREP THEN *of*

2 **Crocks** are plates, cups, saucers, bowls, etc, especially ones made of earthenware rather than china; a rather old-fashioned or literary use. EG *She was sorting soiled sheets and damaged crocks.* N COUNT : USU PL = crockery

3 If you describe a car, bicycle, or other vehicle as a **crock**, you mean that it is very old and falling to pieces; an informal use in British English. EG *I didn't know that Jack ever used his old crock of a bike.* N COUNT : USU+ SUPP = wreck, crate

4 If you describe a person as an old **crock**, you mean that they are old and weak; an informal use in British English. N COUNT : ADJ+N = wreck

crockery /krɒkə⁰ri¹/ refers to plates, cups, saucers, bowls, etc, used at mealtimes. EG *...a sink overflowing with dirty crockery.* N UNCOUNT = dishes

crocodile /krɒkədaɪl/, **crocodiles**. 1 A **crocodile** is a very large meat-eating reptile which lives in rivers in tropical parts of the world, such as Africa and India. Crocodiles have a broad head, large strong jaws with very sharp teeth, and thick scales that cover their body. EG *Crocodiles are the largest of all living reptiles.* N COUNT

2 You also use the word **crocodile** to describe a long line of people walking in pairs along a road or N COUNT

pavement, especially schoolchildren on a school outing; used mainly in informal British English.

crocodile tears are tears or other expressions of grief that are not genuine or sincere. N PLURAL

crocus /krəʊkəs/, **crocuses**. A **crocus** is a very small plant which has narrow leaves, and white, yellow, or purple flowers. Crocuses flower early in spring, and are often planted in parks and gardens. EG *Under the trees in early spring time the crocuses are as bright as splinters of coloured glass.* N COUNT

croft /krɒft/, **crofts**. A **croft** is a small piece of land, especially in Scotland, which is owned and farmed by one family and which provides them with food. EG *He's spent the last 30 years on a croft.* ▸ also used of the house on the croft. EG *...an old croft at the sea's edge.* N COUNT ⇑ farm ▸ N COUNT ⇑ house

crofter /krɒftə/, **crofters**. A **crofter** is the owner or tenant of a croft or small farm, especially in Scotland. N COUNT ⇑ farmer

croissant /krwʌsɒŋ/, **croissants**. A **croissant** is a crescent-shaped piece of light, buttery, pastry that is usually eaten for breakfast, especially in France. EG *Every morning they baked their own croissants.* N COUNT

crone /krəʊn/, **crones**. A **crone** is an old woman; a literary word that is used offensively in informal English. EG *...an aged crone in a floral apron.* N COUNT

crony /krəʊni[1]/, **cronies**. A **crony** is a close friend, or someone with whom you spend a lot of time; a rather old-fashioned and informal word. EG *...a farewell drink with his cronies... He was a geologist, rated by his cronies as the best in the business.* N COUNT : USU POSS+N

crook /krʊk/, **crooks, crooking, crooked**. 1 A **crook** is a dishonest person, especially a criminal or thief; an informal use. EG *The accountants turned out to have been crooks... She called me a lousy crook.* N COUNT

2 The **crook** of your arm or leg is the soft inside part where you bend your elbow or knee. EG *The baby was now lying absolutely motionless in the crook of her left arm... She buried her face in the crook of her arm.* N COUNT+*of*: USU SING

3 If you **crook** a part of your body, especially your arm or a finger, you bend it. EG *She crooked her little finger... He backed away a little, his arms crooked, his fingers outspread.* V+O ⇑ bend

4 A **crook** is also a long pole with a large hook at the top, which a Christian bishop carries in religious services. • **by hook or by crook**: see **hook**. N COUNT

crooked /krʊkɪd[2]/. 1 Something that is **crooked** is bent or twisted. EG *My back is so crooked and painful that I cannot stand upright. ...narrow, crooked streets.* ADJ QUALIT

2 A **crooked** smile or grin is one that is uneven and bigger on one side of your mouth than on the other. EG *He smiled, showing his small pearly teeth in a crooked grin.* ◇ **crookedly**. EG *The grey-haired man smiled crookedly as Grant passed him.* ADJ QUALIT = lopsided ◇ ADV WITH VB

3 Someone who is **crooked** is dishonest or involved in crime. EG *...a crooked cop... Most crooked businesses rely on substantial tax evasion.* ADJ QUALIT = bent ≠ honest

croon /kru:n/, **croons, crooning, crooned**. If you **croon**, 1 you sing or hum quietly and gently. EG *The baby sat there, crooning to himself and throwing sand at the picnic basket.* 2 you say something in a sweet gentle voice, especially something that is sentimental, flattering, or not quite true; used showing disapproval. EG *'You little charmer,' he crooned, 'Hollywood should see you.'... 'Women were always the healers,' Judy crooned, but Martha silently disagreed.* V OR V+O / V, OR V+QUOTE

crooner /kru:nə/, **crooners**. A **crooner** is a male singer who sings sentimental ballads; an old-fashioned word. N COUNT

crop /krɒp/, **crops, cropping, cropped**. 1 A **crop** is 1.1 a plant that is grown regularly and in large quantities on farms, in fields, etc. EG *The population is dependent upon a simple crop, wheat... There stretched vast fields of crops growing in different colours.* 1.2 the plants that you collect at harvest time when they are fully grown and ready to be stored, processed, or sold. EG *They get two crops of rice a year... The commune produced a varied crop of cotton, fruit, and vegetables.* 1.3 animals or their produce that you need and use, and that you obtain by work and care. EG *We had only half the usual honey crop last summer... Next year's crop of kids, calves, and chicks will be poor.* 1.4 an amount of something that has grown in a particular place, often in a place where you do not want it to grow; used humorously in informal English. EG *You've got a splendid crop of hair... ...cracked white china cups with fabulous crops of mould.* 1.5 a group of similar people or things that have all emerged or been produced at the same time; an informal use. EG *What do you think of the current crop of school-leavers?... Every day provides its crop of reasons for delay and hesitation.* N COUNT : USU PL / N COUNT : USU SING, IF+PREP THEN *of* = harvest / N COUNT+SUPP : USU SING ⇑ produce / N PART : USU SING / N PART : USU SING = batch

2 If you **crop** something, 2.1 you produce or grow it in large quantities in order to store, process, or sell it. EG *I specialise in cropping a particular kind of small potato.* 2.2 you use a particular area for growing crops. EG *I knew that unless I could crop this field, I couldn't keep it... In central Nigeria, the land is cropped continuously for six years and then left fallow.* 2.3 you collect crops at harvest time. EG *There was all that barley to be cropped before the storm broke.* V-ERG : IF V THEN +A / V+O = cultivate / V+O

3 When an animal such as a cow or a goat **crops** grass, leaves, etc, it eats it. EG *Our goat was cropping the hedge, her tail swishing... This kind of clover is easily cropped by animals.* V+O ⇑ eat = graze

4 If your hair **is cropped**, it is cut short, close to the head. EG *Her grey hair was cropped close to her skull... ...a boy with closely cropped fair hair and small, merry, blue eyes.* ▸ used as a noun. EG *Her straight grey hair was cut in a crop.* V+O : USU PASS ▸ N SING : a+N ⇑ hairstyle

5 If you **crop** something such as a photograph, you cut the edges off it, usually because you want to frame it or use only part of it. EG *The photograph had been so cropped that the head of the man in it was excluded.* V+O = trim

6 A **crop** is also a kind of bag in a bird's neck where food goes before it is completely digested. EG *You always find bits of gravel in a dead bird's crop.* N COUNT : USU SING

crop up. If something **crops up**, often something difficult or unpleasant, it happens or appears suddenly and unexpectedly; used in informal English. EG *There was one word that cropped up in each of the reports... I can come now, unless any other problems crop up... Has anything cropped up in the week that we should talk about?* PHRASAL VB : V+ADV ⇑ occur = pop up

cropper /krɒpə/; an informal word. If you say that someone **has come a cropper**, you mean 1 that they have had an unexpected, embarrassing, and disastrous failure. EG *Despite all his cheating, he came a cropper in the exams... You've really come a cropper on that one.* 2 that they have accidentally and painfully fallen down. EG *She slipped and came a cropper on her backside.* PHR : VB INFLECTS ⇑ fail / PHR : VB INFLECTS

croquet /krəʊkɪ[3]/ is a game played mainly in Britain in which the players use long-handled wooden mallets to hit wooden balls through a series of metal arches that are stuck firmly into a grass lawn. N UNCOUNT

croquette /krəʊket, krɒ-/, **croquettes**. A **croquette** is a savoury item of food, made by taking a small amount of mashed potato, fish, etc, rolling it in breadcrumbs, and frying it. EG *He ate all the potato croquettes in sight... ...salmon croquettes.* N COUNT = rissole

cross /krɒs/, **crosses, crossing, crossed; crosser, crossest**. 1 If you **cross** a room, road, country etc or **cross** to or into it, you move or travel to the other side of it or sometimes across a border into the next country. EG *He crossed the room slowly... I wanted to prove a woman could cross a desert... We cross by night and then we catch the train... He stood up at once and crossed to the door... Where and how did you cross into Swaziland?* • to **cross that bridge when** you **come to it**: see **bridge**. • to **cross** someone's **palm** with silver: see **palm**. V+O, OR V : USU +A = go across, traverse

2 Roads and bridges that **cross** an area of land or water go across it. EG *The highways cross endless wastelands of charred stumps.* V+O ⇑ cover, traverse

3 Lines, roads, railways, etc that **cross** meet and go across each other. EG *Still farther south, the way is crossed by Brewer Street... And where the two lines cross is where he is.* • to **cross** someone's **path**: see **path**. V+O, OR V ⇑ join

4 If you say that a person or an organization **crosses** something such as a boundary or a limit, especially one that is normally considered to be difficult or important, you mean that they have gone beyond that particular point in their work, life, etc. EG *There is no easy way of crossing difficult social frontiers... But last week the 37-year-old sportswoman crossed a bold new threshold.* V+O = overcome, go beyond

5 If an expression or emotion **crosses** someone's face, it appears briefly on their face. EG *A spasm of anger crossed her face... A flicker of unconcealed distaste crossed his features.* V+O ⇑ show on

6 If something **crosses** your **mind**, you think of it. EG *The thought never crossed my mind... It had not crossed my mind to tell them I was leaving.* PHR : VB INFLECTS, USU+ REPORT-CL/ *to*-INF

7 A Christian **cross** is a shape that has a long vertical line with a shorter horizontal line that goes across it near the top. Because Jesus Christ died on a cross of this shape, it is the most important symbol of the Christian faith and stone or wooden crosses are used, for example, in churches, to mark graves, etc. EG *We started to walk slowly among the white crosses looking at the names... ...Saxon crosses of the early eleventh century... She wore a tiny golden cross... There was a heavy ornate cross on the wall.* ● See also **Red Cross.** N COUNT

8 The **Cross** means the cross on which Jesus Christ died. N PROPER : *the*+N

9 When Christians **cross** themselves, they make the shape of a cross over the top half of their body by moving their hand. EG *She crossed herself.* ● **cross my heart (and hope to die)**: see **heart.** V+O (REFL)

10 If you **cross** your arms or legs, you put one on top of the other. EG *She sat back and crossed her legs... They often sit with one knee crossed over the other knee... He perched on the edge of her desk, with his arms crossed.* V+O : IF+PREP THEN *over*

11 If you say that you **are crossing** your **fingers** about something, you mean that you are hoping that everything will happen as you want it to. Sometimes you do not say anything at all, but simply put one finger on top of another to indicate your hope. EG *The organiser has to cross her fingers and hope... Fingers crossed!* PHR : VB INFLECTS ⇑ wish

12 If you **cross** a cheque, postal order, etc, you draw two parallel lines across it to indicate that it must be paid into a bank account and cannot be cashed. V+O ⇑ mark

13 Someone who is **cross** is rather annoyed, irritated, and angry. EG *It's no good getting cross with her... He was looking very red and rather cross... When she saw him, the cross expression on her face was dramatically transformed... I was being facetious and Grandmother got crosser and crosser.* ADJ QUALIT : USU PRED
◇ **crossly**. EG *'Don't ask me,' the post office lady replied, crossly.* ◇ ADV WITH VB

14 If you **cross** someone, you annoy them or make them angry by opposing them in some way, especially by interfering with their plans or wishes; a formal or literary use. EG *I do know that anyone who crosses me after such a day had better be careful.* V+O ⇑ challenge = mess with

15 A **cross** is also **15.1** an unpleasant or difficult situation or person that you have to deal with or endure. EG *We all have our cross I suppose... Paul tended to regard his brother as one of many crosses life had imposed on him.* N COUNT : USU USED AS O/C ⇑ burden **15.2** a written mark in the shape of the letter X or a plus sign that is used to give information of some kind, for example to indicate that an answer to a question is wrong, that a particular thing on a list is the one you are choosing, or to mark the position of something on a map. EG *They mark them with a red cross... The reader has to indicate, with a cross or a tick, the answer... Pencil a tiny cross where you need a hole.* N COUNT ≠ tick

16 If you say that something is a **cross** between one thing and another, you mean that it is neither one thing nor another, but a mixture of both. EG *A Barbary duck is a cross between a wild duck and an ordinary duck... It resembled a cross between a lunatic asylum and a cotton mill.* N COUNT : USU SING, IF+PREP THEN *between* = hybrid, combination

17 If you **cross** one animal or plant with another, you cause it to breed with another of a different species, in order to produce offspring that are a mixture of both parents; a technical use. EG *It has been crossed with L candidum to produce L testaceum.* V+O, OR V+O+A *(with)* : RECIP

18 Material that **is cut on the cross** is cut diagonally rather than straight. EG *This dress is cut on the cross.* PHR : VB INFLECTS

cross off. If you **cross off** one or more words on a list, you draw a line through them to indicate that someone or something is no longer required, needed, involved in an activity, etc. EG *I crossed my name off the list.* PHRASAL VB : V+O+ADV/PREP = delete

cross out. If you **cross out** one or more words on a page, you draw a line through them, usually because they are wrong or because you do not want people to read them. EG *Now and then he frowned, crossed something out and rewrote it... I crossed out 'Unpublished' and made it 'Works in preparation'.* PHRASAL VB : V+O+ADV = delete

crossbar /krɒsbɑː/, **crossbars**; also spelled with a hyphen. A **crossbar** is 1 a horizontal piece of wood that is attached to two upright pieces of wood, such as the top part of the goal in the game of football. N COUNT 2 the horizontal metal bar that goes between the handlebars and the saddle on a man's or boy's bicycle. N COUNT

crossbones /krɒsbəʊnz/. See **skull and crossbones.**

crossbow /krɒsbəʊ/, **crossbows.** A **crossbow** is a weapon consisting of a small bow fixed across a piece of wood, which releases an arrow with great power when you press a trigger. Crossbows were used in medieval times for hunting and in battle, but are now used mainly in sport. N COUNT ⇑ weapon

cross-Channel is used to describe travel, communications, etc across the English Channel between England and France, Belgium, or Holland, especially when this involves travelling by boat. EG *...a cross-Channel trip... ...the cross-Channel ferry.* ADJ CLASSIF : ATTRIB

cross-check, cross-checks, cross-checking, cross-checked. If you **cross-check** something such as results or data, you use a different method from the one originally used, in order to check that the results or data are correct. EG *Until the information has been carefully assembled, cross-checked and evaluated, none of it will be reliable.* V+O = validate, corroborate

cross-country. 1 If something goes **cross-country,** it uses paths to cross fields and the open countryside or uses less important roads, railway lines, etc, rather than the main routes. EG *...a cross-country bicycle trip... He walked cross-country to the hospital... The train journey back was a tedious cross-country affair lasting over three hours.* ADJ CLASSIF : ATTRIB, OR ADV AFTER VB ≠ by road

2 **Cross-country** or a **cross-country race** refers to the sport of running when it takes place on paths across fields and the open countryside instead of along roads or around a running track. EG *He won a cup for cross-country in Bangalore in 1944... I'm in training for a cross-country run... ...a 10 mile cross-country race.* N UNCOUNT, OR N SING WITH DET

cross-cultural means dealing with or involving two or more different cultures. EG *...cross-cultural data... ...Donnison's influential cross-cultural study of housing policy.* ADJ CLASSIF : ATTRIB ⇑ wide-ranging

cross-examination, cross-examinations. **Cross-examination** or a **cross-examination** is the questioning of someone such as a witness during a trial in a court of law about the evidence they have already given, often in order to prove that it is false, mistaken, or misleading. EG *Mr Fairbairn, in cross-examination, took the matter further... Kruger was shielded from cross-examination.* N UNCOUNT/ COUNT

cross-examine, cross-examines, cross-examining, cross-examined. 1 If you **cross-examine** someone such as a witness during a trial in a court of law, you question them about the evidence they have already given, often in order to prove that it is false, mistaken, or misleading. EG *If he had gone into the witness box he would have been cross-examined on any evidence he gave.* V+O ⇑ interrogate

2 If you **cross-examine** someone about something, you ask them a lot of detailed questions about it. EG *Mary knew the operas by heart and would cross-examine him about every performance.* V+O+A *(about/ on)* ⇑ interrogate

cross-eyed. If someone is **cross-eyed,** they have eyes that look towards each other. EG *...a short, dark, cross-eyed man.* ADJ QUALIT ⇑ squint

crossfire /krɒsfaɪə/; also spelled with a hyphen. 1 **Crossfire** is gunfire, for example in a battle, that comes from two different places but that is aimed at the same point. N UNCOUNT ⇑ fire

2 If you **are caught in the crossfire,** you become involved in an unpleasant situation in which people are arguing with each other, although you do not want to be involved or to say which of them is right. EG *...the general dilemma of a radical caught in the crossfire of the dispute over socialism.* PHR : VB INFLECTS

crossing /krɒsɪŋ/, **crossings.** A **crossing** is 1 a place where people can cross a road safely. EG *The pedestrian crossing was clear... ...one-way traffic systems and light-controlled crossings.* ● See also **zebra crossing.** N COUNT ⇑ pedestrian way 2 a place where a road and a railway meet and cross over each other. ● See also **level crossing.** N COUNT ⇑ junction 3 a journey by boat or ship to a place N COUNT on the other side of a sea, ocean, etc. EG *...the night crossing... It was a very rough crossing.*

cross-legged. If someone is sitting **cross-legged**, they are sitting with one leg placed over the other. ADV AFTER VB, OR ADJ CLASSIF

cross-purposes. If people are **at cross-purposes**, there is a misunderstanding or disagreement between them because they are talking or thinking about different things, although they do not realize it. EG *They are bound to be at cross-purposes... They were talking at cross-purposes.* PHR : USED AS AN A

cross-question, cross-questions, cross-questioning, cross-questioned. If you **cross-question** someone, you ask them a lot of questions about something. EG *I can't bring myself to cross-question the child about her activities... I heard them cross-questioning her thoroughly.* V+O ⇑ interrogated = cross-examine

cross-reference, cross-references, cross-referencing, cross-referenced. A **cross-reference** is a note at one place in a book, such as a dictionary or encyclopedia, that tells the reader that there is relevant or more detailed information at another place in it. EG *In my encyclopedia there is a cross-reference from whale to mammal.* N COUNT ⇑ index, annotate ▸ used as a verb. EG *No one had cross-referenced the forms before.* ▸ V+O

cross-roads. **Cross-roads** is both the singular and the plural form. 1 A **cross-roads** is a place where two roads meet and cross each other. EG *At the first cross-roads a policeman stepped into the road and stopped us.* N COUNT ⇑ junction

2 If you say that someone or something is **at a cross-roads**, you mean that they have reached a very important stage in their life or development. EG *Ecology stands at a cross-roads at present.* PHR : USED AS AN A

cross-section, cross-sections. 1 A **cross-section** is a piece or slice of something, which is made by cutting across it, usually at right angles; also used of a drawing of the cross-section. EG *...a cross-section of a human brain... ...a pipe of varying circular cross-section.* N COUNT+SUPP, OR N UNCOUNT

2 A **cross-section** of something such as the population, community, or opinion, is a typical or representative sample of it as a whole. EG *It is work that attracts a remarkable cross-section of the public... ...well over a hundred people representing a broad cross-section of the community.* N COUNT : USU SING, USU+*of*

crosswind /krɒswɪnd/, **crosswinds**. A **crosswind** is a strong wind that blows across the direction that vehicles such as cars, ships, or aircraft are travelling in, and that makes it difficult for them to keep moving steadily forward. N COUNT ⇑ wind

crosswise /krɒswaɪz/. If something is **crosswise**, it goes from one corner of a thing to the opposite corner. EG *Her umbrella was clutched crosswise against her bosom.* ADV = diagonally

crossword /krɒswɜ:d/, **crosswords**. A **crossword** or a **crossword puzzle** is a word game in which you work out the answers to clues, and write the answers in the white squares of a pattern of small black and white squares that is contained inside a larger square. EG *I do the quick crossword on the back page first... Before going to sleep, he filled in another crossword puzzle.* N COUNT

crotch /krɒtʃ/, **crotches**. 1 Your **crotch** is the part of your body between the tops of your legs. EG *He is carrying a stack of books, which reach from the level of his crotch to just under his chin.* N COUNT : USU POSS+N IN SING

2 The **crotch** of a pair of trousers, pants, etc is the part that covers the area between the tops of your legs. EG *There were grains of sand in the crotch of her swimming costume.* N COUNT : IF+ PREP THEN *of*

crotchet /krɒtʃɪ[1]t/, **crotchets**. A **crotchet** is a musical note that has a time value equal to two quavers or half a minim. It is often used to represent one beat. N COUNT = quarter note

crotchety /krɒtʃɪ[1]ti[1]/. Someone who is **crotchety** is rather grumpy and easily irritated. EG *...the most crotchety judge in Cape Town.* ADJ QUALIT ⇑ irritable

crouch /kraʊtʃ/, **crouches, crouching, crouched**. 1 If you **crouch** or **crouch** down, you are in or move to a position in which your legs are bent under you so that you are close to the ground and slightly leaning forwards. You often crouch because you are frightened or are hiding from someone. EG *Wet and frightened, they crouch there wondering what to do next... There was an enormous cat crouching on the counter... He crouched down among the tangled foliage.* ▸ used as a noun. EG *He slowly sank back into a crouch on the floor.* V : USU+A ⇑ bend down ▸ N COUNT : USU SING

2 If you **crouch** over someone or something, you bend over them so that you are very near to them. EG *...her stout form crouched over a typewriter.* V : USU+A = huddle

croup /kru:p/ is a disease which children sometimes suffer from that makes it difficult for them to breathe and causes them to cough a lot. N UNCOUNT, OR N SING : *the*+N ⇑ illness

croupier /kru:pɪə/, **croupiers**. A **croupier** is the person in charge of a particular gambling table in a casino, who collects the bets and pays money to the people who have won. N COUNT

crouton /kru:tɒn/, **croutons**. **Croutons** are small pieces of toasted or fried bread that are added to soup just before you eat it. EG *Crunchy croutons add interest to a smooth creamy soup.* N COUNT : USU PL

crow /krəʊ/, **crows, crowing, crowed**. 1 A **crow** is a large, black bird which has a loud, harsh cry. There are several different types of crow. N COUNT

2 If you say that a place is a certain distance away **as the crow flies**, you mean that the distance stated is correct if you travel there in a straight line. Usually, however, this is not possible, so the actual journey to the place involves a greater distance. EG *It was only about eight miles as the crow flies.* PHR : USED AS AN A = direct

3 When a cock utters a loud sound early in the morning, it **crows**. EG *The cocks crowed again.* V ◊ **crowing**. EG *It was an hour before the first crowing of the cocks.* ◊ N UNCOUNT

4 If you **crow** about or over something, you keep telling people proudly or triumphantly about it; an informal use, often showing disapproval. EG *I do wish he'd stop crowing over his success... Now perhaps that is something to crow about.* V : USU+A *(over/about)* ⇑ boast, gloat

5 When people, especially babies, **crow**, they make little, happy sounds. EG *She crowed with pleasure and put out her fat little hands.* V = coo

crowbar /krəʊbɑ:/, **crowbars**. A **crowbar** is a heavy iron bar which is used as a lever or for forcing things open. N COUNT ⇑ tool

crowd /kraʊd/, **crowds, crowding, crowded**. 1 A **crowd** is 1.1 a large group of people who have gathered together, for example because something unusual or interesting has happened or is happening, or in order to listen to a speech, take part in a political demonstration, etc. EG *A big crowd had gathered... The crowd was silent... She vanished into the crowd... The court case attracted large crowds.* N COUNT = gathering, mass, throng

1.2 a large group of people who have paid to watch a game or sport. EG *...a typical British football crowd... The umpire blew his whistle, and the crowd roared.* N COUNT ⇑ audience = supporters, fans, onlookers

2 In informal English, you can say **a whole crowd of**, **crowds of**, and **a crowd of** to mean a large amount or a great many. EG *'Who's coming?'– 'A whole crowd of people.'... All day crowds of children kept turning up... There was quite a crowd of them there.* PHR+N IN PL : USED AS N PART = a lot of ≠ few

3 You say **three's a crowd** when you are describing a situation where two people want to spend time alone together but another person keeps trying to join them. You can also use it to warn someone that they are not welcome. EG *Two's company, three's a crowd... Three's a crowd, Hilary–can't you take a hint?* PHR

4 If a group of people **crowd** round or **crowd** about someone or something, they gather closely together around that person or thing. EG *All of the women crowded about her as she wept and moaned... The boys crowded round him... We crowded round eagerly, then felt disappointed.* V+A *(about/round)* = collect, congregate ≠ disperse

5 If a group of people **crowd** a place, they fill it completely so that there is no room to move. EG *Mobs of movie stars were crowding the bar.* V+O = cram into

6 If a group of people or things **crowd** in or into a place, too many of them try to get in at the same time. EG *The TV men crowded in, examining our equipment... So many thoughts of Christopher were now crowding into her mind, all at once.* V+A *(in/into)* = pile, pour, flood

7 If you **crowd** people or things into a place, you try to fit them into a space which seems to be too small for them. EG *He helped his dad and brother crowd the animals into a truck... Reporters and photographers were crowded into the lobby.* V+O+A *(in/into)* = cram, squeeze, push

8 If you **crowd** someone, you make them feel uncomfortable by moving too close to them or by making them very aware that you are watching them closely; an informal use. EG *Stop crowding me, I'm working as fast as I can!* V+O ⇑ pressurize

9 A **crowd** is also a group of friends, or a set of people who share the same interests or occupations; an informal use. EG *You'll always meet quite a good crowd down in the pub... They were mostly women, the usual crowd... Our crowd all comes from Ipswich.* N COUNT+SUPP = lot, bunch

10 You can say **'Join the crowd!'** to someone to inform them that you have already had the same experience as they have, and that there are a lot of other people who share your experiences too; an informal expression. EG *Oh, you're unemployed now are you? So am I-join the crowd.* CONVENTION

11 If you **follow the crowd, move with the crowd**, or **go with the crowd**, you think or behave in exactly the same way as everyone else, so that other people often consider you boring; an informal expression used showing disapproval. EG *Don't expect anything original from him-he just follows the crowd.* PHR : VB INFLECTS ⇑ conform, copy ≠ be unique

crowd in. If things **crowd in** on you, they upset you in a way that occupies all your attention, causing you to feel completely surrounded and unable to escape from them. EG *All the things and places that I loved so well keep crowding in on me now in this gloomy bedroom.* PHRASAL VB : V+ADV, USU+*on* ⇑ overwhelm = flood in

crowd out. To **crowd** someone or something **out** means to deliberately take up so much space that they are forced to leave or move away. EG *I tried to keep my place in the queue, but they crowded me out.* PHRASAL VB : V+O+ADV ⇑ displace = push out

crowded /kraudɪ²d/. 1 A place that is **crowded** is 1.1 very full of people. EG *The bar was very crowded... The centre of Birmingham was crowded with shoppers... ...crowded pavements.* 1.2 inhabited by a lot of people. EG *Liverpool's crowded conditions... The risk of epidemics may be slightly higher in crowded urban areas.* ADJ QUALIT : IF+PREP THEN *with* = crammed ≠ deserted; ADJ QUALIT = overpopulated

2 If you feel **crowded**, you feel uncomfortable because there are too many people too close together in the same place. EG *It was crowded in our room... Nobody seemed to mind being hot or crowded.* ADJ QUALIT

3 If your life, your mind, etc is **crowded**, it is very full of things, activities, or events. EG *His mind was crowded with memories... It's a very, very crowded life, there's always something to be done.* ADJ QUALIT : IF+PREP THEN *with* = full ≠ empty

crown /kraun/, **crowns, crowning, crowned.** 1 A **crown** is 1.1 a circular ornament for the head, usually made of gold and precious jewels. Kings and queens wear crowns at official ceremonies. 1.2 a circle for the head, often made of leaves or flowers, which is given to someone as a prize or a mark of distinction at a special ceremony. EG *Amid much chanting, a crown was awarded to the best poet.* N COUNT; N COUNT : USU+SUPP ⇑ award

2 The **Crown** is the monarchy, regarded as an institution concerned with the government of a country rather than as an individual king or queen. EG *All land in Scotland is ultimately owned by the Crown... ...a senior Minister of the Crown.* N PROPER : *the*+N

3 To **crown** someone means 3.1 to officially give them the power and status of king or queen by placing a crown on their head in a special ceremony. EG *The Emperor was crowned by the Pope.* 3.2 in very informal English, to hit them on the head; often used as a threat. EG *I'll crown him if he does!* V+O, OR V+O+C ⇑ appoint; V+O = brain

4 If something **crowns** something else, it is situated on or round the top of it; a literary use. EG *Sarah climbed the steep slope up to the shattered rocks that crowned the stronghold... ...a head crowned with coils of black hair.* V+O

5 Your **crown** is the top part of your head, at the back. EG *The crown of his head is completely bald.* N COUNT : USU WITH POSS

6 The **crown** of a hat is the part which covers the top of your head. EG *...a straw hat with the crown detached on one side.* N COUNT ≠ brim

7 The **crown** of a hill is the top of it, especially when it is gently rounded. N COUNT : USU WITH POSS

8 A **crown** is also 8.1 an old British coin that was worth 5 shillings. 8.2 an artificial top piece for a broken tooth, usually made of gold or porcelain. EG *I'm having a gold crown fitted on one of my back molars.* N COUNT; N COUNT ⇑ cap

9 When dentists **crown** a tooth that is broken, they fit an artificial crown on it. V+O ⇑ caps

10 An achievement, event, or quality that **crowns** something is the most successful, exciting, or beautiful part of it which often makes it perfect or complete. EG *The evening was crowned by a dazzling performance from Maria Ewing.* ▸ used as a noun. EG *The crown of her career was her election onto the Board of Directors.* ◊ **crowning.** EG *These major new discoveries are the crowning achievement of 16 years of research... Her hair is indeed her crowning glory.* V+O ⇑ culminates = perfects; ▸ N SING WITH DET; ◊ ADJ CLASSIF : ATTRIB ⇑ overriding

11 You can say **to crown it all** in order to introduce and emphasize the final item in a list or the final event in a series of events, because you think it is the best, worst, or most extreme in some way; used in informal English. EG *And to crown it all, he had chocolate cake for tea.* PHR : USED AS ADV SEN = to cap it all

crown court, crown courts. A **crown court** is, in England and Wales, a court in which criminal cases are tried by a judge and jury rather than by a magistrate. EG *He was committed for trial at Knightsbridge Crown Court.* N COUNT ⇑ court

crowned head, crowned heads. A **crowned head** is a king or queen who is the ruler of their country. N COUNT = monarch

crown jewels. The **crown jewels** are the crown, sceptre, and other jewels which are used on important official occasions by the King or Queen. N PLURAL : USU *the*+N ⇑ regalia

Crown Prince, Crown Princes. A **Crown Prince** is a prince who will be king of his country when the present king or queen dies. N COUNT ≠ regent

Crown Princess, Crown Princesses. A **Crown Princess** is 1 the wife of a Crown Prince. 2 a princess who will be queen of her country when the present king or queen dies. N COUNT; N COUNT ≠ regent

crow's feet are little lines of wrinkles on the skin at the outside corner of some people's eyes. EG *She had a maze of crow's feet when she smiled.* N PLURAL

crucial /kru:ʃə⁰l/. Something that is **crucial** is extremely important, especially in connection with a particular situation or event in the future. EG *It was a crucial issue to women... Success or failure here would be crucial to his future prospects... He believes this work is crucial for the welfare of the family.* ◊ **crucially.** EG *Everything has been taken away, including, most crucially, their sense of their own worth.* ADJ QUALIT ⇑ essential; ◊ ADV WITH VB

crucible /kru:sɪbə⁰l/, **crucibles.** A **crucible** is a pot in which metals or other substances can be melted or heated up to very high temperatures. N COUNT = melting pot

crucifix /kru:sɪfɪks/, **crucifixes.** A **crucifix** is a cross with a figure of Christ on it. N COUNT

crucifixion /kru:sɪfɪkʃə⁰n/, **crucifixions.** A **crucifixion** is a way of killing people which was common in the Roman Empire, in which they were tied or nailed to a cross and left there to die. ▸ The **Crucifixion** was the death of Christ by this method. EG *The Crucifixion is the supreme symbol of Christianity.* N COUNT/UNCOUNT ⇑ execution; ▸ N PROPER : *the*+N

crucify /kru:sɪfaɪ/, **crucifies, crucifying, crucified.** To **crucify** someone means 1 to kill them by tying them or nailing them to a cross and leaving them to die there. 2 to punish them severely; an informal use. EG *If he catches us he'll crucify us.* V+O ⇑ execute; V+O

crude /kru:d/, **cruder, crudest.** 1 Something such as a method or idea that is **crude** is simple and unsophisticated; often used showing disapproval. EG *This is a crude oversimplification... ...the crude methods of military administration... ...the crudest kind of racial prejudice.* ◊ **crudely.** EG *The situation can be expressed, crudely, by a mathematical equation.* ◊ **crudeness.** EG *...crudeness of representation.* ◊ **crudity** /kru:dɪti¹/. EG *...the crudity of the draughtsmanship in these sketches.* ADJ QUALIT ≠ complex; ◊ ADV WITH VB; ◊ N UNCOUNT; ◊ N UNCOUNT

2 Something that is **crude** is made from very simple parts and put together in a simple way. EG *The bombs which destroyed these cities were very crude.* ◊ **crudely.** EG *Everyone was dressed in crudely sewn shorts and shirts.* ADJ QUALIT ≠ complex, sophisticated; ◊ ADV

3 Someone who is **crude** speaks or behaves in a rude and often offensive way. EG *Do you have to be so crude?* ▸ used of someone's behaviour or actions. EG *...the crude behaviour of schoolchildren.* ◊ **crudely.** EG *I am not, as you so crudely put it, 'pissed'.* ◊ **crudity.** EG *I never expected such crudity from you.* ADJ QUALIT = vulgar; ◊ ADV WITH VB; ◊ N UNCOUNT

crude oil is oil that is in a natural state and has not yet been processed or refined. EG *The Soviet Union was the world's leading crude oil producer.* N UNCOUNT ≠ refined oil

cruel /kru:əl/, **crueller, cruellest.** 1 Someone who is **cruel** deliberately causes pain or hardship to people or animals and shows no pity. EG *You are a cruel, spiteful person... He was cruel to her.* ▸ used of someone's behaviour or actions. EG *She says the* ADJ QUALIT : IF+PREP THEN *to* ⇑ unkind ≠ kind; ▸ ADJ QUALIT *cruellest things.* ◇ **cruelly**. EG *Cruelly she said it would be no fun if I accompanied her.* ◇ ADV WITH VB

2 Something that is **cruel** is very harsh and causes people pain or hardship. EG *They don't have the ability to survive in this cruel world... The winters there were really cruel.* ◇ **cruelly**. EG *We had a cruelly long time to wait.* ADJ QUALIT ≠ mild ⇑ unpleasant harsh ◇ ADV

cruelty /kruəlti¹/, **cruelties**. **Cruelty** is behaviour that deliberately causes pain or hardship to people or animals and shows no pity. EG *The slaves accused their masters of cruelty... ...cruelty to animals.* ▸ used to refer to an instance of such behaviour. EG *They suffered beatings and other cruelties.* N UNCOUNT = abuse, harshness ▸ N COUNT : USU PL = torment

cruet /kru:ɪt/, **cruets**. A **cruet** is a container that holds several small pots or bottles for salt, pepper, mustard, etc and is used at mealtimes. N COUNT ⇑ salt and pepper

cruise /kru:z/, **cruises, cruising, cruised**. 1 A **cruise** is a holiday during which you travel on a ship and visit lots of places. EG *He was on a world cruise.* ▸ used as a verb. EG *They spent the summer cruising in the Greek islands.* N COUNT ⇑ voyage ▸ V : USU+A

2 If vehicles such as cars or ships **cruise**, they move at a constant speed that is comfortable and unhurried. EG *The taxi cruised off down the Cromwell Road... The new model has a high fifth gear for economical cruising.* V : USU+A ≠ hurry

3 People sometimes use **cruise** to refer to cruise missiles. EG *He does not think the deployment of cruise and Pershing a wise thing.* N UNCOUNT

cruise missile, cruise missiles. A **cruise missile** is a missile which carries a nuclear warhead and which is guided by a computer as it flies. It can be launched from the land, sea, or air. N COUNT

cruiser /kru:zə/, **cruisers**. A **cruiser** is 1 a large fast warship. 2 a motor boat which has a cabin for people to live or sleep in. N COUNT N COUNT

crumb /krʌm/, **crumbs**. 1 A **crumb** is a very small piece of dry food, especially from bread, cake, or biscuits. EG *She dusted the biscuit crumbs from her fingers.* N COUNT : USU PL ⇑ bit

2 A **crumb** of information, knowledge, comfort, etc is a very small amount of it. EG *They eagerly gathered each crumb of information that he let drop... She provided a crumb of hope.* N PART ⇑ morsel

3 Some people say **'crumbs'** to express surprise or anxiety; an old-fashioned use in British English. EXCLAM = gosh

crumble /krʌmbə⁰l/, **crumbles, crumbling, crumbled**. 1 If you **crumble** something soft or brittle or it **crumbles**, it breaks into lots of little pieces. EG *I crumbled an empty snail shell in my fingers... This bread crumbles ever so easily.* ● **that's the way the cookie crumbles**: see **cookie**. V-ERG ⇑ break up

2 When something such as a building or cliff **crumbles**, it breaks or disintegrates into lots of small pieces because of decay. EG *The villages are crumbling into ruin... Most of the paint had crumbled off.* V ⇑ falls

3 When something such as a society, organization, or relationship **crumbles**, it begins to fail or come to an end. EG *States had disappeared, dynasties crumbled, but the village community had persisted... We live in an age of crumbling values... ...the slow crumbling of my faith.* V = die, disintegrate

4 A **crumble** is a pudding made of fruit covered with a crumbly mixture of flour, butter, and sugar, which is baked and usually eaten hot. EG *...apple crumble.* N COUNT : USU MOD+N

crumbly /krʌmbli¹/, **crumblier, crumbliest**. Something that is **crumbly** is easily broken into lots of little pieces. EG *...hot, crumbly rolls.* ADJ QUALIT

crummy /krʌmi¹/, **crummier, crummiest**. If you say that something is **crummy**, you mean that it is of very bad quality; an informal word. EG *...a crummy little flat... By day, Las Vegas is the crummiest town on earth.* ADJ QUALIT = ropey, tacky

crumpet /krʌmpɪt/, **crumpets**. 1 A **crumpet** is a round, flat, bread-like cake with holes in one side, which is toasted and eaten hot with butter, jam, etc, mainly in Britain. N COUNT ⇑ cake

2 **Crumpet** is an offensive term used by some men to refer to women who they consider to be attractive. N UNCOUNT ⇑ female

crumple /krʌmpə⁰l/, **crumples, crumpling, crumpled**. 1 If you **crumple** something such as paper or cloth or it **crumples**, it becomes full of untidy creases and folds, for example by squashing it. EG *...crumpling the piece of paper in his hands... That dress will crumple if you pack it in the case.* ◇ **crumpled**. EG *He was unshaven and dressed in crumpled clothes.* V-ERG ⇑ crease ◇ ADJ QUALIT = rumpled

2 To **crumple** means to collapse suddenly in an untidy and helpless way; used especially of a person's body or face as the result of a sudden shock or loss of strength. EG *He crumpled into a heap... She burst into tears and crumpled on to her chair... Daddy's face crumpled when she told him.* V : USU+A

crumple up. If you **crumple up** a piece of paper, you screw it into a ball. EG *She looked at the scrap of paper, crumpled it up, and threw it into the wastebasket.* PHRASAL VB : V+O+ADV = screw up

crunch /krʌntʃ/, **crunches, crunching, crunched**. 1 If you **crunch** something hard such as a bone, a biscuit, or a sweet, you crush it noisily between your back teeth. EG *Like most dogs, she loved to crunch bones... She made a loud crunching sound.* V OR V+O

2 If you **crunch** something such as stones or glass or it **crunches**, it makes a crushing or breaking noise, for example because you step on it. EG *I crunched a wine glass underfoot... The snow would crunch beneath our steps.* ▸ used as a noun. EG *She could hear the crunch of footsteps upon the gravel... There was a crunch of breaking wood.* V-ERG ⇑ crush ▸ N COUNT+SUPP : USU SING ⇑ sound

3 You say **if it comes to the crunch** or **when it comes to the crunch** when you are considering what you would do if the situation became so serious that you were forced to decide something or to take action; an informal expression. EG *If it came to the crunch, he was prepared to let her go.* PHR : VB INFLECTS = if need be

crunchy /krʌntʃi¹/, **crunchier, crunchiest**. 1 Food that is **crunchy** is hard or crisp so that it makes a noise when you eat it. EG *It's the nuts that make it so crunchy.* ADJ QUALIT = brittle

2 Gravel or snow that is **crunchy** makes a noise when you step on it. EG *We walked along the crunchy gravel.* ADJ QUALIT ⇑ noisy

crusade /kru:seɪd/, **crusades, crusading, crusaded**. A **crusade** is 1 a set of activities that you carry out over a period of time for a particular cause that you feel strongly about. EG *...a crusade in defence of individual liberty... He was deeply involved with the anti-drugs crusade... ...the great crusade to fight and conquer cancer.* ▸ used as a verb. EG *We must crusade for better communication... Is this the fearless, crusading journalist we once knew?* 2 one of the holy wars that were fought by Christians in Palestine against the Muslims in the eleventh, twelfth and thirteenth centuries. N COUNT+SUPP : USU SING ⇑ campaign ▸ V N COUNT : USU PL ⇑ war

crusader /kru:seɪdə/, **crusaders**. A **crusader** is 1 someone who is involved in activities to make people aware of a particular social or political issue or to change a particular situation that they feel strongly about. EG *...a moral crusader.* 2 a knight who fought in the Christian holy wars against the Muslims in Palestine in the eleventh, twelfth, and thirteenth centuries. N COUNT+SUPP ⇑ campaigner N COUNT

crush /krʌʃ/, **crushes, crushing, crushed**. 1 If you **crush** something, 1.1 you press it or squeeze it very hard so that you break it or destroy its shape. EG *The jaws snapped shut around her, crushing bones and flesh... He gave the impression of being able to crush a grown man in those hairy arms.* 1.2 you make it into a powder by pressing it or grinding it between two hard surfaces. EG *I wondered if the reddish powder was crushed rubies... ...crushed ice.* V+O = crush V+O

2 If you **crush** something such as paper or cloth or it **crushes**, you spoil its flat, neat appearance by pressing it or squeezing it and making it creased. EG *Her dress was somewhat crushed... ...a crushed piece of paper... This material crushes very easily.* V-ERG = crumple

3 To **crush** something such as an army or a political organization means to defeat it completely. EG *Large numbers of troops were sent into enemy territory to crush the guerrillas... The government still think they can crush the union.* ◇ **crushing**. EG *It was a crushing result for the Labour Party.* V+O = squash ◇ ADJ CLASSIF : ATTRIB

4 If something such as an event or a piece of news **crushes** someone, it shocks them or upsets them so much that they think they will never recover. ◇ **crushing**. EG *The final lecture was interrupted by the crushing news of President Kennedy's death.* ◇ **crushed**. EG *She saw that he was hurt and crushed.* V+O = devastate ◇ ADJ CLASSIF ◇ ADJ CLASSIF

5 If you **are crushed** against other people or things, you are pushed or pressed against them, for example in a crowd. EG *They were crushed at a small table... Women were crushed up against men... He thought* V+O : USU PASS = squashed

that walking was much better than standing, hot and crushed, in a bus.

6 A **crush** is **6.1** a dense crowd of people. EG *I found myself in a crush of people... A reporter made his way through the crush.* N COUNT : USU SING **6.2** a strong feeling of attraction or love for someone that does not last very long; used especially to describe the feelings of teenagers. EG *I had a crush on the violin master... She scorned the girls who had crushes on football heroes.* N COUNT : IF + PREP THEN *on* ⇑ fancy for

crush barrier, crush barriers; also spelled with a hyphen. A **crush barrier** is a fence in the middle of a large crowd, for example at a football match, which divides the crowd and helps to prevent people from being pressed too closely together. N COUNT

crust /krʌst/, **crusts**. 1 A **crust** is **1.1** a hardened layer of something, especially on top of a softer or wetter substance. EG *There was some sort of brownish crust over the remains in the saucepan... The snow had a fine crust on it.* N COUNT : USU SING **1.2** the hard crispy outside part of a loaf of bread. EG *...egg sandwiches with the crusts cut off.* N COUNT/ UNCOUNT **1.3** the cooked pastry on top of a pie. EG *...pie crust.* N COUNT/ UNCOUNT + SUPP

2 The **crust** of a planet is the outer layer of its surface, which consists mainly of rock. EG *The continuous movements of the earth's crust are, to our eyes, imperceptible.* N COUNT + SUPP ⇑ casing

3 See also **upper crust**.

crustacean /krʌsteɪʃəⁿn/, **crustaceans**. A **crustacean** is an animal with a hard outer shell and several pairs of legs, which usually lives in water. Crabs, lobsters, and shrimps are crustaceans. N COUNT : USU PL ⇑ shellfish

crusted /krʌstɪ²d/. Something that is **crusted** is covered with a substance in a hard crust. EG *The lane was crusted with cow dung.* ADJ CLASSIF : PRED, IF + PREP THEN *with* = caked

crusty /krʌsti¹/, **crustier, crustiest**. 1 Something that is **crusty** has a hard, crisp outside layer. EG *Serve the soup hot with crusty bread... ...crusty snow.* ADJ QUALIT

2 Someone who is **crusty** is impatient and easily irritated. EG *...a crusty old gentleman.* ADJ QUALIT ⇑ irritable

crutch /krʌtʃ/, **crutches**. A **crutch** is 1 a support like a stick, which someone leans on with their arms in order to help them to walk, usually when they have injured their foot or leg. EG *She came walking in on crutches, her foot still in a cast... The old man used his stick as a crutch.* N COUNT 2 a person or a thing that gives you help or support. EG *The book was simply a crutch to my memory... He didn't want that mental crutch... ...one of the crutches of British democracy, an independent press.* N COUNT 3 the same as a crotch.

crux /krʌks/. The **crux** of a problem, argument, etc is the most important or difficult part of it which has an effect on everything else. EG *Here we come to the crux of the matter... Here lies the crux of the whole problem of industrial relations.* N SING WITH DET : USU *the* + N + *of*

cry /kraɪ/, **cries, crying, cried**. 1 When you **cry**, you produce tears, usually because you are unhappy, frightened, or hurt, but sometimes because you are laughing a lot. EG *Helen began to cry... Madeleine's eyes filled with tears. 'Oh don't cry', said Florrie... They cried for their mothers... The boys cried with laughter.* V = shed tears ≠ laugh ▸ used as a noun. EG *She felt a lot better after a good cry.* ▸ N SING ● If you **cry** your **eyes out**, you cry a lot and for a long time. EG *A little girl came in, crying her eyes out.* ● PHR : VB INFLECTS ● If you **cry** yourself **to sleep**, you cry until you fall asleep. ● PHR : VB INFLECTS

2 If you **cry** or **cry** out, **2.1** you call out loudly because you are frightened, unhappy, or in pain. EG *He cried for help... He never cried out although he was in pain... I heard Mary cry out in fright.* V : IF + ADV THEN *out* ⇑ yell out **2.2** you speak loudly, often because you are excited, surprised, or afraid. EG *'Come on!' he cried... 'Oh look!' she cried, seeing the ticket... He cried out angrily, 'Get out of my house!'* V + QUOTE = shout ≠ whisper

3 People sometimes say **'For crying out loud'** when they are annoyed or surprised; an informal expression. CONVENTION = good grief

4 A **cry** is **4.1** a loud, high sound that you make with your voice and that expresses an emotion such as fear, pain, or pleasure. EG *When she saw him she uttered a cry of surprise... She gave a little cry... His cry of alarm was heard across the road.* N COUNT : IF + PREP THEN *of* ⇑ shriek **4.2** a shout, usually made in order to attract someone's attention. EG *We heard cries of 'Help! Please help me!' coming from the river... ...cries of triumph.* N COUNT : IF + PREP THEN *of* **4.3** something that is said loudly and in public, for example to give people information about something or to urge them to do something. EG *The cries of the market traders were all around... ...battle cries... 'India for the Indians' was their cry.* N COUNT + SUPP = shout **4.4** the sound that a bird or other animal makes. EG *A sea bird flapped upwards with a hoarse cry... We heard the cries of the night owls.* N COUNT ⇑ call ▸ used as a verb. EG *The birds cried in alarm and small animals scattered.* ▸ V

5 If you are **in full cry**, EG *you are talking eagerly and continuously about something. He was in full cry when the hall suddenly emptied.* PHR : USED AS AN A ⇑ in midstream

6 People or animals that are **in full cry** after someone or something are chasing eagerly after them. EG *The hounds followed in full cry.* PHR : USED AS AN A = in hot pursuit

7 Something that is **a far cry** from something else is very different from it. EG *The tropical grasslands are a far cry from the lush green pastures of Ireland.* PHR : USED AS C + *from* ≠ similar

cry down. If you **cry down** something, you express a very low opinion of it; an informal expression. EG *He was always crying down his son's abilities.* PHRASAL VB : V + O + ADV = belittle ≠ praise

cry off. When you **cry off**, you change your mind and decide not to do something that you had arranged or agreed to do; an informal expression. EG *She cried off at the last moment.* PHRASAL VB : V + ADV ⇑ evade = cancel

cry out against. If you **cry out against** something, you complain about it because you do not approve of it. EG *People are crying out against the new laws.* PHRASAL VB : V + ADV + PREP

cry out for. If one thing **is crying out for** another, it needs it very much. EG *There is a vast surplus of workers crying out for employment.* PHRASAL VB : V + ADV + PREP ⇑ want

cry-baby, cry-babies. If you say that someone is a **cry-baby**, especially a young child, you mean that they cry a lot for no good reason; an informal word used showing disapproval. EG *You're a lot of cry-babies and sissies.* N COUNT : ALSO VOC

crying /kraɪɪŋ/. 1 **Crying** is the sound that a baby makes when he or she is unhappy, hungry, tired, etc. EG *They worry about the baby's crying.* N UNCOUNT, OR ADJ CLASSIF : ATTRIB

2 If there is a **crying** need for something to be done. there is a very great need for it, especially for it to be done urgently. EG *We still haven't answered one crying need in education.* ADJ CLASSIF : ATTRIB ⇑ urgent

3 If you say that something is **a crying shame**, you are emphasizing what a great shame it is, often when you are annoyed about it. PHR : USED AS C ⇑ unfortunate

crypt /krɪpt/, **crypts**. A **crypt** is an underground room beneath a church or cathedral, especially one that is used as a chapel or a burial place. N COUNT ⇑ cellar

cryptic /krɪptɪk/. Words that are **cryptic** are mysterious because they contain a hidden meaning or suggest a secret that is difficult to understand. EG *The message sent to him had been too cryptic... I didn't ask what this cryptic remark was intended to convey.* ADJ QUALIT ⇑ puzzling ◇ **cryptically**. EG *'I have taken precautions,' she said cryptically.* ◇ ADV WITH VB ▸ **Cryptic** is used of a type of crossword that has difficult clues with hidden meanings rather than simple straightforward ones. EG *Shall we do the cryptic clues or the quick ones?* ▸ ADJ CLASSIF

crystal /krɪstəˀl/, **crystals**. 1 A **crystal** is **1.1** a mineral that has formed into a regular symmetrical shape. Each mineral has crystals of a particular shape. EG *...crystals of copper sulphate... ...snow crystals... These stones are real diamonds found in crystal form.* N COUNT + SUPP : USU PL **1.2** a small irregular piece of something hard, which looks like a real crystal but is not exactly symmetrical. Crystals like these are commercially produced and are usually used in products which dissolve in water, such as bath salts. N COUNT + SUPP : USU PL ⇑ chip **1.3** a transparent piece of glass or plastic that fits over the face of a watch or clock. N COUNT ⇑ cover

2 **Crystal** is **2.1** a rock that is clear and transparent like ice. N UNCOUNT ▸ A **crystal** is a small piece of this rock, used in jewellery or ornaments. EG *Crystals glittered in her ears... The throne has a beautiful inlay of agate, onyx, and crystal.* ▸ N COUNT ⇑ gem **2.2** very high quality glass, usually with its surface cut into many planes so that it twinkles in the light. EG *He slammed down his glass of whisky so hard that he chipped the crystal... ...a shimmering crystal chandelier.* N UNCOUNT

3 **Crystal** water or air is clear, bright, and transparent like glass; a literary word. EG *When you get up there in that cool crystal air, somehow you find you can really breathe... Gertrude swam in the crystal pool.* ADJ CLASSIF : ATTRIB ≠ murky

crystal ball, crystal balls. A **crystal ball** is a ball made of clear glass which is used by fortune-tellers, who claim that they can see things that are N COUNT : USU SING going to happen in the future when they look into it. EG *I peered into my crystal ball.*

crystal clear. Something that is **crystal clear** is **1** absolutely clear and transparent like glass. EG *...blue skies and crystal clear air.* **2** extremely clear in sound. EG *Her voice was crystal clear.* **3** very easy to understand. EG *He challenged every point which he did not find crystal clear... I made my position crystal clear that I would never agree to vote for him.* ADJ CLASSIF / ADJ CLASSIF / ADJ CLASSIF ≠ garbled

crystalline /krɪstəᵒlaɪn/. Something that is **crystalline 1** is clear, bright, and sparkling like crystal; a literary word. EG *The light here has a crystalline quality I have not seen in any other place.* **2** is in the form of crystals or contains crystals; a technical term in chemistry. EG *...a crust of hard crystalline rock.* ADJ CLASSIF ≠ drab, dull / ADJ CLASSIF

crystallize /krɪstəᵒlaɪz/, **crystallizes, crystallizing, crystallized**; also spelled **crystallise**. **1** If you **crystallize** something such as an opinion or idea or it **crystallizes**, it becomes fixed and definite in your mind. EG *This involvement has helped me to crystallize my criticisms of the women's movement... ...a role in producing and crystallizing attitudes to leadership... This was how my thoughts began to crystallize.* ◊ **crystallization** /krɪstəᵒlaɪzeɪʃəᵒn/. EG *...the crystallisation of our wants.* V-ERG = fix, clarify, settle / ◊ N UNCOUNT

2 If you **crystallize** a substance or it **crystallizes**, it turns into crystals. EG *When the syrup begins to crystallize, pour it into moulds.* V-ERG ⇑ solidify

crystallized /krɪstəᵒlaɪzd/ fruits, sweets, etc are covered in sugar which has been melted and then allowed to go hard. ADJ CLASSIF : ATTRIB

CSE, CSE's. **CSE** is a group of examinations in various subjects which some children in Britain take at the age of fifteen or sixteen; an abbreviation for 'Certificate of Secondary Education'. CSE will be replaced by GCSE in 1988. EG *They can take that course one year after CSE.* ▸ also used to refer to one of these examinations or to a pass in one of them. EG *Wendy'll only be doing CSE's... He left school with 6 CSE's.* N UNCOUNT ⇑ qualification / ▸ N COUNT ⇑ exam

CS gas is a gas which causes you to cry and makes breathing painful. It is sometimes used by the army in war or to control a crowd which is rioting. N UNCOUNT ⇑ tear gas

cub /kʌb/, **cubs**. A **cub** is **1** a young wild animal such as a lion, wolf, or bear. EG *...a two-month-old leopard cub.* **2** the same as a cub scout. EG *He's joining the cubs this year.* N COUNT ⇑ baby / N COUNT

Cuban /kjuːbən/, **Cubans**. **1** Something that is **Cuban** belongs or relates to Cuba or to its people. EG *He became the first President of the new Cuban republic.* ADJ CLASSIF

2 A **Cuban** is someone who comes from Cuba. N COUNT

cubby-hole /kʌbi¹ həʊl/, cubby-holes. A **cubby-hole** is a very small room or space for storing things; an informal word. EG *He was given a miserable little cubby-hole to work in.* N COUNT

cube /kjuːb/, **cubes, cubing, cubed**. **1** A **cube** is a solid object with six square surfaces which are all the same size. ▸ also used to refer to a piece of something, especially food, in the shape of a cube. EG *...cubes of bread... ...ice cubes.* ● See also **stock cube**. N COUNT ⇑ shape / ▸ N COUNT+SUPP ⇑ piece

2 The **cube** of one number is another number that is produced by multiplying the first number by itself twice. For example, the cube of 2 is 8. N COUNT : USU SING, *the*+N+*of* ⇑ product ≠ cube root

3 When a number **is cubed**, it is multiplied by itself twice; for example, 3 cubed is 3 x 3 x 3, which is 27. 3 cubed is usually written as 3^3. V+O : USU PASS ⇑ multiply

cube root, cube roots. The **cube root** of one number is another number that makes the first number when it is multiplied by itself twice. For example the cube root of 8 is 2. N COUNT : USU SING, *the*+N+*of* ≠ cube

cubic /kjuːbɪk/ is used in units of volume to indicate that you are measuring length, width, and height. For example, a cubic metre is the equivalent of something a metre long, a metre high, and a metre wide. ADJ CLASSIF : ATTRIB

cubicle /kjuːbɪkəᵒl/, **cubicles**. A **cubicle** is a small enclosed area in a public building such as a swimming pool, with walls on three sides and a door or curtain on the other. Cubicles are used for dressing and undressing without being seen. EG *There were two long rows of small cubicles.* N COUNT ⇑ enclosure

cubism /kjuːbɪzəᵒm/ is a style of art, begun in the early twentieth century, in which objects are represented as if they could be seen from several different positions at the same time, using many lines and geometrical shapes. EG *Cubism is represented by Picasso and Braque.* ◊ **cubist**. EG *The Cubists discovered a new way of representing reality. ...cubist paintings.* N UNCOUNT / ◊ N COUNT

cub reporter, cub reporters. A **cub reporter** is a young reporter for a newspaper who is still being trained in his or her job. EG *He started, at sixteen, as a ten-dollar-a-week cub reporter.* N COUNT = junior

cub scout, cub scouts. The **cub scouts** are a club which is the junior version of the boy scouts, for boys between the ages of 8 and 11. EG *They stood in their Cub Scout uniforms.* ▸ A **cub scout** is a member of this club. N PLURAL / ▸ N COUNT ⇑ boy scout

cuckold /kʌkəᶞld/, **cuckolds, cuckolding, cuckolded**. **1** A **cuckold** is a man whose wife is deceiving him by having an affair with another man; a literary or old-fashioned word. EG *That girl is making him a cuckold.* **2** If a woman **cuckolds** her husband, she deceives him by having an affair with another man; a literary or old-fashioned word. EG *He had kicked her out for cuckolding him.* N COUNT : ALSO VOC / V+O ⇑ betrays

cuckoo /kʊkuː/, **cuckoos**. **1** A **cuckoo** is a grey bird that has an easily recognizable call of two quick notes, the first note higher than the second, and that lays its eggs in other birds' nests. ▸ also used to represent the sound that a cuckoo makes. N COUNT / ▸ CONVENTION ⇑ tweet

2 If you say that someone is **cuckoo**, you mean that they are a little bit mad; an informal use. EG *If you ask me, the old girl's gone quite cuckoo.* ADJ QUALIT : PRED = batty, loony

cuckoo clock, cuckoo clocks. A **cuckoo clock** is a pretty clock with a door from which a toy cuckoo pops out and makes a little noise each time the clock chimes. N COUNT

cucumber /kjuːkʌmbə/, **cucumbers**. A **cucumber** is a long thin vegetable, often used in salads, that has a green skin and is white and moist inside. N COUNT

● Someone who is as **cool as a cucumber** is extremely calm and unemotional; an informal expression. ● PHR : USED AS A/C

cud /kʌd/. **1 Cud** is food that has been eaten by a cow, sheep, or other animal with more than one stomach. The cud has been partly digested by one stomach, and comes back into the animal's mouth to be chewed again before it goes into the other stomach. N UNCOUNT

2 When animals such as cows or sheep **chew the cud**, they slowly chew their partly digested food over and over again in their mouth before finally swallowing it. PHR : VB INFLECTS = ruminate

3 If you **chew the cud**, you think about something slowly and carefully. PHR : VB INFLECTS

cuddle /kʌdəᵒl/, **cuddles, cuddling, cuddled**. When you **cuddle** someone, you put your arms round them and hold them close as a way of showing your affection. EG *A baby must be cuddled a lot.* ▸ used as a noun. EG *Give them a few cuddles and talk nicely to them.* V OR V+O : RECIP ⇑ hug / ▸ N COUNT

cuddle up. When you **cuddle up** to someone, you sit or lie as near to them as possible and you cuddle them; an informal expression. EG *They tried to cuddle up and get warm under the bedclothes... There was a woman cuddled up close to him... In the back seat, Jenny was cuddled up against me.* PHRASAL VB : V+ADV, USU+A ⇑ nestle = snuggle

cuddly /kʌdli¹/, **cuddlier, cuddliest**. People, animals, or toys that are **cuddly** are soft or furry so that you like cuddling them; used showing approval. EG *...cuddly hamsters and rabbits... ...cuddly toys.* ADJ QUALIT

cudgel /kʌdʒəᵒl/, **cudgels, cudgelling, cudgelled**; also spelled **cudgeling** and **cudgeled** in American English. **1** A **cudgel** is a thick short stick used for hitting people; an old-fashioned word. EG *...drunken peasants with cudgels.* N COUNT ⇑ club

2 If you **take up cudgels, take up the cudgel** or **carry the cudgel** for someone or something, you speak, act, or fight in support of them. EG *The Scottish Nationalists were once again carrying the cudgel for their country... Brown took up the cudgels on his behalf.* PHR : VB INFLECTS ⇑ campaign

3 To **cudgel** someone means **3.1** to beat them repeatedly with a thick short stick. **3.2** to punish or torment them by repeatedly insulting or abusing them. EG *He began to cudgel the dissidents into obedience.* V+O / V+O ⇑ beat = batter

4 If you are **cudgelling** your **brains**, you are thinking hard about something or trying to remember something you have forgotten; an informal expression. EG PHR : VB INFLECTS ⇑ think

Cudgelling her brains, Stella was trying to remember where she had last seen him.

cue /kjuː/, **cues, cueing, cued.** 1 A **cue** is 1.1 something that is said or done by a performer that serves as a signal for another performer to begin speaking or doing something. EG *When she coughs, it's my cue to get up out of the chair... The violinist was late for her cue.* ▸ used as a verb. EG *He resumes his place in the circle, cueing another actor into his place.* [N COUNT : USU + POSS, USU + to-INF] [▸ V+O] 1.2 anything that serves as a signal for some action. EG *They started yawning, so that was our cue to leave.* [N COUNT : USU + POSS, USU + to-INF; = hint]

2 If you **take** your **cue** from someone, you use their behaviour as an indication of what you should do or how you should behave in a particular situation. EG *Michael took his cue from the Duke's tone.* [PHR : VB INFLECTS]

3 If you say that something happened **on cue**, you are emphasizing that it happened just when it was most likely to happen, or just after you have been thinking or saying that it might happen. EG *Then, right on cue, the coach broke down... As if on cue, the girl dashed for the door.* [PHR : USED AS AN A; ↑ on time]

4 A **cue** is also a long, thin wooden stick with a leather tip at one end. You use a cue to hit the ball when you are playing billiards, snooker, or pool. [N COUNT; ↑ pole]

cuff /kʌf/, **cuffs, cuffing, cuffed.** 1 A **cuff** is 1.1 the end part of a sleeve, especially a shirt sleeve, which is thicker than the rest of the sleeve. EG *When ironing shirts, I only did the collars and cuffs... Fassler turned from the window, pushed his cuff back, and frowned at his watch.* [N COUNT] 1.2 the bottom part of a trouser leg, which is turned up; used mainly in American English. EG *The sand got down my collar and up the trouser cuffs.* [N COUNT : USU PL; = turn-up]

2 **Cuffs** means the same as handcuffs; an informal use. EG *The prisoner could hear the iron cuffs and chains being unlocked.* [N COUNT : USU PL]

3 If you **cuff** someone or **cuff** their hands, you fasten handcuffs on their wrists. EG *He lay face down, his hands cuffed behind him.* [V+O; ↑ handcuff]

4 If you are speaking **off the cuff**, you are speaking spontaneously, without preparing what you are going to say or thinking about it beforehand. EG *I can't answer that question off the cuff.* [PHR : USED AS AN A; = impromptu; ≠ prepared]

5 If you **cuff** someone, you hit them with your hand, usually in a light, friendly way; an informal word. EG *Sally cuffed my head lightly.* ▸ used as a noun. EG *...a cuff on the head.* [V+O; ↑ knock] [▸ N COUNT : USU SING]

cufflink /kʌflɪŋk/, **cufflinks**; also spelled as two words and with a hyphen. **Cufflinks** are small decorative objects used for holding together shirt cuffs around the wrist. [N COUNT : USU PL; ↑ jewellery]

cuisine /kwɪziːn/. 1 A country's or a district's **cuisine** is the style of cooking which is most characteristic of it. EG *...the delights of the Paris cuisine.* [N UNCOUNT + SUPP]

2 The **cuisine** of a particular restaurant is the range of food that is served in it, especially when it is cooked with great skill; used showing approval. EG *This restaurant is renowned for its cuisine.* [N SING : POSS+N; = cooking]

cul-de-sac /kʌldəsæk, kʊl-/, **cul-de-sacs.** A **cul-de-sac** is 1 a short road which is closed at one end by houses or by a barrier of some kind, so that traffic cannot drive through it. EG *...the inconspicuous cul-de-sac that contains the residence of the Prime Minister.* [N COUNT : USU SING; = dead end] 2 a place, especially a little town, where nothing interesting happens. EG *I plan to retire to a quiet cul-de-sac where there's not much life.* [N SING WITH DET; ↑ hole]

culinary /kʌlɪnəºri¹/ means concerned with kitchens or cooking, especially good cooking. EG *Each son has certain culinary specialities which he enjoys making... ...their culinary skills.* [ADJ CLASSIF : ATTRIB]

cull /kʌl/, **culls, culling, culled.** 1 If you **cull** something such as ideas or information, you gather them together and then choose which of them you need or want. EG *The story is culled from legend... Fanny read many a book to cull a theme for her essay.* [V+O : IF+PREP THEN from; ↑ take]

2 To **cull** animals means to kill the weaker animals in a herd or group in order to reduce their numbers or keep them at a particular level. EG *If you have a flock of ewes it is best to cull them before mating.* ▸ used as a noun. EG *...a big elephant cull in Zimbabwe.* [V+O] [▸ N COUNT; ↑ killing]

culminate /kʌlmɪneɪt/, **culminates, culminating, culminated.** If a situation, process, or action **culminates** in something, it has a particular effect or result after a period of gradual development. EG *The struggle between King and Parliament had culminated in the Civil War... We were in the forefront of the events which culminated in the riots of May and June 1968... ...demonstrations and strikes which culminated in one hundred students being arrested.* [V : USU + A (in); ↑ end]

culmination /kʌlmɪneɪʃəºn/. The **culmination** of something is the final effect or outcome of a gradual process or development. EG *Marriage is seen as the culmination of a successful relationship... British entry into the European Community was the culmination of a long commitment to European unity.* [N SING : USU the +N+of; ↑ climax; = conclusion]

culottes /kjuːlɒts/ are knee-length women's trousers that look rather like a skirt. [N PLURAL : ALSO a pair of+N]

culpable /kʌlpəbəºl/. If someone is **culpable**, they are responsible for something wrong or unpleasant that has happened and should take the blame for it; a formal word. EG *Was Hearst culpable? To what extent?... You can't make me culpable for their mistakes.* ◇ **culpability** /kʌlpəbɪlɪti¹/. EG *...the sensitive subject of the vet's culpability.* [ADJ CLASSIF : PRED, IF+PREP THEN for; = guilty; ≠ innocent] [◇ N UNCOUNT]

culprit /kʌlprɪt/, **culprits.** 1 A **culprit** is someone who has committed a crime or done something wrong, and who therefore has to take the blame for it. EG *'You have no excuse whatever,' the judge told the culprit... The main culprits were caught and heavily sentenced.* [N COUNT; = offender]

2 If you say that a particular thing is the **culprit**, you mean that it is the cause of problems or trouble. EG *Fat is a major culprit in causing cancers of the bowel and womb... Thirty-two per cent of all women are over-weight, the main culprits being fats and sugar.* [N COUNT]

cult /kʌlt/, **cults.** A **cult** is 1 a religious group which worships a particular saint or performs particular rituals, especially if their beliefs and behaviour are considered strange, unnatural, or harmful; often used showing disapproval. EG *...the inspired priest of an exotic cult... The cult of the Virgin Mary flourished in medieval times... The 'Moonies' cult gained adherents at an alarming rate.* [N COUNT : USU SING : IF+PREP THEN of; ↑ religion, sect] 2 a particular person, object, or activity that becomes very popular or fashionable, especially for a short period of time. EG *The Beatles became the heroes of a world-wide cult... Mae West seems to have become something of a cult figure over the last few years.* [N COUNT : USU SING : IF+PREP THEN of; ↑ fashion; = fad, craze]

cultivate /kʌltɪveɪt/, **cultivates, cultivating, cultivated.** 1 If you **cultivate** land, you prepare it and grow crops on it. EG *She and her husband cultivated several fields and had herds of cattle.* ◇ **cultivated.** EG *Only 1 per cent of the cultivated area was under irrigation.* ◇ **cultivation** /kʌltɪveɪʃəºn/. EG *Some extra land is being brought under cultivation in Asia.* [V+O; = farm, till] [◇ ADJ CLASSIF] [◇ N UNCOUNT]

2 If you **cultivate** a particular crop, you grow it. EG *His craze for gardening turned out to be an attempt to cultivate marijuana.* ◇ **cultivation.** EG *...the cultivation of wheat.* [V+O; = tend] [◇ N UNCOUNT : USU+SUPP]

3 If you **cultivate** a feeling, idea, or attitude in yourself or in someone else, you try hard to develop it and make it stronger. EG *One should cultivate a sense of humour about one's importance... He was anxious to cultivate the trust of moderate Tories.* ◇ **cultivation.** EG *The cultivation of good taste is our main objective.* [V+O; = foster] [◇ N UNCOUNT + of]

4 If you **cultivate** someone, you try hard to develop a friendship with them, sometimes for dishonest reasons or in order to gain some advantage; often used showing disapproval. EG *Roland began cultivating a retired Army colonel... Their cooperation is vital, so cultivate them assiduously.* ◇ **cultivation.** EG *...the cultivation of important men.* [V+O; = work on] [◇ N UNCOUNT + of]

cultivated /kʌltɪveɪtɪ²d/. 1 Someone who is **cultivated** shows that they have had a good education by their behaviour, especially by the way that they speak. EG *He is a cultivated man with a soft, rich voice... ...his cultivated Southern English accent.* [ADJ QUALIT; = refined; ≠ uncouth]

2 **Cultivated** plants are ones which have been developed for growing on farms or in gardens. EG *Cultivated plants do not flourish in an acidic soil.* [ADJ CLASSIF : USU ATTRIB; ≠ wild; = tended]

3 See also **cultivate.**

cultivator /kʌltɪveɪtə/, **cultivators.** A **cultivator** is 1 a tool or machine which is used to break up the earth or to remove weeds, for example in a garden or field. [N COUNT] 2 someone who prepares the ground and grows crops in it. [N COUNT]

cultural /kʌltʃəºrəl/ means 1 relating to a particular society and its ideas, customs, and art. EG *The* [ADJ CLASSIF : USU ATTRIB] *social institutions and cultural traditions of these peoples differed greatly... ...cultural links and influences.* ◇ **culturally**. EG *We must try to understand his culturally determined view of women... They had little in common culturally with us.* **1.2** involving or concerning music, literature, and the other arts. EG *...cultural activities such as plays, concerts, and poetry readings... ...the narrow limits of her cultural world.* ◇ **culturally**. EG *...an elegant and culturally vital life.*

◇ ADV

ADJ CLASSIF : ATTRIB
⇑ artistic

◇ ADV+ADJ

cultural desert, cultural deserts. If you describe a place as a **cultural desert**, you mean that there is very little artistic or intellectual activity there; an informal expression. EG *Birmingham is a great cultural desert.*

N COUNT
≠ cultural oasis

culture /kʌltʃə/, **cultures, culturing, cultured**. **1** **Culture** or a **culture** consists of the ideas, customs, and art that are produced or shared by a particular society. EG *He was a fervent admirer of Roman and Greek culture... ...the great cultures of Japan and China.*

N COUNT/ UNCOUNT+SUPP

2 A **culture** is a particular society or civilization, especially one considered in relation to its ideas, its art, or its way of life. EG *Infanticide was practised by many early cultures... ...the rich history of African civilizations and cultures.*

N COUNT+SUPP

3 **Culture** is **3.1** the intellectual and artistic aspects of a society. EG *The war brought about great changes in culture and attitudes.* **3.2** the arts considered as a group, for example art, music, and literature, together with activity or interest in them. EG *He was specially interested in culture and history... Culture was not very high in the city's list of priorities.* **3.3** the quality of being well-mannered and well-educated, especially when you have a good knowledge of the arts and an interest in them. EG *Kingsley had evidently been a man of culture... Beneath the veneer of culture and civilization there was something very savage about her.*

N UNCOUNT
⇑ discernment

N UNCOUNT

N UNCOUNT
= refinement

4 Physical **culture**, beauty **culture**, etc is the development of your body or the improvement of your physical appearance, for example by doing exercises or having particular types of treatment. EG *They have developed their bodies by physical culture.*

N UNCOUNT : MOD +N

5 The **culture** of bees, silkworms, fish, etc is the practice of keeping, rearing, and breeding them for the substance that they produce. EG *The monk was an expert on bee culture... The culture of silkworms.*

N UNCOUNT+ SUPP
= tending, husbandry

6 A **culture** is also a group of bacteria or a group of cells taken from a person or animal, which are grown in a laboratory as part of an experiment, for example to see if a particular disease is present. EG *One of his assistants was careless about a culture of chicken cholera germs... ...blood cultures.* ▸ used as a verb. EG *...techniques whereby cells and tissues of plants may be cultured under aseptic conditions.*

N COUNT : USU+ SUPP
⇑ growth

▸ V+O

cultured /kʌltʃəd/. Someone who is **cultured** has good manners, is well educated, and knows a lot about the arts and is interested in them. EG *They were intelligent, cultured people... ...a highly cultured man.*

ADJ QUALIT
= cultivated, refined

cultured pearl, cultured pearls. A **cultured pearl** is a pearl that is deliberately created by putting sand, grit, etc into an oyster. EG *She wore the string of cultured pearls he had given her.*

N COUNT
≠ real pearl

culture shock ; also spelled with a hyphen. **Culture shock** is a feeling of anxiety, loneliness, and confusion that people sometimes experience when they first arrive in another country or live with people from another culture. EG *It was still a culture shock to arrive in Calcutta.*

N UNCOUNT/N COUNT
⇑ surprise

culvert /kʌlvət/, **culverts**. A **culvert** is a water pipe or sewer that crosses under a road or railway. EG *The water poured through a culvert under the highway.*

N COUNT

-cum- is placed between two nouns to form a compound noun describing something or someone as being partly one thing and partly another. EG *The light in the barn-cum-garage was on... ...a dining-cum-living room... ...a sort of teacher-cum-lexicographer.*

cumbersome /kʌmbəsəm/ is used to describe **1** things which are difficult to carry, wear, or handle, because they are very large and heavy. EG *...a cumbersome piece of machinery... Our costumes were hot and cumbersome.* **2** an activity, process, or system which is very slow, complicated, and inefficient. EG *Such a description is rather cumbersome and open to misunderstanding... The country was handicapped by its more cumbersome system of development... ...a cumbersome, slow computer system.*

ADJ QUALIT
= unwieldy
≠ delicate

ADJ QUALIT
= clumsy

cumbrous /kʌmbrə⁹s/ means the same as cumbersome; a very formal word. EG *...cumbrous protective clothing.*

ADJ QUALIT

cumin /kʌmɪn/; also spelled **cummin**. **Cumin** is a sweet-smelling spice used in cooking, especially Indian cooking.

N UNCOUNT

cummerbund /kʌməbʌnd/, **cummerbunds**. A **cummerbund** is a wide sash worn round the waist as part of a man's evening dress.

N COUNT

cumulative /kjuːmjə⁴lətɪv/. Something that is **cumulative** keeps increasing steadily in quantity, degree, or rate of development. EG *Is scientific knowledge cumulative, or isn't it?... Her anger achieved a cumulative momentum of its own.*

ADJ CLASSIF
⇑ successive

cumulus /kjuːmjə⁴ləs/, **cumuli**. **Cumulus** is a type of thick, fluffy, white cloud formed when hot air rises very quickly. EG *Around midday, the fog lifted and puffy cumulus clouds appeared across the sky.*

N UNCOUNT/ COUNT

cunning /kʌnɪŋ/. **1** Someone who is **cunning** has the ability to plan things cleverly in order to achieve what they want, often by deceiving or tricking other people; usually used showing disapproval. EG *Richard may not be all that bright, but he is certainly cunning... On their second raid they were more cunning.* ▸ used also of someone's behaviour. EG *...a singularly cunning manoeuvre on Kurt's part... He knew nothing of the desperate and cunning means employed to get him out of his job.*

ADJ QUALIT
⇑ clever
= artful, deceitful
≠ naive, stupid

2 **Cunning** is the ability that someone has to plan things cleverly in order to achieve what they want, often by deceiving or tricking other people; often used showing disapproval. EG *She was a woman of diabolical cunning... They achieved their aim by stealth and cunning... I did not realise with what cunning Hamilton had planned his departure.*

N UNCOUNT
⇑ cleverness
= sharpness

3 If you describe something as **cunning**, for example the way that something happens in nature, or the way that an artist creates a particular effect, you are expressing admiration for the beauty, skill, or efficiency that is involved. EG *The tropical rainforest is a cunning solution to this problem... The third movement of the symphony makes cunning use of glockenspiels and whistles.*

ADJ QUALIT
= smart
≠ clumsy

4 You can also describe someone as **cunning** when you mean that they are sweet and cute; used in American English.

ADJ QUALIT
≠ gross

cunt /kʌnt/, **cunts**. **1** A **cunt** is a very rude and offensive word that refers to a woman's vagina.

N COUNT

2 If someone calls another person a **cunt**, they are being very offensive and showing how much they hate or despise that person.

N COUNT : ALSO VOC

cup /kʌp/, **cups, cupping, cupped**. **1** A **cup** is **1.1** a small, round container, usually with a handle, from which you drink liquids such as tea and coffee. EG *John put his cup and saucer on the coffee table... ...a bone china cup... ...a paper cup.* ▸ also used to refer to the liquid inside a cup or the amount of liquid that it contains. EG *I've just made some tea. Would you like a cup?... To clean chrome and paintwork: Mix 2 cups paraffin with 1 cup methylated spirit.* **1.2** something which is small, round, and hollow in shape like a cup. EG *She shook a little powder into each cup of her bra... ...an egg cup.*

N COUNT

▸ N PART

N COUNT : USU+ SUPP
⇑ holder

2 A **cup** is also a prize given to the person or team that wins a game or competition, especially in sport. The cup is usually made of metal and shaped like a cup, with a handle on each side of it and a long, thin piece of metal underneath it which joins on to a flat base. EG *He went up to receive his silver cup for the long jump.* ▸ often used in the title of a sports contest or competition, especially when the prize is a cup. EG *On Saturday Manchester City plays Tottenham Hotspur in the F.A. Cup.*

N COUNT
⇑ trophy

▸ N SING : ALSO IN TITLE
⇑ match

3 If you **cup** something in your hands or with your hands, you hold it with your hands touching all round it. EG *....his hands were cupped around his lighter... He cupped her breast with his hand.*

V+O : USU+A, OR V+A

4 **Cup** is a drink that consists mainly of wine, champagne, or fruit juice and has a number of other ingredients added to it. EG *I had just finished my second glass of fruit cup... We had a lovely champagne cup at her wedding.*

N MASS
⇑ punch

cupboard /kʌbəd/, **cupboards**. A **cupboard** is a piece of furniture which has one or two doors at the front and usually shelves inside it. It is used for keeping things in, such as cups and saucers, tins of food, or clothes. EG *...a well-stocked kitchen cupboard... ...the linen cupboard... I rushed into the kitchen and began opening cupboards and drawers.* N COUNT
• **a skeleton in the cupboard**: see **skeleton**.

cupboard love is the sudden or extremely friendly or loving behaviour of one person to another, especially of a child towards one of its parents, in order to get something that he or she wants. N UNCOUNT ⇑ fawning

Cup Final, Cup Finals. 1 A **Cup Final** is the last match in a football or cricket competition, when the two winners from the previous rounds play against each other to decide who will win the cup for that year. N COUNT ⇑ game
2 The **Cup Final** is, in Britain, the last match of the Football Association Cup soccer competition. It is held every year in London. EG *...the Cup Final at Wembley.* N COUNT : USU *the*+N ⇑ event

cupful /kʌpfʊl/, **cupfuls**. A **cupful** is the amount which one cup can hold. EG *...a cupful of brown rice... Dissolve two cupfuls of sugar in half a cup of water.* N PART+N UNCOUNT/N IN PLURAL

cupid /kjuːpɪd/, **cupids**. 1 **Cupid** is the Roman god of love, the son of the goddess Venus. He is usually drawn as a baby boy with wings and a bow and arrow. N PROPER
2 A **cupid** is a picture or statue of a pretty little boy with wings, often holding a bow and arrow. EG *...a big mirror with little carved cupids at each corner.* N COUNT ⇑ image

cupidity /kjuːpɪdɪti[1]/ is a greedy desire for money and possessions; a formal word. EG *Appeals to human cupidity reach their lowest point in TV give-away shows.* N UNCOUNT = avarice

cupola /kjuːpələ/, **cupolas**. A **cupola** is a roof or part of a roof that is shaped like a round bowl turned upside-down, usually with a pointed spire in the centre. EG *...the golden cupolas of the Kremlin.* N COUNT ⇑ dome

cuppa /kʌpə/, **cuppas**. A **cuppa** is a cup of tea; used mainly in informal British English. EG *What about a cuppa?... ...their morning cuppa.* N COUNT : *a*/POSS +N

cup-tie, cup-ties. In sport, especially football, a **cup-tie** is a match between two teams who are competing in a competition in which the prize is a cup. The winner of one match plays the winner of another, and so on until two teams reach the Cup Final. N COUNT ⇑ game

curable /kjʊərəbə[0]l/. If a disease or illness is **curable**, it can be cured. EG *Infant blindness can be curable later in life.* ADJ CLASSIF

curacy /kjʊərəsi[1]/, **curacies**. A **curacy** is the position held by a curate or the work that a curate has to do. EG *...Somerset, where my father had his first curacy.* N COUNT ⇑ job

curate /kjʊərə[1]t/, **curates**. A **curate** is a clergyman in the Church of England who helps the vicar or rector in charge of a parish. EG *...a humble curate in a small country village.* N COUNT

curative /kjʊərətɪv/ means having the power to cure people's illnesses or problems. EG *Our clinic deals with preventive rather than curative treatment... ...the curative power of herbal remedies.* ADJ CLASSIF : ATTRIB = healing, remedial

curator /kjʊə[0]reɪtə/, **curators**. A **curator** is someone who is in charge of the objects or works of art in a museum, art gallery, etc. EG *...the curator of the Louvre.* N COUNT : IF+ PREP THEN *of* ⇑ caretaker

curb /kɜːb/, **curbs, curbing, curbed**. 1 If you **curb** something, you control it and keep it within fixed limits. EG *A man must decide either to curb his appetites or to surrender to them... ...proposals to curb the powers of the Home Secretary.* ▸ used as a noun. EG *This requires a curb on public spending.* V+O ⇑ counter, check ≠ further ▸ N COUNT : IF+ PREP THEN *on*
2 If you **curb** someone, for example a child who is behaving badly, you act firmly to control them and make them behave properly. EG *Children whose instincts are to rebel often get curbed by their teachers.* V+O = restrain ≠ indulge
3 A **curb** is the same as a kerb; used in American English. EG *She sat down suddenly at the curb... I pulled up at the curb.* N COUNT : USU SING, *the*+N

curd /kɜːd/, **curds**. **Curds** are the thick white substance which is formed when milk turns sour. It is used for making cheese: compare **whey**. N COUNT : USU PL ⇑ food

curdle /kɜːdə[0]l/, **curdles, curdling, curdled**. 1 If milk **curdles** or something **curdles** it, it becomes sour and has little white bits floating in it. EG *The acidity of some coffee can cause the milk to curdle... The effect of acid on milk is to curdle it.* V-ERG ⇑ separate
2 If something **curdles** your **blood** or your **blood curdles**, you are extremely frightened or shocked. EG *He heard a list of atrocities that curdled the blood in his veins... ...a thought which is enough to make the blood curdle.* • See also **bloodcurdling**. PHR : VB INFLECTS ⇑ terrify = scare to death

cure /kjʊə/, **cures, curing, cured**. 1 If someone or something **cures** an illness or injury, they cause it to end or disappear, usually by medical treatment. EG *An illness can be cured. Death, however, remains incurable... There are few remaining diseases that these modern drugs cannot cure... It was reputedly used as a folk medicine to cure snake-bite.* V+O = heal, remedy
2 If someone or something **cures** a person, they make that person well again after an illness or injury. EG *They swore that she had cured them... Her patients appeared to be cured... This therapy does not cure at once.* V OR V+O = heal
3 A **cure** is 3.1 a medicine, medical treatment, or other treatment that cures people or their illnesses. EG *These pills are cures for various illnesses... There's no known cure for a cold.* N COUNT : IF+ PREP THEN *for* = remedy 3.2 the act of curing an illness or injury. EG *I'm interested in the cure of cancer.* N COUNT : IF+ PREP THEN *of* 3.3 something that removes or ends a problem. EG *I told the mother that the only cure for her daughter's unhappiness was to leave home.* N COUNT/ UNCOUNT : IF+ PREP THEN *for* = solution
4 If someone or something **cures** a problem, they remove or end it and improve the situation in some way. EG *The bishop had done nothing to cure the widespread lack of faith... It is love that cures, not money.* V+O = solve, mend
5 If an action or event **cures** someone of a habit or an attitude, it causes them to give it up. EG *Joining the Labour Party began to cure me of such ideas... The shock of losing my purse cured me of all my former absent-mindedness.* V+O+A *(of)* ⇑ release
6 If you **cure** food, tobacco, or animal skins or they **are cured**, they are treated by being dried, smoked, or salted them so that they can be used for a long time and do not rot. EG *After taking out the meat, they scraped and cured the hides... He had a young goat's skin curing in his hut... ...honey-cured ham.* V-ERG ⇑ preserve

curé /kjʊəreɪ/, **curés**. A **curé** is a parish priest in France. N COUNT

cure-all, cure-alls. A **cure-all** is something that people think will solve all your problems or all the problems in a particular situation. EG *Lowering of interest rates has been presented by the media as a kind of universal cure-all.* N COUNT : USU SING ⇑ solution = panacea

curfew /kɜːfjuː/, **curfews**. 1 A **curfew** is a rule or law which states that people must stay inside their houses after a particular time at night. Governments sometimes impose a curfew on all civilians, for example during a war or a period of political unrest. A curfew can also be used by an institution as a punishment for an individual person. EG *An emergency curfew was enforced... After seven in the evening, the curfew became total.* N COUNT : USU SING ⇑ restriction
2 **Curfew** or a **curfew** is the time after which you will be punished if you are found outside your house when there is a curfew. EG *He had gone into a shop ten minutes after the curfew to buy some tobacco... It's against the criminal law of the state to be in the street after curfew.* N COUNT : USU SING : NEEDS NO DET ⇑ deadline

curio /kjʊərɪəʊ/, **curios**. A **curio** is an object such as a small ornament which is unusual and fairly rare. Curios are often sold in antique shops and are collected by some people. EG *...curios and souvenirs... ...curio shops.* N COUNT ⇑ oddity

curiosity /kjʊərɪɒsɪti[1]/, **curiosities**. 1 **Curiosity** is 1.1 the desire that someone has to know about things and to learn as much as possible about them. EG *Thirteen-year-olds no longer have the curiosity of a six-year-old about letters and writing... ...the curiosity and perception of the born reporter... She looked at me, eyes wide open and full of curiosity.* N UNCOUNT ⇑ interest, inquisitiveness ≠ indifference 1.2 the desire to know about other people's private life; often used showing disapproval. EG *She showed an insatiable curiosity for my past... 'Let me ask you something, Larry. Just out of curiosity.'... His curiosity got the better of him.* N UNCOUNT ⇑ interference = nosiness
2 A **curiosity** is an object that is unusual, interesting, and fairly rare. EG *Her house was full of things that were not just old but were real curiosities... ...a little curiosity shop.* N COUNT ⇑ oddity
3 If you refer to someone as a **curiosity**, you mean N COUNT

that they are considered to be slightly strange or old-fashioned. EG *They stared at me casually now; I was still a curiosity, but an increasingly familiar one... Our explanation singled us out, in 1967, as curiosities.*

curious /kjʊərɪəs/. 1 Someone who is **curious** is 1.1 interested in things and eager to learn as much as possible about them. EG *My sister and I were curious children and delighted in finding out all sorts of things... ...the most rewarding of all museums for the curious Londoner... She was curious to see what would happen.* ◊ **curiously**. EG *They stopped and looked at her curiously.* 1.2 eager to find out things about other people's private life; often used showing disapproval. EG *He seemed awfully curious about Robertson's day-to-day routine... Everyone around is too curious, and too concerned to let anything pass unnoticed.* ◊ **curiously**. EG *But why on earth did you agree? I asked curiously.*
ADJ QUALIT ≠ disinterested; ◊ ADV WITH VB; ADJ QUALIT = nosy; ◊ ADV WITH VB

2 Something that is **curious** is 2.1 unusual and interesting. EG *Not long after our arrival, a curious thing happened... I have to talk about it simply because it is so curious.* ◊ **curiously**. EG *She had a curiously husky voice.* 2.2 difficult to explain because you cannot understand why it happens or what causes it. EG *There was a curious certainty about her... It is curious how two such different problems can be solved so similarly... ...the curious way he had of making questions not sound like questions.* ◊ **curiously**. EG *Curiously, Hearst worked energetically during his mental breakdown... Curiously enough, there is a book just out by him.*
ADJ QUALIT = odd; ◊ ADV; ADJ QUALIT = odd; ◊ ADV SEN

curl /kɜːl/, **curls, curling, curled**. 1 **Curls** are pieces of hair, especially on a person's head, that are shaped in curves and circles. EG *...dark red curls... She looked so pretty in those wigs with curls on them... I went to the party with my hair in curls.* ▸ used as an uncount noun. EG *He now wore his hair shorter and it had lost its curl.*
N COUNT : USU PL ⇑ ringlets; ▸ N UNCOUNT = bounce

2 If you **curl** someone's hair, you make curls in it. EG *He was wearing long curled hair with an Indian headband.*
V+O ⇑ style ≠ straighten

3 If your hair **curls**, it naturally forms itself into curves and circles as it grows. EG *She had dark, curling hair just beginning to go grey... Her hair appeared to curl naturally.*
V

4 A **curl** is also a curved, spiral shape. EG *We could see a few curls of smoke in the distance.*
N COUNT : USU+SUPP

5 If something **curls** or you **curl** it, 5.1 it becomes curved or rounded in shape. EG *They've got toes which curl round like this... Her white hands were curled around the cup.* 5.2 it moves in circles or spirals in a particular direction. EG *Smoke was curling out of kitchen chimneys... The moving belt curled over like a snake and entered a large hole in the wall.*
V-ERG : USU+A ⇑ curve, clutch; V-ERG : USU+A = spiral, twist

6 If a person or animal is **curled** or they **curl** themselves **into a ball**, they lie or move into a position in which they form a rounded shape. EG *She would lie curled on her side, her knees drawn up... The kitten curled into a ball, wrapping its tail around its paws.*
V, OR PHR : VB INFLECTS ⇑ curve ≠ stretch

7 When something flat, such as a leaf or a piece of paper, **curls**, its edges bend towards the centre, usually because it is old. EG *The trees were dead; their bark was curling and falling away... He found a piece of cheese, dried and curled with age.*
V : USU+A = shrivel ≠ lie flat, straighten

8 If you **curl** your lip or your lip **curls**, you move your upper lip slightly upwards or to one side, as a way of showing contempt, scorn, or anger. EG *Posy's lip curled at this suggestion.* ▸ used as a noun. EG *My upper lip shaped itself into a tiny curl of contempt.*
V-ERG ⇑ twist; ▸ N SING WITH DET

curl up. 1 If you **curl up**, you lie down bringing your arms, legs, and head in towards your stomach, for example because you sleep in that position or in order to protect yourself from danger. EG *He was lying curled up with his back to us... She could see the cat curled up asleep on the sofa.*
PHRASAL VB : V+ADV = roll up ≠ stretch out

2 When something flat, such as a leaf or a piece of paper, **curls up**, its edges bend towards the centre, usually because it is old. EG *Her photographs have long been discarded and curl up, yellowing, in some dusty drawer.*
PHRASAL VB : V+ADV

curler /kɜːlə/, **curlers**. **Curlers** are small plastic or metal tubes used for shaping people's hair into curls. You wet your hair and wind pieces of hair round each curler. As your hair dries, it becomes curly, and you remove the curlers. EG *In her short, dark hair were rows of pink plastic curlers... When she took her curlers out she looked much younger.*
N COUNT : USU PL = roller

curlew /kɜːljuː/, **curlews**. A **curlew** is a large brown bird with long legs and a long curved beak. Curlews live near water and have a very distinctive cry. EG *...the searing wail of the curlew.*
N COUNT

curling tongs are metal devices that look rather like scissors and are used for shaping people's hair into curls. The curling tongs are heated and placed in people's wet hair, which becomes curly as it dries.
N PL : ALSO *a pair of*+N

curly /kɜːliˡ/, **curlier, curliest**. 1 Hair that is **curly** is full of curls. EG *She shook her short curly blonde hair... Her hair was slightly longer and curlier than that of the other girls in the office.*
ADJ QUALIT ⇑ wavy ≠ straight

2 Something that is **curly** is curved, circular, or spiral in shape; used mainly in informal English. EG *What are these curly bits of paper for?... ...dark green curly leaves... ...curly-toed shoes.*
ADJ QUALIT ≠ straight

currant /kʌrənt/, **currants**. 1 **Currants** are small dried grapes, used especially in cakes. EG *...dried fruits such as currants, raisins and dried apricots.*
N COUNT : USU PL ⇑ raisin

2 **Currant** refers to several different soft fruits, such as red currants or black currants. EG *The currants were at their best, clusters of red, black and white hanging from the branches... ...the soothing properties of blackcurrant juice.* ▸ also used of the bushes on which they grow. EG *She was a great gardener and had planted currants, white and red... The currant bushes were heavy with fruit.*
N COUNT : USU PL ⇑ fruit; ▸ N COUNT : USU BEFORE N ⇑ bush

currency /kʌrənsiˡ/, **currencies**. 1 The **currency** of a country is 1.1 the system of money that is used in it. EG *Sterling has once again become one of the stronger currencies... The world currency markets are in a turmoil at the moment.* 1.2 the coins and banknotes that are used in it. EG *Do you change foreign currency?... I took a few traveller's cheques and bits of odd currency.*
N COUNT : USU+SUPP ⇑ exchange; N UNCOUNT ⇑ money

2 If ideas, expressions, and customs have **currency**, they are used and accepted by many people at a particular time. EG *They have seen many of their basic ideas gain wide currency... This rumour had a certain currency during the 1970's.*
N UNCOUNT ⇑ acceptance

current /kʌrənt/, **currents**. 1 A **current** is 1.1 a steady and continuous flowing movement of some of the water in a river or lake, or in the sea, which may move faster or in a different direction from the water around it. EG *The child had been swept out to sea by the current... We learnt about the Gulf Stream and which way the currents flow.* 1.2 a steady flowing movement of air in a particular direction. EG *A steady current of heated air rose all day from the mountain top.* 1.3 a flow of electricity through a wire or circuit. EG *There was a powerful electric current running through the wires... Switch off the mains current.* 1.4 a general tendency within a group of people to adopt a particular opinion or way of behaving. EG *...the powerful currents of opinion which sway men's minds... ...the fickle currents of theory and fashion.*
N COUNT ⇑ flow, tide; N COUNT : USU+*of*, OR AFTER N ⇑ flow; N COUNT; N COUNT+SUPP ⇑ trend

2 Something that is **current** is happening, being done, or being used in the present period of time. EG *Our current methods of production are far too expensive... At the current rate of growth, this should prove a valuable investment... ...the current issue of the Science Review... The conversation shifted onto what is current in art and music and theater.* ◊ **currently**. EG *The World Health Organisation is currently holding its annual assembly in Geneva... ...experiments currently in progress... This is currently the case with most computers.*
ADJ CLASSIF; ◊ ADV ⇑ now

3 Ideas, expressions, and customs that are **current** are generally accepted and used by most people. EG *The words 'light pollution' are in current use only among astronomers... ...the beliefs and ideals current in a particular age.*
ADJ CLASSIF ⇑ common

current account, current accounts. A **current account** is a personal bank account from which you may take out money at any time using your cheque book or your computerized card; used mainly in British English. EG *It's not usual to be paid interest on your current account.*
N COUNT = checking account ≠ deposit account

current affairs. 1 **Current affairs** are political and social events which are of international importance or interest and which are discussed in newspapers and on television and radio programmes. EG *...the personalization and over-simplification of current affairs... ...the BBC's current affairs programmes.*
N PLURAL ⇑ news = current events

2 **Current affairs** is the name given to a subject which is studied at school, in which children learn about the important things that are happening in the world. N UNCOUNT

curriculum /kərɪkjə⁴ləm/, **curriculums, curricula**. The plural can be either **curriculums** or **curricula**. A **curriculum** is 1 all the different courses of study that are taught in a school, college, or university. EG *...the school curriculum... Some authorities are introducing environmental themes into school curricula... Social studies have now been added to the curriculum.* N COUNT ⇑ syllabus 2 one particular course of study that is taught in a school, college, or university. EG *...our English curriculum.* N COUNT ⇑ syllabus

curriculum vitae, curricula vitae. Your **curriculum vitae** is a brief written account of the main events of your life. It includes personal details about yourself, your education, and the jobs you have had. You are often asked to send a curriculum vitae when you are applying for a job. N COUNT : USU SING ⇑ history, summary, biography = CV

curried /kʌrɪd/ food has been flavoured with curry powder or hot spices. EG *...curried eggs. ...huge dishes of curried chicken.* ADJ CLASSIF : ATTRIB ⇑ spiced

curry /kʌri¹/, **curries, currying, curried**. 1 **Curry** is an Indian dish made with hot spices. EG *This is how I make a vegetable curry.* N MASS ⇑ food ▸ used as a verb. EG *Leave the lamb for three days in wine and vinegar and then curry it.* ▸ V+O ⇑ cook

2 If you **curry favour** with someone such as your boss, you try to please them by praising them or doing things to help them, so that they will notice you and will approve of you; used showing disapproval. PHR : VB INFLECTS, IF + PREP THEN *with* ⇑ flatter = suck up

3 When you **curry** a horse, you clean, brush, and comb it. V+O = dress down

curry powder, curry powders. **Curry powder** is a powder made of a mixture of spices, which you add to food in order to make a curry. N UNCOUNT/COUNT ⇑ spice

curse /kɜːs/, **curses, cursing, cursed**. 1 If you **curse**, you say obscene or blasphemous things because you are angry about something. EG *He missed the ball and cursed violently.* V ⇑ speak = swear ▸ used as a noun. EG *I don't know a word of Italian except a few curses... With a curse he disentangled his head from the netting.* ▸ N COUNT ⇑ utterance = obscenity

2 If you **curse** someone, **2.1** you say insulting or obscene things to them because you are angry with them. EG *I was cursing him under my breath for his carelessness... James cursed himself for being a clumsy fool.* V+O (NG/REFL) : IF + PREP THEN *for* = swear at **2.2** you ask a supernatural power to cause something very unpleasant to happen to them. EG *...the scene in 'King Lear' when Goneril is cursed by Lear.* V+O = damn ▸ used as a noun. EG *She screamed at him curses he had not heard in years, old country curses from their childhood... There is a curse on this family.* ▸ N COUNT : IF + PREP THEN *on/upon*

3 If you **curse** something, you complain angrily about it, especially using obscene language. EG *I cursed the orders that brought me here to the coast... Cursing my plight, I tried to find shelter for the night.* V+O = bemoan

4 A **curse** is something or someone that causes a great deal of trouble or harm. EG *Loneliness in old age is the curse of modern society... Mediocrity is the curse of democracy.* N COUNT : USU SING, IF + PREP THEN *of* ⇑ problem = bane

5 People sometimes used to refer to menstruation as the **curse**; an old-fashioned, informal use. N SING : *the*+N

cursed. The word **cursed** can be pronounced either /kɜːsɪd/ or /kɜːst/. 1 Someone who is **cursed** is suffering as the result of a curse. EG *The descendants of Ham were cursed for ever.... They believe that every dead enemy is cursed.* ADJ CLASSIF = damned

2 If you are **cursed with** something, you are very unlucky in having it. EG *She was cursed with four daughters.* ADJ CLASSIF : PRED + *with* = burdened with

cursory /kɜːsə⁰ri¹/. A **cursory** glance, examination, etc is brief, and one in which you do not pay much attention to detail. EG *They signed with only a cursory glance at what I had written... They made their decision after only cursory consideration of the available options.* ADJ QUALIT : USU ATTRIB ⇑ quick = desultory, perfunctory ≠ detailed ◊ **cursorily**. EG *He opened the lids of the boxes and glanced cursorily at the contents.* ◊ ADV WITH VB = briefly

curt /kɜːt/, **curter, curtest**. 1 If someone is **curt**, they speak or reply in a brief and rather rude way. EG *He had been curt with Gertrude.* ADJ QUALIT = abrupt ▸ used of someone's behaviour. EG *The sick man gave a curt shrug of amusement.* ▸ = abrupt ◊ **curtly**. EG *Marsha said curtly, 'You're supposed to be on watch'.* ◊ **curtness**. EG *His tone was characterised by curtness and dryness.* ◊ N UNCOUNT = bluntness

curtail /kə⁵teɪl/, **curtails, curtailing, curtailed**. 1 If you **curtail** something, for example the amount of money that you spend on something, you reduce it. EG *Countries are under pressure to curtail public expenditure... Participation by Turkey and Greece was drastically curtailed.* V+O = cut back

2 If you **curtail** something such as someone's power or freedom, you restrict it. EG *The power of university rectors has been curtailed... ...further legislation to curtail basic union rights.* V+O = reduce

curtailment /kə⁵teɪlmə²nt/. The **curtailment** of something is the act of reducing or restricting it; a formal word. EG *...the curtailment of military aid from the US... ...the curtailment of liberty.* N UNCOUNT : USU +*of* = limiting

curtain /kɜːtə⁰n/, **curtains, curtaining, curtained**. 1 A **curtain** is a large piece of material which hangs from the top of a window. You pull it across the window when you want to keep light out or prevent people from seeing you. EG *She went over to the window and pulled back the curtain... He drew the curtains.* N COUNT ⇑ screen

2 In a theatre, the **curtain** is **2.1** the large piece of material that hangs in front of the stage, hiding it until a performance begins. EG *There was a burst of applause as the curtain went up... She fainted as the curtain fell on the second act.* N COUNT, OR N SING : *the*+N ⇑ screen **2.2** the time when the curtain is pulled back or up at the beginning of a performance; a technical term. EG *We're rushing to make the eight o'clock curtain... Curtain time is 8 p.m.* N SING WITH DET ⇑ start

3 In a theatre, **the last curtain** or **the final curtain** is the end of a performance when the curtain is lowered or closed for the last time. EG *After the last curtain they went round to see Bernhardt.* PHR : USU USED AS O

4 You also use **curtain** to refer to something which hangs down thickly and which it is difficult to see through or get past. EG *A much denser curtain of reeds and bulrushes stretches across the water... They found a piglet caught in a curtain of creepers... ...an impenetrable curtain of blonde hair.* ● See also **Iron Curtain.** N UNCOUNT + SUPP ⇑ barrier

curtain off. If you **curtain off** part of a room, you separate it from the rest of the room by hanging a curtain across the room. EG *The other end of the room had been curtained off.* PHRASAL VB : V + O + ADV ⇑ shut off

curtain call, curtain calls; also spelled with a hyphen. In a theatre, when actors take a **curtain call**, they come forward to the front of the stage after a performance in order to receive the applause of the audience. EG *Last night we took four curtain calls.* N COUNT = bow

curtained /kɜːtə¹nd/. A **curtained** window, door, or other opening has a curtain hanging across it. EG *The curtained stage was empty... Off from the living-room behind curtained French doors was a bedroom.* ADJ CLASSIF : USU ATTRIB

curtain-raiser, curtain-raisers. A **curtain-raiser** is 1 a short play that is performed before a longer, more important one; a technical expression. EG *It should make a nice curtain-raiser.* N COUNT 2 a relatively minor event that is like a major one that happens after it. EG *The Dieppe landing was a curtain-raiser to the invasion.* N COUNT = prelude

curtsy /kɜːtsi¹/, **curtsies, curtsying, curtsied**; also spelled **curtsey**. When a woman or a girl **curtsies**, she lowers her body briefly, bending her knees and holding her skirt with both hands, as a way of showing respect for an important person. EG *It was customary then for our children to curtsy to the gentry... The ladies curtsied deeply to him.* V : IF + PREP THEN *to* ▸ used as a noun. EG *I bobbed him a curtsy.* ▸ N COUNT

curvaceous /kɜːveɪʃəs/. You say that a woman's body is **curvaceous** when it has curves that make it pleasing to look at; used showing approval. EG *The next instant a long curvaceous body was leaning up against mine. ...a curvaceous blonde.* ADJ QUALIT = shapely ≠ skinny

curvature /kɜːvətjə/. The **curvature** of something is its curved shape, especially when this shape is part of the circumference of a circle; a technical word. EG *...the curvature of the earth... ...the centre of curvature of the curve.* N UNCOUNT : IF + PREP THEN *of* = curving

curve /kɜːv/, **curves, curving, curved**. 1 A **curve** is a smooth, gradually bending line, for example part of the edge of a circle. EG *The beach stretched away before them in a gentle curve... They* N COUNT = bend *reached the curve of the drive... The pines gave way to a curve of marshland.*

2 When something **curves**, **2.1** it has the shape of a curve. EG *The lane curved round to the right... A stone wall curved back on either side of the iron-work gates.* ◇ **curving**. EG *...endless curving streets.* — V+A; ⇑ bend

2.2 it moves in a curve, for example through the air. EG *The missile curved gracefully towards its target... The twins' car curved in towards the filling station.* — V+A; ⇑ move; = turn

3 A woman's **curves** are the curved parts of her body; an informal use. EG *She was wearing a low strapless dress that hugged her curves cleverly.* — N PLURAL; = contours

curved /kɜːvd/. A **curved** object has the shape of a curve. EG *...the curved tusks of a walrus... ...a cylinder containing dozens of curved blades.* — ADJ QUALIT; ⇑ bent; ≠ straight

curvy /kɜːviˡ/, **curvier, curviest**. **Curvy** means the same as 1 curvaceous. EG *Gill was too curvy to model... ...a curvy young woman in a tight dress.* **2** curved. EG *...a settee with only one curvy end.* — ADJ QUALIT; ADJ QUALIT

cushion /kʊʃəⁿn/, **cushions, cushioning, cushioned**. 1 A **cushion** is **1.1** a fabric case filled with soft material, which you put on a seat in order to make it more comfortable. EG *...a big divan covered with cushions... ...cushion covers.* — N COUNT; ⇑ pad

1.2 a soft pad or barrier, especially one that stops something hitting something else violently. EG *He pointed to the fleshy cushion at the base of his thumb... The device floats on a cushion of air.* — N COUNT : USU + SUPP

2 To **cushion** something such as a collision means to make it less violent by being between the two things when one thing hits the other. EG *The pile of branches cushioned his fall... ...the cushioning effect of a solid row of fenders.* — V+O; ⇑ soften

3 To **cushion** the effect of something unpleasant means to reduce it. EG *A cut in income tax would cushion the blow of sharp price increases.* ▸ used as a noun. EG *...that reassuring cushion of economic growth... The scheme provided a cushion against threats of compulsory redundancy.* — V+O; = soften, lessen; ▸ N COUNT : USU SING; ⇑ buffer

cushy /kʊʃiˡ/, **cushier, cushiest**. In informal English, a **cushy** job or task is one that you can do very easily. EG *The poor have no savings and no cushy, pensionable positions... ...that nice cushy job in the bank.* — ADJ QUALIT; ⇑ easy; = jammy

cuss /kʌs/, **cusses, cussing, cussed**. **Cuss** means the same as curse, in old-fashioned informal English. EG *Maybe he'll cuss at it and hit it with a wrench... They found her lying on her bed yelling and cussing.* — V OR V+O; = curse

cussed /kʌsɪd/ is used to describe behaviour in which someone is deliberately unco-operative. EG *...a cussed refusal to give him what he wanted.* ◇ **cussedness**. EG *The reason appears to be pure cussedness.* — ADJ QUALIT; = obstinate, pig-headed; ◇ N UNCOUNT

custard /kʌstəd/ is a sweet yellow sauce made from milk and eggs or from milk and a powder, which you eat with fruit and puddings. EG *Her mother passed round plates of jelly and custard... ...custard powder.* — N UNCOUNT

custard pie, custard pies. A **custard pie** or a **custard tart** is a flat open pie filled with custard. Clowns and comedians sometimes throw custard pies at each other. — N COUNT

custodial /kʌstəʊdiəl/ means relating to the custody of a person or people; a formal word. EG *...various offences, some of which called for custodial sentences... ...day care which is educational and not just custodial.* — ADJ CLASSIF; ⇑ restrictive

custodian /kʌstəʊdiən/, **custodians**. A **custodian** is someone who is in charge of a building or the objects in a building, for example the historical objects in a museum. EG *He was living there as a sort of temporary custodian... ...the custodian of the Ricardian tablets.* — N COUNT; ⇑ guardian; = keeper

custody /kʌstədiˡ/. 1 **Custody** is the legal right to keep and look after a child, especially the right given to the child's father or mother when they become divorced. EG *Desiree was sure to get custody of both children... Almost always divorce courts award custody to mothers.* — N UNCOUNT; ⇑ care

2 If you are **in custody**, you have been arrested and are being kept in prison until you can be tried in a court. EG *I was remanded in custody... ...people who have been quite wrongly held in custody.* — PHR : USED AS AN A; ⇑ detained

custom /kʌstəⁿm/, **customs**. 1 A **custom** is **1.1** a traditional activity or festivity, especially one that takes place at the same time every year. EG *...a charming old custom still practised... My wife likes all the old English customs.* — N COUNT; = tradition

1.2 something that the people of a community or society always do in particular circumstances because it is regarded as the right thing to do. EG *It is the custom to take chocolates or fruit when visiting a patient in hospital... As was the custom, we sent invitations to everyone... His behaviour was utterly out of line with custom and practice.* — N COUNT : USU the+N, OR N UNCOUNT; ⇑ rule; = convention

1.3 something that someone usually does in a particular situation or at a particular time of day. EG *....her grandmother's custom to call her servants by their surnames... It is Howard's custom to take his class for coffee afterwards.* — N COUNT : USU SING, POSS+N; ⇑ habit; = wont

2 The **customs** is the place at a border, airport, or harbour where people arriving from a foreign country have to declare goods that they bring with them. EG *At Kennedy airport I went through the customs... I followed her into the customs building... We went into the arrivals lounge for passport and customs clearance.* ● See also **Customs and Excise**. — N PLURAL : PL FORM WHEN MOD; N PLURAL; ⇑ checkpoint

3 **Custom** is the practice of regularly buying things from a particular shop or tradesman; a rather formal word. EG *We hope to have the pleasure of your custom on future occasions... We get a lot of custom from foreigners... I shall take my custom elsewhere.* — N UNCOUNT; ⇑ trade; = patronage

customary /kʌstəməⁿriˡ/. 1 Something that is **customary** is usually done in a particular situation or at a particular time of the day or year. EG *It is apparently not customary to preserve the scripts... It is customary for them to appear in some green garment... ...the customary Christmas party.* ◇ **customarily**. EG *...the civil exchange of letters which customarily marks the departure of a minister... ...the numbers of flags that customarily fly along the south driveway.* — ADJ CLASSIF; = usual, habitual; ◇ ADV WITH VB; = commonly

2 Someone's **customary** behaviour is their usual behaviour. EG *Peter had never seen her so shaken out of her customary calm... His customary good humour was apparently restored.* — ADJ CLASSIF : ATTRIB, USU AFTER POSS

3 The **customary** way of doing something is the usual way of doing it. EG *Some might think it best to use the customary methods of the old society... She was rewarded in the customary way.* — ADJ CLASSIF : ATTRIB; = regular

4 The **customary** time for something is the time at which it usually happens or is usually done. EG *At the customary hour the doctor knocked on my door.* — ADJ CLASSIF : ATTRIB; = regular

custom-built. Something that is **custom-built** is built according to someone's special requirements. EG *The Council provided them with custom-built homes.* — ADJ CLASSIF; ≠ standard

customer /kʌstəmə/, **customers**. 1 A **customer** is someone who buys something, especially from a shop. EG *There were two customers in the shop... She's one of our regular customers.* — N COUNT; = client

2 An awkward **customer**, a cool **customer**, etc is someone who you think behaves in a awkward way, a cool way, etc; an informal use. EG *He's a queer customer–I can't make him out at all... You're a cool customer.* — N COUNT : ADJ+N; ⇑ person; = character

customize /kʌstəmaɪs/, **customizes, customizing, customized**; also spelled **customise**. If you **customize** something, especially a car, you change its appearance in order to make it look special or unusual. EG *They were customizing some twelve vehicles a month... ...a Rolls Royce that he'd bought and then had customized.* — V+O; ⇑ alter

custom-made. Something that is **custom-made** is made according to your special requirements. EG *He wears custom-made shirts... ...custom-made cars.* — ADJ CLASSIF

Customs and Excise is a British government department which is responsible for collecting duty on imported goods and for collecting taxes on some goods produced in Britain. EG *The Customs and Excise must be notified... ...a retired Customs and Excise officer.* — N PROPER

cut /kʌt/, **cuts, cutting**. The form **cut** is used in the present tense and is the past tense and past participle of the verb. 1 If you **cut** something, **1.1** you push a knife or similar tool completely through it in order to remove a piece of it. EG *She cut the cake and gave me a piece... ...a few job adverts cut from the Times.* ▸ used as an adjective. EG *Make the sandwiches from fresh, thinly cut rye bread.* ● to **cut no ice**: see **ice**. — V+O; ▸ ADJ CLASSIF : ATTRIB

1.2 you push a knife or similar tool into it in order to mark it, damage it, or remove something from it. EG *His wife killed herself by cutting her* — V+O, OR V+A (into); = slit *wrists.* ▸ used as a noun. EG *He made a deep cut in the woodwork.* ▸ N COUNT = gash

2 If you **cut** yourself or **cut** a part of your body, you accidentally injure yourself on a sharp object so that your skin is broken and you bleed. EG *I've often had accidents and cut myself... Robert cut his knee quite badly.* ▸ used as an adjective. EG *His hand was badly cut... Blood was flowing from his cut forehead.* ▸ used as a noun. EG *I had some cuts and bruises but I'm OK... Stryker dabbed the cut on his cheek.* V+O (NG/REFL) ▸ ADJ CLASSIF ▸ N COUNT ⇑ wound = gash

3 To **cut** through something such as water means to move or pass through it as if you were cutting it with a knife. EG *The big canoe was cutting through the water... We were making our way down a path that cut through the pine forest.* V+A *(through)*, OR V+O = carve

4 If you **cut** across or **cut** through a place, you go through it because it is the shortest route to another place. EG *I wanted to cut across country for the next hundred miles.* ● See also **short-cut**. V+A *(across/through)*

5 If you **cut** the amount of money or time that you spend on something, you reduce it. EG *We intend to cut arms spending... She reckoned she cut her costs by half... His lunchtime had been cut by eleven minutes.* ▸ used as a noun. EG *...a campaign against the tax cuts... ...a cut in government spending.* ● to **cut your losses**: see **loss**. ● See also **power cut**. V+O = slash ▸ N COUNT : USU PL, IF+PREP THEN *in/of* ⇑ reduction

6 If you **cut** part of something that someone has written, you do not print or broadcast it, for example because it might offend other people. EG *Her publishers insisted on cutting several stories out of her memoirs.* ▸ used as a noun. EG *Make a few minor changes and cuts in the play.* V+O : USU+A *(from/out/out of)* ⇑ remove = edit out ▸ N COUNT : USU PL

7 If you **cut** something that you do regularly, you stop doing it. EG *For a while he cut his meetings and going out.* V+O = drop

8 If you **cut** someone's hair, you remove parts of it with scissors, especially in order to make it look tidy. EG *Tell him to get his hair cut.* ▸ used as a noun. EG *He is having a cut and blow-dry.* ● See also **crew cut**. V+O ⇑ shorten ▸ N COUNT = haircut

9 When you **cut** your fingernails or toenails, you shorten them using scissors. EG *They cut their fingernails twice a week.* V+O = trim

10 To **cut** a lawn, hedge, etc means to remove the ends of the grass stalks, branches, etc in order to create a tidy effect. EG *We need a lawn mower to cut the grass... I'm hot and tired from cutting brambles.* V+O = trim

11 To **cut** a garment means to cause it to have a particular shape by cutting the material. ▸ used as an adjective. EG *...superbly cut clothes... That coat is not cut right at all, the shoulders shouldn't be like that.* V+O : USU+A ▸ ADJ CLASSIF ⇑ designed

12 To **cut** a jewel means to cut flat surfaces on it in order to reveal its beauty or make it the right shape for jewellery. ▸ used as an adjective. EG *The Star of India is 530 carats and the biggest cut diamond ever.* V+O ▸ ADJ CLASSIF : ATTRIB

13 When the director of a film says **cut**, he wants the actors and the camera crew to stop filming. EG *Cut! That scene was perfect.* CONVENTION

14 When a singer or musician **cuts** a record, they cause the record to be made by having one of their performances recorded on it; a technical word. EG *Fifty years after his first record, he cut a final album... He had an even more compelling recording, cut in his earliest years.* V+O ⇑ make

15 When a baby or young child **cuts** a tooth, a new tooth starts to grow out through the gum. EG *The twins cut their first tooth the same day.* V+O = get

16 To **cut** something also means to be in the middle of it, dividing it into two parts. EG *A metal gate cut the path in half.* V+O+A ⇑ divide = bisect

17 If you **cut** a pack of playing cards, you divide it into two. EG *First the pack is shuffled and cut.* V+O

18 In informal English, someone's **cut** is their share of an amount of money that has been obtained, usually in a dishonest way. EG *They had each been promised a cut of the total.* N SING WITH DET ⇑ proportion

19 A **cut** is also a large piece of meat which is ready for cooking. EG *The cuts are already trimmed to slice into steaks.* N COUNT = joint

20 If you **cut** someone who you know or **cut** them **dead**, you ignore them, for example when you pass them in the street. EG *She will go into a sulk and cut you for days.* V+O, OR PHR : VB INFLECTS = snub

21 If you **cut** someone **short**, you stop them saying something by interrupting them. EG *Lally cut her short. 'Don't give the story away,' she said.* PHR : VB INFLECTS = interrupt

22 In informal English, to **cut and run** means to leave a situation very quickly when it starts to get difficult; used showing disapproval. EG *I might have known he'd cut and run.* PHR : VBS INFLECT = run off

23 Something or someone that is **a cut above** other things or people of the same kind is better than the other things or people. EG *I think she's a cut above the others.* PHR : USED AS C ⇑ superior

24 If you say that something **cuts both ways**, you mean that it has two different effects which tend to cancel each other out. EG *That cuts both ways, you know.* PHR : VB INFLECTS

25 You say **to cut a long story short** in order to tell someone that you originally are going to give a short summary of what you originally intended to say, because you have realized that it will take too long to say it all. EG *Well, to cut a long story short, they went.* PHR : USED AS ADV SEN ⇑ briefly

26 If you say that someone **cuts** a strange **figure**, **cuts** an impressive **figure**, etc, you mean that they appear strange, impressive, etc. EG *...an old stockbroker who cuts a considerable figure in the City... The State does not cut a very convincing figure as Santa Claus.* ● See also **cutting**. PHR : VB INFLECTS

cut across. If an issue or problem **cuts across** something that separates two groups of people and makes them hostile to each other, it is so important to both groups that it makes the thing that separates them seem unimportant. EG *Issues, however, tended to cut across party lines... ...the development of institutional arrangements cutting across ethnic barriers.* PHRASAL VB : V+PREP, HAS PASS = transcend, cross

cut back. If you **cut back** something such as expenditure or **cut back on** it, you reduce it. EG *Congress cut back the funds... The factory has cut back its work force by 50%... Other countries have cut back on high-priced Mexican oil.* ● See also **cutback**. PHRASAL VB : V+O+ADV, V+ADV+PREP, OR V+ADV

cut down. **1** If you **cut down** an activity or **cut down on** it, you do it less often. EG *Save time for yourself by cutting your shopping down to twice a week... She had cut down on smoking.* PHRASAL VB : V+O+ADV, OR V+ADV+PREP ⇑ reduce

2 If you **cut down** a tree, you cut through its trunk so that it falls to the ground. EG *A quarter of forestry reserves had been cut down by 1974... How much is it going to cost us to cut all these trees down?* PHRASAL VB : V+O+ADV ⇑ remove = fell

3 If you **cut** someone **down to size**, you do something that shows them that they are less clever or less important than they think they are. EG *That should cut her down to size.* PHR : VB INFLECTS ⇑ humble

cut in. If you **cut in**, you interrupt someone when they are speaking. EG *'You have to employ a professional,' cut in the Englishman quietly... Mrs Travers began a reply, but Mrs Patel cut in again... Mr Peel cut in on their speculations in a tone of hurt surprise.* PHRASAL VB : V+ADV, OR V+ADV+QUOTE

cut off. **1** To **cut** someone or something **off** means to separate or isolate them from things that they are normally connected to. EG *The battalions found themselves pinned down and cut off... The town was cut off... We have cut ourselves off from the old ways of thinking.* ▸ used as an adjective. EG *Many mothers feel cut off during the day... Mary feels cut off from the central life of the village.* PHRASAL VB : V+O (NG/REFL)+ADV, IF+PREP THEN *from* ▸ ADJ CLASSIF : PRED, IF+PREP THEN *from* = isolated

2 To **cut** something **off** means to stop providing it to someone. EG *People have been suggesting that we should cut off economic aid... Gas supplies had now been cut off... Do you know why they cut off her money?* PHRASAL VB : V+O+ADV = discontinue

3 If you **cut off** someone's hair, you remove most of it by cutting it, especially when they have grown it long. EG *One day she had it all cut off, like a boy's, to save trouble.* PHRASAL VB : V+O+ADV = lop off

4 If you **cut** someone **off** or **cut off** what they are saying, you stop them saying it. EG *I waved my hand to cut him off... 'Jenny, I'm sorry.'–'Stop.' She cut off my apology.* PHRASAL VB : V+O+ADV

5 To **cut** someone **off** also means to disconnect them when they are having a telephone conversation. EG *Don't complain when they cut you off by mistake.* PHRASAL VB : V+O+ADV

6 to **cut off your nose to spite your face**: see **nose**. ● See also **cut-off**.

cut out. **1** If you **cut out** part of something, you remove it by using a tool with a sharp edge. EG *Badly decayed timber should be cut out and replaced... There were pictures of animals cut out of magazines and tacked to the wall.* ● See also **cut-out**. PHRASAL VB : V+O+ADV ⇑ excise

2 If you **cut out** part of something that someone has written, you do not print or broadcast it, for example PHRASAL VB : ORDER V+ADV+

because it might offend other people. EG *He cut out all the references to the baron being a fool.* ○ ⇑ remove = omit

3 If you **cut out** something that you are doing or saying, you stop doing or saying it. EG *He ought to cut out the drinking... 'Look,' he said, 'let's cut out all this encounter-group rubbish.'... Cut it out!* PHRASAL VB: V+O+ADV

4 If you **cut** someone **out** of an activity, job, etc, you do not allow them to do it. EG *He'll cut you out of the operation completely... I don't think I should be cut out of the trip.* PHRASAL VB: V+O+ADV, IF+PREP THEN *of* = exclude

5 If you **cut** someone **out of** your **will**, you change your will so that they no longer receive any of your money or possessions. EG *He was not cutting his brothers and sisters out of his will.* PHR: VB INFLECTS ⇑ disinherit

6 If an object **cuts out** the light or the view, it is between you and the light or the view, so that you are in the dark or cannot see the view. EG *Great trees soar above to cut out most of the light.* PHRASAL VB: V+O+ADV = keep out

7 If an engine **cuts out**, it suddenly stops working. EG *The engine's cut out again.* ● See also **cut-out**. PHRASAL VB: V+ADV

8 If you are **cut out** for something or are **cut out** to do it, you have the qualities that will make you able to do it. EG *I'm not really cut out for this kind of work.* PHR+*for/to*-INF: USED AS C = suitable

9 to **have your work cut out**: see **work**.

cut up. 1 If you **cut** something **up**, you cut it into several pieces. EG *You start the lesson by cutting up a worm... He has to have his food cut up for him.* PHRASAL VB: V+O+ADV = dissect

2 If you are **cut up** about something that has happened, you are very unhappy because of it. EG *She's still terribly cut up about her sister's death.* PHR: USED AS C, IF+PREP THEN *about* = upset

cut-and-dried. A **cut-and-dried** answer, solution, etc is clear and obvious, without any possibility of doubt or need for further questions. EG *There is no cut-and-dried formula which can answer these questions.* ADJ QUALIT = clear-cut

cutback /kʌtbæk/, **cutbacks.** A **cutback** is a reduction in something, especially in the number of people that a firm or organization employs. EG *In the defence industries sudden cutbacks and layoffs are common... ...the cutback in public services.* N COUNT: USU+SUPP, IF+PREP THEN *in*

cute /kjuːt/, **cuter, cutest**; used especially in American English. 1 Someone or something that is **cute** is very pretty; used showing approval. EG *What a cute little girl... Wouldn't it look cute on her?.. He lives in the cutest little house you ever saw.* ADJ QUALIT = sweet

2 If you describe someone as **cute**, you mean that you find them attractive, often in a sexual way. EG *She laughed and said, 'You're cute. What's your name?'... He reckoned she was 'a cute dish' and old enough for a bit of fun.* ADJ QUALIT ⇑ appealing = sweet

3 Someone who is **cute** acts wisely in business or in their dealings with other people; used showing approval. EG *He's cute enough to know that you can't take on the military and win.* ADJ QUALIT ⇑ clever = shrewd

4 You describe something as **cute** when it is intended to be attractive, but you think it is sentimental or tasteless. EG *The wallpaper was decorated with flowers and cute domestic animals.* ADJ QUALIT = sweet, coy

cut glass; often used before another noun, spelled with a hyphen. 1 **Cut glass** is glass that has patterns cut into its surface. EG *Wash delicate china or cut glass by hand.* ▸ used as an adjective. EG *Diana had a cut-glass bowl full of marble eggs.* N UNCOUNT ▸ ADJ CLASSIF: USU ATTRIB

2 A **cut-glass** accent is an upper-class English accent; an informal use. EG *They laughed uproariously at me when they heard my cut-glass vowels.* ADJ CLASSIF: ATTRIB = impeccable

cutlass /kʌtləs/, **cutlasses.** A **cutlass** is a curved sword with one sharp edge that used to be used by sailors. EG *The leader already had his cutlass in his hand.* N COUNT

cutlery /kʌtləri[1]/ refers to the knives, forks, and spoons that you eat your food with. EG *They provide crockery, cutlery and bed linen.* N UNCOUNT = knives and forks

cutlet /kʌtlə[2]t/, **cutlets.** A **cutlet** is 1 a small piece of meat, which is like a chop and which is usually fried or grilled. EG *I'm sure somebody would like another cutlet... ...veal cutlets.* 2 vegetables, nuts, shellfish, etc fried or grilled together in a small lump like a meat cutlet. EG *...a nut cutlet... ...prawn cutlets.* N COUNT: USU+SUPP; N COUNT+SUPP

cut-off, cut-offs. A **cut-off** or a **cut-off point** is the level or limit at which you decide that something should stop happening. EG *Forty-five is our cut-off, and we'll only go that high if we really have to... We thought it was already past the cut-off point.* N COUNT

cut-out, cut-outs. A **cut-out** is 1 an automatic device that turns off a motor or engine, for example because there is something wrong with it. EG *Poole brought his fist down on the alarm cut-out... ...a cut-out to prevent the battery from overcharging.* 2 a shape that has been cut from card or cardboard. EG *...a cut-out of a girl... ...two cardboard cut-outs.* N COUNT: USU+SUPP; N COUNT+SUPP

cut-price is used to describe something that is for sale at a reduced price. EG *Ignore the jar of cut-price stuff on the top... We enjoy going shopping and taking advantage of cut-price offers.* ADJ CLASSIF

cutter /kʌtə/, **cutters.** 1 **Cutters** are a tool that you use for cutting through something thin, especially wire. EG *He took a pair of wire cutters from his pocket... I cut the peg with bolt cutters.* N PLURAL ⇑ scissors

2 A **cutter** is 2.1 a tool for cutting things. EG *He snipped off the end of his cigar with a silver cutter... ...a glass cutter.* 2.2 a person whose job involves cutting things, for example cloth for clothing. EG *She tried bribing a cutter for patterns of a rival's new spring models.* 2.3 a boat. There are different types of cutter. EG *They quickly boarded the cutter... ...an Italian customs cutter.* N COUNT; N COUNT ⇑ worker; N COUNT

cut-throat describes behaviour in which people want the same thing and do not care if they harm each other in getting it. EG *It's a cut-throat business with a lot of money involved... ...cut-throat competition.* ADJ QUALIT: USU ATTRIB = ruthless

cutting /kʌtɪŋ/, **cuttings.** 1 A **cutting** is 1.1 a piece of writing which has been cut from a newspaper or magazine. EG *Lynn would look through the piles of cuttings and newsletters... ...press cuttings.* 1.2 a part of a plant, for example a leaf or part of a stem, that you cut from the plant and use in order to grow a new plant. EG *If he couldn't get cuttings of rare shrubs honestly, he was not above stealing them... They are easy roses to grow from cuttings.* 1.3 a narrow valley cut through a hill so that a railway line can pass through. EG *...a railway cutting.* N COUNT: USU PL = clipping; N COUNT: USU PL ⇑ clipping; N COUNT ⇑ thoroughfare

2 A **cutting** remark is an unkind remark that is likely to hurt someone's feelings. EG *I thought of the cutting remarks I'd been about to make... Does this sound cutting? It's not meant to be.* ADJ QUALIT = sarcastic, biting ≠ flattering

cuttlefish /kʌtə[0]lfɪʃ/, **cuttlefishes. Cuttlefish** can also be used as the plural form. A **cuttlefish** is an animal with a hard internal shell that lives close to the bottom of the sea near a coast. EG *The cod's staple diet includes Norway lobster, squid and cuttlefish.* ▸ also used to refer to the shell. EG *...a cuttlefish stuck between the bars of the bird cage.* N COUNT ⇑ mollusc ▸ N COUNT/UNCOUNT

CV, CV's. CV is an abbreviation for 'curriculum vitae.'

cwt. The plural form can be **cwt** or **cwts. Cwt** is an abbreviation for 'hundredweight'. EG *...75 cwt of wheat.* N COUNT: NUM+N

-cy, -cies. -cy is added 1 at the end of some adjectives, nouns, and verbs in place of -te, -t, and -tic in order to form nouns. EG *...intimate→intimacy... ...secret→secrecy.* 2 at the end of some nouns referring to people with a particular rank or post in order to form other nouns that refer to this rank or post. EG *...viscount→viscountcy... ...captain→captaincy... ...chaplain→chaplaincy.* SUFFIX: FORMS NOUNS; SUFFIX: FORMS NOUNS

cyanide /saɪənaɪd/ is a highly poisonous substance. EG *...a ball of cotton wool soaked in cyanide.* N UNCOUNT ⇑ poison

cybernetics /saɪbənetɪks/ is a science in which control systems in electronic and mechanical devices are studied and compared to biological systems. EG *...the world of cybernetics... ...the Cybernetics Department.* N UNCOUNT

cyclamen /sɪkləmə[2]n/, **cyclamens.** A **cyclamen** is a plant with white, pink, or red flowers. N COUNT/UNCOUNT

cycle /saɪkə[0]l/, **cycles, cycling, cycled.** 1 If you **cycle**, you ride a bicycle. EG *I decided to cycle into town instead of taking the bus... You must be tired after cycling all that distance.* ◇ **cycling.** EG *We recommend cycling as a good form of exercise.* V: USU+A ⇑ travel ◇ N UNCOUNT ⇑ activity

2 A **cycle** is 2.1 a bicycle. EG *A standard tool kit comes with the cycle and is stored under the seat... ...a cycle shop.* 2.2 a motorcycle; used in American English. EG *A car engine is more complex and inaccessible than a cycle engine.* N COUNT = bike; N COUNT ⇑ vehicle = motorbike

3 A **cycle** is also 3.1 a series of events or processes that is repeated again and again, always in the same order. EG *...the endless cycle of the seasons... ...the economic cycle of prosperity and recession... ...the inflationary cycle.* 3.2 a single complete movement in an electrical, electronic, or mechanical process that consists of a continuous repetition of these movements. EG *...50 cycles per second.* 3.3 a series of N COUNT+SUPP = sequence, repetition; N COUNT: USU PL; N COUNT+SUPP

plays, songs, poems, etc written by the same person and intended to be performed or read one after the other. EG *...the controversial Ring cycle at Bayreuth.*

cyclic /saɪklɪk, sɪklɪk/ means the same as cyclical. EG *...a cyclic process... ...cyclic variation.* ADJ CLASSIF

cyclical /sɪklɪkəˡl/. A **cyclical** process is a process that happens again and again in cycles. EG *...cyclical fluctuations in investment... This sequence may be cyclical.* ADJ CLASSIF = cyclic

cyclist /saɪklɪst/, **cyclists**. A **cyclist** is someone who rides a bicycle. EG *The road was crowded with cyclists.* N COUNT

cyclone /saɪkləʊn/, **cyclones**. A **cyclone** is a violent storm in which air circulates rapidly in a clockwise direction. EG *The island was hit by two successive cyclones in a matter of ten days.* N COUNT

cygnet /sɪgnəˀt/, **cygnets**. A **cygnet** is a young swan. N COUNT

cylinder /sɪlɪndə/, **cylinders**. A **cylinder** is 1 a shape or an object with flat circular ends and long straight sides. EG *...two cylinders of the same diameter.* N COUNT 2 a piece of machinery with this shape, especially one in an engine in which a piston moves backwards and forwards. EG *The cylinder is getting too much gas and not enough air... ...a five cylinder engine.* N COUNT ⇑ part

cylindrical /sɪlɪndrɪkəˡl/. Something that is **cylindrical** is shaped like a cylinder. EG *...a cylindrical pipe.* ADJ CLASSIF = tubular

cymbal /sɪmbəˡl/, **cymbals**. A **cymbal** is a thin circular brass object that is used as a musical instrument. You hit it with a stick or hit two cymbals together, making a loud noise. EG *...the clashing of the cymbals.* N COUNT : USU PL

cynic /sɪnɪk/, **cynics**. A **cynic** is someone who believes that people always behave in a selfish way. EG *Pareto was a cynic, disillusioned by the society of his day... The cynic is so negative in all his attitudes.* N COUNT ⇑ pessimist

cynical /sɪnɪkəˡl/. **Cynical** attitudes and behaviour are the attitudes and behaviour of someone who believes that people act selfishly and who always expects people to act like this. EG *You are taking a rather cynical view of marriage... ...men who become cynical about women... Don't be so grumpy and cynical about it all.* ◊ **cynically**. EG *Grant smiled cynically.* ADJ QUALIT ⇑ contemptuous ≠ idealistic, naive ◊ ADV

cynicism /sɪnɪsɪzəˡm/ is an attitude towards people in which you always expect them to act in a selfish way. EG *I was hoping for evidence of interest, but found only cynicism... The mood of political cynicism and despair deepened.* N UNCOUNT ⇑ doubt, bitterness

cypher /saɪfə/, **cyphers**. See **cipher**.

cyphered /saɪfəd/. See **ciphered**.

cypress /saɪprəs/, **cypresses**. **Cypress** can also be used as the plural form. A **cypress** is an evergreen tree. EG *The shadow of the cypress swayed across the lawn... ...green meadows flanked with towering cypresses.* ▸ used to refer to wood taken from this tree. EG *...a giant cypress raft.* N COUNT ⇑ conifer ▸ N UNCOUNT ⇑ wood

Cypriot /sɪprɪət/, **Cypriots**. 1 A **Cypriot** is someone who comes from Cyprus. EG *The Cypriots are ready to fight.* N COUNT

2 Something that is **Cypriot** belongs or relates to Cyprus or to its people. ADJ CLASSIF

cyst /sɪst/, **cysts**. A **cyst** is a growth containing liquid that appears inside your body or under your skin. EG *I was told I had a small cyst.* N COUNT

cystitis /sɪstaɪtɪs/ is an infection of your bladder; a technical term in medicine. N UNCOUNT

czar /zɑː/. See **tsar**.

czarina /zɑːriːnə/. See **tsarina**.

czarist /zɑːrɪst/. See **tsarist**.

Czech /tʃɛk/, **Czechs**. 1 A **Czech** is a person who comes from Czechoslovakia. EG *There were several expatriate communities of Poles and Czechs.* N COUNT

2 **Czech** is one of the two main languages spoken in Czechoslovakia. EG *Czech and Slovak are very closely related.* N UNCOUNT

3 **Czech** means the same as Czechoslovak. EG *It's an old Czech custom.* ADJ CLASSIF

Czechoslovak /tʃɛkəˢsləʊvæk/. Something that is **Czechoslovak** belongs or relates to Czechoslovakia or to its people. EG *...the Czechoslovak frontier.* ADJ CLASSIF

Czechoslovakian /tʃɛkəˢsləˢvækɪən/ means the same as Czechoslovak. ADJ CLASSIF = Czech

Dd

D, d /diː/, **Ds, d's**. 1 **D** is the fourth letter of the English alphabet. N COUNT

2 **D**, in music, is the second note in the scale of C major. N COUNT/UNCOUNT

3 If you get a **D** as a mark for a piece of work or in an exam, your work is considered to be below average or poor. N COUNT/UNCOUNT = delta

4 **d.** is an abbreviation for 'died' which is written in front of dates, for example on memorials or in reference books. EG *Henry Smith, d. 1892.*

5 **d.** was a written abbreviation meaning 'penny' or 'pence' in Britain before decimal currency was introduced in 1971. N AFTER NUM

6 **D** or **d** is also an abbreviation for other words beginning with D or d, such as 'daughter', 'delete', or 'dimension'.

7 **D** or **d** is the Roman numeral for 500.

'd is 1 a short form of 'would' that is used in spoken English. It is added to a pronoun or noun which is the subject of a verb. For example, 'she would' can be shortened to 'she'd'. EG *She'd be sure to see it... I knew there'd be trouble.* 2 a short form of 'had' that is used in spoken English, especially when 'had' is an auxiliary verb. It is added to a pronoun or noun which is the subject of a verb. For example, 'he had gone' can be shortened to 'he'd gone'. EG *She'd got restless... I'd heard it many times.*

d' is a short form of 'do' in spoken English, used especially before 'you' in questions. EG *D'you know him?*

D.A., D.A.s. A **D.A.** is a lawyer in the U.S. who works for the state and prosecutes people on behalf of it; an abbreviation for 'District Attorney'. EG *If you want to understand the meaning of this law, go to the D.A.* N COUNT

dab /dæb/, **dabs, dabbing, dabbed**. 1 If you **dab** a substance from a surface, you remove it with quick, light strokes. If you **dab** a substance onto a surface or if you **dab** a surface with a substance, you put the substance onto the surface with quick, light, strokes. EG *He gently dabbed the sweat from Joe's upper lip... She dabbed some powder on her nose... She dabbed the wound with TCP.* V+O+A ⇑ apply

2 A **dab** of something is a small amount that is put onto a surface. EG *She returned wearing a dab of rouge on each cheekbone.* N PART = touch

3 A **dab** is also a small flat fish with rough scales. N COUNT

4 Someone's **dabs** are their fingerprints; used in very informal British English. N PLURAL : USU POSS+N

5 If you are a **dab hand** at something, you are very good at doing it; used in informal British English. EG *She is a dab hand at finding excuses for their mistakes.* PHR : USED AS C, N INFLECTS, +*at*

dab at. If you **dab at** something, you touch it several times using quick, light movements, as if you are trying to clean it. EG *She dabbed at her mouth with the lace handkerchief.* PHRASAL VB : V+PREP

dabble /dæbəˡl/, **dabbles, dabbling, dabbled**. 1 If you **dabble** in an activity or subject, you are slightly interested or involved in it in a way that is not very serious and that does not take up a lot of time. EG *They dabble in right-wing politics... ...a wealthy dilettante dabbling in science.* V+A *(in)*

2 If you **dabble** your fingers or toes in water or another liquid, you put them into it and move them about. EG *The children sat dabbling their toes in the pool.* V+O+A = paddle

dabbler /dæblə/, **dabblers**. A **dabbler** is someone who is slightly interested or involved in an activity N COUNT ⇑ amateur or subject in a way that is not very serious and that does not take up a lot of time; often used showing disapproval. EG ...*this farmer and intellectual dabbler.*

dace /deɪs/. **Dace** is both the singular and the plural form. A **dace** is a freshwater fish. N COUNT

dachshund /dækshʊnd/, **dachshunds**. A **dachshund** is a small dog that has very short legs, a long body, and long ears. N COUNT

Dacron /deɪkrɒⁿn, dæk-/ is a trademark. It is a synthetic polyester fibre or fabric. N UNCOUNT

dad /dæd/, **dads**. People often call their father **dad** in informal English. EG *Hey, Dad, what's for dinner?... My dad doesn't like going there.* N PROPER/VOC : ALSO N COUNT

daddy /dædi¹/, **daddies**. Children often call their father **daddy** in informal English. EG *I could swim when I was five. Daddy taught me.* N PROPER/VOC : ALSO N COUNT = dad, pa

daddy-longlegs. **Daddy-longlegs** is both the singular and the plural form. A **daddy-longlegs** is a harmless flying insect with very long legs. N COUNT = cranefly

dado /deɪdəʊ/, **dados**. A **dado** in a room is the lower part of a wall, below a rail fixed to the wall, especially when this part is decorated in a different way from the upper part. N COUNT

daemon /diːmə⁰n/, **daemons**. See **demon**. N COUNT

daffodil /dæfədɪl/, **daffodils**. A **daffodil** is a yellow trumpet-shaped flower that has a long stem and that blooms in the spring. N COUNT

daft /dɑːft/, **dafter, daftest**. **Daft** is an informal word used in British English. **1** If you say that someone is **daft**, you mean that they are stupid or not sensible. EG *Don't be daft... I wouldn't be that daft.* ADJ QUALIT : USU PRED ⇑ foolish = silly, barmy

2 A **daft** action or way of behaving is one that seems silly or stupid, often in a way that makes other people laugh. EG *The manager got them to do daft things at the first show.* ADJ QUALIT ⇑ foolish = crazy, mad

3 If you say that someone is **daft** about a particular thing or person, you mean that the thing or person mentioned is very important to them. EG *I was daft about him, you know... He's daft about football.* ADJ QUALIT : PRED+*about* = crazy about

dagger /dægə/, **daggers**. A **dagger** is a weapon like a knife which is sharp on both edges and has a pointed end. ● If two people are **at daggers drawn**, they are having an argument and are very angry with each other. EG *We are still at daggers drawn with the Foreign Ministry over this.* ● If you **look daggers** at someone, you look very angrily at them. N COUNT ● PHR : USED AS AN A ⇑ hostile = fighting ● PHR : VB INFLECTS

dago /deɪgəʊ/, **dagos**. **Dago** is a very offensive word for a person from Spain, Portugal, Italy, or South America. N COUNT ⇑ foreigner

dahlia /deɪlɪ⁰jə/, **dahlias**. A **dahlia** is a garden flower with a lot of brightly coloured petals. N COUNT

daily /deɪli¹/, **dailies**. **1** Something that happens or is done **daily** happens or is done every day. EG *Clean the tray daily... He wrote to her almost daily... Harold was in almost daily consultation with other world leaders... Fights are a daily hazard.* ADV WITH VB, OR ADJ CLASSIF : ATTRIB

2 Daily also means relating to a single day or to one day at a time. EG *Daily wage rates were around two dollars... We went about our daily lives as if nothing had happened.* ADJ CLASSIF : ATTRIB

3 A **daily** newspaper or a **daily** is a newspaper that is published every day of the week except Sunday. EG *When you get your daily paper which bit do you read first? No mention of the scandal was printed in any of Friday's dailies.* ADJ CLASSIF : ATTRIB, OR N COUNT

4 A **daily** is also a woman who is employed to come to a house to clean it; used in informal British English. EG *Our daily comes in on Mondays and Fridays.* N COUNT ⇑ cleaner = charlady

dainty /deɪnti¹/, **daintier, daintiest**. A **dainty** movement, person, or object is small, neat, or pretty; often used to describe women and their movements. EG ...*walking with neat, dainty steps... ...those two dainty, well-dressed women.* ◊ **daintily**. EG *Miss Jackson raised a plump arm, fingers daintily extended.* ADJ QUALIT ⇑ delicate = refined, petite ≠ clumsy ◊ ADV WITH VB

daiquiri /daɪkɪri¹, dæk-/, **daiquiris**. A **daiquiri** is a drink made with rum, lime juice, sugar, and ice. N COUNT ⇑ cocktail

dairy /dɛəri¹/, **dairies**. **1** A **dairy** is **1.1** a shop or company that sells milk and food made from milk, such as butter and cheese. EG *He ran his father's dairy in Amesville.* **1.2** a room or building on a farm where milk is kept or where cream, butter, and cheese are made. N COUNT; N COUNT

2 Dairy is used to refer to **2.1** foods, such as butter, cream, and cheese, that are made from milk. EG *We now produce surpluses of meat, dairy products, and wine.* **2.2** the use of cattle to produce milk rather than meat. EG *The dairy industry dominates the beef market... He owns a dairy herd of 105 cattle.* N BEFORE N ⇑ food; N BEFORE N

dairymaid /dɛərɪ¹meɪd/, **dairymaids**. A **dairymaid** was a girl or woman who milked cows and did other work on a farm; an old-fashioned word. N COUNT

dairyman /dɛərɪ¹mə³n/, **dairymen**. A **dairyman** is a man who looks after cows and does other work on a farm. N COUNT

dais /deɪɪs/. A **dais** is a platform in a hall or meeting room that is higher than the floor of the room and is often used by someone who is talking to all the other people in the room. N SING WITH DET = rostrum

daisy /deɪzi¹/, **daisies**. A **daisy** is a small wild flower, often found in short grass, that has a yellow centre and white petals. There are also some larger kinds of daisies grown as garden flowers. ● If you say that someone **is pushing up daisies**, you mean that they are dead and have been buried; an informal humorous expression. ● **fresh as a daisy**: see **fresh**. N COUNT ● PHR : AUX INFLECTS

daisy chain, daisy chains; also spelled with a hyphen. A **daisy chain** is a string of daisies that have been joined together by their stems to make a necklace; used in British English. N COUNT ⇑ garland

daisywheel /deɪzɪwiːl/, **daisywheels**. A **daisywheel** is a small flat disc which has letters on thin stalks around its edge and which is the part of an electric typewriter or word processor that prints the letters. It is also a printer or typewriter which has this kind of printing device. N COUNT

dale /deɪl/, **dales**. **1** A **dale** is a valley; an old-fashioned word, now used mainly in place-names in Northern England. EG ...*the Yorkshire Dales.* N COUNT : ALSO IN NAMES AFTER N

2 If you say that you went **up hill and down dale**, you mean that you went somewhere by a long, slow, or winding route. PHR : USED AS AN A

dalliance /dælɪəns/ is the behaviour shown by two people who are flirting with each other; an old-fashioned word. N UNCOUNT ⇑ flirtation

dally /dæli¹/, **dallies, dallying, dallied**. **1** If you **dally**, you act or move very slowly, wasting time; an old-fashioned use. EG *The children dallied in the lane.* V ⇑ delay = dawdle

2 If you **dally** with an idea or plan, you think about it but not in a serious way. EG *I'm dallying with the idea of giving up my job.* V+A *(with)* ⇑ consider = toy with

3 If someone **dallies** with you, they flirt with you; an old-fashioned use. V+A *(with)*

Dalmatian /dælmeɪʃə⁰n/, **Dalmatians**. A **Dalmatian** is a large dog with short, smooth, white hair and black or brown spots. N COUNT

dam /dæm/, **dams, damming, dammed**. **1** A **dam** is a wall that is built across a river or stream in order to stop the flow of the water and make a lake behind it. EG *It can take three years to build a dam... They drove up to Boulder Dam in the moonlight.* ▸ used to refer to the lake that is formed in this way. EG *He had drowned in the dam while bathing.* N COUNT : ALSO IN NAMES AFTER N ⇑ barrier ▸ N COUNT

2 To **dam** a river or stream means to build a dam across it. EG ...*men who picked cotton and dammed rivers and built railroads.* V+O ⇑ block

3 A **dam** is also the mother of an animal such as a horse, goat, or sheep; a technical term in breeding livestock. N COUNT

dam up. **1** To **dam up** a river means to cause it to become blocked. EG *The rubbish had dammed up the creek so that it had overflowed.* PHRASAL VB : V+O+ADV ⇑ block

2 If you **dam up** your feelings, you keep strong control of yourself and do not allow your feelings to show. PHRASAL VB : V+O+ADV ⇑ suppress = bottle up

damage /dæmɪdʒ/, **damages, damaging, damaged**. **1** To **damage** something means **1.1** to harm or spoil it physically, so that it does not work properly or does not look as good as it did before. EG *A fire had severely damaged part of the school... Repairs were made on mud huts that had been damaged by the big rains.* **1.2** to have a harmful effect on it and to make it weaker or less successful, etc. EG *Unofficial strikes were damaging the British economy... Their failures in this area have damaged their self-confidence and credibility...* ◊ **damaging**. EG *The incident was damaging to his career and reputation.* V+O; V+O ⇑ affect = harm ≠ improve ◊ ADJ QUALIT : IF+PREP THEN *to/for*

2 Damage is **2.1** physical harm that is caused to something, especially harm that stops it working properly or makes it look less good. EG *The earthquake caused damage estimated at 300 million* N UNCOUNT : IF+ PREP THEN *to* = devastation

pounds... I agreed to help pay for the damage to the floor and the ceiling... A post-mortem showed the damage done to the liver. **2.2** a harmful effect that something has on a particular thing. EG *He could not repair the damage done to the party's standing and credibility... ...psychological damage.* N UNCOUNT : IF + PREP THEN *to* = harm
● If you say **the damage is done**, you mean that it is too late now to prevent the harmful effects of something which has already been done. ● PHR : AUX INFLECTS

3 When a court of law awards **damages** to someone, it orders money to be paid to them by a person who has damaged their reputation or property, or who has injured them. EG *He finally got £4,000 in damages.* N PLURAL ⇑ compensation

4 If you say to someone **What's the damage?** you are asking them how much you have to pay; an informal expression. CONVENTION

damask /dæməsk/ is a type of heavy cloth, usually silk or linen, which is used for tablecloths, curtains, etc. N UNCOUNT

dame /deɪm/, **dames**. **1** A **dame** is a woman; used in informal American English, especially by men. EG *The dame wore a veil.* N COUNT

2 In Britain, **Dame** is a title given to a woman as a special honour because of important service or work that she has done. EG *In tomorrow's programme Dame Flora Robson looks back on fifty years in the theatre.* N COUNT IN TITLES

dammit /dæmɪt/. See **damn**.

damn /dæm/, **damns, damning, damned**. **1 Damn, damn you, damn it,** and **dammit** are swear words which people sometimes use to express anger or annoyance. EXCLAM = blast ▸ used as an adjective. EG *We kept tripping over pieces of wood which some damn fool had carelessly left lying about.* ▸ ADJ CLASSIF : ATTRIB = blasted, bloody

2 Damn is also used, in very informal English, for emphasis. EG *I knew damn well what he was going to say.* ADV + ADJ/ADV = bloody, damned

3 If you say that someone does not **give** or **care a damn** about something, you mean that they do not care at all about it; a very informal expression. PHR : VB INFLECTS, USU WITH BROAD NEG

4 If you say that something is not **worth a damn**, you mean that it is not worth even a small amount; a very informal expression. PHR : USED AS C, USU WITH BROAD NEG

5 As near as damn it means very nearly indeed; a very informal expression. EG *It'll take two weeks, as near as damn it.* PHR : USED AS AN A

6 If someone **is damned** for something bad that has happened, they are blamed for it and considered to be worthless or untrustworthy because of it. EG *The government emerged from the early 1970s damned for total failure to control money growth.* ● See also **damned, damning**. V + O : ONLY PASS, IF + PREP THEN *for* ⇑ blame = condemn

damnable /dæmnəbəᵒl/. Something that is **damnable** is very unpleasant and a great nuisance; a rather old-fashioned word. EG *It's a damnable business... ...this damnable itching.* ADJ QUALIT ⇑ awful = dreadful ◇ **damnably**. EG *The medical fees would still be damnably expensive.* ◇ ADV

damnation /dæmneɪʃəᵒn/. **1** If you say **damnation**, you are expressing anger about something; an old-fashioned swear word. EXCLAM = blast, dammit

2 If someone suffers **damnation**, they are condemned to stay in hell for ever after death because of their sins. EG *...eternal damnation.* N UNCOUNT

damned /dæmd/. **1 Damned** is a swear word that you use **1.1** to let people know that you are angry. EG *He's got a damned cheek to ask me for money when he knows I'm broke.* ADJ CLASSIF : ATTRIB **1.2** to emphasize what you are saying. EG *I don't know what you're talking about, and I'm damned sure you don't either.* ADV + ADJ/ADV

2 If you say that you **are damned if** you are going to do something, you mean that you do not intend to do it and think it is unreasonable for someone to expect you to do it; a very informal expression. PHR : AUX INFLECTS

3 If you say **I'll be damned** or **I'm damned**, you are expressing surprise at something. EG *'Well I'm damned,' he said. 'I never thought you'd do it.'* EXCLAM = blow me

4 People who are **damned** have been condemned to stay in hell for ever after they have died. EG *...the damned souls suffering the torments of hell for all eternity.* ADJ CLASSIF ▸ The **damned** is used to refer to damned people. EG *The painting portrayed the damned burning in hell.* ▸ N PLURAL : *the* + N

damnedest /dæmdɪ²st/. **1** The **damnedest** means the most amazing and surprising in an agreeable way; an old-fashioned, informal word. EG *New York is full of the damnedest eccentrics.* ADJ QUALIT : SUPERL, ATTRIB, *the* + ADJ

2 If you **do** your **damnedest**, you try as hard as you can to do something. EG *I'll have to do my damnedest to find out what really happened.* PHR : VB INFLECTS

damn-fool is a swear word meaning very stupid. EG *Another one of his damn-fool ideas!* ADJ QUALIT : ATTRIB

damning /dæmɪŋ/. Something that is **damning** proves or suggests very strongly that someone is guilty of a particular thing. EG *New and damning evidence has recently been uncovered... The Mail considered his statement damning enough to publish in full.* ADJ QUALIT

damp /dæmp/, **damper, dampest; damps, damping, damped**. **1** Something that is **damp** is slightly wet. EG *The building was cold and draughty and damp... She wiped the table with a damp cloth.* ADJ QUALIT = moist ◇ **dampness**. EG *...the cold and dampness of winter.* ◇ N UNCOUNT ⇑ wetness
● **a damp squib**: see **squib**.

2 Damp is slight wetness; used especially of the slight wetness that occurs in the air after it has been raining or the wetness that occurs on the walls of old houses. EG *Keeping the cold and damp outside is a problem with old houses.* ● See also **rising damp**. N UNCOUNT = dampness

3 If you **damp** something, you make it slightly wet. EG *The material should be damped before ironing.* V + O = dampen

damp down. **1** To **damp down** something means to reduce its liveliness, violence, or urgency. EG *Neighbouring countries had been of little or no help in damping down the crisis.* PHRASAL VB : V + O + ADV ⇑ subdue = dampen

2 If you **damp down** a fire, you make it burn more slowly, especially by reducing the flow of air to it. PHRASAL VB : V + O + ADV

damp course, damp courses; also spelled with a hyphen. A **damp course** is a layer of waterproof material which is put into the bottom of a wall to prevent wetness from rising. N COUNT = damp-proof course

dampen /dæmpəᵒn/, **dampens, dampening, dampened**. **1** To **dampen** something or **dampen** it **down** means to reduce its energy, liveliness, or violence. EG *The prospect of an election in no way dampened Benn's spirits... The 1948 agreement served to dampen controversy... High interest rates further dampened down the economy.* V + O ⇑ subdue

2 If you **dampen** something, you make it slightly wet. EG *I'll have to dampen the shirt before ironing it.* V + O

damper /dæmpə/, **dampers**. **1** If someone or something **puts a damper on** something or **acts as a damper on** something, they have an effect on it which stops it being as enjoyable or as successful as it should be; an informal expression. EG *If the strategy puts even a small damper on terrorism, the effort will have been worthwhile.* PHR : VB INFLECTS ⇑ discourage

2 A **damper** is **2.1** a small sheet of metal in a fire, boiler, furnace, etc that can be moved to increase or reduce the amount of air that enters. N COUNT ⇑ regulator **2.2** a device in a piano or similar musical instrument which makes the sound less loud by restricting the movement of the strings. N COUNT ⇑ mute

damply /dæmpli¹/. If you do something **damply**, you do it in an unenthusiastic way. EG *Marsha smiled damply... The onlookers applauded apathetically, a little damply.* ADV WITH VB

damp-proof course, damp-proof courses. A **damp-proof course** is the same as a damp course. N COUNT

damsel /dæmzəᵒl/, **damsels**. A **damsel** is a young, unmarried woman; an old-fashioned literary word. N COUNT ⇑ girl = maiden

damson /dæmzəᵒn/, **damsons**. A **damson** is a small, sour purple plum; also used of the tree that damsons grow on. EG *...damson jam.* N COUNT

dance /dɑːns/, **dances, dancing, danced**. **1** When you **dance**, you move your body and feet in a way which follows a rhythm, usually in time to music. EG *She had never learned to dance... He was glad that Bob hadn't danced with Margaret.* V

2 A **dance** is **2.1** a series of rhythmic movements of your body and feet, which you usually do in time to music. EG *Before we knew it, we were doing this dance.* N COUNT ⇑ movement **2.2** a piece of music which people can dance to, for example a tango or a waltz. EG *The band played all my favourite dances.* N COUNT **2.3** a social event where people can dance with each other. EG *I hated the big formal dances at college.* N COUNT

3 If you **dance** a particular kind of dance, you do it. EG *She danced an Irish jig... That evening they danced every dance together.* V + O ⇑ perform

4 Dance is **4.1** the art of performing dances as a public entertainment. EG *They are supreme artists of dance and theatre.* N UNCOUNT **4.2** the activity of performing a dance. EG *The teacher wrote the story and inter-* N UNCOUNT ⇑ movement *preted it in dance... I hated my Saturday morning dance classes.*

5 If you **dance** along, you jump and skip as you go along, usually because you are happy or excited. EG *Ralph danced out into the street.* V+A

6 If you say that something **dances**, you mean that it moves about, or seems to move about, lightly and quickly. EG *The colours danced and glistened in the crisp dawn light... The bubbles just danced up and down while I scrubbed the clothes.* V: USU+A ⇑ move = leap, dart

7 If you **dance attendance on** someone, you treat them with a lot of respect and do every little job that they ask you to, especially because they have authority over you. PHR: VB INFLECTS = suck up to

8 If you **lead** someone **a merry** or **a pretty dance,** you make them do things over a long period of time which cause them problems and do not benefit them in any way. PHR: VB INFLECTS

9 to **dance to** someone's **tune**: see **tune**. • to **make a song and dance about** something: see **song and dance**.

dance floor, dance floors; also spelled with a hyphen. A **dance floor** is a part of the floor in a restaurant or night club where guests can dance. N COUNT

dance hall, dance halls; also spelled with a hyphen. A **dance hall** is a large room or building where people pay to go and dance, usually in the evening. N COUNT = ballroom

dancer /dɑːnsə/, **dancers**. A **dancer** is 1 a person who earns money by dancing. EG *He always wanted to be a Broadway dancer.* 2 a person who dances. EG *The musicians began packing their instruments as the last dancers drifted off the floor... He is not a very good dancer.* N COUNT ⇑ performer; N COUNT

dance studio, dance studios. A **dance studio** is a place where people pay to learn how to dance. N COUNT

dancing /dænsɪŋ/. 1 **Dancing** is the performance of dances as a profession, an art, or an activity. EG *The music and dancing lasted for hours... ...a dancing teacher.* N UNCOUNT

2 If someone has **dancing** eyes, their eyes are bright and lively, and they look as if they are just about to laugh. EG *There was one very lively woman with dancing black eyes.* ADJ CLASSIF: ATTRIB = twinkling

dandelion /dændəˈlaɪən/, **dandelions**. A **dandelion** is a wild plant or weed which has yellow flowers with lots of thin petals. After the flowers, it has seeds arranged in a fluffy ball at the top of the stem. N COUNT

dandified /dændɪfaɪd/. A man who is **dandified** thinks a lot about his appearance and always dresses in very smart clothes; an old-fashioned word. ADJ QUALIT ⇑ vain = foppish

dandruff /dændrəᵒf/ is small white pieces of dead skin that can be seen in someone's hair or that fall from their hair. EG *Miss Maltravers has dandruff.* N UNCOUNT

dandy /dændiˈ/, **dandies; dandier, dandiest**. 1 A **dandy** is a man who thinks a great deal about his appearance and always dresses in smart clothes; an old-fashioned word which is used showing disapproval. EG *...a yacht full of upper-class dandies drinking sherry.* N COUNT

2 Something that is **dandy** is very good; an informal American use. EG *The chocolate-coated cherries are dandy, Mrs Breslow.* ADJ QUALIT = great

Dane /deɪn/, **Danes**. A **Dane** is a person who comes from Denmark. N COUNT

danger /deɪndʒə/, **dangers**. 1 **Danger** is the possibility that someone may be harmed or killed. EG *The child is too young to understand danger... There was widespread danger of disease... My friends were round me. I was in no danger... Danger! Keep away!* N UNCOUNT ≠ safety

2 A **danger** is something or someone that can hurt or harm you. EG *Cigarette smoking is a danger to health... They warned us of the dangers of making assumptions.* N COUNT = hazard

3 If someone is **on the danger list**, they are extremely ill, usually in hospital, and may die. PHR: USED AS AN A

4 If someone is **out of danger**, they are still ill but are not expected to die. PHR: USED AS AN A

5 If there is a **danger** that something unpleasant will happen, it is possible that that thing will happen. EG *There was a danger that she might marry the wrong man... There is a danger of war and holocaust.* N UNCOUNT+SUPP ⇑ possibility

6 If you say **'There's no danger of that'**, you mean that you do not think that the thing referred to will happen. CONVENTION

danger money is extra money that is paid to someone for doing dangerous work. EG *He deserves to get danger money for that job.* N UNCOUNT

dangerous /deɪndʒəᵒrəs/. Something that is **dangerous** is able or likely to hurt or harm you. EG *Never run towards a dangerous animal... It is dangerous to drive with a dirty windscreen.* ◇ **dangerously**. EG *He drives very dangerously... She was dangerously close to the fire.* ADJ QUALIT ≠ safe; ◇ ADV

dangle /dæŋgəᵒl/, **dangles, dangling, dangled**. 1 When something **dangles** or when you **dangle** it, it hangs or swings loosely; used of things which are held or attached at one end. EG *Huge wooden earrings dangled from her ears... Charlie was leaning across my desk dangling the long roll of paper.* V-ERG ⇑ hang = swing

2 If you **keep** someone **dangling**, you make them wait in a state of uncertainty before you tell them something; an informal expression. PHR: VB INFLECTS

3 If you **dangle** something attractive before someone, you offer it to them when you are trying to persuade them to do something. EG *...a newspaper editor dangling his cheque book before thirsty writers.* V+O+A *(before/in front of)* = flap

Danish /deɪnɪʃ/. 1 **Danish** means relating to or concerned with Denmark, its people, or their language. ADJ CLASSIF

2 **Danish** is the language spoken in Denmark. N UNCOUNT

3 The **Danish** are the people of Denmark. EG *The Danish were waiting for official confirmation of the report.* N PLURAL: *the*+N

Danish pastry, Danish pastries. A **Danish pastry** is a type of cake consisting of a rich pastry and a sweet filling such as apple or almond paste. N COUNT

dank /dæŋk/, **danker, dankest**. Something that is **dank** is unpleasantly damp and cold; used especially of underground places such as cellars or caves or of the air in such places. EG *I slept in the dank basement room.* ADJ QUALIT = clammy

dapper /dæpə/. A man who is **dapper** is small and has a very neat and clean appearance. ADJ QUALIT = spruce

dappled /dæpəᵒld/. 1 Something, especially an animal, that is **dappled** is marked with spots that are a different and usually darker colour than their background. EG *...a dappled calf.* ADJ CLASSIF ⇑ spotted = mottled

2 **Dappled** is also used to describe light or shadow that is made up of patches of light and shadow. EG *...dappled leafy sunlight.* ▸ used of things that this light and shadow falls on. EG *...the sun-dappled sea floor.* ADJ CLASSIF

dare /deə/, **dares, daring, dared**. **Dare** is used both as a main verb and as a semi-modal. For information about its uses as a semi-modal, see □ at the end of this entry. 1 If you **dare** to do something that needs courage or **dare** do it, you have enough courage to do it, and you actually do it. EG *For a long while no one dared even to whisper... She did not dare to look at him... Who dares to speak for the people?... He dared not show that he was pleased... We're so late I daren't look at my watch... I can't do that–I simply wouldn't dare.* V+*to*-INF, OR SEMI-MODAL: USU +BROAD NEG, SEE □ BELOW

2 You talk about someone **daring** to do something when you are shocked and angry that they are doing it, because they have no right to do it. EG *'Yes!' he cried, 'the Prime Minister dares to talk about prosperity, when millions of people are out of work.'* • If you say **don't you dare** do something, you are telling someone not to do it and letting them know that you are angry. EG *Don't you dare throw it away.* • You say **how dare you** when you are very shocked and angry about something that someone has done. EG *How dare you speak to me like that!* V: USU+*to*-INF/INF: USU WITH BROAD NEG; • PHR: USU+INF; • PHR+INF: VB INFLECTS

3 You say **dare I say it** when you know that what you are going to say will disappoint someone. EG *The British singers were, dare I say it, very poor.* PHR

4 If you say **I dare say** or **I daresay**, you mean that you think something is very probably true. EG *Well, I daresay you've spent all your money by now... It's worth a few pounds, I dare say, but no more.* PHR ⇑ I expect = I suppose

5 If you **dare** someone to do something dangerous or frightening, you challenge them to do it. EG *I dare you to spend the night in the graveyard... She looked round fiercely, daring them to contradict.* V+O: USU+*to*-INF

6 A **dare** is a challenge which one person gives to another to do something dangerous or frightening. EG *It was many years since James Bond had accepted a dare... I jumped off the wall for a dare.* N COUNT: USU SING

DARE □ In this dictionary **Dare** is described as a SEMI-MODAL because it is used like the modals in some ways but not in all. See also □ at MODAL. 'Dare' also has a complete range of uses as a main verb, but this box only concerns 'dare' as a semi-modal. See paragraph 1 of the entry for DARE for examples of 'dare' used as a semi-modal, and paragraphs 1, 2, and 5 for 'dare' used as a main verb. **Dare** as a semi-modal behaves in the following ways: **1** It is followed by an infinitive without *to*, as in *I didn't* ***dare*** *send it... I only once* ***dared*** *cross a major road.* **2** It inflects and has the forms *dare, dares,* and *dared.* **3** *Dare* can be used before the subject to form questions, as in ***Dare*** *she tell him that?* In this case it does not inflect, and the only form that can be used is *dare.* **4** *Dare, dared,* and *dares* can be used before the negative *not*, as in *The government* ***dares*** *not interfere with him.* **5** *Dare* can be joined with the shortened form of the negative *n't* as in *I* ***daren't*** *go far away... She* ***daren't*** *go upstairs.* In this case it does not inflect, and the only form that can be used is *dare.* **6** *Dare* can be used without an infinitive after it to refer back to a previous verbal group, as in *Those questions we'd all like to ask but don't* ***dare***... *'All right! You can look!'–'I don't dare,' she said.*

daredevil /dɛədɛvəˀl/, **daredevils.** A **daredevil** is a person who enjoys doing dangerous things. EG *...a daredevil motorcycle rider.* — N COUNT = madcap

daren't /dɛənt/ is a spoken form of 'dare not'.

daresay /dɛəseɪ/. See **dare**.

daring /dɛərɪŋ/. **1** Someone who is **daring** is **1.1** willing to do things that might be dangerous. EG *Be a bit more daring.* ▸ used of people's actions. EG *...a daring raid.* ◇ **daringly.** EG *One of the boys very daringly bent down and touched it.* — ADJ QUALIT ⇑ courageous = bold ≠ cautious; ◇ ADV
1.2 willing to do or say things which are new and which might shock or anger other people. EG *He was the most daring of contemporary writers of fiction.* ▸ used of things, actions, and behaviour. EG *...a daring and original proposition.* — ADJ QUALIT ⇑ audacious = bold ≠ timid

2 Daring is the courage to do things which might be dangerous or which might shock or anger other people. EG *...the efficiency and daring shown by our armed forces.* — N UNCOUNT ⇑ courage = nerve ≠ caution

dark /dɑːk/, **darker, darkest. 1** When it is **dark,** there is not enough light to see properly, for example because it is night. EG *Luckily it was too dark for anyone to see me blushing... It will not be dark for half an hour yet... The living room was dark and empty.* ◇ **darkness.** EG *The lights went out and the hall was plunged into darkness.* ● **pitch dark**: see **pitch-black.** — ADJ QUALIT ≠ light; ◇ N UNCOUNT

2 The **dark** is any place where there is not enough light to see. EG *He was sitting in the dark at the back of the theatre... They aren't afraid of the dark.* — N SING : the+N = darkness ≠ light

3 If you do something **before dark**, you do it before the sun sets and night begins. If you do something **after dark,** you do it when night has begun. EG *I want to get there before dark... We'll be back after dark.* — PHR : USED AS AN A

4 Something that is **dark** is a colour that has a lot of brown, grey, or black tones in it. EG *...a little patch of dark wood... ...a man in an elegant dark suit.* ▸ used to describe colours. EG *It was a large room with a high ceiling and rich, dark red curtains.* — ADJ QUALIT ≠ light; ▸ ADJ QUALIT : ATTRIB+ADJ COLOUR ≠ light

5 If you say that someone has **dark** hair, eyes, or skin, you mean that they have brown or black hair, eyes, or skin. EG *She was slender and had long dark hair... ...sad dark eyes.* — ADJ QUALIT

6 Someone who is **dark** has brown or black hair, brown eyes, and sometimes a brown or black skin. EG *He was a tall, dark, and undeniably handsome man.* — ADJ QUALIT ≠ fair

7 A **dark** period of time is unpleasant or frightening. EG *We would refer to them later as the dark days of the campaign... The war came, and with it a much darker chapter in my life* — ADJ QUALIT : USU ATTRIB ⇑ sad = black ≠ happy

8 A **dark** place or area is mysterious and not fully known about. EG *There are still some undiscovered dark corners of the world... ...darkest Africa.* — ADJ QUALIT : ATTRIB

9 Dark ideas or thoughts are sad, and show that you are expecting something unpleasant to happen. EG *His mind was occupied with dark worries and gloomy speculations.* — ADJ QUALIT : USU ATTRIB ⇑ pessimistic = gloomy

10 Dark looks or remarks make you think that the person giving them wants to harm you or that something horrible is going to happen. EG *I had some dark looks from the dreaded Glyn Williams.* ◇ **darkly.** EG *Another of the men hinted darkly that there would be violence.* — ADJ QUALIT : USU ATTRIB ⇑ evil = sinister; ◇ ADV

11 If you **keep** something **dark,** you keep it secret. EG *Keep it dark–don't spread it around.* — PHR : VB INFLECTS

12 If you are **in the dark** about something, you do not know anything about it. EG *I am quite in the dark about all this.* — PHR : USED AS AN A ⇑ ignorant

dark age, dark ages. 1 A **dark age** is a period in which there is a lack of culture and progress in a society and people are ignorant. EG *We may be entering a new dark age.* **2** The **Dark Ages** are the period of European history between about 500 A.D. and about 1000 A.D. — N COUNT ⇑ era ≠ golden age; N PLURAL : the+N

darken /dɑːkəˀn/, **darkens, darkening, darkened. 1** If a place or the sky **darkens** or if it is **darkened** by something, it becomes darker, for example because of shadows, clouds, or because it is nearly night. EG *The autumn sky darkened... The road was darkened by great elms.* — V-ERG ≠ brighten

2 When you **darken** something or when it **darkens,** it becomes darker in colour. EG *Rub in linseed oil to darken the wood.* — V-ERG ≠ lighten

3 If something **darkens** a situation or event, it makes it seem less hopeful or enjoyable than it should be. EG *Nothing must darken this happy day.* — V+O ⇑ sadden = cloud

4 If you tell someone **never to darken** your **door** again, you are telling them to go away and never come to your house again; an old-fashioned or literary expression. — PHR : VB INFLECTS

darkened /dɑːkəˀnd/. A **darkened** building has no lights in it and so it is dark. EG *...a darkened four-storey house.* — ADJ CLASSIF : USU ATTRIB ≠ well-lit

dark glasses are glasses which have special dark-coloured lenses to protect your eyes in the sunshine. EG *He always wore dark glasses.* — N PLURAL = shades, sunglasses

dark horse, dark horses. If you say that someone is a **dark horse,** you mean that very little is known about them. Usually this is because they have not told anyone anything about themselves, for example where they come from or what they intend to do. EG *She's a bit of a dark horse.* — N COUNT : USU USED AS C ⇑ person = mystery

darkie /dɑːkiˡ/, **darkies**; also spelled **darky.** A **darkie** is a very offensive word for someone who has brown or black skin. — N COUNT ⇑ person

darkish /dɑːkɪʃ/ means quite dark in colour. EG *We'll give the boat a darkish blue hull.* — ADJ CLASSIF ≠ lightish

darkroom /dɑːkruˀm/, **darkrooms.** A **darkroom** is a room from which all normal daylight has been excluded and which is lit only by red light, so that photographs can be developed there. — N COUNT ⇑ room

darling /dɑːlɪŋ/, **darlings. 1** You call someone **darling** if you love them or like them very much. EG *Oh Harold darling, I am sorry. I didn't mean to upset you... You're looking absolutely marvellous, darling.* — N COUNT/VOC = dearest, dear

2 In some parts of Britain, people call other people **darling** as a sign of friendliness. — N COUNT : USED AS VOC

3 Darling is used to describe someone or something that you love or like very much. EG *...her darling baby brother... The darling old man used to come up and stay in the Grand Hotel... ...a darling little cottage.* — ADJ CLASSIF : ATTRIB = beloved, dear

4 If you say that someone is a **darling,** you mean that they are very helpful or likeable; an informal expression. EG *Now this Molly, she's a darling, and she reminds me of my grandmother.* ● You can say **be a darling** to someone you know very well when you are asking them to do something for you. EG *Be a darling and get my cigarettes from the bedroom.* — N SING : a+N, USU USED AS C = angel; ● PHR ⇑ please

5 The **darling** of a group of people is someone who is especially liked by that group. EG *She quickly became the darling of the crowds.* — N COUNT : WITH POSS ⇑ person = favourite

darn /dɑːn/, **darns, darning, darned. 1** When you **darn** something made of wool, you mend a hole in it by sewing long stitches across the hole and weaving other long stitches in and out across them, so that the hole is filled in. EG *I don't want to darn your socks.* — V OR V+O ⇑ repair

2 A **darn** is a part of a sock or other piece of clothing that has been darned. EG *I still wear this jumper, even though it's full of darns.* — N COUNT

3 People sometimes use **darn** or **darned** to emphasize what they are saying, often when they are irritated or rather annoyed; an informal expression. EG *It's a darned cheek to go and tell her just like that.* — ADV+ADJ/ADV, OR ADJ CLASSIF : ATTRIB

4 If you say **darn it,** you are letting people know that you are annoyed or angry about something; an informal expression. EG *Oh darn it, Etta, I'm fed up.* — EXCLAM

darning /dɑːnɪŋ/ is clothes such as socks, pullovers, etc, that need to be mended by being darned. EG *...piles of knitting and darning.* — N UNCOUNT ⇑ clothing = mending

dart /dɑːt/, **darts, darting, darted. 1** If a person or animal **darts** somewhere, they move suddenly — V : USU+A = flit, spring and quickly. EG *Butterflies were darting from one scarlet flower to another... She darted forward and kissed Mary on the cheek.* ▸ used as a noun. EG *The boy made a quick dart across the road.* ▸ N COUNT = dash

2 If you **dart** a glance or look at something, you look at it very quickly. EG *She darted a glance sideways at her teacher.* V+O+A

3 A **dart** is a small fold which is sewn in a piece of clothing so that it fits better. EG *You never saw so many darts in a bodice!* N COUNT

4 A **dart** is also a small object with a sharp point which can be thrown or shot; used as a weapon or in a game. EG *They killed the elephants with tiny, poisoned darts.* N COUNT

5 **Darts** is a game in which you throw darts at a special board which has numbers on it. EG *He took part in a darts match in his local pub.* N UNCOUNT

dartboard /dɑːtbɔːd/, **dartboards**. A **dartboard** is a circular board with numbers on it which is used as the target in a game of darts. N COUNT ⇑ board

dash /dæʃ/, **dashes, dashing, dashed**. 1 If you **dash** somewhere, you run or go there quickly and suddenly. EG *People dashed out into the street to see what was happening... I spent all day dashing around trying to do my Christmas shopping.* ● If you say that you **have to dash** or you **must dash**, you mean that you are in a hurry and have to leave immediately. EG *I'm sorry, I can't stay, I've got to dash.* V+A ⇑ hurry = race, rush ● PHR

2 A **dash** is 2.1 a sudden, quick run or journey to a place. EG *He made a dash for the door... ...a quick dash to London.* ● If you **make a dash for it**, you run away very quickly, for example because someone is trying to catch you. EG *We'll have to make a dash for it.* 2.2 a short fast race; used in American English. N COUNT: USU SING ● PHR: VB INFLECTS ⇑ flee = run for it N COUNT

3 A **dash** of something is 3.1 a small quantity of something which you add when you are preparing food or mixing a drink. EG *Some soups are delicious served cold with a dash of cream.* 3.2 a small amount of an extra quality that is found in something and that often makes it more interesting or distinctive. EG *Her articles usually contain a dash of wry humour.* N PART+N UNCOUNT: USU SING = hint N PART+N UNCOUNT: USU SING ⇑ quantity = touch

4 **Dash** is a mixture of stylishness, enthusiasm, and courage; an old-fashioned use. EG *He rides with a certain amount of dash.* ● If you say that someone **cuts a dash**, you mean that they have an attractively stylish appearance or bold manner; an old-fashioned expression. N UNCOUNT = flair ● PHR: VB INFLECTS ⇑ impress

5 If you **dash** something somewhere, you throw or push it violently, often so hard that it breaks. EG *She picked up his photograph, dashed it to the ground, and stamped on it... He suddenly dashed the magazine aside angrily.* V+O+A = sweep

6 If an event or person **dashes** someone's hopes or expectations, it destroys them by making it impossible that the thing that is hoped for or expected will ever happen. EG *Our hopes that a solution would be found were dashed when the management refused to negotiate.* V+O ⇑ destroy = shatter

7 A **dash** is also 7.1 a short, straight, horizontal line (-) that is used in writing, for example before and after a sentence that occurs within another sentence, or where the writer breaks off suddenly in the middle of a sentence. 7.2 the short, straight horizontal line which is used to represent the long sound in Morse code. N COUNT ⇑ punctuation mark N COUNT ⇑ symbol ≠ dot

8 You say **dash** or **dash it** or **dash it all** when you are rather annoyed about something; an old-fashioned informal expression. EXCLAM = drat, blast

9 A **dash** is also a dashboard. N COUNT

10 See also **dashing**.

dash off. If you **dash off** something such as a letter or a poem, you write it very quickly and without thinking about it very much. EG *His essay seemed to have been dashed off in seconds.* PHRASAL VB: V+O+ADV

dashboard /dæʃbɔːd/, **dashboards**. The **dashboard** in a car or other vehicle is the panel facing the driver's seat where most of the instruments and switches are. N COUNT = dash

dashing /dæʃɪŋ/. Someone who is **dashing** is very stylish and attractive in a way that shows they have a lot of energy and confidence. EG *She felt very dashing in her wide-brimmed hat with the big feather.* ▸ also used of things. EG *...a dashing pair of tan shoes.* ADJ QUALIT ⇑ showy ≠ dowdy

dastardly /dæstədli[1]/. A **dastardly** action is wicked and planned to hurt someone; an old-fashioned word. EG *...a dastardly crime.* ▸ also used of people. EG *...a dastardly villain.* ADJ QUALIT ⇑ bad

data /deɪtə, dɑːtə/ is information, usually in the form of facts or statistics that you can analyse, or that you use to do further calculations. **Data** is sometimes used as a plural noun, with **datum** as the singular. EG *The data was still being processed at the Census Office... He does not have adequate data.* N UNCOUNT/N PLURAL

data bank, data banks; also spelled with a hyphen. A **data bank** is the same as a database. N COUNT

database /deɪtəbeɪs/, **databases**. A **database** is a collection of data that is stored in a computer in a way that enables people to get information out of it very quickly. N COUNT

data processing; also spelled with a hyphen. **Data processing** is the series of operations that are carried out on data, especially by computers, in order to present, interpret, or obtain information. N UNCOUNT

date /deɪt/, **dates, dating, dated**. 1 A **date** is a specific time that can be named, for example a particular day or a particular year. EG *What's the date today?... No date was announced for the talks... What dates in April would you be free?* N COUNT

2 When you **date** something, you give the date when it began or when it was made. EG *The specialist can date many rocks... The statue was found near a sandal dated at 6000BC... From that moment we may date Britain's start back on the road to recovery.* ● See also **carbon dating**. V+O

3 When you **date** something such as a letter or a cheque, you write that day's date on it. EG *The letter was dated September 18 1952.* V+O

4 **At a later date** or **at some future date** means at some time in the future, although you do not know exactly when it will be. PHR: USED AS AN A

5 If something has happened or been true **to date**, it has happened or been true until the present time. EG *We need a simple record of what has happened to date.* PHR: USED AS AN A ⇑ yet = so far

6 If something **dates**, it goes out of fashion and becomes unacceptable to modern tastes. EG *He's a great fashion designer, his stuff doesn't date.* ● See also **dated**. V: NO IMPER = age

7 If your ideas or the things that you like or can remember **date** you, they show that you are quite old or older than the people you are with. V+O: NO IMPER

8 A **date** is also 8.1 an appointment to do something, for example go to a social event. EG *She couldn't go because of a theatre date.* 8.2 an appointment you have to go out with someone of the opposite sex, for example your girlfriend or boyfriend; an informal use. EG *Sorry I can't come–I have a date with Jill.* N COUNT: USU+SUPP N COUNT: IF+PREP THEN *with*

9 Your **date** is a person of the opposite sex that you have a date with; used mainly in American English. EG *Who's your date tonight?* N COUNT: USU POSS+N = boyfriend, girlfriend

10 If you **are dating** someone of the opposite sex, you go out regularly with them; used especially in American English. EG *Jenny told them she was dating me.* V+O = go out with

11 A **date** is also a small, dark-brown, sticky fruit with a stone inside. Dates grow on palm trees in hot countries. ▸ A **date** or a **date palm** is a tree on which dates grow. N COUNT

12 See also **out-of-date, up-to-date**.

date back. If something **dates back** to a particular time, it was made or started at that time. EG *The present city hall dates back to only the 1880s.* PHRASAL VB: V+ADV, IF+PREP THEN *to* = date from

date from. If something **dates from** a particular time, it started or was made at that time. EG *These stones dated from the days of the dinosaurs.* PHRASAL VB: V+PREP = date back

DATE □ This entry gives some ways of expressing dates. The following examples show ways of talking about dates. A date can be written as 'July 10', 'July 10th', '10 July' or '10th July', but is usually pronounced 'July the tenth' or 'the tenth of July'. However, 'July 10' is sometimes pronounced 'July ten' in American English. The year and the month are often left out of dates when it is clear which year or month you are referring to. The day of the week is usually mentioned before the rest of the date, and the year is usually mentioned after the day and month. EG *'What date is it?'–'It's the 30th today'... ...Tuesday May the thirteenth... ...Monday the fifth of April... They married on December 9, 1913... Labour was defeated in the General Election of 19 June 1970... The case was heard in the High Court in February 1910... They lived together from December of that year until June of 1970... Where were you on the nights of February 4th and 7th?... The paper he hands me has a 1975 date.* In British English, you can mention the month either after or before the day, but in American English it is more common to mention the month first. This is especially important when dates are written just as a series of numbers, since a date such as 10/7/86 usually means July 10th 1986 in British English, but it means October 7th 1986 in American English. In British English, you usually say that something happens **on** a particular day, for example 'It happened on Thursday', but in American English you can also leave out 'on' and say 'It happened Thursday'. If you refer to the twenties, you are referring to the years between 1920 and 1929. If you refer to the 1840's, you are referring to the years between 1840 and 1849. The early sixties are the years between 1960 and 1965, and the late sixties are the years between 1965 and 1969. EG *...in Stockholm in the thirties... I went on a computer training course in the nineteen fifties.* In the following examples, the speaker or writer is referring to things that usually happen on a particular day or that repeatedly happen then. EG *I'm terribly busy on Saturdays... On Monday nights, the pupils go to the local cinema... ...every Tuesday for the next few months... I've never worked on a Saturday in my whole life.*

dated /deɪtɪ²d/. Something that is **dated** seems old-fashioned, although it may have been fashionable and modern some years ago. EG *The play is rather dated now.* ADJ QUALIT

date of birth, dates of birth. Your **date of birth** is the exact date on which you were born, including the year. EG *Give your full name, age, date of birth, and home address.* N COUNT : USU WITH POSS

dative /deɪtɪv/. In the grammar of some languages, for example Latin, the **dative** case is a case used for a noun when it is the indirect object of the verb. It is also used with some prepositions. ▸ used as a noun. EG *...a noun in the dative.* ADJ CLASSIF ▸ N SING : *the*+N

daub /dɔːb/, **daubs, daubing, daubed**. When you **daub** a substance such as mud or paint onto something, you spread it onto that thing quickly or carelessly. EG *The children had daubed paint all over the walls... The side of the building was daubed with slogans.* V+O+A ⇑ smear = plaster

daughter /dɔːtə/, **daughters**. 1 Someone's **daughter** is their female child. EG *My daughter is only sixteen... Joyce was the daughter of the butcher... They have a delightful teenage daughter.* N COUNT ⇑ offspring

2 **Daughter** is used to describe something which comes from something else and is very like it. EG *It has several daughter languages, including English and German... Each daughter cell receives a complete duplicate set of genes.* N BEFORE N

3 If you describe a woman as a **daughter** of a particular place or event, you mean that she comes from that place or that she is as she is because of that event. EG *She is a true daughter of Liverpool.* N COUNT+SUPP

daughter-in-law, daughters-in-law. Someone's **daughter-in-law** is the wife of their son. N COUNT ⇑ relation

daunt /dɔːnt/, **daunts, daunting, daunted**. If something or someone **daunts** you, they make you feel slightly afraid or worried about whether you can succeed in what you are doing. EG *He was daunted by the high quality of work they expected.* ◊ **daunting**. EG *It is a daunting prospect for a party so recently formed... She was a fine though somewhat daunting director.* V+O ⇑ discourage = scare ◊ ADJ QUALIT ⇑ discouraging = intimidating

dauntless /dɔːntlɪ²s/. Someone who is **dauntless** is brave and not easily frightened or discouraged; a rather literary word. EG *Alfred's mother was a dauntless woman.* ADJ QUALIT = fearless ≠ cowardly

dawdle /dɔːdə⁰l/, **dawdles, dawdling, dawdled**. If you **dawdle**, you spend more time than is necessary in doing something or in going somewhere. EG *Come on, don't dawdle!* V ⇑ delay = lounge

dawn /dɔːn/, **dawns, dawning, dawned**. 1 **Dawn** is the time of day when light first appears in the sky, before the sun rises. EG *We got up at dawn... By the time the dawn came, the weather had calmed... We drank and laughed and talked until dawn.* N UNCOUNT/COUNT = daybreak ≠ dusk

2 When the day **dawns**, the sky begins to grow light after the night. EG *The first day of the holidays dawned bright and fair.* V ⇑ begin = break

3 The **dawn** of a period of time or a situation is the beginning of it; a literary word. EG *This marked the dawn of a new era in human history.* N SING : *the*+N+*of*

4 If something **is dawning**, it is beginning to develop or appear; a literary word. EG *She wrote of the dawning hopes of reconciliation in Western Europe.* V = awakening

dawn on. If a fact or idea **dawns on** you or **dawns upon** you, you realise it. EG *Then it dawned on me that they were speaking Spanish... The awful truth dawned upon him.* PHRASAL VB : V+PREP

dawn chorus, dawn choruses. The **dawn chorus** is the singing of birds at dawn. N COUNT : USU SING

day /deɪ/, **days**. 1 A **day** is 1.1 one of the seven twenty-four hour periods of time in a week. EG *The attack occurred about six days ago... Nobody has seen them for days... Can you go any day of the week? What about Monday?... Take the tablets three times a day.* N COUNT 1.2 the time when it is light, and not night. EG *It's just before dawn: almost day... The days and nights are of equal length at this time of year.* N UNCOUNT/COUNT ≠ night

1.3 the time during each period of twenty-four hours when you are not sleeping, especially the time when you are working. EG *What would be for you a typical working day?... He just sits there all day doing nothing.* N COUNT : USU SING

2 You can refer to a particular **day** or to particular **days** as a way of referring to a particular period in history. EG *In Shakespeare's day, women's parts were played by male actors... This is the main problem of the present day... She wrote in the early days of the republic... Are students interested in religion these days?* N UNCOUNT/COUNT+SUPP ⇑ age

3 The **day** of a particular person or thing is the time when that person or thing is especially successful or important. EG *The day of the silent film has passed.* N COUNT+SUPP = heyday

4 **Day** is used in the names of special days, for example Christmas Day, New Year's Day, and Armistice Day. N COUNT IN NAMES AFTER N

5 If you say that something will happen **any day now**, you mean that it will happen soon, probably in the next few days. EG *I am expecting to hear from them any day now.* PHR : USED AS AN A

6 If you **call it a day**, you decide to stop doing something and leave it to be finished later; an informal expression. EG *We called it a day and went home.* PHR : VB INFLECTS

7 If something happens **day and night** or **night and day**, it happens all the time without stopping. EG *The factories were working continuously day and night throughout the year.* PHR : USED AS AN A

8 If you say that something happens **day in, day out**, you mean that it happens every day without changing, and is perhaps boring. EG *She worked day in, day out, cleaning and washing and cooking, with never a break.* PHR : USED AS AN A = continually

9 When people talk about **the good old days**, they are referring to a time in the past when they think that life was better than it is now. EG *Things would soon get back to normal like in the good old days.* PHR : USED AS O/S/C

10 **In this day and age** means in modern times. EG *Even in this day and age the old attitudes persist.* PHR : USED AS AN A

11 If something **makes** your **day**, it makes you feel very happy; an informal expression. EG *Her smile somehow makes my day.* PHR : VB INFLECTS ⇑ please

12 If you say that you want to **make a day of it**, you mean that you want to spend the whole day, not just part of it, doing whatever it is you are talking about; an informal expression. PHR : VB INFLECTS

13 If you say that something will happen **one day** or **some day** or **one of these days**, you mean that it will happen or might happen at some future time. EG *We're all going to be old one day... I'd like to go to China some day... You'll have an accident one of these days if you drive like that.* PHR : USED AS AN A

14 You say that a particular thing happened **one day** when it is not important exactly when it happened. EG *Then one day she wrote to say she wanted to meet me in London.* PHR : USED AS AN A

15 If you say that it is **one of those days**, you mean that it is a day when everything seems to go wrong; an informal expression. EG *It was one of those days: I burnt my hand at breakfast, missed the bus, and then it rained.* PHR : USED AS C

16 If you say **that'll be the day** when someone has mentioned a particular event or situation, you mean that you think that it is very unlikely to happen; an informal expression. EG *'When I'm rich...'-'That'll be the day!'* CONVENTION = some hope

17 If you say **those were the days**, you are talking about a time in the past when you think that things were better, and you are feeling sad that that time has finished. EG *'Those were the days,' she sighed. 'We didn't have a care in the world.'* CONVENTION

18 If it is a year, month, etc **to the day** since a particular thing happened, it is exactly a year, PHR : USED AS AN A

month, etc since it happened. EG *It's a year to the day since she died.*

19 **To this day** means until and including today. EG *I kept my promise, and to this day I have never told anyone her secret.* PHR : USED AS AN A

20 If a particular person, group, or thing **wins the day**, they win a battle, competition, or struggle. If a particular person, group, or thing **loses the day**, they are defeated. EG *There was never any doubt about which team would finally win the day.* PHR : VB INFLECTS

21 The word **day** is also used in the following expressions, which are explained at other places in this dictionary. • **it's early days yet: see early.** • **at the end of the day: see end.** • **late in the day:** see **late.** • **the other day:** see **other.** • **to pass the time of day:** see **time.**

daybreak /deɪbreɪk/ is the time in the morning when light first appears. EG *A streak of pink on the horizon told him that daybreak was near... They got up at daybreak.* N UNCOUNT = dawn

day care is care that is provided for small children during the day while their parents are at work. EG *Private nurseries provide day care for a quarter of the children under five... ...a day care centre... ...inadequate day-care facilities.* N UNCOUNT : USU BEFORE N

daydream /deɪdri:m/, **daydreams, daydreaming, daydreamed**; also spelled with a hyphen. 1 A **daydream** is 1.1 a series of pleasant thoughts, especially about things that you would like to happen. EG *He drifted off into another daydream.* N COUNT = reverie 1.2 a hope or ambition that is unlikely to be achieved. EG *I hated school. My daydream has always been to go back as a celebrity.* N COUNT ↑ wish = pipe dream

2 When you **daydream**, you think about pleasant things for a period of time. EG *Boys and girls daydream about what they want to be.* V : IF+PREP THEN about/of = muse, wonder

daylight /deɪlaɪt/, **daylights.** 1 **Daylight** is 1.1 the light that there is during the day before it gets dark. EG *We've got at least two more hours of daylight... It looks different in daylight... They began to spend almost all the daylight hours up on deck.* N UNCOUNT ≠ night 1.2 the time of day when it begins to get light. EG *The ship sailed into harbour before daylight on 1 May.* N UNCOUNT

2 If a crime is committed **in broad daylight**, it is committed during the day rather than when it is dark. EG *The car was stolen in broad daylight.* PHR : USED AS AN A

3 If you **knock** or **beat the living daylights out of** someone, you hit them very hard many times; an informal expression. PHR : VB INFLECTS ↑ attack

4 If something **scares the living daylights out of** you, it frightens you very much; an informal expression. PHR : VB INFLECTS ↑ frighten

daylight robbery. If you think that someone charges too much money for something, you can describe this action as **daylight robbery**; an informal expression. N UNCOUNT ↑ overcharging

daylight saving is the practice which exists in some countries of setting the clocks one hour later than the normal local time, so that the evenings stay light for longer. N UNCOUNT

day nursery, day nurseries. A **day nursery** is a place where children who are too young to go to school can be left all day while their parents are at work. N COUNT = crèche

day off, days off. A **day off** is a day when you do not have to go to work even though it is usually a working day. EG *She doesn't go to work on Thursdays: it's her day off.* N COUNT ≠ workday

day of reckoning. The **day of reckoning** is a day or time in the future when people will be punished for what they have done wrong. EG *The day of reckoning had not yet come for him.* N SING : the+N

day pupil, day pupils; also spelled with a hyphen. A **day pupil** is a pupil who goes to a boarding school but lives at home. N COUNT ≠ boarder

day release; also spelled with a hyphen. **Day release** is a system in which workers spend one day each week at a college, so that they can study a subject connected with their work; used in British English. EG *I'd like to see a compulsory day release scheme brought in.* N UNCOUNT

day return, day returns. A **day return** is a train or bus ticket which allows you to go somewhere and come back on the same day for a lower price than an ordinary return ticket; used in British English. N COUNT

day school, day schools. A **day school** is a school where all the pupils go home in the evening and do not live at the school. N COUNT ≠ boarding school

daytime /deɪtaɪm/; also spelled with a hyphen. **Daytime** is the part of a day between the time when it gets light and the time when it gets dark. EG *The forests were dark as night even in the daytime... He held a daytime job as a shop assistant.* N SING : the+N, OR N UNCOUNT ↑ period ≠ night time

day-to-day means happening every day as part of ordinary life. EG *This is very much part of the day-to-day life of all human beings... We discussed the day-to-day running of the schools.* ADJ CLASSIF : ATTRIB = daily, routine

day-trip, day-trips; also spelled without a hyphen. A **day-trip** is a journey for pleasure to a place and back again on the same day. N COUNT = excursion

day-tripper, day-trippers; also spelled without a hyphen. A **day-tripper** is someone who makes a day-trip. N COUNT

daze /deɪz/, **dazed.** 1 If someone is **in a daze,** they are feeling very confused or upset. EG *I left the ranch in a daze... Karen had been in a daze all the way to London.* PHR : USED AS AN A = in a dream

2 If someone **is dazed** by something, for example by something that happens or by a blow on the head, they are unable to think clearly. EG *She was dazed by the news.* ◇ **dazed.** EG *He seemed dazed and bewildered... He had a dazed expression on his face.* V+O : ONLY PASS ◇ ADJ QUALIT = stunned

dazzle /dæzəᵒl/, **dazzles, dazzling, dazzled.** 1 If someone or something **dazzles** you, you are extremely impressed by their skill, qualities, or beauty. EG *She had without question been dazzled by the evening's performance... He refused to be dazzled by the vocabulary of the sociologists.* ◇ **dazzling.** EG *She gave him a dazzling smile... The scandal cut short his dazzling ministerial career... We are on the threshold of even more dazzling achievements.* V+O : USU PASS, OR V ↑ impress = bewitch ◇ ADJ QUALIT ↑ impressive = brilliant

2 The **dazzle** of something is 2.1 a sudden brightness that makes it impossible for you to see properly for a short time. EG *They both blinked in the sudden dazzle.* N UNCOUNT, OR N SING : the+N ↑ light = glare 2.2 a quality, for example beauty or skill, which is impressive and attractive. EG *...the dazzle of high technology.* N SING WITH DET : USU the+N ↑ brilliance

3 If a bright light **dazzles** you, it makes you unable to see properly for a short time. EG *She flinched as though a bright light had suddenly dazzled her eyes.* ◇ **dazzling.** EG *Marsha shut her eyes against the dazzling sun.* V+O : USU PASS, OR V ↑ blind ◇ ADJ CLASSIF ↑ blinding

DC is used to refer to an electric current that always flows in the same direction; an abbreviation for 'direct current'. N UNCOUNT : USU BEFORE N

D-day is the day that is chosen for the beginning of an important activity such as a military operation. EG *It's two days to D-day and he's getting worried.* N UNCOUNT

DDT is a poisonous substance which is used for killing insects. N UNCOUNT ↑ poison

de- is sometimes added 1 to a verb, changing the meaning of the verb to its opposite. EG *...sensitize→desensitize... ...nationalize→denationalize.* PREFIX 2 to a noun, making it a verb and giving it the meaning of removing the thing described by the noun. EG *...forest→deforest... ...ice→de-ice.* PREFIX

deacon /di:kən/, **deacons.** A **deacon** is 1 a member of the clergy, for example in the Church of England, who is lower in rank than a priest. N COUNT 2 a person who is not ordained but who assists the minister in some Protestant churches. EG *He's a deacon of the Methodist Church.* N COUNT

deaconess /di:kənɛˈs/, **deaconesses.** A **deaconess** is a woman who is not ordained but who works for a church such as the Church of England and takes some church services. N COUNT

deactivate /di:æktɪveɪt/, **deactivates, deactivating, deactivated.** If you **deactivate** a bomb or other explosive device, you make it harmless by removing the active part of it. V+O ↑ disarm ≠ prime

dead /dɛd/. 1 A person, animal, or plant that is **dead** is no longer living. EG *I thought you were dead... He was shot dead in a gunfight... Mary threw away the dead flowers... They found the dog howling over the two dead bodies.* ADJ CLASSIF ↑ deceased ▸ The **dead** is used to refer to people who are dead. EG *I try to forget the dead.* ▸ N PLURAL : the+N

2 Land or water that is **dead** contains no living things. EG *Scientists are certain that Mars is a dead planet.* ADJ CLASSIF ↑ barren

3 If a part of your body goes **dead**, you cannot feel any sensation in it for a short time. EG *My arm's gone dead.* ADJ CLASSIF : PRED = numb

4 If you are **dead** to something, you are incapable of feeling or understanding it. EG *She is dead to all reason where her children are concerned.* ADJ CLASSIF : PRED+*to* ⇑ impervious

5 If you feel **dead**, you feel very tired and have no energy left; an informal use. EG *I don't know what's wrong today, I'm absolutely dead.* ADJ CLASSIF : PRED = shattered

6 A place that is **dead** has very little activity going on in it. EG *Most holiday resorts are pretty dead during the winter.* ADJ QUALIT ⇑ quiet ≠ lively

7 Something that is **dead** is no longer being used or is finished. EG *A dead cigar lay in the ashtray... Is this glass dead?... The subject is not dead; people are not going to stop discussing it now.* ADJ CLASSIF ⇑ extinct

8 A **dead** language is no longer spoken or written as a means of communication, although it may still be studied. ADJ CLASSIF ⇑ obsolete ≠ living

9 A telephone or piece of electrical equipment that is **dead** no longer has any electrical power and so is not functioning. EG *The phone went dead... Of course the car won't start; the battery's completely dead!* ADJ CLASSIF : PRED ⇑ unresponsive

10 You can describe something, for example a rock or a statue, as **dead** to emphasize that it is not alive. ADJ CLASSIF = lifeless

11 A **dead** sound or colour is dull rather than lively or bright. EG *They talked on in those flat, dead, robot voices... The room was redone in an unattractive dead white.* ADJ CLASSIF

12 **Dead** can mean complete or absolute, especially with the words 'centre', 'silence', and 'stop'. EG *There was dead silence in the bedroom... The table was placed in the dead centre of the room.* ADJ CLASSIF : ATTRIB ⇑ absolute

13 In informal English, **dead** also means **13.1** precisely or exactly. EG *It landed dead in the middle of the pond... We arrived at dead on four o'clock... I was staring dead ahead.* ADV+ADJ/ADV : ALSO+PREP **13.2** very or very much. EG *It's dead easy... He was sitting dead drunk in a corner... They were dead against the idea at first.* ADV+ADJ/ADV : ALSO+PREP = ever so

14 If something stops **dead**, it stops quickly and suddenly rather than gradually. EG *As soon as it reached him it stopped dead.* ADV AFTER VB

15 The **dead** of night or winter is the middle part of it, when it is darkest or coldest. EG *...at dead of night... ...in the dead of winter.* N UNCOUNT+*of* : USU *the*+N

16 If you feel **half dead**, you feel very tired or ill and very weak. EG *She was half dead with exhaustion.* PHR : USED AS C

17 If you say that someone is **dead from the neck up**, you mean that they are very stupid; an informal expression. PHR : USED AS C

18 If you say **'Over my dead body'**, you mean that you feel very strongly that something that has just been mentioned should not happen, and that you will do everything you can to prevent it; an informal expression. EG *'Roger and I are going to get married.'–'Over my dead body!'* CONVENTION

19 If you say that you **wouldn't be seen dead** in a particular place or doing a particular thing, you mean that you would never go to that place or do that thing because you think it is awful or unfashionable; an informal expression. EG *I wouldn't be seen dead in a hat like that.* PHR

20 If someone **rises** or **is raised from the dead**, they come back to life after they have died; a rather literary expression. EG *Christians believe that Christ rose from the dead.* PHR : VB INFLECTS

21 If someone is **dead to the world**, they are asleep; an informal expression. PHR : USED AS C ≠ awake

22 **drop dead:** see **drop.** • **a dead loss:** see **loss.**

deadbeat /dɛdbiːt/, **deadbeats**; also spelled with a hyphen. **1** A **deadbeat** is a person who is lazy or does not want to be part of ordinary society; an informal word used mainly in American English. N COUNT = drop-out

2 If you are **dead-beat**, you are very tired and have no energy left; used in informal English. EG *I knew I'd be dead beat in the morning.* ADJ CLASSIF = shattered

dead duck, dead ducks. Something that is a **dead duck** has absolutely no chance of succeeding or surviving; used in informal British English. EG *That plan's a dead duck.* N COUNT : IF SING *a*+N, USU USED AS C ⇑ failure = non-starter

deaden /dɛdə°n/, **deadens, deadening, deadened.** If something **deadens** a feeling or a sound, it makes it less strong so that you feel it less or hear it less. EG *Drugs deaden the pangs of hunger... ...the deadening effect of alcohol.* V+O ⇑ reduce = dull ≠ heighten

dead end, dead ends; also spelled with a hyphen.
1 A street that is a **dead end** does not lead anywhere because there is no way out at one end. N COUNT = cul-de-sac

2 A job or course of action that is a **dead end** does not lead to further developments. EG *Her work on new methods of heat production proved to be a dead end... ...a dead-end job.* N COUNT

deadening /dɛdə°nɪŋ/. Something that is **deadening** destroys people's enthusiasm and creativity, usually because it is very boring. EG *...the deadening boredom of my routines... ...degrading, deadening tasks.* ADJ QUALIT = soul-destroying ≠ stimulating

dead heat, dead heats. If a race ends in a **dead heat**, more than one competitor arrives at the finishing line at exactly the same time, so that there is more than one winner. N COUNT ⇑ draw

deadline /dɛdlaɪn/, **deadlines.** A **deadline** is a time or date before which a particular job or task must be finished. EG *We must meet the deadline... The 6.30 p.m. deadline approached.* N COUNT ⇑ limit

deadlock /dɛdlɒk/ is a state of affairs in an argument or dispute in which neither side is willing to give in at all and so no agreement can be reached. EG *The meeting between management and unions ended in deadlock... The Government was blamed for the political deadlock.* N UNCOUNT ⇑ suspension = stalemate

deadlocked /dɛdlɒkt/. If a situation is **deadlocked**, no agreement can be reached because neither side will give in at all. EG *The East-West meeting has been deadlocked for eight months.* ADJ CLASSIF ⇑ suspended = at an impasse

deadly /dɛdli^1/, **deadlier, deadliest. 1** Something that is **deadly** is **1.1** likely or able to cause someone's death. EG *This is one of nature's deadliest poisons... A dose of 0.004 gm is deadly to man... ...a deadly attack on the air base.* ADJ CLASSIF ⇑ fatal = lethal **1.2** very effective either as a means of opposing someone or in a way which makes fun of someone or which hurts their feelings. EG *This was the deadliest insult he could hear... She argued with deadly logic.* ADJ QUALIT = devastating **1.3** very dull and boring; an informal use. EG *Our maths classes are pretty deadly.* ADJ QUALIT

2 **Deadly** is used to emphasize the extent to which something has an unpleasant or undesirable quality. EG *The air was deadly cold... She thought he was joking but he was deadly serious.* ADV+ADJ/ADV ⇑ extremely = horribly

3 **Deadly** means absolute or complete in an unpleasant way. EG *There was deadly silence.* ADJ QUALIT : USU ATTRIB

deadpan /dɛdpæn/. If you do something in a **deadpan** way or if you look **deadpan**, you appear to be serious and are hiding the fact that you are joking or teasing someone. EG *He gave his deadpan grin... She looked at me deadpan.* ADJ CLASSIF, OR ADV WITH VB = straight-faced

dead weight, dead weights; also spelled with a hyphen. A **dead weight** is **1** a load which is particularly heavy to lift because it does not lift itself up at all. EG *Keeping him upright was no easy task, for he was practically a dead weight.* N COUNT ⇑ weight **2** something that makes change or progress difficult. EG *...the dead weight of tradition.* N COUNT : USU SING

dead wood; often spelled as one word. People or things that have been used for a very long time and that are no longer useful can be referred to as **dead wood**. EG *Low profits gave the company an excuse to clean out the dead wood.* N UNCOUNT

deaf /dɛf/, **deafer, deafest. 1** Someone who is **deaf** is **1.1** unable to hear anything, especially because of illness or injury. EG *...a school for deaf children... I had an infection of the ears that made me deaf for some time.* ADJ CLASSIF ⇑ handicapped ◇ **deafness.** EG *They finally diagnosed her deafness when she was thirteen.* ◇ N UNCOUNT **1.2** unable to hear very well, especially because of old age. EG *He was very deaf and didn't like having to make conversation.* ADJ QUALIT = hard of hearing

2 The **deaf** are people who are completely or almost completely deaf. EG *She goes to a school for the deaf.* N PLURAL : *the*+N

3 If you say that someone is **as deaf as a post,** you mean that they are completely deaf or very deaf; an informal expression. PHR : USED AS AN A = stone deaf

4 If someone is **deaf** to something, they refuse to pay attention to it. EG *The headmaster was deaf to their complaints.* ADJ QUALIT : PRED+*to* ⇑ impervious

5 If you **turn a deaf ear** to something that someone says, you refuse to pay attention to it. EG *Young people sometimes seem to turn a deaf ear to the words of their anxious parents.* PHR : VB INFLECTS, IF+PREP THEN *to* ⇑ ignore

deaf-aid, deaf-aids; also spelled without a hyphen. A **deaf-aid** is a hearing aid; used in British English. N COUNT

deafen /dɛfə°n/, **deafens, deafening, deafened.** If you **are deafened** by a noise, it is so loud that you cannot hear anything else at the same time. EG *She was momentarily deafened by the din.* V+O : USU PASS ⇑ overpower ◇ **deafening.** EG *We were awakened by a deafening roar from outside... The noise was deafening.* ◇ ADJ CLASSIF = ear-splitting

deaf-mute, deaf-mutes; also spelled as two words. A **deaf-mute** is a person who is unable to hear or speak.
N COUNT

deal /diːl/, **deals, dealing, dealt. 1 A good deal** or **a great deal** of something is a lot of it. EG *There was a great deal of concern about energy shortages... They talked a great deal... We learnt a good deal from her.*
QUANTIF ⇑ quantity

2 A **deal** of something is a large amount of it; used in rather informal English. EG *We had a deal of trouble that day.*
QUANTIF = a lot

3 A **deal** is an agreement or arrangement that is made, especially in business. EG *It was probably the best business deal I ever did... If you do not come, I shall presume the deal is off.*
N COUNT = transaction

4 If you say that someone has a particular kind of **deal**, you mean that they are treated in that way or are in that position. For example, if they have a bad deal, they are unfortunate. EG *He has had a lousy deal out of life... She wrote books urging a new deal for women.* ● **a raw deal:** see **raw.**
N COUNT : ADJ+N ⇑ treatment

5 If you say **big deal**, you are letting people know that you do not think something is as important, interesting, or unusual as someone else thinks it is; an informal expression. EG *'I walked sixteen miles yesterday.'–'Big deal!'*
EXCLAM = so what

6 When you **deal** a blow to someone or something, you inflict it or give it. EG *The growth of modern industry had dealt a heavy blow to their way of life.*
V+O+O, OR V+O +A *(to)* = administer

7 Someone who is involved in drug **dealing** or who **deals** in illegal drugs sells them.
V : IF+PREP THEN *in*

8 When you **deal** playing cards, you give them out to the players in a game of cards. EG *He dealt them each six cards.*
V, V+O, V+O+O, OR V+O+A *(to)* ⇑ distribute

9 If it is your **deal** in a game of cards, it is your turn to deal the cards.
N SING : POSS+N ⇑ distribution

10 See also **dealings** and **wheeling and dealing.**

deal in. If a person, company, or shop **deals in** a particular type of goods, their business involves buying or selling those goods. EG *The shop deals only in trousers.*
PHRASAL VB : V+ PREP ⇑ trade = handle

deal out. 1 If you **deal out** something, especially a punishment, to someone, you inflict it on them. EG *Beatings and other cruelties were dealt out to those who had been captured.*
PHRASAL VB : V+ O+ADV, IF+ PREP THEN *to* = mete out

2 When you **deal out** playing cards, you give them out to the players in a game of cards.
PHRASAL VB : V+ O+ADV

deal with. 1 When you **deal with** something that needs attention, for example a situation or a problem, you do what is necessary to achieve the result you want. EG *They learned to deal with any sort of emergency... The Finance Officer deals with all the finances of the university.*
PHRASAL VB : V+ PREP, HAS PASS = handle

2 If a book, speech, film, etc **deals with** a particular thing, it has that thing as its subject or is concerned with it. EG *The film deals with a strange encounter between two soldiers.*
PHRASAL VB : V+ PREP, HAS PASS

3 If you **deal with** a particular person or organization, you have business relations with them. EG *I would never deal with that company on principle.*
PHRASAL VB : V+ PREP, HAS PASS ⇑ trade

dealer /diːlə/, **dealers. 1** A **dealer** is **1.1** a person or organization whose business involves buying and selling things. EG *By trade he was a dealer in antique furniture.*
N COUNT : USU+ SUPP ⇑ trader

1.2 someone who illegally sells drugs that are banned by law.
N COUNT

2 The **dealer** in a game of cards is the person who gives out the cards to the other players.
N COUNT

dealings /diːlɪŋz/. Someone's **dealings** with a person or organization are the relations that they have with them or the business that they do with them. EG *Ford insists that Carter's dealings with him have been totally correct... He was questioned about his past business dealings.*
N PLURAL : IF+ PREP THEN *with*

dealt /delt/ is the past tense and past participle of **deal.**

dean /diːn/, **deans.** A **dean** is **1** a university or college teacher who has administrative control over a large area of study such as science or arts and who often has special responsibility for the welfare and behaviour of students.
N COUNT

2 a priest in the Church of England and some other Christian churches who is the main administrator of a cathedral or large church.
N COUNT : ALSO IN TITLES

deanery /diːnəri[1]/, **deaneries. 1 Deanery** means connected with the responsibilities of a dean. EG *...diocesan and deanery affairs.*
N BEFORE N

2 A **deanery** is the place where a dean lives.
N COUNT

dear /dɪə/, **dearer, dearest; dears. 1** You call someone **dear** as a sign of affection. EG *If you want a drink, dear, you'll have to fix it yourself... How are you, dear?... What would you like, Shirley dear?*
N VOC = love

2 You address someone as 'my **dear** fellow', **'dear** girl', 'my **dear** Richard', etc when you know them and are fond of them. You can also use expressions like this in an arrogant way that indicates that you think you are superior to the person you are addressing. EG *My dear fellow, I really am sorry.*
ADJ CLASSIF : ATTRIB

3 Dear is usually written at the beginning of a letter, followed by the name or title of the person you are writing to. EG *'Dear Mr Jones,' he began... Dear Sir... Dear Mum, I was glad to get your letter, which arrived yesterday.*
ADJ CLASSIF : ATTRIB

4 Dear is used of someone or something that you think of with affection. EG *'Dear old Aunt Elizabeth,' she thought, 'she's never had much luck'... He's a dear friend and colleague of mine... ...a dear little mouse.*
ADJ CLASSIF : ATTRIB

5 You describe someone as a **dear** when you are fond of them and think that they are nice. EG *That old lady down the road is such a dear.*
N COUNT = love, pet

6 If something is **dear** to someone or **dear** to someone's heart, they care very deeply about it. EG *This cause is very dear to her heart... Sussex was very dear to him.*
ADJ QUALIT : PRED+*to* ⇑ precious

7 You say **dear, oh dear, dear me,** etc when you are sad, disappointed, or surprised about something. EG *Oh dear! That reminds me. I should have phoned him today... 'Dear, dear,' said Spence, 'it sounds rather like you did something very silly.'*
EXCLAM

8 Something that is **dear** costs a lot of money. EG *I can't afford it. It's too dear... Firewood is now getting dearer, as supplies dwindle.*
ADJ QUALIT : PRED = expensive ≠ cheap

9 If something that someone does **costs** them **dear,** they suffer a lot as a result of it.
PHR : VB INFLECTS

dearest /dɪərɪ[2]st/. **1** You call someone **dearest,** or use **dearest** if you are speaking about them, when you are very fond of them. EG *It's too late now, my dearest... Lynn, dearest, what are you saying?... ...my dearest Alan.*
N VOC, OR ADJ QUALIT : SUPERL, ATTRIB = darling

2 Dearest is used of something which is very important to you. EG *His dearest wish was to become a civil servant... The portrait is one of the Gallery's dearest treasures.* ● **nearest and dearest:** see **near.**
ADJ IN SUPERL

dearie /dɪəri[1]/; also spelled **deary. 1 Dearie** is used in informal English as a friendly or sometimes condescending form of address. EG *'Oh, come off it, dearie,' the man said... Shall I put these in your bag, dearie?*
N USED AS VOC = love

2 You say **dearie me** when you are sad, disappointed, or surprised about something; an informal expression.
EXCLAM

dearly /dɪəli[1]/. **1** If you love someone or something **dearly** or would **dearly** like to do or have something, you love them very much or would very much like to do or have it. EG *I loved him dearly... I dearly wish I had more money... ...Jennifer Talgarth, dearly beloved wife of Robert Talgarth.*
ADV WITH VB ⇑ greatly

2 If you **pay dearly** for doing something, you suffer a lot as a result of it. EG *He paid dearly for his mistake.*
PHR : VB INFLECTS

dearth /dɜːθ/. If there is a **dearth** of something, there is not enough of it. EG *There is a dearth of good children's plays.*
N SING WITH DET : IF+PREP THEN *of* = shortage

deary /dɪəri[1]/, **dearies.** See **dearie.**

death /deθ/, **deaths. 1 Death** is the permanent end of the life of a person or animal, when the heart stops beating and all other functions of the body and brain stop too. EG *After the death of her parents she went to live with her aunt... Different societies have different attitudes to life and death... He bled to death before anyone found him... What was the cause of death?* ● See also **brain death.**
N UNCOUNT ≠ birth

2 A **death** is the loss of a person's life. EG *The two deaths in the accident could have been prevented.*
N COUNT = fatality

3 A particular kind of **death** is a particular way of dying. EG *He died a most horrible death.*
N COUNT+SUPP ⇑ end

4 The **death** of something such as a custom or institution is the permanent end of it. EG *Will computers lead to the death of the printed word as we know it?*
N SING : *the*+N+ *of* ⇑ cessation

5 If someone is **at death's door,** they are very ill indeed.
PHR : USED AS AN A

6 If you warn someone that they will **catch** their **death** or **catch** their **death of cold,** for example when they are about to go out in cold, wet weather,
PHR : VB INFLECTS

you mean that they will be very cold and probably become very ill; an informal expression.

7 If you will **fight to the death** for something, you will do anything to achieve or preserve it, even if you suffer as a consequence. EG *He would fight to the death for a principle he believed in.* PHR : VB INFLECTS

8 A **fight to the death** is a fight or struggle which is intended to go on until one of the two people or groups involved is killed or defeated. PHR : USED AS C/O

9 If someone looks or feels **like death warmed up**, they look or feel very ill or tired; an informal expression. PHR : USED AS AN A

10 If someone or something **frightens, scares,** or **worries** you **to death**, they frighten, scare, or worry you very much. EG *He was frightened to death of his teacher.* PHR : VB INFLECTS ⇑ terrify

11 If you say that you are **sick to death** of something or **bored to death**, you mean that you feel very angry about it or very bored. EG *I'm sick to death of those kids.* PHR : USED AS C ⇑ fed up

12 If you **work** someone **to death**, you make them work very hard indeed. PHR : VB INFLECTS

13 If you say that someone **will be the death of** you, you mean that they repeatedly do things which upset you or which you disapprove of. PHR : AUX INFLECTS ⇑ annoy

14 If someone **is put to death**, they are executed. EG *...found guilty of treason and put to death.* PHR : VB INFLECTS

deathbed /dɛθbɛd/, **deathbeds**; also spelled with a hyphen and as two words. Someone's **deathbed** is the bed that they are lying in when they die or are about to die. EG *The whole family has been summoned to her death-bed.* ● If you do something **on** your **deathbed**, you do it as you are dying. EG *He repented on his death bed.* N COUNT, USU WITH POSS ● PHR : USED AS AN A

deathblow /dɛθbləʊ/; often spelled with a hyphen. A **deathblow** is an event or action which puts an end to something, for example a plan, an experiment, or someone's hopes. EG *The resignation of the two top people dealt a deathblow to the project.* N SING WITH DET : IF + PREP THEN *to*

death certificate, death certificates. A **death certificate** is an official certificate signed by a doctor which states the cause of a person's death. N COUNT

death duty, death duties; also spelled with a hyphen. **Death duties** are a tax which has to be paid on the money and property which belonged to someone who has died. N COUNT : USU PLURAL

death knell; also spelled with a hyphen. When you say that the **death knell** of a particular thing is tolling or being sounded, you mean that something has happened that means that it will end soon. EG *A diplomatic crisis would sound the death knell of any hopes of disarmament... ...the death knell of their way of life.* N SING : WITH *the*/POSS

deathly /dɛθli[1]/ means characteristic of a dead person in some way, for example as cold, pale, or quiet as a dead person. EG *He was deathly white... A deathly hush lay in the streets... Her feet were deathly cold.* ADJ CLASSIF : ATTRIB, OR ADV + ADJ

death mask, death masks; also spelled with a hyphen. A **death mask** is a model of someone's face, which is made soon after they have died by pressing wax over the face, allowing it to harden before removing it, and then using it as a mould. N COUNT ⇑ likeness

death penalty. The **death penalty** is the punishment of death used in some countries for people who have committed serious crimes such as murder. EG *The state of California has now abolished the death penalty.* N SING : *the*+N

death row is the part of a prison which contains the cells for criminals who have been sentenced to death; used in American English. N UNCOUNT

death sentence, death sentences. A **death sentence** is a punishment of death given by a judge to someone who has been found guilty of a serious crime such as murder. EG *He commuted two of the death sentences to life imprisonment.* N COUNT

death throes; also spelled with a hyphen. 1 **Death throes** are violent, uncontrolled movements which people sometimes make while they are dying, especially if they are suffering great pain. EG *His death throes were watched by his family.* N PLURAL ⇑ movements

2 The **death throes** of something are its final stages, just before it fails completely or ends. EG *The project was in its death throes.* N PLURAL

death toll, death tolls; also spelled with a hyphen. The **death toll** of an accident, disaster, or war is the number of people who die in it. EG *The death toll stood at 111 with nearly 200 more people still trapped.* N COUNT

death trap, death traps; also spelled with a hyphen. A place or vehicle that is a **death trap** is in such bad condition that it might cause someone's death. EG *These timber houses are an absolute death trap if they catch fire.* N COUNT ⇑ hazard

death warrant, death warrants; also spelled with a hyphen. 1 A **death warrant** is an official document which orders that someone is to be executed as a punishment for a crime. N COUNT

2 If you say that someone **is signing** their own **death warrant**, you mean that they are behaving in a way which will result in a lot of trouble for them and which might cause their ruin or death. EG *Using energy in this extravagant way is tantamount to signing our own death warrant.* PHR : VB INFLECTS

death-watch beetle, death-watch beetles. A **death-watch beetle** is a type of beetle that digs into wood, for example in old houses, and makes a tapping noise. N COUNT

death wish; also spelled with a hyphen. A **death wish** is a conscious or unconscious desire to die or be killed. N SING WITH DET

deb /dɛb/, **debs.** In Britain, a **deb** is a young woman from the upper or upper-middle classes who has started going to social events with other young people; an abbreviation for 'debutante'. N COUNT = debutante

debacle /deɪbɑːkə[0]l, dɪ-/, **debacles**; also spelled **débâcle**. A **debacle** is an event that is a complete failure because it has not been planned properly or because plans have gone wrong. EG *I couldn't afford to make the same mistake again after the debacle of the TV series... The year ended with the British and French debacle at Suez.* N COUNT = fiasco ≠ triumph

debar /di[1]bɑː/, **debars, debarring, debarred.** If you are **debarred** from doing something, you are prevented from doing it by a law or regulation; a formal word. EG *He was consistently debarred from attending the meetings.* V+O : IF + PREP THEN *from* = prohibit ≠ allow

debase /di[1]beɪs/, **debases, debasing, debased.**

1 To **debase** something means to reduce its value or quality. EG *The author creates an image of love that debases the emotion itself... The quality of life can only be debased by such a system.* V+O : USU PASS ⇑ devalue = degrade

2 If you **debase** yourself, you act in a way that is shameful or humiliating. EG *It's absurd for journalists to debase themselves in this way.* V+O (REFL) ⇑ degrade = shame, humiliate

debasement /di[1]beɪsmə[2]nt/ is the action of reducing the value or quality of something so that it is seen as worthless. EG *...the glorification of one race, and the consequent debasement of another.* N UNCOUNT ⇑ devaluation = degradation

debatable /di[1]beɪtəbə[0]l/. A statement or opinion that is **debatable** is not absolutely certain, because different people have different points of view about it. EG *It is debatable how many hungry people there are in the world... Many of his other assertions are highly debatable.* ADJ QUALIT ⇑ uncertain = questionable

debate /di[1]beɪt/, **debates, debating, debated.**

1 A **debate** is a discussion about a subject on which people have different views. EG *I think the debate between us about these difficult issues has been worthwhile... The treaty was signed after many days of intensive debate... ...the nuclear power debate now being conducted in Britain.* N COUNT

2 If a fact or statement is **in debate**, different people have different opinions about it. EG *The identity of the author of the letters is still in debate.* PHR : USED AS AN A ⇑ uncertain = in doubt

3 If you say that an idea is **open to debate**, you do not know whether it is true or not. EG *Whether he will be on time is open to debate.* PHR : USED AS C ⇑ uncertain = debatable

4 A **debate** is also a formal discussion, for example in a parliament, in which people express different opinions about a particular subject and then vote on it. EG *Will the U.N. debate on whaling accomplish anything?... He enjoyed spending his time in Parliament listening to debates.* N COUNT : IF + PREP THEN *on/over/about*

5 If people **debate** a topic, they discuss it fairly formally. EG *The meeting debated the motion that 'Murderers should be hanged'... She listened to him as he debated with his staff on the problems in the factory.* ◊ **debating.** EG *He learned the art of debating by discussing the issues of the day with his father.* ◊ **debated.** EG *The morality of war is a much debated subject.* V+O, OR V : IF + PREP THEN *with* ◊ N UNCOUNT ◊ ADJ CLASSIF : ATTRIB

6 If you **debate** what to do or whether to do something, you think or talk about possible courses V + REPORT-CL, OR V + -ING

of action before deciding exactly what you are going to do. EG *While I was debating what to do the phone rang... He turned round, debating whether to go back... He debated heating up the stew.*

debater /di¹beɪtə/, **debaters**. A **debater** is someone who takes part in a debate. EG *He's a brilliant debater, but has no strong principles.* — N COUNT

debauch /di¹bɔːtʃ/, **debauches, debauching, debauched**. To **debauch** someone means to influence them so that they become bad or corrupt, especially sexually; an old-fashioned or formal word. EG *She told me the way she had been debauched.* — V+O; = lead astray

debauched /di¹bɔːtʃt/. Someone who is **debauched** behaves in a way that is bad, corrupt, or not socially acceptable, for example because they drink a lot of alcohol or are sexually promiscuous; an old-fashioned word. EG *Americans find it difficult to accept the sort of debauched aristocratic society that Congreve draws.* — ADJ QUALIT; = depraved, degenerate

debauchery /di¹bɔːtʃəri¹/ is behaviour that is bad, corrupt, or not socially acceptable; used especially to refer to drunkenness and sexual promiscuity. EG *...eyes dull with debauchery.* — N UNCOUNT; ⇑ corruption; = decadence

debilitate /dɪ¹bɪlɪteɪt/, **debilitates, debilitating, debilitated**. **1** If something such as an illness **debilitates** you, it causes your body or mind to become gradually weaker. EG *You could end up totally debilitated.* — V+O; ⇑ weaken; = disable

◇ **debilitating**. EG *...the most debilitating and demoralizing of illnesses.* — ◇ ADJ QUALIT

2 To **debilitate** an organization or government means to make its authority or effect gradually weaker. — V+O; ⇑ weaken

◇ **debilitating**. EG *The Conservative Party feared a debilitating reform of the House of Lords.* — ◇ ADJ QUALIT

◇ **debilitated**. EG *...the shabby and debilitated economy which is this government's true memorial.* — ◇ ADJ QUALIT

debility /dɪ¹bɪlɪti¹/ is a weakness of a person's body or mind, especially one caused by an illness. EG *He affected a manner of extreme languor and debility... They say I have a nervous debility.* — N UNCOUNT : USU +SUPP; ≠ strength

debit /debɪt/, **debits, debiting, debited**. **1** If someone or something **debits** your bank account, money is taken from it in order to pay for something that you have bought or to repay money that you owe. EG *It will instantaneously debit the owner's account at a central computer.* — V+O; ≠ credit

2 A **debit** is a record of the money which is taken out of your bank account, for example when you write a cheque. EG *...an account that shows £300 on the debit side and £50 on the credit side.* — N COUNT; ≠ credit

debonair /debə⁷neə/. Someone who is **debonair** is pleasantly confident, charming, and well-dressed; used especially of men. EG *Boylan looked debonair and at ease.* — ADJ QUALIT; ≠ shabby, seedy

debrief /di¹briːf/, **debriefs, debriefing, debriefed**. If someone such as a soldier, diplomat, or astronaut is **debriefed**, they are asked to give a report on a mission or task that they have just completed. EG *When he returns to Mexico City he'll be debriefed by an officer from the Miami station.* — V+O : USU PASS; ⇑ interrogate; ≠ brief

◇ **debriefing**. EG *Prior arrangements are made for immediate debriefing at a safe site.* — ◇ N UNCOUNT

debris /deɪbri¹, debri¹/ is **1** a mass of pieces of bricks, metal, concrete, etc which are left after something large, such as a building or aeroplane, has been destroyed. EG *The General emerged from the debris and shook glass splinters from his lapel... ...an erupting storm throwing debris skyward at nearly one kilometre a second.* — N UNCOUNT; ⇑ wreckage; = rubble, detritus

2 a mass of loose stones and earth, sometimes including the remains of dead animals or plants. — N UNCOUNT

debt /det/, **debts**. **1** A **debt** is a sum of money that you owe someone. EG *You must spend less until your debts are paid off.* — N COUNT

2 If you **run up a debt** or **debts**, you have borrowed money. EG *He had run up more debts for food supplies.* — PHR : VB INFLECTS

3 Debt is the state of owing money. EG *The new motorway was financed by increasing government debt.* — N UNCOUNT

4 If you are **in debt** or get **into debt**, you owe money. EG *Father had been heavily in debt for a long time... He spent more and more money, getting deeper and deeper into debt.* — PHR : USED AS AN A; ⇑ owing; ≠ in credit

5 If you are **out of debt**, you no longer owe money to anyone. EG *I was out of debt for the first time in seven years... Scott's novels were written to get him out of debt.* — PHR : USED AS AN A; ≠ in debt

6 A **debt** is also a feeling of gratitude towards someone for something that they have done for you, and a feeling that you owe them something. EG *He repaid his debt of gratitude to Jane by helping her mother... We owe a debt to the Royal Shakespeare Company for its magnificent production of 'King Lear'.* — N COUNT : USU SING

7 If you are **in** someone's **debt**, you are grateful to them for something that they have done for you, and you feel that you must do something for them in return; a formal expression. EG *We are in your debt, Dr Marlowe.* — PHR : USED AS AN A; = indebted

debtor /detə/, **debtors**. A **debtor** is a person who owes money. — N COUNT; ≠ creditor

debug /di¹bʌg/, **debugs, debugging, debugged**. When you **debug** a computer program, you look for the faults in it and correct them so that it will run properly. EG *Alan spent hours debugging the program.* — V+O; ⇑ rectify; = put right

debunk /diːbʌŋk/, **debunks, debunking, debunked**. If you **debunk** an idea or belief, you show that it is false or not important. EG *Later he spent years debunking spiritualists.* — V+O; ⇑ criticize; = ridicule

debut /deɪbjuː, debjuː/, **debuts**. The **debut** of a singer, musician, footballer, etc is their first public performance or recording. EG *It was a Wagner opera with which you made your debut, wasn't it?... Joan Armatrading made her debut album in 1973.* — N COUNT; ⇑ launch; ≠ swan song

debutante /debjə⁴tɑːnt, -tænt/, **debutantes**. In Britain, a **debutante** is a young woman from the upper or upper-middle classes who has started going to social events with other young people; an old-fashioned word. EG *...rich playboys and debutantes.* — N COUNT; = deb

Dec. is an abbreviation for December.

decade /dekeɪd, dɪ²keɪd/, **decades**. A **decade** is a period of ten years. Decades usually begin with years ending in 0, for example 1980 to 1989. EG *Natural gas was very important a decade or so ago... By the end of the decade he had acquired international notoriety... ...the 1970s, designated the decade of disarmament by the United Nations.* — N COUNT

decadence /dekədə²ns/ is the state of living or behaving in a way that shows lower standards, especially lower moral standards, than in a previous time; used showing disapproval. EG *...the indubitable decadence of the professional Fine Art tradition.* — N UNCOUNT

decadent /dekədə²nt/. If you say that someone or something is **decadent**, you mean that they have low standards, especially low moral standards; used showing disapproval. EG *The gaudy casinos seemed even more decadent.* — ADJ QUALIT

decaffeinated /di¹kæfə¹neɪtɪ²d/. **Decaffeinated** coffee has had most of the caffeine removed from it. — ADJ CLASSIF : USU ATTRIB

decamp /di¹kæmp/, **decamps, decamping, decamped**. If you **decamp**, you go away from somewhere secretly or suddenly. EG *I came home to find Nell and Caro had decamped to Wytham without warning.* — V : IF+PREP THEN *to/from*; ⇑ leave; = abscond

decant /dɪ²kænt/, **decants, decanting, decanted**. If you **decant** wine, sherry, etc, you pour it slowly from its bottle into another container before serving it. EG *She decanted some vintage port.* — V+O

decanter /dɪ²kæntə/, **decanters**. A **decanter** is a glass bottle or jug that you use for serving wine, sherry, etc. — N COUNT

decapitate /di¹kæpɪteɪt/, **decapitates, decapitating, decapitated**. To **decapitate** someone means to kill them by cutting off their head; a formal word. — V+O : USU PASS; = behead

decapitation /di¹kæpɪteɪʃə⁰n/ is the cutting off of someone's head; a formal word. EG *The poor were hanged, but the wealthy were entitled to death by decapitation.* — N UNCOUNT; ⇑ execution; = beheading

decathlon /dɪ²kæθlə⁷n/, **decathlons**. A **decathlon** is a sporting competition in which athletes compete in 10 different sporting events. EG *...Daley Thompson, winner of the decathlon in the 1984 Olympics.* — N COUNT

decay /dɪ²keɪ/, **decays, decaying, decayed**. **1** When something such as a plant, a piece of wood, or a piece of meat **decays**, it becomes rotten and unusable. EG *The cabbages had already started to decay.* — V; ⇑ rot; = decompose

▸ used as a noun. EG *Dental decay in children in Britain has almost reached epidemic levels.* — ▸ N UNCOUNT

◇ **decayed**. EG *Badly decayed timber should be cut out and replaced.* — ◇ ADJ QUALIT

◇ **decaying**. EG *...a smell of decaying meat.* — ◇ ADJ CLASSIF : ATTRIB

2 If something such as a social or political institution — V

decays, it gradually becomes weaker or more corrupt. EG *The human world, being what it is, could only decay in the course of time.* ▸ used as a noun. EG *The fabric of modern society is no more immune from decay than were its predecessors... ...creeping political decay.* ◇ **decaying**. EG *...the decaying centres of Europe's big industrial cities.* ▸ N UNCOUNT ⇑ disintegration ◇ ADJ CLASSIF : ATTRIB

decease /di'siːs/. Someone's **decease** is their death; a legal term. EG *Upon your decease the capital will pass to your grandchildren.* N SING : WITH POSS

deceased /di'siːst/. 1 The **deceased** is used to refer to a particular person who has recently died; a legal term, also used in formal English. EG *It appeared that the deceased had increased his life insurance shortly before the accident.* N SING : the+N

2 A **deceased** person is one who has recently died; used in formal English. EG *The relatives of the deceased couple have been notified by the Police.* ADJ CLASSIF = dead ≠ living

deceit /dɪsiːt/ is behaviour that is deliberately intended to make people believe something which is not true. EG *It was then that I acquired the habit of deceit.* N UNCOUNT/COUNT ⇑ dishonesty = duplicity ≠ frankness

deceitful /dɪsiːtful/. Someone who is **deceitful** behaves in a dishonest way by making other people believe something that is not true. EG *We are, in a sense, being deceitful, but we cannot be said to be lying.* ▸ used of people's behaviour. EG *There was nothing wrong or deceitful in the spirit of her words.* ◇ **deceitfully**. EG *She had deceitfully lured the military commandant to her house.* ◇ **deceitfulness**. EG *...yet another example of his deceitfulness.* ADJ QUALIT = sly, misleading ≠ truthful ▸ = devious ◇ ADV WITH VB ◇ N UNCOUNT

deceive /dɪsiːv/, **deceives, deceiving, deceived**. 1 If you **deceive** someone, you make them believe something that is not true, usually in order to get some advantage for yourself. EG *In my experience litigants nearly always deceive their solicitors... She deceived me into coming here.* V+O : IF+PREP THEN *into* ⇑ mislead = fool

2 If you **deceive** yourself, you do not admit to yourself something that you know is true. EG *They try to deceive themselves that everything is all right... I have never deceived myself about the merits of my work.* V+O (REFL) ⇑ mislead = delude

3 If something **deceives** you, it gives you a wrong impression and makes you believe something that is not true. EG *There was a haggard look about his eyes which did not deceive Doctor Chevington.* V+O ⇑ mislead = fool

decelerate /diːsɛləreɪt/, **decelerates, decelerating, decelerated**. When a vehicle or machine **decelerates** or when someone in a vehicle **decelerates**, they begin to gradually go slower. EG *He decelerated as he came to the corner.* ◇ **deceleration** /di'sɛləreɪʃə⁰n/. EG *The jets begin their gentle but steady deceleration.* V ⇑ slow ≠ accelerate ◇ N UNCOUNT ⇑ decrease

December /di'sɛmbə/ is the twelfth and last month of the year in the Western calendar. EG *We gave quite a big party early in December.* N UNCOUNT

decency /diːsə⁰nsi'/, **decencies**. 1 **Decency** is 1.1 the quality of being sensible and following accepted moral standards. EG *They tried to restore some sense and decency to the Administration.* 1.2 behaviour that shows kindness and generosity towards people. EG *They were full of kindness and decency to each other.* N UNCOUNT ⇑ respectability = propriety N UNCOUNT ⇑ goodness = honesty

2 If you say that someone did not **have the decency** to do something, you mean that there was a particular action which they did not do but which you believe that they ought to have done. EG *Why hadn't they had the decency to ask him if he'd like to join in?* PHR : VB INFLECTS

3 The **decencies** are the standards of behaviour that people think are acceptable; a formal use. EG *Picasso seemed to lack a sense of the artistic decencies proper to an old man.* N PLURAL = proprieties

decent /diːsə⁰nt/. 1 **Decent** is used to describe something which is 1.1 considered to be of an acceptable standard or quality. EG *...decent wages... They are incapable of expressing themselves in decent English... It was several weeks before I got a decent night's rest.* ◇ **decently**. EG *The farm animals are decently treated, decently fed, and killed as humanely as possible.* 1.2 morally correct or acceptable. EG *I would get her back as soon as a decent amount of time had elapsed after the wedding.* ◇ **decently**. EG *They only want the chance to live their lives decently.* ADJ QUALIT ⇑ reasonable = proper ◇ ADV WITH VB = reasonably ADJ CLASSIF : USU ATTRIB = respectable ◇ ADV = respectably

2 If you **do the decent thing**, you do something which you do not really want to do, but which you feel morally obliged to do. EG *The union concerned may expect you to do the decent thing and become a member of it.* PHR : VB INFLECTS

3 Someone who is **decent** is honest and behaves in a way that most people approve of. EG *You have the loyal support of all decent people.* ADJ QUALIT : ATTRIB = upright

4 If you say that something is **decent** of someone, you mean that they have done something that is useful or helpful to you; a fairly informal use. EG *It was jolly decent of him to think of me.* ADJ QUALIT : PRED+*of* ⇑ good = nice

5 If someone is **decent**, they are wearing enough clothes so that they will not feel embarrassed if people see them; often used humorously. EG *You can't come in yet, I'm not decent!* ADJ CLASSIF : PRED ⇑ dressed ≠ nude

decentralize /di'sɛntrəlaɪz/, **decentralizes, decentralizing, decentralized**; also spelled **decentralise**. To **decentralize** a large organization means to move some departments or branches away from a central administrative area to other places around the country. EG *He wanted to decentralise and diversify the BBC.* ◇ **decentralized**. EG *...a decentralized regime.* ◇ **decentralization** /di'sɛntrəlaɪzeɪʃə⁰n/. EG *They promised decentralization of local government within 5 years.* V+O ⇑ change ≠ centralize ◇ ADJ CLASSIF ◇ N UNCOUNT

deception /di'sɛpʃə⁰n/, **deceptions**. 1 A **deception** is something that you say or do which is intended to deceive people. EG *He would quickly have seen through Mary's deceptions... You must forgive my little deception.* N COUNT ⇑ ruse = trick

2 **Deception** is the act of deceiving someone or the state of being deceived by someone. N UNCOUNT

deceptive /di'sɛptɪv/. If something is **deceptive**, it encourages you to believe something which is not true. EG *Beth knew that its fragile appearance was deceptive.* ◇ **deceptively**. EG *It all looks deceptively simple.* ADJ QUALIT ⇑ seeming = misleading ◇ ADV

deci- is added to the beginning of nouns referring to measurements in order to form nouns meaning one-tenth as large. For example, a decilitre is one-tenth of a litre. PREFIX

decibel /dɛsɪbɛl/, **decibels**. A **decibel** is a unit of measurement which describes how loud a sound is. EG *A new airport, with its high decibel levels and pollutants, may still be constructed here.* N COUNT

decide /di'saɪd/, **decides, deciding, decided**. 1 If you **decide** to do something, you choose to do it, usually after you have thought carefully about the other possibilities. EG *What made you decide to get married?... 'Where are you going on holiday this year?'-'I don't know, I can't decide.'... She decided that she would leave her money to him... He has a month to decide whether he's going to stay... I'm glad you decided against a career as a waiter.* V : USU+A/REPORT-CL/*to*-INF = make up one's mind

2 If something **decides** you to do something, it is the reason that causes you to choose to do it. EG *It was this which finally decided me to come to India... What decided you against a career in journalism?* V+O : USU+A/REPORT-CL/*to*-INF ⇑ convince = persuade

3 If a person or group of people **decides** something, they choose what something should be like or how a particular problem should be solved. EG *The case is to be decided by the International Court.* V+O ⇑ determine = decree

4 If an event or fact **decides** something, it makes it certain that a particular choice will be made or that there will be a particular result. EG *Charlton's goal decided the match... It was the mention of possible profits that decided the issue... I suppose that shouldn't be a deciding factor.* V+O ⇑ resolve = settle

5 If you **decide** that something is true, you form that opinion about it after considering the facts. EG *He decided that the doorbell was broken... I can't decide whether I like him or not.* V+REPORT-CL ⇑ conclude

decide on. If you **decide on** or **upon** something, you choose it from two or more possibilities. EG *He decided on a career in the army.* PHRASAL VB : V+PREP, HAS PASS = settle for

decided /di'saɪdɪ²d/. 1 **Decided** means very obvious and noticeable. EG *He thought that their plan held very decided dangers.* ADJ QUALIT : ATTRIB = definite ≠ possible

2 If you hold **decided** views about something, you have very strong and definite opinions about it. EG *She has very decided views on abortion.* ADJ QUALIT ⇑ emphatic ≠ vague

decidedly /di'saɪdɪ²dli'/. 1 **Decidedly** means to a great extent and in a way that is very obvious. EG *The men looked decidedly uncomfortable.* ADV+ADJ/ADV ⇑ extremely = distinctly

2 If you say something **decidedly**, you say it in a way that lets people know that you have strong views about something and are unlikely to change your ADV WITH VB ⇑ emphatically

mind. EG *'It's time things were altered,' said Mrs Moffat decidedly.*

deciduous /di'sɪdju:əs/. A tree or bush that is **deciduous** loses its leaves in the autumn every year. ADJ CLASSIF ≠ evergreen

decimal /dɛsɪmə⁰l/, **decimals**. 1 A **decimal** system involves counting in units of ten. EG *It worked on the decimal rather than the binary system... ...the new decimal currency.* ADJ CLASSIF: ATTRIB

2 A **decimal** is a fraction that is written in the form of a dot followed by one or more numbers which represent tenths, hundredths, and so on: for example .5, .51, .517. EG *By the age of eleven, children should know what percentages are and what decimals are.* N COUNT

decimalize /dɛsə'məlaɪz/, **decimalizes, decimalizing, decimalized**; also spelled **decimalise**. To **decimalize** something such as a money system means to change it to a decimal system. V+O
◇ **decimalization** /dɛsə'mə⁰laɪzeɪʃə⁰n/. EG *Many old people were confused by decimalization.* ◇ N UNCOUNT

decimal point, decimal points. A **decimal point** is the dot that separates the whole part of a number from its decimal parts. EG *All you have to do is move the decimal point one digit to the left.* N COUNT

decimate /dɛsɪmeɪt/, **decimates, decimating, decimated**. To **decimate** something such as a group of people or animals means to destroy a very large number of them. EG *The war cost millions of lives and decimated three generations... Last year's freezing weather decimated our bird population.* V+O = wipe out, annihilate
◇ **decimation** /dɛsɪmeɪʃə⁰n/. EG *There are indications of the decimation of several species.* ◇ N UNCOUNT+of

decipher /di'saɪfə/, **deciphers, deciphering, deciphered**. If you **decipher** a piece of writing or a message, you work out what it says, even though it is very difficult to read or understand. EG *Archaeologists laboured to decipher the clay tablets.* V+O = decode

decision /di'sɪʒə⁰n/, **decisions**. 1 A **decision** is a choice that you make about what you think should be done or about which is the best of various alternatives. EG *I think that I made the wrong decision... The actual investment decisions are taken by boards of directors... Shortly afterwards the government announced its decision on the future of the railways.* N COUNT: IF+PREP THEN *on/about*

2 **Decision** is 2.1 the act of deciding something or the need to decide something. EG *Philip laced up his shoes slowly, delaying the moment of decision... The burden of decision lies on her shoulders.* N UNCOUNT ⇑ choice 2.2 the ability to decide quickly and definitely what to do. EG *The examiner felt that his driving lacked concentration and decision... He pulled on his coat with decision and stepped out into the storm.* N UNCOUNT ⇑ resolution = decisiveness

decision-making is the process of or the responsibility for making decisions, especially in a large organization or in government. EG *They set up a workers' co-operative, where decision-making was shared by all... Pensioners should be involved in all decision-making which affects them... ...the decision-making process.* N UNCOUNT ⇑ management

decisive /di'saɪsɪv/. 1 If a fact, action, or event is **decisive**, it makes it certain that a particular choice will be made or that there will be a particular result. EG *Three factors had a decisive influence on the paper's editorial policy... The government fought two decisive battles against the miners' union.* ADJ CLASSIF ⇑ crucial = conclusive ≠ inconclusive
◇ **decisively**. EG *She defended her seat and was decisively re-elected in the general election.* ◇ ADV WITH VB

2 If someone is **decisive**, they have or show an ability to make quick decisions in a difficult or complicated situation. EG *He isn't decisive enough to be a good leader.* ADJ QUALIT ⇑ positive ≠ hesitant ◇ **decisively**. EG *'That's a job for Peter,' she said decisively.* ◇ ADV WITH VB ◇ **decisiveness**. EG *Will he ever learn to show decisiveness at work?* ◇ N UNCOUNT

deck /dɛk/, **decks, decking, decked**. 1 A **deck** on a ship, bus, or other vehicle is a downstairs or upstairs area on it. EG *I made my way to the upper deck... They got on the bus and sat on the top deck.* N COUNT ⇑ floor

2 The **deck** of a ship is the top part of it that forms a floor in the open air which you can walk on. EG *The spray blew all over the deck... I'm going back up on deck...* N SING: *the*+N, OR *on*+N ● **Below decks** means the part of a ship that is underneath the deck. EG *The captain was asleep in a bunk below decks.* ● PHR: USED AS AN A

3 The **deck** on a record player is the part that includes the revolving disc on which you place the records. EG *They stole books, records, stereo deck, the lot.* N COUNT

4 A **deck** of cards is a pack of playing cards. EG *He took out his deck of cards and shuffled them.* N COUNT

5 If you **clear the decks**, you finish the work that you are doing and put everything away so that you are ready for the next job; an informal expression. PHR: VB INFLECTS

6 If you **hit the deck**, you fall to the ground; an informal expression. PHR: VB INFLECTS

7 If you **deck** something or someone, you decorate them with pretty or unusual things; an old-fashioned word. EG *He decked the room with streamers.* V+O+A *(with)* ⇑ adorn = festoon

deck out. If you **deck** something or someone **out**, you decorate them or make them look attractive, for example for a special occasion. EG *The exhibition hall was decked out with flowers... I decked myself out in a suit and tie.* PHRASAL VB: V+O+ADV, USU PASS +A *(in/with)* ⇑ adorn = dress up

deckchair /dɛktʃɛə/, **deckchairs**. A **deckchair** is a light folding chair with a wooden frame and a canvas seat. Deckchairs are used mainly in the garden, at the seaside, or on a ship. N COUNT ⇑ chair

-decker is used after adjectives like 'single' and 'double' to indicate how many levels or floors something has. For example, a single-decker bus has only one floor, and a double-decker sandwich is made of three layers of bread with two layers of filling between them. COMB: FORMS NOUNS OR ADJ CLASSIFS

deckhand /dɛkhænd/, **deckhands**. A **deckhand** is a person who does the cleaning and other work on the deck of a ship. EG *He worked as a deckhand on the lake steamers.* N COUNT ⇑ seaman

declaim /di'kleɪm/, **declaims, declaiming, declaimed**. If you **declaim**, you speak dramatically, as if you were acting in a theatre. EG *'I am a true patriot,' he declaimed.* V, OR V+O/REPORT-CL/QUOTE = declare

declamatory /di'klæmətə⁰rɪ/. Something that is **declamatory** is spoken dramatically, as if in a theatre; also used of a dramatic style of writing. EG *The style is often declamatory and repetitive.* ADJ QUALIT ⇑ forceful = theatrical

declaration /dɛkləreɪʃə⁰n/, **declarations**. A **declaration** is 1 a firm, emphatic statement which shows that you have no doubts about what you are saying. EG *The Prime Minister faced the electorate with the declaration that inflation would be halved in two years... He seemed to be embarrassed by her declaration of love.* N COUNT: USU+REPORT-CL/*of* 2 an official announcement or statement. EG *They gave a press conference the day after the declaration was signed... ...formal declarations of war... ...the Declaration of Independence.* N COUNT: IF+PREP THEN *of* 3 a written statement about something which you have signed and which can be used as evidence in a court of law. EG *She signed the declaration on the form.* N COUNT

declaratory /di'klærətə⁰ri¹/. If something is **declaratory**, it states things firmly and often with some authority. EG *...the declaratory tone of the editorial.* ADJ QUALIT ⇑ firm

declare /di'klɛə/, **declares, declaring, declared**. 1 If you **declare**, you say something firmly and in a way that shows that you believe it is true. EG *Never before in her life, she declared, had she tasted such food as this... They were heard to declare that they would never steal again.* V+REPORT-CL/QUOTE = announce, assert

2 If you **declare** an attitude or intention, you make it known to other people by expressing it clearly. EG *He declared his intention to fight the election... The Labour Party declared its support for the Campaign for Nuclear Disarmament.* V+O ⇑ say = proclaim, state

3 If you **declare** yourself as having a particular attitude or intention, you state clearly that you have this attitude or intention. EG *He declared himself strongly in favour of the action we were taking.* V+O (REFL)+C = profess

4 If you **declare** something, you state officially that it exists or is the case. EG *War was declared on the enemy... The government declared a state of emergency... At his trial he was declared innocent... The clerk declared her duly elected to the committee.* V+O, V+O+C, OR V+REPORT-CL ⇑ announce

5 If you **declare** goods that you have bought abroad or money that you have earned, you say how much you have bought or earned so that you can pay tax on it. EG *'Have you anything to declare?'-'No, nothing'.* V+O

6 If you say **'Well, I declare'**, you are letting people know that you are surprised at something; an old-fashioned expression. EXCLAM = goodness me

declare against. If you **declare against** something, you say that you are opposed to it. EG *They have declared against all war.* PHRASAL VB: V+PREP ⇑ state = oppose

declare for. If you **declare for** something, you say that you are in favour of it. EG *A small group declared for the king.* PHRASAL VB: V+PREP = support

declassify /di:klæsə'faɪ/, **declassifies, declassifying, declassified.** If information or documents **are declassified**, it has been officially stated that they are no longer secret. EG *Most cabinet papers are declassified after thirty years.* ◊ **declassification** /di:klæsə'fə'keɪʃə'n/. — V+O : USU PASS ⇑ reveal = release ≠ classify; ◊ N UNCOUNT

decline /di'klaɪn/, **declines, declining, declined.** 1 If something **declines**, it becomes less in quantity, importance, or strength. EG *The number of congress members declined from 371 to 361... In that one month, the crime rate sharply declined... Since 1971 the party's influence has declined.* ◊ **declining.** EG *...a country with an ever-increasing population and a steadily declining income per head... ...a sign of Britain's declining power.* — V ⇑ decrease = diminish ≠ increase; ◊ ADJ CLASSIF : ATTRIB ⇑ decreasing

2 If you **decline** something or **decline** to do something, you politely refuse to accept it or do it; a fairly formal word. EG *He has declined the invitation... Mr Santos declined to comment on the news... When he asked me to dance, I declined politely.* — V, V+O, OR V+ to-INF

3 **Decline** is the condition or process of becoming less in quantity, importance, or quality. EG *The loosening of family ties has led to the decline of respect and belief in authority... There is a discernible decline in confidence... The city's population is in decline.* — N UNCOUNT/ COUNT : USU SING ⇑ decrease ≠ increase

4 If something is **on the decline**, it is gradually decreasing in importance or becoming less powerful. EG *Many forms of organized religion seem to be on the decline.* — PHR : USED AS AN A

5 If something goes or falls **into decline**, it begins to become gradually less important, less strong, or less powerful. EG *After the war, the British ship-building industry fell into decline.* — PHR : USED AS AN A

decode /di:kəʊd/, **decodes, decoding, decoded.** 1 If you **decode** a message that has been written or spoken in a code, you change it into ordinary language. EG *The last word of the message, when it was decoded, read 'goodbye'.* — V+O ⇑ translate = decipher

2 If you **decode** a word which is unfamiliar to you, you learn and understand its meaning. — V+O

décolletage /deɪkɒltɑ:ʒ/. If you refer to a woman's **décolletage**, you are referring to a very low neckline on her dress or blouse. — N SING : USU POSS +N

décolleté /deɪkɒlteɪ/, **décolletés**; also spelled **décolletée.** If you refer to a woman's **décolleté**, you are referring to the fact that she is wearing a dress or blouse with a very low neckline that does not cover her shoulders. ▸ used as an adjective to describe a dress or blouse like this. EG *...a yellowish décolleté lace blouse.* — N COUNT; ▸ ADJ CLASSIF ⇑ revealing

decolonize /di:kɒlənaɪz/, **decolonizes, decolonizing, decolonized**; also spelled **decolonise.** To **decolonize** a country that was formerly a colony means to give it political independence. EG *We believe that these countries should be decolonized.* ◊ **decolonization** /di:kɒlənaɪzeɪʃə'n/. EG *Some African leaders wanted radical decolonization.* — V+O ⇑ release ≠ colonize; ◊ N UNCOUNT

decompose /di:kə'mpəʊz/, **decomposes, decomposing, decomposed.** If something that has died **decomposes**, it changes chemically and begins to rot. EG *...thousands of bodies everywhere, decomposing, putrefying.* — V ⇑ decay = rot

decomposition /di:kɒmpəzɪʃə'n/ is the process of rotting that takes place when living matter dies and changes chemically. — N UNCOUNT ⇑ decay

decompression /di:kə'mpreʃə'n/ is 1 the reduction of the force on something that is caused by the weight of the air. 2 the process of bringing someone back to the normal pressure of the air after they have been underwater and under greater pressure. EG *...a decompression chamber.* — N UNCOUNT; N UNCOUNT

decongestant /di:kə'ndʒestənt/, **decongestants.** A **decongestant** is a medicine which helps someone who has a cold to breathe more easily. — N COUNT

decontaminate /di:kəntæmɪneɪt/, **decontaminates, decontaminating, decontaminated.** To **decontaminate** something means to clean it by removing all radioactivity, germs, dangerous substances, etc. EG *The boat was decontaminated several times.* ◊ **decontamination** /di:kəntæmə'neɪʃə'n/. EG *...teams of observers and decontamination experts.* — V+O ≠ contaminate; ◊ N UNCOUNT ⇑ purification

decor /deɪkɔ:/. The **decor** of a house, room, or stage is the way in which it is furnished and decorated. EG *...a richly sumptuous example of eighteenth-century decor.* — N UNCOUNT : USU +SUPP ⇑ decoration

decorate /dekə'reɪt/, **decorates, decorating, decorated.** 1 If you **decorate** something, you make it more attractive by adding some kind of ornament to it. EG *The walls of her bedroom were decorated with pictures of popstars.* — V+O ⇑ improve = adorn

2 If you **decorate** a building or room, you put new paint or wallpaper on the walls, ceiling, and woodwork. EG *...a newly decorated room.* ◊ **decorating.** EG *She was working on the house, doing decorating and minor repairs.* — V OR V+O ⇑ improve; ◊ N UNCOUNT

3 If someone **is decorated**, they are given a medal or other honour as an official reward for something that they have done. EG *He was decorated with the George Cross.* — V+O : USU PASS

decoration /dekə'reɪʃə'n/, **decorations.** 1 **Decoration** is 1.1 a particular feature that is added to something in order to make it look more attractive. EG *...nightdresses that are white and plain, free of all decoration... They put Christmas decorations up all around the house.* 1.2 the way a room or building looks, especially with regard to its furniture, wallpaper, and ornaments. EG *Her house had the style of decoration typical of the 1920s... I like the interior decorations.* — N UNCOUNT/ COUNT; N UNCOUNT/ COUNT = decor

2 A **decoration** is something, such as a medal, which is given to someone as an official honour or reward. — N COUNT = award

decorative /dekə'rətɪv/. Something that is **decorative** is intended to look pretty or attractive. EG *...decorative objects... Our costumes for the play were impressive and decorative, though uncomfortable.* — ADJ QUALIT ⇑ beautiful = ornamental

decorator /dekəreɪtə/, **decorators.** A **decorator** is a person who paints houses or puts wallpaper on the walls, usually as a job. • See also **interior decorator.** — N COUNT ⇑ worker

decorous /dekə'rəs/. Behaviour that is **decorous** is very polite and calm and does not offend people. EG *He gave his wife a decorous kiss.* ◊ **decorously.** EG *...teenage lovers strolling decorously.* — ADJ QUALIT ⇑ correct = demure; ◊ ADV

decorum /dɪ'kɔ:rəm/ is behaviour that people consider to be correct and polite; a fairly formal word. EG *Your sense of decorum may be shocked by this.* — N UNCOUNT = propriety ≠ impropriety

decoy /di:kɔɪ/, **decoys, decoying, decoyed.** 1 A **decoy** is 1.1 an object or trick that is used to lead someone or something away from where they intended to go, especially so that you can catch them or kill them. EG *Then the soldiers began to chase the decoys down to the place of ambush.* 1.2 a model of a bird that is used to attract wild birds towards it so that people can study them or shoot them. — N COUNT ⇑ diversion = bait, dummy; N COUNT ⇑ dummy

2 If you **decoy** someone or something, you lead them away from where they intended to go by means of a trick, especially so that you can catch them or kill them. EG *Eight of the missiles were decoyed away from targets.* — V+O+A ⇑ divert = lure

decrease /di'kri:s/, **decreases, decreasing, decreased.** 1 When something **decreases** or when you **decrease** it, it becomes less in quantity, size, or strength. EG *Over a seven-year period the number of marriages has decreased by forty percent... Physiologists in Paris found they could decrease the size and activity of the prostate gland.* — V-ERG ⇑ change = diminish, lessen ≠ increase

2 A **decrease** is the process of something becoming less in quantity, size, or strength, or the amount by which it becomes less. EG *The decrease in size was gradual... ...the decrease in the bank rate from 7% to 5.5%.* — N COUNT, IF + PREP THEN *in/of* ⇑ change = reduction ≠ increase

decreasing /di'kri:sɪŋ/. Something that is **decreasing** is growing less in quantity, size, or strength. EG *It was a life of increasing labour and decreasing leisure.* ◊ **decreasingly.** EG *The parliamentary forum becomes a decreasingly effective democratic institution.* — ADJ CLASSIF : ATTRIB ⇑ changing ≠ increasing; ◊ ADV+ADJ = less and less

decree /di'kri:/, **decrees, decreeing, decreed.** 1 If someone **decrees** that something must happen, they decide or state this officially. EG *The minister decreed that there should be a full investigation.* — V+REPORT-CL = rule

2 A **decree** is 2.1 an official order or decision, especially one made by a king, queen, or other ruler. 2.2 a judgement made by a law court; used especially in American English. — N COUNT = edict; N COUNT ⇑ ruling

decree absolute, decrees absolute. A **decree absolute** is the final order made by a court in a divorce case which ends a marriage completely. — N COUNT : USU SING

decree nisi /di'kri: naɪsaɪ/, **decrees nisi.** A **decree nisi** is an order made by a court which states that a divorce must take place at a certain time in — N COUNT : USU SING the future unless a good reason is produced to prevent this.

decrepit /di'krεpɪt/. Something that is **decrepit** is very old and in bad condition. EG *...the jagged shapes of the decrepit houses opposite.* ADJ CLASSIF = ramshackle

decrepitude /di'krεpɪtju:d/ is the state of being very old and in bad condition; a formal word. EG *...in the late stages of decrepitude and decay.* N UNCOUNT ⇑ age = ruin

decry /di'kraɪ/, **decries, decrying, decried.** If you **decry** something such as an idea or someone's action, you condemn it; a fairly formal word. EG *They are always decrying the people who govern Scotland from Westminster.* V+O = denounce ≠ support

dedicate /dεdɪkeɪt/, **dedicates, dedicating, dedicated.** 1 If you **dedicate** yourself to something, you decide to give a lot of time and effort to it because you think that it is important. EG *She dedicated herself to the anti-nuclear movement.* V+O (REFL)+A (to) ⇑ devote = commit

2 If you **dedicate** something such as a book, play, or piece of music to someone, you mention their name, for example in the front of a book or when a play or piece of music is performed, as a way of showing affection or respect for them. EG *She dedicated her first book to her sister... The next record is dedicated to Bill, who lives in Croydon.* V+O+A (to)

3 When people **dedicate** a church or other public building to a particular person or group of people, they have a formal ceremony to show that the building will always be associated with that person or group. EG *St George's Chapel is dedicated to the dead of 1914-18.* V+O

dedicated /dεdɪkeɪtɪ²d/. 1 If you are **dedicated** to something, you believe that it is right and worthwhile, and give a lot of time and effort to it. EG *...people dedicated to social or political change... He was dedicated to his job.* ADJ QUALIT+to ⇑ devoted = committed

2 Someone who is **dedicated** works very hard at something such as their job, or believes strongly in the importance of a particular ideal. EG *...a dedicated surgeon... They are both dedicated vegetarians.* ADJ QUALIT ⇑ devoted = committed

dedication /dεdɪkeɪʃə⁰n/, **dedications.** 1 If you show **dedication** to something, you show deep interest in it or put a lot of energy into it, because you believe it is important, right, or worthwhile. EG *I admired her dedication... ...their dedication to social work.* N UNCOUNT ⇑ devotion = commitment

2 A **dedication** is 2.1 a message which is written at the beginning of a book or a statement which is sometimes made before a play or piece of music is performed, as a sign of affection or respect for someone. 2.2 a ceremony during which a church or other public building is dedicated to someone. N COUNT; N COUNT

deduce /dɪdju:s/, **deduces, deducing, deduced.** If you **deduce** something or **deduce** that something is true, you reach that conclusion because of other things that you know to be true. EG *Morris deduced that he was in the presence of the Head of Department... What do you deduce from the fact that the request was actually made?* V+O/REPORT-CL ⇑ reason = work out, infer

deduct /di'dʌkt/, **deducts, deducting, deducted.** When you **deduct** an amount from a total, you subtract it from the total. EG *Tax will be deducted automatically from your wages.* V+O ⇑ take away ≠ add

deduction /di'dʌkʃə⁰n/, **deductions.** 1 A **deduction** is 1.1 a conclusion that you have reached about something because of other things that you know to be true. EG *It is difficult to believe, yet the logic of the deduction is undeniable.* 1.2 an amount that has been subtracted from a total. EG *Nearly forty per cent of their income is taken in tax and national insurance deductions.* N COUNT = inference; N COUNT

2 **Deduction** is 2.1 the process of reaching a conclusion about something because of other things that you know to be true. EG *If the battery is dead the horn will not work; that is deduction, not guesswork.* N UNCOUNT ⇑ reasoning = analysis

2.2 the act or process of subtracting an amount of money from a total amount. EG *I had forgotten to take into account deduction of interest.* N UNCOUNT ⇑ subtraction

deductive /di'dʌktɪv/ is used to describe a method of reasoning where conclusions are deduced logically from other things that are already known. EG *...the deductive procedure of testing statements in physics.* ADJ CLASSIF : USU ATTRIB = analytical

deed /di:d/, **deeds.** 1 A **deed** is something that is done with a particular purpose, especially something that is very good or very bad. EG *He talked to her of the brave deeds his son would do when he grew up... What we want as a nation is not words but deeds... She made it crystal clear in word and deed.* ● If you **do** your **good deed for the day**, you do something to help someone; an informal expression. N COUNT : USU+SUPP, OR and+N ⇑ act; ● PHR : VB INFLECTS

2 A **deed** is also a piece of paper on which the terms of an agreement are written, especially an agreement concerning the ownership of land or a building. N COUNT+SUPP ⇑ document

deed box, deed boxes; also spelled with a hyphen. A **deed box** is a strong case or box, often made of metal, in which deeds and other official, legal, or important papers are kept. N COUNT

deed poll. If you change your name **by deed poll**, you change it officially and legally. PHR : USED AS AN A

deem /di:m/, **deems, deeming, deemed.** If you **deem** something to be true or **deem** something to have a particular quality, you consider that this is the case; a formal word. EG *This was deemed to detract from the dignity of the republic... I did hope that my work would be deemed worthy, as before.* V+O+C/to-INF : USU PASS ⇑ think = judge

deep /di:p/, **deeper, deepest; deeps.** 1 If something is **deep**, 1.1 it extends a long way down from the ground or from the top surface of something. EG *The sea is not very deep there... You should have dug a deeper hole... The wound was so deep it needed stitches.* ▸ used as an adverb. EG *He forced the knife in deeper... They dug deep down into the earth.* ◇ **deeply.** EG *Her skin was deeply wrinkled.* 1.2 it extends or measures a lot from front to back; used especially with reference to the space inside an object or a place. EG *The cupboard was very deep.* 1.3 it is far from the surface or edges of something. EG *Very little is known about the deep interior of the earth... ...deep in the forest.* 1.4 it moves a long way towards the end of a sports pitch, tennis court, etc. EG *Borg's serve was deep... He kicks the ball deep into United's half.* ADJ QUALIT ≠ shallow; ▸ ADV WITH VB : ALSO+A; ADJ QUALIT ≠ shallow; ADJ QUALIT; ADJ QUALIT OR ADV ≠ short

2 **Deep** is used in measurements to indicate the distance between the top and bottom of something or between its front and back. EG *The river was 3 metres deep there... The shelf is 30 cm deep.* ADJ AFTER N

3 If you say that things or people are two, three, etc **deep**, you are saying how many rows or layers of them there are. EG *People were standing three deep on either side of the street.* ADV : NUM+ADV

4 You use **deep** to emphasize the seriousness, strength, importance, or degree of something. EG *This was a matter of deep concern... Frank was still in deep financial trouble... Our hearts go out to you in deepest sympathy... He stared with deep admiration at the woman beside him.* ◇ **deeply.** EG *...deeply divided over the terms of the surrender... She loved her husband deeply... ...deeply religious people.* ADJ QUALIT : USU ATTRIB = profound; ◇ ADV = profoundly

5 If you experience or feel something **deep** or **deep down** inside you, you feel it very strongly although you do not necessarily show it. EG *Deep in his mind he knew he was at fault... Deep down he is as frightened as you are.* ADV OR PHR : USED AS AN A = inwardly

6 If you are in a **deep** sleep, you are sleeping peacefully and it is difficult to wake you. EG *About three in the morning I awoke from a deep sleep.* ◇ **deeply.** EG *I slept deeply and dreamlessly.* ADJ QUALIT : ATTRIB ≠ light; ◇ ADV

7 A **deep** gaze or look seems to see right into your mind. EG *His deep penetrating gaze troubled her... Marge looked deep into my eyes.* ◇ **deeply.** EG *They looked deeply into each other's eyes.* ADJ QUALIT : ATTRIB, OR ADV; ◇ ADV WITH VB

8 A **deep** breath or sigh uses or fills the whole of your lungs. EG *She took a deep breath and put her head under the water.* ◇ **deeply.** EG *She sighed deeply.* ● If you **take a deep breath** before doing something dangerous or frightening, you try to make yourself feel strong and confident. EG *Just take a deep breath and knock on the door.* ADJ QUALIT : ATTRIB; ● PHR : VB INFLECTS

9 A **deep** colour is strong and fairly dark. EG *The building was surrounded by a deep green lawn... He had deep blue eyes the colour of cornflowers.* ADJ QUALIT : USU +ADJ COLOUR ≠ pale

10 A **deep** sound is a low one. EG *He sang this in a deep voice... ...a deep growling roar.* ADJ QUALIT ≠ high

11 If you describe someone or something as **deep**, you mean that they have a lot of serious qualities which are not necessarily obvious at first. EG *She's an extraordinary woman: very deep... I have no deep thoughts, no profound philosophy.* ADJ QUALIT ≠ shallow, superficial

12 If you are **deep** in debt, you have a lot of debts. EG *This drove the company deeper and deeper into debt.* ADV+in/into

13 The word **deep** is also used in the following expressions. 13.1 If you are **deep in thought**, you are thinking very hard about something and are not PHR : USED AS AN A

aware of things that are happening around you. EG *He was soon so deep in thought that he forgot all about her.* 13.2 If you are **in deep water**, you are in a difficult or awkward situation. EG *If you do that you'll find yourself in deep water.* 13.3 If you say that something **goes** or **runs deep**, you mean that it is very important and serious. EG *The crisis in the prisons goes deep.* 13.4 If you **go off the deep end**, you lose your temper and suddenly become very angry; an informal expression. 13.5 If you **jump in at the deep end**, you choose to do the most difficult part of a task straight away. 13.6 If you are **thrown in at the deep end**, you are put in a completely new situation or given something difficult to do without any help or preparation.

PHR : USED AS AN A; PHR : VB INFLECTS; PHR : VB INFLECTS; PHR : VB INFLECTS; PHR : USU USED AS C

14 The **deep** means the sea; a literary use. — N SING : the+N

15 The **deeps** refers to a place that is far below the surface of the earth; an old-fashioned use. EG *...the coalminers toiling away in the black deeps.* — N PLURAL : the+N = depths

deepen /diːpəⁿn/, **deepens, deepening, deepened.** 1 If people **deepen** something, they cause it to become greater in measurement from the surface to the bottom. EG *The authority wants to spend £7 million to widen and deepen the River Soar.* — V+O

2 Something such as a river or a sea **deepens** where the bottom begins to slope downwards. EG *The sea deepens gradually.* — V

3 If a situation or emotion **deepens**, it becomes stronger and more intense. EG *The crisis deepened... He waited a couple of hours in gradually deepening despair, then gave up and went home.* — V ↑ intensify

4 If you **deepen** your knowledge or understanding of a subject, or if your knowledge **deepens**, you learn more about it and become more interested in it. EG *Their principal object was to deepen man's understanding of the universe.* — V-ERG ↑ increase = expand

5 When light or a colour **deepens**, it becomes darker. EG *The dusk deepened into night.* — V : IF+PREP THEN into/to

6 When a sound **deepens** or when you **deepen** it, it becomes lower in tone. EG *The engine sound deepened from a steady whine to a thunderous roar.* — V-ERG

deep freeze, deep freezes. A **deep freeze** is the same as a freezer. — N COUNT

deep-fry, deep-fries, deep-frying, deep-fried. If you **deep-fry** food, you fry it in a large amount of fat or oil. EG *...deep-fried chicken and chips.* — V+O

deep-rooted; also **deeply rooted**. A **deep-rooted** idea, belief, feeling, etc is so firmly fixed in a person or a society that it is difficult to destroy or change. EG *...a deep-rooted prejudice that runs through our society.* — ADJ QUALIT = ingrained

deep-sea. **Deep-sea** activities take place in the areas of the sea that are a long way from the coast. EG *...deep-sea diving.* — ADJ CLASSIF : ATTRIB ≠ inshore

deep-seated. Something that is **deep-seated** is caused by an attitude, condition, or idea that is very strong and unchanging. EG *He pointed to a deep-seated crisis of the whole economy... He had his own deep-seated fears of their intentions.* — ADJ CLASSIF ↑ fixed = deep-rooted

deep-set. **Deep-set** eyes have deep sockets. EG *...her deep-set grey eyes.* — ADJ CLASSIF ≠ bulging

deer /dɪə/. **Deer** is both the singular and the plural form. A **deer** is a large, four-legged wild animal that eats grass and leaves. A male deer usually has large, branching horns. — N COUNT

de-escalate /diːɛskəleɪt/, **de-escalates, de-escalating, de-escalated**. If an unpleasant situation or problem **de-escalates**, it becomes less intense and less dangerous or harmful. EG *They are looking for something to de-escalate the problem.* — V-ERG ↑ reduce ≠ aggravate, worsen

deface /dɪˈfeɪs/, **defaces, defacing, defaced.** If people **deface** something such as a wall or a notice, they deliberately damage it by writing or drawing unpleasant or offensive things on it. EG *...windows being broken, posters being defaced.* — V+O : USU PASS ↑ spoil = damage

de facto /deɪ fæktəʊ/ is used to say that something is true or exists, even though it was not planned or intended; a formal expression. EG *...a de facto tax increase for practically everybody... The result is, de facto, a one party system.* — ADJ CLASSIF : ATTRIB, OR ADV ↑ in fact ≠ de jure

defamation /dɛfəmeɪʃəⁿn/ is the damaging of someone's good reputation by saying something bad and untrue about them; a formal word. EG *...charges of defamation of character, slander, and libel... He let it be known that he would sue for defamation.* — N UNCOUNT ↑ damage

defamatory /dɪˈfæmətəⁿriˡ/. Speech or writing that is **defamatory** is likely to damage someone's good reputation by saying something bad and untrue about them; a formal word. EG *...politically defamatory literature.* — ADJ CLASSIF ↑ injurious

defame /dɪˈfeɪm/, **defames, defaming, defamed.** If you **defame** someone or something, you say something bad and untrue about them; a formal word. — V+O ↑ malign = slander

default /dɪˈfɔːlt/, **defaults, defaulting, defaulted.** The word **default** is also pronounced /diːfɔːlt/ in paragraph 3. 1 If you **default** on something that you are legally supposed to do, such as make a payment or appear in court, you fail to do it. EG *He had been right to default on that loan.* — V : IF+PREP THEN on/in

2 **Default** is a failure to do something that you are legally supposed to do, such as make a payment or appear in court. EG *After all, deferred payment is better than default.* — N UNCOUNT

3 A **default** position is something that happens or that you can do if nothing better happens. — N BEFORE N = fall-back

4 If something happens or is caused **by default**, it happens only because something else which might have prevented it has not happened. EG *He is responsible either through bad design or by default... Fascism did not emerge by default but by evolution.* — PHR : USED AS AN A

5 If something happens **in default of** something else, it happens because that other thing does not exist or has not been provided; a formal expression. EG *In default of convincing economic arguments the proposals are likely to be rejected.* — PREP ↑ lacking = without

defaulter /dɪˈfɔːltə/, **defaulters**. A **defaulter** is someone who does not do something that they are legally supposed to do, such as make a payment at a particular time, or appear in a court of law. — N COUNT ↑ offender

defeat /dɪˈfiːt/, **defeats, defeating, defeated.** 1 If you **defeat** someone, you win a victory over them in a contest such as a battle, game, or argument. EG *The French defeated the English troops... United were defeated by Rangers in the semi-final.* — V+O = beat ≠ lose to

2 If you **defeat** someone in an election or if you **defeat** a proposal or a motion in a debate, you win by receiving the most votes. EG *He won the by-election, only to be defeated at the general election... The motion was defeated by 221 votes to 152... The House of Lords defeated the amendment.* — V+O : USU PASS = beat

3 If a task or a problem **defeats** someone, it is so difficult to do or to understand that it causes them to be unsuccessful. EG *It is a task which at present defeats too many children.* — V+O

4 If someone or something **defeats** something else, they cause it to fail. EG *Moral instruction thus defeats its own purpose... He would like to have seen the strike defeated.* — V+O ↑ frustrate = thwart

5 **Defeat** is the state of being beaten in a battle, competition, election, etc, or of failing to achieve what you wanted to. EG *The bad weather contributed to the defeat of the navy... There was a faint air of defeat in the room... Her friend finally gave up in defeat... He would never admit defeat.* — N UNCOUNT ↑ failure

6 A **defeat** is a contest or situation in which you lose or fail to achieve what you wanted to. EG *These defeats came as a particular setback for Thorne.* — N COUNT ↑ failure

defeatism /dɪˈfiːtɪzəⁿm/ is a way of thinking or talking which suggests that you expect to be unsuccessful. EG *We were accused of defeatism and lack of faith.* — N UNCOUNT ↑ pessimism ≠ optimism

defeatist /dɪˈfiːtɪst/, **defeatists**. A **defeatist** is someone who thinks or talks in a way that suggests that they expect to be unsuccessful. ▸ used as an adjective. EG *I was in a defeatist mood when he told me the result.* — N COUNT ↑ pessimist; ▸ ADJ CLASSIF ↑ pessimistic

defecate /dɛfəˈkeɪt/, **defecates, defecating, defecated**. When people and animals **defecate**, they get rid of waste matter from their body through the anus; a formal word. ◇ **defecation** /dɛfəˈkeɪʃəⁿn/. — V ↑ discharge = excrete; ◇ N UNCOUNT

defect, defects, defecting, defected. The word **defect** is pronounced /diːfɛkt/ when it is a noun, and /dɪˈfɛkt/ when it is a verb. 1 A **defect** is a fault or imperfection in a person or thing. EG *Some were in very good condition but others had small defects... ...the defects of Western society.* — N COUNT : IF+PREP THEN in/of = flaw

2 If you **defect**, you leave your country, political party, or other group, and join an opposing country, party, or group. EG *He and his son defected in April this year.* ◇ **defection** /dɪˈfɛkʃəⁿn/, **defections**. EG — V, IF+PREP THEN from/to ↑ desert = escape; ◇ N COUNT/

The number of defections has increased in recent years... The army has dwindled through defection. (UNCOUNT ⇑ desertion)

defective /dɪˈfektɪv/. If something is **defective**, it is imperfect and therefore does not work properly. EG *One of the engines was found to be seriously defective.* (ADJ CLASSIF ⇑ faulty)

defector /dɪˈfektə/, **defectors**. A **defector** is someone who leaves their country, political party, or other group, and joins an opposing country, party, or group. (N COUNT : USU+SUPP ⇑ deserter)

defence /dɪˈfens/, **defences**; also spelled **defense** in American English. **1 Defence** is **1.1** action that is taken to protect someone or something against attack. EG *They carried sticks for defence rather than aggression... The trade union is organizing for the defence of jobs and wages.* (N UNCOUNT ⇑ protection) **1.2** the system and organization of a country's armies and weapons. EG *How much of our national income is allocated to defence?... The government is limiting the increase in defense spending to 7.5 per cent... Britain was taking a proper share in her own defence.* (N UNCOUNT ⇑ militarization) ● If you **come to** someone's **defence**, you help them by doing something to protect them. EG *No one came to her defence as the crowd surged forward.* (● PHR : VB INFLECTS)

2 A **defence** is **2.1** a quality or possession that someone or something has and that they can use to protect themselves. EG *The jellyfish has had to develop this deadly poison as a defence.* (N COUNT, IF+PREP THEN *of/against* ⇑ guard) **2.2** a way of behaving or thinking which protects you emotionally and stops you showing weakness. EG *If you use cynicism as a defence you soon lose all sense of moral values.* (N COUNT, IF+PREP THEN *of/against* ⇑ guard = shield) **2.3** something that you say or write which supports ideas or actions that have been criticized or questioned. EG *His economists have drawn up a defence of monetary policy... Brown, in defence, said that it was his boss who was violent.* (N COUNT, OR *in*+N, IF+PREP THEN *of/against* ⇑ statement = justification ≠ attack)

2.4 the process in a court of law of denying a charge which has been made against someone. EG *He decided to conduct his own defence... ...her much-publicized defences of left-wing dissidents.* (N COUNT : USU+SUPP, IF+PREP THEN *of/against*)

3 The **defence** is the case that is presented by a lawyer for the person in a trial who has been accused of a crime; also used sometimes to refer to this person and his or her lawyers. EG *He gave evidence for the defence in the Hennessy case.* (N SING : *the*+N ≠ prosecution)

4 The **defences** of a country or region are all its armed forces and weapons. EG *No defences would survive a nuclear attack.* (N PLURAL)

5 The **defence** in a football team, hockey team, etc is the group of players who try to stop the opposing players scoring a goal or a point. EG *Arsenal's defence is very strong this season.* (N COUNT : USU+SUPP ≠ attack)

defenceless /dɪˈfensləs/; also spelled **defenseless** in American English. If someone or something is **defenceless**, they are weak and unable to defend themselves properly. EG *...attacks on defenceless civilians.* (ADJ QUALIT = helpless) ◇ **defencelessness**. (◇ N UNCOUNT)

defence mechanism, defence mechanisms. A **defence mechanism** is a way of behaving or thinking which is not conscious or deliberate and is an automatic reaction to unpleasant actions or feelings such as anxiety or fear. (N COUNT)

defend /dɪˈfend/, **defends, defending, defended**. **1** If you **defend** someone or something, **1.1** you take some action in order to protect them against danger or violence. EG *I persuaded my mother that I was capable of defending myself against danger.* (V+O (NG/REFL) = guard) **1.2** you do or say something that is intended to help them to survive or continue, for example when their rights or existence are threatened. EG *They were merely defending the national interest... You're defending the wrong cause for the right reason.* (V+O ⇑ protect = champion)

2 If you **defend** a person or their ideas or actions, you argue in support of them when they have been criticized. EG *It is a point of view which will be awfully hard to defend... The minister defended himself in the House of Commons.* (V+O (NG/REFL) ⇑ justify)

3 If people **defend** a place or country, they protect it against attack by using military force. EG *Important advances had been made in preparations to defend the Federal Republic... The country needs a stronger army to defend itself.* (V+O (NG/REFL))

4 If someone, especially a lawyer, **defends** a person who has been accused of something, they argue in a court of law that the charges are not true. EG *He was determined to have lawyers of his own choice to defend him... She defended herself successfully in court.* (V+O (NG/REFL))

5 If a champion **defends** his or her title or championship, he or she plays a match or a game against someone who will become the new champion if they win. EG *McGuigan defended his title in Dublin... He decided on a rematch with Muhammad Ali rather than defending against Ken Norton.* (V OR V+O)

defendant /dɪˈfendənt/, **defendants**. A **defendant** is the person who has been accused of a crime in a case in a court of law. EG *She was faced with the difficult task of pleading for a defendant who was obviously guilty.* (N COUNT ≠ plaintiff)

defender /dɪˈfendə/, **defenders**. **1** If someone is a **defender** of a particular idea, belief, or person that has been criticized, they argue or act in support of that idea, belief, or person. EG *They were staunch defenders of social democracy... ...an outspoken defender of eccentric right-wing views.* (N COUNT : IF+PREP THEN *of* ⇑ supporter = champion)

2 A **defender** in a game such as football or hockey is a player whose main task is to try and stop the other side scoring. EG *It was unclear who the light really favoured, attackers or defenders.* (N COUNT)

defense /dɪˈfens/. See **defence**.

defensible /dɪˈfensəˈbəˀl/. An idea, opinion, system, etc that is **defensible** is able to be defended because people feel that it is right or logical. EG *The most morally defensible distribution system is one based on income.* (ADJ QUALIT ⇑ justifiable)

defensive /dɪˈfensɪv/. **1** You use **defensive** **1.1** to describe things that are designed for or capable of defending a country or area by military force. EG *These measures are only aimed at limiting the increase of defensive weapons.* (ADJ CLASSIF : ATTRIB ≠ offensive) **1.2** to describe things that are intended to protect someone or something. EG *The canals often overflow their banks and rise above defensive dykes built to contain them... We hope that employer organizations can be persuaded not to adopt defensive positions.* (ADJ CLASSIF : ATTRIB ⇑ protective)

2 If someone is **on the defensive**, they are acting in a way that is intended to protect themselves or their own interests. EG *The business sector is on the defensive.* (PHR : USED AS AN A)

3 Someone who is **defensive** acts in a way that is intended to hide their weaknesses. EG *The women's liberation movement has made them very defensive about their masculinity...* ▸ used of people's behaviour. EG *He had the defensive humour of a lonely man.* (ADJ QUALIT) ◇ **defensively**. EG *'I'm in no hurry,' said Rudolph defensively.* (◇ ADV WITH VB) ◇ **defensiveness**. EG *His defensiveness was positively embarrassing.* (◇ N UNCOUNT)

defer /dɪˈfɜː/, **defers, deferring, deferred**. **1** If you **defer** an event or action, you change the time at which it is due to happen and arrange for it to happen at a later date. EG *The company will defer payment for whatever length of time you require... Philip laced up his shoes slowly, deferring decision.* (V+O, OR V+ING ⇑ postpone = put off) ◇ **deferred**. EG *...a deferred pension.* (◇ ADJ CLASSIF)

2 If you **defer** to someone, you accept their opinion or do what they want you to do, even though you do not agree with it yourself, because you respect them or their authority. EG *No longer did MPs defer to the Speaker... She was rude to most and deferred to nobody.* (V+A *(to)* ⇑ submit)

deference /defərəns/ is polite and considerate behaviour that you show to someone because you have a lot of respect for them or for their authority. EG *She is treated with deference... I refused to discuss the matter out of deference to my employer.* (N UNCOUNT : IF+PREP THEN *to* ⇑ regard ≠ scorn)

deferential /defərenʃəˀl/. Someone who is **deferential** shows respect and regard for someone else's opinions and wishes. EG *They were polite and deferential as always.* (ADJ QUALIT ⇑ respectful ≠ scornful) ◇ **deferentially**. EG *'What work do you do sir?' he asked deferentially.* (◇ ADV WITH VB)

deferment /dɪˈfɜːməˀnt/, **deferments**. **Deferment** is the changing of the time or date when something is supposed to happen so that it will happen at a later time or date; a formal word. EG *Further deferment will not be allowed.* (N UNCOUNT/COUNT ⇑ postponement)

deferral /dɪˈfɜːrəˀl/, **deferrals**. **Deferral** is the same as deferment. (N UNCOUNT/COUNT)

defiance /dɪˈfaɪəns/. **1 Defiance** is behaviour or attitudes which show that you are not willing to obey someone or to behave in the expected way. EG *The demonstration is a gesture of defiance against an allegedly corrupt society.* (N UNCOUNT ⇑ protest = rebellion ≠ compliance)

2 If you do something **in defiance of** someone or (PREP) something, you do it even though you know that there are rules which say that you are not allowed to do it. EG *The houses were erected in defiance of all building regulations.*

defiant /di'faɪənt/. If you are **defiant**, you show aggression or independence by refusing to obey someone or refusing to behave in the expected way. EG *He was brought up to be aggressive and defiant.* ▸ used of people's behaviour. EG *Her tone was defiant... The girl sat down with a defiant look at Judy.* ◇ **defiantly**. EG *She announced defiantly that she intended to wait until he returned.* ADJ CLASSIF ⇑ aggressive = rebellious ≠ submissive ◇ ADV WITH VB

deficiency /di'fɪʃənsi'/, **deficiencies**. 1 **Deficiency** in something, especially something that your body needs, is a lack or shortage of it. EG *...vitamin deficiency... ...deficiencies in personnel and equipment.* N COUNT/UNCOUNT+SUPP ≠ surfeit

2 A **deficiency** that someone or something has is a weakness or imperfection in them. EG *The deficiency of the answers was obvious to everybody.* N COUNT/UNCOUNT+SUPP = inadequacy

deficient /di'fɪʃənt/. 1 If someone or something is **deficient** in a particular thing, they do not have the full amount of it that they need in order to function normally or work properly. EG *Many old people admitted to hospital are deficient in vitamin C.* ADJ CLASSIF : USU PRED+*in* ⇑ lacking = short of

2 Someone or something that is **deficient** is not good enough for a particular purpose or standard. EG *...increasingly deficient public services.* ADJ QUALIT ⇑ imperfect = inadequate

deficit /defɪsɪt, dɪfɪsɪt/, **deficits**. A **deficit** is the amount by which something is less than what is required or expected, especially the amount by which the total money received is less than the total money spent. EG *The balance of payments showed a deficit for the first time in 15 years... ...a deficit of six million pounds.* • If an account or a person, organization, country etc is **in deficit**, money is owed because they have spent more than they have received. EG *A country in deficit abroad should raise its interest rates.* N COUNT ⇑ shortage ≠ surplus • PHR : USED AS AN A ⇑ in debt

defile /di'faɪl/, **defiles, defiling, defiled**. The word **defile** is also pronounced /di:faɪl/ for paragraph 2. 1 If you **defile** something that people think is important or holy, you do something to it or say something about it which is offensive. EG *To defile the sacred is therefore the gravest form of blasphemy.* V+O ⇑ spoil = desecrate

2 A **defile** is a very narrow valley or passage, usually through mountains; a formal or literary use. N COUNT = pass

definable /di'faɪnəbə⁰l/. Something that is **definable** can be explained in a precise and clear way. EG *Is it your view that there is a constant entity definable as virtue?... ...a tradition that may be curable but not legally definable.* ADJ CLASSIF

define /di'faɪn/, **defines, defining, defined**. 1 If you **define** something, you show, describe, or state clearly what it is and what its limits are, or what it is like. EG *Roland Buck asked Dr Kossou to define the problems discussed by the ministers... The boundaries given me in girlhood were strictly defined... They had something significant in common. I tried to define what it was.* ◇ **defined**. EG *Each object had clearly defined functions.* V+O = set out, specify ◇ ADJ CLASSIF

2 If you **define** a word or expression, you explain its meaning, for example in a dictionary. EG *Can you define 'thought' first of all... The Oxford Dictionary defines the 'sportsman' as: a good fellow, a person who is fair to opponents.* V+O

3 If an object **is defined**, its visible outline is clearly shown. EG *The picture was sharp and cleanly defined... ...cameras that could define with astonishing accuracy objects as small as a woodshed.* V+O : USU PASS = delineate

definite /defɪnɪt/. 1 If something is **definite**, 1.1 it is firm, clear, and precise, and unlikely to be changed. EG *They have very definite and pronounced views on this topic... In this school there is a definite plan to separate boys from girls... There's a definite date for the wedding.* ◇ **definitely**. EG *I haven't definitely decided on law school.* 1.2 it has a precise and specific form or position. EG *It had a definite form and shape.* 1.3 it is certainly true rather than guessed or imagined. EG *There was no definite evidence... Neither of these opinions proves anything definite.* 1.4 it is obvious enough for there to be no doubt about it. EG *I had a definite advantage... Certainly, there was a definite relationship between racism and fascism.* ADJ QUALIT = positive ≠ vague ◇ ADV WITH VB ADJ QUALIT : ATTRIB ADJ QUALIT ⇑ sure = certain ≠ doubtful ADJ QUALIT : ATTRIB ⇑ noticeable = clear

2 Someone who is **definite** behaves or talks in a firm, confident way. EG *Some parents are afraid to be definite and firm.* ADJ QUALIT

definite article, definite articles. The **definite article** is a term used in grammar for the word 'the'. In this dictionary 'the' is described as DET. See **the** and □ at DET. N COUNT ⇑ determiner

definitely /defɪnɪtli'/ means certainly and without any doubt; often used to emphasize how certain you are about what you are saying. EG *They were definitely not for sale... Yes, we definitely need a car park... 'Are you going to Greece this summer?'–'Definitely.'* ADV SEN

definition /defɪnɪʃə⁰n/, **definitions**. 1 A **definition** is a statement explaining the meaning of a word or expression, especially in a dictionary. EG *There is no clear definition of schizophrenia.* • If you say that something has a particular quality **by definition**, you mean that it has this quality simply because it is what it is. EG *Street life is, by definition, a life lived in public... 'Happenings' are, almost by definition, crimes or disasters.* N COUNT ⇑ explanation • PHR : USED AS AN A = per se

2 **Definition** is the quality of being clear and distinct. EG *They lack definition and identity as a class.* N UNCOUNT ⇑ clarity

definitive /də²fɪnɪtɪv/. 1 Something that is **definitive** provides a firm conclusion that cannot be questioned. EG *The possible permutations were endless and the definitive commentary became an impossibility.* ◇ **definitively**. EG *'Hearts of Darkness' will definitively establish McCullin the journalist as McCullin the artist.* ADJ CLASSIF = conclusive ◇ ADV WITH VB ⇑ firmly = conclusively

2 A book, performance, etc that is **definitive** is thought to be of a very high quality and has become an example or standard which other similar things are compared to. EG *Olivier's was, to my mind, the definitive Macbeth... He has written the definitive study of Hooker.* ADJ CLASSIF = ultimate

deflate /di'fleɪt/, **deflates, deflating, deflated**. 1 If you **deflate** someone or something, you say or do something which makes them appear less important than they think they are or less confident than they were. EG *...a mischievous desire to deflate the reputation of some contemporary.* ◇ **deflated**. EG *If that left us feeling deflated, worse was to come.* V+O ⇑ diminish = debunk ≠ glorify ◇ ADJ CLASSIF = crestfallen ≠ uplifted

2 If someone with power **deflates** a country's economy, they reduce the amount of economic activity that goes on there. EG *He was forced to deflate the economy still further.* V+O ⇑ decrease = run down ≠ expand

3 When a tyre, balloon, etc **deflates**, or when you **deflate** it, all the air comes out of it. EG *...a series of bubbling sounds as the balloon deflated.* V-ERG ≠ inflate, blow up

deflation /di'fleɪʃə⁰n/ is 1 a reduction in economic activity that leads to lower levels of industrial output, employment, investment, trade, profits, and prices. EG *They began a process of economic deflation.* 2 a feeling of disappointment or sadness that you get, often after you have finished doing something that was exciting. EG *I detected a slight air of deflation after the ceremony.* N UNCOUNT ⇑ decrease ≠ reflation N UNCOUNT

deflationary /di'fleɪʃə⁰nə⁰ri'/. A **deflationary** economic policy or measure is one that is intended to, or is likely to, cause deflation. EG *...a mildly deflationary budget.* ADJ CLASSIF : USU ATTRIB ≠ inflationary, reflationary

deflect /di'flekt/, **deflects, deflecting, deflected**. 1 If you **deflect** something such as criticism, you act in a way that prevents it from being directed towards you or affecting you. EG *They gave the police misleading information, deflecting attention from planned crimes... He would always deflect any criticism of the place he loved.* V+O ⇑ divert = fend off

2 If you **deflect** someone from something, you cause them to change from a course that they were intending to take by putting pressure on them or by offering them something desirable. EG *Benn felt that Labour should not be deflected from its expansionist aims... He was intent on only one subject and would not be deflected from it by her petty preoccupations.* V+O : IF+PREP THEN *from* ⇑ divert = sidetrack, turn

3 When something **deflects** or when you **deflect** it, you make it go in a slightly different direction from the way it was going before, for example by hitting or pushing it. EG *Our goalie deflected their shot... Most of its particles are deflected.* V-ERG ⇑ turn

deflection /di'flekʃə⁰n/, **deflections**. A **deflection** is 1 an action of making something go in a slightly different direction from the way in which it was going before. EG *Shilton's deflection led to the first goal.* 2 the amount by which something is turned away from its original course or moved from its N UNCOUNT/COUNT ⇑ turning N COUNT

original position; a technical term in physics. EG *This is the deflection with both forces acting.*

deflower /di:flaʊə/, **deflowers, deflowering, deflowered.** When a woman **is deflowered**, she has sexual intercourse with a man for the first time; a literary word. V+O : USU PASS

defoliant /di:fəʊliənt/, **defoliants.** A **defoliant** is a chemical used on trees and plants which makes all their leaves fall off. EG *...the first to use defoliants in military operations.* N COUNT

defoliate /di:fəʊlieɪt/, **defoliates, defoliating, defoliated.** If you **defoliate** plants, you make all their leaves fall off, especially by using a defoliant. EG *The airforce used it for defoliating the jungle.* V+O ⇑ strip
◊ **defoliation** /di:fəʊlieɪʃəⁿn/. ◊ N UNCOUNT

deforest /di:fɒrɪ²st/, **deforests, deforesting, deforested.** If an area **is deforested**, all the trees there are cut down or destroyed. EG *The Amazon Basin is quickly becoming deforested.* V+O : USU PASS
◊ **deforestation** /di:fɒrə²steɪʃəⁿn/. EG *Deforestation is by no means a new phenomenon.* ◊ N UNCOUNT

deform /di¹fɔ:m/, **deforms, deforming, deformed.** 1 If something **deforms** someone or something, it causes them to have an unnatural shape or appearance, sometimes because of illness or injury. EG *Badly fitting shoes can deform the feet.* V+O : USU PASS ⇑ damage = cripple
◊ **deformed.** EG *The drug may have caused deformed babies.* ◊ ADJ QUALIT ⇑ misshapen
2 If you **deform** something, you make it appear ugly. EG *Why do painters have to deform everything they see?* V+O ⇑ spoil = distort

deformation /di:fɔ:meɪʃəⁿn/, **deformations.** 1 A **deformation** is a part of the body which has not developed, or which has developed in an unnatural way. EG *Doctors are looking for a common cause of these deformations.* N COUNT ⇑ defect = deformity
2 **Deformation** is the result of abnormal development or changes in a part of the body. EG *Victims suffered progressive deformation of the bones.* N UNCOUNT ⇑ malformation

deformity /di¹fɔ:mɪti¹/, **deformities.** 1 A **deformity** is a part of the body which is not properly developed because of injury or illness. EG *Any scars or deformities frightened her.* N COUNT ⇑ defect
2 **Deformity** is the condition of having a part of the body not properly developed because of injury or illness. EG *Many cases of deformity and death occurred in the villagers who ate the fish.* N UNCOUNT ⇑ damage

defraud /di¹frɔ:d/, **defrauds, defrauding, defrauded.** If someone **defrauds** you, they take something away from you or stop you from getting something that belongs to you by means of tricks and lies. EG *He was charged with conspiracy to defraud.* V OR V+O : IF+PREP THEN *of* ⇑ rob = cheat

defray /di¹freɪ/, **defrays, defraying, defrayed.** If you **defray** someone's costs or expenses, you give them money which represents an amount that they have spent, for example while they have been doing something for you or acting on your behalf; a formal word. EG *It was not enough to defray the extra cost.* V+O ⇑ pay = reimburse

defrost /di¹:frɒst/, **defrosts, defrosting, defrosted.** 1 When you **defrost** a fridge or freezer or when it **defrosts** itself, you switch it off or press a special switch so that the ice inside it can melt. EG *Defrost your refrigerator regularly.* V+O (NG/REFL)
2 When you **defrost** frozen food, or when it **defrosts**, you allow it to become unfrozen so that you can eat it or cook it. EG *You must defrost a frozen chicken before you cook it... Has the meat defrosted yet?* V-ERG ⇑ thaw ≠ freeze

deft /deft/, **defter, deftest.** A **deft** movement is made in a very quick or skilful way. EG *She pushed the child forward with a deft shove to her shoulders... ...cutting the edges away with deft movements of the knife.* ▸ used of people and their hands. EG *The deft fingers massaged his scalp.* ADJ QUALIT = adept ≠ awkward, clumsy; ▸ = nimble
◊ **deftly.** EG *She deftly tilted the pot on its hinged base.* ◊ ADV WITH VB
◊ **deftness.** EG *He performed the mixing of drinks with remarkable deftness.* ◊ N UNCOUNT ⇑ skill

defunct /dɪfʌŋkt/. If something is **defunct**, it no longer exists or it no longer works properly. EG *...the now defunct Campaign Against Racial Discrimination... It isn't true that the British aircraft industry is defunct.* ADJ CLASSIF ⇑ non-existent ≠ active, flourishing

defuse /di¹fju:z/, **defuses, defusing, defused.** 1 If you **defuse** a dangerous or tense situation, you calm it by taking away the trouble which is causing it. EG *It is up to you to defuse the situation... They were unwilling to yield the concessions that would defuse the dispute.* V+O = neutralize ≠ fuel
2 If someone **defuses** a bomb, they remove the fuse from it so that it cannot explode. V+O ≠ fuse

defy /di¹faɪ/, **defies, defying, defied.** 1 If you **defy** a person or a law, you refuse to obey them or do not behave in the expected way. EG *If we had defied him on this question it would have cost us our jobs... They are wrong to defy the order of the Court.* V+O = disobey ≠ obey
2 If you **defy** someone to do something, you challenge them to do it when you think that they will be unable to do it or too frightened to do it. EG *I defy anyone to disprove it.* V+O+*to*-INF = dare
3 If something **defies** description, understanding, etc, it has qualities which are so extreme or surprising that it is extremely difficult for you to understand or explain it. EG *This helps explain many things that otherwise defy analysis... The vastness of space defied comprehension.* V+O : NO PASS, NO IMPER ⇑ frustrate ≠ permit

degeneracy /dɪdʒenərəsi¹/ is behaviour which many people think is shocking or disgusting. EG *It's a part of the degeneracy of the age.* N UNCOUNT = decadence

degenerate, degenerates, degenerating, degenerated. The word **degenerate** is pronounced /di¹dʒenəreɪt/ when it is a verb, and /di¹dʒenərə¹t/ when it is an adjective or a noun. 1 If someone or something **degenerates**, they become worse in quality, behaviour, appearance, or intelligence. EG *The British economy might degenerate into permanent recession... The conversation degenerated to a personal attack.* V : IF+PREP THEN *into/to* ⇑ worsen = sink
2 If someone or something is **degenerate**, they have or show low standards of morality or behaviour; used showing disapproval. EG *...the less degenerate men of earlier times.* ADJ QUALIT = decadent, depraved
3 A **degenerate** is someone who behaves in a way that many people find shocking or disgusting. EG *The world is full of degenerates.* N COUNT ⇑ delinquent

degeneration /dɪdʒenəreɪʃəⁿn/ is the process of becoming worse in quality, behaviour, appearance, or intelligence. EG *This disease causes physical and mental degeneration.* N UNCOUNT ⇑ deterioration

degenerative /di¹dʒenərətɪv/. A **degenerative** disease or condition is one which is getting worse. EG *...degenerative arthritis.* ADJ CLASSIF

degradation /degrədeɪʃəⁿn/ is 1 a state of poverty and dirtiness. EG *They forgot the squalor and degradation around them.* N UNCOUNT = squalor 2 a humiliating experience that causes someone to lose other people's respect and good opinion. EG *...the degradation of individuals... They subjected themselves to every degradation for him.* N UNCOUNT : USU +SUPP, OR N COUNT = debasement 3 the process of causing the quality of something to become worse. EG *...a significant degradation in command and control.* N UNCOUNT + SUPP ⇑ deterioration

degrade /di¹greɪd/, **degrades, degrading, degraded.** 1 Something that **degrades** someone causes people to have less respect for them. EG *...films that degrade women... They degraded themselves by performing unnatural tricks.* V+O (NG/REFL) ⇑ lower = debase, cheapen
◊ **degrading.** EG *He denounced the 'vicious and degrading cult of violence'.* ◊ ADJ QUALIT ⇑ lowering
2 To **degrade** something means to cause it to become worse in quality. EG *Industrial expansion must necessarily degrade the planet.* V+O ⇑ worsen

degree /di¹gri:/, **degrees.** 1 A **degree** is the amount to which something is felt or the extent to which it happens. EG *She admits to a degree of prejudice... The whole population has suffered although in different degrees and in different ways... The number of police carrying guns has increased to an alarming degree... Work interested him to such a degree that he thought about nothing else... To some degree you can control the car in a skid... More often than not the change is only a matter of degree.* N COUNT+SUPP, OR *of*+N
● If something happens **by degrees**, it happens in such a slow and gradual way that you hardly notice it. EG *Only by degrees did it dawn on him.* ● PHR : USED AS AN A ⇑ slowly = gradually
2 A **degree** is also 2.1 a unit of measurement that is used to measure temperature; often written as "°" after a number, for example 23°. EG *The temperature was still 23 degrees centigrade... I think it's eighty degrees outside.* N COUNT 2.2 a unit that is used to measure the angles in a circle and also to measure latitude and longitude; often written as ", for example 50. EG *The control arm swings a full 90 degrees from vertical to horizontal... The yacht was 20 degrees off course... Cyclones frequently form between the lati-* N COUNT ⇑ unit

tudes of 8 and 15 degrees north or south of the equator.
3 A **degree** at a university or polytechnic is a course of study that you take there, or the qualification that you get when you have passed the course. EG *He had taken a degree in Music at Cambridge... I did my first degree at the University of Ohio... A university degree may give one a head-start in getting a job.* N COUNT
4 See also **third degree**.

-degree combines with ordinal numbers in order to form adjectives 1 that indicate how serious a crime is; used in American English. EG *They were found guilty of first-degree murder.* COMB : FORMS ADJ CLASSIFS 2 that indicate how seriously someone is injured when they have been burned. EG *She suffered third-degree burns.* COMB : FORMS ADJ CLASSIFS

dehumanize /diːhjuːmənaɪz/, **dehumanizes, dehumanizing, dehumanized**; also spelled **dehumanise**. 1 Something that **dehumanizes** people takes away from them the qualities which are often thought of as being best in human beings, such as kindness and individuality. EG *It is said that science will dehumanise people.* V+O ◊ **dehumanizing**. EG *...the harmful and dehumanizing effect of retirement.* ◊ ADJ CLASSIF ◊ **dehumanization** /diːhjuːmənaɪzeɪʃəⁿn/. EG *...the threat of dehumanisation.* ◊ N UNCOUNT
2 If an activity **is dehumanized**, it is made dull and mechanical, with no originality or variation. EG *...the dehumanized requirements of the colonial society.* V+O : USU PASS

dehydrate /diːhaɪdreɪt/, **dehydrates, dehydrating, dehydrated**. 1 When something such as food **is dehydrated**, all the water is removed from it, often in order to preserve it. V+O : USU PASS ⇑ dry ◊ **dehydrated**. EG *...a dehydrated beef stew dinner.* ◊ ADJ CLASSIF
2 If you **are dehydrated**, you lose too much water from your body so that you feel weak or ill. V+O : USU PASS ⇑ dry ◊ **dehydrated**. EG *They may develop fever from becoming dehydrated.* ◊ ADJ QUALIT ◊ **dehydration** /diːhaɪdreɪʃəⁿn/. EG *...suffering from dehydration after the race.* ◊ N UNCOUNT

deify /diːɪfaɪ, deɪ-/, **deifies, deifying, deified**. If you **deify** someone or something, you consider them to be a god and treat them as an object of worship; a formal word. EG *The African wildcat was tamed and deified by the ancient Egyptians.* V+O ⇑ exalt = enshrine ◊ **deification** /diːɪfɪkeɪʃəⁿn, deɪ-/. ◊ N UNCOUNT ⇑ exaltation

deign /deɪn/, **deigns, deigning, deigned**. If you **deign** to do something, you do it reluctantly and in a way which clearly shows other people that you think you are really too important to do such a thing. EG *Occasionally I would deign to read one of her ridiculous editorials.* V+*to*-INF ⇑ condescend = stoop

deity /diːɪtɪ, deɪ-/, **deities**. A **deity** is a god or goddess. EG *I accepted this Deity as the only one... ...temples to the elemental deities.* N COUNT : USU+SUPP

déjà vu /deɪʒæ vuː/ is the feeling that you have already experienced in the past exactly the same sequence of events as is happening at the present moment. N UNCOUNT ⇑ repetition

dejected /dɪ¹dʒektɪ²d/. If you are **dejected**, you feel miserable or unhappy, especially because you have just been disappointed by something. EG *Parker won the nomination and the dejected Hearst returned to New York... He had a dejected, saddened look.* ADJ QUALIT = depressed, dispirited ≠ cheerful ◊ **dejectedly**. EG *'I can't do it,' said the girl dejectedly.* ◊ ADV WITH VB = miserably

dejection /dɪ¹dʒekʃəⁿn/ is a feeling of sadness that you get, for example, when you have just been disappointed by something. EG *Each day brought on a more profound dejection.* N UNCOUNT = gloom

de jure /deɪdʒʊəreɪ/ is used to say that something is true or exists because of a law; a technical term in law. EG *...the de facto, if not the de jure ruler.* ADJ CLASSIF : ATTRIB ⇑ legal ≠ de facto

dekko /dekəʊ/. If you **have a dekko at** something, you look at it; an informal expression used in British English. EG *Let's have a dekko at the bathroom.* PHR : VB INFLECTS ⇑ look

delay /dɪ¹leɪ/, **delays, delaying, delayed**. 1 If you **delay** something, you do not do it until a later time. EG *Try and persuade them to delay some of the changes... She would delay starting divorce proceedings for six months.* V+O, OR V+ING = postpone ≠ bring forward
2 If something **delays** you, it causes you to slow down or be late. EG *The mountains may delay the army's advance... I'm afraid I was slightly delayed.* V+O = hold up
3 If you **delay** doing something, 3.1 you fail to do it immediately or by a certain time, often because you cannot make your mind up quickly enough. EG *Don't delay too long... If you delay in claiming they won't pay you.* V OR V+-ING ⇑ wait = hesitate, hold back 3.2 you deliberately take longer than necessary to do it. EG *They're delaying in the hope that they won't have to pay.* V OR V+-ING ⇑ wait = hang on
4 A **delay** is 4.1 a period of time during which an action or event is not allowed to happen until a later time. EG *They were arguing for a delay in introducing the new law... We shall inform you without delay.* N COUNT, OR *without*+N ⇑ interval 4.2 a situation in which an action or event cannot happen immediately and which can cause someone or something to be late. EG *The delays were caused by events beyond our control... This interruption caused delay.* N COUNT/ UNCOUNT = hold-up
5 **Delay** is a failure to do something immediately, for example if you cannot make up your mind quickly enough. EG *There was no time left for delay or hesitation.* N UNCOUNT

delaying /dɪ¹leɪɪŋ/. **Delaying** tactics or actions are intended to prevent something from happening immediately in order to give you more time for what you want to do. EG *These were clearly no more than delaying tactics.* ADJ CLASSIF : ATTRIB

delectable /dɪ¹lektəbəⁿl/. 1 If you say that someone is **delectable**, you mean that they are very attractive, especially in a sexual way; a rather literary or informal use. EG *...the delectable Miss Haynes.* ADJ QUALIT
2 Food that is **delectable** is very pleasant and tasty. EG *'It's delectable,' I said, sipping it.* ADJ QUALIT = delicious

delectation /diːlekteɪʃəⁿn/ is very great pleasure and amusement; a formal word. EG *Some of our greatest music was written for the discerning delectation of a vast audience of musical amateurs.* N UNCOUNT

delegate, delegates, delegating, delegated. The word **delegate** is pronounced /deləgət/ when it is a noun, and /deləgeɪt/ when it is a verb. 1 A **delegate** is a person who is chosen to vote or make decisions on behalf of a group of other people, especially at a conference or a meeting. EG *All the different branches of the union elect delegates to the annual conference.* N COUNT = representative
2 If you **delegate** someone to do something, you give them the duty of acting on your behalf by making decisions, voting, or doing some particular work. EG *The Bishop delegated me to approach the local press.* V+O : USU+*to*-INF ⇑ authorize = appoint
3 If you **delegate** duties, responsibilities, or power, you give them to someone else so that they can act on your behalf. EG *I employ staff and delegate all household tasks... Authority for the use of the weapons had already been delegated to U.S. Commanders... He is no longer prepared to delegate.* V OR V+O ⇑ transfer

delegation /delɪ²geɪʃəⁿn/, **delegations**. 1 A **delegation** is a group of delegates who have been chosen to represent a larger group of people. EG *There was also a delegation from the British Isles.* N COUNT = deputation
2 **Delegation** is the giving of duties, responsibilities, or power to someone else so that they can act on your behalf. N UNCOUNT

delete /dɪ¹liːt/, **deletes, deleting, deleted**. If you **delete** something that has been written down, you cross it out or remove it. EG *The '6' had been deleted altogether.* V+O = strike out ≠ insert ◊ **deletion** /dɪliːʃəⁿn/, **deletions**. EG *Please underline any words for deletion.* ◊ N UNCOUNT/ COUNT

deleterious /delə¹tɪərɪəs/. Something that is **deleterious** has a harmful effect on a person or thing; a formal word. EG *Many women breast-feed several babies with no deleterious effect on their figures.* ADJ QUALIT ≠ beneficial

deliberate, deliberates, deliberating, deliberated. The word **deliberate** is pronounced /dɪ¹lɪbərət/ when it is an adjective, and /dɪ¹lɪbəreɪt/ when it is a verb. 1 If you do something that is **deliberate**, you have planned it or decided on it beforehand and therefore do it intentionally rather than by accident. EG *He told his mother a deliberate lie... He wondered if her silence was deliberate... In many restaurants there is a deliberate policy of discouraging smoking.* ADJ CLASSIF = intentional ≠ accidental ◊ **deliberately**. EG *The terms of the agreement were left deliberately vague... Advertisements are often deliberately written in bad English.* ◊ ADV WITH VB
2 An action or movement that is **deliberate** is done slowly and carefully. EG *His manner was quiet, his speech deliberate... She played the part in a deliberate manner without any feeling of urgency.* ADJ QUALIT = unhurried ≠ rushed ◊ **deliberately**. EG *He climbed the stairs slowly and deliberately.* ◊ ADV = steadily
3 If you **deliberate**, you think about something seriously and carefully, especially before making a V, OR V+REPORT-CL

very important decision. EG *I deliberated whether or not to accept his offer... After deliberating for 28 hours, the union decided to end the strike.*

deliberation /dɪˈlɪbəreɪʃəⁿn/, **deliberations**. 1 **Deliberation** is careful and often lengthy consideration of a subject. EG *After considerable deliberation, I decided to change my job.* N UNCOUNT ⇑ thought

2 If you say or do something with **deliberation**, you do it slowly and carefully. EG *John, with great deliberation, put his books into his briefcase... 'It's the vacation,' she repeated, speaking with deliberation, as if to a stupid child.* N UNCOUNT: with+N ⇑ care

3 **Deliberations** are formal discussions. EG *The deliberations at Versailles led to a peace agreement... I left the committee to its deliberations.* N PLURAL

deliberative /dɪˈlɪbəⁿrətɪv/. A **deliberative** group or organization has the task of considering and discussing problems or important questions. EG *...a deliberative assembly such as Congress.* ADJ CLASSIF: ATTRIB

delicacy /delɪkəsiˈ/, **delicacies**. 1 If someone or something has the quality of **delicacy**, they are small, graceful, and attractive. EG *...ballads praising feminine delicacy, beauty and fragility.* N UNCOUNT ⇑ fineness ≠ clumsiness

2 If something such as a problem has the quality of **delicacy**, it is difficult and needs careful and tactful treatment. EG *I've got here a matter of exceptional delicacy.* N UNCOUNT ⇑ difficulty

3 If you do or say something with **delicacy**, you do it or say it carefully and tactfully because you do not want to offend people or because you want to avoid things which you consider to be rude or unpleasant. EG *He does it with great delicacy and finesse... Delicacy prevented her from approaching him.* N UNCOUNT = tact

4 A **delicacy** is something that is considered especially nice to eat, but too expensive for people to eat often or in large quantities. EG *...artichokes, smoked fish, and other tangy delicacies.* N COUNT ⇑ food = dainty

delicate /delɪkəˈt/. 1 Something that is **delicate** 1.1 is small and graceful or attractive. EG *She had long delicate fingers... The panel was decorated by an inlay of the most delicate floral design... ...delicate ballet steps.* ◇ **delicately**. EG *The princess took the pot delicately from him... ...delicately veined pale skin.* ADJ QUALIT ⇑ beautiful = dainty ≠ clumsy ◇ ADV WITH VB 1.2 has a colour, taste, or smell which is pleasant and not strong or intense. EG *...a delicate pale cream colour... ...a delicate mushroom sauce.* ADJ QUALIT ⇑ subtle ≠ strong 1.3 is fragile and needs to be handled carefully. EG *...delicate china... Wash delicate fabrics in cold water.* ADJ QUALIT: ATTRIB ⇑ weak

2 Someone who is **delicate** 2.1 is not healthy and strong, but becomes ill easily. EG *I think she was delicate; her health was not good.* ADJ QUALIT ⇑ weak 2.2 uses words carefully in order to avoid offending other people. ◇ **delicately**. EG *She had delicately hinted at his inadequacy.* ADJ QUALIT ⇑ cautious ◇ ADV WITH VB 2.3 is careful to avoid anything which they consider to be rude, improper, or unpleasant. EG *He was as delicate in his undressing and showering as a nun.* ADJ QUALIT: USU PRED = modest

3 A **delicate** situation or problem is difficult and needs very careful and tactful treatment. EG *...a very delicate social and political balance... ...the delicate sphere of race relations.* ◇ **delicately**. EG *...highly sensitive and delicately balanced economic systems.* ADJ QUALIT: ATTRIB = sensitive, tricky ◇ ADV+PAST PART

4 A **delicate** sense or scientific instrument is capable of noticing very small changes or differences. EG *Bees have a delicate sense of smell.* ADJ QUALIT: ATTRIB ⇑ sensitive ≠ crude

delicatessen /delɪkətesəⁿn/, **delicatessens**. A **delicatessen** is a shop that sells high quality foods such as cheeses and cold meats that are imported from other countries. N COUNT

delicious /dɪˀlɪʃəs/. 1 Food that is **delicious** has a very pleasant taste or smell. EG *This trout is delicious.* ◇ **deliciously**. EG *It is one of the most deliciously tender of all vegetables.* ADJ QUALIT ◇ ADV+ADJ

2 Something or someone that is **delicious** is very nice, attractive, or pleasant. EG *He was indulging in a delicious feeling of pleasure... I saw the most delicious girl there... She stayed to savour the delicious spectacle.* ◇ **deliciously**. EG *The sun felt deliciously warm.* ADJ QUALIT: USU ATTRIB ⇑ pleasing = delightful ◇ ADV+ADJ

delight /dɪˈlaɪt/, **delights, delighting, delighted**. 1 **Delight** is a feeling of very great pleasure. EG *Kate wrote to me of her delight that I was now so happy... Frank discovered to his delight that the kitten was real... Her father is rubbing his hands with delight at the news... My sister gave a shriek of delight.* N UNCOUNT ≠ displeasure

2 If someone **takes a delight** or **takes delight** in doing something, they get a lot of pleasure from doing it. EG *He takes delight in annoying me.* PHR: VB INFLECTS, USU+in+-ING ⇑ enjoy

3 A **delight** is someone or something that gives you great joy or pleasure. EG *I was four when I first discovered the delights of feeding ducks... Mrs Travers was a delight to interview.* N COUNT: IF+PREP THEN of

4 If something **delights** you or if you **are delighted** by it, it gives you a lot of pleasure. EG *I was delighted by her brilliant performances as Ophelia... The thought of death neither distressed nor delighted her.* V+O: USU PASS ⇑ please ≠ disappoint

5 If you **delight** in something or at something, you get a lot of pleasure from it. EG *Morris delighted in hard manual work... Be prepared for friends who delight in breaking bad news... He delighted at the prospect of leaving home.* V+A (in/at) ⇑ enjoy = rejoice

delighted /dɪˈlaɪtɪˀd/. If you are **delighted**, you are extremely pleased and excited about something. EG *He was grinning, delighted with his achievement... He was delighted to meet them again... ...a delighted grin.* ◇ **delightedly**. EG *The children laughed delightedly at the antics of the chimpanzees.* ADJ QUALIT: USU PRED = thrilled ◇ ADV WITH VB

delightful /dɪlaɪtful/. Something or someone that is **delightful** is very pleasant and attractive. EG *What a delightful flat you have!... Her children really are delightful.* ◇ **delightfully**. EG *His new novel is brief and delightfully readable.* ADJ QUALIT ⇑ pleasing = lovely ≠ horrible ◇ ADV+ADJ

delimit /diˈlɪmɪt/, **delimits, delimiting, delimited**. If you **delimit** something, you fix or establish its limits; a formal word. EG *We need to delimit the scope of our discussion.* V+O

delineate /diˈlɪniˈeɪt/, **delineates, delineating, delineated**. If you **delineate** something such as an idea or an argument, you describe it or define it, often in a lot of detail; a formal word. EG *The principal problems can be delineated... Liberty must be firmly and clearly delineated.* ◇ **delineation** /diˈlɪniˈeɪʃəⁿn/. EG *...Freud's delineation of the unconscious.* V+O = outline, draw ◇ N UNCOUNT/COUNT

delinquency /dɪˀlɪŋkwənsiˈ/, **delinquencies**. **Delinquency** is behaviour in which someone does things which are illegal or violent. EG *The incidence of violence and delinquency in Western society is increasing rapidly... The court took into account his former delinquencies.* • See also **juvenile delinquency**. N UNCOUNT/COUNT ⇑ criminality

delinquent /dɪˀlɪŋkwənt/, **delinquents**. Someone who is **delinquent** repeatedly commits minor crimes; used especially of young people. EG *Most delinquent children have deprived backgrounds.* ▸ used as a noun. EG *A few months of this may deter some potential delinquents.* • See also **juvenile delinquent**. ADJ CLASSIF ▸ N COUNT ⇑ offender

delirious /dɪlɪrɪəs/. Someone who is **delirious** is 1 unable to think or speak in a rational way, usually because they are very ill and have a fever. EG *She was delirious with the fever.* 2 extremely excited and happy. EG *He sang before delirious crowds in a movie theatre.* ◇ **deliriously**. EG *A deliriously joyful boy came whooping into the village.* ADJ CLASSIF: USU PRED ⇑ rambling ADJ QUALIT = ecstatic ◇ ADV+ADJ

delirium /dɪlɪrɪəm/. 1 If someone is suffering from **delirium**, they are not able to think or speak in a rational way because they are very ill and have a fever. N UNCOUNT ⇑ illness

2 **Delirium** is also a very excited and unusually happy state. EG *The congregation went into delirium.* N UNCOUNT = ecstasy

delirium tremens /tremenz, triː-/ is the same as DT's. N UNCOUNT

deliver /dɪˀlɪvə/, **delivers, delivering, delivered**. 1 If you **deliver** something, 1.1 you take it to someone's house, office, etc. EG *The postman at last delivered the letter we had been waiting for... The eggs were delivered from the farm along with the milk... Most of the big stores will deliver if you ask them.* V OR V+O ⇑ bring 1.2 you give it to someone; a formal use. EG *If there is a divorce the husband delivers over to his wife exactly half of his wealth... Chance delivered his enemy into his hands.* V+O+A = surrender

2 If you **deliver** a lecture or speech, you give it in public. EG *He earned his living by delivering lectures throughout the country... He delivered an emotional speech on the horrors of war... The jury delivered a verdict of 'guilty'.* V+O ⇑ utter

3 When someone **delivers** a baby, they help a woman who is giving birth to the baby. EG *The doctor agreed to deliver her baby at home.* • If you say that V+O • PHR: VB

a woman **was delivered of** a baby, you mean that she gave birth to it; a formal expression. INFLECTS

4 If someone **delivers** you from something, they rescue or save you from it; a formal use. EG *They came to deliver the people from tyranny.* V+O: IF+PREP THEN *from* = release

5 When someone **delivers** a blow to someone else, they hit them; a literary use. EG *She delivered a hard blow to his stomach.* . V+O, IF+PREP THEN *to*

6 When you **deliver** something that you have promised to do or make, you do it or make it. EG *The government promised reform of the tax laws but failed to deliver it.* ● If you say that someone has **delivered the goods**, you mean that they have done something that they promised to do. EG *They failed to deliver the goods and things were as bad as ever.* V OR V+O ● PHR: VB INFLECTS

deliverance /di'lɪvərəns/ is rescue from captivity, danger, or evil; an old-fashioned word. EG *He felt optimistic after his deliverance from the threat of physical violence... He entertained hopes of future deliverance.* N UNCOUNT+SUPP = release

delivery /dɪ'lɪvəri'/, **deliveries**. 1 **Delivery** or a **delivery** is the bringing of letters, parcels, or other goods to someone's house or to another place where they want them. EG *All goods must be paid for before delivery... I had to pay a hundred pounds deposit and the remainder on delivery... The debate coincided with the delivery of a petition against hanging.* N UNCOUNT

2 A **delivery** is also something that is delivered to someone. EG *We ordered an extra delivery of coal.* N COUNT

3 Someone's **delivery** is the way in which they give a speech or lecture. EG *His delivery was clear and pleasant to listen to.* N UNCOUNT: USU +SUPP

4 **Delivery** is also the process of giving birth to a baby. EG *She had a difficult delivery... Husbands are encouraged to be present at the delivery and see the baby being born.* N COUNT/UNCOUNT

5 **Delivery** from a difficult situation or from captivity is rescue from it; a literary use. EG *He prayed for delivery from his captors.* N UNCOUNT, IF+PREP THEN *from* = deliverance

dell /del/, **dells**. A **dell** is a small valley which has trees growing in it; a literary word. N COUNT

delouse /di:laus, -lauz/, **delouses, delousing, deloused**. If you **delouse** a person or an animal, you get rid of lice from their body, hair, or fur. V+O ⇑ cleanse

delphinium /delfɪnɪəm/, **delphiniums**. A **delphinium** is a large garden plant with a tall stem and blue flowers which grow along its stem. N COUNT ⇑ flower

delta /deltə/, **deltas**. 1 A **delta** is an area of low, flat land shaped like a triangle, where a river splits and spreads out into several branches before entering the sea. N COUNT

2 **Delta** is the fourth letter of the Greek alphabet, sometimes used as a mark or grade given for a student's work. N COUNT/UNCOUNT

delude /di'lju:d/, **deludes, deluding, deluded**. If you **delude** someone, you make them believe something that is not true. EG *Sometimes you can be deluded into thinking that everything is going well... He deludes himself if he thinks that the company will support him.* V+O (NG/REFL) ⇑ deceive

deluge /delju:dʒ/, **deluges, deluging, deluged**.
1 A **deluge** is a sudden, very heavy fall of rain. EG *The rain turned to a deluge.* N COUNT = downpour

2 If rain **deluges** a place, it falls very heavily there, sometimes causing floods. EG *A rainstorm deluged the city.* V+O = flood

3 A **deluge** of things is a large number of them which all arrive or are presented at the same time. EG *...a deluge of petitions to the Tsar... ...the deluge of new knowledge.* N COUNT: IF+PREP THEN *of* ⇑ lot = flood

4 If you **are deluged** with things, a large number of them all arrive or are presented at the same time, with the result that you feel overwhelmed. EG *...pupils deluged with facts... They were deluged with requests to play the song.* V+O: USU PASS+*with* = inundated

delusion /di'lu:ʒən/, **delusions**. 1 A **delusion** is something that you believe to be true or to be happening, but which is not true or not happening. EG *She was beginning to drink more under the delusion that she had somehow become immune to it... Was this a delusion of persecution?* N COUNT ⇑ illusion

2 **Delusion** is the state of believing things that are not true. N UNCOUNT ⇑ illusion

delusive /di'lu:sɪv/. Something which is **delusive** makes you believe something that is not true. EG *...the heady but delusive scent of victory.* ADJ CLASSIF: ATTRIB ⇑ unreal

de luxe /di' lʌks/ is used to describe something that is better in quality than something ordinary of the same kind and that looks beautiful and expensive; often used in the names of products such as cars. EG *...a de luxe version of the Ford Escort.* ADJ CLASSIF: ATTRIB, OR ADJ AFTER N = luxury ≠ ordinary

delve /delv/, **delves, delving, delved**. 1 If you **delve** into something, you try to discover new information about it. EG *Andrew's presence meant she couldn't delve too deeply into the past... One must delve more deeply to find the reasons.* V+A ⇑ research = dig

2 If you **delve** inside something such as a cupboard or a bag, you search inside it. EG *Cathy passed it to him and he delved carefully among its contents.* V+A = rummage

demagogic /deməgɒgɪk/. If you say that someone is **demagogic**, you mean that they are typical of or like a demagogue; used showing disapproval. EG *...social unrest would be eliminated, thus making demagogic dictators less likely.* ADJ CLASSIF

demagogue /deməgɒg/, **demagogues**. A **demagogue** is a political leader who tries to win support by appealing to people's emotions rather than by rational arguments; used showing disapproval. N COUNT

demagogy /deməgɒgi'/ is a method of political rule which involves appealing to people's emotions rather than using rational arguments. N UNCOUNT ⇑ government

demand /di'ma:nd/, **demands, demanding, demanded**. 1 If you **demand** something, you ask for it very forcefully. EG *The policeman demanded to see their identity cards... She had been demanding that he visit Scotland more often... I demand to see a doctor... They are demanding still higher wages.* V+O/REPORT-CL/*to*-INF = insist on

2 If you **demand**, you insist that someone tells you something. EG *'What have I done?' he demanded.* V+REPORT-CL/QUOTE

3 If one thing **demands** another, it requires the other as a necessary part of a process or activity. EG *He has most of the qualities demanded of a leader... It demands a good supply of skilled workers.* V+O ⇑ require

4 A **demand** is a firm request for something. EG *They are afraid about what might happen if they refused his demands... My demand for a clean towel had upset them... He resisted demands that a censorship board be established.* N COUNT+SUPP

5 If there is **demand** for something, a lot of the public want to buy it or have it. EG *The problem is that the demand for health care is unlimited... There has been a general increase in demand.* ● If something is **in demand** or **in great demand**, it is very popular and a lot of people want to buy it or have it. EG *They were always in demand and were widely read.* N UNCOUNT: IF+PREP THEN *for* ⇑ need ● PHR: USED AS AN A

6 The **demands** of an activity or process are all the essential things required by it. EG *The body's fuel demands are very low... ...the demands of family life.* N PLURAL: IF+PREP THEN *of* = needs

7 **Demands** made on someone or something are things that they are required to do which need a lot of time, energy, or money spent on them. EG *The industrial system has always made heavy demands on those working in it... Thus inflation puts extra demands on the State purse.* N COUNT: USU PL ⇑ requirements

8 If something is available **on demand**, you can have it whenever you need it or ask for it. EG *Your money is available on demand... ...abortion on demand.* PHR: USED AS AN A

demanding /di'ma:ndɪŋ/. 1 Something that is **demanding** requires a lot of your time, energy, or attention. EG *It is a very wearing and demanding job.* ADJ QUALIT = taxing, rigorous

2 People who are **demanding** are not easily satisfied or pleased. EG *...an impatient and demanding public.* ADJ QUALIT = difficult

demarcate /di:ma:keɪt/, **demarcates, demarcating, demarcated**. If you **demarcate** something, you establish its boundaries or limits in order to separate it from other things of the same type; a formal word. V+O

demarcation /di:ma:keɪʃən/ is the separation that is established, for example, between two areas or between the various jobs that have to be done in a particular place of work. EG *The demarcation line which separated East and West is shown on the map... There are more changes in areas of demarcation, manning levels, etc.* N UNCOUNT

demean /di'mi:n/, **demeans, demeaning, demeaned**. 1 If you **demean** yourself, you do something which makes people have less respect for you. EG *He will lose face with the boss by having to demean himself in this way.* V+O (REFL) ⇑ lower = debase, humiliate

2 To **demean** someone or something means to reduce the amount of respect that people have for them. EG *By lying he had demeaned his office.* V+O ⇑ diminish = degrade

demeaning /di1mi:nɪŋ/. An action that is **demeaning** is one which makes people lose some of the respect that they have for you. EG *Acting in a play, on the other hand, was considered socially demeaning.*
ADJ QUALIT ⇑ lowering = degrading

demeanour /di1mi:nə/; also spelled **demeanor** in American English. Your **demeanour** is the way you behave and the impression that this gives people about the sort of person you are; a formal word. EG *The man was polite and his general demeanour had the air of a clergyman.*
N UNCOUNT : USU POSS+N ⇑ behaviour = bearing

demented /di1mentɪ2d/. Someone who is **demented** behaves in a strange or violent way, often because of a mental illness or because of extreme emotional stress. EG *The man was a simple soul and plainly demented.* ◊ **dementedly**. EG *Bob grinned dementedly, thinking I was trying to be funny.*
ADJ CLASSIF ⇑ mad = deranged
◊ ADV

dementia /dɪmenʃɪ0ə/ is a serious illness of the mind; a medical term.
N UNCOUNT

demerara sugar /deməreərə ʃʊgə/ is a crunchy, light brown kind of sugar which usually comes from the West Indies.
N UNCOUNT

demerit /di1merɪt, di:merɪt/, **demerits**. The **demerits** of something are its faults or disadvantages; a formal word. EG *...a discussion on the merits and demerits of the play.*
N COUNT : USU PL = flaw

demijohn /demɪdʒɒn/, **demijohns**. A **demijohn** is a large bottle with a short narrow neck, which is used in making wine.
N COUNT ⇑ container

demilitarize /di:mɪlə1təraɪz/, **demilitarizes, demilitarizing, demilitarized**; also spelled **demilitarise**. When an area **is demilitarized**, all military forces are removed from it. EG *...a demilitarized zone.* ◊ **demilitarization** /di:mɪlə1təraɪzeɪʃə0n/.
V+O
◊ N UNCOUNT

demise /di1maɪz/. **1** The **demise** of something that used to be successful or important is its eventual failure. EG *They had themselves contributed to the demise of the student movement.*
N SING WITH DET +SUPP ⇑ end = death

2 The **demise** of someone is their death; an old-fashioned, formal use. EG *The demise of Mrs Wright came as a great shock.*
N SING WITH DET

demist /di1mɪst/, **demists, demisting, demisted**. If you **demist** a car windscreen, you remove the condensation from it, usually by blowing warm air over it.
V+O ⇑ clear

demo /deməʊ/, **demos**. A **demo** is a demonstration; an informal word used in British English. EG *He is always going on demos.*
N COUNT

demob /di:mɒb/, **demobs, demobbing, demobbed**. To **demob** means the same as to demobilize; an informal word used in British English.
V+O : USU PASS

demobilize /di1məʊbɪlaɪz/, **demobilizes, demobilizing, demobilized**; also spelled **demobilise**. If someone **is demobilized**, they are released from one of the armed forces. EG *The troops were stationed around the country before being demobilised.* ◊ **demobilization** /di1məʊbɪlaɪzeɪʃə0n/. EG *HQ are dealing with the complex problem of demobilisation.*
V+O : USU PASS ⇑ discharge
◊ N UNCOUNT

democracy /dɪ2mɒkrəsi1/, **democracies**. **1 Democracy** is **1.1** a system of government in which people choose their rulers by voting for them in elections. EG *I suppose it takes time for true democracy to work... One important element of democracy is its notion that majority opinion should prevail.*
N UNCOUNT

1.2 a system of running organizations, businesses, groups, etc, in which each member is entitled to vote and participate in management decisions. EG *...industrial democracy.*
N UNCOUNT : USU MOD+N

2 A **democracy** is a country in which the people choose their government by voting for it. EG *...a parliamentary democracy... Yugoslavia has suffered as much as any western democracy from wage inflation.*
N COUNT : USU MOD+N

democrat /deməⁿkræt/, **democrats**. **1** A **Democrat** is **1.1** a member or supporter of the Democratic Party in the United States of America. EG *...a liberal Democrat from Wisconsin... For many years a group of powerful southern Democrats dominated Congress.* **1.2** a member or supporter of a particular political party which has the word 'democrat' or 'democratic' in its title. EG *On Friday they released a kidnapped Democrat politician.*
N COUNT ≠ Republican
N COUNT : USU MOD+N

2 A **democrat** is also a person who believes in the ideals of democracy, personal freedom, and equality. EG *He is just what he claims he is, a natural democrat.*
N COUNT

democratic /deməⁿkrætɪk/. **1** A country, government, or political system that is **democratic** has representatives who are elected by the people. EG *The country was going over to a different form of democratic government... They vote freely, as they do in genuinely democratic countries.* ◊ **democratically**. EG *...a democratically elected government.*
ADJ CLASSIF
◊ ADV

2 Something that is **democratic** is based on the idea that everyone should have equal rights and should be involved in making important decisions. EG *We must help them as they struggle to build a more democratic society... Management is having to become more democratic in style.* ◊ **democratically.** EG *Once a decision has been democratically discussed it must be adhered to.*
ADJ QUALIT ≠ undemocratic
◊ ADV ≠ undemocratically

3 A **Democratic** campaign, majority, plan, etc is one that involves the Democratic Party, which is one of the two main political parties in the United States of America. EG *...the campaign for the Democratic presidential nomination of 1968.*
ADJ CLASSIF : ATTRIB ≠ Republican

4 Democratic is also used in the titles of some other political parties. EG *...The Social Democratic Party.*
ADJ CLASSIF : ATTRIB

democratize /dɪ2mɒkrətaɪz/, **democratizes, democratizing, democratized**; also spelled **democratise**. If people **democratize** something such as a country or an institution, they make it more democratic; a formal word. EG *They decided they must democratize their procedures.* ◊ **democratization** /di1mɒkrətaɪzeɪʃə0n/. EG *A Soldiers' Charter was drawn up, calling for the democratization of the armed forces and trade unions.*
V+O
◊ N UNCOUNT : USU+SUPP

demography /di1mɒgrəfi1/ is the study of the changes in numbers of births, deaths, marriages, and diseases in a community over a period of time.
N UNCOUNT ⇑ science

demolish /di1mɒlɪʃ/, **demolishes, demolishing, demolished**. **1** If people **demolish** something such as a building, they knock it down or destroy it completely. EG *Terry Street was demolished a few years ago.*
V+O = knock down

2 If you **demolish** someone's idea, argument, or belief, you prove that it is wrong. EG *He soon demolished Mr Stewart's suggestions.*
V+O ⇑ destroy = disprove, refute

demolition /deməlɪʃə0n, di:-/, **demolitions**. **1** The **demolition** of a building is the act of knocking it down. EG *...the demolition of the old YMCA building... They underwent courses in radio communication, demolition, and sabotage.*
N UNCOUNT/COUNT ⇑ destruction

2 The **demolition** of an argument, idea, or belief is the act of proving that it is incorrect. EG *The Times began its demolition with an editorial by Lovat Fraser.*
N UNCOUNT/COUNT ⇑ destruction = refutation

demon /di:mə0n/, **demons**. A **demon** is **1** an evil spirit. EG *Can we explain the universe without resorting to gods or demons?* **2** an evil force which is believed to influence people's behaviour. EG *A kind of demon seized her and she could not resist being extraordinarily rude to him.* **3** a person who concentrates very hard on or is very skilled at an activity and puts a lot of energy into it. EG *She worked like a demon all through rehearsals... She's a demon squash player.*
N COUNT = devil
N COUNT = fiend
N COUNT : USU BEFORE N = virtuoso

demoniac /di1məʊnɪæk/; also **demoniacal** /di:mənaɪəkə0l/. **1** A **demoniac** or **demoniacal** person is evil, as though he or she were possessed by a devil.
ADJ CLASSIF : ATTRIB = demonic, wild

2 A **demoniac** or **demoniacal** activity is wild and uncontrolled. EG *...demoniac fury... ...audible for a moment even above the demoniacal hooting.*
ADJ CLASSIF : ATTRIB

demonic /di1mɒnɪk/. Something that is **demonic** is evil or very unpleasant. EG *...a demonic sense of humour... There was, behind Guy's suave superiority, something demonic, something which could be cruel.*
ADJ CLASSIF = cruel, diabolic

demonstrable /dɪ2mɒnstrəbə0l/. Something that is **demonstrable** can be shown or proved to be true. EG *The demonstrable fact was that the company was losing money... This is demonstrable by the fact that plants will die when placed in the dark.* ◊ **demonstrably**. EG *Their vehicles are demonstrably more reliable than ours.*
ADJ CLASSIF ⇑ verifiable
◊ ADV AFTER VB = manifestly

demonstrate /demənstreɪt/, **demonstrates, demonstrating, demonstrated**. **1** If someone or something **demonstrates** a fact, theory, or principle, they make it clear to people. EG *This example is enough to demonstrate the general principle... Her latest book demonstrates how important freedom is.*
V+O/REPORT-CL ⇑ show = illustrate, prove

2 If you **demonstrate** something to someone, you
V+O

show them how to do it or use it by doing it or using it in front of them while you explain what you are doing. EG *She is demonstrating a new kind of cooker in London... She has been demonstrating how you make bread.*

3 If you **demonstrate** a particular skill, quality, or feeling, you reveal that you have it. EG *She has not demonstrated much generosity.* V+O ⇑ show = display

4 When people **demonstrate**, they take part in a march or a meeting which is intended to show their opposition to, or their support for, something. EG *Why don't you go and demonstrate outside the Embassy?... They are demonstrating for a 15 per cent wage rise.* V ⇑ protest

demonstration /dɛmənstreɪʃəⁿn/, **demonstrations**. A **demonstration** is 1 a public meeting or march which is held by people who want to show their opposition to something or their support for something. EG *...a student demonstration... There was a series of demonstrations against the visit.* N COUNT ⇑ protest = demo 2 a talk or explanation by someone who shows you how to do or use something, or how something works. EG *The woman giving the demonstration spoke in a loud voice... ...the first public demonstration of television.* N COUNT 3 a proof by someone that something exists or that something such as a theory or principle is right. EG *It was an unforgettable demonstration of the power of reason.* N COUNT/UNCOUNT ⇑ proof 4 a display or expression of an emotion. EG *...spontaneous demonstrations of physical affection.* N COUNT/UNCOUNT

demonstrative /di²mɒnstrətɪv/, **demonstratives**. 1 Someone who is **demonstrative** shows their feelings very freely. EG *They are very strange and demonstrative people.* ▸ used of people's behaviour. EG *Their greetings and farewells were excessively demonstrative.* ADJ QUALIT ⇑ expressive ≠ reserved, restrained

2 **Demonstrative** is a term used in grammar for words such as *this* and *that*. The demonstratives are a subgroup of determiners and in this dictionary they are described as DET. See **this**, **that**, and ☐ at DET. N COUNT ⇑ determiner

demonstrator /dɛmənstreɪtə/, **demonstrators**. A **demonstrator** is 1 a person taking part in a public meeting or march to show their opposition to something or their support for something. EG *There was a battle between police and demonstrators lasting all afternoon.* N COUNT ⇑ protester 2 a person, usually in a shop, who shows people how a machine or device works by operating it themselves and explaining what they are doing. N COUNT ⇑ salesperson

demoralize /di¹mɒrəlaɪz/, **demoralizes**, **demoralizing**, **demoralized**; also spelled **demoralise**. If something **demoralizes** someone, it makes them lose so much confidence in what they are doing that they want to give up. EG *People are demoralised by the present climate of political opinion.* ◊ **demoralized**. EG *...the stream of desperate and demoralized people seeking work.* ◊ **demoralization** /di¹mɒrəlaɪzeɪʃəⁿn/. EG *...the growing national mood of self-doubt and demoralisation.* V+O : USU PASS ⇑ weaken = dishearten ≠ encourage ◊ ADJ QUALIT ◊ N UNCOUNT

demote /di¹məʊt/, **demotes**, **demoting**, **demoted**. If someone **demotes** you, they give you a lower rank or a less important position, often as a punishment. EG *He was demoted to the rank of ordinary soldier.* ◊ **demotion** /di¹məʊʃəⁿn/, **demotions**. EG *Some months after my demotion we met in a corridor.* V+O = relegate ≠ promote ◊ N UNCOUNT/COUNT : USU POSS +N = relegation

demotic /di¹mɒtɪk/. 1 **Demotic** is used to describe something that is typical of or used by ordinary people; a formal use. EG *...television, that most demotic of the arts.* ADJ CLASSIF : USU ATTRIB ⇑ common

2 **Demotic** is the spoken form of the modern Greek language. N UNCOUNT

demur /dɪmɜː/, **demurs**, **demurring**, **demurred**; a formal word. 1 If you **demur**, you say that you do not agree with something or will not do something. EG *Only the journalist demurred, and he was an economist... The boys demurred at the suggestion.* V ⇑ object = protest ≠ agree

2 If you do something **without demur**, you do it immediately and without making any objection. EG *Without demur, he gave me the three appointments I asked for.* PHR : USED AS AN A ⇑ willingly ≠ reluctantly

demure /di¹mjʊə/. Someone who is **demure** is quiet, rather shy, and behaves very correctly; used especially of young women and children. EG *...torn between her and his demure fiancée.* ▸ used of people's behaviour. EG *She sipped her coffee with a demure air of righteousness.* ◊ **demurely**. EG *She sat down and put the large, creamy napkin demurely on her lap.* ADJ QUALIT ⇑ prim = decorous ▸ ⇑ prim = proper ◊ ADV

demystify /diːmɪstɪfaɪ/, **demystifies**, **demystifying**, **demystified**. If you **demystify** something, you make it easier to understand by giving a clear explanation of it. EG *I began working to demystify some of our society's myths.* V+O ⇑ explain = rationalize

den /dɛn/, **dens**. 1 A **den** is the home of certain types of wild animals such as lions or foxes. N COUNT = lair

2 Your **den** is a small, quiet room in your house where you can go to carry on a hobby or to read, work, or study without being disturbed. EG *...the privacy of a furnished den in his basement.* N COUNT

3 A **den** is also a secret place where people meet, usually for a dishonest purpose. EG *...he finds himself in a den of frightful ruffians.* N COUNT : IF+ PREP THEN *of*

denationalize /diːnæʃəⁿnəlaɪz/, **denationalizes**, **denationalizing**, **denationalized**; also spelled **denationalise**. If people **denationalize** an industry or business, they transfer it into private ownership so that it is no longer owned and controlled by the state. EG *There were plans to denationalise the steel industry.* ◊ **denationalization** /diːnæʃəⁿnəlaɪzeɪʃəⁿn/. V+O ⇑ sell off = privatize ≠ nationalize ◊ N UNCOUNT

denial /dɪ²naɪəl/, **denials**. 1 A **denial** of something such as an accusation is a statement that it is not true. EG *He made a personal denial of all the charges against him... The government's policy of denial was a clear reflection of the position... His denials were once more believed.* N COUNT ≠ admission

2 The **denial** of something that you think people have a right to is a refusal to let them have it, usually by a person or group in authority. EG *They protested against the continued denial of civil liberties.* ● See also **self-denial**. N UNCOUNT : IF+ PREP THEN *of* ⇑ prevention

denier /dɛnjə/ is a measure of the fineness of the nylon or silk thread that is used, for example, in making stockings and tights. EG *...a pair of 15 denier stockings.* N UNCOUNT : NUM+N

denigrate /dɛnɪ²greɪt/, **denigrates**, **denigrating**, **denigrated**. If you **denigrate** someone or something, you criticize them unfairly because you believe that they are not as good or efficient as other people think they are. EG *To assert this is to denigrate the effectiveness of the police.* ◊ **denigration** /dɛnɪ²greɪʃəⁿn/. EG *...its denigration of the role of the individual.* V+O ⇑ criticize = belittle ≠ praise ◊ N UNCOUNT : USU+*of*

denim /dɛnɪm/, **denims**. 1 **Denim** is a strong cotton cloth which is used to make clothes such as jeans and skirts. Denim is usually blue. EG *...a denim jacket.* N UNCOUNT : USU BEFORE N

2 **Denims** are clothes, especially trousers, which are made of denim. EG *...youths wearing denims and T-shirts.* N PLURAL

denizen /dɛnɪzəⁿn/, **denizens**. A **denizen** of a particular place is a person, animal, or plant that lives or grows in this place; a literary word. EG *...that aged denizen of Dye's Hole.* N COUNT : IF+ PREP THEN *of* ⇑ inhabitant = resident

denomination /di¹nɒmɪneɪʃəⁿn/, **denominations**. A **denomination** is a particular religious group which has slightly different beliefs from other groups within the same faith. EG *...Bibles of all denominations.* N COUNT

denominational /di¹nɒmɪ²neɪʃəⁿnəl, -ʃənəⁿl/. **Denominational** institutions, groups, or events belong to or are organized by a particular religious denomination. EG *...a need for denominational education.* ADJ CLASSIF : USU ATTRIB

denominator /di¹nɒmɪ²neɪtə/, **denominators**. A **denominator** is the number which appears under the line in a fraction. It is the amount by which you should divide the top number. EG *In the fraction 5/7 7 is the denominator.* N COUNT : USU *common*+N

denote /di¹nəʊt/, **denotes**, **denoting**, **denoted**. If one thing **denotes** another, 1 it is a sign or indication of it. EG *...a great wrinkling of brows that denoted difficult thought... My identity was denoted by a plastic label on my wrist.* V+O/REPORT-CL = indicate 2 it represents it by using a sign or symbol. EG *We're using 'R' to denote the function.* V+O = represent 3 it represents it clearly and obviously. EG *'Basic', as its name denotes, is a very straightforward set of instructions.* ◊ **denotation**. V+O ⇑ show = indicate ◊ N UNCOUNT

denouement /deɪnuːmɒn/, **denouements**; also spelled **dénouement**. A **denouement** is the explanation of something that has previously been unclear or that has been kept secret, especially at the end of a book or a play. EG *It was the preparation for this denouement in the second act that impressed me most.* N COUNT : USU SING = ending

denounce /di'naʊns/, **denounces, denouncing, denounced.** If you **denounce** a person or an action, you criticize them severely and publicly because you feel strongly that they are wrong or evil. EG *A mass meeting at Carnegie Hall denounced him as a traitor... He denounced the practice of heart transplants.* V+O, OR V+O+A (as) = condemn ≠ praise

dense /dens/, **denser, densest.** 1 Something that is **dense** contains a lot of things or people in a small area. EG *There was a dense crowd waiting to see the Pope pass by... We fought our way through dense forest.* ◊ **densely.** EG *...the most densely populated region in the country.* ADJ QUALIT ⇑ thick ≠ sparse; ◊ ADV WITH VB (USU PAST PART)

2 **Dense** fog or smoke is difficult to see through because it is very heavy and dark. ADJ QUALIT ⇑ thick

3 A book or film that is **dense** is difficult to understand because it contains a lot of information and ideas. EG *He has produced a dense and difficult film... His latest writing is dense and rough.* ADJ QUALIT = concentrated

4 Someone who is **dense** is stupid, and takes a long time to understand simple things; an informal use. EG *He is so dense that he never understands anything I say to him.* ADJ QUALIT : PRED = thick, obtuse

density /densɪti¹/, **densities.** 1 **Density** is 1.1 the amount to which something is filled with people or things. EG *Australia has a very low population density... By 1971 Britain had the highest density of tractors in the world.* 1.2 the relation of the mass of a substance or an object to its volume; a technical term in physics. EG *...the density of water.* N UNCOUNT/COUNT+SUPP ⇑ concentration; N UNCOUNT/COUNT

2 The **density** of a book, film, etc, is the concentrated way in which it contains information and ideas. EG *...the sort of density that Theroux's earlier novels had.* N UNCOUNT+SUPP ⇑ concentration

dent /dent/, **dents, denting, dented.** 1 If you **dent** the surface of something, you make a hollow dip in it by hitting it. EG *I drove into a post and dented the bumper slightly... He pulled back the covers and dented the pillow a little.* ◊ **dented.** EG *...a dented green Cadillac.* ▸ used as a noun. EG *...new car owners searching for dents and scratches.* V+O ≠ smooth, flatten; ◊ ADJ CLASSIF; ▸ N COUNT

2 If something **dents** your ideas or your pride, it makes you realize that your ideas are wrong, or that you are not as good or successful as you thought. EG *It also dented my notion that it never rains in Cairo.* V+O ⇑ damage = knock

3 If something **makes a dent in** something else, it reduces it considerably. EG *The operation had made a major dent in the trade of protected wildlife.* PHR : VB INFLECTS ⇑ reduce

dental /dentə⁰l/ is used to describe things that relate to teeth and the activities involved in caring for them or learning about them. EG *I had undergone a rather serious dental operation.* ADJ CLASSIF : ATTRIB

dentist /dentɪst/, **dentists.** A **dentist** is a person who is qualified to examine and treat people's teeth. ▸ The **dentist's** is used to refer to the surgery or clinic where a dentist works. N COUNT; ▸ N SING : the+N

dentistry /dentɪstri¹/ is the work done by a dentist. N UNCOUNT

dentures /dentʃəz/ are artificial teeth used by people who no longer have all their own teeth. N PLURAL = false teeth

denude /di'nju:d/, **denudes, denuding, denuded.** If something **is denuded,** 1 the covering is taken away from it. EG *Both bunks had been completely denuded of sheets and blankets.* ◊ **denuded.** EG *...the denuded hills.* 2 its protection or its important qualities are taken away. ◊ **denuded.** EG *The policy change was to leave the country denuded of adequate air defence... ...a land denuded of its richness.* V+O : IF+PREP THEN of; ◊ ADJ CLASSIF; V+O : USU PASS; ◊ ADJ CLASSIF = stripped

denunciation /di'nʌnsieɪʃən/, **denunciations. Denunciation** is severe public criticism of someone or something that you believe is wrong or evil. EG *...the denunciation of state involvement by Mr Wilson.* ▸ used as a count noun. EG *...his denunciations of the errors of the previous government.* N UNCOUNT : IF+PREP THEN of = condemnation; ▸ N COUNT+SUPP

deny /dɪ'naɪ/, **denies, denying, denied.** 1 When you **deny** something, you say that it is not true. EG *He denied that he was involved and demanded an apology... ...yet people couldn't deny it... Green denied doing anything illegal.* V+O/REPORT-CL/ING ⇑ contradict ≠ affirm, admit

2 If you **deny** someone something that they need or want, you prevent them from having it. EG *The government exploited their labour while denying them social equality... He has also denied you access to some information.* V+O+O = refuse

3 If you **deny** someone or something, you say that they have no connection with you or do not belong to you; an old-fashioned use. EG *Jesus knew that his disciple Peter would deny him before his death.* V+O ⇑ disown = disclaim ≠ admit

deodorant /di:əʊdə⁰rənt/, **deodorants. Deodorant** is a liquid or spray that you can use to hide or prevent the smell of perspiration on your body. N MASS ⇑ chemical

deodorize /di:əʊdə⁰raɪz/, **deodorizes, deodorizing, deodorized**; also spelled **deodorise.** If you **deodorize** something, you hide or remove unpleasant smells from it; a formal word. ◊ **deodorized.** EG *Deodorized towels can cause allergic reactions.* V+O ⇑ freshen; ◊ ADJ CLASSIF

depart /di'pɑ:t/, **departs, departing, departed.** 1 When someone or something **departs** from a place, 1.1 they leave it. EG *The rescue ship departed from the area as quickly as possible... They watched the visitor depart as quietly as he had come.* 1.2 they leave it at the beginning of a journey. EG *The Blue Express was scheduled to depart at six... ...a number of us departed for an afternoon outing... He felt like a man who was departing into the unknown.* V : IF+PREP THEN from; V : USU+A = set off ≠ get back, return

2 If you **depart** from a traditional or accepted way of doing something, you start acting or behaving in a slightly different way. EG *Children born in this country are British and we ought not to depart from that principle... ...their unwillingness to depart from traditional practice.* V+A (from) ⇑ deviate = stray, break away

departed /di'pɑ:tɪ²d/. If you talk about **departed** friends or relatives, you mean that they are dead; a formal word. EG *Let us pray for our departed friends.* ▸ The **departed** is used to refer to someone who has recently died. ADJ CLASSIF : USU ATTRIB = late; ▸ N SING : the+N ⇑ person

department /di'pɑ:tmə²nt/, **departments.** 1 A **department** is 1.1 one of the sections in a large organization such as a business, hospital, university, etc. EG *He'll have to go to the casualty department and have this stitched... ...the foreign exchange department of a merchant bank... He was head of a very large department of physics.* 1.2 one of the sections of a government which is responsible for the administration of a particular area of policy. EG *The Defence Department is well aware of experiments into germ warfare... Women stood protesting outside the local office of the Department of Health.* N COUNT+SUPP ⇑ section; N COUNT+SUPP : ALSO IN NAMES ⇑ section

2 If you say that something **is** someone's **department**, you mean that it is a task which they are responsible for; an informal expression. EG *I don't want to know about the gardening, that's not my department.* PHR : VB INFLECTS

departmental /di:pɑ:tmentə⁰l/ is used to describe the activities, responsibilities, and possessions of a department, for example a government department, or a department in a large organization. EG *The departmental office was full of people... There's a departmental meeting this afternoon.* ADJ CLASSIF : ATTRIB

department store, department stores. A **department store** is a large shop which is divided into a lot of different sections and which sells many different kinds of goods. N COUNT

departure /di'pɑ:tʃə/, **departures.** 1 **Departure** or a **departure** is 1.1 the act of going away from somewhere. EG *She packed her case ready for departure... He rose and walked slowly away, his departure as unnoticed as his arrival had been... The premature departure of the visitors was worrying.* 1.2 the act of leaving a place at the beginning of a journey. EG *...on the eve of my departure for Cape Town... It'll tell you all the departure times.* N COUNT/UNCOUNT : IF+PREP THEN from/of = leaving ≠ arrival; N COUNT/UNCOUNT : IF+PREP THEN from/for

2 An action that is a **departure** from the usual or accepted way of behaving is one that is being done differently from the usual or accepted way. EG *Does the Chancellor's budget represent a departure from stated Government policy?... ...condemned by many as a departure from normal scientific method.* N COUNT/UNCOUNT : IF+PREP THEN from ⇑ change = deviation

3 A new or fresh **departure** is a start on a new course of action or a new direction that your life or work is now taking. EG *Transport was an entirely new departure for him... Do you think Doris Lessing made a genuinely new departure in her last novel?* N COUNT : ADJ+N

depend /di'pend/, **depends, depending, depended.** 1 If you **depend** on someone or something, you need them in order to be able to survive physically, financially, or emotionally. EG *We in the United Kingdom have depended heavily on coal both for industrial and domestic use... The doctors actually depended on the money that they were paid by the patients... Our lives and those of all other animals depend on oxygen... At college Julie had seemed to depend upon Simon more and more.* V+A (on/upon) = rely

2 If you can **depend** on a person, organization, or V+A (on/upon)

law, you know that they will support you or help you when you need them. EG *I knew I could depend on you... This country is an ally you can depend on.*

3 If you say that something **depends** on something else, or that it **depends**, you mean that what you are saying might only happen or be true if the circumstances are right for it. EG *The success of the meeting depends largely on whether the chairman is efficient... How should you report this event? Well it depends which newspaper you work for... 'What will you do?'–'I don't know. It depends.'*
V+A *(on)*, *it*+V+, OR *it*+V+REPORT-CL : NO IMPER; ⇑ be contingent

4 You use **depending on** to say that the result or truth of something will be affected and determined by the particular factors involved. EG *This training takes a variable time, depending on the chosen speciality... There are, depending on the individual, a lot of different approaches.*
PREP

dependable /di'pɛndəbə⁰l/. If someone or something is **dependable**, you can be sure that they will always act consistently or sensibly, or be ready to help you when they are needed. EG *He's very organized and dependable... ...dependable Austrian cigarette lighters.* ◇ **dependably.** EG *The steam engines were throbbing along as dependably as ever.*
ADJ QUALIT; ⇑ trustworthy; = reliable; ◇ ADV WITH VB; = reliably

dependant /di'pɛndənt/, **dependants**; also spelled **dependent**. A **dependant** is someone who does not have any money of their own and depends financially on someone else, usually another person in their family who has a job. EG *There are approximately 12 million migrants with their dependents living in the EEC countries... You can get an extra pension for adult dependants.*
N COUNT

dependence /di'pɛndəns/; also spelled **dependance** in American English. **Dependence** or **dependency** is **1** a constant and regular need that someone has for something in order to be able to survive or operate properly. EG *The strategy involves dependence on Western imported technology... They discussed the increasing dependence of police forces on computers... She fought off alcoholism and dependence on painkilling drugs.* **2** the need that someone has for another person, especially for emotional security. EG *His dependence on her grew with the years... They had a bond between them of mutual dependence and love.*
N UNCOUNT+*on/upon*; = reliance, dependency; N UNCOUNT : IF+PREP THEN *on/upon*; ⇑ need; ≠ independence

dependency /di'pɛndənsi¹/, **dependencies**. A **dependency** is a country which is controlled by another country. EG *Britain was a Roman dependency for a long period.*
N COUNT

dependent /di'pɛndənt/. **1** If a country, society, etc, is **dependent** on something, it needs that thing in order to be able to survive economically or politically. EG *West Europe was still heavily dependent on Middle Eastern oil... ...small businesses dependent upon old industries.*
ADJ CLASSIF : PRED+*on/upon*; = reliant

2 If you are **dependent** on someone or something, you need them in order to be able to survive physically, financially, or emotionally. EG *At first, a patient may feel very dependent on the nurses... ...those who are entirely dependent for their welfare on the public services.*
ADJ QUALIT : IF+PREP THEN *on/upon*; = reliant

3 See also **dependant**.

depict /di'pɪkt/, **depicts, depicting, depicted**. If you **depict** someone or something, **1** you represent them in a work of art such as a drawing or painting. EG *Haselden's cartoon depicted the British lion roaring triumphantly... ...an art calendar depicting some ancient legend.* **2** you describe or explain what you think they are really like. EG *She went on to depict the revolution as an abstract general state... Tressell was one of several writers who depicted those conditions at the turn of the century.*
V+O; ⇑ show; = portray; V+O, OR V+O+A *(as)*; = portray

depiction /di'pɪkʃə⁰n/, **depictions**. A **depiction** of something is a picture or a written description of it. EG *...Byzantine depictions of the burial of Christ.*
N COUNT

depilatory /dɪ²pɪlətə⁰ri¹/ is used to describe something which removes hair from your body. EG *...a jar of depilatory cream.*
ADJ CLASSIF : ATTRIB; ⇑ remover

deplete /di'pli:t/, **depletes, depleting, depleted**. If you **deplete** something, you reduce the amount of it that is available to be used. EG *We must be careful as we deplete our stocks of non-renewable resources.* ◇ **depletion** /di'pli:ʃə⁰n/. EG *...the depletion of raw material reserves.*
V+O; = run down; ≠ increase; ◇ N UNCOUNT : USU+SUPP

deplorable /di'plɔ:rəbə⁰l/. Something that is **deplorable** is extremely bad or unpleasant; a fairly formal word. EG *It's deplorable!... How did these deplorable conditions come about?* ◇ **deplorably.** EG *The children behaved deplorably at tea time.*
ADJ QUALIT; = appalling; ◇ ADV; ⇑ badly; = dreadfully

deplore /di'plɔ:/, **deplores, deploring, deplored**. When you **deplore** something, you condemn it because you feel it is wrong or immoral; a fairly formal word. EG *Doctors are the first to deplore long waiting lists for admission to hospital... There are many of us who deplore this lack of responsibility.*
V+O; ⇑ disapprove; ≠ praise

deploy /di'plɔɪ/, **deploys, deploying, deployed**. When a country **deploys** troops, resources, or equipment, it organizes them so that they are in a position or condition where they can be used immediately. EG *Oman could deploy regular forces of some 15,000... The decision was to deploy 572 Pershing and Cruise missiles.*
V+O

deployment /di'plɔɪmə²nt/. The **deployment** of troops, resources, or equipment is the organization and preparation of them so that they are ready for immediate action.
N UNCOUNT; ⇑ preparation

depopulate /di:pɒpjə⁴leɪt/, **depopulates, depopulating, depopulated**. If something **depopulates** an area, it greatly reduces the number of people living there. EG *The arrival of the conquerors depopulated large parts of Central and South America.* ◇ **depopulated.** EG *...the landscape has a depopulated and dreamlike air.* ◇ **depopulation** /di:pɒpjə⁴leɪʃə⁰n/. EG *...the depopulation of the city centre.*
V+O : USU PASS; ◇ ADJ CLASSIF; ◇ N UNCOUNT

deport /di'pɔ:t/, **deports, deporting, deported**. If a government **deports** someone, it sends them out of the country because they have committed a crime or because it believes that they do not have the right to be there. EG *He was deported to France... Even if they didn't put her in jail, they would deport her.* ◇ **deportation** /di:pɔ:teɪʃə⁰n/, **deportations**. EG *...prepared to risk prison or deportation.*
V+O; ⇑ eject; = expel; ◇ N UNCOUNT/COUNT; = expulsion

deportment /di'pɔ:tmə²nt/. Your **deportment** is the way you behave, especially the way you walk and move; an old-fashioned word. EG *He observes their deportment carefully.*
N UNCOUNT; = bearing

depose /di'pəʊz/, **deposes, deposing, deposed**. If someone, especially a political leader, **is deposed**, they are removed from their job or position. EG *They wanted Baldwin to be deposed as leader of the Party.*
V+O : USU PASS; ⇑ remove; = oust

deposit /di'pɒzɪt/, **deposits, depositing, deposited**. **1** If something **deposits** something such as a mineral on a surface or in the ground, it leaves a layer of it there over a period of time as a result of a chemical or geological process. EG *The sea that deposited the limestone in these hills has long since disappeared.* ▸ used as a noun. EG *Spray starch tends to leave a nasty brown deposit on the base of the iron... ...rich mineral deposits.*
V+O; ▸ N COUNT : USU PL

2 If something **deposits** someone or something somewhere, it puts them down or leaves them there, often in a rough or ungraceful way. EG *A gust of wind caught her hat and deposited it out of reach... ...a helicopter which deposits him, eight minutes later, at the airport.*
V+O : USU+A; = drop

3 When you **deposit** something somewhere, you put it where it will be safe until it is needed again. EG *He deposited the case in the left luggage office.*
V+O : USU+A

4 When you **deposit** a sum of money, you pay it into a bank account or other savings account, usually with the intention of leaving it there for some time. EG *Work out what your tax should be and deposit this money in a savings account.*
V+O; ⇑ put; = pay in; ≠ withdraw

5 A **deposit** is also **5.1** a sum of money which is in a bank account or other savings account and which will probably be left there for some time. EG *Most banks are paying 11 ¼% on deposits of more than £5,000.* **5.2** a sum of money which is part of the full price of something such as a car or a house, and which you pay when you agree to buy it. EG *We won't be getting married until we've saved enough for the deposit on a house.* **5.3** a sum of money which you pay when you start renting something such as a car or a flat. The money is returned to you if you do not damage what you have rented. **5.4** a sum of money which you have to pay if you want to be a candidate in a parliamentary election in Britain. The money is returned to you if you receive more than 15% of the votes. EG *The National Front candidate lost his deposit.*
N COUNT; ≠ withdrawal; N COUNT : USU SING; ⇑ payment; = down payment; N COUNT : USU SING; ⇑ payment; N COUNT; ⇑ stake

deposit account, deposit accounts. A **deposit account** is a type of bank account in which the amount of money in it increases because it earns interest. N COUNT

deposition /dɛpəzɪʃəⁿn, diːpə-/, **depositions.** 1 **Deposition** is a geological process which causes layers of minerals to be formed in the ground or on the surface of the earth over a period of time. EG *For the most part rocks are not built up by deposition but broken down by erosion.* N UNCOUNT ⇑ build-up ≠ erosion

2 The **deposition** of a political leader is the removal of him or her from office. N UNCOUNT

3 A **deposition** is a formal written statement, made for example by a witness to a crime, which can be used in a court of law if the witness cannot be present. N COUNT ⇑ testimony

depot /dɛpəʊ/, **depots.** 1 A **depot** is 1.1 a place where large supplies, especially of raw materials or essential equipment, are kept until they are needed. EG *...airfields and supply depots.* N COUNT ⇑ store 1.2 a large building or yard where buses or railway engines are kept when they are not being used. N COUNT ⇑ garage

2 A **depot** is also a bus station or a railway station; used especially in American English. EG *The Greyhound bus depot is only a few blocks from here.* N COUNT

deprave /di¹preɪv/, **depraves, depraving, depraved.** A person or thing that **depraves** someone has a morally bad or evil influence on them. EG *This book is likely to deprave youngsters.* V+O = corrupt

depraved /di¹preɪvd/. **Depraved** behaviour is morally bad or evil. EG *In those days, dancing was considered 'depraved'.* ▸ used of people. EG *I was imprisoned at eighteen among the most depraved criminals on the island* ADJ QUALIT = corrupt ▸ = corrupt ≠ pure

depravity /di¹prævɪti¹/ is moral corruption. EG *...its brothels, its opium parlours, its depravity.* N UNCOUNT

deprecate /dɛprə¹keɪt/, **deprecates, deprecating, deprecated.** If you **deprecate** something, you speak critically about it because you disapprove of it; a formal word. EG *They definitely deprecated education for the masses.* V+O ⇑ criticize = condemn, denigrate ≠ support

deprecating /dɛprəkeɪtɪŋ/ means the same as deprecatory. EG *Heissman waved a deprecating hand.* ◊ **deprecatingly.** EG *'Of course,' he said deprecatingly, 'it's very vague.'* ADJ QUALIT ◊ ADV AFTER VB

deprecatory /dɛprəkeɪtəⁿri¹/. A **deprecatory** attitude or gesture shows that you disapprove of something. EG *With a deprecatory grunt, Mrs Haze stooped to pick up the offending sock.* ADJ QUALIT ⇑ critical = disapproving

depreciate /di¹priːʃieɪt/, **depreciates, depreciating, depreciated.** When something **depreciates**, it loses some of its original value. EG *...an investment that was certain to depreciate.* ◊ **depreciation** /di¹priːsi¹eɪʃəⁿn/. EG *There remains, of course, the risk of capital depreciation.* V ⇑ decrease = devalue ◊ N UNCOUNT+SUPP

depredation /dɛprɪdeɪʃəⁿn/, **depredations. Depredations** are attacks which are made in order to steal or destroy something; an old-fashioned word. EG *...the depredations of the enemy.* N COUNT/UNCOUNT ⇑ attack

depress /di¹prɛs/, **depresses, depressing, depressed.** 1 If someone or something **depresses** you, they make you feel sad and hopeless. EG *It depressed me to visit her in hospital... ...the inner city where parents are depressed by bad housing and shortage of money.* V+O = sadden ≠ cheer

2 If something **depresses** prices, wages, etc, it causes them to fall in value. EG *It would create mass unemployment, depress profits and increase public sector borrowing... The current oil glut has depressed prices still more.* V+O ⇑ lower = bring down ≠ boost

depressed /di¹prɛst/. 1 If you are **depressed**, you are sad and feel that you cannot enjoy anything. EG *I realised I was becoming increasingly depressed and apathetic.* ADJ QUALIT ⇑ unhappy = despondent

2 A place that is **depressed** does not have enough trade, business, or economic activity. EG *This book illustrates the effects of living in depressed city areas.* ADJ QUALIT = run-down ≠ thriving

3 Something that is **depressed** has its central part slightly lower than the rest of its surface. EG *She had a rather depressed breast bone.* ADJ QUALIT ⇑ sunken

depressing /di¹prɛsɪŋ/. Something that is **depressing** makes you feel sad and disappointed, often because you realize that something that you hoped would happen will not happen. EG *This was depressing news... The general political outlook was a depressing one for Labour.* ◊ **depressingly.** EG *It was all depressingly clear.* ADJ QUALIT ⇑ dispiriting = disheartening ≠ hopeful ◊ ADV

depression /di¹prɛʃəⁿn/, **depressions.** 1 **Depression** is a mental state in which you feel extremely unhappy and have no enthusiasm for anything. EG *He would tenderly coax the poor girl out of her depression... ...worrying himself into a state of depression.* N UNCOUNT/COUNT = despondency ≠ euphoria

2 A **depression** is 2.1 a time of great reduction in the activity of a country's industries or economy, which causes a lot of unemployment and poverty. EG *...during the world-wide economic depression... ...the depression of the twenties and thirties.* N COUNT ⇑ decline = slump 2.2 an area on the surface of something such as the ground which has become lower than the rest of the surface because of pressure that has been put on it. EG *There was a depression on the seat of the armchair where she had been sitting.* N COUNT ⇑ dip = hollow ≠ mound 2.3 a mass of air that has a low pressure and that often causes rain. EG *...a depression moving in from the east.* N COUNT

depressive /di¹prɛsɪv/, **depressives.** 1 Something that is **depressive** causes you to feel sad and lacking in energy. EG *...the depressive streak in her nature.* ADJ CLASSIF = gloomy, depressing

2 A **depressive** is a person who often suffers from depression. EG *...a manic depressive.* N COUNT : USU ADJ+N

deprivation /dɛprɪ²veɪʃəⁿn/, **deprivations.** If you suffer **deprivation**, you do not have or are prevented from having something that you want or need. EG *...She led a life of comparative deprivation... They suffer from deprivation of political and civil rights... ...punishable by deprivation of freedom for a period of six months.* N UNCOUNT/COUNT ⇑ lack = poverty

deprive /di¹praɪv/, **deprives, depriving, deprived.** If you **deprive** someone of something that they want or need, you take it away from them, or you prevent them from having it. EG *I was to be deprived temporarily of my friends' company... 'I'm not trying to deprive you of the necessities of life,' I explained.* V+O+A *(of)*

deprived /di¹praɪvd/. If someone or something is **deprived**, they do not have the things that people consider to be essential in life, for example acceptable living conditions or education. EG *We have proved that deprived children benefit from playgroups... ...children from deprived backgrounds... ...the most socially deprived area in England.* ADJ QUALIT ⇑ disadvantaged = underprivileged

dept, depts. Dept is an abbreviation for 'department'; used especially as part of a name. EG *...Dept of Chemistry.* N COUNT : ALSO IN NAMES

depth /dɛpθ/, **depths.** 1 The **depth** of something is 1.1 the distance between its top and bottom surfaces, or the distance downwards from a surface. EG *None of the lakes was more than a few yards in depth... The water has frozen to a depth of 2 metres.* N UNCOUNT/COUNT 1.2 the distance between the front and back of it. EG *The depth of the cupboard was 40 centimetres.* N UNCOUNT/COUNT

2 The **depth** of a situation or emotion is the great extent to which it is serious or worrying. EG *The depth of his concern was evident enough... No one really understands the depth of the crisis.* N UNCOUNT+SUPP ⇑ intensity = profundity

3 The **depth** of someone's knowledge is the great amount that they know. EG *I was impressed by her depth of knowledge.* N UNCOUNT ⇑ extent ● If you deal with a subject **in depth**, you deal with it very thoroughly and consider all the aspects of it. EG *I would like to talk in some depth about things that seem important.* ● PHR : USED AS AN A = in detail

4 The **depth** of a colour is its quality of richness and strength. EG *There is an astonishing depth of colour in this painting.* N UNCOUNT+SUPP = intensity

5 The **depth** of a sound is how high or low it is. EG *The depth of the engine note varied.* N UNCOUNT+SUPP ⇑ pitch

6 The **depths** are the places that are a long way below the surface of the sea or earth; a literary use. EG *It sank slowly into the depths of the water.* N PLURAL : *the*+N

7 The **depths** of the countryside are the parts of it which are very remote and far from towns and cities. N PLURAL+SUPP : *the*+N

8 The **depths** of someone or something are their serious or interesting aspects which are not immediately obvious and which you have to think about carefully before you can fully understand them. EG *There were depths to him she had never guessed... She planned to explore the depths of philosophy and religion.* N PLURAL ⇑ aspect

9 If you are in the **depths** of an unpleasant emotion, you feel that emotion very strongly. EG *He was in the depths of despair.* N PLURAL

10 If something happens in the **depths** of a difficult or unpleasant period of time, it happens in the middle and most severe or intense part of it. EG *Their clothes were of thin cotton cloth, even in the depths of winter.* N PLURAL

11 If you are **out of** your **depth**, you are 11.1 in water that is deeper than you are tall, with the result that you cannot stand up but have to swim. EG *Don't go out of your depth in the sea.* PHR : USED AS AN A 11.2 in a situation that is much too difficult for you to be able to cope with it. EG *I was out of my depth in that class.* PHR : USED AS AN A ⇑ lost

depth charge, depth charges. A **depth charge** is a type of bomb which explodes under water and which is used especially to destroy enemy submarines. N COUNT

deputation /dɛpjəˈteɪʃəⁿn/, **deputations.** A **deputation** is a small group of people who have been asked to speak to someone on behalf of a larger group of people, especially in order to make a complaint. EG *In 1932 he had brought a deputation of the unemployed right into the Council Chamber.* N COUNT = delegation

depute /dɪpjuːt/, **deputes, deputing, deputed.** If you **depute** someone for something or **depute** someone to do something, you instruct or authorize them to do it on your behalf; a formal word. EG *Norman and I were deputed for the unpleasant task.* V+O+A *(for)*/ *to*-INF ⇑ appoint = delegate

deputize /dɛpjəˈtaɪz/, **deputizes, deputizing, deputized**; also spelled **deputise**. If you **deputize** for someone, you do something on their behalf, for example attend a meeting. EG *The budget was delivered by Mr Lynch, deputizing for Mr Haughey.* V : IF+PREP THEN *for* ⇑ act = stand in

deputy /dɛpjəˈtɪ/, **deputies.** A **deputy** is 1 a person whose job is the second most important in an organization such as a business or government department. A deputy often represents the boss when he or she cannot be present. EG *He and his deputy had cooperated very well... ...the former Deputy Chairman of the Commission.* N COUNT : ALSO USED IN TITLES ⇑ assistant 2 a person who is given the authority to act or take decisions for someone else. EG *My boss went off on a motoring holiday leaving no address and no deputy.* N COUNT ⇑ delegate

derail /diˈreɪl/, **derails, derailing, derailed.** If a train **is derailed**, it comes off the track on which it is running. EG *The train was derailed four miles outside Manchester.* V+O : USU PASS

derailment /diˈreɪlməˀnt/, **derailments.** A **derailment** is an accident in which a train comes off the track on which it is running. N COUNT/ UNCOUNT

deranged /diˈreɪndʒd/. Someone who is **deranged** behaves in a wild and uncontrolled way, often as a result of mental illness. EG *He's probably slightly deranged... They would do anything at all to prevent deranged fanatics from obtaining weapons.* ADJ QUALIT ⇑ disordered = crazy

derangement /diˈreɪndʒməˀnt/ is the state of being mentally ill and unable to think or act in a controlled way; an old-fashioned word. EG *The author suffers from derangement and insanity.* N UNCOUNT ⇑ disorder

derby /dɑːbiˈ/, **derbies.** 1 The **Derby** is a famous English horse race which takes place every year. N PROPER : *the*+N

2 A **derby** is a sporting event between teams from the same area or city. EG *52,000 fans turned out for the derby between Liverpool and Everton.* N COUNT ⇑ match

3 A **derby** is also a bowler hat; used in American English. EG *...a round-faced old man in a derby and a shabby overcoat.* N COUNT

derelict /dɛrəˈlɪkt/. 1 A place or building that is **derelict** is empty and in a bad state of repair because it has not been used or lived in for a long time. EG *... a derelict tower block.* ADJ CLASSIF ⇑ abandoned

2 A **derelict** is a person who has no home or job and who has to live on the streets; a formal use. N COUNT

dereliction /dɛrəˈlɪkʃəⁿn/. If a building or a piece of land is in a state of **dereliction**, it is deserted or abandoned. EG *The building is still much as it was after being salvaged from dereliction.* N UNCOUNT ⇑ desertion

dereliction of duty is deliberate or accidental failure to do what you should do as part of your job; a formal expression. EG *I call that a grave dereliction of duty.* N SING WITH DET ⇑ failure

deride /diˈraɪd/, **derides, deriding, derided.** If you **deride** someone or something, you mock them because you think that they are stupid or have no value. EG *His sense of superiority makes him deride her opinions.* V+O ⇑ laugh at = ridicule

de rigueur /də rɪgɜː/. A possession or habit that is **de rigueur** is fashionable and therefore necessary for anyone who wants to avoid being considered old-fashioned or unusual. EG *Calculators as thin as biscuits are de rigueur for businessmen.* ADJ CLASSIF : PRED ⇑ required = obligatory

derision /diˈrɪʒəⁿn/ is an attitude of contempt that you have for someone or something. EG *Americans speak with derision of those who are lazy.* N UNCOUNT ⇑ ridicule

derisive /diˈraɪsɪv/. Someone or something that is **derisive** shows an attitude of contempt or ridicule. EG *Maureen rocked with derisive laughter.* ◊ **derisively.** EG *The press were derisively rejecting the peace terms.* ADJ QUALIT ⇑ contemptuous = mocking ◊ ADV WITH VB

derisory /diˈraɪzərɪ/. Something that is **derisory** is so small or insufficient for its purpose that it is not worth considering seriously. EG *Its budget of around 12 million pounds is derisory... They did what they could with the derisory forces available.* ADJ QUALIT ⇑ ridiculous = absurd

derivation /dɛrəˈveɪʃəⁿn/, **derivations.** A **derivation** is the original form or meaning of something, especially a word. EG *...the derivation of a person's name.* N COUNT/ UNCOUNT ⇑ origin

derivative /dɪrɪvətɪv/, **derivatives.** 1 A **derivative** is something such as a language or idea which has developed from something else, such as another language or idea. EG *...the modern derivative of the fairy story.* N COUNT ⇑ development

2 Something that is **derivative** is not new or original but has been developed from something else; used showing disapproval. EG *...the most deadening, dull, derivative work he'd ever seen.* ADJ QUALIT ≠ original

derive /diˈraɪv/, **derives, deriving, derived.** 1 If you **derive** something from someone or something, you get it from them; a fairly formal use. EG *They derive enormous pleasure from their grandchildren... I myself derive no real satisfaction from my labours.* V+O : IF+PREP THEN *from* = draw, gain

2 If you say that something **derives** or **is derived** from something else, you mean that it develops from something else. EG *The word 'detergent' is derived from the Latin word for 'cleaner'... Wealth derives from political power.* V-ERG+A *(from)* ⇑ originate

dermatitis /dɜːmətaɪtɪs/ is a disease which makes your skin red and painful. N UNCOUNT

derogatory /dɪrɒgətəⁿriˈ/. A **derogatory** remark or comment shows what a low opinion you have of someone or something. EG *He might make derogatory comments... It's a highly derogatory name.* ADJ CLASSIF ⇑ critical = disparaging

derrick /dɛrɪk/, **derricks.** A **derrick** is 1 a simple crane that is used to move cargo on a ship. N COUNT 2 a tower built over an oil well which is used to raise and lower the drill. N COUNT

derv /dɜːv/ is the fuel that is used in diesel cars and lorries. EG *The industry consider that derv has been too expensive.* N UNCOUNT = diesel oil

dervish /dɜːvɪʃ/, **dervishes.** A **dervish** is a member of a Muslim religious group which has a very active and lively dance as part of its worship. EG *He whirled through the door like a dervish.* N COUNT

descale /diːskeɪl/, **descales, descaling, descaled.** When you **descale** a kettle, you remove the hard layer which is formed inside it as a result of the action of the chemicals that are in water. V+O ⇑ clean

descant /dɛskænt/, **descants.** A **descant** is a tune which is played or sung above the main tune in a piece of music. EG *I thought we'd try the descant in the second verse only.* N COUNT

descend /diˈsɛnd/, **descends, descending, descended.** 1 If you **descend** or if you **descend** something, you move downwards from a higher to a lower level; a fairly formal use. EG *The valley becomes more exquisite as we descend... They descended the stairs... The lift descended one floor.* V OR V+O = go down ≠ rise

2 If a mood or atmosphere **descends** on people, it affects them by spreading among them; a literary use. EG *A sinister silence descended upon the office... Gloom began to descend on all of them.* V : USU+A *(on/ upon)* ⇑ befall = fall

3 If you **descend** on a place or on a group of people, you arrive suddenly, usually without being invited. EG *The Vikings descended on the Saxon coast... The whole family descended on us without any warning.* V : USU+A *(on/ upon)* = invade

4 If night, dusk, or darkness **descends**, it starts to get dark; a literary use. EG *A damp, reddish dusk descended... He hardly noticed the descending darkness.* V = fall

5 If you **descend** to something or **descend** to doing something, you behave in a way that is considered unacceptable or unworthy of you. EG *Once again the firm had descended to the vulgarity of using nude pictures for advertising... All too soon they will descend to spreading scandal and gossip.* V+A *(to)* ⇑ lower = stoop, sink

6 See also **descended, descending, descent.**

descendant /di'sendə²nt/, **descendants.** A **descendant** is a person or animal that is descended from an individual or group that lived a long time ago. EG *They were descendants of a forest-living ape.* — N COUNT ≠ ancestor

descended /di'sendɪ²d/. 1 If you say that you are **descended** from a particular person, you mean that this person lived a long time ago and is related to you by being one of your ancestors. EG *Caroline's family were descended from three French Huguenot brothers.* — ADJ CLASSIF: PRED+*from*

2 An animal that is **descended** from another sort of animal has developed from the original sort into a different animal. EG *Darwin concluded that men were descended from apes.* — ADJ CLASSIF: PRED+*from* ⇑ derived

descending /di'sendɪŋ/ means progressing in order from the highest to the lowest point on a scale. EG *Arrange the numbers in descending order.* — ADJ CLASSIF: ATTRIB ≠ ascending

descent /di'sent/, **descents.** 1 A **descent** is 1.1 a movement from a higher to a lower level or position. EG *He saw an aircraft high to the east making a very steep descent.* — N COUNT: USU SING ⇑ drop ≠ ascent. 1.2 a surface that slopes downwards, for example the side of a steep hill. — N COUNT. 1.3 a change from a better to a worse condition in life, such as a change to a lower status in society. EG *The family had made the swift descent from gentility to near-poverty.* — N SING WITH DET ⇑ decline ≠ rise. 1.4 a change in your personal behaviour so that you do things which are considered to be unacceptable or unworthy of you. EG *My father, in a rare descent to cattiness, condemned him after he had gone.* — N SING WITH DET: IF+PREP THEN *from/to/into* ⇑ lowering

2 Your **descent** is the ancestry that your family has, for example their nationality or social status. EG *...Americans of Irish descent... Our family can claim royal descent.* — N UNCOUNT+SUPP ⇑ lineage = origin

describe /dɪ²skraɪb/, **describes, describing, described.** 1 If you **describe** something such as an event or a place, you give an account of what it is like, sometimes in great detail. EG *He had come to imagine America from the ways it had been described to him... He described how he escaped from prison.* — V+O/REPORT-CL ⇑ recount

2 If you **describe** a person or thing, you explain in words what they look like. EG *Can you describe your son?... The man described what he had seen.* — V+O/REPORT-CL

3 If you **describe** someone or something as having a particular quality or as being of a particular type, you say that they have that quality or are that type. EG *Neighbours described Mrs Smith as being a very religious woman... His ideas could hardly be described as original... He describes himself as 'ordinary'.* — V+O (NG/REFL) +A *(as)* ⇑ typify = label

4 If something **describes** a particular shape, it forms that shape or makes a movement that follows the exact line of that shape; a formal use. EG *The rainbow described a perfect arc in the sky.* — V+O ⇑ outline = draw

description /dɪ²skrɪpʃə⁰n/, **descriptions.** 1 A **description** is an account of someone or something which explains what they are or what they look like. EG *...a detailed description of the film star's house... The book is worth reading for the descriptions alone... His article contains brief descriptions of some of his ideas.* — N COUNT: IF+PREP THEN *of*

2 **Description** is the act of saying what people or things look like or feel like. EG *The relationships in his family are so complex that description is almost impossible... Her new novel spends more time on description than it should.* — N UNCOUNT ⇑ explanation. ● If you say that something is **beyond** or **past description**, you mean that there is so much of it that you will not try to say exactly how much there is, or that it is of such good quality that you cannot describe it. EG *Gold beyond description had been found.* — ● PHR: NG+PHR

3 If something is of a particular **description**, it is considered to belong to the general class of items that are mentioned. EG *Her dress was too tight to have concealed a weapon of any description... I want to know about telephone expenses, salaries, everything of that description.* — N SING WITH DET: AFTER *of* ⇑ type = kind

descriptive /dɪ²skrɪptɪv/. 1 Writing, speech, or painting that is **descriptive** is intended to explain or describe what someone or something is like or what they look like. EG *...a descriptive article about Venice.* — ADJ QUALIT ⇑ explanatory. ◇ **descriptively.** EG *The book is descriptively accurate but not very interesting.* — ◇ ADV

2 A subject that is **descriptive** deals with what is found to be true rather than what we believe ought to be true. EG *He studied descriptive linguistics at Edinburgh... Sociology is a descriptive science.* — ADJ CLASSIF ≠ prescriptive

desecrate /desɪkreɪt/, **desecrates, desecrating, desecrated.** If someone **desecrates** something which is considered to be sacred or very special, they deliberately damage or insult it. EG *Vandals desecrated the altar with chalk and paint.* — V+O = defile. ◇ **desecration** /desəkreɪʃə⁰n/. EG *...the desecration of religious sites in Nigeria.* — ◇ N UNCOUNT

desegregate /di:segrɪ¹geɪt/, **desegregates, desegregating, desegregated.** To **desegregate** something such as a place, institution, or service means to officially cease keeping the people who use it in separate groups according to their race, religion, or sex. EG *They had to do something about desegregating the schools.* — V+O ≠ segregate. ◇ **desegregation** /di:segrəgeɪʃə⁰n/. — ◇ N UNCOUNT

desensitize /di:sensɪtaɪz/, **desensitizes, desensitizing, desensitized;** also spelled **desensitise.** If you **desensitize** someone, you cause them to react less strongly than they used to react to things such as pain, anxiety, or other people's suffering. EG *A parent doesn't want the school to desensitize his or her children.* — V+O = deaden, harden ≠ sensitize

desert, deserts, deserting, deserted. The word **desert** is pronounced /desə⁵t/ when it is a noun, and /di¹zɜ:t/ when it is a verb. 1 A **desert** is 1.1 a large area of land where there is very little water or rain, no trees, and very few plants. EG *...the Sahara Desert... ...the hot desert sand.* — N COUNT: ALSO IN NAMES AFTER N ⇑ region. 1.2 any place which is considered to be bad for people because things connected with it are not interesting, exciting, or beneficial in any way. EG *Our modern towns are concrete deserts created by modern planning at its worst.* — N COUNT+SUPP = wilderness, wasteland

2 If people or animals **desert** a place, they leave it, with the result that it becomes empty. EG *Even the butterflies deserted the open space.* — V+O = abandon. ◇ **deserted.** EG *They drove home through the deserted, windy streets... ...a deserted village.* — ◇ ADJ CLASSIF ≠ crowded

3 If one person **deserts** another, they leave them and no longer help or support them. EG *She deserted her family and ran away with him.* — V+O = abandon ≠ stand by. ◇ **desertion** /di¹zɜ:ʃə⁰n/. EG *She could get a divorce on the grounds of desertion.* — ◇ N UNCOUNT/COUNT

4 If you **desert** something such as a political party or idea, you stop supporting it. EG *Enough Conservatives were prepared to desert their party to allow the bill to be passed.* — V+O ⇑ leave = abandon ≠ support. ◇ **desertion.** — ◇ N UNCOUNT

5 If a quality or attribute such as courage or a sense of humour **deserts** you, it is no longer there when you need it or want it. EG *His appetite had deserted him.* — V+O ⇑ fail

6 If you **desert** or you **desert** a job, you leave that job without permission, especially when it is a job in the armed forces. EG *...journalists who had deserted in droves to the Daily Express.* — V OR V+O. ◇ **desertion.** EG *...the increasing number of arrests and executions for desertion.* — ◇ N UNCOUNT/COUNT

7 Your **just deserts** are the unpleasant things that happen to you, which you deserve because you have done something wrong. EG *I've got no sympathy for him, it was no more than his just deserts.* — PHR: USED AS C OR O ⇑ retribution

deserter /di¹zɜ:tə/, **deserters.** A **deserter** is someone who leaves their job in the armed forces without permission. — N COUNT

desert island, desert islands. A **desert island** is a small tropical island, where nobody lives. EG *...marooned on a desert island.* — N COUNT

deserve /di¹zɜ:v/, **deserves, deserving, deserved.** If you **deserve** something or you **deserve** to do or have something, you should be rewarded, punished, or treated in some particular way because of your qualities, achievements, or actions. EG *These people deserve recognition for their talents... The play deserves to be read... He has been so awful he deserves whatever he gets.* — V+O/*to*-INF/-ING ⇑ merit = warrant

deserved /di¹zɜ:vd/. You obtain or receive something that is **deserved** because you have certain qualities or have done something which makes you worthy of it. EG *It was a richly deserved honour... They took a well deserved break.* — ADJ QUALIT: USU AFTER ADV ⇑ merited. ◇ **deservedly.** EG *The first prize was won, and most deservedly, by Mrs Jones.* — ◇ ADV

deserving /di¹zɜ:vɪŋ/. 1 Someone or something that is **deserving** has certain qualities which make you think that they should be helped, rewarded, or — ADJ QUALIT = worthy praised; a formal use. EG *Let us not forget the deserving poor... The proceeds will be given away to a deserving charity.*

2 If you are **deserving of** something, you have certain qualities or you have done something which makes you worthy of being treated in a particular way; a formal use. EG *...those who see their behaviour as deserving of punishment.*
PHR : USED AS C
= meriting

desiccated /dɛsɪkeɪtɪ²d/. **1** Something that is **desiccated** has lost all the moisture that was in it; a formal word. EG *...hunks of desiccated skin and fat.*
ADJ CLASSIF
⇑ dried
= dehydrated

2 Desiccated food has been dried in order to preserve it. EG *...desiccated coconut.*
ADJ CLASSIF
⇑ dried

desiccation /dɛsɪkeɪʃə⁰n/ is the process of becoming completely dried out; a formal word. EG *The animals were lucky to avoid death by desiccation.*
N UNCOUNT
⇑ dehydration

design /di¹zaɪn/, **designs, designing, designed. 1** When you **design** something, **1.1** you plan and create a picture of it in your mind and you make a detailed drawing of it from which it can be built or made. EG *The house was designed by local builders... Who designed the costumes?... ...beautifully designed toys.*
V+O
1.2 you plan, prepare, and decide on all the details of it. EG *Series of tests have been designed to assess mathematical ability... They wanted to design English courses.*
V+O, OR V+O+to-INF : USU PASS
⇑ create

2 Design is **2.1** the process and art of creating, planning, and making detailed drawings of something. EG *...graphic and industrial design... I did part-time design work at home for many years.*
N UNCOUNT
⇑ creation
2.2 the way in which something has been planned and made, including what it looks like and how well it works. EG *The awkward design of the handles made it difficult to use the scissors.*
N UNCOUNT

3 A **design** is **3.1** a drawing which is produced to show what something should look like and how you would like it to be built or made. EG *He had the opportunity of submitting a design for the new building... His design was rejected.*
N COUNT
= plan
3.2 a pattern of lines, flowers, or other objects which is used to decorate something. EG *They painted flowered designs on the walls... She bought curtains and wallpaper with the same design.*
N COUNT : USU+SUPP
3.3 the intention that a person has in their mind when they are doing something. EG *He failed in his design to become Prime Minister... Did it happen by accident or by design?... She made no secret of her designs.*
N COUNT : OR *by*+N

4 If you **have designs on** someone or something, you want that person or thing very much and are prepared to act in an extreme way in order to get what you want. EG *She insisted she had absolutely no designs on any of the males in the department.*
PHR : VB INFLECTS
⇑ desire

5 If something **is designed** for a purpose, it is intended for that purpose. EG *His style of teaching was designed to shock his students... The laws were designed to protect women from attack by men.*
V+A *(for)*, OR V+O+*to*-INF : ONLY PASS

designate, designates, designating, designated. The word **designate** is pronounced /dɛzɪ²gneɪt/ when it is a verb, and /dɛzɪ²gnət/ when it is an adjective. **1** When you **designate** someone or something, **1.1** you give them a particular description, name, or title, often because you are formally giving them a particular task or role. EG *The area was promptly designated a national monument... Much of this is designated as parkland.*
V+O (NG/REFL)+A *(as)*, OR V+O (NG/REFL)+C
= label
1.2 you formally choose them to do a particular job. EG *The President designated Hussein as his successor... I had been designated to read the lesson.*
V+O+C, V+O+*to*-INF, OR V+O+A *(as)*
= nominate

2 Designate is used of someone who has been formally chosen to do a particular job, but has not yet started doing it. EG *Mr Bell had been Attorney General designate for no more than twenty-four hours.*
ADJ AFTER N
= elect

designation /dɛzɪgneɪʃə⁰n/, **designations.** A **designation** is a description, name, or title that is given to a person or thing; a formal word. EG *No one would dare to apply the designation 'OAP' to a retired judge.* ▸ used as an uncount noun. EG *I was referring to the designation of 1960 as 'Africa year'.*
N COUNT
▸ N UNCOUNT

designer /di¹zaɪnə/, **designers.** A **designer** is a person whose job is to design things by making drawings of them. EG *The designers have put a more powerful engine into the new car... His daughter wants to be a dress designer.*
N COUNT
⇑ worker

designing /di¹zaɪnɪŋ/. **1 Designing** is art and work that you do when you design things. EG *My brother made a career of dressmaking and designing.*
N UNCOUNT
= design

2 Someone who is **designing** is cunning and prepared to use any method, either honest or dishonest, to get what they want; used showing disapproval. EG *His sister is a very designing girl.*
ADJ QUALIT
= scheming
≠ naive

desirable /di¹zaɪərəbə⁰l/. **1** Something that is **desirable** is worth having or doing because it is useful, necessary, or popular. EG *After an injury an X-ray is often desirable... ...one of the most desirable residences in London... Make any changes that you think desirable.* ◊ **desirably.** EG *...one of the most prestigious and desirably located universities in America.* ◊ **desirability** /di¹zaɪrəbɪlɪti¹/. EG *We cannot question the desirability of strong trade unions... ...its desirability as building land.*
ADJ QUALIT
≠ undesirable
◊ ADV
◊ N UNCOUNT : USU+SUPP
= value

2 Someone who is **desirable** is sexually attractive. EG *He found his wife no longer desirable.* ◊ **desirability.** EG *He was conscious of her desirability and warmth.*
ADJ QUALIT
◊ N UNCOUNT
= allure

desire /di¹zaɪə/, **desires, desiring, desired. 1** If you **desire** something, you want it very much indeed. EG *He passionately desired to continue his career... They may come if they so desire.* ◊ **desired.** *This did not produce the desired effect.*
V+O/*to*-INF : NO CONT, NO IMPER
◊ ADJ CLASSIF

2 If you **desire** someone, you want to have sex with them. EG *He still desired her.*
V+O : NO CONT, NO IMPER

3 A **desire** is a strong feeling that you want to do something or to get something. EG *He had not the slightest desire to go on holiday... This could help us to understand our own desires and needs.*
N COUNT : USU SING+*to*+-INF
⇑ wish
= urge, longing

4 Desire for someone is a strong feeling of wanting to have sex with them. EG *She no longer has any desire for her husband.*
N UNCOUNT/COUNT+*for*

5 If you say that someone or something is your **heart's desire**, you mean that you want that person or thing very much; a literary expression.
PHR : USED AS C OR O, POSS+N

6 If you say that something **leaves much, a lot,** or **a great deal to be desired**, you mean that it is not as good as it should be. EG *His work left much to be desired... I thought the baritone left a lot to be desired.*
PHR : VB INFLECTS
⇑ bad

desirous /di¹zaɪərəs/. If you are **desirous** of something, you want it very much; a formal word. EG *Is Miss Paget desirous of travelling to London?*
ADJ QUALIT : PRED+*of*
⇑ wishful
= hopeful

desist /dɪzɪst/, **desists, desisting, desisted.** If you **desist** from doing something, you stop doing it; a formal word. EG *They ought to desist from such foolish activities... Reason and duty commanded him to desist.*
V : IF+PREP THEN *from*
≠ persist

desk /dɛsk/, **desks.** A **desk** is a table which has a flat or sloping top and often has drawers, at which you can sit in order to write or work. EG *He placed his hands on the desk.* ▸ used to refer to the reception desk in a hotel, office, etc. EG *I enquired at the desk.*
N COUNT
▸ N COUNT : USU *the*+N

desk clerk, desk clerks. A **desk clerk** is a receptionist in a hotel; used especially in American English.
N COUNT

desolate, desolates, desolating, desolated. The word **desolate** is pronounced /dɛsə⁷lət/ when it is an adjective, and /dɛsə⁷leɪt/ when it is a verb. **1** Something that is **desolate** is empty of people and lacking in comfort. EG *The house looked desolate, ready to be torn down... ...dark and desolate caves.*
ADJ QUALIT
= bleak

2 If someone is **desolate**, they feel very sad, lonely, and without hope. EG *For him, helpless and desolate, it already seemed as good as over.*
ADJ QUALIT
⇑ lonely
= wretched

3 To **desolate** a place means to make it empty and uncomfortable, especially by doing something violent and destructive; a literary use. EG *They had desolated it; they had trampled his lovely rose garden.* ◊ **desolated.** EG *He took a last look back into the desolated room.*
V+O
◊ ADJ QUALIT : PRED

desolated /dɛsə⁷leɪtɪ²d/. If you are **desolated** by something, you are very shocked and saddened by it. EG *She was desolated at the loss of her husband.*
ADJ QUALIT : PRED, USU+*at/by*
= devastated

desolation /dɛsə⁷leɪʃə⁰n/ is **1** a quality of a place which makes it seem empty and frightening. EG *...the horror and desolation of the camp.*
N UNCOUNT
= bleakness
2 the act of causing a place to become empty and frightening by doing something violent and destructive. EG *...the desolation of the planet by nuclear action.*
N UNCOUNT
= devastation
3 a feeling of great unhappiness and despair. EG *It can only have added to their desolation.*
N UNCOUNT
= misery

despair /dɪ²spɛə/, **despairs, despairing, despaired. 1 Despair** is the feeling that everything is wrong and that nothing can improve. EG *I was in despair, all hope gone... He felt close to despair... ...feelings of failure and despair.*
N UNCOUNT
⇑ gloom
= desperation
≠ hope

2 If you **despair**, you feel that everything is wrong and that nothing will improve. EG *I had to resist the temptation to despair... She despaired at the thought of it.*
V : IF+PREP THEN *at* ≠ hope

3 If you **despair** of something, you feel that there is no hope that it will happen or improve. EG *She had despaired of completing her thesis... ...people who despair of American society.*
V+A *(of)* ≠ hope

despairing /dɪ²speəːrɪŋ/. If you feel **despairing**, you feel very unhappy and have no hope that things will improve. EG *Life was very difficult and I was often quite despairing.* ▸ used of people's actions and behaviour. EG *...despairing cries from the children.* ◊ **despairingly.** EG *She sighed despairingly.*
ADJ QUALIT = disheartened; ▸ = dismayed; ◊ ADV WITH VB

despatch /dɪspætʃ/. See **dispatch**.

desperado /dɛspərɑːdəʊ/, **desperadoes, desperados.** The plural can be either **desperadoes** or **desperados**. A **desperado** is someone who does illegal, violent things without worrying about the danger; an old-fashioned word.
N COUNT

desperate /dɛspə⁰rə¹t/. **1** If you are **desperate**, you are in such a bad situation that you are willing to try anything to change it. EG *She was frightened, desperate with fright.*
ADJ QUALIT

2 A **desperate** action is one that you take when you are in such a bad or frightening situation that you feel it is the only thing that you can try. EG *She killed him in a desperate attempt to free herself... There were more violent, rapid blows and desperate screams.* ◊ **desperately.** EG *He will fight even more desperately if trapped... 'We must,' he said desperately.*
ADJ QUALIT = panic-stricken, reckless; ◊ ADV WITH VB

3 If you are **desperate** for something or **desperate** to do something, you want or need it very much indeed. EG *She was desperate to find a satisfying job... I was desperate for the money.*
ADJ QUALIT : PRED, USU+*for/to*+-INF ⇑ eager

4 A **desperate** person is violent and dangerous. EG *He was taken hostage by a gang of desperate men.*
ADJ QUALIT

5 A **desperate** situation is very difficult, serious, or dangerous. EG *The situation had become desperate; we were rapidly running out of money.*
ADJ QUALIT ⇑ grave = critical

desperately /dɛspə⁰rə¹tli¹/ means very greatly, seriously, or intensely. EG *I desperately wanted to be on my own... I know how desperately busy you always are... She was desperately ill.*
ADV = dreadfully

desperation /dɛspəreɪʃə⁰n/ is the feeling that you have when you are in such a bad situation that you will try anything to change it. EG *Sam's desperation grew worse as his exams approached... 'Let's get out,' he said in desperation.*
N UNCOUNT = alarm

despicable /dɛspɪkəbə⁰l, dɪspɪk-/. A person or action that is **despicable** is extremely nasty, cruel, or evil. EG *He is too nice a man to do anything as despicable as murder.* ◊ **despicably.** EG *He behaved despicably!*
ADJ QUALIT ⇑ unworthy = contemptible; ◊ ADV

despise /dɪ²spaɪz/, **despises, despising, despised.** If you **despise** something or someone, you dislike them because you think that their quality, standard, or behaviour is very low. EG *They hate and despise you... He thoroughly despised his job.*
V+O (NG/REFL)

despite /dɪ²spaɪt/. **1** You use **despite** to introduce a fact which makes the other part of the sentence surprising. EG *Despite the difference in their ages they were close friends... The cost of public services has risen steeply despite a general decline in their quality.*
PREP = in spite of

2 If you do something **despite** yourself, you do it although you did not really intend or expect to. EG *Rose, despite herself, had to admit that she was hungry.*
PREP+REFL = in spite of

despoil /dɪ²spɔɪl/, **despoils, despoiling, despoiled.** To **despoil** a place means to make it less attractive, valuable, or important by taking things away from it or by destroying it; a formal word. EG *They can sell them back at twice the price and despoil the land that you have conserved.*
V+O ⇑ strip = rob, plunder

despondency /dɪ²spɒndə²nsi¹/ is a strong feeling of unhappiness caused by difficulties which you feel you cannot overcome; a fairly formal word. EG *He was unable to hide his despondency.*
N UNCOUNT = dejection

despondent /dɪ²spɒndə²nt/. If you are **despondent**, you are unhappy because you have been experiencing difficulties that you think you will not be able to overcome; a fairly formal word. EG *She looked despondent and ashamed.* ◊ **despondently.** EG *Mrs Paul sat despondently on an office chair.*
ADJ QUALIT = dejected, downcast ≠ heartened; ◊ ADV

despot /dɛspɒt/, **despots.** A **despot** is a ruler or other person who has a lot of power and who uses it unfairly or cruelly.
N COUNT = tyrant

despotic /də²spɒtɪk/ is used to describe people or their behaviour when they use their power over other people in an unfair or cruel way. EG *...oppression by despotic governments.*
ADJ QUALIT ⇑ unjust = tyrannical

despotism /dɛspə⁷tɪzə⁰m/ is cruel and unfair government by a ruler or rulers who have a lot of power. EG *...ruthless centralized despotism.*
N UNCOUNT ⇑ rule = tyranny

dessert /dɪzɜːt/, **desserts.** **Dessert** is sweet food served at the end of a meal, especially fruit. EG *For dessert there was ice cream... The dessert was pineapple.*
N UNCOUNT/COUNT ⇑ food = sweet

dessert spoon, dessert spoons; also spelled as one word. A **dessert spoon** is a spoon which is oval in shape and about twice as big as a teaspoon. ▸ also used to refer to the amount of something that it can hold. EG *Add two dessertspoons of salt.*
N COUNT; ▸ N COUNT ⇑ measurement

destination /dɛstɪneɪʃə⁰n/, **destinations.** The **destination** of someone or something is the place to which they are going or being sent. EG *I reached my destination around half-past two.*
N COUNT ⇑ goal

destined /dɛstɪnd/. **1** If something is **destined** to happen or if someone is **destined** to do something, that thing is planned and will definitely happen. EG *The station was destined for demolition... We believe we are destined to bring a new principle into history.*
ADJ CLASSIF : USU PRED+*to*-INF/*for* = intended

2 If you are **destined** for a particular place, you are travelling towards that place. EG *...a flight load of passengers destined for New York.*
ADJ CLASSIF : USU PRED+*for* = bound

destiny /dɛstɪ¹ni¹/, **destinies.** **1** A person's **destiny** is everything that happens to them during their life, including what will happen in the future, especially when it is considered to be controlled by someone or something else. EG *We know we are in control of our own destiny... Many of them accepted their destiny.*
N COUNT+SUPP : USU SING = fate

2 **Destiny** is the force which some people believe controls the things that happen to you in your life.
N UNCOUNT = fate

destitute /dɛstɪtjuːt/. Someone who is **destitute** has no money or possessions; a formal word. EG *It left her both childless and destitute.*
ADJ QUALIT ⇑ poor ≠ rich

destitution /dɛstɪtjuːʃə⁰n/ is the state of having no money or possessions; a formal word.
N UNCOUNT ⇑ poverty

destroy /dɪ²strɔɪ/, **destroys, destroying, destroyed.** **1** To **destroy** something means **1.1** to cause so much damage to it that it is completely ruined or does not exist any more. EG *Several apartment buildings were destroyed by the bomb... I destroyed the letter as soon as I had read it.* **1.2** to cause it not to exist any more. EG *There are some who would like to destroy the State and its instruments of power... I don't wish to destroy a life-long friendship... You're destroying all my faith in the medical profession.*
V+O; V+O = demolish ≠ build up

2 If you **destroy** an animal, you kill it, either because it is dangerous or because it is ill. EG *During the epidemic farmers had to destroy entire herds of cattle.*
V+O

3 If a person or an event **destroys** someone, they ruin their life by making them so depressed that there seems to be no hope for them in the future. EG *The loss of his business and of his wife finally destroyed him.* ● See also **soul-destroying**.
V+O = wreck

destroyer /dɪ²strɔɪə/, **destroyers.** **1** A **destroyer** is a small, heavily armed warship.
N COUNT ⇑ ship

2 Something or someone that is described as a **destroyer** destroys things or people. EG *Floods, cyclones, and earthquakes are the major destroyers.*
N COUNT ≠ creator

destruction /dɪ²strʌkʃə⁰n/ is the act of destroying something, or the state of being destroyed. EG *...the possibility of nuclear destruction... It will cause pollution and the destruction of our seas and rivers.*
N UNCOUNT = annihilation ≠ creation

destructive /dɪ²strʌktɪv/. Something that is **destructive** causes or is capable of causing great damage, harm, or injury. EG *This rocket has sufficient destructive power to blow a battleship to pieces... Jealousy is destructive and undesirable.* ◊ **destructiveness.** EG *...a monster of great potential destructiveness.* ◊ **destructively.** EG *They were destructively hostile to what they couldn't understand.*
ADJ QUALIT ⇑ harmful ≠ constructive; ◊ N UNCOUNT; ◊ ADV

desultory /dɛsəltə⁰rɪ/. Something that is **desultory** is done or happens in an unplanned and disorganized way, and without enthusiasm; a formal word. EG *There were some desultory attempts to defend him.* ◊ **desultorily.** EG *He began to look desultorily for another apartment.*
ADJ QUALIT ⇑ weak = half-hearted ≠ energetic; ◊ ADV WITH VB

det. is 1 an abbreviation for 'detached'; used especially in advertisements for houses which are for sale. 2 an abbreviation for 'detective'; used as part of a person's title. EG *Det. Chief Inspector Wallace.*

> **DET** □ In this dictionary DET is used in the grammar notes beside entries to mean 'determiner'. A DET is usually the first word in a noun group and can only have a PREDET such as *such, half* or *both* in front of it. It cannot be used with another DET. Some DETS can only come before particular types of noun and this is shown in the grammar notes beside individual entries. Note that two DETS, *this* and *that*, have plural forms, *these* and *those*, which are used before plural nouns. No other DETS inflect. See also □ at DETPOSS. Examples are **a** and **every**. EG *...a woman... ...such a nice letter... I'm sorry* **every** *room is occupied... The committee meets* **every** *two months.*

detach /di'tætʃ/, **detaches, detaching, detached.** 1 If you **detach** one thing from another that it is fixed to, you remove it. EG *The handle of the saucepan can be detached.* — V+O+*from* ⇑ separate ≠ attach

2 If you **detach** yourself from a person or place, you leave them; a rather formal use. EG *It took quite a time for Daintry to detach himself from the bar.* — V+O (REFL)+*from* = prise

3 If you **detach** yourself from something, you feel less involved in it or less concerned about it than you used to. EG *...learning to detach ourselves from the world.* — V+O (REFL) : IF +PREP THEN *from* = free

detachable /di'tætʃəbə⁰l/. Something that is **detachable** is designed or made so that it can be removed from a larger object. EG *...detachable collars.* — ADJ CLASSIF ⇑ removable

detached /di'tætʃt/. 1 A **detached** house is one that is not joined to any other house. — ADJ CLASSIF ⇑ separate

2 Something that is **detached** is no longer joined to anything. EG *On one side of the island was a huge rock, almost detached.* — ADJ CLASSIF ⇑ separate

3 Someone who is **detached** is not personally involved in something or has no emotional interest in it. EG *I tried to be detached... ...the detached view that writers must take.* — ADJ QUALIT ⇑ disinterested = objective

detachment /di'tætʃmə²nt/, **detachments.** 1 **Detachment** is the feeling that you have of not being personally involved in something or of having no emotional interest in it. EG *She studied the blood with detachment... ...his strange detachment from the world about him.* — N UNCOUNT ⇑ disinterest = aloofness

2 A **detachment** is a group of soldiers who are sent away from the main group to do a special job. EG *The task of these detachments was to defend the bridge.* — N COUNT = detail

detail /di:teɪl/, **details, detailing, detailed.** 1 A **detail** is 1.1 an individual fact, piece of information, or visual feature which you notice when you look at something carefully or remember when you think about it. EG *I can still remember every single detail of that night... He described it correctly down to the smallest detail... There are still a few details to talk over.* — N COUNT : IF+ PREP THEN *of/ about* 1.2 a criticism, fact, or suggestion that is not of major importance to what is being discussed. EG *But those were details; what was important was that the rate of work failed to increase.* — N COUNT ⇑ irrelevance = trifle 1.3 a part of a painting that is printed separately, often enlarged so that the smaller features can be clearly seen. — N COUNT ⇑ extract

2 **Detail** consists of all the small features which are often not noticed when people first look at or think about something. EG *He has a marvellous eye for detail... Attention to detail is vital in this job.* — N UNCOUNT = minutiae

3 If you **go into details, go into the details,** or **go into detail** about something, you explain it thoroughly, including all the small pieces of information. EG *I don't want to go into detail about the actual methods used... There is no need to go into details of the ghastly massacre.* — PHR : VB INFLECTS : IF+ PREP THEN *of/ about*

4 If you examine or discuss something **in detail,** you do it thoroughly and carefully, taking account of all the small points which need to be considered. EG *The implications of this theory are examined in detail in chapter 12... We'll talk about it in more detail later on.* — PHR : USED AS AN A = in depth ≠ superficially

5 **Details** about someone or something are facts or pieces of information about them. EG *You can get details of nursery schools from the local authority.* — N PLURAL : IF+ PREP THEN *of/ about* = particulars

6 If you **detail** things, you list them, giving fairly full information about each item on the list. EG *Howard can detail for you the changes that have occurred.* — V+O

7 If you **detail** someone to do a task or job, you officially order them to do it. EG *Scotland Yard detailed an officer to guard his house.* — V+O+*to*-INF

8 A **detail** is also a small group of soldiers, sailors, or airmen who have been given a particular task to do. — N COUNT ⇑ squad

detailed /di:teɪld/. Something that is **detailed** contains or shows a great number of details. EG *We really need a detailed map of the area... They gave a detailed account of what they had seen.* — ADJ QUALIT ⇑ thorough ≠ vague

detain /di'teɪn/, **detains, detaining, detained.** If you **detain** someone, 1 you force them to stay in a place when they want to leave it. EG *We shall be obliged to detain you here while we continue the investigation.* — V+O ⇑ confine = hold, keep 2 you delay them, for example by talking to them. EG *Well, I needn't detain you any longer.* — V+O = keep

detainee /di:teɪni:/, **detainees.** A **detainee** is someone who is held prisoner by a government because of his or her political views or activities. — N COUNT

detect /di'tekt/, **detects, detecting, detected.** If you **detect** something, 1 you notice it or know that it is there, even when it is not very obvious. EG *These animals seem able to detect a shower of rain falling five miles away... Ellen thought she detected a flicker of irony in Hooper's voice.* — V+O = sense 2 you find it. EG *The submarines had to be detected and destroyed.* — V+O = locate

detectable /di'tektəbə⁰l/. Something that is **detectable** can be noticed or discovered. EG *The differences may be subtle but they will be detectable.* — ADJ QUALIT

detection /di'tekʃə⁰n/ is 1 the act of noticing or sensing something. EG *The main detection device is sonar.* — N UNCOUNT ⇑ discovery 2 the fact of something being discovered in a particular place, especially when it is supposed to be hidden. EG *The submarines were able to withdraw without detection.* — N UNCOUNT ⇑ discovery 3 the work of investigating a crime in order to find out what has happened and who committed it. EG *It was clear that he preferred criminal detection to political work.* — N UNCOUNT : USU +SUPP ⇑ investigation

detective /di'tektɪv/, **detectives.** A **detective** is someone whose job is to discover what has happened in a particular situation and to find the people involved, especially when a crime has been committed. Some detectives work in the police force and others work privately. EG *He was being followed by a private detective... She was interviewed by Detective Inspector Andrews.* — N COUNT

detector /di'tektə/, **detectors.** A **detector** is an instrument which is used to find or measure something. EG *...a metal detector.* — N COUNT : USU+ SUPP

detente /deɪtɑ:nt/; also spelled **détente. Detente** is a state of friendly relations between two countries when previously there had been problems between them; a formal word. EG *We support a policy of detente.* — N UNCOUNT ⇑ reconciliation

detention /di'tenʃə⁰n/ is 1 the arrest or imprisonment of someone, especially for political reasons. EG *It was obvious to his colleagues that his detention was politically motivated... Detention without trial was introduced in 1971... He died in detention.* — N UNCOUNT ⇑ captivity 2 a punishment for naughty schoolchildren, who are made to stay at school after the other children have gone home. — N UNCOUNT/ COUNT

detention centre, detention centres. A **detention centre** is a kind of prison for young people where they are only kept for short periods of time. — N COUNT = remand home

deter /di'tɜ:/, **deters, deterring, deterred.** To **deter** someone means to persuade them not to do something or to prevent them from doing it, by making it difficult for them to do or by showing them that the result would be painful or unpleasant for them. EG *The punishment did not deter him... The existence of such discrimination may deter more women from seeking work... Benn was not deterred by the hostile reaction.* — V+O : IF+PREP THEN *from* ⇑ dissuade = discourage ≠ encourage

detergent /di'tɜ:dʒə²nt/, **detergents. Detergent** is a chemical substance, usually in the form of a powder or liquid, which is used for washing things such as clothes or dishes. EG *Wash it with hot water and detergent... Synthetic detergents generally work very well in hard water.* — N MASS

deteriorate /di'tɪərɪəreɪt/, **deteriorates, deteriorating, deteriorated.** If something **deteriorates,** 1 it becomes worse in condition or quality. EG *His sight had begun to deteriorate.* — V ⇑ worsen ◇ **deterioration** /di'tɪərɪəreɪʃə⁰n/. EG *She had suffered progressive deterioration of health.* — ◇ N UNCOUNT 2 it becomes more difficult or unpleasant. EG *The situation continues to deteriorate... The weather had indeed* — V ⇑ worsen *deteriorated.* ◇ **deterioration.** EG *This speeded the deterioration of our relationship.* ◇ N UNCOUNT

determinant /di'tɜːmɪnənt/, **determinants.** A **determinant** is something that controls or influences what will happen; a formal word. EG *...the historical determinants of this development... The determinant for hair colour is called a gene.* N COUNT ⇑ cause

determination /di'tɜːmɪneɪʃəⁿn/. 1 **Determination** is the quality that you show when you have decided to do something and you will not let anything stop you. EG *Going 60 days without alcohol takes a lot of determination... Seeing my determination to leave, she demanded her money.* N UNCOUNT ⇑ decision = resolution

2 The **determination** of something is the act of deciding or settling it. EG *She is responsible for the determination of wage levels within this company.* N SING : *the*+N+*of* = setting

determine /di'tɜːmɪn/, **determines, determining, determined.** 1 If something **determines** a situation or result, it causes or controls it. EG *Economic factors determine the progress which a society can make... Men's ideas were determined by religion.* V+O ⇑ control = decide

2 To **determine** something or to **determine** that something is the case means to find out the facts about it. EG *It was in the public interest to determine exactly what happened... An X ray determined that no bones were broken.* V+O ⇑ decide = ascertain, discover

3 To **determine** something means to decide or settle it. EG *He has no greater right than her to determine how their money should be spent... The date of the match is yet to be determined.* V+O ⇑ fix

4 If you **determine** to do something, you make a firm decision to do it; a formal use. EG *He now determined to become commander-in-chief of the forces.* V+*to*-INF ⇑ decide = resolve ≠ hesitate

determined /di'tɜːmɪnd/. 1 If you are **determined** to do something, you have made a firm decision to do it and will not let anything stop you. EG *He is determined to win in the end... I was determined not to say a word.* ▸ used of people's actions. EG *They made continued and determined efforts to find and destroy enemy headquarters.* ◇ **determinedly.** EG *She determinedly kept the conversation going.* ADJ QUALIT : USU +*to*-INF = resolved ▸ ADJ QUALIT = stubborn ◇ ADV = resolutely

2 Someone who is **determined** cannot easily be stopped from doing what they want to do. EG *My grandfather was an impetuous, determined man.* ADJ QUALIT = resolute ≠ weak

determiner /di'tɜːmɪnə/, **determiners.** In grammar, a **determiner** is a word that is used before a noun to select which instance of the noun you are talking about or to identify it. Words which are determiners have DET in the grammar note beside the entry. See □ at DET. N COUNT

determinism /di'tɜːmɪnɪzəⁿm/ is the belief that all acts, decisions, and events are the results of things that have already happened, and that these acts, decisions, and events cannot be altered. ◇ **determinist.** N UNCOUNT ≠ free will ◇ N COUNT

deterministic /di'tɜːmɪnɪstɪk/. A theory or view that is **deterministic** is based on the ideas of determinism. ADJ QUALIT

deterrence /di'terəns/ is the prevention of war by having weapons to use as a threat to people who might be enemies. EG *They argued that our policy of deterrence was still justified.* N UNCOUNT ≠ encouragement

deterrent /di'terənt/, **deterrents.** 1 A **deterrent** is 1.1 something that prevents you from doing something by making you afraid of what will happen to you if you do it. EG *Severe punishment is the only true deterrent.* 1.2 a weapon or set of weapons designed to prevent potential enemies from attacking by making them afraid to do so. EG *...the nuclear deterrent.* N COUNT ⇑ dissuasion ≠ encouragement N COUNT

2 A **deterrent** effect has the effect of discouraging people from doing certain things. EG *It is claimed that harsh retribution has deterrent value.* ADJ CLASSIF = cautionary

detest /di'test/, **detests, detesting, detested.** If you **detest** someone or something, you dislike them very much. EG *They detest the thought of living elsewhere.* ◇ **detestation** /diːtesteɪʃəⁿn/. EG *...his detestation of petty rules.* V+O = loathe ≠ love ◇ N UNCOUNT = loathing

detestable /di'testəbəⁿl/. Someone or something that is **detestable** is very unpleasant and deserves to be disliked very strongly. EG *...a stepson he found altogether detestable.* ADJ QUALIT = loathsome ≠ adorable

dethrone /di'θrəʊn/, **dethrones, dethroning, dethroned.** If a king, queen, or other powerful person **is dethroned**, they are removed from their position of power. EG *It was a question of resigning or being dethroned.* V+O : USU PASS ⇑ remove = depose

detonate /detə'neɪt/, **detonates, detonating, detonated.** If you **detonate** a device such as a bomb or it **detonates**, it explodes. EG *The leading group was to detonate anti-tank and anti-personnel mines... The whole lot would detonate in quite a spectacular display.* V-ERG = explode

detonation /detə'neɪʃəⁿn/, **detonations.** 1 A **detonation** is a large or powerful explosion. EG *Few people survived the immediate effects of the detonation.* N COUNT

2 **Detonation** is the action of causing a device such as a bomb to explode. EG *...the possible detonation of a nuclear weapon.* N UNCOUNT = explosion

detonator /detəⁿneɪtə/, **detonators.** A **detonator** is a small amount of explosive or a piece of electrical or electronic equipment which is used to explode a bomb or other explosive device. N COUNT

detour /diːtʊə/, **detours.** A **detour** is a route which is not the shortest way from one place to another but which you take because you want to avoid a problem such as a traffic jam, or because you want to see something on the journey. EG *Road signs indicate detours ahead... As usual, he made a detour to pass the house where Miss Lenaut lived.* N COUNT ⇑ diversion

> **DETPOSS** □ In this dictionary DETPOSS is used in the grammar notes beside entries to describe a group of determiners, *my, your, his, her, its, our,* and *their,* which show who something or someone belongs to or who they relate to. These words are sometimes called possessives. A DETPOSS is generally the first element in a noun group but it can have a PREDET such as *all, half,* or *both* in front of it. It cannot be used with other determiners such as *the* and *this.* An example is **my.** EG *I've left* **my** *bag at the inn... ...***my** *green shoes... ...all* **my** *aches.*

detract /di'trækt/, **detracts, detracting, detracted.** If one thing **detracts** from another, it makes it seem less good than people have thought it to be or than it really is. EG *This fact did not detract from her sense of achievement.* V+A *(from)* ⇑ lessen ≠ enhance

detractor /di'træktə/, **detractors.** A **detractor** of a person, idea, achievement, etc is someone who does or says things which make that person, achievement, or idea seem less good than they really are. EG *He was already aware that his detractors were active.* N COUNT : POSS+N ⇑ critic ≠ defender

detriment /detrə'məⁿnt/. 1 If something happens **to** the **detriment** of something or **to** someone's **detriment**, it causes harm or damage to them. EG *This discovery has been exploited to the detriment of the poor peasants.* PHR : USED AS AN A

2 If something happens **without detriment to** someone or something, it does not harm or damage them. EG *The land could be reclaimed without detriment to conservation.* PHR : USED AS AN A

detrimental /detrɪmentəⁿl/. Something that is **detrimental** has very harmful or damaging effects. EG *...actions which could be detrimental to the company and its shareholders... ...the detrimental effects of the government's incomes policy.* ADJ QUALIT : IF+PREP THEN *to* = damaging ≠ beneficial

detritus /dɪ'traɪtəs/ is the small pieces of rubbish that remain when an event has finished or when something has been used. EG *He walks through the party detritus.* N UNCOUNT+SUPP ⇑ remains = debris

de trop /də trəʊ/. Something or someone that is **de trop** is not wanted, because they are unsuitable or not necessary in a certain situation; a formal word. EG *They'll use all their favourite ploys to make you feel uncomfortable and de trop.* ADJ QUALIT : PRED ⇑ unwanted = unwelcome

deuce /djuːs/, **deuces.** **Deuce** is the score in a game of tennis when both players have forty points. One player has to win two points in succession to win the game. N UNCOUNT/COUNT ⇑ score = forty all

devalue /diːvæljuː/, **devalues, devaluing, devalued.** 1 To **devalue** something or someone means to think that they are unimportant or ordinary and not give them the respect that they deserve. EG *Scientific expertise has been devalued.* ◇ **devalued.** EG *I felt devalued and depressed.* V+O ⇑ lessen ◇ ADJ QUALIT

2 To **devalue** the currency of a country means to reduce its exchange value, usually in order to encourage exports and discourage imports; a technical term in economics. EG *The President has devalued the dollar.* ◇ **devaluation** /diːvæljuːeɪʃəⁿn/. EG *...the* V+O ◇ N UNCOUNT/

devaluation of sterling in November 1967... Devaluation had put Concorde's future in doubt. COUNT

devastate /dɛvəsteɪt/, **devastates, devastating, devastated.** 1 If something **devastates** an area or a place, it damages it very badly or destroys a lot of the things that are there. EG *A hurricane had devastated the plantation... Their offices were devastated by fire.*
V+O : USU PASS ⇑ damage = decimate

2 To **devastate** something means to destroy it completely. EG *The country's agriculture has been devastated by lack of investment.*
V+O : USU PASS

devastated /dɛvəsteɪtɪ^{2}d/. If you are **devastated** by something, you are very shocked and upset by it. EG *We were devastated by her decision... I was devastated when she had to leave.*
ADJ CLASSIF : PRED = desolated

devastating /dɛvəsteɪtɪŋ/. Something that is **devastating** 1 destroys or severely damages something. EG *...devastating bombing raids... Modern intensive farming has had devastating effects on our wild animals and plants.*
ADJ QUALIT = lethal, disastrous, fatal

2 shows that a particular argument or point of view is wrong. EG *He thought of the devastating witticisms with which he would destroy his opponents.*
ADJ QUALIT

◊ **devastatingly**. EG *The author demolished these arguments briefly and devastatingly.*
◊ ADV

3 makes you feel very shocked and upset. EG *It was a devastating announcement.*
ADJ QUALIT

4 is very good or beautiful; an informal word. EG *That's her most devastating insight.*
ADJ QUALIT = brilliant

◊ **devastatingly**. EG *She was devastatingly beautiful.*
◊ ADV = stunningly

devastation /dɛvəsteɪʃə^{0}n/, **devastations**. **Devastation** is severe and widespread destruction or damage. EG *...the threat of nuclear devastation.*
N UNCOUNT/ COUNT

develop /dɪvɛləp/, **develops, developing, developed.** 1 When something **develops**, it grows or expands over a period of time, especially so that it changes from its original form into a form which is stronger, larger, more complicated, etc. EG *The bud develops into a flower... Her friendship with Harold developed slowly... Birds' feathers developed from reptilian scales.*
V-ERG ⇑ change = form, grow ≠ regress

◊ **developed**. EG *They have very small limbs with only two fully developed toes on each.*
◊ ADJ QUALIT = formed

2 If a problem or difficulty **develops**, it comes into existence and then becomes more intense or severe. EG *A new crisis began to develop... Chaos began to develop on the roads.*
V ⇑ begin = break out

3 If a country **develops**, it changes from a poor or agricultural country to an industrial country which is able to produce more wealth and which has a more complex economic and political system. EG *When the great civilizations developed, art began to flourish.*
V ⇑ advance = arise

◊ **developed**. EG *Programmes of overseas aid for the less developed countries were mounted by the U.S.... ...administrators from Britain and other developed countries.*
◊ ADJ QUALIT ≠ backward, underdeveloped

◊ **developing**. EG *Several industrialized nations are already supplying developing countries with new technology.*
◊ ADJ CLASSIF : ATTRIB = young

4 If you **develop** a business or industry, you make it grow bigger and more successful. EG *We had hopes of developing tourism on quite a big scale... Large-scale industry was developed in the region... Teachers can also help to develop public library services.*
V+O = expand

5 To **develop** an area of land means to build houses or factories on it, especially in order to make it more useful or profitable. EG *They began to develop a new industrial site near the river.*
V+O ⇑ utilize

6 If you **develop** a particular habit, personal quality, or physical feature, you begin to have it and it then becomes stronger or more noticeable. EG *She developed an enormous appetite... He can only develop self-confidence if he's told he is good.*
V+O ⇑ get = acquire

7 If you **develop** a skill, ability, or quality, you improve it by working hard at it. EG *He needed to develop his reading further.*
V+O = build up

8 To **develop** an illness or fault means to become affected by it. EG *Every winter I developed a bad cough... Write to the manufacturer if the machine develops the same fault again.*
V+O ⇑ get

9 To **develop** a new machine means to gradually add details, improvements, etc to an initial design or idea in order to make it better and more advanced. EG *Their outstandingly smooth-running engine was developed from a petrol motor.*
V+O = evolve

10 If you **develop** an idea or an argument, you make it clearer and more detailed in your mind, usually by speaking or writing about it. EG *He was developing quite a reasonable point of view as he talked to me.*
V+O ⇑ form = formulate, expand

◊ **developed**. EG *He had well developed opinions on schooling.*
◊ ADJ QUALIT : ADV+ADJ

11 To **develop** photographs means to make negatives or prints from a photographic film. EG *I would like to have these pictures developed.*
V+O = process

12 To **develop** a story or a character means to gradually reveal or explain all the details of it. EG *The narrative is developed with great skill and efficiency.*
V+O = unfold

13 To **develop** a theme or melody in a piece of music means to add details to the basic melody; a technical term in music.
V+O ⇑ expand

developer /dɪvɛlə^{7}pə/, **developers**. 1 A **developer** is 1.1 a person or a company that buys land in order to build new buildings, factories, roads, etc on it. EG *Villagers are protesting about the destruction of their beautiful landscape by the developers.*
N COUNT

1.2 someone whose physical or mental growth occurs at a different rate from others of the same age; used especially of children. EG *...a late developer.*
N COUNT : ADJ+N

1.3 someone who develops an idea, design, etc. EG *The developers were determined to make their product as reliable as possible.*
N COUNT+SUPP ⇑ creator = designer

2 **Developer** is a chemical used for developing photographs or films.
N UNCOUNT

development /dɪvɛlə^{7}pmə^{2}nt/, **developments**. 1 **Development** is 1.1 the gradual growth or formation of something, especially a process in which a person or thing matures, changes, or advances to another stage. EG *...language development... The full development of an idea may well take years... It is interesting to trace his development as a craftsman.*
N UNCOUNT+ SUPP

1.2 the growth or expansion of something such as a firm or an industry. EG *Some people expect rapid economic development in Pakistan.*
N UNCOUNT+ SUPP

1.3 the process or result of making a basic design gradually better and more advanced. EG *...a major long-term expansion of engine development and production has started... Today we have a vast and growing research and development industry... What have been the major developments in aircraft engines in the last decade?*
N UNCOUNT/ COUNT ⇑ innovation

1.4 the process of making an area of land or water more useful or profitable. EG *The company is providing finance for oil drilling and development in the North Sea... ...Japanese ventures for the development of Siberia.*
N UNCOUNT+ SUPP

2 A **development** is 2.1 an event or incident which has recently happened and is likely to have an effect on the present situation. EG *Recent developments in Latin America suggest that the situation may be improving... I had to start taking some note of political developments.*
N COUNT ⇑ change

2.2 an area of houses or buildings which have been built by property developers. EG *Many people live in new housing developments.*
N COUNT

developmental /dɪvɛlə^{7}pmɛntə^{0}l/ is used to describe the activities and processes of different types of development. EG *...the vital period of developmental growth.*
ADJ CLASSIF : USU ATTRIB

deviance /diːvɪəns/ is behaviour which is different from what people normally consider to be acceptable. EG *Children as a group often discourage deviance in words or actions.*
N UNCOUNT ⇑ abnormality ≠ conformity

deviant /diːvɪənt/, **deviants**. 1 **Deviant** behaviour or thinking is different from what people normally consider to be acceptable. EG *To light a cigarette in company is becoming a deviant act... These beliefs are labelled deviant by the majority.*
ADJ QUALIT ⇑ abnormal ≠ normal

▸ used of people and groups. EG *...the politically deviant group is bound together by a total ideology.*
▸ ADJ QUALIT

2 A **deviant** is someone whose behaviour or beliefs are different from what people normally consider to be acceptable.
N COUNT ⇑ nonconformist

deviate /diːvɪeɪt/, **deviates, deviating, deviated**. To **deviate** means to change your ideas or behaviour so that they are different from what you used to think or do or from what people usually consider to be acceptable. EG *He has not deviated from his view that war can never be justified... These minority groups are people who deviate from the arbitrary norms.*
V : IF+PREP THEN *from* ≠ adhere to

deviation /diːvɪeɪʃə^{0}n/, **deviations**. **Deviation** is 1 a difference or change in behaviour from what people consider to be normal or acceptable. EG *A crime is a deviation from generally accepted standards of behaviour.*
N COUNT/ UNCOUNT = deviance

2 a belief held by followers of a particular political philosophy which is different in
N COUNT/ UNCOUNT

some way from the usually accepted beliefs of that philosophy. EG *The totalitarian sees any deviation from the new order as persistent corruption.* **3** the difference between the value of one number in a series of numbers and the average value of all the numbers in the series; a technical term in statistics. = departure / N COUNT

device /di'vaɪs/, **devices**. **1** A **device** is **1.1** an object that has been invented for a particular purpose, for example for recording or measuring something. EG *...an electronic device small enough to be slipped into the pocket... A computer is a device for handling or processing information... There have been over a hundred patented devices to extract energy from the waves.* **1.2** a method of getting what you want or getting something done, especially by behaving in a particular way. EG *She would stoop to any device to lay her hands on Sir John's money... We use conscious and unconscious devices to avoid pain... They used television advertising as a device for stimulating demand.* N COUNT : USU+SUPP = gadget; N COUNT+SUPP ⇑ means = ploy

2 If you **leave** someone **to their own devices**, you leave them alone without giving them anything to do. EG *The children were left to their own devices... Left to my own devices I'd eat the whole cake.* PHR : VB INFLECTS

devil /dɛvə⁰l/, **devils**. **1** In Christianity, the **Devil** is the most powerful and important evil spirit. EG *They vowed to renounce the Devil and all his works.* N PROPER : the+N = Satan

2 If you ask **who the devil, where the devil, why the devil**, etc, you are emphasizing how angry, annoyed, or surprised you are. EG *What the devil is she doing now?* PHR : WH+PHR = on earth

3 A **devil** is **3.1** an evil spirit. EG *All you believe in is angels and devils and eternal damnation.* **3.2** someone who seems to you to be unpleasant or evil; used in informal English. EG *Do you know what those devils have done? They've broken every window in the greenhouse.* N COUNT; N COUNT

4 If you call someone a lucky **devil**, a silly **devil**, etc, you are telling them what your opinion of them is. EG *You lucky devil!–I wish I was going... The poor devil died of a heart attack.* N COUNT : ADJ+N = bugger

5 If you say to someone **be a devil**, you are encouraging them to do something which you know they would like to do but which they think they should not do. EG *'Shall I have another drink?'–'Go on, be a devil!'* CONVENTION

6 Better the devil you know than the devil you don't is a saying that means that you would prefer to deal with someone you already know, even though you do not like them, than with someone you know nothing about. PHR

7 If you say you are **between the devil and the deep blue sea**, you mean that you are in a difficult situation where you have to choose between two equally unpleasant courses of action. PHR : USED AS AN A

8 If someone has **the luck of the devil**, they are extremely lucky; an informal expression. EG *That girl has the luck of the devil!* PHR : USED AS O

9 People say **talk of the devil** when someone who they were talking about arrives unexpectedly. EG *Well, talk of the devil!* CONVENTION

10 If you have **the devil of a time** doing something or if there is **a devil of a mess**, you have a very difficult time or there is a very bad mess. EG *I had the devil of a time trying to find out what happened... We got into a devil of a muddle.* PHR : USED AS O = a hell of a

devilish /dɛvə⁰lɪʃ/. **1** A **devilish** idea or action is a cruel or very unpleasant one. EG *What devilish impulse moved you to this?* ADJ QUALIT : USU ATTRIB = fiendish

2 Devilish is also used to emphasize how extreme or complicated something is. EG *It was devilish hard to explain.* ◊ **devilishly**. EG *He's had good luck, but he's also devilishly clever.* ADV+ADJ/ADV = fiendishly; ◊ ADV

devilry /dɛvə⁰lri¹/ is mischievous and lively behaviour, especially behaviour that is likely to cause trouble; an old-fashioned word. EG *It never entered my head that there was devilry afoot.* N UNCOUNT ⇑ wickedness

devil's advocate, devil's advocates. A **devil's advocate** is someone who, in a discussion or debate, supports an opposing or unpopular point of view in order to make the argument more interesting rather than because they really believe it. N COUNT ⇑ proponent

devious /di:vɪəs/. **1** Someone who is **devious** is dishonest and secretive, often in a complicated way. EG *He was as devious as his adversary was ruthless... Not until it's too late does he learn quite how devious both sides can be.* ▸ used of behaviour. EG *...consultants who are prepared to use devious means to justify their actions.* ◊ **deviousness**. EG *He had found a technical loophole of such deviousness that I laughed aloud.* ADJ QUALIT = deceitful, sly ≠ straightforward; ◊ N UNCOUNT

2 A **devious** route, path, or way makes many changes in direction rather than going in the straightest possible line from one place to another. EG *She led him by devious ways to the meeting place.* ADJ QUALIT ⇑ indirect = tortuous

devise /di'vaɪz/, **devises, devising, devised**. If you **devise** a plan, system, or machine, you have the idea for it and you work out how you could create it and use it. EG *Year by year we devise more precise instruments with which to observe the planets... It has been necessary to devise a system of universal schooling.* V+O ⇑ conceive = invent

devoid /di'vɔɪd/. If someone or something is **devoid** of a quality or thing, they have absolutely none of it. EG *He was devoid of any talent whatsoever... Such plans have been almost entirely devoid of social content.* ADJ QUALIT : PRED+of ⇑ without = lacking

devolution /di:və⁷lu:ʃə⁰n/ is the transfer of some authority or power from a central organization or government to smaller organizations or government departments. EG *There was a case for devolution for Scotland and Wales... ...the decentralization and devolution of the BBC during the 1950s.* N UNCOUNT

devolve /di'vɒlv/, **devolves, devolving, devolved**. **1** If you **devolve** a job, duty, or privilege to a person or group that is less important or powerful than you are, you transfer it to them. EG *Central government is facing growing pressures to devolve authority on the regions... Should we try to devolve responsibility down to factory level... ...the methods by which authority can be devolved to local and regional communities.* V+O+A (to/on/upon)

2 If a job, duty, or privilege **devolves** upon a person or group, it is transferred to them from a more important or powerful person or group. EG *The necessity for making great decisions devolves, not upon him, but upon those others.* V+A (upon/on) ⇑ be transferred

devote /di'vəʊt/, **devotes, devoting, devoted**. If you **devote** yourself or your time, energy, or effort to something, you use that time, energy, or effort for a particular purpose. EG *They have devoted all their time to helping the sick... He devoted himself to his studies... ...ensuring that adequate resources are devoted to capital investment.* V+O (NG/REFL) +A (to) ⇑ give = dedicate

devoted /di'vəʊtɪ²d/. **1** Someone who is **devoted** to a person loves that person very much. EG *...a devoted husband and father... He's devoted to his mother.* ADJ QUALIT : IF+PREP THEN to ⇑ loyal

2 Devoted is used to describe activities which involve great effort, concentration, and dedication. EG *...years of devoted research... Practice and devoted care will bring their reward.* ADJ QUALIT : ATTRIB = dedicated

devotee /dɛvə⁶ti:/, **devotees**. **1** A **devotee** of a subject or activity is someone who is very enthusiastic about it. EG *The building has an enormous appeal for devotees of history.* N COUNT : IF+PREP THEN of = fan

2 A **devotee** is a member of a religious group. EG *The devotees worship three times a day.* N COUNT = believer

devotion /di'vəʊʃə⁰n/, **devotions**. **1 Devotion** is **1.1** great love, affection, or admiration for someone or something. EG *She was helped by the devotion of a brilliant husband and loving family... Their devotion to their children is plain to see.* **1.2** the state or act of giving all your time or energy to a particular activity. EG *It demands total devotion to the cause.* **1.3** the activity of religious worship. EG *We watched them kneel in devotion.* N UNCOUNT : IF+PREP THEN to ⇑ loyalty = dedication; N UNCOUNT : IF+PREP THEN to; N UNCOUNT

2 Someone's **devotions** are the prayers that they say, often silently, during a period of worship. EG *I must return to my devotions.* N PLURAL

devotional /di'vəʊʃə⁰nəl, -ʃənə⁰l/. **Devotional** activities or writings are those which relate to religious worship. EG *Readers expecting a devotional work are likely to be shocked.* ADJ CLASSIF : ATTRIB ⇑ religious

devour /di'vaʊə/, **devours, devouring, devoured**. **1** When one animal or insect **devours** another, it eats it. EG *The ants devour the defenceless larvae.* V+O ⇑ eat

2 When a person **devours** something, they eat it quickly and with great eagerness. EG *He devoured a whole tin of beans.* V+O = wolf

3 If you **devour** a book, magazine, etc, you read it quickly and with great eagerness. EG *As a boy I devoured Scott's novels... He had devoured the newspapers sent out to him from England.* V+O ⇑ absorb

4 If you **are devoured** by an emotion, you feel it very strongly and it influences your behaviour and attitudes a great deal. EG *He was devoured by jealousy.* V+O : ONLY PASS ⇑ be consumed

devouring /di'vaʊəriŋ/. A **devouring** interest or activity has a power which is so great that it takes complete control of someone or causes the destruction of something. EG *...an intense and devouring flame of passion... ...the devouring needs of a fast-changing world.* ADJ QUALIT : USU ATTRIB ⇑ powerful = consuming

devout /di'vaʊt/. Someone who is **devout** believes in God or a religion very deeply and shows this belief in the way that they live, for example by keeping religious rules very strictly. EG *She was a devout Catholic.* ▸ used of behaviour. EG *...rational and devout conduct.* ▸ The **devout** is used to refer to people who are devout. EG *The walls there are carved copiously by the devout.* ADJ QUALIT = staunch ▸ N PLURAL : the+N

devoutly /di'vaʊtli'/. 1 **Devoutly** is used to emphasize how sincerely or deeply you hope or wish for something; a formal use. EG *I devoutly hope that it is not some infection.* ADV WITH VB ⇑ really = sincerely

2 **Devoutly** also means in a way that shows deep religious belief. EG *A small boy knelt devoutly among the leaves.* ADV WITH VB

dew /dju:/ is small drops of water that form on the ground and other surfaces outdoors during the night. EG *His shoes were wet with dew.* N UNCOUNT

dewlap /dju:ləp/, **dewlaps**. A **dewlap** is a loose fold of skin that hangs under the throat of animals such as cows and dogs. N COUNT ⇑ flesh

dewy /dju:i'/, **dewier, dewiest**. Something that is **dewy** is wet with dew. ADJ QUALIT

dewy-eyed. Someone who is **dewy-eyed** is innocent and inexperienced. EG *She and Dan were still dewy-eyed enough to think that they would get full compensation.* ADJ QUALIT = starry-eyed

dexterity /dɛksterɪti'/ is the skill of using your hands, or sometimes your mind, to do something well; used showing approval. EG *I was unable to do anything which required manual dexterity... He was a master with this knife, and used it with dexterity and a sense of power.* N UNCOUNT = adroitness ≠ clumsiness

dexterous /dɛkstrəs/; also spelled **dextrous**. Someone who is **dexterous** is very skilful and clever with their hands. EG *Man, being dexterous of hand and inventive of mind, built shelters... He was dextrous and quick.* ◊ **dexterously**. EG *They tossed them dexterously into the baskets on their backs.* ADJ QUALIT = adroit ◊ ADV WITH VB

dextrose /dɛkstrəʊz, -trəʊs/ is a natural form of sugar that is found in fruits, honey, and in the blood of animals. N UNCOUNT ⇑ glucose

dhoti /dəʊti/, **dhotis**. A **dhoti** is a long loose covering for the lower part of the body, worn by men in India. EG *...a threadbare cotton dhoti.* N COUNT ⇑ loin cloth

diabetes /daɪəbi:tɪs, -ti:z/ is an illness in which someone has too much sugar in their blood. N UNCOUNT

diabetic /daɪəbɛtɪk/, **diabetics**. 1 A **diabetic** is a person who suffers from diabetes. N COUNT

2 **Diabetic** medicine, treatment, conditions, etc, are intended for or affect people who have diabetes. EG *...in a diabetic coma... ...diabetic chocolate.* ADJ CLASSIF : ATTRIB

diabolic /daɪəbɒlɪk/ is used to describe something that people think is caused by or belongs to the Devil; a formal word. EG *...the hysterics that led to suspicion of diabolic possession.* ADJ CLASSIF ⇑ devilish = satanic

diabolical /daɪəbɒlɪkəl/. 1 Something that is **diabolical** is extremely unpleasant and annoying; an informal use. EG *It gave men the pretext for all sorts of diabolical behaviour... This weather's diabolical!* ADJ CLASSIF ⇑ bad = dreadful

2 **Diabolical** is used to emphasize how bad or extreme you think something is; an informal use. EG *What a diabolical nerve he has, coming in here like that!* ◊ **diabolically**. EG *It was diabolically dangerous.* ADJ CLASSIF = incredible ◊ ADV

3 **Diabolical** also means the same as diabolic. ADJ CLASSIF

diadem /daɪədɛm/, **diadems**. A **diadem** is a small crown with precious stones in it. N COUNT

diagnose /daɪəgnəʊz/, **diagnoses, diagnosing, diagnosed**. To **diagnose** an illness or a problem means to discover and identify exactly what is wrong. EG *Routine tests will diagnose the condition accurately... The doctor has diagnosed it as rheumatism... She diagnosed bronchitis... Fortunately, the fault was diagnosed early.* V+O, OR V+O+A (as)

diagnosis /daɪəgnəʊsɪs/, **diagnoses**. **Diagnosis** is the discovery and identification of what is wrong with someone who is ill or with something that is not working properly. EG *Joan's fever led to a diagnosis of pneumonia... He's quite sure his diagnosis will be confirmed.* N UNCOUNT/COUNT

diagnostic /daɪəgnɒstɪk/. **Diagnostic** equipment, methods, or systems are used for discovering what is wrong with people who are ill or with things that do not work properly. EG *...computerized medical diagnostic devices.* ADJ CLASSIF

diagonal /daɪægənəl/, **diagonals**. 1 A **diagonal** line goes in a slanting direction away from another line. EG *There was a diagonal red line on the label.* ▸ used as a noun. EG *...giant diagonals on the side of the ship.* ◊ **diagonally**. EG *We drove onto the base and then shot diagonally across the airfield.* ADJ CLASSIF = oblique ▸ N COUNT ◊ ADV

2 A **diagonal** is a straight line that joins two opposite corners in a flat four-sided shape such as a square; a technical term in geometry. N COUNT

diagram /daɪəgræm/, **diagrams**. A **diagram** is a simple drawing consisting mainly of lines that is used, for example, to explain how a machine works. EG *...a simple diagram showing compass directions... ...a circuit diagram of a transistor amplifier.* N COUNT : USU+SUPP

diagrammatic /daɪəgrəmætɪk/. Something that is **diagrammatic** is arranged or drawn as a diagram. EG *The other factors can be shown in diagrammatic form.* ADJ CLASSIF : USU ATTRIB

dial /daɪl/, **dials, dialling, dialled**; also spelled **dialing, dialed** in American English. 1 A **dial** is 1.1 an indicator on the front of an instrument such as a clock or a meter which shows you the time or the measurement that the meter has recorded. EG *...the luminous dial of his watch... Make sure that the figures on the dial can be seen in direct sunlight.* 1.2 the controlling part of a piece of equipment such as a radio or a time switch which you can move in order to select and change the radio frequency or the timing that you require. EG *The man was still fiddling with dials and buttons... Hodges flicked the dial on the radio to 1850 kilohertz.* 1.3 the panel or indicator on a piece of equipment which tells you at what frequency, speed, or timing the equipment has been set to work. EG *The dial of the central heating stood at 75.* 1.4 the circle on a telephone that has holes in it and numbers behind the holes. You use the dial in order to select the telephone number that you want to call. N COUNT; N COUNT ⇑ control = knob, tuner; N COUNT; N COUNT ⇑ control

2 If you **dial** or you **dial** a number, you move the circle on the front of a telephone in order to phone someone. EG *Jim dialled his home number... I found the necessary coins and dialled... She dialled the operator to ask about a taxi.* ▸ also used by some people to refer to the action of pressing the buttons on a push-button telephone. V OR V+O ⇑ contact = ring, phone ▸ V OR V+O

dialect /daɪəlɛkt/, **dialects**. A **dialect** is a form of a language that is spoken by a particular group of people, especially those living in one area. It has different pronunciations, words, and grammar from other forms of the language. EG *...the old anonymous ballads written in northern dialect... ...odd dialects of a tribal language.* N COUNT, OR in+N

dialectic /daɪəlɛktɪk/, **dialectics**. 1 The **dialectic** is 1.1 the philosophical system of asserting truth by resolving the differences that exist between factors in a particular situation. 1.2 all the differences that exist between factors in a particular situation and the way in which these differences are resolved. EG *...a powerful weapon in the dialectic and strategies of his marriage.* N SING : the+N; N SING : the+N+SUPP

2 **Dialectics** is a form of logic, especially used as a method of reasoning. EG *They know a lot; they shine in dialectics.* N UNCOUNT

dialectical /daɪəlɛktɪkəl/ is used to describe situations, theories, and methods which depend on resolving opposing factors. EG *It had to happen, it had a kind of dialectical inevitability.* ADJ CLASSIF : USU ATTRIB

dialling code, dialling codes. A **dialling code** is a telephone number which you dial before someone's personal number in order to be connected to the right area, town, or village. EG *The dialling code for Birmingham is 021.* N COUNT = code

dialling tone, dialling tones. The **dialling tone** is the noise which you hear when you pick up a telephone receiver and which means that you can dial the number you want. N COUNT

dialogue /daɪəlɒg/, **dialogues**; also spelled **dialog** in American English. 1 **Dialogue** is communication or discussion between people or groups of people such as governments or political parties. EG *The* N UNCOUNT/COUNT+SUPP *union continued to seek dialogue with the authorities... And so the dialogue between rich nations and poor grows more tense and strident... The North-South dialogue will be resumed in October at an international conference in Geneva.*

2 A **dialogue** is **2.1** a conversation between two people which takes place in a book, a film, or a play. EG *He knew he could improve the dialogue... ...500 words of newspaper text or movie dialogue.* **2.2** a conversation between two people. EG *Their dialogue was interrupted by Philip's voice... ...talking to each other in a very energetic dialogue.* N COUNT/UNCOUNT; N COUNT

dial tone, dial tones. A **dial tone** is the same as a dialing tone; used in American English. N COUNT

diameter /daɪæmə¹tə/, **diameters**. The **diameter** of a round object is the length of a straight line that can be drawn across it or through the middle of it. EG *He measured the diameter of this artery... ...a giant planet over 30,000 miles in diameter... Its diameter might have been about twenty feet.* N COUNT, OR *in*+N ⇑ measurement

diametrically /daɪəmetrɪkli¹/. If you say that two things are **diametrically** opposed, you are emphasizing that they are absolutely and completely different from each other. EG *The two systems are diametrically opposed... We held almost diametrically opposing points of view.* ADV = totally

diamond /daɪəmənd/, **diamonds**. **1** A **diamond** is **1.1** a hard, bright, precious stone made of pure carbon. Diamonds are used in jewellery and for cutting substances that are very hard. EG *...a ring containing a diamond the size of a pigeon's egg... ...mink coats and diamond brooches... ...diamond mines.* **1.2** a shape with four straight sides of equal length, but with two opposite angles less than 90 and the other two opposite angles more than 90. N COUNT ⇑ gem; N COUNT

2 Diamonds are jewellery such as necklaces, bracelets, etc, which have diamonds set into them. EG *I'm going to wear my diamonds tonight.* N PLURAL

3 Diamonds is one of the four suits of cards in a pack of playing cards. Each card in the suit is marked with one or more red symbols in the shape of a diamond. N UNCOUNT/COUNT

diamond jubilee, diamond jubilees. A **diamond jubilee** is the sixtieth anniversary of an important event. N COUNT

diamond wedding, diamond weddings. Someone's **diamond wedding** is their sixtieth wedding anniversary. N COUNT

diaper /daɪəpə/, **diapers**. A **diaper** is a piece of soft towel or absorbent paper, worn by babies around their bottoms; used in American English. N COUNT

diaphanous /daɪæfənəs/. Cloth or fabric that is **diaphanous** is very fine or thin and almost transparent. EG *Each window had its own diaphanous blind.* ADJ CLASSIF = gauzy, sheer

diaphragm /daɪəfræm/, **diaphragms**. **1** Your **diaphragm** is a muscle between your lungs and your stomach. It is used especially when you breathe deeply. EG *He blew into the shell with air from his diaphragm.* N COUNT

2 A **diaphragm** is also a circular rubber or plastic contraceptive device that a woman places inside her body in order to prevent sperm from entering her uterus. N COUNT = cap

diarist /daɪərɪst/, **diarists**. A **diarist** is a person who records things in a diary which is later published. EG *...the Victorian diarist Francis Kilvert.* N COUNT ⇑ writer

diarrhoea /daɪərɪə/; also spelled **diarrhea** in American English. **Diarrhoea** is an illness in which people get rid of a lot of faeces which are much more liquid than usual. EG *If you're lucky you'll suffer nothing worse than sickness and diarrhoea.* N UNCOUNT = the runs ≠ constipation

diary /daɪəri¹/, **diaries**. A **diary** is a book which has a separate space or page for each day of the year. You use a diary to write down your appointments and things you have to do in the future, or to record what happens in your life day by day. EG *He got out his diary and made a note in it... Her diary gives an account of what happened.* • If you **keep a diary**, you regularly write down your experiences, thoughts, and feelings in a diary. EG *I haven't kept a diary since I was at school.* N COUNT : USU POSS+N; • PHR : VB INFLECTS

diaspora /daɪæspə⁸rə/. A **diaspora** is a dispersion or spreading of people from a particular nation or culture; a formal word. EG *Moreover, every nationality had a diaspora, often spread far beyond its homestead.* N SING WITH DET ⇑ spread

diatribe /daɪətraɪb/, **diatribes**. A **diatribe** is an angry speech or written article which is extremely critical of certain ideas or activities or of a particular person or group of people. EG *...a cynical diatribe against all human sentiments.* N COUNT : USU+SUPP ⇑ criticism = attack

dice /daɪs/, **dices, dicing, diced. Dice** is both the singular and the plural form of the noun. **1** A **dice** is a small cube made of wood, plastic, or ivory, which has one or more spots on each of its six sides, and which is used in games to provide random numbers. EG *They roll dice each morning to see who will make the coffee.* N COUNT

2 Dice is a game which is played using dice. EG *Some men were drinking, some were playing dice or cards.* N UNCOUNT

3 If you **dice with death**, you do something that involves a lot of risk or danger. EG *...dicing with death on the high seas.* PHR : VB INFLECTS

4 When you **dice** food, you cut it into small cubes. EG *Remove the chicken joint from the stock, dice the flesh, and place in a clean saucepan.* ◇ **diced**. EG *I bought some diced lamb to make a stew.* V+O ⇑ chop; ◇ ADJ CLASSIF

dicey /daɪsi¹/, **dicier, diciest**. Something that is **dicey** is slightly dangerous or uncertain; an informal word. EG *Hitch-hiking's a bit dicey in this area.* ADJ QUALIT = risky

dichotomy /daɪkɒtə⁷mi¹/, **dichotomies**. A **dichotomy** is a difference between two things, especially things that are opposite to each other, which is so great that you cannot imagine how they can be reconciled; a formal word. EG *In terms of ultimate truth a dichotomy of this sort has little meaning.* N COUNT : USU SING ≠ agreement

dickens /dɪkɪnz/. **The dickens** is used in questions after words like 'what', 'where', and 'why' to emphasize the fact that you are confused, surprised, or annoyed; an informal and rather old-fashioned expression. EG *Why the dickens should the boy have any of my money?* PHR : WH+PHR = the devil

Dickensian /dɪkenzjən/ conditions, buildings, or equipment are considered to be very old-fashioned or unpleasant. EG *The prisons are worse than Dickensian.* ADJ QUALIT ⇑ old-fashioned

dicky /dɪki¹/, **dickies; dickier, dickiest**. **1** A **dicky** is a piece of cloth which men sometimes wear to fill in the open neck of a jacket so that it looks as if they have a shirt or a jumper on. EG *...bishops with purple dickies.* N COUNT

2 Something that is **dicky** is weak or unlikely to work properly; an informal use. EG *...a dicky heart.* ADJ QUALIT = dodgy

dicky-bird, dicky-birds. **1** When adults are talking to children, they sometimes call birds **dicky-birds**. EG *Look at the pretty dicky-birds.* N COUNT ⇑ bird

2 If you say that you won't say a **dicky-bird** about something, you mean that you won't say anything at all about it; an informal use. PHR : USED AS O

Dictaphone /dɪktəfəʊn/, **Dictaphones**; a trademark. A **Dictaphone** is a tape recorder on which you can record letters so that they can be typed later. EG *He dictated a message onto the Dictaphone.* N COUNT ⇑ machine

dictate, dictates, dictating, dictated; the word **dictate** is pronounced /dɪkteɪt/ when it is a verb, and /dɪkteɪt/ when it is a noun. **1** If you **dictate** something, **1.1** you say or read it aloud for someone else to write down. EG *It took him a long time to dictate this letter... I was proposing to dictate a story by telephone.* **1.2** you state what must happen in certain circumstances and you have the power to enforce it. EG *Landlords can dictate their own conditions when letting their houses... The printers tried to dictate how he should run his business... The law dictated that his right hand should be cut off.* V OR V+O; V OR V+O/REPORT-CL ⇑ command = prescribe

2 If you **dictate** to someone, you tell them what they should do. EG *His last attempt to dictate to the Prime Minister was a total failure... The unions are hardly in a position to dictate to the Labour party.* V+A *(to)*

3 A **dictate** is **3.1** an order which you have to obey. EG *They obeyed the union's dictates and went on strike... These were allocated by dictate of the central government.* **3.2** a principle or rule which you consider to be extremely important. EG *You condemn me for following the dictates of my conscience... His behaviour challenges one of the oldest and most powerful dictates of human society.* N COUNT OR *by*+N; N COUNT+SUPP

dictation /dɪkteɪʃə⁰n/, **dictations**. **1 Dictation** is **1.1** the speaking or reading aloud of words for someone else to write down. EG *Jill took down a story from Frank's dictation.* **1.2** the words or information that someone says or reads aloud for someone else N UNCOUNT; N UNCOUNT to write down. EG *I hated it if I ever had to take dictation from him.* **1.3** the giving of orders in a forceful and commanding way. EG *The group resented dictation from above.* N UNCOUNT

2 A **dictation** is a test in which people have to write down a text that is read aloud to them. This is to assess their ability to understand and spell a language. EG *Our teacher was always giving us French dictations... She usually did well on dictation.* N COUNT/UNCOUNT

dictator /dɪkteɪtə/, **dictators**. A **dictator** is **1** a ruler who has complete power in a country, especially power which was obtained by force; used showing disapproval. EG *Many of these countries are run by dictators... He behaves as if he were dictator of England.* **2** someone who acts as if they had complete power over people or things. EG *He can be a dictator in his own house if he wants to.* N COUNT = tyrant; N COUNT = tyrant

dictatorial /dɪktətɔːrɪəl/. **1 Dictatorial** means caused, controlled, or used by a dictator. EG *He helped to finance dictatorial regimes all over the world.* ADJ QUALIT = autocratic

2 Dictatorial power or behaviour involves giving orders and telling people what to do in a forceful, commanding, and often unfair way. EG *...the dictatorial power of central committees.* ▸ used of people. EG *He was a dictatorial, bad-tempered old man.* ADJ QUALIT = tyrannical, despotic

dictatorship /dɪkteɪtəʃɪp/, **dictatorships**. **1 Dictatorship** is **1.1** government by a dictator. EG *Democracy soon gave way to dictatorship... ...a military dictatorship.* **1.2** complete and absolute power or authority that is held by a dictator or a political group. EG *...the dictatorship of the proletariat.* N UNCOUNT/COUNT; N UNCOUNT+SUPP = tyranny

2 A **dictatorship** is a country which is ruled by a dictator or by a very authoritarian government. EG *There was no chance that Jamaica would become a dictatorship.* N COUNT

diction /dɪkʃən/ is the clarity with which someone speaks or sings. EG *What was so striking was her magnificent diction.* N UNCOUNT ⇑ articulation

dictionary /dɪkʃənərɪ/, **dictionaries**. A **dictionary** is **1** a book in which the words of a language are listed alphabetically and their meanings are explained. **2** a book in which words in one language are listed alphabetically and are followed by words which have the same meaning in another language. EG *...an English-French dictionary.* **3** any alphabetically ordered reference book on one particular subject or limited group of subjects. EG *...the Dictionary of National Biography.* N COUNT = lexicon; N COUNT; N COUNT+SUPP

dictum /dɪktəm/, **dictums, dicta**. The plural can be either **dictums** or **dicta**. A **dictum** is **1** a formal statement made by someone who has authority. EG *...the General's dictum that 'only patriotic, honest citizens would be allowed these privileges.'* **2** a saying that describes an aspect of life in an interesting or wise way. EG *His dictum always was, 'If a job's worth doing, it's worth doing well'.* N COUNT = pronouncement; N COUNT = maxim

did /dɪd/ is the past tense of **do**.

didactic /dɪdæktɪk/; a formal word. **1** Something that is **didactic** is intended to teach people a moral lesson. EG *Do you think it is necessary for theatre to be didactic?* ◊ **didactically**. EG *I don't say didactically that experience can only be gained first-hand.* ADJ QUALIT ⇑ instructive; ◊ ADV WITH VB

2 Someone who is **didactic** is very eager to teach people things even if nobody seems very interested in learning them. EG *He tends to be rather didactic.* ADJ QUALIT

diddle /dɪdəl/, **diddles, diddling, diddled**. If you **diddle** someone, you take money from them dishonestly or unfairly; an informal word, used especially in British English. EG *You've been diddled!* V+O ⇑ cheat = swindle

didn't /dɪdənt/ is the usual spoken form of 'did not'.

die /daɪ/, **dies, dying, died**. **1** When people, animals, and plants **die**, they stop living. EG *Neil's mother died of pneumonia when he was four... He died a disappointed man.* ▸ **Die** can also be used with 'death' as an object. EG *I don't believe Davis died a natural death.* V OR V+C ≠ be born; ▸ V+O : NO PASS

2 If someone **is dying**, they are so ill or so badly injured that they will not live very much longer. EG *An old woman dying of cancer was taken into hospital.* V : ONLY CONT ≠ recover

3 When things **die**, they function or burn more and more slowly and eventually stop completely. EG *He watched his cigarette die in the ashtray... The plane came to a halt, propellers dying.* V

4 When emotions or facial expressions **die**, they disappear completely, usually after a period of becoming less and less intense, noticeable or successful. EG *True love never dies... His smile died.* V

5 If you say that you **nearly died** or that you **could have died**, you mean that you felt very shocked, surprised, or embarrassed about something that happened; an informal expression. EG *I nearly died when he said that.* PHR : VB INFLECTS

6 If you are **dying of** thirst, **dying of** hunger, etc, you are very thirsty, very hungry, etc; an informal expression. EG *I'm dying of thirst... I was dying of boredom.* PHR : AUX INFLECTS

7 If you are **dying** for something or **dying** to do something, you want very much to have it or to do it; an informal expression. EG *I'm dying for a drink... They were all dying to go to Paris.* PHR+*for/to*-INF : AUX INFLECTS = long

8 If an idea or custom **dies hard**, it changes or disappears very slowly. EG *Colonial traditions die hard... Deeply entrenched views die hard.* PHR : VB INFLECTS

9 A **die** is a specially shaped or patterned block of metal which is used to press or cut other metal into a particular shape. N COUNT ⇑ stamp

10 If you say that **the die is cast**, you mean that an important decision that affects your future has been made and you can do nothing now to change it. PHR : VB INFLECTS

11 See also **dying**.

die away. If a sound **dies away**, it gradually becomes weaker or fainter and finally disappears altogether. EG *Now that the cheers had died away, the circus tent seemed oddly quiet.* PHRASAL VB : V+ADV ⇑ weaken = fade

die back. If a plant **dies back**, its leaves die but its roots remain alive. PHRASAL VB : V+ADV

die down. If something **dies down**, it becomes very much quieter or less intense. EG *She waited until the laughter had died down... The wind has died down quite a lot.* PHRASAL VB : V+ADV ⇑ diminish

die out. If something **dies out**, it becomes less and less common and eventually disappears completely. EG *Traditional grocers' shops are fast dying out now that there are so many supermarkets... The golden eagle is in danger of dying out.* PHRASAL VB : V+ADV ⇑ disappear

diehard /daɪhɑːd/, **diehards**. A **diehard** is someone who is very strongly opposed to change and new ideas. EG *With the exception of a few diehards, the committee welcomed the proposals for reform.* N COUNT ⇑ reactionary ≠ innovator

diesel /diːzəl/, **diesels**. **1** A **diesel** is a vehicle which has a diesel engine. EG *This year one car in ten sold in Italy will be a diesel.* N COUNT

2 Diesel or **diesel oil** is the heavy oil used in a diesel engine. N UNCOUNT

diesel engine, diesel engines. A **diesel engine** is an internal combustion engine in which oil is burnt by very hot air. Diesel engines are often used in trains, buses, or lorries. N COUNT

diet /daɪət/, **diets, dieting, dieted**. **1** A **diet** is **1.1** the food that a person or animal eats regularly. EG *Her diet consisted of bread and lentils... Dogs need a regular, balanced diet.* ▸ used as an uncount noun. EG *Correct diet is so important.* **1.2** a special restricted range of food that a doctor tells a person to eat in order to improve their health. EG *He has to have a special diet because of his kidney condition.* N COUNT; ▸ N UNCOUNT; N COUNT : USU+SUPP

2 If you are on a **diet**, you are eating special kinds of food because you want to lose weight. EG *'Have a biscuit.'-'No thanks, I'm on a diet.'* ▸ used as an adjective. EG *Saccharin is the main sweetener for diet drinks.* N COUNT ⇑ plan; ▸ ADJ CLASSIF : ATTRIB

3 If you **are dieting**, you are eating special kinds of food because you are trying to lose weight. EG *I'm going to start dieting after Christmas.* V = slim ≠ overeat

dietary /daɪətərɪ/ describes the food that people or animals eat or need. EG *We are working on changing dietary habits.* ADJ CLASSIF : USU ATTRIB ⇑ eating

dietician /daɪətɪʃən/, **dieticians**. A **dietician** is someone whose job is to advise people about what they should or should not eat in order to be healthy. N COUNT

differ /dɪfə/, **differs, differing, differed**. **1** If two or more things **differ**, they are unlike each other in some way. EG *Modern cars differ from the early ones in many major ways... Although our looks differ, we are both physically attractive.* V : IF+PREP THEN *from* ⇑ be unlike ≠ resemble

2 If people **differ** about something, they do not agree with each other about it. EG *We differ about moral standards... This is basically where we differ.* V = disagree ≠ agree

3 If people **agree to differ**, they agree to accept the fact that they will never have the same opinion about something and so stop arguing about it. PHR : VB INFLECTS

4 You say **'I beg to differ'** when you want to say CONVENTION politely that you disagree with someone; a formal expression.

difference /dɪfəᵒrəns/, **differences**. 1 A **difference** is a quality in something which makes it unlike something else. EG *Is there much difference between British and European law?... There is an essential difference between computers and humans... Look at their difference in size.* N COUNT/UNCOUNT: IF+PREP THEN *between/in/of* = dissimilarity ≠ similarity

2 The word **difference** is also used in the following expressions. **2.1 With a difference** means unusual and interesting; used showing approval. EG *...a farmhouse with a difference.* PHR: USED AS AN A **2.2** If you say that something **makes no difference** or **does not make any difference**, you mean that it is not important whether it is done or not or whether it happens or not. EG *An extra few days would make no difference... Never mind, it doesn't make any difference.* PHR: VB INFLECTS, IF+PREP THEN *to* **2.3** If you say that something **makes all the difference**, you mean that it helps you succeed or achieve what you are trying to do. EG *That extra money would have made all the difference.* PHR: VB INFLECTS

3 A **difference** is also the amount by which one number or quantity is less than another. EG *What is the difference between 10 and 20?* N SING WITH DET: IF+PREP THEN *between* ● If you agree to **split the difference**, you agree on an amount or price which is halfway between two suggested amounts or prices. EG *I offered him £500, and he wanted £600, so we split the difference and settled on £550.* ● PHR: VB INFLECTS ⇑ divide

4 If people have a **difference** or have their **differences**, they are disagreeing or arguing. EG *The talks collapsed because of irreconcilable differences among them.* N COUNT ⇑ disagreement = dispute

different /dɪfəᵒrənt/. 1 Someone or something that is **different** is **1.1** not like someone or something else in one or more ways. EG *The meeting was different from any that had gone before... His message is very little different to theirs.* ◊ **differently**. EG *He made me feel differently... ...two kinds of differently shaped cells.* ADJ QUALIT: IF+PREP THEN *from/to* ⇑ unlike ◊ ADV WITH VB **1.2** unusual and not like others of the same kind. EG *'What do you think of it?'–'It's different, but I don't really like it.'* ADJ QUALIT = original

2 Two or more **different** things are separate and distinct from each other although they are the same kind of thing. EG *She has accounts with two different banks.* ADJ CLASSIF: ATTRIB

differential /dɪfərenʃəᵒl/, **differentials**. A **differential** is 1 a difference between two values in a scale; a technical term in mathematics or economics. N COUNT 2 a difference between rates of pay for different types of work, especially work done by people in the same industry or company; used in British English. EG *They claim that their differentials have been narrowed by inflation.* N COUNT

differentiate /dɪfərenʃieɪt/, **differentiates, differentiating, differentiated**. 1 If you **differentiate** between things or you **differentiate** one thing from another, you recognize or show the difference between them. EG *How can you differentiate between moral and religious questions?* V+O, V+A (*between*), OR V+O (NG/REFL)+A (*from*) = distinguish

2 Something that **differentiates** one thing from another is the quality or aspect that makes it different. EG *What differentiates a sculpture from an object?* ◊ **differentiation** /dɪfərenʃieɪʃəᵒn/. EG *We aim for the greatest possible differentiation of the product from those of other manufacturers.* V+O, OR V+O+A (*from*) ⇑ separate = distinguish ◊ N UNCOUNT

difficult /dɪfɪkəᵒlt/. 1 Something that is **difficult** causes you a lot of problems, usually because it is not easy to do, understand, or solve. EG *Many youngsters find it difficult to get jobs... It was difficult for Brody to resist the temptation... That's a very difficult question.* ADJ QUALIT: USU + *to*-INF, IF+PREP THEN *for* = hard ≠ easy

2 Someone who is **difficult** is not easy to like or to have a good relationship with, because they are unreasonable or unpredictable in the way they behave. EG *All thirteen-year-olds are difficult.* ADJ QUALIT ⇑ problematic = awkward

difficulty /dɪfɪkəˡlti¹/, **difficulties**. 1 A **difficulty** is something that is a problem for you. EG *There are lots of difficulties that have to be overcome... The main difficulty is a shortage of time.* N COUNT ⇑ obstacle

2 If something causes **difficulty**, it causes problems because it is not easy to do or understand. EG *This can cause difficulty... ...questions of varying difficulty.* N UNCOUNT

3 If you **have** or **find difficulty** doing something, you are not able to do it easily. EG *I was having difficulty breathing... I had no difficulty in getting in touch with him.* PHR+*in*/-ING: VB INFLECTS

4 If you do something **with difficulty**, you have to make a lot of effort to do it because it is not easy for you. EG *She spoke with difficulty.* PHR: USED AS AN A

5 If you are **in difficulty** or **in difficulties**, you are in a situation in which you are struggling. EG *He went to the aid of a swimmer in difficulty.* PHR: USED AS AN A

diffidence /dɪfɪdəˀns/ is the quality that some people have of being shy and not enjoying talking about themselves or being noticed by other people. EG *...his natural diffidence... She walked up with some diffidence.* N UNCOUNT ⇑ shyness = reserve

diffident /dɪfɪdəˀnt/. Someone who is **diffident** is rather shy and does not enjoy talking about themselves or being noticed by other people. EG *She stood in the doorway, diffident and abashed.* ◊ **diffidently**. EG *He expressed himself politely and diffidently.* ADJ QUALIT = hesitant, self-effacing ≠ confident ◊ ADV WITH VB

diffuse, diffuses, diffusing, diffused. The word **diffuse** is pronounced /dɪfjuːz/ when it is a verb, and /dɪfjuːs/ when it is an adjective. 1 When light **diffuses** or when something **diffuses** light, the light spreads in a lot of directions and shines faintly over a wide area rather than shining brightly in just one place. EG *The light was diffused by oak and birch leaves... The curtains did not keep out the diffused lamplight from the street below.* V-ERG ⇑ spread = scatter

2 If you **diffuse** knowledge, information, etc or if it **diffuses**, it spreads over a wide area or to a lot of people. EG *Printing presses have diffused information throughout the world.* ◊ **diffusion** /diˡfjuːʒəᵒn/. EG *...the diffusion of scientific knowledge.* V-ERG ⇑ spread = circulate ◊ N UNCOUNT

3 If a liquid or gas **diffuses**, it moves and spreads over an area or through a space or substance. EG *Ink diffuses through water.* ◊ **diffusion**. V: USU+A ◊ N UNCOUNT

4 Something that is **diffuse** is **4.1** vague and not easy to understand or explain. EG *...a vague and diffuse sense of envy... Modern anarchism has become increasingly diffuse.* ADJ QUALIT ⇑ obscure = imprecise **4.2** not directed towards one place or concentrated in one place but spread out over a large area. EG *...a broad, diffuse organization... ...a faint and diffuse glow of light.* ADJ QUALIT = scattered ≠ concentrated

dig /dɪg/, **digs, digging, dug**. 1 When people or animals **dig**, they push a spade, their hands, their paws, etc into the ground, usually in order to make a hole or to move some of the earth to a different place. EG *I was digging my brother's garden... This animal can dig faster than any cat or dog... It was decided that a new well must be dug.* ▸ used as a noun. EG *You ought to give the garden a good dig.* V OR V+O ▸ N SING: *a*+N

2 If you **dig** into something, you search in it for something that you are looking for. EG *Thomas dug into the bag and pulled out a sandwich.* V, OR V+A = delve

3 If you **dig** one thing into another or if one thing **digs** into another, you press the first thing hard into the second. EG *She dug her needle into her sewing... My corset was digging into my stomach.* ● to **dig** your **heels in**: see **heel**. V-ERG+A = jab, poke

4 If you say that you **dig** something, you mean that you like it and understand it; an old-fashioned, informal expression. V OR V+O

5 A **dig** is **5.1** an archaeological excavation. EG *There's a very interesting dig going on near Bath.* N COUNT **5.2** a spiteful or unpleasant remark which is intended to hurt, anger, or embarrass someone; an informal use. EG *Whenever she can, she takes a dig at me.* N COUNT: IF+PREP THEN *at* ⇑ gibe

6 If you give someone a **dig** in part of their body, you poke them with your finger or your elbow. EG *She gave me a dig in the ribs.* N COUNT ⇑ touch = jab

7 Your **digs** are, a room in someone else's house which you pay to live in for a short time; used in British English. EG *When I was working in Sheffield, I lived in digs.* N PLURAL: *in*+N ⇑ accommodation = lodgings

dig at. If you **dig at** someone, you make a spiteful or unpleasant remark which is intended to hurt or upset them. PHRASAL VB: V+PREP ⇑ gibe = get at

dig in. 1 If you **dig** something **in** or **into** the ground, you mix it into the soil by digging. EG *She was digging compost into the vegetable patch.* PHRASAL VB: V+O+ADV/PREP ⇑ incorporate

2 If people, especially soldiers, **dig in** or **dig** themselves **in**, they dig trenches and prepare themselves for an attack by the enemy. PHRASAL VB: V+ADV, OR V+O (REFL)+ADV

3 If you tell someone to **dig in**, you are telling them to start eating; an informal expression in British English. PHRASAL VB: V+ADV = tuck in

dig out. 1 If you **dig** someone or something **out** of somewhere, you get them out after a certain amount PHRASAL VB: V+O+ADV/PREP of effort or difficulty. EG *They were stranded in a snowdrift and had to be dug out... She dug the splinter out of his finger.* (of) ⇑ remove

2 If you **dig** something **out**, you find it after it has been hidden or stored for a long time. EG *We had dug out our tour books and maps ready for the holiday.* PHRASAL VB : V+O+ADV = root out

dig up. 1 If you **dig** something **up**, you remove it from the ground where it has been buried. EG *They dug up his body and returned it to the church.* PHRASAL VB : V+O+ADV

2 If you **dig up** information or facts, you discover something that has not previously been widely known. EG *The journalists dug up some hair-raising facts about the company.* PHRASAL VB : V+O+ADV = dredge up

digest, digests, digesting, digested. The word **digest** is pronounced /dɪ⁵dʒest/ when it is a verb, and /daɪdʒest/ when it is a noun. 1 When you **digest** food, the food passes through your stomach and is broken down so that your body can use it. EG *I just cannot digest cheese or eggs... ...a supply of easily digested food.* V+O ⇑ break down

2 If you **digest** information, you think about it, understand it, and remember it. EG *The report contains too much to digest at one reading.* V+O ⇑ assimilate = absorb

3 A **digest** is a collection of things that have been written, which are put together and published again in a more concise form. N COUNT : USU+SUPP

digestible /dɪ⁵dʒestəbə⁰l/. Food that is **digestible** is able to be digested easily. EG *He cut up the meat into small, easily digestible pieces.* ADJ QUALIT ≠ indigestible

digestion /dɪ⁵dʒestʃə⁰n/, **digestions.** 1 **Digestion** is the process of digesting food. EG *A good walk aids digestion.* N UNCOUNT

2 Your **digestion** is the system in your body which digests your food. EG *His digestion had always been poor.* N COUNT = digestive system

digestive /dɪ⁵dʒestɪv/, **digestives.** 1 **Digestive** is a trademark for a biscuit that is made from wholemeal flour; used in British English. EG *...a packet of Digestives... ...Digestive biscuits.* N COUNT

2 **Digestive** means relating to the digestion of food. EG *...the body's digestive juices... ...the digestive system.* ADJ CLASSIF : ATTRIB

digger /dɪgə/, **diggers.** A **digger** is a machine that is used for digging. EG *...a mechanical digger.* N COUNT ⇑ excavator

digit /dɪdʒɪt/, **digits.** A **digit** is 1 a finger, thumb, or toe; a formal word. EG *His only clean digit, a pink thumb, slid into his mouth.* 2 a written symbol for any of the ten numbers from 0 to 9. EG *Move the decimal point one digit to the left.* N COUNT; N COUNT

digital /dɪdʒə¹tə⁰l/. **Digital** devices such as watches or clocks give information by displaying numbers rather than by using hands that move round a dial: compare **analogue.** EG *...a digital display... In extremes of temperature the display on a digital watch may fade.* ADJ CLASSIF ⇑ numerical

digital computer, digital computers. A **digital computer** is one which uses a binary system to represent the information it processes, so that the information is represented in an exact form. Compare **analogue computer.** N COUNT

digital recording, digital recordings. A **digital recording** is a sound recording made using a high quality technique which breaks down the sound into thousands of very small signals. N COUNT

dignified /dɪgnɪfaɪd/. Someone who is **dignified** has the quality of being quietly or calmly impressive and worthy of respect. EG *The director of the school was a white-haired, dignified gentleman.* ADJ QUALIT = stately

dignify /dɪgnɪfaɪ/, **dignifies, dignifying, dignified.** 1 If one thing **dignifies** another, it makes it impressive. EG *They stood admiring the broad steps that dignified the front of the mansion.* V+O : NO IMPER ⇑ elevate = ennoble

2 To **dignify** someone or something means to make them seem more respectable or valuable than they really are by giving them a name or title that sounds important. EG *His arrogance and rejection of convention cannot be dignified as a rebellion against authority.* V+O : NO IMPER ⇑ elevate

dignitary /dɪgnɪtə⁰ri¹/, **dignitaries.** A **dignitary** is a person who is considered to be important because they have a high rank in government or in the Church. N COUNT : USU PL = VIP

dignity /dɪgnɪti¹/. 1 **Dignity** is 1.1 behaviour or an appearance which is serious, calm, and controlled; used showing approval. EG *There was something impressive about Julia's quiet dignity... I tried to sit through the laughter with some dignity.* N UNCOUNT ⇑ pride = poise, control 1.2 the quality of being worthy of respect. EG *Don't discount the importance of human dignity... A lot of nonsense is often talked about the dignity of labour.* N UNCOUNT : USU +SUPP ⇑ value

2 Someone's **dignity** is the sense that they have of their own importance. EG *He danced a step or two, then remembered his dignity and stood still.* N SING : POSS+N = self-esteem • If someone **stands on** their **dignity**, they insist on behaving in a very correct way or on being treated in a way that does not damage their sense of self-importance. EG *He was very careful to stand on his dignity when he became the director.* • PHR : VB INFLECTS • If something is **beneath** your **dignity**, you consider yourself to be too important to do it. EG *He considered the job beneath his dignity.* • PHR : USED AS AN A

digress /daɪgres/, **digresses, digressing, digressed.** If you **digress**, you move away from the subject you are talking or writing about and talk or write about something less relevant, usually for a short time. EG *I will digress slightly at this stage... To make this clear, I must digress.* V : IF+PREP THEN *from* ⇑ turn away ◇ **digression** /daɪgreʃə⁰n/. EG *This long digression has led me away from my main story.* ◇ N COUNT/UNCOUNT

dike /daɪk/. See **dyke.**

dilapidated /di¹læpɪdeɪtɪ²d/. A building that is **dilapidated** is old and in a generally bad condition. EG *Each flight of stairs led to a tier of flats more dilapidated than the last.* ADJ QUALIT = run-down, decrepit

dilate /dɪ⁵leɪt/, **dilates, dilating, dilated.** When your eyes **dilate** or when you **dilate** them, they become wider or bigger. EG *Her eyes dilated and grew darker in the dim saloon.* V-ERG ⇑ expand = widen ≠ contract ◇ **dilated.** EG *She smiled, her eyes bright and dilated.* ◇ ADJ QUALIT = wide

dilatory /dɪlətə⁰ri¹/. Someone or something that is **dilatory** is slow and causes delay; a fairly formal word. EG *Decades of dilatory Western involvement had made no impact... He was of the opinion that Jefferson would soon remove his dilatory commander.* ADJ QUALIT ≠ brief

dilemma /dɪ⁵lemə/, **dilemmas.** A **dilemma** is a difficult situation in which you have to choose between two or more alternatives. EG *That's a dilemma that we haven't yet solved... But it put me in a difficult moral dilemma.* • **on the horns of a dilemma**: see **horn.** N COUNT ⇑ difficulty = quandary

dilettante /dɪlɪtɑːnti¹/, **dilettantes, dilettanti.** The plural can be either **dilettantes** or **dilettanti.** A **dilettante** is someone who seems interested in a subject, especially in art, but who does not really know very much about it; used showing disapproval. EG *He is really a dilettante rather than a working photographer.* N COUNT ⇑ amateur = dabbler

diligence /dɪlɪ²dʒə²ns/ is careful and conscientious hard work. EG *I'd been hoping to impress my new boss with my diligence.* N UNCOUNT ⇑ effort = industry

diligent /dɪlɪ²dʒə²nt/. Someone who is **diligent** works hard in a careful and conscientious way. EG *He was a diligent kindly man, loved by his constituents.* ▸ used of behaviour or activities. EG *I have no doubt that diligent research will produce results.* ADJ QUALIT = meticulous ◇ **diligently.** EG *He read the Bible even more diligently.* ◇ ADV WITH VB

dill /dɪl/ is a herb with yellow flowers and a strong sweet smell. It is used in cooking. N UNCOUNT ⇑ plant

dilute /daɪlj⁰uːt/, **dilutes, diluting, diluted.** 1 When you **dilute** a liquid, you add water or another liquid to it in order to make it less concentrated. EG *Dilute the rennet with 1/2 pint of cold water... Strain off the liquid and dilute to taste.* V+O ⇑ weaken

2 Liquid that is **dilute** is very thin and weak, usually because it has had water added to it. EG *Paula fed the lamb on very dilute milk.* ADJ QUALIT : USU ATTRIB ≠ concentrated

3 If someone or something **dilutes** a belief, principle, or quality, they make it weaker and less effective. EG *I enquired if this might not dilute the excellence of the universities.* V+O ⇑ weaken = water down ◇ **dilution** /daɪlj⁰uːʃə⁰n/. EG *They objected to what they saw as the dilution of revolutionary principles.* ◇ N UNCOUNT

dim /dɪm/, **dimmer, dimmest; dims, dimming, dimmed.** 1 Something that is **dim** is 1.1 rather dark and does not reflect or give out much light. EG *He looked around in the dim light... ...a dim hallway on the second floor... The room was dim and apricot-coloured.* ADJ QUALIT ≠ bright, strong ◇ **dimly.** EG *...the dimly lit department store.* ◇ ADV ◇ **dimness.** EG *...in the dimness of the church.* ◇ N UNCOUNT 1.2 not very easy to see, either because it is in shadow or darkness, or because it is a long way away. EG *Bernard peered angrily at the dim figure by* ADJ QUALIT ⇑ obscure = hazy ≠ clear *the bus-stop.* **1.3** very vague and unclear in your mind, and often difficult to remember. EG *...with a dim awareness of some strange virtue.* ◇ **dimly.** EG *He still retains, however dimly, a recollection of better times.* ADJ QUALIT : USU ATTRIB ◇ ADV WITH VB = vaguely ≠ clearly

2 If your future or your prospects are **dim**, you have no reason to feel hopeful or optimistic. EG *Prospects for the company are by no means dim.* ADJ QUALIT = gloomy, grim

3 If your eyes are **dim**, you cannot see very well. ● to **take a dim view of** something: see **view**. ADJ QUALIT

4 Someone who is **dim** is not very intelligent; an informal use. EG *Have you ever met anyone quite so dim?* ADJ QUALIT ⇑ stupid = thick

5 If you **dim** a light or it **dims**, it becomes less bright. EG *Someone dimmed the lights and turned up the music... The orchestra fell silent as the oil lamp dimmed and the curtain rose.* V-ERG ⇑ lower

6 If your emotions or hopes **dim** or if they **are dimmed**, they become less intense and less optimistic. EG *The elation of the brothers could not be dimmed... These hopes were somewhat dimmed by the results of the party conference.* V-ERG ⇑ weaken = dampen

7 If your eyes **dim** or something **dims** them, they become weaker or unable to see clearly. EG *Even the policeman's eyes were momentarily dimmed with tears.* V OR V+O ⇑ weaken = cloud

8 If your thoughts or memories **dim**, they become less clear in your mind. EG *Even after sixty years, his memories of the war had not dimmed.* V ⇑ weaken = fade

dime /daɪm/, **dimes**. A **dime** is an American coin worth ten cents. N COUNT

dimension /dɪ⁵menʃə⁰n/, **dimensions**. **1** A particular **dimension** of a situation is an aspect of it or factor in it which influences the way you understand the situation. EG *Most of us were Catholic, and this added an extra dimension to the tension... There are international dimensions to our problems in Britain.* N COUNT : USU+SUPP = side, angle

2 The **dimensions** of a situation or problem are the extent or scope of it. EG *...a growing awareness of the true dimensions of the threat... The dimensions of the problems of navigation seemed unimportant by comparison.* N COUNT/UNCOUNT+SUPP ⇑ size

3 A **dimension** is a measurement in space such as length, width, or height. N COUNT

4 The **dimensions** of something are its size. EG *...the dimensions of a standard brick... Many of these plants grew to magnificent dimensions.* N COUNT : USU PL = proportions

dimensional /dɪ⁵menʃə⁰nəl, -ʃənə⁰l/. See **two-dimensional, three-dimensional.**

diminish /dɪmɪnɪʃ/, **diminishes, diminishing, diminished**. **1** When something **diminishes**, or when something **diminishes** it, it becomes reduced in size, volume, importance or intensity. EG *As she turned the knob, the sound diminished... Familiarity with the routine did not diminish the horror of living in prison... National autonomy is visibly diminishing in the modern world.* ◇ **diminished.** EG *...clear evidence of diminished social tension.* ◇ **diminishing.** EG *Recent discoveries underline mankind's diminishing importance as a species.* V-ERG ⇑ decrease ◇ ADJ QUALIT ◇ ADJ QUALIT ⇑ decreasing = declining

2 If you **diminish** someone or something, you talk about them or treat them in a way that makes them appear less important than they really are. EG *The critics considered only the undesirable qualities in the artist's work, while ignoring or at best diminishing the more desirable ones... I felt very considerably diminished, a complete and utter idiot.* V+O ⇑ devalue = belittle

diminished responsibility. If a court of law accepts that someone did something illegal in a state of **diminished responsibility**, it is considered that the person was mentally ill at the time and should not be punished too severely. N UNCOUNT

diminution /dɪmɪnjuːʃə⁰n/ is reduction in size, volume, intensity, or importance. EG *They were experiencing constant diminution of funds.* N UNCOUNT : IF+PREP THEN *of/in*

diminutive /dɪmɪnjuːtɪv/ means very small. EG *These birds have fragile, diminutive legs.* ADJ CLASSIF = tiny

dimmer /dɪmə/, **dimmers**. **1** A **dimmer** or a **dimmer switch** is a switch that allows you to gradually change the brightness of an electric light. N COUNT

2 Dimmer is the comparative of **dim**.

dimple /dɪmpə⁰l/, **dimples**. A **dimple** is a small hollow in someone's cheek or chin that you can see when they smile. EG *She still had that dimple he could remember from twelve years ago.* N COUNT

dimpled /dɪmpə⁰ld/. Something that is **dimpled** has small hollows in it. EG *...a large pond dimpled with raindrops... ...the child's dimpled face.* ADJ CLASSIF

dimwit /dɪmwɪt/, **dimwits**. A **dimwit** is an ignorant, stupid person; an informal word. EG *He was an absolute dimwit.* N COUNT : ALSO VOC ⇑ fool = twit

din /dɪn/, **dins, dinning, dinned**. A **din** is a very loud and unpleasant noise that lasts for a long time. EG *...the muffled din of the jet engines... They were unable to sleep because of the din coming from the bar.* N COUNT = row

din into. If you **din** something **into** someone, you teach them something by repeating it to them over and over again in a forceful, determined way. EG *I had it dinned into me at school.* PHRASAL VB : V+O+PREP = drum into

dine /daɪn/, **dines, dining, dined**. When you **dine**, you have dinner; a fairly formal word. EG *They arrived at seven in the evening, in time to dine at a splendid Hungarian restaurant... We dine at half past eight... The following day I dined with the President and a dozen members of Congress.* V ⇑ eat

dine in. If you **dine in**, you have dinner at home. EG *We always dine in on Thursdays.* PHRASAL VB : V+ADV

dine on. If you **dine on** or **dine off** a particular sort of food, you have it for dinner; an old-fashioned or formal expression. EG *They dined on mince, as there was nothing else in the house.* PHRASAL VB : V+PREP ⇑ eat

dine out. If you **dine out**, you have dinner away from your home, for example at a restaurant or at someone else's home. EG *By seven he was showering in his own flat before dining out in the West End.* PHRASAL VB : V+ADV ⇑ eat = eat out ≠ dine in

dine out on. If you **dine out on** a particular event or experience, you tell interesting stories about it when you are having dinner in someone else's house. EG *You'll dine out on it for weeks, won't you, old boy?* PHRASAL VB : V+ADV+PREP

diner /daɪnə/, **diners**. A **diner** is **1** someone who is having dinner in a restaurant. **2** a small, cheap, restaurant; used in American English. N COUNT N COUNT

ding-dong /dɪŋ dɒŋ/, **ding-dongs**. **1 Ding-dong** is used to represent the sound made by a bell. N UNCOUNT/COUNT

2 A **ding-dong** is a lively quarrel or fight; used in informal English. EG *There was a bit of a ding-dong outside the pub when we arrived.* N SING : a+N

3 A **ding-dong** contest is one in which first one person seems to be winning, and then the other person. EG *...the ding-dong nature of the two party system.* ADJ CLASSIF : ATTRIB ⇑ fluctuating

dinghy /dɪŋi¹/, **dinghies**. A **dinghy** is a small open boat that you sail or row. N COUNT

dingo /dɪŋgəʊ/, **dingoes**. A **dingo** is a wild Australian dog. N COUNT

dingy /dɪndʒi¹/, **dingier, dingiest**. **1** A building or place that is **dingy** is rather dark and depressing, and does not seem to have been well looked after. EG *We drove through some of the dingiest streets of the town.* ◇ **dinginess.** ADJ QUALIT = drab, mean ≠ spruce ◇ N UNCOUNT

2 Clothes, curtains, etc that are **dingy** are dirty or faded. EG *She wore a bit of dingy red ribbon in her hair.* ADJ QUALIT ⇑ dull = drab

dining car, dining cars; also spelled with a hyphen. A **dining car** is a carriage on a train where passengers can have a meal. N COUNT ⇑ restaurant

dining room, dining rooms; also spelled with a hyphen. The **dining room** is the room in a house where people have their meals, or a room in a hotel where meals are served. N COUNT : USU *the*+N

dining table, dining tables; also spelled with a hyphen. A **dining table** is a table that is used for having meals on. N COUNT

dinner /dɪnə/, **dinners**. **1 Dinner** is the main meal of the day. In Britain, many working-class people use the word **dinner** to refer to the meal that they have at midday, and many middle-class people use the word **dinner** to refer to the meal that they eat in the evening. EG *Tell him his dinner's in the oven... They had a quiet dinner together... I haven't had dinner yet... After dinner we all went into the drawing-room.* N COUNT/UNCOUNT

2 A **dinner** is **2.1** a formal social occasion, often held in someone's honour, at which an evening meal is served. EG *Mrs Thatcher attended a dinner at the Mansion House last night.* **2.2** the same as a dinner party. EG *There's more fun in throwing a cocktail party than in having a dinner for six.* N COUNT ⇑ celebration = banquet N COUNT

dinner dance, dinner dances; also spelled with a hyphen. A **dinner dance** is a social event that usually takes place in the evening at a hotel or N COUNT restaurant where a large number of people come to have dinner and to dance.

dinner jacket, dinner jackets; also spelled with a hyphen. A **dinner jacket** is a man's black jacket that is worn with a bow tie at formal social events. N COUNT = tuxedo

dinner party, dinner parties; also spelled with a hyphen. A **dinner party** is a social event where a small number of people are invited to have dinner and spend the evening together at someone's house. EG *I happened to meet his boss at a dinner party... How about giving a dinner-party?* N COUNT ↑ gathering

dinner service, dinner services; also spelled with a hyphen. A **dinner service** is a set of plates and dishes that are used for serving meals. N COUNT ↑ crockery

dinner table, dinner tables; also spelled with a hyphen. A **dinner table** is a table which is being used or which is going to be used during a meal. EG *She was setting the dinner-table... His parents won't allow books at the dinner table.* ▸ The **dinner table** is also used to refer to the time during which people are eating their dinner. EG *They were endlessly discussed over the dinner-table.* N COUNT ▸ N SING : the+N

dinnertime /dɪnətaɪm/; also spelled with a hyphen. **Dinnertime** is the time when dinner is eaten, either at about midday or early in the evening. N UNCOUNT

dinosaur /daɪnəsɔː/, **dinosaurs**. A **dinosaur** was a large reptile which lived in prehistoric times and which is now extinct. There were many kinds of dinosaur, some of which were very large indeed. N COUNT

dint /dɪnt/. If you achieve a result **by dint of** something, you achieve it by means of that thing; an old-fashioned expression. EG *He was laid up for several days, but by dint of purging and blood-letting, recovered.* PREP

diocesan /daɪɒsɪsən/ means of or relating to a diocese. EG *...the diocesan newspaper.* ADJ CLASSIF : ATTRIB

diocese /daɪə⁷sɪs/, **dioceses**. A **diocese** is the area over which a bishop has control. N COUNT

dioxide /daɪɒksaɪd/. See **carbon dioxide.**

dip /dɪp/, **dips, dipping, dipped**. **1** If you **dip** something or if it **dips** into a liquid, it goes into the liquid for a short time and then quickly comes out again. EG *He dipped his finger into the jar of syrup... You can clean copper with half a lemon dipped in salt and vinegar.* V-ERG : IF+PREP THEN in/into ↑ immerse

2 If you **dip** into something such as a bowl or your pocket, you put your hand into it so that you can take something out of it. EG *The rice was served in a small dish which they dipped into with their hands... She dipped deep in her raincoat pocket again.* V+PREP (in/ into) ↑ plunge

3 If something **dips**, it makes a downward movement, usually quite quickly. EG *You can see the bird's head dip as its mate approaches... The aeroplane circled quickly, dipped, and flew directly over us... In the arctic summer the sun scarcely dips below the horizon.* ▸ used as a noun. EG *The bird made tiny dips and nods of its head.* V ↑ dive = bob ▸ N COUNT = bob

4 If a road, railway line, or path **dips**, it goes down quite suddenly to a lower level. EG *The railway line climbs and dips between thick forests.* ▸ used as a noun. EG *She stared down the dip in the road between the cliffs.* V ↑ descend ▸ N COUNT

5 When sheep or other farm animals **are dipped**, they are put into a liquid containing disinfectant for a short time, in order to kill harmful insects which live on their bodies. ◇ **dipping**. EG *...a dipping tank.* V+O ↑ disinfect ◇ N UNCOUNT

6 If an amount, rate, etc **dips** below a certain level, it goes just below that level, usually only for a short period of time. EG *This summer her time for the race dipped under one minute.* ▸ used as a noun. EG *There has been a slight dip in the stock market this year.* V+PREP (below/ under) ↑ sink = drop ▸ N COUNT

7 A **dip** is a thick creamy mixture which you scoop up with raw vegetables or biscuits and eat. EG *I'll make two sour cream dips for the party.* N COUNT ↑ food

8 A **dip** is also a liquid with chemicals in it which animals or things can be dipped in to disinfect or clean them. EG *...sheep dip... Leave them in the silver dip for five minutes.* N COUNT : USU+ SUPP

9 If you have a **dip**, you go for a quick swim in the sea, a river, or a swimming pool. EG *I think I'll take a dip before the tide comes in.* N COUNT ↑ bathe

10 If you **dip** your headlights, you make the beams of your car's headlights shine downwards and towards the side of the road, so that drivers coming towards you do not have your headlights shining straight into their eyes; used mainly in British English. V+O ↑ lower = dim

11 A **dip** into a book is a brief look at it without reading or studying it seriously. EG *...a very superficial dip into Victorian literature.* ▸ used as a verb. EG *He hadn't read Homer, but he had dipped into him occasionally.* N COUNT+PREP (into) ▸ V+PREP (in/ into)

12 If you **dip into** your **savings, purse**, or **pocket**, you spend money. EG *I'll have to dip into my savings, if I'm going to buy a record player.* PHR : VB INFLECTS

dip in. If you tell someone to **dip in**, you are inviting them to take their share of something nice, especially food. EG *Dip in, everybody!–The food's on the table.* PHRASAL VB : V+ ADV

dip. is a written abbreviation for **diploma.**

diphtheria /dɪpθɪərɪə, dɪf-/ is a dangerous infectious disease which causes fever and difficulty in breathing and swallowing. N UNCOUNT

diphthong /dɪpθɒŋ, dɪf-/, **diphthongs**. A **diphthong** is a vowel in which the speaker's tongue changes position while it is being pronounced, so that the vowel sounds like a combination of two other vowels. The vowel sound in 'tail' is a diphthong. N COUNT ↑ sound

diploma /dɪpləʊmə/, **diplomas**. A **diploma** is a qualification which a student may be awarded by a university or college. A diploma is not as high as a degree. EG *Are you on the degree course or the diploma course?... She has a diploma in agriculture.* N COUNT

diplomacy /dɪpləʊməsi¹/ is **1** the management of relations between countries. EG *The crisis developed into a matter of high-level diplomacy between the two embassies.* **2** the skill involved in negotiating agreements between countries on particular problems or aspects of international relations. EG *...the diplomacy of U.S. minister Woodford in Madrid.* **3** the skill of being tactful and saying or doing things without offending people. EG *You will need to employ a great deal of tact and diplomacy to put this young man politely in his place.* N UNCOUNT ↑ negotiation; N UNCOUNT; N UNCOUNT ↑ tact

diplomat /dɪplə⁶mæt/, **diplomats**. A **diplomat** is **1** a senior official who negotiates with another country on behalf of his or her own country, usually working as a member of an embassy. EG *Nigerian diplomats were saying privately that their confidence in the strategy was ebbing.* **2** someone who is skilful at being tactful and saying and doing things that do not offend people. EG *William was a good diplomat as well as musician.* N COUNT; N COUNT

diplomatic /dɪplə⁶mætɪk/. **1 Diplomatic** means relating to diplomacy and diplomats. EG *The government was reluctant to endanger its trade and diplomatic links with America and Britain... We are looking for a peaceful, diplomatic solution.* ADJ CLASSIF : USU ATTRIB

2 Someone who is **diplomatic** is able to be tactful and say or do things without offending people. EG *The secretary was poised and diplomatic on the telephone.* ◇ **diplomatically**. EG *Diplomatically, he checked into a hotel in London rather than one near her home.* ADJ QUALIT ↑ courteous ◇ ADV WITH VB

diplomatic corps. The **diplomatic corps** is the group of all the diplomats who work in one city or in one country. EG *...the smart areas where the diplomatic corps and the industrialists live.* N SING : the+N

diplomatic immunity is the freedom from legal action and from paying taxes that a diplomat has in the country in which he or she is working. EG *He should have been prosecuted for drunken driving, but he was able to claim diplomatic immunity.* N UNCOUNT ↑ exemption

diplomatic service. The **diplomatic service** is the government department that employs diplomats to work in foreign countries. N PROPER : the+ N

dipper /dɪpə/, **dippers**. A **dipper** is a large spoon or small bowl, especially one with a long handle, which is used for taking some of the liquid out of a container. EG *You use a dipper of smooth polished wood for tasting the whisky as it is being distilled.* ● See also **big dipper**. N COUNT ↑ scoop

dipstick /dɪpstɪk/, **dipsticks**. A **dipstick** is a metal rod which has notches on one end, so that the amount of liquid in a container can be measured, especially a rod with which you can measure the amount of oil that there is in a car engine. EG *Check the level of the oil with the dipstick.* N COUNT

dir. is a written abbreviation for 'director'. EG *Dirs: J A King, F C Brunton, R A Ward.*

dire /daɪə/ is used to emphasize how serious, important, or terrible a situation is. EG *...dire warnings by the Prime Minister... They are all countries in dire misery... ...the dire consequences of his actions.* ADJ CLASSIF : USU ATTRIB ↑ urgent

direct /dɪ⁵rɛkt/, **directs, directing, directed.** 1 **Direct** means moving or aimed in a straight line towards a place or object, without changing direction and without stopping, for example in a journey. EG *Can you tell me if there are any direct flights to Athens?...* ▸ used as an adverb. EG *You can't go to Manchester direct, you have to change trains at Birmingham.* ◇ **directly.** EG *I actually pointed a gun at someone.–Well, not directly at them.* — ADJ CLASSIF = through; ▸ ADV WITH VB; ◇ ADV WITH VB

2 If something is in **direct** heat or sunlight, it is in strong heat or sunlight and has nothing between it and the source of the heat or the sunlight to protect it. EG *This sweater should be dried away from direct heat.* — ADJ CLASSIF : ATTRIB

3 A **direct** action is one which does not involve an intermediate stage or action or another person. EG *More and more firms pay their employees by direct transfer into their bank accounts... ...the direct intervention of the managing director... ...a direct result of this information... This is not an area over which the government has any direct control.* ▸ used as an adverb. EG *Some of the money comes direct from industry.* ◇ **directly.** EG *They denied having negotiated directly or indirectly with the terrorists... You can pay directly from your bank account.* — ADJ CLASSIF : ATTRIB; ▸ ADV WITH VB = straight; ◇ ADV WITH VB ≠ indirectly

4 **Direct** also means likely or intended to have an immediate effect on someone, in such a way that there can be no doubt about what is being done. EG *It is not advice but direct help... The change in the union's leadership verges on a direct challenge to the government.* — ADJ CLASSIF : ATTRIB ⇑ clear = outright ≠ indirect

5 Someone who is **direct** talks or behaves in a very honest and open way, especially when other people might be more careful or tactful. EG *He is very direct and he prefers others to be the same.* ◇ **directly.** EG *I said as much to her, in fact.–Well, not directly, not in so many words.* ◇ **directness.** EG *Such directness embarrassed John.* — ADJ QUALIT = frank, blunt; ◇ ADV WITH VB ⇑ openly; ◇ N UNCOUNT = frankness

6 If you **direct** something somewhere, you send or aim it there; a rather formal use. EG *A steady volume of brochures was directed at East Germany... He asked for his mail to be directed to his home address.* — V+O+A *(at/to/towards)*

7 If you **direct** your attention or efforts to something or someone, you concentrate on that thing or person. EG *This is a fundamental question to which we should all be directing our attention... Defence efforts were directed to the development of new aircraft.* — V+O+A *(at/to/towards)* ⇑ focus = turn

8 If you **direct** a remark or a look at someone, you say something to them or look at them. EG *I thought her words were directed against me.* — V+O+A *(at/to/towards/against)* ⇑ aim

9 If you **direct** someone somewhere, you tell them how to get there. EG *Can you direct me to the cemetery?* — V+O : IF+PREP THEN *to* = point

10 The person who **directs** a project or a group of people is responsible for leading and organizing it or them. EG *She had directed a major mathematics project.* ◇ **direction.** EG *We are building our own houses under the direction of a builder.* — V+O ⇑ supervise = lead, head; ◇ N UNCOUNT = leadership

11 The person who **directs** a film, play, or television programme is in charge of it and organizes the way it is made and performed: compare **produce.** EG *I asked George Rylands to direct Hamlet... I was beginning to want to try my hand at directing.* — V OR V+O ⇑ supervise

12 If you **direct** someone to do something, you tell them to do it; a formal use. EG *The nurse gave me a hospital dressing gown and directed me to sit in the waiting room.* — V+O+*to*-INF = instruct

13 A **direct** descendant of a person is someone who is descended from that person through their parents, grandparents, etc and not through aunts, uncles, or cousins. EG *She claimed to be a direct descendant of Queen Victoria.* — ADJ CLASSIF : ATTRIB

14 See also **direction, directly.**

direct action is something that you do, for example going on strike or demonstrating, in order to put pressure on an employer or government and to show what you want. EG *We had to decide what forms of direct action should be used.* — N UNCOUNT

direct current. See **DC.**

direct hit, direct hits. A **direct hit** is the hitting of a target exactly with a bomb, bullet, or other missile. EG *We fire off dummy missiles and direct hits are recorded by flashes of light.* — N COUNT ≠ miss

direction /dɪ⁵rɛkʃə⁰n/, **directions.** 1 A **direction** is the general line that someone or something is moving or pointing in. EG *We were trying to get to London but we had somehow ended up going in the opposite direction... A very loud crash came from the direction of the kitchen... The plate fell to the floor, sending bits of china flying in all directions.* — N COUNT : USU+SUPP

● Someone's **sense of direction** is their ability to know approximately where they are or where they should go even when they are in an unfamiliar place. — ● PHR

2 A **direction** is also the general way in which something develops or progresses. EG *The government has to guide the general direction of the economy... I think we've got to change the law in that direction at least... The students' tutor may well guide them in one direction or another.* — N COUNT : USU+SUPP

3 **Directions** are instructions that tell you what to do, how to do something, or how to get somewhere. EG *You should follow the directions that your doctor gives you... John had been given no directions as to what to write... In the end I asked a policeman for directions.* — N PLURAL

4 The **direction** of a film, play, or television programme is the work that the director does while it is being made. EG *This film has brilliant sound effects, excellent direction, and a very good performance from William Hurt.* — N SING : USU *the*+N

5 See also **direct.**

directional /dɪ⁵rɛkʃə⁰nəl, -ʃənə⁰l/; a technical word. 1 Something that is **directional** points in a particular direction. EG *Howard follows the arrows and directional marks.* — ADJ CLASSIF : USU ATTRIB

2 A **directional** piece of equipment receives or transmits radio signals more strongly from some directions than others. — ADJ CLASSIF : USU ATTRIB

directive /dɪ⁵rɛktɪv/, **directives.** A **directive** is an instruction that is given by someone in authority and that must be obeyed; a formal word. EG *The government is obliged to take action because of EEC directives.* — N COUNT ⇑ order

directly /dɪ⁵rɛktli¹/. 1 If something is **directly** above something, below something, or in front of something, it is in exactly that position. EG *The sun was almost directly overhead... A man left the house and I saw him pass directly in front of the window... I've lived in a small house whose door opened directly onto the street.* — ADV = straight, immediately

2 If something will happen **directly**, it will happen very soon. EG *She's in a meeting at the moment but she will be here directly.* — ADV WITH VB = shortly

3 If you do something **directly**, you do it immediately and without doing anything else or going anywhere else first. EG *Newly married girls go directly to live in the village of their new husband.* — ADV WITH VB = straight, at once

4 You also use **directly** to say that as soon as one thing is done, another thing happens. EG *Directly he heard the door close he picked up the telephone.* — CONJ SUBORD = as soon as

5 See also **direct.**

direct object, direct objects. See **object.**

director /dɪ⁵rɛktə/, **directors.** A **director** is 1 someone who has responsibility for organizing and leading a group of people who are working together. EG *Mr Adrian Oliver, director of the excavation, said yesterday that work was progressing well... He became artistic director of the Sadlers Wells ballet in 1978.* — N COUNT ⇑ leader

2 someone who is on the board of a company or business organization or in charge of a government organization. EG *She was the newest and youngest director on the board... He had a connection with CIA director William J. Casey.* — N COUNT ⇑ executive

3 someone who decides how a play, film, or television programme shall be performed or made. EG *I talked to the film critic and television director, Christopher Crook.* — N COUNT ⇑ supervisor

directorate /dɪ⁵rɛktə¹rət/, **directorates.** A **directorate** is 1 a board of directors in a company or organization. EG *...the first meeting of a new directorate.* — N COUNT

2 a part of a government department which is responsible for one particular thing. EG *...the Rural Affairs Directorate.* — N COUNT+SUPP ⇑ section

director general, director generals, directors general. The plural can be either **director generals** or **directors general**; also spelled with a hyphen. The **director general** of a large organization such as the BBC is the person who is in charge of it. — N COUNT : USU SING

directorial /dɪ⁵rə²ktɔːrɪəl/ means relating to company directors or their work. EG *He was about to begin his directorial duties.* — ADJ CLASSIF : ATTRIB ⇑ executive

Director of Public Prosecutions. In England and Wales, the **Director of Public Prosecutions** is a lawyer employed by the government to decide whether there is enough evidence to prosecute — N PROPER : *the*+N someone who has been accused of a crime. The Director of Public Prosecutions also gives other advice to the government on criminal law matters.

directorship /dɪ⁵rektəʃɪp/, **directorships**. A **directorship** is the job or position of a company director. EG *Ten people held between them as many as 400 directorships.* — N COUNT

directory /dɪ⁵rektəⁿri¹/, **directories**. A **directory** is a book which gives lists of facts, for example people's names, addresses, and telephone numbers, or the names and addresses of business companies, usually arranged in alphabetical order. — N COUNT

directory enquiries is a service which you can telephone if you want to find out a person's telephone number. EG *I'll ring directory enquiries.* — N UNCOUNT

direct rule is a system in which a central government rules a province which has had its own parliament or law-making organization in the past. — N UNCOUNT

direct tax, direct taxes. A **direct tax** is a tax which a person or organization pays directly to the government, for example income tax. — N COUNT ≠ indirect tax

direct taxation is a system in which a government raises money by means of direct taxes. — N UNCOUNT

dirge /dɜːdʒ/, **dirges**. A **dirge** is a slow, sad, or mournful song or other piece of music, sometimes played or sung at funerals. — N COUNT = lament

dirndl /dɜːndəⁿl/, **dirndls**. A **dirndl** is a very wide skirt which is tightly gathered at the waist. — N COUNT

dirt /dɜːt/. **1 Dirt** is **1.1** dust, mud, or stains on a surface or fabric, which you remove in order to keep the surface or fabric clean. EG *These carpets are cheap, tough and don't show dirt... Use the liquid for stubborn dirt on cooker enamel.* — N UNCOUNT = grime, filth **1.2** the earth on the ground, especially when it is muddy or dusty. EG *He drew a circle in the dirt with a stick... ...vehicles spattered in red dirt.* — N UNCOUNT **1.3** information about someone that could harm their reputation or career if it becomes known; used in informal English. EG *He was checking out the way the newsmen got the dirt.* — N SING : the+N = scandal

2 If you **treat** someone **like dirt**, you treat them unfairly and with no respect. EG *Some of the kids treat her like dirt.* — PHR : VB INFLECTS ⇑ maltreat

dirt-cheap. Something that is **dirt-cheap** is very cheap indeed; used in informal English. EG *We have lots of dirt-cheap pieces of technical equipment.* — ADJ CLASSIF ▸ used as an adverb. EG *We bought it dirt-cheap.* — ▸ ADV WITH VB

dirt road, dirt roads. A **dirt road** or **dirt track** is a road or track made from earth without any gravel laid on it. — N COUNT

dirty /dɜːti¹/; **dirtier, dirtiest; dirties, dirtying, dirtied**. **1** Something that is **dirty** is marked or covered with stains, spots, or mud, and needs to be cleaned. EG *He wiped his face with a dirty arm... Use a damp sponge to remove dirty or sticky marks from the walls.* — ADJ QUALIT = grubby ≠ clean

2 To **dirty** something means to cause it to become dirty. EG *Too much town driving had dirtied the spark plugs.* — V+O = soil, foul up

3 Dirty colours have a greyish tone. EG *There was a thrash of water, dirty white against the brown current.* — ADJ CLASSIF : ATTRIB ⇑ impure

4 A **dirty** action is unfair or immoral, involving a dishonest way of doing something; used showing disapproval. EG *He claimed he was asked to do a dirty job for the government... They even played a dirty trick or two.* ▸ used of people. EG *They've got some dirty players in their team.* — ADJ QUALIT : USU ATTRIB = underhand ≠ fair

5 Dirty jokes, books, language, etc, refer to sex in a way that many people find offensive. EG *Blue movies and dirty books were banned.* — ADJ QUALIT ⇑ obscene = smutty

6 If you give someone a **dirty** look, you look at them in a way which shows that you are angry or annoyed with them; an informal use. — ADJ QUALIT : ATTRIB = filthy

7 Dirty is used informally before words of criticism to emphasize that you do not approve of someone or something. EG *You're a dirty liar.* — ADJ CLASSIF : ATTRIB = filthy

8 The word **dirty** is also used in the following informal expressions: **8.1** If you **do** someone's **dirty work**, you do a task for them that is dishonest or unpleasant and that they do not want to do themselves. EG *I shall never do his dirty work again.* — PHR : VB INFLECTS **8.2** If someone **does the dirty on** you, they do something that is unfair or harmful to you; used in British English. — PHR : VB INFLECTS **8.3** If you refer to a man as a **dirty old man**, you mean that he shows a strong interest in sexual matters in a way that many people find offensive; used showing disapproval, sometimes humorously. — PHR : USU USED AS C, N INFLECTS **8.4** A **dirty weekend** is a weekend during which two people who are not married to each other go away together, for example to a hotel, and have sex; an informal expression. EG *...a dirty weekend in Brighton.* — PHR : USED AS O, N INFLECTS **8.5** You say that an expression is **a dirty word** with a group of people when it refers to something, especially an idea, that they strongly dislike or strongly disagree with. EG *'High rise' had become almost a dirty word among architects.* — PHR : USED AS C

dis-. **1 Dis-** is added to some verbs that describe processes in order to form verbs describing the opposite processes. EG *...appear→disappear... ...connect→disconnect... ...arm→disarm.* — PREFIX

2 Dis- is also added to some words that describe states, qualities, or attitudes in order to form words describing the opposite states, qualities, or attitudes. EG *...similar→dissimilar... ...agree→disagree... ...belief→disbelief.* — PREFIX

disability /dɪsəbɪlə¹ti¹/, **disabilities**. **1** A **disability** is a permanent physical or mental injury or illness that restricts the way that someone can live their life. EG *She's always cheerful, in spite of her disabilities.* — N COUNT = handicap

2 Disability is the state of suffering from a physical illness or injury that restricts the way that you can live your life; a formal use. EG *This attitude condemns children to death or disability.* — N UNCOUNT = incapacity

disable /dɪseɪbəⁿl/, **disables, disabling, disabled**. If something **disables** someone, it injures them physically or mentally and restricts the way that they can live their life, especially by making it difficult for them to move about. EG *The disease disables thousands every year.* — V+O ⇑ injure = cripple

disabled /dɪseɪbəⁿld/. Someone who is **disabled** has an illness or an injury that restricts the way that they can live their life, especially by making it difficult for them to move about. EG *She has to look after a severely disabled relative... ...disabled ex-servicemen.* — ADJ QUALIT ⇑ handicapped ≠ fit, healthy ▸ The **disabled** is used to refer to people who are disabled. EG *There are some extraordinary chairs for the disabled nowadays.* — ▸ N PLURAL : the+N = the handicapped

disablement /dɪseɪbəⁿlmə²nt/ is the state or process of being or becoming disabled. EG *..the dread of crippling disablement.* — N UNCOUNT ⇑ handicap

disabuse /dɪsəbjuːz/, **disabuses, disabusing, disabused**. If you **disabuse** someone of something, you tell them or persuade them that what they believe is in fact untrue; a rather formal word. EG *'Well, I think I can disabuse you of that notion,' he said solemnly.* — V+O, OR V+O+A (of) ⇑ enlighten

disadvantage /dɪsə³dvɑːntɪdʒ/, **disadvantages**. **1** A **disadvantage** is a factor in someone's character or in a situation which causes difficulties or problems. EG *This inability was obviously an enormous disadvantage... The disadvantage of this plan was that it needed more people.* — N COUNT ⇑ obstacle = drawback

2 The word **disadvantage** is also used in the following expressions: **2.1** If you are **at a disadvantage**, you are in a situation where you cannot succeed easily because you have a problem or difficulty that other people do not have. EG *Those pupils who had poor memories were at a disadvantage.* — PHR : USED AS AN A = hampered, held back **2.2** If something **puts** you **at a disadvantage**, it causes problems for you which prevent you from succeeding easily in what you want to do, in comparison with others who are trying to do the same thing. EG *Interest-rate restrictions had put banks at a disadvantage in competing with the money markets.* — PHR : VB INFLECTS **2.3** If something **is to** your **disadvantage** or **works to** your **disadvantage**, it creates difficulties for you. EG *Having my uncle as my boss worked to my disadvantage.* — PHR : VB INFLECTS

disadvantaged /dɪsə³dvɑːntɪdʒd/. People who are **disadvantaged** live in bad conditions and do not get a good education or have a reasonable standard of living. EG *...disadvantaged children... ...disadvantaged sections of the community.* — ADJ QUALIT ⇑ poor = underprivileged ▸ used of places and situations. EG *This may make up for the disadvantaged homes they come from.* — ▸ = deprived

disadvantageous /dɪsædvɑːnteɪdʒəs/. Something that is **disadvantageous** is harmful or likely to cause problems for you. EG *These factors made the 1976 agreement disadvantageous to the British.* — ADJ QUALIT : IF+ PREP THEN to ≠ beneficial

disaffected /dɪsəfektɪ²d/. People who are **disaffected** no longer fully support something such as an organization or political ideal which they previously supported. EG *The party won a by-election, then gained four disaffected UP members.* — ADJ QUALIT = alienated

disaffection /dɪsəfɛkʃəⁿn/ is the attitude that people have when they stop supporting something such as an organization or political ideal. EG *He was accused of sowing dissent and disaffection among the troops.* N UNCOUNT = alienation

disagree /dɪsəgriː/, **disagrees, disagreeing, disagreed. 1** If you **disagree** with someone or **disagree** with what they say, you do not accept that what they say is true or correct. EG *I disagree completely with John Taylor... I disagree with much of what he says... You know he and I disagree about it... Isn't it fairest to say that we disagree?* V OR V+A (with/about/over) ⇑ differ ≠ agree

2 If you **disagree** with a particular action or proposal, you disapprove of it and believe that it is wrong. EG *Benn disagreed with the abandonment of the project.* V+A (with) ⇑ oppose

3 If two stories, accounts, totals, or other things **disagree**, they are different or produce different results, and therefore cannot both be true or correct. EG *These figures disagree with last week's results... The two statements disagree.* V : IF+PREP THEN with ⇑ differ ≠ match, tally

4 If a particular food or drink **disagrees** with you, it makes you feel unwell; a fairly informal use. EG *Oranges and chocolate disagree with me, they give me migraine.* V+A (with)

disagreeable /dɪsəgriːəbəⁿl/. **1** Something that is **disagreeable** is rather unpleasant and makes you feel unhappy or annoyed. EG *...a disagreeable encounter with Mrs Baggot... ...tests which are disagreeable, humiliating, and agonizing.* ◊ **disagreeably.** EG *They were disagreeably surprised to find him still there.* ADJ QUALIT ≠ agreeable, pleasant; ◊ ADV

2 Someone who is **disagreeable** is unfriendly or unhelpful. EG *There were some disagreeable people around, it was true... Stop being so disagreeable!* ◊ **disagreeably.** EG *Why did he have to behave so disagreeably?* ADJ QUALIT; ◊ ADV AFTER VB

disagreement /dɪsəgriːmə²nt/, **disagreements. 1 Disagreement** is **1.1** the act of saying or showing that you object to something such as a proposal. EG *There was no disagreement and the motion was passed unanimously... There was little disagreement over what needed to be done.* N UNCOUNT : USU +PREP ⇑ conflict = argument **1.2** the state of not being able to reach a decision about something because not everyone involved finds it acceptable. EG *Key areas of disagreement remained.* N UNCOUNT ≠ agreement ● If people are **in disagreement**, they have different opinions about something. EG *Many experts find themselves in total disagreement.* ● PHR : USED AS C ⇑ conflict

2 Disagreement is also differences between two or more accounts, results, totals, etc, which indicate that they cannot all be correct. EG *There is much disagreement evident in this field of research... There was little disagreement between the results of the two tests.* N UNCOUNT/COUNT : USU+SUPP

3 A **disagreement** is a dispute or argument in which two or more people cannot agree about something among themselves. EG *They are divided by disagreements about specific points of policy... I guess you could call it a family disagreement... I can't recall that we ever had a serious disagreement about business.* N COUNT : USU+SUPP

disallow /dɪsəlaʊ/, **disallows, disallowing, disallowed.** If something **is disallowed**, it is not allowed or accepted officially, because it has not been done correctly. EG *The appeals were disallowed by the electoral court.* V+O ⇑ reject ≠ permit

disappear /dɪsəpɪə/, **disappears, disappearing, disappeared. 1** If someone or something **disappears**, they **1.1** go somewhere where you can no longer see them. EG *I saw him disappear round the corner... She disappeared down the corridor... Diana disappeared to heat the soup.* V OR V+A = vanish, go off **1.2** go away somewhere where nobody can find them. EG *I used to disappear for hours up high trees... In short I shall disappear. You will hear nothing from me again.* V ⇑ hide = abscond

2 To **disappear** also means to stop existing or happening. EG *Some newspapers are going to disappear as a result of this strike... His approval can disappear as fast as it appears... After all, it was only the dinosaurs that disappeared, not the whole of animal life.* V ⇑ die out

disappearance /dɪsəpɪərəns/, **disappearances. 1** The **disappearance** of a person is a situation in which they cannot be found and nobody knows where they have gone or where they have been taken to. EG *No one would enquire too closely into the disappearance of such an unimportant person.* N COUNT/UNCOUNT : USU the+N+of

2 The **disappearance** of an object is a situation in which it cannot be found because it has been lost or stolen. EG *He mentioned the disappearance of his passport to the manager.* N SING WITH DET : USU the+N +of = loss

3 The **disappearance** of a type of thing, person, or animal is a process in which the type becomes less common and finally no longer exists. EG *This could lead to their total disappearance within fifty or sixty years.* N UNCOUNT+SUPP = extinction

disappoint /dɪsəpɔɪnt/, **disappoints, disappointing, disappointed. 1** When things or people **disappoint** you, they do not satisfy you because they are not as good or as reliable as you had hoped, or do not do what you want them to do. EG *The answer must have disappointed him... You disappoint me: I had expected you to behave more responsibly.* V+O ≠ gratify

2 If something **disappoints** someone's hopes or expectations, it prevents something happening which they had planned or wanted to happen. EG *I could not help suspecting that it would disappoint Thomas's expectations of an inheritance.* V+O = destroy ≠ fulfil, realize

disappointed /dɪsəpɔɪntɪ²d/. If you are **disappointed**, you are rather sad because something has not happened or because something is not as good or as pleasant as you had hoped. EG *He was disappointed that the other side had won... He died a disappointed man... I was disappointed to learn that the fee would be only fifteen pounds.* ADJ QUALIT : USU +REPORT-CL/to-INF/in/with/at = disheartened

disappointing /dɪsəpɔɪntɪŋ/. Something that is **disappointing** is unsatisfactory, because it is not as good, as pleasant, or as numerous as you had expected it to be. EG *The results have generally been disappointing... They have been somewhat disillusioned by the disappointing progress of the EEC.* ◊ **disappointingly.** EG *...a disappointingly small number of Swiss francs.* ADJ QUALIT ⇑ unsatisfactory ≠ satisfying; ◊ ADV

disappointment /dɪsəpɔɪntmə²nt/, **disappointments. 1 Disappointment** is the state of feeling disappointed. EG *She was doomed to disappointment: they could never have succeeded... To my disappointment, she came with her mother.* N UNCOUNT : USU +SUPP ⇑ sadness ≠ satisfaction

2 A **disappointment** is an event, person, or situation which is not as good or as successful as you had hoped and which makes you feel disappointed. EG *He said it was a disappointment, but not a disaster... This may prove a disappointment to the party.* N COUNT = let-down ≠ success

disapproval /dɪsəpruːvəⁿl/. If you feel or show **disapproval** of something or someone, you feel or show that you do not like them or do not approve of them. EG *Clarissa gave a snort of disapproval... He has never disguised his disapproval of the President.* N UNCOUNT : IF+PREP THEN of = condemnation

disapprove /dɪsəpruːv/, **disapproves, disapproving, disapproved.** If you **disapprove** of something or someone, you feel or show that you do not like them or do not approve of them. EG *The other directors disapproved of his methods... 'Why can't I smoke?'–'Because I disapprove, that's why.'* V : IF+PREP THEN of ⇑ resent ≠ approve

disapproving /dɪsəpruːvɪŋ/. A **disapproving** action, expression, etc shows that you do not approve of something or someone. EG *...a group of women with disapproving expressions.* ◊ **disapprovingly.** EG *He shook his head disapprovingly.* ADJ QUALIT ⇑ hostile ≠ approving; ◊ ADV WITH VB

disarm /dɪsɑːm/, **disarms, disarming, disarmed. 1** If you **disarm** a person or group of people, you take away all their weapons. EG *They set out to disarm the various terrorist groups.* V+O ≠ arm, rearm

2 If a country **disarms**, it gives up the use of weapons, especially nuclear weapons. EG *He argues that if we unilaterally disarm then they will do likewise.* V ≠ arm

3 If you **disarm** someone who is angry or hostile, you do or say something which pleases or amuses them and which causes them to stop being angry or hostile. EG *Perhaps it was the French accent that disarmed her.* V+O ⇑ placate = pacify

4 If you **disarm** criticism, you do or say something that prevents people from criticizing you. EG *Like orthodox Christianity, it can disarm all criticism by reference to its own holy writings.* V+O : IF+PREP THEN by = neutralize

disarmament /dɪsɑːməmə²nt/ is the act of reducing the number of weapons, especially nuclear weapons, that a country has. EG *The 381 delegates voted for unilateral disarmament.* N UNCOUNT : USU MOD+N, OR BEFORE N

disarmer /dɪsɑːmə/, **disarmers. Disarmers** are people who try to persuade a government to ban the use of nuclear weapons. N COUNT : USU MOD+N ⇑ pacifist

disarming /dɪsɑːmɪŋ/. If someone or something is **disarming**, they cause you to feel less anger or hostility than you originally felt. EG *There was a disarming air of informality.* ◊ **disarmingly**. EG *He smiled disarmingly.* — ADJ QUALIT ⇑ soothing; ◊ ADV ≠ infuriatingly

disarrange /dɪsəreɪndʒ/, **disarranges, disarranging, disarranged**. To **disarrange** something means to make it untidy. EG *Already she could feel the wind disarranging her hair.* — V+O ⇑ disorder = mess up

disarray /dɪsəreɪ/. **in disarray**. 1 If an army, organization, or group of people is **in disarray**, they are badly organized and not prepared for action. EG *The group was thrown into disarray when the grant was stopped... The party was in disarray as the election approached.* — PHR : USED AS AN A

2 If your hair, clothes, etc are **in disarray**, they are in a very untidy state. EG *My hair was in hopeless disarray... Everything in his apartment was in disarray.* — PHR : USED AS AN A = dishevelled

disassociate /dɪsəsəʊʃieɪt/, **disassociates, disassociating, disassociated**. If you **disassociate** yourself from something or someone, you show that you are not connected with them, usually in order to avoid trouble or blame. — V+O (NG/REFL) +A *(from)* = dissociate

disaster /dɪzɑːstə/, **disasters**. 1 A **disaster** is 1.1 a very bad accident such as an earthquake or an air crash, especially one in which a lot of people are killed. EG *It was the latest in a string of hotel disasters... She was in Mexico City when the disaster happened... The city suffered the worst US air disaster since 1979.* — N COUNT = catastrophe
1.2 something which you think is extremely bad or unacceptable. EG *Now he must come to grips with the disaster that is the national economy... His last day at work was a disaster... This government's policy on education is an unmitigated disaster.* — N COUNT ⇑ failure = mess

2 **Disaster** is something which has very bad consequences for you. EG *To challenge him directly would be to invite disaster... No one can think clearly when disaster strikes... ...a capacity for facing and surviving disaster.* — N UNCOUNT ⇑ misfortune

disastrous /dɪzɑːstrəs/. 1 A **disastrous** event is extremely bad in its results and consequences. EG *In 1974 famine came in the wake of disastrous floods.* ◊ **disastrously**. EG *Exports fell disastrously in the first half of the year.* — ADJ QUALIT = devastating; ◊ ADV

2 If you say that something that someone does is **disastrous**, you mean that it fails very badly. EG *He made a disastrous attempt to direct 'Antony and Cleopatra'.* ◊ **disastrously**. EG *We performed disastrously.* — ADJ QUALIT = catastrophic; ◊ ADV WITH VB

disavow /dɪsəvaʊ/, **disavows, disavowing, disavowed**. If you **disavow** something, you say that you are not connected with it or responsible for it; a formal word. EG *He had refused to disavow his attitudes on human rights.* — V+O ⇑ deny = disown

disband /dɪsbænd/, **disbands, disbanding, disbanded**. If someone **disbands** a group of people, or if the group **disbands**, it stops operating as a single unit. EG *After twenty years the organization was disbanded... They began to disband.* — V-ERG = split up ≠ unite

disbelief /dɪsbəˈliːf/ is your attitude when you do not believe that something is true. EG *He stared at us in disbelief.* — N UNCOUNT

disbelieve /dɪsbəˈliːv/, **disbelieves, disbelieving, disbelieved**. 1 If you **disbelieve** someone or **disbelieve** something that they say, you do not believe that what they say is true. EG *There is no reason to disbelieve him... I never disbelieved their story.* — V+O = doubt ≠ believe

2 If you **disbelieve** in something, you do not believe that it exists or that it works. EG *I have always disbelieved in telepathy... Can you disbelieve in something you don't know about?* — V+A *(in)* ≠ believe

disburse /dɪsbɜːs/, **disburses, disbursing, disbursed**. To **disburse** an amount of money means to pay it out, usually from a fund which has been collected for a particular purpose; a rather formal word. EG *During 1974, £213m was disbursed in regional development grants.* — V+O = pay out ≠ collect

disbursement /dɪsbɜːsməˀnt/, **disbursements**; a formal word. 1 **Disbursement** is the paying out of a sum of money, especially from a fund. — N UNCOUNT ⇑ payment

2 A **disbursement** is a sum of money that is paid out. — N COUNT

disc /dɪsk/, **discs**; also spelled **disk** in American English. A **disc** is 1 a flat circular object. — N COUNT 2 a small flat object of any shape. EG *...an identity disc.* — N COUNT 3 one of the thin, circular pieces of cartilage which separates the bones in your back. EG *I had slipped a disc... One third of the spine is made up of these discs.* ● See also **slipped disc**. — N COUNT 4 a gramophone record. EG *They regularly bought one or more discs every week.* ● See also **compact disc**. — N COUNT

discard /dɪskɑːd/, **discards, discarding, discarded**. If you **discard** someone or something, you get rid of them or have nothing more to do with them because you no longer want them or need them. EG *Should they discard the present system entirely?... They ate food discarded by the soldiers.* ◊ **discarded**. EG *She sympathized with his discarded lovers.* — V+O = ditch; ◊ ADJ CLASSIF = cast-off

discern /dɪsɜːn/, **discerns, discerning, discerned**; a formal word. If you can **discern** something, 1 you are aware of it and know what it is. EG *He is unable to discern what is actually happening... It is impossible to discern the extent of his links with the Mafia.* — V+O/REPORT-CL ⇑ perceive = make out 2 you can just see it, but not clearly. EG *I could dimly discern his figure.* — V+O = make out

discernible /dɪsɜːnəbəˀl/. If something is **discernible**, you can see it or be aware of it. EG *They are just random dots. There is no discernible shape of any kind.* ◊ **discernibly**. EG *The director's role discernibly changes.* — ADJ QUALIT : IF+ PREP THEN *in* ⇑ noticeable; ◊ ADV WITH VB = visibly

discerning /dɪsɜːnɪŋ/. Someone who is **discerning** has good judgement and can decide which things of a particular kind are good and which are bad; used showing approval. EG *Discerning readers have been praising this writer for years.* ▸ used of qualities and behaviour. EG *She had a discerning taste for opera.* — ADJ QUALIT = discriminating; ▸ ADJ QUALIT

discernment /dɪsɜːnməˀnt/ is the ability to be able to judge which things of a particular kind are good and which are bad. EG *...her intuitive discernment.* — N UNCOUNT ⇑ judgement

discharge, discharges, discharging, discharged. The word **discharge** is pronounced /dɪstʃɑːdʒ/ when it is a verb, and /dɪstʃɑːdʒ/ when it is a noun. 1 When someone **is discharged** from hospital, prison, or one of the armed services, they are officially allowed to leave. EG *He was discharged from hospital last week... He had been discharged from the army after having malaria.* ▸ used as a noun. EG *The midwife will come and see you 48 hours after your discharge from hospital.* — V+O : USU PASS = release; ▸ N UNCOUNT : USU POSS+N, IF+ PREP THEN *from* = release

2 If you **are discharged** from a job, you are dismissed from it. EG *They were discharged for dishonesty.* — V+O : USU PASS, IF+PREP THEN *from*

3 If someone **discharges** their duties or responsibilities, they carry them out satisfactorily; a formal use. EG *He is unable to discharge the powers and duties of his office.* — V+O ⇑ carry out = perform

4 If you **discharge** a debt, you pay someone all the money that you owe them; a formal use. EG *He discharged all his debts before he died.* — V+O = settle

5 If you **discharge** something from inside a place, you send it out or allow it to come out; a formal use. EG *One female insect may discharge as many as 400 million eggs... ...facilities for ships to discharge their catches.* — V+O

6 If you **discharge** a gun, you fire it; an old-fashioned use. EG *Next moment he discharged his own weapon.* — V+O

7 When there is a **discharge** of a substance, the substance is sent out or allowed to come out from inside somewhere, often accidentally; a formal use. EG *...the discharge of mercury from industrial premises... Carbon monoxide discharge is high.* ▸ A **discharge** is the substance that comes out in this way. EG *...a mild cold with a clear nasal discharge... These discharges go out in the form of waves.* — N COUNT/ UNCOUNT : USU+ SUPP; ▸ N COUNT : USU +SUPP ⇑ emission

disciple /dɪsaɪpəˀl/, **disciples**. 1 If you are someone's **disciple**, you are influenced by their teachings and try to follow their example. EG *Not even a committed disciple could think it an impressive document... Lenin was the disciple of Marx but not his slave.* — N COUNT ⇑ follower

2 The **disciples** were the twelve close followers of Jesus Christ during his lifetime. EG *Jesus sent two of the disciples on ahead.* — N COUNT : USU *the*+N IN PL ⇑ follower

disciplinarian /dɪsɪplɪnɛərɪən/, **disciplinarians**. A **disciplinarian** is a person who believes in imposing strict rules of behaviour and in punishing severely anyone who disobeys the rules. EG *...a stern disciplinarian.* — N COUNT = martinet

disciplinary /dɪsɪplɪnəriˈ/. **Disciplinary** matters, measures, or actions are concerned with making sure that people obey rules or regulations and that — ADJ CLASSIF : USU ATTRIB ⇑ corrective they are suitably punished if they do not. EG *...a new disciplinary code... He has no disciplinary problems in his class.*

discipline /dɪsɪplɪn/, **disciplines, disciplining, disciplined.** 1 **Discipline** is 1.1 the practice of making people obey strict rules of behaviour and of punishing them when they do not obey them. EG *Some prisoners were charged with serious breaches of discipline... It is a valuable aid in imposing discipline on children.* — N UNCOUNT
1.2 the quality of being able to behave and work in a controlled way which involves obeying a strict set of rules. EG *She was holding back with iron discipline... ...men of responsibility and discipline.* — N UNCOUNT = self-control
2 The **discipline** of a particular situation or activity is the necessity of acting in a strictly controlled way according to a set of expected rules or standards that this situation or activity involves. EG *...the disciplines and incentives of the competitive market... In this way, the girls learned the disciplines of motherhood... She needs the discipline of having to write an essay every week.* — N COUNT/UNCOUNT
3 If you **discipline** yourself or **discipline** someone else to do something, you train yourself or that person to behave and work in a strictly controlled and regular way. EG *Clearly they will have to play a large part in disciplining themselves.* — V+O (NG/REFL)
4 To **discipline** someone also means to punish them for something that they have done wrong. EG *Laura was not disciplined for this incident... The company is not going to discipline anybody after all.* — V+O
5 A **discipline** is a particular area of study, especially a subject of study in a college or university; a formal use. EG *They are prepared to take candidates from any academic discipline.* — N COUNT : USU MOD+N

disciplined /dɪsɪplɪnd/. The people involved in a **disciplined** organization, activity, or system behave in a controlled way according to a strict set of rules of behaviour. EG *...a disciplined society with rigid social rules... Baker looks as if he lives a disciplined life.* ▸ used of people. EG *She is disciplined, punctual, and kind... The motive is to mould the child into a disciplined adult.* — ADJ QUALIT = ordered; ▸ = self-controlled

disc jockey, disc jockeys; also spelled **disk jockey** in American English. A **disc jockey** is someone who plays and introduces pop records on the radio or at a disco. — N COUNT = D.J.

disclaim /dɪskleɪm/, **disclaims, disclaiming, disclaimed.** If you **disclaim** knowledge of something, **disclaim** responsibility for something, etc, you you say that you did not know about it, are not responsible for it, etc; a formal word. EG *In this way the planner can disclaim responsibility for the consequences... Rich men tend to disclaim their wealth... Tess disclaimed any knowledge of it.* — V+O ⇑ reject

disclaimer /dɪskleɪmə/, **disclaimers.** A **disclaimer** is a statement in which someone says that they did not know about something or that they are not responsible for something; a formal word. EG *They thought I was making the usual disclaimers.* — N COUNT ⇑ denial

disclose /dɪskləʊz/, **discloses, disclosing, disclosed.** 1 If you **disclose** information that has been secret, you tell people about it. EG *Northcliffe's attempt to disclose the truth was systematically blocked.* — V+O/REPORT-CL = reveal ≠ conceal
2 If you **disclose** something that has been hidden, you make it possible for people to see it, for example by removing a cover. EG *The screen fell back with a crash and disclosed a yawning opening in the sand.* — V+O ⇑ reveal = uncover

disclosure /dɪskləʊʒə/, **disclosures. Disclosure** is the act of causing people to know information that was previously secret. EG *It will involve more disclosure of company information.* ▸ A **disclosure** is the information that is made known. EG *There were more disclosures about Casey in the press.* — N UNCOUNT = revelation ≠ concealment; ▸ N COUNT

disco /dɪskəʊ/, **discos.** A **disco** is 1 a club where young people go to dance to pop records, which are usually played by a disc jockey. EG *We need a disco in this town.* — N COUNT = discotheque
2 a party at which people dance to pop records which are played by a disc jockey. EG *Our youth club's got a disco on tonight.* — N COUNT = discotheque

discolour /dɪskʌlə/, **discolours, discolouring, discoloured**; also spelled **discolor** in American English. If something **discolours** or if it **is discoloured** by something else, part of its original colour is lost or changed, especially in an unpleasant, patchy way. EG *The pans may discolour inside... The heat would discolour the paint.* — V-ERG ⇑ change
◊ **discoloured.** EG *...a row of small discoloured teeth.* — ◊ ADJ QUALIT
◊ **discoloration** /dɪskʌləreɪʃə⁰n/. EG *The deficiency may show as a purplish discoloration in seedlings.* — ◊ N UNCOUNT

discomfit /dɪskʌmfɪt/, **discomfits, discomfiting, discomfited.** If you **are discomfited** by something, it causes you to feel slightly embarrassed or confused; a rather literary word. EG *I was discomfited to find that he was still there... Jefferson looked discomfited.* — V+O : USU PASS ⇑ embarrass = disconcert

discomfiture /dɪskʌmfɪtʃə/ is a feeling of slight embarrassment or confusion; a literary word. EG *She seemed delighted at my momentary discomfiture.* — N UNCOUNT

discomfort /dɪskʌmfə⁸t/, **discomforts.** 1 **Discomfort** is 1.1 a painful feeling in part of your body when you have been hurt slightly or when you have been uncomfortable for a long time. EG *They can't stand physical discomfort.* — N UNCOUNT ⇑ pain = suffering
1.2 a feeling of worry caused by shame or embarrassment. EG *Her letter caused him some discomfort.* — N UNCOUNT ⇑ unease
2 **Discomforts** are conditions which cause you to feel physically uncomfortable. EG *The physical discomforts of filming do not worry me unduly.* — N COUNT+SUPP = inconvenience

disconcert /dɪskə⁷nsɜːt/, **disconcerts, disconcerting, disconcerted.** If something **disconcerts** you, it makes you feel uneasy or embarrassed. EG *The cat's cold stare disconcerted me.* — V+O : USU PASS ⇑ worry = unnerve

disconcerting /dɪskə⁷nsɜːtɪŋ/. Something that is **disconcerting** makes you feel uneasy or embarrassed. EG *The old man had this disconcerting habit of pausing before he spoke.* — ADJ QUALIT = unnerving, off-putting
◊ **disconcertingly.** EG *The diary begins disconcertingly: Today is my last day on earth.* — ◊ ADV

disconnect /dɪskə⁷nɛkt/, **disconnects, disconnecting, disconnected.** 1 If you **disconnect** something from something else, you separate the two things. EG *Make sure you have disconnected the hose from the tap.* — V+O : IF+PREP THEN *from* = detach
2 If you **disconnect** a piece of apparatus, you detach it from its supply of gas or electricity. You usually do this when you want to repair or move it. EG *Removal firms won't disconnect any gas or electrical apparatus.* — V+O ≠ connect
3 If the gas or electricity board **disconnects** you or **disconnects** your supply of gas or electricity, the board stops the supply of gas or electricity to your house, usually because you are about to move to another house or because you have not paid your bills. EG *The Gas company wrote to Mrs Bullon saying she was to be disconnected in two days.* — V+O : USU PASS = cut off ≠ connect
4 If a telephone operator **disconnects** people who are speaking on the telephone, he or she breaks the connection that they have so that they are unable to continue their conversation. EG *Then the operator disconnected us... I think we've been disconnected.* — V+O = cut off ≠ connect

disconnected /dɪskə²nɛktɪ²d/. Remarks that are **disconnected** do not relate to each other in a logical way and are therefore difficult to understand. EG *He sometimes exchanged disconnected remarks with her... He continued in rambling, disconnected sentences.* — ADJ QUALIT = disjointed, random

disconsolate /dɪskɒnsələ¹t/. Someone who is **disconsolate** is very unhappy and depressed. EG *Disconsolate passengers waited by the ticket office.* — ADJ QUALIT = woebegone
◊ **disconsolately.** EG *She was standing disconsolately in the middle of the room.* — ◊ ADV WITH VB = woefully

discontent /dɪskə⁷ntɛnt/, **discontents.** 1 **Discontent** is the feeling that you have when you are not satisfied with the way that you are being treated. EG *What are the causes of the current discontent?... There are signs of discontent with pay and conditions.* — N UNCOUNT : USU +SUPP = dissatisfaction
2 **Discontents** are reasons that you have for not feeling satisfied with the situation that you are in; a rather formal use. EG *The intelligentsia transmitted their discontents to the masses.* — N COUNT : USU PL = grievance

discontented /dɪskə⁷ntɛntɪ²d/. If you are **discontented**, you are not satisfied with the situation that you are in. EG *Most of the people he saw looked discontented.* — ADJ QUALIT : IF+PREP THEN *with* ⇑ unhappy = fed up
◊ **discontentedly.** EG *She huddled her shawl discontentedly round her shoulders.* — ◊ ADV WITH VB

discontinue /dɪskə⁷ntɪnjuː/, **discontinues, discontinuing, discontinued.** If you **discontinue** something that you have been doing regularly, you stop doing it. EG *We have decided to discontinue production of television sets... Fanny wanted to discontinue her visits to the mill.* — V+O

discontinuity /dɪskɒntɪnju:ɪti¹/, **discontinuities**; a formal word. 1 **Discontinuity** in a process is a lack of smooth or continuous development. EG *We must see this period as one of discontinuity.* N UNCOUNT

2 A **discontinuity** is a break that occurs in a developing process. EG *...the discontinuities in men's lives.* N COUNT+SUPP = gap

discontinuous /dɪskə⁷ntɪnju:əs/. A process that is **discontinuous** happens in stages with intervals between them, rather than continuously. ADJ CLASSIF ⇑ divided

discord /dɪskɔ:d/, **discords**. 1 **Discord** is disagreement, argument, and unpleasantness between people. EG *I don't want to risk introducing a note of discord into the evening.* N UNCOUNT = disharmony

2 A **discord** is a combination of musical notes which sound unattractive when they are played at the same time. EG *His unbearable discords were more than I could take.* N COUNT ⇑ disharmony

discordant /dɪskɔ:də⁰nt/. 1 Something that is **discordant** is strange or unpleasant because it does not fit in with other things. EG *The suit of armour on the ground floor may seem to strike a discordant note.* ADJ QUALIT = grating

2 A **discordant** sound contains two or more musical notes that sound unattractive when they are played together. ADJ QUALIT

discotheque /dɪskə⁶tɛk/, **discotheques**. A **discotheque** is the same as a disco. N COUNT

discount, discounts, discounting, discounted. The word **discount** is pronounced /dɪskaʊnt/ when it is a noun and when it is the verb in paragraph 2. When it is the verb in paragraph 3, it is pronounced /dɪskaʊnt/. 1 A **discount** is a reduction in the usual price of something. EG *They stayed in places that gave discounts to students... Companies gain membership at discount rates.* N COUNT

2 If a shop **discounts** an amount or percentage from something that they are selling, they deduct the amount or percentage from the usual price. EG *I can discount ten per cent for you.* V+O = knock off

3 If you **discount** an idea, fact, or theory, you consider that it is not true, not important, or not relevant. EG *This must therefore be discounted as a way out of their difficulties... So this approach must not be totally discounted.* V+O ⇑ reject = ignore

discourage /dɪskʌrɪdʒ/, **discourages, discouraging, discouraged**. 1 If someone or something **discourages** you, they cause you to lose your enthusiasm or willingness to do something. EG *She did all she could to avoid discouraging him... Don't be discouraged.* ◊ **discouraging**. EG *Her comments were not in the least discouraging.* ◊ **discouraged**. EG *Whenever I feel discouraged or depressed, I read that letter.* V+O ≠ encourage; ◊ ADJ QUALIT; ◊ ADJ QUALIT : USU PRED

2 If someone or something **discourages** you from doing something, they make you less willing or less likely to do it. EG *She had been forced to discourage him from saying any more... The rain discouraged us from going out.* V+O : IF+PREP THEN *from* ⇑ deter = put off

discouragement /dɪskʌrɪdʒmə²nt/, **discouragements**. 1 **Discouragement** is the act of trying to persuade someone not to do something. EG *I encountered opposition and discouragement as well as support and understanding.* N UNCOUNT ≠ encouragement

2 A **discouragement** is something that makes you unwilling to do something because you are afraid of the consequences. EG *Submarines in the Mediterranean were a constant discouragement to naval movements.* N COUNT = deterrent

discourse, discourses, discoursing, discoursed. The word **discourse** is pronounced /dɪskɔ:s/ when it is a noun, and /dɪskɔ:s/ when it is a verb. **Discourse** is a formal word. 1 A **discourse** is a serious talk or piece of writing which is intended to teach or explain something. EG *She embarked on a discourse about the town's origins.* N COUNT ⇑ communication = disquisition

2 **Discourse** is spoken or written communication between people, especially serious conversation about a particular subject. EG *This happens every time you enter into discourse with your colleagues.* N UNCOUNT

3 If someone **discourses** on a subject, they talk in an authoritative way about it. EG *Howard discoursed on a topic he had grown greatly interested in.* V+A *(on/upon)* ⇑ speak

discourteous /dɪskɜ:tɪəs/. Someone who is **discourteous** is rude and has no consideration for the feelings of other people; a rather formal word. EG *He was quite the most discourteous young man I have ever met.* ▸ used of situations and behaviour. EG *I realised I had allowed a discourteous pause to develop.* ◊ **discourteously**. EG *We were discourteously ignored.* ADJ QUALIT; ▸ = impolite; ◊ ADV WITH VB

discourtesy /dɪskɜ:tə¹si¹/ is rude and ill-mannered behaviour; a formal word. EG *Any other attitude smacked of discourtesy.* N UNCOUNT = rudeness

discover /dɪskʌvə/, **discovers, discovering, discovered**. 1 When someone **discovers** something that they did not know about before, they find out about it. EG *Then we discovered a way to get rid of it... He had since discovered that this statement was wrong.* V+O/REPORT-CL ⇑ learn

2 If you **discover** someone or something, you find them, either by accident or because you have been looking for them. EG *He was dead for three weeks before anyone discovered him... One of the patrols had discovered a small arms cache.* V+O : USU+A = unearth

3 If someone **discovers** a place, substance, or fact which nobody knew about before, they are the first person to find it or find out about it. EG *Columbus discovered the largest island in the Caribbean... Penicillin was discovered by Alexander Fleming.* V+O

4 When you say that someone **discovered** a particular activity or subject, you mean that they tried doing it or studying it for the first time and that they enjoyed it. EG *She discovered the joy of writing... I discovered photography in the Royal Air Force.* V+O ⇑ learn

5 When a actor, musician, etc who is not well-known **is discovered**, someone recognizes that they have talent and helps them in their career. EG *Ellen Terry had been first discovered by William Poel.* V+O : USU PASS ⇑ find

discoverer /dɪskʌvərə/, **discoverers**. The **discoverer** of something is the first person to find out about it. EG *Who was the discoverer of the electron?* N COUNT : USU *the*+N, IF+PREP THEN *of*

discovery /dɪskʌvə⁰ri¹/, **discoveries**. 1 When someone makes a **discovery**, 1.1 they find out about something that they did not know about before. EG *Other rulers of recent times have made the same discovery... ...the discovery by the US intelligence Bureau of a spy ring... ...discoveries of undercover attacks.* ▸ used as an uncount noun. EG *Further discovery can be made by the patient about his own condition.* N COUNT : USU+SUPP; ▸ N UNCOUNT : USU+SUPP 1.2 they are the first person to discover a place, substance, or scientific fact that no one knew about before. EG *The discovery of adrenalin came about through a mistake... New scientific discoveries are being made every day... Printing itself depended on the much earlier Chinese discovery of paper-making.* ▸ used as an uncount noun. EG *Scientific discovery goes on... ...the great voyages of discovery in the 15th century.* N COUNT : USU+SUPP; ▸ N UNCOUNT : USU+SUPP 1.3 they recognize that an actor, musician, etc who is not well-known has talent. EG *Half a dozen times a year they make discoveries - of a new actress, dancer, comedian.* N COUNT

2 When the **discovery** of people or objects happens, someone finds them, either by accident or as a result of looking for them. EG *...the hunting for meat, the discovery of things to eat... ...my discovery of these books.* N COUNT : USU+SUPP

discredit /dɪskrɛdɪt/, **discredits, discrediting, discredited**; a formal word. 1 If someone or something **discredits** a particular person or group, they cause this person or group to lose the respect of other people by showing that they have done something wrong or cannot be relied on. EG *His intention was clearly to discredit Mr Campbell... ...the discrediting of trade union leaders.* ◊ **discredited**. EG *Its leaders have become discredited.* V+O ⇑ disparage = bring into disrepute; ◊ ADJ QUALIT

2 If someone or something **discredits** an idea or belief, they make the idea or belief appear false or doubtful. EG *Scientific discoveries have discredited religious belief... Unfortunately, modern research tends to discredit the legend.* ◊ **discredited**. EG *...discredited theories.* V+O ⇑ question; ◊ ADJ QUALIT = rejected

3 If something that someone has done is **to** their **discredit**, it causes people to lose respect for them. EG *It was to Monty's discredit that he refused to believe them.* PHR : USED AS A

discreditable /dɪskrɛdɪtəbə⁰l/. **Discreditable** behaviour is not acceptable because people consider it to be shameful and wrong; a formal word, used showing disapproval. EG *It is a mistake to suppose that there is anything discreditable in this.* ADJ QUALIT ⇑ bad = disreputable

discreet /dɪskri:t/. 1 **Discreet** behaviour involves being tactful in an awkward situation in order to avoid causing embarrassment or difficulties for other people. EG *I can guarantee that Perry would be discreet... They specialize in the discreet and gentle-* ADJ QUALIT ⇑ careful ≠ indiscreet *manly management of money... I waited in the car at a discreet distance.* ◊ **discreetly.** EG *I left the letter with him and went out discreetly.* ◊ ADV

2 Someone who is **discreet** is careful not to give too much information about subjects which are considered to be secret, personal, or private. EG *She is very discreet. She has never told me anything about it.* ▸ used of what someone says. EG *The account was too discreet to mention what Mrs Waller's reaction may have been.* ADJ QUALIT : USU PRED ⇑ cautious ▸ ADJ QUALIT

3 Something that is **discreet** does not draw attention to itself. EG *It was a discreet flat in a quiet street.* ADJ QUALIT ⇑ quiet

discrepancy /dɪskrɛpənsi¹/, **discrepancies.** If there is a **discrepancy** between two things that ought to be the same, there is actually a difference between them. EG *There was a striking discrepancy between the suicide rates of the cities... There were some discrepancies in his various accounts.* N COUNT : IF+ PREP THEN *between/in*

discrete /dɪskriːt/. **Discrete** ideas or things are separate and distinct from each other. EG *The company was divided into a number of relatively small, discrete units... These computers operate in a series of discrete steps.* ADJ CLASSIF : USU ATTRIB ≠ connected

discretion /dɪskrɛʃən/. 1 **Discretion** is the quality of behaving in a quiet and controlled way without drawing attention to yourself or giving away personal or private information. EG *I am prepared to vouch for your discretion... The servants moved around the house with discretion.* N UNCOUNT ⇑ caution = tact

2 If you are able to use your **discretion** in a particular situation, you have the freedom and authority to use your judgement to decide what to do. EG *The medical profession should have an area of discretion in what it does... Believe it or not, I do have discretion over the job of chief of police.* N UNCOUNT

3 If something is **at the discretion of** a person or group, it can only happen if that person or group gives their permission. EG *Prisoners may have writing materials, but only at the discretion of the authorities... We may, at our discretion, transfer the balance of the account.* PHR : USED AS AN A

discretionary /dɪskrɛʃənəᵒrɪ/. Something that is **discretionary** allows a person or organization the freedom to judge what should be done in a particular case without having to follow a precise instruction or set of rules. EG *These payments are discretionary... The Commission also has discretionary power to award extra funds.* ADJ CLASSIF ≠ mandatory

discriminate /dɪskrɪmɪneɪt/, **discriminates, discriminating, discriminated.** 1 If you can **discriminate** between two things, you recognize that they are different and understand the differences between them. EG *This computer lacks the ability to discriminate between speech and other sounds... It teaches him to discriminate between right and wrong.* V, OR V+A *(between/ among)* ⇑ differentiate = distinguish

2 If someone or something **discriminates** against a person or group, the person or group is treated less well than other people or groups. If someone or something **discriminates** in favour of a person or group, the person or group receives better treatment than other people or groups. EG *The divorce laws discriminated against women and working people... She claims she has been discriminated against in pay... Employers are encouraged to discriminate in favour of minority groups.* V, OR V+A *(against/in favour of)*

discriminating /dɪskrɪmɪneɪtɪŋ/. Someone who is **discriminating** has the ability to recognise things that are of good quality; used showing approval. EG *It was a small but discriminating audience.* ADJ QUALIT = discerning

discrimination /dɪskrɪmɪneɪʃəⁿn/. **Discrimination** is 1 the practice of treating one person or group of people less fairly or less well than other people or groups. EG *He spoke out against racial discrimination... They heard appalling stories of discrimination against women.* 2 the ability to recognize and understand the differences between two things. EG *These robots are capable of only rudimentary shape discrimination.* 3 awareness of what is good or of high quality. EG *He showed a total lack of discrimination in the way he decorated his room.* N UNCOUNT : USU +SUPP; N UNCOUNT : USU +SUPP; N UNCOUNT = discernment

discriminatory /dɪskrɪmɪnətəᵒri¹/. Something that is **discriminatory** is unfair in the way it treats one person or group when compared with the way it treats other people or groups. EG *He has fought these discriminatory proposals.* ADJ CLASSIF ⇑ unequal

discursive /dɪskɜːsɪv/. If a style of writing is **discursive**, it includes a lot of information or opinions that are not necessarily relevant; a rather formal word. EG *They complained that my writing was becoming too discursive.* ADJ QUALIT = rambling

discus /dɪskəs/, **discuses.** 1 A **discus** is a heavy round plate of wood and metal, about 25 centimetres in diameter, which athletes try to throw as far as they can in sports competitions. N COUNT

2 The **discus** is the event or the sport of throwing the discus. EG *She's in the discus and the 100 metres.* N SING : *the*+N

discuss /dɪskʌs/, **discusses, discussing, discussed.** If you **discuss** something, 1 you consider it thoroughly, from different points of view, by talking to someone else about it. EG *They said they had an important matter to discuss with you... The meeting discussed the problems of poor families.* 2 you write or talk about it in detail. EG *In this morning's lecture I will be discussing the education system in Britain... How does the economic state of the country relate to the problems discussed in the previous chapter?* V+O = talk over; V+O ⇑ consider = go into

discussion /dɪskʌʃəⁿn/, **discussions.** 1 **Discussion** is the act of talking or writing about something in detail and from several points of view. EG *There was much discussion about the new driving laws... Her answers allowed an opportunity for discussion... They joined a discussion group on the problems of teaching English.* ● If something is **under discussion** it is still being considered and talked about and no decision has yet been reached. EG *The weapons system under discussion could destroy the whole of Europe.* N UNCOUNT = debating ● PHR : USED AS AN A ⇑ unsettled

2 A **discussion** is a conversation, speech, or piece of writing in which a subject is considered in detail, from several points of view. EG *John Lyons will be taking part in a discussion on 'Language and Communication'... We have had discussions with Members of Parliament about the new immigration laws.* N COUNT = debate

disdain /dɪsdeɪn/, **disdains, disdaining, disdained.** 1 If you feel **disdain** for someone or something, you dislike them because you think that they are inferior or unimportant. EG *They don't attempt to conceal their disdain for foreigners... The intellectuals tend to view this effort with disdain.* ▸ used as a verb. EG *Young people disdain anything so old-fashioned.* N UNCOUNT : IF+ PREP THEN *for* ⇑ contempt = scorn ▸ V+O = scorn

2 If you **disdain** to do something, you do not do it, because you feel that it is not important enough or not worthy of you. EG *Claire disdained to reply.* V+*to*-INF = scorn

disdainful /dɪsdeɪnful/. If someone is **disdainful**, they dislike something or someone because they think that they are inferior or unimportant. EG *Economists tend to be disdainful of their colleagues in other social disciplines.* ◊ **disdainfully.** EG *She looked away disdainfully.* ADJ QUALIT : IF+ PREP THEN *of* ⇑ contemptuous = scornful ◊ ADV WITH VB = scornfully

disease /dɪziːz/, **diseases.** 1 **Disease** or a **disease** is an illness in people, animals, or plants which is caused by bacteria or infection, rather than by an accident. EG *...women and children ravaged by disease... I have a rare eye disease... ...infectious diseases.* N UNCOUNT/ COUNT

2 A **disease** is also an attitude or habit that several people have and that is thought to be unnatural or harmful; often used humorously. EG *You've caught the disease of the profession, suspicion... ...the English disease of being nice to everyone.* N COUNT+SUPP = sickness

diseased /dɪziːzd/. 1 Something that is **diseased** is affected by a disease. EG *His hand was diseased and covered with white spots... ...an old diseased tree.* ADJ CLASSIF

2 If you say that someone's mind is **diseased**, you mean that it is not normal or balanced. EG *...the product of a diseased imagination.* ADJ CLASSIF ⇑ unbalanced = sick

disembark /dɪsɪ²mbɑːk/, **disembarks, disembarking, disembarked.** 1 If you **disembark** from a ship, aeroplane, or bus, you leave it by getting out of it and going on to the land or on to the ground. EG *Half the passengers disembarked at Cherbourg.* ◊ **disembarkation** /dɪsembɑːkeɪʃəⁿn/. EG *Disembarkation will begin in three minutes.* V : USU+A *(from)* ≠ embark ◊ N UNCOUNT

2 If you **disembark** things from a ship, you unload them onto the shore. EG *They were disembarking equipment in Northern France.* ◊ **disembarkation.** V+O : USU+A ≠ embark ◊ N UNCOUNT

disembodied /dɪsɪ²mbɒdɪd/. **Disembodied** means 1 separated from or existing without a body. EG *...a disembodied head.* 2 seeming not to be attached to or to come from anyone. EG *Dawlish's disembodied hands reached into the circle... ...disembodied voices.* ADJ CLASSIF : USU ATTRIB; ADJ CLASSIF : USU ATTRIB

disembowel /dɪsɪ²mbaʊəl/, **disembowels, disembowelling, disembowelled**; also spelled **disemboweling, disemboweled** in American English. To **disembowel** people or animals means to remove their internal organs, especially their stomach, intestines, and bowels. V+O ⇑ mutilate

disenchanted /dɪsɪntʃɑːntɪ²d/. If you are **disenchanted** with something, you are disappointed with it and no longer believe that it is good or worthwhile. EG *She is now thoroughly disenchanted with this world.* ADJ QUALIT ⇑ disillusioned

disenchantment /dɪsɪntʃɑːntmə²nt/ is the feeling of being disappointed with something and no longer believing that it is good or worthwhile. EG *There is growing disenchantment with school.* N UNCOUNT ⇑ disillusionment

disenfranchise /dɪsɪ²nfræntʃaɪz/, **disenfranchises, disenfranchising, disenfranchised**. To **disenfranchise** someone means to take away their right to vote. EG *...small, marginal, disenfranchised minority groups.* V+O ⇑ deprive

disengage /dɪsɪ²ngeɪdʒ/, **disengages, disengaging, disengaged**. 1 If you **disengage** something, you separate it from something which it has become attached to. EG *Melanie smiled and attempted to disengage her arms from his grip.* V+O : IF+PREP THEN *from* = extricate

2 If two armies or navies **disengage**, they stop fighting and move away from one another. EG *The first platoon made their way to the next position as the second began to disengage.* V ≠ engage

disengagement /dɪsɪ²ngeɪdənt/ is a process by which people gradually stop being involved in an activity or an organization. EG *There is a movement in the United States towards a degree of disengagement in Europe... They were now clearly embarking on the process of disengagement from the Party.* N UNCOUNT : IF+PREP THEN *from*

disentangle /dɪsɪ²ntæŋgə⁰l/, **disentangles, disentangling, disentangled**. 1 If you **disentangle** something, you remove it from a place where it has become twisted with or surrounded by other objects. EG *It took him some time to disentangle a pound note from the other crumpled paper in his pocket.* V+O : IF+PREP THEN *from* ⇑ free = liberate, extricate

2 If you **disentangle** wool, string, rope, etc, you remove knots and tangles from it. V+O OR V+O (REFL)

disequilibrium /dɪsiːkwɪlɪbrɪəm/ is a state in which things are not stable or certain, but are likely to change suddenly; a formal word. EG *...the inherent disequilibrium of the economy.* N UNCOUNT ≠ stability

disestablish /dɪsɪ²stæblɪʃ/, **disestablishes, disestablishing, disestablished**. To **disestablish** a church or religion means to take away its official status, so that it is no longer recognised as a national institution; a formal word. V+O ≠ establish

disestablishment /dɪsɪ²stæblɪʃmə²nt/. The **disestablishment** of a church or religion is the act of taking away its official status; a formal word. N UNCOUNT

disfavour /dɪsfeɪvə/, **disfavours**; also spelled **disfavor** in American English; a formal or old-fashioned word. 1 **Disfavour** is 1.1 dislike or disapproval of someone or something; a formal word. EG *He viewed the killing of baby seals with disfavour.* N UNCOUNT : USU *with*+N 1.2 the state of being disliked or disapproved of by someone, especially someone who has authority over you. EG *He fell into disfavour with his superiors.* N UNCOUNT : USU *in/into*+N+*with*

2 A **disfavour** is an unkind or unhelpful act. EG *You have done me a great disfavour.* N COUNT = disservice

disfigure /dɪsfɪgə/, **disfigures, disfiguring, disfigured**. 1 To **disfigure** someone or to **disfigure** a part of their face means to spoil the appearance of their face or part of their face. EG *His nose was disfigured in an accident.* V+O : USU PASS = scar

2 To **disfigure** an object or a place means to spoil its appearance. EG *Non-disposable wastes have disfigured the landscape.* V+O

disfigurement /dɪsfɪgəmə²nt/, **disfigurements**. A **disfigurement** is something, for example a scar, that spoils a person's appearance. EG *Kay didn't care about her husband's disfigurement.* N COUNT+SUPP ⇑ blemish = deformity

disgorge /dɪsgɔːdʒ/, **disgorges, disgorging, disgorged**. 1 If something **disgorges** its contents, it empties them out. EG *...factories disgorging effluent into the river.* V+O

2 If you say that a vehicle or building **disgorges** people, especially a lot of people, you mean that the people leave the vehicle or building. EG *The buses disgorge crowds on to the pavements... The beaches were full of landing craft disgorging troops.* V+O ⇑ emit ≠ swallow up

disgrace /dɪsgreɪs/, **disgraces, disgracing, disgraced**. 1 **Disgrace** is a state in which people disapprove of you and stop respecting you, because of your behaviour. EG *She could not bear the disgrace of anyone knowing what she had done... His son had brought disgrace on the whole family.* N UNCOUNT = shame, dishonour ● If someone is **in disgrace** other people disapprove of them and do not respect them because of something that they have done. EG *Jane was in disgrace... He was driven in disgrace into the wilderness.* ● PHR : USED AS AN A

2 You say that something, for example a state of affairs, is a **disgrace** when you find it completely unacceptable. EG *The state of Britain's roads is a disgrace!* N SING : a+N = scandal

3 You say that someone **is a disgrace to** someone else when their behaviour causes the other person to feel ashamed. EG *He was a disgrace to the regiment.* PHR : VB INFLECTS

4 If you **disgrace** yourself or **disgrace** someone else, you behave in such a way that you cause yourself or someone else to be disapproved of strongly by other people. EG *They have disgraced the whole school... John disgraced himself last night at the party.* V+O (NG/REFL) ⇑ shame = discredit

5 If you **are disgraced**, you are disapproved of or condemned because of your actions, with the result that people no longer respect you. EG *Jacob learned that his daughter had been disgraced... The party leader was disgraced in the revolution.* V+O : ONLY PASS = discredited

disgraceful /dɪsgreɪsful/. If you say that something such as behaviour or a situation is **disgraceful**, you disapprove of it strongly, and feel that the person or people responsible should be ashamed of it. EG *They haven't had a wash and their clothes are disgraceful... You should inform everyone of these dangerous and disgraceful conditions.* ◊ **disgracefully**. EG *He had behaved disgracefully.* ADJ CLASSIF = shocking ◊ ADV = shamefully

disgruntled /dɪsgrʌntə⁰ld/. If you are **disgruntled**, you are cross and dissatisfied because things have not happened the way that you wanted them to happen. EG *They might win support from among disgruntled Tory voters... They are disgruntled because no additional shares were issued.* ADJ QUALIT ⇑ unhappy

disguise /dɪsgaɪz/, **disguises, disguising, disguised**. 1 A **disguise** is something that you wear or other alterations that you make to your appearance in order to avoid being recognized by people. EG *I woke up, got dressed, and struggled with my disguise... You'll never get away with it. They'll see through that disguise in a minute.* N COUNT ⇑ costume

2 **Disguise** is the use of disguises in order to avoid being recognized. EG *He's a master of disguise... Disguise is your only hope.* N UNCOUNT ● If you are **in disguise**, you are not wearing your usual clothes or you have altered your appearance in other ways, so that people will not recognize you. EG *He might be an agent in disguise.* ● PHR : USED AS AN A

3 If you **disguise** yourself, you put on clothes which make you look like someone else or alter your appearance in other ways, so that people will not recognize you. EG *He decided he would disguise himself as a doctor.* V+O (REFL) : IF +PREP THEN *as/with* ⇑ dress up

4 If you **are disguised** as someone else, you have altered your appearance to make yourself look like the other person, especially by wearing the kind of clothes that they wear. EG *He escaped disguised as a girl.* V+O (NG/REFL) +A (*as*) : ONLY PASS ⇑ dressed up

5 If you **disguise** something, 5.1 you change its appearance, sound, taste, etc so that people do not recognize it. EG *The natural colour of her skin was not quite disguised by the cosmetics she had applied... He managed to disguise his voice.* V+O : IF+PREP THEN *by/with* = camouflage 5.2 you hide it because you do not want other people to know about it. EG *It proved difficult to disguise her anxiety.* V+O

6 If you say that something is **a blessing in disguise**, you mean that it seems unpleasant or unfortunate at first but eventually leads to something good happening. PHR : USED AS C

disgust /dɪsgʌst/, **disgusts, disgusting, disgusted**. 1 **Disgust** is a feeling of very strong dislike for something or someone, for example because of their appearance or behaviour. EG *He couldn't hide his disgust... Clarissa gave a snort of disgust.* N UNCOUNT = distaste, aversion ● If you do something **in disgust**, you do it because you feel a strong sense of dislike and shock at something that someone has done. EG *Johnson got up in disgust.* ● PHR : USED AS AN A

2 To **disgust** someone means to make them feel a strong sense of dislike and disapproval. EG *He disgusted Simon by spitting.* V+O : IF+PREP THEN *with/by*

disgusted /dɪsgʌstɪ²d/. If you are **disgusted**, you feel a strong sense of dislike and disapproval at something. EG *Thomas grew more and more disgusted... Kunta was disgusted with his own impulsiveness.* ◊ **disgustedly**. EG *Jake spat disgustedly.* — ADJ QUALIT ⇑ ashamed = revolted; ◊ ADV WITH VB

disgusting /dɪsgʌstɪŋ/; used showing disapproval. Something that is **disgusting** is 1 extremely unpleasant and offends you. EG *The place smelled disgusting... I hate you. You're disgusting.* 2 completely unacceptable. EG *It is disgusting the way taxes keep going up.* — ADJ QUALIT = revolting; ADJ QUALIT = dreadful

dish /dɪʃ/, **dishes, dishing, dished.** 1 The **dishes** are all the plates, cups, saucers, etc that you use during a meal and that have to be washed afterwards. EG *When are you going to do the dishes?... Rudolph stayed to dry the dishes after his mother had washed them.* — N PLURAL : USU *the*+N ⇑ crockery

2 A **dish** is a shallow container, often with a lid, in which you can serve food at a meal or which you can use for cooking. EG *The vegetables were in separate china dishes... ...a baking dish.* ▸ **Dish** is also used to refer to the food inside it or the amount of food it contains. EG *Ida brought a fresh dish of kidneys.* — N COUNT

3 A **dish** is also food that is prepared in a particular way and served as a meal or as part of a meal. EG *I waited for a moment, wondering what special dish she might prepare... He began experimenting with dishes of his own invention.* — N COUNT : USU+SUPP = recipe

dish out; an informal expression. 1 To **dish out** things means to give a lot of them away in a very generous manner. EG *I was dishing out gold cufflinks.* — PHRASAL VB : V+O+ADV ⇑ distribute

2 To **dish out** a punishment or strong criticism means to give it to someone. EG *I had to be able to withstand anything the warder could dish out.* — PHRASAL VB : V+O+ADV ⇑ inflict

3 To **dish out** something also means to distribute or deliver it to several people, especially when it is something that is unpleasant or not wanted. EG *He was burdened with endless paperwork dished out by bureaucrats, and he hated it.* — PHRASAL VB : V+O+ADV ⇑ give = dole out

4 To **dish out** food means to serve it at the beginning of a meal. EG *Shall I dish out the potatoes, then?* — PHRASAL VB : V+O+ADV

dish up. To **dish up** food means to put it into serving dishes or onto people's plates so that it is ready to eat at the beginning of a meal; an informal expression. EG *Mother dished up Sunday breakfast.* — PHRASAL VB : V+O+ADV ⇑ serve

disharmony /dɪshᵒɑːməni¹/. When there is **disharmony**, people disagree about important things and this causes an unpleasant atmosphere; a formal word. EG *There is a certain undercurrent of disharmony between them.* — N UNCOUNT ≠ tension

dishcloth /dɪʃklɒθ/, **dishcloths**. A **dishcloth** is a cloth which you use for wiping plates, saucepans, cutlery, etc when you are washing them after a meal. EG *Louisa, holding a dishcloth in her hand, stepped out of the kitchen.* — N COUNT ⇑ cloth

disheartened /dɪshɑːtᵊnd/. If you are **disheartened**, you feel disappointed about something and have less confidence or less hope about it than you did before. EG *He had felt depressed and disheartened.* — ADJ QUALIT = discouraged

disheartening /dɪshɑːtᵊnɪŋ/. If something is **disheartening**, it makes you feel disappointed and less confident or less hopeful. — ADJ QUALIT ≠ encouraging

dishevelled /dɪʃevəᵒld/; also spelled **disheveled** in American English. If you describe someone's hair, clothes, or appearance as **dishevelled**, you mean that it is very untidy. ▸ used of people. EG *...a wild, dishevelled little girl of eight.* — ADJ QUALIT = bedraggled; ▸ ADJ QUALIT

dishonest /dɪsɒnɪ²st/. Someone who is **dishonest** is not truthful, honest, or able to be trusted. EG *He was dishonest in the actual performance of his duties.* ▸ used of behaviour. EG *They are all victims of that kind of dishonest behaviour.* ◊ **dishonestly**. EG *In my opinion, they have acted dishonestly.* — ADJ QUALIT ⇑ bad = deceitful; ◊ ADV WITH VB

dishonesty /dɪsɒnə¹sti¹/ is behaviour in which someone deceives people, for example by telling lies or cheating. EG *It would have been unfair to accuse him of dishonesty.* — N UNCOUNT ≠ honesty

dishonour /dɪsɒnə/, **dishonours, dishonouring, dishonoured**; also spelled **dishonor** in American English. **Dishonour** is a rather formal word. 1 **Dishonour** is a feeling of shame because you have been involved in something illegal, dishonest, or shameful and because other people no longer respect you. EG *There are men who prefer death to dishonour... They felt that the family would suffer some slight dishonour.* — N UNCOUNT/N SING WITH DET = disgrace ≠ prestige

2 If you **dishonour** someone, you cause them to feel ashamed and to lose the respect of other people. EG *She dishonoured him by taking a lover.* — V+O ⇑ shame = disgrace

3 If a bank **dishonours** a cheque, it refuses to pay the money that has been promised on it because the person does not have enough money in his or her account. — V+O ≠ honour

dishonourable /dɪsɒnərəbəᵒl/. Someone who is **dishonourable** is not honest and does things which you consider to be morally unacceptable; used showing disapproval. EG *There is something very dishonourable about him.* ▸ used of behaviour. EG *I think it is dishonourable to maintain your seat in Parliament under the circumstances.* ◊ **dishonourably**. EG *Stephen would never behave dishonourably.* — ADJ QUALIT ⇑ shameful ≠ honourable; ▸ ADJ QUALIT; ◊ ADV WITH VB

dishwasher /dɪʃwɒʃə/, **dishwashers**. A **dishwasher** is an electrically operated machine that washes and dries plates, saucepans, cutlery, etc. — N COUNT

dishwater /dɪʃwɔːtə/ is water that plates, saucepans, cutlery, etc have been washed in. EG *The dishes were washed without soap so that the dishwater could be used on the garden.* ● If you say that a cup of tea is **as weak as dishwater** or **like dishwater**, you mean that it is very weak and does not have enough flavour. — N UNCOUNT/N SING : *the*+N; ● PHR : USED AS C ⇑ weak

dishy /dɪʃɪ¹/. A woman describes a man as **dishy** when she thinks that he is very good looking and sexually attractive; an informal word in British English. EG *I saw this really dishy bloke down at the Post Office.* — ADJ QUALIT = gorgeous

disillusion /dɪsə¹luːʒəᵒn/, **disillusions, disillusioning, disillusioned**. 1 If something or someone **disillusions** you, they make you disappointed by showing you that something that you thought was true or good is not really true or good. EG *I hate to disillusion him.* — V+O ⇑ disappoint

2 **Disillusion** is the same as disillusionment. — N UNCOUNT

disillusioned /dɪsə¹luːʒəᵒnd/. If you are **disillusioned** with something, you are disappointed, because it is not as good as you had expected it to be. EG *Many social democrats were disillusioned with his leadership... My father was now thoroughly disillusioned with me... He was not bitter, just disillusioned.* — ADJ QUALIT = disenchanted

disillusionment /dɪsə¹luːʒəᵒnmə²nt/ is the disappointment that you feel when you discover that something is not as good as you had expected it to be. EG *A sense of disillusionment and fear began to creep in... There is considerable disillusionment with monetarism in Whitehall.* — N UNCOUNT ⇑ disappointment = disenchantment

disincentive /dɪsɪnsentɪv/, **disincentives**. A **disincentive** is something which discourages people from behaving or acting in a particular way; a rather formal word. EG *Any further increase in benefits would be a disincentive to work.* — N COUNT : IF+PREP THEN *to* ≠ incentive

disinclination /dɪsɪŋklɪneɪʃəᵒn/ is a feeling that you do not want to do a particular thing; a rather formal word. EG *There is a natural disinclination to go out on winter evenings.* — N UNCOUNT : USU +*to*-INF ⇑ dislike

disinclined /dɪsɪŋklaɪnd/. If you are **disinclined** to do something, you do not want to do it. EG *I was disinclined to say anything to anybody.* — ADJ QUALIT : PRED : USU+*to*-INF = reluctant

disinfect /dɪsɪnfekt/, **disinfects, disinfecting, disinfected**. If you **disinfect** something, you clean it using a substance that kills germs. EG *Let me wash those cuts and disinfect them.* — V+O

disinfectant /dɪsɪnfektənt/, **disinfectants**. **Disinfectant** is a substance that kills germs and that you use for cleaning kitchens and bathrooms and also for cleaning wounds. EG *Rinse it with clear water and disinfectant.* — N MASS ⇑ cleaner

disingenuous /dɪsɪndʒenju⁴əs/. Someone who is **disingenuous** is slightly dishonest and insincere. EG *He wasn't being disingenuous.* ▸ used of actions and behaviour. EG *'Do you mean,' she asked with a disingenuous smile, 'that it was John?'* ◊ **disingenuously**. — ADJ QUALIT ⇑ untruthful = devious ≠ candid; ◊ ADV WITH VB

disinherit /dɪsɪnherɪt/, **disinherits, disinheriting, disinherited**. If you **disinherit** someone such as your son or daughter, you arrange that they will not become the owner of your money and property after your death, usually because they have done something that you do not approve of; a fairly formal word. EG *Her father disowned and disinherited her.* — V+O ⇑ dispossess

disinherited /dɪsɪnherɪtɪ²d/. You say that people are **disinherited** when they have lost their cultural — ADJ CLASSIF, OR N SING : *the*+N or social traditions. EG *As a minority group, they remain trapped, disinherited, and despised.*

disintegrate /dɪsɪntɪ²greɪt/, **disintegrates, disintegrating, disintegrated.** 1 If something **disintegrates**, it becomes seriously weakened, and is divided or destroyed. EG *They had seen their marriages or homes disintegrate under its influence... All around me, I could feel morale disintegrating.* V OR V+A ⇑ collapse = crumble
◊ **disintegration** /dɪsɪntɪ²greɪʃə⁰n/. EG *...the disintegration of old-style politics.* ◊ N UNCOUNT ⇑ breakdown
2 If an object **disintegrates**, it breaks into many small pieces or parts and is destroyed. EG *Both ships simply seemed to disintegrate... The bird disintegrated into a few pathetic feathers.* ◊ **disintegration.** EG *The debris from the disintegration rained across a 250 mile stretch.* V ⇑ collapse = fall apart ≠ fuse ◊ N UNCOUNT

disinter /dɪsɪntɜː/, **disinters, disinterring, disinterred.** 1 If you **disinter** something, you start using it again after it has not been used for a long time; often used humorously. EG *An entertaining historical play was disinterred.* V+O = resurrect
2 When a dead body **is disinterred**, it is dug up from out of the ground. V+O : USU PASS = exhume

disinterest /dɪsɪntə⁰rɪ²st/. If there is **disinterest** in something, people are not interested in it. EG *The slogans were greeted with laughter, scepticism, or disinterest... ...the Government's fundamental disinterest in conservation.* N UNCOUNT ≠ enthusiasm

disinterested /dɪsɪntə¹rɪ²stɪ²d/. 1 Someone who is **disinterested** is not involved in a particular situation or not likely to benefit from it and is therefore able to act in a fair and unselfish way. EG *...compassionate and disinterested groups of people... So you can see I'm a disinterested observer.* ▸ used of behaviour and attitudes. EG *Many people remember his disinterested help to unknown writers.* ◊ **disinterestedly.** EG *We reason disinterestedly from the facts we observe.* ◊ **disinterestedness.** ADJ QUALIT = impartial ≠ biased ▸ = objective ◊ ADV WITH VB ◊ N UNCOUNT
2 If you are **disinterested** in something, you are not interested in it. Some users of English believe that it is not correct to use **disinterested** with this meaning. EG *Her mother had always been disinterested in her.* ◊ **disinterestedly.** EG *I watched disinterestedly as the train pulled into the station.* ADJ QUALIT ⇑ indifferent = uninterested ≠ enthusiastic ◊ ADV WITH VB

disjointed /dɪsdʒɔɪntɪ²d/. **Disjointed** words, thoughts, or ideas are not presented in a smooth or logical way and are therefore difficult to understand. EG *We listened to her voluble but disjointed account.* ADJ QUALIT ⇑ incoherent = bitty

disk /dɪsk/, **disks.** 1 A **disk** is a flat circular metal plate which is used to store large amounts of information for use by a computer. ● See also **floppy disk.** N COUNT = disc
2 See also **disc.**

dislike /dɪslaɪk/, **dislikes, disliking, disliked.** 1 If you **dislike** someone or something, you consider them to be unpleasant and do not like them. EG *She disliked the theatre... I grew to dislike working for the cinema... From what I know of him I dislike him intensely.* V+O ⇑ hate ≠ care for
2 **Dislike** is the feeling that you do not like someone or something. EG *They have been united in their dislike of authority... A mounting wave of dislike and anger rose within me.* ● If you **take a dislike to** someone or something, you begin to dislike them. EG *She had taken an unconcealed dislike to me.* N UNCOUNT : IF+ PREP THEN *of/ for* ⇑ hatred PHR : VB INFLECTS
3 Your **dislikes** are the things that you do not like. EG *She has her likes and dislikes, as we all have.* N COUNT : USU PL ≠ favourite

dislocate /dɪslə⁷keɪt/, **dislocates, dislocating, dislocated.** 1 If you **dislocate** a bone or joint in your body, you put it out of its normal position, usually in an accident. EG *My hip felt as if I had dislocated it.* V+O ⇑ displace
2 If something such as a business or routine **is dislocated**, something happens to spoil its usual order so that it no longer works properly. EG *The whole thing was dislocated by the sudden computer failure.* V+O = disrupt

dislocation /dɪslə⁷keɪʃə⁰n/ is a situation in which the usual state of affairs has been changed in a way that is disturbing or disruptive. EG *...the dislocation of traffic caused by the construction of the Thames Barrier.* N UNCOUNT ⇑ change = disruption

dislodge /dɪslɒdʒ/, **dislodges, dislodging, dislodged.** If you **dislodge** something from a particular place, you remove it, usually with effort or difficulty. EG *I had to tug quite hard in order to dislodge the hook... I might have dislodged the earth and stones as I moved.* V+O = shift

disloyal /dɪslɔɪə⁰l/. Someone who is **disloyal** helps the enemies or opponents of someone who they are expected to support, such as their family, their friends, or their country. EG *'You were disloyal to the country,' he replied... They want stronger action taken against disloyal newspapers.* ADJ QUALIT : IF+ PREP THEN *to* = unfaithful ≠ true

disloyalty /dɪslɔɪə⁰lti¹/ is behaviour in which someone is disloyal to their family, their friends, or their country. EG *She never spoke to him–that would have shown disloyalty to her mother.* N UNCOUNT : IF+ PREP THEN *to* ≠ faithfulness

dismal /dɪzmə⁰l/. Something that is **dismal** is 1 sad and depressing. EG *Hunter Road was miles away, in an even more dismal district... ...that rather dismal melody.* ◊ **dismally.** EG *The weather had broken and rain now fell dismally.* 2 very poor in quality. EG *...dismal conjuring tricks.* ADJ QUALIT = dreary, bleak ◊ ADV ADJ QUALIT = abysmal

dismantle /dɪsmæntə⁰l/, **dismantles, dismantling, dismantled.** 1 If you **dismantle** a machine or structure, you carefully undo all its parts so that it is in pieces. EG *They are so constructed that they may be dismantled if necessary.* V+O = take apart ≠ build
2 To **dismantle** an organization or political system means to cause it to stop functioning by gradually reducing its power or purpose. EG *They've been accused of dismantling the welfare state.* V+O ⇑ destroy ≠ build up

dismay /dɪsmeɪ/, **dismays, dismaying, dismayed.** 1 **Dismay** is a strong feeling of fear, worry, or sadness that is caused by something unpleasant and unexpected. EG *Ambassadors spoke of the problems with dismay... We were ushered, to our dismay, into a small room.* N UNCOUNT : USU *to*+ WITH *the/* POSS = alarm
2 If something or someone **dismays** you, they make you feel afraid, worried, or sad. EG *I was homesick and dismayed by the quiet of the country... Last month he dismayed his colleagues by refusing the offer.* V+O ⇑ upset = disconcert

dismember /dɪsmɛmbə/, **dismembers, dismembering, dismembered**; a formal word. 1 To **dismember** a person or animal means to pull off or cut off its arms and legs. EG *You can dismember an animal as large as a cow with a knife like that.* V+O
2 To **dismember** a country or area of land means to divide it into smaller parts. EG *Nor was England about to dismember the empire of the previous king.* V+O = carve up

dismemberment /dɪsmɛmbəmə²nt/; a formal word. **Dismemberment** is 1 the pulling off or cutting off of the arms and legs of a person or animal. EG *The murder was followed by dismemberment and decapitation.* 2 the dividing of a country or area of land into smaller parts. EG *...the dismemberment of the empire.* N UNCOUNT N UNCOUNT = partitioning

dismiss /dɪsmɪs/, **dismisses, dismissing, dismissed.** 1 If you **dismiss** something, 1.1 you decide or say that it is not important enough for you to think about or consider. EG *The problems can no longer be dismissed... I'm not dismissing this as a thing that wasn't worth doing... We shouldn't dismiss them just because they're old-fashioned.* V+O ⇑ reject = discount, ignore **1.2** you refuse to continue thinking about it. EG *And then as suddenly as the idea had risen, he dismissed it... She dismissed him from her mind.* V+O = banish
2 When an employee **is dismissed**, their employer tells them that they are no longer needed to do the job that they have been doing. EG *An individual cannot now be dismissed for non-membership of a union.* V+O : USU PASS ⇑ discharge = sack ≠ recruit
3 If someone in authority **dismisses** you, they tell you that they you can go away from them. EG *Dismissing the other children, she told Anthony to stay behind.* V+O ⇑ release
4 When a judge **dismisses** a case against someone, he or she formally states that there is no need for a trial, usually because there is not enough evidence for the case to proceed. EG *Smollett asked the judge to dismiss the charges against his client... Her lawyer asked to have the case dismissed.* V+O ⇑ reject = throw out

dismissal /dɪsmɪsə⁰l/, **dismissals. Dismissal** is 1 the act of telling an employee that he or she is no longer needed to do the job that he or she has been doing. EG *On one occasion the committee discussed the dismissal of a teacher... Her dismissal came at a bad time for her... The industrial tribunal heard several cases of unfair dismissal.* N COUNT/ UNCOUNT : IF+ PREP THEN *of/ from* = sacking 2 the rejection of something such as an idea or a set of values. EG *He found this dismissal of the computer's potential quite illogical.* N UNCOUNT ≠ acceptance

dismissive /dɪsmɪsɪv/. If you are **dismissive** of someone or something, you show that you think that they are not important or that they have no value. EG *You seemed dismissive of him, too.* ▸ used of behaviour and actions. EG *She looked up with a dismissive smile of contempt.* ◊ **dismissively.** EG *'Thanks,' Dixon said dismissively.*
ADJ QUALIT: IF + PREP THEN *of* ⇑ rejecting = scornful; ◊ ADV WITH VB

dismount /dɪsmaʊnt/, **dismounts, dismounting, dismounted.** If you **dismount** from a horse or a bicycle, you get down from it so that you are standing next to it; a formal word, sometimes used humorously. EG *The police officer dismounted from his bicycle.*
V: IF + PREP THEN *from* = get off ≠ get on

disobedience /dɪsəbiːdɪəns/ is behaviour that involves deliberately not doing what someone tells you to do, or what a rule or law says that you should do. EG *The authoritarian sees disobedience as a crime to be deterred... Disobedience is treated with special harshness.*
N UNCOUNT ⇑ opposition

disobedient /dɪsəbiːdɪənt/. If you are **disobedient,** you deliberately do not do what someone in authority tells you to do or what a rule or law says that you should do. EG *Peter was disobedient to his parents... She wore the air of a disobedient child.*
ADJ QUALIT = rebellious ≠ obedient

disobey /dɪsəbeɪ/, **disobeys, disobeying, disobeyed.** When someone **disobeys** a person or an order, they deliberately do not do what they have been told to do. EG *It never occurred to them that they could disobey their parents... I moaned all the time about it, but I could not disobey... His orders had been disobeyed.*
V OR V+O ⇑ oppose ≠ obey

disobliging /dɪsəblaɪdʒɪŋ/. People who are **disobliging** are unwilling to do the things that you want them to do. EG *He had a somewhat spiteful and disobliging nature.*
ADJ QUALIT = unhelpful

disorder /dɪsɔːdə/, **disorders.** **1 Disorder** is **1.1** a state of untidiness in which it is difficult to find anything. EG *The room was in dreadful disorder... Her desk is normally in a state of disorder... There was disorder among the papers on his desk.* **1.2** a state of being badly prepared or organized for a particular task. EG *Their forces advanced in some disorder for thirty kilometres... Opposition was so strong that the government retreated in total disorder.* **1.3** violence or rioting in public. EG *...a serious risk of public disorder... ...this drastic remedy for lawlessness and disorder.* ▸ used as a plural noun. EG *...a renewal of civil disorders in several cities.*
N UNCOUNT = chaos; N UNCOUNT = disarray; N UNCOUNT: USU MOD+N; ▸ N PLURAL: USU MOD+N

2 A **disorder** is an illness or disability which affects someone's mind or body. EG *There was evidence of a kidney disorder... ...a specialist in various forms of mental disorders.*
N COUNT/UNCOUNT: USU + SUPP

disordered /dɪsɔːdəd/. **1** Something that is **disordered** is untidy and not neatly arranged. EG *There were too many things in the small disordered room.*
ADJ QUALIT ≠ neat

2 Someone who is mentally **disordered** or who has a **disordered** mind is mentally ill. EG *More training in the care of mentally disordered patients was needed.*
ADJ CLASSIF ⇑ ill = disturbed

disorderly /dɪsɔːdəli/. **1** Something that is **disorderly** is very untidy because nobody has tried to arrange it neatly. EG *They go upstairs to their disorderly bedroom... Her belongings now lie scattered once again in a disorderly mess.*
ADJ QUALIT = disordered ≠ neat

2 If a person or a group of people is **disorderly,** they behave in an uncontrolled and violent way. EG *The police attempted to disperse the disorderly crowd.*
ADJ QUALIT = unruly ≠ orderly

3 If someone is charged with being **drunk and disorderly,** they are accused of being drunk and behaving in a noisy, offensive, or violent way in public; a legal expression. EG *He was arrested for being drunk and disorderly.*
PHR: USED AS C

disorganize /dɪsɔːgənaɪz/, **disorganizes, disorganizing, disorganized;** also spelled **disorganise.** If someone **disorganizes** something that has been carefully arranged, they spoil it so that it does not work properly. EG *I'm too busy. You'll disorganize my whole morning schedule.*
V+O ⇑ disrupt ≠ order

disorganized /dɪsɔːgənaɪzd/. Something that is **disorganized** is badly planned or arranged. EG *It was a bit disorganized, but there were one or two very fine scenes.*
ADJ QUALIT

disorient /dɪsɔːrɪɛnt/, **disorients, disorienting, disoriented.** **Disorient** means the same as disorientate.
V+O

disorientate /dɪsɔːrɪɛnteɪt/, **disorientates, disorientating, disorientated.** If something **disorientates** you, you no longer know in what direction anything is, including the direction that you have come from. ◊ **disorientated.** EG *We've taken so many turnings I'm completely disorientated.* ◊ **disorientation** /dɪsɔːrɪɛnteɪʃən/.
V+O: USU PASS ⇑ confuse; ◊ ADJ QUALIT: USU PRED ⇑ confused; ◊ N UNCOUNT

disown /dɪsəʊn/, **disowns, disowning, disowned.** If you **disown** someone or something, you say that you no longer want to have any connection with them or any responsibility for them. EG *Her father disowned and disinherited her.*
V+O ⇑ reject ≠ acknowledge

disparage /dɪspærɪdʒ/, **disparages, disparaging, disparaged.** If you **disparage** someone or something, you refer to them in a way which shows that you do not have a good opinion of them; a rather formal word. EG *Other newspapers in the country tended to disparage this as 'weak liberalism'.*
V+O ⇑ criticize = denigrate ≠ laud

disparagement /dɪspærɪdʒmənt/. **Disparagement** is the act of speaking about someone or something in a way which shows that you do not have a good opinion of them; a rather formal word. EG *He made a noise of disparagement.*
N UNCOUNT ⇑ criticism

disparaging /dɪspærɪdʒɪŋ/. A **disparaging** remark or comment is critical and scornful of someone or something. EG *He had been making disparaging remarks about Otto's talents.* ◊ **disparagingly.** EG *She spoke very disparagingly of the new house.*
ADJ QUALIT = snide; ◊ ADV WITH VB

disparate /dɪspərət/. Things that are **disparate** are clearly different from each other in quality or type; a rather formal word. EG *...a link between these very disparate aspects of scientific research... The level of talent seems so disparate.*
ADJ QUALIT ≠ similar

disparity /dɪspærəti/, **disparities.** If there is **disparity** or a **disparity** between two or more things, there is a noticeable difference between them; a rather formal word. EG *The disparity in inflation rates in 1976 caused many problems... They aim to reduce economic disparities between the rich and poor countries.*
N COUNT/UNCOUNT: IF + PREP THEN *between/in* = imbalance

dispassionate /dɪspæʃənɪt/. Someone who is **dispassionate** is able to make fair and sensible decisions that are not influenced by their emotions. EG *The dispassionate observer can only be puzzled by this phenomenon.* ▸ used of behaviour and actions. EG *...a spirit of inquiry and dispassionate analysis.* ◊ **dispassionately.** EG *The facts were often there, if one chose to look dispassionately.*
ADJ QUALIT = impartial ≠ emotional; ◊ ADV

dispatch /dɪspætʃ/, **dispatches, dispatching, dispatched;** also spelled **despatch.** **1** If you **dispatch** someone to a place, you send them there for a particular reason or in order to carry out a particular task; a formal use. EG *The supervisor would dispatch a crew to repair the damage... The cruiser despatched boats to rescue the survivors... My sister was dispatched to our grandmother in Scotland.* ▸ used as a noun. EG *The emergency required the dispatch of special forces.*
V+O; ▸ N SING WITH DET + *of*

2 If you **dispatch** a message, letter, or parcel, you send it to a particular person or destination; a formal use. EG *He sat down to write and despatch the instructions to the bankers... Invitations were despatched... This load had actually been dispatched three months previously.*
V+O: USU + A ≠ receive

3 A **dispatch** is **3.1** a special report that is sent to a newspaper by a journalist who is in a different town or country. EG *I picked up the paper and read a dispatch from a correspondent in Delhi.* **3.2** a message or report that is sent, for example, by army officers or government officials to their headquarters. EG *We were bringing dispatches from Captain Sydney Smith.* ● If a soldier **is mentioned in dispatches,** he or she is considered to have been extremely brave in a battle, and is recommended for a medal.
N COUNT; N COUNT ⇑ missive; ● PHR: VB INFLECTS

4 To **dispatch** a person or an animal means to kill them; an old-fashioned use. EG *Huntsmen claim that deer are always humanely despatched with a shotgun.*
V+O

5 To **dispatch** a job or task means to finish it quickly and efficiently without wasting time; an old-fashioned use. EG *She managed to despatch her business with Mr Partridge in time to catch the evening flight back.*
V+O = finish off

6 If you do something with **dispatch,** you do it very quickly; an old-fashioned use. EG *She ordered it to be done with the maximum of despatch.*
N UNCOUNT ⇑ speed = alacrity

dispel /dɪspel/, **dispels, dispelling, dispelled.** To **dispel** particular beliefs or feelings means to destroy or remove them. EG *I'm sorry to have to*
V+O = banish

dispel your romantic notions... All such doubts were now dispelled.

dispensable /dɪspe̲nsəbəl/. If someone or something is **dispensable**, they are not really needed. EG *These were dispensable luxuries.*
ADJ QUALIT ≠ essential

dispensary /dɪspe̲nsəri/, **dispensaries**. A **dispensary** is a place, for example in a hospital, where medicines are prepared and given out.
N COUNT

dispensation /dɪspenseɪ̲ʃən/, **dispensations**; a formal word. 1 **Dispensation** is 1.1 the issuing of something, especially from a position of authority. EG *...a 'public security' commission for the dispensation of justice... ...the dispensation of treatment on a rigid schedule.* 1.2 special permission to do something that is normally not allowed. EG *For years, royal dispensation was required to hunt here.* ▸ used as a count noun. EG *I have had a special dispensation... You don't even have to obtain a dispensation.*
N UNCOUNT; N UNCOUNT : IF + VB THEN *to*-INF; ▸ N COUNT : IF + VB THEN *to*-INF

2 A **dispensation** is a religious or political system that has authority at a particular time. EG *They are better off under the new dispensation.*
N COUNT : USU MOD + N ↑ regime

dispense /dɪspe̲ns/, **dispenses, dispensing, dispensed**. 1 To **dispense** something means 1 to divide it into parts or portions and distribute it; a formal use. EG *The charity has been given a large sum of money to dispense as it sees fit.*
V+O = allocate

2 Someone who **dispenses** medicine prepares it and distributes it, especially in a chemist's shop. EG *The firm has been dispensing ointments and lotions for generations... ...a dispensing chemist.* 3 To **dispense** a system or public service means to administer it or provide it; a formal use. EG *The people in charge of health and welfare had ceased to dispense either.*
V+O; V+O

dispense with. If you **dispense with** something, you stop using it or get rid of it altogether, especially because you no longer need it. EG *His knowledge of foreign affairs is too precious to be dispensed with... Wouldn't it be logical to dispense with all weaponry?*
PHRASAL VB : V + PREP, HAS PASS ↑ abandon = discard

dispenser /dɪspe̲nsə/, **dispensers**. A **dispenser** is a machine or container which provides a single item or a fixed quantity of something either automatically or by someone pressing a lever, button, etc. EG *...cash dispensers.*
N COUNT + SUPP ↑ distributor

dispersal /dɪspɜ̲ːsəl/ is the spreading of people or things over a wide area. EG *The explosion led to the widespread dispersal of a poisonous chemical into the atmosphere.*
N UNCOUNT ↑ spreading = dispersion

disperse /dɪspɜ̲ːs/, **disperses, dispersing, dispersed**. 1 When something **disperses** or when you **disperse** it, it spreads over a wide area. EG *By now, most of the pieces had dispersed on the tide... Building tall chimneys to disperse the smoke is no solution at all.* ◇ **dispersed**. EG *He has ties with many widely dispersed friends of his brother.*
V-ERG ↑ spread = scatter; ◇ ADJ QUALIT = scattered

2 When a group of people **disperses** or when someone **disperses** them, the group moves apart and the people leave in different directions. EG *I had seen many crowds dispersed by policemen... The foot soldiers rapidly dispersed and vanished into the woods.*
V-ERG ↑ move = break up

dispersion /dɪspɜ̲ːʃən/. **Dispersion** is the spreading of people or things over a wide area; a rather formal word. EG *The dispersion of troops was efficiently accomplished.*
N UNCOUNT ↑ spreading = dispersal

dispirited /dɪspɪ̲rɪtɪd/. If you are **dispirited**, you have lost your enthusiasm and excitement. EG *She sounded genuinely dispirited... The Party is dispirited and divided.* ◇ **dispiritedly**. EG *He looked about dispiritedly at the small untidy kitchen.*
ADJ QUALIT ↑ discouraged = disheartened; ◇ ADV WITH VB = dejectedly

dispiriting /dɪspɪ̲rɪtɪŋ/. Something that is **dispiriting** causes you to lose your enthusiasm and excitement. EG *...the first dismal, dispiriting day of November.*
ADJ QUALIT ↑ saddening = depressing

displace /dɪspleɪ̲s/, **displaces, displacing, displaced**. 1 If one thing **displaces** another, it forces the other thing out of its present place or position and occupies that place itself. EG *These resources can quickly displace nuclear power... I think this Government is going to be displaced sooner than that.*
V+O : NO IMPER ↑ move = supplant, dislodge

2 If a person or group of people **is displaced**, they are moved away from the area where they live, often by force. EG *This family has been displaced three times by urban demolition.*
V+O : NO IMPER

displacement /dɪspleɪ̲smənt/. **Displacement** is 1 the removal of something from its usual place or position by something which then occupies that place or position. EG *New techniques led to the displacement of the Fine Art tradition.* 2 the forcing of people away from the area or country where they live. EG *...the painful displacement of large masses of people.* 3 the weight or volume of a liquid that is displaced by an object submerged or floating in it, for example the weight of water displaced by a ship floating in it; a technical use.
N UNCOUNT; N UNCOUNT ↑ movement; N UNCOUNT ↑ replacement

display /dɪspleɪ̲/, **displays, displaying, displayed**. 1 If you **display** something that you want people to see, you put it in a particular place, for example in a museum or in a shop window, where it can be seen easily. EG *There were cakes displayed in the front window... ...a small museum where they could display the collection. His attention was caught by the photographs displayed outside.* ▸ used as a noun. EG *The new models are on display in gas showrooms... It was possible to have these photographs for display.*
V+O : USU+A ↑ show = exhibit; ▸ N UNCOUNT : USU+A ↑ show

2 To **display** something also means to show it proudly to people because you want them to admire it. EG *He thrust his chest out, displaying his organiser's badge.*
V+O = flaunt

3 If you **display** a characteristic, quality, or emotion, you behave in a way which shows that you have it. EG *His article had displayed a positive attitude to public ownership... As usual he was trying to display his concern about pollution.* ▸ used as a noun. EG *...a spontaneous display of friendship and affection... In a brief display of courtesy, he offered her his seat.*
V+O ↑ manifest = demonstrate ≠ conceal; ▸ N COUNT : IF + PREP THEN *of*

4 When a computer **displays** information, it shows it on a screen. EG *The computer will not only display the text, but speak it.*
V+O ↑ show

5 A **display** is 5.1 an arrangement of things, for example in a shop window, that is designed to attract people's attention. EG *A display of paperbacks was spread out on the pavement.* 5.2 a public performance or other event which is intended to entertain people. EG *...a firework display... This is one of fifty such displays being mounted over the next few days.* 5.3 an electronic device for representing information in a visual way, for example a screen connected to a computer. EG *Each number would appear on the display.*
N COUNT : IF + PREP THEN *of*; N COUNT ↑ spectacle; N COUNT

displease /dɪspli̲ːz/, **displeases, displeasing, displeased**. If something **displeases** you, it makes you annoyed or rather angry. EG *He could hurt me very badly if I displeased him.*
V+O ↑ anger = annoy ≠ please

displeased /dɪspli̲ːzd/. 1 If you are **displeased**, you are annoyed or rather angry about something that has happened. EG *Don seemed displeased... She didn't sound displeased.*
ADJ QUALIT : PRED + *with* ≠ pleased

2 If you are **displeased** with someone, you are rather angry with them because of something that they have done. EG *Smith has become displeased with some members of the staff.*
ADJ QUALIT : PRED ≠ pleased

displeasure /dɪsple̲ʒə/. A person's **displeasure** is a feeling of anger or annoyance that he or she has about something that has happened. EG *None of them actually dared to voice their displeasure... His policy was to minimize every risk of incurring her displeasure.*
N UNCOUNT ≠ delight

disport /dɪspɔ̲ːt/, **disports, disporting, disported**. If you **disport** yourself, you amuse yourself in a happy and energetic way; an old-fashioned word, now used humorously. EG *They could be seen disporting themselves in the fashionable discotheques.*
V+A OR V+O (REFL)+A

disposable /dɪspəʊ̲zəbəl/. 1 Something that is **disposable** is designed to be thrown away after it has been used. EG *...a disposable cigarette lighter... More parents now use disposable nappies for their babies.*
ADJ CLASSIF = throwaway

2 Your **disposable** income is the amount of your salary that you have left after you have paid income tax, social security contributions, etc. EG *Real disposable income is expected to rise again this year.*
ADJ CLASSIF ↑ usable

3 **Disposable** also means available to be used in whatever way you want. EG *They simply don't have enough disposable leisure time to come to the museum.*
ADJ CLASSIF : ATTRIB ↑ available

disposal /dɪspəʊ̲zəl/. 1 If you have something **at** your **disposal**, you are able to use it whenever you want, and for whatever purpose you want. EG *I had a car with a driver permanently at my disposal... He also had at his disposal a fully equipped laboratory... The whole building has been put at our disposal.*
PHR : USED AS AN A ↑ available

2 **Disposal** is the act or process of getting rid of something that is no longer wanted or needed by
N UNCOUNT : IF + PREP THEN *of*

putting it in a suitable place. EG *There is the problem of the safe disposal of radioactive waste... The kitchen was fitted with an electric waste disposal unit... Arrangements must be made for the disposal of the body.*

dispose /dɪspəʊz/, **disposes, disposing, disposed. dispose of. 1** If you **dispose of** something that you no longer want or need, you get rid of it by putting it in a suitable place, by giving it away, or by selling it. EG *They encourage consumers to dispose of partially worn out goods... Miles of telex tape had to be disposed of... She disposed of her shares three weeks ago.* PHRASAL VB : V+PREP, HAS PASS ≠ keep

2 If you **dispose of** a problem, a task, or a question, you succeed in dealing with it. EG *That, then, is the first point disposed of... He was glad he had disposed of the first question.* PHRASAL VB : V+PREP, HAS PASS ⇑ deal with

3 To **dispose of** a person or an animal means to kill them. EG *The king was disposed of quite painlessly... I disposed of one of the rats that came nosing round the hut.* PHRASAL VB : V+PREP, HAS PASS

disposed /dɪspəʊzd/. **1** If you are **disposed** to do something, you are willing or eager to do it. EG *Neither country seemed disposed to escalate their quarrel any further.* ADJ QUALIT : PRED+to-INF = inclined

2 If you are well **disposed** or favourably **disposed** to someone or to something that they want, you have a good opinion of them and are likely to let them have what they want. EG *The Queen is favourably disposed to your plea... The paper was well disposed towards the regime.* ADJ QUALIT : PRED, ADV+ADJ +to ⇑ inclined

3 If things are **disposed** in a particular way, they are arranged in that way; a formal use. EG *The choir was disposed in the most original way, with half the singers at the back of the hall.* ADJ CLASSIF : PRED+A

disposition /dɪspəzɪʃəⁿn/, **dispositions**; a rather formal word. **1** Someone's **disposition** is **1.1** the way that they tend to behave or feel. EG *My boss was of an exceptionally nervous disposition... ...a natural disposition to feelings of panic.* N UNCOUNT : USU +SUPP ⇑ nature = bent **1.2** their desire or tendency to do something at a particular time. EG *There was no apparent disposition to recognize the grim facts of life... Dixon had been showing a disposition to tremble and stagger.* N UNCOUNT+to-INF, OR N COUNT ⇑ willingness = inclination

2 The **disposition** of something is the way that it has been arranged or laid out. EG *You had best discuss with her the disposition of the furniture... ...the disposition of the rooms.* N COUNT : the+N +of ⇑ arrangement

dispossess /dɪspəⁱzes/, **dispossesss, dispossessing, dispossessed.** If you **are dispossessed** of something that you own, especially land or buildings, it is taken away from you. EG *She and her husband would be dispossessed of the house and left destitute.* V+O : USU PASS, IF+PREP THEN of ⇑ take away = rob, strip ◇ **dispossessed.** EG *In theory, the dispossessed tenants could find jobs elsewhere.* ◇ ADJ CLASSIF ▸ The **dispossessed** are people who are dispossessed. EG *...the needy and the dispossessed.* ▸ N PLURAL : the +N

disproportion /dɪsprəpɔːʃəⁿn/. **Disproportion** or a **disproportion** is a state in which two things are unequal; a formal word. EG *...the disproportion between philosophical and political developments.* N UNCOUNT/COUNT : IF+PREP THEN between ⇑ imbalance

disproportionate /dɪsprəpɔːʃəⁿnət/. Something that is **disproportionate** does not correspond in amount or size to something else. EG *The job seemed to take a disproportionate amount of time.* ADJ QUALIT ⇑ unequal = inordinate, excessive ◇ **disproportionately.** EG *There may be disproportionately high costs.* ◇ ADV ⇑ unequally

disprove /dɪspruːv/, **disproves, disproving, disproved.** If someone **disproves** an idea, belief, or theory, they show that it is not true. EG *They can neither prove nor disprove that it is genuine.* V+O/REPORT-CL = refute ≠ confirm

disputation /dɪspjʊteɪʃəⁿn/, **disputations. Disputation** is discussion on a subject which people cannot agree about; a formal word. EG *After much public disputation the plans were approved.* N UNCOUNT = debate ▸ used as a count noun. EG *...endless meetings, disputations and clashes.* ▸ N COUNT = argument

dispute, disputes, disputing, disputed. The word **dispute** is pronounced /dɪspjuːt/ when it is a noun and /dɪspjuːt/ when it is a verb. **1** A **dispute** is **1.1** a disagreement between a group of workers and their employer, usually about pay or conditions. EG *Industrial disputes are still a problem... The movement has promised to provide support for workers in dispute.* N COUNT, OR in+N **1.2** an argument between two or more people. EG *The couple lived happily together without disputes... An old dispute with a neighbour had resurfaced.* N COUNT, OR in+N = quarrel **1.3** a fight to try to win control of something such as an area of land. EG *...a revival of old border disputes.* N COUNT, OR in+N = conflict

2 Dispute is disagreement about the facts or truth of something. EG *The principle areas of dispute have concerned the nature and structure of these two societies... There has been much dispute, and the question is certainly not yet settled.* N UNCOUNT ≠ consensus

3 If something is **in dispute**, people are questioning it or arguing about it. EG *Her ability to do the job is not in dispute... ...a member whose right to sit in the House of Commons is in dispute.* PHR : USED AS AN A ⇑ uncertain = in question

4 If something is **beyond dispute**, it is clearly true and cannot be denied by anyone. EG *The reason was very simple and beyond dispute.* PHR : USED AS AN A ⇑ undeniable

5 If you **dispute** a fact, statement, or theory, you say that you think that it is not correct or true. EG *Officials quickly disputed the study... I don't dispute that children need love.* V+O/REPORT-CL = question ≠ accept

6 When people **dispute**, they argue with each other. EG *Three of the group are disputing with the other four.* V : IF+PREP THEN with ⇑ disagree

7 When people or animals **dispute** something, they fight for control or ownership of it. EG *They continued to dispute the ownership of the territory.* V+O = contest

disqualification /dɪskwɒlɪfɪkeɪʃəⁿn/, **disqualifications. Disqualification** or a **disqualification** is the act of stopping someone from taking part in an event, activity, or competition. EG *He is liable to disqualification from all official events.* N UNCOUNT/COUNT : IF+PREP THEN from

disqualify /dɪskwɒlɪfaɪ/, **disqualifies, disqualifying, disqualified.** When someone **is disqualified**, they are officially stopped from taking part in a particular event, activity, or competition, usually because they have done something wrong. EG *If the complaint is upheld he could be disqualified from election for three years.* V+O : IF+PREP THEN from ⇑ bar

disquiet /dɪskwaɪət/, **disquiets, disquieting, disquieted**; a formal word. **1 Disquiet** is a feeling of worry or anxiety. EG *Many physicists expressed extreme disquiet about the proposal.* N UNCOUNT = uneasiness

2 If something **disquiets** you, it makes you feel anxious. EG *The intensity of his anger disquieted me.* V+O ⇑ worry ◇ **disquieting.** EG *There was a disquieting moment as I got up to return to my office.* ◇ ADJ QUALIT ⇑ worrying

disquisition /dɪskwɪzɪʃəⁿn/, **disquisitions.** A **disquisition** is a detailed explanation of a particular subject; a formal word. EG *This is no place to enter into a lengthy disquisition on recent trends.* N COUNT ⇑ treatise

disregard /dɪsrɪ²gɑːd/, **disregards, disregarding, disregarded.** If you **disregard** something, you ignore it or do not take account of it. EG *We are not honest men of science if we disregard the facts... We disregarded the notice about not walking on the grass.* V+O ⇑ ignore ▸ used as a noun. EG *Senator Watt shows disregard for the protection of the environment... ...his total disregard of the rules that governed the conduct of visiting diplomats.* ▸ N UNCOUNT : IF +PREP THEN for ⇑ indifference ≠ respect

disrepair /dɪsrɪ²peə/. If something is **in disrepair**, it is broken or badly looked after, and needs to be repaired. EG *The weather was bad, the ships in disrepair... The house fell into disrepair.* PHR : USED AS AN A

disreputable /dɪsrepjə⁴təbəⁿl/. If someone or something is **disreputable**, they are not considered to be respectable or trustworthy. EG *Keep away from Ash and his disreputable friends... I lived a somewhat disreputable life.* ADJ QUALIT = dubious ≠ respectable

disrepute /dɪsrɪ²pjuːt/. **1** If something is brought **into disrepute** or if it falls **into disrepute**, it loses its good reputation, because it is connected with activities that people do not approve of. EG *The allegations will bring British parliamentary government into disrepute.* PHR : USED AS AN A

2 If something is **in disrepute**, people have a very poor opinion of it. EG *Nowadays, he and his paintings are in disrepute.* PHR : USED AS AN A ⇑ in disfavour

disrespect /dɪsrɪ³spekt/. If someone shows **disrespect**, they speak or behave in a way that shows lack of respect for a person, law, or custom. EG *I don't think he intended any disrespect... Citizens showed increasing disrespect for the forces of law and order.* N UNCOUNT : IF+PREP THEN for = contempt ≠ respect

disrespectful /dɪsrɪ¹spektⁿfə⁴l/. If you are **disrespectful**, you show no respect in the way that you speak or behave to someone. EG *She told me I was disrespectful...* ▸ used of behaviour. EG *My father said it would be disrespectful for Tom to change his* ADJ QUALIT ≠ respectful name. ◊ **disrespectfully**. EG *What have I ever done to make you treat me so disrespectfully?* ◊ ADV WITH VB

disrobe /dɪsrəʊb/, **disrobes, disrobing, disrobed**. When someone **disrobes**, they remove their clothes; a formal word, sometimes used humorously. EG *As she disrobed she threw each garment to the audience.* V, OR V+O

disrupt /dɪsrʌpt/, **disrupts, disrupting, disrupted**. 1 If you **disrupt** an event, system, or process, you cause difficulties that prevent it from proceeding or operating easily or peacefully. EG *There have been many attempts to disrupt meetings organized by their opponents... ...tightly organized groups of people who disrupt the workings of society.* V+O ⇑ disturb = upset ≠ assist

disruption /dɪsrʌpʃə⁰n/, **disruptions**. When there is **disruption** of an event, system, or process, it is prevented from proceeding or operating easily or peacefully. EG *...the disruption of rail communications... ...kids who are a potential source of disruption in lessons.* ▸ used as a count noun. EG *There are likely to be more strikes and more disruptions.* N UNCOUNT ⇑ disturbance ▸ N COUNT = upheaval

disruptive /dɪsrʌptɪv/. If someone is **disruptive** or if their behaviour is **disruptive**, they prevent something from operating easily or peacefully. EG *She was expelled from her grammar school as a disruptive influence... The effects of the struggle will be violent and disruptive.* ADJ QUALIT ≠ orderly

dissatisfaction /dɪssætɪsfækʃə⁰n/ is the state of feeling dissatisfied. EG *There is widespread dissatisfaction with the existing political system... Low wages were mentioned as the main cause for dissatisfaction... He said this in a tone of deep dissatisfaction.* N UNCOUNT : IF+ PREP THEN *with* ≠ satisfaction

dissatisfied /dɪssætɪsfaɪd/. If you are **dissatisfied**, you are not contented, or not pleased with something. EG *All of them had been dissatisfied with their lives... The result has left everybody dissatisfied... There are a large number of dissatisfied graduates.* ADJ QUALIT : IF+ PREP THEN *with* ⇑ disappointed ≠ satisfied

dissect /dɪ⁵sekt/, **dissects, dissecting, dissected**. 1 When the body of a dead person or animal **is dissected**, it is carefully cut up so that it can be examined scientifically. EG *Each specimen is carefully dissected.* ◊ **dissection** /dɪ⁵sekʃə⁰n/, **dissections**. EG *...the dissection of an earthworm.* V+O ⇑ cut up ◊ N UNCOUNT/ COUNT ⇑ cutting

2 When something such as a theory or piece of writing **is dissected**, it is examined very carefully so that people can discover its faults or understand it better; a rather formal use. EG *The book was dissected and discussed endlessly.* ◊ **dissection**. V+O = analyse ◊ N UNCOUNT

dissemble /dɪsembə⁰l/, **dissembles, dissembling, dissembled**. When people **dissemble**, they hide their real motives, emotions, etc; a literary word. EG *It was not in her nature to dissemble.* V ⇑ deceive = lie

disseminate /dɪsemɪneɪt/, **disseminates, disseminating, disseminated**. To **disseminate** information or knowledge means to distribute it to many people or organizations. EG *The agency would collect and disseminate information... ...a Research and Development Corporation for disseminating technology.* ◊ **dissemination** /dɪsemɪneɪʃə⁰n/. EG *...the dissemination of information.* V+O = spread ◊ N UNCOUNT : USU+*of*

dissension /dɪsenʃə⁰n/ is disagreement, arguments, and quarrels. EG *These problems can create dissension in the home... The garrison was already weakened by dissension and defeatism.* N UNCOUNT ⇑ disagreement = conflict

dissent /dɪsent/, **dissents, dissenting, dissented**. 1 **Dissent** is strong disagreement or dissatisfaction with a proposal or with established ideas or values. EG *The new leadership would tolerate no dissent from the party line... ...voices of dissent... All healthy societies can tolerate dissent.* N UNCOUNT ⇑ protest ≠ agreement

2 When people **dissent**, they express strong disagreement or dissatisfaction with established ideas or values. EG *Every individual has the right to dissent.* V ⇑ protest

3 If you **dissent** from something, you say that you do not agree with it; a formal use. EG *I dissent from the idea that universities should be concentrating on the natural sciences.* ◊ **dissenting**. EG *The only dissenting voice was Michael Foot's.* V OR V+A (*from*) : NO IMPER ≠ agree ◊ ADJ CLASSIF : ATTRIB

dissenter /dɪsentə/, **dissenters**. A **dissenter** is someone who expresses disagreement with established values or who believes that an idea or opinion is wrong. EG *Dissenters are frequently declared insane.* N COUNT ⇑ protester

dissertation /dɪsəteɪʃə⁰n/, **dissertations**. A **dissertation** is 1 a long essay that you do as part of a degree or other qualification. EG *We spend the final term writing our dissertations.* 2 a long, formal speech or piece of writing. EG *They printed three short editorials instead of one long dissertation... ...a fascinating dissertation by Dr Timothy Leary.* N COUNT N COUNT

disservice /dɪssɜːvɪs/, **disservices**. When you do someone a **disservice**, you do something that harms them. EG *I think George did a real disservice to the trade union movement... He had already done her a disservice by showing too much affection.* N COUNT : USU SING, IF+PREP THEN *to* OR *in/by* +-ING ⇑ wrong ≠ favour

dissident /dɪsɪdə²nt/, **dissidents**. 1 **Dissidents** are people who disagree with and criticize their government or a powerful organization, especially when this is an unusual or dangerous thing to do. EG *...political dissidents... ...the dissident movement in Poland.* N COUNT ⇑ critic

2 **Dissident** means disagreeing with or criticizing a particular system or powerful organization, especially when this might be difficult or dangerous. EG *Trotskyism began as a form of dissident communism.* ADJ CLASSIF : ATTRIB ⇑ critical

dissimilar /dɪsɪmɪlə/. If one thing is **dissimilar** to another, or if two things are **dissimilar**, they are very different from each other or have particular features which are very different. EG *...a group of very dissimilar people... Our Careers Library is not dissimilar to that found in most universities... Their understanding of the world is not so dissimilar from our own.* ADJ QUALIT : IF+ PREP THEN *to/ from/in* ⇑ unlike

dissimilarity /dɪsɪmɪlærɪti¹/, **dissimilarities**. 1 If there is **dissimilarity** between two or more things, they are different from each other in particular ways. EG *You will have noticed the dissimilarity between our organization and the others.* N UNCOUNT : IF+ PREP THEN *between* ≠ resemblance

2 A **dissimilarity** is one of the ways in which two things are different from each other. EG *...the dissimilarities in their characters... Important dissimilarities are often ignored.* N COUNT : IF+ PREP THEN *in/ between* = difference

dissimulate /dɪsɪmjəleɪθ/, **dissimulates, dissimulating, dissimulated**. When people **dissimulate**, they hide their true feelings and motives, especially by lying; a formal word. EG *They learned to conceal, to dissimulate, and to cheat officials.* ◊ **dissimulation** /dɪsɪmjəleɪʃə⁰n/. EG *He was incapable of either dissimulation or duplicity.* V ⇑ deceive ◊ N UNCOUNT ⇑ deception

dissipate /dɪsɪpeɪt/, **dissipates, dissipating, dissipated**; a formal word. 1 When something **dissipates** or when you **dissipate** it, it disappears completely. EG *Gradually the fog dissipated as the sun came up... The heat had to be dissipated by elaborate cooling systems... Their enthusiasm dissipated.* V OR V+O ⇑ break up = disperse

2 When someone **dissipates** money, time, or effort, they waste it in a foolish way. EG *He managed to dissipate his fortune by the time he was thirty... The pursuit of pleasure threatened to dissipate his energies.* V+O

dissipated /dɪsɪpeɪtɪ²d/. Someone who is **dissipated** has harmed their health by spending too much time drinking alcohol and enjoying other physical pleasures. EG *He was looking rather shabby and dissipated.* ▸ Used of people's behaviour. EG *At university he led a very dissipated life.* ADJ QUALIT = debauched, dissolute

dissipation /dɪsɪpeɪʃə⁰n/. 1 The **dissipation** of something such as a feeling is the process by which it disappears or is made to disappear; a formal use. EG *By talking to her mother she managed to bring about the dissipation of all her fears.* N UNCOUNT ⇑ disappearance

2 The **dissipation** of money, time, or effort is the wasting of it; a formal use. EG *We must learn to prevent the dissipation of valuable resources such as oil and gas.* N UNCOUNT ⇑ waste

3 **Dissipation** is also the leading of a dissipated life, or the state of being dissipated. EG *His years of dissipation soon ruined his health... He had an easy, confident manner and an air of mild dissipation.* N UNCOUNT = debauchery

dissociate /dɪsəʊʃɪeɪt, -sɪ-/, **dissociates, dissociating, dissociated**. 1 If you **dissociate** yourself from something or someone, you show that you are not connected with them, usually in order to avoid trouble or blame. EG *Bailey dissociated himself from this group.* V+O (NG/REFL) +A (*from*) ⇑ separate = divorce ≠ associate

2 If you **dissociate** something from something else, you begin to regard the two things as separate from each other. EG *I've tried, but I can't dissociate her from what she did.* V+O+A (*from*) ≠ associate

dissolute /dɪsəluːt/. Someone who is **dissolute** does not care at all about morals and lives in a way that is ADJ QUALIT ⇑ amoral considered to be wicked and immoral; used showing disapproval.

dissolution /dɪsəluːʃəⁿn/ is 1 the act of breaking up officially an organization or institution, or of formally ending a Parliament. EG *They advocated the dissolution of the Council... We had to wait for the dissolution of Parliament.* 2 the act of officially ending a formal agreement, for example a marriage or a business arrangement. 3 a process in which something becomes weaker and then disappears. EG *Progress has led only to the the dissolution of societies.*
N UNCOUNT: IF+PREP THEN *of* ⇑ break-up
N COUNT: USU SING+SUPP
N UNCOUNT: IF+PREP THEN *of*

dissolve /dɪzɒlv/, **dissolves, dissolving, dissolved.** 1 If you **dissolve** something such as a powder in a liquid, you put it into the liquid so that it becomes mixed with the liquid. EG *Dissolve the sugar in the water.* ◊ **dissolved.** EG *Add the dissolved gelatine to the mixture.*
V+O: IF+PREP THEN *in* ⇑ liquefy
◊ ADJ CLASSIF ⇑ liquefied

2 If something such as a powder **dissolves** in a liquid, it becomes mixed with the liquid. EG *Stir over a low heat until the sugar has dissolved.*
V

3 When an organization or an institution **is dissolved,** it is officially ended or broken up. EG *The Government on Friday approved a Bill to outlaw and dissolve all secret societies... The campaign was dissolved in 1963.*
V+O

4 When Parliament **is dissolved,** it is formally ended, so that elections for a new Parliament can be held. EG *Parliament was dissolved on 30th April.*
V+O

5 When a marriage or business arrangement **is dissolved,** it is officially ended. EG *She never saw him again, after their marriage was dissolved.*
V+O

6 If something such as a problem **dissolves** or **is dissolved,** it becomes weaker and disappears. EG *The tension between black and white dissolved... A social revolution is needed to dissolve the legacy of colonialism.*
V OR V+O ⇑ disappear = weaken

dissolve into. If you **dissolve into** tears or laughter, you begin to cry or laugh, because you cannot control yourself. EG *Some of the young ladies dissolve very easily into tears... Eileen dissolved into giggles.*
PHRASAL VB: V+PREP ⇑ collapse

dissonance /dɪsənəns/ is a lack of agreement or harmony between things; a formal word. EG *...this dissonance of colours.*
N UNCOUNT: USU +SUPP ≠ harmony

dissuade /dɪsweɪd/, **dissuades, dissuading, dissuaded.** If you **dissuade** someone from doing something or from believing something, you persuade them not to do it or not to believe it. EG *Nothing that Brenda said could dissuade him from the feeling that he was a failure.*
V+O, OR V+O+A *(from)* = discourage

distance /dɪstəns/, **distances, distancing, distanced.** 1 The **distance** between two points or places is the amount of space between them. EG *Did he run short distances or long distances?... The town is some distance from the sea... Watford is within walking distance of London.*
N COUNT/UNCOUNT+SUPP ⇑ interval

2 **Distance** is the fact of being far away in space, time, or social status. EG *With modern communications, the world seems smaller and distance doesn't matter so much... Distance from the event should make the memories less painful... Social distance can be difficult to overcome.*
N UNCOUNT ⇑ remoteness ≠ closeness

3 If you are **at a distance** from something, or if you see it, remember it, etc **from a distance,** you are a long way away from it in space or time. EG *It is wise to stay at a distance from the cobras... From a distance, he heard Jack's whisper... Remembering this disaster at a distance, I now feel sure that it was not her fault.*
PHR USED AS AN A

4 The **distance** is any point in space which is far away. EG *The mountain looked miles away in the distance... She stood on deck gazing into the middle distance.*
N SING: *in/into+the*+N

5 If you **go the distance** in a race or sports competition, you continue running or playing until the end of the race or match; an informal expression. EG *Even though the race course was in very bad condition, all the horses went the distance.*
PHR: VB INFLECTS ⇑ finish

6 **Distance** is also detachment and remoteness in the way someone behaves so that they do not seem friendly; a formal use. EG *Beneath her distance and aloofness lay, I thought, a heart of gold.*
N UNCOUNT: USU POSS+N = reserve

7 If you **distance** yourself from someone or something or **are distanced** from them, you become less involved with them, especially in your thoughts or feelings. EG *My husband distances himself from what he does not like in me... In some strange way the birth of the baby seemed to distance us.*
V+O (NG OR REFL): IF+PREP THEN *from* ⇑ detach

8 If you **keep** your **distance** from something or someone, 8.1 you do not become involved with them. EG *The local people kept their distance... They were careful to keep their distance from the official Party.*
PHR: VB INFLECTS

8.2 you do not get physically close to them; an old-fashioned use. EG *Keep your distance, or I'll shoot!*
PHR: VB INFLECTS

distant /dɪstənt/. 1 **Distant** means very far away. EG *News arrived of an invasion in a distant part of the country... The roar of the sea became very distant as they walked towards the town.*
ADJ QUALIT = faraway ≠ nearby

2 A **distant** journey is one in which you go to a place which is very far away. EG *She embarked on a distant journey.*
ADJ CLASSIF: ATTRIB = long

3 An event or time that is **distant** is very far away in the future or in the past. EG *And at some distant point in the future it is conceivable that people will no longer have to work.*
ADJ QUALIT = faraway ≠ near

4 A **distant** relative is one who you are not closely related to. EG *He was a distant relative of the Archbishop.*
ADJ QUALIT: ATTRIB ≠ close

5 Someone who is **distant** 5.1 is cold and emotionally detached. EG *I always thought of my parents as being rigid, distant, and unloving.* 5.2 is not concentrating on what they are doing because they are thinking about other things. EG *His eyes took on a glazed, distant look.*
ADJ QUALIT
ADJ QUALIT ⇑ vacant

distantly /dɪstəntli¹/. 1 If you see or hear something **distantly,** you hear or see it faintly because it is far away. EG *From the other end of the street, he could distantly see a figure waiting outside the door... The sound of a recorder was distantly audible.*
ADV ⇑ vaguely

2 If something happens **distantly,** it happens in a place that is far away; a literary use. EG *Children laughed distantly in other rooms.*
ADV

3 If you are **distantly** related to someone, you are related to them but not closely. EG *She was distantly connected on her mother's side with the Rothschilds.*
ADV+PAST PART ≠ closely

4 If you do something **distantly,** 4.1 you do it in a cold and emotionally detached way. EG *He behaved very distantly.* 4.2 you do it in a way that shows that you are not concentrating on what you are doing but are thinking about something else. EG *She carried on with her work, smiling distantly.*
ADV AFTER VB ⇑ coldly
ADV AFTER VB = distractedly

distaste /dɪsteɪst/ is a dislike of something which you consider to be disgusting or immoral. EG *He wore an expression of distaste... ...his distaste for money.*
N SING WITH DET +SUPP

distasteful /dɪsteɪstful/. If you find something **distasteful,** you find it disgusting or immoral. EG *There were aspects of his character which I found distasteful... Unnecessary slaughter of animals is distasteful to most people.* ◊ **distastefully.** EG *He noticed the blood on his hands and grimaced distastefully.*
ADJ QUALIT: IF+PREP THEN *to* = offensive
◊ ADV WITH VB

distemper /dɪstɛmpə/ is 1 paint which dissolves in water and which can be used for decorating. EG *My bedroom was painted with pink distemper.* 2 a dangerous and infectious disease that can be caught by animals, especially dogs. EG *I was treated like a dog with distemper.*
N UNCOUNT
N UNCOUNT

distend /dɪstɛnd/, **distends, distending, distended.** If a part of a person's or animal's body **distends** or if something **distends** it, it becomes swollen and unnaturally large; a formal or medical term.. EG *The camel had a large lump which distended her milk vein.* ◊ **distended.** EG *He had a grossly distended stomach.*
V OR V+O ⇑ enlarge
◊ ADJ QUALIT = bloated

distension /dɪstɛnʃəⁿn/, **distensions**; also spelled **distention** in American English. A **distension** is a swelling in a person's or animal's body; a medical term. EG *The baby cannot consume enough milk to relieve the distension.*
N COUNT/UNCOUNT ⇑ enlargement

distil /dɪstɪl/, **distils, distilling, distilled**; also spelled **distill** in American English. 1 When a liquid **is distilled,** it is heated until it evaporates and then cooled until it becomes liquid again. This is usually done in order to purify it. ◊ **distilled.** EG *You should always use distilled water in car batteries.* ◊ **distillation** /dɪstɪleɪʃəⁿn/. EG *...research groups specialising in distillation processes.*
V+O
◊ ADJ CLASSIF ⇑ purified
◊ N UNCOUNT

2 When whisky or other strong alcoholic drinks **are distilled,** they are made by a process of distilling. ◊ **distillation.**
V+O
◊ N UNCOUNT

3 If you **distil** something from many experiences or thoughts or from many things that you have read, you derive it from them. EG *Allinson's three books are distilled from many insights.* ◊ **distilled.** EG
V+O: USU+A *(from)* ⇑ extract = cull

...filling his mind with distilled knowledge. ◇ **distillation**. EG *...an idiosyncratic distillation of Marxism.* ◇ N COUNT : USU a+N+of

distiller /dɪstɪlə/, **distillers**. A **distiller** is a person or a company that makes whisky or similar strong alcoholic drinks by a process of distilling. N COUNT ⇑ manufacturer

distillery /dɪstɪləri[1]/, **distilleries**. A **distillery** is a place where whisky or a similar strong alcoholic drink is made by a process of distilling. N COUNT

distinct /dɪstɪŋkt/. 1 If something is **distinct** from something else of the same type, it is recognizably different or separate from it. EG *...a tree related to but quite distinct from the European beech... ...a pressure group whose interests were quite distinct from those of the workers they employed... The word 'nationalism' is used in at least three distinct senses.* ADJ QUALIT : IF+PREP THEN *from*

● If you say that you are talking about one thing **as distinct from** another, you are indicating exactly what thing or type of thing you are talking about by contrasting it with something else. EG *It's an economy based on the peasant as distinct from an industry-dominated economy.* ● PREP = as opposed to

2 If something is **distinct**, you can hear or see it clearly. EG *What he was saying was far from distinct... The town looked distinct and toylike in the pure morning air.* ◇ **distinctly**. EG *She heard a voice distinctly calling, 'Jimmie.'* ADJ QUALIT : USU PRED ⇑ clear ≠ vague ◇ ADV

3 If an idea, thought, or intention is **distinct**, it is clear and definite. EG *Claudius was the first to invade Britain with distinct and successful intentions of conquest... We were incapable of clear and distinct ideas.* ADJ QUALIT : USU ATTRIB ≠ muddled

4 **Distinct** also means great enough in amount or degree to be noticeable or important. **Distinct** is often used simply to give emphasis to a noun. EG *After what happened in that country there is a distinct possibility of a coup d'état... The group setting has several distinct advantages over the traditional one.* ◇ **distinctly**. EG *Bernardette looked distinctly wobbly.* ADJ QUALIT : ATTRIB ⇑ definite = undeniable ◇ ADV+ADJ/ADV

distinction /dɪstɪŋkʃə⁰n/, **distinctions**. 1 A **distinction** is 1.1 the classification of two or more similar things as different and the recognition of the features which make them different. EG *Do other countries have the same distinction between amateur and professional?* 1.2 a difference between two things. EG *Look at them closely when they occur separately and the distinction between them is then clear... The distinction between a bush and a shrub is very fine... Are there not always distinctions of dialect within a language?* N SING WITH DET +*between* N COUNT : IF+PREP THEN *between*

2 If you **draw** or **make a distinction**, you say that two things are different. EG *You seem to be making a careful distinction between being a Christian and being a member of a church.* PHR : VB INFLECTS = distinguish

3 **Distinction** is the quality of excellence, superiority, and merit. EG *He is a man of distinction in his own country... It has quiet distinction with a definite touch of fashion.* N UNCOUNT

4 A **distinction** is also 4.1 a mark of respect or of a highly regarded position in society. EG *I had the great distinction of being invited to speak at the conference.* 4.2 a mark of recognition for a very high level of achievement, often in an examination or contest. N UNCOUNT/COUNT = honour N COUNT

distinctive /dɪstɪŋktɪv/. Something that is **distinctive** has a special quality or qualities which makes it easily recognizable and different from other things of the same type. EG *Irene had a very distinctive voice, extremely clear and ringing... The language Xhosa has a variety of distinctive click sounds... He would shamble in with his distinctive walk, a kind of shuffle.* ◇ **distinctively**. EG *...a distinctively Black-African culture.* ◇ **distinctiveness**. EG *...decreasing the cultural distinctiveness of these groups.* ADJ QUALIT = singular ≠ ordinary ◇ ADV ◇ N SING WITH DET+SUPP

distinguish /dɪstɪŋgwɪʃ/, **distinguishes, distinguishing, distinguished**. 1 If you can **distinguish** one thing from another thing or **distinguish** between two things, you can see or understand the difference between them. EG *During his illness he found it difficult to distinguish reality from dreams... The child was unable to distinguish between the letters b and p.* V+O, OR V+A *(between)* ⇑ separate

2 To **distinguish** between two things also means to draw attention to the difference between them in order to classify them for a particular purpose. EG *When studying language, we have to distinguish between speaking and writing.* V+A *(between)* = differentiate

3 If a particular feature **distinguishes** one thing from another thing, it causes the two things to be regarded as different. EG *What distinguishes totalitarian governments from authoritarian ones?* ◇ **distinguishing**. EG *Striped skin is a distinguishing feature of tigers.* V+O+A *(from)* ⇑ identify ≠ equate ◇ ADJ CLASSIF : ATTRIB

4 If you can **distinguish** something, you can just see, hear, or taste it although it is very difficult to detect. EG *The photograph was poor and few details could be distinguished.* V+O ⇑ identify

5 If you **distinguish** yourself, you do something very well or behave in a way that causes other people to praise you or to think highly of you. EG *...young men who had distinguished themselves in battle.* V+O (REFL) ⇑ excel

distinguishable /dɪstɪŋgwɪʃəbə⁰l/. If something is **distinguishable**, 1 you can see or understand that it is different from other things of the same type. EG *These cars are readily distinguishable from assembly-line cars... ...a rural aristocracy that is barely distinguishable from the rural peasantry... They were already a distinguishable breed.* 2 you can see or hear it in conditions when it is difficult to see or hear anything, for example because it is dark or noisy. EG *Only the shine of their metal was distinguishable in the gloom.* ADJ CLASSIF : PRED : IF+PREP THEN *from* ⇑ recognizable ADJ CLASSIF : PRED ⇑ detectable

distinguished /dɪstɪŋgwɪʃt/; used showing approval. 1 If you describe someone as **distinguished** or describe their work or career as **distinguished**, you mean that they have been very successful in their work or career and therefore have a high reputation. EG *His grandfather had been a distinguished professor at the University... General Ravencroft had had a most distinguished career.* ADJ QUALIT = celebrated ≠ unimpressive

2 You also describe someone as **distinguished** or describe their appearance as **distinguished** when they appear very noble and dignified. EG *She was still beautiful and distinguished... Several distinguished ladies were pointed out to me.* ADJ QUALIT = illustrious

distort /dɪstɔːt/, **distorts, distorting, distorted**. 1 If you **distort** a statement or an argument, you change it so that its meaning becomes different. EG *I don't think I'm distorting his argument... Prior knowledge of the old idea may well distort or inhibit the new one.* V+O ⇑ misrepresent = twist

2 If something that you can see or hear **is distorted**, its appearance or sound is changed so that it seems strange or unclear. EG *His voice was distorted by crackling... It will obviously distort the signal.* V+O ⇑ deform

3 If an object **distorts** or **is distorted**, it becomes twisted into a different shape. EG *Their faces would all distort in panic... Metals, and other objects were scorched and distorted.* ◇ **distorted**. EG *...her distorted limbs.* V-ERG : USU PASS ⇑ twist = contort ◇ ADJ QUALIT

distortion /dɪstɔːʃə⁰n/, **distortions**. **Distortion** is 1 the changing of the meaning or purpose of something into something that you strongly disapprove of. EG *...this kind of distortion of history... ...deliberate distortion of an old idea... Cubism appeared to most people to be a distortion of reality.* ▸ used as a count noun. EG *...the grotesque distortions put about by the media.* 2 the changing of the appearance or sound of something in a way that makes it seem strange or unclear. EG *We want to keep the amount of distortion to an absolute minimum.* ▸ used as a count noun. EG *This kind of filtering produces certain kinds of distortions.* N UNCOUNT ⇑ alteration ▸ N COUNT N UNCOUNT/COUNT ▸ N COUNT

distract /dɪstrækt/, **distracts, distracting, distracted**. If something **distracts** you or **distracts** your attention, it takes your attention away from what you are doing or thinking about. EG *It distracted them from their work... Everyone's attention was easily distracted.* V+O : IF+PREP THEN *from* ⇑ divert

distracted /dɪstræktɪ²d/. If you are **distracted**, you are not concentrating properly because you are anxious or preoccupied about something. EG *During classes he was distracted and strangely troubled.* ▸ used of people's actions and behaviour. EG *She could see from his distracted look that he was worried.* ◇ **distractedly**. EG *She began looking distractedly about her.* ADJ QUALIT ⇑ inattentive = abstracted ◇ ADV WITH VB = anxiously ≠ calmly

distracting /dɪstræktɪŋ/. If something is **distracting**, 1 it helps you to stop thinking about your everyday problems; used showing approval. EG *I find films both relaxing and distracting.* 2 it causes you to stop concentrating properly on something; used showing disapproval. EG *Sub-titles can be very distracting.* ADJ QUALIT ADJ QUALIT ⇑ annoying = disruptive

distraction /dɪstrækʃəⁿn/, **distractions**. 1 A **distraction** is 1.1 something that turns people's attention away from something. EG *The government needed foreign adventure as a distraction from domestic discontent.* ▸ used as an uncount noun. EG *She needed to work without interruption or distraction.* 1.2 an activity that is not serious, and which is intended to amuse you. EG *Her playing had been reduced to the level of a gentle living room distraction.*
N COUNT : IF+PREP THEN *from* ⇑ diversion
▸ N UNCOUNT
N COUNT ⇑ diversion = amusement

2 If something or someone **drives** you **to distraction**, they annoy you continually so that you eventually become angry. EG *She was driven nearly to distraction by my failure to practise often enough.*
PHR : VB INFLECTS ⇑ annoy ≠ please

distraught /dɪstrɔːt/. If someone is **distraught**, they are so upset and worried that they cannot think clearly. EG *He saw at once how distraught I was... He was distraught with fury.*
ADJ QUALIT = frantic ≠ rational

distress /dɪstres/, **distresses, distressing, distressed**. 1 Distress is 1.1 a state of extreme unhappiness or worry. EG *Some people show signs of distress when they move house... He was in an extreme state of distress when his wife left him.* 1.2 the state of being in great pain. EG *The baby's distress is caused by teething.* 1.3 a state of suffering that is caused by not having enough money, food, or other necessary things. EG *How can we prevent such poverty, hardship, and distress?* 1.4 the state of needing help urgently because you are in a very dangerous situation. EG *The ship sent out a distress signal... ...an aircraft in distress.*
N UNCOUNT ⇑ suffering = anxiety
N UNCOUNT ⇑ suffering
N UNCOUNT ⇑ hardship
N UNCOUNT ⇑ emergency

2 If you **distress** someone, you upset them by doing or saying something that causes them to feel unhappy or alarmed. EG *I'm sorry if I've distressed you by asking all this.*
V+O = worry

distressed /dɪstrest/. Someone who is **distressed** is 1 upset because something unpleasant or alarming has happened or is about to happen. EG *She was distressed about my having to leave home.* 2 in a great deal of pain. EG *Ovett dropped out of the race, clearly distressed and having difficulty breathing.*
ADJ QUALIT = worried
ADJ QUALIT

distressful /dɪstresful/. Something that is **distressful** causes you to feel very sad. EG *They were very distressful memories to her.*
ADJ QUALIT ⇑ upsetting = distressing

distressing /dɪstresɪŋ/. Something that is **distressing** causes you to feel extremely worried, alarmed, or unhappy. EG *He had found her tears very distressing... It was a distressing experience for me.* ◊ **distressingly**. EG *The number of emergency telephones was distressingly inadequate.*
ADJ QUALIT ⇑ worrying = upsetting
◊ ADV

distribute /dɪstrɪbjuːt/, **distributes, distributing, distributed**. 1 If you **distribute** something such as leaflets or badges, you hand them out or deliver them to several people. EG *The leaflets were to be distributed by hundreds of high school students... I'll get it duplicated and then distribute it.*
V+O ⇑ give out = hand out

2 When goods **are distributed**, they are supplied to shops, garages, cinemas, and other businesses. EG *British Leyland distribute their cars throughout the world... BBC programmes are distributed in many countries.*
V+O : USU+A

3 To **distribute** something also means to share it among the members of a particular group. EG *Fuel resources are very unevenly distributed... ...creating and then distributing new wealth.*
V+O

distribution /dɪstrɪbjuːʃəⁿn/, **distributions**. **Distribution** is 1 the delivering of something to several people or organizations. EG *He can help you with the printing and distribution of your election address... His job is to organize the distribution of money to students... Unions took strike action to stop the production and distribution of the local newspaper.* 2 the sharing out of something among a particular group. EG *The conference discussed the fair distribution of income and wealth.*
N SING : USU *the*+N+OF
N UNCOUNT/N COUNT+SUPP ⇑ allocation

distributor /dɪstrɪbjəᵗtə/, **distributors**. 1 A **distributor** is a person or company that supplies goods to shops, garages, cinemas, or other businesses. EG *He's an importer and distributor by trade.*
N COUNT ⇑ supplier = wholesaler

2 The **distributor** in a car or other motor vehicle is a device that sends electric current to the spark plugs in the engine.
N COUNT

district /dɪstrɪkt/, **districts**. 1 A **district** is 1.1 a particular area of a town or country, especially one which has special or recognizable features. EG *She lived off the main shopping district in a back lane... ...doctors in country districts... ...a working class district of Paris... ...the Lake District.* 1.2 an area of a town or country which has been given official boundaries for the purpose of administration. EG *...Colchester District Council... The death must be registered in the district of the hospital where death took place.*
N COUNT+SUPP, ALSO IN NAMES AFTER N
N COUNT+SUPP : ALSO IN NAMES

2 **The district** is the area which surrounds a particular place, for example the villages and countryside around a town, or the streets and houses around your home. EG *They went to dances and gymkhanas all over the district... The village hall was the social hub of the district.*
N SING : *the*+N = locality

district attorney, district attorneys. A **district attorney** is the same as a D.A.
N COUNT

district nurse, district nurses. In Britain, a **district nurse** is a nurse who goes to people's houses to give them medical treatment. EG *Ask your family doctor, district nurse, or health visitor.*
N COUNT

distrust /dɪstrʌst/, **distrusts, distrusting, distrusted**. 1 If you **distrust** someone, you are very suspicious of them because you cannot trust them. EG *He keeps his savings under his mattress because he distrusts the banks.* ◊ **distrusted**. EG *He is probably the most distrusted statesman in Europe.*
V+O ⇑ doubt = mistrust
◊ ADJ QUALIT = mistrusted

2 **Distrust** is the feeling of suspicion that you have for someone who you do not trust. EG *They view one another with considerable distrust... ...a total distrust of the power of the central authority.*
N UNCOUNT : IF+PREP THEN *of* = mistrust

distrustful /dɪstrʌstful/. If you are **distrustful** of someone or **distrustful** of their behaviour, you do not trust them. EG *Both parties were distrustful of the President's policy... It was better to be too distrustful than not cautious enough.*
ADJ QUALIT : IF+PREP THEN *of* = mistrustful

disturb /dɪstɜːb/, **disturbs, disturbing, disturbed**. 1 If you **disturb** someone, you interrupt their peace or privacy, for example by asking them to do something that is not convenient, or by waking them up. EG *Sorry to disturb you, but can I use your telephone?... If she's asleep, don't disturb her.*
V+O = disrupt

2 If something **disturbs** you or **disturbs** your state of mind, it makes you feel upset or worried. EG *They kill animals in a way that would disturb the ordinary towndweller... It disturbs me profoundly that you so misuse your talents... There were many things at this time that disturbed our domestic happiness.*
V+O = bother, distress

3 If something **is disturbed**, its shape or position is changed. EG *The dent his body had made in the sand had not been disturbed... There were no currents to disturb the fine sediments on the river bed.*
V+O

4 If something pleasant or peaceful **is disturbed**, it is spoiled or unsettled. EG *His air of dignified calm was seldom disturbed... Nothing disturbed the stillness of the afternoon.*
V+O = disrupt

5 If someone is accused of **disturbing the peace**, they are accused of behaving in a noisy and unpleasant way in public; a legal expression. EG *Residents complained that tramps were littering the beaches and disturbing the peace.*
PHR : VB INFLECTS

disturbance /dɪstɜːbəns/, **disturbances**. 1 **Disturbance** is 1.1 a state in which someone is unhappy and emotionally upset. EG *A replacement may mean misery and emotional disturbance for a child.* 1.2 the act of spoiling or disrupting something which was previously in a calm and well-ordered state. EG *These proposals involved the least disturbance of the existing order.*
N UNCOUNT+SUPP
N UNCOUNT+SUPP ⇑ interruption

2 A **disturbance** is an incident or event in which people behave violently in public. EG *After two weeks of urban violence, the disturbances spread to more than 30 cities.*
N COUNT ⇑ disruption = trouble

disturbed /dɪstɜːbd/. 1 Someone who is **disturbed** is very upset emotionally and needs special care or treatment. EG *He must have been very disturbed to require electric shock therapy... ...emotionally disturbed youngsters.*
ADJ QUALIT ⇑ mad = unbalanced

2 You also say that someone is **disturbed** when they are very worried or anxious as a result of an unpleasant incident. EG *He clearly felt disturbed about the assassination.*
ADJ QUALIT ⇑ upset

3 If you describe something such as a period of time or a relationship as **disturbed**, you mean that it is unsatisfactory, because the people involved are unsettled and unhappy. EG *He was determined not to marry after his own unhappy, disturbed childhood... She had a disturbed relationship with her parents.*
ADJ QUALIT ⇑ unhappy ≠ harmonious

disturbing /dɪstɜːbɪŋ/. Something that is **disturbing** makes you feel worried, upset, or alarmed. EG *She has written two disturbing books.* ◊ **disturbingly**. EG
ADJ QUALIT = worrying
◊ ADV+ADJ/

There is a disturbingly large number of individuals who can't read. ADV

disunite /dɪsjʊnaɪt/, **disunites, disuniting, disunited.** If something **disunites** a group of people who have previously had the same ideas and intentions, it causes disagreement and division among them; a fairly formal word. EG *The success of the campaign was in disuniting the ruling party.* V+O ⇑ divide = split ≠ unite

◇ **disunited.** EG *Disunited governments are not good for the country.* ◇ ADJ QUALIT = split

disunity /dɪsjuːnəˈtiˈ/ is lack of agreement among people which prevents them from working together effectively; a fairly formal word. EG *This could provoke serious disunity in the party... There is considerable disunity within the Churches on this issue.* N UNCOUNT : IF+PREP THEN *in/within/among* ⇑ division = discord

disuse /dɪsjuːs/ is the state of being no longer used. EG *These methods have gradually fallen into disuse in the post-war years... His vocal organs began to deteriorate from disuse.* N UNCOUNT ⇑ neglect ≠ use

disused /dɪsjuːzd/. A **disused** place or building is no longer used for its original purpose and is now empty. EG *It was stored in a disused lorry factory... ...a disused airfield near Lincoln.* ADJ CLASSIF = abandoned ≠ working

ditch /dɪtʃ/, **ditches, ditching, ditched.** 1 A **ditch** is a long narrow channel cut into the ground at the side of a road, field, etc, often containing water. EG *My headlights shone over a broad ditch of water... They were kept busy digging ditches.* N COUNT

2 If you **ditch** someone, you end a relationship with them, for example you stop employing them because you no longer need them, or stop having a sexual relationship with them; an informal use. EG *He would willingly, at this point, have ditched her... I think you're trying to ditch your secretary.* V+O = drop, abandon

3 If you **ditch** something that is no longer of any use to you, you abandon it or get rid of it; an informal use. EG *He had decided to ditch the car.* V+O ⇑ shed = dump

4 See also **last-ditch.**

ditchwater /dɪtʃwɔːtə/. If you say that something or someone is **as dull as ditchwater**, you mean that they are extremely boring; a rather old-fashioned informal expression. PHR : USED AS C ⇑ uninteresting

dither /dɪðə/, **dithers, dithering, dithered.** 1 When someone **dithers**, they hesitate because they are unable to make a quick decision about something. EG *After dithering about helplessly for a bit, he picked up the phone.* V : IF+PREP/ADV THEN *about* = shilly-shally

2 If someone is **in a dither**, or **all of a dither**, they are excited and confused, and cannot decide what to do; an informal expression. EG *He's in a terrible dither, poor soul.* PHR : USED AS AN A

ditto /dɪtəʊ/. 1 **Ditto** is used to represent the word or phrase that you have just used in order to avoid repeating it, for example in a list. In written lists, **ditto** can be represented by the symbol " underneath the word that you want to repeat. EG *...a cupboard door with mirror, a bathroom door ditto.* ⇑ same = do

2 **Ditto** is also used to say that you think the same way about something as someone else; an informal use. EG *'I've had enough of this film.'–'Ditto. Let's go, shall we?'* CONVENTION = likewise

ditty /dɪtiˈ/, **ditties.** A **ditty** is a short and simple song or poem; an old-fashioned word, sometimes used humorously. N COUNT

diurnal /daɪɜːnəᵒl/. **Diurnal** activities happen during the daytime; a formal word. EG *His domestic life had led him to strictly diurnal habits, and by sundown he was always asleep.* ADJ CLASSIF ≠ nocturnal

divan /dɪvæn/, **divans.** 1 A **divan** or **divan bed** is a bed that has a thick base under the mattress. EG *A rumpled divan was the only furniture in the room... She was sitting on a divan with her shoes off.* N COUNT

2 A **divan** is also a long soft seat that has no back or arms and that is meant to be placed next to a wall. N COUNT = sofa

dive /daɪv/, **dives, diving, dived.** American English uses the form **dove** for the past tense. 1 If you **dive**, you 1.1 jump head-first into water with your arms held straight above your head. EG *She dived into the water and swam energetically away.* ▸ used as a noun. EG *She plunged straight into the pool with a graceful dive.* V : IF+PREP THEN *into* ▸ N COUNT 1.2 go under the surface of the water, especially the sea, with special breathing equipment. EG *They go diving off the west coast of Scotland.* V : USU+A

2 When birds and animals **dive**, they go down head-first quickly and steeply through the air or through water. EG *The fin-back whale can dive to a depth of 500 metres... Terns flicker and dive against the hazy sunset.* ▸ used as a noun. EG *The falcon went into a rapid dive, swooping to a kill.* V : USU+A = plummet ▸ N COUNT

3 If you **dive** into something such as a bag, you put your hand or hands into it quickly in order to get something out. EG *He suddenly dived into the chest and produced a silk shirt... The tourists began to dive for their cameras.* V+A

4 If you **dive** in a particular direction, you jump forwards or to one side, for example to get out of the way or to catch something. EG *He dived after the ball as it rolled under the hedge.* ▸ used as a noun. EG *He made a dive for the ball.* V+A ▸ N COUNT+SUPP

5 If you **dive** into a shop, a wood, a crowd of people, etc, you move quickly into it. EG *We dived into the Underground to escape the rain.* V+A ⇑ leap = plunge

6 If you **dive** into an activity, you start doing it enthusiastically and without any preparation. EG *Don't dive headlong into a task which you know you can't complete.* V+A *(into/in)* ⇑ begin = rush

7 A **dive** is a bar or club which is not considered to be respectable; used informally and showing disapproval. EG *We went into a smoky dive for a cheap lunch.* N COUNT : USU MOD+N

8 You say **'Dive in'** as a way of inviting people to start eating a meal you have prepared for them. PHR

9 See also **diving.**

diver /daɪvə/, **divers.** 1 A **diver** is 1.1 a person who works or explores under water or at the bottom of the sea, using special breathing equipment. EG *The police have sent down divers to look for the body.* N COUNT ⇑ swimmer

1.2 a person who takes part in the sport of diving. EG *She was a remarkable diver.* N COUNT

2 See also **divers.**

diverge /daɪvɜːdʒ/, **diverges, diverging, diverged.** 1 If two or more things **diverge**, they become different from one another. EG *...these countries whose history and circumstances widely diverge... This is where our interests diverge.* V ⇑ differ

2 If something **diverges** from the truth, a standard, a theory, etc, it does not conform to it or fit it. EG *We all know women who sharply diverge from this generalization.* V+A *(from)*

3 If two or more roads, paths, etc have been going together in the same direction and then they **diverge**, they move apart and go in different directions. EG *The routes of these two journeys have been diverging.* V : IF+PREP THEN *from* ⇑ separate ≠ converge

divergence /daɪvɜːdʒəns/, **divergences. Divergence** is a difference between two or more things, attitudes, opinions, etc that are usually expected to be similar to each other. EG *There is an inseparable divergence of interest... Perhaps more important were divergences in equipment... There was much greater divergence on how to handle the crisis.* N UNCOUNT/COUNT ≠ convergence

divergent /daɪvɜːdʒənt/. Things that are **divergent** are different from each other. EG *It is a country where there are widely divergent ethnic and religious groups... There will always be divergent views on the right emphasis in this matter.* ADJ QUALIT

divers /daɪvəz/. **Divers** things or groups are of many different kinds or qualities; an old-fashioned or formal word. EG *...tourist offices of divers nationalities... Divers approaches to the problem were attempted.* ADJ CLASSIF : ATTRIB ⇑ many = varying

diverse /daɪvɜːs, daɪvɜːs/. 1 If a group, range, or choice of things is **diverse**, it is made up of a wide variety of things. EG *...the most numerous and diverse group of all animals, the insects... ...a man of diverse talents... She had a genuine love of literature in all its diverse forms.* ADJ QUALIT ⇑ various

2 People, ideas, objects, etc that are **diverse** are very different or separate from each other. EG *...celebrities as diverse as Bob Dylan, Bob Hope, and Ronald Reagan... ...artists from diverse parts of the country.* ADJ QUALIT

diversify /daɪvɜːsəˈfaɪ/, **diversifies, diversifying, diversified.** When someone **diversifies** something or **diversifies**, they increase the variety of something, especially the variety of the products that they make. EG *He was determined to diversify the Post Office's services... Many car manufacturers are diversifying as rapidly as they can.* V OR V+O = branch out ≠ specialize

◇ **diversification** /daɪvɜːsəˈfɪkeɪʃəᵒn/. EG *We want to encourage the diversification of rural employment.* ◇ N UNCOUNT

diversion /daɪvɜːʃəᵒn/, **diversions.** 1 A **diversion** is 1.1 an action or event that attracts your attention away from what you are doing or concentrating on. N COUNT = distraction

EG *A diversion was caused when Mrs Kaul's chauffeur came back with the flowers... Billy created a most welcome diversion by bringing in a shrew.* **1.2** a special route arranged for traffic to follow when the normal route cannot be used. EG *You can't go on, there's a diversion.* [N COUNT = detour] **1.3** an activity that you do for pleasure; an old-fashioned use. EG *Hunting was one of Dad's favourite diversions... ...meaningless activities and empty diversions.* [N COUNT = amusement]

2 Diversion or a **diversion** is the changing of the direction that something is following or the changing of the purpose that it is intended to have. EG *Inflation and diversion of investment were having a bad effect... Possible diversions of the troop convoys were considered.* [N COUNT ⇑ change]

diversionary /daɪvɜːʃənəri'/. **Diversionary** activity is intended to attract someone's attention away from something else which you do not want them to think about or know about. EG *His speech was widely viewed as a diversionary tactic to disguise the real situation... This was clearly a diversionary proposal.* [ADJ CLASSIF: ATTRIB ⇑ distracting]

diversity /daɪvɜːsə'ti'/, **diversities**. **Diversity** is **1** a range of difference of condition, quality, or type. EG *The balance and diversity of nature is threatened... The U.S.A. is a country of enormous size and diversity... His writing displays the diversities of human character and capacity... The banking industry will benefit from a new diversity of financial services.* [N UNCOUNT/COUNT ⇑ variety] **2** the state or quality of being different or varied. EG *We should work toward even greater diversity.* [N UNCOUNT ⇑ variation]

divert /daɪvɜːt/, **diverts, diverting, diverted**.
1 If you **divert** something, **1.1** you cause it to be used for a different purpose or activity. EG *We feel it desirable to divert funds from armaments to health and education... If you don't use it, you can divert the money into savings.* [V+O+A] **1.2** you change the course or direction that it is following. EG *We got held up with all the firemen and police diverting the traffic... Reinforcements can be diverted from Europe to other areas.* [V+O: USU+A = re-route]

2 If something or someone **diverts** you, they entertain or amuse you; an old-fashioned use. EG *In Europe you may be diverted to discover some old favourite TV serials... For some time he diverted himself by identifying the other sounds he could hear.* [V+O (NG/REFL)]

divest /daɪvest/, **divests, divesting, divested**; a formal word. **1** If you **divest** yourself of a belief, you stop believing it. EG *They will have to divest themselves of the notion that they have that power.* [V+O (REFL)+A (of) = rid]

2 If you **divest** yourself of something that you are carrying or wearing, you take it off or put it down. EG *She divested herself of her bag.* [V+O (REFL)+A (OF) = relieve]

3 If you **divest** someone or something of a role, function, or quality, you take it away from them. EG *...divesting public housing of its welfare role... Here, the pursuit of strangers is divested of romance.* [V+O+A (of) ⇑ strip]

divide /di'vaɪd/, **divides, dividing, divided**. **1** When something **divides** or **is divided**, it becomes separated into two or more distinct or smaller parts. EG *...an attempt to divide the country into two social classes... At this stage of development the cells begin to divide rapidly.* [V-ERG ⇑ separate = split ≠ join] • If something **is divided in** or **into** sections or parts, it has been separated so that it now consists of two or more sections or parts. EG *The houses in Florence St are almost all divided into flats... The exam is divided in two parts... Economically, the world is divided into two main groups.* [• PHR: VB INFLECTS]

2 If you **divide** something among people or groups, you separate it into a number of parts or portions and distribute these parts or portions to the people or groups. EG *He divided the rest of his property among his brothers and sisters.* [V+O: IF+PREP THEN among/between = share out]

3 If something **divides** two areas or **divides** an area into two, it forms a barrier or boundary which keeps the two areas separate from each other. EG *A line of rocks seemed to divide the cave into two.* [V+O: USU+A]

4 If people **divide** over something or if something **divides** people, it causes strong disagreement between them. EG *This question is dividing the people of Wales... Americans are dividing into two camps over this issue... Beliefs run very deep and religion can either unite or divide.* [V-ERG ≠ unify, unite] • You use **divide and rule** to refer to a policy or technique which is intended to keep someone or an organization in a position of power by causing disagreements within a group of people who might otherwise unite against the person or organization. EG *...the well-proven policy of 'divide and rule'.* [• PHR]

5 If you **divide** a larger number by a smaller number or **divide** a smaller number into a larger number, you calculate how many times the smaller number can fit exactly into the larger number. EG *Divide 35 by 7... Divide 7 into 35... 35 divided by 7 is 5... This total is then divided by 52 to arrive at your weekly payment.* [V+O: IF+PREP THEN into/by, OR V+A (by/into)]

6 A **divide** is **6.1** a significant distinction between two groups, which causes the two groups to be considered as very different and separate. EG *The divide between rich and poor was great.* [N COUNT: USU SING = gulf, rift] **6.2** a moment in time or a point in a process when there is a complete change from one situation to another. EG *The invention of the wheel was the second great divide in human history.* [N COUNT: USU SING = watershed] **6.3** a line of high ground between areas that are drained by different rivers; used in American English. EG *They camped on a windswept Kansas divide.* [N COUNT ⇑ ridge = watershed]

divide off. If something **divides** two things **off**, it forms a barrier that keeps them completely separate. EG *Huge iron gates divide off the east end of the church.* [PHRASAL VB: V+O+ADV]

divide up. If you **divide** something **up**, you **1** separate it into completely separate groups or parts. EG *Film divides motion up into a series of static images.* [PHRASAL VB: V+O+ADV, IF+PREP THEN into = break up] **2** share it out among a number of people or groups in approximately equal parts. EG *The proceeds had to be divided up among about four hundred people.* [PHRASAL VB: V+O+ADV = share out]

divided /di'vaɪdɪd/. **1** If something is **divided**, it contains or involves two or more opposing ideas, opinions, etc. EG *My mind is divided... Public opinion was divided... Many children suffer from divided loyalties when their parents are divorced.* [ADJ CLASSIF = split]

2 If a group of people is **divided**, they strongly disagree about something. EG *The conference was divided on many issues.* [ADJ CLASSIF: IF+PREP THEN on/over]

dividend /dɪvɪdənd/, **dividends**. **1** A **dividend** is **1.1** an amount of money that represents part of a company's profits, which it pays to people who have shares. EG *In 1977 the company paid a dividend of 15p a share.* [N COUNT] **1.2** an extra benefit that you did not expect to get. EG *The welfare state was regarded as a kind of dividend from economic growth.* [N COUNT ⇑ advantage = bonus]

2 If something **pays dividends**, it brings advantages at a later date. EG *It may pay dividends later... The time she had spent learning German now paid dividends.* [PHR: VB INFLECTS = pay off]

divider /di'vaɪdə/, **dividers**. **1** A **divider** is something which forms a barrier between two areas of space or two groups of people. EG *Open shelving makes a most attractive room divider... The two-tier education system is a great social divider.* [N COUNT: USU+SUPP]

2 Dividers are an instrument used for measuring lines and for marking points along them. Dividers consist of two pointed arms joined at one end and look rather like a pair of compasses. EG *...a pair of dividers... ...navigational dividers.* [N PLURAL: ALSO a pair of+N]

dividing line, dividing lines. A **dividing line** is a distinction or set of distinctions which marks the difference between two types or groups and keeps them separate. EG *The dividing line between wants and needs is a hard one to define.* [N COUNT: IF+PREP THEN between]

divination /dɪvɪneɪʃən/ is the art or practice of determining what will happen in the future. EG *...some sort of gift of second sight or divination.* [N UNCOUNT ⇑ foretelling]

divine /di'vaɪn/, **divines, divining, divined**. **1** Something that is **divine** has the qualities of a god or goddess or results from the actions of a god or goddess. EG *At this moment he feels painfully vulnerable to divine retribution... ...the notion that he is created in the Divine Image... These men had all been operating under divine inspiration.* [ADJ CLASSIF ⇑ holy ≠ human] ◇ **divinely**. EG *...a divinely appointed prophet.* [◇ ADV]

2 A **divine** is a priest who specializes in the study of theology. [N COUNT]

3 If you **divine** something that you did not know before, you discover or learn it by guessing, because you have no evidence; a fairly literary word. EG *No watcher could have divined that the quiet English tourist was really an assassin... She had divined something about me.* [V+O/REPORT-CL = guess]

4 You describe something as **divine** when you like or enjoy it very much; an old-fashioned informal use. EG [ADJ QUALIT = heavenly]

Isn't it divine in the sun? ◊ **divinely**. EG *We were fantastically and divinely alone.* ◊ ADV

diving /daɪvɪŋ/. **Diving** is 1 the activity of working or exploring underwater or at the bottom of the sea, using special breathing equipment. 2 the sport or activity in which you jump into water head-first with your arms held straight above your head. EG *I was never any good at diving.*
N UNCOUNT — N UNCOUNT ⇑ jumping

diving board, diving boards. A **diving board** is a board high above a swimming pool or other area of water from which people can dive into the water.
N COUNT

divinity /dɪvɪnɪti¹/, **divinities**. 1 **Divinity** is 1.1 the study of religion. EG *...a Bachelor of Divinity... My daughter is studying divinity.* 1.2 the quality of being divine. EG *The divinity of the Pharoah was not doubted in ancient times.*
N UNCOUNT = theology — N UNCOUNT ⇑ holiness

2 A **divinity** is a god or goddess. EG *...pagan divinities... Perhaps, after all, they have found a divinity to worship.*
N COUNT

divisible /dɪvɪzə¹bə⁰l/. 1 A number that is **divisible** can be divided by another number. EG *Each of these numbers is divisible by two.*
ADJ CLASSIF : PRED, IF + PREP THEN *by*

2 Something that is **divisible** can be separated into two distinct parts or subjects. EG *When the atom was found to be divisible it seemed that it might have an indivisible core.*
ADJ CLASSIF : PRED : IF + PREP THEN *into/from*

division /dɪvɪʒə⁰n/, **divisions**. 1 **Division** is 1.1 the act of separating a large unit into two or more distinct parts, especially parts which are noticeably different from each other. EG *...the division of physical science into chemistry and physics... This division of the world into developed and undeveloped nations is a gross simplification... ...the division of hours into minutes.* 1.2 the separation of something into parts which are distributed among two or more people or things. EG *There were bitter battles after his death over the division of his money.* 1.3 the process of doing arithmetic calculations by dividing one number into another number. EG *A child who can't do division shouldn't be in this class.* ● See also **long division**.
N UNCOUNT : IF + PREP THEN *into* ⇑ separation = split — N UNCOUNT = distribution — N UNCOUNT ≠ multiplication

2 A **division** is 2.1 a difference that exists between two groups or ideas which appear to be opposed to each other. EG *There's a considerable division between left and right in the British Labour Party... In fact, there is a division of opinion among the leaders of the movement... Class divisions become evident very early in a child's life.* 2.2 a group of departments in a large organization whose work is done in the same geographical area or is connected with similar tasks. EG *He is now a senior vice president in the international division of the bank... ...the BBC's engineering division... The Metropolitan Police Thames Division has its headquarters here.* 2.3 a group of military units which fight as a single unit. EG *Two tank divisions led the attack.* 2.4 a smaller area or unit that is formed within a large one. EG *She has a special camera bag, with divisions for each different lens.* 2.5 a vote in the British Parliament where the members of parliament go into separate rooms to record their vote. EG *The house passed it without division, after a generally harmonious debate.* 2.6 one of the groups of teams which make up a football league or other sports league. In each division the teams are considered to be approximately the same standard and they all play against each other during the season. EG *United used to be always top of the First Division.*
N COUNT : IF + PREP THEN *of/between/among* = split — N COUNT : USU MOD + N ⇑ department — N COUNT : USU MOD + N — N COUNT ⇑ section — N COUNT/UNCOUNT — N COUNT : USU MOD + N

divisional /dɪvɪʒə⁰nəl, -ʒənə⁰l/. **Divisional** is used to describe a division in a large organization or in an army. EG *Captain Pomfret was summoned to divisional headquarters... ...the divisional education office in Caxley.*
ADJ CLASSIF : ATTRIB ⇑ departmental

division of labour. A **division of labour** is a way of organizing a society or a household so that each member has a particular task to do and therefore contributes to the running of the society or household.
N UNCOUNT/COUNT ⇑ system

division sign, division signs. A **division sign** is the symbol ÷ used between two numbers to show that the first number has to be divided by the second.
N COUNT

divisive /di¹vaɪsɪv/. Something that is **divisive** has the effect of dividing people into two or more groups and of causing hostility between them. EG *The two-tier school system was seen as divisive by many people.*
ADJ QUALIT ≠ unifying

divorce /dɪvɔːs/, **divorces, divorcing, divorced**. 1 A **divorce** is a formal ending of a marriage by law. EG *Though she obtained a civil divorce, she's still married in the eyes of the church... Mrs Flanagan had been called as a witness in the divorce case... ...a regime under which divorce is prohibited.*
N COUNT/UNCOUNT ⇑ separation

2 If one person **divorces** another or if two people **divorce**, they separate from each other and their marriage is legally ended. EG *If she wants to divorce him, she has my sympathy... When my parents divorced, I went to live with my uncle.* ◊ **divorced**. EG *The head of the household was a divorced lady with two children... What can you expect of a divorced man?*
V, OR V + O — ◊ ADJ CLASSIF ⇑ separated

3 **Divorce** is a separation between two things which is, or is likely to be, permanent. EG *...the divorce between the ideal and the real... This divorce of art from technology is completely unnecessary... The divorce between power and morality is total.*
N UNCOUNT : IF + PREP THEN *between/of*

4 If you **divorce** something from something else, you cause the two things to be considered as very different and separate from each other. EG *I don't think it is possible to divorce sport from politics.* ◊ **divorced**. EG *Research still remained divorced from construction... The condition of the roads could not be divorced from other aspects of transport.*
V + O : USU PAST PART, IF + PREP THEN *from* = dissociate — ◊ ADJ CLASSIF : PRED, IF + PREP THEN *from*

divorcee /di¹vɔːsiː/, **divorcees**. A **divorcee** is a person, especially a woman, who is divorced.
N COUNT

divot /dɪvət/, **divots**. A **divot** is a small piece of grass and earth which is dug out accidentally, for example by a golf club.
N COUNT ⇑ turf

divulge /daɪvʌldʒ/, **divulges, divulging, divulged**. If you **divulge** a piece of information or **divulge** that it is true, you tell someone about it so that it is no longer a secret. EG *I shall divulge the details to no one... The woman divulged that her name was Mrs Musprat.*
V + O/REPORT-CL ⇑ disclose = reveal ≠ withhold

Diwali /dɪwɑli¹/ is a Hindu festival of light that is celebrated in the autumn.
N UNCOUNT

D.I.Y. is the activity of making or repairing things yourself, instead of buying things ready-made or paying a workman to do the work for you; an abbreviation for 'do-it-yourself'. EG *D.I.Y. experts... She was doing some DIY over the weekend.*
N UNCOUNT

dizzy /dɪzi¹/, **dizzier, dizziest; dizzies, dizzying, dizzied**. 1 If you feel **dizzy**, you feel 1.1 that you are losing your balance and are about to fall. EG *She started to feel dizzy and had to lie down... She was having dizzy spells.* ◊ **dizziness**. EG *She was overcome by nausea and dizziness.* ◊ **dizzily**. EG *The pain smashed him dizzily to the floor.* 1.2 slightly confused and unable to think clearly. EG *She was sick and dizzy with grief... They emerged from the lecture, dizzy with facts.*
ADJ QUALIT ⇑ unsteady = giddy — ◊ N UNCOUNT — ◊ ADV WITH VB — ADJ QUALIT : PRED + *with* = light-headed

2 If something **dizzies** you, it causes you to feel unsteady or confused. EG *They had been dizzied by the pace of technological change.*
V + O

3 You can use **dizzy** with words like 'height' and 'peak' to emphasize that the level of something is very high indeed. EG *Sugar rose from 8 cents a pound in 1970 to a dizzy peak of 47 cents... ...the dizzy heights of joyous success.*
ADJ QUALIT : ATTRIB = giddy

D.J., D.J.s. **D.J.** is an abbreviation for 'disc jockey' and 'dinner jacket'.

djinn /dʒɪn/, **djinns**. A **djinn** is the same as a genie.
N COUNT

DNA is an acid in the chromosomes in the centre of the cells of living things. DNA determines the particular structure and functions of every cell and is responsible for characteristics being passed on from parents to their children.
N UNCOUNT

do /duː/, **does, doing, did, done; dos**. **Do** functions as both a main verb and as an auxiliary verb. The meanings of 'do' as an auxiliary are given in paragraph 1. For further information about 'do' as an auxiliary, see ☐ at the end of the entry. The meanings of 'do' as a main verb are given in paragraphs 2 to 20. The meaning of 'do' as a noun are given in paragraphs 21 and 22. 1 **Do** is used as an auxiliary in the following ways. 1.1 to form the negative of main verbs, by putting 'not' or 'n't' after the auxiliary and before the main verb in its infinitive form. EG *She did not appear to be listening... It doesn't matter... You don't have to go.* 1.2 to form questions, by putting the subject after the auxiliary and before the main verb in its infinitive form. EG *Did he go to the fair... What did he say?... Do the British*
AUX : SEE ☐ BELOW — AUX : SEE ☐ BELOW

take sport seriously? **1.3** to give emphasis to the main verb when there is no other auxiliary. EG *People do in fact make mistakes... It does seem a bit cold in here... I did have a map somewhere but I must have lost it.* **1.4** as a polite or formal way of inviting someone to do something. EG *Do sit down... Do have some more tea...' Do help yourself to anything you want.* **1.5** as a way of trying to persuade someone to do something. EG *Do write to me when you get to Kuala Lumpur... Do take care when you cross the main road.* **1.6** with a negative to tell someone not to behave in a certain way. EG *Don't you play the wise old professor with me!... Oh don't you start!* AUX : SEE □ BELOW; AUX : ONLY IMPER, SEE □ BELOW; AUX : ONLY IMPER, SEE □ BELOW; AUX + *not* : ONLY IMPER, SEE □ BELOW

2 If someone or something **does** a particular activity, they perform it and finish it. EG *We did quite a lot of work yesterday... We are expected to do a lot of reading... I did all the usual things to raise money... I had never done anything which required manual dexterity... All we have to know is what the device does, not how it does it... Every decade there is a census which is done in detail.* V+O

3 You use **do** with some nouns when you are talking about performing an activity or task, usually a common one. For example, 'do your teeth' means 'brush your teeth', 'do the flowers' means 'arrange the flowers'. EG *Who's going to do the washing up?... I do the cooking and Brian does the cleaning... Have you done your homework yet?* V+O

4 You can use **do** in a clause at the beginning of a sentence to give special emphasis to the information that comes at the end of the sentence. EG *All they do is discuss the past... I think what he's done is to accept his own limitations... The least I can do is to hide the chocolates.* V+O

5 If you **do** a lot, a little, etc with something, you make use of it in the way indicated. EG *He did as much with the material as he could... You can do whatever you like with it.* V+O+A *(with)*

6 If you **are doing** something, you are busy or active in some way, or have planned an activity for some time in the future. EG *What are you doing tonight?... He just sits there all day doing nothing.* V+O

7 If you **do** something about a problem, you take action to try to solve it. EG *They promised that they were going to do something about immigration... There's nothing I can do about it... We're doing all we can... She was desperately ill and very little could be done for her.* V+O : IF+PREP THEN *about*

8 If an action or event **does** a particular thing, it has that result or effect. EG *Their policies have done more harm for the working class than ours... They are afraid of what it might do to the children.* V+O ⇑ achieve

9 If you talk about how much something **does** for someone, you are talking about how much it changes them, helps them, or suits them. EG *I think home life does a lot for you... I asked Salman Rushdie what winning would do for his career as a novelist... That hat does nothing for you.* V+A *(for)* ⇑ improve

10 If you ask someone what they **do**, you want to know what their job or profession is. EG *What do you want to do when you leave school?... I wonder what his father does.* V+O : *what*+S+VB

11 If you say that someone or something **does** well or badly, you are talking about how successful or unsuccessful they are. EG *I didn't do very well in my exams... It all depends how the Labour Party do at this next election... Well done, Andrew... I think on the whole we don't do too badly.* V+A (ADV) ⇑ achieve

12 If a person or organization **does** a particular service, they provide that service. EG *Do you do ferry bookings to Ireland?... We can do travellers cheques.* V+O ⇑ offer

13 If you **do** a museum, city, country, etc, you visit it as a tourist. EG *Americans do London in an afternoon.* V+O

14 If you **do** a subject, you study it at school or college. EG *We haven't done any Shakespeare yet.* V+O

15 If you **do** a particular person or role, you mimic that person or act that role. EG *She does a marvellous elderly aunt.* V+O

16 If you threaten to **do** someone, you are threatening to hit them or hurt them badly; used in very informal English. EG *I'll do you if you don't stop that.* V+O

17 If you say that someone or something **does** a particular speed, amount, or rate, you mean that they are able to achieve it. EG *He can do 120 miles per hour in that car.* V+NUM

18 If you say that something will **do** or will **do** you, you mean that it is sufficient in quantity or quality to meet your requirements or to satisfy you. EG *This pen will do... Two thousand pounds will do me very well.* V OR V+O : *will/would*+VB ⇑ suffice

• If you say that something **will not do** or **will never do** you mean that it is not suitable or satisfactory. EG *That will never do... That kind of answer would hardly have done.* • PHR : VB INFLECTS ⇑ unacceptable

19 If you say **that will do** to a child, you are telling them to stop behaving in the way that they are. EG *That will do, Jonathan.* CONVENTION

20 The word **do** is also used in the following expressions. **20.1** If you **do** your **best** to achieve something, you try as hard as you can to achieve it. EG *We do our best to make sure it's up to date information.* **20.2** If you ask someone **what** they **did with** something, you are asking them where they put it, what they spent it on, etc. EG *What did you do with the keys?... What did you do with that £10 I gave you?* **20.3** If you say that something is **the thing to do** or **the best thing to do,** you mean that it would be a very good idea to do it. EG *The best thing to do is come in tomorrow morning.* **20.4** If you ask **what** someone or something **is doing** in a particular place, you are asking why they are there and expressing surprise that they are there. EG *What are you doing here, Francis?... What is a telephone doing in a Victorian Conservatory in this film?* **20.5** If you talk about what you **can do for** someone, you are talking about how you can help them. EG *Now, what can I do for you?... Send him down and we'll see what we can do.* **20.6** If you ask **how** someone **is doing**, you are asking if their life is going well and if they are healthy and happy. EG *How are you doing? She always wants to know how you've been doing, always talking about you.* **20.7** **How do you do** is used as a formal way of greeting someone when you meet them. When one person says 'how do you do', the other person also answers 'how do you do'. **20.8** If someone is **badly done by**, they are treated in an unfair way. EG *James felt he had been badly done by.* **20.9** If you say that someone **would do well** to do something, you mean that they ought to do that thing. EG *She would do well to steer clear of men.* **20.10** If you say that one thing **has to do with** or **is to do with** another thing, you mean that the two things are connected or that the first thing is about the second thing. EG *This book has to do with married life... He's something to do with the Foreign Office... This main basic argument has got nothing to do with agriculture... Mind your own business–it's got nothing to do with you... It's got something to do with an economic crisis.* **20.11** If you say that you **could do with** something, you mean that you need it or would benefit from it. EG *I think we could all do with a good night's sleep... The staff could probably do with some more money.* **20.12** If you feel **done in**, you feel completely exhausted; used in informal English. **20.13** **easier said than done**: see **easy.** • **to make do**: see **make.** • **no sooner said than done**: see **soon.** PHR : VB INFLECTS; PHR : VB INFLECTS; PHR : USED AS C/S/O; PHR : AUX INFLECTS, USU+A; PHR; PHR : AUX INFLECTS; CONVENTION; PHR : USED AS C; PHR+*to*-INF; PHR : AUX INFLECTS; PHR ⇑ want; PHR : USED AS C ⇑ tired = dead beat

21 A **do** is a party, dinner party, or other social event; a fairly informal use. EG *We're going to a formal do tonight.* N COUNT

22 The **dos and don'ts** are the things which you must and must not do in a particular situation. EG *There are plenty of dos and don'ts in this contract.* PHR : USED AS C/O/S ⇑ rules

do away with. To **do away with** something means to get rid of it. EG *Our medicines have not done away with disease... It would be nice to do away with all the paperwork that is usually involved.* PHRASAL VB : V+ADV+PREP ⇑ finish

do down. If you **do** someone **down**, you make other people think that that person is unpleasant or unsuccessful by criticizing them; an informal expression. EG *He'll do you down if he can... Don't do yourself down.* PHRASAL VB : V+O+ADV ⇑ discredit

do for. If something **does for** you or you **are done for**, it has a very serious and harmful effect on your life; an informal expression. EG *If I can't finish this report I'm done for.* PHRASAL VB : V+PREP, HAS PASS ⇑ ruin

do in. To **do** someone **in** means to kill them; an informal expression. EG *They might do you in while you're sleeping.* PHRASAL VB : ORDER V+O+ADV = murder

do out. 1 If you **do out** a cupboard or other place, you clean it and tidy it; an informal expression. EG *I must do out these cupboards tomorrow.* PHRASAL VB : V+O+ADV

2 If you **do out** a room or building, you make it look nice, for example by decorating it; an informal expression. EG *The bedroom was done out in pale blue.* PHRASAL VB : V+O+ADV ⇑ decorate

do out of. If you **do** someone **out of** something, you unfairly cause them not to have or get something that they were expecting to have; an informal expression. EG *He did me out of £500.* — PHRASAL VB : V+O+ADV+PREP ⇑ deprive

do over. 1 If you **do** something **over**, you perform a task again from the beginning; used mainly in informal American English. EG *That essay was no good, I'll have to do it over.* — PHRASAL VB : V+O+ADV ⇑ repeat

2 If you **do over** a house, you redecorate it and change its furnishings; used mainly in informal American English. EG *Mrs Kennedy did over the White House.* — PHRASAL VB : V+O+ADV

3 If someone **does** a place **over**, they rob it; an informal expression — PHRASAL VB : V+O+ADV

4 If you **do** someone **over**, you hurt them badly, for example by hitting or kicking them; an informal expression. EG *I'm going to get someone to do him over.* — PHRASAL VB : ORDER V+O+ADV = beat up

do up. 1 If you **do** something **up**, you fasten it. EG *I can't do my top button up... He did his shoelaces up.* — PHRASAL VB : V+O+ADV

2 If a woman **does** her hair **up**, she arranges it so that it is tied or fastened close to her head rather than hanging loosely. EG *Judy's hair, which she did up in a plain bun, was grey.* — PHRASAL VB : V+O+ADV = put up

3 If you **do up** an old building, you decorate and repair it so that it is in a better condition and looks more modern. EG *The theatre was horrible, done up as cheaply as possible.* — PHRASAL VB : V+O+ADV ⇑ renovate

4 If something is **done up**, it is covered in material or paper, like a parcel. EG *I gave her a box, nicely done up in flowered paper.* — PHRASAL VB : V+O+ADV, USU PASS

do without. If you **do without** something, you manage or survive in spite of not having it. EG *Many Victorian households did without a bathroom altogether... If you don't have cigarettes, you must simply do without.* — PHRASAL VB : V+PREP, HAS PASS

> **DO** □ **Do** can be used both as a main verb and as an auxiliary. The meanings of the auxiliary, described as AUX in the grammar notes, are given in paragraph 1 of the entry for **do**. **Do** used as an auxiliary behaves in the following ways: **1** It is followed by a verb in the infinitive without *to*. Examples are *I **do** agree with him... They **did** get a bit worried about me.* **2** It inflects and has the forms: *do, does,* and *did.* **3** *Do, does,* and *did* are used before the subject in questions, as in *Where **did** they go?...**Does** she still want to come?* **4** *Do, does,* and *did* are used before the negative *not*, as in *We **did** not remember the way.* The word *not* has a shortened form *n't* which can be added to *do, does* and *did*, as in *I **don't** like her... She **didn't** have much money.* **5** It can be used to stand for, and refer back to, a previous verbal group, as in *She meets lots more people than I **do**... I like cooking and so **does** John.* **6** It is used in question tags, as in *She made a lot of mistakes, **didn't** she... Buses start at 4 o'clock in Birmingham, **don't** they?... You don't know her, **do** you?* **7** It is not used with another auxiliary or a modal in a verbal group.

do. is a written abbreviation for 'ditto', used in lists, accounts, etc.

d.o.b. is a written abbreviation for 'date of birth', used especially on official forms.

doc /dɒk/, **docs**. You can refer to a doctor as **doc**; an informal word. EG *Have you been to see the doc?* — N COUNT/VOC : ALSO IN TITLES

docile /dəʊsaɪl/. A person or animal that is **docile** is quiet, not aggressive, and easily controlled. EG *The prisoners were grateful and docile.* ◊ **docilely**. EG *He made the beast turn aside and trot docilely away.* ◊ **docility** /də'sɪlɪ'ti'/. EG *I am always surprised at the docility our pupils show when punished.* — ADJ QUALIT ⇑ submissive; ◊ ADV WITH VB; ◊ N UNCOUNT

dock /dɒk/, **docks, docking, docked**. 1 A **dock** is 1.1 an enclosed area in a harbour where ships go to be loaded, unloaded and repaired. EG *The ship entered the dock to a fanfare of trumpets.* — N COUNT. 1.2 a row of docks, with all the sheds, offices and other buildings which are needed to repair, load and unload ships. EG *He went to the London Docks and spent two days trying to get a job... During the war women worked on the farms, on the docks and in the factories... Much of the vast dock area in Glasgow has been closed.* — N COUNT : USU PL = dockyard, shipyard

2 If a ship is **in dock**, it is waiting to be repaired in a dock. EG *The Queen Elizabeth II was in dock for major repairs.* — PHR : USED AS AN A

3 If a ship **docks** or if you **dock** a ship, you bring it into a dock at the end of a voyage. EG *It was raining the morning they docked at Southampton... I sailed slowly because I didn't want to dock my boat in the dark.* — V OR V-ERG : USU +A

4 If two spacecraft **dock** or if you **dock** them, they join together in space. — V-ERG

5 The **dock** is the place in a law court where the person accused of a crime stands or sits. EG *He explained from the dock why he thought his parents should die... He thought about the other people who should have been in the dock at his side.* — N SING : *the*+N

6 If you **dock** someone's wages or money, you take some of the money away or reduce the amount of money that you give them. EG *His wages were docked to pay for the equipment he had broken... She lent her daughter 5 pounds and then docked her pocket money until the debt was paid off.* — V+O

7 If a vet **docks** the tail of an animal, most of the tail is cut off. — V+O ⇑ remove

8 A **dock** is also a plant with big leaves which grows wild by the roadside in Britain and some other northern countries. — N COUNT/UNCOUNT

docker /dɒkə/, **dockers**. A **docker** is a person who works in the docks, loading and unloading ships. EG *He drew attention to the rising unemployment among dockers.* — N COUNT ⇑ worker

docket /dɒkɪt/, **dockets, docketing, docketed**; used mainly in British English. 1 A **docket** is a certificate or ticket which shows the contents of a parcel, cargo or something else that has to be delivered. It also proves who the parcel, cargo, etc belongs to. EG *He stuffed the docket for the second case into his back pocket.* — N COUNT

2 If someone **dockets** a parcel, cargo, etc, they attach a docket to it. EG *They had been examined, categorized, docketed.* — V+O ⇑ label

dockland /dɒklænd/, **docklands**. The **dockland** of a town or city is the area around the docks. EG *He lived and worked in the Liverpool dockland.* — N COUNT/UNCOUNT

dock worker, **dock workers**; also spelled as one word. A **dock worker** is a person who works in the docks, loading and unloading ships. — N COUNT = docker

dockyard /dɒkjɑːd/, **dockyards**. A **dockyard** is a place where ships are built, maintained, and repaired. — N COUNT = dock, shipyard

doctor /dɒktə/, **doctors, doctoring, doctored**. 1 A **doctor** is 1.1 someone who is qualified in medicine and treats people who are ill. EG *She felt so ill we had to call the doctor... I went to see Doctor Barker this morning.* — N COUNT/VOC : ALSO IN TITLES ▸ The **doctor's** is used to refer to the surgery or clinic where a doctor works. — ▸ N SING : *the*+N. 1.2 someone who has been awarded the highest academic or honorary degree by a university. EG *He is a doctor of philosophy.* — N COUNT : ALSO IN TITLES ⇑ scholar

2 If someone **doctors** something, they change it in order to deceive people or to make it more suitable. EG *I'm sure he's doctored the figures... We all realized the play needed a certain amount of doctoring.* — V+O

3 If someone **doctors** food or drink, they add a poison or drug to it. — V+O

4 To **doctor** an animal, especially a dog or cat, means to castrate or sterilize it. — V+O : USU PASS ⇑ neuter

doctoral /dɒktə°rəl/. A **doctoral** thesis or piece of research is written or done in order to obtain a doctor's degree. EG *...a doctoral dissertation.* — ADJ CLASSIF : ATTRIB

doctorate /dɒktə°rə't/, **doctorates**. A **doctorate** is a doctor's degree. EG *...Dr Edwards, a painter with a doctorate in art, psychology and education.* — N COUNT

doctrinaire /dɒktrɪnɛə/, **doctrinaires**. A person or attitude that is **doctrinaire** insists on particular principles or theories without allowing arguments against them and without considering any practical problems; a formal word, used showing disapproval. EG *Their attitudes were condemned as doctrinaire.* — ADJ QUALIT ⇑ dogmatic ≠ broad minded

doctrinal /dɒktraɪnə°l/. **Doctrinal** is used to describe something that is related to doctrines; a formal word. EG *The discussions had collapsed under the weight of doctrinal arguments between rival factions.* — ADJ CLASSIF : USU ATTRIB

doctrine /dɒktrɪn/, **doctrines**. A **doctrine** is a principle or belief, or a set of principles or beliefs, which is thought by its supporters to be absolutely true and therefore the only one acceptable. EG *In Britain we have this very well-established doctrine of parliament being sovereign... ...his ignorance of Christian doctrine... Their doctrines led them to believe in their own moral supremacy.* — N COUNT/UNCOUNT

document /dɒkjəmə'nt/, **documents, documenting, documented**. 1 A **document** is one or more pieces of paper with writing on them which provide an official record or official evidence about — N COUNT something. EG *He studied some official documents relating to the nineteenth century... He was issued with travel documents which allowed him to fly back to the United States.*

2 To **document** something means to write about it in a detailed and factual way, or to record this information in another way, for example on film. EG *He won a prize for documenting the horrors of war in different African countries... The films tried to document the development of the railways... These incidents are the first documented cases of shark attacks on bathers in Australia... The life of Byron is remarkably well documented.* V+O : USU PASS ⇑ record = report, chronicle

documentary /dɒkjəᶦmentəᵒriᶦ/, **documentaries**. 1 A **documentary** is a film or radio or television programme which provides factual information about a particular subject. EG *They made a documentary about the life of William Shakespeare... ...documentary films.* N COUNT

2 **Documentary** evidence is based on documents rather than people's opinions. EG *There is plenty of documentary evidence on the Roman Empire.* ADJ CLASSIF : ATTRIB ⇑ written = concrete

documentation /dɒkjəᶦmenteɪʃəᵒn/ consists of documents which are supplied to provide proof or evidence of something. EG *His story was supported by a great deal of documentation.* N UNCOUNT

dodder /dɒdə/, **dodders, doddering, doddered**. To **dodder** means to walk in an unsteady and shaky way, especially because of old age. V : USU+A = totter

doddering /dɒdərɪŋ/. Someone who is **doddering** walks in an unsteady and shaky way, especially because of old age. EG *She was doddering and frail.* ADJ QUALIT = doddery

doddery /dɒdəriᶦ/. Someone who is **doddery** walks in an unsteady and shaky way, especially because of old age. ADJ QUALIT = doddering

doddle /dɒdəᵒl/. A **doddle** is a job, task, exam, etc that you find very easy to do; an informal word. EG *This should be a doddle.* N SING : a+N = cinch

dodge /dɒdʒ/, **dodges, dodging, dodged**. 1 If you **dodge**, you move suddenly out of the way or out of reach in order to avoid being hit, caught, or seen. EG *He was scrambling to his feet, dodging and ducking to escape more blows... He stopped the car and dodged into the post office.* ▸ used as a noun. EG *...with a quick dodge to the right.* V : USU+A ▸ N COUNT : USU +SUPP

2 If you **dodge** something, you 2.1 avoid it by quickly moving aside or out of reach so that it cannot hit or reach you. EG *The Minister had to dodge flying tomatoes.* 2.2 avoid thinking about it or dealing with it. EG *This issue should not be dodged... We cannot dodge this accusation.* V+O, V+A+O, OR V+-ING+O = duck; V+O, OR V+-ING +O = evade

3 If you **dodge** something unpleasant, such as paying taxes, you avoid doing it, especially by deceit. EG *He's been trying to dodge going to school by pretending to be ill.* V+O, OR V+-ING +O = avoid

4 A **dodge** is a cunning and often deceitful trick which someone uses in order to avoid having to do something EG *He had tried all sorts of dodges to avoid being called up.* N COUNT = scheme

dodgem /dɒdʒəᵒm/, **dodgems**; used in British English. A **dodgem** or **dodgem car** is a small electric car with a wide rubber bumper all round that people can ride in at a fairground. The dodgem cars are driven in an enclosed space and people try to steer them so that they avoid each other or so that they crash into each other. EG *Let's go on the dodgems.* N COUNT : USU PL

dodger /dɒdʒə/, **dodgers**. A **dodger** is someone who avoids an obligation or duty, such as paying taxes, by using trickery or deceit. EG *He was accused of being a tax dodger.* N COUNT : USU+ SUPP

dodgy /dɒdʒiᶦ/; an informal word. 1 Someone who is **dodgy** has a character that you suspect is dishonest. EG *There's something dodgy about him.* ADJ QUALIT ⇑ untrustworthy

2 Something that is **dodgy** seems rather risky, dangerous, or unreliable. EG *It's a rather dodgy plan.* ADJ QUALIT ⇑ uncertain

dodo /dəʊdəʊ/, **dodos, dodoes**. The plural can be either **dodos** or **dodoes**. 1 A **dodo** was a very large bird that was unable to fly. Dodos are now extinct. N COUNT

2 If you say that something is **as dead as a dodo**, you are emphasizing that it no longer exists. PHR : USED AS AN C

3 A **dodo** is also someone who is silly or foolish; an informal use. EG *She was made to feel like an inarticulate dodo.* N COUNT ⇑ fool = dope

doe /dəʊ/, **does**. A **doe** is an adult female rabbit, hare, or deer. N COUNT ≠ buck

doer /du:ə/, **doers**. A **doer** is a person who does jobs promptly and efficiently and does not spend much time thinking about them. EG *She is one of the doers of this world.* N COUNT

does /dʌz/ is the third person singular in the present tense of 'do'.

doesn't /dʌzəᵒnt/ is the usual spoken form of 'does not'.

doff /dɒf/, **doffs, doffing, doffed**. If you **doff** your hat or coat, you take it off; an old-fashioned word. V+O ⇑ remove ≠ don

dog /dɒg/, **dogs, dogging, dogged**. 1 A **dog** is 1.1 a very common four-legged animal that is often kept by people as a pet or used to guard or hunt things. There are a lot of different breeds of dog. EG *Their dog started barking at me.* 1.2 a male dog, wolf, fox, or other animal that is related to the dog. 1.3 a man who seems to you to be unpleasant and evil or harmful; an informal use. EG *He let her down, the dirty dog.* 1.4 something that is unsatisfactory or of poor quality; used in informal American English. EG *This car's a dog.* N COUNT; N COUNT; N COUNT : USU ADJ QUALIT+N = rat; N COUNT

2 If you **dog** someone, you follow them very closely and never leave them. EG *He's been dogging me all day.* V+O, OR V+O+A

3 If things such as problems or injuries **dog** you, they are with you all the time. EG *Bad luck had dogged me all year... The tour was dogged by injury and loss of confidence.* V+O ⇑ follow = plague

4 The **dogs** is a sports meeting where dogs, especially greyhounds, race and people bet on which dog will win; used in informal British English. N PLURAL : the+ N

5 The word **dog** is also used in the following expressions. 5.1 To **treat** someone **like a dog** means to treat them very badly. EG *All the prison guards treated us like dogs.* 5.2 **A dog's life** is a very miserable and unpleasant life. EG *It's a dog's life being a football manager.* 5.3 If someone tells you to **let sleeping dogs lie**, they mean that you should not disturb things which seem satisfactory because if you do you will cause trouble. 5.4 If you say **'love me, love my dog'**, you are telling someone that they must accept you as you are, with all your faults. 5.5 If you say **'You can't teach an old dog new tricks'**, you mean that some people, especially old people, are reluctant to try new ways of doing things. 5.6 If you say **'Every dog has its day'**, you mean that everyone has, at some point in their life, a period of time when they are successful or lucky. 5.7 If you say **'give a dog a bad name'**, you mean that once someone has got a bad reputation, that is the way that people always think of them. 5.8 If you say that **dog eats dog** in a particular situation, you mean that each person wants to succeed and is willing to harm others in order to achieve this. 5.9 If someone is dressed up **like a dog's dinner**, they are dressed in a very smart but showy way; used in informal British English. 5.10 If you **put on the dog**, you behave in an unpleasant, grand way that suggests you think that you are much more important or intelligent than anyone else; used in informal American English. 5.11 If you say that something **is going to the dogs**, you mean that it is losing the good qualities that it had. EG *This country is going to the dogs!* 5.12 ● to fight **like cat and dog: see cat.** ● **raining cats and dogs: see rain.** PHR : VB INFLECTS; PHR : USED AS C; PHR : VB INFLECTS; PHR; PHR; PHR; PHR; PHR; PHR : USED AS AN A; PHR : VB INFLECTS = put on airs; PHR : VB INFLECTS ⇑ deteriorate

6 See also **dogged**.

dogcart /dɒgkɑ:t/, **dogcarts**; often spelled with a hyphen. A **dogcart** is a light cart with two wheels pulled by a horse, which people can ride in. N COUNT

dog-collar, dog-collars; also spelled without a hyphen. A **dog-collar** is 1 a white collar that fastens at the back of the neck, worn by priests and ministers of the Christian Church; an informal use. 2 a collar worn by a dog. N COUNT; N COUNT

dog-eared. A book or piece of paper that is **dog-eared** has been used so much that the corners of the pages are turned down or torn. ADJ QUALIT ⇑ old = tatty

dogfight /dɒgfaɪt/, **dogfights**. A **dogfight** is 1 a fight between fighter planes, in which they fly close to one another and manoeuvre very fast. 2 a fight between dogs, especially one that has been organized by human beings for entertainment, although in many countries this is illegal. N COUNT ⇑ battle; N COUNT

dogfish /dɒgfɪʃ/. **Dogfish** is both the singular and the plural form. A **dogfish** is a small shark. There are several kinds of dogfish. N COUNT

dogged /dɒgɪd/ means showing determination to continue with something however difficult it is. EG ADJ CLASSIF : ATTRIB

...*his dogged refusal to admit defeat... ...dogged determination.* ◊ **doggedly**. EG *They persisted doggedly in their campaign against the law.* ◊ **doggedness**.
◊ ADV WITH VB
◊ N UNCOUNT

doggerel /dɒgə^{0}rəl/ is poetry which is silly or funny, often written quickly and not intended to be serious. EG *She wrote some doggerel on the subject in 1883.*
N UNCOUNT

doggie /dɒgi^1/, **doggies**; also spelled **doggy**. **Doggie** is a child's word for a dog.
N COUNT

doggie paddle; also spelled with a hyphen. The **doggie paddle** or **dog paddle** is a swimming stroke in which the arms and legs are moved up and down rapidly, with short strokes under the water; an informal term. The doggie paddle is often used by children who are learning to swim.
N UNCOUNT : USU *the*+N
= dog paddle

doggo /dɒgəʊ/. If you **lie doggo**, you lie still and keep very quiet so that people will not find you; an informal expression. EG *I lay doggo in my tent.*
PHR : VB INFLECTS
⇑ hide

doggone /dɒgɒn/ is an informal American word that is used to emphasize what you are saying. EG *It's a doggone shame.*
ADJ CLASSIF : ATTRIB
= darn

doggy /dɒgi^1/, **doggies**. See **doggie**.
N COUNT

dog-house. If you are **in the dog-house**, you are in disgrace and people are annoyed with you; an informal expression. EG *Poor Nigel is in the dog-house.*
PHR : USED AS AN A

dogleg /dɒglɛg/, **doglegs**. A **dogleg** is a sharp bend, especially one in a road.
N COUNT

dogma /dɒgmə/, **dogmas**. A **dogma** is a belief or a system of beliefs which is accepted as true and which people are expected to accept, without questioning it. EG *He had no time for political or other dogmas... ...Christianity in the early days when there was less dogma.*
N COUNT/UNCOUNT : USU+SUPP

dogmatic /dɒgmætɪk/. Someone who is **dogmatic** is convinced that they are right and gives their personal opinions without looking at the evidence and without considering that other opinions might be justified. EG *He was so dogmatic about it that I almost believed what he was saying... His friends were all intensely dogmatic political theoreticians... She was not impressed by his dogmatic assertions.* ◊ **dogmatically**. EG *'This stone,' he said dogmatically, 'is far older than the rest.'*
ADJ QUALIT
⇑ opinionated
= categorical
◊ ADV WITH VB
= categorically

dogmatism /dɒgmətɪzə^{0}m/ is a strong and confident assertion of opinion, which is made without looking at the evidence and without considering that different opinions might be justified. EG *His education has taught him a distrust of dogmatism.* ◊ **dogmatist**. EG *England inherited the worst dogmas and dogmatists of the women's movement from America.*
N UNCOUNT
◊ N COUNT

dogmatize /dɒgmətaɪz/, **dogmatizes, dogmatizing, dogmatized**; also spelled **dogmatise**. If you **dogmatize** about something, you speak or write in a very dogmatic and arrogant way, as if you feel certain that you are right and other people are wrong; a fairly formal word.
V : IF+PREP THEN *about*
= pontificate

do-gooder, do-gooders. A **do-gooder** is someone who does things which they think will help other people, although others think that they are interfering; used showing disapproval.
N COUNT
⇑ benefactor

dog paddle means the same as doggie paddle.
N UNCOUNT

dogsbody /dɒgzbɒdi^1/, **dogsbodies**. A **dogsbody** is a person who has to do all the unpleasant or boring jobs that nobody else wants to do; an informal British word. EG *He was employed as a general dogsbody on the project.*
N COUNT
⇑ menial

dog-tired. If you are **dog-tired**, you are extremely tired; used in informal English. EG *I was dog-tired that evening.*
ADJ CLASSIF : PRED
= exhausted

doily /dɔɪli^1/, **doilies**. A **doily** is a small, round piece of paper or cloth that has a pattern of tiny holes in it, which you put on a plate under something such as a cake. EG ...*a lace doily.*
N COUNT
⇑ mat

doings /duːɪŋz/. Someone's **doings** are their activities at a particular time. EG *He gave an admiring account of Larry's doings.*
N PLURAL : USU POSS+N

do-it-yourself. See **D.I.Y**. EG *You can get them from good do-it-yourself shops.*
N UNCOUNT

doldrums /dɒldrəmz/. If an activity or situation is **in the doldrums**, it is very quiet and nothing new or exciting is happening. EG *The American market is as much in the doldrums as the British one... By and large, athletics were in the doldrums during the 1960s.*
PHR : USED AS AN A
⇑ inactive
= in a rut

dole /dəʊl/, **doles, doling, doled**. In Britain, the **dole** is money that is given by the government to people who are unemployed. It is given at regular intervals, for example every two weeks. EG *How much is the dole now, 20 quid?... There was no dole for farm labourers.* ● Someone who is **on the dole** is registered as unemployed and receives money regularly from the government. EG *They made him redundant but he wouldn't go on the dole... He's spent the last year on the dole.*
N SING : *the*+N
⇑ welfare
● PHR : USED AS AN A

dole out. If you **dole** something **out**, you give a certain amount of it to each person or animal in a group. EG *The children dole out their sandwich crusts to the ducks.*
PHRASAL VB : V+O+ADV
= dish out

doleful /dəʊlfʊl/. A **doleful** expression, manner, voice, etc is depressing and miserable. EG *'Things are getting desperate,' he said in a doleful monotone.* ▸ used of people. EG ...*his rapid transformation from senator to doleful night-club comic.* ◊ **dolefully**. EG *Hogan nodded dolefully.*
ADJ QUALIT
⇑ unhappy
= mournful
▸ ADJ QUALIT
◊ ADV WITH VB

doll /dɒl/, **dolls, dolling, dolled**. A **doll** is **1** a child's toy which looks like a small person or baby. **2** a girl or young woman, especially one who is pretty; used especially in informal American English. EG *Who's the doll over there?*
N COUNT
N COUNT : ALSO VOC

doll up. If a woman **dolls** herself **up**, she puts on smart or fashionable clothes in order to try and look attractive for a particular occasion; used in informal English. EG *She dolled herself up to meet her new boyfriend.* ◊ **dolled up**. EG *She was all dolled up in the latest fashion.*
PHRASAL VB : V+O (REFL/NG)+ADV
⇑ dress
◊ ADJ QUALIT

dollar /dɒlə/, **dollars**. A **dollar** is a unit of money used in the USA, Canada, and other countries, which is divided into one hundred smaller units called cents. EG *They spent half a million dollars on the campaign... Ethel gave him a dollar bill... The pound fell more than 25 per cent against the dollar.*
N COUNT : USU NUM+N, OR N SING : *the*+N
= buck

dollop /dɒləp/, **dollops**. A **dollop** of soft or sticky food is a small amount of it served in a lump in a casual way. EG ...*stew with beans, topped up with a dollop of mashed potato.*
N PART+N UNCOUNT

doll's house, doll's houses. A **doll's house** is a toy in the form of a small house, which children can use when they are playing with dolls.
N COUNT

dolly /dɒli^1/, **dollies**. **1 Dolly** is a child's word for a doll.
2 A **dolly** or **dolly bird** is a young woman who is considered to be very pretty but not very intelligent; used in informal British English. EG *He was too busy chasing the teenage dollies of Paris.*
N COUNT : ALSO VOC
N COUNT

dolphin /dɒlfɪn/, **dolphins**. A **dolphin** is a mammal which lives in the sea and looks like a large fish with a pointed mouth.
N COUNT

dolt /dəʊlt/, **dolts**. A **dolt** is a stupid person. EG *You would have to be a complete dolt to miss the turn-off.*
N COUNT, ALSO VOC

-dom is added to some adjectives and nouns in order to form other nouns that refer to human states or conditions. EG ...*free→freedom... ...serf→serfdom... ...star→stardom.*
SUFFIX : FORMS N UNCOUNTS

domain /də^{7}meɪn/, **domains**. A **domain** is **1** a particular area of activity or interest. EG *This question comes into the domain of philosophy... The ultimate responsibility in this domain, as in all others, lay with the chairman.* **2** an area over which someone or something has control or influence. EG *His domain extended to New York... The Arctic remains the domain of the polar bear.*
N COUNT+SUPP
= sphere
N COUNT : WITH POSS
= kingdom

dome /dəʊm/, **domes**. A **dome** is **1** a round roof that is built on a flat circular base. EG *The last stone of the dome of St Peter's was put in place in 1590... ...the huge dome of Central Hall.* **2** any object that has a similar shape to a dome, for example a man's bald head. EG *A band of frizzy grey hair encircled his bald dome.*
N COUNT
N COUNT

domed /dəʊmd/. Something that is **domed** is in the shape of a dome. EG ...*a typical example of traditional architecture with its superb domed roofs.*
ADJ CLASSIF
⇑ rounded

domestic /də^{6}mɛstɪk/, **domestics**. **1 Domestic** political activities, events, and situations happen or exist within one particular country. EG ...*half an hour of world and domestic news... ...foreign and domestic policy... The company needs to acquire domestic sources of oil and natural gas.* ◊ **domestically**. EG *Only 9m tonnes of coal will be produced domestically this year.*
ADJ CLASSIF : USU ATTRIB
= home
≠ foreign
◊ ADV

2 Domestic duties and activities are concerned with the running of a home and family. EG *We share our money and the domestic chores... ...a work load that is quite impossible to combine with domestic respon-*
ADJ CLASSIF : ATTRIB
⇑ home
= household

sibilities... ...a scene of cleanliness and domestic efficiency.

3 Domestic items and services are intended to be used in people's homes rather than in factories or offices. EG *...advanced domestic appliances... ...a domestic supply of water... The country depended heavily on coal both for industrial and domestic use.* ADJ CLASSIF: ATTRIB ≠ industrial

4 A **domestic** situation or atmosphere is one which involves a family and their home. EG *Everything sounded very peaceful and domestic... He was not prepared to sacrifice this principle in the interests of domestic harmony.* ADJ CLASSIF: USU ATTRIB

5 Someone who is **domestic** enjoys being at home and running a family. EG *She was never a very domestic sort of person.* ◊ **domestically.** EG *He's not very domestically inclined.* ADJ QUALIT ◊ ADV

6 A **domestic** animal is one that is not wild and is kept on a farm to produce food or in someone's home as a pet. ADJ CLASSIF ⇑ tame

7 A **domestic** or a **domestic help** is a person who is paid to come to help with the work that has to be done in a house such as the cleaning, washing, and ironing. EG *Should the women quit their jobs and become domestics?* N COUNT ⇑ helper = servant

domesticate /də⁶mɛstɪkeɪt/, **domesticates, domesticating, domesticated.** **1** If someone **domesticates** animals or plants that are usually wild, they bring them under control and use them to produce food or as pets. EG *Our ancestors domesticated various plant and animal species.* ◊ **domesticated.** EG *There were no domesticated animals for ploughing... Cats and ferrets became fully domesticated species.* ◊ **domestication.** EG *The domestication of the horse was a significant factor.* V+O ⇑ tame ◊ ADJ CLASSIF: USU ATTRIB ◊ N UNCOUNT

2 If you **domesticate** someone, you get them used to helping with the tasks that need to be done around the house, such as cooking, washing, and sewing. EG *All my attempts to domesticate Chris came to nothing.* ◊ **domesticated.** EG *He thinks that it is unmanly to be domesticated.* V+O ⇑ train ◊ ADJ QUALIT

domesticity /dəʊmɛstɪsə¹ti¹/ is the state of living at home with your family. EG *I had put off settling down to such domesticity... Any atmosphere of domesticity has long vanished.* N UNCOUNT

domestic science is the study of cooking, needlework, and other household skills, usually learned at school. N UNCOUNT

domicile /dɒmɪsaɪl/, **domiciles.** Your **domicile** is the place where you live; a formal or legal word. EG *She took me to what was apparently her own domicile.* N COUNT+SUPP ⇑ residence = home

domiciled /dɒmɪsaɪld/. If you are **domiciled** in a particular place, you live there; a formal or legal word. EG *She is regarded as domiciled in the UK.* ADJ CLASSIF: PRED, USU+A ⇑ resident

dominance /dɒmɪnəns/. **1** The **dominance** of a person or thing is the power or control that they have over a person, place, or group. EG *The treaty gave them dominance of the sea routes... It was to be even longer before their dominance over the party was eroded.* N UNCOUNT: IF+PREP THEN *of/over* = control

2 If something has **dominance** in a situation, it is the most important or noticeable element in the situation. EG *Agriculture, the original basis of civilization, has lost its dominance in nation after nation... ...the dominance of economics among the social sciences.* N UNCOUNT: USU +SUPP ⇑ importance

dominant /dɒmɪnənt/. Someone or something that is **dominant** IS **1** more powerful, important, or noticeable than other things of its kind. EG *Chapter three examines the dominant feature of the campaign... ...the television experts who play a dominant role in moulding public opinion... As long as the need for food, clothing and shelter is dominant they will continue to work.* **2** the most influential person or group in a particular relationship or society. EG *She is the dominant partner in their marriage.* ADJ QUALIT; ADJ QUALIT ≠ submissive

dominate /dɒmɪneɪt/, **dominates, dominating, dominated.** **1** If someone or something **dominates** a situation or event, they have great influence or control over it by being the most powerful or significant element in it. EG *These issues dominated the election... That sort of job doesn't dominate your whole existence for twenty-four hours a day.* ◊ **domination** /dɒmɪneɪʃə⁰n/. EG *They were delighted by the company's increasing domination of the UK market.* V+O = rule ◊ N UNCOUNT

2 If a person or country **dominates** another place or group of people, they have a great deal of power over the place or people and use this power to govern them. EG *This nation, with its great armies, seemed likely to dominate the whole of Western Europe.* ◊ **domination.** EG *The domination of Europe over the rest of the world has long since declined.* V+O ◊ N UNCOUNT

3 If you **dominate** a person or a group of people, you have so much power over them that you influence everything that they do. EG *The older women were not permitted to dominate the younger male members of the family.* ◊ **domination.** EG *It was a relationship not of co-operation but of domination.* V OR V+O ⇑ control ≠ submit ◊ N UNCOUNT ≠ submission

4 If something **dominates** an area, it is so large or tall that it can be seen from all over that area. EG *The valley was dominated by the huge Benedictine abbey.* V+O

dominating /dɒmɪneɪtɪŋ/. Someone who is **dominating** has a very strong personality and influences the people around them a great deal. EG *He was a rather aggressive and dominating character.* ADJ QUALIT ⇑ influential = forceful ≠ meek

domineering /dɒmɪnɪərɪŋ/. Someone who is **domineering** tries to control other people without any consideration for their feelings or opinions. EG *Many of her women friends also had domineering husbands.* ADJ QUALIT ⇑ influential = overbearing ≠ meek

Dominican /dəmɪnɪkən/. A **Dominican** person or thing **1** belongs to or relates to the Christian religious order founded by St Dominic. EG *...a Dominican monk... At the Dominican Church I joined the line and filed inside.* **2** comes from, belongs to, or relates to the Dominican republic. ADJ CLASSIF; ADJ CLASSIF

dominion /də⁶mɪnjən/, **dominions.** **1 Dominion** is the authority that someone in a position of power has over other people. EG *Political dominion paved the way for the destruction of the traditional industries... They now had virtually undisputed dominion over a large part of southern India... They have a plan for the achievement of world dominion.* N UNCOUNT: IF+PREP THEN *over*

2 A **dominion** is an area of land that is controlled by a ruler. EG *...the great imperial dominions of the nineteenth century.* N COUNT

3 A **Dominion** was one of the nations which belonged to the British Commonwealth in former times but which had their own government. EG *The Dominions did not want Free Trade.* N COUNT ⇑ nation

domino /dɒmɪnəʊ/, **dominoes.** **1** A **domino** is a small rectangular block, often made of wood, which is marked with two groups of spots on one side. Dominoes are used used for playing various games. EG *...a set of dominoes.* N COUNT

2 Dominoes is a game in which players put dominoes onto a table in turn, usually by matching the number of spots. EG *They played dominoes all night.* N UNCOUNT

don /dɒn/, **dons, donning, donned.** **1** If you **don** clothing, you put it on; a fairly literary use. EG *The other two men donned white cotton gloves.* V+O = put on ≠ doff

2 A **don** is **2.1** a lecturer at Oxford or Cambridge University. EG *Dons at Oxford are expected to live in college.* **2.2** a lecturer at any university. EG *...a don at the Ankara faculty of political science.* N COUNT; N COUNT ⇑ teacher

donate /dəʊneɪt/, **donates, donating, donated.** If you **donate** something to a person or an organization such as a charity, you give it to the person or organization without asking for anything in return. EG *The van was donated to us by a local firm... It seemed unfair to ask my family to donate money to such a project.* V+O: IF+PREP THEN *to* ≠ receive

donation /dəʊneɪʃə⁰n/, **donations.** **1** A **donation** is something which someone gives to a charity or other organization that they wish to support. EG *They received a large donation from one of the unions... He made a generous donation to our campaign fund... The rest of the money we get from donations.* N COUNT: IF+PREP THEN *to/from* ⇑ gift = contribution

2 The **donation** of something is the giving of it to a person or organization without asking for anything in return. EG *Much was made of the donation of this sum of money.* N UNCOUNT

done /dʌn/. **1 Done** is the past participle of **do.**

2 A task or activity that is **done** has been completed successfully. EG *When her errand was done she ran home.* ADJ CLASSIF: PRED ⇑ finished

3 If you say that something is **over and done with,** you mean that it is completely finished and that you do not want to have to think about it any more. EG *The whole thing's over and done with.* ● **done to a turn:** see **turn.** PHR: USED AS C

4 You say **'done'** when you are accepting a deal you CONVENTION have been offered or a bet that someone has made with you. EG *'Shall we say £20 then?'–'Done!'*

Don Juan /dɒn dʒuːən/, **Don Juans**. A **Don Juan** is a man who has seduced many women. N COUNT

donkey /dɒŋki¹/, **donkeys**. 1 A **donkey** is an animal which is like a horse but which is smaller and has longer ears. N COUNT ⇑ ass

2 If you say that someone can **talk the hind legs off a donkey**, you mean that they talk a great deal without stopping and without letting other people say anything; an informal expression. EG *My aunt could talk the hind legs off a donkey!* PHR : VB INFLECTS

3 If you say that something has been happening for **donkey's years**, you mean that it has been happening for a very long time; an informal expression. EG *He introduced me to a friend he'd known for donkey's years... She's been there donkey's years.* PHR : USED AS AN A = ages

donkey jacket, donkey jackets; also spelled with a hyphen. A **donkey jacket** is a thick, warm jacket, which workmen often wear. N COUNT

donkey work is hard work which is not very interesting; used in informal English. EG *Nobody tells me anything that's interesting. I just do the donkey work.* N UNCOUNT = drudgery

donnish /dɒnɪʃ/. Someone who is **donnish** is considered to be rather serious and clever; used in British English. EG *I hope you're not too donnish, Tom.* ▸ used of a person's behaviour. EG *It seemed that he might look forward to a donnish life devoted to private study.* ADJ QUALIT = studious ▸ ADJ QUALIT

donor /dəʊnə/, **donors**. A **donor** is 1 someone who gives a part of their body or some of their blood to be used by doctors to help a person who is ill. EG *There is still a shortage of kidney donors... ...a blood donor scheme.* 2 someone who gives something to a charity or other organization that they wish to support. EG *About half this amount comes from individual donors and bequests.* N COUNT+SUPP ≠ recipient; N COUNT ⇑ giver = benefactor

don't /dəʊnt/ is the usual spoken form of 'do not'.

doodah /duːdɑː/, **doodahs**. You can use **doodah** to refer to something whose name you have forgotten or do not know; an informal word. EG *Pass me the doodah will you?* N COUNT ⇑ thing

doodle /duːdə⁰l/, **doodles, doodling, doodled**. 1 A **doodle** is a drawing or pattern that you make while you are thinking about something else or when you are bored. EG *He made a few doodles with a ballpoint on the back of the bill.* N COUNT

2 If you **doodle**, you make little drawings or patterns while you are thinking about something else, or when you are bored. EG *I used to doodle on my papers.* V ⇑ draw

doom /duːm/, **dooms, dooming, doomed**. 1 **Doom** is a terrible future state or event which you cannot prevent. EG *I felt a sense of doom... ...prophets of doom.* N UNCOUNT ⇑ fate

2 To **doom** someone or something means to cause them to have a very unpleasant or disastrous future which they cannot avoid. EG *What doomed him was the verdict of 'guilty'... He was doomed to unemployment by his ill-health.* V+O : IF+PREP THEN *to* OR + *to*-INF = condemn

doomed /duːmd/. 1 If something is **doomed** to happen, or if you are **doomed** to a particular state, something unpleasant is certain to happen, and you can do nothing to prevent it. EG *We are, most of us, doomed to unhappiness... He was doomed to be killed in a car crash.* ADJ CLASSIF : PRED+*to*/*to*-INF ⇑ fated = destined

2 Someone or something that is **doomed** is certain to fail or be destroyed, whatever they do to try and prevent it. EG *They informed the Prime Minister that his government was doomed... He was a propeller maker. Now that is a doomed trade if ever there was one.* ADJ CLASSIF ⇑ fated = ill-starred

doomsday /duːmzdeɪ/. **Doomsday** is 1 a day or time when you know that something terrible or unpleasant will happen. EG *Doomsday happens in every family sometimes.* 2 in the Christian religion, the last day of the world, on which God will judge everyone. EG *The trumpets of Doomsday will echo from the heavens... The Congress could howl till Doomsday with no hope of getting any more from the President.* N UNCOUNT; N PROPER

door /dɔː/, **doors**. 1 A **door** is 1.1 a swinging or sliding piece of wood, glass, or metal, which is used to close the entrance to a building, room, cupboard, etc. EG *My friend knocked on the door... I closed the door behind me... He opened the car door and got out... The police had gone around to the back door.* N COUNT

1.2 the space in a wall which a door can close and by which you enter a building or room. EG *As they passed through the door, they saw Tom at the end of the room.* 1.3 the entrance to a large building such as a shop, hotel, theatre, etc. EG *I'll meet you outside the main door at ten o'clock... A crowd had gathered at the door.* N COUNT ⇑ opening = doorway; N COUNT

2 The word **door** is also used in the following expressions. 2.1 When you **answer the door**, you go and open the door because a visitor has knocked on it or rung the bell. 2.2 If you **see** someone **to the door**, you go to the door of your home, office, etc with a visitor when they leave. EG *I will see you to the door.* 2.3 If you **show** someone **the door**, you ask them to leave your home, office, etc because you are very angry with them. 2.4 If someone is **on the door**, they have the job of waiting by the door of a building such as a nightclub and collecting tickets or checking on the people who come in. EG *There were two large men on the door.* 2.5 If you **shut** or **slam the door in** someone's **face**, you prevent them from finding something out by refusing to give them information or to answer their questions. EG *We tried to find out what really happened, but doors were constantly shut in our faces.* 2.6 If something **opens the door to** a new situation, it makes that new situation possible. EG *This new discovery will open the doors to prosperity.* 2.7 If something **closes the door on** a possible situation or action, it makes it unlikely that that situation or action can happen. EG *He closed the door on the possibility.* 2.8 If someone **gets in by the back door**, they succeed in getting a job or entering a place by unofficial methods. 2.9 If you **lay** something **at** someone's **door**, you blame them and say that they were responsible for something unpleasant that has happened. EG *Responsibility for the strike was laid at the door of the employers.* 2.10 When you are **out of doors**, you are not inside a building, but in the open air. EG *A great deal of time is spent out of doors, and the children lead an active, healthy life.* 2.11 If you say that something happens **two** or **three doors up** or **down**, you mean that it happens in the house that is the second or third one away from yours as you go along the street; an informal expression. EG *The man who lives three doors up complained about our dog.* 2.12 The person who lives **next door** to you lives in the house or flat that is next to yours. EG *You shouldn't have any problem with the people next door.* 2.13 **at death's door**: see **death**. PHR : VB INFLECTS; PHR : VB INFLECTS = see out; PHR : VB INFLECTS; PHR : USED AS AN A; PHR : VB INFLECTS ⇑ obstruct; PHR : VB INFLECTS ⇑ permit; PHR : VB INFLECTS ⇑ prevent; PHR : VB INFLECTS; PHR : VB INFLECTS ⇑ attribute; PHR : USED AS AN A ≠ indoors; PHR : USED AS AN A; PHR : USED AS AN A

3 **from door to door**. 3.1 If someone goes **from door to door**, they go along a street calling at each house in turn, trying to sell something or persuade people to vote for them. EG *He went from door to door, trying to sell brushes.* ● see also **door-to-door**. 3.2 If you talk about a journey or distance **from door to door**, you mean from the place where the journey starts to the place where it finishes. EG *The journey took us three hours from door to door.* PHR : USED AS AN A = house to house; PHR : USED AS AN A

doorbell /dɔːbel/, **doorbells**. A **doorbell** is a bell on the outside of a house which you can ring so that the people inside know that you are there and that you want to see them. N COUNT = bell

door-handle, door-handles. A **door-handle** is the handle on a door which operates the mechanism that holds the door shut. You turn the door-handle to open or close the door. N COUNT

doorknob /dɔːnɒb/, **doorknobs**. A **doorknob** is a round handle on a door which you turn in order to open the door or which you can hold when you close the door. N COUNT ⇑ knob

doorman /dɔːmə³n/, **doormen**. A **doorman** is a person whose job is to stay by the main entrance of a large building, and who opens and closes the door for people, or who helps visitors to the building. N COUNT ⇑ guard

doormat /dɔːmæt/, **doormats**. A **doormat** is 1 a mat which you put by a door so that people can wipe their shoes on it before coming into the house or room. 2 someone who lets other people treat them badly, and who does not complain; an informal expression. EG *Ever since then you've treated me like a doormat.* N COUNT; N COUNT ⇑ weakling

doorstep /dɔːstep/, **doorsteps**. A **doorstep** is a step in front of a door that leads into a building from the outside. ● If something is **on your doorstep**, it is N COUNT = step ● PHR : USED AS very near to where you live. EG *He certainly didn't want an airport on his doorstep.* AN A ⇑ close

doorstop /dɔːstɒp/, **doorstops**. A **doorstop** is something such as a heavy object or a special hook that you use to keep a door open and prevent it closing. N COUNT

door-to-door. **Door-to-door** activities involve going from one house to another along a street, for example in order to try and sell something. EG *...a door-to-door salesman.* ADJ CLASSIF : ATTRIB = house-to-house

doorway /dɔːweɪ/, **doorways**. A **doorway** is a space in a wall where a door opens and closes and through which you enter a building or room. EG *A child stood in the doorway.* N COUNT ⇑ opening

dope /dəʊp/, **dopes, doping, doped**. 1 In informal English, **dope** is 1.1 an illegal drug such as marijuana or cannabis. EG *...twelve year old dope addicts... ...streets free of crime and dope peddling.* N UNCOUNT 1.2 a medicine or drug. EG *...enough dope to knock the average man unconscious.* N UNCOUNT 1.3 information that you are not really supposed to have, but which you get from someone who you can trust. EG *We got the dope on the latest offer from Morgan.* N SING WITH DET : IF+PREP THEN *on* = gen, info

2 If someone **dopes** a person or an animal, they give them a drug that will improve their ability, for example in a race or other sporting competition. EG *They discovered that the horse had been doped.* V+O

3 If someone **dopes** you or **dopes** your food or drink, they put a drug into your food or drink in order to make you unconscious for a while, usually because they have bad intentions towards you. EG *He doped her drink... She had been doped and kidnapped.* V+O

4 If someone **is doped** or **is doped up**, they are in a state where they cannot think clearly because they are under the influence of drugs. EG *The girls were doped to the eyeballs... They are all so doped up they wouldn't know a war had started.* V+O : ONLY PASS, OR PHRASAL VB : V+O+ADV, ONLY PASS

5 A **dope** is a person who you think is stupid. EG *This is what the guy means, isn't it, you dope... What did that dumb dope mean saying it was nothing important?.* N COUNT : ALSO VOC = idiot

dopey /dəʊpi[1]/; an informal word. Someone who is **dopey** is 1 sleepy, as though they have been drugged. EG *Luckily for Louisa she just felt dopey when she woke up the next morning... They were still too dopey to take any notice of us.* ADJ QUALIT = groggy 2 rather silly. EG *She's all right, but her brother's a bit dopey.* ADJ QUALIT ⇑ idiotic

dorm /dɔːm/, **dorms**. A **dorm** is the same as a dormitory; an informal word. N COUNT

dormancy /dɔːmənsi[1]/ is the state of being dormant; a formal word. N UNCOUNT ⇑ inactivity

dormant /dɔːmənt/. Something that is **dormant** is not active, growing or being used at the present time but able to be active later on. Animals, plants, volcanoes and organizations can be dormant, but not humans. EG *The idea had lain dormant in Britain during the fifties... He proposed to mobilise this dormant reserve of experience... The fertilised egg in the uterus still remains dormant.* ADJ CLASSIF ⇑ inactive

dormer /dɔːmə/, **dormers**. A **dormer** or **dormer window** is a window that is built upright in a sloping roof. N COUNT

dormitory /dɔːmə[1]tə[0]ri[1]/, **dormitories**. 1 A **dormitory** is 1.1 a large bedroom where several people sleep, for example in a boarding school. EG *I lay in bed in the dormitory crying under the sheet.* N COUNT 1.2 a building in a college or university where students live; used in American English. N COUNT ⇑ hostel

2 Most of the people who live in a **dormitory** town or suburb travel to work in another, larger town nearby; used in British English. EG *Basingstoke is trying to get rid of its image as a dormitory town... ...a dormitory suburb.* N BEFORE N ⇑ subsidiary

dormouse /dɔːmaʊs/, **dormice**. A **dormouse** is a small mouse which is found in southern England and Wales. People think of it as being a very sleepy animal. N COUNT ⇑ rodent

dorsal /dɔːsə[0]l/. **Dorsal** means relating to the back of a fish or animal; a technical word. EG *Its dorsal fin broke water.* ADJ CLASSIF : ATTRIB

dosage /dəʊsɪdʒ/, **dosages**. A **dosage** is the total amount of a medicine or drug that should be taken over a period of time. EG *It should be administered in 25 mg tablets, with a maximum daily dosage of 150 mg.* N COUNT : USU SING

dose /dəʊs/, **doses, dosing, dosed**. 1 A **dose** is 1.1 a measured amount of a medicine or other substance which is intended to be taken at one time. EG *She refused her daily dose of medicine... This is lethal to rats in small doses.* N COUNT 1.2 an amount of something unpleasant which you have to accept even though you do not want to. EG *Newspapers dispensed large doses of nationalism to their readers during the war.* N COUNT+SUPP

2 If you **dose** someone or **dose** yourself, you give someone a certain amount of a medicine or drug, or take a certain amount of it yourself. EG *Of course he drank, and he dosed himself with pills... Feverish patients were dosed with quinine.* V+O (NG/REFL) : IF+PREP THEN *with* ⇑ administer

dose up. If you **dose** someone **up**, you give them a large amount of a medicine or drug. EG *We'll dose her up with it and see how she responds.* PHRASAL VB : V+O (NG/REFL)+ADV

doss down /dɒs daʊn/, **dosses down, dossing down, dossed down**. If you **doss down** somewhere, you sleep there for a short time, usually in an uncomfortable place; an informal expression, used in British English. EG *...a rusty stretcher where he had dossed down once or twice.* PHRASAL VB : V+ADV

dosser /dɒsə/, **dossers**. A **dosser** is a city person who does not have a permanent home and sleeps outside in the streets or in cheap and uncomfortable hotels; an informal word, used in British English. N COUNT ⇑ tramp

doss-house, **doss-houses**; also spelled without a hyphen. A **doss-house** is a kind of cheap hotel in a city for people who have no home and very little money; an informal expression, used in British English. N COUNT ⇑ lodging

dossier /dɒsieɪ, -sɪə/, **dossiers**. A **dossier** is a collection of papers containing information on a particular event, or on a person such as a criminal or a spy. EG *All records of all meetings, files, and dossiers must be destroyed... We have a hefty dossier on his exploits in the war.* N COUNT

dot /dɒt/, **dots, dotting, dotted**. 1 A **dot** is 1.1 a very small round mark which is used, for example, as the top part of the letter i, as a full stop, or as a decimal point. EG *She painted little black dots for the clown's eyes... ...parallel lines and rows of dots.* N COUNT 1.2 something that is very small or distant and which looks like a dot. EG *Beneath the smoke was a dot that might have been a ship... A dot of light glowed on the roof.* N COUNT = speck, spot 1.3 the small round mark which is used to represent the short sound in Morse code. N COUNT

2 If you **dot** something, you put a very small, round mark on it or above it. For example, when you write the letter 'i', you dot it. V+O ● If you **dot the i's and cross the t's**, you deal with all the remaining small details that need to be dealt with before something is completely finished. EG *They'd want to dot the i's and cross the t's before signing the agreement.* ● PHR : VB INFLECTS

3 When things **dot** a place or an area, they are scattered or spread all over it. EG *Countless fishing villages dot the coast.* V+O = speck ◊ **dotted**. EG *The hills are dotted with quiet little towns.* ◊ ADJ CLASSIF : PRED+*with*

4 If you arrive somewhere **on the dot**, you arrive there at exactly the time that you were supposed to. EG *She'll be here on the dot.* PHR : USED AS AN A

5 **The year dot** is used in informal English to mean a very long time ago. EG *Way back in the year dot, we all ate with our fingers.* PHR : USED AS O

dotage /dəʊtɪdʒ/. If someone is **in** their **dotage**, they are very old and becoming weak. EG *Will you look after me in my dotage?* PHR : USED AS AN A

dote /dəʊt/, **dotes, doting, doted**. If you **dote** on someone or something, you show them a great deal of love and care to an extent which other people think in excessive. EG *The Duchess of Marlborough doted on him.* V+A (*on/upon*) ≠ loathe

doting /dəʊtɪŋ/ means showing a lot of love for someone or something. EG *Parents used to buy extra copies to send to doting relatives elsewhere.* ADJ CLASSIF : USU ATTRIB = adoring

dotted /dɒtɪ[2]d/. 1 **Dotted** lines are lines which are made of a row of dots. EG *The boundaries are shown on the map by dotted lines .* ADJ CLASSIF : USU ATTRIB ≠ continuous

2 If you **sign on the dotted line**, you formally agree to something that has been suggested to you, often by actually signing an official document. EG *Getting them to sign on the dotted line won't be easy.* PHR : VB INFLECTS ⇑ agree

3 Something that is **dotted** is covered with large dots. EG *...a dotted red bow-tie.* ● See also **dot**. ADJ CLASSIF = spotted

dotty /dɒti[1]/, **dottier, dottiest**; used in informal British English. 1 Someone who is **dotty** is slightly mad or likely to do strange things. EG *The old girl is* ADJ QUALIT = nutty *slightly dotty... She really could be very dotty sometimes.*

2 If you are **dotty** about something, you are very enthusiastic about it. EG *Her uncle was still dotty about roses.* ADJ QUALIT: PRED+about = crazy

double /dʌbəºl/, **doubles, doubling, doubled.** 1 If you say that something is **double** the amount, size, strength, etc, of something else, you mean that it is twice as large or twice as strong as the other thing or amount. EG *The boy was double the size of his sister... They need to eat double that amount... He'll think we're millionaires and start charging us double... We paid her double what she was getting before... If you buy them in Egypt you pay double or three times as much as you pay here.* PREDET OR QUANTIF ≠ half

2 **Double** is used to describe something which **2.1** is twice as large in amount, number, or size as it was or as it usually is. EG *They are aiming for a double share of the market by 1989.* ADJ CLASSIF: USU ATTRIB ≠ half **2.2** includes or is made of two things of the same kind. EG *The double doors facing the window were open... The egg had a double yolk... It is illegal in Britain to park on double yellow lines.* ADJ CLASSIF: USU ATTRIB ≠ single **2.3** is intended to be used by two people. EG *The house has three double bedrooms... Double tickets for the dance are £15 each.* ADJ CLASSIF: USU ATTRIB **2.4** is in two layers instead of one, because it has been folded. EG *The blanket had been folded double.* ADJ CLASSIF

3 A **double** whisky, **double** gin, etc has two measures in the same glass. EG *I ordered a double vodka and orange.* ▸ used as a noun. EG *A bottle of whisky was produced and three doubles were poured.* ADJ CLASSIF: ATTRIB ▸ N COUNT

4 **Double** is used when you are spelling a word or telling someone a number to show that a letter or digit is repeated. EG *'Apple' is spelt a, double p, l, e... My phone number is 9, double 3, 2, 4.* ADJ CLASSIF: ATTRIB ⇑ twice

5 When something **doubles** or when you **double** it, it becomes twice as great in number, amount or size. EG *The world population is doubling every thirty-five years... The average baby doubles its birth weight at about five months.* V-ERG ⇑ increase ≠ halve

6 If you **double** something, you fold it in half so that you make two layers. EG *She doubled the blanket before putting it on the bed.* V+O

7 A **double** is **7.1** someone who replaces an actor or actress, for example during dangerous parts of a film or play. EG *My first job was as Sophia Loren's double in an air-crash scene.* N COUNT ⇑ substitute = stand-in **7.2** someone who looks exactly like another person. EG *I saw your double in the street last night.* N COUNT: POSS+N = twin

8 If a person or thing **doubles** as someone or something else, they have a second job or purpose as well as their main one. EG *Her secretary doubled as her housekeeper... This bedroom doubles as a study.* V+A *(as)* ⇑ deputize

9 If you **double**, you change direction suddenly. EG *The tiny animal doubles, stops, and then finally runs back.* V ⇑ turn

10 **Doubles** is a game, for exampie in tennis or badminton, in which two teams of two players play against each other on the same court. EG *Didn't Roche and Newcombe win the doubles that year?... I enjoy playing doubles.* N UNCOUNT ≠ singles

11 If you do something **at the double** or **on the double**, you do it very quickly or immediately; an informal expression. EG *They marched down the street at the double... We shall have to go on the double.* PHR: USED AS AN A

12 If you are **seeing double**, there is something wrong with your eyes, and you can see two images instead of one. EG *He began to see double.* PHR: VB INFLECTS

13 When you **bend double**, you bend the top half of your body downwards a long way. EG *Jack was bent double... The guitar player bent double over her instrument.* PHR: VB INFLECTS

14 **in double figures**: see **figure**.

double back. If you **double back**, you turn and go back in the direction that you came from. EG *When nobody was watching, they doubled back.* PHRASAL VB: V+ADV ⇑ return

double back on. When a line **doubles back on** itself, it bends in the middle, so that the second half of it is parallel to the first half. EG *The queue doubled back on itself.* PHRASAL VB: V+ADV+PREP

double up. 1 If you **double up**, you use the same thing, for example the same room or car, as someone else. EG *There weren't enough offices for everyone, so we had to double up.* PHRASAL VB: V+ADV ⇑ share

2 If something **doubles** you **up**, or if you **double up** or **double over**, you bend your body quickly or violently, for example because you are laughing a lot or because you are feeling a lot of pain. EG *He doubled up with laughter, holding his stomach... I was doubled up in pain... She was doubled over, her whole face distorted with pain.* PHRASAL VB: V-ERG+ADV

double agent, double agents. A **double agent** is someone who works as a spy for a particular country or organization, but who also works for its enemies. N COUNT

double-barrelled; also spelled **double-barreled** in American English. 1 A gun that is **double-barrelled** has two barrels. ADJ CLASSIF

2 A name that is **double-barrelled** has two parts which are joined by a hyphen, for example 'Miss J. Heydon-Smith'. ADJ CLASSIF ⇑ hyphenated

double bass, double basses. A **double bass** is the largest musical instrument in the violin family. N COUNT

double bed, double beds. A **double bed** is a bed that is designed for two people to sleep in. N COUNT

double bill, double bills. A **double bill** is a theatre or cinema performance in which there are two main items on the programme. N COUNT

double bluff, double bluffs. A **double bluff** is an attempt to deceive someone by saying exactly what you intend to do when you know that they will assume you are lying. EG *Perhaps, he thought, it was a kind of double bluff.* N COUNT/UNCOUNT ⇑ deception

double-breasted. A jacket or coat that is **double-breasted** has two very wide sections at the front which overlap when you button them up. ADJ CLASSIF ≠ single-breasted

double-check, double-checks, double-checking, double-checked; also spelled without a hyphen, especially when used as a noun. If you **double-check** something, you examine or test it a second time to make sure that it is completely correct, safe, etc. EG *She double-checked her bag to make sure she'd got everything.* ▸ used as a noun. EG *In spite of all his double-checks, he hadn't noticed that the door wasn't locked.* V OR V+O/REPORT-CL ▸ N COUNT

double chin, double chins. A **double chin** is a fold of loose skin under the chin. EG *He had a red-tipped nose and the hint of a double chin.* N COUNT: USU SING

double cream is very thick cream; used in British English. N UNCOUNT

double-cross, double-crosses, double-crossing, double-crossed; also spelled without a hyphen. If someone **double-crosses** you, they pretend to you that they are doing what you had planned or agreed together, when in fact they are doing the opposite; an informal expression. EG *You want me to double-cross the man I work for?* ▸ used as a noun. EG *I suddenly realized that it was a double-cross.* V+O ⇑ betray ▸ N COUNT

double-dealing is behaviour which is deliberately deceitful. EG *They even accused each other of double-dealing.* N UNCOUNT = duplicity

double-decker, double-deckers. 1 A **double-decker** or **double-decker bus** is a bus that has two floors. N COUNT

2 **Double-decker** items or structures have two layers instead of one. EG *...a double-decker sandwich.* ADJ CLASSIF: ATTRIB

double Dutch; also spelled with a hyphen. **Double Dutch** is talk or writing that you cannot understand at all; an informal expression in British English. EG *It all sounded a bit like double-Dutch to me.* N UNCOUNT = gibberish

double-edged. 1 A comment that is **double-edged** can be understood in two different ways, so that you can, for example, say something which sounds like a compliment but which is in fact quite rude. EG *She made a very double-edged remark about my work.* ADJ QUALIT ⇑ ambiguous = barbed

2 A blade that is **double-edged** has two sharp edges. ADJ CLASSIF

double entendre /du:bəºl ɑ:ntɑ:ndrə/, **double entendres**; also spelled with a hyphen. A **double entendre** is a word or phrase that has two meanings, one of which is not polite and often sexual; used mainly in formal or literary English. EG *They mouthed outrageous double-entendres in crystal clear Edwardian accents.* N COUNT

double-glaze, double-glazes, double-glazing, double-glazed. If you **double-glaze** a house or a window, you fit the windows with a second layer of glass in order to keep the inside of the house warmer or quieter. EG *Is it really worth double-glazing your house?* V+O

double-glazing consists of the second layers of glass which you fit to each of the windows in a house in order to keep the inside of the house warmer or N UNCOUNT quieter. EG *The additional cost of building a house with double-glazing is very small indeed.*

double-jointed. Fingers that are **double-jointed** can bend easily both backwards and forwards. ADJ CLASSIF ⇑ flexible

double negative, double negatives. A **double negative** is a grammatical construction in which two negatives are used. In English, only one negative is needed, and double negatives, for example 'I didn't never say that', are considered to be incorrect. N COUNT

double-park, double-parks, double-parking, double-parked. If someone **double-parks**, they park a car in a road by the side of another parked car, with the result that the other car is prevented from driving away. V OR V+O ⇑ park

double-quick. If something happens **double-quick** or in **double-quick time**, it happens very quickly indeed. EG *The police arrived double-quick, and arrested him... They had the rest of us locked up in double-quick time.* ADV, OR ADJ CLASSIF

double room, double rooms. A **double room** is a bedroom for two people, especially in a hotel. N COUNT

double standard, double standards. A **double standard** is a set of principles that allows more freedom of behaviour to one group of people than to another. EG *There were inequalities between men and women and a double standard of morality.* N COUNT

doublet /dʌblə¹t/, **doublets.** A **doublet** is a short, tight-fitting jacket which was worn by men in former times. N COUNT

double-take, double-takes; also spelled without a hyphen. If you **do a double-take**, you react to something only after a delay. EG *When I told him the news, he did a double take.* PHR : VB INFLECTS

double-talk; also spelled without a hyphen. **Double-talk** is talk that can deceive people or is difficult to understand because the things which are said have two possible meanings. N UNCOUNT

double vision is a medical condition that makes you see a single object as two separate objects, and that is caused by an illness or by drinking too much alcohol. EG *He suffered from double vision.* N UNCOUNT

doubly /dʌbli¹/. You use **doubly** 1 to emphasize that something exists or happens to a greater degree than usual. EG *We were doubly disappointed that Jane didn't come either... They were doubly confident after this that he would win.* ADV ⇑ especially 2 to show that there are two aspects or features that are having an influence on a particular situation. EG *He is doubly disadvantaged, both by his age and his nationality... When inflation is accompanied by unemployment, this is doubly true.* ADV ⇑ twice over

doubt /daʊt/, **doubts, doubting, doubted.** 1 A **doubt** about something is a feeling of uncertainty about it, for example not knowing whether it is true or possible. EG *There was still a doubt in my mind... Both these claims raise doubts... Frank had no doubts about the outcome of the trial... ...but we have serious doubts.* N COUNT : USU PL, IF+PREP, THEN *about* = misgiving ≠ certainty ▸ used as an uncount noun. EG *As I drove to East London I had moments of doubt that I was doing the right thing.* ▸ N UNCOUNT

2 **Doubt** is used in the following phrases: 2.1 If you say that **there is no doubt** or **little doubt** or **not much doubt** about something, you mean that you feel certain that what you are saying is true. EG *There's no doubt that it's going to be difficult... There is little doubt about what is being portrayed.* PHR : USU+A *(about/of/as)*/REPORT-CL 2.2 If you say **no doubt about it**, you are confirming that something is definitely true. EG *Rose was mad, there was no doubt about it.* PHR : USED AS ADV SEN, OR CONVENTION 2.3 If you say that you **have no doubt** about something, you mean that you feel certain about it. EG *They were, I have no doubt, quite indifferent to you... I have no doubt that there will be plenty of youngsters... So if it is a revolution, and I have no doubt that it is, how do we stand in this country?* PHR : VB INFLECTS, USU+A *(about/of)*/REPORT-CL 2.4 If something **leaves no doubt** that something is true, it makes it completely clear or obvious that it is true. EG *The marks left no doubt that the boy had died a violent death.* PHR : VB INFLECTS, USU+A *(as to/)*/REPORT-CL 2.5 You use the expressions **without doubt**, **without a doubt**, and **without a slightest doubt** to emphasize that what you are saying is definitely true. EG *Hugh Scanlon became without doubt one of the most powerful men in Britain... My experience tells me that without the slightest doubt this wood has been processed with lime.* PHR : USED AS ADV SEN 2.6 If something is shown or proved to be true **beyond all doubt** or **beyond a doubt**, it is shown to be definitely true. EG *We have established the ownership beyond all doubt.* PHR : USED AS ADV SEN 2.7 If something is **in doubt** or **open to doubt**, it is considered to be uncertain or unreliable. EG *Devaluation had put Concorde's future in doubt... Its effectiveness is not in doubt.* PHR : USED AS AN A ⇑ unsure 2.8 To **cast doubt** on something means to cause people to suspect that it might not be true or reliable. EG *The new evidence cast overwhelming doubt on Christine's story.* PHR : VB INFLECTS, IF+PREP THEN *on* 2.9 If you are **in doubt** about something, you feel unsure or uncertain about it. EG *...but do check if you're in any doubt... I was left in no doubt that the weather had indeed deteriorated... If in doubt, try the Royal Free Hospital... When in doubt, trust your instincts.* PHR : USED AS AN A, IF+PREP THEN *about/as to* 2.10 If you say that you **have** your **doubts** about something, you mean that you do not think it is completely convincing and find it hard to accept. EG *I must admit I had my doubts... I continued to have my doubts about this... I had my doubts, but dutifully signed the form.* PHR : VB INFLECTS, USU+A *(about)*/REPORT-CL 2.11 If you **give** someone **the benefit of the doubt**, you accept that what they say is true, although you are not completely convinced by it. EG *They decided to give the President the benefit of the doubt.* PHR : VB INFLECTS

3 You use **no doubt** 3.1 to say that you think that something is certain or very likely. EG *As Jennifer has no doubt told you, we are leaving tomorrow... These are problems I have discussed before, and no doubt will discuss again.* PHR : USED AS ADV SEN = undoubtedly 3.2 to suggest that, although you accept that something is probably true, you do not think that it is very important. EG *This is no doubt true enough within certain limits, but we cannot accept it wholeheartedly... All this is, no doubt, wise advice, yet nobody seems to pay any attention to my feelings about it.* PHR : USED AS ADV SEN

4 If you **doubt** whether something is true or possible, you believe that it is probably not true or possible. EG *I very much doubt whether they knew... I doubt if they will ever want vanilla pudding again... Maybe he changed his mind, but I doubt it... I began to seriously doubt that it would be possible to elude the police.* V+REPORT-CL ⇑ disbelieve ≠ believe

5 If you **doubt** something, you believe that it might not be true or genuine. EG *They inwardly doubted the facts... Some of our members doubt the value of demonstrations... He had the courage to doubt, where all the others piously believed.* V, OR V+O ⇑ disbelieve = mistrust

6 If you **doubt** someone or **doubt** their word, you think that they are perhaps not telling the truth. EG *Why should I doubt him?... I apologized for having doubted his word.* V+O ⇑ disbelieve = mistrust

doubter /daʊtə/, **doubters.** A **doubter** is someone who has doubts, especially about their religion or a political system. N COUNT ≠ believer

doubtful /daʊtful/. 1 Something that is **doubtful** 1.1 seems unlikely or uncertain. EG *The organisation has a doubtful future... How long this would continue into the future was doubtful... It is doubtful, however, whether the Chairman would approve.* ADJ QUALIT : USU PRED = debatable 1.2 does not seem genuine. EG *She is being offered a painting with a doubtful signature.* ADJ QUALIT = questionable ◇ **doubtfully.** EG *A magnificent painted ceiling, doubtfully ascribed to Holbein, survives.* ◇ ADV WITH VB

2 If you are **doubtful** about something, you feel unsure or uncertain about it. EG *I was a little doubtful about accepting... He was doubtful that he could ever manage it... Segal is doubtful whether we're meant to take all this very seriously.* ADJ QUALIT : USU PRED+A *(about/of)*/REPORT-CL = dubious ◇ **doubtfully.** EG *Ralph looked at him doubtfully.* ◇ ADV+VB

Doubting Thomas /daʊtɪŋ tɒmə³s/, **Doubting Thomases.** A **Doubting Thomas** is a person who refuses to believe something until they see full proof or evidence of it. N COUNT ⇑ doubter

doubtless /daʊtlɪ²s/ means probably or quite certainly. EG *But he prospers, doubtless because of a certain strain of ruthlessness... She made a detailed point which, though doubtless true, did not advance the argument.* ADV SEN, OR ADV = no doubt

dough /dəʊ/, **doughs. Dough** is 1 a fairly firm mixture of flour, water, and sometimes also sugar and fat, which can be cooked, with various other ingredients, to make things such as pastry, bread, or biscuits. EG *He began to shape the dough into rolls.* N MASS 2 money; an informal word. EG *How the hell could we scrape up enough dough to pay him off.* N UNCOUNT = cash

doughnut /dəʊnʌt/, **doughnuts.** A **doughnut** is a small cake of sweet, bread-like dough cooked in hot fat. Doughnuts usually have a filling of jam or cream. N COUNT

Some are in the shape of a ring with a hole in the middle.

doughty /dauti[1]/, **doughtier, doughtiest**. Someone who is **doughty** is brave, determined, and not easily defeated; an old-fashioned word. EG *...such a doughty fighter.* — ADJ QUALIT = staunch

doughy /dəui[1]/, **doughier, doughiest**. Something that is **doughy** has a thick and sticky texture, like dough. EG *The old man took up the doughy mass and placed it upon the hot stone.* — ADJ QUALIT

dour /duə/. 1 Someone who is **dour** has a rather severe and unfriendly manner. EG *...the dour little preacher... Harris had been dour when they last met.* — ADJ QUALIT = sullen
▸ used of someone's expression or behaviour. EG *When she faced me again, it was with her usual dour expression.* — ▸ ADJ QUALIT

dourly /duəli[1]/. If you smile or say something **dourly**, you smile or say it in a way that makes you seem rather severe and unfriendly. EG *'Yes,' said Christopher, smiling dourly.* — ADV WITH VB

douse /daus/, **douses, dousing, doused**; also spelled **dowse**. 1 If you **douse** a fire or a light, you stop it burning or shining. EG *He doused the lamp, and we made our way back to the house.* — V+O ⇑ extinguish = put out

2 If you **douse** someone or something, you throw a lot of water or other liquid over them. EG *His head had been doused with water... She had doused herself with perfume.* — V+O ⇑ wet = drench

dove, doves. The word **dove** is pronounced /dʌv/ for paragraphs 1 and 2, and /dəuv/ for paragraph 3.
1 A **dove** is a bird of the pigeon family which makes a soft cooing sound. Doves are often used as a symbol of peace. EG *There were white doves on the lawn.* — N COUNT

2 If you call someone, especially a politician, a **dove**, you mean that they are in favour of taking a peaceful and trustful attitude towards rivals in international affairs. — N COUNT ⇑ pacifist ≠ hawk

3 **Dove** is the past tense of **dive** in American English.

dovecote /dʌvkəut/, **dovecotes**; also spelled **dovecot**. A **dovecote** is a box, shelter, or part of a house built for doves or pigeons to live in. — N COUNT

dove-grey means greyish brown in colour. EG *The sky had been a dull dove-grey... ...an elegant document printed on dove-grey paper.* — ADJ COLOUR, OR N UNCOUNT ⇑ grey

dovetail /dʌvteɪl/, **dovetails, dovetailing, dovetailed**. 1 If two things **dovetail** or if one thing **dovetails** with another, the two things fit together or are compatible with each other in a very neat way. EG *The two schedules dovetailed together without friction... Every scientist feels elated when the numbers dovetail.* — V OR V+A (*with*): RECIP = match

2 A **dovetail** or **dovetail joint** is a wedge-shaped joint used in carpentry for fitting two pieces of wood tightly together. — N COUNT

dowager /dauədʒə/, **dowagers**. A **dowager** is 1 a woman who has received a title from her dead husband. EG *...the dowager Countess of Derby.* 2 a rich or grand-looking old lady. EG *...like one of those old dowagers taking the waters.* — N COUNT: ALSO IN TITLES; N COUNT

dowdy /daudi[1]/, **dowdier, dowdiest**. If someone is **dowdy**, they are wearing dull and unfashionable clothes. EG *She felt dowdy as she came through the door.* — ADJ QUALIT ≠ chic, smart

dowel /dauəl/, **dowels**. A **dowel** is a short, thin piece of wood or metal which is used for joining larger pieces of wood or metal together. — N COUNT ⇑ pin

down /daun/, **downs, downing, downed**. 1 **Down** is used in phrasal verbs, for example 'bring down' and 'water down', and after some other verbs such as 'calm', 'close', and 'write'. See individual verb and phrasal verb entries for such uses, which are not treated here.

2 **Down** is used when you refer to movement or position in the following ways: **2.1** to say that something moves in a direction that is towards the ground or towards a lower level. EG *Do you need help in lifting your suitcase down from the rack?... I was about to slam the car door, wind down the glass, wave to Louise... It rolled along the pavement and then disappeared down a drain... The rain came down in sheets... I managed to creep down into the living room without anyone seeing me... She pulled up her sock, which had slipped down.* — PREP OR ADV AFTER VB ≠ up
2.2 to say that you are looking or pointing in a direction that is towards the ground or towards a lower level. EG *She nodded and looked down... She had her head down and she didn't see him... The dog lopes back, its tail hanging down.* — ADV AFTER VB = downwards ≠ up
2.3 to say that something moves through, along, or in something in a direction that is towards a lower level. EG *They walked down the stone steps leading to the river bank... The van started to roll down the hill.* — PREP ≠ up
2.4 to say that something is facing towards the ground. EG *Philip lay face down on the floor.* — ADJ AFTER N = downwards
2.5 to say that something is situated in a position that is lower than where you are or lower in relation to something else. EG *Can you see anything down there?... He could see the house down below, at the bottom of the hill.* — PREP, OR ADV ≠ up
2.6 to say that something is destroyed or damaged and falls to the ground. EG *Once he built a house in a week. It fell down a week later... Two men are trying to cut down a very large tree... It seems that he burnt down his school when he was seventeen.* — ADV AFTER VB
2.7 to say that something is lower or closer to the ground by a particular number of levels. EG *The salt is on the third shelf down... ...the documentation department three floors down.* — ADV AFTER N ≠ up
2.8 to say that something extends from the top of something else towards or to the bottom of it. EG *...a jumper with a stripe down the middle... A girl with a blonde pigtail down her back came out of the house next door... She was running her finger down a list of names.* — PREP, OR ADV AFTER VB
2.9 to say that something is put onto a surface. EG *Put that book down a second and look at this... David slammed the phone down angrily.* — ADV AFTER VB
2.10 to say that you eat or drink something, or that it remains in your stomach, especially when you feel ill and have difficulty in eating or drinking without being sick. EG *He bravely drank it down... I'm finding it hard to get food down... This time the cognac stayed down.* — PREP, OR ADV AFTER VB
2.11 to say that something has been folded into an appropriate closed or open position. EG *...driving your sports car around Britain with the roof down, soaking up the sun.* — ADV AFTER VB, OR ADV AFTER N ≠ up

3 If something or someone moves **up and down, 3.1** they go repeatedly upwards and then downwards. EG *I was so happy I jumped up and down and shouted.* — PHR: USED AS AN A
3.2 they move repeatedly in one direction and then in the opposite direction. EG *The prisoner marched boldly up and down... She was looking up and down the main street.* — PHR, OR PHR+NG: USED AS AN A

4 **Down** also means **4.1** along a river or stream in the direction that is towards the sea. EG *We can go down the river on a boat and have a picnic.* — PREP ≠ up
4.2 along a road, path, etc towards another place. EG *He walked down the road reading a newspaper... 'Where is it?'-'Down the corridor on the left, sir'... The library is halfway down the street on the left hand side.* — PREP
4.3 to or in another place, especially one which is thought of as being lower on a map or as being in the south. EG *Arthur and Mary decided to travel down by coach... Did you have a good trip down?... It's more expensive down south... ...the consultant down here who got interested is a Mr Baillie... There's a man down in Baltimore who does that.* — ADV AFTER VB, OR PREP
4.4 to or in a particular place; used in informal spoken English. EG *I'm going down the pub... I'm sure I could get a job down London.* — PREP

5 If an amount of something is **down** or goes **down**, it is decreasing or has been reduced. EG *One thing is sure, prices never go down... Sheila said that she was trying to get her weight down... ...you can keep down consumption of goods... Tourism is down 40 percent... By the time a baby is 6 months old, the average weight gain is down to a pound a month.* — ADV AFTER VB ≠ up

6 You also use **down 6.1** to say that something has continued throughout a particular period of time. EG *It had been occupied as a palace by all our kings and queens down to James I... There has been a chapel here down all the years my family has lived in this house.* — ADV+PREP, OR PREP = through
6.2 to say that something involves all the levels of a hierarchy from the highest ones to the lowest. EG *...everyone from the managing director down.* — ADV AFTER N ≠ up

7 If something is **down** on paper, it is written on it. EG *That date wasn't down on our news sheet.* — ADJ CLASSIF: PRED+PREP

8 If you are **down for** something, your name is on a list for that particular thing and so it is planned that you will do it. EG *Well, I'm down for physics but not on Wednesdays.* — PREP ⇑ registered

9 If you say **'Down!'** to a dog, you are telling it to sit or lie. EG *Down, boy!* — CONVENTION

10 If you say **'Down with'** something or someone, you — PHR+NG

are saying that you dislike them and want to get rid of them. EG *Down with Imperialism!*

11 In a game or competition, if someone is **down** by a particular number of points, they are losing by that number of points. EG *Eastfield were two down at half-time.* — ADV AFTER VB ≠ up

12 If you say that there are a particular number of things **down** and a particular number **to go**, you are saying how many of the things have already been dealt with and how many remain to be dealt with. EG *One down, five to go.* — CONVENTION ⇑ finished

13 If something is true **down to** or **right down to** the details that you are mentioning, it is true including even those small details. EG *She could describe what the other women in the room are wearing, right down to the colour of their stockings.* — PREP

14 If you **down** food or drink, you eat or drink it quickly. EG *I poured him a glass of Scotch and he downed it at a gulp.* — V+O ⇑ swallow

15 If you are **down** with an illness, you have that illness; an informal use. EG *She's down with the flu... He came down with appendicitis.* — ADV : VB+ADV+*with* ⇑ ill

16 If you are feeling **down**, you are feeling unhappy; used in informal English. EG *I'm feeling a bit down today.* — ADJ QUALIT : PRED = depressed

17 If you **have a down on** someone, you disapprove of them or do not like them. EG *Everybody seems to have a down on the unfortunate director.* — PHR : VB INFLECTS

18 If a computer system is **down**, it is not functioning and so you cannot use it. EG *The computer's down again.* — ADJ CLASSIF : PRED ⇑ unavailable

19 The **Downs** are an area of low grassy hills in the South of England. EG *They all enjoy walking enormous distances over the Downs... ...the South Downs.* — N PLURAL : USU *the*+N

20 **Down** is **20.1** small soft feathers that grow on young birds and that are sometimes used to fill duvets or quilts. EG *The chicks are covered with down when they emerge from the egg.* — N UNCOUNT **20.2** very fine hair. EG *...the fine down on her cheek.* — N UNCOUNT

21 • **ups and downs**: see **up**.

down-and-out, down-and-outs. A **down-and-out** is a person who has no job and no home and who has no hope of getting work or finding somewhere to live. EG *His research took him among the down-and-outs in the city of Liverpool.* — N COUNT = tramp

down at heel; also spelled with hyphens. Someone or something that is **down at heel** looks in bad condition, because of lack of money. EG *He looked somewhat down at heel... ...a crumbling, Victorian resort, slightly down at heel, full of ghosts.* — ADJ QUALIT = shabby ≠ new

downbeat /daʊnbiːt/. Something or someone that is **downbeat** is deliberately casual and restrained; used in informal English. EG *Johnny was hurt that Nino should be so downbeat.* — ADJ QUALIT

downcast /daʊnkɑːst/. 1 If you are **downcast**, you are feeling sad and pessimistic. EG *Cameron seemed unusually downcast and taciturn.* — ADJ QUALIT = dejected

2 If your eyes are **downcast**, you are looking towards the ground, usually because you are feeling sad or embarrassed. EG *He stood still with his eyes downcast... With downcast eyes I explained that I was not the person they all thought I was.* — ADJ CLASSIF = lowered ≠ raised

downer /daʊnə/, **downers**; used in informal English. 1 A **downer** is a drug that causes you to feel sleepy or very calm, for example a barbiturate drug. — N COUNT ≠ upper

2 If you are **on a downer**, you are feeling depressed and pessimistic. — PHR : USED AS AN A

downfall /daʊnfɔːl/. 1 The **downfall** of an institution or person is their failure or ruin, when they have previously been successful or powerful. EG *...the downfall of a dictator.* — N UNCOUNT : USU WITH POSS

2 Something that is the **downfall** of a particular person or thing is the thing that causes the person or thing to be ruined or to fail. EG *Bad publicity was our downfall.* — N UNCOUNT : USU WITH POSS ⇑ ruin

downgrade /daʊngreɪd/, **downgrades, downgrading, downgraded**; also spelled with a hyphen. If you **downgrade** something, you make it less important, less valuable, or less prestigious. EG *The European allies were reluctant to downgrade the nuclear element in deterrence... We are downgrading the quality of our lives.* — V+O ⇑ lower ≠ upgrade

downhearted /daʊnhɑːtɪ²d/. If you are **downhearted**, you are feeling sad and discouraged. EG *Don't be too downhearted.* — ADJ QUALIT ⇑ depressed = dejected

downhill /daʊnhɪl/. 1 If something is moving **downhill**, it is moving down a slope towards a lower point. EG *The children were racing downhill on their sledges.* — ADV AFTER VB ⇑ downwards

2 **Downhill** skiing is skiing in which you go down a slope, especially a prepared slope. — ADJ CLASSIF : USU ATTRIB

3 If a thing or situation is going **downhill**, it is changing and becoming less pleasant or less acceptable. EG *Journalism is going downhill nowadays... Believe me, after age thirty it's all downhill.* — ADV AFTER VB

4 **Downhill** means easier to do or to manage than before. EG *It was downhill all the way after that.* — ADJ CLASSIF : USU PRED

Downing Street is used to refer to the Prime Minister or the British government. EG *The idea was not well received at Downing Street.* — N PROPER

down-market; also spelled without a hyphen. Something such as a product or service that is **down-market** is popular and cheap and not very good in quality. EG *We sell a lot of down-market books... Chichester has gone distinctly downmarket.* — ADJ QUALIT, OR ADV AFTER VB ⇑ lowbrow ≠ upmarket

down payment, down payments; also spelled with a hyphen. A **down payment** is a sum of money which is part of the total cost of something and which is paid immediately when you buy the thing. The remaining amount can be paid later. — N COUNT = deposit

downpour /daʊnpɔː/, **downpours**. When there is a **downpour**, a lot of rain falls fast and heavily. EG *It was the heaviest downpour ever recorded.* — N COUNT

downright /daʊnraɪt/ is used to give emphasis to a particular aspect of a person or situation, especially one which is unpleasant or alarming. EG *Some of the jobs were downright disgusting... ...accusing them of fraud, avarice, and downright misrepresentation.* — ADV, OR ADJ CLASSIF : ATTRIB = out and out

Down's syndrome. If a baby is born with **Down's syndrome**, it has less than normal intelligence and develops a flat forehead and nose and sloping eyes. — N UNCOUNT = mongolism

downstairs /daʊnsteəz/. 1 If you go **downstairs** in a building, you go down towards the ground floor, usually down a staircase. EG *He went downstairs and into the kitchen.* — ADV AFTER VB ≠ upstairs

2 If something or someone is **downstairs** in a building, they are on the ground floor or on a lower floor than you are. EG *Arthur isn't downstairs; he is asleep in bed... My aunt's photograph still stood on the piano downstairs.* — ADV AFTER VB, OR ADJ AFTER N ⇑ below ≠ upstairs

3 A **downstairs** room or object is one which is situated on the ground floor or a lower floor of a building. EG *Jenny's on the downstairs phone.* — ADJ CLASSIF : ATTRIB ≠ upstairs

4 If you refer to a person **downstairs**, you are referring to someone who lives in a flat or room on the ground floor or on a lower floor of a building. EG *I had to leave the baby with the woman downstairs.* — ADJ AFTER N ⇑ below ≠ upstairs

downstream /daʊnstriːm/ means towards or nearer to the mouth of a river, from a point further up the river. EG *The soil from the river banks is washed downstream.* — ADV WITH VB ≠ upstream

down-to-earth; also spelled without hyphens. Something or someone that is **down-to-earth** is concerned with doing practical things and solving problems in a practical way, rather than with abstract theories. EG *...his warm, down-to-earth manner... He had much more down-to-earth reasons.* — ADJ QUALIT ⇑ realistic = practical

downtown /daʊntaʊn/ means in or to the centre part of a large town or city, where the shops and places of business are. EG *May has given up shopping in downtown Belfast... We went downtown to buy a new pair of shoes.* — ADV WITH VB, OR ADJ CLASSIF : ATTRIB ⇑ central

downtrodden /daʊntrɒdəⁿn/. **Downtrodden** people have been oppressed so much that they no longer have the ability or the energy to rebel. EG *This country has the most poverty-stricken and downtrodden population in the world.* — ADJ QUALIT = cowed

downturn /daʊntɜːn/, **downturns**. A **downturn** is a decline in the economy or in the success of a company or industry. EG *The downturn in inflation has only taken place in the last three months... There will be a similar downturn in manufacturing and industry.* — N COUNT : USU SING ≠ upturn

down under; also spelled with a hyphen. **Down under** is used to refer to Australia or New Zealand; used in informal British English. EG *...my cousin from down under.* — PHR : USED AS O/A

downwards /daʊnwədz/; also **downward**. 1 If something moves, looks, etc **downwards** or **downward**, it moves or looks down towards the ground. EG *He kept his head on one side as he spoke, looking downward... Beneath them lie more layers extending downwards for thousands of feet... Read from the top* — ADV AFTER VB, OR ADV AFTER N = down ≠ upward, upwards *downwards... I saw my old dad lying face downward on the floor.*

2 A **downward** movement or look moves or points down towards the ground. EG *She made a bold downward stroke with the paint brush... ...a downward glance.* ADJ CLASSIF : ATTRIB ≠ upward

3 You use **downwards** or **downward** to say that something falls to a lower level or point on a scale. EG *The nations of the West seem to have begun the slow spiral downwards into decay... The USA revised downward its grain output forecast... The long term trend in the male suicide rate is downwards.* ADV AFTER VB = down ≠ upward, upwards

▸ **Downward** can be used as an adjective. EG *...a downward trend in inflation... This can cause a downward spiral in economic activity.* ▸ ADJ CLASSIF : USU ATTRIB ≠ upward

downwind /daʊnwɪnd/. 1 If something moves **downwind**, it moves in the same direction as the direction the wind is blowing in. EG *The sparks drifted downwind.* ADV AFTER VB ≠ upwind

2 If you are **downwind** of something, the wind passes over it before reaching you. EG *He was downwind of the fire and could smell the food.* ADV AFTER VB : IF+PREP THEN of

downy /daʊni[1]/, **downier, downiest**. Something that is **downy** is 1 filled with or covered with small soft feathers. EG *...thick downy feather beds.* 2 covered with very fine hairs. EG *Her skin was slightly downy.* ADJ CLASSIF; ADJ QUALIT ⇑ hairy

dowry /daʊəri[1]/, **dowries**. A woman's **dowry** is money and goods which are a gift from her father to the man that she marries. EG *...a carved chair which was part of Maria's dowry.* N COUNT ⇑ property

dowse /daʊs/, **dowses, dowsing, dowsed**. 1 When someone **dowses**, they search for underground water or minerals using a special stick called a divining rod. V : USU+*for*

2 See also **douse**.

doyen /dɔɪən/, **doyens**; a fairly formal word. The **doyen** of a group or profession is the oldest and most experienced and respected member of it. EG *...the doyen of fashion journalism.* N COUNT : USU SING, *the*+N+*of* ⇑ veteran

doyenne /dɔɪən/, **doyennes**; a fairly formal word. The **doyenne** of a group or profession is the woman who is the oldest and most experienced and respected member of it. N COUNT : USU SING, *the*+N+*of* ⇑ veteran

doz. is a written abbreviation for 'dozen'.

doze /dəʊz/, **dozes, dozing, dozed**. When you **doze**, you sleep lightly or for a short period, especially during the daytime. EG *While the adults doze, the young play.* ▸ used as a noun. EG *I fell into a short doze at about ten o'clock.* V = snooze; ▸ N COUNT = nap

doze off. If you **doze off**, you fall into a light sleep, especially during the daytime. EG *He dozed off in front of the fire.* PHRASAL VB : V+ADV = nod off

dozen /dʌzəⁿn/, **dozens**. **Dozen** is used as the plural form if it is preceded by a number or expression referring to a number. See ☐ at **number** and **measurement**. 1 If you have a **dozen** things, you have twelve of them. EG *...a dozen eggs... The drive was cluttered with half a dozen cars... ...a few dozen grass mats.* NUM : *a*/NUM+*dozen*

2 A **dozen** or **dozens** can be used to refer vaguely to a large number, usually when you are exaggerating. EG *I've told you a dozen times now!... There had been dozens of attempts at reform.* NUM : BEFORE N, OR NUM IN PL, USED AS N PART = many

3 ● to **talk nineteen to the dozen**: see **nineteen**. ● See also **baker's dozen**.

dozy /dəʊzi[1]/, **dozier, doziest**. 1 If you are **dozy**, you are feeling sleepy and not very alert. EG *They lay still and dozy for another hour or so.* ADJ QUALIT = drowsy

2 Someone who is **dozy** is rather stupid and slow to understand things; an informal use. EG *Not like that, you dozy fool!* ADJ QUALIT

Dr, Drs. **Dr** is a written abbreviation for 1 doctor; used before a person's name. EG *Dr. Franz was an economist of some standing... ...Drs Miles, Dick, and Jamieson.* 2 Drive; used in street names. EG *...Clarendon Dr.* N IN TITLES : HAS PL; N IN NAMES

drab /dræb/, **drabber, drabbest**. 1 Something that is **drab** is dull and not exciting to look at or experience. EG *We went into the drab old building... Life was now drab compared with the more exciting life style overseas.* ◊ **drabness**. EG *...the ugliness and drabness of most people's surroundings.* ADJ QUALIT = dreary ≠ exciting; ◊ N UNCOUNT

2 **Drab** is a dull brown colour. ADJ COLOUR

3 See also **dribs and drabs**.

drachma /drækmə/, **drachmae, drachmas**. The plural can be either **drachmae** or **drachmas**. The **drachma** is the unit of money used in Greece. N COUNT

draconian /dreɪkəʊnɪən/. **Draconian** laws or measures are extremely harsh or drastic; used showing disapproval. EG *There has been an overall growth in population, despite some draconian efforts to contain it.* ADJ CLASSIF : ATTRIB ⇑ harsh

draft /drɑːft/, **drafts, drafting, drafted**. 1 A **draft** is an early version of a letter, book, or speech which you are going to write, containing only the broad ideas and not the details. EG *He showed me the draft of an article he was writing... ...the change from the first draft to the final printed version.* N COUNT : USU+SUPP ⇑ outline

2 When you **draft** a letter, book, or speech, you write the first version of it. EG *They sat down and drafted a letter to the local newspaper... The President drafted a bill which he presented to Congress.* V+O = compose

3 The **draft** is the practice of ordering people to serve in the armed forces, usually for a limited period of time; used in American English. EG *He left America so that he could avoid the draft... He received his draft card three months after he left school.* N SING : *the*+N = conscription

4 If you **are drafted**, you are ordered to serve in the armed forces; used in American English. EG *I was drafted into the navy... He took a temporary job while he was waiting to be drafted.* V+O : USU PASS = conscripted

5 If you **draft** people somewhere, you move them to another place so that they can do a specific job. EG *Extra staff were drafted from Paris to Rome to arrange the President's visit... He hoped to draft in a force of 20,000 guerrillas to help overthrow the government.* V+O, OR V+A *(in)*

6 A **draft** is also a written order for payment of money by a bank, especially from one bank to another. EG *I arranged for a draft for £500 to be available in Rome... I was paid by draft... ...cheques, bankers' drafts, or letters of credit.* N COUNT, OR *by*+N

7 See also **draught**.

draft dodger, draft dodgers. A **draft dodger** is someone who avoids joining the armed forces when normally they would be obliged to join; used in American English. N COUNT

draftee /drɑːftiː/, **draftees**. A **draftee** is a person who serves in the armed forces because they have been ordered to, rather than because they volunteered; used in American English. N COUNT ⇑ soldier = conscript

draftsman /drɑːftsmən/, **draftsmen**. See **draughtsman**.

draftsmanship /drɑːftsmənʃɪp/. See **draughtsmanship**.

drafty /drɑːfti[1]/, **draftier, draftiest**. See **draughty**.

drag /dræg/, **drags, dragging, dragged**. 1 If you **drag** something along, you pull it along the ground slowly and with difficulty, usually because it is too heavy or too big to carry. EG *He watched her drag a chair across the room to join them... He listened as the body was dragged up the stairs.* V+O : USU+A = lug, haul

2 If you **drag** someone or something into a particular place or position, you pull them there roughly and using force. EG *He grabbed her and dragged her away... They overturned a car and dragged out the driver... A lot of the plants had been dragged up by the roots.* V+O+A = haul

3 If you **drag** someone somewhere they do not want to go, you make them go there. EG *I'm sorry to drag you to the telephone, but something awful has happened.* V+O+A ⇑ take

4 If you **drag** your foot or another part of your body, you let it touch the ground and be pulled along behind you as you move. EG *He moved slowly, dragging his sore foot... The bird tried to get him away from her nest by dragging a wing as if it had been injured.* V+O ⇑ pull = trail

5 If you **drag** yourself somewhere, you move there slowly and with difficulty. EG *I was able to use the table to drag myself shakily to my feet... Even though she felt ill, she managed to drag herself down to the shops.* V+O (REFL)+A = force

6 If you **drag** along, **drag** around, etc, you go somewhere slowly, usually because you do not want to go. EG *I dragged along behind my sisters who were chatting happily... She found herself dragging around the park with Maria moaning about her children.* V+A = trail

7 If you **drag** yourself away from something, you V+O (NG/REFL)

force yourself to move or to leave somewhere when you do not want to leave. EG *Jack dragged his eyes away from the girl... They could not drag themselves away from the party.* +A (away)

8 If a period of time or an event **drags**, it is very boring and seems to last a long time. EG *The part of the play which drags is the last half-hour... The day was dragging, and I was beginning to wonder if night would ever come.* V = go on

9 When people **drag** a lake or river, they pull nets or hooks across the bottom of it in order to look for something which is lost or missing. EG *I told her I was leaving because I didn't want the police dragging the river for my body.* V+O = dredge

10 If something is a **drag** on the development or progress of something, it slows it down and makes it more difficult. EG *She feels that her children have been a real drag on her career.* N SING : a+N+on ⇑ handicap

11 If you say that something is a **drag**, you mean that it is a nuisance or is very dull; used in informal English. EG *She thought that wearing school uniform was a real drag... It was a drag to drive 30 kilometres to work every day.* N SING : a+N ⇑ nuisance = bore

12 **Drag** is the wearing of women's clothes by a male entertainer. EG *I went to his new show, but I don't find drag funny.* N UNCOUNT ● If a man, especially a male entertainer, is **in drag**, he is wearing women's clothes. ● PHR : USED AS AN A

13 **Drag** is also the resistance to the movement that is experienced by something that is moving through air or through a fluid; a technical term in engineering. N UNCOUNT

14 If you take a **drag** on a cigarette or pipe that you are smoking, you take in air through it; used in informal English. EG *He smiled and took a drag on his pipe.* N COUNT = draw, puff

15 If you **drag** your **heels** or **drag** your **feet**, you delay doing something or do it very slowly because you do not want to do it. EG *It's quite clear that the Government have been dragging their feet over this bill.* PHR : VB INFLECTS = hang back

drag down. 1 Someone who **drags** someone else **down** reduces them to an inferior social status or to lower standards of behaviour. EG *His mother hates me. She thinks I drag him down.* PHRASAL VB : V+O+ADV ⇑ demean

2 Something that **drags** you **down** makes you feel weak or depressed. EG *That bout of flu really dragged me down... I felt dragged down by the obligations I had.* PHRASAL VB : V+O+ADV ⇑ weaken

drag in. If you **drag in** a particular thing, you mention it when it is not really relevant to the conversation. EG *They disapproved of my dragging in his wealth.* PHRASAL VB : V+O+ADV

drag into. To **drag** something or someone **into** an event or situation means to involve them in it when it is not necessary or not desirable. EG *I pointed out that it was the politicians who were dragging politics into sport, not the sportsmen... That's no reason for dragging you into it.* PHRASAL VB : V+O+PREP = bring into

drag on. If an event or process **drags on** or **drags along**, it progresses very slowly. EG *Some legal cases drag on for many years... His divorce was dragging along... The weeks dragged on, but no one ever came to see me.* PHRASAL VB : V+ADV ⇑ last

drag out. 1 If you **drag** something **out**, you make it last for longer than is necessary. EG *We did not know how to prevent them from dragging out the talks.* PHRASAL VB : V+O+ADV ⇑ prolong = spin out

2 If you **drag** something **out** of someone, you persuade them to tell you something that they do not want to tell you. EG *The truth had to be dragged out of him.* PHRASAL VB : V+O+ADV

drag up. If someone **drags up** an unpleasant event or an old story from the past, they mention it when it is not really necessary, and so remind people of it. EG *There's no need to drag that up again.* PHRASAL VB : V+O+ADV = bring up

dragon /drægən/, **dragons**. 1 In stories and legends, a **dragon** is an animal like a big lizard. It has wings and claws and breathes out fire. N COUNT

2 If you call a woman a **dragon**, you mean that she is fierce and unpleasant; a fairly informal use. N COUNT

dragonfly /drægənflaɪ/, **dragonflies**. A **dragonfly** is a brightly-coloured insect with a long thin body and two pairs of wings, which is often found near slow-moving or still water. N COUNT

dragoon /drəguːn/, **dragoons, dragooning, dragooned**. A **dragoon** was a soldier in old European armies. Dragoons usually fought on horseback but were also trained to fight on foot. N COUNT

dragoon into. If you **dragoon** someone **into** something that they do not want to do, you force them to do it. EG *She seems to have this ghastly need to dragoon us all into her schemes.* PHRASAL VB : V+O+PREP = bully

drain /dreɪn/, **drains, draining, drained**. 1 If you **drain** something, you make a liquid, especially water, gradually flow out of it until there is none left. EG *It is important to drain the wound.* V+O ⇑ empty

2 If a liquid **drains** somewhere, it it flows there gradually. EG *All the sewage drains off into the river... The seas drained away and the sea bed became dry... These veins drain the blood from the brain.* V-ERG+A

3 If something **drains**, it becomes dry, because water or other liquid is dripping or flowing off it. EG *Put those plates on the rack to drain.* V ⇑ drip

4 If you **drain** wet land, you dry it by causing water to gradually flow out of it, usually so that it can be used for agriculture. EG *It was marsh once, drained by Henry VIII for a deer park... The clay was drained and much of it turned into bricks.* V+O = dry out ≠ flood

5 If you **drain** a glass, you empty it by drinking what is in it. EG *Mary picked up the glass and drained it... He drained what was left of his drink.* V+O

6 If the colour **drains** from your face, you become very pale. EG *Slowly the red drained from Jack's cheeks.* V+A (from) ⇑ fade = ebb

7 If a feeling **drains** away or **drains** out of you, it gradually becomes less strong until you no longer feel it. EG *He felt the tension drain out of him... Gradually he feels his reluctance draining away.* V+A ⇑ fade = melt

8 If something **drains** someone's strength, energy, or resources, it gradually uses them up. EG *The project is already draining the charity's funds.* V+O ⇑ use up = exhaust

9 If something **drains** you, it leaves you feeling physically and emotionally exhausted. EG *This kind of work drains you.* V+O ⇑ weaken ◇ **drained**. EG *She looked tired and drained after visiting him in prison.* ◇ ADJ QUALIT = worn out

11 If something is a **drain** on your resources, it gradually uses them up. EG *The banks suddenly are facing a very large drain on their funds... ...a heavy drain on military manpower.* ● See also **brain drain**. N SING : a+N+on

12 A **drain** is 12.1 a pipe that carries water or sewage away from a place. EG *...laying drains under fields.* N COUNT

12.2 a metal grid set into the pavement or road through which rainwater can collect into the drainage system. EG *He dropped the keys down a large drain set into the pavement.* N COUNT

13 If you say that something goes or is thrown **down the drain**, you mean that it is wasted. EG *That's just money down the drain.* PHR : USED AS AN A ● If a business is **going down the drain**, it is being ruined or is failing financially. EG *He wrote to tell me that his business had just gone down the drain.* ● PHR : VB INFLECTS ⇑ fail = go bust, fold

drainage /dreɪnɪdʒ/ is 1 the system of pipes, drains or ditches that are used for draining water or other liquids. EG *Massive big drainage ditches take the water away.* N UNCOUNT 2 the act or process of draining or the way in which something drains. EG *Good drainage doesn't mean dry soil... Bad drainage caused the land to be flooded.* N UNCOUNT

draining board, draining boards; also spelled with a hyphen. A **draining board** is the place on a sink unit where things such as cups, plates, cutlery, etc are put to drain after the washing up. N COUNT

drainpipe /dreɪnpaɪp/, **drainpipes**; also spelled as two words. A **drainpipe** is a large pipe through which unwanted water or sewage flows into a drainage system. EG *There were several broken and leaking drainpipes and gutters.* N COUNT

drake /dreɪk/, **drakes**. A **drake** is a male duck. N COUNT

dram /dræm/, **drams**. A **dram** is a small measure of an alcoholic drink such as whisky; used especially in Scottish English. EG *Would you care for a dram?* N COUNT

drama /drɑːmə/, **dramas**. 1 A **drama** is 1.1 a serious play for the theatre, television, or radio. EG *I remember her acting in a drama called The Garden Party.* N COUNT ⇑ work 1.2 a situation that contains interest and excitement, like a play. EG *...a human drama.* N COUNT

2 You use the word **drama** to refer to 2.1 plays in general, or a number of plays which have a similar style, especially those written during a particular period of history. EG *...drama, music, and painting... ...an expert on modern poetic drama.* N UNCOUNT = theatre 2.2 work that is connected with plays and the theatre, such as N UNCOUNT

acting or producing. EG *She went in for drama... She enjoyed two years at drama school.* **2.3** the quality of being interesting and exciting which a situation has. EG *...the drama of politics.*
N SING WITH DET ⇑ excitement

dramatic /drəmætɪk/, **dramatics.** 1 A **dramatic** change or event happens suddenly and is very noticeable and surprising. EG *I expect to see dramatic improvements.* ◊ **dramatically.** EG *The way in which information is transmitted has changed dramatically.*
ADJ QUALIT ⇑ sudden = marked; ◊ ADV = radically

2 An event, situation, or thing that is **dramatic** is very exciting, interesting, and impressive. EG *Landing on the moon was one of the most dramatic scientific adventures of this century.*
ADJ QUALIT

3 If something that you say or do is **dramatic**, it is said or done suddenly, and in a way that is intended to impress or surprise people. EG *'Look!' she said, flinging open the lid with a dramatic gesture.* ◊ **dramatically.** EG *He paused dramatically.*
ADJ QUALIT = theatrical, stirring; ◊ ADV AFTER VB

4 **Dramatic** also means connected with the theatre or written in the form of a play. EG *...Browning's dramatic works.*
ADJ CLASSIF : ATTRIB

5 You use the word **dramatics** to refer to **5.1** activities concerned with the theatre, such as acting in plays or producing them, usually as an amateur. EG *Both of them are involved in amateur dramatics.*
N UNCOUNT = theatricals

5.2 behaviour which seems to show too much emotion, and which you think is done deliberately in order to impress people. EG *George's dramatics were beginning to irritate me.*
N PLURAL : the/POSS+N = histrionics

dramatis personae /drɑːmətɪs pəsəʊnaɪ/. The **dramatis personae** of a play are all the characters in that play; a formal expression.
N PLURAL : the+N = cast

dramatist /dræmətɪst/, **dramatists.** A **dramatist** is someone who writes plays. EG *He knew all the major English novelists, poets and dramatists.*
N COUNT ⇑ writer = playwright

dramatize /dræmətaɪz/, **dramatizes, dramatizing, dramatized**; also spelled **dramatise.** 1 If you **dramatize** a book or story, you rewrite it as a play. EG *His ambition is to dramatise the great works of literature.* ◊ **dramatization** /dræmətaɪzeɪʃəⁿn/, **dramatizations.** EG *It was a dramatization of the story of Ali Baba.*
V+O; ◊ N COUNT ⇑ production

2 If you **dramatize** an event or situation, you try to make it seem more serious, more important, or more exciting than it really is. EG *The conflict has been dramatized in the newspapers... Oh dear! You do dramatise.*
V OR V+O ⇑ exaggerate

drank /dræŋk/ is the past tense of **drink.**

drape /dreɪp/, **drapes, draping, draped.** 1 If you **drape** a piece of cloth somewhere, you arrange it there so that it hangs down and looks attractive or so that it covers something. EG *He brought out a shawl which he began to drape carefully over Gertrude's shoulders... They have draped banners across trees and bushes.*
V+O+A

2 If something **is draped** with or in a piece of cloth, it is covered by it, usually in an attractive way. EG *...coffins draped with American flags... The lectern was draped in white silk sheets.*
V+O : IF+PREP THEN with/in ⇑ cover = swathe

3 If a piece of cloth **drapes** something, it covers it. EG *Dust sheets draped the corridors.*
V+O ⇑ cover

4 If you **drape** a part of your body somewhere, you lay it there in a relaxed way. EG *Their feet were draped over the empty seats in front of them.*
V+O+A = dangle

5 A **drape** is a curtain; used in American English. EG *The drapes were drawn and the lights turned off.*
N COUNT : USU PL

draper /dreɪpə/, **drapers.** A **draper** is someone who has a shop which sells cloth; used in British English. EG *...a draper's shop.* ▸ The **draper** or the **draper's** is used to refer to the shop itself.
N COUNT

drapery /dreɪpəⁿri¹/, **draperies.** 1 You can refer to cloth or clothing that hangs in folds as **drapery** or **draperies.** EG *...the idealized drapery of Renaissance saints... A little wind fluttered her silk draperies as she leant forward... Crimson draperies were looped along the walls.*
N UNCOUNT OR N PLURAL

2 **Draperies** are also thick curtains. EG *Karen ran to the window and pulled the draperies back.*
N PLURAL

3 **Drapery** is also, in British English, cloth or things made from cloth that you can buy in a draper's shop or in a department store. EG *...the drapery department.*
N UNCOUNT

drastic /dræstɪk/. 1 A **drastic** course of action is very strong and severe and is usually taken urgently to solve a problem. EG *This may force the Government to take drastic measures... This drastic step may result in the loss of everything.*
ADJ QUALIT = extreme

2 A **drastic** change is one that is very significant and noticeable. EG *...the recent drastic decline in flat-building... Everybody should be encouraged to make drastic changes in their eating habits and life-style.* ◊ **drastically.** EG *Because of the snow, visibility was drastically reduced.*
ADJ QUALIT = dramatic; ◊ ADV = severely

drat /dræt/; a mild, old-fashioned swear word. You say **'drat'**, **'drat it'**, **'drat the man'**, etc when you are annoyed about something.
EXCLAM

draught /drɑːft/, **draughts**; also spelled **draft** in American English. 1 A **draught** is **1.1** a current of air, usually one coming into a room or a vehicle. EG *The draught from the window stirred the papers on her desk... They used to open the windows and doors to create a draught... She found herself a draught-free corner to sit in.*
N COUNT ⇑ wind

1.2 a large amount of water or air, which you swallow or breathe in all at one time. EG *I made a trip to the bathroom for a draught of water... He gulped the brandy down in one draught... He stood there drinking in great draughts of the scented air.*
N COUNT : USU+SUPP

1.3 a medicine in the form of a liquid which you drink; a formal or rather old-fashioned use. EG *I shall give them a sleeping draught before we go out... ...a healing draught.*
N COUNT+SUPP

2 **Draught** beer is beer which is kept in barrels rather than bottles.
ADJ CLASSIF : USU ATTRIB

3 Beer that is **on draught** is kept in and served from a barrel and not from a bottle. EG *We have Guinness on draught.*
PHR : USED AS AN A = on tap

4 **Draughts** is a game for two people, played with 24 round pieces on a board; used in British English.
N UNCOUNT = checkers

5 A **draught** is also one of the round pieces which are used in the game of draughts; used in British English.
N COUNT

6 A **draught** animal is one which pulls heavy loads, for example on a farm. EG *Oxen are very good draught animals.*
ADJ CLASSIF : ATTRIB

draughtboard /drɑːftbɔːd/, **draughtboards.** A **draughtboard** is a board divided into 64 squares, on which the game of draughts is played; used in British English.
N COUNT = checkerboard

draughtsman /drɑːftsmən/, **draughtsmen**; also spelled **draftsman** in American English. A **draughtsman** is 1 someone who is very skilled at drawing. EG *He trained himself as a draughtsman and is now a professional cartoonist.*
N COUNT ⇑ artist

2 someone whose job is to prepare very detailed drawings of machinery, equipment, or buildings. EG *My father worked as a draughtsman in a shipyard.*
N COUNT

draughtsmanship /drɑːftsmənʃɪp/; also spelled **draftsmanship** in American English. **Draughtsmanship** is the ability to draw well or the act of drawing. EG *The draughtsmanship of the forgery was excellent.*
N UNCOUNT ⇑ artistry

draughty /drɑːfti¹/, **draughtier, draughtiest**; also spelled **drafty** in American English. A room or building that is **draughty** has cold air blowing through it. EG *The building was cold and draughty and damp and dirty.*
ADJ QUALIT

draw /drɔː/, **draws, drawing, drew, drawn.** 1 When you **draw** or when you **draw** something, you use a pencil, pen, crayon, etc to make a picture, pattern, or diagram which usually shows only the outlines of something. EG *She used to draw funny pictures of everybody during lessons... He sat there, drawing the tree... We ought to draw a map... He admits that he can't draw.*
V OR V+O ⇑ depict

2 When a vehicle **draws** away, **draws** out, **draws** off, etc, it moves away, out, off, etc smoothly and steadily. EG *The cab drew away from the kerb... The car drew out into the middle of the road... Before she could reach the bus stop, the bus had drawn off... The bus drew to a halt.*
V+A ⇑ move

3 If you **draw** away, near, etc, you move away, near, etc; a fairly formal use. EG *He began to draw away... As the people draw near they can hear the deep growling roar... When we drew level I smiled... The slave drew back in fear.*
V+A

4 If you **draw** someone somewhere, you lead them there, perhaps by touching them gently. EG *She drew her into the back room... He drew me aside, and whispered in my ear.*
V+O+A

5 If an event or period of time is **drawing** near, or **drawing** closer, it is approaching. EG *Their wedding day was drawing nearer all the time.*
V+A = approach

6 When an event or period of time **draws to an end**
PHR : VB

or **draws to a close**, it finishes. EG *The meeting drew to an end.* INFLECTS = finish

7 If you **draw** something from a particular place or in a particular direction, you pull it there with a smooth movement. EG *He draws the document from its folder... She drew the comb lightly through her hair... The man drew back his fist and punched him hard in the face... I shivered, and drew my coat closer around me... He drew on his socks.* V+O+A

8 If an animal **draws** a cart or other vehicle, it pulls it. EG *She saw two-wheeled and four-wheeled vehicles drawn by huge animals.* V+O ⇑ pull = haul

9 If you **draw** a curtain or blind, you pull it across a window, either to cover or to uncover it. EG *He drew the curtains... A neighbour saw that his curtains weren't drawn back... She drew down the blinds, and turned the light on.* V+O

10 If someone **draws** a gun, knife, or other weapon, they pull it out of its holder, so that it is ready to use. EG *He was ever ready to draw his sword... She drew on me, but I was too quick for her.* V OR V+O : IF+ PREP THEN *on* ⇑ pull out

11 To **draw** a tooth means to pull it out; an old-fashioned use. EG *They drew all the lion's teeth.* V+O = extract

12 If you **draw** a deep breath, you breathe in deeply once. V+O

13 To **draw breath** means to take a break from what you are doing. EG *I've hardly had time to draw breath today.* PHR : VB INFLECTS ⇑ rest

14 To **draw** something such as water or energy from a particular source means to take it from that source. EG *There was a well outside where we drew water to drink... They draw electricity from the national power network.* V+O : USU+A

15 If something that hits you or presses part of your body **draws** blood, it cuts your skin so that it bleeds. V+O

16 If you **draw** money out of a bank, building society, or savings account, you take it out from where it is kept so that you can use it. EG *He drew fifty pounds from his savings account.* V+O+A = withdraw

17 If you **draw** a cheque, you use it to obtain money or goods; a technical term in banking. EG *She drew a cheque on her account.* V+O = cash

18 If you **draw** a salary or a sum of money, you receive it regularly. EG *She draws a good salary each month.* V+O

19 To **draw** something means to choose it or to be given it by chance, as part of a competition, game, or lottery. EG *The duchess drew the name of the winner... Brazil have drawn Spain in the semi-final of the Cup.* V+O

20 A **draw** is **20.1** an act of choosing or being given something by chance. EG *The draw for the next round will be made on Monday.* N COUNT ⇑ selection **20.2** a competition where people pay money for numbered or named tickets, then some of those tickets are chosen by chance, and the owners are given prizes. N COUNT = raffle

21 If you say that something is **the luck of the draw**, you mean that it is the result of chance and you cannot do anything about it. PHR : USED AS C

22 To **draw** something from a particular thing or place means to take or get it from that thing or place. EG *The plan drew strength from its simplicity... The committee members are drawn from all sections of the local community.* V+O+A *(from)* = tap

23 If you **draw** a particular conclusion, you decide that that conclusion is true. EG *What conclusions do you draw from all this?* V+O = infer

24 If you **draw** a distinction, comparison, parallel, etc, you make it or mention it. EG *He never hesitates to draw comparisons... He drew a parallel between unemployment and suicide rates.* V+O

25 If someone **draws** a particular reaction, they get that reaction when they do something. EG *The police drew praise for their cool handling of the riots... The Government's action drew an angry response.* V+O = attract

26 If you **draw attention** to something or **draw** someone's **attention** to it, you make someone aware of it or make them think about it. EG *He drew attention to the rising unemployment rates... I drew her attention to her dirty fingernails.* PHR+*to* : VB INFLECTS = point out

27 If something **draws** you, **27.1** it is so interesting or noticeable that you look at it or move towards it. EG *The noise of the radio draws the children... The film was drawing huge crowds.* V+O = attract **27.2** it attracts you very strongly. EG *She was shy, and perhaps he was drawn to her for that reason.* V+O

28 A **draw** is also a person, place, show, or event that attracts a lot of people to come and see it; a fairly informal use. EG *The main draw in Agra is of course the Taj Mahal.* N COUNT : USU SING = attraction

29 If someone will not **be drawn** or refuses to **be drawn**, they will not reply to questions in the way that you want them to, or will not reveal information or their opinion. EG *I asked him, but he refused to be drawn.* V+O : ONLY PASS, USU INF WITH BROAD NEG

30 In a game or competition, if one person or team **draws** with or against another one, or if two people or teams **draw**, they have the same number of points at the end of the game. EG *Brazil and Spain drew in the World Cup... Brazil drew against Spain.* V+A *(with/against)*, V, OR V+O = tie

31 A **draw** is also a result of a game or competition in which two or more people draw. EG *The match ended in a goalless draw.* N COUNT = tie

32 • to **draw a blank**: see **blank**. • **at daggers drawn**: see **dagger**. • to **draw** someone's **fire**: see **fire**. • to **draw the line**: see **line**. • to **draw lots**: see **lot**. • See also **drawing, drawn**.

draw in. 1 If you say that the evenings or nights **are drawing in**, you mean that it is becoming dark at an earlier time in the evening, because autumn or winter is approaching. PHRASAL VB : V+ADV

2 When a train **draws in**, it arrives at a station and stops. PHRASAL VB : V+ADV

3 If you **draw** someone **in** or **draw** someone **into** something, you cause them to become involved with it. EG *I quite by chance got drawn into a kind of party downstairs... Peter drew her into the discussion.* PHRASAL VB : V+O+ADV/PREP ⇑ involve = rope in

4 If you **draw in** breath, you breathe deeply. EG *She drew in her breath.* PHRASAL VB : V+O+ADV

draw off. If you **draw off** a quantity of liquid, you take it, usually through a pipe or tube, from a larger quantity. EG *She drew off some of the beer, to see if it was ready to drink.* PHRASAL VB : V+O+ADV

draw on. 1 If a period of time **draws on**, it gets nearer or passes. EG *The evening drew on, and Andrew and I got drunk.* PHRASAL VB : V+ADV = advance

2 If you **draw on** something, you make use of it in order to do something. EG *The company can draw on their vast reserves to pay for the project.* PHRASAL VB : V+PREP, HAS PASS

3 When someone **draws on** a cigarette, they breathe in through it and so inhale the smoke. PHRASAL VB : V+PREP, HAS PASS

draw out. 1 When a train **draws out**, it starts moving and leaves the station. EG *The guard blew his whistle, and the train drew out.* PHRASAL VB : V+ADV = pull out

2 If you **draw out** something such as a sound, you make it longer. EG *'Ah,' she said, smiling, drawing out the 'ah'.* PHRASAL VB : V+O+ADV ⇑ lengthen

3 If you **draw** information **out** of someone, you get them to tell it to you. EG *It was impossible to draw the truth out of him.* PHRASAL VB : V+O+ADV = elicit

4 If you **draw** someone **out**, you make them feel less nervous and more willing to talk. EG *Why not make conversation with them, draw them out, make them laugh and feel at ease?* PHRASAL VB : ORDER V+O+ADV

draw up. 1 When you **draw up** a document, list, or plan, you prepare it and write it out. EG *A charter was drawn up, setting out their policies... I was busy drawing up plans for the new course.* PHRASAL VB : V+ADV+O = formulate

2 When a car or other vehicle **draws up**, it comes to a particular place and stops. EG *Just before eleven a bus drew up.* PHRASAL VB : V+ADV = pull up

3 If you **draw up** a chair, you move it nearer to a person or place, for example so that you can watch something or join in with something. EG *Three rows of chairs had been drawn up in front of a small stage... He drew his stool up to the table.* PHRASAL VB : V+O+ADV = pull up

4 If you **draw** yourself **up**, you make your back very straight, rather than stooping. EG *He drew himself up to his full height.* PHRASAL VB : V+O (REFL)+ADV

draw upon. If you **draw upon** something, you make use of it in order to do something. EG *One had to draw upon some knowledge of human psychology.* PHRASAL VB : V+PREP, HAS PASS

drawback /drɔːbæk/, **drawbacks**. A **drawback** is an aspect of something or someone that makes them less good, less pleasant, or less useful. EG *This machine has a major drawback from the technological point of view... Her only drawback is that she's so stupid.* N COUNT : USU+SUPP ⇑ problem = disadvantage

drawbridge /drɔːbrɪdʒ/, **drawbridges**. A **drawbridge** is a bridge that can be pulled up, for example to prevent people from getting into a castle or to allow ships to pass underneath it. N COUNT ⇑ bridge

drawer /drɔːə/, **drawers**. **1** A **drawer** is part of a desk, chest, or other piece of furniture which is N COUNT

shaped like a box and can be pulled out so that you can put things in it or take things out of it. EG *The document had always been kept in a drawer in his study.* • See also **chest of drawers, bottom drawer**.
2 Drawers are a piece of underclothing that you wear on the lower part of your body; an old-fashioned word. EG *...a pair of drawers.* N PLURAL : ALSO *a pair of*+N = knickers

drawing /drɔ:ɪŋ/, **drawings**. 1 A **drawing** is a picture made with a pencil, pen, crayon, etc which usually shows only the outlines of something. EG *On the cover was a drawing of five students... I looked at the pen and ink drawings.* N COUNT
2 Drawing is the skill or work of drawing pictures, patterns, or maps. EG *She had a real passion for drawing and painting.* N UNCOUNT

drawing board, drawing boards; also spelled with a hyphen. 1 A **drawing board** is a large flat board, often fixed to a metal frame so that it looks like a desk, on which you place your paper when you are drawing or designing something. N COUNT
2 If you say **'back to the drawing board'**, you mean that something you have made or done has not been successful and that you must start again or try another idea. PHR : USED AS AN A, OR CONVENTION

drawing pin, drawing pins; also spelled with a hyphen. A **drawing pin** is a short nail with a broad, flat top which is used for fastening papers or pictures to a board, wall, or other surface; used in British English. N COUNT = thumb tack

drawing room, drawing rooms; also spelled with a hyphen. A **drawing room** is a room, especially a large room in a large house, where people sit and relax, or entertain guests; a rather old-fashioned word. EG *The vicar escorted her back to the drawing-room.* N COUNT

drawl /drɔ:l/, **drawls, drawling, drawled**. If someone **drawls**, they speak slowly and not very clearly, with the vowel sounds of the words lengthened. EG *She shifted lazily on the sofa and drawled, 'If you want a drink, dear, you'll have to get it yourself.'* V OR V+QUOTE
▸ used as a noun. EG *He was complaining in his Montana cowboy's drawl.* ▸ N SING WITH DET+SUPP

drawn /drɔ:n/. 1 **Drawn** is the past participle of **draw**.
2 A **drawn** curtain or blind has been pulled across a window or down over a window so that it covers it. EG *Someone was pacing back and forth behind the drawn blind.* ADJ CLASSIF
3 If someone or their face looks **drawn**, their face is thin and they look very tired, ill, worried, or unhappy. EG *There was a drawn and haggard look about his eyes... She was a bit drawn.* ADJ QUALIT = pinched

-drawn combines with words such as 'horse' or 'tractor' to indicate that something is pulled by a particular kind of animal or vehicle. EG *...a horse-drawn carriage.* COMB : FORMS ADJ CLASSIFS

drawn-out. Something that is **drawn-out** takes more time than is usual or more time than you would like. EG *He was tired of the long drawn-out arguments.* ADJ QUALIT ⇑ long = protracted

drawstring /drɔ:strɪŋ/, **drawstrings**; also spelled with a hyphen. A **drawstring** is a cord that goes through a seam round an opening, for example at the top of a bag or a pair of trousers. When the cord is pulled tighter, the opening gets smaller. EG *...a drawstring bag... ...trousers with a drawstring waist.* N COUNT : USU SING

dray /dreɪ/, **drays**. A **dray** is a large flat cart with four wheels which is pulled by horses. N COUNT

dread /dred/, **dreads, dreading, dreaded**. 1 If you **dread** something which is going to happen or which may happen, you feel very unhappy and worried about it because you know or think that it will be very unpleasant. EG *She had begun to dread these excursions... Everything you dread doing you must do straight away... They dreaded him coming... I dread to see him fail.* V+O/*to*-INF/-ING/REPORT-CL ⇑ fear
2 Dread is a feeling of great anxiety and fear about something that is going to happen or that may happen. EG *He spoke of his growing dread of getting old.... Terror and dread fall upon them... ...his dread that the child would be infected with the disease.* N UNCOUNT : IF+ PREP THEN *of*, OR N+REPORT-CL
3 If you say that you **dread to think** what might happen or what is happening, you mean that you are worried about it and think that it is likely to be unpleasant or undesirable. EG *I dread to think what goes on in these schools... I dreaded to think what he might do.* PHR : VB INFLECTS
4 Dread means terrible and greatly feared; an old-fashioned use. EG *She went blind of the dread disease.* ADJ CLASSIF : ATTRIB

dreaded /dredɪ[2]d/ means terrible and greatly feared. EG *Consumption was the most dreaded disease of the time... I doubt if he would want to meet the dreaded General van den Bergh.* ADJ CLASSIF

dreadful /dredful/. 1 Something that is **dreadful** is very bad or unpleasant, or of very low quality. EG *The weather was dreadful... She had a dreadful effect on me... ...that dreadful man!* ADJ CLASSIF = awful
2 Dreadful is also used to emphasize the degree or extent of something bad. EG *I was basically a dreadful coward... It'll be a dreadful waste.* ADJ CLASSIF : ATTRIB

dreadfully /dredfuli[1]/ means 1 very or to a very great extent. EG *The three girls were dreadfully dull companions... She was dreadfully upset... I'm so dreadfully sorry... She was most dreadfully sick all day.* ADV+ADJ/ADV = awfully, terribly **2** in a very bad or unpleasant way. EG *He had behaved dreadfully.* ADV WITH VB ⇑ badly

dream /dri:m/, **dreams, dreaming, dreamed, dreamt**. The forms **dreamed** and **dreamt** are both used as the past tense and past participle of the verb.
1 A **dream** is **1.1** an imaginary series of events that you experience in your mind while you are asleep. EG *In his dream he was sitting in a theatre watching a play... Sam has bad dreams because soon he will be going to prep school... I had a strange dream about you and me last night.* N COUNT : IF+ PREP THEN *of*/*about* ⇑ unreality **1.2** a situation or event which you often think about because you would very much like it to happen, but which you know is probably not possible. EG *My dream was to farm in the American style... His dream of becoming President had come true... These problems can be evaded by retreat into a dream world.* • See also **pipe dream**. N COUNT : IF+ PREP THEN *of*, OR N+REPORT-CL ⇑ wish = fantasy **1.3** a situation or event that does not feel real, especially because it is very strange or unpleasant. EG *'This must stop,' I said politely, feeling this was a bad dream.* N COUNT+SUPP : USU SING **1.4** a state of mind in which you do not concentrate properly on what you are doing because you are thinking about other more pleasant things. EG *He acted like a man in a dream... He lived in dream and fantasy.* N COUNT/UNCOUNT ⇑ reverie
2 When you **dream**, **2.1** you see imaginary pictures and events in your mind while you are asleep. EG *That night I dreamt that I was beaten up by Ernest Hemingway... She was either with Allen or in bed dreaming about him.* V : IF+PREP THEN *of/about*, OR V+REPORT-CL **2.2** you think about a particular situation or event that you would very much like to happen, but which you know is probably not possible. EG *He dreamed of having a car... When you are young you dream about all sorts of things.* V : IF+PREP THEN *of/about*, OR V+REPORT-CL ▸ You can also **dream** a dream. EG *They no longer dream the anarchist dream of society without the State.* ▸ V+O **2.3** you imagine that you saw, heard, or experienced something, when in fact you did not. EG *He must have been dreaming... I seem to have dreamt it.* V OR V+O/REPORT-CL
3 If you say that someone **would not dream of** doing something or **would never dream of** doing something, you mean that they would never do it because they think it is wrong or is not possible or suitable for them. EG *A lot of the boys would never dream of going away for residential courses.* PHR : VB INFLECTS
4 If you say that someone **never dreamed** that something would happen, you mean that they did not think that it would happen or would not have believed it. EG *Those who founded the Cathedrals never dreamed that they would have been put to such uses.* PHR
5 If you describe something as a particular person's **dream**, you mean that it would be ideal for that person and that he or she would like it very much. EG *It was an astonishing sight, a sort of poacher's dream come true... Europe was a young man's dream.* N SING : *a*+POSS+N = paradise
6 If you say that something is a **dream**, you mean that it is wonderful; an informal use. EG *The food is a dream.* N SING : *a*+N ⇑ perfection
7 Dream is used to describe something that you think is wonderful, especially something that you thought you would never be able to have or experience. EG *It was a dream house that he knew she would love... ...trekking east and south on dream holidays.* ADJ CLASSIF : ATTRIB = ideal, fabulous
8 The word **dream** is also used in the following expressions. **8.1** If you describe something as being **beyond** your **wildest dreams**, you mean that it is better than you could have imagined or hoped for. EG *...a salary beyond their wildest dreams... ...enriching mankind beyond our wildest dreams.* PHR : USED AS AN A **8.2** If you say PHR : USED AS AN

that someone could not imagine a particular thing **in** their **wildest dreams**, you mean that it is extremely strange or unlikely. EG *Which junior civil servant, in his wildest dreams, could ever conjure up such a scheme?* **8.3** If you do something **like a dream** or if something happens **like a dream**, you do it perfectly or it happens perfectly. EG *I have also been told that I cooked like a dream... The whole thing went like a dream.* **8.4** If you describe someone or something as the person or thing **of** your **dreams**, you mean that you consider them to be ideal or perfect. EG *...the man of their dreams.*
A, USU+BROAD NEG; PHR : USED AS AN A = brilliantly; PHR : NG+PHR

dream up. If you **dream up** a plan or idea, especially one that is complicated or unpleasant, you work it out or create it in your mind. EG *He would never dream up a desperate scheme like that on his own.*
PHRASAL VB : ORDER V+ADV+O ⇑ conceive = devise

dreamer /driːmə/, **dreamers**. A **dreamer** is someone who hopes or believes that pleasant things will happen, although they are not likely to, rather than being realistic and practical. EG *...the poet, the romantic, the inscrutable dreamer.*
N COUNT ⇑ escapist ≠ realist

dreamily /driːmɪli[1]/. If you do something **dreamily**, you do it slowly and without concentrating on it because you are thinking about something else. EG *He stared dreamily around him... 'It's worth a lot of money,' she said dreamily.*
ADV = absently

dreamless /driːmlə[2]s/. **Dreamless** sleep is very deep and peaceful, and without dreams. EG *He lay down again and soon fell into a mercifully dreamless sleep.*
ADJ CLASSIF = sound

dreamlike /driːmlaɪk/ is used to describe things or situations that seem strange and unreal. EG *There was a dreamlike quality to the scene... Already the landscape has a depopulated and dreamlike air.*
ADJ QUALIT = unreal

dreamt /drɛmt/ is a past tense and past participle of **dream**.

dreamy /driːmi[1]/, **dreamier, dreamiest**. **1** If you say that the expression on someone's face is **dreamy**, you mean that they look as if they are thinking about something very pleasant. EG *...a little dreamy smile of pure content... A dreamy look came into the mother's eyes.*
ADJ QUALIT ⇑ content = faraway

2 A sight or sound that is **dreamy** seems very gentle, as if it were in a dream. EG *...a dreamy, not quite recognizable music... They talked to each other in gentle, dreamy voices.*
ADJ QUALIT = soft, lazy

3 A person or idea that is **dreamy** is very imaginative or creative, but not very practical. EG *It was the same Judy, wild-eyed, dreamy, volatile as ever... No doubt, some will say it is dreamy, escapist, or utopian.*
ADJ QUALIT = idealistic

4 If you say that something is **dreamy**, you mean that you think it is wonderful; an informal use. EG *The desk girl asked us if we owned those groovy, dreamy motorcycles outside.*
ADJ QUALIT = fantastic

5 See also **dreamily**.

dreary /drɪəri[1]/, **drearier, dreariest**. Something that is **dreary** is very dull and uninteresting and makes you feel bored or depressed. EG *They don't realise how dull and dreary their world is... He offered me a game of chess and I spent a dreary hour in achieving a draw.* ◊ **drearily**. EG *He was dressed drearily in grey.*
ADJ QUALIT = boring, dismal; ◊ ADV

dredge /drɛdʒ/, **dredges, dredging, dredged**. To **dredge** a harbour or river means to clear or search it using a special machine which removes unwanted things from the bottom and sides of it.
V+O = drag

dredge up. If you **dredge up** a piece of information, you remember it although you learnt it a long time ago. EG *...all these old verses that we seem to dredge up from early memories.*
PHRASAL VB : V+O+ADV ⇑ recall = dig up

dredger /drɛdʒə/, **dredgers**. A **dredger** is a boat which is fitted with a special machine used to clear or enlarge harbours, rivers, etc.
N COUNT

dregs /drɛgz/. **1** The **dregs** of a liquid are the last drops left at the bottom of the container it is in, and any little solid bits that have sunk to the bottom. EG *She had drunk her coffee down to the dregs... I finished the dregs of my tea.*
N PLURAL ⇑ waste

2 The **dregs** of a society or institution are the people in it who are the most useless or bad; used showing disapproval. EG *...the dregs of humanity.*
N PLURAL+SUPP : *the*+N

drench /drɛntʃ/, **drenches, drenching, drenched**. To **drench** something or someone means to make them completely wet. EG *When Tom was tired of being drenched I turned the water off.* ◊ **drenched**. EG *Scores of drenched but hopeful people were still waiting... Joseph was drenched with sweat.* ◊ **drenching**. EG *...drenching rains.*
V+O : USU PASS = soak ≠ dry; ◊ ADJ QUALIT = soaked; ◊ ADJ CLASSIF

dress /drɛs/, **dresses, dressing, dressed**. **1** A **dress** is a piece of clothing worn by a woman or girl which covers her body and whose hem reaches to somewhere on her legs. EG *She was wearing a short black dress.*
N COUNT ⇑ garment = frock

2 You can refer to clothes in general as **dress**. EG *More money is spent on dress than on books... They started to wear western dress.*
N UNCOUNT

3 You can refer to the special clothes that you wear for a particular occasion as a particular kind of **dress**. EG *He was wearing battle dress.* ● See also **evening dress**, **fancy dress**, full dress, **morning dress**.
N UNCOUNT+SUPP : MOD+N = attire

4 **Dress** is used to describe the special clothes that you wear for very formal occasions. EG *They were wearing full dress uniform... ...a dress suit.*
ADJ CLASSIF : ATTRIB ⇑ formal

5 When you **dress** or when you **dress** yourself, you put on your clothes. EG *When he had shaved and dressed, he went down to the kitchen.*
V OR V+O *(REFL)* ⇑ cover ≠ undress

6 If someone **dresses** in a particular way, they usually wear that style of clothes. EG *He still dressed like the bank manager he had been... I really must try to make him change the way he dresses.*
V OR V+A

7 When you **dress** someone, for example a child, you put clothes on him or her. EG *He helped her dress the children.*
V+O ⇑ cover ≠ undress

8 If you **dress** for a particular occasion, you put on formal clothes for that occasion. EG *They always dressed for dinner.*
V+A *(for)* ⇑ change

9 If you **dress** a salad, you cover it with a mixture of oil, vinegar, herbs, etc to make it taste nicer. EG *Don't dress the salad until we are ready to eat.*
V+O

10 When someone **dresses** a wound, they clean it and cover it with a bandage. EG *She carried him to her house, where his wounds were dressed.*
V+O ⇑ treat = tend

11 To **dress** meat, poultry, or fish means to prepare it for selling and cooking by cleaning it and removing bits that you cannot eat. EG *...dressed crab.*
V+O

12 See also **dressed, dressing**.

dress down. **1** If you **dress down**, you wear clothes that are suitable for a particular occasion but that are less smart than the clothes you usually wear; used in British English.
PHRASAL VB : V+ADV ≠ dress up

2 If you **dress** someone **down**, you scold them. EG *The Foreign Minister was dressed down in public.*
PHRASAL VB : ORDER V+O+ADV = reprimand

3 See also **dressing-down**.

dress up. **1** If you **dress up** or **dress** yourself **up**, you put on different clothes from the ones you usually wear, either in order to disguise yourself or so that you look smarter than usual. EG *He dressed up as a pig... That evening they both dressed themselves up in fancy clothes... I can't be bothered to dress up this evening.* ◊ **dressed up**. EG *...a man dressed up in a soldier's uniform.* ● If you are **all dressed up**, you are wearing very smart, fashionable clothes; an informal expression. EG *She was glad that she was all dressed up and had done her hair that morning.*
PHRASAL VB : V+ADV, OR V+O (REFL)+ADV; ◊ ADJ CLASSIF; ● PHR : USED AS C ⇑ smart = dolled up

2 If you **dress** someone **up**, you give them special clothes to wear in order to make them look smarter or disguise them. EG *He booked hundreds of new courtiers and dressed them up in armour.*
PHRASAL VB : ORDER V+O+ADV

3 If you **dress** something **up**, you make it seem more attractive, interesting, or acceptable than it really is. ◊ **dressed up**. EG *The offer was simply an old one dressed up in new terms.*
PHRASAL VB : V+O+ADV; ◊ ADJ CLASSIF : PRED

4 See also **dressing-up**.

dressage /drɛsɑːʒ/ consists of making the horse you are riding perform controlled movements in response to your signals, especially in a competition.
N UNCOUNT

dress circle; also spelled with a hyphen. The **dress circle** is the first floor balcony in a theatre. EG *We sat in the dress circle.*
N SING : *the*+N

dressed /drɛst/. **1** If you are **dressed**, you are wearing clothes rather than being naked, or wearing ordinary clothes rather than pyjamas or a night-dress. EG *Both men were fully dressed.*
ADJ CLASSIF : PRED = clothed

2 If you **are dressed** in a particular way, you are wearing clothes of a particular kind or colour. EG *He was dressed in a black suit... ...neatly dressed workers... A woman dressed in white came up to me.*
ADJ CLASSIF : IF+PREP THEN *in* = clad, attired

3 If someone is **dressed to kill**, they are wearing very smart or glamorous clothes because they want people to notice them and think them very attrac-
PHR : USED AS C

tive; an informal expression. EG *She arrived at the party, dressed to kill as usual.*
4 When you **get dressed**, you put on your clothes. EG *I woke up and got dressed.* PHR : VB INFLECTS

dresser /drɛsə/, **dressers**. 1 A **dresser** is 1.1 a chest of drawers, usually with a mirror on the top; used mainly in American English. EG *He walked round the beds to the dresser and opened a drawer.* N COUNT
1.2 a piece of furniture in living rooms and kitchens, which has cupboards or drawers in the lower part and shelves in the top part; used in British English. EG *...the blue and white plates on the stripped pine dresser.* N COUNT ⇑ cupboard 1.3 someone who works in a theatre and helps the actors and actresses to dress. N COUNT
2 Someone who is a smart **dresser**, a scruffy **dresser**, etc wears clothes of the kind or quality indicated; an informal use. EG *He was always a smart dresser.* N COUNT : ADJ+N

dressing /drɛsɪŋ/, **dressings**. A **dressing** is 1 a covering that is put on a wound to protect it while it heals. EG *Dr Macdonald will be here later to attend to the dressings.* N COUNT ⇑ bandage 2 a mixture of oil, vinegar, herbs, etc, which you pour over a salad to make it taste nicer. EG *What kind of dressing would you like on your salad?... These oils are ideal for cooking, frying, and salad dressings.* N MASS : USU+SUPP ⇑ sauce

dressing-down. If someone gives you a **dressing-down**, they tell you how foolish you have been or how badly you have behaved. EG *The Duke gives him a severe dressing-down for his drunkenness.* N SING WITH DET = scolding

dressing gown, dressing gowns; also spelled with a hyphen. A **dressing gown** is a piece of clothing in the form of a loose-fitting coat which you wear when you are not dressed in your ordinary clothes, often over pyjamas or a nightdress, for example when you have just got out of bed. N COUNT : USU POSS+N = robe

dressing room, dressing rooms; also spelled with a hyphen. A **dressing room** is a room in a theatre, film studio, or television studio where a performer can get dressed and put on his or her make-up. N COUNT ⇑ changing room

dressing table, dressing tables; also spelled with a hyphen. A **dressing table** is a small table with drawers underneath it and a mirror on top of it which is used in a bedroom. EG *She sat at the dressing table wiping off the last of her make-up.* N COUNT

dressing-up is the activity of putting on special or different clothes, especially as part of a game played by children in which they pretend to be different people. N UNCOUNT ⇑ pretence

dressmaker /drɛsmeɪkə/, **dressmakers**; also spelled with a hyphen. A **dressmaker** is someone, usually a woman, who makes clothes for herself or for other people. N COUNT ⇑ seamstress

dressmaking /drɛsmeɪkɪŋ/; also spelled with a hyphen. **Dressmaking** is the activity or work of making clothes. N UNCOUNT ⇑ sewing

dress rehearsal, dress rehearsals; also spelled with a hyphen. The **dress rehearsal** of a play, opera, or show is the final rehearsal before it is performed, in which the performers wear their costumes and the lights and scenery are all used in the way that they will be used in the proper performance. N COUNT

dress shirt, dress shirts; also spelled with a hyphen. A **dress shirt** is a special shirt which men wear on formal occasions with a dinner jacket and a black bow tie. N COUNT

dressy /drɛsi¹/, **dressier, dressiest**. **Dressy** clothes are elegant clothes which you wear on formal occasions; a fairly informal word. EG *The men had worn suits and ties, the women simple but dressy clothes.* ADJ QUALIT ▸ used also of people who wear or are wearing such clothes. EG *...a group of dressy ladies.* ▸ ADJ QUALIT : ATTRIB ▸ used also of occasions when such clothes are worn. EG *It's going to be a fairly dressy wedding.* ▸ ADJ QUALIT : ATTRIB

drew /druː/ is the past tense of **draw**.

dribble /drɪbəºl/, **dribbles, dribbling, dribbled**. 1 When something **dribbles** over something else or when you **dribble** it, it falls or spills in small drops or tiny pieces. EG *Pieces of pie and orange juice dribbled down Uncle Harold's chin... His hand trembled as he held the spoon, dribbling sugar all over the tablecloth.* V-ERG : USU+A ⇑ fall = trickle
2 A **dribble** of something is a small amount of it which is falling or dripping somewhere. EG *There was a dribble of water running down the wall... ...dribbles of dried blood.* N PART ⇑ trickle
3 If you **dribble**, you let saliva trickle from your mouth. EG *He wore thick glasses, and dribbled.* V
4 **Dribble** is saliva that is trickling from your mouth. EG *Tears and dribble ran down his face.* N UNCOUNT
5 When a player **dribbles** the ball in a game of football, basketball, etc, he or she kicks it or taps it several times in quick succession in order to keep it moving. V+O ⇑ move
6 If people or animals **dribble** to or from a particular place, they go or come slowly and in small numbers. EG *...the children dribbling back from school.* V+A ⇑ travel = trickle

dribs and drabs /drɪbz əⁿn dræbz/. If people or things arrive **in dribs and drabs**, they arrive in small numbers over a period of time rather than arriving all together; an informal expression. EG *The food came in dribs and drabs.* PHR : USED AS AN A

dried /draɪd/. 1 **Dried** food or milk has had all the water removed from it and so will last for long periods of time. EG *Dried milk is very useful when you go camping... ...dried herbs.* ADJ CLASSIF : ATTRIB = dehydrated
2 **Dried** is the past tense and past participle of **dry**.

dried fruit, dried fruits. **Dried fruit** is fruit that has been preserved by being dried; used especially to refer to currants, raisins, or sultanas, which are kinds of dried grapes. N MASS

dried-up. 1 Someone who is **dried-up** looks old, small, and very wrinkled, and also often looks as if they are bad-tempered and unpleasant. EG *A little dried-up old man came to the door.* ADJ CLASSIF = wizened, withered
2 See also **dry up**.

drier /draɪə/, **driers**. See **dryer**.

drift /drɪft/, **drifts, drifting, drifted**. 1 When something **drifts** somewhere, 1.1 it is carried there by the movement of wind or water. EG *A tiny fishing boat was drifting slowly along... The rain ceased and the clouds drifted away.* V+A ⇑ move = float 1.2 it moves there slowly or gradually, and often without any purpose. EG *The crowd started to drift away.* V+A = scatter 1.3 it moves there in a smooth and effortless way. EG *The car drifted round the corner.* V+A = sail
2 **Drift** is the movement of a mass of water such as a river. EG *The drift of the current took us downstream.* N UNCOUNT ⇑ flow
3 A **drift** of something is an amount of it which is suspended in the air or in water or is being carried along by the movement of wind or water. EG *The valley was visible here and there between drifts of mist... ...swirling drifts of flies.* N PART = cloud
4 If snow **drifts**, it builds up into piles as a result of the movement of wind or water. EG *They can't stop the snow drifting.* V ⇑ pile up
5 A **drift** is a mass of snow or something else that has built up into a pile as a result of the movement of wind or water. EG *The road was edged with snow drifts... Their bodies lie rotting in drifts on the surface of the streams.* N COUNT : USU+SUPP
6 If something **drifts**, it progresses or develops in a way that is not planned or controlled. EG *She didn't want to let the conversation drift... Our Party has drifted for long enough.* V ⇑ wander
7 A **drift** is also 7.1 a movement of people or animals away from somewhere or something or towards somewhere or something, especially one that has become a pattern. EG *We have to stop the drift of workers from the countryside.* N COUNT : USU+*of* = shift 7.2 a general change or development. EG *The drift towards house ownership continues... I think there's a general drift back towards science.* N SING WITH DET +SUPP ⇑ trend = shift
8 Someone who **drifts** or who **drifts** around travels about from place to place without a plan and has no settled job and no settled way of life. EG *He drifted about from job to job.* V OR V+A *(around/about)* ⇑ wander
9 The **drift** of an argument or speech is the general point that is being made in it. EG *I was able to follow his drift pretty well... He had only just caught up with the general drift of the conversation.* N COUNT ⇑ meaning

drift off. If you **drift off** to sleep, you gradually fall asleep. EG *I watched him drifting off as the music played.* PHRASAL VB : V+ADV = doze off

drifter /drɪftə/, **drifters**. A **drifter** is a person who does not stay in one place or in one job for very long. EG *She was a drifter. No family, no close friends.* N COUNT

driftwood /drɪftwʊd/ is wood which is floating on the surface of the sea, a river, etc, or which has come from it onto the shore. EG *...an old piece of driftwood he had picked up on the beach.* N UNCOUNT

drill /drɪl/, **drills, drilling, drilled**. 1 A **drill** is 1.1 a tool or machine that is used for making holes. N COUNT

EG ...*an electric drill.* **1.2** a way of teaching something by means of repetition, or an exercise designed for this purpose. EG ...*spelling drills.* — N COUNT

1.3 a way of training a group of people, especially soldiers, to do something, by making them practise it repeatedly, or an exercise designed for this purpose. EG ...*battle drills... ...a drill sergeant.* — N COUNT/UNCOUNT

1.4 a routine exercise whose purpose is to save lives by showing people what to do in a dangerous situation. EG *At the beginning of each term there was a fire drill.* — N COUNT : MOD+N

2 When you **drill** into something or when you **drill** a hole, you make a hole using a drill. EG *A hole had already been drilled... Be careful not to drill into gas pipes.* — V OR V+O, USU+A; ⇑ bore

3 When someone **drills** for oil or water or when they **drill**, they make a deep hole in the ground or in the floor of the sea in order to find oil or water. EG *Most of the men had experience in drilling off the coast... They've started to drill for water.* — V OR V+A *(for)*; ⇑ excavate

4 If you **drill** people, you try to teach them something using repetitive exercises. EG *He doesn't believe in drilling a class for more than ten minutes a day.* — V+O : IF+PREP THEN *in*; ⇑ train

5 When soldiers **drill** or when someone **drills** them, they practise certain actions or movements repeatedly. EG *He was not pleased at having to drill a squad of new recruits... He had to put on the uniform, drill, and go to war.* — V-ERG

6 The **drill** is the correct or usual way of doing something; used in old-fashioned British English. EG *What's the drill for lunch?* — N SING : *the*+N; = procedure

7 Drill is a strong cotton cloth which is often used to make uniforms. EG *She was dressed in khaki drill.* — N UNCOUNT; ⇑ cloth

drill into. If you **drill** something **into** someone, you force them to learn it or understand it by repeating it many times. EG *Somehow we have to drill into them the importance of saving energy.* — PHRASAL VB : V+O+PREP; = drum into

drily /draɪli¹/. See **dry**.

drink /drɪŋk/, **drinks, drinking, drank, drunk. 1** When you **drink** something or **drink**, you take liquid into your mouth and then swallow it. EG *We sat drinking coffee, smoking cigarettes, and talking... She brought him a cup of tea and he drank eagerly... They drank a bottle of champagne.* — V OR V+O; ⇑ consume

2 To **drink** means to drink alcohol, especially regularly or in large quantities. EG *She said she didn't smoke or drink... You shouldn't drink and drive... I never drink alone.* — V

3 If you **drink** yourself into a particular state or condition, you drink so much alcohol that you get into that state or condition. EG *She had been drinking herself into a stupor for at least six hours... They are drinking themselves to death.* — V+O (REFL)+A *(into/to)*/C

4 A **drink** is **4.1** an amount of a liquid which you drink or which is suitable for drinking. EG *I asked her for a drink of water... Lynne brought me a hot drink.* ▸ often used to refer to an alcoholic drink. EG *He poured himself a drink... I'm going to have a drink with some friends this evening... The drinks were served in the sitting room.* — N COUNT

4.2 a small amount of liquid which you swallow in one go. EG *She took a drink of her whisky and smiled at him.* — N COUNT : USU *a*+N IN SING; = mouthful

5 Drink is alcohol, for example beer, wine, or whisky. EG *There was plenty of food and drink at the party... They drowned their troubles in drink... We are trying to keep him away from drink.* — N UNCOUNT

6 The **drink** is, in informal English, the sea. — N SING : *the*+N

7 If you **drink** someone **under the table** when drinking alcohol, they become too drunk to go on drinking before you do. — PHR : VB INFLECTS

8 If someone **takes to drink**, they start to drink a lot of alcohol regularly, for example because they are depressed. — PHR : VB INFLECTS

9 If you say to someone **'what are you drinking?'**, you are asking them what they would like to drink. — CONVENTION

10 to **drink** someone's **health**: see **health**.

drink in. If you **drink in** something that you see or hear, you pay a lot of attention to it and enjoy it. EG *He stood still, drinking in the beauty of the countryside... She drank in every word that the professor spoke.* — PHRASAL VB : V+O+ADV; ⇑ absorb; = take in

drink to. When you **drink to** someone or something, you raise your glass and say their name before drinking, as a way of showing that you hope they will be happy or successful. EG *They agreed on their plan and drank to it.* — PHRASAL VB : V+PREP; ⇑ toast

drink up. When you **drink up** or when you **drink up** an amount of liquid, you finish it completely. EG *Drink up. It's time to go... The two of them drank up a whole bottle of gin.* — PHRASAL VB : V+ADV, OR V+O+ADV

drinkable /drɪŋkəbə⁰l/. **1** Water that is **drinkable** is clean and safe for drinking. — ADJ CLASSIF

2 Wine or beer that is **drinkable** tastes nice and is pleasant to drink. EG *They have a good range of drinkable wines at reasonable prices.* — ADJ QUALIT

drinker /drɪŋkə/, **drinkers. 1** Someone who is a tea **drinker**, a coffee **drinker**, etc drinks the liquid mentioned. — N COUNT : MOD+N

2 Someone who is a **drinker** drinks alcohol, especially in large quantities. EG *I'm not really a drinker, but I would like a glass of wine please... He became a heavy drinker when his wife died.* — N COUNT; ≠ teetotaller

drinking /drɪŋkɪŋ/. **1 Drinking** is the activity of drinking alcohol. EG *There had been some heavy drinking at the party.* — N UNCOUNT

2 Drinking means related to alcohol and the consumption of alcohol. EG *Many people think that the drinking laws in Britain are stupid.* — ADJ CLASSIF : ATTRIB

3 Drinking friends or people are people who enjoy drinking alcohol regularly. EG ...*one of his drinking companions... I'm not really a drinking man.* — ADJ CLASSIF : ATTRIB

drinking fountain, drinking fountains; also spelled with a hyphen. A **drinking fountain** is a device which supplies water for people to drink in places such as streets, parks, or schools. — N COUNT

drinking water; also spelled with a hyphen. **Drinking water** is water which it is safe to drink. — N UNCOUNT

drip /drɪp/, **drips, dripping, dripped. 1** A **drip** is **1.1** a slow succession of drops of liquid falling from somewhere. EG *There's a drip coming from the ceiling... The drip, drip, drip of the tap was driving her mad.* — N COUNT; ⇑ drop

1.2 a piece of medical equipment by which a liquid is passed in small drops through a tube directly into a patient's bloodstream. — N COUNT

2 When liquid **drips** or when you **drip** it, it falls in individual small drops. EG *The rain was dripping down our necks... He dripped a few eye drops into his eyes.* — V-ERG; ⇑ drop; = dribble

3 When something, for example a tap or someone's nose, **drips**, drops of liquid fall from it. EG ...*the dripping of the cold water tap.* — V

4 If you call someone a **drip**, you mean that they are rather stupid and dull and lacking in enthusiasm; an informal use. — N COUNT

drip-dry. Clothes, sheets, etc that are **drip-dry** are made of a fabric that dries free of creases when it is hung up wet. EG ...*drip-dry shirts.* — ADJ CLASSIF

dripping /drɪpɪŋ/. **1** Someone or something that is **dripping** wet is very wet. EG *Judy came out of the bathroom, still dripping wet.* — ADJ CLASSIF; = soaking

2 Dripping is the fat which comes out of meat when it is fried or roasted, and which can be used for frying food in. — N UNCOUNT

drive /draɪv/, **drives, driving, drove, driven.**

1 When you **drive** or when you **drive** a vehicle, you operate and control it so that it works and goes where you want it to. EG *It is her turn to drive the car home through the snow... Two of them have never learned to drive.* — V OR V+O

2 When you **drive** somewhere, you travel there in a car or other vehicle. EG *We thought we'd drive down to the seaside for the day... He saw the accident but drove on.* — V+A

3 If you **drive** someone somewhere, you take them there in a car or other vehicle. EG *Can I drive you to the airport?... I used to get driven straight home after work.* — V+O+A; ⇑ convey

4 A **drive** is **4.1** a journey by car, van, etc. EG *My son has a car but he never takes me for a drive... It'll be a thirty mile drive.* — N COUNT; ⇑ trip

4.2 a piece of hard ground, or sometimes a private road, that leads from the road to a person's garage or front door. EG *There were several cars already parked in the drive when they arrived... A private drive leads up from the road to the palace.* — N COUNT; ⇑ approach

5 If something **drives** a machine, it supplies the power that makes it work. EG *Steam can be used to drive generators... They use liquid hydrogen now to drive some of the rockets.* — V+O

6 Drive is the power supplied by the engine to particular wheels in a car or other vehicle to make the vehicle move. EG *Generally, front wheel drive is more stable and predictable than rear wheel drive... I can only get up there in four-wheel drive.* — N SING : MOD+N

7 If you **drive** something, for example a post or a nail, into something else, you push it in or hammer it in using a lot of effort. EG *She stood in front of a stake driven into the gravel.* V+O+A

8 If you **drive** a ball somewhere in a game of football, cricket, or golf, you kick or hit it quite hard. V+O+A ⇑ propel

9 If wind **drives** snow or rain, it forces it to move in a slanting direction rather than falling straight down. EG *The snowflakes were driven into my face by a gale.* V+O : USU+A = blow

10 If you **drive** people or animals to or from a place, you make them go to or from that place. EG *We were driven into dark dungeons and left there... This could give the police an excuse to drive them out of their homes.* V+O+A

11 To **drive** someone into a particular state or situation means to force them into that state or situation. EG *The farming venture drove the company into debt... These are the lengths to which decent men are driven by the boring jobs they have to do... Going on holiday with these horrible kids will drive me mad.* V+O+C, OR V+O+A ⇑ force

12 If a desire or feeling **drives** someone, it encourages them or motivates them. EG *A man driven by greed or envy loses his sense of justice.* V+O : USU PASS ⇑ motivate

13 **Drive** is the motivation and persistence to try new things and to do things well. EG *Joanna's energy and drive only made me feel more exhausted.* N UNCOUNT = impetus

14 A **drive** is also 14.1 a very strong need or desire in human beings that makes them act in particular ways. EG *This hormone is mainly responsible for our sex drive... He paints because of his drive to create something beautiful.* N COUNT ⇑ urge 14.2 a special effort made by a group of people for a particular purpose. EG *The Poles launched a tremendous investment drive... There is a new anti-pornography drive.* N SING WITH DET +SUPP 14.3 a large-scale attacking move by an army. N COUNT 14.4 a stroke, especially in tennis or golf, in which a ball is hit hard to make it travel a long way. N COUNT

15 **Drive** is also used in the names of some streets. EG *The address is 33 Laurel Drive.* N SING : USED IN NAMES AFTER N

16 When you **drive home** a point, you try to force someone to understand or accept it. EG *I tried to drive home the point that we couldn't afford a new car.* PHRASAL VB : V+O+ADV

17 If you ask **what** someone **is driving at**, you are asking what they are trying to say or what they are saying indirectly. EG *What are you driving at?... She knew at once what I was driving at.* PHR

18 ● to **drive a hard bargain**: see **bargain**. ● See also **driving**.

drive away. If you **drive** an animal or person **away**, you act in such a way that the animal or person is forced to go away. EG *We smoked constantly hoping to drive away the mosquitoes.* PHRASAL VB : V+O+ADV ⇑ repel = fend off

drive off. If you **drive off** someone or something, you force them to go away and to stop attacking you or threatening you. EG *They claimed they had driven off a major force.* PHRASAL VB : V+O+ADV ⇑ repel

drive out. If you **drive out** someone or something, you force them to leave or disappear. EG *The whole point of exorcism is to drive out evil spirits... Successful businesses will always drive out those which are badly managed.* PHRASAL VB : V+O+ADV ⇑ expel

drive-in, drive-ins. A **drive-in** is a restaurant, cinema, or other place offering a service, where people stay in their cars while using the service provided. N COUNT ▸ used as an adjective. EG *...a drive-in cinema.* ▸ ADJ CLASSIF

drivel /drɪvəᵒl/, **drivels, drivelling, drivelled**; also spelled **driveling** and **driveled** in American English. You describe something that is written or said as **drivel** when you think it is very silly; an informal word. EG *You do talk drivel sometimes!* N UNCOUNT = rubbish

drivel on. If someone **drivels on**, they talk for a long time about things that are boring or irrelevant; an informal expression. EG *She spent an hour drivelling on about it.* PHRASAL VB : V+ADV = rabbit on

driven /drɪvəᵒn/ is the past participle of **drive**.

driver /draɪvə/, **drivers**. A **driver** is a person who drives a car, bus, taxi, or train. EG *Her father was a bus driver... Most drivers would like to have radios in their cars.* ● See also **back-seat driver**. N COUNT

driver's licence, driver's licences; also spelled **driver's license** in American English. A **driver's licence** is the same thing as a driving licence. N COUNT

drive shaft, drive shafts; also spelled with a hyphen. A **drive shaft** is a shaft in a car or other vehicle that transfers power from the gear box to the wheels. N COUNT

driveway /draɪvweɪ/, **driveways**. A **driveway** is a piece of hard ground that leads from the road to a person's garage or front door. EG *The car turned into a dark driveway.* N COUNT = drive

driving /draɪvɪŋ/. 1 **Driving** is the way you drive a car or your ability to drive a car. EG *She was found guilty of dangerous driving... I failed my driving test three times.* N UNCOUNT

2 In the front of a car, the **driving** door and the **driving** seat are on the side where the driver sits. EG *The man got out of the driving seat and went round to the passenger door.* ADJ CLASSIF : ATTRIB ≠ passenger

3 If someone is **in the driving seat**, they are in control of a situation. PHR : USED AS AN A

4 **Driving** is used to describe a person, influence, force, etc that has a strong effect on a situation and makes things change. EG *He certainly couldn't be called a driving politician... They claim that the union is the driving force behind the revolution.* ADJ CLASSIF : ATTRIB ⇑ moving

5 **Driving** rain or snow falls fast and heavily, usually in a slanting direction. EG *The driving snow had increased... ...a driving blizzard.* ADJ CLASSIF : ATTRIB

driving licence, driving licences; also spelled **driving license** in American English. A **driving licence** is a card showing that you are qualified to drive because you have passed a driving test. N COUNT ⇑ permit = driver's licence

driving school, driving schools. A **driving school** is a business that employs instructors who give people lessons in how to drive a car. N COUNT

drizzle /drɪzəᵒl/, **drizzles, drizzling, drizzled**.
1 **Drizzle** is very light, fine rain, almost like mist. EG *He walked back home through the fine drizzle that was now falling.* N UNCOUNT

2 If it **is drizzling**, it is raining very lightly. EG *It had rained all day and was still drizzling.* V : USU *it*+V ⇑ rain

droll /drəʊl/. Something or someone that is **droll** is amusing; a rather old-fashioned word. ADJ QUALIT

drollery /drəʊləriⁱ/ is humour; a rather old-fashioned word. N UNCOUNT

dromedary /drʌməᵒdərɪ, drɒm-/, **dromedaries**. A **dromedary** is a camel which has one hump. N COUNT

drone /drəʊn/, **drones, droning, droned**. 1 To **drone** means to make a low, monotonous humming or buzzing noise. EG *The engine droned on and on as we flew northward.* V = whine, hum ▸ used as a noun. EG *...the steady drone of the traffic.* ▸ N SING WITH DET

2 A **drone** is a male bee. EG *The queen is likely to mate with two or three drones.* N COUNT

drone on. If someone **drones on**, they talk boringly about something for a long time in a low, monotonous voice. EG *I remember him droning on about how important it was to study literature.* PHRASAL VB : V+ADV : IF+PREP THEN *about* ⇑ talk

drool /druːl/, **drools, drooling, drooled**. 1 To **drool** means to let saliva fall from your mouth, without being able to stop it. EG *He used to drool at the corners of his mouth.* V = dribble, slobber

2 **Drool** is saliva that falls from your mouth. EG *Bibs are useful for keeping drool off a baby's clothes.* N UNCOUNT = dribble

3 If you **drool** over someone or something, you look at them with great pleasure because you think they are very attractive or nice; an informal use. EG *You go around in that bikini and Gaskell's drooling over you all the time.* V : IF+PREP THEN *over/at* = moon

droop /druːp/, **droops, drooping, drooped**. If something **droops**, it hangs or leans downwards with no strength or firmness. EG *His shoulders drooped and his head hung to his chest... His eyelids drooped as though he was on the verge of sleep.* V ⇑ hang = sag ◇ **drooping**. EG *...a full, drooping moustache.* ◇ ADJ CLASSIF ⇑ hanging

droopy /druːpiⁱ/, **droopier, droopiest**. Something that is **droopy** hangs down limply. EG *...the waiter with the droopy moustache.* ADJ QUALIT = wilting ≠ stiff

drop /drɒp/, **drops, dropping, dropped**. 1 If you **drop** something, 1.1 you let it fall by mistake. EG *He bumped into a chair and dropped his cigar... Careful! Don't drop it!* V+O ⇑ release 1.2 you let go of it deliberately so that it falls on or in a particular place. EG *Planes dropped bombs all through the night... She poured herself some whisky and dropped in a few ice cubes.* V+O

2 If something **drops**, it falls straight down. EG *The stone dropped to the bottom of the pond... The bottle dropped out of the suitcase.* V ⇑ fall

3 If the ground **drops**, it goes down so that it is at a V : USU+A

lower level. EG *The ocean floor dropped steeply fifty yards from the shore.*

4 If you **drop** into a particular position or place, you lower your body quickly into that position or place. EG *She closed her eyes and dropped into a chair... She dropped down onto her knees.* — V+A

5 To **drop** also means fall down because you are exhausted, very ill, or dead. EG *She scrubbed and polished until she dropped.* — V; = collapse

6 If a level or amount **drops**, it becomes less. EG *The temperature of their bodies dropped ten degrees... As the car approaches the bend, the speed drops to seventy.* ▸ used as a noun. EG *Unemployment means a serious drop in income for many people.* — V: USU+A; ⇑ decrease; = fall; ≠ rise; ▸ N COUNT+SUPP: USU SING

7 If your voice **drops** or if you **drop** your voice, it becomes less loud. EG *Bill's voice dropped when he saw his father on the other side of the room... They dropped their voices as they entered the church.* — V-ERG; ⇑ lower; ≠ raise

8 If you **drop** a person or thing somewhere, you take them there, for example by car, and leave them there. EG *He ordered his taxi to drop him at the corner of the street... We'd better drop the parcel over to Jane's house tomorrow.* — V+O; ⇑ deliver

9 If you **drop** something you are doing, using, dealing with, or discussing, you stop doing it or dealing with it, or abandon it. EG *Most of the charges were dropped when Brown pleaded guilty... I was certain he would drop everything to help... 'Have you apologized to her?'–'Look, just drop it, all right?'* ● If you **let** something **drop**, you abandon it and do not continue doing it. EG *I've been thinking about my French course. I don't think I'm going to let it drop now.* — V+O; ● PHR: VB INFLECTS; ⇑ discontinue

10 If you **drop** someone, you are no longer friendly towards them; an informal use. — V+O; = ditch

11 If a player **is dropped** from a team, he or she is no longer included in the team. — V+O; ⇑ exclude

12 To **drop** a sound or word means to leave it out and not say it. EG *Drop the 'sir', will you?–My name's Mr Defoe.* — V+O; ⇑ omit; = skip

13 If you **drop** a hint or piece of advice, you give it to someone in a casual way. EG *Don't drop hints about promotion or pay increases to your boss... It's up to you to drop a word of warning in her ear.* — V+O; ⇑ utter

14 To **drop** a game in a sports competition means to lose it. EG *He's dropped one game so far.* — V+O

15 If you **drop** to a lower position in a competition, you fall to a lower position. EG *He has dropped to fifth place.* — V+A *(to)*

16 In knitting, when you **drop** a stitch, a loop of wool comes off the knitting needle with the result that a hole appears in the knitting. — V+O

17 A **drop** is a small amount of liquid shaped like a little ball. EG *A drop of blood slid down his leg... ...rain drops... He carried the bucket of water without spilling a drop.* — N COUNT

18 A **drop** of a liquid is a very small amount of that liquid; an informal use. EG *A little drop of scotch would be very welcome... 'Do you have milk in your tea?'–'Just a drop thank you'.* — N PART; = dash

19 A **drop** is also **19.1** the distance between a high point and a low point; used of the vertical part of an object, for example a wall or the face of a cliff. EG *The cliff plunged in a vertical drop of 300 feet... I wouldn't jump off that wall. It's quite a drop to the ground.* — N SING WITH DET **19.2** a delivery of something from a vehicle, especially from an aeroplane. EG *They are requesting air drops of essential foodstuffs... I would have done fifteen drops today, but my van ran out of petrol.* — N COUNT: USU+SUPP **19.3** in informal English, a place where something, for example a letter or a message, can be left. EG *...a mail drop.* — N COUNT: USU+MOD **19.4** a small round sweet. EG *He sucked peppermint drops.* — N COUNT: MOD+N

20 **Drops** are a kind of medicine which you take drop by drop in your ears or eyes. EG *I'll get some eye drops for her at the chemist.* — N COUNT: USU PL

21 The word **drop** is also used in the following expressions. **21.1** If you **drop** someone **a line** or **a note**, you write them a short letter; a fairly informal expression. EG *I'll drop you a line tomorrow.* — PHR: VB INFLECTS **21.2** If you **drop a brick** or **drop a clanger**, you say something tactless or inappropriate. — PHR: VB INFLECTS **21.3** To **drop dead** means to die, especially suddenly. EG *Our member of parliament dropped dead at a public meeting.* — PHR: VB INFLECTS **21.4** If you say **'drop dead'** to someone, you are indicating in a rude way that you dislike them very much and want them to go away. — CONVENTION **21.5** If you say that something is **a drop in the ocean**, you mean that it is a very small amount compared to the amount required and will have very little effect. EG *Ten pounds is only a drop in the ocean. We need thousands.* — PHR: USED AS C **21.6** If you do something **at the drop of a hat**, you do it quickly and without hesitating. EG *When she's drunk, she's liable to burst into song at the drop of a hat.* — PHR: USED AS AN A; ⇑ suddenly

drop away. If support or interest **drops away**, it becomes less strong. EG *Public interest in the royal marriage has dropped away... Trade Union support dropped away.* — PHRASAL VB: V+ADV; ⇑ decrease; = wane

drop back. If someone who is moving along **drops back**, they go slower so that they end up in a position behind someone else or behind other people who are going in the same direction. EG *The two-motor cycles dropped back to take up position at the rear of the convoy.* — PHRASAL VB: V+ADV

drop by. To **drop by** means to visit someone informally; a fairly informal expression. EG *If there's anything you want to see, just drop by.* — PHRASAL VB: V+ADV; = drop round

drop in. If you **drop in** on someone or **drop in**, you visit them informally, usually without having arranged it before; a fairly informal expression. EG *I thought I'd just drop in and see how you were... I dropped in on her during the afternoon.* — PHRASAL VB: V+ADV, IF+PREP THEN *on*; = pop in

drop off. **1** If you **drop off** to sleep or **drop off**, you go to sleep, usually without intending to. EG *He has a habit of dropping off in front of the television... I dropped off to sleep in the middle of the lecture.* — PHRASAL VB: V+ADV, IF+PREP THEN *to*; = doze off

2 If you **drop** someone **off**, you take them in a vehicle to a place where they want to go and leave them there. EG *I can drop Daisy off on my way home.* — PHRASAL VB: V+O+ADV; ⇑ transport

3 If support or interest **drops off**, it becomes less strong. — PHRASAL VB: V+ADV

drop out. **1** If you **drop out** of an institution or group or **drop out**, you leave it without telling anyone or without finishing a course or task. EG *The boys had dropped out of school and gone to work... There are only seven people left in the group–five dropped out last month.* — PHRASAL VB: V+ADV: IF+PREP THEN *of*

2 If a word or expression **drops out** of the language, it is no longer used. EG *Today the word 'teeny-bopper' has virtually dropped out of usage.* — PHRASAL VB: V+ADV+*of*

3 See also **drop-out.**

drop round; a fairly informal expression. **1** To **drop round** means to visit someone or go somewhere casually, without making any formal arrangement to do so. EG *I'll drop round when I've finished the shopping.* — PHRASAL VB: V+ADV, USU+A/*to*-INF; = drop by

2 If you **drop** something **round**, you take it to a person's home for them. EG *Bill can drop your books round on his way home.* — PHRASAL VB: V+O+ADV

droplet /drɒplɪ²t/, **droplets.** A **droplet** is a very small drop of liquid. — N COUNT; ⇑ drop

drop-out, drop-outs; an informal word usually used showing disapproval; also spelled as one word. A **drop-out** is **1** a person who rejects social customs and accepted ways of behaving such as working hard and wearing smart clothes. EG *This part of town is full of hippies and dropouts.* — N COUNT; ⇑ dissenter **2** someone who has left school or college before they have finished their studies. — N COUNT; ⇑ dissenter

dropper /drɒpə/, **droppers.** A **dropper** is a small glass tube with a hollow rubber part on one end which you use for drawing up and dropping small amounts of liquid. — N COUNT

droppings /drɒpɪŋz/ are the faeces of some small and medium-sized animals and birds. EG *...mouse droppings.* — N PLURAL

dropsy /drɒpsi¹/ is a medical condition in which parts of the body fill up with fluid. Dropsy can be caused by various diseases. — N UNCOUNT

dross /drɒs/ is **1** the waste material that floats on the surface of a metal such as gold that has been melted. — N UNCOUNT **2** anything that is of a very poor quality. EG *We can't publish this dross.* — N UNCOUNT; = rubbish

drought /draʊt/, **droughts.** **1** **Drought** is lack or shortage of rainwater. EG *...the effects of famine and drought.* — N UNCOUNT

2 A **drought** is a long period of time during which no rain falls. EG *...natural disasters such as droughts, earthquakes, or typhoons.* — N COUNT

drove /drəʊv/, **droves.** **1** **Drove** is the past tense of **drive.**

2 A **drove** is a very large group, especially of people. EG *They were trying to maintain law and order* — N COUNT: ALSO N +*of*+N COUNT IN *amongst the droves of injured citizens... They would come in droves to see Australia's natural wonder.* PL = horde

drown /draʊn/, **drowns, drowning, drowned.**
1 When someone **drowns** or when something **drowns** them, they die because they have gone under water or another liquid and cannot breathe. EG *A man fell from a bridge and drowned... A boy was drowned this morning... The ship sank within minutes, drowning all the passengers on board.* V-ERG

2 To **drown** someone means to kill them by holding their head under water or another liquid so that they cannot breathe. EG *I couldn't make myself drown the poor animal.* V+O

3 If someone **drowns** their **sorrows**, they drink alcohol in order to forget something sad or terrible that has happened to them. EG *He was drowning his sorrows in a bottle of whiskey.* PHR : VB INFLECTS

4 If water **drowns** a place, it covers it completely. EG *This could also cause the melting of ice at the poles, drowning many of the world's cities.* V+O ⇑ cover = inundate

5 If you **drown** food or drink, you put a lot of a particular liquid on it or in it and so hide its flavour. V+O = drench

6 If something **drowns** a sound or **drowns** it **out**, it is so loud that it makes it impossible to hear that sound properly. EG *His words were drowned by loud cheers from the crowd... The noise from the aeroplane drowned out the voice from the loudspeaker.* V+O : USU PASS, OR PHRASAL VB : V+O+ADV

drowse /draʊz/, **drowses, drowsing, drowsed.** To **drowse** means to be almost asleep or just asleep for a while because you feel very calm and relaxed. EG *She drowsed in the sun.* V ⇑ sleep

drowsy /draʊzi^1/, **drowsier, drowsiest.** 1 If you feel **drowsy**, you feel sleepy in a way which leaves you unable to think clearly or do anything. EG *Things were quiet for a while and I became pleasantly drowsy... These tablets will make you drowsy.* ADJ QUALIT ⇑ sleepy
◇ **drowsiness.** EG *A pleasant drowsiness fell upon him.* ◇ N UNCOUNT ◇ **drowsily.** EG *'That's how it began,' she answered drowsily.* ◇ ADV WITH VB

2 Something that is **drowsy** is so peaceful that it makes you feel relaxed and sleepy. EG *He thought of home, of drowsy fields and villages baking in the sun.* ADJ QUALIT

drudge /drʌdʒ/, **drudges.** A **drudge** is a person who has to work hard at a job which is not very important or interesting. N COUNT

drudgery /drʌdʒəri^1/ is work that is not enjoyable to do because it is hard or boring, and does not give the person who does it any importance in society. EG *...the monotonous drudgery of the assembly line.* N UNCOUNT = grind

drug /drʌg/, **drugs, drugging, drugged.** 1 A **drug** is 1.1 a chemical which is given to a person in order to treat or prevent an illness or disease. EG *This drug is prescribed to treat hay fever.* N COUNT ⇑ medicine 1.2 a substance that is illegal in many countries which some people smoke or inject into their blood because it has a stimulating effect or because they are addicted to it. EG *They had reason to believe that the girl was on drugs... I don't think she takes drugs... ...the problems of drug addiction.* N COUNT : USU PL ⇑ chemical = narcotic 1.3 an activity which you enjoy so much that you want to do it more and more. EG *Travelling has become a drug for me: I just can't stop!.* N COUNT ⇑ obsession = addiction

2 To **drug** someone means to give them a chemical substance in order to make them become sleepy or unconscious. EG *All three dogs lay quiet having been slightly drugged... We drugged the camel until it was unconscious.* ◇ **drugged.** EG *She spoke as if half asleep or drugged... ...a drugged sleep.* V+O = sedate, dope ◇ ADJ CLASSIF = doped

3 To **drug** food or drink means to deliberately mix a chemical substance with it which will cause the person who eats or drinks it to become sleepy or unconscious. ◇ **drugged.** EG *They were sleeping heavily under the effect of the drugged sweets she had given them.* V+O ⇑ contaminate = dope ◇ ADJ CLASSIF = doped

druggist /drʌgɪst/, **druggists.** A **druggist** is a person who is qualified to prepare and sell drugs and medicines; used in American English. ▸ also used of the shop where a druggist works. EG *Is there a druggist round here?* N COUNT = pharmacist

drugstore /drʌgstɔ:/, **drugstores.** A **drugstore** is a shop where a large range of things are sold, including medicines, and where you can also buy and eat simple meals; used in American English. N COUNT

druid /dru:ɪd/, **druids.** A **druid** is a priest of a religion which was followed in Britain, Ireland, and France before Christianity. N COUNT

drum /drʌm/, **drums, drumming, drummed.**
1 A **drum** is 1.1 a musical instrument consisting of a skin stretched tightly over the end of a round frame which you beat with sticks or with your hands. EG *She started to beat her drum, singing a native song... He plays the drums superbly.* N COUNT 1.2 a large cylindrical container that is used to contain or transport fuel. EG *...oil drums.* N COUNT 1.3 a hollow cylindrical structure that turns and is used in a machine or to wind wire or rope. EG *The bands are brought into contact with the rotating drums.* N COUNT ⇑ cylinder

2 If you **drum** your fingers or **drum** with your fingers, you hit a surface such as a table or desk top with the ends of your fingers, making a continuous beating sound. EG *He drummed his fingers on the desk... He was waiting, drumming on the table with his fingers.* V OR V+O ⇑ strike = tap

3 If something **drums**, it makes a beating noise because it is regularly hitting a surface or object. EG *The rain started to drum on the roof.* ◇ **drumming.** EG *There was the sound of a tremendous drumming of hoofs inside the van.* V = tap, beat ◇ N UNCOUNT

4 See also **drumming.**

drum into. If you **drum** something **into** someone or **drum** something **in**, you tell someone something many times so that they will eventually listen, understand, or remember it. EG *These facts had been drummed into him.* PHRASAL VB : V+O+ADV/PREP = din into

drum out. To **drum** someone **out** of a club, society, or other organization means to force them to leave it. EG *He was drummed out of the club.* PHRASAL VB : V+O+ADV ⇑ expel = banish

drum up. If you **drum up** support, you do things that attract and win people's support. EG *We were busy canvassing and drumming up support.* PHRASAL VB : ORDER V+ADV+O

drumbeat /drʌmbi:t/, **drumbeats.** A **drumbeat** is the sound of a beat on a drum. EG *He faintly heard the drumbeats and the shouting of dancers in the distance.* N COUNT

drum major, drum majors. A **drum major** is a sergeant in the army who is in charge of the drummers in a military band, or who leads the band when they are marching. N COUNT ⇑ soldier

drum majorette, drum majorettes. A **drum majorette** is a girl or young woman who marches with others at the front of a band in a procession. Drum majorettes wear uniforms and carry sticks which at intervals they throw into the air and catch. N COUNT

drummer /drʌmə/, **drummers.** A **drummer** is a person who plays the drums in a band, group, or orchestra. N COUNT ⇑ musician

drumming /drʌmɪŋ/ is the action of playing the drums. • See also **drum.** N UNCOUNT

drum roll, drum rolls; also spelled with a hyphen. A **drum roll** is a series of drumbeats that follow each other so quickly that they make a continuous sound. A drum roll is sometimes used to introduce someone as they come onto the stage in a theatre. N COUNT

drumstick /drʌmstɪk/, **drumsticks.** A **drumstick** is 1 a stick used for beating a drum. N COUNT 2 the lower part of the leg of a bird such as a chicken which is cooked and eaten. N COUNT : USU MOD+N

drunk /drʌŋk/, **drunks.** 1 If someone is **drunk**, they have consumed so much alcoholic drink that it is difficult for them to speak clearly, move properly, work, etc. EG *He had decided that he was never going to get drunk in his whole life... I knew Dan was slightly drunk and I wasn't impressed... He was often so drunk he couldn't write a word.* • See also **blind drunk.** ADJ QUALIT ⇑ intoxicated = inebriated ≠ sober

2 A **drunk** is 2.1 someone who frequently gets drunk. EG *Today, San Francisco has more drunks than any other American city.* N COUNT = drunkard 2.2 someone who is drunk. EG *The drunk stared at me furiously.* N COUNT

3 If you are **drunk** with a strong emotion, sensation, or experience, you are in a state of great excitement because of it. EG *She returned to England in May 1913 drunk with the freedom she had tasted.* ADJ CLASSIF : PRED, + *with/on* ⇑ excited = intoxicated ≠ calm

4 **Drunk** is also the past participle of **drink.**

drunkard /drʌŋkəd/, **drunkards.** A **drunkard** is someone who frequently gets drunk; used showing disapproval. EG *Her husband was a drunkard who seldom earned any money.* N COUNT = drunk

drunken /drʌŋkə^{0}n/. 1 **Drunken** is used to describe events and situations that are caused by or that involve people who are drunk. EG *...a place where a long drunken party had just broken up... ...drunken* ADJ CLASSIF : ATTRIB = boozy ≠ sober

whoops of laughter... Several members of the company collapsed immediately in a drunken stupor.
2 A **drunken** person is drunk or is frequently drunk. EG *They recommended stiffer penalties for drunken drivers... His thoughts wobbled like a drunken man's.* ◊ **drunkenly**. EG *...filthy children whose parents fought drunkenly with each other in the street.* — ADJ QUALIT: ATTRIB = inebriated ≠ sober; ◊ ADV

drunkenness /drʌŋkənəˀs/ is the habit of being frequently drunk. EG *They acquired a reputation for drunkenness and crime.* — N UNCOUNT ≠ sobriety

dry /draɪ/, **drier, dryer, driest; dries, drying, dried. Drier** and **dryer** are both used as the comparative form of the adjective. The adverb can be spelled **dryly** or **drily**. **1** Something that is **dry** has no water or other moisture on it or in it. EG *They threw onto the fire some dry branches... Polish it with a dry cloth... He was rubbing himself dry with her towel... Is the paint dry yet?* ◊ **dryness**. EG *The dryness of the ground showed that it had not rained for a long time.* • If you say that something is **as dry as a bone**, you mean that it is very dry indeed. EG *The earth seemed as dry as a bone.* — ADJ QUALIT ≠ damp, moist, wet; ◊ N UNCOUNT; • PHR: USED AS A C
2 When something **dries** or when you **dry** it, it becomes dry. EG *He dried his feet with the towel... The washing hung drying in the sun... Leave it to dry.* — V-ERG
3 When you **dry** the dishes after a meal, you wipe the water off the plates, knives, cups, etc when they have been washed, using a cloth. EG *I'll wash up and you can dry... He dried the dishes carefully.* — V OR V+O = wipe, dry up
4 A river, lake, or well that is **dry** is empty of water, usually because of hot weather and lack of rain. EG *By early summer the river was almost dry and there were no fish in it... What shall we do if the well runs dry?* — ADJ QUALIT
5 An oil-well that is **dry** is no longer producing any oil. — ADJ CLASSIF ⇑ disused
6 If you say that a cow is **dry**, or that a woman's breasts are **dry**, you mean that they are no longer able to provide milk. — ADJ CLASSIF
7 Weather, a period of time, or a place that is **dry** has little or no rainfall. EG *The night was dry and clear... These plants will need watering in dry weather... This is a dry area that only gets a few months' rain a year.* ◊ **dryness**. EG *I hadn't planned on the sudden dryness–the lack of grass for the animals.* — ADJ QUALIT ≠ wet; ◊ N UNCOUNT ≠ wetness
8 If you are **dry**, you are thirsty and need to drink something; an informal use. EG *I'm so dry I could drink anything.* — ADJ QUALIT: PRED = parched
9 If your mouth or throat is **dry**, it has little or no saliva in it, and so feels very unpleasant. EG *My throat was dry, and my head ached.* ◊ **dryness**. EG *The dryness in my mouth vanished.* — ADJ QUALIT ≠ moist; ◊ N UNCOUNT
10 A cough that is **dry** does not produce any phlegm. — ADJ CLASSIF
11 If your eyes are **dry**, they are not full of tears. EG *No normal person could watch this film with dry eyes.* — ADJ CLASSIF ≠ tearful
12 A place that is **dry** is one where there are laws or rules which forbid anyone to drink, sell, or buy alcoholic drink; an informal use. EG *The country is dry and no liquor is allowed.* — ADJ CLASSIF
13 Dry humour is very amusing, but in a subtle and clever way that does not make you actually laugh aloud. EG *She had a good sense of humour and I enjoyed her dry accounts of her work experiences.* ◊ **drily**. EG *She said drily that he looked just as stupid as he behaved.* ◊ **dryness**. EG *She remarked with some dryness on the fact that no-one was working.* — ADJ QUALIT ⇑ witty = ironic, wry; ◊ ADV; ◊ N UNCOUNT = irony
14 A voice that is **dry** is cold or dull, and does not express any emotions. EG *He suggested in a cool dry voice that perhaps they had better leave.* ◊ **drily**. EG *'I suppose I shall have to resign.' she said drily.* — ADJ QUALIT = flat; ◊ ADV
15 A piece of writing or a speech that is **dry** is dull and uninteresting. EG *I thought the book was very dry.* • If you say that something is **as dry as dust**, you mean that it is very dull and uninteresting. EG *Her lectures are as dry as dust.* — ADJ QUALIT = uninspired; • PHR: USED AS A C
16 Dry bread is bread which is plain and not covered with butter or jam. EG *He managed to swallow a little soup and dry toast.* — ADJ CLASSIF
17 Sherry or wine that is **dry** does not have a sweet taste. EG *They were drinking dry white wine.* — ADJ CLASSIF ≠ sweet
18 A sound that is **dry** is rough, sharp, or crackling, and not smooth. EG *The branch snapped with a dry cracking noise.* — ADJ QUALIT = harsh
19 If an actor or actress **dries**, he or she forgets his or her lines in a play. — V
20 high and dry: see **high**.

dry out. **1** If something **dries out** or **dries off**, it loses all the water or moisture that was in it or on it. EG *You should let that wood dry out before you use it for anything... The clothes soon dried off in the sun.* — PHRASAL VB: V-ERG+A
2 If someone **dries out** or **is dried out**, they are cured of alcoholism; a fairly informal use. EG *They sent him to a special hospital to dry out.* — PHRASAL VB: V-ERG+A ⇑ cure

dry up. **1** If something **dries up** or if something **dries** it **up**, it loses all the water or moisture that was in it. EG *The heat had dried up the grass.* ◊ **dried-up**. EG *She looked at the dried up piece of cake with disgust.* — PHRASAL VB: V-ERG+A; ◊ ADJ QUALIT = stale
2 If a river, lake, or well **dries up**, it becomes empty of water, usually because of hot weather and the lack of rain. EG *The pool dried up in the late summer.* ◊ **dried-up**. EG *They came upon a dried-up oasis.* — PHRASAL VB: V+ADV ≠ flood; ◊ ADJ CLASSIF
3 When you **dry up** after a meal or **dry up** the dishes, you wipe the water off the plates, knives, cups, etc when they have been washed, using a cloth. EG *I started to dry up a cup rather slowly.* — PHRASAL VB: V+ADV, OR V+O+A
4 If you **dry up** when you are speaking, you stop speaking in the middle of what you were saying, because you do not know or cannot remember what to say next. EG *Halfway through the speech she dried up completely.* — PHRASAL VB: V+ADV ≠ continue
5 If something **dries up**, it stops being productive. EG *They were worried that the oil well would dry up... The market for luxury goods dried up during the recession.* — PHRASAL VB: V+ADV ⇑ fail = run out
6 If you say **'dry up'** to someone, you are telling them in a rather rude way to stop talking and be quiet. — CONVENTION = shut up
7 See also **dried-up, drying-up**.

dry-clean, dry-cleans, dry-cleaning, dry-cleaned. To **dry-clean** clothes or other things made of cloth means to clean them using a liquid chemical and not water. — V+O ≠ wash

dry cleaner, dry cleaners. A **dry cleaner** is someone who has a shop where clothes and other things made of cloth can be dry-cleaned. ▸ You can also refer to the shop as the **dry cleaner** or the **dry cleaner's**. EG *Take it to the dry cleaner's.* — N COUNT

dry-cleaning is **1** the action or work of dry-cleaning things, for example clothes. EG *...a dry-cleaning shop.* **2** clothes and other things made of cloth that have been dry-cleaned, or that are going to be dry-cleaned. — N UNCOUNT; N UNCOUNT

dry dock, dry docks. A **dry dock** is a place in a harbour from which water can be removed after a ship has entered it, so that the ship can be repaired or finished. — N COUNT

dryer /draɪə/, **dryers**; also spelled **drier**. **1** A **dryer** is **1.1** a machine for drying clothes. **1.2** a hairdryer. — N COUNT; N COUNT
2 Dryer and **drier** are the comparative forms of **dry**.

dry-eyed. Someone who is **dry-eyed** is not crying. EG *Then, dry-eyed, he turned and walked away.* — ADJ CLASSIF ≠ tearful

dry ginger is a fizzy, ginger-flavoured drink that is used for mixing with whisky or other alcoholic drinks. — N UNCOUNT ⇑ mixer

dry goods are cloth, thread, and other things that are sold at a draper's shop; used in American English. — N PLURAL = haberdashery

drying-up. Drying-up or the **drying-up** is the task of drying plates, knives, cups, etc after they have been washed. EG *We helped with the drying-up.* — N UNCOUNT, OR N SING WITH DET

dry land is land; used when contrasting it with the sea or the air. EG *We'll soon be on dry land again.* — N UNCOUNT = terra firma

dry rot is a serious disease of wood. It is caused by a fungus and causes wood to decay. EG *If you suspect that you have dry rot in your house call a surveyor.* — N UNCOUNT

dry-stone wall, dry-stone walls. A **dry-stone wall** is a wall that has been built by skilfully fitting stones together without using any mortar. — N COUNT

DT's /diːtiːz/. If an alcoholic has the **DT's**, he or she cannot stop his or her body from shaking, is unable to think clearly, and may see and feel things which do not exist. — N PL: the+N = shakes

dual /djuːəl/. **1 Dual** means having two parts, functions, or aspects in the same situation or unit. EG *Wages have, as already noted, a dual function in the economy... ...another example of her dual personality... ...dual purpose furniture, such as bed-settees... ...dual nationality.* — ADJ CLASSIF: ATTRIB ⇑ double ≠ single
2 Dual is used to describe two separate things that are of the same kind or that do the same job, but that are not exactly the same. EG *This factory has a system of dual rates of pay for the same job.* — ADJ CLASSIF: ATTRIB ⇑ different

dual carriageway, dual carriageways. A **dual carriageway** is a road which has two lanes of traffic travelling in each direction with a strip of grass or concrete down the middle to separate the two lots of traffic; used in British English. N COUNT/ UNCOUNT

dualism /dju:ᵊlɪzᵊm/ is the state of having two main parts or aspects, or the belief that something has two main parts or aspects; a formal word. EG *...the old dualism of God and the devil... He seeks a dualism such as mind and matter.* N UNCOUNT ⇑ plurality

dub /dʌb/, **dubs, dubbing, dubbed.** 1 To **dub** someone or something a particular name means to give them that name, especially as a nickname or as a way of describing them. EG *Some locals have dubbed it Dracula's castle... London was dubbed 'the insurance capital of the world'.* V+O+C, OR V+O +A *(as)* = christen

2 If a film or soundtrack **is dubbed**, the soundtrack you hear is not the actors speaking, but other actors speaking a different language. EG *The series sells in forty-seven countries and is dubbed into six languages... Later on, probably a different voice will be dubbed in.* V+O : USU PAST PART ⇑ change

dubbin /dʌbɪn/ is a kind of thick grease that is rubbed into leather to make it soft and waterproof; used in British English. N UNCOUNT

dubious /dju:bɪəs/. 1 Something that is **dubious** is not considered to be completely honest or safe, and therefore cannot be trusted or approved of. EG *The take-over was executed after some dubious manoeuvres by James... As regards civil rights, he has a very dubious record indeed... ...goods of dubious origin.* ADJ QUALIT ⇑ doubtful = questionable, suspect

2 If you are **dubious**, you are not completely sure about something and have not yet made up your mind about it. EG *He was dubious about Baker's choice of pilot.* ◊ **dubiously.** EG *The others looked at him dubiously, not quite knowing how much to believe.* ADJ QUALIT ⇑ uncertain = unsure ≠ positive ◊ ADV

3 **Dubious** qualities are considered to be bad rather than good. EG *He was also possessed of the dubious distinction of being Gerran's son-in-law... They were not the first to use these chemicals in military operations. This dubious honour goes to the British.* ADJ QUALIT : ATTRIB ⇑ uncertain = questionable

ducal /dju:kᵊl/ places or things belong to or are connected with a duke. EG *...trees that would not have disgraced a ducal park.* ADJ CLASSIF : ATTRIB

duchess /dʌtʃɪ²s/, **duchesses.** A **duchess** is a woman who has a rank equivalent to a duke, or who is a duke's wife or widow. EG *...a memorial put up by the Duchess of Marlborough.* N COUNT : ALSO IN TITLES

duchy /dʌtʃi¹/, **duchies.** A **duchy** is the area of land that is owned or ruled by a duke. EG *...the Grand Duchy of Luxembourg.* N COUNT : ALSO IN NAMES ⇑ territory = dukedom

duck /dʌk/, **ducks, ducking, ducked.** 1 A **duck** is **1.1** a very common water bird with short legs, webbed feet, a short neck, and a large flat beak. There are many kinds of duck, either wild or kept for their eggs, meat, or feathers. N COUNT **1.2** a female duck. The male is called a drake. N COUNT

2 **Duck** is the meat of a duck when it is cooked and eaten. EG *...wild duck in orange sauce.* N UNCOUNT

3 If you **take to** something **like a duck to water**, you discover that you are naturally good at it or that you like it very much. EG *They have taken to the idea like ducks to water.* PHR : VB INFLECTS

4 If you say that something is **like water off a duck's back**, you mean that it has absolutely no effect at all. EG *My suggestions were like water off a duck's back.* PHR : USED AS A C ⇑ ineffective

5 If you **duck**, **5.1** you move your head or the top half of your body quickly downwards, especially in order to avoid being seen or hit by something. EG *My own technique with a cricket ball was to duck... He ducked his head.* V OR V+O **5.2** you go quickly under water, or dip your head quickly under water, for a short time. EG *She ducked under and came up with a large shell.* V OR V+O : USU+A ⇑ plunge = dive

6 To **duck** into a particular place means to move quickly into that place, especially in an attempt to escape danger. EG *When they see you coming, they duck into their holes.* V+A ⇑ disappear = dive

7 If you **duck** something such as a blow, you avoid it by ducking. EG *He managed to duck the blow.* V OR V+O = dodge

8 If you **duck** someone, you force them or their head under water for a short time. EG *They duck you right under.* V+O : USU+A ⇑ immerse

9 If you **duck** a duty or responsibility, you are careful to avoid it, especially because you are afraid of it or because you don't like it. EG *She has a tendency to duck responsibility.* V+O = shirk

duck out. If you **duck out** of something that you are supposed to do, you avoid doing it, especially by making an excuse. EG *It was too late to duck out of going with them.* PHRASAL VB : V+ ADV, USU+*of* = back out

ducking /dʌkɪŋ/, **duckings.** If you give someone a **ducking**, you push them under water. EG *The child got a nasty ducking.* N COUNT ⇑ wetting

duckling /dʌklɪŋ/, **ducklings.** A **duckling** is a young duck. N COUNT ⇑ duck

ducks and drakes. When someone plays **ducks and drakes**, they throw a flat stone across an area of water in such a way that the stone bounces across the surface. N UNCOUNT

duct /dʌkt/, **ducts.** A **duct** is **1** a pipe, tube, or channel which is intended to carry a liquid or gas. EG *The generator is positioned outside the water duct.* N COUNT : USU+SUPP **2** a tube in your body which carries liquid such as tears or bile; a formal use. EG *The condition is caused by an obstructed tear duct.* N COUNT+SUPP

dud /dʌd/, **duds.** Something that is **dud** does not work in the way that it is supposed to, and is therefore useless. EG *He'd stepped on a dud mine.* ▸ used as a noun. EG *I had discovered that the grenade was a dud.* ADJ CLASSIF ⇑ inoperative ▸ N COUNT : IF SING *a*+N

dud cheque, dud cheques. A **dud cheque** is a cheque which is not worth any money because the person who wrote it does not have any money in his or her bank account. N COUNT

dude /dju:d/, **dudes**; used in informal American English. A **dude** is **1** a man; an old-fashioned use. EG *...every damn dude in the platoon.* N COUNT **2** a black man who dresses in a showy style. N COUNT

dude ranch, dude ranches. A **dude ranch** is an American farm where people can have holidays during which they can do activities such as riding or camping. N COUNT ◊ N UNCOUNT

dudgeon /dʌdʒᵊn/. If you are **in high dudgeon**, you are very angry or resentful, usually because your feelings have been hurt by what someone has said or done. EG *He slammed the door and went off in high dudgeon.* PHR : USED AS A/C = fuming

due /dju:/, **dues.** 1 If something is **due** at a particular time, it is expected to happen, be done, or arrive at that time. EG *We were due in London at 2 a.m.... The committee was due to meet on 22 August... The cars were due in thirty-five minutes... The next issue of the magazine is due out in December.* ADJ CLASSIF : PRED, USU+A/ *to*-INF

2 **Due** attention, consideration, etc is the proper, reasonable, or deserved amount of it under the circumstances. EG *In designing the machines due attention was paid to the people who would work them... He paused a moment, giving my comments due consideration... ...failing to exercise due care and control of the child.* ADJ CLASSIF : ATTRIB+N UNCOUNT ⇑ reasonable = proper

3 You say **with due respect** when you are about to disagree politely with someone. EG *With all due respect, I think you will find that the situation is not as you have described.* PHR : USED AS AN A

4 If you say that something will happen or take place **in due course**, you mean that you cannot make it happen any quicker and it will happen when the time is right for it. EG *The people we love die, as we shall ourselves in due course... There is no doubt that every home will have a computer in due course.* PHR : USED AS AN A = eventually

5 Something that is **due**, or that is **due** to someone, is owed to them, either as a debt or because they have a right to it. EG *That money was due to me and I have not had it... Do not forget to claim any additional pension you are due under the state scheme... Old people expect to be treated with the respect due to their age and experience.* ▸ used as a preposition, especially in American English. EG *We made the telephone calls due us from the police station.* ● If you say **'credit where credit's due'**, you are admitting that you ought to praise someone for something that they have done or for a good quality that they possess. EG *I don't like her but, credit where credit's due, she is a good teacher.* ADJ CLASSIF : PRED, IF+PREP THEN *to* ▸ PREP ● PHR

6 **To give** someone their **due** means to admit that there are some good things about them, even though there are things that you do not like about them. EG *To give him his due he had no idea that he was making you angry... The BBC, give them their due, actually asked him to appear on a television programme.* PHR : USED AS ADV SEN = be fair

7 **Dues** are sums of money that you pay regularly to an organization that you belong to, such as a club or N PLURAL ⇑ money

trade union, for your membership fees. EG *Most union members pay their dues willingly.*

8 If an event is **due to** something, it happens or exists as a direct result of that thing. EG *His death was due to natural causes... My desire to act was due to Laurence Olivier's performance in 'Hamlet'.* — PREP ↑ because of

9 You can say **due to** to introduce the reason for something happening. Some speakers of English believe that it is not correct to use **due to** in this way. EG *Due to repairs, the garage will be closed next Saturday.* — PREP = owing to

10 Due north, south, east, or west means exactly in the direction mentioned. EG *They were travelling due east, out into the hills.* — ADV ↑ exactly = precisely

duel /djuːəl/, **duels, duelling, duelled**; also spelled **dueling** and **dueled** in American English. **1** A **duel** is **1.1** a formal fight between two people in which they use guns, swords, or other weapons in order to settle a quarrel. EG *Feelings were so intense that they fought a duel.* — N COUNT **1.2** a situation, event, or activity, in which two people or groups are involved in a struggle or conflict. EG *...a duel between central and local government.* — N COUNT ↑ contest

2 To **duel** means to fight a duel. EG *Duelling was made illegal.* — V

duet /djuːɛt, djuːɛt/, **duets**. A **duet** is a song or other piece of music sung or played by two people. EG *I don't think I know of any duets for piano and trumpet.* — N COUNT

duff /dʌf/, **duffs, duffing, duffed**; used in informal British English. Something that is **duff** is useless or broken. EG *It might look all right, but I'll bet you it's a duff one.* — ADJ CLASSIF : PRED

duff up. If you **duff** someone **up**, you fight them and injure them, usually using your fists. EG *They dragged him into the alley and duffed him up.* — PHRASAL VB : ORDER V+O+ADV = beat up

duffel /dʌfəl/, **duffels**; also spelled **duffle**. A **duffel** is the same as a duffel coat. — N COUNT

duffel bag, duffel bags; also spelled **duffle bag**. It is also spelled with a hyphen. A **duffel bag** is a bag shaped like a cylinder and made of strong cloth such as canvas. Duffel bags have string at one end which is used to close the bag and to carry it with. EG *He threw his stuff in a duffel bag and left.* — N COUNT

duffel coat, duffel coats; also spelled **duffle coat**. It is also spelled with a hyphen. A **duffel coat** is a heavy coat that fastens with rod-shaped buttons and loops, and usually has a hood. EG *...a shapeless black duffel coat.* — N COUNT

duffer /dʌfə/, **duffers**. A **duffer** is someone who is unable to learn what someone else is trying to teach them or who is unable to do something well or properly; an informal word. EG *I'm a complete golfing duffer.* — N COUNT

duffle /dʌfəl/. See **duffel**.

dug /dʌg/ is the past tense and past participle of **dig**.

dugout /dʌgaʊt/, **dugouts**. A **dugout** is **1** a canoe that is made by hollowing out a log. — N COUNT **2** a shelter made by digging a hole in the ground and then covering it or tunnelling so that the shelter has a roof over it. Dugouts are usually made by soldiers. — N COUNT

duke /djuːk/, **dukes**. A **duke** is **1** a nobleman who has a rank just below that of a prince. EG *She was a good friend of six British dukes... ...the Duke of York.* — N COUNT : ALSO IN TITLES

2 the prince or ruler of a small independent state. EG *...the Duke of Upper Saxony.* — N COUNT : ALSO IN TITLES

dukedom /djuːkdəm/, **dukedoms**. A **dukedom** is **1** the rank or title of a duke. — N COUNT **2** the land owned by a duke. EG *So he became heir to a dukedom.* — N COUNT

dulcet /dʌlsɪt/. **Dulcet** sounds are gentle and pleasant to listen to; a literary word, often used humorously. EG *Her dulcet tones came over the airwaves.* — ADJ CLASSIF : ATTRIB = sweet

dull /dʌl/, **duller, dullest; dulls, dulling, dulled**. **1** Someone or something that is **dull 1.1** does not seem to have any interesting features. EG *I thought the book dull and unoriginal... It's a terribly dull place; nothing much goes on here at all... I found that he was the same dull sedate person he had always been.* — ADJ QUALIT ↑ uninteresting = boring, dreary ◊ **dullness**. EG *...the dullness of his life.*

1.2 is not very lively or energetic. EG *I often feel dull and awkward when I go to parties... She became dull and silent during the last part of the long journey.* — ADJ QUALIT ↑ listless ≠ vivacious ◊ **dully**. EG *'How long will I have to be away from home?' he asked dully.* — ◊ ADV WITH VB ◊ **dullness**. EG *A strange dullness had replaced her usual cheerfulness.* — ◊ N UNCOUNT

2 Light or a colour that is **dull** is rather dark. EG *The sea had been a dull grey... The whole canyon is in dull shadow... ...a dull glow.* — ADJ QUALIT : ATTRIB ◊ **dully**. EG *The lights of the houses gleamed dully on the hillside.* — ◊ ADV WITH VB ↑ dimly

3 Dull weather is rather cloudy. EG *It's very dull today but I don't think it'll rain.* — ADJ QUALIT = overcast

4 Sounds that are **dull** are not very clear or loud. EG *Instead of the dull boom we expected there was a terrible crack... There was a dull thud as his head hit the floor.* — ADJ CLASSIF ≠ sharp ◊ **dully**. — ◊ ADV

5 Feelings or pain that are **dull** are not very clear or sharply defined. EG *The dull ache in her belly began again... Because he was fat, he hated school games with a dull passion.* — ADJ CLASSIF : ATTRIB ≠ acute ◊ **dully**. EG *His ankle throbbed dully as the blood rushed to it.* — ◊ ADV WITH VB

6 Someone who is dull is not very intelligent and learns things very slowly. EG *...the dullest boy in the class... ...these factors affect both intelligent and dull children.* — ADJ QUALIT ↑ stupid = slow ◊ **dullness**. EG *Her dullness and his impatience made it impossible for her to learn from him.* — ◊ N UNCOUNT

7 A knife that is **dull** has a blade that is not sharp; a fairly formal use. EG *What use is a knife with a dull blade?* — ADJ QUALIT ↑ blunt ≠ sharp

8 If something **dulls** a pain, emotion, or feeling, it causes it to be felt less intensely. EG *In her experience, the taking of food dulled pain... Her sensitivity is dulled.* — V+O ↑ lessen = numb

9 If something **dulls** or if you **dull** something, it becomes darker or less lively. EG *His eyes dulled.* — V-ERG ≠ brighten

dullard /dʌləd/, **dullards**. A **dullard** is a person who is stupid and unimaginative; an old-fashioned word. EG *...an incompetent, bumbling dullard.* — N COUNT = dimwit, blockhead

duly /djuːli/. **1 Duly** is used to say than an action or process has been done in the proper, correct, or expected way. EG *She was declared duly elected to Parliament... Don't worry. Everything has been duly taken care of.* — ADV ↑ properly

2 If something **duly** happens, it happens at the proper or expected time. EG *De Gaulle duly attended the ceremony at the appointed time... The book duly appeared in March as had been promised... I was expecting the question which he duly asked.* — ADV WITH VB

dumb /dʌm/, **dumber, dumbest**. **1** Someone who is **dumb** is **1.1** completely unable to speak. EG *She was deaf and dumb from birth.* — ADJ CLASSIF **1.2** not able or willing to say anything for a short while, for example because they are angry, shocked, or surprised. EG *The girl stood, dumb and sullen... We were struck dumb with horror and grief.* — ADJ CLASSIF : PRED ↑ silent **1.3** not very clever or intelligent; an informal, offensive use. EG *They used to call you dumb if you worked on a farm.* — ADJ QUALIT ↑ stupid = dim ≠ clever

2 Something that is **dumb** is **2.1** done or expressed without words. EG *Silence can upset some people who interpret it as dumb insolence... He was in a dumb rage.* — ADJ CLASSIF : ATTRIB ↑ silent **2.2** silly and annoying; an informal use showing disapproval. EG *All they bought me was this dumb T-shirt... ...in order to prevent dumb mistakes later on.* — ADJ QUALIT = stupid

3 You can refer to animals as **dumb** animals to emphasize that they cannot speak to people and perhaps that they are helpless. — ADJ CLASSIF

dumbbell /dʌmbel/, **dumbbells**; also spelled with a hyphen. A **dumbbell** is **1** a short bar with weights on either side which people use for physical exercise to strengthen their arm and shoulder muscles. — N COUNT **2** a stupid person; an informal use, mainly in American English. EG *They had watched many a dumbbell turn into a national hero on the baseball pitch.* — N COUNT ↑ fool = dummy

dumbfounded /dʌmfaʊndɪd/. If you are **dumbfounded**, you are so surprised that you are unable to speak. EG *He was watching, dumbfounded, when suddenly he heard a scream... ...a circle of dumbfounded police officers.* — ADJ CLASSIF : USU PRED

dumbly /dʌmli/. If you do something **dumbly**, you do it without saying anything, for example because you are afraid or because you do not understand. EG *Numb with fear, the men followed dumbly the order to sit down... For a moment he stared dumbly at the wall.* — ADV WITH VB

dumbo /dʌmbəʊ/, **dumbos**. If you call someone a **dumbo**, you mean that they are rather stupid; an informal word. — N COUNT : ALSO VOC ↑ fool = dope

dumbstruck /dʌmstrʌk/. If you are **dumbstruck**, you are so shocked or surprised that you cannot speak. — ADJ CLASSIF : USU PRED = dumbfounded

dumb waiter, dumb waiters; also spelled with a hyphen. A **dumb waiter** is a lift used to carry things, such as food or dishes, from one floor of a building to another. — N COUNT

dum-dum /dʌm dʌm/, **dum-dums**. A **dum-dum** or a **dum-dum bullet** is a bullet that is very soft or hollow at the front and that causes large and serious wounds because it breaks into small pieces when it hits someone. N COUNT

dummy /dʌmi¹/, **dummies**. 1 A **dummy** is 1.1 a large model that looks like a human being and is used, for example, to display clothes in a shop. EG *I like the dress that's on the dummy... ...a ventriloquist's dummy.* N COUNT 1.2 a model or imitation of something that has been made to look similar to the real thing or to show some of its characteristics. N COUNT 1.3 in British English, a rubber object that a baby is given to suck so that it feels comforted and stays quiet. N COUNT

2 **Dummy** means not real but used, made, or carried out as if it were real. EG *The cannon was loaded with dummy shells... They used several dummy firms for the arms deal.* ADJ CLASSIF : ATTRIB = fake ≠ genuine

3 A **dummy** or **dummy hand** is a hand of cards in a game of bridge which is placed on the table where all the players can see it. N COUNT

4 If you call someone a **dummy**, you mean that you think they are very stupid; an informal use. N COUNT : ALSO VOC

dummy run, dummy runs. A **dummy run** is a trial or test procedure, which is carried out in order to see if something works properly and if there are any problems. EG *Let's do a dummy run on the computer and see if the program works.* N COUNT = trial run

dump /dʌmp/, **dumps, dumping, dumped**. 1 If you **dump** something, 1.1 you unload it or throw it down in a careless manner. EG *They came back with armful of dry things and dumped them on the fire... She dumped her bag on Judy's table.* V+O : USU+A ↑ put = drop 1.2 you throw it away or leave it somewhere because you do not want it any more. EG *They dumped a load of rubbish in the river... The stolen car was found dumped in one of the side streets.* V+O : USU+A ↑ dispose of = ditch ◊ **dumping**. EG *...the dumping of acid wastes in the North Sea.* ◊ N UNCOUNT

2 If a firm or company **dumps** goods, it sells large qualities of them at prices far below their real value, usually in another country, in order to gain a bigger market share or to keep prices high in the home market. EG *Drugs or chemicals that are banned in Western countries are often dumped in Third World countries.* V+O : USU+A ↑ sell

3 To **dump** computer data or part of a computer's memory means to copy it from one storage system of a computer onto another, such as from disc to magnetic tape; a technical term. V+O

4 A **dump** is 4.1 a place where rubbish is left, sometimes without permission, for example on open ground outside a town. EG *Twelve tons of toxic waste have been discovered on an old rubbish dump in Kent.* N COUNT = tip 4.2 a place where an army stores food, weapons, or ammunition temporarily while it is stationed in a particular place. EG *The ammunition dump was hit by a shell.* N COUNT ↑ store 4.3 a place which is very ugly and unpleasant to live in; an informal use. EG *It's a real dump.* N COUNT = hole, slum 4.4 the act or process of copying data or memory from one storage system onto another; a technical term in computing. N COUNT ↑ copy

5 If you **dump** someone somewhere, you let them get out of a vehicle there after you have taken them there; an informal use. V+O+A = drop

6 If you are **down in the dumps**, you are feeling very depressed and miserable; an informal expression. PHR : USED AS A C ↑ unhappy

dumper truck, dumper trucks; also spelled with a hyphen. A **dumper truck** is a truck whose carrying part can be tipped backwards so that the load falls out. N COUNT = dump truck

dumping ground, dumping grounds. 1 A **dumping ground** is a place where rubbish is left, sometimes without permission, for example on open ground outside a town. N COUNT

2 If you say that a place is a **dumping ground** for a particular thing, you mean that that thing is left there, usually in large quantities, because it is no longer wanted. EG *This country has become a dumping ground for every sort of surplus military hardware.* N COUNT+*for* ↑ store = repository

dumpling /dʌmplɪŋ/, **dumplings**. A **dumpling** is 1 a small lump of dough that is cooked with meat and vegetables. N COUNT 2 a pudding consisting of an apple or other fruit covered in a sweet dough and cooked. N COUNT ↑ pudding

dump truck, dump trucks. A **dump truck** is the same as a dumper truck. N COUNT

dumpy /dʌmpi¹/, **dumpier, dumpiest**. Someone who is **dumpy** is short and fat. EG *...a cross, dumpy woman.* ADJ CLASSIF

dun /dʌn/. Something that is **dun** is of a dull grey-brown colour. EG *...a flat, dun stretch of ground.* ADJ COLOUR

dunce /dʌns/, **dunces**. A **dunce** is a person who is stupid and finds it difficult or impossible to learn what someone is trying to teach them; used showing disapproval. EG *He was such a dunce at school.* N COUNT : ALSO VOC = dimwit

dune /djuːn/, **dunes**. A **dune** is a hill of sand near the sea or in a sand desert. EG *The wind carves it into gulleys and later into sand dunes.* N COUNT

dung /dʌŋ/ is faeces from animals, especially from large animals such as cattle and horses. EG *...fresh buffalo dung.* N UNCOUNT ↑ excrement

dungarees /dʌŋgəᵒriːz/ are trousers that are attached to a piece of cloth which covers your chest and which has straps going over your shoulders. N PLURAL : ALSO *a pair of*+N ↑ clothing

dungeon /dʌndʒəᵒn/, **dungeons**. A **dungeon** is a dark underground prison or prison cell in a castle. EG *They were driven into dark dungeons, straight off the battlefield.* N COUNT ↑ cellar

dunk /dʌŋk/, **dunks, dunking, dunked**. 1 If you **dunk** something such as a biscuit or a piece of bread in a drink or in soup, you dip it into the drink or soup before eating it. EG *He used to dunk his biscuits in his tea.* V+O : USU+A

2 If you **dunk** something in a liquid, you put it in the liquid, especially for a particular purpose and for a short time. EG *Just dunk it thoroughly in white spirit for five minutes.* V+O+A *(in)* ↑ dip

duo /djuːəʊ/, **duos**. A **duo** is 1 two musicians or singers who play music or sing together as a pair. EG *...a world-famous singing duo.* N COUNT 2 two people together, especially people who have something in common; an informal use. EG *When they're together they make a frightening duo.* N COUNT+SUPP = pair

duodenal /djuːəˢdiːnəᵒl/ means relating to or contained in the duodenum; a medical term. EG *...a duodenal ulcer.* ADJ CLASSIF : ATTRIB

duodenum /djuːəˢdiːnəᵒm/, **duodenums**. Your **duodenum** is the part of your small intestine just below your stomach; a medical term. N COUNT

dupe /djuːp/, **dupes, duping, duped**. 1 If someone **dupes** you, they trick you, often in order to make you do something which they want you to do, but which you do not want to do. EG *I was duped into opening my heart and expressing my thoughts... The people could see how they had been duped.* V+O : IF+PREP THEN *into* : USU PASS ↑ deceive = con, fool

2 A **dupe** is someone who is tricked by someone else. EG *I couldn't decide whether he was a dupe or a scoundrel.* N COUNT

duplex /djuːplɛks/, **duplexes**. 1 Something such as a device or process that is **duplex** has two parts; a technical term. EG *This stimulates a duplex transaction.* ADJ CLASSIF : USU ATTRIB = dual, two-fold

2 In American English, a **duplex** is 2.1 a semi-detached house. EG *The house was an older duplex encircled by nicely shaped hedges.* N COUNT = semi 2.2 a flat which has rooms on two floors. N COUNT

duplicate, duplicates, duplicating, duplicated. The word **duplicate is pronounced** /djuːplɪkət/ when it is a noun and an adjective, and /djuːplɪkeɪt/ when it is a verb. 1 To **duplicate** something written or drawn means make exact copies of it, often using a special machine such as a photocopier. EG *The story was typed and duplicated... ...a duplicating machine.* V+O ↑ copy = photocopy

2 **Duplicate** is used to describe things that have been made as an exact copy of other things, usually in order to serve the same purpose. EG *It could be driven away by someone with a duplicate key... We would have to build a duplicate city for the new urban millions.* ADJ CLASSIF : ATTRIB ↑ identical

3 A **duplicate** is something that is identical to something else because it has been copied exactly. EG *We get a written draft, a duplicate, which you use if the first one's lost.* N COUNT ↑ copy

4 If you have something **in duplicate**, you have two identical copies of it. EG *Usually now we ask for a draft in duplicate.* PHR : USED AS A/C

5 If you **duplicate** something that has already been done, you repeat or copy it. EG *...an oversight that would allow candidates to duplicate material in two answers... We really haven't duplicated the old system.* V+O ◊ **duplication** /djuːplɪkeɪʃəᵒn/. EG *There had been some duplication of effort involved.* ◊ N UNCOUNT

duplicator /dju:plɪkeɪtə/, **duplicators**. A **duplicator** is a machine which makes copies of writing or drawings from a specially prepared original. EG *You can use the typewriter or duplicator.* N COUNT

duplicity /dju:plɪsɪti[1]/ is speech or action that has the aim of making people believe something which is not true. EG *I was trying to plan some way of tackling her duplicity.* N UNCOUNT ⇑ deceit = deception ≠ honesty

durable /djʊə[0]rəbə[0]l/. Something that is **durable** is strong and lasts a long time without breaking or becoming weaker. EG *...buyers looking for well-finished and durable products.* ◊ **durability** /djʊə[0]rəbɪlɪti[1]/. EG *You should always consider the durability of a product... ...the durability of their love.* ADJ QUALIT = tough; ◊ N UNCOUNT ⇑ endurance = strength

duration /djʊreɪʃə[0]n/. 1 The **duration** of an event or state is the length of time during which it happens or exists. EG *I shall be away for the duration of the holiday* N SING : the+N+of

2 If you say that something will happen **for the duration**, you mean that it will happen for as long as the event or activity which is being talked about continues. EG *Now the storm has started I shall have to put up with you for the duration.* PHR : USED AS AN A

duress /djʊə[0]rɛs/ is physical or moral pressure that is used to make someone do something which they do not want to do. EG *...a decision made early in life under duress.* N UNCOUNT : under+N

Durex /djʊə[0]rɛks/. **Durex** is both the singular and the plural form. **Durex** is a British trademark for a contraceptive sheath. N COUNT

during /djʊə[0]rɪŋ/. Something that happens **during** a period of time 1 happens continuously or several times from the beginning to the end of that period of time. EG *I worked in Littlewoods during the summer holidays last year... Fry had worked a great deal with her at Oxford during the war... She heated the place during the winter with a huge wood furnace... I take mild tranquillisers every night during the week.* PREP ⇑ in

2 happens or develops gradually from the beginning to the end of that period of time. EG *During my fast I had lost fifteen pounds in weight... Both characters had to age during the course of the play... No credible generation of artists has emerged during the 1970s.* 3 happens at some point in the course of that period of time. EG *He had died during the night... Disease broke out during the journey... She left Bengal during the late spring of 1740.* PREP ⇑ in; PREP ⇑ in

dusk /dʌsk/ is the time just before night when the daylight has almost gone but when it is not completely dark; a fairly literary word. N UNCOUNT, OR N SING : the+N

dusky /dʌski[1]/, **duskier, duskiest**; a literary or formal word. 1 A place, time of day, or light that is **dusky** is rather dark or shadowy. EG *He returned to the dusky room... ...the late, dusky summer evening... ...in the dusky light of the morning.* ADJ CLASSIF = dim ≠ bright

2 **Dusky** means rather dark in colour. EG *...dusky blond hair... Heavy gold earrings gleamed against her dusky cheeks.* ADJ QUALIT

dust /dʌst/, **dusts, dusting, dusted**. 1 **Dust** is 1.1 very small dry particles of earth or sand. EG *A fine red dust covered everything... Each car threw up a cloud of white dust from the road... The hot wind had brought down dust clouds from the Sahara... Lying face down in the dust, he cried for his dead son.* 1.2 the very small pieces of dirt which you find inside buildings, for example on furniture, floors, or lights. EG *Children don't care about mess or dust as long as they feel they are loved... She wrote 'I love you' in the dust on the coffee table.* 1.3 a fine powder which consists of very small particles of a substance such as gold, wood, or cloth. EG *The autumn sun sparkled on the pavements like gold dust... We cut some of the wood to dust.* N UNCOUNT; N UNCOUNT; N UNCOUNT

2 If you **allow the dust to settle** or **let the dust settle**, you let a situation calm down before you try to do anything else; an informal expression. PHR : VB INFLECTS ⇑ wait

3 If something **bites the dust**, it fails and stops working; an informal and humorous expression. EG *My vacuum cleaner's finally bitten the dust.* PHR : VB INFLECTS

4 When you **dust** or when you **dust** something such as furniture, you remove dust from it, usually using a cloth. EG *He dusted all the furniture and then polished it... She spent the day dusting and cleaning.* V OR V+O ⇑ clean

5 If you **dust** something with a fine substance such as powder, you cover it lightly with that substance. EG *She put on lipstick and dusted her face with powder.* V+O : IF+PREP THEN with

6 If you **dust** a fine substance such as powder onto something, you cover or sprinkle the object with that substance. EG *He dusted a powder onto his roses to kill all the insects.* V+O : USU+A

dust down. If you **dust** something **down**, you remove dust from it, usually with a brush or a cloth. EG *They dusted down the whole house before they started decorating.* PHRASAL VB : V+O+ADV ⇑ clean

dust off. If you **dust** dirt **off** something, you take it off, usually using a cloth or a brush. EG *She dusted every bit of dirt off her dining table.* PHRASAL VB : V+O+ADV ⇑ clean

dustbin /dʌstbɪn/, **dustbins**. A **dustbin** is a large, round container with a lid which people put their rubbish in and which is usually kept outside their house; used mainly in British English. N COUNT = trash can

dustcart /dʌstka:t/, **dustcarts**; also spelled with a hyphen. A **dustcart** is a lorry into which the dustmen put the rubbish from people's dustbins; used in British English. N COUNT = garbage truck

duster /dʌstə/, **dusters**. A **duster** is a cloth which you use for removing dust from furniture, ornaments, or other objects. N COUNT

dust-jacket, dust-jackets; also spelled without a hyphen. A **dust-jacket** or a **dust-cover** is a loose paper cover which is put on a book to protect it. It often contains information about the book and its author. EG *They put his photograph on the dust-jacket of his first novel.* N COUNT : USU+SUPP

dustman /dʌstmə[3]n/, **dustmen**. A **dustman** is a person whose job is to empty the rubbish from people's dustbins and take it away to be disposed of; used in British English. N COUNT ⇑ worker = garbage collector

dustpan /dʌstpæn/, **dustpans**. A **dustpan** is a small flat container made of metal or plastic, into which you sweep dust and dirt with a brush. N COUNT

dustsheet /dʌstʃi:t/, **dustsheets**; also spelled with a hyphen. A **dustsheet** is a large cloth which is used to cover objects such as furniture in order to protect them from dust; used in British English. N COUNT

dust-up, dust-ups; also spelled as one word. A **dust-up** is a quarrel that often involves some fighting; an informal word. EG *John was in a bit of a dust-up outside the pub last night.* N COUNT

dusty /dʌsti[1]/, **dustier, dustiest**. 1 Something that is **dusty** is 1.1 covered with, or full of, tiny bits of earth or sand, usually because there has been no rain for a long time. EG *We rode along a dusty mountain track in Morocco... The day was very hot and very dusty.* 1.2 covered with the kind of dust that is found in houses. EG *...a room full of dusty, broken furniture... The goods in the shop window were dusty.* ADJ QUALIT ⇑ dry; ADJ QUALIT ⇑ dirty

2 A **dusty** colour is dull and has a slightly grey tinge. EG *She was wearing a dress of dusty blue.* ADJ QUALIT+COLOUR

Dutch /dʌtʃ/. 1 A person or thing that is **Dutch** comes from the Netherlands or is connected with the Netherlands or its people. ADJ CLASSIF

2 **Dutch** is the language that is spoken in the Netherlands. N UNCOUNT

3 The **Dutch** are the people of the Netherlands. EG *The Germans and the Dutch were not represented at the conference.* N PLURAL : the+N

4 If two or more people **go Dutch**, each of them pays their own bill, for example in a restaurant, rather than one person paying for both of them or all of them; an informal expression. EG *She insisted upon going Dutch.* PHR : VB INFLECTS = share the cost

5 See also **double Dutch**.

Dutch cap, Dutch caps. A **Dutch cap** is a circular rubber contraceptive device used by women. N COUNT = diaphragm

Dutch courage is the courage that you get by drinking alcoholic drinks; an informal expression. N UNCOUNT

Dutchman /dʌtʃmə[3]n/, **Dutchmen**. A **Dutchman** is a man who is a native of the Netherlands. N COUNT

Dutchwoman /dʌtʃwʊ[1]mə[0]n/, **Dutchwomen**. A **Dutchwoman** is a woman who is a native of the Netherlands. N COUNT

dutiful /dju:tɪfʊl/. If you are **dutiful**, you do everything that you are expected to do. EG *He was a dutiful son.* ◊ **dutifully**. EG *He dutifully said his prayers every night.* ADJ QUALIT = obedient; ◊ ADV WITH VB

duty /dju:ti[1]/, **duties**. 1 **Duty** is all the work that you have to do because it is part of your job or your position in society. EG *He reported for duty at the manager's office... I had to do jury duty last month.* N UNCOUNT

2 If someone such as a policeman or a nurse is **on duty** at a particular time, they are working at that time. If they are **off duty** at a particular time, they PHR : USED AS A/C

are not working at that time. EG *There were only two prison wardens on duty when the riot started.*
3 A **duty** is a task which you have to do because it is part of your job or position in society. EG *Nursing auxiliaries help qualified nurses with their basic duties.* N COUNT
5 If you say that something is your **duty**, you mean that you feel you ought to do it because it is right or because it is part of a code of behaviour that you believe in. EG *As a doctor, it was my duty to preserve life... She did her duty and cared for her ageing parents for ten years... This young woman obviously has no sense of duty.* N COUNT: WITH POSS, OR N UNCOUNT = obligation
6 Duty or a **duty** is a tax which you pay to the government on goods that you buy. EG *The government increased the duty on petrol... Customs duties are collected at the border.* N UNCOUNT/COUNT+SUPP

duty-bound. If you are **duty-bound** to do something, you are obliged to do it because it is felt to be right; a formal word. EG *You are duty-bound to stay by her sick bed.* ADJ CLASSIF: PRED+*to*-INF

duty-free. **1 Duty-free** goods are sold at airports, on ships, etc at a cheaper price than usual because you do not have to pay the tax that is usually paid when the goods are brought into a country. EG *...duty-free cigarettes.* ADJ CLASSIF ⇑ tax-free
2 If you buy goods **duty-free**, you buy them at a cheaper price than usual because you do not have to pay the tax that is usually paid when goods are brought into a country. ADV WITH VB ⇑ tax-free

duty-free shop, duty-free shops. A **duty-free shop** is a shop, for example at an airport, where you can buy duty-free goods. N COUNT

duvet /du:veɪ/, **duvets**. A **duvet** is a large bag filled with feathers or similar material which you use to cover yourself in bed instead of a sheet and blankets; used in British English. N COUNT = quilt

duvet cover, duvet covers. A **duvet cover** is a washable cover for a duvet. N COUNT

dwarf /dwɔ:f/, **dwarfs, dwarfing, dwarfed**. **1** If something **dwarfs** a person or object, it is a lot bigger than them and makes them look very small. EG *David was dwarfed by a huge bare desk... Commercial buildings are now beginning to dwarf the city churches.* V+O: USU PASS = tower over
2 Dwarf is used to describe plants or animals which are much smaller than normal. EG *...little trimmed dwarf Japanese Bonsai trees... ...dwarf breeds of dog.* ADJ CLASSIF: ATTRIB = miniature
3 A **dwarf** is **3.1** a person who is much smaller than the usual size. EG *There are some children who remain as dwarfs because they lack a particular hormone.* N COUNT ⇑ midget ≠ giant **3.2** an imaginary creature in fairy stories and legends who is like a small ugly man and often has magical powers. N COUNT

dwarfish /dwɔ:fɪʃ/. Someone or something that is **dwarfish** is surprisingly small. EG *...a dwarfish man with nimble hands.* ADJ QUALIT ⇑ tiny ≠ gigantic

dwell /dwɛl/, **dwells, dwelling, dwelled, dwelt**. **Dwelled** and **dwelt** are both used as the past tense and past participle of the verb. If you **dwell** somewhere, you live there; a formal word. EG *He had gone off to the Himalayas and had dwelt there for some years.* V+A ⇑ reside
dwell on. If you **dwell on** something or **dwell upon** it, you think, speak, or write about it a great deal. EG *She began to dwell on memories of how her mother had lived her life... His mind often dwelt upon the fact that there were only two more weeks before he had to join the army.* PHRASAL VB: V+PREP, HAS PASS = brood about, think about

dweller /dwɛlə/, **dwellers**. A city **dweller**, slum **dweller**, etc is a person who lives in the kind of place or house indicated. EG *They are hoping to provide Western-style housing for all their city dwellers.* N COUNT: MOD+N = resident

dwelling /dwɛlɪŋ/, **dwellings**. A **dwelling** or a **dwelling place** is a place where someone lives; an old-fashioned or formal word. EG *...hillside cave dwellings... They will be given a choice of various dwelling places.* N COUNT ⇑ home

dwelt /dwɛlt/ is the past tense and past participle of **dwell**.

dwindle /dwɪndə⁰l/, **dwindles, dwindling, dwindled**. If something **dwindles**, **1** it becomes smaller, less strong, or less in number. EG *Her money had dwindled away to nothing... The number of people going to the cinema seems to dwindle steadily.* V+A = diminish, decline ≠ increase ◊ **dwindling**. EG *Actors are playing to dwindling audiences as interest in the theatre diminishes.* ◊ ADJ QUALIT **2** it becomes less important. EG *After losing the war, the dynasty began to dwindle.* V

dye /daɪ/, **dyes, dyeing, dyed**. **1** If you **dye** something such as hair or cloth, you change its colour by soaking it in a special liquid. EG *She mixed finely pounded indigo leaves to dye her cloth deep blue.* V+O ◊ **dyed**. EG *...a woman with dyed red hair.* ◊ ADJ CLASSIF
2 A **dye** is a substance made from plants or chemicals which is mixed into a liquid and used to change the colour of something such as cloth or hair. EG *There are four basic dyes... Dip them in a yellow dye... ...a tin of dye powder.* N MASS ⇑ colouring

dyed-in-the-wool means having very strong opinions about something which you refuse to change. EG *He spoke as a dyed-in-the-wool aristocrat himself.* ADJ CLASSIF: ATTRIB = diehard

dyer /daɪə/, **dyers**. A **dyer** is a person whose job is to dye things. EG *There were blacksmiths, tanners, dyers, and weavers.* N COUNT

dying /daɪɪŋ/. **1 Dying** is the present participle of **die**.
2 A **dying** person or animal is very ill and likely to die soon. EG *She walked away and left a dying man.* ADJ CLASSIF: ATTRIB
3 The **dying** are people who are so ill or so badly injured that they will not live very much longer. EG *He is out there in France, tending the dying in the trenches.* N PLURAL: *the*+N
4 Dying is used to describe something which happens at the time when someone dies, or is connected with that time. EG *She begged him with her dying breath to look after his little sister... He swore he would remain faithful until his dying day.* ADJ CLASSIF: ATTRIB
5 A **dying** tradition or industry is becoming less important. EG *Coal is by no means a dying industry.* ADJ CLASSIF: ATTRIB

dyke /daɪk/, **dykes**; also spelled **dike**. **1** A **dyke** is a thick wall that is built to stop water flooding onto very low-lying land from a river or from the sea. N COUNT
2 A **dyke** is a lesbian; an informal and offensive use. N COUNT

dynamic /daɪnæmɪk/, **dynamics**. **1** Someone who is **dynamic** is full of energy or full of new and exciting ideas. EG *The new President of Mexico is a dynamic and able man.* ADJ QUALIT ⇑ forceful = energetic ▸ used of people's actions or ideas. EG *They have rejected my suggestions but seem to have no dynamic alternatives to offer.* ▸ ADJ QUALIT ◊ **dynamically**. EG *We would like to see them participate more dynamically.* ◊ ADV = actively
2 A **dynamic** is a force of society, history, or the mind that produces change; a technical term. EG *The conference discussed land shortage and the dynamics of rural society... The population explosion imports its own dynamic into the world economy.* N COUNT
3 Dynamic is used to describe something which relates to a force which produces power or movement; a technical term. ADJ CLASSIF: ATTRIB ◊ **dynamically**. EG *This is a government-approved, dynamically tested car restraint.* ◊ ADV
4 Dynamics is the scientific study of motion, energy and forces; a technical term. N UNCOUNT

dynamism /daɪnəmɪzə⁰m/ is the quality that someone has when they are full of energy or full of new and exciting ideas. N UNCOUNT

dynamite /daɪnəmaɪt/, **dynamites, dynamiting, dynamited**. **1 Dynamite** is an explosive that is made by soaking something such as sawdust with nitroglycerin. EG *...rebels wielding sticks of dynamite.* N UNCOUNT
2 To **dynamite** something means to blow it up by using dynamite. EG *They dynamited the houses... Their most famous coup was the dynamiting of the King David Hotel.* V+O ⇑ blow up
3 If you say that something or someone is **dynamite**, you mean that they are very dangerous or exciting. EG *In the wrong hands this report could be dynamite... Haldane the philosopher was still political dynamite.* N UNCOUNT

dynamo /daɪnəməʊ/, **dynamos**. **1** A **dynamo** is a device that uses the movement of a machine or vehicle to produce electricity. Dynamos are used in cars and can be used on a bicycle to provide the power for its lights. N COUNT
2 If you call someone a **dynamo**, you mean that they are very energetic and are always busy and active. EG *Her mother, a restless human dynamo, could never bear the stay in one house for more than a year.* N COUNT

dynastic /daɪnæstɪk/ means typical of or relating to a dynasty. ADJ CLASSIF

dynasty /dɪnəsti¹/, **dynasties**. A **dynasty** is 1 a series of rulers of a country who all belong to the same family. EG *The dynasty he founded ruled for 700 years.* 2 a period of time during which a country is ruled by members of the same family. EG *Colonization took place during the Habsburg dynasty.* — N COUNT; N COUNT+SUPP ⇑ era

dysentery /dɪsəⁿntri¹/ is an infection in a person's intestines that causes severe diarrhoea, in which blood and mucus are mixed with a person's faeces. — N UNCOUNT ⇑ illness

dyslexia /dɪsleksɪə/ is difficulty with reading which a person has because of a slight disorder of the brain; a technical term. — N UNCOUNT

dyslexic /dɪsleksɪk/. Someone who is **dyslexic** has difficulty with reading because of a slight disorder of the brain; a technical term. — ADJ CLASSIF

dyspepsia /dɪspepsɪə/ is the same as indigestion; a formal or technical term. — N UNCOUNT

dyspeptic /dɪspeptɪk/. Someone who is **dyspeptic** is suffering from indigestion or often suffers from it; a formal or technical term. — ADJ CLASSIF

dystrophy /dɪstrəfi¹/. See **muscular dystrophy**.

Ee

E, e /iː/, **E's, e's**. 1 E is the fifth letter of the English alphabet. — N COUNT

2 E, in music, is the third note in the scale of C major. — N COUNT/ UNCOUNT

3 E or e is also an abbreviation for various words beginning with E or e, such as 'English', 'east', or 'eastern'.

each /iːtʃ/. 1 If you refer to **each** thing or **each** person in a group, you are referring to every member of the group and considering them as individuals. EG *Each county is subdivided into several districts... Each day Kunta felt a little worse... The average walk for water is five miles each way... She kept a card index for each child... If you have more than one employer, you will need a certificate for each one.* ▸ used as a pronoun. EG *There were peaches, pears, and apricots. I opened two tins of each, six in all... They were all just sitting there, each of them thinking private thoughts.* — DET+N COUNT IN SING; ▸ PRON : IF+ PREP THEN *of*

2 **Each** is used to emphasize that you are referring to every individual thing or person in a group. EG *We each have our private views about it... He counted out five wads of twenty notes each... He offered me the tin of biscuits and my sister and I had one each.* — PRON

3 **Each other** is used when you are saying that each member of a group does something to the others or has a particular connection with all the others. EG *She and John looked at each other... They've known each other for years and years... We know each other's minds very well.* — PRON = one another

eager /iːgə/. 1 If you are **eager** for something or to do something, you want to have or do it very much. EG *The majority were moderate, and eager to express their opinions... People eager for a quick cure are likely to be disappointed.* ◊ **eagerness**. EG *...my eagerness to learn.* — ADJ QUALIT : PRED+*for/ to*-INF = keen, impatient; ◊ N UNCOUNT = impatience

2 If you look or sound **eager**, you look or sound as if you expect something interesting or enjoyable to happen. EG *He looked round the circle of eager faces... The eager crowd streamed into the halls of the court.* ◊ **eagerly**. EG *They began to talk eagerly.* ◊ **eagerness**. EG *...the vitality and eagerness of a normal toddler.* — ADJ QUALIT ⇑ expectant = excited; ◊ ADV WITH VB; ◊ N UNCOUNT = enthusiasm

eagle /iːgəⁿl/, **eagles**. An **eagle** is a large, strong bird that lives by eating small animals. There are several different kinds of eagle. ● If you say that someone has an **eagle eye**, you mean that they are very good at noticing small details. EG *She read each page with an eagle eye.* — N COUNT; ● PHR : USED AS O

ear /ɪə/, **ears**. 1 The **ears** of a person or animal are the two matching parts of their body, one on each side of their head, with which they hear sounds. EG *The ball dropped down past his right ear and into the neck of his shirt... They have large eyes, but only small ears... He leaned over and whispered something in Philip's ear.* — N COUNT

2 If you have an **ear for** music or language, you are able to hear its sounds accurately and to interpret them or reproduce them well. EG *...his marvellous ear for the sound of words.* — N SING WITH DET : IF+PREP THEN *for* ⇑ ability

3 The word **ear** is often used to refer to people's willingness to listen to what someone is saying. EG *He tried to give a sympathetic ear to her complaints... Do not close your ears to that little clicking noise in the hope that it will go away... ...listening with eager ear to the threats of big business.* — N COUNT/ UNCOUNT : USU+ SUPP ⇑ hearing

4 The **ears** of a cereal plant such as wheat or barley are the parts at the top of the stem, which contain the seeds or grains and are used for food. — N COUNT

5 The word **ear** is also used in the following informal expressions. **5.1** If you say that someone is **all ears**, you mean that they are ready and eager to listen. EG *Tell me about the party.–I'm all ears.* — PHR : USED AS C = listening **5.2** If you say that someone's **ears are flapping**, you mean that they are listening very hard to something that is being said, even though it has nothing to do with them. — PHR : VB INFLECTS **5.3** If you say that something goes **in one ear and out the other**, you mean that what has been said is forgotten immediately. — PHR : USED AS AN A **5.4** If you **keep** or **have** your **ear to the ground**, you make sure that you are well informed about other people and their opinions or activities. — PHR : VB INFLECTS **5.5** If someone says that you will be **out on** your **ear**, they mean that you will be or may be thrown out or dismissed suddenly and unpleasantly. EG *You'll find yourself out on your ear if you go on like this... Seconds later they were out on their ears.* — PHR : USED AS AN A = fired **5.6** If you **play by ear** or **play** a piece of music **by ear**, you play music by relying on your sense of tune and harmony or on your memory, rather than by reading printed music. EG *In fact I can only play by ear and have never been able to read music.* — PHR : VB INFLECTS **5.7** If you **play it by ear**, you decide what to say or do in a situation by responding to events rather than by following a plan which you have decided on in advance. EG *I've no idea what they're going to say, so I'll have to play it by ear.* — PHR : VB INFLECTS ⇑ improvise **5.8** If someone gives you a **thick ear**, they punch or slap you on the side of your head; an expression used in British English. EG *You'll get a thick ear if you don't stop it.* — PHR : USED AS O **5.9** If you **turn a deaf ear** to someone or something, you take no notice of what is being said. EG *Young people sometimes seem to turn a deaf ear to the words of their anxious parents.* — PHR : VB INFLECTS ⇑ ignore **5.10** If you are **up to your ears in** something, it is taking up all your time, attention, or resources. EG *She was up to her ears in paint, but made me very welcome... She was up to her ears in debt.* — PHR : USED AS AN A **5.11** If you listen to something or someone **with only half an ear**, you do not give full attention to what is being said. — PHR : USED AS AN A **5.12** ● **a flea in the ear**: see **flea**. ● **wet behind the ears**: see **wet**.

earache /ɪəreɪk/; also spelled with a hyphen. **Earache** is a pain in the inside part of your ear. — N UNCOUNT, OR N SING : *an*+N

eardrum /ɪədrʌm/, **eardrums**; also spelled with a hyphen. Your **eardrum** is a thin piece of tightly stretched skin inside your ear, which vibrates when sound waves reach it so that signals are carried along the nerves connecting your eardrum to your brain, enabling you to hear sounds. — N COUNT ⇑ membrane

earful /ɪəful/. If you say that you gave someone an **earful**, you mean that you spoke angrily to them for quite a long time; an informal word. EG *I gave him an earful on how he had oppressed me all our married life... If anyone touched him, they'd get an earful.* — N SING : *an*+N ⇑ rebuke = mouthful

earl /ɜːl/, **earls**. An **earl** is a British nobleman who ranks below a marquess and above a viscount. EG *The earl and countess are taking breakfast... ...the Earl of Essex.* — N COUNT : ALSO IN NAMES BEFORE N

earldom /ɜːldəᵊm/, **earldoms**. An **earldom** is the rank or state of being an earl. N COUNT

earlier /ɜːliᶦə/ is the comparative of **early**. It is also used to refer to a point or period in time before the present or before the one that you are talking about. EG *Her parents had died of cholera four years earlier... I had seen Komis earlier in the evening... ...as I said earlier... I mentioned that problem earlier on... Mr Habib will resume his earlier efforts to reach a settlement... ...in earlier times, when this fashion was popular.* ADV AFTER VB, OR ADJ QUALIT : COMPAR ≠ later

earliest /ɜːliᶦɪᶻst/ is the superlative of **early**. EG *The components of the earliest computers were large and mechanical... One of my earliest memories is of a total eclipse of the sun.* ADJ QUALIT : SUPERL ⇑ first ● **At the earliest** means not before the date or time mentioned. EG *'When can you get here?'-'Six o'clock at the earliest'... No developments were expected before the second half of August at the earliest.* ● PHR : USED AS AN A ⇑ soonest

earlobe /ɪələʊb/, **earlobes**; also spelled with a hyphen. Your **earlobes** are the soft, rounded parts of your ears, which hang down below the rest. N COUNT = lobe

early /ɜːliᶦ/, **earlier, earliest. 1 Early** means **1.1** near the beginning of a day. EG *I got up early and ate my breakfast... ...very early in the morning... ...in the early morning mist.... ...in the early hours of 4 August.* ADV AFTER VB, OR ADJ QUALIT ≠ late **1.2** near the beginning of a week, year, or other period of time. EG *It was early evening when we finished... ...early last week... ...in early December... ...early in 1915.* ADV+ADV/PREP, OR ADJ QUALIT : ATTRIB **1.3** near the beginning of a period in history or in the history of something such as the world, a society, or an activity. EG *...in the early 1980s... Pyle had enlisted early in the war... Their role in the strike had become evident early on... ...in the early days of railways.* ADV+ADV/PREP, OR ADJ QUALIT : ATTRIB **1.4** near the beginning of someone's life. EG *Mrs Dunn taught all her children to read at an early age... The men realized this quite early on in their lives.* ADV+ADV/PREP, OR ADJ QUALIT : ATTRIB ⇑ young **1.5** near the beginning of something such as a piece of work or a process. EG *This is in a very early stage of development... ...in those early chapters, when he's writing about his family... I don't know. It's too early to say.* ADV+ADV/PREP, OR ADJ QUALIT : ATTRIB **1.6** before the time that was arranged or expected. EG *The day's practice ended early because of bad light... He knew he was three minutes early.* ADV AFTER VB/NG **1.7** happening at a younger age than normal, or happening before the normal time. EG *After her husband's early death she supported her family single-handed... We had an early lunch.* ADV AFTER VB, OR ADJ QUALIT : ATTRIB = premature **1.8** flowering or cropping before or at the beginning of the main season. EG *...early flowers such as daffodils and crocuses... ...a nice crop of early potatoes.* ADV AFTER VB, OR ADJ QUALIT : ATTRIB ≠ late

2 As early as means at a particular time or period that is surprisingly early. EG *As early as 1978 the United States had taken steps to counteract this.* PHR+NUM/NG

3 If you answer that it is **early days** to a question about something, you mean that it is too soon for you to be completely sure about it; used in spoken English. EG *'How has it worked out?'-'Well, it's early days yet to say whether it works.'* ● **bright and early**: see **bright**. ● **early night**: see **night**. PHR : USED AS C

early-warning. An **early-warning** system is a system that is supposed to give a warning at the earliest possible moment of something bad that is likely to happen, for example a system of radar stations which are supposed to give a warning if an enemy has launched missiles against your country. ADJ CLASSIF : ATTRIB ⇑ alarm

earmark /ɪəmɑːk/, **earmarks, earmarking, earmarked**; also spelled with a hyphen. **1** If something **is earmarked** for a particular purpose, it has been reserved for that purpose. EG *The fund contained more than $300,000 earmarked for sensitive political projects... Choice sites are earmarked long before they become vacant.* V+O : USU PASS, IF+PREP THEN *for* = set aside

2 If something has the **earmarks** of a particular thing, it has features which enable you to recognize it as being of a particular type. EG *It had the earmarks of something prepared for a past college exam... This had all the earmarks of a moral dilemma.* N PLURAL : USU+*of* ⇑ characteristics = hallmarks, signs

earn /ɜːn/, **earns, earning, earned. 1** If you **earn** money, you receive money in return for work that you do. EG *The average worker, earning $15,058 in 1981, now pays $5,523 in taxes... I'm not earning any money... They have to earn a living somehow.* V OR V+O = make

2 If something **earns** money, it brings or produces money as profit or interest. EG *Something is uneconomic when it fails to earn an adequate profit... ...to earn the foreign currency that their country badly needs.* V+O ⇑ provide

3 If someone or something **earns** a particular thing, they gain or deserve it because of their actions or qualities. EG *...a system that would earn the hatred of the world: Apartheid... He has earned his place in history.* V+O = merit

earner /ɜːnə/, **earners**. An **earner** is someone or something that earns money or produces profit. EG *...a reliable wage earner... ...when the woman is either the major or the sole earner.* N COUNT : USU MOD+N

earnest /ɜːnɪᶻst/. **1** Someone who is **earnest** is very sincere and serious in what they say or do, believing that their actions are important and often unable to see when something is funny or ridiculous. EG *She was an earnest but clumsy nurse... She was approached by an earnest young man from the University.* ADJ QUALIT ≠ frivolous ▸ used of people's actions, hopes, and beliefs. EG *Her deliberate and earnest efforts proved successful... ...an earnest Victorian report on the sordid night life... It is my earnest wish that you use this money to further your research.* ◊ **earnestness**. EG *...speaking with great earnestness.* ◊ N UNCOUNT

2 If you are **in earnest**, you are sincere in your intentions. EG *He was a likeable young man, and very much in earnest about what he came to say... Is the President in earnest about the desire to negotiate?* PHR : USED AS AN A = serious

3 If something is done or happens **in earnest**, it happens to a much greater extent and more seriously than before. EG *Work on the tunnel began in earnest soon after... Then she started crying in earnest.* PHR : USED AS AN A ≠ half-heartedly

earnestly /ɜːnɪᶻstliᶦ/. **1** If you say something **earnestly**, you say it very seriously, often because you believe that it is important or are trying to persuade someone else to believe it. EG *'Are you sure you can manage it?' she asked earnestly... He was in a corner of the room talking earnestly to Julie.* ADV WITH VB

2 If you do something **earnestly**, you do it in a thorough and serious way, intending to succeed. EG *You must promise that you will go into it seriously and earnestly.* ADV WITH VB ⇑ thoroughly = wholeheartedly

earnings /ɜːnɪŋz/. Your **earnings** are the sums of money that you earn by working. EG *The Equal Pay Act has failed to bring women's earnings up to the same level.* N PLURAL = income, wages

earnings-related. An **earnings-related** payment or benefit provides higher or lower payments according to the amount a person was earning while working. EG *In that year the government introduced its earnings-related pension scheme.* ADJ CLASSIF ⇑ regulated

earphone /ɪəfəʊn/, **earphones**. A set of **earphones** is a piece of equipment which changes electrical signals into sounds. The earphones fit over your ears, so that you can listen to music, speech, etc in private. EG *Pressing his hands more firmly over the earphones, he listened again... Around his neck was a pair of earphones.* N COUNT : USU PL ⇑ device = headphones

earpiece /ɪəpiːs/, **earpieces**; also spelled with a hyphen. **1** The **earpiece** of a telephone receiver, hearing aid, or other device is the part that is held up to or put into your ear. It changes electrical signals into sound. N COUNT

2 The **earpieces** of a pair of glasses are the parts which fit over your ears to keep the glasses on. N COUNT

earplug /ɪəplʌg/, **earplugs**; also spelled with a hyphen. An **earplug** is a small piece of soft material such as wax or cotton wool which you put into your ear to keep out noise, water, or cold air. N COUNT, USU PL ⇑ plug

earring /ɪərɪŋ/, **earrings**; also spelled with a hyphen. An **earring** is a piece of jewellery, often one of a pair, which people wear in or hanging down from the lobes of their ears. N COUNT

earshot /ɪəʃɒt/. If you are **within earshot** of something, you are close enough to hear what is being said. If you are **out of earshot**, you are not close enough to hear what is being said. EG *There were too many people within earshot... Bond stood within earshot of the desk... Luckily, Amy was out of earshot.* PHR : USED AS AN A

ear-splitting. An **ear-splitting** noise is very loud. EG *...an ear-splitting screech... The crash was ear-splitting.* ADJ CLASSIF

earth /ɜːθ/, **earths, earthing, earthed. 1** The **earth** is **1.1** the planet on which we live. EG *The earth moves around the sun... The oceans cover 70% of the* N PROPER : *the*+N *earth's surface... The Rift Valley marks a weakness in the earth's crust... They have vanished from the face of the earth.* ▸ This planet is also referred to as **Earth**. EG *Unlike Earth, Jupiter has no features to break up its surface... ...man's life on Earth.* **1.2** the land surface on which we live and move about. EG *For twenty minutes the earth shook.* ▸ N PROPER / N SING : the+N = ground

2 Earth is the substance on the land surface of the earth, for example clay or sand, in which plants grow. EG *Trees and shrubs may be the only thing holding earth on the steeper slopes... ...a cliff of naked red earth... He was pulling dead roots from the dusty earth.* N UNCOUNT = soil

3 An **earth** is a hole in the ground in which an animal such as a fox lives. N COUNT

4 The **earth** in an electric plug or piece of electrical equipment is the wire in it through which electricity can pass into the ground and which makes the equipment safe even if something goes wrong with it. EG *Cut the neutral and live wires about 1 inch long, leaving the earth a bit longer.* N COUNT : USU SING = ground

5 If an electric plug or piece of electrical equipment **is earthed**, it has been fitted with a wire through which electricity can pass into the ground in order to make the equipment safe. EG *My stereo isn't earthed.* V+O : USU PASS

6 On earth is used for emphasis **6.1** with words such as 'how', 'why', 'what', or 'where', or with negatives. It is often used in questions to suggest that there is no obvious or easy answer to the question being asked or the problem being mentioned. EG *What on earth are you talking about?... How on earth do we raise half a million dollars?... He was wondering what on earth he should do... There's no reason on earth why it shouldn't work.* **6.2** after a noun group that contains a superlative adjective in order to emphasize the adjective. EG *He regarded film-making as the most glamorous job on earth... ...one of the most difficult people on earth.* ● **Like nothing on earth** is used to suggest that something is very unusual and often extremely unpleasant; an informal expression. EG *It tasted like nothing on earth... They looked like nothing on earth... The cut bled like nothing on earth.* PHR : USED AS AN A, WITH WH OR BROAD NEG / PHR : USED AS AN A = around / ● PHR : USED AS AN A

7 The word **earth** is also used in the following expressions. **7.1** If you **come back to earth**, you stop day-dreaming and think about or recognize reality and real facts, especially when these are unpleasant. EG *I came back to earth with a thud, my brilliant plans crashing around me.* **7.2** If you say that something costs **the earth** or that you paid **the earth** for it, you mean that it costs or cost a very large amount of money; an informal expression. EG *If you go to a commercial photographer he'll charge the earth for it.* **7.3** If you say that someone **has gone to earth**, you mean that they are hiding so that their enemies cannot find them. EG *The guerrillas dispersed and went to earth.* **7.4** If you **promise** someone **the earth**, you promise them everything that they want; an informal expression. EG *All the election manifestos promise the earth.* **7.5** If you **run** someone or something **to earth**, you find them after searching for them for a long time. EG *He went off to meet John, who he had finally run to earth.* PHR : VB INFLECTS = wake up / PHR : USED AS AN A ⇑ a lot = a fortune / PHR : VB INFLECTS ⇑ hide / PHR : VB INFLECTS / PHR : VB INFLECTS

8 The word **earth** is also used in the following expressions, which are explained at other places in this dictionary. ● **hell on earth:** see **hell.** ● **to move heaven and earth:** see **heaven.** ● **the salt of the earth:** see **salt.** ● See also **down-to-earth.**

earth-bound; also spelled as one word. **1** If something is **earth-bound**, it is unable to leave the surface of the earth by flying. EG *...earth-bound insects.* ADJ CLASSIF ⇑ grounded

2 If you say that someone is **earth-bound**, you mean that they do not have enough imagination to think how things might be different. EG *...to make comprehensible to our earth-bound senses a vision of divine order.* ADJ QUALIT ⇑ dull = limited

earthen /ɜ:θəⁿn/ means **1** made of clay that is baked so that it becomes hard. EG *The traditional breakfast of porridge was cooked in earthen pots.* **2** made of hard earth; used especially of floors. EG *The earthen floor was covered with rugs and cushions.* ADJ CLASSIF : ATTRIB / ADJ CLASSIF : ATTRIB = dirt

earthenware /ɜ:θəⁿnwɛə/. **Earthenware** bowls, pots, or other things are made of clay that is baked so that it becomes hard. EG *She bought a small earthenware bowl... ...an old earthenware pot.* ▸ used as a noun. EG *The earthenware included rice pots with a round base.* ADJ CLASSIF : ATTRIB = earthen / ▸ N UNCOUNT

earthly /ɜ:θli¹/. **1 Earthly** means happening in the material world of our life on earth and not in any spiritual life or life after death. EG *She believed that our earthly life is all that matters... We may speculate about either end of our earthly existence.* ADJ CLASSIF : ATTRIB ⇑ worldly ≠ spiritual

2 Earthly is used in questions and negative statements to suggest that it would be surprising to disagree with an action or opinion or the reasons for it. EG *There is no earthly reason for me to dislike her... I failed to see what earthly purpose this could serve.* ADJ CLASSIF : ATTRIB = possible

earthquake /ɜ:θkweɪk/, **earthquakes**. An **earthquake** is a shaking of the ground caused by movement of the earth's crust. N COUNT ⇑ tremor

earth-shattering. Something that is **earth-shattering** is very surprising or shocking. EG *...an earth-shattering discovery.* ADJ CLASSIF ⇑ important = momentous

earthwork /ɜ:θwɜ:k/, **earthworks**. **Earthworks** are large mounds of earth that have been built for defence, especially mounds which were built a very long time ago. EG *The earthworks commanded a view of the valley floor.* N COUNT : USU PL ⇑ bank

earthworm /ɜ:θwɜ:m/, **earthworms**. An **earthworm** is a common kind of worm with a long body. Earthworms live under the ground, moving through the soil and breaking it up. N COUNT ⇑ worm

earthy /ɜ:θi¹/. **1** Someone who is **earthy** is open and direct in their talk, especially about subjects which other people avoid or feel ashamed about; often used showing approval. EG *'I love these simple, earthy types,' Clarissa said... ...a buxom, earthy, attractive girl.* ▸ used of a way of thinking or talking. EG *...earthy commonsense.* ◇ **earthiness**. EG *There was an appealing earthiness about her.* ADJ QUALIT ⇑ natural ≠ coy, refined / ◇ N UNCOUNT

2 Something that is **earthy** looks, smells, or feels like earth. EG *...earthy colours... ...the subtle, earthy fragrance of wild thyme.* ADJ QUALIT

earwig /ɪəwɪg/, **earwigs**. An **earwig** is a small, thin brown insect that has a pair of pincers at the back end of its body. N COUNT

ease /i:z/, **eases, easing, eased**. **1 Ease** is lack of difficulty. EG *The greater ease and frequency of divorce were also discussed... The boxes are designed to fit one inside the other for ease of transportation... She performed this trick with ease.* N UNCOUNT : IF+ PREP THEN *of/with* ⇑ facility ≠ difficulty

2 Ease is also the state of being very comfortable and able to live as you want, without any worries or care. EG *...a life of ease and luxury.* N UNCOUNT ⇑ comfort

3 If you are **at ease** or **at your ease**, you are feeling confident and comfortable, and are able to talk to people without feeling worried or anxious. EG *He was at ease with strangers... I was never at ease in the part until almost the end of the run... My smiling face set her at ease.* PHR : USED AS AN A ≠ awkward

4 If you are **ill at ease**, you are rather uncomfortable, anxious or worried. EG *He was ill at ease with people whom he didn't understand... Brody felt ill at ease and patronized.* PHR : USED AS C = awkward

5 To **ease** an unpleasant situation means to reduce the degree of unpleasantness or difficulty that has been caused by a particular problem. EG *The bungalows were built in 1946 to ease the housing shortage after the last war... Community groups were making efforts to ease tensions in the area.* V+O = alleviate ≠ aggravate

6 When something **eases** or when you **ease** it, it becomes less in degree, quantity, speed, or intensity. EG *The snow had eased... My grip had eased... He had taken the drugs to ease the pain... Her words helped to ease his grief.* V-ERG ⇑ decrease

7 If you **ease** something somewhere, you move it slowly, carefully, and gently in a particular direction or towards a particular place. EG *Gary eased back his chair... I came in at the back and started easing my way through the crowd... He threw his bag onto the back seat of the car and eased himself in.* V+O (NG/REFL) +A

8 At ease or **stand at ease** is an order given to a group of soldiers or policemen to stand with their feet apart and their hands behind their backs. CONVENTION = stand easy

ease off. If something **eases off** it becomes less in degree, quantity, speed, or intensity. EG *The pace of our activity gradually eased off.* PHRASAL VB : V+ ADV ⇑ decrease = slacken

ease up. **1** If you **ease up** on someone, you treat them less severely; an informal expression. EG *Come on, ease up on those kids a bit; they've had a hard day!* PHRASAL VB : V+ ADV : IF+PREP THEN *on* = go easy

2 If something **eases up**, it becomes less in degree, PHRASAL VB : V+

quantity, speed, or intensity. EG *The rain has eased up a bit now–we could make a dash for the car.* ADV ⇑ decrease

easel /iːzəl/, **easels**. An **easel** is a wooden frame that supports a picture which an artist is painting or drawing. N COUNT

easily /iːzɪli/. 1 You use **easily** 1.1 to emphasize that something is very likely to happen. EG *She might easily decide to cancel the whole thing... Dishwashers may easily ruin wood or hand-painted china.* ADV WITH VB = well 1.2 to emphasize that there can be no doubt that something is the case. EG *This car is easily the most popular model.* ADV WITH VB = by far 1.3 to say that something happens more quickly than is usual or normal. EG *He tired very easily... It didn't rot very easily, and it was cheap.* ADV WITH VB

2 Other meanings of **easily** can be found in the entry for **easy** in paragraphs 1 and 5.

east /iːst/. The word **east** is often spelled with a capital letter, especially for paragraph 5. 1 The **east** is 1.1 the direction which you look towards in the morning in order to see the sun rise. EG *Ben noticed the first faint streaks of dawn in the east.* N SING : *the*+N ≠ west 1.2 the part of a place, country, or region which is towards the east. EG *There was a good rail link with the East... The south and east of the Square have been rebuilt... The political divisions between North, West, and East are so well established that they seem unlikely to be broken down.* N SING : *the*+N

2 **East** means towards the east or to the east of a place or thing. EG *They were heading almost due east, out into the wild hills... Remains have been found farther east in Java, and in China... There were areas of open country east of the river.* ADV AFTER VB = eastward ≠ west

3 The **east** part of a place, country, or region is the part which is towards the east. EG *He did say something about her having gone on a safari in East Africa... The Beagle sailed down the east coast of South America... ...the Labour MP for Salford East.* ADJ CLASSIF : ALSO IN NAMES = eastern

4 An **east** wind blows from the east. EG *There was a cold blue sky and a biting east wind.* ADJ CLASSIF : ATTRIB

5 The **East** is also used to refer to 5.1 the USSR and other communist countries in the eastern part of Europe. EG *He urged a balance of forces between East and West... It was hailed as a breakthrough in East-West relations.* N SING 5.2 the countries in the southern and eastern part of Asia, including India, China, and Japan, which have a different culture and different traditions from Europe and the USA. EG *He was looking for new routes for the profitable spice trade with the East... He was deeply interested in meditation, the East, and yoga.* N SING : *the*+N = Far East, Orient • See also **Far East**, **Middle East**, **Near East**.

eastbound /iːstbaʊnd/. **Eastbound** roads, cars, trains, etc lead or are travelling towards the east. EG *Morris slouched in the seat of his eastbound aircraft... The eastbound carriageway of the M4 was blocked for 2 hours.* ADJ CLASSIF ≠ westbound

Easter /iːstə/ is a Christian religious festival when Christians celebrate the death and resurrection of Christ. EG *School holidays are at Christmas, Easter and during the summer.* N UNCOUNT

Easter egg, Easter eggs. An **Easter egg** is an egg that is given as a present at Easter. It is usually a chocolate egg or a hen's egg with a painted shell. N COUNT

easterly /iːstəli/. 1 An **easterly** point, area, or direction is to the east or towards the east. EG *We walked out to the most easterly point of the ridge.* ADJ QUALIT = eastern ≠ westerly

2 An **easterly** wind blows from the east. EG *...the bitter easterly wind.* ADJ CLASSIF

eastern /iːstən/. The word **eastern** is often spelled with a capital letter. **Eastern** means 1 in or from the east of a region or country. EG *He was the mayor of a small town in Eastern Portugal... ...the eastern shores of Lake Tanganyika... ...an eastern route.* ADJ CLASSIF : ATTRIB 2 coming from or associated with the people or countries of the East, such as India, China, or Japan. EG *It was in Bengal in the nineteenth century that Eastern and Western cultures merged... ...Eastern philosophy.* ADJ CLASSIF : ATTRIB = Oriental 3 coming from or associated with the countries in the east of Europe and the USSR. EG *The electronic technology of the West had outstripped that of the Eastern bloc.* ADJ CLASSIF : ATTRIB = communist

easterner /iːstənə/, **easterners**. An **easterner** is a person who was born in or who lives in the eastern part of a place or country, especially an American from the East Coast of the USA. EG *Like many another easterner, he was impressed by the California style.* N COUNT

easternmost /iːstənməʊst/. The **easternmost** part of an area or the **easternmost** thing in a line is the one that is farther towards the east than any other. EG *...the easternmost promontories of the region.* ADJ CLASSIF : ATTRIB ≠ westernmost

East German, East Germans. 1 **East German** means belonging or relating to the German Democratic Republic, which is also called East Germany. EG *...East German cars.* ADJ CLASSIF

2 An **East German** is a person who comes from the German Democratic Republic. N COUNT

eastward /iːstwəd/, **eastwards**. **Eastward** or **eastwards** means towards the east. EG *The two cousins hurried eastward against the sharp wind... They travelled eastwards round the Mediterranean.* ADV AFTER VB ≠ westward ▸ **Eastward** is also used as an adjective. EG *...a grassy eastward slope.* ▸ ADJ CLASSIF : ATTRIB

easy /iːzi/, **easier, easiest**. 1 Something that is **easy** is able to be done without difficulty or effort, because it is not complicated and causes no problems. EG *The house is easy to keep clean, easy to heat... How easy is it in Britain for novelists to get their work published?... ...an easy ten-minute walk... This new dancing looked easy... Admission to a tour of Parliament is easier on days when the House is not sitting.* ADJ QUALIT = simple ≠ difficult ◇ **easily**. EG *A baby buggy can be easily carried on a bus or in a car... I like the French yoghurts which can easily be obtained in supermarkets.* ◇ ADV WITH VB ◇ **easiness**. ◇ N UNCOUNT

2 You can say **easier said than done**, or **more easily said than done**, when you feel that although someone's advice may be good in theory, it would be difficult to actually do what they suggest. EG *'Just tell him how you feel.'–'Ha! Easier said than done!'* CONVENTION

3 If you say that something is **easy** or too **easy**, you are criticizing someone because you believe that they have simply accepted or done the most obvious or least difficult thing, and have not considered the situation carefully enough. EG *I think that's a bit too easy an answer... That's easy for you to say, you have so much energy... It is only too easy to believe that one is misunderstood.* ADJ QUALIT

4 You can use the word **easy** in expressions such as **far from easy, none too easy**, and **no easy task**, in order to emphasize that you think that something is very difficult. EG *It was no easy matter to divert her attention... Resolving their differences will take time and will be far from easy... It was not easy to see how anything could be done about it.* PHR : USED AS C

5 If you say that something is **as easy as pie**, you are saying and emphasizing in an informal way that it is very easy to do. PHR : USED AS C

6 **Easy** also means relaxed and without any emotional tension, strain, or pressure. EG *He had an easy temperament... It was an easy, rambling conversation... They have a natural, easy confidence in themselves.* ADJ QUALIT : ATTRIB ≠ tense ◇ **easily**. EG *...a friendly man who talked freely and easily.* ◇ ADV WITH VB

7 If you **take it easy** or **take things easy**, you relax and do not do very much at all; an informal expression. EG *You must realise that you've not been well and you have to take it easy for a bit... I've retired and I'm going to take things easy for a while.* PHR : VB INFLECTS ⇑ rest

8 If you say that you are **easy** about something, you mean that you do not have a strong opinion about it and do not mind what happens; used in informal British English. EG *'Do you want to go out tonight?'–'I'm easy; it's up to you.'* ADJ CLASSIF : PRED, IF+PREP THEN *about*

9 If you say that you are not **easy** or do not feel **easy** about something, you mean that you are not sure that it is correct or justified. EG *I never felt easy about Freud's Oedipus theory.* ADJ CLASSIF : PRED, WITH BROAD NEG, IF+PREP THEN *about*

10 Something that is **easy** on your ear, eye, stomach, etc, is very pleasant to listen to, look at, eat, etc; an informal use. EG *He said that she was easy on the eye, and he liked having her around... It's easy on the brains but hell on the feet.* ADJ QUALIT : PRED+*on*

11 **Easy** also means comfortable and without any troubles or worry. EG *I wanted to leave you to make life easier for you... Oh yes, we're all for having it as easy as possible.* ADJ QUALIT = simple

12 An **easy** victim or **easy** prey has very little defence against bad treatment or attack. ADJ QUALIT : ATTRIB ⇑ unprotected

13 **Easy** is also used in the following informal expressions. 13.1 If you **go easy on** something, you avoid using too much of it. EG *Go easy on the salt, it's* PHR : VB INFLECTS

bad for your heart. **13.2** If you **go easy on** someone, you treat them less severely than you think they deserve to be treated. EG *Go easy on him for a while, he's got a lot of family problems.* **13.3** If you say **'Easy does it'**, you are telling someone to be careful and not to use too much effort, especially when they are moving something large and awkward. **13.4** **'Easy come, easy go'** means that the person referred to does not care much about money and possessions. PHR : VB INFLECTS = ease up on; CONVENTION = steady; CONVENTION

14 Stand easy is an order given to a group of soldiers on parade, instructing them to stand in a relaxed way with their feet apart. CONVENTION

easy chair, easy chairs. An **easy chair** is a large, comfortable chair in which you can relax. N COUNT

easy-going. Someone who is **easy-going** is not easily annoyed, worried, or upset by problems or other people's actions; used showing approval. EG *My father was a gentle, easy-going person.* ADJ QUALIT ⇑ tolerant = even-tempered

easy touch. An **easy touch** is the same as a soft touch; an informal expression. N SING : an+N

eat /iːt/, **eats, eating, ate, eaten.** 1 When you **eat** something or when you **eat**, you put food into your mouth, chew it, and swallow it. EG *She had never eaten Chinese food before... He was too tired even to eat.* V OR V+O ⇑ consume

2 To **eat** also means to have a meal. EG *He said he would eat at his hotel.* V : USU+A

3 If something **is eating** you, it is making you worried or anxious; an informal use. EG *What's eating you, Professor Zapp?* V+O : USU CONT ⇑ trouble = bother

4 In informal English, **eats** are food. EG *You bring the drinks and I'll arrange the eats.* N PLURAL

5 The word **eat** is also used in the following informal expressions. **5.1** If you **eat like a horse**, you have a very large appetite and always eat a lot. EG *There's nothing wrong with her-she eats like a horse.* **5.2** If you say **'I could eat a horse'**, you mean that you are extremely hungry. **5.3** If you **have** someone **eating out of** your **hand**, you have them completely under your control. EG *She has her boss eating out of her hand.* PHR : VB INFLECTS; PHR; PHR : AUX INFLECTS ⇑ obedient

6 The word **eat** is also used in the following expressions, which are explained at other places in this dictionary. • to **eat** your **hat**: see **hat** . • to **eat** someone **out of house and home**: see **house.** • to **eat** your **words**: see **word.**

eat away. To **eat** something **away** means to slowly reduce it or remove it by rubbing against it or by chemical action. EG *He showed them where the waves were eating the walls away... The silver was eaten away.* PHRASAL VB : V+O+ADV = wear away

eat in. When you **eat in**, you have a meal at home rather than go out to a restaurant. PHRASAL VB : V+ADV

eat into. 1 If rust, acid, etc, **eats into** something, it attacks and destroys its surface. EG *Rust had eaten right into the metal.* PHRASAL VB : V+PREP, HAS PASS ⇑ destroy

2 To **eat into** time, energy, resources, etc, means to gradually spend or use them up. EG *Trivial interruptions tend to eat into the working day.* PHRASAL VB : V+PREP, HAS PASS ⇑ use up

eat out. When you **eat out**, you have a meal at a restaurant instead of at home. EG *Do you eat out a lot in London?* PHRASAL VB : V+ADV

eat up. 1 If you **eat up** or **eat** something **up**, you eat everything that you are given to eat. EG *We greedily ate up a whole plate of food that we didn't really want.* PHRASAL VB : V+O+ADV ⇑ consume = polish off

2 To **eat** time, money, fuel, etc, **up** means to use it or consume it in great quantities. EG *Rising costs were eating up most of the profits.* PHRASAL VB : V+O+ADV

3 If you **are eaten up** with jealousy, curiosity, desire, etc, you feel it very intensely; an informal expression used showing disapproval. EG *She was eaten up with envy.* PHRASAL VB : ONLY PASS = consumed

eatable /iːtəbə⁰l/. Something that is **eatable** is good enough or tasty enough for a person to eat and enjoy. EG *The food here is barely eatable.* ADJ CLASSIF = edible

eaten /iːtə⁰n/ is the past participle of **eat.**

eater /iːtə/, **eaters.** An **eater** is 1 a person or animal that eats particular things or in a particular way. EG *Birds were once primarily fruit eaters.* 2 in informal English, a variety of apple, pear, or other fruit which is usually eaten raw rather than cooked. N COUNT : MOD+N; N COUNT

eating /iːtɪŋ/. An **eating** apple or pear is one that is usually eaten raw rather than cooked. ADJ CLASSIF : ATTRIB

eau-de-cologne /əʊdəˈkələʊn/ is a fairly weak, sweet-smelling perfume. EG *He sprayed a little eau-de-cologne over himself.* N UNCOUNT

eaves /iːvz/. The **eaves** of a house are the lower edges of its roof. EG *...racks of drying fish hang under the eaves of farmhouses.* N PLURAL : the+N

eavesdrop /iːvzdrɒp/, **eavesdrops, eavesdropping, eavesdropped.** If you **eavesdrop**, you listen to what other people are saying without them knowing that you are doing so. EG *Some journalists will always try to eavesdrop on the private conversations of the royal family.* V : IF+PREP THEN on = spy

eavesdropper /iːvzdrɒpə/, **eavesdroppers.** An **eavesdropper** is a person who listens secretly to what other people are saying; used showing disapproval. N COUNT

ebb /ɛb/, **ebbs, ebbing, ebbed.** 1 When the tide or the sea **ebbs**, its level is falling. EG *Fish react to the state of the tide as it ebbs and flows.* V ⇑ retreat

2 The **ebb** of the sea or tide is one of the regular periods, about two per day, when it is falling to a lower level. EG *...the stormy ebb and flow of the sea... They set sail on the ebb tide.* • The tide is described as being **on the ebb** when it is falling to a lower level. EG *They ran aground while the tide was on the ebb, and were stuck for eight hours.* N SING : the+N ⇑ recession; • PHR : USED AS AN A ⇑ receding ≠ coming in

3 If a feeling or a person's strength **ebbs**, it becomes weaker and gradually disappears; a fairly literary use. EG *Only then did the strength ebb from his fingers... After a while he felt his strain and confusion, even his body's pains, begin to ebb.* V ⇑ disappear = drain

4 If someone or something is **at a low ebb**, they are not being very successful or profitable. EG *George's fortunes at this time were also at a low ebb, nudging bankruptcy... By the 1960s Catholic politics were at a low ebb.* PHR : USED AS AN A = suffering

5 You talk about **the ebb and flow of** something when you want to describe a situation in which periods of progress and success are followed by periods of trouble or difficulty. EG *In the ebb and flow of political struggle it was inevitable that one of them would go under.* PHR : USED AS O ⇑ fluctuation = ups and downs

ebb away. If a feeling or a person's strength **ebbs away**, it gradually becomes weaker until it disappears completely. EG *Their rage ebbed away, to be replaced by a mounting fear.* PHRASAL VB : V+ADV ⇑ disappear = subside

ebony /ɛbəniˡ/, **ebonies.** 1 **Ebony** is a very hard, heavy, dark-coloured wood that is used for making furniture and other things. EG *...ebony hairbrushes.* ▸ **Ebony** is also used to refer to the tree from which this wood comes. N UNCOUNT; ▸ N COUNT ⇑ tree

2 Something that is **ebony** is a very deep, black colour. EG *She had cropped hair and ebony eyes.* ADJ COLOUR

ebullience /iˡbʌliˡəns/ is the quality of being lively and full of enthusiasm or excitement; a formal word. EG *Their Irish ebullience made them outgoing and spontaneous.* N UNCOUNT ⇑ liveliness = exuberance

ebullient /iˡbʌliˡənt/. Someone who is **ebullient** is lively and full of enthusiasm or excitement; a formal word. EG *Even Lewis, that most ebullient of men, looked downcast.* ADJ QUALIT = exuberant

eccentric /ɪ²ksɛntrɪk/. 1 Someone who is **eccentric** has habits or opinions that other people think strange and peculiar. EG *Living here in the capital city was a noble, if slightly eccentric, Frenchman... ...eccentric right-wing views.* ▸ used of a person's behaviour, clothing, etc. EG *They were dressed in strangely eccentric clothing... Perhaps I did look a little eccentric at that stage.* ◊ **eccentrically.** EG *He lived alone, and, it was said, ate rarely and eccentrically.* ADJ QUALIT ⇑ different = weird ≠ orthodox, conventional; ◊ ADV ⇑ strangely ≠ conventionally

2 An **eccentric** is a person who has habits or opinions or who wears clothes which other people think strange and peculiar. EG *She was a mild eccentric, an amusing oddity.* N COUNT = oddball

eccentricity /ɛksɛntrɪsɪtiˡ/, **eccentricities.** 1 **Eccentricity** is unusual behaviour that other people consider strange and peculiar. EG *She emphasized his eccentricity to the detriment of his truly remarkable achievements... He had not approved the eccentricity of Rose's behaviour.* N UNCOUNT ⇑ strangeness ≠ conventionality

2 An **eccentricity** is a habit or attitude which other people think is strange and peculiar. EG *Davis in the staid office was conspicuous by his eccentricities... These little habits are the origins of quirks and eccentricities that appear in later behaviour.* N COUNT : USU PL = idiosyncrasy

ecclesiastic /ɪ²kliːziæstɪk/, **ecclesiastics.** An **ecclesiastic** is a priest or clergyman in the Christian Church; a formal or old-fashioned word. N COUNT

ecclesiastical /ɪ²kliːziæstɪkə⁰l/ means belonging to or connected with the Christian Church or its priests and ministers. EG *He fell into disfavour with his ecclesiastical superiors.* ADJ CLASSIF ⇑ religious

echelon /ɛʃə⁰lɒn/, **echelons**. An **echelon** is 1 a level of power or responsibility in an organization, together with the people at that level. EG *...the higher echelons of Whitehall.* N COUNT+SUPP = rank 2 a military formation in which soldiers, vehicles, ships or aircraft follow each other but are spaced out sideways so that they can see ahead of them. EG *...the first echelon of the assault force.* N COUNT : USU+SUPP

echo /ɛkəʊ/, **echoes, echoing, echoed**. 1 An **echo** is 1.1 a sound which is caused when a loud, sharp noise, for example a scream, is reflected off a surface such as a cliff or the walls of a building. EG *Judy found herself listening to the last echo of her shoes clicking on the marble floors... They were the only seats not affected by the echo.* N COUNT = reverberation 1.2 an expression of an attitude or opinion which has already been expressed by someone else. EG *The echo of public sentiment in Congress was inevitable.* N COUNT : USU+of ⇑ repetition 1.3 one of a number of small details or features which remind you of something else. EG *But still some echoes of the old ways linger... It's a story with echoes but not imitations of Waugh.* N COUNT : USU+of ⇑ reminder = trace

2 A sound that **echoes** is reflected off a surface, such as a cliff or the walls of a building, so that it can be heard again after the original sound has stopped. EG *The cry echoed back from the pink granite of the mountain... The noise of our footsteps seemed to go echoing around the walls.* V : USU+A = bounce

3 A place that **echoes** is one in which a particular sound continues or is repeated in it after the original sound has stopped. EG *The bamboo grove echoed with bird calls and the screams of monkeys.* V : USU+A = ring, resound ◇ **echoing**. EG *They took us to a hotel with empty echoing halls.* ◇ ADJ CLASSIF

4 If you **echo** something that someone else has said, 4.1 you express your agreement with their attitude or opinion. EG *This was a view echoed by Mr Healey in a Sunday Times article... As Party Treasurer, he echoed the gut feeling of the trade unions.* V+O 4.2 you repeat words or sounds which the other person has just said or made. EG *'They lived in the open air, simply under a tree.'–'Under a tree,' echoed Etta in amused distaste... He let out his spare breath with a little gasp that was echoed by his audience.* V+O (NG/QUOTE)

5 If something **echoes** something else, it is a copy of a particular detail or feature of it. EG *The masonry colours and shapes echo those of the jungle-clad mountains of South America... The listeners were echoing the rhythm with slight tilts of their bodies.* V+O = reproduce

6 To **echo** also means to continue to be discussed and be important or influential in a particular situation or amongst a particular group of people. EG *We will try to examine some of those causes which still echo and re-echo throughout our 'affluent' society... People who were baptized or buried here have names that still echo beyond their parish.* V+A = resound

éclair /ɪ²klɛə/, **éclairs**. An **éclair** is a long thin cake made of very light pastry, which is filled with cream and usually has chocolate on top. N COUNT

eclectic /ɪ²klɛktɪk/ means choosing what seems to be best or most useful from several different sets of ideas or beliefs, rather than following one complete set of ideas or beliefs only; a formal word. EG *...a doctrine that drew upon an eclectic mixture of both Western and Asian thought.* ADJ QUALIT ⇑ mixed = selective ▸ used as a noun. EG *As far as art is concerned, I'm an eclectic.* ▸ N COUNT ⇑ person

eclecticism /ɪ²klɛktɪsɪzə⁰m/ is the principle or practice of choosing what seems to be best or most useful from several different sets of ideas or beliefs; a formal word. EG *We have noted before the eclecticism of the populist theories.* N UNCOUNT

eclipse /ɪ¹klɪps/, **eclipses, eclipsing, eclipsed**. 1 An **eclipse** of the sun is an occasion when the moon comes between the earth and the sun, so that for a short time you cannot see part or all of the sun. An **eclipse** of the moon is an occasion when the earth comes between the sun and the moon, so that for a short time you cannot see part or all of the moon. EG *One of my earliest memories is of a total eclipse of the sun.* N COUNT ⇑ obscuring

2 If someone or something suffers an **eclipse**, they lose some or all of their importance, influence, or prestige, usually because someone or something new has become more popular or famous. EG *Painters and sculptors were protesting against their eclipse... This led to the eventual eclipse of the decorative, 'flat' style of painting.* N SING : USU WITH POSS ⇑ decline = deposition ● If something is **in eclipse** or is going **into eclipse**, it is or is becoming much less important or influential than it previously was. EG *Then came the final confrontation between a European power in eclipse and its misgoverned colony.* ● PHR : USED AS AN A = in decline

3 If something **eclipses** something else, the first thing is more important or influential than the second thing, so that the second thing is no longer noticed. EG *Cameroon has been careful not to let the energy boom eclipse more mundane economic progress... It is the second biggest newspaper group in the country, eclipsed only by the Argus Company.* V+O ⇑ overshadow = top, outshine

ecological /ɪːkəlɒdʒɪkə⁰l/. 1 **Ecological** means involved with or concerning the pattern and balance of relationships between plants, animals, people, and their environment. EG *Use of nitrogen fertilizers has damaged the ecological balance in some of the world's lakes... ...the local ecological impact of removing all the vegetation.* ADJ CLASSIF : ATTRIB ⇑ environmental ◇ **ecologically**. EG *It was an ecologically sound system of farm management.* ◇ ADV+ADJ/ADV

2 **Ecological** groups, movements, and people are concerned with the preservation of the environment and natural resources and improving the quality of life. EG *The poll forecasts a significant loss of voters from the SDP to ecological and anti-nuclear groups.* ADJ CLASSIF : ATTRIB ⇑ environmental

ecologist /i¹kɒlə⁷dʒɪst/, **ecologists**. An **ecologist** is 1 a person who studies the pattern and balance of relationships between plants, animals, people, and their environment. EG *...amateur ecologists.* N COUNT ⇑ scientist 2 a person who believes that the environment and natural resources should be used properly and be preserved, rather than be exploited wastefully. EG *Many people–individuals, church groups, far leftists, ecologists, Welsh Nationalists–are fighting this policy.* N COUNT = conservationist

ecology /i¹kɒlədʒi¹/. **Ecology** is 1 the pattern and balance of relationships between plants, animals, people, and their environment in a particular region. EG *Herbicides used in the 1970s caused damage to the ecology that would take a hundred years to heal... The tourists had no knowledge of desert ecology or the effect that their very presence had on the landscape.* N UNCOUNT 2 the study of the relationships between plants, animals, people, and their environment, and the balances between these relationships. EG *...the most recent research in ecology.* N UNCOUNT ⇑ science

economic /iːkənɒmɪk, ɛk-/ means 1 concerned with economics and with the organization of the money, industry, and trade of a country, region, or social group. EG *What has gone wrong with the economic system during the last ten years?... ...all aspects of social, political and economic life... ...a period of economic and industrial crisis.* ADJ CLASSIF : ATTRIB ⇑ financial ◇ **economically**. EG *Katanga was extremely unevenly developed economically... Are we going to be saved economically by our natural gas supplies?* ◇ ADV ⇑ financially 2 relating to services, businesses, etc, that produce a profit. EG *We have to keep fares high enough to make it economic for the service to continue.* ADJ QUALIT ⇑ profitable = cost-effective

economical /iːkənɒmɪkə⁰l, ɛk-/. 1 Something that is **economical** does not require a lot of money to operate, for example a car that only uses a small amount of petrol. EG *This system was extremely economical because it ran on half-price electricity.* ADJ QUALIT ⇑ cheap ≠ expensive ◇ **economically**. EG *This courier service could be most economically operated.* ◇ ADV WITH VB ⇑ cheaply

2 If someone is **economical**, they spend money carefully and sensibly and do not waste it on unnecessary things. EG *She thought of herself as an economical housewife.* ADJ QUALIT ⇑ careful ≠ extravagant ◇ **economically**. EG *We live very economically.* ◇ ADV WITH VB = frugally

3 **Economical** also means using the minimum amount of time, effort, language, etc, that is necessary. EG *She spoke in short, economical sentences... How could the most economical use of our time be organized?* ADJ QUALIT ⇑ minimal = efficient ◇ **economically**. EG *The book is very economically written, but very warm.* ◇ ADV

economics /iːkənɒmɪks, ɛk-/ is 1 the study of the production of wealth and the consumption of goods and services in a society, and the organization of its money, industry, and trade. EG *Economics is the oldest of the social sciences... She had a degree in economics.* N UNCOUNT ⇑ science ● See also **home economics**. 2 the system of organizing the money, production, and trade of a country, region, or social group. EG *...the* N PLURAL : WITH POSS *economics of the timber trade... The big pitfall in Mitterand's economics may prove to be in nationalization.*

economist /iˈkɒnəmɪst/, **economists**. An **economist** is a person who studies, teaches, or writes about economics. EG *...the ideas of the great English economist, J M Keynes.*
N COUNT

economize /iˈkɒnəmaɪz/, **economizes, economizing, economized**; also spelled **economise**. If you **economize**, you save money by spending it very carefully and not buying expensive things. EG *Don't economize on things which will hardly save you any money... If you're really going to buy a car, we'll have to economize on other things.*
V: IF+PREP THEN *on* = cut costs ≠ splash out

economy /iˈkɒnəmiˈ/, **economies**. 1 An **economy** is the system according to which the money, industry, and trade of a country or region are organized. EG *New England's economy is still largely based on manufacturing... All Western economies are competing against each other.*
N COUNT

2 A country's **economy** is the wealth that it gets from business and industry. EG *Unofficial strikes were damaging the British economy... These businesses contribute hundreds of millions of pounds to the economy of the country.*
N COUNT: USU *the*+N IN SING

3 **Economy** is 3.1 careful spending or the careful use of things in order to save money. EG *The mania for economy had struck even here... His seaside shack was small, for reasons of economy... I switched off all the lights as an economy measure.*
N UNCOUNT ⇑ saving ≠ extravagance

3.2 the use of the minimum amount of time, effort, words, etc, that is necessary to achieve something, so that nothing is wasted. EG *The apparent economy of effort is an illusion... ...economy of language.*
N UNCOUNT+*of*

4 If you make **economies,** you take action in order to save money, by not spending money on unnecessary things. EG *Make some stringent economies, be as frugal as a monk.*
N COUNT ⇑ saving ≠ extravagance

5 **Economy** can be used to describe 5.1 cheap services, such as travel that has no luxuries or extras. EG *I'll have to travel economy class.*
ADJ CLASSIF: ATTRIB

5.2 large-size packages of goods which are cheaper than the normal-sized packages on sale. EG *Buy our new economy packs of 100.*
ADJ CLASSIF: ATTRIB = family

ecosystem /iːkəʊsɪstəᵊm, ɛkəʊ-/, **ecosystems**. An **ecosystem** is all the plants and animals that live in a particular area together with the complex relationship that exists between all of them and their environment; a technical word. EG *...the intricate prairie ecosystem... ...highly sensitive and delicately balanced ecosystems.*
N COUNT

ecstasy /ɛkstəsiˈ/, **ecstasies**. 1 **Ecstasy** is 1.1 an extreme emotional feeling of very great happiness. EG *His big face was transfixed in ecstasy... She trained for years in order to experience the ecstasy of singing.*
N UNCOUNT/ COUNT = rapture

1.2 an extreme emotional state of any kind. EG *She worked herself into an ecstasy of self-pity.*
N COUNT/ UNCOUNT = frenzy

2 If you are **in ecstasies** about something, or if you go **into ecstasies** about it, you are or you become very excited about it. EG *...Kathleen, whose mere proximity would send him into ecstasies.*
PHR USED AS AN A ⇑ excited = raving

ecstatic /iˈkstætɪk/ means showing or feeling great enthusiasm and happiness. EG *Eddie was ecstatic over his new rifle... He felt a wild ecstatic happiness.* ◊ **ecstatically**. EG *Clarissa listened ecstatically.*
ADJ QUALIT ⇑ enthusiastic = rapturous, euphoric ◊ ADV

ecumenical /iːkjuːmɛnɪkəᵊl, ɛk-/ is used to describe activities, ideas, and movements which try to unite different Christian Churches; a formal word. EG *...an ecumenical institute... Both chaplains work as part of an ecumenical team.* ◊ **ecumenically**.
ADJ CLASSIF ◊ ADV

ecumenicism /iːkjuːmɛnɪsɪzəᵊm, ɛk-/ is the belief that all the different branches of the Christian Church should co-operate and be united. EG *The church here has managed to practise ecumenicism for years.*
N UNCOUNT

ecumenism /iːkjuːmɛnɪzəᵊm, ɛk-/ is the same as ecumenicism.
N UNCOUNT

eczema /ɛksɪᵊmə/ is an uncomfortable skin disease which makes your skin itch and become rough and sore. EG *The commonest form of allergy in babies is eczema.*
N UNCOUNT ⇑ dermatitis

ed., eds. ed. is an abbreviation for 'editor'. EG *...Frank Field (ed.) 'Education and the Urban Crisis'.*
N COUNT

-ed is 1 added to verbs to form their past tense or their past participle. If the verb ends in -e, one of the -e's is dropped. If the verb ends in -y, it is usually changed to -i- before -ed. EG *...walk→walked... ...behave→behaved... ...carry→carried.*
SUFFIX

2 added to nouns to form adjectives that describe someone or something as having a particular feature or features. EG *...hood→hooded... ...hump→humped... ...pattern→patterned.*
SUFFIX: FORMS ADJS

3 added to nouns or verbs combined with other words, to form compound adjectives. EG *...shape→shaped→cone-shaped... ...colour→coloured→tomato-coloured.*
SUFFIX: FORMS ADJS

eddy /ɛdiˈ/, **eddies, eddying, eddied**. 1 To **eddy** means to move round and round in unexpected directions, without any clear direction, intention, or plan. EG *The wind whipped and eddied around the buildings.*
V: USU+A = swirl

2 An **eddy** is a a movement in water or in the air which goes round and round instead of flowing in one continuous direction. EG *...every trick and eddy of the tide.*
N COUNT ⇑ current = twist

edge /ɛdʒ/, **edges, edging, edged**. 1 An **edge** is 1.1 the physical limit of an object or place, for example the line that you see where one thing stops and another thing begins. EG *Little children played in the sand at the water's edge... The bird had a white stripe along the front edge of each wing... The paper was old and yellowed and flaking at the edges... They lived in a cottage on the edge of the moors.*
N COUNT: IF+ PREP THEN *of* = border, rim

1.2 the narrow side of a flat, solid object. EG *The line was as straight and as thin as the edge of a ruler.*
N COUNT: IF+ PREP THEN *of*

1.3 the sharp side of the blade of a knife or an axe. EG *I picked up the knife and sharpened the edge.*
N COUNT

2 If something **is edged** with a particular thing, that thing forms a border for it. EG *...a beautiful garden edged with flowering trees.*
V+O: USU PASS+ *with*

3 If someone or something **edges** away from or towards a particular place or person, they move very slowly in that direction. EG *He edged away from the thug... I edged my way to the window.*
V+A, OR V+O+A = inch

4 The **edge** of something is the point at which something different, especially something bad, may start to happen. EG *The world had been brought to the edge of war... He seemed so out of control, so close to the edge, that I believed he could kill.*
N SING: *the*+N, USU+*of* = brink

5 An **edge** to someone's voice is a quality of sharpness, bitterness, or controlled anger in it. EG *There was a new edge to his voice now, and he spoke louder.*
N SING: *an*+N, IF +PREP THEN *to*

6 **On edge**. 6.1 If you are **on edge**, you are tense, nervous, and unable to relax. EG *Father comes home on edge because of troubles that he's having in his work.*
PHR: USED AS AN A

6.2 If something **sets** your **teeth on edge**, you find it extremely unpleasant. EG *Her voice set my teeth on edge.*
PHR: VB INFLECTS ⇑ irritate = grate

7 If something or someone has an **edge** on or over something or someone else, they have an advantage that makes them stronger or more likely to be successful than the other thing or person. EG *Social pressures have the edge over bureaucratic ones.*
N SING WITH DET: IF+PREP THEN *over*

8 If you say that someone or something has **edge**, you mean that they have a powerful effect, for example on the way that people think. EG *There's little edge to this book.*
N UNCOUNT ⇑ power = bite

9 If something **takes the edge off** a situation, usually an unpleasant one, it weakens its effect on people or things. EG *His smile took the edge off her anger.*
PHR: VB INFLECTS = blunt ≠ whet

-edged means having a particular number of edges, or having edges of a particular colour, size, or shape. EG *A blue-edged handkerchief... ...a sharp-edged knife... ...a seven-edged coin.*
COMB: FORMS ADJS

edgeways /ɛdʒweɪz/. In informal English, if you say that you **cannot get a word in edgeways**, you mean that you are unable to say anything because someone else is talking so much.
PHR

edging /ɛdʒɪŋ/, **edgings**. An **edging** is something that is put along the borders or sides of something else in order to make it look attractive. EG *The square, with its edging of chestnut trees, looked clean and fresh in the spring sunshine.*
N COUNT: USU SING ⇑ border = fringe

edgy /ɛdʒiˈ/, **edgier, edgiest**. When you are **edgy**, you are nervous, anxious, and likely to lose control of your feelings; an informal word. EG *Rick seemed very edgy.*
ADJ QUALIT ⇑ agitated = on edge

edible /ɛdɪbəᵊl/. Something that is **edible** is safe to eat and not poisonous. EG *All parts of the plant are edible... ...edible mushrooms.* ◊ **edibility** /ɛdəbɪlɪtiˈ/. EG *...to guarantee the edibility of smoked salmon.*
ADJ CLASSIF ≠ inedible ◊ N UNCOUNT

edict /iːdɪkt/, **edicts**; a formal word. An **edict** is 1 a firm, authoritative command or instruction. EG *I told*
N COUNT ⇑ order

the factory inspector we would defy his edict. **2** a public order or instruction given by a government or other authority, which everyone must obey. EG *...an edict from the Pope himself... He was banned by Government edict.* — N COUNT/UNCOUNT = decree

edifice /ɛdɪfɪs/, **edifices**. An **edifice** is **1** a large and impressive building. EG *She walked past the school, a huge Victorian edifice that loomed up over the other buildings.* — N COUNT ⇑ structure **2** a system of beliefs or a traditional institution; a formal use. EG *The whole edifice of modern civilization is beginning to sway... ...a towering edifice of images and symbols.* — N COUNT : USU + SUPP ⇑ structure

edify /ɛdɪfaɪ/, **edifies, edifying, edified**. To **edify** someone means to make them into a better person by explaining something to them or giving them useful information; a formal word. EG *...a series of popular talks intended to edify and entertain.* — V+O : NO IMPER ⇑ teach = instruct, improve
◇ **edifying**. EG *...not a very edifying experience.* — ◇ ADJ QUALIT
◇ **edification** /ɛdɪfɪkeɪʃəⁿn/. EG *...books bought for instruction or edification.* — ◇ N UNCOUNT

edit /ɛdɪt/, **edits, editing, edited**. **1** If you **edit** a text such as an article or a book, you examine it and make corrections to it so that it is suitable for publishing. EG *I type and edit and index stuff for Derek's friends.* ◇ **editing**. EG *...one of the standard textbooks on editing.* ◇ **edited**. EG *This is the edited text.* — V OR V+O ⇑ correct; ◇ N UNCOUNT; ◇ ADJ CLASSIF
2 If you **edit** a book or series of books, you collect several pieces of writing by different authors and prepare them for publishing. EG *He edits a sociology series for a paperback publisher... ...'The Save and Prosper Book of Money,' edited by Margaret Allen.* — V+O
3 If you **edit** a film or a television or radio programme, you choose some of what has been filmed or recorded and arrange it in a particular order. EG *We edited the film together... He got his first taste of editing a daily programme.* — V+O ⇑ prepare
4 Someone who **edits** a newspaper, magazine, or other regular publication is in charge of it. EG *The men who own and edit newspapers are neither better nor worse than the people who read them.* — V+O ⇑ oversee = run
5 An **edit** is the process of examining and correcting a text so that it is suitable for publishing; a technical term in publishing. EG *The first edit took over a month.* — N COUNT ⇑ correction

edit out. If you **edit** something **out**, you take out parts of a text, film, etc, for example because they are not necessary or because they might be offensive to some people. EG *We had to edit out the expletives.* — PHRASAL VB : V+O+ADV ⇑ exclude = cut

edition /ɪ²dɪʃəⁿn/, **editions**. An **edition** is **1** a particular version of a book, magazine, or newspaper that is printed at one time. EG *...the city edition of the New York Times... The Macmillan edition is out of print.* — N COUNT+SUPP **2** the total number of copies of a particular book, newspaper, etc that are printed at one time. EG *It was published in a limited edition.* — N COUNT+SUPP **3** a single television or radio programme that is one of a series about a particular subject: compare **episode** . EG *Tonight's edition of Kaleidoscope begins at a quarter to ten.* — N COUNT : IF + PREP THEN *of*

editor /ɛdɪtə/, **editors**. An **editor** is **1** a person who is in charge of a newspaper or magazine and who decides what will be published in each edition of it. EG *Peter Smith, editor of a local newspaper... She was appointed editor two years ago.* — N COUNT ⇑ journalist **2** a journalist who is responsible for a particular section of a newspaper or magazine. EG *The foreign editor had gone home, leaving his deputy in charge... The venerable literary editor of a quarterly magazine.* — N COUNT : USU MOD+N, IF + PREP THEN *of* **3** a person whose job is to check articles, stories, novels, etc, and make changes and corrections before they are published. EG *She's a very good editor and cuts much more energetically than I do.* — N COUNT **4** a person who prepares a film, or a radio or television programme by selecting some of what has been filmed or recorded and putting it in a particular order. — N COUNT **5** a computer program that enables you to make alterations and corrections to stored data. EG *...a screen editor.* — N COUNT

editorial /ɛdɪtɔːrɪəl/, **editorials**. **1 Editorial** means **1.1** involved in preparing a newspaper, magazine, book, etc, for publication. EG *Hearst expanded his editorial staff... He increased the editorial budget substantially.* — ADJ CLASSIF : ATTRIB **1.2** involving the attitudes, opinions, and contents of a newspaper, magazine, television programme, etc. EG *...a limited measure of editorial control over State television and radio... ...the paper's editorial policy.* — ADJ CLASSIF : ATTRIB ◇ **editorially**. EG *The Daily Mirror said editorially that the Pope was 'mistaken'.* — ◇ ADV
2 An **editorial** is an article in a newspaper which gives the opinion of the editor or publisher on a topic or item of news. EG *'It is not every day,' said the Church Times in an editorial, 'that a bishop makes such a statement'... ...a humorous article on the editorial page.* — N COUNT

editorialize /ɛdɪtɔːrɪəlaɪz/, **editorializes, editorializing, editorialized**; also spelled **editorialise**. If someone such as a journalist **editorializes**, he or she expresses an opinion rather than stating facts, especially in an article which is supposed to be reporting facts rather than giving opinions. ◇ **editorializing**. EG *This later editorializing style is very well integrated with the humorous beginning... In spite of all the editorializing, it was well worth reading.* — V ⇑ opine; ◇ ADJ CLASSIF : ATTRIB, OR N UNCOUNT

editorship /ɛdɪtə⁸ʃɪp/. The **editorship** of a newspaper or magazine is the position and authority of its editor. EG *Conditions on the paper were considerably improved under McPherson's editorship... Then came promotion to editorship of the magazine.* — N SING WITH DET : USU WITH the/POSS ⇑ leadership

educate /ɛdjə⁴keɪt/, **educates, educating, educated**. To **educate** someone means **1** to teach them over a long period, especially at a school or college, so that they gain knowledge and understanding in several subjects. EG *Many more schools are needed to educate the young... He was educated at Eton... He was sent home as being impossible to educate.* — V+O, OR V **2** to give them an education, for example by paying for it or by sending them to a particular school. EG *He had paid out good money to educate Julie at a boarding school in Yorkshire.* — V+O **3** to teach them better ways of doing something or a better way of living. EG *Not enough is being done to educate smokers about the benefits of stopping the habit.* — V+O = inform

educated /ɛdjə⁴keɪtɪ²d/. Someone who is **educated** has or shows a high standard of learning. EG *The villagers respected me because I was an educated man.* — ADJ QUALIT ⇑ learned ≠ illiterate

educated guess, educated guesses. An **educated guess** is a guess which is based on a certain amount of knowledge and therefore likely to be correct. EG *You'll get three opinions, the best of them an educated guess.* — N COUNT ⇑ deduction

education /ɛdjə⁴keɪʃəⁿn/ is **1** the system of teaching people, usually at a school or college. EG *I think this government's policy on higher education is a disaster... Only a small proportion of our children stay in full-time education after the age of 16... Examinations play a large part in education.* — N UNCOUNT **2** the gradual process by which a person gains knowledge and understanding through learning. EG *Your education is important to me... Education should be a preparation for life.* — N UNCOUNT **3** the knowledge or training that you have gained through formal and systematic study. EG *Wealth and education seem to be what you need to be successful in life.* — N UNCOUNT ≠ illiteracy **4** the field of study concerned with theories and methods of teaching. EG *She's a lecturer in education.* — N UNCOUNT **5** the general area of work that is concerned with teaching people, especially in school or college. EG *There is scope for women in welfare, child care and education.* — N UNCOUNT

educational /ɛdjə⁴keɪʃəⁿnəl, -ʃənəⁿl/ means **1** concerned with and related to education. EG *A university is an educational institution... National wealth depends to a high degree on a country's educational standards... ...educational cuts.* ◇ **educationally**. EG *She was sent to a special school for the educationally subnormal.* — ADJ CLASSIF; ◇ ADV **2** teaching you something that you did not know before. EG *It was a very educational experience.* — ADJ QUALIT = educative

educationalist /ɛdjə⁴keɪʃəⁿnəlɪst/, **educationalists**. An **educationalist** is a specialist in the theories and methods of education. — N COUNT ⇑ teacher

educationist /ɛdjə⁴keɪʃəⁿnɪst/, **educationists**. An **educationist** is the same as an educationalist. — N COUNT ⇑ teacher

educative /ɛdjə⁴kətɪv/. An **educative** quality or activity is one that teaches you something that you did not know before. EG *Our primary function is still an educative one.* — ADJ CLASSIF

educator /ɛdjə⁴keɪtə/, **educators**. An **educator** is a person who educates people. EG *...the sociologist and educator, Dr Richard Saunders.* — N COUNT ⇑ teacher

Edwardian /ɛdwɔːdi¹ən/ is used to refer to the style of architecture, dress, etc that was popular in — ADJ CLASSIF ⇑ period

Britain at the beginning of the 20th century. EG ...*Edwardian England.*

-ee is added to verbs of doing in order to form nouns that refer to a person to whom the action is being done. EG ...*pay→payee... ...employ→employee.* SUFFIX : FORMS N COUNTS

EEC /iː iː siː/ is the abbreviation for 'European Economic Community': an organization of Western European countries, including the UK, that have joint policies on matters such as trade and agriculture. N PROPER : the+N = Common Market

eel /iːl/, **eels**. An **eel** is a long, thin, snake-like fish. Some types of eel are cooked and eaten. N COUNT

e'er /ɛə/ means ever; a poetic word. ADV

eerie /ɪəri¹/, **eerier, eeriest**. Something that is **eerie** is strange and frightening. EG ...*the only person in that eerie place... ...the eerie feeling that someone was watching me.* ◇ **eerily**. EG *The crowd fell eerily silent... The lights gleamed eerily.* ADJ QUALIT = creepy ◇ ADV ⇑ strangely = uncannily

efface /i¹feɪs/, **effaces, effacing, effaced**. 1 If someone or something **effaces** a mark, they rub it out or wipe it off so that it cannot be seen; a formal word. EG *In the sand, all the footprints had effaced one another.* V+O ⇑ remove = erase

2 If you **efface** a wrong or unpleasant feeling or action, you replace it by a better one. EG *He'd hoped to efface the memory of an embarrassing speech... ...to efface the faults of five decades.* V+O ⇑ remove = blot out

3 If you **efface** yourself, you behave in a modest way or in such a way that you avoid being noticed. EG *He would have to efface himself before his visitor.* ● See also **self-effacing**. V+O (REFL) = humble

effect /i¹fɛkt/, **effects, effecting, effected**. 1 An **effect** is 1.1 a change that is caused in a person or thing by another person or thing. EG ...*the effect of noise on people in the factories... ...the effect on a man of a woman crying... ...the effects of the detonation... This has the effect of separating students from teachers.* N COUNT : IF+PREP THEN on = result, consequence 1.2 a physical change or feeling in your body that is caused by an illness or drug. EG ...*the effects of sea-sickness... My arm went numb, then the effect passed off... ...under the effect of the anaesthetic.* ● See also **side-effect**. N COUNT 1.3 an impression that a speaker or artist deliberately creates by their style. EG *Irony was the effect he worked for in conversation... Don't move, or you'll destroy the whole effect.* N COUNT : USU SING ● If you do something **for effect**, you do it in order to impress people and to draw attention to yourself. EG *Here she paused for effect.* ● PHR : USED AS AN A = dramatically

2 **Effect** is the power to influence a situation in the way that you want. EG *Ordinary fire-fighting equipment could have little or no effect upon such an inferno... He pulled hard, but without any noticeable effect.* N UNCOUNT = impact

3 If you say that something is done **to good effect, to no effect**, etc, you are indicating how successful or impressive the action is. EG *He uses his distinctive voice to great effect... I did try, although to little effect.* PHR : USED AS AN A

4 A person's **effects** are the things that they have with them at a particular time, for example when they are arrested or admitted to hospital, or the things that they owned when they died; a formal use. EG *His personal effects would be returned to the bereaved family.* N PLURAL : POSS +N ⇑ possessions = belongings

5 The **effects** in a film are the specially created sounds and scenery. ● See also **special effects, sound effects**.

6 You add **in effect** to a statement or opinion that is not precisely accurate, but which you feel is a reasonable description or summary of a particular situation. EG *In effect he has no choice... What in effect I'm saying is that he couldn't write a novel.* PHR : USED AS ADV SEN = effectively

7 You use **to this effect, to that effect**, or **to the effect that** to indicate that a statement is a summary of something that was said or written, and not the actual words used. EG ...*a rumour to the effect that he had been drunk... He shouted 'No, you fool, the other way!' or words to that effect.* PHR : NG+PHR

8 If you **effect** something that you are deliberately trying to achieve, you succeed in causing it to happen; a fairly formal use. EG *Production was halted until repairs could be effected... ...to effect the rescue of the prisoner... He did it himself, thereby effecting a considerable saving in time and money.* V+O ⇑ cause

9 If you **put, bring**, or **carry** a plan or idea **into effect**, you cause it to happen in practice. EG *Signing the agreement was one thing, putting it into effect was another.* PHR : VB INFLECTS

10 If a law, policy, etc **takes effect, comes into effect**, or **goes into effect** at a particular time, it officially begins to act, apply, or be valid from that time. EG *The tax cuts take effect on July 1st... Professor Master's resignation takes effect from next October...* PHR : VB INFLECTS, USU+A ⇑ begin

11 You can also say that something **takes effect** when it starts to produce the results that are intended. EG *It takes time for policies to take effect... The anaesthetic is taking effect now.* PHR : VB INFLECTS = work

12 If you say that something will happen **with immediate effect** or **with effect** from a particular time, you mean that it will begin to act, apply, or be valid immediately or from the stated time; a formal use. EG *Your salary will be increased with immediate effect... ...with effect from April.* PHR : USED AS AN A

effective /i¹fɛktɪv/. 1 Something that is **effective** 1.1 works well and produces the results that were intended. EG ...*effective ways of reducing pollution... ...an effective incomes policy... In order to be effective we need your support.* ◇ **effectiveness**. EG *Methods vary dramatically in effectiveness.* ADJ QUALIT ⇑ good = successful ≠ ineffective ◇ N UNCOUNT 1.2 is so impressive that it attracts people's attention. EG *I remember her making a most effective entrance in a play I saw.* ADJ QUALIT = striking

2 **Effective** also means having a particular role or result in practice, though not officially or in theory. EG *He assumed effective command of the armed forces... ...the effective leader.* ADJ CLASSIF : ATTRIB = actual

3 When something such as a law or an agreement becomes **effective**, it begins officially to act, apply, or be valid. EG ...*a ceasefire, to become effective as soon as accepted by the rebels.* ADJ CLASSIF : PRED = operative

effectively /i¹fɛktɪvli¹/. 1 **Effectively** means in a manner that works well, so as to produce the results that were intended. EG ...*an attempt to make the system work more effectively.* ADV WITH VB = efficiently

2 You can also use **effectively** with a statement to indicate that it is not precisely accurate, but that you feel it is a reasonable description or summary of a particular situation. EG *The television was on, effectively ruling out conversation... The illness of any one of them would effectively prevent all of them from going.* ADV WITH VB = in effect

effectual /i¹fɛktʃʊ⁰əl/. An **effectual** action, plan, etc, is one that succeeds in producing the results that were intended; a formal word. EG *The law would have to be very tough indeed to be effectual.* ◇ **effectually**. EG *He hacked less effectually at several boards.* ADJ QUALIT = effective ≠ ineffectual ◇ ADV WITH VB

effeminacy /i¹fɛmɪnəsi¹/. If you refer to a man's or boy's **effeminacy**, you mean that he behaves, looks, or sounds like a woman or girl; used showing disapproval. EG *His timidity, his slight effeminacy, were worrying.* N UNCOUNT ⇑ femininity ≠ manliness

effeminate /i¹fɛmɪnə¹t/. A man or boy is described as **effeminate** if he behaves, looks, or sounds like a woman or girl; used showing disapproval. EG *They find European males slightly effeminate... 'Who?' he said, in an effeminate mincing voice.* ADJ QUALIT ⇑ feminine = womanish

effervescence /ɛfəvɛsə⁰ns/ is 1 the releasing of bubbles of gas by a liquid. N UNCOUNT 2 the quality of being lively and enthusiastic in your behaviour. EG *Kitty's letter gave a calm appraisal of Tom's effervescence.* N UNCOUNT ⇑ liveliness

effervescent /ɛfəvɛsə⁰nt/. 1 An **effervescent** liquid is a liquid that releases bubbles of gas. EG ...*a slightly effervescent wine which is very agreeable... ...an effervescent drink.* ADJ QUALIT ⇑ gassy = sparkling

2 Someone who is **effervescent** is lively and enthusiastic in their behaviour. EG ...*a very effervescent personality.* ADJ QUALIT = bubbly

effete /i¹fiːt/ means weak and powerless; used showing disapproval. EG ...*the effete, preposterous Anthony Blanche... West European nations have become 'effete'.* ◇ **effeteness**. ADJ QUALIT ≠ vigorous ◇ N UNCOUNT

efficacious /ɛfɪkeɪʃəs/. Something that is **efficacious** is successful in solving a problem or achieving an aim; a formal word. EG *Cameron's remedy had been remarkably efficacious... These lotions, usually efficacious in cases of prickly heat, seemed slow in having any beneficial results.* ADJ QUALIT ⇑ effective = efficient

efficacy /ɛfɪkəsi¹/ is the ability to do something or do it well and produce the results that were intended; a formal word. EG ...*doubts over the efficacy of his* N UNCOUNT : USU WITH POSS ⇑ effectiveness *leadership... ...the efficacy of our policy... ...the efficacy of prayer.*

efficiency /iˈfɪʃəⁿnsiˈ/ is 1 the quality of being able to do a task successfully and without wasting time or energy. EG *...an increase in business efficiency... ...improve the efficiency of their reading... Her efficiency in developing ideas.* 2 the difference between the amount of energy a machine needs to make it work, and the amount it produces; a technical term in physics and engineering. EG *Electricity is produced at something like 30% efficiency from the power station... ...the efficiency of the battery.*

N UNCOUNT ⇑ effectiveness = competence; N UNCOUNT/COUNT ⇑ ratio

efficient /iˈfɪʃəⁿnt/. A person, machine, organization, etc that is **efficient** does a job well and successfully, without wasting time or energy. EG *Engines and cars can be made more efficient... You need a very efficient production manager... Nationalized industries could be efficient and successful.* ◇ **efficiently.** EG *You must work more efficiently... ...if a business is being efficiently run... ...turbines operate efficiently at higher speeds.*

ADJ QUALIT ⇑ effective ≠ useless, wasteful; ◇ ADV ⇑ effectively = competently

effigy /ɛfɪdʒiˈ/, **effigies**. 1 An **effigy** is 1.1 a roughly made figure or dummy, often ugly or funny, that represents someone you hate or despise. EG *The students burned effigies of the president.* 1.2 a statue or carving of a famous person; a formal use. EG *...his tombstone, with an elaborately carved effigy of him as a knight in armour... ...a coin with her effigy on it.*

N COUNT ⇑ image; N COUNT = image

2 If you burn or hang a person **in effigy**, you burn or hang a figure or dummy that represents them, because you hate or despise them. EG *Poor Sir Ralph got himself burned in effigy by farmers... Chicago bosses were hanged in effigy.*

PHR : USED AS AN A

efflorescence /ɛflɔːrɛsəⁿns/; a literary word. **Efflorescence** is 1 the blooming of flowers on a plant, especially when this happens suddenly. EG *...the efflorescence of tropical weed... ...the efflorescence of early summer.* 2 a period of artistic activity of high quality. EG *...the efflorescence of literature in the same period... ...a brief sculptural efflorescence.*

N UNCOUNT ⇑ flowering; N UNCOUNT + SUPP = upsurge

effluent /ɛfluənt/, **effluents**. **Effluent** is liquid waste material that comes out of factories or sewage works; a formal word. EG *...poisoned by industrial waste and untreated effluent... ...rivers receiving effluents from the textile industry.*

N UNCOUNT/COUNT

effort /ɛfət/, **efforts**. 1 **Effort** is 1.1 energy in the form of thought, action, time, or money that people or organizations use in their work. EG *...a change in the direction of scientific effort... ...a bonus to reward initiative, skill and effort... ...a waste of effort... Little effort has been made to investigate this claim.* 1.2 an unusual amount of physical or mental energy that you need in order to do something, because it is painful or difficult. EG *Robert spoke with effort... He frowns with mental effort, but the sums won't make sense.*

N UNCOUNT = endeavour; N UNCOUNT ⇑ difficulty

2 An **effort** is 2.1 a particular attempt to do something by using energy in the form of thought, action, time, or money. EG *...the efforts of governments to restrain inflation... They have joined forces in an effort to topple the government... ...efforts at forming a new coalition... She thanked them for their efforts on her behalf... Daintry made one more effort to escape.* 2.2 a particular action or activity that is done by a group of people in order to achieve something. EG *We could raise money for the war effort.*

N COUNT : USU + SUPP ⇑ try; N COUNT : MOD + N ⇑ campaign = drive

3 If you describe an object or an action as an **effort** of a particular kind, you mean that it has been done with difficulty, and that the results are not very good. EG *His portrait of Debbie was a rather amateurish effort.*

N COUNT : ADJ + N = endeavour

4 The word **effort** is also used in the following expressions. 4.1 If you say that something such as an action is **an effort**, you mean that an unusual amount of physical or mental energy is needed to do it. EG *Getting up was an effort... With practice, it becomes less of an effort.* 4.2 If you do something by **an effort of will**, you need courage or determination to do it, because it is difficult or painful. EG *At times a great effort of will was needed to go to work.* 4.3 If you **make the effort** to do something, you use the extra energy that is needed to do it, even though you may not really want to. EG *Mothers had to make the effort to go out to a play area with their children.* 4.4 If you say that something is **worth the effort**, you mean that it will justify the energy that you have spent or will spend on it. EG *It's not worth the effort to get them to do the washing up.*

PHR : USED AS C ⇑ difficult; PHR : USED AS O/S; PHR : VB INFLECTS ⇑ try; PHR : USED AS C

effortless /ɛfətlɪˀs/. 1 An **effortless** action or achievement is one that is done easily, without using much energy. EG *...moving up the steps with apparently effortless ease... His rise in politics appears to have been effortless.* ◇ **effortlessly.** EG *He even finished his MA thesis, almost effortlessly... ...floating effortlessly on the water.*

ADJ QUALIT ⇑ easy ≠ laborious; ◇ ADV WITH VB

2 An **effortless** quality is a quality that a person has naturally and has not had to learn. EG *...the effortless superiority of the man... ...that apparently effortless style and ready smile.*

ADJ QUALIT ⇑ natural = easy ≠ forced

effrontery /iˈfrʌntəⁿriˈ/ is bold, rude, or cheeky behaviour. EG *He has the effrontery to use my lighter without asking... For sheer brazen effrontery, Ernest takes some beating.*

N UNCOUNT

effulgence /iˈfʌldʒəns/ is brightness of light; a literary word. EG *In the evening sunshine they glow with a salmon-coloured effulgence.*

N UNCOUNT + SUPP ⇑ radiance = aura

effusion /iˈfjuːʒəⁿn/, **effusions**; a formal or literary word. An **effusion** is 1 a sudden pouring out of light, liquid, etc. EG *...a tremendous effusion of colour, the last glow.* 2 the expression of your emotions or ideas with more enthusiasm and for longer than is usual or expected. EG *Her gesture checked my effusion, which would have led to nothing anyway... If the rumour is contradicted, this effusion would be in vain.*

N COUNT/UNCOUNT; N COUNT/UNCOUNT = outburst

effusive /iˈfjuːsɪv/. A person who is **effusive** expresses pleasure, gratitude, or approval enthusiastically. EG *Mrs Schiff was less effusive in her congratulations...* ▸ used of a person's behaviour. EG *...an effusive welcome.* ◇ **effusively.** EG *The doctor thanked him effusively.*

ADJ QUALIT ⇑ enthusiastic = fulsome; ◇ ADV = profusely

EFL /iː ɛf ɛl/ is an abbreviation for 'English as a Foreign Language'; used to describe books, courses of study, and teachers that are involved with the teaching of English to people whose first language is not English. EG *...EFL dictionaries... ...an EFL teacher.*

N UNCOUNT, OR N BEFORE N ⇑ subject

e.g. /iː dʒiː/ is an abbreviation that means 'for example'; it is used before a noun, or as a conjunction introducing another sentence. EG *Reasonable work expenses, e.g. trade union subscriptions, fares, and overalls, will be taken into account... They try to make them fit their own private interests, e.g. by appealing to different sections of the community.*

= for instance

egalitarian /iˈgælɪtɛərɪən/. An **egalitarian** idea, system, person, or society is one that expresses or supports the belief that all people are equal and should have the same rights and opportunities; a formal word. EG *The new educational facilities must lead to a far more egalitarian society... ...an egalitarian tax structure... ...egalitarian principles.* ▸ used as a noun to refer to a person. EG *...kind, intelligent and an egalitarian to his fingertips.*

ADJ QUALIT; ▸ N COUNT

egalitarianism /iˈgælɪtɛərɪənɪzəⁿm/ is the belief that all people are equal and should have the same rights and opportunities, or the practice of this belief.

N UNCOUNT

egg /ɛg/, **eggs**. 1 An **egg** is 1.1 an oval or rounded object produced by female birds. It has a hard shell and contains a baby bird which later emerges by breaking the shell. Some animals, insects, and other creatures also lay eggs like birds. EG *...birds' eggs... The alligator then lays her eggs in it... These eggs hatch into larvae.* 1.2 a hen's egg considered as food. You break the shell and eat the contents, usually after cooking. EG *...a dozen eggs, a jar of pickles, and some bread... They always had bacon and egg for breakfast.* 1.3 a hard, oval object made so that it resembles a hen's egg. EG *...chocolate eggs... ...holding up the marble egg and looking at it.* • See also **Easter egg**. 1.4 a cell produced in the body of a female animal, that can develop into a baby if it is fertilized by a male reproductive cell. EG *Another egg descends into the uterus... During fertilization the sperm and the egg combine.*

N COUNT ⇑ embryo; N COUNT/UNCOUNT ⇑ food; N COUNT + SUPP ⇑ shape; N COUNT = ovum

2 The word **egg** is also used in the following informal expressions. 2.1 If you have **egg on your face**, you have been made to appear foolish. EG *He accumulated egg on his face thicker than any president since Eisenhower.* 2.2 If you **put all your eggs in one basket**, you are relying on one particular action or decision, instead of trying several things at once and leaving yourself an alternative if one of them fails. EG

PHR : USED AS O; PHR : VB INFLECTS

The government could not afford to put all its economic eggs in one basket again. **2.3** In British English, **'Don't teach your grandmother to suck eggs'** is used to suggest that someone is trying to tell you how to do something when you already know how to do it. **2.4** If you say that something will happen **as sure as eggs is eggs**, you mean that you are absolutely certain that it will happen. EG *If we decide to have a picnic, it'll rain, as sure as eggs is eggs.* **2.5** • **a chicken and egg situation**: see **chicken**. PHR : VB INFLECTS / PHR : USED AS AN A ⇑ certainly = for sure

egg on. If you **egg** someone **on**, you encourage them to do something foolish or daring. EG *Egged on by Iago, Othello makes up his mind to kill Desdemona.* PHRASAL VB : V+O+ADV = urge on

eggcup /ɛgkʌp/, **eggcups**. An **eggcup** is a small container in which you can put a boiled egg while you eat it. N COUNT

egghead /ɛghɛd/, **eggheads**. An **egghead** is someone who you disapprove of because you think they are too interested in ideas and theories, and not enough in practical actions; an informal word. EG *...the pompous egghead!* N COUNT = highbrow

eggplant /ɛgplɑːnt/, **eggplants**. An **eggplant** is an aubergine; used especially in American English. N COUNT/ UNCOUNT

eggshell /ɛgʃɛl/, **eggshells**. **1** An **eggshell** is the hard covering round the egg of a bird or animal. N COUNT/ UNCOUNT

2 Eggshell also means **2.1** delicate in structure and easily broken. EG *...wooden legs carved with that same eggshell elegance.* **2.2** having a dull painted surface or producing a dull surface. EG *...eggshell paint... ...an eggshell finish.* ADJ CLASSIF : ATTRIB / ADJ CLASSIF : ATTRIB

egg-timer, egg-timers. An **egg-timer** is a device that helps you measure the time needed to boil an egg. It usually consists of a small glass cylinder with sand in it. The cylinder has a narrow section in the middle, and when the egg-timer is turned upside down, the sand trickles through the middle for about three minutes, the length of time that it takes to boil an egg. N COUNT

egg whisk, egg whisks. An **egg whisk** is a device used in cooking for beating eggs, cream, etc into a light, fluffy state. N COUNT

ego /iːgəʊ, ɛgəʊ/, **egos**. Your **ego** is your opinion of your own worth and the influence that this has on your self-confidence. EG *It was a blow to my ego, and meant I would have to look for a new job... He quite possibly possessed the most colossal ego of modern times.* N COUNT : USU POSS/MOD+N

egocentric /iːgəʊsɛntrɪk, ɛg-/. If you are **egocentric**, you think only of yourself and what you want, and do not consider the wishes of other people. EG *...egocentric and authoritarian adults.* ADJ QUALIT ⇑ selfish ≠ considerate

◇ **egocentricity** /iːgəʊsɛntrɪsɪti[1], ɛg-/. EG *He was accused of pathological egocentricity.* ◇ N UNCOUNT ⇑ selfishness

egoism /iːgəʊɪzə⁰m, ɛg-/ is the same as egotism. N UNCOUNT

egoist /iːgəʊɪst, ɛg-/, **egoists**. An **egoist** is the same as an egotist. N COUNT

egoistic /iːgəʊɪstɪk, ɛg-/ means the same as egotistic. ADJ QUALIT

egomania /iːgəʊmeɪnɪə, ɛg-/ is a state of mind or a way of behaving in which a person thinks only of his or her own desires or interests, and does not care about harming other people in order to get what he or she wants. EG *He was eaten up with conceit, violent egomania.* N UNCOUNT

egomaniac /iːgəʊmeɪnɪæk, ɛg-/, **egomaniacs**. An **egomaniac** is a person who thinks only of himself or herself and who does not care about harming other people in order to get what he or she wants. N COUNT

egotism /iːgətɪzə⁰m, ɛg-/ is a set of attitudes or behaviour that show that you only care about yourself, or that you believe that you are more important than other people. EG *It was a piece of blatant egotism.* N UNCOUNT ⇑ self-interest ≠ altruism

egotist /iːgətɪst, ɛg-/, **egotists**. An **egotist** is a person who acts selfishly and believes that he or she is more important than other people; used showing disapproval. EG *She was already so much the egotist that her eyes were blind to anyone or anything but herself.* N COUNT

egotistic /iːgətɪstɪk, ɛg-/. The form **egotistical** is also used. If you are **egotistic**, you believe that you and your own needs, ideas, etc, are more important than other people and their needs, ideas, etc; used showing disapproval. EG *Success makes a man egotistic... She was supremely egotistical at heart.* ADJ QUALIT ⇑ self-centred ≠ altruistic

ego trip, ego trips. An **ego trip** is an action or a series of actions that someone does for their own satisfaction and enjoyment, often one that shows that they think they are more important than other people; used showing disapproval. EG *He's on another one of his ego trips.* N COUNT

Egyptian /ɪ[1]dʒɪpʃə⁰n/. **1 Egyptian** means belonging to or connected with Egypt, its people, or its language. EG *...the Egyptian government.* ADJ CLASSIF

2 An **Egyptian** is someone who comes from Egypt, especially a man. EG *...a student named Hamid, an Egyptian with big dark eyes.* N COUNT ⇑ person

eh /eɪ/. You say **eh 1** when you are asking someone to reply to you or to agree with you. EG *Here in an official capacity, eh?... 'Looks good, eh?' he asked exuberantly... Who knows we're here? Eh?* **2** when you are asking someone to repeat what they have just said because you did not hear it the first time. EG *'Tell me.'–'Eh?'–'Does she drink?'... 'Well, I still have a chequebook.'–'Eh?'–'I said I still have a chequebook.'... He looked up vaguely from the paper. 'Eh?' he said.* = pardon

eiderdown /aɪdədaʊn/, **eiderdowns**. An **eiderdown** is a bed covering, placed on top of sheets and blankets, that is filled with small soft feathers or warm material. N COUNT = quilt

eight /eɪt/, **eights**. **Eight** is the number 8: see ☐ at NUMBER, AGE, DATE, MEASUREMENT, MONEY, and TIME. EG *...eight months of exile.* • See also **figure of eight.** NUM

eighteen /eɪtiːn/ is the number 18: see ☐ at NUMBER, AGE, DATE, MEASUREMENT, MONEY, and TIME. NUM

eighteenth /eɪtiːnθ/ The **eighteenth** item in a series is the one that you count as number eighteen: see ☐ at NUMBER, AGE, and DATE. EG *The last major addition to the building came in the early eighteenth century.* ORDINAL

eighth /eɪtθ/, **eighths**. **1** The **eighth** item in a series is the one that you count as number eight: see ☐ at NUMBER, AGE, and DATE. EG *In his room back on the eighth floor he unpacked and changed.* ORDINAL

2 An **eighth** is one of eight equal parts of something. EG *It was about an eighth of an inch thick.* N COUNT ⇑ fraction

eighth note, eighth notes. An **eighth note**, in music, is a quaver; used in American English. N COUNT

eightieth /eɪti[1]ɪθ/. The **eightieth** item in a series is the one that you count as number eighty: see ☐ at NUMBER and AGE. EG *I saw him at his eightieth birthday party.* ORDINAL

eighty /eɪti[1]/, **eighties**. **Eighty** is the number 80: see ☐ at NUMBER, AGE, DATE, MEASUREMENT, and MONEY. EG *Sibelius' Second Symphony was written more than eighty years ago.* NUM

eisteddfod /aɪstɛdfɒd/, **eisteddfods**. An **eisteddfod** is a Welsh festival at which competitions are held in music, poetry, drama, and art. N COUNT

either /aɪðə, iːðə/. **1** You use **either 1.1** in front of the first of two or more alternatives, when you are stating the only possibilities or choices that there are. The other alternatives are introduced by 'or'. EG *I was expecting you either today or tomorrow... You either love him or you hate him... Either you eat your spinach or you go without ice cream.* **1.2** in a negative statement in front of the first of two alternatives, when you are emphasizing that the negative statement refers to both the alternatives. EG *Dr Kirk, you're not being either frank or fair... I wouldn't dream of asking either Mary or my mother to take on the responsibility.* CONJ COORD ≠ neither / CONJ COORD

2 You can also use **either 2.1** to refer to one of two things, people, or situations, when you want to say that they are both possible and it does not matter which one is chosen or considered. EG *One speech by either of them stating the facts would have ended his uncertainty. Either is acceptable... What are your views, either or both of you?* ▸ used as a determiner. EG *If these arguments were sound, then either one of two conclusions might be drawn... Either way, I can't lose.* **2.2** in a negative statement to refer to each of two things, people, or situations, when you are emphasizing that the negative statement includes both of them. EG *'Which one do you want?'–'I don't want either.'... Some are without upper limbs, some without lower, some without either... There was no sound from either of the flats.* ▸ used as a determiner. EG *She could not see either man.* PRON : SING, IF+PREP THEN *of* ⇑ any ≠ neither / ▸ DET+N COUNT IN SING / PRON : IF+PREP THEN *of*, WITH BROAD NEG ⇑ any / ▸ DET+N COUNT IN SING, WITH BROAD NEG

3 You can use **either** by itself at the end of a negative statement **3.1** to indicate that there is a ADV : WITH similarity between a person or thing that you have just mentioned and one that was mentioned earlier, for example when the same fact is true about both of them. EG *'I haven't got that address.'–'No, I haven't got it either'... I can't play golf either... I knew that John wouldn't want to go out and I didn't think Eileen would either.* **3.2** to indicate that you are adding an extra piece of information to a previous statement that you have made. EG *Not only was he ugly, he was not very interesting to talk to either... He doesn't have all his facts right either.* BROAD NEG / ADV : WITH BROAD NEG = what's more

4 You can use **either** to introduce a noun that refers to each of two things when you are talking about both of them. EG *The two ladies sat in large armchairs on either side of the stage... I passed some kids playing football using coats as goals at either end of the street... In either case the answer is the same.* DET+N COUNT IN SING

ejaculate /ɪ'dʒækjə'leɪt/, **ejaculates, ejaculating, ejaculated.** **1** When a man **ejaculates**, he discharges semen through his penis. V ↑ discharge ◊ **ejaculation** /ɪ'dʒækjə'leɪʃə°n/. ◊ N UNCOUNT

2 If you **ejaculate**, you suddenly say or shout something, for example because you are very surprised; an old-fashioned, literary use. EG *'Stout man!' ejaculated Mr Annett.* ◊ **ejaculation**. EG *He screamed, an ejaculation of hopelessness.* V+QUOTE = exclaim / ◊ N UNCOUNT/COUNT

eject /ɪ'dʒekt/, **ejects, ejecting, ejected.** **1** To **eject** something means to push or send it out, usually with force. EG *The machine ejected a handful of cigarettes... Some ants eject formic acid when irritated.* ◊ **ejection** /ɪ'dʒekʃə°n/. V+O ↑ throw out = emit / ◊ N UNCOUNT

2 To **eject** someone means to force them to leave a particular place or position. EG *If someone is trying to enter your house by force you can eject him by force... We reserve the right to eject without notice any objectionable person.* ◊ **ejection**. V+O : USU+A ↑ throw out = remove, expel / ◊ N UNCOUNT

ejector seat, ejector seats. An **ejector seat** is a special seat which can throw the pilot out of a fast military aeroplane in an emergency. N COUNT

eke /iːk/, **ekes, eking, eked.** If you **eke** something **out**, you make your supply of it last as long as possible, by being careful to using no more than is necessary. EG *Migrants send home cash that helps eke out low village incomes.* ● If you **eke out a living** or **an existence**, you manage to survive in a difficult situation in which you have very little food, money, etc. EG *In his early days he eked out a precarious living from designing book jackets... These unfortunate creatures eke out a miserable existence.* PHRASAL VB : V+O+ADV = stretch / ● PHR : VB INFLECTS

elaborate, elaborates, elaborating, elaborated. The word **elaborate** is pronounced /ɪ'læbərət/ when it is an adjective, and /ɪ'læbəreɪt/ when it is a verb. **1** Something that is **elaborate** is **1.1** very complex because it has a lot of different parts. EG *...elaborate cooling systems... ...the elaborate network of canals or water storage tanks... ...elaborate apparatus for digesting cellulose.* **1.2** made with a lot of detailed artistic designs. EG *...the elaborate embroidered and jewelled headdress... The south side of the church is elaborate, decorated with fine stone carvings.* ◊ **elaborately**. EG *Every inch of its surface was elaborately decorated.* ADJ QUALIT ↑ complicated = intricate ≠ simple / ADJ QUALIT = ornate ≠ plain / ◊ ADV = richly

2 **Elaborate** systems, behaviour, or ceremonies consist of many different actions or rules that have to be done or obeyed carefully and in a particular order. EG *The Coptic Pope is chosen by his own Church in an elaborate ceremony... In some countries, the elaborate appeals procedures can delay the final outcome of a court case for several years.* ADJ QUALIT ↑ complicated = intricate ≠ simple

3 **Elaborate** plans, methods, etc, are carefully planned or organized with great attention to detail. EG *...elaborate precautions on the part of the French police... Elaborate preparations were being made to get me over to Tokyo.* ADJ QUALIT : USU ATTRIB ↑ detailed = extensive

4 If you **elaborate** something or **elaborate on** something that you have already mentioned, **4.1** you provide more details about it, in order to make it clearer and more understandable. EG *It isn't a statement I want to elaborate on... Some of these points will have to be further elaborated as we go along.* ◊ **elaboration** /ɪ'læbəreɪʃə°n/. EG *An elaboration of this idea will follow in Chapter 12.* **4.2** you develop a system, plan, or theory by making it more complicated and more effective. EG *Bees have taken this basic arrangement and elaborated it to an extreme degree.* ◊ **elaboration** /ɪ'læbəreɪʃə°n/. EG *...the elaboration of an ideology or rule.* V+O, OR V+A (on) ↑ explain = expand / ◊ N UNCOUNT / V+O = refine / ◊ N UNCOUNT

élan /eɪlɑːn, -læn/ is a quality or type of behaviour that is both energetic and confident; a literary word. EG *She walked into the room with a certain élan.* N UNCOUNT ↑ confidence = flair, dash

elapse /ɪ'læps/, **elapses, elapsing, elapsed.** When time or a period of time **elapses**, it passes or goes by; a formal word. EG *Too much time had elapsed since I had attempted any serious study... A century and a half elapsed before typewriters became commercially available.* V = go by

elastic /ɪ'læstɪk/. **1** **Elastic** is a rubber material that stretches when you pull it and returns to its original size and shape when you let it go. Elastic is often used in clothes to make them fit tightly, for example round the waist. EG *It snapped back like a piece of elastic... ...a pair of elastic knickers.* N UNCOUNT

2 Something that is **elastic** is able to stretch easily and then return to its original size and shape. EG *...a softer, more elastic and lighter material... Inside the pad is a soft, elastic sort of bladder.* ADJ QUALIT ↑ flexible = stretchy ≠ rigid

3 **Elastic** ideas, policies, etc, are able to change in order to suit new circumstances or conditions as they arise. EG *Liberal policy was sufficiently elastic to accommodate both views.* ADJ QUALIT ↑ flexible = adaptable ≠ fixed

elastic band, elastic bands. An **elastic band** is a thin circle of very stretchy rubber that you can put around bundles of things such as papers in order to hold them together. N COUNT = rubber band

elasticity /iːlæstɪsɪti¹, ɪlæstɪsɪti¹/ is **1** the ability to change and adapt in order to suit new circumstances or conditions as they arise. EG *These simple methods possess a certain elasticity as to their practical application.* **2** the ability of a material or substance to return to its original shape and size after it has been stretched. EG *We set up an experiment to measure the elasticity of the thread.* N UNCOUNT ↑ flexibility ≠ rigidity / N UNCOUNT+SUPP ↑ flexibility = stretch

elated /ɪ'leɪtɪ²d/. When you are **elated**, you are extremely happy and excited. EG *Judy, suddenly elated, gave his hand a squeeze... Her hands were still shaking, but she felt elated, excited.* ADJ QUALIT : USU PRED = exhilarated ≠ deflated

elation /ɪ'leɪʃə°n/ is a feeling of great happiness that is caused by such things as success, relief, or enjoyment. EG *This little incident filled me with considerable elation.* N UNCOUNT = delight

elbow /elbəʊ/, **elbows, elbowing, elbowed.** **1** An **elbow** is **1.1** the part of a person's arm where the upper and lower halves of the arm are joined. EG *She sat with her elbows on the table, resting her head on her hands.* **1.2** the part of a sleeve that covers your elbow. EG *He was wearing an old suit whose jacket had worn through at the elbows.* N COUNT ↑ joint / N COUNT

2 If you **elbow** someone aside or to one side, you use one of your elbows to push them out of the way. EG *He stood in the doorway but she elbowed him to one side and walked out... I elbowed my way through the crowd to the front of the hall.* V+O+A = jostle

elbow grease is the strength and energy that you use when doing physical work like rubbing or polishing; an informal expression. EG *Removing all the old paint can be extremely hard work and involves lots of elbow grease.* N UNCOUNT = effort

elbow room; also spelled with a hyphen. **Elbow room** is the freedom in a particular place or situation to do what you want to do or need to do; an informal expression. EG *I needed a little more elbow room to do the job properly.* N UNCOUNT ↑ space

elder /eldə/, **elders.** **1** The **elder** of two people is the one who was born first. EG *He had none of his elder brother's charm... Posy was the elder of the two... The elder Jaykar was very gentle with his son.* ADJ CLASSIF : USU the+ADJ ≠ younger

2 A person's **elder** is someone who is older than them, especially when they are quite a lot older; a fairly formal use. EG *Their father had taught them to show respect towards their elders... She was my elder by some two years.* N COUNT : USU WITH POSS = senior ≠ junior

3 An **elder** is **3.1** a fairly old member of a tribe who has influence and authority. EG *Eddie was a respected elder of the tribe.* **3.2** a person who holds a position of responsibility in some Christian churches. EG *...one of the Elders of the Mormon church.* **3.3** a bush or small tree which has groups of small white flowers and red or black berries. EG *She started to walk down the winding path through the elders.* N COUNT ↑ senior / N COUNT / N COUNT ↑ shrub = elderberry

elderberry /eldəberi¹/, **elderberries.** An **elderberry** is one of the edible red or black berries that N COUNT ↑ berry grow on an elder bush or tree. ▸ also used to refer to the bush or tree itself.

elderly /ɛldəli¹/. 1 **Elderly** people are old; often used as a polite way to refer to old people. EG *The coach was full of elderly ladies having a good time.* ADJ QUALIT ≠ young

▸ The **elderly** is used to refer to people who are elderly. EG *...the elderly and the frail... ...unless the elderly are adequately cared for.* ▸ N PLURAL : the +N = the aged

2 Something that is **elderly** is rather old or old-fashioned and therefore no longer as good or efficient as when it was new, or not as good or efficient as a modern form of it. EG *The ship was still under way, her elderly oil-fired steam engines throbbing along. ...a tired, worn-out, elderly organization.* ADJ QUALIT : USU ATTRIB = out dated ≠ modern

elder statesman, elder statesmen. An **elder statesman** is 1 an old and respected politician or former politician who still has influence because of his or her experience. EG *Beaverbrook and Lloyd George were among the elder statesmen who attended these functions.* N COUNT 2 an experienced member or former member of a company or other organization who still has influence because of his or her experience. N COUNT

eldest /ɛldı²st/. The **eldest** person in a group of people, especially the children in a family, is the one who was born before all the others. EG *Her eldest son was killed in the First War... Gladys was the eldest of four children.* ADJ CLASSIF : USU the+ADJ ▸ used in informal English as a noun. EG *Saul, Emily's eldest, has just got married.* ▸ N SING : POSS+N

elec. is an abbreviation for 'electric' or 'electricity'.

elect /i¹lɛkt/, **elects, electing, elected**. 1 When people elect someone to represent them, they choose him or her to act as their representative, by voting. EG *They met to elect a president... Why should we elect him Mayor?... You could be elected as a member of Parliament... Two women have been elected to the council.* ◇ **elected**. EG *...a democratically elected government.* V+O, OR V+O+C, OR V+O+A (as/to) = appoint ◇ ADJ CLASSIF : ATTRIB

2 If you **elect** to do something, you choose to do it; a formal use. EG *...the questions he had elected to answer in the exam... They may elect to opt out of the scheme.* V+to-INF ⇑ decide

3 **Elect** is added after words such as 'president' or 'governor' to indicate that a person has been elected to the post but has not officially started to carry out the duties involved; a formal use. EG *...the President elect.* ADJ AFTER N ⇑ chosen

election /i¹lɛkʃə⁰n/, **elections**. 1 An **election** is an organized process in which people vote to choose a person or group of people to represent them in parliament, on a committee, etc, or to hold an official position such as president or chairman of a group. EG *Labour did badly in the election... Unemployment was a key issue during the last election campaign... I may vote for her at the next election.* ● See also **by-election, general election**. N COUNT/UNCOUNT ⇑ choice

2 The **election** of a particular person or group of people, their success in an election, as a result of which they gain political power or take up an official position in an organization. EG *...within two months of her election as Tory leader... ...his election to the chairmanship... ...after the election of Mr Heath's government in 1970.* N SING : USU WITH POSS ⇑ installation

electioneering /i¹lɛkʃə⁰nıər⁰ıŋ/ means the activities that politicians and their supporters carry out in order to persuade people to vote for them or for their political party in an election, for example making speeches and visiting voters in their homes. EG *He continued his electioneering tour.* N UNCOUNT ⇑ campaigning

elective /i¹lɛktıv/. An **elective** post, committee, etc is one to which people are appointed as a result of winning an election. EG *Blacks began to win elective offices, many of them becoming mayors.* ADJ CLASSIF ⇑ democratic

elector /i¹lɛktə/, **electors**. An **elector** is a person who has the right to vote in an election. EG *...the democratic right of electors to choose their own MP... ...a petition signed by 10,357 electors of Bristol South East.* N COUNT : USU PL = voter

electoral /i¹lɛktə⁰rəl/ means intended for an election, happening in an election, or resulting from an election. EG *...a contribution to their electoral funds... He helped lay the foundations of electoral success.* ◇ **electorally**. EG *Labour leaders believed it would be electorally popular.* ADJ CLASSIF : ATTRIB ◇ ADV

electoral register, electoral registers. An **electoral register** or **electoral roll** is an official list of all the people who have the right to vote in an election. EG *She has flatly refused to go on the electoral register in Ripon.* N COUNT : USU the+N

electorate /i¹lɛktə⁰rə¹t/, **electorates**. The **electorate** of a country or area is all the people in it who have the right to vote in an election. EG *The Government was responsible to the electorate as a whole... ...constituencies with small electorates.* N COUNT : USU SING, USU the+N

electric /i¹lɛktrık/. 1 An **electric** device or machine works by using electricity. EG *I switched on the electric fire... ...its grimy walls and naked electric light bulbs... ...an electric motor... ...an electric fan.* ADJ CLASSIF

2 An **electric** current, voltage, etc is one that is produced by electricity. EG *There was a powerful electric current running through the wires.* ADJ CLASSIF : ATTRIB

3 An **electric** plug, socket, etc is one that is designed to carry electricity. EG *Check light bulbs and electric plugs... The electric wiring is dangerous... ...fixed near a suitable electric socket.* ADJ CLASSIF : ATTRIB

4 If you describe the atmosphere as **electric**, you mean that people are in a state of great emotional excitement. EG *When she came on stage the atmosphere was already electric.* ADJ CLASSIF ⇑ tense = feverish

electrical /i¹lɛktrıkə⁰l/. 1 **Electrical** devices or machines work by using electricity. EG *...electrical appliances such as dishwashers and washing machines... ...electrical equipment.* ◇ **electrically**. EG *...electrically operated windows.* ADJ CLASSIF ◇ ADV

2 **Electrical** systems or components supply or use electricity. EG *The trouble is in the electrical system... ...electrical fittings... Each chip consisted of about ten electrical components.* ADJ CLASSIF : ATTRIB

3 **Electrical** energy is energy in the form of electricity. EG *Chemical energy in the battery is turned into electrical energy.* ◇ **electrically**. EG *The electrically charged layer in the upper atmosphere.* ADJ CLASSIF : ATTRIB ◇ ADV

4 **Electrical** industries, engineers, etc are involved in the production of electricity or electrical goods. EG *...the electrical and mechanical engineering industries.* ADJ CLASSIF : ATTRIB

electric blanket, electric blankets. An **electric blanket** is a blanket with wires inside it, which carry an electric current that keeps the blanket warm. N COUNT

electric-blue. Something that is **electric-blue** is very bright blue in colour. EG *...electric-blue dragonflies.* ▸ used as a noun. EG *The sofa set was in electric blue.* ADJ COLOUR ▸ N UNCOUNT

electric chair. The **electric chair** is a method of execution, used especially in the United States, in which a person being executed is strapped to a special chair and killed by a powerful electric current which is passed through his or her body. N SING : the+N ⇑ device

electrician /ılɛktrıʃə⁰n, i:lɛk-/, **electricians**. An **electrician** is a person whose job is to install and repair electrical equipment. N COUNT

electricity /ılɛktrısıti¹, i:lɛk-/. **Electricity** is 1 a form of energy that is used for heating and lighting, and to provide power for machines in houses and factories. EG *They generate the electricity in power stations... ... powered by electricity from a battery.* N UNCOUNT 2 the supply of electricity to homes and factories. EG *There were no telephones and no electricity... How can we reduce our electricity and gas bills?* N UNCOUNT

electric shock, electric shocks. An **electric shock** is a sudden painful feeling that you get when you touch something which is connected to a supply of electricity. Strong electric shocks can kill people. N COUNT ⇑ jolt

electrify /i¹lɛktrıfaı/, **electrifies, electrifying, electrified**. 1 An event that **electrifies** someone makes them feel very excited and surprised. EG *...the news that had electrified the world... ...electrified by these events, Rosa could not speak.* ◇ **electrifying**. EG *Kennedy had made an electrifying speech.* V+O ≠ bore ◇ ADJ QUALIT = exciting

2 A region of a country that **is electrified** is supplied with electricity. EG *Only 30 per cent of the villages are electrified...* ◇ **electrification** /i¹lɛktrıfıkeıʃə⁰n/. EG *Rural electrification has reached only about 5 per cent of the country.* V+O : USU PASS ⇑ supply ◇ N UNCOUNT

3 When a railway system or railway line **is electrified**, electric cables are put over the tracks, or electric rails beside them, so that the trains can be powered by electricity. EG *British Rail plans to electrify over 50 per cent of its network...* ◇ **electrification**. EG *...railways investing heavily in electrification.* V+O, OR V ⇑ adapt ◇ N UNCOUNT ⇑ adaptation

4 If someone **electrifies** a fence or other barrier, they connect it to a supply of electricity, so that a V+O ⇑ charge

person or animal that touches it will get an electric shock. ◇ **electrified.** EG *...electrified wire-netting.* ◇ ADJ CLASSIF

electro- is added to words to form other words that refer to electricity or to electrical processes. EG *chemical → electro-chemical... magnetic → electro-magnetic.* PREFIX

electrocute /i¹lɛktrə⁶kju:t/, **electrocutes, electrocuting, electrocuted.** 1 If you **electrocute** yourself or if you **are electrocuted**, you are accidentally killed or badly injured by touching something that is connected to a source of electricity. EG *Don't touch that wire, you'll electrocute yourself!... ...he fell and was electrocuted on the rails.* ◇ **electrocution** /i¹lɛktrə⁶kju:ʃə⁰n/. EG *They somehow managed to escape electrocution when they cut through the power cable...* V+O (REFL/NG) ⇑ be killed ◇ N UNCOUNT

2 If a criminal **is electrocuted**, he or she is executed by means of an electrical apparatus. ◇ **electrocution.** V+O ◇ N UNCOUNT

electrode /i¹lɛktrəʊd/, **electrodes.** An **electrode** is a small piece of metal or other substance that is used to take an electric current to or from a source of power, a piece of equipment, or a living body. EG *...a heating effect which flows from one electrode to another.* N COUNT ⇑ part

electrolysis /ɪlɛktrɒlɪsɪs, iːlɛk-/ is the process of passing an electric current through a substance in order to produce chemical changes in the substance; a technical term in physics. EG *...hydrogen generated from water by electrolysis.* N UNCOUNT

electrolyte /i¹lɛktrəlaɪt/, **electrolytes.** An **electrolyte** is a substance, usually a liquid, which electricity can pass through. EG *...batteries that functioned perfectly when a new electrolyte, copper sulphate, was added.* N COUNT

electromagnetic /i¹lɛktrəʊmægnɛtɪk/ is used to describe electrical and magnetic forces or effects. EG *X-rays are electromagnetic waves... ...energy in the form of electromagnetic radiation.* ADJ CLASSIF

electron /i¹lɛktrɒn/, **electrons.** An **electron** is a tiny particle of matter that is smaller than an atom and has a negative electrical charge; a technical term in physics. N COUNT

electronic /ɪlɛktrɒnɪk, iːlɛk-/, **electronics. Electronic** is an adjective and **electronics** is a noun. 1 An **electronic** device is one that has transistors, silicon chips, or valves which control and change the electric current passing through the device. EG *...the dramatic reduction in size and complexity of electronic components... ...electronic equipment.* ADJ CLASSIF

2 An **electronic** process or activity involves the use of electronic devices. EG *...constant electronic surveillance before boarding an airplane.* ◇ **electronically.** EG *Each vehicle might be electronically tracked.* ADJ CLASSIF : USU ATTRIB ◇ ADV

3 **Electronics** is 3.1 the technology of using transistors, silicon chips, or valves, especially in the manufacture of devices such as radios, televisions, and computers. EG *...modern developments in electronics... ...the British electronics industry.* 3.2 equipment that consists of electronic devices. EG *The boat carries a mass of sophisticated electronics.* N UNCOUNT ⇑ science; N PLURAL

electroplate /i¹lɛktrəʊ⁰pleɪt/, **electroplates, electroplating, electroplated.** To **electroplate** something means to put a layer of silver or other metal on it by dipping it in a special liquid through which an electric current is passed; a technical term. V+O ⇑ coat

elegance /ɛlɪgəns/. If a person or thing has **elegance**, it has a pleasing and graceful appearance, manner, or style. EG *...the elegance of classical ballet... The street had retained some of its old elegance.* N UNCOUNT ⇑ beauty ≠ clumsiness

elegant /ɛlɪgənt/. 1 Someone or something that is **elegant** is pleasing and graceful in appearance. EG *...the little church with its elegant square tower... ...an elegant dark suit... ...a tall, elegant woman.* ◇ **elegantly.** EG *Her umbrella is elegantly capped with a glass knob... ...an elegantly dressed woman.* ADJ QUALIT ⇑ beautiful = stylish, smart ◇ ADV = tastefully

2 An idea, statement, or plan that is **elegant** is simple, clear, and clever. EG *The plan was imaginative in conception and elegant in form... His proposal has an elegant simplicity.* ◇ **elegantly.** EG *...elegantly described in precise mathematical language.* ADJ QUALIT = refined ≠ clumsy ◇ ADV WITH VB ⇑ simply

elegiac /ɛlɪdʒaɪə³k/. Something that is **elegiac** expresses or shows sadness; a literary word. EG *His paintings are never reflective or elegiac... ...an elegiac mood.* ADJ CLASSIF ⇑ sad

elegy /ɛlɪdʒi¹/, **elegies.** An **elegy** is a sad poem, often about someone who has died. EG *...a romantic elegy on the fate of his mistress.* N COUNT = lament

element /ɛlə¹mə²nt/, **elements.** 1 An **element** of something is a single part which combines with others to make up a whole. EG *The different elements in the play are hard to balance properly... ...the basic elements of a job... ...analysis into component elements.* N COUNT+SUPP = constituent ≠ whole

2 A particular **element** of a situation, activity, or process is an important quality or feature that it has or needs. EG *Surprise would be an essential element in any such action... You must bring the human element into it... The time element was the catch.* N COUNT+SUPP = factor

3 The **elements** of a subject or activity are the first and most important things that you need to know about it. EG *He had troubles with the very elements of reading.* N PLURAL+SUPP ⇑ essentials = basics

4 Particular **elements** within a society or organization are groups of people who have similar aims, beliefs, or habits. EG *...sympathetic elements outside the party... ...the younger elements in the armed forces. ...a danger that the dynamic element in the community will go elsewhere.* N COUNT+SUPP : USU PL ⇑ group ≠ individual

5 If something has an **element** of a particular quality or emotion, it has a certain amount of this quality or emotion. EG *Nonetheless, it contains an element of truth... Perhaps there was some element of jealousy... ...to add an element of suspense and mystery to my novels.* N PART+N UNCOUNT

6 An **element** is 6.1 a substance that consists of only one type of atoms; a technical term in chemistry. For example, gold, oxygen, and carbon are all elements. EG *If hydrogen is removed from water, the element that remains is oxygen.* 6.2 a metal part in an electric fire, water heater, etc, which changes the electric current into heat. EG *You need a new element in the kettle.* N COUNT ≠ compound; N COUNT : USU SING

7 The **elements** are the weather conditions, especially when it is stormy weather. EG *...the minimum of shelter and protection against the elements... The elements were wild.* N PLURAL : *the*+N

8 If you are **in** your **element**, you are in a situation or doing something that you really enjoy and do well. If you are **out of** your **element**, you are in a situation or doing something that you do not enjoy or do not do very well. EG *She's really in her element now... He felt totally out of his element.* PHR : USED AS AN A

elemental /ɛlə¹mɛntə⁰l/. An **elemental** idea or feeling is one that is simple and basic but forceful; a fairly literary word. EG *...outbursts of elemental rage... ...the elemental underlying truth... ...an elemental aspect of his work.* ADJ QUALIT ≠ sophisticated

elementary /ɛlə¹mɛntə⁰ri¹/. Something that is **elementary** 1 is very simple and straightforward, involving only the most basic ideas or actions that are absolutely necessary for it to exist. EG *Most towns had taken some elementary precautions of a civil defence nature... ...elementary democracy.* 2 is of a simple standard, concerning the ideas, rules, or methods that you learn when you first begin to study a subject. EG *I did both elementary maths and additional maths at 'O' level... ...books at very elementary levels... He is less likely to make elementary errors.* ADJ QUALIT = initial; ADJ QUALIT ⇑ basic ≠ advanced

elementary school, elementary schools. In America, an **elementary school** is a school where children are taught for the first six or eight years of their education. N COUNT = primary school

elephant /ɛlɪfənt/, **elephants.** An **elephant** is a very large four-legged animal with a long, flexible nose called a trunk, which it uses to pick up things. An adult elephant has tusks of ivory at each side of its mouth. Elephants are found in India and Africa. ● See also **white elephant.** N COUNT

elephantine /ɛlɪfæntaɪn/. Something that is **elephantine** resembles or is suitable for an elephant, for example by being rather clumsy or by being very large and easy to see. EG *...an elephantine parody of the marriage service... He walked with a curious elephantine stealth.* ADJ CLASSIF : USU ATTRIB

elevate /ɛlɪveɪt/, **elevates, elevating, elevated.** 1 If you **elevate** someone or something to a particular status or position, you give them greater V+O+A *(to/into)* : NO IMPER importance or status than they really deserve. EG *Some people elevate football into a religion.*

2 To elevate **something** means to lift it up so that it is higher than the surrounding area. EG *Earth movements in the past elevated great areas of the seabed.*
V+O = raise ≠ lower

elevated /ɛlɪveɪtɪ2d/. 1 A person or a job or role that is **elevated** is very important or of very high rank. EG *It is in keeping with your elevated position in the profession.*
ADJ QUALIT : ATTRIB = exalted ≠ lowly

2 If thoughts or ideas are **elevated**, they are on a higher level morally or intellectually than that usual in ordinary life. EG *Let's discuss it on a slightly more elevated plane.*
ADJ QUALIT = lofty ≠ pedestrian

3 If land or buildings are **elevated** they are raised up higher than the surrounding area.
ADJ CLASSIF ≠ lowered

elevation /ɛli1veɪʃə0n/, **elevations**. 1 the **elevation** of someone or something is 1.1 the act of raising them to a position of greater importance or higher rank. EG *...the elevation of the standards of the average man... ...the elevation of man to divinity.*
N SING : *the*+N+*of*
1.2 the promotion of someone to an important position or job or to a particular rank in society. EG *His elevation to the peerage caused great surprise.*
N SING : WITH POSS, USU+*to* ≠ demotion

2 An **elevation** is 2.1 a piece of ground that is higher than the area around it. EG *I was on a slight elevation and could see the whole length of the gorge.*
N COUNT = hill ≠ dip
2.2 the front, back or side of a building, or a drawing of one of these; a technical term in architecture. EG *This drawing shows the front elevation.*
N COUNT+SUPP : USU SING

3 The **elevation** of a place is its height above sea level. EG *...a fairly flat plateau at an elevation of about a hundred feet.*
N COUNT : USU SING = altitude ≠ depth

elevator /ɛlə1veɪtə/, **elevators**. An **elevator** is 1 a lift that carries people up and down inside buildings; used especially in American English.
N COUNT
2 a machine used for lifting heavy objects and goods, for example in a warehouse.
N COUNT

eleven /ɪlɛvə0n/, **elevens**. 1 **Eleven** is the number 11: see ☐ at NUMBER, AGE, DATE, MEASUREMENT, MONEY, and TIME. EG *The flight had been postponed until eleven o'clock the next morning.*
NUM

2 An **eleven** is a team of eleven people in football, cricket, hockey, etc. EG *Richard's been picked for the first eleven.*
N COUNT : USU MOD+N

elevenses /ɪlɛvə0nzɪz/ is a light snack that you have in the middle of the morning, for example a cup of tea or coffee and biscuits; an informal word used in British English. EG *I went indoors to put on the kettle for our elevenses.*
N UNCOUNT

eleventh /i1lɛvə0nθ/, **elevenths**. 1 The **eleventh** item in a series is the one that you count as number eleven: see ☐ at NUMBER, AGE, and DATE. EG *...the eleventh floor of the building.*
ORDINAL

2 An **eleventh** is one of eleven equal parts of something.
N COUNT : USU+*of*

eleventh hour. The **eleventh hour** is the last possible moment before something happens. EG *I was asked, at the eleventh hour, to step in and direct the play... We are hoping for an eleventh-hour political settlement.*
N SING : *the*+N = last minute

elf /ɛlf/, **elves**. An **elf** is a small magical person in fairy stories who plays tricks on people.
N COUNT

elfin /ɛlfɪn/. 1 If you say that someone looks **elfin**, you mean that they have small, delicate features.
ADJ CLASSIF : ATTRIB

2 **Elfin** is also used to describe things that belong to elves or that are said to have been made by elves.
ADJ CLASSIF : ATTRIB

elicit /i1lɪsɪt/, **elicits, eliciting, elicited**. 1 If you **elicit** a response or a reaction, you cause it to happen by saying or doing something. EG *She went round the ward, talking to each woman in turn but eliciting little response from any of them... Threats to reinstate the tax elicited jeers in Brussels.*
V+O : IF+PREP THEN *from* ⇑ cause = provoke

2 If you **elicit** a piece of information, you find it out by asking careful questions; a formal use. EG *In five minutes she had elicited all the Herriard family history.*
V+O/REPORT-CL ⇑ discover = extract

elide /i1laɪd/, **elides, eliding, elided**. If you **elide** a part of a word, you do not pronounce it when you are speaking; a technical term in linguistics.
V+O

eligible /ɛlɪdʒə1bə0l/. 1 Someone who is **eligible** for something is qualified or suitable to take part in it, receive it, or be connected with it, for example because they are of the correct age. EG *You may even be eligible for a grant to help you study... Not all applicants are legally eligible to work in the United States.*
ADJ CLASSIF : IF+PREP THEN *for/to-INF*
◊ **eligibility** /ɛlɪdʒəbɪlɪti1/. EG *...the eligibility of applicants.*
◊ N UNCOUNT

2 An **eligible** man or woman is not yet married and considered to be a suitable partner. EG *...the deliciously eligible bachelor who was organizing the party.* ◊ **eligibility**.
ADJ QUALIT = marriageable
◊ N UNCOUNT

eliminate /i1lɪmɪneɪt/, **eliminates, eliminating, eliminated**; a fairly formal word. 1 To **eliminate** something means to remove it completely, especially when it is something that you do not want or need. EG *It is not safe to eliminate all fat and starches from the diet... ...a co-ordinated plan to eliminate illiteracy by 1980... Poverty must be eliminated.*
V+O = eradicate, cut out
◊ **elimination** /i1lɪmɪneɪʃə0n/. EG *Elimination of this squalor is the main object of socialist policies.*
◊ N UNCOUNT

2 If you **eliminate** something from a group or list, you remove it, usually because you have just learned that it is unsatisfactory in some way. EG *He continued testing hypotheses and eliminating them or confirming them...*
V+O = rule out ≠ include
◊ **elimination**. EG *It's a process of elimination... ...the elimination of spelling errors.*
◊ N UNCOUNT : IF+PREP THEN *of*

3 When a person or team **is eliminated** from a competition, they are defeated and so take no further part in the competition. EG *Four minor candidates were eliminated in the first round.*
V+O : USU PASS = knock out

3 To **eliminate** someone means to kill them in order to stop them causing problems; an informal use. EG *Out of six attempts to eliminate him, three were exposed immediately.*
V+O ⇑ kill = liquidate, assassinate
◊ **elimination**. EG *...the swift, quiet elimination of some sixty of their leaders.*
◊ N UNCOUNT : IF+PREP THEN *of*

elision /i1lɪʒə0n/ is the leaving out of the sound of some part of a word when it is spoken; a technical term in linguistics.
N UNCOUNT

elite /ɪ3li:t/, **elites**. 1 An **elite** is a group of the most powerful, rich, or talented people in a place or community. EG *...a small intellectual elite.*
N COUNT ≠ the masses

2 **Elite** people or organizations are considered to be the best of their kind. EG *...a small group of elite investment bankers... He's one of the few people who went through both the elite training establishments.*
ADJ CLASSIF : ATTRIB = top, select

elitism /ɪ3li:tɪzə0m/ is 1 the belief that a society or country should be ruled by a small group of people who are superior to everyone else. EG *This kind of elitism is even more marked in public schools.*
N UNCOUNT ≠ egalitarianism
2 a system of government in which a society or country is ruled by a small group of people who are considered to be superior to everyone else. EG *The elements of elitism in the present system are likely to remain.*
N UNCOUNT ≠ egalitarianism
3 the feeling of superiority someone has when they believe they are part of an elite. EG *...the elitism which almost inevitably insinuates itself in the minds of such people.*
N UNCOUNT ⇑ awareness

elitist /ɪ3li:tɪst/, **elitists**. 1 **Elitist** people, systems, or ideas practise or support elitism. EG *It had been a very elitist society... They have a very much more selective and elitist system at the top... ...elitist arguments...*
ADJ CLASSIF : USU ATTRIB ⇑ select ≠ egalitarian

2 An **elitist** is a person who believes that a society or country should be ruled by a small group of people who are superior to everyone else. EG *In some ways he's quite like you–an elitist.*
N COUNT ≠ egalitarian

elixir /ɪ2lɪksɪə/, **elixirs**. An **elixir** is 1 an imaginary liquid that is considered to have magical powers, for example to cure illness, keep people young, turn ordinary metals into gold, etc. EG *...their search to find the elixir of life.*
N COUNT : IF+PREP THEN *of*
2 an alcoholic drink; a humorous use. EG *Captain Imrie's own private elixir. For emergency use only.*
N COUNT : USU SING ⇑ alcohol

Elizabethan /ɪ2lɪzəbi:θə0n/. Something or someone that is **Elizabethan** happened, was made, or lived in England when Elizabeth the First was Queen, in the second half of the sixteenth century. EG *...the unique nature of Elizabethan painting.*
ADJ CLASSIF : USU ATTRIB

elk /ɛlk/, **elks**. **Elk** can also be used as the plural form. An **elk** is the largest type of deer, sometimes two metres high at the shoulder and with big, flattened antlers.
N COUNT = moose

ellipse /i1lɪps/, **ellipses**. An **ellipse** is an oval shape like a flattened circle.
N COUNT

ellipsis /ɪ2lɪpsɪs/, **ellipses** /ɪ2lɪpsi:z/. **Ellipsis** is the missing out of one or more words from a sentence when the sentence can be understood without them; a technical term in linguistics.
N UNCOUNT/COUNT ⇑ omission

elliptic /i1lɪptɪk/ means the same as elliptical.
ADJ CLASSIF

elliptical /ɪ2lɪptɪkə0l/. 1 Something that is **elliptical** has an oval shape like a flattened circle.
ADJ CLASSIF = elliptic
◊ **elliptically**.
◊ ADV WITH VB

2 Speech or writing that is **elliptical** is difficult to
ADJ QUALIT

understand, or easily misunderstood, because some words have been missed out. ◊ **elliptically**. ◊ ADV WITH VB

elm /ɛlm/, **elms**. An **elm** is a type of tall tree that has broad leaves which it loses in winter. ▸ **Elm** is also used to refer to the wood of the elm tree, which is hard and heavy. N COUNT/ UNCOUNT

elocution /ɛləkjuːʃə[0]n/ is the art of speaking clearly in public with a standard accent. EG *He taught elocution at a junior college.* N UNCOUNT ⇑ speech

elongate /iːlɒŋgeɪt/, **elongates, elongating, elongated**. If you **elongate** something or if it **elongates**, you stretch it so that it becomes longer; a formal word. EG *Rise up on your toes and elongate the complete length of your spine.* V-ERG ⇑ lengthen = stretch ≠ shorten

elongated /iːlɒŋgeɪtɪ[2]d/. Something that is **elongated** is very long and thin. EG *Their bodies are thin and elongated.* ADJ QUALIT ⇑ long ≠ squat

elongation /iːlɒŋgeɪʃə[0]n/, **elongations**. The **elongation** of something is the process of making it longer. EG *...the elongation of the circles into ellipses.* N UNCOUNT/ COUNT ⇑ lengthening ≠ contraction

elope /i[1]ləʊp/, **elopes, eloping, eloped**. When one person **elopes** with another or when two people **elope**, they go away secretly together in order to get married, usually without their parents' permission. EG *They eloped a month before Tom's graduation.* V OR V+A (*with*) : RECIP ⇑ run away

elopement /i[1]ləʊpmə[2]nt/, **elopements**. An **elopement** is an act of eloping. EG *He had read of her elopement while at Oxford.* N COUNT/ UNCOUNT

eloquence /ɛləkwəns/ is **1** the ability to speak and write well and in a convincing way. EG *He may have inherited his eloquence from his father, a Christian preacher.* N UNCOUNT = fluency **2** the art of speaking or writing well and in a convincing way. EG *But the eloquence and fluent imagery of that period never returned.* N UNCOUNT

eloquent /ɛləkwə[2]nt/. **1** Speech or writing that is **eloquent** is well expressed and effective in persuading people. EG *His stories were eloquent and funny... The speech was eloquent.* ◊ **eloquently**. EG *They spoke eloquently of their concern.* ADJ QUALIT ⇑ persuasive = expressive; ◊ ADV WITH VB

2 A person who is **eloquent** is good at speaking and able to persuade people; used showing approval. EG *He was tall, eloquent, and had noticeably fine manners.* ADJ QUALIT ⇑ persuasive

3 Behaviour that is **eloquent** shows feelings and reactions very clearly and obviously although nothing is spoken or written. EG *No one spoke but the faces were eloquent in their malevolent pleasure at my confusion.* ◊ **eloquently**. EG *She pushed eloquently at her untouched pastry.* ADJ QUALIT ⇑ expressive; ◊ ADV WITH VB

else /ɛls/. **1** You use **else** after words such as 'anywhere', 'someone', 'what', and 'little', to mean **1.1** other than this. EG *I don't like it here. Let's go somewhere else... I'm too tired. Somebody else will have to go... The experience of China was unlike anything else that had ever happened to me... I had nothing else to do... I always enjoy going to someone else's house.* ADJ : PRON/ADV +ADJ **1.2** more than this. EG *Stop her before she says anything else... Everyone else is downstairs... What else do you want to know?... Who else was there living in the house?... Her past medical history included hay-fever but little else.* ADJ : PRON/ADV +ADJ

2 You can say **'if nothing else'** to indicate that what you are mentioning is, in your opinion, the only good thing in a particular situation. EG *It was a fine publicity stunt if nothing else... If nothing else, we should have a good laugh.* PHR : USED AS ADV SEN = at least

3 You use **or else 3.1** when you want to mention the unpleasant effects or results of a particular action or event. EG *Either you stop drinking, or else the children and I will leave you... You've got to be very careful or else you'll miss the turn-off into our drive.* CONJ COORD = otherwise **3.2** to mention the second of two possibilities when you are not sure if the first possibility is true or not. EG *I think I was at school in Switzerland, or else I was staying with a school friend during the vacation... He's got some fierce hangover, or else he hasn't slept in a month.* CONJ COORD **3.3** in informal spoken English, to threaten someone when you are warning them not to do something. EG *Don't talk to me like that again, or else.* PHR : USED AT END OF SENTENCE AS ADV SEN

elsewhere /ɛlswɛə/means in or to another place or other places. EG *I will say good day to you and take the matter up elsewhere... This gesture is popular in Europe and elsewhere... Elsewhere in the tropics, rainfall is notoriously variable and unreliable... I shall go elsewhere.* ADV ≠ here

ELT /iː ɛl tiː/ is the abbreviation for 'English Language Teaching'. N UNCOUNT

elucidate /i[1]luːsɪdeɪt/, **elucidates, elucidating, elucidated**. If you **elucidate** something, you make it clear and understandable by explaining it fully, especially when it has not been understood before; a formal word. EG *...a lesson elucidating the points that have been made in the previous lecture.* ◊ **elucidation** /i[1]lj[0]uːsɪdeɪʃə[0]n/. EG *These are issues which deserve more thorough elucidation.* V+O ⇑ explain = clarify; ◊ N UNCOUNT ⇑ explanation

elude /i[1]luːd/, **eludes, eluding, eluded**; a formal word. **1** If a fact or idea **eludes** you, you do not succeed in understanding it, realizing it, or remembering it. EG *Yet new ideas may for ever elude them... The new subject matter eluded these artists.* V+O : NO PASS ⇑ escape = evade

2 If you **elude** someone or something, you avoid them or escape from them. EG *I had to learn how to elude him, outsmart him... I was hopelessly preoccupied with problems of eluding the police.* V+O = evade

elusive /i[1]luːsɪv/. Something or someone that is **elusive** is difficult to find, achieve, describe, or remember. EG *Their camouflage and nocturnal habits make long-eared owls elusive... Happiness is an elusive quality... Poppy seeds are slate grey in colour and have an elusive taste.* ◊ **elusively**. ◊ **elusiveness**. ADJ QUALIT; ◊ ADV; ◊ N UNCOUNT

elves /ɛlvz/ is the plural of **elf**.

em- is a form of **en-** that is used before b-, m-, and p-. EG *...bitter→embitter.* PREFIX

emaciated /i[1]meɪsɪeɪtɪ[2]d/. A person or animal that is **emaciated** is extremely thin and weak because of illness or lack of food. ADJ QUALIT = skeletal

emaciation /imeɪsɪeɪʃə[0]n/ is the state of being extremely thin and weak because of illness or lack of food. EG *They starved themselves into a state of emaciation.* N UNCOUNT ⇑ thinness

emanate /ɛməneɪt/, **emanates, emanating, emanated**. If a quality, idea, feeling, etc, **emanates** from you, or if you **emanate** such a quality, feeling, or idea, it comes from you or was originally started by you; a formal word. EG *These ideas are said to emanate from Henry Kissinger... He emanates concern... A dim glow of light still emanated from the room.* ◊ **emanation** /ɛməneɪʃə[0]n/. V+A (*from*), OR V+O ⇑ disseminate = radiate; ◊ N UNCOUNT

emancipate /i[1]mænsɪpeɪt/, **emancipates, emancipating, emancipated**. To **emancipate** someone means to free them from social, political, or legal restrictions that are considered to be degrading or unnecessary, or from having to do degrading work; a formal word. EG *Some housewives do not wish to be emancipated... ...a government determined to emancipate the poor.* ◊ **emancipation** /i[1]mænsɪpeɪʃən/. EG *Marx spoke of the emancipation of mankind.* V+O = liberate; ◊ N UNCOUNT : IF+PREP THEN *of*

emasculate /i[1]mæskjə[4]leɪt/, **emasculates, emasculating, emasculated**. If someone or something **is emasculated**, their strength or power is removed so that they become weak or ineffective. EG *...measures designed to emasculate worker militancy.* ◊ **emasculation** /i[1]mæskjə[4]leɪʃə[0]n/. V+O ⇑ weaken ≠ strengthen; ◊ N UNCOUNT

embalm /ɪ[2]mbɑːm/, **embalms, embalming, embalmed**. If a dead person **is embalmed**, various spices, oils, or chemicals are put on their body to preserve it and prevent it from decaying. EG *They embalmed his body and put it in a coffin.* V+O

embankment /ɛmbæŋkmə[2]nt/, **embankments**. An **embankment** is a thick wall or mound of earth that is built to carry a road or railway over an area of low ground, or to prevent water from a river or the sea from flooding the area. EG *The car ran up an embankment covered with grass... ...a railway embankment... ...Chelsea Embankment.* N COUNT : ALSO IN NAMES AFTER N

embargo /ɛmbɑːgəʊ/, **embargoes, embargoing, embargoed**. **1** An **embargo** is an order that is made by a government to stop trade with another country. EG *The states imposed an embargo on oil shipments... ...his decision to lift the grain embargo... They would not enforce a trade embargo with any member nations.* N COUNT : IF+ PREP THEN *on*

2 To **embargo** goods or transport means to officially prohibit them going to another country. EG *...embargoing arms sales to South Asia... They embargoed five more Sicilian ships carrying 6.6 million gallons of wine.* V+O = ban

embark /ɪ[2]mbɑːk/, **embarks, embarking, embarked**. When someone **embarks** on a ship, they go on board before the start of a voyage. EG *She had* V : USU+A ≠ disembark *embarked on the S.S. Gordon Castle at Tilbury...* ◊ **embarkation** /ɛmbaːkeɪʃəⁿn/. EG *They returned to their port of embarkation, Toulon.* ◊ N UNCOUNT

embark on. 1 If you **embark on** or **upon** something, especially something new, difficult, or exciting which may take a long time to finish, you start doing it. EG *Peru embarked on a massive programme of reform... ...the decision to embark upon a new translation of the Bible... ...embarking on his favourite story of the secret valley.* PHRASAL VB : V+PREP, HAS PASS = begin, undertake

2 If you **are embarked on** or **upon** a course of action, you have already started doing it. EG *We are already embarked on a course which will change our lives considerably.* PHRASAL VB : V+O+PREP : ONLY PASS

embarrass /ɪ²mbærəs/, **embarrasses, embarrassing, embarrassed.** 1 To **embarrass** someone means to make them feel shy, ashamed, or guilty about something. EG *He didn't want to talk either, which embarrassed her... It embarrasses me even to think about it... He had been highly embarrassed by this confession.* V+O

2 To **embarrass** a politician, political party, government, or other public group means to cause political problems for them. EG *The march could embarrass the government.* V+O ⇑ upset

embarrassed /ɪ²mbærəst/. A person who is **embarrassed** feels shy, ashamed or guilty about something. EG *I felt really embarrassed about it... She had been too embarrassed to ask her friends.* ▸ used of people's behaviour or actions. EG *'I'm sorry,' she added with an embarrassed laugh... They were met with embarrassed silence.* ADJ QUALIT : USU PRED ▸ ADJ QUALIT : ATTRIB ⇑ awkward = uncomfortable

embarrassing /ɪ²mbærəsɪŋ/. Something that is **embarrassing** makes you feel shy, ashamed, or guilty. EG *He said something that would be embarrassing for me to repeat... This put the Americans in an embarrassing position.* ◊ **embarrassingly.** EG *Their possessions were embarrassingly few.* ADJ QUALIT ◊ ADV

embarrassment /ɪ²mbærəsmə²nt/, **embarrassments.** 1 **Embarrassment** is a feeling of shyness, shame, or guilt. EG *His cheeks were hot with embarrassment... ...her embarrassment at having to visit me... He pulled off his cap and bowed gently, to my embarrassment and surprise.* N UNCOUNT : IF+PREP THEN *at/of* ⇑ emotion

2 An **embarrassment** is an action, event, or situation which causes problems for a politician, political party, government, or other public group. EG *For Labour, it was a political embarrassment.* N COUNT : USU+SUPP ⇑ problem

3 If you refer to a person as an **embarrassment**, you mean that you disapprove of them but cannot avoid your connection with them. EG *Unfortunately, he was an embarrassment to so many people.* N SING : *an*+N ≠ asset

4 **Embarrassment** is also a difficult situation that you are in because of lack of money. EG *He was suffering considerable financial embarrassment.* N UNCOUNT+SUPP ⇑ problem

embassy /ɛmbəsi¹/, **embassies.** An **embassy** is 1 a group of government officials, headed by an ambassador, who work in a foreign country and represent their government in that country. EG *She was attached to the Canadian embassy... ...a request by the Argentine Embassy.* 2 a building in which an ambassador and his or her officials work. EG *They went to a reception at the Soviet Embassy in Delhi.* N COUNT : ALSO IN NAMES AFTER N; N COUNT : ALSO IN NAMES AFTER N

embattled /ɪ²mbætəⁿld/. 1 An **embattled** area or country is one that is involved in fighting a war, especially when it is surrounded by its enemies. ADJ CLASSIF = beleaguered

2 A person, group, or organization that is **embattled** is having a lot of problems or difficulties. EG *...supporting an embattled Labour Government... The modern mother feels embattled.* ADJ CLASSIF ⇑ troubled = beset

embed /ɪ²mbɛd/, **embeds, embedding, embedded.** 1 If an object **is embedded** in a mass of surrounding substance, it is fixed there firmly and deeply. EG *He examined the locks; both were embedded in the woodwork... ...its rudder embedded in mud... ...several thorns embedded in his arms.* V+O : USU PASS+*in* ⇑ fix = stick

2 If something such as an attitude or feeling **is embedded** in a society or in someone's personality, it has become a permanent and noticeable feature of it. EG *...racist ideas which had become so deeply embedded. ...a deeply embedded feeling of guilt.* V+O : USU PASS ⇑ fix = root

embellish /ɪ²mbɛlɪʃ/, **embellishes, embellishing, embellished.** 1 If something **is embellished** with other things such as decorations, the decorations are added to it to make it more attractive. EG *Hampton Court was already embellished with masterly paintings... ...a dress embellished with tiny circular mirrors.* V+O : USU PASS+*with* ⇑ decorate = adorn

2 To **embellish** a story or account of something means to make it more interesting by adding details which are possibly untrue. ◊ **embellished.** EG *...embellished accounts of the day's events.* V+O = embroider ◊ ADJ QUALIT

embellishment /ɪ²mbɛlɪʃmə²nt/, **embellishments.** An **embellishment** is 1 a decoration added to something to make it seem more attractive. EG *...a flat surface that seemed to cry out for decorative embellishments... ...public tasks such as construction, artistic embellishment and maintenance of the city.* N COUNT/UNCOUNT ⇑ addition = frill

2 a detail added to a story or account of something to make it seem more interesting, even if it is not actually true. EG *...the exact truth without any exaggerations or embellishments... ...copying articles from other papers and repeating them with embellishments.* N COUNT ⇑ addition = frill

ember /ɛmbə/, **embers.** The **embers** of a fire are small pieces of partly burned coal, wood, etc that remain and glow with heat after the fire has finished burning. EG *I watched her stare into the embers of the fire...* N COUNT : USU PL ⇑ remains

embezzle /ɪ²mbɛzəⁿl/, **embezzles, embezzling, embezzled.** If someone **embezzles** money, they take or use it illegally for their own purposes, when it belongs to a company or organization that they work for. EG *For years he'd been embezzling very large sums of money from the company.* ◊ **embezzlement.** EG *...embezzlement by public officials.* V+O, OR V+A ⇑ steal = misappropriate ◊ N UNCOUNT

embitter /ɪ²mbɪtə/, **embitters, embittering, embittered.** If someone **is embittered**, they feel anger and despair because of the harsh, unpleasant, and unfair things that have happened to them. EG *Internment camps had done nothing to harden or embitter her.* ◊ **embittered.** EG *He appeared a profoundly disappointed and embittered man... People on the dole queue may become embittered and unemployable.* ◊ **embittering.** EG *...an embittering experience.* V+O : USU PASS ⇑ sadden = sour ◊ ADJ QUALIT = bitter ◊ ADJ QUALIT

emblazon /ɪ²mbleɪzəⁿn/, **emblazons, emblazoning, emblazoned.** If designs, words, or letters **are emblazoned** on something, they are clearly drawn, printed, or sewn on it. EG *...sweatshirts emblazoned with the name of their college... ...a flag on which the imperial double-headed eagle was emblazoned.* V+O : USU PASS+A *(on/with)* ⇑ decorate

emblem /ɛmblə²m/, **emblems.** An **emblem** is 1 a design or object that has been chosen as a symbol representing an organization such as a country, a sports club, or a business company. EG *There was a small golden emblem on his tie... The Bald Eagle remains the proud emblem of the USA.* 2 something that represents a quality or idea. EG *...an emblem of kingship... ...an emblem of some deep truth.* N COUNT : USU+SUPP = insignia; N COUNT+SUPP ⇑ symbol = mark

emblematic /ɛmbləmætɪk/. Something, such as an object in a painting, that is **emblematic** of something else, such as an abstract idea, stands for it or represents it. EG *...the emblematic function of this type of art... We began to replace our old things withnew items, emblematic of our new identification.* ADJ CLASSIF ⇑ representative

embodiment /ɪ²mbɒdi¹mə²nt/. A person, organization, or thing that is the **embodiment** of a quality or idea shows or expresses the quality or idea to a high degree. EG *She was the embodiment of loyalty... To the alchemists, gold was the embodiment of incorruptibility.* N SING WITH DET : USU+*of* ⇑ expression = epitome

embody /ɪ²mbɒdi¹/, **embodies, embodying, embodied.** 1 A person, organization, or thing that **embodies** an idea or quality contains and expresses it as an important feature in what they say or do. EG *These proposals were embodied in the Industrial Relations Act... ...the institutions which embody traditional values... They expect their leaders to embody their aspirations.* V+O ⇑ express = manifest

2 Something which **embodies** people or things includes them as part of its structure or organization. EG *The three corps embodied sixteen armoured brigades.* V+O ⇑ include

embolden /ɪ²mbəʊldəⁿn/, **emboldens, emboldening, emboldened.** If a fact or event **emboldens** someone, it increases their self-confidence so that they feel able to take some further action. ◊ **emboldened.** EG *Emboldened by this success, he* V+O : USU PASS ⇑ encourage ◊ ADJ QUALIT :

had begged a further favour... Thus emboldened, the President challenged the Democrats in Congress. PRED ⇑ encouraged = heartened

embolism /ɛmbəlɪzə⁰m/, **embolisms**. An **embolism** is a blockage in a vein or artery in the body of a person or animal, caused by a blood clot or air bubble; a technical term in medicine. EG *Although he had been partly paralysed by an air embolism, he had survived.* N COUNT : USU+SUPP

embossed /ɛmbɒst/. A design or group of letters or words that is **embossed** on something is added to it in such a way that it stands up or sticks out from the surface. EG *The words were embossed in gold at the base of the portrait... ...embossed chinaware and cutlery.* ADJ CLASSIF ⇑ raised

embrace /ɪ²mbreɪs/, **embraces, embracing, embraced**. 1 When you **embrace** someone or something, you put your arms around them and hold them tightly, usually in order to show your love or affection for them. EG *Before she could embrace him he stepped away... They laughed and embraced... We embraced each other.* ▸ used as a noun. EG *They greeted us with warm embraces... Sam and Eric, locked in an embrace, were fighting each other.* V OR V+O ▸ N COUNT = hug

2 If something **embraces** a group of people, things, or ideas, it includes them in a larger group or category. EG *It embraces elements of chemistry, physics, and engineering... ...the extended family, embracing several generations.* V+O ⇑ include

3 If you **embrace** a religion, political system, or idea, you start believing wholeheartedly in it. EG *She embraced the Catholic faith.* V+O ⇑ adopt ≠ renounce

embrasure /ɪ²mbreɪʒə/, **embrasures**. An **embrasure** is 1 an opening in a wall where a window or door is fixed, when it is wider on the inside than on the outside; a technical term in architecture. 2 an opening in the wall of a castle or other fortification, through which defenders could shoot at their enemies. N COUNT ⇑ hole; N COUNT

embrocation /ɛmbrə⁶keɪʃə⁰n/, **embrocations**. **Embrocation** is a liquid which is rubbed onto the body to reduce pain from aches or bruises. N MASS = liniment

embroider /ɪ²mbrɔɪdə/, **embroiders, embroidering, embroidered**. 1 If you **embroider** something such as a cloth or piece of clothing, you sew a decorative design onto it. EG *She embroidered it with figures of winged creatures...* ◇ **embroidered**. EG *...an embroidered shirt... ...a veil embroidered with red and blue flowers.* V OR V+O; ◇ ADJ QUALIT

2 If you **embroider** a story or account of something, or **embroider** on it, you try to make it more interesting by adding details to it from your imagination. EG *This mystery of the sea has been retold and embroidered... Ancient writers have embroidered on these early reports.* ◇ **embroidered**. EG *...a wildly distorted and embroidered version of an anecdote.* V+O, OR V+A (on) ⇑ add = embellish; ◇ ADJ QUALIT = embellished

embroidery /ɪ²mbrɔɪdə⁰ri¹/, **embroideries**. **Embroidery** is 1 cloth, clothing, or other material on which designs have been sewn. EG *She began folding up her embroidery.* 2 the act or process of sewing designs on cloth or other material. EG *...Jane's first attempts at embroidery.* N COUNT/UNCOUNT; N UNCOUNT

embroil /ɪ²mbrɔɪl/, **embroils, embroiling, embroiled**. If someone **is embroiled** in something, they have become deeply involved in it, so that it causes them many problems or difficulties. EG *They were deeply embroiled in a fiery discussion... It would be foolish to become embroiled in this struggle... This course would inevitably embroil the Party with the unions.* V+O : USU PASS, IF+PREP THEN in ⇑ involve = entangle

2 If someone **is embroiled** with another person, they are involved in a relationship with them that causes problems for them. EG *She got embroiled with some young man much younger than her.* V+O : USU PASS, IF+PREP THEN with = entangle

embryo /ɛmbrɪəʊ/, **embryos**. 1 An **embryo** is an unborn animal or human being in the very early stages of development, in humans up to the third month of pregnancy: compare **foetus**. EG *...the cell of a human embryo... ...snake embryos.* N COUNT ⇑ beginning

2 Something that is **in embryo** is at a very early stage of its development. EG *The electron microscope has been around, in embryo at any rate, for a long time.* PHR : USED AS AN A ⇑ rudimentary

3 The word **embryo** also means in a very early stage of development. EG *An embryo sand dune is formed... ...the survivors of the massacre who now staff the embryo government.* ADJ CLASSIF : ATTRIB

embryonic /ɛmbrɪɒnɪk/. Something that is **embryonic** is at a very early stage in its development; a formal word. EG *Embryonic peasant movements began to emerge.* ADJ CLASSIF : ATTRIB ⇑ rudimentary

emend /i¹mɛnd/, **emends, emending, emended**. To **emend** a piece of writing means to remove mistakes from it. ◇ **emendation** /iːmɛndeɪʃə⁰n/. V+O ⇑ improve; ◇ N UNCOUNT/COUNT

emerald /ɛmə⁰rəld/, **emeralds**. 1 An **emerald** is a precious stone which is clear and bright green. EG *...an emerald necklace.* N COUNT ⇑ gem

2 **Emerald** also means bright green in colour. EG *...glorious emerald silk.* ADJ COLOUR

emerge /i¹mɜːdʒ/, **emerges, emerging, emerged**. To **emerge** means 1 to come out from an enclosed space such as a room or vehicle or from a position where you could not be seen. EG *I saw the woman emerge from a shop... The chick becomes independent as soon as it emerges from its shell... A figure emerges from the crowd.* V : IF+PREP THEN from/out of

2 If you **emerge** from a particular state of mind or of existence, such as sleep, you change from one state to another, for example by waking from sleep. EG *He seemed to emerge from his reverie.* V+A (from) ⇑ wake

3 If you **emerge** from a difficult or unpleasant experience, you come to the end of it. EG *There was little chance of them emerging from imprisonment as better or wiser individuals.* V+A (from)

4 If a fact or result **emerges** from a period of thought, discussion or investigation, it becomes known as a result of it. EG *One really interesting thing emerged from this research... It emerged that she had been drinking.* V, V+REPORT-CL, OR V+A (from) = transpire

5 If something large and complex such as an industry or economic or political system **emerges**, it comes into existence over a long period of time. EG *Large-scale industry emerged only gradually as technology evolved.* V ⇑ develop = appear

emergence /ɪmɜːdʒəns/. The **emergence** of something is the process or event of its coming into existence. EG *...the emergence of new ideas.* N SING : USU the+N+of

emergency /i¹mɜːdʒənsi¹/, **emergencies**. 1 An **emergency** is an unexpected and difficult or dangerous situation, especially an accident, which arises suddenly and which requires quick action to deal with it. EG *The bells were only supposed to be used in emergencies... We have personnel and facilities for any emergencies...* ● **state of emergency**: see **state**. N COUNT = crisis

2 An **emergency** action is one that is done or arranged quickly and not in the normal way, because an emergency has occurred. EG *The plane made an emergency landing... They were holding emergency talks... ...emergency repairs.* ADJ CLASSIF : ATTRIB ⇑ unforeseen

3 **Emergency** equipment or supplies are those intended for use in an emergency. EG *...emergency supplies of food... ...an emergency exit.* ADJ CLASSIF : ATTRIB

emergency services. The **emergency services** are the organizations whose responsibility it is to take quick action to deal with emergencies when they occur, especially the fire brigade, the police, and the ambulance service. N PLURAL : USU the+N

emergent /i¹mɜːdʒənt/; a fairly formal word. 1 An **emergent** country is one that has recently become independent. EG *...the needs of underdeveloped and emergent countries.* 2 An **emergent** idea, political movement, social group, etc is one that is coming into existence and beginning to have a strong influence on people. EG *...an emergent industrial middle-class.* ADJ CLASSIF : ATTRIB ⇑ developing; ADJ CLASSIF : ATTRIB ⇑ developing = emerging

emeritus /i¹mɛrɪtəs/ is used with a professional title to indicate that the person bearing it has retired but keeps the title as an honour. EG *...Emeritus Professor of Anthropology... Their emeritus chairman is Father Basil Wrighton... ...the Professor Emeritus of Theology.* ADJ CLASSIF : ATTRIB, OR ADJ AFTER N : USU USED IN TITLES ⇑ honorary

emery /ɛməri¹/ is a hard grey metal, which is often ground to a powder that is stuck onto paper, cardboard, or cloth to make a tool for smoothing or polishing surfaces. N UNCOUNT ⇑ abrasive

emery board /ɛməri¹ bɔːd/, **emery boards**. An **emery board** is a long, narrow piece of wood or cardboard with a rough surface, which women use for smoothing and shaping their fingernails. N COUNT ⇑ file

emetic /ɪmɛtɪk/, **emetics**. 1 An **emetic** is something that is given to someone to swallow, in order to make them vomit. N COUNT

2 Something that is **emetic** makes you vomit. ADJ CLASSIF

emigrant /ɛmɪgrənt/, **emigrants**. An **emigrant** is a person who has left their own country to live in another country. N COUNT ≠ immigrant

emigrate /ɛmɪgreɪt/, **emigrates, emigrating, emigrated**. If you **emigrate**, you leave your native country to live in another country: compare **migrate**, **immigrate**. EG *He and his mother received permission to emigrate to Canada... He had emigrated from Germany in the early 1920's.* V: IF+PREP THEN *from/to* = move
◊ **emigration** /ɛmɪgreɪʃəⁿn/. EG *These people sought salvation in mass emigration... ...her emigration to France.* ◊ N UNCOUNT ⇑ journey

émigré /ɛmɪgreɪ/, **émigrés**. An **émigré** is someone who has left their country for political reasons; a formal or literary word. EG *...revolutionary émigrés from Russia.* N COUNT ⇑ emigrant

eminence /ɛmɪnəˀns/. **1 Eminence** is the quality of being very well-known and highly respected. EG *Jimmie was a man of some local eminence... ...a mathematician of eminence.* N UNCOUNT ⇑ repute = prominence
2 Your **Eminence** is the title of respect that you use when you are addressing a Roman Catholic cardinal. N COUNT: DETPOSS+N

eminent /ɛmɪnənt/. **1** An **eminent** person is well-known, important, and respected, especially because they are very good at their profession; used showing approval. EG *One of the most eminent scientists in Britain... The committee has 10 members, each eminent in his or her particular field.* ADJ QUALIT ⇑ famous = prominent, noted
2 In formal English, an eminent quality is one that is very great in degree or very noticeable. EG *You showed eminent good sense in coming to us.* ADJ QUALIT
◊ **eminently**. EG *Children are eminently practical... All you want is to go home and get a good night's sleep, which you eminently deserve.* ◊ ADV: USU+ADJ = strongly

emir /ɛmɪə/, emirs. An **emir** is a Muslim ruler, especially in South-West Asia and West Africa. N COUNT ⇑ leader

emirate /ɛmɪərɪˀt/, **emirates**. An **emirate** is a country that is ruled by an emir. N COUNT ⇑ land

emissary /ɛmɪsəⁿrɪ¹/, **emissaries**. An **emissary** is a person who is sent by a government or leader to another government or leader for a particular purpose, especially as a messenger; a formal word. EG *...the emissary of a vast revolutionary organization.* N COUNT = envoy

emission /ɪ¹mɪʃəⁿn/, **emissions**. An **emission** of something such as gas or radiation is the release of it into the atmosphere; a formal word. EG *The reduction in emissions of sulphur and nitrogen oxides is vital... ...emissions of mercury into the atmosphere.* N COUNT/UNCOUNT: USU+SUPP+A = discharge

emit /ɪ¹mɪt/, **emits, emitting, emitted**; a fairly formal word. **1** To **emit** a sound or noise means to produce it so that other people can hear it. EG *He was heard to emit heartbroken sighs... Some satellites send out signals almost continuously, others emit short bursts.* V+O = give out
2 If something emits heat, light, or a smell, it sends it out by means of a physical or chemical process. EG *The fireball emits a first heat wave lasting only a fraction of a second.* V+O ⇑ produce = give out
3 To **emit** something also means to release it from the place in which it is contained. EG *When a boil is lanced it emits pus... ...a machine which emitted cartons of orangeade when money was inserted.* V+O = discharge

emollient /ɪ¹mɒljənt/, **emollients**. An **emollient** is a liquid or cream which you put on your skin to soften it; a formal word. N MASS

emolument /ɪ¹mɒljəⁿməˀnt/, **emoluments**. An **emolument** is money or some other form of payment which a person receives for doing work; a formal word. EG *Emoluments earned by UK residents abroad may be taxed.* N COUNT: USU PL ⇑ income = wage

emotion /ɪ¹məʊʃəⁿn/, **emotions**. **1** An **emotion** is a feeling such as fear, love, hate, anger, or jealousy, which can be caused by the situation that you are in or the people you are with. EG *He began to feel a welcome new emotion: pride... Chopin aroused very complicated emotions in her... She looked around her room without emotion.* N UNCOUNT/COUNT
2 Emotion is the part of a person's character that consists of their feelings as opposed to their thoughts. EG *...the split between reason and emotion... How deeply intertwined were his emotion and his judgement.* N UNCOUNT ≠ reason

emotional /ɪ¹məʊʃəⁿnəl, ʃənəⁿl/. **1 Emotional** means concerned with your emotions and the way that you are feeling rather than with your physical health or condition. EG *There are obviously emotional problems too... ...intolerable emotional stress... Emotional states can affect our hormone levels.* ADJ CLASSIF: USU ATTRIB ⇑ mental = psychological ≠ physical
◊ **emotionally**. EG *He felt physically and emotionally exhausted... ...emotionally disturbed youngsters.* ◊ ADV
2 An **emotional** situation or issue is one that causes people to have strong feelings. EG *The disarmament issue became a tensely emotional one.* ADJ QUALIT = emotive
◊ **emotionally**. EG *...an emotionally charged atmosphere.* ◊ ADV
3 An **emotional** person or attitude is influenced by feelings rather than by rational thinking. EG *...their own emotional approach to life... I think the Welsh are a much more emotional people.* ADJ QUALIT ≠ rational
◊ **emotionally**. EG *Intellectually, I have no doubt he is right. Emotionally, I don't think he'll succeed.* ◊ ADV WITH VB, OR ADV SEN ≠ rationally
4 If someone is or becomes **emotional**, they show their feelings very openly, especially because they are upset. EG *He could be very emotional at such moments and would weep freely... Nell was far more emotional about it than he was.* ADJ QUALIT: USU PRED ⇑ demonstrative

emotive /ɪ¹məʊtɪv/. Something that is **emotive** is likely to make people feel strong emotions. EG *Destruction of the world's forests is now an emotive issue... Sir John was tough and used extremely emotive language.* ADJ QUALIT ⇑ evocative

empathize /ɛmpəθaɪz/, **empathizes, empathizing, empathized**; also spelled **empathise**. If you **empathize** with someone, you understand their situation, problems, and feelings, perhaps because the situation that they are in is one which you have been in yourself. EG *Josh had understood. At last he empathized with the woman's dilemma.* V: IF+PREP THEN *with* ⇑ feel

empathy /ɛmpəθi¹/ is the ability to share another person's feelings and emotions as if they were your own. EG *She could see our sadness, our empathy with the pain she was surely suffering... Lawrence had real sensitivity, real empathy.* N UNCOUNT ⇑ affinity = sympathy

emperor /ɛmpəⁿrə/, **emperors**. An **emperor** is a man who rules an empire or is the head of state in an empire. EG *The company was chartered by the Emperor of Austria in 1711.* N COUNT: ALSO IN TITLES, USU *the*+N ⇑ ruler

emphasis /ɛmfəsɪs/, **emphases** /ɛmfəsi:z/. **Emphasis** is **1** special or extra importance that is given to an activity, statement, event, or situation. EG *...a setting where the emphasis is on parental care... Too much emphasis is being placed on basic research.* N UNCOUNT/COUNT, IF+PREP THEN *on/upon* = stress
2 extra force that you put on a word or phrase when you are speaking in order to make it seem more important. EG *'Do you really want to study philosophy?' the professor asked, slowly and placing emphasis on each word.* N UNCOUNT/COUNT ⇑ stress

emphasize /ɛmfəsaɪz/, **emphasizes, emphasizing, emphasized**; also spelled **emphasise**. To **emphasize** something means to indicate strongly that it is particularly important or significant. EG *John went on to emphasise a point I'd already made... Mr Thompson was at pains to emphasize that he was threatening nobody... I keep emphasizing how dramatically things have changed.* V OR V+O/REPORT-CL ⇑ express = underline, stress

emphatic /ɪ²mfætɪk/. **1** An opinion or point that is **emphatic** is expressed very strongly, because the speaker thinks that it is important. EG *Their reply was too emphatic for anyone to doubt them... ...an emphatic and written refutation.* ADJ QUALIT ⇑ forceful ≠ hesitant
2 If you are **emphatic**, you use forceful language, showing that you believe that what you are saying is important. EG *But Wendy was emphatic. 'You must do it,' she said... Pat was emphatic about how valuable the course had been for her.* ADJ QUALIT: PRED = insistent
3 An **emphatic** way of speaking is one in which you speak slowly and carefully, adding extra stress to many words in order to make them sound more important. EG *My father read English verse with the emphatic stress of his own classical schooldays.* ADJ CLASSIF: ATTRIB ⇑ heavy = weighty

emphatically /ɛmfætɪkəⁿli¹/. **1** If you say something **emphatically**, you say it using forceful language, showing that you believe that what you are saying is important. EG *'That'll be the day,' said Foster emphatically... He emphatically defended the proposition that we could make further savings... I agree most emphatically.* ADV WITH VB ⇑ forcefully
2 Emphatically is used with descriptions to suggest that there can be no doubt about the truth of the description. EG *The sign is now used by protestors to signify something emphatically different... She is emphatically not a recluse.* ADV+ADJ/*not* ⇑ very = manifestly

empire /ɛmpaɪə/, **empires**. An **empire** is **1** a number of nations that are separate but that are all N COUNT

controlled by the government or ruler of one particular country. EG *...the ancient empires of Russia, Austria and Turkey.* **2** a group of companies, often controlled by one person, which have a wide influence over a particular area of activity. EG *His publishing empire was flourishing.*
N COUNT : USU MOD+N

empirical /ɪ^{2}mpɪrɪkə^{0}l/. **Empirical** knowledge, study, etc, relies on practical experience rather than theories. EG *...the empirical study of anatomy.*
ADJ CLASSIF : USU ATTRIB ≠ theoretical
◇ **empirically.** EG *The theory could be tested empirically.*
◇ ADV WITH VB, OR ADV SEN

empiricism /ɛmpɪrɪsɪzə^{0}m/ is the belief that people should rely on practical experience rather than theories as a basis for knowledge and in order to deal with problems; a term in philosophy.
N UNCOUNT ⇑ practicality
◇ **empiricist, empiricists.** EG *He would have defined himself as an empiricist.*
◇ N COUNT

emplacement /ɪ^{2}mpleɪsmə^{2}nt/, **emplacements.** An **emplacement** is a specially prepared position, usually strong and fortified, from which a heavy gun can be fired; a technical military word. EG *...massive gun emplacements on top of the cliffs.*
N COUNT : USU AFTER N

employ /ɪ^{2}mplɔɪ/, **employs, employing, employed.** **1** If you **employ** someone, you pay them to work for you. EG *The factory employed a total of forty workers... There are still more people employed in textiles than in computers... He was employed as a research assistant.*
V+O, OR V+O+A (as) : USU PASS

2 If you are **in** someone's **employ**, you work for them; a formal expression. EG *The company has 450,000 workers in its employ.*
PHR : USED AS AN A

3 To **employ** something for a particular purpose means to use it in order to do something or achieve something. EG *If nuclear weapons are employed the world will be destroyed... You will need to employ a great deal of tact and diplomacy.*
V+O, OR V+O+A (as)

4 If you say that someone would **be better employed** doing something else, you mean that they should spend their time doing something that is more useful and necessary than what they are doing at the moment. EG *You would be better employed tidying your room!*
PHR+-ING/CONJ (if)

employable /ɪ^{2}mplɔɪəbə^{0}l/. Something or someone that is **employable** is capable of being employed or used in a job. EG *...She has no employable skills.*
ADJ CLASSIF ≠ unemployable

employee /ɛmplɔɪiː, ɪ^{2}mplɔɪiː/, **employees.** An **employee** is a person who is paid to work for an organization or for another person. EG *...an employee of the state... ...a BBC employee.*
N COUNT ⇑ worker ≠ employer

employer /ɪ^{2}mplɔɪə/, **employers.** An **employer** is a person who has other people working for him or her, or a company that people work for. EG *Some employers are reluctant to take on new workers... She was in trouble with her employer.*
N COUNT ≠ employee

employment /ɪ^{2}mplɔɪmə^{2}nt/ is **1** work that you do in order to earn money. EG *Village crafts used to provide a good deal of employment... He had retired from regular employment.*
N UNCOUNT ≠ unemployment
2 the fact or condition of employing people. EG *They called for the employment of members of minority groups... ...better conditions of pay and employment.*
N UNCOUNT
3 the availability of jobs for the population of a town, area, or country. EG *They were asking for guarantees of full employment and wages.*
N UNCOUNT ≠ unemployment

employment agency, employment agencies. An **employment agency** is an organization that earns money by helping people to find work.
N COUNT

emporium /ɛmpɔːrɪəm/, **emporiums** or **emporia.** An **emporium** is a large shop that sells a lot of different things; an old-fashioned or formal word.
N COUNT = department store

empower /ɪ^{2}mpaʊə/, **empowers, empowering, empowered.** If someone is **empowered** to do something, they have the legal authority or power to do it; a formal word. EG *The Act of 1936 empowered the police to ban political processions... His assistant will be empowered to act on his behalf in less weighty matters.*
V+O+*to*-INF : USU PASS ⇑ authorize

empress /ɛmprɪ^{2}s/, **empresses.** An **empress** is a woman who rules an empire; also used to refer to the wife of an emperor. EG *...the Empress Elizabeth of Russia.*
N COUNT : ALSO IN TITLES, USU *the*+N

emptiness /ɛmp^{0}ti^{1}nɪ^{2}s/. **1** A feeling of **emptiness** is an unhappy or frightening feeling that nothing is worthwhile, especially one which arises because you are very tired or have just experienced something upsetting. EG *This way of life can lead only to self-destruction and emotional emptiness... You are left with this sort of numb emptiness.*
N UNCOUNT

2 Emptiness is the state of affairs when an area or space has nothing in it. EG *...the Galapagos Islands isolated in the emptiness of the Pacific.*
N UNCOUNT

3 An **emptiness** is a very large area of land, sea, or space that has nothing in it; a literary use. EG *I felt very alone and very small suddenly in this great emptiness.*
N COUNT : USU SING

empty /ɛmp^{0}ti^1/, **emptier, emptiest; empties, emptying, emptied.** **1** A place or vehicle that is **empty** has no people or things in it. EG *The room was empty... We drove along apparently empty streets... As far as the eye could see the desert was empty.*
ADJ QUALIT ≠ full

2 A container that is **empty** no longer has anything in it. EG *She dropped two empty Coca-Cola bottles into a wastebasket... He noticed that Meadows' glass was empty... She took the envelope, now empty of money, and laid it on the table.* ▸ used as a noun, usually referring to bottles. EG *She put the empties in the dustbin.*
ADJ CLASSIF : IF+PREP THEN *of* ≠ full
▸ N COUNT : USU PL

3 If someone's hands are **empty,** they are not holding or carrying anything.
ADJ CLASSIF ≠ full

4 A gesture, threat, or relationship that is **empty** has no real value, meaning, or effectiveness. EG *They ignored his threats as empty rhetoric... ...an empty and foolish gesture... Their marriage has been empty for years.*
ADJ QUALIT ⇑ meaningless = barren

5 If you describe a person's life or a period of time as **empty,** you mean that it has nothing interesting or important in it. EG *His life was empty and meaningless... How shall I exist during the empty days ahead?*
ADJ QUALIT ⇑ lacking = dreary

6 If you feel **empty,** you feel unhappy and have no energy, usually because you are very tired or have just experienced something upsetting. EG *He felt empty and beaten.*
ADJ QUALIT : PRED = numb

7 If you **empty** a container, you remove the contents from it, especially by taking, pouring, or tipping them out. EG *She picks up an ashtray and empties it into a wastepaper basket... The he emptied the gun of bullets... Empty his pockets, Rudi...*
V+O : USU+A ≠ fill

8 If you **empty** a substance or object out of a container, you remove it from the container. EG *You ought to empty the water out of those boots... Two men carrying a wooden keg emptied its contents into the opening.*
V+O+A

9 A speech, debate, or performance that **empties** a place causes the audience to leave in large numbers, especially because they are very bored. EG *The average debate on this subject was still guaranteed to empty the House of Commons.*
V+O = clear ≠ fill

10 If a room or container **empties,** everything or everyone that is in it goes out of it. EG *The play was over and the auditorium began to empty... ...problems about half-full baths emptying at such and such a rate.*
V : IF+PREP THEN *of* ≠ fill

11 A river that **empties** into a lake or sea flows into it. EG *I wondered where the Hwang Pu emptied into the mighty Yangtze.*
V+A *(into)* ⇑ flow

empty-handed. If you come back from somewhere **empty-handed,** you have failed to get what you hoped to get or were expected to get. EG *You wouldn't want us to come back empty-handed, would you?... He walked back to the filling-station empty-handed.*
ADJ CLASSIF : USU PRED ⇑ unsuccessful

empty-headed. If you say that someone is **empty-headed,** you mean that they do not think sensibly and often do silly or stupid things. EG *He was putting on an act to impress an empty-headed girl.*
ADJ QUALIT = feather-brained

Empyrean /ɛmpɪ^{5}riːən/. The **Empyrean** is the sky; a literary word. EG *...soaring up into the Empyrean.*
N SING : *the*+N

emu /iːmjuː/, **emus.** An **emu** is a large Australian bird with long legs. Emus can run fast, but cannot fly.
N COUNT

emulate /ɛmjə^{4}leɪt/, **emulates, emulating, emulated.** If you **emulate** something or someone, you imitate them because you admire them very much; a formal word. EG *He is forever trying to emulate people like Howard Hawks... ...a management system that has been envied and emulated worldwide.*
V+O = copy
◇ **emulation** /ɛmjə^{4}leɪʃə^{0}n/. EG *...the unconscious emulation of social fashions.*
◇ N UNCOUNT ⇑ imitation

emulsifier /ɪ^{1}mʌlsɪfaɪə/, **emulsifiers.** An **emulsifier** is a substance used in food manufacturing which helps to combine liquids of different thicknesses. EG *...food additives such as thickeners, flavour enhancers, emulsifiers, colourings, to name a few.*
N COUNT

emulsify /ɪ'mʌlsɪfaɪ/, **emulsifies, emulsifying, emulsified.** When two liquids of different thicknesses **emulsify** or when something **emulsifies** them, they combine; a technical term in the food industry. V-ERG ⇑ mix

emulsion /ɪ'mʌlʃəⁿn/, **emulsions, emulsioning, emulsioned. 1 Emulsion** is a substance that is used to make photographic film sensitive to light; a technical term in photography. EG *There was a fault in the photographic emulsion.* N UNCOUNT/COUNT ⇑ coating
2 Emulsion or **emulsion paint** is a water-based paint, which is not shiny when it dries. It is used for painting walls and ceilings. EG *...dark brown carved wood set against white emulsion.* N UNCOUNT ⇑ paint
3 If you **emulsion** something, you paint it with emulsion paint. EG *...an ordinary, flat emulsioned wall.* V+O

en- is **1** added to adjectives or nouns that refer to human states or conditions, to form verbs that describe putting someone into one of these states or conditions. EG *...rich→enrich... feeble→enfeeble.* PREFIX **2** added to nouns that refer to places or things, to form verbs that describe putting someone or something into or onto one of these places or things. EG *...cage→encage... tomb→entomb... throne→enthrone.* PREFIX

enable /ɪ'neɪbəⁿl/, **enables, enabling, enabled.**
1 If someone or something **enables** you to do something, they give you the opportunity to do it. EG *Contraception enables women to plan their families... Such safety systems would probably have enabled the pilot to land without mishap... This would enable me to go to Canada.* V+O+to-INF = allow ≠ prevent
2 To **enable** someone to do something also means to give them permission or the right to do it. EG *...to enable former peers to sit in the Commons if elected.* ◊ **enabling.** EG *Clearly some enabling legislation is called for.* V+O+to-INF = allow ≠ forbid ◊ ADJ CLASSIF : ATTRIB
3 To **enable** something to happen means to make it possible for it to happen. EG *The shell has to be slightly porous to enable oxygen to pass in.* V+O+to-INF = allow ≠ prevent

enact /ɪ'nækt/, **enacts, enacting, enacted. 1** When a government or authority **enacts** a law or bill, they officially pass it, so that it becomes legal; a technical term in law and politics. EG *The Tories are trying to enact a 'nationality' bill... Many states have enacted battered-child laws.* V+O ≠ rescind
2 f people **enact** a story or play, they perform it by acting. EG *They enacted tales of feudal princes and magic birds.* V+O = act out

enactment /ɪ'næktməⁿnt/, **enactments. 1** The **enactment** of a law is The process in a parliament or legislative assembly by which it is agreed upon and made official. EG *They succeeded in forcing the Bill's acceptance and immediate enactment.* N UNCOUNT/COUNT ⇑ passing
2 The **enactment** of a play, story, or character is the performance of it by an actor or group of actors. EG *...his dramatic enactment of Marcus's plight.* N UNCOUNT

enamel /ɪ'næməⁿl/, **enamels, enamelling, enamelled**; also spelled **enameling** and **enameled** in American English. **1 Enamel** is **1.1** a substance like glass which can be heated and put onto metal, glass or pottery in order to decorate or protect it. EG *...coloured enamel bowls from Yugoslavia... ...an ashtray made of blue enamel.* N UNCOUNT **1.2** a hard, shiny paint that is used especially for painting metal and wood. EG *...a small unopened can of red enamel.* N UNCOUNT **1.3** the hard white substance that forms the outer part of a tooth. EG *I chipped the enamel on my front tooth when I fell over.* N UNCOUNT ⇑ coating
2 If you **enamel** something, you decorate it or cover it with enamel. ◊ **enamelled.** EG *...a line of enamelled blue pennants.* V+O ◊ ADJ CLASSIF : ATTRIB

enamoured /ɪ'næməd/; also spelled **enamored** in American English. **1** If you are **enamoured** of something, you are very impressed by it and like it very much. EG *I was, of course, always enamoured of the theatre.* ADJ QUALIT : PRED, USU+of = keen on
2 If you are **enamoured** of a person, you are in love with them. EG *He became enamoured of a sixteen-year-old girl in New York.* ADJ QUALIT : PRED, USU+of

encamp /ɪ'ŋ'kæmp/, **encamps, encamping, encamped.** When people **encamp**, they set up their camp; a formal word. EG *His tribe had encamped for the summer up at the quarry... The army was encamped outside the walls.* V : USU+A = camp

encampment /ɪ'ŋ'kæmpməⁿnt/, **encampments.** An **encampment** is a group of tents or other shelters put together in one place, for example by soldiers or gypsies. EG *We made our way down to the encampment below.* N COUNT = camp

encapsulate /ɪ'ŋ'kæpsjə'leɪt/, **encapsulates, encapsulating, encapsulated.** If something **encapsulates** certain facts, ideas, etc, it represents all the most important aspects of those facts or ideas in a very small space or in a single object or event. EG *...an edict of 1503 which encapsulates the history of the continent... There's always a lot more than can be encapsulated in a questionnaire.* V+O ⇑ contain = encompass

encase /ɪ'ŋ'keɪs/, **encases, encasing, encased.** When a container or covering **encases** something, it holds or keeps the thing completely inside it. EG *Lynn glanced at the felt boots that encased Posy's feet... The crab is encased in bone.* V+O : IF PASS THEN+A (in) ⇑ cover

enchant /ɪ'ntʃɑːnt/, **enchants, enchanting, enchanted. 1** If someone or something **enchants** you, they fill you with a feeling of great delight. EG *Her charisma managed to enchant the audience.* ◊ **enchanted.** EG *Both her listeners were quite enchanted... Morris Zapp was less than enchanted with his view.* V+O ◊ ADJ QUALIT = thrilled
2 To **enchant** someone or something also means to put a magic spell on them, especially in fairy stories. ◊ **enchanted.** EG *...an enchanted island.* V+O ◊ ADJ CLASSIF

enchanter /ɪ'ntʃɑːntə/, **enchanters.** An **enchanter** is a person who uses magic to put spells on people and things in fairy stories. N COUNT = sorcerer

enchanting /ɪ'ntʃɑːntɪŋ/ means attractive, delightful, and charming in appearance or behaviour. EG *...the most enchanting smile... He could be very enchanting but also rather forbidding.* ◊ **enchantingly.** EG *She was enchantingly pretty, too pretty perhaps.* ADJ QUALIT ⇑ pleasant ◊ ADV : USU+ADJ

enchantment /ɪ'ntʃɑːntment/, **enchantments. 1 Enchantment** is the feeling of great delight that something very beautiful or mysterious gives you. EG *Those woods where he played as a boy still retained for him a secret, subtle enchantment.* N UNCOUNT = magic
2 An **enchantment** is a magic spell, for example in fairy stories. N COUNT

enchantress /ɪ'ntʃɑːntrɪs/, **enchantresses.** An **enchantress** is **1** a woman who men find extremely attractive and fascinating. EG *...dark enchantresses in black lace.* N COUNT **2** in fairy stories, a woman who uses magic to put spells on people and things. N COUNT = witch

encircle /ɪ'nsɜːkəⁿl/, **encircles, encircling, encircled.** To **encircle** someone or something means to completely surround or enclose them. EG *David walked into the room, encircled by guards... Access to the area was provided by the M5 and M6 motorways, which encircle Birmingham... 'Not now,' she said, encircling me with her arms.* V+O

enclave /ɛŋ'kleɪv/, **enclaves.** An **enclave** is a place or area that is surrounded by areas which are completely different in some important way, for example because they are inhabited by people of a different nationality or a different culture. EG *...the original population was now reduced to a tiny handful of islands and enclaves... ...a city with an enclave of posh shops and a ring of poorer suburbs.* N COUNT : USU+SUPP

enclose /ɪ'ŋ'kləʊz/, **encloses, enclosing, enclosed. 1** To **enclose** an object or an area means to surround it with something solid so that it is separate from everything that is outside. EG *The fence that enclosed the house was painted white... This parcel was enclosed in something clear and shiny.* ◊ **enclosed.** EG *The reaction takes place extremely rapidly within an enclosed space.* V+O : IF+PREP THEN in/with = contain ◊ ADJ CLASSIF = confined
2 If you **enclose** something with a letter, you put it in the same envelope. EG *I enclose a small cheque... Write to them enclosing a stamped addressed envelope.* ◊ **enclosed.** EG *Many thanks for your letter and the enclosed leaflet, which looks quite interesting.* V+O : IF+PREP THEN in/with ⇑ insert ◊ ADJ CLASSIF

enclosed /ɪ'ŋ'kləʊzd/. An **enclosed** community, existence, etc, is kept separate from the normal and typical activities of the outside world. EG *Growing up at Charleston wasn't a particularly enclosed existence for Quentin... They lived in an enclosed community.* ADJ QUALIT : USU ATTRIB ⇑ separated = sheltered

enclosure /ɪ'ŋ'kləʊʒə/, **enclosures.** An **enclosure** is **1** an area of land that is surrounded by a wall or fence and that is used for a particular purpose. EG *...the public enclosure of a racecourse... We were led to a fenced enclosure.* N COUNT **2** something that is put in the N COUNT same envelope as a letter. EG *The letter said there was an enclosure, but they obviously forgot to put it in.*

encode /ɪ²ŋ'kəʊd/, **encodes, encoding, encoded**. If you **encode** a message or some information, you put it into a code. EG *Messages can be encoded for greater security.* — V+O = code ≠ decode

encompass /ɪ²ŋ'kʌmpəs/, **encompasses, encompassing, encompass**. 1 If someone or their activity **encompasses** certain things, they have a wide range that includes all those things. EG *She actually encompasses themes such as Judaism in her last novel... ...a policy which encompasses all aspects of conservation... New York's public education system encompasses nearly 900 schools.* — V+O ⇑ include = cover

2 If something **encompasses** an area of land, it completely covers or surrounds it. EG *...a landscape encompassing perhaps 200 square miles... ...the European world empires which, between them, encompassed the earth.* — V+O ⇑ cover

encore /ɒŋkɔː/, **encores, encoring, encored**. 1 An **encore** is a short extra performance at the end of a longer one, which an entertainer gives because the audience asks for it. EG *What shall I sing as an encore?* — N COUNT

2 To **encore** someone means to ask them to perform an encore. EG *We were encored five times.* — V+O = call back

3 **Encore** is the word shouted by an audience when they want a performer to perform an encore. — CONVENTION = more

encounter /ɪ²ŋ'kaʊntə/, **encounters, encountering, encountered**. 1 If you **encounter** someone who you do not know or do not know very well, you meet them, especially when it is unexpected and unplanned; a formal use. EG *At the beginning of their journey they encounter an English couple.* — V+O : NO CONT = run into

2 If you **encounter** problems or difficulties, you experience them. EG *One still encounters general resistance to this idea... They've never encountered any discrimination.* — V+O = meet with

3 To **encounter** something means to meet or experience it, often for the first time. EG *Evolution could proceed as organisms encountered new environments... ...remote native tribes that had never previously encountered white men.* — V+O

4 An **encounter** is 4.1 a casual or unexpected meeting. EG *We've just had a very strange encounter with a civil servant!* — N COUNT : IF+PREP THEN *with* 4.2 a difficult or dangerous meeting. EG *I don't propose to describe that encounter; it was too painful... He beamed his way through a series of frosty encounters with his leading opponents.* — N COUNT : IF+PREP THEN *with/between* 4.3 a particular type of experience. EG *...sexual encounters... ...encounters with new ideas.* — N COUNT : IF+PREP THEN *with*

encourage /ɪ²ŋ'kʌrɪdʒ/, **encourages, encouraging, encouraged**. 1 If you **encourage** someone, 1.1 you tell them that what they are doing is good and that they should continue to do it. EG *He seemed to like me and encouraged me.* — V+O, OR V+O+*to*-INF 1.2 you give them the courage or confidence to do something. EG *Her husband encouraged her to get a car... Her success encouraged me to try the same thing.* — V+O+*to*-INF, OR V+O = prompt ≠ dissuade ◊ **encouraged**. EG *Jack felt encouraged.* — ◊ ADJ QUALIT = emboldened

2 If someone or something **encourages** a particular activity, 2.1 they support it actively and help it to happen. EG *Group meetings in the factory were always encouraged... Attendance every day was encouraged.* — V+O : USU PASS ⇑ approve 2.2 they stimulate it and cause it to increase. EG *Could the Scarman Report encourage racism?... This encouraged the growth of Marxism.* — V+O

encouragement /ɪ²ŋ'kʌrɪdʒmə²nt/. If someone gives you **encouragement**, they tell you that what you are doing is good and that you should continue to do it. EG *All I need is some encouragement!* — N UNCOUNT ⇑ support

encouraging /ɪ²ŋ'kʌrɪdʒɪŋ/. Something that is **encouraging** gives hope, courage, or confidence to someone. EG *I don't find what you've just said very encouraging.* — ADJ QUALIT ⇑ hopeful = promising ◊ **encouragingly**. EG *She spoke encouragingly about the company's sales figures.* — ◊ ADV WITH VB

encroach /ɪ²ŋ'krəʊtʃ/, **encroaches, encroaching, encroached**. 1 To **encroach** on or upon something means to slowly take possession or control of it, so that someone else loses it bit by bit. EG *This new law doesn't encroach on the rights of the citizen.* — V : USU+A (*on/upon*) ⇑ trespass = intrude

2 If something **encroaches** on or upon land, it gradually moves over it or covers more and more of it. EG *The steppe was encroached upon by the advancing wild wheat.* — V : USU+A (*on/upon*) ⇑ move

encroachment /ɪ²ŋ'krəʊtʃmə²nt/, **encroachments**. An **encroachment** is an act of taking all or part of something away from someone or something. EG *...encroachments of civil liberties... ...an encroachment on their property.* — N COUNT/UNCOUNT : IF+PREP THEN *on/of/upon* ⇑ violation

encrustation /ɪ²ŋ'krʌsteɪʃə⁰n/, **encrustations**. An **encrustation** is 1 a layer that has built up on a surface during the course of a very long period of time. EG *...encrustations of moss.* — N UNCOUNT 2 a layer of jewels, gold, silver, etc, that is decorating something. EG *...the waist-length plumes, the encrustations of gold lace.* — N UNCOUNT/COUNT : IF+PREP THEN *of*

encrusted /ɪ²ŋ'krʌstɪ²d/. If a surface is **encrusted** with something, it has a layer or crust of that thing on it. EG *At that time, the whole continent was encrusted with ice... These things are gold and silver, and most of them are encrusted with jewels... I gazed out at the snow-encrusted landscape.* — ADJ QUALIT : IF+PREP THEN *with* ⇑ cover

encumber /ɪ²ŋ'kʌmbə/, **encumbers, encumbering, encumbered**. If something **encumbers** you, it prevents you from moving or doing what you want easily and freely. EG *I was so encumbered with clothes I just couldn't run... The soldiers were encumbered with women and children.* — V+O : USU PASS+A (*with*) ⇑ prevent = burden

encumbrance /ɪ²ŋ'kʌmbrəns/, **encumbrances**. An **encumbrance** is something or someone that encumbers you. EG *If he overstayed his welcome he would become a hated encumbrance.* — N COUNT = burden

encyclical /ɛnsɪklɪkə⁰l/, **encyclicals**. An **encyclical** is an official letter written by the Pope and sent to all Roman Catholic bishops, usually in order to make a statement about the official teachings of the Church. — N COUNT

encyclopedia /ɛnsaɪklə⁶piːdɪə/, **encyclopedias**; also spelled **encyclopaedia**. An **encyclopedia** is a book or set of books in which facts about many different subjects or about one particular subject are arranged for reference, usually in alphabetical order. EG *They made us read whole pages of the encyclopedia... ...the last volume of the encyclopedia.* — N COUNT

encyclopedic /ɛnsaɪklə⁶piːdɪk/; also spelled **encyclopaedic**. If something is described as **encyclopedic**, it is very full, complete, and thorough in the amount of knowledge or information that it has. EG *She knew her subject with encyclopedic thoroughness.* — ADJ QUALIT ⇑ comprehensive = exhaustive

end /ɛnd/, **ends, ending, ended**. 1 The **end** of a period of time, an event, or an experience is the last part of it or the final point in it.. EG *...at the end of August... ...one afternoon near the end of my stay... We will leave that till the end.* — N SING : *the*+N, USU WITH POSS = close ≠ beginning

2 An **end** to something or the **end** of it is the act or result of stopping it so that it does not continue any longer. EG *...an immediate end to all armed attacks... They were advised to try and bring the sit-in to an end... That was the end of the matter.* — N COUNT : USU SING, IF+PREP THEN *to/of* ⇑ stop = close

3 An **end** is 3.1 one of the two extreme points of something long and narrow. EG *...sharpen a stick at both ends... The table was set for six, two at each side and one at each end... Ellen and Hooper were sitting at opposite ends of the couch... ...a door at the other end of the room.* — N COUNT+SUPP ⇑ extremity 3.2 the point on something long and narrow that is farthest away from you or from the point where it is attached to something else. EG *The end of its tail quivered... The gas dried her hair up and frizzled the ends.* — N COUNT : IF+PREP THEN *of* ⇑ extremity = tip 3.3 the part of something that is left after the rest has been used or destroyed, especially something that is long and narrow in shape. EG *...cigarette ends... ...the unburnt ends of branches.* — N COUNT : USU+SUPP = remains

4 The **end** of a book, film, speech, etc, is the last part of it. EG *I wept at the end of the book... She read the first draft from beginning to end.* — N COUNT, OR *to*+N = conclusion ≠ beginning

5 The other **end** is one of two places that are connected because people are communicating with each other by telephone or writing, or are travelling from one place to the other. EG *The phone at the other end rang... There was an awkward interval of silence at both ends. Then he wrote to me again.* — N COUNT+SUPP

6 A particular **end** of an activity or relationship is a particular part, aspect, or area of it. EG *I'm surprised at how well John keeps up his end of the conversation... Chris took care of the day-to-day running of the company and I looked after the business end.* — N COUNT+SUPP ⇑ part

7 An **end** is also the purpose for which something is done or towards which you are working. EG *...their use of industrial power for political ends... To that* — N COUNT : USU MOD+N

end the committee is trying to develop a formula which will be acceptable to all concerned. ● If you consider something to be **an end in itself**, you do it because it seems desirable and not because it is likely to achieve anything lasting or useful. EG *He regarded violence as an end in itself.* ● PHR : USED AS C

8 End is also used to refer to either of the two extreme points of a scale or of something that you are considering as a scale or a line. EG *...at the other end of the social scale... There is support at both ends of the political spectrum in many countries.* N COUNT+SUPP

9 A person's **end** is their death, especially when referring to the way that they die; a literary use. EG *He did not deserve such a cruel end.* N COUNT : USU SING

10 When a situation or period of time **ends**, it stops and continues no longer. EG *The current agreement ends on November 24... He took her out a couple of times before term ended... The day ended in uncertainty and gloom.* V : USU+A ⇑ stop = finish ≠ begin

11 When someone **ends** an activity, they cause it to stop and prevent it from continuing any longer. EG *He refused to end his nine-week-old hunger strike... That ended the discussion.* V+O = terminate ≠ start ◊ **ending**. EG *...the ending of all manufacture and testing of nuclear weapons.* ◊ N SING : *the*+N

12 If a situation or event **ends** in a particular way, it has that particular result. EG *...a desperate initiative which ended in failure... A row broke out which ended with Colley's being shot... Where will it all end?* V+A

13 When a speech, piece of writing, activity, etc **ends** or when someone **ends** it, it stops in a particular way. EG *The play ends with all the children playing and reciting... She ended a polemical article with the sentence, 'Art corrupts.'... Jaykar ended on a dry laugh. Her telegram ended 'Please return immediately'.* V OR V-ERG+A *(with/on)*/QUOTE ⇑ finish = conclude ≠ begin

14 An object that **ends** with or in something has a particular thing on its tip or point, or as its last part. EG *Each finger ends with a sharp claw, not a flat blunt nail.* V+A *(with/in)* ⇑ finish = terminate

15 A journey, road, river, etc, that **ends** at a particular place stops there and goes no further. EG *They watched the harbor where their journeys had ended... The trail ends one mile from Bakewell.* V : USU+A ⇑ stop ≠ begin

16 If you say that something **ends** at a particular point, you mean that it is true or exists up to that point, and no further. EG *It was quite impossible to know where the truth ended and falsehood began.* V+A ⇑ be = stop ≠ begin

17 The word **end** is also used in the following expressions. **17.1** You say **at the end of the day** when you are talking about what happens after a long series of events or what appears to be the case after you have considered the relevant facts; an informal expression. EG *The question at the end of the day is whether the house is actually worth that amount.* PHR : USED AS AN A ⇑ finally = ultimately

17.2 If something is **at an end**, it is finished and will not continue. EG *The service was nearly at an end.* PHR : USED AS AN A

17.3 If you say that something **is the end**, you are expressing how impatient or annoyed you are with a situation, person or thing; an informal expression used in British English. EG *This is the end... He's the absolute end.* PHR : VB INFLECTS = be the limit **17.4** If you do something **to the bitter end** or **to the very end**, you do it for as long and to as great an extent as you possibly can, especially when you find this unpleasant. EG *We have always pursued everything to the bitter end.* PHR : USED AS AN A **17.5** If something **comes to an end**, it stops. EG *And here the story comes to an end.* PHR : VB INFLECTS **17.6** If someone **ends it all**, they commit suicide. EG *She obviously wasn't interested in him, and he had decided to end it all.* PHR : VB INFLECTS **17.7 To the end of time** means for ever. EG *I will love you to the end of time.* PHR : USED AS AN A **17.8** If you consider something to be **the end of the world**, it is something that seems really terrible and that you find very upsetting. EG *Well that's not the end of the world.* PHR : USED AS C, USU WITH BROAD NEG = calamity **17.9 In the end** means finally, after a considerable time, and often as a result of the previous situation. EG *She went back to England, I believe, in the end... They kept on raising the price and in the end he got thirty thousand for it.* PHR : USED AS AN A = eventually **17.10** If you **keep** or **hold** your **end up**, you show bravery and competence in dealing with a difficult or frightening situation. EG *Once there, he felt he should keep his end up and never be frightened of speaking for himself.* PHR : VB INFLECTS ≠ chicken out **17.11** If you **make ends meet**, you are able to manage financially because you have just enough money for your needs. EG *Many were finding it difficult to make ends meet, especially those with young children.* PHR : VB INFLECTS **17.12 No end** means a lot; an informal expression. EG *She had no end of trouble at school... It upset me no end.* PHR : USED AS N PART OR AS AN A = a great deal

18 On end. 18.1 Something that is **on end** is upright, instead of in its normal or natural position, for example lying down, flat, or on its longest side. EG *He asked them to stand an egg on end.* PHR : USED AS AN A ≠ prone **18.2** When something happens for days or weeks **on end**, it happens continuously and without stopping for the amount of time that is mentioned or specified. EG *I don't see anybody for weeks on end.* PHR : USED AS AN A ⇑ consecutively = at a time

19 The word **end** is also used in the following expressions, which are explained at other places in the dictionary. ● to **burn the candle at both ends**: see **candle**. ● **in at the deep end**: see **deep.** ● **to go off the deep end**: see **deep.** ● to **make** your **hair stand on end**: see **hair.** ● **a means to an end**: see **mean.** ● to **be on the receiving end**: see **receive.** ● the **end of the road**: see **road.** ● to **get the wrong end of the stick**: see **stick.** ● **at the end of** your **tether**: see **tether.** ● the **thin end of the wedge**: see **wedge.** ● to be at your **wits' end**: see **wit.** ● See also **dead end, ending, loose end, never-ending,** and **odds and ends.**.

end up. 1 If you **end up** somewhere, you eventually arrive there, even though you did not originally intend to go there. EG *Many of their friends and neighbours have ended up in prison for terrorist activities.* PHRASAL VB : V+ADV+A = wind up **2** If you **end up** doing something or **end up** in a particular state, you do it or get to that state even though you did not originally intend to. EG *We ended up taking a taxi there... If we go on in this way, we shall end up with millions and millions of unemployed.* PHRASAL VB : V+ADV+A/-ING = finish up

endanger /ɪ²ndeɪndʒə/, **endangers, endangering, endangered.** If you **endanger** something, you cause it to be in a dangerous situation where it might be destroyed or damaged. EG *They claimed the herbicides did not endanger human life... The security of the country was not endangered.* V+O ⇑ risk = jeopardize ≠ secure ◊ **endangered.** EG *He's always argued that the whale is an endangered species.* ◊ ADJ QUALIT

endear /ɪ²ndɪə/, **endears, endearing, endeared.** If something **endears** you to someone or if you **endear** yourself to them, you become popular with them and well liked or loved by them. EG *Needless to say, this sort of talk did not endear him to Mr Nixon... The King did not endear himself to the ministers.* V+O (NG/REFL) +A *(to)*

endearing /ɪ²ndɪərɪŋ/. If a person or their behaviour is **endearing**, it causes you to feel very fond of them. EG *...a slightly foolish but wonderfully endearing smile.* ADJ QUALIT ⇑ likeable = appealing ◊ **endearingly.** EG *...endearingly childish behaviour.* ◊ ADV : USU+ADJ

endearment /ɪ²ndɪəmə²nt/, **endearments.** An **endearment** is a loving or affectionate word or phrase that you say to someone you love. EG *He held me close to him, murmuring endearments... ...terms of endearment.* N COUNT/UNCOUNT

endeavour /ɪ²ndɛvə/, **endeavours, endeavouring, endeavoured**; also spelled **endeavor** in American English. **Endeavour** is a formal word. **1** If you **endeavour** to do something, you try very hard to do it. EG *He endeavoured to adopt a positive but realistic attitude... We do endeavour to assess any case on its merits.* V+*to*-INF = strive

2 An **endeavour** is an attempt to do a particular thing, especially something new or original. EG *...the history of scientific endeavours... We must wish ourselves good fortune in our endeavours.* N COUNT = effort

3 Endeavour is hard work and effort in attempting to do things, especially new or original things. EG *...this exciting new field of endeavour. ...our pride in human endeavour and success.* N UNCOUNT ⇑ effort

endemic /ɛndɛmɪk/. A condition or illness that is **endemic** in a particular place is found naturally or commonly among the people there; a formal word. EG *Until the 1940's, malaria was endemic in Ceylon... ...Africa's endemic poverty... Violent class conflict is endemic in our society.* ADJ CLASSIF : IF+PREP THEN *in/to* ⇑ common = prevalent

ending /ɛndɪŋ/, **endings.** An **ending** is **1** the last part of a book, story, play, or film; used especially when you are considering the way that the story ends. EG *The best kind of story is the one with a happy ending.* N COUNT = conclusion **2** the last part of a word. EG *...words that had the same ending, such as 'wanted', 'wor-* N COUNT ≠ beginning *ried', and 'killed'.* 3 the tip or end of something, such as a nerve. EG *...nerve endings.* N COUNT+SUPP

endive /ɛndaɪv/, **endives**. 1 An **endive** is a plant with crisp, curly leaves that are eaten in salads. N COUNT/UNCOUNT

2 **Endive** is chicory; used in American English. N UNCOUNT

endless /ɛndlɪ²s/. 1 If something is **endless**, it seems as if you will never reach the end of it because it is very large or lasts for a very long time. EG *They spend their time in an endless search for food... Mr Starke would ask endless repetitive questions... ...the perfect, languorous, endless hot summer that we all dream of.* ◇ **endlessly**. EG *In Bombay, every citizen seems endlessly on the move... She used to nag me endlessly about the family's money.* ADJ CLASSIF : USU ATTRIB ↑ unlimited = interminable ◇ ADV WITH VB ↑ continually = perpetually

2 An area of land that is **endless** is very large and has few changes in its appearance, vegetation, etc. EG *...an endless sandy waste... The forest is an endless woven carpet of dense, dark green.* ADJ CLASSIF : USU ATTRIB = continuous

endocrine /ɛndə⁶krɪ⁵n/ refers to the system of glands that secrete hormones directly into the bloodstream, such as the pituitary or thyroid glands; a technical term in medicine. ADJ CLASSIF : ATTRIB

endorse /ɪ²ndɔːs/, **endorses, endorsing, endorsed**. 1 If you **endorse** someone or something, you say publicly that you support or approve of them. EG *The Germans and Italians endorsed the plan... Delegates will be invited to endorse unilateral nuclear disarmament.* V+O = back

2 If someone's driving licence **is endorsed**, an official record is made on it that they have been found guilty of a driving offence. EG *He was ordered to pay a fine of £200 and his licence was endorsed.* V+O : USU PASS ↑ mark

3 When you **endorse** a document, you write a note or comment on it. EG *If you want a receipt the account should be sent intact, endorsed 'receipt required.'* V+O ↑ mark

4 When you **endorse** a cheque, you write your name on the back of it so that it can be paid into someone else's bank account. V+O

endorsement /ɪ²ndɔːsmə²nt/, **endorsements**. 1 An **endorsement** is 1.1 a formal or public statement that you support or approve of something or someone. EG *The Pope has issued his fullest endorsement ever of the Solidarity trade union movement.* N COUNT/UNCOUNT : IF+PREP THEN *of* 1.2 a note on someone's driving licence saying that they have been found guilty of a driving offence. EG *He's already got three endorsements.* N COUNT/UNCOUNT : IF+PREP THEN *of*

2 If you make an **endorsement** of a document or cheque, you write a note on the document or write your name on the back of the cheque. N COUNT/UNCOUNT : IF+PREP THEN *of* ↑ writing

endow /ɪ²ndaʊ/, **endows, endowing, endowed**. 1 If someone or something **is endowed** with particular qualities, abilities, or characteristics that are considered to be good or remarkable, they have them or are given them. EG *Nature has endowed the Cobra Lily with the means of catching its own food... Eugene O'Neill had been endowed with Clark Gable looks.* V+O : USU+A *(with)*, USU PASS ↑ give = bless

2 If someone **endows** a person or institution, they give them a large amount of money so that they can receive a certain annual income or pay for a project, building, etc. EG *He personally endowed a ward in Manhattan General Hospital... It was a richly endowed school.* V+O ↑ support

endowment /ɪ²ndaʊmə²nt/, **endowments**. 1 An **endowment** is a gift of money that is made to an institution such as a school or hospital in order to provide it with an annual income. EG *Every penny of our endowment is spent on equipment.* N COUNT ↑ provision = settlement

2 If someone has an **endowment** of a particular quality or ability, they possess it as a natural quality or ability; used in formal English. EG *She had, moreover, a reasonable endowment of intelligence.* N COUNT = portion

endowment policy, endowment policies. An **endowment policy** is an insurance policy which will give you a sum of money after a certain number of years. EG *This policy offers life-time cover with flexibility to convert to an endowment policy.* N COUNT

end product, end products; also spelled with a hyphen. An **end product** is something that is produced or achieved by means of a particular activity or process. EG *It's a tough course with a fairly tough exam, so that the end-product is a really worthwhile qualification.* N COUNT, USU SING

end result, end results; also spelled with a hyphen. The **end result** of a process or activity is the final outcome produced by it. EG *This sense of one's own worth is the end result of years of loving, sensitive care.* N COUNT : USU SING ↑ outcome = culmination

endurance /ɪ²ndj⁰ʊərəns/ is the ability to experience an unpleasant or painful situation for a period of time calmly and patiently. EG *They admired the troops for their courage and endurance... The practice of law was boring me beyond endurance... ...a test of human endurance.* N UNCOUNT = stamina, patience

endure /ɪ²ndj⁰ʊə/, **endures, enduring, endured**. 1 If you **endure** a painful or difficult situation, you bear it calmly and patiently. EG *You must be ready to endure hardships and even death... Sam could hardly endure this delay... It was more than I could endure.* V+O ↑ experience = face

2 If something **endures**, it continues to exist without any loss in quality or importance. EG *Certain kinds of relationships endure longer than others... ...a city which will endure for ever.* ◇ **enduring**. EG *...one of Hollywood's most enduring and respected actors... ...hopes for an enduring peace.* V ↑ last = survive ◇ ADJ QUALIT : USU ATTRIB = lasting

endways /ɛndweɪz/. Something that is **endways** to something else is placed at right angles to it. EG *The cottage is built endways to the road.* ADV WITH VB

enema /ɛnɪmə/, **enemas**. An **enema** is a liquid which is put into a person's rectum in order to empty their bowels, for example before an operation is performed. N COUNT

enemy /ɛnəmi¹/, **enemies**. 1 If someone is your **enemy**, 1.1 they hate you or want to harm you. EG *I have many enemies... He didn't have an enemy in the world... These creatures have no natural enemies.* N COUNT = foe ≠ friend 1.2 they are opposed to you and to what you think or do. EG *He is one of the most formidable enemies of the regime... ...an enemy of society.* N COUNT : IF+PREP THEN *of* ↑ opponent ≠ friend

2 The **enemy** is an army or other force that is opposed to you in a war, or a country with which your country is at war. EG *After a fierce battle the enemy had been forced back a thousand yards... ...enemy aircraft.* N COUNT, OR N SING : *the*+N = foe ≠ ally

energetic /ɛnədʒɛtɪk/. 1 Someone or something that is **energetic** has or shows a lot of enthusiasm and determination to succeed. EG *He is an energetic campaigner in the cause of road safety... ...an energetic programme of applied research.* ◇ **energetically**. EG *This right is not merely questioned but energetically denied.* ADJ QUALIT ↑ enthusiastic = lively ≠ apathetic ◇ ADV WITH VB ↑ strongly

2 An **energetic** activity involves a lot of physical movement and power. EG *Do something energetic, play golf, swim, or ski.* ◇ **energetically**. EG *...acrobats energetically tumbling across the stage.* ADJ QUALIT = active ◇ ADV WITH VB ↑ vigorously

energize /ɛnədʒaɪz/, **energizes, energizing, energized**; also spelled **energise**. If something **energizes** you, it gives you the enthusiasm and determination to do something. EG *...a sparkling friendliness which had a curious energizing effect on Tom.* V+O ↑ encourage

energy /ɛnədʒi¹/, **energies**. 1 **Energy** is 1.1 the ability and strength to do active physical things and the feeling that you are full of physical power and life. EG *You must eat to give you energy... It was several seconds before I could muster the energy to get up and switch the machine off... This sequence combines the elegance of classical ballet with the energy of modern dance.* N UNCOUNT 1.2 the determination and enthusiasm to achieve something and the belief that you will succeed; used showing approval. EG *Michael praised Tony's diligence, energy and imagination... ...a woman of energy and ambition.* N UNCOUNT ↑ strength

2 Your **energies** are the amount of effort and attention that you have available to use in order to achieve something. EG *Men like Muhammed Abdu poured their energies into religious reform... You would be wiser to direct your emotional energies into social rather than amorous activities.* N COUNT : POSS+N, SING = PL ↑ capability = efforts

3 **Energy** is also the power from electricity, coal, wind, etc that makes machines work. EG *Wood is an efficient source of energy... ...the energy crisis... ...Britain's current nuclear energy programme.* N UNCOUNT

enervated /ɛnəveɪtɪ²d/. If you feel **enervated**, you feel that you have lost your strength and liveliness. EG *I leaned back, already enervated.* ADJ QUALIT ↑ tired = drained

enervating /ɛnəveɪtɪŋ/ If you feel that something is **enervating**, you feel that it takes away your strength and liveliness. EG *...a particularly enervating day.* ADJ QUALIT ↑ tiring = draining

enfant terrible /ɑːfɑː terɪbl/, **enfants terribles**. An **enfant terrible** is a clever but unconven- N COUNT ↑ prodigy tional person whose unusual behaviour or ideas cause anger or embarrassment among their friends or colleagues; a literary term. EG *Jacques Derrida was an enfant terrible of the French intelligentsia.*

enfeebled /ɪ²nfiːbə⁰ld/. Someone or something that is **enfeebled** has become very weak. EG *...enfeebled through age... ...an enfeebled state of mind... ...an enfeebled economy.* — ADJ QUALIT = weakened ≠ strengthened

enfold /ɪ²nfəʊld/, **enfolds, enfolding, enfolded**; a formal word. 1 If you **enfold** someone or something, you hold them close in a very gentle, loving way. EG *Their arms reached out to enfold him.* — V+O : IF+PREP THEN *in* = embrace

2 Something that **enfolds** something else covers it or is wrapped around it. EG *...this darkness that continually enfolds me.* — V+O : IF+PREP THEN *in* ⇑ surround = cloak

enforce /ɪ²nfɔːs/, **enforces, enforcing, enforced**. 1 If people in a position of authority **enforce** a law or a rule, they make sure that it is obeyed, usually by punishing people who do not obey it. EG *...the government's inability to apply and enforce its own laws and regulations.* — V+O ⇑ implement

2 If you **enforce** a particular condition, you force it to be done or to happen without anyone having an opportunity to avoid or prevent it. EG *Our belief was that workers had a right to enforce a closed shop.* — V+O : IF+PREP THEN *on* ⇑ force

◊ **enforced**. EG *...a life of enforced inactivity.* — ◊ ADJ CLASSIF

enforceable /ɪ²nfɔːsəbə⁰l/. Something that is **enforceable** can be enforced. EG *...a civil contract enforceable by law.* — ADJ CLASSIF : IF+PREP THEN *by*

enforcement /ɪ²nfɔːsmə²nt/. If someone carries out an **enforcement** of an act or rule, they enforce it. EG *...the enforcement of discipline.* — N UNCOUNT : IF+PREP THEN *of*

enfranchise /ɪ²nfræntʃaɪz/, **enfranchises, enfranchising, enfranchised**. To **enfranchise** someone means to give them the right to vote in elections; a formal word. EG *...the reform Acts of 1884 and 1918 enfranchised working men and women.* — V+O ⇑ entitle

enfranchisement /ɛnfræntʃaɪzmə²nt/ is the condition of someone being enfranchised; a formal word. EG *...the enfranchisement of the masses.* — N UNCOUNT

engage /ɪ²ŋ¹geɪdʒ/, **engages, engaging, engaged**; a fairly formal word. 1 If you **engage** in an activity, you do it or are involved in doing it. EG *It was considered inappropriate for a former President to engage in commerce... The work we're engaged on is a study of heat transfer.* — V+A *(in/on/upon)*

2 If something **engages** you or your attention or interest, it keeps you interested in it and thinking about it. EG *Boredom has a chance to develop if the child's interest is not engaged... ...a social policy which engages the hearts and minds of men.* — V+O ⇑ attract = capture

3 If you **engage** someone **in conversation**, you have a conversation with them. EG *This allowed him to engage the woman in further conversation.* — PHR : VB INFLECTS ⇑ talk = involve

4 If you **engage** someone to do a particular job, you appoint them to do it. EG *No continental opera would engage an English singer... The only alternative left to us is to engage the services of an outsider.* — V+O, OR V+O+A *(as)* ⇑ employ = hire

5 When a part of a machine or other mechanism **engages** or when you **engage** something in a machine or other mechanism, it moves into a position where two or more parts fit together. EG *Press the lever until you hear the magazine catch engage.* — V-ERG : ALSO V OR V+A *(with)* : RECIP

6 If a military force **engages** the enemy, it attacks them and starts a battle. EG *...forces waiting to engage the US strike fleet.* — V OR V+O : RECIP ⇑ attack

7 See also **engaged, engaging**.

engaged /ɪ²ŋ¹geɪdʒd/. 1 When two people are **engaged**, they have agreed to marry each other. EG *A week later, Tony became engaged to Caroline... They were not officially engaged.* — ADJ CLASSIF : IF+PREP THEN *to* ⇑ promised

2 If a telephone or telephone line is **engaged**, it is already being used by someone else so that you are unable to get through. EG *Receptionists' telephones are always engaged... 'Is there any answer?'-'It's engaged.'* — ADJ CLASSIF : USU PRED = busy

3 If a public toilet is **engaged**, it is already being used by someone else. — ADJ CLASSIF : PRED

engagement /ɪ²ŋ¹geɪdʒmə²nt/, **engagements**. An **engagement** is 1 an arrangement that you have made to do something at a particular time; used in formal English. EG *Mr Baverstock is regretfully unable to accept your invitation. He pleads a prior engagement... I keep my engagement book in my office.* — N COUNT = appointment 2 an arrangement that has been made for an actor, musician, or other performer to perform somewhere on a particular occasion. EG *This part in Romeo and Juliet was Ellen's last professional engagement in London... His lecture bureau had booked seventy-odd engagements for him.* — N COUNT = booking 3 an agreement that two people have made with each other to get married. EG *All that remained was to announce their engagement and fix the date of the wedding.* ▸ used to refer to the period of time during which two people are engaged before they get married. EG *...a letter which she wrote to Harold during their engagement.* — N COUNT : USU SING, USU POSS+N ⇑ time 4 a battle with an enemy. EG *There are valuable lessons to be learned from the first engagements with the enemy.* — N COUNT

engagement ring, engagement rings. An **engagement ring** is a ring worn by a woman when she is engaged to be married. — N COUNT

engaging /ɪ²ŋ¹geɪdʒɪŋ/. Someone who is **engaging** is pleasant and charming. EG *...this harmless and engaging young man... ...an engaging frankness.* — ADJ QUALIT ⇑ nice

engender /ɪ²ndʒɛndə/, **engenders, engendering, engendered**. If someone or something **engenders** a particular feeling, atmosphere, or situation, they cause it to occur; a formal word. EG *This engenders a sense of responsibility.* — V+O = foster

engine /ɛndʒɪn/, **engines**. An **engine** is 1 a machine that uses heat or other kinds of energy to produce power, especially in order to make a vehicle move. EG *He couldn't get his engine started so he left the car at home... ...a jet engine... ...engine oil.* — N COUNT 2 a large vehicle that pulls a railway train. EG *...British Rail's latest high-speed engine... ...a steam engine.* — N COUNT = locomotive

-engined means having an engine or engines of a particular type or number. EG *...a twin-engined patrol plane... ...petrol-engined cars.* — COMB : FORMS ADJS

engineer /ɛndʒɪnɪə/, **engineers, engineering, engineered**. 1 An **engineer** is 1.1 a skilled person who uses scientific knowledge to design and construct machinery, engines, electrical devices, or roads and bridges. EG *...a brilliant young mining engineer.* — N COUNT 1.2 a person who repairs mechanical or electrical devices such as telephones or central heating systems. EG *The telephone engineers can't come until Wednesday.* — N COUNT ⇑ worker 1.3 a soldier who is in a regiment in the army which is responsible for building bridges, roads, etc. EG *...truly heroic work by army engineers.* — N COUNT

2 To **engineer** a building, bridge, etc means to construct it following scientific principles and methods. EG *Thus the core of a building might be engineered to last twenty-five years.* — V+O = build

3 If you **engineer** an event or situation, you arrange or cause it in a clever or indirect way, especially in order to obtain some advantage for yourself. EG *She had engineered the whole excursion.* — V+O, OR V+O+*to*-INF = rig

engineering /ɛndʒɪnɪərɪŋ/ is the activities and work involved in designing and constructing machinery, engines, electrical devices, or roads and bridges. EG *Why don't many girls go into science or engineering?... ...a major engineering feat.* ● See also **civil engineering, genetic engineering**. — N UNCOUNT ⇑ science

English /ɪŋglɪʃ/. 1 **English** means belonging or relating to England, or to its people or language. It is also sometimes used to mean belonging or relating to Great Britain. EG *...the English language.* — ADJ CLASSIF

2 **English** is 2.1 the language that is spoken by people who live in Great Britain and Ireland, the United States, Canada, Australia, and many other countries. EG *Half the letter was in Swedish and the rest in English.* — N UNCOUNT 2.2 the study of the English language or of English literature. EG *Karen obtained A levels in English, French, and Geography.* — N UNCOUNT ⇑ subject

English breakfast, English breakfasts. An **English breakfast** is a breakfast which consists of cooked food, such as bacon and eggs, in addition to toast and marmalade and tea or coffee. EG *The ticket (£50 for two) includes a full English breakfast and a bottle of champagne.* — N COUNT/UNCOUNT

Englishman /ɪŋglɪʃmə³n/, **Englishmen**. An **Englishman** is a man who comes from England or Great Britain. — N COUNT ⇑ man

Englishwoman /ɪŋglɪʃwʊ¹mə⁰n/, **Englishwomen**. An **Englishwoman** is a woman who comes from England or Great Britain. — N COUNT ⇑ woman

engrave /ɪ²ŋ¹greɪv/, **engraves, engraving, engraved**. 1 If you **engrave** something with a design or inscription or if you **engrave** a design or inscription on it, you cut the design or inscription into its surface. EG *It was prettily engraved with flowers on* — V+O+A *(with)*, V+O/QUOTE, OR V+O/QUOTE+A *(on)* *the back... Get a skilful jeweller to engrave on the bracelet the name of your child... They engraved on it, 'Dedicated to the Lord'.* ◊ **engraved.** EG *...Victorian engraved glass.* ◊ ADJ CLASSIF

2 To **engrave** something such as designs or pictures means to print them on paper from a metal or wooden plate on which they have already been cut. EG *Her name was engraved at the top of the sheet of watermarked paper.* ◊ **engraved.** EG *We received engraved invitations to the wedding.* V+O, OR V+O+A (on) ◊ ADJ CLASSIF

3 If something **is engraved** on your mind, memory, heart, etc, it is fixed permanently there, so that you feel that you will never forget it. EG *This episode remains sharply engraved on my mind.* V+O/QUOTE+A (on): USU PASS = etched

engraver /ɪ²ŋ¹greɪvə/, **engravers.** An **engraver** is someone who cuts designs or inscriptions on metal, glass, wood, etc. EG *He learnt to be a wood engraver.* N COUNT

engraving /ɪ²ŋ¹greɪvɪŋ/, **engravings.** 1 An **engraving** is 1.1 a picture that has been printed from an engraved plate. EG *Most of my pictures are etchings, engravings or screen prints.* 1.2 a picture or design that has been cut into metal, glass, wood, etc. EG *...steel engravings.* N COUNT; N COUNT

2 **Engraving** is the art or skill of an engraver. N UNCOUNT

engrossed /ɪ²ŋ¹grəʊst/. If you are **engrossed** in something, it completely holds your attention and interest, and you are not thinking about anything else at all. EG *She was engrossed in her book.* ADJ QUALIT: PRED, IF+PREP THEN *in* = absorbed ≠ bored

engrossing /ɪ²ŋ¹grəʊsɪŋ/. Something that is **engrossing** is so interesting that you do not want to do or think about anything else. EG *...two of the most engrossing books I have ever read.* ADJ QUALIT = absorbing

engulf /ɪ²ŋ¹gʌlf/, **engulfs, engulfing, engulfed.** 1 To **engulf** something means to completely cover and hide it. EG *The house was soon engulfed in flames.* V+O

2 If a feeling or emotion **engulfs** you, you are so affected by it that you cannot feel or think about anything else. EG *Finally panic engulfed him... ...a world engulfed in hatred and intolerance.* V+O ⇑ affect = swamp

enhance /ɪ²nhɑːns/, **enhances, enhancing, enhanced.** To **enhance** something means to improve its value, quality, or attractiveness. EG *Will it enhance my reputation?... The nutritional value of rice is enhanced by baking it with milk.* V+O

enhancement /ɪ²nhɑːnsmə²nt/. The **enhancement** of something is the improvement of it in relation to its value, quality, or attractiveness. N UNCOUNT

enigma /ɪ²nɪgmə/, **enigmas.** An **enigma** is a person, thing, or situation that is mysterious, puzzling, and difficult to understand. EG *In spite of all our investigations it remains an enigma... She's a riddle–an enigma.* N COUNT ⇑ mystery = puzzle

enigmatic /ɛnɪgmætɪk/. Something that is **enigmatic** is mysterious, puzzling, and difficult to understand. EG *Donne is the most enigmatic of all our poets... ...an enigmatic smile.* ◊ **enigmatically.** EG *'You can try,' he said enigmatically.* ADJ QUALIT ≠ obvious ◊ ADV WITH VB

enjoin /ɪ²ndʒɔɪn/, **enjoins, enjoining, enjoined;** a formal word. 1 If you **enjoin** someone to do something, you order them to do it, especially when you are in a position of authority. EG *He enjoined them to be fierce and uncompromising... They were enjoined to be submissive.* V+O+*to*-INF ⇑ tell = command, instruct

2 If you **enjoin** a particular kind of behaviour on someone, you order or recommend that they behave in that way, especially when you are in a position of authority. EG *Zoe put a finger to her lips to enjoin silence... This religion enjoins poverty upon all its followers.* V+O: IF+PREP THEN *on/upon* = impose

enjoy /ɪ²ndʒɔɪ/, **enjoys, enjoying, enjoyed.** 1 If you **enjoy** something, 1.1 you find pleasure and satisfaction in doing or experiencing it. EG *I enjoyed the holiday enormously... She is someone who loves people and enjoys life... Painting is something that I really enjoy doing.* 1.2 you are lucky enough to have something, for example a right, benefit, or privilege. EG *They enjoyed exceptional living standards... He was well aware of the privileges he enjoyed.* V+O, OR V+-ING ⇑ like ≠ dislike; V+O = possess

2 If you **enjoy** yourself, you are very happy and take great pleasure in the situation that you are in. EG *He is thoroughly enjoying himself.* V+O (REFL)

enjoyable /ɪ²ndʒɔɪəbə⁰l/. Something that is **enjoyable** gives you pleasure and satisfaction. EG *We had an enjoyable day at Poole.* ◊ **enjoyably.** EG *This book tells you how you can live simply and enjoyably.* ADJ QUALIT = pleasant ◊ ADV

enjoyment /ɪ²ndʒɔɪmən²t/, **enjoyments.** 1 **Enjoyment** is the feeling of pleasure and satisfaction that you have when you do or experience something that you enjoy. EG *...the enjoyment that reading brings... Do you think I do it for enjoyment?* N UNCOUNT

2 The **enjoyment** of something such as an advantage or a privilege is the benefit of having it. EG *...the enjoyment of wealth.* N UNCOUNT+SUPP ⇑ possession

3 An **enjoyment** is an activity that gives you pleasure. EG *His enjoyments in life are limited to fighting, shooting, and drinking.* N COUNT

enlarge /ɪ²nlɑːdʒ/, **enlarges, enlarging, enlarged.** 1 When you **enlarge** something or when it **enlarges**, it becomes bigger. EG *The original Norman windows were enlarged by Christopher Wren... The pores enlarge and secrete more oil... Mrs White was then free to enlarge the scope of her activities.* ◊ **enlarged.** EG *The leaders met to discuss the aims for the new, enlarged EEC...* V-ERG ⇑ expand ◊ ADJ QUALIT

2 To **enlarge** a photograph means to develop a bigger print of it. EG *We had some of our wedding photos enlarged.* V+O = blow up

enlarge on. If you **enlarge on** or **enlarge upon** a subject, you give a lot of details about it when you are speaking or writing; a formal expression. EG *He enlarged on the glorious future he had in mind.* PHRASAL VB: V+PREP, HAS PASS ⇑ talk = expand on

enlargement /ɪ²nlɑːdʒmə²nt/, **enlargements.** 1 The **enlargement** of something is the action or process of making it bigger. EG *...the enlargement of crowded hospitals... We must resist the enlargement of existing university programmes.* N SING: *the*+N+*of* ⇑ expansion

2 **Enlargement** is also the state of something that has become bigger. EG *The chest X-ray showed moderate enlargement of the heart.* N UNCOUNT

3 An **enlargement** is a photograph that has been made bigger. EG *...poster-sized enlargements.* N COUNT

enlighten /ɪ²nlaɪtə⁰n/, **enlightens, enlightening, enlightened.** To **enlighten** someone means to give them more knowledge and greater understanding about something. EG *The object of the exercise is to amuse and enlighten the general reader.* ◊ **enlightening.** EG *I find her enlightening to talk to... It was a most enlightening book.* V+O ⇑ inform ◊ ADJ QUALIT = illuminating

enlightened /ɪ²nlaɪtə⁰nd/. If you describe someone or something as **enlightened**, you mean 1 that they deal with problems and tasks in a good way, which brings benefits without causing unnecessary harm or suffering for other people; used showing approval. EG *Our enlightened social policies are much admired all over the world... ...a more enlightened approach to part-time farming.* 2 that they possess knowledge about things in general, and are free from false or mistaken beliefs. EG *...pious and enlightened men.* ADJ QUALIT ≠ ignorant; ADJ CLASSIF ≠ ignorant

enlightenment /ɪ²nlaɪtə⁰nmə²nt/ means the act of enlightening or the state of being enlightened. EG *These talks were intended to bring culture and enlightenment to the hearers.* N UNCOUNT ≠ ignorance

enlist /ɪ²nlɪst/, **enlists, enlisting, enlisted.** 1 If someone **enlists** or **is enlisted**, they join the army, navy, or air force. EG *He had enlisted in the Marines... They were enlisted into the 21st Regiment.* V-ERG: IF+PREP THEN *in/into*

2 If you **enlist** someone or their help, you persuade them to help or support you in something you are trying to do. EG *He enlisted Nick's help... He enlisted the aid of another back-bench Conservative.* V+O: IF+PREP THEN *in*, OR+*to*-INF = drum up

enlisted /ɪ²nlɪstɪ²d/. An **enlisted** man or woman is a member of the American army or navy who is below the rank of an officer. EG *...two officers and four enlisted men.* ADJ CLASSIF

enlistment /ɪ²nlɪstmə²nt/ is the act of joining the army, navy, or air force. EG *...enlistment in the Air Force.* ▸ An **enlistment** is the period of time for which someone is a member of one of the armed forces. EG *...a normal five-year enlistment.* N UNCOUNT ▸ N COUNT ⇑ period

enliven /ɪ²nlaɪvə⁰n/, **enlivens, enlivening, enlivened.** To **enliven** events, situations, or people means to make them more lively or cheerful. EG *Tea was a hilarious meal, much enlivened by Malcolm.* V+O = brighten ≠ depress

en masse /ɒn mæs/. If a group of people do something **en masse**, they do it all together and at the same time. EG *They threatened to resign en masse.* ADV WITH VB

enmeshed /ɪ²nmɛʃt/. If you are **enmeshed** in a situation, you are involved in it, even though you do not want to be, and you find it difficult or impossible to escape from it. EG *He felt he was being enmeshed* ADJ QUALIT: PRED, USU+*in* = caught up *in the family business against his will... The whole country was enmeshed in turmoil.*

enmity /ɛnmɪti¹/, **enmities**. **Enmity** is a feeling of anger or hatred for a person that you strongly disagree with. EG *...his long-standing enmity for Mr Baldwin... Tribal enmities have been inflamed by the new ruling.* N UNCOUNT/COUNT = hostility ≠ love

ennoble /ɪ²nəʊbə⁰l/, **ennobles, ennobling, ennobled**. 1 To **ennoble** someone means to make them a member of the nobility. EG *He was subsequently ennobled as Lord Beaumont of Whitley.* V+O ⇑ elevate

2 To **ennoble** something means to make it more noble, honourable and dignified. V+O ⇑ elevate

ennui /ɒnwi:/ is a feeling of tiredness, boredom, and dissatisfaction that is caused by a lack of excitement or activity; a literary word. N UNCOUNT

enormity /i¹nɔ:mɪti¹/, **enormities**. 1 If you refer to the **enormity** of something such as a problem or difficulty, you are referring to its very large size or extent and its seriousness. EG *We were really not aware of the enormity of that problem... Smith did not seemingly grasp the enormity of the danger involved.* N SING : *the*+N, IF+PREP THEN *of* = magnitude

2 An **enormity** is something that is considered to be a terrible crime or sin; a fairly formal word. EG *I had at last been forgiven for some of my own enormities.* N COUNT

enormous /i¹nɔ:məs/. 1 Something that is **enormous** is extremely large in size or amount. EG *There was an enormous cat crouching on the counter eating fish... There is an enormous amount of hard work in child care.* ADJ QUALIT = massive

2 **Enormous** is also used to emphasize the great scale or extent of something. EG *To his enormous delight he was elected MP for Bristol South... ...an enormous success.* ADJ QUALIT = huge

enormously /i¹nɔməsli¹/. You use **enormously** to emphasize the scale or extent of something. EG *It has increased enormously the demand for food in the third world... I became enormously fond of her... He had a blurred impression of being in an enormously long room.* ADV

enough /i¹nʌf/. 1 **Enough** is used in front of a noun to say that a quantity is as much as you need in order to achieve a particular purpose or result. EG *I haven't enough room... I don't think I've really got enough information on that to speak confidently.* ▸ used as a pronoun. EG *I've got five thousand dollars–I hope it's enough... I had not seen enough of his work.* ▸ In formal English, used after a noun. EG *The fact that he did so much is proof enough that Mary's ideas were relevant to him.* DET+N UNCOUNT/PLURAL = sufficient ▸ PRON : IF+PREP THEN *of* ▸ DET AFTER N

2 If you say something such as 'I've had enough', 'I've seen enough' or 'I've heard enough', you mean that you do not want to see or hear any more. EG *I didn't want to stay in Germany any longer. Two years was enough... With all respect, I think you have said enough... I've got enough to worry about... We've made enough of a mess of Northern Ireland.* ▸ used as a determiner. EG *Don't ask me to help you, I've got enough problems of my own.* ▸ used as an adverb. EG *They've suffered enough already.* PRON : IF+PREP THEN *of* ▸ DET+N UNCOUNT/PLURAL ▸ ADV AFTER VB

3 If you say that someone or something is 'old enough', 'fast enough', or 'large enough', you mean that they can do, achieve, or be the particular thing that is mentioned, because of their age, speed, or size. EG *He was old enough to understand... We were close enough to be able to see their faces... The student isn't trying hard enough.* ADV AFTER ADJ/ADV/VB = sufficiently

4 If you say that someone or something is 'sincere enough' or 'common enough', you are saying that although you admit that something or someone is sincere or common, you are not prepared to state just how sincere or common they actually are. EG *She sounded sincere enough, but I couldn't take any chances... That's a common enough experience... That would suit Godley well enough.* ADV AFTER ADJ/ADV = fairly

5 You use expressions such as **oddly enough**, **strangely enough**, and **interestingly enough** in order to comment on a piece of information and to say that it seems especially odd, strange, or interesting. EG *Oddly enough, I do believe you... Funnily enough, old people seem to love bingo... I think, interestingly enough, America is now dependent on Africa for 40% of its oil imports.* PHR : USED AS ADV SEN

6 The word **enough** is also used in the following expressions. 6.1 If you say **'Enough is enough'** to someone, you mean that you want them to stop what they are doing, for example to stop criticizing you. CONVENTION

6.2 **Enough said** means that what you have just said is sufficient to make a particular point clear, and there is no need to say any more. CONVENTION = say no more

6.3 If you say that you **have had enough**, you mean that you are unhappy and dissatisfied with a situation and you want it to stop. EG *I've had enough... He seemed to have had enough of talk about wars and wounds.* PHR : AUX INFLECTS, IF+PREP THEN *of* = be fed up

6.4 You say **that's enough** to tell someone, especially a child, to stop behaving in a particular way, usually when you think they are being silly or unpleasant. EG *'That's enough!' the doctor said sharply.* CONVENTION

6.5 **fair enough**: see **fair**. • **sure enough**: see **sure**.

en passant /ɒm¹ pæsɑ:ŋ/. If you deal with or speak about something **en passant**, you do it quickly and briefly while you are doing something else, especially because you do not think it is important or significant; a rather literary expression. EG *She felt that it was unimportant and could be dealt with en passant.* ADV WITH VB = cursorily ≠ in detail

enquire /ɪ²ŋ¹kwaɪə/, **enquires, enquiring, enquired**. See **inquire**.

enquirer /ɪ²ŋ¹kwaɪərə/, **enquirers**. See **inquirer**.

enquiry /ɪ²ŋ¹kwaɪəri¹/, **enquiries**. See **inquiry**.

enrage /ɪ²nreɪdʒ/, **enrages, enraging, enraged**. If something **enrages** you, it makes you very angry indeed. EG *She chose a quotation that she knew would enrage him... She was enraged by these remarks.* ◇ **enraged**. EG *He raced back towards the forest with the enraged dogs at his heels... He got up, suddenly enraged.* V+O ⇑ anger = rile ◇ ADJ QUALIT ⇑ angered

enraptured /ɪ²nræptʃəd/. Someone who is **enraptured** is filled with fascination, joy, and delight about something; a literary word. EG *We would gaze enraptured at the sunsets.* ADJ CLASSIF ⇑ joyful = ecstatic

enrich /ɪ²nrɪtʃ/, **enriches, enriching, enriched**. 1 To **enrich** something means to improve the quality or value of something by adding something else to it. EG *Libraries were enlarged and enriched by new books... General debates on public affairs can greatly enrich our parliamentary system.* ◇ **enriched**. EG *...enriched breakfast cereals.* V+O : IF+PREP THEN *with* = enhance ≠ impoverish ◇ ADJ QUALIT

2 To **enrich** someone means to increase the amount of money that they have. EG *The purpose of the colonies was to enrich the colonists and the Spanish realm.* V+O ≠ beggar

enrichment /ɪ²nrɪtʃmə²nt/ is the act of enriching someone or something or the state of being enriched. N UNCOUNT ≠ impoverishment

enrol /ɪ²nrəʊl/, **enrols, enrolling, enrolled**; also spelled **enroll** and **enrolls** in American English. If you **enrol** or **are enrolled** at a college or other institution or on a course, you join it by being officially registered and by paying a fee. EG *He had gone to college to enrol on an art course... I enrolled at the University of Vienna.* V-ERG = register

enrolment /ɪ²nrəʊlmə²nt/, **enrolments**; also spelled **enrollment** in American English. 1 **Enrolment is** the act of enrolling or the state of being enrolled at an institution or on a course. EG *...the enrolment of Prince Charles at the University.* N UNCOUNT = registration

2 An **enrolment** is the number of people who are enrolled at an institution or on a course. EG *University enrolments had risen by 50 per cent.* N COUNT ⇑ membership

en route /ɒn ru:t/. If something happens **en route** to somewhere, it happens on the way there or between two places. EG *You'll see plenty to interest you en route.* ADV AFTER VB

ensconce /ɪ²nskɒns/, **ensconces, ensconcing, ensconced**. If you **ensconce** yourself or **are ensconced** in a particular place, you put yourself there firmly and comfortably, with no immediate intention of moving away. EG *I knew she'd ensconce herself in the corner by the fire... Karl was happily ensconced at West Point.* V+O (NG/REFL) +A *(in/at)* = install

ensemble /ɒnsɒmbə⁰l/, **ensembles**. An **ensemble** is 1 a group of things or people considered as a whole rather than as separate individuals. EG *It is better to consider the buildings as an ensemble than individually.* 2 all the clothes that you are wearing at a particular time, especially if you have chosen them carefully so that they look nice together. EG *A black silk tie completed the ensemble.* 3 a small group of musicians who regularly play or sing together. EG *The Amadeus Quartet is one of the most famous ensembles in the world.* N COUNT : USU SING; N COUNT : USU SING = outfit; N COUNT

enshrine /ɪ²nʃraɪn/, **enshrines, enshrining, enshrined.** To **enshrine** something, such as a political idea or a legal right, means to contain and protect it, especially within a society or legal system. EG *The universities' autonomy is enshrined in their individual charters.* V+O : USU PASS

enshroud /ɪ²nʃraʊd/, **enshrouds, enshrouding, enshrouded.** To **enshroud** something means to cover it completely so that it can no longer be seen; a formal or literary word. EG *Gases and debris enshrouded the centre of the explosion.* V+O = shroud

ensign /ɛnsaɪn/, **ensigns.** An **ensign** is **1** a flag flown on a ship to show what country that ship belongs to. ● See also **white ensign, red ensign. 2** a junior officer in the United States Navy. **3** a junior officer in the British army until the late nineteenth century. N COUNT : USU+SUPP; N COUNT; N COUNT

enslave /ɪ²nsleɪv/, **enslaves, enslaving, enslaved. 1** To **enslave** someone means to make them into a slave. EG *He was enslaved and ill treated.* V+O : USU PASS ≠ free
◊ **enslaved.** EG *...slave-owning governments and enslaved peoples.* ◊ ADJ CLASSIF
2 To **enslave** a person or society means to trap them in a situation from which they cannot escape. EG *Men were enslaved by developing industrialism.* V+O : USU PASS

enslavement /ɪ²nsleɪvmə²nt/ is **1** the act of making someone into a slave or the state of being a slave. EG *...the systematic enslavement and exploitation of the masses.* **2** the state of being caught or trapped in a situation from which it is difficult to escape. EG *...enslavement to the status quo.* N UNCOUNT : USU WITH POSS ⇑ oppression; N UNCOUNT : IF+PREP THEN *to* = tie

ensnare /ɪ²nsnɛə/, **ensnares, ensnaring, ensnared. 1** If you **ensnare** an animal, you catch it in a trap or snare. V+O = snare
2 If you **ensnare** someone, you gain power or control over them, especially by using dishonest or devious methods. EG *A look would ensnare and enchant her completely... I decided to try to ensnare Mr Peake into doing it.* V+O = trap

ensue /ɪ²nsj⁰uː/, **ensues, ensuing, ensued.** If something **ensues**, it happens immediately after another event, especially as a result of it. EG *Death might ensue within seven weeks... Inevitably, a shouting match ensued between us and the bus driver.* V ⇑ happen = follow

ensuing /ɪ²nsj⁰uːɪŋ/ means happening immediately afterwards. EG *He had half killed the policeman in the ensuing fight... ...the ensuing months.* ADJ CLASSIF : ATTRIB ⇑ following

ensure /ɪ²nʃʊə, -ʃɔː/, **ensures, ensuring, ensured.** To **ensure** something or **ensure** that something happens means to make certain that it happens. EG *The first duty of the state is to ensure that law-abiding people are protected from crime... The door did not lock, but at least it ensured a reasonable amount of privacy.* V+O/REPORT-CL ⇑ guarantee = assure

entail /ɪ²nteɪl/, **entails, entailing, entailed.** If something **entails** something else, the second thing follows necessarily and inevitably from the first. EG *Balancing the budget would entail public spending cuts of thirteen billion pounds... The move entailed radical changes in lifestyle.* V+O : IF+PREP THEN *in* ⇑ require = involve, mean

entangle /ɪ²ntæŋgə⁰l/, **entangles, entangling, entangled. 1** If something **is entangled** in something else, such as a rope, wire, or net, it is caught in it very firmly. EG *Suddenly she was entangled in the seaweed.* ◊ **entangled.** EG *...the mass of entangled boughs... ...veils of black netting entangled with silver paper.* V+O : USU PASS, IF+PREP THEN *in/with* = enmeshed ◊ ADJ CLASSIF
2 If you **are entangled** in something, you are involved in difficulties from which it is hard to escape. EG *They became entangled in a mass of contradictions... The country became entangled in a grave economic crisis.* V+O : USU PASS, IF+PREP THEN *in* ⇑ involved = embroiled
3 If you **are entangled** with someone, you are involved in a relationship with them that causes problems or difficulties. EG *She got entangled with a pretty awful crook herself... A professional should do his work and not become entangled emotionally.* V+O : USU PASS, IF+PREP THEN *with*

entanglement /ɪ²ntæŋgə⁰lmə²nt/, **entanglements.** An **entanglement** is a relationship with someone, often a sexual one; used showing disapproval. EG *For years Uncle Tom avoided entanglements. Then he met his match in Effie Mansell.* N COUNT/UNCOUNT : IF+PREP THEN *with*

entente /ɒntɒnt/, **ententes.** An **entente** or an **entente cordiale** is a friendly agreement between two or more countries. EG *The entente between Britain and France shows signs of breaking down.* N COUNT/UNCOUNT : IF+PREP THEN *with/between* ⇑ friendship

enter /ɛntə/, **enters, entering, entered**; a fairly formal word. **1** To **enter** means to come into or go into a particular place. EG *They stopped talking as soon as they saw Brody enter... The island ends in vertical cliffs, the streams entering the sea by waterfalls.* V OR V+O = come in ≠ leave
2 To **enter** an organization or institution means to become a member of it. EG *I could not enter the university without Latin... He entered Parliament in 1950.* V OR V+O = join
3 If you **enter** a particular activity or situation, you become involved in it. EG *She entered politics and was MP for Little Stansmere... She had entered my world.* V+O, OR V+A *(into)* = come into
4 If something new **enters** a situation, it is suddenly added to it, often rather unexpectedly. EG *A note of resolution entered the bishop's voice... A new factor unfortunately has entered trade union negotiations.* V+O, OR V+A *(into)* = creep into
5 To **enter** a new period of time or process means to begin it. EG *I entered my second year at university... The industry entered a period of lower growth.* V+O, OR V+A *(into)* = go into
6 If you **enter** a competition, race, or examination, you take part in it. EG *I entered one or two competitions and won prizes... Exxon, the largest oil company, may enter the takeover game.* V OR V+O ⇑ participate
7 If you **enter** someone else for a race or competition, you register their name with the organizers so that they can take part. EG *They had pooled their meagre savings to enter the horse in the Derby.* V+O, OR V+O+A *(in/into)*
8 To **enter** something in a notebook, register, financial account, etc, means to write it down. EG *Enter it in the cash book.* V+O, OR V+O+A *(in/for)* = record

enter into. 1 When you **enter into** something important, serious, or complicated, you start to do it or to become involved in it, expecting that it will take a long time to be completed. EG *No correspondence will be entered into... The Labour Government refused to enter into negotiations... The particulars are too long to enter into here.* PHRASAL VB : V+PREP, HAS PASS
2 Something that **enters into** something is an important or necessary consideration or factor in it. EG *Obviously personal relationships enter into balances of power... Money doesn't enter into it at all... Calling on my mother didn't enter into our original plan.* PHRASAL VB : V+PREP, HAS PASS ⇑ affect come into

enter upon. When you **enter upon** something, you start to do it or become involved in it; a rather formal expression. EG *Brandt entered upon this new policy in the 1960s.* PHRASAL VB : V+PREP, HAS PASS = embark on

enterprise /ɛntəpraɪz/, **enterprises. 1** An **enterprise** is **1.1** a company or business. EG *...large industrial enterprises... ...India's most famous capitalistic enterprise, the Tata steel firm.* **1.2** something new, difficult, or important that you do or try to do. EG *He said he had doubts about the whole enterprise.* N COUNT : USU+SUPP; N COUNT : USU+SUPP ⇑ deed = venture
2 Enterprise is **2.1** a system of business, especially one in a particular country. EG *This has done much to cripple national enterprise.* **2.2** the ability to think of new and effective things to do, together with an eagerness to do them; used showing approval. EG *...men of enterprise, energy, and ambition.* N UNCOUNT : USU+SUPP; N UNCOUNT ⇑ boldness = initiative

enterprising /ɛntəpraɪzɪŋ/. Someone who is **enterprising** shows the ability to think of new things to do and has an eagerness to do them. EG *You are no longer the enterprising cook that once you were.* ADJ QUALIT ⇑ inventive = adventurous

entertain /ɛntəteɪn/, **entertains, entertaining, entertained. 1** To **entertain** people or to **entertain** means **1.1** to do things which other people, especially an audience, enjoy and find interesting or amusing. EG *We entertained the guests with a detailed description of the party... A series of popular talks intended to inform and entertain.* **1.2** to give someone food and hospitality, for example by inviting them to your house. EG *She never entertained... He had a beautiful house and entertained all the eminent people.* V OR V+O = amuse; V OR V+O
2 If you **entertain** an idea or suggestion, you allow yourself to consider it as possible or as worth thinking about seriously. EG *I wondered what on earth could have led me to entertain so ludicrous a suspicion.* V+O : NO IMPER = harbour

entertainer /ɛntəteɪnə/, **entertainers.** An **entertainer** is a person whose job is to amuse and please audiences, for example by telling jokes, singing, or dancing. EG *She was one of the last entertainers to survive from the Edwardian music hall.* N COUNT ⇑ performer

entertaining /ɛntəteɪnɪŋ/. **1** People or things that are **entertaining** are amusing and full of interest and ADJ QUALIT = fun

therefore give people pleasure. EG *Films should be entertaining... She is full of entertaining stories.*
2 **Entertaining** is hospitality that you give to guests. EG *Public relations executives usually have more entertaining to do than, say, personnel managers... ...business entertaining.* N UNCOUNT

entertainment /ɛntəteɪnmə²nt/, **entertainments.** 1 **Entertainment** is shows, performances, films, etc, that people watch for pleasure. EG *...the entertainment business... He performs magical tricks for entertainment... This was not Morris's idea of an evening's entertainment.* N UNCOUNT
2 An **entertainment** is a performance which people watch for pleasure. EG *Jennifer O'Neill heads the cast of this original entertainment.* N COUNT = show

enthral /ɪ²nθrɔːl/, **enthrals, enthralling, enthralled**; also spelled **enthraling** and **enthraled** in American English. To **enthral** someone means to hold their attention and interest completely, for example by showing or telling them something which pleases or delights them. EG *Daniel was enthralled by the book.* ◊ **enthralling.** EG *...all the enthralling details of a well-equipped wedding.* V+O : USU PASS, IF+PREP THEN *by/with* = engross, captivate ◊ ADJ QUALIT = riveting

enthrone /ɪ²nθrəʊn/, **enthrones, enthroning, enthroned.** 1 When kings, queens, or bishops **are enthroned**, they officially take on their role during a ceremony in which they are placed on a throne; used in formal English. V+O : USU PASS ⇑ instal = crown
2 To **enthrone** an idea means to give it a prominent place in your life or thoughts because you consider it to be very important; used in formal English. EG *They wanted to help their Russian brethren to enthrone socialism.* V+O, OR V+O+A : USU PASS ⇑ exalt = elevate

enthronement /ɪ²nθrəʊnmə²nt/, **enthronements.** An **enthronement** is 1 a ceremony to mark the start of the reign of a king, queen, or bishop. EG *...the enthronement of George Neville as Archbishop of York.* 2 the act of giving something a prominent place in your life or thoughts because you consider it to be very important. EG *...the enthronement of reason.* N COUNT : USU *the*+N+*of* ⇑ installation; N SING WITH DET +SUPP ⇑ elevation

enthuse /ɪ²nθj⁰uːz/, **enthuses, enthusing, enthused.** 1 If you **enthuse** over something, you talk about it in a way that shows that you are excited and pleased about it. EG *She was enthusing innocently but trivially over something that had caught her eye... 'Brilliant,' he enthused.* V+A *(over/about)*, OR V+QUOTE = rave
2 If something **enthuses** you, you feel excited and enthusiastic about it. EG *...a speech which will certainly enthuse Labour's activists.* V+O : USU PASS ⇑ stimulate = encourage

enthusiasm /ɪ²nθj⁰uːziæzə⁰m/, **enthusiasms.** 1 **Enthusiasm** is great eagerness to be involved in a particular activity, because it is something you like and enjoy or that you think is important. EG *Some years ago he had embarked with great enthusiasm on an ambitious critical project... ...her enthusiasm for the theatre.* N UNCOUNT/COUNT = passion
2 An **enthusiasm** is an activity or subject that interests you a great deal and that you spend a lot of time on. EG *Pop music, together with football, is the chief enthusiasm of the post-war average man.* N COUNT : USU+SUPP ⇑ interest = passion

enthusiast /ɪ²nθj⁰uːziæst/, **enthusiasts.** An **enthusiast** is a person who is very interested in a particular activity or subject and who feels strongly about it. EG *...a great soccer enthusiast.* N COUNT : USU+SUPP = fanatic

enthusiastic /ɪ²nθj⁰uːzi¹æstɪk/. If you are **enthusiastic** about something, you show a lot of excitement, eagerness, or approval of it by the way that you behave and talk. EG *Sarah is very enthusiastic about learning to read... Enthusiastic crowds filled the streets.* ▸ used of things that people do and say. EG *The response was enthusiastic.* ◊ **enthusiastically.** EG *I responded very enthusiastically.* ADJ QUALIT : IF+PREP THEN *about* ⇑ eager = excited, exuberant ◊ ADV

entice /ɪ²ntaɪs/, **entices, enticing, enticed.** If you **entice** someone away from a particular thing, place, or activity to another one, you attract them away from the first one to the second one. EG *He enticed his former employer into another dice game... An attempt is being made to entice otters back to the river.* V+O = lure, tempt

enticing /ɪ²ntaɪsɪŋ/. Something that is **enticing** is extremely attractive and has the effect of tempting you. EG *Tanya's invitation seemed too enticing to refuse.* ◊ **enticingly.** ADJ QUALIT = tempting ◊ ADV WITH VB

entire /ɪ²ntaɪə/ is used to refer to 1 the whole of something, including all the details, parts, or aspects of it. EG *That fact alone changed the entire situation... I had resolved to tell nobody, to shoulder the entire burden myself... He took to pieces and reassembled an entire engine.* 2 the whole of a particular period of time. EG *He retired at the age of 62, having spent his entire career on Wall Street... That was the only time in my entire life that I was off this farm.* 3 the whole of a particular place or area. EG *There's a huge geological fault running through the entire State... We've covered the entire wall with beer mats.* ADJ CLASSIF : ATTRIB; ADJ CLASSIF : ATTRIB; ADJ CLASSIF : ATTRIB

entirely /ɪ²ntaɪəli¹/. 1 **Entirely** means 1.1 completely and only in the way mentioned, without anyone or anything else being included or involved. EG *It was entirely the work of these women's organizations... In its early days the school was attended almost entirely by 'problem' children... It was the most heavenly stew, made entirely of parsnips and herbs.* ADV = exclusively
1.2 all the time and without any exception or change. EG *We all lived out our lives entirely on the farm.* ADV WITH VB
2 **Entirely** is also used to emphasize what you are saying. EG *I must say I agree entirely... McGovern had told them something entirely different from what he had told me... It seems to me the change was not entirely an improvement... He seemed entirely at ease.* ADV = totally

entirety /ɪ²ntaɪərɪti¹/. If something is used or affected in a particular way **in its entirety**, the whole of it is used or affected in that way, without any exception. EG *If published it must be published in its entirety... The agricultural surplus was taken over almost in its entirety by the ruler.* PHR : USED AS AN A ≠ in part

entitle /ɪ²ntaɪtə⁰l/, **entitles, entitling, entitled.**
1 If something **entitles** you to have something or do something, it gives you the right to have it or do it. EG *Their educational qualifications entitle them to a higher salary... Women aged 60 and over are entitled to free prescriptions.* V+O+A *(to)* : USU PASS = qualify
2 If a book, film, painting, etc is **entitled**, for example, 'Sunrise', this means that its title is 'Sunrise'. EG *...a report entitled 'Attitudes Towards Geriatrics.'* V+O+C *(NAME)* : USU PASS ⇑ name

entitlement /ɪ²ntaɪtə⁰lmə²nt/, **entitlements. Entitlement** to something is the right to have it or do it; a formal word. N UNCOUNT/COUNT

entity /ɛntɪti¹/, **entities.** An **entity** is a complete, separate thing that is not divided and that is not part of anything else; a formal word. EG *When do children start being aware of themselves as separate entities?* N COUNT : USU+SUPP ⇑ individual

entomb /ɪ²ntuːm/, **entombs, entombing, entombed**; a fairly formal word. 1 If something **is entombed**, it is buried or trapped underground. EG *The site is now entombed in the foundations of a block of luxury flats.* V+O : USU PASS = bury
2 When a person's dead body **is entombed**, it is put into a grave or tomb. EG *...the linen cloth in which the body of Christ was entombed.* V+O : USU PASS = bury

entomology /ɛntə⁶mɒlədʒi¹/ is the study of insects. ◊ **entomologist, entomologists.** N UNCOUNT ◊ N COUNT

entourage /ɒnturɑːʒ/, **entourages.** The **entourage** of someone famous or important is the group of assistants, servants, or other people who travel with them. EG *Among his entourage was a retired general.* N COUNT : USU WITH POSS = retinue

entrails /ɛntreɪlz/. The **entrails** of people or animals are their inside parts, especially their intestines. N PLURAL = guts

entrance, entrances, entrancing, entranced. The word **entrance** is pronounced /ɛntrəns/ when it is a noun, and /ɪ²ntrɑːns/ when it is a verb. 1 An **entrance** is a way into a place, for example a door or gate. EG *...the entrance to the National Gallery... We camped near the entrance of the water-filled gorge.* N COUNT : IF+PREP THEN *to/into/of* ⇑ opening = entry
2 Someone's **entrance** is 2.1 their arrival in a room or building. EG *She had only broken off to acknowledge our entrance.* 2.2 the way that they arrive in a room, especially when they try to be noticed and admired. EG *The ripples created by her entrance had not yet subsided... Her father would make a sudden, startling entrance.* 2.3 their coming on to the stage when they are in a play; a technical term in the theatre. EG *I remember her making a most effective entrance in a melodramatic play.* N COUNT : USU POSS+N; N COUNT : USU POSS+N ⇑ arrival ≠ exit; N COUNT : USU POSS+N = entry ≠ exit
3 If you gain **entrance** to a particular place, you are able to go in it. EG *I denied him entrance... They must produce identity cards before they can gain entrance to the proceedings.* N UNCOUNT : IF+PREP THEN *to/into* ⇑ access = entry
4 If you gain **entrance** to a particular profession, society, or institution, you are accepted as a member of it. EG *Entrance to the professions is open to many* N UNCOUNT : IF+PREP THEN *to/into*

more people... *She had failed her college entrance exams.*

5 If you are given an **entrance** to a particular activity, system, or group of people, you are given a means of becoming involved with it. EG *His father's reputation gave him an entrance to a wide circle of people.*
N SING WITH DET : IF + PREP THEN *to/into* ⇑ access = introduction

6 If something **entrances** you, it causes you to feel delight and wonder. EG *The novelties and souvenirs simply entranced her.* ◇ **entranced**. EG *Everyone sat entranced.* ◇ **entrancing**. EG *He had the most entrancing generosity.*
V+O : USU PASS = captivate ◇ ADJ QUALIT ◇ ADJ QUALIT

entrance fee, entrance fees. An **entrance fee** is a sum of money which you pay before you enter a cinema, museum, etc, or which you have to pay in order to join an organization. EG *He used to look at the pictures outside cinemas, unable to afford the entrance fee.*
N COUNT = entry fee

entrant /ɛntrənt/, **entrants**. An **entrant** is 1 a person who has recently become or is about to become a member of an institution, such as a university. EG *400,000 hopeful entrants sat university entrance exams.* 2 a person who is taking part in a competition. EG *Each entrant plays the music of their choice.*
N COUNT; N COUNT ⇑ participant = competitor

entrap /ɪ²ntræp/, **entraps, entrapping, entrapped**. If you **entrap** someone or something, you trap them by tricking or deceiving them; a formal word.
V+O : IF + PREP THEN *in*, USU PASS

entrapment /ɪ²ntræpmə²nt/ is the practice of arresting someone by using unfair or illegal methods; a technical term in law. EG *...victims of entrapment and government misconduct.*
N UNCOUNT/UNCOUNT

entreat /ɪ²ntriːt/, **entreats, entreating, entreated**. If you **entreat** someone to do something, you ask them very humbly and seriously to do it; a formal word. EG *He entreated her not to be angry.*
V+O, OR V+O+*to*-INF = implore

entreaty /ɪ²ntriːti¹/, **entreaties**. An **entreaty** is a humble and serious request; a formal word. EG *Nobody listened to my entreaties... Entreaty failed, so I tried threats.*
N COUNT/UNCOUNT = pleading

entrée /ɒntreɪ/, **entrées**. 1 The **entrée** to a particular place or group of people is the right to enter that place or to be accepted and welcomed by that group. EG *I have the entrée into his house... She hopes one day to regain her entrée to polite society.*
N SING WITH DET + SUPP ⇑ acceptance

2 An **entrée** is the main course of a meal or, in very formal banquets, a dish eaten immediately before the main course. EG *He ordered the most expensive hors d'oeuvre and entrée that the restaurant offered... ...during the lull between the entrée and dessert.*
N COUNT ⇑ course

entrench /ɪ²ntrɛntʃ/, **entrenches, entrenching, entrenched**. If something such as power, a custom, or an idea **is entrenched**, it is firmly and strongly established, so that it would be difficult to change it. EG *He was well entrenched, but the final power in the business lay with someone else. The Nationalists entrenched their power further by adding six seats to the Parliament.* ◇ **entrenched**. EG *...strongly entrenched ideas... ...the entrenched power of the landed nobility.*
V+O : USU PASS = strengthen ◇ ADJ QUALIT : USU ADV + ADJ

entrenchment /ɪ²ntrɛntʃmə²nt/, **entrenchments**. An **entrenchment** is a series of trenches which are dug for defence by soldiers in war.
N COUNT ⇑ earthworks

entrepreneur /ɒntrəprənɜː/, **entrepreneurs**. An **entrepreneur** is a person who sets up business deals in order to make a profit. EG *Entrepreneurs with a belief in the future potential of the market... ...a creative entrepreneur.*
N COUNT ⇑ businessman

entrepreneurial /ɒntrəprənɜːrɪəl/ means having the qualities that are needed for people to succeed as entrepreneurs. EG *...competitive, entrepreneurial capitalism.*
ADJ QUALIT : ATTRIB ⇑ commercial

entropy /ɛntrəpi¹/ is, in formal English, a state of disorder, confusion, and disorganization.
N UNCOUNT = chaos

entrust /ɪ²ntrʌst/, **entrusts, entrusting, entrusted**. If you **entrust** something important to someone or **entrust** them with it, you give them the responsibility of looking after it or dealing with it. EG *Children are too young to be entrusted with family money... It was a task the Foreign Secretary had entrusted to him.*
V+O+A *(to/with)* ⇑ trust

entry /ɛntri¹/, **entries**. 1 An **entry** is 1.1 a way into a place, for example a door or gate. EG *...the pretty screen at the entry to Hyde Park... The entry is up the Royal Staircase.* 1.2 a brief note or group of figures written in a diary or account book or put onto a computer. EG *Let me look up the entries for mid-June.* 1.3 a short article about something or someone in a dictionary or encyclopedia. EG *I was in the library looking up the entry for the French President in the Encyclopaedia Britannica.* 1.4 a piece of work, such as a story or drawing, or the answers to a set of questions, which you complete in order to take part in a competition. EG *Here are some extracts from the five winning entries.* 1.5 the total number of people taking part in an event or competition, or joining an institution or school class. EG *In 1914 the entry for the Championship had grown to 194... The sixth form entry went down slightly this year.*
N COUNT : USU SING = way in, entrance; N COUNT + SUPP; N COUNT + SUPP = reference; N COUNT = submission; N COUNT : USU SING

2 A person's **entry** is 2.1 their arrival in a particular place. EG *At Derek's entry a few heads turned.* 2.2 the way that they arrive in a room, especially when they try to be noticed and admired. EG *He made his entry as Napoleon.*
N COUNT; N COUNT ⇑ arrival = entrance

3 If you are allowed **entry** into a country, a building, etc, you are allowed to go in it. EG *Many of his associates were deported from, or refused entry to, Britain... The gallery will be open Sunday afternoons from next weekend. Entry will be free.*
N UNCOUNT ⇑ access = admission

4 The words **no entry** are used on signs to indicate that you are not allowed to go into a particular area or through a particular door or gate. EG *There was a 'no entry' sign on the gate.*
= no thoroughfare

5 Someone's **entry** into a particular society or group is their joining of it. EG *He succeeded in negotiating British entry into the European Community... It provided the occasion for his entry into national politics.*
N UNCOUNT : IF + PREP THEN *to/into* = entrance

6 **Entry** in a competition is the act of taking part in it. EG *Entry is free to all readers... Send the completed entry form to the magazine by 10th December 1986.*
N UNCOUNT, OR N BEFORE N ⇑ participation

7 The **entry** of information into a computer is the process of putting it in. EG *They welcomed this new system for rapid data entry.*
N UNCOUNT : USU + SUPP = input

entry fee, entry fees; also spelled with a hyphen. An **entry fee** is an entrance fee.
N COUNT

entryism /ɛntri¹ɪzə⁰m/ is the policy or practice of trying to gain political power by joining and taking over an existing political party, rather than by establishing a new party or by using other means.
N UNCOUNT ⇑ infiltration

entwine /ɪ²ntwaɪn/, **entwines, entwining, entwined**. If you **entwine** something in something else, you twist it in and around that thing. EG *One second later her fingers were entwined in my own.*
V-ERG : USU PASS, IF + PREP THEN *in/with*

enumerate /ɪ¹njuːməreɪt/, **enumerates, enumerating, enumerated**. When you **enumerate** a list of things, you name each one in turn. EG *I don't quite know where to begin in enumerating the innovations.* ◇ **enumeration** /ɪ¹njuːməreɪʃə⁰n/.
V+O ⇑ state ◇ N UNCOUNT

enunciate /ɪ¹nʌnsieɪt/, **enunciates, enunciating, enunciated**; a formal word. 1 When you **enunciate** a word or part of a word, you pronounce it clearly. EG *You must enunciate your consonants more clearly.* ◇ **enunciation** /ɪ¹nʌnsieɪʃə⁰n/. EG *...the art of vocal enunciation.*
V, OR V+O/QUOTE = articulate ◇ N UNCOUNT

2 When you **enunciate** a thought, idea, or plan, you express it very clearly and precisely. EG *No one doubts his ability to enunciate policies which connect with popular need.* ◇ **enunciation**. EG *...Rutherford's enunciation of atomic structure.*
V+O/QUOTE ◇ N UNCOUNT ⇑ expression

envelop /ɪ²nvɛləp/, **envelops, enveloping, enveloped**. To **envelop** something means to cover, surround, or enclose it completely. EG *She was enveloped in an ill-fitting sacklike garment... ...that certain honesty that seems to envelop everything he does.*
V+O = engulf

envelope /ɛnvələup, ɒn-/, **envelopes**. An **envelope** is a rectangular paper cover in which a letter is sent to someone through the post. EG *The solicitor took a sealed envelope from the folder... She opened the envelope and drew out the contents.*
N COUNT

enviable /ɛnviəbə⁰l/ is used to describe things, qualities, or situations that you wish you had yourself. EG *...a nice man, whose job was not as enviable as it appeared to be... She learned to speak foreign languages with enviable fluency... You are in a position that many would consider enviable.*
ADJ QUALIT ⇑ attractive = superb

envious /ɛnvɪəs/. Someone who is **envious** of someone else envies them. EG *Ralph watched them, envious and resentful.* ▸ used of people's behaviour and expressions. EG *Envious glances were cast at Anne.*
ADJ QUALIT = jealous, covetous

◇ **enviously**. EG *They were watched enviously by the rest of the crowd.* ◇ ADV WITH VB

environment /ɪ²nvaɪrən⁰mə²nt/, **environments**. 1 Someone's **environment** is 1.1 all the circumstances, people, things, and events around them that influence their life. EG *A child can easily adjust to changes in its environment... Could the college provide a stimulating environment?... It was cruel to plunge her into such a totally alien environment and culture... Are we more influenced by environment or heredity?* 1.2 the particular surroundings in which they live or exist, especially a region that has particular land, sea, or weather conditions. EG *There could scarcely be a less promising environment for an amphibian than the desert... Science offers us total mastery over our environment and over our destiny.* N COUNT/UNCOUNT : USU+SUPP = surroundings; N COUNT : USU SING+SUPP = habitat

3 The **environment** is the natural world of land, sea, air, plants, and animals that exists around towns and cities. EG *We are fighting pollution to protect the environment... ...the Secretary of State for the Environment.* N SING : the+N ⇑ nature

environmental /ɪ²nvaɪrən⁰mentə⁰l/ means 1 concerned with or relating to the natural world in which we live. EG *...the environmental group Greenpeace... ...pesticides, herbicides, and all kinds of environmental pollutants.* ◇ **environmentally**. EG *...a worldwide campaign against the environmentally unacceptable use of pesticides.* 2 relating to or caused by the surroundings in which a person or animal lives. EG *Clearly it is responding to environmental change or stimuli... Corals are very demanding in their environmental requirements.* ◇ **environmentally**. ADJ CLASSIF : ATTRIB; ◇ ADV+ADJ/ADV; ADJ CLASSIF : ATTRIB; ◇ ADV

environmentalist /ɪ²nvaɪrən⁰mentəlɪst/, **environmentalists**. An **environmentalist** is a person who wants to protect and preserve the natural environment, for example by preventing pollution. EG *Environmentalists have been protesting about the destruction of Amazon rain forests.* N COUNT = conservationist

environs /ɪ²nvaɪrənz/. The **environs** of a place are the area immediately surrounding it. EG *...the national press that inhabits Fleet Street and its environs... ...the environs of Istanbul.* N PLURAL WITH POSS ⇑ surroundings = neighbourhood

envisage /ɪ²nvɪzɪdʒ/, **envisages, envisaging, envisaged**. If you **envisage** a situation or state of affairs, you imagine it as being true, real, or likely to happen, especially in the future. EG *The last forecast envisaged inflation falling to about 10 per cent... The party envisages that socialism can come without civil war.* V+O/REPORT-CL ⇑ foresee

envision /ɪ²nvɪʒə⁰n/, **envisions, envisioning, envisioned**. If you **envision** something, you envisage it; used in American English. V+O/REPORT-CL

envoy /envɔɪ/, **envoys**. An **envoy** is 1 someone who is sent as a messenger, especially from one government to another. EG *The U.S. special envoy made a surprise announcement.* 2 a diplomat in an embassy who is immediately below the ambassador in rank. N COUNT = emissary; N COUNT

envy /envi¹/, **envies, envying, envied**. 1 **Envy** is the feeling you have when you wish you could have the same thing or quality that someone else has. EG *Her undisputed good looks caused envy and admiration.* N UNCOUNT ⇑ emotion

2 If you **envy** someone, you wish that you had the same things or qualities that they have. EG *You know, I envy a person like Jaykar very much... It would be unfair to envy him his good fortune.* V+O, OR V+O+O ⇑ desire

3 If a thing or quality is **the envy of** a particular person, they wish very much that they could have or achieve it. EG *Such a good time would be the envy of many of today's marathon runners.* ● **green with envy**: see **green**. PHR : USED AS C

enzyme /enzaɪm/, **enzymes**. An **enzyme** is a chemical substance that is found in living creatures which produces changes in other substances without being changed itself, for example the digestive enzymes in your stomach; a technical term in biology and medicine. EG *...a rare enzyme deficiency.* N COUNT ⇑ catalyst

eon /iːə⁷n/, **eons**. See **aeon**.

EP /iː piː/, **EPs**. An **EP** is a record which is designed to be played at either 33 rpm or 45 rpm and which lasts for about 8 minutes on each side; an abbreviation for 'extended play'. N COUNT

epaulet /epəlɛ¹t/, **epaulets**; also spelled **epaulette**. An **epaulet** is a decoration worn on the shoulder of certain uniforms, especially military ones. EG *There were narrow gold epaulets at the shoulders of his tunic.* N COUNT

ephemeral /ɪ¹femə⁰rəl/. Something that is **ephemeral** lasts only for a very short time; a fairly literary word. EG *...the ephemeral nature of fads and fashions.* ADJ QUALIT ⇑ transitory

epic /epɪk/, **epics**. 1 An **epic** is a book, poem, or film which is longer or larger than others of its type, and which tells a story of heroic deeds. EG *...the latest James Bond epic... ...a historical epic of great richness.* N COUNT : USU MOD+N

2 Something that is described as **epic** is considered to be very impressive or ambitious. EG *...the beginning of that epic 6,000 mile retreat... ...his triumphant return after his epic voyage.* ADJ CLASSIF ⇑ great

epicentre /epɪ¹sentə/, **epicentres**. The **epicentre** of an earthquake is the place where the earthquake starts. EG *We could see that the damage was worse as the epicentre was approached.* N COUNT

epicure /epɪkjʊə/, **epicures**. An **epicure** is a person who enjoys eating food which is of very good quality; a formal, old-fashioned word. N COUNT = gourmet

epidemic /epɪdemɪk/, **epidemics**. An **epidemic** is 1 the occurrence of a disease which affects a very large number of people living in an area and which spreads quickly to other people. EG *...an influenza epidemic... There was an epidemic of yellow fever in Philadelphia.* 2 the rapid development and spread of something. EG *When tennis became fashionable there was an epidemic of white socks and canvas shoes.* N COUNT : USU+SUPP ⇑ outbreak; N COUNT+SUPP ⇑ outbreak

epidermis /epɪdɜːmɪs/. Your **epidermis** is the thin, protective, outer layer of your skin. EG *These cells are just under the epidermis.* N SING : the/POSS +N

epiglottis /epɪglɒtɪs/, **epiglottises** or **epiglottides**. Your **epiglottis** is the thin flap at the back of your tongue which closes when you swallow food in order to prevent the food from going down your windpipe. N COUNT

epigram /epɪgræm/, **epigrams**. An **epigram** is a short saying or poem which expresses an idea in a very clever and amusing way. EG *...brilliant epigrams of his own invention.* N COUNT

epigrammatic /epɪgrəmætɪk/. Something that is **epigrammatic** is like an epigram. EG *...almost epigrammatic jokes.* ADJ CLASSIF ⇑ snappy

epilepsy /epɪlepsi¹/ is a disease in which causes a person suddenly to lose consciousness and have violent fits. EG *He couldn't take that job at the zoo because of his epilepsy.* N UNCOUNT/COUNT ⇑ condition

epileptic /epɪleptɪk/, **epileptics**. 1 **Epileptic** means caused by epilepsy or suffering from epilepsy. EG *He fell into my arms in an epileptic fit.* 2 An **epileptic** is a person who suffers from epilepsy. ADJ CLASSIF : ATTRIB; N COUNT

epilogue /epɪlɒg/, **epilogues**. An **epilogue** is a passage or speech which is added to the end of a book or play as a conclusion. EG *The novel ends with an epilogue in the form of a poem.* N COUNT ≠ prologue

Epiphany /ɪ¹pɪfəni¹/ is a Christian festival held on January 6th, which commemorates the arrival of the three wise men who came to see Jesus Christ soon after he was born. N UNCOUNT

episcopal /ɪ¹pɪskəpə⁰l/; often spelled with a capital letter, especially for paragraph 2. 1 **Episcopal** is used to describe the activities, duties, responsibilities, etc, of a bishop or bishops. ADJ CLASSIF : ATTRIB

2 An **Episcopal** Church is one which is governed by bishops. EG *...the hierarchy of the Episcopal Church.* ADJ CLASSIF : ATTRIB

Episcopalian /ɪ¹pɪskəpeɪlɪən/. 1 **Episcopalian** means belonging to an Episcopal Church. EG *They were married by an Episcopalian minister in Boston.* ADJ CLASSIF : ATTRIB ⇑ Christian

2 An **Episcopalian** is a member of an Episcopal church. N COUNT ⇑ Christian

episode /epɪsəʊd/, **episodes**. 1 An **episode** is a period or event in which something exciting, sad, or important has happened. EG *A wartime episode had demonstrated his judgement of men... Has this episode changed your way of working or your attitude?... A series of isolated episodes from history.* N COUNT : USU MOD+N ⇑ happening

2 An **episode** of a book or play is one part of it when it is appearing in several parts over a period of time, for example on television, on the radio, in a magazine, etc. EG *At the end of the first episode the kidnapper finally makes an appearance... Subsequent episodes will go out on Tuesdays on ITV.* N COUNT = instalment

episodic /epɪsɒdɪk/. Something that is **episodic** occurs at irregular and infrequent intervals; a formal word. ADJ QUALIT = intermittent, sporadic

epistle /ɪ'pɪsə⁰l/, **epistles**. 1 An **epistle** is a letter; a formal word, sometimes used humorously. EG *...a smudged, greasy, and tear-stained epistle which I received the other day.* N COUNT

2 An **Epistle** is also one of the books in the New Testament which were originally written as letters to early Christians by the apostles. EG *...the First Epistle to the Corinthians.* N COUNT+SUPP ⇑ letter

epistolary /ɪ²pɪstələ⁰ri¹/. An **epistolary** novel or story is one that is presented in the form of a series of letters; a formal word. EG *There's a whole chapter on how to write an epistolary novel.* ADJ CLASSIF : ATTRIB

epitaph /ɛpɪtɑːf, -tæf/, **epitaphs**. An **epitaph** is a short description, thought, or message about someone who is dead, often written on their gravestone. EG *He began to collect old books of epitaphs.* N COUNT ⇑ inscription

epithet /ɛpɪθɛt/, **epithets**. An **epithet** is an adjective or short, descriptive phrase which is used in praise or criticism of someone. EG *No one could have denied to him the epithet of handsome... ...the most vulgar kind of racial epithets.* N COUNT : USU+SUPP

epitome /ɪ'pɪtəmi¹/. The **epitome** of something is the thing that is considered to be the most typical example of its sort; a formal word. EG *His wealth of knowledge made him seem ageless and the epitome of a philosopher... ...the very epitome of Eastern grace and confidence.* N SING : *the*+N+*of* ⇑ example = model

epitomize /ɪ'pɪtəmaɪz/, **epitomizes, epitomizing, epitomized**; also spelled **epitomise**. If something **epitomizes** something else, it is a perfect or very typical example of this thing. EG *His failure epitomizes that of the whole movement... Conrad's novel epitomised both the good and the evil in Victorian society.* V+O ⇑ exemplify = typify

epoch /iːpɒk/, **epochs**. An **epoch** is a long period of time which is marked by an important event or series of events, often causing a great change in people's lives. EG *We are at the end of one historical epoch, and at the dawn of another.* N COUNT+SUPP = age

epoch-making. Something that is **epoch-making** is considered to be extremely important or significant. EG *...Needham's epoch-making account of Chinese science and civilization.* ADJ CLASSIF = momentous ≠ petty

eponymous /ɪ'pɒnɪməs/. An **eponymous** hero or heroine is the character in a play or book whose name is the title of that play or book; a literary term. EG *...Cedric, the eponymous hero of Little Lord Fauntleroy.* ADJ CLASSIF : ATTRIB

Epsom salts /ɛpsə⁰m sɔːlts/ is a white powder which you can mix with water and drink as a medicine to help you empty your bowels. N PLURAL ⇑ purgative

equable /ɛkwəbə⁰l/. Someone who is **equable** is always fair and reasonable, even in difficult circumstances. EG *'Oh yes, sir.' Bond's voice was patient, equable.* ADJ QUALIT ◊ **equably**. EG *'Ladies first, Hans,' says William equably.* ◊ ADV WITH VB

equal /iːkwəl/, **equals, equalling, equalled**; also spelled **equaling** and **equaled** in American English. 1 If two things are **equal** or if one thing is **equal** to another, they are 1.1 the same in size, number, or amount. EG *The cake was divided into twelve equal parts... Mix together equal parts of coarse salt and soda crystals. A table-tennis ball is roughly equal in size to a golf ball.* ADJ QUALIT : IF+PREP THEN *to* ⇑ identical ≠ unequal 1.2 of the same standard. EG *...cars that are at least equal to the imports.* ADJ QUALIT : IF+PREP THEN *to* = comparable

2 **Equal** is used with a noun that describes a feeling or quality to say that this feeling or quality is present to the same extent as in another person or thing. EG *The prevailing creed is held with equal fervour by all political parties.* ADJ CLASSIF : ATTRIB as much

3 If you treat people on an **equal** basis or give them **equal** rights, you treat them all in the same way and consider them to have the same rights as each other without considering their sex, status or race. EG *There is a trend towards equal opportunities for men and women.* ADJ CLASSIF : ATTRIB = identical ≠ unequal

4 If you say that people are or should be **equal**, you mean that everyone has or should have the same rights and opportunities as each other. EG *All men are equal.* ADJ CLASSIF : PRED ⇑ alike

5 Someone who is your **equal** has the same ability, status, or rights and responsibilities as you have. EG *...his intellectual equals... Women should be the legal equals of men.* N COUNT : WITH POSS ⇑ peer

6 If someone is **equal** to a particular job or situation, they have the necessary ability, strength or courage to deal successfully with it. EG *The staff are not equal to all these demands.* ADJ CLASSIF : PRED+*to*

7 If something **equals** a particular number or amount, it is the exact equivalent of it. EG *79 minus 14 equals 65... The standard dry measure then in use equalled twenty litres.* V+C

8 To **equal** something or someone means to be as good, to do as well, or in some other way to be of the same standard as them. EG *Few cars can equal a Ferrari for speed... ...specialized institutions, of which many now equalled the universities in repute.* V+O = match, rival

9 If you say that one thing **equals** another thing, you are comparing them and saying that they are both as remarkable as each other. EG *My respect for your intelligence is only equalled by my admiration for your integrity... I had seen nothing to equal the extravagance of her flowers.* V+O : USU+BROAD NEG ⇑ match

10 If you are **on equal terms** with someone or two people do something **on equal terms**, neither person has any advantage over the other or is regarded as being superior or better in any way. EG *This law enables British shipbuilders to compete on equal terms with foreign yards. He was the first black man I got to know on equal terms.* PHR : USED AS AN A on a level

11 If you say **'Other things being equal'**, you mean that a situation is or will be the case if nothing unexpected happens or if there are no other factors which affect it. EG *This would lead, other things being equal, to a price increase of not less than 2%... Education is a good thing, other things being equal.* PHR : USED AS ADV SEN

12 If something **has no equal**, there is nothing that is as good as it or that reaches the same standard. EG *...an act of charity that has no equal in modern times.* PHR : VB INFLECTS = be unsurpassed

equality /ɪ'kwɒlɪti¹/ is the same status, rights and responsibilities for all the members of a society, group or family. EG *Equality was a matter of official policy... ...equality of opportunity... Equality does not guarantee happiness in love.* N UNCOUNT ≠ inequality

equalize /iːkwəlaɪz/, **equalizes, equalizing, equalized**; also spelled **equalise**. 1 To **equalize** something such as a situation means to give everyone the same rights or opportunities in a particular area, for example society, education, wealth, etc. EG *It was thought that comprehensive schools would help to equalize society... Capital taxation will play a major part in equalizing the distribution of wealth.* V+O, OR V ⇑ balance = level ◊ **equalization** /iːkwəlaɪzeɪʃə⁰n/. EG *...the equalization of wealth through taxation.* ◊ N UNCOUNT

2 In a game such as football, if a team or player **equalizes**, they score a goal that makes the score of the two teams equal. EG *England equalized at the beginning of the second half.* V

equalizer /iːkwəlaɪzə/, **equalizers**. In a game such as football, an **equalizer** is a goal that makes the score of the two teams equal. EG *The equalizer came only minutes before the final whistle.* N COUNT

equally /iːkwəli¹/. 1 **Equally** means 1.1 in sections, amounts, or spaces, that are the same size as each other. EG *The fence posts should be equally spaced. On his death the land was divided equally between them.* ADV WITH VB ⇑ evenly ≠ unequally 1.2 to the same degree or extent as other people. EG *Men and women must become equally responsible for bringing up children... ...two equally qualified men.* ADV+ADJ/ADV 1.3 to the same degree or extent as someone or something else that has already been mentioned. EG *Irene was equally brilliant in timing and expertise... The sky seemed equally endless and desolate... Another tree of the same species, equally enormous, grew a stone's throw further on.* ADV+ADJ/ADV = just as

2 **Equally** is also used to introduce another comment on the same topic, which balances or contrasts with the previous comment. EG *Each country must find its own solution to unemployment.-Equally, each must find its own way of coping with inflation.* ADV SEN = by the same token

equals sign, equals signs. An **equals sign** is the sign =, which is used in arithmetic to indicate that two numbers or sets of numbers are equal. N COUNT ⇑ symbol

equanimity /ɛkwənɪmɪti¹/ is a calm state of mind and attitude to life, so that you never lose your temper or become very upset; a formal word. EG *They were content to accept their defeat with equanimity.* N UNCOUNT : USU *with*+N ⇑ calmness

equate /ɪ'kweɪt/, **equates, equating, equated**. If you **equate** a particular thing with something else, you say or believe that it is similar to or equal to this other thing. EG *They equated socialism with the* V+O+A (*with/to*) = identify *welfare state... It is imperative that war should on no account be equated with glory.*

equation /i¹kweɪʒəⁿn/, **equations**. An **equation** is 1 a mathematical statement saying that two amounts or values are the same, for example 6x4=12x2. EG *The solution can be expressed, crudely, by a mathematical equation.* 2 a situation or problem in which two or more parts have to be considered together so that the whole situation or problem can be understood or explained. EG *We have to consider the demand and the supply side of the economic equation.* — N COUNT; N COUNT

equator /i¹kweɪtə/. The **equator** is an imaginary line drawn round the middle of the earth at an equal distance from the North Pole and the South Pole. EG *The Galapagos lie scattered across the equator.* — N PROPER : the+N

equatorial /ɛkwətɔːrɪəl/. Something that is **equatorial** is near or at the equator. EG *Too much rain is the problem of the equatorial lands in the Amazon and Congo basins.* — ADJ CLASSIF : USU ATTRIB

equerry /ɪ²kweri¹/, **equerries**. An **equerry** is an officer of a royal household or court who acts as a personal assistant to a member of the royal family. — N COUNT

equestrian /ɪ²kwestrɪən/. **Equestrian** means connected with the activity of riding horses. EG *...a colossal equestrian statue of the Duke of Wellington... ...equestrian gloves.* — ADJ CLASSIF : USU ATTRIB

equidistant /iːkwɪdɪstənt/. A place that is **equidistant** from two other places is the same distance away from each of these places. EG *These places on the Continent lay conveniently equidistant between Lionel's various offices.* — ADJ CLASSIF : PRED; ↑ positioned

equilateral /iːkwɪlætəⁿrəl/. A shape or figure that is **equilateral** has sides that are all the same length; a mathematical term. EG *...a tiny equilateral triangle.* — ADJ CLASSIF

equilibrium /iːkwɪlɪbrɪəm/, **equilibria**; a formal word. 1 **Equilibrium** is 1.1 a balance existing between several different influences or aspects of a situation so that none is more important or powerful than another. EG *I believe this state of equilibrium, evident at the end of the second year, will be maintained.* 1.2 a calm state of mind and attitude to life in which you are able to control your feelings and emotions so that you are never very angry or upset for a long time. EG *Change in the world around us disturbs our inner equilibrium.* — N UNCOUNT/COUNT; N UNCOUNT = composure ≠ turmoil

2 If something is **in equilibrium** it is in a state or condition in which no influence or aspect of a situation is more important or powerful than another. EG *We must reduce the rise of unemployment in order to keep the economy in equilibrium.* — PHR : USED AS AN A; ↑ stable

equine /ɛkwaɪn/ means 1 connected with or relating to horses. EG *...research into equine health.* 2 looking like a horse. EG *...a long, slightly equine face.* — ADJ CLASSIF; ADJ QUALIT

equinox /iːkwɪnɒks, ɛk-/, **equinoxes**. An **equinox** is one of the two days in the year when day and night are of equal length. EG *...the autumn equinox.* — N COUNT : USU MOD+N; ≠ solstice

equip /ɪ²kwɪp/, **equips, equipping, equipped**. 1 If someone **equips** you with something, or if you **equip** yourself with it, you obtain it for a particular purpose. EG *They will equip themselves with a great variety of computerised gadgets... You will be equipped with all the weapons you need.* — V+O (NG/REFL) : IF+PREP THEN with/for = supply

◊ **equipped**. EG *...a large and well equipped army.* — ◊ ADJ QUALIT

2 If something **is equipped** with a particular device, it contains that device. EG *The card will be equipped with a built-in computer chip... Not all microscopes are equipped to do this.* — V+O : USU PASS

3 If something **equips** you for a particular task or experience, it prepares you mentally for it, especially by educating you in a particular way. EG *His contribution to the boy's welfare was to equip him for the world in which he would live... Kindness will not equip them to stand on their own feet.* — V+O (NG/REFL) : IF+PREP THEN for

◊ **equipped**. EG *He did not think himself equipped to comment... They were plainly ill equipped to deal with the situation.* — ◊ ADJ QUALIT : PRED, USU ADV+ADJ = fit

equipment /i¹kwɪpməⁿnt/ consists of the things which are used for a particular purpose, for example a hobby or job. EG *...basic kitchen equipment... This is an important piece of equipment... A fair amount of money goes on equipment and research expenditure... They exported a million dollars' worth of stereo equipment.* — N UNCOUNT

equipoise /ɛkwɪpɔɪz/ is a balance existing between several different influences or aspects of a situation so that none is more important or powerful than another; a formal word. — N UNCOUNT = equilibrium

equitable /ɛkwɪtəbəⁿl/. Something that is **equitable** is fair and reasonable in a way that gives equal treatment to everyone. EG *...economic growth of a more balanced and equitable kind.* ◊ **equitably**. EG *Land would inevitably become more equitably distributed.* — ADJ QUALIT = just; ◊ ADV

equity /ɛkwɪti¹/ is 1 the quality of being fair and reasonable in a way that gives equal treatment to everyone. EG *...an assurance of equity and social justice.* 2 the principle used in law which allows a fair judgement to be made in a case where the existing laws do not provide a reasonable answer to the problem; a technical term in law. — N UNCOUNT = fairness; N UNCOUNT

equivalence /i¹kwɪvələns/. If there is **equivalence** between two things, they have the same use, function, size, or value. EG *Can we establish the equivalence of these two values?* — N UNCOUNT = correspondence

equivalent /i¹kwɪvələ²nt/, **equivalents**. 1 An **equivalent** is something that has the same use or function as something else. EG *...Kabutocho, Japan's equivalent of Wall Street... A good quilt can be the equivalent of at least three blankets.* — N COUNT : IF+PREP THEN of

2 **Equivalent** means having the same use, function, size, or value as something else. EG *Women were paid less than men doing equivalent work... His job was roughly equivalent to that of the State Department's chief.... I wonder if they have equivalent institutions in other countries.* — ADJ CLASSIF : USU PRED, IF+PREP THEN to/of = similar ≠ different

equivocal /i¹kwɪvəkəⁿl/. 1 If you say something which is **equivocal**, it is deliberately vague or ambiguous because you want to avoid speaking the truth; a formal word. EG *She gave an equivocal reply.* ▸ used of people. EG *He found me equivocal on the subject.* — ADJ QUALIT ≠ unequivocal; ▸ ADJ QUALIT : USU PRED

2 **Equivocal** behaviour, attitudes, and events are difficult to understand, interpret, or explain. EG *The anarchists' attitude to violence is so often equivocal and subjective.* — ADJ QUALIT ≠ unequivocal

equivocate /i¹kwɪvəkeɪt/, **equivocates, equivocating, equivocated**. When someone **equivocates**, they deliberately use vague and ambiguous language in order to deceive people or to avoid speaking the truth. EG *For Adams the temptation to equivocate was especially strong.* ◊ **equivocation** /i¹kwɪvə⁷keɪʃəⁿn/. EG *'Wishy-washy liberal equivocation,' she shouted.* — V = hedge; ◊ N UNCOUNT

er /ə, ɜː/ is used to represent 1 the sound that people make when they hesitate, especially while they decide what to say next. EG *And it was not until 1845 that, er, Texas became part of the USA... 'Do you want the coach from Cardiff?'-'Er, yes.'* 2 the sound that people make when they want to attract someone's attention before speaking. EG *Er, ladies and gentlemen, dinner is served.*

-er. You add **-er** 1 to adjectives that have one or two syllables in order to form comparative adjectives. It is also added to some adverbs that do not end in -ly in order to form comparative adverbs. EG *...hard→harder... ...big→bigger... ...simple→simpler... ...pretty→prettier... ...soon→sooner.* 2 to verbs to form nouns which refer to a person, animal, or thing that does the action described by the verb; for example a reader is someone who reads and a money-saver is something that saves money. EG *...rob→robber... ...question→questioner... ...cleanse→cleanser.* 3 to words to form nouns which refer to a person who is associated or involved with the thing described by the word; for example a pensioner is someone who is entitled to a pension. EG *...teenage→teenager... ...backbench→backbencher.* 4 to nouns to form nouns or adjectives which refer to things with a particular characteristic or feature; for example a three-wheeler is a vehicle with three wheels. EG *...double-decker... ...eight-pounder.* 5 to words to form nouns which refer to a person with a particular job. EG *...miner... ...hairdresser... ...steelworker.* 6 to the names of places to form nouns which refer to a person who comes from that place. EG *...New Zealand→New Zealander... ...London→Londoner... ...island→islander.* — SUFFIX : FORMS ADJS/ADVS IN COMPAR; SUFFIX : FORMS NOUNS; SUFFIX : FORMS NOUNS; SUFFIX : FORMS NOUNS OR ADJ CLASSIFS; SUFFIX : FORMS N COUNTS; SUFFIX : FORMS N COUNTS

era /ɪərə/, **eras**. An **era** is a continuous period of time that is considered as a single unit because it has a particular feature that makes it notable. EG *Such cases have been rare in the post-war era... We are moving swiftly into the era of the temporary prod-* — N COUNT : USU+SUPP = age *uct... Her candidacy marked the beginning of a new era for the party.*

eradicate /ɪrædɪkeɪt/, **eradicates, eradicating, eradicated.** To **eradicate** something means to destroy it completely; a formal word. EG *Why should I be against measures attempting to eradicate the problem altogether?... ...positive and overt efforts to eradicate every trace of discrimination.* ◊ **eradication** /ɪ²rædɪkeɪʃə⁰n/. EG *...the eradication of apartheid.* — V+O = eliminate, wipe out; ◊ N UNCOUNT = removal

erase /ɪreɪz/, **erases, erasing, erased.** 1 If you **erase** a thought or feeling, you destroy it completely so that you can no longer remember something or no longer feel a particular emotion. EG *Although he is now a wealthy man he cannot erase the memories of childhood... The whisky erased any uneasiness and soon we were chatting as old friends.* — V+O = blot out

2 If you **erase** sound which has been recorded on a tape or information which has been stored in a computer, you completely remove or destroy it. EG *We cannot erase the recording... You can erase those two files.* — V+O = wipe, delete

3 If you **erase** writing, you remove it from somewhere, especially by rubbing it with a rubber or a cloth. — V+O = wipe out

4 To **erase** something also means to destroy or remove it completely so that it no longer exists; a formal use. EG *The process of weathering has erased most craters.* — V+O

eraser /ɪreɪzə/, **erasers.** An **eraser** is a piece of rubber used for rubbing out writing; used especially in formal or American English. EG *Try to remove dirt marks with an eraser.* — N COUNT = rubber

erasure /ɪreɪʒə/, **erasures.** 1 An **erasure** is a letter or word that has been removed from a text by being rubbed out; a formal use. EG *Every detail of it was written with scarcely an erasure or correction.* — N COUNT

2 The **erasure** of something is the complete loss or destruction of it. — N UNCOUNT : USU +SUPP

ere /ɛə/ is an old-fashioned or poetic word that means the same as 'before' when it is used to refer to time. EG *Sam well knew this habit of hers and had ere now taken advantage of it.* — PREP OR CONJ SUBORD

erect /ɪrɛkt/, **erects, erecting, erected.** 1 If you **erect** a building, wall, etc, you build it; a formal use. EG *It would be splendid to erect a memorial to the 42nd regiment... This is the famous La Punta Fortress, erected to shield Havana from the French and English armies.* — V+O = construct, build, put up

2 If you **erect** something, you fit the pieces of it together and put it in an upright position, so that it is ready to be used. EG *Six policemen started to erect a roadblock... Thirty camp-beds had to be erected in the canteen each night... This type of chair, easily erected or folded away, is ideal for use in the garden.* — V+O = put up ≠ take down

3 If you **erect** a political or social system or institution, you create it. EG *The mission of socialism was not to erect a conglomeration of separate nations... I don't want to see a system like that erected.* — V+O = set up

4 **Erect** means in a straight and upright position. EG *Humans walk erect on their hind legs... In the door, small but erect, stood an old man... She held herself erect, trembling slightly.* ◊ **erectly.** EG *Each plant begins by growing erectly.* — ADJ QUALIT; ◊ ADV WITH VB

5 If an animal's tail or ears are **erect**, they are stiff and sticking out or up, rather than hanging down or lying flat. EG *For a dog, an erect tail indicates aggression.* — ADJ CLASSIF : ATTRIB = rigid ≠ drooping

6 If a man's penis or a woman's nipples are **erect**, they are stiff, swollen, and sticking up or out. — ADJ CLASSIF

erection /ɪrɛkʃə⁰n/, **erections.** 1 If a man has an **erection**, his penis is stiff, swollen, and sticking up. — N COUNT

2 The **erection** of something is the act of building it or placing it in an upright position. EG *...the erection of a gravestone.* — N UNCOUNT : USU +SUPP = putting up

ergo /ɜːgəʊ/ is a formal or humorous word which means the same as 'therefore'. — ADV SEN = so, hence

ergonomics /ɜːgənɒmɪks/ is the study of how working conditions, machines, and equipment can be arranged, in order that people can work with them more efficiently. — N UNCOUNT

ermine /ɜːmɪn/ is expensive white fur that comes from stoats. — N UNCOUNT

erode /ɪ¹rəʊd/, **erodes, eroding, eroded.** 1 If rock or soil **erodes** or **is eroded** by the weather, sea, or wind, it cracks and breaks so that it is gradually destroyed. EG *Rain and rivers eroded the soft sandstones... Kimberly would be sliding down into it if the edges started eroding.* — V-ERG : USU PASS

2 If someone's power, authority, rights, etc **erode** or **are eroded**, they are gradually destroyed or removed; a formal use. EG *International confidence in the dollar has eroded... Our freedom is being eroded by quite well meaning and insidious bureaucrats.* — V-ERG : USU PASS

erode away. 1 If rock or soil **erodes away** or **is eroded away**, it cracks and breaks so that it is gradually destroyed completely. EG *The deposits that had accumulated on the mountainside were eroded away.* — PHRASAL VB : V-ERG + ADV, USU PASS = wear away

2 If someone's power, authority, rights, etc **erode away** or **are eroded away**, they are gradually destroyed or removed completely. EG *You would think colonialism of this kind would have eroded away... Our sovereign right to legislate has been eroded away.* — PHRASAL VB : V-ERG + ADV, USU PASS

erogenous /ɪ¹rɒdʒɪnəs/. An **erogenous** part of your body is one where sexual pleasure can be felt or caused; a formal word. EG *...an erogenous zone.* — ADJ QUALIT

erosion /ɪ¹rəʊʒə⁰n/ is 1 the gradual destruction and removal of rock or soil in a particular area by rivers, the sea, or the weather. EG *Floyd has reported severe and destructive soil erosion and progressive loss of plant nutrients.* 2 the gradual destruction or removal of a person's power, rights, authority, etc. EG *...the gradual erosion of individual freedom.* 3 a gradual reduction in the number of people or things in a particular group. EG *They will have to go a long way before there is much erosion of the numbers out of work.* — N UNCOUNT : USU +SUPP = weathering; N UNCOUNT + SUPP; N UNCOUNT + SUPP

erotic /ɪ¹rɒtɪk/. 1 Activities and situations that are **erotic** involve sexual desire and feelings. EG *She had loved him with a wild erotic joy... ...erotic dreams.* ◊ **erotically.** EG *He found her loose dress erotically appealing.* — ADJ QUALIT; ◊ ADV

2 Paintings, books, films, etc, that are **erotic** describe or show situations that involve naked people or sexual acts, usually in a skilful and artistic way, and are often intended to produce feelings of sexual pleasure. EG *...an anthology of erotic verse... ...erotic photographs.* — ADJ QUALIT

erotica /ɪ¹rɒtɪkə/ are works of art that show and describe naked people and sexual activity, usually in a skilful and artistic way, and are often intended to arouse sexual feelings in the viewer or reader: compare **pornography**. — N UNCOUNT

eroticism /ɪ¹rɒtɪsɪzə⁰m/ is 1 the erotic quality of a book, picture, sculpture, etc. EG *The powerful eroticism of the book was a revelation.* 2 sexual interest and excitement. EG *...the helpless rapture of adolescent eroticism.* — N UNCOUNT; N UNCOUNT

err /ɜː/, **errs, erring, erred.** 1 If you **err**, you make a mistake; an old-fashioned, formal use. — V
● When you say **to err is human**, you mean that it is natural for human beings to make mistakes. — ● PHR

2 If you **err on the side of** something, you tend to support a particular way of behaving in what you say or do. EG *Often one finds that advisers err on the side of caution.* — PHR : VB INFLECTS

errand /ɛrənd/, **errands.** An **errand** is a short trip that you make in order to do a job for someone, for example when you go to a shop to buy something for them. EG *As children grow older, they enjoy going on errands... Colonel Burr sent me on an errand to the Register's office.* ● If you **run an errand** for someone, you do or get something for them, usually by making a short trip somewhere. EG *It was the children's job to run errands.* — N COUNT; ● PHR : VB INFLECTS ⇑ help

errant /ɛrənt/; a formal word. 1 **Errant** is used to describe someone whose behaviour or actions are considered unacceptable or wrong by other people. EG *They came straight up to me, like errant children, begging forgiveness... ...errant capitalist intellectuals.* — ADJ CLASSIF : ATTRIB

2 **Errant** is also used to describe a husband or wife who is unfaithful to his or her partner. EG *...laws that compel an errant husband to support his ex-wife.* — ADJ CLASSIF : ATTRIB

errata /ɪ²rɑːtə/ are the mistakes that are made during the printing of a book; a formal word. — N PLURAL

erratic /ɪ²rætɪk/. Something that is **erratic** does not follow a regular pattern, but happens at unexpected times or moves along in an irregular way. EG *...a dreadful symbol of the country's erratic attempts to move into the future... I made my erratic way through the dining saloon.* ◊ **erratically.** EG *The boat* — ADJ QUALIT ≠ steady; ◊ ADV *was now rolling, erratically and violently, through almost fifty degrees.*

erroneous /ɪ²rəʊnɪəs/. Beliefs, opinions, methods, etc, that are **erroneous** are incorrect or only partly correct. EG *Criminal law is founded on the erroneous belief that every man is a responsible human being... This idea seemed to me totally erroneous.*
ADJ QUALIT = mistaken ≠ accurate

◊ **erroneously.** EG *Textbooks have erroneously called this an oxygen deficit machine.*
◊ ADV WITH VB = mistakenly

error /ɛrə/, **errors**. An **error** is something you have done which is considered to be incorrect or wrong, or which should not have been done. EG *His own country had made the same strategic error... The doctor committed an appalling error of judgement... ...errors in grammar... A degree of error is inevitable in guides such as this.* ● See also **trial and error**.
N COUNT/UNCOUNT = mistake

2 If you do something **in error** or if it happens **in error**, you do it or it happens because you have made a mistake, especially in your judgement. EG *Another innocent village had been wiped out in error.*
PHR : USED AS AN A

ersatz /ɛəzæts, ɜː-/. Something that is described as **ersatz** is an imitation of an expensive substance such as coffee or silk, usually because the real substance is either too expensive or too difficult to obtain; used showing disapproval. EG *It tasted more like ersatz coffee to me.*
ADJ CLASSIF : USU ATTRIB ⇑ substitute = fake ≠ authentic

erstwhile /ɜːstwaɪl/. You use **erstwhile** to describe someone or something that used to have the job, position, or role indicated, but no longer has it; a formal and old-fashioned word. EG *My erstwhile brother-in-law wants to see me.*
ADJ CLASSIF : ATTRIB = former

erudite /ɛrudaɪt/. People or books that are **erudite** have or show great academic knowledge; used showing approval. EG *...one of the most erudite political philosophers of his age... ...erudite works.*
ADJ QUALIT = learned, scholarly

erudition /ɛruːdɪʃə⁰n/ is great academic knowledge; a formal word, used showing approval. EG *...a thinker of great originality and immense erudition.*
N UNCOUNT = learning

erupt /ɪ¹rʌpt/, **erupts, erupting, erupted**. 1 When a volcano **erupts**, it throws out a lot of hot, molten lava, ash, and steam in a violent and destructive way. ◊ **eruption** /ɪ¹rʌpʃə⁰n/, **eruptions.** EG *...a volcano on the point of eruption.*
V : NO IMPER ⇑ burst = explode
◊ N COUNT/UNCOUNT

2 If something such as fire or a loud sound **erupts** from somewhere, it suddenly comes out of it in a surprising or frightening way. EG *A burst of gunfire erupted from Fort Esther... Again laughter erupted from the children.* ◊ **eruption**.
V+A (from) = burst out
◊ N COUNT

3 If war or fighting **erupts**, it suddenly begins in a surprising and violent way. EG *...the urban riots that erupted this summer in Britain... Fighting and plundering and arson have erupted all over the city.* ◊ **eruption**. EG *...the eruption of a major war between the super-powers.*
V = break out, explode
◊ N COUNT : USU +of

4 When a place, meeting, or group of people **erupts**, the people involved suddenly become very disorganized and violent. EG *US cities may erupt in protest against the latest Reagan policies... The demonstration erupted into a brutal battle between police and students.* ◊ **eruption**. EG *...the spontaneous eruption of the masses, when they sense a crisis.*
V+A = break out, explode
◊ N COUNT : USU +of

5 If a new situation or movement **erupts**, it suddenly happens in a surprising and unexpected way. EG *Spontaneous discussion erupted about colour prejudice... The women's movement erupted, and sex roles started breaking down... A strange new society is apparently erupting in our midst.* ◊ **eruption**. EG *...the eruption of religious sects in the seventeenth century.*
V ⇑ happen = break out
◊ N COUNT : USU +of

6 If a sore or spot **erupts** on your skin, it suddenly appears there. EG *Skin sores resembling burns erupted on parts of her body.* ◊ **eruption**. EG *...an eruption of pimples.*
V : USU+A ⇑ appear
◊ N COUNT : USU +of

-ery; also spelled **-ry**. The suffix **-ery** is added to some nouns that refer to objects of a particular kind, to form nouns that refer to groups or collections of these objects. EG *...machine→machinery... ...jewel→jewellery... ...weapon→weaponry... ...gadget→gadgetry.*
SUFFIX : FORMS NOUNS

-es is added in place of '-is' at the end of some nouns to form plurals. EG *...crisis→crises... ...hypothesis→hypotheses... ...oasis→oases.* ● See also **-s**.
SUFFIX : FORMS NOUNS IN PLURAL

escalate /ɛskəleɪt/, **escalates, escalating, escalated.** If a bad or unpleasant situation **escalates** or if someone **escalates** it, it becomes greater in size, seriousness, or intensity. EG *There is a danger that the conflict might escalate to a nuclear confrontation... By so doing, we escalate the problems.*
V-ERG = worsen, increase

◊ **escalation** /ɛskəleɪʃə⁰n/, **escalations.** EG *...a steady escalation of violence.*
◊ N COUNT/UNCOUNT

escalator /ɛskəleɪtə/, **escalators**. An **escalator** is a moving staircase on which people can go from one level to another without walking.
N COUNT

escalope /ɛskəlɒp/, **escalopes**. An **escalope** is a thin boneless slice of meat, especially veal.
N COUNT

escapade /ɛskəpeɪd/, **escapades**. An **escapade** is an adventurous, daring, or naughty act or incident that causes trouble. EG *He was involved in covering up the Watergate escapade... The whole school knew every detail of this mad escapade.*
N COUNT ⇑ adventure = exploit

escape /ɪ²skeɪp/, **escapes, escaping, escaped**.
1 If you **escape** a situation or duty that you think is dangerous, unpleasant, or difficult, you succeed in avoiding it. EG *How does one escape from the influence of such dominating ideas... Goodness knows how I escaped being like that... Ralph walked in the rear, thankful to have escaped responsibility for a time.*
V, V+-ING, V+A (from), OR V+O : NO PASS ⇑ avoid

2 If you **escape** from a person, situation, or feeling which you do not like or which you are afraid of, you succeed in getting away from them. EG *Many crossed the border to escape the carnage in their homeland... She would marry the first man who asked her, in order to escape her father.*
V, V+A (from), OR V+O : NO PASS

3 If you **escape** or **escape** from a place such as a prison, you succeed in getting away from there, even though people are trying to keep you there by force. EG *In 1966 the master spy George Blake escaped from prison... Even if he managed to escape, where would he run?* ◊ **escaped.** EG *...escaped convicts.*
V : IF+PREP THEN from/out of/to
◊ ADJ CLASSIF

4 If you **escape**, 4.1 you get away from a place or person when someone is trying to catch you, for example if you have just committed a crime. EG *This enabled him not only to complete the mission, but to escape unharmed... The two other burglars were tipped off by a lookout and escaped.* 4.2 you survive something unpleasant or dangerous, such as an attack or a natural disaster. EG *Fortunately we all escaped unscathed... The minister escaped without a scratch.*
V, V+A (from), OR V+O : NO PASS
V+C, OR V+A

5 If something **escapes** you or **escapes** your notice or attention, it remains unknown, unnoticed, or forgotten. EG *And there's a major point that seems to have escaped you, Captain Imrie... I doubt that that such tactics escaped their notice.*
V+O = elude

6 Gases, heat, liquids, etc that **escape** come out from a physical object, channel, or container which is intended to hold them. EG *...a hissing sigh, rather like the sound of air escaping from a tyre.*
V, OR V+A (from) ⇑ emerge

7 If you describe a situation or activity as an **escape**, you mean that it is a way of avoiding something which you think is dangerous, unpleasant, or difficult. EG *To be ill is the honourable way out, the escape from intolerable emotional stress... Reading is an escape from reality... Paris would be an escape from the provincialism I detested... There can be no escape for the man who does not conform.*
N COUNT/UNCOUNT : IF+PREP THEN from ⇑ release = refuge

8 An **escape** is an act of escaping from a particular place or situation. EG *They were now enabled to make their escape... It was a daring escape... She had nourished dreams of escape herself, once.*
N UNCOUNT/COUNT : IF+PREP THEN from/to

9 An **escape** of gas or liquid is a leak of it from a pipe or container.
N COUNT

escapee /ɪ²skeɪpiː/, **escapees**. An **escapee** is a person who has escaped, especially from prison. EG *There has been a steady stream of escapees.*
N COUNT ≠ detainee

escapism /ɪ²skeɪpɪzə⁰m/ is activity that helps you to think about pleasant or fantastic things instead of the uninteresting or unpleasant aspects of your everyday life. EG *Thinking about the future is a form of escapism... His films are pure escapism.*
N UNCOUNT ⇑ fantasy

escapist /ɪ²skeɪpɪst/, **escapists**. 1 **Escapist** is used to describe ideas, stories, films, etc that help you to think about pleasant or fantastic things instead of the uninteresting or unpleasant aspects of your everyday life. EG *It is accepted by all as light, escapist, television stuff... The film is an escapist fantasy.*
ADJ QUALIT = diverting

2 An **escapist** is someone who thinks a lot about imaginary things in order to avoid thinking about their ordinary life.
N COUNT ⇑ dreamer ≠ realist

escapologist /ɛskəpɒlədʒɪst/, **escapologists**. An **escapologist** is someone who entertains audiences
N COUNT ⇑ entertainer

by being tied up and placed in a dangerous situation, such as a tank full of water, and escaping from it while the audience watches.

escarpment /ɪ²skɑːpmə²nt/, **escarpments**. An **escarpment** is a wide, steep slope on a ridge or mountain. N COUNT

eschew /ɪ²stʃuː/, **eschews, eschewing, eschewed**. If you **eschew** something, you deliberately avoid doing it or becoming involved in it; a formal word. EG *Evans eschewed costly ideas such as financing new prisons... A civilized leader must eschew violence.* V+O = shun

escort, escorts, escorting, escorted. The word **escort** is pronounced /ɛskɔːt/ when it is a noun, and /ɪ²skɔːt/ when it is a verb. **1** An **escort** is **1.1** a person or vehicle that travels with someone in order to protect or guard them. EG *...a police escort... We set off on our march, under escort of course.* ▸ used as a verb. EG *He had supplied soldiers to escort the miners to the mountains.* N COUNT, OR *under*+N : USU MOD+N ▸ V+O **1.2** a person who accompanies another person of the opposite sex to a social event, especially when they are not emotionally involved with each other. EG *I was wearing a fur coat and my escort was, I think, in a dinner jacket.* ▸ used as a verb. EG *John would be only too pleased to escort you, I'm sure.* N COUNT ⇑ companion ▸ V+O

2 If you **escort** someone, you accompany them somewhere, especially in order to make sure that they leave a place or get to their destination. EG *He escorted me to the door... The vicar escorted her back to the drawing-room... The ship had been refuelled and escorted out of Moroccan waters.* V+O+A

-ese is **1** added to the names of countries in order to form nouns and adjectives. EG *...China→Chinese... ...Japan→Japanese... ...Congo→Congolese.* SUFFIX : FORMS NOUNS/ADJS **2** added to adjectives, nouns, or the names of places to form uncount nouns that refer to unattractive or confusing ways of writing or speaking; used showing disapproval. EG *...legal→legalese... ...telegraph→telegraphese... ...Brooklyn→Brooklynese.* SUFFIX : FORMS N UNCOUNTS

Eskimo /ɛskɪməʊ/, **Eskimos**. The plural can be either **Eskimos** or **Eskimo**. **1** An **Eskimo** is a member of the group of peoples who live in Alaska, Northern Canada, eastern Siberia, and other parts of the Arctic. N COUNT

2 Eskimo is the language spoken by Eskimos. N UNCOUNT

ESL /iː ɛs ɛl/ is an abbreviation for 'English as a second language'.

esophagus /iːsɒfəgəs/. See **oesophagus**.

esoteric /ɛsəʊtɛrɪk/. Something that is **esoteric** is understood only by a small number of people, especially because they have special knowledge or particular tastes and interests; a formal word. EG *It is written in an esoteric script that few people can read... The arguments are rather esoteric... There are indications that his esoteric popularity may be ebbing.* ADJ QUALIT = obscure ≠ well known

ESP /iː ɛs piː/ is an abbreviation for **1** 'English for specific purposes' or 'English for special purposes'; the technique of teaching English to students who need it for a particular job or profession or for some other purpose. N UNCOUNT **2** 'extra-sensory perception'. N UNCOUNT

esp. is a written abbreviation for 'especially'. EG *Everyone in the area, esp. children under 5, is at risk.*

especial /ɪ²spɛʃə⁰l/ means the same as special; a formal word. EG *He took especial care to vary his routine... This sculpture is of especial importance.* ADJ QUALIT : ATTRIB

especially /ɪ²spɛʃə⁰li¹/. **1** You use **especially** to emphasize **1.1** the importance of something when it is a member of a group which has just been mentioned. EG *They don't trust anyone. Especially people in our position... Children's bones and organs, especially, are very sensitive to radiation.* ADV SEN = particularly **1.2** a characteristic of something which has just been mentioned. EG *He loved young people, especially if he thought they had talent... I'm not attracted to sociology, especially the way it's taught here.* ADV SEN = particularly

2 Especially also means much more than usually or normally. EG *I tried to appear especially cheerful for her benefit... They didn't seem to find it especially hard to do these exams.* ADV+ADJ/ADV = particularly

Esperanto /ɛspərænṭəʊ/ is an invented language which consists of parts of several languages, and which was designed to help people from different countries communicate easily with each other. N UNCOUNT

espionage /ɛspɪənɑːʒ/ is the activity of finding out the political, military, industrial, etc secrets of your enemies or rivals by using spies. EG *The Swiss government threatened to throw them in jail for espionage.* N UNCOUNT = spying

esplanade /ɛspləneɪd/, **esplanades**. An **esplanade** is a wide, open road where people walk for pleasure, especially by the sea in seaside towns. EG *She would meet me for lunch in the King's Hotel on the Esplanade.* N COUNT = promenade

espousal /ɪ²spaʊzə⁰l/. The **espousal** of a particular policy, cause, or plan is the act of strongly supporting it; a formal word. EG *This espousal of disarmament lost him many friends.* N SING WITH DET +SUPP : USU+*of* ⇑ support

espouse /ɪ²spaʊz/, **espouses, espousing, espoused**. If you **espouse** a particular policy, cause, or plan, you become very interested in it and give your support to it; a formal word. EG *The ideas she espoused were incomprehensible to me.* V+O

espresso /ɛsprɛsəʊ/, **espressos**. **Espresso** is a coffee drink that is made by forcing steam or boiling water through ground coffee beans. N MASS ⇑ coffee

esprit de corps /ɛspriːdəkɔː/ is a feeling of loyalty and pride that is shared by the members of a group who consider themselves to be different from other people in some special way; a formal expression. N UNCOUNT

espy /ɪ²spaɪ/, **espies, espying, espied**. If you **espy** something, you see or notice it; an old-fashioned or humorous word. EG *Peter went right in and at this point espied the briefcase in the corner of the room.* V+O

Esq. is a written abbreviation for 'esquire'. EG *J. F. Walton, Esq., 52 Leicester Road, London EC3.*

-esque is added to the names of famous people, for example writers, composers, or painters, in order to form adjectives that describe something as being written, composed, painted, etc in a similar style to theirs. EG *...Pinter→Pinteresque... ...Mahler→Mahleresque.* SUFFIX : FORMS ADJS

esquire /ɛskwaɪə/ is a formal title that can be used after a man's name if he has no other title, especially on an envelope that is addressed to him. N IN TITLES : AFTER NAME = Esq.

-ess is used at the end of some nouns that refer to women or to female animals. EG *...actress... ...waitress... ...princess... ...lioness.* SUFFIX : FORMS N COUNTS

essay /ɛseɪ/, **essays, essaying, essayed**. **1** An **essay** is **1.1** a short piece of writing on one particular subject that is written by a student. EG *I had to produce an essay on Herrick for my tutor.* N COUNT **1.2** a short piece of writing on one particular subject that is written by a writer for publication. EG *...a volume of essays... I read some of his political essays.* N COUNT

2 If you **essay** something, you try to do it; a formal use. EG *She essayed a smile.* V+O = attempt

essayist /ɛseɪɪst/, **essayists**. An **essayist** is a writer who writes essays for publication. EG *...the best political essayist in the country today.* N COUNT

essence /ɛsə⁰ns/, **essences**. **1** The **essence** of something is its basic, central, and most important characteristic which gives it an individual identity. EG *Competition is the essence of all games... London has changed a good deal, though her essence, it seems to me, has remained undisturbed.* N SING WITH DET : USU WITH POSS = soul

2 You use the expression **in essence** when you are talking about the most important or central aspect of an idea, situation, event, etc. EG *But this is not in essence a book about religion... ...a technique capable of solving what have become in essence sociological and political problems.* PHR : USED AS ADV SEN = essentially, fundamentally

3 If you say that something **is of the essence**, you mean that it is absolutely necessary in order for a particular action to be successful. EG *Timing is of the essence in the art market.* PHR : VB INFLECTS = vital, crucial

4 Essence is a concentrated liquid that is used for flavouring food. EG *...brandy essence.* N MASS : USU+SUPP

essential /ɪ¹sɛnʃə⁰l/, **essentials**. **1** Something that is **essential** is considered to be extremely important or extremely necessary for a particular situation or activity. EG *It is essential to set your targets realistically... Land is essential for food and for work... It is absolutely essential that you continue... Qualifications are not essential, but some previous experience is useful... A degree is by no means an essential journalistic qualification.* ADJ QUALIT : IF+PREP THEN *for*/*to* = vital

2 Essential is also used to describe the most basic or important aspect of something, especially when you consider this aspect to be very typical. EG *...the* ADJ QUALIT : ATTRIB = fundamental *essential feature of the situation... The people around me translate the essential points of the lectures into English.*

3 An **essential** is something that you consider to be extremely important or necessary for the situation you are in or for the activity you are trying to do. EG *...other essentials such as fuel and clothing... I always considered a washing machine an essential.* N COUNT : USU PL ≠ luxury

4 **Essentials** are the most important principles, ideas, or facts involved in a particular subject. EG *Their laws deal with essentials, not appearances.* N PLURAL ≠ trivia

5 You use **in essentials** or **in all essentials** to say that you are not describing something in great detail, but are referring to the main aspects of it. EG *What Hal had written had been 'in all essentials a piece of fiction'... His development, in essentials, was the same as that of poor John.* PHR : USED AS ADV SEN = basically, essentially

essentially /ɪ'se̲nʃəli/. You use **essentially** 1 to say what you think is the most important and relevant feature of someone or something, and to say that you are not describing it in detail. EG *Phyllis was essentially a soft, caring person... The argument is essentially a technical one... Essentially, what you're saying is that a teacher shouldn't be seen to agree with this.* ADV SEN = basically 2 to emphasize a particular quality that something or someone has, and to say that you think this quality is their most important one. EG *This is a new and essentially fertile idea... We were living in a country not essentially different from our own.* ADV+ADJ = really

3 to indicate that what you are saying is true in general terms, and that other, more detailed factors, are not necessary for you to be able to make your point. EG *Such theories are essentially correct... Pat Branson essentially stopped eating.* ADV ⇑ broadly = basically

-est. You add **-est** to adjectives that have one or two syllables in order to form superlatives. It is also added to some adverbs that do not end in -ly. EG *...hard→hardest... ...big→biggest... ...simple→simplest... ...pretty→prettiest.* SUFFIX : FORMS ADJS/ADVS IN SUPERL

establish /ɪ'stæblɪʃ/, **establishes, establishing, established**. 1 If someone **establishes** a system, organization, or state of affairs, they create it and set it up in a way that is intended to be permanent. EG *A just, ordered society without a bureaucracy has yet to be established... There he had set out to establish his own business... They had already established a clear superiority.* V+O = set up, found

◊ **established**. EG *...his distrust of established authority... Though illegal, this was a well-established custom among the prisoners.* ◊ ADJ CLASSIF : ATTRIB

2 If you **establish** contact or communications with a group of other people, 2.1 you make the arrangements necessary to allow you to talk to them. EG *At six o'clock they managed to establish radio contact with the survivors.* V+O : IF+PREP THEN *with/between* = set up 2.2 you start to have discussions with them. EG *The proposal to establish contact with pressure groups was warmly welcomed... A solid relationship and a mutual trust were established very early between them.* V+O : IF+PREP THEN *with/between* ⇑ create = set up

3 If you **establish** that something is the case, you discover facts that show that it is certainly true. EG *I understand you've so far been unable to establish the cause of death... A court of enquiry established that there were faults on both sides.* V+O/REPORT-CL = determine

4 If you **establish** yourself as something, you become firmly associated with a particular kind of activity, often because you are known to do it well. EG *The third world has established itself as a low-cost manufacturer... The Liberals established themselves as the major alternative.* V+O (REFL) : IF +PREP THEN *as* ◊ **established**. EG *They took over an existing restaurant with an established clientele... ...several established carpenters.* ◊ ADJ QUALIT

5 If you **establish** your reputation as something, you cause people to have a particular opinion of you, often because you have done something very well. EG *He immediately established his reputation as a radical... ...the performances that established his international reputation.* V+O : IF+PREP THEN *as* = set up

establishment /ɪ'stæblɪʃmənt/, **establishments**. 1 The **establishment** of an organization or system is the act of creating it for a particular purpose. EG *...the establishment of free trade unions... The establishment of legal minimum pay is one of the objectives.* N SING : *the*+N+*of* = creation

2 An **establishment** is a shop, business, or some other sort of institution. EG *At least one establishment in Savile Row now sells clothes off-the-peg... The Government opened up its research establishments to industry.* N COUNT+SUPP

3 You use the **establishment** to refer to 3.1 a group of people in a country who have power and influence, especially civil servants and businessmen rather than politicians. The establishment is generally opposed to making changes to the existing political and social order. EG *It taught me more about the British Establishment... ...a pillar of the French Establishment.* N SING : *the*+N 3.2 a group of people who have power in a particular organization or area of activity. EG *...the financial establishment... The university establishment couldn't tolerate him.* N SING : *the*+ADJ CLASSIF+N

estate /ɪ'ste̲ɪt/, **estates**. 1 An **estate** is 1.1 a large area of land in the country, together with the property on it, which is owned by one person, family, or organization; used especially to refer to a country house and the farms and cottages nearby. EG *He bought an estate near Oxford... The colonel returned to his estate in Somerset for the weekend.* N COUNT 1.2 a large area of land, usually in or near a city, which has factories or houses on it; used in British English. EG *Singapore's industrial estates are comparable to those of any Western city... ...a housing estate.* N COUNT : ALSO IN NAMES AFTER N

2 Someone's **estate** is 2.1 all the money and property that they leave behind them when they die. EG *He divided his estate among his four brothers.* N COUNT : POSS+N 2.2 their position in society or among a particular group of people, which is judged by the amount of financial, social, or political power that they have; used in formal English. EG *So low had Suzuki's estate fallen that his own cabinet ministers disregarded his wishes.* N SING : POSS+N = standing

3 An **estate** is also an estate car; used in British English. N COUNT

estate agent, estate agents. An **estate agent** is someone who works for a company that sells houses and land for people; used in British English. N COUNT = realtor

estate car, estate cars. An **estate car** is a car which has a long body with a door at the back end and space behind the back seats; used in British English. N COUNT = station wagon

esteem /ɪ'sti̲:m/, **esteems, esteeming, esteemed**. 1 **Esteem** is admiration and respect that you feel towards another person; an old-fashioned and formal use. EG *I know the high esteem and friendship you feel for our colleague here... Zapp had no great esteem for his fellow labourers.* ● See also **self-esteem**. N UNCOUNT, OR N SING WITH DET

2 If you **hold** someone or something **in high esteem** or **in great esteem**, you admire and respect them very much. EG *This organization was one which he held in high esteem.* PHR : VB INFLECTS

3 If you **esteem** someone or something in a particular way, you have a particular opinion about them; used in formal or old-fashioned English. EG *I esteem him nothing but a fool.* V+O+C ⇑ think = deem

esteemed /ɪsti̲:md/. **Esteemed** is used to describe someone who you greatly admire and respect; a formal or old-fashioned word. EG *...our esteemed employer, Otto Gerran.* ADJ QUALIT ⇑ honoured = revered

esthete /i̲:sθi:t/. See **aesthete**.

esthetic /ɛsθe̲tɪk/. See **aesthetic**.

estimable /e̲stɪməbəl/. Someone or something that is **estimable** deserves respect and admiration; a formal word. EG *...valuable and estimable characteristics.* ADJ QUALIT ⇑ good = worthy

estimate, estimates, estimating, estimated. The word **estimate** is pronounced /e̲stɪmət/ when it is a verb, and /e̲stɪmeɪt/ when it is a noun. 1 If you **estimate** an amount or quantity, you calculate it approximately. EG *It has been estimated that four-fifths of the children in these schools will suffer... The hurricane caused damage estimated at 300 million pounds.* V+REPORT-CL, V+O+*to*-INF, OR V+O+A *(at)* ⇑ guess = reckon ◊ **estimated**. EG *In 1975 there were an estimated 6,000 children in community homes... Its estimated cost has climbed to a staggering £35 billion.* ◊ ADJ CLASSIF

2 If you **estimate** something, you make a judgement about it based on the available evidence. EG *She was estimating Anne's attitude to Tim... How would you estimate our chances?... He estimated he would do the hundred miles by noon.* V+O/REPORT-CL, OR V+O+*to*-INF = assess

3 An **estimate** is 3.1 an approximate calculation of an amount or quantity. EG *According to some estimates the number of farms has increased by 50 per cent... Moscow has clearly revised downward its* N COUNT = assessment

crop estimate from 230 million to 200 million tons.
3.2 a judgement about a person or situation which you make based on the available evidence. EG *Thomas wasn't living up to anyone's estimate of him... I've had to revise my estimate somewhat in her favour.* N COUNT : USU WITH POSS = assessment
3.3 a formal statement from a manufacturer, builder, plumber, etc which tells you how much a particular job is likely to cost. EG *It is a good idea to get at least two written estimates to compare costs.* N COUNT
4 You say **at a rough estimate** to indicate that the quantity or amount you are talking about is not exact, but is based on your approximate calculation. EG *It will take three years, at a rough estimate.* PHR : USED AS ADV SEN

estimation /ɛstɪmeɪʃəⁿn/, **estimations**; a formal word. 1 Your **estimation** of a person or situation is an opinion or impression that you have formed about them. EG *His comments were, in my estimation, correct and most useful... Their children's estimation of them will gradually get lower.* N SING : USU WITH POSS
2 An **estimation** is an approximate calculation of something that can be measured. EG *...an estimation of the speed of the air leaving the lungs.* N COUNT : IF + PREP THEN *of*

estranged /ɪ²streɪndʒd/. 1 If you are **estranged** from your husband or wife, you are no longer living with them. EG *Lionel and his estranged wife had never had children... He was thirty-five years old and estranged from his second wife.* ADJ CLASSIF : IF + PREP THEN *from*
2 If you are **estranged** from your family or friends, you have quarrelled with them and are not on speaking terms; a formal use. EG *He knows I am estranged from my father; he does not know why.* ADJ QUALIT : IF + PREP THEN *from* = alienated

estrangement /ɪ²streɪndʒmə²nt/, **estrangements**. **Estrangement** is the state of being estranged from someone or the length of time for which you are estranged; a formal word. EG *...his estrangement from his son... This sense of isolation and estrangement was easy enough to understand.* N UNCOUNT/COUNT ⇑ separation = alienation

estrogen /ɛstrədʒən, iːstrə-/. See **oestrogen**.

estuary /ɛstjuəⁿri¹/, **estuaries**. An **estuary** is the wide part of a river near where it joins the sea. N COUNT : ALSO IN NAMES AFTER N

et al. /ɛt æl/. The expression **et al.** is used after a name or a list of names to indicate that other people are also involved. EG *...an admirable paper by Harris et al.*

etc (pronounced the same as 'et cetera') is a written abbreviation for 'et cetera'; used at the end of a list to indicate that there are other items, events, or situations which you could mention if you had enough time and space, in addition to the ones which you have mentioned. EG *...window frames, floorboards, beams, etc... She had to empty bed pans, do the cleaning, make beds etc, etc.* = and so on

et cetera /ɪ²tsɛtəⁿrə/. See **etc**.

etch /ɛtʃ/, **etchs, etching, etched**. 1 If you **etch** a design or pattern on a surface, you cut it into the surface by using acid or by using a knife, chisel, etc. EG *I really enjoy etching... I read stories etched on the gravestones.* ◊ **etched**. EG *...an etched glass door.* V OR V+O = score ◊ ADJ CLASSIF
2 If shadows, lines, etc **etch** a surface, they mark it, and look as though they might have actually been cut into the surface. EG *Outside, icy branches etch lacy designs on the frosted window panes... The dry air etched his face full of fine lines.* V+O
3 If something **is etched** on your mind or memory, it has made a very strong impression on you so that you feel you will never forget it. EG *It will remain permanently etched on my memory... Some memories are etched with surprising clarity.* V+O : USU PASS = imprint

etching /ɛtʃɪŋ/, **etchings**. An **etching** is a picture printed from a metal plate that has had a design cut into it with acid. EG *His etchings and drawings never went out of fashion.* N COUNT

eternal /i¹tɜːnəⁿl/. 1 Something that is **eternal 1.1** lasts for ever. EG *...the promise of eternal bliss... For our Nordic ancestors, hell was the land of eternal cold.* ◊ **eternally**. EG *The door to Heaven stands eternally open, my son... Something remained eternally unspoiled in him.* **1.2** seems to last for ever, especially because it is boring or annoying. EG *Can't you stop this eternal quarrelling?... Bobby was the eternal practical joker.* ◊ **eternally**. EG *...the eternally recurring difficulties of his sick wife.* ADJ CLASSIF = everlasting ◊ ADV = forever ADJ CLASSIF = perpetual ◊ ADV + ADJ/ADV
2 **Eternal** truths, values, etc, never change and are believed to be always true and relevant in all situations. EG *...an unchanging society which lives by eternal principles.* ◊ **eternally**. EG *Political theories are not eternally valid.* ADJ CLASSIF = immutable, absolute ◊ ADV + ADJ/ADV

eternal triangle. You use the **eternal triangle** to refer to an emotional relationship involving love and jealousy between two men and a woman or two women and a man. N SING : *the*+N

eternity /i¹tɜːnɪti¹/, **eternities**. 1 **Eternity** is time without an end or a state of existence outside time, especially the state which some people believe they will pass into after they have died. EG *The preacher promised us eternity.* N UNCOUNT
2 An **eternity** is a period of time which seems to be very long indeed, usually because during that time you are experiencing something very boring or unpleasant; an informal use. EG *What an eternity ago that seems!.. I lay there for an eternity, retching and gasping.* N COUNT : IF SING *an*+N = age

ether /iːθə/. 1 **Ether** is a colourless liquid that burns easily. It is used in industry as a solvent and in medicine as an anaesthetic. N UNCOUNT
2 The **ether** is the air; a literary or formal use. EG *...a stutter of Morse code whispering through the ether.* N SING : *the*+N

ethereal /i¹θɪərɪəl/. Something that is **ethereal** is so light and delicate that it seems almost supernatural; often used showing approval. EG *...her ethereal beauty.* ADJ QUALIT ⇑ unearthly = fragile

ethic /ɛθɪk/, **ethics**. 1 An **ethic** of a particular kind is an idea or moral belief that influences the behaviour, attitudes, and philosophy of life of a group of people. EG *...the American 'frontier' ethic of expansion and opportunity... ...the Protestant work ethic.* N SING WITH DET +SUPP = principle
2 **Ethics** are moral beliefs and rules about right and wrong. EG *...a conscious, rational, scientific code of ethics... ...the basic ethics which any religion sets forward.* N PLURAL = morality
3 Someone's **ethics** are the moral principles about right and wrong behaviour which they believe in. EG *She despised his business ethics.... ...the dubious ethics of publishing information gained by deception or burglary.* N PLURAL + SUPP
4 **Ethics** is the study of questions about what is morally right and wrong. EG *...lectures on Church History, Ethics, and Systematic Theology.* N UNCOUNT

ethical /ɛθɪkəⁿl/ means 1 influenced by or arising from a system of moral beliefs about right and wrong. EG *They don't have any ethical codes to follow... ...an ethical problem... He had no real ethical objection to drinking.* ◊ **ethically**. EG *I found Captain Imrie's proposal distasteful and ethically objectionable.* 2 morally right when considered in relation to a system of beliefs about right and wrong. EG *It has never seemed so ethical and so right as it does now.* ADJ CLASSIF : USU ATTRIB = moral ◊ ADV + ADJ/ADV ADJ QUALIT ≠ unethical

Ethiopian /iːθɪəʊpɪən/, **Ethiopians**. 1 **Ethiopian** means belonging or relating to Ethiopia, or to its people or language. ADJ CLASSIF
2 An **Ethiopian** is a person who comes from Ethiopia. N COUNT

ethnic /ɛθnɪk/. 1 **Ethnic** means connected with or relating to different racial groups of people, especially when referring to the native people of a particular region or to racial minorities within a particular country or city. EG *...the ethnic composition of the voters of New York... ...ethnic minorities.* ◊ **ethnically**. EG *These people are geographically and ethnically distant from us.* ADJ CLASSIF : USU ATTRIB ⇑ national ◊ ADV + ADJ/ADV
2 **Ethnic** clothes, music, food, etc, are characteristic of the traditions of a particular ethnic group, and very different from what is usually found in modern Western culture; used showing approval. EG *She's really into ethnic music these days.* ADJ QUALIT = traditional

ethnographic /ɛθnə⁶græfɪk/. Something that is **ethnographic** is connected with or relates to ethnography. ADJ CLASSIF ⇑ anthropological

ethnography /ɛθnɒgrəfi¹/ is the branch of anthropology in which different cultures are studied and described. N UNCOUNT

ethnology /ɛθnɒlədʒi¹/ is the branch of anthropology in which the organization and cultures of different races of people are studied and compared. ◊ **ethnologist, ethnologists**. EG *...one of the world's most distinguished ethnologists.* ◊ **ethnological** /ɛθnə⁶lɒdʒɪkəⁿl/. N UNCOUNT ◊ N COUNT ◊ ADJ CLASSIF

ethos /iːθɒs/. An **ethos** is the set of ideas and attitudes that is associated with a particular group of people or a particular type of activity. EG *The working-class ethos of 'togetherness'... ...the prevailing social ethos.* N SING WITH DET : USU + SUPP

etiquette /ɛtɪkɛt/ is a set of customs and rules for polite behaviour, especially in a particular class of people or in a particular profession. EG *May I ask your opinion on a question of etiquette?* N UNCOUNT = manners

-ette is added to the names of objects to form nouns that refer to similar, but smaller, objects. EG *...statue→statuette... ...kitchen→kitchenette.* SUFFIX: FORMS N COUNTS

etymological /ɛtɪmə⁶lɒdʒɪkə⁰l/ means concerned with or relating to etymology. EG *...an etymological dictionary.* ◊ **etymologically**. ADJ CLASSIF ◊ ADV

etymology /ɛtɪmɒlədʒi¹/, **etymologies**. 1 **Etymology** is the study of the origins and historical development of words. N UNCOUNT

2 The **etymology** of a particular word is its history. N COUNT

eucalyptus /ju:kəlɪptəs/, **eucalyptuses**. **Eucalyptus** can also be used as the plural form. A **eucalyptus** is an evergreen tree that is grown to provide timber, gum, and an oil that is used in medicines. EG *...a forest of pines and eucalyptus.* N COUNT/UNCOUNT

Eucharist /ju:kərɪst/, **Eucharists**. The **Eucharist** is the Christian religious ceremony in which Christ's last meal with his disciples is remembered and celebrated. EG *...celebrating the Eucharist.* N SING: *the*+N, OR N COUNT

Eucharistic /ju:kərɪstɪk/ means concerned with or relating to the Eucharist. ADJ CLASSIF

eugenics /ju:dʒɛnɪks/ is the study of how to improve the human race by carefully selecting parents who will produce stronger children; a scientific term. EG *...the problems and ethical issues arising out of eugenics.* N UNCOUNT

eulogize /ju:lə⁷dʒaɪz/, **eulogizes, eulogizing, eulogized**; also spelled **eulogise**. If you **eulogize** something or **eulogize** over it, you praise it very much; a formal word. EG *...a new brand of literature that eulogized peasant life... On 28 May 1356, Bishop Henry was eulogizing over what Geoffrey had done.* V+A, V+O, OR V+O+A *(as)*

eulogy /ju:lə⁷dʒi¹/, **eulogies**. A **eulogy** is a speech or piece of writing that praises someone or something very much; a formal word. EG *...the various eulogies that have been written about the Queen Mother... For ten years he had heard nothing but eulogy.* N COUNT/UNCOUNT = panegyric

eunuch /ju:nək/, **eunuchs**. A **eunuch** is a man who has been castrated. Eunuchs were often employed in the past to guard women in Eastern countries. N COUNT

euphemism /ju:fɪ¹mɪzə⁰m/, **euphemisms**. A **euphemism** is a polite word or expression that people use when they are talking about something which they or other people find unpleasant or embarrassing, such as sex, bodily functions, war, etc. EG *'Escort' is the jail euphemism for a guard... 'Defence aid' is the modern euphemism for guns and ammunition.* N COUNT

euphemistic /ju:fɪ¹mɪstɪk/. Language that is **euphemistic** uses polite words or expressions when referring to things that people find unpleasant or embarrassing. ◊ **euphemistically**. EG *Then came what the French euphemistically call 'the events of May'–the student revolution.* ADJ QUALIT ◊ ADV WITH VB

euphoria /ju:fɔ:rɪə/ is a feeling of great happiness and elation. N UNCOUNT

euphoric /ju:fɒrɪk/. If you are **euphoric** you feel great happiness and elation. ADJ QUALIT ⇑ happy

Eurasian /juəreɪʃə⁰n, -ʒə⁰n/, **Eurasians**. 1 **Eurasian** means concerned with or relating to both Europe and Asia. ADJ CLASSIF

2 A **Eurasian** is a person who has one European and one Asian parent; an old-fashioned use. N COUNT, OR ADJ CLASSIF

eureka /jʊri:kə/. Someone might say **'eureka'** when they suddenly discover something such as the answer to a problem, or when they solve a mystery; an old-fashioned or humorous word. EXCLAM

Euro- is added to words to form other words that describe something which is connected with Europe or with the EEC. EG *...communism→Eurocommunism... ...dollar→Eurodollar... ...MP→Euro-MP.* PREFIX

Europe /jʊərəp/. **Europe** is 1 the continent which is joined to Asia in the east, and which is to the north of Africa and the Mediterranean Sea and to the east of the Atlantic Ocean; also used to refer to the people who live in Europe. EG *...the western coasts of Europe and Africa... Among them were some of the most notable political thinkers in Europe.* N PROPER 2 all of Europe except for the United Kingdom; used in British English. EG *Are our British dramatists equally unknown in Europe?* N PROPER = The Continent 3 the same as the EEC. EG *I gather that you are very much in favour of Britain being in Europe.* N PROPER

European /jʊərəpɪən/, **Europeans**. 1 **European** means coming from or relating to Europe. ADJ CLASSIF: USU ATTRIB

2 A **European** is a person who comes from Europe. EG *She was the only European living in the neighbourhood.* N COUNT

euthanasia /ju:θəneɪzɪə/ is the practice of killing someone painlessly in order to relieve their suffering when nothing can be done to help them, for example when they have an incurable illness. EG *He is totally against euthanasia.* N UNCOUNT = mercy killing

evacuate /i¹vækju⁴eɪt/, **evacuates, evacuating, evacuated**. 1 If someone **is evacuated**, they are sent to a place of safety, away from a building, town, or area where there is danger. EG *I was evacuated to Swindon... Tell them you intend to evacuate the children... They will be evacuated tomorrow night.* ◊ **evacuation** /i¹vækju⁴eɪʃə⁰n/, **evacuations**. EG *...arrangements for the evacuation of children.* V+O: USU PASS ⇑ relocate ◊ N UNCOUNT/COUNT ⇑ relocation

2 If people **evacuate** a place or if they **are evacuated**, they move out of it for a period of time, especially because it is dangerous. EG *The entire complex was being evacuated... During the war Westminster was evacuated four times... We grabbed sleeping bags and evacuated.* ◊ **evacuation**. EG *Orders went out to prepare for the evacuation of the city.* V+O: USU PASS, OR V ⇑ leave = clear ◊ N UNCOUNT/COUNT

evacuee /i¹vækju⁴i:/, **evacuees**. An **evacuee** is someone who has been sent away from a place because it is too dangerous, especially in war. EG *We crowded into the village hall, to await the arrival of the evacuees from Liverpool.* N COUNT

evade /i¹veɪd/, **evades, evading, evaded**. 1 If you **evade** something, 1.1 you find a way of not doing something that you really have to do. EG *...his desire to evade paying unnecessary tax... ...children who evade reading and writing.* V+O, OR V+-ING ⇑ avoid = dodge 1.2 you avoid talking about something or dealing with something important. EG *With great skill they evade the problem altogether... He had found a loophole which allowed him to evade responsibility... She never ever lied to us or evaded any question.* V+O = duck 1.3 you move in such a way as to avoid meeting someone or to avoid being touched or hit by someone or something. EG *He circled the table like one trying to evade the smoke from a bonfire... He caught her arm before she could evade him, drawing her towards him.* V+O = escape

2 If something such as success, glory, or love **evades** you, you never manage to achieve it. EG *Military glory had evaded him on his last campaign... Beauty and truth evade her.* V+O = elude

evaluate /i¹vælju⁴eɪt/, **evaluates, evaluating, evaluated**. If you **evaluate** something, you decide on its significance, value, or quality after carefully studying its good and bad features. EG *He was asked to evaluate the situation... ...the children's performance in school, as evaluated by their teachers... He's the kind of individual that's very hard to evaluate.* V+O ⇑ judge = assess

evaluation /i¹vælju⁴eɪʃə⁰n/, **evaluations**. An **evaluation** is a decision about the significance, value, or quality of something, based on a careful study of its good and bad features. EG *...a realistic evaluation of the working of Britain's economy... I attempted an honest evaluation of my own life.* N COUNT/UNCOUNT = appraisal

evanesce /ɛvənɛs/, **evanesces, evanescing, evanesced**. To **evanesce** means to disappear gradually from sight or memory; a formal or literary word. EG *...an apparition evanescing into darkness.* V+A = fade

evanescent /ɛvənɛsə⁰nt/. Something that is **evanescent** gradually disappears from sight or memory; a formal or literary word. EG *...evanescent wants and desires.* ADJ CLASSIF

evangelical /i:vændʒɛlɪkə⁰l/. People and beliefs that are **evangelical** are Christian and emphasize the importance of the four gospels and the need for personal belief in Christ in order to obtain salvation. EG *...an article about evangelical Christianity... ...a minister who is evangelical and charismatic in his beliefs.* ADJ CLASSIF ⇑ Christian

evangelism /i¹vændʒəlɪzə⁰m/ is the teaching of Christianity, especially to people who are not Christians. EG *Many of these students are involved in evangelism.* N UNCOUNT

evangelist /iˈvændʒəlɪst/, **evangelists**. An **evangelist** is a person who travels from place to place in order to try to convert people to Christianity. EG *...Joseph Booth, a white evangelist from the United States.* N COUNT

evangelize /iˈvændʒəlaɪz/, **evangelizes, evangelizing, evangelized**; also spelled **evangelise**. To **evangelize** means to try to convert people to Christianity. V OR V+O

evaporate /iˈvæpəreɪt/, **evaporates, evaporating, evaporated**. 1 When a liquid **evaporates**, some of it disappears because it has changed from a liquid state to a gas state, for example because it has been heated. EG *Boil until the carrots are tender and all the water has evaporated... Near the equator, the sun evaporates greater quantities of water.* V-ERG = vaporize ≠ condense
◊ **evaporation** /iˈvæpəreɪʃəⁿn/. EG *...incredibly fast evaporation.* ◊ N UNCOUNT
2 If a feeling or attitude **evaporates**, it gradually becomes less and eventually disappears completely. EG *All the glamour of the past nine weeks evaporated... Outraged public opinion, which fuelled the movement, had evaporated.* V = melt away

evaporated milk is thick unsweetened milk from which some water has been removed. N UNCOUNT

evasion /iˈveɪʒəⁿn/, **evasions**. 1 **Evasion** of something is the act of not doing something that you are supposed to do, especially when it is something that is required by law. EG *He is guilty of gross tax evasion... ...the evasion of death duties... ...an evasion of our responsibilities.* N UNCOUNT/ COUNT : IF+ PREP THEN *of* ⇑ avoidance
2 **Evasion** is also the deliberate act of avoiding talking about something or of dealing with something important. EG *His answer was a predictable example of parliamentary evasion... ...a growing pattern of reticence and evasion.* N UNCOUNT/ COUNT ⇑ avoidance

evasive /iˈveɪsɪv/. If you are being **evasive**, or give **evasive** answers, you are deliberately trying to avoid talking about something. EG *Victor became evasive, and told us that he had nothing more to say... ...a civil but evasive answer.* ADJ QUALIT ◊ **evasively**. EG *The Count had answered evasively.* ◊ ADV WITH VB ◊ **evasiveness**. EG *There was a certain evasiveness in Mary's relies.* ◊ N UNCOUNT
2 If you **take evasive action**, you deliberately move away from people or things so that you do not have to meet or touch them. EG *It might be necessary to take evasive action.* PHR : VB INFLECTS

eve /iːv/, **eves**. The **eve** of a particular event or occasion is the day before it. EG *It was a devastating attack on the eve of the election.* ● See also **Christmas Eve, New Year's Eve**. N COUNT : USU SING, USU+SUPP ⇑ period

even /iːvəⁿn/, **evens, evening, evened**. 1 You use the word **even** 1.1 to suggest that what comes just after or just before it in the sentence is rather surprising. EG *The hotel had everything. There was even a swimming pool... She liked him even when she was quarrelling with him... I shall give the details to no one, not even to you... No one dared even to whisper... A fire could be built on the rocks. On the sand, even.* ADV SEN 1.2 with comparatives, to emphasize the fact that something is greater in degree than the thing you have just mentioned or are about to mention. EG *I must be even more tired than I thought... Tomorrow might be even better... Barber had something even worse to tell me.* ADV+ADJ/ADV IN COMPAR = still 1.3 when you are adding a word which is more extreme than the one you have just used but which is actually a more accurate description of something. EG *People seemed content, even happy... It seemed that the captain was upset, even agitated.* ADV = indeed
2 **Even** is also used in the following expressions. 2.1 You use **even if** or **even though** to introduce a clause which appears to partly contradict the main clause in the sentence, but that does not actually affect the truth of the main clause. EG *Even if you disagree with her, she's worth listening to... Very good work, even if I do say so myself... I was always rather afraid of men, even though I had lots of boyfriends.* CONJ SUBORD 2.2 You use **even so** to introduce a surprising statement which is the opposite to what you would normally expect to be true; usually used in spoken English. EG *He smokes and drinks, but even so I bet he'll live till he's a hundred... This could lead you up some blind alleys. Even so, there's no real cause for concern.* ADV SEN = nevertheless
2.3 You use **even now** or **even then** to say that it is surprising that something is true at the time you are talking about, when you consider what has already happened. EG *Even now, after a week alone in the house, she still expected to hear his key in the front door... I often lend her money even now... I raised an eyebrow at what even then were outrageous prices... I suppose we looked very odd, even then.* PHR : USED AS ADV SEN 2.4 You also use **even then** to say that something is the case in spite of what has just been stated or whatever the circumstances may be. EG *He says that the only chance of a place on the course is if you achieve good A-level results and get the fees together. Even then, he's not promising.* ADV SEN
3 If one thing happens **even as** something else happens, they both happen at exactly the same time; a formal or literary use. EG *Even as he spoke, he realized that he had forgotten her name... The idea may mature even as it is being tried out.* CONJ SUBORD = while
4 A temperature, rhythm, rate, etc that is **even** stays at about the same level without much change or variation. EG *...an even body temperature... The oars were going in a fierce, even rhythm.* ADJ QUALIT = steady ◊ **evenly**. EG *Mary was breathing quietly and evenly.* ◊ ADV
5 Surfaces that are **even** are smooth and flat. EG *...a nice even surface... The road wasn't very even.* ADJ QUALIT = level
6 If your teeth are **even** they are regular and well-formed. ADJ QUALIT ≠ crooked
7 Something that is **even** has been arranged or shared out so that there is an equal amount or number in each place, or so that the spaces between things are about equal. EG *The distribution of land was much more even than, say, in the Middle East or in Latin America.* ADJ QUALIT ◊ **evenly**. EG *Public investment in agriculture has not been evenly spread... Opinion seems to be fairly evenly divided.* ◊ ADV = equally
8 If a contest or competition is **even**, it is equally balanced between the two sides who are taking part. EG *This has been a pretty even contest.* ADJ QUALIT ≠ one-sided ◊ **evenly**. EG *Government and rebel soldiers are evenly matched.* ◊ ADV WITH VB
9 If you are **even** with someone, in informal English, 9.1 you do not owe them anything, such as money or a favour. EG *I'll give you two pounds and then we're even.* ADJ CLASSIF : PRED 9.2 you have caused them the same amount of harm or annoyance as they have caused you. EG *He'd sworn at me and I'd sworn at him. Now we were even.* ADJ CLASSIF : PRED, IF+PREP THEN *with*
10 If you say that you are going to **get even** with someone, you mean that you are going to cause them the same amount of harm or annoyance as they have caused you. EG *Just you wait–I'll get even with you!* PHR : VB INFLECTS, IF+ PREP THEN *with*
11 If your voice is **even**, you are speaking in a very controlled way which makes it difficult for people to tell what your feelings are. EG *Ralph surprised himself, not so much by the quality of his voice, which was even, but by the bravado of his intention.* ADJ QUALIT = steady, calm ◊ **evenly**. EG *Vaughan said evenly, 'Trust me, Martin. You won't be sorry.'* ◊ ADV WITH VB
12 If you say that there is an **even** chance of something happening, or that the odds or chances are **even**, you mean that the probability of it happening is exactly the same as the probability of it not happening. EG *She would have had only an even chance of being saved... I should think the odds are about even.* ADJ CLASSIF = fifty-fifty
13 **Evens** is used to describe something which people bet on, such as a horse in a race, which is thought to be just as likely to succeed as to fail; a technical term in betting and sport. EG *Silver Star is the evens favourite.* ADJ CLASSIF : ATTRIB
14 An **even** number can be divided exactly by the number two. EG *I want to invite an even number of people... Houses with even numbers are on the right, odd numbers on the left.* ADJ CLASSIF ≠ odd
15 ● to **break even**: see **break**. ● **on an even keel**: see **keel**.

even out. When something **evens out** or when you **even it out**, its distribution becomes more equal, especially because some of it has gone from one place to another. EG *In Asia, irrigation systems help to even out the supply of water over the growing season... No amount of 'social engineering' will even out the world's unfairness.* PHRASAL VB : V-ERG+ADV = balance out

even up. To **even up** a contest or game means to make it more equally balanced than it was, because previously one side was better or stronger than the other. EG *Frank and I will change sides. That should even things up a bit.* PHRASAL VB : V+O+ADV = balance

even-handed. Someone who is **even-handed** is completely fair, especially when they are judging or testing other people. EG *He had been a fair and even-handed assessor.* ◊ **even-handedly**. EG *She dispensed justice even-handedly.* ◊ **even-handedness**. ADJ QUALIT = impartial ◊ ADV WITH VB ◊ N UNCOUNT

evening /iːvnɪŋ/, **evenings**. 1 The **evening** is the part of each day between the end of the afternoon and the time when you go to bed. EG *It's a lovely summer evening, go out and enjoy it before bedtime... Will she be in later this evening?... She left on Tuesday evening.* ▸ used in front of a noun. EG *He was silently finishing his evening meal.* N COUNT/UNCOUNT ⇑ period ▸ N BEFORE N

2 A particular kind of **evening** is an entertainment or activity that takes place during an evening. EG *Tell me about the meditation evenings that you go to.* N COUNT+SUPP

3 If it is a particular time **in the evening**, it is between the end of the afternoon and midnight. EG *He arrived about six in the evening.* PHR : USED AS AN A = p.m.

evening class, evening classes; also spelled with a hyphen. An **evening class** is an educational class for adults that is held in the evening. EG *I am now going to evening classes once a week.* N COUNT

evening dress, evening dresses. 1 An **evening dress** is a special dress, usually a long one, that a woman wears on a formal occasion in the evening. N COUNT

2 **Evening dress** consists of the formal clothes worn by people at formal occasions that take place in the evening. N UNCOUNT ⇑ outfit

evening star. The **evening star** is the planet Venus, that shines brightly in the sky just after sunset. N SING : *the*+N

evensong /iːvəⁿnsɒŋ/ is the evening service in the Church of England. N UNCOUNT

event /iˡvent/, **events**. 1 An **event** is 1.1 something that happens, especially when it is unusual or important. EG *Next day the newspapers reported the event... ...the most important event in family life... ...the events leading up to the war... ...the course of events.* ▸ used in the plural to refer to a whole situation. EG *Events now moved swiftly... The authorities were quite unable to control events.* 1.2 a planned and organized occasion, for example a social gathering or a sports match. EG *...the Berkeley Ball, a major annual social event... ...the sponsoring of sports events.* 1.3 one of the races or competitions that are part of an organized occasion, especially in sports. EG *Lord Exeter presented the medals for this event... ...a team event.* N COUNT ▸ N PLURAL N COUNT N COUNT ⇑ competition

2 You say **in the event of** something, **in the event that** something happens, **in that event**, etc when you are talking about a possible future situation, especially when you are planning what to do if it does occur; used in formal English. EG *In the event of a tie, the winner will be decided by the toss of a coin... In the unlikely event that they give you any real trouble, give me a ring... In that event, we would probably take the matter to court.* PHR

3 You say **at all events** or **in any event**, after you have been discussing a situation, in order to indicate that the statement you are making is true or likely, in spite of anything that has happened or may happen. EG *At all events, it seems that the lunch might be cancelled... In any event, government was faced with the prospect of widespread protest.* PHR : USED AS ADV SEN = anyway

4 You say **in the event**, after you have been discussing what could have happened in a particular situation, in order to indicate that you are now describing what actually did happen; a formal expression. EG *In the event, it turned out to be rather fun... ...a scepticism which in the event proved abundantly justified... In the event, there were no further casualties.* PHR : USED AS ADV SEN = in fact

even-tempered. Someone who is **even-tempered** is usually calm and does not easily get angry. EG *She was a happy, even-tempered woman.* ADJ QUALIT = placid

eventful /iˡventfʊl/. Something that is **eventful** is full of interesting, exciting, or important events. EG *...the most exhausting and eventful day of his life... My social life at that time was so eventful.* ADJ QUALIT = busy

eventual /iˡventʃʊ⁰əl/ means happening or being achieved at the end of a situation or process. EG *...the company's eventual collapse in 1971... ...anxiety about the eventual outcome... The eventual aim is to cut out the waste.* ADJ CLASSIF : ATTRIB ⇑ final = ultimate

eventuality /iˡventʃʊælɪti¹/, **eventualities**. An **eventuality** is a possible future event or result, often one that is unpleasant or surprising; a formal word. EG *He was ready for any eventuality... ...an eventuality that no one had foreseen... We are insured against all eventualities.* N COUNT = contingency

eventually /iˡventʃʊ⁰əli¹/ means 1 in the end, especially after a lot of delays, problems, or arguments. EG *Eventually, in the afternoon, they got through to the hospital... Rodin eventually agreed that Casson was right.* 2 at the end of a situation or process or as the final result of it. EG *The three firms eventually became Imperial Airways... His activities eventually led him into politics.* ADV ⇑ finally = at last ADV ⇑ finally

ever /evə/. 1 **Ever** means at any time in the future, or at any time in the past. It always adds some degree of emphasis and is used in the following ways: 1.1 in negative sentences, questions, conditional structures, and with words expressing uncertainty such as 'doubt'. EG *I don't think I'll ever be homesick here... Nothing like it had ever been built before... Have you ever been to Paris?... I shall kill you if you ever mention my visits here... He was unlikely ever to have seen her.* • If you say **did you ever** do something or **have you ever** done something, you are expressing surprise or shock at something you have just seen, heard, or experienced, and expect people to agree with you. EG *Have you ever seen such big ears?... Did you ever hear anything like it?.* 1.2 with superlatives, often when you are exaggerating, and in comparisons, especially when you are comparing a present situation with the past or the future. EG *...one of the best novels ever written... I am happier than I have ever been... He's better than you'll ever be... ...more women working than ever before.* ADV ≠ never • PHR : AUX INFLECTS ADV : COMPAR/SUPERL+ADV

2 **Ever** also means all the time. It is used in the following ways: 2.1 in expressions like 'ever-increasing' and 'ever-present', to show that something exists all the time or continues doing something or being something all the time. EG *...an ever-increasing prison population... ...an ever-present sense of danger... ...his ever open notebook... Achievement has come to be ever more important to the scientist.* 2.2 in order to introduce a quality that a person usually shows all the time, before you go on to talk about a particular situation when they showed it. EG *Ever unpredictable, Tallulah could be angry one moment and calm the next... Ever hopeful, McKellen never gave up on the cinema... Ever the optimist, I thought everything would be okay.* COMB : FORMS ADJS = always, constantly ADV+ADJ/NG = always

3 **Ever** is used in informal English in order to give emphasis in the following ways: 3.1 after 'never', in order to emphasize that something never happens, never has happened, or never will happen; used especially in spoken English. EG *She never ever wears a hat... I will never talk to him. Ever.* 3.2 with superlatives to emphasize strong approval or disapproval; used especially in spoken English. EG *They're the sweetest kids ever... It was the most awful film ever.* 3.3 in comparative structures when you want to emphasize that something still has a particular quality to a great degree. EG *She looked frailer than ever... The news is as awful as ever.* 3.4 in order to emphasize statements that you make when you are very angry. EG *I was a fool ever to marry you... This is the last time I ever want to see you... Don't you ever come here again!* 3.5 in questions, often when you do not really expect an answer, in order to emphasize your surprise at something that has been said or something that has happened. EG *'I'm sorry. I'd rather not say.'–'Why ever not?'... Who ever would have thought that?... How ever did you manage it?... Where ever have you been?* 3.6 in order to emphasize an exclamation that is in the form of a question. EG *'You like girls, don't you?'–'Do I ever!'* ADV : *never*+ADV ADV : SUPERL+ADV ADV : COMPAR+ADV ADV ADV : WH+ADV = on earth ADV

4 You use **ever since** when you want to say that something started being true at a particular time in the past, and to emphasize that it is still true now or to emphasize the long period of time it has been true for. EG *'How long have you lived here?'–'Ever since I was married.'... Jack has loved trains ever since his boyhood... We have been devoted friends ever since.* CONJ SUBORD, PREP, OR ADV WITH VB

5 The word **ever** is also used in the following expressions. 5.1 You use the expression **all** someone **ever does** when you want to emphasize that they do the same thing all the time or very often; used showing disapproval. EG *All she ever does is make jam.* 5.2 You say **as ever** in order to indicate that someone's behaviour is not at all unusual because PHR PHR : USED AS ADV SEN

they behave like that all the time or very often. EG *The children, as ever, were down in the recreation room.* **5.3** You often find **ever after** at the end of children's stories, especially fairy tales. It indicates that the situation at the end of the story continued for a long time. EG *They lived happily ever after.* **5.4** **Ever so** and **ever such** are used to emphasize what you are saying, especially when you are expressing enthusiasm or gratitude; used in informal spoken English. EG *They are ever so kind... Thank you ever so much... They're ever such nice people... It's ever such a nice day.* **5.5** If you say that someone **hardly ever** does something, you mean that they do it very rarely. EG *I hardly ever drink.* **5.6** **Yours ever** or **Ever yours** are written at the end of a letter before you sign your name, as an informal and friendly way of ending the letter. EG *Yours ever, Harry.* **5.7** See also **forever**.

PHR : USED AS AN A | PHR = very | ADV BRD NEG | CONVENTION

evergreen /ɛvəgriːn/, **evergreens**. An **evergreen** is a tree or bush which has green leaves all the year round. EG *...forests of evergreens.* ▸ used as an adjective. EG *...a small evergreen shrub.*

N COUNT | ▸ ADJ CLASSIF ≠ deciduous

everlasting /ɛvəlɑːstɪŋ/. Something that is **everlasting** continues to exist for a long time and may never come to an end; a literary word. EG *...the everlasting snows of the mighty Himalayas... It promises only everlasting misery for the tiny community... Hawkins, to his everlasting credit, refused... Grant us life everlasting. Amen.* ◇ **everlastingly**. EG *He was everlastingly optimistic.*

ADJ CLASSIF, OR ADJ AFTER N = eternal | ◇ ADV = forever

evermore /ɛvəmɔː/ means for all the time in the future; a formal or literary word, sometimes used in prayers. EG *Watch over us, now and for evermore.*

ADV = always

every /ɛvri[1]/. **1 Every** is used to refer to each member of a particular group of more than two things or people, when you are emphasizing that you are considering them all. EG *She spoke to every person at that party... Posy changed the subject every time it was raised... He read every one of my scripts... I have answered every single question.*

DET+N COUNT IN SING

2 Every is used to emphasize that you are talking about the whole of something by referring to each of the smaller parts of it. EG *I loved every minute of it... She's taken the whole lot! Every drop of it!... He washed off every bit of dirt.*

DET+N COUNT IN SING

3 Every is used to refer to all the members of a group of people or set of things that there may possibly be. EG *The crowd was of all ages and every colour... They are willing to help at every opportunity... They are encouraged in every way.*

DET+N COUNT IN SING

4 Every is used when you talk about frequency **4.1** in order to say that something happens at regular periods of time. EG *They met every day... We go to Mass every Sunday... The government changes every 5 years... I visit her about once every six months.* **4.2** in expressions such as 'every now and then' in order to indicate that something happens occasionally; by using **every**, you make the activity seem slightly more frequent and regular. EG *Every now and then she would cry out... ...every now and again... ...every once in a while... Every so often, she spends a weekend in London.*

DET ⇑ each | DET+A

5 If you say, for example, that something happens **every second** day, **every other** day, or **every alternate** day, you mean that it happens on one day in each period of two days. EG *It seemed easier to shave every second day... We only save enough money to take a real vacation every other year.* ● If you say that something happens **every third** day, **every fourth** year, etc, you mean that it happens on one day in each period of three days, in one year in each period of four years, etc.

PHR+NG | ● PHR+NG

6 Every is used in front of a number when you are considering how many things or people within a group are affected by something, or when it is the second number in a comparison. EG *One woman in every two hundred is a sufferer... Five out of every six hectares of land were unused... Since 1976, nine women have lost jobs for every five men.*

DET : NUM+ PREP+DET+ NUM

7 Every is used to emphasize that you are confident that a feeling, quality, or action is correct, necessary, or will happen in a particular situation. EG *I have every expectation of good crops... Guibaud had every reason to be pleased... They show every sign of continuing to advance... We have every right to marry.* ● If you say that someone or something is **every bit as** good, true, etc **as** someone or something else, you are defending or supporting the first person or thing, because other people think they are less good, true, etc; an informal use. EG *She believes she is every bit as good as you are.*

DET+N COUNT IN SING ≠ no | ● PHR ⇑ equally

everybody /ɛvribɒdi[1]/. See **everyone**.

everyday /ɛvrideɪ/. **Everyday** is used to describe something which **1** forms a regular and basic part of normal life, and is not especially interesting or unusual. EG *People could resume a normal everyday life... ...their role in everyday affairs... ...things which were common and everyday to him but luxuries to them... I rarely run out of everyday food.* **2** happens or is used each day. EG *Exercise is part of my everyday routine... ...everyday home activities like cooking... The furniture was threadbare from everyday use.*

ADJ CLASSIF = ordinary | ADJ CLASSIF : ATTRIB ⇑ regular = day-to-day

everyone /ɛvriwə[ə]n/. The form **everybody** is also used. **Everyone** and **everybody** are used when you are talking about people. **1** You use **everyone** and **everybody** to refer to all the people in a particular group, usually of more than two. EG *Everybody in the office laughed... She was genuinely interested in everyone she met... ...everyone except Dana... ...a small organization where everyone knows everyone else... Has everybody eaten as much as they want?*

PRON INDEF ≠ no one, nobody

2 You use **everyone** and **everybody** to refer generally to all people in the world. EG *Everybody has his dream... Everyone has their own ideas about it... You can't please everyone... Everyone knows that.*

PRON INDEF ≠ no one, nobody

3 You use **everyone** and **everybody** when you want to refer to a large number of people. EG *Everyone is waiting to see his new film... Everyone knew Eddie... Everybody kept asking where you were... What's the point of having a Jaguar, if everybody else has one?*

PRON INDEF ≠ no one, nobody

everything /ɛvriθɪŋ/. **Everything** is used when you are talking about things, ideas, actions, situations, etc. **1** You use **everything** to refer in general terms to all the objects, actions, activities, or facts in a particular situation that you are talking about. EG *I don't agree with everything he says... A vet is supposed to know about everything from a cow to a mouse... I will arrange everything... Dust slowly covered everything.*

PRON INDEF ≠ nothing

2 You use **everything** to refer to all possible or likely actions, activities, or situations when you are making a general statement about them. EG *That's your answer to everything... The twins did everything alike... You think of everything.*

PRON INDEF ≠ nothing

3 You use **everything** to refer to a whole situation or to life in general, especially in relation to the way it is changing or the way it is affecting you. EG *Is everything all right?... Everything's fine... Everything went on just as before.*

PRON INDEF : USU USED AS S = things

4 You use **everything** to refer to a general atmosphere that exists in a situation. EG *Everything is quiet... Here everything was bustle and talk.*

PRON INDEF : USU USED AS S = all

5 You use **everything** to emphasize an aspect or quality that you consider to be very striking or important. EG *There is everything wrong with this place... This has nothing to do with terrorism and has everything to do with politics.*

PRON INDEF ≠ nothing

6 You use **everything** to refer to something that you consider to be the most important and valuable thing in your life. EG *Money isn't everything... She means everything to me.*

PRON INDEF = all ≠ nothing

7 You say **and everything** after a particular thing or list of things in order to indicate that they are only examples and that other things may have been involved; used in informal English. EG *I've argued with him and everything, but he won't listen!... We bought a huge window–the frame, glass and everything–for just a few dollars.*

everywhere /ɛvriwɛə/. **Everywhere** is used especially when you are talking about places. **1** You use **everywhere** to refer in general terms to a whole area or all the places in a particular area. EG *Everywhere in Asia it is the same... People everywhere are becoming aware of the problem.*

ADV

2 You use **everywhere** to refer to all the places that someone or something goes to, when you are speaking in general terms rather than considering specific places. EG *Everywhere I went, people were angry or suspicious... She always carried a gun with her everywhere.*

ADV WITH VB

3 You use **everywhere** to refer to lots of places or a very large area, when you are exaggerating or emphasizing the number of places or the size of the

ADV AFTER VB

area. EG *Today videos are everywhere... I was looking everywhere for Jenny... Jack's been everywhere.*
4 You use **everywhere** to make a general statement about a situation that exists in all places in the world. EG *The laws of nature are the same everywhere... Children everywhere love to have stories read to them.* ADV

evict /iˈvɪkt/, **evicts, evicting, evicted**. To **evict** someone means to officially force them to leave a house that they are occupying, because they have broken a law or contract. EG *...attempts to evict families from their homes... Being a good tenant, he can't be evicted... Indians have been evicted from their traditional lands.* V+O

eviction /iˈvɪkʃən/, **evictions**. **Eviction** is the act or process of officially forcing someone to leave a house or piece of land. EG *...seeking Barnett's eviction from the Malibu house... The family faces eviction for non-payment of rent... ...an eviction notice.* N UNCOUNT/COUNT

evidence /ɛvɪdəns/, **evidences, evidencing, evidenced**. 1 **Evidence** is 1.1 anything that you see, experience, read, or are told that causes you to believe that something is true or has really happened. EG *In China, we saw evidence everywhere that a real effort was being made to promote tourism.... Later we got evidence of another leak... There is no evidence to suggest it will occur... He gave no evidence for his statement... ...the historical evidence.* N UNCOUNT : USU +SUPP 1.2 the information which is used in a court of law to try to prove something and which is obtained from documents, objects, or witnesses; a technical term in law. EG *There was no real evidence against Davis... The photograph was part of the evidence in a divorce case.* N UNCOUNT/COUNT 1.3 the way a person behaves in a particular situation, which shows what they feel or think about it. EG *He was hoping for evidence of interest but found only cynicism... If he was irritated by his cameraman, he showed no evidence of it.* N UNCOUNT : USU +SUPP = sign, indication
2 If you **give evidence** in a court of law or an official enquiry, you officially tell facts that you know about people or events, or describe an occasion at which you were present. What you say helps the court or enquiry to reach a final decision. EG *The doctor gave evidence at an inquest... He had given evidence for the defence in the Lady Chatterley case... She will give evidence to a committee of enquiry.* PHR : VB INFLECTS = testify ● If something you say **is held in evidence**, it is officially written down, especially by the police, and may be used as evidence in a court of law. EG *These things have been noted and will be held in evidence.* ● PHR : AUX INFLECTS
3 If someone or something is **in evidence**, they are present and can be clearly seen in a particular situation. EG *The servants were never in evidence... Lawlessness was particularly in evidence in the towns.* PHR : USED AS AN A = noticeable
4 If a particular feeling, ability, attitude, etc **is evidenced** by something, it is shown to exist; used in formal English. EG *Boredom is often evidenced among college students... You evidenced no talent for music... We were attracting a growing number of females, as evidenced by the formation of the Women's Section.* V+O : USU PASS = demonstrate, exhibit

evident /ɛvɪdənt/. If something such as a feeling, attitude, or reason is **evident**, it is easily noticed or understood. EG *She took a sip with evident enjoyment... Their exact purpose was not always evident to observers... This is most strikingly evident in the field of economics... It was evident that his faith in the Government was severely shaken.* ADJ QUALIT = clear, obvious

evidently /ɛvɪdəntliˈ/ is used 1 to indicate that you think something is true but that you are not sure, because you do not have enough information or proof. EG *They said it would come last week, but evidently they had failed to send it... Evidently he feared I was going to refuse... ...a list of names referring, evidently, to her class at school.* ADV SEN = clearly 2 to say that something is obviously true, for example because you have seen proof of it yourself. EG *I found her in bed, evidently in great pain... You are evidently a craftsman... She was evidently excited.* ADV SEN = plainly 3 to introduce a statement or opinion and to emphasize that it is true or correct; a formal use. EG *Evidently, such men are usually powerful and wealthy... Evidently, a sculpture must exist as an object.* ADV SEN = clearly

evil /iːvəl/, **evils**. 1 **Evil** is 1.1 a powerful force that is believed to cause wicked and bad things to happen. EG *...the conflict between good and evil... ...the forces of evil and darkness... There was never any trace of evil in her–she was good all through.* N UNCOUNT 1.2 all the wicked and bad things that happen in the world. EG *...the good and the evil in Victorian Britain... He felt pain as he contemplated the evil in the universe.* N UNCOUNT
2 An **evil** is a very unpleasant or harmful situation or activity. EG *Taxation is a necessary evil in my view... ...social evils... ...a sermon on the evils of drink.* N COUNT : USU+SUPP
3 Someone who is **evil** is very wicked by nature and takes pleasure in doing things that harm other people. EG *I've known for years that Molly was really evil.* ADJ QUALIT ⇑ bad ≠ good
4 Something that is **evil** 4.1 causes a great deal of harm to people and is regarded as morally bad. EG *Slavery was the most evil and inhumane system of labour ever devised... No political system is evil unless it involves force and cruelty.* ADJ QUALIT ⇑ harmful = wicked 4.2 is influenced by the devil. EG *...an evil and dreadful and sinister place... This prayer was believed to protect a man from possession by evil spirits while he slept.* ADJ CLASSIF
5 If you describe something as **evil**, you mean that it is very unpleasant. EG *...the evil noise of the underground trains... ...an evil smell.* ADJ QUALIT = foul ◇ **evilly**. EG *The kitchen stank powerfully and evilly of rotting fish.* ◇ ADV
6 An **evil** hour or **evil** day is a time that you think will be a very unpleasant experience or when something unpleasant will happen. EG *It is my duty to keep off the evil day of her marriage as long as I can.* ADJ QUALIT : ATTRIB

evildoer /iːvəldu:ə/, **evildoers**. An **evildoer** is a person whose behaviour is wicked and who causes harm and suffering to others. N COUNT ⇑ wrongdoer

evil eye. The **evil eye** is the magical power to cast a spell on someone or something by looking at them, so that bad things happen to them; also used to refer to the actual look that someone with this power gives to someone or something. EG *She gave me the evil eye.* N SING : the+N ⇑ look

evince /iˈvɪns/, **evinces, evincing, evinced**. If someone **evinces** a feeling or quality, they show it very clearly; used in formal English. EG *I have never heard one of our boys evince any interest in the movement.* V+O

evocation /iːvəkeɪʃən/, **evocations**. An **evocation** is an act of evoking an emotion, memory, or response; a formal word. EG *It was disturbing, this evocation of her young self... ...nostalgic evocations of rural America... ...the wealth of visual evocation which the novel offers.* N COUNT/UNCOUNT : USU+SUPP

evocative /iˈvɒkətɪv/. Something that is **evocative** produces memories, emotions, and responses in people. EG *...an evocative description.* ADJ QUALIT ◇ **evocatively**. EG *Old photographs are evocatively displayed round the building.* ◇ ADV

evoke /iˈvəʊk/, **evokes, evoking, evoked**. To **evoke** a particular emotion, memory, reaction, etc, means to cause it to be felt, expressed, or recalled. EG *The quarrel seemed to evoke the bitterest passions... He had never quite lost the sense of wonder evoked by the sight of his own home.* V+O ⇑ produce

evolution /iːvəlu:ʃən/ is 1 a process of gradual change that takes place over many generations, during which animals, plants, insects, etc, slowly change some of their physical characteristics. EG *The processes of evolution are still going on among plants, birds, and animals... ...the evolution of the human species... The Darwinian theory of evolution is really very ancient.* N UNCOUNT 2 a process of gradual and uninterrupted change and development in a particular situation over a period of time. EG *Cultural and social evolution has now become extremely rapid... ...the evolution of parliamentary democracy.* N UNCOUNT+SUPP

evolutionary /iːvəlu:ʃənəriˈ/ means relating to the process of gradual change and development in animals, plants, insects, etc. EG *...the evolutionary process... ...evolutionary theory.* ADJ CLASSIF : ATTRIB

evolve /iˈvɒlv/, **evolves, evolving, evolved**. 1 When animals, plants, insects, etc **evolve**, they gradually change and develop into different forms. EG *Once more the continent was cut off and its animals evolved in isolation... The early fish have evolved into some 30,000 different species.* V OR V+O : IF+PREP THEN *into/in/from*
2 If something **evolves** or you **evolve** it, it gradually develops and changes over a period of time into something different and usually more advanced. EG *I think that this policy must have evolved over time... Good planting schemes can take years to evolve...* V-ERG ⇑ change = develop

How did Giotto evolve this very personal and original style?

ewe /juː/, **ewes**. A **ewe** is a female adult sheep. N COUNT

ewer /juːə/, **ewers**. A **ewer** is a large jug with a wide opening; an old-fashioned word. N COUNT

ex /ɛks/. Someone's **ex** is their ex-wife, ex-husband, ex-girlfriend, etc. N SING : POSS+N

ex- is added to nouns and adjectives that refer to people and things to show that the person or thing no longer has the characteristic described by the noun or adjective. EG *...British→ex-British... ...serviceman→ex-serviceman... ...wife→ex-wife.* PREFIX = former

exacerbate /ɪ[2]gzæsəbeɪt, ɪ[2]ksæs-/, **exacerbates, exacerbating, exacerbated**. To **exacerbate** something means to make it a lot worse; a formal word. EG *Withholding aid only exacerbates the situation.* V+O = worsen, aggravate

exact /ɪ[2]gzækt/, **exacts, exacting, exacted**. **1** Something that is **exact** is **1.1** accurate, correct, and specific rather than based on a guess or an approximation. EG *He noted the exact time and place on the sketch... He searched his vocabulary for the exact word to define his feelings.* ADJ CLASSIF ↑ right = precise ≠ approximate **1.2** correct and complete in every detail. EG *...an exact replica of Hamburg airport... The ceremony had to be performed in an exact manner and with dignity.* ADJ CLASSIF = precise ≠ rough

2 You say **to be exact** to indicate that you are now giving more detailed information or a slight correction that relates to what you have been saying. EG *There was a double bed: a big panel bed, to be exact, with a Tuscan rose chenille spread... I had a hunch that this would be possible, or to be more exact, could see no reason why it should not be so.* PHR : USED AS ADV SEN = in fact

3 **Exact** is used to emphasize that something is very similar to something else that you have just been talking about, or that it has a precise and close relationship with it. EG *That was the exact type of moccasin I was trying to describe to you... It is the exact opposite of Pop art.* ADJ CLASSIF : ATTRIB

4 Someone who is **exact**, especially in their work, is very careful and detailed in their thinking and methods. EG *...a modest man and an exact and patient scientist.* ADJ QUALIT = meticulous

5 An **exact** science is one that is based on measurement and formulation of laws rather than on description and classification, for example maths or physics. EG *History is not an exact science.* ADJ CLASSIF : ATTRIB

6 When someone **exacts** something, they demand and obtain it from someone else, especially because they are in a superior or more powerful position; a formal use. EG *They exacted absolute obedience from their followers... The sum he had exacted on occupying the city was not unreasonable.* V+O : IF+PREP THEN *from*

exacting /ɪ[2]gzæktɪŋ/. If someone or something is **exacting**, they demand hard work and a great deal of care. EG *The task proved to be exacting... Both were tireless workers and exacting bosses... The state of repair failed to measure up to their exacting standards.* ADJ QUALIT = rigorous

exactitude /ɪ[2]gzæktɪtjuːd/ is the quality of being very accurate and careful. EG *He copied the words which followed with exactitude... ...military exactitude.* N UNCOUNT = accuracy

exactly /ɪ[2]gzæktli[1]/. **1** **Exactly** means with complete accuracy and precision. EG *I don't know exactly where it is, but it's in the south of France... Sam answered the owl's cry, imitating it exactly... You've exactly one hour to do those.* ADV = precisely ≠ roughly

2 You can use **exactly** to emphasize the truth of a statement, or the similarity or close relationship that something has with something else. EG *He's exactly like a little baby... I think the computer presents exactly that challenge... That's exactly what they told me.* ADV = just, precisely

3 If you say **'exactly'**, you are agreeing with someone or emphasizing that what they have said is correct. EG *'Do you mean that we are stuck here?'–'Exactly, my dear.'... 'You were told you wouldn't be able to go if you'd lost your tickets?'–'Exactly, yes.'* CONVENTION = just so, precisely

4 You use **not exactly** **4.1** to indicate that a word is not quite what you mean, or that a situation is not quite as has been stated, especially when it is explained more accurately in the following statement. EG *He didn't exactly block me, but he didn't move either... He was ineffective, not exactly a weakling, but ineffective... 'She's taken the day off.'–'Is she sick?'–'Not exactly.'* ADV : ALSO USED AS CONVENTION **4.2** to suggest in a rather ironic, sarcastic, or humorous way, that the opposite of what is being said is true. EG *His father was not exactly poor: he left 10 million pounds... The divorce wasn't exactly amiable.* ADV

exactness /ɪ[2]gzæktnɪ[2]s/ is the quality of being accurate and very precise. EG *He chose to express himself delicately and with great exactness.* N UNCOUNT = precision

exaggerate /ɪ[2]gzædʒəreɪt/, **exaggerates, exaggerating, exaggerated**. **1** If you **exaggerate**, you say something which is more than the true facts, for example because you want to emphasize how impressive or important something is. EG *I am exaggerating a little... She did not exaggerate about the height of the tower... I don't think it is possible to exaggerate the power of television.* V OR V+O ◊ **exaggeration** /ɪ[2]gzædʒəreɪʃə[0]n/, **exaggerations**. EG *Isn't that a bit of an exaggeration?... One can speak, without exaggeration, of a peaceful revolution.* ◊ N COUNT/UNCOUNT

2 If something **exaggerates** a situation, quality, feature, etc, it makes the situation, quality, feature, etc appear more obvious or more important than it really is. EG *The figures quoted here tend to exaggerate the inequality between rich and poor... Ballet exaggerates ordinary body movements.* V+O ◊ **exaggeration**. EG *He spoke with a mocking exaggeration of my accent.* ◊ N COUNT/UNCOUNT

exaggerated /ɪ[2]gzædʒəreɪtɪ[2]d/. Something that is **exaggerated** is or seems larger, better, worse, or more important than it actually needs to be. EG *Brody heaved an exaggerated sigh... I considered this remark exaggerated but complimentary... ...an exaggerated swing of the hips.* ADJ QUALIT = overdone ◊ **exaggeratedly**. EG *...an exaggeratedly intense smile... Her features moved slowly, exaggeratedly, like a bad actress.* ◊ ADV

exalt /ɪ[2]gzɔːlt/, **exalts, exalting, exalted**; a formal word. To **exalt** someone means **1** to praise them very highly. EG *Some historians exalt Churchill as a war leader.* V+O = extol **2** to raise them to a higher position in society. EG *The Prime Minister exalted many of his friends.* V+O = elevate

exaltation /ɛgzɔːlteɪʃə[0]n/; a formal word. **Exaltation** is **1** an intense feeling of great joy and happiness. EG *...peasants in a state of religious exaltation.* N UNCOUNT **2** the act of praising something or someone very highly. EG *...the exaltation of nature and the soil.* N UNCOUNT

exalted /ɪ[2]gzɔːltɪ[2]d/; a formal word. Someone who is **exalted** is **1** very high in rank or importance. EG *I had never met so exalted a person... They were men who owed their exalted positions to politics rather than experience.* ADJ QUALIT = prominent **2** full of joy and happiness. EG *I spread my arms wide and felt joyous and exalted and free.* ADJ QUALIT = exultant

exam /ɪ[2]gzæm/, **exams**. An **exam** is an official and formal test that you take to show your knowledge or ability in a particular subject or to obtain a qualification. EG *After the third term we'll be sitting the exam... ...chemistry exams... ...exam results.* N COUNT = examination

examination /ɪ[2]gzæmɪneɪʃə[0]n/, **examinations**. **1** An **examination** is an official and formal test that you take to show your knowledge or ability in a particular subject or to obtain a qualification; a more formal word than 'exam'. EG *...a three-hour written examination... ...examination results.* N COUNT

2 See also **examine**.

examine /ɪ[2]gzæmɪn/, **examines, examining, examined**. **1** If you **examine** something, **1.1** you look carefully or closely at it. EG *I examined the lighter, then handed it back... She sat back in a chair and examined her fingernails.* V+O = inspect, scrutinize ◊ **examination** /ɪ[2]gzæmɪneɪʃə[0]n/, examinations. EG *Mrs Oliver applied herself to an examination of the address book.* ◊ N UNCOUNT/COUNT = inspection **1.2** you officially look at or inspect every part of it as carefully as possible in order to discover something about it. EG *Divers were sent down to examine the hull... Government experts were still examining the wreckage of the plane.* V+O = go over ◊ **examination**. EG *A detailed examination was made of the plane's flight recorder... The weapon was taken away for examination.* ◊ N COUNT/UNCOUNT = inspection

2 If a doctor **examines** you or a part of your body, he or she looks at your body or at a particular part of it in order to make sure that you are healthy. EG *We stayed with her until the doctor examined her... An optician is qualified to examine your eyes and prescribe glasses.* V+O ◊ **examination**. EG *A full examination of the chest failed to reveal anything... There are three consulting-rooms and two examination rooms.* ◊ N UNCOUNT/COUNT = check-up

3 When people **examine** an idea, proposal, plan, etc, they consider or discuss it very carefully. EG *The* V+O = investigate *committee has been examining whether Mr Grantham's letter contravenes the Offical Secrets Act... It is necessary to examine this claim before we proceed any further... His novel examines the borderline between fact and fiction.* ◊ **examination.** EG *...an important case which merits closer examination... Self-criticism calls for a constant examination of values and attitudes.* ◊ N UNCOUNT/COUNT

4 To **examine** someone means to find out how much they know by asking them questions or by making them take an exam. EG *These pupils were examined in a total of 39 subjects.* V+O OR V ⇑ test

examiner /ɪ²gzæmɪnə/, **examiners**. An **examiner** is a person who sets or marks an exam. EG *...the values and requirements of examiners.* N COUNT

example /ɪ²gzɑːmpə⁰l/, **examples**. **1** An **example** of something is a particular situation, event, object, person, etc, often one of a number of similar things, that illustrates a point you are making, or that supports an argument, theory, or opinion. EG *London and Liverpool are examples of a policy of decentralization... Primary fuels: examples of these are crude oil, coal and natural gas... Professional people, doctors, lawyers, booksellers–just to mention a few examples–are sprinkled all over the city... Could you give me an example of an application of this principle?* N COUNT

2 You use **for example** to introduce and emphasize something that illustrates a point you are making, or that supports an argument, theory, or opinion. EG *Japan, for example, has two languages... In our library we have quite a lot of newspapers, The Times, for example, and the New York Times... This file contains a sheet of paper with a list of names, addresses and telephone numbers that are important to you. For example: doctor; dentist; vet; garage, and so on... Although no one can claim that the probation service is well paid, there have been improvements and the work is now better paid than, for example, most teaching posts.* ADV SEN = for instance

3 An **example** of a particular class of objects, style, etc, is something that has many of the typical features of such a class or style, and that you consider clearly represents it. EG *It's a very fine example of traditional architecture... The most commonly cited example of a primitive device is the abacus... He brought along several examples of his work for her to look at... There's a particularly good example in the middle of the book.* N COUNT

4 An **example** is a person, or their way of behaving or acting in a particular situation, that inspires or encourages other people to behave or act in a similar way. EG *...a shining example to progressive people everywhere... Pizzaro did, of course, have the example of Cortes to inspire and guide him, too... Children then see an example of successful co-operation which they can copy... They are presumably as capable of profiting by example as any others.* N COUNT : ALSO *by*+N

5 If you **follow** someone's example, you behave in the same way as they did in the past, or in a similar way, especially because you think it is a good idea or you have been encouraged or inspired by it. EG *He published a written protest, and invited others to follow his example... A number of people followed Reverend Shuttleworth's example and were subsequently arrested.* PHR : VB INFLECTS

6 If you **set an example**, you encourage or inspire people by your behaviour to behave or act in a similar way to the way that you do or have done in a particular situation. EG *She set such a good example to us all... I suppose the kind of example I'm setting her is one which undermines authority.* PHR : VB INFLECTS

7 If you **make an example of** someone, you punish them severely as a warning to other people, so that people will be afraid and will not commit the same crime or behave in the same way. EG *It was decided to make an example of some of the top conspirators.* PHR : VB INFLECTS

8 An **example** is a clause or sentence in a dictionary that comes after the definition of a particular word and that illustrates the way the word is used. EG *Examples are printed in italics.* N COUNT = illustration

exasperate /ɪ²gzɑːspəreɪt/, **exasperates, exasperating, exasperated**. If someone or something **exasperates** you, they annoy you and make you feel rather frustrated or upset. EG *She frequently exasperates her friends.* ◊ **exasperated.** EG *He had an exasperated look on his face... She was getting more and more exasperated.* ◊ **exasperating.** EG *I have seldom had a more exasperating day.* ◊ **exasperation** /ɪ²gzɑːspəreɪʃə⁰n/. EG *He looked at the little boy in exasperation... I was almost crying from exasperation.* V+O ◊ ADJ QUALIT ◊ N UNCOUNT

excavate /ɛkskəveɪt/, **excavates, excavating, excavated**. **1** When people **excavate** a piece of land, they remove earth carefully from it and look for very old things such as pots, bones, or buildings which are buried there, in order to discover information about the past. EG *The Project has excavated and partially restored the hilltop fort... He excavated at many sites in Kenya and Tanzania.* ◊ **excavation** /ɛkskəveɪʃə⁰n/, **excavations**. EG *...the excavation of a Neolithic lake village... Further excavations had to wait until the following year.* V OR V+O ⇑ dig ◊ N COUNT/UNCOUNT

2 To **excavate** also means to dig a hole in the ground, for example in order to build something there. EG *The turtles burrow deep into the sand and excavate a small chamber... They were excavating an underground helicopter base at the time.* V OR V+O

excavator /ɛkskəveɪtə/, **excavators**. An **excavator** is a very large machine that is used for digging, for example on a building site. N COUNT

exceed /ɪ²ksiːd/, **exceeds, exceeding, exceeded**. **1** If something **exceeds** a particular amount or number, it is greater or larger than the amount or number. EG *Average annual temperatures exceed 20 centigrade... His gross income will very likely exceed £900,000 this year... Sales exceeded all expectations.* V+O = top

2 If you **exceed** a limit or rule, you go beyond it, even though you are not supposed to or it is against the law. EG *A motorist was caught exceeding the speed limit... The company is not allowed to exceed its budget... You were exceeding your duty in opening those letters.* V+O = go over

exceedingly /ɪ²ksiːdɪŋli¹/ means very or very much; a rather old-fashioned word. EG *The Colonel was exceedingly wealthy... Doug is an exceedingly amiable fellow.* ADV+ADJ/ADV = enormously

excel /ɪ²ksɛl/, **excels, excelling, excelled**. If someone **excels** in something or **excels** at it, they are very good at doing it. EG *We want to improve, to excel... He excels at sports... It is in this area of running that women excel... They had excelled in acts of inhumanity.* V : IF+PREP THEN *at/in* = shine ≠ fail

excellence /ɛksələns/. **1 Excellence** is the quality of being very good at something. EG *Sports is an area in which excellence is still treasured... The job has new responsibilities and a new standard of excellence to maintain.* N UNCOUNT

2 See also **par excellence**.

Excellency /ɛksələnsi¹/, **Excellencies**. You use **Excellency** when you are referring to or addressing officials of very high rank, for example ambassadors or governors. EG *His Excellency is willing to see you now... Will that be all, your Excellency?... Good morning, Excellency.* N WITH PL IN TITLES : USU DETPOSS+N

excellent /ɛksələnt/. **1** Something that is **excellent** is very good indeed. EG *I think the teaching at the school is excellent... That's an excellent idea... Her work was always excellent.* ◊ **excellently.** EG *The system works excellently... There are some excellently preserved fossils here.* ADJ QUALIT ◊ ADV

2 You can say **excellent** to show that you approve of something. EG *'We'll come round in the morning.'–'Excellent. I'll see you then'.* EXCLAM ⇑ good

except /ɪ²ksɛpt/, **excepts, excepting, excepted**. **1** You use **except** in order to introduce the only things, people, or ideas that your main statement does not apply to. EG *Anything, except water, is likely to block a sink... All the boys except Piggy started to giggle... He no longer went out, except when Jeannie forced him... I knew nothing about Judith except what I'd heard at second hand... I didn't see him, except casually, in two months... There was little I could do except wait... I can scarcely remember what we ate, except that it was plentiful and simple.* PREP OR CONJ SUBORD = apart from, save ≠ including

2 Except for is used to introduce the only things, people, or ideas that prevent your main statement from being completely true. EG *The classroom was silent, except for the busy scratching of pens on paper... The room was very cold and, except for Morris, entirely empty... Except for emergencies I* PREP = apart from, excepting ◊ ADJ QUALIT *have found it easier not to expect any help from my children.*

3 You can also use **except** to introduce a reason or excuse that you have for not doing something or for not completely agreeing with a statement. EG *I'd tell you about it, except it would probably put you to sleep... I even felt like apologizing to them except that they wouldn't know what I was talking about.* CONJ SUBORD : USU+REPORT-CL = only

4 To **except** something means to regard it as not included in a general statement, judgement, or rule. EG *Most of the reviews saved my embarrassment a little by excepting the script from their general criticism of the film... Men! I hate them! Present company excepted, of course.* V+O = exclude ≠ count

excepting /ɪ²ksɛptɪŋ/ is used to introduce the only things, people, or ideas that prevent your main statement from being completely true. EG *He was the only human male for a couple of miles around (excepting an old stone-deaf handyman).* PREP OR CONJ SUBORD

exception /ɪ²ksɛpʃə⁰n/, **exceptions**. **1** An **exception** is a particular thing, person, or situation that is not included in a general statement, judgement, or rule. EG *I think we have more paper per employee in this department than in any other, perhaps with the exception of Planning... Women, with a few prominent exceptions, are conspicuous by their absence in politics... As always with human behaviour, there are exceptions to this general rule.* N COUNT : IF+ PREP THEN *of/to*

2 You use **without exception** to indicate that the statement you are making is true in all cases. EG *Without exception these measures would be costly... Almost without exception, the fastest-growing cities are in Africa.* PHR : USED AS ADV SEN

3 If you **take exception to** something, you feel offended or annoyed by it, usually with the result that you complain about it. EG *There are three things you've just said that I want to take exception to... I take exception to being called 'love'.* PHR : VB INFLECTS = object

exceptionable /ɪ²ksɛpʃə⁰nəbə⁰l/. Something that is **exceptionable** causes you to feel offended or annoyed, usually with the result that you complain about it. EG *What I do find really quite exceptionable in his argument is the idea that a woman is unfit to run a company.* ADJ QUALIT = objectionable

exceptional /ɪ²ksɛpʃə⁰nəl, ʃənə⁰l/. **1** Someone who is **exceptional** is unusually talented, clever, or gifted. EG *She was an exceptional teacher... ...an exceptional mathematician... My brother isn't exceptional; there are plenty of youngsters like him.* ▸ used of a person's abilities and achievements. EG *...an act of exceptional daring.* ADJ QUALIT = extraordinary, rare

2 Exceptional situations, incidents, cases, etc, are unusual and only likely to happen very rarely. EG *Permission will be granted only in very exceptional circumstances... There is no provision in the basic pension for exceptional needs.* ADJ QUALIT ⇑ unusual ≠ normal

exceptionally /ɪ²ksɛpʃə⁰nəli¹/. You can use **exceptionally** **1** to emphasize that something has a particular quality to a very high degree indeed. EG *...an exceptionally fine meal... February had been exceptionally wet.* **2** to indicate that what you are talking about is unusual and only likely to happen very rarely. EG *Exceptionally, some causes do bring on to the streets large numbers of people.* ADV+ADJ/ADV = extraordinarily; ADV SEN ≠ normally

excerpt /ɛksɜːpt/, **excerpts**. An **excerpt** is a short piece of writing or music which is taken from a larger piece, such as a book or symphony. EG *Here are a few excerpts from her diary.* N COUNT : IF+ PREP THEN *from* ⇑ part = extract

excess, excesses. The word **excess** is pronounced /ɛksɛs/ when it is an adjective, and either /ɪ²ksɛs/ or /ɛksɛs/ when it is a noun. **1** An **excess** of something is a larger amount than is actually needed, allowed, or usual. EG *Inflation results from an excess of demand over supply... This report should discourage us all from eating an excess of fat.* N SING : *an*+N, USU+*of* = surfeit

2 In excess of means more than a particular amount; a rather formal expression. EG *Only a few years ago interest rates in excess of 20 per cent would have been unthinkable.* PREP = above, over

3 Excess is used to describe something which is more than is actually needed, allowed, or usual. EG *Exercise can at least help the body to burn off excess calories... The body promptly gets rid of excess water through the urine.* ADJ CLASSIF : ATTRIB = surplus

4 If you do something **to excess**, you do it too much; used showing disapproval. EG *He spent all his time alone in the flat, cleaning and tidying it to excess... Don't eat to excess.* PHR : USED AS AN A

5 Excess is behaviour that is unacceptable because it is considered too extreme or immoral. EG *...a life given up to excess or the search for excitement.* N COUNT/ UNCOUNT

6 Excesses are acts or actions which are very extreme, irresponsible, cruel, immoral, etc. EG *I'm tired of hearing of your mother's excesses... ...the excesses of the French Revolution.* N PLURAL

excessive /ɪ²ksɛsɪv/ is used to describe things that are considered to be too great, too large, or too extreme. EG *Excessive rainfall washes out valuable minerals from the soil... Their profits can only be described as excessive... ...excessive pessimism.* ◊ **excessively**. EG *He laughed excessively, even holding his sides... He walked excessively fast.* ADJ QUALIT; ◊ ADV

exchange /ɪ²kstʃeɪnd⁰ʒ/, **exchanges, exchanging, exchanged**. **1** If two or more people **exchange** things of a particular kind, they give them to each other at the same time. EG *They hardly exchanged a word... The three of us exchanged addresses... We exchanged greetings over the wall... The boys were ready to exchange blows.* V+O

2 If you **exchange** something or **exchange** it for something else, you replace it with something else, especially something that is better or more satisfactory. EG *We will be glad to exchange damaged goods... The sales girl refused to exchange the sweater... Their rags were exchanged for new clothing... She exchanged the jewels for money.* V+O : IF+PREP THEN *for* = change

3 If you **exchange** your house or job with someone, you live or work in the place where they normally live or work, while they live or work where you normally live or work. EG *The Ingrams exchanged houses with some friends who live in London... I'm Philip Swallow–exchanging with Professor Zapp.* V OR V+O : IF+ PREP THEN *with*

4 An **exchange** is **4.1** the act of doing or giving something to another person at the same time as they do or give something to you. EG *...an almost imperceptible exchange of glances... ...a direct and personal exchange of views... ...a polite exchange of information.* **4.2** the act of temporarily going to live in another person's house or doing another person's job at the same time as they go to live in your house or do your job. EG *...the exchange of visiting teachers... What are the advantages of a holiday home exchange?* **4.3** a brief conversation, usually an angry one; a formal use. EG *Our exchange was heated and soon a confrontation had brewed... Throughout these exchanges I had a curious feeling of detachment.* **4.4** an event during a war when armies or nations use weapons against each other; a military use. EG *...the nightmare of unrestricted nuclear exchange.* N COUNT : IF+ PREP THEN *of* ⇑ transfer; N COUNT ⇑ interchange; N COUNT; N COUNT/ UNCOUNT

5 in exchange. **5.1** You use **in exchange** to say that something is done or given in return for something else. EG *They helped him. In exchange, he was to provide them with information.* **5.2** If you give a person something **in exchange for** something else, you give it to them because they are giving the other thing to you. EG *They were given food, shelter and clothes in exchange for two years labour without wages... They sold chemicals and textiles in exchange for agricultural products.* PHR : USED AS AN A; PREP = in return for

6 An **exchange** is also **6.1** a place where people trade and do business with each other. EG *...the Corn Exchange.* **6.2** the same as a telephone exchange. EG *Get the exchange to call their number.* N COUNT : ALSO IN NAMES; N COUNT

7 See also **foreign exchange**, **stock exchange**, **telephone exchange**.

exchange rate, exchange rates. An **exchange rate** is the rate at which a sum of money of one country's currency is exchanged for an equivalent sum of money of another country's currency. N COUNT

Exchequer /ɪ²kstʃɛkə/. The **Exchequer** is the department in the British government which is responsible for receiving, issuing and accounting for money belonging to the state. ● See also **Chancellor of the Exchequer**. N PROPER : *the*+ N

excise, excises, excising, excised. The word **excise** is pronounced /ɛksaɪz/ when it is a noun, and /ɪ²ksaɪz/ when it is a verb. **1 Excise** is a tax that the government of a country puts on goods which are produced for sale in that country. ● See also **Customs and Excise**. N UNCOUNT : USU BEFORE N

2 If you **excise** something, you remove it completely; a formal or technical use. EG *The lump was excised and a series of tests done.* V+O = cut out

excitable /ɪ²ksaɪtəbə⁰l/. Someone who is **excitable** is rather nervous and becomes excited very easily. EG *...a wavy-haired child who was a little excitable.* ADJ QUALIT = temperamental
◊ **excitability** /ɪ²ksaitə¹bɪlɪ¹ti¹/. ◊ N UNCOUNT

excite /ɪ²ksaɪt/, **excites, exciting, excited.** 1 If something or someone **excites** you, 1.1 they give you strong feelings of happiness, nervousness, worry, etc that make you unable to relax. EG *'What happened, doctor?'–'Don't excite yourself, please. Everything is normal.'* V+O (NG/REFL) 1.2 they make you very interested and enthusiastic. EG *The idea of journalism excited me... He is like a modern Luther. Theological debate excites him.* V+O = stimulate 1.3 they cause you to feel sexual desire. EG *Why does the way she walks excite me so much?* V+O = arouse
2 If something excites a particular feeling, emotion, or reaction, it causes it to happen. EG *These rumours excited the suspicion of corruption in the Civil Service... The experiment excited much admiration... One paragraph in particular excited his interest.* V+O = arouse
3 If something **excites** an organ, tissue, or nerve in your body, it causes a response in it, or increases its activity; a technical use. V+O = stimulate

excited /ɪ²ksaɪtɪ²d/. If you are **excited**, you are 1 so happy that you are full of energy and cannot relax, especially because you are looking forward to an enjoyable and special event and cannot stop thinking about it. EG *He was so excited he could hardly sleep... There were hundreds of excited children to meet us... He sat back and looked at the water with bright, excited eyes.* ADJ QUALIT ◊ **excitedly.** EG *They were excitedly discussing plans for a party at the weekend... They turned to each other, laughing excitedly.* ◊ ADV WITH VB 2 sexually aroused or stimulated. EG *As the female approaches, the male becomes greatly excited.* ADJ QUALIT

excitement /ɪ²ksaɪtmə²nt/, **excitements. Excitement** is the state of being excited; also used of something that causes you to be excited. EG *Struggling to conceal his excitement, he accepted her invitation... The arrival of the colour TV made Dr O'Shea quite ill with excitement... ...the excitement of going to the moon... But the excitements of the day were not over.* N UNCOUNT/COUNT

exciting /ɪ²ksaɪtɪŋ/. Something that is **exciting** causes you to feel very excited and interested. EG *Growing up in the heart of London was exciting... It did not seem a very exciting idea.* ADJ QUALIT ◊ **excitingly.** EG *Life was excitingly unpredictable.* ◊ ADV

excl. is a written abbreviation for 'excluding' and 'exclusive'; used especially in advertisements.

exclaim /ɪ²ksklеɪm/, **exclaims, exclaiming, exclaimed.** When you **exclaim**, you speak suddenly, loudly, or emphatically because you are excited, shocked, or angry. EG *'Oh, you poor child!' exclaimed Mrs Socket... 'Desiree! What are you doing here?' she exclaimed... All of the women exclaimed at how well formed the baby was.* V+QUOTE/REPORT-CL, OR V: IF+PREP THEN *at/over* = cry out

> **EXCLAM** □ In this dictionary EXCLAM is used in the grammar notes beside entries to mean 'exclamation'. It is used beside words and expressions which you say when you are reacting to something that has been said or to something that has happened, usually to show that you feel pain, anger, anxiety, fear, etc. The definition tells you what context the EXCLAM is used in. Examples are **ouch!**, **big deal!**, and **crikey!**

exclamation /ɛkskləmeɪʃə⁰n/, **exclamations.** An **exclamation** is a sound, word, or sentence that is spoken suddenly, loudly, or emphatically and that expresses excitement, admiration, shock, or anger. EG *He drew back with a sharp exclamation... They embraced him with exclamations of joy.* N COUNT = cry

exclamation mark, exclamation marks. An **exclamation mark** is the sign (!) which is used in writing to show that a word, phrase, or sentence is an exclamation. N COUNT

exclamation point, exclamation points. An **exclamation point** is an exclamation mark; used in American English. N COUNT

exclude /ɪ²ksklu:d/, **excludes, excluding, excluded.** 1 If you **exclude** something, 1.1 you deliberately do not include it in a piece of work, discussion, activity, etc. EG *This Act explicitly excluded from its provisions cases of death by murder... For the moment we will exclude the special case of the religious wars.* V+O: IF+PREP THEN *from* ⇑ omit ≠ include 1.2 you reject a possibility after considering it carefully in the process of discovering the truth or a solution to a problem. EG *Valid thinking must exclude alternatives at every step... A fake call from some local phone box was not excluded.* V+O: IF+PREP THEN *from*
2 If you **exclude** someone, you prevent them from entering a place or taking part in an activity. EG *...jobs from which the majority of workers are excluded.* V+O (NG/REFL): IF+PREP THEN *from* = debar ≠ admit

excluding /ɪ²ksklu:dɪŋ/ is used to say that someone or something is not included in the group of people or things that you are referring to. EG *We are open seven days a week, excluding Christmas Day... She was feared by everyone in the hotel, not excluding Freddie.* PREP = excepting

exclusion /ɪ²ksklu:ʒə⁰n/. 1 **Exclusion** is the act of deliberately not including something or of preventing something from being included. EG *We will be concentrating on one subject with the deliberate exclusion of other distracting matters.* N UNCOUNT: USU WITH POSS ⇑ omission
2 You say that something happens **to the exclusion of** something else, to show that it happens to such a great extent or in such a dominant way that there is no room for anything else to be considered or to be present. EG *...the ability to concentrate on a problem to the exclusion of all other matters.* PREP
3 **Exclusion** is also the act of preventing someone from entering a place or taking part in an activity. EG *...their exclusion from the rights and liberties that others enjoy... ...the laws relating to the admission and exclusion of aliens.* N UNCOUNT: USU WITH POSS

exclusive /ɪ²ksklu:sɪv/, **exclusives.** 1 Something that is **exclusive** is 1.1 limited to people who have a lot of money or who belong to a high social class, and is therefore not available to everyone. EG *...a rather exclusive gathering of top executives and their wives... ...an exclusive residential district.* ADJ QUALIT = select 1.2 used or owned by only one person or group, and not shared with anyone else. EG *They have exclusive use of the machine... You should have informed us it was your exclusive property.* ADJ CLASSIF: ATTRIB ≠ shared
2 If two things are **exclusive** or are mutually **exclusive**, they are separate and very different from each other, so that there seems to be no connection between them, or it seems impossible for them to exist together. EG *There is no reason why these two functions should be mutually exclusive.* ADJ CLASSIF = incompatible
3 An **exclusive** story in a magazine or newspaper is one that is published only in that particular paper and in no other. EG *...an exclusive interview.* ADJ CLASSIF: ATTRIB ▸ used as a noun. EG *The story was a Times exclusive.* ▸ N COUNT = scoop
4 Financial terms or arrangements that are **exclusive** do not include all the charges or all the facilities or services offered. EG *...at a rate of £70 per week, exclusive of VAT... Our terms are exclusive.* ADJ CLASSIF: PRED, IF+PREP THEN *of* = excluding

exclusively /ɪ²ksklu:sɪvli¹/ is used to refer to situations or activities that involve only the thing or things mentioned, and nothing else. EG *The pygmy ant-eater lives exclusively on termites... The style is exclusively western.* ADV = only, entirely

excommunicate /ɛkskəmju:nɪkeɪt/, **excommunicates, excommunicating, excommunicated.** If a Roman Catholic is **excommunicated**, it is publicly and officially stated that the person is no longer allowed to be a member of the Roman Catholic church. This is a punishment for some very great wrong that they have done. EG *She was excommunicated by Cardinal Manning.* V+O ⇑ expel

excommunication /ɛkskəmju:nɪkeɪʃə⁰n/, **excommunications. Excommunication** is the state of being excommunicated or the act of excommunicating someone. N UNCOUNT/COUNT ⇑ expulsion

excrement /ɛkskrɪ¹mə²nt/ is the solid waste matter that is passed out of a person or animal's body through their bowels; a formal word. EG *The road was filled with camel and donkey excrement.* N UNCOUNT = faeces

excrescence /ɪ²kskrɛsə⁰ns/, **excrescences.** An **excrescence** is a lump or growth on the surface of an animal or plant; a formal or technical word. N COUNT

excreta /ɪ²kskri:tə/ is waste matter such as urine, sweat, or faeces, which is passed out of a person or animal's body; a formal word. N UNCOUNT ⇑ waste matter

excrete /ɪ²kskri:t/, **excretes, excreting, excreted.** When you **excrete** waste matter from your body, you get rid of it, for example by sweating or going to the lavatory. EG *Water is excreted from the body in urine.* V OR V+O ⇑ eliminate ◊ **excretion** /ɪ²kskri:ʃə⁰n/, **excretions.** ◊ N UNCOUNT/COUNT

excruciating /ɪ²kskru:ʃieɪtɪŋ/. Something that is **excruciating** is 1 extremely painful. EG *I had the* ADJ QUALIT: USU most excruciating cramp in my leg. ◊ **excruciatingly**. EG *Walking was excruciatingly painful.* **2** extremely difficult to bear or to cope with, usually because it is very sad, unpleasant, or embarrassing. EG *...a home which had come to be associated with excruciating unhappiness.* ◊ **excruciatingly**. EG *It was an excruciatingly humiliating experience.*

ATTRIB / ◊ ADV / ADJ QUALIT / ◊ ADV+ADJ/ADV

exculpate /ɛkskʌlpeɪt, ɪkskʌlpeɪt/, **exculpates, exculpating, exculpated**; a formal word. If you **exculpate** someone, you show that they are not guilty of doing something wrong, or at fault or to blame for something bad that has happened. EG *In 1956 he was legally exculpated.*

V+O : IF+PREP THEN *from* / ⇑ clear / = exonerate

excursion /ɪ²kskɜːʃə⁰n, -ʒə⁰n/, **excursions**. **1** An **excursion** is **1.1** a short journey, especially one that you make for a particular purpose. EG *...a shopping excursion... ...midnight excursions to deserted beaches.* **1.2** a short journey that is organized by a holiday company, tourist organization, etc, so that people can visit an interesting place. EG *You could go on a day excursion to the nearby island of Aegina.*

N COUNT / ⇑ trip / = outing / N COUNT / = outing

2 An **excursion** into something is an attempt to develop or understand a new idea or something that you have not experienced before. EG *...a rare excursion into contemporary music.*

N COUNT : IF+PREP THEN *into* / ⇑ journey

excusable /ɪ²kskjuːzəbə⁰l/. If something is **excusable**, you can forgive it. EG *He made an excusable mistake.*

ADJ QUALIT / = forgivable

excuse, excuses, excusing, excused. The word **excuse** is pronounced /ɪ²kskjuːs/ when it is a noun, and /ɪ²kskjuːz/ when it is a verb. **1** An **excuse** is a reason which you give in order to explain why something has been done or has not been done, or in order to avoid doing something. EG *You don't have to make any excuses to me... The government had no excuse to be ignorant of it... There is no excuse for this happening in a new building... He kept finding excuses not to go home... He had found the perfect excuse for retiring early.*

N COUNT : IF+PREP THEN *for* / ⇑ explanation / = justification

2 If you **excuse** yourself or someone else, you provide reasons or a justification for your actions or behaviour, especially when other people disapprove of the way you have behaved. EG *I'm not going to try and justify or excuse myself... I hope you're not excusing him... Within five minutes he was excusing himself.*

V+O (NG/REFL) / ⇑ explain / = justify

3 If you **excuse** your behaviour, you explain or justify it, especially when other people disapprove of the way you have acted or behaved. EG *The Vice President admitted taking bribes, excusing it as momentary weakness... We'll do it better tomorrow, I told myself, excusing our idleness.*

V+O : IF+PREP THEN *as*

4 If you **excuse** someone for something wrong that they have done, you forgive them for it. EG *I could never excuse him for being so rude... Such delays cannot be excused... I excused him much of his prejudice because I liked him.*

V+O : IF+PREP THEN *for*, OR V+O+O / = pardon

5 If you **excuse** someone from a duty or responsibility, you free them from it. EG *She asked to be excused from acting that evening... ...a certificate excusing him from games at school... You can apply to be excused payment if your earnings are low.*

V+O : USU PASS, IF+PREP THEN *from* / = exempt

6 If you ask someone to **excuse** you, you are asking them to allow you to leave. EG *You'll have to excuse me; I ought to be saying goodnight... Will you excuse me just a second?... This is where I ought to excuse myself.*

V+O (NG/REFL)

7 excuse me. You can use the expression **excuse me** in the following ways: **7.1** to get someone's attention, especially when you are about to ask them a question. EG *'Excuse me,' he said, 'but is there a fairly cheap restaurant near here?'.* **7.2** when you are disagreeing with someone or expressing a different or contradictory point of view. EG *Excuse me, but with all respect, I think you have misunderstood.* **7.3** to apologize to someone when you have disturbed or interrupted them. EG *Well, excuse me for disturbing you at home... Excuse me butting in.* **7.4** to indicate that you don't want to talk to someone. EG *Excuse me, I'm busy.* **7.5** to indicate that you are about to leave the room, usually just for a short while. EG *'Excuse me.' He stood up. 'I have to make a telephone call.'* **7.6** to apologize when you have done something slightly embarrassing or impolite, such as burping, hiccupping or sneezing. **7.7** when you are asking someone to repeat what they have just said; used in American English.

PHR / = pardon me / PHR / = sorry / PHR+-ING/*for* / = sorry / PHR / = sorry / CONVENTION / = pardon me / CONVENTION / = pardon me / CONVENTION / = sorry

ex-directory. In Britain, if a person or his or her telephone number is **ex-directory**, the number is not listed in the telephone directory, and the telephone company will refuse to give it to people who ask for it.

ADJ CLASSIF

execrable /ɛksɪkrəbə⁰l/. Something that is **execrable** is very bad or unpleasant; a formal word. EG *Why do tourists come here? The food is execrable, the hotels lousy.*

ADJ QUALIT / = abysmal

execute /ɛksɪkjuːt/, **executes, executing, executed**. **1** To **execute** someone means to kill them as a punishment for a serious crime. EG *...the last woman to be executed in Britain... ...a month or two later they executed the king.* ◊ **execution** /ɛksɪkjuːʃə⁰n/, **executions**. EG *...the execution of Charles I... The rebel faced capture and possible execution... The executions were carried out at dawn.*

V+O : USU PASS / = put to death / ◊ N COUNT/UNCOUNT

2 If you **execute** something such as a plan, you do it in the way that has been planned, agreed, or requested; a formal use. EG *Never once did I doubt that I would be able to execute my plans... ...a carefully premeditated and carefully executed crime.* ◊ **execution**. EG *He was arrested on a charge of obstructing a police officer in the execution of his duty.*

V+O / = carry out, implement / ≠ abort, cancel / ◊ N UNCOUNT / = implementation

3 If you **execute** a difficult action or movement, you successfully perform it. EG *The pilot began to execute a series of playful aerobatics... The dance was very skilfully executed.* ◊ **execution**.

V+O / ◊ N UNCOUNT

4 If you **execute** a work of art, you create it. EG *His pictures are executed with tremendous humour... The other one was executed in gold thread on a dark red background.* ◊ **execution**.

V+O : USU PASS / ◊ N UNCOUNT

5 If you **execute** a legal document such as a will, you carry out the instructions that are contained in it; a technical term in law. EG *The will was duly executed... But they did not execute the warrant immediately.*

V+O

executioner /ɛksɪkjuːʃə⁰nə/, **executioners**. An **executioner** is a person who has the job of executing criminals.

N COUNT / = hangman

executive /ɪ²gzɛkjə⁴tɪv/, **executives**. **1** An **executive** is someone who is employed by a business at a senior level. Executives decide what the business should do, and ensure that it is done. EG *...a senior executive... ...business executives.*

N COUNT / ⇑ manager

2 The **executive** sections and tasks of an organization are concerned with the making of decisions and with ensuring that decisions are carried out. EG *...the executive function of actually running the business... ...our executive board.*

ADJ CLASSIF : ATTRIB

3 Executive goods are expensive, fashionable, and designed or intended for people who are executives or who are at the same social or economic level as executives; an informal use. EG *She swivels back and forth in her executive chair... ...the fashionable executive two-litre car.*

ADJ CLASSIF : ATTRIB

4 The **executive** of an organization such as a political party is a committee within that organization that has the authority to make decisions and that ensures that these decisions are carried out. EG *...the Party's National Executive... ...the executive of the National Union of Teachers... Five executive members resigned.*

N COUNT : IF SING, VB CAN BE SING OR PL

5 The **executive** is the part of the government of a country that is concerned with carrying out decisions or orders, as opposed to the part that makes laws or the part that deals with criminals: compare **legislature** and **judiciary**. EG *...the highest reaches of the judiciary and the executive... ...the executive branch of government.*

N SING : *the*+N

executor /ɪ²gzɛkjə⁴tə/, **executors**. An **executor** is someone whose name you write in your will when you want them to be responsible for dealing with your affairs after your death; a technical term in law. EG *It was my duty as her executor to go through her personal papers.*

N COUNT / ⇑ appointee

exegesis /ɛksɪdʒiːsɪs/, **exegeses** /ɛksɪdʒiːsiːz/. An **exegesis** is an explanation and interpretation of a piece of writing, especially a religious piece of writing, after very careful study; a technical term. EG *...a lengthy exegesis on classical Marxist theory.*

N COUNT

exemplar /ɪ²gzɛmplɑː/, **exemplars**; a formal word. An **exemplar** is **1** a typical example of a group or class of things. EG *Ostensibly, he is a walking exemplar of change.* **2** someone or something that is

N COUNT : IF+PREP THEN *of* / N COUNT : IF+

considered to be so good that they should be copied or imitated; used showing approval. EG *They are the pillars of society, our exemplars of success and social attainment.* PREP THEN *of* = model

exemplary /ɪ²gzɛmpləri¹/. **1** If you describe someone or something as **exemplary**, you mean that you consider them to be excellent or extremely good. EG *He had been an exemplary father... He was possessed of an exemplary patience.* ADJ QUALIT : USU ATTRIB

2 An **exemplary** punishment is an unusually harsh one which is intended to discourage other people from committing similar crimes. EG *He was singled out for the exemplary punishment of execution.* ADJ CLASSIF : USU ATTRIB ⇑ deterrent

exemplify /ɪ²gzɛmplɪfaɪ/, **exemplifies, exemplifying, exemplified. 1** To **exemplify** a situation, quality, class of objects, etc, means to be a typical example of it. EG *Perhaps above all other groups teachers exemplify the virtues of the middle class.* V+O = typify

2 If you **exemplify** something, you give an example of it. EG *I'm going to try and exemplify one or two of these points.* ◊ **exemplification** /ɪ²gzɛmplɪfɪkeɪʃə⁰n/, **exemplifications.** EG *You could make the point more clearly with further exemplification.* V+O = illustrate ◊ N COUNT/UNCOUNT = illustration

exempt /ɪ²gzɛmp⁰t/, **exempts, exempting, exempted. 1** If you are **exempt** from a particular rule, duty, or obligation, you are not affected or bound by it. EG *Harold was exempt from military service... These houses are exempt from paying rates.* ADJ CLASSIF : PRED, USU+*from* ⇑ freed = excused

2 To **exempt** a person or thing from a particular rule, duty, or obligation means to state officially that they are not bound or affected by it. EG *The new rules exempt such loans from capital transfer tax... They made efforts to exempt him from responsibility.* ◊ **exemption** /ɪ²gzɛmp⁰ʃə⁰n/, **exemptions.** EG *...exemption from jury service... ...tax exemptions for home-owners.* V+O : IF+PREP THEN *from* ⇑ free = excuse ◊ N UNCOUNT/COUNT ⇑ freedom

exercise /ɛksəsaɪz/, **exercises, exercising, exercised. 1 Exercises** are **1.1** a series of energetic movements which you do in order to get fit or remain healthy. EG *...gymnastic exercises... ...breathing exercises.* **1.2** a series of movements or repeated actions which you do in order to practise for a particular activity, such as playing a musical instrument. EG *I always start my singing practice with scales and exercises... Every morning the whole cast had to do exercises.* **1.3** operations or manoeuvres that are performed by a section of the army, navy, or air force. EG *They're carrying out fleet exercises somewhere off the North Cape... ...peacetime exercises and training.* N COUNT : USU PL ⇑ movement; N COUNT : USU PL ⇑ practice; N COUNT : USU PL ⇑ operation

2 An **exercise** is a short piece of work that you do, for example in school, which is designed to help you learn a particular mental skill such as arithmetic. EG *Can we proceed now with exercise five?... ...spelling exercises.* N COUNT ⇑ practice

3 An **exercise** in something is an activity which is planned to achieve a particular purpose. EG *...the first large-scale exercise in computer modelling... The rally was organized by the state as an exercise in patriotism.* N COUNT : IF+ PREP THEN *in*

4 Exercise is energetic movement that you do to keep healthy or train for a sport. EG *The horses emerged to the park for exercise... I have had all the exercise I need for one day.* N UNCOUNT ⇑ exertion

5 When you **exercise**, you move your body energetically in order to get fit and to remain healthy. EG *Often I could not fall asleep unless I exercised to the point of exhaustion.* V

6 If you **exercise** authority, rights, responsibilities, etc, you use them well or effectively. EG *They already exercise considerable influence in all western countries... They had no intention of exercising restraint... ...a book designed to help you exercise the right to buy your council house.* V+O

7 The **exercise** of authority, a right, a responsibility, etc, is the careful and effective use or practice of it. EG *The exercise of personal responsibility is encouraged.* N SING : *the*+N+*of* ⇑ operation

8 If something **exercises** you or your mind, you think or talk about it a great deal, especially because you are worried or concerned about it. EG *The question put by Mary had exercised many a group of gossiping faculty members... This problem has much exercised the minds of academics as well as politicians.* V+O ⇑ concern = occupy

exercise book, exercise books. An **exercise book** is a small book with blank pages that pupils and students use for doing their schoolwork. N COUNT ⇑ notebook

exert /ɪ²gzɜːt/, **exerts, exerting, exerted. 1** If someone or something **exerts** influence, authority, pressure, etc, they use it in a strong or determined way, especially in order to produce an effect on someone or something. EG *His teachings still exert a strong influence on his former students... The social pressures exerted by a small community are enormous.* V+O : USU+A

2 If you **exert** yourself, you make a physical or mental effort to do something. EG *He had to exert himself to make conversation with the visitor.* V+O (REFL) ⇑ try = force

exertion /ɪ²gzɜʃə⁰n/, **exertions. Exertion** is physical effort or exercise. EG *Her head throbbed with exertion... I was weakened by my exertions.* N UNCOUNT/COUNT

ex gratia /ɛksgreɪʃə/. An **ex gratia** payment or grant is one that is given as a favour or gift and not because it is legally necessary; a formal or legal term. ADJ CLASSIF ⇑ voluntary

exhale /ɪ²gzh⁰eɪl/, **exhales, exhaling, exhaled.** When you **exhale**, you breathe out the air that is in your lungs. EG *He exhaled slowly and smiled... He exhaled another great billow of cigar smoke.* ◊ **exhalation** /ɛgzəleɪʃə⁰n/, **exhalations.** EG *...a soft exhalation of breath.* V OR V+O ≠ inhale ◊ N UNCOUNT/COUNT

exhaust /ɪ²gzɔːst/, **exhausts, exhausting, exhausted. 1** To **exhaust** someone means to make them so tired, either physically or mentally, that they have no energy left. EG *She exhausted Nell both nervously and physically.* ◊ **exhausted.** EG *All three men were hot, dirty, and exhausted... She was too exhausted to argue... He stumbled and fell, exhausted.* ◊ **exhausting.** EG *...a difficult and exhausting job.* V+O (NG/REFL) ⇑ tire = drain ◊ ADJ QUALIT = worn out ◊ ADJ QUALIT

2 If you **exhaust** something such as money or food, you use it up or finish it completely. EG *They soon exhausted the food resources of the surrounding area.* V+O = drain

3 If you **exhaust** a subject or topic, you talk about it so much that there is nothing else to say about it. EG *When the subject had been thoroughly exhausted, everyone went home.* V+O ⇑ deal with

4 An **exhaust** or an **exhaust pipe** is a pipe which carries the gas or steam out of the engine of a car, lorry, motorbike, etc. N COUNT

5 Exhaust is the gas or steam that is produced when the engine of a car, lorry, motorbike, etc is running, and that has to be allowed to escape. N UNCOUNT

exhaustible /ɪ²gzɔːstə¹bə⁰l/. Something that is **exhaustible** exists only in a limited quantity. EG *...possible long term shortages of exhaustible resources.* ADJ CLASSIF ≠ inexhaustible

exhaustion /ɪ²gzɔːstʃə⁰n/ is the state of being so tired that you have no energy left. EG *She was almost fainting with exhaustion.* N UNCOUNT ⇑ tiredness

exhaustive /ɪ²gzɔːstɪv/. An **exhaustive** study or search is thorough and complete. EG *He studied the problem in exhaustive detail... This list is by no means exhaustive.* ◊ **exhaustively.** EG *...exhaustively researched evidence.* ADJ QUALIT = comprehensive ◊ ADV

exhibit /ɪ²gzɪbɪt/, **exhibits, exhibiting, exhibited. 1** If you **exhibit** a particular quality, ability, or feeling, it can be easily seen or noticed by other people; a formal use. EG *He still exhibited signs of stress... Different sectors within the same society exhibit different rates of change.* V+O = show, display

2 When something such as a picture or sculpture **is exhibited**, it is put in a public place such as a museum or art gallery, so that people can come to look at it. EG *The paintings are exhibited in chronological sequence... I exhibited some tapestries I had done in America.* V+O : USU PASS = display

3 When artists **exhibit**, they show their work in public. EG *She was still working and exhibiting last year.* V

4 An **exhibit** is **4.1** something that is put on show to the public in a museum or art gallery. EG *Our local museum has over a thousand exhibits.* **4.2** something that a lawyer shows in court as evidence in a legal case. EG *Exhibit number two is a pocket diary belonging to the accused.* N COUNT ⇑ object; N COUNT : ALSO N+NUM ⇑ object

5 If you **exhibit** something to someone, you show it to them in order to make them believe you or admire you. EG *Glenn exhibited the rat's tooth to all his friends... They exhibited their supposedly occult powers.* V+O : IF+PREP THEN *to* = display

exhibition /ɛgzɪbɪʃə⁰n/, **exhibitions**. 1 An **exhibition** is a collection of pictures, sculptures, or other things in a public place where people can come to look at them. EG *Did you see the Shakespeare exhibition?... ...exhibition galleries.* — N COUNT ⇑ show

2 **Exhibition** is the showing of pictures, sculptures, or other things in a public place. EG *The film was refused a licence for public exhibition... ...the exhibition of her work.* — N UNCOUNT ⇑ show = display ● If something is **on exhibition**, it is being shown in a public place. EG *Cecil Beaton's war photographs are on exhibition at the Imperial War Museum.* — ● PHR : USED AS AN A = on view

3 An **exhibition** of rudeness, arrogance, etc is very rude behaviour, very arrogant behaviour, etc. EG *...an exhibition of petulance and arrogance.* — N COUNT+SUPP ⇑ show

4 An **exhibition** of skill, talent, etc is something that someone does, which shows how skilled, talented, etc they are at doing something. EG *...a remarkable exhibition of musicianship.* — N COUNT+SUPP ⇑ show

5 If you **make an exhibition of** yourself, you behave very stupidly or rudely in public, so that other people notice you and disapprove of you. — PHR : VB INFLECTS

6 In Britain, an **exhibition** is also a small amount of money that is given as a prize to students in some private schools and colleges. — N COUNT = award

exhibitionism /ɛgzɪbɪʃə⁰nɪzə⁰m/ is 1 a type of behaviour in which someone tries to get people's attention all the time, especially by boasting or by trying to make people notice their talents and abilities; used showing disapproval. — N UNCOUNT ◇ **exhibitionist, exhibitionists**. EG *As a child I was inclined to be an exhibitionist.* — ◇ N COUNT ⇑ show-off 2 a type of behaviour, usually the result of psychological problems or mental illness, in which a man deliberately reveals his genitals in public places, especially in front of women; a technical term. — N UNCOUNT ◇ **exhibitionist, exhibitionists**. — ◇ N COUNT

exhibitor /ɪ²gzɪbɪtə/, **exhibitors**. An **exhibitor** is a person whose work is being shown in an exhibition. EG *Flanagan was also a prominent exhibitor in a large-scale exhibition.* — N COUNT ⇑ participant

exhilarate /ɪ²gzɪləreɪt/, **exhilarates, exhilarating, exhilarated**. If something **exhilarates** you, it gives you a strong feeling of happiness and excitement. EG *The refugees were exhilarated by the news... This city exhilarates and stimulates me.* — V+O : USU PASS ⇑ excite = thrill ◇ **exhilarated**. EG *No longer cold, he felt exhilarated with cleanliness.* — ◇ ADJ QUALIT ◇ **exhilarating**. EG *...an exhilarating experience.* — ◇ ADJ QUALIT

exhilaration /ɪ²gzɪləreɪʃə⁰n/ is a strong feeling of excitement and happiness. EG *There was a sense of exhilaration about being alone on the beach.* — N UNCOUNT

exhort /ɪ²gzɔ:t/, **exhorts, exhorting, exhorted**. If you **exhort** someone to do something, you try hard to persuade them to do it; a formal word. EG *I exhorted the men not to drink too much.* — V+O ⇑ advise = entreat ◇ **exhortation** /ɛgzɔ:teɪʃə⁰n/, **exhortations**. EG *...fervent exhortations to revolutionary action... ...a rhetorical, almost poetic, work of exhortation.* — ◇ N COUNT/UNCOUNT ⇑ persuasion = invocation

exhume /ɛksh⁰ju:m/, **exhumes, exhuming, exhumed**. To **exhume** a dead person's body means to take it out of the ground where it is buried so that you can examine it, especially in order to find out how the person died; a formal word. — V+O ⇑ dig up = disinter ≠ bury ◇ **exhumation** /ɛgzju:meɪʃə⁰n/, **exhumations**. EG *He never liked being present at exhumations, but it was part of his job.* — ◇ N COUNT/UNCOUNT

exigency /ɛksɪdʒənsi¹, ɪ²gzɪdʒənsi¹/, **exigencies**. The **exigencies** of a situation or a job are the difficulties that you have to deal with as part of it; a formal word. EG *...the exigencies of the war... ...the exigencies of her profession.* — N COUNT : USU PL = demands ▸ used as an uncount noun. EG *The government was compelled by military exigency to introduce many reforms.* — ▸ N UNCOUNT

exigent /ɛksɪdʒənt/; a formal word. 1 Something that is **exigent** needs immediate attention or action. — ADJ QUALIT = urgent

2 Someone who is **exigent** asks or expects other people to do more than it is reasonable to expect them to do. EG *She became even more exigent over his pronunciation.* — ADJ QUALIT = demanding

exiguous /ɪ²gzɪgju:əs/. If something is **exiguous**, there is very little of it; a formal word. EG *He invested his exiguous savings in ordinary shares.* — ADJ QUALIT = meagre

exile /ɛgzaɪl, ɛksaɪl/, **exiles, exiling, exiled**. 1 **Exile** is the state of being forced to live away from your country, especially for political reasons. EG *He lived here in exile... ...eight whole months of exile.* — N UNCOUNT = banishment

2 To **exile** someone means to send them away from their own country so that they have to live somewhere else, especially for political reasons. EG *I was exiled from Ceylon for a year.* — V+O ◇ **exiled**. EG *The exiled King Umberto had asked for a personal representative to accompany him.* — ◇ ADJ CLASSIF

3 An **exile** is someone who has been exiled. EG *...political exiles.* — N COUNT ⇑ expatriate

exist /ɪ²gzɪst/, **exists, existing, existed**. 1 To **exist** means 1.1 to be present in the world or universe as a real, living, or actual thing and not, for example, to be something that people have imagined or made up, or something that has disappeared or been destroyed. EG *That word doesn't exist in English... Communities who live by hunting and gathering still exist... Nobody can actually know God exists, but we believe he exists... I got a present from an aunt in Hungary whom I didn't know existed... Within our society there still exist rampant nationalism and racism.* — V : NO CONT 1.2 to live, especially under difficult conditions or with very little food or money. EG *How we're to exist out here I don't know... She existed only on milk.* — V : USU+A = survive

2 See also **existing**.

existence /ɪ²gzɪstəns/, **existences**. 1 **Existence** is the state of being real, alive, or actual, rather than being something that people have imagined or made up. EG *Do you believe in the existence of God?... There are those who argue that the existence of nuclear weapons has reduced the risk of war... It will be much faster than any submarine now in existence... These institutions do not come into existence except as a result of state policy... In the course of evolution, dinosaurs simply passed out of existence.* — N UNCOUNT ≠ non-existence

2 You refer to someone's way of life as an **existence** when they live under difficult conditions. EG *These unfortunate creatures eke out a miserable existence... The family lived a more or less vagabond existence.* — N COUNT+SUPP

existent /ɪ²gzɪstənt/. You can describe something as **existent** when it exists; a formal word. EG *...an attempt to refine the existent machinery to make it even more efficient.* — ADJ CLASSIF ≠ non-existent

existential /ɛgzɪstɛnʃə⁰l/ means relating to human existence and experience; a formal word. — ADJ CLASSIF : ATTRIB

existentialism /ɛgzɪstɛnʃə⁰lɪzə⁰m/ is a modern philosophical belief which stresses the importance of human experience, and says that everyone is responsible for the results of their own actions; a technical term. — N UNCOUNT ⇑ philosophy

existentialist /ɛgzɪstɛnʃə⁰lɪst/, **existentialists**. An **existentialist** is a person who agrees with the philosophy of existentialism; a technical term. EG *...the writings of the Existentialists.* — N COUNT ▸ used as an adjective. EG *...an existentialist approach.* — ▸ ADJ CLASSIF

existing /ɪ²gzɪstɪŋ/ is used to describe something which is now in use or in operation, especially when you are contrasting it with something which is planned for the future. EG *We have to find ways of making the existing system work better... Many members of my party are not satisfied with the existing press laws.* — ADJ CLASSIF : ATTRIB = present

exit /ɛgzɪt, ɛksɪt/, **exits, exiting, exited**. 1 An **exit** is 1.1 a door in a public building such as a theatre, large shop, railway station, etc, through which people can leave. EG *He hurried towards the exit... ...the fire exit.* — N COUNT = way out ≠ entrance 1.2 an act of leaving a place. EG *Her exit was perfectly timed.. Opposition councillors staged a mass exit after ten minutes... He made a hasty exit from the Men's Room.* — N COUNT ⇑ departure ≠ arrival 1.3 a point on a motorway where traffic can leave it or join it. EG *I missed my exit from the motorway and had to drive on another four miles.* — N COUNT

2 If you **exit** from somewhere, you leave there. EG *I exited from the surgery.* — V : IF+PREP THEN *from*

exit visa. An **exit visa** is an official stamp in someone's passport, or an official document, which allows them to leave a particular country. — N COUNT ⇑ permit

exodus /ɛksədəs/. When there is an **exodus**, a lot of people leave a place together. EG *...the exodus of senior politicians and public figures from London in the summer... These measures are likely to increase poverty and speed up the exodus to the cities.* — N SING WITH DET ⇑ departure ≠ influx

ex officio /ɛx əfɪʃɪəʊ/ is used to indicate that someone is entitled to something because of their rank, office or position; used in formal English. EG *...an ex officio member of the University Council.* — ADJ CLASSIF : ATTRIB, OR ADV

exonerate /ɪ²gzɒnəreɪt/, **exonerates, exonerating, exonerated**. To **exonerate** someone means to demonstrate officially that they are not responsible for something wrong or unpleasant that has happened; a formal word. EG *Although he was eventually exonerated, he never recovered from the strain of the trial. ...to exonerate me from the crimes they had charged me with.* V+O : IF+PREP THEN *from* = clear ≠ blame, convict

exorbitant /ɪ²gzɔːbɪtənt/. If you describe something as **exorbitant**, you mean that it is much bigger or much more expensive than it should be. EG *She charged them an exorbitant rent... ...exorbitant prices.* ◊ **exorbitantly**. EG *Even a house of this size seems exorbitantly large by our standards.* ADJ QUALIT ⇑ high = excessive ◊ ADV+ADJ/ADV

exorcism /ɛksɔːsɪsə⁰m/, **exorcisms**. **Exorcism** is 1 the removing of evil spirits from a place or person. EG *They called in a priest to perform the exorcism.* ◊ **exorcist, exorcists**. EG *They felt they had to call in an exorcist.* 2 the process of getting rid of unhappy or painful memories and emotions. N UNCOUNT/COUNT ◊ N COUNT N UNCOUNT/COUNT ⇑ eradication

exorcize /ɛksɔːsaɪz/, **exorcizes, exorcizing, exorcized**; also spelled **exorcise**. 1 To **exorcize** an evil spirit or demon means to force it to leave a particular place or person by means of special prayers and ceremonies. V+O ⇑ expel

2 To **exorcize** a place or person means to force an evil spirit or demon to leave them by means of special prayers and ceremonies. V+O ⇑ free

3 If you **exorcize** a painful or unhappy memory, you succeed in removing it from your mind. V+O ⇑ remove

exotic /ɪ²gzɒtɪk/. Something that is **exotic** is strange, unusual, and interesting because it comes from a distant country. EG *...rich exotic foods... ...exotic places in Southern Mexico.* ◊ **exotically**. ADJ QUALIT ◊ ADV

expand /ɪ²kspænd/, **expands, expanding, expanded**. 1 If you **expand** something, or if it **expands**, 1.1 it becomes greater in number or amount. EG *...major measures to expand the Royal Air Force... Between 1960 and 1970 the city's population expanded by 12 per cent.* 1.2 it becomes larger in size. EG *Natural materials expand with heat and contract with cold and damp... He breathed deeply, his lungs fully expanded.* V-ERG ⇑ increase ≠ decrease V-ERG ⇑ enlarge

2 If a business **expands**, it becomes bigger and more successful. EG *His retail business in Darlington expanded rapidly between the wars.* V = grow

expand on. If you **expand on** or **expand upon** something, you give more information or details about it when you write or talk about it. EG *This highly relevant observation is expanded on by Dr. White... I went on to expand upon this theme.* PHRASAL VB : V+PREP, HAS PASS = enlarge on

expanse /ɪ²kspæns/, **expanses**. An **expanse** of sea, sky, etc is a very large amount of it that you can see from a particular place. EG *...a wide expanse of blue sky.* N COUNT+*of* ⇑ area = stretch

expansion /ɪ²kspænʃə⁰n/ is the process of becoming greater in size, number, or amount. EG *...the rapid expansion of British agriculture... ...economic expansion.* N UNCOUNT ⇑ increase = growth

expansionism /ɪ²kspænʃə⁰nɪzə⁰m/ is the policy of expanding the economy of a particular country, or the land that it rules; used showing disapproval. EG *Their expansionism continued successfully for several centuries.* ◊ **expansionist**. EG *...expansionist policies.* N UNCOUNT ◊ ADJ CLASSIF

expansive /ɪ²kspænsɪv/. 1 If you are **expansive**, you are willing to talk a lot, because you are happy and relaxed. EG *That week had made him jovial and expansive.* ◊ **expansively**. EG *'Have another drink, help yourself,' he said expansively.* ◊ **expansiveness**. EG *The locals started to regret their earlier expansiveness.* ADJ QUALIT ⇑ talkative ◊ ADV WITH VB ◊ N UNCOUNT

2 Something that is **expansive** is very large or extensive; a formal use. EG *...expansive ambitions.* ADJ CLASSIF : ATTRIB

expatiate /ɪ²kspeɪʃieɪt/, **expatiates, expatiating, expatiated**. If you **expatiate** on or about something, you write or speak in detail or at great length about it; a formal word. V+A *(on/upon/about)* ⇑ expand = enlarge on

expatriate /ɛkspætri¹ɪ³t/, **expatriates**. An **expatriate** is someone who is living in a country which is not their own. EG *...British expatriates.* ▸ used as an adjective. EG *...an expatriate American.* N COUNT ⇑ foreigner ▸ ADJ CLASSIF : ATTRIB

expect /ɪ²kspɛkt/, **expects, expecting, expected**. 1 If you **expect** something to happen, you believe that it will happen, because of what you know about the situation. EG *Nobody expected the strike to succeed... The talks are expected to last two or three days... Panic here and there was only to be expected... The journey was not as nice as Clarissa had expected.* V+O/*to*-INF/REPORT-CL, OR V+O+*to*-INF = anticipate

2 If you **expect** something, 2.1 you believe that it is going to happen or arrive, because you have been told that it will. EG *Rodin was expecting an important letter from France... We are expecting rain.* ◊ **expected**. EG *We would resist this expected attack... The expected income is eight-tenths of this amount.* 2.2 you believe that it is your right to get it or have it done for you. EG *We expect sincerity from our politicians... I expect no sympathy... They expect to have the door opened for them.* V+O ◊ ADJ CLASSIF V+O/*to*-INF/REPORT-CL, OR V+O+*to*-INF

3 If you **expect** a person, you are waiting for them to arrive, because you have invited them or arranged to see them. EG *She would expect him at eight... He was clearly not expected to dinner this evening.* ◊ **expected**. EG *...ushering in the expected guest.* V+O : USU+A ◊ ADJ CLASSIF

4 If you **expect** someone to do something, you require them to do it as a duty or obligation, for example as part of their work. EG *He is expected to put his work before his family... I'm sure she doesn't expect you to take the plane... We stood there, not knowing what was expected of us.* ◊ **expected**. EG *...an expected formality.* V+O+*to*-INF ◊ ADJ CLASSIF

5 If you **expect** to do something, you plan to do it or hope to achieve it. EG *He expects to be home after lunch... I don't expect to be in England very long... We expect to sell 70,000 by September.* V+*to*-INF

6 If you say that a woman **is expecting**, you mean that she is pregnant. V : ONLY CONT

7 If you say **'I expect'**, you mean that you think that what you are saying is likely to be proved correct. EG *'I expect that's Mrs Oliver's,' said Celia... I expect it'll be in the attic upstairs.* PHR : USED AS ADV SEN, USU+REPORT-CL

8 If you say **'What can you expect?'** or **'What do you expect?'** you mean that there is nothing surprising about a person's behaviour or a situation, because they have occurred before and could be predicted. EG *What could you expect from a family like that?* PHR

expectancy /ɪ²kspɛktənsi¹/ is the feeling that something exciting or interesting is about to happen; a formal word. EG *...an air of expectancy... There had been such a sense of expectancy beforehand.* ● See also **life expectancy**. N UNCOUNT ⇑ hope = anticipation

expectant /ɪ²kspɛktənt/. 1 If someone is **expectant**, they are excited because they think something interesting is about to happen. EG *The assembly, sensing a crisis, was tensely expectant... ...an expectant hush.* ◊ **expectantly**. EG *She looked at him expectantly.* ADJ QUALIT ⇑ waiting = eager ◊ ADV WITH VB

2 An **expectant** mother or father is someone whose baby is going to be born soon. ADJ CLASSIF : ATTRIB ⇑ future

expectation /ɛkspɛkteɪʃə⁰n/, **expectations**. An **expectation** is 1 a strong hope that something will happen or that you will get something that you want. EG *The plan has succeeded beyond our expectations... Living standards and expectations are increasing... Harold soon abandoned any expectation that Vita would take an interest.* 2 a strong belief that something is likely to happen. EG *I was watched in the expectation that I would go too far.* 3 a strong belief that something or someone is likely to be a particular kind of thing or person. EG *Her mother turned out to be, against all expectations, a young redhead.* 4 a strong belief that someone should behave in a particular way. EG *You're so busy living up to other people's expectations... ...women with expectations of old-fashioned gallantry.* N COUNT : SING=PL = aspiration N COUNT N COUNT : SING=PL N COUNT : USU PL, SING=PL

expectorant /ɛkspɛktərənt/, **expectorants**. An **expectorant** is a cough medicine that helps to loosen phlegm in your chest; a formal or medical term. N COUNT

expediency /ɪ²kspiːdɪənsi¹/. **Expediency** or **expedience** is usefulness or convenience in a particular situation, often gaining an immediate advantage while ignoring moral principles or later effects; a formal word. EG *...a matter of military expediency... We are sacrificing the long-term interest to short-term expediency... The government is torn between principle and expediency... His policies were dictated by expedience.* N UNCOUNT ⇑ suitability

expedient /ɪ²kspiːdɪənt/, **expedients**; a formal word. 1 An **expedient** is an action or plan that achieves a particular purpose, but may not be morally acceptable. EG *Incomes controls were used only as a short-term expedient.* N COUNT = measure

2 Something that is **expedient** is useful or convenient in a particular situation. EG *They adopt the measures* ADJ QUALIT

they regard to be most expedient... The President did not find it expedient to attend the meeting.

expedite /ɛkspɪdaɪt/, **expedites, expediting, expedited.** If you **expedite** something, you cause it to be done more quickly; a formal word. EG *We must do more to expedite development... This helped to expedite the army's withdrawal.* — V+O ⇑ hasten = speed up

expedition /ɛkspɪdɪʃəⁿn/, **expeditions.** An **expedition** is 1 an organized journey, usually involving several people, that is made for a particular purpose such as exploration. EG *...the British expedition to Mount Everest... The men were away on a hunting expedition.* ▸ The **expedition** is also used to refer to the people who make such a journey. EG *The expedition set out from St Louis.* 2 a short journey or outing that you make for pleasure. EG *I often go off on little expeditions when I have an afternoon off... ...a shopping expedition... ...sightseeing expeditions.* — N COUNT; N COUNT = excursion

expeditionary force /ɛkspɪdɪʃəⁿnəʳrɪ fɔːs/, **expeditionary forces.** An **expeditionary force** is a group of soldiers who are sent to fight in a foreign country; a military term. — N COUNT

expeditious /ɛkspɪdɪʃəs/ means quick and efficient; a formal word. EG *...the most expeditious method of obtaining reduced hours.* ◊ **expeditiously.** EG *The reports will be examined as expeditiously as possible.* — ADJ QUALIT; ◊ ADV WITH VB

expel /ɪ²kspɛl/, **expels, expelling, expelled.** 1 If someone **is expelled** from a school or organization, they are officially told that they no longer belong to it, for example because they have broken the rules very seriously. EG *He had been expelled from his previous schooi for stealing... 200 party members were expelled or resigned.* — V+O : USU PASS ⇑ dismiss = throw out

2 If someone **is expelled** from a place, they are made to leave it, often by force. EG *Peasants were expelled from their villages.* — V+O : USU PASS+A ⇑ displace = evict

3 To **expel** something means to force it out from a container or from your body. EG *Water is sucked in at one end and expelled at the other... She sank into her chair, expelling her breath in a long sigh.* — V+O

expend /ɪ²kspɛnd/, **expends, expending, expended.** If you **expend** energy, time, or money, you spend it or use it; a formal word. EG *They expend large sums of money to maintain this beach... ...the energy expended in this operation... They were expending every ounce of effort.* — V+O

expendable /ɪ²kspɛndəbəⁿl/, **expendables**; a formal word. 1 A person who is **expendable** may be dismissed or allowed to die because they are no longer considered to be necessary or important in a particular situation. EG *Mr Conrad, you are not expendable... My part would be played and I would become expendable... ...expendable airborne units.* — ADJ CLASSIF ⇑ unnecessary = disposable ≠ vital

2 Something that is **expendable** may be thrown away, abandoned, or destroyed because it is no longer necessary or useful. EG *The land is expendable; the people must go somewhere.* ▸ used as a noun. EG *...food supplies or other expendables.* — ADJ CLASSIF ⇑ unimportant = inessential; ▸ N COUNT

expenditure /ɪ²kspɛndɪtʃə/, **expenditures**; a formal word. **Expenditure** is 1 the amount of money that is spent on a particular thing or in a particular situation. EG *We restricted our expenditure on food... The government has had to cut down on public expenditure... ...tax expenditures.* 2 the using of money, energy, or time for a particular purpose. EG *...the expenditure of millions of pounds on inquiries... This was done expertly, with a minimum expenditure of energy.* — N UNCOUNT/COUNT = spending; N UNCOUNT+SUPP ⇑ use = outlay

expense /ɪ²kspɛns/, **expenses.** 1 **Expense** is the money that something costs you or that you need to spend in order to do something. EG *...the roads they're building at vast expense... Cut down on expenses until all your debts are paid off... ...household expenses... It's well worth the expense.* ● If you **go to great expense** to do something, you spend a lot of money in order to achieve it. EG *The Government has gone to great expense to set up procedures.* — N UNCOUNT/COUNT ⇑ cost = expenditure; ● PHR : VB INFLECTS

2 **Expenses** are amounts of money that you spend while doing something in the course of your work, which will be paid back to you afterwards. EG *The Executive Committee have their travelling expenses paid... Good. Now for the question of your expenses and fee.* — N PLURAL

3 If you do something **at** someone's **expense,** 3.1 they pay the money for you to do it. EG *...flying everywhere first class at the company's expense... He circulated the document at his own expense to the world's leading newspapers.* 3.2 you say or do something to make fun of them or to make them seem foolish. EG *He was unkind to people, making jokes at their expense.* — PHR : USED AS AN A; PHR : USED AS AN A

4 If you do something **at the expense of** something else or someone else, you do it in a way that harms them or reduces their importance. EG *Economic growth must not be pursued at the expense of environmental pollution... They increase their own income at the expense of the rural masses.* — PREP

expense account, expense accounts; also spelled with a hyphen. An **expense account** is an arrangement that is made by the company you work for, which allows you to spend their money on things that are part of your job, for example travelling or looking after their clients. EG *As an executive, you will be entitled to an expense account.* ▸ used as an adjective. EG *...an expense-account lunch.* — N COUNT; ▸ ADJ CLASSIF : ATTRIB

expensive /ɪ²kspɛnsɪv/. Something that is **expensive** costs a lot of money. EG *...expensive clothes... 'Vogue' was more expensive than the other magazines... It would be too expensive to alter existing lighting.* ◊ **expensively.** EG *Sheila was very expensively dressed... We can do that fairly easily and not too expensively.* — ADJ QUALIT = costly ≠ cheap; ◊ ADV ≠ cheaply

experience /ɪ²kspɪərɪəns/, **experiences, experiencing, experienced.** 1 **Experience** is 1.1 knowledge or skill in a particular job which you have gained because you have worked at the job for a long time. EG *I had no military experience... ...in my experience as a teacher... ...experience of working with children... He was senior to me in experience... She's had nine months experience.* 1.2 the state or process of feeling something or being affected by it. EG *The experience of colour is wholly subjective... ...the experience of fear.* 1.3 all the events, knowledge, and feelings that make up an individual's life or the character of a society. EG *Everyone learns best from his own experience... ...speaking from personal experience.* — N UNCOUNT ⇑ practice; N UNCOUNT+SUPP ⇑ sensation; N UNCOUNT

2 An **experience** is something that happens to you or something that you do, especially something important that affects you. EG *The funeral was a painful experience... ...my later experiences in the village.* — N COUNT+SUPP

3 If you **experience** a situation or problem, it happens to you or you are affected by it. EG *Similar problems have been experienced by other students... They are experiencing a population explosion... Few of the soldiers had experienced combat.* — V+O ⇑ undergo = face

4 If you **experience** an emotion or a physical feeling, you have it or feel it. EG *He experienced a pang of sadness... They experienced a mild burning sensation.* — V+O ⇑ feel

experienced /ɪ²kspɪərɪənst/. Someone who is **experienced** is skilled or knowledgeable in a particular job because they have worked at it for a long time. EG *She is an experienced lecturer... We need someone more experienced... My colleagues are less experienced in history.* — ADJ QUALIT

experiential /ɪ²kspɪərɪɛnʃəⁿl/ means relating to or resulting from experience; a very formal word. EG *...a personal, experiential reality.* — ADJ CLASSIF

experiment /ɪ²kspɛrə¹mə²nt/, **experiments, experimenting, experimented.** 1 An **experiment** is 1.1 a scientific test which is done in order to prove that a theory is true or to discover what happens to something in particular conditions. EG *...the results of a scientific experiment... ...new information gathered by observation or experiment... ...experiments in physics.* 1.2 the trying out of a new idea or method in order to see what it is like and what effect it has. EG *...the failure of this great experiment in industrial democracy.* — N COUNT/UNCOUNT; N COUNT/UNCOUNT ⇑ trial

2 If you **experiment** with something or **experiment** on it, you do a scientific test on it in order to prove that a theory is true or to discover what happens to it in particular conditions. EG *In 1939 he experimented with young rats.* ◊ **experimentation** /ɪ²kspɛrə¹mɛnteɪʃəⁿn/. EG *...a place for medical experimentation.* — V; ◊ N UNCOUNT ⇑ testing = research

3 To **experiment** also means to try out a new idea or method to see what it is like and what effects it has. EG *...small businesses anxious to experiment with computers... It's well worth experimenting to produce good cakes... Your willingness to experiment* — V

does you credit. ◊ **experimentation.** EG *...experimentation with cut-out shapes.* ◊ N UNCOUNT

experimental /ɪ²kspɛrə¹mɛntə⁰l/. Something that is **experimental 1** uses new ideas or methods. EG *The college is noted for its experimental forms of teaching... It's a very experimental novel.* ADJ QUALIT = innovative ◊ **experimentally.** EG *...the first parking meters, introduced experimentally in Soho in 1958.* ◊ ADV WITH VB **2** uses, is used in, or results from scientific experiments. EG *There is some experimental detail which seems to back this up... ...an experimental psychologist.* ADJ CLASSIF ◊ **experimentally.** EG *These are then measured experimentally and the results compared.* ◊ ADV WITH VB **3** is done in order to see what it is like, or what effects it has. EG *One of them gave an experimental tug at Clarissa's bag.* ADJ CLASSIF ⇑ exploratory = tentative ◊ **experimentally.** EG *He passed his tongue experimentally over his teeth.* ◊ ADV WITH VB

experimenter /ɪ²kspɛrə¹mɛntə/, **experimenters**. An **experimenter** is **1** someone who does scientific tests in order to prove a theory or discover what happens to things in particular conditions. EG *Experimenters have licences granted by the Home Office.* N COUNT ⇑ scientist
2 someone who likes trying new ideas or methods. N COUNT

expert /ɛkspɜːt/, **experts**. **1** An **expert** is **1.1** a person who is very skilled at doing something. EG *What an expert can do in minutes may take you hours... ...experts in various skills... Experts were called in to dismantle the bomb.* N COUNT = specialist **1.2** a person who has studied a particular subject and knows a lot about it. EG *...an expert on Eastern philosophy... ...the financial expert who writes in The Times... ...experts in obscure subjects... Experts say the company will fail.* N COUNT = specialist
2 Someone who is **expert** at doing something is very skilled at it. EG *Only expert acrobats can master these activities... They have to be expert at dealing with any problems that arise.* ADJ QUALIT = practised ◊ **expertly.** EG *Burke drove expertly and fast in and out of the traffic... They'd been expertly repaired.* ◊ ADV ⇑ skilfully
3 If you say that someone has **expert** hands or an **expert** eye, you mean that they are very skilful or experienced in using their hands or eyes for a particular purpose. EG *He rubbed his expert hands over the wound... ...not noticeable except to the expert eye... He ran an expert eye over the photographs.* ADJ CLASSIF: ATTRIB = trained
4 **Expert** advice, opinion, or help is advice, opinion, or help that is given by someone who has studied a subject thoroughly or is very skilled at a particular job. EG *We would like an expert opinion... Get expert treatment from a specialist... The appliance needs expert attention.* ADJ CLASSIF: ATTRIB ⇑ professional = specialist

expertise /ɛkspɜːtiːz/ is special skill or knowledge that is acquired by training, study, or practice; a formal word. EG *...his professional expertise... ...the technical expertise of the two Spanish firms.* N UNCOUNT: USU +SUPP = know-how

expiate /ɛkspɪeɪt/, **expiates, expiating, expiated**. If you **expiate** guilty feelings or bad behaviour, you do something to indicate that you are sorry for what you have done; a formal word. EG *He hoped to expiate his guilt over leaving her... Her frightful behaviour to Stephanie must be expiated.* V+O ⇑ redeem = atone for ◊ **expiation** /ɛkspɪeɪʃə⁰n/. EG *He sought expiation for what he had done.* ◊ N UNCOUNT = atonement

expiration /ɛkspɪreɪʃə⁰n/, **expirations**. **1** The **expiration** of a period of time is its ending; a formal use. EG *...expiration of the legal waiting period... ...after the expiration of seven academic years.* N UNCOUNT
2 **Expiration** is also the action of breathing air out of your lungs; a formal or medical use. N COUNT/UNCOUNT

expire /ɪ²kspaɪə/, **expires, expiring, expired**.
1 When something **expires**, it reaches the end of the period of time for which it is valid or during which it is allowed to exist. EG *My passport is due to expire in three months... The lease on the house had expired... The Government's term of office expired in 1979.* V ⇑ cease = run out
2 When someone **expires**, they die; a literary use. EG *The old lady expired within the hour.* V = pass away

expiry /ɪ²kspaɪəri¹/. The **expiry** of a period of time is its ending, especially in relation to legal documents, agreements, etc that stop being valid at the end of that time. EG *The French licences have no expiry date... ...the expiry of the period of study.* N UNCOUNT ⇑ end = expiration

explain /ɪ²ksplеɪn/, **explains, explaining, explained**. **1** If you **explain** something, you give details about it or describe it so that it can be understood. EG *John went on to explain the legal situation... He began explaining to her how a pawn ticket worked... Mrs Travers explained that the girl used to be a prostitute.* V OR V+O/QUOTE/REPORT-CL, V+A (to), OR V+O+A (to)
2 To **explain** also means to give people reasons for a particular event or situation that they do not understand or do not approve of. EG *If the battery was dead, that would explain why he couldn't call on the radio... Just a minute. Let me explain... He never wrote to me to explain his decision... When he calmed down, he explained himself.* V OR V+O (NG/REFL)
explain away. If you **explain away** a mistake or a situation that you are responsible for, you give reasons for it in order to say that it is not very important or that it is not really your fault. EG *He was seen on TV later, explaining away his department's latest blunder.* PHRASAL VB: V+O+ADV ⇑ dismiss

explanation /ɛksplәneɪʃə⁰n/, **explanations**. An **explanation** is **1** something that tells you why a particular event or situation happened. EG *There was no reasonable explanation for her decision... ...explanations of why the communication failed.* N COUNT ⇑ account **2** something that describes a situation in detail. EG *It is hard to give a simple explanation of Rose Gibbon's job... ...a scientific explanation of the universe.* N COUNT ⇑ description

explanatory /ɪ²ksplænətə⁰ri¹/ statements are intended to make people understand something by describing it or giving the reasons for it; a formal word. EG *They produce free explanatory leaflets on heating... Davis sent an explanatory letter.* ADJ CLASSIF ⇑ descriptive

expletive /ɪ²ksplіːtɪv/, **expletives**. An **expletive** is a rude word or expression such as 'Damn!' which you say loudly and suddenly when you are annoyed, excited, or in pain; a formal word. N COUNT ⇑ exclamation

explicable /ɛksplɪkəbə⁰l, ɪ²ksplɪk-/. Something that is **explicable** can be explained and understood because it is logical or sensible; a formal word. EG *His behaviour is explicable only in terms of his origins... For no explicable reason your mind goes blank.* ADJ QUALIT ⇑ understandable ≠ inexplicable

explicate /ɛksplɪkeɪt/, **explicates, explicating, explicated**. To **explicate** something means to explain it and make it clear; a formal word. EG *...informal activities that help the student define, explicate and test his values.* V+O = clarify

explicit /ɪ²ksplɪsɪt/. **1** An opinion or attitude that is **explicit** has been expressed clearly, so that there is no doubt about what is meant. EG *...the explicit support of the Prime Minister... Don't leave without explicit permission!... Facing failure means accepting explicit criticism from others.* ADJ QUALIT ⇑ clear ≠ unspoken ◊ **explicitly.** EG *...explicitly violent scenes.* ◊ ADV ◊ **explicitness.** ◊ N UNCOUNT
2 Someone who is **explicit** says something very clearly and exactly, so that nobody is in any doubt about what is meant. EG *She could, however, be more explicit with Peter... Let's be explicit... She was not explicit about what she really felt.* ADJ QUALIT ⇑ clear = frank ≠ vague ◊ **explicitly.** EG *This was explicitly admitted by the Premier.* ◊ ADV = openly

explode /ɪ²ksplәʊd/, **explodes, exploding, exploded**. **1** If an object such as a bomb **explodes** or if you **explode** it, it bursts loudly and with great force, often causing damage or injury. EG *A bomb had exploded in the next street... In 1974 India exploded a nuclear device... Clear the harbour before the ship explodes.* V-ERG
2 If something **explodes**, **2.1** it makes a sudden very loud noise; used in literary English. EG *The thunder exploded again... A branch exploded with a sharp crack.* V ⇑ bang **2.2** it appears suddenly and brightly; used in literary English. EG *Sunlight exploded, flooding everything... The hawthorn was exploding white and pink along the hedges.* V ⇑ appear = break out **2.3** it increases suddenly and rapidly in importance or seriousness. EG *The discontent will explode into prison riots before long... The issue has exploded because an MP is involved.* V ⇑ develop = erupt **2.4** it increases rapidly in number or amount. EG *The population was still exploding.* V ⇑ increase = multiply
3 If someone **explodes**, they express strong feelings suddenly and violently. EG *She picked up her newspaper and exploded with rage... The Judge exploded: 'Who are you?'... I expected Sheila to explode again into laughter.* V+A/QUOTE = erupt
4 If you say that someone or an animal **explodes** in some way, you mean that they move suddenly and energetically in the way mentioned; used in literary English. EG *The fighter suddenly explodes with a series of blows and kicks.* V+A = burst out
5 If someone **explodes** a theory, they prove that it is wrong or impossible. EG *I could explode some of the* V+O ⇑ disprove = destroy

myths about him... The book fails to explode the assumption that religious experience is abnormal.

exploit, exploits, exploiting, exploited. The word **exploit** is pronounced /ɪksplɔɪt/ when it is a verb, and /ɛksplɔɪt/ when it is a noun. 1 If someone **exploits** you, they treat you unfairly by using your work or your ideas and giving you very little money or anything else in return; used showing disapproval. EG *They would help to exploit and repress their own people... Adults exploit children far too often... Of course she's not exploiting me!* ◇ **exploitation** /ɛksplɔɪteɪʃəⁿn/. EG *...to protect the public from commercial exploitation... ...the exploitation of children in factories.* — V+O; ⇑ mistreat; = take advantage of; ◇ N UNCOUNT

2 If you **exploit** something such as a raw material, an idea, or someone's ability, you develop it in order to make money out of it. EG *Slate was exploited commercially... You can exploit a talent which you already possess... Everyone is seeking to exploit opportunities for improving efficiency.* ◇ **exploitation**. EG *...the comprehensive exploitation of the Earth's resources.* — V+O; ⇑ use; ◇ N UNCOUNT + of

3 Someone's **exploits** are the brave, interesting, or humorous actions that they have done at a particular time. EG *...his exploits in the War... ...the exploits of Alexander the Great... ...laughing at Midge's exploits.* — N COUNT : USU PL +SUPP; ⇑ deed

exploitable /ɪ²ksplɔɪtəbəⁿl/. 1 Something that is **exploitable** can be used as a basis for making money. EG *...commercially exploitable forest... ...the fear of missing exploitable talent.* — ADJ CLASSIF; ⇑ usable

2 People who are **exploitable** can be made to work for very low pay. EG *...a large and easily exploitable work force.* — ADJ QUALIT

exploitative /ɪ²ksplɔɪtətɪv/. If you describe a person, company, or other organization as **exploitative**, you mean that they treat people unfairly because they are interested only in making money; a formal word used showing disapproval. EG *Foreign capital was exploitative and a menace to national sovereignty... ...exploitative employment agencies.* — ADJ QUALIT

exploiter /ɪ²ksplɔɪtə/, **exploiters**. An **exploiter** is a person who uses people or things in order to make money, often in an uncaring way. EG *...the misuse of power by property-hungry exploiters... The first serious exploiters of Lebanon timber were the Phoenicians.* — N COUNT; ⇑ user

exploratory /ɪ²ksplɒrətəⁿri¹/; a fairly formal word. An **exploratory** action or investigation 1 is done in order to assess a situation or people's opinions before deciding on a course of action. EG *They will begin exploratory talks on a new grain agreement... ...forecasts and exploratory calculations.* 2 is done in order to find out what is in a particular place. EG *An early exploratory expedition had failed... ...exploratory digging in southern Iraq.* — ADJ CLASSIF = preliminary; ADJ CLASSIF = investigative

explore /ɪ²ksplɔː/, **explores, exploring, explored**. 1 If you **explore** a place, you travel there because you have not been there before, or because nobody else has been there before, in order to find out what it is like. EG *Between the wars, he explored three continents by canoe... Every part of the island has been explored.* ◇ **exploration** /ɛkspləreɪʃəⁿn/, **explorations**. EG *...voyages of exploration... ...underwater exploration... ...the exploration of space.* — V+O; ◇ N UNCOUNT/COUNT

2 If you **explore** something with a part of your body, you cause that part of your body to touch and move about over it to feel what it is like. EG *With widespread hands he explored the grass around him.* — V+O; = investigate

3 If you **explore** an idea, method, or suggestion, you think about it carefully and try it out or discuss it with other people in order to assess whether it is possible or a good idea. EG *The conference explored the possibility of closer trade links... Stop the tape and explore the implications of what you've heard... ...issues that the group had already explored.* ◇ **exploration**. EG *...a fundamental exploration of the main alternatives... ...ideas in need of further exploration.* — V+O; = examine, investigate; ◇ N UNCOUNT/COUNT = investigation

4 If people **explore** an area for something such as oil or minerals, they study the area and do tests on the land or dig holes in it because they hope to find oil, minerals, or something else of value there. ◇ **exploration**. EG *Mining companies have neglected exploration in developing countries... ...exploration for fossil fuels... ...exploration and exploitation of offshore oil.* — V OR V+O; ⇑ search; ◇ N UNCOUNT/COUNT

explorer /ɪ²ksplɔrə/, **explorers**. An **explorer** is someone who travels to places about which very little is known, in order to discover what is there. EG *...an Arctic explorer... ...explorers, climbers, and journalists.* — N COUNT; ⇑ traveller

explosion /ɪ²ksplәʊʒəⁿn/, **explosions**. An **explosion** is 1 a sudden, violent, loud burst of energy, for example one caused by a bomb. Explosions often result in damage or injury. EG *Twenty men were killed in the explosion... ...the areas hit by the nuclear explosion... ...an explosion in a chemical plant.* 2 an act of deliberately causing a bomb or similar device to explode. EG *...the explosion of nuclear devices in the atmosphere... ...over a thousand nuclear explosions had been conducted since 1945.* 3 a large and rapid increase in the number or amount of something. EG *The population explosion may yet have disastrous effects... ...the explosion of job opportunities... ...an explosion in demand for telephones.* 4 a sudden and violent expression of someone's feelings, especially anger. EG *The explosion is avoided when Chris turns and walks away... ...an explosion of rage.* 5 a sudden and serious outbreak of political protest or violence. EG *...the explosion of mass protest... The explosion was precipitated by the police raids.* 6 a sudden very loud noise. EG *He drove off, with a loud explosion from his exhaust... ...an explosion of loud laughter.* — N COUNT = blast; N COUNT = detonation; N COUNT+SUPP; N COUNT = outburst; N COUNT ⇑ upheaval = eruption; N COUNT = burst

explosive /ɪ²ksplәʊsɪv/, **explosives**. 1 An **explosive** is a substance or device which causes something such as a bomb to explode. EG *The heat set off some explosive... ...searching premises for explosives, gelignite, and firearms.* — N COUNT/UNCOUNT

2 Something that is **explosive** 2.1 is capable of exploding or is likely to explode under particular conditions. EG *...a very powerful explosive device.* 2.2 involves an explosion or results from it. EG *Modern bullets produce an explosive effect upon impact... ...measuring the explosive power.* ◇ **explosively**. EG *Sodium reacts explosively with water.* 2.3 happens suddenly and makes a loud noise. EG *...the explosive thunderclap of sound... The final applause was explosive.* 2.4 happens, develops, or increases in number very suddenly and rapidly. EG *...the explosive growth in world population... ...the explosive renaissance of the British Theatre.* — ADJ CLASSIF; ADJ CLASSIF ⇑ violent; ◇ ADV WITH VB; ADJ QUALIT = deafening; ADJ QUALIT ⇑ rapid

3 An **explosive** situation is likely to have difficult, serious, or dangerous effects. EG *Unemployment has become the most explosive political issue... ...dangerously explosive international repercussions.* ◇ **explosiveness**. — ADJ QUALIT ⇑ unstable = sensitive; ◇ N UNCOUNT

4 If you describe someone as **explosive**, you mean that they tend to express their anger suddenly and violently. EG *...an explosive temper.* ◇ **explosively**. EG *'A good kid!' he said explosively, and as though shocked by his own show of emotion.* — ADJ QUALIT = fierce; ◇ ADV WITH VB

exponent /ɪ²kspәʊnənt/, **exponents**; a formal word. 1 An **exponent** of an idea, theory, or plan is a person who supports and explains it, and who tries to persuade other people that it is a good idea. EG *Mr Heath is not the only exponent of this ideal... ...the leading exponents of apartheid.* — N COUNT+SUPP ⇑ supporter = advocate

2 An **exponent** of a particular skill or activity is a person who is good at it. EG *...the supreme exponent of the English humorous essay... ...the living exponents with whom an audience comes into contact.* — N COUNT+SUPP ⇑ expert

exponential /ɛkspə⁶nɛnʃəⁿl/ means growing or increasing very rapidly; a formal word. EG *Computer technology is embarking on a period of exponential growth.* ◇ **exponentially**. EG *Money spent by Education Authorities has risen exponentially.* — ADJ CLASSIF ⇑ rapid; ◇ ADV WITH VB

export, exports, exporting, exported. The word **export** is pronounced /ɛkspɔt/ when it is a noun, and /ɪ²kspɔt/ when it is a verb. 1 The **export** of a product or raw material is the sale and sending of it to another country. EG *...the export of agricultural produce... Germany banned all exports of uranium... They grow coffee, cotton and bananas for export... ...a thriving export trade.* — N UNCOUNT ≠ import

2 An **export** is a product or raw material which is sold and sent to another country. EG *Production of coal, a major export, is down sharply... ...one third of exports from industrial nations go to the developing countries.* — N COUNT ⇑ commodity ≠ import

3 To **export** products or raw materials means to sell them to another country. EG *Africa is exporting beef to Europe... Raw materials are exported at low* — V OR V+O ≠ import

prices... The firm exports 90 per cent of its production...

4 To **export** ideas or values means to introduce them into another country and encourage people there to accept them or adopt them. EG *The values of today's Europeans are now exported by them to all parts of the world.*
V+O ⇑ spread ≠ import

exportable /ɪ²kspɔtəbə⁰l/ means suitable to be exported. EG *...a greater share of the exportable surplus... ...exportable cultural achievements.*
ADJ CLASSIF ⇑ marketable

exporter /ɛkspɔtə/, **exporters**. An **exporter** is a country, firm, or person that sells and sends goods to another country. EG *Britain is now a net exporter of all three cereals... ...the company's position as a leading exporter.*
N COUNT ⇑ seller ≠ importer

expose /ɛkspəʊz/, **exposes, exposing, exposed**. **1** To **expose** something that is usually hidden means to uncover it and make it visible. EG *The mouth opens to expose a great number of sharp teeth... The rocks are exposed at low tide... His shirt was open, exposing the blue and red lines of the tattoo on his chest.*
V+O ≠ conceal

2 To **expose** a person or animal to something dangerous or unpleasant means to put them in a situation in which it might harm them. EG *They had been exposed to radiation... The creature stands out in the open, exposed to attack... Amphibians cannot expose themselves directly to the sun.*
V+O (NG/REFL) +A (to) ≠ shield, protect

3 If someone **is exposed** to an idea or feeling, they are given experience of it, or introduced to it, especially when it is new to them. EG *We were exposed to the latest theories on child care... We are all of us exposed to grief.*
V+O (NG/REFL) +A (to) : USU PASS

4 To **expose** a person or situation means to reveal the truth about them, especially when it involves dishonest or shocking behaviour that has been kept secret. EG *...the political scandals he could expose... He was eventually exposed in the perjury case.*
V+O = denounce

5 A man who **exposes** himself shows people his genitals in a public place, usually because he is mentally or emotionally disturbed.
V+O (REFL) ⇑ show = flash

exposé /ɛkspəʊzeɪ/, **exposés**. An **exposé** is a piece of writing which reveals the truth about a situation or person, especially when it involves dishonest or shocking behaviour that has been kept secret. EG *...a lucid exposé of the hypocrisy surrounding the payment... ...an exposé which triggered off a parliamentary debate.*
N COUNT ⇑ revelation = disclosure

exposed /ɪ²kspəʊzd/. If a place is **exposed**, it has no natural protection against bad weather or enemies, for example because it has no trees or is on very high ground. EG *The house is in a very exposed position... ...the most exposed of seaside promenades... When the animal has left the exposed feeding grounds it is safe from attack.*
ADJ QUALIT ⇑ open ≠ sheltered

exposition /ɛkspə⁶zɪʃə⁰n/, **expositions**; a formal word. An **exposition** is **1** a detailed explanation of an idea or a discussion of a problem. EG *The paper contained a clear exposition of the theory of evolution.* **2** an exhibition in which goods, works of art, etc are shown to the public. EG *...the Montreal Exposition of 1967.*
1: N COUNT ⇑ description = account
2: N COUNT

expostulate /ɪ²kspɒstjə⁴leɪt/, **expostulates, expostulating, expostulated**; a formal word. If you **expostulate**, you express strongly your disagreement with someone or your dissatisfaction with something that they have done. EG *He was expostulating with the porter... Sir William Bull expostulated against this policy of suppression... Morris expostulated, 'How many times have you said that!'* ◇ **expostulation** /ɪ²kspɒstjə⁴leɪʃə⁰n/, **expostulations**. EG *They planned to stay for another six weeks in spite of Thomas's furious expostulations.*
V OR V+QUOTE ⇑ object = remonstrate
◇ N UNCOUNT/COUNT ⇑ objection

exposure /ɪ²kspəʊʒə/, **exposures**. **1 Exposure** is **1.1** the state of being in a position or situation in which something affects you or influences you very strongly, usually in a harmful way. EG *He was suffering from exposure to nuclear radiation... Exposure to the air had bleached his hair... The body cannot cope with sudden exposure to stress... ...an age when youngsters are receiving maximum exposure to new ideas.* **1.2** the harmful effect on a person's body caused by very cold weather, sometimes resulting in their death. EG *The group's leader died of exposure on the mountain.*
1.1: N UNCOUNT : IF+PREP THEN *to* ≠ protection
1.2: N UNCOUNT ⇑ condition = hypothermia

2 Exposure is also **2.1** the revealing of the truth about a situation or person, especially when it involves dishonest or shocking behaviour that has been kept secret. EG *She concealed it from her parents, fearing that exposure would mean the banishment of Rosamund... ...the public exposure of a president who was threatened with impeachment.* **2.2** a lot of publicity that is given by television, newspapers, etc to a person or event. EG *...giving the widest possible exposure to scenes of casualties and damage... He had, in a few short days of intense exposure, become a folk hero.*
2.1: N UNCOUNT ⇑ revelation
2.2: N UNCOUNT = coverage

3 In photography, an **exposure** is **3.1** a single photograph, especially one on a length of film that is used to take several photographs. EG *...a camera capable of taking a hundred exposures before the film needs changing.* **3.2** the amount of light that is allowed to enter a camera when taking a photograph, which is controlled by the speed of the shutter and the size of the opening. EG *...pictures of aircraft at very slow exposures.*
3.1: N COUNT
3.2: N COUNT/UNCOUNT

expound /ɪ²kspaʊnd/, **expounds, expounding, expounded**. If you **expound** an idea or opinion, you give a clear and detailed explanation of it; a formal word. EG *He expounded his latest theory to his students.*
V+O ⇑ explain

express /ɪ²ksprɛs/, **expresses, expressing, expressed**. **1** If you **express** an idea or feeling, **1.1** you put it into words by speaking or writing. EG *He expressed his sorrow and regret to the King... We are anxious that students' views should be expressed... ...if I may express an opinion.* ◇ **expressed**. EG *He didn't have the courage to defy his father's expressed will.* **1.2** you show it in the look on your face or in your behaviour. EG *A child's feelings are often expressed by crying... Her eyes expressed annoyance... They hooted their car horns to express their disapproval.*
1.1: V+O ⇑ utter = voice
◇ ADJ CLASSIF : ATTRIB
1.2: V+O = convey

2 When you **express** yourself, **2.1** you put ideas into words, especially openly or clearly, by speaking or writing them. EG *He could express himself more freely outside the office... ...junior clerks incapable of expressing themselves in decent English... I expressed myself better in French.* **2.2** you show your thoughts or feelings by your actions or by artistic activities. EG *She expresses herself through art... ...the way Italians express themselves in music... The children had a big open space in which to express themselves.*
2.1: V+O (REFL) : USU+A ⇑ explain
2.2: V+O (REFL) : USU+A ⇑ reveal

3 If an idea or feeling **expresses** itself in some way, it can be clearly seen in someone's actions or in its effects on a situation. EG *The logic expressed itself in the Government's decision... That increased confidence expressed itself in other ways.*
V+O (REFL) : USU+A ⇑ show = manifest

4 If you **express** a quantity or mathematical problem in symbols or equations, you write it using these symbols or equations; a technical use. EG *Express T in terms of these variables... Express it in the form A plus J equals B... Here it is expressed as a percentage.*
V+O : USU+A ⇑ describe = represent

5 An **express** command or order is one that is clearly and deliberately stated, usually in writing; a formal use. EG *This may not be published save by the express direction of the School... The action was taken on his express order.* ◇ **expressly**. EG *Jefferson had expressly asked her to invite Freeman... The Charter expressly forbids the building of any chapel.*
ADJ CLASSIF : ATTRIB = explicit ≠ implicit
◇ ADV WITH VB = explicitly, specifically

6 An **express** intention or purpose is a deliberate and specific one that you have before you do something. EG *She came with the express purpose of causing trouble.* ◇ **expressly**. EG *They bought the house expressly for her... He does not cry expressly to annoy you!*
ADJ CLASSIF : ATTRIB
◇ ADV WITH VB

7 Express is used in British English to describe special services which are provided by companies or organizations such as the Post Office, in which things are sent or done faster than usual for a higher price. EG *...an express letter... Send it by express delivery... We also have an express laundry service.* ▸ used as an adverb. EG *This letter is very important. Please send it express.*
ADJ CLASSIF : ATTRIB ⇑ fast
▸ ADV WITH VB ⇑ quickly

8 An **express** or **express train** is a fast train which stops at very few stations. EG *...the Orient Express... The express for Paris was waiting to go.*
N COUNT : ALSO IN NAMES AFTER N

9 An **express** is also a fast bus or coach which goes from one place to another directly or with very few stops.
N COUNT

expression /ɪ²ksprɛʃə⁰n/, **expressions**. **1** In this dictionary, the word **expression** is used to refer to any groups of two or more words, for example phrases or sentences, that are being considered as one unit.

2 An **expression** is **2.1** a word or phrase that is usually used in a particular situation or by particular people, and that you are quoting, explaining, or commenting on. EG *She's always using slang expressions... I think they're full of-if you'll pardon the expression-bull... The expression is 'fly in the ointment'.* **2.2** a symbol or equation which represents a quantity or problem; a technical use in mathematics. EG *This gives us an expression for the mean value.* — N COUNT ⇑ phrase; N COUNT

3 The **expression** of ideas or feelings is **3.1** the act of putting them into words by speaking or writing. EG *We parted with many expressions of goodwill... His speech provoked expressions of support from MPs of all parties... ...the freedom of expression of the press.* **3.2** the act of showing them through your actions or through artistic activities. EG *Giving and sharing are spontaneous expressions of joy... His carvings that have become one of the finest expressions of African art... The act was a legitimate expression of his duty as a police officer.* **3.3** the way in which they show themselves in things that happen. EG *All political parties are but the expression of class interest... These sentiments found expression in the formation of the London Industrial Development Board.* — N COUNT/UNCOUNT : IF+PREP THEN *of* ⇑ utterance; N COUNT : IF+PREP THEN *of* = manifestation; N UNCOUNT : USU +SUPP = manifestation

4 Your **expression** is the way that your face looks at a particular moment. It shows what you are thinking or feeling. EG *When I saw the expression on his face, I realised how angry he was... His facial expressions made us laugh... I couldn't see Helen's expression, because her head was turned.* ▸ used as an uncount noun. EG *Anthony's face showed not a flicker of expression.* — N COUNT+SUPP ⇑ look; ▸ N UNCOUNT = emotion

5 **Expression** is the ability to show feeling when you are acting, singing, or playing a musical instrument. EG *Their playing of Beethoven was full of expression.* — N UNCOUNT

expressionism /ɪ²kspre̲ʃə⁰nɪzə⁰m/ is a style of art, literature, and music, which uses symbolism and exaggeration in order to represent emotions as opposed to physical reality; a technical term. ◊ **expressionist, expressionists.** — N UNCOUNT; ◊ N COUNT

expressionless /ɪ²kspre̲ʃə⁰nlɪ²s/. If someone's face or voice is **expressionless**, it shows no emotional feelings; often used showing disapproval. EG *His face was completely expressionless... She gave me an oddly expressionless look... ...expressionless brown eyes... ...an expressionless voice.* ▸ used of artistic performances. EG *He played the viola in an accurate, expressionless way.* — ADJ QUALIT = blank ≠ expressive

expressive /ɪ²kspre̲sɪv/. 1 Something that is **expressive** indicates clearly a person's feelings or intentions. EG *She had given Lynn an expressive glance... ...one crude expressive syllable... He had an expressive face.* ◊ **expressively**. EG *He drew a finger expressively across his throat.* ◊ **expressiveness**. EG *...a glare that gave her face a startling expressiveness.* — ADJ QUALIT ⇑ revealing; ◊ ADV WITH VB; ◊ N UNCOUNT

2 Someone's **expressive** ability is their ability to speak or write clearly and interestingly. EG *It is not easy to evaluate a child's expressive powers in an exam.* — ADJ CLASSIF ⇑ communicative

3 If something is **expressive** of particular ideas or qualities, it has features which indicate or demonstrate them; a formal use. EG *The election result seemed expressive of their organizational superiority.* — ADJ QUALIT : PRED+*of* ⇑ indicative

expressway /ɪ²kspre̲sweɪ/, **expressways**. An **expressway** is a wide road that is specially designed so that a lot of traffic can move along it very quickly; used mainly in American English. EG *...a four-lane expressway... ...the Long Island Expressway.* — N COUNT : ALSO IN NAMES AFTER N

expropriate /ɛkspr**əʊ**prɪeɪt/, **expropriates, expropriating, expropriated**; a formal word. 1 If a government or other authority **expropriates** money or other property, they take it away from its owners for public use. EG *The surplus will be expropriated by the government.* ◊ **expropriation** /ɪ²kspr**əʊ**prɪ**eɪ**ʃə⁰n/. EG *...the expropriation of land.* — V+O = seize; ◊ N UNCOUNT

2 If someone **expropriates** money or other property, they take it away from its owners illegally for their own use. EG *The funds had been expropriated by Darcy.* ◊ **expropriation.** — V+O = steal; ◊ N UNCOUNT

expulsion /ɪ²kspʌ̲lʃə⁰n/, **expulsions**; a formal word. **Expulsion** is 1 the expelling of someone from a school, university, or organization. EG *...his expulsion from the university... He risked lifetime expulsion from international athletics for larceny.* **2** the expelling of someone from a place, often by force. EG *...the temporary expulsion of military advisers.* **3** the expelling of something from a container or from your body. EG *Her lips quivered with each expulsion of breath.* — N UNCOUNT/COUNT; N UNCOUNT/COUNT; N UNCOUNT/COUNT+SUPP = discharge

expunge /ɪ²kspʌ̲ndʒ/, **expunges, expunging, expunged**. To **expunge** something means to remove it completely, for example from a piece of writing or from your memory, because it causes problems or bad feelings; a formal word. EG *...his battle to expunge the clause from the contract... He had tried to expunge memories of the failure.* — V+O = erase

expurgate /ɛ̲kspəgeɪt/, **expurgates, expurgating, expurgated**. To **expurgate** a piece of writing means to remove parts of it before it is published in order to avoid offending or shocking people; a formal word. ◊ **expurgated**. EG *Even Shakespeare was dangerous, except in the expurgated version.* — V+O = bowdlerize; ◊ ADJ CLASSIF

exquisite /ɪ²kskwɪ̲zɪt, ɛ̲kskwɪzɪt/. Something that is **exquisite** 1 is extremely beautiful in appearance. EG *She has the most exquisite face... The city has two small but exquisite harbours.* ◊ **exquisitely**. EG *Their children were exquisitely dressed.* **2** demonstrates a high degree of artistic skill or style. EG *...the exquisite jewellery of the Aztecs... ...exquisite craftsmanship... This next letter is translated from her exquisite French.* ◊ **exquisitely**. EG *...exquisitely carved statuettes.* **3** is extremely pleasant and polite. EG *...a man with exquisite manners... ...the exquisite courtesy of simple folks... ...his usual exquisite tact.* ◊ **exquisitely**. EG *...his exquisitely polite voice.* **4** is greater in effect because it happens at the right time or in a suitable way; a literary use. EG *With exquisite condescension he stated, 'I have passed your message on.'... ...the exquisite irony of the situation.* ◊ **exquisitely**. EG *...an exquisitely comical effect... He left a pause, exquisitely timed to show he was joking.* **5** is felt very strongly and is greatly appreciated. EG *...the exquisite pleasure of being free... ...sipping the water slowly with exquisite relief.* ◊ **exquisitely**. EG *His tongue was exquisitely sensitive.* — ADJ QUALIT = delightful; ◊ ADV; ADJ QUALIT = beautiful; ◊ ADV; ADJ QUALIT = perfect; ADJ QUALIT ⇑ appropriate; ◊ ADV; ADJ QUALIT ⇑ intense; ◊ ADV

ex-serviceman, ex-servicemen. An **ex-serviceman** is a man who used to be in a country's army, navy, or air force; used in British English. — N COUNT ⇑ person

ext. is written on business letters to indicate someone's telephone extension number in an office. EG *Ring the Information Bureau (928-5000 ext. 7430)... She can be contacted on Ext. 2307.* — N SING+NUM

extant /ɛkstæ̲nt, ɛ̲kstənt/. Something that is **extant** still exists in spite of being very old; a formal word. EG *...one Spanish law that is still extant in California... ...according to an extant document... ...the old but now no longer extant structure.* — ADJ CLASSIF ⇑ existing

extemporize /ɪ²kstɛmpərɑɪz/, **extemporizes, extemporizing, extemporized**; also spelled **extemporise**. If you **extemporize**, you speak, act, or perform something immediately, without any rehearsing or preparation; a formal word. EG *Certain performers are funnier when they extemporize.* — V OR V+O = ad lib

extend /ɪ²kste̲nd/, **extends, extending, extended**. 1 If something **extends** for a particular distance, it continues to exist for that distance from a point or central area. EG *The road now extends two kilometres beyond the River... ...empires which extended over large areas... A red carpet extended all the way to the sidewalk.* — V+A = reach, stretch

2 If something **extends** from a surface or from the main part of something, it sticks out from it. EG *...chalk boulders extending from the cliffs.* — V+A = protrude

3 If something **extends** for a period of time, it continues for that time. EG *His working day often extends well into the evening... ...the end of a saga extending over thirty years.* — V+A = last

4 If something **extends** to other people, ideas, or activities, it includes or affects them. EG *The consequences of unemployment extend well beyond the labour market... His radicalism did not extend to the sphere of economics... This tendency extends even into old age.* — V+A ≠ be restricted

5 If you **extend** something, **5.1** you make it bigger or longer than it was before. EG *Have you ever thought of extending your house?... They aren't sure whether or not to extend the runway.* **5.2** you cause it to exist or be valid for a longer period of time. EG *The* — V+O ⇑ enlarge; V+O ⇑ prolong

authorities extended her visa... It was repaired from time to time to extend its life... ...extending loan repayment times. ◊ **extended.** EG *Albery gave me an extended contract... ...extended news bulletins on TV... ...going home on extended leave.*
◊ ADJ CLASSIF : ATTRIB

5.3 you cause it to include or affect more people, ideas, or activities than it did before. EG *It is designed to extend people's knowledge of modern methods... Import controls were extended to the paper industry... Congress wants the law extended to cover all states.*
V+O ⇑ increase

5.4 you spread it out or unfold it. EG *The cloth can be extended into a hood.*
V+O+A ⇑ stretch

6 If you **extend** a part of your body, you straighten it or stretch it out. EG *He sat in the boat with his arms extended along its sides.*
V+O

7 If you **extend** something to someone, **7.1** you hold it out for them to take; a formal use. EG *I extended the document to the judge... He extended his hand, and Brody shook it.*
V+O : IF+PREP THEN *to/towards* = proffer

7.2 you offer it to them in a polite or friendly way. EG *The invitation she had extended was promptly accepted... Industrialists will extend a warm welcome to him.*
V+O : IF+PREP THEN *to* = give

7.3 you give it to them or make it available to them in order to help them. EG *Aid in the form of food and housing was extended to those in need... ...the tradition of extending asylum to refugees... The banks agreed to extend credit for the purchase of new equipment.*
V+O : IF+PREP THEN *to* = grant

8 If something **extends** you or if you **extend** yourself, you have to use all your ability or strength. EG *Simon was never really extended at school... Athletes were more interested in extending themselves to the limits of their abilities.*
V+O (NG/REFL) = stretch

extendable /ɪ^{2}kste̱ndəbə^{0}l/. Something that is **extendable 1** can be made longer in length. EG *Some species have small extendable tentacles... ...an extendable ladder.*
ADJ CLASSIF

2 can be made to exist or be valid for a longer period of time. EG *The tenancy of the Lodge was only extendable on a weekly basis.*
ADJ CLASSIF

extension /ɪ^{2}kste̱nʃə^{0}n/, **extensions. 1** An **extension** is **1.1** a new room or building which is added to an existing building or group of buildings. EG *...a new extension to the library... Some house extensions need planning permission.*
N COUNT ⇑ wing

1.2 an extra period of time for which something continues to exist or be valid, usually as a result of official permission. EG *I had applied for an extension to our visas... He asked for extension of his residence permit.*
N COUNT/UNCOUNT

1.3 a development that includes or affects more people, ideas, or activities. EG *...the extension of bombing to the British mainland... Nationalist leaders demanded the extension of democratic rights... The role of women within the family and, by extension, within the community, has changed.*
N COUNT/UNCOUNT

1.4 a part which is connected to a piece of equipment in order to make it reach something further away. EG *Unroll the extension lead and put the vacuum plug into the socket... ...an extension ladder.*
N COUNT, OR N BEFORE N

1.5 one of two or more telephones in a building, all of which have the same number. EG *I'm thinking of getting an extension in the bedroom.*
N COUNT ⇑ telephone

1.6 a telephone that is connected to the switchboard of a company or institution, and that has a special number. EG *Call me at the university, extension 2251... Make sure the switchboard have your correct extension.*
N COUNT, OR N+NUM

2 In Britain, **extension** colleges and courses arrange teaching and examinations for people who cannot attend full-time courses. EG *...the National Extension College... ...the University Extension Service.*
ADJ CLASSIF : ATTRIB, ALSO USED IN NAMES ⇑ part-time

extensive /ɪ^{2}kste̱nsɪv/. Something that is **extensive 1** covers a large physical area. EG *...an extensive Roman settlement in north-west England... If the rash is extensive, call the doctor.*
ADJ QUALIT

2 is very great in effect. EG *Many buildings suffered extensive damage in the blast... The device had undergone extensive testing.* ◊ **extensively.** EG *The aircraft were extensively modified.*
ADJ QUALIT = severe; ◊ ADV WITH VB

3 contains many details, ideas, or items on a particular subject. EG *...a very extensive reading list... We had fairly extensive discussions... ...extensive television coverage... ...an extensive knowledge of aeronautics.* ◊ **extensively.** EG *I have quoted extensively from it.*
ADJ QUALIT ⇑ detailed = comprehensive; ◊ ADV WITH VB

extent /ɪ^{2}kste̱nt/. **1** The **extent** of something is its length, area, or size. EG *...the extent of the solar system... The door opened to the extent of its short tight chain... ...to expand the empire to its largest extent.*
N SING : WITH POSS ⇑ dimension

2 The **extent** of a situation or difficulty is its size or scale. EG *We reported the extent of local damage and casualties... The full extent of the problem is not yet known... They will benefit from it to the same extent as the Japanese.*
N SING : WITH the/POSS ⇑ amount

3 You use expressions such as **to a large extent, to some extent,** or **to a certain extent** in order to indicate that something is partly true, but not entirely true. EG *The community is, to a very large extent, a closed one... To some extent his warnings have proved absolutely correct... Well I think to a certain extent it's true.*
PHR : USED AS ADV SEN ≠ entirely

4 You use expressions such as **to what extent, to that extent,** or **to the extent that** when you are discussing how true a statement is. EG *To what extent are diseases linked with genes?... The aim of the policy was to deal with inflation, and to that extent it had considerable success... A computer is intelligent only to the extent that it can store information.*
PHR

5 You use expressions such as **to the extent of, to the extent that,** or **to such an extent that** in order to indicate that a situation has reached an interesting or difficult stage, and that someone has done or is likely to do something surprising or dangerous. EG *They are prepared to fight for their rights, even to the extent of going on strike... The party lost all appeal and purpose to the extent that by 1949 it chose to disband itself... Sanitary conditions had deteriorated to such an extent that there was widespread danger of disease.*
PHR

extenuate /ɪ^{2}kste̱nju^{4}eɪt/, **extenuates, extenuating, extenuated.** If something **extenuates** a wrong action, it causes it to be judged less seriously by giving reasons that partly excuse it; a formal word. ◊ **extenuating.** EG *It was essential to have a complete dossier, with every extenuating circumstance, before issuing a verdict.* ◊ **extenuation** /ɪ^{2}kste̱nju^{4}e̱ɪʃə^{0}n/. EG *Without that extenuation, he would have been jailed.*
V+O ⇑ reduce = mitigate; ◊ ADJ CLASSIF : ATTRIB; ◊ N UNCOUNT

exterior /ɪ^{2}kstɪ̱ərɪə/, **exteriors. 1** The **exterior** of something is its outside surface. EG *The rooms in the town hall were as grand as the exterior... Keep your car exterior in good condition... ...the exterior of a space capsule.*
N COUNT

2 Your **exterior** is your usual appearance or behaviour, especially when it is very different from your character. EG *Beneath his professional doctor's exterior, he was wildly fun-loving and reckless... Dirk's surly exterior concealed a warm and generous nature.*
N COUNT+SUPP ≠ inner self

3 You use **exterior** to refer to something that is situated or happening outside something or someone. EG *Exterior drains must be kept clear... ...the exterior approaches to the prison... ...the objects of the exterior world.*
ADJ CLASSIF : ATTRIB = external

exterminate /ɪ^{2}kstɜ̱:mɪneɪt/, **exterminates, exterminating, exterminated.** If a group of animals or people **is exterminated**, all of the animals or people are killed. EG *Fishing must stop before the species is exterminated... Their job is to exterminate rats and mice... The inhabitants were tortured to death or exterminated by starvation.* ◊ **extermination** /ɪ^{2}kstɜ̱:mɪne̱ɪʃə^{0}n/. EG *We have to think of a way to prevent the extermination of these beautiful creatures.*
V+O ⇑ kill = wipe out; ◊ N UNCOUNT ⇑ destruction

exterminator /ɪ^{2}kstɜ̱:mɪneɪtə/, **exterminators.** An **exterminator** is a person whose job is to kill animals such as rats or mice, because they are a nuisance or a danger. EG *...a rodent exterminator.*
N COUNT : USU MOD+N

external /ɪ^{2}kstɜ̱:nə^{0}l/, **externals. 1 External** means **1.1** happening, coming from, or existing outside a particular place, person, or area of activity. EG *...the external walls of the chimneys... ...customs which they see as alien and external to their village world... They did it in response to external pressures.* ◊ **externally.** EG *Internally and externally, the colonial world is conditioned by its situation in a world system.*
ADJ CLASSIF : USU ATTRIB, IF+PREP THEN *to* = outer; ◊ ADV WITH VB = outwardly

1.2 involving or intended for foreign countries. EG *...the nation's £27 billion external debt... ...the French External Relations Minister... ...the BBC external service.*
ADJ CLASSIF : ATTRIB, ALSO IN NAMES ⇑ outside

1.3 happening or existing in the world in general and affecting you in some way. EG *New social arrangements in the external world erupt into our lives... ...external reality... ...something beyond our genes and external events.*
ADJ CLASSIF : ATTRIB ⇑ outside

2 External examiners, accountants, etc come into an organization from outside in order to do a job there that must be done fairly and impartially. EG *External*
ADJ CLASSIF : ATTRIB

examiners have been quick to notice this trend... Their accounts are audited by a firm of external auditors.

3 An **external** part of an animal's body is on the outside of its body, or is attached to the outside. EG *The tadpoles have feathery external gills... The external skeleton is highly versatile.* ● A medicine that is **for external use** is intended to be used only on the outside of your body, and not to be eaten or drunk. EG *For external use only.* — ADJ CLASSIF : ATTRIB ↑ outer; ● PHR : USED AS AN A ↑ outer

4 When you talk about **externals** or **the externals**, you are referring to the features of a situation that are obvious but unimportant; a formal use. EG *The popular historian is concerned only with externals... Your generation knows all about the externals... Misled by externals, he had failed to see the truth.* — N PLURAL : ALSO *the*+N ↑ superficial

externalize /ɪ²kstɜːnəlaɪz/, **externalizes, externalizing, externalized**; also spelled **externalise**. If you **externalize** your ideas or feelings, you express them in words or actions; a formal word. EG *Their discontent was externalised in political action... He tried to externalize his thoughts in pencilled images... Her cold anger was not externalized in any gesture or change in voice.* — V+O

extinct /ɪ²kstɪŋkt/. 1 An **extinct** species of animal or plant no longer has any living members. EG *The wolf is now nearly extinct... The species will be made extinct by the end of this century.* ▸ used of groups of people. EG *...tribes that had become extinct.* — ADJ CLASSIF : USU PRED ↑ dead = wiped out

2 If a particular kind of worker, way of life, or type of activity is **extinct**, it no longer exists because of changes in society. EG *We can expect the farm worker to become extinct in the near future.* 3 An **extinct** volcano does not erupt or is unlikely to erupt. — ADJ CLASSIF : USU PRED; ADJ CLASSIF ≠ active

extinction /ɪ²kstɪŋk⁰ʃə⁰n/ is 1 The **extinction** of a species of animal or plant is the death or destruction of all its remaining members, so that the species no longer exists. EG *...the extinction of some plant and animal species... Bears and wolves were hunted to extinction... Apes are in danger of extinction... ...plants threatened with extinction.* — N UNCOUNT

2 When the **extinction** of a particular way of life or type of activity occurs, people no longer have that way of life or take part in that activity. EG *...an attractive way of life now threatened with extinction... ...the extinction of private ownership.* — N UNCOUNT ↑ ending = abolition

extinguish /ɪ²kstɪŋgwɪʃ/, **extinguishes, extinguishing, extinguished**; a formal word. 1 If you **extinguish** a fire or a light, you stop it burning or shining. EG *...a new method of extinguishing forest fires... Someone had extinguished the lights in the kitchen... An air hostess made him extinguish his cigar.* — V+O = put out

2 If someone or something **extinguishes** an idea or feeling, they destroy it so that it no longer exists. EG *We have to extinguish the memory of the defeat... Her spark of hope was extinguished... The first sight of Betty extinguished every thought of the music.* — V+O ↑ eliminate = banish

extinguisher /ɪ²kstɪŋgwɪʃə/, **extinguishers**. See **fire extinguisher**.

extn. is written on business letters to indicate someone's telephone extension number in an office. EG *He may be contacted on Extn 2241.* — N SING+NUM

extol /ɪ²kstəʊl/, **extols, extolling, extolled**. If you **extol** an idea, quality, or person, you praise them enthusiastically, often in order to make other people like or approve of them; a formal word. EG *She continued to extol the virtues of equality... Luce continued to extol MacArthur and his policy... Ancient customs were extolled as a better guide to living... Mrs Datchet had been extolling the splendours of the lake.* — V+O, OR V+O+A *(as)* = laud

extort /ɪ²kstɔːt/, **extorts, extorting, extorted**. 1 If someone **extorts** money from you, they get it from you using force, threats, or other unfair or illegal means. EG *They extorted every penny from us... Moneylenders offer help, but extort a heavy price.* — V+O : IF+PREP THEN *from* ↑ extract = squeeze

2 To **extort** also means to get something from another person with difficulty; a literary use. EG *It was the first surprised look I managed to extort from that old knowing face... It is no good trying to extort promises.* — V+O : IF+PREP THEN *from* ↑ extract

extortion /ɪ²kstɔːʃə⁰n/. 1 **Extortion** is the crime of obtaining something from someone, especially money, by using force or threats. EG *...a criminal specializing in extortion and armed robbery... He faces trial on extortion charges.* — N UNCOUNT

2 You also describe someone's behaviour as **extortion** if you think they are trying to obtain more money for something than it is worth; used showing disapproval. EG *'It's extortion,' she said. 'He's not worth this much.'* — N UNCOUNT = robbery

extortionate /ɪ²kstɔːʃə⁰nət/. You describe something as **extortionate** when it is bigger or more costly than you consider to be fair; used showing disapproval. EG *...a worker making extortionate demands upon the employer... ...extortionate profits... ...bars where the music is loud and the drinks extortionate.* — ADJ QUALIT ↑ high = excessive

extra /ɛkstrə/, **extras**. 1 You use **extra** 1.1 to describe a thing, person, or amount that is added to others of the same kind. EG *If you're cold put an extra pullover on... Take an extra pair of shoes and a sweater... Extra land is being brought under cultivation... A hundred extra postmen are being taken on.* — QUANTIF ↑ further = additional

1.2 to describe an amount of money that is more than the normal or expected amount. EG *Ask if there will be any extra costs... ...an extra £2.80 a week... Send 25p extra for postage and packing... You have to pay extra for breakfast.* — QUANTIF, OR ADV AFTER VB = additional

2 An **extra** is 2.1 something that is not necessary in a situation, activity, or object, but that makes it more comfortable, useful, or enjoyable. EG *The only extras she used were cheese and mixed herbs... With the extras, the car cost £4,000... They miss the extras which most other children take for granted.* 2.2 an additional amount of money that is added to the price that you have to pay for something. EG *There are no extras to pay... Service charges may be shown as extras.* 2.3 a person who plays an unimportant part in a film, for example as a member of a crowd. EG *...laughing like extras in a bad film... Even the extras were dressed like kings and queens.* — N COUNT ↑ addition = luxury; N COUNT ↑ charge; N COUNT ↑ actor

3 You can also use **extra** to say that something such as a person's behaviour has more of a particular quality than usual. EG *He was extra polite to his superiors... She took extra trouble this time.* — ADV+ADJ/ADV ↑ very = especially

extra- is sometimes added 1 to adjectives in order to form other adjectives, especially when someone such as an advertiser wants to say that a product has more of a particular quality than usual; an informal use. EG *...large→extra-large... ...long→extra-long... ...special→extra-special.* 2 to adjectives in order to form other adjectives that describe something as not being part of something else; a formal use. EG *...parliamentary→extra-parliamentary... ...territorial→extra-territorial.* — PREFIX ↑ very; PREFIX ↑ outside

extract, extracts, extracting, extracted. The word **extract** is pronounced /ɪ²kstrækt/ when it is a verb and /ɛkstrækt/ when it is a noun. 1 When a person or an animal **extracts** something from a particular place, they pull it out using force or skill. EG *He tried to extract his pole from the mud... They have sharp claws for extracting grubs from holes... The new corks still have to be extracted with a corkscrew... That tooth should be extracted at once.* — V+O : IF+PREP THEN *from* ↑ withdraw = pull out

2 If you **extract** something, you take it carefully and deliberately out of a container; a literary use. EG *Mrs. Oliver extracted a small notebook from her bag... He reached into his pocket and extracted a bundle of notes... He took out an envelope, extracted a document and handed it to me.* — V+O : IF+PREP THEN *from* ↑ withdraw = take out

3 To **extract** a raw material means to get it from the ground or from another substance by using machines or industrial processes. EG *The Japanese extract ten million tons of coal each year... ...the cost of extracting the silicon.* ◇ **extraction**. EG *...industries involved in mineral extraction.* — V+O = produce; ◇ N UNCOUNT

4 If you **extract** information or a particular response from someone, you get it from them with difficulty, because they are unwilling to say or do what you want. EG *Sir James had extracted from Francis a fairly detailed account... ...apologies extracted under threat of legal action.* — V+O : IF+PREP THEN *from* = elicit

5 If someone **extracts** an advantage from a situation, they use the situation in order to gain the advantage, often in an unfair or dishonest way. EG *They will extract the maximum propaganda value from this affair.* ◇ **extraction**. EG *...the extraction of profit from their labour.* — V+O+A *(from)* ↑ obtain; ◇ N UNCOUNT = extortion

6 If you **extract** facts or ideas from a large amount of information, you study the information carefully and — V+O : IF+PREP THEN *from*

choose the facts that are important for your purpose. EG ...*the habit of trying to extract causes and effects... I extract moral values from what I read.*

7 An **extract** is 7.1 a part of a piece of writing, speech, or music that is printed, spoken, or played separately, for example in order to demonstrate something or to give an example of someone's style. EG ...*extracts from 'The Sunday Times'... I would like to quote two extracts from the book... ...extracts from that tape... I think these extracts show that the proposals are ill-conceived.* 7.2 a substance that has been obtained using a scientific process. EG ...*obtaining from that extract a crude mixture of compounds... ...the extracts of certain plants and barks.* — N COUNT : IF + PREP THEN *from* ⇑ passage = excerpt; N COUNT ⇑ product

extraction /ɪ²kstræ̲kʃə⁰n/, **extractions.** 1 At the dentist's, if you have an **extraction**, the dentist pulls out one of your teeth. EG *Few patients need an extraction.* — N COUNT/UNCOUNT ⇑ removal

2 Your **extraction** is the country or people that your family originally comes from; a formal use. EG *Alistair was of Scottish extraction... His father was Irish by extraction.* — N UNCOUNT ⇑ descent

3 Other meanings of **extraction** can be found in the entry for **extract**.

extractor /ɪ²kstræ̲ktə/, **extractors.** 1 An **extractor** is 1.1 a person or machine involved in obtaining raw materials. EG ...*timber extractors.* 1.2 a device that squeezes liquid out of something. EG ...*a juice extractor.* — N COUNT; N COUNT

2 An **extractor** or **extractor fan** is a device that is fixed to a window or wall to draw smells, steam, or hot air out of a room or building. — N COUNT

extra-curricular /ɛ̲kstrə kərɪ̲kjə⁴lə/; also spelled as one word. **Extra-curricular** activities are student activities that are not part of the course that they are doing, for example sports or hobbies. EG ...*informal, extra-curricular discussions about politics... We offer a wide range of extracurricular activities.* — ADJ CLASSIF

extradite /ɛ̲kstrədaɪt/, **extradites, extraditing, extradited.** To **extradite** someone means to officially send them back to their own country so that they can be tried in a court of law for a crime that they have been accused of; a formal word. EG *They have refused to extradite the terrorists... The Americans want to extradite him.* — V+O = send back

◊ **extradition** /ɛ̲kstrədɪ̲ʃə⁰n/, **extraditions.** EG *France requested their extradition from the United States... ...extradition proceedings.* — ◊ N UNCOUNT/COUNT

extramarital /ɛ̲kstrəmæ̲rɪtə⁰l/. You use **extramarital** to refer to close relationships between a married person and another person who is not their husband or wife; a formal word. EG ...*an extramarital affair.* — ADJ CLASSIF : USU ATTRIB

extra-mural. You use **extra-mural** to refer to 1 people, departments, or courses in a college or university, which are involved mainly with part-time students. EG ...*the Department of Extra-mural Studies... ...extra-mural lecturers.* 2 activities done by someone from an organization that are not part of their official duties. EG *He co-ordinates most of the extra-mural activities.* — ADJ CLASSIF : USU ATTRIB; ADJ CLASSIF : USU ATTRIB = outside

extraneous /ɪ²kstre̲ɪnɪəs/. Something that is **extraneous** exists, happens, or concerns things outside the situation or subject that you are talking about; a formal word. EG *We need to be absolutely clear about all this and avoid all extraneous issues.* — ADJ CLASSIF : IF + PREP THEN *to* = irrelevant

extraordinary /ɪ²kstrɔ̲ːdə⁰nə⁰ri¹/. 1 Someone or something that is **extraordinary** 1.1 has some special or extreme quality. EG *My grandfather was a most extraordinary man.* ◊ **extraordinarily.** EG ...*an extraordinarily beautiful girl... ...the extraordinarily successful copying machine.* 1.2 is unusual or surprising in a particular situation. EG *What an extraordinary thing to say... It was the most extraordinary behaviour for a policeman.* ◊ **extraordinarily.** EG *The bomb caused extraordinarily high levels of radiation.* — ADJ QUALIT = exceptional; ◊ ADV+ADJ/ADV; ADJ QUALIT ⇑ different = remarkable; ◊ ADV+ADJ/ADV = remarkably

2 An **extraordinary** meeting is arranged specially to deal with a particular situation or problem, rather than happening regularly; a formal use. EG *An Extraordinary General Meeting of the Union will debate the proposal... ...this month's extraordinary party congress.* — ADJ CLASSIF ⇑ special

extrapolate /ɪ²kstræ̲pə⁶leɪt/, **extrapolates, extrapolating, extrapolated.** If you **extrapolate**, you examine known facts and use logic or reason in order to calculate a quantity or make statements about what is likely to happen in the future; a formal word. EG *To assess future needs, the Department simply extrapolated past demand trends... ...the inadequacy of extrapolating from the experience of English-speaking students.* — V OR V+O : IF + PREP THEN *from*

extrapolation /ɪ²kstræ̲pə⁶le̲ɪʃə⁰n/, **extrapolations;** a formal word. 1 **Extrapolation** is the act or process of extrapolating. EG *Avoid the disasters predicted by continuous extrapolation.* — N UNCOUNT = inference

2 An **extrapolation** is a quantity, idea, or calculation which is the result of extrapolating from existing ones. EG ...*one simple extrapolation from existing technology... ...simple extrapolations from current events.* — N COUNT : IF + PREP THEN *from*

extra-sensory perception is an ability that some people think exists, by which people can feel or know things that they could not have felt or known through the ordinary senses such as touch, sight or hearing. — N UNCOUNT

extraterrestrial /ɛ̲kstrətɪ¹rɛ̲strɪəl/, **extraterrestrials.** 1 **Extraterrestrial** means happening, existing, or coming from somewhere beyond the planet Earth; a formal use. EG *Extraterrestrial activity will be limited to exploration... ...a concentrated search for extraterrestrial life.* — ADJ CLASSIF : USU ATTRIB ≠ earthly

2 An **extraterrestrial** is a living creature that some people think exists or may exist in another part of the universe. EG ...*the first to contact intelligent extraterrestrials... What would extraterrestrials look like?* — N COUNT = alien

extravagance /ɪ²kstræ̲və¹gəns/, **extravagances.** 1 **Extravagance** is the spending of more money than is reasonable or than you can afford, often on things that you do not really need. EG *The African states were shocked at such extravagance... It is easy to criticize governments for extravagance and waste.* — N UNCOUNT ⇑ excess

2 An **extravagance** is an act of extravagant behaviour, especially spending more money than is reasonable or than you can afford. EG *In the quiet streets of Bloomsbury, commercial development would be an unjustifiable extravagance... It was a little extravagance of my father to buy new plants every year.* — N COUNT ⇑ excess

extravagant /ɪ²kstræ̲və¹gənt/. 1 Someone who is **extravagant** 1.1 spends more money than is reasonable or than they can afford, often on things they do not really need. EG *He said his wife was extravagant... I was simply too extravagant for the company's good.* ◊ **extravagantly.** EG *I lived extravagantly, taking cabs everywhere.* 1.2 uses more of something than is reasonable. EG *She considered him extravagant with electricity.* 1.3 is extreme in their behaviour and likely to do foolish or harmful things. EG *Mother was extravagant and romantic... ...a reckless, extravagant, disreputable fellow.* — ADJ QUALIT ⇑ wasteful ≠ thrifty; ◊ ADV; ADJ QUALIT = wasteful; ADJ QUALIT = profligate

2 Something that is **extravagant** 2.1 costs more money than is reasonable or than you can afford. EG ...*extravagant and often harmful luxuries... ...extravagant gifts.* ◊ **extravagantly.** EG ...*merchandise known to be extravagantly priced.* 2.2 uses more of something than is reasonable. EG ...*machines that are extravagant in their requirements of energy... The car is an extravagant consumer of land.* — ADJ QUALIT ⇑ costly; ◊ ADV; ADJ QUALIT ⇑ wasteful = inefficient

3 **Extravagant** behaviour is extreme behaviour that is often done for a particular effect. EG ...*people whose admiration is extravagant and often insincere... He raised his eyebrows in extravagant surprise... She treated me with extravagant contempt.* ◊ **extravagantly.** EG *Harold was extravagantly affectionate with his daughters... ...extravagantly eccentric behaviour.* — ADJ QUALIT = exaggerated; ◊ ADV+ADJ/ADV

4 **Extravagant** ideas are unrealistic and impractical; used showing disapproval. EG *You have the most extravagant ideas... ...extravagant expectations.* — ADJ QUALIT

5 **Extravagant** entertainments, designs, etc are elaborate and impressive. EG ...*extravagant feather patterns... ...extravagant musical entertainments.* ◊ **extravagantly.** EG ...*the extravagantly elaborate funerals.* — ADJ QUALIT; ◊ ADV+ADJ/ADV

extravaganza /ɪ²kstræ̲vəgæ̲nzə/, **extravaganzas.** An **extravaganza** is a public activity or performance which takes place in a very elaborate, colourful, and expensive way. EG ...*spaceship-inspired extravaganzas... ...extravaganzas at Cardiff Castle.* — N COUNT+SUPP ⇑ entertainment

extreme /ɪ²kstri̲ːm/, **extremes.** 1 **Extreme** means very great in degree or intensity. EG *He died in* — ADJ CLASSIF : ATTRIB *extreme poverty... Large numbers of old people suffer extreme discomfort each winter... You must proceed with extreme caution... Extreme cold can wake a hibernating animal.* ◇ **extremely**. EG *...an extremely difficult and dangerous task... Ralph and I have always got on extremely well... He played an extremely important part in the revolution.* ◇ ADV+ADJ/ ADV : USU+ADJ

2 Extreme situations and behaviour are much more severe or unusual than you would expect. EG *People are capable of surviving in extreme conditions... Baby battering is the most extreme example of such behaviour... Their methods may seem extreme to many parents.* ADJ QUALIT

3 Extreme opinions, beliefs, or political movements are unacceptably severe or unreasonable; used showing disapproval. EG *...extreme views... ...the extreme Right Wing of the Party.* ADJ QUALIT ≠ moderate

4 The **extreme** point, edge, or end of something is its furthest point, edge, or end. EG *...the extreme south of the country... ...the extreme tip of the bullet.* ADJ CLASSIF : ATTRIB ⇑ far

5 An **extreme** of behaviour is a type or example of behaviour which is considered to be so exaggerated that it is unacceptable; used showing disapproval. EG *There's now a danger that we're going to the other extreme and being too lenient... Society does not tolerate the extremes of human behaviour.* N COUNT : IF+ PREP THEN *of*

6 If you **go to extremes**, **take** something **to extremes**, or **carry** something **to extremes**, you do or say something in a way that is considered unacceptable, unreasonable, or foolish. EG *We had to go to extremes to get any reaction... That's taking generosity to extremes... Surely we can have clean air and water without carrying any policy to extremes?* PHR : VB INFLECTS

7 You use **in the extreme** to give emphasis to an adjective, especially when you want to say that something is undesirable or very surprising; a formal expression. EG *I thought the suggestion dangerous in the extreme... Her manner was friendly and welcoming in the extreme.* PHR : USED AS AN A ≠ in the least

extremis /ɪ²kstriːmɪs/. See **in extremis**.

extremism /ɪ²kstriːmɪzə⁰m/ is the behaviour or beliefs of extremists. EG *...the political extremism which brought their country close to civil war.* N UNCOUNT ≠ moderation

extremist /ɪ²kstriːmɪst/, **extremists**. An **extremist** is a person who wishes to bring about political or social change by doing things that other people consider too severe or disruptive, especially by using violence; used showing disapproval. EG *A bomb planted by Nationalist extremists seriously injured an army officer.* ▸ used as an adjective. EG *...an extremist splinter group... ...minor political parties with extremist views.* N COUNT : USU PL ⇑ activist ≠ moderate ▸ ADJ CLASSIF ≠ moderate

extremity /ɪ²kstrɛmɪti¹/, **extremities**. **1** The **extremity** of a situation is the degree to which it is severe or unacceptable. EG *...a mumble that suggested the extremity of drunkenness... ...the extremity of the tragedy.* N UNCOUNT/ COUNT = height

2 If you talk about the **extremity** of someone's ideas or beliefs, you mean that they are very extreme and unacceptable. EG *...the extremity of this racialist position.* N UNCOUNT ≠ moderation

3 An **extremity** is **3.1** the furthest end or edge of something; a formal use. EG *...the northern extremity of the west wing.* N COUNT **3.2** a very serious situation; a formal use. EG *She tried to remember how things had ever reached such an extremity.* N COUNT ⇑ degree

4 Your **extremities** are the ends or outermost parts of your body, especially your hands and feet. EG *The warmth spread outwards till it reached his extremities.* N PLURAL : USU POSS+N

extricate /ɛkstrɪkeɪt/, **extricates, extricating, extricated**. **1** If you **extricate** yourself or another person from a difficult or serious situation, you free yourself or the other person from it. EG *She found it impossible to extricate herself from the relationship.* V+O (NG/REFL) : USU+*from* = disentangle
◇ **extrication** /ɪ²kstrɪkeɪʃə⁰n/. ◇ N UNCOUNT

2 If you **extricate** yourself or someone else from a place where they are trapped or caught, you free yourself or the other person from the place. EG *He once more extricated himself from this embrace... It was exceedingly difficult to extricate her from the hole.* ◇ **extrication**. V+O (NG/REFL) : USU+*for* = liberate ◇ N UNCOUNT

extrovert /ɛkstrəvɜːt/, **extroverts**. An **extrovert** is a person who is very active, lively, and sociable, and who finds it easy to talk to other people and make friends. EG *If, however, you are an extrovert you are quite likely to enjoy it.* ▸ used as an adjective. EG *He had thought her gay, insensitive, extrovert... ...a rather extrovert student.* N COUNT ≠ introvert ▸ ADJ QUALIT

extrude /ɪ²kstruːd/, **extrudes, extruding, extruded**. To **extrude** something means to force or squeeze it out through a small opening; a formal word. V OR V+O

extrusion /ɪ²kstruːʒə⁰n/, **extrusions**. **Extrusion** is the act or process of extruding something; a formal word. N UNCOUNT/ COUNT ⇑ squeezing

exuberance /ɪ²gzjuːbə⁰rəns/ is behaviour which is energetic, excited, and cheerful. EG *She always greeted him with the same exuberance.* N UNCOUNT = enthusiasm

exuberant /ɪ²gzjuːbə⁰rənt/. If you are **exuberant**, you are full of energy, excitement, and cheerfulness. EG *...the exuberant director of the Theatre Royal.* ▸ used of people's behaviour. EG *He ran to Fanny and gave her an exuberant kiss.* ◇ **exuberantly**. EG *Children danced exuberantly around the tree.* ADJ QUALIT ⇑ lively ◇ ADV WITH VB

exude /ɪ²gzjuːd/, **exudes, exuding, exuded**; a formal word. **1** If you **exude** a particular quality, feeling, etc, you seem to have it or feel it to a great extent. EG *She exuded vitality, enthusiasm, and generosity... The rider did not speak, but exuded panic.* V+O ⇑ give off = ooze

2 If something **exudes** a liquid or smell or if a liquid or smell **exudes** from it, the liquid or smell comes out slowly and steadily. EG *Some frogs exude a poisonous chemical from their skins.* V-ERG = give off

exult /ɪ²gzʌlt/, **exults, exulting, exulted**; a formal word. If you **exult**, **1** you feel and show great happiness and pleasure because of some triumph or success that you have had. EG *I both trembled and exulted at my fortune.* ◇ **exultation** /ɪ²gzəlteɪʃə⁰n/. EG *He spoke with an air of suppressed exultation. Dixon guessed with growing exultation that this must be the painting he had been searching for.* **2** you speak in a way which indicates how pleased or proud you are of something that has happened. EG *'I've never played golf like I did last week,' he exulted.* **3** you get great pleasure from something. EG *He exulted in the title of the Napoleon of Fleet Street.* V : USU+A ⇑ rejoice ◇ N UNCOUNT = jubilation V+QUOTE ⇑ say = crow V : USU+A = glory

exultant /ɪ²gzʌltənt/. If you are **exultant**, you feel very happy and triumphant; a formal word. EG *This made her mildly exultant.* ▸ used of a person's behaviour. EG *Her tone was loud, exultant.* ◇ **exultantly**. EG *She laughed again, exultantly.* ADJ QUALIT ▸ = jubilant ◇ ADV WITH VB

eye /aɪ/, **eyes, eyeing** or **eying, eyed**. **1** An eye is **1.1** one of the two organs on the face of a person, animal, or bird that are used for seeing. EG *She went into hospital for an operation on her left eye... After a while my eyes became accustomed to the dark.* N COUNT ⇑ organ **1.2** the part of an eye which you can see when you look at someone's face. EG *...blue eyes... She opened her eyes.* N COUNT **1.3** the area of skin around an eye. EG *My eyes are always swollen after I've been crying.* N COUNT

2 If you **eye** something, you look at it carefully or suspiciously. EG *They eyed each other's newly bought shoes... Posy was eyeing the man thoughtfully.* V+O : NO IMPER

3 If you say that someone has an **eye** for something, you mean that they can recognize or see it clearly and make good judgements about it. EG *The mechanic looked at the car engine with a practised eye... This artist has a marvellous eye for detail... It was their eye for profit that made them successful.* N SING : USU *a*+ MOD+N, OR *an*+ N+*for* ⇑ discrimination

4 An **eye** is also **4.1** anything which seems to look at things in the way that an eye does, for example a camera. EG *The events of the war took place under the eye of a television camera.* N SING WITH DET : USU+SUPP **4.2** one of the dark spots on a potato which new stems grow out of. N COUNT **4.3** a small metal loop which a hook fits into to make a fastening on a piece of clothing. EG *Her skirt was fastened with hooks and eyes.* N COUNT

5 The **eye** of a needle is the small hole at one end of it which the thread passes through. N COUNT

6 The **eye** of a storm, tornado, or hurricane, is the calm centre of it. EG *...the eye of a storm... ...the eye of a hurricane.* N SING : *the*+N+ *of*

7 The word **eye** is also used in the following expressions. **7.1** If you are **all eyes**, you are very observant and looking round eagerly; an informal expression. EG *The children were all eyes at the circus.* PHR : USED AS C ⇑ interested **7.2** If you say that something happens **before**, **in front of**, or **under** your **eyes**, it happens where you can see it very clearly, and you are emphasizing that it is surprising or unpleasant. EG *Her father was murdered before her very eyes.* PHR : USED AS AN A **7.3** If you **cast** or **run** your **eye over** something, you look or glance quickly at it. EG *He ran his eye over the newspaper article.* PHR : VB INFLECTS

7.4 If something **catches** your **eye**, you suddenly notice it. EG *The flowers in your window caught my eye.* **7.5** If you **catch** someone's **eye**, you do something to attract their attention, so that you can speak to them or ask them to do something. EG *Can you catch the waiter's eye?* **7.6** If you **clap**, **lay**, or **set eyes on** someone or something, you see them; an informal expression. EG *She was the most extraordinary person I had ever laid eyes on.* **7.7** If someone **has** their **eye on** you, they are watching you and making judgements about you. EG *I've had my eye on you for a long time.* **7.8** If you say that something appears to be true **to** someone's **eyes** or **in** someone's **eyes**, you mean that this is their opinion, although other people might disagree with you. EG *The habits of strangers sometimes seem peculiar to our eyes... Her children could do no wrong in her eyes.* **7.9** If you **keep** your **eyes open** or **keep an eye out for** someone or something, you are looking or watching for them carefully; an informal expression. EG *You'll have to keep your eyes open for trouble tonight.* **7.10** If you **keep** your **eyes peeled** or **skinned**, you are constantly watching for something; an informal expression. EG *Keep your eyes peeled for pickpockets on Oxford Street.* **7.11** If you **keep an eye on** something or someone, you watch them and make sure that they are safe, especially while the person who owns them or normally looks after them is absent. EG *Can you keep an eye on the baby while I go shopping?* **7.12** If you **look at** or **see** something **through** a particular person's **eyes**, you understand it in the same way that they do. EG *Try looking at the world through a child's eyes.* **7.13** If you **make eyes at** someone, you look at them in a way that indicates that you are attracted to them; an informal expression. EG *He was making eyes at the waitress.* **7.14** If you say that there is **more** to a situation **than meets the eye**, you mean that it is more complicated than you originally thought. **7.15** If you **only have eyes for** a particular person, you are especially interested in them, for example because you are in love with them. EG *He only had eyes for me.* **7.16** If you do or go into something **with** your **eyes open**, you are aware of the problems and difficulties that you are likely to face. EG *He went into the job with his eyes open.* **7.17** If something **opens** your **eyes**, it makes you aware for the first time that something is different from the way that you thought it was. **7.18** If you **see eye to eye** with someone, you agree with them and share the same opinions and views. EG *She doesn't see eye to eye with her parents.* **7.19** If you **shut** or **close** your **eyes to** something, you ignore it. EG *It is foolish to shut our eyes to the effects of unemployment.* **7.20** If you **cannot take** your **eyes off** someone, you are unable to stop looking at them, for example because you find them very attractive. EG *He could not take his eyes off her throughout the meal.*

PHR : VB INFLECTS (7.4) · PHR : VB INFLECTS ⇑ signal (7.5) · PHR : VB INFLECTS (7.6) · PHR : VB INFLECTS ⇑ observe (7.7) · PHR : USED AS AN A (7.8) · PHR : VB INFLECTS ⇑ expect (7.9) · PHR : VB INFLECTS ⇑ watch (7.10) · PHR : VB INFLECTS = look after (7.11) · PHR : VB INFLECTS (7.12) · PHR : VB INFLECTS = ogle (7.13) · PHR : USED AS C (7.14) · PHR : VB INFLECTS (7.15) · PHR : USED AS AN A (7.16) · PHR : VB INFLECTS (7.17) · PHR OR PHR+A *(with)* : RECIP, VB INFLECTS (7.18) · PHR : VB INFLECTS (7.19) · PHR (7.20)

8 If you are **up to** your **eyes in** something, you are extremely busy because of it; an informal expression. EG *Sal is still up to her eyes in kids and housework.* — PHR : USED AS AN A

9 If you are **doped** or **drugged up to** your **eyes**, you have taken so many drugs that you cannot think clearly or move properly; an informal expression. EG *She's doped up to the eyes with valium.* — PHR : USED AS C

10 If you **cry** your **eyes out**, you are crying very much because you are very upset; an informal expression. EG *A little girl was crying her eyes out.* — PHR : VB INFLECTS = sob

11 If you say **that's one in the eye** for someone, you mean that something unpleasant has just happened to them which you feel they deserve; an informal expression. — PHR + *for* + N PROPER/NG

12 You use **an eye for an eye** or **an eye for an eye and a tooth for a tooth** when you are talking about the idea that it is right that someone should be treated in the same harsh way that they have treated someone else, and that there should be no mercy for them. — PHR : USED AS C/O ⇑ revenge

13 If you say that someone's **eyes are too big for** their **stomach**, you mean that they are greedy because they have taken more food than they can actually eat; a humorous expression. — PHR : VB INFLECTS

14 If you say that someone **has an eye to the main chance** or **has an eye for the main chance**, you mean that they are ambitious and always aware of good opportunities when they happen; often used showing disapproval. — PHR : VB INFLECTS

15 You say **my eye** in order to express scorn or disagreement; an old-fashioned informal expression. EG *A rose, my eye! That's a geranium!.* — PHR ⇑ nonsense

16 See also **black eye**, **cross-eyed**, **private eye**, **shut-eye**.

17 The word **eye** is also used in the following expressions, which are explained at other places in this dictionary. • to **turn a blind eye**: see **blind**. • to **feast your eyes**: see **feast**. • to **look someone in the eye**: see **look**. • to **meet someone's eyes**: see **meet**. • **in the twinkling of an eye**: see **twinkling**.

eye up. If someone **eyes** you **up**, they look at you in a way that indicates that they think that you are attractive; an informal expression. EG *He's been eyeing me up all evening.* — PHRASAL VB : V + O + ADV ⇑ ogle

eyeball /aɪbɔːl/, **eyeballs**. A person's or animal's **eyeball** is the round part of their eye that is in the shape of a sphere. In humans, eyeballs are usually white with a coloured centre. — N COUNT

eyebrow /aɪbraʊ/, **eyebrows**. **1** Your **eyebrows** are the lines of hair which grow in an arch above each of your eyes. — N COUNT

2 If something causes you to **raise an eyebrow** or to **raise** your **eyebrows**, it causes you to feel surprised, shocked, or disapproving. EG *Eyebrows were raised at their behaviour... This comment raised hardly an eyebrow in the medical profession.* — PHR : VB AND N INFLECT ⇑ disapprove

eye-catching. Something that is **eye-catching** is so noticeable that people look at it. EG *...an eye-catching poster.* — ADJ QUALIT

-eyed combines with words such as 'blue', 'dark', or 'wild' to indicate that the person or animal described has eyes of a particular colour, expression, or quality. EG *...dark-eyed children... She was feverish and wild-eyed.* — COMB : FORMS ADJS

eyeful /aɪfʊl/, **eyefuls**. **1** An **eyeful** of dust, liquid, etc is an amount of it which has got into someone's eye. EG *...an eyeful of sand.* — N PART

2 If you get an **eyeful** of someone or something, you have a good look at them; a very informal expression. EG *So what you got was an eyeful of my wife.* — N SING : *an* + N, USU + *of*

3 If men refer to a woman as an **eyeful**, they mean that they find her very attractive; a very informal word. — N SING : *an* + N

eyelash /aɪlæʃ/, **eyelashes**. Your **eyelashes** are the hairs which grow on the edge of your upper and lower eyelids. — N COUNT

eyelet /aɪlɪ²t/, **eyelets**. An **eyelet** is a small hole with a metal or leather ring round it, which is made in cloth. You can put cord, rope, or string through it, for example in the sails of a boat or in the flaps of tents. — N COUNT

eyelid /aɪlɪd/, **eyelids**. **1** Your **eyelids** are the two flaps of skin which cover your eyes when they are closed. EG *...his lower eyelid.* — N COUNT ⇑ flap

2 If you **don't bat an eyelid** when something happens, or if you do something **without batting an eyelid**, you remain completely calm and are not at all shocked or surprised; an informal expression. EG *She didn't bat an eyelid when she was given the bill.* — PHR : VB INFLECTS, OR PHR USED AS AN A ⇑ react

eye-opener, eye-openers. If you say that something is an **eye-opener**, you mean that you find it very surprising and that you learn something from it which you did not know before. EG *The book is quite an eye-opener.* — N SING : USU *an* + N, USED AS C ⇑ surprise = revelation

eye patch, eye patches; also spelled with a hyphen. An **eye patch** is a piece of material which you wear over your eye when you have damaged or injured it. — N COUNT ⇑ covering

eyepiece /aɪpiːs/, **eyepieces**; also spelled with a hyphen. The **eyepiece** of a microscope or telescope is the piece of glass at one end, where you put your eye in order to look through the instrument. — N COUNT ⇑ lens

eye-shadow; also spelled without a hyphen. **Eye-shadow** is a substance which you can paint on your eyelids in order to make them a different colour. — N COUNT ⇑ cosmetic

eyesight /aɪsaɪt/. Your **eyesight** is your ability to see. EG *His eyesight was excellent... ...poor eyesight.* — N UNCOUNT ⇑ vision

eye socket, eye sockets; also spelled with a hyphen. Your **eye sockets** are the two bony parts on either side of your face, which hold your eyeballs. — N COUNT

eyesore /aɪsɔː/, **eyesores**. If you say that something is an **eyesore**, you mean that it is extremely ugly. EG *It's an architectural eyesore.* — N COUNT : USU USED AS C

eye strain; also spelled with a hyphen and as one word. **Eye strain** is pain that you feel around your eyes or at the back of your eyes when you are very tired or should be wearing glasses. N UNCOUNT ⇑ pain

eye tooth, eye teeth; also spelled with a hyphen and as one word. 1 Your **eye teeth** are the two pointed teeth towards the front of your upper jaw. N COUNT ⇑ canine
2 If you say that you would **give** your **eye teeth** for something, you mean that you want it very much and you would do anything to get it; an informal expression. EG *I'd give my eye teeth for such a lot of money.* PHR : VB INFLECTS, USU + *for/to*-INF

eyewash /aɪwɒʃ/, **eyewashes**; also spelled with a hyphen. 1 **Eyewash** is a liquid which you use for bathing your eyes when they are sore. N UNCOUNT ⇑ lotion
2 If you say that something is **eyewash**, you mean that it isn't true or that you don't believe it; an informal, slightly old-fashioned use. EG *That report is a load of old eyewash.* N UNCOUNT, USU USED AS C ⇑ nonsense = rubbish

eyewitness /aɪwɪtnɪ¹s/, **eyewitnesses**; also spelled with a hyphen and as two words. An **eyewitness** is a person who has seen an event and can therefore describe it, for example in a law court. EG *The lawyer had an eyewitness to give evidence... ...an excellent eye-witness description of the collision.* N COUNT ⇑ witness

eyrie /ɪəri¹, ɛəri¹, aɪəri¹/, **eyries**. An **eyrie** is 1 the nest of an eagle, falcon, or other similar bird, that is usually built high up in rough, mountainous country. N COUNT
2 a place, such as a house or a castle, that is built high up and is difficult to reach. N COUNT = refuge

Ff

F, f /ɛf/, **Fs, f's, ff.**. The form **ff.** is used for the plural of the abbreviation in paragraph 4. 1 **F** is the sixth letter of the English alphabet. N COUNT
2 **F**, in music, is the fourth note in the scale of C major. N COUNT/UNCOUNT
3 **F** is an abbreviation for 'Fahrenheit', written after a number when a temperature is expressed as a particular number of degrees Fahrenheit. EG *...when the outside temperature is 30°F.*
4 **f.** is an abbreviation for 'following'. It is written after a page or line number in a cross-reference in order to indicate that you are referring to both the page or line mentioned and the next one. You use **ff.** when you are referring to the page or line mentioned and two or more following pages or lines. EG *For further discussion of this point, see pages 56f.*
5 **F** or **f** is also an abbreviation for other words beginning with F or f, such as 'female', 'feminine', 'franc', and 'false'.

fab /fæb/. If you say that something is **fab**, you are expressing your approval of it; an informal word. ADJ QUALIT = great

fable /feɪbə⁰l/, **fables**. A **fable** is 1 a story that is intended to teach a moral lesson. Fables often have animals as the main characters. EG *It was so clearly a moral fable.* N COUNT 2 a story that people tell, especially one that is based on traditional ideas, beliefs, or memories rather than scientific or historical facts. EG *There is, however, some truth in this fable... ...a dream that developed like a fable or a myth.* N COUNT = legend 3 a statement or explanation that is untrue. EG *...the fable that the Nationalist Government had firm popular support.* N COUNT ⇑ lie = fiction

fabled /feɪbə⁰ld/. If something is **fabled**, it is well known because a lot of stories are told about it. EG *The greatest of all its cities was the fabled Timbuktu.* ADJ CLASSIF : ATTRIB ⇑ famous = legendary

fabric /fæbrɪk/, **fabrics**. 1 **Fabric** is cloth or other material produced by weaving cotton, nylon, wool, silk, or other threads together. There are many different kinds of fabrics. They are used for making things such as clothes, curtains, and sheets. EG *If you aren't certain what fabric you are trying to dye, don't guess... These fabrics are specially imported from Italy and France.* N COUNT/UNCOUNT
2 The **fabric** of a society or way of life is its basic structure and the customs and beliefs that are associated with it, which makes it stable and secure. EG *...the priests who upheld the fabric of Roman society.* N SING : *the*+N, USU+*of* = foundations
3 The **fabric** of a building, especially a church or large house, is all its walls and roof and the materials with which it is built. EG *This amount was enough to maintain the fabric of the house.* N SING : *the*+N+SUPP ⇑ structure

fabricate /fæbrɪkeɪt/, **fabricates, fabricating, fabricated**. 1 If you **fabricate** something such as a story or piece of evidence, you deliberately invent it even though it is untrue, in order to deceive people. EG *They fabricated evidence and threatened witnesses.* V+O = fake
2 If you **fabricate** an object, 2.1 you make it from whatever materials are available. EG *Some of the parts broke and new ones had to be fabricated out of scrap iron.* V+O 2.2 you manufacture it for the first time; a formal use. V+O ⇑ make

fabrication /fæbrɪkeɪʃə⁰n/, **fabrications**; a formal word. 1 A **fabrication** is a false story or piece of evidence that someone has deliberately invented in order to deceive people. EG *The story was a fabrication, she insisted.* N COUNT ⇑ lie
2 **Fabrication** is the deliberate invention of a false story or piece of evidence. EG *...the problem of what truth means and how it differs from falsehood and fabrication.* N UNCOUNT
3 The **fabrication** of an object is the process of manufacturing or producing it. EG *...shipped to a sister company for fabrication into fuel rods.* N UNCOUNT : USU +SUPP = manufacture

fabulous /fæbjə⁴ləs/. 1 If you say that something is **fabulous**, 1.1 you are expressing your admiration or approval of it; an informal use. EG *She's got a fabulous figure.* ADJ QUALIT = fantastic 1.2 you are expressing a general sense of pleasure and wellbeing; an informal use. EG *I feel absolutely fabulous.* ADJ QUALIT = fantastic 1.3 you are saying that it is very large or wonderful. EG *...the tale of a woman saint of fabulous beauty... Many of their cities were centres of fabulous wealth.* ADJ CLASSIF : ATTRIB = extraordinary ◇ **fabulously**. EG *She is fabulously wealthy.* ◇ ADV+ADJ/ADV
2 **Fabulous** creatures, places, or things occur in stories and legends, but are not true or real. EG *...the door was carved with fabulous beasts... ...the towers and turrets of some fabulous city.* ADJ CLASSIF : ATTRIB ⇑ fictitious = mythical

façade /fæsɑːd/, **façades**. 1 The **façade** of a building, especially a large one, is its front wall or the wall that faces the street. EG *...the ornate façade of the Palace.* N COUNT
2 A **façade** is an outward appearance which is deliberately false and gives you a wrong impression about someone or something. EG *These are the grim facts which lie behind the façade of gaiety... The unity of the Party was a façade.* N SING WITH DET = pretence, show

face /feɪs/, **faces, facing, faced**. 1 Your **face** is the front part of your head from your chin to the top of your forehead, where your mouth, eyes, nose, and other features are. EG *She had a smooth, un-lined face... Tears were pouring down her face... They were both red in the face from running.* N COUNT = countenance
2 If your **face** is happy, sad, serious, etc, you have a happy, sad, or serious expression. EG *The girl's face was unhappy... ...looking at her with a puzzled face.* N COUNT : USU ADJ+N = countenance
3 The word **face** is used in the following expressions.
3.1 If you **put on a brave face** or **a good face**, you try not to show how unhappy, afraid, or upset you really are. PHR : VB INFLECTS 3.2 If you have **a long face**, you look very unhappy or serious. EG *I saw her going about with a long face.* PHR : USED AS O 3.3 If you **make** or **pull a face**, you show your dislike, disgust, or defiance by means of your expression. EG *The children made faces at the teacher... He saw her make a sudden face of disgust.* PHR : VB INFLECTS = grimace 3.4 If you cannot **keep a straight face**, you cannot stop yourself from smiling or laughing. EG *I found it hard to keep a straight face.* PHR : VB INFLECTS
4 The **face** of a cliff or a mountain, or of an object such as a gemstone, is a surface or side of it, N COUNT : USU+*of*

especially a vertical surface. EG *...the black cliff of the north face of the Eiger.*

5 The **face** in a mine is the part of the rock from which miners dig coal, metal, etc. N COUNT : USU the+N

6 The **face** of a clock or watch is the surface with the numbers or hands on it, which shows the time. N COUNT = dial

7 The **face** of a playing card is the side which has symbols, pictures, or numbers printed on it. N COUNT ⇑ front

8 If someone or something is **face down**, their face or front points downwards. If they are **face up**, their face or front points upwards. EG *Philip lay face down on the floor... Lay three cards face up on the table.* PHR : USED AS C/A

9 The **face** of a place is its physical appearance; a rather literary use. EG *The face of a city can change completely in a year.* N SING : the+N+of

10 Expressions such as **the face of the earth** or **the face of the world** are ways of referring to the whole of the world or the whole of the place mentioned. EG *The appearance of the flowers transformed the face of the world... ...the densest cluster of human beings on the face of the globe.* PHR : USU USED AS O ● If you say that someone or something **disappeared** or **vanished off the face of the earth**, you mean that they disappeared without any reason, and that you have no idea where they are now. ● PHR : VB INFLECTS

11 If you refer to the **face** of something such as an activity, belief, or system, you are referring to one particular aspect of it, in contrast to other aspects. EG *As far as photographers are concerned, the close-up lens has changed the face of their profession... I think the general face of industrial relations is changing... ...the ugly face of Liberalism.* N SING : the+N+of

12 The word **face** is also used in the following expressions. **12.1** If you **lose face** or suffer a **loss of face**, you do something or experience something which damages your reputation and makes you lose people's respect. EG *She wanted to end the affair without too much loss of face.* PHR : VB INFLECTS, OR PHR : USED AS O **12.2** If you do something in order to **save face**, you do it in order to avoid damaging your reputation and losing people's respect. EG *He had to resign, to save face.* PHR : VB INFLECTS

13 If someone or something **faces** a particular thing, person, or direction, they are positioned opposite the other thing or person or are looking in that direction. EG *The two boys faced each other... ...the houses facing the river... Most seats on London buses face forward.* V+O, OR V+A

14 If you **face** a group of people, you stand in front of them for a particular purpose. EG *I'm nervous. I've never faced a class of children before.* V+O = confront

15 If you **face** something difficult or unpleasant, or if you **are faced** with it, it is going to affect you and you have to deal with it. EG *It is the biggest problem he has ever faced... You are faced with a choice of loyalties... She was now facing bankruptcy.* V+O : USU PASS+with ⇑ experience

16 If you **face** the truth, a fact, or a problem, you accept that it is true or really exists and respond to it in a suitable way, although you would prefer to ignore it. EG *We simply must face facts... He was willing to face the truth... It is something that has to be faced.* V+O ⇑ acknowledge ● You say **'Let's face it'** when you are stating a fact or making a comment about something which is unpleasant or which you do not really want to admit. EG *Let's face it, we all cheat in exams.* ● PHR : USED AS ADV SEN

17 If you can't **face** something, you do not want to do it or accept it, and do not like thinking about it because it is too difficult or serious. EG *She could not really face speaking to them... I'm sorry, I just couldn't face the idea of going back there.* V : MODAL+V+O/-ING, USU WITH BROAD NEG = cope with

18 If you **face** a charge or punishment, you have been accused of a particular crime or are going to receive a particular punishment. EG *She faced criminal charges for deceiving the State... If they are found guilty they will face a sentence of ten years in prison.* V+O

19 If you **are faced** with something wrong that you have done, evidence for it is produced and you are accused of it. EG *Even when faced with the broken vase or spilt milk, most children will continue to protest their innocence.* V+O : USU PASS+with = be confronted

20 If you **face** part of a garment that you are making, for example the neckline or armhole of a dress, you make it look neat and strengthen it by stitching a piece of fabric along the edge and turning this to the inside. V+O ⇑ line

21 If you **face the music**, you put yourself in a position where you know you will be criticized or punished for something that you have done; an informal expression. EG *I had to go back home and face the music.* PHR : VB INFLECTS

22 If a situation **blows up** or **explodes in** your **face**, it goes wrong unexpectedly, with the result that you suffer considerably; an informal expression. EG *Miller's plans blew up in his face.* PHR : VB INFLECTS = misfire

23 If an action or belief **flies in the face of** accepted ideas, it seems to oppose or contradict them. EG *The proposal to introduce identity cards flies in the face of so many British political traditions.* PHR : VB INFLECTS = go against

24 If you do not **have the face** to do something, you feel too embarrassed or guilty to do it; an informal expression. EG *I don't have the face to tell him to leave.* PHR+to-INF : VB INFLECTS, USU WITH BROAD NEG = have the nerve

25 If you do something **in the face of** a particular problem or difficulty, you do it even though this problem or difficulty exists. EG *They carry on smiling in the face of adversity.* PREP

26 If you cannot **look** someone **in the face**, you are too ashamed or embarrassed to look at them directly. EG *I could never look my son in the face again if I lied to him.* PHR : VB INFLECTS, USU WITH BROAD NEG

27 You say **on the face of it** when you are expressing an opinion in order to emphasize that the opinion may change when you know or think more about the subject. EG *On the face of it, it sounds like a good idea.* PHR : USED AS ADV SEN ⇑ apparently

28 If you **set** your **face against** something, you oppose it strongly. PHR : VB INFLECTS

29 If you **show** your **face** somewhere, you go there and see people that you know. EG *She felt she could never show her face in the town again.* PHR : VB INFLECTS, USU+A = be seen

30 If you say something **to** someone's **face**, you say it openly in their presence. EG *They certainly didn't say what they were thinking to my face.* PHR : USED AS AN A ⇑ directly

31 See also **face to face, facing, full-face, volte-face.**

32 The word **face** is also used in the following expressions, which are explained at other places in this dictionary. ● **blue in the face**: see **blue.** ● to **shut** or **slam the door in** someone's **face**: see **door.** ● **egg on your face**: see **egg.** ● **shut your face**: see **shut.** ● a **slap in the face**: see **slap.** ● to **cut off your nose to spite your face**: see **spite.** ● **face value**: see **value.** ● to **wipe the grin** or **smile off** someone's **face**: see **wipe.**

face down. If you **face** someone **down**, you oppose them or beat them by being confident and looking at them boldly; used in American English. EG *She didn't argue with him, she just faced him down.* PHRASAL VB : V+O+ADV

face out. If you **face** a person or situation **out**, you deal with them or it by behaving firmly or defiantly; used in British English. EG *We'll face this crisis out.* PHRASAL VB : V+O+ADV ⇑ handle

face up to. If you **face up** to a difficult situation, you accept it and deal with it. EG *They had to face up to many setbacks.* PHRASAL VB : V+ADV+PREP = cope with

face cloth, face cloths; also spelled with a hyphen. A **face cloth** is the same as a face flannel. N COUNT

face cream, face creams; also spelled with a hyphen. **Face cream** is a thick substance that you rub into your face in order to clean or soften it. N MASS

-faced combines with adjectives in order to form other adjectives that describe someone's face or expression. EG *He was a plump red-faced young man... They were stiff-faced with defiance.* COMB : FORMS ADJS

face flannel, face flannels; also spelled with a hyphen. A **face flannel** is a small cloth made of towelling which you use for washing yourself; used in British English. N COUNT = face cloth

faceless /feɪslɪ²s/. If you describe someone or something as **faceless**, you mean that they are dull and boring and have no character or individuality; used showing disapproval. EG *...faceless bureaucrats in the Civil Service.* ADJ CLASSIF : USU ATTRIB = anonymous

face lift, face lifts. 1 A **face lift** is an operation in which a surgeon tightens the skin on someone's face in order to make them look younger. N COUNT

2 If you give a place or thing a **face lift**, you do something that will make it look better or more attractive. N COUNT : USU SING

face pack, face packs. A **face pack** is a thick substance which you spread on your face, allow to dry for a short time, and then remove, in order to clean your skin thoroughly. N COUNT

face powder, face powders. Face powder is a very fine, soft, flesh-coloured powder that you put on your face in order to make it look smoother. N MASS ⇑ cosmetic

face-saver, face-savers. A **face-saver** is an action or excuse which prevents damage to your reputation or the loss of people's respect for you. N COUNT

face-saving. A **face-saving** action is one which prevents damage to your reputation or the loss of people's respect for you. EG *...a face-saving compromise.* ADJ CLASSIF : ATTRIB ⇑ redeeming

facet /fæsɪ²t/, **facets.** 1 A **facet** of something is a single part or aspect of it. EG *Tact was just one facet of his talents as a captain.* N COUNT : IF + PREP THEN *of* = feature

2 The **facets** of a diamond or other precious stone are the flat surfaces that have been cut on its outside. N COUNT

facetious /fəsiːʃəs/. If someone is **facetious**, they make amusing remarks, often in a clever or critical way or at inappropriate times. EG *He was being facetious and Grandmother got crosser and crosser.* ▸ used of what someone says or writes. EG *...a facetious remark.* ◊ **facetiously.** EG *We hid our nervousness in jokes–Frank suggesting facetiously that the office might be better called a dormitory.* ADJ QUALIT = flippant, frivolous ≠ serious ◊ ADV WITH VB

face to face. 1 If you are **face to face** with someone, you are in their presence or you meet them and can talk to them or look at them directly. EG *I suddenly came face to face with Karen... ...face to face encounters.* PHR : USED AS AN A, IF + PREP THEN *with*

2 If you are brought **face to face** with a difficulty, you cannot avoid it and have to deal with it. EG *Being alone can bring people face to face with their problems.* PHR : USED AS AN A, IF + PREP THEN *with*

facial /feɪʃə⁰l/, **facials.** 1 **Facial** means appearing on or being part of your face. EG *...their lack of facial hair... ...facial expressions.* ◊ **facially.** EG *He reminded him facially of a man he once knew.* ADJ CLASSIF : ATTRIB ◊ ADV WITH VB

2 A **facial** is a beauty treatment in which your face is massaged, and creams and other substances are rubbed into it. N COUNT

facie. See **prima facie.**

facile /fæsaɪl/. A **facile** remark, argument, or feeling is one which is simple and obvious, and which indicates lack of careful, intelligent thinking; used showing disapproval. EG *...facile replies... It is facile to point out that no such relationship exists.* ADJ QUALIT = simplistic, easy

facilitate /fəsɪlɪteɪt/, **facilitates, facilitating, facilitated.** To **facilitate** an action or process means to make it easier for it to happen or be done; a fairly formal word. EG *...legislation to facilitate the sale of businesses... This trend has been facilitated by recent changes in the economic structure.* V + O ⇑ help

facility /fəsɪlɪti¹/, **facilities.** 1 **Facilities** are the equipment, buildings, services, etc that are provided for a particular activity or purpose. EG *She had no cooking facilities in her room... ...the lack of play facilities for young children... The central facility is the library... Only six countries had the facilities and know-how to produce advanced weapon systems of this kind.* N COUNT : USU PL + SUPP

2 A **facility** is something useful but not essential such as an additional service provided by an organization or an extra feature on a machine, which you can use if you want or need to. EG *They ask for a 6 million pounds loan facility as working capital... A tape recorder like this has a tape slide facility, and you can attach this to a projector.* N COUNT + SUPP ⇑ advantage

3 If you have a **facility** for something such as learning languages, you find it easy or do it well. EG *Meehan began to learn German, and having a facility for languages, was soon fluent in it... Not everyone easily acquires facility in foreign languages.* N COUNT/ UNCOUNT : USU SING + *for/in* ⇑ skill = quickness

4 If you do something with **facility**, you do it easily and well. EG *They had all learned to read and write with great facility.* N UNCOUNT = proficiency

facing /feɪsɪŋ/, **facings.** 1 **Facing** is fabric which is stitched inside the cuffs, collars, or seams of a piece of clothing in order to make them look neat and strengthen them. N UNCOUNT ⇑ reinforcement

2 The **facings** of a uniform, jacket, coat, etc are its collar and cuffs when they are made of a different fabric from the main part. N PLURAL ⇑ edgings

3 A **facing** on a wall is a layer of stone, concrete, or other material that is spread over its surface in order to make it look attractive. N COUNT/ UNCOUNT ⇑ coating

facsimile /fæksɪmɪli¹/, **facsimiles.** A **facsimile** of a book or document is an exact reproduction of it. N COUNT ⇑ copy

fact /fækt/, **facts.** 1 Something that actually happened or happens can be described or referred to as **fact** or a **fact.** EG *How much of the novel is fiction and how much is fact?... I don't know whether the rumour was based on fact or not... This service has now gone, victim of the economic facts of life.* N UNCOUNT/ COUNT ⇑ reality

2 A **fact** is 2.1 an item of knowledge that is true and that can be proved. EG *Scientific hypotheses are not facts.* 2.2 a piece of information or a detail about something or someone. EG *Meadows was handed every fact–names, ages, and charges lodged... The report is several pages long and full of facts and figures... It may help you to know the full facts of the case.* ● If you tell a child **the facts of life,** you tell him or her about sexual intercourse and explain how babies are born. N COUNT N COUNT ● PHR : USU USED AS O

3 If you say **the fact that, a fact which, this fact,** etc, you are referring to a situation or state of affairs that you have just mentioned or are about to mention, and suggesting that it is true. EG *There wasn't a great deal of warmth owing to the fact that Smithy had left the door open... They had waited in vain, a fact which was repeatedly explained to them... He is really not amused but wishes to hide the fact.* PHR

4 The word **fact** is also used in the following expressions. 4.1 **In fact, in point of fact,** or **in actual fact** means in reality or in truth; often used as emphasis, or when you are asking whether something really is true or really has happened. EG *Is this in fact going to affect relationships between Britain and Europe?... We were asked to have a look at this seed and we did in fact do that... In point of fact, they arrived an hour early... This is, in fact, what happened.* 4.2 You say **in fact, in actual fact, as a matter of fact,** or **in point of fact** to emphasize or to introduce a contradiction or an opinion which is different from something that has just been said. EG *'I couldn't communicate with you.'–'As a matter of fact,' Landy said, 'I believe you could'... In actual fact, this book wasn't the book I was looking for... I thought he could speak the language fluently, whereas in actual fact that wasn't the case at all... In fact, I'm not at all sure that Freud was correct.* 4.3 You say **in fact, in actual fact,** or **in point of fact** to introduce or to indicate more detailed information which is related to what you have just been saying. EG *We were allowed, in fact expected, to write our papers in English... It was terribly cold weather–a blizzard in fact... I don't think Mrs Rosentelle mentioned it. In fact I don't think she knew... This isn't very interesting–in fact I think it's remarkably dull.* 4.4 You say **as a matter of fact** to introduce or to indicate information which is related to something that has just been said but which may surprise the listener. EG *'How's Richard?'–'That's all over as a matter of fact'... As a matter of fact I just got given that this afternoon... These are the first ones I've seen as a matter of fact.* PHR : USED AS ADV SEN = actually PHR : USED AS ADV SEN = actually PHR : USED AS ADV SEN PHR : USED AS ADV SEN = actually

5 **the fact is.** 5.1 You can say **the fact is** to introduce a statement, especially when you would rather not admit it but you are forcing yourself to be honest. EG *The fact is, I don't really want to go... Fact is, we are rivals.* 5.2 You can say **the fact is** or **the fact of the matter is** to introduce a statement which summarizes what you have just said and emphasizes the truth and reality of what you are saying. EG *The fact is that child rearing is a long, hard job... The fact of the matter is Cynthia said she'd meet me there and she didn't turn up.* PHR : VB INFLECTS = actually PHR : VB INFLECTS

6 You say **the fact remains** that something is the case when you want to emphasize that this must be realized and accepted. EG *People may have forgotten their true meaning but the fact remains that they exist.* PHR : VB INFLECTS + REPORT-CL = nevertheless

7 You say **that's a fact** or **and that's a fact** to emphasize a statement that you have just made; an informal expression. EG *The whole world is going to want to meet him, that's a fact.* PHR

8 When you say **is that a fact?,** you are asking if something you have just heard is true because you found it surprising or interesting; an informal expression. EG *'She got married last year.'–'Is that a fact?'* CONVENTION

9 When you say that you know something **for a fact,** you mean that you are absolutely sure that it is true. EG *I know for a fact that there's a place in town where you can get them.* PHR : USED AS AN A = for sure

fact-finding; also spelled without a hyphen. A **fact-finding** trip or mission is one whose purpose is to find out information about a particular situation, especially for an official group. ADJ CLASSIF : ATTRIB ⇑ exploratory

faction /fækʃəⁿn/, **factions**. 1 A **faction** is an organized group of people within a larger group or organization, who actively oppose some of the ideas of the larger group and fight for their own ideas. EG *Two months later a faction calling itself the 'New Opposition' issued a circular to all members... ...warring religious factions.* N COUNT: IF SING, VB CAN BE SING OR PL = camp

2 **Faction** is 2.1 argument and strong disagreement within a group. EG *...petty political faction.* N UNCOUNT 2.2 writing that deals with true events, but that describes them using the techniques of fiction. N UNCOUNT

factitious /fæktɪʃəˢs/. Something that is **factitious** is artificial, as opposed to being natural or genuine; a formal word. ADJ CLASSIF

factor /fæktə/, **factors**. 1 A **factor** is a single part that combines with others to form the cause of something. EG *Youth unemployment is a major contributing factor to this problem... The scale of industry was the crucial factor determining the rate of growth... In today's world, social and economic factors are inextricably linked.* N COUNT

2 If an amount increases or decreases by a **factor** of a stated number, it becomes that number of times bigger or smaller. EG *The amount of energy used has gone up by a factor of eight... ...higher by a factor of 50%.* N SING WITH DET: IF + PREP THEN *of*

3 A **factor** of a whole number is a smaller whole number which can be multiplied with another whole number to produce the first whole number. EG *2 and 5 are factors of 10.* N COUNT: IF + PREP THEN *of*

4 You can use **factor** to refer to a particular level on a scale of measurement. EG *This type of quilt has a high warmth factor... The factor 2 suntan oil is for skin that tans easily... ...a higher wind chill factor.* N SING WITH DET + SUPP ⇑ degree

factory /fæktəⁿriˡ/, **factories**. 1 A **factory** is a large building or group of buildings where goods are made in large quantities, usually with the use of machines. EG *The workers left the land to work in the factories and mills... ...the average skilled factory worker... ...a carpet factory.* ▸ used to refer to the people who work in a factory. EG *A local factory phoned us one day with a problem.* N COUNT

2 The **factory floor** refers to the area where the ordinary workers in a factory work, rather than the people who run it, and to the workers themselves. EG *...negotiations involving workers on the factory floor.* PHR: USU PREP + N ⇑ place

3 You refer to a place as a **factory** when something is being produced or dealt with there in large quantities; often used humorously. EG *Our entire house has turned into a jam factory.* N COUNT: USU MOD + N = production line

factory farming /fæktəⁿriˡ fɑːmɪŋ/ is a system of animal farming which involves keeping animals indoors with very little space for each one, and giving them special foods so that they grow more quickly or produce more eggs or milk. N UNCOUNT

factory ship, factory ships. A **factory ship** is a large fishing boat which has equipment for processing the fish that are caught, for example by cleaning or freezing them, before it returns to port. N COUNT

factotum /fæktəʊtəⁿm/, **factotums**. A **factotum** is a servant who is employed to do a wide variety of jobs for someone; a formal word. N COUNT

fact sheet, fact sheets. A **fact sheet** is a piece of paper with information about a particular subject, especially a summary of information that has been given on a radio or television programme. EG *Write to this address for our fact sheet on National Savings certificates.* N COUNT ⇑ leaflet

factual /fæktʃʊⁿəl/. Something that is **factual** is concerned with facts or contains facts, rather than giving theories or personal interpretations. EG *The other speakers made factual, sober speeches... He could store in his mind an enormous amount of factual information... It is best to be as short, clear, and factual as possible.* ADJ CLASSIF = exact

faculty /fækəⁿltiˡ/, **faculties**. 1 A **faculty** is 1.1 the ability to do something that a normal, healthy person can, especially to see, hear, remember, or reason. EG *She was in full command of all her faculties... I kept my mental and critical faculties alive... ...the faculty of sensation.* N COUNT: USU PL = power 1.2 an ability which a particular person has. EG *...people who develop the faculty for looking at things in different ways.* N COUNT: IF + PREP THEN *for/of* = knack

2 In some universities or colleges, a **faculty** is a group of related departments. EG *...the head of the Law Faculty... He continued to haunt the corridors of the Faculty of Arts for some months... ...faculty parties.* N COUNT: ALSO IN NAMES ⇑ section ▸ The **faculty** is also used to refer to the staff who belong to it. EG *...the long row of chairs where the faculty sit.* ▸ N SING: *the* + N: IF SING, VB CAN BE SING OR PL

fad /fæd/, **fads**. A **fad** is something which a person or a group of people is very enthusiastic about, but with which they become bored very quickly. EG *The interest in things Japanese is not just a passing fad... ...the skateboard fad.* N COUNT ⇑ interest = craze

faddy /fædiˡ/, **faddier, faddiest**. Someone who is **faddy** has very strong likes and dislikes which you think are unreasonable; used showing disapproval. EG *He's rather faddy about his food.* ADJ QUALIT = fussy

fade /feɪd/, **fades, fading, faded**. 1 When a coloured object **fades** or when light **fades** it over a period of time, it gradually becomes paler in colour. EG *The wallpaper may have faded... How can I stop the sun from fading the carpet?... ...fading photographs.* V-ERG = discolour ◇ **faded**. EG *...an old man in a clean, faded, blue shirt... ...addresses written in faded ink.* ◇ ADJ QUALIT

2 When something that you are looking at **fades**, it slowly becomes less bright or clear until it disappears. EG *The ghostly figure fades... As the picture fades, a choir starts singing... Already the mountains are fading in the evening light.* V ⇑ disappear = melt away

3 A **fade** in a television programme or film is the slow disappearance of a particular picture on the screen, for example when the programme or film ends. EG *...a close-up fade against a stormy sky.* N COUNT

4 When the light **fades**, it slowly becomes darker, usually because the sun is going down. EG *We reached the cottage as the light was fading... I was trying to get a good look at him in the fading light.* V ⇑ decrease

5 When a sound or radio signal **fades**, it slowly becomes less loud or strong until you cannot hear or receive it. EG *The applause gradually faded.* V ⇑ disappear = die away

6 When something such as a feeling or a memory **fades**, it slowly becomes less great, intense, strong, or important, and might end completely. EG *My anger faded... Soon interest in the story will fade... This allows time for the memory of the last disaster to fade... The incident had faded from her mind... Britons refused to acknowledge their fading influence.* V ⇑ disappear = recede, dwindle ◇ **faded**. EG *...Europe's faded aristocracy.* ◇ ADJ CLASSIF

7 When someone's looks **fade** over a period of time, they gradually look older and more tired, although previously they had looked fresh and young. EG *Her looks had faded.* V ⇑ worsen = wither

8 When someone's smile **fades**, they slowly stop smiling. V ⇑ disappear

9 If someone **fades** somewhere, they quietly go there with the result that you can no longer see them. EG *He sensed Pavel fade back into the crowd again.* V + A ⇑ disappear = slip

10 If someone **is fading**, they are slowly dying; a rather literary use. EG *The king was fading fast.* V: USU CONT ⇑ die

fade away. 1 If someone **fades away** over a period of time, they become weaker and die. EG *He was fading quietly away day by day... She'd fade away and die, that's what she'd do.* PHRASAL VB: V + ADV = waste away

2 When something **fades away**, it slowly becomes less great, intense, strong, or important until it ends completely. EG *Your new-found enthusiasm for running will soon fade away... If the traditional English policeman faded away, I'd be very sorry... After ten or fifteen minutes the attack faded away.* PHRASAL VB: V + ADV = die out

fade in. When someone **fades in** a particular picture on television or in a film, or when they **fade in** a sound that is being broadcast or recorded, that picture or sound slowly becomes brighter or louder until it is able to be seen or heard. PHRASAL VB: V + O + ADV

fade out. 1 When something **fades out**, it slowly becomes less great, intense, strong, or important until it ends completely. EG *This sort of protest tends to fade out through its own foolishness.* PHRASAL VB: V + ADV = fizzle out

2 When a sound or radio signal **fades out**, it slowly becomes less loud or strong until you cannot hear it or receive it. EG *The sound of the chopper had faded out.* PHRASAL VB: V + ADV = die away

3 When someone **fades out** a particular picture on television or in a film, or **fades out** a sound that is being broadcast or recorded, that picture or sound slowly becomes less bright or loud until it is unable to be seen or heard. PHRASAL VB: V + O + ADV

faeces /fiːsiːz/; also spelled **feces** in American English. **Faeces** is the solid waste substance that people and animals get rid of from their body, for example when a person goes to the toilet; a formal or technical word. N UNCOUNT = excrement

faff about /fæf əbaʊt/, **faffs about, faffing about, faffed about.** If you say that someone is **faffing about** or **faffing around**, you mean that they are doing something in a very disorganized way or doing lots of unnecessary things and not really achieving very much; used in informal British English. EG *He's been faffing about all morning.* — PHRASAL VB : V+ADV = mess about

fag /fæg/, **fags, fagging, fagged.** 1 A **fag** is 1.1 in informal British English, a cigarette. EG *I just slipped out for a packet of fags.* — N COUNT 1.2 in very informal American English, a homosexual; an offensive use. — N COUNT
2 If you say that a particular task is a **fag**, you mean that it is boring or tiring and you do not really want to do it; an informal use. EG *You may find it a bit of a fag to dig up every weed.* — N SING : a+N, USED AS C ⇑ nuisance = pain
3 At some British public schools, a **fag** is a younger boy who has to do jobs for an older boy. EG *He was my fag at Eton.* — N COUNT ⇑ servant
4 A younger boy who **fags** for an older boy at a British public school has to do jobs for him. — V : IF+PREP THEN *for*
5 See also **fagged.**

fag end, fag ends; an informal expression, also spelled with a hyphen. 1 A **fag end** is the last bit of a cigarette, which people throw away when they have smoked the rest. — N COUNT = stub
2 The **fag end** of something is the last or worst part of it. EG *...the fag end of the day.* — N COUNT+*of*

fagged /fægd/. If someone is **fagged** or **fagged out**, they are very tired; used in very informal British English. EG *'You look fagged to death,' said Kate.* — ADJ QUALIT : PRED = knackered

faggot /fægət/, **faggots.** 1 In very informal American English, a **faggot** is a homosexual man; an offensive use. — N COUNT/VOC
2 In British English, **faggots** are balls of chopped meat, bread, and herbs which have been cooked. EG *...faggots and peas.* — N COUNT : USU PL
3 A **faggot** is also a bundle of sticks for burning as fuel on a fire; an old-fashioned use. — N COUNT

Fahrenheit /færənh⁰aɪt/. A temperature that is stated as a particular number of degrees **Fahrenheit** has been measured on a scale in which water freezes at 32 degrees and boils at 212 degrees. EG *The temperature won't drop below sixty-five degrees Fahrenheit... 'It's nine degrees Centigrade.'–'What's that in Fahrenheit?'* — N UNCOUNT : USU NUM+*degrees*+N ⇑ system

fail /feɪl/, **fails, failing, failed.** 1 If someone **fails** to achieve something that they were trying to achieve, or if their attempt **fails**, they do not succeed in doing it. EG *The England team failed to win a place in the finals... She failed in her attempt to swim to France... The attempt to bribe the clerk had failed... This technique seldom fails.* — V, OR V+*to*-INF ≠ succeed ◊ **failed.** EG *...a failed novelist.* — ◊ ADJ CLASSIF : ATTRIB
2 If someone **fails** a test or examination, they do not reach the standard that is required. EG *I failed my driving test twice... He failed the written paper... 'Did you pass?'–'No, I failed.'* — V OR V+O = flunk ≠ pass
3 If an examiner **fails** you in a test or examination, he or she decides that you have not reached the standard that is required. EG *One of the examiners wanted to fail him.* — V+O ≠ pass
4 A **fail** is a piece of work that is below the required standard in a test or examination. — N COUNT ≠ pass
5 If someone or something **fails** to do a particular thing that they should have done, they do not do it. EG *He had been fined five pounds for failing to complete a national census form... She had changed so much that he failed to recognize her... This never failed to annoy her.* — V+*to*-INF ⇑ omit ● You say **'I fail to see'** in order to introduce a statement which indicates that you do not agree with the point of what someone has just said. EG *I fail to see what that's got to do with it.* — ● PHR+REPORT-CL
6 **without fail.** 6.1 You say that something happens **without fail** when you want to emphasize that it always happens. EG *In the afternoon he would without fail take a nap lasting from two to four hours.* — PHR : USED AS AN A = religiously 6.2 You say that something will happen **without fail** when you want to emphasize that it will definitely happen. EG *I shall kill you, without fail, if you ever mention my visits here.* — PHR : USED AS AN A = for certain
7 If something **fails,** 7.1 it stops working properly or does not do what it is supposed to do. EG *Her lighter failed... The brakes failed and his car crashed into a tree... Their crops have failed again this year.* — V 7.2 it becomes unable to continue in operation or in existence. EG *Four local companies have failed this year.* — V = close down ◊ **failed.** EG *...his involvement in the failed New Orleans firm... ...a failed democracy.* — ◊ ADJ CLASSIF 7.3 it becomes less strong, great, or effective and might become completely useless. EG *They go and read to people whose sight is failing... He shouted orders until his voice failed... In a few hours the light would fail.* — V ⇑ weaken
8 When a supply of something **fails,** it runs out and there is no more of it that can be used. EG *You may find that the milk supply is failing rapidly and the baby is quite hungry... Ralph's breath failed and the horn fell silent.* — V = run out
9 If someone **fails** you, they do not do what you had expected or trusted them to do or what they have a duty to do for you. EG *Our leaders have failed us... You can trust me, sir. I've never failed you yet... She feels that she must have failed him somehow.* — V+O = let down
10 If someone **fails** in their duty, their responsibilities, etc, they do not do everything that they have a duty or a responsibility to do. EG *I would be failing in my duty to my family if I did not try to ensure their safety.* — V+A *(in)* = want
11 If a quality or ability that you have **fails** you or if it **fails**, it is not great or good enough in a particular situation to enable you to do what you need or want to do. EG *At the last minute his courage failed him... His usually inventive imagination had failed for once.* — V OR V+O = desert
12 If you say that **words fail** you, you mean that you are so surprised, shocked, or angry that you cannot think of anything to say. EG *Looking at them, words failed him.* — PHR : VB INFLECTS, USU+PRON

failing /feɪlɪŋ/, **failings.** 1 A **failing** is a fault or unsatisfactory feature. EG *The present system has many failings... Being rude was one of Cindy's failings.* — N COUNT = shortcoming
2 Something that is **failing** is becoming weaker or less effective, and is likely to end completely or become useless. EG *...failing marriages... He had given up acting because of failing health.* — ADJ CLASSIF : ATTRIB
3 You say **'failing that'** to introduce an alternative to what you have just said, in case what you said is not true or impossible. EG *Wear evening dress or, failing that, a suit.* — PREP ⇑ lacking

fail-safe. Something that is **fail-safe** is designed or made in such a way that nothing dangerous can happen if a part of it goes wrong. EG *...a fail-safe system.* — ADJ CLASSIF

failure /feɪljə/, **failures.** 1 **Failure** is a lack of success in doing or achieving something, or in a particular area of activity. EG *The attempt ended in failure... The break-up of his marriage left him with a vague feeling of failure... They seemed doomed to failure... These factors are crucial in determining the success or failure of this great experiment.* — N UNCOUNT ≠ success
2 A **failure** is an unsuccessful person, action, or thing. EG *The meeting was a failure... I felt such a failure.* — N COUNT = flop
3 Someone's **failure** to do a particular thing is the fact that they do not do it although you expected them to do it or think that they should have done it. EG *His friends remarked on his failure to appear at the party... ...his apparent failure to grasp this fact.* — N UNCOUNT/COUNT+*to*-INF ⇑ omission
4 When there is a **failure**, 4.1 something stops working or does not do what it is supposed to do. EG *...engine failure... My mother had heart failure... The storm caused a power failure... Crop failures are common.* — N UNCOUNT/COUNT+SUPP ⇑ deficiency 4.2 something is no longer able to continue in operation or in existence. EG *...the failure of the bank where he kept his money.* — N UNCOUNT/COUNT+SUPP = collapse
5 When there is a **failure** of a quality or ability that you have, you cannot do what you need or want to do because the quality or ability is not great or good enough. EG *...a sudden failure of nerve.* — N UNCOUNT/COUNT = loss

fain /feɪn/. If someone says that they would **fain** do something, they mean that they would like to do it; a very old-fashioned word. EG *The Prime Minister himself would fain wait upon him at breakfast.* — ADV : MODAL+ADV+INF ⇑ gladly

faint /feɪnt/, **fainter, faintest; faints, fainting, fainted.** 1 A sound, colour, feeling, idea, etc that is **faint** has very little strength or intensity. EG *Her voice had a faint American accent... ...a faint glow of pearl coloured light... There was a faint smell of gas... There was a faint feeling of unrest at the table... Her ears were alert for the faintest sound... Her cries grew fainter.* — ADJ QUALIT ⇑ weak = slight ◊ **faintness.** EG *The problem is exacerbated by the image's faintness.* — ◊ N UNCOUNT
2 A **faint** attempt at something is one that is done, made or performed without proper effort and with — ADJ QUALIT = half-hearted

little enthusiasm. EG *There were, at first, a few faint protests... It was the only faint attempt at a joke.*
3 If you **faint**, you lose consciousness for a short time, especially because of hunger, pain, heat, or shock. EG *He nearly fainted from the pain.* — V; ⇑ collapse = pass out
4 Someone who is **faint** is weak and unsteady as if they are about to lose consciousness. EG *He began to feel faint.* ◊ **faintness**. EG *...headaches, fits, faintness, and other related symptoms.* — ADJ QUALIT; ◊ N UNCOUNT
5 A **faint** is a temporary loss of consciousness. EG *She fell to the ground in a dead faint.* — N COUNT; ⇑ collapse

faintest /feɪntɪst/. You use **faintest** in negative statements such as 'I haven't the faintest idea', or 'you haven't got the faintest chance of winning', to emphasize that, for example, you have absolutely no idea what to do, or that someone has no chance at all of winning. EG *He simply didn't have the faintest idea what to do... She had not the faintest notion of what he was talking about... I never felt the faintest desire to cry.* — ADJ QUALIT: SUPERL, ONLY ATTRIB; = slightest, remotest

faint-hearted. If someone or their behaviour is **faint-hearted**, they are not very confident and do not try very hard because they are afraid of failing. EG *The picket was well-intentioned, but faint-hearted... It was a pretty faint-hearted attempt, if you ask me.* — ADJ QUALIT; = irresolute, feeble ≠ bold
▸ The **faint-hearted** is used to refer to people who are faint-hearted. EG *It is not recommended for the faint-hearted.* — ▸ N PLURAL: *the*+N; = squeamish

faintly /feɪntli[1]/. **1** You use **faintly** to reduce the effect of an adjective or a statement, by saying that it applies only to a very slight degree. EG *It was faintly possible... They were faintly amused... In the public mind, the clubs are faintly absurd.* — ADV+ADJ; ⇑ slightly = mildly
2 If someone does something or if something happens **faintly**, it happens with very little strength or intensity. EG *She turned and smiled faintly... The stars still glowed faintly in the sky.* — ADV WITH VB; = weakly

fair /fɛə/, **fairer, fairest; fairs**. **1** Something that is **fair** is reasonable according to a generally accepted standard or idea about what is right and just. EG *It wouldn't be fair to disturb the children's education at this stage... Ten pounds. I think that would be a fairer price... Be fair, darling. It's not their fault... This isn't fair on anyone, but it does happen... Does he do his fair share of the household chores?... That is a very fair point I think... In a very crude sense, it is fair to say that people who are geographically mobile probably achieve greater success in life.* — ADJ QUALIT
2 Someone or something that is **fair** gives the same or equal treatment to everyone concerned, especially without allowing personal feelings to influence judgements. EG *They are very fair, looking at problems from both sides before reaching any conclusions... Dr Kirk, you're not being either frank or fair: you know you don't like me... The trials accorded to them were fair... No judge, however fair-minded, was going to split up a pair of twins.* — ADJ QUALIT; ⇑ impartial = equitable, just
3 You use **fair enough** **3.1** when you want to say that a statement, decision, or action seems reasonable to a certain extent, but that perhaps there is more to be said or done. EG *All this is fair enough, but it touches only the surface of the problem.* — PHR: USED AS C OR ADV SEN; = true **3.2** when you want to acknowledge what someone has just said and to indicate that you understand it. EG *'Oh yes, just go ahead.'-'Fair enough. Right, thank you...' 'I've decided to scrap this plan.'-'Oh, fair enough.'* — CONVENTION; = okay
4 You say **fair's fair** when you want to suggest that it is reasonable and right that a particular action should happen. EG *Come on, fair's fair. He's always giving you lifts. Why don't you offer to take your car for once?* — CONVENTION; = be reasonable
5 When someone **plays fair**, they behave or act in a reasonable and honest way. EG *I think we can trust this company to play fair; not like the last one... Each country undertook to maintain the treaty and play fair by it.* ● See also **fair play**. — PHR: VB INFLECTS; ⇑ be honourable
6 You use the word **fair** in expressions such as **to be fair**, **I must be fair**, etc when you want to add a favourable comment about someone or something that you have just mentioned and to correct an unfair, unreasonable, or false impression that you might have given. EG *Last month there were over a thousand bankruptcies in the private sector. To be fair, by no means all of these were due to government policies.* — PHR USED AS ADV SEN
7 fair and square. **7.1** If you tell someone something **fair and square**, you say it in a clear, honest, and direct way. EG *He told me fair and square what the position was.* — PHR: USED AS AN A **7.2** If you hit something **fair and square**, you hit it directly, firmly, and in the middle. — PHR: USED AS AN A
8 A **fair** amount, degree, size, or distance is quite a large amount, degree, size, or distance. EG *He must have made a fair amount of money... It is necessary to have a fair degree of competence... We've got a fair number of postgraduate students... We have a fair size garden and we might as well make use of it... He was able to see a fair way.* — ADJ CLASSIF: ATTRIB; ⇑ great = considerable ≠ meagre
9 A **fair** guess, assessment, idea, etc is one that is likely to be correct. EG *I had a pretty fair idea of the answer to this question.* — ADJ QUALIT: ATTRIB; ⇑ good = shrewd
10 If you describe someone or something as **fair**, you mean that they are about average in standard or quality, neither very good nor very bad. EG *She was only a fair cook... It received fair to good reviews.* — ADJ CLASSIF; = indifferent
11 Someone who is **fair**, or who has **fair** hair, has light coloured hair. EG *My daughter has three children actually, and they're all fair... She had long fair hair... He was a slim, fair-haired boy.* — ADJ QUALIT; ⇑ blonde
12 Fair skin is very pale and usually burns easily in the sun. EG *The sun's rays can be very harmful, beating on unprotected fair skin.* — ADJ QUALIT
13 A person or place that is **fair** is attractive and rather beautiful; an old-fashioned use. EG *The fair lady of some brave knight of old... ...this fair city of ours.* — ADJ QUALIT; = lovely
14 When it is **fair**, the weather is pleasant, dry, and fine; used especially on barometer readings, shipping forecasts, etc. EG *It will be fair and warm... ...a fair mid-June evening.* — ADJ CLASSIF; ⇑ good
15 A **fair** is **15.1** in British English, a form of public entertainment held in a large open area. At fairs you can ride on various machines for amusement or try and win prizes in games of skill or luck. Fairs often travel from one town to another. — N COUNT: ALSO IN NAMES AFTER N; = funfair **15.2** a country market where animals and farm produce are displayed and sold. EG *My pig won first prize at Skipton Fair.* — N COUNT: ALSO IN NAMES AFTER N **15.3** the same as a fete. EG *...our local school fair... ...a village fair.* — N COUNT
16 A book **fair**, trade **fair**, etc is an exhibition of goods produced by a particular industry. A fair of this kind is usually held in a large building for a period of two or three days, and is intended mainly for the people involved with that industry and not for the general public. EG *The Leipzig Trade Fair.* — N COUNT: MOD+N, ALSO IN NAMES AFTER N

fair copy, fair copies. A **fair copy** of a piece of writing is a neat copy of it that has no mistakes or alterations. — N COUNT

fair game. If you say that someone is **fair game**, you mean that they have behaved so badly that you are justified in criticising them. — N UNCOUNT: USED AS C; ⇑ target

fairground /fɛəgraʊnd/, **fairgrounds**. A **fairground** is a large open area where a fair is being held, where you can ride on various machines for amusement or try and win prizes at games of skill or luck. — N COUNT; ⇑ site

fairly /fɛəli[1]/. **1 Fairly** means **1.1** to quite a large or reasonable degree. EG *The information was fairly accurate... I wrote the first part fairly quickly... It's fairly complicated... ...it's fairly heavy.* — ADV+ADJ/ADV; = pretty **1.2** to a very great degree or extent; a literary use. EG *The young children fairly flew up and down the rows of fruit, filling the baskets really quickly... One window fairly blazed in the late afternoon light.* — ADV WITH VB; ⇑ really = positively
2 You use **fairly** to say that something you say or do is reasonable according to generally accepted ideas about what is right or acceptable. EG *Ten years ago the typical diesel car could fairly have been described as sluggish and noisy.* — ADV WITH VB; ⇑ reasonably = justifiably
3 If you treat people **fairly** or if you do something **fairly**, you treat everyone equally and do not allow personal feelings to influence your judgement; used showing approval. EG *We want it to be fairly distributed.* — ADV WITH VB; = equally

fairness /fɛənəs/. **1 Fairness** is **1.1** the quality of being reasonable according to generally accepted ideas about what is right. EG *They question my fairness and competence in every possible way.* — N UNCOUNT **1.2** the quality of treating all people equally without allowing personal feelings to influence judgements. EG *There is not fairness for women in this country.* — N UNCOUNT; = justice
2 You use **fairness** in expressions such as **in fairness to, out of all fairness**, etc when you want to add a favourable comment about someone or something that you have just mentioned and to correct an — PHR: USED AS ADV SEN

unfair, unreasonable, or false impression that you might have given. EG *In fairness to the students it must be pointed out that they did work very hard on the project.... I think out of all fairness I should say that the majority behaved very well... It must be said in fairness that Frank played an important role in all this.*

fair play. Actions or decisions that are reasonable according to a generally accepted feeling or belief about what is right are referred to as **fair play**. EG *They appealed to his sense of fair play and common justice.* N UNCOUNT ⇑ justice

fair sex. If you talk about the **fair sex**, you are referring to women in general; an old-fashioned or humorous expression. N SING : *the*+N

fairway /fɛəweɪ/, **fairways**. The **fairway** on a golf course is the long strip of short grass between every tee and green; a technical term. N COUNT : USU *the*+N

fair-weather. You use **fair-weather** to refer to someone who takes part in a particular activity or offers help to someone only when it is easy or pleasant for them to do so; used showing disapproval. EG *A fair-weather friend... A fair-weather sailor.* ADJ CLASSIF : ATTRIB ≠ staunch, reliable

fairy /fɛəri^{1}/, **fairies**. **1** A **fairy** is an imaginary creature in children's stories and folk tales. Fairies are imagined as tiny, delicate women or girls, often with wings, who have magical powers. N COUNT = sprite

2 In very informal English, a **fairy** is a male homosexual; an offensive term. N COUNT/VOC

fairyland /fɛəri^{1}lænd/, **fairylands**. **1 Fairyland** is the imaginary place where fairies live. N UNCOUNT

2 If you describe a place as a **fairyland**, you mean that it has a delicate beauty. EG *By night, the scene is a brilliant fairyland of blazing neon lights.* N COUNT : USU SING = wonderland

fairy lights are small, coloured electric lights that are hung up as decorations, for example on a Christmas tree. N PLURAL

fairy tale, **fairy tales**; also spelled with a hyphen. A **fairy tale** or **fairy story** is **1** a story, usually for children, in which magical things happen because some of the characters are fairies or other imaginary people. N COUNT **2** a story or explanation which is not true and which is told in order to deceive someone. EG *Better to tell the truth, rather than tell a fairy story and have to change it later.* N COUNT ⇑ untruth = tall story

fait accompli /feɪt ɔ^{3}kɔ^{8}mpliː/, **faits accomplis**. Something that is a **fait accompli** has already been done and cannot be changed, however much you want to change it; a formal expression. EG *The development could be kept secret until it was a fait accompli, after which it would not matter... I was presented with a fait accompli.* N COUNT : USU SING ⇑ fact

faith /feɪθ/, **faiths**. **1** If you have **faith** in someone or something, you have a strong feeling of confidence, trust, and optimism about that person or thing. EG *I had faith in Al–I knew he could take care of me... You're destroying all my faith in the medical profession... The experience gave me faith that people can change... I've got faith in human nature.* N UNCOUNT+*in*/REPORT-CL

2 A **faith** is a particular religion such as Christianity, Buddhism, Islam, etc. EG *...prejudice against a minority with a different faith... His children were raised in the Catholic faith... ...clergymen of many faiths.* N COUNT : USU+SUPP ⇑ belief

3 Faith is also a strong religious belief in a particular God. EG *She had deep religious faith... Christians who have lost their faith may still observe certain rules of Christian morality.* N UNCOUNT

4 If someone breaks **faith** with a belief, ideal, or organization that they support, they stop acting in a way that supports that belief, ideal, or organization. If they keep **faith** with it, they continue to support it even when it is difficult for them to do so. EG *They chose to break faith with millions of decent, proud, hard working citizens... You must keep faith and show no shame.* N UNCOUNT = loyalty

5 If you do something in **good faith**, your reasons for doing it are honest and sincere and you do not intend to harm anyone. EG *The two doctors were acting in good faith, the law insisted... Accusations were made as to the good faith of many involved.* N UNCOUNT : USU *in*+N ⇑ honesty

faithful /feɪθfʊl/, **faithfuls**. **1** Someone who is **faithful** to a person, organization, or idea remains firm in their support for that person, organization, or idea. EG *He was awarded a medal as a mark of merit for long and faithful service... We do not doubt that England has a faithful patriot in the Lord Chancellor.* ADJ QUALIT ⇑ supportive = loyal, steadfast ≠ disloyal

◇ **faithfully**. EG *The party rallied round him faithfully.* ◇ ADV WITH VB = loyally

2 The **faithful** or **faithfuls** are people who remain firm in their support for a political party, an organization, an idea, etc. EG *Rumours that were already causing stirrings among the faithful... He sat with thousands of party faithfuls on wooden stands facing the White House... The small cluster of fans were mostly old hockey faithfuls.* N COUNT : USU *the*/MOD+N, SING=PL ⇑ supporter = stalwart

3 The **faithful** are also the group of people who believe in a particular religion. EG *The bishop was condemned because he had led the faithful astray.* N PLURAL : *the*+N ⇑ believers

4 Someone who is **faithful** to their lover or to the person they are married to remains loyal to them by not having a sexual relationship with anyone else. EG *He would never be faithful to you if you married him... Like the faithful wife she was, she did not stay but went straight home.* ◇ **faithfulness**. EG *Rumour had it that she was no model of faithfulness.* ADJ CLASSIF : IF+PREP THEN *to* ≠ unfaithful ◇ N UNCOUNT = fidelity

5 An account or a work of art which is **faithful** to reality or to the original work is one which accurately represents the facts or the original version of the work. EG *Do you think the film adaptation was faithful to the book?... He gave a faithful rendering of the poem.* ◇ **faithfully**. EG *Their slightest move was faithfully described in newspapers and magazines.* ADJ QUALIT : IF+PREP THEN *to* ⇑ accurate = true ◇ ADV WITH VB

6 A **faithful** animal, friend, car, etc is one that you have known or had for a long time and that you can rely on. EG *I drove back to town in that old faithful car of mine... Sometimes Larry and his mates romped with their faithful dogs.* ADJ CLASSIF : ATTRIB ⇑ reliable = trusty

7 You can also use **faithful** to describe someone who does something regularly with dedication or determination. EG *She was a faithful listener to the programme.* ◇ **faithfully**. EG *She practised her part faithfully... This is the tight money policy faithfully pursued by the Federal Reserve Board.* ADJ CLASSIF : ATTRIB ⇑ dedicated = steadfast ◇ ADV WITH VB = steadfastly

faithfully /feɪθfə^{4}li^{1}/. **1** You write **Yours faithfully** before your signature at the end of a formal or business letter when you have started the letter 'Dear Sir' or 'Dear Madam' and have not used the person's name. EG *Yours faithfully, Pamela Brown.* CONVENTION+N PROPER

2 Other meanings of **faithfully** can be found in the entry for **faithful**.

faith healing; also spelled with a hyphen. **Faith healing** is the treatment of a sick person by someone who believes they are able to heal people through prayer and the power of religious faith. N UNCOUNT ⇑ treatment

faithless /feɪθlɪ^{2}s/. Someone who is **faithless** is disloyal or dishonest. EG *The friend had turned out to be faithless.* ADJ CLASSIF = false

fake /feɪk/, **fakes, faking, faked**. **1** A **fake** is something that is not genuine, but that has been made in order to trick people into thinking that it is genuine, or that it is rarer or more valuable than it really is. EG *They swore that the pictures were fakes.* ▸ used as an adjective. EG *His house is full of fake antiques... ...a fake passport.* N COUNT ⇑ reproduction = forgery ▸ ADJ CLASSIF = phoney

2 If someone **fakes** something, they try to make it in such a way that it appears to be valuable, rare, or genuine, although in fact it is not. EG *They did nothing else but apply themselves to faking the fine furniture of the century before... ...two classified documents that contained the faked reports.* V+O ⇑ reproduce

3 Someone who is a **fake** is not what they claim to be, for example by not having the qualifications that they claim to have. EG *Better to give up and admit I'm a fake.* N COUNT ⇑ pretender = impostor

4 If you **fake** a feeling, emotion, or reaction, you pretend that you are experiencing it when you are not. EG *Thomas faked a yawn and stretched... ...real or faked suffering.* V+O = feign

falcon /fɔːl^{0}kən/, **falcons**. A **falcon** is a bird of prey that can be trained to hunt other birds and animals. There are several kinds of falcon. N COUNT

falconer /fɔːl^{0}kənə/, **falconers**. A **falconer** is someone who trains and uses falcons for hunting. N COUNT ⇑ trainer

falconry /fɔːl^{0}kənri^{1}/ is the skill of training falcons to hunt, and the sport of using them to hunt. N UNCOUNT

fall /fɔːl/, **falls, falling, fell, fallen**. **1** If someone or something **falls**, they suddenly move downwards onto or towards the ground, especially by accident. EG *If he tried to move, he would fall off the stool... ...table napkins that had fallen to the floor... The china fell from her hand and shattered on the floor... Large masses of rock are constantly falling into the sea... ...the occasional crash of falling mason-* V : USU+A ry... *Tears fell from Mother's eyes... He raised his arms in a helpless gesture and let them fall again to his sides.* ▸ used as a noun. EG *He was rushed to hospital after a 40-foot fall... ...paying no heed to the steady fall of his tears.* ▸ N COUNT ⇑ drop

2 If someone or something **falls** after they have been in an upright or standing position, they become unbalanced, with the result that they drop to the ground and end up lying lengthways or in a heap. EG *She lost her balance and would have fallen if she hadn't supported herself... It was shattered by a falling tree.* ▸ used as a noun. EG *He asked her if she had had a fall.. He had a nasty fall on the way out of the supermarket.* ◊ **fallen**. EG *Ralph sat on a fallen trunk... The hyenas leapt on the fallen zebra.* V = topple ▸ N COUNT : USU SING ◊ ADJ CLASSIF : ATTRIB

3 If a building, bridge, or other structure **falls**, it collapses onto the ground because it has been damaged. EG *They were waiting for the bridge to fall.* ◊ **fallen**. EG *No attempt could be made to rescue people trapped inside the fallen buildings.* V = collapse ◊ ADJ CLASSIF : ATTRIB

4 When rain, snow, etc **falls**, it comes down from the sky. EG *A light drizzle began to fall... Five inches of snow had fallen... Big drops of rain fell.* V ⇑ descend

5 A **fall** of snow, soot, or another substance is a large amount of it that has fallen to the ground. EG *A heavy fall of snow last night has blocked many minor roads... There has been a fall of soot, indicating that the chimney needs sweeping.* N COUNT : USU+SUPP

6 If a blow or a weapon **falls** somewhere, it lands on or hits that place. EG *Tom moved in and let the blow fall on his left shoulder.* V : IF+PREP THEN *on* ⇑ hit = land

7 If you say that something long such as clothes or hair **is falling** to the ground, or to someone's shoulders, etc, you mean that it is hanging downwards towards the point mentioned. EG *His wavy, reddish hair falls to his shoulders.* V : USU+A ⇑ hang = cascade

8 The **fall** of something long such as a piece of clothing or a curtain is the way that it hangs. N SING WITH DET : USU+*of*

9 If something **falls** open, it opens accidentally. EG *Her housecoat kept falling open... The book fell open at the chapter on farming.* V+A

10 If you **fall** into or out of somewhere, you move there hurriedly and in a disorganized or rough way. EG *...the crush of humanity that falls out of the opening doors... She eventually got home and fell into bed.* V+A = tumble

11 When someone in a position of authority or power **falls**, they are suddenly removed from their position. EG *The regime had fallen.* ▸ used as a noun. EG *...a debate which led to the Government's fall... ...the rise and fall of the Roman Empire.* V = topple ▸ N SING WITH DET : WITH POSS ⇑ collapse

12 If a place, group, or organization **falls**, it is captured or taken over by someone else, and passes into their control. EG *Greater London will fall to Labour with a swing of only 2.8%... The city fell after a siege lasting three months.* ▸ used as a noun. EG *...the fall of the Bastille.* V ⇑ be taken ▸ N SING WITH DET : WITH POSS

13 If someone **falls** in battle or as a result of disease, they are killed; a literary use. EG *...the brave young men who have fallen in the struggle... After a few days, yet more began to fall of hunger and exhaustion.* V : USU+A ⇑ die = perish

14 If an idea, claim, or attempt **falls**, it is proved to be useless or ineffective. EG *But the air effort stood or fell on the retention of secure bases... All religion stands or falls on the claim that divine reality cannot be experienced by man.* V : USU+A ⇑ fail ≠ stand

15 If barriers or feelings of awkwardness between people **fall**, people allow themselves to become more open or honest about their feelings. EG *The barriers fell and we could see the fear in his eyes.* V = drop

16 If someone's guard **falls**, the care with which they have been defending or protecting themselves fails for a short period of time and they become weaker against attack. EG *My guard fell for a second, and he smacked me in the jaw.* V = drop

17 If something **falls** in amount, quantity, value, or strength, it diminishes and becomes less or weaker. EG *The value of the dollar has fallen... Oil consumption in the region fell by 24%... Living standards were falling... ...aircrew strength had fallen very low... The wind rises and then falls as the storm passes by.* ▸ used as a noun. EG *...a 3 per cent fall in industrial output... ...a fall in moral standards.* ◊ **falling**. EG *Nations were uneasy about their falling birth rates.* V ⇑ decrease = drop ▸ N COUNT : USU SING+*in* ◊ ADJ CLASSIF = dwindling

18 When a sound **falls**, it becomes quieter or lower in pitch. EG *Their voices could be heard rising and falling even before they appeared.* V

19 If words or sounds **fall** from someone's lips or mouth, they are spoken by this person; a literary use. EG *What words had fallen from the lips of Mr Smythe?* V+A *(from)* = issue

20 If silence, sadness, fear, etc **falls** on a group of people, they become silent, sad, afraid, etc. EG *A hush would fall among the villagers as they sat around the fire... All of these ills have fallen upon us.* V : USU+A = descend

21 When light or shadow **falls** on an object, place, or area, it covers it. EG *A ray of light from the corridor fell across the floor... A shadow fell over her book and she looked up.* V+A ⇑ cover

22 When night or darkness **falls**, night begins and it becomes dark. EG *We settled down to wait until darkness fell.* V ⇑ occur

23 The **fall** of night is the time when night begins; a rather literary use. N SING : *the*+N+*of*

24 When someone **falls** asleep, ill, in love, or into some other state, they pass into the particular state or condition mentioned. EG *After a while I fell asleep... They'd met at university and fallen in love... Their ideas had simply fallen into disuse and been forgotten... Doctor Percival had fallen silent... He has fallen a victim to hysterical exhaustion.* V+C/A ⇑ become

25 If something **falls** into a particular classification, grouping, or area of consideration, it is classified, grouped, or considered in this way. EG *My work really falls into three parts... The present case falls outside our jurisdiction... Most decision making falls in the grey area between these two extremes.* V+A = come

26 If a celebration or other special event **falls** on a particular day or date, it occurs on that day or date. EG *This year Easter Day falls on March 30th.* V+A = be

27 The **fall** of events is the way that things happen, especially when they seem to happen by chance. EG *...events caused by thoughts and emotions, not by the chance fall of symbols... ...the fall of the dice.* N SING

28 According to the Bible, the **fall** was the occasion when Adam and Eve sinned and God made them leave the Garden of Eden. EG *...the fall of man... ...Adam before the fall.* N PROPER : *the*+N, IF+PREP THEN *of*

29 You can refer to a waterfall as the **falls**. EG *They went fishing below the falls and caught half a dozen trout... ...Niagara Falls.* N PLURAL, ALSO IN NAMES

30 In American English, the **fall** is the autumn. EG *...two years later, in the fall of 1941.* N COUNT : USU *the*+N IN SING

31 A **fall** in judo is the act of throwing your opponent to the floor. N COUNT

32 A **fall** in wrestling is the act of forcing your opponent's back to the floor and holding it there. EG *He had won by a single fall.* N COUNT

33 When a wicket **falls** in cricket, the fielding team get a batsman out. V = go

34 The word fall is also used in the following expressions. **34.1** If something **falls to bits** or **falls to pieces**, it is so old or damaged that it gradually breaks into different parts. EG *The boots issued to them had all fallen to bits by the end of the year.* PHR : VB INFLECTS = disintegrate

34.2 If someone's **face falls**, they suddenly look upset or disappointed. EG *His face fell at the news... ...a ring of fallen faces.* PHR : N AND VB INFLECT **34.3** If you **fall at** someone's **feet**, you kneel in front of them, perhaps in order to express great respect for them or to ask them for forgiveness. EG *He falls at her feet to beg her forgiveness.* PHR : VB INFLECTS

34.4 If someone or something **falls into** the **hands** or **clutches** of someone else, they are captured or become controlled or owned by that person. EG *The party was falling into the hands of extremists... Cottage after cottage falls into the hands of retired Londoners.* PHR : VB INFLECTS **34.5** If someone **falls to** their **knees**, they suddenly kneel down, especially to express great respect or repentance or because they are afraid. EG *The crowd outside fell to their knees.* PHR : VB INFLECTS

35 The word **fall** is also used in the following expressions, which are explained at other places in this dictionary. • to **fall flat**: see **flat**. • to **fall on** your **feet**: see **foot**. • to **fall foul of** someone: see **foul**. • to **fall off the back of a lorry**: see **lorry**. • to **fall into place**: see **place**. • to **fall short**: see **short**. • to **fall into step**: see **step**. • to **fall by the wayside**: see **wayside**.

36 See also **fallen**.

fall about. If you say that people **are falling about**, you mean that they are very amused by something; PHRASAL VB : V+ADV an informal expression. EG *When he complained that it was unfair, they fell about laughing.*

fall apart. 1 If something **falls apart**, it breaks into pieces, usually because it is weak, old, or badly made. EG *Clothing which lasts a little while and then falls apart... Fragile materials that simply fall apart after a short time.* PHRASAL VB : V+ ADV = disintegrate

2 If an organization or system **falls apart**, it becomes disorganized and unable to work effectively. EG *The conference fell apart when the President refused to participate... The nation is falling apart.* PHRASAL VB : V+ ADV = collapse

3 If you say that someone is **falling apart**, you mean that they are becoming emotionally disturbed and are unable to think normally and calmly because they are in such a difficult or unpleasant situation; an informal expression. EG *It was something to do, it kept you from falling apart.* PHRASAL VB : V+ ADV = go to pieces

fall away. 1 If something **falls away** from a surface which it has been attached to, it breaks off and becomes unattached. EG *Patches of plaster had fallen away between the windows.* PHRASAL VB : V+ ADV, USU+PREP = fall off

2 Where land **falls away** it slopes gently downwards. EG *I got to the ridge expecting to see a gentle slope falling away in front of me.* PHRASAL VB : V+ ADV ⇑ slope

3 If a quality or type of behaviour **falls away** from someone, they no longer have that quality or behave in that way. EG *His film star affectations had fallen away... Paradise, where all their earthly infirmities would fall away.* PHRASAL VB : V+ ADV ⇑ disappear

4 If the degree, amount, or rate of something **falls away**, it diminishes and becomes less or smaller. EG *During the general strike, the party's membership fell away.* PHRASAL VB : V+ ADV = fall off

fall back. 1 If an army **falls back** during a battle or war, it retreats. EG *They fell back in confusion, surprised by the direction of attack.* PHRASAL VB : V+ ADV ⇑ withdraw = retreat

2 If you **fall back**, you move quickly away from someone because they have upset or frightened you. EG *I watched him fall back in horror.* PHRASAL VB : V+ ADV, USU+*in*+N UNCOUNT

fall back on. If you **fall back on** a particular solution or way of doing something, you choose it because it is easy, obvious, or safe, although it is not necessarily the best. EG *He invariably falls back on sentimental clichés about peace and 'nature'... Often you give up and fall back on easier solutions.* PHRASAL VB : V+ ADV+PREP = resort to

fall behind. 1 If you **fall behind** when you are moving with a group of other people, you start to move more slowly than they do, so that everyone else gets further and further ahead of you. EG *He began to limp and fell so far behind that the Captain decided to let him rest.* PHRASAL VB : V+ ADV = lag, trail

2 If someone or something **falls behind**, they do not achieve the standard of success or effectiveness that was expected of them or that is achieved by other people or similar things. EG *...children who fall behind with their reading.* PHRASAL VB : V+ ADV ⇑ fail

3 If a process **falls behind** or if you **fall behind**, the process is not completed, or you do not produce something when it is due. EG *The programme had fallen so far behind that there was little chance of meeting the deadline... Unfortunately, we have fallen behind with the payments.* PHRASAL VB : V+ ADV

fall down. 1 If someone or something **falls down** when they have been in an upright or standing position, they become unbalanced and drop to the ground. EG *He tripped and fell down.* PHRASAL VB : V+ ADV ⇑ fall = fall over

2 If something such as a building or bridge **falls down,** it collapses to the ground and breaks into pieces because it is old, weak, or damaged. EG *That shelter might fall down if the rain comes back.* PHRASAL VB : V+ ADV = collapse

3 If you say that a building is **falling down**, you mean that it is in a very bad condition and is in danger of collapsing. EG *The house was cheap because it was falling down.* PHRASAL VB : V (-ING)+ADV

4 An idea, argument, etc **falls down** when there is a weakness in it which becomes evident in a particular situation. EG *In one area only did the comparison fall down... In that particular instance the argument falls down.* PHRASAL VB : V+ ADV ⇑ fail ≠ work

fall for; used in informal English. 1 If you **fall for** someone, you are strongly attracted to them and start loving them. EG *He fell for her the moment he set eyes on her... ...masculine types that women traditionally fall for.* PHRASAL VB : V+ PREP ⇑ desire

2 If you **fall for** something that is not true, you are tricked into believing it. EG *The working class were not going to fall for this one.* PHRASAL VB : V+ PREP, HAS PASS = swallow

fall in. 1 If something such as a roof or ceiling **falls in**, it collapses and falls to the ground. EG *The roof of the house was about to fall in.* PHRASAL VB : V+ ADV = cave in

2 If soldiers, scouts, or other people in a procession **fall in**, they get into a line one behind the other. EG *Pick up your gear and fall in... As he began to march around the lawn, people fell in behind him.* PHRASAL VB : V+ ADV ⇑ follow = line up

fall into. 1 If you **fall into** discussion, conversation, or an argument etc with someone, you start talking or arguing etc with them. EG *We fell into conversation as the train pulled out of the station.* PHRASAL VB : V+ PREP = get into

2 If you **fall into** a particular mood or way of behaving, you get into that mood or start behaving in that way. EG *He fell into that strange mood of speculation.* PHRASAL VB : V+ PREP = lapse into

fall in with. If you **fall in with** an idea, plan, system, etc, you accept it and do not try to change it. EG *I didn't know quite how to deal with that remark except to fall in with it.* PHRASAL VB : V+ ADV+PREP = go along with

fall off. 1 If something **falls off** the surface to which it was attached, it becomes loose and separates from that surface. EG *At this stage their scales fall off.* PHRASAL VB : V+ ADV/PREP ⇑ drop

2 If the degree, amount, or rate of something **falls off**, it diminishes and becomes less or smaller. EG *The flow of western capital is falling off just when it is most needed... We knew that the numbers of overseas students would fall off drastically.* • See also **falling-off.** PHRASAL VB : V+ ADV ⇑ decrease = fall away

fall on or **fall upon.** 1 If something **falls on** someone or something, it comes down accidentally from a higher position onto them, often causing injury or damage. EG *I just opened the cupboard and they fell on my head.* PHRASAL VB : V+ PREP

2 If something unpleasant **falls on** someone, it happens to them; a literary use. EG *All of these ills have fallen upon us.* PHRASAL VB : V+ PREP, HAS PASS

3 If a responsibility or duty **falls on** someone, it becomes their responsibility or duty. EG *It would fall on her to make the final decision.* PHRASAL VB : V+ PREP = fall to

4 If someone **falls on you,** they hug you and embrace you eagerly and joyfully because they are very happy or excited. EG *People were falling on each other in delight and tears.* PHRASAL VB : V+ PREP = seize

5 If someone who is attacking you **falls on** you, he or she attacks you suddenly and violently. EG *Terrorist groups were falling indiscriminately upon men and women in the street.* PHRASAL VB : V+ PREP ⇑ attack = set upon

6 If your eyes **fall on** someone or something, you see or notice them. EG *His gaze fell on a small white bundle... His eyes fell on Laing, who was hunched in a corner.* PHRASAL VB : V+ PREP = light on

fall out. 1 If something such as hair or a tooth **falls out**, it becomes loose and separates from your body. EG *After about two weeks, the victim's hair starts to fall out.* PHRASAL VB : V+ ADV ⇑ loosen

2 If something **falls out** of a container, it drops from there onto the ground, usually by accident. EG *It must have fallen out when I opened my bag at the bus stop.* PHRASAL VB : V+ ADV

3 If you **fall out** with someone, you have an argument and stop being friendly with them. EG *I've fallen out with certain members of the band... Everybody stands to lose if the partners fall out.* PHRASAL VB : V+ ADV, OR V+ADV +A (*with*) : RECIP ⇑ disagree

4 When soldiers or people in a parade or formation **fall out**, they leave their positions and the formation is broken up. EG *The men fell out.* PHRASAL VB : V+ ADV ⇑ disperse

5 See also **fallout.**

fall over. 1 If someone or something **falls over** from an upright or standing position, they become unbalanced and fall to the ground, lying lengthways or in a heap. EG *He pushed back his chair so hard that it fell over.* PHRASAL VB : V+ ADV = topple over

2 If you **are falling over** yourself to do something, you are very keen to do it; an informal expression. EG *Producers were falling over themselves to hire girls who had acting experience... Governments are falling over each other to win valuable export contracts.* PHR+0 (REFL/ NG)+*to*-INF ⇑ rush

fall through. If an arrangement, plan, deal, etc **falls through**, it fails or is unsuccessful before it can be completed. EG *We arranged to book a villa and it fell through... Any number of things could lead to a sale falling through.* PHRASAL VB : V+ ADV ⇑ fail ≠ come off

fall to. 1 If a responsibility or duty **falls to** someone, it becomes their responsibility or duty. EG *That task fell to Mrs Isabel Travers... It fell to Philip Crow to act the part of host.* PHRASAL VB : V+ PREP = fall on

2 If someone **falls to** doing something, they start doing it, although it is not a very sensible thing for them to be doing. EG *The party fell instead to blaming the voters.* PHRASAL VB: V+PREP, USU-ING = begin

fall upon. See **fall on.**

fallacious /fəleɪʃəs/. If an idea, argument, or reason is **fallacious**, it is wrong because it is based on a fallacy; a formal word. EG *This point of view is exposed as fallacious in her new book.* ADJ CLASSIF ⇑ erroneous

fallacy /fæləsi[1]/, **fallacies**; a formal word. A **fallacy** is **1** an idea which many people believe to be true but which is in fact false because it is based on incorrect information or faulty reasoning. EG *...a complex mass of facts, fallacies and emotive opinions... It is a total fallacy that painters inspire other painters.* N COUNT ⇑ error = misconception **2** a weakness and lack of logic or good sense in an argument or piece of reasoning. EG *There are logical fallacies in the information they are all absorbing... Mrs Lennon unwittingly touched upon the fallacy in the argument.* N COUNT/UNCOUNT = flaw

fallen /fɔːlən/. **1 Fallen** is the past participle of **fall.**

2 The **fallen** are soldiers who have died in battle; a fairly literary expression. N PLURAL: *the*+N

3 Some people use **fallen** to describe people or angels after the time when they sinned and were punished by God; an old-fashioned, literary, or religious use. EG *...Satan and his fallen angels... ...fallen man.* ADJ CLASSIF: ATTRIB ≠ holy, saintly

4 A **fallen** woman is considered to have lost her respectability and virtue because she has had sex with someone who she is not married to; an old-fashioned term. ADJ CLASSIF: ATTRIB ⇑ immoral ≠ virtuous

5 Other meanings of **fallen** can be found in the entry for **fall.**

fallen arches. If you have **fallen arches,** the hollow part at the bottom of each of your feet has become flat and does not support the rest of your foot properly when you walk. N PLURAL

fall guy, fall guys. A **fall guy** is someone who has been tricked by another person and used by them so that the other person could get something deceitfully; an informal expression. N COUNT = sucker

fallible /fælɪbə[0]l/; a formal word. **1** If you say that someone is **fallible**, you mean that their judgement or knowledge is not perfect and they may make mistakes. EG *He was only human, fallible, might have misjudged her.* ◇ **fallibility** /fælɪbɪlɪti[1]/. EG *...human fallibility.* ADJ QUALIT ≠ infallible ◇ N UNCOUNT

2 If you say that something is **fallible**, you mean that it is not perfect and it may be wrong. EG *...human memory being as fallible as it is... It is a very fallible method.* ◇ **fallibility.** ADJ QUALIT ≠ infallible ◇ N UNCOUNT

falling-off. If there is a **falling-off** of an activity, there is a decrease in the amount or intensity of it. EG *There was a definite falling-off of active interest... A falling-off in business was expected.* N SING WITH DET: IF+PREP THEN *of/in* = decline

falling star, falling stars. A **falling star** is the same as a meteor. N COUNT

fallopian tube /fələʊpɪən tjuːb/, **fallopian tubes.** A woman's **fallopian tubes** are the pair of tubes in her body along which eggs pass from her ovaries to her uterus. N COUNT

fallout /fɔːlaʊt/ is the radiation that affects a particular place or area after a nuclear explosion has taken place. EG *Exposure to radioactive fallout would be much worse than previously anticipated.* N UNCOUNT

fallow /fæləʊ/. **1 Fallow** land, or land that has been left **fallow**, has been dug or ploughed but nothing has been sown or planted in it, so that its quality or strength has a chance to improve. ADJ CLASSIF ⇑ unused

2 A **fallow** period is a time when not very much is being achieved. EG *They have their creative and their fallow times.* ADJ CLASSIF: USU ATTRIB ⇑ inactive

fallow deer; the form **fallow deer** is used for both the singular and the plural. A **fallow deer** is a small deer that has a reddish coat which develops white spots in summer. N COUNT

false /fɒls, fɔːls/, **falser, falsest. 1** If a statement is **false**, it is not true. For example, the statement '2+2=5' is false. EG *The statement may be true or false... What you're saying is false... The accusation is false and unjust.* ◇ **falsely.** EG *Other Ministers are being accused quite falsely of licentious behaviour.* ADJ CLASSIF = wrong ≠ true ◇ ADV WITH VB

2 If something such as an idea, impression, or action is **false**, it is mistaken or based on a wrong belief or understanding. EG *Perhaps this assumption is false... I picked up a false impression of him right away... ...wrongful arrest and false imprisonment.* ADJ CLASSIF = wrong ≠ right, true

3 If something is **false**, **3.1** it is not real or genuine, but it is intended to seem real. EG *...false teeth... When the architect started to reconstruct the building, a false wall was discovered in the wine cellar... She travelled under a false name.* ADJ CLASSIF: USU ATTRIB ≠ real **3.2** it is not sincere and is intended to deceive; used showing disapproval. EG *...their false promises.* ● **under false pretences**: see **pretence.** ADJ CLASSIF: USU ATTRIB = deceitful ≠ true

4 If someone is **false**, **4.1** their character or general behaviour is insincere and deceitful. EG *She wants to convince herself that I'm false and fake.* ADJ QUALIT ⇑ dishonest **4.2** they pretend to have particular feelings and attitudes, usually in such an obvious way that people notice the pretence; used showing disapproval. EG *He's very false.* ▸ used of people's behaviour. EG *Her voice sounded prissy and false.* ◇ **falsely.** EG *Her voice was falsely bright.* ◇ **falseness.** EG *He could have detected any falseness on her part.* ADJ QUALIT = affected, insincere ≠ genuine, sincere ◇ ADV ◇ N UNCOUNT **4.3** they are unfaithful or disloyal, especially to a lover or friend; used showing disapproval. EG *What a false friend she turned out to be.* ADJ CLASSIF ≠ true **4.4** If you **are false to** someone or something, you betray them; used showing disapproval. EG *They have not been true to themselves, and therefore they are false to everyone else.* PHR: VB INFLECTS ≠ be true to

false alarm, false alarms. A **false alarm** is a situation where you think something dangerous is about to happen, but then discover that you were mistaken, for example when a fire alarm goes off by accident. EG *We've had more trouble with false alarms than actual arson... They think it was all some kind of false alarm.* N COUNT

falsehood /fɒlshʊd, fɔːl-/, **falsehoods. 1 Falsehood** is the quality or fact of being untrue or of being a lie. EG *She needs to learn what truth means and how it differs from falsehood and fabrication... The Inquiry was set up to establish the truth or falsehood of the various rumours and reports.* N UNCOUNT ⇑ untruth ≠ truth

2 A **falsehood** is a lie; a formal use. EG *There is more to dishonesty than uttering falsehoods.* N COUNT = untruth

false move, false moves. A **false move** is an action or movement which turns out to be a mistake and which can put you in a position of great risk or danger. EG *Barbara soon realized that this was a false move... One false move, and I might have slipped two hundred feet.* N COUNT: USU SING

false start, false starts. A **false start** is **1** an attempt to start something, such as a speech, project, or plan, which fails because you were not properly prepared or ready to begin. EG *After a few false starts, we managed to get the company off the ground... ...natural speech with all its hesitations, false starts, and coughs.* N COUNT **2** a beginning of a race when one competitor moves before the starter has given the signal. EG *They finally got under way after three false starts.* N COUNT

falsetto /fɒlsetəʊ/, **falsettos.** A **falsetto** is a high-pitched singing or speaking voice that is higher than a person's normal voice. EG *I heard him singing in a clear, high falsetto... ...a high falsetto whine.* N COUNT

falsify /fɒlsɪfaɪ, fɔːl-/, **falsifies, falsifying, falsified.** If you **falsify** something, you change it, add details to it that are not true, or misrepresent it in order to deceive people. EG *He had taken part in falsifying some official documents... The same name will be on the document, but with the personal details falsified.* ◇ **falsification** /fɒlsɪfɪkeɪʃə[0]n, fɔːl-/, **falsifications.** EG *The falsification of the records has now been exposed.* V+O ◇ N COUNT/UNCOUNT

falsity /fɒlsɪti[1], fɔːl-/, **falsities. 1 Falsity** is **1.1** the quality or fact of being untrue. EG *I'm not interested in the truth or falsity of what you're saying.* N UNCOUNT = untruth **1.2** the quality or fact of being deceitful or pretending to have particular feelings or attitudes; used showing disapproval. EG *Charlotte did not notice the falsity of all the everyday conventions and rules of etiquette.* N UNCOUNT ⇑ falseness

2 A **falsity** is a false or deceitful action or situation. EG *This is an age of polite falsities.* N COUNT = lie

falter /fɒltə, fɔːltə/, **falters, faltering, faltered. 1** If something **falters**, it loses power or strength in an uneven way, or no longer makes much progress. EG *...when the demand for commodities began to falter in 1974... ...should the engines falter and the plane lose height... It seemed to awaken an interest which never faltered... Their progress does not falter.* V = waver, hesitate

2 If you **falter**, you become unsure about what to do. EG *From that moment onwards he never faltered in his resolve... She gave me a look of so much anguish, I almost faltered.* V : IF+PREP THEN *in* = waver, hesitate

3 If you **falter** when you are speaking, you speak in a weak and hesitant way. EG *The harsh voice never faltered... 'What happened?'–'It's...' Bixby faltered.* V OR V+QUOTE = hesitate

4 If you **falter** when you are moving, you stop moving easily and steadily, and move uncertainly and hesitantly instead. EG *Looking to his left, he saw Percy Hopkins faltering... His steps faltered; his body sagged as if he'd been knifed.* V = hesitate, pause

faltering /fɒltəºrɪŋ, fɔːl-/. A **faltering** attempt or effort is hesitant and uncertain because you are nervous or do not really know what to do. EG *She made faltering attempts to write letters in German... ...Britain's faltering steps towards a fourth television channel.* ADJ QUALIT = tentative

fame /feɪm/ is the state or fact of being very well-known. EG *The fame of the Omega workshops spread very quickly... She was jealous of Ellen's enormous fame... He rose rapidly to fame... It was sure to bring fame and fortune to its originator.* N UNCOUNT = renown

famed /feɪmd/. If people, places, or things are **famed**, they are very well-known. EG *...another great church, famed for its flower festivals...* In the thirteenth century, it was one of the famed cities of Europe. ADJ QUALIT : IF+PREP THEN *for* = renowned, famous

familial /fəmɪlɪəl/. **Familial** means relating to families in general, or typical of a family; a formal word. EG *...the need for independence on a personal and familial level.* ADJ CLASSIF : USU ATTRIB

familiar /fəmɪljə/, **familiars**. **1** If someone or something is **familiar** to you, you are able to recognize them or know them well because you have seen, heard, or experienced them before. EG *My name was now familiar to millions of people... Gradually I began to recognize familiar faces... The man was a stranger, yet there was something familiar about him.* ◊ **familiarity** /fəmɪljærɪti¹/. EG *...the familiarity of the surroundings.* ADJ QUALIT : IF+PREP THEN *to* = well-known ≠ strange, unfamiliar ◊ N UNCOUNT

2 If you are **familiar** with something, you know or understand it well. EG *I am of course familiar with your work... ...to become familiar with affairs of state.* ◊ **familiarity**. EG *...her familiarity with these things.* ADJ QUALIT : PRED+*with* ≠ unfamiliar ◊ N UNCOUNT+*with*

3 If you behave in a **familiar** way towards someone, you treat them in an informal way that is appropriate only between close friends, and so may be considered offensive by anyone who is not a close friend. EG *I can't stand that familiar tone he uses when he talks to young women.* ◊ **familiarly**. EG *He spoke of them casually and familiarly by their first names.* ◊ **familiarity**. EG *...in terms of familiarity and affection... ...insolent familiarity.* ● If you **are on familiar terms** with someone, you know them well and do not need to behave formally towards them. EG *You're on familiar terms already, I see... They are almost certainly not on familiar terms with any of the teachers.* ADJ QUALIT = intimate ≠ distant ◊ ADV ◊ N UNCOUNT ● PHR OR PHR+A (*with*) : RECIP, VB INFLECTS

4 Your **familiars** are your close friends; an old-fashioned use. EG *Rhoda and Kathy were equals, not to say familiars.* N PLURAL = intimates

5 A **familiar** is a cat, bird, or other animal which, according to folk tales, is supposed to live with a witch or devil and share their magic powers. N COUNT

familiarity /fəmɪljærɪti¹/. **1 Familiarity breeds contempt** is a saying which refers to the fact that if you know someone very well, or if you are often in a particular situation, you can easily lose respect for that person or become careless in that situation. PHR

2 Other meanings of **familiarity** can be found in the entry for **familiar**.

familiarize /fəmɪljəraɪz/, **familiarizes, familiarizing, familiarized**; also spelled **familiarise**. If you **familiarize** yourself with something, or if someone **familiarizes** you with it, you learn about it and start to understand it. EG *She had familiarized herself with a great deal of native lore... ...to familiarize their colleagues with the principles.* V+O (REFL/NG) +A (*with*) : USU O(REFL) ⇑ teach

family /fæmɪºli¹/, **families**. **1** A **family** is **1.1** a group of people that consists of parents and their children. EG *...an English family on holiday in Germany... Each apartment could house a family of six... ...the Adams Family.* ● See also **nuclear family**. **1.2** a group of related species of animals or plants. EG *The weaver bird is a member of the sparrow family.* N COUNT : IF SING, VB CAN BE SING OR PL; N COUNT : USU+SUPP

2 Your **family** is **2.1** your husband or wife and children, or your brothers, sisters, and parents; sometimes used to refer to your other relations too, including aunts, uncles, cousins, and grandparents. EG *What about your family? Do they live in Leicester?... ...workers and their families.* ▸ used as an uncount noun. EG *They had known our parents for years before we were born, so they got to be almost family.* **2.2** your children, especially when they are young. EG *It's often very difficult for mothers to get back to work after raising a family... ...mothers with large families.* **2.3** all the people of previous generations who were related to you. EG *Her mother's family had lived for generations in Norfolk... There was a history of mental illness in the family.* N COUNT : USU POSS+N : IF SING, VB CAN BE SING OR PL ⇑ group; ▸ N UNCOUNT : USED AS C; N COUNT : IF SING, VB CAN BE SING OR PL; N COUNT : IF SING, VB CAN BE SING OR PL

3 You can use **family** to describe **3.1** things that belong to or are shared by a particular family. EG *Buddy Westerman's father loaned him the family car... Ben lived in Bermondsey and worked in the family business.* **3.2** things that are suitable to be used or enjoyed by parents and children together. EG *The Mini Metro isn't really designed to be a family car... With a programme like this you're appealing to a family audience.* N BEFORE N ⇑ communal; N BEFORE N

4 If a woman is **in the family way**, she is pregnant; an old-fashioned and informal expression. PHR : USED AS AN A

family doctor, family doctors. A **family doctor** is the same as a GP; used in British English. EG *Family doctors have no time these days to make regular calls.* N COUNT

family man, family men. A **family man** is **1** a man who is very fond of his wife and children and likes to spend a lot of time with them. **2** a man who has a wife and children. EG *Wages are so low in relation to the cost of living that a family man cannot survive on them.* N COUNT; N COUNT ≠ bachelor

family name, family names. Your **family name** is your surname. EG *...a tomb with our family name inscribed on it.* N COUNT

family planning is the practice of using contraception to control the number of children you have. EG *...family planning clinics.* N UNCOUNT = birth control

family tree, family trees. A **family tree** is a chart that shows all the people in your family over many generations and their relationships with one another. N COUNT

famine /fæmɪn/, **famines**. **Famine** is a serious shortage of food in a country which may cause many deaths. EG *Wars, earthquakes, famine, and disease... During the famine of 1929 he was afraid his family wouldn't survive.* N UNCOUNT/COUNT ⇑ disaster

famished /fæmɪʃt/. If you are **famished**, you are extremely hungry; an informal word. EG *He must be absolutely famished.* ADJ CLASSIF = ravenous, starving

famous /feɪməs/. Someone or something that is **famous** is very well known. EG *...a famous writer... The city has been most famous for its cloth... The collapse of Britain's most famous company shocked the entire country.* ADJ QUALIT : IF+PREP THEN *for* = well-known

famously /feɪməsli¹/. **1** You use **famously** to refer to the fact that someone or something is well-known. EG *...a good place for poets, most famously Larkin and Douglas Dunn.* ADV OR ADV SEN

2 If you **get on famously** with someone, you are both very friendly with each other and enjoy meeting and being together. EG *She and Smithy should meet up, they'd get on famously.* PHR : VB INFLECTS, IF+PREP THEN *with*

fan /fæn/, **fans, fanning, fanned**. **1** If you are a **fan** of a particular sport or of someone famous such as a singer, you like them very much and are very interested in them. EG *I was a Beatles fan... ...football fans... The fans were already screaming with delight.* N COUNT : USU+SUPP = supporter

2 Fan mail or **fan** letters are letters that are received by famous people such as singers or film stars from people who admire them. N BEFORE N ⇑ admiring

3 A **fan** is **3.1** a flat object that you wave in order to move the air and make yourself feel cooler, especially one that is made of a folded piece of paper or cloth, and that opens out into a flat semicircular shape. EG *...Japanese fans... Its tail was spread out like a fan.* **3.2** an electric or mechanical device that has several blades which turn round in order to create a current of air. Fans can be used to keep a room cool or to get rid of unpleasant smells. EG *I lay there watching the rotations of the ceiling fan... ...electric fans.* ● If someone says that **the shit hit the fan**, they mean that there was suddenly a lot of N COUNT; N COUNT; ● PHR : VB INFLECTS trouble or angry arguments; a rude or very informal expression. EG *I said, 'I'm gay.' Then the shit really hit the fan.*

4 You can also use **fan** to describe anything that has the shape of a wide 'V' with a semicircle above it, rather like an open fan. EG *...a lovely fan of foam on the edge of a tide.* — N COUNT : USU+ *of*

5 If you **fan** yourself or your face when you are hot, you wave a fan or something that has the same effect as a fan in order to make yourself feel cooler. EG *She took up some sheets of typewritten paper and fanned herself with them.* — V+O (REFL/NG) ⇑ cool

6 If you **fan** a fire, you wave something flat next to it in order to make it burn more strongly. — V+O ⇑ stimulate

7 If a wind or draught **fans** a fire, it makes it burn more strongly. EG *The rush of air fed and fanned the fires.* — V+O ⇑ stimulate

8 If someone **fans** a feeling such as fear, hatred, or passion, they deliberately act in a way that will increase the fear, hatred, or passion that people already feel. EG *They succeeded in fanning public resentment against him... Public hysteria fanned fears of an invasion.* ● **to fan the flames**: see **flame**. — V+O ⇑ provoke = increase, stir up

fan out. 1 If a group of people or things **fan out**, they move forwards away from a particular point in different directions. EG *The five of us fanned out at intervals of not more than fifteen feet... The others fanned out in line of search.* — PHRASAL VB : V+ADV = spread out

2 If something **fans out** or if you **fan** it out, it spreads out or opens out into a flat shape. EG *The dead birds lay with their wings fanned out... Animals make themselves look fierce by fanning out furry crests.* — PHRASAL VB : V-ERG+ADV = unfurl

fanatic /fənætɪk/, **fanatics**. A **fanatic** is 1 a person whose behaviour is considered to be very extreme, especially in the way they support particular religious or political ideas; used showing disapproval. EG *They would do anything at all to prevent dangerous fanatics from obtaining their weapons.* — N COUNT = extremist 2 a person who is very enthusiastic about a particular activity, sport, or way of life; used in informal English. EG *The owner of the hotel is a sports fanatic.* — N COUNT : USU+MOD+N = devotee

fanatical /fənætɪkəᵒl/. Someone who is **fanatical** or **fanatic** feels very strongly about something and behaves in a way that is considered to be extreme and unreasonable. EG *...fanatical rebels... He was a fanatic hunter.* ▸ used of actions, behaviour, or beliefs. EG *His campaign became increasingly fanatical... Bill inspired fanatical devotion in his pupils.* — ADJ QUALIT = zealous

◊ **fanatically**. EG *He was fanatically against intervention in the war.* — ◊ ADV

fanaticism /fənætɪsɪzəᵒm/ is fanatical behaviour or the quality of being fanatical. EG *Clem's eyes gleamed with fanaticism.* — N UNCOUNT = zeal

fan belt, fan belts; also spelled with a hyphen. A **fan belt** is a belt in a car engine that drives the fan which keeps the engine cool. — N COUNT

fancier /fænsɪə/, **fanciers**. 1 An animal or plant **fancier** is a person who breeds animals or plants of a particular type or who is very interested in them. EG *...a pigeon fancier.* — N COUNT : MOD+N ⇑ lover

2 **Fancier** is also the comparative form of **fancy**.

fanciful /fænsɪful/. 1 An idea that is **fanciful** is not based on reality. EG *She had a fanciful notion that germs were waiting to pounce on her... Their interpretations are often fanciful.* ▸ used of people. EG *'I am being fanciful,' Fanny thought wearily.* — ADJ QUALIT ⇑ imaginary = curious, whimsical

2 Something that is **fanciful** is unusual and elaborate rather than plain and simple; used showing disapproval. EG *...fanciful architecture... He considered this name far too fanciful.* — ADJ QUALIT = extravagant

fan club, fan clubs. A **fan club** is an organized group of people who all admire the same pop singer, film star, etc, and who arrange trips to concerts, publish newsletters for club members, etc. — N COUNT, ALSO IN NAMES AFTER N PROPER

fancy/fænsiˡ/, **fancies, fancying, fancied; fancier, fanciest**; used in informal English except for the meanings in paragraphs 9, 10, and 11. 1 If you **fancy** something, you want to have it or to do it. EG *She fancied a flat of her own... Do you fancy a cup of tea?... I don't fancy going back to that dreary house alone.* — V+O/-ING ⇑ desire

2 If you **fancy** someone, you feel attracted to them, especially in a sexual way. EG *I'll bet anything she fancied you.* — V+O ⇑ desire

3 If you **fancy** yourself, you think that you are very attractive, clever, or good at something; used showing disapproval. EG *Fancies himself, doesn't he?... I've heard that this man Bond fancies himself with a pistol.* — V+O (REFL)

4 If you **fancy** yourself as a particular kind of person, you like the idea of being that kind of person. EG *When I was a student I rather fancied myself as a Socialist... She fancies herself as a linguist.* — V+O (REFL)+A *(as)*

5 A **fancy** is a liking or desire for someone or something, especially one that does not last long. EG *Where did he get this fancy for pineapples?... ...whims and fancies.* — N COUNT = craving

6 If you **take a fancy to** someone or something, you start liking them, usually for no understandable reason. EG *Fortunately she took a fancy to me.* — PHR : VB INFLECTS

7 If something **takes** your **fancy** or **tickles** your **fancy**, you like it quite a lot when you see it or think of it. EG *He bought a vase that had taken his fancy... The idea of being a waitress rather tickled her fancy.* — PHR : VB INFLECTS = appeal, attract

8 You say **'fancy'** when you want to express surprise or disapproval. EG *Fancy seeing you here!... Fancy him remembering... Fancy old Harrington a tax cheat!... 'Fancy!' she said. 'Three miles just for a bucket of water!' 'You're in hospital.'-'Well, fancy that.'* — EXCLAM, OR EXCLAM+-ING = imagine

9 If you **fancy** that something is the case, you think or suppose that it is so. EG *I fancied I could hear a baby screaming... They fancied themselves to be Europeans... I don't know how long we can hold out. Not long, I fancy.* — V+REPORT-CL, OR V+O (REFL)+*to*-INF = imagine

10 A **fancy** is also an idea that is unlikely or untrue; a formal use. EG *I'd had a childhood fancy that I would one day be famous... It is difficult to separate fact from fancy.* — N COUNT/UNCOUNT = fantasy

11 **Fancy** is also uncontrolled imagination. EG *...indulging in a flight of fancy... He paints whatever his fancy suggests.* — N UNCOUNT

12 Something that is **fancy** is **12.1** special, unusual, and elaborate, for example with a lot of decoration. EG *...fancy hats... He prefers good plain food: nothing fancy... You should hear the fancy excuses some of them make!* — ADJ QUALIT = extravagant ≠ plain, simple **12.2** very expensive or of very high quality. EG *He took her out to dinner at a fancy place in London.* — ADJ QUALIT = high-class, posh

13 A **fancy** price is higher than what is usual, fair, or reasonable. EG *They charge fancy prices there.* — ADJ QUALIT = inflated

14 **Fancies** are small sweet cakes which have a lot of decoration. — N PLURAL

fancy dress is clothing that you wear for a party at which everyone dresses up to look like a character from a story or like a particular kind of person such as a policeman or a waitress. EG *Everyone will be in fancy dress... ...a fancy dress ball.* — N UNCOUNT ⇑ costume

fancy-free. Someone who is **fancy-free** is free to do what they like, especially because they have no responsibilities or are not married. EG *There I was, footloose and fancy-free.* — ADJ CLASSIF ⇑ uncommitted = carefree

fancy man, fancy men. A woman's **fancy man** is her lover or boyfriend; used in rather old-fashioned and informal English showing disapproval. — N COUNT : USU POSS+N

fancy woman, fancy women. A man's **fancy woman** is his lover or girlfriend; used in rather old-fashioned and informal English showing disapproval. — N COUNT : USU POSS+N

fandango /fændæŋgəu/, **fandangos**. A **fandango** is a Spanish dance in which two people dance very close together. — N COUNT

fanfare /fænfɛə/, **fanfares**. A **fanfare** is a short, loud tune, usually played on a trumpet or trumpets to announce a special event, for example the arrival of an important person. EG *The bride's arrival was greeted with a fanfare by the State Trumpeters.* — N COUNT ⇑ signal

fang /fæŋ/, **fangs**. If an animal has **fangs**, it has long sharp teeth. EG *Most snakes withdraw their fangs after striking... The wolf sank its fangs into his leg.* — N COUNT : USU PL ⇑ tooth

fanlight /fænlaɪt/, **fanlights**. A **fanlight** is a small window over a door. EG *...the stained glass fanlight above the front door.* — N COUNT

fanny /fæniˡ/, **fannies**. 1 Someone's **fanny** is their bottom; a rude word used in informal American English. — N COUNT : USU POSS+N

2 A woman's **fanny** is her genitals; a rude word used in informal British English. — N COUNT : USU POSS+N

fantasize /fæntəsaɪz/, **fantasizes, fantasizing, fantasized**; also spelled **fantasise**. If you **fantasize**, you think about a pleasant event or situation which you would like to happen but which is unlikely to happen. EG *She had fantasized that she and Wendy* — V, V+REPORT-CL, OR V+A *(about)* ⇑ dream = daydream *would live in this house... More than once he fantasized about buying a Renoir.*

fantastic /fæntæstɪk/. 1 If you say that something is **fantastic**, you mean that you think it is very good and you like it very much or are very pleased about it; an informal use. EG *He took a bite of meat, chewed it, savoured it, and said, 'Fantastic!'... I think it's a fantastic film!... You're pregnant? That's fantastic!* EXCLAM, OR ADJ QUALIT = fabulous, terrific, wonderful

2 A **fantastic** amount or quantity is an extremely large one; an informal use. EG *Dr O'Shea seemed to spend a fantastic amount of time on the road... Patterson's make a fantastic profit on this.* ADJ QUALIT : ATTRIB ⇑ great = terrific, vast
◇ **fantastically**. EG *The divorce rate is fantastically high here.* ◇ ADV+ADJ/ADV

3 Something that is **fantastic** or **fantastical** is strange and wonderful. EG *...the bright fantastic birds... ...fantastic images of gods.* ◇ **fantastically**. EG *Fantastically coloured and exotic birds.* ADJ QUALIT = exotic ◇ ADV+ADJ/ADV

4 A statement or story that is **fantastic** is very strange and very difficult to believe. EG *The truth is scarcely less fantastic than the fable... He happened to be very much in love with her–fantastic though that may seem.* ADJ QUALIT = unbelievable, incredible, extraordinary

5 An idea, plan, etc that is **fantastic** is very unlikely to happen or be possible. ADJ QUALIT

fantasy /fæntəsi[1]/, **fantasies**. 1 A **fantasy** is 1.1 a pleasant situation or event that you think about and hope will happen, although it is unlikely to happen. EG *That's supposed to be every schoolgirl's fantasy... ...Joy's fantasies about a voyage up the Nile.* N COUNT ⇑ idea = dream, fancy **1.2** something that people believe to be true, but which in fact is not true. EG *There is a fantasy that enormous amounts of money are wasted by the council.* N COUNT = misconception

2 You can refer to a story or situation that someone creates from their imagination and that is not based on reality as **fantasy**. EG *To a small child, fantasy and reality are very close to each other... The play is a nice mixture of fantasy and hard headed realism.* N UNCOUNT/COUNT ⇑ fiction = unreality

3 **Fantasy** is also the activity of imagining things. EG *Everyone should indulge in fantasy on occasions. ...the place where fantasy is given free rein.* N UNCOUNT

far /fɑː/, **farther, farthest; further, furthest**. **Far** has two comparatives, **farther** and **further**, and two superlatives, **farthest** and **furthest**. **Farther** and **farthest** are used mainly in relation to paragraph 1, and are dealt with here. **Further** and **furthest** are dealt with in separate entries. **1 Far** means a long distance from somewhere, something, or someone. EG *He sat as far away from the others as possible... They had rented a villa not far from Hotel Miranda... ...bits of white cloud drifting far above... He never hit the ball very far... ...a little farther south.* ADV ≠ close, near ▸ used as an adjective; an old-fashioned or literary use except in the comparative or superlative form. EG *...at the farthest possible point from the aisle... ...tickets to far places.* ▸ ADJ QUALIT = remote ● **Far and wide** or **far and near** means in a very large number of places or over a very large area or distance. EG *The bang was heard far and wide... People would come from far and wide.* ● PHR : USED AS AN A ⇑ everywhere

2 You use **far** after 'how' to ask questions about distance, and in the expression 'as far as' when you are mentioning a distance by stating the place reached. EG *How far is Amity from here?... He asks us how far we have come... Vita and Rosamund went with Harold as far as Bologna.* ADV : *How*+ADV, OR *as/so*+ADV+*as*

3 The **far** north, south, east, west of a country, continent, or other area is the part of it that is the greatest distance from the centre in the direction stated. EG *...in the far north of the country... ...living in China's far west.* ADJ CLASSIF : ATTRIB = extreme

4 When there are two things of the same kind in a place, the **far** one is the one that is the greater distance from you. EG *...at the far end of the room... ...on the far side of the river.* ADJ CLASSIF : ATTRIB = other ≠ near

5 A time or event that is **far** off in the future or past is a long time from the present or from a particular point in time. EG *The Fourth of July isn't far off... ...as far back as the twelfth and thirteenth centuries... ...if we look far into the future... Control over the mind is not as far off as we think.* ADV+ADV/PREP

6 **Far** also means much, or to a great extent or degree; often used when referring to change or progress, or in negative statements. EG *Interest rates will not come down very quickly or very far because of the level of government borrowing... Few of their closest friends would trust them very far... An adverse decision could push the minister farther along the path of union reform.* ADV WITH VB ⇑ greatly

7 You can also use **far** after 'how' to ask questions about extent or degree, and in the expressions 'as far as' and 'so far as' when referring to the extent to which something is possible. EG *How far are you going to tax people who don't own cars?... I think we need a couple of years to see how far the present government's policies are successful... ...fitting in with her methods as far as possible... It might be reflected in the environment so far as the circumstances of the time permitted.* ADV : *How*+ADV, OR *as/so*+ADV+*as* ⇑ much

8 You ask or say how **far** someone or something gets, goes, or is taken, as a way of referring to the level of achievement that they have reached in a situation or to the degree to which they take action in it. EG *How far have you got with the work?... Only those ideas which pass this test get as far as a practical trial... This opposition cannot take us very far.* ADV WITH VB

9 Someone who goes **a bit far**, takes something **too far**, pushes someone **too far**, etc behaves in an unacceptable or extreme way. EG *Sometimes the press went too far and suffered accordingly... The chastening of the trade unions, if not taken too far, will have been a salutary experience... In 1963 he unwisely pushed the Americans too far... That is probably going a bit far.* PHR : USED AS AN A = over the top

10 If you say that someone **goes as far as** to do a particular thing or **goes so far as** to do it, you mean that what they do seems surprising or extreme. EG *The directors went so far as to stage actual killings... Our pest officers will even go as far as tackling foxes... She wouldn't actually go so far as to say she is glad it happened.* PHR : VB INFLECTS, USU+*to*-INF/-ING

11 When you say how **far** you would go, you are referring to the degree to which you are willing to agree or to commit yourself in a conversation. EG *I think that's really as far as I would want to go... I wouldn't go as far as Kingsley.* ADV : *as/so*+ADV+*as*

12 **Far** also means very much. It is used to give emphasis in front of comparative adjectives and adverbs, in front of 'too', and also in front of verbs, adjuncts, or adjectives that refer to or describe progress, comparison, or difference. EG *...a far greater problem... I enjoyed it far more than I expected to... I have been talking far too much... ...a suicide rate far in excess of the national average... ...electronic techniques, in which the firm had so very far outstripped its rivals over the last few years... My ideas on foreign policy were far removed from those of the Government... The reality fell far short of the promise.* ADV : ADV+COMPAR, ADV+*too*+ADJ/ADV, OR ADV+VB/A/ADJ ⇑ greatly = very much, decidedly

13 You use **far** in expressions such as **by far**, **far and away**, etc to emphasize that someone or something is much better, worse, greater, etc than anything else or than another thing that has been mentioned. EG *She was by far the camp's best swimmer... ...by far the greater part of the prosecution's evidence... This is far and away the most important point... Mr Gerran is by far and away the biggest share holder.* PHR+SUPERL/COMPAR, OR COMPAR+PHR+*than*

14 Someone or something that is **not far wrong, not far out, not far off**, or **not far short** is almost correct. EG *...an answer that's not far wrong... He hadn't been so far out at that, for Antonio had died.* PHR : USED AS C/A ⇑ right

15 When you say that someone will **not go far wrong** with a particular thing or course of action, you mean that it is likely to be generally successful or satisfactory. EG *For a white wine you will not go far wrong with Soave... They are convinced that they cannot go far wrong so long as they obey the law.* PHR : VB INFLECTS ⇑ succeed

16 **far gone**. Someone or something that is **far gone** is in an advanced state or at an advanced stage of a particular condition. EG *It's a psychological thing, maybe too far gone for any of us to help... ...a young woman, far gone in the family way.* PHR : USED AS C

17 **far from**. **17.1** You use **far from** to emphasize that something is not a particular thing or does not do a particular thing, often when you are making a contrast with what people expect or think. EG *His hands were far from clean... Nell was very far from poor... The first day was a nightmare–but it was far from a total disaster... Far from speeding up, the tank slithered to a halt... You weren't my choice, not that I'm against you, far from it, but my first choice was Holliday... It is not that Irish Americans are ungenerous. Far from it.* PHR+ADJ/ADV/NG/-ING, OR PHR+*it* ⇑ not **17.2** Something that is **far** PREP

from a particular thing is completely different or separate from it. EG *Though with hindsight she realises this was far from the truth... I think literature isn't so far from the sciences as it is often represented as being.*

18 You say **far be it from me** to disagree, or **far be it from me** to interfere, criticize etc in order to make your disagreement, interference, or criticism seem less hostile or personal. EG *Far be it from me to disagree... Far be it from me to criticize her; I just think she's behaved extremely badly.* PHR + to-INF

19 as far as or **so far as**. **19.1** When you say that something is the case **as far as** a particular thing **is concerned** or **as far as** it **goes**, you mean that your statement or opinion applies only to that thing. EG *He has a reasonable similarity to yourself, at least as far as the head and face is concerned... I'm not really perceptive as far as literature goes, I much prefer history.* PHR : USED AS ADV SEN **19.2** You say **as far as I am concerned** when giving an opinion to emphasize that it is your opinion and that other people may disagree with you. EG *This is all nonsense as far as I am concerned.* PHR : USED AS ADV SEN **19.3** You say **as far as I know, so far as I remember** etc, when you are introducing or making a statement to say that you think it is true, but that there might be other factors that you have forgotten or do not know about. EG *We only had one paper as far as I remember, one three-hour essay... 'Is he alone?'–'As far as she knows'... As far as they could see, the room was empty.* CONJ SUBORD **19.4** When you say that something is satisfactory **so far as** it **goes** or **as far as** it **goes**, you mean that it is satisfactory only to a limited extent. EG *The essay's all right as far as it goes.* PHR : USED AS ADV SEN

20 You say **in so far as** or **insofar as** to introduce a clause in which you mention something that is relevant to what you have just said or what you are about to say, for example something that gives its extent or gives a reason for it. EG *I think it is better that we trust each other in so far as we can while our business association lasts... She had felt complete sympathy with the movement insofar as she perceived it... That is to be feared in so far as it threatens to dissipate man's energies.* CONJ SUBORD

21 So far means **21.1** only a limited distance. EG *They only went so far into the forest that day before turning back.* PHR : USED AS AN A **21.2** up until the present point in a situation, story, or account. EG *What do you think of the story so far?... It's gone well so far... So far only two bodies have been discovered.* PHR : USED AS AN A = to date ● You say **so far so good** to express satisfaction with the way that a situation or activity is progressing, developing, or happening. EG *I tied him quickly to a tree. So far so good. Then I hurtled back to the settlement.* ● CONVENTION

22 Thus far means up until the present point in a situation, story, or account; used in formal English. EG *Thus far, Wall Street, at least, has been notably unimpressed.* PHR : USED AS AN A

23 You can describe people with extreme left-wing or right-wing political views as the **far** left or the **far** right. EG *The far left has solidly backed the Republican cause... ...groups on the far right.* ADJ CLASSIF : ATTRIB

24 ● **a far cry from**: see **cry**. ● **few and far between**: see **few**. ● **to go far**: see **go**.

faraway /fɑːəweɪ/; also spelled with a hyphen or as two words. **1** Something that is **far away**, or a **faraway** place, sound, etc, is a long distance from you or from a particular place or person. EG *I no longer felt the need to travel to faraway places... They heard the faraway sound of a waterfall... A train hoots far away.* ADJ CLASSIF : ATTRIB, OR ADJ QUALIT : PRED = far-off, distant ≠ nearby

2 If your thoughts are **far away** or if you have **faraway** thoughts, you are thinking or dreaming about something that is very different from the situation around you. EG *Going down in the elevator, my thoughts were far away... She had a faraway look in her eyes.* ADJ CLASSIF : ATTRIB, OR ADJ QUALIT : PRED = distant

farce /fɑːs/, **farces**. **1** A **farce** is a humorous play in which the characters become involved in ridiculous and unlikely situations. N COUNT

2 Farce is the style of acting and writing that is used in this kind of play. N UNCOUNT ⇑ drama

3 If you describe an event as a **farce**, you mean that it is extremely disorganized and ridiculous; used showing disapproval. EG *My history classes were a farce.* N COUNT = shambles

farcical /fɑːsɪkəºl/. If you describe a situation or event as **farcical**, you mean that it is completely ridiculous. EG *The inquest had been largely farcical anyway... There was the farcical episode with Mr Brooks and the Daily Recorder.* ADJ QUALIT = ludicrous

fare /fɛə/, **fares, faring, fared**. **1** A **fare** is the money that you pay for a journey that you make, for example, in a bus, train or taxi. EG *How much is your bus fare home?... He spends fifty pounds a month on fares to work.* N COUNT : IF SING, USU the/POSS+N ⇑ payment

2 Taxi drivers sometimes refer to their passengers as **fares**. EG *My last fare wanted to go to the airport.* N COUNT : USU POSS+N

3 The **fare** served at a restaurant, cafe, etc is the food that is served there; a rather old-fashioned use. EG *The village pub serves up more interesting fare than some of the hotels in town.* N UNCOUNT

4 If you say that someone **fares** well or badly, **4.1** you are referring to the degree of success they achieve in a particular situation or activity; a rather old-fashioned use. EG *All fourteen branch candidates fared ill in the council election... How would an 8-stone boxer fare against a 14-stone boxer?* V+A : USU WITH BROAD NEG = get on **4.2** you are referring to how well or badly they are treated; an old-fashioned use. EG *Even the dog under the table fares better than we do.* V+A : USU WITH BROAD NEG ⇑ do

Far East. The **Far East** is used to refer to all the countries of Eastern Asia, including China, Japan, North and South Korea and Indochina. N PROPER : the+N = Orient

farewell /fɛəwel/, **farewells**. **Farewell** means goodbye; a rather old-fashioned or literary word. EG *Farewell, my dear child... It would grieve them not to bid you farewell.* ▶ used as a noun. EG *Next day we said fond farewells to Jim and Pam Moffatt.* CONVENTION ≠ hello ▶ N COUNT

far-fetched. An idea, suggestion, etc that is **far-fetched** is unlikely to be true or practical. EG *This vision of high growth and low inflation is not as far-fetched as it sounds.* ADJ QUALIT = unrealistic, improbable ≠ realistic

far-flung. Something that is **far-flung 1** spreads over a very large area. EG *Mali's enormous wealth came from its far-flung trade routes in salt and gold and copper.* ADJ CLASSIF : ATTRIB **2** is a very long distance away. EG *...in a far-flung corner of the Empire.* ADJ CLASSIF : ATTRIB

farm /fɑːm/, **farms, farming, farmed**. **1** A **farm** is a large area of land, together with the buildings on it, that is used for growing crops or raising animals, usually in order to sell them. EG *The eggs were delivered from the farm along with the milk... He works on a farm... ...a farm labourer... ...farm buildings.* N COUNT ⇑ business

2 If you **farm**, you use and cultivate land to grow crops or raise animals, usually in order to sell them and make a living. EG *My stepson farms in the beautiful Alexander Valley.* V OR V+O ⇑ work

3 A mink **farm**, fish **farm**, etc is a place where someone raises a particular kind of animal or fish in large quantities in order to sell them commercially. EG *...an oyster farm... ...a mink farm... ...a fish farm.* N COUNT : USU AFTER N ⇑ business

farm out. If you **farm out** work to people, you send it to them to do. EG *She has more knitting orders than she can cope with, so she farms them out to little old ladies with lots of spare time.* PHRASAL VB : V+O+ADV ⇑ give = delegate

farmer /fɑːmə/, **farmers**. A **farmer** is a person who owns or manages a farm. N COUNT

farm-hand, farm-hands. A **farm-hand** is a person who is employed by a farmer to work on a farm. N COUNT ⇑ labourer

farmhouse /fɑːmhaʊs/, **farmhouses**. A **farmhouse** is the main house on a farm, usually where the farmer lives. N COUNT ⇑ house

farming /fɑːmɪŋ/ is the practice or business of growing crops or raising animals on a farm. EG *Their economy is still largely based on manufacturing, farming, and tourism... ...sheep farming... ...modern farming methods.* N UNCOUNT ⇑ agriculture

farmland /fɑːmlænd/, **farmlands**. **Farmland** is land which is farmed, or which is suitable for farming. EG *...a country house set in 1,500 acres of forest and farmland... ...gently rolling farmlands.* N UNCOUNT/COUNT

farmyard /fɑːmjɑːd/, **farmyards**. A **farmyard** is the small enclosed area of land around or between the buildings on a farm. N COUNT ⇑ yard

far-off. **1** A time that is **far off** or a **far-off** time is a long time from the present. EG *...in those far-off days when people still bought fish for their cats... The day is not far off when manufacturers will be producing the same line of products for sale everywhere.* ADJ QUALIT = distant, remote

2 Something that is **far off**, or a **far-off** place, is a long distance from you or from a particular person or place. EG *...a far-off country... ...far off along the beach.* ADJ QUALIT, OR ADV WITH VB = faraway ≠ nearby

far-out; also spelled as two words. If you describe something as **far-out**, 1 you mean that it is unusual or strange, and very different from other things of the same kind. EG *That may sound far out, but it had happened a couple of times before... The possibility of creating new, far-out forms of man for space exploration.* 2 you mean that you think it is excellent; an informal use. EG *You got four tickets for the concert?–Far-out!*
ADJ CLASSIF : ATTRIB, OR ADJ QUALIT : PRED = bizarre, way-out
ADJ CLASSIF, OR EXCLAM = fantastic

far-reaching. Actions events or changes that are **far-reaching** have a very wide influence and affect a great number of things. EG *It could have far-reaching implications for the country's economy... ...many far-reaching changes in the social structure.*
ADJ QUALIT = extensive, sweeping

farrier /færiə/, **farriers**. A **farrier** is a person who fits horseshoes onto horses.
N COUNT

farrow /færəʊ/, **farrows, farrowing, farrowed**. When a female pig **farrows**, she gives birth to piglets; a technical term.
V

far-sighted. 1 If you say that someone is **far-sighted**, you mean that they understand what is likely to happen in the future, and consequently makes wise decisions and plans; used showing approval. EG *...far-sighted and sensitive political leaders.* ▸ used of plans and actions that are based on this understanding. EG *...the far-sighted plans which were laid at that time.*
ADJ QUALIT ≠ short-sighted

2 In American English, **far-sighted** means the same as long-sighted.
ADJ QUALIT

fart /fɑːt/, **farts, farting, farted**; a rude word. 1 If someone **farts**, they allow air to be forced out of their body through their anus. ▸ used as a noun.
V
▸ N COUNT

2 If you call someone an old **fart**, you are indicating that you think that they are boring and that you do not respect them; an offensive expression.
N COUNT : USU MOD+N

fart about or **fart around**. If you say that someone **is farting about** or **is farting around**, you mean that thy are wasting time doing silly things instead of doing what needs to be done; used in very informal English.
PHRASAL VB : V+ADV = mess around

farther /fɑːðə/ is the comparative of **far**.

farthest /fɑːðɪ²st/ is the superlative of **far**.

farthing /fɑːðɪŋ/, **farthings**. 1 A **farthing** is a coin that is no longer used which was worth a quarter of a penny in old British currency.
N COUNT

2 If you say **'it doesn't matter a brass farthing'** or 'I don't care a brass farthing', you are emphasizing that something does not matter and that you do not care about it at all; an old-fashioned and informal expression. EG *It does not matter a brass farthing if they get messy or not.*
PHR

fascia /feɪʃə/, **fascias**. 1 The **fascia** in a car is the part surrounding the instruments and dials; a fairly formal word.
N COUNT = dashboard

2 The **fascia** on a shop front is the flat surface above the shop window, on which the name of the shop is written.
N COUNT

fascinate /fæsɪneɪt/, **fascinates, fascinating, fascinated**. If something **fascinates** you, it interests and delights you so much that your thoughts tend to concentrate on it. EG *I love history, it fascinates me... Herschel was fascinated by astronomy... Both girls and boys become fascinated with marriage and having babies.* ◇ **fascinated**. EG *She stared, fascinated, as the blood flowed out of her.* ◇ **fascinating**. EG *It's a fascinating book... ...a truly fascinating country.* ◇ **fascinatingly**. EG *It's a fascinatingly interesting theory.*
V OR V+O : USU V+O = intrigue ≠ bore
◇ ADJ QUALIT
◇ ADJ QUALIT
◇ ADV OR ADV SEN

fascination /fæsɪneɪʃəⁿn/, **fascinations**. 1 **Fascination** is the state of being greatly interested in and delighted by something. EG *He watched in fascination as her rickety loom wove the beautiful patterns... He just stared with a kind of numb fascination at the writhing man.*
N UNCOUNT = absorption

2 A **fascination** is something that fascinates people. EG *Here is one of the fascinations that this ancient land holds for us.*
N COUNT ⇑ attraction

fascism /fæʃɪzəⁿm/ is a right-wing political philosophy that believes in the importance of having a powerful dictator and state control. Nationalistic feelings are encouraged and political opposition is not allowed.
N UNCOUNT

fascist /fæʃɪst/, **fascists**. 1 A **fascist** is someone who believes in fascism. EG *...the alliance with the British Fascists.*
N COUNT ⇑ person

2 A **fascist** group or organization believes in or follows the principles of fascism. EG *...fascist countries.*
ADJ CLASSIF

3 People sometimes refer to a person who holds extreme right-wing views as a **fascist**.
N COUNT/VOC

fashion /fæʃəⁿn/, **fashions, fashioning, fashioned**. 1 The **fashion** in which someone does something or in which something happens is the way in which it happens or is done. EG *We talked in an animated fashion... He joined his hands together in Indian fashion and gave a little bow... He greeted us warmly in his usual friendly fashion.* ● See also **parrot fashion**.
N COUNT+SUPP, OR *in*+MOD+N = manner

2 Something that is done **after the fashion of** a particular person is done in a way that is typical of this person. EG *Leibnitz was another child prodigy who, after the fashion of his kind, was writing Greek and Latin from an early age.*
PREP

3 If you say that something was done **after a fashion**, you mean that it was done, but not very well. EG *He changed the baby's nappies after a fashion... The water was running into his eyes, but he could still see after a fashion.*
PHR : USED AS AN A = just about

4 **Fashion** is the styles of clothing, hairstyles, make-up, etc, that change quickly as people's ideas and tastes change. EG *There were 100 models promoting Italian fashion... The fashion industry responded to the new mood of feminism.*
N UNCOUNT

5 A **fashion** is a particular style of clothing, hairstyle, etc that is popular at a particular time. EG *I gather mini skirts are the fashion again now... French boutiques sell the latest Parisian fashions.*
N COUNT

6 A **fashion** is also an activity, attitude, way of behaving, etc that is popular with a lot of people at a particular time. EG *It may be the fashion at the moment to be in favour of decentralization.... These four young Beatles set the fashion for a generation.*
N COUNT/UNCOUNT ⇑ interest = trend

7 If a style, colour, way of behaving, etc is **in fashion**, it is popular and considered to be currently fashionable. If it is **out of fashion**, it is considered to be unfashionable. EG *Exotic fruits are coming into fashion... Capability and efficiency seem to be coming back into fashion... Platform shoes are back in fashion again... She never ever wears a hat. They're out of fashion... Open-plan offices are going out of fashion.*
PHR : USED AS AN A = in vogue ≠ out of date

8 If you **fashion** something, you make it in a particular shape using your hands; a rather formal or old-fashioned use. EG *The artist fashioned out of clay a grinning skeleton..*
V+O = model

9 If someone or something **fashions** you, your attitudes, or your future, they have an influence on you which affects your development; a formal use. EG *We fashion our children into believers in the status quo.*
V+O = mould

fashionable /fæʃəⁿnəbəⁿl/. 1 Styles of clothing, ideas, etc that are **fashionable** are generally popular and copied or used by a lot of people at a particular time. EG *He put on one of his habitual striped shirts that were fashionable in 1963... It is fashionable at the moment to say how inadequate the government is... He knows all about these fashionable people like Chomsky and Saussure.* ◇ **fashionably**. EG *...a tall, lean young man of thirty-four, his hair fashionably long.*
ADJ QUALIT = in ≠ unfashionable
◇ ADV

2 If a restaurant, club, area, etc is **fashionable**, it is currently popular among the richer people in society. EG *It lies in one of the less fashionable parts of the city... ...Au Grand Choix, the newest New York fashionable restaurant.*
ADJ QUALIT = smart

fast /fɑːst/, **faster, fastest; fasts, fasting, fasted**. 1 Something or someone that is **fast** moves, does something, or happens with great speed. EG *...a fast car... ...fast communications... Relationships today tend to change at a faster pace than ever before.* ▸ used as an adverb. EG *I ran as fast as I could... The music went faster and faster... News travels pretty fast... ...fast-flowing upland streams.*
ADJ QUALIT = quick, swift, rapid ≠ slow
▸ ADV WITH VB

2 You can use **fast** to ask about the speed of something, even if it is moving quite slowly. EG *...looking out of the windows to see how fast we were going.*
ADV WITH VB : AFTER *how* = quickly

3 If you say that someone or something is **fast** becoming something, or that something is **fast** developing, disappearing, etc, you mean that the process mentioned is happening with great speed. EG *We are fast becoming a nation fed on canned food... The time was fast approaching when I would have to*
ADV WITH VB (-ING) = quickly, rapidly ≠ gradually, slowly

leave... Such cultures are fast disappearing from the face of the earth.

4 A **fast** road or a **fast** lane on a motorway is designed for vehicles to travel along quickly. EG *This guy passed me in the fast lane doing at least 100 mph... It's a fast road; there's no speed limit.*
ADJ CLASSIF: ATTRIB ≠ slow

5 A **fast** surface for sports such as tennis is one which enables a ball to move especially quickly after it has bounced. EG *He found the grass courts at Wimbledon much faster than he'd expected.*
ADJ QUALIT ≠ slow

6 If things happen or are repeated **fast**, they happen or come quickly one after the other. EG *The footsteps were too fast and heavy to be his mother's.* ▸ used as an adverb. EG *Vivi's tears and memories, spilling so fast, half the words not understood.*
ADJ QUALIT: USU PRED ▸ ADV WITH VB = rapidly ≠ slowly

7 If you do something **fast**, or if something happens **fast**, you do it, or it happens, very soon and without any delay. EG *She needed medical help fast... Treat stains as fast as possible.* ▸ used as an adjective. EG *I only got a fast return on my investment once.*
ADV AFTER VB ▸ ADJ QUALIT: ATTRIB

8 If you say to someone **'not so fast'**, you are telling them not to act so soon or to be so sure of success because what they assume will happen may not actually take place. EG *'Jones, Marsh and Barrett,' I told her. 'Not so fast–I'm not a partner yet.'*
CONVENTION ⇑ wait = hold on

9 An activity or action that is **fast** takes only a short time to do or happen. EG *Give your guests a fast tour of the house... We had a fast game of tennis before breakfast.*
ADJ QUALIT = quick ≠ leisurely

10 If a watch or clock is **fast**, it is working too quickly and shows a time that is later than the real time.
ADJ QUALIT: PRED ⇑ wrong ≠ slow

11 Fast photographic film is very sensitive and can be used for taking pictures when there is not very much light. EG *You have to use fast film for this.*
ADJ QUALIT

12 Something that is fixed or held **fast** is firmly fixed, held, or fastened. EG *I struggled to free myself but my leg was stuck fast.* ● If you **make** something **fast**, you tie it firmly to something else. EG *He made it fast to a bracket on the side.*
ADV AFTER VB = tightly ● PHR: VB INFLECTS

13 If you **hold fast**, **13.1** you grip something very tightly because you do not want to let go of it. EG *He was holding fast with his left hand to a strap.* **13.2** you continue doing or thinking the same thing as before, especially when someone is trying to make you give it up. EG *He was determined to hold fast to both kinds of art... ...the feminists held fast in the face of considerable opposition.*
PHR: VB INFLECTS; PHR: VB INFLECTS = hang on ≠ give up

14 Someone who is **fast asleep** is completely and thoroughly asleep. EG *The girl was lying fast asleep on the sofa.*
PHR: USED AS C ≠ wide awake

15 If colours or dyes are **fast**, they will not come out of a piece of cloth when it gets wet. EG *Are the colours fast?*
ADJ CLASSIF: PRED ⇑ fixed = permanent

16 A **fast** way of life is one which involves a lot of enjoyable and expensive or dangerous activities; used especially of young people or the way they live. EG *...the desire for a fast life... She wanted to move in the fast set.*
ADJ QUALIT: USU ATTRIB ⇑ active

17 A **fast** woman is one who shows boldness and lack of modesty in sexual relationships; used showing disapproval. EG *It would stigmatize her for life as a fast woman.*
ADJ QUALIT: USU ATTRIB ⇑ immoral = forward, loose

18 If you **play fast and loose** with someone, you behave in an unreliable, irresponsible, or insincere way towards them. EG *He had played fast and loose with her affections.*
PHR: VB INFLECTS = trifle with

19 If you **pull a fast one**, you cheat or deceive someone, especially in a deal involving money; an informal expression. EG *He tried to pull a fast one on me.*
PHR: VB INFLECTS

20 If you **fast**, you eat no food for a period of time, especially for a religious reason. EG *He fasts for a whole day every week.* ▸ used as a noun. EG *During my fast I had lost fifteen pounds.*
V ⇑ abstain ▸ N COUNT

21 ● to **make a fast buck**: see **buck**. ● **hard and fast**: see **hard**. ● **thick and fast**: see **thick**.

fast breeder reactor, fast breeder reactors. A **fast breeder reactor** or a **fast breeder** is a kind of nuclear reactor that produces more plutonium than it needs to use for the purposes of generating electricity.
N COUNT

fasten /fɑ:sə⁰n/, **fastens, fastening, fastened.** **1** When you **fasten** something, or when it **fastens**, you do it up or close it with a device such as a button, hook, strap, or clasp. EG *He fastened his seat-belt... I shut the door and fastened the bolt... This dress fastens at the back.*
V-ERG ≠ undo, unfasten

2 If you **fasten** one thing to another, you attach it to the other thing, for example with a piece of string or tape. EG *Bowman caught hold of the short lever which was fastened to the valve... He had an electrode fastened to his wrist.*
V+O+A

3 If someone or something **fastens** their teeth, hands, etc around or onto something, they take hold of it tightly with their teeth or hands. EG *He wished that he could fasten his hands around the throat of the dog.*
V-ERG+A

fasten on. 1 If you **fasten** your attention **on** something, you think about that thing rather than about anything else. EG *Your attention is fastened on that one event... Once she had fastened on to a scheme she did not let go.*
PHRASAL VB: V+PREP, OR V+O+PREP

2 If someone **fastens on** to you, they keep following, talking to, or staying with you, when you want them to go away. EG *The doctor had fastened on to an official of the Yugoslav embassy.*
PHRASAL VB: V+PREP = latch onto ≠ ignore

fasten up. If you **fasten** something **up**, you do it up or close it completely, for example by using buttons or straps. EG *Fasten your coat up.*
PHRASAL VB: V+O+ADV ≠ unfasten, undo

fasten upon. To **fasten** your attention **upon** something means the same as to fasten your attention on it. EG *His mind fastened upon it now: escape.*
PHRASAL VB: V+PREP, HAS PASS

fastener /fɑ:sə⁰nə/, **fasteners.** A **fastener** is a device such as a button, zip, or safety pin that fastens something, especially clothing.
N COUNT ⇑ fastening

fastening /fɑ:sə⁰nɪŋ/, **fastenings.** A **fastening** is something such as a clasp, cord, or latch that fastens something. EG *No fastenings are visible or exposed to the weather.*
N COUNT

fast-food is hot food that is prepared and served quickly after you order it. EG *...a chain of fast-food restaurants.*
N UNCOUNT ⇑ convenience food

fastidious /fæstɪdɪəs/; a formal word. Someone who is **fastidious 1** pays great attention to detail because they like everything to be very neat, accurate, and orderly. EG *He was very fastidious about his personal correspondence... She has a fastidious and incisive intellect...* ◊ **fastidiously.** EG *The process was fastidiously checked and re-checked.* ◊ **fastidiousness.** EG *...a growing feeling for privacy and a growing fastidiousness.* **2** is concerned about cleanliness to an extent that is considered to be too fussy; used showing disapproval. EG *He flushed the toilet with his pointed boot, too fastidious to touch the lever with his hand.* ◊ **fastidiously.** EG *Hfastidiously exammied the glass.* ◊ **fastidiousness.**
ADJ QUALIT = fussy ≠ careless; ◊ ADV; ◊ N UNCOUNT; ADJ QUALIT ⇑ careful; ◊ ADV; ◊ N UNCOUNT

fastness /fɑ:stnɪ²s/, **fastnesses.** A **fastness** is a safe place, usually one that is difficult to get to; a literary word. EG *...this island fastness.*
N COUNT+SUPP = stronghold

fat /fæt/, **fatter, fattest; fats. 1** A person or animal that is **fat** has a lot of flesh on their body that they do not need. EG *My father is fat–he weighs over fifteen stone... She was fatter than when he last saw her.* ◊ **fatness.** EG *Resistance to disease has nothing to do with fatness.*
ADJ QUALIT ⇑ large = overweight ≠ thin, slim; ◊ N UNCOUNT

2 Fat is **2.1** the extra flesh that animals and humans have under their skin, which is used to store energy and to help keep them warm. EG *Asiatic sheep turn their food into fat and store it... Fat dripped from the roasting joint of beef.* **2.2** a solid or liquid substance obtained from animals or vegetables, which is used in cooking. EG *Rub the fat into the flour.* **2.3** a substance contained in foods such as cheese and butter, which forms an energy store in your body. EG *Your doctor may recommend limiting the fat and starch in your diet.*
N UNCOUNT; N MASS; N MASS ⇑ nutrient

3 Something that is **fat** is very thick or wide. EG *They published their conclusions in one fat volume of a report.*
ADJ QUALIT: USU ATTRIB ≠ thin, slim

4 A **fat** profit, fee, wallet, etc is one which involves or contains a large amount of money; an informal use. EG *This made a fat profit for the manufacturer.*
ADJ QUALIT: ATTRIB = hefty ≠ slim

5 A **fat** period of time is one during which you earn or receive a lot of money. EG *Even in the fat years a farmer has to bear the lean years in mind.*
ADJ QUALIT = prosperous ≠ lean

6 Someone who has **grown fat** on something has become very rich as a result of it. EG *Merchants in Boston had grown fat on the trade from the campus.*
PHR: VB INFLECTS, IF+PREP THEN *on*

7 You use **the fat of the land** to refer to the best and richest part of things, or a rich, comfortable lifestyle. EG *They're living off the fat of the land.*
PHR

8 If you say that **the fat's in the fire**, you mean that
PHR

something has happened which will start a lot of trouble; an informal expression.

9 If you say that something which someone has said or done is a **fat lot of good**, you mean that it is not at all good or useful; an informal expression. EG *A fat lot of good thieving did you... 'Then we should know what the time was.'-'A fat lot of good that would be!'... 'A fat lot you tried,' said Jack contemptuously.*
PHR : USED AS O

10 If you say that there is a **fat chance** of something happening, you mean that you do not believe that it will happen; an informal expression. EG *'Just give us our money back and we'll leave.'-'Fat chance,' the usher said.*
CONVENTION, OR N SING : a+N = some hope

11 If you say that someone can't get something into their **fat** head, you are saying in a rude way that you think that they are stupid. EG *Can't you get it into your fat head, I'm not going to do it!*
ADJ CLASSIF : ATTRIB = thick

fatal /feɪtəˀl/. **1** Something that is **fatal** is very important or significant, and likely to have an unwanted effect on future events. EG *I made the fatal mistake of letting her talk me into it... Analyse your fatal weakness and stamp it out.* ◇ **fatally**. EG *He had to deliver up what turned out to be the fatally incriminating tape.*
ADJ CLASSIF ⇑ serious; ◇ ADV

2 A **fatal** accident, illness, etc causes someone's death. EG *He had a fatal accident with a gun... Patients will face possible fatal delays if the unit is closed.* ◇ **fatally**. EG *In December four Manhattan men were fatally stabbed.*
ADJ CLASSIF ⇑ deadly; ◇ ADV = mortally

fatalism /feɪtəlɪzəˀm/ is belief in a power which controls everything that happens in a way that human beings cannot prevent or change. EG *Fatalism is the real controlling force... ...the fatalism with which people are encouraged to accept these received truths.* ◇ **fatalist, fatalists**. EG *She was a committed fatalist.*
N UNCOUNT; ◇ N COUNT

fatalistic /feɪtəlɪstɪk/. Someone who is **fatalistic** believes that human beings cannot influence or control events. EG *I suddenly became fatalistic, resigning myself to the inevitable.* ▸ used of attitudes, remarks, etc that express this belief. EG *...the almost fatalistic foreboding of the Prison Service itself... They speak in a deadpan and fatalistic way about the loss of friends and family.*
ADJ QUALIT = resigned, deterministic

fatality /fətælɪti¹/, **fatalities**. **1** A **fatality** is a death caused by an accident or by violence. EG *The last duty-related fatality to a local policeman occurred in 1957.*
N COUNT

2 Fatality is the feeling or belief that human beings cannot influence or control events. EG *The modern world is dominated by a sense of fatality.*
N UNCOUNT

fate /feɪt/, **fates**. **1 Fate** is a power that is believed to control and decide everything that happens, in a way that people cannot prevent or change. EG *Fate was against me... I eagerly accepted the job fate offered me.*
N UNCOUNT = destiny

2 The **Fates** are the three goddesses who, according to the belief of the ancient Greeks, have the power to control and decide everything that happens. EG *It was here that the Fates laid him low.*
N PLURAL : the+N

3 Someone's **fate** is what happens to them. EG *Their factory closed down, and several other companies suffered a similar fate... Rick decided to stay until we knew what Dookie's fate would be.*
N COUNT : USU POSS+N = lot

fated /feɪtɪ²d/. If you say that someone is **fated** to do something, or that an event is **fated**, you mean that this event or action has been planned or decided by fate and there is nothing that can be done to avoid or change it. EG *We were fated to dislike one another... Once it had happened, it seemed fated.*
ADJ CLASSIF : USU PRED, USU+to-INF = destined

fateful /feɪtful/. If an action or a time when a particular event occurred is described as **fateful**, it is considered to have an important, and often disastrous, effect on future events. EG *And so to the fateful day of the election... ...a fateful decision... The Prime Minister made his fateful announcement.*
ADJ QUALIT : USU ATTRIB = momentous

fathead /fæthˀɛd/, **fatheads**. If you refer to someone as a **fathead**, you mean that they are stupid; an offensive word. EG *Should my income suffer because some fathead swears in front of a prospective parent?*
N COUNT = idiot, fool

father /fɑːðə/, **fathers, fathering, fathered**. **1** Your **father** is the man who is one of your parents. EG *My father was born in London... He becomes worried if his mother or father are annoyed with him... The participants are actually father and daughter... ...families where fathers are away a lot of the time... Father called him Buster Billy.* ▸ **Father** is also used to address your father. EG *Don't you want to know my news, Father?*
N COUNT = dad; ▸ N PROPER/VOC

2 When a man **fathers** a child, he makes a woman pregnant. EG *He fathered two children.*
V+O = beget

3 Our ancestors are sometimes referred to as our **fathers**.
N PLURAL = forefather

4 The **father** of something is the man who invented or started it. EG *Chaucer is often said to be the father of English poetry... ...the founding fathers of the University.*
N COUNT : the+N +of

5 The city **fathers** are people who hold important and respected positions in a community. EG *The city fathers rejected the plans for a new theatre.*
N COUNT : MOD+N, USU PL

6 Father is used in a literary way as part of the name of something that is thought of as an old man. EG *...Father Thames... ...Old Father Time.*
N IN NAMES BEFORE N

7 Father is also used to address or refer to a priest in some Christian churches, particularly the Catholic and Orthodox Churches. EG *'Good afternoon, father.'-'My son,' the priest answered solemnly... ...the kind of religion which Father Drew preaches.*
● See also **Holy Father**.
N IN TITLES : ALSO VOC

8 Father is also another name for God. EG *Heavenly Father, hear our prayers.*
N PROPER = Lord

Father Christmas. **Father Christmas** is an imaginary old man who has a long, white beard and wears a red coat. He is believed by children to visit them at Christmas to bring all their presents.
N PROPER = Santa Claus

father figure, father figures; also spelled with a hyphen. Someone who is a **father figure** is thought of as taking the place of a father and being the person you can turn to for advice, support, guidance, and help. EG *In terms of sculpture, Moore was a father figure.*
N COUNT

fatherhood /fɑːðəhud/ is the state of being a father. EG *...attitudes to fatherhood.*
N UNCOUNT = paternity

father-in-law, fathers-in-law. Someone's **father-in-law** is the father of their husband or wife.
N COUNT

fatherland /fɑːðəlænd/, **fatherlands**. Someone's **fatherland** is the country in which they or their ancestors were born. EG *...thinking of the fatherland... They were fighting for their fatherland.*
N COUNT ⇑ mother country

fatherless /fɑːðəlɪ²s/. If someone is **fatherless**, their father has died, or they are brought up by their mother without a man in the family and without seeing their father regularly.
ADJ CLASSIF

fatherly /fɑːðəli¹/. A **fatherly** action or attitude is one that shows feelings that are thought to be typical of a warm, kind, and protective father but which perhaps could be considered patronizing. EG *Let me give you some fatherly advice.*
ADJ QUALIT : USU ATTRIB = paternal ≠ motherly

Father's Day is the third Sunday in June, celebrated in honour of fathers.
N UNCOUNT

fathom /fæðəˀm/, **fathoms, fathoming, fathomed**. **1** A **fathom** is a measurement of 1.8 metres or 6 feet, used when describing the depth of water.
N COUNT

2 If you **fathom** something or **fathom** it **out**, you understand it as a result of thinking carefully about it. EG *I couldn't fathom the meaning of her remarks... ...X-ray photography, used to fathom such mysteries as honeybee navigation.*
V+O/REPORT-CL : ALSO+A (out) = work out

fathomless /fæðəˀmlɪ²s/. Something that is **fathomless** cannot be measured or understood because it gives the impression of being very deep, obscure, or complicated. EG *Its use is inexhaustible. Fathomless!... She looked at him with calm, fathomless eyes... ...a fathomless truth.*
ADJ CLASSIF = unfathomable

fatigue /fəti:g/, **fatigues, fatiguing, fatigued**.

1 Fatigue is a feeling of extreme physical or mental tiredness. EG *Finally, her mind gave in to fatigue and she fell asleep... I was covered with freezing mud and shaking with fatigue.*
N UNCOUNT = exhaustion ≠ liveliness

2 If something **fatigues** you, it makes you feel extremely tired; a formal use. EG *By the end of term my wife and I are thoroughly fatigued.* ◇ **fatigued**. EG *'How boring it all is,' she said, in a voice fatigued to the point of desperation.*
V+O : USU PASS = exhaust; ◇ ADJ QUALIT = exhausted ≠ lively

3 Fatigues are clothes that soldiers wear when they are doing routine jobs or when they are on the battlefield. EG *I use old army fatigues. They're cheap, tough and don't show the dirt... They all had their fatigue shirts off.*
N PLURAL

4 Fatigue in metal, wood, etc is a weakness in it that is caused by repeated stress. Fatigue can sometimes cause the metal, wood, etc to break. EG *...thermal*
N UNCOUNT

changes and forces of internal fatigue common to all metals.

fatless /fætlɪ²s/. Food that is **fatless** does not contain any fat. EG *...a fatless fruit cake.* ADJ CLASSIF ≠ fatty

fatted /fætɪ²d/. If you **kill the fatted calf**, you have a great celebration to welcome a person you have not seen for a long time; an old-fashioned expression. PHR : VB INFLECTS ⇑ celebrate

fatten /fætə⁰n/, **fattens, fattening, fattened.** 1 If you **fatten** an animal or person, or if they **fatten**, they become fatter as a result of eating more. EG *Soya is excellent for fattening pigs... Most hill farmers cannot fatten their lambs off in their first summer.* • See also **fattening**. V-ERG

2 To **fatten** also means to become richer. EG *...while Western and Eastern bloc nations fatten on gigantic arms sales to the poorer countries.* V OR V+O

fatten up. If you **fatten up** an animal, you feed it more food so that it reaches the weight that you want it to be. EG *They take twice as long to fatten up as European cattle... Go on, have some more–you look as if you need fattening up.* PHRASAL VB : V+O+ADV = feed up

fattening /fætə⁰nɪŋ/. Food that is **fattening** is considered to make people fat easily. ADJ QUALIT ≠ slimming

fatty /fæti¹/, **fatties; fattier, fattiest.** 1 A fat person is sometimes called a **fatty**; an offensive term. EG *I wrote about being a fatty... Shut up, Fatty.* N COUNT : ALSO VOC

2 Food that is **fatty** contains a lot of fat or too much fat. EG *The goose was a little fatty to his taste.* ADJ QUALIT = greasy

3 **Fatty** tissues, **fatty** acids, etc, contain or consist of fat; a technical term. EG *...the ability of the body to store residues in fatty tissues... Coconut oil is very high in saturated fatty acids... ...a fatty deposit which builds up on the walls of the arteries.* ADJ CLASSIF : ATTRIB

fatuous /fætjuəs/. A remark, action, plan, etc that is **fatuous** is considered to be very silly indeed, showing no sign of intelligence or thought, even though perhaps the person responsible for it does not realize this. EG *...'Not for the ears of ladies', or some such fatuous remark... Television commercials seem more smug and fatuous than ever... ...the government's fatuous games plan for 'limited' war.* ADJ QUALIT = foolish, stupid, inane

◇ **fatuously.** ◇ ADV

faucet /fɔːsɪt/, **faucets.** In American English, a **faucet** is a tap. N COUNT ⇑ device

fault /fɔːlt/, **faults, faulting, faulted.** 1 If a bad or undesirable situation is a particular person's **fault**, he or she is considered to be the cause of it or to have responsibility for it. EG *This was all Jack's fault... It was entirely my own fault... It's their fault... It's all the fault of a girl called Sarah...* N SING WITH DET : USU POSS

2 A **fault** is a mistake in what someone is doing or in what they have done. EG *He flushed, conscious of a fault... However, she muffed that too through no fault of her own.* N COUNT = error

3 If you are **at fault**, you are mistaken in a particular action, sometimes with the result that you are to blame for an event or situation. EG *We failed to explain that to the public and we are at fault in that... It was 1976, I believe, if my memory is not at fault.* PHR : USED AS AN A = wrong ≠ right

4 A **fault** in something, for example a person's character or a system, is a weakness or imperfection in it. EG *I knew my past much better than she did–and my faults... Two of the great achievements of our country are the NHS, with all its faults, and the Open University... Perhaps that's a fault in Anthony. Yet the fault lies not in him but in the system.* • **For all** someone's or something's **faults** is an expression used to say that although someone or something has obvious faults, they also have good or positive qualities. EG *For all her faults, Tallulah's countless friends tolerated and even adored her.* N COUNT = flaw, failing • PHR

5 A **fault** on a machine or in a structure is a broken part or a mistake in the way it was made. EG *Send it back to the manufacturer if the machine develops the same fault... Technicians laboriously tried to find and remedy faults.* N COUNT = defect

6 If you **fault** someone, you criticize them because you believe that there is something wrong in what they are doing or in what is happening. EG *You can't fault their psychology... I couldn't fault him on that one.* V+O, IF+PREP THEN *with/on* = find fault with

7 If you **find fault** with something or someone, you look for mistakes and complain about them. EG *Those who find fault with it do so chiefly on political grounds.* PHR : VB INFLECTS ⇑ criticize = knock

8 A **fault** is also a large crack in the surface of the earth; a technical term. EG *...a huge geological fault running through the entire State.* N COUNT

9 **To a fault** means much more than is usual or necessary; used of people's good qualities. EG *So, obedient to a fault, as I always am, I got it... Generous to a fault, he was noted for his hospitality.* PHR AFTER ADJ ⇑ excessively

10 A **fault** in tennis is a service that is wrong according to the rules. If the ball lands or bounces outside the proper area, the line judge shouts 'Fault!' EG *McEnroe served six double faults in the third set.* N COUNT

faultless /fɔːltlɪ²s/. Something that is **faultless** is perfect and has no mistakes at all. EG *He was accosted by two men who spoke to him in faultless German... He went over his homework and found it faultless.* ◇ **faultlessly.** EG *Victoria never learnt to speak English faultlessly.* ADJ CLASSIF = immaculate ≠ flawed ◇ ADV ⇑ perfectly

faulty /fɔːlti¹/. A machine, piece of equipment, etc that is **faulty** is imperfect and not working properly. EG *We traced the trouble to a faulty transformer.* ADJ CLASSIF = defective

faun /fɔːn/, **fauns.** A **faun** is an imaginary creature which is like a man with goat's legs and horns. N COUNT

fauna /fɔːnə/. Animals, especially the animals in a particular area, are referred to in technical or formal language as **fauna**. EG *...the flora and fauna of Africa.* N PLURAL ⇑ wildlife

faux pas /fəʊ pɑː/. **Faux pas** is both the singular and the plural form. A **faux pas** is a socially embarrassing action or mistake; a formal word. EG *They behaved as if they were fearful of committing a faux pas.* N COUNT = gaffe

favour /feɪvə/, **favours, favouring, favoured;** also spelled **favor** in American English. 1 If you regard something or someone with **favour**, you like, support, or agree with them. EG *I think the company will look with favour on your plan... ...a newer strategy which found increasing favour in the seventies... Is this just an attempt to win his favour?* N UNCOUNT ⇑ liking = approval, sympathy

2 If you show **favour** to a particular person or group, you are unfair by treating them more kindly than you treat other people. EG *The women were shown no favour and had to do the same tasks as the men.* N UNCOUNT = favouritism

3 **in favour.** 3.1 If you are **in favour** of something, you support it and think that it is a good thing or that it should happen. EG *They are in favour of reforming the tax laws... I'm all in favour of nuclear reactors... Will those in favour please raise their hands.* PHR : USED AS AN A, IF+PREP THEN *of* ≠ against 3.2 If you make a judgement **in** someone's **favour** or if you speak **in** their **favour**, you say that they are right or good. EG *The umpire ruled in her favour... There is a lot that can be said in their favour.* PHR : USED AS AN A ≠ against 3.3 Something that is **in** someone's **favour** helps them or gives them an advantage. EG *The odds were in their favour... The system is biased in favour of young people... The current is in our favour.* PHR : USED AS AN A 3.4 If something is rejected **in favour of** something else, the second thing is done, taken, or dealt with instead of the first one. EG *The plans for a new airport have been scrapped in favour of an extension to the old one.* PREP = for

4 If something such as an idea is **out of favour** with a particular person, that person does not like, support, or agree with it, although they used to. If something is **in favour** with a person, that person likes, supports, or agrees with it. EG *Their views are very much out of favour now.* PHR : USED AS AN A

5 A **favour** is something that you do for someone even though you do not have to do it, often because they ask you to do it and you want to help them. EG *Do me a favour, Grace. Don't say anything about this... I've come to ask a favour.* • You reply **'Do me a favour!'** to someone who has asked a question as an emphatic way of saying no and suggesting that it was a silly question to ask; a very informal expression. EG *'Did you tell her it wasn't yours?'–'Do me a favour!'* N COUNT = kindness • CONVENTION = you're joking!

6 If you **favour** something, you like that thing more than the other choices available. EG *Most observers favour the second view... The men seemed to favour the flat cap or the beret.* ◇ **favoured.** EG *The most favoured explanation was that the car's brakes had failed.* V+O = opt for, prefer ◇ ADJ QUALIT = popular

7 Something, for example a particular set of circumstances, that **favours** a person or event make it easier for that person to do something or for that event to happen. EG *The weather favoured the attacking army.* V+O = benefit, aid

8 If you **favour** someone, you treat them better or more kindly than you treat other people, often V+O ⇑ like

unfairly, when you should treat them all equally. EG *Parents sometimes favour the youngest child in the family... The referee mustn't give the impression of favouring one side or the other.* ◇ **favoured**. ◇ ADJ QUALIT

9 If you **favour** someone with your attention, your presence, etc, you give them that thing; a formal use. EG *The minister favoured us with an interview... I cannot say why he thinks this is so, for he does not favour us with his reasoning.* V+O+A *(with)* = honour

10 When a woman gives her **favours** to a man she allows him to have sex with her; a formal use. EG *She sometimes took money in return for her favours.* N PLURAL

11 to **curry favour**: see **curry**.

favourable /feɪvəʳrəbəᵒl/. **1** If your opinion about something or your reaction to something is **favourable**, you like or agree with that thing. EG *Her request met with a favourable response... ...favourable reviews.* ▸ used of people. EG *We found that most people were favourable to the idea.* ◇ **favourably**. EG *Many reacted favourably to the plan.* ADJ QUALIT : IF + PREP THEN *to* = good, positive ≠ negative ▸ ADJ QUALIT ◇ ADV WITH VB

2 Something that is **favourable 2.1** causes a particular person or thing to be liked or approved of or makes them more likely to be. EG *...the favourable impression created by his brother... We must try to present our profession in a more favourable light.* ◇ **favourably**. EG *Her application had impressed him very favourably.* **2.2** helps a particular person or thing or makes success more likely. EG *This creates an atmosphere favourable to expansion... She waited for a favourable moment to broach the subject.* ◇ **favourably**. EG *Other European countries, more favourably placed, were able to expand.* ADJ QUALIT = agreeable ≠ unfavourable ◇ ADV WITH VB = well ADJ QUALIT ⇑ helpful = beneficial ◇ ADV WITH VB

3 If you make a **favourable** comparison between one thing and another, you say that the first is better than or as good as the second. ◇ **favourably**. EG *He was always being compared favourably to his sister... We want to know how favourably it compares with services in other countries.* ADJ QUALIT ◇ ADV WITH VB ≠ unfavourably

favourite /feɪvəᵒrɪt/, **favourites**. **1** Your **favourite** thing of a particular type is the one you like most. EG *What is your favourite television programme?... She's one of my favourite writers... This was a favourite expression of his.* ▸ used as a noun. EG *Liquorice was his favourite.* ADJ CLASSIF ⇑ best = pet ▸ N COUNT : USU POSS+N

2 A person who is the **favourite** of someone in authority is treated with special kindness or given special privileges. N COUNT : USU POSS+N = pet

3 The **favourite** in a race or contest is the person, animal, or thing that is expected to win. EG *The favourite came second... Which team are favourites to win the cup?* N COUNT : IF SING USU *the*+N ≠ outsider

favouritism /feɪvəᵒrɪtɪzm/ is the practice of unfairly helping or favouring one person or group much more than another. EG *There must be no favouritism in the allocation of contracts.* N UNCOUNT = partiality

fawn /fɔːn/, **fawns, fawning, fawned**. **1** Something that is **fawn** is a pale yellowish brown colour. EG *...a fawn overcoat.* ADJ COLOUR

2 A **fawn** is a very young deer. EG *They looked up like startled fawns.* N COUNT

3 When you **fawn** on someone, especially someone more powerful than yourself, you insincerely treat them as if you think they are wonderful in order to make them like you and perhaps give you something. EG *...courtiers who had once flattered and fawned on him.* V : IF+PREP THEN *on* = dance attendance

4 When a dog **fawns** on someone, it behaves in a very friendly and affectionate way towards them. V : IF+PREP THEN *on*

faze /feɪz/, **fazes, fazing, fazed**. Something that **fazes** someone upsets or disturbs them. EG *Nothing seemed to faze them.* V+O = throw

FBI /ɛf biː aɪ/. The **FBI** is an agency of the American Department of Justice that investigates crimes in which a national law is broken or in which the country's security is threatened; an abbreviation for 'Federal Bureau of Investigation'. N PROPER : *the*+N

fealty /fiːltiˡ/, **fealties**. When someone swore **fealty** in former times to their ruler or lord, they promised to be loyal to him or her. N UNCOUNT/COUNT = allegiance

fear /fɪə/, **fears, fearing, feared**. **1 Fear** or a **fear** is the unpleasant feeling you have when you think that you are in danger. EG *They huddled together, quaking with fear... He lay there, flooded with pain, fear, and hatred... She was brought up with no fear of animals.* N UNCOUNT/COUNT ⇑ emotion = dread

2 If you **fear** someone or something, you are frightened because you think that they will harm you. EG *...a woman whom he disliked and feared... He fears nothing.* V+O/-ING/*to*-INF = be scared of

3 If you **fear** something unpleasant or undesirable, you think that it is likely to happen or to have happened and feel worried about this. EG *An epidemic of plague was feared... The new countries fear that their new-found independence might be lost... 'What about the doors?' Harris asked, fearing the worst.* V+O/REPORT-CL ⇑ anticipate

4 A **fear** is a thought that something unpleasant might happen or might have happened. EG *Her one fear was that one day he would give it up... Talk about your hopes and fears to your friends... My worst fears were quickly realized.* N COUNT = anxiety

5 If you are **in fear of** doing or experiencing something unpleasant or undesirable, you think that you might be going to do it or experience it and are very worried. EG *Sometimes I am in fear of losing my sanity.* PHR+-ING = afraid of

6 If you take a particular course of action **for fear of** something, you take it because you do not wish that thing to happen. EG *They did not mention it for fear of offending him... Few of us are prepared to admit to being happy for fear that we will be thought stupid.* PHR+*of*+-ING/NG, OR PHR+REPORT-CL = in case, lest

7 If you **fear** for something, you think that it might be in danger and are very worried. EG *Morris began to fear for the life of Mrs Reilly... She feared for her daughters.* ▸ used as a noun. EG *They had fears for their health.* V+A *(for)* ▸ N UNCOUNT/COUNT+*for*

8 Never fear and **fear not** are old-fashioned or formal ways of telling someone not to be worried or frightened. EG *But never fear. Virtue was rewarded.* CONVENTION

9 If there is a **fear** of something unpleasant or undesirable happening, there is a possibility that it will happen. EG *There is less fear of them refusing if they are asked publicly.* N UNCOUNT+*of* = risk, chance

10 You reply **no fear** when someone asks whether you will do something as an emphatic way of saying no; a very informal expression. EG *'Are you going out?'-'On a night like this? No fear!'* CONVENTION = not likely

11 If you **fear** to do something, you do not wish to do it. EG *Some pilgrims ventured no further than this, fearing to disturb the priest.* ▸ used as a noun. EG *...this fear of wasting money on a new idea.* V+*to*-INF ▸ N UNCOUNT/COUNT

12 If you say that you **fear** that something is the case you mean that you are sorry or distressed that it is the case; a formal use used when you want to be very polite. EG *I fear I do not know the answer to that... It is usually, I fear, the parents who are responsible... 'So you cannot tell me anything more?'-'I fear not.'* V+REPORT-CL, V OR V+*not/so* = regret to say

13 If you **put the fear of God into** someone, you threaten them with severe punishment if they do not do what you tell them to do; an informal expression. PHR : VB INFLECTS ⇑ intimidate

fearful /fɪəful/. **1** Someone who is **fearful** is afraid of something or afraid of doing something. EG *A fearful person is a weak person... ...parents who are fearful of letting their feelings take over.* ◇ **fearfully**. EG *The boys looked at each other fearfully.* ADJ QUALIT = frightened, scared ≠ confident ◇ ADV WITH VB = nervously

2 Something that is **fearful** is very unpleasant or bad. EG *This led to all sorts of fearful consequences.* ◇ **fearfully**. ADJ QUALIT = dire ◇ ADV WITH VB

3 Fearful is also used to emphasize that something is very bad; an informal use. EG *I've just had a fearful row with my parents... They were making a fearful racket.* ADJ CLASSIF : ATTRIB = frightful, terrible

fearfully /fɪəfəᵒliˡ/ means extremely; an informal, rather old-fashioned word. EG *It was fearfully hot.* ADV+ADJ/ADV = dreadfully

fearless /fɪəlɪˢs/. Someone who is **fearless** is not afraid at all. EG *...fearless reporters.* ◇ **fearlessly**. EG *If provoked, it defended itself fearlessly.* ADJ CLASSIF ◇ ADV

fearsome /fɪəsəm/. Something that is **fearsome** is terrible or frightening; a formal word. EG *The dog had a fearsome set of teeth.* ADJ QUALIT = formidable

feasible /fiːzəbəᵒl/. Something that is **feasible** can be done, made, or achieved. EG *The electric car is technically feasible... Godley's proposals are not feasible.* ◇ **feasibility** /fiːzəbɪlɪtiˡ/. EG *He was talking about the feasibility of setting up a military government... ...feasibility studies.* ADJ QUALIT ⇑ possible = practicable ◇ N UNCOUNT : IF+PREP THEN *of*

feast /fiːst/, **feasts, feasting, feasted**. **1** A **feast** is a large and special meal to which several people are invited. EG *...a wedding feast... 'Delightful,' he said as he surveyed the feast before him.* N COUNT = banquet

2 If you **feast**, you take part in a feast. EG *The poor* V

starve while the rich feast. ◊ **feasting**. EG *The dancing and the feasting went on for hours.*
◊ N UNCOUNT

3 If someone **is feasted**, a feast is given in their honour. EG *Sir Gawain was feasted in the great hall.*
V+O : IF+PREP THEN *on*

4 To **feast** on or off a particular type of food means to eat a large amount of it with great enjoyment. EG *Flies feast on rotting flesh... He sprawled there, feasting off cold roast duck.*
V : IF+PREP THEN *on/off* = gorge

5 If you **feast** your **eyes on** or **upon** something, you look at it for a long time with great attention because you like it very much or are very pleased to see it. EG *I feasted my eyes upon her lovely face.*
PHR : VB INFLECTS ⇑ stare

6 A **feast** of something is a large number of a particular type of thing, or something that is very good and enjoyable. EG *These elements combine to make a feast of entertainment.*
N COUNT : USU+SUPP ⇑ abundance

7 A **feast** or a **feast day** is a day on which a special religious celebration takes place; a technical term. EG *...feasts like Christmas and Easter.*
N COUNT = festival

feat /fiːt/, **feats**. A **feat** is an impressive and difficult act or achievement. EG *He received a medal for his heroic feat... The construction of this bridge was a brilliant feat of engineering.*
N COUNT

feather /feðə/, **feathers, feathering, feathered**. 1 A **feather** is one of the very light things that form the covering on a bird's body. A feather consists of lots of soft or smooth hairs on each side of a thin stiff centre. EG *...a pink dress trimmed with ostrich feathers... ...a great feather bed.* ● **as light as a feather**: see **light**.
N COUNT

2 If you **feather** something, you cover it with feathers or stick feathers onto it. ● **to tar and feather** someone: see **tar**.
V+O

3 You describe two or more people as **birds of a feather** when you think that they have similar characters, beliefs, interests, etc.
PHR : USED AS C = kindred spirits

4 If something you have done is **a feather in** your **cap**, it is an achievement that other people admire you for. EG *If he clinches this deal, that'll really be a feather in his cap!*
PHR : USED AS C ⇑ success

5 Someone who **feathers** their **nest** makes or obtains a lot of money over a period of time, especially in a dishonest way, so that they are able to live a very comfortable life.
PHR : VB INFLECTS = line one's pocket

6 When you **feather** your oars as you are rowing a boat, you turn them so that the flat parts are parallel with the surface of the water.
V OR V+O

7 See also **feathered**.

feather-bedding is the practice of allowing work to be done slowly or inefficiently so that the jobs of all the employees of a firm are protected; an informal expression used showing disapproval. EG *...the feather-bedding of agriculture.*
N UNCOUNT

feather boa, feather boas. A **feather boa** is a kind of long, thin scarf made of soft feathers.
N COUNT

feather-brained. Someone who is **feather-brained** is rather silly and forgetful.
ADJ QUALIT

feather duster, feather dusters. A **feather duster** is an object that is used for dusting. It consists of a bunch of feathers attached to a stick.
N COUNT

feathered /feðəd/. Something that is **feathered** has feathers on it. EG *...girls in feathered head-dresses... ...our feathered friends.*
ADJ CLASSIF : USU ATTRIB = plumed

featherweight /feðəweɪt/, **featherweights**. A **featherweight** is 1 a professional boxer who weighs between 53.5 and 57 kilograms, which is one of the lowest weight ranges. 2 someone or something that does not weigh very much. 3 someone or something that is of very little importance.
N COUNT / N COUNT / N COUNT

feathery /feðəᵒriˡ/. Something that is **feathery** 1 has an edge divided into lots of thin parts so that it looks soft. EG *...the tops of feathery palm trees.* 2 is soft and light. EG *...feathery flakes of ashes.*
ADJ QUALIT = fringed / ADJ QUALIT = fluffy

feature /fiːtʃə/, **features, featuring, featured**. 1 A **feature** of something is a particular part of it or characteristic that it has, which you notice because it seems important or interesting. EG *But the most important feature of our work must be parental involvement... Career guidance discussions were a feature of our final year... They both hit upon the same idea for the chief feature of their designs... Every car will come with built-in safety features.*
N COUNT : IF+PREP THEN *of/in* ⇑ part

2 Someone's **features** are their eyes, nose, mouth, and other parts of their face; used especially when you are describing what sort of emotions they are showing or what they look like. EG *A flicker of distaste crossed his features... He was slightly taller than me, with very regular features.*
N PLURAL = countenance

3 When a person, film, exhibition, etc **features** something or when it **features** in a particular thing, it is included as an important part of that thing and is very noticeable. EG *This film features two of my favourite actors... This is not the first time he has featured in allegations of violence... ...a sign outside a cafe featuring a one-legged pirate.*
V+O, OR V+A *(in)* ⇑ show

4 If you **feature** a particular thing that you are selling, you display it or advertise it more than the other things you are selling.
V+O = promote

5 A geographical **feature** is something noticeable in a particular area of country, for example a hill, river, or valley. EG *Many birds certainly follow major geographical features... ...the natural features of the landscape.*
N COUNT+SUPP : USU PL ⇑ characteristic

6 A **feature** is also 6.1 a special article in a newspaper or magazine, usually one that does not deal with an actual news event. EG *Only the other week the local newspaper ran a feature on drug abuse... Out of this interview I got a feature article.* 6.2 a special programme on radio or television that is not part of a series, and which is usually about a serious subject. 6.3 a full-length film that is shown in a cinema. EG *I believe it's the first long feature film that he has made... He was in some feature with Ava Gardner.*
N COUNT : IF+PREP THEN *on* / N COUNT : IF+PREP THEN *on* / N COUNT

featureless /fiːtʃəlɪˢs/. Something that is **featureless** has no interesting features or characteristics. EG *...a featureless expanse of sand... ...featureless rooms.*
ADJ CLASSIF = nondescript

Feb. is an abbreviation for February.

febrile /fiːbraɪl/. **Febrile** behaviour is intensely and nervously active; a literary word. EG *...her febrile state of creativity.*
ADJ QUALIT = feverish

February /februəriˡ/ is the second month of the year in the Western calendar. EG *The case was heard in the High Court in February 1910.*
N UNCOUNT

feces /fiːsiːz/. See **faeces**.
N UNCOUNT

feckless /feklɪˢs/. Someone who is **feckless** lacks determination or strength, and is unable to do anything properly; a formal word. EG *...children with drunken or feckless parents.*
ADJ QUALIT ⇑ weak = incompetent

fecund /fiːkənd, fek-/. A living thing or place that is **fecund** is fertile; a literary word. EG *...fecund soil.* ◊ **fecundity** /fekʌndɪtiˡ/.
ADJ QUALIT / ◊ N UNCOUNT

fed /fed/ is the past tense and past participle of **feed**.

federal /fedəᵒrəl/. 1 A **federal** country or system of government is one which consists of a group of states controlled by a central government. The central government deals with things concerning the whole country, such as foreign policy, but each state has its own local powers and laws. EG *...a huge, federal country like the U.S.A... ...the Federal Republic of Germany.*
ADJ CLASSIF : ATTRIB

2 **Federal** also means belonging or relating to the central government of a federal country rather than to one of the states within it. EG *The company might find the federal government on its side... Mr Stans will be brought to a federal court.*
ADJ CLASSIF : ATTRIB

federalism /fedəᵒrəlɪzəᵒm/ is belief in or support for a federal system of government, or this system itself. EG *...a party dedicated to federalism.* ◊ **federalist, federalists**.
N UNCOUNT / ◊ N COUNT

federate /fedəreɪt/, **federates, federating, federated**. When a group of states or societies **federates**, it becomes a federation.
V-ERG ⇑ unite

federation /fedəreɪʃəᵒn/, **federations**. A **federation** is 1 a federal country. EG *...the proposal to form a federation out of Northern and Southern Rhodesia.* 2 a group of societies or other organizations which have joined together, usually because they share a common interest. EG *It is a federation of 20 regional unions... ...the National Federation of Women's Institutes.*
N COUNT / N COUNT : ALSO IN NAMES = association, league

fed up. Someone who is **fed up** is unhappy, bored, or tired of something, especially something that they have been experiencing for quite a long time; an informal expression. EG *I should think they're getting pretty fed up with him by now... You sound a bit fed up.*
ADJ QUALIT : PRED, IF+PREP THEN *with/about* ⇑ miserable = cheesed off

fee /fiː/, **fees**. A **fee** is 1 a sum of money that you pay to be allowed to do something. EG *...an entrance fee... ...a registration fee.* 2 the amount of money that a person or organization is paid for a particular job or service that they provide. EG *...a fee of one*
N COUNT ⇑ payment / N COUNT ⇑ payment

thousand pounds... Agencies charge a fee to find an au pair.

feeble /fi:bəºl/, **feebler, feeblest**. 1 Someone who is **feeble** 1.1 has very little strength or energy. EG *The creature is physically feeble, with poor vision and dull senses.* ◇ **feebly**. EG *He waved his hands feebly... He smiled feebly.* **1.2** is afraid to do things and is easily controlled or influenced by other people. EG *The management was feeble and cowardly.* ADJ QUALIT = weak, puny; ◇ ADV WITH VB; ADJ QUALIT ⇑ weak = ineffectual

2 Something that is **feeble** 2.1 does not have much power, force, or strength. EG *...the feeble light of the bulb in the hallway... 'Hello,' he said in a feeble voice.* ◇ **feebly**. EG *The heater glowed feebly in the far corner.* **2.2** is not effective, good, or convincing. EG *Their attempts at conversation grew even feebler... ...feeble excuses... ...a feeble joke.* ◇ **feebly**. EG *'They seemed all right to me,' I explained feebly.* ADJ QUALIT = weak, puny; ◇ ADV WITH VB; ADJ QUALIT ⇑ weak; ◇ ADV WITH VB

feeble-minded. Someone who is **feeble-minded** is unable to think or understand things very quickly. ADJ QUALIT = slow-witted

feed /fi:d/, **feeds, feeding, fed**. 1 If you **feed** a baby, a person who is helpless, or an animal, you give them food, in some cases actually putting the food into their mouth. EG *She fed the baby some milk... He had just come back from feeding the ponies with sugar... Garbage was carefully saved and fed to the pig.* ◇ **feeding, feedings**. EG *His feeding time was still an hour away.* V+O (NG/REFL): IF+PREP THEN *with/on*, V+O+A *(to)*, OR V+O+O; ◇ N UNCOUNT/COUNT

2 When an animal or baby **feeds**, it eats something. EG *Not all bats feed on insects... The baby feeds when it is hungry.* V: IF+PREP THEN *on/off*

3 When a baby or animal has a **feed**, it is given food. EG *What time is the next feed?* N COUNT ⇑ meal

4 **Feed** is the food that is given to an animal or baby. EG *They're growing crops for use as animal feed.* N MASS

5 If you **feed** a person or a group of people such as your family or a community, you supply or prepare food for them. EG *The farmers grew too little to feed even their own families... Are you feeding yourself properly?* ● To **bite the hand that feeds** you: see **hand**. ● **a mouth to feed**: see **mouth**. V+O (NG/REFL) ⇑ provide for

6 A **feed** also means a meal; an informal use. EG *She gave us a slap-up feed.* N COUNT

7 If you **feed** a plant, you give it substances that will make it grow well. V+O: IF+PREP THEN *with/on*

8 If you **feed** something, or **feed** something else to it, you supply it with what it needs in order to operate, grow, or exist. EG *We use their natural resources to feed the factories of Europe... The fires were being fed by escaping gas... Nothing feeds fear so much as ignorance.* V+O: IF+PREP THEN *with/on*, V+O+O, OR V+O+A *(to)* = fuel

9 If something such as a feeling, system, or process **feeds** on a particular thing or on itself, it continues or becomes greater or stronger because of the existence of that thing. EG *Once the process has been started it feeds on itself... Anger feeds on disappointment.* V+A *(on)* = thrive

10 If something **is fed** into or through something else, it is put into it. EG *Extra gas was to be fed into the pipeline... This new data is fed into the computer... I kept feeding coins into the meter... ...when you feed a current through the coil.* V+O: IF+PREP THEN *into/in/through* ⇑ supply

11 The **feed** in a machine is the part of it by which or through which it is supplied with something such as fuel. EG *...the petrol feed.* N COUNT ⇑ mechanism

feedback /fi:dbæk/. 1 **Feedback** consists of comments and information about something that someone has done. It tells them whether or not it was successful or liked. EG *The more feedback we get from viewers, the better.* N UNCOUNT ⇑ response

2 **Feedback** occurs in a machine or system when part of the power, sound, or information that is produced goes back into the machine or system; a technical term. EG *They reduced the amount of feedback by moving the microphone.* N UNCOUNT ⇑ return

feeder /fi:də/, **feeders**. 1 A baby or animal that is a slow **feeder**, a fussy **feeder**, etc feeds in the way described. EG *...a baby who is a listless, sleepy feeder.* N COUNT: ADJ+N ⇑ eater

2 A **feeder** is a minor road, railway line, or air route that leads to a major one. N COUNT ⇑ link

feeding-bottle, feeding-bottles. A **feeding-bottle** is a small bottle with a special rubber top through which a baby can suck milk or another liquid. N COUNT

feeding ground, feeding grounds. The **feeding ground** of a group of birds or animals is the place where they find food and eat. N COUNT: SING=PL

feel /fi:l/, **feels, feeling, felt**. 1 If you **feel** a particular emotion, sensation, physical state, or attitude, you experience it. EG *I felt angry... I was feeling hungry and sleepy... Are you feeling all right now, John?... People feel safer in well-lit streets... Mrs Oliver felt a sudden desire to burst out crying... He felt a sudden pain in his left leg... She felt a fool... I felt like a murderer... He felt as if he hadn't slept at all.* ● **feel free**: see **free**. V+C, V+O, OR V+A *(like, as if, as though)*

2 If you **feel** a physical object, you touch it deliberately with your hand, so that you learn what it is like, for example what shape it is or whether it is rough or smooth. EG *I reach down and feel the aluminium side cover of the engine... Eric felt his face. 'I'm all rough. Am I bleeding?'* ▸ used as a noun. EG *Have a feel of this.* V+O; ▸ N SING: a+N

3 If an object **feels** heavy, light, rough, soft, smooth, hot, cold, etc when you touch it, you notice that it has the physical quality mentioned. EG *How does it feel, warm or cold?... His fork felt heavy... It looks and feels like a normal fabric.* ▸ used as a noun. EG *...the cool feel of armchair leather... This gives their surface a curious prickly feel.* V+C, OR V+A *(like)*: NO CONT ⇑ seem; ▸ N SING WITH DET+SUPP = texture

4 If an experience, event, or situation **feels** good, strange, different, etc, it seems to you to have the quality mentioned. EG *It felt good to be back... At first it felt strange working with such a great man... It felt as if it would never end... It felt like tea time.* V+C, OR V+A *(like/as if)*: USU *it*+V

5 You say that it **feels** warm or cold, or like winter, summer, etc, when you are describing the weather, usually when you have been outside and experienced it yourself. EG *It feels lovely and warm in the garden... It feels like autumn.* ● If you say that it **feels like rain** or **snow**, you mean that you think it is going to rain or snow. V: *it*+V+C OR *it*+V+A *(like/as if)* = be; ● PHR: VB INFLECTS

6 If you **feel** something on your skin, you are aware that it is present or happening. EG *They felt the wind on their damp faces... He felt a sting on his elbow... Every one of them felt an itching in their feet... She felt his hand pat hers... He could feel the warm blood pouring down his face.* ● Someone who **feels the cold** feels cold easily, and feels very unhappy when they are cold. V+O: NO CONT; ● PHR: VB INFLECTS ⇑ suffer

7 If you **feel** yourself doing something or being in a particular state, you are aware that something is happening to you which you are unable to control. EG *Rudolph could feel himself blushing... Langtry felt himself thrown into the air... He felt himself sliding into obsession... I felt myself being drawn into an argument I would rather have avoided... Ralph felt his lips twitch.* V+O (REFL/NG) +-ING, PAST PART, OR INF

8 If you **do not feel** yourself, you feel slightly ill. EG *I don't really feel myself today.* PHR: VB INFLECTS+REFL

9 If you **feel** something such as the presence of someone or something, you become aware of it, even though you cannot see or hear it. EG *He had felt Binta's presence in the hut... I felt his eyes upon my back as I left the room... I could feel the tension in the room.* V+O: USU+A, NO CONT ⇑ perceive = sense

10 If you **feel** that something is the case, you have a strong idea in your mind that it is the case, although this idea is based on intuition rather than on evidence. EG *He felt I was making a terrible mistake... I feel I'm neglecting my duty... They did not feel that they were doing anything wrong... He felt sure that his technique would work... He felt himself to be a failure.* ● to **feel** something **in** your **bones**: see **bone**. V+REPORT-CL, V+C+REPORT-CL, OR V+O+*to*-INF: NO CONT ⇑ believe = sense

11 If you **feel** that you should or must do something, you think that you should or must do it. EG *I felt I should do something to help them... I felt obliged to invite him in... We felt it our duty to make it public... He felt it necessary to explain why he had come.* V+REPORT-CL, V+C+*to*-INF, OR V+*it*+C+*to*-INF: NO CONT

12 If you **feel** a particular way about something, you have that opinion about it or that attitude or reaction to it. EG *She knew how I felt about totalitarianism... He felt strongly about what he regarded as unfairness.* V+A: IF+PREP THEN *about*, NO CONT

13 You say that you **feel** that you want to do something to say and emphasize that you want and intend to do it. EG *I feel I'd like to say something about what happened last week... I felt that I wanted to see him at least once more.* V+REPORT-CL: NO CONT

14 If you **feel like** having something or doing something, you want to have it or do it because you are in the right mood for it and think you would enjoy it. EG *Whenever I felt like talking they were ready to* PHR: VB INFLECTS = fancy

listen... I feel like a stroll... I feel like a drink... I felt like saying, 'Why don't you shut up?'

15 If you **feel** the effect or result of something, you experience it. EG *The consequences of the computer revolution will be felt in the short-term future... We shan't feel the effect of the change for some years... The strength of the mass movement will be felt in Parliament.* V+O = notice

16 The **feel** of something, for example a place, is the general impression that it gives you. EG *The Brazilian Amazon has the feel of a tropical wild west... This had a very different feel about it.* N SING WITH DET +SUPP = atmosphere ● If you **get the feel of** something, for example a place or a new activity, you become familiar with it. EG *I spent the first week talking to people and generally getting the feel of the place.* ● PHR : VB INFLECTS = get used to

17 Someone who **is feeling** their **way** is learning about a new situation and so is behaving more cautiously than they normally would. EG *I'd like to stick to the plan because I'm still feeling my way.* PHR ⇑ uncertain

18 See also **feeling, felt.**

feel around. If you **feel around** somewhere or in something, you use your hands rather than your eyes to find things there. EG *He unbuttoned the coat and felt around in his jacket.* PHRASAL VB : V+ADV = grope, fumble

feel for. **1** If you **feel for** an object you try to find it by using your hands rather than your eyes. EG *She felt in her bag for her key... A finger felt for the nerve spot below the ear.* PHRASAL VB : V+PREP ⇑ search for

2 If you **feel for** someone, you have sympathy for them. EG *Boy, I feel for you guys.* PHRASAL VB : V+PREP

feeler /fi̲:lə/, **feelers.** **1** An insect's **feelers** are the two thin stalks on its head with which it touches and senses things around it. EG *It has two feelers at the front of the head.* N COUNT : USU PL = antenna

2 If you **put** or **have feelers out**, you suggest something in an informal and tentative way in order to discover what people's reaction will be, or in order to find out something. EG *Already feelers were out about another script.* PHR : VB INFLECTS

feeler gauge, feeler gauges; also spelled with a hyphen. A **feeler gauge** is a thin metal strip of a particular thickness that is used to measure a narrow gap. N COUNT ⇑ tool

feeling /fi̲:lıŋ/, **feelings.** **1** A **feeling** is an emotion, such as anger or happiness. EG *...strong feelings of jealousy... A feeling of panic was rising in him... She had the most horrible guilty feeling... I didn't like him and I was sure the feeling was mutual.* N COUNT : USU+SUPP

2 Your **feelings** are the things that you think and feel about something but do not necessarily express to other people, for example your emotions or your attitudes towards other people. EG *She dare not express her feelings... He was unsure of his real feelings... They cannot put their feelings into words... She tried to hide her feelings as much as possible.* N PLURAL : USU POSS+N ⇑ thoughts

3 **Feeling** is a way of thinking and reacting to things which is emotional and spontaneous rather than logical and rational. EG *...the difference between reason and feeling... She cried out in a voice rich in real feeling, 'It means so much to me!'* N UNCOUNT = emotion

4 **Feeling** for someone is sympathy and caring for them. EG *He may be moved by feeling for his fellow-citizens... ...a community of feeling.* N UNCOUNT : IF+PREP THEN *for* ⇑ concern

5 A **feeling** of, for example hunger or tiredness is a physical sensation that you experience. EG *Soon many of them noticed an itchy feeling on parts of the body exposed... He had the most appalling depression, accompanied by feelings of nausea, and a bitter, dry mouth.* N COUNT+SUPP

6 **Feeling** in part of your body is the ability to experience the sense of touch in this part of the body. EG *I've lost the feeling in my left arm... He lost all feeling in his legs.* N UNCOUNT

7 A **feeling** is also a sensation that you experience both physically and emotionally. EG *There was no feeling in the world as good as being airborne.* N COUNT+SUPP

8 If you have a **feeling** about something, **8.1** you have an opinion, thought, or idea about it that is based on your intuition rather than on things you know. EG *My feeling is that it would work very well... I had a feeling that no one thought I was sufficiently good... I'm not sure, but I have a nasty feeling that it's here at home... I got the feeling that it was intended to kill them stone dead... My own feelings would be very much that schools have to make these decisions for themselves.* N COUNT : USU+REPORT-CL, SING=PL = impression **8.2** you have an idea that something is going to happen or that something is true, although you have no proof or no logical reason for believing it. EG *It might be bad. He just had a feeling about it... There's nothing in it of course. Just a feeling.* N SING : a+N

9 Your **feeling** about something is also your general attitude towards it or the view that you have about it. EG *Americans had, and have, a quite different feeling about the press... As Party Treasurer, he echoed the gut feeling of the trade unions... You can keep her in touch with grass roots feelings in the company... Socialist feeling was very strong in the village.* N COUNT/UNCOUNT : USU SING+SUPP

10 A **feeling** is also the way in which you see and think about yourself or the situation you are in. EG *You would no longer have this feeling of being surrounded by hostility.* N SING WITH DET +SUPP = consciousness

11 If you have a **feeling** for something, you have an understanding of it. EG *He went to get a feeling for the situation at first hand... I have always had a tremendous feeling for Russian literature.* N SING : a+N+*for*

12 The **feeling** that a place has or that a book, play, etc creates is the atmosphere that it has or creates. EG *The place did have a real medieval feeling... A lot of people remark on the happy kind of feeling at the factory... There was a tremendous feeling of urgency and excitement.* N SING WITH DET +SUPP = feel

13 If you **hurt** someone's **feelings**, you upset them by something that you say or do. EG *He spoke gently; he didn't want to hurt her feelings... I don't go around deliberately hurting people's feelings.* PHR : VB INFLECTS

14 If you **have mixed feelings** about something or someone, you feel uncertain about them because you can see both good and bad points about them. EG *She had mixed feelings about pregnancy... Most executives have mixed feelings about whether trade unions are a 'good thing'.* PHR : VB INFLECTS : IF+PREP THEN *about* ⇑ be uncertain

15 **Bad feeling** is resentment, bitterness, or anger which exists between people, for example after they have had an argument. EG *This only gives rise to more resentment, bad feeling and aggravation... There was bad feeling between them.* PHR : USED AS O ⇑ hostility ≠ goodwill

16 **Hard feelings** are feelings of anger or bitterness towards someone who you have had an argument with or who has upset you. EG *She got up at once and, without any apparent hard feelings, walked out.* PHR : USU USED AS O = resentment

17 You say **'I know the feeling'** to say that you understand and sympathize with the problem or difficult experience that someone is telling you about. EG *'I don't hold my liquor very well.' Ellen nodded. 'I know the feeling.'* CONVENTION

feet /fi̲:t/ is the plural of **foot.**

feign /fe̲ın/, **feigns, feigning, feigned.** If you **feign** an emotion or feeling, you behave as if you are experiencing this emotion or feeling in order to deceive people; a literary word. EG *She knew that her efforts to feign cheerfulness weren't convincing... 'I thought you must know,' Dixon said with feigned surprise.* V+O ⇑ pretend = affect

feint /fe̲ınt/, **feints, feinting, feinted.** **1** A **feint** is a misleading action or movement, especially in boxing, intended to confuse or deceive your opponent. EG *The contest becomes mainly one of feint and counter-feint.* N UNCOUNT/COUNT ⇑ distraction = play ▸ used as a verb. EG *The two bulls, after a great deal of skilful feinting, withdrew to opposite ends of the field.* ▸ V OR V+O = manoeuvring

2 **Feint** is used to refer to paper that has pale lines across it for writing on. EG *...a pad of narrow feint.* N UNCOUNT

felicitous /fı²lı̲sıtəs/. Something such as a word, expression, or image that is **felicitous** is particularly suitable, appropriate, and well-chosen. EG *Nationalization is a word which is neither very felicitous nor free from ambiguity... ...an example of the felicitous conjunction of poetry and image.* ADJ QUALIT = happy, fitting

felicity /fı²lı̲sıti¹/, **felicities**; a formal or literary word. **1** **Felicity** is **1.1** great happiness and pleasure. EG *It has little or nothing to do with the felicity of marriage.* N UNCOUNT = bliss **1.2** the quality of being good, pleasant, or desirable. EG *...small moments of architectural madness and felicity amidst acres of monotony.* N UNCOUNT = grace

2 **Felicities** are particularly suitable or well-chosen remarks. N COUNT : USU PL

feline /fi̲:laın/, **felines.** **1** **Feline** means belonging or relating to the cat family. ADJ CLASSIF

2 A **feline** is an animal that belongs to the cat family. EG *...information on the care of felines.* N COUNT ⇑ mammal

3 Someone who is described as **feline** resembles a cat in appearance or in the graceful, quiet way that ADJ QUALIT = slinky they move or behave. EG *On the screen she had a feline feminine charm that made her irresistible.*

fell /fel/, **fells, felling, felled.** 1 A **fell** is a mountain, hill, or moor, especially in the North of England. EG *...recent floods in the fell country... ...the sheep on the fell tops.* N COUNT, OR N BEFORE N

2 If you **fell** a tree, you cut it down. V+O

3 If you **fell** someone, you knock them down, for example in a fight. EG *This blow would have felled most men.* V+O = floor

4 **with one fell swoop**: see **swoop**.

5 **Fell** is also the past tense of **fall**.

fellow /feləʊ/, **fellows**; also spelled **fella** or **feller** in informal English for paragraphs 1 and 2. **Fella** and **feller** are both pronounced /felə/. 1 A **fellow** is a man; an informal term often used affectionately, especially in rather old-fashioned English. EG *Doug is an exceedingly amiable fellow... My dear fellow, I really am sorry... What do you other fellers have to say?... Okay fellas, we're doing fine.* N COUNT : ALSO VOC = chap

2 A woman's **fellow** is her boyfriend or lover; an informal use. EG *You didn't expect me to say it in front of her fellow, did you?* N COUNT : POSS+N ⇑ man = bloke

3 **Fellow** is used to describe a person or people who have something in common with you, for example because they are doing the same job, work for the same company, have the same nationality, or simply because they too are human beings. EG *I've always trusted my fellow men... You will soon feel at ease with your fellow students or workers... During the flight I had a conversation with a fellow passenger.* ADJ CLASSIF : ATTRIB

4 Your **fellows** are the people who share work or an activity with you or who are like you in some way. EG *He sought the approval of his fellows... People have given their lives to save their fellows.* N PLURAL : POSS +N ⇑ associates = comrades

5 A **fellow** of a society or academic institution is a member of it. EG *...Sir George Porter, Fellow of the Royal Society.* N COUNT : ALSO IN TITLE

fellow feeling is sympathy and friendship that exists between people who have shared similar experiences or difficulties. N UNCOUNT

fellowship /feləᵘʃɪp/, **fellowships.** 1 **Fellowship** is a feeling of friendship that people have when they are talking or doing something together and sharing their experiences. EG *We meet regularly for fellowship... There is a great amount of good fellowship and love in people.* N UNCOUNT ⇑ companionship

2 A **fellowship** is a group of people that join together for a common purpose or interest. EG *Healy set up a new body, the Socialist Fellowship.* N COUNT+SUPP ⇑ society

3 A **fellowship** at a university is a post which involves research work. N COUNT

felon /felən/, **felons.** A **felon** is a person who is guilty of a felony; a legal term. N COUNT ⇑ criminal

felony /feləni[1]/, **felonies.** **Felony** or a **felony** is a very serious crime such as murder or armed robbery; a legal term. N UNCOUNT/ COUNT

felt /felt/. 1 **Felt** is the past tense and past participle of **feel**.

2 **Felt** is also a material made from wool or other fibres packed tight together to form a thick cloth. EG *...an old brown felt hat.* N UNCOUNT

felt-tip, felt-tips. A **felt-tip** or a **felt-tip pen** is a pen which has a thin piece of fibre for a nib. EG *Jane is wondering if you know where her felt tips are.* N COUNT

fem. is an abbreviation for 'female' or 'feminine'.

female /fiːmeɪl/, **females.** 1 A **female** is 1.1 an animal that belongs to the sex that can have babies. EG *The male fertilizes the female's eggs.* ▸ used as an adjective. EG *A female toad may lay 20,000 eggs each season.* 1.2 a woman or girl; a formal or technical use which some people find offensive. EG *...a lone female staying at a hotel... ...the new liberated female... ...a perfect job for ambitious females.* ▸ used as an adjective. EG *There are only nineteen female members of the government... I could see a small female figure coming towards us.* N COUNT ≠ male ▸ ADJ CLASSIF ≠ male N COUNT ⇑ human ▸ ADJ CLASSIF ≠ male

2 Something that is **female** concerns, relates to, or affects women rather than men. EG *...female inventions... ...the cause of female equality... ...the decline in traditionally female areas of work.* ADJ CLASSIF : ATTRIB = women's ≠ male

3 **Female** is a group or category that represents females. EG *The old stereotypes of male and female are increasingly being questioned.* ▸ used as an adjective. EG *...the female sex.* N UNCOUNT ≠ male ▸ ADJ CLASSIF ≠ male

4 A **female** plant or part of a plant contains or consists of the part that will become the fruit when it is fertilized; a technical term. ADJ CLASSIF

5 The **female** part of a device or piece of equipment is one of two parts which fit together. The male part is pressed into a hole in the female part; a technical term. ADJ CLASSIF ≠ male

feminine /femɪnɪn/. 1 Something that is **feminine** relates to or is considered typical of women, in contrast to men. EG *Society hasn't regarded science or engineering as feminine occupations... He had feminine handwriting.* ADJ QUALIT ⇑ female ≠ masculine

2 Someone or something that is **feminine** has qualities that are considered to be characteristic of women, especially in terms of being delicate, pretty, or gentle. EG *She became very coquettish and feminine... I dress my daughter in feminine clothes and she wears ribbons in her hair.* ADJ QUALIT ⇑ female ≠ masculine

3 A **feminine** noun, pronoun, etc, in some languages, belongs to a particular class of nouns, pronouns, etc. Words that are feminine have sets of inflections which are different from those of masculine and neuter words. ADJ CLASSIF

femininity /femɪnɪnɪti[1]/. **Femininity** is 1 the fact of being a woman. EG *Masculinity has certain characteristics and femininity has others.* 2 qualities that are considered to be feminine, especially those qualities which are considered to be attractive to men. EG *The fashion industry responded to the new mood of femininity by creating a new look.* N UNCOUNT ≠ masculinity N UNCOUNT ≠ masculinity

feminism /femɪnɪzəᵘm/. **Feminism** is 1 the political belief that women should have the same rights, power, and opportunity that men have, and that the present situation should be changed to give them equality with men. 2 the social movement based on this belief. N UNCOUNT ⇑ doctrine N UNCOUNT = women's lib

feminist /femɪnɪst/, **feminists.** A **feminist** is a person who believes in and supports feminism, especially one who actively campaigns to achieve change. EG *Claudia thought of herself as a feminist... Lucy was a feminist member of a radical group.* ▸ used as an adjective. EG *...the feminist response to the new law.* N COUNT ▸ ADJ CLASSIF

femme fatale /fæm fətæl, -tɑːl/, **femmes fatales.** A woman who is referred to as a **femme fatale** is a mysterious, attractive and seductive woman who leads men into dangerous or difficult situations by her charm. N COUNT = charmer

femur /fiːmə/, **femurs, femora.** The plural can be either **femurs** or **femora**. Your **femur** is the large bone in the upper part of your leg. N COUNT

fen /fen/, **fens.** An area of low, flat, very wet land is referred to as **fen** or the **fens**. EG *...areas of marsh and fen... The landscape of the fens is utterly flat and strangely wild.* N COUNT/ UNCOUNT

fence /fens/, **fences, fencing, fenced.** 1 A **fence** is a barrier between two areas of land, made of wood or wire supported by posts. EG *A football had come over the fence from the playing fields... ...a row of fence posts.* N COUNT

2 If you **fence** an area of land, you surround it with a fence. EG *I helped him fence a part of the garden.* ◊ **fenced.** EG *...a fenced rectangle of ten acres.* V OR V+O : USU V+O ◊ ADJ CLASSIF

3 If you **sit on the fence**, you avoid supporting a particular side in a discussion or argument. PHR : VB INFLECTS

4 A **fence** in show jumping or horse racing is a frame or artificial hedge that horses have to jump over. N COUNT ⇑ obstacle = hurdle

5 When two sportsmen **fence**, they use special thin swords to fight as a sport: see **fencing**. V

6 If you say that two people **are fencing** when they are talking to each other, you mean that they are answering each other's remarks cleverly but evasively, often because each of them is trying to get an advantage over the other one; a formal use. EG *We fenced like this for a while, weighing each other up.* V OR V+A (with) : RECIP = spar

7 A **fence** is also a person who receives and then sells stolen property; an informal word. N COUNT

fence in. 1 If you **fence** something **in**, you surround it completely with a fence. EG *It stands on a sloping road which is fenced in by iron railings.* PHRASAL VB : V+O+ADV

2 If someone or something **fences** you **in**, they are so close to you that you are or feel you are unable to move or leave. PHRASAL VB : V+O+ADV ⇑ restrict = hem in

fence off. If you **fence off** an area of land, you build a fence round it. EG *The railway line was fenced off.* PHRASAL VB : V+O+ADV ⇑ separate

fencing /fensɪŋ/. **Fencing** is 1 a sport in which two competitors fight each other using very thin swords. N UNCOUNT

The ends of the swords are covered, and the competitors wear protective clothes, so that they do not hurt each other. 2 materials, for example wood or wire, that are used to make fences. EG *...cedar wood fencing.* — N UNCOUNT : USU +SUPP

fend /fɛnd/, **fends, fending, fended.** If you have to **fend for yourself**, you have to look after yourself without relying on help from anyone else. EG *Grown up children should leave home and fend for themselves.* — PHR : VB INFLECTS = support yourself

fend off. 1 If you **fend off** someone who is attacking you, you use your arms or something such as a stick to defend yourself from their blows. EG *He raised his arms to fend off the blows.* — PHRASAL VB : V+O+ADV ⇑ repel = ward off

2 If you **fend off** unwanted questions, enquiries, problems, people, etc, you deal with them in a defensive way to prevent yourself being affected or harmed by them. EG *It was the first time Daniel had spoken, except to fend off questions... He was continually fending off unwanted meals.* — PHRASAL VB : ORDER V+ADV+O = fight off

fender /fɛndə/, **fenders.** A **fender** is 1 a low metal wall around a fireplace, which stops any coals that fall out of the fire from rolling onto the carpet. 2 a fireguard. 3 a solid but soft object, such as an old tyre or a coil of rope, which hangs over the side of a boat to protect it when it comes alongside other boats or a harbour wall. 4 a wing of a car; used in American English. — N COUNT ⇑ guard; N COUNT; N COUNT ⇑ buffer; N COUNT

fennel /fɛnə⁰l/ is a plant with a crisp rounded base and feathery leaves. It can be eaten as a vegetable or used as a herb. — N UNCOUNT

feral /fɛrəl, fɪə-/ means wild or uncultivated; used especially to describe animals that used to be kept by people but have now become wild again; a formal word. EG *Very young feral kittens may settle well into domestic life. ...the feral instinct.* — ADJ CLASSIF : ATTRIB

ferment, ferments, fermenting, fermented. The noun in paragraph 1 is pronounced /fɜːmɛnt/, and the verb in paragraph 2 is pronounced /fə⁵mɛnt/. 1 **Ferment** is excitement and unrest caused by change or uncertainty. EG *Portugal was in ferment... ...the reason for the present ferment in education... All the political ferment has produced a new leadership.* — N UNCOUNT = commotion, upheaval

2 When wine, beer, fruit, dough, etc **ferments**, a chemical change takes place in it. EG *Cover it up and leave it to ferment... Don't try bottling it as it may still be fermenting.* ◊ **fermented.** EG *...the whiff of fermented apples... ...jars full of half-fermented rhubarb wine.* ◊ **fermentation**/fɜːmɛnteɪʃə⁰n/, **fermentations.** EG *Fermentation ceases when a certain amount of sugar has been converted to alcohol... ...yeast from a previous fermentation.* — V-ERG ⇑ react; ◊ ADJ CLASSIF : ATTRIB; ◊ N UNCOUNT/COUNT

fern /fɜːn/, **ferns.** **Fern** can also be used as the plural form. A **fern** is a plant that has long stems with feathery leaves. There are many different types of fern, none of which produce flowers. — N COUNT

ferocious /fərəʊʃəs/. 1 An animal or person that is **ferocious** behaves in a very violent and cruel way. EG *...the shrieks of someone caught by some ferocious animal...* ▸ used of actions and behaviour. EG *The stillness was broken by the ferocious barking of a dog... ...a ferocious assault... ...a ferocious expression.* ◊ **ferociously.** — ADJ QUALIT = fierce, savage; ◊ ADV WITH VB

2 A **ferocious** war, argument, or other form of conflict involves a great deal of aggression, bitterness, and determination. EG *...two years of bitter and ferocious fighting... ...Nicholson's ferocious criticisms of the civil service... This had produced a ferocious atmosphere of competition.* ◊ **ferociously.** — ADJ QUALIT ⇑ determined = fierce, savage; ◊ ADV WITH VB

3 A **ferocious** knife, dagger, etc is one that looks especially sharp and able to do a lot of damage. EG *They were armed with ferocious daggers... ...a gateway with ferocious spikes.* — ADJ QUALIT ⇑ dangerous = vicious

4 Something that is described as **ferocious** is so strong or extreme that it is unpleasant or unacceptable. EG *By midday, the heat is just ferocious... No doubt the ferocious climate had an influence on the customs.* ◊ **ferociously.** EG *The play has been ferociously cut.* — ADJ QUALIT = fierce; ◊ ADV = savagely

ferocity /fərɒsɪti¹/ is the quality of being violent, or aggressive and intense. EG *The attack was resumed with a new ferocity at first light... He had never heard such ferocity in a man's voice.* — N UNCOUNT ⇑ strength = intensity

ferret /fɛrɪt/, **ferrets, ferreting, ferreted.** 1 A **ferret** is a small, white, fierce animal related to the weasel, which is kept by people for hunting rabbits and rats. — N COUNT

2 If you **go ferreting**, you hunt rats or rabbits with ferrets. — V

3 If you **ferret** about in something, you search busily in it by pushing and pulling things about; an informal expression. EG *Do stop ferreting about and come and sit down!* — V+A = rummage

ferret out. If you **ferret out** information about something, you discover it by searching very thoroughly and with determination; an informal expression. — PHRASAL VB : V+O+ADV ⇑ find = unearth

ferrous /fɛrəs/ means containing or relating to iron. EG *...ferrous metals... ...ferrous sulphate.* — ADJ CLASSIF : ATTRIB

ferrule /fɛruːl, -əl/, **ferrules.** A **ferrule** is a metal or rubber cap or band that is fixed onto the end of a stick or post to prevent it splitting or wearing down. — N COUNT ⇑ tip

ferry /fɛri¹/, **ferries, ferrying, ferried.** 1 A **ferry** is a boat that transports passengers and sometimes also vehicles, usually across rivers or short stretches of sea. EG *The ferry wasn't terribly busy... We got back to London by train and ferry... ...car ferries and steamers... ...Channel ferry crossings.* — N COUNT, OR *by*+N = ferryboat

2 To **ferry** people or goods somewhere means to transport them; usually used when the journeys are done regularly. EG *They were ferried from one state building to another... The newspaper reported on Friday that the plane had been ferrying military supplies.* — V+O : USU+A ⇑ take

ferryboat /fɛri¹bəʊt/, **ferryboats.** A **ferryboat** is a boat used as a ferry. EG *I had hoped we might find an unofficial ferryboat crossing or footbridge.* — N COUNT = ferry

fertile /fɜːtaɪl/. 1 Land or soil that is **fertile** is able to support the growth of a lot of strong healthy plants. EG *...valleys so fertile that three crops a year can grow... ...the light, fertile soil of this sparsely populated land.* ◊ **fertility** /fɜːtɪlɪti¹/. EG *They use cow dung as fuel instead of using it to maintain soil fertility.* — ADJ QUALIT ⇑ productive = rich ≠ barren; ◊ N UNCOUNT ⇑ productivity

2 A **fertile** mind or imagination is able to produce a lot of good or original ideas. EG *Clearly, we are in the realm of fertile imagination rather than historical record... His fertile brain worked away on the idea of a universal cure.* ◊ **fertility.** EG *It's a very experimental novel. It has incredible fertility of invention.* — ADJ QUALIT : USU ATTRIB ⇑ productive = lively, creative; ◊ N UNCOUNT+SUPP

3 A situation or environment that is **fertile** in relation to a particular activity is especially suitable for and helpful to the success of this activity. EG *Britain is not fertile ground for news magazines.* — ADJ QUALIT = productive

4 A person or animal that is **fertile** is able to reproduce and have babies or young. EG *...fertile women with several children.* ◊ **fertility.** EG *Women could not advance without full control of their fertility... Fertility rates have continued to decline.* — ADJ QUALIT ⇑ productive; ◊ N UNCOUNT

fertilize /fɜːtɪlaɪz/, **fertilizes, fertilizing, fertilized;** also spelled **fertilise.** 1 When an egg, a plant, or a female **is fertilized**, the sperm joins with the egg, or pollen from one plant comes into contact with the reproductive part of another, causing the process of reproduction to begin. EG *...a tree which somehow manages to feed and fertilize itself... The males fertilise the eggs as they are laid... The eggs are immediately fertilized by the male's sperm.* ◊ **fertilized.** EG *The fertilised egg remains where it is for one more week.* ◊ **fertilization** /fɜːtɪlaɪzeɪʃə⁰n/. EG *...the small amount of pollen necessary for fertilization.* — V+O : USU PASS = inseminate; ◊ ADJ CLASSIF; ◊ N UNCOUNT = insemination

2 To **fertilize** land means to spread manure or a chemical mixture on it in order to make plants grow well. EG *...foods grown on land that is fertilised by manure.* — V+O ⇑ nourish

fertilizer /fɜːtɪlaɪzə/, **fertilizers;** also spelled **fertiliser.** **Fertilizer** is a substance such as manure or a chemical mixture that you spread on the ground in order to make plants grow more successfully. EG *This requires greater use of fertilizer... Soon the cost of the fertilizer will be greater than the profit from the crop. ...producing vegetables without the use of fertilizers and pesticides.* — N MASS ⇑ supplement

fervent /fɜːvənt/. Someone who is **fervent** about something has or shows strong feelings about it, and is very sincere and enthusiastic about it. EG *...a fervent belief in God... He had been one of Lily's most fervent admirers... ...a fervent supporter of Britain's membership of the EEC.* ◊ **fervently.** EG *'Oh, I am glad!' Scylla said fervently... Both of them fervently believed in the document.* — ADJ QUALIT = passionate, ardent; ◊ ADV WITH VB = devoutly

fervid /fɜːvɪd/ means the same as fervent; a formal use. EG *...full of fervid and misplaced loyalties.* ADJ QUALIT : ATTRIB

fervour /fɜːvə/; also spelled **fervor** in American English. **Fervour** for something is a very strong feeling for or belief in it; a formal word. EG *...a tide of patriotic fervour... 'She's marvellous,' said Mrs Moffatt with fervour.* N UNCOUNT ⇑ emotion = enthusiasm

festal /fɛstəl/ means relating to a festival or celebration; a formal word. EG *...as though some primitive festal act was taking place.* ADJ CLASSIF : ATTRIB = festive

fester /fɛstə/, **festers, festering, festered.** 1 If a wound **festers**, it becomes infected. EG *...a painful, festering sore.* V ⇑ decay = suppurate

2 If a difficult or unpleasant situation, feeling, or thought **festers**, it grows worse and is characterized by increasing bitterness, anger, and hatred. EG *...allowing inner cities to fester and become breeding grounds for hatred and violence... His memories festered into hate... ...an anger that must find outlet or fester inwardly.* V ⇑ deteriorate

festival /fɛstɪvəˀl/, **festivals.** A **festival** is 1 an organized event or series of events such as musical concerts or drama productions. EG *...an amateur performance at the Edinburgh Festival... This year the San Sebastian Film Festival has been paying homage to Zeffirelli.* N COUNT : ALSO IN NAMES AFTER N 2 a date or time of the year when people have a holiday from work and celebrate some special event, especially a religious event. N COUNT

festive /fɛstɪv/. Something that is **festive** is full of colour and happiness and so is appropriate to a holiday or celebration. EG *The atmosphere is really festive and friendly... ...at Christmas time or on other festive occasions.* ADJ QUALIT ⇑ happy = joyous

festivity /fɛstɪvɪtiˡ/, **festivities.** 1 **Festivity** is the celebration of something and the atmosphere of happiness and enjoyment that is a result of this. EG *...a spirit of joy and festivity... He entered the village almost unobserved amid the general festivity.* N UNCOUNT

2 **Festivities** are the things that are arranged and done to celebrate something. EG *The week is crammed with festivities... Ash enjoyed the wedding festivities as much as anyone.* N PLURAL ⇑ event = celebrations

festoon /fɛstuːn/, **festoons, festooning, festooned.** If you **festoon** something with decorations, lights, or other things, you spread or hang these things over it in large numbers in order to decorate it. EG *The counters were festooned with rainbow coloured scarves... The garden was festooned with coloured lights.* V+O : USU PASS+ with = garland, bedeck

fetal /fiːtəˀl/. See **foetal.**

fetch /fɛtʃ/, **fetches, fetching, fetched.** 1 If you **fetch** something or someone, you bring them from somewhere by going there in order to get them. EG *My mum goes to work in the morning and fetches me on her way home... He fetched a bucket of water from the pond... I went and fetched another glass... I don't want you to fetch anything for me... His brother had to be sent to fetch him back.* V+O, V+O+O, OR V+O+A *(for)*

2 To **fetch and carry** means to perform simple and often boring tasks for someone, such as collecting and carrying things for them. PHR : VBS INFLECT

3 If something that is being sold **fetches** a particular sum of money, it is sold for this amount of money. EG *His pictures fetch very high prices... He had decided to sell the machinery for what it would fetch.* V+O = get, bring

4 If you **fetch** someone a blow, you hit them; an informal usage. V+O+O

5 see also **fetching, far-fetched.**

fetch up. If you **fetch up** somewhere, you arrive there; used especially when you have not planned where you are going; an informal expression used mainly in American English. PHRASAL VB : V-ERG+ADV = land up

fetching /fɛtʃɪŋ/. A woman or a piece of clothing that looks **fetching**, looks attractive. EG *Melanie looked remarkably fetching this evening in a white dress.* ◊ **fetchingly.** EG *She was in her early twenties and fetchingly pretty.* ADJ QUALIT = captivating ◊ ADV WITH VB

fete /feɪt/, **fetes, feting, feted.** 1 A **fete** is an event that is usually held outdoors and includes competitions, entertainments, and the selling of second-hand or homemade goods. EG *The money was raised through a summer fete... ...the church fete.* N COUNT = bazaar

2 If someone **is feted**, a public welcome is provided for them in honour or admiration of what they have achieved. EG *In New York, Karen Blixen was being feted by everyone who knew her work.* V+O : USU PASS = fuss over

fetid /fɛtɪd, fiː-/. Something, especially water, that is **fetid** has a strong, very unpleasant smell; a formal word. ADJ CLASSIF = rank

fetish /fɛtɪʃ, fiːtɪʃ/, **fetishes.** A **fetish** is 1 a strong liking or need for a particular object or activity which gives a person sexual pleasure and excitement. EG *Stealing knickers is a well recognized minor fetish.* N COUNT ⇑ obsession = fixation 2 an activity that you have an extremely strong liking for or that you do a great deal; used to suggest that your interest in something is excessive. EG *Cleanliness is almost a fetish with her.* N COUNT = mania

fetishism /fɛtɪʃɪzəᵒm, fiː-/ is the condition of having a fetish. N UNCOUNT

fetlock /fɛtlɒk/, **fetlocks.** A horse's **fetlock** is the back part of its leg, just above the hoof, which sticks out and has longer hairs on it. N COUNT

fetter /fɛtə/, **fetters, fettering, fettered.** 1 If something **fetters** you, it prevents you from behaving in a free and natural way. EG *...the forces that fetter our souls... This does not mean that we wish to fetter the trade union movement.* ▸ used as a noun. EG *They will run wild freed from the fetters of control.* V+O ⇑ restrict = inhibit ▸ N COUNT : USU PL = shackles

2 A **fetter** is also one of a pair of chains for a prisoner's feet, used especially in former times. N COUNT : USU PL = shackle

fettle /fɛtəˀl/. If someone or something is **in fine fettle**, they are in very good condition or health; an informal expression. PHR : USED AS AN A = on form

fetus /fiːtəs/, **fetuses.** See **foetus.**

feud /fjuːd/, **feuds, feuding, feuded.** A **feud** is a long-lasting and bitter quarrel or dispute between two people or groups. EG *There was a long-standing feud between Kurt and Fullarton... His feud with the Premier proceeded remorselessly.* ▸ used as a verb. EG *The two families had been feuding for years.* N COUNT = vendetta ▸ V OR V+A *(with)* : RECIP

feudal /fjuːdəˀl/ means relating to the system or the time of feudalism. EG *...feudal lords... ...a feudal society.* ADJ CLASSIF : ATTRIB

feudalism /fjuːdəˀlɪzəᵒm/ is a system in which people are given land and protection by lords and work and fight for the lords in return. N UNCOUNT

fever /fiːvə/, **fevers.** 1 If you have a **fever** when you are ill, you have a body temperature that is higher than usual and a quick heartbeat. EG *Nancy got a fever which eventually shot up to 106 degrees.* ● See also **hay fever, rheumatic fever, scarlet fever.** N COUNT/ UNCOUNT

2 A **fever** is also used to refer to extreme excitement or agitation about something. EG *Everyone was in a fever of excitement... He stayed calm through the fever of the campaign... His father had succumbed to the Chinese fever for gambling.* N COUNT : USU+ SUPP = frenzy

fevered /fiːvəd/ means the same as feverish. EG *The intervening hours were spent in a fevered guessing game as to what the message would be... The men lay sick on the deck, rubbing fevered chests and foreheads.* ADJ CLASSIF : ATTRIB

feverish /fiːvəᵒrɪʃ/. 1 **Feverish** emotion is characterized by extreme agitation or excitement. EG *There was a kind of feverish excitement in his voice.* ◊ **feverishly.** EG *I stood at the living-room window, feverishly awaiting my darling's return.* ADJ QUALIT ⇑ agitated = frenzied ≠ calm ◊ ADV WITH VB = impatiently

2 **Feverish** activity is done extremely quickly, often in a state of agitation because you want to finish it as soon as possible. EG *The next few hours were a feverish race against time.* ◊ **feverishly.** EG *They worked so feverishly that there was no time for talk.* ADJ QUALIT : ATTRIB ⇑ energetic = frantic ◊ ADV WITH VB = frenetically

3 If you are **feverish**, you are suffering from a fever. EG *He felt flushed, almost feverish... She looked feverish.* ADJ QUALIT ⇑ hot

fever pitch; also spelled with a hyphen and as one word. If something is at **fever pitch**, it is characterized by a state of extreme excitement. EG *Our excitement reached fever pitch on the day of the wedding.* N UNCOUNT ⇑ peak = delirium

few /fjuː/, **fewer, fewest.** 1 **Few** is used 1.1 to refer to a small number of units of time when you are considering an approximate period of time. EG *During the first few weeks, I didn't understand a word... I'll get this play typed out in the next few days... Every few weeks he and his wife would ask Brody.* ADJ CLASSIF : ATTRIB 1.2 to refer to a small number of things in a series of things. EG *The first few poems are very good.* ADJ CLASSIF : ATTRIB 1.3 to refer to a small number of things or people when the number is smaller than you would expect. EG *Very few people survived... There are fewer trains late at night... Changes in policy were few.* ▸ used as a pronoun. EG *Many of us tried but* QUANTIF+N IN PL ≠ many ▸ PRON *very few succeeded... Few of them ever reach their potential... Few small businesses apply for them and even fewer obtain them.*

2 A few things or people means a small number of them, but not very many. EG *I'll be going to London for a few days... He will try it a few more times... These creatures are only a few centimetres long... ...a few hundred pounds.* ▸ used as a pronoun. EG *A few were smoking... 'I know lots of ways,' and I told him a few... We had started to develop some friendships with a few of them.*
QUANTIF+N IN PL ⇑ some ▸ PRON

3 As few as is used when stating a number to suggest that it is surprisingly small. EG *Some centipedes have more than two hundred legs and some have as few as eight.*
PHR+NUM ⇑ only

4 No fewer than is used when stating a number to suggest that it is surprisingly large. EG *No fewer than five cameramen lost their lives.*
PHR+NUM = as many as

5 Quite a few, a good few, and **not a few** are expressions used to say that you are referring to quite a lot of things or people, but not an unusually large number. EG *We had quite a few friendly arguments... I spent a good few years of my life there.*
QUANTIF+N IN PL ⇑ many = several

6 Things that are **few and far between** occur very infrequently, or are very uncommon. EG *The really top fashion houses are few and far between unless you go abroad.*
PHR : USED AS C ⇑ rare = scarce

7 If you **have had a few too many** or **have had a few,** you have drunk too many alcoholic drinks; an informal expression.
PHR : VB INFLECTS ⇑ drink

8 The **few** means a small set of people when they are thought of as separate from the majority, especially because they share a particular opportunity or quality which the others do not have. EG *We are seeing a concentration of wealth and power in the hands of the few... He finally appeared to delight the few of us who remained.*
N PLURAL : *the*+N ⇑ minority

fey /feɪ/. Someone who is **fey** behaves in a vague, strange, and rather silly way. EG *They may well have been irritatingly fey at times.* ▸ used of people's ideas and behaviour. EG *...her fey imaginings.*
ADJ QUALIT = whimsical

fez /fez/, **fezzes**. A **fez** is a round, red hat which has a flat top with a tassel hanging from it and no brim.
N COUNT ⇑ cap

ff. **1** When **ff.** is written after a particular page, line, etc has been mentioned, it means 'and the following pages, lines, etc'. EG *See p. 28 ff.*
2 ff is a written abbreviation for 'fortissimo'.

fiancé /fiˈɒnseɪ/, **fiancés**. A woman's **fiancé** is the man to whom she is engaged to be married.
N COUNT : USU POSS+N

fiancée /fiˈɒnseɪ/, **fiancées**. A man's **fiancée** is the woman to whom he is engaged to be married.
N COUNT : USU POSS+N

fiasco /fiˈæskəʊ/, **fiascos**. American English uses the spelling **fiascoes** for the plural form. An action or attempt that fails completely can be described or referred to as a **fiasco**. EG *The meeting was a fiasco... ...as a result of the recent Janet Cooke fiasco.*
N COUNT ⇑ disaster, blunder

fiat /faɪəᵊt/, **fiats**. A **fiat** is an official order given by someone in authority; a formal word.
N COUNT

fib /fɪb/, **fibs, fibbing, fibbed**; an informal word.
1 A **fib** is a small lie which is not very important. EG *Clearly either Waddell or Carmichael was telling fibs.*
N COUNT

2 If you are **fibbing**, you are telling lies. EG *It isn't true! You're fibbing!*
V ⇑ lie

fibber /fɪbə/, **fibbers**. A **fibber** is someone who tells fibs; an informal word.
N COUNT ⇑ liar

fibre /faɪbə/, **fibres**; also spelled **fiber** in American English. **1** A **fibre** is a thin thread of a natural or artificial substance, especially one that is used to make cloth or rope. EG *Wigs were woven of long fibres.*
N COUNT

2 A particular **fibre** is a type of cloth or other material that is made from or consists of threads. EG *...the development of artificial fibres... There was a big demand for cotton fibre.*
N COUNT/UNCOUNT

3 Fibre is parts of plants or seeds which you eat that your body cannot digest. Fibre is useful because it makes food move quickly through your body. EG *Scientists are recommending people to eat more fibre.*
N UNCOUNT = roughage

4 A **fibre** is also a thin piece of flesh like a thread which connects nerve cells in your body or which muscles are made of. EG *...a simple network of nerve fibres.*
N COUNT : USU MOD+N ⇑ tissue

5 Moral **fibre** is the quality of being brave and determined to do what is right. EG *We must cure the widespread lack of faith and moral fibre.*
N UNCOUNT+SUPP ⇑ strength

6 If you say that you feel something with every **fibre** of your being, you mean that you feel it very deeply; a literary use. EG *I love my country with every fibre of my being.*
N COUNT+SUPP

fibreglass /faɪbəglɑːs/; also spelled **fiberglass** in American English. **Fibreglass** is **1** plastic strengthened with short, thin threads of glass. EG *...the fibreglass deck of the boat.* **2** a material made from short, thin threads of glass which can be used to keep heat in.
N UNCOUNT; N UNCOUNT

fibre optic /faɪbərᵒ ɒptɪk/, **fibre optics**. **Fibre optic** is an adjective and **fibre optics** is an uncount noun. **1 Fibre optics** is the use of long thin threads of glass to carry information in the form of light.
N UNCOUNT

2 Fibre optic means relating to or involved in fibre optics. EG *...a fibre optic cable.*
ADJ CLASSIF : ATTRIB

fibrous /faɪbrəs/. Something that is **fibrous** contains a lot of fibres or fibre, or looks like fibres. EG *They eat a great deal of fibrous twigs and woody material.*
ADJ CLASSIF ⇑ stringy

fibula /fɪbjəˈlə/, **fibulae, fibulas**. The plural can be either **fibulae** or **fibulas**. The **fibula** is the outer bone of the two bones in your leg between the knee and the ankle; a technical term in medicine.
N COUNT

fickle /fɪkəᵒl/. **1** Someone who is **fickle** keeps changing their mind about what they like or want; used showing disapproval. EG *She was extremely fickle.*
◇ **fickleness**. EG *...the fickleness of public taste.*
ADJ QUALIT = capricious; ◇ N UNCOUNT

2 If a wind or the weather is **fickle**, it changes often and suddenly.
ADJ QUALIT ⇑ unstable

fiction /fɪkʃəᵒn/, **fictions**. **1 Fiction** refers to books or stories about people and events invented by the author, rather than books about real events or things. EG *Her interests include painting and reading fiction... He was a fiction writer mainly... Happy marriages may be more common in fiction than in real life.* See also **science fiction**.
N UNCOUNT ⇑ literature

2 A statement or account that is **fiction** is not true. EG *You can't tell the difference between truth and fiction.*
N UNCOUNT ⇑ invention

3 A **fiction** is something that you say or pretend is true but in fact is not. EG *...the replacement of facts by comforting fictions... We had to keep up the fiction of being a normal couple.*
N COUNT ⇑ deceit = lie

fictional /fɪkʃəᵒnəl, -ʃənəᵒl/. **1** A **fictional** character, thing, or event is one that occurs in a story, play, or film but never actually existed or happened. EG *...a musical about a fictional composer called Moony Shapiro.*
ADJ CLASSIF ⇑ invented = literary

2 Fictional means relating to fiction or involving the telling of an invented story. EG *...a clever fictional device... ...the fictional treatment of adultery.*
ADJ CLASSIF : USU ATTRIB

3 Something that is **fictional** does not exist or is not the case, although it is said or thought to exist or be the case. EG *Its internal unity was in large measure fictional.*
ADJ CLASSIF = fictitious

fictionalization /fɪkʃəᵒnəlaɪzeɪʃəᵒn/, **fictionalizations**. A **fictionalization** is a fictionalized account of a real event.
N COUNT/UNCOUNT ⇑ adaptation

fictionalize /fɪkʃəᵒnəlaɪz/, **fictionalizes, fictionalizing, fictionalized**; also spelled **fictionalise**. If you **fictionalize** an account of something that actually happened, you tell it as a story, with some details changed or added. ◇ **fictionalized**. EG *...a fictionalized autobiography.*
V+O ⇑ adapt; ◇ ADJ CLASSIF

fictitious /fɪktɪʃəs/. **1** Something that is **fictitious** is false or does not exist, although it is said or thought to be real or true or to exist. EG *They bought the materials under fictitious names.*
ADJ CLASSIF ⇑ invented = non-existent

2 A **fictitious** character, thing, or event is one that occurs in a story, play, or film but never actually existed or happened.
ADJ CLASSIF ⇑ invented

fiddle /fɪdəᵒl/, **fiddles, fiddling, fiddled**. **1** If you **fiddle** with something, you keep moving it or touching it with your fingers with small movements, for example because you are nervous or bored. EG *He sat nervously fiddling with his spectacles.*
V : USU+A *(with)* = fidget

2 If you **fiddle** with a machine or other object, you move or adjust parts of it in order to make it work properly or until it is how you want it to be. EG *He cursed as he fiddled with the volume control.*
V : USU+A *(with)* = twiddle

3 If you **fiddle** with something that does not belong to you, you move it or interfere with it. EG *Have you been fiddling with my things?*
V+A *(with)* = meddle, tamper

4 If someone **fiddles** something, they alter it dishonestly or illegally or arrange it so that they get money or some other benefit for themselves; an informal
V+O = fix, cook

use. EG *I think the bill is being fiddled... Pity we can't fiddle the books... He had fiddled the figures in the transaction.* ◊ **fiddling**. EG *A lot of fiddling goes on in many companies.* ◊ N UNCOUNT

5 A **fiddle** is a dishonest action or scheme in which a person gets money for himself or herself; an informal use. EG *Laing had worked some fiddle and hadn't minded being caught.* N COUNT = fraud, swindle

6 Someone who is **on the fiddle** is getting money by doing dishonest or illegal things. PHR : USED AS A/C

7 A **fiddle** is a violin, especially one used to play folk music; an informal use. N COUNT

8 Someone who **plays second fiddle** to someone else has a less important or less powerful position than them. EG *In the young child's eyes father plays second fiddle.* PHR : VB INFLECTS, IF + PREP THEN *to* ↑ be subordinate

9 If you say that someone **is fiddling while Rome burns**, you mean that they are not dealing with a serious or dangerous situation that exists but instead are doing useless things or pretending that nothing is wrong. PHR : VB INFLECTS, USU CONT

10 See also **fiddling**.

fiddle about, fiddle around. 1 If you **fiddle about** or **fiddle around**, you waste time by doing things without any particular plan or purpose, so that you do not achieve anything. EG *I spent about two hours just fiddling about.* PHRASAL VB : V + ADV, IF + PREP THEN *with*

2 If you **fiddle about** or **around** with a group of things, you change their position many times in an attempt to find an arrangement that satisfies you. EG *He had been fiddling about with drawings for the news sheet.* PHRASAL VB : V + ADV, USU + A *(with)* ↑ move

3 If you **fiddle about** or **around** with something, you keep moving it or touching it with your fingers with small movements, for example because you are nervous or bored. PHRASAL VB : V + ADV, USU + A *(with)* = fidget

fiddler /fɪdlə/, **fiddlers**. A **fiddler** is 1 a person who plays the violin, especially one who plays folk music. N COUNT ↑ violinist 2 a person who dishonestly alters something or tells lies in order to get money; an informal use. N COUNT = cheat

fiddlesticks /fɪdəᵒlstɪks/. You say **fiddlesticks** when you are annoyed because something has gone wrong, or to say that you totally disagree with someone; an old-fashioned word. EXCLAM

fiddling /fɪdlɪŋ/. Something that is **fiddling** is small or unimportant and difficult to do. ADJ QUALIT = petty

fiddly /fɪdliˡ/, **fiddlier, fiddliest**. A task or object that is **fiddly** is annoyingly difficult to do, use, or handle, for example because it involves small or complicated objects. EG *It is a very fiddly job... Beech nuts are tasty but fiddly to eat.* ADJ QUALIT ↑ awkward

fidelity /fɪdelɪtiˡ/ is 1 the quality of remaining firm in your beliefs or ideas or in your friendships with people; a formal use showing approval. EG *...fidelity to basic principles... There's nothing like a dog's fidelity.* N UNCOUNT : IF + PREP THEN *to* ↑ adherence = faithfulness 2 the state of having only one sexual partner, especially your husband or wife; used showing approval. EG *...buying each other wedding rings, demanding fidelity.* N UNCOUNT : IF + PREP THEN *to* ↑ morality = faithfulness 3 the degree of accuracy of a report, translation, or adaptation; a formal use. N UNCOUNT 4 See also **high fidelity**.

fidget /fɪdʒɪt/, **fidgets, fidgeting, fidgeted**. 1 If you **fidget**, you keep moving your hands or feet slightly or changing your position slightly, for example because you are nervous or bored. EG *The children are starting to fidget.* V ↑ be restless = shuffle

2 A **fidget** is a person, especially a child, who keeps fidgeting. N COUNT

3 Someone who has the **fidgets** keeps fidgeting. N PLURAL

4 Someone who **is fidgeting** to do something behaves in a restless way that shows they are eager and impatient to do it. EG *Mr Annett was fidgeting to begin.* V + *to*-INF : ONLY CONT

5 If you **fidget** with something, you keep moving it or touching it with your fingers with small movements, for example because you are nervous or bored. EG *She fidgeted with her gloves.* V + A *(with)* = fiddle

fidget about. If you **fidget about**, you keep changing your position slightly, for example because you are nervous or bored. PHRASAL VB : V + ADV ↑ be restless

fidgety /fɪdʒɪtiˡ/. Someone who is **fidgety** keeps fidgeting, for example because they are nervous or bored. ADJ QUALIT = restless, jittery

fie /faɪ/ is an old-fashioned exclamation used to express disapproval. EG *Fie on you!* EXCLAM : IF + PREP THEN *on*

fief /fiːf/, **fiefs**. A **fief** was in former times a piece of land given to someone by their lord, to whom they had a duty to provide particular services in return. N COUNT = serf

field /fiːld/, **fields, fielding, fielded**. 1 A **field** is an area of land on which a crop is grown or an area of rough grass, especially one where animals such as cows, sheep, or horses are kept. EG *...a corn field... ...fields of wheat... We pitched our tent in a field... We saw people working together in the fields.* N COUNT

2 A sports **field** is an area of grass which is used for playing a sport such as football, rugby, or hockey. EG *The garden was as big as a football field... Come on, lads, get on the field!* N COUNT = pitch

3 An oil **field**, gas **field**, etc is an area of land or sea bed under which oil, gas, etc is found. EG *...oil and gas fields... They have been given a 950 million dollar loan to develop the Forties field... ...the diamond fields of Kimberley.* N COUNT + SUPP USU MOD + N

4 A snow **field**, lava **field**, etc is a large area of land always covered by the substance mentioned. N COUNT + SUPP

5 Fighting or other military action in a war takes place in the **field** or on the **field** of battle. EG *They needed a more effective way of using military forces in the field... ...the field artillery.* N SING : *the* + N

6 A particular **field** is a particular subject or area of activity or interest. EG *He doesn't seem to have done much in the political field... She is an expert in this field... Insects were my father's particular field of study.* N COUNT + SUPP = sphere

7 The **field** is used in expressions such as **hold the field** and **lead the field** when referring to success or importance in a particular area of activity in which there is competition. EG *The explanation of migration that holds the field today is known as the Todaro model... At one point his ideas led the field.* N SING : *the* + N

8 A **field** trip, **field** scientist, **field** study, etc involves or is involved in research or testing that is done in a real, natural environment rather than in a theoretical way or in controlled conditions. EG *We could say we were on an extended field trip... ...field studies of individuals following immigration.* N BEFORE N ↑ practical ● Something that is studied or tested **in the field** is studied or tested in a real, natural environment. EG *...projects and programmes that have been tried and proved in the field... We will study their natural history in the field.* ● PHR : USED AS AN A

9 When you **field** a ball that has been hit, especially in cricket or baseball, you catch it or stop it. V OR V + O

10 The team that **is fielding** in a game of cricket, baseball, or rounders is the team that is having a turn at trying to catch or stop the ball, rather than batting. EG *This didn't make me popular with the fielding side.* V : USU CONT

11 If you **field** a question or remark, you deal with it, usually skilfully. EG *Most of them were not interested in fielding questions about it.* V + O

12 If a sports club **fields** a particular number or type of players, the players play for the club and represent it in matches. EG *We're fielding a good team this season.* V + O

13 If someone **fields** a particular number or type of people or things, they make use of them in order to achieve something. EG *They can field 1,000 helicopters and 3,000 armoured vehicles.* V + O

14 A magnetic **field**, gravitational **field**, force **field**, etc is the area in which that particular force is strong enough to have an effect. EG *A gibbon is better adapted than a man for life in a low gravitational field.* N COUNT + SUPP USU MOD + N

15 Your **field** of vision, **field** of view, or visual **field** is the whole area that you can see without turning your head or that you can see from a particular position. EG *A brown figure dressed in red crept into her field of vision... Its eyes are mounted so as to give it an extremely wide field of view.* N COUNT + SUPP

16 Your **field** of fire is the area within which you can hit something you fire at from a particular position. EG *...tanks with considerable depth to their fields of fire.* N COUNT + SUPP USU + *of*

17 The **field** is a way of referring to all the horses or people taking part in a particular race. EG *On the third round, Sy was leading the field with Hiawatha.* N SING : *the* + N, VB CAN BE SING OR PL ↑ group

18 On a flag, shield, or coin, the **field** is the background. EG *On a field of blue was a cross.* N COUNT + SUPP USU SING

19 If you **have a field day** you have a very pleasant time doing something that you have been given an opportunity to do in a very active way. EG *The local papers had a field day.* PHR : VB INFLECTS

20 If you **play the field**, you have a number of different romantic or sexual relationships, often before deciding who to marry; an informal expression. PHR : VB INFLECTS

fielder /fiːldə/, **fielders**. A **fielder** is a player in cricket, baseball, or rounders who is fielding or one who has a particular skill at fielding. EG *The ball soared over the fielders' heads... He's an excellent fielder.* N COUNT

field event, field events. A **field event** is an athletics contest such as the high jump or throwing the discus or javelin, rather than a race. N COUNT ≠ track event

field-glasses; also spelled without a hyphen. **Field-glasses** are binoculars. EG *Their field glasses were pointed towards the opposite windows and roofs.* N PLURAL : ALSO *a pair of*+N

field hockey is the same as hockey; used in American English. N UNCOUNT ⇑ sport

field marshal, field marshals; also spelled with a hyphen and as one word. A **field marshal** is an officer in the army who has the highest rank. EG *...Field Marshal Montgomery... He had been personally interrogated by the Field Marshal.* N COUNT : ALSO IN TITLES

fieldmouse /fiːldmaʊs/, **fieldmice**; also spelled with a hyphen. A **fieldmouse** is a mouse with a long tail that lives in fields and woods. N COUNT

field sports. Hunting, shooting birds, and fishing with a rod are referred to as **field sports** when they are done mainly for pleasure. N PLURAL = blood sports

field-test, field-tests, field-testing, field-tested. If you **field-test** a new piece of equipment, you test it in a real, natural environment. EG *It hasn't been field-tested yet.* ▸ used as a noun. EG *It has undergone several field-tests.* V+O ▸ N COUNT

fieldwork /fiːldwɜːk/ is the gathering of information about something directly. EG *The course included a lot of fieldwork.* N UNCOUNT ⇑ research

fiend /fiːnd/, **fiends**. **1** A **fiend** is a person who is extremely wicked or cruel; an old-fashioned or literary use. EG *I have no idea who this murderous fiend may be.* N COUNT = devil, monster

2 A health **fiend**, car **fiend**, etc is a person who is very keen on or interested in the thing mentioned. EG *He's a fresh air fiend.* N COUNT : AFTER N = fanatic

fiendish /fiːndɪʃ/. **1** Someone who is **fiendish** is cruel and enjoys being cruel. EG *He was filled with a fiendish glee at seeing his pupils struggle with the sums he set them... ...a fiendish despot.* ADJ QUALIT

2 A **fiendish** plan, action, or device is very clever or imaginative; an informal use. EG *It was just a fiendish plan to keep their minds off asking for more money.* ADJ QUALIT : USU ATTRIB = cunning

3 A **fiendish** problem or task is very difficult and challenging; an informal use. ADJ QUALIT : USU ATTRIB

fiendishly /fiːndɪʃli¹/. **1** **Fiendishly** is used to emphasize how difficult something is; an informal use. EG *This effect is fiendishly hard to achieve.* ADV+ADJ/ADV

2 **Fiendishly** also means cruelly. EG *Fiendishly laughing, they had insisted on coming too.* ADV WITH VB

fierce /fɪəs/, **fiercer, fiercest**. **1** An animal or person that is **fierce** is very aggressive or angry. EG *...fierce dogs... ...a fierce warrior.* ◇ **fiercely**. EG *'Don't assume anything!' said Martha fiercely.* ADJ QUALIT ◇ ADV WITH VB

2 Something that is **fierce** **2.1** involves very strong feelings or great and energetic activity. EG *After a fierce battle the enemy had been forced back... ...the fierce loyalty of these people... There will be fierce resistance if this is attempted.* ◇ **fiercely**. EG *This plan was fiercely resisted by the ranchers... ...a fiercely dedicated group of people.* **2.2** is very intense, great, or strong. EG *...fierce heat... ...a fierce storm.* ◇ **fiercely**. EG *The fire was blazing fiercely.* ADJ QUALIT ⇑ intense ◇ ADV ⇑ intensely ADJ QUALIT ◇ ADV

fiery /faɪəri¹/, **fierier, fieriest**. **1** Something that is **fiery** **1.1** is burning strongly or contains or involves fire. EG *...clouds of fiery gas... ...the fiery pits of hell.* **1.2** is bright red in colour. EG *The tonsils become fiery red and swollen.* ADJ CLASSIF : USU ATTRIB ADJ QUALIT = flaming

2 A drink or food that is **fiery** makes your mouth or throat feel as if it is burning. EG *Johnny gulped down the fiery liquid.* ADJ QUALIT : USU ATTRIB

3 A **fiery** person behaves or speaks with great energy, feeling, and passion, often angrily. EG *...this fiery young man... ...a fiery and uncompromising speech... Her fiery temper got the better of her.* ADJ QUALIT : USU ATTRIB ⇑ passionate

fiesta /fiːestə/, **fiestas**. A **fiesta** is a time of public entertainment and parties on a special religious day, especially in Spain or Latin America. N COUNT ⇑ celebration

fife /faɪf/, **fifes**. A **fife** is a small pipe-shaped musical instrument. N COUNT

fifteen /fɪftiːn/, **fifteens**. **1** **Fifteen** is the number 15: see □ at NUMBER, AGE, DATE, MEASUREMENT, MONEY, and TIME. EG *We were married for fifteen years.* NUM

2 A **fifteen** is a rugby football team. EG *Alan's got into the first fifteen.* N COUNT : USU ORD+N, VB CAN BE SING OR PL

fifteenth /fɪftiːnθ/. The **fifteenth** item in a series is the one that you count as number fifteen: see □ at NUMBER, AGE, and DATE. EG *The palace is supposed to have been built in the late fifteenth century.* ORDINAL

fifth /fɪfθ/, **fifths**. **1** The **fifth** item in a series is the one that you count as number five: see □ at NUMBER, AGE, and DATE. EG *We were sent to another office on the fifth floor.* ORDINAL

2 A **fifth** is one of five equal parts of something. EG *Only one fifth of the surface area of Africa is farmland.* N COUNT : USU+*of* ⇑ fraction

3 In music, a **fifth** is the interval between two notes on a musical scale when there are three notes separating them. N COUNT : USU SING

fifth columnist, fifth columnists. A **fifth columnist** is someone who secretly supports and helps the enemies of the country or organization they are in. N COUNT ⇑ traitor

fiftieth /fɪfti¹əθ/. The **fiftieth** item in a series is the one that you count as number fifty: see □ at NUMBER and AGE. EG *...the fiftieth anniversary of the Russian Revolution.* ORDINAL

fifty /fɪfti¹/, **fifties**. **Fifty** is the number 50: see □ at NUMBER, AGE, DATE, MEASUREMENT, MONEY, and TIME. EG *He pointed to some low buildings about fifty yards away.* NUM

fifty-fifty. **1** When something, for example money or property, is divided **fifty-fifty** between two people, each person gets half of it. EG *Profits were to be split fifty-fifty between the two men.* ▸ used as an adjective. EG *It was a fifty-fifty deal.* ADV WITH VB ⇑ equally ▸ ADJ CLASSIF

2 If the chances of something happening are **fifty-fifty**, it is as likely that it will not happen as that it will happen. EG *He realistically admitted his chances of victory to be 'fifty-fifty'... This bird may have little better than a fifty-fifty chance of survival.* ADJ CLASSIF = even

fig /fɪg/, **figs**. **1** A **fig** is a soft sweet fruit which is full of tiny seeds, is often eaten dried, and grows in hot countries; used also of the tree that it grows on. N COUNT

2 You say that someone **doesn't care a fig** or **doesn't give a fig** about something to say and emphasize that they do not care about it at all. EG *You don't really care a fig about status.* PHR : VB INFLECTS

fig., figs. **1** **Fig.** is an abbreviation for 'figure'; used to refer to a particular diagram or as part of a heading of a diagram. EG *The piston is then brought into a horizontal position (see fig. 3).* N COUNT : USU+NUM

2 **Fig.** is also an abbreviation for 'figurative'.

fight /faɪt/, **fights, fighting, fought**. **1** If you **fight** something, you try in a determined way to prevent it or stop it happening. EG *We intend to fight racism... You can't fight against progress... ...the great crusade to fight and conquer cancer.* ▸ used as a noun. EG *...the fight against illegal drugs... ...the fight against inflation.* V+O, OR V : IF+PREP THEN *against* ⇑ resist ▸ N COUNT : IF+PREP THEN *against* = battle

2 If you **fight** for something, you try in a determined way to get it or achieve it. EG *They will fight for their rights... Workers will have to fight to participate in the country's economic growth.* ▸ used as a noun. EG *...the fight for equality.* V : USU+*for*/*to*-INF ⇑ strive = battle ▸ N COUNT : IF+PREP THEN *for*

3 If you **fight**, **3.1** you take part in a battle or a war. EG *He had fought in the First World War... People used to fight each other over religion... The men were going off to fight a battle.* ▸ used as a noun, especially to refer to a battle to get control of a particular place. EG *...the critical fight for Venlo.* ◇ **fighting**. EG *We were only metres away from the fighting.* **3.2** you try to hurt someone, for example by hitting them with your fists, while they try to hurt you in a similar way. EG *The children continued to fight... Sam and Eric were fighting each other... I learned how to fight other boys... He was always fighting with his brother.* ▸ used as a noun. EG *There would be fights sometimes between the workers.* **3.3** you take part in a boxing match. EG *Cooney had signed to fight Mike Weaver... Tomorrow he fights against the reigning champion.* ▸ used as a noun. EG *It was his fourth fight since the summer.* **3.4** you quarrel with another person. EG *They fought about money... It's nice not having to fight you about housework.* ▸ used as a noun. EG *'That's my trouble at parties,' says Miss Callendar, 'I get into fights.'* V OR V+O : IF+PREP THEN *with/against* ▸ N COUNT ◇ N UNCOUNT V OR V+O : IF+PREP THEN *with/against* = wrestle ▸ N COUNT V OR V+O : IF+PREP THEN *against* = take on ▸ N COUNT V OR V+O : IF+PREP THEN *about/over* ⇑ disagree ▸ N COUNT = row

4 If you **fight** someone for something, for example V OR V+O : IF+

an important job, you compete with them for it. EG *He was nominated by the Republicans to fight Hearst for the post of governor.* ▸ used as a noun. EG *...that memorable fight for the presidency.* PREP THEN *against* = challenge ▸ N COUNT+*for* = contest

5 If you **fight** an election in a particular place, you are a candidate in the election and try to win it. EG *It takes a great deal of money to fight a general election... He successfully fought Smethwick for Labour.* V+O

6 If you **put up a fight**, you fight strongly against someone who is stronger than you are. PHR : VB INFLECTS

7 Fight is the desire or ability to keep fighting. EG *They still have a lot of fight left in them.* N UNCOUNT = resistance

8 If you **fight** your **way** somewhere, you get there with great difficulty, for example because there are a lot of people or difficulties in your way. EG *She had reached me only after fighting her way through a huge crowd.* PHR : VB INFLECTS = battle

9 When you **fight** an emotion or desire, you try very hard not to feel it, show it, or act on it. EG *He fought the urge to cry.* V+O = resist

10 Someone who **is fighting for** their **life** is making a great effort to stay alive, either when they are being physically attacked or when they are very ill. EG *He is fighting for his life.* PHR : VB INFLECTS

11 When you **fight for breath**, you try to breathe but find it very difficult. PHR : VB INFLECTS

12 Someone who is **fighting fit** is very fit or healthy. PHR : USED AS C

13 If you have a **fighting chance** of doing or achieving something, it is possible that you will do or achieve it, but not very likely. EG *We've still got a fighting chance of winning the contract.* PHR : USED AS O = hope

14 • to **fight a losing battle**: see **lose**. • to **fight fire with fire**: see **fire**. • to **fight shy of** something: see **shy**. • See also **dog-fight**.

fight back. **1** If you **fight back** against someone who has attacked you or made difficulties for you, you try to protect yourself and stop them or beat them. EG *Our forces were fighting back desperately... The importing countries could fight back with laws of their own.* PHRASAL VB : V+ADV ⇑ respond = resist

2 When you **fight back** an emotion or a desire, you try very hard not to feel it, show it, or act on it. EG *She fought back the tears... I waited, fighting back my fear.* PHRASAL VB : ORDER V+ADV+O = hold back

fight down. When you **fight down** an emotion or a desire, you try very hard not to feel it, show it, or act on it. EG *He had to fight down the impulse to sneak out.* PHRASAL VB : ORDER V+ADV+O

fight off. **1** If you **fight off** something, for example an illness or an unpleasant feeling, you succeed in getting rid of it and in not letting it overcome you. EG *We can fight off most minor ailments... For most of the time she was fighting off despair.* PHRASAL VB : V+O+ADV ⇑ repel = ward off

2 If you **fight off** someone who has attacked you, you succeed in driving them away by fighting them. PHRASAL VB : V+O+ADV

fight out. When two people or groups **fight** something **out,** they fight or argue until one of them wins and so the matter they were fighting or arguing about is settled. EG *The European nations were fighting it out on the battlefields... These decisions were fought out between contending groups.* PHRASAL VB : V+O+ADV ⇑ decide = thrash out

fighter /faɪtə/, **fighters**. **1** A **fighter** or a **fighter plane** is a fast military aircraft that is used for destroying other aircraft. N COUNT

2 A **fighter** is also **2.1** a person who keeps trying to achieve things and who is not put off by difficulties or opposition. N COUNT ≠ pushover **2.2** a person who physically fights another person. N COUNT ⇑ combatant

3 See also **fire fighter, freedom fighter, prize fighter.**

fig leaf, fig leaves; also spelled with a hyphen and as one word. A **fig leaf** is a large leaf which comes from the fig tree. A fig leaf is sometimes used in painting and sculpture to cover the genitals of a nude body. N COUNT

figment /fɪgmə°nt/, **figments**. If something is a **figment** of someone's imagination, it does not really exist and they are just imagining it. EG *I thought this man Broum was another figment of your imagination.* N COUNT : USU USED AS C, USU+*of* = product

figurative /fɪgə°rətɪv/. **1** If you use a word or expression in a **figurative** sense, you use it with a more abstract or imaginative meaning than its ordinary one. EG *He imprisoned her, in a figurative sense.* ADJ CLASSIF = metaphorical

2 Figurative art is a style of art in which people and things are shown as they actually look. ADJ CLASSIF

figuratively /fɪgə°rətɪvli[1]/. **1 Figuratively** is used in a sentence to indicate that a word or expression is being used in a figurative sense rather than in its most physical and ordinary one. EG *A majority of men figuratively still live in the twelfth century.* ADV WITH VB, OR ADV SEN ≠ literally

2 Someone who is speaking **figuratively** is using a particular word or expression in a figurative sense. EG *'She said I killed him.'-'She was speaking figuratively.'* ADV WITH VB, OR ADV SEN = metaphorically

figure /fɪgə/, **figures, figuring, figured**. **1** A **figure** is **1.1** a particular amount expressed as a number, especially one that is given as a statistic in a piece of information. EG *Recent government figures show that there are 135,000 families with four or more children... ...unemployment figures... The figure for 1983 was as low as 23 per cent... We decided on a figure of ten thousand.* N COUNT • When you **put a figure on** an amount, you say exactly how much it is. EG *They said defence spending should be raised but put no figure on the increase they wanted.* • PHR : VB INFLECTS ⇑ state **1.2** any of the ten written symbols from 0 to 9 that are used to represent a number. EG *He wrote the date in figures at the top of the paper... ...a three-figure number.* N COUNT ⇑ symbol = digit • An amount or number that is in **double figures** is between ten and ninety-nine. EG *The rate of inflation remains in double figures.* • PHR : USED AS O, USU PREP+O • An amount or number that is in **single figures** is between nought and nine. EG *We want inflation brought down to single figures.* • PHR : USED AS O, USU PREP+O

2 Arithmetic can be referred to in informal English as **figures**. EG *He has a better head for figures than I ever had.* N PLURAL = numbers

3 You refer to someone that you can see as a **figure** when you cannot see them clearly, for example because they are a long way away or because it is dark, or when you are describing them. EG *Far away down the road I could see a small female figure advancing towards us... ...a lean figure dressed in a grey top hat... The sturdy figure of Joe Shaw appears.* N COUNT ⇑ person = form

4 When you describe someone as **a fine figure of a man** or **woman**, you mean that they are quite tall and strong-looking in an attractive way. PHR : USED AS C ⇑ good-looking

5 In art, a **figure** is a person who is in a drawing or a painting or a statue of a person. N COUNT

6 Someone who is referred to as a **figure** of a particular kind is a person who is well-known and important in some way. EG *He was a key figure in the independence struggle... ...one of the great theatrical figures of our time... He's a controversial figure... The incident made her a national figure.* N COUNT+SUPP = personality

7 Someone who is regarded as, for example, a mother **figure** or a hero **figure** by someone else is regarded as the type of person stated or suggested. EG *She was a mother figure for him... ...authority figures.* N COUNT : MOD+N ⇑ symbol

8 Someone who is a **figure of fun** is often laughed at in an unkind way. PHR : USED AS C

9 Your **figure** is the shape of your body. EG *She's got a fabulous figure... He was always worrying about his figure.* N COUNT : USU POSS+N • If you **keep** your **figure**, you stay slim. If you **lose** your **figure**, you become rather fat. • PHR : VB INFLECTS

10 A **figure** is also a drawing or diagram that is used to explain or illustrate information that is being given; often used with a number to refer to a drawing or diagram. EG *This led to the development of a new type of machine (see Figure 8).* N COUNT : USU+NUM ⇑ illustration

11 In geometry, a **figure** is a shape, especially a regular shape. EG *A hexagon is a six-sided figure.* N COUNT

12 A **figure** in, for example, dancing or ice skating is a movement that follows a particular shape or pattern. N COUNT ⇑ movement

13 If you **figure** that something is the case, you think or guess that it is the case, especially after considering the matter quite carefully; an informal use used especially in American English. EG *They figured it was better to stay where they were... She brought a torch, as she figured he might need it.* V+REPORT-CL = reckon

14 If you say 'that **figures**' or if you say that it **figures** that something is the case, you mean that the fact referred to is not surprising and is what you would expect to happen; an informal expression. EG *'The subject never came up.'-'That figures.'* *that*+V OR V+REPORT-CL = make sense

15 In American English, when you **figure**, you work out the answers to sums; an old-fashioned expression. EG *...the ability to read, write and do simple figuring.* V OR V+O

16 To **figure** in something means to appear or be included in it. EG *Loneliness figures quite a lot in his* V : USU+*in* = feature

conversation... The photograph had figured as part of the evidence in the trial.
17 to **cut a figure**: see **cut**.

figure on. If you **figure on** something, you plan that it will happen or assume that it will happen when making your plans; an informal expression used mainly in American English. EG *How soon are you figuring on getting married?... We'd figured on you helping us.* — PHRASAL VB : V+PREP, HAS PASS

figure out. **1** If you **figure out** a solution to a problem, the answer to a question, or the reason for or nature of something, you work it out so that you understand it; an informal expression used especially in American English. EG *She had not yet figured out what she was going to do... We tried to figure out a way to see them... I just can't figure him out.* — PHRASAL VB : V+ADV+O/REPORT-CL = suss out
2 If you **figure out** the answer to a sum, you work it out; an informal expression used in American English. — PHRASAL VB : V+O+ADV = work out

figure eight, figure eights. A **figure eight** is the same as a figure of eight; used in American English. — N COUNT

figurehead /fɪgəhɛd/, **figureheads**. **1** Someone who is the **figurehead** of a movement or organization is its leader, often one who has little real power. EG *The party's president had become merely a figurehead.* — N COUNT
2 A **figurehead** is also a large wooden model of a person that was put just under the pointed front of a sailing ship in former times. — N COUNT ⇑ effigy

figure of eight, figures of eight. A **figure of eight** is something, for example a knot or a movement done by a skater, that has the shape of the number 8. — N COUNT

figure of speech, figures of speech. A **figure of speech** is an expression or word that is used with a figurative rather than a literal meaning. EG *When he wrote of the 'two nations' he was not employing a figure of speech but identifying a fact of life.* — N COUNT = turn of phrase

figure skating is skating in an attractive pattern, usually with spins and jumps included. — N UNCOUNT

figurine /fɪgəriːn/, **figurines**. A **figurine** is a small ornamental model of a person. — N COUNT = statuette

filament /fɪləmə²nt/, **filaments**. A **filament** is a very thin piece or thread of something; used especially to refer to the piece of wire inside a light bulb. EG *...traditional filament bulbs... ...filaments of algae.* — N COUNT

filch /fɪltʃ/, **filches, filching, filched**. When you **filch** something, you steal it; an informal word. EG *The letters had been filched from the private files of John D. Archbold.* — V+O : USU+*from* = pilfer

file /faɪl/, **files, filing, filed**. **1** A **file** is **1.1** a box, large envelope, or folded piece of card in which someone keeps letters or other documents that belong together, for example because they are about one subject. EG *...eight standard cardboard files... Put it in a 'do later' file.* ● See also **box file**. — N COUNT ⇑ container **1.2** the written information in a file. EG *...a very dull file about crime statistics... Casson finished reading the file and grimaced.* — N COUNT = dossier **1.3** a collection of information about a particular person or thing. EG *Get me the personal file on Viktor Kowalski... Perhaps they've lost my file... Without access to the files of a good Secret Service, this is difficult.* — N COUNT = dossier
2 Something that is **on file** or **on the files** or on someone's **files** is recorded or kept in a file or in a collection of information. EG *These notes were on file... I don't know who his dentist is. It's not on the files. The police had both men on their files.* — PHR : USED AS AN A
3 If you **file** a document, you put it in the correct file. EG *Bills are not filed under B but under U for unpleasant.* — V+O : IF+PREP THEN *under* ⇑ store
4 In computing, a **file** is a set of related data that has its own name and that can be handled as one item by referring to it by this name. — N COUNT ⇑ store
5 When you **file** a formal or legal accusation, complaint, or request, you make it officially. EG *They have made this accusation in a lawsuit they have filed... The wife is then forced into filing for divorce... Adoption papers were duly filed by Mr and Mrs White in May 1974.* — V+O, OR V+A *(for)* ⇑ register
6 When someone **files** a report or a news story, they send or give it to their employer. EG *I had filed two stories for my paper.* — V+O = submit
7 When a group of people **files** somewhere, they walk one behind the other in a line. EG *They filed out in silence.* — V+A ⇑ go
8 A **file** of people is a line of people who are walking or standing one behind the other. EG *...the file of passengers coming down the steps... They walked in a file down the hill.* ● A group of people who are walking or standing **in single file** or **single file** are in a line, one behind the other. EG *We were crossing the bridge now, in single file.* — N COUNT : IF SING, VB CAN BE SING OR PL; ● PHR : USED AS A
9 A **file** is also a hand tool consisting of a long piece of steel with rough surfaces, sometimes with a handle, which is used for rubbing hard objects to make them smooth, shape them, or cut through them. ● See also **nail file**. — N COUNT
10 If you **file** an object, you smooth it, shape it, or cut it with a file. EG *Kitty sat at the kitchen table filing her fingernails... He had filed through the bars and escaped.* — V+O, OR V+A
11 See also **rank and file**.

file away. **1** If you **file** a document **away**, you put it in the correct file. — PHRASAL VB : V+O+ADV
2 When you **file away** a fact or idea, you pay careful attention to it, intending to remember or think about it again later. EG *Dan carefully filed away this added reason for hating Joe Parker.* — PHRASAL VB : V+O+ADV = note

filial /fɪljəl/ means relating to the status, duties, etc of a son or daughter. EG *...a sense of duty or filial obligation. ...lacking in filial affection.* — ADJ CLASSIF

filibuster /fɪlɪbʌstə/, **filibusters, filibustering, filibustered**. A **filibuster** is a long slow speech or a series of long slow speeches. Filibusters are used, especially in the U.S.A., as a method of preventing laws from being passed by the legislature, because the debating time runs out before the debate is over, so that a vote cannot be taken. EG *I could not prolong a filibuster indefinitely.* ▸ used as a verb. EG *We had agreed that we would not filibuster... Filibustering is not technically allowed at Westminster.* — N COUNT ⇑ strategy = delay; ▸ V = delay

filigree /fɪlɪgriː/ is delicate ornamental designs made with gold or silver wire. EG *You might look at some of the embroidery and filigree silver.* — N UNCOUNT

filing cabinet, filing cabinets; also spelled with a hyphen. A **filing cabinet** is a piece of office furniture, usually made of metal, and having deep drawers in which files are kept. — N COUNT ⇑ cupboard

filing clerk, filing clerks; also spelled with a hyphen. A **filing clerk** is a person whose job is to file documents in an office. — N COUNT ⇑ employee

Filipino /fɪlɪpiːnəʊ/, **Filipinos**. **1** A **Filipino** is a person who comes from the Philippines. — N COUNT
2 **Filipino** means belonging to or coming from the Philippines. EG *...the Filipino people.* — ADJ CLASSIF = Philippine

fill /fɪl/, **fills, filling, filled**. **1** If you **fill** something, you put a large amount of a substance or a lot of things into it, with the result that it is full. EG *Fill the teapot with boiling water... Can you fill me a bucket of water, please?* — V+O : IF+PREP THEN USU *with/for*, OR V+O+O ≠ empty
2 If something **fills** a space or area, it is so big, or is present in such large numbers or amounts that it seems as if the whole space is occupied. EG *Enthusiastic crowds filled the streets.* ◊ **filled**. EG *They entered a large hall filled with rows of desks.* — V+O ⇑ occupy = crowd; ◊ ADJ CLASSIF : PRED+*with*
3 If something or a place or area **fills**, it becomes full of things, people, or a substance. EG *Madeleine's eyes filled with tears... The place of assembly filled quickly.* — V : IF+PREP THEN *with* ≠ empty
4 If you **fill** a crack or hole, you put a substance into it in order to make the surface smooth again. EG *Small wall cracks can be filled with plaster.* — V+O : IF+PREP THEN *with* = seal
5 If a sound, smell, or light **fills** a space, the air, etc it is very strong or noticeable. EG *The familiar smell of dust filled the air... The tropical sun fills the room with light... A chatter of German and French filled his ears.* — V+O : IF+PREP THEN *with* = flood
6 If something **fills** you with an emotion, or if an emotion **fills** you, you experience this emotion strongly and suddenly. EG *His son's lies filled him with anger and contempt... A wave of panic filled her.* ◊ **filled**. EG *He was filled with resentment.* — V+O : IF+PREP THEN *with* = engulf; ◊ ADJ QUALIT
7 To **fill** something with a particular quality or thing means to cause it to have a lot of that quality or thing. EG *He wanted someone or something that would fill his life with meaning again... ...tutors who go around filling our heads with all these ideas.* — V+O+A *(with)* = charge
8 If you **fill** a period of time with a particular activity, you spend the time in this way. EG *People must fill their time 'healthily' and 'meaningfully'.* — V+O+A = occupy
9 If something **fills** a need or a gap, it puts an end to this need or gap by existing or being active. EG *The* — V+O ⇑ stop

SDP Liberal Alliance filled the political vacuum... This book fills a major gap.

10 Something that **fills** a role or position performs a particular function or has a particular place within a system. EG *It has filled this role in a most satisfactory way for many years.* V+O = fulfil

11 If someone **fills** a job vacancy, **11.1** they accept a job that they have been offered. EG *The remaining 37,000 posts were filled by Africans.* V+O = take up **11.2** they choose someone to do the job. EG *The election to fill his vacated post took place the following week.* V+O = assign

12 If you have your **fill** of something, you eat, drink, laugh, watch, etc as much or for as long as you want or need. EG *They could eat their fill of honey... When she had laughed her fill, she told him he was too late.* N SING : DET/POSS +N, IF+PREP THEN *of*

13 If you **have had your fill of** something, you do not want to experience or do it any more. EG *I'd had my fill of storms... I have had my fill of Hamlet now.* PHR+NG/-ING : VB INFLECTS = be sick of

14 If you **fill** yourself with food, you eat so much that you do not feel hungry. EG *You can't expect to lose weight if you keep filling yourself with chocolate.* V+O (REFL/NG) = stuff

15 A play, film, or performer that **fills** a theatre, concert hall, or cinema attracts a very large audience. EG *...those great actors whose names alone could fill a theatre.* V+O = pack

16 When the wind **fills** a sail, or when the sail **fills**, the sail becomes rounded rather than hanging loosely. V-ERG = swell

17 When a dentist **fills** someone's tooth, he or she puts a filling in it. V+O ⇑ plug

18 If you **fill** an order or a prescription, you provide the things that are asked for; used mainly in American English. EG *The bartender went back to fill the order.* V+O ⇑ supply

19 • to **fill the bill**: see **bill**. • See also **filling**.

fill in. 1 If you **fill in** a crack or a hole, you put a substance into it so that the surface becomes level. PHRASAL VB : V+O+ADV

2 If you **are filling in** time, you are using time that is available by doing something that is not very important. EG *Derrick thought he would fill in the waiting time by seeing the world.* PHRASAL VB : ORDER V+ADV+O = use

3 If you **fill in** a form, you write information in the spaces on it. EG *We filled in all the customs forms... Fill in your name and address.* PHRASAL VB : V+O+ADV

4 If you **fill in** a shape, you paint or draw all over the space inside the lines so that it becomes covered with colour. EG *She drew a circle and filled it in.* PHRASAL VB : V+O+ADV = shade in

5 If you **fill** someone **in**, **5.1** you give them more details about something that you know about. EG *I'll fill you in on the details now... Come on back to the house and I'll fill you in.* PHRASAL VB : V+O+ADV ⇑ inform **5.2** you beat them up; a very informal use. PHRASAL VB : V+O+ADV

6 If you **fill in** for someone, you do the work or task that they normally do because they are unable to do it. EG *One of the other girls is sick and I said I'd fill in.* PHRASAL VB : V+ADV, IF+PREP THEN *for* = stand in

fill out. 1 If you **fill out** a form, you write information in the spaces on it. EG *I've filled out the death certificate.* PHRASAL VB : V+O+ADV ⇑ write

2 If a fairly thin person **fills out**, they become fatter. EG *He'd filled out a lot since I'd last seen him.* PHRASAL VB : V+ADV

fill up. 1 If you **fill up** a container, you put a large amount of a substance or a lot of things into it, with the result that it is full. EG *Fill it up, please.* PHRASAL VB : V+PREP, HAS PASS

2 If something **fills up** a space or area, it is so big, or is present in such large numbers or amounts that it seems as if the whole space is occupied. EG *The computer was massive, filling up a whole room.* PHRASAL VB : V+O+ADV ⇑ occupy = take up

3 If a place or area **fills up**, it becomes full of things, people, or a substance. EG *His office began to fill up with people.* PHRASAL VB : V+ADV, IF+PREP THEN *with* ⇑ fill

4 If you **fill up** a period of time with a particular activity, you spend the time in this way. EG *The idea was to fill up the day with meaningless activities.* PHRASAL VB : V+PREP, HAS PASS = take up

5 If you **fill** yourself **up** with food, you eat so much that you do not feel hungry. EG *No filling up with sandwiches, beer, and chips!* PHRASAL VB : V+O (REFL/NG), OR V+ADV

6 A type of food that **fills you up** makes you feel that you have eaten a lot, even though you have only eaten a small amount. EG *Wholemeal bread fills you up better than white.* PHRASAL VB : V+O+ADV

7 If you **fill up** a form, you complete it, giving all the information that is requested. EG *Sorry to interrupt, but I've some forms to fill up.* PHRASAL VB : V+O+ADV ⇑ write = fill out

-filled combines with nouns in order to form adjectives which indicate that something contains or is full of the thing mentioned. EG *She stared at me with tear-filled eyes... ...gas-filled tanks... ...his twisted hate-filled face.* COMB : FORMS ADJS

filler /fɪlə/, **fillers**. **Filler** is a substance used for filling cracks or holes, especially in walls, car bodies, or wood. N UNCOUNT

filler cap, filler caps; also spelled with a hyphen. A **filler cap** is the lid that covers the hole through which you put petrol or oil into a vehicle. N COUNT

fillet /fɪlɪt/, **fillets, filleting, filleted**. 1 **Fillet** is a strip of tender meat, especially beef, that has no bones in it. EG *...fillet of beef... ...two fillet steaks.* N UNCOUNT/COUNT

2 A **fillet** of fish is the side of a fish with the bones removed. EG *...a fillet of plaice.* N COUNT/UNCOUNT

3 When you **fillet** fish or meat, you prepare it by cutting it to take the bones out. V+O

filling /fɪlɪŋ/, **fillings**. 1 A **filling** is a small amount of metal or sometimes plastic that a dentist puts in a hole in a tooth to prevent further decay. EG *She has lots of fillings.* N COUNT ⇑ plug

2 A **filling** for a cake, pie, chocolate, or sandwich is an edible substance or mixture that is put inside it. EG *...delicious chocolates with cream fillings.* N MASS ⇑ contents

3 The **filling** of a quilt, cushion, or sleeping bag is the soft substance that is put inside it to make it warm or comfortable. N MASS ⇑ contents

4 Food that is **filling** makes you feel full when you have eaten it. ADJ QUALIT ⇑ substantial

filling station, filling stations; also spelled with a hyphen. A **filling station** is a place where you can buy petrol and oil for your car. EG *I stopped at a filling station.* N COUNT = petrol station

fillip /fɪlɪp/, **fillips**. A **fillip** is a sudden improvement or increase in excitement or energy. EG *The choice of films is wide and gives an added fillip to the classroom lessons.* N COUNT : USU SING

filly /fɪli[1]/, **fillies**. A **filly** is a young female horse. N COUNT

film /fɪlm/, **films, filming, filmed**. 1 A **film** is moving pictures shown on a screen, especially at a cinema, that tell a story, or sometimes show a real situation or series of events. EG *Shall we go and see a film?... The film was shot largely on location... She made a film about Egypt.* N COUNT

2 When you **film** or when you **film** someone or something, you use a camera to take moving pictures which can be shown on a screen or on television. EG *The TV crews couldn't film at night... Joan ran ahead to film us as we crossed the bridge... He is intending to film Tagore's novel 'The Home and the World'... I was filming a scene outside.* V OR V+O

3 **Film** of something is moving pictures of a real event that are shown on television or on a screen. EG *The broadcast began with close-up film of babies crying.* N UNCOUNT = footage

4 **Film** or a **film** is also a long narrow flat piece of plastic that is used in a camera to take photographs. EG *I used half a roll of film taking pictures... I need a new film for my camera... ...a moment preserved for ever on film.* N UNCOUNT/COUNT

5 The making of cinema films, considered as a form of art or a business, can be referred to as **film** or **films**. EG *The age of film was probably over by 1950... I enjoyed working in films.* N UNCOUNT/COUNT

6 A **film** of powder, liquid, or grease is a very thin layer of it on the surface of something. EG *They were like letters seen through a film of tears.* N COUNT : USU SING+SUPP = veil

7 Plastic **film** is a very thin sheet of plastic, used especially to wrap and cover things. EG *...transparent wrapping film.* N UNCOUNT+SUPP ⇑ covering

8 See also **filming**.

film over. 1 If your eyes **film over**, they become covered with a very thin layer of tears. PHRASAL VB : V+ADV

filming /fɪlmɪŋ/ is the activity of making a film including, for example the acting, directing, and operating of the cameras. EG *I found filming terribly exhausting.* N UNCOUNT

film star, film stars. A **film star** is a famous actor or actress who appears in films. N COUNT ⇑ celebrity

film-strip, film-strips. A **film-strip** is a series of still pictures on a piece of film that are shown one after the other on a screen. EG *...an educational film-strip company.* N COUNT = slides

filmy /fɪlmi[1]/, **filmier, filmiest**. A fabric or substance that is **filmy** is very thin and almost transparent. EG *...a filmy black nightie.* ADJ CLASSIF = gauzy

filter /fɪltə/, **filters, filtering, filtered**. 1 To **filter** a substance means to pass it through a device which is designed to remove certain particles con- V-ERG ⇑ purify tained in it. EG *Water and soil would have to be filtered many times to remove any radioactive matter.*

2 A **filter** is 2.1 a device through which a substance is passed when it is being filtered. 2.2 a device through which sound or light is passed and which blocks or reduces particular sound or light frequencies. N COUNT; N COUNT

3 If light or sound **filters** into a place it comes in faintly or slowly, either through a small or partly covered opening, or from a long distance away. EG *Light filtered into the room... Sounds of cheering filtered in through the closed window.* V+A ⇑ get = seep

4 When news or information **filters** through to people, it gradually reaches them. EG *Disturbing rumours filtered back from the East... The word filtered through about the death camps.* V+A ⇑ get = trickle

5 A traffic **filter** is a traffic signal or lane which controls the movement of traffic wanting to turn left or right. ▸ used as a verb. EG *...traffic waiting to filter to the right.* N COUNT; ▸ V : USU+A

6 A **filter** cigarette is the same as a filter-tipped cigarette. EG *He was chain-smoking his habitual filter cigarettes.* N BEFORE N

filter out. To **filter out** something from a substance means to remove it from the substance by passing the substance through a filter. EG *The first part of the problem would involve filtering out some of the tar particles.* PHRASAL VB : V+O+ADV

filter tip, filter tips; also spelled with a hyphen. A **filter tip** is a small device at the end of a cigarette that reduces the amount of nicotine that passes into the smoker's body. N COUNT

filter-tipped. A **filter-tipped** cigarette has a filter tip. ADJ CLASSIF

filth /fɪlθ/. **Filth** is 1 a disgusting amount of dirt. EG *...the filth and decay of the villages.* 2 language or behaviour that is felt to be very disgusting and rude. EG *Our children should not be exposed to filth like that.* 3 written material or pictures that represent naked people or sex in what is thought to be a crude and offensive way. EG *That filth should never be shown on television.* N UNCOUNT; N UNCOUNT = smut; N UNCOUNT = smut

filthy /fɪlθi¹/, **filthier, filthiest**. 1 Something that is **filthy** is 1.1 very dirty indeed. EG *...a really filthy oven... I noticed his filthy and torn sweater.* 1.2 morally very unpleasant and disgusting, sometimes concerning sexual matters. EG *I caught her reading a filthy book... That's a filthy thing to say... ...the dishonesty that prevails in this filthy world we have to live in.* ◇ **filthiness**. ADJ QUALIT; ADJ QUALIT ⇑ immoral; ◇ N UNCOUNT

2 If the weather is **filthy**, it is raining or snowing, and perhaps very cold and windy; an informal use. ADJ QUALIT ⇑ bad

3 Someone who is **filthy rich** is very rich indeed; an informal expression. PHR : USED AS C = loaded

fin /fɪn/, **fins**. A fish's **fin** is a flat object like a small wing sticking out of its body. It helps the fish to swim and to keep its balance. N COUNT ⇑ limb

final /faɪnə⁰l/, **finals**. 1 In a series of events, things, or people, the **final** one is the last one. EG *...on the final morning of the festival... We made our second and final attempt to beat the record... The final letter was very vague. Possibly an R.* ADJ CLASSIF : ATTRIB

2 **Final** also means 2.1 happening at the end of an event or series of events. EG *The final applause was explosive... ...a final summing up.* 2.2 the greatest or most severe that is possible; used of abstract things. EG *He paid the final penalty for his crime... The final irony is that he died two days before it was completed.* ADJ CLASSIF : ATTRIB; ADJ CLASSIF : ATTRIB = ultimate

3 If a decision, authority, or situation is **final**, it cannot be changed or questioned. EG *The judges' decision is final... You'd be insane to let him have the final say.* ADJ CLASSIF ⇑ definitive

4 The **final** of a competition or tournament is the last game or contest which takes place and which decides the winner of the whole competition or tournament. EG *England beat West Germany in the World Cup Final... We've done well to get to the Final.* N COUNT+SUPP

▸ You can also refer to the last few games or contests as the **finals**. EG *There is a long way to go before the World Cup Finals in Spain... We hope to qualify for the finals.* ▸ N PLURAL : *the*+N

5 When a student takes his or her **finals**, he or she takes the last and most important examination in a university or college course. N PLURAL : *the*/POSS+N ⇑ examinations

6 The **final** edition of a daily newspaper is the last edition to be printed on a particular day. ▸ used as a noun. EG *The story appeared in the late final.* ADJ CLASSIF; ▸ N COUNT

finale /fɪnɑːli¹/, **finales**. The **finale** of a show or piece of music is the last section of it, especially when this is exciting or impressive. EG *The finale was a spectacular dance involving all the members of the cast.* N COUNT ⇑ end = climax

finalise /faɪnəlaɪz/. See **finalize**.

finalist /faɪnəlɪst/, **finalists**. A **finalist** is someone who takes part in the final of a competition or tournament. EG *...an Olympic finalist.* N COUNT ⇑ competitor

finality /faɪnælɪti¹/ is the quality of ending or deciding something in a definite and unchangeable way. EG *Margaret said quietly but with finality: 'Well, we'll just have to disagree over this'... ...the finality of death.* N UNCOUNT

finalize /faɪnəlaɪz/, **finalizes, finalizing, finalized**; also spelled **finalise**. If you **finalize** something that you are arranging or organizing, you complete and agree on all the arrangements. EG *I'm now hoping to finalize things with the builders early next week... They would like the deal to be finalized before I release any keys.* V+O = settle

finally /faɪnəli¹/. 1 If someone **finally** does something, or if something **finally** happens, it is done or happens after quite a long period of time, sometimes a longer time than it should have done. EG *One of them stared at me for a long time and finally asked whether I was Angela Davis... It was Mr Heath's incomes policy which finally led to his downfall... When John finally arrived, he said that he had lost his way... They finally realized that the whole thing was a joke.* ADV = eventually

2 You use **finally** 2.1 to say that something is last in a series of actions or events. EG *Trotsky lived in turn in Turkey, France, Norway and finally Mexico.* 2.2 in speech or writing when you want to introduce a final point, ask a final question, or mention a final item. EG *Finally, Carol, are you encouraged by the direction education is taking?... Let's come finally to the question of pensions.* ADV+VB/NG = lastly; ADV SEN = lastly

finance /fɪnæns, faɪnæns/, **finances, financing, financed**. 1 If you **finance** a particular project or purchase, you provide the money, loans, or grants that are necessary to pay for it. EG *A private company will finance and build the pipeline... ...a special job-creation programme to be financed by increased taxes.* V+O = fund

2 **Finance** for a project or purchase is the money, loans, credits, or grants that are used to pay for it. EG *Obtaining finance from him may be vital to the whole enterprise... ...replacing private finance by government money... We couldn't get the finance for it.* N UNCOUNT

3 **Finance** is also the management of money, loans, credit, and investment, especially on a national level. EG *....the dangerous political arena of public-sector finance... ....a successful job in high finance.* N UNCOUNT ⇑ business

4 You can refer to the amount of money that you have and how well it is organized as your **finances**. EG *Whether it can be done depends, of course, on your finances.* N PLURAL : POSS+N = resources

financial /fɪ⁵nænʃə⁰l/ means relating to or involving money. EG *The company was in deep financial difficulties... Let's talk in purely financial terms... ...the country's financial condition.* ◇ **financially**. EG *The venture was not financially successful... We are able to be financially independent.* ADJ CLASSIF ⇑ economic; ◇ ADV+ADJ

financial year, financial years. The **financial year** is a period of twelve months, used by government, business, and other organizations according to which they plan and assess their budgets, profits, etc. In Britain, the financial year used by government for tax collection starts on 5th April. N COUNT

financier /fɪ⁵nænsɪə/, **financiers**. A **financier** is a person, company, or government that provides finance for projects or enterprises. EG *...an American financier and art collector... America and Russia were both possible financiers of the Aswan High Dam.* N COUNT ⇑ backer

finch /fɪntʃ/, **finches**. A **finch** is a small bird with a short strong beak that usually eats seeds. There are many kinds of finch. N COUNT

find /faɪnd/, **finds, finding, found**. 1 If you **find** someone or something, 1.1 you discover or get what you have been looking for as a result of searching for it. EG *Put things in a place where you can find them* V+O, V+O+O, OR V+O+A *(for)* = locate *quickly and easily... I think I'm lost, I can't find the bridge... He went back to his room to find his watch... His body has not been found.* **1.2** you discover something or someone unexpectedly or accidentally. EG *What an amazing restaurant to find in such a place... When she got home she found a six-page letter from David... He walked to the riverbank one day and found a crocodile trapped in a net... She looked up to find Tony standing there.* **1.3** you succeed in achieving something or in getting something that you need. EG *He cannot find work... She said she would find an electrician for us.*

V+O

V+O, V+O+O, OR V+O+A *(for)* ⇑ get

2 If you **find** the answer to a problem, you work out the answer by thinking logically. EG *There is a genuine effort to find a solution... We can now find the area of this triangle.*

V+O ⇑ learn = arrive at

3 If you **find** that something is the case, you become aware of it or discover that it is the case. EG *When I woke up, I found that I could not move my legs... Sue arrived at eleven-thirty, only to find that everyone had gone... He found it hard to make friends... I found him to be much younger than I expected... He was so frightened he found it almost impossible to speak.*

V+REPORT-CL OR V+O+C/*to*-INF

4 If you say that something **is found** in a particular place, you mean that this place is where it is or where it lives or exists. EG *Four different species of lungfish are found in Africa... There are no reptiles to be found here... You can find the National Portrait Gallery just off Trafalgar Square... You'll find details of these programmes in The Radio Times.*

V+O : USU PASS+A

5 If you **find** your **way** somewhere, you successfully get to or away from a place by choosing the right way to go. EG *Just tell me how to get there and I'll find my own way... She had turned on the lamp so that he could find his way out without bumping into anything.*

PHR+A : VB INFLECTS

6 If something **finds** its **way** somewhere, it eventually comes to a place which is regarded as suitable or for which it was intended. EG *Most of my ideas find their way into the wastepaper basket... I doubt whether much of the money found its way to Bernadette.*

PHR+A : VB INFLECTS ⇑ end up

7 If you say that you **find** that something has a particular quality, you are expressing your opinion about it. EG *I found him a disappointment... I don't find that funny at all... I thought I would find it very difficult to give people advice... A character that's mad, I find, is a very difficult character to write about... I find myself in almost total agreement with Tony... Do you find that there are a lot more fires in the summer?*

V+O (NG/REFL) +C/A, OR V+ REPORT-CL ⇑ think

8 If you **find** yourself doing something, you are doing it without deciding or intending to do it. EG *He found himself giggling quite uncontrollably.*

V+O (REFL)+ -ING/A = discover

9 If you **find** pleasure, enjoyment, comfort, etc in a particular thing or activity, you experience the feeling mentioned as a result of this thing or activity. EG *I found comfort in his words... Much pleasure is to be found in mathematics.*

V+O+A *(in)*

10 If you **find** the time or money to do something, you succeed in making or obtaining enough time or money to do it. EG *Some families cannot even find enough money for basic needs... How do you find time to write these books?*

V+O : IF+PREP/ VB THEN *for/ to*-INF ⇑ get

11 If something **finds** its target, it arrives at the target for which it was intended. EG *Nine of the fifteen missiles had found their targets.*

V+O = reach

12 If a particular time of the day **finds** someone doing something, that person is doing the thing mentioned at that time; a rather literary use. EG *Sunday afternoon found Andrew sleeping happily in an armchair... Every morning found her squatted comfortably before her hut.*

V+O+C/A = see

13 If a person who has been on trial is **found** guilty or **found** not guilty, the court, or the jury, decides that the person is guilty or innocent. EG *He was found guilty of murder.*

V+O+C : USU PASS ⇑ decide = judge

14 If a particular thing **finds expression in** something else, its ideas or attitudes are represented or put into words or action by this other thing. EG *'Love your neighbour as yourself' finds practical expression in Anne's daily life.*

PHR : VB INFLECTS

15 You also use **find** in a letter to make a polite enquiry about the health or circumstances of the person you have sent the letter to. EG *I hope this letter finds you in good health.*

V+O : NO PASS, NO CONT, NO IMPER

16 Something that is a **find** is **16.1** something valuable, interesting, or useful which has been discovered after a search or an investigation. EG *An active volcano on one of Jupiter's moons could be the greatest find of the planetary exploration programme.* **16.2** a person or place that is very suitable for a particular purpose and that you have discovered by accident. EG *They've got this new singer, and she's a real find.*

N COUNT : USU USED AS C = discovery

N SING WITH DET : USU USED AS C = discovery

17 If you say to someone **'Take me as you find me'** or **'You'll have to take us as you find us'**, you mean that they have to accept you as you are and that you cannot make any special changes to please them. This expression is often used to refer also to the state of tidiness of the place in which you live.

PHR

18 The word **find** is also used in the following expressions, which are explained at other places in this dictionary. • to **find fault**: see **fault**. • to **find favour**: see **favour**. • to **find** your **tongue**: see **tongue**. • to **find** your **feet**: see **foot**.

find for. When a judge **finds for** one of the people contesting a court case, he or she comes to a judgement in favour of this person. EG *The judge had found for the husband.*

PHRASAL VB : V+ PREP, HAS PASS

find out. 1 If you **find out** something, you learn something that you did not already know, especially by making a deliberate effort to do so. EG *I found out the train times... I'm only interested in finding out what the facts are... We found out that she was wrong.*

PHRASAL VB : V+ ADV+O/REPORT-CL = discover

2 If you **find** someone **out**, you discover that they have been telling lies, doing something dishonest, or doing something that they should not be doing. EG *The manager had found him out and was going to sack him... I'm the sort of man who's always found out.*

PHRASAL VB : ORDER V+O+ ADV, USU PASS = rumble

finder /faɪndə/, **finders. 1** The **finder** of something is the person who finds it.

N COUNT

2 You say **'finders keepers'** to suggest that because you have found something you have the right to keep it rather than give it back to the person who lost it.

CONVENTION

finding /faɪndɪŋ/, **findings. 1** Someone's **findings** are the information they get or the conclusions they come to as the result of an investigation or some research. EG *Tell me about your findings... ...the findings of the committee... One very alarming finding was that the children had been suffering from lead poisoning.*

N COUNT : USU PL ⇑ discovery

2 The **findings** of a court are the decision that it reaches after a trial or an inquiry into some matter. EG *He mentioned the findings of the European Court on a similar appeal.*

N COUNT : USU PL ⇑ judgement = verdict

fine /faɪn/, **finer, finest; fines, fining, fined. 1** Something that is **fine** is very good indeed or of very good quality. EG *From the top there is a fine view... Paul Scofield gave a fine performance... It is, I believe, the finest English painting of its time... They use only the finest ingredients.* ◇ **finely.** EG *...finely written novels.*

ADJ QUALIT = excellent ≠ mediocre, poor

◇ ADV WITH VB = exquisitely

2 If you say that you are **fine**, you mean that you are in good health and reasonably happy; usually said in answer to a question. EG *'How are you?'-'Fine thanks'... 'Is Sam all right?'-'He's fine'.*

CONVENTION ⇑ well = okay

3 If you say that something is **fine**, you mean that it is very satisfactory or suitable. EG *'Do you want it stronger than that?'-'No, that's fine'... The temperature is fine.* ▸ used as an adverb. EG *We get on fine... I was doing fine.*

ADJ CLASSIF : USU PRED ⇑ acceptable = okay

▸ ADV WITH VB = okay

4 Someone, especially someone who is in control of a discussion, says **'fine'** to show that a particular subject has been dealt with satisfactorily and does not need to be discussed further. EG *Any questions on this? No? Fine.*

CONVENTION ⇑ right = good

5 You say **'fine'** or **'that's fine'** to show that you do not object to an arrangement, action, or situation that has been suggested or mentioned. EG *'How about the two of us taking a little stroll down the garden?'-'Fine'... 'I'll be back by supper time.'-'Fine'... Everything is under control, but if you want to come out that's fine by me... The house needed a lot of work doing to it. That was fine with him.*

CONVENTION = okay, all right

6 Something that is **fine** is also very narrow or thin or consists of very narrow threads or pieces. EG *These pins are very fine and won't split the wood... My hair is too fine... ...a fine-nibbed pen... The lemon peel must be cut very fine.* ◇ **fineness.** EG *...stretching the dough to a gauze-like fineness.*

ADJ QUALIT ≠ coarse, thick

◇ N UNCOUNT = thinness

7 A **fine** powder, mist, etc consists of very small bits or particles. EG *...handfuls of fine sand... The rain was falling as a fine mist.* ◇ **finely**. EG *...finely chopped meat.* — ADJ QUALIT : USU ATTRIB; ◇ ADV ≠ coarsely

8 A **fine** sieve, net, etc is one that has very small holes. — ADJ QUALIT : USU ATTRIB

9 A **fine** adjustment, detail, distinction, etc is very delicate, subtle, small, or exact. EG *...this fine adjustment to an individual's pace of learning... Their eyes are trained to see the fine detail... The hunter's senses must be fine.* ◇ **finely**. EG *...the hazards of meddling with these finely balanced systems.* ◇ **fineness**. EG *His hand emphasizes the fineness of the points he is stressing.* — ADJ QUALIT = refined; ◇ ADV = subtly; ◇ N UNCOUNT = subtlety

10 A **fine** object is beautiful and delicate in appearance and structure, and of very high quality. EG *...fine pieces of china... The women have high cheekbones and fine features... ...fine white linen.* ◇ **finely**. EG *...finely sewn linen shirts.* — ADJ QUALIT : USU ATTRIB ⇑ good = dainty; ◇ ADV = exquisitely

11 A **fine** person or thing is considered to be very grand and important. EG *Will I shame you in front of your fine friends?* — ADJ QUALIT : ATTRIB

12 **Fine** is also used to show, in a rather humorous or sarcastic way, that you are rather angry or upset about a situation or about the way that someone has behaved. EG *You're a fine one to talk!... They sacked me. A fine reward for trying to preserve academic standards.* — ADJ QUALIT ⇑ upsetting = nice

13 You describe the weather as **fine** when it is not raining, especially when it is also sunny. EG *They sat on the verge if it was fine and on the benches inside the shop if it was wet... ...a fine summer's day.* — ADJ CLASSIF = pleasant

14 A **fine** is a punishment, especially one given by a court of law, in which the guilty person is ordered to pay a specific sum of money; also used to refer to the sum of money itself. EG *He paid a £10,000 fine for income tax evasion... ...a parking fine.* — N COUNT

15 If you **fine** someone, you punish them by ordering them to pay a fine. EG *The three demonstrators were fined £5 each for breach of the peace... He was heavily fined.* — V+O

16 If you **cut it a bit fine**, you allow only just enough time for something, with the result that there may not be enough time if difficulties occur. EG *'I've said we'll deliver next Friday.'-'That's cutting it a bit fine, isn't it?'* — PHR : VB INFLECTS

17 **not to put too fine a point on it**: see **point**.

fine down. If you **fine down** something such as a theory or criticism, you gradually make it more precise or exact. EG *He needs to fine down his theory a bit.* — PHRASAL VB : V+O+ADV ⇑ refine = hone

fine art, fine arts. **1** Painting and sculpture, in which objects are produced that are beautiful rather than useful, can be referred to as the **fine arts** or as **fine art**. EG *Few people here are interested in the Fine Arts... He decided to enrol on a fine art course.* — N PLURAL, *the*+N, OR N UNCOUNT ⇑ art

2 Objects which are made by artists to be looked at and admired rather than used are referred to as **fine art**. EG *This philosophy is reflected in the Fine Art of that era.* — N UNCOUNT ⇑ objects

3 ● to **get** something **down to a fine art**: see **art**.

fine print. The **fine print** of a contract or agreement is the part of it written in very small print, especially when this is considered as referring to unfavourable conditions which the person signing the contract might overlook. — N UNCOUNT = small print

finery /faɪnəºriˡ/ is clothing and jewellery that is beautiful and impressive and is usually worn only on special occasions. EG *The ladies were dressed up in all their finery... She has a love of finery.* — N UNCOUNT

finesse /fɪnɛs/. If you do something with **finesse**, you do it with great skill and elegance or subtlety. EG *The matter had been handled by Eddie with tact and finesse.* — N UNCOUNT = polish

fine-tooth comb. If you **go over** or **through** something **with a fine-tooth comb** or **fine-toothed comb**, you look at it very carefully and consider every detail of it. EG *They went over the company's records with a fine-tooth comb but could find nothing wrong.* — PHR : VB INFLECTS ⇑ examine

finger /fɪŋgə/, **fingers, fingering, fingered**. **1** Your **fingers** are the four long jointed parts at the end of your hand; sometimes used to include the thumbs too. The word **finger** is not used in the singular to refer to a thumb. EG *She ran her fingers through the cool grass... ...the wedding ring on her finger... He held the handkerchief between his finger and thumb.* — N COUNT ⇑ digit

2 The **fingers** of a glove are the parts that a person's fingers fit into. — N COUNT ⇑ part

3 A **finger** of something such as smoke or land is an amount of it that is shaped like a finger. EG *...a finger of black smoke rose up from the chimney.* ● See also **fish finger**. — N COUNT+*of*

4 If you **finger** something, you touch or feel it with your finger or fingers. EG *Eric fingered his split lip.* — V+O

5 A **finger** of a strong alcoholic drink is an amount of it which, when it is in a glass, is the same size as the width of a person's finger. EG *He poured out three fingers of whisky.* — N COUNT : ALSO N+*of*+N UNCOUNT ⇑ measure = tot

6 The word **finger** is also used in the following expressions. **6.1** If you **get your fingers burnt** or **burn your fingers**, you suffer because something you did or were involved in was a failure or a mistake. EG *He got his fingers burnt over the sale of the business.* — PHR : VB INFLECTS **6.2** If you say that someone did not or must not **lay a finger on** a particular person or thing, you mean they did not or must not touch or harm that person or thing at all. EG *He didn't lay a finger on you... If you so much as lay a finger on that car, I'll kill you!* — PHR : VB INFLECTS **6.3** If you do not **lift a finger** or **raise a finger** to do something, especially to help someone, you make no attempt to do it. EG *He's never raised a finger to help you with the baby.* — PHR : VB INFLECTS **6.4** If someone **has a finger in every pie** or **in** the **pie**, they are involved in many activities or in a particular activity. EG *But many other countries have fingers in the pie.* — PHR : VB+*finger* INFLECTS **6.5** If you **point the finger** or **point a finger at** someone, you blame them or accuse them of something. EG *The party has pointed an accusing finger at the antics of its left wing... Who am I to start pointing the finger?* — PHR : VB INFLECTS **6.6** If you **point the finger of scorn, the finger of suspicion**, etc **at** someone, you talk about them in a way that shows the feeling mentioned. — PHR : VB INFLECTS **6.7** You tell someone to **pull** their **finger out** or to **get** their **finger out** as an informal and fairly angry way of telling them to start doing some work or making an effort. EG *Come on! Pull your finger out, for goodness sake!* — PHR : VB INFLECTS **6.8** If you **put** your **finger on** something, for example a reason or problem, you see and identify exactly what it is. EG *He immediately put his finger on what was wrong.* — PHR : VB INFLECTS **6.9** If you **put the finger on** a particular person, you tell someone, usually the police, that that person has done something illegal or wrong; an informal expression. — PHR : VB INFLECTS **6.10** If something **slips through** your **fingers**, you fail to catch it or get it, especially when you have been very near to it. EG *Happiness seemed to slip through his fingers.* — PHR : VB INFLECTS = elude **6.11** If you say that you are **all fingers and thumbs**, you mean that you are being very clumsy at doing something with your hands, for example tying a knot. — PHR : USED AS C **6.12** If you can **twist** someone **round** your **little finger**, you can persuade them to do anything that you ask them to. EG *Sue can twist her father round her little finger.* — PHR : VB INFLECTS **6.13** ● to **work** your **fingers to the bone**: see **bone**. ● to **cross** your **fingers**: see **cross**. ● to **have green fingers**: see **green**.

finger bowl, finger bowls. A **finger bowl** is a small bowl with water in it which you can wash your fingers in during a formal meal. — N COUNT

fingering /fɪŋgəºrɪŋ/ is the method of using the most suitable finger to play each note when you are playing a musical instrument, especially the piano. EG *I haven't learnt the fingering for this piece yet.* — N SING : *the*+N

fingermark /fɪŋgəmɑ:k/, **fingermarks**. A **fingermark** is a mark which is made when someone puts a dirty or greasy finger onto a clean surface. EG *You've put fingermarks all over my mirror.* — N COUNT ⇑ mark

fingernail /fɪŋgəneɪl/, **fingernails**; also spelled with a hyphen. Your **fingernails** are the thin hard areas that cover the end of each of your fingers. — N COUNT = nail

finger painting; also spelled with a hyphen. **Finger painting** is painting, done mainly by small children, in which the paint is put onto the paper with the fingers rather than with a brush. — N UNCOUNT/COUNT

fingerprint /fɪŋgəprɪnt/, **fingerprints, fingerprinting, fingerprinted**. **1** A **fingerprint** is a mark made by a person's finger which shows the lines on the skin. Every person's fingerprints are different from every other person's and so they can be used to identify criminals. EG *He was careful, leaving no fingerprints.* — N COUNT = print ● When the police **take** a person's **fingerprints**, they make that person press their fingers onto an inky pad and then onto paper, so that they know what that person's fingerprints — ● PHR : VB INFLECTS look like. EG *He was photographed and had his fingerprints taken.*

2 If the police **fingerprint** a person, they take that person's fingerprints. V+O

3 If the police **fingerprint** an object, they put a layer of special dust on it so that any greasy fingerprints that are on it can be seen. V+O

fingertip /fɪŋgətɪp/, **fingertips**; also spelled with a hyphen. **1** Your **fingertips** are the ends of your fingers. EG *I probed through his hair with my fingertips and found a lump... The chairman nodded and put his fingertips together.* N COUNT: USU PL ⇑ end

2 Someone who is, for example, professional or an artist **to their fingertips** or **to the fingertips** is the thing mentioned in every way possible. EG *She was professional to her fingertips, disciplined, and punctual... He was a gentleman to his fingertips.* PHR: USED AS AN A ⇑ completely

3 If you have something **at your fingertips**, you can reach or make use of it quickly and easily. EG *...with computers at your fingertips... Have your cash at your fingertips!* PHR: USED AS AN A ⇑ available = to hand

4 If you have particular information **at your fingertips**, you know it very well and can easily remember it and give it. EG *Mrs Hoyland Leach had the facts at her fingertips.* PHR: USED AS AN A = ready

finicky /fɪnɪki[1]/. Someone who is **finicky** is fussy and does not like many things; used showing disapproval. EG *He was a very finicky eater.* ADJ QUALIT

finis /fɪnɪs/ means 'the end'; usually written at the end of a book or film.

finish /fɪnɪʃ/, **finishes, finishing, finished. 1** If you **finish**, or **finish** something that you are doing or dealing with, you reach the end of it, so that there is no more for you to do or deal with. EG *I've just finished reading that book... Aren't you ever going to finish the ironing?... When he had finished, he closed the file.* V OR V+O/-ING

2 When you **finish** something that you are making or producing, you reach the end of making or producing it, so that it is complete. EG *The building was finished in 1962... I have to finish a report tonight... They were eager to see the finished product.* V+O ● When you put the **finishing touches** or **a finishing touch** to something, you add or do the last things or thing that must be added or done to it in order to make it complete. EG *He was sitting at the kitchen table putting the finishing touches to his own DIY computer.* ● PHR: USED AS O

3 When something such as a course, film, sale, etc **finishes**, especially at a planned time, it ends. EG *He's looking forward to going home when his course finishes... It starts in October and finishes in June... 'Heat and Dust' finishes at the Odeon on Friday.* V: USU+A

4 When you **finish** by doing or saying a particular thing, you do or say it as the last part of an event or series of actions. EG *Can I just finish with a final question... We finished dinner with hot pumpkin pie... He finished the argument by walking out of the room.* V OR V+O, IF+PREP THEN *with/by* = conclude, end

5 The **finish** of something is the end of it or the last part of it. EG *I missed the finish of the match... I have worked for the firm all these years and I intend to be there at the finish... It is a piece of communication from start to finish.* N SING: USU *the* +N, IF+PREP THEN *of* = conclusion

6 Someone who **finishes** work or school at a particular time, stops working or studying at that time. EG *I finish work at 3.* V+O: USU+A ⇑ stop

7 When you **finish** something that you have been eating, drinking, or smoking, you eat, drink, or smoke the last part of it. EG *Brody finished his sandwich... She finished her cigarette.* V OR V+O, USU V+O

8 If you **finish**, you reach the end of saying something. EG *Don't interrupt, William. Let me finish... In a voice broken with emotion, he finished: 'God bless America.'* V OR V+O/QUOTE = conclude

9 If you **finish** first, second, etc in a race or competition, you end it in the position stated. EG *It was Montclair who finished first... He first came into prominence when he finished fifth in the 1967 US Open.* V+A (USU ORDINAL), OR V+O+A (USU ORDINAL) = come

10 The **finish** of a race is the end of it. EG *It looks like being a close finish.* N COUNT

11 If the surface of something that has been made has a particular kind of **finish**, it has the appearance or texture mentioned. EG *The paintwork was shocking–a really gritty finish... Metallic finish is standard.* N COUNT/UNCOUNT: USU+SUPP ⇑ surfacing

12 **A fight to the finish** is one in which one of the people or groups fighting is killed or completely defeated. EG *It will be a fight to the finish.* ▸ used as a verb. EG *...young men settled arguments by fighting to the finish with battle-axes.* PHR: USED AS O OR C ▸ PHR: VB INFLECTS

13 See also **finished**.

finish off. 1 When you **finish off** someone or something that is already badly injured or damaged, you kill or destroy them. EG *The captain finished him off with his revolver.* PHRASAL VB: V+O+ADV = dispatch

2 When you **finish off** something that you are doing, you reach the end of it by doing the last part of it. EG *I've had problems finishing off the job... He had finished off his thesis.* PHRASAL VB: V+O+ADV = complete

3 When you **finish off** by doing or saying a particular thing, you do or say it as the last part of an event or series of actions. EG *He always finished off with his favourite song.* PHRASAL VB: V+ADV, OR V+O+ADV = conclude

4 When you **finish off** something that you have been eating or drinking you eat or drink the last part of it with the result that there is none left. EG *He finished off the wine with a couple of swallows.* PHRASAL VB: V+ADV, OR V+O+ADV = polish off

finish up. 1 If you **finish up** in a particular place, or in a particular state or condition, you are in that place, state, or condition at the end of something you do or experience. EG *She'll be going on tour, starting in Southampton and finishing up in London... They all finished up stranded on the beaches.* PHRASAL VB: V+ADV = wind up, end up

2 If you **finish up** doing a particular thing or as a particular thing, the thing stated is what you are doing or what you are at the end of your career. EG *They finished up serving in a shop... Maybe you too will finish up as Prime Minister.* PHRASAL VB: V+ADV, USU+-ING/A = wind up

3 When you **finish up** something that you have been eating or drinking you eat or drink the last part of it so that there is none left. PHRASAL VB: V+O+ADV

finish with. If you **finish with** someone or something, you stop dealing with them, being involved with them, or being interested in them. EG *I haven't finished with you yet... I thought I had finished with the play for ever.* PHRASAL VB: V+PREP, HAS PASS

finished /fɪnɪʃt/. **1** Someone who is **finished** with something is no longer doing it or dealing with it or is no longer interested in it. EG *He won't be finished for at least half an hour... Marion was not finished with Paul yet... He was finished with marriage.* ADJ CLASSIF: PRED, IF+PREP THEN *with*

2 Something that is **finished** no longer exists or is no longer happening. EG *All that is finished now... The shooting was almost finished.* ADJ CLASSIF: PRED = over

3 Someone or something that is **finished** is no longer important, powerful, or effective. EG *If that happens, Richard is finished... He declared that the printed word was finished.* ADJ CLASSIF: PRED

4 An object that is **finished** in a particular way has been given a particular appearance or decoration. EG *...a well finished and durable product... It was finished in knotty pine... ...specially finished fabrics.* ADJ CLASSIF

finishing school, finishing schools. A **finishing school** is a private school where rich or upper-class young women are taught behaviour and skills that are considered to be suitable for them. EG *I met him while at finishing school last year in Switzerland.* N COUNT/UNCOUNT

finite /faɪnaɪt/. **1** Something that is **finite** has a particular size or has a limit beyond which it cannot increase or develop; a formal use. EG *We have a finite number of places... ...a finite but unbounded universe.* ADJ CLASSIF

2 A **finite** verb is one that inflects according to person, tense, mood, etc, rather than being, for example, an infinitive or a participle; a technical term in grammar. ADJ CLASSIF

fink /fɪŋk/, **finks.** A **fink** is someone who tells the authorities that a person they know has done something illegal or wrong; an informal American word, used showing disapproval. N COUNT = grass

Finn /fɪn/, **Finns.** A **Finn** is a person who comes from Finland. N COUNT

Finnish /fɪnɪʃ/. **1** A person or thing that is **Finnish** belongs to or relates to Finland, or to its people or language. ADJ CLASSIF

2 **Finnish** is the language that is spoken by people who live in Finland. N UNCOUNT

fiord /fiːɔːd/. See **fjord**.

fir /fɜː/, **firs.** A **fir** or a **fir tree** is a tall, pointed tree, usually an evergreen, that has thin needle-like leaves N COUNT and produces cones. Firs grow mainly in cool countries. EG *...fir cones.*

fire /faɪə/, **fires, firing, fired. 1 Fire** is the hot, bright flames produced by things that are burning. Fire can destroy or damage many things. EG *Picture books show our ancestors discovering fire.* N UNCOUNT

2 Fire or a **fire** is an occurrence of uncontrolled burning which destroys buildings, forests, crops, etc. EG *A fire had severely damaged part of the school... ...a forest fire... His neighbour's house is not insured against fire... A paraffin heater can be a dangerous fire risk.* N COUNT/ UNCOUNT

3 A **fire** is **3.1** a burning pile of wood, coal or other fuel that you have made and set light to, for example in order to keep yourself warm or to cook food over. EG *There were two armchairs drawn up to the fire... He gathered firewood, lit a fire and cooked a meal.* N COUNT
3.2 a device that uses electricity or gas to give out heat and warm a room. EG *She switched on the electric fire.* N COUNT

4 The word **fire** is also used with the general sense of something that is burning in the following expressions. **4.1** If something **catches fire**, it starts burning. EG *Will the house catch fire?* PHR **4.2** To **fight a fire** means to try to put it out. EG *He has spent a lifetime fighting fires.* PHR : VB INFLECTS **4.3** If you say that you can only **fight fire with fire**, you mean that you can only deal with someone who is attacking you or causing you problems by using similar methods to the ones they are using. PHR : VB INFLECTS **4.4** Something that is **on fire** is burning and being damaged or destroyed by an uncontrolled fire. EG *The house is on fire!* PHR : USED AS AN A **4.5** If you say that part of your body, for example your mouth or chest, is **on fire**, you mean that it feels very painful or sore. EG *Her throat was on fire.* PHR : USED AS AN A ⇑ hurt = burn **4.6** Someone who is **playing with fire** is doing something or is involved in something that is dangerous and may result in great harm for them. EG *He doesn't realize he's playing with fire.* PHR : VB INFLECTS
4.7 If you **set fire to** something or if you **set it on fire**, you start it burning in order to damage or destroy it. EG *He set fire to the church... A small hut was set on fire.* PHR : VB INFLECTS = ignite **4.8** • **the fat's in the fire**: see **fat**. • **out of the frying pan into the fire**: see **frying pan**. • to get on **like a house on fire**: see **house**. • **there's no smoke without fire**: see **smoke**.

5 If someone **fires** a gun or a bullet, or if they **fire**, a bullet is sent from a gun that they are using. EG *I fired three or four times in quick succession... I haven't fired a gun in years... Few had ever fired a shot in anger... ...an artillery gun that could fire a nuclear shell.* V OR V-ERG ⇑ shoot ◇ **firing**. EG *Then, abruptly, the firing stopped.* ◇ N SING WITH DET : *the*+N

6 Shots fired from a gun or guns can be referred to as **fire**. EG *Then there was a burst of automatic rifle fire... The men on the beach were under fire.* N UNCOUNT

7 The word **fire** is used with the general sense of shots fired from a gun in the following expressions.
7.1 If you **draw the fire of** someone who is shooting or about to shoot, you fire at them or attract their attention in order to make them shoot at you, usually so that they will not shoot at someone else. EG *They were waiting by the bridge, drawing the fire of the enemy artillery.* PHR : VB INFLECTS **7.2** If you **hold** your **fire**, you stop shooting or wait before you start shooting. EG *Johnson ordered his men to hold their fire.* PHR : VB INFLECTS **7.3** If you are in someone's **line of fire**, you are between them and the thing that they are aiming their gun at. EG *Two people strayed into his line of fire and got killed.* PHR : PREP+ POSS+PHR ⇑ position **7.4** If you **open fire** on someone, you start shooting at them. EG *This was the signal for the marksmen to open fire on the President's car.* PHR : VB INFLECTS, IF+ PREP THEN *on* **7.5** If you **return fire** or you **return** someone's **fire**, you shoot back at someone who has shot at you. EG *Keep in cover and return fire with mortars and machine-guns.* PHR : VB INFLECTS

8 If something **hangs fire**, it does not progress or develop for a period of time. EG *At that point the matter had hung fire for more than half a year.* PHR : VB INFLECTS

9 If you **fire** an arrow, you send it from a bow. EG *Robin had fired all his arrows.* V+O = shoot

10 If you **fire** questions or suggestions at someone, you say a lot of them quickly, one after another. EG *...a host of questions which are being fired at him.* V+O : IF+PREP THEN *at* ⇑ shoot

11 Someone's **fire** can also mean strong criticisms made by them. EG *Oliver, of course, would be concentrating his fire on me, as usual.* N UNCOUNT : POSS +N • If you **come under fire** from someone, they criticize you strongly. EG *He could come under fire from Liberal councillors if he goes ahead with his plan.* • PHR : USED AS AN A • If you are **in the firing line**, you are being criticized or blamed for something. EG *The Government found itself in the firing line over its proposals.* • PHR : USED AS AN A

12 If you **fire** someone with enthusiasm or **fire** their imagination, you make them feel full of enthusiasm about something. EG *He lacked imagination and could not fire the imagination of others... ...inspiring ideals that could fire the followers of his party with enthusiasm.* V+O ⇑ excite = inspire

13 Fire is also energy and enthusiasm. EG *Everything he said was delivered with the fire and idealism of a man of twenty, not forty... The chairman of the African group brought new fire to the debate.* N UNCOUNT ⇑ excitement = inspiration

14 Someone who is **on fire** with enthusiasm or passion is very enthusiastic or excited about something. PHR : USED AS AN A, IF+PREP THEN *with*

15 If an employer **fires** someone, he or she dismisses them from their job. EG *Graffman fired him for incompetence... She was fired on the spot.* V+O = sack

16 When the engine of a motor vehicle **fires**, an electrical spark is produced which causes the fuel to burn and the engine to work. EG *The engine isn't firing.* V

17 If you **fire** a clay object, as part of the process of making it, you heat it at a high temperature in a special oven. EG *When a pot has been formed it must be fired.* V+O ⇑ bake ◇ **firing, firings**. EG *With most glazed ware there are two firings.* ◇ N COUNT/ UNCOUNT

fire away. You say **fire away** to someone, when you know that they want to say something, as a way of showing that you are ready for them to say it. EG *'I was hoping to bring up a point.'-'Well fire away.'* CONVENTION = go ahead, shoot

fire off. If you **fire off** a shot, you send a bullet or other missile from a gun. EG *The sniper popped up and fired off a single round.* PHRASAL VB : V+ O+ADV

fire alarm, fire alarms; also spelled with a hyphen. A **fire alarm** is a device that makes a noise, for example with a bell, to warn people when there is a fire. N COUNT

firearm /faɪərɑːm/, **firearms**. A **firearm** is a gun, especially a pistol. EG *He got a fourteen-year sentence for illegal possession of firearms.* N COUNT : USU PL ⇑ weapon

fireball /faɪəbɔːl/, **fireballs**. A **fireball** is a ball of fire, for example one at the centre of a nuclear explosion. N COUNT

firebomb /faɪəbɒm/, **firebombs**; also spelled with a hyphen. A **firebomb** is a bomb that is made in a particular way so that it burns after it has exploded. EG *Sixteen youths were charged with throwing fire-bombs.* N COUNT = incendiary device

firebrand /faɪəbrænd/, **firebrands**. A **firebrand** is a person who is very active, especially in politics, and who tries to make other people take action, often in a way that causes trouble. EG *He is represented by the media as a dangerous firebrand.* N COUNT = activist

firebreak /faɪəbreɪk/, **firebreaks**. A **firebreak** is an area of open land in a wood or forest, which is intended to stop a fire from spreading. N COUNT

firebrick /faɪəbrɪk/, **firebricks**. A **firebrick** is a type of brick which cannot be damaged by heat and which is used to line furnaces. N COUNT/ UNCOUNT

fire brigade, fire brigades; also spelled with a hyphen. The **fire brigade** is an organization which has the job of putting out fires. EG *Call the fire brigade.* N SING : *the*+N, OR N COUNT

firecracker /faɪəkrækə/, **firecrackers**; also spelled with a hyphen. A **firecracker** is a firework that makes several loud bangs when it is lit. EG *People set off strings of firecrackers.* N COUNT ⇑ device

-fired combines with nouns referring to a fuel to indicate that something uses the type of fuel stated. EG *...oil-fired central heating... ...coal-fired power stations.* COMB : FORMS ADJ CLASSIFS

fire drill, fire drills. When a **fire drill** takes place in a particular building, the people who work or live there practise what to do if there is a fire. N COUNT/ UNCOUNT ⇑ practice

fire-eater, fire-eaters; also spelled as two words.
1 A **fire-eater** is a performer who puts flaming rods into his or her mouth to entertain people. N COUNT
2 If you call someone a **fire-eater**, you mean that they are very quarrelsome. N COUNT

fire engine, fire engines; also spelled with a hyphen. A **fire engine** is a large vehicle that carries firemen and equipment for putting out fires. N COUNT

fire escape, fire escapes; also spelled with a hyphen. A **fire escape** is a metal staircase or ladder N COUNT ⇑ exit on the outside of a building, to be used for escaping from a building when there is a fire.

fire extinguisher, fire extinguishers; also spelled with a hyphen. A **fire extinguisher** is a metal cylinder which contains water or chemicals at high pressure for putting out fires. N COUNT ⇑ device

fire fighter, fire fighters; also spelled with a hyphen. A **fire fighter** is a fireman or a person who helps to put out a large fire. N COUNT

fire-fighting; also spelled as two words. **Fire-fighting** is the work of putting out fires. EG *...individual attempts at fire-fighting... ...fire-fighting equipment.* N UNCOUNT

firefly /faɪəflaɪ/, **fireflies**. A **firefly** is an insect that glows in the dark. N COUNT ⇑ beetle

fireguard /faɪəgɑːd/, **fireguards**; also spelled with a hyphen. A **fireguard** is a screen made of strong wire mesh that you put round a fire so that young children cannot accidentally burn themselves and to prevent burning wood or coal falling out. N COUNT

fire hydrant /faɪə haɪdrənt/, **fire hydrants**; also spelled with a hyphen. A **fire hydrant** is a pipe in the street from which firemen can obtain water for putting out a fire, or a post that shows where this pipe is. N COUNT = fireplug

fire-irons; also spelled without a hyphen. **Fire-irons** are tools that you use for putting coal or wood on a fire, or for cleaning the fireplace. N PLURAL

firelight /faɪəlaɪt/ is the light that comes from a fire that you have lit. EG *His face looked ruddy in the firelight.* N UNCOUNT : USU *the*+N

fire lighter, fire lighters. A **fire lighter** is a small block of a material which burns easily, used to start a fire burning. N COUNT

fireman /faɪəmə³n/, **firemen**. A **fireman** is a person whose job is to put out fires. Firemen also rescue people or animals who are trapped in cars, railings, trees, etc. EG *Firemen turned their hoses on the flames.* N COUNT

fireplace /faɪəpleɪs/, **fireplaces**. A **fireplace** is a place at the bottom of a wall in a room, usually with an opening into a chimney, where a fire can be lit or has been put. Fireplaces usually have a shelf above them and bricks, tiles, or stone round them. EG *A fire was going in the fireplace... There was a portrait of his wife over the marble fireplace.* N COUNT = grate, hearth

fireplug /faɪəplʌg/, **fireplugs**. A **fireplug** is the same as a fire hydrant; used in American English. N COUNT = standpipe

firepower /faɪəpaʊə/; also spelled with a hyphen. The **firepower** of an army, ship, tank, or aircraft is the amount of ammunition it can fire. EG *They have greatly increased the offensive firepower of their fleet.* N UNCOUNT ⇑ capability

fireproof /faɪəpruːf/, **fireproofs, fireproofing, fireproofed**; also spelled with a hyphen. **1** Something that is **fireproof** cannot be damaged by fire. EG *...fireproof clothing.* ADJ CLASSIF

2 If you **fireproof** something, you make it fireproof. EG *The stables were all fireproofed.* V+O

fire-raising is the act of deliberately starting a fire in order to damage or destroy something, usually a building. N UNCOUNT = arson

fire sale, fire sales; also spelled with a hyphen. A **fire sale** is a sale in which goods are sold cheaply because the shop or warehouse they were in has been damaged by fire. EG *We got them at fire-sale prices.* N COUNT

fire service, fire services. The **fire service** is an organization which has the job of putting out fires. EG *There was a quick response from the police, the ambulances, and the fire service.* N SING : *the*+N, OR N COUNT = fire brigade

fireside /faɪəsaɪd/. If you sit by the **fireside** in a room, you sit near the fire. EG *...sitting comfortably by his fireside... He ran to join his father at the fireside... ...a fireside chat.* N COUNT : USU SING ⇑ place = hearth

fire station, fire stations. A **fire station** is a building where fire engines are kept, and where firemen wait until they are called to put out a fire. N COUNT

fire-storm, fire-storms. When a **fire-storm** occurs in a place that is burning after being bombed, strong winds rush into it to take the place of the hot air that is rising, causing the blaze to burn uncontrollably. N COUNT

fire trap, fire traps. If you describe a building as a **fire trap**, you mean that it is a building that could easily catch fire or one from which it would be difficult to escape if there was a fire. N COUNT

fire-watching is the job of looking out for fires that have started, especially as the result of bombing during wartime. N UNCOUNT

firewater /faɪəwɔːtə/ is very strong alcoholic drink such as whisky; an informal word, usually used humorously. N UNCOUNT

firewood /faɪəwʊd/ is wood that has been cut into pieces so that it can be burned on a fire. EG *...a bundle of firewood.* N UNCOUNT

firework /faɪəwɜːk/, **fireworks**. **1** A **firework** is a small object with chemicals inside it that burns with coloured flames, sparks, or smoke when you light it, and often makes loud noises too. Large numbers of fireworks are lit to entertain people on special occasions. EG *...a firework display in Hyde Park... A few loud fireworks went off.* N COUNT

2 Fireworks are a firework display. EG *I had gone to watch the fireworks, one Fourth of July.* N PLURAL : PL FORM WHEN MOD

3 An exciting and impressive performance, speech, or piece of writing can be referred to as **fireworks**. EG *...James Joyce's verbal fireworks.* N PLURAL : USU+SUPP

4 Fireworks are also angry arguments or words. EG *There'll be fireworks when the boss finds out.* N PLURAL

firing squad, firing squads. A **firing squad** is a group of soldiers who are ordered to shoot and kill a person who has been found guilty of committing a crime. EG *I would line them up in front of a firing squad... He faces death by firing squad.* N COUNT, OR *by*+N

firm /fɜːm/, **firmer, firmest; firms, firming, firmed**. **1** A **firm** is an organization which sells or produces something or which provides a service which people pay for. EG *The firm has not been doing well recently... He was a partner in a firm of solicitors in Holborn... ...insurance firms.* N COUNT = company

2 Something that is **firm 2.1** does not change much in shape when it is pressed but is not completely hard. EG *Bake the cake for about an hour until it is firm and brown... I like a firm mattress.* ◇ **firmly**. EG *...a small, firmly stuffed settee.* ◇ **firmness**. EG *...the firmness of his body.* **2.2** does not shake or move when weight or pressure is put on it because it is resting flat on a surface or because it is strongly made. EG *Make sure that you have a strong firm ladder.* ◇ **firmly**. EG *Each block rested firmly and squarely on the block below it.* **2.3** is fixed or held so that it cannot move easily. EG *She wound a bandage around the splint till it was firm... He put sticky tape round it to hold it firm.* ◇ **firmly**. EG *The moustache was stuck firmly in place.* ADJ QUALIT ⇑ solid = stiff ◇ ADV ◇ N UNCOUNT ADJ QUALIT ⇑ steady ◇ ADV ADJ QUALIT : PRED = secure ◇ ADV = securely

3 A **firm** grasp or push is done with quite a lot of force or pressure, and in a controlled way. EG *His handshake was firm and solid... I took a firm hold on the rope.* ◇ **firmly**. EG *He held her arm, not hard, but firmly... She closed the door firmly.* ◇ **firmness**. ADJ QUALIT ⇑ strong ◇ ADV ◇ N UNCOUNT

4 A **firm** band or tie round something holds it with quite a lot of pressure. EG *...a firm bandage.* ADJ QUALIT = secure

5 A **firm** decision or opinion is definite and unlikely to change or be changed. EG *They want a firm decision by next Monday... ...a person with firm views on a variety of matters... Have they set a firm date for the wedding?* ▸ used of a person. EG *I am a firm believer in this philosophy.* ◇ **firmly**. EG *His sister was firmly of the belief that he was crazy.* ◇ **firmness**. ADJ QUALIT ⇑ positive ▸ ADJ QUALIT ◇ ADV = strongly ◇ N UNCOUNT

6 Firm evidence or information is based on facts and is definitely true. EG *No firm evidence had come to light... By the weekend came firm news.* ADJ QUALIT ⇑ certain

7 Someone who is **firm** behaves in a way that shows that they are not going to be persuaded to change their mind, or that they are in control. EG *Our present state of affairs demands firm leadership... 'No,' said Mother in a firm voice... He was very firm about it.* ◇ **firmly**. EG *Actors must be dealt with firmly... I shall tell her quite firmly that it is not any business of hers.* ◇ **firmness**. EG *'This is what I want,' said Mrs Oliver, with firmness and determination.* ● Someone who **stands firm** refuses to change their mind or to give in. EG *The Americans refused to stand down. The British also stood firm... The Government should stand firm against such threats.* ADJ QUALIT = decisive ◇ ADV = definitely ◇ N UNCOUNT ● PHR : VB INFLECTS, IF+PREP THEN *against*

8 If something, for example a basis for a particular thing or someone's control over a particular thing, is **firm**, it is strong and unlikely to be ended or removed. EG *The guerrillas soon established a firm foothold in the area... We have not given these kids any firm foundations on which to build... He had taken a firm grip on the management side of the* ADJ QUALIT ⇑ secure = solid

paper. ◇ **firmly**. EG *The trend is already firmly established.*
◇ ADV ⇑ securely

9 If something relating to finance and trade is **firm**, it is not decreasing in value or amount. EG *Investment remained firm despite the average 1.8% growth rate... The pound held firm against the dollar.*
ADJ CLASSIF ⇑ steady

10 If you **firm** soil, you press it so that it is fairly solid rather than loose.
V+O

firm up. If you **firm up** a part of your body, you make it firmer and less fat, for example by exercising. EG *This exercise will help to firm up those flabby thighs.*
PHRASAL VB : V+O+ADV

firmament /fɜ:məmə[2]nt/. The **firmament** is the sky or the heavens; an old-fashioned or literary word.
N SING : *the*+N

first /fɜ:st/, **firsts**. **1** The **first** thing, person, event, or period of time is the one that happens or comes before all the others of a similar type: see □ at **number**, **age**, and **date**. EG *...the first man in space... ...the first two years of life... ...January the first... I was the first to recover.*
ORDINAL ≠ last, final

2 If someone does something **first**, they do it before anyone or anything else. EG *Ralph spoke first... When people get their newspaper, which page do they read first?*
ADV WITH VB ≠ last

3 First is also used **3.1** when you say what happened before all the other things in a situation or series of events. EG *First I went to see the editor of the Dispatch... He turned his head first to one side, then to the other.* **3.2** when indicating that a particular thing should be done before something else. EG *'Sit down and eat.'–'Give me some matches first'... But first I had to get a visa.*
ADV WITH VB ≠ finally; ADV WITH VB

4 If something is described as the **first**, or the **first** for a particular person, it has never happened before or has never been done or experienced before by anyone or by that person. EG *If it's her first baby, she can't help feeling anxious... For the first time in our lives something really exciting has happened... ...first-time visitors to the Soviet Union... The proposals–the first for 22 years–are extremely radical.* ▸ used as a noun. EG *It's a first for me, too.*
ORDINAL; ▸ N COUNT

5 When something **first** happens, it has not happened before and this is the first time that it has happened; often used to emphasize the introduction or creation of something. EG *Vita and Harold first met in the summer of 1910... 'The Sheltering Sky' was first published in 1949... ...when they first introduced 'O' levels.*
ADV WITH VB

6 The **first** someone heard of or saw of a particular thing was the first time they heard of or became aware of it, or the first example of it that they saw. EG *The first Mr Walker knew about it was when he saw it in the local paper.*
PRON : *the*+PRON+REPORT-CL ≠ last

7 The time when someone **first** did something is the early part of a situation or activity. EG *When he first came he would hardly speak to anyone.*
ADV WITH VB ⇑ initially

8 First is used to describe the early signs or parts of something that suggest that it will develop into something bigger, more serious, etc. EG *...the first thin flakes of snow... ...the first rumblings of discontent.*
ORDINAL+N IN PL

9 Your **first** reaction to something is the way you feel or react immediately after experiencing it, which is often different from the way you feel about it later. EG *My first instinct was to resign.... My first reaction to this device was one of alarm.*
ORDINAL+N = initial

10 You use **at first** when you are talking about what happens in the early stages of an event or experience, or just after something else has happened, in contrast to what happens later. EG *At first I was reluctant... He couldn't at first work out why the room seemed different.*
PHR : USED AS AN A = initially

11 From the first means ever since something started. EG *From the first, its size and grandeur caught the public imagination.*
PHR : USED AS AN A ⇑ always

12 From first to last means from the beginning of something until the end. EG *He was in control of the project from first to last.*
PHR : USED AS AN A = throughout

13 You use **first** in speech or writing **13.1** when you want to give a reason, make a point, or mention an item that will be followed by others connected with it. EG *There were several reasons for this. First, four submarines had been sighted.* ● You can also say **first off** to give a reason or make a point in this way; used in informal English. EG *First off, there's the matter of the swimming-pool.* **13.2** when you are giving a list and want to refer to the thing or person that you are mentioning or describing first. EG *There are two main critical areas. The first is food.* **13.3** when you have mentioned two things, to refer to the one you mentioned first. EG *The first man said: 'Security Police-Special Branch'... She wore a blouse and skirt, but the first was too tight and the second too ample.*
ADV SEN = firstly; ● PHR : USED AS AN A ⇑ firstly; ORDINAL : *the*+ORDINAL ≠ last; ORDINAL : USU *the*+ORDINAL ≠ last

14 If you do something **first thing**, or **first thing** at night, in the afternoon, etc, you do it at the beginning of the day or at the beginning of the part of the day mentioned, before you do anything else. EG *...a nauseating sight, especially first thing in the morning... I would look it up and tell her first thing tomorrow.*
PHR : USED AS AN A, USU+A

15 The **first** thing, person, or place in a row or line is the one nearest to you or to something else. EG *They took their seats in the first three rows... They stopped beside the first of the trees.*
ORDINAL ≠ last

16 First is also **16.1** used of the person or thing that comes above all the others in a series, order, or list, especially because it is better, more basic, etc than the others. EG *My pig won first prize at Skipton Fair... There are now 22 teams in the first division... Let's get down to first principles.* **16.2** used when referring to the thing that is considered to be the main and most important one. EG *The first duty of the state is to ensure that law and order prevail... I am a draughtsman first and a painter second.* **16.3** used in the title of someone's job or position to indicate that they are higher in rank than someone else. EG *...the First Lord of the Treasury... ...the first mate.*
ORDINAL ≠ last; ORDINAL = chief; ORDINAL : BEFORE N ⇑ chief

17 If you **put** someone or something **first**, you treat or consider them as more important than anything or anyone else. EG *Put your career first... The new Bill puts the rights of children first.*
PHR : VB INFLECTS = give priority

18 Someone or something that **comes first** is treated or considered as more important than anything else. EG *Your family and children must always come first.*
PHR : VB INFLECTS = have priority

19 A **first** is an honours degree of the highest standard. EG *He got a first in French.*
N COUNT : IF+PREP THEN *in*

20 First is the first gear in a series of gears in a car or other vehicle. EG *I had to change down into first.*
N UNCOUNT

21 In order to emphasize your determination not to do a particular thing, you can say that rather than do it, you would do something else **first**. EG *He's never getting me to do his dirty work again. I'd die first.*
ADV AFTER VB

22 The word **first** is also used in the following expressions. **22.1** If you experience or learn something **at first hand**, you experience it yourself or learn it directly rather than being told about it by other people. EG *He had learned about electronic warfare at first hand.* **22.2 First come, first served** is used to say that a group of people or things will be dealt with or given something in the order in which they arrive. EG *Applications will be dealt with on a first come, first served basis.* **22.3** You say **'first things first'** to introduce something that should be done or dealt with before anything else because it is the most important. EG *Rodin held up his hand. 'First things first, gentlemen. Are we willing to accept the proposals?'* **22.4 First and last** is used when referring to the thing, person, or characteristic that is definitely the most important one. EG *The first and last thing about my Aunt Gladys is that she is an eccentric.* ● **first and foremost**: see **foremost**. **22.5** If you say that you **do not know the first thing about** something, you mean that you know absolutely nothing about it. EG *You are talking about a subject you don't know the first thing about.* **22.6** If you **do not have the first idea** about something, you have no understanding of it at all. EG *She didn't have the first idea how to start the car.*
PHR : USED AS AN A; PHR; PHR; PHR : BEFORE N, OR USED AS AN A ⇑ main; PHR : VB INFLECTS; PHR : VB INFLECTS

-first combines with nouns like 'head' and 'feet' to say that someone moves with the part that is mentioned pointing in the direction in which they are moving. EG *Then we shove him in head first.*
COMB : FORMS ADVS

first aid is simple medical treatment given as soon as possible to a person who is injured or who suddenly becomes ill. EG *The wounded were given first aid... ...my first-aid kit.*
N UNCOUNT

first-born. Someone's **first-born** is their first child; a rather literary word. EG *David was the first-born... ...his first-born son.*
N SING WITH DET, OR ADJ CLASSIF : ATTRIB

first-class; also spelled without a hyphen. **1** If you describe something or someone as **first-class**, you mean that they are excellent and of the highest quality. EG *...a first-class administrator.*
ADJ QUALIT = first-rate

2 **First-class** is used to describe something that is in the group considered to be of the highest standard. EG *...a first class honours degree in applied chemistry... Am I the worst cricketer ever to play first class cricket?* ADJ CLASSIF : ATTRIB

3 A **first-class** ticket allows you to travel in the best type of accommodation on a train, aircraft, or ship. EG *...a first-class rail ticket... ...the privilege of flying everywhere first class.* ADJ CLASSIF, OR ADV AFTER VB

4 **First-class** postage is the quicker and more expensive type of postage. EG *Two first-class stamps, please... I sent it first class on Friday.* ADJ CLASSIF, OR ADV AFTER VB

first cousin, first cousins. Someone's **first cousin** is their cousin, in contrast to their second cousin. N COUNT

first-day cover, first-day covers. A **first-day cover** is an envelope on which a set of special stamps has been stuck and which is post-marked on the first day that the stamps were issued. N COUNT

first-degree. A **first-degree** burn or murder is one of the least bad or severe kind. ADJ CLASSIF : ATTRIB

first-ever. Something that is the **first-ever** one of its kind has never happened before. EG *...the first-ever Piccadilly Festival.* ADJ CLASSIF : ATTRIB = very first

first floor, first floors. The **first floor** of a building is 1 the floor of a building immediately above the one at ground level; used in British English. EG *...on the first floor of the Museum... ...a first-floor suite.* N COUNT : USU the+N 2 the ground floor; used in American English. N COUNT : USU the+N

first fruits. The **first fruits** of a project or activity are the earliest results or profits. EG *The first fruits are likely to be trivial.* N PLURAL

first-hand. **First-hand** information or experience is gained or learned directly, rather than from other people or from books. EG *They have first-hand experience of charitable organizations.* ADJ CLASSIF : ATTRIB, OR ADV

First Lady, First Ladies. 1 The **First Lady** in a country or state is the wife of the president or state governor, or a woman who performs the official duties normally performed by the wife. EG *The Ivory Coast's First Lady was beautifully dressed.* N COUNT : USU the+N IN SING

2 A woman who is referred to as the **first lady** of something is considered to be better than any other at the thing mentioned. EG *...the acknowledged first lady of rock and roll.* N COUNT+of : USU SING

first language, first languages. Someone's **first language** is the language that they learnt first and speak best; used especially when they speak more than one language. N COUNT = native language

firstly /fɜːstli¹/. You use **firstly** 1 in speech or writing when you want to give a reason, make a point, or mention an item that will be followed by others connected with it. EG *There are two reasons. Firstly I have no evidence whatever that the original document has been destroyed.* ADV SEN = first 2 when you refer to the earliest in a series of events; some people consider this use to be incorrect English. EG *Jim Smith was elected firstly to the District Council and then to the Regional Council.* ADV WITH VB = initially, first

first name, first names. Your **first name** is the first of the names that were given to you when you were born. You can also refer to all of your names except your surname as your **first names**. EG *Nobody called Daintry by his first name because nobody knew it... I was on first-name terms with them.* N COUNT = Christian name, given name

first night, first nights. The **first night** of a show, play, or performance is the first public performance of it. EG *...the first night of 'Pacific Overtures'... We all had first-night nerves.* N COUNT

first offender, first offenders. A **first offender** is a person who has been found guilty of a crime for the first time. N COUNT ⇑ criminal

first person. The **first person** refers to yourself when you are speaking or writing, and is expressed as 'I' or 'we' with the form of a verb which is used with 'I' or 'we'. EG *Charles is the first person storyteller of the book... ...a narrative in the first person.* N SING : the+N

first-rate. Something that is **first-rate** is excellent and of the highest quality. EG *...a first-rate golfer... ...first-rate performances.* ADJ CLASSIF = first class

first school, first schools. A **first school** is a school for children aged between five and eight or nine. N COUNT

First World War. The **First World War** or the **First War** is the major war that was fought between 1914 and 1918 in Europe. EG *He had fought in the First World War.* N PROPER : the+N = Great War

fiscal /fɪskə⁰l/. 1 **Fiscal** is used to describe something that relates to government or public money, especially taxes. EG *...fiscal policies... ...fiscal controls.* ADJ CLASSIF : ATTRIB ⇑ financial

2 See also **procurator fiscal**.

fiscal year, fiscal years. The **fiscal year** is the same as the financial year; used in American English. N COUNT

fish /fɪʃ/, **fishes, fishing, fished**. **Fish** is most commonly used as the plural form, but **fishes** is also sometimes used. 1 A **fish** is a creature that lives in water and has a tail and fins. There are many different kinds of fish. EG *We stayed there all day but we didn't catch any fish... ...a shoal of fish... ...collections of minerals, insects, fishes, and birds.* N COUNT

2 **Fish** is the flesh of a fish eaten as food. EG *...different ways of cooking fish... ...fish and chips.* N UNCOUNT

3 If you **fish**, you try to catch fish, either for food or as a form of sport or recreation. EG *They went fishing and caught half a dozen trout... The beach is a good place to fish from... ...a trawler fishing off the coast of Iceland.* V : IF+PREP THEN for

4 If you **fish** a particular area of water, you try to catch fish in it. EG *It was the first trawler ever to fish those waters.* V+O

5 If you **fish** for information or praise, you try and get it from another person in an indirect way. EG *I think he was just fishing for compliments.* V+A (for) ⇑ seek

6 If you **fish** something out of something or from somewhere, you take or pull it out, often after searching for it for some time; an informal use. EG *According to the police, more bodies have been fished out of the canal... I fished out my passport from the bottom of the bag.* V+O+A ⇑ extract = haul

7 If you feel **like a fish out of water**, you do not feel comfortable or relaxed because you are in an unusual or unfamiliar situation. PHR : USED AS AN A = awkward

8 Someone who **drinks like a fish** drinks a lot of alcohol; an informal expression. PHR : VB INFLECTS

9 If you say that **there are other fish in the sea**, you mean that even though a relationship or deal with someone has failed, there are other people with whom you may be successful. PHR

fish and chip shop, fish and chip shops. A **fish and chip shop** is a place where you can buy fried fish, fishcakes, sausages, chips, etc to take away and eat. N COUNT

fishcake /fɪʃkeɪk/, **fishcakes**. A **fishcake** is a mixture of fish and mashed potato that is made into a flat round shape, covered in breadcrumbs and fried. N COUNT ⇑ food

fisherman /fɪʃəmə³n/, **fishermen**. A **fisherman** is a person who catches fish, usually as a job, but sometimes for sport. N COUNT

fishery /fɪʃə⁰ri¹/, **fisheries**. A **fishery** is an area of the sea where fish are caught in large quantities for commercial purposes. EG *...the offshore fisheries of Iceland.* N COUNT : USU PL

fish finger, fish fingers; also spelled with a hyphen. **Fish fingers** are small oblong pieces of fish, covered in breadcrumbs and usually sold in frozen form. N COUNT ⇑ food

fishing /fɪʃɪŋ/ is the sport, hobby, or business of catching fish. EG *Fishing has been a profitable industry for the town in recent years... We did a bit of fishing at the weekend... ...a small fishing boat.* N UNCOUNT, OR N BEFORE N

fishing rod, fishing rods; also spelled with a hyphen. A **fishing rod** is a long thin pole that has a line and hook attached to it and is used for catching fish. N COUNT

fishing tackle; also spelled with a hyphen. **Fishing tackle** consists of all the equipment that is used in the sport of fishing, such as fishing rods, lines, hooks, and bait. N UNCOUNT

fish knife, fish knives; also spelled with a hyphen. A **fish knife** is a knife that has a broad blade without a sharp edge and is used when you eat fish. N COUNT

fishmonger /fɪʃmʌŋgə/, **fishmongers**. A **fishmonger** is a shopkeeper who sells fish; used in British English. N COUNT ▸ The **fishmonger** or the **fishmonger's** is used to refer to a shop where fish is sold. EG *I've got to go to the fishmonger's.* ▸ N SING : the+N

fish slice, fish slices; also spelled with a hyphen. A **fish slice** is a kitchen tool which consists of a flat part with slits in it attached to a handle. It is used for turning or serving fish or other food that is cooked in a frying pan. N COUNT ⇑ utensil

fishwife /fɪʃwaɪf/, **fishwives**. If you refer to a woman as a **fishwife**, you mean that she is a coarse or bad-tempered woman with a loud voice; an offensive use. N COUNT = shrew

fishy /fɪʃi¹/, **fishier, fishiest**. 1 A **fishy** taste or smell reminds you of fish. EG *It smells very fishy in here.* ADJ QUALIT

2 If something seems **fishy** to you, you feel that someone is not telling the truth or behaving completely honestly; an informal use. EG *There was something a bit fishy about his explanation... It all sounds rather fishy to me.* ADJ QUALIT = suspicious, dubious

fission /fɪʃə⁰n/. Nuclear **fission** is the splitting of the nucleus of an atom to produce a large amount of energy or cause a large explosion. N UNCOUNT

fissure /fɪʃə/, **fissures**. A **fissure** is a deep crack in something, especially in rock or in the ground. N COUNT = crevice

fist /fɪst/, **fists**. Your hand is referred to as your **fist** when you have bent your fingers in towards the palm in order to hit someone, to make an angry gesture, or to hold something. EG *She screamed and hit me with her fist... Ralph clenched his fist... I shook my fist... The Marine held it tightly in his fist.* ● **hand over fist**: see **hand**. N COUNT

fistful /fɪstful/, **fistfuls**. A **fistful** of things is the number of them that you can hold in your fist. EG *He handed me a fistful of letters.* N PART ⇑ amount

fisticuffs /fɪstɪkʌfs/ is fighting in which people try to hit each other with their fists; an old-fashioned word. EG *I do not choose to engage in fisticuffs with you.* N UNCOUNT = brawling

fit /fɪt/, **fits, fitting, fitted; fitter, fittest**. In American English the form **fit** is used in the present tense and sometimes also as the past tense and past participle of the verb. 1 If something **fits** a particular person or thing, or **fits**, it is the right size and shape to go on that person or to go on, in, or next to that thing, and is neither too big nor too small. EG *The box has got a nice lid which fits... The sheets are made in several sizes to fit different sizes of bed... He was wearing pyjamas which did not fit him.* ● **if the cap fits**: see **cap**. V OR V+O

2 If something **fits** well, closely, etc, it is the size indicated in relation to the thing it is on, in, or next to. EG *The boots fitted Rudolph perfectly... Make sure that the jacket on the hot water cylinder fits snugly.* V+A, OR V+O+A
● If something, especially a piece of clothing, **fits like a glove** or **fits** someone **like a glove**, it fits perfectly. ● PHR : VB INFLECTS

3 If something is a good **fit**, it fits. If it is a bad **fit**, it does not fit. EG *She tried the dress on. It was a perfect fit.* N SING WITH DET : USU *a*+ADJ +N

4 If you **are fitted** for a particular piece of clothing, you try it on so that the person who is making it can see where it needs to be altered. EG *She's at her dressmaker's being fitted for a suit.* V+O : USU PASS, IF+PREP THEN *for*

5 If something or a group of things **fits** into or onto something else, it is small enough to be able to go in it or on it. EG *All my clothes fit into one suitcase... The chapel was so small that only twenty-six people could fit in.* V+A

6 If something **fits** somewhere, it can be put there or is designed to be put there, and is just the right size and shape. EG *The metal cover fits over the tap... ...the hole into which the pole fitted... ...a set of bowls designed to fit one inside the other.* V : USU+A = go

7 If you **fit** something into, onto, or next to something else, you put it into the right hole or space, where it belongs. EG *Philip fitted his key into the lock... The upper strut was fitted into place... He unwrapped the parts of the rifle, fitting it together piece by piece.* V+O+A ⇑ place = slot

8 If you **fit** something such as a piece of equipment or an extra part to a particular thing, or **fit** that thing with it, you fix it to or in that thing. EG *Castors can be fitted to a bed to make it easier to pull or push... There may be no one around who can fit the new lock... The kitchen has been fitted with a stainless steel sink.* V+O : USU+A *(to/with)* ⇑ provide

9 If something such as an idea or subject **fits** something or **fits** in, it is able to be part of that thing or is consistent with it or compatible with it. EG *This would fit the theory that he was in fact a spy... Perhaps he killed her himself. But that didn't fit... It's difficult to know where books of this kind fit in... ...a nurse who is willing to fit in with your way of doing things... That didn't fit their lifestyle.* ● **to fit the bill**: see **bill**. V : USU+A OR V+O

10 If you **fit** something into a category, system of ideas, etc, you work out where its right place is in it. EG *There are always some opinions which do not fit into any of the categories available... ...trying to fit it into his scheme of things.* V+O (NG/REFL) +A *(in/into)* = slot

11 If something **fits** a particular person or thing, it is appropriate or suitable for them or it. EG *...the Governor's attempt to make the punishment fit the unspeakable crime... The description fits women far better than it fits men... Does this plan fit our present and future needs?* V+O ⇑ correspond to

12 Someone or something that is **fit** for a particular person or thing is good enough or suitable for that person or thing. EG *We are here to see that the houses are fit for human habitation... ...a world fit for heroes to live in... She regarded herself as fit only to be a governess... She's not fit to live... It is a fit object for love.* ◇ **fitness**. EG *Their fitness for responsibility was not in doubt.* ADJ CLASSIF : USU PRED+*for/to*-INF = worthy ◇ N UNCOUNT+ *for/to*-INF

13 If you **fit** someone or something for a particular task or role, you make them good enough or suitable for it; a formal use. EG *The humble man will ask: What fits me to make so momentous a decision?... She must fit herself for the honour of being a wife.* V+O (NG/REFL) +*for/to/to*-INF ⇑ prepare

14 Someone who **sees fit** or **thinks fit** to do a particular thing decides that it is the right thing to do; often used to suggest that you do not agree with that decision. EG *In its report the committee saw fit to make no reference whatever to this... The Trust has been given a considerable sum to dispense as it sees fit.* PHR : VB INFLECTS, USU+ *to*-INF = choose

15 If you say that someone is **fit** to do something, you mean that they seem likely to do it; an informal use, often used as an exaggeration to emphasize the intensity with which something is done. EG *Casson looked fit to explode.* ▸ used as an adverb. EG *I laughed fit to burst... The boy was yelling fit to wake the dead.* ADJ CLASSIF : PRED+*to*-INF = about, ready ▸ ADV AFTER VB +*to*-INF ⇑ enough

16 Someone who is **fit** is healthy and able to do physical activities without getting tired. EG *He felt relaxed and fit after his holiday... They're both fit and well... She works hard at keeping herself fit.* ◇ **fitness**. EG *They were trained to a peak of physical fitness.* ● Someone who is as **fit as a fiddle** is very fit; an informal expression. ● **fighting fit**: see **fight**. ● **not in a fit state**: see **state**. ADJ QUALIT ◇ N UNCOUNT ● PHR : USED AS C ⇑ healthy

17 If someone has a **fit**, they suddenly lose consciousness and their body makes sudden uncontrollable movements. EG *He seemed to be having some kind of fit... ...an epileptic fit.* ● If you say that someone will **have a fit** when they hear about something, you mean that they will be very angry or shocked. EG *My father would have a fit if he found out.* N COUNT = seizure ● PHR : VB INFLECTS = go mad

18 If you have a **fit** of coughing, laughter, etc, you suddenly start doing the thing mentioned in an uncontrollable way and find it very difficult to stop doing it. EG *She'd had a coughing fit and we had to hit her on the back quite hard... She threw a fit of hysterics.* ● Someone who is **in fits** is laughing uncontrollably. EG *He had us all in fits with tales of his schooldays.* N COUNT+SUPP ⇑ episode = bout ● PHR : USED AS AN A = in stitches

19 If you have a **fit** of rage, panic, unhappiness, etc, you feel the emotion mentioned very strongly for a short time. EG *In a fit of rage, he had flung Paul's violin out of the window... He was plagued with fits of depression.* N COUNT+*of* ⇑ episode = outbreak

20 Something that happens or progresses **in fits and starts** or **by fits and starts** keeps happening or progressing and then stopping again. EG *There is no easy way of coping with orders that come in fits and starts throughout the year.* PHR : USED AS AN A = erratically

21 See also **fitted, fitting, fitter**.

fit in. 1 If you **fit** something or someone **in**, you manage to find time to do it or to deal with it or them. EG *You seem to fit in an enormous amount every day... I can fit you in on the 9th.* PHRASAL VB : V+O+ADV = squeeze in

2 If you **fit in** or **fit into** a particular group, you seem to belong there because you are similar to the other people in it. EG *You can't bring outsiders into a place like this; they wouldn't fit in... These children are unable to fit into ordinary society when they leave school.* PHRASAL VB : V+ADV/PREP

fit out. If you **fit** someone or something **out** or you **fit** them **up**, you provide them with equipment and other things that they need. EG *He started to fit out a ship in secret... They would fit them out in combat uniforms.* PHRASAL VB : V+O+ADV, IF+PREP THEN *in/with* = kit out

fitful /fɪtful/. Something that is **fitful** happens for irregular periods of time or occurs at irregular times, rather than being continuous. EG *He dozed off into a fitful sleep.* ◊ **fitfully**. EG *A pallid moon shone fitfully between the ragged clouds.*
ADJ CLASSIF = broken; ◊ ADV WITH VB

fitment /fɪtmə[2]nt/, **fitments**. A **fitment** is a piece of furniture, for example a cupboard, which is fixed to the wall of a room but which can be removed. EG *...kitchen fitments.*
N COUNT ⇑ furnishing

fitted /fɪtɪ[2]d/. 1 Someone who is **fitted** to do something or for something has the right qualities for it. EG *She began to wonder if she was fitted for the role of motherhood... Those best fitted to the work will be chosen.*
ADJ QUALIT : PRED + to-INF/ for/to = suited

2 A **fitted** piece of clothing is designed so that it is the same size and shape as your body rather than being loose. EG *Dolly wore a nice grey dress with fitted bodice and flared skirt.*
ADJ CLASSIF : ATTRIB = tailored

3 A **fitted** sheet has the corners sewn so that they fit over the corners of the mattress and do not have to be folded.
ADJ CLASSIF : ATTRIB

4 A **fitted** carpet covers the floor completely and is fixed into place.
ADJ CLASSIF : ATTRIB

5 A **fitted** piece of furniture, for example a cupboard, is designed to fill a particular space and is fixed in place. EG *...fitted shelves.*
ADJ CLASSIF : ATTRIB = built-in

6 A **fitted** kitchen or bedroom is one in which the furniture is fixed in place and all the pieces match each other.
ADJ CLASSIF : ATTRIB ⇑ furnished

fitter /fɪtə/, **fitters**. A **fitter** is someone whose job is to put together, adjust, or install machinery or equipment. EG *He got a job as mate to an electrical fitter in the Dockyard.*
N COUNT ⇑ worker

fitting /fɪtɪŋ/, **fittings**. 1 Something that is **fitting** is right or suitable. EG *She said that I was the eldest and that it was fitting that I should go first... We should offer fitting thanks to God.* ◊ **fittingly**. EG *The speech was fittingly solemn.*
ADJ QUALIT = proper; ◊ ADV

2 A **fitting** is one of the smaller parts on the outside of a piece of equipment or furniture, for example a handle or a tap. EG *...a bath with brass fittings... They make fittings for car dashboards... ...polished steel light fittings.*
N COUNT ⇑ component

3 **Fittings** are things, for example cookers or electric fires, that are fixed inside a building, but that can be removed if you move house. EG *Make sure you know what fixtures and fittings will be left at your new home.*
N PLURAL ⇑ installations

4 If someone has a **fitting**, they try on a piece of clothing that is being made for them to see if it fits. EG *I've got a fitting next week for my wedding dress.*
N COUNT

5 A shoe in a wide or narrow **fitting** is made for a wide or narrow foot; used in British English. EG *This shoe is a bit tight: have you got it in a wider fitting?*
N COUNT : ADJ + N ⇑ size

-fitting combines with adjectives or adverbs such as 'close', 'loose', or 'tightly' to show that something is the size indicated in relation to the thing it is on, in, or next to. EG *...a close-fitting lid... ...tightly-fitting suits.*
COMB : FORMS ADJS

five /faɪv/, **fives**. 1 **Five** is the number 5: see ☐ at NUMBER, AGE, DATE, MEASUREMENT, MONEY, and TIME. EG *Five inches of snow had fallen.*
NUM

2 **Fives** is a ball game in which you hit the ball with your hands or a bat against three walls of a court.
N UNCOUNT ⇑ sport

five o'clock shadow, five o'clock shadows. If a man has a **five o'clock shadow**, his chin and the sides of his face look dark because his beard has grown a little during the day after he has shaved in the morning.
N COUNT : USU SING

fiver /faɪvə/, **fivers**. A **fiver** is five pounds or five dollars, or a note of this value; an informal word. EG *You owe me a fiver, old chap... She took a fiver from her purse.*
N COUNT

fix /fɪks/, **fixes, fixing, fixed**. 1 If you **fix** something to a particular thing, or in a particular position, you attach it firmly to that thing, or you place it firmly in that position, so that it cannot move or be moved. EG *He had the sign fixed to the gate... She fixed a jewelled brooch on her dress... The spades and forks of the men still stood fixed in the ground... The screws had been fixed into place with a blob of glue.*
V+O+A ⇑ secure

2 If something **is fixed in** your **mind** or **brain**, you remember it very well, because it is very important, interesting, or unusual. EG *The scene was firmly fixed in all our minds... I fixed the name firmly in my brain.*
PHR : VB INFLECTS

3 If you **fix** your eyes or attention on something, or **fix** something with your eyes, you look at it or think about it with complete attention. EG *She fixed her brown eyes upon him... The thoughts of every American mind are fixed upon the President... The cop fixed him with a solemn stare.* ◊ **fixed**. EG *The intruder met with fixed glares from the citizens.* ◊ **fixedly** /fɪksə[1]dli[1]/. EG *She stared fixedly at the drops of rain sliding down the glass.*
V+O+A (on/ upon/with) ⇑ concentrate; ◊ ADJ CLASSIF : ATTRIB; ◊ ADV AFTER VB = intently

4 If you **fix** the date or amount of something, you decide what it will definitely be. EG *All that remained was to fix the date of the wedding... These weekly amounts are fixed at the start of every tax year... The meeting is fixed for the 11th.* ◊ **fixed**. EG *You pay your landlord a fixed charge for heating.*
V+O = set; ◊ ADJ CLASSIF = set

5 If you **fix** the exact time or position of something, you find out or prove exactly what it is. EG *It is impossible to fix the exact moment in time when it happened.*
V+O = establish

6 If you get a **fix** on your position, for example when you are on a ship, you find out exactly where you are, using instruments such as a compass or radar. EG *I'm trying to get a fix on where we are... If he could only take a fix in one direction.*
N COUNT

7 If you **fix** a dye, photograph, or drawing, you treat it with a chemical so that the colours or lines do not run or become blurred.
V+O

8 If you **fix** something such as a machine which is damaged or which will not work properly, you repair it. EG *I fixed a small leak in the roof... I learned how to fix radios in the Army... He spent the afternoon getting his car fixed.*
V+O = mend

9 If you **fix** something, especially your hair or make-up, you make small changes to it in order to make it look neater or more suitable or attractive. EG *She went to the cloakroom to fix her hair... The girls were just finishing fixing the Dining Room for a dance.*
V+O ⇑ improve = tidy

10 If you say that you will **fix** something, you mean that you will make all the arrangements necessary to make it possible or easy, especially for someone else. EG *Leave it to me. I'll fix it. Someone will look after the kids... I could fix it with Rosemary.*
V+O ⇑ arrange = organize

11 If you **fix** something such as a race or a competition, you make unfair or illegal arrangements relating to it, so that a particular competitor will win or lose; an informal use. EG *We tossed for it, but I fixed it so that Rick won... I had seen many horse races that had been fixed over the years.* ▸ used as a noun. EG *It's a fix!* ◊ **fixed**. EG *It's a fixed trial.*
V+O = rig; ▸ N SING : a+N; ◊ ADJ CLASSIF

12 If you **fix** someone or their activities, you stop their activities permanently, for example by using violence on them; a very informal use. EG *We really fixed Mr Nickerson.*
V+O = put paid to

13 If you **fix** a drink or food for someone, you make it or prepare it for them. EG *Would you like me to fix you a drink?... She fixed herself a plate of food.*
V+O, V+O (NG/ REFL) + O, OR V+ O+A (for)

14 If you are in a **fix**, you are in a difficult situation, especially one that you have caused for yourself; a fairly informal use. EG *Could you lend me a fiver? I'm in a bit of a fix.*
N COUNT : USU a +N IN SING = jam, tight spot

15 A **fix** is also an injection of an addictive drug such as heroin; an informal use. EG *He looked like he needed a fix.*
N COUNT = shot

16 See also **fixed**.

fix on. If you **fix on** or **fix upon** a particular thing, you decide that it is the one you want and will have. EG *Have you fixed on a date for the party yet?*
PHRASAL VB : V+ PREP, HAS PASS ⇑ choose = set

fix up. 1 If you **fix** someone **up** with something they need, you provide it for them. EG *They told me that they could fix me up with tickets... Can I stay at your place till I get fixed up?*
PHRASAL VB : V+ O (NG/REFL) + ADV, IF + PREP THEN with

2 If you **fix** someone or something **up**, you make the arrangements that they need or that are necessary. EG *The holiday is all fixed up, you'll be pleased to hear... I fixed the kids up to go down to the zoo.*
PHRASAL VB : V+ O+ADV, USU+A

3 If you **fix** something **up**, **3.1** you build it very quickly or roughly, for example because you need it at once or need it for only a short time. EG *We tried to fix up a shelter from the wind... I've fixed up this sort of wire barricade.* **3.2** do work that is necessary in order to make it more suitable or attractive. EG *He was fixing up his new flat, ready to move in.*
PHRASAL VB : V+ O+ADV ⇑ erect = rig up; PHRASAL VB : V+ O+ADV ⇑ improve = do up

fixated /fɪkseɪtɪ[2]d/. Someone who is **fixated** on a particular thing thinks about it to an extreme and excessive degree. EG *He remains fixated on objects which remind him of his mother.*
ADJ CLASSIF

fixation /fɪkseɪʃə⁰n/, **fixations**. A **fixation** is an extreme and excessive interest in something or love of someone or something. EG *The child may develop a mother fixation... ...fixations on brothers or sisters... ...the sport fixation of the British.* [N COUNT: USU + SUPP; = obsession]

fixative /fɪksətɪv/, **fixatives**. **Fixative** or a **fixative** is 1 a liquid used to preserve the surface of a drawing, photograph, etc. EG *You should spray it with fixative.* [N UNCOUNT/COUNT] 2 a liquid used to hold things in place, for example dentures. [N UNCOUNT/COUNT]

fixed /fɪkst/. 1 A **fixed** amount, position, pattern, method, etc always stays the same. EG *The signal goes on sounding at fixed intervals... ...a fixed pattern of behaviour.* [ADJ CLASSIF; ⇑ invariable = set]

2 A **fixed** idea or desire is one which you will not change your mind about, although perhaps you should. EG *Children can be raised without fixed ideas and prejudices... It was his fixed ambition to see his brother ruined.* [ADJ QUALIT; ⇑ inflexible = set]

3 A **fixed** smile or other facial expression does not change and looks artificial. EG *She kept a fixed smile on her face.* [ADJ CLASSIF: ATTRIB; ⇑ rigid]

4 Someone who has **no fixed abode** or **no fixed address** does not have a permanent place to live; a formal use. EG *Mr Sims, 21, of no fixed abode, was remanded in custody for a further week.* [PHR: USED AS O]

5 See also **fix**.

fixings /fɪksɪŋz/ are extra items that are used to decorate or complete something, especially a meal; used in American English. EG *The rich food and its fixings lie heavy on the stomach.* [N PLURAL; = trimmings]

fixity /fɪksɪti¹/. The **fixity** of a person's gaze, concentration, or attitude is the quality it has of not changing or weakening. EG *...the fixity of his stare... He showed a remarkable fixity of purpose.* [N UNCOUNT: USU + *of*]

fixture /fɪkstʃə/, **fixtures**. 1 A **fixture** is 1.1 a piece of furniture or equipment, for example a bath or sink, which is fixed inside a house or other building and which is usually left in place when you move. EG *Make sure you know what fixtures and fittings will be left at your new home... ...the light fixture on the ceiling.* [N COUNT; ≠ moveable] 1.2 a sports event, for example a football match, which has been arranged to take place on a particular date; used in British English. EG *We had to cancel a lot of fixtures... Most athletic clubs produce their own fixture lists.* [N COUNT]

2 Someone or something that is a **fixture** in a particular place or group is always there and seems likely to be there always in the future. EG *It was Old Mary, a fixture at Richmond Hill... Pool seems likely to become a fixture in working-class pubs.* [N COUNT: USU USED AS C; ⇑ feature]

fizz /fɪz/, **fizzes, fizzing, fizzed**. 1 If a liquid, especially a drink, **fizzes**, it produces lots of little bubbles of gas and makes a hissing sound. [V; ⇑ bubble]

2 If something **fizzes**, it makes a hissing sound. EG *The firework fizzed for a while and went out.* [V; = sizzle]

3 **Fizz** is 3.1 the quality of being fizzy. EG *This lemonade has lost its fizz.* [N UNCOUNT] 3.2 fizzy white wine, especially champagne. [N UNCOUNT]

fizzle /fɪzə⁰l/, **fizzles, fizzling, fizzled**. To **fizzle** means to make a weak hissing or bubbling sound. EG *The fire fizzled and spat.* [V; = sputter]

fizzle out. If something starts off strongly and then **fizzles out**, it ends in a weak or disappointing way. EG *The strike fizzled out after three days... It wasn't long before interest in it fizzled out.* [PHRASAL VB: V + ADV; ⇑ end = peter out]

fizzy /fɪzi¹/, **fizzier, fizziest**. A **fizzy** drink or other liquid is full of little bubbles of gas and makes a hissing sound. EG *...fizzy lemonade.* [ADJ QUALIT]

fjord /fjɔːd/, **fjords**; also spelled **fiord**. A **fjord** is a strip of sea that comes into the land between high cliffs, especially in Norway. [N COUNT: ALSO IN NAMES AFTER N]

flab /flæb/ is loose flesh on the body of someone who is fat. EG *She was ashamed of her flab... ...formerly athletic bodies that have gone to flab.* [N UNCOUNT]

flabbergasted /flæbəgɑːstɪ²d/. Someone who is **flabbergasted** is extremely surprised. EG *'Well!' I exclaimed, flabbergasted at Doctor Martin's deceit.* [ADJ CLASSIF; = dumbfounded]

flabby /flæbi¹/. 1 Something that is **flabby** is not as firm as it should be, but loose or soft instead. EG *...his long, flabby face... ...wilting spinach and flabby turnips.* [ADJ QUALIT]

2 Someone who is **flabby** 2.1 has loose flesh and muscles rather than firm ones because they have not taken enough exercise. EG *He was a flabby, pale-faced bachelor.* [ADJ QUALIT; ⇑ overweight = flaccid] 2.2 is weak and lazy in character. EG *...the flabby, hesitant, misguided leaders of the party.* [ADJ QUALIT] ◇ **flabbiness**. EG *...a speech of exceptional flabbiness.* [◇ N UNCOUNT]

flaccid /flæsɪd/. Something that is **flaccid** is soft and loose or limp, rather than firm. [ADJ QUALIT]

flag /flæg/, **flags, flagging, flagged**. 1 A **flag** is 1.1 a piece of cloth which can be attached to a pole and which is used as a sign, signal, or symbol of something, especially of a particular country. Flags are a particular colour or have a particular pattern or design on them. EG *The flag flying over our building was the Union Jack... Their coffins were draped with American flags... He hoisted the flag of surrender... The guard blew his whistle and waved his flag.* [N COUNT] 1.2 a small piece of paper or cloth attached to a stick or pin which is sold on a flag day or used as a marker, for example on a map on which you are planning military action. EG *You can tell where our divisions are posted by the position of the flags on the map.* [N COUNT; ⇑ tag]

2 You refer to the **flag** of a particular country as a way of referring to the country itself and its values or power. EG *This invasion is a hideous insult to our flag... He loved athletics, the flag, and capitalism... ...the people that lived under the flag of the British Empire.* [N COUNT + SUPP: USU SING; ⇑ symbol]

3 You refer to the **flag** of a particular cause or belief as a way of referring to that cause or belief. EG *The flag of peace hung in tatters.* [N SING + SUPP; = banner]

4 If you do something **with flags flying**, you do it in a triumphant or confident way. EG *She not only survived the ordeal but came out with flags flying.* [PHR: USED AS AN A; ⇑ triumphantly]

5 If you **fly the flag** or to **keep the flag flying**, you show that you are proud of your country, especially when you are in a foreign country or when few other people do. EG *I try to fly the flag, and buy British, and all that.* [PHR: VB INFLECTS]

6 If you **flag** or your spirits **flag**, you begin to lose enthusiasm or energy. EG *I started to flag a bit after a while... We must not flag in our efforts to fight crime... Your spirits may flag when faced with this new task.* [V; ⇑ tire = falter, weaken] ◇ **flagging**. EG *She tried to revive their flagging energies.* [◇ ADJ CLASSIF; = failing]

7 A **flag** is also the same as a flagstone. [N COUNT]

flag down. If you **flag down** a vehicle, especially a taxi, you wave at it as a signal for the driver to stop. EG *We flagged down the tractor and clambered aboard.* [PHRASAL VB: V + O + ADV; = hail]

flag day, flag days; also spelled with a hyphen. A **flag day** is a day on which people collect money for a charity from people in the street and give them a small badge or paper flag to show that they have given money. [N COUNT]

flagellate /flædʒə²leɪt/, **flagellates, flagellating, flagellated**; a formal word. If someone **flagellates** themselves or someone else, 1 they beat themselves or the other person, for example as an act of religious penance. EG *...a painting of a saint flagellating himself.* [V + O (NG/REFL)] ◇ **flagellation** /flædʒɛ¹leɪʃə⁰n/. [◇ N UNCOUNT] 2 you criticize yourself or them very severely. EG *I did not like the way he flagellated me in his speech.* [V + O (NG/REFL); = castigate]

flagged /flægd/. A **flagged** path or area of ground is paved with flagstones. [ADJ CLASSIF]

flagon /flægə⁰n/, **flagons**. A **flagon** is 1 a wide bottle in which cider or wine is sold. [N COUNT] 2 a jug with a narrow neck in which water or another drink is served. [N COUNT]

flagpole /flægpəʊl/, **flagpoles**. A **flagpole** is a tall pole on the ground, or on the top or side of a building, with ropes attached to it, on which a flag can be displayed. EG *A flagpole flew the French flag.* [N COUNT; ⇑ pole = flagstaff]

flagrant /fleɪgrənt/ is used to describe a bad or shocking action, situation, or attitude that is very obvious and not concealed in any way. EG *...a flagrant violation of human rights... ...flagrant injustices.* [ADJ QUALIT: ATTRIB; = blatant, glaring] ◇ **flagrantly**. EG *...a series of news stories that flagrantly broke the British censorship... The present distribution of wealth in the world is flagrantly unjust.* [◇ ADV; = blatantly]

flagship /flægʃɪp/, **flagships**. 1 A **flagship** is the most important ship in a fleet of ships, especially the one on which the commander of the fleet is sailing. EG *...a replica of Christopher Columbus's flagship.* [N COUNT; ⇑ ship]

2 The **flagship** of a group of things that are owned or produced by a particular organization is the most important one. EG *Bentley's flagship is his restaurant* [N COUNT: USU WITH POSS; ⇑ asset]

in Bishopgate... ...the BBC's flagship news programme.

flagstaff /flægstɑ:f/, **flagstaffs**. A **flagstaff** is the same as a flagpole. N COUNT

flagstone /flægstəun/, **flagstones**. **Flagstones** are big, flat, square pieces of stone which are used for paving. EG *At last she was walking on the flagstones of Venice.* N COUNT : USU PL = flag

flag-waving is the expression of patriotic feelings in an excessively loud or exaggerated way. EG *All this flag-waving disgusts me.* ▸ used as an adjective. EG *...flag-waving patriots.* N UNCOUNT = jingoism ▸ ADJ CLASSIF : ATTRIB

flail /fleɪl/, **flails, flailing, flailed**. 1 If you **flail** your arms or legs about or if they **flail**, they wave about in an energetic but uncontrolled way. EG *The baby flailed her little arms around... One flailing arm caught him across the cheek... His hands flailed the air about his head.* V-ERG = thresh, thrash

2 If you **flail** someone, you beat them, for example with a stick. V+O

3 A **flail** is a tool which consists of a piece of wood or metal that can swing freely from a handle. Flails are used to thresh grain. N COUNT

flair /flɛə/. If you have **flair** or a **flair** for doing a particular thing, you have a natural ability to do it well. EG *It was apparent to everyone that he had a flair for this branch of law... Wilson was impressed by his political flair.* N SING WITH DET : IF+PREP THEN *for*, OR N UNCOUNT = talent

2 **Flair** is the ability to do things in an original, interesting, and stylish way. EG *He has flair, which his party desperately needs.* N UNCOUNT = panache

flak /flæk/ is 1 a large number of explosive shells that are being fired at an aircraft or a group of aircraft. EG *I saw one of the Dakota transports hit by flak.* 2 severe criticism; an informal use. EG *He can expect to receive a lot of flak for this decision.* N UNCOUNT ⇑ gunfire N UNCOUNT

flake /fleɪk/, **flakes, flaking, flaked**. 1 A **flake** of something is a small thin piece of it, especially one that has broken off a larger piece. EG *...large fluffy flakes of snow... ...oat flakes... Flakes of plaster had fallen from the ceiling.* N COUNT : ALSO N +*of*+N UNCOUNT

2 If something, for example paint, **flakes**, small thin pieces of it come off. EG *The paint was flaking off the walls... ...the dry, flaking skin of her hands.* V = peel

3 If you **flake** fish or other food, you break it into small thin pieces. EG *Remove all skin and bones, and flake the fish... Simmer very gently until the fish flakes easily.* ◊ **flaked**. EG *...flaked almonds.* V-ERG ◊ ADJ CLASSIF

flake out. If you **flake out**, you collapse, go to sleep, or lose consciousness, usually because you are very tired; an informal expression. EG *When I got to the top I just flaked out.* ◊ **flaked out**. EG *I was lying flaked out on my bed.* PHRASAL VB : V+ADV ◊ ADJ CLASSIF : PRED

flak jacket, flak jackets; also spelled with a hyphen. A **flak jacket** is a thick sleeveless jacket that soldiers and policemen sometimes wear to protect themselves against bullets. N COUNT

flaky /fleɪki[1]/. Something that is **flaky** breaks easily into flakes or tends to come off in flakes. EG *The car was flaky with rust... This gives the pastry a flaky texture.* ADJ QUALIT

flaky pastry is a rich pastry consisting of very thin layers. N UNCOUNT

flambé /flæmbeɪ/, **flambés, flambéing, flambéed**. If you **flambé** food, you serve or cook it in flaming brandy. EG *...flambéed steaks.* V+O

flamboyance /flæmbɔɪəns/ is 1 behaviour that is very noticeable, confident, and exaggerated. EG *James was a gentle man, despite his flamboyance.* 2 the quality of being brightly coloured or of a very noticeable shape or design. N UNCOUNT N UNCOUNT ⇑ distinctiveness

flamboyant /flæmbɔɪənt/. 1 Someone who is **flamboyant** behaves in a very noticeable, confident, and exaggerated way. EG *He has been accused of being too flamboyant on stage... My father was capable of flamboyant generosity.* ADJ QUALIT = extravagant

2 Something that is **flamboyant** is very brightly coloured or of a very noticeable shape or design. EG *...a flamboyant quilted bathrobe.* ADJ QUALIT = dazzling

flame /fleɪm/, **flames, flaming, flamed**. 1 A **flame** is a hot bright quantity of burning gas that comes in a pointed stream from something that is burning or on fire. EG *The flames and smoke rose hundreds of feet into the air... He turned to put his cigarette to the flame of his lighter... The aircraft disappeared in a ball of brilliant yellow flame.* N COUNT/ UNCOUNT

2 Something that is **in flames** is on fire. EG *My parents' home was in flames.* PHR : USED AS AN A

3 If something **goes up in flames**, it starts to burn fiercely and is destroyed. EG *In seconds the factory had gone up in flames.* PHR

4 If something **bursts into flames**, it suddenly starts burning fiercely. EG *The satellite burst into flames and disintegrated.* PHR : VB INFLECTS ⇑ burn

5 To **flame** means 5.1 to suddenly start burning brightly, or more brightly than before. EG *The gas-fire began to flame blue and gold.* 5.2 to be, or to suddenly become, bright red. EG *The trees flamed scarlet against the grass... Sally's cheeks flamed and her eyes glittered.* V OR V+C = flare V OR V+C = blaze

6 You refer to a **flame** of passion, desire, anger etc as a way of referring to a strong feeling that someone has; a literary use. EG *...the flame of passion that has been lit in their souls.* N COUNT+*of* = fire

7 If you **fan the flames** or you **add fuel to the flames**, you make a situation more intense or extreme in some way. EG *Both films will be big hits and fan the flames of his success... Without doubt these rumours added further fuel to the flames.* PHR : VB INFLECTS ⇑ encourage

8 See also **old flame**.

flamenco /flə[3]mɛŋkəu/, **flamencos**. A **flamenco** is a Spanish dance that is danced to a special type of guitar music. N COUNT/ UNCOUNT

flameproof /fleɪmpru:f/. Something that is **flameproof** is made of a substance that is not easily damaged by fire or heat. ADJ CLASSIF = fireproof

flame-thrower, flame-throwers; also spelled as two words. A **flame-thrower** is a gun that can send out a stream of burning liquid and is used as a weapon or for clearing plants from an area of ground. N COUNT

flaming /fleɪmɪŋ/. 1 **Flaming** is used to describe something that is burning and producing a lot of flames. EG *...bursting shells and planes diving down with flaming wings.* ADJ CLASSIF : ATTRIB

2 Something that is **flaming**, or **flaming** red or orange, is bright red or orange in colour. EG *...the gorgeous flaming sunsets... Her hair was flaming red, her skin white.* ADJ CLASSIF : ATTRIB = fiery

3 A **flaming** argument or temper is very angry and passionate. EG *We had a flaming row.* ADJ CLASSIF : ATTRIB

4 **Flaming** is a mild swear word used to emphasize what you are saying, especially when you feel strongly about something or are annoyed. EG *'Any chance of a cup of tea?'–'Flaming heck! Give me a chance!'... The flaming car's locked.* ADJ CLASSIF : ATTRIB = blooming

flamingo /flə[3]mɪŋgəu/, **flamingos, flamingoes**. The plural can be either **flamingos** or **flamingoes**. A **flamingo** is a bird with pink feathers, long thin legs, a long neck, and a curved beak. Flamingos live near water in warm countries. N COUNT

flammable /flæməbə[0]l/. Chemicals, gases, cloth, or other things that are **flammable** catch fire and burn easily. EG *Hydrogen is highly flammable.* ADJ QUALIT = inflammable

flan /flæn/, **flans**. A **flan** is an open tart made of pastry or cake and filled with fruit or something savoury. N COUNT

flange /flændʒ/, **flanges**. A **flange** is a projecting edge on an object used for strengthening it or for attaching it to another object. N COUNT

flank /flæŋk/, **flanks, flanking, flanked**. 1 An animal's **flank** is its side, between the ribs and the hip. N COUNT

2 A **flank** of an army or fleet is one side of it when it is organized ready for battle. EG *...reinforcements for the northern flank.* N COUNT

3 The side of anything large can be referred to as its **flank**. EG *...the south flank of St. James's Park.* N COUNT : USU+SUPP

4 If something **is flanked** by something, it has the thing mentioned at one side or at both sides of it. EG *Billy was seated at one end of the table, flanked by the two women... ...an old-fashioned bed, flanked on both sides by marble-topped tables.* V+O : USU PASS+ *by/with*

flannel /flænə[0]l/, **flannels, flannelling, flannelled**; also spelled **flanneling, flanneled** in American English. 1 **Flannel** is a lightweight cloth woven from wool or from a synthetic material and used especially for making clothes. EG *...a grey flannel suit.* N UNCOUNT, OR N BEFORE N

2 **Flannels** are men's trousers made of flannel. EG *He wore flannels and a faded blue tweed jacket.* N PLURAL : ALSO a pair of+N

3 A **flannel** is a small piece of towelling cloth that you use for washing yourself; used in British English. N COUNT = face cloth

4 If you refer to something that someone has said as N UNCOUNT

flannel, you mean that they talked a lot but deliberately avoided telling you what you wanted to know; an informal use. EG *He gave us no flannel; on the contrary, he was very helpful.* ▸ used as a verb. EG *Why do politicians have to flannel all the time?* ▸ V

flannelette /flænəˈlet/ is a soft cloth made from cotton and used especially for making sheets and nightclothes. N UNCOUNT, OR N BEFORE N

flap /flæp/, **flaps, flapping, flapped**. **1** If a piece of cloth or paper **flaps** or if you **flap** it, it moves quickly up and down or from side to side, often making a snapping sound. EG *...a young man, dressed in long robes which flapped in the breeze... She leant out of the window and furiously flapped the blanket.* V-ERG ↑ wave

2 If a bird **flaps** its wings or if its wings **flap**, the wings move quickly up and down. EG *...huge brown birds flapping their wings... The pheasant flapped around for a few seconds.* V-ERG OR V+A

3 If you **flap** your arms, you move them quickly up and down as if they were the wings of a bird. V+O ↑ wave

4 A **flap** of skin, cloth, paper, etc is a flat piece of it that can move freely up and down or from side to side because it is held or attached by only one edge. EG *...looking out through a tent flap at the night sky... ...black shiny caps, with broad flaps at the back to protect their necks.* N COUNT : IF + PREP THEN *of*

5 A **flap** on the wing of an aircraft is the area along the edge of the wing that can be raised or lowered to control the movement of the aircraft. N COUNT

6 A **flap** is a sudden noisy movement made by a bird's wing or by a piece of paper or cloth. EG *With a couple of flaps, the swan took off from the lake.* N COUNT

7 Someone who is **in a flap** is in a state of great excitement, worry, or panic. EG *My parents were understandably in a flap about it all.* PHR : USED AS AN A = agitated

flapjack /flæpdʒæk/, **flapjacks**. **1 Flapjack** is a thick chewy biscuit made from oats, butter, and syrup or treacle; used in British English. N UNCOUNT

2 A **flapjack** is the same as a pancake; used in American English. N COUNT

flare /fleə/, **flares, flaring, flared**. **1** A **flare** is a small device that produces a bright flame and is usually used as a signal. Flares can be shot into the air or used to mark a particular spot. EG *He stood ready to fire a warning flare.* N COUNT

2 If fire or a flame **flares** or **flares up**, it suddenly burns with much larger flames. EG *The candle flared to a bright light... He stood watching it flare up until the last shred was consumed.* V OR PHRASAL VB : V+ADV ↑ blaze

3 If something such as violence, conflict, or anger **flares** or **flares up**, it suddenly starts or becomes more violent. EG *From time to time violence flared... Panic flared up in her... ...when an international crisis flared up... The conflict flared up into civil war.* V OR PHRASAL VB : V+ADV = blow up, erupt

4 Something that **flares** or **flares out** spreads outwards at one end to form a wide shape. EG *She pirouetted, making the skirt flare out... The long feathered tail flared out behind it.* V OR PHRASAL VB : V+ADV ↑ broaden

5 Flares are trousers which are very wide towards the lower part of the leg. N PLURAL : ALSO *a pair of*+N

flared /fleəd/. **Flared** skirts or **flared** trousers are shaped so that they become very wide towards the bottom of the leg or towards the hem. EG *...a grey dress with fitted bodice and flared skirt.* ADJ CLASSIF : ATTRIB

flash /flæʃ/, **flashes, flashing, flashed**. **1** A **flash** of light is a very bright light which comes suddenly and disappears immediately, like lightning in a storm. EG *Suddenly there was a flash and a zigzag of forked lightning... ...the flash of a long knife slicing through the air.* N COUNT : IF+ PREP THEN *of* = gleam, glint

2 If a light **flashes** or if you **flash** a light, it shines with a sudden bright light, especially as quick, regular flashes of light. EG *I'll flash my headlight to make sure he sees us... Sheet lightning flashed on and off like a faulty neon sign... Photographers with flashing lights jumped out of the shadows.* V-ERG = beam, glare

3 Flash is the use of flashbulbs to give more light when taking a photograph. EG *I think this needs flash.* N UNCOUNT

4 A **flash** is also the same as a torch; used in American English. N COUNT = flashlight

5 If something **flashes** past or through somewhere, it moves very fast, almost too fast for you to see it properly; used especially of things that are brightly coloured or shiny. EG *Bright birds flash through the air... Something white flashed past the van.* V+A *(by/past/ through)* = dart, flick

6 If something happens or is done **in a flash**, it happens immediately and suddenly, and lasts only a very short time. EG *In a flash the elder sister recognized the truth... I was out of the room in a flash... The incident was over in a flash.* PHR : USED AS AN A

7 If someone reacts to something by doing something **quick as a flash** they react very quickly indeed. EG *'How dare you tell me what to do!' he snapped back, quick as a flash... Quick as a flash, Claud pulled the paper bag out of his pocket.* PHR : USED AS C/A = smartly

8 If something **flashes** through or into your mind, or if a picture **flashes** onto a screen, it appears suddenly and then immediately disappears. EG *The pictures flashed onto the screen... A vision of Hooper's smiling face flashed across her mind... It flashed through his mind that he might never get back.* V+A ↑ pass

9 A **flash** of a particular emotion or experience is something that you experience suddenly and unexpectedly. EG *She had a flash of anger at being taken for granted... Sarah guessed it with a flash of intuition... ...all those awkward little flashes of guilt.* N COUNT+SUPP : USU+*of*+N UNCOUNT = moment, spark

10 If someone's eyes **flash**, they express a sudden strong emotion, especially anger. EG *Her eyes flashed as she demanded to know what I was laughing at... 'How dare you!' he answered with flashing eyes.* ▸ used as a noun. EG *There was a reproachful flash in her eyes.* V OR V+O : USU V = blaze ▸ N SING WITH DET+SUPP

11 If you **flash** a look or a smile at someone, you look at them suddenly in the way mentioned. EG *He flashed a conspiratorial grin at the other two... Several people flashed glances of recognition at me.* V+O+A *(at)*, OR V+O+O = dart

12 If you **flash** something, you show it to people quickly and then put it away again. EG *She flashed her identification at the guards.* V+O : USU+A

13 If you **flash** information or news to a particular place, you send it quickly by computer, satellite, telex, etc. EG *The computer immediately flashes the information to a control centre... The news had been flashed to all the neighbouring countries.* V+O+A

14 Something that has a **flash** of a particular colour on it has a small patch of bright colour on it. EG *Her jumper is green with a flash of pink on the back.* N COUNT+*of* = spot

15 Something that looks **flash** looks expensive, fashionable, and new; an informal use. EG *Her new car looks really flash.* ADJ QUALIT ↑ smart = swish

16 A man who **is flashing** deliberately exposes his penis to people in public, usually because he has a form of mental illness; an informal term. V : ONLY CONT

17 If you describe an achievement or success as a **flash in the pan**, you mean that it is not likely to be repeated and is not an indication of future achievements or successes. EG *The team's good results at the beginning of the season seem to have been a flash in the pan.* PHR : USED AS C

18 See also **news flash**.

flash back. **1** If your thoughts **flash back** to something, you have a sudden vivid memory of something that has happened in the past. EG *My mind flashed back to what the sisters had said about their mother, all those years ago.* PHRASAL VB : V+ ADV, IF+PREP THEN *to* ↑ return = go back

flashback /flæʃbæk/, **flashbacks**. A **flashback** is **1** a scene in a film or a passage in a novel, play, etc that suddenly returns to events in the past. N COUNT **2** a sudden memory of a past experience which comes to you very vividly. N COUNT

flashbulb /flæʃbʌlb/, **flashbulbs**. A **flashbulb** is a small lightbulb that can be fixed to a camera and that makes a large flash of light so that you can take photographs indoors. N COUNT

flash burn, flash burns. A **flash burn** is a burn that you get if you are near an extremely bright, hot flash, for example a flash caused by an exploding bomb. N COUNT

flashcard /flæʃkɑːd/, **flashcards**. A **flashcard** is a card with a word or words written on it that is used to teach children how to read. N COUNT

flashcube /flæʃkjuːb/, **flashcubes**. A **flashcube** is a small cube containing four flashbulbs, which turns on the top of a camera so that you can take four photographs without changing the bulb. N COUNT

flasher /flæʃə/, **flashers**; an informal word. **1** A **flasher** on a vehicle is a signal light which flashes to show that the vehicle is going to turn left or right. EG *People use their nearside flashers when they're going to stop.* N COUNT = indicator

2 A **flasher** is a man who deliberately exposes his penis to people in public, usually because he has a form of mental illness. N COUNT ↑ exhibitionist

flash flood, flash floods; also spelled with a hyphen. A **flash flood** is a sudden rush of water over dry land, usually caused by a great deal of rain. N COUNT

flashgun /flæʃgʌn/, **flashguns**; also spelled with a hyphen. A **flashgun** is a device that you can attach to, or that is part of, a camera and that causes a flashbulb to work automatically when the shutter opens. N COUNT

flashing /flæʃɪŋ/ is waterproof material used to cover joins in a roof that might otherwise leak. EG *Someone got up on our roof and stripped away all the lead flashing.* N UNCOUNT

flashlight /flæʃlaɪt/, **flashlights**. A **flashlight** is 1 a torch, especially a large one. EG *I could see the beam of his flashlight waving around in the dark... ...a pocket flashlight.* 2 a device containing a flashbulb that you use with a camera to take photographs indoors; an old-fashioned use. EG *The cameras click and the flashlights flash.* 3 any flashing light that is used as a signal. N COUNT ⇑ light; N COUNT ⇑ light; N COUNT

flashpoint /flæʃpɔɪnt/, **flashpoints**; also spelled as two words, especially in paragraph 2. 1 A **flashpoint** is 1.1 the moment at which emotional or political conflict reaches a climax and becomes violent. EG *The crisis in that troubled country neared a flashpoint last week.* 1.2 a place which people think is dangerous because political trouble may start there and then spread to other towns or countries. EG *This country is another very possible flashpoint, precisely because it is so weak.* N COUNT; N COUNT ⇑ site = trouble spot

2 The **flash point** of a substance is the lowest temperature at which it will produce sufficient vapour to ignite when a small flame is put close to it. N COUNT : USU SING

flashy /flæʃi¹/, **flashier, flashiest**. Something that is **flashy** is so smart, bright, and expensive that you find it unpleasant and perhaps vulgar; an informal word. EG *...a flashy sports car.* ◊ **flashily**. EG *He was dressed rather more flashily than usual.* ADJ QUALIT ⇑ ostentatious; ◊ ADV WITH VB = loudly

flask /flɑːsk/, **flasks**. A **flask** is 1 a small flat bottle made of glass or metal and used for holding alcoholic drink such as brandy or whisky that you want to carry with you. EG *Chevington took out a flask of brandy and poured a measure.* ● See also **hip flask**. 2 a glass bottle with a narrow neck and a bowl-shaped bottom, used especially in chemistry for boiling liquids or preparing gases. 3 the same as a Thermos flask; an informal use. N COUNT : ALSO N + *of* + N UNCOUNT ⇑ container; N COUNT; N COUNT

flat /flæt/, **flats; flatter, flattest**. 1 A **flat** is a set of rooms for living in, usually on one floor and part of a larger building. A flat usually includes a kitchen and bathroom. EG *...they rented a furnished flat in Rummidge... ...a ground floor flat... ...a block of flats.* N COUNT ⇑ dwelling = apartment

2 Something that is **flat** 2.1 is level and horizontal rather than sloping, curved, or round. EG *He believes that the earth is flat... The ceiling of the Sistine Chapel is not flat... Use a saucepan with a flat base.* ADJ QUALIT

2.2 has no raised or hollow parts, such as lumps, bumps, or wrinkles. EG *He took the handkerchief and smoothed it flat... ...the flatter part of the island.* 2.3 is not as round or pointed as things of that kind usually are. EG *...a huge man with a broad flat nose... She is rather flat-chested.* ADJ QUALIT ⇑ smooth; ADJ QUALIT

3 If something is in a position **flat** against or on a surface, it is not curved or bent, but all of it is touching that surface. EG *He was lying flat on his back... The rest of us pressed flat against the walls... She let the blade of her oar rest flat upon the water.* ADV AFTER VB : USU + PREP ⇑ level

4 Something that is **on the flat** is on level ground. EG *Was the car parked on the flat?* PHR : USED AS AN A

5 The **flat** of an object is the flat surface of it. EG *He struck the water with the flat of one of his oars.* N COUNT : IF SING *the* + N, USU + *of*

6 An object that is **flat** is not very tall or deep in relation to its length and width. EG *...a flat, round basket.* ADJ QUALIT = shallow, low

7 Something that folds **flat** can be folded into a flat shape so that it takes up less space. EG *The bed folds flat to store away.* ADJ QUALIT : PRED

8 **Flat** shoes have no heels or very low heels. EG *...old flat red leather shoes.* ADJ QUALIT

9 A **flat** tyre, ball, or balloon has not enough air or no air at all inside. ADJ CLASSIF

10 A **flat** is also a tyre that does not have enough air in it. N COUNT

11 If you are **flat** broke or **flat** out of money, you have absolutely no money; an informal expression. ADV

12 If you do something **flat out**, you do it as fast or as hard as you can; an informal expression. EG *Our staff are working flat out.* PHR : USED AS AN A

13 A **flat** refusal, denial, or rejection is definite and firm, and not likely to be changed. EG *He has issued a flat denial of these allegations.* ◊ **flatly**. EG *She has flatly refused to go.* ● You say **'and that's flat'** to emphasize a refusal, denial, or rejection. EG *You can't have it, and that's flat!* ADJ CLASSIF; ◊ ADV WITH VB; ● PHR

14 Something that is done in a particular amount of time **flat** is done in exactly or not more than the stated length of time; used to emphasize the speed at which something happens. EG *They will be able to hit the targets in four minutes flat.* ADV AFTER N/NUM

15 If someone says something in a **flat** voice, or if they make a **flat** statement, they do not express any emotion. EG *Arnold went on, his voice flat, neither menacing nor inviting... ...not an accusation, just a flat statement.* ◊ **flatly**. EG *'I see,' Boylan said flatly.* ADJ QUALIT = unemotional; ◊ ADV WITH VB

16 A performance, piece of writing, etc that is **flat** is not exciting or interesting. EG *If the actors are word-perfect, I think it makes everything flat and dull... The writing is mostly flat.* ADJ QUALIT ⇑ dull = unexciting

17 If an event or attempt to do something **falls flat**, it is unsuccessful and does not produce the desired effect or reaction. EG *His little joke fell flat... It's pointless spending time on work which might fall quite flat.* PHR : VB INFLECTS ⇑ fail = flop

18 A **flat** sound or colour is dull and lacks variety or richness. ADJ QUALIT

19 **Flat** paint is dull or matt rather than shiny and glossy. EG *You'll need two coats of white paint, the first flat and the second glossy.* ADJ CLASSIF ⇑ dull = matt

20 A **flat** in music is a note or key that is a semitone lower than the note or key which is described by the same letter. It can be represented by the symbol '♭' after the letter. EG *This piece has a lot of flats in it... ...the Scherzo in B flat minor... I played E flat by mistake.* N COUNT, OR ADJ AFTER N

21 A **flat** note or a musical instrument that is **flat** is very slightly lower in pitch than it should be. EG *The tenor was a bit flat... Just don't play flat on 'Stardust'.* ADJ QUALIT, OR ADV WITH VB

22 A **flat** rate or price is one that is fixed at a single rate or price which is the same for everyone whatever the circumstances are. EG *All the passengers pay a flat fare of 50p... We charge a flat rate of £2.00... ...flat-rate contributions.* ADJ CLASSIF : ATTRIB = standard

23 A drink that is **flat** has lost the bubbles of gas it previously contained. EG *This beer's flat.* ADJ QUALIT

24 A **flat** battery has lost some or all of its electrical charge. EG *The batteries have gone flat.* ADJ CLASSIF = dead

25 Someone who has **flat** feet has feet with arches that are too low. ADJ CLASSIF : ATTRIB

26 A low flat area of uncultivated land, especially a marsh, can be referred to as **flats** or a **flat**. EG *...townships built on treeless salt flats.* N COUNT : USU PL, USU MOD + N

27 If trade or business is **flat**, it is slow and not at all busy. ADJ QUALIT

28 Something that is **as flat as a pancake** is very flat or unusually flat. EG *Norfolk is as flat as a pancake.* PHR : USED AS C

29 **in a flat spin**: see **spin**.

flat cap, flat caps. A **flat cap** is the same as a cloth cap. N COUNT

flatfish /flætfɪʃ/, **flatfishes**. The plural can be either **flatfish** or **flatfishes**. A **flatfish** is a sea fish that has a wide, flat body, for example a plaice or sole. N COUNT

flat-footed. Someone who is **flat-footed** 1 has feet with arches that are too low. 2 is unable to move quickly, easily, or gracefully. EG *I'm a rather flat-footed dancer, I'm afraid.* 3 is rather clumsy, stupid, or insensitive in what they say or do. EG *That's typical of his flat-footed approach to things!* ADJ CLASSIF; ADJ QUALIT ⇑ awkward; ADJ QUALIT ≠ sensitive, tactful

flatiron /flætaɪən/, **flatirons**. A **flatiron** is an old type of iron that was heated on a fire or stove rather than by electricity. N COUNT

flatlet /flætlɪ²t/, **flatlets**. A **flatlet** is a small flat. EG *There's a flatlet for rent in Bridge Road.* N COUNT

flatmate /flætmeɪt/, **flatmates**; also spelled with a hyphen. Your **flatmate** is a person who shares a flat with you. N COUNT

flat racing is horse racing which does not involve jumping over fences. N UNCOUNT

flatten /flætə⁰n/, **flattens, flattening, flattened**. 1 If you **flatten** something, or if it **flattens** or **flattens out**, it becomes flat or flatter. EG *The steel rod had been slightly flattened... ...flattened paper cups... ...a bulldozer flattening out the ruts in the* V-ERG, OR PHRASAL VB : V-ERG + ADV *road... ...where the foothills flattened out to meet the Bay shore.*

2 If you **flatten** something, especially a building or a crop, you destroy it by knocking or pushing it down. EG *The slums have been flattened.* V+O ⇑ crush

3 If you **flatten** yourself against something, you press yourself flat against it, for example in order not to be seen. EG *She flattened herself against the door.* V+O (REFL)+A

4 If you **flatten** someone, 4.1 you make them fall over by hitting them very violently or suddenly. EG *I watched Carpentier flatten Wells in 73 seconds.* 4.2 you defeat them completely in a contest or argument. EG *Her questions completely flattened me.* V+O ⇑ knock over; V+O = crush

flattened /flætəᵒnd/ is used to describe something which has a flatter shape than normal. EG *...a grotesque creature with a flattened body... ...the flattened 'X' symbol.* ADJ CLASSIF

flatter /flætə/, **flatters, flattering, flattered.** 1 If you **flatter** someone, you tell them or imply that they are more attractive, important, or clever than they really are in order to please them or persuade them to do something. EG *Jamie was as good at flattering others as he was at praising himself... You flatter me. I'm not that important.* V OR V+O : USU V+O ⇑ compliment

2 If you **are flattered** that someone has done something, you are pleased and made to feel rather important by the way that they have behaved towards you, especially when this is unexpected. EG *I was flattered that he remembered my name... I'm all the more flattered to be invited to your home.* V+O, OR V+O+REPORT-CL, USU PASS

◇ **flattered.** EG *I couldn't decide whether I felt flattered or threatened.* ◇ **flattering.** EG *They listened to him with a flattering interest.* ◇ ADJ QUALIT ◇ ADJ QUALIT

3 If you **flatter** yourself that something is the case, you believe, perhaps wrongly, something good about yourself or your abilities. EG *I rather flatter myself I've been reserved for a better fate... I flatter myself on being a good judge of character.* V+O (REFL)+REPORT-CL, OR V+O (REFL) : IF+PREP THEN on

4 Something that **flatters** you makes you appear more attractive. EG *That dress doesn't flatter her, does it?* ◇ **flattering.** EG *That's a very flattering dress!... 'We saw a lot of pictures of Wellington.'–'Were they flattering?'* V+O = suit ◇ ADJ QUALIT

flatterer /flætərə/, **flatterers.** A **flatterer** is someone who flatters people. EG *'You look really nice in that dress.'–'Flatterer!'* N COUNT/VOC ⇑ person

flattery /flætəᵒri¹/ consists of flattering words or behaviour. EG *He was immune to the flattery of political leaders.* N UNCOUNT ⇑ compliment

flatties /flæti¹z/ are shoes with no heels or with very low heels; an informal word. N PLURAL

flatulence /flætjə⁴ləns/ is too much gas in a person's stomach or bowels, which causes an uncomfortable feeling. N UNCOUNT = wind

flaunt /flɔːnt/, **flaunts, flaunting, flaunted.** If you **flaunt** your valuable possessions, abilities, or qualities, you display them in a very obvious way in order to try to obtain other people's admiration or to shock them. EG *They flaunt their engagement rings... He claimed his wife had flaunted her infidelity... ...his public arrogance and the flaunting of his criminal wealth.* V+O ⇑ show off

flautist /flɔːtɪst/, **flautists.** A **flautist** is someone who plays the flute, especially as their job. N COUNT ⇑ musician

flavour /fleɪvə/, **flavours, flavouring, flavoured**; also spelled **flavor** in American English. 1 The **flavour** of a particular food or drink is the taste that it has. EG *...the flavour of the honey... Do you think that improves the flavour?* N COUNT/UNCOUNT

2 The **flavour** that something has is a quality of it which seems either to be special to it or to remind you strongly of something else. EG *Pimlico has its own peculiar flavour and atmosphere... ...drama with an African flavour.* N UNCOUNT/COUNT : USU+SUPP = feel

3 If you **flavour** food or drink with something, you add this thing to the food or drink to give it a particular taste. EG *...stock flavoured with herbs or onions... Hops have been used for flavouring beer since the ninth century.* V+O : IF+PREP THEN with

flavouring /fleɪvəᵒrɪŋ/, **flavourings. Flavouring** is a substance that is added to food or drink to give it a particular taste. EG *It contains monosodium glutamate and other artificial flavourings.* N UNCOUNT/COUNT

flavourless /fleɪvələ¹s/. Food that is **flavourless** has a boring and uninteresting taste. EG *...gigantic insipid tomatoes, huge flavourless lettuces.* ADJ QUALIT

flaw /flɔː/, **flaws.** 1 A **flaw** in something such as cloth, glass, or a design or pattern is a fault or mark in it that should not be there. EG *There's a flaw in this cloth, but it's a tiny one.* N COUNT : IF+PREP THEN in

2 A **flaw** in something such as a plan, theory, or argument is a mistake in it, which causes it to be less effective or valid. EG *The Bill contained a flaw which made it, initially, unworkable... Did you spot the flaw in his argument?* N COUNT : IF+PREP THEN in = fault

3 A **flaw** in someone's character is an undesirable quality that they possess which spoils the rest of their good qualities. EG *Some flaw in my nature has made me indifferent to slander.* N COUNT : IF+PREP THEN in = failing

flawed /flɔːd/. Something that is **flawed** has a fault, mistake, or mark in it. EG *We are all flawed in some way... ...trying to find ways of improving their flawed arguments.* ADJ CLASSIF = defective

flawless /flɔːlɪ²s/. Something that is **flawless** is perfect and has no flaws. EG *It had been a flawless day. ...a flawless performance... ...a flawless complexion.* ADJ CLASSIF = immaculate

flax /flæks/ is a plant with blue flowers. Its stem is used for making thread, rope, and cloth, and its seeds are used for making linseed oil. N UNCOUNT

flaxen /flæksəᵒn/. **Flaxen** hair is pale yellow in colour. ADJ COLOUR

flay /fleɪ/, **flays, flaying, flayed.** 1 If you **flay** a dead animal, you cut the skin off it. V+O

2 If you **flay** someone, you beat them very hard with a stick or a whip, so that some of their skin comes off. EG *When I catch him I'll flay him alive!* V+O ⇑ flog

3 If you **flay** someone, you criticize them severely and attack their beliefs, policies, or actions. EG *Marx expended much energy in flaying these various brands of socialism.* V+O

flea /fliː/, **fleas.** 1 A **flea** is a very small jumping insect that has no wings and feeds on the blood of humans and animals. EG *The cat's got fleas.* N COUNT

2 If you send someone away **with a flea in** their **ear**, you speak to them angrily and reject their suggestion or attempt to do something. EG *Don't blame me if you come back with a flea in your ear!* PHR : USED AS AN A ⇑ criticize = rebuke

flea market, flea markets. A **flea market** is an outdoor market selling cheap second-hand goods and sometimes also antiques. N COUNT

fleapit /fliːpɪt/, **fleapits.** A **fleapit** is an old, shabby cinema or theatre; an informal word used in British English. N COUNT

fleck /flɛk/, **flecks, flecking, flecked.** 1 A **fleck** is 1.1 a small mark, or a small amount of something that appears as a small mark, that is a different colour from its background. EG *Its egg is green with irregular flecks of white... Little flecks of white powder floated on top.* 1.2 a pattern of small marks of a particular colour. EG *His coat is blue with a grey fleck.* N COUNT : USU N+of+N UNCOUNT = speck; N COUNT, OR N SING : a+N

2 Something that **is flecked** with something is marked or covered with small flecks of it. EG *...the eyes, dull grey, and flecked with dots of milky white.* V+O : USU PASS+A (with) = spatter, speckle

fled /flɛd/ is the past tense and past participle of **flee.** V

fledgling /flɛdʒlɪŋ/, **fledglings.** 1 A **fledgling** is a young bird that has its feathers and is learning to fly. N COUNT

2 You use **fledgling** to describe a person or organization that is new or inexperienced. EG *...fledgling industries.* ADJ CLASSIF : ATTRIB

flee /fliː/, **flees, fleeing, fled.** To **flee** from something or someone, or to **flee** a person or place means to run quickly away from the person, place, or thing mentioned, especially because of danger or fear. EG *Local tribesmen fled in fear... He had to flee to Tanzania... Along with thousands of others, he fled the country... The city's population prepared to flee the heat for the relative cool of the rivers.* V OR V+O : NO PASS ⇑ escape

fleece /fliːs/, **fleeces, fleecing, fleeced.** 1 A sheep's **fleece** is the coat of wool that covers it. N COUNT

2 A **fleece** is the wool, in a single piece, that is cut off one sheep during shearing. N COUNT ⇑ coat

3 If you **fleece** someone, you get a lot of money from them by tricking or overcharging them; an informal use. EG *The pensioners feel they are being fleeced.* V+O IF+PREP THEN of ⇑ cheat

fleecy /fliːsi¹/. Something that is **fleecy** is 1 made of a soft, slightly fluffy material. EG *...a nylon tracksuit with a fleecy lining.* 2 light, soft and fluffy in appearance. EG *...fleecy clouds.* ADJ CLASSIF : USU ATTRIB; ADJ QUALIT

fleet /fliːt/, **fleets.** 1 A **fleet** is a group of ships organized to do something together, for example to N COUNT : USU MOD+N fight battles or to catch fish. EG *Britain had to increase her battle fleet... ...a trawling fleet.*

2 A **fleet** of vehicles is a group of them, especially when they all belong to a particular organization or business, or when they are all going somewhere together. EG *We bought our own fleet of vans... Fleets of buses take them the rest of the way.* N COUNT : ALSO N + *of* + N IN PL

fleeting /fliːtɪŋ/ is used to describe something which lasts only for a very short time. EG *I got only fleeting glimpses of them... ...the fleeting, passing contacts of city life.* ◇ **fleetingly**. EG *...a way to assert personality and power, however fleetingly.* ADJ QUALIT ⇑ brief = passing ◇ AD WITH VB

Fleet Street is a street in London where some British newspapers have their offices; often used to refer to these newspapers and to the journalists who work for them. EG *Things in Fleet Street are very bad just now... ...a possible Fleet Street job.* N PROPER

Flemish /flɛmɪʃ/. 1 **Flemish** is used to describe something which belonged or related to the region of Flanders in northern Europe, especially in medieval times. EG *...Flemish masterpieces.* ADJ CLASSIF

2 **Flemish** is a language that is spoken by some of the people who live in Belgium. N UNCOUNT

flesh /flɛʃ/, **fleshes, fleshing, fleshed**. 1 **Flesh** is 1.1 the soft part of a person's or animal's body between the bones and the skin. EG *...pig's flesh... These thorns stick in bare flesh like tacks.* N UNCOUNT 1.2 human skin and the human body, especially when being considered in a sexual way. EG *...the whiteness of her flesh.* N UNCOUNT

2 The **flesh** of a fruit or vegetable is the soft inner part of it. EG *Cut the avocado in half and remove the flesh.* N UNCOUNT = pulp

3 **Flesh** is also used, especially in the expression 'flesh and blood', to refer to people and the condition of being human and alive. EG *I'm only flesh and blood!... Dreams of universal justice are obstructed by flesh and blood... This is more than flesh and blood can bear!* N UNCOUNT

4 Someone who is your **own flesh and blood** is someone who is a member of your family or a close relative. EG *You are my flesh and blood. I would never do anything to hurt you.* PHR : VB CAN BE SING OR PL = kin

5 The **flesh** is used to refer to sensual or sexual feelings and desires. EG *...sins of the flesh... ...the comforts and pleasures of the flesh.* N SING : *the* + N

6 If you say **'the spirit is willing but the flesh is weak'** you mean that although you are willing to do something, you are too tired or weak to be able to do it. PHR

7 If you meet or see someone **in the flesh** you actually meet or see them, rather than, for example, seeing them in a film or on television. EG *I went up to the Cotton Club to see the great man in the flesh.* PHR : USED AS AN A = in person

8 If you **put flesh on** something, you add details and more information to it. EG *This book puts flesh on the knowledge most of us have about the inequalities of society.* PHR : VB INFLECTS = fill out

9 • **a pound of flesh**: see **pound**.

flesh out. If you **flesh** something **out**, you add details and more information to it. EG *Those are the main points I'll be talking about. Now I'll flesh them out for you.* PHRASAL VB : V + O + ADV ⇑ develop

flesh-coloured. Something that is **flesh-coloured** is yellowish pink in colour. ADJ COLOUR

fleshly /flɛʃli¹/ means relating to sensual and sexual feelings and desires. EG *...a particularly luscious and fleshly poem.* ADJ QULAIT = bodily, carnal

fleshpot /flɛʃpɒt/, **fleshpots**. A **fleshpot** is a place such as a strip club, massage parlour, or brothel, where people go for sexual pleasure. EG *...the fleshpots of Soho.* N COUNT : USU PL

flesh wound, flesh wounds. A **flesh wound** is a wound that breaks the skin but does not damage the bones or any of the body's important internal organs. N COUNT

fleshy /flɛʃi¹/, **fleshier, fleshiest**. 1 Someone who is **fleshy** has a lot of flesh on their body or on a particular part of their body. EG *...a broad-shouldered, rather fleshy individual... ...broad, fleshy jowls.* ADJ QUALIT ⇑ fat

2 Something that is **fleshy** consists of flesh or looks or feels like flesh. EG *Each of these fins has a fleshy base supported internally by bones.* ADJ CLASSIF

3 **Fleshy** leaves or fruits are thick and have a soft, pulpy inner part. ADJ QUALIT

flew /fluː/ is the past tense of **fly**.

flex /flɛks/, **flexes, flexing, flexed**. 1 A **flex** is two or three wires covered in a tube of plastic that carry electricity from a plug to an electrical appliance. EG *The flex isn't long enough.* N COUNT/UNCOUNT

2 If you **flex** your muscles or parts of your body, you bend, move, or stretch them for a short time in order to exercise them. EG *He eased his boots off and flexed his toes in front of the stove.* V+O

flexible /flɛksɪbəºl/. 1 A **flexible** object or material can be bent easily without breaking. EG *The tube is flexible but tough.* ◇ **flexibility** /flɛksəbɪlɪti¹/. EG *Clearly the paper had sufficient flexibility to be easily moulded around an object.* ADJ QUALIT = supple ◇ N UNCOUNT = suppleness

2 Something or someone that is **flexible** is able to change easily and adapt to different conditions and circumstances as they occur. EG *We need a more flexible decision-making system... This is a flexible arrangement... ...flexible working hours... People today must be far more flexible.* ◇ **flexibly**. EG *This makes it easier for a large school to schedule more flexibly.* ◇ **flexibility**. EG *This called for some flexibility of approach... ...the flexibility of a modern computer... ...an economic system that does provide some scope for flexibility.* ADJ QUALIT ◇ ADV WITH VB ◇ N UNCOUNT

flexitime /flɛksi¹taɪm/ is a system that allows employees to vary the time that they start or finish work, provided that an agreed total number of hours are spent at work each week, month, or some other period. N UNCOUNT

flibbertigibbet /flɪbətɪdʒɪbɪt/, **flibbertigibbets**. Someone, especially a woman, who is referred to as a **flibbertigibbet** is foolish and talkative and cannot be trusted to be sensible or serious about anything. N COUNT ⇑ idiot

flick /flɪk/, **flicks, flicking, flicked**. 1 If something **flicks** in a particular direction, it moves with a short, sudden movement, often repeatedly. EG *When it feeds, its huge tongue flicks in and out of its tiny mouth... ...watching the windscreen wipers flick forwards and back... He flicked out his wrist and frowned at his watch... The keeper's head flicked round.* ▸ used as a noun. EG *...a quick upward flick of the arm.* V-ERG + A = jerk ▸ N COUNT = jerk

2 If you **flick** something away or off something else, you make it move quickly away by hitting or pushing it sharply with a little movement of your finger, hand, or something else. EG *He got up and flicked the dust from his suit... Her hand flicked away the tear... She sat there, flicking ash into the ashtray... He shook his head as if he was flicking off beads of sweat.* V+O+A ⇑ brush

3 If you **flick** something such as a whip or a towel, or **flick** something with it, you throw it out quickly to its full length and suddenly pull it back, especially in order to make it hit something. EG *He flicked their bare arms with a tea towel.* ▸ used as a noun. EG *He gave a flick of the whip.* V+O : IF + PREP THEN *with* ▸ N COUNT : IF + PREP THEN *of*

4 If you **flick** pages over or back, or you **flick** through pages, you turn them quickly, especially with your thumb. EG *Flora opened her diary and flicked through the pages... He flicked over the last page.* ▸ used as a noun. EG *...a quick flick through the pages.* V+O, V+A *(through)*, OR V+O+A *(back/over)* = flip ▸ N COUNT + SUPP : USU SING

5 If you **flick** something, you hit it sharply with one of your fingernails by pressing your thumb against the finger and suddenly releasing it. EG *It should give a high 'ping' when flicked with a fingernail... I flicked the hollow door with my finger.* ▸ used as a noun. EG *Give it a flick.* V+O ▸ N COUNT

6 If you **flick** a switch or catch, or **flick** on an electrical appliance, you press the switch or catch sharply so that it moves into a different position and works the equipment. EG *Bradshaw walked to his desk and flicked on the lamp... Karen flicked the safety catch off her rifle... Put your fingers in and flick open the catch of the door... He flicked a couple of light switches.* V+O : USU + A *(on/off)* = click

7 The **flicks** is the cinema; an old-fashioned informal use. EG *Sometimes she just went to the flicks... What's on at the flicks?* N PLURAL : *the* + N

flick through. If you **flick through** a magazine, book, pile of letters, etc, you look at it quickly, turning over pages or individual items to get a brief idea of what it contains. EG *He flicked through the passport, not understanding a word.* PHRASAL VB : V + PREP, HAS PASS = leaf through

flicker /flɪkə/, **flickers, flickering, flickered**. 1 If a light or flame **flickers**, it shines unsteadily, with sudden changes in strength and brightness. EG *The candle flickered by the bed... She was reading by* V ⇑ flutter the flickering light of the T.V. ▸ used as a noun. EG *A faint flicker of lightning lit the room.* ▸ N COUNT

2 A **flicker** of emotion or feeling is one that is experienced or visible only faintly and for a very short time. EG *There was a flicker of fear in the man's eyes... ...the quick flicker of pain... A flicker of annoyance crossed the face.* ▸ used as a verb. EG *Disapproval flickers across her face... The thought had flickered through my brain.* N COUNT: USU SING+of+N UNCOUNT ▸ V+A

3 If something **flickers**, it makes a single light, quick movement or a series of such movements. EG *His eyes kept flickering towards the huge silk purse... Not once did he flicker so much as an eyelid... Swarms of blue dragonflies flicker and hover in the glades.* ▸ used as a noun. EG *'Maybe,' she said, with a flicker of a smile... Even as he watched it, it gave the faintest flicker to its tail.* V OR V+O: IF V USU+A ▸ N COUNT: IF+ PREP THEN *of* ⇑ trace

flick-knife, flick-knives; also spelled as two words. A **flick-knife** is a knife with a blade that is hidden in the handle and that springs out when a button is pressed. N COUNT

flier /flaɪə/. See **flyer**.

flight /flaɪt/, **flights**. 1 A **flight** is 1.1 a journey made by flying, especially in an aeroplane. EG *It had been his first flight... ...the flight of a bird across a city window... The new flight path was fed into the plane's computer.* N COUNT 1.2 an aeroplane that is taking passengers on a particular journey. EG *I had an hour to wait for my flight to London... Can you tell me what time Flight No. 172 arrives in Jeddah?... He bought a ticket for New York on the next flight out.* N COUNT, OR N+ NUM

2 **Flight** is the action of flying, or the ability to fly. EG *They have lost the power of flight... This reduces drag when the bird is in flight... Supersonic flight is very expensive.* N UNCOUNT ⇑ motion

3 A **flight** of birds is a group of them flying together. EG *A flight of duck in formation creaks swiftly over.* N PART+N IN PLURAL

4 **Flight** is also the act of running away from a particular place or avoiding a particular situation which you feel is dangerous or unpleasant. EG *He was born at sea during his parents' flight from the revolution.* N UNCOUNT: USU +SUPP ● If you **put** someone **to flight**, you make them run away from you; a rather old-fashioned expression. ● PHR: VB INFLECTS ● To **take to flight** or to **take flight** means to run away from something. EG *When the police arrived the thieves took flight.* ● PHR: VB INFLECTS = flee

5 A **flight** of steps or stairs is a set of steps or stairs that lead from one level to another without changing direction. EG *She led the way down a short flight of steps... She sounded as though she had just run up two flights of stairs.* N COUNT: USU N +of+N IN PL

6 An idea or statement that is very imaginative but complicated, silly, or impractical can be referred to as a **flight** of fancy, imagination, rhetoric, etc. EG *Despite his occasional flights of emotion and fancy, he is an astute politician.* N COUNT+*of*

flight deck, flight decks; also spelled with a hyphen. 1 The **flight deck** of an aircraft carrier is the flat open surface on the deck where aircraft take off and land. N COUNT

2 The **flight deck** of a large aeroplane is the area at the front where the pilot works and where all the controls are. N COUNT ⇑ cabin = cockpit

flightless /flaɪtlɪ²s/. A **flightless** bird or insect is unable to fly because it does not have the necessary type of wings. EG *On the islands of the Indian Ocean, huge flightless pigeons evolved.* ADJ CLASSIF: ATTRIB

flight lieutenant, flight lieutenants. A **flight lieutenant** is an officer in the British air force of the rank below squadron leader. N COUNT: ALSO IN TITLES

flight recorder, flight recorders; also spelled with a hyphen. The **flight recorder** on an aeroplane the same as the black box. N COUNT

flighty /flaɪti¹/, **flightier, flightiest**. Someone, especially a woman, who is **flighty** is not very serious or reliable and keeps changing from one activity, idea, or partner to another. EG *...the disrespectful way in which these flighty females carry out their duties.* ADJ QUALIT = capricious, fickle

flimsy /flɪmzi¹/, **flimsier, flimsiest; flimsies**. 1 Something that is **flimsy** is weak because it is made of a weak material, or badly made. EG *Poor people can afford only flimsy houses of wood, mud, and straw... All the women had to wear were flimsy shoes.* ADJ QUALIT

2 **Flimsy** cloth or clothing is thin and does not give much protection. EG *They stood shivering in flimsy white muslin gowns.* ADJ QUALIT

3 A **flimsy** excuse or **flimsy** evidence is not very good or convincing. EG *Helen invented a flimsy excuse to take her out of the house... The evidence against him was flimsy.* ADJ QUALIT ⇑ weak = feeble

4 **Flimsy** or a **flimsy** is thin paper on which a copy of a piece of typing is produced when carbon paper is used. EG *He took the folded sheet of flimsy... I found the flimsy of the report we were talking about.* N UNCOUNT/ COUNT

flinch /flɪnt⁰ʃ/, **flinches, flinching, flinched**. 1 If you **flinch** when you are startled or hurt, or when you suddenly see or hear something frightening or upsetting, you make a small sudden movement without meaning to. EG *The children flinched as the cold rain splashed them... He flinched every time she spoke to him... He let the match burn down to his thumb and forefinger without flinching.* V = wince

2 If you **flinch** from something unpleasant, you are unwilling to do it or think about it, or you avoid doing it. EG *...men who would not flinch from assassinating a president... They flinched from the prospect of starting again in a new place.* V: IF+PREP THEN *from* ⇑ shun

fling /flɪŋ/, **flings, flinging, flung**. 1 If you **fling** something somewhere, you throw it there using a lot of force. EG *He flung a football at me... She took off her hat, flinging it on the grass.* V+O+A = hurl

2 If you **fling** yourself somewhere, you move or jump there suddenly and with a lot of force. EG *He flung himself down at Jack's feet... Charlotte flung herself forward into the water with a great splash.* V+O (REFL)+A = throw oneself

3 If you **fling** a part of your body, especially your arms or head, in a particular direction, you move it suddenly, often in an uncontrolled and violent way. EG *He screamed with pain, flinging his free hand up to cover his eyes... The woman flung her arms around him and kissed him... She flung back her head.* V+O+A = throw

4 If you **fling** someone to the ground or into a particular place or position, you push them very roughly so that they fall over or are forced into that place or position. EG *He flung her to the ground... He let her go with an abruptness that almost flung her on the grass.* V+O+A = throw, hurl

5 If you **fling** something into a particular place or position, you put it there in a quick and careless or aggressive way. EG *When he had finished reading, he flung the paper back on to his lectern... She was busy picking up some last-minute necessities and flinging them into her handbag... The door was flung open by the manager.* V+O+A = toss, chuck, sling

6 If someone **flings** you into prison, they put you in prison quickly and perhaps roughly or without doing it in the proper legal way. EG *Why are they looking at us as if they'd like to fling us all in jail?* V+O+A = clap, throw

7 If you **fling** a remark at someone, you say it in an aggressive way. EG *'I will sell the house anyway,' he flung at her one night... She flung a sarcastic comment in his direction.* V+O+A, OR V+A +QUOTE = hurl

8 If you **fling** yourself into a particular activity, you begin it with a lot of effort and energy. EG *She flung herself into her work.* V+O (REFL)+A *(into)* = throw

9 A **fling** is 9.1 a short period of energetic activity or enjoyment, especially one that is the last one that you will have an opportunity to do or have. EG *It was as if nature was having one last fling before the summer... The boys must have their fling.* N COUNT 9.2 a brief romantic relationship, often a sexual one, which neither of the people involved feels seriously about; a fairly informal use. EG *She had a brief fling while her husband was away.* N COUNT = affair

10 **Fling** can be used instead of 'throw' in many expressions that usually contain 'throw'. Most of these expressions are explained in this dictionary at the noun in the expression.

fling off. If you **fling off** your clothes, you take them off very quickly and carelessly. EG *She ran into the bedroom, where she flung off her dress and took out a clean one.* PHRASAL VB: V+ O+ADV = throw off

fling on. If you **fling on** your clothes, you put them on very quickly and carelessly. PHRASAL VB: V+ O+ADV

fling out. 1 If you **fling out** something that you do not want, you get rid of it from your home, for example by putting it in a dustbin. EG *When we moved house we flung out loads of books.* PHRASAL VB: V+ O+ADV ⇑ discard = turf out

2 If you **fling out** a remark, you say it in a rather PHRASAL VB: V+

aggressive way. EG *They lurk about, ready to fling out their routine insults.* O+ADV, OR V+ADV+QUOTE = hurl

flint /flɪnt/, **flints**. 1 **Flint** or a **flint** is a very hard, greyish-black stone that is used, for example, for building. EG *Embedded in the limestone are nodules of flint... ...a wall made of flints... ...the grey flint parish church.* N UNCOUNT/COUNT

2 A **flint** is a small piece of flint which can be struck with a piece of steel to produce sparks and used to light a fire or cause a gun to fire. N COUNT ⇑ stone

flintlock /flɪntlɒk/, **flintlocks**. A **flintlock** is a type of gun that was used in former times, in which sparks struck from a flint in it would light gunpowder and cause the gun to fire. N COUNT

flinty /flɪnti[1]/. 1 A **flinty** person is uncaring and impossible to persuade to be kind. EG *The colonel was a short, balding man with flinty eyes.* ADJ QUALIT = hard-hearted

2 A **flinty** building or piece of land is made of flints or contains flints. ADJ CLASSIF : ATTRIB

flip /flɪp/, **flips, flipping, flipped**. 1 If you **flip** through a book or file, you turn the pages or documents very quickly, in order to find a particular one or to get an idea of the contents. EG *Renshaw flipped through the book... She flipped through a card-index.* V+A *(through)* = flick

2 If you **flip** a switch, or if you **flip** a device or machine on or off, you turn it on or off by pressing or turning the switch quickly. EG *I reach forward and flip the headlight switch... Flip on the engine... He flipped off the outside light.* V+O, OR V+O+A *(off/on)* = flick

3 If you **flip** something over or into a different position, you turn it or move it into that position with a quick push. EG *Flip the fish on its back... He looked through the notebook, quickly flipping over the pages... He flipped open his notebook... She took the box and flipped the metal clasps off the sides.* V+O+A = flick

4 If you **flip** something somewhere, you hit it sharply, often from underneath with your thumb, so that it moves there through the air, often turning over and over as it moves. EG *He tore off the metal tab and flipped it into the garbage can... Tom flipped a toffee in the air... He flipped the boy a coin.* V+O+A, OR V+O+O ⇑ toss = flick

5 If you **flip** something, you hit it sharply with your finger. EG *He flipped his finger against a glass on the table.* ▸ used as a noun. EG *He gave the letter a little contemptuous flip with his fingers.* V+O = flick ▸ N COUNT ⇑ blow

6 If you **flip**, you suddenly become extremely upset or angry because of something that has happened; an informal use. EG *Her employers said they might prosecute. She flipped.* V = freak

7 If someone is being **flip** or says something **flip**, what they say shows that they are not taking something as seriously as they should. EG *I don't mean to sound flip, but it could be worse, you know... ...Jennifer's usual flip repartee.* ADJ QUALIT = flippant

8 **Flip** is an exclamation used in informal British English to express annoyance. EXCLAM = bother, blow

9 See also **flipping**.

flip-flop, flip-flops. **Flip-flops** are sandals, usually made of rubber, which are held on your foot by a V-shaped strap that goes between your big toe and the toe next to it. N COUNT : USU PL ⇑ shoe

flippancy /flɪpənsi[1]/ is saying flippant things. EG *'This is no time for flippancy,' he said angrily.* N UNCOUNT = frivolity

flippant /flɪpənt/. If someone is **flippant** or says something **flippant**, what they say shows that they are not taking something as seriously as they should. EG *Colin's tone was flippant but his dark eyes were serious... John was offended by the doctor's flippant attitude... ...flippant answers.* ADJ QUALIT = frivolous

flipper /flɪpə/, **flippers**. 1 The **flippers** of an animal that lives in water, such as a seal or a penguin, are the two or four flat limbs it has which it uses for swimming. N COUNT : USU PL ⇑ limb

2 **Flippers** are flat pieces of rubber that you can wear on your feet to help you swim more quickly, especially underwater. N COUNT : USU PL ⇑ aid

flipping /flɪpɪŋ/. You use **flipping** to emphasize what you are saying, especially when you are annoyed; an informal word used in British English. EG *It's flipping impossible!* ADJ CLASSIF : ATTRIB, OR ADV+ADJ/ADV = flaming

flip side; also spelled with a hyphen. The **flip side** of a gramophone record is the side that does not have the main song on it. N SING : *the*+N ⇑ back = b side

flirt /flɜːt/, **flirts, flirting, flirted**. 1 If you **flirt** with someone, you behave as if you are sexually attracted to them, in a not very serious way. EG *She flirted with the barman.* V : IF+PREP THEN *with*, RECIP = dally ◇ **flirtation** /flɜːteɪʃə[0]n/, **flirtations**. EG *He had a mild flirtation with two Danish blondes... She had a gift for flirtation.* ◇ N COUNT/UNCOUNT : IF+PREP THEN *with* = dalliance

2 Someone who is a **flirt** flirts a lot. EG *She had declared Miss Harlowe to be a shocking flirt.* N COUNT : USU SING

3 If you **flirt** with the idea of doing or having something, you consider doing or having it, without making any definite plans. EG *You need to flirt with alternatives... Burlington has flirted for years with the idea of a wood-burning electrical generator.* ◇ **flirtation**. EG *...his brief flirtation with the idea of public service.* V+A *(with)* = toy ◇ N COUNT/UNCOUNT

flirtatious /flɜːteɪʃəs/. Someone who is **flirtatious** behaves towards someone else as if they are sexually attracted to them, in a not very serious way. EG *...a pretty and flirtatious twenty-five-year-old... She kept giving him flirtatious looks.* ADJ QUALIT = provocative

flit /flɪt/, **flits, flitting, flitted**. 1 If you **flit** about or **flit** to a particular place, you fly or move quickly from one place to another, with small light movements. EG *Bats flitted about in the darkening sky... Mr Annett was already there, flitting about the hall from one side to the other... The birds flitted into a pomegranate tree.* V+A = buzz, whizz

2 If an expression **flits** across your face or an idea **flits** through your mind, it is there for a short time and then goes again. EG *An expression of pain flitted across her face... A picture of three boys walking along the bright beach flitted through his mind.* V+A = flash

3 If someone or something **flits** from one thing or situation to another, they do not deal with one thing or stay in one situation for long, but quickly go on to another one. EG *...the butterfly mind which flits from idea to idea... ...this mysterious person who flits in and out of my life.* V+A = dart

4 If you do a **flit**, you secretly leave the place where you have been living; an informal use. N COUNT : USU SING

float /fləʊt/, **floats, floating, floated**. 1 Something that **floats** lies on or just below the surface of a liquid when it is put in it, rather than sinking. EG *Empty things float.* V

2 If something is **floating** in a liquid, or if you **float** it, it is in the liquid, on or just below the surface, and is being supported by it or moving slowly along in it. EG *Simon was floating in the water with his eyes closed... There was seaweed floating on the surface of the water... They floated logs down the river... ...a floating restaurant.* V-ERG : USU+A ⇑ lie

3 A **float** is 3.1 a light object that is used to help someone or something float. EG *The children still learning to swim are holding on to floats.* N COUNT 3.2 a small object attached to a fishing line which floats on the water and moves when a fish takes the bait. N COUNT

4 Something that **floats** in or through the air hangs in it or moves slowly and gently through it or around in it. EG *Thistledown floats across the field... He turned his wallet upside down and six dollar bills floated down on to the table... ...floating banners.* V : USU+A = waft, drift

5 If a sound **floats** somewhere quite far away, it can be heard as a rather soft or faint sound by people there; a literary use. EG *The sound went floating out on the air... His voice floated into the room from downstairs.* V+A ⇑ travel = carry

6 If you **float** somewhere, 6.1 you walk there very lightly and gracefully. EG *She floated up to me to ask if I was Mr Braddock.* V+A = glide, waft 6.2 you are in a particular place or situation, or you do something, without any particular purpose or in a vague way. EG *Her mind was floating somewhere apart from her body... Dreams of future glory floated through her head... He spent his days floating from activity to activity.* V+A = drift

7 If you **float** a project, plan, or idea, you suggest it or start it off. EG *One suggestion floated at Rome was that western and African states should collaborate... She could either sink or float a project with one word.* V+O = initiate, launch

8 If a company director **floats** his or her company, he or she starts to sell shares in it to the public. V+O

9 If a government **floats** its country's currency, or if the currency **floats**, its value in relation to other currencies is allowed to change freely; a technical term in economics. EG *Sterling should be allowed to float.* V-ERG ≠ fix

10 A **float** is also 10.1 a lorry on which displays and people in special costumes are carried in a festival procession. EG *Nuns and priests had organized a float whose theme was the Holy Family.* N COUNT ⇑ vehicle 10.2 a small N COUNT : USU

amount of coins and notes of low value that someone gets before they start selling things so that they are able to give customers change if necessary. EG *Have you got the float ready for the jumble sale tomorrow?* SING ⇑ money

11 See also **milk float**.

float around. A rumour or idea that is **floating around** is often heard or talked about. EG *There are a lot of weird ideas floating around at the moment.* PHRASAL VB : V+ADV ⇑ spread = go around

floating /fləʊtɪŋ/. 1 A **floating** voter or vote is a person who is not a firm supporter of any political party. EG *She was all too familiar with the dilemma of attracting the floating voter.* ADJ CLASSIF : ATTRIB ≠ loyal

2 If a city or area has a **floating** population, people are constantly moving away and new people arriving. ADJ CLASSIF : ATTRIB = transitory

flock /flɒk/, **flocks, flocking, flocked.** 1 A **flock** of birds, sheep, or goats is a group of them. EG *We were followed by a whole flock of sea gulls... Shepherds moved with their flocks to lowland pastures... They owned two goats and a flock of sheep.* N PART+N IN PLURAL

2 A **flock** of people or things of the same type is a group or number of them. EG *A flock of barges sailed past... A flock of memories fought for my attention.* N PART+N IN PLURAL ⇑ set

3 A clergyman's **flock** is the group of Christians who come to his church or live in the area that he has responsibility for; a rather old-fashioned use. EG *The duty of the pastor is to look after his flock.* N COUNT : POSS+N, IF SING VB CAN BE SING OR PL = congregation, parish

4 If people **flock** to a particular place or event, a very large number of them go there, usually because it is interesting or attractive in some way. EG *The startled lunch guests flocked to the windows... Crowds flocked to see the treasures... Miss Clare's old pupils would soon be flocking round her again.* V+A ⇑ gather = crowd, flood, pour ≠ file

5 **Flock** wallpaper has a soft furry pattern on it. ADJ CLASSIF

6 A **flock** mattress or pillow is stuffed with small pieces of cloth. N BEFORE N

floe /fləʊ/. See **ice floe**.

flog /flɒg/, **flogs, flogging, flogged.** 1 If you **flog** something, you sell it; an informal word used in British English. EG *We thought we might be able to flog it to someone.* V+O : IF+PREP THEN *to*, OR V+O+O ≠ buy

2 If you **flog** someone, you hit them very hard with a whip or stick as a punishment for something which they have done. EG *Frequently slaves were flogged.* V+O = lash

◊ **flogging, floggings.** EG *He was sentenced to receive a public flogging.* ◊ N UNCOUNT/COUNT

3 If you say that someone is **flogging a dead horse,** you mean that they are trying to achieve something impossible; an informal expression. PHR : VB INFLECTS

4 Something, for example a joke or idea, that has been **flogged to death** has been mentioned or used so often that it is no longer interesting or useful; an informal expression. PHR : VB INFLECTS ⇑ exhausted

5 If you **flog** yourself or your car **to death** or **into the ground,** you work very hard or drive your car very hard and roughly, so that you are exhausted or your car is worn out; used in informal English. EG *He buys a new car, flogs it into the ground, and then buys another one.* PHR : VB INFLECTS

flood /flʌd/, **floods, flooding, flooded.** 1 If there is a **flood**, a large amount of water covers an area of land or a place which is usually dry, for example when a river overflows or a pipe bursts. EG *In September 1975, floods in north-eastern India made 233,000 people homeless... ...an annual cycle of drought alternating with flood... We had a flood upstairs.* N COUNT/UNCOUNT : ALSO SING=PL = deluge

2 A **flood** is also a large amount of water that flows very fast. EG *Moments later, the flood subsided to a trickle.* ● See also **flash flood**. N COUNT = spate, torrent

3 If something **floods** a place that is usually dry, or if the place **floods**, it becomes covered with water. EG *The dam collapsed, flooding an area of five thousand square miles... The rice fields were flooded... When we took the plug out the kitchen flooded.* V-ERG = deluge

4 If a river **floods** or if it **floods** an area beside it, it overflows, usually after very heavy rain. ● A river that is **in flood** is overflowing because it has more water in it than normal. V OR V+O ● PHR : USED AS AN A = flooding

5 If a liquid **floods** a particular thing, especially a person's body or part of it, a large quantity of it is in that thing or flows through it. EG *They painfully swallowed the saliva that flooded their mouths... The engine is flooded with petrol and cannot operate properly.* V+O : IF+PREP THEN *with*

6 A **flood** of things, or of something, is a large number of them, or a large amount of it, that comes or occurs. EG *She received a flood of grateful telegrams and letters... ...the flood of refugees... There followed a great flood of indignation in the newspapers.* N COUNT : USU SING+*of* = torrent

7 If people or things **flood** into a particular place, they come there in large numbers. EG *This brought more and more migrants flooding into the cities... Calls for assistance flooded into the emergency services.* V+A = pour

8 If you **flood** a place with a particular type of thing, you fill it with so many of them that it cannot hold or deal with any more. EG *Manufacturers have been flooding India with imports from Britain.* ● If a manufacturer or a particular type of goods **floods the market**, a large number of goods are put on sale at the same time, often at a cheap price. EG *Cheap plastic bowls and buckets flood the market.* V+O : IF+PREP THEN *with* ⇑ saturate ● PHR : VB INFLECTS

9 If an emotion, feeling, or thought **floods** you, or **floods** back, you suddenly feel it or remember it very strongly; a fairly literary use. EG *The jealousy which flooded her took away all the strength she had... He lay there, flooded with pain, fear, and hatred... Relief flooded over him... The memories flooded back as we passed the old school.* V+O : USU PASS+*with*, OR V+A = pour, surge

10 If light **floods** a place or **floods** into it, it suddenly fills it. EG *Daylight flooded the room.* V+O, OR V+A *(into)*

11 If your face **floods** with red or if redness **floods** it, it suddenly becomes red in colour because you are embarrassed or angry. EG *Her skin flooding with maroon, she lowered her eyelids... A flush spread over her, flooding her neck and face.* V-ERG : IF V USU +A *(with)* ⇑ blush = flush

12 Someone who is **in floods of tears** is crying a lot. EG *...after a night spent in floods of tears.* PHR : USED AS AN A

flood out. If people are **flooded out**, they have to leave their homes because of a flood. PHRASAL VB : V+O+ADV, USU PASS

floodgates /flʌdgeɪts/. If someone or something **opens the floodgates**, they make it possible for a large number of people to do a particular thing for the first time, or for someone to express their feelings. EG *This opened the floodgates of revolution.* PHR : VB INFLECTS

flooding /flʌdɪŋ/. If **flooding** occurs, an area of land that is usually dry is covered with water when a river or lake overflows or after very heavy rain. EG *There has been heavy rain in many areas, resulting in widespread flooding.* N UNCOUNT

floodlight /flʌdlaɪt/, **floodlights, floodlighting, floodlit.** 1 **Floodlights** are very powerful lamps that are used outside to light public buildings, sports grounds, etc in the dark. EG *He walked to the Temple to see it once again, this time under the floodlights.* N COUNT : USU PL

2 If a building or place **is floodlit**, it is lit by floodlights. EG *The cathedral is floodlit at night.* V+O : USU PASS

floor /flɔː/, **floors, flooring, floored.** 1 The **floor** of a room is the flat part of it that you walk on. EG *A brown suitcase lay on the floor... ...the bathroom floor... The book fell to the floor.* N COUNT : USU SING, USU *the*+N ⇑ ground ≠ ceiling

2 The **floor** of a valley, forest, sea, etc is the ground at the bottom of it. EG *The fish has markings that enable it to blend in with the ocean floor.* N COUNT+SUPP : USU *the*+MOD+N IN SING ⇑ surface

3 The **floor** of a vehicle is the bottom surface of it inside. EG *I shot off with the accelerator pedal flat on the floor.* N COUNT

4 A **floor** of a building is all the rooms that are on a particular level. EG *My office is on the second floor... ...on the top floor... ...a ground floor flat.* N COUNT = storey

5 The **floor** in a place such as a club or disco is the area where people dance. EG *As the last dancers drifted off the floor, Boylan was still at the bar.* N COUNT : USU *the*+N IN SING ⇑ place

6 The **floor** of a stock exchange is the large open area where trading is done. N COUNT+*of*

7 The **floor** is also used to refer to the place where official debates and discussions are held, especially between members of parliament or councillors. EG *He stated his position openly on the floor of the House.* N COUNT : USU *the*+N IN SING

8 If someone has the **floor** in a debate or discussion, they have the right to speak. EG *You now have the floor for the next five minutes.* N SING : *the*+N

9 If a remark or question **floors** you, you are completely unable to answer it or are surprised and confused by it. EG *Bing appeared to be floored by this casual remark.* V+O = stump

10 If you **floor** someone, you hit them so hard that they fall over. EG *I could cheerfully have floored her with my weighty inkstand.* V+O = swipe, wallop

11 If you **hold the floor**, you talk to a group of people for a period of time. EG *Captain Imrie had been holding the floor for over an hour.* PHR : VB INFLECTS

12 If you **take the floor**, 12.1 you start dancing at a dance or disco. EG *Everyone was amazed when he took the floor with Jenny.* PHR : VB INFLECTS **12.2** you start speaking in a debate or discussion. PHR : VB INFLECTS

13 If you **wipe the floor with** someone, you defeat them completely in a competition, fight, or discussion; an informal expression. EG *He wiped the floor with both the Americans and the Canadians.* PHR : VB INFLECTS

14 See also **floored, flooring, dance floor.** ● **Factory floor**: see **factory.** ● **Shop floor**: see **shop.**

floorboard /flɔːbɔːd/, **floorboards.** A **floorboard** is one of the long pieces of wood that a floor is made of. EG *The floorboards creaked.* N COUNT : USU PL ⇑ plank

floored /flɔːd/. A room that is **floored** with a particular material has a floor made of that material. EG *The attic is floored with pine planks.* ADJ CLASSIF : PRED + *with/in*

flooring /flɔːrɪŋ/ is the material that is used to make the floor of a room. EG *...stone flooring.* N UNCOUNT

floor show, floor shows; also spelled with a hyphen and as one word. A **floor show** is a series of performances by dancers, singers, or comedians at a night club. N COUNT ⇑ entertainment

floozy /fluːzi¹/, **floozies.** A **floozy** is a woman or girl who is rather immoral and whose appearance is rather vulgar and untidy; an informal word. N COUNT

flop /flɒp/, **flops, flopping, flopped.** 1 If you **flop** into a chair, onto the ground, etc, you sit or lie down loosely and heavily because you are tired. EG *He flopped down on the bed and read for a while... She flopped into an armchair with a drink.* V+A = collapse

2 If something **flops** onto or against something else, it falls there, moves about, or bounces loosely and rather heavily. EG *His blond hair flopped over his brow... She tipped the pan over and a dozen fish flopped out.* V : USU+A

3 Something that is a **flop** is completely unsuccessful. EG *His first play was a disastrous flop.* ▸ used as a verb. EG *One of their space projects flopped this week.* N COUNT ▸ V

4 See also **belly flop.**

floppy /flɒpi¹/, **floppier, floppiest.** Something that is **floppy** is loose rather than stiff, and tends to hang downwards. EG *...ladies in floppy hats... She wears a big floppy bow on her blouse.* ADJ QUALIT = droopy, limp

floppy disk, floppy disks. A **floppy disk** is a small flexible magnetic disk used for storing data and programs. Floppy disks are used with microcomputers. N COUNT

flora /flɔːrə/. Plants, especially the plants growing in a particular area, are referred to as **flora** in technical or formal English. EG *...the unnecessary destruction of the flora and fauna of our countryside.* N PLURAL OR N UNCOUNT

floral /flɔːrəᵒl/. 1 A **floral** piece of clothing, carpet, birthday card, etc has a pattern or picture of flowers on it. EG *...floral dresses... ...floral wallpaper.* ADJ CLASSIF : USU ATTRIB

2 You also use **floral** to describe something that contains flowers or is made of flowers. EG *...floral decorations.* ADJ CLASSIF : ATTRIB

florid /flɒrɪd/. 1 Something that is **florid** is complicated and extravagant rather than plain and simple; often used showing disapproval. EG *...florid verse... ...a spectacularly florid cast-iron hatstand.* ADJ QUALIT ⇑ ornate = ornamented

2 Someone who is **florid** always has a red face. EG *He was a large, cheerful man, with a florid complexion.* ADJ QUALIT = ruddy

florin /flɒrɪn/, **florins.** A **florin** was a British coin that was worth two shillings. N COUNT ⇑ money

florist /flɒrɪst/, **florists.** A **florist** is a person who has a shop that sells indoor plants and bunches of flowers. EG *A florist's van came with flowers.* ▸ The **florist** or the **florist's** is also used to refer to the shop where flowers are sold. EG *He used to send her daffodils or gladioli–whatever was cheap at the florist.* N COUNT ▸ N SING : *the*+N ⇑ retailer

floss /flɒs/ is soft threads of some kind, for example hair. EG *Spiders exude a silky floss... Use dental floss to clean between your teeth.* ● See also **candy floss.** N UNCOUNT

flotation /fləʊteɪʃəᵒn/, **flotations.** 1 The **flotation** of a company is the selling of shares in it to the public. N UNCOUNT/ COUNT

2 A **flotation** tank or compartment helps something to float because it is filled with air or gas. N BEFORE N

flotilla /flətɪlə/, **flotillas.** A **flotilla** is a group of small ships, usually military ships. EG *His immediate concern was the flotilla of minesweepers several miles ahead.* N COUNT

flotsam /flɒtsəm/. 1 **Flotsam** or **flotsam and jetsam** is rubbish or wreckage, for example bits of wood, that is floating on the sea or has been left by the sea on the shore. EG *They searched for several weeks for identifiable flotsam from the lost planes.* N UNCOUNT ⇑ debris

2 People who do not have homes or jobs and perhaps have had to leave their own country or area may be referred to as **flotsam** or **flotsam and jetsam.** EG *They counted themselves as wanderers, misfits, flotsam and jetsam.* N UNCOUNT = vagrants, waifs

flounce /flaʊns/, **flounces, flouncing, flounced.** 1 If someone, usually a woman, **flounces** somewhere, they walk quickly, with big, exaggerated movements, in a way which suggests that they are angry or upset. EG *She had flounced from the classroom vowing never to return.* V+A

2 A **flounce** is a quick, vigorous movement that you make, especially when you are leaving, for example to show that you do not care about something. EG *Mrs Baggot bustled off with a flounce of her striped poplin skirts.* N COUNT : USU SING

3 A **flounce** is also a big frill round the bottom of a skirt, dress, tablecloth, etc or round the neck or sleeves of a dress or blouse. EG *She wore a wide, whirling skirt with a flounce at the hem.* N COUNT ⇑ decoration

flounder /flaʊndə/, **flounders, floundering, floundered. Flounder** can also be used as the plural form of the noun. 1 If you **flounder** in a place, you move in an energetic, uncontrolled way in an attempt to go somewhere or to stay upright, for example when in water or mud. EG *Ahead, men were floundering in the dark swamps... He floundered towards the shore.* V : USU+A ⇑ struggle

2 If you **flounder**, 2.1 you are unable to think what to say or to decide what to do. EG *Suddenly she asked me: 'What do you think of Jeremy?' I floundered for a moment.* V = dither **2.2** you are in difficulties. EG *The economy continues to flounder.* V = waver

3 A **flounder** is a flat edible fish. N COUNT

flour /flaʊə/, **flours, flouring, floured.** 1 **Flour** is a white or brown powder that is made by grinding grain, usually wheat, and that is used to make bread, cakes, pastry, etc. EG *Add the remaining flour to make a soft dough.* N UNCOUNT

2 If you **flour** something, you cover it with a thin layer of flour. ◇ **floured.** EG *Place the dough on a floured board.* V+O ◇ ADJ CLASSIF : ATTRIB ⇑ powdered

flourish /flʌrɪʃ/, **flourishes, flourishing, flourished.** 1 If something **flourishes**, it continues to exist or function and is successful, active, or widespread, or develops quickly and strongly. EG *Parliamentary democracy cannot possibly flourish in such circumstances... While some international bodies have flourished, others have virtually collapsed... The arts flourished.* ◇ **flourishing.** EG *Flourishing industries had been destroyed... He is alive and flourishing.* V = bloom, thrive ◇ ADJ QUALIT = booming, thriving

2 If a plant or a type of animal **flourishes**, it grows well or is healthy because the conditions it is in are right for it. EG *In these waters, bacteria flourish... There were two or three palm trees flourishing in the promenade gardens.* V

3 If you **flourish** an object, you wave it about in a way that makes people notice it. EG *She rushed in flourishing a document.* V+O = brandish

4 A **flourish** is 4.1 a bold waving or sweeping movement, especially one that is intended to make people notice you. EG *Jack drew his knife again with a flourish.* N COUNT : USU SING = gesture **4.2** a curly line or piece of decoration. EG *...a signature embellished with flourishes.* N COUNT **4.3** a fancy or extravagant action or part of something. EG *He decorated his discourse with quaint flourishes of style and Latin quotations... The old man hated unnecessary flourishes in business matters.* N COUNT ⇑ touch

floury /flaʊəᵒri¹/. 1 Something that is **floury** is covered with flour or tastes of flour. EG *She wiped her floury hands on her apron.* ADJ QUALIT ⇑ dusty

2 **Floury** potatoes go fluffy and break up when they are cooked. ADJ QUALIT ⇑ soft ≠ waxy

flout /flaʊt/, **flouts, flouting, flouted.** If you **flout** something such as a law, an order, or an accepted way of behaving, you deliberately disobey it or do not follow it. EG *Be prepared to flout convention... Our rulers know now that we're prepared to flout their laws if forced.* V+O = disregard

flow /flǝʊ/, **flows, flowing, flowed.** 1 If a liquid, or something that moves smoothly like a liquid, **flows** in a particular direction, it moves steadily and continuously in a stream. EG *The river flows south-west to the Atlantic Ocean... The tears flowed down his cheeks... They have blood flowing in their veins... ...a current flowing in a circuit... Its antennae vibrate as the air flows over them.* ▸ used as a noun. EG *New channels are deliberately cut to alter the flow of the water... The blood flow is cut off... Heavy rains in October 1978 brought mud flows down the mountain.* V : USU+A = stem ▸ N COUNT : USU SING+SUPP = stem

2 If a number of people, pieces of information, ideas, etc **flow** from one place to another, they move steadily and freely. EG *European scientists, engineers, and technicians are flowing into the United States.* ▸ used as a noun. EG *We are seeing a growing flow of farmers and peasants into the cities... There's a good flow of information.* V : USU+A ▸ N COUNT+SUPP : USU SING

3 When traffic **flows** through the streets of a town or city, it moves steadily and without difficulty. EG *...traffic flowing down the streets of Helsinki.* ▸ used as a noun. EG *There was a noisy flow of traffic.* V : USU+A ▸ N COUNT+SUPP : USU SING

4 When the tide or the sea **flows**, the waves gradually reach higher and higher up the beach until high tide. EG *...an ebbing and flowing sea tide.* ▸ used as a noun. EG *...the stormy ebb and flow of the sea.* V = rise, surge ▸ N SING : *the*+N ≠ ebb

5 If a quality or an expression of feeling **flows** from someone or something, it comes from them strongly and continuously or in a natural way. EG *The humblest apologies flowed from him... In ancient China all authority flowed from the Emperor... From confession flows repentance and from repentance forgiveness.* ▸ used as a noun. EG *Who would condemn her for a constant flow of pity towards both males?* V+A *(from)* ▸ N COUNT+SUPP : USU SING+*of*

6 If someone's words **flow**, they are spoken smoothly and continuously without hesitation. EG *Her words flowed on, in perfect sentences.* ▸ used as a noun to refer to these words or their quality of smoothness. EG *She can keep up a non-stop flow of baby talk... 'Flow' and naturalness is necessary for good reading.* V ⇑ progress ▸ N UNCOUNT, OR N SING WITH DET : USU+*of* ⇑ continuity

7 Someone who is **in full flow** is talking fluently and easily and seems likely to go on talking for some time. EG *He stopped me when I was in full flow.* PHR : USED AS AN A

8 If events, situations, or periods of time **flow** one after the other, they happen or are experienced one after the other smoothly, without a break. EG *The days flowed imperceptibly into one another... Things and places flow through our lives at an increasingly fast rate.* V+A ⇑ progress

9 If someone's hair or clothing **flows** about them, it hangs freely and loosely. EG *She let her hair down so that it flowed darkly over her shoulders.* ◊ **flowing.** EG *...women in long flowing robes.* V+A ◊ ADJ QUALIT

10 If something **flows** or if a place is **flowing** with it, there is a lot of it available. EG *When Kwong was two years old, the money ceased to flow... ...a traditional view of Jamaica, an island flowing with liquor and luxury.* V : IF+PREP THEN *with*

flow chart, flow charts. A **flow chart** or a **flow diagram** is a diagram which represents a sequence of actions in a particular process or activity and shows the way they follow on from each other. N COUNT

flower /flaʊǝ/, **flowers, flowering, flowered.** 1 A **flower** is 1.1 the part of a plant which is often brightly coloured, grows on a stem, and only survives for a short time. EG *The hawthorn has white flowers in June followed by orange-red berries.* N COUNT = bloom, blossom **1.2** a stem of a plant with one or more flowers on it when it has been picked, usually with others, for example to give as a present or to put in a vase. EG *...a bunch of flowers... My sister always picked the flowers and arranged them herself.* N COUNT : USU PL

2 **Flowers** are small plants that are grown for their flowers as opposed to trees, vegetables, shrubs, etc. EG *He cleared up the mess and planted flowers on the station banks. ...a flower garden.* N COUNT : USU PL

3 When a plant is **in flower** or when it has come **into flower**, its flowers have appeared and opened. EG *The daffodils are in flower... The roses are just coming into flower.* PHR : USED AS AN A ⇑ flowering = in bloom, out

4 When a plant or tree **flowers**, its flowers appear and open. EG *...all will grow in shade, although they flower and fruit most freely in sun.* V : NO IMPER = bloom, blossom

5 When an idea, artistic style, or political movement **flowers**, it develops fully and becomes popular or successful. EG *Liberties need to grow and flower in times of peace.* V : NO IMPER, USU+A

6 Someone or something that is described as the **flower** of something is the best part or example of it; a literary use. EG *...the flower of the nobility and the first lady of the land... ...a woman in the flower of her youth.* N SING : *the*+N+*of*

7 See also **flowered, flowering.**

flowerbed /flaʊ⁵ebɛd/, **flowerbeds**; also spelled with a hyphen and as two words. A **flowerbed** is an area of ground in a garden or park which has been specially prepared so that flowers can be grown in it. N COUNT

flowered /flaʊǝd/. **Flowered** paper or cloth has a pattern of flowers on it. EG *It was nicely done up in flowered paper.* ADJ CLASSIF ⇑ patterned = floral, flowery

flowering /flaʊǝ⁰rɪŋ/, **flowerings.** 1 The **flowering** of something such as an idea or artistic style is the development of its popularity and success. EG *...the eventual flowering of certain moral values.* N COUNT+SUPP : USU+*of* = blossoming

2 **Flowering** shrubs, trees, or plants are those which are planted mainly for the decorative quality of the flowers that they produce. ADJ CLASSIF : ATTRIB

flower people; also spelled with a hyphen. The **flower people** were people who belonged to a cult of the late 1960s advocating peace and love, using the flower as a symbol of these beliefs. N PLURAL = hippies

flowerpot /flaʊǝpɒt/, **flowerpots.** A **flowerpot** is a small container that is usually made of plastic or clay and round or square in shape. Flowerpots are used for growing plants in. N COUNT = pot

flowery /flaʊǝ⁰ri¹/. 1 A **flowery** perfume, wine, or smell has a strong sweet smell. EG *She was liberally dosed with a flowery perfume.* ADJ QUALIT ⇑ fragrant

2 A **flowery** pattern or fabric has a lot of flowers drawn or painted on it. EG *Her mother was a big woman in a flowery apron.* ADJ CLASSIF = flowered

3 **Flowery** speech or writing contains long and complicated words and literary expressions. EG *...his fondness for dramatic courtroom gestures and flowery speech.* ADJ QUALIT = elaborate, fancy

flown /flǝʊn/ is the past participle of **fly.**

fl. oz is a written abbreviation for 'fluid ounce'. EG *Add 3 fl oz methylated spirit.* N COUNT : USU NUM+N

flu /flu:/ is an illness which is similar to a bad cold but more serious. It often makes you feel very weak and your muscles ache. EG *We had to cancel it because Mummy had flu... I was too weak from the flu to work.* N UNCOUNT = influenza

fluctuate /flʌktjʊeɪt/, **fluctuates, fluctuating, fluctuated.** 1 If the rate, speed, or cost of something **fluctuates**, it is irregular and changes a lot. EG *...adjusting the supply to suit the fluctuating demand for heat... Although prices fluctuated between 1929 and 1972, overall the trend was downward.* ◊ **fluctuation** /flʌktjʊeɪʃǝ⁰n/, **fluctuations.** EG *...fluctuations in temperature... ...avoiding the fluctuations of the money market.* V : NO IMPER ⇑ vary ◊ N COUNT/UNCOUNT : IF+PREP THEN *in/of*

2 If behaviour, an attitude, or the condition or state of something **fluctuates**, its nature changes often and quite noticeably. EG *Friendships blossomed, fluctuated, and died... ...fluctuating opinions... ...local co-operatives, capable of quick response to rapidly fluctuating local needs.* ◊ **fluctuation.** EG *Climatic fluctuations are already playing an important role... ...sharp fluctuations in policy.* V : NO IMPER = oscillate ◊ N COUNT/UNCOUNT : IF+PREP THEN *in/of*

flue /flu:/, **flues.** A **flue** is a pipe or shaft that acts as a chimney taking fumes and smoke away from a boiler or stove. N COUNT

fluency /flu:ǝnsi¹/ is the quality or the state of being fluent. EG *She could speak German with great fluency... ...the clarity and fluency of his diction... ...subjects that require fluency in the written word.* N UNCOUNT : IF+PREP THEN *in/of*

fluent /flu:ǝnt/. 1 Someone who is **fluent** in a particular language, or who speaks **fluent** Spanish, French, Russian, etc can speak or write the language easily and correctly, with no hesitation or inaccuracy. EG *She was fluent in Spanish... It was hard to find people who spoke fluent Portuguese.* ◊ **fluently.** EG *The boy still spoke both languages as fluently as ever.* ADJ QUALIT : IF+PREP THEN *in* ◊ ADV WITH VB

2 Someone whose speech, reading, or writing is **fluent** speaks, reads, or writes easily, smoothly and clearly with no hesitation or mistakes. EG *Fluent readers rarely stop at an unknown word... Rage was making him fluent; the words came easily, in a rush.* ◊ **fluently.** EG *He wrote fluently and without erasures.* ADJ QUALIT = eloquent, articulate ◊ ADV WITH VB

fluff /flʌf/, **fluffs, fluffing, fluffed**. 1 **Fluff** is small pieces of soft, light, woolly thread bunched together. Fluff is usually found in a place where you do not want it to be, for example on smart clothes or in dusty corners of a room. EG *He brushed some fluff from his jacket.* — N UNCOUNT ⇑ material

2 If you **fluff** things such as cushions or feathers, or if you **fluff** them **up** or **fluff** them **out**, you get lots of air into them, for example by shaking or brushing them, in order to make them seem larger and the texture softer and lighter. EG *The little birds faced each other, fluffing their feathers... She fluffed her hair out in big waves... Fluff up the egg-white with a fork.* — V+O, OR V+O+A (out/up) ⇑ puff out

3 **Fluff** is also very soft, newly grown hair or fur such as the hair found on a young animal. EG *...a tiny creature covered with black fluff.* — N UNCOUNT ⇑ down

4 If you **fluff** something that you are trying to do, you are unsuccessful or you do it badly; an informal use. EG *They used to get very cross if I fluffed my lines... She fluffed her exams.* — V+O ⇑ fail = bungle

fluffy /flʌfi[1]/, **fluffier, fluffiest**. 1 Something that is **fluffy** is 1.1 very soft and woolly. EG *...a lovely fluffy little kitten... ...a fluffy jumper.* ◊ **fluffiness**. EG *Just feel the fluffiness, I adore it.* 1.2 covered with fluff. EG *You can't go out like that-your suit's all fluffy!* — ADJ QUALIT; ◊ N UNCOUNT; ADJ QUALIT

2 A cake or other food that is **fluffy** is very light because it has a lot of air trapped inside the particles. — ADJ QUALIT

fluid /flu:ɪd/, **fluids**. 1 A **fluid** is a liquid; used especially in technical or medical English. EG *If fluid seeps out at the top, it may corrode the case... Death may result from loss of fluids... ...petrol and cleaning fluids.* ▸ used as an adjective. EG *After a month and a half it was still completely fluid at the centre.* — N COUNT/UNCOUNT ⇑ substance; ▸ ADJ CLASSIF : PRED

2 **Fluid** movement is relaxed, smooth, and graceful, without any sudden movements. ◊ **fluidity** /flu:ɪdɪti[1]/. — ADJ QUALIT; ◊ N UNCOUNT = fluency

3 A situation, arrangement, idea, etc that is **fluid** does not have any fixed pattern or structure and is likely to change often. EG *...the inability of regimental commands to handle a fluid situation... Opinion in the trade unions is very fluid as regards this question.* ◊ **fluidity**. EG *...the fluidity of the learning situation.* — ADJ QUALIT = variable; ◊ N UNCOUNT

fluid ounce, fluid ounces. A **fluid ounce** is a measurement of liquid. There are twenty fluid ounces in a British pint, and sixteen in an American pint. — N COUNT

fluke /flu:k/, **flukes**. Something that is a **fluke** is something good that has happened accidentally rather than by being planned or arranged; an informal word. EG *Getting that job was a fluke... The police have stumbled on this man by a fluke.* — N COUNT : USU SING ⇑ luck

flummox /flʌmәks/, **flummoxes, flummoxing, flummoxed**. If someone **is flummoxed**, they are confused and do not know what to do or say. EG *Mrs Partridge looked a little flummoxed... He completely flummoxed me.* — V+O : USU PASS ⇑ overwhelm

flung /flʌŋ/ is the past tense of **fling**.

flunk /flʌŋk/, **flunks, flunking, flunked**; an informal word. 1 If you **flunk** an exam or a course, you fail to reach the required standard. EG *He flunked all his science courses.* — V OR V+O

2 If an examiner **flunks** someone, he or she gives them a low mark or assessment for an exam or course, so that they fail it. EG *Who is he? Some PhD student I flunked?* — V+O

flunk out. If you **flunk out**, you are dismissed from a school or college because your work is not good enough; used in American English. EG *You're gonna flunk out if you just sit there watching me study!* — PHRASAL VB : V+ADV

flunkey /flʌŋki[1]/, **flunkeys**; also spelled **flunky**; an informal word. A **flunkey** is 1 a man who acts as a servant in a large house and who wears ceremonial dress. 2 a person who follows or stays close to someone who is powerful or important and who does small, unimportant jobs for them in the hope of being rewarded; used showing disapproval. — N COUNT; N COUNT = sycophant, toady

fluorescence /flʊәrɛsә[0]ns/ is the very bright appearance that fluorescent things have, as if light is shining from them. — N UNCOUNT

fluorescent /flʊәrɛsә[0]nt/. 1 Something that is **fluorescent** has a very bright appearance when light is directed onto it, as if it is actually shining itself. EG *...a fluorescent orange circle fixed to a belt... ...fluorescent paint.* — ADJ CLASSIF ⇑ glowing

2 A **fluorescent** light is usually in the form of a long strip and shines with a very hard, bright light. — ADJ CLASSIF : USU ATTRIB

fluoridation /flʊәrɪdeɪʃә[0]n/ is the action or process of adding fluoride to a water supply; a formal word. EG *...literature that claims that fluoridation is harmful.* — N UNCOUNT

fluoride /flʊәraɪd/ is a mixture of chemicals that is sometimes added to a water supply because it is thought to be good for people's teeth. — N UNCOUNT

flurried /flʌrɪd/. Someone or something that is **flurried** is confused and disorganized because they are being rushed. EG *The child wandered about, deserted, flurried and bewildered... This flurried christening proved unnecessary.* — ADJ QUALIT = flustered

flurry /flʌri[1]/, **flurries**. 1 A **flurry** is a short rush of vigorous activity or action. EG *There was the usual flurry of activity in the hall... The decision raised a flurry of objections... There was a flurry of wings and a bird flew out... This threw the officials into a flurry.* — N COUNT : USU + of ⇑ bustle

2 A **flurry** of something such as snow or wind is a small amount of it that suddenly appears for a short time and moves in a rushed, swirling way. EG *Snow flurries had been predicted... The wind came at them in a flurry... Their front runners collided, sending up a flurry of sparks.* — N COUNT : IF + PREP THEN of = whirl

flush /flʌʃ/, **flushes, flushing, flushed**. 1 If you **flush** or if something **flushes** you, your face goes red because you are embarrassed or because you feel hot or unwell. EG *The captain looked at him, and flushed... The wine had flushed her face and throat.* ◊ **flushed**. EG *Her face was suddenly hot and flushed.* ▸ used as a noun. EG *He looked at her with shining eyes and there was a flush in his cheeks.* — V OR V+O ⇑ blush; ◊ ADJ QUALIT; ▸ N SING WITH DET

2 When you **flush** a toilet or when it **flushes**, the handle is pressed or pulled and the toilet bowl fills with water. EG *She heard the toilet flush... He presses the handle, and flushes the lavatory.* — V-ERG ⇑ operate

3 If you **flush** something down the toilet, you put it into the toilet bowl and operate the handle so that it is washed away. — V+O+A ⇑ dispose

4 If you **flush** something such as a pipe, you clear it or clean it by forcing water or another fluid through it. — V+O

5 Something that is **flush** with a surface is completely flat against or along the surface. EG *The trigger had been sawn off flush with the surface of the breech.* — ADJ CLASSIF : IF + PREP THEN with = level

6 If you **flush** people or things out of a place, you force them to come out. EG *They went into the area to flush out guerrillas who were sheltering there... ...secrets which Cobb will painstakingly flush out.* — V+O+A (from/out/out of) ⇑ draw out

7 Someone who is **flush** has plenty of money or something else that is pleasant, useful, or attractive. EG *I could do with borrowing a fiver, if you're feeling flush... Flush with funds, they could afford to buy all the raw materials they wanted.* — ADJ CLASSIF : PRED, IF + PREP THEN with = replete ≠ lacking, starved

8 A **flush** of something is a sudden or intense feeling of excitement or pleasure about something. EG *A nation in the full flush of economic prosperity.* — N COUNT : USU SING + of ⇑ surge

9 A **flush** of something is also a large amount of it that appears suddenly or quickly. EG *The frogs feast on the great flush of insects that have come with the rain.* — N SING WITH DET + of ⇑ burst = flood

10 In a game of cards, a **flush** is a hand of cards which are all of the same suit. • See also **royal flush**. — N COUNT

flushed /flʌʃt/. Someone who is **flushed** with success, excitement, etc is very excited or pleased as a result of achieving the thing mentioned. EG *He hurried flushed with victory into the office... ...the tribal chieftain, victorious in battle, flushed with success.* — ADJ CLASSIF : IF + PREP THEN with ⇑ filled

fluster /flʌstә/, **flusters, flustering, flustered**. If you **fluster** someone, you make them feel nervous and confused by rushing them and preventing them from concentrating on what they are doing. EG *Go away, you're flustering me.* ◊ **flustered**. EG *The teacher grew flustered and curiously cross... He was so flustered he forgot it.* ▸ used as a noun. EG *...doing several things at once and not getting in a fluster... ...kids who say what they think without fluster or hate.* — V+O : USU PASS ⇑ bother; ◊ ADJ QUALIT; ▸ N UNCOUNT, OR N SING : a+N

flute /flu:t/, **flutes**. A **flute** is a musical instrument made of metal or wood in the shape of a long tube with holes in it. You play it by blowing over a hole at one end while holding the instrument sideways to your mouth. — N COUNT ⇑ wind instrument

fluted /flu:tɪ[2]d/. Something that is **fluted** has a decoration consisting of long inward curving col- — ADJ CLASSIF ⇑ decorated umns or grooves cut or shaped into it. EG *...fluted columns... ...tall fluted glasses.*

flutist /flu:tɪst/, **flutists**. A **flutist** is the same as a flautist; used in American English. N COUNT ⇑ musician

flutter /flʌtə/, **flutters, fluttering, fluttered**. 1 If something **flutters** or if you **flutter** it, it waves up and down or from side to side in small quick movements. EG *His long robe fluttered a little in the wind... Courting male birds flutter their wings like chicks.* ◊ **fluttering**. EG *She sighed with relief, pressing a fluttering hand to her chest.* ▸ used as a noun. EG *He let her pass after one flutter of her long dark eyelashes.* V-ERG ⇑ quiver ◊ ADJ CLASSIF ▸ N COUNT : USU SING ⇑ quiver

2 If something light such as a small bird or insect or a piece of paper **flutters**, it moves through the air making small fast movements. EG *Dragonflies with dark wings flutter over the flowers... The letter fluttered from his hands and down to the steps.* ◊ **fluttering**. EG *Their flight is very different from the fluttering of bats.* ▸ used as a noun. EG *The noise would send a flutter of pigeons skywards.* V : USU+A ⇑ fly = float ◊ N UNCOUNT ▸ N SING WITH DET

3 If you **flutter** from one place to another or if you **flutter about**, you walk or move quickly and nervously. EG *Unable to sit down, she would flutter and fidget about from room to room.* V, OR V+A (about) : IF+PREP THEN *from* = flit

4 If you are in a **flutter**, you are in a very nervous, confused, or excited state. EG *'Good gracious me!' she cried, all of a flutter... He suddenly felt surprise and a flutter of panic.* N SING WITH DET : IF+PREP THEN *of* = dither

5 If something causes a **flutter**, it makes people interested and excited. EG *...revelations which caused a mild flutter among the readers of certain papers.* N SING WITH DET = flap

6 If your heart or stomach **flutters**, you experience a strong feeling of excitement or anxiety. EG *Her heart fluttered. 'Oh Tusker, it's so expensive.'... His heart fluttered with fear.* V : USU+A ⇑ tremble

7 If you have a **flutter**, you have a small bet on something such as a horse race; an informal use. N COUNT ⇑ gamble

flux /flʌks/. 1 Something that is in a state of **flux** is characterized by constant changes. EG *...the opportunities presented by this period of flux... ...years of political flux and turmoil.* N UNCOUNT

2 Something that is referred to as a **flux** is being considered as a flowing mass. EG *...a flux of people and traffic... ...the need to give some shape to the flux of experience.* N SING WITH DET : IF+PREP THEN *of* = stream

fly /flaɪ/, **flies, flying, flew, flown**. 1 A **fly** is a small insect with two wings. There are many kinds of flies, and the most common are black in colour. EG *They headed home, swatting at the biting flies that buzzed around their bodies.* N COUNT

2 When a bird, insect, or aircraft **flies**, it moves through the air. EG *No other creature can fly as far, or for as long as birds... The aircraft was flying above thick fog... The day my canary flew away I cried.* V : USU+A

3 If you **fly** somewhere, you travel there in an aircraft. EG *You can fly from Cardiff to Ostend... His relations came flying in from every corner of the earth.* ◊ **flying**. EG *Flying is the only way to travel.* V : USU+A ◊ N UNCOUNT

4 When someone **flies** an aircraft, they control its movement in the air. EG *Once I was flying my plane and ran into a storm over San Francisco.* ◊ **flying**. EG *Why don't you take up flying?* V OR V+O = pilot ◊ N UNCOUNT

5 If you **fly** someone or something somewhere, you send them there by plane. EG *Exotic fruits were specially flown in for the occasion.* V+O+A

6 If you **fly** an ocean or an area of land, you travel over it in an aircraft or hot air balloon. EG *Next year he's hoping to fly the Atlantic in a hot air balloon.* V+O ⇑ cross

7 If something **flies** about, it moves about freely and loosely, for example in the way that long hair moves about in the wind. EG *He jumped onto the platform with his cloak flying.* V : USU+A

8 If you **fly** a kite or if a kite **flies**, it is made to rise into the air and move about in the wind on the end of a piece of rope or string. V-ERG

9 When a flag is **flying**, it is displayed at the top of a pole. EG *All the flags were flying and the sun was shining.* • to **fly the flag**: see **flag**. V-ERG ⇑ display

10 If you **fly** in a particular direction, you move there with a lot of speed or force. EG *She came flying into the room... His glasses flew off and smashed on the rocks... She went flying down Princes Street... The door to Brody's office flew open.* V+A ⇑ hurtle

11 If you **send** someone or something **flying**, or if they **go flying**, they fall over with a lot of force. EG *He almost sent Eddie flying one day... I tripped over his foot and went flying.* PHR : VB INFLECTS

12 If you say that you have to **fly**, you mean that you have to leave a person or a place in a great hurry. EG *I'm sorry, I must fly... By the time they returned, their prisoner had flown.* V = dash

13 If you say that **time is flying**, you mean that the time is passing very quickly. PHR : VB INFLECTS

14 If rumours or stories are **flying**, they are being discussed a great deal and by a lot of people within a short period of time. EG *Rumours were flying in official circles.* V

15 The front opening on a pair of trousers is referred to as the **fly** or the **flies**. It is usually a zip or row of buttons behind a band of cloth. EG *She started to button up the flies of her shorts... ...a man with his fly open.* N COUNT : SING=PL

16 A **fly** used in fishing is a model of a small winged insect that is usually made of silk or nylon and is used as a bait. N COUNT

17 If you **fly** at someone or **let fly** at them, you attack them, either physically by hitting them, or with words by insulting them. EG *She looked at him as though she were about to fly at his face... One day the man flew at me in a temper... He really let fly on the subject of racism.* V+A *(at)*, OR PHR : VB INFLECTS = let rip

18 If you say that someone **wouldn't harm a fly** or **'wouldn't hurt a fly**, you mean that they are very kind and gentle. PHR

19 If you say that **there are no flies on** someone, you mean that they are not stupid and that they cannot be tricked easily. PHR

20 If people are **dropping like flies** or **dropping off like flies**, large numbers of people are dying within a short period of time. EG *People were dropping like flies from diabetes, malnutrition, and heart disease.* PHR : VB INFLECTS

21 The word **fly** is also used in the following expressions, which are explained at other places in this dictionary. • **a fly in the ointment**: see **ointment**. • **as the crow flies**: see **crow**. • **sparks fly**: see **spark**. • **the bird has flown**: see **bird**. • to **fly in the face of** something: see **face**. • to **fly off the handle**: see **handle**. • See also **flying**.

fly into. If you **fly into** a rage, a panic, or other physical expression of strong emotion, you suddenly feel and show this emotion very strongly. EG *She flies into a temper if I make a mistake... She flew into a rage and screamed out with all her might... He flew into a panic.* PHRASAL VB : V+PREP

flyaway /flaɪəweɪ/. **Flyaway** hair is very soft and fine. EG *This shampoo is recommended for flyaway hair.* ADJ QUALIT

flyblown /flaɪbləʊn/. Something that is **flyblown** is covered with dirty spots or marks, or generally dirty or in bad condition. EG *She took two cakes out of the flyblown display case.* ADJ CLASSIF = pock-marked

flyby /flaɪbaɪ/, **flybys**. A **flyby** is the same as a flypast; used in American English. N COUNT

fly-by-night. A **fly-by-night** business or person in business is unreliable because they are interested only in making money very quickly, and not necessarily legally or honourably; an informal word. ADJ CLASSIF : ATTRIB = shady

flyer /flaɪə/, **flyers**; also spelled **flier**. 1 A **flyer** is a pilot of an aircraft or helicopter. EG *She was taking tea with some dashing young flyers.* N COUNT = airman

2 A bird or insect that is a **flyer** of a particular quality or kind flies in the way mentioned. EG *Hawkmoths are among the swiftest insect flyers.* N COUNT : USU+SUPP

3 See also **high-flyer**.

fly-fishing; also spelled without a hyphen. **Fly-fishing** is is a kind of fishing in which a silk or nylon model of a small winged insect is used as bait. N UNCOUNT = angling

flying /flaɪɪŋ/. 1 If you take a **flying** leap or jump, you jump forward, for example over something, after running forward. EG *She rushed forward and took a flying leap at the fence.* ADJ CLASSIF : ATTRIB = soaring

2 A **flying** animal has wings and is able to fly. EG *...flies and other flying insects.* ADJ CLASSIF : ATTRIB

3 If a person or thing **gets off to a flying start**, the person starts something very well, for example a race or a new job, or the thing starts very well. EG *He got off to a flying start but slowed down towards the end of the race.* • **with flying colours**: see **colour**. PHR : VB INFLECTS

flying buttress, flying buttresses. A **flying buttress** is an arch and vertical column that supports the outside of a wall, especially the wall of a large church. N COUNT ⇑ support

flying doctor, flying doctors. A **flying doctor** is a doctor, especially in Australia, who travels by aircraft to visit patients who live in distant or isolated areas. N COUNT

flying fish, flying fishes. **Flying fish** can also be used as the plural form. A **flying fish** is a type of fish that lives in warm seas. It has large fins that enable it to move forward in the air when it jumps out of the water. N COUNT

flying picket, flying pickets. A **flying picket** is a trade union member or group of trade union members that travels to different factories, offices, etc during a strike in order to persuade people there to go on strike. N COUNT

flying saucer, flying saucers. A **flying saucer** is a round flat spacecraft from another planet, which some people believe they have seen. N COUNT = UFO

flying squad, flying squads. The **flying squad** is a group of police officers who are always ready to travel quickly to the scene of a serious crime. N COUNT : USU *the*+N, IF SING, VB CAN BE SING OR PL

flying visit, flying visits. A **flying visit** is a visit that only lasts a very short time. EG *I'm afraid this will only be a flying visit, as I have to be back in London tonight.* N COUNT

flyleaf /flaɪliːf/, **flyleaves**. The **flyleaf** of a book is a page at the front that has nothing printed on it, or just the title and the author's name. EG *'To Aunt Agnes' was written in a bold hand on the flyleaf.* N COUNT

flyover /flaɪəʊvə/, **flyovers**. A **flyover** is a structure which carries one road over the top of another road. N COUNT = overpass

flypaper /flaɪpeɪpə/ is a long piece of sticky paper that you hang up in a room in order to catch flies. N UNCOUNT

flypast /flaɪpɑːst/, **flypasts**. When a **flypast** takes place on a ceremonial occasion or as a display, a group of aircraft fly through the sky in a special formation. N COUNT

flysheet /flaɪʃiːt/, **flysheets**. The **flysheet** of a tent is the waterproof outer part that covers the inner part and protects it from rain. N COUNT ↑ cover

flywheel /flaɪwiːl/, **flywheels**. A **flywheel** is a heavy wheel that is part of a machine and makes it work at a steady speed. N COUNT ↑ wheel

foal /fəʊl/, **foals, foaling, foaled**. 1 A **foal** is a very young horse. N COUNT

2 A female horse that is **in foal** is pregnant. PHR

3 When a female horse **foals**, it gives birth. V

foam /fəʊm/, **foams, foaming, foamed**. 1 **Foam** is 1.1 lots of small bubbles of air together in a mass, formed when air is mixed in with a liquid. EG *She could see the line of white foam where the waves broke on the beach... ...the pale yellow foam on their coffee.* N UNCOUNT = froth 1.2 a substance that consists of a mass of very small bubbles formed in a chemical so that it is suitable to be used for a particular purpose. EG *Willy squeezed shaving foam from an aerosol and patted it on his chin... ...a foam carpet cleaner.* N UNCOUNT

2 **Foam** or **foam rubber** is soft rubber full of small holes which is used, for example, to make mattresses and cushions. EG *...foam mattresses.* N UNCOUNT

3 If a liquid **foams**, it is full of small bubbles and is often moving. EG *He poured foaming champagne into her glass... The icy cold water foamed over the side of the boat.* V : USU+A ↑ bubble

4 If a person or animal **foams at the mouth** or if their **mouth foams**, a mass of small bubbles comes from their mouth, for example because they are ill or very angry. EG *He looked like a madman, foaming at the mouth... Its ears were back; its mouth foamed.* PHR : VB INFLECTS = froth

foamy /fəʊmi¹/, **foamier, foamiest**. 1 A liquid that is **foamy** has a mass of small bubbles on its surface or consists of a mass of bubbles. EG *The sea was all glossy and pale and foamy like ginger beer.* ADJ QUALIT = frothy

2 Something such as blossom or lace that is **foamy** is pale in colour and made up of light delicate parts or strands; a literary use. EG *...foamy clusters of cream-coloured flowers.* ADJ QUALIT = frothy

fob /fɒb/, **fobs, fobbing, fobbed**. A **fob** is a chain which is used for attaching a watch to a man's waistcoat, or an ornament attached to such a chain. EG *...a watch fob.* N COUNT

fob off. If you **fob off** someone who needs something or is asking for something, you give them something that is not very good or is not really what they wanted, although you pretend it is. EG *He may try to fob you off with a prescription for pills... She felt she was being fobbed off.* PHRASAL VB : V+O+ADV, USU+*with* ↑ deceive = put off

fob off on. If you **fob off** something unwanted or inferior **on** someone, you persuade them to buy it or accept it, usually in a dishonest way. EG *She managed to fob her old car off on an unsuspecting buyer.* PHRASAL VB : V+O+ADV+PREP = unload on

focal /fəʊkəºl/ is used 1 to describe something relating to the point where a number of rays or lines meet. EG *...the focal crossroads, grandly named the 'Place des Nations'.* ADJ CLASSIF : ATTRIB ↑ central 2 to describe something that is very important. EG *In most developing countries, the state is a focal institution.* ADJ CLASSIF : ATTRIB = central

focal point, focal points. 1 Something that is a **focal point** is the thing that someone concentrates on or pays most attention to. EG *Their family is the focal point of their lives... These problems provide the focal point for two new plays by Michael Abbenset.* N COUNT ↑ centre = core

2 The **focal point** of a lens or mirror is the point where the rays of light from it meet; a technical term in optics. N COUNT

focus /fəʊkəs/, **foci, focuses, focusing, focused**. The spellings **focusses, focussing,** and **focussed** are also used. The plural of the noun can be either **foci** or **focuses**. 1 If you **focus** your eyes or an instrument such as a camera or telescope, or if it **focuses**, you adjust your eyes or the instrument so that you can clearly see the thing you want to look at. EG *His eyes, bandaged for twenty-four hours, would not focus... He tried to focus his eyes on a painting above Ellen's head... Each man was focusing a large telescope.* V-ERG : IF+PREP THEN *on* ↑ adjust

2 If a photograph or an instrument such as a telescope through which you are looking is in **focus**, the edges of what you see are clear and sharp. If it is out of **focus**, they are fuzzy and blurred. EG *The only part of the picture which was in clear focus was a small child... The camera was a bit out of focus when I took that one... I'm just trying to get the focus right.* N UNCOUNT : USU PREP+N, OR N COUNT

3 If you **focus** rays of light, or if they **focus** on something, they pass through a lens or are reflected from a mirror and meet at a particular point. EG *He took the glass and focused the sun on some dried wood.* V-ERG : IF+PREP THEN *on* ↑ direct

4 The **focus** of a number of rays is the point at which they meet after passing through a lens or being reflected. N COUNT

5 If you **focus** your attention on something, you look at it or think about it carefully and concentrate on it. EG *As we cannot study all resources, I propose to focus attention on one... Attention focussed on Jack.* V-ERG : USU+*on* = centre

6 Someone or something that is the **focus** of attention or interest is the person or thing to which special attention is being paid or on which everyone is concentrating. EG *Changes in the urban environment are once again the focus of public interest and discussion... This story is used as a focus for discussion... He expected to be the evening's chief focus of attention.* N SING WITH DET : USU+*of* ↑ object

7 Someone's **focus** on a particular thing is special attention that they pay to it. EG *The focus on money and position tends to foster rivalry... A shift in focus had occurred away from issues of civil liberty.* N UNCOUNT = emphasis

fodder /fɒdə/. 1 **Fodder** is food that is given to animals such as cows or horses. N UNCOUNT ↑ food

2 People or things that are **fodder** for a particular thing are considered to be useful for only the purpose indicated. EG *Its people are cannon fodder in wars with bordering states... The documents were useless-waste-basket fodder.* N UNCOUNT+SUPP ↑ material

foe /fəʊ/, **foes**. Someone's **foe** is their enemy; an old-fashioned or formal word. EG *He was succeeded by his political foe, Taylor... The guard challenged him. 'Who goes there? Friend or foe?'* N COUNT

foetal /fiːtəºl/; also spelled **fetal**. **Foetal** is used to describe something relating to or like a foetus. EG *The drug may cause foetal abnormalities... I was curled up in a foetal position.* ADJ CLASSIF : ATTRIB

foetus /fiːtəs/, **foetuses**; also spelled **fetus**. A **foetus** is an unborn animal or human being in its later stages of development. EG *...the fluid that surrounds the growing foetus in the womb.* N COUNT

fog /fɒg/, **fogs, fogging, fogged**. 1 When there is **fog**, there are tiny drops of water in the air which form a thick cloud and make it difficult to see things. EG *I hate driving in fog... Then the fog came down... Winter brought the fogs.* N UNCOUNT, OR N COUNT : *the*+N, USU SING ↑ mist

2 A **fog** is also an unpleasant cloud of something such as smoke inside a building or room. EG *They all* N SING WITH DET : USU+SUPP

smoked cigarettes, and there was a constant nicotine fog.

3 If something made of glass, for example a window, **fogs** or **fogs up**, it becomes covered with steam so that it is difficult to see through. EG *Through the fogged window he saw Denton stop... My glasses are all fogged up.* V, OR PHRASAL VB : V+ADV ⇑ cloud

4 Someone who is in a **fog** is confused and unable to understand something or think clearly. EG *...bewildered scholars who stumble about in a fog... Gradually the fogs of ignorance and clumsiness cleared.* N COUNT ⇑ confusion

fog bank, fog banks; also spelled with a hyphen. A **fog bank** is an area of thick fog, especially at sea. N COUNT

fogbound /fɒgbaʊnd/; also spelled with a hyphen. Something such as an airport that is **fogbound** cannot operate as usual, because of fog. ADJ CLASSIF ⇑ immobilized

fogey /fəʊgi¹/, **fogeys**; also spelled **fogy**. A **fogey** is a boring, old-fashioned person; an informal word. EG *Don't be such an old fogey!* N COUNT : USU *old*+N, ALSO VOC

foggy /fɒgi¹/, **foggier, foggiest**. **1** When it is **foggy**, there is fog. EG *Tomorrow it will be cold, cloudy, and foggy... ...a damp and foggy climate... ...a foggy day.* ADJ QUALIT ⇑ misty

2 If you say that you **haven't the foggiest** or you **haven't the foggiest idea**, you emphasize that you do not know something; an informal expression. EG *I haven't the foggiest idea what it is.* PHR : VB INFLECTS

foghorn /fɒghɔːn/, **foghorns**. A **foghorn** is a loud horn that is used to warn ships about the position of land and other ships in fog. N COUNT ⇑ horn

fog lamp, fog lamps. A **fog lamp** or a **fog light** is a special, powerful light on a car or other vehicle which you use when you are driving in fog. N COUNT

fogy /fəʊgi¹/. See **fogey**.

foible /fɔɪbəºl/, **foibles**. A **foible** is a habit or characteristic that someone has which is considered rather strange, foolish, or bad but which is also considered unimportant and allowable. EG *Their foibles were treated with indulgence.* N COUNT = idiosyncrasy

foil /fɔɪl/, **foils, foiling, foiled**. **1 Foil** is metal in the form of a sheet as thin as paper. It is used especially to wrap food in and keep it fresh. EG *Wrap cakes in foil before storing them... ...aluminium foil... ...the foil wrapper of a bar of chocolate.* N UNCOUNT

2 If you **foil** someone's plan or attempt at something, you prevent them from being successful. EG *Their attempt to recapture Calais was foiled by a traitor... He had planned to leave at four, but he was foiled by Mrs Harlowe, who rang for tea.* V+O = thwart

3 Something that is a **foil** for something else makes its good qualities more noticeable when the two things are experienced together, because of the great difference between them. EG *She had bronzed skin, for which her yellow swimsuit was a perfect foil... Cranberries are fairly sharp, but a good foil to fat meat.* N COUNT : IF+ PREP THEN *for/to* = contrast, complement

4 A **foil** is also a thin light sword used in fencing, which has a button on its tip to prevent injury. N COUNT

foist /fɔɪst/, **foists, foisting, foisted. foist on.** If you **foist** something **on** someone, you force them to have it or experience it. EG *They were not out to foist their ideas and views on the people... Goodness knows what type of manager they might foist on us.* PHRASAL VB : V+ O+PREP = impose

fold /fəʊld/, **folds, folding, folded**. **1** If you **fold** something such as a piece of paper or cloth, you bend one part of it so that it covers another part, often pressing the edge so that it stays in place. EG *Fold the sheet and blankets back at the top... There was a piece of paper folded in two.* V+O : USU+A

2 If you **fold** something or if you **fold it up**, you make it into a smaller, neat shape by folding it several times. EG *Bedding should be folded and left for removal men to pack... They folded the tent neatly... The husband folded his newspaper into a neat rectangle... She folded up some shirts.* ◊ **folded**. EG *She took the folded blanket and spread it out.* V+O, V+O+A *(up)* ≠ open out ◊ ADJ CLASSIF : ATTRIB

3 A **fold** in a piece of paper or cloth is **3.1** a bend that you make in it when you put one part of it over another part, usually pressing the edge so that it stays in place. EG *You need to make three folds in the paper along lines A, B, and C.* N COUNT **3.2** the curved shape made by a piece of cloth when it is not lying flat. EG *The soft light fell on the folds of her dress... The curtains hung in bulging folds.* N COUNT

4 If you **fold** or **fold** up something such as an umbrella or specially designed piece of furniture or equipment, you make it smaller or change its shape by causing parts of it to close up or bend. EG *The bed can be easily erected or folded away... He folded back the partition... The pram had its hood folded down... This is a well designed easel which folds up quickly and neatly.* V-ERG : USU+A ≠ put up

5 If you **fold** something such as your hand or a piece of material around an object, you wrap it around the object. EG *A sheet of paper had been folded around the whole bundle... She folded the napkin sides up around the bowl... He produced a small pebble and folded my hand over it... I found a tiny tooth folded in a little piece of paper.* V+O+A

6 If you **fold** your arms or hands, you bring them together and cross or link them, for example over your chest or in your lap. EG *Fold your arms and sit up straight!... She sat erectly, her hands folded on her black skirt.* V+O ⇑ intertwine

7 If you **fold** part of your body, you bend it or put it close to the main part of your body, especially in a resting position. EG *The bird folded its wings... She sank back again, one leg folded under her.* V+O

8 If the petals of a flower **fold** or **fold up**, they close and come together in the centre of the flower. EG *The buds folded up against the light.* ◊ **folded**. EG *...inside the folded petals of a flower.* V OR V+A *(up)* = furl ◊ ADJ CLASSIF

9 If a business or organization **folds** or **folds up**, it closes or ceases to exist as a result of failure. EG *She had known too many businesses fold up through bad management... The project folded.* V-ERG OR V-ERG +A *(up)* ⇑ stop = collapse

10 The **fold** is used to refer to the home, or to an organization or group to which you feel a sense of belonging. EG *Renounce the devil and return to the fold... Many did enter the fold of the Labour Party.* N COUNT : USU *the*+N IN SING

11 A **fold** is also a small area of a field which is enclosed by a wall or fence and in which sheep can be put, for example to protect them at night. N COUNT

12 A **fold** in a line of rock beneath the earth's surface is a bend in the line which has been caused by movement of the earth's crust. N COUNT

13 See also **folding**.

fold in. 1 In cooking, when you **fold** a substance **into** another substance, or when you **fold** it **in**, you put the first substance into the second substance very gently and mix the two together. EG *Fold the flour into the batter using a metal spoon... Beat the egg whites until stiff and fold in 2oz sugar.* PHRASAL VB : V+ O+ADV/PREP ⇑ add

-fold combines with a number **1** to indicate that something has the stated number of kinds or parts. EG *The problems were two-fold: it was difficult to get finance, and there weren't enough trained people available.* COMB : FORMS ADJ CLASSIFS **2** to indicate that something is multiplied by the stated number of times. EG *Even if we multiplied it ten-fold that would be thirty per cent.* COMB : FORMS ADVS

fold-away. A **fold-away** piece of furniture or equipment is one that is specially designed so that it can be folded into a smaller shape for convenience or storage. EG *...a fold-away table.* ADJ CLASSIF : ATTRIB = collapsible

folder /fəʊldə/, **folders**. A **folder** is a thin piece of cardboard folded into the shape of a container or cover, in which you can keep loose papers. EG *The solicitor took a sealed envelope from the folder on his desk.* N COUNT

folding /fəʊldɪŋ/. A **folding** table, bicycle, umbrella, etc is designed so that you can fold it into a smaller shape to make it easier to carry or store. EG *Amy was sitting on her folding stool which she always carried with her... ...folding steps. ...folding doors.* ADJ CLASSIF : ATTRIB = collapsible

folding money is the same as paper money; used in American English. N UNCOUNT = notes

fold-up. A **fold-up** piece of furniture or equipment is one that is specially designed so that it can be folded into a smaller shape for convenience or storage. EG *...fold-up desks... ...fold-up bicycles.* ADJ CLASSIF, ATTRIB = collapsible

foliage /fəʊli¹ɪdʒ/. **1** The green leaves of a plant are referred to as its **foliage**. EG *Pollution has stripped the trees of their foliage.* N UNCOUNT

2 Leaves together with the small stems, twigs, and branches which they are attached to are also referred to as **foliage**. EG *We carried armfuls of foliage to the bonfire.* N UNCOUNT

folio /fəʊli¹əʊ/, **folios**. A **folio** is a book made with paper of a large size, used especially in the earlier centuries of European printing. EG *...a copy of Shakespeare's first folio of 1623... ...a folio volume of Italian paintings.* N COUNT

folk /fəʊk/, **folks**. **1 Folk** are people; sometimes used showing affection. EG *She was like all the old* N PLURAL : USU MOD+N *folk, she did everything in strict rotation... ...country folk are a suspicious lot... Nearly all English Department folk here, I guess.... Mrs Hogan and I are having some folks round for drinks on Sunday.*

2 Your **folks** are your close family, especially your mother and father; used especially in American English. EG *I don't even have time to write letters to my folks.*
N PLURAL : USU POSS+N ⇑ parents = kin

3 You use **folks** as a term of address in informal English when you are addressing several people. EG *That's all for tonight, folks.*
N VOC = everyone

4 **Folk** music, art, custom, etc is considered to be traditional or typical of a particular community or nation, representing the culture and feelings of the ordinary people there. EG *...this gem of Russian folk wisdom... It was reputedly used as folk medicine to cure snake bites... ...one of the folk songs he had learnt in childhood.*
ADJ CLASSIF : ATTRIB

folklore /fəʊklɔː/ is the traditional stories, customs, habits, etc of a particular community or nation. EG *Island folklore still recounts the story of the raft... ...exhibitions of archaeology, history and folklore.*
N UNCOUNT ⇑ knowledge

folksy /fəʊksi[1]/. Something that is **folksy** is simple and has a style that is characteristic of folk craft and tradition. EG *...her full and folksy long skirt.*
ADJ QUALIT

follicle /fɒlɪkə[0]l/, **follicles**. A **follicle** is one of the small hollows in the skin which hairs grow from.
N COUNT

follow /fɒləʊ/, **follows, following, followed**. **1** If you **follow** someone or something that is moving or travelling, **1.1** you move along behind them. EG *He followed Sally into the yard.... Come on! Follow me!... Lynn got up and made for the stairs. Marsha followed... They followed after me.* **1.2** you go after them without them knowing in order to catch them or find out where they are going. EG *He must have known he was followed... Follow that car.* **1.3** you go to the place that they have recently gone to, and where they are now staying. EG *He followed them to Venice.*
1.1: V OR V+O ⇑ accompany ≠ precede
1.2: V+O = tail
1.3: V OR V+O

2 If an event, activity, or period of time **follows** a particular thing, it happens or comes after this thing; used especially when the events or things are related in some way. EG *In the days that followed, Keith and his mates could talk of nothing else... We now have two introductory sessions, followed by a personal interview... ...the day following the assassination.*
V OR V+O ≠ precede

3 If a particular thing happens **followed** by something else, this thing happens first and then the other thing happens. EG *We voted first, and were followed by the French and the Russians... Use carbon tetrachloride, followed by soap and warm water.*
V+O : USU PASS+BY

4 If you **follow** something with something else, or **follow** it **up** with something else, you do or say something after you have just done or said something else. EG *By 1880 Walker had to open an office in London and follow it with a bottling hall... He followed up this criticism of the Government's record with a personal attack on the Prime Minister... He murmured the word quietly and with great venom, following up with a string of oaths.*
V+O+A *(by/with)*, OR V+O+A *(up)*+A*(by/with)* = chase

5 You use **followed by** to say what comes after something else in a list or ordered set of things. EG *The main product is the vacuum cleaner, followed by washing machines and tumble dryers.*
V+O : ONLY PASS *+by*

6 If you say that something **follows**, you mean that **6.1** it happens as a result of something else. EG *Many advantages would follow if the tree could grow tall... Hunger and poverty followed upon the ruthless operation of this system.* **6.2** it is true or is the case as a logical result of something else being true or being the case. EG *Just because they are old, it doesn't follow that they have to be patronized... ...it doesn't necessarily follow... A disturbing conclusion followed from that.* **6.3** it comes next in a piece of writing or speech, or after another part of it. EG *I learned most of what follows from a parlourmaid called Louise... Several paragraphs followed to the effect that things were getting worse...*
6.1: V : IF+PREP THEN *from/on/upon* = ensue
6.2: V OR V+REPORT-CL : USU *it*+V, IF +PREP THEN *from* ⇑ lead from
6.3: V OR V+O = ensue

7 You use **as follows** to introduce **7.1** a list of people or things or a section of writing or speech. EG *The contents are as follows: one black desk, one grey wastepaper bin, two red and black chairs... It can be summed up as follows: 'Man is a creation of God, and has been given the earth.'* **7.2** a description or explanation of the way that something is done. EG *File your correspondence roughly as follows... The amount of benefit you are entitled to will be worked out as follows.*
7.1: PHR : USED AS AN A = like this, thus
7.2: PHR : USED AS AN A = thus

8 If you **follow** a path, river, line, or set of signs, you go along beside it or from one sign to another, using it or them to show you which direction to go in. EG *We followed a path up along the creek... We followed arrows pointing through subterranean passages.*
V+O : USU+A ⇑ track

9 If you **follow** a particular route or course, you go somewhere by this route or course. EG *Follow the route marked on the map to the church.*
V+O ⇑ use

10 If the edge or surface of something **follows** something else that is next to it, this edge or surface has the same shape as the thing next to it. EG *The boundary follows the Rio Grande river.*
V+O

11 If something **follows** a particular shape or pattern, it has this shape or is in a particular position; used of something long and thin or of a number of things considered to be in a line. EG *The streets follow irregular patterns.*
V+O

12 If you **follow** something with your eyes, you watch it as it moves or you look along a line that it indicates. EG *Its eyes followed her everywhere she moved... Eric and the others could follow the man's finger as it moved across the map... Ralph shaded his eyes and followed the jagged outline of the crags up towards the summit.*
V+O : USU+A ⇑ observe

13 Something that **follows** a particular course of development happens or develops in this way; used especially when you are comparing two things. EG *Frogs have followed a very different line of development... Their debut album follows the pattern set by their singles.*
V+O

14 If you **follow** or **follow out** advice, instructions, a diagram, etc, you do something in the way indicated or advised. EG *She promised to follow his advice... She knew she could trust him to follow out her instructions... This forced them to follow a tight money policy... The diagrams were simple and easy to follow.*
V+O, OR V+O+A *(out)* = carry out

15 If you **follow** what someone else has done, you do it too because you think it is a good thing or because you want to copy them. EG *Other banks tended to follow the trend set by the major ones... Where America leads, the UK tends to follow.*
V OR V+O : USU V+O

16 If you **follow** someone in what you do, you do the same thing or job as they did previously. EG *Is it very difficult to follow Edith Evans in the part?... Michael Manley followed his father into politics.*
V+O

17 If you **follow** something such as an explanation or a plot of a story, **17.1** you understand it and the way its parts relate to each other. EG *He could not really quite follow what Dr Hochstadt was attempting to say... They were having some difficulty in following the plot... He didn't quite follow... You follow me?* **17.2** you listen to it or watch it with great attention. EG *I could see he was following the play attentively.*
17.1: V OR V+O : USU WITH BROAD NEG
17.2: V+O

18 If you **follow** something, **18.1** you take an interest in it and keep informed about what happens. EG *One man who follows its fortunes closely is Christopher Poll... ...the thousands of American couples who followed the case with great interest.* **18.2** you see how each one of a succession of connected events, people, or things came one after the other. EG *...we can follow the history of life through the strata.*
18.1: V+O
18.2: V+O = trace

19 A story, film, or TV programme that **follows** someone or something is about their experiences over a particular period of time. EG *Her story follows an English family on a Rhine holiday... The story follows the events of one Christmas term.*
V+O ⇑ concern

20 If you **follow** a score or written copy of a play, you read it while you listen to it being performed. EG *He liked to follow the score of the music.*
V+O

21 If you **follow** a particular religion, political belief, or leader, you have the religion or belief or you support the leader mentioned. EG *They followed Cromwell during the fighting... Most of them follow the Buddhist faith.*
V+O ⇑ adhere to

22 If you **follow** a particular job, hobby, or way of life, you have this job, hobby, or way of life. EG *He was unable to follow his trade without a union card... Others have been prepared to follow a life of austerity.*
V+O = carry on, practise

23 If you **follow** a particular idea or if you **follow** it **through**, you study or think about it and all its implications to discover whether it is correct or appropriate. EG *He was asked to follow a particular*
V+O, OR V+O+A *(through)*

line of research... Tempting though it may be to follow this point through, it is not really relevant.

24 In a meal or on a menu, the course that is to **follow** is the next course of the meal. EG *I'll have the steak, and ice cream to follow.*
PHR : USED AS AN A

25 The word **follow** is also used in the following expressions, which are explained at other places in this dictionary. ● to **follow suit**: see **suit**. ● to **follow in** someone's **footsteps**: see **footstep**. ● to **follow the crowd**: see **crowd**. ● to **follow** your **nose**: see **nose**. ● to **follow hard on the heels of** something: see **heel**. ● See also **following**.

follow through. 1 If you **follow through** an action or planned series of actions, you complete it. EG *...offensive action, swiftly followed through to the early attainment of an advantage.*
PHRASAL VB : V+O+ADV, OR V+ADV

2 If you **follow through** in a sport such as golf, tennis, or football, you complete the movement of hitting a ball by continuing to move your arm or leg in the same curve after you have hit the ball. EG *You're not following through after playing the stroke.*
PHRASAL VB : V+ADV

3 See also **follow-through**.

follow up. If you **follow up** something that has been said, suggested, or discovered, you try to find out more about it or to take action about it. EG *It's an idea which has been followed up by a group of researchers at Birmingham... I followed up an advertisement for a second-hand Volkswagen.* ● See also **follow-up**.
PHRASAL VB : V+O+ADV = investigate

follower /fɒləʊə/, **followers**. A **follower** of a particular person, group, or belief is someone who supports or admires this person, group, or belief. EG *...Freud and his followers... ...the followers of Chinese communism.* ● See also **camp follower**.
N COUNT : USU WITH POSS = adherent

following /fɒləʊɪŋ/, **followings**. **1** The **following** day, week, etc refers to the next period of time or event that comes after the one of the same kind that has just been mentioned. EG *He died the following day... She intended to come to see the play on the following Friday.*
ORDINAL : *the*+ORDINAL+N ≠ previous

2 Following is also used **2.1** to indicate that something happens after an event and perhaps as a result of it. EG *...the election of Harold Wilson to the leadership following Gaitskell's death in February 1963... Following that outburst, the general was banished.*
PREP
2.2 to refer to something that is about to be said or written. EG *This could be achieved in the following way... Where are the following: Madrid, Thursday Island, Lima, the Azores... The following appeared in the German magazine Stern.*
ORDINAL : *the*+ORDINAL

3 A person or organization that has a **following** has a group of people who support or admire their beliefs, actions, or aims. EG *She has a keen following among rock fans... This religion is too stark to attract a large following.*
N COUNT : USU SING

4 If a boat or vehicle has a **following** wind, the wind is moving in the same direction as the boat or vehicle. EG *Fortunately we had a following wind that day.*
ADJ CLASSIF : ATTRIB ⇑ favourable

follow-my-leader is a children's game in which one child is followed by all the others in a line, and his or her actions are copied.
N UNCOUNT

follow-on, follow-ons. A **follow-on** is the act of following someone or something that has gone on ahead. EG *He proposed an early start for the first group with a follow-on of two more groups the next day.*
N UNCOUNT/COUNT ⇑ movement

follow-through, follow-throughs. A **follow-through** is **1** the completion of an action or planned series of actions. EG *This wouldn't halt the attack but it would at least blunt the follow-through.* **2** the completion of a movement such as hitting a ball. EG *He held his follow-through pose for 10 seconds.*
N COUNT : USU SING; N COUNT : USU SING

follow-up, follow-ups. A **follow-up** visit, programme, etc is done as a continuation or second part of something done previously. EG *There will be a follow-up programme next month to report on the progress made... He needed follow-up treatment from a specialist doctor.* ▸ used as a noun. EG *This conference is a follow-up to an earlier one in Gabon.*
ADJ CLASSIF : ATTRIB; ▸ N COUNT/UNCOUNT

folly /fɒli¹/, **follies**. **1** If you say that a particular action or way of behaving is **folly** or a **folly**, you mean that it is foolish. EG *It would be folly to continue... There is no limit to the folly of mankind... The government persisted in its folly.*
N UNCOUNT/COUNT = foolishness

2 A **folly** is an imitation castle, temple, or other unusual building that is built as a decoration in a large garden or park.
N COUNT

foment /fəment/, **foments, fomenting, fomented**. If someone or something **foments** trouble, especially trouble of a political nature, they cause it to develop; a formal word. EG *...the art of fomenting distrust between your two opponents.*
V+O = stir up

fond /fɒnd/, **fonder, fondest**. **1 Fond** is used to describe someone or something that shows or expresses a strong feeling of affection for a person or thing. EG *His fond parents looked on with a triumphant smile... ...looking at me with fond eyes... Absence makes the heart grow fonder.* ◊ **fondly**. EG *He used to gaze at the old car fondly... She was fondly known as 'Little Madge'.* ◊ **fondness**. EG *I recall with fondness a young woman I met in Corsica.*
ADJ QUALIT : ATTRIB ⇑ loving = adoring; ◊ ADV WITH VB; ◊ N UNCOUNT = affection

2 If you are **fond** of someone, you like them very much and have an emotional feeling for that person which is not quite as strong as love. EG *'I've always been terribly fond of you,' she said.* ◊ **fondness**. EG *I had noticed his growing fondness for her.*
ADJ QUALIT : PRED+*of*; ◊ N UNCOUNT

3 If you say that you are **fond** of something, you mean that you like it or you like doing it very much. EG *Etta was fond of shopping... His mouth was full of sponge cake of which he was particularly fond... I'm not enormously fond of Shaw's plays...* ◊ **fondness**. EG *...my fondness for red wine.*
ADJ QUALIT : PRED+*of*; ◊ N UNCOUNT

4 If you say that someone is **fond** of doing something, you mean that they do it often and that you are rather critical of them for doing it. EG *He was fond of pointing out that children in the past were to be seen and not heard.* ◊ **fondness**. EG *His fondness for name-dropping was irritating to say the least.*
ADJ QUALIT : PRED+*of* = partial to; ◊ N UNCOUNT

5 Fond is also used to refer to something that is foolishly hoped for because it is unlikely to happen. EG *Shaking my head over my fond fancies, I tottered back to bed... ...fond hopes.* ◊ **fondly**. EG *I fondly believed that we could succeed.*
ADJ CLASSIF : ATTRIB = absurd, silly; ◊ ADV WITH VB = naively

fondant /fɒndənt/, **fondants**. A **fondant** is a sugar sweet that seems to melt in your mouth.
N COUNT

fondle /fɒndəᵊl/, **fondles, fondling, fondled**. If you **fondle** someone or something, you touch them gently with a stroking movement, usually to show your love or affection for them. EG *Mothers and fathers must have a chance to fondle their new babies.*
V+O = pet, caress

fondue /fɒndju:/, **fondues**. A **fondue** is a hot sauce, often made with cheese, which you dip small pieces of bread, meat, or vegetable into and eat. There are several kinds of fondue.
N COUNT/UNCOUNT

font /fɒnt/, **fonts**. A **font** in a church is a bowl which holds the water used for baptisms.
N COUNT

food /fu:d/, **foods**. **1 Food** is what people and animals eat and what living things cannot grow without. EG *There was little money left for food or clothing... Take all the food out... ...food supplies... She eats the plainest of foods... ...health foods... ...baby foods... ...breakfast food.*
N MASS ⇑ nourishment

2 If you **are off** your **food**, you have very little or no appetite, usually because you are ill.
PHR : VB INFLECTS

3 If something is **food for thought** or **food for reflection**, it causes your mind to be active, especially by making you think about the way it will affect future events. EG *This supplies food for reflection about the future of the nation... The accident gave drivers food for thought.*
PHR : USED AS O ⇑ material

food chain, food chains. A **food chain** is a series of living things which are considered as being linked because each thing feeds on the thing below it in the series.
N COUNT

food mixer, food mixers; also spelled with a hyphen. A **food mixer** is a piece of electrical equipment which is used in the kitchen for mixing food such as cake mixture.
N COUNT ⇑ device

food poisoning; also spelled with a hyphen. **Food poisoning** is an illness giving you sickness and diarrhoea, caused by eating food that has gone bad.
N UNCOUNT = gastro-enteritis

foodstuff /fu:dstʌf/, **foodstuffs**. **Foodstuff** or a **foodstuff** is a substance which is used as food or used to make a particular food. EG *...foodstuffs such as cookies, candies, and sugar.*
N COUNT/UNCOUNT : USU PL

fool /fu:l/, **fools, fooling, fooled**. **1** If you refer to someone as a **fool**, you mean that they have behaved in a very silly or unintelligent way. EG *Just look what you've done! You stupid fool!... I was a fool. I should have gone when you gave me the chance... She was*
N COUNT, ALSO VOC = idiot

sharp-witted and no fool... He was not fool enough to think that the job would be easy.

2 If you **make a fool of** someone, you make them seem silly by telling people about something stupid that they have done, or by tricking them in some way. EG *They threatened to publish his letters to her and make a fool of him before the world.* — PHR : VB INFLECTS ⇑ ridicule

3 If you **make a fool of** yourself, you behave in a way that makes other people think that you are silly or lacking in judgement. EG *He had never learned to dance and was not prepared to make a fool of himself.* — PHR : VB INFLECTS = show yourself up

4 If you say **'more fool you'** when you have heard what someone has done or plans to do, you mean that you think they have done something unwise which will be of disadvantage to them or to someone else. EG *'I decided to accept it.'–'More fool you, I wouldn't go, no matter how much they offered me.'* — CONVENTION

5 If you **play the fool** or **act the fool**, you behave in a playful, childish, and foolish way, usually in order to make other people laugh. EG *I must seriously ask you not to play the fool.* — PHR : VB INFLECTS = muck about

6 A **fool** is also a person whose job is to do silly things to make people laugh; used especially of a person in former times who was employed in the court of a king or queen. — N COUNT ⇑ entertainer = jester

7 **Fool** is used to describe an action that is stupid or silly; an informal or offensive use, used especially in American English. EG *...somebody making a damn fool speech... This is the kind of fool thing a reader might suppose I did.* — ADJ CLASSIF : ATTRIB

8 If you **fool** someone, you deceive or trick them. EG *The tribesmen weren't fooled by the government's fine-sounding edicts... The pilot releases a flare which fools the missile's guidance system... I was fooled into thinking that she loved me... She certainly had me fooled.* — V+O (NG/REFL) = con, hoodwink

9 **Fool** is a dessert made of fruit, eggs, sugar, and cream that are whipped together to make a light, frothy substance. EG *...a raspberry fool.* — N MASS : USU MOD +N = whip

fool around. 1 If you **fool around** or **fool about**, you behave in a playful, childish, and silly way, often in order to make people laugh. EG *He was always fooling about.* — PHRASAL VB : V + ADV, IF + PREP THEN *with* = lark about

2 If you **fool around**, you behave in a silly, dangerous, or irresponsible way without having thought seriously and carefully about what you are doing. EG *...that fellow you told me about, the one who's fooling around with your wife... I don't want to have to fool around trying to dock two boats in the dark.* — PHRASAL VB : V + ADV, IF + PREP THEN *with* = mess around

foolery /fu:lə^{0}ri^{1}/ is foolish behaviour. EG *...if Nell will stop this foolery of sleeping on the sitting-room sofa.* — N UNCOUNT/ COUNT = silliness

foolhardy /fu:lhɑ:di^{1}/. **Foolhardy** behaviour is foolish because it involves doing something that is too risky. EG *It was considered rather foolhardy for him to quit his job... It would be foolhardy to try.* — ADJ QUALIT ⇑ stupid = rash
◇ **foolhardiness**. — ◇ N UNCOUNT

foolish /fu:lɪʃ/. **1** If your behaviour or action is **foolish**, it is not sensible and shows a lack of good judgement. EG *It would be foolish to suppose that it is an easy thing to change one's faith.* — ADJ QUALIT ⇑ stupid = silly, unwise
▸ used of people. EG *How foolish I was not to have gone earlier to my doctor.* — ▸ = silly
◇ **foolishly**. EG *Foolishly, I allowed myself to be influenced by their arguments... They have acted a little foolishly.* — ◇ ADV, OR ADV SEN
◇ **foolishness**. EG *Have I killed him by my foolishness?* — ◇ N UNCOUNT = folly

2 Someone or something that is **foolish** is so silly, ridiculous, and thoughtless that people are likely to laugh at them. EG *They looked foolish... It is a wildly romantic and foolish book.* — ADJ QUALIT = stupid
◇ **foolishly**. EG *...laughing somewhat foolishly... After 92 years would the piece appear foolishly melodramatic?* — ◇ ADV = ridiculously
◇ **foolishness**. — ◇ N UNCOUNT

foolproof /fu:lpru:f/. Something such as a plan or a machine that is **foolproof** is so well designed, easy to understand, or easy to use that it cannot go wrong or be used wrongly. EG *...a foolproof identification system... The machine was foolproof as drivers would be unable to alter the readings.* — ADJ QUALIT

foolscap /fu:lskæp/ is paper which is about 34 centimetres by 43 centimetres in size. EG *...three sheets of foolscap... ...foolscap paper.* — N UNCOUNT

fool's errand, fool's errands. A **fool's errand** is something that a person does and that they eventually realize is useless. EG *It was a fool's errand; he'll never change his mind.* — N COUNT

fool's gold is a substance that is found in rock and that looks rather like gold. — N UNCOUNT ⇑ mineral

fool's paradise. If you say that someone is living in a **fool's paradise**, you mean that they are in a state of great happiness which is threatened by change, but they are not aware of this threat. — N SING : a + N ⇑ fantasy

foot /fʊt/, **feet; foots, footing, footed.** The plural of the noun is **feet**. The form **foot** can also be used as a plural in paragraph 8 if you are stating measurements or if the noun is in modifier position. **Foots** is the third person singular of the verb. **1** Your **foot** is the part of your body that is at the end of your leg and that you stand on. EG *She's got very small feet... He kept on running in spite of the pain in his foot... ...hopping from one foot to another on the hot sand... It fell to the floor at her feet.* — N COUNT ⇑ extremity

2 If you go somewhere **on foot**, you walk, rather than using any form of transport. EG *The city should be explored on foot... You have to get off the train at the frontier and cross on foot.* — PHR : USED AS AN A ⇑ walking

3 If you get **to** your **feet**, jump **to** your **feet**, etc, you stand up. EG *He rose hurriedly to his feet and ran from the room... She scrambled to her feet... I helped my sister to her feet.* — PHR : VB INFLECTS

4 When you are **on** your **feet**, you are standing up. EG *Posy was on her feet and demanding that everyone listen to her... I need a rest–I've been on my feet all day!* — PHR : VB INFLECTS

5 A **foot** brake, pump, etc is operated by your foot rather than by your hand. — ADJ CLASSIF : ATTRIB

6 A **foot** patrol or a **foot** soldier moves or operates on foot, rather than in a vehicle or on horseback. — ADJ CLASSIF : ATTRIB

7 The **foot** of something is **7.1** the part at the bottom or base of it. EG *I stood at the foot of the stairs and shouted up to her... We camped at the foot of some hills... The body was found close to the foot of the cliffs... ...at the foot of the page.* — N SING : *the* + N, IF + PREP THEN *of*
7.2 the lower end of something such as a bed, where you put your feet. EG *He sat at the foot of his son's bed... ...at the foot of the grave.* — N SING : *the* + N, IF + PREP THEN *of*

8 A **foot** is also a unit for measuring length, equal to 12 inches or 30.48 centimetres. EG *We were only a few feet away from the edge of the cliff... The planes flew at 65,000 feet... ...a 40-foot fall... ...a small hill about 400 feet high... She's five foot eight inches tall.* — N COUNT ⇑ measurement

9 If you **set foot** in a place, you go there. EG *He lived in Paris for years without ever setting foot in the Louvre... It starts raining whenever we set foot out of doors.* — PHR : VB INFLECTS ⇑ visit

10 When someone or something is **on** their **feet** again after an illness or a difficult period of time, they have recovered and returned to a normal condition. EG *We just want to see you on your feet again... ...an economic programme to put the country back on its feet.* — PHR : USED AS AN A ⇑ healthy

11 If you say that someone is **dragging** their **feet**, you mean that they are being deliberately slow in taking any action or making any decisions; used showing disapproval. EG *The government have been dragging their feet on this matter.* — PHR : VB INFLECTS ⇑ delay

12 If you **fall on** your **feet**, you have good luck and are successful even when conditions are unfavourable. — PHR : VB INFLECTS

13 If you say that someone is **finding** their **feet**, you mean that they are starting to feel confident in a new situation. EG *It'll probably be a week or two before he finds his feet.* — PHR : VB INFLECTS = settle in

14 Someone who **has** their **feet on the ground** has a sensible and practical attitude towards life, and does not have unrealistic ideas. EG *These advocates of freedom have not got their feet on the ground.* — PHR : VB INFLECTS

15 If you **start off on the wrong foot** when you are involved in a new situation, meeting new people, etc, you make a bad or unsuccessful start. EG *He got off on the wrong foot by turning up late for his first day at the office.* — PHR : VB INFLECTS

16 Someone who **never puts a foot wrong** never makes any mistakes. — PHR WITH BROAD NEG : VB INFLECTS

17 If you **put** your **feet up**, you relax by sitting or lying with your feet supported by something. EG *She likes to put her feet up after a day's work.* — PHR : VB INFLECTS ⇑ rest

18 If someone **puts** their **foot down**, they assert their authority to prevent something from happening. EG *She'll have to put her foot down... When they started asking me to work at weekends, I decided to put my foot down.* — PHR : VB INFLECTS = be firm

19 If you **put** your **foot in it**, you cause embarrass- — PHR : VB ment by doing or saying something tactless; an informal expression. EG *He really put his foot in it.* INFLECTS = boob

20 If someone has to **stand on** their **own two feet**, they have to be independent and manage their lives without help from other people. EG *The camp gives the children an opportunity to stand on their own feet... Stand on your own two feet man!* PHR : VB INFLECTS

21 If someone is **under** your **feet**, they are in your way and being a nuisance to you. EG *The children are always under my feet... She told us to get out from under her feet.* PHR : USED AS AN A

22 If you **foot it**, you walk or run rather than travelling in a vehicle; an informal expression. EG *We decided to foot it, rather than wait for the next bus.* PHR : VB INFLECTS

23 If you **foot the bill** for something, you pay for it. EG *Who's going to foot the bill for the damage?* PHR : VB INFLECTS

24 A **foot** in poetry is one of the basic units of rhythm into which a line of poetry is divided. N COUNT

25 The word **foot** is also used in the following expressions, which are explained at other places in this dictionary. • **from head to foot**: see **head**. • **hand and foot**: see **hand**. • to **have** or **get cold feet**: see **cold**. • to **sweep** someone **off** their **feet**: see **sweep**.

footage /fʊ̱tɪdʒ/ of a particular event is a film of it or the part of a film which shows this event. EG *...some spine-chilling footage on the effects of nuclear war.* N UNCOUNT

foot-and-mouth disease is a serious disease that affects cattle, sheep, pigs, and goats, in which blisters are formed in the animal's mouth and around its hooves. N UNCOUNT

football /fʊ̱tbɔ:l/, **footballs**. **1 Football** is **1.1** a game played between two teams of eleven players who kick a ball around a field in an attempt to score goals. EG *I go and watch football most weekends... The children are playing football in the garden... ...a football match.* N UNCOUNT = soccer **1.2** any of various similar games played with a round or oval ball which is kicked, thrown, or carried in an attempt to score goals or reach the opposing team's goal line. Rugby, American football, and Australian Rules football are all types of football. N UNCOUNT

2 A **football** is a large ball filled with air, which is used in games of football. N COUNT

footballer /fʊ̱tbɔ:lə/, **footballers**. A **footballer** is a person who plays football, especially as a profession. N COUNT ⇑ player

football pools are the same as the pools: see **pool**. N PLURAL

footbridge /fʊ̱tbrɪdʒ/, **footbridges**. A **footbridge** is a narrow bridge for people travelling on foot. N COUNT

-footed combines with an adjective, noun, or number to indicate that a person or animal has feet of a particular kind, or that they have a particular number of feet. EG *...bare-footed children... Ducks are web-footed... ...a four-footed animal.* COMB : FORMS ADJS

-footer, -footers. **-footer** combines with a number to indicate that a person or thing is a particular number of feet in length or height. EG *The boat we used was a fourteen-footer with an outboard motor.* COMB : FORMS N COUNTS

footfall /fʊ̱tfɔ:l/, **footfalls**. A **footfall** is the sound that is made by someone walking each time they take a step; a literary word. EG *Suddenly he heard heavy footfalls behind him.* N COUNT ⇑ noise

foothill /fʊ̱thɪl/, **foothills**. A **foothill** is a hill or a fairly low mountain at the base of a higher mountain or range of mountains. EG *...exploring the foothills of the Himalayas.* N COUNT : USU PL ⇑ area

foothold /fʊ̱thəʊld/, **footholds**. A **foothold** is **1** a place such as a ledge, crevice, or hollow where you can safely put your foot when climbing. EG *...scrabbling with my feet to find a foothold.* N COUNT **2** a strong or favourable position from which further advances or progress may be made. EG *It was necessary to find a way to gain a foothold in the organization... The guerillas established a firm foothold by offering protection against the government.* N COUNT

footing /fʊ̱tɪŋ/. **1** You refer to someone's **footing** when you are referring to their position and whether they have their feet firmly and safely placed on a surface. EG *He lost his footing, and stumbled to the floor... When you reach the rocks, be sure of your footing before you let go... She could not gain her footing, the water was too deep and too fast.* N UNCOUNT : USU POSS+N = balance

2 If something is on a particular kind of **footing**, it is established, happens, or functions on a basis of the kind mentioned. EG *We've had to get this on a more official footing... The transition to a war footing had really gone very smoothly... The funds should be made available on a wider footing.* N SING WITH DET +SUPP = level

3 If you are on a particular kind of **footing** with someone, you have that kind of relationship or friendship with them. EG *The school's constitution puts parents on an equal footing with staff... She knew all the neighbours but had never got onto a really intimate footing with any of them.* N SING : a+ADJ+ N+with

footlights /fʊ̱tlaɪts/. The **footlights** in a theatre are the lights that are in a row along the front of the stage. N PLURAL ⇑ illumination

footling /fu̱:tlɪŋ/. Something that is **footling** is very unimportant and not worth taking seriously; a rather old-fashioned word, used showing disapproval. EG *Don't let's have a lot of footling excuses for not going.* ADJ QUALIT = paltry

footloose /fʊ̱tlu:s/. Someone who is **footloose** has no responsibilities or commitments and so is free to do what they want and go where they want. EG *...numerous footloose young men from other villages... She's still footloose and fancy-free.* ADJ CLASSIF = fancy-free ≠ tied down

footman /fʊ̱tmə³n/, **footmen**. A **footman** is a male servant who does various jobs such as opening doors or serving food at table, and who often wears a special uniform. N COUNT ⇑ employee

footmark /fʊ̱tmɑ:k/, **footmarks**. A **footmark** is a mark that someone's foot or shoe has made on a surface. EG *...the marks of wheels, hoof-prints and footmarks.* N COUNT = footprint

footnote /fʊ̱tnəʊt/, **footnotes**. A **footnote** is **1** a note at the bottom of a page in a book which provides more detailed information about something that is mentioned on that page. EG *...a lengthy footnote to the last three sections of this chapter.* N COUNT ⇑ comment **2** a comment that you add to give extra information about what you have just been saying. EG *There is a footnote to the invention of the lightning conductor... As a footnote, I should say that he did not actually visit the place himself.* N COUNT **3** an extra later event or development that is fairly unimportant. EG *In terms of the history of art it's just a footnote... All post-1945 economics consists of footnotes to Keynes.* N COUNT ⇑ detail

footpath /fʊ̱tpɑ:θ/, **footpaths**. A **footpath** is a path for people to walk on, especially in the countryside. EG *...the footpath by the river.* N COUNT ⇑ way

footplate /fʊ̱tpleɪt/, **footplates**. A **footplate** is the platform on a steam locomotive where the driver and fireman stand. N COUNT

footprint /fʊ̱tprɪnt/, **footprints**. A **footprint** is a mark in the shape of a foot that a person or animal makes in or on a surface. EG *There were no footprints or any signs of how the burglars got in... ...fresh footprints in the snow.* N COUNT : USU PL = footmark

footsie /fʊ̱tsi¹/. If someone **plays footsie** with you, they touch your feet with their own feet, for example under a table, often as a playful way of expressing their romantic or sexual feelings towards you; an informal expression. PHR+with : VB INFLECTS ⇑ flirt

footslogging /fʊ̱tslɒgɪŋ/. If you are **footslogging** round somewhere, you walk long distances and become very tired. EG *...footslogging around the shops all afternoon.* ▸ used as a noun. EG *The job involves a lot of footslogging.* V : USU CONT+ PREP = trudging ▸ N UNCOUNT

footsore /fʊ̱tsɔ:/. If you are **footsore**, you have sore or tired feet after walking a long way. EG *She was tired and footsore and desperately weary of travelling.* ADJ QUALIT : USU PRED ⇑ aching

footstep /fʊ̱tstɛp/, **footsteps**. A **footstep** is the sound or mark that is made by someone walking each time their foot touches the ground. EG *They heard footsteps and turned... A door was closed softly, footsteps passed along the corridor above.* N COUNT : USU PL • If you **follow in** someone's **footsteps**, you do the same things as they did earlier. EG *She is following in her sister's footsteps... Japan's success with this technology has encouraged other countries to follow in its footsteps.* • PHR : VB INFLECTS ⇑ emulate

footstool /fʊ̱tstu:l/, **footstools**. A **footstool** is a low stool that you can rest your feet on when you are sitting in a chair. N COUNT

footway /fʊ̱tweɪ/, **footways**. A **footway** is a path for people to walk on, for example alongside a bridge or river. N COUNT ⇑ towpath

footwear /fʊ̱twɛə/ refers to things that people wear on their feet such as shoes, boots, or sandals. EG *...the footwear industry.* N UNCOUNT

footwork /fʊtwɜːk/ is 1 the way in which you move your feet, especially in sports such as boxing, football, or tennis, or in dancing. EG *...attention to footwork, angle of the racket, smoothness of strokes.* 2 the way in which you behave in a situation and deal with it. EG *...an economic system that will require some fancy footwork indeed.* N UNCOUNT ⇑ skill; N UNCOUNT = handling

foppish /fɒpɪʃ/. A man who is **foppish** is vain and dresses in fancy, elegant clothes; an old-fashioned word. ADJ QUALIT

for /fɔː/. **For** is used as a preposition after some verbs, nouns, and adjectives in order to introduce extra information. It is also used with some verbs that have two objects in order to introduce the second object. The following paragraphs show the commonest structures in which **for** is used. 1 If something is **for** someone, it is intended to be given to them or to be used by them. EG *She held out the flowers and said, 'They're for you.'... The villagers had bought it for me... He left a note for her on the table... The lounge bar catered for tourists.* PREP

2 If something is done **for** someone, it is done in order to help or benefit them. EG *I am doing everything I can, for all of you... What can I do for you?... It was for her own good... He often cooked for himself.* PREP

3 If you act **for** a particular group or organization, you represent them. EG *Mr Weinberger was speaking for the administration... ...the Labour MP for Oldham West.* PREP

4 If you work or do a job **for** someone, you are employed by them. EG *She's a nurse working for the health service... I was already writing for magazines... It's fun working for him.* PREP

5 You use **for** when you state or explain the purpose of an object, action, activity, etc. EG *I had two knives with me, one for leather work and one for skinning animals... The mug had been used for mixing flour and water... I walked two miles there and back for a couple of pails of water... The boys were digging for bait... I am going to apply for a job... We met for lunch... I'm having treatment for my hay fever.* PREP

6 You use **for** after words such as 'reason' or 'cause', or when you say why something happens in a particular way. EG *Money is the primary reason for a young man's leaving the village... There are no real grounds for optimism... I teased him for using such language... He is serving life sentences for the murder of 13 women... They apologized for being silly... This area is famous for its spring flowers.* PREP

7 You can use **for** to introduce a clause which gives the reason why you made the statement in the main clause; a fairly formal use. EG *They were surprised, for it was almost ten o'clock... This was where he spent a great deal of his free time for he had nowhere else to go... They filed out of the hotel sadly, for there was still so much left to say.* CONJ SUBORD = as, because, since

8 You can use **for** to introduce the cause of the fact that you have just mentioned; a fairly formal use. EG *I could not sleep for the pain in my leg... His department was shut down for lack of funds.* PREP = because of

9 **For** is the preposition that has to be used after some nouns, adjectives, or verbs in order to introduce more information. EG *Trade Unions are reintroducing proposals for a 35 hour week... ...their reputation for being fierce and warlike... ...his designs for the engine... She'll be responsible for all the illustrations... You had to be ready for any emergency... They were aiming for a double share by 1985... The Social Security office will arrange for it to be paid to you.* PREP, OR CONJ SUBORD

10 You use **for** when you make a statement about something in order to say how it affects or relates to someone or what their attitude to it is. EG *I knew it was difficult for him to talk like this... It was a frightening experience for a boy... The only thing that matters for me is other people... For him the survival of his people has always been the most important thing.* PREP, OR CONJ SUBORD

11 You can use **for** to mention a fact or particular aspect of something that you are considering. EG *For social justice, this system could hardly be improved on.* PREP

12 You use **for** when you say that an aspect of something or someone is surprising in relation to other aspects of them. EG *She wore rather too much make-up for her age... He's very young for a doctor.* PREP

13 If you feel a particular emotion **for** someone, 13.1 you feel it in relation to them. EG *He even felt a belated pity for Anthony... I felt sorry for my wife... ...Kurt's contempt for people.* **13.2** you feel it on their behalf. EG *I'm delighted for you... He felt very sad for her.* PREP; PREP

14 You use **for** after words such as 'time', 'space', 'money', or 'energy' when you say how much there is or whether there is enough of it in order to be able to do or use a particular thing. EG *There was room for a small table... There's a place on the shelf for it... We've only got two hours for the exam... He didn't have the concentration required for doing the puzzle.* PREP

15 If you say that something lasts or continues **for** a particular length of time, you are saying how long it lasts or continues. EG *I have known you for a long time... Redundancy money does not last for ever... This is the first competition for 22 years... They were able to stay for a while.* PREP ⇑ during

16 If you say that something continues or stretches **for** a particular distance, you are saying how far it continues or stretches. EG *We drove on for another few miles... Black cliffs rose sheer out of the water for a hundred feet or more.* PREP

17 If you give someone something **for** Christmas, **for** their birthday, or **for** some other occasion, or if you receive or do something **for** this occasion, you give it, receive it, or do it on that occasion. EG *For Christmas, my mother and father gave me a bicycle... We went to the pictures for my birthday.* PREP

18 If something happens or is planned **for** a particular date, day, or time, it happens or is planned to happen then. EG *The meeting has been scheduled for August 30... I've made an appointment for next Tuesday... It was time for tea.* PREP

19 You use expressions such as **for the first time** and **for the last time** when you are talking about how often something has happened. EG *For the first time in our relationship I felt completely happy... I met them for the second time last week.* PHR : USED AS AN A

20 If you leave **for** a particular place or if you take a bus, train, plane, or boat **for** a place, you are going there. EG *200,000 labourers fled their villages for Australia and Canada... We headed for the tunnel to the M4... It happened early one morning before he left for the fields.* PREP

21 If something is bought, sold, or done **for** a particular price or amount, that price or amount is the cost of buying, selling, or doing it. EG *They were forced to sell their house for less than its original price... You can buy the paperback for about two pounds... India spent about £300 million in cash for 1.5 million metric tons of wheat.* PREP

22 If you say that you are **for** a particular activity, you mean that this is what you want or intend to do. EG *Who's for a drink?... I'm for bed.* PREP

23 If you say that something is **not for** you, you mean that you do not think that it is appropriate or suitable for you; a fairly formal expression. EG *Peace and prayer were not for him in his present mood.* PHR + NG : USED AS C

24 If you are **for** something, you are in favour of it. EG *There was a majority of 294 for war, with only 6 voting against... Are you for or against?* • If you are **all for** something, you are very much in favour of it. EG *'Shall we go then?'–'Yes, I'm all for it.'* PREP, OR ADV AFTER N/NUM/BE; • PHR + NG : USED AS C

25 You use **for** after words such as 'argue', 'case', 'evidence', or 'vote' in order to introduce the thing that is being supported or proved. EG *Very conflicting evidence for and against nuclear energy power is being given at the enquiry... This looked like a rather good case for the existence of telepathy... I had to vote for him on principle... ...the fight for equality.* PREP ≠ against

26 If something is **for** sale, hire, use, etc, it is available to be sold, hired, or used. EG *It was for sale... There were boats for hire... These books are for use in the library only.* PREP

27 You use **for** when you state the second part of a ratio. EG *About nine women have lost jobs for every five men.* PREP

28 If one word or expression has the same meaning as a second word or expression, you can say that the first one is another word or expression **for** the second one. EG *Rubella is the technical term for German Measles.* PREP

29 You use **for** in cross-references when you mention information which will be found somewhere else. EG *For more details see pages 4 and 5... For further information write to the head office.* PREP

30 If you **are for it** or if you **are in for it**, you are going to be in trouble because of something you have done; an informal expression. EG *Nell was for it.* ● **as for:** see **as.** ● **but for:** see **but.** ● **for all:** see **all.** — PHR : VB INFLECTS

forage /fɒrɪdʒ/, **forages, foraging, foraged. 1** When animals **forage**, they search for food. — V

2 If someone **forages** for something, they search busily for it. EG *We went down to the kitchen to forage for snacks... She couldn't resist foraging around for paintings.* — V : IF+PREP THEN *for* = rummage

3 Forage crops are grown as food for cattle and horses. — N UNCOUNT : USU BEFORE N

foray /fɒreɪ/, **forays. 1** If a group of soldiers make a **foray** into an area, they make a quick attack, usually in order to steal supplies. — N COUNT : USU+A = raid

2 If someone makes a **foray** to a particular place, they make a short journey to go there, especially to do something in particular. EG *From time to time he made forays to the pavement booksellers... The days pass with gentle forays into the sea or pool.* — N COUNT+A = excursion

3 If you make a **foray** into a particular area of activity, you try it and become involved in it for a short while. EG *There have been some forays into the trade by small companies... It was his first foray into politics.* — N COUNT+*into* = sortie

forbade /fəbæd, -beɪd/ is the the past tense of **forbid**.

forbear /fɔːbeə/, **forbears, forbearing, forbore, forborne.** If you **forbear** from doing something, you do not do it although you have the opportunity or the right to do it; a formal word. EG *He would continue to forbear from claiming his marital rights... He forbore to use them in that way, for they were his friends.* — V : IF+PREP/VB THEN *from/ to-INF/-ING* ⇑ abstain = forswear

forbearance /fɔːbeərəns/ is self-control, kindness, and forgiveness which is shown to someone who has done something wrong. EG *He cast aside his Christian forbearance and forgiveness... The policy was forbearance, to avoid armed intervention.* — N UNCOUNT ⇑ patience

forbearing /fɔːbeərɪŋ/. Someone who is **forbearing** shows forbearance. EG *She remembers her mother as mild and forbearing.* — ADJ QUALIT ⇑ patient

forbid /fə^8bɪd/, **forbids, forbidding, forbade, forbidden. 1** If you **forbid** someone to do something, or if you **forbid** an activity, you order that it must not be done. EG *I forbid you to tell her... They had obtained a court order forbidding the sale... The Charter expressly forbade the building of any chapel or retreat on the land.* — V+O, OR V+O+O/*to*-INF

2 If something **forbids** a particular course of action, event, etc, it makes it impossible for this to happen or be done. EG *His fatherly concern forbids him to leave the house at such a time... Mexico City's altitude forbids such exertions.* — V+O, OR V+O+O/*to*-INF = prohibit, prevent

3 If you say **'God forbid!'** or **'Heaven forbid!'** that a particular thing should happen or be done, you mean that you think it would be a very bad thing and you hope that it will not happen. EG *God forbid that anything should happen to my father... It should be done by someone but not, heaven forbid, by that Franklyn fellow!* — PHR : USED AS ADV SEN, OR EXCLAM

forbidden /fə^8bɪdə^0n/. **1** Something that is **forbidden** must not be done, especially because of a rule, law, or order. EG *...smoking is strictly forbidden... It is forbidden to bathe in the sea here.* — ADJ CLASSIF : USU PRED = prohibited

2 A **forbidden** place, or a place that is referred to as **forbidden** ground or territory, is one that you are not allowed to visit or enter. EG *...penetrating the forbidden North.* — ADJ CLASSIF : USU ATTRIB ⇑ prohibited

3 A **forbidden** subject, or a subject that is referred to as **forbidden** ground or territory, is one that you are not allowed to mention or talk about. EG *...a visitor brave enough to touch upon the forbidden subject.* — ADJ CLASSIF : USU ATTRIB ⇑ taboo

forbidden fruit, forbidden fruits. Forbitten fruit is a source of pleasure which you are not allowed to enjoy. EG *He will grow up and taste of the forbidden fruit.* — N COUNT/ UNCOUNT : SING=PL

forbidding /fə^8bɪdɪŋ/. Someone or something that is **forbidding** has a severe, unfriendly, or threatening appearance. EG *He looked rather stern and forbidding in his official photographs... ...a bleak, forbidding stretch of grey water.* ◊ **forbiddingly.** EG *There was something forbiddingly prison-like about the cluster of buildings.* — ADJ QUALIT = ominous, stern; ◊ ADV = ominously

force /fɔːs/, **forces, forcing, forced. 1** If you **force** someone to do something, you make them do something they do not want to do, for example by threatening them or taking action that makes it impossible for them not to do it. EG *Ought he to be forced out of the Presidency?... She forced herself to kiss her mother's cheek... ...the campaign to force the closure of the factory... They forced a confession out of him... Marsha forced her brain to work.* — V+O (NG/REFL), OR V+O (NG/REFL)+ *to*-INF/A

2 If you **force** something **on** or **upon** someone, you make them accept, use, or deal with something when they would prefer not to. EG *...the missiles which the Americans are forcing, he believes, upon Britain... I forced some more of the salt and water on him.* — V+O+A *(on/ upon)* ⇑ coerce

3 If a situation or event **forces** you to do something, it makes it necessary for you to do something that you would not otherwise have done. EG *Weekend gales forced him to change his plans... He asked me if I was clever. I was forced to admit that I was not... Setbacks can be a good thing, forcing you out of your complacency.* — V+O+*to*-INF/A ⇑ cause = compel, oblige

4 If you **force** something into a particular position, you use a lot of strength to make it move there. EG *I forced his head back... Topson forced open the tin of bacon... They forced David into a small room.* — V+O : USU+A = prize

5 If you **force** a lock, a door, or a safe, you break the lock violently in order to open it. EG *They had to force the lock on the trunk.* — V+O

6 If you **force** your **way** through or into somewhere, you have to push or break things that are in your way in order to get there. EG *He forced his way through the undergrowth... A number of them forced their way into the office of the Vice-Chancellor.* — PHR+A : VB INFLECTS

7 If you use **force** to do something or if it is done by **force**, strong and violent physical action is taken in order to achieve it. EG *Hitler's aim was to impose his ideology by force... We have renounced the use of force to settle our disputes.* — N UNCOUNT = violence

8 The **force** with which someone hits or moves something is the amount of power that is used. EG *I hit him with all the force I could muster... The force of an earthquake can be measured quite accurately.* — N SING WITH DET = strength

9 Someone or something that is referred to as a **force** has a considerable effect or influence on a situation or on people or things. EG *Britain is re-establishing itself as a powerful force in world affairs... Nationalism was rapidly becoming a dangerous force... Managers need more freedom to respond to market forces... ...the forces of evil.* — N COUNT

10 The **force** of something is the powerful effect or quality that it has. EG *She at once saw the force of this argument... This is what he had been arguing with great force for many years.... ...if the planet was exposed to the full force of ultraviolet rays.* — N UNCOUNT ⇑ strength

11 A **force** in physics is the pulling, attracting, or pushing effect that something has on something else. EG *The force acting on the particle is constant... It was as if he were drawn by some force as strong as gravity... ...magnetic forces.* — N COUNT/ UNCOUNT

12 The word **force** is used before a number to indicate a wind of a particular speed or strength, especially a very strong wind. EG *...a force nine gale... The ship had engine failure in a Force Ten.* — N COUNT : N+ NUM

13 If you **force** something such as a process or decision, you make it happen more quickly. EG *I don't want to force things, but we will have to reach a decision soon... We will have to force the issue I think.* — V+O ⇑ press

14 If you **force** fruit or vegetables, you make them grow faster or earlier in the year than normal by giving them extra heat. EG *...forced rhubarb.* — V+O ⇑ accelerate

15 If you **force** a smile, you manage, with an effort, to smile. — V+O

16 If something happens **by force of** a particular quality, action, set of circumstances, etc, it happens because of the nature or intensity of that quality, action, or set of circumstances. EG *By sheer force of will, he fought the urge to go after them... They overwhelmed the guards by sheer force of numbers.* — PREP

17 If you do something from **force of habit**, you do it because you have always done it in the past, rather than because you have thought carefully about it. EG *Many of them stayed from force of habit until the shooting began... 'You shouldn't have switched the light off.'–'Oh, sorry. Force of habit.'* — PHR

18 A law, rule, or system that is **in force** exists or is being used. EG *We will look at any arrangements that are in force at that point in time.* — PHR : USED AS AN A = in effect, in operation

19 When people do something **in force**, they do it in — PHR : USED AS AN large numbers. EG *Animal rights campaigners turned up in force.* A

20 A **force** of soldiers or armed people is an organized group of soldiers or armed military vehicles. EG *They were able to hold off a superior attacking force... ...the French security forces.* N COUNT : USU SING=PL

21 The **forces** means the army, the navy, or the air force, or all three. EG *...someone who died as a result of service in the forces.* N PLURAL : the+N = armed forces

22 The **force** is sometimes used to mean the police force. EG *He was always threatening to leave the force... It was certainly nothing like working for a metropolitan force.* N SING : USU the+N ⇑ organization

23 If you **join forces** with someone, you work together in order to achieve a common aim or purpose. PHR : VB INFLECTS

24 • See also **air force, labour force, peace-keeping forces, task force, tour de force, workforce.** • to **force** someone's **hand**: see **hand**.

25 See also **forced**.

force back. If you **force back** an emotion or desire, you manage, with an effort, not to experience it. EG *He forced back the strong urge to stroke her.* PHRASAL VB : V+O+ADV ⇑ fight = suppress

forced /fɔ:st/. 1 **Forced** describes 1.1 something that you do only because someone else makes you do it. EG *They promised to abolish forced labour... ...a forced marriage.* ADJ CLASSIF : ATTRIB ≠ voluntary 1.2 something that is done only because it is made necessary by a situation or event, especially an unexpected one. EG *...a forced landing.* ADJ CLASSIF : ATTRIB

2 Something that is **forced** is done or shown with an effort rather than being genuine and spontaneous. EG *His face crinkled into a forced smile... The forced joviality of a football team trying to show how confident they are... The conversations had been stiff, forced, and uncomfortable.* ADJ QUALIT ⇑ false = contrived, strained

3 An explanation or comparison that is **forced** is unlikely and unnatural. EG *...a rather forced interpretation.* ADJ QUALIT

force-feed, force-feeds, force-feeding, force-fed. If you **force-feed** a person or animal, you make them eat or drink by pushing food or drink down their throat. EG *Prisoners who went on hunger strike were force-fed.* V+O

forceful /fɔ:sful/. 1 Someone who is **forceful** expresses their opinions and wishes in a strong, emphatic, and confident way; used showing approval. EG *Rothermere was a forceful, able man.* ADJ QUALIT ⇑ powerful ▸ used of actions and behaviour. EG *...his forceful and successful advocacy of increased defence spending.* ▸ ⇑ powerful ◇ **forcefully**. EG *Her commitment could have been more forcefully expressed.* ◇ ADV WITH VB ◇ **forcefulness**. ◇ N UNCOUNT

2 Something that is **forceful** has a very powerful effect and causes you to think or feel something very strongly. EG *It made a very forceful impression on me.* ADJ QUALIT ⇑ great = strong ◇ **forcefully**. EG *It forcefully struck the bishop that this was very unusual.* ◇ ADV WITH VB = forcibly

3 A **forceful** point or argument in a discussion is one that is good, valid, and convincing. EG *She tried to recall the other forceful points he had expounded to her.* ADJ QUALIT = strong

forcemeat /fɔ:smi:t/ is the same as stuffing. N UNCOUNT

forceps /fɔ:sɪps/ are an instrument consisting of two long narrow arms in the form of pincers or tongs. Forceps are used by a doctor to hold something firmly and are sometimes used to help deliver a baby. N PLURAL

forcible /fɔ:səbəl/. 1 **Forcible** action involves physical force or violence. EG *...the forcible imposition of military control... ...legislation to limit forcible treatment of patients.* ADJ CLASSIF : USU ATTRIB ◇ **forcibly**. EG *Half-caste children were taken forcibly from their mothers.* ◇ ADV WITH VB = by force

2 A **forcible** reminder, example, or lesson is one that is very powerful. EG *Today we had a forcible reminder of the continuing strife there.* ADJ QUALIT : ATTRIB ◇ **forcibly**. EG *She reminded me forcibly of her mother at the same age... This fact was brought home to me forcibly by a personal experience.* ◇ ADV WITH VB = strongly

3 A **forcible** expression of an opinion or wish is expressed in a strong and emphatic way. EG *The survey made certain very forcible recommendations.* ADJ QUALIT : USU ATTRIB ◇ **forcibly**. EG *This point has been forcibly expressed also by Marxist-Leninists.* ◇ ADV WITH VB ⇑ strongly

4 A **forcible** argument is good, valid, and convincing. EG *It's a forcible argument.* ADJ QUALIT : USU ATTRIB

ford /fɔ:d/, **fords, fording, forded**. 1 A **ford** is a shallow place in a river or stream where it is possible to cross safely on foot, in a vehicle, etc, and without using a boat. N COUNT ⇑ crossing

2 If you **ford** a river or stream, you cross it at a shallow point without using a boat. V+O

fore /fɔ:/. 1 If someone or something comes **to the fore** in a particular situation or group, they suddenly become important or popular. EG *Andrew Young came to the fore during the Civil Rights marches of the 1960s... ...student revolts that pushed Marxist-Leninism to the fore in Europe.* PHR : USED AS AN A ⇑ appear = surface

2 **Fore** is used to refer to parts at the front of an animal, ship, or aircraft. EG *...the fore and hind wings of the dragonfly... They set about clearing away the big fore derrick and testing the winch.* ADJ CLASSIF : ATTRIB ⇑ front

forearm /fɔ:rɑ:m/, **forearms**. Your **forearm** is the part of your arm between your elbow and your wrist. N COUNT ⇑ arm

forebear /fɔ:beə/, **forebears**. Your **forebears** are your ancestors; a formal word. EG *...the lands from which their forebears had been driven.* N COUNT : USU PL ⇑ relative = ancestor

foreboding /fɔ:bəʊdɪŋ/, **forebodings**. **Foreboding** is a strong feeling that something terrible is going to happen. EG *Their pitiless laughter filled me with foreboding... They would find something there that would justify all their forebodings and apprehensions.* N UNCOUNT/COUNT ⇑ fear

forecast /fɔ:kɑ:st/, **forecasts, forecasting, forecasted**. The forms **forecast** and **forecasted** are both used as the past tense and past participle of the verb. 1 A **forecast** is a prediction or statement of what is expected to happen in the future, especially in relation to a particular event or situation. EG *The last Treasury forecast envisaged inflation falling to about 10 per cent... Their profit forecasts were over-optimistic... ...forecasts of military involvement in British politics.* N COUNT : USU+SUPP

2 If you **forecast** future events, you say what you think is going to happen in the future. EG *It is almost impossible to forecast the future development of a very young child... In 1974 the Worker's Press forecast large-scale unemployment and pay cuts.* V+O = predict

3 A weather **forecast** is a specially prepared and presented statement telling people what the weather is expected to be like; used also to refer to the television or radio programmes in which this information is presented. EG *What's the forecast for the next few days?... Forecasts of mild weather reduced the demand for holidays abroad.* N COUNT ▸ used as a verb. EG *Some nice warm weather had been forecast... We now have vastly improved forecasting of storms, freezes, droughts, and smog.* ▸ V+O ⇑ predict

foreclose /fɔ:kləʊz/, **forecloses, foreclosing, foreclosed**. If the person or organization that lent someone money **forecloses**, they take possession of the property that was bought with the borrowed money, for example because regular repayments have not been made; a technical term. EG *My bank foreclosed on me.* V : IF+PREP THEN on, OR V+O ⇑ repossess

forecourt /fɔ:kɔ:t/, **forecourts**. The **forecourt** of a large building or a petrol station is the open area at the front of it. EG *They started across the hotel's cobbled forecourt.* N COUNT

foredoomed /fɔ:du:md/. If you say that something is **foredoomed**, you mean that it was intended by fate to be unsuccessful or unlucky. EG *An intelligent film is not necessarily foredoomed to failure.* ADJ CLASSIF ⇑ condemn

forefather /fɔ:fɑ:ðə/, **forefathers**. Your **forefathers** are your ancestors, especially your male ancestors. EG *...the laws of our forefathers.* N COUNT : USU PL ⇑ ancestor = forebear

forefinger /fɔ:fɪŋgə/, **forefingers**. Your **forefinger** is the finger that is next to your thumb. EG *...the tips of your thumb and forefinger.* N COUNT ⇑ finger = index finger

forefoot /fɔ:fʊt/, **forefeet**. A four-legged animal's **forefeet** are its two front feet. EG *It swims by paddling with its webbed forefeet and steering with its hind feet.* N COUNT ⇑ foot

forefront /fɔ:frʌnt/. Something that is in or at the **forefront** of a situation is in the most important and exciting part of it where things are controlled and where new developments are taking place. EG *This was to place the company in the forefront of computer manufacture... Since 1972, he has brought Jamaica to the forefront of world politics.* N SING : the+N, USU+of ⇑ front = fore, vanguard

forego /fɔ:gəʊ/, **foregoes, foregoing, forewent, foregone**; also spelled **forgo**. If you **forego** something, especially something that seems desirable, you voluntarily do not have or take it; a fairly formal word. EG *Lilian Braithwaite very kindly* V+O ⇑ sacrifice = go without *agreed to forego her holiday and continue in the play.*

foregoing /fɔːgəʊɪŋ/. You can refer to what has just been stated or mentioned as the **foregoing**; a formal word. EG *How can ideas such as the foregoing be taken seriously?... In the foregoing we have seen how people differ in their approach to problems.* ▸ used as an adjective. EG *I am indebted to the ideas of Bob Waller for much of the foregoing analysis.* N SING : the+N ⇑ this = the above ▸ ADJ CLASSIF : ATTRIB, WITH the

foregone /fɔːgɒn/. 1 **Foregone** is the past participle of **forego**.

2 If a particular result is **a foregone conclusion**, it is certain to happen. EG *The outcome of both votes was assumed to be a foregone conclusion.* PHR : USED AS C

foreground /fɔːgraʊnd/. 1 The **foreground** of a picture or of a scene you are looking at is the part or area that is or seems nearest to you. EG *...the woman in the foreground who's dressed in a floral dress... The spire of St Patrick's dominates the foreground.* N SING : USU the+N ≠ background

2 Someone or something that is in the **foreground** is having a lot of attention paid to them. EG *Today Glenn has receded from the foreground of public attention.* N SING : USU the+N = focus

forehand /fɔːhænd/, **forehands**. 1 A **forehand** is a shot or stroke in a game such as tennis in which the palm of your hand faces the direction in which you are hitting the ball. EG *...a forehand return.* N COUNT ≠ backhand

2 The **forehand** of a tennis player, squash player, etc is the same side as the hand in which they are holding the racket. EG *Send the return deep to your opponent's forehand.* N COUNT : USU WITH POSS ≠ backhand

forehead /fɒrɪd, fɔːhɛd/, **foreheads**. Your **forehead** is the flat area at the front of your head above your eyebrows but below where your hair grows. EG *He wiped his forehead with the back of his hand.* N COUNT = brow

foreign /fɒrɪ³n/. 1 Something that is **foreign** belongs to or relates to a country that is not your own. EG *...a policy of restricting foreign imports... ...children from foreign countries... ...foreign holidays... ...foreign-owned mines.* ADJ CLASSIF = overseas

2 **Foreign** also means dealing with or concerning countries which are not your own. EG *...a country whose foreign policy is based on economics... ...the Belgian Foreign Minister... He had come to India as a foreign correspondent.* ADJ CLASSIF : ATTRIB ⇑ external

3 A **foreign** object or substance is something that has come into something else, usually by accident, and should not be in it; a formal use. EG *...offences relating to the sale of food containing foreign matter... Our eyes act instinctively against the entry of foreign objects.* ADJ CLASSIF : ATTRIB ⇑ extraneous

4 Something that is **foreign** to a particular person or thing is 4.1 not characteristic of them; a formal use. EG *He again fell into that strange gloomy mood that was usually so foreign to him... I heard cars in the distance. Such a foreign, incongruous sound in the desert.* 4.2 unfamiliar to them, and seems strange; a formal use. EG *This way of waging war was foreign to their thinking.* ADJ QUALIT : IF+PREP THEN to ⇑ atypical = alien ADJ QUALIT : IF+PREP THEN to = alien

foreign body, foreign bodies. A **foreign body** is an object that has come into something else, usually by accident, and should not be in it; a formal expression. EG *...a complaint about a foreign body in some food.* N COUNT

foreigner /fɒrɪ³nə/, **foreigners**. A **foreigner** is 1 a person who belongs to a country that is not your own. EG *More than a million foreigners visit the United States every year.* 2 a person who has come into a community or other group of people from outside it and does not seem to belong there. EG *I am still a foreigner in this village.* N COUNT ⇑ stranger N COUNT : USU USED AS C ⇑ outsider = stranger

foreign exchange is the system by which one country's currency is changed into another country's currency. EG *The pound fell on foreign exchange markets.* ▸ used also of foreign currency which is obtained by this system. EG *Coffee is the region's major source of foreign exchange.* N UNCOUNT

Foreign Office. The **Foreign Office** is the government department, especially in Britain, which has responsibility for the government's dealings and relations with foreign governments. N PROPER : the+N

foreknowledge /fɔːnɒlɪdʒ/ is knowledge of an event or situation before it actually happens. N UNCOUNT = anticipation

foreleg /fɔːlɛg/, **forelegs**. The **forelegs** of an animal are its two front legs. EG *It has short silky fur, powerful forelegs, and a stumpy tail.* N COUNT ⇑ limb

forelock /fɔːlɒk/, **forelocks**. A **forelock** is a piece of someone's hair that falls over their forehead. People of low social class used to pull their forelocks to show respect for people of a higher class. EG *People began to move aside, touching their forelocks.* N COUNT

foreman /fɔːmə³n/, **foremen**. 1 A **foreman** is a person, especially a man, in charge of a group of workers. EG *The foreman swore at one of the workers.* N COUNT ⇑ leader = supervisor

2 The **foreman** of a jury is the person who is chosen as their leader. N COUNT

foremost /fɔːməʊst/. 1 **Foremost** means most important or best. EG *Some new organizations were emerging and foremost among these was CND... ...the company's foremost materials expert.* ADJ CLASSIF : IF PRED THEN+PREP ⇑ first = uppermost

2 **First and foremost** means more than anything else; used when referring to the characteristic, person, or thing that is more important than any other. EG *Rugby is first and foremost a team game... So, first and foremost, remember that fish are live creatures with feelings.* PHR : USED AS ADV SEN = above all

3 The **foremost** thing or part of something is the one that is nearest the front. EG *This is the foremost compartment of the ship.* ▸ used as an adverb. EG *He jabbed the brushes into the ground bristles foremost.* ADJ CLASSIF ⇑ first ▸ ADV WITH VB

forename /fɔːneɪm/, **forenames**. A **forename** is a first name. N COUNT ≠ surname

forensic /fərɛnsɪk/ means 1 relating to the discovery of information about a crime by scientifically examining objects involved in it. EG *...forensic medicine... He telephoned Detective Inspector Cook at the forensic department.* 2 relating to the profession of being a lawyer; a formal use. EG *He spoke at great length and with great forensic skill.* ADJ CLASSIF : ATTRIB ⇑ scientific ADJ CLASSIF : ATTRIB

foreordain /fɔːrɔːdeɪn/, **foreordains, foreordaining, foreordained**. If you say that something **is foreordained**, you mean that you believe that fate or God has planned that it will happen, and you are sure that it will; a formal word. V+O : USU PASS = fated, destined

forepart /fɔːpɑːt/, **foreparts**. The **forepart** of something, especially an animal, is the front part of it; a formal word. EG *The forepart and head remain raised.* N COUNT : the+N, USU+of

foreplay /fɔːpleɪ/ is activity such as kissing and stroking when it takes place before sexual intercourse. N UNCOUNT ⇑ sex = petting

forerunner /fɔːrʌnə/, **forerunners**. The **forerunner** of someone or something is 1 a thing or person that happened or existed before them and that is similar in some way. EG *...the forerunners of the International Socialists... The power of the smaller engine is equal to that of its 1.6 forerunner.* 2 a thing or person that is a sign of what is going to happen in the future. EG *They are obviously no freak of nature. They are the forerunner of things to come.* N COUNT : IF+PREP THEN of ⇑ ancestor = precursor N COUNT : IF+PREP, THEN of = harbinger

foresee /fɔːsiː/, **foresees, foreseeing, foresaw, foreseen**. If you **foresee** something, you know or have the opinion that it is going to happen. EG *The coming of the silicon chip could not have been foreseen by any of the computer pioneers... Do you foresee any problems with the new system?... He foresaw that public indignation might lead to the plan being scrapped.* V+O/REPORT-CL ⇑ see = predict

foreseeable /fɔːsiːəbə³l/. 1 **the foreseeable future**. 1.1 If you say that something will happen **in the foreseeable future**, you mean that you think it will happen fairly soon. EG *There is little hope that this will occur in the foreseeable future.* 1.2 If you say that something will happen **for the foreseeable future**, you mean that you think that it will continue to happen for a long time, and you cannot see any chance of it ending. EG *This seems likely to remain the pattern for the foreseeable future.* PHR : USED AS AN A PHR : USED AS AN A

2 If something is **foreseeable**, you can see that it is going to happen or that it is likely to happen. EG *This will land the man concerned in a perfectly foreseeable catastrophe.* ADJ QUALIT = predictable

foreshadow /fɔːʃædəʊ/, **foreshadows, foreshadowing, foreshadowed**. Something that **foreshadows** something else shows or suggests that it is going to happen. EG *These later movements had, as we have seen, been foreshadowed in much of the work of the late 1950s.* V+O ⇑ indicate = presage

foreshore /fɔːʃɔː/, **foreshores**. The **foreshore** is the part of the shore that is between the points reached by the high tide and the low tide. N COUNT

foreshorten /fɔːʃɔːtəⁿn/, **foreshortens, foreshortening, foreshortened**. Something that **is foreshortened** is drawn or seen from such an angle that its ends appear closer together than they really are. ◇ **foreshortened**. EG *...the foreshortened bulks of two old women, seen from above.* — V+O ⇑ compact; ◇ ADJ CLASSIF ⇑ compacted

foresight /fɔːsaɪt/ is the ability to see what is likely to happen in the future, and the practice of taking this into consideration when you do things. EG *Throughout his career he showed remarkable foresight.* — N UNCOUNT = vision

foreskin /fɔːskɪn/, **foreskins**. A man's **foreskin** is the skin that covers the end of his penis. — N COUNT

forest /fɒrɪ²st/, **forests**. 1 A **forest** is a large area where trees grow close together. EG *They had their picnic in a clearing in the forest... ...animals that live in woodland or thick forest... ...Sherwood Forest.* — N COUNT/UNCOUNT ⇑ woodland

2 A **forest** of tall or narrow objects is a group of them standing or sticking upright. EG *'Who wants to clean the blackboard for me?' said Mrs Root. A forest of hands went up.* — N PART ⇑ mass

forestall /fɔːstɔːl/, **forestalls, forestalling, forestalled**. If you **forestall** someone or **forestall** something that they were intending or likely to do, you realize what they were intending to do and prevent them from doing it by doing something else first. EG *He was about to speak but she forestalled him... It was believed that this action would forestall any further discussion of economic intervention.* — V+O = anticipate, pre-empt

forester /fɒrɪstə/, **foresters**. A **forester** is a person whose job is to look after the trees in a forest and to plant new ones. — N COUNT

forestry /fɒrɪstri¹/ is the science or skill of growing and taking care of trees in forests, especially in order to obtain wood. — N UNCOUNT

foretaste /fɔːteɪst/, **foretastes**. If you describe something as a **foretaste** of something else, you mean that it is smaller in degree or amount than the second thing, but is similar to it and shows you what it is going to be like. EG *The episode was a foretaste of the bitter struggle that was to come... The haggling in Geneva this week gives a foretaste of the discussions that will follow.* — N COUNT : USU a +N+*of* = sample

foretell /fɔːtel/, **foretells, foretelling, foretold**. If you **foretell** something, you say correctly that it will happen in the future; a rather literary word. EG *...the destiny foretold by the ancient prophets... If only the planners of 1960 had been able to foretell these remarkable changes.* — V+O/REPORT-CL = predict, prophesy

forethought /fɔːθɔːt/ is the practice of thinking carefully about what will be needed, or about what the consequences of something will be. EG *To pass the time, I played patience with cards which I had had the forethought to bring with me.* — N UNCOUNT ⇑ planning

foretold /fɔːtəʊld/ is the past participle of **foretell**.

forever /fəˢrevə/. The form **for ever** is also used, except in paragraphs 4 and 5. 1 Something that will happen or continue **forever** will always happen or continue, without ever ending. EG *She would remember his name forever... They thought that their empire would last forever... ...the feeling that the prairie goes on forever... Are you ready to link up your life with mine for ever and ever?* — ADV WITH VB = evermore, eternally

2 Something that has changed or gone **forever** has changed or gone completely and permanently. EG *In the latter half of the 19th century, Japan changed forever... They will vanish forever into the grey twilight... ...a world from which he was forever exiled.* — ADV WITH VB = for good

3 You say that something takes **for ever** or lasts **for ever** to emphasize that it takes or lasts a very long time, or seems to; an informal use. EG *The next minutes lasted for ever... I had been walking for ever.* — ADV WITH VB = ages

4 If someone or something is **forever** doing a particular thing, they do it often; an informal use. EG *Babbage was forever spotting trivial errors in their calculations... They are forever being knocked down by cars.* — ADV WITH VB (-ING) = consistently

5 Someone who is **forever** kind, cheerful, etc always has or shows the quality mentioned; an informal use. EG *...the forever cocky James Cagney.* — ADV+ADJ/ADV = eternally

6 You can say **forever** after the name of a group, person, place, etc to indicate that you support or admire them. EG *The band were playing 'The stars and stripes forever'... 'Swallows and Amazons forever,' she cried.* — ADV AFTER N = long live

forewarn /fɔːwɔːn/, **forewarns, forewarning, forewarned**. If you **forewarn** someone, you warn them in advance that something is going to happen. EG *We were forewarned that the food would be unusual.* — V+O/REPORT-CL OR V+O+REPORT-CL ⇑ caution

forewent /fɔːwent/ is the past tense of **forego**.

foreword /fɔːwɜ²d/, **forewords**. The **foreword** of a book is an introduction by the author or by someone else. EG *Professor Zim, in his foreword to The Milton Papers, praises the book's boldness.* — N COUNT = preface

forfeit /fɔːfɪt/, **forfeits, forfeiting, forfeited**. 1 If you **forfeit** something, 1.1 you lose it or are forced to give it up because you have broken a rule or done something wrong. EG *Violation of this contract makes them liable to forfeit £50... He has forfeited the right to be the leader of this nation.* 1.2 you give it up voluntarily, especially so that you can achieve something. EG *They were persuaded to forfeit some of their income.* — V+O ⇑ surrender; V+O ⇑ surrender

2 A **forfeit** is something that you have to give up because you have done something wrong. EG *...his reluctance to exact from them a forfeit they could not pay.* — N COUNT = penalty, price

3 If something of yours **is forfeit**, you will have to lose it or give it up because you have done something illegal or wrong. EG *Her own life might well be forfeit for having tried to save him.* — PHR : VB INFLECTS

forfeiture /fɔːfɪtʃə/ is the action of forfeiting something. — N UNCOUNT : IF+PREP THEN *of*

forgave /fɔːgeɪv/ is the past tense of **forgive**.

forge /fɔːdʒ/, **forges, forging, forged**. 1 A **forge** is a place where someone makes metal goods such as horseshoes or old-fashioned farm equipment by hand. EG *Go and work for Mr Gladwell at the forge.* — N COUNT : USU SING ⇑ workshop

2 If you **forge** metal, especially iron, or you **forge** an object out of metal, you heat the metal, and hammer and bend it into the shape you want. — V+O : IF+PREP THEN *from/into* ⇑ work = fashion

3 If you **forge** something, especially an alliance or relationship, you create it with a lot of hard work, hoping that it will be strong or lasting. EG *They forged links with the French Communist Party... We need to forge an alliance between them and the workers.* — V+O = form

4 If you **forge** money, documents, paintings, etc, you copy them or make them so that they look genuine in order to deceive people. EG *I learnt how to forge someone else's signature... ...a forged passport.* — V+O = counterfeit

5 If you **forge** forward, you move forward in a steady powerful way. EG *We forged steadily northward.* — V+A

forge ahead. If you **forge ahead**, you make a lot of progress, or you make more progress than someone else. EG *They forged ahead, leaving countries like Britain behind.* — PHRASAL VB : V+ADV

forger /fɔːdʒə/, **forgers**. A **forger** is a person who forges money, documents, paintings, etc. EG *I think we're dealing with the work of a forger.* — N COUNT ⇑ criminal

forgery /fɔːdʒəⁿri¹/, **forgeries**. 1 **Forgery** is the crime of forging money, documents, paintings, etc. EG *She was prosecuted for passport forgery.* — N UNCOUNT ⇑ fraud

2 A **forgery** is a forged document, banknote, painting, etc. EG *The documents were forgeries.* — N COUNT = counterfeit

forget /fəget/, **forgets, forgetting, forgot, forgotten**. 1 If you **forget** something or **forget** how to do something, you are unable to think of it or think how to do it, even though you have known it, experienced it, or been able to do it in the past. EG *I never forget a face or a name... Sue was afraid that she had forgotten how to ride a bicycle... It was a marvellous occasion and I shall never forget it... Dan had written his fourth or fifth play, I forget which now.* ◇ **forgotten**. EG *...a long forgotten event in her past.* — V+O/REPORT-CL/-ING : NO CONT ≠ remember; ◇ ADJ CLASSIF

2 If you **forget** something, you do not think about it, for example because you are thinking about other things or because it is unimportant. EG *He often forgot what he was supposed to be doing... I forgot all about him for several years... Don't forget that I worked for her once... Oh yes, of course. I was forgetting... His aching muscles forgotten, Paul bolted home.* — V+O/REPORT-CL, OR V+A ⇑ overlook
● You say **not forgetting** a particular person or thing when adding that person or thing at the end of a list. EG *On the first floor, there's a library and a drawing room, not forgetting the music room.* — ● PHR ⇑ and
● You say **'and don't you forget it!'** to someone after making a statement to emphasize that they must behave in the way implied by that statement, for — ● PHR = okay?, alright?

example by showing respect. EG *It's my house and my record player, and don't you forget it!*

3 If you **forget** something such as a birthday, an appointment, or a duty, you do not do what you should do because you do not think about it at the right time. EG *I meant to see her about it on Friday morning, but I forgot all about it... Don't forget to send in your entries by Wednesday to this address... He forgot my birthday again this year.* V+O/REPORT-CL, V+A (about), OR V+to-INF ⇑ omit = neglect

4 If you **forget** something that you had intended to bring or buy, you do not bring or buy it because you did not think about it at the right time. EG *Sorry to disturb you–I forgot my key... 'Don't forget the bag,' she said.* V+O/REPORT-CL, V+A (about), OR V+to-INF : NO CONT ⇑ omit

5 If you **forget** something or someone, you deliberately put them out of your mind and do not think any more about them. EG *If you want my advice I think you ought to forget her... In terms of turnover, we can forget any idea of competing with the big companies.* ● You say **'forget it'** in reply to someone as a way of telling them not to worry or bother about something, or when you cannot be bothered to repeat something, or as an emphatic way of saying no to a suggestion. EG *'What do I owe you for lunch?'–'Forget it.'... 'Sorry, what did you say?'–'Forget it.'... 'I'll take the small truck.'–'And leave me to drive the other one? Forget it.'* V+O/REPORT-CL, V+A (about), OR V+to-INF ⇑ reject ● CONVENTION ⇑ never mind

6 If you **forget** yourself, you behave in an uncontrolled or unacceptable way, which is not the way in which you usually behave; a fairly formal use. EG *'Oh darling!' cried Judy, forgetting herself.* V+O (REFL) ⇑ misbehave

forgetful /fəgetful/. 1 Someone who is **forgetful** often forgets things. EG *Be sure to remind your uncle–you know how forgetful he is.* ◇ **forgetfulness.** EG *She often hesitated, from forgetfulness.* ADJ QUALIT ◇ N UNCOUNT ⇑ amnesia

2 Someone who is **forgetful** of a particular thing does not think about it or notice it. EG *Fiona, forgetful of the time, was still working away in the library.* ADJ QUALIT+of

forget-me-not, forget-me-nots. A **forget-me-not** is a small plant with tiny blue flowers. N COUNT ⇑ flower

forgettable /fəgetəbə⁰l/. Something that is **forgettable** is not unusual or special in any way. EG *...thousands of entirely forgettable men working at obscure jobs in the city.* ADJ QUALIT ⇑ ordinary

forgivable /fəgɪvəbə⁰l/. If you say that something bad or unacceptable is **forgivable**, you mean that you can understand it and can forgive it in the circumstances. EG *Her lack of sympathy was perhaps forgivable. Missing bricks would have been forgivable in an old building, but not in a brand new house!* ◇ **forgivably.** EG *She was furious, forgivably so in the circumstances.* ADJ CLASSIF = pardonable ◇ ADV

forgive /fəgɪv/, **forgives, forgiving, forgave, forgiven.** 1 If you **forgive** someone who has done something wrong, or **forgive** a bad deed that someone has done, you stop being angry with them and no longer want to punish them. EG *Julie would never have forgiven him... I forgive you... Sins cannot be undone, only forgiven... I forgave him everything... They had forgiven their host his delayed arrival... He has never forgiven the newspaper for printing this story.* V+O : IF+PREP THEN for, OR V+O+O = pardon

2 **Forgive** is used in polite expressions like 'forgive me', 'forgive my ignorance', and 'forgive the language', to reduce the directness of what you are saying, and to apologize in a mild way for saying something that might seem rude, silly, or too complicated. EG *Forgive my ignorance, but who is Jane Fonda?... It was clearly a lymphoma, if you'll forgive my medical jargon... We may not agree about this but forgive me, Geoffrey, I think we could at least discuss it.* PHR : USED AS ADV SEN = excuse, pardon

3 If you say that someone could **be forgiven** for doing something, you mean that this behaviour or reaction is likely and expected because of the circumstances involved. EG *One could be forgiven for being hesitant about putting Norman in charge... The family could be forgiven for thinking that we were still in London.* V : MODAL+V+O, USU PASS = excused

4 If you **forgive** someone a debt, you say that they do not have to pay you the money that they owe you. EG *I forgave you the whole amount you owed me.* V+O+O ⇑ excuse

forgiveness /fəgɪvnɪ²s/. If you ask someone for their **forgiveness**, you ask them to forgive you for something wrong that you have done. EG *I have to ask your forgiveness... They are not always sure of forgiveness.* N UNCOUNT = pardon

forgiving /fəgɪvɪŋ/. Someone who is **forgiving** is willing to forgive. EG *...a forgiving father... This made it easy for her to be forgiving.* ADJ QUALIT = merciful

forgo /fɔːgəʊ/. See **forego**.

forgot /fəgɒt/ is the past tense of **forget**.

forgotten /fəgɒtə⁰n/ is the past participle of **forget**.

fork /fɔːk/, **forks, forking, forked.** 1 A **fork** is 1.1 a tool with which you eat food. It consists of three or four prongs on the end of a handle. 1.2 a large tool that you use for digging in the soil when you are gardening. It consists of three or four long prongs attached to a long handle. ● See also **pitchfork**. N COUNT ⇑ cutlery N COUNT

2 If you **fork** food into your mouth or onto something, you use a fork to pick up food and eat it or put it somewhere. EG *She glumly forked her way through endless risottos... ...forking the meat and slapping it into sandwiches.* V+O

3 If you **fork** earth or plant material somewhere, you turn it over or put it somewhere using a fork. EG *He could see Mr Willett forking dead vegetation onto the smoking bonfire.* V+O+A

4 A **fork** in a road, path, river, or branch of a tree is the point at which it divides into two parts in the shape of a 'Y'. EG *When you come to the fork, turn left... The pigeon remained where it was, wedged in the fork of a branch.* ▸ used as a verb. EG *Near the dead tree, the trail forks... When you reach the junction, fork left.* N COUNT ⇑ junction ▸ V

5 One of the **forks** in a road, path, river or branch of a tree is one of the two parts of it after it has divided at a fork. EG *The men took the fork that led on past the village... Take the left fork.* N COUNT+SUPP

6 The **forks** on a bicycle or motorbike are the two pieces of metal below the handlebars, to which the front wheel is attached. N PLURAL ⇑ prong

fork out. If you **fork out** for something, you pay money for it; an informal expression. EG *His old man's forked out at last... ...the fortune I had already had to fork out on her education.* PHRASAL VB : V+ADV, USU+A

forked /fɔːkt/. Something that is **forked** divides into two parts in the shape of a 'Y'. EG *...an adder's forked tongue.* ADJ CLASSIF ⇑ divided

forked lightning is lightning that is seen as jagged lines of light dividing into two or more parts near the ground. EG *Suddenly there was a flash and a zig-zag of forked lightning.* N UNCOUNT

fork-lift truck, fork-lift trucks. A **fork-lift truck** or a **fork-lift** is a small vehicle with two movable arms on the front that are used to lift heavy loads. N COUNT

forlorn /fəlɔːn/. 1 Someone or something that is **forlorn** is lonely and unhappy. EG *The child looked pathetically forlorn.* ▸ used of behaviour. EG *...a forlorn cry... ...a forlorn voice.* ◇ **forlornly.** EG *He was still standing forlornly by the ticket office.* ADJ QUALIT = desolate, wretched ◇ ADV WITH VB

2 A place that is **forlorn** looks deserted and not cared for. EG *...this grimy, forlorn industrial town... The house looked bare and forlorn.* ◇ **forlornly.** EG *...a house standing forlornly on the hillside.* ADJ QUALIT = forsaken ◇ ADV WITH VB

3 A **forlorn** attempt or hope is one that is desperate and without any expectation of success. EG *...forlorn attempts to patch up the victims of our industrial mistakes. ...in the forlorn hope of achieving full employment.* ◇ **forlornly.** ADJ CLASSIF : ATTRIB ◇ ADV WITH VB

form /fɔːm/, **forms, forming, formed.** 1 A particular **form** of something is a type or kind of it. EG *He begged for any form of transport that would take him to the ferry... The symptoms take various forms... I never touch alcohol in any form... Taxation in one form or another has been with us for a very long time.* N COUNT

2 The **form** in which a particular thing occurs or is expressed is one of the ways in which it occurs or can be expressed. EG *Coal is a form of carbon... She didn't like the form in which the questions were written... She is taking lots of exercise in the form of walks or swimming.* N COUNT : USU+SUPP ⇑ way

3 Something that **takes the form of** a particular thing happens or is expressed in the particular manner or style indicated. EG *The broadcast took the form of an interview... Their unease took the form of extreme hostility.* PHR : VB INFLECTS ⇑ appear

4 When something or someone **forms** a particular shape they move or are arranged in such a way that this shape is made. EG *Her body and bare limbs formed a Z... ...they formed a ring to keep her warm... At 9 a.m. they opened their doors, outside* V-ERG, OR V+O (REFL)+A ⇑ make

which long queues had formed... The men formed themselves into a line.

5 When you **form** a particular shape or letter, you create it in the shape indicated. EG *It could so easily be a badly formed A.* — V+O ⇑ make

6 The **form** of something is its shape or pattern, rather than its size or texture. EG *The middle finger was touching the end of the thumb in the form of a letter O.* — N COUNT

7 The word **form** can also be used to refer to the outside shape or appearance of a person or thing; a rather literary use. EG *She gazed with deep affection at his slumbering form... We saw a slender ghostly form detaching itself from the shelter of a square.* — N COUNT ⇑ body = figure

8 When something **takes form** it begins to be visible and to have a clear shape or outline. EG *I could see the streets of Cape Town take form as the ship sailed into Table Bay.* — PHR : VB INFLECTS = appear

9 In order to describe the shape, structure, or function of a particular thing, you can say that it **forms** something that has this shape, structure, or function. EG *The black leather chair folds back to form a couch... There were some red rocks forming a kind of cave... The steep hills form a backdrop to the city.* — V+O ⇑ make

10 The things, people, features, etc that **form** a particular thing are the things or people that this thing consists of. EG *The contents of the house will form the basis of a major exhibition... The five western nations that drew up the plan formed the bulk of the UN peace-keeping force.* — V+C ⇑ be = constitute

11 If you **form** an organization, committee, company, etc, you organize and start it. EG *The League was formed in 1959... The leadership broke away to form a separate organization... ...a young radical section formed... There were a number of groups forming themselves into cooperatives... He sent for Ramsay MacDonald on 24 January 1924 to form a government.* — V-ERG

12 When something natural **forms**, it begins to exist and develop. EG *The islands are volcanic and were formed comparatively recently... A great scab had formed on his right knee... We ended up at a large pool that was formed by the flood-water crashing through the children's play area.* — V-ERG

13 If you **form** something, for example an idea, a relationship with someone, or a habit, you begin to have and to develop it. EG *This was at variance with the impression I'd formed of Otto... He becomes wary of forming another close relationship... He formed the habit of taking long solitary walks.* — V-ERG

14 Something that **forms** a person's character and personality has a strong influence on them and causes them to develop in a particular way. EG *They were formed within this tradition... I suppose the experience with Nell formed me.* — V+O

15 A **form** is a paper on which there are particular questions and spaces marked where you should write the answers. Forms usually ask you to give details about yourself, for example when you are applying for a job, or joining an organization. EG *At the counter he had to fill in the form... Just sign the booking form there for me please.* — N COUNT

16 A **form** in a school is a class; used especially with a number to refer to a particular class or age group of children. EG *...the fifth form... She's in Form 5.* — N COUNT : USU WITH NUM/ORD

17 A **form** is also a long low seat without a back. EG *Children sat on forms at the front of the hall.* — N COUNT = bench

18 A particular **form** of a word is the particular way in which it is represented in writing or speech which shows, for example, whether it is singular or plural, or past or present. EG *He hasn't grasped the difference between the simple form and the continuous form.* ▸ used as a verb. EG *How do you form the past tense?* — N COUNT+SUPP ⇑ version; ▸ V+O

19 **Form** in something such as a work of art or piece of writing is the structure and arrangement of it, in contrast to its subject or contents. — N UNCOUNT

20 **Form** in sport is the ability and success of an animal or person over a period of time. EG *He gambles regularly–pretends to be a judge of form and to win quite a lot... D'Oliveira had a slump in form and was considered out of the running.* — N UNCOUNT

21 Someone who is **on form** is performing their usual activity very well. Someone who is **off form** is not performing as well as they usually do. EG *She was on form right through the tournament... I thought he was a bit off form today, didn't you?... You've got to be on good form before you can do that.* — PHR : USED AS AN A = out of form

22 If you say that it is bad **form** to behave in a particular way, you mean that it is rude and impolite. EG *It is bad form to keep the clergyman waiting too long.* — N UNCOUNT : ADJ +N ⇑ behaviour = manners

23 Something that is done **as a matter of form** has been done because it was considered usual or expected. EG *They continued sneaking a few spies over the river as a matter of form.* — PHR : USED AS AN A

24 If someone's behaviour is **true to form** it is what is expected and is typical of that person. EG *They lobbied Watson who, true to form, made an instant decision... Otto's luck was running true to form.* — PHR : USED AS A/C

form up. When a group of things **form up**, they move into position in lines. EG *The yachts formed up in Hampton Roads.* — PHRASAL VB : V-ERG+ADV = draw up, line up

formal /fɔːməºl/. **1** **Formal** speech or behaviour is very correct and serious rather than relaxed and friendly, and is used for example in official situations or when you are talking to someone important. In this dictionary, language of this kind is indicated by the use of the word 'formal' in definitions. EG *'How is your mother?' Daintry asked with formal politeness... ...the formal handshake... The letter was stiff and formal.* ◊ **formally**. EG *Everyone was formally lined up to meet the king.* ◊ **formality** /fə[3]mælɪti[1]/. EG *The elders conversed with strict formality when children were around... They reacted against the formality of their predecessors.* — ADJ QUALIT; ◊ ADV WITH VB; ◊ N UNCOUNT ⇑ correctness

2 A **formal** statement, decision, action, etc is one that is officially declared, done, or accepted so that it becomes publicly known or recognized. EG *No formal declaration of war had been made... It will have to go to the Houses of Parliament for formal approval... A formal enquiry was made... I have the formal responsibility for planning... We have many formal procedures for celebrating these occasions.* ◊ **formally**. EG *He had already formally announced his candidacy... They're now formally engaged... The rules are formally set out in a book.* — ADJ CLASSIF : ATTRIB ⇑ public = official; ◊ ADV WITH VB

3 **Formal** occasions are ones at which people wear smart clothes and behave correctly in accordance with particular conventions. EG *Foreign leaders are expected to attend a formal dinner at Buckingham Palace... The dances held at the embassy were formal affairs... Their wedding had been formal and formidable.* — ADJ QUALIT ⇑ conventional

4 **Formal** clothes are very smart clothes that are suitable for formal occasions. ◊ **formally**. EG *He dressed rather formally.* ◊ **formality**. EG *Her clothes have a formality which makes it impossible to judge her age.* — ADJ QUALIT; ◊ ADV WITH VB; ◊ N UNCOUNT ⇑ smartness

5 Something that is done, written, or studied in a **formal** way has a very ordered, organized style or method. EG *...a formal mathematical approach... My Marxism has never been a formal, organized study... The whole play is performed in a formal style.* — ADJ QUALIT

6 A **formal** garden or room is arranged in a very regular and controlled way, especially according to certain conventions of design. EG *Holland House and its formal gardens... Here is, quite simply, grass and trees and paths; no formal flowerbeds... We came out among the high buildings into a formal square.* ◊ **formally**. EG *And so we move on to the formally composed semi-circle of the Victoria Memorial.* — ADJ QUALIT; ◊ ADV WITH VB ⇑ regularly

7 **Formal** education or training is given officially in a school, college, etc. EG *Many great discoverers like Faraday had no formal education at all... No formal qualifications are necessary.* ◊ **formally**. EG *They are formally taught.* — ADJ CLASSIF : ATTRIB ⇑ official; ◊ ADV WITH VB

8 **Formal** is also used to describe something that appears to be true or to exist rather than what is really true or what really exists. EG *We cannot operate with as much freedom as our formal powers might appear to suggest.* ◊ **formally**. EG *The Sixties were dominated, even if only formally, by politics.* — ADJ CLASSIF ⇑ apparent; ◊ ADV WITH VB ⇑ apparently

9 See also **formality**.

formaldehyde /fə[3]mældɪhaɪd/ is a strong-smelling gas, used especially to preserve specimens in biology. — N UNCOUNT

formalise /fɔːməlaɪz/. See **formalize**.

formalism /fɔːməlɪzəºm/ is a style, especially in art, in which great attention is paid to the outward form or appearance rather than to the inner reality or true significance of things. EG *I think that as a doctrine formalism has done damage.* ◊ **formalist**. — N UNCOUNT; ◊ N COUNT

EG *My quarrel with the formalists is about the nature of sculpture itself.*

formality /fɔ⁸:mælɪti¹/, **formalities**. 1 A **formality** is a formal action or procedure that is conventionally carried out as part of an activity or event. EG *The pre-funeral formalities had to be attended to.* N COUNT ⇑ convention

2 A procedure or action that is referred to as a **formality** is done because it has to be done, even though its result will not affect the final result. EG *He knew the interview was just a formality.* N COUNT ⇑ rule

3 See also **formal**.

formalize /fɔːməlaɪz/, **formalizes, formalizing, formalized**; also spelled **formalise**. If you **formalize** a plan, idea, arrangement, etc, you make it clear and official. EG *His major role is to formalize the distribution of money to individuals... Their marriage vows will be formalized.* V+O ⇑ organize

format /fɔːmæt/, **formats**. The **format** of something is the way and order in which it is arranged and presented. EG *The author of the article had resented the changes I had made in its format and tone... They're already producing material in all kinds of different formats.* N COUNT ⇑ arrangement = layout

formation /fɔ⁸meɪʃə⁰n/, **formations**. 1 The **formation** of an organization, company, system, etc is the act or process of organizing and starting it. EG *He had played a major role in the formation of the United Nations... Since its formation, the company had made losses of £9.5m.* N UNCOUNT+SUPP = establishment

2 If things are in a particular **formation**, they are arranged in a particular order or pattern. EG *...aircraft flying in formation.* N COUNT/UNCOUNT ⇑ arrangement

3 The **formation** of an idea, habit, relationship, etc is the process of developing and firmly establishing it. EG *This procedure effectively prevents the formation of new ideas.* N UNCOUNT+SUPP ⇑ development

4 The **formation** of something natural is its origin and development. EG *This shows how much the mother's feelings have to do with the formation of milk... It's all part of the physical process of rock formation.* N UNCOUNT+SUPP

5 A rock or cloud **formation** is rock or cloud of a particular shape or structure. EG *...beautiful rock formations in underground caves.* N COUNT ⇑ group

formative /fɔːmətɪv/. A **formative** period of time or influence is one which has an important and lasting influence on a person's character and attitudes. EG *...a suburb of Cambridge is where I spent my formative years... This person may well become the most formative influence on the young child's developing personality.* ADJ CLASSIF: ATTRIB ⇑ developing

-formed combines with adverbs to indicate that something has reached a particular stage of growth or development. EG *...a fully-formed frog.* COMB: FORMS ADJS = developed

former /fɔːmə/. 1 **Former** is used to describe 1.1 someone who used to have a particular job, position, or role, but no longer has it. EG *The guide showed us the old home of former President Theodore Roosevelt... ...a former army officer.* ADJ CLASSIF: ATTRIB = one-time 1.2 something which someone used to have or which used to be a particular thing. EG *They have lost much of their former authority... They have been relocated quite near to their former homes... The college was in fact a former mansion.* ADJ CLASSIF: ATTRIB ⇑ earlier 1.3 a situation or period of time which came before the present one. EG *A selection of items published in former years was put out in book form.* ADJ CLASSIF: ATTRIB ≠ later

2 When two people, things, or groups have just been mentioned, you refer to the one that was mentioned first as the **former**. EG *The former believe in a strong centralized government... There is a widespread conspiracy to conceal the former and exaggerate the latter.* ▸ used as an adjective. EG *Lack of space forbids the former alternative.* N SING/PLURAL: *the*+N ≠ latter ▸ ADJ CLASSIF: *the*+ADJ+N

-former, -formers. **-former** combines with ordinal numbers to refer to a child who is in a particular year at school; used especially in British English. EG *They have all the skills we expect of fifth-formers.* COMB: FORMS N COUNTS

formerly /fɔːməli¹/. You use **formerly** to say that something happened, existed, or was the case at a time before the present time, but it no longer happens, exists, or is the case. EG *Some of my salesmen formerly worked for this rival concern... A sinister silence descends upon your formerly busy office... The ships would thus not be as dependent as formerly on return journeys to Black Sea ports... Lake Malawi, formerly Lake Nyasa, is 450 miles long.* ADV = previously

Formica /fɔːmaɪkə/; a trademark. **Formica** is a hard plastic that is used for covering kitchen worktops, tables, etc. N UNCOUNT

formidable /fɔːmɪdəbə⁰l/. Something or someone that is **formidable** is 1 rather frightening because it is difficult to do, deal with, or overcome. EG *No one is willing to take on the formidable task of changing the whole structure... He had earned the reputation of being a formidable opponent... ...her formidable grandmother.* ◊ **formidably**. EG *...a formidably difficult task.* ADJ QUALIT = daunting, intimidating ◊ ADV 2 very impressive because it is so good or great. EG *...the formidable army of brains that are at the Prime Minister's disposal... Nelson's portrait is said to be a formidable likeness.* ◊ **formidably**. EG *The jeeps came with army drivers, each formidably armed.* ADJ CLASSIF = prodigious ◊ ADV = prodigiously

formless /fɔːmlɪ²s/. Something that is **formless** 1 does not have a clear or definite physical shape. EG *...a group of formless shapes.* ADJ CLASSIF = amorphous 2 does not have a clear structure, or is not detailed; used of ideas, feelings, etc. EG *The apprehension had been shapeless, formless, completely lacking in detail.* ADJ CLASSIF = nebulous, vague

formula /fɔːmjə⁴lə/, **formulae, formulas**. The plural can be either **formulae** /fɔːmjə⁴liː/ or **formulas** in paragraph 1. In paragraph 2 the plural is **formulas**. 1 A **formula** is 1.1 a short group of letters, numbers, or other symbols which represents a scientific or mathematical rule. EG *He knew the formula for converting kilometres into miles... It all fits together with the precision of a mathematical formula.* N COUNT 1.2 a plan or set of rules that is thought up as a way of dealing with a particular problem, or of creating something. EG *There is no magic formula which, once learned, can thereafter be applied to every situation.... ...a peace formula... Each must find its own formula for the distribution of national income.* N COUNT: USU SING = proposal, solution 1.3 a list of substances which tells you what amounts to mix together in order to make another substance. EG *The formula for the new glue is a closely guarded secret.* N COUNT: USU SING ⇑ recipe

2 A **formula** is also an expression which is often used in a particular situation, especially one that has come to sound stupid and meaningless. EG *They liked to begin a paper with some formula like, 'I want to raise some questions that need answers.'* N COUNT: USU SING ⇑ phrase = cliché

3 **Formula** is used followed by a number to indicate a particular type of racing car or something relating to that type of car. EG *...Formula 1 racing.* N UNCOUNT+NUM

4 **Formula** is a powder which you mix with water to make a milky drink for babies; used in American English. N UNCOUNT ⇑ baby food

formulaic /fɔːmjə⁴leɪɪk/. A **formulaic** way of saying something has been used many times before in similar situations. EG *...formulaic expressions in Homer.* ADJ CLASSIF ⇑ fixed = set

formulate /fɔːmjə⁴leɪt/, **formulates, formulating, formulated**. 1 If you **formulate** something such as a plan or proposal, you invent it, thinking about the details carefully. EG *We had formulated our own strategy... ...the need to formulate a policy that will promote rather than hinder peace.* ◊ **formulation** /fɔːmjə⁴leɪʃə⁰n/, **formulations**. EG *...the formulation of a common foreign policy.* V+O ⇑ put together = work out ◊ N UNCOUNT/COUNT

2 If you **formulate** a thought, opinion, etc, you express it or describe it using particular words. EG *She made a promise to herself that she could not formulate in words... 'Public affluence and private squalor,' was how he formulated it.* ◊ **formulation, formulations**. EG *May I suggest the formulation 'Can we come to order, persons?'* V+O = encapsulate ◊ N UNCOUNT/COUNT

fornicate /fɔːnɪkeɪt/, **fornicates, fornicating, fornicated**. To **fornicate** means to have sex with someone who you are not married to; a formal or Biblical word used showing disapproval. ◊ **fornication** /fɔːnɪkeɪʃə⁰n/. V OR V+A *(with)*: RECIP ◊ N UNCOUNT

forsake /fə⁸seɪk/, **forsakes, forsaking, forsook, forsaken**; a fairly literary word. 1 If you **forsake** a person or place, you leave them when you should have stayed, or stop helping them or looking after them. EG *Don't forsake me in my hour of need!... ...not quite knowing why their leaders have forsaken them.* ◊ **forsaken**. EG *...a dusty, forsaken prairie village.* V+O = abandon, desert ◊ ADJ CLASSIF

2 If you **forsake** something, you stop doing it or using it. EG *Not that I want the girls to forsake their* V+O ⇑ reject

boisterous ways... Forsaking sober suits, they wore shorts and T-shirts.

3 To **forsake** something means to leave it or go away from it. EG *A porter forsook the shelter of the inn doorway and brought my bags in... Her mellow tranquillity forsook her then forever.* V+O = abandon

forswear /fɔˢswɛə/, **forswears, forswearing, forswore, forsworn**. If you **forswear** something, you stop doing it, having it, or using it, or you promise that you will. EG *Harold had forsworn fighting.* V+O ⇑ give up

forsythia /fɔːsaɪθɪə/ is a bush that has yellow flowers on it in the spring before the leaves have grown. N UNCOUNT/COUNT ⇑ shrub

fort /fɔːt/, **forts**. **1** A **fort** is a strong building or a place with a wall or fence around it where soldiers can stay and be safe from the enemy. N COUNT: ALSO IN NAMES

2 If you **hold the fort** for someone, you look after things for them while they are somewhere else. EG *Will you hold the fort for an hour?* PHR: VB INFLECTS, IF + PREP THEN *for*

forte /fɔːteɪ/, **fortes**. **1** If a particular activity is your **forte**, you are very good at it. EG *Cooking is hardly my forte.* N COUNT: POSS + N = strong point

2 A piece of music that is played **forte** is played loudly; a technical term in music. ADV WITH VB ≠ piano

forth /fɔːθ/; a rather formal or old-fashioned word. **1** When someone or something goes or is sent **forth**, they leave a particular place and move in a forward or outward direction away from it. EG *...the story of a tiny island which had sent forth her sons to conquer the world... The goats came bounding forth from their pens.* ADV AFTER VB ≠ back

2 When something is brought **forth**, it is brought out into a place where you can see it. EG *He reaches into his shiny leather briefcase, and brings forth a blue cardboard file... I found her dragging a slide-projector forth from a classroom.* ADV AFTER VB

3 When pieces of information, opinions, etc are put **forth**, they are made known to other people or written down. EG *The Welsh bishops met, discussed the matter, and put forth their conclusions... ...a book that sets forth the efforts of the early explorers to reach the East.* ADV AFTER VB

4 When words or signs of emotion are sent **forth**, they are spoken or shown in some way. EG *He flung forth an obscure prayer across the flowing stream... His eyes sent forth such signals of anguish that her heart melted.* ADV AFTER VB = out

5 If you say, when referring to a particular time, that **from** that time **forth** something has been or will be the case, you mean that it has been or will be the case ever afterwards, beginning from that time. EG *From that day forth the bishop was a marked man.* PHR: USED AS AN A ⇑ for ever

6 • **and so forth**: see **so**. • **back and forth**: see **back**. • to **hold forth**: see **hold**.

forthcoming /fɔːθkʌmɪŋ/; a fairly formal word. **1** A **forthcoming** event is planned to happen soon. EG *I wrote to the Minister asking his advice on the forthcoming presidential election.* ADJ CLASSIF: ATTRIB ⇑ future

2 If something is **forthcoming**, it is given or made available by someone, especially when it is needed. EG *No evidence of this was forthcoming... If Baker has his way the money will be forthcoming.* ADJ CLASSIF: PRED

3 Someone who is **forthcoming** willingly gives information about something when you ask them. EG *He was disinclined to talk about that: nor was he forthcoming on the way in which he had risen to power.* ADJ QUALIT: PRED = communicative

forthright /fɔːθraɪt/. Someone who is **forthright** shows clearly and strongly what they think and feel. EG *He had a reputation for being a bit forthright.* ▸ used of speech, actions, and behaviour. EG *Mr Wilson condemned the invasion in the most forthright terms... ...his forthright opposition to the Boer War.* ADJ QUALIT = blunt, direct

forthwith /fɔːθwɪθ, -wɪð/ means immediately; a formal word. EG *He would take up his new duties forthwith.* ADV WITH VB ⇑ now = at once

fortieth /fɔːtɪ²θ/. The **fortieth** item in a series is the one that you count as number forty: see ☐ at NUMBER and AGE. EG *...the fortieth president of the United States.* ORDINAL

fortification /fɔːtɪfɪkeɪʃəⁿn/, **fortifications**. **1** **Fortifications** are buildings, walls, ditches, etc that are built to protect a place against attack. EG *...a network of coastal fortifications.* N COUNT: USU PL

2 See also **fortify**.

fortified wine, fortified wines. **Fortified wine** is an alcoholic drink such as sherry or port that is made by mixing wine with a small amount of brandy or strong alcohol. N MASS

fortify /fɔːtɪfaɪ/, **fortifies, fortifying, fortified**. **1** If you **fortify** a place, you make it more able to resist an attack, for example by building a wall or ditch round it. EG *He spent his spare time fortifying the house against attacks... ...the tiny fortified town.* V+O ⇑ strengthen

◇ **fortification** /fɔːtɪfɪkeɪʃəⁿn/. EG *He drew plans for the fortification of Florence.* ◇ N UNCOUNT

2 Something that **fortifies** you, especially a drink or food, makes you feel stronger and more full of energy, courage, or determination. EG *Fortified with tea, he spoke slowly about his ordeal... To fortify himself, he began thinking about how pleased his wife would be... The effect of this was to fortify them in their resolve to try to save the party.* V+O (NG/REFL) ⇑ strengthen

◇ **fortification**. ◇ N UNCOUNT

3 Something that **fortifies** something, for example an idea or intention, makes it stronger or firmer. EG *Those Pioneer images had fortified the conventional idea that Jupiter's atmosphere was well ordered... The harrowing episode fortified her resolve to protest against such injustices.* ◇ **fortification**. V+O = strengthen; ◇ N UNCOUNT

4 Food that **is fortified** with a substance that people need has an amount of that substance added to it. EG *...a cereal fortified with iron and vitamins.* V+O: USU PASS = enrich

◇ **fortification**. ◇ N UNCOUNT

fortissimo /fɔːtɪsɪməʊ/. A piece of music that is played **fortissimo** is played very loudly; a technical term in music. EG *The band continued playing fortissimo.* ▸ used as an adjective. EG *...a fortissimo passage of the score.* ADV WITH VB ≠ pianissimo; ▸ ADJ CLASSIF

fortitude /fɔːtɪtjuːd/. If someone shows **fortitude** when they experience something unpleasant or painful, they do not complain and remain brave and calm. EG *Cal bore his pain with commendable fortitude.* N UNCOUNT ⇑ courage = stoicism

fortnight /fɔːtnaɪt/, **fortnights**. A **fortnight** is a period of two weeks. EG *He borrowed it a fortnight ago... I went to Rothesay for a fortnight... ...at the end of his fortnight's stay in London.* N COUNT: USU SING

fortnightly /fɔːtnaɪtli¹/. **1** Something that is **fortnightly** happens or appears once a fortnight or every fortnight. EG *...a fortnightly newspaper... ...fortnightly visits.* ▸ used as an adverb. EG *The therapy group meets fortnightly.* ADJ CLASSIF; ▸ ADV AFTER VB

2 **Fortnightly** means relating to or consisting of a period of a fortnight. EG *...for four or five days in each fortnightly cycle.* ADJ CLASSIF

fortress /fɔːtrɪ²s/, **fortresses**. A **fortress** is a castle or other large strong building, or a well-protected place, which is intended to be difficult for enemies to enter. EG *...the massive fortress built into the rock.* N COUNT

fortuitous /fəˢtjuːɪtəs/. A **fortuitous** event or result happens completely by chance. EG *It is more likely to be a fortuitous discovery than the result of a concerted effort to find it.* ADJ QUALIT ⇑ accidental = coincidental

fortunate /fɔːtʃə⁴nɪ¹t/. **1** Someone who is **fortunate** has good luck or has something good. EG *...those who are fortunate enough to get jobs... I have been unusually fortunate in my parents and teachers... Other, less fortunate, children died much earlier.* ADJ QUALIT ⇑ lucky

2 A **fortunate** event happens by chance and is good for a particular person. EG *...a fortunate choice... It was fortunate indeed for Mr Fox that he decided to wait.* ADJ QUALIT ⇑ lucky

fortunately /fɔːtʃə⁴nətli¹/ is used to introduce or indicate a statement about an event or situation that is good. EG *I was afraid Peggy would be disappointed, but fortunately she didn't seem to mind... Fortunately such occurrences are fairly rare... Fortunately for us, the damage was only slight.* ADV SEN ⇑ luckily = happily

fortune /fɔːtʃəⁿn/, **fortunes**. **1** **Fortune** or good **fortune** is good luck, success, or good experiences. Bad **fortune** is bad luck or lack of success. EG *It would be unfair to envy him his good fortune... ...people who did not have the fortune to live in Britain... ...protection against ill fortune and disaster.* N UNCOUNT

2 You refer to the way that someone is treated by **fortune** or by the **fortunes** of war, history, etc as a way of referring to the good or bad luck that they have. EG *Fortune had been kind to him... But the fortunes of war turned against them.* N UNCOUNT, OR N PLURAL + *of* = fate

3 Someone or something's **fortunes** are the extent to N PLURAL: WITH which they are doing well or being successful. EG *In the following years, Victor's fortunes improved considerably... Once again the fortunes of England are low.* POSS

4 Someone who **tells** your **fortune** looks at something, for example the lines on your hand or playing cards, and tells you what they think these indicate will happen to you in the future. PHR : VB INFLECTS ⇑ predict

5 If you have a **fortune**, you have a very large amount of money. EG *His father left him an immense fortune... Her father had made a fortune in scrap metal.* N COUNT = wealth

6 You refer to a sum of money as a **fortune** or a small or tidy **fortune** when you think it is a very large amount of money. EG *She earns a fortune... That suit had cost me a small fortune.* N SING : a+N = bomb, mint

fortune-teller, fortune-tellers. A **fortune-teller** is a person who tells people's fortunes. N COUNT ⇑ clairvoyant

forty /fɔːti[1]/, **forties.** **Forty** is the number 40: see □ at NUMBER, AGE, DATE, MEASUREMENT, MONEY, and TIME. EG *We have a nursery school for forty children... ...women in their forties.* ● **forty winks**: see **wink.** NUM

forum /fɔːrəm/, **forums.** **1** A **forum** is a place, situation, or group in which people exchange ideas and discuss issues, especially important public issues. EG *...parliament's role as a forum for debate... The journal serves as a regular forum for the interchange of information and ideas... The next programme will be a listeners' forum in which you can air your views.* N COUNT : USU SING ⇑ meeting place

2 In ancient Roman towns, the **forum** was a square where people met to discuss business and political matters. N COUNT ⇑ meeting place

forward /fɔːwəd/, **forwards, forwarding, forwarded.** **1** If someone or something moves, looks, or faces **forward** or **forwards**, they move, look, or face in a direction that is in front of them. EG *Ralph took a sudden step forward... The seats face forward... I reach forward and flip the headlight switch... John peered forward through the twilight... Suddenly she leaned forward.* ADV AFTER VB ≠ backwards ▸ **Forward** is also used as an adjective. EG *...the impetus of his forward movement.* ▸ ADJ CLASSIF : ATTRIB ≠ backward ● **backwards and forwards**: see **backwards.**

2 If you bring something or move **forward** or **forwards**, you bring it or move towards a particular person or place. EG *Salesmen rush forward to serve her... He pulled forward a chair, and the man sat down.* ADV AFTER VB ≠ backwards

3 **Forward** also means in a position near the front of something such as a building or a vehicle. EG *I like to have the seat quite far forward when I'm driving... He was sitting in a forward pew this morning.* ADJ CLASSIF ≠ back

4 Something that is **forward of** a particular thing or place is in front of it or further ahead, especially on a ship or aircraft. EG *...a bulky item of cargo immediately forward of the one behind which we were sheltering.* PREP

5 If you look or go **forward** in time, you look or go into the future. EG *When I was your age I could only look forward.* ADV AFTER VB ▸ used as an adjective. EG *...forward planning.* ▸ ADJ CLASSIF : ATTRIB ● to **look forward to** something: see **look.**

6 If you put a clock or watch **forward**, you change the time shown on it so that it shows a later time, for example when the time changes to summer time. EG *I set my watch forward once again.* ADV AFTER VB ≠ back

7 If you say, when referring to a particular time, that **from** that time **forward** something was the case, you mean that it was the case ever afterwards, beginning from that time. EG *From this point forward I tried to acquire the information I needed.* PHR : USED AS AN A = forth

8 **Forward** or **forwards** is also used to indicate that something changes or develops so as to improve or become more modern. EG *They had to be persuaded that there was a better way forward by closer cooperation... Obviously it's a great step forward for you... We're interested in moving society forward into a better world.* ADJ AFTER N, OR ADV WITH VB ≠ backwards

9 You say how far **forward** a project is as a way of saying how far it has progressed. EG *We're no further forward than we were two weeks ago.* ADJ CLASSIF : PRED, ADV+ADJ ≠ behind

10 Something or someone that is brought **forward** or comes **forward** is suggested or offered as suitable for a particular purpose. EG *Various theories have been put forward... I once brought forward a motion that swearing be abolished by law... More than 700 people have come forward so far.* ADV AFTER VB

11 If a piece of film or music is played **forwards** or **forward**, or if a book is read **forwards**, it is played or read from the beginning towards the end rather than from the end towards the beginning. ADV AFTER VB = backwards

12 If you **forward** a letter or piece of information to someone, you send it on to them, especially when they have asked you to do this when they move to a different address. EG *Would you mind forwarding my mail to this address?... Any information is to be forwarded to Sergeant Ayr.* V+O

13 If you **forward** something, you cause it to progress or improve. EG *He's hoping to forward his career by this move.* V+O = further

14 Someone who is **forward** speaks boldly to people in a way that is thought to be disrespectful. EG *'I told her she ought to slim.'–'That was very forward of you.'* ADJ QUALIT ◊ **forwardness.** EG *I am conscious of my forwardness in applying to you.* ◊ N UNCOUNT

15 In football, rugby, or hockey, a **forward** is a player whose job is to try to score goals rather than to defend their own goal. EG *He's built like a rugby forward.* N COUNT ≠ back

forwarding address, forwarding addresses. A **forwarding address** is an address that you give to someone when you go and live somewhere else so that they can send your mail on to you. EG *She had gone to Spain, leaving no forwarding address.* N COUNT

forward-looking. Someone who is **forward-looking** thinks about the future or has modern ideas. EG *As a publisher, Ernest Benn was forward-looking and imaginative.* ADJ QUALIT ≠ backward-looking

forwent /fɔːwent/ is the past tense of **forgo.**

fossil /fɒsəl/, **fossils.** A **fossil** is the hardened remains of a prehistoric animal or plant that are found inside a rock. N COUNT

fossil fuel, fossil fuels. A **fossil fuel** is a fuel such as coal, oil, or peat that is formed from the decayed remains of plants or animals. N MASS

fossilize /fɒsɪlaɪz/, **fossilizes, fossilizing, fossilized**; also spelled **fossilise.** **1** If the remains of an animal or plant **fossilize** or **are fossilized**, they become hard and form fossils, instead of decaying completely. EG *...fossilised human bones... Brains do not fossilize.* V-ERG : USU PASS = ossify ◊ **fossilization** /fɒsɪlaɪzeɪʃən/. EG *...the physical and chemical conditions necessary for fossilisation.* ◊ N UNCOUNT = ossification

2 If ideas, attitudes, or ways of behaving **are fossilized**, they are fixed and unlikely to change, in spite of changing situations or circumstances. EG *...its obsolete, fossilised ways and immovable conservatism.* V-ERG : USU PASS = set, inflexible

foster /fɒstə/, **fosters, fostering, fostered.** **1** **Foster** parents are people who take someone else's child into their family for a period of time, by arrangement with an official authority, without becoming the child's legal parent. A **foster** child is the child who they look after. EG *Not enough time or trouble is taken in introducing foster children to their new families... ...her foster mother.* ADJ CLASSIF : ATTRIB ⇑ temporary ▸ used of the system of providing children with foster parents. EG *Their children are in foster care.*

2 If you **foster** a child, you take someone else's child into your family for a period of time, without becoming the child's legal parent: compare **adopt.** EG *When they are fostered, boys have more behaviour problems than girls... People who can't have children of their own sometimes foster... ...fostered children.* V OR V+O ⇑ look after ◊ **fostering.** EG *...fostering arrangements.* ◊ N UNCOUNT

3 If you **foster** something such as an activity or idea, you help its development or growth by encouraging people to do or think it. EG *The local council has a policy of fostering music, drama, and crafts... The industrialism of the nineteenth century fostered a harsh, crude life-style... ...a popular image, fostered by the media.* V+O = promote

fought /fɔːt/ is the past tense of **fight.**

foul /faʊl/, **fouler, foulest; fouls, fouling, fouled.** **1** If something is **foul**, **1.1** it is unpleasant because it is dirty or decayed. EG *The water in the pools became tepid and foul... We spent a grim night in a very foul cabin.* ADJ QUALIT = filthy **1.2** it is unpleasant and not at all enjoyable or successful. EG *I've had a really foul day at work... It's such foul luck for you all.* ADJ QUALIT = rotten **1.3** it is evil and wicked. EG *...a foul crime.* ADJ QUALIT = base, vile

2 If you say that you will do something **by fair means or foul**, you are prepared to use any means at all in PHR : USED AS AN A order to get what you want and you do not care if your behaviour is dishonest and unfair.

3 **Foul** weather is unpleasant, windy, and stormy with a lot of rain or snow. ADJ QUALIT ⇑ bad

4 **Foul** language is offensive and contains unacceptable words such as swear words and rude words related to sex or other bodily functions. EG *I won't have you using such foul language in my house!* ADJ QUALIT ⇑ bad = coarse, obscene
▸ used of people who use foul language, or of their way of thinking. EG *What a foul mind you've got!* ▸ = filthy

5 If someone has a **foul** temper, they become angry or violent very suddenly and easily. ADJ QUALIT : USU ATTRIB

6 If you **fall foul of** someone, or if you **run foul of** them, you do something which makes them angry or annoyed with you. EG *He was found drowned in a river after falling foul of local poachers.* PHR : VB INFLECTS ⇑ anger

7 If you **foul** something, 7.1 you make it dirty. EG *The deck would soon be fouled with the blood from their backs... ...a tern lying on a beach, fouled by oil.* V+O = soil 7.2 you drop faeces onto it. EG *...an elector who was complaining about dogs fouling the pavement.* V+O = soil

8 If something **fouls** a mechanism, device, net, etc it accidentally becomes twisted or knotted around it and prevents it from working properly. EG *The boat's engine stopped because some weed had fouled the propeller... They fouled their nets on these underwater obstructions... Suddenly the rope started coming too fast. It fouled on the winch.* V-ERG ⇑ block = snag

9 If a player **fouls** in a game or sport, or if they **foul** another player, they do something which is not allowed according to the rules. V OR V+O

10 A **foul** is an act in a game of sport that is not allowed according to the rules. EG *The England team's record of fouls was among the worst.* N COUNT ⇑ infringement ▸ used as an adjective. EG *If the white ball goes into a pocket in snooker, it is a foul shot.* ▸ ADJ CLASSIF : ATTRIB ≠ acceptable

foul up. If you **foul up** something such as a plan, you spoil it by doing something wrong or stupid; used in informal English. EG *So many good projects have been fouled up by elementary mistakes in planning.* • See also **foul-up**. PHRASAL VB : V+O+ADV ⇑ ruin = mess up

foul-mouthed. If someone is **foul-mouthed**, their language is offensive and contains unacceptable words such as swear words and rude words related to sex or other bodily functions. EG *...eight noisy foul-mouthed women, all shouting at once.* ADJ QUALIT = obscene, abusive

foul play is 1 criminal violence or activity that results in a person's death. EG *There was no evidence of foul play; many people die from accidental poisoning.* N UNCOUNT ⇑ murder 2 unfair or dishonest behaviour; used showing disapproval. EG *He would be willing to use any ruse, any dirty trick, any amount of foul play to get what he wanted.* N UNCOUNT = skulduggery

foul-up, foul-ups. A **foul-up** is a state of disorder or trouble which is the result of mistakes or carelessness; used in informal English. EG *The Centre hates that kind of foul-up.* N COUNT = mess

found /faʊnd/, **founds, founding, founded**. 1 **Found** is the past tense and past participle of **find**.

2 If someone **founds** an institution, company, organization, etc, they set it up, often by providing the necessary money. EG *The Constituency Labour Party was founded in 1918 by Walter Ayles and others... The following year they founded a magazine called Socialist Review.* • See also **founding**. V+O ⇑ start = establish, form

3 If someone **founds** a town, important building, or other place, they begin to build it or cause it to be built. EG *The theatre was founded in 1720, but rebuilt by Nash in 1820... Cortes founded Mexico City.* V+O ⇑ start

4 If something **is founded** on a particular thing, such as a source of support or strength, it is based on it. EG *A political system founded on force alone is an uneasy and fragile arrangement... The settlement was founded upon facts.* • See also **wellfounded**. V+O+A, USU PASS = be built

5 If you **found** metal or glass, you make it into a particular shape by melting it and pouring it into a mould. V+O

foundation /faʊndeɪʃᵊn/, **foundations**. 1 The **foundation** or **foundations** of something such as a belief or way of life is the basic idea, attitude, or experience on which that belief or way of life is built. EG *Respect for the law is the very foundation of civilised living... The industrial revolution was firmly built on the foundations of an agricultural revolution... This early training gave her a very firm foundation.* N COUNT+SUPP = basis

2 The **foundations** of a building or other structure are the layer of bricks, concrete, etc below the ground that it must be built on so that it is solidly supported. N PLURAL

3 The **foundation** of an institution, company, organization, etc, is the fact or act of setting it up. EG *There have been continued financial problems since the foundation of the university.* N SING : the+N+of = founding DET

4 A **foundation** is an organization, often set up by the legacy of a person who has died, which provides money for a special purpose such as research or a charity. EG *...the National Foundation for Educational Research... In America they have many different foundations and bequests.* N COUNT : ALSO IN NAMES

5 If a story, idea, or argument has no **foundation**, there are no facts to support it and prove that it is true. EG *This theory seems to have no foundation in physical observation and experiment... The suggestion that I am about to resign is absurd and without foundation.* N UNCOUNT : USU WITH BROAD NEG ⇑ evidence = basis, justification

6 **Foundation** or **foundation cream** is a skin-coloured cream that a woman puts on her face before putting on the rest of her make-up. N MASS

foundation course, foundation courses. In Britain, a **foundation course** is a course that you do at some colleges and universities in order to prepare you for a longer or more advanced course. N COUNT

foundation stone, foundation stones; also spelled with a hyphen. A **foundation stone** is a large smooth block of stone built into a large public building near the bottom. The foundation stone is usually unveiled at a ceremony when the building is complete, and it usually has words cut into it which record the occasion. EG *The foundation stone was laid by the Duke of Edinburgh.* N COUNT

founder /faʊndə/, **founders, foundering, foundered**. 1 The **founder** of an institution, organization, building, etc is the person who sets it up, or causes it to be built, perhaps by providing the necessary money. EG *Thomas Kemp, the founder of Kemp Town.* N COUNT : USU WITH POSS

2 If something **founders**, it fails because of a particular point, difficulty, or problem. EG *His arguments foundered on the Norfolk case of 1302... Without their assistance the arrangement would have foundered pretty quickly.* V = break down

3 If a ship **founders**, it fills with water and sinks. V : USU+A

founder member, founder members. A **founder member** of a club, group, or organization is one of the original members, often one who was involved in setting it up. EG *...Geoff Carlsson, a founder member of the Socialist Review group.* N COUNT : USU+of

founding /faʊndɪŋ/. 1 **Founding** is used to refer to the time that an institution or organization is first set up. EG *The organization held its founding conference in Birmingham... He made moving reference to the party's founding philosophy.* ADJ CLASSIF : ATTRIB ⇑ initial

2 The **founding** of an institution, company, organization, etc, is the fact or activity of setting it up. EG *He opposed the founding of the National Gallery.* N SING : the+N+of = foundation

founding father, founding fathers. The **founding father** of an institution, organization, idea, etc is the person who sets it up or who first it; a literary expression. EG *...the founding fathers of the university. If economics has a founding father, it is Smith.* N COUNT : USU PL = founder

2 The **Founding Fathers** of the United States were the members of the American Constitutional Convention of 1787. N PLURAL

foundling /faʊndlɪŋ/, **foundlings**. A **foundling** is a baby which has been abandoned by its parents, often in a public place, and then been found by someone; an old-fashioned word. N COUNT ⇑ outcast

foundry /faʊndri[1]/, **foundries**. A **foundry** is a place where metal or glass is melted and formed into particular shapes. N COUNT ⇑ factory

fount /faʊnt/. If you describe a person or thing as the **fount** of something, you are saying that they are an important source or supply of it; a literary word. EG *...the Encyclopaedia Britannica, the fount of all knowledge... ...the prime fount of business opportunity in almost all countries.* N SING WITH DET +of

fountain /faʊntɪn/, **fountains**. 1 A **fountain** is an ornamental feature in a pool or lake which consists of a spray or jet of water that is forced up into the air by a pump. It is often part of a specially built pool and is sometimes in the form of a statue. EG *...the fountain in the courtyard of the mosque... ...a sunken* N COUNT ⇑ structure *garden with a pond and a fountain playing.* ● See also **drinking fountain, soda fountain.**

2 A **fountain** of something is a powerful jet or spray of it going up into the air. EG *A fountain of blood shot up... ...sudden shattering fountains of red fireballs and flames.* N COUNT+*of* ⇑ flow = shower

3 If you describe something as a **fountain**, you are saying that it seems light, bright, and flowing, like the spray of water in a fountain; a literary use. EG *...the full fountain of white blossom.* N COUNT : USU+*of* = cascade

4 If you describe a person or thing as a **fountain** of something, you are saying that they are an important source or supply of it; a literary use. EG *Regions such as Africa have proved to be the fountain of many new ideas about the causes of cancer.* N SING WITH DET +*of* = fount

fountain pen, fountain pens; also spelled with a hyphen or as one word. A **fountain pen** is a pen with a nib that is supplied with ink from a container inside the pen. N COUNT

four /fɔː/, **fours**. 1 **Four** is the number 4: see □ at NUMBER, AGE, DATE, MEASUREMENT, MONEY, and TIME. EG *His mother died when he was four and he was brought up by an aunt... ...a four-mile walk.* NUM

2 A **four** is 2.1 a narrow racing boat that is rowed by a team of four people. 2.2 a team of four people, or a group of four people or things. N COUNT N COUNT

3 If you are **on all fours**, you are crawling or leaning on your hands and knees. EG *Claud slipped through the hedge on all fours and I followed.* PHR : USED AS AN A

four-letter word, four-letter words. A **four-letter word** is a short word that people consider to be rude or offensive, usually because it refers to sex or other bodily functions. N COUNT = swear-word

four-ply wool, rope, wood, etc has four layers or strands. ADJ CLASSIF

four-poster, four-posters; also spelled without a hyphen. A **four-poster** or a **four-poster bed** is a large old-fashioned bed that has a tall post at each corner and curtains that can be drawn around it. N COUNT

foursome /fɔːsəm/, **foursomes**. A **foursome** is a group of four people or things. EG *We functioned well as a foursome.* N COUNT

four-square. If something is **four-square**, 1 it looks solid and square in shape. EG *...a four-square house, with corner turrets and battlements.* 2 it is straight and placed or balanced firmly on something. EG *...with his regulation chef's hat four-square on his greying clipped hair.* 3 it is strong and steady, and unlikely to be affected by changing situations. EG *...the four-square rock-like quality of the old religion.* ADJ CLASSIF; ADJ CLASSIF, OR ADV = squarely; ADJ CLASSIF = solid

fourteen /fɔːtiːn/ is the number 14: see □ at NUMBER, AGE, DATE, MEASUREMENT, MONEY, and TIME. EG *He was the eldest of a family of fourteen children.* NUM

fourteenth /fɔːtiːnθ/. The **fourteenth** item in a series is the one that you count as number fourteen: see □ at NUMBER, AGE, and DATE. EG *...their son's fourteenth birthday.* ORDINAL

fourth /fɔːθ/, **fourths**. 1 The **fourth** item in a series is the one that you count as number four: see □ at NUMBER, AGE, and DATE. EG *My mother died just before my fourth birthday.* ORDINAL

2 A **fourth** is 2.1 one of four equal parts of something. EG *They conceded him three-fourths or more of the spending cuts he sought.* 2.2 the interval between two notes on a musical scale when there are two notes separating them. N COUNT : USU+*of*; N COUNT : USU SING

fourth dimension. The **fourth dimension**, in physics, is time. The other three dimensions are length, breadth, and height. N SING : *the*+N

fourthly /fɔːθli[1]/. You use **fourthly** when you want to make a fourth point or to give a fourth reason that is connected with three points or reasons which you have already stated. EG *Fourthly, there will need to be a guarantee of full employment.* ADV SEN

Fourth of July. The **Fourth of July** is a holiday in the United States when people celebrate the Declaration of Independence in 1776. N SING : *the*+N = Independence Day

fowl /faʊl/, **fowls**. **Fowl** can also be used as the plural form. A **fowl** is a bird, especially one that is hunted or that can be eaten as food, such as a duck or chicken. There are many kinds of fowl. EG *...guinea fowl.* N COUNT/ UNCOUNT

fox /fɒks/, **foxes, foxing, foxed**. 1 A **fox** is a wild animal which looks like a dog and has reddish-brown fur, a pointed face and ears, and a thick tail. EG *...the footprints of wildcats, badgers and foxes.* N COUNT

2 If something is made of **fox**, it is made from the fur and skin of a fox. EG *...a shaggy red fox coat.* N UNCOUNT

3 If you call someone a **fox**, you are saying that they do things in clever ways, such as by deceiving people or by being dishonest and secretive; used showing disapproval. EG *It was probably the Colonel's doing, and the wily old fox was making damn sure he didn't leave any tracks.* N COUNT = devil

4 If something **foxes** you, it causes you a lot of difficulty, so that you cannot understand or complete it; an informal use. EG *When you get a piece of handwriting which really foxes you, you have a very careful look at it... The computers were foxed by the calculations.* V+O = baffle, stump

foxglove /fɒksglʌv/, **foxgloves**. A **foxglove** is a tall plant that has pink or white flowers shaped like bells growing up the stem. N COUNT

foxhole /fɒkshəʊl/, **foxholes**. A **foxhole** is a small pit that soldiers dig as a shelter from the enemy and from which they can shoot. N COUNT

foxhound /fɒkshaʊnd/, **foxhounds**. A **foxhound** is a type of dog that is trained to hunt foxes. N COUNT

fox-hunting is a sport in which people, riding horses, chase foxes across the countryside. They use foxhounds to track down the foxes. N UNCOUNT

foxy /fɒksi[1]/, **foxier, foxiest**. If someone is **foxy**, they are deceitful in a clever, secretive way. EG *...a certain foxy gentleman.* ▸ used of someone's appearance or behaviour. EG *He cast a foxy glance at her.* ADJ QUALIT = artful ▸ = sly

foyer /fɔɪeɪ, fɔɪə/, **foyers**. A **foyer** is the large area where people meet or wait just inside the main doors of a theatre, cinema, hotel, etc. N COUNT : USU *the*+N = lobby

Fr. is 1 a written abbreviation for 'French' and 'franc'. 2 a written abbreviation for 'Father'; used in titles before the name of a Catholic priest.

fracas /frækɑː/. A **fracas** is a rough, noisy quarrel or fight. EG *They got involved in another fracas.* N SING WITH DET

fraction /frækʃə[0]n/, **fractions**. A **fraction** is 1 a tiny amount or proportion of something. EG *The door opened a fraction... My new job pays just that fraction more... For a fraction of a second I hesitated.* 2 an exact division of a figure that is used in arithmetic. For example, ½ and are both fractions of 1. EG *The output voltage is a certain fraction of the input voltage.* N PART ⇑ bit; N COUNT : IF+ PREP THEN *of*

fractional /frækʃə[0]nəl, -ʃənə[0]l/. If something is **fractional**, it is very small in size or degree. EG *...a fractional hesitation.* ◊ **fractionally**. EG *They're only fractionally different.* ADJ QUALIT = minute; ◊ ADV = marginally

fractious /frækʃə[0]s/. If someone, especially a child, is **fractious**, they become upset or angry very quickly about small unimportant things, often because they are tired. EG *She was fractious with other children.* ▸ used of a person's behaviour. EG *...in a fractious mood.* ADJ QUALIT = irritable ▸ = cantankerous

fracture /fræktʃə/, **fractures, fracturing, fractured**. 1 A **fracture** is a slight crack or break in something, especially a bone. EG *...a fracture of the left shoulder blade... ...small fractures in the rock.* N COUNT

2 If something such as a bone **fractures** or **is fractured**, it gets a slight crack in it. EG *...serious injuries such as broken ribs, smashed kidneys, and fractured skulls... The vibration of the bells is said to fracture the towers that they hang in.* V-ERG

3 To **fracture** something means to harm or damage it; a fairly formal use. EG *His reputation for integrity was permanently fractured.* V+O = impair

fragile /frædʒaɪl/. 1 If something is **fragile**, 1.1 it is easily spoilt or harmed, and therefore needs to be treated carefully. EG *...extremely fragile economies... A fragile peace had been reached.* ◊ **fragility** /frə[3]dʒɪlɪti[1]/. EG *...the fragility of their communications links.* 1.2 it is thin or delicate, and therefore easily broken or damaged. EG *...constructions built of fragile materials that simply fall apart after a short period of time.* ◊ **fragility**. 1.3 very delicate or fine in appearance. EG *...the castle with its fragile turrets.* ADJ QUALIT = delicate, tenuous; ◊ N UNCOUNT; ADJ QUALIT = flimsy ≠ tough; ADJ QUALIT = dainty

2 If you feel **fragile**, you feel weak, for example because you are ill or because you have drunk too much alcohol; an informal expression. EG *You're looking a bit fragile this morning.* ADJ QUALIT = delicate

fragment, fragments, fragmenting, fragmented. The word **fragment** is pronounced /frægmə[2]nt/ when it is a noun, and /frægment/ when it is a verb. 1 A **fragment** of something is a small piece or part of it. EG *...a small fragment of black, fossilized bone... I tried to scoop up the broken* N COUNT : USU+ *of/from* = bit, scrap *fragments... This was only a fragment out of a long conversation with John.*

2 If something **fragments** or **is fragmented**, it breaks or separates into small pieces. EG *There was a threat that the entire body might fragment... Farms are constantly being fragmented into smaller and smaller holdings.* ◇ **fragmentation** /frægmɛnteɪʃə⁰n/. EG *This led to its fragmentation into eight independent parties.* V-ERG = split up; ◇ N UNCOUNT = split

fragmentary /frægmə²ntə⁰ri¹/. Something that is **fragmentary** is made up of small or unconnected pieces. EG *...the fragmentary evidence for this history.* ADJ QUALIT = sketchy

fragmented /frægmɛntɪd/. Something that is **fragmented** consists of a lot of different things or parts which seem unconnected with each other. EG *It's a book that is very fragmented and very complicated in its structure... ...the disordered, fragmented world of the sixties.* ADJ QUALIT ⇑ bitty = disjointed

fragrance /freɪgrəns/, **fragrances**. A **fragrance** is a pleasant or sweet smell. EG *...the deep, musky fragrance of the mangroves.* N COUNT : USU + SUPP = scent

fragrant /freɪgrənt/. Something that is **fragrant** has a pleasant, sweet smell. EG *...fragrant flowers... ...her mass of fragrant hair.* ADJ QUALIT

frail /freɪl/, **frailer, frailest**. 1 Someone who is **frail** is not very strong or healthy. EG *...a frail old man.* ADJ QUALIT ⇑ weak = delicate

2 Something that is **frail** is easily broken or damaged. EG *...a frail structure.* ADJ QUALIT = fragile

frailty /freɪlti¹/, **frailties**. 1 If you refer to the **frailties** or **frailty** of people, you are referring to their weaknesses. EG *...our many vanities and frailties... ...human frailty.* N COUNT : USU PL, OR N UNCOUNT = imperfection

2 **Frailty** is the condition of being weak in health. EG *...the advanced age and frailty of some of the inhabitants.* N UNCOUNT : IF + PREP THEN *of*

frame /freɪm/, **frames, framing, framed**. 1 A **frame** is 1.1 a hollow structure inside which you can fit something such as a window, door, or picture, or across which you can stretch something such as embroidery or canvas. Frames are usually rectangular and made of wood or metal. EG *...gold-painted picture frames... The name plate was screwed into the door frame immediately below the bell... She lifted the cushions from the bamboo chair frame and put them aside.* ● See also **cold frame**. N COUNT ⇑ edge **1.2** a piece of equipment made of bars, for example one used by old or ill people to support themselves while they walk, or an arrangement of bars for children to climb and play on. N COUNT ⇑ apparatus **1.3** the general context which forms the background to something which you are discussing or considering. EG *These stories are all set safely in a nice domestic frame.* N COUNT + SUPP

2 The **frame** of a pair of glasses is the wire or plastic part which holds the lenses in place. EG *They wore sunglasses with black frames.* N COUNT

3 A **frame** of a cinema film is one of the many separate photographs of which it is made up. EG *They ran the film through at about fifty thousand frames per second.* N COUNT

4 Your **frame** is your body, considered as a complete structure. EG *His big frame was gaunt and weak... A sharp tingling sensation ran through her whole frame.* N COUNT : USU POSS + N IN SING

5 A **frame** building is built with a frame of wooden posts which are joined together by boards or filled with bricks. EG *...a cluster of old wooden frame houses.* N BEFORE N

6 If you **frame** something such as a picture or photograph, you put it in a frame. EG *Are you having your picture professionally framed?* ◇ **framed**. EG *There were framed snaps of family and friends on her desk.* V+O : USU PASS; ◇ ADJ CLASSIF

7 If something **is framed** by a particular thing, it is surrounded by it in a way that emphasizes it and its shape. EG *He had a fine powerful face, framed in a mass of long grey hair... She stood framed in the doorway of the dining-room.* V+O : USU PASS

8 If you **frame** something such as a set of rules, a plan, or a system, you create and develop it; a fairly formal use. EG *The military plan will be framed tomorrow... What previous documents have they drawn upon in framing their constitution?* V+O = formulate

9 If you **frame** something such as a document or statement in a particular kind of language, you express it in that way. EG *Laws are invariably framed in tortuous jargon.* V+O+A = couch

10 If someone **frames** you, they pretend that you have committed a crime by deliberately lying or inventing evidence. EG *For goodness sake–don't you see? We've been framed!* V+O ⇑ implicate = set up

frame of mind, frames of mind. Your **frame of mind** is the mood that you are in, which causes you to have a particular attitude to something. EG *I'm not in the right frame of mind for riddles, Tana.* N COUNT : USU SING = humour

frame of reference, frames of reference. A **frame of reference** is a particular set of beliefs, ideas, or observations on which you base your judgement of things. EG *Their frame of reference was totally American.* N COUNT ⇑ outlook

frame-up, frame-ups. A **frame-up** is a situation where someone pretends that an innocent person has committed a crime by deliberately lying or inventing evidence; an informal word. EG *The girl snorted that it was a frame-up and went off in search of the true culprit.* N COUNT = set-up

framework /freɪmwɜːk/, **frameworks**. A **framework** is 1 a structure that forms a support or frame for something. EG *There are nine large panels set in a richly carved framework.* N COUNT 2 a particular set of rules, ideas, or beliefs which you use in order to deal with problems or to decide what to do. EG *You can't make decisions without an ethical framework... They were able to absorb these changes within the framework of traditional institutions and ideas.* N COUNT : USU + SUPP ⇑ structure = frame of reference

franc /fræŋk/, **francs**. The **franc** is one of the different units of money of France, Switzerland, Belgium, and of some other countries where French is spoken. EG *The franc plunged to its lowest rate against the dollar for a year... It cost twenty thousand Belgian francs.* N COUNT : USU NUM + N, OR N SING : *the* + N ⇑ currency

franchise /fræntʃaɪz/, **franchises**. 1 **Franchise** is the right to vote in an election, especially one in which people elect a parliament. EG *...a policy of universal franchise.* N UNCOUNT, OR N SING WITH DET

2 A **franchise** is an authority that is given by a company to someone, allowing them to sell its goods or services. EG *...a farm equipment franchise.* N COUNT

frank /fræŋk/, **franker, frankest; franks, franking, franked**. 1 If someone is **frank**, they state or express things in an open, honest, and straightforward way. EG *John was perfectly frank with him.* ▸ used of the things that they say or their behaviour. EG *...a really frank discussion... She looked at him with frank eyes.* ◇ **frankness**. EG *He certainly seemed to be speaking with complete frankness.* ADJ QUALIT; ▸ = candid; ◇ N UNCOUNT = sincerity

2 To **frank** a letter or parcel means to put a mark on it that shows that the proper charge has been paid or that no stamp is needed. V+O

frankfurter /fræŋkfɜːtə/, **frankfurters**. A **frankfurter** is a type of smoked sausage. N COUNT

frankincense /fræŋkɪnsɛns/ is a substance that is burned as incense and is obtained from a tree. N UNCOUNT

frankly /fræŋkli¹/. 1 You use **frankly** when you are stating an opinion to emphasize that you mean what you are saying, even though the person you are speaking to may not like it. EG *Frankly, this has all come as a bit of a shock... It is frankly absurd... Quite frankly, I am too miserable to care.* ADV SEN = honestly

2 If you say or do something **frankly**, you say or do it in an open, honest, and straightforward way. EG *He asked me to tell him frankly what I wished to do.* ADV WITH VB = candidly

frantic /fræntɪk/. 1 If you are **frantic**, you are behaving in a wild and desperate way because you are frightened or worried. EG *We were frantic with worry.* ▸ used of people's behaviour. EG *...a frantic yell.* ◇ **frantically**. EG *...frantically searching for David.* ADJ QUALIT = distraught; ◇ ADV WITH VB = desperately

2 If an activity is **frantic**, things are done hurriedly and in an energetic but disorganized way. EG *...frantic activity... ...after a frantic week of high-level discussions.* ◇ **frantically**. ADJ QUALIT = hectic; ◇ ADV WITH VB

fraternal /frə³tɜːnə⁰l/ means having strong links of friendship and support with another group of people; a rather formal word. EG *Fraternal greetings were received from the Communist Party of the Soviet Union... ...towards a more fraternal and co-operative society.* ADJ CLASSIF = brotherly

fraternity /frə³tɜːnɪti¹/, **fraternities**. 1 **Fraternity** is the quality or activity of showing friendship and support to other people, who you think of as your brothers. EG *...liberty, equality, and fraternity.* N UNCOUNT = brotherhood

2 A **fraternity** is 2.1 a group of people who have the same profession or the same interests. EG *It's well-known amongst the computing fraternity... ...the elite of the banking fraternity... ...the boating fraternity.* 2.2 in American English, a society of male students formed for social purposes.
N COUNT : USU MOD+N = crowd; N COUNT

fraternize /frætənaɪz/, **fraternizes, fraternizing, fraternized**; also spelled **fraternise**. 1 If you **fraternize** with someone, you associate with them in a friendly way. EG *Ash fraternized with their sons and grandsons.*
V OR V+A (*with*) : RECIP = hobnob, mix

2 **Fraternizing with the enemy** is the offence of meeting and talking with enemies of your country, for which soldiers can be punished. EG *...punished for being off base and fraternizing with an enemy civilian.*
PHR : VB INFLECTS

fratricidal /frætrɪsaɪdə⁰l/. A **fratricidal** activity is one in which people kill members of their own society or social group. EG *They do not want a repetition of fratricidal collectivization and forced industrialization.*
ADJ CLASSIF

fratricide /frætrɪsaɪd/ is the crime of killing your brother.
N UNCOUNT

fraud /frɔːd/, **frauds**. 1 **Fraud** is the crime of gaining money or other benefits by deceit or trickery. EG *His closest adviser is under indictment for fraud.*
N UNCOUNT

2 A **fraud** is 2.1 something that deceives people in a way that is illegal or immoral. EG *The official investigation into the election frauds hadn't even begun.* 2.2 someone who pretends to be someone else or to have skills, abilities, or a status which they do not really possess. EG *He said he painted a little, the old fraud... I feel a bit of a fraud whenever people assume we're legally married.*
N COUNT = swindle; N COUNT = fake, impostor

fraudulence /frɔːdjə⁴ləns/ is the quality of being fraudulent. EG *He was aware of the fraudulence of what he was proposing.*
N UNCOUNT

fraudulent /frɔːdjə⁴lənt/. Something that is **fraudulent** is deliberately deceitful, dishonest, or untrue. EG *We were facing a fraudulent murder charge... The promise Mrs Haze had made was a fraudulent one... The election was fraudulent.*
ADJ CLASSIF = phoney

fraught /frɔːt/. 1 If a situation or action is **fraught** with problems or possibilities, it is filled with them. EG *Even this modest aim was fraught with problems... Any further moves would be fraught with danger... ...stares that were fraught with meaning.*
ADJ CLASSIF : PRED+*with* ⇑ full = charged

2 If someone is **fraught**, they are very worried or anxious. EG *Everyone's rather tense and fraught.* ▸ used of situations or actions. EG *It was a fraught evening altogether.*
ADJ QUALIT = uptight; ▸ = trying

fray /freɪ/, **frays, fraying, frayed**. 1 If something such as cloth or rope **is frayed**, or if it **frays**, its threads or strands become worn, loose, or broken. EG *His shirts were frayed... ...the fraying edge of the carpet.* ◇ **frayed**. EG *...frayed jeans.*
V-ERG; ◇ ADJ QUALIT

2 If your nerves **fray** or your temper **frays**, you feel irritable and nervous because of mental strain and anxiety. EG *Tempers were fraying... Nerves get frayed.*
V-ERG

3 The **fray** is an exciting or challenging activity, situation, or argument that you are involved in. EG *I returned to the fray with renewed vigour... She publicly joined the fray because of her interest in theatre.*
N SING : *the*+N = battle

frazzle /fræzə⁰l/; an informal word. 1 If you are **worn to a frazzle**, you are exhausted and irritable because of worry, problems, or overwork.
PHR : USED AS C = knackered

2 If something is burned **to a frazzle**, it is burned because it has been cooked for too long.
PHR : USED AS AN A

frazzled /fræzə⁰ld/; an informal word. 1 If you are **frazzled**, you are exhausted and often confused or irritable because of worry, problems, or overwork. EG *...a frazzled mother of five.*
ADJ QUALIT = harassed

2 If something is **frazzled**, it is burned or dried up because it has been cooked for too long or because it has been in the sun for too long. EG *I was frazzled and burned black by the sun.*
ADJ QUALIT

freak /friːk/, **freaks, freaking, freaked**. 1 A **freak** is 1.1 someone who is considered unusual because of their behaviour or attitudes; used showing disapproval. EG *A woman is considered a freak if she puts her career first... Ordinary people can become mentally ill; they are not freaks and many recover.* 1.2 a person or thing that is physically abnormal in some way. EG *...hair-raising freaks, including a two-headed Indian... ...freak potatoes.* 1.3 someone who is very enthusiastic about a particular thing; an informal use. EG *He was a real cleanliness freak.*
N COUNT = monster; N COUNT = mutant; N COUNT : MOD+N = fan, nut

2 A **freak** event or action is one that is very unusual and very unlikely to happen. EG *My mother died in a freak accident, struck by lightning at a picnic... Through some freak mechanical flaw all my coins came tumbling back... ...a freak rainstorm.*
N BEFORE N = bizarre, chance

3 If someone **freaks, freaks out**, or **is freaked out**, they are extremely surprised, upset, or angry, or they feel confused, for example because of drugs; an informal use. EG *His roommate freaked out on LSD and burned their place down... He'd freaked a little and become violent... Well, I'm freaked out by what we're seeing.*
V-ERG, OR PHRASAL VB : V-ERG+ADV

freakish /friːkɪʃ/. If something is **freakish**, it is unusual or unnatural, and therefore remarkable. EG *...an isolated, freakish event... ...freakish-looking people.* ◇ **freakishly**. EG *It was a sunny day, freakishly warm for the time of year.*
ADJ QUALIT = fantastic, strange; ◇ ADV = abnormally

freaky /friːki¹/, **freakier, freakiest**. If someone or something is **freaky**, they are very unusual in some way; an informal word. EG *The whole thing was freaky.*
ADJ QUALIT = weird, peculiar

freckle /frekə⁰l/, **freckles**. **Freckles** are small light brown spots on someone's skin, especially on their face. EG *She had red hair and freckles.*
N COUNT : USU PL ⇑ spot

freckled /frekə⁰ld/. If a part of your body is **freckled**, it has freckles on it. EG *...her freckled face.*
ADJ CLASSIF ⇑ spotted

free /friː/, **frees, freeing, freed; freer, freest**. 1 Someone or something that is **free** is not restricted, controlled, or limited, for example by rules, customs, or other people. EG *Within the EEC there is of course free movement of labour... ...free trade... We are free to regard such a view as mistaken... It's their free choice, they got married... Older children roamed free... Part of the disc was cut out to allow free passage backwards of the bolt.*
ADJ CLASSIF ≠ controlled, limited, restricted

2 A **free** society, press, election, etc is not controlled by the government, with people having the right to express any opinion. EG *We can't do that if we haven't got a free press and access to information... ...free speech... ...the richest and freest country in the world.*
ADJ CLASSIF ≠ restricted

3 If you **free** someone or something, you stop them from being restricted or controlled by rules. EG *They wanted to see the colonies freed.*
V+O = liberate

4 Someone who is **free** is no longer a prisoner or a slave. EG *One prisoner in seven had been set free... ...the slave who escapes and becomes a free man.*
ADJ CLASSIF OR ADV WITH VB ≠ captive

5 If you **free** a prisoner or a slave, you let them go, take them out of prison, or give up your ownership of them. EG *They were freed yesterday by their kidnappers unharmed.*
V+O = release

6 If you **free** a person or thing of something that is unpleasant or restricting, you remove it from them. EG *...the attempt to free France of the Dictator... The man who refuses to decide is not thereby freed from responsibility.*
V+O (NG/REFL) : USU+A ⇑ liberate

7 A person or thing that is **free** of something unpleasant or unwanted does not have it or is not affected by it. EG *The area will be reasonably free of pollution by the year 2000... I was free of my previous paranoia... I have not found them freer from prejudice than an ordinary judge would be.*
ADJ QUALIT : PRED+*of/from* ⇑ without

8 If you **free** someone or something, you cause them to become available for a task or purpose when they were previously unavailable. EG *We all stand on two feet rather than four, freeing our hands... Local authorities can remove parental rights, freeing many more children for adoption... The child could attend a day nursery part time, freeing two days for the stressed mother.*
V+O ⇑ release

9 If you have a **free** period of time or are **free** at a particular time, you are not working or occupied then. EG *They don't have much free time... Are you free for lunch?... 'There's one evening you've got to keep free,' says Howard. 'Next Monday. Come to a party.'*
ADJ CLASSIF ⇑ available ≠ busy, occupied

10 Something such as a place or seat that is **free** is not being used or occupied by someone, or is not reserved for someone to use. EG *Is that seat free?*
ADJ CLASSIF ⇑ available = vacant

11 A sum of money or type of goods that is **free** of tax or duty is one that you do not have to pay tax on. EG *Such payments are free of Capital Gains Tax.*
ADJ CLASSIF : PRED+*of/from* = exempt

12 If something is **free**, you can have it or use it
ADJ CLASSIF

without paying for it. EG *The coffee was free... ...a free gift... Children can get into the museum free.*

13 for free. 13.1 If you do something or get something **for free**, you do it without being paid or get it without having to pay for it. EG *I said I'd work for free... I got it for free.* PHR : USED AS AN A = for nothing **13.2** You say you will tell someone something **for free** to emphasize how strongly you feel about it. EG *And I'll tell you this for free; I'm having nothing more to do with it!* PHR : USED AS AN A = for nothing

14 Something that is moved **free** is moved so that it is no longer attached to or trapped by something. EG *It was stapled to the others and she tugged to get it free... I shook my jacket free and hurried off.* ADV WITH VB, OR ADJ CLASSIF : PRED ⇑ away = loose

15 If you **free** something, you remove or loosen it from the place in which it has been fixed or trapped. EG *He freed his arms... He freed himself from the phone booth.* V+O ⇑ release = extricate

16 The **free** end of something long is the end that is not attached to anything. EG *He clicked the free end of the dog's chain round a thick pole.* ADJ CLASSIF ⇑ loose

17 When someone is using one hand or arm to hold or move something, their other hand or arm is referred to as their **free** one. EG *...buttoning his overcoat with his free hand.* ADJ CLASSIF ≠ occupied

18 Someone who is **free** with something gives or uses a lot of it; sometimes used showing disapproval. EG *They do not need unions at all: employers have been free with benefits to keep them out... She is too free with her tongue.* ADJ QUALIT : PRED+*with* ⇑ generous

19 If you **make free with** something that belongs to someone else, you use it a lot in a way that is considered unacceptable. EG *She accused him of making free with her money.* PHR : VB INFLECTS ⇑ exploit

20 A **free** translation roughly expresses the meaning of the original piece of writing but is not an exact translation. ADJ QUALIT ⇑ approximate

21 You say **feel free** to someone who has asked you if they may do something as an informal way of giving your permission. EG *'Is it OK if I take this one?'–'Yeah, feel free.'* PHR : ONLY IMPER = go ahead

22 See also **freely**, **fancy-free**, **scot-free**. ● **free of charge**: see **charge**. ● **to give someone a free hand**: see **hand**.

-free combines with nouns to form adjectives that mean not having, not involving, or not affected by the thing mentioned. EG *Each submarine reported a trouble-free launch... ...error-free computer programs.* COMB : FORMS ADJS ⇑ without

free agent, free agents. Someone who is a **free agent** can do whatever they want to do because they are not responsible to or for anyone. N COUNT ⇑ person

free-and-easy. Someone or something that is **free-and-easy** is casual, informal, and tolerant. EG *...a free-and-easy, give-and-take relationship.* ADJ QUALIT = easy-going

freebie /fri̲ːbiˈ/, **freebies**. A **freebie** is something that you are given without having to pay for it; an informal word. N COUNT ⇑ gift

freedom /fri̲ːdəm/, **freedoms**. **1 Freedom** is **1.1** the right to express any political or religious opinion and live or act without the government or another country interfering. EG *In the world of today political freedom is still rare... ...freedom of speech... The people of this country are ripe for freedom... ...legislation restricting the freedoms of the working class.* N UNCOUNT/ COUNT = liberty **1.2** the state of being able or allowed to do what you want to do without being restricted by anything or anyone. EG *They had been given complete freedom to photograph what they chose... Will you allow them freedom of choice or will you interfere?... Children are getting more freedom with every generation.* N UNCOUNT/ COUNT = liberty **1.3** the state of not being a prisoner or a slave. EG *...twisting his body wildly in another break for freedom... Many slaves buy their freedom with what they save from farming.* N UNCOUNT = liberty ≠ captivity **1.4** the condition of being able to move about. EG *The bar still had some freedom of vertical movement.* N UNCOUNT

2 Freedom from something unpleasant is the state of being without it or not being affected by it. EG *...freedom from hunger and starvation... ...forty years freedom from income tax.* N UNCOUNT+ *from* ⇑ release

3 Someone who is given the **freedom** of a particular place is given the right to use it as if it were their own, or is given special privileges in it. EG *They were given the freedom of the city after their Olympic success... You have the freedom of my house and gardens.* N SING : *the*+N+ *of*

freedom fighter, freedom fighters. A **freedom fighter** is a person who belongs to a group that is trying to overthrow the government of their country using violent methods; used showing approval. EG *One man's rebel is another man's freedom fighter.* N COUNT

free enterprise is an economic system in which businesses compete for profit without much government control. EG *I am a believer in free enterprise.* N UNCOUNT ⇑ capitalism

free fall. In parachuting, **free fall** is the part of the jump before the parachute opens. N UNCOUNT ⇑ fall

free-floating things or people are able to move freely and are not controlled or directed by anything. EG *...free-floating satellites.* ADJ CLASSIF : ATTRIB ⇑ unrestricted

Freefone /fri̲ːfəʊn/ is a system in Britain which allows you to phone particular organizations without paying for the call. You ask the operator for Freefone and give a special number. EG *For enquiries about your telephone bill ask for Freefone 8904.* N UNCOUNT

free-for-all, free-for-alls. A **free-for-all** is **1** a disorganized fight or argument in which everybody joins in. EG *The fight turned into a free-for-all.* N COUNT = riot **2** a situation in which several people or groups are trying to get something for themselves and there are no controls on how they do it. EG *This would result in a free-for-all on wage bargaining.* N COUNT

free form. A **free form** work of art or piece of music has not been created according to a standard style or convention. EG *...a modern free form bronze of Icarus.* ADJ CLASSIF : ATTRIB

freehand /fri̲ːhænd/. A **freehand** drawing is drawn without using instruments such as a ruler or a pair of compasses. ▸ used as an adverb. EG *She drew it freehand.* ADJ CLASSIF ≠ aided ▸ ADV WITH VB

freehold /fri̲ːhəʊld/, **freeholds**. **1** If you have the **freehold** of a building or piece of land, it is yours for life and there are no conditions regarding your ownership: compare **leasehold** . EG *The person with the freehold has absolute title to the land.* N UNCOUNT/ COUNT

2 If a building or piece of land is **freehold**, you can own it for life. EG *...freehold property.* ADJ CLASSIF

free house, free houses. A pub that is a **free house** is not owned by a particular brewery and can sell whatever beers it chooses to sell. N COUNT ⇑ public house

free kick, free kicks. When there is a **free kick** in a game of football, the ball is given to a member of one side to kick without opposition because a member of the other side has broken a rule. N COUNT ⇑ penalty

freelance /fri̲ːlɑːns/, **freelances, freelancing, freelanced**. **1** A **freelance** journalist, photographer, etc, or someone who does **freelance** work is not employed by one organization, but is paid for each piece of work they do by the organization they do it for. EG *Eddie used to be a freelance photographer... 'Which publication are you representing?'–'I'm freelance.'... ...freelance writing.* ADJ CLASSIF ⇑ independent = self-employed ▸ used as an adverb. EG *Much of the work is taken on part-time or freelance by married women.* ▸ ADV WITH VB ▸ used as a noun. EG *'Are you employed by Collins?'–'No, I'm a freelance.'* ▸ N COUNT ⇑ worker

2 If you **freelance**, you do freelance work. EG *You could always freelance.* V

freeloader /fri̲ːləʊdə/, **freeloaders**. A **freeloader** is someone who takes advantage of the generosity of other people to provide them with food, accommodation, etc; used mainly in American English. N COUNT = sponger

free love is the practice of having sexual relationships without marrying, often several relationships at the same time; an old-fashioned expression. N UNCOUNT = permissiveness

freely /fri̲ːliˈ/. **1 Freely** means in large quantities or often, especially without restraint. EG *He's a bachelor. Lives alone. Spends fairly freely... ...perspiring freely... The argument was freely used that to do so would only diminish confidence.* ADV WITH VB = liberally

2 Someone or something that can move or act **freely** is not restricted, controlled, or limited by anything or anyone. EG *We were allowed to mix freely with the villagers... He couldn't move his shoulders freely when he put it on... British goods were allowed to move freely from one Indian state to another.* ADV WITH VB

3 If you can talk **freely**, you can talk without needing to be careful about what you say. EG *We are all comrades here and I may talk freely.* ADV WITH VB = frankly ≠ cautiously

4 Something that is **freely** available can easily be obtained, especially because there is a lot of it about. EG *These drugs are freely available in most cities.* ADV+ADJ = readily

5 Something that is given or done **freely** is given or done willingly. EG *One cent bled from the master was worth a million given freely by anyone else.* — ADV WITH VB ≠ grudgingly

freeman /fri:mə³n/, **freemen**. Someone who is a **freeman** of a particular city has been given the freedom of that city as a special honour. — N COUNT : IF + PREP THEN *of* ⇑ person

Freemason /fri:meɪsə⁰n/, **Freemasons**. A **Freemason** is a member of a large secret society whose members promise to help each other and use a system of secret signs to recognize other members. — N COUNT = mason

freemasonry /fri:meɪsə⁰nri¹/. 1 **Freemasonry** is the natural friendly feeling that exists between people who are of the same kind. EG *A happy freemasonry exists between expense account fiddlers.* — N UNCOUNT ⇑ understanding

2 **Freemasonry**. Freemasonry is the organization of the Freemasons and their beliefs and practices. — N UNCOUNT

free pardon, free pardons. If someone who has been found guilty of a crime is given a **free pardon**, they are allowed to go free because new evidence shows that they did not commit that crime. — N COUNT

free pass, free passes. A **free pass** is an official document that allows a person to travel or to enter a particular building without having to pay. — N COUNT ⇑ permit

free port, free ports. A **free port** is a port or airport where goods can be brought in from foreign countries without payment of duty if they are going to be exported again. — N COUNT

Freepost /fri:pəʊst/ is a system in Britain by which an organization pays the postage when someone writes to them. 'Freepost' is written on the envelope as part of the address. EG *Return it to: Lloyds Bank PLC, FREEPOST, Birmingham.* — N UNCOUNT

freer /frɪə/ is the comparative of **free**.

free-range means relating to a system of keeping hens in which they can move and feed freely on an area of open ground. EG *...free-range eggs.* — ADJ CLASSIF

freesia /fri:zɪə/, **freesias**. A **freesia** is a plant with fragrant yellow, pink, white, or purple tubular flowers. — N COUNT/UNCOUNT ⇑ flower

free spirit, free spirits. Someone who is a **free spirit** is independent and lives as he or she wants to live rather than in a conventional way; used showing approval. — N COUNT : USU USED AS C ⇑ person = maverick

freest /fri:ɪ²st/ is the superlative of **free**.

free-standing. A **free-standing** piece of furniture or other object is not fixed to anything or stands on its own away from other things. EG *...a free-standing bath.* — ADJ CLASSIF ≠ fixed

freestyle /fri:staɪl/. 1 **Freestyle** is used to describe sports competitions, especially in swimming, wrestling, and skiing, in which competitors can use any style or method that they like when they take part. EG *She won the 100 metres freestyle.* — N SING WITH DET, OR N BEFORE N

2 **Freestyle** is a way of swimming in which you lie on your stomach, kick your legs, and swing one arm forward over your head and then the other. EG *He began doing laps in an easy freestyle.* — N UNCOUNT = crawl

freethinker /fri:θɪŋkə/, **freethinkers**. A **freethinker** is someone who works out their own ideas rather than accepting generally accepted views. — N COUNT ⇑ independent

freeway /fri:weɪ/, **freeways**. In America, a **freeway** is a road which has several lanes and controlled places where vehicles join it, so that people can travel quickly. EG *...driving on a California freeway.* — N COUNT

freewheel /fri:wi:l/, **freewheels, freewheeling, freewheeled**. If you **freewheel**, you travel, usually downhill, on a bicycle without using the pedals, or in a vehicle without using the engine. — V ⇑ move = coast

freewheeling /fri:wi:lɪŋ/; also spelled with a hyphen. A **freewheeling** person behaves in a casual way without feeling restricted by rules or accepted ways of doing things. EG *...all the trappings one associates with free-wheeling urban youth... ...the versatility of his poetic, freewheeling style.* — ADJ CLASSIF : ATTRIB ⇑ unrestricted = free-and-easy

free will. 1 If you believe in **free will**, you believe that people have a choice in what they do and that their actions have not been decided in advance by God or Fate. EG *...the notions of predestination and free will.* — N UNCOUNT

2 If you do something **of your own free will**, you do it by choice and not because you are forced to do it. EG *He has come back of his own free will.* — PHR : USED AS AN A = voluntarily

freeze /fri:z/ **freezes, freezing, froze, frozen**.
1 If a liquid **freezes** or something **freezes** it, it becomes solid because of low temperatures. EG *Anti-freeze prevents the water in the radiator from freezing overnight and cracking the cylinder... The pond usually freezes in the winter.* — V-ERG ⇑ solidify

2 If you **freeze** something such as food, you preserve it by storing it at a temperature below freezing point. EG *You can profit by buying and freezing local produce when plentiful... Bakery freezes extremely well.* ● See also **deep freeze**. — V-ERG : IF V THEN USU + A

3 If a substance such as earth **freezes** or something **freezes** it, it becomes hard because low temperatures have caused the moisture in it to freeze. — V-ERG ⇑ harden

4 If something such as a pipe or machine **freezes** or something **freezes** it, it becomes blocked or stiff with ice or frozen liquid. EG *No home can be comfortable if pipes are frozen or burst.* — V-ERG = ice over

5 If you say that it will **freeze**, you are saying that the weather will become so cold that the temperature will fall below freezing point. EG *I think it'll freeze tonight.* ▸ used as a noun. EG *...the forecasting of storms, freezes, droughts, smog.* — V : *it* + AUX + V = ice over; ▸ N COUNT

6 If you **freeze**, you become unpleasantly cold. EG *So he opens the window and she freezes.* — V

7 If you **freeze** when you are moving, you suddenly stop and become completely still and quiet. EG *A soft tap at the front door broke the glass. She froze... Harsh flashlight froze Delaney.* — V-ERG = halt ≠ move

8 If you **freeze** a film, you stop it, for example because you want to look at an individual frame in it. — V + O

9 To **freeze** something such as wages, prices, or numbers means to state officially that they will not be allowed to increase for a fixed period of time. EG *Various attempts to control or freeze wages have failed... The powers could indicate their willingness to move towards disarmament by immediately freezing their atomic armaments at current levels.* ▸ used as a noun. EG *...a proposed 30 month pay freeze... ...a freeze in the nuclear arms race.* — V + O ⇑ control = fix; ▸ N COUNT + SUPP ⇑ control

10 If you **freeze** something such as a bank account, fund, or property, you obtain a legal order which states that it cannot be used or sold for a particular period of time. EG *These associations have been hit hard by the freezing of their funds and the imprisoning of several leaders.* — V + O ⇑ stop

11 If a process or way of life **freezes** or **is frozen** by something, it seems to stop developing and does not change. — V-ERG : USU PASS = set, stick

12 ● See also **freezing, frozen**.

freeze out. If you **freeze** someone out of an activity or situation, you prevent them from being involved in it by creating difficulties or by being unfriendly. EG *Producers try to freeze out parasitic middle men.* — PHRASAL VB : V + O + ADV ⇑ exclude = force out

freeze over. If something **freezes over** or if it **is frozen over**, it becomes covered with a layer of ice or other frozen substance. EG *The lakes were frozen over last winter.* — PHRASAL VB : V-ERG + ADV, USU PASS ⇑ freeze = ice over

freeze up. If something **freezes up** or if it **is frozen up**, it becomes completely covered or blocked with ice. EG *It was so cold last winter that even the river froze up... The lock has frozen up.* ● See also **freeze-up**. — PHRASAL VB : V-ERG + ADV, USU PASS = ice up

freeze-dried food has been preserved by a process of rapid freezing and drying. — ADJ CLASSIF

freeze-frame, freeze-frames. 1 A **freeze-frame** from a film is an individual picture from it, produced by stopping the film at that point. EG *...a freeze-frame of Finney reaching out to Keaton.* — N COUNT ⇑ photograph = still

2 The **freeze-frame** on a video is a device that allows you to stop the film, for example to look at an individual picture. — N COUNT : USU SING ⇑ facility

freezer /fri:zə/, **freezers**. A **freezer** is a large container like a fridge in which you can store food for long periods of time since the temperature inside is kept below freezing point. — N COUNT ⇑ appliance = deep freeze

freeze-up, freeze-ups. When a **freeze-up** occurs, ice completely covers or blocks something such as a pipe, machine, or river. EG *We kept the water moving enough to prevent a complete freeze-up.* — N COUNT ⇑ blockade

freezing /fri:zɪŋ/. 1 If something is **freezing**, it is very cold indeed. EG *It's freezing outside... ...a freezing wind... ...sleeping out of doors in the freezing cold... The water was black and freezing.* — ADJ CLASSIF = icy, arctic

2 If you say that you are **freezing**, you mean that you feel unpleasantly cold. EG *Let's get out of here. I'm freezing.* — ADJ CLASSIF : PRED = frozen

3 **Freezing** also means freezing point. EG *The air temperature was now well below freezing.* — N UNCOUNT

freezing point; also spelled with a hyphen. 1 Freezing point is 0 Celsius, the temperature at which water freezes; often used when talking about the weather. EG *The temperature was well above freezing point.* N UNCOUNT = freezing

2 The **freezing point** of a particular substance is the temperature at which it freezes. N COUNT: IF+ PREP THEN *of*

freight /freɪt/, **freights, freighting, freighted**. 1 **Freight** is 1.1 goods that are transported by ships, aeroplanes, or trains. EG *Eight thousand tons of freight were being landed each day... He worked as a freight handler on the railroads.* N UNCOUNT = cargo

2 If something is sent **freight**, it is sent as part of a larger load, so that the cost of transporting it is less. EG *I sent an expensive tape recorder on ahead, air freight.* ADV AFTER VB

3 When goods **are freighted**, they are transported in large quantities over a long distance. EG *Much of the fish sold in England is freighted overland from Scotland.* V+O = send

freight car, freight cars. A **freight car** is a wagon on a train in which goods are transported; used in American English. N COUNT

freighter /freɪtə/, **freighters**. A **freighter** is a large ship or aeroplane that is designed for carrying freight. N COUNT

freight train, freight trains. A **freight train** is a train on which goods are transported; used in American English. N COUNT

French /frent⁰ʃ/. 1 **French** means belonging or relating to France, its people, or their language. ADJ CLASSIF

2 **French** is the language that is spoken by people who live in France and in parts of some other countries, including Belgium, Canada, and Switzerland. N UNCOUNT

3 The **French** are the people who live in France. N PLURAL

French bean, French beans. **French beans** are long, rounded green beans which you cook and eat as a vegetable. N COUNT: USU PL = haricot bean

French bread is bread which is baked in long, thin, crusty loaves. N UNCOUNT

French Canadian, French Canadians. 1 A **French Canadian** is a Canadian whose native language is French. N COUNT

2 **French-Canadian** means belonging or relating to people who come from the part of Canada where French is spoken. ADJ CLASSIF

French door, French doors. **French doors** are the same as French windows. N COUNT: USU PL

French dressing is a thin sauce made of oil, vinegar, and spices which you put on salad. N UNCOUNT = vinaigrette

French fries are long, thin pieces of potato fried in oil or fat. EG *'Chicken?' I said encouragingly. 'Perhaps some French fries?'* N PLURAL = chips

French horn, French horns. A **French horn** is a musical instrument which consists of a long metal tube wound round in a circle with a funnel at one end. You play it by blowing down the tube and moving valves in order to obtain different notes. N COUNT

French loaf, French loaves. A **French loaf** is a long, thin loaf of bread. N COUNT

Frenchman /frent⁰ʃmə³n/, **Frenchmen**. A **Frenchman** is a man who comes from France. N COUNT

French polish is a type of varnish which is painted onto wood so that the wood has a hard, shiny surface. N UNCOUNT

French window, French windows. **French windows** are a pair of glass doors which you go through into a garden or onto a balcony. N COUNT: USU PL, SING=PL = French door

Frenchwoman /frent⁰ʃwʌ¹mə⁰n/, **Frenchwomen**. A **Frenchwoman** is a woman who comes from France. N COUNT

frenetic /frɪ²netɪk/. You describe activities as **frenetic** when they are lively, energetic, and rather wild. EG *It generated much excitement and frenetic activity.* ◊ **frenetically**. EG *They continued to dance frenetically.* ADJ QUALIT = frantic, feverish ◊ ADV WITH VB

frenzied /frenzɪd/. **Frenzied** activities or actions are wild, excited, and uncontrolled. EG *Will this push him too far and lead to a frenzied attack?... She was climbing now with a sort of frenzied haste.* ▸ used of people. EG *...a frenzied mob of over a thousand students.* ◊ **frenziedly**. EG *His heart was beating frenziedly.* ADJ QUALIT = demented, desperate ▸ = hysterical ◊ ADV WITH VB = frantically

frenzy /frenzi¹/, **frenzies**. **Frenzy** or a **frenzy** is 1 violent or wild behaviour that results from losing control of your feelings. EG *They were whipping up nationalist frenzy among the excitable crowds... There was a a squeal of pain, and the child hopped round in a frenzy.* 2 great excitement about something that is shown in the way that you behave. EG *They were singing in a frenzy of joy... ...a frenzy of kissing and champagne cork popping.* N COUNT: USU SING, OR N UNCOUNT

frequency /friːkwənsi¹/, **frequencies**. 1 **Frequency** is 1.1 the rate at which something happens, for example the number of times it happens in a particular period of time. EG *Serious disasters appear to be increasing in frequency... This idea crops up with increasing frequency in the writings of scientists... The most common British town birds, in order of frequency are: (1) the sparrow; (2) the pigeon.* N UNCOUNT 1.2 the fact that something happens often. EG *We are concerned at the high incidence of disease and the frequency of death in the district.* N UNCOUNT

2 The **frequency** of a sound wave or a radio wave is the rate at which it vibrates. If a sound wave is at a high frequency, you hear it as a high-pitched noise. If it is at a low frequency, you hear it as a low-pitched noise; a technical term. EG *Most of the sounds we hear have frequencies of around several hundred vibrations a second... The wave itself was of very low frequency.* N COUNT/UNCOUNT

frequent, frequents, frequenting, frequented. The word **frequent** is pronounced /friːkwənt/ when it is an adjective, and /fri¹kwent/ when it is a verb. 1 If something is **frequent**, it often happens or you often see it. EG *George's absences were frequent... The purchase of a new car is a relatively frequent occurrence in the life of the average American... Etta was a frequent visitor there... ...some of the more frequent wild flowers of Britain.* ADJ QUALIT = common

2 If you **frequent** a particular place, you often go there and spend time there; a fairly formal use. EG *Jo liked to frequent the bars... She had a fashionable house which was frequented by all sorts of grand people.* V+O = visit

frequently /friːkwəntli¹/. If something happens or occurs **frequently**, it happens or occurs often. EG *We went out frequently... The baby was fed as frequently as possible... The promises were made less and less frequently.* ADV WITH VB

fresco /freskəʊ/, **frescoes**. A **fresco** is a picture that is painted on a plastered wall when the plaster is still wet. N COUNT

fresh /freʃ/, **fresher, freshest**. 1 **Fresh** is used to describe a further thing or a further amount of something, especially when it replaces or is added to the original one, or when it is being considered instead of the original one. EG *He poured himself a fresh drink... It took only seconds to extract the spent cartridge and insert a fresh one... Rose had given him fresh instructions... You and I could make a fresh start... There is fresh fighting in the border region.* ADJ CLASSIF: ATTRIB ⇑ new

2 Something that is **fresh** has been made, done, obtained, or experienced recently, and has not yet changed in any way or been disturbed. EG *I had seen the sharp fresh footprints in the snow... Some of the scars were fresh... Memories of three Indian-Pakistani wars are fresh in both countries.* ADJ QUALIT ⇑ recent

3 If food is **fresh**, 3.1 it has been picked, gathered, or made recently, and has not gone bad or stale. EG *I love the smell of fresh bread.* ADJ QUALIT 3.2 it is raw and has not been preserved, for example by freezing or drying. EG *Fruits and vegetables can be fresh, canned, frozen, or dried.* ADJ CLASSIF ⇑ untreated

4 If you describe something as **fresh**, you mean that 4.1 it is different from anything else in a new, exciting, or admirable way; used showing approval. EG *She treats the subject in a very fresh and exciting way... He has a fresh approach.* ◊ **freshness**. EG *This gives the early part of the novel freshness and charm.* ADJ QUALIT = original, novel ≠ hackneyed ◊ N UNCOUNT = originality 4.2 it has a pleasant, bright appearance and looks as if it has been recently made, cleaned, or cared for; used showing approval. EG *...fresh white paint.* ◊ **freshness**. ADJ QUALIT = clean ◊ N UNCOUNT

5 If something smells, tastes, or feels **fresh**, it is clean, cool, or refreshing; used showing approval. EG *The air is cool and fresh... A piece of grated lemon peel gives a fresh flavour to almost anything.* ◊ **freshness**. ADJ QUALIT = tangy ◊ N UNCOUNT

6 **Fresh** water is water that is not salty, especially water that you find in streams, springs, reservoirs, etc. EG *There's not much fresh water on the island.* ADJ CLASSIF ⇑ pure

7 If you say that the weather is **fresh**, you mean that ADJ QUALIT

it is fairly cold and windy. EG *It's a bit fresh this morning, isn't it?... ...a fresh spring morning.* ⇑ cool = nippy

8 If you say that the wind is **fresh**, you mean that it is fairly strong. ADJ QUALIT = brisk

9 **Fresh** colours are clear, bright, and fairly light; used showing approval. EG *Her dress was a fresh pink.* ADJ QUALIT : ATTRIB

10 If someone has a **fresh** face or complexion, their skin is pink and healthy; used showing approval. ADJ QUALIT : ATTRIB

11 If you feel **fresh**, you feel full of energy and enthusiasm, and so ready to deal with things. EG *Try to be as fresh as possible when you tackle top-priority jobs.* ◇ **freshness**. ADJ QUALIT = alert, rested ≠ tired ◇ N UNCOUNT

12 If someone is **fresh** with you, they behave or speak in a way that is too friendly and therefore disrespectful; an informal expression, used showing disapproval. ADJ QUALIT = forward

13 If you are **fresh** from a particular place or experience, you have just come from that place or you have just had that experience. EG *He had the manner of one fresh from a dangerous safari... You know what these fabrics smell like when they come fresh off the mills.* ADJ CLASSIF : PRED+PREP = straight

14 If you are **fresh out of** something, you have just run out of it and you have none left; an informal expression. EG *We're fresh out of chilis.* PHR+NG : USED AS C

15 If someone or something looks or feels **as fresh as a daisy**, they look or feel very fresh, lively, or smart. EG *She looked as fresh as a daisy in her crisp white frock.* PHR : USED AS C

fresh- is added to past participles in order to form adjectives which describe something as having been recently made or done. EG *...a vase of fresh-cut flowers... ...fresh-frozen orange juice.* PREFIX

fresh air is the air outside; used especially when this is considered to be good for you. EG *Get out in the fresh air... What you need is plenty of sun and fresh air.* N UNCOUNT, OR N SING : *the*+N

freshen /frɛʃəⁿn/, **freshens, freshening, freshened**. 1 If you **freshen** something, you make it clean and pleasant in appearance or smell. EG *The brief rainstorm about midnight had done little to freshen the air.* V+O ⇑ improve = clear

2 If the wind **freshens**, it increases in strength and becomes fairly strong. V

freshen up. 1 If you **freshen up** or **freshen** yourself **up**, you wash your hands and face and make yourself look neat and tidy. EG *Sarah and Barry returned to their hotel to freshen up.* PHRASAL VB : V+ADV, OR V+O (REFL)+ADV

2 If you **freshen** something **up**, you make it clean and pleasant in appearance or smell. EG *New wallpaper and curtains will freshen up the place.* PHRASAL VB : V+O+ADV = smarten up

fresher /frɛʃə/, **freshers**. A **fresher** is a student at a university or college who has just started his or her first year there; an informal word in British English. EG *...three freshers of Edinburgh University.* N COUNT = freshman

freshly /frɛʃli¹/. If something is **freshly** made or done, it has been recently made or done. EG *...freshly squeezed orange juice... The body was lowered into the freshly dug hole.* ADV WITH VB (PAST PART) = newly

freshman /frɛʃmə³n/, **freshmen**. A **freshman** is a student who is in his or her first year at university or college; used in American English. EG *I searched the crowds of freshmen for others who were black... He had finished his freshman year of science.* N COUNT = fresher

freshwater /frɛʃwɔ:tə/. **Freshwater** means living in or containing water that is not salty, usually in contrast to sea water. EG *...freshwater prawns... ...freshwater pools.* ADJ CLASSIF : ATTRIB ≠ salt water

fret /frɛt/, **frets, fretting, fretted**. 1 When someone **frets** or **is fretting**, they are worried or unhappy about something. EG *He was constantly fretting about their financial situation... Don't fret, there's plenty more where that came from.* V-ERG, OR V+O (NG/REFL) : IF+PREP THEN *about/over* ⇑ worry

2 The **frets** on a stringed instrument such as a guitar are the metal ridges across its neck that show you where to put your fingers on the strings to make different notes. N COUNT ⇑ mark

3 See also **fretted**.

fretful /frɛtfʊl/. If someone is **fretful**, they complain a lot, because they are unhappy about something. EG *...a restless, fretful baby.* ▸ used of behaviour. EG *...the baby's fretful crying... 'I want to go home,' said the old lady in a fretful tone.* ◇ **fretfully**. ADJ QUALIT = peevish ◇ ADV WITH VB

fretted /frɛtı²d/. A **fretted** wooden or stone object has been decorated by cutting bits out of it. EG *...the fretted roof of the station arch.* ADJ CLASSIF : ATTRIB

fretwork /frɛtwɜ:k/ is wood or metal that has been decorated by cutting bits of it out to make a pattern. EG *...fretwork bookcases.* N UNCOUNT, OR N BEFORE N ⇑ decoration

Freudian /frɔɪdıən/ means relating to the ideas and methods of the psychiatrist Freud, especially to his ideas about people's subconscious sexual feelings. EG *...the Freudian concept of infant sexuality.* ADJ CLASSIF : USU ATTRIB

Freudian slip, Freudian slips. If someone accidentally says something that indicates what their subconscious feelings are, especially their sexual feelings, this is referred to as a **Freudian slip**. N COUNT ⇑ mistake

Fri. is an abbreviation for 'Friday'.

friable /fraɪəbəⁿl/. **Friable** soil is easily broken up rather than being hard; a formal or technical word. ADJ CLASSIF = crumbly

friar /fraɪə/, **friars**. A **friar** is a member of one of several Catholic religious orders. In the Middle Ages, friars used to beg for their food and travel from place to place preaching about Christianity. N COUNT

fricassee /frıkəsi¹/, **fricassees**. A **fricassee** consists of pieces of meat, especially chicken or veal, cooked and served in a white sauce. EG *...chicken fricassee.* N COUNT/UNCOUNT : USU+SUPP ⇑ meal

friction /frıkʃəⁿn/, **frictions**. 1 **Friction** is 1.1 the force that makes it difficult for an object to slide over something. EG *The overall efficiency of the machine is higher because there is less friction.* **1.2** the rubbing of an object against something. EG *...the friction of the toes against the front of the running shoe.* N UNCOUNT ⇑ resistance; N UNCOUNT = chafing

2 **Friction** is also disagreement and arguments between people. EG *These decisions can cause friction... When Joan returned to work, the friction between them increased... Family frictions can interfere with a child's schoolwork.* N UNCOUNT/COUNT = conflict

Friday /fraɪdı/, **Fridays**. **Friday** is one of the seven days of the week. It is the day after Thursday and before Saturday. EG *I wasn't able to be present on Friday... You'll be away next Friday won't you, Alan?* ● See also **girl Friday, Good Friday**. N UNCOUNT/COUNT

fridge /frıdʒ/, **fridges**. A **fridge** is a large metal container which is kept cool, usually by electricity, so that food that is put in it stays fresh. EG *He put the milk back in the fridge.* N COUNT = refrigerator

friend /frɛnd/, **friends**. 1 A **friend** is someone who you know well and like, but who is not related to you. EG *He was my best friend at Oxford... A close friend told me about it... She later married Shaw's great friend Harley Granville-Barker... ...an engineer friend of mine... ...an old friend of the family... Isabel and I are just good friends.* N COUNT ⇑ acquaintance

2 If you are **friends** with someone, you are their friend and they are yours. EG *I used to be friends with the people who ran the local shop... We became great friends... Stay friends with Parry.* ● If two people who have quarrelled want to **be friends**, they want to forgive each other and behave in a friendly way to each other. EG *Let's forget our differences and be friends.* N PLURAL : USED AS C, IF+PREP THEN *with*; ● PHR OR PHR+A (*with*) : RECIP, VB INFLECTS = make up

3 If you **make friends** with someone or **make a friend** of them you begin a friendship with them. EG *She made friends with Reg... He found it hard to make friends... If we're lucky, we make friends of them.* PHR : VB INFLECTS, IF+PREP THEN *with/of*

4 The **friends** of a country, a cause, or a famous politician are the people and organizations who help and support them. EG *You have friends, you know, both in this country and in France... It is the cause all friends of Ireland should support.* N PLURAL : IF+PREP THEN *of* ⇑ supporter = ally

5 You also say that someone is a **friend** when they are on your side, for example in a war, and are therefore not dangerous to you. EG *You can leave your arms out there, we're all friends here... I was among friends... Who goes there–friend or foe?* N COUNT : IF+PREP THEN *of/to* = ally ≠ enemy

6 The word **friend** is also used in the following expressions. **6.1** People sometimes address other people as **friend** or as **my friend**, especially when they are speaking in a humorous way. EG *'Fear not, my friend,' said Groucho, 'it's only money.'... This is the truth I'm telling you, my friends.* **6.2** You can refer to someone who your listeners know about as **our friend** or **our old friend** when you are speaking humorously or sarcastically. EG *Everest presented a challenge to our friend Hilary... I had a feeling that it might be our old friends the CIA.* **6.3** The expression **my honourable friend** is used by British Members of Parliament to refer to each other in Parliament. **6.4** The expression **my learned friend** is used by British VOC = comrade; PHR : USED AS S OR O; PHR : USED AS S OR O; PHR : USED AS S OR O

lawyers to refer to each other in law courts. **6.5** You can also refer to something that is very useful or familiar to you as your **friend**. EG *Lots of the pictures are old friends to me... Use your old friend the microscope.* N COUNT

7 A **Friend** is a Quaker. This term is preferred by Quakers themselves. N COUNT

friendless /frendlɪ²s/. Someone who is **friendless** has no friends. EG *...a friendless stranger.* ADJ CLASSIF = lonely

friendly /frendli¹/, **friendlier, friendliest; friendlies.** **1** Someone who is **friendly** behaves in a pleasant, kind, warm way as if they are or would like to be your friend. EG *The women had been friendly to Lyn... Malawians seemed to be the friendliest people in the world.* ▸ used of behaviour. EG *She smiled at him in a friendly way... He gave me a friendly pat on the shoulder.* ◊ **friendliness**. EG *The friendliness was gone from his voice.* ADJ QUALIT = amiable ◊ N UNCOUNT

2 If you are **friendly** with someone or have a **friendly** relationship with them, you are friends or behave to each other like friends. EG *You need to be on friendly terms with him... Relations between them had not always been close or friendly... A salesman got friendly with him.* ADJ QUALIT = chummy, matey

3 You say that people are **friendly** to someone when they support or encourage them. EG *...a big corporation very friendly to the President.* ◊ **friendliness**. EG *One of New England's great strengths is its friendliness to entrepreneurs.* ADJ QUALIT + *to* ◊ N UNCOUNT + *to*

4 You describe a country, government, etc as **friendly** when it is on your side rather than being an enemy. EG *...neutral and friendly governments.* ▸ used of things that belong to such a country or government. EG *...a friendly port.* ADJ CLASSIF : USU ATTRIB = allied ≠ enemy, hostile

5 You describe places or objects as **friendly** when they cause you to feel comfortable and safe. EG *...a small vault lit by friendly lamps... ...the still, friendly waters of the lagoon.* ADJ QUALIT ⇑ reassuring = welcoming

6 A **friendly** argument, fight, or sports match is one in which the people involved are amusing themselves rather than seriously trying to win. EG *We had quite a few friendly arguments.* ADJ QUALIT = amicable ≠ serious

7 A **friendly** is a sports match in which the players play in order to practise and have fun, without caring who wins; used in British English. EG *They were called 'friendlies' but they were really tough matches.* N COUNT

8 To get **friendly** with someone also means to start behaving towards them in a sexual way; an informal use. EG *I didn't want to spoil a promising relationship by getting too friendly too soon.* ADJ QUALIT : PRED ⇑ intimate = familiar

friendly society, friendly societies. In Britain, a **friendly society** is an organization to which people regularly pay small amounts of money and which then gives them money when they retire or when they are ill. N COUNT

friendship /frendʃɪp/, **friendships**. **1** A **friendship** is a relationship between two or more friends. EG *Their friendship was as close as ever it had been... ...the ability to form friendships... My friendship with her had taught me a great deal.* ● If you **strike up a friendship** with someone, you and they start being friends. EG *Alice and I struck up a friendship immediately.* N COUNT ● PHR OR PHR + A (*with*) : RECIP, VB INFLECTS = make friends

2 **Friendship** is the relationship of being friends, or the feelings that friends have for each other. EG *Friendship is based on shared interests... He underestimated the power of friendship.* N UNCOUNT = affection

3 If you have someone's **friendship**, they are your friend. EG *He lost Britten's friendship... The friendship of your boss is vital.* N SING : WITH POSS = support

4 **Friendship** or a **friendship** is also a relationship between two countries in which they help and support each other. EG *I have always defended our alliance and friendship with America... He was strenuous in his efforts to promote Anglo-German friendship.* N UNCOUNT/COUNT ≠ hostility

frieze /friːz/, **friezes**. A **frieze** is a decoration high up on the walls of a room or just under the roof of a building. It consists of a long strip of paper with a picture or pattern on it or a long panel of carving. N COUNT

frig /frɪg/, **frigs, frigging, frigged**; a swear word. If someone says that you **are frigging about** or **are frigging around**, they mean that you are wasting time when you should be doing a task or job. PHRASAL VB : V + ADV = mess around

frigate /frɪgət/, **frigates**. A **frigate** is a fairly small naval ship that can move fast, especially one that is used for protecting other ships. N COUNT

frigging /frɪgɪŋ/; a swear word. People use the swear word **frigging** before a noun when they are expressing their anger or annoyance about something. ADJ CLASSIF : ATTRIB = bloody

fright /fraɪt/, **frights**. **1** **Fright** is a sudden feeling of fear, for example the fear that you feel when something surprises you unpleasantly or when you are very anxious or nervous about something. EG *I heard Amy cry out in fright... He was paralysed with fright.* ● If you **take fright** at something, you are suddenly frightened by it, and want to run away or to stop doing whatever you are doing. EG *The horse had taken fright and bolted.* ● See also **stage fright**. N UNCOUNT = terror ● PHR : VB INFLECTS = panic

2 A **fright** is an experience which makes someone suddenly feel afraid. EG *She had given him a fright too, to judge from the way his mouth hung open... Because she had got a fright she sounded angry at first.* ● If you get **the fright of** your **life**, you are suddenly very frightened by something. N COUNT : USU SING ● PHR : USED AS O

3 If you say that someone looks a **fright**, you mean that they look very strange or unattractive, for example because of the clothes that they are wearing; an informal use. EG *I want to be presentably clothed in winter, instead of looking a fright.* N COUNT : USU SING = sight, mess

frighten /fraɪtə⁰n/, **frightens, frightening, frightened**. If something **frightens** you, it causes you to suddenly feel afraid, anxious, or nervous. EG *The situation was beginning to frighten me... The thunder so frightened the horse that it galloped down the road.* ● If something **frightens the life out of** you, **frightens the wits out of** you, or **frightens** you **out of** your **wits**, it causes you to feel suddenly afraid or gives you a very unpleasant surprise. EG *The car was fitted with a very loud horn to frighten the wits out of people.* V + O = scare ● PHR : VB INFLECTS ⇑ startle

frighten away. **1** If you **frighten away** a person or animal or **frighten** them **off**, you make them frightened so that they run away and do not come any closer. EG *He waved his torch to frighten away some animal, probably a hyena... We were waving our arms to frighten the donkeys off the premises.* PHRASAL VB : V + O + ADV = scare off

2 To **frighten away** or **frighten off** a person also means to make them nervous so that they decide not to become involved with a particular person or activity. EG *I suppose you've been frightened off attempting any more partnerships.* PHRASAL VB : V + O + ADV ⇑ repel

frighten into. If you **frighten** someone **into** something, you make them so frightened that they do something which they might not otherwise have done. EG *'Don't you dare,' he said, frightening her into silence.* PHRASAL VB : V + O + PREP, HAS PASS ⇑ force

frighten out of. If you **frighten** someone **out of** something, you make them so frightened that they do not do something that they had intended to do. EG *She refused to be frightened out of going.* PHRASAL VB : V + O + PREP, HAS PASS ⇑ intimidate

frightened /fraɪtə⁰nd/. If you are **frightened**, **1** you are afraid because of something that has just happened or that you think may happen. EG *The men led their frightened families to safety... They stared at him with frightened eyes... When you were a child, were you frightened of the dark?* **2** you are nervous or anxious about something. EG *I was frightened of making a fool of myself... I am frightened to look... They were frightened there would be another earthquake.* ADJ QUALIT = scared ADJ QUALIT : PRED, USU + *of*/ *to*-INF/REPORT-CL = afraid

frightening /fraɪtə⁰nɪŋ/. If something is **frightening**, it makes you feel afraid, anxious, or nervous. EG *...the most frightening sight he had ever seen... It is frightening to think what damage it would do.* ◊ **frighteningly**. EG *It was happening frighteningly fast.* ADJ QUALIT = scary ◊ ADV = alarmingly

frightful /fraɪtfʊl/. **1** If you describe something as **frightful**, you are saying that it is very bad, serious, or unpleasant; an informal use. EG *There's been a frightful mistake... It's a frightful poem... The smell was frightful.* ADJ QUALIT = dreadful

2 **Frightful** is also used in informal English to emphasize what you are saying. EG *It seems a frightful nuisance... Not a frightful lot has happened.* ◊ **frightfully**. EG *I'm frightfully sorry... He's not frightfully popular.* ADJ CLASSIF : ATTRIB ⇑ great = awful ◊ ADV = awfully

frigid /frɪdʒɪd/. **1** If a woman is **frigid**, she finds it difficult to become sexually aroused. EG *I was depressed, withdrawn and sexually frigid.* ◊ **frigidity** ADJ QUALIT ⇑ unresponsive ◊ N UNCOUNT

/frɪdʒɪdɪti¹/. EG *The toughest problem to treat is frigidity.*
2 A **frigid** place is very cold indeed. EG *We moved out into the frigid wilderness... They extended their hands into the frigid pool.* ADJ QUALIT = icy
3 You also say that the atmosphere in a place is **frigid** when it seems formal and unfriendly. EG *There was a frigid silence round the table.* ◊ **frigidity**. ADJ QUALIT = icy ◊ N UNCOUNT

frill /frɪl/, **frills**. 1 A **frill** is 1.1 a long narrow strip of fabric with many folds in it which is sewn along the edge of something as a decoration, for example along the edge of a cushion or round the neckline of a blouse. N COUNT 1.2 a strip of paper that has lots of small slits cut along one edge and that is used to decorate something. N COUNT
2 The **frills** are the parts of something that are not essential, but that are added to make it more interesting, pleasant, comfortable, or decorative. EG *The car is a basic model with no frills such as a cassette player or sunshine roof.* N COUNT : USU PL ⇑ addition

frilled /frɪld/. If a piece of clothing, cushion, curtain, etc is **frilled**, it is decorated with a frill or frills. EG *She wore a white frilled blouse and a velvet jacket.* ADJ CLASSIF

frilly /frɪli¹/. If a piece of clothing, cushion, curtain, etc is **frilly**, it has a lot of frills on it. EG *...a frilly nightdress.* ADJ QUALIT

fringe /frɪndʒ/, **fringes, fringing, fringed**. 1 A **fringe** is 1.1 a short border of hair which is cut so that it hangs over your forehead. N COUNT 1.2 a decoration used on clothes, curtains, lampshades, etc, which consists of a strip of fabric with a lot of hanging threads that are sometimes knotted or twisted together. N COUNT/UNCOUNT
2 The **fringe** of a place is the outside edge of it, or the part that is farthest from its centre. EG *Enemy helicopters were flying around the fringes of the zone... They stopped on the fringe of the crowd.* N COUNT : SING=PL = perimeter
3 The **fringes** of an activity are its minor and less important parts, rather than its main and central part. EG *We have been living too long on the bloodless fringes of the action... ...two agents on the fringes of espionage activities.* N COUNT : USU PL +SUPP = periphery ≠ mainstream
4 A **fringe** is also 4.1 a group of people who belong to a political party but who do not share all the ideas of the party. EG *He belongs to the radical fringe of the Labour Party.* N SING WITH DET : USU+SUPP 4.2 actors who perform plays which are very unusual or unconventional. EG *Julie's work in fringe theatre has led her into some peculiar situations.* ● See also **lunatic fringe**. N SING WITH DET : USU+SUPP = avant-garde ≠ mainstream

fringe benefit, fringe benefits. **Fringe benefits** are extra things that you get from a particular job, for example a car, a house, or free insurance which you are given in addition to your salary. N COUNT : USU PL = perk

fringed /frɪnd⁰ʒd/. 1 If clothes, curtains, or lampshades are **fringed**, they are decorated with a fringe. ADJ CLASSIF
2 If a place or object is **fringed** with something, that thing forms a border around it or is situated along its edges. EG *Her eyes were fringed with unusually long lashes... The square was floodlit at night and fringed by guest houses.* ADJ CLASSIF + *with/by* ⇑ edge

frippery /frɪpəri¹/, **fripperies**. Objects are referred to as **frippery** or **fripperies** when they are cheap, vulgar, and do not serve any useful purpose; used showing disapproval. EG *...the mass manufacture of fripperies and novelties of all kinds... ...a case full of frippery.* N UNCOUNT/N PLURAL

Frisbee /frɪzbi¹/, **Frisbees**. **Frisbee** is a trademark for a light plastic disc that one person throws to another as part of a game. N COUNT

frisk /frɪsk/, **frisks, frisking, frisked**. 1 If someone **frisks** you, they search you with their hands in order to see if you have a weapon, drugs, or something else hidden in your clothes; an informal use. EG *The 200-strong audience was frisked on arrival.* ▸ used as a noun. EG *He gave Michael a thorough frisk for a weapon.* V+O ⇑ inspect ▸ N COUNT ⇑ inspection
2 When animals or people **frisk**, they move or jump and run about in a happy, energetic way. EG *The children ran about the lawn frisking like lambs.* V = frolic

frisky /frɪski¹/, **friskier, friskiest**. A **frisky** animal or person is energetic and high-spirited, and wants to have fun. EG *...frisky young ponies... I felt frisky, as if I might break into a dance.* ADJ QUALIT ⇑ lively

frisson /friːsɒn/, **frissons**. A **frisson** is a short, sudden feeling of excitement or fear. EG *...a little frisson of excitement.* N COUNT : USU+SUPP = thrill

fritter /frɪtə/, **fritters, frittering, frittered**. A **fritter** is a slice of fruit, vegetable, or other food which is dipped in batter and then fried. EG *...corn fritters.* N COUNT : USU+SUPP
fritter away. If you **fritter away** something such as time or money, you waste it by spending it in a foolish way, a little bit at a time. EG *It is all too easy to fritter away the best hours of the day shopping.* PHRASAL VB : V+O+ADV = squander

frivolity /frɪvɒlɪti¹/, **frivolities**. 1 **Frivolity** is activities that are amusing and fairly silly, rather than serious and sensible. EG *There were occasional outbreaks of frivolity... Todd shunned such frivolity.* N UNCOUNT ⇑ fun = gaiety
2 **Frivolities** are things or activities which are amusing and fairly silly, rather than useful or serious. EG *No one could spare the time for such frivolities.* N COUNT : USU PL ⇑ foolishness

frivolous /frɪvələs/. 1 If someone is **frivolous** or if their behaviour is **frivolous**, they behave in a silly or light-hearted way, rather than being serious and sensible; often used showing disapproval. EG *He laughed and became frivolous and made light of it all... This is a frivolous way of attacking the problem.* ADJ QUALIT = flippant ≠ sensible
2 **Frivolous** objects and activities are amusing and fairly silly, rather than useful or serious. EG *I spend a lot of my salary on frivolous things.* ADJ QUALIT ≠ serious, important

frizz /frɪz/, **frizzes, frizzing, frizzed**. 1 If you **frizz** your hair, you brush or perm it so that it has a lot of stiff, wiry curls. ◊ **frizzed**. EG *Her hair is frizzed and pretty.* V+O ⇑ style ◊ ADJ CLASSIF
2 A **frizz** of hair is hair that has a lot of stiff, wiry curls. N COUNT ⇑ mass

frizzle /frɪzə⁰l/, **frizzles, frizzling, frizzled**. If something **frizzles** or if it **is frizzled**, it becomes burned and crisp or hard, because of very strong heat. EG *The gas dried up her hair and frizzled the ends.* ◊ **frizzled**. EG *...frizzled bacon.* V-ERG = scorch ◊ ADJ CLASSIF

frizzy /frɪzi¹/, **frizzier, frizziest**. **Frizzy** hair is very thickly and stiffly curled. EG *He was broad and muscled, with frizzy red hair.* ADJ QUALIT ⇑ curly

fro /frəʊ/. **to and fro**: see **to**.

frock /frɒk/, **frocks**. A **frock** is a woman's or girl's dress; an old-fashioned word. N COUNT

frock coat, frock coats. A **frock coat** is a long coat that was worn by men in the 19th century. N COUNT

frog /frɒg/, **frogs**. 1 A **frog** is a small creature with smooth skin, big eyes, and long back legs which it uses for jumping. Many frogs live near water. N COUNT ⇑ amphibian
2 A **Frog** is a French person; an informal and offensive word. N COUNT
3 If you **have a frog in** your **throat**, you cannot speak properly because your throat is partly blocked by phlegm; an informal expression. PHR

frogging /frɒgɪŋ/, **froggings**. The **frogging** on the front of a coat or uniform is a series of decorative fastenings that are usually made out of braid. N UNCOUNT/COUNT ⇑ decoration

frogman /frɒgmə³n/, **frogmen**. A **frogman** is someone who works underwater, especially in order to mend or search for something. Frogmen wear special rubber suits and shoes, and carry equipment to help them to breathe underwater. N COUNT = diver

frog-march, frog-marches, frog-marching, frog-marched. If you **are frog-marched** somewhere, you are taken there by force, with one person holding each of your arms so that you are almost carried there. EG *I was frog-marched down to the police station.* V+O : USU+A = drag

frogspawn /frɒgspɔːn/ is a soft, jelly-like substance which contains the eggs of a frog. N UNCOUNT

fro-ing. See **to-ing and fro-ing**.

frolic /frɒlɪk/, **frolics, frolicking, frolicked**. 1 When people **frolic**, they play about or behave in a lively, happy, and carefree way. EG *They dashed and frolicked about... We frolicked in the sun.* V : USU+A = romp
2 **Frolic** or a **frolic** is lively, happy, and carefree behaviour. EG *It was nothing but a frolic.* N COUNT

from /frɒm/. 1 You use **from** when you say where something was made or originates, or where someone first lived. EG *This water came from a spring... ...wisps of smoke from a small fire... She came from Ilford.* PREP ⇑ out of
2 You use **from** when you mention the place that someone leaves in order to go somewhere else. EG *They drove down from Leeds in the van... He had to flee to Tanzania. From Tanzania, Mr Otunnu went on to Oxford... We scrambled from our trucks and ran after them.* PREP
3 You use **from** when you mention the organization PREP

where someone works or to which they belong. EG *This is Mr Castle from the office... ...representatives from the Ancient Monuments board.*

4 If you are away **from** a place or if you have gone **from** it, you are not there or you have left it. EG *They were away from home... He was absent from school for two weeks.* PREP

5 If you return **from** a particular activity, you return after doing or experiencing it. EG *I went to meet my children from school... The men had not as yet come back from fishing.* PREP

6 If you take or move something **from** a particular place or thing, you take it out or remove it. EG *She pours whisky from the bottle into two small tumblers... Carmody picks up the books from beside his chair... We went around clearing rubbish from the fields... His arm drops from Jenny's shoulders... This amount will be deducted from your pension... Four from seventeen leaves thirteen.* PREP

7 If something is taken **from** you, it is removed or stolen, and you no longer have it. EG *I was too big to have money taken from me like this... Everything had been stripped from us, even hope.* PREP

8 If you get something **from** a particular place or person, you obtain or buy it there. EG *He bought the car from Ford's of Dagenham... He says he'd have to borrow the money from his wife... You can get leaflet M.11 from a post office.* PREP

9 If you get a letter, parcel, or telephone call **from** someone, they have sent it to you or they have telephoned you. EG *She got a card from them yesterday.* PREP

10 If you see, hear, or do something **from** a particular position, you are in that position when you see, hear, or do it. EG *From the top of the bus you could look down on people below... From here you cannot see the water itself... From upstairs there was the sound of the radio... The door was opened from within.* PREP

11 If something hangs or projects **from** a particular thing, it is attached to it or held by it, and sticks out from it or hangs down from it. EG *From his left hand dangled Piggy's broken glasses... He carried water in two buckets hanging from a bamboo pole across his shoulders... The brackets stick out too far from the wall.* PREP

12 You use **from** when you express distances or when you say how far something stretches. EG *From our back door to their back door was just a few yards... There's a tunnel beneath the ocean from Hokkaido to Honshu... From Parkington I still had a hundred miles to go.* PREP

13 You use **from** when you mention the substance that something is made out of. EG *All the shafts were cut from heavy planks of wood... They would have been made from iron smelted with charcoal.* PREP

14 You use **from** when you mention the book, play, film, etc that something is a part of. EG *I was quoting from a newspaper article... She could hear him through the door, singing a song from his latest film.* PREP

15 You use **from** when you mention where you got a particular piece of information. EG *The farmers knew about our union activities from their grooms and gardeners... He said the rumour came from you.* PREP = through

16 If you get a particular kind of behaviour or reaction **from** someone, they behave or react in that way towards you. EG *He was always sure of sympathy from his mother-in-law... 'And what started the quarrel?'–'An insult. From him.'* PREP

17 If something happens **from** a particular time or point, it begins to happen then. EG *From November 1980, the amount of money you receive may be less... She was deaf and dumb from birth... We had no rain from March right through to October... ...from nine in the morning till 5 p.m.... From the eighteenth century on, great private palaces sprang up all over the country.* PREP

18 If something is **from** a particular occasion or time or if it is left over **from** then, it belongs to that occasion or time. EG *She washes the dishes from last night... I've still got work to do from last month... I've just got the photographs from last year's holiday.* PREP

19 If something changes or develops **from** a particular amount, thing, or state, it was previously that amount or thing or it was in that state before the change. EG *They agreed to enlarge the national committee from 17 members to 30... It is impossible to translate satisfactorily from one language to another... All the trees are grown from seed... The farmers had turned from crops to cattle.* PREP

20 You use **from** after words that mean 'prevent', 'forbid', or 'not do' in order to mention the thing that is prevented, forbidden, or not done. EG *They made an attempt at both rallies to prevent me from being heard... He could be disqualified from election for three years... She was wearing a lilac gauze scarf to keep her hair from flying... You should phone up to see if you can be excused from paying.* PREP

21 If something is hidden **from** you, you cannot see it or you are not told about it. EG *He tries to hide it even from me... The truth had been kept from me.* PREP

22 You use **from** when you refer to a difference between two things or people. EG *It seemed to him to be no different from any other brain he had seen... Can you tell a poisonous mushroom from an edible one?* PREP

23 You use **from** when you state the cause of a particular event, action or state. EG *He died in prison. From pneumonia... She had been suffering from a severe headache... From sheer nervousness she said a few more stupid things... My eyes hurt from the wind.* PREP ⇑ because of

24 You use **from** when you mention something which leads to or results in a particular event, action, or fact. EG *The committee's inquiry arose from representations made by Basildon District Council... It's a spin-off from military and space research... No new jobs will result from it.* PREP ⇑ out of

25 You use **from** when you state the reasons or basis for a particular judgement, opinion, or conclusion. EG *I could see from her face that she felt disappointed... From what I can gather, this was a real freak accident... From the way she immediately shut up, I sensed that she did not approve... I was speaking from bitter personal experience... ...from a personal point of view.* PREP

26 You use **from** in structures with 'to' when you describe ranges, for example when you are stating maximum and minimum amounts, or the possible varieties of something. EG *The process takes anything from two to five weeks... From 50,000 to 500,000 people died... The flowers may be anything from light carmine to crimson... A vet is supposed to know about everything from a cow to a mouse.* PREP+NG+*to*+NG

frond /frɒnd/, **fronds**. A **frond** is a long leaf or piece of seaweed which has an edge divided into lots of thin parts. EG *...palm fronds... The curtains were moving slowly, like huge fronds of seaweed.* N COUNT

front /frʌnt/, **fronts, fronting, fronted. 1** The **front** of something is the part of it that is closest to you or that faces you, or that is more important because it is the part that you normally see or use. EG *They wore jackets with high lapels and six buttons down the front... I had red claw gashes down my neck and front... Their fangs are placed at the front of the upper jaw... She came crawling out of a trapdoor in the front of the stage.* ▸ used as an adjective. EG *One of his front teeth was gone.* N COUNT+SUPP: USU SING ≠ back ▸ ADJ CLASSIF: ATTRIB

2 A **front** room, window, garden, etc is on the side of a building that faces the street. EG *I took him into the front room for a quick sherry... She walked out the front gate.* ▸ used as a noun. EG *Miss Vernon's post office was at the front of her cottage.* ADJ CLASSIF: ATTRIB ≠ back ▸ N COUNT: USU *the*+N IN SING

3 The **front** of a car or lorry is the part where the driver sits. EG *The cop searched the front of the car.* ▸ used as an adjective. EG *The front seats are comfortable.* N COUNT: USU *the*+N IN SING ▸ ADJ CLASSIF: ATTRIB

4 The **front** of a piece of paper is the side which contains the most important writing or pictures. EG *Most of my key work seems to be on the front of old envelopes.* N COUNT: USU *the*+N IN SING ≠ back

5 The **front** page or **front** cover of a newspaper or magazine is the outside part on which the first words or pictures are printed. EG *The Sunday Express had a headline on the front page: 'Child's Body Found in Wood'... Every woman's magazine has a picture of a woman on the front cover.* ADJ CLASSIF: ATTRIB ≠ back

6 in front. 6.1 Someone or something that is **in front** is moving along or situated ahead of a particular person or thing, or is further forward than them with nothing in between. EG *Jaykar walked in front and Sudhir and Bal behind him... ...an American lady in the row in front.* PHR: USED AS AN A ≠ behind **6.2** Someone or something that is **in front** or **up front** is in the place or position which is PHR: USED AS AN A nearest to the front of something, for example to the front of a vehicle. EG *She got into the bus and sat up front near the driver.* **6.3** Someone who is **in front** in a competition or contest is in a winning position. PHR : USED AS AN A

7 in front of. 7.1 A person or object that is **in front of** something is close to the front part of it or ahead of it, with nothing in between. EG *A car drew up in front of the house... I'd spend whole evenings just sitting in front of the television set.* PREP ≠ behind **7.2** If something is **in front of** you, you are facing it and it is very near you. EG *Grilled trout was put in front of them... You should have your notes in front of you... There was a man standing in front of me.* PREP = before **7.3** If you write something **in front of** a particular word, you write it to the left of that word. EG *Put the little word 'de' in front of your name.* PREP = before **7.4** If you do or say something **in front of** someone else, you do or say it when they are present and can therefore see or hear what you are doing or saying. EG *I couldn't tell you in front of Sam... He thought they had conspired to discredit him in front of Hogan... They will all have to sign in front of a magistrate.* PREP = before

8 In a seaside town, the **front** is a road next to the sea. EG *After tea we'd walk along the front a bit.* N SING : the+N

9 In a war, the **front** is a line where two opposing armies are facing each other. EG *He was given three days' leave before going to the Western front.* N COUNT : USU the+N

10 When you say that something happens on a particular **front**, you mean that it happens with regard to a particular situation or field of activity. EG *On the purely intellectual front, little advance has been made... Computers are advancing on a variety of fronts... Has anything happened on that front?* N COUNT : USU+SUPP

11 On the home front or **on the domestic front** means with regard to your own country rather than foreign countries. EG *On the home front, the big pitfall in his economics may be the problem of inflation.* PHR : USED AS AN A

12 If someone puts on a particular kind of **front**, they try to appear to have that feeling or quality, although they do not have it. EG *I knew, of course, that this carefree attitude was only a front. ...presenting a united front to the world... He put on a bold front.* N SING : USU a+MOD+N = face

13 An organization or activity that is a **front** for an illegal or secret activity is used to hide it. EG *The hotel is just a front for organized prostitution.* N COUNT

14 In meteorology, a **front** is the line where a mass of cold air meets a mass of warm air. • See also **cold front, warm front.** N COUNT

15 The word **Front** is often used in the titles of political organizations with a particular aim. EG *...the Mozambique Liberation Front.* N COUNT : ALSO IN NAMES AFTER N

16 A building that **fronts** a particular place or **fronts** onto it is next to it and faces it. EG *This beach has two restaurants fronting it... ...houses that front directly onto little brick-paved courtyards.* V+O, OR V+A (onto) = face

17 An organization that **is fronted** by a particular person is led by that person. V+O : USU PASS ↑ head

frontage /frʌntɪdʒ/, **frontages**. A **frontage** of a building is a wall which faces a street. EG *...the early Victorian frontage of the Treasury.* N COUNT : USU MOD+N = front

frontal /frʌntəᵒl/. **1** A **frontal** attack is direct and obvious. EG *I never believed in frontal attack either in war or politics... ...a frontal assault.* ADJ CLASSIF : ATTRIB

2 Frontal also means **2.1** in or relating to a person's forehead; a formal or medical use. EG *...the frontal lobes of your brain.* ADJ CLASSIF : ATTRIB **2.2** involving the front of someone's body. EG *There was frontal nudity on stage and screen.* ADJ CLASSIF : ATTRIB

front bench, front benches. The **front bench** or the **front benches** are British members of Parliament who are ministers in the Government or who hold official positions in an opposition party. EG *...the debating strength of the front bench... He was appointed front-bench spokesman on transport.* N COUNT : the+N, USU SING=PL

frontbencher /frʌntbɛntᵒʃə/, **frontbenchers**. A **frontbencher** is a front-bench member of Parliament. EG *...a Tory frontbencher.* N COUNT

front door, front doors. The **front door** of a house or other building is the main door, which is usually in the wall that faces a street. N COUNT

frontier /frʌntɪə/, **frontiers**. **1** A **frontier** is a border between two countries, or between a country and an area of wild, unclaimed land. EG *...the four thousand mile frontier between the United States and Canada... There have been large-scale military manoeuvres on the frontier... ...a frontier town.* N COUNT

2 The **frontiers** of something, especially knowledge, are the limits of it or a boundary that exists between it and something else. EG *They are doing work on the frontiers of discovery... Human acts have repercussions far beyond the frontiers of the human world... This is an easy way of crossing different social frontiers.* N COUNT+SUPP : USU PL ↑ border

frontiersman /frʌntɪəzməᵊn, frʌntɪəz-/, **frontiersmen**. A **frontiersman** was a man who lived in a part of North America where settlers had only just come to live, especially near the frontier of wild, unclaimed land. N COUNT

frontispiece /frʌntɪspiːs/, **frontispieces**. The **frontispiece** of a book is a picture at the beginning, opposite the page with the title on. N COUNT : USU SING

front line, front lines; often used before another noun and spelled with a hyphen. **1** The **front line** is the place where two opposing armies are facing each other and where fighting is going on. EG *We came to within a mile and a half of the front line... ...front-line troops.* N COUNT : USU the+N IN SING

2 Someone who is **in the front line** has to play a very important part in defending or achieving something. EG *He found himself in the front line, having to defend the Government's record.* PHR : USED AS AN A

front man, front men. A **front man** is **1** someone, especially someone respectable, who represents a particular group and acts on their behalf. EG *Mohamed was the comparatively respectable front man of the team.* N COUNT **2** someone who presents a television or radio programme. N COUNT ↑ presenter

front-page. A **front-page** article or picture appears on the front page of a newspaper because it is very important or interesting. EG *He was exposed two days later by a front-page piece in the New York Times.* ADJ CLASSIF : ATTRIB

front-runner, front-runners. In a competition or contest, the **front-runner** is the person who seems most likely to win it. EG *...George Smith, the current front-runner for the job.* N COUNT = favourite

frost /frɒst/, **frosts, frosting, frosted**. **1** If there is **frost** or a **frost**, the temperature outside falls below freezing point, tiny ice crystals form, and the ground becomes white. EG *There was a touch of frost this morning... ...the severe frost damage to Brazil's coffee plantations... ...the first frosts of autumn.* N UNCOUNT/COUNT ↑ weather

2 Frost is also the thin whitish covering of ice crystals that forms on things when there has been a frost. EG *The lawn was sparkling with frost.* N UNCOUNT ↑ deposit

3 When someone says that there are a particular number of **degrees of frost**, they mean that the temperature is that number of degrees below freezing point. EG *You can expect six degrees of frost tonight.* PHR : NUM+PHR

frost over. When something made of glass **frosts over** or **frosts up**, it becomes covered with frost. EG *It must have been cold last night, my windscreen's frosted over.* • See also **frosted, frosting.** PHRASAL VB : V+ADV

frostbite /frɒstbaɪt/ is a condition in which your fingers, toes, etc become seriously damaged as a result of being very cold. EG *The old woman died of exposure and frostbite.* N UNCOUNT

frostbitten /frɒstbɪtəᵒn/. If someone or a part of their body is **frostbitten**, they are suffering from frostbite. ADJ CLASSIF ↑ injured

frosted /frɒstɪ²d/. **1 Frosted** glass has had its surface roughened so that you cannot see through it clearly. EG *...frosted glass partitions.* ADJ CLASSIF : USU ATTRIB ↑ opaque

2 Frosted also means **2.1** covered with frost; a literary use. EG *...frosted grass.* ADJ CLASSIF **2.2** covered with something that looks like frost. EG *...a gown frosted with diamonds.* ADJ CLASSIF : IF+PREP THEN with **2.3** covered with icing; used in American English. ADJ CLASSIF = iced

frosting /frɒstɪŋ/ is the icing on a cake; used in American English. N UNCOUNT

frosty /frɒstiˡ/, **frostier, frostiest**. **1** You say that the weather is **frosty** when the temperature is below freezing but it is not snowing. EG *...a still and frosty night... The air was frosty.* ADJ QUALIT ↑ cold

2 You describe the ground or an object as **frosty** when it is covered with frost. EG *I could feel the crisp frosty grass underfoot.* ADJ QUALIT

3 You describe someone's behaviour as **frosty** when they are unfriendly or disapproving. EG *The banker's voice became frosty.* ADJ QUALIT = cold, icy ◇ **frostily**. EG *He smiled frostily.* ◇ ADV WITH VB ◇ **frostiness**. EG *She was well known for her frostiness with men who paid her compliments.* ◇ N UNCOUNT

froth /frɒθ/, **froths, frothing, frothed.** 1 **Froth** consists of lots of small bubbles together in a mass. It forms when air is mixed with a liquid. EG *The big canoe was cutting through the water with froth curling at her bow.* — N UNCOUNT = foam

2 If a liquid **froths**, it is full of small bubbles. EG *He looked down and saw the water frothing at his feet... ...buckets of frothing creamy milk.* — V : USU+A = foam

3 **froth at the mouth. 3.1** If a person or animal **froths at the mouth**, a mass of small bubbles comes from their mouth, because they are ill. EG *He was rolling on the floor, frothing at the mouth.* — PHR : VB INFLECTS **3.2** You also say that someone **is frothing at the mouth** when they are very angry; an informal use. — PHR : VB INFLECTS

4 **Froth** is also something which seems attractive and fun but has no real worth. EG *Some people think that the West End is all froth and glitter.* — N UNCOUNT

frothy /frɒθi[1]/, **frothier, frothiest.** A **frothy** liquid has lots of bubbles in it or on its surface. EG *...a frothy milk shake.* — ADJ QUALIT

frown /fraʊn/, **frowns, frowning, frowned.** When someone **frowns**, their eyebrows become drawn together, because they are annoyed, worried, or puzzled, or because they are concentrating. EG *He frowned as though deep in thought... He pushed his cuff back and frowned at his watch.* — V ▸ used as a noun. EG *...a middle-aged man with a perpetual worried frown... Sheila's behaviour was attracting disapproving frowns.* — ▸ N COUNT ⇑ expression ◊ **frowning.** EG *...a frowning glance.* — ◊ ADJ CLASSIF

frown upon. If something **is frowned upon** or **is frowned on**, people disapprove of it. EG *Any sign of priggishness is frowned upon by the community... Society frowns upon candour.* — PHRASAL VB : V+PREP, HAS PASS

froze /frəʊz/ is the past tense of **freeze**.

frozen /frəʊzəºn/ 1 **Frozen** is the past participle of **freeze**.

2 If a lake, river, etc is **frozen** or **frozen over**, its surface has turned into ice because the temperature has been below freezing point. EG *...the silence of the frozen lake... He was found in the frozen canal... Part of the Missouri was frozen over.* — ADJ CLASSIF

3 If the ground is **frozen**, it has become very hard because the temperature has been below freezing point. EG *The land is still frozen.* — ADJ CLASSIF

4 **Frozen** food has been preserved by freezing it; usually used of food that you buy. EG *...a packet of frozen peas... ...a frozen chicken.* — ADJ CLASSIF : USU ATTRIB

5 If you are **frozen**, you are very cold. EG *We were frozen–we only had our pyjamas on.* ▸ used of a part of your body. EG *She blew on her frozen fingers.* — ADJ QUALIT

6 If you are **frozen** with fear, terror, etc, you cannot move because you are so frightened. EG *The chained men sat frozen with terror... He heard someone coming and lay frozen.* — ADJ CLASSIF : USU PRED+*with* ⇑ rigid

frugal /fruːgəºl/. 1 People who are **frugal** or who live **frugal** lives do not eat much or spend much money on themselves. EG *Be as frugal as a monk... She lived a careful, frugal life.* — ADJ QUALIT ⇑ careful = parsimonious ◊ **frugally.** EG *Happiness, he said, lay in working hard and living frugally.* — ◊ ADV WITH VB ⇑ cheaply ◊ **frugality** /fruːgælɪti[1]/. EG *...a people known for their self-reliance and frugality.* — ◊ N UNCOUNT = parsimony

2 A **frugal** meal is small and inexpensive. EG *He went into the kitchen to prepare his frugal breakfast.* — ADJ QUALIT

fruit /fruːt/, **fruits, fruiting, fruited.** The plural of the noun can be either **fruit** or **fruits**, but it is usually **fruit**. 1 A **fruit** is something that you can eat that grows on a tree or bush. It has soft or firm flesh, and contains seeds or a stone. Oranges, bananas, and grapes are fruit. Fruit is eaten either raw or cooked, usually as a dessert. EG *They always buy the very best and freshest fruit and vegetables... She bit into the fruit... Bananas and citrus fruits are the country's only cash crops... ...acres of fruit trees.* — N COUNT/UNCOUNT ⇑ food

2 A **fruit** is also something containing seeds or a stone that grows on a tree, bush, or flowering plant and that is not normally eaten by people; a technical term. EG *The mountain ash has red fruits.* — N COUNT/UNCOUNT

3 When a tree or bush **fruits**, it produces fruit; a technical term. EG *This is an excellent variety which always fruits well.* — V

4 A tree or bush that is **in fruit** has fruit growing on it. — PHR : USED AS AN A

5 You can refer to everything that grows and that can be eaten or used by people as the **fruits** of the earth, the **fruits** of nature, etc; a literary use. EG *The fruits of nature belong to all mankind.* — N PLURAL/UNCOUNT : USU+*of* ⇑ produce

6 You can refer to the results of something as the **fruits** or the **fruit** of it, especially when these results are good or pleasant. EG *They had reached a time of life when most people would be reaping the fruits of their labour.* — N PLURAL/UNCOUNT : USU+*of*

7 If an action **bears fruit**, it produces good results. EG *The government predicts that their measures will start to bear fruit soon and inflation rates will come down.* — PHR : VB INFLECTS ⇑ succeed

8 See also **dried fruit, first fruits, forbidden fruit**.

fruitcake /fruːtkeɪk/, fruitcakes; also spelled as two words. **Fruitcake** or a **fruitcake** is a cake that contains dried fruit. — N UNCOUNT/COUNT

fruit cocktail, fruit cocktails. A **fruit cocktail** is a mixture of pieces of different kinds of fruit which is usually eaten as the first course of a meal. — N COUNT/UNCOUNT ⇑ starter

fruitful /fruːtfʊl/. Something that is **fruitful** 1 produces a lot of good and useful results. EG *There's been a very fruitful collaboration between British Rail and ourselves... This is proving a very fruitful area of research at present.* — ADJ QUALIT = profitable ◊ **fruitfully.** EG *We want to help women to use their childbearing years more fruitfully.* — ◊ ADV WITH VB ⇑ usefully **2** produces a lot of fruit, crops, or young. EG *They believe that their god makes the trees flourish and the earth fruitful.* — ADJ QUALIT ⇑ fertile

fruition /fruːɪʃəºn/. When a plan, hope, or action comes to **fruition**, the thing that was planned or hoped for happens or comes into existence; a formal word. EG *At last his efforts were coming to fruition.* — N UNCOUNT ⇑ fulfilment

fruitless /fruːtlɪ[2]s/. Something that is **fruitless** is useless and does not result in the achievement of anything. EG *...a prolonged and fruitless industrial dispute... His quest proved fruitless.* — ADJ QUALIT = vain

fruit machine, fruit machines. A **fruit machine** is a slot machine used for gambling which pays out money if particular symbols, usually of fruit, appear together when it is operated; used in British English. — N COUNT = one-armed bandit

fruit salad, fruit salads. Fruit salad is a mixture of pieces of different kinds of fruit in juice which is eaten as a dessert. — N UNCOUNT/COUNT

fruity /fruːti[1]/, **fruitier, fruitiest.** 1 Something that is **fruity** smells or tastes of fruit. EG *...fruity fragrances... ...cheap, fruity wines.* — ADJ QUALIT

2 A **fruity** laugh or voice is rich and deep; used showing approval. — ADJ QUALIT

3 A **fruity** remark or story refers in a humorous way to things relating to sex; an informal use. EG *His remarks were far too fruity to be put down on paper.* — ADJ QUALIT ⇑ rude = lewd

frump /frʌmp/, **frumps.** When people refer to a woman as a **frump**, they mean that she is old-fashioned, dull, and uninteresting. — N COUNT

frustrate /frʌstreɪt/, **frustrates, frustrating, frustrated.** 1 If something **frustrates** you, it makes you feel upset and angry because you are unable to deal with the difficulties and problems it gives you. EG *The lack of money and facilities depressed and frustrated him... It always frustrates me when I can't afford the time to get involved and help out.* — V+O ⇑ annoy = irk ≠ encourage ◊ **frustrated.** EG *...a job in which you feel frustrated and unhappy.* — ◊ ADJ QUALIT ◊ **frustrating.** EG *There must be nothing more frustrating than having a job you don't enjoy.* — ◊ ADJ QUALIT = irritating ◊ **frustration** /frʌstreɪʃəºn/, **frustrations.** EG *She lay on the floor, screaming with frustration... ...the frustration of feeling caught in a trap... The reactions were the product of pent-up frustrations.* — ◊ N UNCOUNT/COUNT ⇑ feeling

2 If something **frustrates** something such as a plan, an event, or the progress of something, it results in it not taking place or not succeeding. EG *Improvements in the economy could be frustrated by industrial disruption... ...their unrivalled skill at delaying and frustrating changes of which they disapproved.* — V+O ⇑ prevent = block, thwart ◊ **frustrated.** EG *So many frustrated poets end as pipe-smoking teachers... ...popular belief, which associates suicide with frustrated love.* — ◊ ADJ CLASSIF = unfulfilled ◊ **frustration.** EG *There is nothing more damaging for society than the frustration of hopes.* — ◊ N UNCOUNT = disappointment

fry /fraɪ/, **fries, frying, fried.** 1 When you **fry** food, you cook it in a pan that contains hot fat or oil. EG *Ellen was frying an egg for her breakfast.* — V-ERG ◊ **fried.** EG *She was forbidden to eat fried food or anything with fat.* — ◊ ADJ CLASSIF ⇑ cooked

2 **Fry** are very small, young fish. EG *The fry remain in the streams for a few weeks.* ● See also **small fry**. — N PLURAL

fry up. If you **fry up** food, you fry it, especially in order to make a quick, casual meal; an informal expression. EG *Make yourself useful and fry up some bacon.* ● See also **fry-up**. — PHRASAL VB : V+O+ADV ⇑ cook

frying pan, frying pans. 1 A **frying pan** is a flat metal pan with a long handle, in which you fry food. N COUNT

2 If you say that to do a particular thing would be to jump **out of the frying pan into the fire**, you mean that to do it would not improve the situation, and might make things worse. EG *There they go, leaping merrily out of the frying pan into the fire.* PHR : USED AS AN A

fry-up, fry-ups. A **fry-up** is a meal consisting of food that has been fried; an informal expression in British English. N COUNT

ft is a written abbreviation for **foot** or **feet.** EG *...280,000 sq. ft. of office space... An 80ft viaduct straddles the river Wye.* N COUNT : NUM + N ⇑ measurement

fuchsia /fjuːʃə/, **fuchsias.** A **fuchsia** is a plant or a small bush which has pink, purple, or white flowers. The flowers are often two-coloured, and hang downwards, with their outer petals curved backwards. N COUNT

fuck /fʌk/, **fucks, fucking, fucked**; an extremely rude word, which most people find offensive. It is only used in very informal English, usually spoken English, and most speakers do not use it at all. 1 **Fuck** and **fucking** are used as swear words **1.1** in order to emphasize a word or phrase. **1.2** in order to emphasize something that makes you feel angry or annoyed.

2 **Fuck all** is used to mean 'nothing at all'. PHR : AS O OR C

3 To **fuck** someone means to have sex with them. V OR V+O : RECIP
▸ used as a noun. ▸ N COUNT

fuck about. To **fuck about** or **fuck around** means to behave in a way that is silly, stupid, or unnecessary and that annoys other people; a very rude expression. PHRASAL VB : V+ADV, OR V+O+ADV

fuck off is an insulting and offensive way of telling someone to go away. PHRASAL VB : V+ADV, USU IMPER

fuck up. If you **fuck** something **up**, you make a mess of it; a very rude expression. PHRASAL VB : V+O+ADV

fuddled /fʌdəld/. If you are **fuddled**, you are confused and unable to think clearly. EG *I was fuddled with drink... You have some fuddled idea that each of us carries his own destiny.* ADJ QUALIT = hazy

fuddy-duddy /fʌdi¹dʌdi¹/, **fuddy-duddies.** You describe people as **fuddy-duddy** when they are old-fashioned and dull in their appearance or attitudes; used showing disapproval. EG *...two old fuddy-duddies.* N COUNT/VOC = stuffed shirt
▸ used as an adjective. EG *They consider boxer shorts old-fashioned and fuddy-duddy.* ▸ ADJ QUALIT = square

fudge /fʌdʒ/, **fudges, fudging, fudged.** 1 **Fudge** is a soft brown sweet that is made from butter, milk, and sugar. N UNCOUNT

2 If you **fudge** something, you avoid making a clear and definite decision, distinction , or statement about it. EG *We will always fudge issues while we can... There must be no fudging the figures.* V+O

fuel /fjʊəl/, **fuels, fuelling, fuelled**; also spelled **fueling, fueled.** 1 **Fuel** is something such as wood, coal, oil, or petrol that is burned in order to provide heat or power. EG *The cost of fuel is a major worry for old people... ...alternative fuel for aircraft... There is neither fuel nor food in the house... ...the use of fuels such as coal and oil.* • See also **fossil fuels.** N MASS ⇑ material

2 When a machine or vehicle **is fuelled** by a particular fuel, the fuel is used in it in order to make it work. EG *Heat can be supplied from boilers fuelled by domestic refuse.* V+O : USU PASS ⇑ power

3 If something **fuels** a situation that is already difficult or unpleasant, it makes the situation worse. EG *This budget fuels inflation and cuts our living standard... ...rumours of street fighting and violence, fuelled by the press.* V+O ⇑ worsen = encourage

4 If something **adds fuel to** a difficult or unpleasant situation, or **adds fuel to the flames**, it makes the situation worse. EG *It will only add fuel to the class war.* PHR : VB INFLECTS = exacerbate

fug /fʌg/. A **fug** is an airless, usually smoky and rather smelly atmosphere; an informal word, mainly used in British English. EG *...a thick fug of cigarette smoke.* N SING WITH DET = fog

fugitive /fjuːdʒɪtɪv/, **fugitives.** 1 A **fugitive** is someone who is running away or hiding, especially someone who is trying to avoid being caught by the police. EG *...the life of a fugitive in Paraguay... ...federal charges of harbouring a fugitive... ...a fugitive from injustice.* N COUNT ⇑ runaway
▸ used as an adjective. EG *...two fugitive German ships... ...the manhunt for a fugitive American.* ▸ ADJ CLASSIF : ATTRIB = escaping

2 **Fugitive** means lasting only for a very short time; a literary use. EG *...fugitive perceptions... ...a fugitive smile... Apart from some rare and fugitive visits, he did not live with us again.* ADJ CLASSIF ⇑ brief

fugue /fjuːg/, **fugues.** A **fugue** is a piece of music that begins with a short, simple tune, which is then repeated by other voices or instrumental parts with small variations according to a particular musical pattern; a technical term in music. N COUNT/UNCOUNT

-ful, -fuls. -ful is added to nouns that refer to containers or objects in order to form countable nouns. Nouns formed in this way refer to the quantity of a substance that the object contains or can hold. EG *...sack→sackful... ...hand→handful... ...cupboard→cupboardful... ...another mouthful of food... ...two teaspoonfuls of salt.* SUFFIX : FORMS N PARTS

fulcrum /fʌlkrəm/, **fulcrums, fulcra.** The plural can be either **fulcrums** or **fulcra.** The **fulcrum** of something that is balancing or being used as a lever is the point at which it is balancing or pivoting. N COUNT ⇑ pivot

fulfil /fʊlfɪl/, **fulfils, fulfilling, fulfilled**; also spelled **fulfill, fulfills.** 1 If you **fulfil** a promise, threat, duty, request, hope, etc, you do what was promised, asked, or expected. EG *They failed to fulfil their promises to revive the economy... Those who have friends in an office may have their requests fulfilled... This limits the ability of many of the smaller organizations to fulfil their obligations... I had fulfilled many of my youthful ambitions.* V+O = carry out, realize

2 If something **fulfils** you, or if you **fulfil** yourself, you feel happy and satisfied with what you are doing or with what you have achieved. EG *This way of life no longer adequately fulfils the individuals concerned... Now that the children have left home I can go out and fulfil myself.* ◇ **fulfilling.** EG *Jobs should be made as creative and fulfilling as possible.* ◇ **fulfilled.** EG *The children gain if both parents are living fulfilled lives.* V+O (NG/REFL) ⇑ satisfy ◇ ADJ QUALIT ⇑ satisfying ◇ ADJ QUALIT

3 If someone or something **fulfils** a particular role or function, they do whatever is required by that role or function. EG *He could no longer fulfil his function as breadwinner for the family... Helicopters fulfilled a variety of roles.* V+O ⇑ perform

fulfilment /fʊlfɪlmə²nt/; also spelled **fulfillment.** 1 **Fulfilment** is a feeling of satisfaction that you get from doing or achieving something, especially something useful. EG *People there do appear to find fulfilment in working for a common goal... There are men who want more fulfilment within the home.* N UNCOUNT

2 When there is **fulfilment** of a promise, threat, request, hope, duty, etc, the promised or expected thing happens. EG *...the partial fulfilment of a dream... ...the fulfilment of our needs.* N UNCOUNT : USU +*of*

full /fʊl/, **fuller, fullest.** 1 Something that is **full** contains as much of a substance or as many objects as it is possible for it to hold. EG *The bucket's almost full... Judy picked up one of the full ashtrays... I had always been lectured about not talking with my mouth full.* ADJ QUALIT ⇑ filled

2 You describe something as being **full** of things or people when it contains a very large number of them. EG *...a long garden full of pear and apple trees... His office was full of policemen... Her eyes were full of tears... The air was full of flying objects.* ADJ QUALIT : PRED+*of*

3 You describe people or things as being **full** of a particular feeling or quality when they have a lot of it and when it seems to be the most important or noticeable thing about them. EG *I was full of confidence... His dark eyes were full of fury and defiance... The papers were suddenly full of news about China... She's full of her own importance.* ADJ QUALIT : PRED+*of*

4 You say that a place or vehicle is **full** when there is no space left in it for any more people or things. EG *All the car parks are absolutely full... Have any table you like. We're not exactly full.* ADJ QUALIT = packed

5 If your hands or arms are **full**, you are carrying or holding as much as you can carry. EG *I'm sorry–my hands are full... He came back with his arms full.* • to **have** your **hands full**: see **hand.** ADJ QUALIT : PRED, IF+PREP THEN *of* ⇑ filled = loaded

6 If you feel **full**, you have eaten or drunk so much that you do not want anything else; a fairly informal use. ADJ QUALIT : PRED ⇑ satiated

7 **Full** also means as great in extent or amount as is possible. EG *...economic policies which would ensure a return to full employment... They'll never be able to make full use of their brains.* ADJ CLASSIF : ATTRIB = complete, maximum

8 Something that provides you with a **full** explanation or **full** details explains or tells you everything that you need to know about a particular matter. EG *I* ADJ CLASSIF : ATTRIB ⇑ complete = detailed

was then given the full story of Andrea's marriage... We'll have full details in next week's programme... Their parents have demanded a full inquiry.

9 You say that something has been done or described **in full** when everything that was necessary has been done or described. EG *The bill has been paid in full... Many of the devices have not been described in full.* PHR : USED AS AN A ⇑ completely = fully

10 Something that is done or experienced **to the full** is done to as great an extent as is possible. EG *She wanted to exploit that opportunity to the full... This prevented him from enjoying his role as father to the full.* PHR : USED AS AN A ⇑ completely = fully

11 If someone has or leads a **full** life, they are very busy, and do a lot of pleasant or interesting things. EG *Everybody has a right to a full life.* ADJ QUALIT

12 You also use **full** **12.1** when you are referring to the whole of something, or to something that has all the parts that it could have or usually has. EG *I haven't got his full name... ...a full English breakfast... ...my last full day in Warsaw... The passenger lounge ran the full width of the ship.* ADJ CLASSIF : ATTRIB ⇑ complete **12.2** in order to emphasize the completeness of a particular quality or characteristic. EG *Here you can see the full squalor of the buildings... I paused to allow the full impact of this to strike home.* ADJ CLASSIF : ATTRIB **12.3** in order to emphasize how great an amount is. EG *For a full week we did not have one square meal... ...a control arm that swings a full 90 degrees.* ADJ CLASSIF : ATTRIB ⇑ whole **12.4** in order to emphasize the directness and force with which someone or something hits, looks at, or falls on something else. EG *My skis struck a woman full in the face... The light from the motorcycle headlight was full upon me.* ADV : VB + ADV + PREP ⇑ right = squarely

13 When a piece of equipment or a machine is **full** on, working at **full** volume, etc it is working at the greatest extent possible. EG *The gas fire was full on... The volume was turned up full.* ADV AFTER VB

14 Someone who is a **full** member, **full** partner, etc has all the rights, status, and importance of a member, partner, etc rather than having only some of these. EG *She wanted to be a full member of the club... He achieved the rank of full professor at the age of thirty.* ADJ CLASSIF : ATTRIB

15 A **full** sound is rich, strong, loud, and resonant; used showing approval. ADJ QUALIT

16 A **full** flavour is strong and rich; used showing approval. EG *...a cheese with a good full flavour.* ADJ QUALIT

17 Something that is in **full** light is in bright, direct light. Something that is in **full** shade or shadow is in very dark shadow. EG *...places that are exposed to full sunshine throughout the day... His face was in full shadow.* ADJ CLASSIF : ATTRIB ⇑ strong = intense

18 **Full** is used to describe soft parts of the body that are rounded and rather large. EG *Her full red lips parted in a faint smile... ...a dress specially designed to flatter the fuller figure.* ADJ QUALIT = plump

19 A **full** skirt or sleeve is wide and has been made from a lot of fabric. EG *She wore a full mid-calf skirt... The sleeves were cut full.* ADJ QUALIT

20 If a piece of clothing is **full** at a particular point, it is rather loose and perhaps too large at that point. EG *The other pair of trousers were a bit full round the seat... It's not full enough across the back.* ADJ QUALIT : PRED + A ⇑ big ≠ tight

21 When the moon is **full**, it appears as a bright circle. EG *Slowly a full moon came up from the horizon.* ADJ CLASSIF

22 You describe people as **full of** themselves when they are pleased with themselves and think that they are very clever, special, or important; used showing disapproval. PHR + PRON REFL : USED AS C ⇑ conceited ≠ modest

23 If you say that someone's heart is **full**, you mean that they are very happy, grateful, generous, or sentimental; a rather literary use. EG *My heart was full, thumping with happiness... She had been able, with a full and generous heart, to return the compliment.* ADJ QUALIT = overflowing

24 If you say that you know **full well** that something is the case, you are emphasizing that you know a fact very well. EG *We know full well that Congress will spend every penny.* PHR : USED AS AN A

25 **Full** is also used in phrases such as 'at full pelt', 'in full cry', 'in full swing', and 'in full view', to emphasize the degree or extent of what is happening. Each of these phrases is explained at the entry for the noun. • to be **full of beans**: see **bean**. • to **come full circle**: see **circle**.

full-back, full-backs. A **full-back** is a defending player in football, hockey, or rugby who stands close to the goal or line that he or she is defending. N COUNT ⇑ defender

full-blooded. **1** **Full-blooded** behaviour and actions are carried out with great commitment and enthusiasm. EG *We have the full-blooded support of the Opposition parties... ...a full-blooded investigation.* ADJ CLASSIF : ATTRIB = vigorous

2 A **full-blooded** person or animal has ancestors of only one race or breed. EG *...a full-blooded Cherokee Indian.* ADJ CLASSIF : ATTRIB ⇑ pure

full-blown means having all the characteristics of a particular type of thing or person. EG *...a full-blown military operation... ...full-blown heart attacks.* ADJ CLASSIF : ATTRIB

full board. If you stay at a hotel that provides **full board**, you can obtain all your meals there. N UNCOUNT

full dress. Someone who is in **full dress** is wearing all the clothes needed for a ceremony or formal occasion. EG *A Zulu in full dress looked magnificent... Round the corner marched a full-dress regiment of soldiers.* N UNCOUNT ⇑ costume

full-face; also spelled as two words, especially when used as an adverb. A **full-face** photograph or portrait is one of someone who is facing you directly rather than having their head turned away or downwards. EG *Send a full-face photograph of yourself... The face is seen both in profile and full face.* ADJ CLASSIF, OR ADV AFTER VB

full-fledged means the same as fully-fledged. ADJ CLASSIF

full-grown. An animal or plant that is **full-grown** has reached its natural size and stopped growing. EG *A full-grown male giraffe can stand over nineteen feet tall... When full grown, the larva will spin a cocoon.* ADJ CLASSIF = adult

full house, full houses. If a theatre has a **full house** for a particular performance, it has as large an audience as it can hold. EG *I can remember when we'd have a full house every night.* N COUNT

full-length. **1** A **full-length** book or film is the normal length for a book or film. EG *Between 1906 and 1910, Vita wrote eight full-length novels.* ADJ CLASSIF : ATTRIB

2 A **full-length** skirt, coat, sleeve, etc is of the greatest normal length for such a piece of clothing. EG *She wears a white full-length raincoat... ...full-length sleeves.* ADJ CLASSIF : ATTRIB ⇑ long

3 **Full-length** curtains or other furnishings reach to the floor. ADJ CLASSIF : ATTRIB

4 A **full-length** mirror or portrait shows the whole of a person. ADJ CLASSIF : ATTRIB

5 Someone who is lying **full-length** is lying down flat and stretched out. EG *He stretched out full-length beside her.* ADV AFTER VB ⇑ extended

full marks. **1** If you get **full marks** in a test or exam, you get everything right and gain the maximum number of marks. N PLURAL

2 If you say that someone gets **full marks** for something, you are praising them for being very clever or for showing some other good quality. EG *Mr Jenkins gets full marks for courage and enterprise... Full marks to you for spotting that.* N PLURAL : IF + PREP THEN *for*

fullness /fʊlnɪ²s/. **1** **Fullness** is the state that something is in when it is full. EG *I've got this feeling of fullness in my stomach all the time.* N UNCOUNT

2 If there is **fullness** in a part of a person's body, the part is large and rounded. EG *A padded bra contributed a fraudulent fullness to her chest.* N UNCOUNT

3 If a sound or flavour has **fullness**, it is rich and strong; used showing approval. EG *...the fullness of the string sound of the continental orchestras.* N UNCOUNT

4 If you say that something will happen **in the fullness of time**, you mean that it will eventually happen after a long time or after a long series of events. EG *He was modelling for the stone effigy which in the fullness of time would adorn his tomb.* PHR : USED AS AN A = finally, one day

full-page. A **full-page** advertisement, picture, or article in a newspaper or magazine takes up a whole page. EG *There's a marvellous full-page picture of Fonteyn and Helpmann.* ADJ CLASSIF : ATTRIB ⇑ large

full-scale. **1** **Full-scale** means having the characteristics of something to the fullest extent. EG *We are prepared for any crisis, including full-scale warfare... The United States will soon resume full-scale negotiations on a new arms pact.* ADJ CLASSIF : ATTRIB

2 A **full-scale** drawing or model is the same size as the thing that it represents. ADJ CLASSIF : ATTRIB

full-size. **1** **Full-size** or **full-sized** means the same as full-grown. EG *A conifer will be full-sized by the time it fifty years old.* ADJ CLASSIF

2 A **full-size** or **full-sized** model or picture is the ADJ CLASSIF :

same size as the thing or person that it represents. EG ...*a full-size plastic doll.* ATTRIB = life-size

full stop, full stops; used in British English. 1 A **full stop** is the punctuation mark (.) which you use at the end of a sentence when it is not a question or exclamation. It is also sometimes put after an abbreviation or initial. EG *Good writing isn't just the ability to put capital letters and full stops in the right places.* N COUNT = period

2 You can say **'full stop'** after you have stated a fact or opinion, to emphasize that you have very strong feelings about it and to say that you are not willing to discuss it any further. EG *You have failed the exam, full stop.* PHR : USED AS ADV SEN = period

3 If you **come to a full stop**, you are not able to proceed any further with something that you are trying to achieve. EG *We have come to a full stop in our efforts to achieve Utopia.* PHR : VB INFLECTS

full-throated. A **full-throated** shout, laugh, etc is very loud. EG *She gave a full-throated laugh.* ADJ CLASSIF : ATTRIB

full-time. 1 **Full-time** work or study involves working or studying for the whole of each normal working week rather than for part of it. EG *Some of them already have a full-time job... We have eight hundred full-time students.* ▸ used as an adverb. EG *Bobbie and I worked full time.* ADJ CLASSIF ▸ ADV AFTER VB

2 If you describe a regular activity or task as **a full-time job**, you mean that it takes up so much of your time that it is like doing a proper job; an informal expression, often used in an exaggerated way. EG *It's a full-time job keeping the path clear of leaves.* PHR : USED AS C

3 In a game of football, hockey, etc, **full time** is the end of the game. EG *The whistle blew for full time.* N UNCOUNT

full up. 1 Something that is **full up** has no space left for any more people or things. EG *The town's full up... The car parks are all full up.* ADJ CLASSIF : PRED

2 If you are **full up**, you have eaten or drunk so much that you do not want to eat or drink anything else; an informal use. ADJ CLASSIF : PRED

fully /fuli¹/. 1 **Fully** means to the greatest degree or extent possible. EG *The secrets of its success are still not fully understood... ...fully automatic washing machines... She had fully intended to leave early.* ADV = completely

2 You use **fully** to say that a process is completely finished. EG *It was weeks before he fully recovered... The snake's young emerge fully formed from the mother... Barber isn't fully trained yet.* ADV WITH VB

3 If you describe, answer, or deal with something **fully**, you do it in such a way that you leave out nothing that should be mentioned or dealt with. EG *She answered his questions fully and candidly... This method is described more fully in the next chapter.* ADV WITH VB = thoroughly

4 **Fully** is also used to emphasize how great an amount is. EG *Fully one-quarter of the workers are Turks... It was fully 200 years since the last element had been discovered.* ADV + NG

fully-fledged /fʌli¹fledʒd/ means having all the characteristics of someone or something, especially as the result of a process of development. EG *By the age of seventeen I was a fully-fledged atheist... The SDP now sees itself as a fully-fledged rival party.* ADJ CLASSIF : ATTRIB ⇑ real

fulminate /fʌlmɪneɪt, fʊl-/, **fulminates, fulminating, fulminated**. If you **fulminate** against someone or something, you criticize them angrily. EG *He paced up and down, fulminating against Thomas.* V : IF + PREP THEN *against/at* = rage, rail

◊ **fulmination** /fʌlmɪneɪʃə⁰n/, **fulminations**. EG ...*the fulminations of preachers in the eighteenth century.* ◊ N COUNT/ UNCOUNT

fulsome /fʊlsəm/. **Fulsome** praise, apology, or gratitude is so exaggerated and elaborate that it sounds insincere; used showing disapproval. EG *They tried to please him with fulsome compliments and extravagant gifts.* ◊ **fulsomely**. EG *'That'll do beautifully, sir,' Michie said fulsomely.* ADJ QUALIT = extravagant ◊ ADV WITH VB = effusively

fumble /fʌmbə⁰l/, **fumbles, fumbling, fumbled**. 1 If you **fumble** when you are trying to do something with your hands, you are clumsy and do not move quickly and efficiently or hold things safely and steadily. EG *His awkwardness made him fumble with the key... He fumbled in his pocket for his whistle.* V : USU + A

2 If you **fumble** when you are trying to say something, you say it in a clumsy and unclear way. EG *What I'm fumbling to say is that I felt different about you.* V OR V + O

fume /fjuːm/, **fumes, fuming, fumed**. 1 **Fumes** are the unpleasant and often unhealthy smoke, gas, or smells that are produced by fires or by things such as chemicals, fuel, or cooking. EG *These fires produce really obnoxious fumes and smoke... He breathed whisky fumes all over my face... To rid clothes of cooking smells or tobacco fumes, hang them in the open air.* N PLURAL

2 If something **fumes**, it produces gas or smoke. EG *Don't bend over the mixture, because it fizzes and fumes.* V

3 If you **fume**, you show or express impatience and anger; an rather informal use. EG *I sat there fuming... 'This is your doing,' she fumed at Jim.* V, OR V + QUOTE = rage

fumigate /fjuːmɪgeɪt/, **fumigates, fumigating, fumigated**. If you **fumigate** something, you disinfect it, for example in order to get rid of germs or insects, by using special chemicals. EG *Your things will probably need fumigating.* ◊ **fumigation** /fjuːmɪgeɪʃə⁰n/. V + O ⇑ purify ◊ N UNCOUNT

fun /fʌn/. 1 **Fun** is something such as an activity or situation that is pleasant and enjoyable and that causes you to feel happy. EG *I think it'll be enormous fun... It's great fun playing with it... She got a lot of fun out of hiking... That would have spoiled the fun.* N UNCOUNT ⇑ enjoyment = sport

2 If you say that someone is **fun**, you mean that they are friendly and humorous and often do interesting or amusing things, so that you enjoy being with them. EG *She was very young, pretty, and great fun... He was fun to be with sometimes... They're both full of fun.* ADJ QUALIT, OR N UNCOUNT

3 If you describe something as a **fun** thing, you mean that you enjoy doing it. If you describe someone as a **fun** person, you mean that you enjoy being with them; used informally, mainly in American English. EG *Those were fun times... It is actually quite a fun read.* ADJ CLASSIF : USU ATTRIB = amusing, lively

4 The word **fun** is also used in the following expressions. **4.1** A **figure of fun** is someone who is considered ridiculous, so that people laugh at them or make jokes about them. PHR : USED AS C **4.2** If you do something **for fun, for the fun of it**, or **for the fun of the thing**, you do it in order to enjoy yourself rather than because it is important or necessary; an informal expression. EG ...*things that you do for fun in your spare time... You don't come to work just for the fun of it.* PHR : USED AS AN A **4.3 Fun and games** means playful behaviour, especially if it involves playing tricks and making jokes; an informal expression, often used showing disapproval. EG *I was sick of their fun and games.* PHR : USED AS O OR C = pranks **4.4** If you **have fun**, you do something that you enjoy and that causes you to feel happy. EG *We had great fun sleeping rough on the beaches... Let me do it, Cyril! Why should you have all the fun?* PHR : VB INFLECTS **4.5** If you do something **in fun** or **out of fun**, you do it as a joke or for amusement, without intending to cause any harm. EG *For goodness sake, don't you see it was just in fun!* PHR : USED AS AN A **4.6** If you **make fun of** someone or something or **poke fun at** them, you laugh at them, tease them, or make jokes about them in a way that causes them to seem ridiculous. EG *Don't make fun of me... I giggled and poked fun at it.* PHR : VB INFLECTS ⇑ ridicule = scoff at **4.7** People say **'What fun!'** when they are expressing excitement about something that they think will be enjoyable. EXCLAM = great

function /fʌŋkᵒʃə⁰n/, **functions, functioning, functioned**. 1 The **function** of an object, activity, job, etc is the role that it has, or the purpose for which it is used. EG *Each object has a single function... The function of reading aloud is to communicate the written word... ...the very difficult functions that languages have to perform.* N COUNT

2 **Function** is used to refer to the way in which something works or operates, especially the way in which a part of the body or a part of a machine works. EG ...*a device to test some aspects of heart function.* N UNCOUNT ⇑ working

3 A **function** is also a large formal dinner, reception, or party, usually held for important people and officials. EG *He was invited to attend some function at his uncle's house.* N COUNT

4 If you say that something is a **function** of another thing, you mean that its precise nature depends on that other thing in some way; a formal use. EG *Intelligence is partly a function of the speed with which the brain processes information.* N COUNT + *of* : USU SING = product

5 A **function** in computing is a sequence of operations that a computer performs, for example when a single key is pressed; a technical use. EG ...*the function keys on the keyboard.* N COUNT

6 A **function** in mathematics is a mathematical N COUNT : IF +

value which is not fixed but which depends on another mathematical value and changes whenever the other value changes; a technical use. PREP THEN *of*

7 The way in which something **functions** is the way in which it works or operates. EG *John has a very good idea of how the civil service functions, because he has been part of it... Today we understand almost everything about the functioning of the heart.* V : USU+A

8 When something such as a machine **is functioning,** it is working or operating in the way that it is supposed to. EG *Quite often the phone didn't function at all... Only one hospital is functioning.* V

9 If something or someone **functions** as a particular thing, they fulfil or perform the purpose or role of that thing. EG *The brain functions as a computer... I was amazed to find myself suddenly functioning as an ambassador from the South.* V+A *(as)* = act

functional /fʌŋkºʃəºnəl, -ʃənəºl/. **1 Functional** means relating to the way in which something works or operates, or relating to how useful it is. EG *We define our relationships with most people in functional terms... It preserved the legal and functional independence of each of the concerns.* ADJ CLASSIF : USU ATTRIB ⇑ operational

◇ **functionally.** EG *His work, therefore, ceases to be functionally necessary.* ◇ ADV

2 If something is **functional, 2.1** it is intended to be useful or practical rather than beautiful or decorative. EG *...an admirably clear and functional design.* ADJ QUALIT

2.2 it works or operates in the way that it is supposed to. EG *How long has the machine really been functional?* ADJ CLASSIF = operational

3 A **functional** illness affects the way in which a part of your body works but does not damage the part itself; a technical term in medicine. ADJ CLASSIF : USU ATTRIB

functionalism /fʌŋkºʃənəlɪzəºm/ is the idea that the most important aspect of something, especially a building or piece of furniture, is its use; a technical or formal word. ◇ **functionalist, functionalists.** EG *This view has been challenged by the functionalists.* N UNCOUNT ◇ N COUNT OR ADJ CLASSIF

functionary /fʌŋkºʃənəºri¹/, **functionaries.** A **functionary** is a person whose job is to do administrative work, especially for a government or a political party. N COUNT ⇑ employee

fund /fʌnd/, **funds, funding, funded. 1 Funds** are amounts of money that are available to be spent, especially money that is given to an organization or person for a particular purpose. EG *Congress cut back the funds for the program... They have spent their scarce funds on expensive housing... ...a public appeal for funds.* N PLURAL = resources, cash

2 A **fund** is an amount of money that is collected or saved, for example to help someone or to enable something to be done. EG *A fund was set up to maintain the buildings... ...the disaster fund... They began to organize a fund for the women.* N COUNT

3 If you have a **fund** of something, you have a lot of it. EG *...a large fund of scientific and technological knowledge... They have a fund of experience to draw on.* N COUNT : USU+ *of* = reserve

4 When a person or organization **funds** something, they provide money for it. EG *The work is being funded both by governments and private industry.* V+O = finance

◇ **funding.** EG *Lack of proper funding is making our job more difficult.* ◇ N UNCOUNT = financing

fundamental /fʌndəmentəºl/, **fundamentals. 1** You use **fundamental 1.1** to indicate that something is an essential feature or part of something. EG *...the fundamental principles on which society is based... ...a grasp of fundamental mathematical concepts... Computers are fundamental to our industrial structure.* ADJ CLASSIF : IF+ PREP THEN *to* = essential, central

1.2 to indicate that something exists at every possible level or in every possible way, and is therefore likely to continue. EG *There is a fundamental incompatibility between them... ...the hollowness and fundamental unsatisfactoriness of this way of life... The differences are in some respects fundamental.* ADJ QUALIT = basic

2 A **fundamental** change affects the basic nature of something. EG *This will bring about fundamental changes in society... ...the fundamental revolution in human values that has occurred.* ADJ CLASSIF : ATTRIB

3 A **fundamental** mistake results from misunderstanding the real or basic nature of something and so has a very great and serious effect. EG *The Administration is making a fundamental error in confusing spending with extravagance.* ADJ CLASSIF : ATTRIB = elementary

4 The **fundamentals** of something, for example of a subject or activity, are its most important and basic parts. EG *...my inability to grasp the fundamentals of physics... Such treatment never gets down to root causes, to fundamentals.* N PLURAL

fundamentalism /fʌndəmentəlɪzəºm/ is the belief in an extreme or old form of a religion or theory. Christian fundamentalism is the belief that everything in the Bible is completely true. N UNCOUNT

◇ **fundamentalist, fundamentalists.** EG *...a fundamentalist preacher.* ◇ N COUNT OR ADJ CLASSIF

fundamentally /fʌndəmentəli¹/. You use **fundamentally 1** to indicate that you are saying what the real or basic nature of something is. EG *It's fundamentally a political satire... Our criminal code is based fundamentally on fear... Yet, fundamentally, we are not a part of the community.* ADV SEN, OR ADV = basically

2 to indicate that something affects or relates to the basic nature of something. EG *They have fundamentally altered the rationale for military spending... I disagreed fundamentally with what the Party stood for.* ADV WITH VB = radically

fund-raising is the activity of collecting money to support a charity, political campaign, organization, etc. EG *...six weeks of active fund-raising... We held a fund-raising cocktail party.* N UNCOUNT

funeral /fju:nəºrəl/, **funerals.** A **funeral** is the service or ceremony that is held when someone has recently died and their body is being buried or cremated. EG *Today is Arthur's funeral... They're having a funeral service at eleven.* N COUNT ⇑ burial

● If someone says to you **'It's your funeral',** they mean that you have made a wrong decision and that you alone will be responsible for its consequences; an informal expression. ● PHR : VB INFLECTS

funerary /fju:nərəri¹/ means relating to funerals, burials, or cremations; a formal word. EG *The funerary ceremonies occupied two days.* ADJ CLASSIF : ATTRIB

funereal /fju:nɪərɪəl/. If you describe something as **funereal**, you mean that it reminds you of funerals or death in a depressing way; used showing disapproval. EG *The atmosphere in the cabin was almost unbearably funereal.* ADJ QUALIT = mournful, gloomy

funfair /fʌnfeə/, **funfairs.** In Britain, a **funfair** is a form of entertainment that consists of large machines on which you can have exciting rides and stalls where you can win things. Funfairs often travel from one place to another. EG *I promised to take them to the funfair on Saturday... ...a funfair Ghost Train.* N COUNT

fungal /fʌŋgəºl/ means caused by, consisting of, or relating to fungus; a formal word. EG *...fungal infections.* ADJ CLASSIF

fungi /fʌŋgaɪ/ is the plural of **fungus.**

fungicide /fʌŋgɪsaɪd/, **fungicides.** A **fungicide** is a chemical that can be used to kill fungus or to prevent it from growing. N COUNT/ UNCOUNT

fungoid /fʌŋgɔɪd/ means consisting of or covered with fungus, or reminding you of fungus; a formal or literary word. ADJ CLASSIF

fungus /fʌŋgəs/, **fungi, funguses.** The plural can be **fungi, funguses,** or **fungus.** A **fungus** is a plant that has no flowers, leaves, or green colouring. Mushrooms and toadstools are fungi. Other types of fungus such as mould and mildew are extremely small, spread quickly over surfaces, and look like a fine powder. N COUNT/ UNCOUNT

funicular railway /fju:nɪkjəºlə reɪlweɪ/, **funicular railways.** A **funicular railway** is a special railway up a very steep hill or mountain. A machine at the top of the slope pulls the carriage up the rails by a steel rope. N COUNT

funk /fʌŋk/, **funks, funking, funked. 1 Funk** is fear or cowardice; an old-fashioned use. EG *Out of sheer funk he had not gone to the party... He was really in a funk.* N UNCOUNT, OR N SING WITH DET

2 If you **funk** something, you avoid doing it because you are afraid; an old-fashioned use. EG *A man who will climb a cliff may funk grasping a snake... We had our chance then, and funked it.* V+O

3 A **funk** is a coward; an old-fashioned use. EG *Maurice spoke, hesitating, not wanting to seem a funk.* N COUNT = drip, sissy

4 **Funk** is also a style of music based on jazz and blues, with a strong, repetitive tune in the bass part of the music. N UNCOUNT

funky /fʌŋki¹/, **funkier, funkiest. 1 Funky** pop music or jazz has a very strong, simple rhythm. ADJ QUALIT

2 Young people used to describe things as **funky** ADJ QUALIT

when they thought they were very good or enjoyable; an informal use.

funnel /fʌnəˡl/, **funnels, funnelling, funnelled**; also spelled **funneling, funneled** in American English. 1 A **funnel** is a cone-shaped object which is wide at the top and has a short tube at the bottom. Funnels are used to pour things into containers by placing the tube into the neck or opening of the container. EG ...*medicines which he had transferred through a funnel from the bottles.* N COUNT ⇑ utensil

2 A **funnel** is also 2.1 something narrow, or narrow at one end, through which a substance flows and is directed. EG *The ravine was a funnel for winds... Try making a funnel of your hands.* N COUNT : USU+SUPP 2.2 a metal chimney on a ship or railway engine powered by steam. EG *The smoke was pouring from the funnel.* N COUNT

3 If something **funnels** or **is funnelled** somewhere, it is directed through a narrow space. EG ...*the funnelling effect of bays, estuaries and straits... Icy blasts funnel down the streets.* V-ERG : USU+A

4 If you **funnel** something from one place to another, you cause it to be transferred continuously in a direct, controlled way. EG *They were planning to funnel aid to the resistance movement.* V+O+A = channel

funnily /fʌnɪliˡ/. 1 You use **funnily enough** to indicate that, although a particular thing is unlikely or unexpected, it does or did happen. EG *I hated the green scarves, although, funnily enough, those were the ones that most people bought.* PHR : USED AS ADV SEN = oddly, strangely

2 If someone does something **funnily**, they do it in a strange way; a fairly informal use. EG *She was walking a bit funnily.* ADV AFTER VB = strangely

funny /fʌniˡ/, **funnier, funniest; funnies**. 1 Something that is **funny** is rather strange, surprising, or puzzling. EG *Some of them have some very funny ideas about war... ...a funny black hat... Have you noticed anything funny about this plane?... Funny how people change... The funny thing is, when they went back it had gone... It's funny but I can always tell who's going to win.* ADJ QUALIT = bizarre, odd

2 **Funny** people, incidents, stories, etc are amusing and makes you smile or laugh. EG *She laughed. 'What's funny?' he asked... Honestly, it looked so funny... He told funny stories and made everyone laugh... ...a genuinely funny man... Don't try to be funny.* ADJ QUALIT = comic, hilarious

3 The **funnies** are comic strips in newspapers; an informal term used mainly in American English. EG *Carol reads the funnies.* N PLURAL : *the*+N

4 You say that someone is **funny** when they are slightly mad; an informal use. EG *She's a bit funny sometimes.* ADJ QUALIT : PRED = odd, peculiar

5 If something **goes funny**, it stops working properly; an informal use. EG *The computer went all funny.* PHR : VB INFLECTS

6 If you feel **funny**, you feel slightly ill; an informal use. ADJ QUALIT : PRED

7 **Funny business** is dishonest or unacceptable behaviour; an informal expression.. EG *Any funny business and the deal's off.* PHR : = tricks

funny bone, funny bones. Your **funny bone** is the part of your elbow that gives you a tingling feeling when it is hit; an informal expression. N COUNT : USU SING = humerus

fur /fɜː/, **furs, furring, furred**. 1 **Fur** is 1.1 the thick and usually soft hair that grows on the bodies of many mammals. EG *Moles have short silky fur.* N UNCOUNT 1.2 the fur-covered skin of an animal that is used to make clothing or rugs. EG ...*a little pink jacket edged with white fur... ...a fur coat... The dog was excited by the smell of the furs they had been packing.* N UNCOUNT/COUNT 1.3 a synthetic fabric that looks like fur and is used, for example to make clothing, soft toys, and seat covers. EG ...*a Russian hat in black nylon fur.* N UNCOUNT = fake fur

2 A **fur** is a coat made from real or synthetic fur, or a piece of fur worn like a shawl or scarf. EG *She had been accused of stealing furs from a department store.* N COUNT ⇑ clothing

3 If an event **makes the fur fly** or **sets the fur flying**, it causes a great argument. EG *That'll really make the fur fly!* PHR : VB INFLECTS

4 **Fur** is also 4.1 a layer of a soft greyish-white substance on a person's tongue caused, for example, by smoking a lot. N UNCOUNT 4.2 a layer of a hard greyish-white substance that sometimes forms on the inside of objects such as kettles or water pipes. N UNCOUNT = scale

5 When a kettle or water pipe **furs** or **furs up**, the inside of it becomes covered with fur. EG *An iron sometimes furs up like a kettle and needs cleaning.* V, OR PHRASAL VB : V+ADV

furbish /fɜːbɪʃ/, **furbishes, furbishing, furbished**. If you **furbish** something, you make it look better, for example by painting or repairing it; a formal word. EG ...*my freshly furbished dining room.* V+O = renovate, restore

furious /fjʊərɪəs/. 1 Someone who is **furious** is extremely angry. EG *I was furious and told them to get out of my house... He was furious with himself for not realizing it sooner.* ADJ QUALIT = livid ◊ **furiously**. EG *'Who is this man?' the Prince exclaimed furiously.* ◊ ADV WITH VB

2 **Furious** is also used to describe something that is done with great energy, effort, speed, or violence. EG ...*a furious battle... ...the furious efforts they were making to catch up... ...the furious speed of technological development.* ADJ CLASSIF : USU ATTRIB ⇑ violent = vigorous ◊ **furiously**. EG ...*huge brown birds flapping their wings furiously to gain height.* ◊ ADV WITH VB = vigorously

furl /fɜːl/, **furls, furling, furled**. When you **furl** something such as an umbrella, sail, or flag, you roll or fold it up because it is not going to be used. V+O ◊ **furled**. EG *His black umbrella was furled tight.* ◊ ADJ CLASSIF

furlong /fɜːlɒŋ/, **furlongs**. A **furlong** is an imperial unit of length that is equal to 220 yards or 201.2 metres. EG *We could predict which horse would win over five furlongs.* N COUNT : USU NUM+N

furnace /fɜːnɪs/, **furnaces**. A **furnace** is 1 a container or enclosed space in which a very hot fire is made, for example to melt metal, burn rubbish, or produce steam. EG *His job was to stoke the furnace.* N COUNT 2 a very hot place; a fairly informal use. EG *The room, which had been so icy in winter, was now a furnace.* N SING

furnish /fɜːnɪʃ/, **furnishes, furnishing, furnished**. 1 If you **furnish** a room or building, you put furniture and furnishings into it. EG *He wanted to be moved to a nursing home where he could furnish his own room.* V+O : IF+PREP THEN *with*

2 If you **furnish** something or **furnish** someone with it, you provide or supply it; a formal use. EG *They were not willing to furnish the necessary troops... Luckily, they have furnished us with a translation.* V+O, OR V+O+A *(with)*

furnished /fɜːnɪʃt/. 1 A **furnished** room or house is available to be rented together with the furniture in it. EG *We are looking for furnished accommodation in the centre of town.* ADJ CLASSIF

2 When you say that a room or house is **furnished** in a particular way, you are describing the kind or amount of furniture that it has in it. EG *The bedroom was scantily furnished... She lived in a poorly furnished flat.* ADJ CLASSIF

furnishings /fɜːnɪʃɪŋz/. The **furnishings** of a room or house are the furniture, and also fittings such as sinks, curtains, or carpets, and decorations such as pictures. EG *The bed and the toilet were the only furnishings in the tiny cell... The furnishings are mostly modern.* N PLURAL ⇑ contents

furniture /fɜːnɪtʃə/. 1 **Furniture** consists of large movable objects such as tables, chairs, or beds that are used in a room for sitting on or for putting things on or in. EG *She arranged the furniture... It's quite trendy to have pine furniture... The only other piece of furniture was an old-fashioned wardrobe.* N UNCOUNT

2 If you describe someone or something as **part of the furniture**, you mean that they have been near you so long or fit in with your surroundings so well that you do not notice that they are there; an informal expression. PHR : USED AS C = fixture

furore /fjʊəʳrɔːriˡ/; also spelled **furor** in American English. A **furore** is a very angry or excited reaction by people to something. EG *The half-hour lecture caused an enormous furore... ...the present furore over drugs.* N SING WITH DET

furrier /fʌrɪə/, **furriers**. A **furrier** is a person who makes or sells clothes made from fur. N COUNT

furrow /fʌrəʊ/, **furrows, furrowing, furrowed**. 1 A **furrow** is 1.1 a long line in the earth, a few inches deep, which a farmer makes so that seeds can be planted in it or so that water for the crops can be made to flow down it. EG ...*a field with parallel furrows running down it.* N COUNT ⇑ trench 1.2 a deep, fairly wide, line in the surface of something. EG *Generations of bare feet had worn a furrow in the floor.* N COUNT 1.3 a deep fold or line in the skin of someone's face. EG *I could tell from the deep furrows in her forehead that she was very disturbed by the news.* N COUNT = wrinkle

2 If someone **furrows** their brow or forehead or if it **furrows**, it has deep folds in it because they are frowning. EG *The pain of the disease caused him habitually to furrow his brow... Sutherland's brow* V-ERG

furrowed. ◊ **furrowed.** EG *...the scholar's furrowed brow.* ◊ ADJ CLASSIF = lined

3 To **furrow** something means to make a deep line along its surface; a literary use. EG *A bullet furrowed the wall beside him.* V+O

furry /fɜ:ri¹/, **furrier, furriest. 1** An animal or part of an animal that is **furry** is covered with thick, soft hair. EG *The lemur has yellow eyes and a long furry tail.* ADJ QUALIT

2 Something that is **furry** has a soft rough texture like fur. EG *Barbara looked smart in a furry coat.* ADJ QUALIT

3 If a person's tongue is **furry**, it is covered with a layer of a soft greyish-white substance. ADJ QUALIT

further /fɜ:ðə/, **furthers, furthering, furthered. Further** is a comparative form of 'far', and also a verb. **1 Further** means more than before or more than something else, or to a greater extent or degree. EG *The Chancellor was forced to deflate the economy still further... The situation was further complicated by uncertainty about the future... He sank further into debt... He had never read further than Chapter LXXIX.* ADV WITH VB

2 If someone or something goes **further** or if someone takes a particular thing **further**, the thing is done to a more advanced or more extensive degree. EG *Now, however, the government are keen to take the matter further... The art of the 1970's went further, abandoning tradition... They never got any further.* ADV WITH VB

3 If you say you will go **further** or take something **further** in a discussion, you mean you will make a more extreme statement or deal with a point more thoroughly. EG *I shall go further and say that Lawrence was playing a double game... I wouldn't want to take it any further at this stage.* ADV WITH VB

4 When you refer to a **further** thing or number of things, or to a **further** amount of something, you are referring to an additional thing, number of things, or amount. EG *Turkey is eager for a further round of talks with Greece.... There were no further casualties... ...a further five hundred pounds... For further information, see leaflet NI.49... I have at this stage no further comment on them... I don't think I've anything further to say.* ADJ CLASSIF, OR ADJ AFTER N ⇑ more = extra

5 You use **further** to introduce a statement that relates to the same general topic and that gives additional information or makes an additional point; a fairly formal use. EG *Davis related that the three girls were pretty; further, that before the ship sailed they had all acquired admirers... He argued that the freedom to join a union does not also imply a freedom not to join. He further argued that the 1980 Act would protect workers more.* ADV SEN

6 Further to is used in business letters in expressions such as 'further to your letter' or 'further to our telephone discussion'. It indicates what you are referring to in the letter; a formal use. EG *Further to your letter of the 16th, I am happy to inform you that I have now received the contract duly signed.* PREP ⇑ with respect to = with reference to

7 Further also means a greater distance than before or than something else. EG *...further along the beach... I walked further than I intended... He closed the book and pushed the candle further from him... Further to the north, the British infantry advanced into the enemy lines.* ▸ used as an adjective. EG *...at the further end of the table.* ADV = farther ▸ ADJ CLASSIF

8 If you tell someone that what you have just said must **not go any further**, you mean that it must not be told to anyone else. EG *'This mustn't go any further.'–'No it won't, I promise.'* PHR : MODAL + PHR ⇑ not spread

9 Further is used in expressions such as 'further back' and 'further on' to refer to a point in time that is earlier or later than the one you are talking about, or earlier or later than the present time. EG *It has its origins much further back in time... Three years further on, Linda has no regrets... Looking further ahead, airfields were to be built.* ADV+ADV

10 If you detain someone **further**, delay something **further**, etc, you do it for an additional length of time. EG *I won't detain you further.* ADV WITH VB

11 If you **further** something, you help it to progress, to be successful, or to be achieved. EG *We are no longer able to further the cause of world revolution... ...a plot by Morris to further his career.* V+O ⇑ assist = advance, promote

furtherance /fɜ:ðəʳrəns/. The **furtherance** of something is the activity of helping it to be successful or be achieved; a formal word. EG *...massive subsidies to cover deficits incurred in the furtherance of anti-inflation policy.* N UNCOUNT ⇑ development = fostering

further education is the education of people who have left school and who are not at a university, polytechnic, or college of higher education; used in British English. EG *The state is pouring money into further education... ...further education courses.* N UNCOUNT

furthermore /fɜ:ðəmɔ:/ is used to introduce a piece of information or opinion that adds to or supports the previous one; a rather formal word. EG *Computer chess games are still a bit expensive, but they are getting cheaper all the time. Furthermore their chess-playing strength is rising.* ADV SEN ⇑ and = moreover, in addition

furthermost /fɜ:ðəməʊst/. The **furthermost** one of a number of similar things is the one that is the greatest distance away from a particular place. EG *We made our way to the furthermost hut.* ADJ CLASSIF : ATTRIB = farthest

furthest /fɜ:ðɪ²st/. **Furthest** is a superlative form of 'far'. **1 Furthest** means to a greater extent or degree than ever before or than anything or anyone else, or more than ever before or than anyone or anything else. EG *...countries where commercialized farming has advanced furthest.* ADV WITH VB, OR ADJ QUALIT : SUPERL ⇑ most

2 The **furthest** one of a number of similar things is the one that is the greatest distance away from a particular place. EG *She sat near the furthest window.* ▸ used as an adverb. EG *...the fields which lay furthest from his farm... It was often those without charts who got the furthest.* ADJ CLASSIF = farthest ▸ ADV

furtive /fɜ:tɪv/. If you are **furtive**, you behave as if you want to keep something secret or hidden. EG *They suddenly looked furtive.* ▸ used of people's behaviour and actions. EG *Fear showed in his eyes, in the furtive darting of his gaze.* ◊ **furtively.** EG *She watched Gertie furtively pencil a note and slip it between the pages.* ADJ QUALIT = secretive ▸ = sly ◊ ADV WITH VB = stealthily

fury /fjʊəri¹/. **1 Fury** is violent or very strong anger. EG *He clenched his fists in fury... There was fury in Miss Lenaut's dark eyes.* N UNCOUNT = rage

2 If you are **in a fury**, you are very angry. EG *When the women heard this, they jumped on Willie in a fury... He flew into a fury and said that the whole thing was disgusting.* PHR : USED AS AN A = in a rage

3 If you run, fight, etc **like fury**, you do so with great energy, strength, or power; a rather old-fashioned expression. EG *Charlie Barret could hit like fury.* PHR : USED AS AN A ⇑ violently

fuse /fju:z/, **fuses, fusing, fused. 1** A **fuse** is **1.1** a safety device in an electric plug or circuit, etc. It is a piece of wire which melts in order to stop the flow of electricity and which prevents fire. **Fuse** is also used to refer to the container that the piece of wire is in. EG *Switch off lamp and mend the fuse again... Has the fuse blown then?* **1.2** a failure in a piece of electrical equipment or in the electricity supply to a building, usually because too much electricity is used; a fairly informal use in British English. EG *There's been a fuse.* N COUNT / N COUNT

2 When a light or some other electric device **fuses** or when you **fuse** it, it stops working because of a fault, especially because too much electricity is being used; used in British English. EG *As usual, several of the street lamps had fused... If the wires had met they would have fused all the lights.* V-ERG

3 A **fuse** is also a device on a bomb or firework which causes a delay before the bomb explodes or firework goes off, so that you can get a safe distance away. It can be a long piece of wire or something more complicated. N COUNT = touch paper

4 When things **fuse** or **are fused**, they join together physically, usually to become one thing. EG *During fertilization the sperm and egg fuse... The two slightly different images on the two retinae are fused in the cortex.* V-ERG : USU PASS ⇑ unite = merge

5 When two pieces of metal **fuse** or when you **fuse** them, they melt because of heat and become joined together. EG *...some pieces of gold coin that had fused together in the blaze.* V-ERG ⇑ combine

6 If something **fuses** two different ideas, subjects, beliefs, etc, it causes them to join together, especially in order to form a pleasing or satisfactory combination. EG *...the attempt to fuse new and old... In this portrait of Henry VII, art and history fuse in inextricable magic.* V-ERG ⇑ combine = blend

fuse box, fuse boxes. A **fuse box** is a box that is usually fixed to a wall in a house or other building and that contains the fuses for all the electric circuits in the building. N COUNT

fused /fjuːzd/. A **fused** plug, kettle, etc, has a fuse in it. ADJ CLASSIF

fuselage /fjuːzɪlɑːʒ/, **fuselages**. The **fuselage** is the main part of an aeroplane, missile, or rocket. It is usually cylindrical in shape. EG *The plane tore through the tops of the elms, the fuselage disintegrating.* N COUNT = body

fuse wire is metal wire used in fuses. N UNCOUNT

fusillade /fjuːzɪleɪd, -lɑːd/. A **fusillade** of shots is a large number of them fired at the same time. EG *They retreated under a fusillade of bullets.* ▸ used of criticism, questions, etc. EG *He faced a fusillade of questions.* N SING WITH DET +*of* ▸ = barrage

fusion /fjuːʒəⁿn/, **fusions**. 1 **Fusion** is the act or process of fusing, or the state of being fused: see **fuse**. EG *The movement's emotional appeal lay in the fusion of radical and socialist ideals.* N UNCOUNT ⇑ union = synthesis

2 A **fusion** is something new that is created by a mixture of different qualities, ideas, or things. EG *...Tagore's fusion of Indian tradition and Western liberalism... The painting is a rich fusion of several elements.* N COUNT ⇑ combination = blend

3 **Fusion** is also the process in which atomic particles combine and produce a large amount of nuclear energy; a technical use. EG *...a fusion bomb.* N UNCOUNT

fuss /fʌs/, **fusses, fussing, fussed**. 1 A **fuss** is anxious or excited behaviour which serves no useful purpose and which is often unwelcome. EG *What is all the fuss about?... The meeting ended without too much fuss.* N SING/UNCOUNT : IF+PREP THEN *about/over* = commotion

2 If you **make a fuss of** someone, you pay a lot of attention to them; used in British English. EG *They like to be flattered and to be made a fuss of... She made a lot of fuss of her baby granddaughter.* PHR : VB INFLECTS

3 If you **fuss**, you behave in a nervous, anxious way about small, unimportant matters and rush around doing unnecessary things. EG *Stop fussing, Mary, and come here... He was a nuisance, always fussing and worrying... She's always fussing about her appearance.* ▸ used as a noun. EG *She is in a fuss because her mother's coming... She gets into a fuss when things go wrong.* V : IF+PREP, THEN *about/over* ⇑ worry = fret ▸ N SING : a+N = flap

4 If there is a **fuss**, people become anxious or angry about something and complain about it; used in informal English. EG *There's certain to be a fuss when Mother knows you've broken her best vase.* N SING : a+N = to-do

5 If you **make a fuss** or **kick up a fuss** about something, you become angry or excited about it and complain; an informal expression. EG *Alan kicked up a great fuss and swore our friendship was at an end... There's no point making a fuss about it.* PHR : VB INFLECTS : IF+PREP THEN *about/over* = get worked up

6 If you **fuss** someone, you make a nuisance of yourself to them when they are busy; an informal use; used mainly in American English. EG *Tim, please, just stop fussing me.* V+O = pester

fuss over. If you **fuss over** someone or something, you pay too much attention to them or show too much concern or affection for them. EG *Matty was inclined to fuss over her health... She is being fussed over too much.* PHRASAL VB : V+PREP, HAS PASS

fusspot /fʌspɒt/, **fusspots**. A **fusspot** is a person who is always complaining and is difficult to please; an informal word. EG *Sit down and stop being such a fusspot, Karen.* N COUNT/VOC = worrier

fussy /fʌsiˈ/, **fussier, fussiest**. 1 People who are **fussy** 1.1 are very concerned with unimportant details and are difficult to please. EG *I hope you're not fussy about garlic.* ◊ **fussiness**. EG *She was upset by his fussiness about his food.* 1.2 get nervous and excited about things that are not important. EG *Feeling over-anxious and fussy I began to question her further.* ◊ **fussily**. EG *She fussily checked all the arrangements.* ADJ QUALIT ◊ N UNCOUNT ADJ QUALIT ◊ ADV WITH VB

2 Clothes and furniture are described as **fussy** when they have too many elaborate details or too much decoration. EG *...fussy lace curtains.* ◊ **fussily**. EG *She was fussily dressed.* ADJ QUALIT = fancy ◊ ADV WITH VB

3 If someone offers you a choice of two things and you say **'I'm not fussy'**, you mean that you would be equally pleased with either thing. EG *'Tea or coffee?'–'I'm not fussy.'* CONVENTION = I don't mind

fusty /fʌstiˈ/, **fustier, fustiest**. Something that is **fusty** 1 is old-fashioned in attitudes or ideas; used showing disapproval. EG *I was sent to a fusty old school in the country.* 2 has a stale smell. EG *The sleeping bag smelt fusty.* ADJ QUALIT = archaic ADJ QUALIT = musty

futile /fjuːtaɪl/. If you think something is **futile**, you think it has no chance of achieving what you want. EG *...a series of costly and futile wars... She knew from experience how futile it was to argue with her father.* ADJ QUALIT = pointless

2 If you say something **futile**, it sounds foolish and has no value. EG *She kept making futile remarks while I was trying to concentrate on the lecture.* ADJ QUALIT = inane

futility /fjuːtɪlɪtiˈ/ is a total lack of purpose or usefulness. EG *She sits there brooding on the futility of human effort... ...the futility of life.* N UNCOUNT

future /fjuːtʃə/, **futures**. 1 The **future** is the period of time that will take place after the present. EG *Industrial unrest will continue into the foreseeable future... We will have to see what the future holds... The offices of the future may well have no typewriters... They look to the future with a certain anxiety.* N SING : the+N

2 You use **in the future** to refer to a period of time after now. This expression is often used with an adjective to indicate that you are thinking about a particular period of time. For example, 'in the distant future' means a long time from now. EG *I can see nothing in the future but boredom and pain... She's not going to get rid of them in the foreseeable future. I don't know what'll happen in the near future... I'm leaving in the not too distant future. ...some mythical date in the distant future.* ● **For the future** means in the future or in preparation for the future. EG *What plans do you have for the future... We've got to meet training requirements for the future.* ● You use **in future** to indicate that you want things to change or to be done differently from now on. You are often criticizing someone and telling them to change their behaviour. EG *Be more careful in future... We will be able to avoid it in future.* PHR : USED AS AN A ● PHR : USED AS AN A ● ADV SEN

3 **Future** is used to describe something that relates to the future. EG *Let's meet again at some future date... ...the need to conserve energy for future generations... She stored it all away for her own future reference.* ADJ CLASSIF : ATTRIB

4 The **future** is what is going to happen, in contrast to what is now happening or what has already happened. EG *We have the future to think of... The future was obscure and peace was not yet in sight... We need to face the future.* N SING WITH DET ⇑ situation

5 Your **future** is what will happen to you, especially in your career. EG *They have to find their own way to whatever political future they might choose... I decided that my future lay in medicine... I'm convinced that there is a sound future in farming.* N COUNT : USU+SUPP

6 If something has a **future**, it is likely to succeed. EG *Members of the public might wonder if this scheme has any future at all... He had faith in its future.* N SING WITH DET = prospects

7 The **future** tense of a verb is the one used when you want to talk about things that will happen, in contrast to things that have happened or are happening. ADJ CLASSIF

futuristic /fjuːtʃərɪstɪk/. Something that is **futuristic** seems very strange and modern, as if belonging to a time in the future when science has made great advances. EG *...a futuristic reference to push-button voting... There was a futuristic weirdness about the place.* ADJ QUALIT = avant-garde

fuzz /fʌz/. 1 **Fuzz** is used to refer to 1.1 short, soft hairs sticking out from a person's skin, especially from their face, arms or legs. EG *...the light, blond fuzz on his cheeks.* 1.2 curly hair that does not have a definite shape. N UNCOUNT = down N UNCOUNT

2 **The fuzz** are the police; an informal expression. EG *'I didn't steal it'–'You tell the fuzz that.'* N SING : the+N

fuzzy /fʌziˈ/, **fuzzier, fuzziest**. 1 Hair that is **fuzzy** sticks up in a firm, soft mass. EG *He's the one with fuzzy red hair.* ADJ QUALIT = frizzy

2 If something is **fuzzy**, it has a covering that feels soft and like fur. EG *When I woke up my tongue and teeth felt fuzzy.* ADJ QUALIT = furry

3 A **fuzzy** photograph, television picture, etc has a blurred outline or shape. EG *The picture is fuzzy.* ADJ QUALIT

4 If your thoughts are **fuzzy** or what you are thinking about is **fuzzy**, you are confused and cannot see an idea clearly or make a decision. ◊ **fuzzily**. EG *I suppose I'm thinking rather fuzzily.* ADJ QUALIT ⇑ unclear ◊ ADV WITH VB

5 You also describe something as **fuzzy** when it is not clearly defined and is indistinct or vague. EG *The difference between the leader and the led has become fuzzy.* ADJ QUALIT

Gg

G, g /dʒiː/, **Gs, g's**. G is used as both the singular and the plural form for paragraph 3. **1 G** is the seventh letter of the English alphabet. N COUNT

2 G, in music, is the fifth note in the scale of C major.

3 A **G** is **3.1** a measurement of the rate of acceleration in something such as a space rocket. One G is equivalent to the earth's gravitational pull. EG *At race speeds drivers are subject to forces of several G as they corner.* N COUNT : USU NUM+N **3.2** a thousand pounds or dollars; a very informal use, mainly in American English. EG *They stole 1000G of equipment.* N COUNT : NUM+N = grand, K

4 G or **g** is also an abbreviation for words beginning with g, such as 'gram,' 'gallon,' or 'German'.

gab /gæb/, **gabs, gabbing, gabbed**; an informal word. **1** If someone **gabs**, they talk a lot without saying anything that is important or useful. EG *What were you two men gabbing about?* V : IF+PREP THEN *about* = natter

2 If you say that someone has **the gift of the gab**, you mean that they have the ability to speak easily, confidently, and in a persuasive way. PHR : USED AS O ⇑ eloquence

gabardine /gæbədiːn/, **gabardines**; also spelled **gaberdine**. **Gabardine** is a fairly thick cloth which is used especially for making coats. EG *...a grey gabardine suit.* N UNCOUNT ▸ A **gabardine** is a coat made from this cloth. ▸ N COUNT ⇑ coat

gabble /gæbəºl/, **gabbles, gabbling, gabbled**; an informal word. **1** If you **gabble**, you say things so quickly that it is difficult for people to understand you. EG *The result was that we gabbled and the audience could barely hear us... 'Look here,' he gabbled, 'It's about the Harvest Festival.'* V : IF+PREP THEN *about*, OR V +O/QUOTE ⇑ speak = babble

2 Gabble is very fast talking that is difficult to understand, especially because a lot of people are all talking at once. EG *There was a gabble of conversation in the pub.* N UNCOUNT ⇑ speech = babble

gable /geɪbəºl/, **gables**. A **gable** is the triangular part at the top of the end wall of a building, between the two sloping sides of the roof. N COUNT

gabled /geɪbəºld/ is used to describe houses that have a gable or gables. EG *...small gabled houses.* ADJ CLASSIF

gad /gæd/, **gads, gadding, gadded**. If you **gad** about or **gad** around, you go to a lot of different places looking for amusement and entertainment; an informal and old-fashioned word. EG *This is hardly the time to be gadding around.* V+A *(about/around)* = gallivant

gadget /gædʒɪ²t/, **gadgets**. A **gadget** is a small machine or device which does something useful. EG *...household gadgets... Never connect an electric gadget to a light socket.* N COUNT = appliance

gadgetry /gædʒɪ²tri¹/ consists of small machines or devices that do something useful. EG *New developments will make the present gadgetry look very old-fashioned.* N UNCOUNT ⇑ machinery

Gaelic /geɪlɪk/. **1 Gaelic** is a language spoken by people in parts of Scotland and Ireland. N UNCOUNT

2 Something that is **Gaelic** is written or spoken in Gaelic, or relates to people who speak Gaelic. EG *...an old Gaelic proverb.* ADJ CLASSIF

gaff /gæf/. If you **blow the gaff** you let someone know a secret that other people do not want them to know, especially by mistake or without meaning to; an informal expression. EG *Was Mrs Welch there when he blew the gaff about the phone call?* PHR : VB INFLECTS ⇑ reveal = blab

gaffe /gæf/, **gaffes**. A **gaffe** is something that you say or do that is considered to be socially incorrect, and that offends or upsets people. EG *I had no idea of the gaffe which I was committing.* N COUNT ⇑ mistake = faux pas

gaffer /gæfə/, **gaffers**; an informal word used in British English. **1** The **gaffer** in a business, a factory, or on a building site is the man in charge, for example the owner or a foreman. EG *You'll have to ask the gaffer.* N COUNT : USU *the*+N IN SING ⇑ supervisor = guvnor

2 Some people use **gaffer** to refer to any man, especially an old man. EG *...an old gaffer not famous for his tact.* N COUNT = fellow

gag /gæg/, **gags, gagging, gagged**. **1** A **gag** is something such as a piece of cloth that is tied round or put inside someone's mouth in order to stop them from speaking or shouting. EG *A gag was taped over his mouth and he could hardly breathe.* N COUNT

2 If someone **gags** you, they tie a piece of cloth round your mouth in order to stop you from speaking or shouting. EG *She was tied up and gagged and left in a locked room.* V+O ⇑ silence

3 If you **gag**, you choke and nearly vomit. EG *Dr. Hutchinson suddenly gagged. 'Too much wine. Forgive me.'* V : NO IMPER = retch

4 In informal English, a **gag** is a joke, especially one told by a professional comedian. EG *Where do you get all these gags?* N COUNT

gaga /gɑːgɑː/. Someone who is **gaga** is senile; a very informal word. EG *She's seventy-seven and rather gaga.* ADJ QUALIT

gaggle /gægəºl/, **gaggles**. **1** A **gaggle** of geese is a group of geese. N PART+N IN PLURAL

2 You can use **gaggle** to refer to a group of people, usually when you want to express disapproval or contempt for them. EG *...a gaggle of critics... ...a gaggle of disorderly little girls.* N PART+N IN PLURAL ⇑ group

gaiety /geɪə²ti¹/ is a feeling or attitude of liveliness and fun. EG *...the grim facts which lie behind the facade of gaiety... ...fresh youthful gaiety.* N UNCOUNT

gaily /geɪli¹/. **1** If you do something **gaily**, you do it in a lively, happy way. EG *Off we set, with Pam chattering gaily all the way... She waved goodbye very gaily, her scarf fluttering in the wind.* ADV WITH VB ⇑ happily = blithely, cheerily

2 Something that is **gaily** coloured or decorated is coloured or decorated in a bright, pretty way. EG *...gaily coloured wrappers for chocolates.* ADV WITH VB ⇑ prettily = brightly

gain /geɪn/, **gains, gaining, gained**. **1** If you **gain** something such as an ability or quality, you gradually get more of it. EG *After a nervous start, the speaker began to gain confidence... She has gained a reputation for toughness... The opposition party is gaining in popularity... This gives you a chance to gain experience.* V+O, OR V+A *(in)* = pick up

2 If you **gain** from something such as an event or situation, you get some advantage or benefit from it. EG *We all hope to gain from the company's recent success... What has Britain gained by being a member of the EEC?... ...the pleasure to be gained from books.* V OR V+O : USU+A = profit

3 A **gain** is **3.1** an advantage or improvement that has been obtained by effort or skill. EG *Unemployment was high despite the gains of the civil rights movement... ...some notable gains in productivity.* N COUNT = advance **3.2** an increase in an amount of something, for example weight or price. EG *The price of gold fell again today following yesterday's gains.* N COUNT

4 If you do something for **gain**, you do it in order to get some advantage or profit for yourself; a rather formal use. EG *He did it as much out of kindness as for financial gain.* N UNCOUNT

5 If something **gains** speed, height, weight, etc, it moves faster, or becomes higher, heavier, etc. EG *The car gained speed as it rolled down the hill... The campaign seems to be gaining momentum... Gaining height, he saw Fairwater like a relief map on the ground below him... He had stopped smoking and had gained thirty pounds.* V OR V+O ⇑ increase = gather

6 If you **gain** a place, you reach it, especially after a lot of hard work or effort; a literary use. EG *I finally gained the shore.* V+O

7 If a clock or watch **gains**, it moves too fast and shows a time that is later than the real time. EG *My watch gains about 10 minutes every day.* V OR V+O ⇑ speed

8 If an idea, political movement, etc, **gains ground**, it gradually becomes more widely known or accepted. EG *Their ideas are gaining ground.* PHR : VB INFLECTS = make headway

9 If you do something in order to **gain time**, you do it in order to give yourself enough time to think of an excuse or a way out of a difficult situation. EG *'It would look nice,' said Judy, to gain time... It was a ruse to gain time.* PHR : VB INFLECTS ⇑ delay

gain on. If you **gain on** someone or something that is moving in front of you, you gradually catch them up. EG *You'll have to drive faster–they're gaining on us... We were gaining on him towards the end of the race.* PHRASAL VB : V+PREP = catch up with

gainful /geɪnfʊl/. Something that is **gainful** is useful or profitable; a formal word. EG ...*gainful employment... ...all manner of professions and gainful pursuits.* ◇ **gainfully.** EG *Clearly there was nothing that could gainfully be said... ...gainfully employed.* — ADJ QUALIT : USU ATTRIB = worthwhile; ◇ ADV WITH VB = usefully

gainsay /geɪnseɪ/, **gainsays, gainsaying, gainsaid.** If something cannot **be gainsaid** or there is no **gainsaying** it, it is true or correct and cannot be denied or contradicted; a formal word. EG *Teachers have expertise that cannot be gainsaid... This was such an evident truth that there was no gainsaying it.* — V+O : USU WITH BROAD NEG = dispute

gait /geɪt/, **gaits.** A **gait** is a particular way of walking; a formal word. EG ...*her habitual gait.* — N COUNT+SUPP : USU SING

gaiter /geɪtə/, **gaiters. Gaiters** are coverings made of cloth, leather, or other material for your legs below your knees. Gaiters were commonly worn in former times, but are now mainly worn by climbers and skiers or as part of an old-fashioned uniform. EG ...*a fat man in breeches and gaiters.* — N COUNT : USU PL

gal /gæl/, **gals. Gal** is used in written English to represent the word **girl** pronounced this way in a particular accent: compare **gel.** EG *Since she's known you she's a different gal... ...a very nice, ladylike gal.* — N COUNT/VOC ⇑ woman = girl

gal. or **gals.** also spelled **gall.** or **galls.** are written abbreviations for 'gallon' or 'gallons'. EG ...*fuel tank capacity: 7 gals.*

gala /gɑːlə, geɪlə/, **galas.** A **gala** is a special public celebration, entertainment, or performance, for example a carnival or festival. EG ...*the special guest on a gala occasion... ...Charity Gala Night at the Royal Opera House... ...a swimming gala.* — N COUNT : ALSO IN NAMES

galactic /gəlæktɪk/ means concerned with or relating to the Galaxy or to galaxies in space. — ADJ CLASSIF : USU ATTRIB

galaxy /gæləksi[1]/, **galaxies. 1** A **galaxy** is a huge group of stars and planets that extends over many millions of miles. EG ...*distant stars and galaxies.* — N COUNT ⇑ system

2 The **Galaxy** is the huge group of stars and planets to which the Earth and the Solar System belong. — N PROPER : the+N

3 If you talk about a **galaxy** of people from a particular profession, you mean a group of them who are all famous or important. EG *I'd never before seen such a galaxy of actors and actresses... ...a galaxy of legal talent.* — N SING WITH DET +of = array

gale /geɪl/, **gales. 1** A **gale** is a very strong wind. EG *There seemed to be a gale blowing all the time... ...a force nine gale.* — N COUNT

2 A **gale** of laughter is the loud noise made by a lot of people when they all laugh at the same time; a rather literary use. EG *It's wonderful to get great gales of laughter when you tell a joke.* — N PART : USU PLURAL+N UNCOUNT ⇑ outburst = explosion

gall /gɔːl/, **galls, galling, galled**; a rather old-fashioned or literary word. **1** If you say that someone has the **gall** to do something dangerous, risky, or dishonest, you mean that they have the courage or boldness to do it; often used showing disapproval. EG *They haven't the gall to steal, nor the stability to work.* — N UNCOUNT, OR N UNCOUNT+toINF = nerve

2 If something **galls** you, it causes you to feel very angry or annoyed. EG *It galled him to have to ask permission to go into town.* — V+O ⇑ anger = irk

gallant /gælənt/; also pronounced /gəlænt/ in rather old-fashioned English for paragraph 2. **1** Someone who is **gallant** is very brave and honourable when they are in danger or great difficulty. EG *They are one of the most distinguished and most gallant peoples in Europe.* ▸ Used of people's behaviour and actions. EG *They have put up a gallant fight for pensioners over the years.* ◇ **gallantly.** EG *Gallantly they battled on.* — ADJ QUALIT = courageous, heroic; ◇ ADV WITH VB = valiantly

2 A man who is **gallant** is kind, polite, and considerate towards other people, especially women. EG *'Allow me,' said the gallant policeman.* ▸ Used of people's actions and behaviour. EG ...*a gallant bow.* ◇ **gallantly.** EG *He gallantly offered to carry her cases to the car.* — ADJ QUALIT = gentlemanly, courteous; ◇ ADV WITH VB = chivalrously

gallantry /gæləntri[1]/ is **1** bravery that is shown by someone who is in danger, especially when they are fighting in a war. EG *He was awarded the Military Cross for conspicuous gallantry in combat.* **2** polite and considerate behaviour towards people, especially women. EG ...*old-fashioned gallantry.* — N UNCOUNT; N UNCOUNT ⇑ politeness

gall bladder, gall bladders; also spelled with a hyphen. Your **gall bladder** is the organ in your body which contains bile and is next to your liver. EG ...*inflammation of the gall bladder.* — N COUNT

galleon /gæliən/, **galleons.** A **galleon** is a sailing ship with three masts. Galleons were used mainly in the fifteenth to seventeenth centuries. EG ...*Spanish galleons.* — N COUNT

gallery /gælə[0]ri[1]/, **galleries. 1** A **gallery** is **1.1** a place that has permanent exhibitions of works of art in it. EG *I'd like a job restoring pictures in the National Gallery.* **1.2** a large room in a museum or art gallery that contains a particular exhibition or display. EG *The main galleries for exhibition lie up the grand stairway.* **1.3** a place rather like a shop where works of art are displayed and sold, often a collection of works of art by the same artist. EG *Two galleries in London kept him gainfully occupied.* **1.4** a raised area at the back or at the sides of a large room or hall. People often stand or sit in the gallery to get a good view of what is happening. EG *We used to sneak into the public gallery at Parliament to listen to the debates.* **1.5** an underground passage in a mine or cave. EG *Before you stretches a long gallery not much more than a metre high.* — N COUNT : ALSO IN NAMES; N COUNT : ALSO IN NAMES; N COUNT : ALSO IN NAMES; N COUNT ⇑ balcony; N COUNT

2 The **gallery** in a theatre or concert hall is a raised area like a large balcony that usually contains the cheapest seats. EG *He used to see his plays from the gallery at His Majesty's Theatre.* ▸ used to refer to the people who sit in the gallery. EG *The gallery always applauded celebrities when they arrived.* ● If you **play to the gallery**, you do something in public in a way which you hope will impress people. EG *If anyone was playing to the gallery, it was the Prime Minister.* — N COUNT : USU the+N IN SING = gods; ▸ ⇑ people; ● PHR : VB INFLECTS

galley /gæli[1]/, **galleys.** A **galley** is **1** a ship used in former times. Galleys had sails and many oars and were often rowed by slaves or prisoners. EG ...*galley slaves.* **2** the kitchen of a ship or an aircraft. EG *I went through to the tiny galley to wash up.* — N COUNT; N COUNT

Gallic /gælɪk/. Something that is **Gallic** belongs to or is associated with France or the French people; a fairly formal word. EG ...*the Gallic nation.* — ADJ CLASSIF

gallivant /gælɪvænt/, **gallivants, gallivanting, gallivanted.** If you **gallivant** about or **gallivant** around, you go to a lot of different places looking for amusement and entertainment; a rather old-fashioned word. EG *You're here to do a job, not go gallivanting around all those country clubs.* — V+A = gad about

gallon /gælən/, **gallons.** A **gallon** is **1** in Britain and many Commonwealth countries, a unit of volume that is equal to eight pints, or 4.55 litres. EG *Three gallons of hot water... He got a gallon jar and filled it with water... The little red car would do fifty miles per gallon.* **2** in America, a unit of volume that is equal to eight American pints, or 3.79 litres. — N COUNT : USU NUM+N; N COUNT : USU NUM+N

gallop /gæləp/, **gallops, galloping, galloped. 1** When a horse **gallops**, it runs very fast so that all four legs are off the ground at the same time in each stride. EG *The horse galloped down the road with his ears flat to his head.* — V : USU+A ⇑ run

2 If you **gallop, 2.1** you ride a horse that is galloping. EG *I galloped bareback... We galloped the horses up to the moor.* **2.2** you run somewhere very fast; an informal use. EG *The doctor thanked him effusively and galloped down the stairs.* **2.3** you do something much more quickly than usual; an informal use. EG *There was no hurry, no need to gallop through the reading.* — V OR V+O : USU+A; V+A = bolt; V+A (through) ⇑ rush = race

3 A **gallop** is **3.1** a ride on a horse that is galloping. EG ...*a brisk morning's gallop.* **3.2** a very fast rate at which you do something, or at which something develops or progresses; an informal use. EG *We had a quick gallop through British history.* — N COUNT; N SING WITH DET = trip

4 At a gallop means **4.1** riding a horse that is galloping. EG *They came up the hill at a full gallop, sweat glistening on their coats.* **4.2** running very fast. EG *The dogs would follow at a gallop, yapping and yelping.* **4.3** happening or developing at a very fast rate; an informal use. EG *Man has mounted the evolutionary ladder at a gallop.* — PHR : USED AS AN A; PHR : USED AS AN A; PHR : USED AS AN A

galloping /gæləpɪŋ/ is used to describe something that is increasing or developing at a very fast rate and is difficult or impossible to control. EG *The oil crisis of the seventies brought galloping inflation on an international scale... ...dying of galloping consumption.* — ADJ CLASSIF : ATTRIB = rampant

gallows /gæləʊz/. **Gallows** is both the singular and the plural form. A **gallows** is a wooden frame used to execute criminals by hanging. — N COUNT = gibbet

gallstone /gɔːlstəʊn/, **gallstones**. A **gallstone** is a small and painful lump which can develop in your gall bladder.
N COUNT

Gallup poll /gæləp pəʊl/, **Gallup polls**. A **Gallup poll** is a survey in which a group of people, specially chosen to represent all the people in a country, are asked for their opinion on something. Gallup polls are especially used to ask people how they will vote in an election, in order to predict the result.
N COUNT, OR *by*+N

galore /gəlɔː/ means existing in very large numbers; an informal and slightly old-fashioned word. EG *There are empty houses galore, many of them owned by the council... ...friendly bars, restaurants, and night clubs galore.*
ADJ AFTER N IN PLURAL = in profusion

galoshes /gəlɒʃɪz/ are waterproof shoes, usually made of rubber, which you wear over your ordinary shoes to prevent them getting wet. EG *He was wearing galoshes and an absurd hat.*
N PLURAL : ALSO *a pair of*+N

galvanize /gælvənaɪz/, **galvanizes, galvanizing, galvanized**; also spelled **galvanise**. To **galvanize** someone means to cause them to do something suddenly, for example by making them feel excited, afraid, or angry. EG *The lecture galvanized several others into action... She became galvanized. She started to run... ...galvanizing support for a wealth tax.*
V+O : USU+A *(into)* ⇑ provoke = rouse, excite

galvanized /gælvənaɪzd/; also spelled **galvanised**. **Galvanized** is used to describe metal, especially iron and steel, which has been covered with zinc in order to protect it, especially from rust. EG *...a small galvanized iron shed... ...galvanized steel wire.*
ADJ CLASSIF : USU ATTRIB

gambit /gæmbɪt/, **gambits**. A **gambit** is 1 an action or set of actions in a situation or game, which you do in order to try to gain an advantage, but which often involves taking a risk. EG *...a good gambit for attracting attention... We discussed the various opening gambits used in chess... His basic gambit is to give them presents a couple of weeks beforehand.*
N COUNT : USU MOD+N = ploy, manoeuvre

2 something you say to someone in order to start a conversation with them, often when you are trying to gain some advantage from them. EG *'Been sick?' I asked. As a conversational gambit it lacked something... ...suitable opening gambits for dinner parties.*
N COUNT : USU MOD+N = line

gamble /gæmbəl/, **gambles, gambling, gambled**. 1 A **gamble** is a risky action or decision that you take in the hope of gaining money, success, or an advantage. EG *We came to a decision, took a gamble, and lost... ...a gamble that paid off for us... ...a logical process rather than a wild gamble.*
N COUNT : USU SING = risk, chance

2 If you **gamble**, 2.1 you take a risky action or decision in the hope of gaining money, success, or an advantage. EG *The company gambled all on the new factory... ...gambling on the assumption that the file had been lost.* 2.2 you bet money in a game such as cards or on the result of a race or competition, especially as a regular activity. EG *Fred gambled his profits away... There was little to do except gamble and drink beer... He gambled heavily on the horses.*
V OR V+O : IF+PREP THEN *on* ⇑ risk
V OR V+O : IF+PREP THEN *on* ⇑ risk

gambler /gæmblə/, **gamblers**. A **gambler** is someone who gambles regularly, for example in card games or horseracing. EG *I'm not a gambler, but I did have a few pounds on the Derby... He had the impassive face of a professional gambler.*
N COUNT ⇑ player = punter

gambling /gæmblɪŋ/ is the act or habit of betting money, for example in card games, horseracing, etc. EG *He used the firm's money to pay off gambling debts... He ran a gambling casino.*
N UNCOUNT

gambol /gæmbəl/, **gambols, gambolling, gambolled**; also spelled **gamboling, gamboled** in American English. If people or animals **gambol**, they run or jump about in a playful way. EG *...with his dogs gambolling round him.*
V : USU+A ⇑ play = romp

game /geɪm/, **games**. 1 A **game** is 1.1 an activity or sport involving skill, knowledge, or chance, in which you follow fixed rules and try to win against an opponent or to solve a puzzle. EG *You need two people to play this game... In a game like tennis, the score is kept by the umpire... ...word games... ...computer games.* 1.2 a particular occasion, usually arranged in advance, on which a game is played. EG *On the hockey pitch Miss Cadogan was umpiring a game... He played in a game of cricket against a team from St Mary's... This was our last game, which we lost 6-3.* 1.3 a part of a match, for example in tennis or bridge, consisting of a fixed number of points. EG *...Game to Becker. Becker leads by four games to one... ...game, set and match.* 1.4 the degree of skill or the style that someone uses when playing a particular game. EG *The worse Dudley's game got, the more his stomach ached... Could computers ever play a decent game of chess?... There is a ruthlessness about his game.* 1.5 the equipment that you need to play a particular indoor game, for example a specially marked board, dice, or special cards. EG *A box of toys, games, books... He'd have games to play with in the nursery.* 1.6 an activity that children do, for example pretending to be someone or using toys. EG *The twins were playing a game with toy oil tankers... Other games were looking in shop windows and making faces.* 1.7 a situation that you do not treat seriously. EG *They think life is a game... He told himself it was only a game, a little revenge.* 1.8 a way of behaving in which a person uses a particular plan, especially in order to gain an advantage. EG *...these games that politicians play... It's a ridiculous game of bluff and counter-bluff... ...the power game.*
N COUNT
N COUNT = match
N COUNT/UNCOUNT
N SING : USU POSS+N ⇑ performance
N COUNT
N COUNT
N COUNT : USU a+N, USED AS C ⇑ joke = jest
N COUNT : USU+SUPP

2 The word **game** is also used in the following expressions. 2.1 If you say **It's all part of the game**, you are telling someone not to be surprised or upset by something, because it is a normal part of the situation that they are in. 2.2 If you beat someone **at their own game**, you use the same methods that they have used, but more successfully, so that you gain an advantage over them. EG *The Japanese were trouncing the West at its own game.* 2.3 If you say **the game is up** or someone's **game is up**, you mean that their secret plans or activities have been revealed and therefore must stop because they cannot succeed. EG *He glanced at Marianne, 'Game's up, love'... The British realized that the game was up.* 2.4 If something or someone **gives the game away**, they reveal the secret of a plan, puzzle, trick, etc and prevent it being successful or enjoyable. EG *I always give the game away–you've only got to look at my face... The key words have been omitted because they would give the game away.* 2.5 If you are **new to** a particular **game**, you have not done a particular activity or been in a particular situation before. EG *I'm a bit new to this game myself.* 2.6 If you say that someone is **playing games** or **playing silly games**, you mean that they are not treating a situation seriously and that you are annoyed with them. EG *Stop playing games, Jeremy!... All she ever does is play silly games.* 2.7 If you say that someone is not **playing the game**, you mean that they are not behaving in a fair or reasonable way in a particular situation. 2.8 If someone asks you **'What's your game?'**, they are suspicious of your behaviour and want to know what your intentions are; an informal expression.
CONVENTION
PHR : USED AS AN A
CONVENTION, OR PHR : VB INFLECTS
PHR : VB INFLECTS ⇑ disclose
PHR : USED AS C ⇑ inexperienced
PHR : VB INFLECTS = mess about
PHR : VB INFLECTS = play fair
CONVENTION

3 **Game** is 3.1 wild animals or birds that are hunted or killed for sport and sometimes cooked and eaten. EG *The men had gone to hunt wild game... ...meat, game and poultry... ...game reserves.* 3.2 a person who you think can be tricked, made to look foolish, or persuaded to do what you want them to. EG *I look easy game... The daughter of a general was after bigger game.*
N UNCOUNT
N UNCOUNT : USU MOD+N = prey

4 If you say that someone is **game** or **game** for something, you mean that they are willing to do something new, unusual or risky. EG *He was certainly game. I put him on the horse and he didn't look at all scared... I'm game for anything!* • See also **gamely**.
ADJ CLASSIF : USU PRED, IF+PREP THEN *for*

5 **Games** are 5.1 an organized event in which competitions in several sports take place. EG *...the ground on which the games were held... ...the Highland Games... ...a gold medal winner in the Olympic Games.* 5.2 in British English, organized sports activities that children do at school. EG *You were always hopeless at games at school... ...a games mistress.*
N PLURAL : *the*+N, ALSO IN NAMES
N PLURAL

6 See also **ball game, fair game, waiting game.** • **the name of the game** : see **name.** • **fun and games** : see **fun.**

gamekeeper /geɪmkiːpə/, **gamekeepers**. A **gamekeeper** is a person who takes care of the wild animals or birds that are kept on someone's land for shooting or hunting. EG *Sir Matthew's gamekeeper raised pheasants.*
N COUNT ⇑ keeper

gamely /geɪmli[1]/ means done bravely or with effort. EG *The vicar rose gamely to the challenge... The bock gamely tries to avoid moralizing.*
ADV WITH VB = resolutely

gamesmanship /geɪmzmənʃɪp/ is the art or practice of winning a game by methods that are not against the rules but are very close to cheating. EG *It is gamesmanship to make a loud noise while your opponent is playing.* N UNCOUNT ⇑ psychology

gaming /geɪmɪŋ/ is the same as gambling, especially at cards or roulette; an formal or old-fashioned word. EG *...gaming clubs... ...the Betting and Gaming Act of 1960.* N UNCOUNT

gamma /gæmə/, **gammas**. **Gamma** is the third letter of the Greek alphabet, sometimes used as a mark or grade given for a student's work. N COUNT/UNCOUNT

gamma rays are a type of electromagnetic radiation that has a shorter wavelength and higher energy than X-rays. N PLURAL

gammon /gæmən/; used mainly in British English. **Gammon** is meat from the back leg or the side of a pig. Gammon is usually fried or grilled like bacon, but can also be smoked or salted like ham. EG *...a piece of gammon... ...gammon rashers.* N UNCOUNT ⇑ pork

gamut /gæmə[4]t/. The **gamut** of something is the wide variety of things that can be included in it. EG *...the entire gamut of London politics... ...a rich gamut of facial expressions.* ● If you **run the gamut** of something, you experience or express the wide variety of things that can be included in it. EG *She ran the gamut of all the illnesses that babies can have... Its snarls ran the gamut from pain to terror.* N SING WITH DET : USU+*of* ⇑ range ● PHR : VB INFLECTS, IF+PREP THEN *of/from..to*

gander /gændə/, **ganders**. A **gander** is a male goose. N COUNT

gang /gæŋ/, **gangs, ganging, ganged**. When **gang** is used as a noun in the singular, it can be used with a singular or a plural verb. A **gang** is **1** a group of criminals who work together to commit crimes. EG *Highly organized gangs of criminals had been operating there for years... ...a gang of terrorists... ...gang bosses.* **2** a group of people, especially young people, who usually go around together and often deliberately cause trouble. EG *They stood around in gangs, frightening people and breaking windows... ...fights with rival gangs... ...violent street gangs.* **3** a group of people who are connected in some way; an informal use. EG *...his gang of dedicated young fellow pianists.* **4** a group of friends who frequently meet socially; an informal use. EG *The whole gang's there–Suzie, Jack, Karen.* **5** a group of workers who work together. EG *...a gang of six labourers clearing weeds... Lorries picked the work gangs up at dusk.* N COUNT; N COUNT = pack; N COUNT = company; N COUNT = crowd; N COUNT = party

gang up. If people **gang up**, they unite against someone else in a fight or argument or for a particular purpose; used in informal English. EG *They are ganging up against you... National groups are ganging up to claim their rights.* PHRASAL VB : V+ADV, USU+A/*to*-INF

gangland /gæŋlə[3]nd/ is used to describe activities or people that are involved in organized crime. EG *They were all gangland killers... ...a New York gangland boss.* ADJ CLASSIF : ATTRIB = underworld

gangling /gæŋglɪŋ/ is used to describe a young person, especially a man, who is tall, thin, and clumsy in their movements. EG *A tall, slender, gangling young man with big feet... ...a gangling twenty-year-old by the name of Pyle.* ADJ CLASSIF = lanky

gangplank /gæŋplæŋk/, **gangplanks**. A **gangplank** is a short bridge or platform that can be placed between the side of a ship or boat and the shore, so that people can get on or off. EG *The gangplank was again lowered and they were put ashore.* N COUNT = ramp

gangrene /gæŋgriːn/ is the decay that can occur in a part of a person's body if the blood stops flowing to it, for example as a result of illness or injury. EG *It was badly infected, but she had ignored it, so gangrene had set in.* N UNCOUNT

gangrenous /gæŋgrɪnəs/ is used to describe a part of a person's body that has been affected by gangrene. EG *They had to amputate the gangrenous leg.* ADJ QUALIT ⇑ rotting

gangster /gæŋstə/, **gangsters**. A **gangster** is a member of an organized group of violent criminals. EG *...muggers, thieves, and gangsters... ...a gangster film.* N COUNT ⇑ criminal

gangway /gæŋweɪ/, **gangways**. A **gangway** is **1** a passage left between rows of seats, for example in a theatre or aircraft, for people to walk along; used mainly in British English. EG *In a fairly empty bus, he had chosen a gangway seat... ...sitting below the gangway in the House of Commons.* **2** a gangplank leading onto a ship. EG *...walking down the gangway to the wharf.* N COUNT = aisle; N COUNT

gantry /gæntri[1]/, **gantries**. A **gantry** is a high metal structure that supports a crane, a set of road signs, railway signals, or other equipment. EG *There was only one metal ladder up to the gantry... The gantry was crammed with photographic lights.* N COUNT

gaol /dʒeɪl/, **gaols, gaoling, gaoled**; used mainly in British English. **1** A **gaol** is the same as a jail. EG *He spent two months in gaol... ...the roof of the gaol... She went to gaol for assault.* N UNCOUNT/COUNT = prison
2 If you **gaol** someone, you jail them. EG *The Judge gaoled her for three months.* V+O

gaoler /dʒeɪlə/, **gaolers**. A **gaoler** is the same as a jailer; used mainly in British English. EG *He escaped from his gaolers.* N COUNT = warder

gap /gæp/, **gaps**. A **gap** is **1** an empty space or hole in the middle of something solid or between two things or people. EG *...a narrow gap in the mountains... She had gaps in her teeth... ...the gap between the two coverings... Fill in the gaps on the diagram.* **2** a period of time when you are not busy or when you stop doing something that you normally do. EG *After a gap of two or three years, she went back to college... ...that five year gap when you didn't sing... This leaves an awkward gap in the afternoon.* **3** the absence of something in a situation that prevents it from being satisfactory or complete. EG *This book fills a major gap... In spite of these gaps, the story remains clear... You may not get a pension if there are gaps in your record.* **4** a great difference between two things, two groups of people, or two sets of ideas. EG *The gap between rich and poor regions widened... ...bridging the gap between pro-government and pro-union members... ...a trade gap of only £450 million.* ● See also **generation gap**. N COUNT : USU+A; N COUNT : USU+A ⇑ interval = hiatus; N COUNT ⇑ deficiency; N COUNT : USU+*between* = gulf

gape /geɪp/, **gapes, gaping, gaped**. **1** If you **gape**, you look at someone or something in surprise, especially with an open mouth. EG *Jackson gaped in astonishment at the result... McPherson gaped. 'You talked to the Chairman?'* ◊ **gaping**. EG *...gaping tourists... They gathered round him with gaping eyes.* V : IF+PREP THEN *at* ⇑ stare = goggle; ◊ ADJ CLASSIF : USU ATTRIB
2 If something **gapes**, it opens wide or comes apart. EG *The front door gaped open... Her lips gaped in laughter... The shirt gapes to reveal his chest.* ◊ **gaping**. EG *The dressing gown had a gaping hole in it... His stomach was a gaping wound... ...poured water down their gaping throats.* V; ◊ ADJ CLASSIF : USU ATTRIB = cavernous

gappy /gæpi[1]/ is used to describe something that contains a lot of gaps, especially people who have gaps in their teeth. EG *She plunged her gappy teeth into it... His speech was gappy.* ADJ CLASSIF

gap-toothed. A **gap-toothed** person has wide spaces between their teeth. EG *...a genial gap-toothed man... ...a gap-toothed grin.* ADJ CLASSIF : USU ATTRIB

garage /gærɑːʒ, -rɪdʒ/, **garages**. A **garage** is **1** a building in which you keep a car, often built next to or as part of a house. EG *It was lying in pieces at home in the garage... He jumped out of the car and opened the garage doors.* **2** a place where you can get your car repaired, buy a car, or buy petrol. EG *It was Sunday and the garage was closed... ...garage mechanics.* N COUNT ⇑ building; N COUNT : ALSO IN NAMES AFTER N ⇑ business

garb /gɑːb/. A person's **garb** is the set of clothes that they are wearing, especially clothes that are in a particular style or are part of a uniform. EG *...a convict in striped prison garb... ...his habitual winter garb of cloak and gloves... ...the standard garb of peasants.* N UNCOUNT+SUPP ⇑ clothing = attire, dress

garbage /gɑːbɪdʒ/ is **1** in American English, rubbish, especially waste from a kitchen. EG *In her home, garbage was fed to the pig... ...the garbage in the streets.* **2** in informal English, ideas and opinions that are of no value or importance. EG *He talked a lot of further garbage on the subject.* N UNCOUNT; N UNCOUNT = tripe

garbage can, **garbage cans**. A **garbage can** is a container that you put rubbish into; an American term. EG *He threw his beer bottle into the garbage can.* N COUNT = dustbin

garbled /gɑːbə[0]ld/ is used to describe something someone says or writes in which the details are confused or wrong, for example because they are nervous or in a hurry. EG *...a garbled version of their love affairs... ...the garbled telephone message.* ADJ QUALIT ⇑ distorted = jumbled up

garden /gɑːdə[0]n/, **gardens, gardening**. **1** A **garden** is a piece of land next to someone's house where they grow flowers, vegetables or other plants, and N COUNT which often includes a lawn. EG ...*having tea one afternoon in the back garden... ...staring over the fence into the neighbour's garden... ...the vegetable garden.* ● **common or garden**: see **common**. ● See also **market garden**.

2 If you **are gardening**, you are doing work in your garden such as weeding or planting. EG *Vita is busy gardening.* ◊ **gardening**. EG *It is too hot to do any gardening... He was good at gardening... ...leisure pastimes like gardening, woodwork, music... ...gardening gloves.* — V: USU CONT ⇑ cultivate; ◊ N UNCOUNT

3 **Gardens** sometimes refers to a place like a park that has areas of plants, trees, and grass, and which people can visit and walk around. EG ...*Kensington Gardens... ...the municipal gardens... ...the botanical gardens.* — N COUNT: ALSO IN NAMES, SING=PL

4 **Gardens** is also used as part of the name of a street. EG *He was our next-door neighbour in Carlton Gardens... ...Sussex Gardens, just up the Edgware Road, near Paddington.* — N IN NAMES

garden centre, garden centres. A **garden centre** is a place where you can buy things for your garden such as plants, gardening tools, and fertilizers. — N COUNT ⇑ shop

gardener /gɑːdəᵒnə/, **gardeners**. A **gardener** is 1 a person who is paid to work in someone else's garden. EG *We had a cook and a gardener.* 2 someone who enjoys working in their garden as a hobby and growing flowers or vegetables. EG *He was not a keen gardener.* — N COUNT ⇑ employee; N COUNT

gardenia /gɑːdiːnɪə/, **gardenias**. A **gardenia** is a large white or yellow flower that has a very pleasant smell; used also of the bush on which it grows. — N COUNT

garden party, garden parties. A **garden party** is a formal party that is held out of doors, especially in a large private garden, during the afternoon. EG ...*wearing colourful hats, as though they were at a garden party... ...a garden party at the commandant's house.* — N COUNT ⇑ function

gargantuan /gɑːgæntju⁴ən/. Something that is **gargantuan** is very large; a formal or literary word. EG ...*a gargantuan meal.* — ADJ QUALIT = mammoth

gargle /gɑːgəᵒl/, **gargles, gargling, gargled**. When you **gargle**, you wash your mouth by filling it with liquid, tilting your head back, and breathing out through your mouth, making a bubbling noise. — V OR V+O ⇑ rinse

gargoyle /gɑːgɔɪl/, **gargoyles**. A **gargoyle** is a decorative stone carving on old buildings. It is usually shaped like the head of a strange and ugly creature, and water drains through it from the roof of the building. — N COUNT ⇑ waterspout

garish /geərɪʃ/. Something that is **garish** is very bright and harsh, and not pleasant or restful to look at; used showing disapproval. EG ...*the garish glow of neon signs... ...a garish yellow tie.* ◊ **garishly**. ◊ **garishness**. — ADJ QUALIT = glaring; ◊ ADV; ◊ N UNCOUNT

garland /gɑːlənd/, **garlands, garlanding, garlanded**. 1 A **garland** is a decoration in the shape of a circle made of flowers and leaves, which is worn round the neck or head. EG *The women put a garland round her neck... ...a picture of the god Ganesh, decorated with a little garland of jasmine.* — N COUNT: ALSO N +of+N UNCOUNT/N IN PL

2 If you **garland** someone, you put a garland of flowers or leaves around their neck. EG *After the show, young girls will garland the guest of honour and the artistes.* ◊ **garlanded**. EG *Jack, painted and garlanded with crimson flowers, sat there like an idol.* — V+O: IF+PREP THEN with ⇑ decorate; ◊ ADJ CLASSIF: USU PRED+with ⇑ decorated

garlic /gɑːlɪk/ is the small round white bulb of an onion-like plant which has a very strong smell and taste and is used in small quantities in cooking to add flavour. EG ...*a crushed clove of garlic.* — N UNCOUNT ⇑ herb

garment /gɑːməˀnt/, **garments**. A **garment** is a piece of clothing, for example a shirt, dress, coat, skirt, or pair of trousers; a fairly formal word. EG *She wore a long smock-like garment in scarlet linen.* — N COUNT

garner /gɑːnə/, **garners, garnering, garnered**. If you **garner** something such as information, you collect it, often with some difficulty or by making an effort; a formal word. EG *A certain amount can be garnered from the British press.* — V+O ⇑ gather = glean

garnet /gɑːnɪˀt/, **garnets**. A **garnet** is a hard shiny stone that is used in making jewellery. — N COUNT ⇑ gem

garnish /gɑːnɪʃ/, **garnishes, garnishing, garnished**. 1 A **garnish** is a small amount of food that you use to decorate cooked or prepared food. EG ...*a garnish of parsley and cream.* — N COUNT/UNCOUNT ⇑ decoration

2 If you **garnish** food, you decorate it with small amounts of different food. EG *Garnish the fish with cucumber slices.* — V+O: IF+PREP THEN with

garret /gærɪˀt/, **garrets**. If you refer to a room as a **garret**, you mean that it is a very small room at the top of a house, usually a room that a lodger lives in for very little rent. EG ...*student garrets in London, or Paris... I found him in a garret in Brixton.* — N COUNT = attic

garrison /gærɪsəᵒn/, **garrisons, garrisoning, garrisoned**. 1 A **garrison** is a group of soldiers whose job is to guard the town or building which they live in. EG *Maize was grown here to feed the garrison.* ▸ used of the buildings which the soldiers live in. — N COUNT: IF SING, VB CAN BE SING OR PL = troops; ▸ N COUNT ⇑ camp

2 To **garrison** a place means to put soldiers there in order to protect it. EG *The Duke, leaving a small force to garrison the town, set out at first light.* — V+O ⇑ guard = man

garrotte /gərɒt/, **garrottes, garrotting, garrotted**; also spelled **garrote** or **garotte**. 1 To **garrotte** someone means to kill them by strangling them or breaking their neck, using a device such as a piece of wire or a metal collar. — V+O

2 A **garrotte** is a piece of wire or a metal collar used to garrotte someone. — N COUNT

garrulous /gærə⁴ləs/. Someone who is **garrulous** talks a great deal, especially about things that are not important. EG ...*his fat, garrulous wife... ...a crowd of garrulous well-wishers.* ◊ **garrulously**. — ADJ QUALIT ⇑ talkative = voluble ≠ taciturn; ◊ ADV WITH VB

garter /gɑːtə/, **garters**. A **garter** is a piece of elastic that was worn mainly in former times round the top of a stocking or sock in order to prevent it slipping down. — N COUNT ⇑ support

gas /gæs/, **gases; gasses, gassing, gassed**. The form **gases** is the plural of the noun; **gasses** is the 3rd person singular, present tense of the verb. 1 **Gas** is 1.1 a substance like air that is neither liquid nor solid and burns easily. It is used as a fuel for fires, cookers, and central heating in people's homes. EG *Today we're going to have a look at gas, coal, and oil, the so-called fossil fuels... He remembered to turn the gas off before leaving home...* ● See also **coal gas, natural gas**. 1.2 any substance that is neither liquid nor solid, for example oxygen or hydrogen. EG *Of course helium is a gas at room temperature.* 1.3 a poisonous gas that can be used as a weapon. EG *There have been many reports of gas being used in war zones... ...deadly nerve gases.* ● See also **tear gas**. 1.4 a gas used for medical purposes, for example to make their patients relax, feel less pain, or go to sleep during an operation; an informal use. EG *I used to hate having gas at the dentist.* ● See also **laughing gas**. — N UNCOUNT ⇑ fuel; N COUNT/UNCOUNT; N MASS; N UNCOUNT = anaestheti[c]

2 **Gas** is also the same as petrol; used mainly in American English. EG *Sorry I'm late. I had to stop for gas.* ● If you **step on the gas** when you are driving a vehicle, you go faster; an informal expression. EG *I wish this guy in front would step on the gas.* — N UNCOUNT = gasoline; ● PHR: VB INFLECTS ⇑ accelerate = speed up

3 To **gas** a person or animal means to kill them by making them breathe poisonous gas. EG *She took a flat in a cheap suburb of Paris and tried to gas herself... About 100,000 men, women and children were gassed.* — V+O (NG/REFL[...])

4 If you **gas**, you talk a lot, especially about things that are not important; an old-fashioned, informal expression. EG *Everybody doesn't have the time to sit around and gas all day the way you do.* — V = rabbit

5 A **gas** is a very lively, amusing, and enjoyable event or situation; used mainly in informal American English. EG *You should have seen his first lesson, it was a real gas.* — N SING: a+N, USED AS C ⇑ laugh = scream

gasbag /gæsbæg/, **gasbags**. If you call someone a **gasbag**, you mean that they talk a lot, especially about things that are not important; an informal and offensive word. EG *I spent three hours with the old gasbag and I couldn't get a word in edgeways.* — N COUNT = windbag

gas chamber, gas chambers; also spelled with a hyphen. A **gas chamber** is a room that has been specially built so that it can be filled with poisonous gas in order to kill people or animals. — N COUNT

gaseous /gæsɪəs, -ʃəs, -ʃɪəs, geɪ-/ is used to describe substances like air which are neither solid nor liquid. EG ...*gaseous oxygen.* — ADJ CLASSIF: ATTRIB ≠ solid, liqui[d]

gas fire, gas fires; also spelled with a hyphen and as one word. A **gas fire** is a fire that has a supply of gas to it, used to heat a room. EG *The gas fire was full on.* — N COUNT

gash /gæʃ/, **gashes, gashing, gashed.** 1 A **gash** is a long and deep cut in the surface of something, for example in someone's skin. EG *Zeleika had a large gash in her head.* — N COUNT : USU+A = wound

2 If you **gash** something, you make a long and deep cut in its surface, for example in someone's skin. EG *He gashed his arm on a window last night.* — V+O = lacerate

gasholder /gæshəʊldə/, **gasholders.** A **gasholder** is a very large metal container that is the size of a building, which stores gas and then supplies it through pipes to buildings which have gas fires, cookers, etc. EG *The view would be all right if it weren't for the gasholder.* — N COUNT = gasometer, gas tank

gasket /gæskɪ²t/, **gaskets.** A **gasket** is a flat piece of soft material that you put between two joined surfaces in a pipe or engine in order to make sure that gas, oil, etc, cannot escape. — N COUNT ⇑ seal

gas light, gas lights; also spelled with a hyphen. A **gas light** is a lamp that produces light by burning gas. EG *She turned up the gas light.* — N COUNT, OR *by*+N

gasman /gæsmə³n/, **gasmen.** A **gasman** is a man whose job is to install and repair gas appliances, read gas meters, etc; an informal word. EG *Don't turn the gas on again until the gasman tells you it's safe to do so.* — N COUNT ⇑ worker

gas-mask, gas-masks; also spelled without a hyphen. A **gas mask** is a device you wear over your face in order to protect you from breathing poisonous gases. EG *Everyone had to carry gas masks around all the time.* — N COUNT

gasoline /gæsəli¹n/ is the same as petrol; used mainly in American English. EG *...soaring gasoline prices.* — N UNCOUNT

gasometer /gə³sɒmɪ¹tə/, **gasometers.** A **gasometer** is the same as a **gasholder**. — N COUNT

gasp /gɑːsp/, **gasps, gasping, gasped.** 1 A **gasp** is a short quick breath of air that you take in through your mouth, especially when you are surprised, shocked, or in pain. EG *He listened to himself breathing in short gasps... ...a gasp of horrified surprise... ...gasps of amazement.* — N COUNT : IF+PREP THEN *of*

2 When you **gasp**, you take a short quick breath through your mouth, especially when you are surprised, shocked, or in pain. EG *He was gasping for air and seemed close to exhaustion... Fanny gasped and turned white... 'Call the doctor!' she gasped.* — V OR V+QUOTE/REPORT-CL/O ⇑ breathe = gulp

3 If you **are gasping** for a drink, you are extremely thirsty; an informal expression. EG *Would you like a cup of tea? You must be gasping.* — V+A *(for)* : ONLY CONT

gas ring, gas rings; also spelled with a hyphen. A **gas ring** is a circular gas pipe on a cooker, which has several holes in it and directs the flames under saucepans, kettles, etc. — N COUNT = burner

gas station, gas stations. A **gas station** is a place where gasoline is sold; an American English term. EG *I spotted you standing by your car at the gas station.* — N COUNT = petrol station

gassy /gæsi¹/, **gassier, gassiest.** Drinks that are **gassy** have a lot of bubbles. EG *This beer's a bit too gassy for my taste.* — ADJ QUALIT ⇑ bubbly = fizzy

gastric /gæstrɪk/ is used to describe processes, pain, or illnesses that occur in the stomach of a person or animal. EG *...gastric upsets... ...a hard-working man with a gastric ulcer.* — ADJ CLASSIF : ATTRIB

gastro-enteritis /gæstrəʊentəraɪtɪ¹s/ is an illness in which your stomach and intestines become swollen and painful; a technical term in medicine. EG *...an attack of gastro-enteritis.* — N UNCOUNT ⇑ ailment

gastronomic /gæstrə⁶nɒmɪk/. Something that is **gastronomic** relates to or is concerned with good food that has been prepared by an expert; a formal word. EG *...the gastronomic reputation of France... ...delicious gastronomic experiences.* — ADJ CLASSIF : ATTRIB

gastronomy /gæstrɒnəmi¹/ is the activity and knowledge involved in preparing and appreciating good food; a formal word. EG *But above all, France is noted for its gastronomy.* — N UNCOUNT

gasworks /gæswɜːks/. The plural form is also **gasworks**. A **gasworks** is a factory where coal is made into gas that can be used in people's homes for heating and cooking. EG *Then the city's gasworks blew up, and the fire began.* — N COUNT

gate /geɪt/, **gates.** 1 A **gate** is 1.1 a door-like structure used outdoors at the entrance to a field, a garden, or the grounds of a building. Gates usually consist of strips of wood or metal on a frame that swings on hinges. EG *The prison gates closed behind him... We reached a little gate in the hedge.* — N COUNT ▸ used of an entrance where there is a gate. EG *The taxi swung in through the gates of the vicarage.* — ▸ N COUNT : USU PREP+N 1.2 an official exit in a large airport which passengers go through on their way to the aeroplane. EG *Passengers on flight BA205 should proceed to gate four.* — N COUNT : USU+NUM

2 **Gate** is used in the names of streets that stand on the site of an old gate into a city. EG *...Queen Anne's Gate.* — N IN NAMES

3 The **gate** at a sporting event such as a football match is the total number of people who attend it; an informal use. EG *The highest gate of the day was at Anfield, where 48,000 saw Liverpool draw one all.* — N COUNT : USU *the*+N ⇑ attendance

gateau /gætəʊ/, **gateaux.** A **gateau** is a very rich and elaborate cake that has cream or fresh fruit in it. EG *...a cream gateau... ...some chocolate gateau.* — N COUNT/UNCOUNT

gatecrash /geɪtkræʃ/, **gatecrashes, gatecrashing, gatecrashed.** If someone **gatecrashes** a party or other social event, they go to it, even though they have not been invited; an informal word. EG *I haven't gatecrashed a party since I was eighteen.* — V OR V+O ⇑ intrude

gatecrasher /geɪtkræʃə/, **gatecrashers.** A **gatecrasher** is a person who goes to a party or other social event without having been invited; an informal word. EG *The party was so boring, even the gatecrashers left early.* — N COUNT ⇑ intruder

gatehouse /geɪthaʊs/, **gatehouses.** A **gatehouse** is a small house next to a gate into a park or estate, usually one in which the park-keeper lives. EG *They used to deliver parcels of food to the man who lived in the gatehouse.* — N COUNT ⇑ house

gatekeeper /geɪtkiːpə/, **gatekeepers.** A **gatekeeper** is a person who is in charge of a gate and who allows people through it; an old-fashioned word. — N COUNT ⇑ employee

gate money is the total amount of money that is paid by the spectators who attend a sporting event such as a football match; an informal term. EG *Gate money accounts for only two thirds of the club's income.* — N UNCOUNT

gatepost /geɪtpəʊst/, **gateposts**; also spelled with a hyphen. A **gatepost** is a post in the ground which a gate is attached to, or which it is fastened to when it is closed. EG *We turned between two big gateposts into what looked like an extensive park.* — N COUNT ⇑ post ● You say **between you, me, and the gatepost** when you are telling someone something that you want them to keep secret; used in informal spoken English. EG *Between you, me and the gatepost, I'm leaving at the end of October.* — ● PHR : USED AS ADV SEN = confidentially

gateway /geɪtweɪ/, **gateways.** 1 A **gateway** is an entrance through a fence, wall, hedge, etc, where there is a gate. EG *They passed through an arched gateway.* — N COUNT = gate

2 A **gateway** to somewhere is a place which you go through because it leads you to a much larger place. EG *The new airport terminal at Sheremetyevo, the gateway to Moscow... It was a natural port, the most convenient gateway to the Continent.* — N COUNT+*to* ⇑ way

3 A **gateway** to something is an activity or qualification that gives you the opportunity to progress into a more important profession, career, or other activity. EG *...a world in which examinations are the gateways to some professions.* — N COUNT+*to* ⇑ entrance = passport

gather /gæðə/, **gathers, gathering, gathered.** 1 If people or animals **gather**, they come together in a group. EG *The children gathered around their teacher... To protect themselves, deer gather together in large herds.* — V-ERG : USU+A = congregate, assemble ◊ **gathering.** EG *The gathering crowd of villagers started to murmur angrily.* — ◊ ADJ CLASSIF : ATTRIB ◊ **gathered.** EG *All the family were gathered to hear the solicitor read the will.* — ◊ ADJ CLASSIF : PRED

2 If you **gather** a number of things, for example after you have spread them out or distributed them, you bring them together again. EG *I gathered my maps together and tucked them into the folder... He gathered his papers and slipped quietly away.* — V+O : USU+A ⇑ collect

3 If you **gather** something, you collect a number of things from different places that are far apart, especially so that you can use them. EG *I gathered the eggs and fed the pigs... They gathered berries, nuts and fruit for food... When we were gathering wood, we saw a squirrel.* — V+O

4 If you **gather** information or evidence, you collect it, especially over a period of time and after hard work. EG *This would give historians and archaeologists an opportunity to gather evidence of this...* — V+O = amass

...new information gathered by observation or experiment... The team worked for about a year and a half to gather data.

5 If you **gather** someone **in your arms**, you take hold of them and put your arms around them, usually because you have strong protective or sexual feelings for them; a fairly formal expression. PHR : VB INFLECTS = embrace

6 If you say that something is **gathering dust**, you mean that it is not being used regularly. EG *My briefcase was already beginning to gather dust.* PHR : VB INFLECTS

7 If something **gathers** speed, momentum, force, etc, it gradually becomes faster or more powerful. EG *The train gathered speed as it left the town... This movement gathered momentum.* V+O ⇑ increase = gain

8 When you **gather** your strength, courage, thoughts, etc, you make an effort to prepare yourself to do or deal with something. EG *She gathered strength and walked on through the gate... Dan, I've been trying to gather courage all week to ring you.* V+O = muster up

9 If you **gather** something, you obtain knowledge or ideas by noticing things about the situation you are in. EG *She did not gather a very clear impression of him... His wife had been ill, I gather, for some time... I gathered that they were not expected to eat with us.* V+O/REPORT-CL, OR PRON+V : USED AS ADV SEN ⇑ get

10 If you **gather** fabric or cloth, you make a row of very small pleats in it by sewing a thread through it and then pulling the thread tight. EG *I've nearly finished gathering the sleeves on my dress.* V+O ⇑ pleat
◇ **gathered**. EG *...a long white dress gathered under the bosom.* ◇ ADJ CLASSIF

11 **Gathers** are very small pleats in a piece of clothing. N PLURAL

12 If you **gather** a loose piece of clothing to you or about you, you pull it close to your body. EG *She gathered her shawl about her shoulders.* V+O+A = draw

gather in. If you **gather** something **in**, you bring a group of things or people safely together into one place. PHRASAL VB : V+O+ADV ⇑ collect

gather up. If you **gather up** a group of things, you bring them together into a group so that they can be moved or handled all together. EG *She watched Willie gather up the papers and stuff them carelessly in his pocket.* PHRASAL VB : V+O+ADV ⇑ collect = assemble

gathering /gæðəᵒrɪŋ/, **gatherings**. 1 A **gathering** is a meeting of people who have come together in the same place, usually for a particular purpose. EG *...a rather exclusive gathering of top businessmen and their wives... ...political and social gatherings.* N COUNT ⇑ group = assembly

2 If you talk about the **gathering** dusk, darkness, or gloom, you mean that the light is gradually decreasing, usually because it is nearly night. EG *We walked up the long Main Street in the gathering dusk.* ADJ CLASSIF : ATTRIB ⇑ increasing = growing

gauche /gəʊʃ/. Someone who is **gauche** is awkward and uncomfortable in the company of other people. EG *...trying to act like a lady, but failing utterly, being still skinny and gauche... Entering politics seemed an absurd goal for one so tongue-tied and gauche.* ADJ QUALIT = graceless, maladroit
◇ **gaucheness**. ◇ N UNCOUNT

gaudy /gɔːdi¹/, **gaudier, gaudiest**. Something that is **gaudy** has too many bright colours; used showing disapproval. EG *...young men in gaudy shirts and jeans.* ◇ **gaudily**. EG *...gaudily painted statues.* ADJ QUALIT = garish ◇ ADV

gauge /geɪdʒ/, **gauges, gauging, gauged**. 1 If you **gauge** an amount or quantity, you measure or calculate it, especially accurately by means of some device. EG *With a modern machine, you can gauge the number of stitches... Meg was able to gauge the distance to an inch... They waited, trying to gauge whether it was dark enough.* V+O/REPORT-CL = determine

2 If you **gauge** people's feelings, actions, or intentions in a particular situation, you carefully consider and judge them. EG *...a method for the teacher to gauge what the child is doing... ...gauging what the people of America wanted... I couldn't gauge how it would affect me... The Times sent reporters out to gauge support for the new party.* V+O/REPORT-CL = assess

3 A **gauge** is 3.1 a device that measures the amount or quantity of something and shows the amount measured. EG *The fuel gauges dropped swiftly towards zero... Bond read the speed gauge... A gauge stuck, giving a wrong reading.* N COUNT : USU MOD+N 3.2 a particular fact or event that can be used to judge a situation or a person's feelings. EG *The increase in attendance was used as a gauge of its success.* N COUNT+SUPP ⇑ sign = measure 3.3 the distance between the two rails on a railway line. EG *On the rail system within the Warsaw Pact, gauges had been standardized.* N COUNT 3.4 the thickness of something, especially metal or wire. EG *...heavy gauge metal.* N COUNT

gaunt /gɔːnt/. 1 Someone who is **gaunt** is so thin that you can see the bones under their skin, usually because they are ill, old, or very tired. EG *She looked very weak, her black face gaunt and drawn... ...his gaunt, slightly stooping figure... ...a gaunt unsmiling nurse.* ADJ QUALIT = emaciated, haggard

2 Something that is **gaunt** looks bare and unattractive. EG *...the gaunt outlines of the houses opposite... The windows were gaunt and narrow.* ADJ QUALIT = stark

gauntlet /gɔːntlɪ²t/, **gauntlets**. 1 **Gauntlets** are long, thick gloves that are worn for protection, for example by factory workers or as part of a uniform. EG *...a motorcyclist wearing steel-studded gauntlets... ...heavily-padded flying gauntlets... The policemen pulled on their white gauntlets.* N COUNT : USU PL

2 The word **gauntlet** is also used in the following expressions. 2.1 If you **throw down the gauntlet** to someone, you say or do something that challenges them to argue, compete, or fight with you. EG *He shouted angrily: 'You have thrown the gauntlet down.'... The assembly threw down the gauntlet to the Tsar.* PHR : VB INFLECTS ⇑ challenge 2.2 If you **pick up** or **take up the gauntlet**, you accept the challenge that someone has made. EG *Wendy now had to pick up the gauntlet thrown down by her mother... He enjoyed picking up the gauntlets thrown down by Trevino and Miller.* PHR : VB INFLECTS ≠ run away 2.3 If you **run the gauntlet**, you go through an unpleasant experience in which a lot of people criticize or attack you. EG *Shouts of 'fascist pigs' greeted those running the gauntlet... They now had to run the gauntlet of rifle fire from the cliffs.* PHR : VB INFLECTS ⇑ endure

gauze /gɔːz/ is a light, soft cloth with tiny holes in it, used especially as a bandage. EG *I taped a gauze square over his cuts... There were curtains of gauze... ...Etta, wearing a lilac gauze scarf... ...gauze nappies.* N UNCOUNT

gauzy /gɔːzi¹/ means light, soft, and thin, so that you can see through it. EG *...a gauzy nightdress... ...a blur of gauzy wings.* ADJ CLASSIF : ATTRIB = filmy

gave /geɪv/ is the past tense of **give**.

gavel /gævəᵒl/, **gavels**. A **gavel** is a small wooden hammer that you bang on a table to get attention when you are officially in charge of a formal event such as a meeting. EG *The chairman rapped sharply with his gavel... ...the banging of the judge's gavel.* N COUNT = mallet

Gawd /gɔːd/ is used in written English to represent the word **God** pronounced this way in a particular accent or tone of voice, especially in phrases expressing boredom, irritation, or shock such as 'Oh Gawd, here we go again' or 'Oh my Gawd'. EXCLAM

gawk /gɔːk/, **gawks, gawking, gawked**. If someone **is gawking**, they are staring at someone or something in a rude, stupid, or unthinking way; an informal word. EG *Come along, girl! Don't just stand there gawking!... They would remain quaint villagers to be gawked at.* V : IF+PREP THEN at ⇑ stare = gape

gawky /gɔːki¹/, **gawkier, gawkiest**. Someone who is **gawky** stands and moves awkwardly and clumsily; used especially of tall people. EG *Her tall, gawky colleague was at the desk... ...a gawky young woman with large grey eyes.* ADJ QUALIT ⇑ awkward = ungainly

gawp /gɔːp/, **gawps, gawping, gawped**. If you **gawp**, you gawk. EG *Don't stand there gawping, come away... She heard the price and gawped in shock.* V : IF+PREP THEN at

gay /geɪ/, **gays; gayer, gayest**. 1 A person who is **gay** is homosexual; used especially by homosexuals themselves or by people who support them. EG *I've told them I'm gay...* ▸ used of organizations and magazines for homosexuals. EG *They have an active Gay Group.* ▸ used as a noun. EG *...a holiday spot for gays... Many gays were worried about the new system.* ◇ **gayness**. EG *He wasn't ashamed of his gayness.* ADJ CLASSIF : USU PRED ▸ ADJ CLASSIF : USU ATTRIB ▸ N COUNT ◇ N UNCOUNT ⇑ homosexuality

2 In slightly more old-fashioned English, a person who is **gay** is 2.1 lively and enjoyable to be with. EG *...gay, innocent Annabel... Sonny was gayer, more cheerful... Well, he's not the gayest of companions.* ADJ QUALIT ⇑ happy 2.2 free from all worries and fears. EG *...the image of the gay bachelor... ...a gay, carefree young woman.* ADJ CLASSIF : ATTRIB

3 A place that is **gay** has a lively atmosphere and is full of interesting things to do and people enjoying themselves. EG *What gay and exciting place are you taking me to?... ...more open-air cafes, brighter and gayer streets at night.* ▸ used of the activities or people involved. EG *You had a gayer time with your* ADJ QUALIT ▸ = merry

parties and discussions... ...streaming out in gay family parties to the races.

4 Something that is **gay** is brightly coloured and pretty to look at. EG *Her dress was gay and flowered... Most of the gay paint had crumbled off... ...gay record covers.* — ADJ QUALIT = bright, colourful

5 Music that is **gay** is lively and pleasant to listen or dance to. EG *... a very gay record, fast and with a lot of rhythm.* — ADJ QUALIT

6 • See also **gaiety** and **gaily**.

gay lib or, in more formal English, **gay liberation** is a political movement organized by homosexuals that tries to make other people in society accept them and treat them more fairly. EG *For homosexuals, gay liberation does not just mean reforms... ...women's liberation and gay lib groups.* — N UNCOUNT ⇑ organization

gaze /geɪz/, **gazes, gazing, gazed.** 1 If you **gaze**, you look steadily at someone or something for a long time because you find them attractive or surprising, or because you are thinking about something else. EG *She turned to gaze admiringly at her husband... He gazed down into the water... I spent most of my time gazing out of the window.* — V+A = stare

2 Someone's **gaze** is the long and steady way they are looking at someone or something. EG *He sat without shifting his gaze from the television... The man met his gaze and smiled patiently... ...the indifferent gaze of the art students... His gaze turned to the field below.* — N COUNT : USU SING ⇑ look

gazelle /gə³zel/, **gazelles.** A **gazelle** is a small antelope with large eyes that moves very quickly and gracefully and lives in Africa and Asia. — N COUNT

gazump /gəzʌmp/, **gazumps, gazumping, gazumped.** If you **are gazumped** by someone, they agree to sell their house to you, but then sell it to someone else who offers to pay a higher price; used mainly in informal British English showing disapproval. — V+O : USU PASS ⇑ mislead

GB is an abbreviation for 'Great Britain'.

GCE /dʒi: si: i:/, **GCEs.** 1 **GCE** is an abbreviation for 'General Certificate of Education'; a system of examinations in Britain which are usually taken at Ordinary level when leaving school and at Advanced level before going to University: see also **A level** and **O level**. EG *...good grades in GCE subjects... Wait until you get to GCE standard.* — N UNCOUNT

2 A **GCE** is a pass in an Ordinary level GCE examination for a particular subject; an informal use. EG *He's got eight GCEs.* — N COUNT = O level

GCSE /dʒi: si: ɛs i:/ is an abbreviation for 'General Certificate of Secondary Education'; a system of examinations in Britain introduced to replace **GCE** Ordinary level and **CSE** examinations in 1988. — N UNCOUNT

gdn is a written abbreviation for 'garden'; used especially in advertisements when describing houses which are for sale.

Gdns is a written abbreviation for 'Gardens'; used in names of streets, especially in addresses and on maps or signs. EG *...56 Acacia Gdns, Hockingham, Surrey.* — N IN NAMES

GDP is an abbreviation for 'gross domestic product'; the total value of goods and services produced within a country in a year; a technical term in economics. — N UNCOUNT

GDR is an abbreviation for 'German Democratic Republic'; another name for East Germany. — N PROPER : *the*+N

gear /gɪə/, **gears, gearing, geared.** 1 A **gear** in a machine or vehicle is 1.1 a device or system which controls the rate at which the energy being used is converted into motion, and often whether the motion is in a particular direction or in the reverse direction. Gears often consists of wheels with teeth around their edges that fit into the teeth of another wheel or into the holes of a chain. EG *...interlocking cogs and gears... John checked the gear on the cycle... ...the grinding of gears while overtaking lorries.* — N COUNT 1.2 the range of speed or power which it has when a particular gear is used. EG *We slow down to first gear and ten miles an hour... A car with a really high top gear.* — N COUNT/UNCOUNT : MOD+N

2 If a vehicle is **in gear**, a gear is connecting the engine to the wheels, and the vehicle will move if the engine is working and the brakes are not on. EG *Leave the car in gear.* — PHR : USED AS AN A

3 If you say that a person, system, or process is in a particular **gear**, you are talking about the speed, energy, or efficiency with which they are working or functioning. EG *It took time to shift back into normal gear for boring routine tasks... She knew how to change gear in order to achieve the right result... The American economy will be in high gear.* — N UNCOUNT : USU +SUPP ⇑ mode

4 The **gear** involved in a particular activity is the equipment, special clothes, etc that you use when you do it. EG *...camping gear... We took off our riding gear... I packed my gear and walked out.* — N UNCOUNT : USU +SUPP = kit

5 If someone or something **is geared** to, towards, or for a particular purpose, they are organized or designed specially in order to achieve that purpose. EG *They were not geared to armed combat... ...a policy geared towards rehabilitation... ...plantations geared for export.* — V+O+A *(to/for/towards)* : USU PASS ⇑ be orientated

gear up. If someone **is gearing up** to a particular activity, or **is geared up** to it, they are preparing to do it. EG *Many football teams are not geared up to attack... They are gearing up to a civil war... Martin and Liz were gearing themselves up to a full-time job.* — PHRASAL VB : V+ADV OR V+O (REFL/NG)+ADV : USU CONT/PASS

gearbox /gɪəbɒks/, **gearboxes.** A **gearbox** is the system of gears in an engine or vehicle. EG *Gearbox whining, our jeep laboured up a hillside... Replace the oil in the gearbox.* — N COUNT ⇑ box

gear lever, gear levers; also spelled with a hyphen. A **gear lever** is the lever that you use to change gear in a car or other vehicle; used mainly in British English. EG *The traffic moves again. Howard pushes the gear lever in.* — N COUNT = gearshift

gearshift /gɪəʃɪft/, **gearshifts**; also spelled as two words. A **gearshift** is the same as a gear lever; used mainly in American English. — N COUNT

gee /dʒi:/. Some people say **gee** or **gee whizz** in order to express a strong reaction to something; used mainly in informal American English. EG *Gee, what fun!... Gee, Ed, that was bad luck.* — EXCLAM = gosh

geese /gi:s/ is the plural of **goose**.

geezer /gi:zə/, **geezers.** Some people use **geezer** to refer to a man; a very informal and rather old-fashioned word. EG *This other geezer comes along and takes his shoes.* — N COUNT = bloke

Geiger counter /gaɪgə kaʊntə/, **Geiger counters.** A **Geiger counter** is a device which detects and measures radioactivity. — N COUNT

geisha /geɪʃə/, **geishas.** A **geisha** is a Japanese woman who is specially trained in music, dancing, and the art of conversation, and whose job is to entertain men. — N COUNT

gel /dʒɛl/, **gels, gelling, gelled**; also spelled **jell** for paragraphs 1 to 3. The noun in paragraph 4 is pronounced /gɛl/. 1 If a liquid **gels**, it changes into a thicker, firmer substance rather like jelly. — V

2 If a vague shape, thought, or idea **gels**, you can see or understand it more clearly and definitely. EG *After talking to you things really began to gel... Gradually, they jelled into definite forms.* — V = focus

3 **Gel** is a thick oily substance, especially one used to keep your hair in a particular style. EG *It's worth experimenting with different creams or gels.* — N MASS

4 **Gel** is used in written English to represent the word **girl** pronounced in a particular way. EG *...a handsome gel... Where's the poor ol' gel to live?* — N COUNT/VOC = girl

gelatine /dʒɛləti¹n/, **gelatines**; also spelled **gelatin**. **Gelatine** is a clear, tasteless substance, usually in the form of a powder, that is used to make liquids become firm. Gelatine is often used in cooking, for example to make jelly. EG *Pour the water into a saucepan and sprinkle in the gelatine... Vegetable gelatines are used for thickening soups.* — N MASS

gelatinous /dʒɪ²læti¹nəs/ is used to describe substances that are like a very thick liquid and often sticky. EG *He put his fork into something gelatinous on his plate... ...eggs laid within gelatinous masses.* — ADJ CLASSIF = gooey, viscous

gelding /gɛldɪŋ/, **geldings.** A **gelding** is a male horse which has been castrated in order to make it less aggressive or to make it jump better in races or competitions. — N COUNT

gelignite /dʒɛlɪgnaɪt/ is an explosive substance that is similar to dynamite. EG *We need a bit of gelignite or a detonator... ...the weapons, the gelignite and so on.* — N UNCOUNT

gem /dʒɛm/, **gems.** A **gem** is 1 a jewel or stone that is used in jewellery. EG *...a bracelet of solid gold, studded with gems... ...the value of the stolen money and gems.* — N COUNT 2 someone or something that you think is especially good or pleasing. EG *...this gem of wisdom... ...a gem like Barbara... This house is a gem.* — N COUNT = treasure

gemstone /dʒemstəʊn/, **gemstones**. A **gemstone** is a jewel or stone used in jewellery. N COUNT

gen /dʒen/, **gens, genning, genned**; used mainly in informal British English. If you say someone has **the gen** on something, you mean that they have all the information about it. EG *Let me have the gen on the deal by lunchtime.* N UNCOUNT : USU *the+N+on* = details

gen up. If you **gen up** on something, you find out as much information as possible about it. EG *He's genning up on the legal position before he signs it.* • See also **genned up**. PHRASAL VB : V+ADV, USU+*on* = mug up

Gen. is a written abbreviation for 'General'; used to indicate a person's rank in the armed forces. EG *...Gen. de Gaulle.* N IN TITLES BEFORE NAME

gendarme /ʒɒndɑːm/, **gendarmes**. A **gendarme** is a member of the French police force. EG *The second car was driven by a gendarme.* N COUNT ⇑ policeman

gender /dʒendə/, **genders**. 1 In formal English, **gender** is the fact of being male or female; used of people and animals. EG *...differences of temperament, race or gender... ...someone of the male gender.* N UNCOUNT/COUNT = sex

2 In grammar, **gender** is used to refer to the classification of nouns in some languages as masculine and feminine, or as masculine, feminine and neuter. The gender of a noun affects the form of determiners, adjectives, and sometimes verbs used with it. N UNCOUNT/COUNT ⇑ category

gene /dʒiːn/, **genes**. A **gene** is a part of a cell in a living thing which controls its physical characteristics, growth, and development. Genes can change and reproduce themselves and are passed on from one generation to another, for example from human parents to their children. N COUNT

genealogical /dʒiːnɪəlɒdʒɪkəˀl/means concerning the history of families; a formal word. EG *...evidence of genealogical relationships... ...answers to genealogical queries.* ADJ CLASSIF : ATTRIB ⇑ historical

genealogy /dʒiːniˈælədʒiˈ/, **genealogies**; a formal word. 1 **Genealogy** is the study of the history of families, especially studying historical documents to find out the relationships between particular people and families. N UNCOUNT

2 A **genealogy** is the history of a particular family over several generations, describing who each person married and who their children were. EG *The family genealogy tells how Moses De Camp of Westfield married Anna Rackham, the daughter of a wool merchant.* ◊ **genealogist, genealogists**. EG *...an amateur genealogist attempting to trace the family of his wife.* N COUNT; ◊ N COUNT

genera /dʒenərə/ is the plural of **genus**.

general /dʒenəˀrəl/. 1 **General** is used to summarize 1.1 a situation or idea, without considering details or exceptions. EG *Their cost rose despite a general decline in their quality... The general standard of education there is very high... I'm sure he'll get the general idea.* ◊ **generally**. EG *His account was generally accurate... Wool and cotton blankets are generally cheapest... The fault generally lies with the management.* 1.2 the appearance or behaviour of someone or something, usually after considering particular details or events. EG *...a woman with a wrinkled face, humped shoulders and a general arthritic appearance... ...stairs covered with cobwebs and a general coating of dust... His general attitude suggested that he regarded me as a fool.* ◊ **generally**. EG *They smile, touch, and generally behave more intimately.* 1.3 several items or activities, when there are too many of them or they are not important enough to mention separately. EG *Put down telephone calls as part of your general business expenses.* ◊ **generally**. EG *She's wonderful for information on things generally.* ADJ CLASSIF : ATTRIB = overall; ◊ ADV OR ADV SEN = on the whole; ADJ CLASSIF : ATTRIB = overall; ◊ ADV WITH VB; ADJ CLASSIF : ATTRIB = miscellaneous; ◊ ADV SEN = in general

2 **General** is used to describe 2.1 something that involves or affects most people, or most people in a particular group. EG *There was a general movement to leave the table at this point... We must move towards 'general and complete disarmament'... ...a topic of general interest.* ◊ **generally**. EG *..a generally accepted definition... When will this material become generally available?* 2.2 a statement that involves only the main features of something and not its details. EG *Fortune tellers are so general in their statements... Principles have to be stated in very general terms... In a very general sense it is based on Roman law.* ◊ **generally**. EG *Perhaps he'd say a few words generally on grants.* 2.3 a statement or opinion that is true or suitable in most situations. EG *As a general rule, consult the doctor if the baby has a temperature... My general advice would be to leave him alone.* ◊ **generally**. EG *You mustn't write this down as if it was generally true... Generally speaking, there are union instructions about such situations.* 2.4 an organization or business that offers a variety of services or goods, not just one particular kind. EG *They spent two weeks at a general hospital and two at a psychiatric unit... ...a general grocery store.* 2.5 a person's job, usually as part of their title, to indicate that they have complete responsibility for the administration of an organization or business. EG *...the general manager of the hotel... She was assistant to the General Secretary... ...the Consul General.* ADJ QUALIT = widespread; ◊ ADV = widely; ADJ QUALIT = vague, loose ≠ specific; ◊ ADV WITH VB; ADJ CLASSIF : ATTRIB ⇑ usual; ◊ ADV+ADJ = typically; ADJ CLASSIF : ATTRIB; ADJ CLASSIF : ATTRIB, ALSO IN TITLES

2.6 a person who does a variety of jobs which require no special skill or training. EG *...unskilled general labourers... They want a general drudge about the place.* 2.7 a person who has an average amount of knowledge or interest in a particular subject. EG *The commentaries were not for the general reader but for the specialist.* ADJ CLASSIF : ATTRIB ⇑ unskilled; ADJ CLASSIF : ATTRIB ≠ specialist

3 You say **in general**, 3.1 to indicate that you are summarizing a situation. EG *They want shorter shifts, and shorter working hours in general... The book looks at life in general and Otto in particular... It will make them in general less satisfied and more envious.* 3.2 to indicate that you are referring to most people or things in a particular group. EG *...his contemptuous attitude to society in general... The prices are comparable with those for Third World products in general.* 3.3 to indicate that a statement is true in most cases. EG *The industrial processes, in general, are based on man-made processes.* PHR : USED AS AN A = generally; PHR : AFTER N = as a whole; PHR : USED AS ADV SEN = ordinarily

4 A **general** is a person who holds a high officer's rank in the armed forces, usually in the army. EG *No one under the rank of general can do that... ...General Ravenscroft... ...the Soviet air generals.* ▸ used in other military titles. EG *...Major General... ...Lieutenant General.* N COUNT : ALSO IN TITLES; ▸ N IN TITLES

general delivery. If you send a letter **general delivery**, you send it to a particular post office, where the person who it is addressed to can collect it; an American term. N UNCOUNT = poste restante

general election, general elections. A **general election** is an election at which all the citizens of a country vote for people to represent them in the national parliament. EG *These issues dominated the 1964 General Election... ...a candidate in the general election of 1974... A general election was called.* N COUNT

generalise /dʒenəˀrəlaɪz/. See **generalize**.

generalissimo /dʒenəˀrəlɪsɪməʊ/, **generalissimos**. A **generalissimo** is a supreme commander of combined military, naval, and air forces, especially one who wields political as well as military power. N COUNT : ALSO IN TITLES

generality /dʒenərælɪtiˈ/, **generalities**; a rather formal word. 1 A **generality** is 1.1 a statement of a principle which is true in most situations and concerns the main features of something rather than the details. EG *He focuses only on specifics, not large generalities... Try not to get lost in generalities.* 1.2 a statement about something of common interest such as the weather, which is not important but is used to begin a conversation or discussion; a rather literary use. EG *After a few nervous generalities about the balmy mornings she began her story.* N COUNT/UNCOUNT = generalization; N COUNT : USU PL = pleasantry

2 You say **in the generality**, when you think you are giving a reasonable summary of a situation. EG *Other people cannot, in the generality, be taken as models of how to live.* PHR : USED AS ADV SEN = as a rule

generalization /dʒenəˀrəlaɪzeɪʃəˀn/, **generalizations**; also spelled **generalisation**. A **generalization** is a statement which says that something is true in most situations or for most people, especially when it is based on very little evidence. EG *It is easy to make sweeping generalizations about someone else's problems... We all know women who diverge from this generalization.* N COUNT/UNCOUNT

generalize /dʒenəˀrəlaɪz/, **generalizes, generalizing, generalized**; also spelled **generalise**. 1 If you **generalize**, you say that something is true in most situations or for most people, especially when you have very little evidence for it. EG *I don't think you can generalize about that.* V ⇑ theorize

2 If you **generalize** something, you use a particular example as the basis for saying that something is V+O

true in most situations or for most people. EG *They want to be the vanguard of the working class, generalizing its experiences.*

generalized /dʒɛnəᵒrəlaɪzd/; also spelled **generalised. 1 Generalized** means involving a large number of people or things. EG *The problem is one of generalized human needs... The sickness became generalized... There cannot be unlimited, generalised growth.* **2** applying to a variety of situations or subjects. EG *...one of those generalised but savage remarks about the futility of love... His comments no longer apply to specific points but have become generalized.* ADJ QUALIT = widespread; ADJ QUALIT = general ≠ specific

general knowledge is information about many subjects or events which you get in a casual way, from reading, television, or talking to people, and not by studying one subject in detail. EG *Her general knowledge is amazing... He's better at reading and general knowledge, but average in arithmetic.* N UNCOUNT ⇑ knowledge

general practice is the work of a doctor who usually treats sick people at a surgery or in their homes, not in a hospital, and who does not specialize in particular illnesses or methods of treatment; used mainly in British English. EG *If he's going into general practice, he must have further training.* N UNCOUNT
▸ used of the place where such a doctor works. EG *Some hospital doctors are also attached to general practices.* ▸ N COUNT ⇑ place

general practitioner, general practitioners. See **GP**.

general public. The **general public** is all the people in a society; used especially by someone in an organization or a specialist in a particular subject, to refer to everyone who is not. EG *The lecture will interest both musicians and members of the general public... A lot of fires could be prevented if the general public were better informed.* N SING : *the*+N, VB CAN BE SING OR PL = populace

general strike, general strikes. A **general strike** is the refusal to work by all or most people in a country or state. EG *...demands for a general strike to force the government to concede.* N COUNT

generate /dʒɛnəreɪt/, **generates, generating, generated. 1** To **generate** a situation or feeling means to cause it to begin, especially when it then continues to exist or develop by itself; a formal use. EG *Technology by itself does not generate new ideas... This book will continue to generate excitement for a long time... Tourism will generate new jobs.* V+O ⇑ produce = give rise to

2 To **generate** a product or a financial gain means to cause it to be produced by a particular process or over a period of time; a formal use. EG *The government alone generates 100,000 reports each year... ...computers that generate bank statements... Investment generates higher incomes.* V+O ⇑ produce

3 To **generate** a form of energy or power means to produce it from fuel or another source of power such as water. EG *...improved methods of generating electricity from fossil fuels... The heat energy that's generated in the reactor is extracted and used elsewhere.* V+O

generation /dʒɛnəreɪʃəᵒn/, **generations. 1** A **generation** is **1.1** all the people in a group or country who are of a similar age, especially when they are considered as having the same experiences or attitudes. EG *...an older generation of intellectuals... ...few actresses of her generation could play the part well... ...the only writer to win the hearts of the new generation... ...a generation that has had no experience of war.* N COUNT+SUPP **1.2** the group of people in your family who share the same position in its history and structure, for example your parents, aunts, and uncles belong to one generation and you, your brothers and sisters, and your cousins belong to another. EG *Her brother Fred, the youngest of that generation, was also a teacher... Property is handed on from generation to generation.* N COUNT **1.3** the period of time, usually considered to be about thirty years, that it takes for children to grow up and become adults and have children of their own. EG *We have had a generation of peace in Europe... They have been advocating this for generations.* N COUNT **1.4** a stage of development in the design and manufacture of machines or equipment. EG *...the so-called fifth generation of computers... ...the new generation of missiles.* N COUNT+SUPP ⇑ set = crop

2 Generation is used to indicate how long members of your family have had a particular nationality. For example, if you are a second generation Australian, your parents were also Australian, but not your grandparents. N SING : ORDINAL +N

3 Generation is also the production of a form of energy or power from fuel or another source of power such as water. EG *Electric power generation had ceased.* N UNCOUNT

generation gap. A **generation gap** is a difference in attitude and behaviour between older people and younger people, which often causes them to argue or be unfriendly to one another. EG *There is no generation gap in this family... In this way they are bridging the generation gap.* N SING WITH DET ⇑ division

generative /dʒɛnəᵒrətɪv/ means capable of producing something; a formal word. EG *...generative powers... ...generative forces... ...generative rules.* ADJ CLASSIF ⇑ productive

generator /dʒɛnəreɪtə/, **generators.** A **generator** is a machine which produces electricity. EG *The electricity generator had broken down... ...diesel generators.* N COUNT

generic /dʒɪ²nɛrɪk/ means referring to, shared by, or typical of a whole group of similar things; a formal word. EG *Software is a generic term for the sets of programs which control a computer... ...generic faults in power plants.* ADJ CLASSIF : USU ATTRIB ⇑ common

generosity /dʒɛnərɒsɪti¹/ is the quality of being generous in your character or behaviour, especially in doing or giving more than is usual or expected. EG *You shouldn't take advantage of his generosity... The house was acquired through the generosity of Dr Hilliard... ...the generosity with which she had shared her ideas.* N UNCOUNT ⇑ kindness

generous /dʒɛnəᵒrəs/. **1** Someone who is **generous 1.1** gives or offers to give more of something, especially money, than is usual or expected. EG *You can give more if you are feeling generous... That's very generous of you... I was a bit too generous with the whisky... You've been most generous with your time.* ADJ QUALIT ⇑ lavish = liberal ≠ stingy
◊ **generously.** EG *She was paid generously to look after the children... Supporters have generously given us three thousand pounds.* ◊ ADV WITH VB = handsomely **1.2** is friendly, helpful, and willing to see the good qualities in someone or something. EG *She was a kind and generous soul... He was unexpectedly generous in his comments on the article... The most generous interpretation is that he didn't know.* ADJ QUALIT ⇑ benevolent = charitable ◊ **generously.** EG *Mrs Hutchins has generously agreed to be with us today.* ◊ ADV WITH VB = kindly

2 Something that is **generous** is much larger in quantity or amount than is usual or necessary. EG *Steve made a generous donation to our campaign fund... ...a generous measure of cognac.* ADJ QUALIT ⇑ lavish = handsome
◊ **generously.** EG *He was providing for them generously in his will... ...a generously illustrated book.* ◊ ADV WITH VB = handsomely

genesis /dʒɛnɪsɪs/. The **genesis** of something is its beginning, birth, or creation; a formal word. EG *I explained the genesis of my idea as well as I could.* N SING : USU WITH POSS = origin

genetic /dʒɪ²nɛtɪk/, **genetics. 1 Genetics** is the study of heredity and how qualities and characteristics are passed on from one generation to another by means of genes. EG *...amazing developments in biochemistry and genetics.* N UNCOUNT ⇑ science

2 Something that is **genetic** is concerned with genetics or with genes. EG *...genetic defects... ...the genetic make-up of the individual.* ◊ **genetically.** EG *...genetically programmed behaviour.* ADJ CLASSIF; ◊ ADV

genetic engineering is the science of changing the genetic structure of a living organism in order to make it stronger or more suitable for a particular purpose. EG *Aren't there dangers associated with genetic engineering?* N UNCOUNT

geneticist /dʒɪ²nɛtɪsɪst/, **geneticists.** A **geneticist** is a person who studies or specializes in genetics. EG *...a plant geneticist.* N COUNT ⇑ scientist

genial /dʒiːnɪəl/. Someone who is **genial** is kind and friendly in appearance or attitude. EG *...a genial but ineffectual man... Since the evening was at an end, he felt quite genial.* ADJ QUALIT ⇑ pleasant = affable ≠ surly ▸ used of someone's behaviour. EG *...a genial comment... ...a genial smile.* ▸ = cordial ◊ **genially.** EG *He waved genially to several people as they passed.* ◊ ADV WITH VB = amiably ◊ **geniality** /dʒiːnɪælɪti¹/. EG *He smiled at them with geniality.* ◊ N UNCOUNT = warmth

genie /dʒiːni¹/, **genies.** A **genie** is a magical being, in stories from Arabia and Persia, that obeys the orders of the person who controls it. EG *He had disappeared overnight, in a puff of dust, like a genie.* N COUNT ⇑ spirit = djinn

genital /dʒɛnɪtəˡl/, **genitals**. 1 Someone's **genitals** are their external sexual organs, for example the penis of a man or the vagina of a woman. N PLURAL = genitalia

2 **Genital** means concerned with a person's external sexual organs. ADJ CLASSIF: ATTRIB

genitalia /dʒɛnɪteɪlɪə/. Someone's **genitalia** are their genitals; a formal word. N PLURAL = genitals

genitive /dʒɛnɪtɪv/. In the grammar of some languages, the **genitive** case is a case used for nouns, pronouns, and other words that indicates a relationship of ownership, possession, or association between one thing and another. ▸ used as a noun. EG *Both the adjective and the noun are in the genitive.* ADJ CLASSIF ▸ N SING: the+N

genius /dʒiːnɪəs/, **geniuses**. 1 **Genius** is 1.1 very great ability or skill in a particular subject or activity. EG *The restless, innovatory genius of an island race of adventurers... ...the British genius for compromise.* N UNCOUNT = flair 1.2 an outstanding quality or character which makes something distinct from everything else. EG *That is the genius of the capitalist system.* N UNCOUNT: USU +of = beauty

2 A **genius** is 2.1 a person who has very great natural ability and talent, especially for art, literature, music, or in scientific research. EG *That man was a genius... He was one of the very greatest scientific and mathematical geniuses.* N COUNT 2.2 a person who is very clever and successful at a particular activity. EG *The principal was a young man and a genius in the way he handled us... He was a genius with flowers.* N COUNT: USU+SUPP = expert 2.3 a person who has a lot of influence over a group of people. N COUNT+SUPP = spirit

genned up /dʒɛnd ʌp/. If you are **genned up**, you have all the details or information about something that you need; used mainly in informal British English. ● to **gen up**: see **gen**. ADJ QUALIT: PRED = well-informed

genocide /dʒɛnəˢsaɪd/ is the deliberate murder of a whole community or race; a formal word. EG *He was a tyrant and guilty of genocide.* N UNCOUNT ⇑ killing

genre /ʒɑːnrə/, **genres**. A **genre** is a type of literature, art, music, etc, which people consider to have the same style or subject; a formal word. EG *...a whole new genre of sentimental fiction.* N COUNT = class

gent /dʒɛnt/, **gents**. 1 A **gent** is the same as a gentleman; an informal and old-fashioned use. EG *They'll behave like real gents... They are very tough gents indeed.* N COUNT

2 A **gents** or the **gents** is a public toilet for men; used mainly in informal British English. EG *He had just got back from the gents.* N COUNT = lavatory

genteel /dʒɛntiːl/; a rather formal or literary word. Someone who is **genteel** 1 is respectable, well-bred, and refined. EG *He came from one of these genteel Calcutta families... ...a genteel eccentric, an amusing oddity.* ▸ used of people's behaviour. EG *She lived a genteel, careful, frugal life.* ▸ The **genteel** refers to people who are genteel. EG *...the rich, the genteel, the powerful.* ADJ QUALIT ▸ ▸ N PLURAL: the+N 2 pretends to be of a higher social class than they actually are, especially in order to impress people. EG *Oh, she was very genteel: she said 'excuse me' whenever she burped.* ▸ used of people's behaviour. EG *...her supposedly genteel accent.* ◊ **genteelly**. EG *She was genteelly swearing.* ADJ QUALIT ◊ ADV WITH VB

gentian /dʒɛnʃəⁿn/, **gentians**. A **gentian** is a small plant with a blue or purple flower shaped like a trumpet which grows in mountain regions. N COUNT

gentile /dʒɛntaɪl/, **gentiles**. A **gentile** is a person who is not Jewish; a technical term. EG *She seemed to regard me, an Englishman and a Gentile, with some suspicion.* ▸ used as an adjective. EG *...the gentile world.* N COUNT ≠ Jew ▸ ADJ CLASSIF ≠ Jewish

gentility /dʒɛntɪlɪtiˡ/; a formal or literary word. **Gentility** is 1 the respectability and high social status of the upper classes. EG *The family had made a swift descent from gentility to near-poverty.* N UNCOUNT ⇑ rank 2 polite and well-mannered behaviour. EG *...the courtesy and gentility of these beautiful girls.* N UNCOUNT = refinement

gentle /dʒɛntəˡl/, **gentler, gentlest**. 1 Someone who is **gentle** is kind, mild, and pleasantly calm in character or behaviour. EG *...a gentle, sweet man... The young woman was gentle and religious... ...a gentle, sensitive nature.* ▸ used of someone's behaviour. EG *Her gentle manner was comforting.* ◊ **gently**. EG *She smiled gently at him... 'You have nothing to worry about,' he said gently.* ◊ **gentleness**. ADJ QUALIT = quiet ≠ tough, wild ▸ = tranquil ◊ ADV WITH VB = softly ◊ N UNCOUNT

2 If someone's voice or expression is **gentle**, it is calm, quiet, and kind. EG *He greeted me with a very gentle voice... She had very gentle blue eyes.* ADJ QUALIT = soft

3 Movements that are **gentle** are even and calm, and do not harm or damage things in any way. EG *...the gentle rocking of his mother's chair.* ◊ **gently**. EG *He patted my hand very gently... I shook her gently and she opened her eyes... She sat gently caressing the baby in her lap.* ◊ **gentleness**. ADJ QUALIT = light ◊ ADV WITH VB = lightly ◊ N UNCOUNT

4 If weather is described as **gentle**, it is pleasant and calm and not harsh or violent. EG *There was a gentle breeze... ...the rain became gentler.* ◊ **gently**. EG *...it rained gently.* ADJ QUALIT = light ◊ ADV WITH VB = softly

5 Scenery or landscapes that are **gentle** have soft, soothing shapes and colours that people find pleasant, relaxing, and calming. EG *...a gentle little landscape... The scenery was gentler, neater, and more ordered than at home. The beach stretched away before them in a gentle wave.* ◊ **gently**. EG *...gently sloping hills.* ADJ QUALIT = pleasing ◊ ADV WITH VB ≠ abruptly

6 **Gentle** jokes, hints, parodies, etc, are quite kind and not malicious or meant to hurt people. EG *...a very gentle parody of American life... ...a gentle hint... When Colonel Daintry's name arose he poked gentle fun at him.* ADJ QUALIT: ATTRIB ⇑ kind = mild ≠ spiteful

gentlefolk /dʒɛntəˡlfəʊk/ are people who come from the middle or upper classes; an old-fashioned word. EG *...a rest home for retired gentlefolk.* N PLURAL = gentry

gentleman /dʒɛntəˡlməˢn/, **gentlemen**. 1 A **gentleman** is 1.1 a man who comes from a family of high social standing. EG *...a country gentleman... City merchant banks still project the image of a gentleman's club... ...the highest class of gentleman farmers.* N COUNT 1.2 a man who is well behaved, educated, and refined in his manners. EG *He is old enough to behave himself like a gentleman... ...the perfect gentleman... He was a terribly nice man–a real gentleman.* N COUNT: USU USED AS C ≠ rogue ● A **gentleman's agreement** or a **gentlemen's agreement** is an informal agreement in which people trust one another to do what they have promised. The agreement is not written down and does not have any legal force. EG *It was a gentleman's agreement. Kurt did not have to sign anything.* ● PHR: USED AS C = understanding

2 You can also use **gentleman** when you want to refer politely to any man, for example a man whose name you do not know, or **gentlemen** when you are addressing a group of men. EG *Lawyer Didlington read the old gentleman's will... If you will excuse me, gentlemen... ...the gentlemen of the Press... ...a continental gentleman... ...her many gentlemen friends.* N COUNT ⇑ man

gentlemanly /dʒɛntəˡlməˢnliˡ/; a rather formal or literary word. 1 If a man is **gentlemanly**, he has perfect manners and is very well-behaved; used showing approval. EG *Arnold had always been so reserved and gentlemanly and had never called her by her first name.* ▸ used of a man's behaviour. EG *...a courteous, gentlemanly gesture.* ADJ QUALIT ⇑ polite = well-mannered ▸ = well-mannered

2 If a man is of **gentlemanly** rank, status, or position, he belongs to a noble family, owns property, and has enough money so that he does not have to work but employs others to work for him. EG *His gentlemanly status was ignored entirely.* ADJ CLASSIF: ATTRIB

gentlewoman /dʒɛntəˡlwʊˡməˢn/, **gentlewomen**; an old-fashioned word. A **gentlewoman** is 1 a woman of high social standing. EG *Skill with the needle was considered a necessary quality of a gentlewoman in the early nineteenth century.* N COUNT = lady 2 a woman who is cultured, educated, and refined in her manners. N COUNT = lady

gentry /dʒɛntriˡ/. The **gentry** are people of high birth and high social status, ranking just below the nobility; a formal and old-fashioned word. EG *He was an extreme right winger from a family of landed gentry... The power of the gentry has gone.* N SING: the+N, OR N UNCOUNT, VB CAN BE SING OR PL ⇑ aristocracy

genuflect /dʒɛnjəˡflɛkt/, **genuflects, genuflecting, genuflected**. If you **genuflect**, you bend one or both knees, especially in church, as a sign of respect for someone or something; a formal word. EG *They both genuflected and crossed themselves.* ◊ **genuflection** /dʒɛnjuːflɛkʃəⁿn/, **genuflections**. V ⇑ kneel ◊ N COUNT/UNCOUNT

genuine /dʒɛnjʊɪn/. 1 Something that is **genuine** is real and exactly what it appears to be, and is not fake or an imitation. EG *The experts decided that the painting was a genuine Constable... ...genuine Ugandan food.* ◊ **genuinely**. EG *...genuinely democratic countries.* ◊ **genuineness**. ADJ CLASSIF = authentic ≠ artificial, imitation ◊ ADV ◊ N UNCOUNT

2 A feeling, emotion, or reaction that is **genuine** is really and truly felt by someone and is not simply displayed in order to deceive someone. EG *She looked* ADJ CLASSIF ⇑ real = sincere

at me in genuine astonishment... ...genuine love. ◊ **genuinely**. EG *I was genuinely angry with him.* ◊ ADV
◊ **genuineness**. ◊ N UNCOUNT
3 If you describe a person as **genuine**, you mean that they are honest, truthful, and sincere in the way they live and in their relationships with other people; used showing approval. EG *They seemed nice, genuine fellows.* ADJ QUALIT

genus /dʒiːnəs/, **genera** /dʒɛnərə/. A **genus** is a class or group of similar things, especially a group of animals or plants that contain several closely related species; a technical term. N COUNT ⇑ family

geographer /dʒɪɒgrəfə/, **geographers**. A **geographer** is a person who studies geography or is an expert in it. N COUNT

geographic /giːə⁶græfɪk/ means the same as geographical; a formal and rather old-fashioned word. EG *...geographic and political boundaries.* ADJ CLASSIF : USU ATTRIB = geographical

geographical /giːə⁶græfɪkə⁰l/. Something that is **geographical** is concerned with or relates to geography. EG *...the characteristics of any geographical region.* ◊ **geographically**. EG *...geographically separated species.* ADJ CLASSIF : USU ATTRIB = geographic ◊ ADV OR ADV SEN

geography /dʒɪɒgrəfi¹/. **1 Geography** is the study of the countries of the world and of such things as land formations, seas, climate, towns and population. N UNCOUNT
2 The **geography** of a place is the way that features such as rivers, mountains, towns, streets, etc, are arranged within it. EG *...the geography of the United States.* N UNCOUNT : USU WITH POSS

geological /giːə⁶lɒdʒɪkə⁰l/ means relating to geology. EG *...an interesting geological site.* ◊ **geologically**. ADJ CLASSIF : USU ATTRIB ◊ ADV

geology /dʒɪɒlədʒi¹/. **1 Geology** is the scientific study of substances such as rock and soil in order to find out about the origin, structure, and history of the earth. ◊ **geologist, geologists**. N UNCOUNT ◊ N COUNT
2 The **geology** of an area is the structure of its land, together with the types of rocks and minerals that exist within it. ◊ N UNCOUNT : USU WITH POSS

geometric /dʒiːə⁶mɛtrɪk/. Something that is **geometric** consists of regular shapes and lines, such as squares and circles. EG *...geometric blocks of concrete... ...the geometric scars of the long canals.* ADJ CLASSIF : USU ATTRIB = geometrical

geometrical /giːə⁶mɛtrɪkə⁰l/. **1** Something that is **geometrical** relates to or involves the principles of geometry. EG *...a purely geometrical problem.* ◊ **geometrically**. EG *The four wooden chairs were arranged geometrically round the square oak table.* ADJ CLASSIF : USU ATTRIB ⇑ mathematical ◊ ADV ⇑ regularly
2 Geometrical can also mean the same as geometric. EG *...abstract geometrical designs.* ADJ CLASSIF : USU ATTRIB

geometry /dʒɪɒmɪ²tri¹/. **1 Geometry** is a mathematical science concerned with the study and measurement of lines, angles, and curves, and with the shapes which are formed when several lines are joined together. EG *...the laws of geometry.* N UNCOUNT ⇑ mathematics
2 The **geometry** of an object is the way that it fits together, especially when it has a very regular shape or pattern; a formal use. EG *...the church's geometry.* N UNCOUNT : USU WITH POSS = layout

geophysical /giːə⁶fɪzɪkə⁰l/ means relating to or concerned with geophysics. ADJ CLASSIF : USU ATTRIB

geophysicist /giːə⁶fɪzɪsɪst/, **geophysicists**. A **geophysicist** is someone who studies or specializes in geophysics. N COUNT ⇑ scientist

geophysics /dʒiːə⁶fɪzɪks/ is the branch of geology that uses physics to examine the earth's structure, climate, oceans, etc. N UNCOUNT

geopolitical /giːə⁶pəlɪtɪkə⁰l/ means relating to or concerned with geopolitics. EG *...those problems are political in nature, not geopolitical.* ADJ CLASSIF : USU ATTRIB ⇑ geographical

geopolitics /dʒiːə⁶pɒlɪtɪks/ is the study of the effect that the geographical position and features of a country have on its politics and its relations with other countries. N UNCOUNT ⇑ geography

Georgian /dʒɔːdʒj⁰ən/ is used in Britain to describe the eighteenth century and the style of architecture, literature, etc that was popular at the time. EG *...a large late Georgian house.* ADJ CLASSIF

geranium /dʒɪ²reɪnɪəm/, **geraniums**. A **geranium** is a plant that is grown in gardens or in pots inside people's houses and has small red, pink, or white flowers. N COUNT

gerbil /dʒɜːbɪ¹l/, **gerbils**. A **gerbil** is a small, furry animal with long back legs that is often kept as a pet. N COUNT ⇑ rodent

geriatric /dʒɛri¹ætrɪk/, **geriatrics**. **1 Geriatric** is used to describe very old people, their illnesses, and their treatment; a technical term in medicine. EG *...a geriatric ward.* ▸ used as a noun. EG *...the treatment of geriatrics in Rio.* ADJ CLASSIF ▸ N COUNT
2 Geriatrics is the study of the illnesses that affect old people and the methods of treating them. N UNCOUNT

germ /dʒɜːm/, **germs**. A **germ** is **1** a very small living thing in food, other substances, or in your body that causes disease. EG *...a flu germ... The germs are easily passed from person to person.* **2** the beginning of an idea or feeling which may become more important. EG *It contains the germ of an idea which might save us... This germ of alarm began to spread.* N COUNT ⇑ organism; N COUNT : USU SING + *of* ⇑ start = seed

German /dʒɜːmən/, **Germans**. **1** Something that is **German** belongs or relates to West Germany, East Germany, their people, or their language. EG *She's German... ...the German economy.* ADJ CLASSIF
2 A **German** is a person who comes from West Germany or East Germany. EG *The Germans offered to help... ...a Frenchman or a German.* N COUNT
3 German is the language that is spoken in West Germany, East Germany, and parts of Austria and Switzerland. EG *They spoke to him in faultless German... ...German lessons.* N UNCOUNT

germane /dʒɜːmeɪn/. Something that is **germane** to a situation or idea is connected with it in an important way; a formal word. EG *It is clearly not germane to present-day conditions... ...issues most germane to socialist policy.* ADJ QUALIT : PRED + *to* = relevant

Germanic /dʒɜːmænɪk/. **1** If you describe someone or something as **Germanic**, you think that their appearance or behaviour is typical of German people or things. EG *...his Germanic nature... ...very Germanic in everything they did.* ADJ QUALIT
2 Germanic is also used to describe the ancient culture and people of northern Europe, and the language they spoke, from which the modern Scandinavian languages and English, German, and Dutch derive. EG *...a Germanic tribe... ...Germanic mythology.* ADJ CLASSIF

German measles is a disease which causes you to have a cough, a sore throat, and red spots on your skin. N UNCOUNT = rubella

germinal /dʒɜːmɪnə⁰l/. Something that is **germinal** is in an early stage of its development, or is causing something else to develop; a formal word. EG *...a germinal force in re-establishing industry.* ADJ CLASSIF = generative

germinate /dʒɜːmɪneɪt/, **germinates, germinating, germinated**. **1** If a seed **germinates** or you **germinate** it, it starts to grow; a technical use. EG *You need cool, moist weather for the seed to germinate.* ◊ **germination** /dʒɜːmɪneɪʃə⁰n/. V-ERG ⇑ start = develop ◊ N UNCOUNT
2 If an idea, plan, or feeling **germinates**, or someone or something **germinates** it, it comes into existence and begins to develop; a formal or literary use. EG *This was enough to germinate the guilt which had lain dormant for years... New concepts germinate before your eyes.* V-ERG ⇑ start = originate

germ warfare is the use of germs in a war in order to cause disease in enemy troops or to destroy crops that they might use as food. EG *This treaty bans germ warfare.* N UNCOUNT = biological warfare

gerontology /dʒɛrə⁷ntɒlədʒi¹/ is the study of the process by which we get old, how our bodies change, and the problems that old people have: compare **geriatrics**. ◊ **gerontologist, gerontologists**. N UNCOUNT ◊ N COUNT

gerrymandering /dʒɛri¹mændə⁰rɪŋ/ is the act of altering political boundaries in order to give an unfair advantage to one political party or group of people; used showing disapproval. N UNCOUNT ⇑ cheating

gerund /dʒɛrə⁹nd/, **gerunds**. In grammar, a **gerund** is a noun formed from a verb and expressing an action or state. In English, gerunds end in -ing. N COUNT

gestalt /gə²ʃtælt/. A **gestalt** is something that you see or think of that has particular qualities when you consider it as a whole which are not apparent when you consider only the separate parts of it; used especially as a technical term in psychology. EG *...patterns from different editions, the gestalt clear, but shifting in size... ...Gestalt psychology.* N SING WITH DET ⇑ pattern

gestation /dʒɛsteɪʃə⁰n/ is **1** the process in human beings and some animals in which babies grow inside their mother's body before they are born, or the period of time during which this process happens; a technical term in biology. EG *...the shortest gestation period in any mammal.* **2** the process in which an idea develops or a plan is carried out; a N UNCOUNT = pregnancy; N UNCOUNT ⇑ development formal or literary use. EG *The road had been sixty years in gestation.*

gesticulate /dʒɛstɪkjə[4]leɪt/, **gesticulates, gesticulating, gesticulated.** If you **gesticulate**, you make movements with your arms or hands, often while you are talking, for example because you are excited or describing something that is difficult to express in words; a rather formal or literary word. EG *We sometimes gesticulate even when talking on the telephone... Stuart gesticulated angrily.* [V; ⇑ move; = gesture]
◊ **gesticulation** /dʒɛstɪkjə[4]leɪʃ[ə]n/, **gesticulations.** EG *...the gesticulations that accompany conversation... There were head-shakings and gesticulations.* [◊ N UNCOUNT/COUNT; = gesture]

gestural /dʒɛstjərəl/ means consisting of or relating to gestures. EG *We share the same kind of gestural language.* [ADJ CLASSIF : ATTRIB]

gesture /dʒɛstʃə/, **gestures, gesturing, gestured.** 1 A **gesture** is 1.1 a movement that you make with a part of your body, especially your hands or your head, to express emotion or information, either instead of speaking or while you are speaking. EG *She made an angry gesture with her fist... He held one hand over his eyes in a gesture of pain.* [N COUNT; ⇑ sign] **1.2** something that you say or do in order to express your attitude or intentions, often something that you know will not have much effect. EG *The only gesture he made was to change its name... The demonstration is a gesture of defiance against the government... She thanked him for his thoughtful gesture.* [N COUNT : USU+SUPP; ⇑ act; = token]
2 If you **gesture**, you use movements of your hands or head in order to tell someone something or draw their attention to something. EG *He gestured at one of the larger suitcases... Frey gestured with his head towards the closed door... He gestured to me to lie down... The operator gestured the Frenchman to a cabin.* [V+REPORT-CL, V+A, OR V+O+A (to); ⇑ signal; = motion]

get /gɛt/, **gets, getting, got** or **gotten. Gotten** is the American form of the past participle of the verb. In most of its uses **get** is a fairly informal word. **1** If someone or something **gets** cold, angry, bored, etc, they become cold, angry, bored, etc. EG *She got massively fat... The sun shone and I got very brown... She began to get suspicious... I was getting quite hungry... If things get any worse you'll just have to come home... Being alone got awfully boring sometimes.* [V+C; = grow]
2 If you **get** yourself, someone, or something into a particular state, you cause yourself or them to be in that state. EG *He got himself into frightful trouble recently... I was getting drunk every night... My father talked about getting in touch with his lawyer... Should religious leaders get involved in politics?... The girl finally got the door open... He got her pregnant.* [V+O (NG/REFL)+C/A]
3 If you **get** someone to do something, you cause them to do it by asking, persuading, or telling them. EG *She gets Stuart to help her clean... We managed to get him to talk about Brighton... I could get someone else to do it.* [V+O+*to*+-INF; = persuade]
4 If you **get** something done, you cause it to be done. EG *I got safety belts fitted... He has to get a tap taken out... It's important to get the ringleaders put on trial.* [V+O+PAST PART]
5 If you **get** somewhere, **5.1** you arrive there. EG *When we got to Firle Beacon we had a bit of a rest... My typewriter had been stolen before I got to the Customs... What time do they get back?... I got there about 8 o'clock.* [V+A; = reach] **5.2** you move in a particular direction or manner. EG *Frankie and Clive were trying to get through the window... Nobody can get past... We got along the street as best we could... They had a terrible job getting down the gangplank.* [V+A; ⇑ go]
6 If you **get** someone or something into a place or position, **6.1** you cause them to move there. EG *I got Allen into his bunk... I have been trying to get him over here for four years... He was trying to get his face in front of the general's.* [V+O+A; = manoeuvre] **6.2** you bring them there. EG *I'll just get it for you... Please get me the documents now... Morris hurried off eagerly to get a cab.* [V+O, V+O (NG/REFL)+O, OR V+O+A (for); = fetch]
7 Get is often used in place of 'be' as an auxiliary verb to form passives. EG *I get asked to so many things... Suppose someone gets killed... He failed to get re-elected... If you have things on the floor, they get trodden on... The difficulties tend to get exaggerated by the media.* [AUX+PAST PART : FORMS PASS; = be]
8 If you **get** something that you want or need, **8.1** you obtain it as a possession or as something that you are going to use. EG *He's trying to get a flat... You can get a dog from a pet shop... He had managed to get himself a large armchair.* [V+O, V+O (NG/REFL)+O, OR V+O+A (for); = acquire] **8.2** you obtain advice, medical treatment, education, etc. EG *You may have to get help... Get advice from your local health department... You can get free dental treatment... Their first priority is to get an education... I told him to get a good lawyer.* [V+O, V+O (NG/REFL)+O, OR V+O+A (for)] **8.3** you obtain something such as sleep or exercise that you need in order to keep your body healthy. EG *Try to get some rest... The children get all the exercise they need... It will do you good to get a breath of fresh air.* [V+O, OR V+O (REFL)+O] **8.4** you obtain a job, a place at a school or college, or a part in a play or film. EG *He got her a job with the telephone company... George Farr might get the editorship... I got the part of Ophelia.* [V+O, V+O (NG/REFL)+O, OR V+O+A (for); = land] **8.5** you obtain a qualification. EG *Are you going to teach French, when you get your degree?... The reason I came to this class was to get my certificate.* [V+O : NO PASS]
9 If you **get** something as a result of an official or legal decision, you obtain it. EG *I am going to get a divorce... Desiree was sure to get custody of both children. He got ten years in jail... They don't have to get planning permission for it... We had to get a temporary five-year licence... He managed to get a week's leave in August.* [V+O, V+O (NG/REFL)+O, OR V+O+A (for)]
10 If you **get** something as a gift or prize, you receive it. EG *I got the anorak for Christmas... Everybody gets a prize in this school.* [V+O : NO IMPER, NO PASS]
11 If you **get** a letter, telephone call, or response from someone, you receive it. EG *She got these letters every day... I got a call from the President... Next day I got an answer from him. I should get an apology.* [V+O : NO IMPER, NO PASS]
12 If you **get** a particular sum of money, you receive it regularly as your wages or salary or as an allowance. EG *He was getting a very low salary... They got a hundred pounds a week... She gets a state retirement pension.* [V+O : NO PASS; = be paid]
13 If you **get** a loan, grant, etc, you are given or lent it for a particular purpose. EG *They found it impossible to get a bank loan... I couldn't get a grant unless I had five years' teaching experience.* [V+O : NO PASS; = obtain]
14 If you **get** a particular result, you obtain it from some action that you take, or from a calculation or experiment. EG *It would take time to get results... How did you get that answer, Ian?... You can get this effect quite easily.* [V+O, OR V+O+O, OR V+O+A (for) : NO PASS; = arrive at]
15 If you **get** a particular price or sum of money for something, you obtain that sum by selling it. EG *She ought to get at least eight pounds for it.* [V+O : IF+PREP THEN *for*, NO PASS; = receive]
16 If an object **gets** a particular price or sum of money, it is sold for that amount of money. EG *His old teapot got two hundred dollars.* [V+O : NO PASS; = fetch]
17 If you **get** food or drink, you eat or drink it. EG *I thought you'd get a nice breakfast at the club... We stopped along the way to get a drink of water.* [V+O : NO PASS]
18 If you **get** a meal, you prepare it. EG *Kate's just getting the dinner.* [V+O : NO PASS]
19 If you **get** a seat, flight, room, etc, you succeed in making a reservation in a theatre, plane, hotel, etc. EG *I rang up to see if I could get seats... I'll try and get a flight tomorrow.* [V+O, V+O+O, OR V+O+A (for); = book]
20 If you **get** the time, chance, or opportunity to do something, you have the time or opportunity to do it. EG *We get little time for sewing... I didn't get a chance to introduce myself.* [V+O : USU+*to*-INF, OR *for*+-ING, NO PASS/IMPER/CONT]
21 If you **get** an idea, impression, feeling, etc, you begin to have an idea that something is true or to have knowledge or understanding of something. EG *I got the impression he'd had a sleepless night... You get the feeling that it could easily happen here... You can get an idea what it's all about... We spent the time talking to people and generally getting the feel of the place.* [V+O : USU+REPORT-CL/*of*, NO PASS, NO IMPER; ⇑ receive; = pick up]
22 If you **get** a particular physical or emotional feeling from an event or experience, the event or experience produces that feeling in you. EG *She got a lot of fun out of sweeping the front porch... I get a real thrill, when I read a piece of his... Poor John will get a surprise... When I opened the door I got a nasty shock... I'm getting a pain in my side.* [V+O : IF+PREP THEN *from/out of*, NO PASS, NO IMPER]
23 If you **get** a look, view, or glimpse of something, you have a view of it. EG *Come back here so you can get a better look... A delivery boy might get a glimpse of him.* [V+O : NO PASS; = catch]

24 If you say that a place **gets** snow, rain, sunshine, etc, you mean that it usually has that type of weather, for example at a particular time of year. EG *We get a lot of sun on the south coast... Scotland will be getting rain this weekend.* V+O : NO PASS, NO IMPER = have

25 If you **get** a mark or grade, you are given it in a test or examination. EG *I got an A minus... You have to get 120 marks to pass.* V+O : NO PASS, NO CONT = obtain

26 If you **get** to do something, **26.1** you gradually reach a stage in which you do it, or in which you have a particular appearance, feeling, or belief. EG *The kids would have a chance to get to know him... The Prime Minister got to hear of the rumours... Every capital city in the world is getting to look like every other... I got to like the whole idea... I got to hate surprises.* V+*to*-INF = come **26.2** you eventually succeed in doing it. EG *We never got to see you play... They all got to play leading roles.* V+*to*-INF, NO IMPER = manage

27 If you **get** to be something, you become a particular kind of person or thing. EG *I'm getting to be an old man, Davis... You may get to be a Cabinet officer... Pegler's manners got to be a national scandal.* V+*to*-INF

28 If you **get** moving, going, working, etc, you begin moving, going, working, etc. EG *We can't seem to get moving... Get digging!* V+-ING = start

29 If you **get** to a particular stage in your life, career, or action, you reach that stage. EG *You have got to an important stage in your career... I got as far as dismantling the plug... I had hoped this conversation wouldn't even get this far... It got to the point where we were having to share desks. We'd only got up to stage three.* V+A = come

30 If it **gets** to a particular time, it is that time. EG *It got to five o'clock... It had got to Christmas morning... It's getting late.* V : *it*+V+*to* ⇑ reach

31 If you **get** a joke or the point of something that is said, you understand it. EG *I tried to tell somebody your joke and they didn't get it... I don't really get the point of the story... 'I don't get you,' he said.* V+O : NO IMPER, NO PASS

32 If you **get** news or information, **32.1** you obtain it, especially by taking some deliberate action in order to obtain it. EG *Harry switched on the radio to get the latest news... I'll try and get the information for you.* V+O, V+O+O, OR V+O+A *(for)* **32.2** you receive it, especially by having it brought to you by another person. EG *He was with us when we got the news.* V+O : NO IMPER, NO PASS

33 If you **get** an illness or disease, you become ill with it. EG *She got chicken pox.* V+O : NO IMPER, NO PASS

34 If you **get** a train, bus, etc, you leave a place on a particular train, bus, etc. EG *We walked to Ipswich and got the train to Colchester... Where do you have to go to get the plane?* V+O : NO PASS = catch, take

35 If you **get** a person or animal, you succeed in catching, killing, or hitting them. EG *Perhaps the police got him in the end... Do you think the shark got Ben?* V+O ⇑ catch = do for

36 If something **gets** to you, it causes you to suffer physically or mentally. EG *The fatigue and backache are getting to me now... What got to them sooner or later was an inability to reconcile these two things.* V+A *(to)* ⇑ affect

37 If someone's behaviour **gets** you, it annoys you. EG *It's the bossiness that gets them... What gets me is the way Janet implies that I'm fascinated by her husband.* V+O : NO CONT/ PASS/IMPER ⇑ annoy = bug

38 If you **get** a newspaper or magazine, you regularly buy it. EG *I used to get 'The Times' but now I get 'The Guardian'.* V+O : NO CONT/ PASS = take

39 If you can **get** a particular radio or television channel, you are able to receive broadcasts from it on your radio or television. EG *We can't get BBC 2.* V+O : NO PASS/ IMPER = pick up

40 If you **get** someone **alone** or **to yourself**, you succeed in meeting them without anyone else being present. EG *She was not a cosy person, except when you could get her alone occasionally... If only I could get you to myself.* PHR : VB INFLECTS ⇑ monopolize

41 You can use **you get** instead of 'there is' or 'there are' to say that something exists, happens, or can be experienced. EG *You get some rather curious effects... In the Finale you get the grandest melody that Sibelius ever wrote.* PHR+NG = you have

42 The word **get** is also used in the following expressions. **42.1** If you say that you are **getting somewhere, getting nowhere**, etc, you are talking about the progress or the lack of progress that you are making. EG *Now we're getting somewhere... You're not getting anywhere with this plan.* PHR : VB INFLECTS **42.2** If you say to someone that a particular type of behaviour **will get** them **nowhere, won't get** them **anywhere**, etc, you are expressing disapproval and advising them not to behave in that way. EG *Rudeness will get you nowhere.* PHR : VB INFLECTS **42.3** If you **get a lot out of** something, **get little out of** something, etc, you experience that amount of pleasure, satisfaction, or stimulation from it. EG *Children get a lot out of these visits... He's not getting the most out of his relationships.* PHR : VB INFLECTS **42.3** If you say **'How lucky can you get?', 'How stupid can you get?'**, etc, you are expressing your surprise that anyone could be as lucky, stupid, etc as the person that you are talking about. EG *How daft can you get?* PHR **42.4 As hot as you can get it, as accurate as you can get it**, etc means as hot or as accurate as it is possible to make it. EG *The fluid is as hot as you can get it.* PHR : USED AS C **42.5 Get stuffed, get knotted, get lost**, etc, are very offensive ways of expressing contempt for someone, disagreement with someone, or refusal to do something. PHR : ONLY IMPER = on your bike

43 The word **get** is also used in the following expressions, which are explained at other places in this dictionary. ● to **get no change** out of somebody: see **change**. ● to **get cracking**: see **cracking**. ● to **get** someone's **goat**: see **goat**. ● to **not get a look in**: see **look-in**. ● to **get the message**: see **message**. ● to **play hard to get**: see **play**. ● to **get used to** something: see **used**. ● to **get in the way**: see **way**. ● to **get out of the way**: see **way**. ● to **get** your **way**: see **way**. ● to **get weaving**: see **weave**.

44 See also **getting, got**.

get about. 1 If you **get about**, you go to a lot of different places as part of your way of life. EG *I can't get about as much as I used to.* PHRASAL VB : V+ ADV = get around

2 To **get about** also means the same as to **get round**. EG *Startling rumours began to get about in next to no time.* PHRASAL VB : V+ ADV, OR V+ADV +REPORT-CL

get across. When something **gets across** or when you **get** something **across**, you succeed in making other people understand it. EG *We managed to get our message across.* PHRASAL VB : V-ERG+ADV ⇑ communicate = get over

get after. To **get after** someone means to try to catch them, especially when they have committed a crime. EG *It is their job to get after the villains as fast as possible.* PHRASAL VB : V+ PREP = pursue

get ahead. If you **get ahead**, you are successful in your career. EG *The bright young man can get ahead quickly in industry.* PHRASAL VB : V+ ADV ⇑ succeed = advance

get along. 1 If you **get along** with someone, you have a friendly relationship with them. EG *They just can't get along together... I used to get along really well with my boss.* PHRASAL VB : V+ ADV+A *(together/with)* : RECIP = get on

2 If you are **getting along** with something such as a task or a machine, you are being successful in doing it or using it. EG *How are you getting along with the new photo-copier?* PHRASAL VB : V+ ADV+A = fare

get around. 1 To **get around** a problem or difficulty means to overcome it. EG *To help get around this problem, some tanks are now equipped with radar.* PHRASAL VB : V+ PREP, HAS PASS = surmount

2 If you **get around** a rule or law, you find a way of doing something that a rule or law is intended to prevent, without actually breaking the rule or law. PHRASAL VB : V+ PREP, HAS PASS = bypass

3 If news **gets around**, it becomes well known as a result of being told to lots of people. EG *The word started to get around about the awful scripts for the new show.* PHRASAL VB : V+ ADV, OR V+ADV +REPORT-CL = get round

4 If you **get around**, you visit a lot of different places as part of your way of life. EG *She must be able to get around.* PHRASAL VB : V+ ADV = get about

get around to. If you **get around to** something, you eventually do something that you would have liked to avoid doing or that you were unable to do before because you were too busy. EG *I only got around to doing this a few days ago.* PHRASAL VB : V+ ADV+PREP

get at. 1 To **get at** something means **1.1** to succeed in reaching it. EG *The goats bent down on their knees to get at the short grass.* PHRASAL VB : V+ PREP, HAS PASS **1.2** to succeed in discovering the truth about something. EG *I must get at the fellow's secret.* PHRASAL VB : V+ PREP, HAS PASS = find out

2 If you **get at** someone, you keep criticizing or teasing them in an unkind way; an informal expression. EG *You're always getting at me.* PHRASAL VB : V+ PREP, HAS PASS = pick on

3 If you ask someone what they **are getting at**, you are asking them to explain what they mean, usually because you think that they are being unpleasant or are suggesting something that is untrue or unfair. EG *I don't know what you are getting at.* PHRASAL VB : V+ PREP = insinuate

get away. 1 If you **get away**, **1.1** you succeed in PHRASAL VB : V+

leaving a place or a person's company. EG *You've got away from home... I was itching to get away.* ADV, USU+*from* **1.2** you go away for a period of time in order to have a holiday. EG *Is there any chance of you getting away this summer?* PHRASAL VB : V+ADV ● If you **get away from it all**, you have a holiday in a place that is very different from the place where you normally live and work. EG *Get away from it all–fly to the sunshine!* ● PHR : VB INFLECTS

2 When someone or something **gets away**, or when you **get** them **away**, they escape. EG *They got away through Mrs Barnett's garden... George Watin got away and is presumed to be living in Spain.* ● See also **getaway**. PHRASAL VB : V-ERG+ADV

3 If you **get away** from something, you do a job or a task differently from the way that it has been done before. EG *They wanted to get away from the rigid timetables of the past.* PHRASAL VB : V+ADV, IF+PREP THEN *from* = break away

4 If you say **you can't get away from it** or **there's no getting away from** something, you are emphasizing the fact that something is true; an informal expression. EG *There's no getting away from the fact that they are better organized than we are.* PHR

5 People sometimes say **'Get away'** or **'Get away with you'** to say to someone that they cannot accept what has just been said because they think that it is foolish or untrue. EG *Get away! We can't have that.* EXCLAM = go on

get away with. If you **get away with** something, you are not punished for doing something that you should not do. EG *Nobody gets away with tearing my coat... He might have bribed her–and got away with it.* ● to **get away with murder**: see **murder**. PHRASAL VB : V+ADV+PREP

get back. 1 If you **get back** to something, **1.1** you are in the same state, condition, or situation that you were in before. EG *Eddie wanted to get back to sleep... Things would soon get back to normal.* PHRASAL VB : V+ADV+*to* = go back **1.2** you start talking again about something that you were talking about before. EG *Let's just get back to the argument... She got back to what she had really come for.* PHRASAL VB : V+ADV+*to* = return **1.3** you start doing something again after you have stopped doing it. EG *He eventually got back to work again... Maybe you could get back into journalism.* PHRASAL VB : V+ADV+*to/into* = go back

2 If you **get** something **back**, you have it again after you have lost it or after someone has taken it from you. EG *He would get back his old job... All he wants to do is get his girl friend back.* PHRASAL VB : V+O+ADV = regain

3 If you **get back**, you move away from a person or a place. EG *If you come near, I'll scream. Get Back!* PHRASAL VB : V+ADV

get by. If you **get by**, you just manage to survive and have a fairly satisfactory life. EG *He had managed to get by without much reading or writing... They slide through life, getting by as best they can.* PHRASAL VB : V+ADV, USU+A = cope

get down. 1 If something **gets** you **down**, it makes you unhappy. EG *The quiet got them down... It isn't just the work that gets her down.* PHRASAL VB : ORDER V+O+ADV = depress

2 If you **get down**, you lower your body until you are sitting or lying on the ground. EG *They got down on their knees... We got down on the ground.* PHRASAL VB : V+ADV : USU+*on* = go down

3 If you **get** something **down**, you write it, especially something that has just been said. PHRASAL VB : V+O+ADV

4 If you **get** food **down**, you swallow it, especially with difficulty; an informal expression. EG *I eventually managed to get it down.* PHRASAL VB : ORDER V+O+ADV

get down to. If you **get down to** something, you begin doing it, especially when it is something that requires a lot of attention. EG *I got down to work... Let's get down to business.* PHRASAL VB : V+ADV+PREP ⇑ start

get in. 1 If a political party or a politician **gets in**, they are elected. EG *What would Labour do if they got in ?... She got in by more than 5,000 votes.* PHRASAL VB : V+ADV

2 If you **get** something **in**, you manage to do it at a time when you are very busy doing other things. EG *The idea was to get in a little golf... They get in all the work they can.* PHRASAL VB : V+O+ADV = fit in

3 To **get** crops or the harvest **in** means to gather them from the land and take them to a particular place. EG *They wanted to get the harvest in.* PHRASAL VB : V+O+ADV = bring in

4 When trains, buses, planes, etc, or the people travelling in them, **get in**, they arrive. EG *What time does the coach get in, do you know?... We get in at five.* PHRASAL VB : V+ADV

5 If you **get** something **in**, you eventually manage to succeed in saying something, usually because a lot of people are talking at the same time or one person is talking non-stop. EG *'What I wanted to say,' I finally got in, 'is that I've a set of instructions at home.'... Tinker had to get in the last word.* ● to **get a word in edgeways**: see **edgeways**. PHRASAL VB : V+O+ADV, OR V+ADV+QUOTE/REPORT-CL = chip in

get in on. If you get in on something, you take part in an activity that other people are already involved in; an informal expression. EG *He even gets in on the photography shows.* PHRASAL VB : V+ADV+PREP ⇑ join in

get into. 1 If you **get into** something such as a conversation, argument, or fight, you begin it with another person or group of people. EG *It usually took that long to get into a serious conversation... I always get into arguments with people.* PHRASAL VB : V+PREP = embark on

2 If you **get into a particular habit or way of doing something,** you have begun to have it. EG *She'd got into the habit of sulking... We tend to get into a certain way of thinking.* PHRASAL VB : V+PREP = develop

3 If you **get into** something, **3.1** you take it up as an interest or a hobby; an informal expression. EG *She got into health foods and astrology.* PHRASAL VB : V+PREP **3.2** you become involved in a particular kind of work or activity. EG *He was determined to get into Federalist politics.* PHRASAL VB : V+PREP

4 If you **get into** a school, college, or university, you are accepted there as a pupil or student. EG *There has been a demand to get into various schools... Darwin failed to get into medical school at Cambridge.* PHRASAL VB : V+PREP ⇑ enter

5 If you ask what has **got into** someone, you mean that they are behaving in an unexpected way; an informal expression. EG *What's got into her?* PHRASAL VB : V+PREP, NO CONT/IMPER/PASS

get in with. If you **get in with** someone, you become friendly with them, often because you think that they can help you because they are rich or important. EG *She takes good care to get in with the people who matter.* PHRASAL VB : V+ADV+PREP ⇑ befriend

get off. 1 If you **get off** a bus, train, etc, you leave it. EG *When the train stopped, he got off... Get off at Mayfield Church.* PHRASAL VB : V+PREP/ADV ⇑ get out

2 If you **get off something,** you move your body from an object that you have been standing, sitting, or lying on. EG *She started to get off the table... He got off his bicycle.* PHRASAL VB : V+PREP

3 If you **get off** a piece of land, you leave a place where you should not be. EG *I told them to get off the university playing fields.* PHRASAL VB : V+PREP = clear off

4 If you **get off, 4.1** you leave somewhere. EG *I have to be getting off now.* ● to **get off on the wrong foot**: see **foot**. ● to **get off to a flying start**: see **flying**. PHRASAL VB : V+ADV **4.2** you are not punished for breaking a law or rule, or are given only a very small punishment. EG *He got off with a £50 fine... He expressed relief that he had got off so lightly.* PHRASAL VB : V-ERG+ADV = be let off

5 If you **get** something **off** something else, you remove it, especially when it is stuck. EG *...stains you can't get off your skin... I can't get the top off.* PHRASAL VB : V+O+ADV/PREP ⇑ remove

6 If you **get** a letter or parcel **off**, you post it. EG *He eventually got his letter off... Try to get that one off early so it reaches them tomorrow.* PHRASAL VB : ORDER V+O+ADV

7 If you **get** a piece of clothing off, you remove it. EG *Get your shirt off and let's have a look at that arm right away.* PHRASAL VB : ORDER V+O+ADV = take off

8 If you **get off** or **get off** to sleep, you succeed in falling asleep in spite of something that makes it difficult for you to sleep. EG *I just couldn't get off last night.* PHRASAL VB : V+ADV, USU+*to* = fall asleep

9 If you **get off** on something, you become very excited by it; a very informal expression. EG *He really enjoys blowing people up–he really gets off on it.* PHRASAL VB : V+ADV+*on* = get high

10 You can say **'Get off', 'Get your hands off'**, etc, to tell someone not to touch something. For example, a woman might say this to a man who is touching her. EG *Get your hands off. And don't call me 'love', thank you... Get your greedy hands off that cake, it's for tomorrow.* PHR : ONLY IMPER

11 If you **tell** someone **where to get off**, you tell someone who is behaving in an arrogant way that they are not as important as they think that they are; an informal expression. EG *I should tell them where to get off, if I were you.* PHR : VB INFLECTS

get off with. If you **get off with** someone, you begin a romantic or sexual relationship with them. EG *Mike thinks I'm trying to get off with his girlfriend.* PHRASAL VB : V+ADV+PREP = make it with

get on. 1 If you **get on** with someone, you have a friendly relationship with them. EG *Mother and I get on very well... The two communities are not prepared to get on together... I have never been able to get on with Cyril.* PHRASAL VB : V+ADV OR V+ADV+A (*together/with*) : RECIP = get along

2 If you **get on** with something, you continue with something that you have started doing or you start something that you were about to do. EG *I get on with my work most weekends... Perhaps we can get on with the meeting.* PHRASAL VB : V + ADV, USU + *with* = press on

3 If you **get on**, **3.1** you have a particular degree of success with something that you are trying to do. EG *I always get on far better if I can draw a diagram... How's he getting on?* PHRASAL VB : V + ADV + A, NO IMPER = manage **3.2** you are successful in your career. EG *She's got to study to get on.* PHRASAL VB : V + ADV, NO IMPER

4 If you **get on** a bus, train, etc, you get into it. EG *She got on the bus every morning... Some new passengers were getting on.* PHRASAL VB : V + PREP/ADV = board

5 If you **get** a piece of clothing **on**, you put it on. EG *Get your coat on... She told them to get their scarves and gloves on.* PHRASAL VB : ORDER V + O + ADV

6 If someone **is getting on**, they are old. EG *Now I'm getting on I find these stairs a little difficult for me.* PHRASAL VB : V + ADV

7 If you say that **time is getting on**, you mean that there is not much time left before something will happen. Often this is a way of saying that something should be done quickly. PHR : AUX INFLECTS

get on to. **1** If you **get on to** a topic, you change to it during a lecture, conversation, etc. EG *That's something we'll get on to in the future... Somehow we got on to grandparents.* PHRASAL VB : V + ADV + PREP = move on to

2 If you **get on to** someone, you contact them in order to ask them to do something or to give them some information. EG *I'll get on to her right away.* PHRASAL VB : V + ADV + PREP

get out. **1** If you **get out** of somewhere, **1.1** you leave a vehicle, room, building, etc. EG *We got out of the car... I got out and examined the right rear wheel... Brody got out of bed... Get out of here!* PHRASAL VB : V + ADV ⇑ leave **1.2** you leave a place because you want to leave it, or because you are made to leave it. EG *I'm going to get out of New York... They told me to get out.* • to **get out while the going is good**: see **going**. PHRASAL VB : V-ERG + ADV = clear out

2 If you **get out** of something such as an organization, you withdraw from it. EG *The Common Market? The sooner we get out the better.* PHRASAL VB : V + ADV = pull out

3 If you **get out**, you go to places and meet people, usually in order to have a more enjoyable or interesting life. EG *Get out and enjoy yourself... You've got to get out and make friends.* PHRASAL VB : V + ADV, USU + A = go out

4 If you **get** something **out**, you take it out of a cupboard, pocket, bag, etc. EG *He got out a book and read... After a few drinks he would get his clarinet out.* PHRASAL VB : V + O + ADV = produce, take out

5 If you **get** a stain **out**, you remove it from a surface or a fabric. EG *I couldn't get the stain out of your green dress... It's got stuff spilt on it you can't get out.* PHRASAL VB : V + O + ADV

6 If you **get out** a report or a statement, you produce it for people to read. EG *The American Cancer Society got out its first report in 1954... Production schedules had to be got out.* PHRASAL VB : V + O + ADV

7 If you **get out** of something, you succeed in avoiding doing something that you do not want to do. EG *She always got out of washing up... We'll do anything to get out of work.* PHRASAL VB : V + ADV + *of* ⇑ avoid

8 If you **get** something **out**, you manage to say something, often with difficulty because, for example, you are out of breath. EG *She couldn't get a word out for the moment... I had barely got out my name.* PHRASAL VB : V + O + ADV

9 If news or information **gets out**, it becomes known. EG *The news got out in the end... The word got out that he would go ahead.* PHRASAL VB : V + ADV, OR V + ADV + REPORT-CL, NO CONT

10 If you **get out** of a habit or particular activity, you stop doing it. PHRASAL VB : V + ADV + *of*

get over. **1** If you **get over** an unpleasant or unhappy experience or an illness, you recover from it. EG *Have you got over the shock?... George did not get over his homesickness for some time... She's just getting over mumps.* PHRASAL VB : V + PREP

2 If you **get over** a problem or difficulty, you overcome it. EG *One mother got over this problem by leaving her baby with someone else.* PHRASAL VB : V + PREP = get around

3 If you **get** your meaning **over**, people understand what you are saying. EG *He got his meaning over to Jo at the fourth time of trying.* PHRASAL VB : V + O + ADV, IF + PREP THEN *to* = get across

get over with. If you **get** something **over with**, you do something unpleasant or tedious that must be done. EG *Can we just get this questioning over with?* PHRASAL VB : V + O + ADV + PREP ⇑ finish

get round. **1** If you **get round** a problem or difficulty, you overcome it. EG *Irving got round the problem in a novel way.* PHRASAL VB : V + PREP, HAS PASS = get over

2 If you **get round** a rule or law, you find a way of doing something that a rule or law is intended to prevent, without actually breaking that rule or law. EG *She knew the ways to get round the rules.* PHRASAL VB : V + PREP, HAS PASS

3 If news **gets round**, it becomes well known as a result of being told to lots of people. EG *The word got round that Morris was going to England.* PHRASAL VB : V + ADV, OR V + ADV + REPORT-CL = get about

4 If you **get round** someone, you persuade them to allow you to do or to have something by pleasing them or by flattering them. EG *She could always get round him in the end.* PHRASAL VB : V + PREP, HAS PASS ⇑ persuade = win over

get round to. If you **get round to** something, you eventually do something that you would have liked to avoid doing or that you were unable to do earlier because you were busy doing other things. EG *It took you six weeks to get round to telling me about Melanie... I didn't get round to taking the examination.* PHRASAL VB : V + ADV + PREP = get around to

get through. **1** If you **get through** something such as a task, you complete it, especially when it requires a lot of effort. EG *It is difficult to get through this amount of work in such a short time... We tried to get through the whole play in two hours.* PHRASAL VB : V + PREP, HAS PASS = wade through

2 If you **get through** a period of time during which something unpleasant is happening, you manage to live through it. EG *They helped me to get through that time... How do John and Sylvia ever get through Minnesota winters?* PHRASAL VB : V + PREP, HAS PASS = survive

3 If you **get through** a large amount of something, you completely use it up. EG *He had got through all his money... I got through about six pounds worth of drink.* PHRASAL VB : V + PREP, HAS PASS = run through

4 If you **get through** to someone, **4.1** you succeed in making them understand something that you are trying to tell them. EG *Howard, how do I get through to you?* PHRASAL VB : V + ADV + *to* ⇑ reach = get **4.2** you succeed in contacting them on the telephone. EG *I finally got through at twenty past ten.* PHRASAL VB : V + ADV

5 If you **get through** or **get through** an examination, you pass it. EG *They haven't got a chance of getting through... He qualifies if he gets through his two subjects this year.* PHRASAL VB : V + ADV/PREP ⇑ succeed

6 If a law or proposal **gets through**, it is officially approved by something such as a parliament or committee. EG *If this new White Paper gets through, there will be no subsidized meals... The bill might not have been able to get through Congress.* PHRASAL VB : V-ERG + ADV/PREP = go through

get together. **1** When people **get together**, they meet in order to discuss something or to spend time together. EG *Workers and supervisors get together to discuss their grievances... Do you think we could get together at Christmas?... Can you get together with Henry to arrange the wedding reception?* • See also **get-together**. PHRASAL VB : V-ERG + ADV, ALSO V + ADV OR V + ADV + A (*with*) : RECIP = come together

2 If you **get** something **together**, you assemble it from several parts, for example you build a machine or you form an organization. EG *He's spent a whole afternoon trying to get the thing together... It now only remained to get the company together.* • to **get** your **act together**: see **act**. PHRASAL VB : V + O + ADV = assemble

3 If you **get** money **together**, you succeed in getting all the money that you need in order to pay for something. EG *Almost all of the children had got the money together themselves... Somehow we have to get the fees together.* PHRASAL VB : V + O + ADV = scrape together

get up. **1** If you **get up**, **1.1** you rise to a standing position when you have been sitting or lying down. EG *I had to get up from my stool... He got up off the floor... Please. Don't get up.* PHRASAL VB : V + ADV, USU + A = stand up **1.2** you get out of bed. EG *You've got to get up at eight o'clock... He was always the last to get up.* PHRASAL VB : V + ADV, OR V + O + ADV = rise

2 If you **get** something **up**, you organize something such as a public event, especially with very little preparation; a rather old-fashioned expression. EG *An impromptu dance was got up in his honour.* PHRASAL VB : V + O + ADV = arrange

3 If you **get** yourself **up** in something, you dress in a particular kind of clothing. EG *...children got up in spaceman outfits... He had got himself up like a U.S. marine.* • See also **get-up**. PHRASAL VB : V + O (REFL) + ADV + *in/like* = rig out

get up to. If you say that someone **gets up to** something, you mean that they do things that you do not approve of. EG *He got up to all sorts of things... When I found out what they used to get up to I was absolutely horrified.* PHRASAL VB : V + ADV + PREP ⇑ do

getaway /gɛ̲təweɪ/, **getaways.** If someone makes a **getaway**, they leave a place in a hurry, especially after committing a crime. EG *I was busy packing up to make my getaway... They leapt aboard the getaway cars.* N COUNT : USU SING ⇑ departure = escape

getting /gɛtɪŋ/. **1 Getting** is the present participle of **get**.
2 In informal English, **getting on for** means the same as nearly. EG *They have getting on for a hundred stores in England... The place must be getting on for four hundred years old.* PHR : V+ADV+PREP

get-together, get-togethers. A **get-together** is an informal meeting or party, usually arranged for a particular purpose. EG *We're having a little get-together to celebrate Helen's promotion.* N COUNT = gathering

get-up, get-ups. A **get-up** is a strange or unusual set of clothes worn by someone on a particular occasion. EG *...Albert Finney in a Mexican get-up smoking a cigar.* N COUNT = outfit, rig

gewgaw /gjᵊu:gɔ:/, **gewgaws**. A **gewgaw** is an attractive and brightly-coloured ornament or piece of jewellery that is of little value; used showing disapproval. EG *...a bag of fancy gewgaws.* N COUNT = trinket

geyser /gi:zə/, **geysers**. A **geyser** is **1** a hole in the Earth's surface from which hot water and steam come out forcefully, usually at irregular intervals of time. EG *...steam geysers and hot water springs... ...volcanoes and geysers.* N COUNT ↑ eruption **2** in British English, a device for providing hot water, usually a large metal container with water pipes and a gas burner inside, fixed to the wall of a bathroom or kitchen. EG *There was a geyser above the bath.* N COUNT ↑ appliance

Ghanaian /gɑ:neɪən/. **1** Something that is **Ghanaian** belongs or relates to Ghana or to its people. EG *...Ghanaian musicians.* ADJ CLASSIF
2 A **Ghanaian** is a person who comes from Ghana. N COUNT

ghastly /gɑ:stli¹/. **1** If you say that someone is **ghastly**, you mean that you do not like them at all, especially because of the way they behave. EG *...those ghastly Hewson-Smarts and their idiot guests... 'Ghastly, isn't she?'* ADJ QUALIT ↑ unpleasant = awful
2 If you say that something is **ghastly**, **2.1** you think that it is vulgar and poor in artistic style. EG *...ghastly scarlet lipstick... ...ghastly office blocks.* ADJ QUALIT = frightful **2.2** you mean that it is very unpleasant to taste, smell, hear, or look at. EG *The empty glasses and full ash-trays were a ghastly sight... ...a ghastly bowl of soup.* ADJ QUALIT = repulsive
3 A **ghastly** experience or situation is one that you find very unpleasant, for example because it makes you unhappy or embarrassed. EG *For a ghastly moment I thought she was going to ask me to stay... We wouldn't be in this ghastly mess if you had kept quiet... ...ghastly long arguments.* ADJ QUALIT = hideous, awful
4 If something is **ghastly** in appearance, it makes you feel afraid, because there is something strange, unnatural, or evil about it. EG *The great fangs gleamed a ghastly white... They jerked through their ghastly dance, the priest, the hangman and the convict.* ADJ QUALIT ↑ frightening = spectral, macabre
5 If someone looks **ghastly**, they look very ill or unhappy. EG *She was crying, blowing her nose and looking simply ghastly.* ADJ QUALIT : PRED = awful
6 If you describe events, situations, or news as **ghastly**, you mean that they involve suffering or death. EG *...the ghastly news of the murder... The scene after the battle was ghastly.* ADJ QUALIT = horrifying, grim
7 Something that is **ghastly** is extremely severe in its effects. EG *They had made a ghastly mistake... ...a new and ghastly economic slump.* ADJ QUALIT : ATTRIB ↑ extreme = serious

gherkin /gɜ:kɪn/, **gherkins**. A **gherkin** is a small green cucumber which has been pickled in vinegar and is eaten as part of a snack or meal. EG *...crisps, gherkins, and cocktail onions.* N COUNT

ghetto /gɛtəʊ/, **ghettos, ghettoes**. The plural can be either **ghettos** or **ghettoes**. A **ghetto** is a part of a town or city in which many poor people or many people of a particular race, religion, or nationality live in isolation from the majority group in the town or city; used showing disapproval. EG *It's about this black kid growing up in the ghetto... ...ghetto life in European cities... ...slums and ghettos.* N COUNT ↑ area

ghost /gəʊst/, **ghosts, ghosting, ghosted**. **1** A **ghost** is a dead person that some people think they see or feel the presence of, and that they usually find frightening. EG *...the ghost of Mrs Dowell... Her ghost would haunt me all my life... I don't believe in ghosts... Do you know any good ghost stories?* • See also **Holy Ghost**. N COUNT ↑ apparition = spook • If you say that someone **looks like** they **have seen a ghost**, you mean that they look very shocked or frightened. • PHR : AUX INFLECTS
2 A **ghost** of something is a faint trace of it; a rather literary word. EG *...a ghost of a smile.* N COUNT + *of* : USU SING
3 If you say that someone has not got **the ghost of a chance** of doing something, you mean that they have very little chance of succeeding in doing it; an informal expression. EG *We have not the ghost of a chance of changing Father's will.* PHR WITH BROAD NEG : USED AS O
4 If you say that someone **has given up the ghost**, you mean that they have died; an informal expression. PHR : VB INFLECTS = die
5 If you say that a machine **has given up the ghost**, you mean that it has stopped working properly and cannot be repaired. EG *The car took us across Europe, only giving up the ghost in the last stages of the journey.* PHR : VB INFLECTS = die, conk out
6 If you **ghost** a book or other piece of writing, you write it for someone, who then puts their name on it. EG *...a famous play, and even that was half ghosted... He published his ghosted memoirs in a Sunday newspaper.* V+O = ghost-write

ghostly /gəʊstli¹/. Something that is **ghostly** is slightly frightening in its appearance or effect, because it does not seem real or natural. EG *He saw them far overhead, ghostly in the moonlight... ...a ghostly laugh... ...ghostly rumbling noises.* ADJ QUALIT = eerie, sinister

ghost town, **ghost towns**. A **ghost town** is a town which was once busy and prosperous but which people no longer live in, especially one where the buildings are still standing. EG *...a ghost town in New Mexico.* N COUNT

ghost-write, ghost-writes, ghost-writing, ghost-wrote, ghost-written; also spelled as one word. If you **ghost-write** an article, speech, or book, you write it for another person, for example a politician or sportsman, who then publishes or uses it as his or her own work. EG *The speech was in fact mostly ghost-written by Stockman.* ◇ **ghost-writing**. EG *...a piece of ghost-writing on Mailer's part.* V+O; ◇ N UNCOUNT ↑ writing

ghost-writer, **ghost-writers**; also spelled as one word. A **ghost-writer** is someone who writes articles, speeches, or books for other people. N COUNT

ghoul /gu:l/, **ghouls**. **1** A **ghoul** is an imaginary evil spirit, especially one which eats dead bodies. N COUNT = fiend
2 If you say that someone is a **ghoul**, you mean that they are interested in things that usually shock or upset other people, such as torture, death, and dead bodies; used showing strong disapproval. N COUNT

ghoulish /gu:lɪʃ/. Something that is **ghoulish** is concerned with torture, suffering, or death; used showing disapproval. EG *Ghoulish rumours race through the community.* ▸ used of people who are interested in such things. EG *...their ghoulish desire for grisly details... ...a ghoulish smile.* ◇ **ghoulishly**. EG *She licked her lips ghoulishly.* ADJ QUALIT ↑ unpleasant = macabre; ▸ = gruesome; ◇ ADV WITH VB

GHQ is an abbreviation for 'General Headquarters': the place where the people work who organize military forces or a military operation; a military term. EG *She agreed to meet him at GHQ at four-thirty.* ▸ used of the people who work there. EG *GHQ would not offer an official estimate.* N UNCOUNT; ▸ N UNCOUNT : VB CAN BE SING OR PL

GI /dʒi: aɪ/, **GIs**. A **GI** is a soldier in the United States army. EG *The GI hadn't removed his cap... Eighty GIs had died in combat.* N COUNT

giant /dʒaɪənt/, **giants**. **1** A **giant** is an imaginary person of great size and strength, especially one mentioned in myths and children's stories. EG *...stories of cruel giants and wicked witches... ...one-eyed giants in Greek legends... ...like a giant's armchair.* N COUNT ↑ creature
2 A very large business company or organization is often referred to as a **giant** in newspapers, magazines, and economic journals. EG *...the electronics giant, Hitachi... ...competition from the American giants.* ▸ used as an adjective. EG *...the giant chemical concern, Hoechst.* N COUNT + SUPP; ▸ ADJ CLASSIF : ATTRIB
3 Anything that is much larger than the usual size can be referred to as a **giant**. EG *...a giant of a man with wavy white hair.* ▸ used as an adjective. EG *...giant Christmas trees... ...the giant Post Office computer.* N COUNT = colossus; ▸ ADJ CLASSIF : ATTRIB = colossal
4 Giant is used as part of the name of some species of animals that are different from similar species in size and other characteristics; a technical term in zoology. EG *...the giant anteater... ...the giant pandas.* ADJ CLASSIF : ATTRIB
5 Giant is also used to describe events or situations that are considered to be very important, especially when they are part of a larger process. EG *...giant steps in the conquest of a disease... ...giant conspiracies to defraud management.* ADJ CLASSIF : ATTRIB ↑ important = major

gibber /dʒɪbə/, **gibbers, gibbering, gibbered.** If you **gibber**, you talk very fast and in a confused manner, often because of fear or madness. EG *...naked men gibbering in their terror... 'I shouldn't have told you,' she gibbered.* ◊ **gibbering.** EG *...a gibbering idiot.*
V OR V+QUOTE = babble; ◊ ADJ CLASSIF : ATTRIB

gibberish /dʒɪbərɪʃ/ is words or ideas that do not make any sense; often used showing disapproval. EG *He was talking gibberish... Could the theory be sheer gibberish?.*
N UNCOUNT ⇑ nonsense

gibbet /dʒɪbɪt/, **gibbets.** A **gibbet** is a gallows; an old-fashioned word.
N COUNT

gibbon /gɪbən/, **gibbons.** A **gibbon** is an animal that lives in southern Asia and looks like a monkey but has no tail.
N COUNT ⇑ ape

gibe /dʒaɪb/, **gibes.** A **gibe** is a jibe.
N COUNT

giblets /dʒɪblɪ[2]ts/ are the parts such as the heart and liver that you remove from inside a chicken or other bird before you cook and eat it. Some people cook the giblets separately to make soup or a sauce.
N PLURAL ⇑ innards

giddy/gɪdi[1]/, **giddier, giddiest. 1** If you feel **giddy,** you feel unsteady and think that you are about to fall over, usually because you are not well or are very tired. EG *He had a headache and felt giddy... He tried to get up and failed, feeling too giddy.* ▸ used of the feeling or the cause of the feeling. EG *It gave him a giddy feeling when he looked out of the window... ...the giddy heat of the garage.* ◊ **giddiness.** EG *...giddiness and sea-sickness.*
ADJ QUALIT : PRED = dizzy, faint; ▸ ADJ QUALIT : ATTRIB = dizzying; ◊ N UNCOUNT = dizziness

2 If something makes you **giddy**, you feel **2.1** slightly worried and confused, because you are thinking hard or cannot understand it properly. EG *It made me giddy to hear so much subtle analysis.* ▸ used of the cause of the feeling. EG *...the giddy heights of responsibility.* **2.2** happy and full of energy. EG *The news made me giddy with excitement.* ▸ used of the feeling or the period of time that it lasts. EG *...the atmosphere of giddy joy... ...after those first giddy weeks at home.*
ADJ QUALIT : PRED = dizzy; ▸ ADJ QUALIT : ATTRIB; ADJ QUALIT; ▸ ADJ QUALIT : ATTRIB = intoxicating

3 In old-fashioned English, someone who is **giddy** is mainly interested in having fun and not in serious matters; used showing disapproval. EG *...her husband's giddy cousin.*
ADJ QUALIT = flighty

gift /gɪft/, **gifts. 1** A **gift** is something that you give someone as a present. EG *Give her a scarf as a gift... ...buying a gift for his hostess... ...the gift of a handful of primroses... ...a gift from the Russian ambassador to Charles II... ...a parting gift.*
N COUNT

2 If someone has a **gift** for doing something, they have a natural ability for doing it. EG *John has a real gift for casual conversation... Rudolf had the gift of being liked by everyone he met... ...his gifts as a storyteller.*
N COUNT : USU SING+*for/of* = talent

3 In informal English, if you say that something is a **gift**, you mean that it is much cheaper or much easier to do than usual. EG *At £50 it was a gift... That exam question was a gift to anyone who'd read the book.*
N SING : a+N = give-away

4 In informal English, if you say that someone thinks that they are **God's gift** to someone or something, you mean that you believe that they are very arrogant and conceited; used showing strong disapproval. EG *He thinks he is God's gift to women.*
PHR : USED AS C

gifted /gɪftɪ[2]d/. Someone who is **gifted 1** has a natural ability to do something well. EG *She was a gifted actress... He was gifted with extraordinary powers of memory... ...the most gifted of all living musicians... She is very gifted at French.* **2** is more intelligent than average; used of children. EG *Even gifted children fail to progress without good teaching.*
ADJ QUALIT = talented; ADJ QUALIT

gift-wrapped means wrapped in pretty paper in order to be given as a present.
ADJ CLASSIF

gig /gɪg/, **gigs. 1** A **gig** is a performance, especially one by pop musicians; an informal use. EG *No group has played a gig there since 1960... They started out doing free gigs in bars.*
N COUNT

2 A **gig** was a small, open carriage that had two wheels and was pulled by one horse. EG *A farmer came in his gig.*
N COUNT

gigantic /dʒaɪgæntɪk/. Something that is **gigantic** is unusually and surprisingly large in size, amount or degree. EG *The entire area looked like a gigantic rubbish heap... ...mistakes on a truly gigantic scale... ...gigantic amounts of money... ...a gigantic effort.* ◊ **gigantically.** EG *...the smooth sides of the mountain rising gigantically from the plain.*
ADJ QUALIT = colossal; ◊ ADV

giggle /gɪgəl/, **giggles, giggling, giggled. 1** If you **giggle**, you make quiet and repeated laughing noises, because you are happy or occasionally because you are nervous or embarrassed. EG *The absurd sound made her giggle... 'Oh dear,' she giggled, 'I'd quite forgotten'... ...giggling helplessly at her own joke.* ▸ used as a noun. EG *...a nervous giggle... We had a good giggle about that.* ● If someone has **the giggles**, they cannot stop giggling; an informal use. EG *This gave Lynn the giggles... ...a fit of the giggles.*
V OR V+QUOTE ⇑ laugh = chuckle, titter; ▸ N COUNT; ● PHR : USED AS O

2 If you say that something is **a giggle** or if you do something **for a giggle**, you mean that you think that it is fun to do and will not do any harm to anyone; an informal expression.
PHR : USED AS C/A = a lark

giggly /gɪgli[1]/. If people are **giggly**, they are happy and amused or slightly nervous. EG *They returned, rather giggly.* ▸ used also of people's behaviour. EG *...a giggly shyness.*
ADJ QUALIT ⇑ amused

gigolo /dʒɪgəʊləʊ/, **gigolos.** A **gigolo** is a man who is paid to be the lover and companion of a rich and usually older woman; used showing disapproval. EG *She had a drunken row with her gigolo.*
N COUNT

gild /gɪld/, **gilds, gilding, gilded. 1** If you **gild** a surface, you cover it in a thin layer of gold or gold paint. ◊ **gilded.** EG *The priest chants before gilded altars... ...the ornate gilded mirror.* ◊ **gilding.** EG *The gilding is thinner than he expected.*
V+O; ◊ ADJ CLASSIF; ◊ N UNCOUNT

2 If something **is gilded**, it appears golden; a literary word. EG *The hedges were gilded by the sun... ...his face gilded in the glow from the stove.*
V+O : USU PASS ⇑ light

3 If you say that someone is **gilding the lily**, you mean that they are spoiling something that is already beautiful or perfect by trying to improve it or by praising it too highly.
PHR : VB INFLECTS ⇑ overdo = spoil

gilded /gɪldɪ[2]d/. If you describe someone as **gilded**, you mean that they are rich and belong to a high social class. EG *...the gilded aristocratic audience... I was an heiress in my gilded youth.*
ADJ CLASSIF : USU ATTRIB ⇑ fortunate = fashionable

gill, gills. The word **gill** is pronounced /gɪl/ for paragraphs 1 and 2, and /dʒɪl/ for paragraph 3. **1** **Gills** are the organs on the sides of fish and other water creatures through which they breathe by taking oxygen from the water.
N COUNT : USU PL ⇑ organ

2 If you say that someone is **pale** or **green about the gills**, you mean that they look sick and ill, often because of shock or fear; an informal expression.
PHR : USED AS C = queasy

3 A **gill** is a unit of measurement for liquids that is equal to a quarter of a pint or 0.142 litres. EG *...a gill of rum.*
N PART+N UNCOUNT

gilt /gɪlt/, **gilts. 1** Something that is **gilt** is covered with a thin layer of gold or gold paint. EG *...three small gilt chairs... ...paintings in dark gilt frames... ...gilt lettering.* ▸ used as a noun. EG *The gilt had been chipped... ...adorned with gilt.*
ADJ CLASSIF : USU ATTRIB ⇑ coated = gilded; ▸ N UNCOUNT ⇑ coating

2 **Gilts** are gilt-edged stocks or securities. EG *Gilts, stocks and shares...*
N COUNT : USU PL ⇑ stock

gilt-edged. Gilt-edged stocks or securities are issued by the government for people to invest in for a fixed period of time at a fixed rate of interest. With gilt-edged stocks there is very little risk of investors losing their money.
ADJ CLASSIF ⇑ secure

gimcrack /dʒɪmkræk/. **Gimcrack** things look attractive but are badly made and so are of little use or value; used showing disapproval. EG *...some flashy gimcrack boat.* ▸ used also of ideas. EG *...gimcrack theories.*
ADJ CLASSIF : ATTRIB = rubbishy

gimlet /gɪmlɪ[2]t/. **1** A **gimlet** is a small sharp tool used for making small holes in wood.
N COUNT

2 If you say that someone has **gimlet** eyes, you mean that they look at things very carefully and notice every detail. EG *His gimlet eyes blinked at her.*
ADJ CLASSIF : ATTRIB ⇑ sharp = piercing

gimmick /gɪmɪk/, **gimmicks.** A **gimmick** is an unusual action, object, or device that is not really necessary or important but whose main purpose is to attract attention, interest or publicity. EG *The manufacturer needed a new sales gimmick... ...fancy gimmicks on the steering column... ...an election gimmick.*
N COUNT ⇑ contrivance

gimmickry /gɪmɪkri[1]/ is actions or objects that are not necessary or important but whose main purpose is to attract attention, interest, or publicity. EG *No legal gimmickry will save the animals... ...computers loaded with gimmickry.*
N UNCOUNT

gimmicky /gɪmɪki[1]/. If you say that something is **gimmicky**, you mean that it contains a lot of things that are not necessary or important but are included
ADJ QUALIT ⇑ superficial

mainly to attract attention, interest, or publicity; an informal word. EG *The production was rather gimmicky... Good ideas become standard, gimmicky ones die quickly.*

gin /dʒɪn/, **gins**. **Gin** is a colourless alcoholic drink made from grain and juniper berries. Gin is usually drunk with tonic water or fruit juice. EG *'A gin and tonic, please.'... ...a dozen empty gin bottles.* N MASS

ginger /dʒɪndʒə/. **1 Ginger** is the root of a certain plant, also sold in the form of a powder, which has a spicy hot flavour and is used in cooking. EG *I added a chopped onion and a little ginger... ...a ginger cake.* N UNCOUNT

2 Ginger is also a bright orange-brown colour. EG *...a man with ginger hair and nervous blue eyes... ...his ginger moustache... ...a young ginger cat.* ADJ COLOUR, OR N UNCOUNT

ginger ale, ginger ales. **Ginger ale** is a fizzy, sweet, non-alcoholic drink that is flavoured with ginger. N MASS

ginger beer, ginger beers. **Ginger beer** is a drink that is made from syrup and ginger and is sometimes slightly alcoholic. N MASS

gingerbread /dʒɪndʒəbrɛd/ is a sweet cake or biscuit that is flavoured with ginger. The biscuits are often made in the shape of a man or an animal. N UNCOUNT

ginger group , ginger groups. A **ginger group** is a group of people who have similar ideas and work together, especially within a larger organization, to try to persuade others to accept or approve of their ideas. EG *...an independent ginger group in the union.* N COUNT = pressure group

gingerly /dʒɪndʒəli¹/. If you do something **gingerly**, you do it in a careful, hesitant manner, usually because you expect it to be dangerous, unpleasant, or painful. EG *They walked gingerly over the rotten floorboards... ...holding it gingerly by its corner... Gingerly she rubbed the wounded spot.* ADV WITH VB ⇑ carefully = tentatively, delicately

gingery /dʒɪndʒəᵒri¹/ means slightly ginger in colour. EG *...his curly gingery locks... ...a gingery tweed jacket.* ADJ COLOUR

gingham /gɪŋəm/ is cloth made of cotton which has a pattern of small squares or stripes, usually in white and one other colour. EG *She was dressed in her brightest gingham... ...a pink gingham shirt... ...gingham checks.* N UNCOUNT

ginseng /dʒɪnsɛŋ/ is the root of a plant found in China, Korea, and America which some people believe is good for your health. N UNCOUNT

gipsy /dʒɪpsi¹/. See **gypsy**. N COUNT

giraffe /dʒəˈrɑːf, -ræf/, **giraffes**. A **giraffe** is a large African animal with a very long neck, long legs, and dark patches on its yellowish skin. N COUNT

gird /gɜːd/, **girds, girding, girded**; an old-fashioned word. **1** If you **gird** yourself with something such as a belt, you fasten it around you. EG *...the cords with which they gird themselves.* V+O (NG/REFL) +A (with)

2 If you **gird** yourself for a fight or contest, you prepare yourself for it. EG *We girded ourselves for the fray.* • If you say that someone is **girding** their **loins** or **girding up** their **loins**, you mean that they are preparing to do something difficult or dangerous. EG *Both sides in the argument were girding their loins.* V OR V+O (REFL) : USU+A • PHR : VB INFLECTS ⇑ prepare = steel yourself

3 If something **is girded** by something else, it is surrounded by it. EG *...as if girded by an invisible wall.* V+O : ONLY PASS = be encircled

girder /gɜːdə/, **girders**. A **girder** is a long, thick piece of steel or iron that is used in the framework of buildings and bridges. N COUNT ⇑ beam

girdle /gɜːdəᵒl/, **girdles, girdling, girdled**. **1** A **girdle** is **1.1** a piece of clothing that fits tightly around the stomach and hips and is worn by women underneath other clothes so that they look slimmer. EG *She didn't wear a girdle any more... ...bras and girdles.* **1.2** a cord or belt that you wear around your waist, sometimes in order to fasten a piece of clothing. EG *...a robe, tied round the waist by a girdle.* N COUNT ⇑ garment = corset; N COUNT

2 If you **girdle** something, you surround it with a circle; a literary word. EG *...the rings which girdle Saturn's surface... ...a mansion girdled by a black path.* V+O = encircle

girl /gɜːl/, **girls**. **1** A **girl** is **1.1** a female child. EG *...a girl of eleven... The boys and girls cheered... ...when you were a little girl... ...a girls' school.* **1.2** someone's daughter, whether they are a child or a woman. EG *She has two girls and a boy... My little girl was called Ida... ...the Talbot girl.* **1.3** a young woman, usually a teenager. EG *...a girl of nineteen... ...calendars showing naked girls... ...a working girl.* **1.4** a man's girlfriend; a rather old-fashioned word. EG *The soldier and his girl... I had a girl in Cornwall.* N COUNT; N COUNT; N COUNT; N COUNT : USU POSS+N IN SING

2 You can refer to a woman of any age as a **girl**, especially when you are talking about a woman who is younger than you or when you are in a position of authority over her; an informal use. EG *...the girl behind the bar... He married a Spanish girl... ...telephone girls.* N COUNT : USU SING

2 You might address a girl or woman as **girl** or **my girl** when she is younger than you or when you are in a position of authority over her. EG *You've got spoiled in your ways, my girl... Be more careful, girl!... My dear girl, what does it matter?* N VOC = lass

4 Women say **girls** when they are talking to or talking about a group of close women friends or women whom they work with; used showing affection. EG *Come on, girls, don't be afraid... ...the other girls at work.* N PLURAL : DET+N, OR VOC = ladies

5 If you refer to a young woman as a **girl Friday**, you mean that she is employed by a business man or woman to be their personal assistant and to do general office work. N COUNT : USU SING

6 See also **head girl, old girl**.

girlfriend /gɜːlfrɛnd/, **girlfriends**. **1** A man's or boy's **girlfriend** is a girl or woman with whom he is having a romantic or sexual relationship. EG *His girlfriend walked out on him.* N COUNT : USU POSS+N ⇑ lover

2 A **girlfriend** is also a female friend. EG *She went to the movies with some girlfriends.* N COUNT ⇑ friend

girl guide, girl guides. **1** The **Girl Guides** is an organization for girls which teaches them to become disciplined, practical, and self-sufficient. N PROPER the+N, VB CAN BE SING OR PL

2 A **girl guide** is a girl who belongs to the Girl Guides. EG *The method I was taught came from a girl guide.* N COUNT

girlhood /gɜːlhʊd/ is the time during which a female human being is a girl, before she becomes an adult. EG *The sisters had both been sponsored in their girlhood by Irving and Ellen Terry.* N UNCOUNT ⇑ youth

girlie /gɜːli¹/. In informal English, **girlie** magazines or calendars are ones that show photographs of naked or almost naked women in a way which is intended to please men but which is offensive to many women. EG *He was reading a girlie magazine.* ADJ CLASSIF : ATTRIB ⇑ pornographic

girlish /gɜːlɪʃ/ means behaving or looking like a girl, especially showing such qualities as playfulness, liveliness, or sweetness. EG *...girlish giggles... She suddenly felt a surge of girlish nervousness.* ADJ QUALIT ⇑ youthful

girl scout, girl scouts. **1** In America, the **Girl Scouts** are an organization similar to the Girl Guides. N PROPER : the+N, VB CAN BE SING OR PL = Girl Guides

2 A **girl scout** is a girl who belongs to the Girl Scouts. N COUNT

giro /dʒaɪrəʊ/, **giros**; used in British English. **1 Giro** is a system in which a bank or post office transfers money from one account to another when they receive instructions to do so. N UNCOUNT ⇑ banking system

2 If someone has a **giro** account, they have an account at a post office which they can use in similar ways to a current account at a bank. N BEFORE N

3 A **giro** or a **giro cheque** is a cheque for a certain amount of money that is given by the government to people who are unemployed or ill. Giros may be cashed at a bank or post office. N COUNT

girth /gɜːθ/, **girths**. **1** The **girth** of something is the measurement around it; a fairly formal word. N COUNT

2 A **girth** is a leather strap which is fastened firmly around the middle of a horse to keep the saddle or load in the right place. N COUNT

gist /dʒɪst/. The **gist** of something is the general meaning or the most important points of a long piece of writing, a speech, or a conversation. EG *I missed the lecture; can you give me the gist of it?* N SING : the+N, USU+of ⇑ summary = drift

give /gɪv/, **gives, giving, gave, given**. **1 Give** is one of the most common verbs in English. It is often used in expressions where it does not have a very distinct meaning of its own, but where most of the meaning is in the noun that follows it. So, for example, 'she gave a smile' means almost the same as 'she smiled.' This structure is often chosen in order to emphasize that an action or event has a definite beginning or end, or in order to be able to add more information about the noun. The following paragraph shows **give** used in this way. **1.1** with nouns that express physical actions. EG *Jill gave an immense sigh... He gave a short laugh... She gave Etta a quick, shrewd glance... Judy gave Bal's hand a squeeze... She gave the door a push.* **1.2** with nouns V+O, OR V+O+O; V+O, V+O+O, OR that express speech actions. By using 'give' you can avoid saying what the report, account, etc, was actually about. EG *They gave her bad news at the hospital... My father gave me all the information I needed... He gave a humorous account of his journey... I don't understand why I couldn't have been given some warning... The Foreign Office said it was unable to give an immediate answer.*

V+O+A *(to)*

1.3 with nouns that express opinions, thoughts, decisions, etc. EG *That's the best advice I can possibly give... She hadn't bothered to give it particular thought... Politeness prevented her mother from giving the real reason... Could you give me a few examples?*

V+O, V+O+O, OR V+O+A *(to)*

1.4 with various swear words to express indifference, dislike, etc; an informal use. EG *He clearly didn't give a damn about his passengers.*

V+O : IF+PREP THEN *about*, USU WITH BROAD NEG

1.5 with nouns that are related to speaking or performing in public. EG *He was due to give a lecture at the Polytechnic that evening... He doesn't often give interviews... No one gave any speeches at the dinner last night... I think Roger Rees gives a remarkable performance in 'Hamlet'... The film is a record of several concerts given by the group in New York.*

V+O, OR V+O+O

2 If you **give** something to someone, **2.1** you offer it to them as a present. EG *I gave Catriona the silver chain I was wearing... What are you giving Rachel for her birthday?* ◊ **giving**. EG *Giving and sharing are spontaneous expressions of love.*

V+O+O, OR V+O+A *(to)*
◊ N UNCOUNT

2.2 you hand it over to them. EG *Joe, give the Colonel another martini... He gave her father some money... The woman gave me a dollar tip.*

V+O+O, OR V+O+A *(to)*
⇑ present

3 If you **give** someone a piece of information or a message, you tell it to them or write it down for them. EG *Castle gave the porter the message... Give my regards to your daughter, Mrs Donovan... Marsha gave her name... Rudolph gave her Julie's number.*

V+O, V+O+O, OR V+O+A *(to)*
⇑ communicate

4 If you **give** someone something that they want or need, **4.1** you provide them with it. EG *We'd love to give you a pay rise, but we are not making enough profit just yet... I was given a large bedroom at the Taj Mahal... She went without giving me time to protest... He gave her a lift back to London... ...a tutor who came to give lessons to my son.*

V+O+O, OR V+O+A *(to)*

4.2 you help them by providing money, time, care, etc, for them. EG *...people who are able to give money to the charities of their choice... He promised to give her any help he could... Much of the aid given has been wastefully used... They won't want to give the rest of their lives to caring for their elderly relations.*

V+O, V+O+O, OR V+O+A *(to)*
⇑ provide

5 If something **gives** you a particular physical or emotional feeling, it produces that feeling in you. EG *The idea gave me pleasure... I thought I'd give you a surprise... Working on the car has given me an appetite... That noise gives me a headache.*

V+O, V+O+O
⇑ cause

6 If something **gives** you a particular idea or impression, it causes you to have that idea or impression. EG *What gave you that idea?... It was Harold who gave me the clue... They tried to give the impression of being detached.*

V+O, OR V+O+O
⇑ suggest

● If something **gives** you **to believe** or **to understand** a particular thing, it causes you to think or believe it. EG *The boys lose out through being given to understand that their emotions must never be shown... We are given to believe that there will be an election soon.*

● PHR : VB INFLECTS

7 If someone **gives** their **life**, they die or are killed; a formal or literary use. EG *People had given their lives to save their fellow men.*

PHR : VB AND N INFLECT
⇑ die

8 If you say that you would **give** your **right arm**, **give** your **eye teeth**, or **give anything** to have or to do something, you are emphasizing how very keen you are to have or to do it. EG *She said she would give anything to stay in China... A dramatist would give his right arm to have Lawrence Olivier act in one of his plays.*

PHR : VB INFLECTS, USU+ *for/to*-INF
⇑ want

9 If you **give** a party, show, etc, you organize it and are usually the host at it. EG *They gave a farewell party for her... Every year he gives a lunch in his garden for his family and friends.*

V+O, V+O+O, OR V+O+A *(for)*
= hold

10 If something **gives** you a particular power, right, rank, etc, you have that power, right, or rank as a result of the official position that you hold or the situation that you are in. EG *His leadership gives him the right to command... Death gave Davis a kind of stature... This gave them standing in the community.*

V+O, V+O+O, OR V+O+A *(to)*
= accord, grant

11 If you **give** someone a particular right, responsibility, or privilege, you allow them that right, responsibility, or privilege because you are in a position of authority. EG *Children in large families are often given responsibility when they are young... His permission was given... This is a generation which expects women to be given equal opportunities with men... The court gave them the custody of the child.*

V+O, V+O+O, OR V+O+A *(to)*
= grant

12 If you **give** something importance, attention, etc, you treat it with the importance or attention that it deserves. EG *Priority will have to be given to unemployment... Teachers are more tolerant than they are often given credit for being... The report was rediscovered and given its full importance.*

V+O+O, OR V+O+A *(to)*
= grant

13 If you **give** something as a cause or reason, you say that it is the cause or reason for a particular situation. EG *13% gave bad housing as their main source of worry.*

V+O, V+O+O, OR V+O+A *(to/as)*
= advance

14 If you **give** an amount, time, or value, you estimate it or offer it based on calculations that have been made. EG *I give him a week before he has a nervous breakdown... The polls had given the President a 10 to 15 point lead... Judging by the wind, the major gave the storm three minutes before it reached us.*

V+O, V+O+O, OR V+O+A *(to)*

15 To **give** a judgement means to formally announce a legal decision. EG *He had been given ten years in prison... The train robbers were given sentences ranging up to 30 years... Judgement was given against him, with costs... The umpire was wrong to give the batsman out.*

V+O, V+O+O, OR V+O+A *(to)*

16 If someone **gives**, they yield and admit that they may be wrong. EG *Someone's got to give, or the miners will be on strike for ever.*

V
= surrender

17 If something **gives**, it collapses or breaks, especially when pulled or put under pressure. EG *His legs gave beneath him... The catch suddenly gave and a hundred and fifty seven empty bottles tumbled onto the floor.*

V
= give way

18 If a woman **gives** herself to a man, she allows him to have sex with her.

V+O (REFL) : IF +PREP THEN *to*

19 Give is the ability that something has to bend or stretch when it is pulled or put under pressure. EG *Be sure that the neck opening has sufficient give to get the vest over the baby's head.*

N UNCOUNT
⇑ elasticity

20 The word **give** is used in the following informal expressions. **20.1** You use **give me** to say that you would rather have one thing than another, especially when you have just mentioned the thing that you do not want. EG *I can't take too much reality. Give me passion, romance... Give me Majorca any day!*

PHR+O

20.2 If you say to someone **'Don't give me that'**, you mean that you do not believe them or that you do not accept what they are saying.

CONVENTION

20.3 You say **'I'll give you that'** to indicate that you admit that someone has a particular characteristic or ability, even if you do not like it very much. EG *You're a bloody good liar, I'll give you that!*

CONVENTION
⇑ I admit

20.4 If someone **gives as good as** they **get**, they fight or argue as well as the person they are fighting or arguing with. EG *They were young enough to give as good as they got in rugby practice.*

PHR : VBS INFLECT
⇑ retaliate

21 The words **give way** are used in the following expressions. **21.1** If something **gives way** to something else, it is replaced by it, especially because it is old-fashioned or the new thing is more important. EG *The old world was giving way to the new... Her look of joy gave way to one of misery... The woods where he picked blackberries were giving way to new brick houses.*

PHR : VB INFLECTS, USU+ *to*
= surrender

21.2 If something **gives way**, it collapses. EG *In an old house the walls might bend or the floors give way... My eyes widened in horror as two of the bridges gave way.*

PHR : VB INFLECTS
= collapse

21.3 If you **give way** to someone or something, you eventually agree to allow someone to do something, even though you really disagree or disapprove. EG *In the long run it proved easier to give way to his demands, though his mother profoundly disliked doing so.*

PHR : VB INFLECTS, USU+ *to*
= give in

21.4 If you **give way** to an emotion, you allow yourself to show how you feel about something, especially by losing control of yourself. EG *He was angry with himself for giving way to tears.*

PHR : VB INFLECTS, USU+ *to*
= give in

21.5 If you **give way** when you are driving a car or other vehicle, you slow down or stop in order to allow other traffic to go in front of you. EG *Give way to traffic coming from the right.*

PHR : VB INFLECTS, IF+ PREP THEN *to*

22 The word **give** is also used in the following expressions, which are explained at other places in this dictionary. ● to **give** someone **hell**: see **hell**. ● to **give notice**: see **notice**. ● to **give** someone **a ring**: see ring. • to **give rise to** something: see **rise**. • to **give vent**: see **vent**.

give away. 1 If you **give** something **away**, you give it to someone, either because you do not want it or because you want to give them a present. EG *She has given away jewellery worth millions of pounds... I could not decide whether to keep the money he left me or give it away.* PHRASAL VB : V+O+ADV ≠ keep

2 If you **give away** information that should be kept secret, you make it known to other people, sometimes by mistake. EG *I didn't feel like giving away more information than I had to... The synopsis doesn't give the plot away.* PHRASAL VB : V+O+ADV ⇑ reveal = divulge • If you **give the game away**, you let people know something that should be kept secret. EG *What are the clues that give the game away?* • PHR : VB INFLECTS ⇑ reveal

3 When someone **gives** a woman **away**, they officially present a bride to her husband at the wedding ceremony. EG *She asked her uncle to give her away.* PHRASAL VB : V+O+ADV

give back. If you **give** something **back**, you return it to its owner or to the person who gave it to you. EG *If I didn't need the money, I would give it back again... It's mine. Give it back.* PHRASAL VB : V+O+ADV

give in. 1 If you **give in**, you admit that you are defeated or that you cannot do something or that you will have to do something you did not want to do. EG *We mustn't give in to threats... I resolved not to give in.* PHRASAL VB : V+ADV, IF+PREP THEN *to* = surrender, yield

2 If you **give** a book or paper **in**, you hand it to someone who has asked for it or who has authority over you, especially a teacher or an official. EG *...students giving in dissertations.* PHRASAL VB : V+O+ADV = hand in

give off. If something **gives off** a substance such as heat, light, smoke, etc, it produces it and sends it out into the air. EG *...the tremendous heat given off by the fire.* PHRASAL VB : V+O+ADV ⇑ produce

give onto. If a door or window **gives onto** a particular place, it has a view of that place, or it goes straight to that place. EG *The narrow Cockpit Steps give onto St. James's Park.* PHRASAL VB : V+PREP = front onto

give out. 1 If you **give out** a number of things, you distribute them to a number of different people. EG *Howard gave out drinks to his guests.* PHRASAL VB : V+O+ADV = hand out

2 If something **gives out**, 2.1 it stops working, usually because it is very old or because it has broken down. EG *The fuse within a plug will give out occasionally.* PHRASAL VB : V+ADV = conk out

2.2 it is completely finished or used up. EG *Turn all the taps on until the water gives out.* PHRASAL VB : V+ADV

3 If news or information is **given out**, it is made known to people. EG *It was given out that the Princess was expecting a baby.* PHRASAL VB : V+O+ADV OR V+O+ADV+REPORT-CL

give over. 1 If something is **given over** to a particular thing, it is set aside for a particular purpose or use. EG *...land given over to agriculture... The response was so great that a whole page had to be given over to readers' letters.* PHRASAL VB : V+O+ADV, USU PASS +*to* ⇑ assign

2 In informal English, if you **give over**, you stop doing something, especially something that is annoying other people. EG *If you don't give over, I'll smack you... She asked me to give over humming.* PHRASAL VB : V+ADV, OR V+ADV+-ING = leave off

3 If you **give** something **over** to someone, you hand it over to them for them to look after it or have responsibility for it. EG *I'm quite thankful to give the business over to the girls now.* PHRASAL VB : V+O+ADV, IF+PREP THEN *to* = relinquish

give up. 1 If you **give up** something, you stop doing it or believing in it. EG *It's unrealistic to give up smoking to save money now... I don't have any intention of giving up politics... She never completely gave up hope.* PHRASAL VB : ORDER V+ADV+O = renounce • If you **give** someone **up for dead**, you believe that they are dead EG HIS BROTHER HAD BEEN GIVEN UP FOR DEAD YEARS AGO. • PHR : VB INFLECTS • If you **give up** your **life**, you die, especially for a particular cause. EG *They were ready to give up their lives for their country.* • PHR : VB AND N INFLECT = die • to **give up the ghost**: see **ghost**. • to **give** something or someone **up as a bad job**: see **job**.

2 If you **give up**, you admit that you cannot solve a problem, puzzle, or joke. EG *I don't know. I give up. What is it?* PHRASAL VB : V+ADV = give in

3 If you **give up** your job, you resign from it. EG *She'd had to give up her job... She was required to give up her throne in the cause of love.* PHRASAL VB : V+O+ADV ⇑ leave = relinquish

4 If you **give up** an object, you allow someone else to have it; a fairly old-fashioned expression. EG *'Give up that book!' she hissed. 'Give it up.'* PHRASAL VB : V+O+ADV = hand over

5 If you **give** a person **up**, you let the police or other people know where that person is hiding. EG *They tortured her, but still she wouldn't give me up.* PHRASAL VB : V+O (NG/REFL)+ADV = betray

give up on. If you **give up on** something, you abandon all hope of doing it or of understanding it. EG *...a kind of mystery that one gives up on.* PHRASAL VB : V+ADV+PREP

give up to. If you **give** yourself or your life **up to** a particular thing, you devote all your time, thought, and energy to it. EG *She gave herself up to an inner vision of happiness... ...a life given up to sexual excess.* PHRASAL VB : V+O (NG/REFL)+ADV+PREP, USU PASS

give-and-take; also spelled without hyphens. **Give-and-take** is 1 a willingness by all the people involved in something to listen to other people's opinions and to compromise where necessary. EG *...a believer in the give-and-take of democracy... ...a free-and-easy, give-and-take relationship.* N UNCOUNT 2 a smoothly flowing exchange of ideas in a conversation, with everyone listening and joining in. EG *...the give and take of the vocal exchanges.* N UNCOUNT

give-away, give-aways; also spelled as one word. A **give-away** is 1 something that allows plans, secrets, or intentions to become known. EG *...'The face of the Seventies' exhibition–the title is the give-away... ...a give-away remark.* N SING WITH DET ⇑ disclosure 2 something that is given free, especially when you buy something else. EG *When I bought perfume yesterday, I got a lipstick as a give-away... ...giveaway Sunday colour magazines.* N COUNT ⇑ gift = freebie

given /gɪvə⁰n/. 1 **Given** is the past participle of **give**.

2 A **given** date or time is one that has been fixed or decided on previously. EG *At a given moment we all cheered.* ADJ CLASSIF : ATTRIB = specified

3 If you talk about **any given** society, **any given** time, etc, you mean the particular society, time, etc that you are discussing. EG *One cannot look at the problems of any given society in isolation from the rest of the world... A majority of the electorate at any given time is concerned with the preservation of the status quo... Often people don't know what's happening at any given moment.* PHR : USED AS MOD = any particular

4 In formal English, **given** the chance, **given** the opportunity, etc means if you have the chance, the opportunity, etc. EG *My husband was a hard worker given the opportunity... She could have done just as well as you have, given the chance... Remember that on radio, given imagination, anything is possible.* PREP

5 If you say **given** a particular thing, or **given that** something is true, you mean if what is mentioned is taken into account. EG *This was the best place to study, given my interest in Kent, Hegel, and Marx... It seems churlish to send him away, given that he wanted to get photographs of Aboriginals at work.* PREP, OR CONJ SUBORD = considering

6 If you are **given** to something, you have a particular habit or tendency. EG *He was given to claiming that he was related to the Queen... ...a family given to bouts of melancholia.* ADJ CLASSIF : PRED+*to* = prone

given name, given names. A **given name** is a person's first name, which they are given at birth in addition to their surname; used especially in American English. N COUNT = Christian name

give or take. If you say **give or take** a few, **give or take** ten, etc, after you have mentioned a particular quantity or amount, you are indicating that the amount you are mentioning is not completely accurate. EG *It's three hundred miles to Edinburgh, give or take ten... The results turned out to be exactly the same, give or take one percent.* PHR+NG = plus or minus

glacé /glæseɪ/. **Glacé** fruits are ones that have been preserved in a thick sugary syrup and then dried. EG *...glacé cherries.* ADJ CLASSIF : ATTRIB ⇑ sugared

glacial /gleɪsjə⁰l/. 1 **Glacial** means relating to glaciers or ice. EG *...a glacial landscape.* ADJ CLASSIF : USU ATTRIB

2 If you describe a person as **glacial**, you mean that they are unfriendly and hostile towards you. EG *She is self-sufficient, composed, and also slightly glacial.* ADJ QUALIT = icy, cold ▸ used of a person's behaviour. EG *...glacial stares.* ▸ = icy

glacier /glæsjə/, **glaciers**. A **glacier** is a huge mass of ice which moves very slowly, often down a mountain valley. N COUNT

glad /glæd/, **gladder, gladdest**. 1 If you are **glad** about something, you are happy and pleased about it. EG *I'm so glad that your niece was able to use the tickets... Ralph was glad of a chance to change the subject.* ADJ QUALIT : PRED, USU+PREP/*to*-INF/THAT-CL = delighted ◇ **gladly**. EG *He gladly accepted their invitation to dinner.* ◇ ADV WITH VB ◇ **gladness**. EG *His heart was filled with joy and gladness.* ◇ N UNCOUNT = happiness

2 If you say that you are **glad** to do something, you mean that you are willing and eager to do it. EG *There are several people coming up to retirement* ADJ QUALIT : PRED+*to*-INF = happy, keen

who would be very glad to work half time... Lexington was only too glad to oblige. ◊ **gladly**. EG *To set you free I would gladly admit to the murder myself.* ◊ ADV WITH VB = willingly

gladden /glædən/, **gladdens, gladdening, gladdened**. If something **gladdens** you, it makes you feel very happy and pleased. EG *He went to tell her how much he had missed her and how it gladdened him to be home... The sight of it would have gladdened Philip Swallow's heart.* V+O ⇑ please = cheer

glade /gleɪd/, **glades**. A **glade** is a grassy space without trees in a wood or forest. EG *...a forest glade.* N COUNT = clearing

gladiator /glædi[1]eɪtə/, **gladiators**. A **gladiator** was a man who, in the time of the Roman Empire, used to have to fight against other men or wild animals in order to entertain an audience. N COUNT ⇑ fighter

glad-rags. Your **glad-rags** are smart clothes which you wear for special occasions such as parties. EG *Go and put your glad rags on!* N PLURAL

glamor /glæmə/. See **glamour**.

glamorize /glæməraɪz/, **glamorizes, glamorizing, glamorized**; also spelled **glamorise**. If you **glamorize** something, you make it look or seem more attractive than it really is. EG *The truth is sometimes glamorised.* V+O ⇑ improve = dress up

glamorous /glæmərəs/. Someone or something that is **glamorous** has glamour. EG *...a photograph of a glamorous model... ...glamorous parts of the world.* ADJ QUALIT ⇑ attractive

glamour /glæmə/ is the charm and excitement that seems to surround an interesting, fashionable, and attractive person, place, or job. EG *Acapulco has lost much of its glamour... ...the superficial glamour of television.* N UNCOUNT ⇑ attractiveness = glitter

glance /glɑːns/, **glances, glancing, glanced**. **1** If you **glance** at something, you look at it very quickly and then look away again immediately. EG *Jacqueline glanced at her watch... I kept glancing in the rear-view mirror to see if we were being followed... Rudolph glanced around to make sure nobody was watching.* V+A

2 If you **glance** through or at a newspaper, report, or book, you spend a short time looking at it without reading it very carefully. EG *During breakfast he reads his letters and glances through the morning paper.* V+A (through/at) ⇑ read = flick

3 A **glance** is a quick look at something. EG *He cast a quick glance at his old friend... The women exchanged glances... He signed the letters with only a cursory glance at what I had written.* N COUNT : IF+PREP USU *at*

4 If you see, tell, recognize, etc, something **at a glance**, you see or notice it immediately, and without having to think or look carefully. EG *He could tell at a glance that she was upset... She recognized at a glance the implication of his statement.* PHR : USED AS AN A ⇑ immediately = at once

5 If you say that something was true or seemed to be true **at first glance**, you mean that it seemed to be true when you first saw it or thought about it, but that your first impression was probably wrong. EG *They looked the same at first glance but in fact they were different.* PHR : USED AS AN A ⇑ initially = at first

5 If the sun **glances** on something shiny or wet, it shines on it and makes it sparkle; a literary word. EG *The sun outside the windows glanced on the knives and forks.* V : USU+A ⇑ shine = glint

glance off. If something **glances off** another object, it hits it at an angle and bounces away in another direction. EG *The ball glanced off his foot into the net.* PHRASAL VB : V+ADV/PREP, HAS PASS IF PREP ⇑ bounce off

glancing /glɑːnsɪŋ/. A **glancing** blow is one that hits something at an angle rather than from directly in front. EG *The glass hit him a glancing blow on the forehead.* ADJ CLASSIF : ATTRIB ⇑ slanting

gland /glænd/, **glands**. A **gland** is an organ in the body which makes chemical substances for the body to use, or that allows substances to be passed out of the body. EG *...the thyroid gland... ...sweat glands.* N COUNT : USU MOD+N

glandular /glændjə[4]lə/. Something that is **glandular** relates to or affects your glands. EG *...glandular fever.* ADJ CLASSIF : USU ATTRIB

glare /gleə/, **glares, glaring, glared**. **1** If you **glare** at someone or something, you look at them with a hard or angry expression on your face. EG *They stopped arguing and glared at each other... He just stood there, glaring and breathing heavily.* ◊ **glaring**. EG *...glaring defiant eyes.* V : IF+PREP THEN *at* = glower ◊ ADJ QUALIT

2 A **glare** is an angry, hard and unfriendly look or expression on someone's face. EG *He shot a suspicious glare at me... ...a glare of hostility.* N COUNT : USU+SUPP ⇑ stare

3 Glare is very bright light that is difficult to look at. EG *The windows were heavily tinted to reduce the glare... ...the glare of the sun.* N UNCOUNT : USU +SUPP

4 If the sun or a light **glares**, it shines with a very bright light which is difficult to look at. EG *...the low sun that glared over the hill... A harsh thin light glared through the windows.* ◊ **glaring**. EG *...the glaring sun.* V : USU+A ⇑ shine = blaze ◊ ADJ QUALIT : ATTRIB

5 If someone is in the **glare** of publicity, public attention, etc, they are constantly being watched and talked about by a lot of people. EG *At home he can relax once he's away from the glare of publicity.* N SING : *the*+N = spotlight

glaring /gleərɪŋ/. **1** If you refer to something as **glaring**, you mean that it is very obvious and easily seen or noticed; used showing disapproval. EG *...glaring inequalities of wealth... ...the glaring weakness of all those arguments.* ◊ **glaringly**. EG *It had become glaringly obvious that he had no idea what he was doing.* ADJ QUALIT : USU ATTRIB ⇑ clear = conspicuous ◊ ADV : USU+ADJ = patently

2 Other meanings of **glaring** can be found at the entry for **glare**.

glass /glɑːs/, **glasses**. **1 Glass** is a hard transparent substance that is easily broken. It is used to make windows, bottles, bowls, etc. EG *He sweeps away the broken glass under the window... They crept up to the glass doors and peeped inside.* N UNCOUNT

2 A **glass** is a container made from glass, which you can drink from and which does not have a handle. EG *I put down my glass and stood up.* ▸ **Glass** is also used to refer to the drink inside it or the amount of drink it contains. EG *We'll just have one glass and go away... He poured Ellen a glass of wine, then filled his own.* N COUNT ▸ N COUNT : ALSO N+*of*+N UNCOUNT ⇑ amount

3 Glass is also used to mean objects made of glass, for example drinking containers and bowls. EG *...a house crammed with beautiful furniture, glass and china.* N UNCOUNT = glassware

4 Glasses are **4.1** two transparent lenses in a metal or plastic frame, that someone with bad eyesight wears in front of their eyes in order to help them see better. EG *He wore thick glasses... ...a rather serious girl with glasses and long hair.* **4.2** binoculars. EG *When he lowered the glasses, he could barely see the boat.* N PLURAL : ALSO *a pair of*+N = spectacles; N PLURAL

5 A **glass** is also **5.1** a mirror; a rather old-fashioned use. EG *The man down the bar caught his eye in the glass and smiled.* **5.2** a barometer. EG *The glass is rising.* N COUNT; N SING WITH DET

6 See also **dark glasses, magnifying glass.**

glass fibre is a cloth made from short thin threads of glass. It is used to keep heat in or to strengthen plastic. N UNCOUNT = fibreglass

glasshouse /glɑːshaʊs/, **glasshouses**. A **glasshouse** is a large greenhouse. EG *...a tropical plant in a glasshouse.* N COUNT ⇑ building

glassware /glɑːsweə/ is objects made of glass, for example bowls, drinking containers, and ornaments. N UNCOUNT = glass

glassy /glɑːsi[1]/. **1** Something that is **glassy** is very smooth and shiny, like glass. EG *...smooth, glassy water.* ADJ CLASSIF ⇑ shining

2 If you describe someone's eyes or the look in their eyes as **glassy**, you mean that they show no feeling, emotion, or understanding in their expression. EG *...a glassy stare... He gazed at the street with dull, glassy eyes.* ADJ QUALIT = blank

glaucoma /glɔːkəʊmə/ is an eye disease which sometimes causes a person to go gradually blind. N UNCOUNT

glaze /gleɪz/, **glazes, glazing, glazed**. **1** If you **glaze** a piece of pottery, you cover it with a thin layer of a special liquid and then put it in a very hot oven so that its surface becomes shiny and nonporous. ◊ **glazed**. EG *...glazed clay pots.* V+O ⇑ coat ◊ ADJ CLASSIF

2 When you **glaze** food such as bread or pastry, you spread a layer of beaten egg, milk, or other liquid onto it before you cook it in order to make its surface shine and look attractive. EG *She glazed the pie with egg and a sprinkling of sugar.* V+O : IF+PREP THEN *with* ⇑ coat = brush

3 A **glaze** is **3.1** a thin layer of liquid that is put on a piece of pottery and that is dried in a very hot oven so that it becomes hard and shiny. EG *There are hundreds of different glazes.* **3.2** a thin layer of beaten egg, milk, or other liquid that you spread onto food in order to make the surface shine and look attractive. EG *Use milk or egg as a glaze for pastry.* N COUNT ⇑ coating; N COUNT ⇑ coating

4 If you **glaze** a window, you fit a sheet of glass into a window frame. V+O

glaze over. If someone's eyes **glaze over**, they PHRASAL VB : V+

become dull in appearance, usually because the person is no longer interested in what they are looking at or being told. EG *I can see people's eyes start to glaze over at the mention of Chomsky.* ADV = go blank

glazed /gleɪzd/. If you describe someone's eyes or the look in their eyes as **glazed**, you mean that their expression is dull or dreamy, especially when they are tired or have difficulty concentrating on something. EG *His eyes took on a slightly glazed, distant look.* ADJ QUALIT = glassy ≠ alert

GLC is an abbreviation for Greater London Council; an organization which, until 1986, was responsible for local government in the London area. N PROPER : *the*+N ⇑ council

gleam /gliːm/, **gleams, gleaming, gleamed.** 1 If an object or a surface **gleams**, it reflects light because it is shiny and clean. EG *He polished the gold until it gleamed... The polished red cello gleamed in the dim light.* ◊ **gleaming.** EG *...the gleaming brass on the altar.* V ⇑ shine = glisten; ◊ ADJ CLASSIF = glistening

2 If a light or the sun or moon **gleams**, it shines faintly; a fairly literary use. EG *The many lighthouses of the islands gleam and wink above the surf.* V = glimmer

2 A **gleam** is 2.1 a pale, clear light. EG *There were no lights on outside but there was a gleam from a window downstairs.* N COUNT : IF+PREP THEN *of* 2.2 the way that something reflects light or shines in light. EG *...a gleam of water... ...a gleam of white silk.* N COUNT : USU SING 2.3 a quick expression that you see briefly on someone's face. EG *A gleam of triumph crossed the older woman's face... ...a gleam of pride... ...a malicious gleam in his eye.* N COUNT : USU SING, IF+PREP THEN *of* = flicker

3 If your face or eyes **gleam**, they show a particular expression. EG *Her face gleamed with one of her rare, soft smiles... His eyes gleamed with pleasure.* V : IF+PREP THEN *with* = shine

glean /gliːn/, **gleans, gleaning, gleaned.** 1 If you **glean** information about something, you find it out slowly and with difficulty. EG *Much of the information he gleaned was of no practical use.* V+O : IF+PREP THEN *from* ⇑ discover = cull

2 If you **glean** grain or **glean** a field, you collect the small amounts of grain that are left behind on a field after the crop has been harvested. EG *...bowls of mixed wheat and oats which she had helped to glean nearly a year ago.* V OR V+O

glee /gliː/ is a feeling of joy and excitement, often caused by someone else's foolishness or failure; sometimes used showing disapproval. EG *...the glee with which the media report scientific calamities... He smiles with a hint of glee.* N UNCOUNT ⇑ pleasure = delight

gleeful /gliːful/. Someone who is **gleeful** is full of joy and excitement, often because of someone else's foolishness or failure. EG *'Perhaps we're lost,' cried Liz, gleeful at the thought.* ◊ **gleefully** . EG *He gleefully rubbed his hands.* ADJ QUALIT ⇑ pleased = exultant; ◊ ADV WITH VB = exultantly

glen /glen/, **glens.** A **glen** is a deep, narrow valley, especially in the mountains of Scotland or Ireland. N COUNT : ALSO IN NAMES

glib /glɪb/, **glibber, glibbest.** Someone who is **glib** talks too quickly and confidently, often making difficult situations sound easy, so that you feel that you cannot trust them; used showing disapproval. EG *MPs are a bit glib, assuming that they can cure all... He was bitter and glib.* ▸ used of people's ideas or what they say. EG *MacIver was always ready with glib promises.* ◊ **glibly.** EG *'Oh well, that's life,' she said glibly.* ADJ QUALIT ⇑ quick; ▸ = slick; ◊ ADV WITH VB = easily

glide /glaɪd/, **glides, gliding, glided.** 1 If you **glide**, you move silently and in a smooth and effortless way. EG *The snake glides smoothly towards its prey... The canoes glided by... Tim glided to the door and down the stairs.* ▸ used as a noun. EG *...a fast glide.* V : USU+A = slip, slide; ▸ N COUNT ⇑ movement

2 When birds or aeroplanes **glide**, they float on air currents. EG *...an owl gliding silently over the fields.* V : USU+A ⇑ fly

glider /glaɪdə/, **gliders.** A **glider** is an aircraft that does not have an engine but flies by floating on air currents. N COUNT

gliding /glaɪdɪŋ/ is the sport or activity of flying in a glider. N UNCOUNT

glimmer /glɪmə/, **glimmers, glimmering, glimmered.** 1 A **glimmer** is a faint, gentle, often unsteady light. EG *The faint, far-off glimmer of the dawn... ...glimmers of light.* N COUNT : IF+PREP THEN *of* = flicker

2 If you see a **glimmer** of interest or emotion in someone or something, you see a faint sign of it in them. EG *He showed no glimmer of interest in them... ...without a glimmer of a smile.* N COUNT+SUPP : USU+*of* = trace

3 To **glimmer** means to produce or reflect a faint, gentle, often unsteady light. EG *The pearl glimmered faintly as she moved... Dawn glimmered through the blinds.* ◊ **glimmering.** EG *...the glimmering night sky.* V ⇑ shine; ◊ ADJ CLASSIF

glimmering /glɪməᵒrɪŋ/, **glimmerings.** A **glimmering** of an idea or emotion is a faint sign of it. EG *...a glimmering of forethought... ...the first glimmerings of hope.* N COUNT+SUPP = glimmer

glimpse /glɪmpᵒs/, **glimpses, glimpsing, glimpsed.** 1 A **glimpse** of something or someone is 1.1 a very brief sight of them, in which you do not see them very well. EG *...the first glimpse I caught of Fanny... ...the fleeting glimpse of a figure hurrying by... ...a glimpse of the morning paper.* N COUNT : IF+PREP THEN *of* ⇑ look 1.2 a brief experience of them or an idea about them that helps you understand or appreciate them better. EG *...glimpses of his kindness... ...glimpses of the future... ...a glimpse into his youth.* N COUNT : IF+PREP THEN *of* = flash

2 If you **glimpse** something, you see it very briefly and not very well. EG *...a village they had glimpsed through the trees... She glimpsed him out of the corner of her eyes.* V+O = catch sight of

3 If you **glimpse** an idea or thought, you briefly experience it or learn something about it so that you understand or appreciate it better. EG *She glimpses something of what life ought to be about... I glimpsed a bleak future.* V+O = perceive

glint /glɪnt/, **glints, glinting, glinted.** 1 If something **glints**, it produces or reflects a quick flash of light. EG *His spectacles glinted in the sunlight... The sun glinted on the walls... His pen glinted as it fell.* ◊ **glinting.** EG *...the glinting water.* V ⇑ shine = glisten; ◊ ADJ CLASSIF

2 If someone's eyes **glint**, they shine and express a particular emotion. EG *Her small green eyes glinted with mockery... His eyes were glinting at her, and a slow smile crossed his face.* = twinkle

3 A **glint** is a quick flash of light. EG *...a few glints of weak, yellow light... ...the glint of water.* N COUNT = gleam

4 A **glint** in someone's eyes is a brightness that expresses a particular emotion. EG *There was no glint of humour in the man's eyes... ...a glint of aggression.* N COUNT ⇑ look = gleam

glisten /glɪsəᵒn/, **glistens, glistening, glistened.** 1 If something **glistens** , it shines or sparkles, usually because it is smooth, wet, or oily. EG *His face glistened with sweat... ...golden sovereigns glistening in the sunlight.* ◊ **glistening.** EG *...glistening lips.* V = gleam; ◊ ADJ CLASSIF : ATTRIB = glossy

2 If someone's eyes **glisten**, they are bright and express a particular emotion. EG *His eyes glisten with contempt.* V = glitter

glitter /glɪtə/, **glitters, glittering, glittered.** 1 If something **glitters**, it shines in a sparkling way, for example when light is reflected off many small pieces of metal. EG *Her jewellery glittered under the spotlight... Stars glittered in a clear sky.* ◊ **glittering.** EG *...glittering Christmas trees.* ● If you say **all that glitters is not gold**, you are warning someone that something which seems attractive or exciting at first may not be as good as they think. V = sparkle, twinkle; ◊ ADJ CLASSIF; ● PHR

2 If someone's eyes **glitter**, they are bright and express a particular emotion. EG *Her eyes glittered as she described these wonders.* ◊ **glittering.** EG *...his glittering eyes wide with alarm.* V = glint; ◊ ADJ QUALIT : ATTRIB = glassy

3 If someone or something **glitters**, they impress you by their appearance, success, or behaviour; a literary use. EG *Mrs Todd glittered at the elegant table.* ◊ **glittering.** EG *...a glittering career... The glittering prize was a holiday in Hawaii.* V = shine; ◊ ADJ QUALIT : ATTRIB

4 **Glitter** is 4.1 a sparkling light, usually one that is reflected. EG *...the glitter of the sea... ...the glitter of coins.* N UNCOUNT = glint 4.2 superficial attractiveness, but actually being of poor quality or of little real use or value. EG *...cheapness and glitter... ...the glitter of consumer gadgetry.* N UNCOUNT = tinsel 4.3 the excitement and glamour that a situation or lifestyle has. EG *...the glitter of the election... ...his life of bluster, glitter and power.* N UNCOUNT 4.4 the brightness in someone's eyes that shows a particular emotion. EG *...the dangerous glitter in her eyes.* N SING : USU *the*+N = glint

glittery /glɪtəᵒriᶦ/. Something that is **glittery** shines with a sparkling light. EG *...glittery jewellery.* ADJ QUALIT

gloaming /gləʊmɪŋ/. The **gloaming** is the dull light in the evening when it is beginning to get dark; a Scots or literary word. EG *Dusk is falling and you are roaming in the gloaming.* N SING : *the*+N = twilight

gloat /gləʊt/, **gloats, gloating, gloated.** If you **gloat**, you show great pleasure at your own success or at other people's failure in an arrogant or uncar- V : IF+PREP THEN *over* ⇑ delight

ing way; used showing disapproval. EG *They were gloating over my bankruptcy... He hadn't come there to gloat.* ◊ **gloating**. EG *...gloating self-satisfaction.*
◊ ADJ CLASSIF

glob /glɒb/, **globs**. A **glob** is, in very informal English, a small amount of something soft or liquid that has a rounded shape. EG *...a glob of milk... ...globs of foam.*
N PART : USU+N UNCOUNT = blob

global /gləʊbə^{ə}l/ means 1 concerning or including the whole world. EG *...the global energy output... ...protests on a global scale.* ◊ **globally**. EG *...half the wheat sold globally.* 2 involving or relating to all the parts or aspects of a situation. EG *These marks give a global picture of their progress... ...a global judgment.* ◊ **globally**. EG *...globally accepted ideas of beauty.*
ADJ CLASSIF : USU ATTRIB; ◊ ADV WITH VB; ADJ CLASSIF : USU ATTRIB = overall; ◊ ADV

globe /gləʊb/, **globes**. 1 The **globe** is used to refer to the Earth, especially when you are emphasizing how big it is or that something is true in many different parts of it. EG *...television pictures seen all over the globe... ...countries on the far side of the globe.*
N SING : the+N = world

2 A **globe is 2.1** a spherical model of the Earth that is usually fixed on a stand and has a map of the world drawn on it. EG *...maps, charts, and globes.* **2.2** any object that is round in shape like a ball. EG *...a series of globes, one inside another... ...the orange globe of the sun.*
N COUNT; N COUNT : USU+SUPP ⇑ sphere

globetrotter /gləʊbtrɒtə/, **globetrotters**. If you refer to someone as a **globetrotter**, you mean that they spend a lot of time visiting places all over the world.
N COUNT

globular /glɒbjə^{1}lə/. Something that is **globular** is round in shape like a ball; a formal word. EG *...a globular helmet... ...the globular front part of the tadpole.*
ADJ CLASSIF : USU ATTRIB = spherical

globule /glɒbjuːl/, **globules**. A **globule** is a tiny round particle of a substance, usually a liquid; a formal word. EG *...a globule of blood... ...tiny globules of gold.*
N PART+N UNCOUNT = droplet

gloom /gluːm/. 1 **Gloom** is a state of partial darkness in which there is still a little light. EG *He peered through the gloom at the dim figure... ...the gloom of their cell.*
N SING : the+N = obscurity

2 **Gloom** is also a feeling of unhappiness or despair. EG *He viewed the future with gloom... Valentina was plunged into deep gloom.* ▸ used of a place or its atmosphere that causes this feeling. EG *...the pervading gloom of the place.*
N UNCOUNT ⇑ sadness; ▸ = desolation

gloomy /gluːmi^{1}/, **gloomier, gloomiest**. 1 If a place is **gloomy**, it is almost dark so that you cannot see very well. EG *...the gloomy mud-walled prison... ...the hallways were mysterious and gloomy.*
ADJ QUALIT = shadowy ≠ light

2 If the weather is **gloomy**, the sky is covered by clouds and the light is very dull. EG *We drove under a gloomy sky, up a winding road... The day was gloomy.*
ADJ QUALIT = overcast

3 If people are **gloomy**, they are unhappy and have no hope. EG *He looked gloomy again... The fishing industry is gloomy about the E.E.C.* ▸ used of people's behaviour. EG *There was a gloomy silence.* ◊ **gloomily**. EG *'Trouble,' Rudolph said gloomily.*
ADJ QUALIT = despondent; ▸ = dismal; ◊ ADV WITH VB

4 If a situation is **gloomy**, it does not give you much hope of success or happiness. EG *He could only see the gloomy possibilities of modern science.*
ADJ QUALIT = dispiriting ≠ promising

glorified /glɔːrɪfaɪd/ means very ordinary in reality, but having a name or title that suggests something of higher quality or greater importance; used showing disapproval. EG *The 'yacht' was a glorified sailing boat.*
ADJ CLASSIF : ATTRIB = jumped-up

glorify /glɔːrɪfaɪ/, **glorifies, glorifying, glorified**. 1 If you **glorify** someone or something, you praise them or make them seem important. EG *His newspapers glorified his charitable donations... A group that glorified the values of law, order, and tradition.* ◊ **glorification** /glɔːrɪfɪkeɪʃə^{ə}n/. EG *...denouncing the glorification of war.*
V+O, OR V+O+A (as) = extol, eulogize; ◊ N SING WITH DET+of

2 If you **glorify** God, you express his greatness by speech or action, for example by singing hymns of praise.
V+O ⇑ worship

glorious /glɔːrɪəs/. 1 Something that is **glorious 1.1** is very beautiful and impressive in appearance and often very colourful or large. EG *...the most glorious flowers ever seen... ...villages in the glorious valleys... What a glorious colour!* ◊ **gloriously**. EG *...gloriously embroidered pictures.* **1.2** makes you feel very happy. EG *...a glorious carefree feeling of joy... We have glorious memories of that holiday.* ◊ **gloriously**. EG *...arriving gloriously dirty and tired.* **1.3** involves great fame or success. EG *...a great and glorious Empire... ...the glorious future opening before them.* ◊ **gloriously**. EG *The soldiers had failed where he had gloriously succeeded.*
ADJ QUALIT ⇑ splendid = magnificent; ◊ ADV; ADJ QUALIT ⇑ wonderful = heavenly; ADJ QUALIT = illustrious; ◊ ADV

2 If you describe the weather as **glorious**, you mean it is hot and sunny. EG *We had glorious sunshine... The weather was glorious.* ◊ **gloriously**. EG *The first few days were gloriously hot.*
ADJ QUALIT = gorgeous; ◊ ADV = marvellously

glory /glɔːri^{1}/, **glories, glorying, gloried**. 1 **Glory** is **1.1** the fame and admiration that you gain by doing something. EG *The warriors valued glory and honour above life itself... I did it for the theatre, not for my own personal glory.* **1.2** the greatness of God.
N UNCOUNT ⇑ approval = prestige; N UNCOUNT

2 If you talk about the **glory** of something, you are referring to **2.1** its great beauty or impressiveness.. EG *The glory had gone from the afternoon... ...the glory of the play.* **2.2** the most beautiful or impressive part or feature of it. EG *The great glory of the castle is the ballroom ceiling.*
N UNCOUNT+SUPP; N UNCOUNT+SUPP = marvel

3 The **glories** of a person, country, etc are **3.1** the occasions on which they have done something famous or admirable. EG *...a shrine to the glories of the French Army... He became sentimental and talked about past glories.* **3.2** the things that people find most attractive about them. EG *...the glories of Venice... ...the glories of French language and literature.*
N PLURAL+SUPP = triumphs; N PLURAL : WITH POSS = splendours

4 If you say that someone is **bathing in reflected glory**, you mean that they are gaining fame or admiration not because of any personal achievement, but because of the success of someone or something that they are connected with. EG *Barnes bathed in the reflected glory of Rolls Royce's triumph.*
PHR : VB INFLECTS

5 If you say that something is done **to the greater glory of** someone or something, you mean that it is done in order to praise them or to increase their fame. EG *...to the greater glory of the Fatherland... The Cathedral would be rebuilt, to the greater glory of God.*
PHR : USED AS AN A ⇑ honouring

glory in. If you **glory in** something, you very much enjoy doing it or being in a particular situation. EG *The women were glorying in this new-found freedom.*
PHRASAL VB : V+PREP, HAS PASS = revel in

gloss /glɒs/, **glosses, glossing, glossed**. 1 A **gloss** is **1.1** a bright shine on the surface of something such as furniture. EG *The wood has a high gloss... ...the harsh gloss of the royal-blue hat.* **1.2** an appearance of attractiveness or good quality which sometimes hides less attractive features or poor quality. EG *...the gloss and glitter of consumer gadgetry... Crowe had added gloss, pace, and colour to Bill's play.* **1.3** the ability to behave in an acceptable and polite way in society. EG *...that middle-class gloss... The social gloss that Sloane lacked.*
N SING WITH DET = sheen; N UNCOUNT = polish; N SING WITH DET +SUPP = polish

2 If you **gloss** a difficult word or someone's ideas, you provide an explanation of them. EG *...lower middle-class backgrounds (Howard will gloss this for you).* ▸ used as a noun. EG *Carmody's gloss of nineteenth-century thought.*
V+O = elucidate; ▸ N COUNT = elucidation

3 **Gloss** is gloss paint.
N UNCOUNT

gloss over. If you **gloss over** a problem, a mistake, or an embarrassing moment, you try and make it seem unimportant by ignoring it or by dealing with it very quickly. EG *'I was leaving anyway,' I said, to gloss over the tense moment... Truffaut glosses over such contradictions.*
PHRASAL VB : ORDER V+ADV+O ⇑ hide = smooth over

glossary /glɒsə^{ə}ri^{1}/, **glossaries**. A **glossary** is an alphabetical list of words or expressions and the special or technical meanings that they have in a particular book, subject, or activity. EG *Glossaries were provided in French and Spanish... ...a Dictionary and Glossary of the Koran.*
N COUNT

gloss paint is paint that forms a shiny surface when it dries.
N UNCOUNT

glossy /glɒsi^{1}/. 1 Something that is **glossy** is **1.1** smooth and shiny. EG *She had glossy brown hair... ...glossy black railings.* **1.2** attractive in appearance but of poor quality or little real use or value; used showing disapproval. EG *...glossy but unsatisfying substitutes for what he really wanted.* ◊ **glossily**. EG *...a glossily packaged product.*
ADJ QUALIT = lustrous; ADJ QUALIT = slick, glittering; ◊ ADV

2 **Glossy** is used to describe books, magazines, and photographs that are produced on expensive, shiny paper, usually in colour. EG *...a glossy booklet... ...a glossy snapshot... ...the glossy pages of Cosmopolitan.*
ADJ QUALIT : ATTRIB

glossy magazine, glossy magazines. A **glossy magazine** is a magazine printed on expensive, shiny paper with colour photographs, usually of fashionable clothes, famous people, expensive houses, etc. EG *...the fashion models you see in glossy magazines... The glossy magazines carried detailed pictures of the Royal Wedding.* N COUNT

glove /glʌv/, **gloves.** 1 A **glove** is a piece of clothing which covers your hand and wrist and has individual sections for each finger. You usually wear gloves to keep your hands warm or dry or to protect them. EG *He pulled his gloves on... Wear rubber gloves or you may scald yourself.* N COUNT: USU PL ● If something **fits like a glove** , it fits exactly. EG *I tried it. The enormous thing fitted like a glove.* ● PHR : VB INFLECTS
2 See also **boxing glove.** ● **hand in glove**: see **hand.**

glove compartment, glove compartments; also spelled with a hyphen. A **glove compartment** is a small cupboard or shelf inside a car below the front windscreen. EG *...a screwdriver in the glove compartment.* N COUNT

gloved /glʌvd/ is used to describe a person's hand when they are wearing a glove. EG *He gripped it with his gloved hands... She bent her gloved fingers over it.* ADJ CLASSIF ⇑ clothed

glow /gləʊ/, **glows, glowing, glowed.** 1 A **glow** is 1.1 a dull, steady light, for example the light produced by a fire when there are no flames. EG *...the glow increased and the branch took fire... ...the blue glow of a police station light... ...the delicate pink glow along the horizon.* N COUNT : USU SING = gleam 1.2 a red colour on a person's face when they are excited about something, or after physical exercise. EG *The conversation brought a glow to her cheeks and a smile to her lips.* N SING WITH DET : USU *a*+N
1.3 a strong feeling of pleasure or satisfaction, often causing a person to have a bright, cheerful expression. EG *His glow of pleasure gave him away... He got a certain glow out of being helpful.* N SING WITH DET : USU+SUPP = thrill
2 If something **glows** 2.1 it produces a dull, steady light. EG *A cluster of stars glowed above us... The bedside lights were glowing beside her.* V ⇑ shine 2.2 it produces heat and a dull reddish light by burning slowly. EG *Only embers glowed in the fire... ...three cigarettes glowing in the dark.* ◇ **glowing.** EG *...glowing coals.* V, OR V+C (ADJ) = smoulder
2.3 it looks bright by relecting light, for example from the sun or a lamp. EG *...children's faces glowing in the light of the camp fire... Its windows glowed yellow and red.* ◇ **glowing.** EG *...the glowing kitchen.* V, OR V+C (ADJ) ⇑ shine
2.4 it is bright, attractive, and colourful or full of colourful things. EG *...the Church glowed with colourful African patterns and fabrics.* ◇ **glowing.** EG *...the glowing colour of its pink fruits.* V, OR V+C = be vibrant ◇ ADJ CLASSIF : ATTRIB
3 If someone **glows,** 3.1 their face looks red or hot because they are excited or have been doing physical exercise. EG *After her exertions, her face glowed with a healthy red sheen.* V : IF+PREP THEN *with* = shine 3.2 they have a bright, cheerful expression because of a pleasant emotion which they feel. EG *Her eyes glowed with a passionate fervour... Aunt Agnes glowed with joy.* V : IF+PREP THEN *with*
4 See also **glowing.**

glower /glaʊə/, **glowers, glowering, glowered.** If you **glower**, you look angrily at someone or something. EG *He glowered resentfully at Ash... She paused, glowering out across the playground.* V : USU+A = glare

glowing /gləʊɪŋ/. A **glowing** description or opinion is one that praises someone or something highly or supports them strongly. EG *...the book, of which I had read such glowing reports... ...an account of them in glowing terms... ...glowing tributes.* ● See also **glow.** ADJ QUALIT ⇑ favourable = rhapsodic

glow-worm, glow-worms; also spelled as one word. A **glow-worm** is a type of beetle. The females and young glow-worms have special organs on their bodies which produce a greenish light. N COUNT ⇑ insect

glucose /gluːkəʊz, -əʊs/is a type of sugar that exists in plants and which animals and people make in their bodies from the food they eat. Glucose provides your body with energy and can also be bought in the form of a powder or tablets. N UNCOUNT

glue /gluː/, **glues, glueing, gluing, glued.** The forms **glueing** and **gluing** are both used as the present participle of the verb. 1 **Glue** is a sticky substance used for joining things together, often for repairing broken things. EG *The hat seems to be stuck on with glue... ...mending things with glue.* N MASS = adhesive
2 If you **glue** one object to another, you stick them together using glue. EG *...gluing messages on to cards... A new piece was glued into place and repainted... Glue the bits together.* V+O+A ● If you say that something is **glued to** something else by a substance that is not glue, you mean that it is firmly fixed. EG *...a chop glued to the plate by a thick sauce... ...his hair glued to his head with hair cream.* ● ADJ CLASSIF : PRED+*to* ⇑ fixed to
3 If you say that someone is **glued to** something, you mean that they are giving it all their attention. EG *They were glued to their TV sets watching the latest news.* ADJ CLASSIF : PRED+*to* ⇑ attentive
4 If you say that someone's eyes are **glued** to something, you mean that they are watching it with all their attention. EG *Their eyes were glued to the scene below... ...keeping his eyes glued on the ball.* ADJ CLASSIF : PRED+*to/on*

glue sniffing is the dangerous practice of inhaling the vapour from glue in order to become intoxicated. N UNCOUNT

gluey /gluːi¹/. Something that is **gluey** is very sticky. EG *...gluey sweets.* ADJ QUALIT

glum /glʌm/, **glummer, glummest.** 1 Someone who is **glum** is sad and quiet, usually because they are disappointed or have lost hope in a particular situation. EG *Don't look so glum... She felt alone and glum... His glum face brightened.* ADJ QUALIT = forlorn ▸ used of people's behaviour. EG *...a glum conversation... ...a glum smile.* ▸ = doleful ◇ **glumly** . EG *'It's no use,' Eddie said glumly... He stared glumly at the window.* ◇ ADV WITH VB = gloomily
2 A place that is **glum** looks dull and unattractive and has a sad atmosphere. EG *...endless glum streets... ...a glum frontier village.* ADJ QUALIT = desolate

glut /glʌt/, **gluts, glutting, glutted.** 1 A **glut** is 1.1 a situation in which there is too much of something, especially goods or raw materials, so that not all of it can be sold or used. EG *The oil glut has forced price cuts... ...the glut in the French wine market.* N COUNT : IF+ PREP THEN *in/of* ⇑ excess = surplus 1.2 a large quantity of something that is more than you need or want. EG *...the enormous glut of detail.* N COUNT : IF+ PREP THEN *of* = torrent
2 If something **is glutted** with goods, raw materials, etc, it is provided with too great a quantity of them. EG *The market may be glutted.* V+O : IF+PREP THEN *with* = swamp, flood
3 If you **glut** yourself, you eat or drink more of something than you really need or want. EG *...watching them glut themselves on cakes... Glutted with bread, he returned.* V+O (REFL) : IF +PREP THEN *on/with* ⇑ fill = gorge

glutinous /gluːtɪnəs/. Something that is **glutinous** is very sticky. EG *...glutinous cakes... The leaves are fairly glutinous.. ...banks of glutinous mud.* ADJ QUALIT

glutton /glʌtə⁰n/, **gluttons.** 1 A **glutton** is someone who eats too much in a greedy way. EG *He is a glutton and a drinker... ...as quickly as a glutton swallows food.* N COUNT ⇑ person
2 If you say that someone is a **glutton** for something, you mean that they enjoy or need it very much. EG *The British must be gluttons for satire.* N COUNT+*for* ● If you say that someone is a **glutton for punishment** , you mean that they seem to enjoy working very hard or doing something that you think is unpleasant. ● PHR : *glutton*INFLECTS, USED AS C = masochist

gluttonous /glʌtə⁰nəs/. A **gluttonous** person is one who eats too much in a greedy way. EG *...over-fed women and their gluttonous husbands.* ADJ QUALIT ▸ used of people's behaviour. EG *...a gluttonous binge on meat.* ▸ = piggish ADV WITH VB

gluttony /glʌtə⁰ni¹/ is the act or habit of eating too much. N UNCOUNT

glycerine /glɪsə⁰ri¹n/; also spelled **glycerin** in American English. **Glycerine** is a thick, sweet, colourless liquid that is used especially in making medicine, explosives, and antifreeze for cars. N UNCOUNT

gm, gms. gm is is an abbreviation for 'gram'. EG *...250 gms of sugar.* N PART : USU NUM+N

GMT is abbreviation for 'Greenwich Mean Time': the standard time in Great Britain which is used to calculate the time in the rest of the world. EG *...at 10.20 hours GMT... ...departs Bermuda 12.42 GMT 17th Jan.* N UNCOUNT : NUMBER+N

gnarled /nɑːld/. 1 A tree or part of a tree that is **gnarled** is twisted and rough as a result of old age. EG *...the gnarled trunks of Scots pine... ...gnarled branches.* ADJ QUALIT
2 A person or a part of their body that is **gnarled** has rough skin that looks swollen and knotty, usually because of old age or from doing hard physical work. EG *...huge, gnarled peasant's hands... She was 75 years old, wrinkled and gnarled.* ADJ QUALIT ⇑ twisted

gnash /næʃ/, **gnashes, gnashing, gnashed.** If you **gnash** your teeth, you rub them together forcefully, usually because you are angry, frustrated, or in pain. EG *I lay gnashing my teeth in despair.* V+O, OR V = grind ◇ **gnashing.** EG *...amid much wailing and gnashing of teeth.* ◇ N UNCOUNT : USU+*of*

gnat /næt/, **gnats**. A **gnat** is a very small flying insect that bites people and usually lives near water. N COUNT = midge

gnaw /nɔː/, **gnaws, gnawing, gnawed**. 1 If people or animals **gnaw** something or **gnaw** at it, they bite it repeatedly. EG *...watching her puppy gnaw a bone... The rats had begun to gnaw at his body... Be careful that the baby doesn't gnaw the paint off furniture.* V+O, OR V: USU +A = chew

2 If animals **gnaw** through something or **gnaw** a hole in something means they keep biting it until it breaks or until a hole is made in it. EG *...gnawing tunnels in wood... The ant tried to gnaw through the thread.* V+A, OR V+O ⇑ bite = chew

If a feeling **gnaws** at you or **gnaws away** at you, it causes you to worry or suffer and is hard to get rid of; a literary word. EG *These desires gnaw away at us constantly... ...a sorrow and longing gnawing at him.* V+A *(at/away)* = nag

◇ **gnawing.** EG *...gnawing guilt... ...gnawing doubts about the future.* ◇ ADJ CLASSIF: ATTRIB

gnome /nəʊm/, **gnomes**. A **gnome** is 1 an imaginary creature in children's stories that is like a very small old man with a beard and pointed hat. Gnomes usually lives underground in these stories. N COUNT 2 a small statue in the shape of a gnome that some people put in their gardens for decoration. EG *...a garden gnome.* N COUNT

gnomic /nəʊmɪk/. Something that is **gnomic** seems to be very wise but is also slightly puzzling; a literary word. EG *...his calm and gnomic face... ...gnomic questions.* ADJ CLASSIF = enigmatic

GNP is an abbreviation for 'Gross National Product'; the total value of all the goods produced and services provided by a country in one year; a technical term in economics. EG *...22 per cent of GNP... ...a GNP per head of $11,000.* N UNCOUNT/COUNT

gnu /nuː/, **gnus**. A **gnu** is a large African antelope. N COUNT

go /gəʊ/, **goes, going, went, gone**. See also separate entries at **going** and **gone**. In most cases the past participle of **go** is 'gone', but occasionally you use 'been': see **been**. 1 In this paragraph, **go** usually expresses physical movement away from you or from the place where you are now. If you **go**, 1.1 you move from one place to another, often in order to do something. EG *I went to Stockholm... She went into the sitting-room... He went to get some fresh milk.* V: USU+A 1.2 you leave somewhere. EG *'I must go,' she said... Our train went at 2.25.* V ◇ **going**. EG *I felt sad at his going.* ◇ N UNCOUNT 1.3 you move in a particular direction, or move a particular distance. EG *A car went by... He went down another street... We've gone about thirty miles.* V+A ⇑ travel 1.4 you leave a place, especially your house, and take part in an activity. EG *Let's go fishing... She's going for a swim.* V+-ING/*for* ● In informal English, if you say that someone **goes** doing something, or if you advise them not to **go** doing something, you are expressing disapproval of the kind of behaviour that you mention. EG *Don't go hiding in the attic... ...the women he goes chasing after.* ● V+-ING

2 If you **go** and do a particular thing, you move from one place to another in order to do the thing, and you do it. EG *I'll go and see him in the morning.* V+*and*+VB: NO CONT ● In informal English, if you say that someone has **gone and** done something, you are expressing annoyance at something foolish that they have done. EG *That idiot Antonio has gone and locked our door.* ● PHR: VB INFLECTS+PAST PART

3 If you **go** to school, church, work, etc, you attend it regularly as part of your normal life. EG *She went to London University... ...whether people go to church or not... Having the crèche enables me to go to work.* V+A *(to)*

4 In this paragraph, **go** is usually followed by an adjective that describes the state or condition of a person or thing, or changes in that state or condition. 4.1 If someone **goes** naked, unarmed, etc, they choose to be in that particular state. EG *What would she think if people went naked?* V+C 4.2 If something **goes** unheard, unseen, etc, it remains in that particular state because people do not notice it or try to change it. EG *Halliday's absence had gone unnoticed... Her decision went unchallenged.* V+C ⇑ continue = remain 4.3 If someone or something **goes** crazy, bankrupt, grey, etc, they change to that particular state, condition, or colour. EG *The village thought we had gone crazy... They let firms go bankrupt... Her hair was going grey.* V+C = become

5 In this paragraph, **go** is usually followed by an adverb which indicates the manner in which something happens or operates, how it changes, or the degree of success it has. 5.1 If a price, number, or measurement **goes** up or down, it changes by becoming higher or lower. EG *The price of food will go up... The average age of farmers has gone down.* V+A ⇑ change 5.2 If you say that a period of time **goes** quickly, slowly, etc, you mean that it seems to pass in that manner. EG *The days went quickly.* V+A ● If workers **go slow**, they deliberately work slowly as a form of protest in order to cause problems for their employers; used in British English. ● See also **go-slow**. ● PHR: VB INFLECTS 5.3 If you say that an event or situation **went** well or badly, or if you ask how it **is going**, you are talking about the degree of success, ease, or difficulty with which it takes place, especially when it was planned beforehand. EG *Everything went pretty smoothly... How did school go?* V+A = work out ● You say **'the way things are going'** before you give your opinion of how a situation will end; an informal expression. EG *The way things are going, we'll be very late.* ● PHR: USED AS ADV SEN ● You can say **'How's it going?'** in informal English as a friendly greeting instead of 'How are you?'. ● CONVENTION 5.4 If you say that a machine or device **is going, is going well, is not going**, etc, you are saying whether it is working properly or not. EG *How is your car going?... The clock won't go.* V OR V+A = function 5.5 If you say that a particular kind of product **is going** well, badly, etc, you mean that you are selling a lot of them, very few of them, etc. EG *The briefcases are going well.* V+A = sell

6 **Go** is used with words such as 'far', 'further', 'beyond' and expressions such as 'some way', 'a long way', etc to indicate that people's actions, claims, or success are surprising, extreme, or that they reach or pass the level mentioned. See also **far, further, beyond** and **way**. 6.1 If you **go** so far as to do something, you do something surprising or extreme. EG *The directors went as far as to stage actual killings... How far should any of us go to get what we want?* V+A = venture 6.2 If you **go** beyond a particular kind of action, you do something more extreme. EG *They wanted to go beyond one-day strikes.* V+A *(beyond)* ⇑ pass 6.3 If an action or idea **goes** beyond something, it is better or more important than that thing. EG *She shows a precision that goes beyond mere cleverness.* V+A *(beyond)*: NO CONT ⇑ advance = reach 6.4 If you say you would **go** so far, further, etc, you are saying how much you agree with someone or support an idea. EG *I wouldn't go that far... I shall go further and say that Lo is a fool.* V+A = commit oneself 6.5 If you say that someone **will go far** or **will go a long way**, you mean that they will be very successful. PHR: AUX INFLECTS+VB 6.6 If you say that something **goes some way** or **goes a long way** towards doing something, you mean that it succeeds in achieving it partly or to a great extent. EG *That goes a long way towards explaining why people dislike the old rectory.* PHR: VB INFLECTS ⇑ help

7 You use **go** in informal English to introduce something you are quoting, imitating, or describing. 7.1 You say or write 'the story **goes**', 'as the saying **goes**', 'How does the proverb **go**?' etc just before you quote it or tell a part or a summary of it. EG *As the song goes: I fell in love with eyes of blue... Very roughly, her theory goes like this.* V+QUOTE/A *(like)* = run 7.2 You say 'the tune **goes**', 'the song **goes**', etc just before you hum, whistle, or sing it or a part of it. EG *It goes something like this.* V+QUOTE/A *(like)* = sound 7.3 You use **go** just before the words or letters that represent a noise that someone or something makes. EG *American sirens which instead of going 'Ow-wow' go 'Whoop-whoop'... It went 'splat' in the water.* V+QUOTE/REPORT-CL/A *(like)*

8 If a bell or alarm **goes**, it makes a noise, usually as a signal for you to do something. EG *When the alarm goes, he has to leave his work.* V = sound

9 If you say that money **goes** in, into, or on something, you mean that it is used for that particular purpose. EG *Most of the aid has gone into urban projects... 40% of his income goes on rent.* V+A *(in/into/on)*

10 If land, buildings, or money **go** to someone, it becomes their property, for example when the previous owner dies. EG *The ranch was going to the girls... Every penny should go to charity.* V+A *(to)* = be left

11 If you say that something **goes** to someone, you mean that it is given or should be given to them. EG *Some of the credit should go to the cameraman... The job is to go to a private contractor.* V+A *(to)*

12 In a lecture, discussion, or book, if you say that you are **going** to a particular point in it, you mean that you want to discuss that point. EG *Can we go to Question Six?... ...going back to your point.* V+A *(to)* = turn

13 If something **goes** with something else, or if two things **go** together, 13.1 they have a pleasing effect V+A *(together/*

when they are placed together. EG *I got the shoes to go with my coat... The colours go so very well together.* **13.2** they are, or are considered to be, the correct things to have together. EG *...the hat that went with the uniform... White wine goes with fish.*

with): RECIP, NO CONT, NO IMPER
V+A (together/with): RECIP, NO CONT
⇑ correspond

14 A **go** is an attempt at doing something. EG *He passed the test first go... Few authors write a book at one go.* • If you **have a go** at something, you try to do it; an informal expression. EG *I'll have a go at mending it... Go on–have a go.* • If you **have a go at** someone, you criticize or attack them, usually in speech or writing; an informal expression used in British English. EG *Flaherty wants to have a go at the British.*

N COUNT = whack
• PHR : VB INFLECTS
• PHR : VB INFLECTS = slate

15 If it is your **go** in a game, it is your turn to do something, for example to play a card or move a piece. EG *It's Pam's go.*

N COUNT : WITH POSS

16 You say **'Go'** quickly and loudly as a signal for people to begin running a race. EG *On your marks. Get set. Go!* • If you say that something happened **from the word go**, you mean that it happened from the very beginning of a situation. EG *She complained from the word go.*

V : ONLY IMPER
• PHR : USED AS AN A

17 If you say that someone is **making a go** of something, you mean that they are being successful, usually in a business or a relationship; an informal expression.

PHR : VB INFLECTS + *of*
⇑ succeed

18 has to go, has got to go. 18.1 If you say that someone **has to go** or **has got to go**, you mean that they must be forced to leave a place or job. EG *The last to be hired had to be the first to go.* **18.2** If you say that something **has to go** or **has got to go**, you mean that you must sell it, get rid of it, or stop using it. EG *It lost three million dollars last year and it has to go.*

PHR : FIRST VB INFLECTS
PHR : FIRST VB INFLECTS

19 to go. 19.1 If you say that there are a number of things **to go**, you mean that they still remain to be dealt with, after you have finished with others in the same group. EG *Eight down and two to go.* **19.2** If you say that there is a period of time **to go**, you mean that this time must pass before something such as an exam or a contract ends or before something happens. EG *There are still two years to go.* **19.3** If you say that there is a particular distance **to go**, you mean that you must travel that distance before arriving somewhere or finishing a race. EG *We had less than three miles to go.* **19.4** If you say that an item of food is **to go**, you mean that it is intended to be taken away and not eaten in the cafe or restaurant you are in; used in American English.

PHR : NUM + PHR = left
PHR : USED AS AN A = left
PHR : USED AS AN A = left
PHR : USED AS C

20 Go is the quality of being active and energetic. EG *...men like Northcliffe, men of go.* • If you say that someone is **on the go**, you mean that they are busy and active; an informal expression. EG *They'll be on the go until they die.* • If you say **'it's all go'**, you mean that you have many things to do and no time to rest; an informal expression.

N UNCOUNT
• PHR : USED AS AN A
• PHR : AUX INFLECTS

21 If someone's sight or hearing is **going**, it is getting worse, and they may become blind or deaf. EG *His hearing is beginning to go... ...people whose eyesight is going.*

V = fail

22 If something such as a light bulb or a part of an engine is **going**, it is no longer working properly and will soon need to be replaced; an informal use. EG *The battery's going.*

V = give out

23 If someone **goes** on television or radio, they take part in a television or radio programme. EG *The princess agreed to go on television... The president went on the air that evening.*

V+A (*on*)

24 If something **goes** in a particular place, **24.1** it is put there. EG *The same engine goes into the new Talbot Tagora.* **24.2** it fits in that place because it is the right size or shape. EG *The silencer went on easily... Her suitcase only just went in the boot.* **24.3** it belongs there, because that is where you normally keep it. EG *That goes in there, and this goes on top of it.*

V+A = be put
V : USU+A = fit
V+A = belong

25 If a road or path **goes** somewhere, it leads to, from, or through a particular place. EG *Off the north side go Burlington Street and Cork Street... That road goes back to the city centre.*

V+A = lead, run

26 If you say that one number **goes** into another number, you are dividing the second number by the first. EG *Six goes into thirty five times... Six into thirty-two goes five with two left over.*

V : NUM + V + *into* + NUM
⇑ divide

27 If you say that someone is **going** or has **gone**, you mean that they are dying or dead, but you do not want to use these words because they upset you or they might upset the person you are talking to.

V = pass away

28 If you **go one better**, you do something better than it had been done before, or obtain something better than you had before or than someone else has. EG *Go one better and use electronic valves... Father went one better and got a colour TV.*

PHR : VB INFLECTS, USU + *and/than* = do better

29 You say **'here goes'** or **'here we go'** just before you start to do something, especially something new, exciting, or dangerous; an informal expression.

CONVENTION

30 You say **there goes** something to express disappointment when something happens to prevent you getting something; an informal expression. EG *There goes my chance of winning the award.*

PHR + NG = bang goes

31 You say **'there you go'** in informal English **31.1** to express annoyance at someone who continues to do something that they know you dislike or that you told them not to do. EG *There you go again. How you talk, honestly.* **31.2** after giving someone something or doing something for them, for example after serving them in a shop. EG *There you go, 20 pence change.* **31.3** after someone tells you about a situation or event, in order to express the opinion that the situation cannot be changed and must be accepted, or that the event is not surprising, because you had expected it. EG *There you go, what did I tell you?*

PHR
PHR
PHR = told you so

32 If someone asks **'Where do we go from here?'**, they mean 'What shall we do next?', usually because a problem has not been solved satisfactorily.

PHR

33 If someone says **'anything goes'**, they mean that anything that people say or do is considered acceptable; an informal expression, often used showing disapproval. EG *Today almost anything goes.*

PHR

34 If you say, for example, **'What I say, goes'**, or **'Whatever I say, goes'**, you mean that you have total authority and must be obeyed or agreed with; an informal expression. EG *Martin wanted the bathroom painted and what Martin says, goes.*

PHR

35 If you do something **as** you **go along**, you do it without preparing it beforehand; an informal expression. EG *I was making it up as I went along... He destroyed the evidence as he went along.*

PHR : USED AS AN A, VB INFLECTS

36 If you say that something **goes to show** or **goes to prove** something, you mean that it shows or proves it, especially when it agrees with your previous opinions or theories but surprises other people. EG *All of which goes to show that people haven't changed.*

PHR + REPORT-CL = confirm

37 You use **'as** things **go'** when describing one thing and comparing it with other things of the same kind; an informal expression. EG *Aluminium is soft and sticky, as metals go.*

PHR : USED AS AN A

38 If you **go all out for** something, you make the greatest possible effort to get it or achieve it; an informal expression.

PHR : VB INFLECTS
⇑ try

39 If you say your **heart goes out to** someone, your **thoughts go out to** someone, etc, you mean that you are thinking in a sympathetic way about someone, for example because they are suffering or doing something very brave; used in formal English.

PHR : VB INFLECTS

40 'Who goes there?' is used by guards or sentries as an official warning when they see or hear something, to indicate that anyone who is there must say who they are, otherwise they may be shot or arrested.

CONVENTION

41 The word **go** is also used in the following expressions, which are explained at other places in this dictionary. • **as far as** something **goes**: see **far.** • **bang goes**: see **bang.** • **easy come, easy go**: see **easy.** • **touch and go**: see **touch.** • to **go easy**: see **easy.** • to **go flying**: see **fly.** • to **go hungry**: see **hungry.** • to **go to town**: see **town.**

go about. 1 If you **go about** a task or problem, you begin to deal with it. EG *She told me how to go about it... ...a sensible way of going about things.*

PHRASAL VB : V + PREP = set about

2 If you **go about** a regular activity such as your job, you continue doing it. EG *He wanted to be left alone to go about his business.* • See also **go around.**

PHRASAL VB : V + PREP
⇑ do
= get on with

go after. If you **go after** something, you try to get it. EG *My husband had gone after a job... Go after a better deal.*

PHRASAL VB : V + PREP
⇑ seek
= try for

go against. 1 If something **goes against** an idea, a person's wishes, etc, it conflicts or disagrees with it. EG *When things go against my wishes, I threaten to resign... The teaching of the Bible clearly goes against it.*

PHRASAL VB : V + PREP, HAS PASS
= conflict with
≠ accord with

2 If you **go against** other people's advice or wishes, you do something different from what you have been

PHRASAL VB : V + PREP
= disregard

told or advised to do. EG *She went against the advice of her Cabinet and called a general election.*

3 If a decision or judgement **goes against** someone, for example in a court of law, it is unfavourable to them, and they lose the case. EG *The verdict went against his brother.* ● to **go against the grain**: see **grain**. PHRASAL VB : V+PREP ≠ favour

go ahead. **1** If someone **goes ahead** with something, they begin to do it or make it, especially after planning, promising, or asking permission to do it. EG *They are going ahead with the missile... 'Would you like to hear it?'–'Go ahead.'* PHRASAL VB : V+ADV, IF+PREP/CONJ THEN *with/and* = proceed

2 If a process or an organized event **goes ahead**, it takes place or is carried out. EG *The unloading had gone ahead very briskly... The May day marches could go ahead.* PHRASAL VB : V+ADV ⇑ begin = proceed

3 If someone **goes ahead** or **goes on ahead**, they go in front of someone else who is going in the same direction or to the same place. EG *You go ahead this time... The minibus went ahead of us... Anthony had gone on ahead.* ● See also **go-ahead**. PHRASAL VB : V+ADV, OR V+ADV+ADV : IF+PREP THEN *of* = precede

go along. **1** If you **go along**, **1.1** you move from one place to another, usually in order to do something. EG *I went along to the recording room... Go along and talk to a solicitor.* PHRASAL VB : V+ADV, IF+PREP/CONJ THEN *to/and* **1.2** you move in a particular way. EG *They go along very slowly.* PHRASAL VB : V+ADV+A

2 If you describe how something is **going along**, you describe how it is progressing. EG *It was going along nicely.* PHRASAL VB : V+ADV+A = progress

go along with. **1** If you **go along with** a rule, decision, or policy, you accept it and obey it. EG *You agreed to go along with the decision.* PHRASAL VB : V+ADV+PREP = abide by

2 If you **go along with** a person or an idea, you agree with the person or idea or accept that what they are saying is true. EG *I am willing to go along with Celli.* PHRASAL VB : V+ADV+PREP

go around. **1** If you **go around** or **go about** in a particular way, you behave or dress in that way, often as part of your normal life. EG *The kids go around barefoot.* PHRASAL VB : V+ADV/PREP+A = go round

2 If you **go around**, **go round**, or **go about** doing something, often something that other people disapprove of, you have the habit of doing it. EG *I don't go around deliberately hurting people's feelings... They're always going round sticking posters on walls.* PHRASAL VB : V+ADV+-ING = make a habit of

3 If you **go around**, **go round**, or **go about** with a person or group of people, you regularly meet them and go to different places with them. EG *Don't go around with them... They go round with their fellow countrymen.* PHRASAL VB : V+ADV+A *(together/with)* : RECIP = associate

4 If a piece of news or a joke is **going around**, **going round**, or **going about**, it is being told by many people in the same period of time. EG *...the gossip that went around years ago... Some jokes go round year after year... ...so many stories going about.* PHRASAL VB : V+ADV/PREP = circulate

5 If a quantity of something will **go around** or **go round**, there is enough of it to be shared among a group of people, or to do all the things for which it is needed. EG *There were never enough textbooks to go around... The money just won't go round... There was always enough food to go round.* PHRASAL VB : V+ADV/PREP, NO CONT, NO IMPER ⇑ suffice

go at. If you **go at** a task or activity, you start doing it in an energetic, enthusiastic way. EG *The breakfast arrived and he went at it like a starving refugee.* PHRASAL VB : V+PREP = attack

go away. If you **go away**, **1** you leave a place or a person's company. EG *She went away to think about it... Go away!* PHRASAL VB : V+ADV **2** you leave a place and spend a period of time somewhere else, especially as a holiday. EG *She had gone away for a few days.* PHRASAL VB : V+ADV

go back. **1** If something **goes back** to a particular time in the past, it was made, built, or started at that time. EG *The shop goes back to 1707.* PHRASAL VB : V+A *(to)* = date from

2 If someone **goes back** to a time in the past, they begin to discuss or consider events that happened at that time. EG *To trace its origins, we have to go back some thirty million years.* PHRASAL VB : V+ADV, IF+PREP THEN *to* = return

go back on. If you **go back on** a promise or agreement, you do not do what you promised or agreed to do. PHRASAL VB : V+ADV+PREP = break

go back to. If you **go back to** a task or activity, you start doing it again after you have stopped doing it for a period of time. EG *She had gone back to staring out of the window.* PHRASAL VB : V+ADV+PREP = resume

go before. **1** Something that has **gone before** an event or subject has happened or been discussed at an earlier time. EG *The meeting was different from any that had gone before... ...a topic which had nothing to do with what had gone before.* PHRASAL VB : V+ADV ⇑ precede

2 When people, problems, or cases **go before** a judge, tribunal, or court of law, they are brought or discussed there as part of an official or legal process so that a decision can be made about them. EG *The matter has gone before a grand jury.* PHRASAL VB : V+PREP = come before

go by. **1** If you say that a period of time has **gone by**, you mean that it has passed. EG *Eight years went by... As time goes by more devices come on to the market.* ● *If you say 'in days* **gone by**' or 'in years **gone by**', you are talking about events that have taken place in the past, often long ago. PHRASAL VB : V+ADV = elapse ● PHR : USED AS AN A

2 If you **go by** a person, book, rule, etc, you use the information or advice that the person, book, or rule gives you in order to do something. EG *I try to go by reason as far as possible... Don't go by what he says.* ● If someone **goes by the book**, they obey rules very strictly and insist on other people doing so as well. PHRASAL VB : V+PREP = follow ● PHR : VB INFLECTS

go down. **1** If you **go down** to a place, you walk or travel there for a short period of time; often used of places that are further south than you or further south in the country. EG *I have to go down to Brighton... I'm going down to the shops.* PHRASAL VB : V+ADV+*to*

2 If you **go down**, you go from one floor of a building to a lower one, especially to the ground floor. EG *I must go down and put on my necklace.* PHRASAL VB : V+ADV, IF+PREP/CONJ THEN *to/and*

3 If you **go down** on your knees or on all fours, you lower your body until it is supported by your knees, or by your hands and knees. PHRASAL VB : V+ADV+*on* = get down

4 When students **go down**, they leave their college or university at the end of a term or at the end of the academic year; used in British English. PHRASAL VB : V+ADV

5 In sport, if a person or team **goes down**, **5.1** they are defeated in a match or contest. EG *Lendl went down by three sets to one.* PHRASAL VB : V+ADV = lose **5.2** they move down to a lower position in an official list, or to a lower division in a league. PHRASAL VB : V+PREP = be relegated

6 When a remark, speech, or artistic performance **goes down** in a particular way, it gets a particular kind of reaction from a person or group of people. EG *The act didn't go down terribly well.* PHRASAL VB : V+ADV+A = be received

7 If you say that something has **gone down**, you mean that its quality or standard has become worse. EG *It's gone down a lot, the food.* PHRASAL VB : V+ADV = deteriorate

8 If you talk about food or drink **going down** well, you mean that it is eaten or drunk with enjoyment; an informal use. EG *A cup of tea would go down nicely.* PHRASAL VB : V+ADV+A

9 When the sun **goes down**, it sets. EG *The sun went down behind the mountains.* PHRASAL VB : V+ADV

10 If a ship **goes down**, it sinks. EG *They all got off before she went down.* PHRASAL VB : V+ADV

11 If the level of something, for example water in a tank, **goes down**, it becomes lower. PHRASAL VB : V+ADV

12 If a computer **goes down**, it stops functioning temporarily; a technical term in computing. PHRASAL VB : V+ADV

go down as. If an event, action, product, etc **goes down as** something, it is regarded, remembered, or recorded in a particular way by someone. EG *Helping your neighbour can go down in the teacher's view as cheating.* ● to **go down in history**: see **history**. PHRASAL VB : V+ADV+PREP = be regarded as

go down with. If you **go down with** an illness or a disease, you catch it; an informal expression. EG *She went down with flu.* PHRASAL VB : V+ADV+PREP = contract

go for. **1** If you **go for** a particular type of product or way of doing something, you choose it. EG *Children go for the brightly-coloured ones... ...a tendency to go for even grander projects.* PHRASAL VB : V+PREP = favour

2 If you **go for** someone or something, you like them very much; an informal use. EG *I really go for him... I don't go for talk like that.* PHRASAL VB : V+PREP = dig

3 If you **go for** someone or something, you attack them. EG *He went for me with the bread-knife... They go for the eyes.* PHRASAL VB : V+PREP

4 If you say that a statement you have made about one person or thing **goes for** another person or thing, you mean that the statement is also true of this other person or thing. EG *The same goes for Bardolph... ...and that goes for India too.* PHRASAL VB : V+PREP = apply to

5 If you say to a person or group of people **'go for it'**, you are encouraging them to increase their efforts to achieve or win something; an informal expression. CONVENTION ⇑ try

go in. **1** If the sun **goes in**, it goes behind a cloud and can no longer be seen. PHRASAL VB : V+ADV

2 If you **go in**, you enter a building, especially your own house. PHRASAL VB : V+ADV

go in for. If you **go in for** a particular activity, you PHRASAL VB : V+

decide to do it as your job, or as a hobby or interest. EG *I thought of going in for teaching.* ADV+PREP = take up

go into. 1 If you **go into** something, 1.1 you describe it fully or in detail. EG *I've gone into this example in some detail... I won't go into what I've suffered.* PHRASAL VB : V+PREP, HAS PASS 1.2 you examine or investigate it in detail. EG *My solicitors are going into the question of my jewellery... ...as one goes more deeply into a subject.* PHRASAL VB : V+PREP, HAS PASS = delve into 1.3 you decide to do it as your job or career. EG *Ever thought of going into journalism?.* PHRASAL VB : V+PREP = take up

2 If someone **goes into** a long speech or lecture, they begin it; often used showing disapproval. EG *He went into a long monologue.* PHRASAL VB : V+PREP = launch into

3 If time, effort, or money **goes into** something, it is spent or used to do it, get it, or make it. EG *Three years of research went into the making of those films.* PHRASAL VB : V+PREP

4 If a vehicle or its driver **goes into** a particular kind of movement, it starts moving in the way mentioned. EG *The plane went into a nose dive... I went into a skid.* PHRASAL VB : V+PREP ⇑ begin

5 If a vehicle or its driver **goes into** another vehicle, it hits the other vehicle. EG *Three cars went into me... I went into the mini in front.* PHRASAL VB : V+PREP = crash into

go off. 1 If you **go off** somewhere, you leave a place, usually in order to do something. EG *He had gone off to work... She went off to look at the flowers.* PHRASAL VB : V+ADV, USU+A

2 If you **go off** someone or something, you stop liking them; an informal use. EG *He's gone off the idea... I think she's going off him a bit.* PHRASAL VB : ORDER V+ADV+O

3 If you **go off**, you fall asleep; an informal use. EG *He went off as soon as his head touched the pillow.* PHRASAL VB : V+ADV

4 If something **goes off**, 4.1 it explodes. EG *I could hear the bombs going off on the other side of the city.* PHRASAL VB : V+ADV 4.2 it makes a sudden loud noise. EG *The alarm went off but he tried to ignore it.* PHRASAL VB : V+ADV 4.3 it stops operating. EG *The light only goes off at night.* PHRASAL VB : V+ADV

5 If an organized event **goes off** in a particular way, it takes place in that way. EG *The meeting went off well.* PHRASAL VB : V+ADV+A = go

6 Food or drink that has **gone off** has become stale, sour, or rotten. PHRASAL VB : V+ADV

go off with. 1 If someone **goes off with** another person, they leave their husband, wife, or lover and have a relationship with that person. EG *My boyfriend went off with my best friend.* PHRASAL VB : V+ADV+PREP = run off with

2 If someone **goes off with** something that belongs to someone else, they leave a place and take it with them. EG *She had let him go off with her papers.* PHRASAL VB : V+ADV+PREP = make off with

go on. 1 If you **go on** doing something, or **go on** with an activity, you continue to do it. EG *I went on writing... They can't go on with their examinations.* PHRASAL VB : V+ADV+-ING/*with* = carry on

2 If you **go on** to do something, you do it after you have finished doing something else. EG *He went on to get his degree... These women go on to have children.* PHRASAL VB : V+ADV+*to*-INF

3 If you **go on** in a particular direction, you continue to walk, drive, etc in that direction. EG *I went on up the hill... You can't go on, there's a diversion.* PHRASAL VB : V+ADV, USU+A = carry on

4 If you **go on** to a place, you go to it from the place that you have reached. EG *We had gone on to Clare's house... Go on home.* PHRASAL VB : V+ADV+A ⇑ proceed

5 If you **go on**, you continue saying something or talking about something. EG *'You know,' he went on, 'it's extraordinary.'... 'Sounds serious,' I said, 'go on.'* PHRASAL VB : V+ADV+QUOTE/*about* = proceed

6 If you **go on** about something, or **go on** at someone, you continue talking to them about the same thing, often in an annoying way; an informal use. EG *I went on at my father to have safety belts fitted... Don't go on about it.* PHRASAL VB : V+ADV+*about/at*, OR V+ADV = keep on, nag

7 If a process or institution **goes on**, it continues to take place or to exist, often for a particular period of time. EG *The fighting had gone on all through the night... We want the theatre to go on.* PHRASAL VB : V+ADV, USU+A ⇑ continue = last

8 If you say that a particular type of activity is **going on**, you mean that it is taking place. EG *There's a big argument going on... A lot of cheating goes on.* • See also **goings-on**. PHRASAL VB : V+ADV ⇑ happen = take place

9 If you say that a period of time **goes on**, you mean that it passes. EG *I get more depressed, as time goes on.* PHRASAL VB : V+ADV ⇑ continue = elapse

10 In informal English, you say **'Go on'** to someone 10.1 to persuade or encourage them to do something. EG *Go on, have a biscuit. ...Go on you'll never know until you try.* PHRASAL VB : V+ADV, ONLY IMPER 10.2 to indicate that you do not believe what they have said. EG *Go on–you're kidding.* PHRASAL VB : V+ADV = get away

11 If you **go on** a piece of information, you base an opinion or judgement on it. EG *It's not much to go on... I'm only going on what I've seen at Mr Gladwell's.* PHRASAL VB : V+PREP, HAS PASS

12 If a device or machine **goes on**, it begins operating. EG *The light goes on automatically.* PHRASAL VB : V+ADV = come on

go on ahead. See **go ahead 3.**

go out. 1 If you **go out** with someone, you spend time with them socially and often have a romantic or sexual relationship with them. EG *My parents wouldn't let me go out with boys... I went out with him a long time ago.* PHRASAL VB : V+ADV+A (*together/with*): RECIP ⇑ socialize

2 If you **go out** to do something, you make a practical effort to achieve it, by going to different places or by contacting people. EG *They went out and inquired into matters themselves... Charities must go out and raise money.* PHRASAL VB : V+ADV+*to/and* = set out

3 If a light **goes out**, it stops shining. EG *The lights went out in the big tent.* • to **go out like a light**: see **light**. PHRASAL VB : V+ADV

4 If something that is burning **goes out**, it stops burning. EG *The fire went out... My cigar's gone out.* PHRASAL VB : V+ADV

5 If information **goes out** from somewhere, it is announced or published, often officially. EG *The news went out from Washington that he was dead... Word went out that he'd arrived.* PHRASAL VB : V+ADV, USU+A = come

6 If a television or radio programme **goes out**, it is broadcast. EG *The series goes out on Tuesday evenings on BBC 2.* PHRASAL VB : V+ADV+A

7 If something **goes out**, it ceases to exist or be used, usually because it is replaced by something else. EG *Steam went out and diesel was introduced.* PHRASAL VB : V+ADV = die out

8 If a quality or feeling **goes out** of someone or something, they no longer have it. EG *Some of the snap has gone out of the market... All the heart seemed to have gone out of him.* PHRASAL VB : V+ADV+*of* = die out

9 When the tide **goes out**, the water in the sea or in a river gradually falls to a lower level until the tide comes in again. PHRASAL VB : V+ADV = recede ≠ come in

go over. 1 If you **go over** to someone or something, you move towards them and reach them. EG *'Mabel,' he said, going over to her... Go over and help him.* PHRASAL VB : V+ADV+*to/and*

2 If you **go over** something, you examine, discuss, or think about it very carefully and systematically. EG *He helped me go over my books... He went over this in his mind.* • See also **going-over**. PHRASAL VB : V+PREP = review

go over to. 1 If someone or something **goes over to** a different way of doing things, they change to it. EG *We went over to the American system... The school will go over to mixed ability teaching.* PHRASAL VB : V+ADV+PREP = switch to

2 If you **go over to** a group of people, a political party, etc, you join them after previously belonging to a group or party with very different aims or ideas. EG *Who was loyal and who had gone over to the other group?... Anyone joining the police is going over to the other side.* PHRASAL VB : V+ADV+PREP = desert to

go round. 1 If you **go round** to someone's house, you go to visit them at their house. EG *We went round one night but they were out.* PHRASAL VB : V+ADV, USU+A

2 If something **goes round**, it turns continuously like a wheel. EG *The tape is still going round.* PHRASAL VB : V+ADV ⇑ turn = revolve

3 See also **go around 2, 3, 4.**

go through. 1 If you **go through** an event or a period of time, especially an unpleasant one, you experience it. EG *Not all girls go through this stage... I'm too old to go through that again.* PHRASAL VB : V+PREP = undergo

2 If you **go through** a lot of things such as papers, clothes, etc, you look at them, usually in order to sort them into groups or to search for a particular item. EG *They went through her things... Go through the files again.* PHRASAL VB : V+PREP, HAS PASS = check

3 If you **go through** a list, story, or plan, you say it or describe it from beginning to end. EG *You'd better go through the names... Could you go through roughly what's required.* PHRASAL VB : V+PREP, HAS PASS = run through

4 If someone **goes through** a series of actions or movements, they perform them, usually as a practice or a test. EG *They watched Pat going through some of the movements she had learned.* • to **go through the motions**: see **motion**. PHRASAL VB : V+PREP, HAS PASS = rehearse

5 If a law, agreement, or official decision **goes through**, it is approved by the people who have the power or authority to do so. EG *The adoption went through.* PHRASAL VB : V+ADV/PREP = be approved

go through with. If you **go through with** a decision or an action, you continue to do what is necessary in order to achieve it or complete it, often even though it involves unpleasant experiences. EG *I didn't go through with the abortion.* PHRASAL VB : V+ADV+PREP ⇑ pursue = proceed with

go towards. If an amount of money **goes towards** something, it is used as part of the cost of that thing. EG *It will go towards a deposit on the flat... £54m went towards investment.* PHRASAL VB : V+PREP

go under. 1 If a business or project **goes under**, it fails. EG *Ten thousand small businesses have gone under.* PHRASAL VB : V+ADV = fold

2 If a boat, ship, or person in a sea or river **goes under**, it sinks below the surface of the water. EG *He thrashed about for some time before he went under.* PHRASAL VB : V+ADV

go up. 1 If you **go up** to a place, you walk or travel there, often in order to do something. EG *We all went up to the pub.* PHRASAL VB : V+ADV+A = go along

2 If you **go up** in a building, you go to a higher floor in it, especially from the ground floor. EG *She went up to her bedroom... We can go up in the elevator.* PHRASAL VB : V+ADV+A ≠ go down

3 If a building, wall, or other structure **goes up**, it is built or fixed in place. EG *Small blocks of flats are going up... Billboards went up all over town.* PHRASAL VB : V+ADV : USU+A

4 If something **goes up**, it explodes or starts to burn, usually suddenly and with great intensity. EG *...if one of those gas tankers goes up... In seconds it had gone up in flames.* ● to **go up in smoke**: see **smoke**. PHRASAL VB : V+ADV

5 If something **goes up**, for example the curtain in a theatre, it is raised. EG *There was a burst of applause as the curtain went up.* PHRASAL VB : V+ADV ⇑ rise

6 When students **go up** to a college or university, they begin studying there, or return there at the beginning of an academic year or term; used in British English. PHRASAL VB : V+ADV, IF+PREP THEN *to*

7 If a shout, a cheer, etc **goes up**, it is made by a lot of people together. PHRASAL VB : V+ADV

8 In sport, if a person or team **goes up**, they move to a higher position in the official list, or move to a higher division in a league. EG *I think Stoke will go up this season.* PHRASAL VB : V+ADV/PREP = be promoted

go with. 1 If one thing **goes with** another thing, 1.1 the two things officially belong together, so that if you get one, you also get the other. EG *The house went with the job.* PHRASAL VB : V+PREP, NO CONT, NO IMPER = accompany 1.2 it is usually found or experienced together with the other thing. EG *...the sigh of satisfaction that goes with pleasant tiredness.* PHRASAL VB : V+PREP, NO CONT, NO IMPER = accompany

2 If someone **goes with** another person, they have sex with that person; an informal use. EG *He never went with other women.* PHRASAL VB : V+PREP = sleep with

go without. If you **go without** something, often something that you have or do regularly, you do not get it or do it. EG *The family went without food all day... If I go a day without practice, I notice it... If they couldn't get coal, they had to go without.* ● to **go without saying**: see **say**. PHRASAL VB : V+PREP/ADV ⇑ lack = do without ≠ have

goad /gəʊd/, **goads, goading, goaded.** 1 If you **goad** someone, you arouse strong feelings of anger, irritation, etc, in them, often causing them to react by doing something. EG *She was being goaded into denouncing and mocking her best friend... Mobs, goaded by blind hatred and fed on fear, tore through the city.* V+O+A *(into)*, OR V+O *(NG/REFL)* : USU+A ⇑ provoke = drive

2 A **goad** is a sharp, pointed stick that is used for driving cattle. N COUNT

goad on. If you **goad** someone **on**, you encourage them. EG *The thought of all that money goaded him on.* PHRASAL VB : ORDER V+O+ADV, USU PASS = spur on

go-ahead. 1 If you give someone the **go-ahead**, or give the **go-ahead** to a plan or project, you give permission or approval to someone to start doing something. EG *He gave the go-ahead for the Manhattan Project... You have the go-ahead from the Prime Minister.* N SING : *the*+N = green light

2 A **go-ahead** person or organization is ambitious and tries hard to succeed, often by using new methods. EG *...its go-ahead young secretary... ...promising a 'dynamic and go-ahead Britain'.* ADJ QUALIT = enterprising

goal /gəʊl/, **goals.** 1 A **goal** in some games such as football or hockey is 1.1 the space into which the players try to get the ball in order to score a point for their team. EG *The ball missed the goal by a few inches.* N COUNT 1.2 an instance in which a player gets the ball into the goal, or the point that is scored by doing this. EG *They beat us by four goals to three.* N COUNT

2 Something that is your **goal** is something that you hope to achieve, especially when much time and effort is needed in order to achieve it. EG *They had at last achieved their goal of landing a man on the Moon... ...social and economic goals.* N COUNT = objective, aim

goalie /gəʊli¹/, **goalies.** A **goalie** is a goalkeeper; an informal word. N COUNT

goalkeeper /gəʊlki:pə/, **goalkeepers.** A **goalkeeper** is the player in a sports team whose job is to guard the goal and stop the other team from getting the ball into the goal. N COUNT = goalie

goal line, goal lines; also spelled with a hyphen. A **goal line** is one of the lines at each end of the pitch in games like football and hockey, on which the goalposts stand. N COUNT

goalpost /gəʊlpəʊst/, **goalposts**; also spelled with a hyphen. A **goalpost** is one of the two upright wooden posts that are connected by a crossbar and form the goal in games like football and hockey. N COUNT

goat /gəʊt/, **goats.** 1 A **goat** is an animal with a beard, horns, and a short tail, which is found in mountain areas or on farms. N COUNT

2 A **goat** is also an unpleasant and bad-tempered old person; an informal use. EG *The old goat could walk fifty miles to my ten.* N COUNT : USU ADJ+N

3 If something **gets** your **goat**, it makes you very annoyed; an informal expression. EG *Don't let them get your goat.* PHR : VB INFLECTS

4 If someone is **acting** or **playing the goat**, they are behaving in a silly way; an informal expression. EG *Stop acting the goat and sit down!* ● to **separate the sheep from the goats**: see **sheep**. PHR : VB INFLECTS = play the fool

goatee /gəʊti:/, **goatees.** A **goatee** is a very short pointed beard that a man wears on his chin but not on his cheeks. N COUNT

goatherd /gəʊthɜ:d/, **goatherds.** A **goatherd** is a person who is responsible for looking after a group of goats. N COUNT

goatskin /gəʊtskɪn/, **goatskins. Goatskin** is leather made from the skin of a goat. N UNCOUNT/COUNT

gob /gɒb/, **gobs.** 1 A person's **gob** is their mouth; a very informal use in British English. EG *You shut your gob!* N COUNT : USU DETPOSS+N

2 A **gob** of something is a mass of something thick and liquid, especially saliva; an informal use. EG *He spat out a big gob of spit.* N COUNT : USU N +*of*+N UNCOUNT = blob

gobbet /gɒbɪ²t/, **gobbets.** A **gobbet** of something soft, especially food, is a small lump or piece of it; an informal word. EG *Most animals simply bolt their food in gobbets.* N PART+N UNCOUNT = chunk

gobble /gɒbə⁰l/, **gobbles, gobbling, gobbled.** 1 If you **gobble** some food, you eat it very quickly and greedily; an informal use. EG *Still hungry, I gobbled a second sandwich.* V+O = wolf

2 When a turkey **gobbles**, it utters a loud sound. V

gobble down. If you **gobble** some food **down** or **gobble** it **up**, you eat all of it very quickly; an informal expression. EG *He gobbled down the two remaining stuffed eggs with satisfaction... ...truck drivers gobbling up hot dogs dripping with mustard.* PHRASAL VB : ORDER V+ADV+O = bolt down

gobbledygook /gɒbə⁰ldi¹gu:k/; also spelled **gobbledegook. Gobbledygook** is a speech or statement, often in very official, formal language, which seems like nonsense to you because you cannot understand it at all; an informal word. EG *All he did was give us a load of gobbledygook.* N UNCOUNT = mumbo jumbo

gobbler /gɒblə/, **gobblers.** A **gobbler** is a turkey; an informal word. N COUNT

go-between, go-betweens. A **go-between** is a person who takes messages between people who are unable or unwilling to meet each other. EG *Fortunately Piero was there to act as a go-between.* N COUNT ⇑ messenger = intermediary

goblet /gɒblɪ²t/, **goblets.** A **goblet** is a type of cup made of metal, pottery, or glass, without handles and usually with a long stem, which you use for drinking alcohol out of. N COUNT ⇑ container

goblin /gɒblɪn/, **goblins.** A **goblin** is a small ugly creature in fairy stories, which usually enjoys causing trouble or harm. N COUNT ⇑ spirit

go-cart, go-carts. A **go-cart** is a small vehicle that children ride in or pull along. N COUNT

god /gɒd/, **gods.** 1 The name **God** is given to the spirit or being who is worshipped as the creator and ruler of the world, especially by Christians, Jews, and Muslims. EG *'Our responsibility is to God alone,' declared the Rabbi... Good luck to you, my boy, and God bless you.* N PROPER/VOC

2 People sometimes use **God** in exclamations to emphasize something that they are saying, or to express surprise, fear, shock, excitement, etc; an informal use that some people find offensive. EG *My God, John, what are you doing here at this hour?... God, he looks awful, Brody thought... I'm frightened. I want to go home. O God I want to go home.* EXCLAM = goodness

3 The word **God** is also used in the following expressions. **3.1** If you say **God help** someone, you are expressing a wish that they will not have to experience something unpleasant or dangerous, especially when you are warning them or when you are remembering your own unpleasant experience. EG *He spoke sharply: 'God help them if that's whom they follow.'* PHR = heaven help **3.2** If you say **God forbid**, you are expressing your hope that something will not happen; a fairly formal expression. EG *God forbid that anything should happen to my father.* EXCLAM, OR PHR + REPORT-CL = heaven forbid **3.3** If you say **God willing**, you mean that something will happen if everything goes well. EG *His plane lands at six-thirty, God willing.* PHR : USED AS AN A **3.4** If you say **what in God's name, how in God's name, why in God's name**, etc, you are emphasizing in the question you are asking how angry, annoyed, or surprised you are. EG *What in God's name are you going to do with a hundred and sixty-five watches?* PHR **3.5** You use **to God** in expressions like **I pray to God, I hope to God**, etc, to emphasize what you are saying; a fairly informal use. EG *I hope to God she'll be happy... I swear to God I never took the money.* PHR : USED AS AN A

4 God knows. 4.1 If you say **God only knows** or **God knows**, you are emphasizing that you don't know something or that you find a fact or event very surprising. EG *His eyes had a yellow tint. God only knew what mixture he had drunk the night before.* PHR + REPORT-CL = heaven only knows

4.2 People sometimes say **God knows** in reply to a question to indicate that they don't know the answer and that they don't care or that they are angry or annoyed; a very informal use. EG *'Where is he now, Mildred?'–'God knows. In the summer-house, I expect.'* EXCLAM

5 If someone **plays God**, they act as if they believe that they have unlimited power and can do anything they want; used showing disapproval. EG *Scientists should never play God.* PHR : VB INFLECTS

6 A **god** is **6.1** one of the spirits or beings that are believed in many religions to have power over a particular part of the world or nature. EG *If they killed the lion, they would be punished by the gods... ...the Saxon god of war.* N COUNT ⇑ deity **6.2** a picture or statue of a particular god. EG *The granite gods glittered in the sunlight.* N COUNT ⇑ image **6.3** someone or something that you admire and think is more important than anything else and that influences you very much. EG *When I was eight years old, my uncles were my gods.* N COUNT = idol

7 The **gods** are the seats in a theatre or concert hall that are very high up and farthest away from the stage; an informal use. EG *We were sitting up in the gods but we could still hear every note.* N PLURAL : *the*+N = gallery

8 The word **God** is also used in the following expressions, which are explained at other places in this dictionary. ● **for God's sake**: see **sake**. ● **God's gift**: see **gift**. ● **please God**: see **please**. ● **thank God**: see **thank**. ● to **put the fear of God into** someone: see **fear**. ● See also **act of God, tin god**.

god-awful; also spelled as one word. **God-awful** is a swear word used to describe something that the speaker thinks is very bad indeed. ADJ CLASSIF : USU ATTRIB = terrible

godchild /gɒdtʃaɪld/, **godchildren**. If someone is your **godchild**, you are their godparent which means that you agreed to take responsibility for their religious upbringing when they were baptized in a Christian church. N COUNT : USU WITH POSS

goddammit /gɒdæmɪt/ is a swear word that is used to express annoyance, anger, irritation, etc; used especially in American English. EXCLAM

goddamn /gɒdæm/; also spelled **goddam**. **Goddamn** is a swear word that is used for emphasis, usually to express a strong emotion such as excitement, anger, irritation, etc; used especially in American English. EXCLAM, ADV, OR ADJ CLASSIF : ATTRIB

goddamned /gɒdæmd/ means the same as goddamn; a swear word. ADV, OR ADJ CLASSIF

goddaughter /gɒdɔːtə/, **goddaughters**; also spelled with a hyphen. A **goddaughter** is a female godchild. N COUNT

goddess /gɒdɪ^{2}s/, **goddesses**. A **goddess** is a female spirit or being that is believed in many religions to have power over a particular part of the world or nature. EG *The river Osun is sacred to the river goddess.* N COUNT ⇑ deity

godfather /gɒdfɑːðə/, **godfathers**. **1** A **godfather** is a male godparent. N COUNT

2 Godfather is sometimes used to refer to a very powerful man who is at the head of a criminal organization. EG *This man was obviously the Godfather, the boss of the outfit.* N SING : DET+N ⇑ leader

god-fearing. Someone who is **god-fearing** is religious and behaves according to the moral rules of their religion. EG *...a God-fearing man who baptized his children in the river.* ADJ QUALIT = godly

god-forsaken; also spelled as one word. A **godforsaken** place is one that is not interesting or pleasant but very depressing. EG *Below us was a godforsaken coast of smooth dark sand.* ADJ CLASSIF : ATTRIB = bleak

godhead /gɒdhɛd/. The **godhead** is the divine nature of God. EG *Art is the godhead as revealed in the works of man.* N UNCOUNT : USU *the*+N

godless /gɒdlɪ^{2}s/. A **godless** person **1** does not believe in God and has no religion. ADJ CLASSIF **2** is very wicked or evil. EG *These men were dirty, drunken, and both godless and lawless.* ADJ CLASSIF = ungodly

godly /gɒdli^1/. Someone who is **godly** is deeply religious and shows obedience to God and to the rules of their religion. ▸ used of people's behaviour and actions. EG *...a godly existence.* ADJ QUALIT = devout

godmother /gɒdmʌðə/, **godmothers**. A **godmother** is a female godparent. N COUNT

godparent /gɒdpɛərənt/, **godparents**. Someone's **godparent** is a man or woman who agrees to take responsibility for their religious upbringing when they are baptized in a Christian church. N COUNT ⇑ sponsor

godsend /gɒdsɛnd/. Something that is a **godsend** arrives or happens unexpectedly and helps you very much in some way. EG *The extra twenty-five dollars a week was a godsend.* N SING : *a*+N = blessing

godson /gɒdsʌn/, **godsons**. A **godson** is a male godchild. N COUNT

-goer /gəʊə/, **-goers**. **-goer** is added to words such as 'theatre', 'church', 'film', etc, to form nouns that refer to people who regularly go to a particular type of place or event. EG *They were both enthusiastic playgoers... I don't hold myself up as a good church-goer.* COMB : FORMS N COUNTS

go-getter, go-getters. A **go-getter** is a person who is very ambitious and energetic. EG *We are forced into competition, forced to be go-getters and achieve great things.* N COUNT = whizz kid

goggle /gɒgə^{0}l/, **goggles, goggling, goggled**. **1** If you **goggle** at something, you stare at it with your eyes very wide open, especially because you are surprised by it; an informal use. EG *She goggled at the dreadful suit... There was no answer from him. He just goggled at her.* V : IF+PREP THEN *at* ⇑ look = gape

2 Goggles are large glasses that fit closely to your face around your eyes to protect them from such things as water, wind, dust, or sparks. EG *She was wearing big green-tinted snow goggles.* N PLURAL

goggle box. The **goggle box** is the television; an informal expression. EG *He sits watching the goggle box all day.* N SING : *the*+N

goggle-eyed. If you are **goggle-eyed**, your eyes are wide open in surprise; an informal word. ADJ CLASSIF ⇑ surprised

go-go is used to describe a type of dancing performed to pop music in pubs, clubs, etc by young women wearing very few clothes. EG *...go-go dancing... Those go-go girls have got you all excited.* ADJ CLASSIF : ATTRIB

going /gəʊɪŋ/. **1** You say that something **is going to** happen, or that you **are going to** do something, **1.1** when you are talking about events that will happen in the future, especially very soon. EG *I'm going to have a baby... I'm going to take a look at the waterfall... He is going to start an employment agency... She told him she was going to leave her job.* PHR : *be* INFLECTS **1.2** when you are making a prediction about what you believe will happen in the future, especially very soon. EG *The Democrats are going to take a beating... this war was not going to last very long... He is going to have to prove his innocence.* PHR : *be* INFLECTS **1.3** to say that you are intending to do something, or that someone else is intending to do something. EG *He was not going to be made a scapegoat.* PHR : *be* INFLECTS = be about to

2 If you **get going**, **2.1** you start doing something, especially after a delay. EG *I'm really getting anxious to get going.* PHR : VB INFLECTS **2.2** you start to move away from a place in order to go somewhere else. EG *I wondered if we'd ever get going.* PHR : VB INFLECTS ⇑ leave

3 If you **keep going**, you continue doing something. EG *This helped him to keep going.* PHR : VB INFLECTS

4 The **going** is the conditions that affect your ability to do something, often when these conditions are unfavourable. EG *When the going gets tough, we run* N SING : *the*+N, OR N UNCOUNT : ADJ+N

back to our parents... It was hard going at first. ● If you **get out while the going is good**, you go away or withdraw from something when it is still possible, while things are going well and before conditions become difficult. EG *Don't you think we ought to get out while the going's good?* ● You say that something is **good going** or **not bad going** when you want to say that it has been done more quickly or more successfully than usual or than expected; used in informal English. EG *That's quite good going.*
● PHR : VB INFLECTS = back out
● PHR : USED AS C

5 The **going** rate or the **going** salary is the usual amount of money that you expect to pay or receive for something such as a service. EG *The going rate is about £1,000 a head... They had stuck out for twice the going salary.*
ADJ CLASSIF : ATTRIB = customary

6 If you describe something as a **going concern**, you mean that it is a business which is operating satisfactorily and doing well and which can be expected to continue in the same way.
PHR WITH DET : N INFLECTS

7 If you **have** something **going for** you, or **have** something **going in** your **favour**, you have a particular advantage, especially when you are trying to achieve something or do better than other people. EG *She had so much going for her in the way of wealth and success.*
PHR : VB INFLECTS

8 You say that something is enough **to be going on with** to indicate that it is satisfactory for present purposes, but that it will be necessary for more to be done or provided in the future. EG *That'll do to be going on with.*
PHR : USED AS AN A = for starters

9 If you say that someone is **going on** a particular age, you mean that they are nearly that age. EG *He's going on fifty.*
PHR : USED AS AN A = pushing

10 See also **go**. ● **comings and goings**: see **coming**.

-going is added to nouns such as 'theatre', 'church', 'film', etc, to refer to the activity of going to a particular type of place or event. EG *It happened during one of our periods of movie-going... His church-going patterns appear orthodox.* ● See also **easy-going, ocean-going**.
COMB : FORMS N UNCOUNTS, OR ADJ CLASSIFS

going-over, goings-over; an informal word. A **going-over** is **1** an examination that you make of something in order to make sure that it is all right. EG *I gave the engine a thorough going-over.* **2** a violent physical attack on someone, especially as a punishment or a warning. EG *The boys gave him a going-over.*
N COUNT = check
N COUNT

goings-on. You use the word **goings-on** to refer to activities that you think are strange or amusing or that you do not approve of. EG *...an amusing story about goings-on at Harry's Bar.*
N PLURAL = happenings

goitre /gɔɪtə/, **goitres**. **Goitre** is a disease of the thyroid gland that makes a person's neck very swollen. ▸ used to refer to the thyroid gland itself. EG *She had a very large goitre.*
N UNCOUNT ⇑ swelling
▸ N COUNT

go-kart /gəʊkɑːt/, **go-karts**. A **go-kart** is a very small motor vehicle with four wheels, used for racing.
N COUNT

go-karting /gəʊkɑːtɪŋ/ is the sport of racing or riding on go-karts.
N UNCOUNT

gold /gəʊld/, **golds**. **1 Gold** is a valuable, yellow-coloured metal that is used for making jewellery, and as an international currency. EG *...gold bracelets... ...a fixed exchange rate for the dollar against gold.*
N UNCOUNT

2 Gold is also **2.1** jewellery and other things that are made of gold. EG *They stole an estimated 12 million pounds worth of gold and jewels.* **2.2** a bright yellow colour. EG *There are white and gold daisies among the grass... ...English autumnal browns and golds.*
N UNCOUNT
N UNCOUNT/ COUNT, OR ADJ COLOUR

3 Something that is **gold** is shiny and yellow-coloured, and looks like gold. EG *...a cap with gold braid all over it... The sign was written in gold letters.*
ADJ CLASSIF = golden

4 A **gold** is a gold medal; an informal use. EG *He won the gold at Amsterdam in 1928.*
N COUNT ⇑ prize

5 The word **gold** is also used in the following expressions. **5.1** If someone or something is **worth** their **weight in gold**, they are so useful, helpful, or valuable that you feel you could not manage without them. EG *The aircraft was going to be worth its weight in gold.* **5.2** If you say that someone has a **heart of gold**, you mean that they are very good, kind, and considerate. **5.3** If you say that a child or an animal is **as good as gold**, you mean that it behaves very well and does not cause you any problems; used showing approval. EG *Her twins are wonderful babies, they're as good as gold!*
PHR : USED AS C = invaluable
PHR : USED AS O
PHR : USED AS C ⇑ obedient

gold dust; also spelled with a hyphen. If you say that something is **like gold dust**, you mean that it is very difficult to obtain, especially because everyone wants it; an informal expression. EG *Biros are like gold dust in this office.*
PHR : USED AS AN A ⇑ rare

golden /gəʊld(ə)n/. **1** Something that is **golden** is **1.1** made of gold. EG *She wore a tiny golden cross.* **1.2** bright yellow in colour and looks rather like gold. EG *...a beautiful girl with bright golden hair.*
ADJ CLASSIF
ADJ COLOUR

2 If you describe something as **golden**, you feel that it is wonderful because it is likely to be successful and rewarding, or because it is the best of its kind. EG *...a golden opportunity... We feel sure your future here is golden... ...the golden girl of British athletics.*
ADJ QUALIT ⇑ favourable = excellent

golden age, golden ages. A **golden age** is a period of time during which a very high level of achievement is reached in a particular subject, especially in art or literature. EG *...the golden age of jazz.*
N COUNT : IF+ PREP THEN *of*

golden handshake, golden handshakes. A **golden handshake** is a large sum of money that a company gives to an employee when he or she retires, as a reward for long service or good work.
N COUNT ⇑ gift

golden jubilee, golden jubilees. A **golden jubilee** is the 50th anniversary of an important or special event.
N COUNT : IF+ PREP THEN *of*

golden rule, golden rules. A **golden rule** is an important thing to remember to do in order to be successful at something. EG *...the golden rules of time management.*
N COUNT ⇑ guideline

golden syrup is a sweet, sticky, yellow liquid that is made from sugar.
N UNCOUNT

golden wedding, golden weddings. A **golden wedding** or a **golden wedding anniversary** is the fiftieth anniversary of a wedding.
N COUNT

goldfish /gəʊldfɪʃ/. **Goldfish** is both the singular and the plural form. A **goldfish** is a small gold or orange-coloured fish which is often kept as a pet in a bowl or a garden pond.
N COUNT ⇑ fish

gold medal, gold medals. If you win a **gold medal**, you come first in a competition, especially a sports contest, and you are given a medal of gold or gold-coloured metal as your prize. Gold medals are also awarded in some activities, such as dancing, to people who have reached a particularly high standard.
N COUNT

goldmine /gəʊldmaɪn/, **goldmines**. If you call a business or activity a **goldmine**, you mean that it is very successful and produces or is likely to produce large profits. EG *The company has bought Cosmopolitan, a future goldmine... Owners of urban property are cashing in on the goldmine produced by the rural exodus.* See also **mine**.
N COUNT : USU SING ⇑ success = treasury

gold-plated. Something that is **gold-plated** is covered with a very thin layer of gold. EG *...a bath with gold-plated taps.*
ADJ CLASSIF ⇑ coated

gold-rimmed is used to describe something that has a golden edge or border, especially a person's glasses that have a frame of gold or gold-coloured metal. EG *...a pair of gold-rimmed reading glasses... ...an enormous gold-rimmed cup.*
ADJ CLASSIF ⇑ edged

goldsmith /gəʊldsmɪθ/, **goldsmiths**. A **goldsmith** is a person whose job is making jewellery and other objects using gold.
N COUNT ⇑ craftsman

golf /gɒlf/ is a game in which you use long sticks called clubs to hit a small, hard ball into holes that are spread out over a large area of grassy land. EG *We played golf at least twice a week... ...a golf ball.*
N UNCOUNT

golf ball, golf balls; also spelled with a hyphen or as one word, especially for paragraph two. **1** A **golf ball** is a small, hard white ball which people use when they are playing golf.
N COUNT

2 A **golfball** or **golfball typewriter** is an electric typewriter in which the letters and symbols are on a round piece of metal that moves across the paper when you type. ▸ This round piece of metal is also referred to as a **golfball**.
N COUNT

golf club, golf clubs; also spelled with a hyphen. A **golf club** is **1** a long, thin, metal stick with a piece of wood or metal at one end that you use to hit the ball in golf. **2** an organization whose members play golf. **3** a place where people play golf.
N COUNT
N COUNT
N COUNT

golf course, golf courses; also spelled with a hyphen. A **golf course** is a large area of grassy land that is specially prepared for playing golf on. It
N COUNT = links

usually has nine or eighteen holes, clearly marked routes to reach them, and deliberately created obstacles such as sand bunkers.

golfer /gɒlfə/, **golfers**. A **golfer** is a person who plays golf for pleasure or as a profession. N COUNT

golfing /gɒlfɪŋ/. 1 **Golfing** is used to describe things that involve the playing of golf or that are used while playing golf. EG *...a golfing holiday... ...a pair of golfing slacks.* N BEFORE N

2 **Golfing** is the activity of playing golf. EG *Ira and the Major were out golfing.* N UNCOUNT

golliwog /gɒli¹wɒg/, **golliwogs**; also spelled **gollywog**. A **golliwog** is a child's toy that looks like a little man with a black face, large white eyes, and spiky black hair. Golliwogs are usually made out of soft material. N COUNT

golly /gɒli¹/, **gollies**. 1 People say **'golly'** to indicate that they are very surprised by something; an informal, slightly old-fashioned use. EG *'Golly!' cried Dot. 'Have you seen the time!'... 'Golly, I didn't know he was an expert.'* EXCLAM = gosh

2 People say **'by golly'** to emphasize that something did happen or should happen; an informal, rather old-fashioned use. EG *He said he'd do it, and by golly he's succeeded.* EXCLAM ⇑ certainly

3 A **golly** is the same as a golliwog. N COUNT

gondola /gɒndələ/, **gondolas**. A **gondola** is a long narrow boat that is used especially in Venice. It has a flat bottom and curves upwards at both ends. A person stands at one end of the gondola and uses a long pole to move and steer it. N COUNT

gondolier /gɒndəli:ə/, **gondoliers**. A **gondolier** is a person whose job is to take people from one place to another in a gondola. N COUNT ⇑ boatman

gone /gɒn/. 1 **Gone** is the past participle of **go**.

2 Someone or something that is **gone** is no longer present or no longer exists. EG *He turned the corner and was gone... The initial enthusiasm was gone... The days are gone when women worked for half pay.* ADJ CLASSIF : PRED ≠ here

3 If you say it is **gone** a particular time, you mean it is later than that time. EG *It's gone tea-time... It was gone eight o'clock when I got home.* PREP = past

goner /gɒnə/, **goners**. If you say that someone is a **goner**, you mean that they are about to die, or in such danger that nobody can save them; an informal, old-fashioned word. EG *'Thanks for rescuing me.'–'I thought you were a goner.'* N COUNT = dead duck

gong /gɒŋ/, **gongs**. A **gong** is a flat, circular piece of metal that you hit with a hammer in order to make a sound like a loud bell, for example as a signal. Gongs are sometimes used as musical instruments. N COUNT

gonna /gɒnə/ is used, especially in written American English, to represent the words **going to** pronounced informally or in a particular accent or tone of voice. EG *'What are we gonna do?'* V+INF

goo /gu:/ is a thick, sticky substance like mud or paste; an informal word. EG *...the goo at the bottom of the tin... ...covered in goo.* N UNCOUNT = gunge

good /gʊd/, **better, best; goods**. See also separate entries at **better** and **best**. 1 Something that is **good** is 1.1 pleasant and enjoyable. EG *They had a good time... ...a really good book... That's good news... ...a good feeling... Hello! It's good to see you.* ADJ QUALIT = great 1.2 of a high quality or standard, often in comparison to other similar things. EG *...a very good school... ...good agricultural land... She put her good shoes on... I get very good marks... She speaks good English.* ADJ QUALIT ≠ bad, poor

2 Someone who is **good** is 2.1 kind to people and always thinks of their feelings and needs. EG *He's always been good to me... How simple and good her gesture seemed... It's good of you to come... Would you be good enough to ask him.* ADJ QUALIT = nice ≠ inconsiderate 2.2 morally correct in their behaviour and character, for example never lying or stealing. EG *There was no trace of evil in her-she was good.* ADJ QUALIT = virtuous ≠ wicked

3 Someone who is in a **good** mood is cheerful and pleasant to be with. EG *I'm in a good mood... ...his natural good humour.* ADJ QUALIT : ATTRIB ⇑ agreeable

4 Someone who has a **good** nature is pleasant and kind. EG *We took full advantage of his good nature.* ADJ QUALIT : ATTRIB

5 A child or animal that is **good** is well-behaved and obedient. EG *Were the kids good?... 'Good dog.'... There's a good boy!* ADJ QUALIT ≠ naughty

6 If you say that a situation or idea is **good**, you think it is desirable, acceptable, or right. EG *It's good that there are places like this... They were taught to share, and that can only be good... We were fighting for a good cause.* ADJ QUALIT = admirable ≠ wrong ● If you say **it is a good thing** or **it is a good job** that something happens or is the case, you mean it is fortunate that it happens or is the case. EG *It's a good thing I wasn't there.* ● PHR : USU + REPORT-CL, VB INFLECTS ⇑ fortunately

7 **Good** is what is considered to be right and desirable according to moral standards or religious beliefs, and is often thought of as a force or power. EG *...the conflict between good and evil... To him 'success' was the highest moral good.* N UNCOUNT, OR N SING WITH DET = virtue ≠ evil ● If you say that someone is **up to no good**, you mean that they are doing or planning to do something dishonest or illegal. ● PHR : USED AS A

8 **Good** music, art, literature, etc is considered to be of high quality and serious rather than light-hearted or popular. EG *...wandering through the West End in search of good theatre.* ADJ CLASSIF : ATTRIB

9 A person's **good** arm, leg, eye, etc is the one that is healthy and strong; used when the other one is weak, injured, or diseased. EG *Claus hung on to him with his good arm.* ADJ CLASSIF : ATTRIB ≠ weak

10 If someone or something has a **good** reputation, name, etc, other people respect them or think highly of them. EG *He hadn't got a very good reputation... ...concern for the family and its good name.* ADJ QUALIT ⇑ honourable ≠ bad

11 If you describe a chance or reason as **good**, you think it is strong or valid and likely to succeed or be believed. EG *They had a good chance of winning the election... The Secretary had several good reasons for his conduct... There was a very good case for introducing a degree in the subject.* ADJ QUALIT = powerful ≠ poor

12 Someone who is **good** at a particular activity is skilful and successful at doing it. EG *Alex is a good swimmer... Was she being a good mother?... He was very good at talking me out of things... Marcus was good with his hands.* ADJ QUALIT = capable, proficient ▸ used of people's actions. EG *Good shot, Hughie.* ▸ = first-rate ● If someone is **no good** or **not any good** at a particular activity, they are not at all skilful or successful at doing it. EG *You were never any good at Latin... I'd be no good as a doctor.* ● PHR : USED AS C, USU + PREP = hopeless, useless

13 You use **good** with a negative or an implied negative to say that something will not succeed or be of any use, especially when you are giving advice to someone, or when you realize this after trying for a period of time. EG *It's no good worrying any more tonight... A fat lot of good that would be!... Even if I came, what good would it do?* ADJ QUALIT : WITH BROAD NEG = use

14 **good for**. 14.1 If a situation is **good for** someone or something, it is likely to be of help, use, or advantage to them. EG *...a climate of confidence which was good for trade... She takes on more work than is good for her... It is also good for cleaning paint brushes.* ADJ QUALIT + *for* ⇑ beneficial ≠ bad 14.2 A person or place that is **good for** something is likely to have it and provide you with it. EG *The river was always good for a trout or two... She must be good for a few pounds.* ADJ QUALIT + *for* 14.3 If you say that someone or something is **good for** a period of time, you mean that they are likely to live or last for that period. EG *The old car is good for another few years yet.* ADJ QUALIT + *for* ⇑ serviceable 14.4 People say **'Good for you'**, **'Good for her'**, etc when they are expressing approval of or support for someone's actions. EG *'I've told him I won't do it.'–'Good for you.'* CONVENTION 14.5 You can say **Good on you** when you mean **Good for you**; an informal expression. CONVENTION

15 If you talk about someone's **good** or the **good** of something, you are discussing what will be of benefit or advantage to them in a particular situation. EG *Casey should quit for the good of the agency... It was for her own good.* N SING : WITH POSS = welfare ● If you say that something will **do** someone or something **good**, you mean that it will improve, help, or benefit them. EG *A sea voyage will do her health good... It'll do you good to get a bit of fresh air!* ● PHR : VB INFLECTS

16 If you describe a situation, time, sign, etc as **good**, you mean that 16.1 it does not involve any problems or difficulties and is likely to result in benefit or success. EG *The picture is far from good... Will this be a good year for honey?... He may be an army officer (not a good sign).* ADJ QUALIT = favourable ≠ bad 16.2 it is suitable for a particular purpose. EG *This is a good holiday for people who want to go exploring... This is as good a time as any to find out.* ADJ QUALIT : ATTRIB = convenient

17 You use **good** before a noun 17.1 to indicate the positive, desirable, or successful aspects of the noun. EG *Develop a good relationship with the staff... Ed and I became good friends... It's good fun... Both* ADJ QUALIT ≠ bad, poor

policies make good sense. **17.2** to indicate a great degree of something desirable, enjoyable, or that you approve of. EG *Take good care of it, won't you?... ...a good range of herbs and spices... ...a good-sized living room.* ADJ QUALIT : ATTRIB ≠ poor

18 You use **good** to emphasize that a great degree, extent, or amount of the following word or expression is involved. EG *One good shake of my head and it would fall off... He took a good long look at it... He must owe them a good ten bucks by now... It would be a good bit cheaper... ...a good while ago... I dug it good and deep.* ADJ QUALIT : ATTRIB

19 You use **good** in the following ways to express your reaction to something. **19.1** You say **'Good'** or **'That's good'** to express pleasure or satisfaction about something that has been said or done. EG *'How is he?'-'He's fine.'-'Good.'... 'Everyone's invited,' says Howard. 'Oh that's good,' says the girl... 'I walked,' said Daisy. 'Good, good. Come in.'* EXCLAM = splendid **19.2** You say **'Good'** or **'Very good'** to someone in order to praise them for answering or doing something correctly or well. EG *'That's where we had the recorder.'-'Very good. You're very observant.'* EXCLAM = well done **19.3** People say **'Good one'** in order to praise something clever or funny that someone has just said or done; an informal expression. CONVENTION = nice one **19.4** People say **'That's a good question'** or **'Good question'** in reply to a question which they do not know the answer to, or when there are problems involved in the answer. EG *'What's that?'-'Good question. I'm not quite sure.'... 'When will it be ready?'-'That's a good question, Larry. We're doing all we can.'* PHR = Goodness knows **19.5** If someone in authority says **'Very good'**, they are giving permission or expressing agreement; a formal use. EG *'He'll be alright now.'-'Very good,' Jayne said, 'Let him go.'* CONVENTION ⇑ right = very well

19.6 People in authority say **'Good'** in a conversation or discussion to indicate that they want to end the topic and start doing or talking about something else. EG *'But I am superstitious.'-'Good. Let's move on to another question.'* CONVENTION ⇑ right = okay

20 If you do something or something happens **for good**, you do it or it happens for the last time or completely and permanently. EG *She retired from the kitchen for good, leaving him in charge... The theatre closed down for good.* PHR : USED AS AN A

21 You use **as good as** before an adjective or a verb in order to indicate that the statement you are making is not quite true but is reasonable in the particular situation, since the effect is almost the same as if the statement was true. EG *Without her glasses she was as good as blind... He had as good as abdicated.* PHR : USED AS AN A ⇑ almost = virtually

22 make good. 22.1 If someone **makes good**, they become successful, important, or rich. EG *He had made good, he had become a big name... The Treasury chief was a local boy made good... He had made good and gone to the States.* PHR : VB INFLECTS ⇑ succeed **22.2** If you **make good** something that you have said you will do, you do it. EG *Alas, she never made good her threat.* PHR : VB INFLECTS **22.3** If you **make good** something that you have damaged or harmed, you try to repair it or remove the harmful effects. EG *Three years was a short time in which to make good the deficiencies.* PHR : VB INFLECTS = put right

23 Someone might say **'Good fellow'** or **'Good chap'** to you in order to persuade you to do something or to emphasize that you are of a lower social class than them; used in rather old-fashioned British English. EG *You may leave me now, my good fellow... Pour out another whisky, Percy, there's a good chap.* VOC

24 You use **good old** with the name of a person, place, or thing when you are referring to them in an affectionate way or praising them. EG *Good old Bessie... ...a letter from good old Washington.* PHR + NG/N PROPER ⇑ dear

25 Goods are things that are made to be sold; used of things that can be moved rather than things like buildings. EG *...a wide range of electrical goods... We must produce goods at competitive prices... ...the demand for goods and services.* N PLURAL = merchandise

26 You say **the goods** to refer to what is expected or required in a particular situation; a fairly informal use. EG *Such an unwieldy banking system is unable to deliver the goods... You can always rely on her to come up with the goods.* N PLURAL : *the*+ N ⇑ requirements

27 Good is used with various other words in expressions of surprise or shock, for example 'Good grief' and 'Good heavens': see **gracious**, **grief**, **heaven**, **lord**.

28 The word **good** is also used in the following expressions, which are explained at other places in this dictionary. • **a good deal**: see **deal**. • **a good few**: see **few**. • **a good sailor**: see **sailor**. • **good deed for the day**: see **deed**. • **good show**: see **show**. • **good turn**: see **turn**. • **the good old days**: see **day**. • **as good as gold**: see **gold**. • **as good as your word**: see **word**. • **for good measure**: see **measure**. • **so far so good**: see **far**. • **in good faith**: see **faith**. • **in good taste**: see **taste**. • **in good time**: see **time**. • **to be in** someone's **good books**: see **book**. • **to get out while the going's good**: see **going**.

good afternoon. People say **'Good afternoon'** in the afternoon when they meet someone, speak to them on the telephone, or introduce a television programme or other event; a polite, fairly formal expression. EG *Good afternoon. Could I speak to Mr Duff, please.* CONVENTION ⇑ hallo

goodbye /gʊdbaɪ/, **goodbyes**; also spelled **goodby** in American English; also spelled with a hyphen. **1** You say **'Goodbye'** to someone when you or they are leaving, at the end of a telephone conversation, or at the end of a TV or radio broadcast. EG *'Goodbye, dear,' Miss Saunders said... We said good-bye to Charlie and walked back... 'It's goodbye from me, Alex Lartey, until next week'.* CONVENTION = bye

2 A **goodbye** is the act of saying goodbye when someone goes away. EG *After saying an awkward goodbye to Helen, I left... They say their goodbyes.* N COUNT = farewell

3 If you **say goodbye** to something that you want or usually have, you accept that you are not going to get it. EG *I had to say goodbye to plain wholesome food... I said goodbye to the whole business.* • to **kiss** something **goodbye**: see **kiss**. PHR : VB INFLECTS

good day. People say **'Good day'** to each other during the day when they meet or sometimes instead of 'Goodbye', when they want to indicate that they want to go away; a very formal, old-fashioned expression. EG *'I see,' he said, 'Then we understand each other. Good day, Monsieur Goossens.'... As he walked in he nodded gravely, and said as he went into his office, 'Good day to you.'* CONVENTION

good evening. People say **'Good evening'** in the evening when they meet, when introducing a TV programme or other event, or sometimes instead of 'Goodbye'; a polite, fairly formal expression. EG *Good evening. Tonight my guests are... Good evening, Mr Castle. I'm sorry I'm so late.* CONVENTION ⇑ hallo

good-for-nothing, **good-for-nothings**. A **good-for-nothing** is a lazy or irresponsible person; used showing disapproval. EG *'That good-for-nothing!' muttered Liz... ...his good-for-nothing son.* N COUNT : USU USED AS C = layabout

Good Friday is the day on which Christians remember the crucifixion of Jesus Christ. It is the Friday before Easter Sunday. N UNCOUNT

good-humoured, better-humoured. Someone who is **good-humoured** is pleasant and cheerful in their attitude and behaviour. EG *The crowds were patient and good-humoured... ...good-humoured, friendly rivalry.* ADJ QUALIT = good-natured

goodie /gʊdi[1]/. See **goody**.

good-looking, **better-looking, best-looking**. Someone who is **good-looking** has an attractive face. EG *He was tall and good-looking... ...a good-looking girl like you.* ADJ QUALIT = personable

good looks. If you talk about someone's **good looks**, you are referring to the attractive appearance of their face. EG *...his striking good looks and charm... She seems to have everything, intelligence, good looks, a comfortable home.* N PLURAL

goodly /gʊdli[1]/. A **goodly** amount or part of something is a fairly large amount or part of it, often more than was expected; a formal word. EG *A goodly part of her income went on travel... ...a goodly number of the alleged spies... He sold it for a goodly sum.* ADJ CLASSIF : ATTRIB = substantial

good morning. People say **'Good morning'** in the morning when they first see each other or when they get to work, and sometimes as a way of saying 'Goodbye'. EG *Good morning, darling. Another beautiful day... Good morning, doctor. I hope we'll see you again soon... She kissed him good morning.* CONVENTION

good-natured. A person or animal that is **good-natured** is naturally friendly and does not easily get angry. EG *...our good-natured policemen... ...a very good-natured and foolish cousin.* ▸ used of behaviour ADJ QUALIT ⇑ pleasant = kindly and actions. EG ...*a good-natured complaint... The sound of good-natured revelry filled the hotel.*

goodness /gʊdnɪ²s/. 1 People say **'My goodness'**, **'Goodness'**, etc to express surprise. EG *My goodness, this is a difficult one... Goodness, look at that!... Goodness me! You look a couple of miseries!* • **thank goodness**: see **thank**. EXCLAM

2 **Goodness** is the quality of being kind, considerate, and helpful. EG ...*a belief in the goodness of human nature... Is this how you repay my goodness?* N UNCOUNT

3 If you ask someone to **have the goodness to** do something, you ask them in a polite way to do it; a very formal expression. EG *Would you have the goodness to pass me the salt?... Perkins had the goodness to start a fire.* PHR : VB INFLECTS

goodnight /gʊdnaɪt/, **goodnights**; also spelled with a hyphen or as two words. 1 You say **'Goodnight'** to someone late in the evening, when you or they are going home, going to bed, or going to sleep, or at the end of a telephone conversation or a TV or radio broadcast. EG *'Goodnight love,' says Flora, shutting her door... We all stood up, said good night, and went to our rooms... 'I have to go now. Good night.' He hung up.* CONVENTION

2 A **goodnight** is the act of saying goodnight to someone. EG *They just left. Not even a goodnight or a thank you for the meal...* ...*a good-night kiss.* N COUNT ⇑ goodbye

goods train, goods trains. A **goods train** is a train that transports goods and not people. N COUNT

goods wagon, goods wagons. A **goods wagon** is a carriage on a train that carries goods and not people. N COUNT = freight train

good-tempered. Someone who is **good-tempered** is cheerful and does not easily get angry or upset. EG ...*an adorable baby, chubby and good-tempered... Cal was usually easy-going and good-tempered.* ADJ QUALIT ⇑ pleasant = good-natured

goodwill /gʊdwɪl/; also spelled with a hyphen and as two words. **Goodwill** is 1 kind feelings or helpful behaviour towards other people. EG *He beamed with such goodwill...* ...*the goodwill and cooperation of all who are involved...* ...*a goodwill gesture.* N UNCOUNT ⇑ kindness = benevolence 2 the popularity and good reputation of a successful business that forms part of its financial worth. EG *Was goodwill taken into consideration in arranging the sale?* N UNCOUNT

goody /gʊdi¹/, **goodies**; also spelled **goodie**; an informal word. 1 People, especially children, say **goody** to express their pleasure or approval of something. EG *Oh goody, there's some cake!* EXCLAM = whoopee

2 A **goody** is 2.1 a person in a situation, especially in a film or book, who works or fights for people or ideas that you approve of. N COUNT : USU PL ≠ villain 2.2 something pleasant, exciting, attractive, or clever. EG *She opened the bag of goodies... His writing contains some real goodies.* N COUNT : USU PL = treat

goody-goody, goody-goodies. A **goody-goody** is a person who behaves extremely well in order to please people in authority; an informal word used showing disapproval. N COUNT ⇑ crawler

gooey /gu:i¹/, **gooier, gooiest**; an informal word used in British English. 1 A **gooey** substance is very soft and sticky. EG ...*a gooey mess.* ADJ QUALIT

2 A **gooey** cake or dessert is very sticky or creamy and usually very sweet. EG ...*gooey fudge sundaes.* ADJ QUALIT

3 If you describe a film or someone's behaviour as **gooey**, you mean that they show or express love in a very sentimental way. EG *The song made her go all gooey.* ADJ QUALIT = slushy

goof /gu:f/, **goofs, goofing, goofed**; an informal word used especially in American English. 1 If you **goof**, you make a foolish mistake and often fail to achieve what you wanted. EG *They had their chance, and they goofed.* V ⇑ blunder = boob

2 If you **goof** or **goof off**, you spend time in a lazy or foolish way, often when you are supposed to be working. EG *He never goofed off into restaurants when he was on patrol... We spent most of August sailing and goofing.* V : USU+A *(off/around)* ⇑ laze = skive

3 A **goof** is 3.1 a foolish person, especially one who is easily deceived. EG *That poor goof wouldn't know.* N COUNT 3.2 a foolish mistake, often one that prevents you achieving what you wanted. EG *What a goof!* N COUNT = boob

goofy /gu:fi¹/, **goofier, goofiest**. Something that is **goofy** is silly or ridiculous, often in a strange or unusual way; an informal word used especially in American English. EG ...*wearing a pair of goofy overalls... It's the sort of goofy idea that Zoe would have.* ADJ QUALIT ⇑ eccentric = loony

gook /gu:k, gʊk/, **gooks**. A **gook** is a very offensive word for a person from a country in the Far East; used in American English. N COUNT

goon /gu:n/, **goons**; an informal word. A **goon** is 1 in British English, a person who behaves in a silly or humorous way. N COUNT/VOC = clown 2 in American English, a person who is paid to hurt or threaten people. EG *Pimps were shot, goons were massacred...* ...*organizing goon squads to intimidate party officials.* N COUNT = thug

goose, /gu:s/, **geese**; **gooses, goosing, goosed**. **Geese** is the plural of the noun. **Gooses** is the third person singular, present tense, of the verb. 1 A **goose** is 1.1 a large bird that has a long neck and webbed feet and makes a loud noise. Geese exist as wild birds, but are also often kept on farms for their meat, eggs, and feathers. EG *A flock of geese honked across the sky, heading south... The barn rang with the cries of geese and turkeys.* N COUNT ⇑ fowl 1.2 a female goose. The male goose is called a gander. N COUNT

2 **Goose** is the meat from a goose that has been cooked. EG ...*roast goose with red cabbage and dumplings.* N UNCOUNT

3 If you call someone a **goose**, you mean that you think they are foolish; used affectionately in informal, rather old-fashioned English. EG *'You goose!'... He thought her a silly goose.* N COUNT/VOC ⇑ fool = clot

4 If you **cook** someone's **goose**, you prevent their plans from succeeding; an informal expression. EG *Will he get a Cabinet post, or has he cooked his own goose?* PHR : VB INFLECTS ⇑ hinder

5 If someone **kills the goose that lays the golden eggs**, they harm or destroy the person or thing that gives them their money, power, or advantage. • **say boo to a goose**: see **boo**. • **wild goose chase**: see **chase**. PHR : VB INFLECTS

6 If you **goose** someone, you poke them playfully between their buttocks, in order to startle them; a very informal expression used in American English. V+O

gooseberry /gʊzbəⁿri¹/, **gooseberries**. 1 A **gooseberry** is a small green berry that grows on a bush, has a sharp taste, and is covered with tiny hairs. You can eat gooseberries or use them to make pies and puddings. N COUNT ⇑ fruit

2 If you say that someone is **playing gooseberry**, you mean that they are an unwelcome third person in the company of two people who are in love with each other and who want to be alone together. EG *I'd hate to play gooseberry to you and your boyfriend.* PHR : VB INFLECTS

gooseflesh /gu:sflɛʃ/; also spelled with a hyphen. **Gooseflesh** is a condition of your skin when you are cold or scared. The hairs on the skin stand up so that it is covered with tiny bumps. EG *The sudden chill raised gooseflesh on the girl's arms...* ...*the gooseflesh which came when Rhoda touched him.* N UNCOUNT = goose pimples

goose pimples; also spelled with a hyphen. **Goose pimples** are the same as gooseflesh. EG *Wild irritation was bringing her out in goose pimples.* N UNCOUNT

goose-step, goose-steps, goose-stepping, goose-stepped. If soldiers **goose-step**, they march in such a way that they lift their legs high and do not bend their knees. EG *Two sentries with white gloves were goose-stepping up and down.* V

Gordian knot /gɔ:dɪən nɒt/, **Gordian knots**. A **Gordian knot** is a very difficult and complicated problem or situation; a formal expression. EG *Planners were busy by-passing the Gordian knot.* N COUNT : USU SING ⇑ difficulty • If you **cut** or **untie** the **Gordian knot** in a particular situation, you solve a difficult problem by taking bold or forceful actions. EG *The way to socialism and democracy was a Gordian knot which could not be cut... A generous system of child benefits unties this Gordian knot.* • PHR : VB INFLECTS

gore /gɔ:/, **gores, goring, gored**. 1 If an animal **gores** someone, it wounds them badly with its horns or tusks. EG ...*if a bull gores someone to death...* ...*gored in the belly by a cow's horn.* V+O ⇑ wound = stab 2 **Gore** is unpleasant-looking blood from a person or animal, for example after they have been involved in an accident. EG ...*lie dying in a pool of black gore...* ...*a horror film full of gore.* N UNCOUNT

gorge /gɔ:dʒ/, **gorges, gorging, gorged**. 1 A **gorge** is a deep, narrow valley with very steep sides, usually where a river passes through mountains or an area of hard rock. EG ...*the lower gorge where the Colorado River runs... The desert road winds through rocky gorges and hills.* N COUNT : ALSO IN NAMES AFTER N ⇑ canyon = ravine

2 If you **gorge** or **gorge** yourself, you eat very V OR V+O (REFL)

greedily until you are so full that you cannot possibly eat any more. EG *They gorged themselves on rich food... The hunters gorged and then rested.*
◊ **gorged**. EG *Hours later, gorged to repletion, he awoke.* ◊ ADJ CLASSIF = glutted

gorgeous /gɔːdʒəs/. 1 If you say something is **gorgeous**, you mean that it gives you a lot of pleasure or enjoyment; an informal use. EG *'Look what David gave me for Christmas.'–'Oh it's absolutely gorgeous.'... We stayed at that gorgeous hotel on Nob Hill.* ADJ QUALIT ⥣ nice = lovely

2 **Gorgeous** weather is very warm and sunny and extremely pleasant. EG *Isn't it a gorgeous day?... We had three weeks of gorgeous weather.* ADJ QUALIT ⥣ good = glorious

3 Something that is **gorgeous** is very attractive and bright to look at. EG *...ruby necklaces, shimmering and gorgeous on beds of green velvet... The night sky was now gorgeous with billions of stars.* ADJ QUALIT = brilliant
◊ **gorgeously**. EG *...gorgeously coloured fancy underwear.* ◊ ADV+ADJ = brilliantly

4 If you say that someone is **gorgeous**, you mean that you think they are extremely attractive or beautiful; an informal use. EG *...the hero embracing his gorgeous bride... 'Hello, gorgeous.'* ADJ QUALIT, ALSO VOC

gorilla /gərɪlə/, **gorillas**. A **gorilla** is an animal which looks like a very large monkey. It has long arms, a black face, and black fur. Gorillas live on the ground in African forests. N COUNT ⥣ ape

gormless /gɔːmlɪ²s/. If you say that someone is **gormless**, you think that they are stupid because they do not understand things very quickly; an informal word used in British English. EG *He is soft and vulnerable, though not gormless.* ADJ QUALIT = witless ≠ quick

gorse /gɔːs/ is a dark green bush that has small yellow flowers and sharp prickles. It grows wild in the countryside or on waste land. EG *...the ferns, the gorse and the bracken... ...gorse bushes.* N UNCOUNT ⥣ shrub

gory /gɔːri¹/, **gorier, goriest**. You use **gory** to describe situations or facts that involve people suffering, being injured, or dying in a horrible way. EG *...the gory details of the police brutality... ...nurses confronted with gory operations such as limb amputation... The film contains no gory violence.* ADJ QUALIT = bloody

gosh /gɒʃ/. You say **'Gosh'** to indicate how surprised you are or how strongly you feel about something; an informal, slightly old-fashioned word. EG *'Thirteen pounds! Gosh that's a lot'... 'Gosh, I'm hungry. Are you?'* EXCLAM = goodness

gosling /gɒzlɪŋ/, **goslings**. A **gosling** is a baby goose. EG *...a newly hatched gosling.* N COUNT

go-slow, go-slows. A **go-slow** is a protest by workers in which they deliberately work slowly in order to cause problems for their employers. N COUNT

gospel /gɒspə⁰l/, **gospels**. 1 A **Gospel** is one of the four books of the Bible which describe the life and teachings of Jesus Christ. EG *...the Gospel according to St Mark.* N COUNT

2 A **gospel** is also a particular way of thinking or a set of ideas that a person or group believes in very strongly and that they urge others to accept. EG *...spreading the pacifist gospel... They continue to preach their gospel of self-reliance.* N COUNT+SUPP = doctrine

3 If you **take** something **as gospel** or **gospel truth**, you believe that it is completely true. EG *You can take it as gospel truth that he is busy.* PHR : VB INFLECTS

4 **Gospel** music is a style of religious music that uses strong rhythms and people singing in harmony. It is especially popular among black Christians in the southern United States. EG *...gospel songs.* ADJ CLASSIF : ATTRIB

gossamer /gɒsəmə/. 1 **Gossamer** is the very light, fine thread that spiders use to make cobwebs. It is often found floating in the air or lying on plants. EG *...shining ends of flying gossamer.* N UNCOUNT

2 **Gossamer** is used to refer to cloth that is very thin and delicate. EG *...a gossamer handkerchief... ...gossamer curtains.* N BEFORE N

gossip /gɒsɪp/, **gossips, gossiping, gossiped**. 1 **Gossip** is informal conversation or information about other people or their actions, often including unkind or disapproving comments about their private affairs. EG *...a nice, chatty letter full of news and gossip... ...spreading scandal and gossip about their colleagues... Gossip had it that she would marry Granby.* N UNCOUNT, OR N SING : *the*+N = rumour

2 A **gossip** is 2.1 a person who enjoys talking informally to people, especially about the private affairs of other people; used showing disapproval. EG *Gossips have insisted that he's more than just another friend... Isn't he a bit of a gossip himself?* N COUNT = scandal-monger 2.2 an informal conversation, especially about other people or local events. EG *What he really enjoys is a good gossip... ...friendly gossips over our garden gates.* N COUNT = chat

3 If you **gossip**, you talk informally with someone, especially about other people or local events. EG *Well, let us not gossip about the past... I mustn't stay gossiping with you any longer... Some gossiping old woman had seen them meet.* V : USU+A = natter

gossip column, gossip columns. A **gossip column** is a part of a newspaper or magazine where the activities and private affairs of famous people are discussed, often in a critical way. EG *Several people made speeches defending his performance. The gossip columns were full of it... A week later, this appeared in his gossip column.* N COUNT

gossipy /gɒsɪpi¹/. 1 A **gossipy** person enjoys gossiping; used showing disapproval. EG *...a lot of gossipy old women.* ADJ QUALIT ⥣ talkative

2 Speech or writing that is **gossipy** is full of news and information about your own affairs or about other people, and written or spoken in a very informal style. EG *Martin's tone became more gossipy, casual... Their observations were slightly malicious and gossipy... ...his rather gossipy book.* ADJ QUALIT = chatty

got /gɒt/. 1 **Got** is the past tense and past participle of **get**.

2 **Got** is often used in spoken English after the verb 'have' in the expression **have got**, when 'have' alone would be correct but more formal. The word **got** itself adds nothing to the meaning of 'have'. The form **have got** looks as if it is the auxiliary 'have' followed by the past participle of the verb 'get', but it is used with the same meanings as the main verb 'have', in the senses of owning or possessing things: see **have**. EG *We haven't got a car... I've got loads of friends... Have you got any brochures on Holland, please?... I've got no regrets about what I did... I've got nothing to hide... That door's got a lock on it... You've got a lot of work to do... He hasn't got time to do that sort of thing... They've got plenty of money... She's got a very good job.* V+O

3 **Got** is also used in the expression **have got to**, which is an informal way of saying 'have to' or 'must'. It is used mainly to indicate that it is necessary that something should be done: see **have**, **must**. EG *We've all got to get up early tomorrow... If you want children you've got to accept the responsibility... You've got to admit that he did it very well... There's got to be some motive... Jenny's got to be here!... If Dolly has got to die, I want to be with her.* V+*to*-INF

Gothic /gɒθɪk/. 1 A building such as a cathedral that is **Gothic** has a style of architecture that is distinguished by tall pillars, high vaulted ceilings, and pointed arches. EG *...carved Gothic doorways.* ADJ CLASSIF ▸ used as an uncount noun. EG *...the transition from Gothic to Renaissance.* ▸ N UNCOUNT

2 **Gothic** is used to describe 2.1 stories in which strange, mysterious adventures happen in dark and lonely places such as the ruins of a castle. EG *...Seven Gothic Tales.* ADJ CLASSIF 2.2 a style of printing or writing in which the letters are very ornate, and which is used especially in signs, book titles, etc. EG *'Hotel Metropole' was inscribed in Gothic letters above the door.* ADJ CLASSIF

gotta /gɒtə/ is used in written English to represent an informal pronunciation of 'got to'. It is an informal way of saying 'have to' or 'must', especially in American English: see **have**, **must**. EG *I gotta get dressed... I've gotta get back.* V+INF

gotten /gɒtə⁰n/ is the past participle of **get** in American English. ● See also **ill-gotten**.

gouge /gaʊdʒ/, **gouges, gouging, gouged**. 1 If you **gouge** something, you make a hole in it with a pointed object, often without being very careful about how you do it. EG *You've gouged a hole in the wall with the end of that pole!* V+O : USU+A ⥣ dig

2 A **gouge** is a big hole that has been made in something. EG *The notice boards had gouges several feet long.* N COUNT

gouge out. If you **gouge** something **out**, you force it out of a hole using your fingers or a sharp instrument. EG *It was revolting; he gouged out his eyes!* PHRASAL VB : V+O+ADV

gourd /gʊəd/, **gourds**. A **gourd** is 1 a type of large fruit that is similar to a marrow or a cucumber; also used of the plant that produces this fruit. N COUNT 2 a N COUNT container that is made from the hard, dry skin of this fruit. EG ...*a gourd full of milk.*

gourmand /gʊəmənd/, **gourmands**. A **gourmand** is a person who enjoys eating and drinking, especially in large amounts. EG *He was an enormous gourmand and gambler as well as a splendid actor.* — N COUNT

gourmet /gʊəmeɪ/, **gourmets**. A **gourmet** is a person who knows a lot about good cooking and wine, and who enjoys eating high quality food. EG *First, for the gourmet, the rainbow trout... ...a gourmet restaurant.* — N COUNT ⇑ expert

gout /gaʊt/. 1 **Gout** is a disease which causes someone's joints to swell painfully, especially in their toes. EG *Gout is a form of arthritis.* — N UNCOUNT

2 A **gout** of something soft and wet is a small amount of it; a formal use. EG ...*gouts of blood.* — N PART+N UNCOUNT

gouty /gaʊti¹/. Someone who is **gouty** suffers from gout. — ADJ QUALIT

Gov. is an abbreviation for 'Governor'. EG ...*Gov. Hugh L. Carey of New York.* — N IN TITLES

govern /gʌvəⁿn/, **governs, governing, governed**. 1 Someone who **governs**, or who **governs** a country or a group of people, rules the country by making and revising the laws, managing the economy, controlling public services, etc. EG *Many civil servants are sure that they can govern better than the politicians... ...a strong, centralized State, governed by a single party.* ◇ **governing**. EG *The actual governing of the town was done by trusted counsellors.* — V OR V+O; ◇ N UNCOUNT

2 Something that **governs** an event or situation has control and influence over it. EG *Poverty governed our lives and behaviour... There are strict rules governing the killing and cooking of kangaroo... ...a battle for the rights of people to govern their own destinies.* — V+O ⇑ rule

3 Something that **governs** the way something works, happens, or develops controls and determines the exact way that it works, happens, or develops. EG *The laws that govern the behaviour of light are universal... Do genes govern all characteristics of an individual?* — V+O = dictate

governess /gʌvənɪ²s/, **governesses**. A **governess** is a woman who is employed by a family to live with them and educate their children. EG ...*a kind of unpaid governess and housekeeper.* — N COUNT ⇑ teacher

governing body, governing bodies. A **governing body** is a committee that is responsible for making and enforcing the rules which control a public organization or group of professional people. EG *He's directly responsible to the governing bodies of the university.* — N COUNT

government /gʌvənⁿmə²nt/, **governments**. 1 A **government** is the group of people who are responsible for governing a country or state at a particular time. EG *The Wilson Government came to power in 1964... ...the government of Mexico... The government has had to cut back on public expenditure.* — N COUNT : VB CAN BE SING OR PL

2 **Government** is 2.1 the departments, ministries, committees, etc that represent the state and that carry out the decisions of the political leaders of a country. EG ...*a cut in government spending... He had some private money besides his government grant.* — N UNCOUNT : USU BEFORE N

2.2 the activities and processes involved in governing a country or state. EG *Government has become much more difficult today... Most of his ministers had no previous experience of government.* — N UNCOUNT ⇑ ruling

2.3 a particular method, style, or system of governing a country or state. EG ...*the principle of government by the majority... ...democratic Government.* — N UNCOUNT+SUPP ⇑ rule

governor /gʌvəⁿnə/, **governors**. 1 A **governor** is 1.1 a person who is responsible for the political administration of a region, especially of a state in the United States of America. EG ...*former Governor John Connally of Texas... His mother begged for an audience with the governor... ...the Governor of New York.* — N COUNT : ALSO IN TITLE ⇑ ruler

1.2 the chief political administrator of a colony. EG ...*Sir Hugh Clifford, governor of the Gold Coast... ...the Governor's Palace.* — N COUNT/PROPER

1.3 a person who is on a committee which controls the conduct and standards of an institution such as a school, hospital, university, etc. EG *Being a School Governor does mean real involvement... ...the Board of Governors.* — N COUNT ⇑ administrator

1.4 the person who is in charge of the administration of a prison. EG ...*that is the view of the governor of Brixton Prison, Michael Selby.* — N COUNT ⇑ head

2 Your **governor** is a man who is in a position of authority over you, for example your employer or your father; an informal use in British English, usually used only by men. EG *I had to accept everything my governor said to me.* — N COUNT/VOC : USU POSS+N ⇑ superior

Governor-General, Governors-General, Governor-Generals. The plural can be either **Governors-General** or **Governor-Generals**. A **Governor-General** is a person who is sent to a former colony as the chief representative of the country which used to control that colony. EG *Instructions had been communicated to the Governor-General.* — N COUNT/PROPER

govt is an abbreviation for 'government'.

gown /gaʊn/, **gowns**. A **gown** is 1 a long dress which women wear on formal occasions. EG *You're going to get flour all over that fancy gown... ...a wedding gown.* — N COUNT ⇑ garment

2 a loose piece of clothing rather like a long cloak, which is usually black in colour and is worn on formal occasions by people such as judges, lawyers, and university students and staff. EG *The Speaker was wearing black breeches, gown and wig... ...a student's gown.* — N COUNT ⇑ robe

GP, GPs. A **GP** is a doctor who does not specialize in any particular area of medicine, but who has a medical practice in which he or she treats all types of illness; an abbreviation for 'general practitioner'. EG ...*the GP's surgery.* — N COUNT = general practitioner

grab /græb/, **grabs, grabbing, grabbed**. 1 If you **grab** something, you take it or pick it up suddenly and roughly. EG *She grabbed my arm... I grabbed her by the shoulders... He grabbed the bottle.* — V+O = seize

2 If you **grab** at something, you make an attempt to take it or pick it up, but you do not always succeed. EG *She fell on her knees to grab at the money.* — V+A *(at)* = snatch

3 If you **grab** something such as food, drink, sleep, etc, you have it or get it quickly, especially when you are in a hurry. EG *I think I'll grab a sandwich... He hoped to grab a few hours sleep at the airport.* — V+O = pick up

4 If you **grab** something such as a chance or opportunity, or **grab** at it, you take advantage of it eagerly. EG *Why didn't you grab the chance to go to New York?... ...an old woman, grabbing at youth.* — V+O, OR V+A *(at)*

5 If something such as an experience, idea, plan, etc **grabs** you, it makes you feel excited and interested; an informal use. EG *No, the idea doesn't grab me.* — V+O ⇑ interest

6 A **grab** at or for an object is a sudden attempt to hold it tightly or pick it up. EG *He made a savage grab for the knife.* — N COUNT = lunge

7 A **grab** at or for something such as power, fame, etc is an attempt to gain it. EG *Their grab for real power in this world was doomed to failure.* — N COUNT = bid

8 If something is **up for grabs**, it is generally available to anyone who is interested; an informal expression. EG *His job is up for grabs.* — PHR : USED AS AN A = free

grace /greɪs/, **graces, gracing, graced**. 1 **Grace** is 1.1 a way of moving which is smooth, controlled, and attractive to watch. EG *She moved with an extraordinary spontaneity and grace... ...Jenny's simplicity and grace.* — N UNCOUNT ⇑ beauty

1.2 a polite and pleasant way of doing things that makes people admire you and be glad to work with you or be with you. EG *He brought to the negotiations his own perceptions, his own grace.* — N UNCOUNT ⇑ sensitivity = refinement

1.3 the ability to behave in a polite and generous way even though you are upset or annoyed about something. EG *I was not handling the experience with any more grace than the rest of the delegation had.* — N UNCOUNT ⇑ behaviour = tact

2 If you do something **with good grace** or **with a good grace**, you do it cheerfully and without complaining, especially when it is something that you do not like doing. If you do something **with bad grace** or **with a bad grace**, you are unwilling to do it and complain about it, especially because you think you should not have to do it. EG *Listen to whatever he says with a good grace... They accept unhappiness with stoic good grace.* — PHR : USED AS AN A

3 If you **have the grace** or **have the good grace** to do something, you behave in a way which shows that you are sorry for doing something wrong or for upsetting someone. EG *At least he had the good grace to drop his smile and look away from me... Her daughter didn't even have the grace to try to hide it.* — PHR : VB INFLECTS+*to*-INF = have the decency

4 The **graces** are the ways of behaving and doing things which are considered polite amongst upper-class people. EG *She tried to emulate the graces of more polished homes... They learn the social graces.* — N PLURAL : *the*+N ⇑ manners

5 Grace also refers to the period of time which remains or an extra period which you are allowed before something happens or before you are expected to do something such as finish a job or pay a bill. EG *We have only a few hours' grace before the soldiers come... The grace period will end soon.*
N UNCOUNT = reprieve

6 If something **graces** a place, it makes the place more pleasant or attractive; a formal use. EG *...plants that grace our conservatories... ...the row of bells which had once graced the portico.*
V+O ⇑ improve = adorn

7 If you say that someone important **graces** an event, you mean that they kindly agree to be present at it; a formal use. EG *He had been invited to grace a function at the evening college... Two English directors graced the board of the company.*
V+O ⇑ attend = honour

8 If you are in the **grace** of a person or organization, you are liked and trusted by them. EG *...a famous television reporter's fall from official grace.*
N UNCOUNT : USU +SUPP ⇑ approval = favour

9 In Christianity and some other religions, **grace** is the kindness that God shows to human beings because He loves them. EG *The struggle cannot be undertaken without divine grace.* ● If you say **'There but for the grace of God go I'**, you are talking about someone who is in an unfortunate situation, and admitting that you could have been in the same situation if the circumstances had been different.
N UNCOUNT ⇑ favour; ● PHR

10 Grace is also a prayer which Christians say or sing before a meal, or sometimes after it, in order to thank God for the food and to ask Him to bless it. EG *The father seemed to be saying grace, for the children bowed their heads... ...a Latin grace.*
N UNCOUNT/COUNT = benediction

11 Grace is used to address or refer to a duke, duchess, or archbishop. EG *His Grace will receive you now... May I assist you, Your Grace?*
N COUNT : DETPOSS+N, USED IN TITLES

12 See also **coup de grace**, **saving grace**. ● **airs and graces**: see **air**.

graceful /greɪsful/. **1** Someone or something that is **graceful** moves in a smooth and controlled way which is attractive to watch. EG *They're very graceful animals... ...graceful dancers... Sydney was tall and graceful.* ▸ used of their movements. EG *She runs up the stairs with her light graceful step.* ◊ **gracefully**. EG *Learn how to move gracefully on a stage... The yacht slid gracefully into the water.*
ADJ QUALIT ⇑ beautiful = elegant ≠ clumsy, gauche; ◊ ADV = elegantly

2 Something that is **graceful** is attractive because it has a very pleasing shape or style. EG *...the graceful little white wooden building... ...graceful curves... ...graceful writing.*
ADJ QUALIT = elegant

3 If a person's behaviour is **graceful**, it is polite, kind, and pleasant, especially in a difficult or embarrassing situation. EG *She turned with graceful solicitude to Anthea... There is no graceful way of refusing.* ◊ **gracefully**. EG *He accepted gracefully and gratefully.*
ADJ QUALIT ≠ grudging, sullen; ◊ ADV WITH VB ≠ grudgingly

graceless /greɪslɪ^{2}s/. **1** Something that is **graceless** is unattractive and has no interest or charm. EG *The dresses were graceless and expensive... ...a large, graceless industrial city.*
ADJ QUALIT ⇑ ugly ≠ elegant

2 If you say that someone is **graceless**, you mean that they behave impolitely, especially when someone has been kind to them. EG *He was so graceless, so eager to shock... It was a bit graceless of her considering the expense I'd incurred on her behalf.*
ADJ QUALIT ⇑ rude = churlish ≠ gracious

gracious /greɪʃəs/. **1** If you say that someone is **gracious**, you mean that they are very polite and pleasant, especially in the way that they treat people who have a lower social position than them; a formal use. EG *She could also be witty, very ladylike and gracious... ...my brief association with the gracious lady many years ago.* ▸ used of people's actions and behaviour. EG *...a gracious smile.* ◊ **graciously**. EG *She accepted the tribute graciously... Her ladyship graciously invited me to come in.* ◊ **graciousness**.
ADJ QUALIT = affable; ◊ ADV WITH VB ≠ grudgingly; ◊ N UNCOUNT

2 Gracious is used to describe the way of life of wealthy people, especially in former times, referring to its luxury and leisure. EG *...places of recreation and gracious living... ...the gracious world of the Forsytes... ...the last remnants of a more gracious era.*
ADJ QUALIT : USU ATTRIB = elegant

3 People use expressions such as **'Good gracious!'**, **'Good gracious me!'**, **'Goodness gracious!'**, etc, in informal and slightly old-fashioned English, **3.1** to express surprise, interest, or annoyance. EG *'Good gracious! I never knew that.'... 'Good gracious me,' he said. 'How absolutely fascinating.'* **3.2** to add emphasize to what they are saying, usually when they are expressing agreement or disagreement with what someone has just said. EG *'You know Jack, don't you?'-'Good gracious, yes.'... 'You're short of money?'-'Good gracious no!'... Good gracious, the school he goes to doesn't matter.*
EXCLAM = good heavens; EXCLAM = heavens

gradation /grədeɪʃə^{0}n/, **gradations**. A **gradation** is a small or slow change, or one of the stages in the process of change. EG *...the subtle colour gradations... ...white bread and wholemeal bread, and many gradations between the two... ...gradations of power.*
N COUNT+SUPP

grade /greɪd/, **grades, grading, graded**. **1** If you **grade** something, you judge or measure the quality of it and give it a number, name, etc that indicates how good or bad it is. EG *...questions about the way wheat was graded... All written work has to be marked and graded... The reports are graded 1 to 6.* ● See also **graded**.
V+O : USU PASS = classify

2 The **grade** of a product is its quality, especially when this has been officially judged or measured. EG *I tried using the ordinary grade petrol... ...low grade energy... ...different grades of paper.*
N COUNT : USU MOD+N

3 Your **grade** in an examination or piece of written work is the mark you get, usually in the form of a letter or number, that indicates your level of achievement. EG *She passed the exams with very good grades... I got grade B... ...the A level grades required to enter university.*
N COUNT : USU MOD+N, OR N+NUM/*A,B,C,D,E* ⇑ result

4 Your **grade** in a company or organization is your level of importance or your rank. EG *...separate dining rooms for different grades of staff... ...recruits from all social grades and every political party... ...a junior executive of a fairly low grade.*
N COUNT+SUPP

5 A **grade** in an American school is a class or a group of classes in which all the children are of a similar age. When you are five years old you go into the first grade and you leave school after the twelfth grade. EG *She had entered the sixth grade at eleven... ...a boy in the second grade.*
N COUNT : USU ORD+N = form, year

6 A **grade** is a slope; used especially in American English. EG *On a steep grade I found myself behind a gigantic truck... We climbed long grades and rolled downhill again.*
N COUNT

7 If someone **makes the grade**, they succeed, especially by reaching a particular standard; an informal expression. EG *You'll make the grade, don't worry.*
PHR : VB INFLECTS

grade crossing, grade crossings. A **grade crossing** is a level crossing; used in American English.
N COUNT

graded /greɪdɪ^{2}d/ is used to describe something that is gently and gradually sloping or changing. EG *...a nicely graded curve... ...a graded series of transformations.*
ADJ CLASSIF : ATTRIB

grade school, grade schools. A **grade school** is a primary school in the United States.
N COUNT/UNCOUNT

gradient /greɪdɪənt/, **gradients**. **1** A **gradient** is a slope or the degree of steepness of a slope; used especially when measuring the steepness of a road or railway line. EG *The floor has a minimum gradient of 1 in 5... The tunnel, two miles long, is on a gradient... ...roads with sharp bends and varying gradients.*
N COUNT

2 The **gradient** of a graph or series of measurements is the rate at which one set of amounts changes in relation to another. EG *...a stable temperature gradient in the tank.*
N COUNT+SUPP = curve

gradual /grædju^{0}əl/. Something that is **gradual** happens or changes over a long period of time rather than suddenly. EG *It's a process of gradual development... In other cases the progress is much more gradual.* ◊ **gradually**. EG *Things change gradually in engineering... Women are taking over gradually.*
ADJ QUALIT ⇑ slow ≠ immediate, sudden; ◊ ADV WITH VB = bit by bit

graduate, graduates, graduating, graduated. The word **graduate** is pronounced /grædjuət/ when it is a noun and /grædjueɪt/ when it is a verb. **1** A **graduate** is **1.1** a student who has successfully completed a first degree at a university or college and has received a certificate that shows this. EG *...a psychology graduate of Stanford University... ...a period of high graduate unemployment... ...ever-increasing numbers of graduates.* **1.2** in the United States, a student who has sucessfully completed high school and has received a certificate or diploma. EG *...a high school graduate.*
N COUNT : IF+PREP THEN *of*; N COUNT+SUPP

2 Graduate also means the same as postgraduate. EG *...graduate students in the philosophy department... ...the graduate prospectus.*
N BEFORE N = postgraduate

3 When a student **graduates**, they have successfully completed a degree course at a university or college
V : USU+A ⇑ pass

and receive a certificate that shows this, usually at a special ceremony. EG *She had recently graduated from law school... He will graduate as a chemical engineer... The young man had graduated a couple of years previously.*

4 In the United States, when someone **graduates** or when a person **graduates** them, they have successfully completed high school and receive a certificate or diploma that shows this, usually at a special ceremony. EG *Gretchen graduated from high school.* — V-ERG : USU+A

5 If you **graduate** from one thing to another, you go from a less important job or position to a more important one. EG *Start on a local paper, and then graduate to a provincial paper... Later they would graduate to really important work.* — V : USU+A *(to/from)* ⇑ rise = progress

graduated /grædʒueɪtɪ²d/ is used to describe 1 something that increases by regular amounts or grades. EG *...graduated pensions... ...a campaign of graduated violence.* — ADJ CLASSIF : USU ATTRIB 2 something that is marked with lines and numbers which show particular measurements. EG *...a graduated flask.* — ADJ CLASSIF : USU ATTRIB

graduate school, graduate schools. A **graduate school** is a department in a North American university or college where postgraduate students are taught. EG *I intended to study philosophy in graduate school... ...the Graduate School of Business at McGill University.* — N UNCOUNT/COUNT

graduation /grædʒueɪʃəⁿn/, **graduations.** 1 **Graduation** is 1.1 the successful completion of a course of study at a university, college, etc, for which you receive a degree or diploma. EG *I'm hoping to get a good job after graduation.* — N UNCOUNT ⇑ finishing 1.2 a special ceremony at university, college, etc, at which degrees and diplomas are given to students who have successfully completed their studies. EG *He had just attended his daughter's graduation.* — N SING : BEFORE N, OR POSS+N

2 A **graduation** is a line or number on a container or measuring instrument which marks a particular measurement. — N COUNT

graffiti /grəˢfiːti¹/. **Graffiti** is both the singular and the plural form. **Graffiti** is words or pictures that are written or drawn on walls, signs, posters, etc in public places. It is usually rude, funny, or contains a political message. EG *...some vulgar graffiti about him in the loo... ...walls covered with graffiti... ...graffiti artists.* — N UNCOUNT, OR N PLURAL ⇑ writing

graft /grɑːft/, **grafts, grafting, grafted.** 1 A **graft** is a piece of healthy skin or bone, or a healthy organ, which is attached to a damaged part of your body by a medical operation in order to replace it. EG *Laverne had gone to Chicago for skin grafts on her thighs.* ▸ used as a verb. EG *...the new veins grafted to his heart.* — N COUNT : USU AFTER N ⇑ transplant; ▸ V : IF+PREP THEN *to/onto*

2 If you **graft** a part of one plant or tree on to another plant or tree, you join them together so that they will become one plant or tree, often in order to produce a new variety. EG *You can graft pears on to white thorn or may trees... Apples are easily grafted.* — V+O : IF+PREP THEN *onto*

3 If you **graft** one idea or system on to another, you try to join one to the other; often used showing disapproval. EG *...modern federal structures grafted on to ancient cultural divisions... ...an introduction grafted upon ideas from a very different source.* — V+O : IF+PREP THEN *on/onto/upon* = transplant

4 **Graft** means hard work; an informal use in British English. EG *...the hard graft of the working men... In his constituency he was noted for his hard graft.* ▸ used as a verb. EG *...after a full day of grafting.* — N UNCOUNT : USU MOD+N = slog; ▸ V

5 **Graft** is also the act of obtaining money dishonestly by using your position of power, especially political power; used in American English. EG *...graft and corruption.* — N UNCOUNT ⇑ corruption

grain /greɪn/, **grains.** 1 A **grain** of wheat, rice, or other cereal crop is a seed from it. EG *...no bigger than grains of rice... ...a hen pecking around for grains of corn.* — N PART+N UNCOUNT

2 **Grain** is a cereal crop, especially wheat or corn, that has been harvested and is used for food or in trade. EG *We had money and surplus grain... ...a recent US decision to lift the grain embargo... World grain prices may start rising again... ...rice, barley and other grains.* — N MASS

3 A **grain** of something such as sand or salt is a tiny hard piece of it. EG *Each grain of sand is different... ...tiny grains of gold.* — N PART+N UNCOUNT = particle

4 A **grain** is also the smallest unit of weight in several systems of measurement; used especially in medicine. EG *Each tablet contains one and a quarter grains.* — N COUNT : USU *a*/NUM+N

5 A **grain** of a quality is a very small amount of it. EG *He did not seem to have a grain of humour... Might there be a tiny grain of logic in my theory?... ...a grain of truth.* — N PART+N UNCOUNT = ounce

6 The **grain** of a piece of wood is 6.1 the natural pattern of lines on its surface. EG *He took the pipe and examined the grain on the bowl... ...the panelling has a finish in various grains.* — N COUNT 6.2 the direction of the fibres in it. It is easier to cut the wood in the same direction as the grain. — N SING : *the*+N

7 If you say that an idea or action **goes against the grain**, you mean that it is very difficult for you to accept it or do it, because it conflicts with your previous ideas, beliefs, or principles. EG *However much it goes against the grain, we are compelled to concede that their methods may succeed.* — PHR : VB INFLECTS ⇑ displease

grained /greɪnd/ is used after adjectives and adverbs to describe substances that consist of particles of a particular size mentioned. EG *...a coarse grained clay... ...a more finely grained substance than lava.* — ADJ CLASSIF ⇑ granulated

grainy /greɪni¹/. 1 A **grainy** photograph looks as if it is made up of lots of spots of colour, which make the lines or shapes in it difficult to see. EG *...the grainy black-and-white of old movies... The reproduction was too grainy to see any detail.* — ADJ QUALIT ⇑ unclear = fuzzy

2 Something that is **grainy** has a rough surface or texture. EG *...the hard, dry, grainy cheese... ...the grainy pitted skin... ...the scrubbed grainy wood of the table.* — ADJ CLASSIF : ATTRIB

gram /græm/, **grams**; also spelled **gramme.** A **gram** is a very small unit of weight. One thousand grams are equal to one kilogram. EG *...500 grams of flour.* — N PART

grammar /græmə/, **grammars.** 1 **Grammar** is 1.1 the rules of a language, concerning the way in which you can put words together in order to make sentences. EG *I need some books to be able to look up the grammar... Is there enough grammar taught in schools?... I hear you've abandoned teaching grammar lessons.* — N UNCOUNT 1.2 the way someone either obeys or does not obey the rules of grammar when they write or speak a language. EG *I'm constantly having to correct their grammar... Take off a full point for any errors in grammar.* — N UNCOUNT ⇑ usage

2 A **grammar** is 2.1 a book that describes the rules of a language. EG *...an old French grammar.* — N COUNT 2.2 a theory that is intended to explain the rules of a language. EG *...the theory of Case Grammar.* — N COUNT/UNCOUNT

grammarian /grəmeərɪən/, **grammarians.** A **grammarian** is a person who specializes in studying and writing books about grammar. — N COUNT ⇑ linguist

grammar school, grammar schools. A **grammar school** is a school in Britain for children aged between eleven and eighteen who have a high academic ability. EG *There are very few grammar schools left of that type.* — N COUNT

grammatical /grəmætɪkəºl/. 1 **Grammatical** is used to describe something that relates to grammar. EG *This sentence is extremely complex in its grammatical structure... ...grammatical exercises.* — ADJ CLASSIF : ATTRIB ⇑ structural ◇ **grammatically.** EG *His English was usually grammatically correct.* — ◇ ADV ⇑ structurally

2 If someone's language is **grammatical**, it is correct, especially because it obeys the rules of grammar. EG *He speaks perfectly grammatical English.* — ADJ QUALIT

gramme /græm/. See **gram.**

gramophone /græməfəʊn/, **gramophones.** A **gramophone** is an old-fashioned type of record player. EG *...an old portable gramophone... ...gramophone records.* — N COUNT ⇑ machine

gran /græn/, **grans.** Your **gran** is your grandmother; an informal word used in British English. EG *I went to stay with my Gran over Christmas.* — N PROPER/VOC : ALSO N COUNT = grandma

granary /grænəri¹/, **granaries.** 1 A **granary** is 1.1 a building which is used for storing grain. — N COUNT 1.2 a region where a large amount of corn is grown. EG *The Ukraine was the granary of Russia.* — N COUNT+SUPP

2 **Granary** bread is bread which contains whole grains of wheat; used in British English. EG *Two granary loaves, please.* — ADJ CLASSIF : ATTRIB

grand /grænd/, **grander, grandest.** 1 Buildings that are **grand** are splendid or impressive in size and appearance; used showing approval. EG *...grand architecture... ...the grand country-house she lived* — ADJ QUALIT = imposing in... ...*a grand baroque palace.* ◇ **grandly**. EG *Its interior is one of the most grandly elegant in Europe.* ◇ ADV

2 Plans and actions that are **grand** are ambitious and intended to achieve important results. EG ...*a grand design that purports to unite disparate elements... With this method we could operate on a really grand scale.* ADJ QUALIT : USU ATTRIB

3 People, jobs, appearances, etc, that are **grand** seem important or socially superior. EG ...*all sorts of grand people... The job isn't as grand as it sounds... She had no grand clothes and did not give parties any more.* ◇ **grandly**. EG *She waved her hand grandly... He announced grandly that he 'had no time for women.'* ADJ QUALIT = posh; ◇ ADV = majestically

4 **Grand** moments, activities, etc have great importance in relation to a particular subject or area of activity. EG *Finally, the grand moment comes when you make your first solo flight... You must not forget that the farmers do grand work of national importance.* ADJ QUALIT : ATTRIB ⇑ important

5 If you describe an activity or experience as **grand**, you mean that it is very pleasant and enjoyable. EG *We've had some grand old times together, haven't we?... It would be a grand adventure.* ADJ QUALIT = great, wonderful

6 You use **grand** in informal spoken English to indicate that you admire or approve of someone or something. EG *'Oh that's grand, that's fine.'... 'Grand girl, Flora,' says Henry, a few minutes later.* ADJ QUALIT = great, wonderful

7 A **grand** total is one that is the final amount of something or the final result of a calculation. EG *In 1886 Levers, the soap firm, spent a grand total of 50 pounds on advertising.* ADJ CLASSIF : ATTRIB ⇑ complete = sum

8 The word **Grand** is often used in the names of buildings, hotels, etc, especially when they are very large. EG ...*the brightly lit Grand Gallery... He used to come up and stay in the Grand Hotel.* ADJ CLASSIF : ATTRIB, IN NAMES ⇑ important

9 A **grand** is 9.1 a thousand dollars or pounds; a very informal use. EG *You will find that ten grand has been transferred into your account. We still need another couple of grand.* 9.2 a grand piano. N COUNT : NUM + N, ONLY SING FORM; N COUNT

grandad /grændæd/, **grandads**; also spelled **granddad**. Your **grandad** is your grandfather; an informal word used in British English. N COUNT/VOC = grandpa

grandaddy /grændædi[1]/, **grandaddies**; also spelled **granddaddy**. Your **grandaddy** is your grandfather; an informal word used in American English. N COUNT/VOC = grandad

grandchild /grænd⁰tʃaɪld/, **grandchildren**. Someone's **grandchild** is the child of their son or daughter. EG *Several of us are m. rried and have children and grandchildren.* N COUNT ⇑ relation

granddaughter /grændɔːtə/, **granddaughters**. Someone's **granddaughter** is the daughter of their son or daughter. N COUNT ⇑ grandchild

grandee /grændiː/, **grandees**. A **grandee** is a Spanish prince of the highest rank; an old-fashioned word. N COUNT ⇑ nobleman

grandeur /grændʒə/ is 1 the quality in something, for example in a building or in scenery, which makes it seem impressive and often elegant and extravagant. EG ...*the delicate restrained grandeur of Robert Adam's Lansdowne House... ...Old Delhi with its esplanades of crumbling grandeur.* 2 great importance and social status that a person has. EG ...*his wealth gave him grandeur... ...delusions of grandeur.* N UNCOUNT ⇑ magnificence = splendour; N UNCOUNT

grandfather /grænd⁰fɑːðə/, **grandfathers**. Your **grandfather** is the father of your father or mother. N COUNT : ALSO N PROPER/VOC

grandfather clock, grandfather clocks. A **grandfather clock** is an old-fashioned type of clock in a tall wooden case which stands upright on the floor. N COUNT = long case clock

grandiloquent /grændɪləkwə[3]nt/. Language or behaviour that is **grandiloquent** uses words that are unnecessarily complicated and difficult to understand, or exaggeratedly impressive gestures; a formal word. EG ...*a grandiloquent announcement... ...a grandiloquent gesture against the system of education.* ◇ **grandiloquently** . EG ...*gesturing grandiloquently.* ADJ QUALIT ⇑ pompous; ◇ ADV WITH VB

grandiose /grændɪəʊs/ is used to describe something which is bigger or more elaborate than necessary and therefore seems ridiculous; used showing disapproval. EG *The rooms inside the town hall were as preposterously grandiose as the exterior... He was always making grandiose plans to sell or mortgage his house.* ADJ QUALIT ⇑ impressive

grand jury, grand juries. A **grand jury** is a jury, usually in the United States, which considers a criminal case in order to decide if someone should be tried in a court of law. EG ...*a hearing before a grand jury.* N COUNT

grandma /grænd⁰mɑː/, **grandmas**. Your **grandma** is your grandmother; an informal word. EG *I got this sweater from my grandma.* N PROPER/VOC : ALSO N COUNT

grandmother /grænd⁰mʌðə/, **grandmothers**. Your **grandmother** is the mother of your father or mother. N COUNT : ALSO N PROPER/VOC ⇑ grandparent

grandpa /grænd⁰pɑː, græmpɑː/, **grandpas**. Your **grandpa** is your grandfather; an informal word. N PROPER/VOC : ALSO N COUNT

grandparent /grænd⁰pɛərənt/, **grandparents**. Your **grandparents** are the parents of your father or mother. EG *My grandparents on my father's side were both Polish.* N COUNT : USU PL ⇑ relation

grand piano, grand pianos. A **grand piano** is a large flat piano that has horizontal strings and that is used especially for giving concerts, making recordings, etc. N COUNT ≠ upright piano

Grand Prix /grɑːn priː/. The plural can be written **Grands Prix**, **Grand Prix**, **Grand Prixs**, or **Grand Prixes**, and is pronounced /grɑːn priː/ or /grɑːn priːz/. A **Grand Prix** is one of a series of races for very powerful racing cars; also used sometimes in the names of competitions in other sports. EG *It reminded me of grinding brakes and screeching tyres at a Grand Prix.* N COUNT ⇑ race

grand slam, grand slams. A **grand slam** is the achievement of winning all the matches or major tournaments in a season in a particular sport, for example in tennis, rugby, etc. EG *Who was the last tennis player to do the grand slam?* N COUNT

grandson /grænd⁰sʌn/, **grandsons**. Someone's **grandson** is the son of their son or daughter. N COUNT ⇑ grandchild

grandstand /grænd⁰stænd/, **grandstands**. A **grandstand** is a covered stand with several rows of seats which provide a good view at racecourses, football grounds, etc. EG ...*a steeply raked grandstand.* N COUNT ⇑ stand

grand tour, grand tours. 1 A **grand tour** is a journey round the main cities of Europe that young men from rich families used to make in former times as part of their education. EG *Part of his education was the traditional Grand Tour which he made with two tutors.* N COUNT

2 If you are given a **grand tour** of a place, you are taken all round it and shown everything. EG *Come round and we'll give you a grand tour of the house!* N COUNT

grange /greɪndʒ/, **granges**. A **grange** is a farmhouse, especially one that has several other buildings attached to it. N COUNT : ALSO IN NAMES ⇑ farm

granite /grænɪt/ is a very hard rock, usually light in colour, which is often used in building. EG ...*a great block of granite.* N UNCOUNT

granny /græni[1]/, **grannies**; also spelled **grannie**. Your **granny** is your grandmother; an informal word. N PROPER/VOC : ALSO N COUNT = grandma

grant /grɑːnt/, **grants, granting, granted**. 1 A **grant** is an amount of money that the government gives to an individual or to an organization for a particular purpose such as education, welfare, home improvements, etc. EG *They get a grant from the council... You may even be eligible for a grant to help you study... ...student grants.* N COUNT ⇑ allowance

2 If you **grant** a sum of money to a person or organization, you give it to them for a particular purpose. EG *Proposals have been made to grant each displaced family £25,000.* V+O+O, OR V+O +A *(to)* = allocate

3 If you **grant** something to someone, you allow them to have it, especially when you have authority, power, or responsibility over them. EG *He was finally granted an exit visa... Until now women have been granted a year's maternity leave after giving birth... Thank you very much for granting me so much of your valuable time.* V+O+O, OR V+O +A *(to)*

4 **take for granted**. 4.1 If you **take it for granted** that something is true, you believe that it is true without thinking about it very much or looking for proof. EG *It is taken for granted that every child should learn mathematics... We take it for granted that knowledge advances rapidly.* 4.2 If you **take** someone or something **for granted**, you benefit from a person or situation without showing that you are grateful. EG *I mean he just takes me absolutely for granted.* PHR : VB INFLECTS, USU + REPORT-CL = assume, presume; PHR : VB INFLECTS

5 If you **grant** that something is true, you admit to someone that it is true, especially when it is embarrassing to you, for example when it indicates that a V+O/REPORT-CL = concede

previous statement of yours is not completely accurate. EG *But I grant that sincerity has its awkward moments... That joy ride, I grant you, was a silly stunt.* ● You use **granted** or **granting** to say that something is true, before you make a comment about it; a fairly formal use. EG *Granted that he's in hospital, he can't do us much harm... Granting that childhood is playhood, how do we adults generally react to this fact?* — ● CONJ SUBORD = given that

granular /grænjəˈlə/. Something that is **granular** is composed of a lot of granules, or has the texture or appearance of being composed of a lot of granules; a fairly formal word. EG *...a granular white surface.* — ADJ CLASSIF = grainy

granulated /grænjəˈleɪtɪˈd/. **Granulated** sugar is sugar which you buy in the form of coarse grains rather than a fine powder. EG *...two level teaspoonfuls of granulated sugar.* — ADJ CLASSIF : USU ATTRIB ⇑ ground

granule /grænjəˈl/, **granules**. A **granule** is a small round piece of something, usually something fairly hard. EG *...polystyrene granules.* — N COUNT ⇑ grain

grape /greɪp/, **grapes**. A **grape** is a small, sweet, round fruit, green or dark purple in colour, which is eaten raw, used for making wine, or dried to make raisins, sultanas, or currants. EG *...a bunch of grapes.* ● **sour grapes**: see **sour**. — N COUNT : USU PL

grapefruit /greɪpfru:t/, **grapefruits**. **Grapefruit** can also be used as the plural form. A **grapefruit** is a large, round fruit, similar to an orange, that has a thick yellow skin and a sharp, slightly bitter taste. — N COUNT ⇑ fruit

grapevine /greɪpvaɪn/, **grapevines**. 1 A **grapevine** is a climbing plant on which grapes grow. — N COUNT

2 The **grapevine** is a way of passing on news or information from one person to another, either in casual conversation or in secret. EG *'How did you know about that?'–'Oh, I heard it on the grapevine.'* — N SING : *the*+N ⇑ channel

graph /grɑ:f, græf/, **graphs**. A **graph** is a mathematical diagram, usually a line or curve, which shows how two or more sets of numbers or measurements are related. EG *At the front of the atlas there's a series of graphs... ...a temperature graph.* — N COUNT = chart

graphic /græfɪk/, **graphics**. 1 Descriptions, accounts, etc, that are **graphic** are very clear, detailed, and easy to understand; used especially of descriptions that contain unpleasant details. EG *...his graphic stories of persecution... Seldom have I read a more graphic, cold-blooded description of a killing than this.* ◇ **graphically**. EG *The history of the economic life of Man graphically illustrates my point.* — ADJ QUALIT = vivid; ◇ ADV WITH VB = clearly

2 Something that is **graphic** is concerned with drawing, especially the use of strong bold lines and colours. EG *...graphic and industrial design... The graphic work owes a good deal to Goya.* — ADJ CLASSIF : ATTRIB ⇑ artistic

3 **Graphics** are drawings and pictures that are composed using simple lines and sometimes strong colours. EG *...exhibitions of graphics from all over the world... ...computer generated graphics.* — N PLURAL ⇑ representations

graphite /græfaɪt/ is a hard black substance that is a form of carbon. It is used to make the centre part of a pencil, used instead of oil in some machines, and is also used in some nuclear reactors. — N UNCOUNT

graphology /græfɒlədʒiˈ/ is the science of examining people's handwriting in order to discover what sort of personality they have. ◇ **graphologist, graphologists**. — N UNCOUNT; ◇ N COUNT ⇑ specialist

graph paper; also spelled with a hyphen. **Graph paper** is paper that has small squares printed on it so that you can use it for drawing graphs. — N UNCOUNT

grapnel /græpnəˈl/, **grapnels**. A **grapnel** is a device which consists of several hooks that are joined together and attached to one end of a rope. Grapnels are used especially in sailing. EG *The grapnel was caught between rocks and we had to cut the rope.* — N COUNT

grapple /græpəˈl/, **grapples, grappling, grappled**. 1 If you **grapple** with someone, you take hold of them and struggle with them, as part of a fight. EG *We grappled with him and took the guns from him.* — V : USU+A *(with)* = wrestle

2 If you **grapple** someone, you seize them and hold them close to you with a strong grip; used in American English. EG *She grappled me again.* — V+O

3 If you **grapple** with a problem or difficulty, you try hard to solve it. EG *I grappled with this moral dilemma.* — V+A *(with)* = struggle

grappling iron, grappling irons. A **grappling iron** is the same as a grapnel. — N COUNT

grasp /grɑ:sp/, **grasps, grasping, grasped**. 1 If you **grasp** something, you take it with your hand and hold it very firmly. EG *Edward grasped Castle's arm... I stood quite still, my hands grasping the edge of the table... He raised his hands above his head, grasping at the escape hatch.* ◇ **grasping**. EG *...long grasping tentacles.* ● See also **grasping**. — V+O, OR V+A *(at/for)*; ◇ ADJ CLASSIF : ATTRIB

2 A **grasp** is a very firm hold or grip. EG *The animal had a powerful grasp.* — N SING WITH DET +SUPP

3 If you **grasp** something that is complicated or difficult to understand, you understand it. EG *The concepts were difficult to grasp... I think I grasped quite soon what was going on.* — V+O/REPORT-CL

4 A **grasp** of something is an understanding of it. EG *He had a sound grasp of tactics... You'd better get a grasp of those techniques.* — N SING WITH DET +SUPP, IF+PREP THEN *of*

5 If you say that something is **within** your **grasp**, you mean that it is very likely that you will achieve it. EG *Success was now within his grasp.* — PHR : USED AS AN A

6 If something is **in** your **grasp**, you hold it or control it. If something escapes or slips **from** your **grasp** or **out of** your **grasp**, you no longer hold it or control it. EG *The thing I had most longed for was in the grasp of Alice McWhirter... They regretted letting her slip from their grasp.* — PHR : USED AS AN A

grasping /grɑ:spɪŋ/. Someone who is **grasping** wants to get and keep as much money as possible and is unwilling to spend it; used showing disapproval. EG *...a grasping woman.* — ADJ QUALIT ⇑ greedy = grabbing

grass /grɑ:s/, **grasses, grassing, grassed**. 1 **Grass** is 1.1 a very common green plant with long, thin, spiky leaves. Grass is eaten by sheep, cows, etc and is often planted over large areas in parks, gardens, and playing fields. EG *My clothes were damp from walking in long grass.* — N UNCOUNT; 1.2 a particular species of grass, usually one that grows wild. EG *...prairie grasses.* — N MASS ⇑ plant; 1.3 in informal English, marijuana. EG *...sitting around smoking grass.* — N UNCOUNT

2 If you talk about the **grass**, you are referring to an area of ground that is covered with grass, for example in your garden. EG *Keep off the grass.* — N SING : *the*+N = lawn

3 If you say to someone **'the grass is always greener on the other side of the fence'**, you are reminding them that other people's situations always seem better or more attractive than your own, but may not really be so. — PHR

4 If you say that someone is being **put out to grass**, you mean they are no longer being employed because they are considered to be too old or no longer useful; a fairly informal expression. EG *You can't put a 32-year-old out to grass.* — PHR : VB INFLECTS = pension off

5 If you **grass** on someone, you give information to the police or other people in authority about something criminal or wrong which that person has done; an informal use. EG *...the rumour that I had grassed on them.* — V : IF+PREP THEN *on* ⇑ betray = inform

6 A **grass** is someone who grasses on someone else; an informal use. EG *Don't trust him–he's a grass.* — N COUNT = informer

grass over. To **grass over** an area of ground means to plant grass all over it. — PHRASAL VB : V+O+ADV

grasshopper /grɑ:shᵊɒpə/, **grasshoppers**. A **grasshopper** is an insect which has long back legs and can jump into the air. Grasshoppers make a sound by rubbing their back legs against their wings. — N COUNT

grassland /grɑ:sləˈnd/, **grasslands**. **Grassland** is land which is covered with grass, especially grass that grows naturally and has not been planted by people. EG *The area around the cave was open grassland... ...tropical grasslands.* — N COUNT/UNCOUNT

grass roots; often used before another noun and spelled with a hyphen. The **grass roots** of an organization or movement are the ordinary people who form the main part of it, rather than its leaders. EG *...to strengthen democracy at the grass roots... You've got to start at the grassroots... ...grass-roots support for the new party.* — N PLURAL : USU BEFORE N, OR PREP+N

grassy /grɑ:siˈ/, **grassier, grassiest**. An area of land that is **grassy** is covered in grass. EG *We rode up a grassy slope.* — ADJ QUALIT

grate /greɪt/, **grates, grating, grated**. 1 A **grate** is a framework of metal bars in a fireplace, which holds the coal or wood. EG *A fire was burning in the grate.* — N COUNT

2 If you **grate** food such as cheese or carrots, you rub a piece of it over a metal tool so that the food is shredded into very small pieces. EG *...grated lemon peel... ...spinach with cream and grated nutmeg.* — V+O = shred

3 When something **grates** or when you **grate** it, it makes a harsh, unpleasant sound because two sur- — V-ERG

faces rub hard and roughly against each other. EG *He could hear her shoes grating on the steps... He grated his teeth.*

4 If a noise or someone's behaviour **grates** on you, it makes you feel irritated. EG *That shrill laugh grated on her mother... 'Go and find her,' she ordered, and her manner grated.* V : IF + PREP THEN *on* ↑ irritate

5 See also **grating**.

grateful /greɪtfʊl/. If you are **grateful** for something pleasant or useful that someone has done or given you, you have warm, friendly feelings towards them and wish to thank them. EG *I am ever so grateful to you for talking to me... I'd be grateful if you could do that... He was grateful that he was still alive.* ▸ used of people's behaviour. EG *...grateful kisses... ...grateful letters.* ◇ **gratefully**. EG *He accepted the money gratefully... 'It's such a help,' she said gratefully.* ADJ QUALIT = thankful; ◇ ADV WITH VB

grater /greɪtə/, **graters**. A **grater** is a metal tool with sharp, raised parts on its surface which is used for grating food. N COUNT ↑ utensil

gratify /grætɪfaɪ/, **gratifies, gratifying, gratified**; a fairly formal word. 1 If you **are gratified** by something, it gives you pleasure or satisfaction. EG *I was gratified to find that I'd had some effect... He was gratified that his guess had been proved right.* ◇ **gratified**. EG *A gratified murmur arose from the crowd.* ◇ **gratifying**. EG *The new plan may be gratifying to the President... It makes a gratifying change... It is gratifying that women do not accept this.* ◇ **gratification** /grætɪfɪkeɪʃəⁿn/. EG *Dull, repetitive work gives no gratification... ...sexual gratification... To my immense gratification, he fell into the trap.* V + O OR V + REPORT-CL/ *to*-INF, USU PASS ↑ please = delight; ◇ ADJ QUALIT; ◇ ADJ QUALIT = pleasing; ◇ N UNCOUNT

2 If you **gratify** your own or another person's desire, you do what is necessary to please yourself or them. EG *Was she merely gratifying her own appetite?... His smallest wish must be gratified... Do gratify our curiosity.* ◇ **gratification**. EG *...action directed towards the gratification of desire.* V + O = satisfy, indulge ≠ deny; ◇ N UNCOUNT = indulgence

grating /greɪtɪŋ/, **gratings**. 1 A **grating** is a flat metal frame with rows of bars across it, which is fastened over a window or over a hole in a wall or the ground. EG *The grating protected a window in the men's room.* N COUNT ↑ grid

2 A **grating** sound is harsh and unpleasant. EG *...a repulsive woman with a grating voice.*

gratis /greɪtɪs, grætɪs, grɑːtɪs/. If something is done or provided **gratis**, it does not have to be paid for. EG *He works gratis for his creditor... It is yours, gratis.* ADJ CLASSIF : PRED, OR ADV = free

gratitude /grætɪtjuːd/ is the feeling of being grateful, or the expression of this feeling. EG *People wish to show their gratitude for the help he has given them... I must express my gratitude to the BBC... Dolly was overwhelmed by gratitude and shame.* N UNCOUNT

gratuitous /grətjuːɪtəs/. An action or behaviour that is **gratuitous** is unnecessary in a particular situation, and usually harmful or upsetting; a formal word used showing disapproval. EG *...gratuitous acts of vandalism... ...gratuitous cruelty.* ◇ **gratuitously**. EG *She had no wish to wound his feelings gratuitously... ...a gratuitously evil act.* ADJ QUALIT = unwarranted, wanton; ◇ ADV = needlessly

gratuity /grətjuːɪti¹/, **gratuities**. A **gratuity** is 1 a gift of money to someone who has done something for you. EG *Is one allowed to offer gratuities to the guides?* 2 in British English, a large gift of money given to someone when they leave their employment, especially when they leave the armed forces. EG *He resigned from the service and applied for a gratuity instead of a pension.* N COUNT = tip; N COUNT

grave, graves; graver, gravest. The word **grave** is pronounced /greɪv/ for paragraphs 1 to 5, and /grɑːv/ for paragraph 6. 1 A **grave** is a place where a dead person is buried. EG *Amy wants to go and see her mother's grave... Flowers had been put on the grave.* N COUNT

2 You can refer to someone's death as their **grave** or to death as the **grave**, especially in expressions such as 'to his grave' and 'from the grave'. EG *Jefferson went to his grave confident that he was right... He drank himself into an early grave... ...ghosts staking their claims from beyond the grave.* N COUNT : USU PREP + MOD + N

3 The word **grave** is also used in the following fairly informal expressions relating to death or disaster. 3.1 If you say that someone **is digging** their **own grave**, you mean that they are doing something foolish or dangerous that will cause their own failure. PHR : VB INFLECTS 3.2 If you say that someone has **one foot in the grave**, you mean that they are so old or ill that they will probably die soon. PHR : USED AS C 3.3 If you say that someone who is dead would **turn in** their **grave**, you mean that they would be very shocked or upset by something that is happening now, if they were alive. EG *My mother must be turning in her grave... Crewe would turn in his grave if that building came down.* PHR : VB INFLECTS 3.4 **from the cradle to the grave**: see **cradle**.

4 A situation or event that is **grave** is very serious, important, and worrying. EG *...grave mistakes... ...a very grave decision... I had the gravest suspicions about the whole enterprise.* ◇ **gravely**. EG *His father was gravely ill... Their policies had gravely damaged industrial relations.* ADJ QUALIT ↑ extreme; ◇ ADV = severely

5 A person who is **grave** is quiet and serious in appearance or behaviour. EG *...a grave, courteous man... ...the pale face, so grave and serene... She returned, looking even graver.* ◇ **gravely**. EG *Roger understood and nodded gravely.* ADJ QUALIT = solemn; ◇ ADV = solemnly

6 A **grave** accent is a symbol that is placed over a vowel in a word in some languages, such as French, to show how the vowel is pronounced. N COUNT : USU SING

gravedigger /greɪvdɪgə/, **gravediggers**. A **gravedigger** is a person whose job is to dig holes for dead people to be buried in, in a cemetery or churchyard. N COUNT

gravel /grævəⁿl/ consists of very small stones that are found, for example, in river beds and are used to cover paths. EG *...the sound of his feet on the gravel... ...an abandoned gravel pit... ...the uneven surface of the gravel road.* N UNCOUNT ↑ stone

gravelled /grævəⁿld/; also spelled **graveled** in American English. A **gravelled** path or road is one with a surface made of gravel. EG *A gravelled terrace surrounded the house... ...the gravelled road leading away from the highway.* ADJ CLASSIF

gravelly /grævəⁿli¹/. 1 An area of land that is **gravelly** is covered in small stones. EG *...gravelly soil... ...birds that live on gravelly shores.* ADJ QUALIT ↑ stony

2 A **gravelly** voice is low and rather rough and harsh. ADJ QUALIT

graven /greɪvəⁿn/. A **graven** image is one that has been carved, especially for use in religious worship; a literary word. ADJ CLASSIF : ATTRIB

graveside /greɪvsaɪd/. The **graveside** is the area around a grave; used especially when talking about the time when a dead person is being buried. EG *At the graveside he made a little speech.* N COUNT : USU *the* + N IN SING

gravestone /greɪvstəʊn/, **gravestones**. A **gravestone** is a large piece of stone that is placed above or near a grave and usually has information on it about the person buried there, and sometimes a prayer. N COUNT ↑ monument = headstone

graveyard /greɪvjɑːd/, **graveyards**. 1 A **graveyard** is an area of land, sometimes near a church, where dead people are buried. N COUNT = cemetery

2 If you call a place a **graveyard**, 2.1 you mean that there are many broken or unwanted things there or that many things have been destroyed there. EG *...that dreaded graveyard of ships, the Bermuda Triangle... ...a graveyard of stolen cars.* N COUNT : USU + SUPP 2.2 you mean that it is very dull and boring, with very few facilities for entertainment; an informal use. EG *Out here it's practically a graveyard.* N COUNT : USU USED AS C = morgue

3 If you call an event or place the **graveyard** of people or their hopes, you mean that people have often failed in such events or in that place; a literary use. EG *Elections are the graveyard of the political prophet... Broadway! Graveyard of a thousand hopes.* N COUNT + *of* ↑ end = death

gravitate /grævɪteɪt/, **gravitates, gravitating, gravitated**. If you **gravitate** towards a particular place, thing, or activity, you are attracted by it and go to it, use it, or get involved in it; a formal word. EG *The best reporters gravitate towards the centres of power... People gravitate toward foods that are cheaper... He gravitated naturally to Newmarket.* V + *towards/to* ↑ move = be drawn

gravitation /grævɪteɪʃəⁿn/ is the force which causes objects to be attracted towards each other because they have mass; a technical term in physics. EG *...the laws of gravitation.* N UNCOUNT

gravitational /grævɪteɪʃəⁿnəl, -ʃənəⁿl/ means relating to or resulting from the force of gravity. EG *...the earth's gravitational force... ...a low gravitational field.* ADJ CLASSIF : USU ATTRIB

gravity /grævɪti¹/, **gravities**. 1 **Gravity** is 1.1 the force which causes things to fall to the ground when you drop them, and to remain on the ground instead N UNCOUNT of floating in the air. EG ...*the law of gravity.* ▸ also used to refer to a similar force of different strength on another planet or a moon. EG ...*an asteroid captured by Jupiter's great gravity.* 1.2 the same as gravitation. • See also **centre of gravity, specific gravity**. ▸ N COUNT/UNCOUNT; N UNCOUNT

2 The **gravity** of a situation or event is its extreme importance and seriousness. EG ...*the gravity of the financial position... ...the gravity of the submarine threat to shipping.* N UNCOUNT : IF + PREP THEN *of*

3 The **gravity** of someone's behaviour or speech is the extremely serious way in which they behave or speak. EG ...*the odd gravity of little girls... 'A very interesting question,' he said with mock gravity.* N UNCOUNT = solemnity

gravy /greɪvi¹/, **gravies**. **Gravy** is a thin sauce made from the juices that come out of meat when you cook it. N MASS

gravy boat, gravy boats; also spelled with a hyphen. A **gravy boat** is a short, narrow jug used for serving gravy. N COUNT

gravy train, gravy trains. If you describe a job, business, or method of obtaining money as a **gravy train**, you mean that you get a lot of money from it without much effort; an informal expression. EG ...*a private gravy train subsidized from public funds... I've been riding the gravy train all my life.* N COUNT : USU SING = goldmine

gray /greɪ/. See **grey**.

graze /greɪz/, **grazes, grazing, grazed**. 1 When an animal **grazes** or you **graze** it, it eats the grass or other plants that are growing in a particular place. EG *The horses graze peacefully... We used to graze sheep on the fields where the corn is now... ...land grazed by sheep and cattle.* V-ERG ⇑ feed

2 If you **graze** a part of your body, you injure the skin by scraping against something. EG *I grazed my legs as he pulled me up.* ◊ **grazed**. EG ...*his grazed knee.* V+O (NG/REFL) = scrape; ◊ ADJ CLASSIF

3 A **graze** is a small wound caused by scraping against something. EG *There was a nasty graze on his knee... ...cuts and grazes.* N COUNT

4 If something **grazes** you, it touches you lightly as it passes you. EG *Jones's shot only grazed him... Something hard grazed the back of his head.* V+O ⇑ rub = brush

grazing /greɪzɪŋ/. **Grazing** or **grazing land** is land on which animals graze or are grazed. EG ...*the lack of good grazing.* N UNCOUNT = pasture

grease /griːs/, **greases, greasing, greased**. 1 **Grease** is 1.1 a thick, oily substance which is put on the moving parts of cars and other machines in order to make them work smoothly. EG *The engine was covered in grease... ...grease-stained mechanics.* N UNCOUNT ⇑ lubricant = oil

1.2 an oily substance that is produced by your skin. EG *His hair looked shiny with grease... ...grease marks on sofa backs and arms.* 1.3 animal fat that is produced by cooking meat or which you use for cooking. EG *Try cooking oil or grease.* N UNCOUNT ⇑ secretion; N UNCOUNT

2 If you **grease** a part of a car, machine, or device, you put grease on it in order to make it work smoothly. EG *Clean and grease the valve thoroughly.* V+O = oil

3 If you **grease** someone's **palm**, you bribe them; an informal expression. EG *The gatekeepers won't let you in unless you grease their palms.* PHR : VB INFLECTS

4 See also **elbow grease**.

grease gun, grease guns. A **grease gun** is a device for forcing grease into special holes in machines so that their moving parts work smoothly. N COUNT

greasepaint /griːspeɪnt/ is an oily substance used by actors as make-up. N UNCOUNT

greaseproof paper /griːspruːf peɪpə/ is a special kind of paper which does not allow grease or oil to pass through it and is used especially in cooking or to wrap food. N UNCOUNT

greasy /griːsi¹, -zi¹/, **greasier, greasiest**. Something that is **greasy** is covered with grease or contains a lot of grease. EG ...*greasy tools... ...her fat greasy hand... ...greasy hamburgers.* ADJ QUALIT ⇑ oily

great /greɪt/, **greater, greatest; greats**. 1 You use **great** to describe something that is 1.1 very large in size, or unusually large. **Great** is more formal than 'big', and is used instead of 'large' when you are particularly impressed by the size. EG *A great tree had fallen across one corner... ...a great black cloud of smoke.* 1.2 large in number or amount, especially more than the average number or amount. EG ...*the great majority of new jobs... There is a great amount of conflict about it... The heat was so great I took off my sweater.* 1.3 important, famous, or exciting. EG ...*the great cities of the Rhineland... ...the great issues of the day.* ◊ **greatness**. EG ...*the greatness of Germany.* ADJ QUALIT : USU ATTRIB = massive, immense; ADJ QUALIT = considerable; ADJ CLASSIF : USU ATTRIB; ◊ N UNCOUNT : USU WITH POSS

2 A person who is described as **great** is successful and famous for their actions, knowledge, or skill. EG ...*a great actor... ...Alexander the Great. ...one of the greatest engineers of this century.* ◊ **greatness**. EG ...*Boltzmann's greatness as a physicist.* ADJ QUALIT : ALSO N PROPER + *the*+ADJ; ◊ N UNCOUNT : USU WITH POSS

3 The **greats** in a particular subject or field of activity are the people who have been most successful or famous in them. EG ...*one of the all-time greats... ...most of the golfing greats.* N PLURAL : USU *the*+N+SUPP = stars

4 You use **great** in informal English 4.1 to express approval, admiration, or excitement. EG *It's a great idea... He was great. I really like him... 'Great,' says Howard. 'That's marvellous.'* 4.2 to express contempt, scorn, or bitterness, by using a sneering tone of voice. EG *'Oh great,' I thought. 'Just what I need.'... If that's what they want to believe in, great.* 4.3 as part of expressions of surprise, shock, or disbelief such as 'Great Heavens' and 'Great Scott'. EG *'Great Heavens!' she cried, seeing me.* ADJ QUALIT OR EXCLAM ⇑ good = terrific; ADJ QUALIT OR EXCLAM; EXCLAM

5 If someone feels **great**, they feel very healthy, energetic, and enthusiastic. EG *My wife isn't feeling so great.* ADJ QUALIT : PRED ⇑ good = well

6 You use **great** for emphasis in the following ways: 6.1 with another adjective, to emphasize the size or quality of something or someone, or your opinion about them; an informal use. EG ...*a great big gaping hole... ...an enormous great grin... Great fat old cow!* 6.2 to emphasize a noun that refers to a quality, emotion, or problem. EG *He switched from one task to another with great difficulty... This is of great importance... Their love of travelling is so great that they are hardly ever at home... The greater the threat, the less tolerance there can be.* 6.3 with a noun that refers to a person with a particular characteristic, interest, quality, etc, to emphasize that characteristic. EG *He was a great friend of Huxley... He was a great womaniser.* ADV + ADJ, OR ADJ CLASSIF : ATTRIB ⇑ very; ADJ QUALIT = extreme; ADJ QUALIT : ATTRIB = terrific

7 **Great** is also used 7.1 as part of the name of a city or road. EG ...*Great Yarmouth... ...Great Marlborough Street.* 7.2 as part of the name of a species of plant or animal when there is another species of the same plant or animal which is smaller and has other different characteristics. EG ...*the great apes... ...a great tit.* ADJ CLASSIF : IN NAMES BEFORE N; ADJ CLASSIF : ATTRIB

8 See also **greater**.

great- is used before nouns that refer to relatives, such as 'aunt' or 'grandson', to indicate that a relative is one generation further away than the one the noun refers to. Your great-aunt is the aunt of your mother or father, and your great-grandson is the grandson of your son or daughter. EG ...*William's great-uncle... ...Great Aunt Alice's recipe... ...our great great grandparents.* PREFIX

Great Britain is the island consisting of England, Scotland, and Wales, which together with Northern Ireland makes up the United Kingdom. N PROPER

greatcoat /greɪtkəʊt/, **greatcoats**. A **greatcoat** is a long thick overcoat that is worn especially as part of a uniform. EG ...*an army greatcoat.* N COUNT ⇑ coat

greater /greɪtə/ is used with or as part of the names of large cities, when you are referring to the whole city including the suburbs and not just to the central area. EG ...*Greater London... ...the eight million people in greater Calcutta.* ADJ CLASSIF : ATTRIB

greatly /greɪtli¹/ is used, in formal English, to emphasize the degree or extent of something. EG *I was greatly influenced by Sullivan... He admired his father greatly... He was not greatly surprised.* ADV = very much, tremendously

Grecian /griːʃ°n/ is used to describe something whose style is like that of things made or used in ancient Greece. EG ...*huge Grecian columns... ...her pink Grecian tunic.* ADJ CLASSIF : USU ATTRIB ⇑ Greek

greed /griːd/ is an eager desire for something, for example food, money, or power, especially for more than is necessary or fair for you to have; used showing disapproval. EG *Inequality has stimulated envy, ambition and greed... ...the glint of greed in his eyes.* N UNCOUNT ⇑ desire = avarice

greedy /griːdi¹/, **greedier, greediest**. Someone who is **greedy** wants something eagerly, for example food, money, or power, especially more of it than they need or than is fair for them to have; used showing disapproval. EG *Don't be greedy... ...the ambitions of greedy lawyers... People got richer and also greedier.* ▸ used of people's behaviour. EG *The* ADJ QUALIT = grasping, avaricious; ▸ = covetous *ring excited her greedy gaze.* ◊ **greedily**. EG *He slurped the soup greedily.* ◊ ADV WITH VB = ravenously

Greek /griːk/, **Greeks**. 1 Something that is **Greek** belongs or relates to Greece, its people, or its culture. EG *A Greek family lived next door.* ADJ CLASSIF

2 **Greek** is the language that is spoken in Greece; used to refer both to the modern language and the language which was used in ancient times. N UNCOUNT

3 A **Greek** is a person who comes from Greece. N COUNT

green /griːn/, **greener, greenest; greens**. 1 Something that is **green** is the colour of grass or leaves. EG *...green and yellow stripes... She had blonde hair and green eyes.* ▸ used as a noun. EG *...a deep green.* ADJ COLOUR ▸ N MASS

2 **Green** signals are used to indicate that there is no danger, or that a person or vehicle may proceed. EG *Accelerate away from the traffic lights when they go green... The guard waved his green flag.* ● If someone in authority gives you a **green light**, they give you permission to do something. EG *The United States gave them a green light to go in... I'm only waiting for the green light from you.* ADJ COLOUR ⇑ safe ● PHR : USED AS O = go-ahead

3 A place that is **green** is covered with grass, plants, and trees and not with houses or factories; used showing approval. EG *...the green Devon countryside... ...lush green meadows.* ◊ **greenness**. EG *...its greenness, its lack of industrialization.* ADJ COLOUR = leafy, verdant ≠ urbanized ◊ N UNCOUNT

4 A **green** is 4.1 an area of land covered with grass, especially in a town or in the middle of a village. EG *...the church, the village green... Between the road and the river is a strip of green.* 4.2 a smooth, flat area of grass around a hole on a golf course. EG *He missed his putts on the first four greens.* ● See also **bowling green, putting green**. N COUNT/UNCOUNT; N COUNT : USU the+N

5 **Green** is used in the names of places. EG *...Winson Green Prison... ...Hatters Green in Sussex.* N IN NAMES

6 **Greens** are the green leaves of vegetables such as spinach or cabbage that are cooked and eaten. EG *Get him to eat freshly cooked potatoes and greens.* N PLURAL

7 Fruits that are **green** are unripe and not ready to be eaten. EG *The green fruits were as hard as rocks.* ADJ QUALIT

8 If a person looks **green**, they look pale and ill, as if they are going to be sick. EG *Hogan went slightly green.* ADJ QUALIT : USU PRED = bilious

9 If a person is **green** with envy, they are very envious indeed. EG *I'm green with envy when I go to Bristol and see their facilities.* ADJ CLASSIF : PRED+with

10 If you say that someone is **green**, you mean that they have had very little experience of life or a particular job. EG *He was very green, he thought he could do it easily... ...green recruits, new to the traditions.* ◊ **greenness**. EG *...a sort of greenness, an underlying innocence.* ADJ QUALIT ⇑ inexperienced = naive, raw ◊ N UNCOUNT

11 If you say that someone has **green fingers** or, in American English, **a green thumb**, you mean that they are very good at gardening and their plants grow well. PHR : USED AS O ⇑ skill

12 **Green** is also used of political movements whose members are particularly concerned about protecting the environment, and of the members themselves and their policies. EG *...green activists.* ▸ used as a noun to refer to members of such movements. EG *...the success of the Greens in Germany.* ADJ CLASSIF : USU ATTRIB ▸ N COUNT : USU PL

greenback /griːnbæk/, **greenbacks**. A **greenback** is an American banknote such as a dollar bill; used in informal American English. N COUNT

green belt, green belts. A **green belt** is an area of land with fields or parks around a town or city, where people are not allowed to build houses or factories by law. N COUNT ⇑ zone

Green Beret, Green Berets. A **Green Beret** is a British or American commando; an informal use. N COUNT

greenery /griːnəʳri¹/ consists of plants or leaves that make a thing or place look attractive. EG *...vases spilling with blossoms and greenery... ...the lush greenery and long white beaches.* N UNCOUNT ⇑ vegetation = foliage

greenfly /griːnflaɪ/, **greenflies**. **Greenfly** can also be used as the plural form. **Greenfly** are small, green, winged insects that damage plants. N COUNT

greengage /griːngeɪdʒ/, **greengages**. A **greengage** is a greenish-yellow coloured plum with a sweet taste. N COUNT

greengrocer /griːngrəʊsə/, **greengrocers**. A **greengrocer** is a shopkeeper who sells fruit and vegetables; used in British English. EG *...your local greengrocer.* ▸ The **greengrocer** or the **greengrocer's** is used to refer to a shop where fruit and vegetables are sold. EG *...a woman at the greengrocer's that morning.* N COUNT ▸ N SING : the+N ⇑ shop

greenhorn /griːnhɔːn/, **greenhorns**; an informal word. A **greenhorn** is 1 in American English, someone who has recently come to live in America. EG *They made him feel a foreigner, a greenhorn.* 2 a person who has had very little experience of life or of a particular job. N COUNT = newcomer; N COUNT = novice

greenhouse /griːnhaʊs/, **greenhouses**. A **greenhouse** is a building in a garden or park which has glass walls and a glass roof and in which you grow plants that need to be kept warm, or protected from winds or frost. N COUNT = glasshouse

greenhouse effect. The **greenhouse effect** is the problem of the gradual rise in temperature in the Earth's atmosphere because heat is absorbed from the sun but cannot leave the atmosphere. N SING : the+N

greenish /griːnɪʃ/ means slightly green in colour. EG *...a jacket of a greenish colour... ...a greenish blue.* ADJ COLOUR = greeny

Green Paper, Green Papers. A **Green Paper** is, in Britain, a document containing ideas about a particular subject that is published by the Government so that people can discuss them before any decisions are made. N COUNT

Green Party. The **Green Party** is a political party that is particularly concerned about protecting the environment. N PROPER : the+N

green pepper, green peppers. A **green pepper** is an unripe pepper that is used in cooking or eaten raw in salads. N COUNT = capsicum

green revolution. The **green revolution** is the increase in agricultural production in developing countries that has been made possible by the use of new types of crops and new farming methods. N SING : the+N

greenroom /griːnru⁴m/, **greenrooms**; also spelled as two words. A **greenroom** is a room in a theatre, television studio, etc where performers can rest. N COUNT

green salad, green salads. A **green salad** is a salad made mainly with lettuce and other green vegetables. N COUNT

greenstuff /griːnstʌf/ means green vegetables that are used for food. N UNCOUNT

Greenwich Mean Time /grenɪtʃ miːn taɪm/. See GMT.

greeny /griːni¹/ means slightly green in colour. ADJ COLOUR

greet /griːt/, **greets, greeting, greeted**. 1 When you **greet** someone, you express friendliness or pleasure when you meet them, or when they arrive somewhere, for example by saying 'Hello' or shaking hands with them. EG *Sarah came out to greet him... He hurried to greet his guests.* V+O = welcome, receive

2 If you **greet** something or someone in a particular way, you express your reaction to them in that way. EG *They will be greeted with shock and surprise... The announcement was greeted by shouts.* V+O : USU+A = meet

3 If something **greets** you, it is the first thing you notice in a particular situation; a rather literary use. EG *The smell of coffee would greet us as we entered.* V+O = hit

greeting /griːtɪŋ/, **greetings**. 1 A **greeting** is something you say or do that expresses your friendliness or pleasure when you meet someone. EG *...a friendly greeting... She smiled in greeting... Ari stopped at their table to exchange greetings.* N COUNT, OR in+N ⇑ salutation

2 You can say **'Greetings'** when you meet someone, as a formal way of saying 'Hello'. EG *'Greetings, Reverend,' he said respectfully.* CONVENTION ⇑ hello

greetings card, greetings cards. A **greetings card** is a folded card with a picture on the front and greetings inside that you give or send to someone, for example on their birthday. EG *Thank you for the anniversary greetings card.* N COUNT

gregarious /grɪ²geəriəs/. 1 Someone who is **gregarious**, enjoys being with other people; a fairly formal use. EG *...a charming and gregarious man whose dinner parties were always lively.* ADJ QUALIT ⇑ sociable = outgoing

2 **Gregarious** animals or birds normally live in large groups. ADJ CLASSIF = social

gremlin /gremlɪn/, **gremlins**. A **gremlin** is a tiny imaginary evil spirit that people say is the cause of a problem, especially in a machine, which they cannot explain properly or locate. EG *Engineers have conquered the gremlins that have plagued front-wheel drive cars.* N COUNT : USU PL

grenade /grɪ²neɪd/, **grenades**. A **grenade** is a small bomb containing explosive or tear gas that can be thrown by hand or fired from a gun. EG *He killed* N COUNT *two policemen with a grenade... ...a hand grenade... ...an anti-tank grenade launcher.*

grew /gru:/ is the past tense of **grow**.

grey /greɪ/, **greyer, greyest; greys, greying**; also spelled **gray** in American English. **1** Something that is **grey** is the colour of ashes or of clouds on a rainy day. Light or pale grey is similar to white, and dark grey is similar to black. EG *...piercing gray eyes... ...a grey flannel suit.* ▸ used as a noun. EG *...subtle grays and silvers.* — ADJ COLOUR; ▸ N MASS

2 Grey is used to describe the colour of people's hair when it changes from its original colour, usually as they get old, and before it becomes white. EG *...the grey-haired driver... ...a small grey beard.* ▸ used of people. EG *...elderly males, grey and balding.* ● If someone or their hair **goes grey** or **turns grey**, their hair starts becoming grey, usually as they get old. EG *She went grey in about a year... ...with dark hair just beginning to turn grey.* — ADJ QUALIT ⇑ grey-haired; ● PHR : VB INFLECTS

3 If someone or their hair **is greying**, their hair is becoming grey, usually because they are getting old. EG *Her hair was greying.* ◊ **greying**. EG *...a small, fierce, greying man... ...greying hair.* — V : ONLY CONT; ◊ ADJ CLASSIF : ATTRIB

4 If someone looks **grey**, their face looks pale, usually because they are tired, ill, or worried. EG *Otto was still looking grey and very tired... Coward walked in with a grey face, saying it was terrible.* ◊ **greyness**. EG *...a greyness about his face.* — ADJ QUALIT = ashen; ◊ N UNCOUNT

5 If the weather is **grey**, there are many clouds in the sky and the light is dull. EG *...grey skies... ...a grey April afternoon.* ◊ **greyness**. EG *...a day of uniform greyness.* — ADJ QUALIT = overcast; ◊ N UNCOUNT = drabness

6 If you describe a situation as **grey**, you mean that it is dull, unpleasant, or difficult. EG *...seeing only grey days ahead... ...a grey predictable routine.* — ADJ QUALIT = bleak

7 If you describe something or someone as **grey**, you mean that they are boring and unattractive, and very similar to other things or other people. EG *Grey men with graphs explain the new voting system... ...this grim, grey city.* — ADJ QUALIT = anonymous

grey area, grey areas. If a situation or aspect of something is a **grey area**, it is not clear how it should be dealt with or it does not seem to belong to a particular category. — N COUNT

greyhound /greɪhaʊnd/, **greyhounds**. A **greyhound** is a dog that has a thin body and long thin legs and that can run very fast. Greyhounds sometimes run in races and people bet on them. — N COUNT

greyish /greɪɪʃ/; also spelled **grayish** in American English. **Greyish** means slightly grey in colour. EG *...the thin, greyish-brown liquid.* — ADJ COLOUR

grid /grɪd/, **grids**. **1** A **grid** is a pattern which consists of straight lines that cross over each other and form a series of squares; also used of anything built or made in this pattern. EG *...abstract designs-parallel lines, squares, grids... ...the grid of small streets... ...the wire grid round the tennis courts.* ● See also **cattle-grid**. — N COUNT = lattice

2 The **grid** or the electricity **grid** in Britain is the network of wires and cables by which electricity is distributed throughout the country, or a part of this network. EG *They draw electricity from the national grid... ...the failure of the northeast power grid.* — N SING : *the*+N

3 Grid maps have lines drawn on them from top to bottom and side to side. The lines are numbered, so that you can refer to any place on the map by using the numbers of the lines. EG *...a large-scale grid map... ...the grid reference.* — N BEFORE N ⇑ measurement

griddle /grɪdəºl/, **griddles**. A **griddle** is a round, flat, heavy piece of metal which is placed on a stove or fire and used for cooking. — N COUNT ⇑ utensil

grief /gri:f/, **griefs**; a formal word. **1 Grief** is extreme sadness. EG *We were struck dumb with horror and grief... He had caused them grief... That helped to ease his grief.* — N UNCOUNT ⇑ distress = anguish

2 A **grief** is something unpleasant that happens which causes someone great sadness or unhappiness. EG *His death was a great grief to Dean... ...the misfortunes and griefs of others.* — N COUNT ⇑ trouble = sorrow

3 If someone or something **comes to grief**, they fail or harm themselves. EG *I ran away once but came to grief... A number of good ideas always come to grief.* — PHR : VB INFLECTS = come unstuck

4 Some people say **'Good Grief'** to express surprise or disbelief. — EXCLAM

grief-stricken /gri:fstrɪkəºn/. If someone is **grief-stricken**, they are extremely sad about something that has happened; a formal word. EG *She had looked so utterly grief-stricken... ...the grief-stricken widow.* — ADJ QUALIT ⇑ upset

grievance /gri:vəns/, **grievances**. A **grievance** is **1** something that has happened or been done which you feel is unfair and complain about. EG *The complainant may well have a genuine grievance... ...a willingness to settle grievances quickly.* **2** a feeling that something that has happened or been done is unfair. EG *...my family's grievance against Mr Geard... Her extravagance had given him a sense of grievance... Colin never harboured a grievance for long.* — N COUNT/UNCOUNT ⇑ complaint; N COUNT/UNCOUNT

grieve /gri:v/, **grieves, grieving, grieved**; a formal word. **1** If you **grieve**, you feel very sad about something that has happened. EG *She was grieving for the dead baby... It is not right to grieve over one's mistakes... I lay there grieving.* — V : IF+PREP THEN *for/over* ⇑ suffer = lament

2 If something **grieves** someone, it causes them to feel very sad. EG *It grieves me to say this, but you must leave now... Her disappointments grieved him... I was grieved to hear that he had been captured.* ◊ **grieved**. EG *...an expression of grieved astonishment... 'Did he complain ?' Daniel asked, in a grieved tone.* — V+O ⇑ upset = pain; ◊ ADJ QUALIT = hurt

grievous /gri:vəs/; a formal word. **1** A **grievous** injury to your body is one that causes you great pain and suffering. EG *...grievous internal wounds that would never heal.* ◊ **grievously**. EG *He had been grievously wounded.* — ADJ QUALIT = serious, severe; ◊ ADV = seriously

2 Something that is **grievous** is extremely serious or worrying in its effects. EG *...a grievous mistake... Her death was a grievous shock... The economic position was grievous.* ◊ **grievously**. EG *The report had been grievously distorted.* — ADJ QUALIT = grave; ◊ ADV = dreadfully

grievous bodily harm. If someone is accused of **grievous bodily harm**, they are accused of causing very serious physical injury to someone; a legal term. EG *...assault with intent to commit grievous bodily harm.* — N UNCOUNT

grill /grɪl/, **grills, grilling, grilled**. **1** When you **grill** food, you cook it using very strong heat directly above or below it. EG *I usually grill or fry beef.* ◊ **grilled**. EG *I had a grilled chop and salad for lunch.* — V-ERG = broil; ◊ ADJ CLASSIF

2 A **grill** is **2.1** a part of a cooker that consists of a metal shelf where food is cooked by strong heat from above. EG *Place the pepper under a hot grill... Arrange the slices on the grill pan.* **2.2** a flat frame of metal bars or a flat metal plate which you put food on and heat over a fire to cook the food. EG *Rub the grill bars with fat to prevent meat sticking.* **2.3** a dish which consists of food that has been grilled, especially meat. EG *I asked for a mixed grill.* **2.4** a restaurant or part of a restaurant where grilled food is served. EG *...Corcoran's Bar and Grill.* **2.5** See also **grille**. — N COUNT : USU SING; N COUNT; N COUNT/UNCOUNT; N COUNT : ALSO IN NAMES

3 If you say the sun **grills** someone or something, you mean that the sun makes them very hot indeed; a fairly literary use. EG *The black lava, grilled by the sun, is painful to walk on... ...the grilling sun.* — V+O ⇑ heat = bake

4 If you **grill** someone about something, you ask them many questions for a long period of time; a fairly informal use. EG *At the police station, she was grilled for twenty-four hours... She had to grill him on the topic of her mother's bleeding stomach.* ◊ **grilling, grillings**. EG *She gave me a grilling about where I'd been.* — V+O ⇑ question = interrogate; ◊ N UNCOUNT/COUNT

grille /grɪl/, **grilles**; also spelled **grill**. A **grille** is a framework of metal bars or wire which is placed in front of something such as a window or a piece of machinery, in order to protect it or to protect people. EG *...an iron grille... ...the protective grille at the back of the set... The post-office lady glowered through the grill.* — N COUNT

grim /grɪm/, **grimmer, grimmest**. **1** A situation or piece of information that is **grim** is unpleasant or difficult and makes people feel unhappy or pessimistic. EG *...the grim facts... ...the grim aftermath of World War I.* ◊ **grimness**. EG *...the grimness of their life.* — ADJ QUALIT ⇑ cheerless = terrible; ◊ N UNCOUNT = harshness

2 A place that is **grim** is unattractive and depressing in appearance. EG *...its grim walls, its dirty gutters.* — ADJ QUALIT = gloomy

3 If a person or their behaviour is **grim**, they are very serious or stern, especially because they are very worried or angry about something. EG *...his grim determination not to cry... ...grim-faced guards.* ◊ **grimly**. EG *'Smoke,' Eddie announced grimly.* — ADJ QUALIT = resolute, stern; ◊ ADV WITH VB

4 If you say that you feel **grim**, you mean that you — ADJ QUALIT : USU feel very ill; an informal use. EG *I felt really grim last week.* PRED

5 If you say that something is **grim**, you mean that it is awful in style or quality; an informal use. EG *The music was grim.* ADJ QUALIT = dreadful

6 If you **hang on** or **hold on like grim death**, you grip something very tightly, usually because you are afraid. PHR : VB INFLECTS ⇑ cling

grimace /grɪmeɪs/, **grimaces, grimacing, grimaced.** A **grimace** is an expression you make by twisting your face in an ugly way because you are displeased, disgusted, annoyed, in pain, etc. EG *Thomas made a little grimace. Perhaps he thought the wine was sour.* ▸ used as a verb. EG *She made a bad gear-change and grimaced... He grimaced with disgust.* N COUNT ▸ V = pull a face

grime /graɪm/ is dirt which gets into your skin and clothes, or which gathers on buildings over a period of several years. EG *The windows were thick with grime.* N UNCOUNT

grimy /graɪmi[1]/. Something that is **grimy** is very dirty. EG *...a grimy office... ...a grimy handkerchief.* ADJ QUALIT = filthy

grin /grɪn/, **grins, grinning, grinned.** **1** If you **grin**, you smile broadly. EG *He grinned at her and laid his hand on hers... He was grinning proudly, delighted with his achievement.* ◇ **grinning.** EG *I turned to see a grinning corporal hunched over a cassette recorder.* V : IF + PREP USU at/with ◇ ADJ QUALIT : ATTRIB ⇑ smiling

2 A **grin** is a broad smile. EG *The pilot was unhurt and climbed out with a cheerful grin... ...a little grin of triumph.* ● to **wipe the grin off** someone's **face**: see **wipe.** N COUNT

3 To **grin and bear it** means to accept a difficult or unpleasant situation without complaining because you know there is nothing you can do to make things better. EG *I'd just have to grin and bear it for the next two hours.* PHR : VBS INFLECTS ⇑ suffer = grit your teeth

grind /graɪnd/, **grinds, grinding, ground.** **1** If you **grind** something such as corn or pepper, you crush it between two hard surfaces or with a machine until it becomes a fine powder. EG *They were grinding white flour for the people of Norfolk... ...freshly ground black pepper.* V+O ⇑ mill

2 If you **grind** something into a surface, you press and rub it hard into the surface using small circular or sideways movements. EG *He ground his cigarette in the ashtray.* V+O+A = work

3 If you **grind** your **teeth**, you rub your upper and lower teeth together as though you are chewing something. EG *Hooper's teeth were clenched, and he ground them the way people do during sleep.* PHR : VB INFLECTS = gnash your teeth

4 If you **grind** something, you make it smooth or sharp by rubbing it against a hard surface or on a machine. EG *There was a knife being ground on a wheel.* V+O ⇑ sharpen

5 If a machine **grinds**, it makes a harsh scraping noise. EG *The lift grinds in the shaft.* ◇ **grinding.** EG *Our washing machine is making a terrible grinding noise.* V ◇ ADJ CLASSIF : ATTRIB = grating

6 If a vehicle **grinds** along, it moves very slowly and noisily. EG *...heavy trucks grinding down the road.* V+A = trundle

7 grind to a halt. 7.1 If a vehicle **grinds to a halt**, it stops slowly. EG *The huge coal cart would grind to a halt at our front door.* **7.2** If a country, economy, process, etc **grinds to a halt** or **a standstill**, it gradually becomes less efficient or less active until it stops, or stops functioning. EG *Why doesn't the whole economy grind to a halt?... The war was grinding to a standstill.* **7.3** If you **bring** something **to a grinding halt** or if it **comes to a grinding halt**, it stops, especially before it was meant to. EG *Things came to a grinding halt Thursday night.* PHR : VB INFLECTS / PHR : VB INFLECTS = run down / PHR : VB INFLECTS = come to a standstill

8 You can refer to routine work which you have to do and which takes a lot of time and effort as the **grind.** EG *They then begin the long and tiresome grind of preparing themselves for college entrance.* N SING WITH DET = labour

9 If you say that something is a **grind**, you mean that it is annoying and inconvenient; an informal use. EG *It'll be a real grind to go on the bus.* N SING : a+N ⇑ nuisance = bind, drag

10 ● to **have an axe to grind**: see **axe.** ● See also **grinding.**

grind away. If you **grind away**, you work very hard; an informal expression. EG *We were grinding away in the library for weeks.* PHRASAL VB : V+ ADV, IF+PREP THEN at

grind down. 1 If you **grind** someone **down**, you treat them very harshly and cruelly, with the result that they do not have the will to resist you. EG *See how the working people of Britain are ground down.* PHRASAL VB : V+ O+ADV

2 If you **grind** something **down**, you make it smooth or sharp by rubbing it against a hard surface or on a machine. PHRASAL VB : V+ O+ADV = polish

grind on. If something **grinds on**, it continues to happen in the same boring way for a long time. EG *He ground on for another half hour... The year grinds on.* PHRASAL VB : V+ ADV ⇑ continue = go on

grind out. A person or machine **grinds** something **out**, for example information or a piece of work, they produce it in a boring or routine manner; a fairly informal expression. EG *It is a data-processing computer which grinds out decisions after computing the information.* PHRASAL VB : V+ O+ADV = churn out

grind up. If you **grind** something up, you completely crush it between two hard surfaces or with a machine until it becomes a fine powder. EG *They would smash the bottles with a hammer until they were ground up.* PHRASAL VB : V+ O+ADV ⇑ pulverize

grinder /graɪndə/, **grinders.** A **grinder** is a device which crushes something into small pieces or makes it into a powder. EG *...a coffee grinder.* N COUNT

grinding /graɪndɪŋ/. You use **grinding** to describe a situation that never seems to change or end, and that makes you feel unhappy, tired, or bored. EG *...grinding poverty.* ◇ **grindingly.** EG *The routine became grindingly familiar.* ADJ CLASSIF : ATTRIB = relentless ◇ ADV+ADJ

grindstone /graɪnd[0]stəun/, **grindstones. 1** A **grindstone** is a large round stone that turns like a wheel and is used for sharpening knives and tools. N COUNT

2 To **keep** your **nose to the grindstone** means to work very hard all the time. PHR : VB INFLECTS

grip /grɪp/, **grips, gripping, gripped. 1** If you **grip** something, you take hold of it with your hand and continue to hold it firmly. EG *Lomax gripped the boy's arm... He gripped the lectern with both hands.* V OR V+O : USU V +O = clasp

2 A **grip** is **2.1** a firm, strong hold on something. EG *I tightened my grip on the handrail... The grip on Casson's right wrist did not slacken.* **2.2** a particular way of holding someone when you are fighting them or trying to control them. EG *This is the old fashioned policeman's grip.* N COUNT : USU SING / N COUNT : USU MOD+N = hold

3 A **grip** on something is power and control over a situation, activity, or person. EG *He now took a firm grip on the management side of the newspaper... She felt herself in the grip of a sadness she could not understand.* N SING WITH DET +SUPP ⇑ hold = grasp

4 If something **grips** you, **4.1** it affects you very strongly. EG *The heartburn gripped him again... He seemed to be gripped by a powerful desire to laugh.* **4.2** it keeps your attention concentrated on it. EG *I'm not really a golfer myself but actually I'm gripped by it.* ◇ **gripping.** EG *...a piece of research which promises to be more gripping than most.* V+O ⇑ seize / V+O : USU PASS ⇑ fascinate ◇ ADJ QUALIT = riveting

5 Grip is the ability to stick to something or stay on a surface without slipping. EG *These new tyres give a much better grip than the old ones.* N SING WITH DET, OR N UNCOUNT ⇑ hold = purchase

6 A **grip** is also **6.1** a bag that is smaller than a suitcase, and that you use when you are travelling. **6.2** a hair-grip. N COUNT = holdall / N COUNT

7 The word **grip** is also used in the following expressions. **7.1** If you **get** or **come to grips with** something such as a problem, you consider it seriously, and start taking the necessary action to deal with it. EG *It's taken us eighteen years to get to grips with our inadequacies.* **7.2** When two people **get to grips**, they start fighting. EG *It wasn't long before they got to grips.* **7.3** If you **get** or **take a grip on** yourself, you make a deliberate effort to control or improve your behaviour or work, for example after you have received a shock or after you have become careless or lazy. **7.4** If you **lose** your **grip**, you become less efficient and less confident, and less able to deal with things. EG *I could see they thought I was losing my grip.* PHR : VB INFLECTS = tackle / PHR : VB INFLECTS / PHR : VB INFLECTS ⇑ control yourself / PHR : VB INFLECTS ⇑ lose control

gripe /graɪp/, **gripes, griping, griped**; an informal word. **1** If you **gripe**, you keep on complaining about something. EG *Don't pay any attention to him; he's always griping about something or other.* V : IF+PREP THEN about/at ⇑ complain = moan

2 A **gripe** is a bitter complaint about something, or the reason for it. EG *Supervisors get together to discuss their gripes.* N COUNT

3 The **gripes** are sudden intense pains in your stomach or bowels. EG *I've got the gripes.* N PLURAL : the+ N

griping /graɪpɪŋ/. A **griping** pain is a sudden, stabbing pain in your stomach or bowels. ADJ CLASSIF : ATTRIB

grisly /grɪzli¹/. Something that is **grisly** is extremely nasty and horrible. EG ...*a grisly experiment.* ADJ QUALIT : USU ATTRIB

grist /grɪst/. If you say that something is **grist to the mill**, you mean that it is useful for a particular situation. EG *You might as well take another exam if you have time–it's all grist to the mill.* PHR : USU USED AS C

gristle /grɪsə⁰l/ is a tough, rubbery substance found in meat, especially in meat of poor quality, which is unpleasant to eat. N UNCOUNT = cartilage

gristly /grɪsə⁰li¹/. Meat that is **gristly** has lots of gristle in it. ADJ QUALIT

grit /grɪt/, **grits, gritting, gritted**. **1 Grit** is **1.1** very small pieces of stone or sand that are often put on roads in winter to make them less slippery. N UNCOUNT **1.2** the determination and courage to continue doing something necessary, even though it is very difficult. EG *I admire his grit.* N UNCOUNT = guts

2 If you **grit** a road or path, you throw grit on it in order to make it less slippery in icy or snowy weather. EG *I expect they'll be gritting the roads tonight.* V+O

3 If you **grit** your **teeth**, **3.1** you press your upper and lower teeth tightly together. EG *I gritted my teeth, but she didn't notice my anger.* PHR : VB INFLECTS **3.2** you make up your mind to carry on even if the situation is very difficult. EG *We'll just have to grit our teeth and carry on.* PHR : VB INFLECTS

4 Grits are coarsely ground grains of corn which are eaten as a dish in the Southern United States. EG ...*a plate of pork chops and grits.* N UNCOUNT ⇑ dish

gritty /grɪti¹/, **grittier, grittiest**. **1** Something that is **gritty** is covered with grit or has a texture that is like that of grit. EG ...*the gritty carpet... ...gritty, chewy Irish bread.* ADJ QUALIT ⇑ rough = grainy

2 Someone who is **gritty** is determined, courageous, and tough. EG ...*a gritty upholder of the law.* ADJ QUALIT

3 A **gritty** description or portrayal of a place shows realistically how tough life there is. ADJ QUALIT

grizzle /grɪzə⁰l/, **grizzles, grizzling, grizzled**; a fairly informal word. **1** If a baby or child **grizzles**, it keeps crying and whining. EG *The baby grizzles all night.* V ⇑ cry = whinge

2 If someone **grizzles**, they continously complain about something in a whining manner. EG *Rhoda was grizzling because she had lost.* V = whine

grizzled /grɪzə⁰ld/. A **grizzled** person or a person with **grizzled** hair has hair that is grey or streaked with grey. EG ...*a grizzled beard.* ADJ CLASSIF : USU ATTRIB

grizzly /grɪzli¹/, **grizzlies**. A **grizzly** or a **grizzly bear** is a large, fierce, greyish-brown bear which lives in Western North America. N COUNT

groan /grəʊn/, **groans, groaning, groaned**. **1** If you **groan**, you make a long, low sound because you are in pain or unhappy, or to indicate that you disapprove of something. EG *The girl groaned in pain... He groaned and rubbed his eyes... His pupils always groaned at his appalling jokes.* V = moan

2 A **groan** is a long, low sound expressing pain, unhappiness, or disapproval. EG *John fell forward with a groan... ...the groans of the wounded... A chorus of groans greeted his joke.* N COUNT = moan

3 If you **groan** something, you say it in a low, unhappy voice. EG *'I'm sick,' he groaned.* V+O/QUOTE = moan

4 If you **groan** about something, you complain about it; an informal use. EG *She was groaning about some essay she had to write.* V+A *(about)* = grumble

5 If a tree or floorboard **groans**, it makes a loud creaking sound. EG *The wind still roared, and the trees groaned.* V ⇑ creak

6 A **groan** is also a loud, creaking sound made when something wooden is pushed or pressed. EG *Eventually I got used to the creaks and groans of the tree outside my window.* N COUNT ⇑ creak

7 If you say that something such as a table **groans** under something, you mean that the thing or quantity of things that is on it is extremely heavy and large. EG *Tables groan under rich exotic foods.* V : IF+PREP THEN *under/beneath* = creak

grocer /grəʊsə/, **grocers**. A **grocer** is a shopkeeper who sells foods such as flour, sugar, and tinned foods, and some other products used in people's homes. EG *She was now married to a grocer in Cedar City.* ▸ The **grocer** or the **grocer's** is also used to refer to a shop where these things are sold. EG *I went over the cobbled road to the grocer's.* N COUNT ▸ N SING : *the*+N ⇑ shop

grocery /grəʊsə⁰ri¹/, **groceries**. **1** A **grocery** is a grocer's shop; used in American English. EG ...*a combined post office and grocery.* N COUNT

2 Groceries are foods such as flour, sugar, and tinned foods. EG ...*a wicker shopping-basket containing groceries... She was adding up her grocery bills.* N PLURAL ⇑ provisions

grog /grɒg/ is a drink made by diluting a strong spirit, such as rum or whisky, with water. N UNCOUNT

groggy /grɒgi¹/, **groggier, groggiest**. Someone who is **groggy** feels weak and is unable to stand or walk properly, for example because they are ill. EG *I was feeling a bit groggy with the injections.* ADJ QUALIT

groin /grɔɪn/, **groins**. Your **groin** is the part of your body where your legs meet. N COUNT : USU SING, POSS+N

groom /gru⁴m/, **grooms, grooming, groomed**. **1** A **groom** is **1.1** someone whose job is to look after the horses in a stable and to keep them clean. N COUNT **1.2** a bridegroom. EG ...*the bride and groom.* N COUNT

2 If you **groom** an animal, you clean its fur, usually by brushing it. EG *We watched two apes grooming each other.* V+O

3 If you **groom** a person, you prepare them for a special job by teaching them the skills they will need. EG *I had been chosen to be groomed as editor.* V+O (NG/REFL) : USU+A *(as/for)* ⇑ train

groomed /gru:md/. Someone who is well **groomed**, beautifully **groomed**, etc is very neat, clean, and smart in appearance. EG *The manager was a beautifully groomed young man.* ADJ QUALIT : USU WITH ADV = turned out

groove /gru:v/, **grooves**. A **groove** is **1** a wide, deep line cut into a surface. EG ...*a steel plate with grooves cut in it.* N COUNT ⇑ line **2** a way in which someone behaves or lives which has remained the same for a long time and is difficult to change. EG *He felt himself slipping into the groove of compulsive self-justification again.* N COUNT+SUPP ⇑ habit

grooved /gru:vd/. Something that is **grooved** has grooves on its surface. EG *The upper jaw is deeply grooved.* ADJ QUALIT = furrowed

groovy /gru:vi¹/. Something that is **groovy** is attractive, fashionable, or exciting; a fairly old-fashioned word. EG *It's quite a groovy game, actually.* ADJ QUALIT ⇑ good

grope /grəʊp/, **gropes, groping, groped**. **1** If you **grope** for something that you cannot see, you try to find it by moving your hands around in order to feel it. EG *I groped for the timetable I had in my pocket... She put the glasses into Piggy's groping hands.* V : USU+A : OFT A *(for)* = fumble

2 If you **grope** your way to a place, you move there, holding your hands in front of you and feeling the way because you cannot see anything. EG *I groped my way out of bed and did my morning exercises... He groped into the kitchen and switched on the light.* V+O+A, OR V+A = feel

3 If you **grope** someone, you touch or grab their body in a rough, sexual way; used in informal English showing disapproval. ◇ **groping, gropings**. EG *Their clumsy gropings seemed meaningless to her.* ▸ used as a noun. EG *He was having a good grope.* V OR V+O : USU V+O ◇ N COUNT ▸ N COUNT

4 If you **grope** for something, for example in order to solve a problem, you try to find or think of something, when you have no real idea what it could be. EG *Economists started to grope around with increasing desperation for explanations of the recession... 'I mean...' She groped for words.* ◇ **groping, gropings**. EG ...*early scientific gropings with radar.* V : USU+A ⇑ search = fumble ◇ N COUNT : USU PL, OR N UNCOUNT

gross /grəʊs/, **grosses, grossing, grossed; grosser, grossest**. The plural form of the noun in paragraph 8 is **gross**. **1 Gross** is used to describe something unacceptable or unpleasant that is very great in amount, degree, or intensity. EG ...*children whose parents are guilty of gross neglect... ...gross inequalities in wealth, power and privilege.* ◇ **grossly**. EG ...*grossly unfair social conditions.* ADJ CLASSIF : ATTRIB = serious ◇ ADV

2 Speech or behaviour that is **gross** shows lack of taste, or is very rude or unacceptable. EG *He felt he had said something gross, indecent.* ◇ **grossly**. EG *He didn't put it quite as grossly as that, but he did make his intention quite plain.* ADJ QUALIT = vulgar ◇ ADV ⇑ bluntly

3 Something that is **gross** is very large and ugly. EG ...*the gross architecture of the Piccadilly frontages... She always wears really gross earrings.* ADJ QUALIT = tasteless

4 A person or animal that is **gross** is extremely fat in an unattractive way. EG ...*like a great, gross beast.* ADJ QUALIT = enormous

5 Gross is also used to describe **5.1** the total amount of something, especially money, before any necessary deductions are made. EG ...*gross income... She earns £20,000 gross.* ADJ CLASSIF : ATTRIB, OR ADV ≠ net **5.2** the total amount of something, after all the relevant amounts have been added together. EG ...*the gross national product.* ADJ CLASSIF : ATTRIB **5.3** the total weight of something, including its container ADJ CLASSIF : ATTRIB, OR ADV or wrapping. EG *Its gross weight is 100g... It weighs 12kg gross.*

6 If you **gross** an amount of money, you earn that amount of money before tax has been deducted. EG *You could gross millions by spending only £400,000.* V+O ⇑ gain

7 The **gross** is the whole amount of something, especially money. EG *...ten per cent of the gross.* N SING : *the*+N

8 A **gross** is a group of 144 things. EG *...five gross of pencils... He bought them by the gross.* N COUNT ⇑ quantity

grotesque /grəʊtesk/. Something that is **grotesque** is **1** very exaggerated in an unpleasant way so that it is ridiculous or frightening. EG *The idea was simply grotesque.* ADJ QUALIT ◇ **grotesquely**. EG *I knew I had been perfectly ridiculous, over-acting grotesquely.* ◇ ADV **2** very ugly in appearance. EG *He was rather grotesque to look at.* ADJ QUALIT = hideous

grotto /grɒtəʊ/, **grottoes, grottos**. The plural can be either **grottoes** or **grottos**. A **grotto** is a small cave with coloured or attractively shaped rocks. N COUNT

grotty /grɒti¹/, **grottier, grottiest**. If you describe something as **grotty**, you mean that you think it is unpleasant or of poor quality; an informal word. EG *...a grotty little play... Women's magazines get grottier and grottier.* ADJ QUALIT ⇑ bad

grouch /graʊtʃ/, **grouches, grouching, grouched**; an informal word. **1** If you **grouch**, you complain about something in a bad-tempered way. EG *He is always grouching about his children.* V : IF+PREP THEN *about* ⇑ complain

2 A **grouch** is someone who is always complaining in a bad-tempered way. EG *I am a grouch before my first cup of coffee.* N COUNT

grouchy /graʊtʃi¹/. Someone who is **grouchy** is very bad-tempered and complains a lot; an informal word. EG *She can be a bit grouchy when she wakes up.* ADJ QUALIT = grumpy ◇ **grouchiness**. ◇ N UNCOUNT

ground /graʊnd/, **grounds, grounding, grounded**. **1** The **ground** is **1.1** the surface of the earth or the floor of a room. EG *He set down his bundle carefully on the ground... He seized a lamp which was on a table and threw it to the ground.* N SING : *the*+N **1.2** the soil and rock on and beneath the earth's surface. EG *The ground all round was very wet and marshy.* N SING WITH DET

2 Something that happens or is situated **above ground** happens or is situated on the surface of the ground. Something that happens or is situated **below ground** or **below the ground** happens or is situated beneath the surface of the ground. EG *They graze above ground during the day... They spend their lives below ground sucking sap from roots.* PHR : USED AS AN A

3 **Ground** is **3.1** land where there are very few buildings or no buildings at all. EG *...a rocky piece of ground... They own all the ground in front of you as far as the next hill.* N UNCOUNT ⇑ country **3.2** land which is considered to be special in some way. EG *The building in question was not holy ground... All countries were concerned to honour it as neutral ground.* N UNCOUNT+SUPP ⇑ place

4 A **ground** is **4.1** an area of land, sea, or air which is used for a particular purpose. EG *They have their own burial ground behind the chapel... This is one of the world's best fishing grounds.* N COUNT+SUPP : USU MOD+N **4.2** an area of land where sport is played, especially football or cricket. EG *...football grounds and open-air sports centres.* N COUNT : MOD+N **4.3** a place or situation in which a particular activity happens. EG *The Army had been an excellent training ground... It became the jumping-off ground for driving through Namibia to South Africa.* N COUNT : MOD+N

5 **Ground** is also used to refer to **5.1** a place or situation in which particular ideas, attitudes, organizations, etc can develop and be successful. EG *This is particularly infertile ground for trade unionism... The Public Schools of England are the breeding ground of snobbery.* N COUNT/UNCOUNT+SUPP = area **5.2** a particular subject or area of experience. EG *We are indeed on dangerous ground... This course covers the same ground as the undergraduate degree in Social Administration.* N UNCOUNT+SUPP

6 Something that is a **ground** for something else or **grounds** for something else is a reason or argument for it to exist or happen. EG *You have no real grounds for complaint... I'm in favour of being in the Common Market for the grounds I've given... Adultery was a ground for divorce.* N COUNT/UNCOUNT+SUPP ● You can use expressions such as **on grounds of, on the grounds that**, and **on the grounds of** to introduce the reason or reasons for a particular action. EG *He was always declining their invitations on grounds of ill health... They refused to participate on the grounds that broader issues should be discussed... They refused to publish the report on the grounds of cost.* ● PHR : USED AS AN A = because

7 **Ground** is used in expressions such as 'gain ground', 'lose ground', and 'give ground' which refer to an advantage that you have in a particular situation, activity, or argument, or to the progress that you are making. EG *Godley's views are gaining political ground... He tried to regain lost ground.* N UNCOUNT ⇑ advantage

8 **On** someone's **own ground** means **8.1** at the place where someone lives or works and where they feel confident. EG *You need to go and see people on their own ground.* PHR : USED AS AN A **8.2** in a subject or area of experience in which someone is an expert. EG *I also intended to beat my father on his own ground.* PHR : USED AS AN A

9 **Grounds** are an area of land or a garden which belongs to someone and which usually surrounds a building. EG *These are private grounds and you are all trespassing... There was a commotion outside the school grounds.* N PLURAL : USU+SUPP = estate

10 **Ground** is used to describe equipment and activities that operate or take place on the surface of the earth and not in the air, especially in the air force or army. EG *My air and ground crew will be stretched beyond the limits... The plane was hit by enemy ground fire.* ADJ CLASSIF : ATTRIB

11 If you **ground** an aircraft or person, you cause them to remain on the ground and not be able to take off. EG *The defences were totally grounded.* V+O

12 When you **ground** a ship or boat or when it **grounds**, it touches the bottom of a lake, river, etc and is not able to move off it. EG *The ship was grounded on a sand bank.* V-ERG = run aground

13 If you **ground** an argument or opinion on something, you use it to justify that argument or opinion. EG *They had grounded their appeal on the common law... The assumption is well grounded in the box office receipts.* V+O+A : USU A *(in/on)* = base

14 If you **ground** someone in a subject, you teach them the basic facts or principles of that subject. EG *He was well grounded in English and Maths.* V+O+A *(in)* : USU PASS

15 The **ground** in an electric plug or piece of electrical equipment is the wire in it through which electricity can pass into the ground and which makes the equipment safe even if something goes wrong with it; used in American English. N COUNT : USU SING = earth

16 **Grounds** are also the small bits of coffee beans which are left at the bottom of a cup or jug when you have drunk the coffee. N PLURAL ⇑ sediment = dregs

17 **Ground** is also the past tense and past participle of **grind**.

18 The word **ground** is also used in the following expressions. **18.1** If you say that a town or building has been burnt or razed **to the ground**, you are emphasizing that it has been completely destroyed. EG *Many villages were razed to the ground... The school was burned down, burned to the ground.* PHR : USED AS AN A **18.2** If you **drive** or **hammer** someone or something **into the ground**, you treat them so severely over a long period of time that they are completely exhausted or destroyed. EG *We'll drive them into the ground as an act of vengeance... He hammered his car into the ground and then bought a new one.* PHR : VB INFLECTS = flatten, destroy **18.3** If you **go to ground**, you hide somewhere where you cannot easily be found. EG *All the people involved have gone to ground in cheap hotels.* PHR : VB INFLECTS **18.4** If you **run** someone or something **to ground**, you find them after a long and difficult search. EG *It was run to ground in the nearby woods.* PHR : VB INFLECTS = hunt down **18.5** If you **prepare the ground**, you make it easier for future actions, activities, developments, etc to happen. EG *Her work prepared the ground for the romantic novel.* PHR : VB INFLECTS = clear the way **18.6** If you **break fresh ground** or **break new ground**, you make a new discovery or start a new activity. EG *There is a political awareness of the need to break fresh ground.* PHR : VB INFLECTS ⇑ innovate **18.7** If you **get** something **off the ground**, you begin something or make it start functioning. EG *There was a hurry to get the new film off the ground.* PHR : VB INFLECTS = get going **18.8** If you **stand** your **ground**, you do not run away from a situation, but face it bravely; used showing approval. EG *As we scrambled out of our tents, they stood their ground.* PHR : VB INFLECTS = stand firm **18.9** If you **hold** your **ground**, you continue to support a particular argument or opinion when other people are opposing you or trying to make you change your mind. EG *Laing held his ground. 'We seek only to reverse the discrimination which already exists.'* PHR : VB INFLECTS = stand firm **18.10** If you **shift** or **change** your **ground**, you change the subject of a conversa- PHR : VB INFLECTS tion or the basis on which you are arguing something. EG *The Left is shifting its ground... Suddenly she shifted ground. 'I can't make out if Nell likes him or not.'* 18.11 If you **cut, sweep,** or **dig the ground from under** someone's **feet**, you destroy their chance of success by your own actions. EG *By challenging the traditional beliefs of mankind we dig away the ground from under our own feet.* 18.12 If something such as a job, life-style, or piece of clothing **suits** someone **down to the ground**, it is completely suitable or appropriate for them; an informal expression. EG *Working mornings only suits me down to the ground.*

PHR : VB INFLECTS = undermine

PHR : VB INFLECTS ⇑ suit

19 • to **have** your **ear to the ground**: see **ear**. • **thick on the ground**: see **thick**. • **thin on the ground**: see **thin**. • See also **grounding**, **home ground**.

groundcloth /graʊndklɒθ/, **groundcloths**. A **groundcloth** is the same as a groundsheet; used in American English. N COUNT ⇑ sheet

ground floor; often used before another noun and spelled with a hyphen. The **ground floor** of a building is the floor that is level or almost level with the ground outside; used in British English. EG *There's a bathroom on the ground floor... She had taken a beautiful ground-floor flat.* N SING

grounding /graʊndɪŋ/. A **grounding** in a subject is a course of instruction in the basic facts or principles of that subject. EG *They would have had a good grounding in literacy.* N SING WITH DET +SUPP : IF + PREP THEN *in* = foundation

groundless /graʊndlɪ²s/. A fear, suspicion, etc that is **groundless** is not based on reason or evidence. EG *Your fears are groundless... His allegations, when investigated, prove groundless.* ADJ QUALIT : USU PRED = unfounded

ground level; also spelled with a hyphen. **Ground level** is used to refer to 1 the floor of a building which is at the same level as the ground, or the ground around it. EG *The lift was stuck at ground level.* 2 the people who have the least status or importance in a company or organization. EG *Dissent was occurring in the executive suite as well as at the ground level of the factory floor... ...ground-level technicians.*

N UNCOUNT = ground floor

N UNCOUNT = shop floor

groundnut /graʊndnʌt/, **groundnuts**. A **groundnut** is a peanut. N COUNT : USU PL ⇑ nut

ground plan, ground plans. A **ground plan** is 1 a plan of the ground floor of a building. 2 a basic plan for future action. N COUNT / N COUNT

ground rent, ground rents; also spelled with a hyphen. **Ground rent** is rent which is paid by the owner of a flat to the owner of the land on which the flat is built. N UNCOUNT/ COUNT

ground rule, ground rules; also spelled with a hyphen. The **ground rules** for something are the basic principles on which future action will be based. EG *An Act of Parliament formally lays down the ground rules upon which such intervention should take place.* N COUNT : USU PL

groundsheet /graʊndʃiːt/, **groundsheets**. A **groundsheet** is a piece of waterproof material which you put on the ground to sleep on when you are camping. N COUNT ⇑ sheet

groundsman /graʊndzmən/, **groundsmen**. A **groundsman** is a person who is paid to maintain a park or sports ground. N COUNT ⇑ gardener

ground staff are people who are paid to maintain a sports ground. EG *As usual the ground staff here have done a magnificent job.* N UNCOUNT : VB CAN BE SING OR PL

groundswell /graʊndswɛl/, **groundswells**; also spelled with a hyphen and as two words. A **groundswell** is the rapid growth and development of a feeling or opinion about something in a society or group of people. EG *...the groundswell of opinion against reform.* N COUNT + SUPP : USU SING ⇑ wave

groundwork /graʊndwɜːk/ is early work on something which forms the basis for further work or study. EG *The previous president had already provided the groundwork for economic progress.* N UNCOUNT : USU *the*+N, IF + PREP THEN *for* ⇑ preparation

group /gruːp/, **groups, grouping, grouped**. 1 A **group** is 1.1 a number of people or things which are together in one place and at one time. EG *...a small group of my schoolmates... They were all standing in an animated group in the centre of the room... ...a group of buildings... ...a group photograph.* 1.2 a set of people who have the same interests or objectives, and who organize themselves to work or act together. EG *A parents' action group has accused the local authority of breaking the law... ...co-operation between small groups of activists.* 1.3 a set of people, organizations, or things, which are considered together because they have something in common. EG *Children of his age group don't usually verbalize at this stage... ...the minority group of countries which have been through the industrial revolution... ...the lower income groups... One whole group of molluscs have single shells.* 1.4 a number of separate commercial or industrial firms which all have the same owner. EG *...the second biggest newspaper group in the country.*

N COUNT : ALSO N +*of*+N IN PL, IF SING VB CAN BE SING OR PL ⇑ gathering

N COUNT + SUPP : IF SING VB CAN BE SING OR PL ⇑ collective

N COUNT + SUPP : IF SING VB CAN BE SING OR PL

N COUNT : USU MOD + N ⇑ conglomerate

2 When you **group** a number of things or people together or when they **group** together, they all come together in one place or within one organization or system. EG *They encouraged workers, consumers and other sections to group together... You should be able to group all of these constants together... The party has 280 members grouped into eleven branches.* V-ERG : USU + A ⇑ organize

3 A **group** is also a number of musicians who perform together, especially ones who play popular music. EG *The film is a record of several concerts given by the group in New York... ...a pop group.* N COUNT = band

4 See also **blood group**, **ginger group**, **pressure group**, **grouping**.

groupie /gruːpi¹/, **groupies**. A **groupie** is someone who is very keen on a particular pop group, singer, or other famous person, and follows them around and tries to meet them. N COUNT ⇑ fan

grouping /gruːpɪŋ/, **groupings**. A **grouping** is 1 a set of people who have the same interests or objectives, and who organize themselves to work or act together. EG *The point of the EEC is that it's very largely an economic grouping.* 2 a set of people, organizations, or things, which are considered together because they have something in common. EG *Lawyers and government officials were the largest groupings.*

N COUNT + SUPP = group

N COUNT + SUPP = group

group practice, group practices. A **group practice** is a small organization of doctors who work together in the same place. N UNCOUNT/ COUNT

group therapy is a form of psychiatric treatment in which people discuss their problems with each other in a group. N UNCOUNT ⇑ therapy

grouse /graʊs/, **grouses, grousing, groused**. **Grouse** is both the singular and the plural form of the noun in paragraph 1. **Grouses** is the plural form of the noun in paragraph 3 and the third person singular, present tense, of the verb. 1 A **grouse** is a small fat bird with feathered feet. Grouse are often reared and shot for sport and can be cooked and eaten. EG *They kept people off their grouse moors.* ▸ used of the flesh of a grouse eaten as meat. EG *...lunching at the Savoy on smoked salmon and grouse.*

N COUNT

▸ N UNCOUNT

2 If you **grouse**, you complain, especially regularly or repeatedly. EG *She never grumbled or groused... 'They don't have to do it every week,' groused Carl.* V, V + QUOTE, OR V + A *(about)* = gripe

3 A **grouse** is also a complaint. EG *His constant grouse was about prices.* N COUNT

grove /grəʊv/, **groves**. 1 A **grove** is a group of trees that are close together, often because they have been planted in this way. EG *On top of the hill was a grove of tall, dark trees... ...the orange grove.* N COUNT

2 **Grove** is often used as part of the name of a street. EG *...60, Westbourne Grove, London.* N IN NAMES

grovel /grɒvə⁰l/, **grovels, grovelling, grovelled**; also spelled **groveling** and **groveled** in American English. If you **grovel**, 1 you behave very humbly towards someone and try to please them, because they are important, or you are frightened, or you want something from them; used showing disapproval. EG *They are going to make you grovel.* ◇ **grovelling**. EG *...a letter of grovelling apology.* 2 you crawl on the floor, for example in order to find something. EG *He was grovelling under his desk for a dropped pencil.*

V ⇑ be humble = crawl

V + A

grow /grəʊ/, **grows, growing, grew, grown**. 1 When a person, an animal, or their body **grows**, their body increases in size and changes physically over a period of time. EG *Babies who are small at birth grow faster... Frogs may grow eight inches long... As my children grew into teenagers, they needed more of my time...* V : USU + A ⇑ increase

2 When someone's hair **grows**, it gradually becomes longer. EG *My hair grew thickly all over my scalp.* V : USU + A

3 If you **grow** your hair, you do not cut it and it gradually becomes longer. V+O ≠ cut

4 If a man **grows** a beard or a moustache, he does not shave his face, and the beard or moustache gradually develops. V+O ≠ shave

5 If someone **grows** mentally, they change and develop in character or attitude. EG *New friends and experiences will help children grow in understanding.* V: USU+A

6 If a plant or tree **grows** in a particular place, **6.1** it is alive there. EG *An oak tree grew at the edge of the lane... ...an open space where bright flowers grew.* V: USU+A ⇑ exist = flourish

6.2 it starts to exist there and increases in size or spreads over a particular area. EG *...an old brick wall with things growing up it... ...fast-growing weeds.* V: USU+A = sprout

7 If you **grow** a particular type of plant, you put seeds or young plants in the ground and look after them because you want the flowers, fruit, or vegetables that they will produce. EG *The district grew peas on a large scale... Both are easy roses to grow from cuttings... Cotton growing expanded in Texas.* V+O = cultivate

8 If someone or something **grows** into a particular state or condition, they change gradually until they are in that state or condition. EG *Some of her ministers are growing impatient... The sun grew so hot that they were forced to stop working... I grew to dislike working for the cinema.* V: USU+C/to-INF/A ⇑ become

9 If an idea or feeling **grows**, it begins to exist and gradually becomes stronger or more important. EG *His fear and his hate grew simultaneously... ...a growing awareness of the problem... Their influence is steadily growing.* V ⇑ develop = increase

10 If one idea, plan, or policy **grows** out of another, it develops from it. EG *Out of this would grow a broad socialist programme... My own idea grew out of seeing this film.* V: USU+A *(out of/from)* ⇑ develop = evolve

11 If the number or amount of something **grows**, it increases. EG *Jobs in industry will grow by 11 per cent... ...a growing body of evidence... I waved, and the applause grew.* V ⇑ increase

12 If a problem or situation **grows**, it becomes more serious or important. EG *Refugees were posing a growing problem.* V ⇑ develop = increase

13 If a place, organization, or thing **grows**, it increases in size, wealth, or importance. EG *The British empire grew as a result of the demands of commerce... Sapporo has grown into a thriving communications centre... ...the fast-growing New York investment bank.* V ⇑ develop = expand

14 See also **grown**.

grow apart. If people who have a close relationship **grow apart**, they gradually start to have different interests and opinions from each other, and their relationship starts to fail. EG *As we travelled together, we started to grow apart.* PHRASAL VB: V+ADV = drift apart

grow away. If you **grow away** from someone, you gradually have fewer interests and opinions in common with them. EG *Cathy grew away from mother.* PHRASAL VB: V+ADV+*from*

grow into. **1** If you **grow into** a job or situation, you gradually learn how to do it or deal with it skilfully. PHRASAL VB: V+PREP

2 If someone, especially a child, **grows into** an item of clothing, they become taller or bigger so that it fits them properly. EG *It's a bit big, but she'll soon grow into it.* PHRASAL VB: V+PREP

grow on. If someone or something **grows on** you, you start to like them more and more; a fairly informal expression. EG *She was someone whose charm grew very slowly on you.* PHRASAL VB: V+PREP

grow out. **1** If you **grow out** of a type of behaviour or an interest, especially one that people consider childish or immature, you stop behaving in that way or having that interest. EG *I've rather grown out of my taste for the bizarre.* PHRASAL VB: V+ADV+*of* = outgrow

2 If someone, especially a child, **grows out** of an item of clothing, they become so tall or big that it no longer fits them properly. PHRASAL VB: V+ADV+*of* = outgrow

grow up. **1** When someone **grows up**, they gradually change from being a child into being an adult. EG *I had grown up in the district... They grew up in the early days of television... Resistance to parents is a part of growing up.* PHRASAL VB: V+ADV ⇑ develop

2 If you tell someone to **grow up**, you are telling them, in an informal and forceful way, to stop behaving in a silly or childish way. EG *Lally said that it was time we all grew up... 'Grow up, Mother.' Jeannie's voice was harsh.* PHRASAL VB: V+ADV, USU IMPER

3 If a place, organization, or idea **grows up**, it starts to exist and becomes larger or more important. EG *Cities grew up as markets, centres of religion or trade... The idea has grown up that science cannot be wrong.* PHRASAL VB: V+ADV = spring up

4 See also **grown-up**.

grower /grəʊə/, **growers**. A **grower** is a person who grows large quantities of a particular plant or crop in order to sell them. EG *...a British lily grower... Growers in the southern counties were making large profits.* N COUNT: USU MOD+N

growing pains are the temporary difficulties and problems that an organization has when it starts to exist, or starts to develop. EG *...a company's growing pains.* N PLURAL: USU WITH POSS = teething troubles

growing season, growing seasons. The **growing season** in a particular country or area is the period in each year when the weather and temperature is usually right for plants and crops to be able to grow. EG *If rains are late, the growing season is cut short.* N COUNT: USU SING

growl /graʊl/, **growls, growling, growled**. **1** When a dog or other animal **growls**, it makes a low rumbling noise, usually because it is angry. EG *The dog growled at me.* ▸ used as a noun. EG *...a sequence of yelps and growls.* V = snarl ▸ N COUNT = snarl

2 If you say that a person **growls** something, you mean that they say it in a low, rough, and rather angry voice; a literary use. EG *'There's a visitor here,' he growled... He growled out a command to her to stop.* ▸ used as a noun. EG *'Now then!' began Arthur in a menacing growl... ...a growl of assent.* V OR V+O/QUOTE ▸ N COUNT

3 If you say that something **growls**, you mean that it makes a deep rumbling noise; a literary use. EG *The thunder still growled in the distance... His stomach started to growl with hunger.* ▸ used as a noun. EG *The engine's pitch changed from a low murmur to an urgent growl.* V = rumble ▸ N COUNT = rumble

grown /grəʊn/. A **grown** man or woman is one who is fully developed and mature, physically and mentally. EG *It requires a child's spontaneity and a grown man's decisiveness.* ADJ CLASSIF: ATTRIB ⇑ adult

-grown is used **1** after adverbs like 'full' or 'half', to form adjectives that describe the size or stage of development that an animal or plant has reached. EG *The caterpillar was full grown... ...two half-grown cubs.* **2** after the name of a plant, to form adjectives that describe a place that is covered by plants of that type. EG *...a moss-grown wall... ...weed-grown terraces.* **3** after a word that tells you the method by which a plant, vegetable, etc was grown, to form adjectives that describe the plant, vegetable, etc. EG *...compost-grown vegetables and fruit... ...a tub-grown tree.* ● See also **home-grown**. COMB: FORMS ADJ CLASSIFS / COMB: FORMS ADJ CLASSIFS / COMB: FORMS ADJ CLASSIFS

grown-up, grown-ups; also spelled as one word when used as a noun. **1** A **grown-up** is an adult; used in informal English, especially by children. EG *We could see a grown-up coming... The boys and girls cheered and grownups applauded.* N COUNT

2 If you say that someone is **grown-up**, you mean **2.1** that they are physically and mentally mature and no longer dependent on their parents or another adult. EG *...older couples, with grown-up children of their own.* **2.2** that they behave in an adult way, especially when they are in fact still a child. EG *Your brother's awfully grown-up for his age.* ADJ CLASSIF / ADJ QUALIT = mature

3 If you say that something is **grown-up**, you mean that it seems suitable for or typical of adults; used in informal English, especially by children. EG *Everybody called me Matt. I thought it sounded grown-up... Grown-up versions may be more sophisticated.* ADJ QUALIT = adult

growth /grəʊθ/, **growths**. **1 Growth** in an industry or other economic activity is the increase in the money being spent on it and the increase in the goods it produces. EG *Science-based industries are key points of growth in the economy... Its economic growth rate is second only to Japan's... Computing remains a growth area.* N UNCOUNT: USU +SUPP, OR BEFORE N = development, expansion

2 The **growth** of an organization is its coming into existence and development in size or importance, with the result that it involves more people. EG *...the growth of political opposition... ...phases of urban growth... Co-operatives are of very recent growth.* N UNCOUNT: USU +SUPP ⇑ development = evolution

3 The **growth** in the number of people or things in a particular place or group, or in the amount of something, is the increase in it. EG *...India's population growth... ...the slower growth of the labour force... ...a growth in research expenditure.* N UNCOUNT+SUPP = expansion

4 The **growth** of a particular attitude or feeling is the gradual development of it and increase in it. EG *...the growth of discontent... ...a growth of moderate opinion... ...the growth of nationalism.* [N SING WITH DET +*of* = heightening]

5 The **growth** of a person or their character is their progress and improvement. EG *It can limit intellectual growth... Marriage traps her growth.* [N UNCOUNT : USU +SUPP ↑ development]

6 **Growth** in a person, animal, or plant is the process of increasing in physical size and development. EG *Only physical growth was necessary for him to claim his heritage... They stunt plant growth and reduce yields.* [N UNCOUNT : USU +SUPP ↑ increase]

7 A **growth** is 7.1 a plant, a part of a plant, or a mass of plants which have recently developed or which developed at the same time. EG *Each year the seaweed growth returns and has to be cleared... ...clearings amid the last year's growths.* [N COUNT/ N UNCOUNT : USU+ SUPP] 7.2 a lump that grows inside or on a person, animal, or plant, and that is caused by a disease or other abnormality. EG *...an ache where a growth was removed... ...secondary growths after an unsuccessful operation.* [N COUNT] 7.3 a short beard on the face of a man who has not shaved recently. EG *...a skinny man with a week's growth of beard on his face.* [N SING WITH DET : USU+SUPP = stubble]

grub /grʌb/, **grubs, grubbing, grubbed**. 1 A **grub** is a young insect which has just come out of an egg and looks like a short fat worm. EG *Each of these eggs hatches out into a tiny grub... ...wasp grubs.* [N COUNT = larva]

2 **Grub** is food; an informal use. EG *Don't expect a lot of free grub.* [N UNCOUNT] ● If someone says **'Grub up'**, they mean that the food that people have been waiting for is now ready to eat; a very informal expression. [● CONVENTION]

3 If you **grub** about or around for something, you search for it, especially by moving things or digging. EG *...grubbing for fallen fruit... The fish grubs around on the river bed... ...grubbing about in the public library for material.* [V : USU+A *(about/around/ for)* = root]

4 If you **grub** something up or **grub** it out, you dig it out of the ground. EG *...grubbing up hedgerows... ...birds grubbing up insects.* [V+O+A *(up/out)* ↑ dig out = uproot]

grubby /grʌbi[1]/, **grubbier, grubbiest**. 1 A person or object that is **grubby** is rather dirty in appearance. EG *...the largest and grubbiest boy... ...grubby exercise books... ...the grubby London streets.* [ADJ QUALIT]

2 If you call an activity or someone's behaviour **grubby**, you mean that it is not proper or acceptable; used showing disapproval. EG *...this grubby circulation war among the newspapers... ...the grubbier aspects of political life.* [ADJ QUALIT = seamy, sordid] ◊ **grubbiness**. EG *...the grubbiness of the campaign.* [◊ N UNCOUNT]

grudge /grʌdʒ/, **grudges, grudging, grudged**. 1 If you have a **grudge** against someone, you have very unfriendly feelings towards them because they have upset you or harmed you, especially feelings which last for a longer time than is reasonable. EG *...someone with a grudge against him... I hope you don't bear me any grudge... He would hold a grudge for years.* [N COUNT : IF+ PREP THEN *against* = grievance]

2 If you **grudge** someone something, or **grudge** doing something, you give it to them or do it very unwillingly. EG *We had to pay £5 for lunch, of which I grudge them every penny... Not that she grudged it to him... She will not grudge doing a bit extra when it's really needed.* [V+O/-ING, V+O+ O, OR V+O+A *(to)* ↑ resent = begrudge]

grudging /grʌdʒɪŋ/. A **grudging** feeling or action is one that is felt or done very unwillingly. EG *...Mrs Pringle's grudging assistance... Others stood watching with grudging respect... ...the grudging way in which the government has reacted.* [ADJ QUALIT ↑ unwilling ≠ charitable, enthusiastic] ◊ **grudgingly**. EG *'Okay,' he said grudgingly, 'I suppose I was to blame.'* [◊ ADV WITH VB]

gruel /grʊəl/ is a simple and cheap food made by boiling oats or another cereal with water or milk. [N UNCOUNT]

gruelling /grʊəlɪŋ/; also spelled **grueling** in American English. Something that is **gruelling** is extremely difficult and requires a lot of effort to do. EG *...the most gruelling part of my trip... ...long hours of gruelling work... The pace is pretty gruelling.* [ADJ QUALIT ↑ demanding]

gruesome /gruːsəm/. Something that is **gruesome** involves or concerns death or injury and is very unpleasant and shocking. EG *...gruesome tales of child murder... ...gruesome scenes of violence.* [ADJ QUALIT = grisly]

gruff /grʌf/. 1 If someone's voice is **gruff**, it sounds low and rough, usually because they are angry or impatient. EG *...his rumpled appearance and gruff voice.* [ADJ QUALIT = harsh ≠ gentle] ◊ **gruffly**. EG *She said gruffly, 'Put on your clothes.'* [◊ ADV WITH VB = roughly]

2 If someone or their behaviour is **gruff**, they seem rather unfriendly or bad-tempered. EG *He was very kind in a gruff sort of way... ...a gruff, soldierly style.* [ADJ QUALIT = brusque] ◊ **gruffness**. EG *Her gruffness put me off.* [◊ N UNCOUNT]

grumble /grʌmbə[0]l/, **grumbles, grumbling, grumbled**. 1 If you **grumble**, you complain about something in a bad-tempered way, usually in a low voice and not forcefully. EG *They will grumble about having to do the work... She never grumbled... 'It's awful,' Posy grumbled.* [V, V+REPORT-CL/ QUOTE, OR V+A *(about)* = moan] ◊ **grumbling**. EG *There was more grumbling at the Cabinet's decision as soon as the news was released.* [◊ N UNCOUNT/ COUNT] ▸ used as a noun. EG *There were angry grumbles from the British ranks.* [▸ N COUNT = complaint]

2 If something **grumbles**, it makes a low continuous sound; a literary use. EG *The train grumbled into motion... ...my grumbling digestive system.* [V = rumble] ◊ **grumbling**. EG *...a low grumbling of thunder from the next valley.* [◊ N UNCOUNT] ▸ used as a noun. EG *...the grumble of a dozen conversations.* [▸ N SING WITH DET+SUPP]

grumpy /grʌmpi[1]/, **grumpier, grumpiest**. Someone who is **grumpy** is bad-tempered, often because they are slightly angry, disappointed, or pessimistic. EG *Don't be so grumpy and cynical about it... Martha looked less grumpy than usual.* [ADJ QUALIT = surly, crotchety] ◊ **grumpily**. EG *'Not far now,' he said grumpily.* [◊ ADV WITH VB] ◊ **grumpiness**. EG *...his grumpiness towards his wife.* [◊ N UNCOUNT]

grunt /grʌnt/, **grunts, grunting, grunted**. 1 If you **grunt**, you make a low rough noise, especially because you are annoyed or uninterested. EG *His father looked up and grunted, then went back to his work... 'What if some shark came along right now?' he grunted.* [V OR V+O/QUOTE] ▸ used as a noun. EG *I answered with a grunt... He gave a sceptical grunt.* [▸ N COUNT : USU SING]

2 When a pig **grunts**, it makes a low rough noise. EG *Wild pigs grunted and snorted.* [V] ▸ used as a noun. EG *It sounded like something between a fox-bark and a pig's grunt.* [▸ N COUNT]

G-string, G-strings. A **G-string** is a narrow band of cloth that is worn between a person's legs to cover up his or her sexual organs, and that is held up by a piece of string round the waist. [N COUNT ↑ garment]

guano /gwɑːnəʊ/ is the excrement of sea birds. It is used as a fertilizer. EG *...rich guano deposits.* [N UNCOUNT ↑ droppings]

guarantee /gærəntiː/, **guarantees, guaranteeing, guaranteed**. 1 If something **guarantees** something else, it is certain to cause that thing to happen or result. EG *Equality does not guarantee happiness in love... This method guarantees seed precisely adapted to the area.* [V+O/REPORT-CL, OR V+O+O = ensure]

2 Something that is a **guarantee** of something else makes it certain that it will happen or that it is true. EG *There is no guarantee that they are telling the truth... He argued that the best guarantee of economic growth was 'the confidence of the business community'.* [N COUNT : USU+ REPORT-CL = assurance]

3 If you **guarantee** something, 3.1 you promise that something will definitely happen, or that you will do or provide something for someone. EG *I'm not guaranteeing that this will work... Advertisers were guaranteed a weekly circulation of 250,000.* [V+O/REPORT-CL/ *to*-INF, OR V+O+ O ↑ say] 3.2 you make sure that it will definitely happen. EG *You should have at least one evening off a week, but you can't guarantee it.* [V+O/REPORT-CL ↑ rely on = depend on]

4 If you say that something **is guaranteed** to happen or have a particular result, you mean that you are certain or fairly sure that it will happen or have the result mentioned. EG *The average colonial debate was still guaranteed to empty the House of Commons.* [V+O+*to*-INF : ONLY PASS]

5 A **guarantee** is also 5.1 a promise that you will do something, or that something will definitely happen. EG *Tory backbenchers want some guarantee that an enquiry will be held.* [N COUNT : USU N +REPORT-CL = assurance] 5.2 a formal written statement of someone's intention to do something, or their acceptance of responsibility in a particular situation. EG *He promptly produced a signed guarantee that if I came to work for him for a couple of months he would cancel the debt.* [N COUNT : USU N +REPORT-CL] 5.3 something valuable which you give to a person to show that you will do what you have promised, especially as part of a legal agreement. EG *They have to provide a financial guarantee.* [N COUNT] 5.4 a written promise by a company that if a product that they sell or work that they do has any faults within a particular time, it will be repaired, replaced, or redone free of charge. EG *Fortunately it's still covered by the manufacturer's guarantee.* [N COUNT ↑ undertaking = warranty]

6 If a company **guarantees** a product or work that they do, they give a written promise that if it has any faults within a particular time it will be repaired, replaced, or redone free of charge. EG *Is it guaranteed?* V+O

7 If you **guarantee** someone, you say that they are suitable or reliable because you know them well. EG *...an Englishman who had been guaranteed to him over the phone by one of his friends.* V+O ⇑ recommend = vouch for

guarantor /gærəntɔː/, **guarantors**. A **guarantor** is a person who gives a guarantee or who is bound by one; a legal term. N COUNT = surety

guard /gɑːd/, **guards, guarding, guarded**. 1 If you **guard** a place, person, or object, you stand near them in order to watch and protect them. EG *Scotland Yard detailed an officer to guard his house.* V+O (NG/REFL): IF+PREP THEN *against/from*

2 If you **guard** someone, you watch them and keep them in a particular place to stop them from escaping. EG *She had been locked in her room and was guarded night and day.* V+O

3 A **guard** is 3.1 a person who is guarding a particular person, place, or object in order to protect them. EG *Another guard was standing by the fence.* N COUNT 3.2 a person who is watching a prisoner to prevent him or her from escaping. EG *Two brothers were charged with killing a prison guard.* N COUNT = warder 3.3 a specially organized group of people, such as soldiers or policemen, that protect or watch someone or something. EG *They will give him an armed guard.* N COUNT: IF SING VB CAN BE SING OR PL 3.4 a person whose job is to travel on a train in order to make sure it arrives and leaves at the correct time. EG *The guard blew his whistle and waved his green flag.* N COUNT

4 If you **guard** something that you do not want to be discovered or changed, you protect or hide it. EG *The professions, as you might expect, guard their secrets closely.* V+O

5 A wall, fence, etc that **guards** a place or thing acts as a protective barrier. EG *A high stone wall guarded the approach to the entrance.* V+O

6 A **guard** is also 6.1 a device which covers a dangerous part of something. EG *When the guard is taken off the motor the machine can't start.* N COUNT 6.2 something that protects a particular part of your body from being hurt. EG *I felt my chin underneath the chin guard of the helmet.* N COUNT ⇑ device

7 The **Guards** is the name of some regiments in the British army. EG *...the Irish Guards.* N PLURAL: *the*+N, USED IN NAMES ⇑ regiment

8 The word **guard** is also used in the following expressions. 8.1 If you **mount guard** or **mount a guard**, you organize people to watch or protect a person or place. EG *The men would arm themselves and mount a guard.* PHR: VB INFLECTS 8.2 If you **stand guard**, you stand near a particular person or place because you are responsible for watching or protecting it. EG *You will be expected to stand guard over the village.* PHR: VB INFLECTS 8.3 If you are **under guard**, you are being guarded. EG *All of them were under military guard.* PHR: USED AS AN A 8.4 Someone who is **on guard** is on duty and responsible for guarding a particular place or person. PHR: USED AS AN A 8.5 If you are **on** your **guard**, you are being very careful because you think a situation might become difficult or dangerous. EG *It is up to you in this situation to be on your guard.* PHR: USED AS AN A ⇑ alert 8.6 If you **lower** your **guard** or **let** your **guard down**, you relax when you should be careful and alert, with the result that you are not properly prepared for a difficult or dangerous situation. EG *He had thought he could finally lower his guard and relax.* PHR: VB INFLECTS 8.7 To **catch** someone **off guard** means to surprise them by doing something or by happening when they are not expecting it. EG *This piece of intelligence caught the Administration off guard.* PHR: VB INFLECTS

9 See also **coastguard, lifeguard, old guard, guarded.**

guard against. If you **guard against** something, you are very careful in order to avoid it happening, or to avoid being affected by it. EG *...ideas which the trained mind of a judge knows to guard against.* PHRASAL VB: V+PREP, HAS PASS = beware of

guard dog, guard dogs. A **guard dog** is a fierce dog that has been specially trained to protect a particular place. N COUNT

guarded /gɑːdɪ²d/. Someone who is **guarded** is careful not to show their feelings or give away information about something. EG *I'm being a bit guarded, I suppose.* ▸ used of someone's behaviour. EG *His statements were guarded.* ◇ **guardedly**. EG *'Do you ever hear from your sister?'–'Sometimes,' Rudolph said guardedly.* ADJ QUALIT ⇑ cautious = cagey ▸ = cagey ◇ ADV: USU WITH VB = cagily

guardian /gɑːdɪən/, **guardians**. A **guardian** is 1 someone who has been legally appointed to look after the affairs of another person, for example a child or someone who is mentally ill. EG *He became the legal guardian of his brother's daughter.* N COUNT: USU WITH POSS ⇑ protector 2 someone who is considered to defend someone or something against danger or bad treatment. EG *Their view that women are the natural guardians of morality is not my view... We are the trustees and guardians of the whole people.* N COUNT: IF+PREP THEN *of* ⇑ defender

guardian angel, guardian angels. A **guardian angel** is a spirit who is believed to protect and to guide a particular person. N COUNT: USU POSS+N

guardianship /gɑːdɪənʃɪp/ is the position of being a guardian. EG *She was placed under her mother's guardianship.* N UNCOUNT: USU WITH POSS ⇑ care

guard-rail, guard-rails. A **guard-rail** is a railing that is sometimes placed along roads, paths, and staircases to protect people. EG *He walked past me and looked over the guard-rail.* N COUNT = barrier

guardsman /gɑːdzmə³n/, **guardsmen**. A **guardsman** is a soldier who is a member of the Guards. EG *...the scarlet coats and bearskins of the guardsmen.* N COUNT

guard's van, guard's vans. The **guard's van** of a train is a small carriage in which the guard travels; used in British English. N COUNT

guava /gwɑːvə/, **guavas**. A **guava** is a round yellow tropical fruit with pink or white flesh and hard seeds. N COUNT

guerrilla /gərɪlə/, **guerrillas**; also spelled **guerilla**. A **guerrilla** is someone who fights as part of an unofficial army, usually against an official army or police force. EG *He had been held a prisoner by the guerrillas... ...guerilla attacks.* N COUNT ⇑ soldier = insurgent

guess /gɛs/, **guesses, guessing, guessed**. 1 If you **guess** something, 1.1 you give an answer or provide an opinion about something when you do not know whether it is correct. EG *We can only guess at the number of deaths it has caused... She guessed that she was fifty yards from shore.* V, V+O/REPORT-CL/QUOTE, OR V+A *(at)* ⇑ conjecture 1.2 you successfully give the correct answer to a problem or question when you actually do not know all the facts or information. EG *How did you guess?... I had guessed the identity of her lover.* V OR V+O ⇑ suppose

2 A **guess** is an attempt to give the answer to something when you do not know all the facts or information. EG *I don't know the name but I'll take a guess at it... I'll give you two guesses.* N COUNT: IF+PREP THEN *at/as to* ⇑ estimate = shot

3 **I guess** is an informal expression used especially in American English. You say **I guess** 3.1 to indicate that you suppose, think, or suspect that something is true or likely. EG *I guess I got the news a day or so late... It looks almost like frost in those fields, but I guess it's just dew... 'What's that?'–'Some sort of blackbird, I guess.'* PHR: USED AS ADV SEN = I suppose 3.2 to indicate that you are reluctantly agreeing with someone. EG *'Sure?'–'I guess so. Nothing else seems to make much sense.'* PHR+*so/not*/REPORT-CL = I suppose 3.3 to indicate what you are thinking, especially when you have just come to a decision. EG *I guess I was thinking out loud... I guess I won't wake him up yet... I guess I must be going now.* PHR+REPORT-CL = I suppose

4 If you **keep** someone **guessing**, you do not tell them what they want to know. EG *I suggest that you keep her guessing.* PHR: VB INFLECTS

5 You say **'guess what'** to draw attention to something exciting, surprising, or interesting that you are about to say; an informal expression. EG *Guess what, you're going to be a granny!... Oh, Albert! Guess what!* CONVENTION

6 You say **at a guess** to indicate that what you are saying is only an estimate or what you believe to be true, rather than being based on fact. EG *At a guess, I'd say she must have got lost.* PHR: USED AS ADV SEN

7 If you say that something is **anyone's guess** or **anybody's guess**, you mean that no-one can be certain about what is really the case or what is really true; an informal expression. EG *What would have happened is anyone's guess... It's anybody's guess how long this has been going on.* PHR: USED AS C

guesswork /gɛswɜːk/ is the process of trying to guess or estimate something without knowing all the facts or information. EG *This is pure guesswork at this stage, of course.* N UNCOUNT = speculation

guest /gɛst/, **guests, guesting, guested**. 1 A **guest** is 1.1 someone who is staying in your home or is at your party or wedding because you have invited them. EG *He opened the door and ushered his guest* N COUNT ⇑ visitor inside... ...wedding guests. **1.2** someone who is taken to a restaurant, theatre, opera, etc by a friend or relation who pays for the meal or tickets. **1.3** someone who is staying in a hotel. EG *The other hotel guests sat under striped umbrellas.* **1.4** someone who visits a place or an organization because they have been invited for a special reason. EG *In fact we're here as guests of the National Theatre... The guest speaker looked absolutely exhausted.* **1.5** someone who appears on a radio or television show because they have been invited to do so. EG *Tonight's star guest is Gene Kelly.* — N COUNT ⇑ person; N COUNT ⇑ visitor; N COUNT ⇑ visitor; N COUNT

2 If someone **guests** on a radio or television show, they appear on the show because they have been invited to do so; a fairly informal use. EG *He's guesting on tonight's show.* — V : USU+A

3 If you say to someone **'be my guest'**, you are giving them permission to do something that they have asked to do. EG *'May I have some more?'-'Be my guest!'* — CONVENTION = feel free

guest book, guest books. A **guest book** is a book in which guests write their names and addresses when they have been staying in someone's house or in a guest house. — N COUNT

guest house, guest houses; also spelled with a hyphen. A **guest house** is a type of small hotel. — N COUNT

guest of honour, guests of honour; also spelled **guest of honor** in American English. The **guest of honour** is the most important guest at a dinner or other social occasion. — N COUNT : USU SING

guest-room, guest-rooms; also spelled without a hyphen. A **guest-room** is a bedroom in someone's house for guests and visitors to sleep in. — N COUNT

guff /gʌf/. If you say that something that is said or written is **guff**, you mean that it is nonsense; an informal word. — N UNCOUNT

guffaw /gəfɔː/, **guffaws, guffawing, guffawed** A **guffaw** is a very loud, hearty laugh. EG *Martin let out a delighted guffaw.* ▸ used as a verb. EG *He guffawed and thumped his friend between the shoulder blades.* — N COUNT; ▸ V

guidance /gaɪdəᵊns/. **1 Guidance** is help and advice, especially from people who are older or more experienced than you are. EG *The college chaplain was available for individual guidance... We would much appreciate guidance from an expert in this field... All he could do was to report to base and await guidance.* — N UNCOUNT

2 Guidance is also used when referring to the controlling of the course of a missile or rocket. EG *..the missile's guidance system.* — N UNCOUNT

guide /gaɪd/, **guides, guiding, guided. 1** A **guide** is **1.1** someone who shows places such as cities or museums to tourists, and who explains their points of interest. **1.2** someone who shows people the way to a particular place, especially as a job in a difficult or dangerous region. **1.3** a guidebook. EG *...an exhaustive guide to New York City.* **1.4** a book which gives you information, advice, or instructions to help you do or understand something. EG *This book is meant to be a practical guide to healthy living.* **1.5** something that can be used to help you plan your actions. EG *The parents can keep in mind, as a rough guide, a 4-hour timetable.* — N COUNT ⇑ courier; N COUNT; N COUNT; N COUNT : IF+PREP THEN *to* = handbook; N SING : a+N

2 If you **guide** someone round a city, museum, etc, you show it to them, explaining points of interest. EG *A young woman guided us on a tour of the museum.* ◇ **guided.** EG *We went on a guided tour of Paris.* — V+O : USU+A; ◇ ADJ CLASSIF

3 To **guide** someone or something means **3.1** to make them move in a particular direction, especially by touching or holding them. EG *He took Julie's arm and guided her through the doorway.* **3.2** to show them the right way or direction. EG *Men crossing the ocean would use the stars to guide them, so that they would not be lost.* — V+O = lead; V+O ⇑ direct

4 If you **guide** someone, **4.1** you direct or influence their actions or decisions. EG *Politicians will in the end always be guided by changes in public opinion.* ◇ **guiding.** EG *The guiding principle of the family was Catholicism.* **4.2** you help them learn something by teaching them or showing them how to do it. EG *Dr Mitra enjoyed guiding me through the infinite variety of Indian social customs.* — V+O; ◇ ADJ CLASSIF; V+O ⇑ show

5 A **Guide** is also, in British English, a Girl Guide. — N COUNT

guidebook /gaɪdbʌk/, **guidebooks**; also spelled with a hyphen and as one word. A **guidebook** is a book which gives information for tourists about a town, area, or country. EG *The guidebook tells us that this is the largest cathedral in France.* — N COUNT ⇑ book

guided missile, guided missiles. A **guided missile** is a missile whose course can be controlled while it is in the air. — N COUNT

guide dog, guide dogs; also spelled with a hyphen. A **guide dog** is a dog that has been trained to lead a blind person. — N COUNT

guideline /gaɪdlaɪn/, **guidelines.** A **guideline** is a piece of official advice about how to do something. EG *The government pay guidelines have proved a godsend to industry... ...guidelines for the control of dogs in public places.* — N COUNT : USU PL

guild /gɪld/, **guilds.** A **guild** is an organization of people who do the same job, or who have the same interests. EG *I belong to a guild of wine butlers... ...Townswomen's Guilds.* — N COUNT : ALSO IN NAMES AFTER N ⇑ association

guilder /gɪldə/, **guilders.** A **guilder** is a unit of money that is used in the Netherlands. — N COUNT : USU a/NUM+N

guildhall /gɪldhɔːl/, **guildhalls.** A **guildhall** is a building near the centre of a town or city where members of a guild used to meet. — N COUNT : USU SING, OR N PROPER

guile /gaɪl/ is the quality of being very cunning and good at deceiving people; a formal or literary word. EG *He was a man without guile.* — N UNCOUNT ⇑ deceit

guileless /gaɪllɪ²s/. Someone who is **guileless** behaves openly and truthfully and does not try to deceive people; a fairly formal word. — ADJ QUALIT ⇑ open = artless

guillotine /gɪlətiːn/, **guillotines, guillotining, guillotined. 1** A **guillotine** is **1.1** a device used to execute people, especially in France in the past. A sharp blade was raised up on a frame and dropped onto the person's neck. EG *Not many French people are in favour of using the guillotine.* **1.2** a device used for cutting and trimming paper. — N COUNT; N COUNT

2 To **guillotine** someone means to kill them using a guillotine. EG *Forty people were guillotined that day.* — V+O ⇑ execute

guilt /gɪlt/ is **1** an unhappy feeling that you have because you think that you have done something wrong, or that you have failed to do something which you should have done. EG *I had agonizing feelings of shame and guilt... Many people still feel a sense of guilt... The children do not feel guilt about sacrifices their mothers or fathers make.* **2** the fact that you have done something wrong or have failed to do something you should have done, or have broken a law. EG *He at last made a public admission of his guilt.* **3** responsibility for doing something wrong or failing to do something which you should have done, or for having broken a law. EG *The guilt was attributed to the dead attaché... He gave no acknowledgement of his portion of guilt for the squandering of lives.* — N UNCOUNT = remorse; N UNCOUNT ⇑ responsibility = culpability; N UNCOUNT = blame

guilt complex, guilt complexes. A **guilt complex** is a feeling of guilt that someone has which they cannot get rid of, and which may eventually lead to mental illness. — N COUNT ⇑ preoccupation

guiltless /gɪltlɪ²s/. If someone is **guiltless**, they have not done anything wrong or have not done a particular wrong thing. EG *Nor were governments guiltless in this matter.* — ADJ CLASSIF

guilty /gɪlti¹/, **guiltier, guiltiest. 1** If you feel **guilty**, you feel unhappy because you think that you have done something wrong or have failed to do something which you should have done. EG *They feel guilty about seeing her so little.* ▸ used of behaviour and expressions. EG *...a guilty grin.* ◇ **guiltily.** EG *Madeleine moved and Ida jumped, guiltily. 'Oh, I'm sorry if I woke you. I tried to be quiet.'* — ADJ QUALIT : IF+PREP THEN *about*, OR+REPORT-CL ⇑ worried; ◇ ADV AFTER VB = sheepishly

2 Guilty is used of an action or fact that you feel guilty about. EG *...a guilty secret... ...guilty pleasures.* — ADJ CLASSIF : ATTRIB

3 If you have a **guilty conscience**, you feel guilty about something that you have done or not done. EG *Some children get a guilty conscience about not learning enough lessons.* — PHR : USED AS O

4 If someone is **guilty, 4.1** they are officially stated to have committed a crime or offence. EG *Mr. Woods pleaded guilty to causing criminal damage at his parents' home... He was found guilty of passing on secret papers to a foreign power... The guilty party should clearly have to pay all the costs.* **4.2** they have done something wrong or failed to do something which they should have done. EG *He was guilty of an important misjudgment... Their parents are guilty of gross neglect, abuse, and cruelty.* — ADJ CLASSIF : IF+PREP THEN *of/to*; ADJ CLASSIF : IF+PREP THEN *of/to* ≠ blameless, innocent

guinea /gɪni¹/, **guineas.** A **guinea** is an old British unit of money that was worth 21 shillings. Guineas — N COUNT : USU a/NUM+N are still sometimes used, for example in auctions. EG *She graciously handed me a cheque for two guineas.*

guinea fowl; also spelled with a hyphen. **Guinea fowl** is both the singular and the plural form. A **guinea fowl** is a large grey African bird. N COUNT

guinea pig, guinea pigs; also spelled with a hyphen. A **guinea pig** is 1 a small, furry animal without a tail. Guinea pigs are often kept as pets. 2 an animal or person that is used in an experiment or test. EG *I'm using the second year as guinea pigs for my new Japanese poetry course.* N COUNT; N COUNT : USU USED AS C OR AN A ⇑ subject

guise /gaɪz/, **guises**. A **guise** is an outward appearance or form which makes something seem new, different, or attractive, especially an appearance which is intended to deceive people. EG *They will form new political groupings, or old ones in new guises... This ploy can take all sorts of seemingly innocent guises... Propaganda is served out to us in the guise of information... A lot of nonsense was talked, under the guise of philosophy.* N COUNT+SUPP

guitar /gɪtɑː/, **guitars**. A **guitar** is a musical instrument that is made of wood and has six strings. You play the guitar by plucking or strumming the strings. EG *Do you play the guitar?... ...guitar music.* N COUNT

guitarist /gɪtɑːr⁰ɪst/, **guitarists**. A **guitarist** is someone who plays the guitar. N COUNT ⇑ musician

gulch /gʌltʃ/, **gulches**. A **gulch** is a long narrow valley with steep sides which has been made by a stream flowing through it; used in American English. EG *...the Grand Gulch.* N COUNT : ALSO IN NAMES = ravine

gulf /gʌlf/, **gulfs**. 1 A **gulf** is 1.1 an important or significant difference between two people, things, or groups. EG *...the widening gulf between the leaders of the party and the ordinary members... The gulf between the cultures was too great to be easily bridged... There was a gulf of ten years between him and his youngest sister.* 1.2 a large area of sea which extends a long way into the surrounding land. EG *...the Gulf of Mexico.* N COUNT : IF+ PREP THEN *between/in* = gap; N COUNT : ALSO IN NAMES ⇑ bay

2 The **Gulf** is used to refer to the Persian Gulf and the countries around it. EG *...the oil of Saudi Arabia and the Gulf... ...the Gulf states.* N PROPER : *the*+ N ⇑ region

Gulf Stream. The **Gulf Stream** is a warm ocean current which flows from the Gulf of Mexico, along the south-east coast of the United States, and north-eastwards in the Atlantic Ocean. N PROPER : *the*+ N

gull /gʌl/, **gulls**. A **gull** is a fairly large bird which has white and grey or black feathers and which lives near the sea. There are several kinds of gull. N COUNT = seagull

gullet /gʌlɪ²t/, **gullets**. A person's or animal's **gullet** is the tube which goes from their mouth to their stomach. N COUNT = oesophagus

gulley /gʌli¹/. See **gully**.

gullible /gʌləbə⁰l/. Someone who is **gullible** is easily tricked because they are too trusting. EG *At that early age she had been gullible and in love.* ◇ **gullibility** /gʌləbɪlɪti¹/. EG *The report throws an interesting light on the gullibility of some Western politicians.* ADJ QUALIT = naive ≠ wary; ◇ N UNCOUNT = credulity

gully /gʌli¹/, **gullies**; also spelled **gulley, gulleys**. A **gully** is a long narrow valley with steep sides. EG *...hilly ridges and deep-sided gullies.* N COUNT = ravine

gulp /gʌlp/, **gulps, gulping, gulped**. 1 If you **gulp** something, you eat or drink it very fast by swallowing large quantities of it at once. EG *The thirsty Frenchman gulps a hasty milkshake... At parties they wolfed your canapés and gulped your gin as if they hadn't eaten for a week.* V+O ⇑ consume = guzzle

2 A **gulp** is the act of swallowing a large quantity of food or drink at once. EG *She took a satisfying gulp of whisky... He drank half the contents of his glass in one gulp.* N COUNT : ALSO N +*of*+N UNCOUNT ⇑ swallow = swig

3 If you **gulp**, you swallow air, often making a noise in your throat as you do so, because you are nervous or excited. EG *It made you gulp once or twice and titter nervously... 'How's it been going?' I gulped.* ▸ used as a noun. EG *'Me?' I said with a gulp.* V OR V+QUOTE ⇑ swallow = gasp; ▸ N COUNT

4 If you **gulp** air, you breathe in a large amount of air quickly through your mouth, for example when you are swimming. EG *It rises every now and then to gulp air from the surface.* ▸ used as a noun. EG *He stopped at last and thankfully breathed in gulps of cold Montana air.* V+O; ▸ N COUNT : ALSO N+*of*+N UNCOUNT

gulp down. If you **gulp** something **down**, you quickly eat or drink it all by swallowing large quantities of it at a time. EG *After gulping down his breakfast in the morning, he hurried to the station... The old man gulped down his coffee.* PHRASAL VB : V+ O+ADV = wolf down

gum /gʌm/, **gums, gumming, gummed**. 1 **Gum** is 1.1 a fairly soft substance, often flavoured, which people chew. EG *He chews gum, and wears a basket-ball hat... The woman took a piece of gum out of her mouth.* 1.2 a substance used to stick a piece of paper or something very light in weight to something else. EG *The trouble was I hadn't got the right gum, so I couldn't stick it down properly.* 1.3 a sticky substance which comes from the eucalyptus tree or from various other trees and shrubs. N UNCOUNT; N UNCOUNT ⇑ adhesive; N UNCOUNT ⇑ resin

2 If you **gum** something to something else, you stick it to something else. EG *I noticed for the first time the false eyelashes gummed together by generous lumps of mascara.* V+O+A

3 A **gum** is a sweet which feels like firm rubber and which usually tastes of fruit. EG *...a fat spotty girl who giggled and sucked a gum while she listened.* N COUNT = gumdrop

4 Your **gums** are the layers of firm, pink flesh inside your mouth, above your top teeth and below your bottom teeth, which cover the bone that your teeth are fixed into. EG *She smiled widely, showing her toothless gums.* N COUNT : USU PL

5 **By gum** is an exclamation used in rather old-fashioned British English to emphasize what you are saying and make your listener realize that you really mean it. EG *And by gum, Judy, I'll see to it that there is some action.* EXCLAM, OR PHR : USED AS ADV SEN = by golly

gum up. 1 If you **gum** something **up**, you prevent it from opening, moving, or operating by covering it in a sticky substance which dries hard. EG *When he woke in the morning his eyes were all gummed up.* PHRASAL VB : V+ O+ADV, USU PASS ⇑ immobilize = clog up

2 To **gum up the works** means to make it impossible for any progress to be made or anything useful to be done; an informal expression. EG *All you do when you go along is mill about and gum up the works.* PHR : VB INFLECTS

gumboot /gʌmbəʊt/, **gumboots**; also spelled with a hyphen. **Gumboots** are long rubber boots which you wear to keep your feet dry. N COUNT : USU PL

gumdrop /gʌmdrɒp/, **gumdrops**. A **gumdrop** is a sweet which feels like firm rubber and tastes of fruit. N COUNT = gum

gummy /gʌmi¹/, **gummier, gummiest**. 1 Something that is **gummy** is sticky. EG *...a special gummy substance.* ADJ QUALIT ⇑ adhesive

2 A **gummy** smile or grin shows the gums of your mouth. EG *She liked to think he had a special gummy grin for her.* ADJ QUALIT

gumption /gʌmp⁰ʃə⁰n/ is the quality of being able to think what it would be sensible to do in a particular situation, and to do it; an informal word. EG *I'd never have had the gumption to do what he had done.* N UNCOUNT ⇑ intelligence = nous, wit

gum tree, gum trees. 1 A **gum tree** is a eucalyptus tree. N COUNT

2 If you say that someone is **up a gum tree**, you mean that they are in a difficult situation which is difficult to get out of; used in informal British English. PHR : USED AS AN A ⇑ stuck = stymied

gun /gʌn/, **guns, gunning, gunned**. 1 A **gun** is 1.1 a weapon which consists of a long metal tube and a compartment in which bullets are placed. The bullets are forced out of the gun by means of a small explosion and fly very quickly through the air. EG *He was carrying a gun... They have guns and will not hesitate to use them.* 1.2 a small device which looks like a gun and which is used to make a sudden loud noise as a signal to start a race. EG *The gun sounded and the race began.* 1.3 a device which you fill with a substance such as paint or grease and which forces the substance out very quickly under pressure. EG *...a glue gun.* N COUNT; N COUNT : USU *the*+N = starting pistol; N COUNT+SUPP

2 If you **gun** an engine or a vehicle, you make it start or go faster by pressing on the accelerator pedal; used in American English. EG *Two white-helmeted officers gunned their engines into life... He gunned the plane down the runway.* V+O : USU+A

3 If you **jump the gun**, you do something before everyone else or before the proper or right time; an informal expression. EG *Newspapers both at home and abroad began to jump the gun and talk about impeachment.* PHR : VB INFLECTS ⇑ be premature

4 If you **stick to** your **guns**, you continue to have your own attitude or opinion about something even though other people are trying to influence you or tell you that you are wrong; an informal expression. PHR : VB INFLECTS ⇑ persevere = stand fast

EG *People who really lean towards strictness should stick to their guns and raise their children that way.*
5 • to **spike** someone's **guns**: see **spike**. • See also **airgun, machine-gun, shotgun, sub-machine gun**.

gun down. If you **gun** someone **down**, you shoot them and injure them severely or kill them. PHRASAL VB : V+O+ADV

gun for. If someone **is gunning for** you, they are trying to find a way to harm you or cause you trouble; an informal expression. EG *I do not wish to have half an army gunning for me.* PHRASAL VB : V+PREP, HAS PASS = after

gunboat /gʌnbəʊt/, **gunboats**. A **gunboat** is a small ship which has several large guns fixed on it. N COUNT ⇑ boat

gundog /gʌndɒg/, **gundogs**. A **gundog** is a dog that has been trained to work with a hunter or game-keeper, especially to find and carry back birds or animals that have been shot. N COUNT ⇑ dog

gunfire /gʌnfaɪə/ is the repeated shooting of guns, especially in a battle. EG *He was praised for his gallantry under gunfire.* N UNCOUNT = fire

gunge /gʌndᵒʒ/ is a soft or sticky mass of something; used in informal British English. EG *It's solidifying into a sort of brown gunge.* N UNCOUNT ⇑ substance = goo

gunman /gʌnməˀn/, **gunmen**. A **gunman** is someone who uses a gun to commit a crime such as murder or robbery. EG *He was shot in the head by a gunman from a passing car.* N COUNT ⇑ criminal

gunmetal /gʌnmɛtəᵒl/ is a dark grey metal which is made of copper mixed with tin and zinc. EG *...one grey gunmetal desk lamp.* N UNCOUNT ⇑ alloy

gunner /gʌnə/, **gunners**. A **gunner** is someone who is trained to maintain and use guns, especially large guns, in an army, navy, or air force. N COUNT ⇑ fighter

gunnery /gʌnəri¹/ is the technique of firing large guns. EG *...a gunnery officer.* N UNCOUNT

gunpoint /gʌnpɔɪnt/. If someone does something to you **at gunpoint**, they are threatening to shoot and kill you if you do not obey them. EG *He held the three men at gunpoint.* PHR : USED AS AN A

gunpowder /gʌnpaʊdə/ is an explosive substance which is used especially to make fireworks. Gunpowder is made from a mixture of potassium nitrate and other substances. N UNCOUNT

gun-runner, gun-runners. A **gun-runner** is someone who takes or sends guns into a country secretly and illegally, especially so that the guns can be used by people who are opposed to their government. N COUNT ⇑ smuggler

gun-running is the activity of taking or sending guns into a country secretly and illegally. N UNCOUNT ⇑ smuggling

gunshot /gʌnʃɒt/, **gunshots**. **1 Gunshot** is used to refer to bullets that are fired from a gun. EG *The house was peppered with gunshot... He died of gunshot wounds.* N UNCOUNT
2 A **gunshot** is the firing of a gun or the sound of a gun being fired. EG *They heard the sounds of gunshots.* N COUNT
3 If you are **out of gunshot**, you are beyond the maximum distance at which a bullet fired from a gun can hit you. If you are **within gunshot**, you are within the maximum distance at which a bullet fired from a gun can hit you. EG *We ran hard until we were out of gunshot.* PHR : USED AS AN A

gunsmith /gʌnsmɪθ/, **gunsmiths**. A **gunsmith** is someone who makes and repairs guns. N COUNT ⇑ person

guppy /gʌpi¹/, **guppies**. A **guppy** is a small, brightly-coloured tropical fish. People sometimes keep guppies in aquariums. N COUNT

gurgle /gɜːgəᵒl/, **gurgles, gurgling, gurgled**. **1** When water **gurgles**, it makes a rippling, bubbling, sound, especially because it is not flowing smoothly EG *We stared into the gloomy crack where water gurgled between the rocks... The waves swept back with a gurgling, sucking sound.* ▸ used as a noun. EG *Now and then we heard a gurgle of water.* V ▸ N COUNT
2 When someone **gurgles**, they make a bubbling sound in their throat when they are breathing or talking, especially because there is liquid in their throat. EG *Kicking and gurgling, his little brother looked up at him.* ▸ used as a noun. EG *...gurgles of pleasure.* V OR V+QUOTE ▸ N COUNT

guru /gu¹ruː/, **gurus**. A **guru** is **1** a religious and spiritual leader and teacher, especially in Hinduism. N COUNT
2 an adviser or intellectual leader of a person or group of people. EG *She has become the guru of many a modern mother-to-be.* N COUNT = mentor

gush /gʌʃ/, **gushes, gushing, gushed**. **1** When liquid or gas **gushes** out of something, it flows out very quickly and in large quantities. EG *Blood gushed from the wounds... Tears were gushing from her closed eyes and down her cheeks.* V+A ⇑ run
2 If someone **gushes**, they express their admiration, praise, or pleasure in such an exaggerated way that other people think they are not sincere. EG *'Amanda!' he gushed. 'How good to see you again.'* ◇ **gushing**. EG *...a large gushing female.* V OR V+QUOTE ⇑ overstate ◇ ADJ QUALIT = effusive
3 A **gush** of liquid or gas is a sudden, rapid flow of it, or a quantity of it that suddenly flows out. EG *...a little gush of blood.* N SING WITH DET : IF+PREP THEN *of*
4 A **gush** of pleasure, enthusiasm, confession, etc is a sudden outburst of speech or emotion. EG *Elise failed to restrain Mrs Trotter's gush of pleasure.* N SING WITH DET : IF+PREP THEN *of*

gusset /gʌsɪt/, **gussets**. A **gusset** is a small strip or triangle of cloth sewn into a garment to make it wider, stronger, or more comfortable. EG *...nylon briefs with a cotton gusset.* N COUNT ⇑ insert

gust /gʌst/, **gusts, gusting, gusted**. **1** A **gust** is a short, strong, sudden rush of wind. EG *...a sudden gust of wind... A gust of icy air struck me... The wind blew in sharp gusts outside.* N COUNT : IF+PREP THEN *of* = blast
2 When the wind **gusts** or when snow or rain **gusts**, it blows with short, strong, sudden rushes of wind. EG *The wind gusted and fell away... Snow gusted past the street lamps.* V : USU+A ⇑ blow = flurry
3 If you feel a **gust** of anger, happiness, longing, etc, you feel the emotion mentioned suddenly and intensely. EG *...a sudden gust of anger... A gust of pure happiness swept through her.* N SING WITH DET +*of* = burst

gusto /gʌstəʊ/ is energetic and enthusiastic enjoyment. EG *We ate with gusto... With all the gusto of the novice, I accepted the responsibility.* N UNCOUNT : USU *with*+N ⇑ enthusiasm = zest

gusty /gʌsti¹/ is is used to describe weather in which there are very strong, irregular winds. EG *...gusty winds... ...a cold gusty day.* ADJ QUALIT = blustery

gut /gʌt/, **guts, gutting, gutted**. **1** A person or animal's **guts** are all the organs inside them. EG *The entire carcass, hide, guts and bones, will quickly be devoured.* N PLURAL = insides
2 When someone **guts** a dead animal or fish, they remove all the organs from inside it, especially before they cook and eat it. EG *...the gutted carcass of a pig.* V+O ⇑ clean
3 The **gut** is the tube inside the abdomen of a person or animal through which food passes while it is being digested. EG *Root vegetables are absorbed more slowly in the gut.* N SING WITH DET = intestine
4 Someone's **gut** is their stomach, especially when it is very large and sticks out; used in informal English showing disapproval. EG *His beer gut was popping the buttons on his shirt.* N SING WITH DET = belly
5 Guts is the will and courage to do something difficult or unpleasant or which might have unpleasant results; an informal use. EG *It takes a lot more guts for a woman to resign than for a man... Sam hasn't got the guts to leave his dad.* N UNCOUNT = nerve
6 Gut is also used to refer to the area inside you where your strongest and deepest feelings are imagined to Exist. EG *He knew, deep down, in the gut, what it was like to be inferior... As Party Treasurer, he echoed the gut feeling of the trade unions.* N SING WITH DET = subconscious
7 If you call someone a **guts** or a greedy **guts**, you mean that they are very greedy and eat a lot of food; an informal use. EG *Come on, greedy guts, you'll be late for school.* N SING/VOC ⇑ person = glutton
8 The **guts** of a machine, building, etc are the inside parts of it; an informal use. EG *...the guts of the department store... ...the vital working parts of a mechanism (the guts of a toaster, for instance).* N PLURAL : USU+*of* = insides
9 To **gut** a building means to destroy the inside of it so that only its outside walls remain. EG *Much of Downing Street has recently been gutted, and entirely rebuilt... The whole house was gutted by fire.* V+O : USU PASS
10 Gut is string made from part of the stomach of an animal. It is used especially to make the strings of tennis rackets or the strings of some musical instruments such as violins. EG *We could just hear the twang of tennis balls bouncing off tightly-strung gut.* N UNCOUNT
11 The word **gut** is also used in the following informal expressions. **11.1** If you **hate** someone's **guts**, you dislike them very intensely. EG *OK, so you hate my guts.* PHR : VB INFLECTS **11.2** If you say that you are going to **have** someone's **guts for garters**, you mean that you are going to punish them or do something unpleasant to them, especially because you are annoyed or angry with them. PHR : VB INFLECTS **11.3** If you **work, run, or scream** PHR : VB

your **guts out**, you work, run, or scream as hard and as much as you possibly can, to the point of being exhausted. EG *He made us flog our guts out to finish on time... A man could scream his guts out in here and never be heard.* INFLECTS ↑ hard

gutless /gʌtlɪ²s/. Someone who is **gutless** has a weak character and lacks courage or determination. EG *...that yellow, gutless worm, Claude.* ADJ QUALIT = spineless

gutsy /gʌtsi¹/; an informal word. Something that is **gutsy 1** expresses a meaning or idea very powerfully and vividly. EG *The play used red-hot, gutsy, four-letter words.* ADJ QUALIT = meaty **2** shows or requires courage or determination. EG *That's so gutsy, you've really got to admire her for doing it.* ADJ QUALIT ↑ courageous = plucky

gutter /gʌtə/, **gutters, guttering, guttered. 1** A **gutter** is **1.1** the edge of a road next to the pavement, where rain water collects and flows away. EG *The motorbike lay on its side in the gutter... ...its lamp-posts, its grim walls, its dirty gutters.* N COUNT ↑ channel **1.2** a plastic or metal channel fixed to the lower edge of the roof of a building, which rain water drains into. EG *...just above the gutter where the tiles were loose.* N COUNT

2 The **gutter** is used to refer to the dirty environment and bad social conditions which poor people live in, especially in cities; used showing disapproval. EG *The fact that they are following in her footsteps and have gone to the gutter should not surprise me... ...a pale little gutter girl.* N SING : *the*+N

3 If a candle **gutters**, it burns unsteadily, often with a weak flame. EG *He walked down the path in the dark, with the candle guttering in the candlestick.* V ↑ burn = sputter

guttering /gʌtə⁰rɪŋ/ consists of the plastic or metal channels fixed to the lower edge of the roof of a building, which rain water drains into. EG *He looked across at the Kirks' unstable guttering.* N UNCOUNT

gutter press. The **gutter press** is used to refer to newspapers and magazines which contain more stories about people's private affairs, and scandals involving sex or violence, than about international, political, or economic affairs; used in informal English showing disapproval. EG *That sort of sensational reporting is typical of the gutter press.* N SING : *the*+N

guttural /gʌtə⁰rəl/ is used to describe sounds which are produced at the back of a person's throat, and are often considered to be rather unpleasant. EG *...a guttural German accent... ...a strange, loud, guttural cry.* ADJ QUALIT ↑ deep = harsh

guv /gʌv/ is sometimes used in very informal British English to address a man, especially a customer or someone you are doing a service for. EG *'For you, Guv,' he yelled, waving a purple envelope.* VOC

guvnor /gʌvnə/, **guvnors. Guvnor** is sometimes used in very informal British English to refer to or address a man who is in a position of authority over you, for example your employer or father. EG *I had to sit in front of my guvnor and he made me fill a form in... Where to, guvnor?* N COUNT : USU SING, ALSO VOC = chief

guy /gaɪ/, **guys. 1** A **guy** is a man or boy; an informal use. EG *...the guy who drove the school bus... He's a nice guy. You'll really like him... We're looking for this guy Evans.* • See also **wise guy**. N COUNT = bloke

2 In informal American English, you can address a group of people as **guys** or **you guys**, whether they are male or female. EG *Hey, you guys! Come back here.* N PLURAL/VOC = you folks

3 A **guy** or **guy rope** is a rope or wire which has one end fastened to a tent or pole and the other fixed to the ground, so that it keeps the tent or pole in position. N COUNT

guzzle /gʌzə⁰l/, **guzzles, guzzling, guzzled**; a fairly informal word. If you **guzzle** something, you drink or eat it quickly and greedily. EG *The Cherry Wine was being guzzled like lemonade.* V OR V+O ↑ consume = knock back

gym /dʒɪm/, **gyms. 1** A **gym** is a gymnasium. EG *He was always at the gym.* N COUNT

2 Gym means gymnastics. EG *We did an hour of gym... She wore a T-shirt and white gym shorts.* N UNCOUNT

gymkhana /dʒɪmkɑːnə/, **gymkhanas**. A **gymkhana** is an event in which people riding horses compete with one another in various competitions and races, for example jumping over special fences. N COUNT

gymnasium /dʒɪmneɪzɪəm/, **gymnasiums**. A **gymnasium** is a building or large room which is used for physical exercise and usually has equipment such as bars, mats, and ropes in it. N COUNT = sports hall

gymnast /dʒɪmnæst/, **gymnasts**. A **gymnast** is someone who is trained in gymnastics, and who usually competes in gymnastic competitions. N COUNT ↑ athlete

gymnastic /dʒɪmnæstɪk/, **gymnastics**. **1 Gymnastics** are physical exercises, often using equipment such as bars, mats, and ropes, that develop your strength, co-ordination, and agility. EG *...a doctor's certificate excusing him from gymnastics at school.* N PLURAL

2 Gymnastic is used to describe things relating to gymnastics. EG *He showed a gymnastic ability one might not have suspected.* ADJ CLASSIF : ATTRIB

gymslip /dɪmslɪp/, **gymslips**. A **gymslip** is a sleeveless dress that schoolgirls used to wear over a blouse or jumper as part of their school uniform; used in British English. N COUNT ↑ garment

gynaecology /gaɪnəkɒlədʒi¹/; also spelled **gynecology. Gynaecology** is the branch of medical science which deals with diseases and medical conditions that only women have; a technical term. EG *I had decided that my future lay in obstetrics and gynaecology.* N UNCOUNT ◇ **gynaecologist, gynaecologists**. EG *...an eminent gynaecologist.* ◇ N COUNT ◇ **gynaecological**. EG *...gynaecological cancer.* ◇ ADJ CLASSIF : ATTRIB

gypsum /dʒɪpsəm/ is a soft white substance which looks like chalk and which is used to make plaster of Paris. N UNCOUNT ↑ mineral

gypsy /dʒɪpsi¹/, **gypsies**; also spelled **gipsy**. A **gypsy** is a member of a race of people who travel from place to place in caravans and earn money in various ways, for example by horse dealing or selling flowers. N COUNT ↑ itinerant = traveller

gyrate /dʒaɪreɪt/, **gyrates, gyrating, gyrated**. To **gyrate** means to turn round and round in a circle, usually very fast. EG *...a small gyrating plastic advertisement for a brand of lager.* V = rotate ◇ **gyration** /dʒaɪreɪʃə⁰n/, **gyrations**. EG *Their bodily gyrations and contortions fascinated him.* ◇ N COUNT/UNCOUNT : USU PL

gyroscope /dʒaɪrə⁶skəup/, **gyroscopes**. A **gyroscope** is a device that contains a disc rotating on an axis that can turn freely in any direction, so that the disc maintains the same position whatever the position or movement of the surrounding structure. N COUNT

Hh

H, h /eɪtʃ/, **Hs, h's** /eɪtʃɪz/. **1 H** is the eighth letter of the English alphabet. N COUNT

2 If you **drop** your **h's**, you pronounce incorrectly words that begin with the letter h, by not pronouncing the h, for example by saying "ere' instead of 'here'. PHR : VB INFLECTS ↑ mispronounce

3 H or **h** is also an abbreviation for various words beginning with 'h', such as 'hour', 'height', 'hospital', and 'hard'.

ha /h⁰ɑː/; also spelled **hah. 1 Ha** and **hah** are written forms representing a sound that people make when they suddenly feel surprised, upset, or annoyed. EG *'Ha!' she said, 'Isn't that wonderful?'* EXCLAM = huh

2 You say **hah** or **ha** when you want to surprise someone or show that you suddenly feel pleased or annoyed; an informal use. EG *'Hah! Scared you, didn't I?'... He laughed bitterly. 'Hah, you don't know what you are saying.'* CONVENTION/EXCLAM = there

3 See also **ha ha**.

ha. is an abbreviation for 'hectare'. N COUNT

habeas corpus /heɪbɪəs kɔːpəs/ is a law that exists in many countries. It states that a person cannot be kept in prison unless he or she has been brought N UNCOUNT ↑ writ before a judge or a magistrate, who must decide whether it is lawful for that person to be kept in prison. EG *It is of little consolation to a poor peasant that habeas corpus exists, if he cannot get a lawyer... Two days later he was released at the habeas corpus hearing.*

haberdasher /hæbədæʃə/, **haberdashers**. A **haberdasher** is 1 in British English, a shop or shopkeeper selling small articles for sewing and dressmaking, for example buttons and zips. 2 in American English, a shop or shopkeeper selling men's clothing. — N COUNT; N COUNT ⇑ tailor

haberdashery /hæbədæʃəʳri¹/ is 1 in British English, small articles used in sewing and dressmaking, sold in a shop. 2 in American English, men's clothing sold in a shop. — N UNCOUNT; N UNCOUNT

habit /hæbɪt/, **habits**. A **habit** is 1.1 something that you do often or regularly. EG *I got into the habit of studying at the Radcliffe Library... Her father had a habit of clearing his throat and looking skyward... The book-purchasing habit could well spread to a far wider population... More out of habit than anything else, I stopped and went in.* 1.2 an action or activity that someone has done many times before and finds it difficult to stop doing, especially when this action or activity is considered to be bad. EG *He has had a lifelong nervous habit of biting his nails... He must not be allowed to form bad habits... It's a hard habit to break.* 1.3 an addiction to a drug such as heroin or cocaine. EG *Groups exist to help those who want to kick the marijuana habit... ...women with heavy heroin habits.* — N COUNT : IF + PREP THEN *of*, OR N UNCOUNT; N COUNT : IF + PREP THEN *of* ⇑ practice; N COUNT + SUPP

2 If you are **in the habit of** doing something, you do it regularly or often. EG *Once a month Castle was in the habit of taking Sarah and Sam for an excursion... I wouldn't like you to think that I am in the habit of making a nuisance of myself.* — PHR + -ING : USED AS AN A

3 If you **make a habit of** doing something or **make** something **a habit,** you decide to do it regularly or often. EG *They made a habit of lunching together twice a week... Having done it once, she made a habit of it.* — PHR + -ING : VB INFLECTS, OR PHR : VB INFLECTS

4 If you say that someone is **a creature of habit,** you mean that they usually do the same thing at the same time each day, rather than doing new and different things. EG *He had not allowed himself to become a creature of habit.* ● **from force of habit:** see **force**. — PHR : USED AS C

5 A **habit of mind** is the kind of thought, feeling, or attitude that someone generally has. EG *Resistance is a natural habit of mind in people who have been oppressed.* — N COUNT : USU USED AS C

6 A **habit** is also a piece of clothing shaped like a long loose dress, which a nun or monk wears. EG *A novice would don the religious habit for a period of three years.* — N COUNT ⇑ garment

habitable /hæbɪtəbəˡl/. **Habitable** means good enough for people to live in. EG *A few flats were made habitable.* ◊ **habitability** /hæbɪtəbɪlɪti¹/. EG *...the habitability of coastal areas and cities.* — ADJ CLASSIF : USU PRED; ◊ N UNCOUNT

habitat /hæbɪtæt/, **habitats**. The **habitat** of an animal or plant is the natural environment in which it normally lives or grows. EG *It was probably brought here from its native Mediterranean habitat by the Romans... ...the open woodland that is their natural habitat.* — N COUNT + SUPP ⇑ surroundings = home

habitation /hæbɪteɪʃəⁿn/, **habitations**. 1 **Habitation** is the human activity of living somewhere. EG *...to see whether the houses are fit for human habitation.* 2 A **habitation** is a place where people live; a fairly formal use. EG *...squalid human habitations... The rocks looked like weird habitations.* — N UNCOUNT = occupation; N COUNT ⇑ dwelling

habitual /həˡbɪtjuᵒəl/. A **habitual** action is one that someone usually or often does, especially when it is considered to be typical or characteristic of them. EG *She rocked rhythmically to and fro in a way that had become habitual in the last few days... 'Sorry I'm late,' David said with his habitual guilty grin.* ▸ used of someone who usually or often does a particular thing. EG *There seem to be two distinct types of habitual criminals. ...a habitual wearer of glasses.* ◊ **habitually**. EG *Anybody who habitually keeps his office door shut is suspect... She wore a habitually severe expression.* — ADJ CLASSIF = standard, customary; ▸ ADJ CLASSIF : ATTRIB = regular; ◊ ADV = persistently

habituate /həˡbɪtjueɪt/, **habituates, habituating, habituated**. If you **are habituated** to something, you get used to it; a formal word. EG *The people of these countries have been habituated to authoritarian traditions.* — V+O : USU PASS + *to* = accustomed

habitué /hæbɪtueɪ/, **habitués**. A **habitué** is someone who often visits a particular place or attends a particular kind of event; a formal word. EG *...nightclub habitués.* — N COUNT : USU + SUPP = regular

hack /hæk/, **hacks, hacking, hacked**. 1 If someone **hacks** something, they cut it using a sharp tool, such as an axe or knife, with strong, rough strokes. EG *They were ambushed in their caravan and stabbed and hacked to death... ...men so evil that they could hack off the heads and hands of their victims.* — V+O = hew

2 If you **hack** something such as a clearing or path from a forest, you create it by cutting down trees and bushes. EG *A few months later they were hacking farms from the forests.* — V+O = carve out

3 A **hack** is a professional writer, journalist, or other creative worker who produces work fast and on a regular basis, without worrying very much about quality; an informal use. EG *It makes no difference whether it's a hack or a great artist... ...a hack writer, scribbling madly to keep to the deadline.* — N COUNT

4 If you refer to something as **hack** work, you mean that it is boring and routine; an informal use. EG *...with a secretary to do all the hack work.* — ADJ CLASSIF : ATTRIB = donkey

5 A **hack** is also 5.1 a horse kept at a riding stable and hired out for people to ride. EG *I knew nothing really about horses, except riding a few hacks.* 5.2 a ride on a hired horse. EG *We went for a hack in the afternoon.* 5.3 a rough or difficult journey. EG *It is a long 120-mile hack over very mixed road surfaces.* — N COUNT; N COUNT : USU SING; N COUNT : USU SING

6 If you **hack** or **go hacking**, you go for a ride on horseback, usually in the country. EG *They had become tired of hacking cross-country on horseback.* — V : USU CONT = riding

hack about. If someone **hacks** the wording of a text **about**, they change it and cut parts out, without caring much about what was originally written. EG *My book's been hacked about terribly by the editor.* — PHRASAL VB : V + O + ADV ⇑ amend

hack at. If you **hack at** something, you try to cut it using strong, rough strokes of an axe or knife. EG *They hacked at the jungle undergrowth with machetes... ...hacking away at the branches.* — PHRASAL VB : V + PREP, HAS PASS = chop at

hack through. 1 If you **hack through** something such as jungle, you move through it by cutting down branches, bushes, and other things that are in your way. — PHRASAL VB : V + PREP, HAS PASS

2 If you **hack through** a piece of work, you work at it quickly, doing each part in order but without caring much how well it is done. EG *I'll just hack my way through the list.* — PHRASAL VB : V + PREP/ADV

hacking /hækɪŋ/. A **hacking** cough is a dry, painful cough with a harsh, unpleasant sound. EG *His hacking cough could be heard next door.* — ADJ CLASSIF : ATTRIB = rasping

hacking jacket, hacking jackets. A **hacking jacket** is a jacket made of tweed with a slit at the bottom on either side and with slanting pockets. Hacking jackets are often worn by people who go riding on horseback. — N COUNT

hackles /hækəᵒlz/. 1 If your **hackles rise**, you begin to feel angry and hostile because of something that has happened. EG *To this day, my hackles rise when I hear actors talking about 'getting laughs'.* — PHR : VB INFLECTS

2 The **hackles** of a dog, cat, etc are the hairs on the back of its neck, which rise when the animal is angry. — N PLURAL

3 The **hackles** of a cock, turkey, pheasant, or other male bird are long feathers on the back of its neck that stand up when it is angry or ready to fight. — N PLURAL

hackneyed /hæknɪd/. A phrase or expression that is **hackneyed** is boring because it has been used many times before. EG *'Of course I love you. With all my heart.' The hackneyed phrase came unintended to his lips.* — ADJ QUALIT ⇑ repeated = clichéd

hacksaw /hæksɔː/, **hacksaws.** A **hacksaw** is a small saw used for cutting metal. — N COUNT ⇑ tool

had /hæd/ is the past tense and past participle of **have**.

haddock /hædək/, **Haddock** is both the singular and the plural form. A **haddock** is a sea fish that you can eat. Haddock are found in the North Atlantic. ▸ used as a uncount noun. EG *Do you want haddock or plaice, dear?... Would you like smoked haddock this evening?* — N COUNT; ▸ N UNCOUNT

Hades /heɪdiːz/, in Greek mythology, was a place under the earth where people's souls went after they had died. — N PROPER = Underworld

hadji /hædʒi¹/, **hadjis**; also spelled **hajji**. A **hadji** a Muslim who has made a pilgrimage to Mecca; also used as a title.
N COUNT : ALSO IN TITLES ⇑ pilgrim

hadn't /hædəⁿt/ is the usual spoken form of 'had not'.

haemoglobin /hiːmə⁶gləʊbɪn, hɛm-/; also spelled **hemoglobin** in American English. **Haemoglobin** is a substance that carries oxygen in red blood cells; a technical term in biology.
N UNCOUNT ⇑ protein

haemophilia /hiːmə⁶fɪlɪə, hɛm-/; also spelled **hemophilia** in American English. **Haemophilia** is an inherited disease, usually affecting men, in which a person's blood does not clot properly, so that they continue to bleed for a long time if they are injured.
N UNCOUNT ⇑ disability

haemophiliac /hiːmə⁶fɪlɪæk, hɛm-/, **haemophiliacs**; also spelled **hemophiliac** in American English. A **haemophiliac** is a person, usually a man, who suffers from haemophilia.
N COUNT

haemorrhage /hɛmə⁰rɪdʒ/, **haemorrhages, haemorrhaging, haemorrhaged**; also spelled **hemorrhage** in American English. A **haemorrhage** is serious bleeding from broken blood vessels inside a person's body. EG *He had died of a brain haemorrhage.* ▸ used as a verb. EG *Manek began to haemorrhage badly.*
N COUNT/ UNCOUNT
▸ V ⇑ bleed

haemorrhoids /hɛmə⁰rɔɪdz/; also spelled **hemorrhoids** in American English. **Haemorrhoids** are swellings that appear in the veins inside a person's anus and then develop into painful growths; the technical term in medicine.
N PLURAL = piles

hag /hæg/, **hags**. A **hag** is an ugly old woman; often used to refer in an offensive way to a woman you dislike. EG *...some old hag of an actress.*
N COUNT = witch, bag

haggard /hægəd/. Someone who is **haggard** has a tired expression and shadows under their eyes, especially because they are ill or have not had enough sleep. EG *There was a drawn and haggard look about his eyes... As she got older she got haggard.*
ADJ QUALIT = careworn

haggis /hægɪs/, **haggises**. **Haggis** is a Scottish dish made from the heart and other internal organs of a sheep or calf, which are all boiled up together with oatmeal and spices in a bag that is usually made from the lining of the animal's stomach.
N UNCOUNT

haggle /hægeⁿl/, **haggles, haggling, haggled**. If you **haggle**, you argue about something, especially about the cost of something that you are buying. EG *They haggled with shopkeepers in the bazaar... His salary was settled after a lot of haggling on both sides.* ▸ used as a noun. EG *...a haggle in the market-place over the price.*
V OR V+A *(with)* : RECIP = bargain, wrangle
▸ N COUNT ⇑ argument = wrangle

hah /hɑː/. See **ha**.

ha ha /hɑː hɑː/. **1 Ha ha** is used in writing to represent the sound that people make when they laugh.
CONVENTION ho, ho!

2 In spoken English, you sometimes say **ha ha** sarcastically, when you are not amused and are only pretending to laugh. EG *I watched as the man made mistakes. 'Ha ha,' I sneered to myself.*
CONVENTION

hail /heɪl/, **hails, hailing, hailed**. **1 Hail** consists of small balls of ice that fall like rain from the sky. EG *The hail battered on the windows.*
N UNCOUNT, OR N SING : *the*+N

2 When it **hails**, hail falls like rain from the sky. EG *It hailed and poured all afternoon.*
V : *it*+V

3 A **hail** of things, usually small objects, is a large number of them that fall down on you at the same time and with great force. EG *He was dead, killed in a hail of bullets.* ▸ used as a verb. EG *Blows hailed down at him from every side.*
N PART = shower
▸ V+A = rain

4 A **hail** of criticism, insults, etc is a large amount of criticism that comes rapidly from a lot of people. EG *I don't think the statue deserved the hail of abuse that greeted it.*
N PART = torrent

5 If you **hail** someone, you call to them, usually by their name, in order to attract their attention or to greet them. EG *A voice hailed him from the steps... The old man looked up and hailed them over to where he sat.* ▸ used as a word of greeting in formal old-fashioned English. EG *Hail to the chief!* ● If you are **within hailing distance** of someone, you are near enough to them so that they will hear you if you shout to them. EG *Tell me when we get within hailing distance of their boat.*
V+O
▸ CONVENTION
● PHR : USED AS AN A, IF+PREP THEN *of* ⇑ near to

6 If you **hail** a taxi or a cab, you wave at it in order to stop it and ask the driver to take you somewhere.
V+O = signal

7 If you **hail** a person, event, or achievement as important, successful, etc, you praise them publicly and declare that they are important or successful. EG *They were hailed as heroes by the entire Labour movement... The discovery was hailed as the scientific sensation of the century.*
V+O+A *(as)* = acclaim

8 Someone who **hails** from a particular place was born there or lives there; a formal use. EG *I hail from America.*
V+A *(from)* = originate

hailstone /heɪlstəʊn/, **hailstones**. A **hailstone** is one of the small balls of ice that fall from the sky when it hails. EG *Enormous hailstones hit the roof.*
N COUNT ⇑ pellet

hailstorm /heɪlstɔːm/, **hailstorms**; also spelled with a hyphen. A **hailstorm** is a storm during which it hails.
N COUNT ⇑ storm

hair /hɛə/, **hairs**. **1** A **hair** is one of the long, fine, thread-like things that grows in large numbers on the top part of your head and on other parts of your body. Hair also grows on the bodies of some other animals. EG *...black hairs on the back of his hands... Its underside is naked except for a few sparse hairs.* ▸ Your **hair** is the large number of hairs that grow in a mass on your head. EG *...a young woman with long blonde hair... I washed my hands and combed my hair. ...hair lotion.*
N COUNT ⇑ strand
▸ N UNCOUNT ⇑ strands

2 Hair is the hair of certain animals that is often used to stuff mattresses or to cover furniture. EG *...mattresses made of foam rubber or hair.*
N UNCOUNT ⇑ stuffing

3 A **hair** is also a very fine thread-like piece of material that grows on parts of some insects and plants. EG *The adult beetle has silken hairs on its body... Once inside the flower, downward pointing hairs prevent the insect from crawling out.*
N COUNT ⇑ strand

4 The word **hair** is also used in the following informal expressions. **4.1** If you say to someone **'Keep your hair on'** when they have become angry about something, you are telling them to keep calm.
CONVENTION = calm down, simmer down

4.2 If you say that you are **tearing** your **hair out**, you mean that you are very angry or upset about a situation that you cannot control. EG *I could see our manager tearing his hair out at the side of the field.*
PHR : VB INFLECTS = go berserk

4.3 If someone **gets in** your **hair**, they annoy you, especially by being with you all the time and stopping you from doing what you want to do. EG *Her younger sister used to be always in her hair.*
PHR : VB INFLECTS

4.4 Something that **makes** your **hair stand on end** or that **makes** your **hair rise** makes you very frightened or worried. EG *She did it with an ease that made his hair stand on end... She read it, and felt the hair rise on the back of her neck.*
PHR : VB INFLECTS ⇑ frightens

4.5 If you **let** your **hair down**, you relax completely and enjoy yourself without worrying about whether you will upset or offend other people.
PHR : VB INFLECTS = loosen up

4.6 If you say that someone has **not a hair out of place**, you mean that they are extremely smart and neatly dressed.
PHR : USED AS O = immaculate

4.7 If someone tells you not to **touch** or **harm a hair on** a person's **head**, they are emphasizing that you must not harm that person in any way. EG *If you harm a hair on his head, I swear I'll kill you.*
PHR : VB INFLECTS, USU WITH BROAD NEG

4.8 If you **don't turn a hair** in a difficult or dangerous situation, you remain completely calm.
PHR : VB INFLECTS

4.9 If you say that someone is **splitting hairs**, you mean that they are making distinctions when the differences between things are very small and not at all important or useful; used showing disapproval. EG *Politicians are always splitting hairs.* ● See also **hair-splitting**.
PHR : VB INFLECTS

hairbrush /hɛəbrʌʃ/, **hairbrushes**; also spelled with a hyphen. A **hairbrush** is a brush that you use to brush your hair.
N COUNT ⇑ brush

haircut /hɛəkʌt/, **haircuts**. **1** If someone has a **haircut**, someone, usually a barber or a hairdresser, cuts their hair for them. EG *I must have a haircut... He needed a haircut.*
N COUNT

2 A **haircut** is the style in which your hair has been cut. EG *The girls had short, neat haircuts.*
N COUNT

hairdo /hɛəduː/, **hairdos**; also spelled with a hyphen. A **hairdo** is the style in which a person's hair has been cut and arranged, especially a woman's hair; an informal word. EG *I went to a salon and had a new hairdo... ...the sudden rise in popularity of Afro hairdos.*
N COUNT

hairdresser /hɛədrɛsə/, **hairdressers**. A **hairdresser** is a person who cuts, washes, and styles people's hair. EG *...a small hairdresser's shop.* ▸ used to refer to a shop in which hairdressers work. EG *There are two hairdressers in the High Street.*
N COUNT ⇑ barber
▸ ⇑ shop

hairdressing /hɛədrɛsɪŋ/ is the occupation or activity of cutting, washing, and styling people's hair. EG *...a small hairdressing business in Barnet.*
N UNCOUNT ⇑ job

hairdryer /hɛədraɪə/, **hairdryers**; also spelled **hairdrier**; also spelled with a hyphen. A **hairdryer** is a machine that you use to dry your hair after you have washed it, by blowing hot air on it. N COUNT

-haired combines with words such as 'red' or 'short' to indicate that someone has hair of the stated kind. EG *...a white-haired old man... ...the long-haired young woman.* COMB: FORMS ADJS

hair-grip, hair-grips. A **hair-grip** is a small metal or plastic clip that women use to hold their hair in position. N COUNT

hairless /hɛəlɪ²s/. A part of a person's body or an animal that is **hairless** has no hair on it. EG *...his hairless chest.* ADJ CLASSIF ≠ hairy

hairline /hɛəlaɪn/, **hairlines**. 1 Your **hairline** is the area on the front part of your head which is the edge of the area where your hair grows. EG *His hairline was receding.* N COUNT: USU SING ⇑ hair

2 A **hairline** crack, gap, etc is one that is very narrow or fine. EG *Hairline cracks in some of the walls had been detected... ...a tiny hairline fracture... ...a neat hairline moustache.* ADJ CLASSIF: ATTRIB ≠ broad, wide

hairnet /hɛənɛt/, **hairnets**. A **hairnet** is a small net that some women wear over their hair in order to keep it tidy. EG *...hair kept in place with an invisible hairnet.* N COUNT

hairpiece /hɛəpiːs/, **hairpieces**. A **hairpiece** is a piece of false hair that some people wear on their head if they are bald or if they want to make their own hair seem longer or thicker. N COUNT ⇑ wig

hairpin /hɛəpɪn/, **hairpins**. A **hairpin** is 1 a thin piece of metal, bent in a U shape, that women use to hold their hair in a particular position. 2 the same as a hairpin bend. N COUNT ⇑ clip; N COUNT

hairpin bend, hairpin bends. A **hairpin bend** is a very sharp bend in a road, where the road turns back in the opposite direction. EG *I was nearly killed on a hairpin bend near Sparrowpit.* N COUNT

hair-raising. A situation or event that is **hair-raising** is very frightening or disturbing. EG *The ride was bumpy and at times hair-raising... We often delivered babies in hair-raising conditions.* ADJ QUALIT = terrifying

hair's breadth. A **hair's breadth** is a very small degree or amount. EG *The bullet smashed the window and missed me by a hair's breadth... A national strike has been averted by no more than a hair's breadth... ...a brilliant election campaign that earned him a hair's breadth victory.* N SING: a+N

hair slide, hair slides; also spelled with a hyphen. A **hair slide** is a decorative clip that girls and women put in their hair to hold it in position. N COUNT

hair-splitting is the act of making distinctions between things or ideas when the differences between them are very small and not at all important or useful; used showing disapproval. EG *They did not take his theoretical hairsplitting seriously.* ▸ used as an adjective to refer to unimportant differences. EG *...hair-splitting distinctions between different kinds of insects.* N UNCOUNT; ▸ ADJ CLASSIF: ATTRIB = petty

hairstyle /hɛəstaɪl/, **hairstyles**. Your **hairstyle** is the style in which your hair has been cut or arranged. EG *...a new hairstyle.* N COUNT

hairy /hɛəri¹/, **hairier, hairiest**. 1 Someone or something that is **hairy** is covered with hair. EG *...a plump child with hairy legs... ...a big, hairy man... The function of a mammal's hairy coat is to insulate the body.* ADJ QUALIT

2 If you describe a situation as **hairy**, you mean that it is exciting, worrying, and rather frightening; a very informal use. EG *It got a little hairy when we drove him to the station with less than two minutes to spare.* ADJ QUALIT = nerve-racking, scary

hake /heɪk/ is a big fish, similar to cod, that is eaten in Europe and North America. N UNCOUNT

halcyon /hælsɪən/. A **halcyon** time is a peaceful or happy one, especially one that you remember later in your life; a formal word. EG *...the halcyon days of his late teens.* ADJ CLASSIF: ATTRIB

hale /heɪl/. If you describe people, especially people who are old, as **hale**, you mean that they are healthy; a literary word. EG *They had hale old parents who lived on farms in the country.* ADJ QUALIT

half /hɑːf/, **halves**. 1 **Half** means one of two equal or approximately equal parts that together make a whole. It is used in a large number of grammatical structures and can be a noun, adjective, adverb, pronoun, or predeterminer. Uses of all of these are shown here. ▸ used as a noun. EG *...the two halves of the brain... ...the second half of August... ...the latter half of the nineteenth century.* ▸ used as an adjective. EG *...a half chicken... ...a half century of German mechanical finesse... The picture wouldn't end for another half hour.* ▸ used as an adverb. EG *The bottle was now only half full... ...his half empty glass... She had already half filled an ashtray.* ▸ used as a pronoun. EG *Roughly half are French and roughly half are from North America... ...some of the money for you, half for me.* ▸ used as a predeterminer. EG *The house was half a mile away... ...half a million men... I was half an hour late... We had only half the normal crop last year... Half his front teeth are missing.* ▸ When **half** is used following a whole number, it is always used with 'a' or sometimes 'one'. EG *...a mile and a half below the surface of the Pacific Ocean... I went to Poland four and a half years ago.* ⇑ part; ▸ N COUNT: USU +of; ▸ ADJ CLASSIF: ATTRIB; ▸ ADV ⇑ part; ▸ PRON ⇑ some; ▸ PREDET

2 The word **half** is also used in the following expressions. **2.1** If something is **in half**, it has been divided into two equal parts. EG *The ticket collector tore it in half.* **2.2** If you change something **by half**, half of the original amount is added to it or is taken away from it. EG *She reckoned she cut her costs by half... They cut the fares by half... The proportion of landless labourers rose by half between 1951 and 1967.* **2.3** If two people **go halves**, they divide the cost of something equally between them. EG *I'll come if we can go halves... Janet is going halves with Cheryl.* **2.4** If you say that someone **never does things by halves**, you mean that they always do things thoroughly and completely. **2.5** You use an expression such as **half a minute** or **half a second**, in informal English, when you are asking someone to wait a short time. EG *Half a minute, let me write it down... I'll only be half a second.* **2.6** **Half measures** is used in expressions such as 'we don't want any half measures' to indicate that you want something to be done fully and thoroughly. PHR: USED AS AN A; PHR: USED AS AN A = by fifty per cent; PHR OR PHR+A (*with*): RECIP, VB INFLECTS; PHR: VB INFLECTS; CONVENTION; PHR: USU USED AS O

3 A **half** is **3.1** one of the two equal periods of time that a football game, rugby match, etc is divided into. **3.2** half a pint of beer, cider, etc; an informal use. EG *...a half of lager.* **3.3** a half-price ticket on a bus or train, especially one for a child. N COUNT: USU ORDINAL+N; N PART; N COUNT

4 If you are **half** English, German, etc, you have one parent or two grandparents who are English, German, etc. EG *She's of mixed parentage: half English, half Dutch.* ADV+ADJ CLASSIF ⇑ part

5 If you talk about your **better half** or your **other half**, you mean your husband or wife; a humorous usage. PHR: POSS+PHR = spouse

6 **Half** is used when you are talking about time to mean thirty minutes after a particular hour: see ☐ at TIME. EG *I reached my destination around half-past two... ...half past six in the morning.* ADV+*past*+NUM

7 You use **half** to say that something is only partly true or partly the case or happens only to a limited extent. EG *She was half smiling through her anxiety... She said nothing as I half helped her to a sitting position... He half expected to see Davis there... His eyes were half-closed... ...a half-built mansion... ...a pale smile that was half apology, half recognition.* ADV = part

8 You sometimes use the word **half** in informal English to emphasize and exaggerate something that you are saying. EG *She was half dead with exhaustion... ...a project which, I knew, already had them worried half into the grave.* ADV = nearly, almost

9 You use **not half** in informal spoken English **9.1** to emphasize an opinion or to emphasize the truth of a statement. EG *You don't half look a mess... You can't half swim... It wasn't half cold down there in the night.* **9.2** instead of 'yes' in order to emphasize how much you agree with something, or how strongly you feel about something. EG *'Did you enjoy it?'–'Not half.'* PHR ⇑ really; CONVENTION

10 If you say that someone is **too clever by half, too** arrogant **by half**, etc, you mean that you disapprove strongly of that particular quality in their behaviour or in their character. EG *He has been too clever by half... She's too pushy by half.* PHR: USED AS C

11 When you use an expression such as **a problem and a half** or **a meal and a half**, you are showing that your reaction to it is either very favourable or very unfavourable. EG *That's a job and a half... Thursday was a day and a half.* PHR: USED AS C

12 The word **half** is also used in the following expressions, which are explained at other places in this dictionary. ● **half the battle**: see **battle**. ● **half an**

ear: see **ear.** • **half a mind**: see **mind.** • **six of one and half a dozen of the other**: see **six.**

half-baked. Ideas, opinions, or plans that are **half-baked** have not been properly thought out, and so are usually stupid or impractical. EG *...your half-baked political opinions.*
ADJ QUALIT

half board. If you stay at a hotel and have **'half board**, you have your breakfast and evening meal at the hotel, but not your lunch.
N UNCOUNT

half-brother, half-brothers. Your **half-brother** is a boy or man who has the same mother or the same father as you have. EG *...her ten-year-old half-brother.*
N COUNT

half-caste, half-castes A **half-caste** or a person who is **half-caste** has parents who come from different races, for example a European father and an Indian mother. EG *Half-caste children were taken forcibly from their parents and sold as slaves.*
N COUNT, OR ADJ CLASSIF = mixed

half cock. If something goes off **half cock** or **at half cock**, it is unsuccessful because it happens before all the proper preparations or arrangements for it have been made.
PHR : USED AS AN A

half-day, half-days; also spelled as two words. A **half-day** is a day when you work only in the morning or in the afternoon, but not all day. EG *Saturday is his half-day.*
N COUNT

half-hearted. Someone or something that is **half-hearted** shows no real effort, interest, or enthusiasm. EG *She became aware of the arm around her and made a half-hearted attempt to break away.* ◇ **half-heartedly.** EG *He continued to lie there, chewing the sweet half-heartedly... I stayed home, studying half-heartedly.*
ADJ QUALIT = feeble
◇ ADV WITH VB = feebly

half-life, half-lives; also spelled without a hyphen. The **half-life** of a radioactive substance is the amount of time that it takes to lose half its radioactivity. This is used as a standard of measurement because radioactive substances take an infinitely long time to decay completely. EG *...a half-life of 200 years.*
N COUNT

half-mast. If a flag is flying **at half-mast**, it is flying not from the top but from the middle of the mast. It is a sign that someone important has died. EG *It was decided that the Union Jack should fly at half-mast from Churchill's death until his funeral.*
PHR : USED AS AN A

half-note, half-notes. A **half-note** is, in American English, a minim.
N COUNT

halfpenny /heɪpni¹/, **halfpennies, halfpence**. The plural can be either **halfpennies** or **halfpence. 1** A **halfpenny** is a small British coin which used to be worth one half of a penny; used also of the amount of money that this coin was worth. EG *...all the penny and halfpenny sweets.*
N COUNT

2 You sometimes use **halfpenny** to mean a very small amount of money. EG *These are the four months when I'm not earning a halfpenny.*
N SING : a+N = cent, bean

half-price. If something is **half-price**, it costs only half what it usually costs. EG *It was extremely economical because it ran on half-price electricity.* ▸ used as an adverb. EG *At 5 o'clock the stall-holders began to sell their wares half-price.*
ADJ CLASSIF ⇑ cheap
▸ ADV WITH VB

half-sister, half-sisters. Your **half-sister** is a girl or woman who has the same mother or the same father as you have. EG *She was his half-sister, I think.*
N COUNT

half-term, half-terms; also spelled as two words. **Half-term** is a short holiday in the middle of a school term. EG *Two more youngsters joined the group before half-term... The half-term holiday flew by.*
N UNCOUNT/COUNT

half-timbered is used to describe old buildings that have wooden beams showing in the brick and plaster walls, both on the inside and the outside of the building.
ADJ CLASSIF ≠ timbered

half-time; also spelled without a hyphen. **Half-time** is the short period of time between the two parts of a sporting event such as a football match, when the players have a short rest.
N UNCOUNT ⇑ break

halftone /hɑːftəʊn/, **halftones**. A **halftone** is an illustration in a newspaper or book that consists of a very large number of very small dots, each of which is either black or white. **2** in American English, a semitone.
N COUNT ⇑ picture
N COUNT ⇑ note

halfway /hɑːfweɪ/; also spelled with a hyphen. **1** If someone or something is **halfway, 1.1** they are at or towards the middle of a place, area of land, or distance between two points. EG *She was half-way up the stairs... His hand was poised halfway to his mouth with an empty pipe.* **1.2** they are at or towards the middle of a period of time or of an event or process. EG *Dr O'Shea usually fell asleep halfway through the programme... It is so easy to stop halfway.*
ADV : USU+PREP/ADV
ADV : USU+PREP/ADV

2 Halfway is used as an adverb to mean fairly or reasonably. EG *No computer could ever be programmed to play a half-way decent game of chess.*
ADV+ADJ/ADV

3 If you **meet** someone **halfway**, you accept some of the points they are making so that you can come to an agreement with them.
PHR : VB INFLECTS ⇑ compromise

half-wit, half-wits. 1 If you call someone a **half-wit**, you are showing that you think they have behaved in a stupid, silly, or irresponsible way; an informal use.
N COUNT = fool, moron

2 A **half-wit** is a person who is not very intelligent; an old-fashioned use.
N COUNT = idiot

half-witted is used, in informal English, to describe behaviour that you think is very stupid, silly, or irresponsible. EG *Well, that was a pretty half-witted thing to do.*
ADJ QUALIT

half-yearly means happening twice a year, with six months between each event. EG *...a half-yearly dividend.*
ADJ CLASSIF : ATTRIB

halibut /hælɪbət/, **halibuts**. A **halibut** is a large flat fish that is very good to eat.
N COUNT/UNCOUNT

halitosis /hælɪtəʊsɪs/. If someone has **halitosis**, they have breath that smells unpleasant, usually because they have a throat infection or decayed teeth.
N UNCOUNT ⇑ condition = bad breath

hall /hɔːl/, **halls. 1** A **hall** is **1.1** the area just inside the front door of a house, into which some of the other rooms open. EG *We began bringing down our suitcases and putting them in the hall.* **1.2** a large building which is used for public events such as concerts, exhibitions, and meetings. EG *...the Royal Festival Hall... We organized a concert in the village hall.* **1.3** a large room which is used for exhibitions, meetings, and other public events. EG *They wanted seats in the front of the hall so they could hear the speeches.* **1.4** a large building where a local government authority has its main offices. EG *If you see a rat, call the town hall and ask for the pest controller... The demonstrators marched on City Hall.*
N COUNT = lobby
N COUNT : ALSO IN NAMES AFTER N
N COUNT
N COUNT : MOD+N, ALSO IN NAMES AFTER N

2 Students who live in **hall** live in university or college accommodation during termtime. EG *I lived in hall during my first and second years.*
PREP+N UNCOUNT, OR N COUNT : ALSO IN NAMES

3 A **hall** is a large house on a country estate in which the owner of the estate usually lives.
N COUNT : ALSO IN NAMES AFTER N

hallelujah /hælɪ²luːjə/; also spelled **halleluiah, alleluia. Hallelujah!** is used by people in church or some other religious place as an exclamation of praise and thanks to God; also sometimes used when someone has eventually succeeded in doing something difficult.
EXCLAM/CONVENTION ⇑ exclamation

hallmark /hɔːlmɑːk/, **hallmarks, hallmarking, hallmarked**. A **hallmark** is **1** the most typical quality or feature of something or someone. EG *Hair or fur is the hallmark of a mammal, just as feathers are of birds... ...the kind of subtlety that was the hallmark of Elgar.* **2** an official mark put on things made of gold, silver, or platinum that indicates the quality of the metal, where the object was made, and who made it. EG *You can tell it's 9 carat gold from the hallmark.* ▸ used as a verb. EG *Is the ring hallmarked?*
N COUNT : USU WITH POSS = trademark
N COUNT
▸ V+O

hallo /hə³ləʊ/. See **hello.**

hall of residence, halls of residence. **Halls of residence** are blocks of rooms or flats, usually built by universities or colleges, in which students live during termtime.
N COUNT ⇑ building

hallowed /hæləʊd/. **1 Hallowed** is used to describe something that is considered to be holy. EG *The church stands on hallowed ground.*
ADJ CLASSIF : ATTRIB

2 If something is **hallowed**, it is respected and revered, usually because it is old, important, or has a good reputation. EG *...those hallowed offices on State Street.*
ADJ QUALIT

Halloween /hæləʊiːn/; also spelled **Hallowe'en. Halloween** is October 31st. It is traditionally said to be the night on which ghosts and witches can be seen, and so children often dress up as ghosts and witches and make lanterns using pumpkins. EG *...the Pumpkin Ball annually held on Halloween at the country club... ...dusty Halloween masks.*
N UNCOUNT

hallstand /hɔːlstænd/, **hallstands**. A **hallstand** is a piece of furniture on which you hang coats and hats.
N COUNT = hall tree

hallucinate /hə³lu:sɪneɪt/, **hallucinates, hallucinating, hallucinated**. If you **hallucinate**, you see things that are not really there, either because you are ill or because you have taken a drug. EG *She barked at me and I knew she must be hallucinating.* — V

hallucination /hə³lu:sɪneɪʃə⁰n/, **hallucinations**. A **hallucination** is the experience of seeing something that is not really there because you are ill or have taken a drug; used also of what you think you see in these circumstances. EG *...a bizarre hallucination... I have not had either visions or hallucinations.* — N COUNT/UNCOUNT ⇑ vision

hallucinatory /hə³u:sɪnətri¹/. Something that is **hallucinatory** is like a hallucination or is the cause of a hallucination. EG *I had a sudden hallucinatory vision of him... There was no question of my having been given a hallucinatory drug.* — ADJ CLASSIF : USU ATTRIB

hallucinogenic /hə³u:sɪnə⁶dʒenɪk/. A **hallucinogenic** drug is one that causes you to hallucinate. — ADJ CLASSIF : USU ATTRIB

hallway /hɔ:lweɪ/, **hallways**. A **hallway** is the entrance hall of a house or other building. — N COUNT = hall

halo /heɪləʊ/, **haloes, halos**. The plural can be either **haloes** or **halos**. **1** A **halo** is a circle of light that is drawn round the heads of saints, angels, or Jesus to show that they are holy. EG *Although appearing to be Christ, the figure bears no halo.* — N COUNT = nimbus

2 A **halo** is also anything which looks like a circle of light round a person or thing. EG *The light behind him made an untidy halo round his pink head... Around the summit of the hill was a halo of small, puffy clouds... ...a halo of hair.* — N COUNT

halt /hɒlt/, **halts, halting, halted**. **1** When you **halt** or when something **halts** you, you stop moving in the direction you were going and stand still. EG *He took a step and halted... Suddenly the drums stopped and the marchers halted... The last thing he wished at this stage was to be halted by a cheery 'Well, fancy seeing you here'... A smart young professional raised an arm to halt a cab.* — V-ERG

2 When something such as growth, development, or activity **halts** or when you **halt** it, it stops completely. EG *If population growth were to halt overnight, the workforce would still go on growing... Successive governments have sought to halt or slow down the inflationary spiral... The firm ran into foreign exchange problems which halted its imports of nylon.* — V-ERG = end

3 If someone or something comes **to a halt**, they stop moving. EG *The car slowed, and came to a halt opposite her.* — PHR : USED AS AN A = to a standstill

4 EG *If something such as growth, development, or activity comes* **to a halt**, it stops completely. EG *Work would screech to a halt if management did that... This brought conversation to a halt.* — PHR : USED AS AN A = to a standstill

5 If you **call a halt** to something such as an activity, you decide not to continue with it. EG *Surely it is time to call a halt to these practices?* — PHR : VB INFLECTS, IF + PREP THEN *to* ⇑ discontinue

6 'Halt!' is a military order to stop walking or marching and stand still; used for example by the person in charge of a parade or by a sentry on guard duty. EG *Parade, halt! Stand at ease!... Halt! Who goes there?* — CONVENTION

7 A **halt** is a very small station on a country railway line, which often consists only of a short platform and no station building. EG *The train stopped at some wayside halt.* — N COUNT

halter /hɒltə, hɔ:l-/, **halters**. A **halter** is a strap made from leather or rope that is fastened round the head of a horse so that it can be led easily. EG *I tied Bub with his halter to the tree.* — N COUNT

halterneck /hɒltənɛk, hɔ:l-/. A woman's **halterneck** dress or top is one that is held in place by a narrow band of cloth which goes from the front of the bodice round the back of the neck, so that no shoulder straps are necessary and her back is bare. — ADJ CLASSIF : USU ATTRIB

halting /hɒltɪŋ, hɔ:l-/. If you speak in a **halting** way, you speak with a lot of pauses because you are uncertain what to say or afraid to speak. EG *We stammered a few polite words in our halting French... ...his halting admission of guilt.* ◇ **haltingly**. EG *He answered haltingly.* — ADJ QUALIT ⇑ unsure = stumbling ≠ fluent; ◇ ADV WITH VB = hesitantly

halve /hɑ:v/, **halves, halving, halved**. **1** When you **halve** something or when it **halves**, it is reduced to half its previous size or amount. EG *This could halve rail fares... If that happened, sales would halve overnight.* — V-ERG ⇑ reduce

2 If you **halve** something, you divide it into two equal parts. EG *Halve the avocado pears and remove the stones.* — V+O

3 Halves is the plural of **half**.

ham /hæm/, **hams, hamming, hammed**. **1 Ham** is meat from the top of one of the back legs of a pig, specially treated so that it can be kept for a long period of time. EG *...slabs of bacon and legs of ham hanging behind the counter... ...a ham sandwich.* — N UNCOUNT

▸ used as a count noun to refer to a joint of this meat or to the back leg of a pig where the joint comes from. EG *Trim the fat off the hams... The most valuable parts of the pig are the two hams.* — ▸ N COUNT ⇑ joint

2 A **ham** is **2.1** a person whose hobby is using special radio equipment to talk to other people with the same hobby, often people in other countries. EG *The signal was picked up by a radio ham who raised the alarm... ...ham radio stations.* — N COUNT ⇑ amateur **2.2** a bad actor or actress who exaggerates every emotion and gesture. — N COUNT

▸ used as an adjective to refer to actors or actresses or to their bad performances. EG *...the worst excesses of nineteenth-century ham acting.* — ▸ ADJ CLASSIF : ATTRIB ⇑ exaggerated

3 If actors or actresses **ham it up**, they exaggerate every emotion and gesture when they are acting, often deliberately because they think that the audience will be more amused. EG *She was obviously hamming it up for the benefit of the watching tourists.* — PHR : VB INFLECTS

hamburger /hæmbɜ:gə/, **hamburgers**. A **hamburger** is a piece of minced meat which has been shaped into a flat disc. Hamburgers are fried or grilled and then eaten, often in a bread roll. — N COUNT ⇑ food

ham-fisted. Someone who is **ham-fisted** is clumsy, usually in the way that they use their hands. EG *Even the most ham-fisted cook can take pleasure in his effort.* — ADJ QUALIT = ham-handed

ham-handed means the same as ham-fisted. EG *...ham-handed governmental interference.* — ADJ QUALIT

hamlet /hæmlɪ²t/, **hamlets**. A **hamlet** is a very small village. — N COUNT

hammer /hæmə/, **hammers, hammering, hammered**. **1** A **hammer** is a tool that consists of a heavy piece of metal at the end of a handle. It is used for hitting things, for example nails into walls , or for breaking things by force. EG *We knocked holes in the tin with a hammer and a big nail.* — N COUNT ● The **hammer and sickle** is the symbol that represents industrial workers and peasants on the flags of communist countries such as the USSR. — ● PHR : *the*+N ● Something that **comes under the hammer** is sold at an auction. EG *His entire collection will come under the hammer at next week's sale.* — ● PHR : VB INFLECTS ● If people are going at something **hammer and tongs**, they are doing it in a very vigorous way; used especially of people arguing violently. — ● PHR : USED AS AN A ⇑ vigorously

2 If you **hammer** something such as a nail, you hit it with a hammer. EG *Give a gentle first tap, then hammer it in... Claude selected two big planks and began to hammer them into a cross.* — V+O = bang

3 If you **hammer** a surface or **hammer** on it, you make a noise by hitting it several times with your fist or hand, often when you are angry. EG *Men used to hammer on our door late at night... He hammered the table and told the Minister he wanted results.* — V+O, OR V+A = thump, bang

4 If you **hammer** something such as an idea into people or you **hammer** at it, you keep repeating it forcefully so that it will have an effect on people. EG *Speakers at meetings up and down the country have hammered the message across... ...ideas hammered into their heads by a stream of movies... Mr Stewart was not to be deflected, and went on hammering at the same point.* — V+O+A *(into)*, OR V+A *(at)* ⇑ force = drive

5 If you **hammer** or **hammer away** at some work or activity, you work at it constantly and with great energy. EG *Why do you hammer at the subject day after day?... They all hammer away at their thesis.* — V+A *(at)*, OR PHRASAL VB : V+ADV, USU+*at* = slog

6 If you **hammer** someone, **6.1** you attack, criticize, or punish them severely. EG *He hammered everybody who didn't subscribe to his views... It is not enough to go on hammering the Government's proposals.* — V+O = slate **6.2** you defeat them completely and easily in a sports match; an informal use. EG *At Lord's that year they hammered the West Indies.* — V+O = thrash

7 If something such as the rain **hammers** down, it is strong and feels or sounds like something beating hard. EG *I was woken by the rain hammering against my bedroom window... With hammering heart I admitted my identity.* — V : USU+A = pound

8 A **hammer** is also 8.1 the part of a gun that moves forward when you pull the trigger and causes the bullet to shoot out of the gun. EG *The hammer clicked back.* 8.2 the part of a piano that hits a string when you press a key. 8.3 a heavy weight attached to a piece of wire, that is thrown as a sport. ▸ also used to refer to the sport itself. EG *The next athletics event is the hammer.* — N COUNT ⇑ device; N COUNT; N COUNT; ▸ N SING : *the*+N

hammer out. If you **hammer** something **out**, you reach an agreement about it after a long or difficult discussion. EG *There will be trouble unless we actually sit down together and hammer out an agreement for the future... ...procedures hammered out over recent years.* — PHRASAL VB : V+O+ADV ⇑ create = thrash out

hammock /hæmək/, **hammocks**. A **hammock** is a piece of strong cloth or netting which is hung between two supports and used as a bed. EG *He went to sleep on the garden hammock.* — N COUNT

hamper /hæmpə/, **hampers, hampering, hampered**. 1 If you **hamper** a person or their actions, you restrict them by making their development, progress, or movement difficult. EG *Legislation can provoke strikes and hamper their settlement... His attempts at change were hampered... They were hampered by a constant stream of visitors... Her heavy skirts hampered her movements.* — V+O ⇑ limit = impede

2 A **hamper** is 2.1 a large basket with a lid, used especially for carrying food in. EG *We packed a big wicker hamper and went for a picnic.* 2.2 a basket containing fine food that is given to people as a present. EG *The firm sent him a hamper every Christmas.* — N COUNT; N COUNT

hamster /hæmstə/, **hamsters**. A **hamster** is a small rodent similar to a mouse, which is often kept as a pet. — N COUNT ⇑ animal

hamstring /hæmstrɪŋ/, **hamstrings, hamstringing, hamstrung**. 1 A **hamstring** is a tendon behind your knee which joins the muscles of your thigh to the bones of your lower leg. EG *...a hamstring injury.* — N COUNT

2 If you **hamstring** someone, you make it very difficult for them to take any action. EG *If you made the law too precise, you would so hamstring the medical profession that the majority of patients would go untreated... I found my activities severely hamstrung by this dependence.* — V+O ⇑ restrict = handicap

hand /hænd/, **hands, handing, handed**. 1 Your **hand** is the part of your body which is at the end of your arm and has four fingers and a thumb, and which you use to hold things and to pick things up. EG *Louise stood shading her eyes with her hand... He took her hand and passionately squeezed it... He conducts using the simplest hand movements.* — N COUNT

2 Your **hand** is also the style in which you write with a pen or pencil; a literary word. EG *He writes, in his neat little hand: 'Happy Birthday, Julia.'* — N SING WITH DET +SUPP = handwriting

3 The **hand** of someone or something is an effective influence that the person or thing has on particular events or on a particular situation. EG *...the hand of fate... ...the hand of God... The hand of the military in shaping government policy was obvious.* — N SING : *the*+N+*of*

4 If you ask someone for a **hand** with something, you ask them to help you in what you are doing. EG *I wonder if you could give me a hand to get my raincoat on?... Do you need a hand with that?* ● To **lend a hand**: see **lend**. — N SING : *a*+N, IF +PREP THEN *with*

5 If a person speaking to an audience asks for a **hand** for someone, they ask the audience to clap loudly, usually to welcome them before they perform something or to applaud them afterwards. EG *Let's give a big hand to Sally for singing so beautifully tonight.* — N SING : *a*+N ⇑ applause

6 If a man asks for a woman's **hand** or for her **hand** in marriage, he asks her or her parents for permission to marry her; an old-fashioned use. EG *The Spanish envoy came to plead for her hand on behalf of the King of Spain... I've told him I have asked for your hand in marriage and that you've rejected me.* — N SING WITH DET : WITH POSS

7 A **hand** is 7.1 someone, usually a man, who does hard physical work, for example in a factory or on a farm, as part of a group of people who all do similar work. EG *...farm hands... All hands on deck!* ● See also **old hand**. 7.2 a long thin piece of metal, plastic, etc, that points to numbers around the edge of a dial, usually on the face of a clock in order to show what the time is. 7.3 the cards that you are holding in your hand at any time in a game of cards, or the cards that are dealt to you at the beginning of the game. EG *...a hand of poker... I've had some lousy hands tonight.* 7.4 a measurement of four inches or about ten centimetres, which is used for measuring the height of a horse from its front hooves to its shoulders. EG *It was a small horse, only fourteen hands.* — N COUNT ⇑ worker = labourer; N COUNT ⇑ indicator; N COUNT; N COUNT : NUM+N

8 **Hand** is used in the following ways after different prepositions. 8.1 Something that is **at hand**, **near at hand**, or **close at hand** is very near in time or place. EG *I picked up a book that happened to lie at hand and read a few pages... The apocalypse stood at hand, the new world waited to be born.* 8.2 If you do something **by hand**, you do it using your hands rather than a machine. EG *I did the sewing by hand.* — PHR : USED AS AN A; PHR : USED AS AN A ⇑ manually

8.3 If you have time **in hand**, you have it free to do what you want before something starts. EG *He arrived with half an hour in hand and went for a walk.* — PHR AFTER N ⇑ spare

8.4 The job, problem, etc **in hand** is the job that you are dealing with at the moment. EG *Let's get on with the job in hand.* 8.5 A situation that you have **in hand** is one that you have under control. EG *The Prime Minister has the situation well in hand.* 8.6 Something that you know **off hand** is something that you know without having to ask anyone else or look up in a book. EG *What time do we get there? Do you know off hand?... I can't think off hand what the answer is.* — PHR : AFTER N, OR USED AS AN A; PHR : USED AS AN A; PHR : USED AS AN A = off the cuff

8.7 Someone or something that is **on hand** is near and ready to help if they are needed. EG *Emergency services were on hand in case there was any trouble.* — PHR : USED AS AN A ⇑ available

8.8 If you make a decision **out of hand**, you make it quickly and suddenly without any thought of changing your mind, especially when you decide to reject something in some way. EG *One might even be inclined to dismiss it out of hand.* 8.9 If you have something **to hand**, you have it with you or near you ready to use when needed. EG *I haven't got one to hand... ...using the material most readily to hand.* — PHR : USED AS AN A ⇑ instantly; PHR : USED AS AN A ⇑ available = handy

9 **Hand** is used in a large number of expressions in its singular form. 9.1 If someone gives you **a free hand**, they give you the freedom to use your own judgement and to do exactly as you wish, especially in your work or duties. EG *The team gave me a free hand in all editorial matters.* 9.2 Someone who treats people with **a heavy hand** is very rough and severe; used for example of the ruler of a country. 9.3 You use **on the one hand** to introduce the first part of an argument or discussion that has two different and opposite points of view. It is always followed later by 'on the other hand'. EG *The firm was accommodating its customers on the one hand and making aggressive demands on the other.* 9.4 You use **on the other hand** to introduce the second part of an argument or discussion that has two different and opposite points of view. EG *John had great difficulties playing cricket. But on the other hand, he was an awfully good rugby player.* 9.5 Someone who is tied **hand and foot** has both their hands and both their feet tied together. EG *They found him unconscious, bound hand and foot.* — PHR : USED AS O = carte blanche; PHR : AFTER PREP; PHR : USED AS ADV SEN; PHR : USED AS ADV SEN ⇑ conversely; PHR : USED AS AN A

9.6 If you work **hand in glove** with someone, you work very closely with them. EG *Health workers are now working hand in glove with midwives in Birmingham.* 9.7 Two people who are **hand in hand** are holding each other's hand, usually while walking or sitting together, with one person's left hand holding the other person's right hand. People often do this to show their affection for each other. EG *They sat on the sofa hand in hand.* 9.8 If you do something such as spend or make money **hand over fist**, you spend or make it quickly and in large amounts. EG *They were making money hand over fist.* 9.9 If you say that you could do something **with one hand tied behind** your **back**, you mean that you think you could do it very easily; an informal expression. 9.10 If you **bite the hand that feeds** you, you are cruel to the person who pays your wages or who has been generous to you. EG *Only a fool bites the hand that feeds him.* 9.11 If you **force** someone's **hand**, you force them to act sooner than they want to or in public when they would prefer to keep their actions secret. EG *I had intended to keep quiet about the deal, but they forced my hand.* 9.12 If a person or a situation **gets out of hand**, you are no longer able to control them. 9.13 Two things that **go hand in hand** with each other are closely connected and cannot be considered separately from each other. EG *Biblical criticism has gone hand in hand with a distrust of dogmatism.* 9.14 If you **have a hand in** something such as an activity, you are involved in it. EG *Derek* — PHR : USED AS AN A, USU+*with* ⇑ together; PHR : USED AS AN A, IF+PREP THEN *with*; PHR : USED AS AN A ⇑ fast = like mad; PHR : USED AS AN A; PHR : VB INFLECTS ⇑ be ungrateful; PHR : VB INFLECTS ⇑ hurry; PHR : VB INFLECTS; PHR OR PHR+A (*with*) : RECIP, VB INFLECTS; PHR : VB INFLECTS

seemed to have had a hand in getting the information... Quellin may have had a considerable hand in it. **9.15** If you ask someone to **hold** your **hand** at an event that you are worried about, you ask them to support you by being there with you; an informal expression. EG *I've got to go to the dentist–will you come and hold my hand?* **9.16** If you **keep** your **hand in** at something such as a skill or hobby, you do it or practise it occasionally in order to remain fairly good at it. EG *I still write the occasional article, just to keep my hand in.* **9.17** If you **know** something **like the back of** your **hand**, you know it extremely well. EG *A London cabbie knows the city like the back of his hand.* **9.18** Someone who **lives from hand to mouth** has hardly enough food or money to live on. EG *We lived from hand to mouth, never knowing where the next meal was coming from.* • See also **hand-to-mouth.** **9.19** If you **show** your **hand**, you show how much power you have and the way you intend to act. EG *Don't show your hand until you have to.* **9.20** If you **take** someone or something **in hand**, you take control or responsibility over them, especially in order to improve them in some way. EG *I'm going to take that boy in hand and teach him a lesson or two.* **9.21** If you **try** your **hand** at an activity or skill, you attempt to do it, especially when it is for the first time. EG *I had tried my hand at milking years ago, when I was about eighteen.* **9.22** If you **turn** your **hand to** something new, especially a practical skill, you learn about it and practise it for the first time. EG *That spring, I turned my hand to photography.* **9.23** • to **be a dab hand** at something: see **dab.** • to **eat out of** someone's **hand**: see **eat.** • to **wait on** someone **hand and foot**: see **wait.**

PHR : VB INFLECTS / PHR : VB INFLECTS / PHR : VB INFLECTS, NO CONT / PHR : VB INFLECTS ⇑ be poor / PHR : VB INFLECTS ⇑ reveal / PHR : VB INFLECTS / PHR : VB INFLECTS, USU + *at* = have a go / PHR : VB INFLECTS = take up

10 Hand is also used in a number of expressions in its plural form. **10.1** You say **'Hands off'** to someone to tell them in an aggressive way not to touch something or interfere with it; an informal expression. EG *That's mine–hands off!... This is my area of responsibility, so hands off!* **10.2** **'Hands up!'** is a command used by gunmen to make people hold both hands above their heads while they point a gun at them. **10.3** Treatment of a particular kind **at the hands of** a person or organization is treatment that is received from them, especially when it is unpleasant. EG *...brutality at the hands of angry, unpredictable parents... The details of his persecution at the hands of officialdom during the war would shock us all.* **10.4** If someone or something is **in the hands** of a person or organization, the person or organization owns them, has power over them, or has responsibility for them. EG *This law leaves much too much power in the hands of the judges... No need to worry about Johanna–she's in safe hands... In January a letter came into the hands of a Senator from Iowa.* **10.5** A responsibility or burden that is **on** your **hands** is one which you have to deal with yourself. When it is **off** your **hands**, it is no longer your responsibility and you do not have to deal with it. EG *They've still got an economic crisis on their hands... Now the kids are off my hands I can write my book.* **10.6** If you are **on** your **hands and knees**, you are kneeling down and bending forward so that your knees, feet, and the palms of your hands are all on the ground. EG *Does he have to crawl on his hands and knees?* **10.7** If a possession **changes hands**, it changes from the ownership of one person to that of another, especially by being sold. EG *Properties are changing hands very rapidly in Selly Oak.* **10.8** If you **get** your **hands on** something, **lay** your **hands on** someone, etc, you manage to find them or obtain them; an informal expression. EG *I wondered how I could lay my hands on the money to buy equipment... That's what happens when the poor get their hands on money.* **10.9** If you **have** your **hands full**, you are very busy and have no time to do anything extra. EG *I'm sorry, I've got my hands full, you'll have to do it yourself.* **10.10** Two people who are **holding hands** are holding each other's hand, usually while walking or sitting together, with one person's left hand holding the other person's right hand. People often do this to show their affection for each other. EG *They never touched in public, they did not hold hands.* **10.11** If you **play right into** someone's **hands**, you do something which they want you to do and which places you in their power in some way. EG *That was a stupid thing to do–you've played right into his hands.* **10.12** If you **wash** your **hands** of someone or something, you refuse to be involved with them any more and to take any more responsibility for them or their actions. EG *It was hypocritical of the company to wash its hands of the deed afterwards.* **10.13** • with your **bare hands**: see **bare.** • to **shake hands**: see **shake.** • to **win hands down**: see **win.**

CONVENTION / CONVENTION / PREP / PHR + SUPP / PHR : USED AS AN A / PHR : USED AS AN A = on all fours / PHR : VB INFLECTS / PHR : VB INFLECTS = get hold of / PHR : VB INFLECTS ⇑ be busy / PHR : VB INFLECTS / PHR : VB INFLECTS / PHR : VB INFLECTS

11 If you **hand** something to someone, you pass it from your hand to their hand. EG *Could you hand me that piece of wood in the corner?... He handed down to Casson the file he held in his hand.* • If you say you **have got to hand it to** someone, you mean that you admire them for their skills or achievements and you think they deserve a lot of praise; an informal expression. EG *You have to hand it to them, they're wonderful entertainers.*

V+O+O, OR V+O +A *(to)* ⇑ give / • PHR : VB INFLECTS

hand around means the same as hand round. EG *I asked her to hand around the sandwiches.* PHRASAL VB : V+O+ADV

hand back. If you **hand** something **back** to someone, you return it to them after you have borrowed or taken it from them. EG *He handed back his room key to the receptionist... I examined the lighter, then handed it back.* PHRASAL VB : V+O+ADV, USU+*to* = give back

hand down. If you **hand down** something such as possessions, skills, or knowledge, you give or leave it to people who belong to a younger generation than you do. EG *Such knowledge was handed down from father to son... This brooch has been handed down in our family for two hundred years.* PHRASAL VB : V+O+ADV, USU PASS ⇑ transfer = pass on

hand in. 1 If you **hand in** something such as homework or a document, you give it to a teacher or some other person in authority, especially in order for it to be read or corrected. EG *In July he handed in the finished version of the novel to the publishers.* PHRASAL VB : V+O+ADV ⇑ submit = give in

2 If you **hand in** your notice or your resignation, you tell your employer, either in writing or in speech, that you no longer wish to work for him or her and are resigning from your job. EG *I was tempted to hand in my resignation at once... I handed in my notice and fled to the relative sanity of the pub.* PHRASAL VB : V+O+ADV = give in, tender

hand on. If you **hand** something **on** to someone, you give it or leave it to them. EG *They handed on to their children the only life they knew... Property is something handed on from generation to generation.* PHRASAL VB : V+O+ADV, USU+*to* = pass on

hand out. 1 If you **hand** something **out** to people, you give each person in a group one of a set of similar or identical things. EG *Make a list of names, see if they're all present, and hand out the books... Birth control pills are handed out with free orange juice in many rural areas.* PHRASAL VB : V+O+ADV ⇑ distribute = give out

2 When people in authority **hand out** something such as advice or punishment, they give it to people and expect them to accept it. EG *The penalties which he handed out last week were extremely unfair.* PHRASAL VB : V+O+ADV = mete out

3 See also **handout.**

hand over. 1 If you **hand** something **over** to someone, you give it to them so that they own it. EG *Samuel was about to hand over large sums of money to his local hospital.* PHRASAL VB : V+O+ADV, USU+*to* = donate

2 When you **hand over** someone such as a prisoner to someone else, you give the control of and responsibility for them to that other person. EG *Britain was under no obligation to hand him over to America... Children are often handed over to the child-minder at seven a.m.* PHRASAL VB : V+O (NG/REFL)+ADV, USU+*to* ⇑ move = turn over

3 If you **hand over** to someone or **hand** something **over** to them, you give them the responsibility for dealing with a particular situation or problem. EG *Sir John handed over to his deputy and left... In 1977 the problem was handed over to a computer.* PHRASAL VB : V+ADV OR V+O+ADV, USU+*to* ⇑ delegate

hand round. When you **hand round** something such as food, you pass it from one person to another in a group. EG *She handed round the cakes.* PHRASAL VB : V+O+ADV = distribute

handbag /hændbæg/, **handbags.** A **handbag** is a small bag with a woman's money, chequebook, keys, etc in it, which she takes with her when she goes out. N COUNT : USU POSS+N IN SING ⇑ bag

handball /hændbɔːl/ is a game, usually played by two teams, in which you hit the ball with the palm of your hand. N UNCOUNT ⇑ sport

handbill /hændbɪl/, **handbills.** A **handbill** is a small printed notice which is used to advertise a particular company, service, or event. EG *...thousands of handbills distributed to shops and offices announcing a revolutionary new accounting system.* N COUNT = leaflet

handbook /hændbʊk/, **handbooks.** A **handbook** is a book that gives you advice and instructions about a particular subject, tool, machine, etc. Handbooks are N COUNT : USU+SUPP, ALSO IN NAMES AFTER N often produced by a particular organization or by the company who make the tool, machine, etc. EG *...the new AA Members' Handbook... ...the official handbook for the airport... Two very clear and comprehensive handbooks are available.*

handbrake /hændbreɪk/, **handbrakes**. A **handbrake** is a brake which is operated by a lever moved by the hand of the person driving a vehicle. EG *Mr Boggis released the handbrake, and began moving slowly down the hill.* N COUNT ⇑ brake

handcart /hændkɑːt/, **handcarts**. A **handcart** is a small two-wheeled cart which is pushed or pulled along and is used for transporting goods. N COUNT ⇑ cart = barrow

handclap /hændklæp/. A **slow handclap** is slow rhythmic clapping by an audience to show that they do not like what they are seeing or hearing and that they want the performer, speaker, etc, to leave; used in British English. PHR : USED AS O ⇑ clap

handcuff /hændkʌf/, **handcuffs, handcuffing, handcuffed**. 1 **Handcuffs** are two metal rings which are fastened together and can be locked round someone's wrists, usually by the police during an arrest. EG *They swept toward me like vultures and clamped handcuffs around my wrists.* N PLURAL = manacles, cuffs

2 If you **handcuff** someone, you put handcuffs around their wrists. EG *Ordering them out of their car, he prepared to handcuff them... They were searched and handcuffed.* V+O : USU PASS ⇑ confine = manacle

-handed. 1 **-handed** combines with 'left' and 'right' to indicate which hand a person usually uses for writing or playing games. EG *I'm left-handed and teachers don't like that.* ▸ used of tools which are made to be used by people who are left- or right-handed. EG *...left-handed scissors.* COMB : FORMS ADJ CLASSIFS ▸ COMB : FORMS ADJ CLASSIFS

2 **-handed** combines with numbers 2.1 to indicate how many hands are needed or used to do something. EG *...a firm two-handed gesture... ...two-handed swords.* 2.2 to indicate how many people are working or are needed for a particular job. EG *...a four-handed cast and a small orchestra... ...running a house and family single-handed.* • See also **short-handed**. COMB : FORMS ADJ CLASSIFS COMB : FORMS ADJ CLASSIFS

handful /hændful/, **handfuls**. 1 A **handful** of something is the amount of it that you can hold in your hand. EG *Roger gathered a handful of stones and began to throw them... ...a few handfuls of rice.* N PART = fistful

2 If there is only a **handful** of people or things, there are not very many of them. EG *The firm employs only a handful of workers, on low incomes... He had published nothing except a handful of essays and reviews.* N PART : SING ⇑ number = few

3 If you describe a person or an animal as a **handful**, you mean that they are difficult to control; an informal use. EG *How old is she?–Eight–I bet she's a handful.* N COUNT : USU a +N IN SING = mischief-maker

handgun /hændgʌn/, **handguns**. A **handgun** is a gun that you can hold, carry, and fire with one hand. N COUNT = pistol

handicap /hændɪkæp/, **handicaps, handicapping, handicapped**. 1 A **handicap** is 1.1 a physical or mental disability that you are born with or that is caused by an illness or accident which prevents you from living a totally normal life. EG *These changes have made the campus an easier place for people with handicaps... One-third of our workforce have significant physical handicaps.* 1.2 an event or situation that makes it difficult for something to happen or for you to do something. EG *His chief handicap is that he comes from a broken home.* N COUNT; N COUNT ⇑ disadvantage = impediment

2 If an event or a situation **handicaps** someone, it makes it difficult for them to act or to do something. EG *The bad weather severely handicapped their performance in the race... We were handicapped by the darkness.* V+O ⇑ restrict = impede, hamper

3 A **handicap** is also 3.1 a disadvantage that is given to someone who is good at a particular sport, in order to make the competition between them and the other competitors more equal. 3.2 an advantage that is given to someone who is not good at golf, in order to make the competition between them and other players more equal. The lower your handicap is, the better a player you are. EG *He's a good golfer, about a seven handicap. What's your handicap?–Fifteen.* N COUNT; N COUNT : USU POSS+N

handicapped /hændɪkæpt/. 1 Someone who is **handicapped** has a physical or mental disability that prevents them living a totally normal life. EG *A journalist friend of his had a handicapped daughter...* ▸ **The handicapped** refers to people who are handicapped. EG *...establishments for the mentally or physically handicapped.* ADJ QUALIT ⇑ disabled ▸ N PLURAL : the +N

2 If a person is **handicapped** in a sport or race, they are given a particular disadvantage in order to make the competition more equal among the people taking part. ADJ CLASSIF

handicraft /hændɪkrɑːft/, **handicrafts**. **Handicrafts** are 1 activities such as embroidery and pottery which involve doing or making things with your hands in a skilful way. EG *...a pretty wife who teaches handicrafts... I've told her about the handicraft class on Saturday mornings.* 2 the objects that are produced by people doing embroidery, pottery, etc. EG *Handicrafts were produced by families to be sold in the local shops.* N COUNT : USU PL ⇑ craft; N COUNT : USU PL

handiwork /hændɪwɜːk/ is 1 something that you have done or made yourself. EG *He stood back and surveyed his handiwork... He felt a certain satisfaction at his handiwork.* 2 work or activities such as embroidery or pottery that involve doing or making things with your hands in a skilful way; a rather old-fashioned use. EG *I would have the children do more handiwork, dramatics, and dancing... Only Aurelia could do that delicate handiwork.* N UNCOUNT : USU POSS+N = work; N UNCOUNT = handicrafts

handkerchief /hæŋkətʃiˈf/, **handkerchiefs**. A **handkerchief** is a small square piece of fabric which you use for blowing your nose. N COUNT = hankie

handle /hændəˈl/, **handles, handling, handled**. 1 A **handle** is 1.1 a small round object or a lever that is attached to a door or window and is used for opening and closing it. EG *He tugged at the metal handle, and it came off in his hand... I was going to screw some handles onto the new bathroom cabinet.* 1.2 the part of an object such as a tool, bag, or cup that you hold in order to be able to pick up and use the object. EG *...a broom handle... ...a letter opener with a leather handle.* N COUNT; N COUNT

2 If you **fly off the handle**, you suddenly and completely lose your temper; an informal expression. PHR : VB INFLECTS

3 If you **handle** something, you hold it and move it about in your hands, especially in order to look at it or to examine it carefully. EG *The child handled the ornaments carefully and seldom broke anything... Glass. Handle with Care.* V+O

4 When you **handle** something such as a weapon, car, or horse, or when it **handles** in a particular way, you are able to use or control it effectively or successfully, especially by using your hands. EG *She had handled a machine gun herself... He could handle his pans like a juggler... This car handles very nicely.* V-ERG : IF V THEN +A

5 If you **handle** a problem, situation, or something that you find difficult to accept, you deal with it successfully. EG *I decided to let Eddie handle the situation... You don't have to come. Hendricks and I can handle it... Abortion was an issue too explosive for him to handle.* ◊ **handling**. EG *His handling of these important issues was condemned by the opposition.* V+O ⇑ manage = cope with; ◊ N UNCOUNT : USU+of = treatment

6 To **handle** something also means 6.1 to have the ability, equipment, etc, to deal with things and events while working or functioning normally. EG *The exchange had more business than it could handle... Last year, they handled 50,000 tons... The walkways should have been strong enough to handle all normal foot traffic.* 6.2 to have responsibility for a particular area of work, usually on someone else's behalf. EG *He handles all the major accounts... ...travel agents that handle British Airways business.* V+O = tackle; V+O ⇑ deal with

7 If you can **handle** people, you build up a good relationship with them so that they respond well to you and usually do what you want them to. EG *The principal was a young man and a genius in the way he handled us.* V+O ⇑ manipulate = deal with

8 If you can **handle** words, numbers, or ideas, you use them with great skill and competence, so that you are able to explain things in an efficient and interesting way. EG *...how you use and handle words... A mathematics test is a test of how you handle figures.* V+O

9 If an event, situation, or fact is or provides a **handle** for something else, you can use it as an excuse, reason, or opportunity for doing something, especially for making other people do what you want. N SING WITH DET *+for*

10 If you talk about someone's **handle**, you mean the title or name they have, especially the code name that a CB user has; an informal use. N COUNT : USU SING

handlebar /hændə⁰lbɑː/, **handlebars**. The **handlebars** of a bicycle consist of a curved metal bar with handles at each end. The handlebars are attached to the front of the bicycle and are turned in order to steer it. EG *Those handlebars are still loose.* N COUNT : USU PL, SING=PL ↑ steering

handler /hændlə/, **handlers**. A **handler** is 1 someone who is in charge of and controls an animal, especially when this is part of their work. EG *They are highly sensitive animals, easily frightened by bad handlers.* N COUNT : USU POSS/MOD+N ↑ keeper 2 someone who deals with a particular type of object as part of their work. EG *...baggage handlers.* N COUNT : USU MOD+N ↑ worker

handmade /hændmeɪd/. If something is **handmade**, it is made by someone using their hands or using tools rather than by machines. EG *...beautiful handmade clothes... ...handmade paper of a quality unknown today.* ADJ CLASSIF

handmaiden /hændmeɪdə⁰n/, **handmaidens**. A **handmaiden** or a **handmaid** is 1 a female servant; an old-fashioned and literary use. N COUNT 2 something which plays a lesser but important supportive role to something else. EG *The Party regarded the trade unions as the handmaid of the political movement.* N COUNT+of/to ↑ subordinate

hand-me-down, hand-me-downs. **Hand-me-downs** are things, especially clothing, which have been used by other people before you and which have been given to you for your use. EG *...my elder sister's hand-me-downs... ...hand-me-down clothes.* N COUNT : USU PL = cast-off

handout /hændaʊt/, **handouts**. A **handout** is 1 a gift of money, clothing, or food, which is given free to poor people by people who are richer than they are or by an organization or charity. EG *We said that we wouldn't be relying on handouts from anyone for our future... 'Tennis star lives off handouts from his parents,' the headlines screamed.* N COUNT ↑ donation 2 a document which gives information about a particular company, event, etc, and is used to publicize that company or event. EG *The handout explains what that means... ...a pile of unread public relations handouts and shiny magazines.* N COUNT = leaflet 3 a paper containing a summary of information or topics which will be dealt with in a lecture or talk. N COUNT

hand-picked; also spelled without a hyphen. If someone is **hand-picked**, they are very carefully chosen by someone in authority for a particular purpose or a particular job. EG *The team were all hand picked.* V+O : USU PASS ▸ used as an adjective. EG *...their own hand-picked guards.* ▸ ADJ CLASSIF = select

handrail /hændreɪl/, **handrails**. A **handrail** is a long piece of metal or wood which is fixed near stairs or high places where people could fall, for people to hold for support as they walk. EG *I had to cling with both hands to the handrails because the wind was so strong.* N COUNT ↑ barrier = railing

handshake /hændʃeɪk/, **handshakes**. If you give someone a **handshake**, you take their right hand with your own right hand and hold it firmly or move it up and down, as a sign of greeting or to show that you have agreed about something such as a business deal. EG *He came to the door to welcome me with a handshake... His handshake was firm and solid.* ● See also **golden handshake**. N COUNT

handsome /hænsəm/. 1 A man who is **handsome** has an attractive face with regular features. EG *He was a tall, dark, and undeniably handsome man... ...a tall driver with a handsome face.* ADJ QUALIT = good-looking

2 A woman who is **handsome** has an attractive, smart appearance, especially with features that are large and regular rather than small and delicate and that are considered to show strength of character. EG *...a strikingly handsome woman.* ADJ QUALIT = majestic

3 A building, garden, etc that is **handsome** is large and well made with an attractive appearance. EG *...handsome big apartment buildings... ...a rather handsome rug... It is a handsome place with green lawns and tall trees.* ◊ **handsomely**. EG *...handsomely proportioned rooms.* ADJ QUALIT = elegant ◊ ADV = elegantly

4 A **handsome** sum of money is a large or generous amount that is often more than you expected. EG *The rate of return on these farmers' outlay was a handsome 57 per cent.* ◊ **handsomely**. EG *The system rewards handsomely those who control capital or land.* ADJ CLASSIF : ATTRIB ↑ good ◊ ADV WITH VB = generously

5 A **handsome** situation, event, action, etc is pleasing to you because of particular good qualities that it has. EG *He had a handsome dinner given in his honour.* ◊ **handsomely**. EG *The centres are handsomely equipped and teaching in them is a pleasure.* ADJ CLASSIF : ATTRIB = splendid ◊ ADV = admirably

handstand /hændstænd/, **handstands**. A **handstand** is an exercise in which you balance yourself upside down on your hands with your body and legs straight up in the air. EG *Mummy, I did three handstands in the playground today.* N COUNT

hand-to-hand. A **hand-to-hand** fight is one in which the people fighting are very close together, fighting with their hands or sometimes with knives. EG *It was hand-to-hand fighting from then on.* ADJ CLASSIF : ATTRIB, OR ADV WITH VB

hand-to-mouth. A **hand-to-mouth** existence is a way of life in which you have hardly enough food or money to live on. ● See also **hand**. ADJ CLASSIF : ATTRIB, OR ADV WITH VB ↑ poor

handwriting /hændraɪtɪŋ/. Someone's **handwriting** is their style of writing which they do with a pen or pencil rather than a typewriter and which can usually be recognized as belonging to them. EG *He looked at his son's laborious handwriting... Handwriting varies from individual to individual.* N UNCOUNT ↑ writing

handwritten /hændrɪtə⁰n/. A piece of writing that is **handwritten** is one that someone has written using a pen or pencil rather than by typing. ADJ CLASSIF

handy /hændi¹/, **handier, handiest**. 1 Something that is **handy** is useful and easy to use or do. EG *An electric kettle is very handy... A pushchair is a handy way to take a young child shopping.* ● *If you say that something will* **come in handy**, you mean that it will be useful; an informal expression. EG *Rick's raft came in handy for shipping camera gear up the river.* ADJ QUALIT = convenient ● PHR : VB INFLECTS

2 Someone who is **handy** with something such as a particular tool is skilful at using it; an informal use. EG *He was handy with an axe... Newmarket was crowded with village boys who had a handy way with horses.* ADJ QUALIT = good

3 A place that is **handy** is nearby and convenient; an informal use. EG *The shops are very handy–only five minutes' walk.* ● If you **keep** something **handy** or **have** something **handy**, you keep it quite near so that you can easily use it when you need it. EG *Keep a spare fuse handy by the fuse box... It's a good idea to have a packet of frozen peas handy.* ADJ QUALIT ↑ close ● PHR : VB INFLECTS

handyman /hændi¹mæn/, **handymen**. A **handyman** is a man who is good at making things or repairing things, especially in his own home. N COUNT

hang /hæŋ/, **hangs, hanging, hanged, hung**. The forms **hang, hangs, hanging, hung** are used for the verb except in paragraph 6 where the forms are **hang, hangs, hanging, hanged**. 1 If you **hang** something in a high place or position or you **hang it up**, you attach it there so that it does not touch the ground. EG *He was hanging his coat in the hall... Howard hangs up his scarf on the hook behind the door.* V+O : USU+A, OR PHRASAL VB : V+O+ADV ↑ suspend

2 Something that **is hanging** or **is hanging up** in a high place or position is attached there so that it does not touch the ground. EG *There are some old tools hanging up in the shed... ...some washing hanging on a line.* V OR PHRASAL VB : V+ADV, USU CONT ↑ suspended

3 Something that **hangs** somewhere is heavy or loose so that it swings slightly or can move freely from the place where it is attached. EG *Her long hair hung over her face... The whole engine was hanging on by only one bolt... ...a silver peace symbol hanging on a chain around her neck.* ● to **hang by a thread**: see **thread**. ● If you **hang** your **head**, you look down at the ground instead of looking at other people, usually because you are upset, ashamed, or embarrassed. EG *'I meant nothing to you,' he said bitterly, hanging his head.* V : USU+A = dangle ● PHR : VB INFLECTS

4 If you **hang** a wall with pictures or other objects, you decorate it by attaching the pictures or objects to it. EG *The walls were hung with some really valuable oil paintings... ...a chamber hung with banners and shields.* ● See also **hanging**. V+O+A (with) : USU PASS ↑ adorn

5 Cloth or clothing that **hangs** in a particular way falls or flows in this way when it is worn or arranged somewhere. EG *Loosely woven material will hang unevenly in curtains... ...altered suits, hanging uneasily around his thin body.* ▸ used as a noun to refer to the way in which the cloth hangs. EG *The weight affects the hang of the material.* V+A ↑ move = fall ▸ N SING : the+N = drape

6 To **hang** someone means to kill them by tying a rope around their neck and taking away the support V+O (NG/REFL)

from under their feet so that they hang in the air. EG *Rebecca Smith was hanged in 1849... He tried to hang himself.* • See also **hanging**.

7 When a butcher **hangs** certain types of meat or when meat **hangs**, it is left to decompose slightly in order to improve the flavour before being cooked. EG *He's very partial to roasted pheasant; he hangs it for eighteen days... ...leaving venison for a week or so to hang.* V-ERG ⇑ mature

8 Something that **hangs** in the air remains there without appearing to move or change position. EG *...white clouds hanging motionless in the sky... The smell of paint hung in the air... Her breath hung round her face.* V+A ⇑ remain = linger

9 Something such as a problem that **hangs** over you or over a situation worries you and makes the situation unpleasant, difficult, or dangerous. EG *...the threat of deportation hanging over me... Question-marks hung over her relationship with Cliff.* V+A *(over)* • A problem or question that **hangs in the air** is a difficult or serious one which concerns people but which they cannot or will not answer. EG *None of them spoke, but the question hung in the air.* • PHR : VB INFLECTS ⇑ remain

10 You say **hang** something to indicate that you are not concerned about something, for example about the consequences of doing something; an informal use. EG *Hang the expense.* V+O : ONLY IMPER = blow

11 You say you're **hanged** if you'll do something in order to emphasize that you are determined not to do it; an informal expression. EG *I'm hanged if I'm going all that way to fetch her.* PHR : USED AS C, USU+*if*

13 If you say **'Hang on in there'** to someone, you are encouraging them to keep trying to do something and not to give up even though it might be difficult; an informal expression used in American English. EG *Grab his attention and then hang on in there.* CONVENTION ⇑ continue ≠ give up

14 If you **hang loose**, you remain calm, happy, or in control of a situation; an informal expression used in American English. CONVENTION

14 If you **get the hang of** something such as a skill or activity, you begin to understand or realize how to do it; an informal expression. EG *Once you have got the hang of it, you'll be alright.* PHR : VB INFLECTS = suss out

hang about. 1 If you **hang about**, you stay in the same place doing nothing, usually because you are waiting for something or someone; an informal expression. EG *Three quarters of a soldier's life is spent hanging about doing nothing.* PHRASAL VB : V+ ADV/PREP

2 If you ask someone to **hang about**, you ask them to wait or stop for a moment what they are doing or saying; an informal expression. CONVENTION

hang around. 1 If you **hang around**, you stay in the same place doing nothing, usually because you are waiting for something or someone; an informal expression. EG *We would have to hang around for a while... Some of the men would be hanging around the doors at opening time.* PHRASAL VB : V+ ADV/PREP ⇑ wait = hang about

2 If you **hang around** with someone, or in a particular place, you spend a lot of time in the company of the person or in the place; an informal expression. EG *I enjoyed hanging around Parliament listening to debates... He was always hanging around his bigger brother... I was becoming more cynical, probably from hanging around with newspapermen.* PHRASAL VB : V+ ADV : USU+A, OR V+PREP ⇑ frequent

hang back. If you **hang back, 1** you stay in a place such as a school or an office after everyone else has gone home. EG *Often I hung back after classes to ask more questions.* **2** you are unwilling or afraid to do something. EG *The rest of the children hung back, watching her.* PHRASAL VB : V+ ADV ⇑ wait = stay behind; PHRASAL VB : V+ ADV ⇑ wait = hesitate

hang on. 1 If you ask someone to **hang on**, you ask them to wait or stop for a moment what they are doing or saying; an informal expression. EG *Hang on a minute... Hang on, I've just got to think about this.* CONVENTION = hang about

2 If you are able to **hang on** in a difficult or dangerous situation, you can just manage to keep living or working there until the situation improves. EG *If they can hang on, things will get better.* PHRASAL VB : V+ ADV = hold out

3 Something that **hangs on** something else depends on it in order to be successful. EG *Everything hangs on money at the moment... It was a tricky area and his own political future hung on it.* PHRASAL VB : V+ PREP

4 If you **hang on** someone's **every word**, you listen very carefully to what they say. EG *He told them stories around the campfire, the boys hanging fascinated on his every word.* PHR : VB INFLECTS

5 If you **hang on** or you **hang onto** something, you hold it very tightly in order to support yourself or protect yourself. EG *We were both hanging onto the side of the boat... Claude moaned, and hung on to Tom's shoulder... Hang on, here we go.* PHRASAL VB : V+ ADV/PREP = hold tight

6 If you **hang on** or you **hang onto** a position or condition that you have such as power or safety, you try hard to keep it when something is threatening it. EG *Fear is a powerful motive for hanging on to power... ...patients who managed to hang on to life for three to four months.* PHRASAL VB : V+ ADV/PREP ⇑ hold = cling on to

hang onto. If you **hang onto** something, **1** you hold it very tightly in your hands to stop someone taking it from you. EG *She hung onto the keys as though her life depended on it.* **2** you keep it even though it may not be useful or valuable. EG *There's no point in hanging onto old letters.* PHRASAL VB : V+ PREP = grip; PHRASAL VB : V+ PREP ⇑ retain

hang out. 1 If you **hang out** clothes that you have washed, you hang them on a clothes line to dry. EG *Mrs Poulter was hanging out her washing.* PHRASAL VB : V+ O+ADV = peg out

2 If you **hang out** in a particular place or area, you live there or spend a lot of time there; an informal expression. EG *I don't hang out at the factory.* • See also **hangout**. PHRASAL VB : V+ ADV+A ⇑ frequent

3 If you **let it all hang out**, you relax completely and enjoy yourself without worrying about hiding your emotions or behaving politely; an informal expression used mainly in American English. EG *After midnight we're gonna let it all hang out.* PHR : VB INFLECTS ≠ repress

hang round means the same as hang around.

hang together. 1 Two people or groups that **hang together** stay with each other and support each other even though they may disagree on some things. EG *We have argued. But we have in the end hung together... The reformists and the hardliners have hung together in the same party.* PHRASAL VB : V+ ADV = stick together

2 Things such as ideas that **hang together** are properly organized and fit together reasonably. EG *All aspects of the struggle hang together.* PHRASAL VB : V+ ADV = correspond

hang up. 1 If you **hang up** or you **hang up** the phone, you end a phone call and put back the receiver. EG *'Thank you. Goodbye.' He hung up... 'Good night.' He hung up the phone.* PHRASAL VB : V+ ADV, OR V+O+ ADV

2 If you **hang up** on someone you are speaking to on the phone, you end the phone call suddenly and unexpectedly by putting back the receiver. EG *He didn't answer. He just hung up on me.* PHRASAL VB : V+ ADV

3 If you **hang up** something that you use for a particular activity, you stop using it because you are giving up the activity. EG *If your one joy is playing squash don't hang up your racquet.* • See also **hang**, **hang-up**, **hung up**. PHRASAL VB : V+ ADV = put away

hangar /hæŋə/, **hangars**. A **hangar** is a large building in which aircraft are kept. N COUNT

hangdog /hæŋdɒg/. Someone who looks **hangdog** has a guilty or ashamed expression on their face. ADJ QUALIT = shamefaced

hanger /hæŋə/, **hangers**. A **hanger** is the same as a coat hanger. EG *He took off his shirt, put it on a hanger, and hung it in the wardrobe.* N COUNT

hanger-on, hangers-on. A **hanger-on** is someone who tries to be friendly and spend a lot of time with a richer or more important person or group, especially for their own advantage; used showing disapproval. EG *...a small group of writers, artists and assorted hangers-on.* N COUNT = parasite

hang-glider, hang-gliders; also spelled without a hyphen. A **hang-glider** is **1** a glider for one person, with which they can fly in the air. It consists of a large piece of cloth over a frame which you hang from in a harness. **2** a person who flies using a hang-glider. N COUNT; N COUNT

hang-gliding is the activity of flying in a hang-glider. N UNCOUNT

hanging /hæŋɪŋ/, **hangings**. **1 Hanging** is the practice of executing people by hanging them. EG *Every one of them was in favour of hanging... ...the hanging debate.* N UNCOUNT ⇑ execution

2 A **hanging** is **2.1** the act or occasion of killing a person by hanging them. EG *The crowds at Tyburn used to find a hanging entertaining.* **2.2** a large piece of cloth that you put as a decoration on a wall or as a curtain over a window. EG *She stared at a Chinese silk hanging on the wall.* N COUNT/ UNCOUNT; N COUNT : USU+ SUPP

3 A **hanging** question or issue is one which has not yet been decided. EG *There's no immediate answer so I just leave it as a hanging question.* ADJ CLASSIF : ATTRIB ⇑ uncertain

hangman /hæŋmə³n/, **hangmen**. A **hangman** is a man whose job is to execute people by hanging them. N COUNT ⇑ executioner

hangout /hæŋaʊt/, **hangouts**. A **hangout** is a place where you like spending a lot of time because you can relax there and meet other people; an informal word. EG *This bar became one of my favourite hangouts... The station served as a hangout for the town derelicts and delinquents.* N COUNT+SUPP = haunt

hangover /hæŋəʊvə/, **hangovers**. A **hangover** is 1 a feeling of sickness and headache that you have in the morning if you have drunk a lot of alcohol the night before. EG *Colin and Mary are suffering from a hangover... He claimed that vodka didn't give you hangovers.* N COUNT ⇑ condition 2 something that results from ideas or attitudes which people had in the past but which are no longer generally held or accepted. EG *This feeling should be attributed to habit, a hangover from earlier, more primitive times.* N COUNT+*from/of* ⇑ remainder = relic

hang-up, hang-ups. A **hang-up** is a feeling of fear or embarrassment about something that makes it very difficult for you to deal with certain situations and ideas; an informal word. EG *He's got a hang-up about flying... ...adolescent hang-ups.* N COUNT = problem, inhibition

hank /hæŋk/, **hanks**. A **hank** is an amount of wool, rope, string, etc that has been loosely wound in a ball or tied together. EG *...spinning wool from a hank onto a wooden spindle.* N COUNT ⇑ length = skein

hanker /hæŋkə/, **hankers, hankering, hankered**. If you **hanker** after something or you **hanker** for something, you have a great desire or longing for it. EG *We always hankered after a bungalow of our own... However much we may hanker after comfort and security, we have to face reality... The miracle I hankered for did happen after all.* V+A *(after/for)* ⇑ want

hankering /hæŋkə⁰rɪŋ/, **hankerings**. A **hankering** for something is a great desire or longing for it. EG *If you give way to this hankering for food you will become fat.* N COUNT+*for* = craving

hanky /hæŋki¹/, **hankies**; also spelled **hankie**. A **hanky** is the same as a handkerchief; an informal word. N COUNT

hanky-panky /hæŋki¹ pæŋki¹/ is improper but not very serious sexual activity between two people; an informal word used humorously. EG *I caught them having a little hanky-panky in the car.* N UNCOUNT ⇑ impropriety

hansom /hænsəm/, **hansoms**. A **hansom** or a **hansom cab** is a horse-drawn carriage with two wheels and a fixed hood. Hansom cabs were used in former times. N COUNT

haphazard /hæphæzəd/. Something that is **haphazard** is not at all organized or arranged according to a plan. EG *They have a most haphazard system of record-keeping... It was done on a haphazard basis.* ADJ QUALIT = casual, careless
◊ **haphazardly**. EG *...amid all the papers haphazardly strewn on desks.* ◊ ADV WITH VB = randomly

hapless /hæplɪ²s/. A **hapless** person is unlucky; a literary word. EG *...the hapless victim of a misplaced murder attempt.* ADJ CLASSIF: ATTRIB = unfortunate

happen /hæpə⁰n/, **happens, happening, happened**. 1 Something that **happens** 1.1 occurs or is done without being planned; usually used of something that cannot be controlled or prevented. EG *The accident happened at 10 o'clock... It happened that I wasn't at home when they called.* V: USU+A 1.2 occurs as the result or effect of a situation or course of action. EG *What would happen if the police found out about this?... I pressed the button, but nothing happened.* V = follow
1.3 is created or achieved over a period of time, often as part of a process of change and development. EG *They said things would soon improve, but this has not happened.* V = materialize
2 Something that **happens** to someone or something is done or takes place with a resulting effect on the person or thing, often one that is unpleasant. EG *If anything happens to the car, you'll have to pay for it.* V+A *(to)* ⇑ be damaging
3 Someone who **happens** to do something does it as a result of chance. EG *If you happen to see Jane, ask her to phone me... There happened to be a policeman on the corner, so I asked him the way..* V+*to*-INF
4 If you say to someone that something **happens** to be true, you give this information to them in a rather indignant way, for example when they have said something about it that makes you cross. EG *You may think that about him, but he happens to be a good friend of mine.* V+*to*-INF ● You say **as it happens** before a statement when the statement is rather surprising. EG *As it happens, I've got my things with me here.* ● PHR: USED AS ADV SEN = actually

happen on. If you **happen on** someone or something, you find them or meet them by chance; an old-fashioned literary expression. PHRASAL VB: V+PREP, HAS PASS

happening /hæpə⁰nɪŋ/, **happenings**. A **happening** is something that happens, often in a way that is unexpected or hard to explain. EG *There have been some strange happenings in the village recently.* N COUNT: USU MOD+N = incident

happy /hæpi¹/, **happier, happiest**. 1 Someone who is **happy** has feelings of pleasure, for example because something nice has happened or because they feel satisfied with their life. EG *I was happy to hear that you passed your exam... This will make the children happy.* ADJ QUALIT ⇑ content = pleased ≠ sad ▸ used of a person's expression. EG *...a happy smile.* ▸ = cheerful ◊ **happily**. EG *We laughed and chatted happily together.* ◊ ADV ◊ **happiness**. EG *Money did not bring happiness.* ◊ N UNCOUNT
2 A time or place that is **happy** is full of happy feelings and pleasant experiences, or has an atmosphere in which people feel happy. EG *We spent many happy hours playing on the beach... Did she have a happy childhood?... It was the happiest day of my life... The school seems to be a happy place.* ADJ QUALIT: USU ATTRIB ⇑ pleasing
3 If you are **happy** about a situation or arrangement, you are satisfied with it, for example because you think that something is being done in the right way. EG *I'm not very happy about the way this decision was reached... Are you happy about the prospect of three more years at university?... She wasn't happy with his work and she made him do it again... He seems quite happy to let things go on as they are.* ADJ QUALIT: PRED, USU+*about/with/*REPORT-CL/*to*-INF = content
4 If you say you are **happy** to do something, you mean that you are very willing to do it. EG *We'll be happy to help if you need us.* ADJ QUALIT: PRED+*to*-INF ◊ **happily**. EG *He said he would happily lend us the money.* ◊ ADV WITH VB = gladly
5 **Happy** is used in greetings to say that you hope someone will enjoy a special occasion. EG *Happy birthday!... Happy New Year!* ● **many happy returns**: see **return**. ADJ QUALIT: USED IN CONVENTIONS
6 A **happy** chance or coincidence is one that results in something pleasant happening. EG *By a happy coincidence, we were all on the same train.* ADJ QUALIT: ATTRIB ⇑ lucky = fortunate ◊ **happily**. EG *Happily, no one was hurt in the accident.* ◊ ADV SEN = fortunately

happy-go-lucky. Someone who is **happy-go-lucky** enjoys life and does not worry about the future. ADJ QUALIT = easy-going

hara-kiri /hærə kɪri¹/ is a Japanese method of suicide in which a man cuts his own stomach open. Hara-kiri was traditionally regarded in Japan as the honourable way to avoid disgrace. N UNCOUNT

harangue /hə³ræŋ/, **harangues, haranguing, harangued**. A **harangue** is a long, forceful speech that someone makes to try and persuade other people to accept their opinions; often used showing disapproval. EG *After the play he delivered a long harangue about how dreadful the English theatre was... Whenever they started their harangues, he simply sat back and stopped listening.* N COUNT: IF+PREP THEN *about/at/against* = tirade ▸ used as a verb. EG *Smith harangued his fellow students and persuaded them to walk out in protest... One of the speakers at the rally started to harangue the crowd against Communism.* ▸ V+O ⇑ speak

harass /hærəs/, **harasses, harassing, harassed**. If you **harass** someone, you trouble them or annoy them, for example by attacking them repeatedly or by causing them as many problems as you can. EG *Some governments have chosen to harass and persecute the rural poor... He stated that unless I ceased harassing Sir William he would not be prepared to defend me.* V+O = hound, pester

harassed /hærəst/. Someone who is **harassed** feels strained because they have too many jobs to do or problems to cope with. EG *Many harassed working mothers will continue to use convenience food, no matter how expensive... As the pressure gets worse, people get more harassed and work is rushed.* ADJ QUALIT = hard-pressed, careworn

harassing /hærəsɪŋ/. Something that is **harassing** makes you feel strained because you have too many jobs to do or problems to cope with. EG *I have had a particularly busy and harassing day.* ADJ QUALIT ⇑ demanding = troublesome

harassment /hærəsmə²nt/ is 1 behaviour which is intended to trouble or annoy someone, for example repeated attacks on them or attempts to cause them problems. EG *Owing to harassment by patrol aircraft, the convoy changed course.* N UNCOUNT ⇑ annoyance = hounding 2 a feeling of strain when you have too many jobs to do or problems to N UNCOUNT = aggravation cope with. EG *Typical signs of overwork are nervous tension, irritability, harassment, severe headaches.*

harbinger /hɑːbɪndʒə/, **harbingers**. A **harbinger** of something that is going to happen in the future is a person or thing that is a sign that it is going to happen or that foretells it; a literary word. EG *The sudden oil price rise was a harbinger of future problems... The Beatles were the harbingers of a new style of living.* — N COUNT : USU + *of* = herald

harbour /hɑːbə/, **harbours, harbouring, harboured**; also spelled **harbor** in American English. **1** A **harbour** is **1.1** an area of water on a coast which is protected from the open sea by land or strong walls, so that boats can be left there safely. EG *...a small hotel overlooking the picturesque fishing harbour of Zeebrugge... Some of the best natural harbours in the world are there.* — N COUNT : ALSO IN NAMES AFTER N ⇑ mooring. **1.2** a place where you are safe and free from danger. EG *...a harbour of refuge.* — N COUNT + SUPP = haven

2 If you **harbour** a hope, fear, or other emotion, you have it in your mind over a long period of time. EG *I was unable to dismiss the fears I harboured for my safety... She begins to harbour resentments that can turn to hate.* — V+O ⇑ feel = hold

3 If you **harbour** someone who is wanted by the police or is in other difficulty, you help them by allowing them to stay secretly in your house. EG *You must remember that she has broken the law, and that you could get into trouble for harbouring her.* — V+O ⇑ protect = shelter

hard /hɑːd/, **harder, hardest**. **1** Something that is **hard 1.1** is very firm and stiff rather than soft to touch, and usually not easily bent, cut, or broken. EG *The green fruits were as hard as rocks... The ground was baked hard.* — ADJ QUALIT = solid ≠ soft ◊ **hardness**. EG *We gave them cushions to ease the hardness of the benches.* — ◊ N UNCOUNT **1.2** is very difficult to do or understand. EG *He found it hard to make friends... I don't see the point in doing it the hard way... That is a very hard question to answer... The exam was extremely hard... ...stories that are hard to understand.* — ADJ QUALIT ≠ easy, simple ● If you are **hard pushed, hard put**, or **hard pressed** to do something, you have great difficulty doing it. EG *We'll be hard pushed to finish this tonight!... Things are changing so quickly these days that we're hard pressed to keep up to date... One would be hard put to think of a better plan.* — ● PHR : USED AS C, USU + *to*-INF ● to **be a hard nut to crack**: see **nut**. ● to **play hard to get**: see **play**. ● to **drive a hard bargain**: see **bargain**. ● See also **hard-pressed**.

2 If you work **hard** doing something, you do it with a lot of effort. EG *He had worked hard all his life... I cannot stand upright any more, no matter how hard I try... She works hard at keeping herself fit.* — ADV WITH VB = doggedly, assiduously

3 Something that is **hard** involves a lot of work and effort. EG *It was very hard work in the shop... This has been a long hard day.* — ADJ QUALIT = exhausting ● Something that **is hard going** is difficult and requires a lot of effort to do. EG *It was hard going at first, over the rough ground.* — ● PHR : VB INFLECTS ⇑ be difficult

4 If you listen, look, or think **hard**, you do it carefully and with a great deal of attention. EG *When I look hard I can make out stars overhead... He listened hard but could hear only silence... Think hard about what I'm offering.* — ADV WITH VB

5 If you move something or push something **hard**, you move or push it with a lot of force. EG *She slammed the door hard behind us... Check that the cord is tight by tugging it hard.* — ADV WITH VB ⇑ strongly = forcefully ▸ used as an adjective. EG *Give it a hard push.* — ▸ ADJ QUALIT = strong

6 If you do something **hard**, you do it strongly or intensely for quite a long time. EG *We laughed so hard she wondered what she had said wrong... ...a baby who cries hard every afternoon or evening... It's still raining hard.* — ADV WITH VB ⇑ a lot

7 If you turn **hard** in a particular direction, you move suddenly and sharply in that direction. EG *At the end of the lane bear hard round to your left... ...forcing the ship to go hard astern.* — ADV : ADV+A ⇑ quickly

8 A person or event that follows **hard** behind another person or **hard** upon another event follows closely behind the person or happens immediately after the event. EG *I hurried off up the steps with my sister hard behind me... It will be difficult to find finance for such a project following hard upon the opening of the new sports centre.* — ADV : ADV+A ● to **follow hard on the heels of** something: see **heel**. ● Something such as a building or street that is **hard by** something else is very close to it. EG *...Cleveland Place, hard by Bruntsfield Square.* — ● PREP ⇑ by = near

9 Someone who is **hard** shows no kindness or sympathy towards other people. EG *She's very hard, no pity for anyone.* — ADJ QUALIT ▸ used of a person's facial expression. EG *...a hard, ironic smile... His hard grey eyes began to soften a little.* — ▸ = cold ◊ **hardness**. EG *A peculiar hardness had settled itself upon her features.* — ◊ N UNCOUNT ● Someone who is **as hard as nails** doesn't care at all about how their actions might hurt or affect other people. EG *That man's as hard as nails: he just sat there and laughed!* — ● PHR : USED AS C = ruthless

10 If you are **hard** on someone, you treat them severely or unkindly. EG *Don't be hard on her... Goodness, that seems a bit hard on the wife.* — ADJ QUALIT : PRED + *on* ▸ used as an adverb. EG *The government's first reaction to the riots was to clamp down hard.* — ▸ ADV WITH VB = heavily ● If you feel **hard done by**, you feel that you have not been treated fairly. EG *He sat in a corner feeling miserable and hard done by.* — ● PHR : USED AS C = wronged ● Someone or something that **is hard hit** by something is affected very severely by it. EG *...schools in South London that have been particularly hard hit by government spending cuts.* — ● PHR : VB INFLECTS ● If you **take** something unpleasant **hard**, you are very upset and severely affected by it. EG *My father was taking the whole thing very hard.* — ● PHR : VB INFLECTS

11 Something that is **hard** on a person or thing affects them in a way that is likely to cause them damage or suffering. EG *Why not get a job as a shop assistant: hard on the feet but it can be more interesting than you think... These rough roads are hard on the car's suspension... The job's OK, but it's a bit hard on the nerves.* — ADJ QUALIT : PRED + *on* = tough

12 A life or period of time that is **hard** is difficult and unpleasant because you have so many problems that you need to struggle constantly to succeed or survive. EG *Their life is extremely hard... Those who have been through hard times are glad to pay back the help they've had.* — ADJ QUALIT = tough ≠ easy ◊ **hardness**. EG *These men were only in their fifties but the hardness of their lives made them look older.* — ◊ N UNCOUNT = harshness

13 The weather or a season that is **hard** is very cold and severe. EG *Hard winters seem now less frequent... ...a hard frost.* — ADJ QUALIT

14 Something such as a colour or sound that is **hard** is harsh or bright and often unpleasant to see or hear. EG *...a hard blue... Kunta made his voice hard.* — ADJ QUALIT

15 **Hard** evidence or facts are definitely true and do not need to be questioned. EG *We have no hard evidence to indicate that he is the culprit... ...they respected accuracy, worshipped hard facts.* — ADJ CLASSIF : ATTRIB = real ≠ questionable

16 Water that is **hard** contains a lot of lime so that it leaves a whitish coating on kettles and soap does not lather well in it. EG *One way to counteract hard water is by using a water softener.* — ADJ QUALIT ≠ soft

17 **Hard** drugs are very strong illegal drugs such as heroin or cocaine. — ADJ CLASSIF : ATTRIB

18 A **hard** sound in phonetics is one such as the letters 'c' or 'g' as they are pronounced in the words 'cat' or 'give', and not as in the words 'cinema' or 'gin'. — ADJ CLASSIF ≠ soft

hard and fast. **1** **Hard and fast** rules cannot be changed and should be obeyed. EG *There isn't any hard and fast rule about the use of hyphens in English.* — ADJ CLASSIF : USU ATTRIB ⇑ clear = strict

2 **Hard and fast** information is information which is definitely true or correct. EG *We have very little hard and fast information on this.* — ADJ CLASSIF : USU ATTRIB ⇑ definite

hardback /hɑːdbæk/, **hardbacks**. A **hardback** is a book which has a stiff hard cover. EG *The publisher proposed to do both a hardback and a cheap paperback edition... The book was published in hardback.* — N COUNT, OR *in* + N ≠ paperback

hard-bitten. **Hard-bitten** people are determined to get what they want without having any sympathy for the people they might hurt or affect. EG *...hard-bitten women... They were given revolutionary and hard-bitten government but also order and security.* — ADJ QUALIT ⇑ tough = hard-nosed

hardboard /hɑːdbɔːd/ is a kind of wood. It is made by pressing very small pieces of wood very closely together and you buy it in thin, flexible sheets. EG *...the thin hardboard walls of the dressing room.* — N UNCOUNT

hard-boiled. **1** A **hard-boiled** egg has been boiled in its shell until the yolk and the white are hard. — ADJ CLASSIF ⇑ cooked

2 People who are **hard-boiled** are tough and do not show their feelings, usually because the experiences they have suffered have made them bitter. EG *...antisocial, hard-boiled youngsters glorying in their reputation as thugs.* — ADJ QUALIT = cynical

hard cash is money in the form of notes and coins as opposed to a cheque or a credit card. — N UNCOUNT

hard core; spelled with a hyphen when used before another noun. **1** A **hard core** of members or the **hard-core** members of a group are the ones who are most involved and concerned with the activities of that group. EG *The years thinned the ranks considerably and left only a hard core of members.* — N SING WITH DET : ALSO + *of* + N IN PL; ⇑ centre

2 Hard core consists of pieces of broken stone that are used as a base on which to build roads. — N UNCOUNT

hard currency, hard currencies. A **hard currency** is one which is unlikely to lose its value and so is considered to be a good one to have or to invest in. EG *Is sterling any longer a hard currency?* — N UNCOUNT/COUNT

hard drink is strong alcoholic drink such as whisky, gin, or brandy. — N UNCOUNT; = spirits

hard-drinking. A **hard-drinking** person is one who frequently drinks large quantities of alcohol. EG *...an impetuous, loud-mouthed, hard-drinking actor.* — ADJ QUALIT : ATTRIB; = boozy

harden /hɑːdən/, **hardens, hardening, hardened. 1** When something **hardens** or when you **harden** it, it becomes stiff or firm. EG *The glue dries very fast and hardens in an hour... This is then dipped in cold water to harden the wax.* — V-ERG; ⇑ solidify; = set

2 When you **harden** your ideas or attitudes or when they **harden**, they become fixed and you become more determined than ever that you will not change them. EG *The organization has hardened its attitude to the crisis.* ◇ **hardening.** EG *It would almost certainly result in a hardening of Allied opposition and determination.* — V-ERG; ⇑ strengthen; ≠ weaken; ◇ N UNCOUNT; = toughening

3 When prices, economies, etc **harden**, they become much more stable than they were. — V; ⇑ stabilize

4 When events **harden** people or when people **harden**, they become less easily affected emotionally and less sympathetic and gentle than they were before. EG *Life in the camp had hardened her considerably... It was a sight that should make even the most hardened ruler open his eyes.* — V-ERG; ⇑ toughen

5 When facts **harden**, they become more certain, definite, and true. EG *As time went by the evidence began to harden.* — V

hardened /hɑːdənd/ means having so much experience of something that you are no longer affected by it in the way that other people would be. EG *The report claims that young people put in prison are corrupted by hardened criminals.* — ADJ CLASSIF : USU ATTRIB

hard-headed. Someone who is **hard-headed** is practical and determined to get what they want, refusing to allow emotions to affect their actions. EG *...this hard-headed brother of mine.* ▸ used also of people's behaviour or attitudes. EG *...a nice mixture of fantasy and hard-headed realism.* — ADJ QUALIT; ▸ = shrewd

hard-hearted. Someone who is **hard-hearted** has no sympathy for other people and does not care if people are hurt or made unhappy. EG *How can you be so hard-hearted?* — ADJ QUALIT; ⇑ uncaring; = callous

hard labour; also spelled **hard labor** in American English. **Hard labour** is physical work which is difficult and tiring, and requires a great deal of effort. In some countries it is used as a punishment for a crime. EG *He was condemned to six months hard labour.* — N UNCOUNT

hard left. You use the expression the **hard left** to describe those members of a left wing political group or party who have the most extreme beliefs about the sort of society they want to create and about the sort of policies their group should adopt to achieve this. — N SING/PLURAL : *the*+N; ⇑ socialists

hard line, hard lines; spelled with a hyphen when used as an adjective. If someone takes a **hard line** on something, they have a firm, uncompromising policy which they refuse to change. EG *He applauded the president's hard line on the issue.* ▸ used as an adjective. EG *The Red Fighters are spreading their hard-line doctrine of revolution.* ● See also **hard luck.** — N COUNT; ⇑ attitude; ▸ ADJ QUALIT : ATTRIB

hardliner /hɑːdlaɪnə/, **hardliners.** A **hardliner** is a person who supports a strict, fixed set of ideas that are often extreme, and who refuses to accept any change in them. EG *Political power in this country alternates between hardliners and moderates within the ruling party.* — N COUNT

hard luck. You might say **'Hard luck'** or **'Hard lines'** to someone to say that you are sorry they have not got or done something that they had wanted to get or do; an informal expression. EG *Did you lose? Hard luck!* — CONVENTION; = tough luck

hard-luck story, hard-luck stories. If you tell someone a **hard-luck story**, you tell them about some awful things that have happened to you in order to get help, sympathy, or money from them. — N COUNT; = sob story

hardly /hɑːdli[1]/. **1 Hardly** adds a negative quality to what you are saying and so means that the thing you are talking about is only just true or is not quite true. EG *I was beginning to like Sam, though I hardly knew him... The boy was hardly more than seventeen or eighteen... I could understand hardly a word.* — ADV BRD NEG; = barely, scarcely

2 Hardly is used with words like 'ever', 'any', 'anyone', etc to mean almost not, almost never, almost none, etc. EG *We meet rarely–hardly ever... She had hardly any money... It's worth hardly anything... There was hardly anywhere to go.* — ADV BRD NEG; = scarcely

3 When you use **hardly** followed by a noun followed by a negative or the word 'without', you lose most of the negative meaning and so the phrase or sentence becomes much more positive in its meaning. EG *Hardly a day goes by when we don't read about murders in the newspaper... Hardly an hour passed without loud shouting from the prisoners.* — ADV BRD NEG; ⇑ not; = scarcely

4 When you say you **can hardly** do something, you mean that it is very difficult for you to do it. EG *I can still hardly believe it... Her bedroom was so small that she could hardly move in it.* — PHR + INF; ⇑ not; = scarcely

5 If you say **hardly** had one thing happened when something else happened, or one thing had **hardly** happened when something else happened, you mean that the first event was followed immediately by the second. EG *Hardly had he uttered the words when he began laughing... The local police had hardly finished their examination when the CID arrived.* — ADV BRD NEG; ⇑ after; = no sooner had

6 Hardly is used in a slightly ironic way to mean not at all, or certainly not. EG *I will hardly need to remind you to be polite to your grandmother... Considering my experience last time, it's hardly surprising that I've stayed away.* — ADV BRD NEG; = scarcely

7 See also **hard.**

hard-nosed. Hard-nosed people are tough and realistic, and take decisions on practical grounds rather than emotional ones; an informal expression. EG *...hard-nosed economists.* ▸ used also of people's behaviour and attitudes. EG *Audiences are favouring a more hard-nosed, realistic acting style.* — ADJ QUALIT; = unsentimental; ▸ = down-to-earth

hard of hearing. If someone is **hard of hearing**, they are not able to hear properly. EG *I'm a little hard of hearing. I don't always catch everything that's said.* — ADJ QUALIT; ⇑ deaf

hard palate, hard palates. Your **hard palate** is the hard top part of the inside of your mouth, from your teeth back towards your throat: compare **soft palate.** — N COUNT

hard porn is pornography that shows sex in a very explicit, violent, or unpleasant way. — N UNCOUNT

hard-pressed. If someone is **hard-pressed**, they are under a great deal of strain and worry, usually because they have not got enough money. EG *...hard-pressed clergymen... Hard-pressed Mexican hotels are lowering their prices.* — ADJ QUALIT; ⇑ anxious; ≠ well off

hard right. You use the expression the **hard right** to describe those members of a right wing political group or party who have the most extreme beliefs about the sort of society they want to create and about the sort of policies their group should adopt to achieve this. — N SING/PLURAL : *the*+N

hard sell. The **hard sell** is a method of selling in which the salesperson puts a lot of pressure on someone to make them buy something. ▸ used as an adjective. EG *I don't like his hard sell approach.* — N SING WITH DET : USU *the*+N; ▸ ADJ CLASSIF : ATTRIB

hardship /hɑːdʃɪp/, **hardships. Hardship** is the situation someone is in when they are suffering from great difficulties and problems in life, often because they do not have enough money. EG *...a period of considerable hardship and unhappiness... Many illnesses in the elderly can result from the hardships they have suffered throughout life.* ▸ used as an adjective. EG *You may be able to get a hardship allowance.* — N UNCOUNT/COUNT; ⇑ difficulty; = privation; ▸ ADJ CLASSIF : ATTRIB

hard shoulder, hard shoulders. The **hard shoulder** is the area at the side of a motorway where you are allowed to stop if your car has broken down. EG *Pull over to the hard shoulder.* — N COUNT : USU *the*+N; ⇑ roadside

hard top, hard tops. A **hard top** is **1** a car with a metal roof which cannot be removed; usually used of a car for which there is a soft top model available. — N COUNT **2** a metal roof which can be put onto a sports car, for example during bad weather, as an alternative to a soft top. — N COUNT

hard up. If you are **hard up**, you have so little money that you cannot really afford to buy the things that you need. EG *I know we're all hard up, but everybody can afford a drink now and then... When you are setting up your own household you may be hard up for a while.* ADJ QUALIT ⇑ poor = broke

hardware /hɑːdweə/. **Hardware** is 1 tools and equipment for use in the home and garden, for example saucepans, screwdrivers, and garden tools. EG *Ask in a hardware shop for clear enamel paint.* N UNCOUNT 2 the machinery of a computer as opposed to the programs that are written for it: compare **software**. EG *Computer technology in all its phases from hardware to software has become less expensive.* N UNCOUNT 3 machinery that is used in war, for example tanks, aircraft, or missiles. EG *The biggest spenders on military hardware are the two super-powers.* N UNCOUNT

hard-wearing; also spelled without a hyphen. Something that is **hard-wearing** is strong and well made so that it lasts for a long time and stays in good condition even though it is used a lot. EG *These blankets are hard-wearing, but not so warm as wool.* ADJ QUALIT ⇑ tough = durable

hardwood /hɑːdwʊd/, **hardwoods**. A **hardwood** is a tree such as an oak tree that produces very strong, hard wood; used also of the wood produced by such a tree which is used for making good quality furniture. EG *Dyewood is a dense Indian hardwood... ...hardwood floors.* N COUNT/UNCOUNT

hardy /hɑːdi[1]/, **hardier, hardiest**. 1 People and animals that are **hardy** are strong and able to endure difficult conditions. EG *Their children are remarkably hardy... ...hardy black-faced sheep.* ADJ QUALIT = robust, tough ≠ weak ◇ **hardiness**. EG *He praised the hardiness of the American character.* ◇ N UNCOUNT

2 Plants that are **hardy** are able to survive frost and cold weather. EG *Strawberries are hardy and easy to grow in all soils.* ADJ QUALIT ⇑ tough

3 If you describe explorers, pioneers, etc as **hardy**, you mean that they are bold and adventurous. ADJ QUALIT = intrepid

hare /heə/, **hares, haring, hared**. 1 A **hare** is an animal like a rabbit but larger with long ears, long legs, and a small tail. Hares can run very fast and are sometimes hunted for their meat. N COUNT ▸ used also of the meat that people eat. EG *I wonder how much hare and venison they sell.* ▸ N UNCOUNT

2 If you **hare** off or **hare** away somewhere, you run off very fast. EG *They took one look at him and hared off.* V+A

harebrained /heəbreɪnd/. If plans or ideas are **harebrained**, they are foolish and not likely to be successful. EG *...harebrained schemes.* ADJ QUALIT = crackpot

harelip /heəlɪp/, **harelips**. If someone has a **harelip**, their upper lip is split slightly because it did not grow properly before they were born. N COUNT/UNCOUNT ⇑ defect

harem /heərəm, hɑːriːm/, **harems**. A **harem** is a group of wives or mistresses belonging to one man, especially in Muslim societies. EG *...a harem of more than a hundred wives.* N COUNT ▸ **Harem** is used also of the part of the house in which they live. EG *The children were brought up in the harem.* ▸ N COUNT ⇑ house

haricot /hærɪkəʊ/, **haricots**. **Haricots** or **haricot beans** are small pale beans that can be cooked and eaten. They are usually sold dried. N COUNT : USU PL ⇑ bean

hark /hɑːk/, **harks, harking, harked**. **'Hark!'** means 'Listen!'; an old-fashioned word. EG *...the Christmas carol, 'Hark! The Herald Angels Sing.'* CONVENTION

hark back. 1 When people **hark back** to something in the past, they remember it or remind someone of it. EG *Increasingly she harked back to our 'dear little cottage'.* PHRASAL VB : V+ADV+*to*

2 When one thing **harks back** to another thing in the past, it is similar to it or takes it as a model. EG *The decorative use of brick here harks back to the old farmhouse style.* PHRASAL VB : V+ADV+*to* ⇑ resemble

harlequin /hɑːlɪkwɪn/, **harlequins**. 1 A **harlequin** or **Harlequin** is a character in an old play who wears a mask and a costume with lots of bright colours and who plays tricks on people. N COUNT/PROPER

2 **Harlequin** means having or being a lot of different colours. EG *...harlequin light... ...a harlequin jacket.* ADJ CLASSIF : ATTRIB

harlot /hɑːlət/, **harlots**. A **harlot** is a prostitute, or a woman who looks or behaves like a prostitute; a literary word used showing disapproval. N COUNT = strumpet

harm /hɑːm/, **harms, harming, harmed**. 1 To **harm** someone means to cause them physical injury, usually on purpose. EG *I stood very still, hoping they wouldn't harm my sister and me... There should be health warnings on things that have harmed a lot of people.* V+O = hurt

2 To **harm** something or perhaps someone means to damage them or make them less effective or successful than they were. EG *Washing cannot harm the fabric... If a father is away for long periods, this can harm a child's psychological development.* V+O

3 **Harm** is 3.1 physical injury to a person or an animal which is usually caused on purpose. EG *He went in danger of physical harm.* N UNCOUNT 3.2 the damage to something which is caused by a particular course of action. EG *Much harm has been done to the earth's environment... Do prisons do more harm than good?... The men had meant no harm.* N UNCOUNT

4 If you say that someone or something will **come to no harm** or that **no harm will come** to them, you mean that they will not be hurt or damaged in any way. PHR : VB INFLECTS

5 If you say that someone or something is **out of harm's way**, you mean that 5.1 they are in a safe place away from danger or from the possibility of being damaged. EG *The presents were now hidden under the sink, out of harm's way.* PHR : USED AS AN A 5.2 they are no longer able to hurt anyone or cause damage because they have been put in a particular place. EG *He's now in prison, safely out of harm's way.* PHR : USED AS AN A

6 You can say **'No harm done'** as an informal way of telling the person you are talking to not to worry about something that has happened because it has not caused any injury or damage. EG *It's all right. No harm done.* CONVENTION

7 If you say **it does no** or **little harm to** do something or **there is no harm in** doing something, you mean that it might be worth doing, and you will not be blamed for doing it. EG *There's no harm in asking... It does no harm to try.* PHR + INF/-ING : VB INFLECTS

8 You say that something will **do** someone **no harm** when you are recommending a course of action which you think is worthwhile, helpful, or useful. EG *A bit of exercise never did anyone any harm... The publicity will do the official Labour candidate no harm at all.* PHR : VB INFLECTS = not hurt

harmful /hɑːmfʊl/. Something that is **harmful** has a bad effect on something else, especially on a person's health. EG *...a natural antibiotic which was harmful to bacteria... The rays of the sun, in excess, can be very harmful... Institutions have harmful effects on children.* ADJ QUALIT = damaging

harmless /hɑːmlɪ[2]s/. 1 Something that is **harmless** is safe to use, touch, or be near. EG *...harmless bacteria... The bomb was rendered harmless.* ADJ QUALIT ≠ harmful ◇ **harmlessly**. EG *The rocket thudded harmlessly to the ground.* ◇ ADV WITH VB

2 Someone or something that is **harmless** is unlikely to annoy other people or make them worried or upset. EG *Your brother seems harmless enough to me... Singing in the bath gives him a little harmless pleasure.* ADJ QUALIT = innocuous, inoffensive ◇ **harmlessly**. EG *His column now deals harmlessly with the antics of film stars and the trivia of television.* ◇ ADV WITH VB

harmonic /hɑːmɒnɪk/, **harmonics**. 1 **Harmonic** means composed, played, or sung using two or more notes which sound right and pleasing together. EG *...the newer harmonic structures he was always reaching for.* ADJ CLASSIF : ATTRIB ⇑ musical

2 A **harmonic** is a musical note which is produced as an overtone of another note. EG *His work exposes in its harmonics a whole region of sound neglected until now.* N COUNT : USU PL

harmonica /hɑːmɒnɪkə/, **harmonicas**. A **harmonica** is a small musical instrument. You play it by moving it across your lips and by blowing and sucking air through it. N COUNT = mouth organ

harmonious /hɑːməʊnɪəs/. 1 A relationship, agreement, discussion, etc that is **harmonious** is friendly and peaceful. EG *The two countries were enjoying tolerably harmonious relationships with one another... ...a generally harmonious debate... ...the possibility of harmonious industrial relations.* ADJ QUALIT = amicable, cordial ◇ **harmoniously**. EG *Harold Walker and I worked harmoniously together.* ◇ ADV WITH VB = amicably

2 Things which are **harmonious** have parts which make up an attractive whole and which are in proper proportion to each other. EG *The different parts of the garden fit together in a harmonious way.* ADJ QUALIT ⇑ co-ordinated = balanced ◇ **harmoniously**. EG *...trees that stooped harmoniously towards the sea.* ◇ ADV WITH VB = agreeably

3 Notes that are **harmonious** produce a pleasant sound when played or sung together. EG *...a harmonious musical chord.* ◊ **harmoniously**.
ADJ QUALIT ≠ discordant
◊ ADV WITH VB

harmonize /hɑːmənaɪz/, **harmonizes, harmonizing, harmonized**; also spelled **harmonise**. **1** If two or more things **harmonize** with each other or if you **harmonize** them, they fit in with each other as part of a system, society, etc. EG *Such events harmonized with one's view of society... The great achievements of the early Catholic church lay in harmonising the deepest impulses of its believers.*
V OR V+A (with) : RECIP, ALSO V-ERG = reconcile

2 If colours, shapes, etc **harmonize**, they form a pleasant group or whole when seen together. EG *...with the dancers' costumes harmonising with their choice in colours.*
V OR V+A (with) : RECIP

3 When people **harmonize**, they agree about issues or subjects in a friendly, peaceful way; a formal use. EG *It's difficult to get the various leaders to harmonize on the important issues.*
V OR V+A (with) : RECIP = concur

4 When someone **harmonizes**, they sing or play notes which are different from the notes in the main tune but which sound right and pleasing with the main tune. EG *He sat down next to the woman with the guitar and started harmonizing.*
V OR V+A (with) : RECIP

harmony /hɑːməni[1]/, **harmonies**. **1** If people are living or working in **harmony** with each other, they are in a state of peaceful agreement and co-operation. EG *Industry and the universities have worked together in harmony... Several incidents damaged this image of racial harmony... ...an example of people living in harmony with their environment.*
N UNCOUNT = accord, unity

2 The **harmony** of a piece of music is the pleasant combination of several different notes of music played or sung at the same time. EG *They sing in harmony... ...the harmonies of Ravel and Debussy.*
N UNCOUNT/COUNT

3 The **harmony** of something is the way in which the parts of it are combined into a suitable and attractive arrangement. EG *The harmony he perceived in the scene was, he knew, ill-founded... The composition of the painting has a pleasing harmony.*
N UNCOUNT = balance, symmetry

harness /hɑːnɪ[2]s/, **harnesses, harnessing, harnessed**. **1** If you **harness** something such as a natural source of energy, you bring it under your control and use it. EG *Techniques harnessing the energy of the sun are being developed... Plans are now underway to trap some of this power and harness it for our own use.*
V+O

2 A **harness** is **2.1** a set of straps which fit under a person's arms and fasten round their body in order to keep a piece of equipment in place or to prevent the person moving from a place. EG *Will's body had been released from the parachute harness and lifted into the ambulance... A seat and harness for a child are essential in a family car.* **2.2** a set of leather straps and metal links fastened round a horse's head or body so that the horse can have a carriage, cart, or plough fastened to it. EG *...a mare in harness.*
N COUNT
N COUNT/UNCOUNT

3 If you **harness** a horse or other animal, you put a harness on it, especially so that it can pull a carriage, cart, or plough. EG *...a dog harnessed to a sledge.*
V+O : IF+PREP THEN *to*

4 People who work **in harness** with each other help each other in their work and co-operate in order to achieve their aim. EG *Ministers work in harness with the civil servants in their ministries.*
PHR : USED AS AN A, IF+PREP THEN *with* ⇑ together

harp /hɑːp/, **harps, harping, harped**. A **harp** is a large musical instrument consisting of a long row of strings stretched from the top to the bottom of a frame, which you play by stroking or plucking the strings with your fingers.
N COUNT

harp on. If you **harp on** a subject or **harp on** about it, you keep on talking about it although other people may be bored hearing it. EG *She continued to harp on the theme of her wasted life... You do harp on so.*
PHRASAL VB : V+PREP/ADV, IF+PREP THEN *about*

harpist /hɑːpɪst/, **harpists**. A **harpist** is a person who plays the harp.
N COUNT ⇑ musician

harpoon /hɑːpuːn/, **harpoons, harpooning, harpooned**. **1** A **harpoon** is a weapon like a spear with a long rope attached to it, which is fired or thrown by people hunting whales or large sea fish.
N COUNT

2 If you **harpoon** a whale or large fish, you hit it with a harpoon.
V+O ⇑ spear

harpsichord /hɑːpsɪkɔːd/, **harpsichords**. A **harpsichord** is a musical instrument which looks like a small piano, but which has strings that are plucked mechanically, rather than hit by hammers, when the keys are pressed.
N COUNT

harpy /hɑːpi[1]/, **harpies**. If you refer to a woman as a **harpy**, you mean that she is very unpleasant, violent, or greedy; a literary word.
N COUNT

harrow /hærəʊ/, **harrows**. A **harrow** is a piece of farm equipment consisting of a row of spikes fixed to a heavy frame. When it is pulled over ploughed land, the spikes break up large lumps of soil.
N COUNT ⇑ implement

harrowing /hærəʊɪŋ/. A situation or event that is **harrowing** is very upsetting or disturbing. EG *...a harrowing experience... It was a harrowing interview... The film is deeply harrowing.*
ADJ QUALIT ⇑ distressing

harry /hæri[1]/, **harries, harrying, harried**. If you **harry** someone, you try and get them to do what you want by constantly telling them or asking them so that they feel anxious or annoyed. EG *I harried her like a spoilt child... He set to work harrying men for donations.* ◊ **harried**. EG *...a waiter with a full tray and a harried expression.*
V+O ⇑ pressurize = hassle
◊ ADJ QUALIT

harsh /hɑːʃ/, **harsher, harshest**. **1** A condition or way of life that is **harsh** is severe and difficult for people to cope with. EG *His family wouldn't survive the harsh winter... He was subjected to the harshest possible conditions.* ◊ **harshness**. EG *...the harshness of their nomadic life.*
ADJ QUALIT ≠ mild
◊ N UNCOUNT = severity

2 Behaviour or actions that are **harsh** are unkind and show no understanding or sympathy. EG *...her harsh, cold, contemptuous attitude... He had no harsh words or even criticism.* ◊ **harshly**. EG *He thinks you've marked his essay rather harshly... Courts deal with rioters quickly and harshly.* ◊ **harshness**. EG *Disobedience is treated with special harshness.*
ADJ QUALIT = hard, severe ≠ lenient
◊ ADV
◊ N UNCOUNT

3 Something that is **harsh** is too hard, bright, or rough to feel pleasant or to be good for something. EG *Never use lavatory cleaner in the bath, it's too harsh... Harsh daylight fell into the room.*
ADJ QUALIT ≠ mild

4 A voice or other sound that is **harsh** sounds rough and unpleasant and often forced. EG *Emily had asthma, and her breathing was harsh and laboured... She spoke in a harsh whisper.* ◊ **harshly**. EG *'What is it?' he said harshly.*
ADJ QUALIT ≠ soft
◊ ADV

harvest /hɑːvɪ[2]st/, **harvests, harvesting, harvested**. **1** The **harvest** is the cutting or picking of crops at the time of year when they are ripe. EG *Their dwindling stock of rice wouldn't last until the harvest... ...harvest time... It was harvest so it was late when he returned.* ▸ used as a verb. EG *...bountiful crops, which would soon be ready for harvesting... We harvested what we could before the rains came.*
N SING : *the*+N, OR N UNCOUNT
▸ V+O ⇑ gather

2 A **harvest** is the crops that have ripened so that they can be cut or picked. EG *Their sons always came home to help bring in the harvest... A bumper harvest is expected this year.*
N COUNT : USU SING

3 If you **harvest** a large number of things, you collect them, often by making great efforts; a literary use. EG *He and his brother harvested more titles than any family living then... Two hundred thousand signatures were harvested in England by Lady Rothschild.*
V+O

4 If you **reap the harvest**, you benefit or suffer from the results of your own past actions or of someone else's. EG *Inevitably it was the new independent states who were to reap the bitter harvest.*
PHR : VB INFLECTS

harvester /hɑːvɪ[2]stə/, **harvesters**. A **harvester** is **1** a machine which cuts ripe wheat, corn, etc in fields and often binds it into bundles. • See also **combine harvester**. **2** a person who cuts and collects the harvest. EG *Using a sickle instead of the traditional knife cuts the average number of harvesters needed by more than half.*
N COUNT
N COUNT

harvest festival, harvest festivals. A **harvest festival** is a special Christian church service held every year to thank God for the harvest.
N COUNT

has /hæz/ is the third person singular of the present tense of **have**.

has-been, has-beens. A **has-been** is a person whose achievements are in the past, and who is now thought to be unimportant and is no longer respected. EG *She was no longer dismissed as a political has-been.*
N COUNT

hash /hæʃ/. **1** If you **make a hash of** a job or a situation, you do the job badly or cause the situation to develop badly, with the result that you cannot achieve what you intended to. EG *At first I thought I would make a terrible hash of it... Be honest, John,*
PHR : VB INFLECTS = bungle

and admit what a hash that stupid idea has made of things.

2 Hash is **2.1** a dish made from meat cut into small lumps and fried with other ingredients such as onions or potato. EG *...corned beef hash.* — N UNCOUNT ⇑ food **2.2** in informal English, hashish. — N UNCOUNT

hashish /hæʃi^{1}ʃ/ is a drug made from the hemp plant which people usually smoke like a cigarette to make them feel relaxed. Hashish is illegal in many countries. — N UNCOUNT

hasn't /hæzə^{0}nt/ is the usual spoken form of 'has not'.

hasp /hɑːsp/, **hasps**. A **hasp** is a flat piece of metal with a slot in it, fastened to the edge of a door or lid. To close the door or lid, you push the slot over a metal loop fastened to the other section and put a padlock through the loop. — N COUNT ⇑ catch

hassle /hæsə^{0}l/, **hassles, hassling, hassled**; an informal word. **1** A **hassle** is **1.1** something that is difficult and annoying to do. EG *Washing is a real hassle in a house with one cold tap... He didn't want to go through all that divorce hassle again.* — N COUNT/UNCOUNT ⇑ trouble = bother **1.2** an argument. EG *We had a long hassle about whether or not to wear boots.* — N COUNT = quarrel

2 If you **hassle** someone, you keep telling them or asking them to do something, in an annoying way. EG *Stop hassling me, will you?* — V+O = pester, nag

hassock /hæsək/, **hassocks**. A **hassock** is a cushion for kneeling on in a church. — N COUNT

haste /heɪst/. **1 Haste** is the quality of doing something quickly, perhaps too quickly. EG *I immediately regretted my haste... The old men began interrupting each other in their haste to explain what had happened.* — N UNCOUNT = hurry

2 If you do something **in haste**, you do it quickly and hurriedly. EG *The reports that the tutors sent in were read in haste.* — PHR : USED AS AN A = hastily

3 To **make haste** means to act quickly in doing something; an old-fashioned expression. EG *Make haste all of you and get ready.* — PHR : VB INFLECTS

hasten /heɪsə^{0}n/, **hastens, hastening, hastened**. **1** If you **hasten** something, you make it happen faster or sooner. EG *Two factors hastened the formation of the new party.* — V+O = accelerate, speed up ≠ delay

2 If you **hasten** to do something, you are quick to do it. EG *On achieving office himself, he hastened to increase the top prize to £25,000.* — V+*to*-INF = hurry

3 If you **hasten** to say something, you quickly add something to what you have just said in order to prevent it being misunderstood. EG *For some–but not, I hasten to add, for me–that made Burgin unacceptable... Mr Nixon hastened to remark that he was not against television.* — V+*to*-INF = be quick

4 If you **hasten** somewhere, you hurry there; a literary use. EG *He hastened back into the forest.* — V+A = rush

hasty /heɪsti^1/, **hastier, hastiest**. **1** An action that is **hasty** is **1.1** sudden, and often done in reaction to something that has just happened. EG *...a hasty departure... There were hasty apologies.* — ADJ QUALIT = swift ◊ **hastily**. EG *Philip hastily changed the subject... Parliament was hastily recalled from recess.* — ◊ ADV WITH VB ⇑ quickly **1.2** quick; used especially of something you would do more slowly if you had the time. EG *...a hasty meal.* — ADJ QUALIT = hurried ◊ **hastily**. EG *He dressed himself hastily.* — ◊ ADV WITH VB ⇑ quickly

2 If you are **hasty**, you act too quickly, without thinking carefully, for example because you are angry. EG *Don't be hasty. It's not so easy to find another job.* ▸ used of a person's behaviour or actions. EG *He made a hasty, unsuitable marriage.* — ADJ QUALIT = rash

hat /hæt/, **hats**. **1** A **hat** is a head covering that often has a brim round it and is usually worn out of doors to give protection from the weather. — N COUNT

2 If you say that you are wearing a particular **hat**, you mean that you are performing the role or job indicated at that time, although you have other roles or jobs. EG *I'm wearing my teacher's hat today.* — N SING WITH DET +SUPP

3 The word **hat** is also used in the following informal expressions. **3.1** If you say you will **eat your hat** if something happens, you are saying in an emphatic way that you do not believe it will happen. EG *If he wins that race I'll eat my hat!* — PHR : VB INFLECTS **3.2** To **hang up** your **hat** means to stop doing the job that you have been doing for a long time. EG *Hang up your hat before this job kills you!* — PHR : VB INFLECTS = throw in the towel **3.3** If you **keep** something **under** your **hat**, you do not tell anyone about it. — PHR : VB INFLECTS **3.4** Something that is **old hat** is so well-known and familiar that it has become uninteresting and boring. — PHR : USED AS C **3.5** If you **pass the hat round**, you collect money from a group of people, for example in order to give someone a present. EG *Whenever someone retires from this office we pass the hat round.* — PHR : VB INFLECTS **3.6** If you say that you **take off** your **hat to** someone, you mean that you admire them for something that they have done. EG *I take my hat off to her for the way she did it.* — PHR : VB INFLECTS ⇑ admire **3.7** If you say that someone **is talking through** their **hat**, you mean that they are talking nonsense. — PHR : VB INFLECTS **3.8 at the drop of a hat**: see **drop**.

hatband /hætbænd/, **hatbands**. A **hatband** is a strip of cloth that is put round a hat above the brim as a decoration. — N COUNT

hatbox /hætbɒks/, **hatboxes**. A **hatbox** is a cylindrical box in which a hat can be carried and stored. — N COUNT ⇑ box

hatch /hætʃ/, **hatches, hatching, hatched**. **1** When a baby bird, insect, or other animal **hatches** or **hatches out**, or when it **is hatched**, it comes out of its egg by breaking the shell. EG *She stays beside the nest and when the young hatch, she brings food to them... The larva hatches out and lives in the soil... ...newly hatched tadpoles.* — V-ERG

2 When an egg **hatches**, it breaks open and a baby bird, insect, or other animal comes out. EG *After ten days, the eggs hatch.* — V

3 If you **hatch** a plot or a scheme or **hatch it up**, you think of it and work it out. EG *I've heard about the grand plot that you two gentlemen are hatching.* — V+O, OR PHRASAL VB : V+O+ADV ⇑ plan

4 A **hatch** is **4.1** an opening in the deck of a ship or in the bottom of a plane, which is used especially during loading and unloading. EG *Both men quickly disappeared down the hatch.* — N COUNT = hatchway ▸ used of the door or cover of this opening. EG *We heard the noise of a hatch being closed.* — ▸ ⇑ cover **4.2** an opening in a wall, especially the one between a kitchen and a dining room which you use to pass food and other things through. — N COUNT = hatchway

hatchback /hætʃbæk/, **hatchbacks**. A **hatchback** is a car with an extra door at the back which opens upwards. EG *It comes in two styles, a five-door hatchback and a four-door saloon.* ▸ used to refer to the door of this car. EG *He opens the hatchback and loads in the suitcase.* — N COUNT

hatchery /hætʃəri^1/, **hatcheries**. A **hatchery** is a place where people control the hatching of eggs, especially fish eggs. — N COUNT ⇑ farm

hatchet /hætʃɪ^{2}t/, **hatchets**. **1** A **hatchet** is a small axe that you can hold in one hand. — N COUNT

2 Someone with a **hatchet** face has a long, narrow face with sharp features. — ADJ CLASSIF : ATTRIB

3 If two people **bury the hatchet**, they become friendly again after a quarrel or disagreement. EG *Now that our fight was over we were glad to bury the hatchet.* — PHR : VB INFLECTS = make it up

hatchet job, hatchet jobs. A **hatchet job** is a violent written or spoken attack on someone or something that harms or destroys them; used in informal English. EG *Stryker had done a hatchet job on him.* — N COUNT

hatchet man, hatchet men. A **hatchet man** is a man who is employed by someone to destroy things or do unpleasant tasks for them; used in informal English. — N COUNT

hatchway /hætʃweɪ/, **hatchways**. A **hatchway** is the same as a hatch. — N COUNT

hate /heɪt/, **hates, hating, hated**. **1** If you **hate** someone or something, you have an extremely strong feeling of dislike for them. EG *You really hate her, don't you?... I hate injustice as much as you do... She was aware of what she was doing and she hated herself for it.* — V+O (NG/REFL) = detest ≠ love ▸ used as a noun. EG *He was a violent bully, destructive, and full of hate... ...highly charged scenes of love and hate.* — ▸ N UNCOUNT = hatred ◊ **hated**. EG *...the most hated man in America... ...an invisible and hated enemy.* — ◊ ADJ QUALIT

2 When you say that you **hate** something such as a particular activity, you mean that you find it very unpleasant. EG *I used to hate going to lectures... I hate Sundays... I hate milk... I hate it when you can't discuss things openly... I would hate to move to another house.* — V+O/*to*-INF/-ING = dislike ≠ love

3 You say **'I hate to disturb you'**, **'I hate to trouble you'**, etc to someone when you are apologizing to them for disturbing them or doing something which they might find unpleasant but which you feel is necessary. EG *I hate to wake you up, but there's something urgent I've got to tell you... I hate having to bother you this early but our daughter is very ill.* — PHR ⇑ sorry

4 You say **'I hate to say it'** to introduce something that you regret having to say because you feel that it is rather unpleasant or should not be the case. EG *There is unfortunately–I hate to say it–a substantial amount of racism still in our cities... I hate having to say it, but I can't see how we can afford to keep the car.* PHR = I'm sorry to say

hateful /heɪtful/. Someone or something that is **hateful** is extremely unpleasant; a rather old-fashioned word. EG *It was going to be a hateful week... Don't be so hateful.* ADJ QUALIT ⇑ awful = horrid

hatpin /hætpɪn/, **hatpins**. A **hatpin** is a metal pin which can be pushed through a woman's hat and through her hair to keep the hat in position. N COUNT ⇑ pin

hatred /heɪtrɪ²d/ is an extremely strong feeling of dislike for someone or something. EG *She felt hatred towards his sister... I have a hatred of all examinations.* N UNCOUNT : IF + PREP, THEN for/ of/towards ≠ love

hatstand /hætstænd/, **hatstands**. A **hatstand** is an upright pole with hooks at the top on which hats can be hung. N COUNT

hatter /hætə/. If you say that someone is **as mad as a hatter**, you mean that they do very foolish or strange things. PHR : USED AS C

hat trick, hat tricks. A **hat trick** is a series of three achievements, especially in a sports match, for example three goals scored by the same person in a football match or three wickets taken by one bowler with consecutive balls in cricket. EG *Robson scored two fine goals and narrowly missed a hat trick.* N COUNT

haughty /hɔːti¹/, **haughtier, haughtiest**. Someone who is **haughty** is very proud and thinks that they are better than other people; used showing disapproval. ▸ used of a person's behaviour or actions. EG *He had an air of haughty aloofness.* ADJ QUALIT = disdainful ≠ humble
◊ **haughtily**. EG *He haughtily ignored his subordinate.* ◊ ADV WITH VB ◊ **haughtiness**. EG *The nobility still preserved their haughtiness.* ◊ N UNCOUNT

haul /hɔːl/, **hauls, hauling, hauled**. 1 If you **haul** someone or something that is heavy or difficult to move, you pull them with a long, steady pull in order to move them to a different place. EG *They hauled the pilot clear of the wreckage... Ralph hauled himself onto the platform... If you haul hard you will divert the fish.* ▸ used as a noun. EG *After each haul on the ropes, they sang.* V+O (NG/REFL) +A, OR V+A ≠ push; ▸ N COUNT ≠ push

2 A **haul** is 2.1 the quantity of something, especially stolen goods, that is obtained as a result of a robbery, fraud, police operation, etc. EG *They have made some spectacular hauls.* N COUNT ⇑ amount 2.2 the quantity of fish caught by someone fishing with a net. EG *...a succulent haul of many kinds of fish.* N COUNT ⇑ catch

3 If you **haul** yourself into a better position, for example in a competition, you achieve the position by making a great effort. EG *Jackson closed with a final round of 66 to haul himself into third place.* V+O (REFL)+A ⇑ move = drag

4 If something such as a journey or a struggle is a **long haul**, it takes a long time and you have to make a big effort. EG *We began the long haul up the cobbled street... ...as women begin the long haul to equality.* PHR : USED AS C/O

5 to **haul** someone **over the coals**: see **coal**.

haul up. If someone **is hauled up** before a court of law or someone who has the power to punish them, they are made to appear before that court or person because they are thought to have broken the law or disobeyed orders. EG *He got hauled up in court for assaulting a student.* PHRASAL VB : V+O+ADV : USU PASS = have up

haulage /hɔːlɪdʒ/ is the business of transporting goods by road. EG *...long-distance haulage drivers.* N UNCOUNT

haulier /hɔːlɪə/, **hauliers**. A **haulier** is a person who runs a business that transports goods by road. N COUNT

haunch /hɔːntʃ/, **haunches**. The **haunch** of an animal or a person is the area of the body which includes the hip, the buttock, and the top part of the leg. EG *He squatted down on his haunches... ...fat antelope haunches roasting over glowing coals.* N COUNT : USU PL

haunt /hɔːnt/, **haunts, haunting, haunted**. 1 A ghost or spirit that **haunts** a place or a person regularly appears in the place, or is seen by the person and frightens them. EG *Their ghosts come back to haunt people... The building was supposed to be haunted by the ghost of a leper woman.* V+O ⇑ appear

2 If something unpleasant **haunts** you, you keep thinking about it or worrying about it over a long period of time. EG *The woman's dark face haunted her... ...a mystery that had haunted me for most of my life.* V+O ⇑ disturb

3 Something that **haunts** a person or organization regularly causes problems for them over a period of time. EG *The paradoxes and inconsistencies which haunt the party came to the surface... Lack of money haunted successive projects.* V+O ⇑ affect = plague

4 A place that is the **haunt** of a particular person is one which they often visit because they enjoy going there. EG *Familiar childhood haunts were the village well and the wood behind the school... This bar is famous as a haunt of bookies and hustlers.* N COUNT+SUPP

haunted /hɔːntɪ²d/. 1 A **haunted** building or other place is one where a ghost regularly appears. EG *...a haunted house.* ADJ CLASSIF

2 Someone who has a **haunted** expression looks very worried or troubled. EG *The woman looked progressively more haunted... Her face took on a haunted quality.* ADJ QUALIT ≠ calm

haunting /hɔːntɪŋ/. Something that is **haunting** has a quality such as great beauty or sadness that makes a strong impression on you and remains in your thoughts. EG *The carol has a primitive strength and haunting simplicity... He repeated the haunting melody.* ADJ QUALIT : USU ATTRIB ⇑ unforgettab[le] = evocative ◊ **hauntingly**. EG *...a misty day, hauntingly romantic.* ◊ ADV

hauteur /əʊtɜː/ is haughtiness; a formal word. EG *...icy aristocratic hauteur.* N UNCOUNT ⇑ attitude

have /hæv/, **has, having, had**. **Have** is used in two main ways: as an auxiliary and as a main verb. The auxiliary uses are shown in paragraphs 1 to 6, and the main verb uses from paragraph 7 to the end. The most common semantic meaning of 'have' is 'possess', and this is explained in paragraph 9. The other common meanings of 'have' are explained from paragraph 10 to the end of the entry. **Have** is often contracted to **'ve, has** to **'s**, and **had** to **'d**. The forms **have, has, having**, and **had** are used in the following ways to express past time. 1 The forms **have** and **has** are used 1.1 when you mention an action that happened in the past but that is still relevant to the present, or when the action happened in the recent past. EG *We have already done that... I've just sold my car... Has she found a job yet?... I've never heard of it.* AUX+PAST PART : SEE □ BELOW 1.2 when you mention an action that continues to happen from the past up until the present. EG *Dental decay in Britain has almost reached epidemic level... I've always supported Mr Heath and I still do... I've been thinking... I haven't been playing football recently.* AUX+PAST PAR[T] OR AUX+*been*+-ING : SEE □ BELOW

2 The form **had** is used to indicate 2.1 that an action or situation occurred at a previous time. **Had** is often used when the clause in which it occurs is less important than another clause nearby. EG *He had known her for two years before he proposed... By 1950 more than half the land had been cleared for pasture... People have already forgotten, or had until last Tuesday.* AUX+PAST PAR[T] OR AUX+*been*-ING : SEE □ BELOW 2.2 that you are reporting what someone said or felt in the past. EG *Officials said that Japan had agreed to restrict car shipments for three years... In half an hour Rudolph felt that he had known her for years.* AUX+PAST PART : SEE □ BELOW

3 **Had** is also used instead of 'if' to begin a clause which refers to a possible situation that is not the actual situation. The main clause uses modal verbs to suggest what might have happened if the situation had been the one that is mentioned. EG *Had his theories been accepted, the world might have been a better place... They could not have produced the consequences that they did had there not been other forces at work.* AUX+NG/*there*/*it*+PAST PART : SEE □ BELOW

4 The form **having** is used to introduce a clause that mentions an action which had already happened before another related action began. EG *We were back in Edinburgh at ten past twelve having driven straight across the bridge again... Quite a few of the shop fronts were still boarded up, having closed down in 1930 or 1931.* AUX+PAST PART : SEE □ SEE BELOW

5 The forms **have, has**, and **had** are used 5.1 with a pronoun at the end of a statement with 'have' in it to make it into a question, especially when you are expecting the other person to agree with you or to answer in a way that confirms what you already think. EG *You've got that, have you? Right... 'Do you want the insurance?'–'We'd better, hadn't we?'... They've got television, haven't they, in the lounges?* SEE □ BELOW 5.2 to stand for the whole of a verb phrase in a SEE □ BELOW

previous clause that consisted of a main verb preceded by **have, has** or **had**. EG *'Has he enjoyed himself?'–'Yes, he has.'... Have I got this the right way up? Yes, I have.*

6 If something **has** still to be done or **has** yet to be done, it is likely to happen in the future. EG *Much has still to be done... ...one ingredient of a compound that had yet to be developed.* AUX+ADV+ to-INF, OR AUX+ to-INF : SEE ☐ BELOW = need

7 Have is frequently used with nouns as objects, where the word 'have' has very little meaning in itself, but where most of the meaning is given by the noun. The function of 'have' is thus to provide a verb for the structure and very little else. In this group there is always an equivalent verb for the 'have + noun' structure, so that 'to have a look' means almost the same as 'to look'. This structure is often chosen in order to emphasize that an action or event has a definite beginning or end, or in order to add more information about the noun. The following paragraph shows 'have' used in this way. **7.1** used with nouns that describe actions. EG *I had a little stroll round the garden this morning... You go and have a look... ...a herd of buffaloes having a bath in the river.* V+O = take **7.2** used with nouns which refer to communication between people. EG *In recent weeks he has been having talks with the bank... We're having a meeting. Come and join in.* V+O = hold **7.3** used with nouns which refer to the effect that one thing has on another. EG *What effect will this have on transportation? ...the very considerable influence which EEC law has on us... If this has no result, try a weak solution of bleach.* V+O **7.4** used to form nouns from verbs. EG *We've had a think about what to do... It's worth having a try... She sat down to have a quiet read.* V+O

8 Have is also used in this structure with some nouns which cannot themselves be used as verbs. Some examples of 'have' used in this way are given here. EG *The children are having a party... It had its first performance last week... They regretted having an October election... Let's have a celebration.* V+O

Note. In the rest of the entry for **have**, there is a relationship between **have** and **got**. Very often **have got** occurs in natural spoken English where **have** alone would also be correct. So you can say 'I have one brother and two sisters' or 'I've got one brother and two sisters'. This is a feature of spoken English, and it seems to arise from the fact that **have** is sometimes an auxiliary and sometimes a main verb. Adding **got** makes its status as an auxiliary quite clear. For further information about this and for more examples see **got**. **Have** sometimes shows grammatical signs of being an auxiliary verb when it is actually being used as a main verb. So that you can say 'Have you any brothers?' or 'Do you have any brothers?', 'I haven't any sisters' or 'I don't have any sisters'. For examples using 'have got', see **got**.

9 Have is used in the following senses to say that something is associated with or belongs to someone or something else. **9.1** If you **have** something such as a car or a house, it belongs to you. EG *What is the point of having a mink coat or a Rolls Royce, if everybody else does too?... Could you bring back my book please, now that you have one yourself.* V+O = possess **9.2** If you **have** a business or company, you own it and run it. EG *...a man who had a bakery in Port Philip... He had a small hotel.* V+O **9.3** If you **have** money or something that earns money for you, it is yours. EG *They don't have any money... My children have had bank accounts since they were eight... Both companies have a 23 percent interest in the well.* V+O = possess **9.4** If you **have** feelings or opinions, you feel or think in that way. EG *Do you have any doubts about it?... We had no regrets at all.* V+O **9.5** If you **have** a particular relationship or role, it is yours. EG *The Scots had more positions of influence than anyone else... We have a role in schools liaison work... He didn't have a very good reputation.* V+O = enjoy **9.6** If you **have** a job, you are employed and are paid. EG *I'm not getting anywhere in this job I have... She felt useless, despite having a successful career of her own.* V+O **9.7** If you **have** something in a particular place, you keep it there. EG *I don't have very much drink in stock... She always has dozens of tins in her cupboards.* V+O+A

10 Have is often used in structures where the meaning would be the same if you used the verb 'be', because you are talking about the attributes that something has. For example, when we say 'The house has a lovely view', we mean 'There is a lovely view when we look out of the windows'. EG *We have a plan... You have no alternative... It's nice to have an excuse... It has no basis at all in Roman law.* V+O

11 If someone or something **has** a particular feature or attribute, it is in them or part of them. EG *He has nice eyes... Jordache had the appearance of a sick man... He had beautiful manners... I have a lot of sympathy with them... We have very good schools in Scotland... ...machines which have dangerous moving parts.* V+O = possess

12 If you **have** a relation, he or she is part of your family. EG *They have one daughter... I have two younger brothers and one sister.* V+O = possess

13 If you **have** a friend, employee, teacher, etc, you know them, you work with them, you go to them for advice, etc. EG *I have loads of friends... How many patients does a doctor normally have on his list?... I had a completely incompetent solicitor.* V+O = possess

14 If you **have** a sudden or unexpected experience, it happens to you. EG *I had the most frightful shock this morning... One night I had an even worse scare... What would happen if you had a crash?* V+O = suffer

15 If you **have** a meal or a drink, you eat or drink it. EG *Come at one-thirty then, while I'm having a sandwich... At least have dinner with me... I had a large whisky.* V+O

16 If you **have** an idea, opinion, etc about a situation, you respond to the situation in some way. EG *She has a very clear sense of what it entails... I have a feeling that you're relying on memory here... I have no opinion to give.* V+O ⇑ possess

17 If a shop, hotel, or company **has** something that you want, it is available for you to buy, rent, or use. EG *Swimming suits? We have them in all shades... I couldn't find a hotel that had a vacant room.* V+O

18 If you **have** people who work for you, you employ them. EG *I don't think that we have reviewers of that calibre on this paper... The Finance Officer has a staff of twenty five people.* V+O

19 If you **have** someone do something or **have** them doing something, you persuade them to do it or you order them to do it. EG *Have that shirt washed and brought round to my room... Will the shop you're buying the machine from have it installed for you?* V+O+ to-INF OR V+O+PAST PART/-ING

20 If you **have** something happen to you or done to you, you are in a situation in which it happens or is done. EG *Children everywhere love to have stories read to them... She had some money stolen... I've an aunt coming this afternoon from Greenock.* V+O+PAST PART/-ING

21 If you **have** a certain amount of time, **21.1** it is available to you. EG *He had only a short time to live... Go back later to refine it–if you have time.* V+O **21.2** you use it in a particular way or at a particular place. EG *We were all having a day by the seaside... I had a boring afternoon... People have been having a hard time lately.* V+O = pass

22 If you **have** a job or task to do, you must do it or you ought to do it. EG *She had a huge department to administer... Make sure elected officials do not have more work than they can manage.* V+O

23 If you **have** someone such as a visitor, a lodger, a workman, etc, they are visiting you or are staying, living, or working in your house or your district. EG *I like to have visitors... I told him that we'd had students living in the house once and found it hell... Why don't we have him over for dinner?* V+O

24 If you **have** someone or something with you, they are accompanying you or with you. EG *I have with me Professor Geoffrey Best, who I hope will help explain this.... He had with him a copy of a London paper.* V+O+A

25 If you **have** something from someone, **25.1** you receive it from them, and you then own it or can keep it. EG *There's something I'd particularly like your sister to have from me... If they fit you, you can have them.* V+O **25.2** you receive something that you want or need to use. EG *Can we have something to wipe our hands on please... If she doesn't have help with shopping, she won't eat at all.* V+O **25.3** you receive help, advice, information, etc from them. EG *I had an invitation to go and talk to the prison officers... I've had some very friendly comments from people... Ask her advice; it'll be well worth having.* V+O

26 If you **have** part of your body in a particular position, it is in that position. EG *She had her head* V+O+A *down and she didn't see him... He had his hand on the girl's arm... Boylan had his back to the window.*

27 If you **have** an illness or disability, you suffer from it. EG *He had a headache every night from this job... She began to have attacks of chest pain... I thought he was having a heart attack.* V+O ⇑ experience = get

28 If you **have** medical treatment such as surgery or drugs, you receive it. EG *They all had an injection when they left Britain... I had a little operation on my spine.* V+O ⇑ undergo

29 If you **have** someone by a part of their body, you are holding them there because you are threatening to hurt or injure them. EG *Jack had him by the hair and was brandishing his knife... She had him by the throat.* V+O+A *(by)* = clutch

30 If a woman **has** a baby, she gives birth to it. EG *My mother had six children in nine years... She's having a baby next month.* V+O ⇑ produce

31 If you **have** something or somewhere **to** yourself, you are the only person there. EG *They had the bar to themselves.* V+O+A *(to)*

32 You sometimes say **'we have'** or **'you have'** to refer to a situation which you want to talk about or which you want people to consider. EG *Energy comes in many different forms: you have mechanical energy, heat, light, electricity, chemical energy, and so on... Suppose you have a row of cells all of which are behaving this way.* V+O : WITH *we/you*

33 You say **'I have'** or **'we have'** when you want to refer to an example of something experienced by a group, society, nation, etc. EG *We had first of all the lorry drivers' strikes, and then we had the local government workers' strikes... One thing about the Croydon by-election is that we have again in the House of Commons someone called William Pitt.* V+O : WITH *I/we*

34 If you use an expression such as **I won't have it** or **I'm not having** something, you mean that you will not allow it to happen. EG *We can't have that... No, I'm not having it. Not in this house.* PHR

35 If you are quoting something that you have heard, you often use an expression such as 'Rumour **has it** that...' or 'as computer jargon **has it**'. By expressing it in this way you show that you do not necessarily agree with what is said or do not like the actual words used. EG *Rumour had it that he had known Otto Gerran a very long time... Gossip had it that she would marry Granby... It's a question of getting the problems out–or debugging as the jargon has it.* PHR : VB INFLECTS : NG + PHR + REPORT-CL, OR *as*+NG+PHR

36 If you **have** to do something, **36.1** you must do it or are forced to do it, without having any choice. EG *We had to learn it in school... There are plenty of jobs; she doesn't have to go to Canada... We all have to have food.* V+*to*-INF = be obliged to **36.2** you need to do it. EG *My brother'll have to take care of you. I'll call him today... Then he had to sit down because he felt dizzy.* V+*to*-INF **36.3** you feel that it is your moral duty to do it. EG *'Did you really kill a Frenchman with a bayonet?' He had to know. 'Yeah,' Jordache said... I have to speak to your father. Is he in?* V+*to*-INF = need

Note. If you do not **have** to do something, there is no need, compulsion, or obligation to do it, but you can do it if you want to.

37 If something **has** to happen, **37.1** it is inevitable that it happens, although you do not want it to happen and are annoyed or upset by it. EG *Just tonight the train had to be late... And now, just when I was sorting things out, this has to come along.* V+*to*-INF **37.2** it is extremely important that action should be taken because a worrying or dangerous situation has arisen. EG *It's been losing about three million dollars a year, and it has to go... The government has to learn the lessons of Ulster.* V+*to*-INF = must

38 You tell someone that they **have** to do something when you are giving them an instruction and telling them how they should act or what they should know. EG *Yes. Now, you have to apply the same concepts there... Again, you have to be careful in what facts you choose... The Department of Publication is on the phone telling him he's going to have to spend another three hundred million dollars.* V+*to*-INF = must

39 If you come to a conclusion about something, you can say that it **has to be** so. EG *You have to be damn sure of yourself, Rudolph thought, to use a word like that... You would have to be a foreigner, and a newcomer at that, not to know this... That has to be the reason.* PHR+C : *have* INFLECTS = must

40 The word **have** is also used in the following informal expressions. **40.1** If you **have it**, you remember something which helps you to solve a problem that has been puzzling you. EG *Yes, that was it, he had it now, it was all coming back to him.* PHR : VB INFLECTS ⇑ recall **40.2** If you **have it in** you, you have abilities and skills which you do not usually use and which other people do not realize you have. EG *I never guessed Rudy had it in him... She spoke with a volubility I never suspected she had in her.* PHR : VB INFLECTS **40.3** If you **give** something **all you have** or you **put everything you have into** something, you use all your energy and skill in doing it. EG *I gave it all I had... Rudolph took a solo on the trumpet, putting everything he had into it.* PHR : VBS INFLECT **40.4** If you **have it in for** someone, you are determined to cause them unpleasantness, because you dislike them or are angry with them. EG *He had it in for me.* PHR : VB INFLECTS **40.5** If you **have it out, have the matter out, have the whole thing out**, etc, you talk to someone about something on which you seriously disagree, because you want to stop arguing or worrying about it. EG *Oh well, let's have it out.* PHR OR PHR + A *(with)* : RECIP, VB INFLECTS **40.6** If you **have** something **over with**, something horrible that was going to happen to you has happened and you no longer need to worry about it. EG *There was a great desire to have it over with.* PHR : VB INFLECTS

40.7 If you **have been had**, you have been tricked by someone who has deliberately deceived you, for example by selling you something at too high a price. PHR : AUX INFLECTS **40.8** If you **are had up for** something, you appear in court for a crime that you have committed or are thought to have committed. EG *He was had up for indecent exposure.* PHR : AUX INFLECTS **40.9** If you **have it off** or **have it away** with someone, you have sex with them; used in very informal British English. EG *I told you she was having it off with him.* PHR OR PHR + A *(with)* : RECIP, VB INFLECTS **40.10** If you say that someone **has had it**, you mean that they will be in trouble because of something they have done. EG *Oh Lord–she's had it now!... You've had it, chum.* PHR : FIRST VB *(have)* INFLECTS **40.11** If you say that you **have had it**, you mean that you are so tired or exhausted that you cannot continue doing something. EG *They both look as if they've about had it.* PHR : FIRST VB *(have)* INFLECTS = be all in **40.12** If you say that something **has had it**, you mean that it is no longer in a good enough condition to work properly or be useful. EG *It's worn out, this piano. It's just had it.* PHR : FIRST VB *(have)* INFLECTS ⇑ be finished

have on. **1** If you **have on** a piece of clothing, you are wearing it. EG *She had on an old bathrobe.* PHRASAL VB : V+O+ADV

2 If you **have on** a piece of equipment such as a radio, television, or hi-fi, it is switched on and you are usually listening to it or watching it. EG *It was encouraging to hear he didn't have the television on all night.* PHRASAL VB : ORDER V+O+ADV

3 If you **are having** someone **on**, you are teasing them by pretending that something is true when it is not true; an informal expression. EG *You're having me on!* PHR : USED AS C

> **HAVE** ☐ **Have** can be used as a main verb and as an auxiliary. The meanings of the auxiliary, described as AUX in the grammar notes, are given in paragraphs 1 to 6 of the entry for **have**. 'Have' used as an auxiliary behaves in the following ways: **1** It is followed by a past participle or by a *to*-infinitive. **2** It inflects. **3** *Have, has,* and *had* are used before the subject in questions, as in ***Has** he arrived yet?... Why **had** she complained?* **4** *Have, has,* and *had* are used before the negative *not*, as in *They **have** not been to Italy.* The word *not* has a shortened form *n't* which can be added to *have, has,* and *had*, as in *You **haven't** finished your homework... It **hasn't** rained for a month.* **5** It can be used to stand for a previous verbal group in which *have* is used as an auxiliary, as in *Have you seen 'Macbeth'?–Yes, we **have**... She has never visited Paris, but I **have**.* **6** It is used in question tags, as in *He has bought a new car, **hasn't** he?... They haven't much time, **have** they?* **7** It can be used with modals and other auxiliaries, as in *They might **have** been fighting.*

haven /heɪvəⁿn/, **havens**. A **haven** is a place where people or animals feel safe and secure. EG *The terrorists feel they have a safe haven from which to operate... They have made the park a haven for weary Londoners.* N COUNT ⇑ shelter = refuge

have-nots. The **have-nots** are people who are poor and have no money or possessions. EG *The next few years are going to be a great deal tougher for the have-nots.* N PLURAL ≠ haves

haven't /hævəⁿnt/ is the usual spoken form of 'have not'.

haversack /hævəsæk/, **haversacks**. A **haversack** is a canvas bag that is usually worn over one N COUNT shoulder. It is used for example by walkers for carrying food and personal belongings or by soldiers for carrying food supplies.

haves /hævz/. The **haves** are people who have a lot of money and possessions. EG *...the haves and the have-nots.* — N PLURAL = rich

havoc /hævək/ is chaos, disorder, and confusion. EG *After the havoc of the war, England had to be rebuilt... He managed this manoeuvre without causing more havoc than a couple of crushed feet... This concentration of airborne firepower wrought havoc with the enemy forces.* — N UNCOUNT
● If one thing **plays havoc with** another, it causes a great deal of disorder and confusion. EG *The anxieties of the last few days had played havoc with his working hours and disrupted his routine... When it comes to definitions, politics certainly plays havoc with the English language.* — ● PHR : VB INFLECTS ⇑ disrupt

haw /hɔː/, **haws, hawing, hawed.** 1 **Haws** are the red berries produced by hawthorn trees in autumn. — N COUNT : USU PL ⇑ berry
2 Writers sometimes use **'haw haw'** to show that one of their characters is laughing, especially in a rather unpleasant or superior way. EG *'He cut himself eating peas last night.'–'Haw haw.'* — EXCLAM ⇑ laugh = tee hee
3 The word **haw** is used as a verb only in the expression 'to hum and haw': see **hum**.

hawk /hɔːk/, **hawks, hawking, hawked.** 1 A **hawk** is a large bird with a short, hooked bill, sharp claws, and very good eyesight. Hawks catch and eat small birds and animals. EG *A hawk hovered, motionless, in the blue sky.* — N COUNT
2 If you **watch** someone **like a hawk**, you watch them very carefully to see what they are doing, especially to see if they do anything wrong. EG *I watched her like a hawk during these first days.* — PHR : VB INFLECTS
3 You use the word **hawk** to describe someone who believes in using force and violence to achieve something rather than using more peaceful or diplomatic methods. EG *It has made him more of a hawk in defence matters than the previous president was... She didn't know whether Chisholm was a hawk or a dove.* — N COUNT ⇑ person ≠ dove
4 If you **hawk** something, you try to sell it by taking it around to various people who might be interested in buying it; often used showing disapproval. EG *His writings were being hawked round German publishers... ...pedlars in historical costumes loudly hawking traditional goods.* — V+O

hawker /hɔːkə/, **hawkers.** A **hawker** is a person who travels from place to place selling things. — N COUNT

hawk-eyed. Someone who is **hawk-eyed** has very good eyesight and seems to see absolutely everything that is happening. — ADJ CLASSIF ⇑ observant

hawkish /hɔːkɪʃ/. Someone who is **hawkish** believes in using force and violence to achieve something rather than using more peaceful or diplomatic methods. EG *His aides evidently feared that he had been too hawkish.* — ADJ QUALIT

hawser /hɔːzə/, **hawsers.** A **hawser** is a large heavy rope, especially one used on a ship. — N COUNT

hawthorn /hɔːθɔːn/, **hawthorns.** A **hawthorn** is a small tree which has sharp thorns and produces white flowers and red berries. EG *There was a mist softening the tangle of the hawthorn... ...a road bordered with hawthorn hedges.* — N COUNT/ UNCOUNT = may

hay /heɪ/. 1 **Hay** is grass which has been cut and dried so that it can be used to feed animals. EG *About 30 or 40 bales of hay were scattered over the barn.* — N UNCOUNT
2 If you say that someone **is making hay while the sun shines**, you mean that they are doing what they want to do now while they have the chance to do it. — PHR : VBS INFLECT
3 If you say that someone **has hit the hay**, you mean that they have gone to bed or to sleep; an informal expression. — PHR : VB INFLECTS = turn in
4 If you say that someone is having **a roll in the hay**, you mean that they are involved in sexual activities with someone; an informal expression. — PHR

haycock /heɪkɒk/, **haycocks.** A **haycock** is a small pile of hay in the shape of a cone, which is left in the field until it is dry. — N COUNT ⇑ haystack

hay fever; also spelled with a hyphen. **Hay fever** is inflammation of the nose and throat, with symptoms similar to those of the common cold. Hay fever affects people who are allergic to the pollen of some grasses or flowers. — N UNCOUNT

haystack /heɪstæk/, **haystacks.** 1 A **haystack** is a large, firmly built pile of hay, often covered with a straw roof to protect it, which is left in the field until it is needed. — N COUNT
2 If you say that trying to find a particular thing is **like looking for a needle in a haystack**, you mean that you are very unlikely indeed to find it. — PHR : USED AS AN A

haywire /heɪwaɪə/. If something goes **haywire**, it becomes completely disordered or out of control; an informal word. EG *A nuclear plant went haywire. For a few days the plant leaked and there was a risk of a catastrophe... That's what you should do when your whole procedure goes haywire, when everything goes wrong.* — ADJ CLASSIF : PRED ⇑ wrong

hazard /hæzəd/, **hazards, hazarding, hazarded.** 1 A **hazard** is something which could be dangerous to you, your health or safety, or your plans or reputation. EG *...a natural hazard, like an earth tremor... Drinking alcohol is a real health hazard if carried to excess... Not infrequently this may present certain hazards for the individual.* — N COUNT ⇑ danger
2 If you **hazard** someone or something, you put them into a situation which might be dangerous for them, because of something you are trying to achieve or a plan you are trying to follow; a formal use. EG *He was absolved from any accusation of hazarding the health of his crew.* — V+O = endanger ≠ protect
3 If you **hazard** or if you **hazard** a guess, you make a suggestion about something which is only a guess and which you know might be wrong. EG *'How much do you think he makes a year?'–'Fifteen thousand,' Rudolph hazarded.–'Much more,' Brad said... As to the author of the letter, I will hazard a guess that it is Howard Ringbaum.* — V+QUOTE/O

hazardous /hæzədəs/. Something that is **hazardous** is dangerous, especially to people's health or safety. EG *...hazardous chemicals... The strait is a difficult stretch of water, too hazardous for small ferries to cross... Breathing asbestos-laden air may be hazardous to health.* — ADJ QUALIT : IF + PREP, THEN *to/for* ≠ safe

haze /heɪz/. 1 If there is **haze** or a **haze**, you cannot see clearly very far into the distance because of the heat of the air or because of the dust or moisture in the air. EG *...in the golden morning haze... Breezes crept over the polished waters beneath the haze of heat.* — N SING WITH DET +SUPP, OR N UNCOUNT
2 If there is a **haze** of something such as smoke or fumes, you cannot see clearly through it. EG *The room became cloudy with a blue haze of smoke.* — N SING WITH DET +SUPP
3 If you are in a **haze**, you cannot think clearly and you have no real idea of how time is passing or of what is happening. EG *He lived for most of the time in a haze of whisky.* — N SING+SUPP : *a* +N = blur

hazel /heɪzəᵊl/, **hazels.** 1 A **hazel** is a small tree which produces nuts that you can eat; also used of the wood of the tree. EG *Throughout most of England oak and hazel used to be the commonest trees.* — N COUNT/ UNCOUNT
2 **Hazel** eyes are greenish-brown in colour. — ADJ COLOUR

hazelnut /heɪzəᵊlnʌt/, **hazelnuts**; also spelled as two words. **Hazelnuts** are nuts from a hazel, which can be eaten. — N COUNT

hazy /heɪziˡ/, **hazier, haziest.** 1 Something that is **hazy**, for example a view or the sky, cannot be seen clearly because of the heat of the air or the dust in it. EG *...a hazy blue view beyond railings on a mountain pass... The afternoon wore on, hazy and dreadful with damp heat.* — ADJ QUALIT ≠ clear
2 If you are **hazy** about things or if ideas, details, etc are **hazy**, you are unclear or confused about them. EG *She was understandably hazy about her mother's origins... The details are getting a bit hazy in my mind now... My memory's a little hazy on this.* — ADJ QUALIT : USU PRED ≠ clear
3 If things seem **hazy** to you or if you feel **hazy**, things do not seem clear or distinct, often because you are not feeling well or have drunk too much. EG *...the hazy outlines of the afternoon drinkers... 'How do you feel now?'–'A lot better thanks. A bit hazy, but otherwise all right.'* — ADJ QUALIT ⇑ blurred ≠ clear
4 A **hazy** colour is pale and misty-looking. EG *...a hazy pale green.* — ADJ QUALIT

H-bomb, H-bombs. An **H-bomb** is a bomb in which energy is released from hydrogen atoms. — N COUNT

he /hiː/ is used as the subject of a verb. 1 You use **he**
1.1 to refer to a man or boy who has already been mentioned or named, or whose identity is known. EG *Bill had flown back from New York and he and his wife took me out to dinner... He was known to all as Eddie.* ▸ used also to refer to a male animal. EG *He won't eat cat food.* — PRON : SING, USED AS S
1.2 to refer to a person whose sex — PRON : SING,

is not known or is not stated, especially after pronouns such as 'someone' or 'nobody', or when you have used a singular noun to refer generally to a particular class or group of people. Some people dislike this use. EG *This will mean that the artist can work in areas in which he is interested... A teacher should do whatever he thinks best.* — USED AS S = they

2 In the Christian religion **He** is used to refer to God or Jesus Christ. — PRON : SING, USED AS S

H.E. is an abbreviation for 'His Excellency' or 'Her Excellency' and is used as part of the title of an important official such as an ambassador. EG *...H.E. The Peruvian Ambassador.* — PHR : USED IN TITLE

head /hɛd/, **heads, heading, headed. 1** Your **head** is the part of your body which has your eyes, mouth, brain, etc in it. EG *She shook her head.* ▸ used also of the same part of an animal's body. EG *...her fingers moving over the fur on the cat's head.* — N COUNT

2 Your **head** is also your mind, and your mental abilities. EG *He's not very good at doing sums in his head... She's been filling my head with new ideas... She has a good head for languages.* — N COUNT : USU SING

3 The **head** of something is **3.1** the top or most important end of it. EG *Howard stood at the head of the stairs... ...the head of the queue... ...the head of the table.* — N SING WITH DET +SUPP **3.2** the part of an object such as a nail or an arrow which is a different shape from the rest of the object. EG *...an arrow head... ...a pin-head.* — N COUNT+SUPP ⇑ end

4 If you are the **head** of something such as a company or organization, you are in charge of it and in charge of the people in it. EG *...the head of the English department.* — N COUNT+SUPP = boss ▸ used as an adjective. EG *...the head gardener... I must telephone head office in London.* — ▸ ADJ CLASSIF : ATTRIB = chief

5 The **head** of a plant is the top part of it, where the leaves or flowers grow clustered together. EG *This lettuce has a good firm head... He cut the dead heads off the roses.* — N COUNT : USU+SUPP

6 The **head** of a page is the top part of it. EG *Write your address at the head of your letter.* — N SING WITH DET : USU+*of*

7 The **head** of a tape recorder is the part of it which touches the magnetic tape and so plays back or records music, speech, etc. — N COUNT

8 The **head** of a spot or boil is the part of it which goes yellow and has pus in it when it is about to burst. — N COUNT

9 The **head** on a glass of beer is the layer of small bubbles on the beer. — N COUNT : USU SING

10 The **head** of a river or stream is the beginning or source of it. EG *...the head of the Thames.* — N COUNT+SUPP : USU SING

11 A **head** of water or of steam is the pressure which it has in an enclosed space. EG *An overheated water tank will build up a head of steam.* — N SING WITH DET +SUPP

12 If you talk about the cost or the amount **a head** or **per head**, you mean the cost or the amount for each person who is there or who is included. EG *It will cost £9 a head.* — PHR : USED AS AN A = per person

13 If someone has fifty **head** of cattle, they have fifty cows. In this sense, **head** is used as the plural form. — N PART : USU NUM+N

14 You can use a **head** to refer to a distance or amount which is equal to the length of a person's or animal's head. EG *The horse won the race by a head... She is half a head taller than her brother.* — N SING : a+N ⇑ amount

15 A **head** is also **15.1** a headmaster, headmistress, or head teacher. EG *I had coffee with the head after school.* — N COUNT **15.2** a headland. EG *...Dunnet Head... ...Beachy Head.* — N IN NAMES **15.3** a heading. EG *They drew up a list under three heads.* — N COUNT **15.4** in informal English, a headache. EG *I've got a rotten head.* — N SING+SUPP : a +N

16 When you are tossing a coin and it comes down **heads**, you can see the side of the coin which has the ruler's head on it. — ADV AFTER VB ≠ tails ▸ You say **'Heads or tails?'** when you are asking someone to guess which side of a coin will be facing upwards after it has been tossed. — ▸ CONVENTION

17 If you **head** a company, organization, etc, you are the person in charge of it. EG *The firm is headed by John Murray.* — V+O : NO IMPER = control

18 When you **head** in a particular direction or when you **head** someone or something in a particular direction, you go or you make them go there. EG *It was so dark that they couldn't see where they were heading... I headed Lolita away... Julie came into the kitchen and headed for the cupboard.* — V+A, OR V+O+A ⇑ move

19 When something **heads** in a particular direction or towards a particular number, it moves towards it. EG *Unemployment is heading towards four million.* — V+A : NO IMPER ⇑ move

20 If someone or something **heads** a line or procession, they are at the front of it. EG *Their car headed the funeral procession.* — V+O : NO IMPER

21 If something **heads** a list or a group, it is at the top of it. EG *The list of cities which spend most on education is headed by London.* — V+O : NO IMPER

22 You can mention the title of a piece of writing by saying what the piece of writing **is headed**. EG *The essay was headed 'Developments in English Syntax.'* — V+O+C : USU PASS

23 When you **head** a ball, you hit it with your head. EG *He could head a ball faster than he could kick it.* — V+O ⇑ strike

24 The word **head** is used in a large number of expressions, some of which are explained here. Other expressions which include the word **head** are explained at other words in the dictionary. **24.1** If someone has **a swollen head**, they are very conceited, usually because of something that has happened or has been said. — PHR : USED AS O **24.2 From head to foot** means all over your body. EG *The child was covered in mud from head to foot.* — PHR : USED AS AN A **24.3** If you are **head over heels in love**, you are very much in love. — PHR : USED AS C **24.4** If you say something **off the top of your head**, you say it without thinking very much about it before you speak. — PHR : USED AS AN A, *head* INFLECTS **24.5** If you tell someone that something is **on** their **own head** or if you say **'On your own head be it'**, you mean that they are totally responsible for any consequences that there might be of the action they intend to take. — PHR : USED AS AN A, OR CONVENTION, N INFLECTS **24.6** If something is **over** someone's **head**, it is too difficult for them to understand. — PHR : USED AS AN A : N INFLECTS **24.7** If you do something **over** someone's **head**, you do it without consulting them. EG *Don't you dare go over my head again.* — PHR : USED AS AN A, N INFLECTS **24.8** If you are laughing, crying, or shouting your **head off**, you are laughing, crying, or shouting very noisily; an informal expression. — PHR : USED AS AN A, N INFLECTS **24.9** If you **bite** or **snap** someone's **head off**, you speak to them very sharply, usually for no good reason; an informal expression. — PHR : VB AND N INFLECT **24.10** If you **bring** something **to a head** or if something **comes to a head**, it reaches a state where you have to do something urgently about it. EG *The argument was brought to a head when her boss refused to talk.* — PHR : VB INFLECTS **24.11** If you **get** a fact or idea **into** your **head**, you realize or think that it is true. If you **get** a fact or idea **into** someone's **head**, you make them realize that it is true. — PHR : VB AND N INFLECT **24.12** If you say that you cannot **get** your **head round** something, you mean that you cannot understand it at all; an informal expression. — PHR : VB AND N INFLECT **24.13** If you **give** someone **their head**, you allow them to do what they want to do, without trying to advise or stop them. — PHR : VB AND N INFLECT **24.14** If alcohol **goes to your head**, it makes you feel drunk. EG *The champagne went straight to my head.* — PHR : VB AND N INFLECT **24.15** If praise or success **goes to** your **head**, it makes you conceited; used showing disapproval. — PHR : VB AND N INFLECT **24.16** If you **keep** your **head**, you remain calm. EG *I managed to keep my head despite the panic all around.* — PHR : VB AND N INFLECT **24.17** If you **lose** your **head**, you panic. EG *He lost his head completely.* — PHR : VB AND N INFLECT **24.18** If you say you could not **make head nor tail of** something, you mean you could not understand it at all; an informal expression. — PHR : VB INFLECTS **24.19** If two or more people **put** their **heads together**, they talk about a problem they have and try to solve it. — PHR : VB INFLECTS ⇑ consult **24.20** If say that you can do something **standing on** your **head**, you mean that you can do it very easily indeed; an informal expression. — PHR : USED AS AN A, N INFLECTS **24.21** If you **take it into** your **head** to do something, you suddenly decide to do it. — PHR : VB AND N INFLECT **24.22** If you say that someone is **off** their **head**, you mean that they are about to do something very foolish or that they do very foolish things; an informal expression. — PHR : VB AND N INFLECT

25 See also **heading**.

head for. If you **are heading for** a particular situation, especially an unpleasant one, you are behaving in such a way that the situation is becoming more and more likely. EG *You're heading for disaster if you carry on smoking so much.* — PHRASAL VB : V+PREP, HAS PASS = be destined for

head off. 1 If you **head off** a person, animal, or vehicle, you make them turn and change the direction they are moving in. EG *We started running and shouting, trying to head off the goats.* — PHRASAL VB : V+O+ADV ⇑ divert

2 If you **head** something **off**, especially something unpleasant, you prevent it from happening. EG *They did this in order to head off possible unrest.* — PHRASAL VB : V+O+ADV = avert

headache /hɛdeɪk/, **headaches**. A **headache** is **1** a pain that you feel in your head. EG *She took an aspirin to relieve her headache.* — N COUNT **2** something that causes you difficulty or worry. EG *Rivalry between the two industries presents a big headache for government.* — N COUNT

headband /hɛdbænd/, **headbands**. A **headband** is a narrow strip of material which you can wear round your head across your forehead, usually to keep hair or sweat out of your eyes.
N COUNT ⇑ band

headboard /hɛdbɔːd/, **headboards**. A **headboard** is an upright board at the end of a bed where your head is.
N COUNT ⇑ board

head boy, head boys. The **head boy** of a school is the boy who is the leader of the prefects and who often represents the school on public occasions.
N COUNT

head count, head counts. If you do a **head count**, you count the number of people present.
N COUNT

headdress /hɛddrɛs/, **headdresses**; also spelled with a hyphen. A **headdress** is something that is worn on a person's head for decoration. EG *The dancers wore face masks and tall head-dresses.*
N COUNT

headed notepaper is notepaper which has the name and address of the person or organization it belongs to printed at the top of each sheet. EG *The doctor sent me a letter on headed notepaper.*
N UNCOUNT

header /hɛdə/, **headers**. A **header** is 1 the act of hitting a ball with your head in football. 2 a jump or dive in a particular direction with your head going first. EG *She took a header into the bushes.*
N COUNT; N SING: a+N = nose dive

head-first; also spelled without a hyphen. 1 If you move in a particular direction **head-first**, your head is the part of your body that is furthest forward as you are moving. EG *He had fallen head-first into the ditch.*
ADV AFTER VB

2 If you rush into something **head-first**, you do it quickly without thinking carefully. EG *She jumped head-first into marriage.*
ADV AFTER VB = headlong

headgear /hɛdgɪə/. You can refer to hats or other things worn on the head as **headgear**.
N UNCOUNT ⇑ clothing

head girl, head girls. The **head girl** of a school is the girl who is the leader of the prefects and who often represents the school on public occasions.
N COUNT

head-hunter, head-hunters; also spelled without a hyphen. A **head-hunter** is a person who tries to persuade someone to leave their job and take another job which has better pay and more status. EG *She was approached by a head-hunter and offered a job with another company.*
N COUNT

heading /hɛdɪŋ/, **headings**. A **heading** is the title of a piece of writing, which is written or printed at the top of the page. EG *Each chapter heading is printed in capital letters... The discussion paper was read out under the heading 'World Fuel Requirements in the 1990's'.*
N COUNT

headlamp /hɛdlæmp/, **headlamps**. A **headlamp** is a headlight.
N COUNT

headland /hɛdlə³nd/, **headlands**. A **headland** is a narrow piece of land which sticks out from the coast into the sea. EG *A road was built across the headland.*
N COUNT

headless /hɛdlɪ²s/. If the body of a person or animal is **headless**, the head has been cut off.
ADJ CLASSIF

headlight /hɛdlaɪt/, **headlights**. **Headlights** are large powerful lights at the front of a vehicle. EG *All the cars had their headlights on.*
N COUNT = headlamp

headline /hɛdlaɪn/, **headlines, headlining, headlined**. 1 A **headline** is the title of a newspaper story, printed in large letters at the top of the story, especially on the front page. EG *The headlines that day were full of news of the kidnapping.*
N COUNT

2 If you **headline** a piece of writing such as a news story, you provide a headline for it. EG *He wrote a long article headlined 'The New Economics'.*
V+O: USU PAST PART, USU+C ⇑ entitle

3 The **headlines** are the main points of the news which are read on radio or television. EG *The news headlines are broadcast on the half hour.*
N PLURAL: USU the+N ⇑ summary

4 Someone who **hits the headlines** suddenly becomes famous because they get a lot of publicity from the media about something. EG *She hit the headlines when she published her second book.*
PHR: VB INFLECTS

headlong /hɛdlɒŋ/. 1 If you move **headlong** in a particular direction, you move fast with your head going before the rest of your body. EG *The frightened elephants ran headlong through the forest.* ▸ used as an adjective. EG *They made a headlong dash for the door.*
ADV AFTER VB; ▸ ADJ CLASSIF: USU ATTRIB

2 If you rush **headlong** into something, you do it quickly without thinking carefully about it. EG *Don't rush headlong into buying new furniture.* ▸ used as an adjective. EG *There was a great unrestrained headlong rush to sell.*
ADV AFTER VB = head-first; ▸ ADJ CLASSIF: USU ATTRIB = reckless

headman /hɛdmə³n/, **headmen**. A **headman** is a chief or tribal leader in a village.
N COUNT

headmaster /hɛdmɑːstə/, **headmasters**. A **headmaster** is a man who is the head teacher of a school.
N COUNT = head

headmistress /hɛdmɪstrɪ²s/, **headmistresses**. A **headmistress** is a woman who is the head teacher of a school.
N COUNT = head

head-on. 1 If two vehicles hit each other or move towards each other **head-on**, they hit each other or move towards each other with their front parts pointing towards each other. EG *The motor cycle ran head-on into the lorry... It was coming at me head-on.* ▸ used as an adjective. EG *...a head-on collision.*
ADV AFTER VB ⇑ head-first; ▸ ADJ CLASSIF

2 A **head-on** conflict, disagreement, etc is firm and direct and has no compromises. EG *The government did not want to risk a head-on confrontation with the unions.* ▸ used as an adverb. EG *It had to meet the threat head-on.*
ADJ CLASSIF: ATTRIB; ▸ ADV AFTER VB ⇑ directly

headphone /hɛdfəʊn/, **headphones**. **Headphones** are a pair of speakers inside pads which you wear over your ears in order to listen to a radio, record player, or tape recorder without other people hearing it. EG *She listened to the record on her headphones.*
N COUNT: USU PL ⇑ earphone

headquarters /hɛdkwɔːtəz/. The **headquarters** of an organization such as the army, police, or a business company are a building or other place where the leaders of the organization work. EG *The bank for which he worked had its headquarters in Paris... The soldier reported to headquarters.*
N PLURAL ⇑ base = HQ

headrest /hɛdrɛst/, **headrests**. A **headrest** is an object which is attached to the back of a seat and which you can lean your head on, especially one on the front seat of a car.
N COUNT ⇑ support

headroom /hɛdru⁴m/ is the space below a roof or a bridge which allows an object to pass or stay underneath it without touching it. EG *There is barely headroom even when he is sitting.*
N UNCOUNT

headscarf /hɛdskɑːf/, **headscarves**. A **headscarf** is a scarf which is worn on the head, especially by women.
N COUNT ⇑ scarf

headship /hɛdʃɪp/, **headships**. A **headship** is the position or job of being a leader, especially a head teacher in a school. EG *Two new headships have been created by the education authority.*
N COUNT

head-shrinker, head-shrinkers. A **head-shrinker** is a psychiatrist; an informal word.
N COUNT

headstand /hɛdstænd/, **headstands**. When someone does a **headstand**, they balance upside down with their head and the palms of their hands on the ground and their legs up in the air.
N COUNT

head start, head starts; also spelled as one word. If you have a **head start** on other people, you have an advantage over them in a competition or race. EG *A university degree would give you a head start in getting a good job.*
N COUNT: USU SING

headstone /hɛdstəʊn/, **headstones**. A **headstone** is a large stone which stands at one end of a grave, usually with the name of the dead person carved on it.
N COUNT = gravestone

headstrong /hɛdstrɒŋ/. Someone who is **headstrong** is determined to do what they want and will not allow anyone to stop them. EG *Luce was stubborn and headstrong.*
ADJ QUALIT = wilful

head teacher, head teachers; also spelled with a hyphen and as one word. A **head teacher** is a teacher who is in charge of a school.
N COUNT

headway /hɛdweɪ/. If you **make headway**, you progress towards achieving something. EG *By the late 1980s their research will probably begin to make headway... The emergency services began to make some headway in restoring order to the devastated area... I find I'm not making much headway with 'War and Peace'.*
PHR: VB INFLECTS

headwind /hɛdwɪnd/, **headwinds**; also spelled with a hyphen. A **headwind** is a wind which blows in the opposite direction to the one in which you are moving. EG *I was cycling against a headwind for 30 miles.*
N COUNT ⇑ wind

headword /hɛdwɜːd/, **headwords**. A **headword** is a word which is followed by a phrase or paragraph which explains the word's meaning, especially in a dictionary. EG *A headword may have more than one meaning.*
N COUNT ⇑ word

heady /hɛdi¹/, **headier, headiest**. 1 A **heady** experience, period of time, idea, etc makes you feel very excited and full of energy. EG *Working in Fleet*
ADJ QUALIT: ATTRIB ⇑ exciting = exhilarating

Street was a heady experience for the young journalist... ...the heady days of the sixties.

2 A **heady** alcoholic drink, atmosphere, etc strongly affects your physical senses, for example by making you feel drunk or excited. EG *I was given a heady mixture of champagne and brandy... The air was heady with the perfume from roses.* ADJ QUALIT = intoxicating

heal /hiːl/, **heals, healing, healed. 1** When a cut, broken bone, or other injury **heals** or **heals up** or when something **heals** it, it becomes healthy and normal again. EG *His leg needs support while the bone is healing... His hoof had healed up... This ointment should heal the cut in no time.* V-ERG, OR PHRASAL VB : V+ADV ⇑ mend

2 If you **heal** someone who has an illness, you make them recover. EG *...success in healing the sick... He had been miraculously healed of his illness.* V OR V+O : USU V+O = cure

3 If you **heal** something, you restore it to its former state after it has been damaged. EG *...damage to the ecology that would take a hundred years to heal... The disagreement has left deep wounds that only time may heal.* V+O = remedy

healer /hiːlə/, **healers**. A **healer** is a person who heals people. N COUNT

health /hɛlθ/. **1** A person's **health** is the condition of their body and the extent to which it is free from illness or able to resist illness. EG *Her health has never been very good... The warning says cigarette smoking is dangerous to your health... The children are all in good health.* N UNCOUNT : USU POSS+N

2 Health is a state in which a person is not suffering from any illness and is feeling well. EG *He was restored to health by good medical care and plenty of rest... Their rosy cheeks were glowing with health.* N UNCOUNT = good health

3 When you **drink to** someone's **health** or **drink** their **health**, you have a drink as a sign of wishing that they will be healthy and happy. EG *We all drank to her health.* PHR : VB INFLECTS = toast

4 The **health** of something such as an organization or a system is its success and the fact that it is working well. EG *The company's health is shown by this year's high profits.* N UNCOUNT : USU +SUPP = prosperity

health centre, health centres. A **health centre** is, in Britain, a building in which the doctors of a particular district have offices where their patients can visit them. N COUNT = surgery

health food, health foods. **Health food** is food which has been made or grown without using any chemicals or artificial ingredients, and which some people eat because they believe it is good for their health. N MASS

healthy /hɛlθiˡ/, **healthier, healthiest. 1** Someone who is **healthy** is well and is not suffering from any illness. EG *...a healthy baby... I'm feeling much healthier since I've started jogging.* ◊ **healthily**. EG *It is perfectly possible to live healthily on a meat-free diet.* ADJ QUALIT = fit, robust ◊ ADV

2 If a feature or quality that you have is **healthy**, it makes you look well or shows that you are well. EG *The children have healthy appetites... ...healthy skin.* ◊ **healthily**. EG *His cheeks were healthily red.* ADJ QUALIT ◊ ADV+ADJ

3 Something that is **healthy** is good for you and likely to make you healthy. EG *...healthy outdoor work... ...healthy seaside air.* ADJ QUALIT ⇑ beneficial = bracing

4 If the condition of something is **healthy**, it is doing well and achieving successful results. EG *The country's economy is fairly healthy.* ADJ QUALIT = thriving

5 A **healthy** amount of something is a large amount that indicates a successful situation. EG *...healthy profits... She had a healthy majority at the last election.* ADJ QUALIT = substantial

6 If you have a **healthy** attitude about something, you show good sense. EG *...a healthy scepticism about the politicians' promises.* ADJ QUALIT = sensible

heap /hiːp/, **heaps, heaping, heaped. 1** A **heap** of things is a pile of them, usually a lot of them in a rather untidy arrangement. EG *Brody picked up the heap of papers and piled them on top of a radiator... ...a compost heap.* N COUNT/PART ⇑ collection = mound

2 If you **heap** things in a pile or you **heap** them **up**, you arrange a quantity of them in a large pile. EG *...food heaped on platters... Heap up the flour round the sides of the bowl... We sat on cushions heaped on the floor.* V+O, OR PHRASAL VB : V+O+ADV

3 If you **heap** praise, criticism, etc on someone or something, you give them a lot of praise or criticism. EG *Film director Kenneth Loach heaped praise on Young Socialists... Burgin heaped scorn on such styles of painting and sculpture.* V+O+A *(on/upon)* = shower

4 Heaps of something or a **heap** of something is a large quantity of it; an informal use. EG *He took heaps of photographs of Vita... We've got heaps of time... There was a heap of information about fish and fishing.* N PART ⇑ lots = loads

5 If you say that something is **heaps** bigger, more interesting, etc than something else, you are saying in an emphatic way that it is very much bigger, more interesting, etc; an informal use. EG *Oh this is heaps better!* ADV+COMPAR

6 If someone falls down or collapses **in a heap**, they fall heavily and untidily and do not move. PHR : USED AS AN A

7 Someone who is at **the bottom of the heap** or at **the top of the heap** is low down or high up in the structure of society or of an organization, considered in terms of their status, their quality of life, and how successful they have been. EG *Single parent families have joined the bottom of the heap in our society... You are still at the bottom of the heap, the most junior of the team.* PHR : USED AS O

heaped /hiːpt/. A container or a surface that is **heaped** with things has a lot of them in it or on it in a pile, especially so many that it cannot hold any more. EG *...heaped baskets waiting for ironing... Add one heaped tablespoon of salt... The desk was heaped with magazines.* ADJ CLASSIF : IF+PREP THEN *with* ⇑ full

hear /hɪə/, **hears, hearing, heard** /hɜːd/. **1** When you **hear** sounds, you are aware of them and are able to recognize or understand them by means of your ears. EG *He heard a distant voice shouting... She could hear clearly... 'What's that noise?'-'I don't hear anything.'... Etta hated to hear Mrs. Hochstadt talk like that.* V OR V+O : NO IMPER ⇑ perceive

2 If you say that you can **hear** something which you heard in the past or which you can easily imagine happening, especially someone saying something, you mean that you are able to imagine hearing it in your mind. EG *He could just hear his brother saying to his wife, 'Isn't my supper ready yet?'* V+O : NO CONT, NO IMPER

3 If you **hear** something such as a lecture or a piece of music, you listen to it. EG *All the relatives were gathered to hear the lawyer read the will... I had the chance to hear her speak in person... You can hear 'A Dark Horse' on Radio Four on Monday.* V+O : NO CONT

4 When a judge or a court **hears** a court case, a legal complaint, etc, they listen to it officially in order to make a decision about it. EG *We hope our plea will be heard... The Court of Inquiry had not yet heard a witness.* V+O

5 If you **hear** from someone, **5.1** you listen to them giving their opinion or information during a debate or discussion. EG *We hear first from a veteran of World War 2... I would have liked to hear more from the patient.* **5.2** you receive a letter or telephone call from them. EG *Very occasionally I hear from her... They'll be delighted to hear from you again.* V+A *(from)* : NO IMPER; V+A *(from)* : NO CONT, NO IMPER

6 If you **hear** some news or information about something or someone, you find it out by someone telling you or by means of radio or television. EG *I was glad to hear that things are quietening down... My first meeting with the woman confirmed everything I had heard about her... 'Haven't you heard?' he screamed. 'He's dead!'... When he came to hear of their difficulties, he volunteered help.* V, V+O/REPORT-CL, OR V+A *(about/of)* : NO CONT, NO IMPER ⇑ learn

7 If you **have heard of** someone or something, you know about them, not in great detail, but enough to know who or what they are. EG *The vast majority of these students had never heard of the Marshall plan... Have you heard of Lewis Baker?* PHR : AUX INFLECTS ⇑ know of

8 If you say that you **have heard** something **before**, you mean that you already know all about it, so it does not surprise you or interest you. EG *I've heard all these arguments before... Yes, we've heard it all before.* PHR : AUX INFLECTS

9 If you say that you **can't hear** yourself **think**, you mean that there is so much noise that you find it very difficult to concentrate or think about anything. EG *I could hardly hear myself think.* PHR : VB INFLECTS

10 If you say **'Do you hear?'** or **'Do you hear me?'** to someone, you are indicating in a firm way that you want them to pay attention to something important that you are saying. EG *A mistake has been made, do you hear me?... Well, I'm not. D'you hear, Sam? I'm not.* PHR

11 If you **won't hear of** someone doing something, PHR : AUX you refuse to let them do it. EG *I offered to pay for myself, but she wouldn't hear of it... Her father had refused to hear of such a thing.* INFLECTS ⇑ reject

12 'Hear hear' is something that people such as politicians say during debates to show that they agree with what the speaker is saying. CONVENTION

hear out. If you **hear** someone **out**, you listen to them without interrupting them until they have finished saying everything that they want to say. EG *It was considered inattentive to hear a speaker out in silence for any length of time.* PHRASAL VB : ORDER V+O+ADV, OR V+ADV +REPORT-CL ≠ interrupt

hearer /hɪərə/, **hearers.** The **hearer** of someone who is speaking is someone who is listening to them; a fairly formal word. EG *He was shocked by the violent reactions of some of his hearers.* N COUNT = listener ≠ speaker

hearing /hɪərɪŋ/, **hearings. 1 Hearing** is the sense which people and animals have that makes it possible for them to be aware of sounds, and to recognize and understand them. EG *My sense of hearing gradually deteriorated... Her limbs were weak, her hearing almost gone.* ● See also **hard of hearing.** N UNCOUNT

2 If you are **in** or **within** someone's **hearing**, you are so close to them that they can hear what you are saying. EG *You shouldn't have said those awful things in the hearing of the waiter... She began to grumble about it within his hearing.* PHR : USED AS AN A

3 A **hearing** is an official meeting which is arranged in order to collect facts about an incident, event, or problem, so that a decision can be made as to whether a further investigation is necessary. EG *There was not a trial but a hearing before a grand jury... On the third day of the hearing he dismissed his Counsel.* N COUNT

4 If you get **a hearing** or **a fair hearing**, you have the opportunity to give your opinion or ideas about a particular subject, especially when other people disagree with you. EG *It was the loudest voice that got a hearing... She believed in giving a fair hearing to all sides of the question.* PHR : USED AS O

hearing aid, hearing aids. A **hearing aid** is a small device worn by people who are rather deaf which magnifies sounds so that they can hear them more easily. EG *She had turned off her hearing aid.* N COUNT = deaf-aid

hearsay /hɪəseɪ/ is information which you have been told by another person or learnt indirectly, but which you do not personally know to be true. EG *We are told (though perhaps it is only hearsay) that he has emigrated to Australia.* N UNCOUNT = rumour ≠ fact

hearse /hɜːs/, **hearses.** A **hearse** is a large car that carries the coffin at a funeral. N COUNT ⇑ vehicle

heart /hɑːt/, **hearts. 1** Your **heart** is the organ in your chest that pumps the blood around your body. EG *She could hear her heart beating... Heavy drinking can cause lethal damage to the liver, heart and kidneys... Her heart condition was much improved by the operation... ...the first successful human heart transplant.* N COUNT

2 You use the word **heart** to refer to the part of your chest that is nearest your heart. EG *Mrs Hochstadt clutched at her heart and shouted to the driver 'Not so fast!'... Stroganov pressed his hand to his heart: 'I swear,' he said.* N COUNT : USU POSS+N IN SING = breast

3 Children often say **'Cross my heart and hope to die'** or just **'Cross my heart'** when they want someone to believe that what they are saying is true or when they are making a promise which they intend to keep. CONVENTION = honest

4 Your **heart** is also used to mean the place where your deepest and strongest feelings and emotions are; a fairly literary use. EG *...the troubled heart of the younger man... I felt that she knew all the secrets of my heart... My heart ached for the lovers... The news filled Sam's heart with deep uneasiness.* N COUNT : USU WITH POSS = bosom, breast

5 You use the word **heart** when you are talking about someone's character and the attitudes that they have towards other people, especially when they are kind and generous. EG *...a wildly passionate nature and a warm, generous heart... He's got a very soft heart, hasn't he... ...a man with more money than sense and more heart than money.* N COUNT/ UNCOUNT : USU SING

6 Heart is used in various expressions to refer to courage and determination. EG *It was a bad time and people were losing heart... No one had the heart to tell her what they really thought... This should give heart to parents who worry about their children.* N UNCOUNT

7 The **heart** of something is the most central and important part of it. EG *...the individualism which lies at the heart of the Christian tradition... ...the heart of the problem... ...lyrics that get right to the heart of the matter.* N COUNT : USU the+N IN SING+of = core

8 The **heart** of a vegetable such as a cabbage or lettuce is its centre leaves. N COUNT+SUPP

9 The **heart** of a place is its centre. EG *Thousands of protesters marched right into the heart of San Francisco... ...a working men's club in the heart of the steel area of Sheffield.* N COUNT : USU the+N IN SING+of

10 A **heart** is also a shape with an outline made up of two curves going upwards and then meeting at a point at the bottom. It is often coloured red or pink and used to represent love. EG *These sweets were in the shapes of hearts, diamonds and spades... ...a heart-shaped region a thousand kilometres across.* N COUNT

11 Hearts is one of the four suits in a pack of playing cards. Each card in the suit is marked with one or more symbols in the shape of a heart. ▸ A **heart** is one of the cards in the suit. EG *I was forced to play my last heart.* N UNCOUNT/ COUNT ▸ N COUNT ⇑ card

12 The word **heart** is also used in the following expressions. **12.1** If you say that someone is a person **after** your **own heart**, you mean that they are the sort of person that you admire and like because of their character, opinions, tastes, etc. EG *He's a man after my own heart.* PHR AFTER NG **12.2** If you say that someone is a particular kind of person **at heart**, you mean that that is what they are really like, however different they may seem to be. EG *He was at heart a kindly and reasonable man... They were townsfolk at heart.* PHR : USED AS AN A = basically **12.3** If you say that someone has a **broken heart**, you mean that they are deeply upset and sad, for example because a love affair has ended unhappily. EG *He said that she had died of a broken heart.* PHR : USED AS O/ S, N INFLECTS **12.4** If you know something such as a poem **by heart**, you have learnt it so well that you can remember it perfectly. EG *I couldn't see the point of learning by heart the dates of forgotten battles.* PHR : USED AS AN A **12.5** If someone has a **change of heart**, their feelings and attitudes about something change and their behaviour shows this. EG *Even if the Government does have a change of heart, a more fundamental problem remains.* PHR : USED AS O, change INFLECTS **12.6** If you have **everything the heart can desire**, you have everything you could possibly want; a rather old-fashioned expression. EG *She was given everything the heart could desire.* PHR : USED AS O, N AND VB INFLECT **12.7** If you say something **from the heart** or **from the bottom of** your **heart**, you are being genuine and sincere. EG *I mean it from the bottom of my heart.* PHR : USED AS AN A ⇑ sincerely **12.8** You say **'Have a heart'** to someone when you think they are asking you to do too much and you want them not to ask so much of you; an informal expression. CONVENTION **12.9** Your **heart's desire** is something that you want very much indeed; a rather old-fashioned expression. PHR : USED AS O/ C/S **12.10** If your **heart is in** your **mouth**, you feel very excited, worried, or frightened. EG *She knocked timidly at the door, her heart in her mouth.* PHR : NOUNS AND VB INFLECT **12.11** If you say that someone's **heart is in the right place**, you mean that they are kind, considerate, and generous. PHR : *heart* AND VB INFLECT **12.12** If your **heart isn't in** something, you have very little enthusiasm for it, usually because you are depressed or are thinking about something else. EG *The children soon sensed that his heart was not in it.* PHR : N AND VB INFLECT **12.13 In** your **heart of hearts** means in your most secret and genuine thoughts and feelings that you will never reveal to people who might want to hurt or harm you. EG *In his heart of hearts, he didn't trust the authorities.* PHR : USED AS AN A ⇑ secretly = deep down **12.14** If you use the expression **two hearts that beat as one**, you are referring to two people who are very close in opinions, feelings, tastes, etc, especially if they are in love with each other. PHR **12.15** If you can do something **to your heart's content**, you can do it as much as you want. EG *Jack could talk and plan to his heart's content, it would make no difference now.* PHR : USED AS AN A, heart INFLECTS **12.16** You say **with all my heart** when you want people to realize how strongly you feel an emotion or believe something. EG *'Wish me luck, Castle.'–'Of course. With all my heart.'... I hated these people with all my heart.* PHR : USED AS AN A, N INFLECTS ⇑ very much = fervently **12.17** If someone **breaks** your **heart**, they make you very sad and unhappy, usually because they end a love affair or close relationship. EG *She must have broken Antonio's heart.* PHR : VB AND N INFLECT ⇑ hurt **12.18** If something **breaks** your **heart**, it makes you feel very sad and depressed; used especially of situations where people are suffering but you can do nothing to help them. EG *It breaks* PHR : VB AND N INFLECT ⇑ hurt *my heart to see you so unhappy.* **12.19** If something is **close to, dear to** or **near to** your **heart**, it is very important to you and you are interested in and concerned about it. PHR : USED AS AN A, N INFLECTS **12.20** If a feeling, action, or gesture **comes from the heart**, it is sincere and genuine. EG *The cheers for Hearst came from the heart.* PHR : VB INFLECTS **12.21** If something **does** your **heart good**, it makes you feel happy and cheerful. EG *It does my heart good to see you in such high spirits.* PHR : VB AND N INFLECT **12.22** If you **harden** or **steel** your **heart against** someone, you become less sympathetic and friendly to them than you were before, usually because they have behaved badly or you have quarrelled. EG *Frieda hardened her naturally soft heart against them.* PHR : VB AND N INFLECT

12.23 When your **heart leaps**, you are so excited about something that your heart suddenly starts beating very fast. EG *My heart leapt. She had remembered!* PHR : N AND VB INFLECT **12.24** If you **lose** your **heart** to someone, you fall in love with them; a fairly literary expression. EG *She lost her heart to a handsome soldier.* PHR : VB INFLECT **12.25** When you **open** your **heart** to someone, you tell them what you really feel and believe. EG *I was duped into opening my heart and expressing my thoughts.* PHR : VB AND N INFLECT, IF + PREP THEN *to* ⇑ talk **12.26** If you **pour out** your **heart** to someone, you tell them all about your feelings, problems, etc, especially if you are in love and are unhappy. EG *He poured out his heart to a French colonel he met in the bar.* PHR : VB AND N INFLECT, IF + PREP THEN *to* **12.27** If you have **set** your **heart on** something, or on doing something, you want it very much or want to do it very much. EG *If you've set your heart on a cat then you'd better start saving up your pocket-money.* PHR : VB AND N INFLECT

12.28 When your **heart sinks**, you suddenly have a very strong feeling of disappointment or unhappiness about something. EG *I found there were six of us auditioning and my heart sank.* PHR : N AND VB INFLECT **12.29** If you **take heart** from something, you feel encouraged and optimistic. EG *Sandy had taken heart from his lucky escape.* PHR : VB INFLECTS **12.30** If you **take** something, especially someone's behaviour, **to heart**, you are deeply affected and upset by it. EG *Don't take it to heart, I'm sure he didn't mean what he said.* PHR : VB INFLECTS **12.31** If you **throw** yourself **heart and soul into** something, you start to do it with a great deal of enthusiasm, dedication, and pleasure. EG *He decided to throw himself heart and soul into some great cause... Mrs Kaul threw herself into her work heart and soul.* PHR : VB INFLECTS **12.32** If you **wear** your **heart on** your **sleeve**, you openly show your deepest emotions, especially your love for someone, rather than keeping them hidden. PHR : VB INFLECTS

heartache /hɑ:teɪk/, **heartaches**; also spelled with a hyphen. **Heartache** is very great sadness and emotional suffering. EG *I was young enough to suffer adolescent heartache... ...all the trials and heartaches that followed.* N UNCOUNT/COUNT

heart attack, heart attacks. **1** A **heart attack** is a serious medical condition in which your heart gives you a great deal of pain and beats in an irregular way. People often die of heart attacks. EG *He had had a heart attack two years earlier.* N COUNT ⇑ seizure

2 You say that someone will have a **heart attack** about something, when you want to emphasize how shocked, surprised, or angry they will be. EG *I swear the old man nearly had a heart attack when he saw my new hairstyle.* N SING : *a*+N = fit

heartbeat /hɑ:tbi:t/, **heartbeats**; also spelled with a hyphen. A **heartbeat** is the regular movement of your heart as it pumps blood around your body. EG *The doctor searched in vain for the least sound of a heartbeat in the baby's chest... She awoke in a state of extreme panic, with rapid heartbeat and heavy breathing... He heard nothing but her heartbeats.* N COUNT/UNCOUNT ⇑ beat

heartbreak /hɑ:tbreɪk/, **heartbreaks**. **Heartbreak** is very great sadness and emotional suffering, especially after the end of a love affair or close relationship. EG *...tragedy and heartbreak... All of Allen's work is about heartbreak.* N UNCOUNT/COUNT ⇑ grief ≠ happiness

heartbreaking /hɑ:tbreɪkɪŋ/. Something that is **heartbreaking** causes you to feel very great sadness or pity. EG *I had a heartbreaking letter from an American friend whose wife has died.* ADJ QUALIT ⇑ sad = heartrending

heartbroken /hɑ:tbrəʊkəⁿn/. Someone who is **heartbroken** is very sad and emotionally upset. EG *She was heartbroken... Sylvia would be heartbroken if one of her cats died.* ▸ used of people's behaviour. EG *...heartbroken sighs.* ADJ QUALIT = broken-hearted

heartburn /hɑ:tbɜ:n/ is a painful burning sensation in your chest, caused by indigestion in your stomach. N UNCOUNT ⇑ pain

-hearted combines with adjectives such as 'kind' or 'cold' to indicate that someone has a particular character or personality or is in a particular mood. EG *She's a kind-hearted person, I've found... Judy suddenly felt light-hearted and happy.* See also **wholehearted, half-hearted.** COMB : FORMS ADJ QUALITS

hearten /hɑ:təⁿn/, **heartens, heartening, heartened.** When something such as good news **heartens** someone, it encourages them and makes them cheerful. EG *Sir Geoffrey was heartened by this and has been describing the debate as 'very encouraging'... I am very heartened by her success in the last election.* ◊ **heartening.** EG *...some heartening news.* V+O : USU PASS ⇑ encourage = cheer ◊ ADJ QUALIT

heart failure is a serious medical condition in which someone's heart does not work as well as it should, sometimes stopping completely so that they die. EG *My mother had heart failure the year before last.* N UNCOUNT ⇑ illness

heartfelt /hɑ:tfɛlt/ is used to describe something that you feel or believe deeply and sincerely. EG *...a heartfelt prayer... ...a heartfelt wish that it will never happen.* ADJ CLASSIF : USU ATTRIB ⇑ sincere = fervent

hearth /hɑ:θ/, **hearths.** **1** A **hearth** is the floor of a fireplace, which sometimes extends into the room. EG *A bright fire was burning in the hearth.* N COUNT ⇑ grate

2 Your **hearth** or the family **hearth** is your home, thought of as a place of warmth and comfort; a fairly formal use. EG *Messages of cheer and comfort from the family hearth reached the soldiers in time for Christmas.* N SING WITH DET : USU *the*+N ● Your **hearth and home** is your home and your family life there. EG *He was reluctant to leave hearth and home and work abroad again.* ● PHR : USED AS O

hearthrug /hɑ:θrʌg/, **hearthrugs**; also spelled with a hyphen. A **hearthrug** is a rug which is put in front of a fireplace. N COUNT

heartily /hɑ:tɪli¹/. **1** If you do something **heartily**, you do it in a loud, cheerful, and enthusiastic way. EG *When he had finished, Etta laughed heartily... 'Now then,' she cried heartily, 'who's for a lovely drink?'* ADV WITH VB ⇑ cheerfully

2 **Heartily** means completely and absolutely. EG *Why should one pretend to like people one actually heartily dislikes?... She had taken up the Open University course again, and he heartily approved.* ADV = thoroughly

heartland /hɑ:tlænd/, **heartlands.** The **heartland** of a country or continent is the most central area of it. EG *...the steppes of the Eurasian heartland... ...the booming industrial heartlands of western Europe.* N COUNT+SUPP ⇑ centre

heartless /hɑ:tlɪ²s/. Someone who is **heartless** is cruel, unkind, and has no sympathy for anyone or anything. EG *'You are a heartless bastard,' she said... ...a shrewd and heartless schemer.* ▸ used of people's behaviour or attitudes. EG *She sat there, mocking me with her heartless eyes.* ◊ **heartlessly.** EG *...while so many defenceless creatures are being heartlessly destroyed.* ADJ QUALIT = hard ≠ kind ◊ ADV

heartrending /hɑ:trɛndɪŋ/; also spelled with a hyphen. Something that is **heartrending** causes you to feel great sadness and pity. EG *Isabel's sigh was heartrending.* ADJ QUALIT ⇑ sad = heart-breaking

heartstrings /hɑ:tstrɪŋz/. When sights, sounds, events, etc **tug at** your **heartstrings**, they cause you to feel very emotional. EG *It's wonderful music–it really tugs at your heartstrings.* PHR : VB INFLECTS

heartthrob /hɑ:tθrɒb/, **heartthrobs**; also spelled with a hyphen. A **heartthrob** is a man who is very physically attractive, so that lots of women fall in love with him. N COUNT ⇑ idol

heart-to-heart, heart-to-hearts. A **heart-to-heart** is an intimate conversation between two people, especially close friends, in which feelings, personal problems, etc are talked about openly. EG *I had quite a heart-to-heart with her last night... Maybe we ought to have a heart-to-heart talk.* N COUNT, OR N BEFORE N

heart-warming; also spelled as one word. Something that is **heart-warming** causes you to feel pleased and very happy. EG *It was a heart-warming spectacle... Is there a sight more heartwarming than a family reunion?* ADJ QUALIT ⇑ pleasing = cheering

hearty /hɑ:ti¹/, **heartier, heartiest.** **1** Something that is **hearty** is loud, cheerful, and friendly. EG *We spent the rest of the evening singing hearty songs... He had a big hearty laugh... There was hearty knocking at the door.* ADJ QUALIT

2 Someone who is **hearty** is cheerful, enthusiastic, and energetic, and speaks loudly, sometimes in a way that annoys people. EG *...hearty soccer fans.* ADJ QUALIT = boisterous

3 Hearty means complete and absolute when it is used of feelings and opinions. EG *My staff and I have a hearty hatred of all examinations... ...a hearty condemnation of Alan's job.* ADJ CLASSIF: ATTRIB ⇑ thorough

4 Hearty meals are large and very satisfying. EG *I had a hearty meal in a crowded diner.* ADJ QUALIT: ATTRIB

heat /hiːt/, **heats, heating, heated. 1** When you **heat** something, you raise its temperature by using, for example, a flame or a special piece of equipment. EG *Don't heat more water than you need... ...accommodation that is exceptionally difficult to heat.* V+O = warm ≠ cool

2 Heat is **2.1** warmth or the quality of being hot. EG *Water retains heat much longer than air... ...loss of body heat... ...the heat from a nuclear blast... Save up to 75 per cent of your heat loss by insulating your roof.* N UNCOUNT **2.2** the temperature of something that is warm or that is being heated. EG *...equivalent to blood heat... ...a valuable method of heat control... I use gas cookers when possible because the heat of the burners is instantly adjustable.* N UNCOUNT+SUPP **2.3** a source of heat, for example a cooking ring or the heating system of a house; used especially when referring to its temperature, or when you are adjusting its temperature. EG *Don't put pans straight on to a high heat... If a room gets too warm, turn down the heat.* N SING WITH DET

3 The **heat** is very hot weather. EG *Because of the intense heat, I slept half inside the tent and half outside... You shouldn't go out in this heat.* N SING WITH DET ● The **heat of the day** is the hottest part of the day, especially when this is very hot. EG *...relaxing in the shade during the heat of the day.* ● PHR: USU USED AS O ⇑ time

4 Heat is also used to mean a state of strong emotional feeling, especially of anger or excitement. EG *Realizing that you wrote it in the heat of emotion I am prepared to forget the matter... 'You're a fool,' Boylan said, without heat.* N UNCOUNT

5 The **heat** of a particular activity or time is the point at which there is the greatest activity and excitement. EG *Last week, in the heat of the election campaign, the Prime Minister left for America!... ...in the heat of the moment.* N SING: *the*+N+*of*

6 A **heat** is a race or competition whose winners qualify to take part in the next one with other winners of similar races or competitions. This continues until one person has won the final race or competition. ● See also **dead heat.** N COUNT

7 When a female animal is **on heat** or **in heat**, she is in a state where she is ready for mating. EG *Bitches on heat can be very messy.* PHR: USED AS A C = in season

8 See also **heated, heating.**

heat up. 1 When something **heats up**, it gradually becomes hotter. EG *The air over the great land mass heats up in summer and rises.* PHRASAL VB: V+ADV = warm up ≠ cool down

2 When you **heat** something **up**, you make it hot; used especially of food which has already been cooked and allowed to go cold, so that you are heating it again. EG *He debated heating up the pot roast.* PHRASAL VB: V+O+ADV = warm up

3 When a situation **heats up**, things start to happen much more quickly and with increased interest and excitement among the people involved. EG *Things were heating up so fast in the US that I felt I should return straight away.* PHRASAL VB: V+ADV ≠ cool off

heated /hiːtɪ²d/. **1** Someone who is **heated** about something is angry and excited about it. EG *He carried on at length and became quite heated in the process.* ▸ used of a discussion or quarrel. EG *...a heated argument.* ◇ **heatedly.** EG *Naturalists argued heatedly about the issue for nearly a century.* ADJ QUALIT ≠ calm ◇ ADV

2 A **heated** piece of equipment is one that has been designed so that it can be made hotter when required by a heating mechanism inside it. EG *...a heated curler set... ...a heated swimming pool.* ADJ CLASSIF: USU ATTRIB

heater /hiːtə/, **heaters.** A **heater** is a piece of equipment or a machine which is used to raise the temperature of something, especially of the air inside a room or a car. EG *...a paraffin heater... ...a water heater... The car soon warms up–the heater's very good.* ● See also **immersion heater.** N COUNT ⇑ appliance

heath /hiːθ/, **heaths.** A **heath** is an area of open land covered with rough grass or heather and with very few trees or bushes. N COUNT

heathen /hiːðəⁿn/, **heathens**; an old-fashioned word. If you say that someone is **heathen,** you mean that they have no religion, or have a religion that is not Christianity, Judaism, or Islam; often used by members of these religions showing disapproval. EG *The ancient heathen inhabitants of this place worshipped many gods.* ▸ used as a noun. EG *He was sent out to convert the heathens.* ADJ CLASSIF = pagan ▸ N COUNT = pagan

heather /hɛðə/ is a low, spreading plant with woody stems, very small spiky leaves, and small purple, pink, or white flowers. Heather grows wild, especially on hills or moorland. N UNCOUNT

heating /hiːtɪŋ/ is **1** the process of heating a building or room, considered especially from the point of view of how much this costs. EG *The rent was £7 a week including heating... We're using solar panels for domestic hot water heating.* N UNCOUNT **2** the system and equipment that is used to heat a building. EG *Try turning down the heating.* ● See also **central heating.** N UNCOUNT

heat-stroke is the same as sunstroke. N UNCOUNT

heatwave /hiːtweɪv/, **heatwaves**; also spelled with a hyphen. A **heatwave** is a period of time during which the weather is much hotter than usual. N COUNT

heave /hiːv/. The forms **heave, heaves, heaving, heaved** are used in paragraphs 1 to 5. The forms **heave, heaves, heaving, hove** are used in paragraph 6 and for the phrasal verb.

1 If you **heave** or if you **heave something that is heavy or difficult to move,** you push, pull, or lift it using a lot of effort. EG *The rock was as large as a small motor car. 'Heave!' cried Jack... I brought the rope around the tree and heaved with all my might... Lee heaved himself with a groan from his chair.* V OR V+O ▸ used as a noun. EG *'One heave', cried Nick, 'that's all it needs.'* ▸ N COUNT ⇑ movement

2 If you **heave** something heavy in a particular direction, you throw it there. EG *He heaved a table at me.* V+O+A

3 If something **heaves,** it moves up and down or in and out with large regular movements. EG *I staggered across the heaving deck... She was in a state of suppressed emotion: heaving breasts and short breaths... His shoulders heaved silently.* V

4 To **heave** also means to vomit or feel sick. ● Something that makes your **stomach heave** makes you feel as though you are going to be sick. EG *The sight of the soapy scum made her stomach heave.* ● PHR: VB AND N INFLECT

5 If you **heave a sigh,** you give a big sigh. EG *They all heaved a sigh of relief when he finally departed.* PHR: VB INFLECTS

6 When something **heaves in sight** or **into view,** it becomes visible to you as it moves nearer to you or as you move nearer to it; a literary expression. EG *The island hove in sight... Our garden was heaving into view.* PHR: VB INFLECTS

heave to. When a boat or ship **heaves to,** it stops moving; a nautical term. PHRASAL VB: V+ADV ⇑ stop

heaven /hɛvəⁿn/, **heavens. 1 Heaven** is a place of eternal happiness where God is believed to live, and where good people are believed to go when they die. Many people imagine that heaven is high in the sky. EG *Do you believe you'll go to heaven?... ...prayer, the meeting place of earth and Heaven... He lifted pious eyes to heaven and sighed deeply.* N PROPER ≠ Hell

2 If you say that something such as a place or a situation is **heaven** or **heaven on earth,** you mean that it gives you a lot of pleasure; a fairly informal use. EG *Mrs Duncan's cottage is just heaven... To have a good publisher at last was heaven... Kelmscott is a heaven on earth.* N UNCOUNT OR PHR: USED AS C = paradise ≠ hell

3 The **heavens** are the sky; a literary use. EG *The moon was high in the heavens... The man continued to gesticulate sadly towards the heavens... ...the creation of the heavens and the earth.* N PLURAL: *the*+N ● If the **heavens open,** it suddenly starts raining very heavily. ● PHR: VB INFLECTS

4 You say **heaven knows,** in fairly informal English, **4.1** to emphasize that you do not know something or that you find something very surprising. EG *Heaven knows what I would do without it... He wandered across Hyde Park and ended up, heaven knows why, in the Geological Museum.* PHR: USU+WH **4.2** to emphasize something that you feel or believe very strongly. EG *Heaven knows I've suffered enough!* PHR: USU+REPORT-CL

5 Heaven is also used in the following fairly informal expressions. **5.1** You say **good heavens** or **heavens** to express surprise or to emphasize that you agree or disagree with someone. EG *Heavens, is that the time?... 'Oh, good heavens, no,' said Etta with a light laugh.* EXCLAM = good grief **5.2** You say **heaven forbid** to emphasize that you very much hope that something will not happen. EG *He wants to come here? Heaven forbid.* CONVENTION **5.3** You PHR+O say **heaven help** someone if they do a particular thing in order to emphasize what a difficult situation they will be in if they do it because nobody will be able to help them. EG *Heaven help her if she goes under in this sea.* **5.4** If you ask what **in heaven's name** something is, where **in heaven's name** someone is, etc, you are asking the question in an emphatic way that shows that you are angry or surprised. EG *What in heaven's name does that mean?* **5.5** If you **move heaven and earth** to do something, you try as hard as you can to do it. EG *Bill moved heaven and earth to get a ticket for the concert.* **5.6** Something that **smells** or **stinks to high heaven** smells very bad indeed. EG *The drains stink to high heaven.* **5.7** • **thank heaven**: see **thank.** • **for heaven's sake**: see **sake.** PHR : AFTER WH = on earth; PHR : VB INFLECTS; PHR : VB INFLECTS ⇑ smell

heavenly /hɛvə⁰nli¹/. Something that is **heavenly 1** relates to heaven or is like heaven. EG *...earthly crime and heavenly punishment.* **2** is very pleasant and enjoyable; an informal use. EG *...a big steaming pot of the most heavenly stew... We spent a heavenly day on the beach.* ADJ CLASSIF : ATTRIB; ADJ QUALIT ⇑ wonderful = blissful

heavenly body, heavenly bodies. A **heavenly body** is a planet, star, moon, or other natural object in space. N COUNT

heaven-sent. Something that is **heaven-sent** is unexpected but very welcome because it happens at just the right time. EG *...the latest heaven-sent triumph of advanced technology.* ADJ CLASSIF ⇑ lucky

heavenward /hɛvə⁰nwəd/; also **heavenwards**. **Heavenward** means towards the sky or to heaven; a literary word. EG *Mr Menzies turned his eyes heavenward... The old lady's husband had departed heavenwards during the night.* ADV WITH VB

heavily /hɛvɪli¹/. If someone says something **heavily**, they say it in a slow way which shows a feeling such as sadness, tiredness, or annoyance. EG *'I don't understand you,' he said heavily... He gave me a long look, then said heavily, 'I've driven all the way from Kei Road to see you.'* • See also **heavy.** ADV WITH VB ⇑ slowly ≠ lightly

heavy /hɛvi¹/, **heavier, heaviest; heavies. 1** Something that is **heavy 1.1** weighs a lot or weighs more than is usual and is often difficult to move. EG *He dumped the heavy suitcases by the door... Water was running in slow heavy drops off his fingertips... It was considerably larger and heavier than the average medical bag.* ▸ used to ask how much something weighs. EG *How heavy are you? About ten stone?* ◇ **heaviness**. EG *She could feel the heaviness of the animal.* **1.2** is great in amount, degree, or intensity; used especially of something that is unpleasant or worrying. EG *There would be heavy casualties... ...a heavy responsibility... ...heavy expenditure.* ◇ **heavily**. EG *It began to rain outside more heavily... He smoked heavily all his life... Hong Kong's prosperity relies heavily on foreign businesses.* **1.3** has a solid, thick appearance rather than being delicate in design. EG *...spectacles with heavy black frames... The clouds were heavy and dark.* ADJ QUALIT ≠ light; ▸ ADJ CLASSIF : PRED, how+ADJ; ◇ N UNCOUNT; ADJ QUALIT; ◇ ADV ⇑ a lot; ADJ QUALIT ≠ light

2 Something that is **heavy** with a quantity of things is full of them or loaded with them; a literary use. EG *The trees were heavy with fruit and blossoms... The air was heavy with the fragrance of lush wild blooms.* ADJ QUALIT : PRED+*with* = laden

3 If a person's breathing is **heavy**, it is unusually loud and deep, for example as a result of physical effort, illness, or emotion. EG *She lay sleeping, her breathing heavy.* ◇ **heavily**. EG *He grabbed the nearest chair and collapsed into it, breathing heavily... She sighed heavily.* ADJ QUALIT; ◇ ADV WITH VB ⇑ deeply

4 If a person has a **heavy** build, their body is large, solid, and strong or slow-moving. EG *He moved across the room quickly, in spite of his heavy build.* ◇ **heavily**. EG *I've never seen anyone so heavily built move quite so fast.* ◇ **heaviness**. EG *He might make a boxer, as far as width and heaviness goes.* ADJ QUALIT : ATTRIB; ◇ ADV WITH VB; ◇ N UNCOUNT ⇑ physique

5 If a person's face or part of their face is **heavy**, it looks sad, tired, or unfriendly, and as if it is weighed down by something. EG *He had a heavy, sullen face... ...her eyes, with their heavy lids.* ADJ QUALIT

6 A substance or material that is **heavy** is thick and solid in texture. EG *The heavy clay soils of the region were almost unworkable... She was wearing a heavy tweed coat.* ADJ QUALIT ≠ light

7 Food that is **heavy** is solid or large in amount and often difficult to digest. EG *I felt so full after that heavy meal... ...a heavy pudding.* ADJ QUALIT = filling ≠ light

8 A **heavy** movement or action **8.1** is one that is done with a lot of force or pressure; used especially of something that is moving downwards in a rather uncontrolled way. EG *The plane was having its undercarriage renewed after a heavy landing... A heavy blow with a club knocked him senseless.* ◇ **heavily**. EG *She walked with me, leaning heavily on my arm... He sat down heavily.* **8.2** is one that is rather slow and not smooth or graceful. EG *He canters away, then subsides into a heavy lumbering trot.* ◇ **heavily**. EG *She heavily hoisted herself to her feet.* ADJ QUALIT : ATTRIB ⇑ forceful ≠ gentle, light; ◇ ADV WITH VB ≠ gently; ADJ QUALIT ≠ sprightly; ◇ ADV WITH VB

9 A **heavy** machine or piece of military equipment is very large and powerful. EG *The army had tanks and heavy artillery.* ADJ CLASSIF : ATTRIB ≠ light

10 Something such as a period of time or a schedule that is **heavy** involves a lot of work, especially too much work, which you cannot easily deal with. EG *I've had a heavy week... My timetable is very heavy this term.* ADJ QUALIT ⇑ busy ≠ easy, light

11 Work that is **heavy** is hard and tiring because it requires a lot of strength or energy. EG *I cannot do heavy work in the fields.* ADJ QUALIT ≠ light

12 A machine or device that is **heavy** on something, especially on fuel, uses a lot of it; an informal use. EG *Our old car was very heavy on petrol.* ADJ QUALIT : PRED+*on* ≠ economical

13 If you are **heavy** on something, you use too much of it, especially in an unskilful or crude way; an informal use. EG *You've been a bit heavy on the mascara, haven't you?* ADJ QUALIT : PRED+*on* = lavish ≠ skimpy

14 Heavy humour is a way of joking that is very obvious and rather unskilful. ADJ QUALIT ≠ subtle

15 Air or weather that is **heavy** is unpleasantly still, hot, and damp or stale. EG *The air was heavy, damply hot... It's heavy today. I think it's going to thunder.* ADJ QUALIT = oppressive ≠ cool, fresh

16 A situation or atmosphere that is **heavy** has a serious quality which makes you feel anxious or sad. EG *The silence continued, breathless and heavy and full of shame.* ADJ QUALIT = oppressive

17 If your heart is **heavy**, you are sad about something. EG *With a heavy heart, I left the house.* ADJ QUALIT ≠ happy

18 A situation that is **heavy** is serious and difficult to cope with; an informal use. EG *It was all a bit heavy yesterday.* ADJ QUALIT

19 A piece of writing or a speech that is **heavy** is difficult to understand because it is written or spoken in a serious, formal, or complicated way. EG *...heavy academic anthropological texts.* ADJ QUALIT ≠ light

20 A **heavy** is a large strong man who is employed to use violence if necessary in order to protect a person or place; an informal use. EG *He had a couple of heavies with him, so we didn't push our luck.* ▸ used as an adjective to refer to a group of these people. EG *Could it be the heavy mob come to beat them up?* N COUNT = tough guy; ▸ ADJ CLASSIF : ATTRIB

21 • **a heavy hand**: see **hand.** • **to make heavy weather of** something: see **weather.**

heavy-duty. A **heavy-duty** machine or other piece of equipment is strong and can be used a lot or used to do very hard work without breaking or wearing out. EG *...heavy-duty machinery.* ADJ CLASSIF : USU ATTRIB = robust ≠ lightweight

heavy-handed. Someone who is **heavy-handed** acts or speaks forcefully or roughly and without any care or thought. ▸ used of a person's actions or behaviour. EG *We are incensed at the government's heavy-handed economic policies.* ADJ QUALIT ⇑ forceful ≠ delicate

heavy industry, heavy industries. **Heavy industry** is industry in which large machines are used to produce a raw material such as steel, or to make large objects. EG *Heavy industry was quailing before foreign competition.* N UNCOUNT/COUNT ≠ light industry

heavy metal is a style of rock music with a strong, fast beat, which is played very loudly on electric guitars and drums. N UNCOUNT

heavy-set. Someone who is **heavy-set** has a large, solid body; used especially in American English. ADJ CLASSIF = thick-set

heavyweight /hɛvi¹weɪt/, **heavyweights. 1** A **heavyweight** is a boxer weighing more than 175 pounds and therefore in the heaviest class; a technical term in boxing. EG *He had been a heavyweight boxing champion.* N COUNT

2 Something such as an issue or a subject that is **heavyweight** is serious and important. EG *...heavyweight current affairs reporting.* ADJ QUALIT ≠ trivial

3 A **heavyweight** substance, for example a **heavyweight** cloth, is thick and heavy. EG *...heavyweight cotton bedspreads.* ADJ CLASSIF : ATTRIB

Hebraic /hiˈbreɪɪk/. Something that is **Hebraic** belongs or relates to the Hebrews and their language or culture. EG *...an ancient Hebraic melody.* ADJ CLASSIF = Hebrew

Hebrew /hiːbruː/, **Hebrews**. 1 **Hebrew** is a language that was spoken by Jews in former times and that is spoken now in Israel in a more modern form. EG *...knowledge of the Old Testament in Hebrew.* N PROPER

2 A **Hebrew** was a person in former times who was Jewish and lived in Israel. ▸ used as an adjective. EG *...the greatest of all the Hebrew prophets.* N COUNT ▸ ADJ CLASSIF

heck /hɛk/; an informal word. 1 If you say 'oh **heck**!', you are expressing slight irritation or surprise. EG *Oh heck! I'd forgotten all about that!* EXCLAM = blast, rats

2 If you say something is **a heck of a** lot, **a heck of a** long time, etc, you are emphasizing that it is a very large amount, a very long time, etc. EG *Jean has done a heck of a lot for us.* PHR+NG

heckle /hɛkəˀl/, **heckles, heckling, heckled**. If you **heckle** or if you **heckle** public speakers or performers, you interrupt them by making loud, unfriendly remarks from the audience. EG *He went to heckle at their meetings.* ◇ **heckling**. EG *Now, now, no heckling please.* V OR V+O = barrack ◇ N UNCOUNT

heckler /hɛkəˀlə/, **hecklers**. A **heckler** is someone who interrupts a public speaker or performer by making loud remarks from the audience. N COUNT ⇑ person

hectare /hɛktɑː/, **hectares**. A **hectare** is a measurement of an area of land, which equals 10,000 square metres, or 2.471 acres. N COUNT : USU NUM+N

hectic /hɛktɪk/. A situation that is **hectic** is very busy and involves a lot of rushed activity. EG *It's been pretty hectic at the office... Monday morning is a hectic time.* ADJ QUALIT ≠ peaceful, quiet

hector /hɛktə/, **hectors, hectoring, hectored**. If you **hector** someone, you try to make them do something by bothering them and talking to them aggressively. EG *Marcus must be left alone, he must not be hectored.* ◇ **hectoring**. EG *Television interviewers were accused of being too aggressive and too hectoring with party officials.* V OR V+O ⇑ persuade = bully ◇ ADJ QUALIT

he'd /hiːd/ is 1 the usual spoken form of 'he had', especially when 'had' is an auxiliary verb. EG *He said he'd told them.* 2 a spoken form of 'he would'. EG *He said that he'd give me a lift.*

hedge /hɛdʒ/, **hedges, hedging, hedged**. 1 A **hedge** is a row of bushes or small trees that form a boundary to a garden, field, or road. EG *We emerged through the hedge into the safety of the lane... ...hawthorn hedges.* N COUNT ⇑ bush

2 If you **hedge** against something unpleasant or unwanted that might affect you, you do something which will protect you from it. EG *This deposit provides a way of hedging against fluctuating interest rates.* ▸ used as a noun. EG *The investment can be seen as a safe hedge against the insane rates of inflation.* V+A *(against)* ▸ N COUNT+*against* ⇑ protection

3 If you **hedge** or if you **hedge** a problem or question, you avoid answering the question or committing yourself to a particular action or decision. EG *We kept on hedging the questions... Politicians are known for hedging on promises... America is hedging a little on its grain embargo.* V : IF+PREP THEN *on*, OR V+O = stall

4 If something **is hedged about, hedged around**, or **hedged in** with things, it is affected by things which prevent or restrict its freedom or natural development. EG *The concessions were hedged around with many restrictions... We feel hedged in by fear... The proposals were hedged in with legal niceties.* V+O+A : ONLY PASS, USU+*with* ⇑ restricted

5 If you **hedge** your **bets**, you reduce the risk of losing a lot by supporting more than one person or thing in a situation where they are opposed to each other. PHR : VB INFLECTS

hedgehog /hɛdʒhɒg/, **hedgehogs**. A **hedgehog** is a small brown animal which has sharp spikes covering its back, and which rolls up into a ball to defend itself. N COUNT

hedgerow /hɛdʒrəʊ/, **hedgerows**. A **hedgerow** is a row of bushes, trees, and plants, usually growing along a bank bordering a country lane or between fields. EG *...tidy hedgerows dividing the green fields.* N COUNT

hedonism /hiːdəˀnɪzəˀm, hɛd-/ is the belief that gaining pleasure is the most important thing in life; a formal word. ◇ **hedonist**. EG *My son, being somewhat of a hedonist, prefers the attractions of the city.* N UNCOUNT ◇ N COUNT ⇑ person

hedonistic /hiːdəˀnɪstɪk, hɛd-/ means relating to hedonism; a formal word. EG *...lives of unending hedonistic delight.* ADJ CLASSIF

heed /hiːd/, **heeds, heeding, heeded**; a formal and old-fashioned word. 1 If you **heed** someone's advice or warning, you pay attention to it and do what they suggest. EG *David wished that he had heeded his father's warnings.* V+O = mind, listen to

2 If you **take heed of** what someone says or if you **pay heed** to them, you pay attention to them and consider carefully what they say. EG *Take heed of these warnings... He ran along the beach, paying no heed to the crowd of people shouting after him.* PHR : VB INFLECTS = take note of

heedless /hiːdlɪˀs/. If you do something **heedless** of another person or thing, you do it without taking any notice of them. EG *She stood glued to the radio, heedless of the ordered bustle about her... He began to put down the rebellion by force, heedless of the military logistics involved... ...heedless passers-by hurrying through the market place.* ADJ CLASSIF : IF+PREP THEN *of* ⇑ regardless

hee-haw /hiː hɔː/ **hee-haws**. **hee-haw** is used in writing to represent the sound that a donkey makes. N COUNT ⇑ bray

heel /hiːl/, **heels, heeling, heeled**. 1 Your **heel** is 1.1 the back part of your foot, just below your ankle. EG *One of his heels had got blistered on the walk.* 1.2 the raised part on the bottom of your shoe at the back. EG *All I could hear was the click of my own heels on the linoleum.* N COUNT N COUNT

2 **Heels** are women's shoes that are raised very high at the back, and that are sometimes considered suitable for formal or evening wear. EG *They walked down a narrow corridor, her heels making a noise like a pony trotting.* N PLURAL

3 The **heel** of a sock, stocking, shoe, etc is the part that covers your heel. N COUNT : IF+PREP THEN *of*

4 The **heel** of your hand is the rounded pad at the bottom of your palm. EG *He squashed the sandwich down with the heel of his hand.* N COUNT+*of*

5 The word **heel** is also used in the following expressions. 5.1 If a person or an animal is walking **at your heels**, they are walking close behind you. EG *There was a black Labrador walking at his heels.* PHR : USED AS AN A 5.2 If you **bring** someone **to heel**, you force them to obey you. EG *...the government's policy of bringing the dissidents to heel by economic sanctions.* PHR : VB INFLECTS ⇑ subdue 5.3 If you **click** your **heels**, you make a sharp sound with the heels of your shoes, especially by knocking them together, often as part of a military salute. EG *He made a smart military turn, clicking his heels.* PHR : VB INFLECTS 5.4 If you **dig** your **heels in**, you refuse to do something such as change your opinions or plans, especially when someone is trying very hard to make you do so. EG *Organizations employing volunteers are beginning to dig their heels in about the new regulations.* PHR : VB INFLECTS

5.5 If you **drag** your **heels**, you do something unwillingly and with deliberate slowness. EG *They're not being obstructive as such, but they're certainly dragging their heels.* PHR : VB INFLECTS ⇑ delay 5.6 If one event or situation **follows hard on the heels of** another, it happens very quickly or immediately after it. EG *Cultural isolation has followed quickly on the heels of economic recession in this country... A second thermal wave follows immediately on the heels of the first.* PHR : VB INFLECTS ⇑ succeed 5.7 If you **tread hard on** someone's **heels** or if you are **hot on** their **heels**, you follow them very close behind. EG *Two little boys were treading hard on her heels, whining for money.* PHR : VB INFLECTS = dog 5.8 If you are **kicking** your **heels** or **cooling** your **heels**, someone is deliberately keeping you waiting, so that you get bored or impatient; an informal expression. EG *The two young men were cooling their heels in his outer office.* PHR : VB INFLECTS ⇑ wait = mark time 5.9 If you **spin on** your **heel, turn on** your **heel**, or **swing on** your **heel**, you suddenly turn round, especially because you are angry or surprised. EG *Miss Lenaut turned on her heel and walked back to her desk... He swung round upon his heel and surveyed the young man.* PHR : VB INFLECTS = spin round

5.10 If you **take to** your **heels**, you run away; a literary expression. EG *As soon as he saw me he took to his heels.* PHR : VB INFLECTS 5.11 Someone who has something such as a group of people **under** their **heel** or **beneath** their **heel** has them in their power and control. EG *Caesar had all Rome under his heel... ...those beneath the invader's heel.* PHR : USED AS AN A

6 • See also **Achilles heel**. • **head over heels**: see **head**.

heel over. When something **heels over**, it leans over very far as if it is about to fall over. EG *Heeling over to the right, the two motorcyclists swept past him.* PHRASAL VB : V+ADV ⇑ lean

hefty /hɛfti¹/, **heftier, heftiest**; an informal word. 1 Someone or something that is **hefty** is very large in size, weight or amount. EG *...a broad, hefty Irish nurse... We sell them at a hefty profit... ...hefty redundancy payments.* ADJ QUALIT = substantial

2 A movement that is **hefty** is forceful and vigorous. EG *I was nearly knocked down by a hefty slap on the back.* ADJ QUALIT = powerful

hegemony /hɪ²gɛmənі¹/ is the domination or control by one country or state over a group of others, especially if it is a member of that group; a formal word. EG *The final key to Europe's world hegemony was her military superiority.* N UNCOUNT

heifer /hɛfə/, **heifers**. A **heifer** is a young cow that has not yet had a calf. N COUNT

height /haɪt/, **heights**. 1 The **height** of a person or thing is its measurement from the bottom to the top. EG *The redwood grows to 100 metres in height... What height are you?... He was of medium height... The animal grew to a height of over a metre and a half... This enables them to grow to considerable heights.* N COUNT+SUPP, OR N UNCOUNT

2 **Height** is the quality of being tall. EG *You'll recognize her because of her height.* N UNCOUNT

3 A particular **height** is the distance that something is above the ground or above something else mentioned. EG *It usually reaches its maximum height of 80,000 feet in about ten minutes... ...attacking aircraft at heights often below sixty metres... The bag of sand had been dropped from about shoulder height... The glider skimmed at tree-top height along and over the ridge... The mooring rings should be fixed at a height of three feet above the high water mark.* N COUNT/UNCOUNT+SUPP • If something **gains height**, it moves to a higher position above the ground. If it **loses height**, it moves to a lower position above the ground. EG *...birds flapping their wings furiously to gain height... The plane began to lose height on its approach to Heathrow..* • PHR : VB INFLECTS ⇑ move

4 A **height** is a high position or place above the ground. EG *...throwing herself off a height... ...dropping from a height... ...fierce fighting on the heights above the bay.* N COUNT : IF PL, ALSO IN NAMES AFTER N

5 The **height** of an activity, situation, etc is the time when it is the most successful, powerful, or intense. EG *The group had at its height 500 members... ...an athlete at the height of training... The crisis was at its height... ...at the height of its power... It is the height of the tourist season.* N SING : WITH POSS = peak

6 If you say that something is the **height** of a particular quality, you are emphasizing that it has that quality to the greatest degree possible; a fairly formal use. EG *It would be considered the height of arrogance... It seemed to me the height of luxury.* N SING : *the*+N+*of* ⇑ maximum

7 If you say that something reaches great **heights**, you mean that it becomes very extreme or intense. EG *Love must soar to the greatest heights of sacrifice... My panic and irritability reached absurd heights... Your pay will never rise to the same heights... ...dizzy heights of joyous success.* N PLURAL+SUPP

heighten /haɪtə⁰n/, **heightens, heightening, heightened**. When something **heightens** a feeling that you have, or when the feeling **heightens**, it increases in degree or intensity. EG *We should try to calm people's fears rather than heighten them through uncertainty... It heightens still further the sense of speed... As their hardship heightened, so did their desperation and anger.* ◊ **heightened**. EG *She is in a state of heightened emotion.* V-ERG ⇑ increase = intensify ◊ ADJ CLASSIF : ATTRIB

heinous /hɛɪnəs, hiː-/. Something that is **heinous** is extremely evil; a formal word. EG *...heinous crimes.* ADJ QUALIT = atrocious

heir /ɛə/, **heirs**. 1 Someone's **heir** is the person who has the right to inherit their money, property, or title when they die. EG *The Prince of Wales is heir to the throne... ...Thompson's son and heir... ...Lord Granby, heir to one of the most magnificent houses in Britain.* N COUNT : IF + PREP THEN *to* ⇑ successor

2 If someone or something **is heir to** a particular quality or condition that developed in the past, they inherit it so that it continues to exist. EG *This is one of the many blights that the city is heir to.* PHR : VB INFLECTS

heiress /ɛərɪ²s/, **heiresses**. An **heiress** is a woman or girl who has the right to inherit property or a title, especially when this involves great wealth. EG *He wanted Thynne's bride, the richest heiress in England... She is born heiress to a fortune in money.* N COUNT : IF + PREP THEN *to*

heirloom /ɛəluːm/, **heirlooms**. An **heirloom** is an ornament or other object that has belonged to a family for a very long time and that has been handed down from one generation to another. EG *...jewels and other family heirlooms.* N COUNT ⇑ object

held /hɛld/ is the past tense and past participle of **hold**.

helicopter /hɛlɪkɒptə/, **helicopters**. A **helicopter** is an aircraft without wings which has one or two sets of large blades which rotate above it and enable it to take off vertically and hover in one position. N COUNT = chopper

heliport /hɛli¹pɔːt/, **heliports**. A **heliport** is an airport for helicopters. N COUNT

helium /hiːlɪəm/ is a gas that is lighter than air and that is used to fill balloons and airships. N UNCOUNT

hell /hɛl/. 1 In Christianity and some other religions, **Hell** is the place where the souls of wicked and evil people go after death, where they will receive eternal punishment. EG *They were afraid of going to Hell when they died.* N PROPER

2 If you say that a particular situation is **hell**, you mean that it is extremely unpleasant, for example because it frightens or depresses you or is full of problems; an informal use. EG *War is hell... It took us eight days of unspeakable hell to walk to the border... I don't know how I've stuck it. It's been hell.* N UNCOUNT = torture

3 **Hell** is a swear word used by some people to express annoyance or to emphasize what they are saying. EXCLAM = blast

4 The word **hell** is also used in the following informal expressions. **4.1** If **all hell breaks loose**, people suddenly begin reacting very strongly about a particular issue or event, often arguing about it and becoming very angry. EG *When Darwin concluded that men were descended from apes, all hell broke loose... If there had been a programme forecasting all this a year ago, all hell would have broken loose.* PHR : VB INFLECTS

4.2 If you say that something will happen **come hell or high water**, you mean that it will certainly happen, in spite of any difficulties that there might be. EG *He said he'd be there, come hell or high water.* PHR : USED AS AN A

4.3 If you say that a place or a situation is **hell on earth**, you mean that you think it is dreadful and that it causes you considerable suffering. PHR : USU USED AS C **4.4** If someone **gives** you **hell** or **makes** your **life hell**, they are very severe and cruel to you, for example by making you work extremely hard, by shouting at you, or by hitting you. EG *I bet these ladies gave their secretaries hell, because they were perfectionists... The director was going to give them hell the moment the curtain came down... He used to make her life hell at rehearsals.* PHR : VB INFLECTS **4.5** Something that **plays hell** or **plays merry hell** with something else has a bad effect on it, for example by damaging it. EG *The new extension will play hell with the plumbing... Thatching is a painful job and plays merry hell with your hands.* PHR : VB INFLECTS ⇑ wreck **4.6** If you **raise hell**, you protest strongly and angrily about a situation in order to persuade other people to correct it or improve it. EG *He intended to raise hell with the housing department.* PHR : VB INFLECTS **4.7** If you say **there'll be hell to pay**, you mean that there will be serious trouble. EG *There'll be hell to pay if we don't get this work done on time.* PHR : FIRST VB INFLECTS **4.8** If you say to someone **'go to hell'**, you are angrily telling them to go away and not talk to you; a rude expression. EG *He'd have told you to go to hell if you'd tried to give him any advice.* CONVENTION = get lost **4.9** If you **'get the hell out** of somewhere, you leave there, usually very quickly; used in American English. EG *Let's get the hell out... Get the hell out of here!* PHR : VB INFLECTS ⇑ get out **4.10** Someone who says **'to hell with'** something is expressing the fact that they have a low opinion of it or that they are angry about it and do not want any more to do with it. EG *To hell with university and scholarship... Let me get rich quick and to hell with society.* PHR **4.11** If you ask **why the hell, who the hell, what the hell**, etc, you are emphasizing how angry, annoyed, or surprised you are. EG *How the hell should I know?... Who the hell do you think you are?... What in hell are you talking about?* PHR = on earth **4.12** If someone says **what the hell**, they are expressing the fact that they don't care about something. EG *I found out that she had a boyfriend. But what the hell? We could still have lunch together.* CONVENTION **4.13** If someone does something **for the hell of it**, they do it for fun or for no particular reason. EG *I don't want to offend people for the hell of it.* PHR : USED AS A = for kicks **4.14** If you say that something is a **hell of a** lot, **one hell of a** mess, etc, you are emphasizing a quality that it has, for example its size or how good or bad it is. EG *There was a hell of a lot of traffic on the roads... From what I can see, Rob,* PHR BEFORE N *you're in a hell of a good position... The government was in one hell of a mess.* **4.15** People say **like hell** to emphasize that they disagree very strongly with someone. EG *'We wouldn't have to bother with anaesthetic.' 'Like hell you wouldn't,' I said.* **4.16** If you say that you work **like hell**, that something is as hard **as hell**, etc, you are emphasizing how strong the action or quality is that you mention. EG *It was beginning to hurt like hell... I worked like hell and got my A levels... It's cold as hell out here... I sure as hell don't like this responsibility.* **4.17** If you say you **wish to hell** or **hope to hell** that something is true, you are emphasizing how strongly you wish or hope it to be true. EG *I wish to hell he was here now... I hope to hell he didn't go alone.* **4.18** If something scares or annoys **the hell out of** you, it scares or annoys you a great deal. EG *He had a way of snapping his fingers that annoyed the hell out of me... You scare the hell out of people.* — CONVENTION, OR PHR : USED AS ADV; PHR : USED AS AN A, OR PHR AFTER ADJ; PHR : VB INFLECTS; PHR

he'll /hi:l/ is the usual spoken form of 'he will'. EG *He'll have to go to hospital, won't he?*

hell-bent. If you are **hell-bent** on doing something, you are very determined to do it, however dreadful the consequences might be. EG *The two sides seem hell-bent on another meaningless trial of strength.* — ADJ CLASSIF : USU PRED+*on*

Hellenic /hɛlenɪk, -li:-/ is used of the people, language, and culture of Ancient Greece. — ADJ CLASSIF : USU ATTRIB

hellish /hɛlɪʃ/; a very informal word. **1** If you describe something as **hellish**, you mean that it is extremely unpleasant. EG *It's hellish being a student without a grant... The hellish traffic swirls all round the church but inside there is calm.* — ADJ QUALIT = diabolical

2 Hellish and **hellishly** mean extremely, or to a very great degree. EG *The Dorchester is hellish expensive in fact... It was a hellishly difficult job... These people are hellishly snobbish.* — ADV+ADJ/ADV = dreadfully

hello /hə²ləʊ/, **hellos**; also spelled **hallo** and **hullo**. **1** You say **'Hello'** to someone **1.1** when you are greeting them or when you are meeting them for the first time in the course of a day. EG *'Hello,' Lynn said. 'Hello,' said the girl... Hallo there, Richard, how are you today?* ▸ used as a noun. EG *Do come over to the table and say hello to the group... He gave me a cheery 'hello' as we passed in the street.* **1.2** at the beginning of a telephone conversation, either when you answer the phone or before you give your name or say why you are phoning. EG *'Hello.'–'Hello. Could I speak to Sue, please?'... He lifted the receiver and said 'Hello,' but no one replied.... 'Parkfield Medical Centre.'–'Hello. I'd like to make an appointment to see one of the doctors.'* — CONVENTION = hi ≠ goodbye; ▸ N COUNT; CONVENTION

2 A radio or television presenter often says **'Hello'** at the beginning of a programme, as part of the introduction. EG *Hello, and welcome to 'Money Box'... Hello. This programme is all about computers.* — CONVENTION

3 You can call **'hello'** to attract someone's attention. EG *The door was open. 'Hello, can I come in?' I called. 'Is anyone here?'* — CONVENTION

4 You sometimes say **'hello!'** when you want to express surprise. EG *'Hullo!' Charlie said. 'What's this?'* — EXCLAM

helm /hɛlm/, **helms**. **1** The **helm** of a boat or ship is its wheel or tiller and the position from which the boat is controlled. EG *The company's chairman took the helm of the huge ship for two minutes.* — N COUNT : USU SING

2 When someone is **at the helm** or when they **take over the helm**, they are in a position of leadership or control. EG *With such a prime minister at the helm one need never fear a dictatorship of generals... He took over the helm of state in 1948.* — PHR : USED AS AN A, OR PHR : VB INFLECTS

helmet /hɛlmɪt/, **helmets**. A **helmet** is **1** a type of hard hat which is worn as protection for the head, for example by motorcyclists, or as part of their uniform by firemen or policemen. ● See also **crash helmet**. **2** an iron or steel hat worn by soldiers in battle. — N COUNT; N COUNT

helmsman /hɛlmsmə³n/, **helmsmen**. The **helmsman** of a boat is the person who is steering it. — N COUNT ⇑ controller

help /hɛlp/, **helps, helping, helped**. **1** If you **help** someone, **1.1** you do part of a job for them so that it can be finished more easily or more quickly. EG *Something went wrong with his machine so I helped him fix it... The old porter helped to carry my sleeping bag... I employed her to help me in the home... Brandt returned to help in the reconstruction of Germany.* **1.2** you give useful advice, information, or sympathy to them when they have a problem or a question. EG *This organization may be able to help you with such information... All local councils aim at helping people with real housing needs... Hello–Can you help? I've been trying to get a London number... We must try to help students to have confidence in their ability.* — V, V+INF/*to*-INF, V+O, OR V+O+INF/*to*-INF = assist, aid; V, V+INF/*to*-INF, V+O, OR V+O+INF/*to*-INF ⇑ advise = assist

2 If something **helps** you, it makes it easier for you to get something or to do something you want to do. EG *It would be a useful qualification to help me in my present job... A diagram does help when one is reading this... I've got about 40 pence, will that help?... Maybe it would help if you took some adult education courses.* — V, V+INF/*to*-INF, V+O, OR V+O+INF/*to*-INF = be of use

3 You say that something **helps** when it makes a difficult or unpleasant situation easier to tolerate or more pleasant, EG *This room is so depressing–I suppose new curtains would help... I get terrible headaches but it helps if I lie down in the dark for a while... I had to wait for over an hour before anybody came, which didn't help any.* — V, V+*to*-INF, OR V+O ⇑ improve

4 If someone **helps** you get something that you need, especially money, they provide you with it. EG *The kids needed new shoes and I wondered whether Social Security could help me.* — V, V+O, OR V+O+INF/*to*-INF

5 If you **help** someone go somewhere or move in some way, you give them support so that they can move more easily. EG *The courier helped everyone out of the coach... I helped Oakley inside... Help me sit up, Lottie.–I can't sleep.* ● If you **help** someone **to their feet**, you help them stand up. — V+O : USU+A, OR V+O+INF = assist; ● PHR : VB INFLECTS

6 If you **help** someone up with something heavy, you help them lift it, for example to a shelf above their head. EG *Can you help me up with this case please?* — V+O+ADV *(up)* : IF+PREP THEN *with*

7 If you **help** someone on or off with a piece of clothing, usually a coat, you help them put it on or take it off. — V+O+ADV *(on/off)*+A *(with)*

8 If one thing **helps** to do something, it is one of several facts or conditions that together result in a particular situation or event. EG *One of the things that can help to keep prices down is high productivity... Having a job helps keep them off the streets... The shock had helped her find her voice.* — V+INF/*to*-INF, OR V+O+INF/*to*-INF ⇑ contribute

9 If you **help** someone to some food or drink, you serve it to them. EG *Can I help you to some more meat?* — V+O+A *(to)*

10 If you **help** yourself, **10.1** you serve yourself some food or drink. EG *Mr Stokes helped himself to some more rum... He helped himself from the sauce boat proffered to him.* **10.2** you take something yourself, rather than have someone give it to you or serve you. EG *Can I borrow a pencil?–Yes, help yourself.* **10.3** you steal something; an informal use. EG *He's been helping himself to the contents of the till again!* **10.4** you try to get yourself out of a difficulty you are in. EG *The provision of financial means to allow communities to begin to help themselves.* — V+O (REFL) : IF+PREP THEN *to*; V+O (REFL); V+O (REFL) : IF+PREP THEN *to*; V+O (REFL)

11 If you **can't help** the way you feel or the way you behave, you cannot control it or change it or stop it happening. EG *You can't help who you fall in love with... You know what his temper's like, he just can't help himself... It was so crowded, I couldn't help leaning on him a little... 'You must stop thinking like that.'–'But I can't help it!'* — V+O (NG/REFL), OR V+ING : AFTER MODAL/BROAD NEG

12 You use the expressions **I can't help but** do something or **I can't help** doing something when you want to emphasize the point you are making in a polite way and not sound rude or abrupt. EG *I cannot help but think that is very important... I can't help feeling that it was a mistake to let him go... He's a chap you couldn't help but admire.* — PHR+INF/ING

13 If you give **help** to someone who has a problem or question, you give them advice, information, or support. EG *The organization gives help and support to single women... Ask the Citizens Advice Bureau if you need help with the letter.* — N UNCOUNT = assistance

14 If you have **help** to do something, you have someone who helps you do it. EG *I do all my shopping and the gardening on my own with no help at all... She needs help to get up the stairs.* — N UNCOUNT = assistance

15 A **help** is someone who is employed to do housework in another person's home. EG *...a mother's help.* — N COUNT = daily

16 If you need **help** with something such as money or accommodation, you need it to be provided for you. EG *It is quite substantial help that we're talking about: many hundreds of pounds... Ask for help with your fares at the Social Security Office.* — N UNCOUNT ⇑ aid

17 Help is the assistance that someone gives when — N UNCOUNT they go to rescue a person who is in danger. EG *One student set off down the mountain for help... I thought I'd better yell for help.*

18 You shout **'help!'** when you are in danger in order to attract someone's attention so that they can come and rescue you. EXCLAM

19 If you say that someone or something is **a help**, **a great help**, **a lot of help**, etc, you mean that they have helped you to do something that you were having difficulty with. EG *He was a great help with some of the problems... The new tablets are a tremendous help... That isn't much help.* PHR : USED AS C ⇑ use

20 If something **is of help**, it makes things better than they might have been. EG *Having a sober mind around might prove to be of some help... The fact that we taught everything has been of help... I sat with my head bent forward but this was of no help either.* PHR : VB INFLECTS

21 You say **'there is no help for it'** when you realize that you are forced to do something that you would prefer not to do. EG *There's no help for it, we'll just have to sell the shop.* PHR : VB INFLECTS

22 You use the expression **so help me God** when you are making a very serious promise, for example in a law court. EG *I swear that I will tell the truth, so help me God.* PHR

help out. 1 If you **help** someone **out**, you lend them some money. EG *Come back at the end of the week if you're still broke and I'll see if I can help you out.* PHRASAL VB : V+O+ADV

2 If you **help out** or **help** someone **out**, you do some work for them. EG *She helped out with the instruction... I was asked to come in for a few days to help them out.* PHRASAL VB : V+ADV, OR V+O+ADV

helper /hɛlpə/, **helpers**. A **helper** is a person who helps another person or group with a job they are doing. EG *All the helpers for this organization are voluntary.* N COUNT = assistant

helpful /hɛlpfʊl/. 1 Someone who is **helpful** is useful to you by doing part of your job for you or by giving you advice or information. EG *She made a special effort to be helpful and polite to Lynne... They were all very pleasant and extremely kind and helpful.* ▸ used also of the information, advice, etc that is given. EG *None of these suggestions is very helpful... I find Adler's theories quite helpful.* ◇ **helpfully**. EG *Doctor Percival said helpfully, 'I'd advise you not to go'.* ◇ **helpfulness**. EG *Children depend mainly on the intuition and helpfulness of adults to get the things that they need.* ADJ QUALIT; ◇ ADV WITH VB; ◇ N UNCOUNT

2 Something that is **helpful** makes a situation more pleasant or more easy to tolerate. EG *It is often helpful during an illness to talk to other sufferers.* ADJ QUALIT = reassuring

helping /hɛlpɪŋ/, **helpings**. A **helping** of food is the amount of it that you get in a single serving. EG *...a second helping of pudding... My mother used to give my older brother larger helpings of cornflakes.* N PART = serving, portion

helpless /hɛlplɪ²s/. If you are **helpless**, 1 you are unable to behave normally or to react normally to a situation because you have no power or strength. EG *He could do nothing, he was helpless... He was helpless to resist... He kept the audience helpless with laughter.* ▸ used also of a person's behaviour or attitudes. EG *...a horribly helpless feeling... ...the sort of helpless situation where there's nothing you can do.* ◇ **helplessly**. EG *His head seemed to sink helplessly down... ...his wrist, which hung helplessly at his side... ...helplessly handicapped children.* ◇ **helplessness**. EG *She took advantage of my utter helplessness.* 2 you have no protection, and cannot defend yourself or anyone else. EG *...a helpless child... ...a chick left in the nest, blind and helpless.* ◇ **helplessly**. EG *...the little boys stretched out so helplessly on the ground... Sir James had no option but to look on helplessly.* ◇ **helplessness**. EG *...the helplessness of childhood.* ADJ QUALIT ⇑ powerless; ◇ ADV WITH VB ⇑ uselessly; ◇ N UNCOUNT; ADJ QUALIT ⇑ vulnerable; ◇ ADV WITH VB; ◇ N UNCOUNT ⇑ vulnerability

helter-skelter /hɛltə skɛltə/, **helter-skelters**. 1 You use **helter-skelter** to describe something that is hurried and disorganized, especially when things happen very quickly, one after the other. EG *...the last minute helter-skelter rush for the bus... Then the film plunges into a helter-skelter account of Melvin's marriage.* ▸ used as an adverb. EG *...pieces of rubbish blowing helter-skelter across the concrete.* ADJ CLASSIF : ATTRIB ⇑ rushed; ▸ ADV WITH VB = pell-mell

2 A **helter-skelter** is a tall piece of apparatus in the form of a spiral which you can slide down for fun, usually in fairgrounds. N COUNT

hem /hɛm/, **hems, hemming, hemmed**. 1 The **hem** of a skirt or dress is the bottom edge of it, which is folded over and sewn to make it neat and to prevent it fraying. N COUNT

2 If you **hem**, you sew the edge of a piece of cloth to make it neat and prevent it fraying. V OR V+O

hem in. If someone **is hemmed in** or if something **hems** them **in**, they are prevented from moving because they are surrounded. EG *The Princess's car was hemmed in by the crowd.* PHRASAL VB : V+O+ADV ⇑ restrict = box in

he-man, he-men. A **he-man** is a strong man, especially one who likes to show everyone how strong he is; an informal word. N COUNT

hemisphere /hɛmɪsfɪə/, **hemispheres**. A **hemisphere** is 1 one half of the earth. EG *First the northern, then the southern hemisphere is inclined towards the sun... ...the greatest empires in the western hemisphere.* 2 one half of the brain. EG *...studies of the brain leading to the conclusion that its hemispheres have separate and distinct functions.* N COUNT ⇑ part; N COUNT ⇑ section

3 one half of a sphere. N COUNT

hemline /hɛmlaɪn/, **hemlines**. The **hemline** of a dress or skirt is the bottom edge of it. N COUNT

hemlock /hɛmlɒk/ is a poison made from a plant which has small white flowers, a spotted stem, and finely divided leaves. N UNCOUNT

hemoglobin /hiːmə⁶gləʊbɪn, hɛm-/. See **haemoglobin**.

hemophilia /hiːmə⁶fɪlɪə, hɛm-/. See **haemophilia**.

hemorrhage /hɛmə⁰rɪdʒ/. See **haemorrhage**.

hemorrhoids /hɛmə⁰rɔɪdz/. See **haemorrhoids**.

hemp /hɛmp/ is a plant grown in Asia, some varieties of which are used to make rope, and others of which are used to produce the drug cannabis. N UNCOUNT

hemstitch /hɛmstɪtʃ/ is a special sewing stitch that you use when you sew a hem. N UNCOUNT

hen /hɛn/, **hens**. A **hen** is 1 a female chicken. People often keep hens for their eggs, which you can cook and eat. EG *She had vegetables, a flower garden, three cows, a dozen hens, and a fine cockerel.* 2 the female of any bird. EG *...a hen pheasant.* N COUNT ⇑ fowl ≠ cock; N COUNT ≠ cock

hence /hɛns/; a formal word. You use **hence** 1 to indicate that you have just given a reason for what you are about to say. EG *The computer has become smaller and cheaper and hence more available to a greater number of people.* 2 after you have mentioned a period of time to mean from now or from this time. EG *The tunnel will open in 1993, seven years hence... ...a few hours hence.* 3 to mean from here; a very formal use. EG *We arrive at the side gate; hence steps lead down to the walled garden.* ADV SEN = thus, therefore; ADV AFTER NG; ADV AFTER NG ≠ thence

henceforth /hɛnsfɔːθ/ means from this time on; used in formal English. EG *He never returned to live in Hanover, and henceforth became 'William' instead of Wilhelm... Henceforth his life would never be the same again.* ADV SEN

henchman /hɛntʃmə³n/, **henchmen**. A **henchman** is someone who supports and obeys without question a person in a position of authority or power, and whose actions are often violent or dishonest; used showing disapproval. EG *He signed the papers and left it to his henchmen to do the work.* N COUNT ⇑ follower

henna /hɛnə/, **hennas, hennaing, hennaed**. 1 **Henna** is a reddish-brown dye that is used especially for colouring hair or skin. It is made from the leaves of a shrub which grows in Asia and North Africa. N UNCOUNT

2 When you **henna** your hair or your skin, you dye it using henna. EG *My hair was still crimson from having been persistently hennaed for seven years.* ◇ **hennaed**. EG *...slightly curly, hennaed hair.* V+O; ◇ ADJ CLASSIF

hen party, hen parties. A **hen party** is a party or gathering at which only women are present; used in informal English. N COUNT ⇑ celebration

henpecked /hɛnpɛkt/. If you describe a man as **henpecked**, you mean that he is completely dominated by a woman, usually his wife, who orders him about and tells him what to do. EG *Macbeth can be seen as the henpecked husband of a domineering wife.* ADJ QUALIT

hepatitis /hɛpətaɪtɪs/ is a serious disease which causes the patient's liver to become inflamed. N UNCOUNT

heptagon /hɛptəgə⁷n/, **heptagons**. A **heptagon** is a geometric shape that has seven straight sides. N COUNT

heptagonal /hɛptægənə⁰l/. An object or shape that is **heptagonal** has seven straight sides. ADJ CLASSIF

her /hɜː/. 1 **Her** is used as the object of a verb or preposition. You use **her** when you are referring to a PRON : SING, USED AS O woman, girl, or female animal who has already been mentioned or named, or whose identity is known. See **she**. EG *I knew your mother. I was at school with her... When she had the interview, they gave her the job... If your child develops a fear of the dark, try to reassure her.* ▸ sometimes used in relation to a nation, ship, or car. EG *The Cadillac was standing next to one of the pumps. 'Fill her up,' Mr Herbert said.*

2 You also use **her** to indicate that something belongs or relates to a woman, girl, or female animal who has already been mentioned or named, or whose identity is known. See **she**. EG *Clarissa jumped to her feet. Her face was very red... She took the clippers from her husband... She's Davis's secretary. Her name is Cynthia.* ▸ sometimes used in relation to a nation, ship, or car. EG *Britain must, of course, expand her air power.* — DETPOSS

3 Her is also used in some titles when you are referring to a woman with that title. EG *...her ladyship... ...Her Majesty the Queen.* — DETPOSS : USED IN TITLES

herald /hɛrəld/, **heralds, heralding, heralded. 1** Something that **heralds** a future event, situation, etc is a sign that it is going to happen or appear. EG *His rise to power heralded the end of the liberal era.* ▸ used as a noun. EG *The festival was the herald of a new age... The Barbican Centre is the herald of the new style of theatrical entertainment.* — V+O ⇑ signal = mark; ▸ N COUNT+*of* = forerunner

2 If an important event or action **is heralded**, announcements have been made about it so that it is publicly known and expected. EG *...the royal couple's much heralded world tour... Every reduction in taxation is heralded as a new achievement... The official opening was highly ceremonial, heralded in the great hall by a fanfare of trumpets.* — V+O, OR V+O+A (*as*) : USU PASS ⇑ announce

3 In former times, a **herald** was a person who delivered and announced important messages and news. — N COUNT ⇑ messenger

4 The word **Herald** is often used in the name of newspapers. EG *...the Daily Herald.* — N IN NAMES

heraldic /hɛrældɪk/ means relating to heraldry. EG *...the heraldic motto.* — ADJ CLASSIF : ATTRIB

heraldry /hɛrəldri[1]/ is the study of coats of arms and of the history of the families who are entitled to have them. — N UNCOUNT

herb /hɜːb/, **herbs**. A **herb** is a plant whose leaves are used in cookery to add flavour to food, or as a medicine. EG *...dried herbs and spices... She set about brewing some herb tea.* — N COUNT

herbaceous /hɜːbeɪʃəˢs/. **Herbaceous** plants are soft and fleshy rather than hard and woody. — ADJ CLASSIF

herbaceous border, herbaceous borders. A **herbaceous border** is a flower bed, especially one with perennial plants in it. — N COUNT

herbal /hɜːbəˢl/ means made from herbs or relating to herbs. EG *...herbal medicine... ...the use of herbal remedies... ...herbal tea.* — ADJ CLASSIF : ATTRIB

herbalist /hɜːbəˢlɪst/, **herbalists**. A **herbalist** is a person who grows or sells herbs that are used in medicine. — N COUNT ⇑ specialist

herbicide /hɜːbɪsaɪd/, **herbicides**. A **herbicide** is a chemical that is used to destroy plants, especially weeds; a technical term. — N COUNT/ UNCOUNT

herbivore /hɜːbɪvɔː/, **herbivores**. A **herbivore** is an animal that only eats plants. — N COUNT

herbivorous /hɛːbɪvərəs/. An animal that is **herbivorous** only eats plants. — ADJ CLASSIF

herculean /hɜːkjəˢliːən/; sometimes written **Herculean**. A **herculean** task, effort, etc is one that requires extremely great strength or effort; a literary word. EG *You must make a herculean effort not to talk to them about it... ...hours of Herculean toil.* — ADJ CLASSIF : ATTRIB ⇑ enormous

herd /hɜːd/, **herds, herding, herded. 1** A **herd** is **1.1** a large group of animals of one kind that live together. EG *He wants his herd delivered to the cattle market in prime condition... A pride of lions killed his entire herd of goats.* — N PART+N IN PLURAL **1.2** a large group of people, especially when they are considered as working as a group rather than as separate individuals. EG *This has the effect of isolating you from the herd... He failed to notice the herd of naked children that followed close behind.* — N PART : USU SING, N+N IN PLURAL = pack

2 If you **herd** people or animals or if you **herd** them **up**, you make them move together to form a group. EG *...men herding cattle... The chained people were herded back into the dark cellar... Walter herded up his goats as quickly as he could.* — V+O, OR V+O+A (*up*) : USU+A = shepherd

herdsman /hɜːdzməˢn/, **herdsmen**. A **herdsman** is a man who looks after a herd of animals such as cattle or goats. — N COUNT ⇑ person

here /hɪə/. **1** You use **here 1.1** when you are referring to the place where you are or a place which has been mentioned and is quite near you. EG *She left here at eight o'clock this morning... You've been here at Sussex for a number of years... I'm going to fetch your dinner in here... I don't know whether you can see from here... It's just near here... Elizabeth, come over here.* — ADV WITH VB, OR ADV AFTER PREP ≠ there **1.2** when you are pointing towards a place that is near to where you are, to draw someone else's attention towards that place. EG *Stand here at this corner... You have to sign here and acknowledge the receipt... Then this moves to here.* — ADV WITH VB, OR ADV AFTER PREP ≠ there

1.3 in order to indicate that the person or thing that you are talking about is the one near you. EG *My friend here loves everything and everybody... What can you do with this thing here?... If you think of anything else, ask the lady here.* — ADV AFTER NG

1.4 when you are referring to the institution or country where you are, or to one that has already been mentioned. EG *No prisoners here are allowed to use the phone... The people here are extremely open.* — ADV AFTER NG ≠ there **1.5** to indicate that something is near you, or that you are holding it, and so it is available for use. EG *There are four letters here for you to sign... I have here a very important message that has just arrived.* — ADV WITH VB

1.6 to indicate that someone is present in a particular place, often for a particular purpose. EG *It's a pleasure to have you here... The Prince of Wales will be here presently... I am here to ask your opinion... You aren't here to talk to me.* — ADV WITH VB **1.7** when you are referring to people in general and their life on Earth. EG *...mysterious questions about our purpose here, about death, and life.* — ADV WITH VB, OR ADV AFTER NG

2 You say **'here's** someone' or **'here comes** someone' in order to draw attention to a person who has just arrived in the place where you are. EG *Here's Doctor Ford to see you... Here she is... Here comes the postman.* — PHR WITH NG

3 You can also use **here 3.1** to refer to a particular situation or point that you are commenting on in a discussion, speech, or piece of writing. EG *I think that what we're talking about here is role-playing... Jo will stop me if I'm wrong here... Two points need stressing here... I think you've got to distinguish here between fact and fiction.* — ADV WITH VB **3.2** to indicate a particular point or stage that has been reached in the development of something. EG *Even here, at a preverbal stage, children were encouraged to express themselves... I want the responsibility to stop here.* — ADV WITH VB **3.3** to refer to a piece of writing. EG *It says here that Liszt loved all of Chopin's work... I have attempted here to describe the Palace of Westminster.* — ADV WITH VB **3.4** to refer to a period of time, a situation, or an event that is present or happening now. EG *The autumn's really here at last... Here is your chance to do well.* — ADV WITH VB

4 You use **here's**, **here is**, **here are**, etc **4.1** to introduce something that you are going to tell someone, or to introduce something such as a piece of music that someone is going to hear. EG *Here are the addresses to which you should apply... Now here is the News... Here's how it's done... ...and to inspire us, here's some more music.* — PHR **4.2** when you are saying that you have just found something. EG *Look here's a package... Roberts, looking at his papers, said 'Here's a good one.'* — PHR **4.3** to introduce and draw attention to something or someone that you are going to talk about. EG *Here is a situation in which our decisions clearly count... Here was a man who knew his own mind... He felt conscious that here was something that suited his nature better.* — PHR = this is

5 You say **here we are**, **here** you **are**, etc in order to emphasize a statement that you are making about someone's character or situation. EG *Here you are, an intelligent and ambitious woman determined to get on in the world... So here we are, living in the California bush above Mill Valley.* — PHR : USED AS ADV SEN

6 You say **'here'**, **'here you are'**, or **'here's** something' when you are offering or giving something to someone. EG *He pushed a piece of paper across the table. 'Here you are. My address.'... Here, hold this while I go and get a newspaper... 'Here's your ticket,' he said, handing it to Thomas... Here's a dollar for you.* — CONVENTION, OR PHR+NG = there

7 You say **'here we are'**, **'here it is'**, etc when you — CONVENTION have just found something that you have been looking for. EG *I'm looking for a green volume containing all of Chopin's works. Here it is.*

8 You say **'here we are'** or **'here I am'** when you have just arrived somewhere. EG *Here we are at last.* CONVENTION

9 You say **'here we go'**, **'here we go again'**, or **'here I go again'** in order to indicate that something is happening again in the way that you expected, especially something unpleasant; an informal use. EG *Mother is drunk again. Here we go... Oh dear, here I go again.* CONVENTION

10 You use **here and there** to indicate that something is happening or situated in several different places in a random and disordered way. EG *Panic here and there was only to be expected... In colour the shell was deep cream touched here and there with fading pink.* PHR : USED AS AN A

11 **Here and now.** **11.1** You use **here and now** to emphasize something that you are saying or something that is happening at the moment. EG *I'll say here and now that I don't believe in ghosts... They have to deal with the problems staring them in the face here and now.* PHR : USED AS AN A **11.2** If you talk about the **here and now**, you are referring to people's life on earth and what happens to them while they are alive, as opposed to what might happen after they die. EG *The only meaning to be found in life is in the here and now, inside ourselves... ...the achievement of material advantage in the here and now.* PHR : USU AFTER PREP

12 You say **'here's to us'**, **'here's to your new job'**, etc as a toast in order to wish success to a venture or happiness to a person. EG *Here's to you, Howard.* CONVENTION

hereabouts /hɪərəbaʊts/. If you say that something is **hereabouts**, you mean that it is near to you or in the same general area as the place where you are. EG *Is there a fellow American hereabouts?* ADV WITH VB = here

hereafter /hɪərɑːftə/; a formal word. **1** The **hereafter** is the life which some people believe exists after you have died. EG *The hereafter for all we know may be an eternal state of boredom.* N SING WITH DET **2** In legal documents, you use **hereafter** to introduce information about what you are going to call something in the document after you have referred to it for the first time. EG *...the South Australia Housing Trust (hereafter called the Trust).* ADV WITH VB

hereby /hɪəbaɪ/. You use **hereby** in formal statements and documents to emphasize that a statement or declaration is official. EG *I hereby resign... Mr Alexander James Quentin Duggan of London W1 is hereby licensed to drive motor vehicles of Groups A and E* ADV WITH VB

hereditary /hɪ[2]rɛdɪtə[0]ri[1]/. **1** A characteristic, illness, etc that is **hereditary** is one that is passed on to a child from its parents before it is born. EG *...a progressive, hereditary disease of certain glands.* ADJ CLASSIF ⇑ genetic

2 A title or position in society that is **hereditary** is one that is passed on as a right from parent to child. EG *He proposed the abolition of the hereditary right to belong to the House of Lords... Their society was based on caste: a man's occupation was hereditary.* ADJ CLASSIF ⇑ inherited ▸ used of a person. EG *Lord Silkin introduced an amendment to allow hereditary peers to become life peers.* ▸ ADJ CLASSIF : ATTRIB

heredity /hɪ[2]rɛdɪti[1]/ is the process by which features and characteristics are passed on from parents to their children before the children are born. EG *Some children seem to be thin by heredity... Do you think we are influenced more by environment or heredity?* N UNCOUNT ⇑ genetics

herein /hɪərɪn/ means in this place, situation, document, etc; a formal word. EG *Herein lies the real danger... ...the undeniable facts contained herein.* ADV WITH VB

hereinafter /hɪəɪnɑːftə/. In legal documents, you use **hereinafter** to introduce information about what you are going to call something in the document after you have referred to it for the first time; a formal word. EG *...holidays operated by Redwood Travel Ltd, hereinafter called the Company.* ADV WITH VB

heresy /hɛrə[1]si[1]/, **heresies**. **Heresy** is **1** a belief, opinion, or way of behaving that most people think is wrong because it disagrees with beliefs that are generally accepted. EG *He decided the public should never hear of such heresy and ordered the Times not to print it... ...bitter complaints about the heresies of the group... In fashion today's vogue is often tomorrow's heresy.* N UNCOUNT/COUNT **2** a belief, opinion, or way of behaving that seriously disagrees with the principles of a particular religion, and which is therefore considered to be a sin. EG *He was tried for heresy in the ecclesiastical courts.* N UNCOUNT/COUNT

heretic /hɛrə[1]tɪk/, **heretics**. A **heretic** is **1** a person who has beliefs or opinions that most people think are wrong because they disagree with beliefs that are generally accepted. EG *His views are portrayed as those of an unrealistic leftist heretic.* N COUNT = rebel **2** a person who belongs to a particular religion, but whose beliefs seriously disagree with the principles held by that religion. EG *They were denounced as heretics and burned at the stake.* N COUNT ⇑ dissenter

heretical /hɪ[2]rɛtɪkə[0]l/. A belief or action that is **heretical** is **1** one that most people think is wrong because it disagrees with beliefs that are generally accepted. EG *...heretical opinions.* ADJ CLASSIF ⇑ unorthodox **2** one that seriously disagrees with the principles of a particular religion. EG *The bishops jailed him for heretical and blasphemous words.* ADJ CLASSIF

heretofore /hɪətuːfɔː/. means before this time; a formal word. EG *I devoted all my heretofore unchannelled enthusiasm to it.* ADV WITH VB = previously

herewith /hɪəwɪð/; a formal word. **1** You use **herewith** to say that you are enclosing something in a letter that you are sending. EG *I herewith return your cheque.* ADV WITH VB

2 Herewith also means the same as hereby. EG *I herewith declare myself Dictator.* ADV WITH VB

heritage /hɛrɪtɪdʒ/. A country's **heritage** is all the qualities, traditions, or features of life that have been continued over many years and passed on from one generation to another; used especially to refer to things that are of historical importance or that have had a strong influence on society. EG *We feel that preserving the history, heritage and culture of the Flint Hills is of vital importance... They are part of the Mexican heritage, like the stone colossus of Tlaloc... ...a building that may one day be part of Britain's national heritage.* N SING WITH DET = inheritance

hermaphrodite /hɜːmæfrədaɪt/, **hermaphrodites**. A **hermaphrodite** is a person, animal, or flower that has both male and female reproductive organs; a technical term. N COUNT

hermetic /hɜːmɛtɪk/ means very tightly closed; used especially of the seals of containers that are so tight that no air can get in; a formal or technical term. EG *It solidified and formed a perfect hermetic seal... They found themselves shut within small hermetic circles.* ADJ CLASSIF : ATTRIB ◇ **hermetically**. EG *...plastic packs of food, hermetically sealed.* ◇ ADV WITH VB = vacuum

hermit /hɜːmɪt/, **hermits**. A **hermit** is a person who lives alone with a very simple life style, away from people and normal society, especially for religious reasons. N COUNT

hermit crab, hermit crabs. A **hermit crab** is a small crab that lives in the empty shells of other shellfish. N COUNT

hernia /hɜːnɪə/, **hernias**. A **hernia** is a medical condition which results in part of your intestine sticking through a weak point in the surrounding tissue, especially as a result of strain or injury. N COUNT/UNCOUNT = rupture

hero /hɪərəʊ/, **heroes**. **1** A **hero** is **1.1** the main male character in a book, play, film, etc who is usually admired or respected for his good qualities. EG *Robert Powell playing Alec, the hero of the play, was very good... ...the trials which the mythological hero must surmount before he reaches the goal... ...Kingsley Amis's hero Jake, in Jake's Thing.* N COUNT **1.2** someone who has done something brave, new, or good, and who is therefore greatly admired by a lot of people. EG *...one of the heroes of the Battle of Britain... Claude was no hero: he'd never die under torture... ...Benn's triumphal return to Parliament as a hero of democracy... ...Charles Lindbergh's world fame as an aviation hero.* N COUNT ⇑ celebrity = champion

2 If you describe someone as your **hero**, you mean that you admire them greatly, usually because of a particular quality or skill that they have. EG *I thought Paul Newman was your hero... Bill Hook was my first rugby hero.* N COUNT : USU SING WITH POSS = idol

heroic /hɪ[2]rəʊɪk/, **heroics**. **1** Actions or behaviour that are **heroic** **1.1** are brave and courageous. EG *...truly heroic work by army engineers.* ADJ QUALIT ▸ used of people. EG *My grandmother, in death, became more heroic.* ◇ **heroically**. EG *They fought heroically until they were finally captured.* ◇ ADV **1.2** involve determination to succeed and deserve admiration. EG *...in spite* ADJ QUALIT ⇑ determined *of heroic and efficient work by German police... ...a heroic stand against undemocratic provocation.* ◇ **heroically**. EG *The boys heroically kept the secret even from their parents.* ◇ ADV

2 A **heroic** story, character, etc involves a hero or relates to a hero's impressive characteristics. EG *They are heroic figures in the fight against cancer... Sports people take on a heroic dimension.* ADJ CLASSIF : ATTRIB

3 **Heroics** are actions, language, or behaviour that are considered to be too grand or brave for the particular situation in which they are used. EG *Contemporary letters record simply and without heroics the story of those four days... If someone points a gun in your face, hand over the money. We don't want any heroics.* N PLURAL

heroin /hɛrəʊɪn/ is a powerful drug which some people take for pleasure, but which they can become addicted to. Doctors sometimes use heroin as an anaesthetic. EG *The girl was unconscious from an overdose of heroin... ...a heroin addict.* N UNCOUNT

heroine /hɛrəʊɪn/, **heroines**. A **heroine** is 1 the main female character in a book, play, film, etc who is usually admired or respected for her good qualities. EG *Tess was Hardy's favourite heroine... ...Adah, the heroine of the book.* N COUNT 2 a woman who has done something brave, new, or good, and who is therefore greatly admired by a lot of people. EG *...the heroine of their great 1967 election triumph... The crowd cheered their heroine again.* N COUNT

heroism /hɛrəʊɪzə⁰m/ is great courage and bravery. EG *...an act of heroism... ...memories of flags and battles, of desperation and heroism.* N UNCOUNT ⇑ quality

heron /hɛrən/, **herons**. A **heron** is a bird which has very long legs, a long beak, and grey and black feathers. Herons live near water. N COUNT

herpes /hɜːpiːz/ is a disease which causes painful red spots to appear on the skin. There are several different types of herpes. N UNCOUNT

herring /hɛrɪŋ/, **herrings**; **herring** can also be used as the plural form. A **herring** is a long silver-coloured fish that lives in large groups in the sea, and that can be eaten. EG *...an appetizing smell of grilled herring.* ● See also **red herring**. N COUNT

herringbone /hɛrɪŋbəʊn/ is a pattern used in fabrics, brickwork, etc which consists of short lines of V shapes. N UNCOUNT

herring gull, herring gulls. A **herring gull** is a large bird that is very common on the coasts of Britain. It has white feathers, black tips on its wings, and pink legs. N COUNT ⇑ seagull

hers /hɜːz/. You use **hers** to indicate that something belongs or relates to a woman, girl, or female animal who has already been mentioned or named, or whose identity is known. It is also sometimes used to refer to something associated with a nation, ship, or car. See **she**. EG *You were an old friend of hers... He grinned at her and laid his hand on hers... She wept bitterly as she told her story. Hers was a difficult case to help.* PRON POSS : SING

herself /hə⁵sɛlf/. 1 You use **herself** as the object of a verb or preposition in order to refer to the same woman, girl, or female animal who is mentioned as the subject of the clause, or as a previous object in the clause. It is also sometimes used in relation to a nation, ship, or car. See **she**. EG *She groaned and stretched herself out flat on the sofa... Barbara stared at herself in the mirror... On the way home Rose bought herself a piece of cheese for lunch.* PRON REFL : SING, USED AS O ▸ You also use **herself** to emphasize the subject or object of a clause, and to make it clear who you are referring to. It is usually used in addition to a subject or object, although it is sometimes used instead of 'her' as an object. EG *Sally herself came back... She could hardly believe it herself... How strange that he should collide with Melanie Byrd herself... Their audience was of middle-aged women like herself.* ▸ PRON REFL : SING

2 If a girl or woman does something **herself**, she does it without any help or interference from anyone else. EG *She had printed the little card herself.* PRON REFL ⇑ alone

he's /hiz/ is the usual spoken form of 'he is' or 'he has', especially when 'has' is an auxiliary verb. EG *He's a reporter... He's going away soon... I hope he's got some money left.*

hesitancy /hɛzɪtənsi¹/. **Hesitancy** or **hesitance** is unwillingness to do something or a doubt about doing it, usually because you feel afraid, embarrassed, or not sure that you can do it properly. EG *...an air of childlike hesitancy.* N UNCOUNT = reluctance

hesitant /hɛzɪtə⁰nt/. If you are **hesitant** about doing something, you do not do it quickly or directly because you are not certain whether you ought to do it or because you do not know how to do it. EG *Some parents are hesitant about usurping the teacher's role... He seemed hesitant to confirm the bad news in the letter.* ▸ used of a person's behaviour. EG *She spoke in a soft, hesitant voice about her past... ...a hesitant, almost boyish smile... His reactions were slow, decisions hesitant.* ◇ **hesitantly**. EG *'Maybe you could teach me,' said Marsha hesitantly... The girl went hesitantly away.* ADJ QUALIT = reluctant ◇ ADV WITH VB = uncertainly

hesitate /hɛzɪteɪt/, **hesitates, hesitating, hesitated**. 1 If you **hesitate**, 1.1 you pause slightly while you are doing something or just before you do it, usually because you are uncertain, embarrassed, or worried about it. EG *She put her hand on the phone, hesitated for a moment, then picked up the receiver... She stood there on the pavement, hesitating, not knowing which way to go... 'Hold out your hands,' he commanded. They hesitated.* V = falter 1.2 you pause slightly while you are speaking or before you speak, for example because you are not sure what to say next or because you are about to give someone some bad news. EG *'No, tomorrow I can't come.' He hesitated, and then he said it. 'I can't come tomorrow because my wife will be back.'... I said: 'What was all that about?' He hesitated. 'I'm sorry. I'd rather not say.'* V = waver

2 If you **hesitate** to do something, 2.1 you are unwilling to do it because you are not quite certain whether it is correct or right. EG *I would hesitate to say precisely what a fantasy is... What about the woman who hesitates to breast-feed because she has to go back to work?... The children had not hesitated to make this point very clear.* V+to-INF 2.2 you do not do it immediately because you are not certain that you ought to do it at all. EG *For a fraction of a second I hesitated to give the address.* V+to-INF

3 You say **'don't hesitate** to call me', **'don't hesitate** to contact us', etc when you are telling someone that they really ought to do something and that they should not worry about disturbing other people if they do. EG *Don't hesitate to go to a doctor if you have any unusual symptoms... If any questions do occur to you, then don't hesitate to write to us in London.* V : IMPER + to-INF

hesitation /hɛzɪteɪʃə⁰n/, **hesitations**. 1 **Hesitation** is 1.1 a pause or slight delay in something that you are doing, usually because you are worried, embarrassed, or uncertain. EG *'Well, no,' Karen said, with some hesitation... 'Not at the moment,' she said after a slight hesitation... They stood in hesitation on the doorstep, each looking very nervous.* N UNCOUNT/COUNT 1.2 an unwillingness to do something because you are worried or embarrassed about it or because you are not sure if you really ought to do it. EG *After some hesitation he agreed to allow me to write the article... The calm voice of authority overrode the teacher's hesitations.* N UNCOUNT/COUNT ⇑ reticence

2 If you **have no hesitation in** saying something, you say it immediately or willingly because you are certain that you are right to say it. EG *I have no hesitation in saying that the Prime Minister has my full support... They had no hesitation in describing the situation as ridiculous.* PHR + -ING : VB INFLECTS

3 If you do something **without hesitation**, you do it immediately and willingly. EG *Even though I hadn't been invited, I went at once without hesitation... We will do our duty without hesitation.* PHR : USED AS AN A

hessian /hɛsɪən/ is a thick rough fabric. It is usually used for making sacks. N UNCOUNT ⇑ textile

heterodox /hɛtə⁰rə⁶dɒks/. Beliefs, opinions, and ideas that are **heterodox** are different from the accepted or official ones; a formal word. ADJ CLASSIF = unorthodox

heterogeneous /hɛtə⁰rə⁶dʒiːnɪəs/. Something that is **heterogeneous** consists of many different types of things; a formal word. EG *Arts and sciences are contained in one heterogeneous collection, the South Kensington Museum... These artists brought with them a heterogeneous assortment of European fashions.* ADJ CLASSIF ⇑ diverse

heterosexual /hɛtə⁰rə⁶sɛksjʊ⁰əl/, **heterosexuals**. 1 A **heterosexual** relationship is a sexual relationship between a man and a woman. ADJ CLASSIF

2 Someone who is **heterosexual** is sexually attracted to people of the opposite sex. EG *I am a white, Anglo-Saxon, heterosexual, happily married female.* ▸ used as a noun. EG *Heterosexuals rarely give their sexuality a second thought.* ADJ CLASSIF ▸ N COUNT ⇑ person

heterosexuality /hɛtə⁰rə⁶sɛksjuælɪti¹/ is sexual attraction or sexual activity between a man and a woman. N UNCOUNT

het up /hɛt ʌp/. If you get **het up**, you get very excited or anxious about something; used in informal English. EG *...when he gets all het up about some business problem... There's no need to get so het up!* ADJ QUALIT : PRED = worked up

heuristic /hjuərɪstɪk/. **Heuristic** methods of learning involve using reasoning and past experience rather than formulas or solutions that are given to you; a formal word. ADJ CLASSIF ⇑ experiential

hew /hjuː/, **hews, hewing, hewed, hewn**; the past participle can be either **hewed** or **hewn**. 1 If you **hew** something solid such as stone, you cut large pieces out of it roughly and without bothering whether the pieces are smooth or finished. EG *They made Him hew out his cross and then dragged Him to Calvary... ...hewn stone.* ● See also **rough-hewn**. V+O : USU+A (out) ⇑ carve = hack 2 If you **hew** one thing out of another, you cut large parts out of it in order to make something new. EG *Excavators have hewn out an underground car park for 1,000 cars.* V+O+A (out/from) = carve out

hexagon /hɛksəgə⁷n/, **hexagons**. A **hexagon** is a geometric shape that has six straight sides. N COUNT

hexagonal /hɛksægənə⁰l/. An object or shape that is **hexagonal** has six straight sides. ADJ CLASSIF

hey /heɪ/. You say or shout **'hey'** when you want to attract someone's attention or show how surprised, interested, or annoyed you are; an informal word. EG *'Hey, Ben!' he called. There was no reply... Hey, Dad, what's for dinner?* CONVENTION = hi

heyday /heɪdeɪ/. A person's, nation's, or organization's **heyday** is the time when they are most powerful, successful, or popular. EG *The Indian cinema turns out films at a rate that not even Hollywood in its heyday matched... ...the heyday of Christianity... I had never been a political animal, even in the heyday of the 1960's.* N SING : USU WITH POSS ⇑ prime = peak

hi /haɪ/; an informal word. You say **'hi'** to someone 1 when you see them or when you meet them for the first time in the course of a day. EG *'Hi, Uncle Harold,' Thomas said... Hi, there, Mr Swallow, good to see you.* CONVENTION = hello 2 when you are trying to attract their attention. EG *Ralph jumped to his feet. 'Hi! You two!'* CONVENTION = hey

hiatus /haɪeɪtəs/, **hiatuses**. A **hiatus** is a pause in which nothing happens, or a gap where something is missing; a formal word. EG *There came a pause, a hiatus. He stared out of the window.* N COUNT : USU SING

hibernate /haɪbəneɪt/, **hibernates, hibernating, hibernated**. 1 Animals or reptiles that **hibernate** spend the winter in a state like a deep sleep in which their temperature, heartbeat, and breathing rate become very low. EG *Because squirrels don't hibernate they need food stores throughout the winter.* ◇ **hibernation** /haɪbəneɪʃə⁰n/. EG *...a brown bear emerging from hibernation.* V ⇑ sleep ◇ N UNCOUNT ⇑ sleeping

2 If you say that someone **is hibernating**, you mean that they go out as little as possible in winter; a humorous use. EG *...the den where he hibernated for three months each year.* V ⇑ retire

hibiscus /haɪbɪskəs/, **hibiscuses**. A **hibiscus** is a plant or bush which has large yellow or red flowers shaped like a bell. The flowers of the hibiscus usually last for only one day. N COUNT

hiccup /hɪkʌp/, **hiccups, hiccupping, hiccupped**; also spelled **hiccough**. **Hiccup** and **hiccough** have the same pronunciation. 1 **Hiccups** are little choking sounds in your throat caused by a quick jerking movement in your chest. You sometimes get hiccups if you have been eating or drinking too quickly. EG *She was still suffering with hiccups.* N COUNT : USU PL ⇑ sound

2 When you **hiccup**, you make little choking sounds in your throat. EG *She turned over on her side, hiccupped once or twice and went to sleep.* V

3 A **hiccup** is a small problem or difficulty, usually one which can be fairly easily put right. EG *We got the car up to the Snowdonia National Park without so much as a hiccup.* N COUNT = hitch

hid /hɪd/ is the past tense of **hide**.

hidden /hɪdə⁰n/. 1 **Hidden** is the past participle of **hide**.

2 Something that is **hidden** is not easily noticed. EG *Such programmes on television may have a hidden danger in that children may confuse them with reality.* ADJ CLASSIF

3 A place that is **hidden** is difficult to find. EG *They would make their camps in hidden valleys or dense woods.* ADJ CLASSIF = concealed

hide /haɪd/, **hides, hiding, hid, hidden**. 1 If you **hide** something, you put it in a place where it cannot easily be seen or found. EG *The women managed to steal and hide a few knives.* V+O = conceal

2 If you **hide** or if you **hide** yourself, you go somewhere where you cannot easily be seen or found. EG *There was nowhere to hide... I walked back a few paces and hid myself in the shadows.* V OR V+O (REFL) ⇑ place = conceal

3 If you **hide** something such as your feelings or information, you keep it a secret, so that no one knows about it. EG *She tried to hide her feelings as much as possible... I couldn't hide this fact from you.* V+O = conceal, cover up

4 If something **hides** an object, it covers it and prevents it from being seen. EG *Much of his face was hidden by a beard... Clouds hid the sun.* V+O = obscure

5 A **hide** is 5.1 a place which is built to look like its surroundings. Hides are used by people who want to watch or photograph animals and birds without being seen by them. N COUNT 5.2 the skin of a large animal such as a cow, horse, or elephant, which can be used for making leather. N MASS = pelt

6 If you say you **haven't seen hide nor hair** of someone, you mean that you have not seen them at all recently; an informal expression. PHR : AUX INFLECTS+*of*

7 If you say that you will **tan** someone's **hide**, you mean that you will punish them by hitting them hard; a rather old-fashioned expression. PHR : VB INFLECTS = beat

8 See also **hidden, hiding**.

hide-and-seek is a game in which one player covers his or her eyes until the other players have hidden themselves, and then he or she tries to find them. N UNCOUNT

hideaway /haɪdəweɪ/, **hideaways**. A **hideaway** is a place where you go to be private and to get away from other people. EG *After stocking up our hideaway with luxuries, we drove up the mountain to watch the sunset.* N COUNT = retreat

hidebound /haɪdbaund/. People who are **hidebound** are unwilling to change their ideas, or to accept new ideas, even when they obviously should do so; used showing disapproval. EG *The members of committees are often hidebound, unimaginative and even incompetent.* ▸ used of people's behaviour and attitudes. EG *He hated the intrigues and jealousies of his colleagues, the hidebound conservatism of his superiors.* ADJ QUALIT ⇑ conservative

hideous /hɪdi¹əs/. If you describe something as **hideous**, you mean that it is extremely unpleasant or ugly. EG *They're not like dogs, they're ugly, hideous brutes... ...the hideous conditions of trench warfare.* ADJ QUALIT = ghastly

hideously /hɪdi¹ʊsli¹/. You use **hideously** 1 to emphasize the degree or extent to which something appears horrible or ugly. EG *His face was quite hideously contorted... ...hideously mutilated bodies.* ADV+ADJ/ADV = atrociously 2 to emphasize the degree or extent to which something rather unpleasant or unacceptable occurs. EG *Such a way of life was, naturally, hideously expensive... He had been hideously embarrassed by this confession... These mechanical methods are hideously slow in terms of what the computer could achieve.* ADV+ADJ/ADV = terribly

hideout /haɪdaʊt/, **hideouts**. A **hideout** is a place where someone goes secretly because they do not want anyone to find them, for example if they are running away from the police. N COUNT = lair

hiding /haɪdɪŋ/, **hidings**. 1 If someone is in **hiding**, they have secretly gone somewhere where they cannot be seen or found. EG *She escaped, and went into hiding... They emerged from hiding, and surrendered to the police.* N UNCOUNT : PREP+N ⇑ seclusion

2 If you give someone a **hiding**, you punish them by hitting them many times; an informal use. EG *He told us to stop, or else we'd get a good hiding.* N COUNT = beating

hiding place, hiding places; also spelled with a hyphen. A **hiding place** is a place where someone or something can be hidden, or where they are hiding. EG *You need to find a new hiding place for that key.* N COUNT

hierarchical /haɪərɑːkɪkə⁰l/. Something that is **hierarchical** is organized into a hierarchy; a formal word. EG *...ancient hierarchical societies.* ADJ QUALIT ≠ egalitarian

hierarchy /haɪərɑːki¹/, **hierarchies**; a formal word. 1 A **hierarchy** is a system of organization in N COUNT which people or things have different ranks or positions depending on how important they are. The most important people or things are at the top of the hierarchy, and the least important are at the bottom. EG *They became very conscious of the lack of females in the hierarchy... ...the hierarchy of the Episcopal Church.*

2 The **hierarchy** is the group of people who have the power in an organization. EG *The university hierarchy decided, apparently, that it was best to ignore the situation.* [N COUNT = powers]

3 Hierarchy involves organizing ideas and beliefs into a formal structure. [N COUNT]

hieroglyph /haɪərəglɪf/, **hieroglyphs**. **Hieroglyphs** are symbols in the form of pictures, which are used in some writing systems, especially that of ancient Egypt. EG *A combination of hieroglyphs represent place names of a conquered location.* [N COUNT = hieroglyphic]

hieroglyphic /haɪərəglɪfɪk/, **hieroglyphics**. **1** A **hieroglyphic** is **1.1** something that has been written, but that you cannot understand because you are not familiar with the symbols that are used. EG *On the blackboards were hieroglyphics which I was told were called logarithms.* [N COUNT] **1.2** a hieroglyph. [N COUNT]

2 Hieroglyphics is a system of writing that uses hieroglyphs. [N PLURAL]

hi-fi /haɪfaɪ/, **hi-fis**. A **hi-fi** is a set of equipment on which you play records and tapes, and which produces stereo sound of very good quality. EG *...listening to classical music on the hi-fi... ...hi-fi equipment...* [N COUNT/UNCOUNT]

higgledy-piggledy /hɪgəldi pɪgəldi/. If things are **higgledy-piggledy**, they are to be found all over the place, in a great muddle or disorder. EG *The books were higgledy-piggledy on the table.* [ADJ QUALIT ⇑ muddled = jumbled] ▸ used as an adverb. EG *He thrust clothes higgledy-piggledy into plastic bags... ...all of it stacked up higgledy-piggledy on the shelves.* [▸ ADV AFTER VB]

high /haɪ/, **higher, highest; highs**. **1** Something that is **high** extends a fairly long way from the bottom to the top when it is upright. You do not use the word **high** to describe people, animals, or plants. EG *...the high walls of the prison... ...a high block of flats... Roofs were blown off and higher buildings suffered extensive damage... Due north lay the highest cliffs of the island.* [ADJ QUALIT ≠ low]

2 You use **high** to say what size something is when it is measured from the bottom to the top. However small it is, you must use the word **high** and not 'low' or 'small'. EG *...a low mud wall about 10 centimetres high... ...fences three metres high... The house was four storeys high... ...a 200 foot high crag.* [ADJ AFTER N : NUM+N+ADJ]

3 If something is **high**, it is a long way above the ground, above sea level, or above someone or something else. EG *The bookshelf was too high for him to reach... It's the highest road in England... We spotted them high up on a hill... He kicked the ball high in the air... It ought to warm up as soon as the sun gets higher in the sky... He raised his arms high.* [ADJ QUALIT ≠ low]

4 You can also use **high** **4.1** when you are referring to large numerical values, or to something which is towards the top of a particular scale. EG *Dogs' hearing is tuned to very high frequencies... Scottish grants are higher than English ones... Ceramic materials will withstand high temperatures... Europeans are now complaining of high American interest rates... Bexhill-on-Sea has the highest proportion of old people of any community... Don't put pans straight on to a high heat.* [ADJ QUALIT ⇑ big ≠ low] ▸ used as a noun. EG *Prices on the stock exchange reached another record high last week... ...ever since interest rates zoomed up to all-time highs.* [▸ N COUNT ⇑ point] **4.2** when you are referring to something which is greater in number or amount than is usual or acceptable. EG *Her works fetch high prices... ...areas of high unemployment... The husband suffered from high blood pressure... The ratio of children to adults is very high.* [ADJ QUALIT ≠ low] **4.3** to emphasize how great in degree or intensity something is. EG *...at times of high anxiety in official quarters... I am prepared to take some exceptionally high risks for that prize... The game requires a high degree of skill... The chances are high that it will be approved... ...a movement which had begun with such high expectations. ...a high fever.* [ADJ QUALIT ≠ low]

5 Someone or something that is **high** in a particular profession or society occupies a very important position, and has great authority, experience, expertise, or influence. EG *She is high enough up in the company to be able to help you... I have consulted a very high legal authority... ...friends in high places... ...high social status... He wanted to take it up at the highest level... ...high-ranking officers.* [ADJ QUALIT]

6 If someone's reputation is **high** or if your opinion of them is **high**, that person is regarded very favourably and is praised very much. EG *We have a very high opinion of you, Miss Jordan... This award is one of the highest honours which can be conferred on anyone in the film industry.* [ADJ QUALIT ⇑ great]

7 If the quality or standard of something is **high**, it is very good indeed. EG *They put on professional concerts and the standard is high... ...high-quality colour photographs... The care of the aged generally is of a high calibre... ... high-grade metals.* [ADJ QUALIT = excellent]

8 A sound, especially the sound of a human voice, that is **high** is close to the top of a particular range of notes. EG *...a high squeaky voice... ...an octave higher.* [ADJ QUALIT ≠ deep, low]

9 When a river is **high**, it contains much more water than usual. EG *The river was high and murky.* [ADJ QUALIT ≠ low]

10 A **high** wind blows hard and with great force. EG *...sheltered in the rock against the high wind.* [ADJ QUALIT ⇑ strong]

11 If someone has **high** principles, **high** standards, etc, they believe in things which are morally good. EG *...a man of high principles and courage... ...families with high ethical standards... ...beautiful women of high character... Compromise is one of the highest human virtues.* [ADJ QUALIT = honourable]

12 Language that is in a **high** style is very formal and literary. EG *...high register language... ...a very high style of speech.* [ADJ QUALIT]

13 If your spirits are **high**, you are happy and confident that the future will be successful. EG *My health was good and my spirits were high... They were not at all depressed, but in high spirits.* [ADJ QUALIT ⇑ good ≠ low]

14 If you are **high** on drugs or alcohol, you are drunk or are under the influence of drugs; an informal use. EG *...getting high on heroin.* [ADJ QUALIT : IF+PREP THEN *on* ⇑ drugged]

15 A **high** is a feeling or mood of great excitement, stimulation, and happiness. EG *The urge to perform is irresistible. It's such a high... I'm on a permanent high these days.* [N COUNT]

16 If something such as food is **high**, it has a very unpleasant smell because it is beginning to rot. EG *I think this cheese is a bit high, even for my taste.* [ADJ QUALIT : PRED ⇑ smelly]

17 If meat is **high**, it has been left for several days before it is eaten. This is done in order to improve its flavour. [ADJ QUALIT = ripe]

18 High also means **18.1** in an advanced and developed state, especially of a complex, successful, or powerful nature. EG *...a successful job in high finance... ...high fashion... The questions he'd asked were at a higher level than other people's.* [ADJ CLASSIF : ATTRIB] **18.2** of an intense emotional nature. EG *You're surely not expecting high adventure here?... ...moments of high drama.* [ADJ CLASSIF : ATTRIB]

19 On high. **19.1** When people refer to God **on high** in hymns and religious language, they are referring to His presence in heaven. EG *Sing praises now to God on high.* [PHR : USED AS AN A] **19.2** If you say that something came from **on high**, you mean that it came from a person or place of great authority or importance; a humorous use. EG *A pronouncement from on high arrived in the office yesterday.* [PHR : USED AS AN A ⇑ above]

20 The word **high** is also used in the following expressions. **20.1** If you are left **high and dry**, you are left in a difficult situation with no one to help you; an informal expression. EG *They pulled out leaving their partners high and dry.* [PHR : USED AS A C ⇑ helpless] **20.2** If you look **high and low** for something, you look for it in every place that you can think of. [PHR : USED AS AN A] **20.3** If you **are having a high old time**, you are enjoying yourself very much; an informal expression. [PHR : VB INFLECTS] **20.4** If you say that **it is high time** something was done, you mean that it should be done immediately before it is too late. EG *It's high time that we did something about improving the situation.* [PHR : VB INFLECTS+REPORT-CL]

21 The word **high** is also used in the following expressions, which are explained at other places in this dictionary. • **in high dudgeon**: see **dudgeon**. • **to high heaven**: see **heaven**. • **come hell or high water**: see **hell**. • **on the high seas**: see **sea**.

-high combines with words such as 'knee' or 'shoulder' to indicate that someone or something reaches as high as the point that is mentioned. EG *The water was waist-high.* [COMB : FORMS ADJ CLASSIFS OR ADVS]

high altar, high altars. The **high altar** in a church is the most important altar there. N COUNT: USU SING

high and mighty. If someone's behaviour is **high and mighty**, they consider themselves to be very important and are confident that their opinions are right; used showing disapproval. EG *There's no need to be so high and mighty about it!* ADJ QUALIT = arrogant, stuck-up

highborn /haɪbɔːn/. Someone who is **highborn** has parents who belong to the nobility. ADJ CLASSIF ⇑ noble

highbrow /haɪbraʊ/, **highbrows**; sometimes used showing disapproval. 1 A book, discussion, etc that is **highbrow** deals with serious subjects in an intellectual way. EG *...highbrow radio programmes... ...highbrow reading matter.* ADJ QUALIT = sophisticated

2 A person who is **highbrow** is interested in serious subjects of an intellectual nature. EG *She complained of my being too highbrow.* ▸ used as a noun. EG *The new magazine should appeal to highbrows everywhere.* ADJ QUALIT ▸ N COUNT

high chair, high chairs; also spelled with a hyphen. A **high chair** is a chair with long legs for a baby or small child to sit in. High chairs usually have a tray attached to the front, and are used at mealtimes. N COUNT

high church; sometimes written **High Church**. Someone or something that is **high church** belongs or relates to a section of the Church of England which emphasizes the importance of ceremony and ritual. EG *...a High Church Mass... ...practising his religion as a devout high church Anglican.* ADJ CLASSIF ⇑ religious

high-class; also spelled without a hyphen. Something that is **high-class** is of very good quality and often considered to be of superior social status. EG *...big hotels and high-class restaurants... She did occasional high-class jobs.* ADJ QUALIT = exclusive

high command. The **high command** is the group that consists of the most senior officers in a nation's armed forces. N SING: *the*+N, VB CAN BE SING OR PL

High Commission, High Commissions. A **High Commission** is an office which houses the High Commissioner and his or her staff. EG *...the acting head of the British High Commission.* N COUNT: IF SING, VB CAN BE SING OR PL ⇑ office

High Commissioner, High Commissioners. A **High Commissioner** is a senior representative who is sent by one Commonwealth country to live in another in order to work as an ambassador. EG *...the Zambian High Commissioner.* N COUNT: ALSO IN TITLES ⇑ official

High Court, High Courts. In England and Wales, the **High Court** is a court of law which deals with serious or important civil cases. EG *The case was heard in the High Court... ...a distinguished High Court judge.* N COUNT: IF SING *the*+N

higher /haɪə/. 1 A **higher** exam or qualification is one of an advanced standard or level. EG *They have their first degrees and are studying for higher degrees... ...a higher diploma.* ADJ CLASSIF: ATTRIB

2 A **higher** type of animal or plant is one with an advanced and complex biological form. EG *...humans and higher primates... They are themselves eaten in turn by higher species.* ADJ CLASSIF: ATTRIB

3 **Higher** is also the comparative form of **high**.

higher education is education or training at universities, colleges, and polytechnics. EG *...the government's policy on higher education... ...higher education grants.* N UNCOUNT

high explosive, high explosives. **High explosive** is an extremely powerful explosive substance such as gelignite or TNT. N UNCOUNT/COUNT

highfalutin /haɪfəluːtə[i]n/. **Highfalutin** behaviour seems false and foolish because it is too grand or important; an informal word. EG *I'm sick of her and her highfalutin ways!* ADJ QUALIT = pretentious

high fidelity; also spelled with a hyphen. A **high fidelity** tape recorder is one of very good quality which produces recordings that are very close to the original sound. EG *...a high-fidelity recording.* ADJ CLASSIF: USU ATTRIB = hi-fi

high-flier, high-fliers. See **high-flyer**.

high-flown. Language that is **high-flown** is considered to be very grand, formal, or literary; often used showing disapproval. EG *...high-flown compliments.* ADJ QUALIT: USU ATTRIB = extravagant

high-flyer, high-flyers; also spelled **high-flier**. A **high-flyer** is someone who is very ambitious and who is likely to be very successful in their career. EG *We offer a tough four-year course for high-flyers.* N COUNT

high-flying. A **high-flying** person is very ambitious and is likely to be successful in their career. EG *They were all very high-flying people, but I think we still managed to impress them.* ▸ used of people's behaviour. EG *...a high-flying life style and an extensive bank account.* ADJ QUALIT: USU ATTRIB

high-handed. Someone who is **high-handed** uses their authority in an unnecessarily forceful way without considering other people's feelings or without asking other people before they act; used showing disapproval. EG *There was really no need for such high-handed behaviour.* ◊ **high-handedness**. EG *The incident was quoted as another example of the high-handedness of the police chief.* ADJ QUALIT ⇑ insensitive = overbearing ◊ N UNCOUNT

high-heeled. Shoes that are **high-heeled** have a narrow high heel at the back. High-heeled shoes are usually worn by women. ADJ CLASSIF ≠ flat

high heels are high-heeled shoes. N PLURAL

high jinks is lively, excited behaviour in which people do things for fun; an informal word. EG *They have learned to expect high jinks as part of the show.* N UNCOUNT = horseplay

high jump. 1 The **high jump** is an athletics event which involves jumping over a raised bar. EG *I was never any good at the high jump at school.* N SING: *the*+N ⇑ sport

2 If you say that someone **is for the high jump**, you mean that they are in trouble and are likely to be severely punished; an informal expression. EG *You'll be for the high jump when your mother finds out!* PHR: VB INFLECTS = be for it

highlands /haɪləndz/ are mountainous areas of land. EG *...the highlands of New Guinea.* N PLURAL ⇑ mountains

high life. The **high life** is an exciting and luxurious way of living involving a great deal of entertainment, going to parties, eating good food, etc. EG *She has a taste for the high life.* N SING: *the*+N ⇑ luxury

highlight /haɪlaɪt/, **highlights, highlighting, highlighted**. 1 If you **highlight** a point, problem, etc, you emphasize it, for example in an article or a book, by drawing special attention to it and explaining its importance in detail. EG *The survey highlighted the needs of working women... This problem was highlighted in her book.* V+O = spotlight

2 If you **highlight** a piece of printed or written text, you mark it with a coloured pen, which allows the words to be read while making them stand out. V+O

3 A **highlight** is 3.1 the most interesting or exciting part of something such as a tour or a series of programmes. EG *The visit provided the real highlight of the morning... ...a typical week's TV highlights selected by Richard Baker.* 3.2 a lighter area of a painting or photograph which shows where the light shines on objects. EG *You need to put the highlight in now.* N COUNT+SUPP = high spot; N COUNT

4 **Highlights** in a person's hair are thin streaks of lighter colour that have usually been made by dyeing parts of the hair. EG *She's just had blonde highlights put in her hair.* N PLURAL

highly /haɪli[1]/. 1 You use **highly** 1.1 before an adjective to emphasize that a particular quality is true to a great degree. EG *It's an extremely simple concept in principle, though highly complex in detail... The report is highly critical of these policies... It's highly improbable that they will accept... ...highly-educated people.* 1.2 to indicate that something is at a level or standard that is towards the top of a scale of importance. EG *...a highly placed negotiator... ...a very highly classified planning document.* ADV+ADJ = very; ADV+ADJ

2 If you praise someone **highly**, speak **highly** of them, etc, you praise them a lot because you admire them or have great respect for them. EG *They spoke highly of a lecturer named Harold Levy... Ross Thompson obviously thought very highly of him... ...a highly regarded senior official.* ADV WITH VB ⇑ well = favourably

highly-strung. Someone who is **highly-strung** is very nervous and easily upset. ADJ QUALIT = excitable

High Mass is a church service held in a Catholic church in which there is more ceremony than in an ordinary mass. N UNCOUNT

high-minded. Someone who is **high-minded** has strong moral principles that are sometimes thought to be too strict. EG *Only the high-minded Evening Post published the letter.* ADJ QUALIT ⇑ good = principled

Highness /haɪnɪ[2]s/, **Highnesses**. You say **Your Highness**, **His Highness**, etc when you address or refer to a member of the royal family other than a king or queen. EG *...Her Royal Highness, Princess Alexandra... This is indeed an honour, your Highness.* N COUNT: DETPOSS+N, USED IN TITLES

high noon means the same as noon; a literary use. N UNCOUNT

high-pitched; also spelled without a hyphen. A sound such as a person's voice that is **high-pitched** is ADJ QUALIT = piercing very high and often shrill in tone. EG ...*a high-pitched whine.*

high point, high points. The **high point** of an event or period of time is the most exciting or enjoyable part of it. EG *His speech was the high point of the evening.* N COUNT : USU+SUPP = highlight

high-powered. 1 A machine or piece of equipment that is **high-powered** is very powerful, sophisticated, or efficient. EG ...*high-powered microscopes... ...high-powered rifles.* ADJ QUALIT

2 An activity that is **high-powered** is of a very advanced and successful nature. EG ...*high-powered advertising... The course is high-powered.* ADJ QUALIT = dynamic

high-rise. **High-rise** buildings are modern buildings which are very tall and have lots of storeys. EG ...*high-rise flats.* ADJ CLASSIF : ATTRIB

highroad /haɪrəʊd/, **highroads**. 1 A **highroad** is a main road. N COUNT

2 The **highroad** to something is the easiest or most successful way to achieve it. EG *Political power is the highroad to self-advancement.* N COUNT+*to* = pathway

high school, high schools. A **high school** is 1 a school in Britain for people aged between eleven and eighteen. EG ...*Plymouth High School for Girls... When she was in high school she had three good friends... ...high school education.* 2 a school in the United States which people go to when they are between fifteen and eighteen years old. N COUNT/UNCOUNT : ALSO IN NAMES AFTER N; N COUNT/UNCOUNT

high season. The **high season** is the time of year when a holiday resort, hotel, tourist attraction, etc receives most visitors. N SING : *the*+N ⇑ period

high-sounding. Language or ideas that are **high-sounding** seem very grand and important, although often they are not at all important; sometimes used showing disapproval. EG ...*altruism and other high-sounding principles.* ADJ QUALIT = high-flown

high-spirited. 1 Someone who is **high-spirited** is very lively and always wants to have fun and adventure. ADJ QUALIT = exuberant

2 A horse that is **high-spirited** is difficult to control because it is very lively, active, or nervous. ADJ QUALIT = frisky

high spot, high spots. The **high spot** of an event or activity is the most exciting or enjoyable part of it. EG *The temple was the high spot of the tour.* N COUNT : USU+SUPP = highlight

high street, high streets. The **high street** of a town is the main street where most of the shops and banks are. EG *They had a little flat off Kensington High Street... A number of businesses have closed their high street shops in Sunderland.* N COUNT : ALSO IN NAMES AFTER N

High summer is the middle of summer. EG *They serve lunches here only in high summer.* N UNCOUNT

high tea. In Britain, **high tea** is a meal, often with cups of tea to drink, that some people eat in the late afternoon rather than supper or dinner later in the evening. EG *The children have high tea at about 5.30, but we don't eat until 8.* N UNCOUNT

high technology; also spelled with a hyphen. **High technology** is the practical use of advanced scientific research and knowledge, especially in relation to electronics and computers, and the development of new advanced machines and equipment. EG ...*a new leap forward into an age of high technology... ...high-technology equipment.* N UNCOUNT ⇑ technology

high-tension. A **high-tension** electricity cable is one which is able to carry a very powerful current. ADJ CLASSIF : ATTRIB

high tide is the time at which the sea is at its highest level on the shore before it starts to fall again according to its regular daily pattern. EG ...*a pool which the sea only reached at high tide... High tide is at 5.03 this morning.* N UNCOUNT

high treason is a very serious crime which involves putting your country or the king or queen in danger. N UNCOUNT

high-up, high-ups. A **high-up** is an important person who has a lot of authority and influence; used in informal English. N COUNT = VIP

high water is the time at which the water in a river or sea is at its highest level as a result of the tide. EG *We'll have to wait for high water before we can reload the boat.* N UNCOUNT

high-water mark, high-water marks. A **high-water mark** is 1 the level reached by the sea at high tide or by a river in a flood. EG *Just below the high-water mark there are thick clumps of green sea-weed.* 2 the highest or most successful stage of achievement in a process. EG *Life in the court of Urbino was one of the high-water marks of western civilization.* N COUNT; N COUNT : USU+SUPP

highway /haɪweɪ/, **highways**. A **highway** is 1 a main road, especially one that connects towns or cities; used in American English. EG ...*inter-state highways.* 2 a road that is a main route for any form of transport. EG *This happens to be a public highway... She was charged with obstructing the highway.* N COUNT; N COUNT

Highway Code. In Britain, the **Highway Code** is an official booklet published by the Department of Transport containing the rules which tell people how to use public roads and how to drive on them safely. N SING : *the*+N ⇑ regulations

highwayman /haɪweɪmə³n/, **highwaymen**. In former times, a **highwayman** was a robber, usually on a horse, who used to stop travellers by threatening to shoot them and then steal their valuable possessions. EG ...*the most famous highwayman, Dick Turpin.* N COUNT ⇑ thief

high wire, high wires; also spelled with a hyphen. A **high wire** is a length of rope or wire stretched tight high above the ground and used for balancing acts. N COUNT = tightrope

hijack /haɪdʒæk/, **hijacks, hijacking, hijacked**. If someone **hijacks** a plane or other vehicle, they illegally take control of it by force while it is on a journey. They do this in order to steal from it, make it travel to a different place, or to make demands on a particular government. EG *A Pan Am aircraft was hijacked on its way to Singapore.* V+O = seize, take over

◇ **hijacking, hijackings**. EG *There had been three hijackings in the previous two weeks.* ◇ N COUNT/UNCOUNT

hijacker /haɪdʒækə/, **hijackers**. A **hijacker** is a person who hijacks a plane or other vehicle. N COUNT ⇑ criminal

hike /haɪk/, **hikes, hiking, hiked**. 1 A **hike** is a long walk in the country that you go on for pleasure. EG *We're going on a four mile hike tomorrow to the lake.* ▸ used as a verb. EG *I've been hiking round Scotland for a month.* ◇ **hiking**. EG *We have maps of the area where we hope to do some hiking.* N COUNT ⇑ journey = trek; ▸ V; ◇ N UNCOUNT = rambling

2 a rise in prices or interest rates; an informal use. EG *The government announced a 300 per cent hike in bread prices.* N COUNT+SUPP

hike up. If you **hike** something **up**, you pull it up with a quick movement. EG *She hiked up her trousers.* PHRASAL VB : V+O+ADV = hitch up

hiker /haɪkə/, **hikers**. A **hiker** is a person who is walking on a hike. N COUNT ⇑ walker

hilarious /hɪleərɪəs/. Something that is **hilarious** is extremely funny and makes you laugh a lot. EG ...*the hilarious tale of how Uncle Harold got stuck in a lift... ...hilarious games of hide-and-seek... I launched into a hilarious account of my arctic adventures.* ADJ QUALIT ⇑ amusing = uproarious

◇ **hilariously**. EG *These words are now hilariously old-fashioned to the young... This novel is hilariously funny.* ◇ ADV+ADJ/ADV = hysterically

hilarity /hɪlærɪti¹/ is great amusement and laughter. EG *The noise of hilarity in the restaurant below kept him awake until the small hours.* N UNCOUNT

hill /hɪl/, **hills**. 1 A **hill** is an area of land that is higher than the land that surrounds it, but not as high as a mountain. EG *I started to walk up the hill towards her... On top of the hill there was a grove of tall, dark trees... ...the Malvern Hills of Worcestershire... ...a lovely region of green hills and valleys.* N COUNT : ALSO IN NAMES AFTER N

2 If you say that someone or something is **as old as the hills**, you mean that they are very old; an informal expression. PHR : USED AS C

hillbilly /hɪlbɪli¹/, **hillbillies**. A **hillbilly** is a person who comes from the mountainous country areas of the south-east United States, especially one who does not seem to be very intelligent or educated; used by people who live in towns showing disapproval. N COUNT

hillock /hɪlək/, **hillocks**. A **hillock** is a small hill. EG *The view was broken up into many little valleys and small hillocks.* N COUNT

hillside /hɪlsaɪd/, **hillsides**. A **hillside** is the sloping side of a hill. EG ...*the steep hillsides of North Wales... ...a hillside town.* N COUNT

hilltop /hɪltɒp/, **hilltops**. A **hilltop** is the top of a hill. EG *They thought they saw something moving on the hilltops... ...the hilltop village of Combe.* N COUNT ⇑ summit

hilly /hɪli¹/, **hillier, hilliest**. Land that is **hilly** has many hills. EG *They drove around the hilly area behind the town.* ADJ QUALIT

hilt /hɪlt/, **hilts**. 1 A **hilt** is the handle of a sword, dagger, or knife. N COUNT

2 If you support or defend someone **to the hilt** or **up to the hilt**, you give them all the support that you can; an informal expression. EG *She had backed me to the hilt in all my projects.* PHR : USED AS AN A

him /hɪm/ is used as the object of a verb or preposition. You use **him** when you are referring to a man, boy, or male animal, or to someone whose sex is not known or stated, who has already been mentioned or named, or whose identity is known. In the Christian religion, **Him** is used to refer to God or Jesus Christ. See **he**. EG *He asked if you'd ring him back when you got in... There's no need for him to worry... 'Let me have those raisins,' Claud said. I gave him the bag.* PRON : SING, USED AS O

himself /hɪmself/. 1 You use **himself** as the object of a verb or preposition in order to refer to the same man, boy, or male animal, or to someone whose sex is not known or stated, who is mentioned as the subject of the clause, or as a previous object in the clause. In the Christian religion, **Himself** is used to refer to God or Jesus Christ. See **he**. EG *Mr Boggis introduced himself... He poured himself a whisky... ...his lack of confidence in himself.* PRON REFL : SING, USED AS O ▸ You also use **himself** to emphasize the subject or object of a clause, and to make it clear who you are referring to. It is usually used in addition to a subject or object, although it is sometimes used instead of 'him' as an object. EG *Forman himself became Minister of International Affairs... His friend looked as miserable as he felt himself... I've just been having a talk with Davis himself... It was easy for a clever young man like himself to make a good living.* ▸ PRON REFL : SING

2 If a man or boy does something **himself**, he does it without any help or interference from anyone else. EG *They had stopped Henry from doing it himself.* PRON REFL : SING ⇑ alone

hind /haɪnd/, **hinds**. 1 An animal's **hind** legs or feet are at the back of its body. EG *Kangaroos' hind legs are enormously powerful.* ● **to talk the hind legs off a donkey**: see **donkey**. ADJ CLASSIF : ATTRIB = rear

2 A **hind** is a female deer, especially one of the red deer family. N COUNT = doe

hinder, hinders, hindering, hindered. **Hinder** is pronounced /hɪndə/ when it is a verb and /haɪndə/ when it is an adjective. 1 If you **hinder** someone or something, **1.1** you make it more difficult for them to do something or for something to happen. EG *Her career was not noticeably hindered by the fact that she had three children... More people have been hindered than helped by his diagnoses... ...a policy that will promote rather than hinder reform.* V+O = impede **1.2** you make it difficult for them to move or advance. EG *...floods and landslides to hinder the enemy... I wrenched at the clothes that hindered me.* V+O = hamper

2 The **hinder** parts of an animal are the hind parts. ADJ CLASSIF

Hindi /hɪndi[1]/ is one of the official languages of India that is spoken by people who live in northern India. N UNCOUNT ⇑ language

hindquarters /haɪndkwɔːtəz/; also spelled with a hyphen and as two words. The **hindquarters** of an animal with four legs are the back part of it, including its two back legs. N PLURAL = rear end

hindrance /hɪndrəns/, **hindrances**. 1 A **hindrance** is a person or thing that makes it more difficult for you to do something. EG *Here new ideas may be more of a hindrance than an asset.* N COUNT : IF + PREP THEN *to* = nuisance

2 **Hindrance** is the act of hindering someone or something. EG *Now they can construct tunnel systems without hindrance.* N UNCOUNT

hindsight /haɪndsaɪt/ is the ability to understand and realize something about an event after it has happened. EG *I was able to attempt a judgement with the benefit of hindsight.* N UNCOUNT

Hindu /hɪnduː, hɪnduː/, **Hindus**. 1 A **Hindu** is a person who believes in Hinduism and follows its teachings. N COUNT

2 Something that is **Hindu** belongs or relates to Hinduism. EG *...Hindu civilization.* ADJ CLASSIF

Hinduism /hɪnduːɪzə[0]m/ is an Indian religion which Indian society is based on. Hinduism has many gods and teaches that people live again after they die. N UNCOUNT

Hindustani /hɪnduːstɑːni[1]/ is a group of northern Indian languages that includes Hindi and Urdu. N UNCOUNT ⇑ language

hinge /hɪndʒ/, **hinges, hinging, hinged**. 1 A **hinge** is a piece of metal, wood or plastic that is used to join a door to its frame or to join two things together so that one of them can swing freely. EG *The front door gaped open, hanging away by its lower hinge.* N COUNT ⇑ device

hinge on. Something that **hinges on** or **hinges upon** one thing or event depends entirely on it. EG *He said everything hinged on what happened to the United States economy.* PHRASAL VB : V+PREP ⇑ depend on

hinged /hɪnd[0]ʒd/. Something that is **hinged** is joined to something, or joined together, by means of a hinge. EG *She lifted the hinged flap of the counter and gestured that he should come through.* ADJ CLASSIF

hink /hɪŋk/, **hinks, hinking, hinked**. If you **hink**, you think hopefully and unrealistically about something. V OR V+REPORT-CL ⇑ imagine

hint /hɪnt/, **hints, hinting, hinted**. 1 A **hint** is a suggestion or clue about something that is made in a very indirect or secretive way. EG *As yet no hint had appeared as to who was going to be the next Foreign Secretary.* N COUNT ● If you **drop a hint**, you suggest something in a very indirect way in the hope that someone will understand it. EG *He had dropped several hints that he knew where Mary had spent the previous evening.* ● PHR : VB INFLECTS ● If you **take a hint**, you understand something that someone is suggesting indirectly to you. EG *She took the hint and left... All right, I can take a hint.* ● PHR : VB INFLECTS

2 If you **hint** or **hint** at something, you suggest in a very indirect way that something is true. EG *I hinted I had had dinner with her last week... I tried to hint that I deserved an increase in salary... The things they said seemed to hint at the possibility of a return to work... Harold hinted at what she had already guessed.* V, V+REPORT-CL/QUOTE, OR V+A (at) ⇑ imply

3 A **hint** is also **3.1** a helpful piece of advice, usually about how to do something. EG *The magazine had the usual hints on fashion and cookery... They gave me a booklet with useful hints for airline passengers.* N COUNT : USU PL = tip **3.2** a very small amount or sign of something. EG *Her smile held a tiny hint of a challenge... The struggle would be difficult, but there was already a hint of victory in the air.* N COUNT : IF + PREP THEN *of* = glimmer

hinterland /hɪntəlænd/, **hinterlands**. The **hinterland** of a piece of coastline or a large river is the area of land behind it or around it. EG *...a small town somewhere in the hinterland of Watermouth.* N COUNT : USU *the*+N IN SING ⇑ land

hip /hɪp/, **hips**. 1 Your **hip** is the area at the side of your body between the top of your leg and your waist. EG *Her waist was slender, her hips curved... She put her hand on her hip.* ▸ used to refer to the bone at this part of the body. EG *She had never been the same after breaking that hip.* N COUNT ⇑ body part

2 A **hip** is a rose hip. N COUNT

3 If you say that someone is **hip**, you mean that they follow all the most modern and recent fashions, for example in clothes and ideas; an informal use. EG *We thought we were so hip in those days.* ● **hip, hip, hurray**: see **hurray**. ADJ QUALIT = trendy

hip-bath, hip-baths; also spelled as two words. A **hip-bath** is a small bath which is big enough for you to sit in but not to lie down in. N COUNT

hip flask, hip flasks; also spelled with a hyphen. A **hip flask** is a small metal container in which brandy, whisky, or other spirits can be carried, usually in the pocket of a jacket. N COUNT ⇑ bottle

hippie /hɪpi[1]/, **hippies**; also spelled **hippy**. A **hippie** is someone who has chosen to live a different sort of life based on peace and love and has rejected conventional ideas about things such as dress and social values. The hippie movement started and was most popular during the 1960's. EG *...hippies in a commune... ...the pop and hippy generation.* N COUNT

hippo /hɪpəʊ/, **hippos**. A **hippo** is a hippopotamus; an informal word. N COUNT ⇑ animal

Hippocratic oath /hɪpə[6]krætɪk əʊθ/, **Hippocratic oaths**. A **Hippocratic oath** is a solemn promise made by newly qualified doctors, saying that they will follow the standards set by their profession and try to save life. N COUNT

hippopotamus /hɪpəpɒtəməs/, **hippopotamuses, hippopotami**. The plural can be either **hippopotamuses** or **hippopotami**. A **hippopotamus** is a large animal with short legs and thick, wrinkled skin without fur. Hippopotamuses like water and live near rivers in tropical Africa. N COUNT

hippy /hɪpi[1]/. See **hippie**.

hire /haɪə/, **hires, hiring, hired**. 1 If you **hire** something, you pay money in order to be allowed to V+O ⇑ rent

use it for a period of time. EG *We hired a car from a local car rental agency and drove across the island... ...the hiring of specialist skills.* ▸ used as a noun. EG *Hire of a van costs a little more but it is worth it.* ▸ N UNCOUNT + SUPP
● Something that is **for hire** is available for use in return for the payment of a sum of money. EG *...boats for hire.* ● PHR : USED AS AN A
2 If you **hire** someone, you pay them to do a particular job for you. EG *Skilled men were hired and construction got under way... You've got to hire a private detective to make enquiries... ...a hired assassin.* V+O ⇑ contract

hire out. If you **hire out** something such as a car or a person's services, you allow them to be used in return for payment. EG *Holborn library hires out reproductions and original pictures... ...people whom they would be glad to hire out on moderate terms.* PHRASAL VB : V+O+ADV = let, rent out

hireling /haɪəlɪŋ/, **hirelings**. A **hireling** is a person who does not care who they work for and who is willing to do something bad or illegal as long as they are paid for it; used showing disapproval. EG *...hireling soldiers.* N COUNT

hire purchase; also spelled with a hyphen. **Hire purchase** is a way of buying goods gradually. You make regular payments to the seller until, after some time, you have paid the full price and the goods belong to you. EG *Have you bought anything on hire purchase?... ...hire-purchase goods.* N UNCOUNT ⇑ credit = HP

hirsute /hɜːsjᵊuːt/. Someone who is **hirsute** is hairy; a formal or literary word. ADJ CLASSIF

his /hɪz/. **1** You use **his** to indicate that something belongs or relates to a man, boy, or male animal, or to someone whose sex is not known or stated, who has already been mentioned or named, or whose identity is known. In the Christian religion, **His** is used to refer to God or Jesus Christ. See **he**. EG *Her husband remained standing. He had his hands in his pockets and a cigarette in his mouth... It's his own fault... He said that his name was Simon... Everything in the village is allocated by the chief on the basis: to each according to his need.* ▸ used as a pronoun. EG *Willie had a job on a new magazine that a friend of his had just started... Tim's car is more reliable than mine, but then his is newer.* DETPOSS ▸ PRONPOSS
2 His is also used in some titles when you are referring to a man with that title. EG *...his Lordship... ...His Majesty.* DETPOSS : USED IN TITLES

hiss /hɪs/, **hisses, hissing, hissed**. **1** If you **hiss**, **1.1** you make a sound like a long 's'. EG *If you shove a hot aluminium frying pan into water it will hiss and perhaps buckle... Hissing with rage, the snake wriggled violently on the ground.* ▸ used as a noun. EG *The soft hiss of roasting meat could be heard clearly.* **1.2** you say something in a strong, angry whisper. EG *He pointed a shaking finger at my friend and hissed through clenched teeth: 'You, you get out!'* V ▸ N COUNT V+REPORT-CL/QUOTE
2 When an audience **hisses** a performance or a person making a speech, they express their disapproval or dislike of it by making long loud 's' sounds. EG *The crowd was expected to hiss or boo every point won by the Americans... The audience hissed me with great gusto... His public appearances were frequently hissed.* V OR V+O ⇑ disapprove

historian /hɪstɔːrɪən/, **historians**. A **historian** is a person who specializes in the study of history, and who writes books and articles about it. EG *...art historians... ...a distinguished historian of religion... No historian has ever doubted the authenticity of these documents.* N COUNT ⇑ scholar

historic /hɪstɒrɪk/. **1** Something that is **historic** is important in history, or likely to be considered important at some time in the future. EG *What we are talking about would have been a historic change... Attlee was able to include an historic compromise.* ADJ QUALIT
2 See also **historical**.

historical /hɪstɒrɪkəᵊl/. **1 Historical** or **historic** people, situations, etc used to exist in the past and are often considered to be a part of history. EG *They had their part to play in the historical process... The historical reason for it is that it was originally a Catholic cathedral... ...actual historical events... ...a historical figure in a work of fiction... ...their historic fear of invasion.* ◊ **historically**. EG *Historically, Labour was strongly opposed to the powers of the Lords.* ADJ CLASSIF : ATTRIB ⇑ past ◊ ADV SEN = traditionally
2 Historical or **historic** books, pictures, etc describe or represent real people, situations, or things that existed in the past. EG *...historical novels... ...an accurate historical representation of what the man looked like... ...peddlers in historical costumes loudly selling traditional goods... The play now has historic rather than aesthetic merit.* ◊ **historically**. EG *The set was historically accurate down to the last detail.* ADJ CLASSIF : ATTRIB ◊ ADV
3 Historical information, discussion, etc has a particular purpose or use in the study of history. EG *...introductory sessions on historical methods... It is documented in the historical archives... ...autographs and manuscripts of historical interest.* ADJ CLASSIF : ATTRIB

history /hɪstəᵊriᶦ/, **histories**. **1 History** is the events of the past, especially when they are seen as a long process which leads up to the present. History can refer to the political, social, and cultural events of the world in general, or it can be concerned with a particular area of activity. EG *...one of the most dramatic moments in Polish history... Those twenty-five minutes were to change the history of France... ...the highest salary in television history... ...the dawn of a new era in human history... We cannot reverse the course of history.* ● Someone who **makes history** does something that is considered to be important and significant in the development of the world or of a particular society. EG *...the people who made history.* ● If you **go down in history**, people in the future remember you because of particular events that have happened or particular actions that you have done. EG *Let the twenty-first century go down in history as the century of planning.* N UNCOUNT ⇑ record ● PHR : VB INFLECTS ⇑ achieve ● PHR : VB INFLECTS, IF + PREP THEN *as* = be remembered
2 History is also **2.1** a subject that is studied in schools, colleges, universities, etc that deals with events that have happened in the past. EG *I adored history and hated geography... It is a history book, not a novel.* ● See also **natural history**. **2.2** the period of time that has passed since people became able to write down information about themselves. EG *...conditions before the dawn of recorded history... ...origins in civilization that preceded written history.* N UNCOUNT N UNCOUNT
3 The **history** that a particular topic or place has is past events which concern it and which are considered to be interesting and significant. EG *Each city has its own peculiarities, its own history and character... ...a name rich with history and with promise... ...a college with a tremendous sporting history.* N UNCOUNT : USU + SUPP
4 A **history** is **4.1** an account or description of the important events that have happened in the past in a particular subject. EG *...a television history of the United States... ...a social history... ...when the history of the space war comes to be written... Their work is rarely covered in the histories or journals of modern American art.* **4.2** a play that contains characters who are intended to represent real people who lived in the past. EG *...Shakespeare's histories... ...a history play.* N COUNT + SUPP N COUNT
5 If someone has a **history** of a particular thing such as an illness or an activity, this thing has been very common or happened frequently in their past. EG *They had a history of radical political activity... They seem to have had no case history of illness... She had a history of premature births... Both he and Nick have similar histories of success.* N COUNT + *of*
6 The **history** of a person or thing is a set of facts that are known about their past and that you can sometimes use to help you estimate how they will behave in the future. EG *I'd like to look at his medical history... ...people's personal histories... Volcanoes have cycles, and according to this one's history, it will probably be quiet for another thirty years.* N COUNT : USU SING WITH POSS
6 If you say that something such as an event or situation is **history**, you mean that it is no longer very important to you because it happened some time ago. EG *Oh, let's forget that. It's all past history and it happened in another country... To everybody else it's history.* N UNCOUNT : USU USED AS C ⇑ unimportant

histrionic /hɪstriᶦɒnɪk/, **histrionics**. **1 Histrionic** behaviour is very dramatic and full of emotion, usually too much to be sincere. EG *...a flamboyant, histrionic gesture.* ◊ **histrionically**. EG *She sighed histrionically.* ▸ **Histrionics** are behaviour of this kind. EG *...the feelings wickedly distended by histrionics.* ADJ QUALIT : ATTRIB = melodramatic ◊ ADV WITH VB ▸ N PLURAL ⇑ behaviour
2 Histrionic also means relating to drama and acting; a formal use. EG *Many critics believe that he has the greatest histrionic talent of the century.* ADJ CLASSIF : ATTRIB

hit /hɪt/, **hits, hitting**. The form **hit** is used in the present tense and is the past tense and past participle of the verb. 1 If you **hit** someone, you touch them quickly using a lot of force with your hand, a stick, or another object, usually in order to hurt them. EG *The vicar was so angry, he hit the burglar on the head with a candlestick... I was hit every Monday morning at school.* ▸ used as a noun. EG *He gave me a hit on the head.* — V+O = strike; ▸ N COUNT = blow

2 If you **hit** something, 2.1 you touch it quickly using a lot of force with a hammer or other object, usually in order to push it firmly into something else. EG *To fix shelves to the wall use a plug punch which you hit with a hammer.* 2.2 you move towards it and touch it violently, usually by accident and causing damage. EG *The truck had hit a wall... The car stopped without hitting me... In the dark I stumbled and hit the back of a chair.* — V+O = strike; V+O = strike

3 If a missile such as a bomb or a bullet **hits** something that it is being aimed at, it moves towards it and reaches it, usually causing great damage. EG *Three ships were hit... The torpedo hit but didn't explode... He reported with satisfaction that none of his men had been hit... It's important that you hit what you shoot at... He has hit the bull's eye and won the prize.* ▸ used as a noun. EG *The tanks were designed to withstand anything except a direct hit... The helicopter had taken eight hits, but somehow managed to land.* — V OR V+O : USU V+O = strike; ▸ N COUNT = strike

4 If you **hit** a ball or other object, you make it move by swinging a bat, racket, or club to touch it with force. EG *He has a capacity for hitting the ball immensely hard... Golf is a game whose aim is to hit a very small ball into an even smaller hole.* ▸ used as a noun. EG *Somebody gets the winning hit in the World Series and he immediately becomes a hero.* — V OR V+O : USU V+O = strike; ▸ N COUNT

5 Something that **hits** a person, place, or thing affects them very badly and therefore causes difficulty or damage. EG *The Opposition protested against budget measures which hit workers' incomes... Spectator sport has been badly hit by the increase in ticket prices... The recession has hit especially hard in Scotland... Unskilled workers will be hit even harder by the rise in the mortgage rate... In May a typhoon hit the Philippines.* — V OR V+O : USU V+O ⇑ affect

6 A shock that **hits** you has a sudden strong effect on you and makes you think about something more deeply. EG *The shock of her death kept hitting me afresh... Suddenly it hit me: my diary had probably been read by everyone in the office.* — V+O ⇑ affect = strike

7 If you **hit** a particular high or low point on a scale of success, health, etc, you reach it. EG *This year's U.S. harvest is projected to hit record levels... The ominous words 'Pound hits new low' appeared daily for weeks... They are alcoholic. They have hit the bottom.* — V+O

8 If you **hit** a particular place, in informal English, you arrive there. EG *It was a great relief when we finally hit the road at the bottom of the mountain... Bear south after you hit the courthouse and you'll find our house two miles further on.* — V+O ⇑ reach

9 A **hit** is 9.1 a play, film, or other entertainment that is very popular and successful. EG *The play became a tremendous hit.* 9.2 a song or tune that becomes very popular, so that large numbers of records of it are sold. EG *They were dancing to the driving beat of a current hit by the Jackson Five... ...a hit single.* 9.3 a clever remark that has a damaging effect on the person or thing it is aimed at. EG *It was evident that that final hit at the opposition was very popular with her government colleagues.* — N COUNT ⇑ success; N COUNT ⇑ pop song; N COUNT : IF + PREP THEN *at* = dig

10 The word **hit** is also used in the following expressions. 10.1 If you **hit a man when he's down**, in informal English, you do or say something nasty and unfair to someone who is in a weak position and cannot fight back. 10.2 If you **hit the roof** or you **hit the ceiling**, in informal English, you show extreme anger about something. EG *She hit the roof when she saw what I'd done.* 10.3 When something that you say to someone **hits home**, they recognize that it is fair and true, even though it may be painful for them to realize. EG *A lot of what he said hit home.* 10.4 If something **hits you for six**, it amazes you and often upsets you. EG *His sudden anger really hit me for six.* 10.5 If you say that someone has **hit the nail on the head**, you mean that what they have said is exactly right. 10.6 If two people **hit it off**, they like each other and become friendly as soon as they meet. EG *David and Mary hit it off well from the start... My mother-in-law and Tom have never hit it off.* 10.7 If you **hit the road**, in informal English, you set out on a journey. EG *We decided we'd hit the road very early the next morning.* 10.8 Someone or something that **hits the headlines** gets a lot of publicity, especially in the news media. EG *One venture that hit the headlines was a British expedition from the North to the South Pole... She first hit the headlines when she decided to elope with a millionaire.* 10.9 If someone **hits the bottle**, in informal English, they start drinking too much. EG *He hit the bottle when his wife left him.* 10.10 If you **hit the sack** or you **hit the hay**, in informal English, you go to bed. EG *Although it was only 10 o'clock, he decided to hit the sack.* 10.11 If you **make a hit** with someone, they like you or are impressed by you when they meet you. EG *He made a hit with Amanda... 'Well,' says Howard, 'you seem to have made a hit.'* — PHR : VB INFLECTS; PHR : VB INFLECTS = explode; PHR : VB INFLECTS; PHR : VB INFLECTS; PHR : VB INFLECTS; PHR OR PHR + A *(with)* : RECIP, VB INFLECTS; PHR : VB INFLECTS ⇑ leave; PHR : VB INFLECTS; PHR : VB INFLECTS; PHR : VB INFLECTS; PHR : VB INFLECTS, IF + PREP THEN *with*

hit back. 1 If you **hit back** at someone or you **hit** them **back**, you hit them in return after they have hit you. EG *Thomas staggered and then hit back.* — PHRASAL VB : V + ADV, OR ORDER V +O+ADV

2 If you **hit back** at someone, you attack or criticize them when they have attacked you or affected you badly. EG *John was obsessed with hitting back at those who had wronged him.* — PHRASAL VB : V + ADV, IF + PREP THEN *at*

hit on. If you **hit on** an idea or you **hit upon** it, you think of it, especially when it is a solution to a problem. EG *He hit on the idea of cutting a hole in the door to allow the cat to get in and out... He had tried on many characters before hitting on the one that fitted him... Twelve years and four restaurants after hitting upon his formula, he was a millionaire.* — PHRASAL VB : V + PREP, HAS PASS = stumble on

hit out. If you **hit out** at someone, 1 you try to hit them, although you may miss them. EG *Ralph hit out at his assailant.* 2 you criticize them strongly because you do not agree with them. EG *The Prime Minister hit out at her colleagues in Europe.* — PHRASAL VB : V + ADV; PHRASAL VB : V + ADV

hit upon. See **hit on**.

hit and miss; also spelled with hyphens. Something that is **hit and miss** happens in an unplanned, casual, or unpredictable way, so that you never know what the result will be. EG *The service in this hotel is very hit and miss... The development of cancer is a hit-and-miss affair, subject to chance.* — ADJ QUALIT = random

hit-and-run is used to describe a car accident in which the person who has caused damage drives away without stopping. EG *...killed in a hit-and-run accident... ...a hit-and-run driver.* — ADJ CLASSIF : ATTRIB

hitch /hɪtʃ/, **hitches, hitching, hitched**. 1 A **hitch** is a slight problem or difficulty which causes a short delay. EG *There had also been one or two technical hitches, such as the curtain not closing promptly... The negotiations continued without a hitch.* — N COUNT = snag

2 If you **hitch** or **hitch** a lift you hitch-hike; used in informal English. EG *He broke out one spring night and hitched south towards Italy... We hitched a ride with some young kids in a Volkswagen.* — V OR V+O : USU A ⇑ travel

3 If you **hitch** something onto something else, you hook it or fasten it there. EG *...ponies hitched to rails... Each wagon was hitched on to the one in front.* — V+O+A

4 If you **get hitched**, you get married; an informal expression. EG *They're getting hitched next week.* — PHR : VB INFLECTS

hitch up. If you **hitch up** a piece of cloth such as a skirt or a curtain, you lift the bottom of it and pull it up into a higher position, for example by tucking it into something. EG *He hitched up his trousers and waded into the river... Her skirt had hitched itself up and was crumpled round her waist.* — PHRASAL VB : V + O + ADV

hitch-hike, hitch-hikes, hitch-hiking, hitch-hiked; also spelled as one word. If you **hitch-hike**, you travel by getting lifts in other people's vehicles, which you ask for by standing at the side of the road with your thumb held out. EG *She went off with a friend intending to hitchhike to Turkey.* — V : USU + A

hitch-hiker, hitch-hikers. A **hitch-hiker** is someone who is hitch-hiking, or someone who hitch-hikes regularly. — N COUNT ⇑ traveller

hi tech. Something that is **hi tech** is designed using the most modern and advanced methods and equipment. — ADJ QUALIT = space age

hither /hɪðə/ is used to describe movement towards the place where you are at present; an old-fashioned word. EG *...my journey hither... He comes hither from Savile Row.* ● Something that moves **hither and thither** moves in all directions; an old-fashioned or — ADV WITH VB, ADV AFTER N = here; ● PHR : USED A literary expression. EG *She ran hither and thither in the orchard.*

hitherto /hɪðətuː/ is used to refer to something that has been true or that has been happening until now; a formal word. EG *She had hitherto been relatively nice to me... Modern technology has solved so many hitherto insoluble problems.* ADV+ADJ ⇑ before = previously

hit list, hit lists. A **hit list** is a list that terrorists or gangsters make, consisting of people they intend to have killed. EG *He may be on a hit list drawn up by terrorists acting for dissidents.* N COUNT

hit man, hit men. A **hit man** is a person who is hired by terrorists or gangsters to kill people. N COUNT ⇑ killer

hit or miss; also spelled with hyphens when used before a noun. Something that is **hit or miss** happens in an unplanned, casual, or unpredictable way, so that you never know what the result will be. EG *We are largely working on a rather hit-or-miss basis at the moment.* ADJ QUALIT

hit parade. The **hit parade** is the list of pop records which have sold most copies over the previous week or month; a rather old-fashioned expression. N COUNT : the+N = the charts

hive /haɪv/, **hives, hiving, hived**. 1 A **hive** is a beehive. EG *There must be fifty or sixty thousand bees in the hive.* N COUNT

2 You describe a place as a **hive** of activity, industry, etc when there is a lot of activity and people are busily working there. EG *Calcutta is a hive of industry and trade... The little office is a hive of activity.* N COUNT+of+N UNCOUNT = powerhouse

3 **Hives** is a disease which causes patches of your skin to become red and very uncomfortable and itchy. N UNCOUNT ⇑ allergy

hive off. If you **hive off** something such as a business, you transfer part of it to new ownership; used especially when a profitable part of a nationalized industry is sold to private industry. EG *...a proposal to hive off London Transport to the private sector.* PHRASAL VB : V+O+ADV

h'm; also spelled **hm**. You say **'h'm'** when you are hesitating, for example because you are puzzled by something or are thinking about something.

HM is the abbreviation for 'Her Majesty's' or 'His Majesty's'; used as part of the name of some British government organizations, or as part of a person's title. EG *HM Customs and Excise must be notified... ...HM Forces.* N IN NAMES/TITLES BEFORE N

HMI /eɪtʃ ɛm aɪ/, **HMI's**. An **HMI** is a government official in Great Britain who is responsible for supervising teaching and administration in schools; an abbreviation for 'Her Majesty's Inspector' or 'His Majesty's Inspector'. EG *There's been a recent HMI's report on foreign language teaching in primary schools.* N COUNT

HMS is used before the names of ships in the British Royal Navy; an abbreviation for 'Her Majesty's Ship' or 'His Majesty's Ship'. EG *He had been in command of HMS Churchill for nearly a year.* N IN NAMES BEFORE N

HNC, HNCs. An **HNC** is a group of examinations in technical subjects such as electronics and engineering, which you can take at a British college or polytechnic; an abbreviation for 'Higher National Certificate'. EG *She's doing an HNC course in electronics.* N COUNT/UNCOUNT ⇑ certificate

ho /həʊ/ is a rather old-fashioned exclamation used to attract people's attention. EG *'Ho!' they shout when they see somebody they know.* • See also **righto**. CONVENTION

• **Ho ho** is used to represent the sound you make when you laugh. • CONVENTION = ha ha

hoard /hɔːd/, **hoards, hoarding, hoarded**. 1 If you **hoard** things, you save or store them, often in secret, because they are valuable or important to you. EG *He hoarded colourful picture books for children... Is it better to spend your money today or hoard every penny in the bank for tomorrow?* V+O = collect

2 A **hoard** is a store of things you have saved that are valuable or important to you and that you do not want other people to have. EG *Not unless there was an emergency would she break into that precious hoard of hers.* N COUNT : IF+PREP THEN of = cache

hoarding /hɔːdɪŋ/, **hoardings**. A **hoarding** is a very large notice board that stands at the sides of roads and is used for displaying advertisements and posters. EG *On the way in from London Airport, I scanned the hoardings for election posters... This advertisement is seen now on the hoardings of nearly every country in the world.* N COUNT : USU PL = billboard

hoarse /hɔːs/, **hoarser, hoarsest**. If your voice is **hoarse**, it sounds rough and unclear, for example because your throat is sore. EG *'Who are you?' he asked in a hoarse voice.* ▸ used of a person with this kind of voice. EG *They can shout themselves hoarse–it won't change anything.* ◇ **hoarsely**. EG *'Go in there,' he whispered hoarsely.* ◇ **hoarseness**. EG *I noticed a peculiar hoarseness in Johnny's voice.* ADJ QUALIT = rasping ◇ ADV WITH VB = harshly ◇ N UNCOUNT

hoary /hɔːri¹/. Someone or something that is **hoary** is 1 greyish white; used especially of a person who has white or grey hair because they are old; a literary use. EG *...an old, hoary Negro... ...a clump of hoary juniper bushes.* 2 very old. EG *They discussed the hoary old problem.* ADJ QUALIT ⇑ grey ADJ QUALIT = ancient

hoax /həʊks/, **hoaxes, hoaxing, hoaxed**. 1 A **hoax** is a trick in which someone tells the police, emergency services, or the public something that is not true, for example that there is a bomb somewhere, or that a forged work of art is genuine. EG *It wasn't a hoax, there really was a fire... The painting had actually been done recently; it was a hoax.* N COUNT = con, prank

2 If you **hoax** someone, you make them believe that something is genuine or really happening when it is not. EG *We've been hoaxed.* V+O : USU PASS ⇑ trick = dupe

hob /hɒb/, **hobs**. A **hob** is a surface on top of a cooker which can be heated and usually contains gas rings or electric rings for putting saucepans on. EG *The stew simmered on the hob.* N COUNT ⇑ device = hotplate

hobble /hɒbə⁰l/, **hobbles, hobbling, hobbled**. 1 If you **hobble**, you walk in an awkward way with small steps, for example because your feet are injured. EG *He hobbled along as best he could.* V : USU+A = limp

2 If you **hobble** an animal or person, you tie their legs together so that they can walk slowly but not run away. EG *They were hobbled by straps around their legs.* V+O = fetter

hobby /hɒbi¹/, **hobbies**. A **hobby** is something that you enjoy doing in your spare time, such as collecting stamps, painting, or bird-watching. EG *In the evening I like to sit down and pursue my hobbies... Music is his chief hobby.* N COUNT ⇑ activity

hobby-horse, hobby-horses; also spelled without a hyphen. 1 You describe a subject or idea as your **hobby-horse** if you have strong feelings on it and like talking about it whenever you have the opportunity. EG *Film censorship is a personal hobby-horse of mine... Oh dear, he's on his hobby-horse again.* N COUNT : USU POSS+N ⇑ topic

2 A **hobby-horse** is a toy that looks like a horse's head on a stick and which a child can pretend to ride like a horse. N COUNT

hobnail boot /hɒbneɪl buːt/, **hobnail boots**. **Hobnail boots** or **hobnailed boots** are heavy boots with short nails put in underneath to make them wear out less quickly. N COUNT : USU PL

hobnob /hɒbnɒb/, **hobnobs, hobnobbing, hobnobbed**. If you **hobnob** with someone, in informal English, you are friendly and spend time with them; used especially when this friendship is new or surprising. V+A (with) ⇑ associate = fraternize

hobo /həʊbəʊ/, **hobos, hoboes**. The plural can be either **hobos** or **hoboes**. **Hobo** is an American word. A **hobo** is 1 a tramp. EG *The old hobo sat slouched in a corner seat.* 2 a worker, especially a farm worker, who goes from place to place in order to find work. N COUNT N COUNT ⇑ labourer

Hobson's choice /hɒbsə⁰nz tʃɔɪs/. You describe a situation as **Hobson's choice** when, although there appear to be alternatives, in fact there is only one thing you can do. EG *I'm afraid it's a case of Hobson's choice.* PHR : USED AS C ⇑ necessity

hock /hɒk/, **hocks, hocking, hocked**. 1 **Hock** is a type of dry white wine from Germany. EG *...a glass of hock.* N MASS

2 An animal's **hock** is the joint in its back leg that points backwards; used especially of horses. N COUNT

hockey /hɒki¹/ is an outdoor game, played between two teams of 11 players who use long curved sticks to hit a small ball and try to score goals. EG *I used to play hockey at school... ...a hockey pitch... ...a hockey stick.* • See also **field hockey, ice hockey**. N UNCOUNT

hocus-pocus /həʊkəs pəʊkəs/ is something that is done or said in order to trick or confuse someone; used showing disapproval. EG *There's been a bit of hocus-pocus going on here... The rest of your question I find rhetorical hocus-pocus.* N UNCOUNT ⇑ trickery

hod /hɒd/, **hods**. A **hod** is a container that workmen on a building site use for carrying bricks. It consists of a box-shaped holder attached to a long handle. N COUNT

hodge-podge /hɒdʒ pɒdʒ/. A **hodge-podge** is a confused or disorderly mixture of different types of things; used in American English. EG *...a hodge-podge of modern building.* N SING WITH DET : IF+PREP THEN *of*

hoe /həʊ/, **hoes, hoeing, hoed**. 1 A **hoe** is a gardening tool with a long handle and a small square blade, which is used to remove small weeds and break up the surface of the soil. N COUNT

2 If you **hoe** or you **hoe** a field, you use a hoe on the weeds or soil there. V OR V+O ⇑ work

hog /hɒg/, **hogs, hogging, hogged**. 1 A **hog** is 1.1 a male pig that has been castrated. N COUNT 1.2 a greedy, dirty, or vulgar person; an informal use. N COUNT = pig

2 If you **hog** something, in informal English, you take all of it in a selfish or impolite way. EG *...a huge lorry hogging the centre of the road... ...hogging the publicity.* V+O = monopolize ≠ share

3 If you **go the whole hog**, in informal English, you do something in the most complete way possible, especially something rather bold or extravagant. EG *I thought I might as well go the whole hog and have my hair dyed as well.* PHR : VB INFLECTS = go to town

Hogmanay /hɒgmənei/ is New Year's Eve in Scotland and the celebrations that take place at that time; a Scottish word. N UNCOUNT

hogwash /hɒgwɒʃ/ If you describe something that someone says as **hogwash**, you mean that it is nonsense; an informal word. EG *This is all hogwash as far as I'm concerned.* N UNCOUNT : USED AS C = codswallop

hoi polloi /hɔɪ pəlɔɪ/. The **hoi polloi** are ordinary people considered as a group, rather than people who are rich, well-educated, or upper-class; used showing disapproval. EG *Avocado pears used to be smart but now the hoi polloi eat them in wine bars.* N PLURAL : *the*+N = riff-raff

hoist /hɔɪst/, **hoists, hoisting, hoisted**. 1 If you **hoist** something heavy somewhere, 1.1 you lift it or pull it up there with your hands. EG *She hoisted the child onto her shoulder... He hoisted the rope over the branch.* V+O+A = heave 1.2 you lift it using a machine such as a crane. EG *...steel modules that can be hoisted by crane... ...a slab that might easily be hoisted into place.* V+O : USU+A = winch

2 If you **hoist** a flag or a sail, you pull it up to its correct high position by means of ropes. EG *The American flag was hoisted.* • **hoist with** your **own petard**: see **petard**. V+O ⇑ lift = run up

3 A **hoist** is a machine for lifting heavy things. EG *...an electric hoist.* N COUNT

hoity-toity /hɔɪti[1] tɔɪti[1]/. Someone who is **hoity-toity** behaves in a proud and haughty way; an informal word used showing disapproval. ADJ QUALIT = snooty

hold /həʊld/, **holds, holding, held**. 1 When you **hold** something, you have it in your hand and you keep it there by putting your fingers firmly round it. EG *I held the picture up to the light... Lomax gave him the gun to hold... Her hands were holding tight to the umbrella... I struggled on, holding the cage tight to my chest.* ▸ used as a noun. EG *She resumed her hold on the rope.* V+O : USU+A, OR V+A (*on to/to*) ▸ N SING WITH DET

2 When you **hold** someone, 2.1 you put your arms round them, usually because you want to show them how much you like them or because you want to comfort them. EG *He held her in his arms... The tears were pouring, and I held her tight, trying to comfort her.* V+O : USU+A = clasp 2.2 you keep them in a particular position by using force. EG *'Hold him!' They got his arms and legs.* V+O = pin down 2.3 you keep them still or under control by using your hands. EG *My sister was holding her puppy.* V+O 2.4 you keep them as a prisoner or hostage and do not allow them to leave. EG *I was held overnight in a cell... The young private had been held a prisoner by the guerrillas.* V+O : USU+A, OR V+O+C ⇑ detain

3 If you **hold** a part of your body or a part of someone else's body, you put your hand on or against it. You often put your hand on part of your own body because it hurts, or because you are worried or upset about something, and on someone else's arm or shoulder in order to comfort or encourage them. EG *Claude lay on his back, moaning, holding his burnt arm... She held her head in her hands... He would wish me luck and hold my arm.* V+O = clasp

4 If you **hold** your body or part of your body in a particular position or manner, you put it into that position and keep it there. EG *Etta held her head back and groaned... Mrs Patel held herself erect.* V+O (NG/REFL) +A

5 **Hold** is frequently used in English to say that someone or something has the particular attitude, position, qualification, etc that is mentioned. It thus takes most of its meaning from the word that follows it. **Hold** is used in the following ways: 5.1 used with words referring to attitudes or feelings. EG *The government is destroying every institution and value they hold dear... They are seeking an excuse to hold their parents in contempt.* V+O+A, OR V+O+C ⇑ regard 5.2 used with nouns such as 'office', 'power', and 'responsibility'. EG *Northcliffe held the power to suppress the riots... She was one of the greatest Prime Ministers who ever held office.* V+O = have 5.3 used with nouns such as 'permit' and 'degree', and other nouns referring to qualifications. EG *She held a BA in psychology... You need to hold a work permit.* V+O = have 5.4 used with nouns such as 'party', 'meeting', 'talks', 'election', and 'trial', showing that people are meeting for formal or informal reasons. EG *In 1945 he decided to hold meetings of party officials... He had promised he would hold elections in June... Mrs Smith is holding a party next week... The UN called for the holding of tripartite talks.* V+O = have 5.5 used with nouns such as 'conversation', 'interview', and 'consultation'. EG *I won't be able to hold a conversation with him... John Morgan had held an interview at a secret rendezvous... Dr Leon would come and hold a surgery there.* V+O = have, conduct 5.6 used with nouns referring to qualities and characteristics. EG *Her face held no sign of fear... The marriage held little promise of happiness for either... We will have to see what the future holds... These legends hold a romantic fascination for many Japanese.* V+O = have, bear

6 If you **hold** a particular opinion or belief about something, you believe that it is true. EG *This soon dispelled any foolish notions they might hold about Baldwin's ability... Marxists hold that people are all naturally creative... I also hold strongly to the idea that the university should seek funding from industry and commerce.* V+O/REPORT-CL, OR V+A (*to*)

7 If you **hold** someone responsible, liable, accountable, etc for something, they will be blamed if anything goes wrong because you have made them responsible for it. EG *I hold you personally responsible... The President is held accountable.* V+O+C ⇑ consider

8 If you **hold** your lead or position in a competition or event, you manage to keep it. EG *He succeeded in holding third position in 49.11 seconds.* V+O = retain

9 If you **hold** or **hold** the line when you have made a telephone call, you wait until the person who has answered the call can put you through to the person you want to speak to. EG *The line's engaged: will you hold?* V OR V+O : IF+PREP THEN *for* = hang on

10 If you **hold** telephone calls for someone else, you do not put them through to the person they are for but instead you take a message for them. EG *Galbraith asked his secretary to hold all phone messages while he took a nap.* V+O

11 If you **hold** something at a particular level, number, or rate, you keep it there and do not allow it to rise or fall. EG *Japan has agreed to hold shipments this year to 1.68 million cars... The speed drops to sixty, then fifty-five and I hold it there.* V+O+A ⇑ maintain

12 If you **hold** a sound or musical note, you continue making it. EG *One of the wind instruments held the note longer than the rest.* V+O = sustain

13 If you **hold** something such as someone's interest or attention, you do or say something which keeps them interested or listening to you. EG *He was finding it a strain to hold his students' attention... It's a great thrill, knowing that you are holding the audience completely.* V+O = grip

14 If you **hold** something such as the departure of a train, you delay it. EG *They'll probably hold the London train if we're late in... Come on, we're holding dinner for you.* V+O = keep back

15 If you can **hold** your drink, you are able to drink large quantities of alcohol without becoming ill or getting drunk. EG *I never did hold my liquor very well.* V+O

16 If people such as an army or a group of fighters **hold** a place, they control it by using force. EG *They only held the fort for three days.* V+O = occupy

17 If an army or a group of fighters **hold** the enemy, they check their progress and prevent them from V+O = hold off

attacking. EG *The available conventional forces could not hold the enemy.*

18 When one thing **holds** another or when it **holds**, the first thing keeps the other fixed in position. EG *There was just a rail or something holding it... ...the glue held.* V OR V-ERG

19 If something **holds** a particular amount of something, it can contain that amount. EG *He brought a tub big enough to hold eighteen gallons... The theatre itself can hold only a limited number of people.* V+O = take

20 If a place **holds** something, it keeps it available for reference or for future use. EG *These places also hold a list of solicitors... He couldn't guess at the amount of gold held in national vaults.* V+O ⇑ store

21 If a place such as a hotel or travel agency **holds** something for you, they keep it reserved for you and do not let anyone else have it. EG *He held the room till half-past six... Do you want me to hold an option for you for 24 hours?* V+O = retain

22 If a vehicle **holds the road** well, it remains in close contact with the road and can be controlled safely and easily. EG *The new car holds the road much better.* ▸ used as a noun. EG *The tyres are so worn they don't have much hold on the road.* PHR : VB INFLECTS = grip ▸ N UNCOUNT = grip

23 If an offer or invitation **holds**, it is still available for you to accept. EG *Will you tell her the offer still holds.* V = stand

24 If your luck **holds** or if the weather **holds**, it remains good and does not change. EG *If my luck continues to hold, I think I've got a fair chance... While colder than usual, the weather held.* V = last

25 If an argument **holds**, it is true or valid. EG *Your argument doesn't hold... These predictions will not hold.* V = stand up

26 If rules and laws **hold**, they exist and remain in force. EG *The same rules hold for everyone.* V = operate

27 A **hold** is a way of keeping part of another person's body in a particular position using your own hands, arms, or legs; used especially in wrestling. EG *They bent each arm upward behind my back in a hold that was impossible to break.* N COUNT = grip

28 On a rock or cliff, a **hold** is a place, such as a small piece of rock which sticks out, where you can put your hand or foot when you are climbing. EG *Everyone had gone from the more popular routes with ledges and holds cleared of debris.* N COUNT = foothold

29 In a ship or aeroplane, a **hold** is a place where cargo or luggage is stored. EG *They used to fish those waters and come back with full holds.* N COUNT ⇑ storeroom

30 If you have a **hold** over someone, **30.1** you know something about them that you can use in order to threaten them or to make them do something for you. EG *The farmer had a hold over me. He had found out about my illegal whiskey still.* **30.2** you have power or control over them or their activities. EG *The party tightened its hold on the union... Black African nations wanted to destroy the white hold on South Africa.* N SING WITH DET +*over* ⇑ power; N SING WITH DET : IF+PREP THEN *on/over* = grip

31 If something has a **hold** over someone, it has a lot of influence which affects or controls their attitude or behaviour. EG *The hold of religion over the Victorians was an important factor... Such principles did indeed exert a hold on the minds of some of the children.* N SING WITH DET : USU+*on/over* = spell

32 **Hold** is used in expressions such as 'get hold', 'grab hold', 'seize hold', or 'take hold', which have the following meanings: **32.1** to put your hand tightly round something and not let go of it. EG *She took hold of my wrist... There was nothing else for me to catch hold of... He still had hold of my jacket.* **32.2** to gain control or possession of something, especially by force. EG *We managed to get hold of Hill 13 again... We must take hold of the power of the state, or we will be crushed.* **33.3** to finally gain complete control or influence over something. EG *Then the fire took hold... Once her monetarist policies took hold, Britain would be back on its feet... Something quite different gets a hold of him.* N UNCOUNT : IF+PREP THEN *of*; N UNCOUNT : IF+PREP THEN *of* = command; N UNCOUNT : IF+PREP THEN *of* = take over

33 Get hold of. 33.1 If you **get hold of** something, you obtain it, especially by borrowing it or by finding it somewhere and keeping it. EG *Can you get hold of a car this weekend?... Anyone who gets hold of that ticket can come in and claim the article.* **33.2** If you **get hold of** information, you find out about it, especially when the people involved do not want others to know about it, or in a way which people do not entirely approve of. EG *Our reporters got hold of the story.* **33.3** If you **get hold of** a fact or a subject, you learn about it and understand it well. EG *Once one has got hold of certain basic facts the rest is comparatively easy.* **33.4** If you **get hold of** an idea, belief, or impression, you have it, especially when it is wrong or when other people disapprove of it. EG *I am afraid they have got hold of the idea that we can solve all their financial problems... It is easy to see how they have got hold of this impression.* **33.5** If you **get hold of** someone, you find out where they are in order to contact them. EG *I've been trying to get hold of you... This friend of mine got hold of me in London.* PHR : VB INFLECTS = get, acquire; PHR : VB INFLECTS ⇑ discover = ferret out; PHR : VB INFLECTS = grasp; PHR : VB INFLECTS = pick up; PHR : VB INFLECTS

34 The word **hold** is also used in the following expressions. **34.1** If you say to people **'Hold everything'**, you are telling them to stop what they are doing, for example because something serious has happened. EG *'Stop!' he cried. 'Hold everything! My leg is caught!'* **34.2** If you **hold forth**, you speak confidently and for a long time about something, especially to a group of people. EG *They sat about drinking wine, and holding forth, as one does at that age... He was holding forth about river-bank erosion.* **34.3** If you say to someone **'Hold it'**, you are telling them to stop what they are doing and to wait. EG *Hold it a moment, will you?.* **34.4** If you **hold still** or **hold steady**, you do not move. EG *'Oh! do hold still!' she cried.* **34.5** If you **hold tight**, you put your hand round or against something in order to prevent yourself from falling over. Someone might say **'Hold tight!'** to you if you are standing on a bus when it is about to move. **34.6** If you say **'There's no holding** someone', you mean that they are very interested in and enthusiastic about an activity and spend a lot of time on it. EG *Now he's got his own computer there's no holding him: he taps away all the time.* **34.7** If you **hold** your **own**, you are able to resist someone who is attacking or opposing you. EG *It assisted them to hold their own against the attacks.* **34.8** If you can do something well enough to **hold** your **own**, you do not appear foolish when you are compared with someone who is generally thought to be very good at it. EG *She was still able to hold her own with the Prime Minister.* **34.9** If you **hold the door** or **hold the door open** for someone, you open a door for them to go through. EG *Go and hold the door for him.* CONVENTION = hold it; PHR : VB INFLECTS, IF+PREP THEN *about/on/to* = spout; CONVENTION = hold on; PHR : VB INFLECTS; PHR : VB INFLECTS = cling on; PHR : *be* INFLECTS; PHR : VB INFLECTS : IF+PREP THEN *against*; PHR : VB INFLECTS; V+O : IF+PREP THEN *for*

35 The word **hold** is used in the following expressions, which are explained at other places in this dictionary. • **no holds barred**: see **bar**. • **to hold** something **at bay**: see **bay**. • **to hold** your **breath**: see **breath**. • **to not hold a candle to** someone: see **candle**. • to **hold** something **in check**: see **check**. • to **hold court**: see **court**. • to **hold fast**: see **fast**. • to **hold the floor**: see **floor**. • to **hold the fort**: see **fort**. • to **hold** your **ground**: see **ground**. • to **be held hostage**: see **hostage**. • to **hold (out) hope**: see **hope**. • to **hold** your **peace**: see **peace**. • to **hold** someone **to ransom**: see **ransom**. • to **hold sway**: see **sway**. • to **hold** your **tongue**: see **tongue**.

hold against. If you **hold** something **against** someone, you let something which they did wrong in the past influence your present attitude towards them and cause you to deal more severely with them than you would otherwise have done. EG *His refusal to cooperate will be held against him... They'll hold that against you when you apply next time.* PHRASAL VB : V+O+PREP

hold back. 1 If you **hold back** or something **holds** you **back**, you hesitate before you do something because you are not sure whether it is the right thing to do. EG *Police have held back from going into a holy place.* PHRASAL VB : V-ERG+ADV = delay

2 If you **hold** someone or something **back**, **2.1** you prevent them from doing something, or you prevent something from happening. EG *If she is ambitious, don't try to hold her back... The rise in living standards has been held back for so long.* **2.2** you keep them under control and prevent them from advancing or spreading. EG *Rows of police held back the crowds.* PHRASAL VB : V+O+ADV = inhibit; PHRASAL VB : V+O+ADV ⇑ restrain

3 If you **hold** something **back**, **3.1** you keep it in reserve to use later. EG *They need the money immediately and cannot hold back their goods to push the price up.* **3.2** you do not tell someone the full details about something. EG *I want the truth, now, with nothing held back.* PHRASAL VB : V+O+ADV ⇑ save; PHRASAL VB : V+O+ADV ⇑ suppress = withhold

4 If you **hold back** something such as tears or laughter, you do not allow yourself to show how you feel. EG *They just couldn't hold back their laughter.* PHRASAL VB : V+O+ADV ⇑ control = contain

hold down. 1 If you **hold** someone **down**, 1.1 you use force to keep them in a particular place and to stop them from moving. EG *It took three men to hold him down.* PHRASAL VB : V+O+ADV ⇑ control 1.2 you keep them under control and do not allow them to have much freedom or power, or many rights. EG *These measures would still not be enough to hold down the rioters.* PHRASAL VB : V+O+ADV = suppress

2 If you are **holding down** a job, you are managing to keep it. PHRASAL VB : V+O+ADV

3 If you **hold down** wages, prices, etc, you keep them at a low rate and prevent them from rising much. EG *The only way to keep down prices was to hold down wages... Did they think that their policy would hold down inflation?* PHRASAL VB : V+O+ADV ⇑ control = keep down

hold in. If you **hold in** something such as an emotion, you do not allow yourself to express it. EG *Women are expected to hold in their anger.* PHRASAL VB : V+O+ADV ⇑ control = suppress

hold off. 1 If you **hold off** something such as an army, you prevent it from coming too close to you. EG *They were able to hold off a very much superior attacking force.* PHRASAL VB : V+O+ADV = fend off

2 If you **hold off** doing something, you delay doing it or delay making a decision about it. EG *He held off making a final decision until the new year.* PHRASAL VB : V+ADV+-ING, OR V+O+ADV = put off

3 If the rain **holds off**, it does not rain when you had expected it to. EG *The rain held off and we had a fine day.* PHRASAL VB : V+ADV

hold on. 1 If you **hold on** or **hold on** to something, 1.1 you put your hand round or against it in order to prevent yourself from falling over. EG *I couldn't put up my umbrella and hold on at the same time... He has to hold onto something to steady himself.* PHRASAL VB : V+ADV, USU+*to* = hang on 1.2 you keep your fingers round it and do not let it fall or let anyone take it from you. EG *Jordan took a step back, holding on to the drawing.* PHRASAL VB : V+ADV, USU+*to* ≠ let go 1.3 you keep it for yourself and do not give it to anyone else. EG *He permitted Rudolph to hold on to the money he earned... Politicians want to hold on to power at all costs.* PHRASAL VB : V+ADV, USU+*to* = hang on 1.4 you look after something which belongs to another person for a period of time; an informal use. EG *Will you hold on to this for me for a couple of days?* PHRASAL VB : V+ADV, USU+*to* = keep

2 If you **hold on** to your beliefs, ideas, or principles, you continue to believe in them and do not change or abandon them if others try to influence you or if circumstances cause you to doubt them. EG *They hold on to these virtues with a rare tenacity... They hold on to their dream.* PHRASAL VB : V+ADV, USU+*to* ⇑ keep = hang on

3 If you **hold on**, 3.1 you force yourself to continue with what you have to do even though you have problems or difficulties and want to give up. PHRASAL VB : V+ADV 3.2 you wait for a short time. EG *Hold on a moment, please... We are only asking you to hold on a little longer.* PHRASAL VB : V+ADV, USU+A = hang on

hold out. 1 If you **hold out** your hand or something you have in your hand, you move it away from your body, usually in order to take something or to give something to someone. EG *Daintry held out his hand for the briefcase... 'John?' Esther held out the phone.* PHRASAL VB : V+O+ADV ⇑ extend

2 If you **hold out** for something, you refuse to accept something which you do not think is adequate, and you continue to demand more. EG *Women all over the country are holding out for more freedom... If you just hold out a little longer you'll win.* PHRASAL VB : V+ADV, IF+PREP THEN *for* ≠ settle, yield

3 If you **hold out** on someone, in informal English, you refuse to give them information that they want. EG *I'm sure he's holding out on them.* PHRASAL VB : V+ADV, IF+PREP THEN *on*

4 If you **hold out**, you manage to resist an enemy or opponent in difficult circumstances and refuse to surrender. EG *The rebels would hold out for ten years.* PHRASAL VB : V+ADV = last out

5 If you **hold out** hope of something happening, you offer hope for the future that something will happen as you want it to. EG *I don't hold out much hope... Science may hold out some prospect of feeding the hungry.* PHRASAL VB : ORDER V+ADV+O

hold over. 1 If you **hold** something **over** someone, you use it in order to threaten them or make them do what you want. EG *He held the letter over her like a threat.* PHRASAL VB : V+O+PREP

2 If you **hold** something **over**, you decide not to discuss or deal with it, until a future date. EG *We'll have to hold that point over until the next meeting.* PHRASAL VB : V+O+ADV ⇑ keep = defer

3 If a play or film is **held over**, performances of it continue for longer than was originally planned. EG *'Rambo' is being held over for a further week.* PHRASAL VB : V+O+ADV = keep on

hold together. 1 When you **hold** people **together** or when they **hold together**, people who have different aims, attitudes, or interests manage to live or work together without arguing or disagreeing. EG *He impressed people by the way he held his constituents together... I hoped the group would hold together.* PHRASAL VB : V-ERG+ADV

2 If something **holds together**, it stays in good condition, so that it is able to be used. EG *The problem now seemed to be whether the car would hold together.* PHRASAL VB : V+ADV

hold up. 1 If you **hold up** your hand or something you have in your hand, you move it upwards into a particular position and keep it there. EG *Ralph held up his hand. 'Why shouldn't we get our own?' he asked... The Englishman held up the rifle.* PHRASAL VB : V+O+ADV ⇑ raise = lift

2 If one thing **holds up** another, it is placed under the other thing in order to support it and prevent it from falling. EG *There were tremendous pillars holding up high ceilings... These books hold the bed up.* PHRASAL VB : V+O+ADV = prop up

3 If something or someone **holds** you **up**, they delay you or make you late. EG *The whole thing was held up about half an hour... These slogans persuaded her to hold up the procession.* PHRASAL VB : V+O+ADV = detain

4 If someone **holds** you **up**, they point a weapon at you in order to make you give them money or valuables. EG *He held me up at the point of a gun... Banks were held up with pistols and sawn-off shotguns.* PHRASAL VB : V+O+ADV = rob

5 If you **hold up** something such as someone's behaviour, you make it known to other people, together with your own attitude, in order to influence them to have the same attitude as you. EG *Their ways are held up to scorn... What do you hold up to the children as being desirable goals?* PHRASAL VB : V+O+ADV+A

6 If equipment or clothing **holds up**, in informal English, it stays in reasonable condition after fairly rough treatment. EG *How did your boots hold up?* PHRASAL VB : V+ADV ⇑ last = fare

7 If theories, beliefs, and arguments **hold up**, they remain convincing after close examination of them. EG *Your argument, though romantically appealing, doesn't hold up.* PHRASAL VB : V+ADV

8 See also **hold-up**.

hold with. If you don't **hold with** an activity or action, you don't approve of it. EG *You know I don't hold with smoking.* PHRASAL VB : V+PREP, WITH NEG

holdall /həʊldɔːl/, **holdalls.** A **holdall** is a large bag, often made of nylon, canvas or leather, in which you put clothes and other things when you are going away from home. EG *He emerged from the night train from London, scuffed leather holdall in one hand.* N COUNT

holder /həʊldə/, **holders.** A **holder** is 1 a container or framework in which you put an object, usually in order to protect it or to keep it in place. EG *I screwed the now useless lamp back in its holder... Its plastic cup was held in a brown plastic holder.* N COUNT 2 a cigarette-holder. EG *She was smoking endless cigarettes from a long black holder.* N COUNT 3 someone who owns or has possession or control of something. EG *I require the licence number and the full name of the holder... ...ticket-holders... The managers operate in the interest of the holders of big blocks of shares.* N COUNT+SUPP ⇑ possessor 4 someone who has a particular opinion or theory. EG *The holder of anti-government opinions is not likely to support such a move.* N COUNT+SUPP

holding /həʊldɪŋ/, **holdings.** 1 If you have a **holding** in a company, you own shares in it. EG *We should sell the government holding in British Gas... The maximum holding is £5,000, or £10,000 for a married couple.* N COUNT+SUPP = investment

2 The **holding** of a place such as a museum, library, or art gallery is the collection of items such as books or paintings which are kept there. EG *...the unparalleled holding of Leonardo drawings.* N COUNT

3 A **holding** is also an area of farm land which is rented or owned by the person who cultivates it. EG *78 per cent of holdings are below 5 hectares.* N COUNT

4 **Holding** is used of an action which is intended to keep a situation under control and to prevent it from becoming worse, but which you intend to follow with more positive measures. EG *The rest of the campaign was a holding operation.* ADJ CLASSIF : ATTRIB

hold-up, hold-ups. A **hold-up** is 1 a situation in which someone is threatened with a weapon in order to make them hand over money or valuables. EG *Seven people were wounded towards the end of July in different hold-ups.* N COUNT = robbery, raid 2 something which causes a delay. EG *He may be delayed by some trifling hold-up in the department.* N COUNT = hitch 3 the stopping or very slow N COUNT movement of traffic, sometimes caused by an accident which happened earlier. EG *I nearly missed my flight owing to a traffic hold-up... ...hold-ups on the M6 motorway.*

hole /həʊl/, **holes, holing, holed.** 1 A **hole** is 1.1 a hollow space in something solid, with an opening on one side. EG *What do you recommend for filling holes and cracks?... First of all dig a deep hole in the ground.* 1.2 the home or hiding place of a mouse, rabbit, or other small animal. EG *It makes its home in holes beneath a river bank... ...a large rabbit hole.* 1.3 an opening in something that goes right through it. EG *The ants got into the hut through a hole in the wall... He was wearing grey socks with holes in them.* • If something is **in holes**, especially fabric or clothing, it has a lot of holes in it. EG *His socks were in holes.*
N COUNT = cavity; N COUNT ⇑ shelter; N COUNT; • PHR : USED AS A C

2 If something that you buy **makes a hole in** your pocket, savings, etc, it uses up a large amount of your money; an informal expression. EG *The new car made a hole in their savings.*
PHR : VB INFLECTS

3 A **hole** in a law, theory, argument, etc is a fault or weakness that it has. EG *The new tax law has several holes in it.* • If you **pick holes in** an argument or theory, you find weak points in it so that it is no longer valid; an informal expression. EG *You can pick holes in most of his arguments.*
N COUNT+SUPP = flaw; • PHR : VB INFLECTS ⇑ criticize

4 You describe a place as a **hole** when it is very unpleasant to live or work in, for example because it is small, dirty, or dark; an informal use. EG *Why don't you leave this awful hole and come to live with me.*
N COUNT = pit, dump

5 If you say that you are **in a hole**, you mean that you are in a difficult or embarrassing situation; an informal expression. EG *If she took the papers she might find herself in the same hole as her boss.*
PHR : USED AS AN A = in a tight spot

6 A **hole** is also 6.1 one of the nine or eighteen sections of a golf course. EG *He invited me to play a few holes of golf with him.* 6.2 one of the places on a golf course that the ball must drop into, usually marked by a flag. EG *It's not easy to guide the ball into a hole 425 yards away.* • If you get **a hole in one** in golf, you get the golf ball into the hole with a single stroke. EG *I've never seen anybody get a hole in one.*
N COUNT ⇑ section; N COUNT = cup; • PHR : USED AS O

7 If something such as a building or ship **is holed**, holes are made in it by guns or other weapons. EG *The buildings were holed by shells... Two ships were holed during the attack.*
V+O ⇑ pierce

8 If you **hole** in a game of golf, you hit the ball so that it goes into the hole. EG *...that superb shot he holed at the seventy-first hole.*
V OR V+O

hole out. If you **hole out** in a game of golf, you finish the course. EG *In the six rounds he played, he never holed out in less than 92.*
PHRASAL VB : V+ADV

hole up. If you **hole up** somewhere or you **are holed up** there, you hide or shut yourself there, usually so that people can't find you or disturb you; an informal expression. EG *San Francisco was where she holed up... The men were holed up on the top floor of the hotel.*
PHRASAL VB : V+ADV+A, OR V+O+ADV+A : ONLY PASS

holiday /hɒlɪdɪ³/, **holidays, holidaying, holidayed.** A **holiday** is 1 a period of time during which you stay away from home travelling, visiting other places, relaxing, and enjoying yourself. EG *I went to Marrakesh for a holiday... Remember to turn off the gas or electricity when you go on holiday... I'll see you when I get back from holiday... Where are you going for your holidays?... ...holiday resorts.* ▸ used as a verb. EG *British colonial rulers continued the tradition of holidaying in the temperate climate of the hill country.* 2 a period of time during which you are not working or attending school, college, or university. EG *The company offers a pension scheme and three weeks paid holiday... They eventually talked me into taking a week's holiday... New Year's Day is a national holiday... ...wages, safety regulations, overtime, and holiday arrangements.* • See also **bank holiday.**
N COUNT, OR *on/from*+N = vacation, break; ▸ V+A ⇑ sojourn; N COUNT/UNCOUNT ⇑ break = leave

holiday camp, holiday camps. A **holiday camp** is a place which provides holiday accommodation in chalets for large numbers of people, and also different kinds of entertainment including fairgrounds, play grounds, swimming pools, discos, and night clubs.
N COUNT

holidaymaker /hɒlɪdɪ³meɪkə/, **holidaymakers;** also spelled with a hyphen. A **holidaymaker** is a person who is away from home on holiday. EG *The sundeck was crowded with holidaymakers in floral dresses.*
N COUNT = tourist

holiness /həʊlɪnɪ²s/. 1 **Holiness** is the state or quality of being holy and dedicated to God. EG *She could feel the holiness of the place.*
N UNCOUNT = sacredness

2 You say **Your Holiness, His Holiness** etc when you address or refer respectfully to the Pope or to leaders of some other religions. EG *...His Holiness Leo XIII.*
N UNCOUNT DET POSS+N USED IN TITLES

holler /hɒlə/, **hollers, hollering, hollered.** If you **holler**, you shout or weep loudly; an informal word. EG *You should have heard him holler!... 'Just checking to see if you're still there,' I hollered... We could hear Grandmother hollering for Ned from the upstairs window.* ▸ used as a noun. EG *I grabbed him and he let out a holler.*
V+QUOTE, OR V : IF+PREP THEN *at/for* = yell; ▸ N COUNT = yell

hollow /hɒləʊ/, **hollows, hollowing, hollowed.**

1 Something that is **hollow** has a space inside it, as opposed to being solid all the way through. EG *...a hollow tube... ...a large hollow container... ...a hollow ball.*
ADJ CLASSIF ≠ solid

2 If you **hollow** something or **hollow it out**, 2.1 you remove the inside part that is solid and you make something new or different by doing this. EG *Then we hollow it out a little... ...a hollowed elephant's tooth.* 2.2 you make a surface curve inwards or downwards. EG *He hollowed out a small dip in the ground... ...a cadaverous face, hollowed by illness.*
V+O, OR PHRASAL VB : V+O+A *(out)* ⇑ excavate; V+O, OR PHRASAL VB : V+O+A *(out)* ⇑ change

3 A surface that is **hollow** curves inwards or downwards. EG *It was in a little hollow place... ...a lean, hollow-cheeked man.*
ADJ QUALIT = concave

4 A **hollow** is 4.1 a hole inside something. EG *It was fifty years since he had discovered the hollow in the tree's trunk.* 4.2 an area of ground that is lower than the ground surrounding it. EG *Davis hid in a hollow surrounded by bracken.*
N COUNT; N COUNT : ALSO IN NAMES AFTER N = depression

5 If you hold something small in **the hollow of your hand**, you hold it on your palm with your fingers curled up slightly.
PHR : USU PREP+PHR = the palm

6 If something such as a situation or an opinion is **hollow**, it has no real value, worth, or effectiveness; a rather literary use. EG *Their independence is hollow... His outward election optimism rang hollow... 'That's what you think.' Even to his own ears, it sounded hollow, childish.* ◊ **hollowness.** EG *...the hollowness of his victory.*
ADJ QUALIT ⇑ false = empty; ◊ N UNCOUNT+SUPP

7 If you say that someone gives a **hollow** laugh or a **hollow** groan, you are describing the way they laugh at something when it is obvious they do not find it funny. EG *...a trick that would have raised hollow groans in the good old days.* ◊ **hollowly.** EG *He laughed hollowly. 'And what a mess we made of that!'*
ADJ CLASSIF : ATTRIB = empty; ◊ ADV WITH VB

8 A **hollow** sound is one that goes on for some time after it has been made, like an echo. EG *The door closed with a hollow clang behind him.* ◊ **hollowly.** EG *His footsteps sounded hollowly on the uncarpeted stairs.*
ADJ QUALIT ⇑ resonant; ◊ ADV WITH VB

9 If you are playing a game and you **beat** your opponent **hollow**, you win the game very easily indeed.
PHR : VB INFLECTS = thrash

holly /hɒli¹/. **Holly** is a small evergreen tree which has hard prickly leaves all year round, and bright red berries in winter. Holly is often used to decorate houses at Christmas. EG *...a sprig of holly... ...a holly hedge.*
N UNCOUNT

Hollywood /hɒlɪwʊd/ is the place in Los Angeles where a large number of American films are made; used also to refer to the part of the American film industry that makes these films. EG *This film has made Clint Eastwood the highest paid star in Hollywood... ...heroines in old Hollywood movies.*
N PROPER

holocaust /hɒləkɔːst/, **holocausts.** A **holocaust** is very large-scale destruction and loss of life, especially in war or by fire. EG *He claimed that the world was about to be consumed in a nuclear holocaust... There is a danger of war and holocaust.*
N COUNT/UNCOUNT

hologram /hɒlə⁶græm/, **holograms.** A **hologram** is a three-dimensional photographic image created by laser beams.
N COUNT

holograph /hɒlə⁶græf, -grɑːf/, **holographs.** A **holograph** is 1 the same as a hologram. 2 a book or document written in the author's own handwriting; a formal use.
N COUNT; N COUNT ⇑ manuscript

hols /hɒlz/. The **hols** are the period of time during which you are not working or are not attending school, college, or university; an informal word. EG
N PLURAL : *the*+N = holidays

She was down from Oxford for the hols... ...the last day of the Christmas hols.

holster /həulstə/, **holsters**. A **holster** is a holder for a pistol or revolver, which is usually worn either on a belt round your waist or on a strap below your arm. EG *She seized an officer's revolver from its holster and shot him dead.* — N COUNT

holy /həuli¹/, **holier, holiest**. 1 Something that is **holy** is related to or connected with God or a particular religion. EG *Do you think of the bible as being a holy book?... Some holy pictures and statues stood on a little shelf.* — ADJ QUALIT = sacred

2 Someone who is **holy** leads a pure and good life which is dedicated to God or to a particular religion. EG *This is one of the reasons why he became so holy.* — ADJ QUALIT

3 If you say that someone is **holier than thou**, you mean that they seem to believe that they are more religious or more moral than anyone else; used showing disapproval. EG *They are always holier than thou, people like that.* — PHR : USED AS C = self-righteous

Holy Communion is the most important religious service in the Christian church, in which people share bread and wine as a symbol of the Last Supper and the crucifixion of Christ. — N PROPER = Mass

Holy Father. The **Holy Father** is the Pope. — N PROPER

Holy Ghost. The **Holy Ghost** is the same as the Holy Spirit. — N PROPER : *the*+N

holy of holies. A **holy of holies** is a place that is so holy or special for some reason that only particular people are allowed to enter; an informal expression. EG *I had been summoned into that holy of holies, the headmaster's study.* — N SING WITH DET

Holy Spirit. In the Christian religion, the **Holy Spirit** is one of the three aspects of God, together with God the Father and God the Son. — N PROPER : *the*+N ⇑ God

Holy Week, Holy Weeks. In the Christian religion, **Holy Week** is the week before Easter, when Christians remember the events leading up to the crucifixion of Christ. — N PROPER/COUNT = Passion Week

Holy Writ is an old-fashioned name for the Bible. — N PROPER

homage /hɒmɪdʒ/ is the way you behave towards someone, usually someone in authority, which shows how much you respect or honour them. EG *The young soldiers gathered to pay homage to the new heroes... Mr Davis accepted the homage of his people with a gracious smile.* — N UNCOUNT : USU +*to*

home /həum/, **homes, homing, homed**. 1 Your **home** is 1.1 the place where you live and feel you belong, usually because that is where your family is. EG *The old man wants to die in his own home.* ▸ used as an adjective. EG *These children are in need of a normal home life.* 1.2 the area or country where you were born or where your home is. EG *For most English children, home is a town or city... Jack dreamed of home from his prisoner-of-war camp.* ▸ used as an adjective. EG *My own home town is thousands of miles away.* — N UNCOUNT/COUNT; ▸ ADJ CLASSIF : ATTRIB; N UNCOUNT/COUNT; ▸ ADJ CLASSIF : ATTRIB

2 **Home** means in or at the place where you live. EG *I'll pick the parcels up on my way home... I want to go home... Here we are, home at last.* — ADV AFTER VB ⇑ dwelling

3 **At home** means 3.1 in your house as opposed to being out somewhere. EG *She went out to work, while he stayed at home to care for the children... I find it very difficult to work at home.* 3.2 in your own country, as opposed to in a foreign country. EG *...recession and mounting unemployment at home... Newspapers both at home and abroad ignored the incident.* 3.3 comfortable and at ease because you feel that you belong where you are. EG *I felt at home at once, because I recognized familiar faces... It lays its eggs in water, but otherwise it is entirely at home on land.* — PHR : USED AS AN A; PHR : USED AS AN A; PHR : USED AS AN A

4 If you say to someone **'Make yourself at home'**, you are inviting them to make themselves comfortable and to do in your house the things that they would do in their own. EG *Make yourself at home. I'll be back in half an hour.* — CONVENTION

5 If you are **at home in** a particular topic or subject, you know about it and are therefore happy to discuss it. EG *He's at home in all the sciences.* — PHR+NG : USED AS AN A

6 **Home** also means 6.1 made or done in the place where you live. EG *Most of the home employment offered to housewives is naked exploitation. ...home-baked bread.* 6.2 relating to your own country as opposed to foreign countries. EG *The government had promised to maintain an expanding home market.* — ADJ CLASSIF : ATTRIB ⇑ domestic; ADJ CLASSIF : ATTRIB = domestic

7 If you **make** your **home** somewhere, you decide to live there. EG *Tramps have made their homes in warehouses on the river bank.* — PHR : VB INFLECTS ⇑ settle

8 When someone **leaves home**, they go to live somewhere else; used especially of young people who have left school and are becoming independent. — PHR : VB INFLECTS

9 If you **bring** something **home to** someone, you make them understand how important or serious it is. EG *We must bring home to everyone the dangers of any other course of action.* — PHR : VB INFLECTS ⇑ impress

10 If an action or event **brings** something **closer to home**, you realize, often for the first time, that you could be affected by it. EG *The missile base brought the fear of nuclear weapons closer to home.* — PHR : VB INFLECTS

11 If you say that something is **nothing to write home about**, you mean that it is not very interesting or exciting; an informal expression. EG *The party was nothing to write home about.* — PHR : USED AS C ⇑ ordinary

12 If you are **home and dry**, you have succeeded in doing something; an informal expression. — PHR : USED AS C

13 A **home from home** is a place in which you feel very happy and at ease, just as if you were in your own home. — PHR : USED AS C

14 A **home** is also 14.1 a house where a number of people live and are looked after, instead of living in their own homes. They usually live there because they are old or ill or have no family to look after them. EG *I thought of starting a home for old ladies... ...a children's home.* 14.2 a place where something begins its existence. EG *...that home of free enterprise, the United States.* — N COUNT ⇑ institution; N SING WITH DET +SUPP

15 If you find a **home** for something, you find a place where it can be kept. EG *Plastic containers make very good homes for geranium cuttings.* — N COUNT+SUPP ⇑ container

16 If you press, drive, or hammer something **home**, 16.1 you push it firmly into position. EG *Push the magazine into the butt of the gun, and press home.* 16.2 you explain it to your listeners as firmly as possible. EG *He raised his voice to drive home the point.* — ADV AFTER VB; ADV AFTER VB ⇑ emphasize

17 A **home** game or match is one that is played on your team's own ground, rather than on the opposing team's ground. EG *They watched every single game, home or away.* — ADJ CLASSIF : ATTRIB ≠ away

18 **Home**, in some games and sports, is the place you have to reach in order to win or to score points. — N UNCOUNT ⇑ base

home in. If something such as a weapon **homes in** or **homes in on** something else, it aims at it and moves towards it with great accuracy. EG *It can thus home in on the target with pinpoint accuracy.* — PHRASAL VB : V+ADV : IF+PREP THEN *on*

home-brew is beer made in someone's home as opposed to in a brewery. — N UNCOUNT

homecoming /həumkʌmɪŋ/, **homecomings**. Your **homecoming** is your return to your home or your country, usually after a fairly long absence. EG *There were 120,000 people at the exiled politician's homecoming.* — N COUNT/UNCOUNT

home economics is a subject studied at school and college in which students are taught how to run a house well and efficiently. — N UNCOUNT

home ground. 1 If you are **on home ground**, 1.1 you are near where you live and so know where you are and where you are going. 1.2 you are discussing a subject you know about and so you feel confident to talk about it. — PHR : USED AS AN A; PHR : USED AS AN A

2 A sports team's **home ground** is their own playing field as opposed to that of other teams. — N COUNT

home-grown fruit and vegetables have been grown in your own garden, area, or country. — ADJ CLASSIF : USU ATTRIB

home help, home helps. A **home help** is a person employed by a local government authority to help people with their housework if they are too ill or too old to do it themselves. EG *We need more hospitals, more home helps, and more nurseries.* — N COUNT ⇑ worker

homeland /həumlə³nd/, **homelands**. 1 Your **homeland** is your native country. EG *Neither country would launch an attack upon the homeland of the other.* — N COUNT

2 The **homelands** are the regions which have been given by the South African government to the black population. Some of these are now independent states, although they are not recognized as such by other countries. EG *...the Transkei and Ciskei homelands.* — N PLURAL

homeless /həumlɪ²s/. If people are **homeless**, they have nowhere to live. EG *Floods in north-eastern India made 233,000 people homeless... ...homeless families.* ▸ The **homeless** is used to refer to people — ADJ CLASSIF ⇑ destitute; ▸ N PLURAL : *th* who have nowhere to live. EG *We were running homes for the homeless.* ◊ **homelessness.** EG *For a growing number of young people, homelessness is becoming a way of life.* +N ◊ N UNCOUNT = destitution

homely /həʊmli¹/. 1 If something is **homely**, it is simple and ordinary, rather like your own home. EG *We stayed in the Hotel Claravallis, a homely and comfortable establishment.* ADJ QUALIT

2 If someone is **homely**, they are not very attractive to look at; used in American English. EG *Paul is a homely, shy, stammering boy.* ADJ QUALIT = plain

home-made; also spelled as one word. Something that is **home-made** has been made in somebody's home, rather than in a shop or factory. EG *He made his breakfast: a slice of homemade bread covered with syrup.* ADJ CLASSIF

Home Office. The **Home Office** is the department of the British Government which is responsible for the police, immigration, and broadcasting. N PROPER : the+N

homeopath /həʊmi¹ə⁶pæθ/, **homeopaths**; also spelled **homoeopath**. A **homeopath** is someone who treats illness by homeopathy. N COUNT ⇑ doctor

homeopathic /həʊmi¹ə⁶pæθɪk/ means relating to or used in homeopathy. EG *...homeopathic remedies.* ADJ CLASSIF ⇑ medical

homeopathy /həʊmi¹ɒpəθi¹/ is a way of treating illness in which the patient is given very small amounts of a drug that produces signs of the illness in healthy people. N UNCOUNT ⇑ treatment

homeowner /həʊməʊnə/, **homeowners**. A **homeowner** is a person who owns the place where they live. N COUNT ⇑ owner

Home Secretary, Home Secretaries. The **Home Secretary** is the member of the British government who is in charge of the Home Office. N PROPER : the+N, OR N COUNT ⇑ politician

homesick /həʊmsɪk/. If you are **homesick**, you are away from home and are feeling unhappy because you are missing your home and your family very much. EG *The smell of the grass made her homesick for her parents' farm... ...a homesick child trying to make friends.* ◊ **homesickness.** EG *...a sudden spasm of homesickness.* ADJ QUALIT ⇑ sad ◊ N UNCOUNT ⇑ sadness

homespun /həʊmspʌn/. 1 Beliefs, opinions, or comments that are **homespun** are simple, uncomplicated, and often not very well thought out. EG *...homespun, down-to-earth views of reality... They believed in simple living and homespun virtues.* ADJ CLASSIF

2 **Homespun** is cloth made from thread that is spun at home rather than in a factory. N UNCOUNT

homestead /həʊmstɛd/, **homesteads**. A **homestead** is a farmhouse and the land around it. N COUNT ⇑ farm

home stretch. The **home stretch** or the **home straight** is 1 the last part of a race. 2 the last part of any activity that lasts for a fairly long time, especially a difficult or boring one. N SING : the+N / N SING : the+N

home time is the time of day when children finish school and go home; an informal word, used especially by young children in school or by teachers talking to young children. N UNCOUNT ≠ school time

home town, home towns. Your **home town** is the town where you were born or spent your childhood. N COUNT

home truth, home truths. **Home truths** are unpleasant facts that you learn about yourself, usually from someone else. N COUNT : USU PL ⇑ fact

homeward /həʊmwəd/ means going towards home. EG *The tank blew up on its homeward journey.* ADJ CLASSIF : ATTRIB

▸ **Homeward** or **homewards** is also used as an adverb. EG *The time had come to drive the goats homewards.* ▸ ADV AFTER VB

homeward-bound. People or things that are **homeward-bound** are on their way home. EG *...homeward-bound commuters... ...homeward-bound ships.* ADJ CLASSIF

homework /həʊmwɜːk/ is 1 school work that teachers give to pupils to do at home in the evening or at the weekend. EG *He never did any homework and he got terrible results in school...* 2 research that someone does in order to find out more about something, usually in preparation for a written article or speech. EG *Aiken did his homework and worked out a convincing commercial case... I've done a bit of homework and found out something about his background.* N UNCOUNT / N UNCOUNT

homey /həʊmi¹/. If you describe a place as **homey**, you mean that you feel comfortable and relaxed there; an informal word used especially in American English. EG *My second flat was more homey than the first.* ADJ QUALIT ⇑ pleasant = cosy

homicidal /hɒmɪsaɪdə⁰l/. Someone who is **homicidal** is dangerous because they are likely to kill someone. EG *...homicidal maniacs.* ▸ used of a person's feelings or behaviour. EG *...homicidal rage.* ADJ CLASSIF = murderous

homicide /hɒmɪsaɪd/, **homicides**. **Homicide** is the murder of one person by another. EG *...countries where theft and homicide are unknown today.* N UNCOUNT/COUNT ⇑ killing

homily /hɒmɪli¹/, **homilies**. A **homily** is a speech or piece of writing in which someone complains about the state of something or tells people how they ought to behave; a formal word. EG *We listened to her homily about the rising cost of living.* N COUNT = sermon

homing /həʊmɪŋ/. 1 A weapon or piece of equipment that has a **homing** system is able to guide itself to a position that it is aimed at. EG *Even small missiles have built-in homing devices.* ADJ CLASSIF : ATTRIB

2 An animal that has a **homing** instinct has the ability to remember and return to a place where it has been in the past, for example where it breeds. EG *They have a highly accurate homing instinct that leads them to sea cliffs.* ADJ CLASSIF : ATTRIB

homing pigeon, homing pigeons. A **homing pigeon** is trained to return to a particular place, especially in races with other pigeons. N COUNT

homoeopath /həʊmi¹ə⁶pæθ/. See **homeopath**.

homogeneity /hɒmə⁶dʒɪniːɪti¹, həʊ-/ is the quality of being homogeneous. EG *...emphasis on the unity of the nation and the homogeneity of society.* N UNCOUNT : USU +SUPP = uniformity

homogeneous /hɒə⁶dʒiːniəs, həʊ-/. A thing or group that is **homogeneous** has parts or members which are all the same or which consist of only one substance. EG *The working class is not quite so homogeneous in its political preference... Amoebae consist of just one more or less homogeneous cell.* ADJ QUALIT = uniform

homogenized /həmɒdʒənaɪzd/ milk has had the cream on top of it broken up so that the cream and milk are evenly mixed. ADJ CLASSIF

homogenous /həmɒdʒənəs/ means the same as homogeneous. ADJ QUALIT

homo sapiens /həʊməʊ sæpɪɛnz/ is used to refer to human beings considered as a type of animal in relation to other animals. EG *Homo sapiens has suddenly become the most numerous of all large animals.* N UNCOUNT ⇑ species = man

homosexual /həʊmə⁶sɛksjuᵘəl, hɒm-/, **homosexuals**. Someone who is **homosexual** is sexually attracted to someone of the same sex as them; used especially of men. ▸ used as a noun. EG *...clubs for homosexuals.* ▸ used of the relationship that homosexuals have. EG *They had a homosexual relationship that lasted for seven years.* ◊ **homosexuality** /həʊmə⁶sɛksjuːælɪti¹, hɒm-/. EG *...the reform of the laws on homosexuality.* ADJ CLASSIF = gay ▸ N COUNT ▸ = gay ◊ N UNCOUNT ⇑ sexuality

Hon. is a written abbreviation for 'honourable' and 'honorary'; used as part of a person's title.

hone /həʊn/, **hones, honing, honed**. 1 If you **hone** something such as a stone, you sharpen it. EG *Grind it down to shape and hone it to a fine edge.* V+O

2 If you **hone** someone or something, you carefully prepare and develop them for a special purpose over a long period of time. EG *...intellectuals honed in the ancient universities to direct the nation.* V+O = groom

honest /ɒnɪst/. 1 Someone who is **honest** about something that concerns them is being completely truthful about it and is not hiding anything. EG *At least you're honest about why you want the money... Be honest, John, and admit what a mess the whole thing is... I'll be quite honest with you, I haven't any faith in myself.* ◊ **honestly.** EG *They must be conscious of this and face it honestly.* ● If you say **'to be honest'** before or after a statement, you are emphasizing what you are saying, often when you are admitting a failure or disagreement. EG *I don't really know to be honest... To be perfectly honest, up until three weeks ago I had never set foot in a nightclub.* ADJ QUALIT : PRED = frank, open ◊ ADV WITH VB ● PHR : USED AS ADV SEN

2 You say **'honest'** before or after a statement to emphasize that you are telling the truth and that you want people to believe you; an informal use. EG *I've got a stinking cold coming on, honest... It's true as I'm sitting here, Mabel, honest it is.* ● See also **honestly**. ADV SEN = honestly, truly

3 Someone who is **honest 3.1** always tells the truth and can therefore be trusted completely. EG *Not all scientists are as honest as Pasteur was.* ▸ used of a person's behaviour, attitudes, or actions. EG *Most of them gave a completely honest explanation about their background... If you want my honest opinion,* ADJ QUALIT ⇑ truthful ▸ = genuine

she'll leave. ◊ **honestly**. EG *Philip had answered them honestly.* **3.2** does not cheat or break the law and can be trusted with money and other valuable things. EG *He's very honest in money matters.* ▸ used of a person's actions or behaviour. EG *He needed to get a job, to get an honest living of any sort.* ◊ **honestly**. EG *If he couldn't get rare shrubs honestly, he was not above stealing them.* **3.3** is open and sincere in their relationships and attitudes. EG *Off-stage she is direct, honest, forceful.* ▸ used of a person's behaviour or actions. EG *...a word of honest indignation... A little honest sensuality never does any harm.*

◊ ADV WITH VB; ADJ QUALIT = scrupulous; ▸ ADJ QUALIT ≠ illegal; ◊ ADV WITH VB; ADJ QUALIT = straight-forward; ▸ = straight-forward

4 If a man **makes an honest woman of** a woman, he marries her, especially when she is pregnant or when he has already been living with her for some time; an old-fashioned expression, often used humorously. EG *He had seduced a girl only once in his life, and he made an honest woman of her later.*

PHR : VB INFLECTS ⇑ marry

5 Some people say **'honest to God'** or **'honest to goodness'** in order to express their annoyance or impatience about something; a rather old-fashioned expression. EG *Honest to God, how can you believe such rubbish?*

CONVENTION, OR PHR : USED AS ADV SEN = good God

honestly /ɒnɪ²stli¹/ is used **1** to emphasize that you really and truthfully believe or feel what you are saying. EG *I'm truly and honestly not that concerned... Do you honestly think this is right?* **2** to emphasize that you are telling the truth and that you want people to believe you. EG *I'll go if you like. I don't mind, honestly... I got all emotional, honestly I did.* **3** to indicate that you are annoyed or impatient. EG *'Honestly,' says Barbara, 'that woman.'... Honestly, Flora, this is getting ridiculous.* ● See also **honest**.

ADV SEN; ADV SEN = honest; CONVENTION, OR ADV SEN = really

honesty /ɒnɪ²sti¹/. **1 Honesty** is the quality of being honest. EG *I sat quietly admiring Claudia's honesty... I insist on complete honesty with the people in my life.* ● If you say something **in all honesty**, you are being completely truthful; often used when you are ashamed about admitting the truth. EG *In all honesty he had to admit that he was glad.*

N UNCOUNT = openness; ● PHR : USED AS ADV SEN ⇑ actually

2 Honesty is also a plant with round flat silvery seed-pods.

N UNCOUNT

honey /hʌni¹/, **honeys**. **1 Honey** is a sweet sticky yellowish substance that is made by bees. People often eat it spread on bread. EG *...steaming tea sweetened with honey.*

N UNCOUNT ⇑ food

2 You call someone **honey** as a sign of affection; used especially in American English. EG *Hi there, honey.*

N VOC = love

3 A **honey** is someone you are very fond of, especially a girl; an informal use. EG *What a honey she is!*

N COUNT : USU USED AS C

honeybee /hʌni¹biː/, **honeybees**. A **honeybee** is a bee that makes honey.

N COUNT ⇑ bee

honeycomb /hʌni¹kəʊm/, **honeycombs**. A **honeycomb** is a wax structure made by bees, which contains lots of six-sided holes where they store the honey that they make.

N COUNT/ UNCOUNT

honeydew melon /hʌni¹djuː mɛlən/, **honeydew melons**. A **honeydew melon** is a type of melon with a yellow skin.

N COUNT

honeyed /hʌnɪd/. If someone speaks **honeyed** words or speaks with a **honeyed** voice, what they say is soft and pleasant to listen to and often makes you feel calmer. EG *She was soothed by his honeyed words.*

ADJ CLASSIF : USU ATTRIB ⇑ sweet

honeymoon /hʌnɪmuːn/, **honeymoons, honeymooning, honeymooned**. **1** A **honeymoon** is **1.1** a holiday taken by a man and a woman who have just got married. EG *They spent their honeymoon at Petersburg, Florida... ...a honeymoon couple.* **1.2** a period of time after the start of a new job or new government when everyone is pleased with the person or people concerned and is nice to them. EG *He had a brief honeymoon with Radio One... The honeymoon period is over.*

N COUNT; N COUNT

2 When a newly married couple **honeymoon** somewhere, they go there on their honeymoon. EG *They had got married in Milan and were honeymooning in Sicily.*

V+A ⇑ holiday

honeysuckle /hʌnɪsʌkə⁰l/. **Honeysuckle** is a climbing plant with sweet-smelling yellow, pink, or white flowers in the shape of long narrow tubes.

N UNCOUNT

honk /hɒŋk/, **honks, honking, honked**. **1** If you **honk** the horn of a vehicle or it **honks**, it produces a short loud sound. EG *She honked her horn when she saw me... Horns honked incessantly.* ▸ used as a noun. EG *I heard the honk of his horn outside.*

V-ERG = hoot; ▸ N COUNT = hoot

2 When a goose **honks**, it makes a short loud noise. EG *The geese were making a frightful honking sound.* ▸ used as a noun. EG *The cackle of chickens and the honk of a goose met their ears.*

V; ▸ N COUNT ⇑ cry

honor /ɒnə/. See **honour**.

honorable /ɒnə⁰rəbə⁰l/. See **honourable**.

honorary /ɒnə⁰rəri¹/. **1** An **honorary** title or membership of a group is given to someone for a special reason without them needing to have the qualifications that are usually necessary. EG *...an honorary degree... The Prince came to receive an honorary fellowship from the college.*

ADJ CLASSIF : ATTRIB ⇑ complimentary

2 Honorary is used to describe an official job that is done without payment. EG *...the honorary Treasurer.*

ADJ IN TITLES

honorific /ɒnərɪfɪk/, **honorifics**. An **honorific** title is one that is given to someone as a sign of respect or honour. ▸ used as a noun. EG *The Japanese language makes a lot of use of honorifics.*

ADJ CLASSIF : ATTRIB; ▸ N COUNT

honour /ɒnə/, **honours, honouring, honoured**; also spelled **honor** in American English. **1 Honour** is a feeling of pride that you have when you believe that you are behaving in the best way so that other people admire or respect you. EG *Don't you know that a debt is a thing of family honour?... He was able to withdraw from the battle with honour in the eyes of his people.*

N UNCOUNT ⇑ self-respect

2 An **honour** is a special award or job that is given to someone, usually because they have done something good or because they are greatly respected by the public. EG *It was a richly deserved honour... He was the youngest boy ever given the honour of carrying the flag... The scientists had received great honours from their country for their services.*

N COUNT ⇑ distinction = tribute

3 If you say you **have the honour** of doing something or **it is** your **honour** to do something, you are saying politely that you are very pleased to be doing it; a formal expression. EG *He is one of the most interesting people I have had the honour of meeting... It's my honour to present Miss Kathleen Jones.*

PHR : VB INFLECTS + *of*, OR CONVENTION : USU + *to*-INF = have the privilege

4 A person who is an **honour** to someone or something brings them respect and a good reputation because of their excellent behaviour. EG *He is an honour to his country.* ● If something that you do **does** you **honour**, it is so good that it makes other people respect you greatly. EG *Her behaviour in such a difficult situation does her honour.*

N SING : *an*+N+*to* = credit; ● PHR : VB INFLECTS

5 If something such as a special event is arranged **in** your **honour**, it is arranged specially for you. EG *I arranged to give a party at my house in her honour... A poem had been composed in my honour.* ● See also **guest of honour, maid of honour.**

PHR : USED AS AN A

6 If something is arranged **in honour of** a particular event, it is arranged in order to celebrate the event. EG *The ceremony was held in honour of the Queen's birthday.*

PREP ⇑ for

7 If a person, especially someone important whom you admire or respect, does you the **honour** of something or grants you an **honour**, they do something for you which you consider to be special and are very grateful for. EG *The king received a request to grant the village the honour of a brief visit... She did me the honour of attending the opening of my exhibition... May I have the honour of the next dance?*

N SING : USU *the* +N+*of* ⇑ favour

8 You address a judge in court as **your honour**. EG *Is there any evidence for this, your honour?*

N VOC

9 Honours is a type of university degree which is of a higher standard than a pass or ordinary degree. EG *He left university with a first class honours degree in French.*

N UNCOUNT

10 If you **do the honours** at a social occasion such as a party, you act as the host or hostess by pouring drinks for people or serving food; an informal expression, often used humorously. EG *Shall I do the honours?*

PHR : VB INFLECTS ⇑ serve

11 If you **honour** someone, **11.1** you give them public praise or a symbol of that praise because they have done something good or brave. EG *The people came to honour their leader... In 1949, he was honoured by the Grand Cross.* ◊ **honoured**. EG *...the honoured dead.* **11.2** you treat them with special attention and respect. EG *The song exhorted them to honour, obey, and support the Chief.* ◊ **honoured**. EG *Rose was the honoured guest, the star... This discovery has the honoured place in the history of science.*

V+O ⇑ acclaim; ◊ ADJ CLASSIF; V+O; ◊ ADJ CLASSIF : ATTRIB = celebrated

12 If you ask someone to **honour** you by doing something, or say you would be **honoured** if they

V+O

would do something, you ask them to do it in very polite formal English. EG *We would be honoured if you would visit us... Would you honour me by dining with me tonight?*

13 If you **honour** something that you have arranged, agreed, or promised, you keep to it and do not change your mind. EG *The government has solemn commitments and must honour them... The policy of wage restraint was honoured by the union.* V+O ⇑ accept = respect

honourable /ɒnəˀrəbəˀl/; also spelled **honorable** in American English. 1 An **honourable** action is one that is worthy of being respected or admired. EG *This is the honourable course open to him: he should resign immediately... Major Vane had always tried to do the honourable thing.* ▸ used of people. EG *...an honourable man.* ◇ **honourably**. EG *He served his master honourably until his death.* ADJ QUALIT = proper ▸ = upright ◇ ADV WITH VB

2 **Honourable** is used as a title before the names of some members of the nobility, judges, and certain other officials. EG *...the Honourable Miss Sparrow.* ADJ IN TITLES = Hon.

honourable member, honourable members. A member of parliament refers to another member as **honourable member** when they are speaking in the House of Commons. EG *'...the honourable member for Malmesbury is mistaken.'* N COUNT ⇑ MP

honourable mention, honourable mentions. If something that you do in a competition is given an **honourable mention**, it receives a mark of special praise although it does not actually win a prize. N COUNT ⇑ commendation

Hons. is a written abbreviation for 'Honours', used after the name of a university degree. EG *...BA Hons. History, Cambridge.*

hooch /huːtʃ/ is alcoholic drink; an informal word. EG *Otto brought out his private hooch supplies.* N UNCOUNT ⇑ alcohol

hood /hʊd/, **hoods.** A **hood** is 1 a part of a coat, cloak, etc which you can pull up to cover your head. It is in the shape of a triangular bag attached to the neck of the coat at the back. EG *He held both sides of the parka hood closed against the snow.* N COUNT ⇑ headgear 2 a bag made of cloth, which is put over someone's head and face so that they cannot be recognized or so that they cannot see. EG *A heavy white cotton hood was over the head of each boy.* N COUNT ⇑ covering 3 a covering on a vehicle or a piece of equipment, which is usually curved and can be moved. EG *He couldn't be bothered to stop to put up the hood... ...a pram which had its hood folded down... ...the hood of a hairdryer.* N COUNT 4 the bonnet of a car; used in American English. EG *...the raised hood, under which I had bent to watch the mechanic at work.* N COUNT : USU the+N

hooded /hʊdɪ²d/. 1 A **hooded** piece of clothing, furniture, etc has a hood. EG *...a hooded duffel coat... She sleeps in her hooded cot.* ADJ CLASSIF : USU ATTRIB ⇑ covered

2 Someone with **hooded** eyes has large eyelids that are partly closed. ADJ CLASSIF : ATTRIB

hoodlum /huːdləm/, **hoodlums.** A **hoodlum** is a violent criminal, especially one who is part of a gang; an informal use. EG *...people who have been knifed and robbed by hoodlums.* N COUNT = thug

hoodwink /hʊdwɪŋk/, **hoodwinks, hoodwinking, hoodwinked.** If you **hoodwink** someone, you trick or deceive them. EG *He is too often hoodwinked by flashy external appearances.* V+O = fool

hooey /huːiˈ/. If you describe something that someone says as **hooey**, you mean that it is nonsense; an informal word. N UNCOUNT : USU USED AS C = codswallop

hoof /huːf/, **hoofs, hooves.** The plural can be either **hoofs** or **hooves**. The **hooves** of an animal such as a horse are the hard bony parts of its feet. EG *I heard the clip clip of the horses' hooves.* N COUNT : USU PL ⇑ foot

hook /hʊk/, **hooks, hooking, hooked.** 1 A **hook** is a bent piece of metal, plastic, etc that is used for catching or holding things, or for hanging things up. EG *Howard hangs up his coat on the hook behind the door... The man wrenched the hook out of the bleeding mouth of the fish... ...curtain hooks.* N COUNT

2 If you **hook** one thing onto another, you attach it there using a hook. EG *One after the other they were hooked to the moving cable.* ● See also **hooked**. V+O : USU+A

3 If you **hook** your arm, leg, or foot round an object, you place it like a hook round the object in order to move it or hold it. EG *She hooked her foot under a cane stool, drawing it nearer.* V+O+A

4 If you **hook** a fish, you catch it with a hook on the end of a line. EG *I've lost every trout I ever hooked.* V+O

5 A **hook** is also 5.1 a short sharp hit with your fist that you make with your elbow bent, usually in a boxing match. EG *He hit the soldier with a short left hook to the head.* N COUNT : USU SING 5.2 a shot in golf that makes the ball move to the player's left instead of straight ahead. N COUNT 5.2 a shot in cricket in which the ball is hit on the player's left side with the bat held horizontally. N COUNT

6 The word **hook** is used in the following expressions.

6.1 If you take a phone **off the hook**, you take the receiver off the part that it normally rests on, so that the phone will not ring. EG *...a telephone with its receiver off the hook.* PHR : USED AS AN A 6.2 Someone who **gets off the hook** manages to get out of the difficult or dangerous situation that they are in. EG *He felt he had got off the hook perhaps too easily.* PHR : VB INFLECTS ⇑ escape 6.3 If you **let** someone **off the hook** or **get** them **off the hook**, you help them so that they are no longer in a difficult or dangerous situation. EG *Don't let him off the hook–he's guilty and you know it.* PHR : VB INFLECTS ⇑ defend 6.4 If you say that you will do something **by hook or by crook**, you mean that you are determined to do it even if it is very difficult; an old-fashioned expression. EG *I'll see her tomorrow by hook or by crook.* ● to **sling** your **hook**: see **sling**. PHR : USED AS AN A = come what may

hook up. If you **hook up** a computer or other electronic machine, you connect it to other similar machines or to a central power supply. ● See also **hook-up**. PHRASAL VB : V+O+ADV, USU PASS

hookah /hʊkə/, **hookahs.** A **hookah** is a Middle Eastern pipe for smoking tobacco or marijuana. It consists of a long flexible stem and a jar of water, through which the smoke is sucked in order to cool it. N COUNT

hook and eye, hooks and eyes. A **hook and eye** is a small metal hook and bar that together form a fastening for clothes such as dresses or skirts. N COUNT : USU PL

hooked /hʊkt/. 1 Something that is **hooked** is shaped like a hook. EG *Its huge hooked claws are extremely dangerous.* ADJ CLASSIF ⇑ curved

2 A **hooked** nose is large and curves out in the middle. ADJ CLASSIF : ATTRIB

3 If you are **hooked** on something, in informal English, 3.1 you like it or enjoy it so much that it takes up a lot of your interest and attention. EG *They're all hooked on the Sound of Music... I had been hooked by an amazing exhibition called 'Two Thousand Years On'... They're the sweetest kids ever. I'm really hooked on those kids.* ADJ QUALIT : PRED, USU+*on* ⇑ attracted 3.2 you are addicted to it. EG *...hooked on drugs... ...truly hooked on the grand life-style.* ADJ QUALIT : PRED

hooker /hʊkə/, **hookers.** A **hooker** is a prostitute; a very informal word. N COUNT

hook-nosed. Someone who is **hook-nosed** has a large nose that curves out in the middle. ADJ CLASSIF

hook-up, hook-ups. A **hook-up** is an electronic or radio connection made between computers, electronic machines, satellites, etc. N COUNT : USU MOD+N

hooky /hʊkiˈ/. A child who **plays hooky** deliberately stays away from school without permission; used in American English. EG *Paul is a shy, stammering boy who plays hooky and keeps to his bedroom practising his guitar.* PHR : VB INFLECTS = play truant

hooligan /huːlɪgən/, **hooligans.** A **hooligan** is a young person who behaves in a noisy and violent way in public places, usually with a group of other similar people; used showing disapproval. N COUNT : ALSO VOC ⇑ youth = yob

hooliganism /huːlɪgənɪzəˀm/ is the behaviour and actions of hooligans. EG *...an increase in football hooliganism.* N UNCOUNT = rowdiness

hoop /huːp/, **hoops.** 1 A **hoop** is 1.1 a large ring made of wood, metal, or plastic. Hoops are often used as children's toys or for animals to jump through at a circus. EG *...boys holding hoops, kites, and marbles.* ● See also **hula hoop**. N COUNT 1.2 one of the small metal arches which players hit the ball through in the game of croquet. N COUNT ⇑ arch

2 If someone makes you **go through the hoops** or **puts** you **through the hoops**, they make you go through an unpleasant or difficult experience or test. EG *He really made me go through the hoops... She and I were going to be put through the hoops together.* PHR : VB INFLECTS

hooped /huːpt/. Something that is **hooped** has hoops or is in the shape of a hoop. EG *...hooped earrings.* ADJ CLASSIF ⇑ circular

hoop-la, hoop-las. The **hoop-la** is a game at a fair in which you try to throw small hoops over objects in order to win them. N COUNT/UNCOUNT

hooray /həˈreɪ/. People sometimes shout **'Hooray!'** when they are very happy and excited. CONVENTION = whoopee

hoot /hu:t/, **hoots, hooting, hooted.** 1 If you **hoot** the horn on a vehicle or it **hoots**, it makes a loud noise on one note. EG *Tug boats hooted at it... He hoots the horn... The horn hooted once.* ▸ used as a noun. EG *I heard a hoot and saw Martin driving by.* V OR V-ERG ⇑ sound = toot ▸ N COUNT

2 If you **hoot**, you make a loud high-pitched noise when you are laughing or showing disapproval. EG *They pointed and hooted with enjoyment... I fled, pursued by the hooting mob.* ▸ used as a noun. EG *At this Etta gave a hoot of laughter... ...booing and hoots of scorn.* V : USU+A = whoop, shriek ▸ N COUNT = snort

3 When an owl **hoots**, it makes a sound like a long 'oo'. EG *Outside, an owl hooted among the pines.* ▸ used as a noun. EG *He heard the hoot of an owl coming from the direction of the wood.* V ▸ N COUNT ⇑ cry

4 If you say that you **don't give a hoot, don't care two hoots**, etc about something, you are emphasizing that you don't care at all about it; used in informal English. EG *It doesn't matter two hoots whether you're married or not.* PHR : VB INFLECTS ⇑ not care

hoot down. If people in an audience **hoot down** someone who is making a speech, they force them to stop talking by making loud noises at them. EG *Scientists who tried to speak at the recent meeting were hooted down.* PHRASAL VB : V+O+ADV = boo

hoot off. If people in an audience **hoot off** someone who is performing on stage, they force them to stop performing and to leave the stage by making loud noises at them. EG *He was hooted off the stage.* PHRASAL VB : V+O+ADV/PREP = boo

hooter /hu:tə/, **hooters.** 1 A **hooter** on a vehicle is a device such as a horn or a siren that makes a hooting noise. EG *The hooter sounded out like a foghorn.* N COUNT

2 Someone's **hooter** is their nose, especially if it is very large; used in very informal British English. EG *He's got a hooter the size of an elephant's.* N COUNT = conk

hoover /hu:və/, **hoovers, hoovering, hoovered.** 1 A **Hoover** is a vacuum cleaner; a trademark. N COUNT

2 If you **hoover** a carpet, you clean it using a vacuum cleaner. EG *She began the daily round of washing and hoovering.* V OR V+O

hooves /hu:vz/ is a plural of **hoof.**

hop /hɒp/, **hops, hopping, hopped.** 1 If you **hop**, you move in small jumps using only one foot. EG *...hopping clumsily up and down in their chains.* ▸ used as a noun. EG *They began jumping up and down together in short hops.* V : USU+A ▸ N COUNT ⇑ jump

2 When birds and some small animals **hop**, they move in small jumps using both feet together. EG *All the birds were hopping about on their perches... A hare hopped straight into the doorway.* ▸ used as a noun. EG *...a bird so heavy that it could make only short, low hops through the brush.* V : USU+A ▸ N COUNT ⇑ jump

3 If you **hop** onto something, out of something, etc, you move onto it or out of it quickly, suddenly, or easily; an informal use. EG *He hopped out of bed... I decided to hop on a plane and go after him... Let's hop in my car and drive out there.* V+A = jump

4 A **hop** is 4.1 a journey that is quick or easy, usually by plane; an informal use. EG *...a fifty-five minute Paris hop.* 4.2 a social dance for lots of people. EG *They always run a dance, a sort of hop, on Sunday night.* N COUNT : USU MOD+N; N COUNT

5 A **hop** is also a flower that is dried and used for making beer. EG *...the hop gardens of Sussex.* N COUNT : USU PL

6 If you tell someone to **hop it**, you are telling them to go away; an informal expression. CONVENTION = beat it

7 If you **catch** someone **on the hop**, you surprise them by doing something when they are not expecting you to; an informal expression. EG *He caught the President's representatives on the hop.* PHR : VB INFLECTS = catch napping

8 If you **keep on the hop** or you **keep** someone **on the hop**, you keep yourself or someone else very busy; used in informal English. EG *He likes to fill his days and keep on the hop.* PHR : VB INFLECTS ⇑ work

9 Someone who is **hopping mad** is very angry or annoyed; an informal expression. PHR : USED AS C = seething

hope /həʊp/, **hopes, hoping, hoped.** 1 If you **hope** that something is true or **hope** for something to happen, you want it to be true or to happen and usually believe that it is possible or likely. EG *Nothing can be done except to wait, hope, and pray... She hoped she wasn't going to cry... He paused, hoping for evidence of interest... I sat down, hoping to remain unnoticed... 'You haven't lost the ticket, have you?'-'I hope not.'... This was less successful than the Russians had hoped.* V : IF+PREP THEN *for*, OR V+REPORT-CL/ *to*-INF

2 If you **hope** to do something, you want to do it and intend to do it if you possibly can. EG *She hoped to leave that evening for her sister's in Scotland... 'You'll be home at six?'-'I hope so.'* V+*to*-INF/ REPORT-CL

3 If there is only one thing that you can **hope** to get, there is only one thing that you feel you have any chance of getting. EG *The only benefits they can hope to gain are through the additional employment... None of them could hope to get rich... That would be too much to hope for.* V+*to*-INF/ REPORT-CL, OR V +A *(for)* ⇑ expect

4 You say **'I hope'** before a negative clause 4.1 when you are being polite and showing your concern that something you are going to say or something you have done will offend or disturb someone. EG *I hope you don't mind me saying this, but I don't like that tie you're wearing... I hope I didn't wake you.* 4.2 in order to make an accusation against someone which you would like them to deny. EG *I hope you're not excusing him... I hope you're not brewing trouble for us.* PHR WITH BROAD NEG = I trust; PHR WITH BROAD NEG = I trust

5 You add **'I hope'** to something that you say in order to make it sound more polite and less abrupt or definite. EG *You are quite well, I hope?... Pieces like that will I hope serve to lighten the evening.* PHR : USED AS ADV SEN = I trust

6 **Hope** is a feeling of desire and expectation that things will go well in the future. EG *He left me with a great deal of hope... She never completely gave up hope... Do you see any cause for hope for a settlement?... ...people who were beyond any hope of salvation.* N UNCOUNT ≠ despair

7 If you have **hopes** of something successful happening in the future, you feel that there is a good chance that it will happen. EG *We have great hopes of his doing well in the future... I have high hopes of getting into parliament.* ● If something **raises** your **hopes**, it gives you a stronger feeling that the future will be as you want it to be. EG *The new agreement raised hopes for conditions of prosperity and harmony.* N PLURAL ⇑ expectations ● PHR : VB INFLECTS ⇑ encourage

8 If there is a **hope** of something successful happening, there is a chance that it will happen. EG *Technical co-operation is the only hope for progress... There was not a hope for them.* N SING WITH DET

9 A **hope** is 9.1 something that you desire. EG *All their hopes were dashed... ...the hopes and dreams of reformers... But it was a forlorn hope.* 9.2 a person or thing that you want to be helpful or successful because you depend on them or base your expectations for the future on them. EG *You're our only hope now... Rudolph was the hope of the family.* N COUNT = aspiration; N COUNT : USU WITH POSS

10 The word **hope** is also used in the following expressions. 10.1 If you **hope for the best**, you hope that everything will happen in the way that you want it to, although there are reasons to fear that it will not. EG *Don't cross your fingers and hope for the best: do something about it!* 10.2 If you **hope against hope**, you hope for something that seems impossible. EG *I fell asleep hoping against hope that I had been wrong.* 10.3 If you do one thing **in the hope** of another thing happening, you do it because you hope that the other thing will happen. EG *Tourists were waiting outside the palace in the hope of getting a look at the king... You do not put two prisoners in a cell in the hope that they will grow to like each other.* 10.4 If you **hold out hope** for something in the future, you give someone a reason to expect that it will happen. EG *The doctor could hold out no hope that she would recover.* 10.5 If you **live in hope** of something happening in the future, you continue to hope that there is a chance of it happening. EG *He's very ill, but we live in hope.* 10.6 If you say that someone doesn't have **a hope in hell** of doing something, you are emphasizing that they have no chance at all of being able to do it; an informal expression. EG *You haven't got a hope in hell of opening it.* 10.7 If you say **what a hope, some hope,** or **not a hope**, you are saying that you think there is no chance that something will happen; used in informal English. EG *He said he'd be here on time. Some hope!* PHR : VB INFLECTS; PHR : VB INFLECTS = pray; PHR+*of*/ REPORT-CL ⇑ hoping; PHR : VB INFLECTS ⇑ assure; PHR : VB INFLECTS; PHR : USED AS O, WITH BROAD NEG; CONVENTION

hopeful /həʊpful/, **hopefuls.** 1 If you are **hopeful**, you are fairly confident that something that you want to happen will happen. EG *He sounded hopeful that she would come... Ever hopeful, McKellen never abandoned the cinema... There was a queue of people hopeful of obtaining the few seats available.* ADJ QUALIT = optimistic

2 Something that is **hopeful** is promising and gives ADJ QUALIT

you the feeling that what you want to happen will happen. EG *The use of volunteers has resulted in the most astonishing and hopeful results... This seems to me to be a hopeful way of tackling the problem.*

3 A **hopeful** action is one that you do in the hope that you will be successful in getting what you want to get. EG *Little groups of beggars made hopeful sorties towards the tourists.* — ADJ CLASSIF = expectant

4 If you refer to someone as a **hopeful**, you mean that they have an ambition that they very much want to achieve and that there is a possibility that they will achieve it. EG *This news was very hard indeed for presidential hopefuls in an election year... Almost a hundred hopefuls stood in a queue outside the theatre.* — N COUNT = aspirant

hopefully /həʊpfəli¹/. 1 If you do something **hopefully**, you do it in a way which shows that you are fairly confident that what you want to happen will happen. EG *He smiled hopefully in their direction... We must proceed hopefully on the basis of what we know... 'Can we come in?' she asked hopefully.* — ADV WITH VB ⇑ confidently = expectantly

2 You say **hopefully** when mentioning something that you hope and are fairly confident will happen. Some careful speakers of English think that this use of **hopefully** is not correct, but it is very frequently used. EG *The new legislation, hopefully, will lead to some improvements... In this university we have two careers advisers, hopefully a third... The submarines had to be detected, and hopefully destroyed.* — ADV WITH VB, OR ADV SEN = with any luck

hopeless /həʊplɪ²s/. 1 If someone feels **hopeless**, they feel desperate because there seems to be no possibility of comfort or success. EG *I walked away in an agony of hopeless grief and pity... She was sitting on the floor, a hopeless figure if ever I saw one... With a hopeless sigh, Dolly turned away.* — ADJ CLASSIF = despairing, forlorn
◊ **hopelessly**. EG *She shook her head hopelessly.* — ◊ ADV WITH VB
◊ **hopelessness**. EG *And what of the tax cuts for the rich, the hopelessness of the poor?* — ◊ N UNCOUNT = despair

2 Something that is **hopeless** is certain to fail or be unsuccessful. EG *I knew my love was as hopeless as ever... The situation was hopeless... His attempt to swim the river was hopeless from the beginning.* — ADJ CLASSIF = impossible

3 If someone is **hopeless** at something, they are unable to do it well; an informal use. EG *He was hopeless at games... I proved to be hopeless as a teacher... She described herself as 'completely hopeless with my hands.'* — ADJ CLASSIF = useless ≠ competent

4 You use **hopeless** to emphasize how bad an event or situation is, especially when you feel that there is not much chance that it will improve. EG *Her room is in a hopeless muddle... ...hopeless extravagance.* — ADJ CLASSIF : ATTRIB = terrible
◊ **hopelessly**. EG *She was hopelessly impulsive... The results, when completed, would be hopelessly out of date... Rescue work continued but was hopelessly inadequate to meet the town's needs.* — ◊ ADV = helplessly

hopper /hɒpə/, **hoppers**. A **hopper** is a device shaped like a large funnel, in which substances such as grain, coal, animal food, or sand can be stored. — N COUNT

horde /hɔːd/, **hordes**. A **horde** is a crowd of people. Hordes are usually very large and excited, and often rather frightening or unpleasant. EG *I never thought I'd be able to control hordes of screaming children... ...rioting hordes... ...the great horde of the unemployed.* — N PART = multitude, mass

horizon /həraɪzə⁰n/, **horizons**. 1 The **horizon** is the line in the far distance where the sky seems to touch the land or the sea. EG *...the smoke on the horizon... ...summers when the sun scarcely dips below the horizon... ...smooth seas stretching from horizon to horizon.* — N COUNT : USU *the*+N IN SING = skyline

2 If something is **on the horizon**, it is almost certainly going to happen or be done quite soon. EG *On the horizon is a new type of drug.* — PHR : USED AS AN A ⇑ coming

3 If something is **over the horizon**, it is almost certainly going to happen or be done at some time in the future, especially after something else has been finished. EG *...the thought that over the horizon is another assignment.* — PHR : USED AS AN A ⇑ coming

4 Your **horizons** are the limits of what you want to do or are interested or involved in. EG *...the spontaneous upsurge and expansion of human horizons... ...the broader issues beyond their own horizons.* — N COUNT : USU PL ⇑ limit = perspective

horizontal /hɒrɪzɒntə⁰l/. 1 Something that is **horizontal** is flat and level with the ground or with a line or surface that you are considering as a base, rather than at an angle to it. EG *...horizontal stripes... ...the whirling horizontal blades of a helicopter.* — ADJ CLASSIF ≠ vertical
◊ **horizontally**. EG *The head turns horizontally from side to side.* ▸ used as a noun. EG *...5 degrees below the horizontal... He lowered her carefully to the horizontal.* — ◊ ADV WITH VB; ▸ N SING : *the*+N

2 **Horizontal** also means affecting or happening at one level in a system or organization. EG *...horizontal divisions of class.* — ADJ CLASSIF ≠ vertical

hormonal /hɔːməʊnə⁰l/ means relating to or involving hormones. EG *...hormonal changes... ...hormonal activity.* — ADJ CLASSIF : USU ATTRIB ⇑ chemical

hormone /hɔːməʊn/, **hormones**. A **hormone** is a chemical in your body that stimulates certain organs of your body. EG *...the male hormone testosterone... We are governed by the hormones that circulate around our bodies.* ▸ used also to refer to drugs made from these human chemicals. EG *...hormone treatment.* ▸ used also to refer to the chemicals that plants produce which control the way they grow. EG *...the five main groups of plant hormones.* — N COUNT; ▸ N COUNT ⇑ drug; ▸ N COUNT

horn /hɔːn/, **horns**. 1 **Horns** are the hard pointed growths that stick out of the top of the heads of animals such as deer, sheep, and goats. EG *...the horns of a bull.* — N COUNT : USU PL ⇑ growth

2 If you **take the bull by the horns**, you do something unpleasant, difficult, or dangerous that you feel you ought to do even though you are nervous or frightened. EG *'Why can't I choose John?'–I grabbed the bull by the horns. 'Because he's horrible, that's why.'* — PHR : VB INFLECTS ⇑ confront = grasp the nettle

3 **Horn** is the hard substance that the horns of animals are made of. People often use horn to make objects such as spoons or ornaments. — N UNCOUNT

4 A **horn** is also **4.1** a musical instrument made out of an animal's horn. You play it by blowing into it. EG *...the trumpeting of five hundred elephant-tusk horns.* — N COUNT **4.2** a musical instrument consisting of a metal pipe or tube that is narrow at one end and wide at the other. You play it by blowing into it. EG *He wasn't bad on the horn... ...the soaring, triumphant horn notes.* — N COUNT **4.3** a hollow curved object that is narrow at one end and wide at the other. EG *...an old drinking horn.* — N COUNT **4.4** a device on cars, trains, and other vehicles that you use to make a loud noise as a signal or warning to other people. EG *A car passed him at top speed, sounding its horn.* — N COUNT = hooter

5 If you are **on the horns of a dilemma**, you have to choose between two things which are both unpleasant or difficult. EG *He was on the horns of a dilemma, precisely the same dilemma which had always worried him.* — PHR : USED AS AN A ⇑ undecided = in a quandary

horned /hɔːnd/ is used to describe animals that have horns or parts of their body that look like horns. EG *...the great horned owl... ...the horned toad.* — ADJ CLASSIF : ATTRIB

hornet /hɔːnɪ²t/, **hornets**. 1 A **hornet** is a large wasp. Hornets live in nests and have a very painful sting. — N COUNT

2 If you describe a situation as **a hornet's nest**, you mean that it is extremely unpleasant or difficult to deal with; an informal expression. — PHR : USED AS O/C

horn-rimmed glasses or spectacles have frames made of plastic that is intended to look like horn. EG *She wore enormous horn-rimmed glasses.* — ADJ CLASSIF

horny /hɔːni¹/, **hornier, horniest**. 1 Something that is **horny** is hard, strong, and made of horn or of a hard substance like horn. EG *It has an armour of horny scales... Their skeleton is flexible and horny.* — ADJ CLASSIF ⇑ bony

2 A **horny** hand has skin that is very hard, tough, or strong. EG *He crunched Philip's fingers in his huge, horny hand.* — ADJ CLASSIF

3 If you describe someone as **horny**, you mean that they are sexually aroused or easily aroused; used in very informal English. — ADJ QUALIT = randy

horoscope /hɒrəskəʊp/, **horoscopes**. Your **horoscope** is information about what is going to happen to you on a particular day or in your life generally, which is based on the position of the stars when you were born. EG *...your personal horoscope... They claimed that their horoscopes were prepared by computer.* — N COUNT ⇑ prediction

horrendous /hə⁷rendəs/. Something that is **horrendous** is **1** very unpleasant and shocking. EG *...the horrendous murder of a prostitute.* — ADJ QUALIT **2** so big or great that you find it extremely unpleasant; a rather informal use. EG *The bill was going to be horrendous... ...battles which achieved so little at such horrendous cost.* — ADJ QUALIT = staggering

horrible /hɒrə¹bə⁰l/; a rather informal word. 1 You describe something as **horrible 1.1** when you do not — ADJ QUALIT like it at all. EG *Everything was very expensive and the hotel was horrible... I've never had such a horrible meal... It was a horrible colour.* **1.2** when it causes you to feel great shock, fear, and disgust. EG *...an imaginary torture, perhaps, but all the more horrible.* ◊ **horribly**. EG *The man had begun to scream horribly.* — ADJ QUALIT = horrific; ◊ ADV WITH VB = hideously

2 Horrible is used to emphasize how awful or unpleasant an experience, event, or situation is. EG *Everything's in a horrible muddle... I've got a horrible suspicion this thing's going to drip...* ◊ **horribly**. EG *I am horribly timid... Lined curtains are nicest but horribly expensive... Everything has gone horribly wrong.* — ADJ QUALIT : ATTRIB; ◊ ADV+ADJ/ADV = frightfully

horrid /hɒrɪd/; a rather informal word. **1** Something that is **horrid** is very unpleasant indeed. EG *Tea always tastes horrid out of Thermos flasks... We had to live in a horrid little flat... Something horrid is going to happen... ...a horrid dream.* — ADJ QUALIT = nasty ≠ nice

2 Someone who is **horrid** behaves in a very unpleasant, nasty way towards other people. EG *She would give her horrid parents one more chance... ...a horrid pimply boy... I don't mean to be horrid to you.* — ADJ QUALIT = beastly ≠ nice

horrific /hə⁷rɪfɪk/. Something that is **horrific** is so bad that people are horrified when they see it or think about it. EG *It was one of the most horrific experiences of my life.* ◊ **horrifically**. EG *Max went berserk and, screaming horrifically, trampled his way through the audience.* — ADJ QUALIT ⇑ nasty = horrifying; ◊ ADV WITH VB = horrifyingly

horrify /hɒrɪfaɪ/, **horrifies, horrifying, horrified**. If someone **is horrified**, they feel dismay or disgust, usually because of something that is said to them or because of some information they receive. EG *I was horrified by the amount of work I had to do... Both Mr. Faulds and his daughter were horrified at the proposal.* ◊ **horrifying**. EG *...horrifying stories... ...an alarming, even horrifying, picture.* ◊ **horrifyingly**. EG *The decision was horrifyingly swift.* — V+O : USU PASS ⇑ shock = appal ≠ delight; ◊ ADJ QUALIT = horrific; ◊ ADV = horrifically

horror /hɒrə/, **horrors**. **1 Horror** is **1.1** a strong feeling of alarm and dismay, often mixed with disgust or disapproval. It is caused by something which you find extremely unpleasant. EG *The boys shrank away from her in horror... To my horror there was a big black spider in the bath... These policies arouse in many people a horror and an anger that cannot be suppressed.* **1.2** a strong feeling of dislike or fear which you get whenever you think about a particular thing and which makes you want to avoid that thing. EG *Despite a fundamental horror of violence, John allowed himself to be drafted into the army.* — N UNCOUNT; N SING : USU *a*/POSS+N+*of* = abhorrence

2 The **horror** of something, especially something that hurts people, is the very great unpleasantness of it, which is often frightening and shocking. EG *They will never forget the blood and horror of the battle.* — N SING : *the*+N+*of*

3 A **horror** is **3.1** an extremely unpleasant experience, especially one in which people are hurt. EG *Sometimes his mind would dwell on the horrors he had been through.* **3.2** someone or something that you think is very ugly or nasty; an informal use. EG *Davenport House is the horror at the corner of the avenue.* **3.3** a child who is very naughty and disobedient; an informal use. EG *Come here, you little horror!* — N COUNT : USU PL; N COUNT = monstrosity; N COUNT/VOC = terror

4 A **horror** film or story is one which is intended to be really frightening. It is often about ghosts, witchcraft, vampires, or imaginary monsters. EG *Did you see the late-night horror movie on Friday?* — N BEFORE N ⇑ suspense

5 Horror of horrors is used in a humorous way to mean something that you consider to be the worst thing that could possibly happen. EG *He paused in mid-sentence, lighting–horror of horrors–a cigarette.* — PHR : USED AS ADV SEN

6 If something gives you **the horrors**, you have a feeling of irrational fear and nervousness caused by something which you know cannot hurt you but which still frightens you; an informal expression. EG *The very sound of an air-raid siren is enough to give my mother the horrors.* — PHR : USED AS O

horror-stricken. Someone who is **horror-stricken** or **horror-struck** feels very great horror or dismay at something that has happened. EG *Roland was horror-stricken at what he'd done.* — ADJ CLASSIF = appalled

hors de combat /ɔ: də kɒmbɑ:/. If someone is **hors de combat**, they have been wounded or injured, and so are unable to take part in something such as a battle or a sport; a formal or literary term. — ADJ CLASSIF : PRED = out of action

hors d'oeuvre /ɔ:dɜ:v/, **hors d'oeuvres**. **Hors d'oeuvres** are different dishes of cold food that have been specially prepared to be eaten before the main course of a meal. EG *...a tray of hors d'oeuvres... I've never had an hors d'oeuvre that I liked.* — N COUNT : USU PL ⇑ dish = starter

horse /hɔ:s/, **horses, horsing, horsed**. **1** A **horse** is a large animal which people ride for enjoyment or for getting from one place to another, and use for pulling ploughs, carts, etc. EG *He was seen riding a horse through the streets of London... In the early twentieth century the internal combustion engine replaced the horse.* — N COUNT

2 When you talk about **the horses**, you mean horse races in which people bet money on the horse which they think will win. EG *I have an occasional flutter on the horses.* — PHR : PREP+PHR

3 A **horse** is also a piece of sports equipment which gymnasts jump over. It is made of wood and the top is covered in a soft material such as leather. — N COUNT : USU *the*+N

4 Horse is the same as heroin; a very informal use. — N UNCOUNT

5 The word **horse** is used in the following expressions, which are explained at other places in this dictionary. ● to **put the cart before the horse**: see **cart**. ● **straight from the horse's mouth**: see **mouth**. ● See also **clothes horse**, **dark horse**, **rocking horse**, and **seahorse**.

horse about. If you **horse about** or **horse around**, you play roughly and rather carelessly, so that you could hurt someone or damage something; used in informal English. EG *He loved to horse around with them in the compound.* — PHRASAL VB : V+ADV = fool about

horseback /hɔ:sbæk/. If you are **on horseback** or are riding **horseback**, you are riding a horse. EG *The crowds were dispersed by policemen on horseback... She played tennis, rode horseback, and shot rapids in a canoe.* ▸ used as an adjective. EG *...horseback riding.* — PHR : USED AS AN A, OR ADV WITH VB; ▸ ADJ CLASSIF : ATTRIB

horse box, **horse boxes**; also spelled with a hyphen. A **horse box** is a vehicle rather like a removal van which is used to take horses from one place to another. — N COUNT = loose box

horse chestnut, **horse chestnuts**; also spelled with a hyphen. A **horse chestnut** is **1** a large tree which has broad leaves and shiny reddish-brown nuts covered with a spiky case. **2** the nut of this tree. A more common name for the nut is **conker**. — N COUNT; N COUNT

horse-drawn. A vehicle that is **horse-drawn** is pulled by one or more horses. EG *She saw a picture of Piccadilly almost jammed with horse-drawn traffic in about 1875.* — ADJ CLASSIF

horseflesh /hɔ:sfleʃ/. **1** If you say that someone is a **good judge of horseflesh** or **a bad judge of horseflesh**, you mean that they are either good or bad at knowing whether a horse is worth buying or training. — PHR : USED AS C

2 Horseflesh or **horsemeat** is meat from a horse, especially when it is fed to other animals or is eaten by people. — N UNCOUNT

horsefly /hɔ:sflaɪ/, **horseflies**. A **horsefly** is a large fly that stings horses, cattle, and people and sucks their blood. — N COUNT ⇑ insect

horsehair /hɔ:sheə/ is hair which is taken from the tail or mane of horses. It was used to stuff mattresses, armchairs, etc, before more modern materials like polyester were available. EG *The Colonel reclined on a horsehair sofa.* — N UNCOUNT

horseman /hɔ:smə³n/, **horsemen**. A **horseman** is a man who is riding a horse, or one who rides horses well. EG *Horsemen would arrive and tether their horses to the rail... He was sent to Curragh Camp in Ireland because he was such a fine horseman.* — N COUNT ⇑ rider = equestrian

horsemanship /hɔ:smə³nʃɪp/ is the ability to ride horses well. — N UNCOUNT ⇑ skill

horseplay /hɔ:spleɪ/ is rough play in which people, often teenagers, push and hit each other quite violently, but do not really want to hurt each other; a rather old-fashioned word. EG *She was engaged in some horseplay involving the hiding of her swimming-costume.* — N UNCOUNT

horsepower /hɔ:spauə/ is a unit of power. It is used for measuring how powerful an engine is. EG *He started up the outboard motor–5 horsepower only, but enough for a fourteen-foot dinghy.* — N UNCOUNT ⇑ measurement

horse racing; also spelled with a hyphen and as one word. **Horse racing** is a sport in which horses ridden by jockeys run in races, sometimes jumping — N UNCOUNT = racing over fences. The owner of the winning horse usually receives a prize of money.

horseradish /hɔːsrædɪʃ/is the white root of a plant similar to a mustard plant. It has a very strong, sharp taste and is often made into horseradish sauce, which is usually eaten with roast beef. N UNCOUNT

horse riding; also spelled with a hyphen and as one word. **Horse riding** is the activity of riding a horse, especially for enjoyment or as a form of physical exercise. EG *She enjoyed yachting and horse riding.* N UNCOUNT ⇑ sport

horse sense; also spelled with a hyphen. **Horse sense** is the same as common sense; used in rather old-fashioned and informal English. EG *He showed his political horse sense in a carefully worded speech.* N UNCOUNT

horseshoe /hɔːsʃuː/, **horseshoes**. A **horseshoe** is 1 a piece of metal shaped like a U, which is fixed with nails to the hard lower surface of a horse's hoof in order to protect it. N COUNT ⇑ shoe 2 something which has the shape or appearance of a horseshoe. Cardboard or plastic horseshoes are sometimes given to people because they are thought to bring good luck. EG *The stream curved round in a glittering horseshoe... ...towering apartment buildings that formed a grand horseshoe around the southern end of the park.* N COUNT

horse show, horse shows; also spelled with a hyphen. A **horse show** is a sporting event in which people riding horses compete in order to demonstrate their skill and control. N COUNT = gymkhana

horse-trading; also spelled without a hyphen. **horse-trading** is the bargaining which takes place unofficially and which often involves exchanges rather than payment. EG *At the beginning of term there is horse trading over timetables.* N UNCOUNT

horsewhip /hɔːswɪp/, **horsewhips, horsewhipping, horsewhipped**. 1 A **horsewhip** is a long thin piece of leather on the end of a short, stiff handle. It is used to train and control horses. N COUNT ⇑ whip

2 If someone **horsewhips** a person or animal, they hit them several times with a horsewhip in order to hurt or punish them. EG *The man was tied to a tree and horse-whipped.* V+O = flog

horsewoman /hɔːswʌ¹mə⁰n/, **horsewomen**. A **horsewoman** is a woman who is riding a horse, or one who rides horses well. N COUNT ⇑ rider

horsey /hɔːsi¹/, **horsier, horsiest**; also spelled **horsy**. 1 Someone who is **horsey** is very keen on horses or is fond of riding horses; used especially of people who spend most of their free time with horses. EG *We watched her show-jumping at a gymkhana, in her horsy phase.* ADJ QUALIT ⇑ enthusiastic

2 If you describe a woman as **horsey**, you are saying in a rather rude way that her face reminds you of a horse, for example because it is long and thin. ADJ QUALIT = equine

horsy /hɔːsi¹/. See **horsey**.

horticultural /hɔːti¹kʌltʃərəl/means concerned with horticulture. EG *...the Royal Horticultural Society.* ADJ CLASSIF ⇑ gardening

horticulturalist /hɔːti¹kʌltʃərəlɪst/, **horticulturalists**. A **horticulturalist** is a person who grows flowers, fruit, and vegetables, especially as their job. N COUNT ⇑ gardener

horticulture /hɔːtɪkʌltʃə/ is the study and practice of growing flowers, fruit, and vegetables. N UNCOUNT

hose /həʊz/, **hoses, hosing, hosed**. 1 A **hose** is 1.1 a long, flexible pipe made of rubber or plastic. Water is directed through a hose in order to put out fires, clean cars, water gardens, etc. EG *...the spray from the hose... ...a fire hose.* N COUNT 1.2 a pipe made of rubber or plastic, along which a liquid or gas flows or is carried, for example from one part of an engine to another. N COUNT

2 If you **hose** something, you wash or water it using a hose. EG *Hose the soil well immediately after planting rose bushes... It's sensible to hose underneath the car in winter.* V+O, OR V : USU +A

3 **Hose** is 3.1 an old-fashioned men's garment that looks like a pair of very tight trousers. N UNCOUNT 3.2 used to refer to tights, socks, stockings, etc; an old-fashioned or technical use. ● See also **panty hose**. N UNCOUNT ⇑ hosiery

hose down. When you **hose** something **down**, you clean it using a hose. EG *Joseph was hosing down the new tractor... Could you not get the sanitation department to hose the place down?* PHRASAL VB : V+O+ADV

hose out. When you **hose** something **out**, you clean the inside of it using a hose. EG *He hosed out the barn.* PHRASAL VB : V+O+ADV

hosiery /həʊzɪ⁰əri¹/ refers to tights, stockings, leotards, etc, especially when they are on sale in shops; a formal or technical term. N UNCOUNT ⇑ clothing

hospice /hɒspɪs/, **hospices**. A **hospice** is a special hospital in which people who are dying are looked after with a great deal of understanding and care. N COUNT : ALSO IN NAMES AFTER N ⇑ home

hospitable /hɒspɪtəbə⁰l, hɒspɪt-/. 1 If you are **hospitable**, you are friendly, welcoming, and generous to your guests or to strangers in the part of the country where you live. EG *Mr Steinberg was a good-natured and hospitable man... People here are really nice. Hospitable. They invite you to their homes for Sunday dinner.* ▸ used of a person's behaviour. EG *...her hospitable invitations.* ◇ **hospitably**. EG *'You must have a drink!' cried Bal hospitably.* ADJ QUALIT = sociable ≠ unfriendly ◇ ADV WITH VB

2 Something that is **hospitable** enables and even encourages particular people, things, processes, etc to live or work in a certain place or area. EG *...a hospitable climate... It seems to make the soil more alkaline and more hospitable to plants.* ADJ QUALIT ⇑ favourable ≠ hostile

hospital /hɒspɪtə⁰l/, **hospitals**. A **hospital** is a place where people who are ill are looked after by nurses and doctors. EG *I was working at the hospital... I used to visit him in hospital... ...a psychiatric hospital.* N COUNT, OR PREP+N UNCOUNT

hospitality /hɒspɪtæli¹ti¹/ is friendly, welcoming behaviour towards guests or towards strangers in your part of the country. EG *I thanked him for his hospitality and his kindness in driving me back to my hotel.* N UNCOUNT ⇑ friendliness

hospitalize /hɒspɪtəlaɪz/, **hospitalizes, hospitalizing, hospitalized**; also spelled **hospitalise**. If someone **is hospitalized**, they are sent or admitted to hospital. EG *I said that her mother was hospitalized and that the situation was grave... The most effective way of stopping this is to hospitalize him for a brief period.* ◇ **hospitalization** /hɒspɪtəlaɪzeɪʃə⁰n/. EG *...the first 60 days of hospitalization.* V+O : USU PASS ◇ N UNCOUNT

host /həʊst/, **hosts, hosting, hosted**. 1 A **host** is 1.1 the person at a party or other social occasion who invited the guests and who looks after them while they are there. EG *There were only three of us to dine– my host, his father and me... Vorster acted the dutiful host, filling up glasses and mixing with his guests.* N COUNT : USU WITH the/POSS 1.2 the country or organization that provides the facilities for an event or function, or that takes people in from another place and gives them somewhere to live. EG *Charnwood Comprehensive are the hosts in this year's Schools Athletic Championships... The attitude of the host community to the refugees was at first hostile... Within a week his host country had supplied him with accommodation.* N COUNT : USU the/POSS+N 1.3 a man who owns or manages an inn; a rather old-fashioned use. N COUNT = landlord 1.4 someone who is in charge of a radio or television programme in which they introduce and talk to important or interesting people. EG *Our host tonight is Janet Street Porter.* ▸ used as a verb. EG *He has been hosting the show for two years.* N COUNT : USU WITH the/POSS ⇑ compere ▸ V+O ⇑ compere

2 A **host** is also a plant or animal which has other smaller plants or animals living on or in it and getting their food from it; a technical use. EG *Each type of flea likes a different sort of host: horses, cats, rats, dogs, humans.* N COUNT

3 A **host** of things is a large number of them. EG *I'm sure the audience has a host of fascinating questions for our team of experts... We visited a whole host of places between Wick and Thurso.* N PART : USU SING = multitude

4 The **Host** is the bread which is used in the Christian church service of Mass or Holy Communion; a technical term. N COUNT : USU the+N IN SING

hostage /hɒstɪdʒ/, **hostages**. A **hostage** is someone who is taken prisoner by an organization or another person and is threatened with injury or death unless people do what that organization or person demands. EG *They were still holding one hostage... They also took other political leaders as hostages.* ● If someone **is taken hostage** or **is held hostage**, they are captured and kept as a hostage. EG *He had been taken hostage by terrorists... They are being held hostage until our demands are met.* N COUNT ● PHR : VB INFLECTS

hostel /hɒstə⁰l/, **hostels**. A **hostel** is a large house, usually owned by a local government authority or a charity, which has beds or rooms that people can rent cheaply to live in for a short time. EG *The young men's hostel in central London has been rebuilt.* N COUNT ⇑ building = home

hostess /həʊstɪ²s/, **hostesses**. A **hostess** is 1 the woman at a party or other special occasion who invited the guests and who looks after them while they are there. EG *My hostess greeted me with* N COUNT : USU WITH the/POSS

unexpected warmth. 2 a woman who is paid by a man to be his partner for an evening at a night club or dance hall. 3 a woman who is employed in a restaurant to take guests to their tables and to make sure the waitresses do their work; used mainly in American English. 4 an air hostess.
N COUNT ⇑ escort / N COUNT / N COUNT

hostile /hɒstaɪl/. 1 Someone who is **hostile** is unfriendly and aggressive. EG *Frank used to be a reserved, almost hostile person... She was surprised and puzzled, but not hostile.* ▸ used of a person's behaviour. EG *I was in a depressed and hostile mood... ...a hostile attitude.*
ADJ QUALIT = antagonistic ≠ sociable

2 People, societies, etc that are **hostile** to a particular person or idea are unfriendly or aggressive because they disagree with or disapprove of them. EG *...a new government that is hostile to us... For many years, these immigrants have lived in a hostile society.* ▸ used of behaviour. EG *The proposal was met with a hostile reaction.*
ADJ QUALIT ⇑ unfavourable ≠ friendly, receptive

3 Situations and conditions that are **hostile** are unpleasant or dangerous. EG *...the continuously hostile weather... ...the problem of running machinery in hostile environments.*
ADJ QUALIT ⇑ unfriendly

4 You use the word **hostile** to describe the people, organizations, etc, that belong to your enemy in a war. EG *...with hostile naval and air forces... ...local rulers who might turn hostile at any time.*
ADJ CLASSIF

hostility /hɒstɪlɪti[1]/, **hostilities**. 1 **Hostility** is behaviour which is unfriendly or aggressive, especially towards particular people or ideas that you disagree with or disapprove of. EG *Their friendship is regarded with suspicion and hostility... American spokesmen made clear their hostility to the new proposals.*
N UNCOUNT = opposition

2 **Hostilities** means behaviour or action that indicates that you have become involved in a battle or war with someone; a formal use. EG *Both sides wanted a cessation of hostilities... ...a highly provocative act, which could result in hostilities escalating out of control.*
N PLURAL = conflict

3 **Hostilities** are feelings of anger and hatred towards someone or something. EG *He needs an outlet for his frustrations and hostilities.*
N PLURAL = resentments

hot /hɒt/, **hotter, hottest; hots, hotting, hotted**. 1 Something that is **hot** has a high temperature. EG *The metal of the tank is so hot I can't touch it... All I want is a hot bath... ...hot water... The back of her neck was hot...*
ADJ QUALIT ≠ cold, cool

2 **Hot** is used to describe the weather or the air in a room or building when the temperature is high. EG *It was terribly hot yesterday... ...a fine, hot August day... Most of her life had been spent in hot, dusty Delhi... The room was hot and smelled of hospitals.*
ADJ QUALIT ≠ chilly, cold

3 If you are **hot**, you feel as if your body is at an unpleasantly high temperature. EG *I'm hot and tired... Hot and perspiring, John toiled up the dusty ascent.*
ADJ QUALIT : PRED ≠ cold

4 If something is **hot**, it has a particular temperature or degree of heat. EG *Enzymes are ineffective in water hotter than 140°F... How hot should the oven be?*
ADJ QUALIT

5 **Hot** food 5.1 is intended to be eaten as soon as it is cooked, as opposed to food that you eat when it has cooled or that you do not cook at all. EG *You could have a hot supper at the inn or a cold supper with us... ...producing two hot meals a day.* 5.2 has a strong, burning taste caused by spices such as chili or cayenne pepper. EG *...hot curries... Soon they were feasting on dried gram, nuts hot with chili powder and puffed rice.*
ADJ CLASSIF : USU ATTRIB ≠ cold / ADJ QUALIT ⇑ spicy

6 In informal English, if you say that someone is **hot** on something, you mean that 6.1 they have a lot of knowledge about a particular subject or skill in a particular activity. EG *Why don't you ask Meg to do it? She's quite hot on that sort of thing... ...which suggested that we weren't so hot at these things as we used to be... The book is good on methodology but not so hot on linguistic theory.* 6.2 they consider something to be very important and are very careful to see that it is done correctly. EG *You'd better check it. They're very hot on spelling mistakes.*
ADJ QUALIT : PRED, USU + *on/at* = good / ADJ QUALIT : PRED, USU + *on/at* ⇑ strict

7 Something such as news or information that is **hot** is new, recent, and fresh; an informal use. EG *...a hot scent... ...news hot off the press.*
ADJ QUALIT

8 In informal English, you can use **hot** to describe something that is 8.1 very exciting and that many people want to see, use, obtain, or become involved with. EG *She couldn't act. Nonetheless, she was a very hot box office attraction indeed... You know, Gordon, I think we're on to a hot one this time.* 8.2 very dangerous and that no one wants to deal with, for example because it has been illegally obtained and is very valuable or famous. EG *The tapes had existed but they were too hot to preserve and had been destroyed... I wouldn't touch it, mate–it's too hot to handle!*
ADJ QUALIT : USU ATTRIB ⇑ popular / ADJ QUALIT : PRED

9 You can describe a situation that is created by a person's behaviour or attitude as **hot** when it is unpleasant and difficult to deal with; an informal use. EG *They're making it hot for me here. I'm going to have to leave.*
ADJ QUALIT : PRED

10 A contest or conflict that is **hot** is intense and involves a great deal of activity and determination; an informal use. EG *This was an indication of just how hot the contest for the leadership had become... The battle over Kevin was likely to grow even hotter.*
ADJ QUALIT = fierce

11 Someone who has a **hot** temper gets angry very quickly and easily. EG *My brother had a hot temper... ...a hot-tempered young man.* ▸ used of reactions caused by anger, embarrassment, or similar emotions. EG *He felt hot tears well up and run down his cheeks... ...vindictive anger and hot shame.*
ADJ QUALIT : USU ATTRIB / ▸ ADJ CLASSIF = bitter

12 The word **hot** is also used in the following expressions in informal English. 12.1 If you are **in hot water** or **get into hot water**, you are in trouble with someone because you have done something wrong. EG *You'll be in hot water when your mother finds out!... We don't want to get them into hot water.*
PHR : USED AS A, OR PHR : VB INFLECTS

12.2 If you **blow hot and cold**, you keep changing your attitude towards something or someone, sometimes being very enthusiastic and at other times expressing no interest at all. EG *The management blew now hot, now cold, now fierce, now conciliatory.* 12.3 If you **go hot and cold** or if something makes you **go hot and cold**, you suddenly feel very worried and frightened about something that you have heard or have thought of. EG *I used to go hot and cold about it because I knew what the implications were.* 12.4 If you are **hot and bothered**, you are so worried and anxious that you cannot think clearly or behave sensibly. EG *It's no use getting hot and bothered about it.*
PHR : VB INFLECTS / PHR : VB INFLECTS / PHR : USED AS C = in a flap

hot up; used in informal English. 1 When something **hots up** or when you **hot it up**, it starts to happen very quickly with a lot of activity and excitement. EG *Now the pace really began to hot up.*
PHRASAL VB : V-ERG + ADV ⇑ intensify

2 If you **hot up** a car, you make it more powerful, for example by adjusting the engine or adding special parts.
PHRASAL VB : V + O + ADV = soup up

hot air refers to claims or promises that are made to impress people but which will probably never happen; used in informal English showing disapproval. EG *His speech was just hot air... ...innumerable explosions of hot air from the opposition parties.*
N UNCOUNT ⇑ talk

hot-air balloon, hot-air balloons. A **hot-air balloon** is a large balloon with a basket underneath in which people can travel. When the balloon is filled with hot air, it rises off the ground and moves through the air.
N COUNT

hotbed /hɒtbɛd/, **hotbeds**. If a place is a **hotbed** of some unpleasant or unacceptable feeling or activity, there is so much of it in the place that everyone seems to be involved in it or affected by it. EG *The universities are hotbeds of intrigue.*
N COUNT : USU + *of*

hot-blooded. Someone who is **hot-blooded** quickly and easily expresses their feelings, especially those of anger or love.
ADJ QUALIT ⇑ passionate

hotchpotch /hɒtʃpɒtʃ/. A **hotchpotch** is a disorderly mixture of different types of things; a rather informal word. EG *...a hotchpotch of uncoordinated schemes.*
N PART : SING = jumble

hot dog, hot dogs. A **hot dog** is a long bread roll which is cut along the middle and has a sausage in it. EG *...truck drivers gobbling up hot dogs dripping with mustard... ...a hot dog stand.*
N COUNT ⇑ snack

hotel /h[o]əʊtɛl/, **hotels**. A **hotel** is a building where people stay, usually for a few nights, paying for their rooms and meals. EG *We drove past hotels and banks to fashionable suburbs... ...the Hilton Hotel.*
N COUNT : ALSO IN NAMES

hotelier /h[o]əʊtɛlɪə/, **hoteliers**. A **hotelier** is a person who owns or manages a hotel.
N COUNT ⇑ manager

hot flush, hot flushes. A **hot flush** is a sudden hot feeling in the skin which women often experience at the time of their menopause; used mainly in British English.
N COUNT

hotfoot /hɒtfʊt/. If someone goes somewhere **hotfoot**, they go there quickly and eagerly; an informal word. EG *...the kindly doctor goes hotfoot to the rescue of suffering mankind.* ADV AFTER VB

hothead /hɒthɛd/, **hotheads**. A **hothead** is someone who does things hastily and without thinking what the consequences will be; used showing disapproval. EG *There was a time when he was regarded as a hothead, a man whose career could be blunted by his rashness.* N COUNT ⇑ person = madcap

hot-headed. Someone who is **hot-headed** acts hastily and without thinking what the consequences will be. ADJ QUALIT = impetuous

hothouse /hɒthaʊs/, **hothouses**; also spelled with a hyphen. 1 A **hothouse** is a heated building, usually made of glass, in which plants and flowers can be grown. EG *There were numerous well-kept hothouses in the grounds.* N COUNT ⇑ greenhouse

2 A **hothouse** is also a place or a situation in which there is intense intellectual or emotional activity, for example by artists or academics. EG *I tend to think about Brighton as a leisure centre and Lewes as a hot-house of amateur historians... ...the hothouse world of classical music... ...people cultivating their feelings in a kind of hothouse atmosphere.* N COUNT

hot line, hot lines. The **hot line** is a special, direct telephone line between the heads of government in different countries so that they can contact each other in an emergency. EG *...the Hot Line telephone link between Washington and Moscow... He got through on the hot line to the head of government in the USSR.* N COUNT : USU the+N

hotly /hɒtli[1]/. 1 If you do something **hotly**, you do it angrily and with determination. EG *...a claim which the United States has hotly denied... ...shoving the boy roughly aside and exclaiming hotly, 'That's my brother.'* ADV WITH VB ⇑ strongly = vehemently

2 If you are being **hotly** pursued, there is someone who is close behind you, moving very quickly, and determined to catch you. EG *I roared off on his motor bike, hotly pursued by the wedding guests on their machines.* ADV WITH VB = closely

hot-plate, hot-plates; also spelled without a hyphen. A **hot-plate** is a flat surface, often on a cooker, which is heated by electricity and on which you can cook food in pans or keep food warm. N COUNT = ring

hotpot /hɒtpɒt/, **hotpots**; also spelled with a hyphen. A **hotpot** is a dish made from a mixture of meat, vegetables, and gravy cooked slowly in the oven. N COUNT/UNCOUNT ⇑ stew

hot potato, hot potatoes; used in informal English. A problem or issue that is a **hot potato** is a very difficult or awkward one that nobody wants to deal with. EG *The subject of abortion became a political hot potato.* • If you **drop** a person or a project **like a hot potato**, you suddenly stop being involved with them. EG *She dropped him like a hot potato when she found out.* N COUNT; • PHR : VB INFLECTS ⇑ disown

hot seat. Someone who is **in the hot seat** is in a position or job in which they have to make very important and difficult decisions for which they will be held responsible; an informal expression. PHR : USED AS AN A

hot spot, hot spots; used in informal English. A **hot spot** is 1 an exciting place where there is a lot of activity or entertainment. EG *...Birmingham's fashionable hot spots.* 2 an area where there is some form of trouble such as fighting or political unrest. N COUNT; N COUNT

hot stuff; used in informal English. 1 If you think someone is **hot stuff**, you find them exciting and attractive, especially sexually. EG *We stood there pretending to be hot stuff.* N UNCOUNT : USU USED AS C

2 Something such as an activity that is **hot stuff** is very popular. EG *Skateboarding is hot stuff in East Anglia.* N UNCOUNT : USU USED AS C

hot-water bottle, hot-water bottles. A **hot-water bottle** is a rubber container which you can fill with hot water and put in a bed to make it warm. N COUNT

hound /haʊnd/, **hounds, hounding, hounded**. 1 A **hound** is a type of dog that is often used for hunting or racing. EG *...large packs of tireless hounds.* N COUNT

2 If you **hound** someone, 2.1 you trouble them by constantly disturbing them or criticizing them. EG *He was hounded by the press.* 2.2 you chase them away. EG *They were hounded out of their small shack in the township.* V+O = persecute; V+O+A = drive

hour /aʊə/, **hours**. 1 An **hour** is a period of sixty minutes. There are twenty-four hours in a day. EG *He spent an hour carefully cleaning the rifle... They slept for two hours... She had left half an hour before... ...a two hour examination paper... The speed increased to nearly sixty miles per hour.* • See also **lunch hour, rush-hour**. N COUNT

2 If you are an **hour** from a place, it will take you an hour to travel there. EG *It was a half hour from the Pinewood Studios... 'How far is it?'–'Less than an hour by train.'* N COUNT : USU+A ⇑ distance

3 A clock that strikes the **hour** strikes when it is exactly one o'clock, two o'clock, etc. EG *...a marble clock which struck the hours and quarters.* N COUNT : the+N

• Something that happens **on the hour** happens at exactly one o'clock, two o'clock, etc. EG *Buses for London leave every hour on the hour.* • PHR : USED AS AN A

4 The **hour** at which something happens is the actual time at which it happens or is supposed to happen; a literary use. EG *It was a good deal after half-past four–the hour when they had been invited... The hour for tea had arrived... It happened between the hours of eleven and twelve.* • See also **eleventh hour, zero hour**. • You can use **at this hour** or **at that hour** to refer to the particular time of day when something happens, especially to emphasize that it is an unusual time or event. EG *The telephone rang. 'At this hour,' Davis complained. 'It's anti-social.'... There was little traffic at this hour... He couldn't remember when he had last risen at that unearthly hour.* N COUNT+SUPP; • PHR : USED AS AN A

5 Someone's **hour** of hardship, happiness, etc is an important time in their life or in a series of events when they are experiencing the feeling or condition mentioned; a literary use. EG *She did not desert him in his dark hours... ...in their hour of need.* N COUNT+SUPP

6 If you do something for **hours**, you do it for a long time, or for a time that seems very long to you. EG *I spent hours gazing at them... We talked for hours and hours about every subject under the sun.* • If you do something **hour after hour** or **for hour after hour**, you do it for a long time without any change. EG *...extreme monotony and boredom as you drive for hour after hour.* N PLURAL = ages; • PHR : USED AS AN A

7 The **hours** of a particular part of the day or night, or the **hours** when you do a particular activity, are that particular time of the day or night. EG *...during the hours of darkness... ...in the very early hours of the morning... Such thoughts filled many waking hours.* • If someone does something **at all hours, at all hours of the day and night**, etc, they do it all the time, or at any time during the day or night. EG *The café serves meals at all hours... They seem to enjoy being rung up at all hours of the day and night.* • If you do something until **the small hours**, you do it until the early morning after midnight. EG *The noise kept him awake until the small hours... In the small hours of the morning, very drunk, they agreed on an answer.* • If you do something **till all hours**, you continue doing it until very late at night. EG *I object to him having the radio on at full blast till all hours of the night.* N PLURAL+SUPP ⇑ period; • PHR : USED AS AN A; • PHR : PREP+PHR ⇑ late; • PHR : USED AS AN A

8 The **hours** that you work, that a business is open, etc are the actual period of time each day that you work or that the business is open. EG *...our demands for shorter working hours... ...business hours... She complains about the hours of her job.* • See also **opening hours**. • If it is **after hours**, it is after the time when business or trade is supposed to have finished; used especially of the time when a pub must stop serving drinks by law. EG *I can't serve you, sir, it's after hours.* • Something that happens **out of hours** happens at a time that is not during the usual hours of business or work. EG *We don't usually keep the lights on out of hours.* N PLURAL; • PHR : USED AS AN A; • PHR : USED AS AN A

9 The **hours** that you keep are the times that you usually go to bed and get up, usually described as early, late, irregular, etc, when compared with most people. EG *They seem to keep unreasonable hours... ...regular hours, home-cooked meals, all the qualities of a settled existence.* N PLURAL : USU+SUPP

hourglass /aʊəglɑːs/, **hourglasses**. An **hourglass** is a device that can be used to measure the passing of an hour in time. It has two glass sections linked by a narrow channel, and sand flows slowly from the top one into the lower one, taking an hour to do so. N COUNT ⇑ timer

hour hand, hour hands. The **hour hand** on a clock or watch is the hand that points to the number of hours that have passed since twelve o'clock. N COUNT ⇑ pointer

hourly /aʊəli¹/. 1 An **hourly** event happens once every hour. EG *The town is served by an hourly bus service.* ▸ used as an adverb. EG *We shall be meeting hourly until six.* [ADJ CLASSIF : ATTRIB] [▸ ADV WITH VB ⇑ regularly]

2 If you are paid **hourly**, you are paid according to the number of hours you work. [ADV WITH VB]

3 **Hourly** earnings are the earnings that you make in one hour. EG *Their average hourly earnings were £5.00.* [ADJ CLASSIF : ATTRIB]

4 If you are doing something **hourly**, you keep doing it again and again. EG *They changed their minds and shifted their votes hourly.* [ADV WITH VB ⇑ constantly]

5 If you are **hourly** expecting something to happen, you are expecting it to happen at any time soon. EG *He was hourly expecting attack by fresh enemy forces.* [ADV WITH VB]

house, houses, housing, housed. The word **house** is pronounced /haʊz/ when it is a verb and /haʊs/ when it is a singular noun. The plural of the noun is pronounced /haʊzi¹z/. 1 A **house** is a building in which people live, usually the people belonging to one family. EG *He has a house in Pimlico... I don't think I can stand being in the house with him for another minute... It only takes 35 minutes from my house.* ▸ **House** is also used to refer to all the people who live together in a house. EG *I stayed awake until the whole house was sleeping... He's the head of the house.* ● See also **boarding house, council house, doll's house, wendy house**. [N COUNT] [▸ N SING : *the*/POSS+N = household]

2 The word **house** is also used in the following expressions. **2.1** If you say you are having **open house**, you mean that any visitors are welcome at your house and they do not need a special invitation to come; an informal expression. EG *It's open house tonight... Come along for a drink, we keep open house on Saturday evenings.* [PHR : USED AS C/O] **2.2** Someone who is **under house arrest** is forbidden by the government to go outside their own home. EG *The nationalist leader remains under house arrest.* [PHR : USED AS AN A] **2.3** If someone staying at your house is **eating** you **out of house and home**, they are making life difficult for you by eating more food than you can afford to provide; an informal expression. [PHR : VB INFLECTS] **2.4** If two people **get on like a house on fire**, they quickly become close friends, for example because they have many interests in common; an informal expression. EG *She got on with him like a house on fire.* [PHR : VB INFLECTS = hit it off] **2.5** If you **keep house**, you stay at home and do the cleaning and cooking, and do not go out to work. EG *He keeps house and I go out to work.* [PHR : VB INFLECTS] **2.6** If someone tells you to **set** or **put** your **own house in order**, they tell you to arrange your own affairs and solve your own problems before you try to tell others how to solve theirs. EG *Put your own house in order before you tell me what to do.* ● to **set up house**: see **set up.** [PHR : VB INFLECTS]

3 A **house** is also **3.1** a building which is used for a special purpose such as an official or business purpose; often used as part of the name of a building. EG *...Broadcasting House... ...New York's Metropolitan Opera House... She was collecting eggs from the chicken house.* ● See also **chapter house, clearing house, White House**. [N COUNT : ALSO IN NAMES AFTER N] **3.2** a place where people go to eat and drink, such as a restaurant or café. EG *We had a quick meal at a cheap eating house... ...a steak house... ...a coffee house.* ● See also **public house**. [N COUNT : MOD+N] **3.3** a company, especially one which publishes books, lends money, or designs clothes. EG *She worked for a small publishing house... ...Paris fashion houses.* [N COUNT : MOD+N] **3.4** a group of people who make laws and govern a country. EG *...the Speaker of the lower house, the House of Assembly... ...twenty-two members drawn equally from both Houses.* ▸ The **House** is often used to refer specifically to one of these groups, for example the House of Commons, the House of Lords, or the House of Representatives. EG *The House switched its attention to another speaker... In the House, he needed a minimum of 26 democratic votes.* [N COUNT ⇑ parliament] [▸ N SING : *the*+N] **3.5** a group of children of different ages in a school who compete against other groups in sports and other activities. Each house usually has a name. EG *Our house won the prize for the best exam results.* [N COUNT : USU POSS/MOD+N] **3.6** a famous and important family, especially the family of a king or queen, including ancestors. EG *...the house of Windsor... She is related to a European royal house.* [N COUNT+SUPP] **3.7** all the people at a debate; a formal use. EG *There was a debate on the motion 'This house would fight for Queen and country'.* [N SING WITH DET] **3.8** the part of a theatre, cinema, or other place of entertainment where the audience sits. EG *We stood at the back of the packed house to listen to an orchestra.* ▸ used also to refer to the people present at a particular performance, or to a particular performance when it is one of many. EG *The house fell silent as the curtain rose... The first house was sold out.* ● See also **full house**. ● If a person or their performance in a play or concert **brings the house down**, the audience claps and cheers loudly for a long time because they are so pleased with the performance; an informal expression. EG *There was one scene which never failed to bring the house down.* [N COUNT] [● PHR : VB INFLECTS]

4 **House** wine is the cheapest wine sold in restaurants, which is not listed by name on the wine list and is not guaranteed to be of a particular type or quality. EG *Usually I have the dry house white wine.* ● If you are given something at a restaurant, hotel, etc **on the house**, it is provided free of charge by the owner; an informal expression. EG *You try some.-It's on the house.* [N BEFORE N ⇑ cheap] [● PHR : USED AS AN A]

5 To **house** someone means to provide a house or flat for them to live in. EG *Too many married couples are waiting to be housed... They are better fed, better housed and better clothed than ever before.* [V+O = accommodate]

6 A building that **houses** something is the place where it is kept or where it happens. EG *This is the building which houses the library... The Castle now houses government receptions and congresses.* [V+O ⇑ contain]

7 A building that **houses** someone is the place where they live or where they are staying. EG *The hotel had housed the journalists during the Nixon visit.* [V+O = put up]

houseboat /haʊsbəʊt/, **houseboats**. A **houseboat** is a small boat which people live on and which usually remains at a particular place on a river or canal. [N COUNT ⇑ boat]

housebound /haʊsbaʊnd/. Someone who is **housebound** is unable to go out of their house, usually because they are ill or cannot walk far. EG *Most of the old people we visit are housebound.* [ADJ CLASSIF ⇑ immobilized]

houseboy /haʊsbɔɪ/, **houseboys**. A **houseboy** is a man or boy who cleans and does other jobs in someone else's house; an old-fashioned word now considered by most people to be offensive. [N COUNT ⇑ servant]

housebreaker /haʊsbreɪkə/, **housebreakers**. A **housebreaker** is someone who enters another person's house, for example by breaking the locks or windows, in order to steal their possessions. [N COUNT ⇑ criminal = burglar]

housebreaking /haʊsbreɪkɪŋ/ is the crime of entering another person's house, for example by breaking the locks or windows, in order to steal their possessions. EG *He was arrested by the police on charges of housebreaking.* [N UNCOUNT = burglary]

housecoat /haʊskəʊt/, **housecoats**. A **housecoat** is a long loose coat that some women wear during the day when they are in their house. [N COUNT ⇑ garment]

housefather /haʊsfɑːðə/, **housefathers**. A **housefather** is a man who looks after a particular group of children in an institution such as a children's home. [N COUNT]

houseful /haʊsfʊl/, **housefuls**. A **houseful** of people or things is a number of them all together in one house, which makes the house very full. EG *A houseful of children is easier than dealing with one lazy husband... You've got quite a houseful.* [N PART ⇑ amount]

house guest, house guests. A **house guest** is a person who is staying at someone's house for a period of time. EG *He was her house guest in Paris.* [N COUNT]

household /haʊshəʊld/, **households**. 1 A **household** is all the people in a family or group who live together in a house. EG *He loved being part of a huge household... Only 8 per cent of households owned a fridge.* [N COUNT]

2 The **household** is everything that is connected with looking after a house and the people who live in it. EG *My daughter managed the entire household including the baby and cooking... Household chores are not just women's work.* [N SING WITH DET ⇑ family]

3 Someone or something that is a **household** name, word, term, etc is very well known and often talked about. EG *William Randolph Hearst was a household name in America.* [N BEFORE N ⇑ familiar]

4 The word **Household** is used in the names of groups of soldiers who have the job of protecting a king or queen and their family. EG *...the Household Cavalry... ...the Port Philip Household Guards.* [N IN NAMES BEFORE N]

householder /hausholdə/, **householders**. A **householder** is a person who is the legal owner or tenant of a house. EG *...a letter addressed to The Householder, 16 Friary Lane.* N COUNT = occupant

housekeeper /hauski:pə/, **housekeepers**. A **housekeeper** is a person whose job is to cook and clean and look after a house for its owner. EG *Some working parents employ a housekeeper... She lived with the family as a kind of unpaid governess and housekeeper.* N COUNT ⇑ servant

housekeeping /hauski:pɪŋ/ is 1 all the work and organization involved in running a home, including cooking and cleaning. EG *Some parts of housekeeping are pleasant... Keep your own private money apart from the housekeeping money.* N UNCOUNT ⇑ management 2 the money which people use to buy food, cleaning materials, and other items that need to be bought regularly for a home. EG *She would go mad and spend all the housekeeping on a new coat or dress.* N UNCOUNT 3 the process of organizing and using the money available for buying general household items. EG *Bad housekeeping has led them into debt.* N UNCOUNT ⇑ managing

house lights are the lights in the part of a theatre or cinema where the audience sits. EG *The house lights came up.* N PLURAL

housemaid /hausmeɪd/, **housemaids**. A **housemaid** is a female servant who cleans and does other work in someone else's house. N COUNT = maid

houseman /hausmə³n/, **housemen**. A **houseman** is a doctor who has a junior post in a hospital; used mainly in British English. EG *She is assisted by housemen, nurses, and consultants.* N COUNT = intern

house martin, house martins. A **house martin** is a small black and white bird with a slightly forked tail, which usually makes its nest under the roof of a building. N COUNT

housemaster /hausmɑ:stə/, **housemasters**. A **housemaster** is a male teacher who is in charge of one of the houses in a school. N COUNT

housemistress /hausmɪstrɪ²s/, **housemistresses**. A **housemistress** is a female teacher who is in charge of one of the houses in a school. N COUNT

housemother /hausmʌðə/, **housemothers**. A **housemother** is a woman who looks after a particular group of children in an institution such as a children's home. N COUNT

House of Commons. The **House of Commons** is the more powerful of the two parts of parliament in Britain or Canada, to which members are elected by the adult population of the country. EG *He made his statement to the House of Commons on April 30... One week later the House of Commons debated the entire business.* N PROPER : *the*+N ≠ House of Lords ▸ used of the building where this part of parliament meets. EG *Look over the road on your left to the House of Commons.* ▸ ⇑ building

house of God, houses of God. A Christian church or chapel is sometimes referred to as a **house of God**. N COUNT : USU SING ⇑ building

House of Lords. The **House of Lords** is the less powerful of the two parts of parliament in Britain, whose members have the right to belong because they come from noble families or hold a special office. EG *...the campaign for the abolition of the House of Lords... ...Archbishops and Bishops, of whom twenty-four sit in the House of Lords.* N PROPER : *the*+N ≠ House of Commons ▸ used to refer to the building where this part of parliament meets. EG *Beyond this, as ante-room to the actual House of Lords, is the Prince's chamber.* ▸ ⇑ building

House of Representatives. The **House of Representatives** is the less powerful of the two parts of Congress in the United States, or the equivalent part of the system of government in some other countries. EG *Last week the House of Representatives approved a $136 billion order.* N PROPER : *the*+N ≠ Senate

house-owner, house-owners; also spelled without a hyphen. A **house-owner** is a person who owns a house. N COUNT ⇑ owner

house-party, house-parties; also spelled without a hyphen. A **house-party** is a party held at a big house in the country, usually at a weekend, where the guests stay for a few days. N COUNT ⇑ party

houseplant /hausplɑ:nt/, **houseplants**; also spelled with a hyphen. A **houseplant** is a plant which grows in a pot indoors. N COUNT

houseproud /hauspraud/. Someone who is **houseproud** spends a lot of time making their house attractive and clean because they are eager for other people to admire it. ADJ QUALIT ⇑ tidy

houseroom /hausru⁴m/. If you say that you **wouldn't give** something **houseroom**, you mean that you do not like it at all and would not want it in your house; an informal expression. PHR : VB INFLECTS

house servant, house servants; also spelled with a hyphen. A **house servant** is a person who works in someone else's house and does their cleaning, cooking, etc. N COUNT

Houses of Parliament. The **Houses of Parliament** are, in Britain, the British parliament which consists of two parts, the House of Commons and the House of Lords. EG *The measure will have to go to the Houses of Parliament.* N PROPER : *the*+N ▸ used to refer to the buildings in London where each part of the British parliament does its work. EG *The road leads to the Houses of Parliament.* ▸ ⇑ buildings ▸ used also to refer to the national parliament in some other countries.

house-to-house. A **house-to-house** activity involves going to all the houses in an area one after another. EG *We've not really got the manpower to do a house-to-house check.* ADJ CLASSIF : ATTRIB = door-to-door

housetop /haustɒp/, **housetops**. A **housetop** is the roof of a house. N COUNT ● If you **shout** or **proclaim** something **from the housetops**, you tell everyone about it in an excited way; a rather literary expression. EG *We must proclaim from the housetops the need for a bold attack.* ● PHR : VB INFLECTS ⇑ publicize

housetrain /haustreɪn/, **housetrains, housetraining, housetrained**; also spelled with a hyphen. If you **housetrain** a pet animal such as a dog or a cat, you teach it to urinate and defecate out of doors or in a special container indoors, rather than on the floor. EG *Housetrain your puppy by saying 'no' in a firm voice.* V+O ⇑ train ◊ **housetrained**. EG *Are the kittens housetrained?* ◊ ADJ CLASSIF

house-warming, house-warmings. A **house-warming** is a party that you give for friends when you have just moved into a new house. EG *When's the house-warming going to be?* N COUNT : USU BEFORE N

housewife /hauswaɪf/, **housewives**. A **housewife** is a married woman who does the cooking, cleaning, and shopping and who does not normally have a full-time paid job outside the home. EG *I was a housewife and mother of two small children.* N COUNT

housework /hauswɜ:k/ is the work that is done in order to look after a home and the people who live there, for example cooking, cleaning, and shopping. EG *The men shared all the housework, including washing and ironing.* N UNCOUNT

housing /hauzɪŋ/, **housings**. 1 **Housing** is 1.1 the buildings and conditions in which people live. EG *...bad housing and poverty in the city... The bungalows were built in 1946 to ease the housing shortage.* N UNCOUNT = accommodation 1.2 the job of providing houses for people to live in. EG *She's very active locally in fields such as education and housing... Carol worked in the housing department of her local authority.* N UNCOUNT = accommodation 2 A **housing** is a case or covering which protects parts of a machine. EG *The engine consists of a housing, power unit, and feedpipes.* N COUNT

housing association, housing associations. A **housing association** is an organization which owns houses and helps its members to rent or buy them more cheaply than usual. EG *Ms West has formed a housing association to build homes for single mothers.* N COUNT

housing development, housing developments. A **housing development** is a housing estate. EG *They live in a housing development for poor families.* N COUNT

housing estate, housing estates. A **housing estate** is a large number of houses or flats built close together at the same time. N COUNT

housing project, housing projects. A **housing project** is the same as a housing estate; used mainly in American English. N COUNT

hove /həuv/ is the past tense and past participle of **heave** in some senses: see **heave**.

hovel /hʌvə⁰l, hɒv-/, **hovels**. 1 A **hovel** is a small hut, especially one which is dirty or needs a lot of repair. EG *They lived in cold and horribly overcrowded hovels, thick with grime.* N COUNT = shack 2 You might refer to a house, room, or flat as a **hovel** if it is dirty, untidy, and in poor condition. EG *I don't know how you can bear to live in this hovel.* N COUNT ⇑ place = dump

hover /hɒvə/, **hovers, hovering, hovered.** 1 To **hover** means to stay in the same position in the air without moving forwards or backwards. Many birds and insects can hover by moving their wings very quickly. EG *...bright little birds that hovered like insects.* — V; ⇑ fly

2 If a person **hovers,** 2.1 they stay in one place and move slightly in a nervous way, for example because they cannot decide what to do. EG *The door opens and a figure hovers uncertainly in the frame... His hand was hovering over the telephone.* — V : USU+A; = linger 2.2 they are in an uncertain or unsettled situation or state of mind. EG *We hovered between the two possibilities... The socialists believe themselves to be hovering on the brink of a major victory.* — V : USU+A; = teeter

hovercraft /hɒvəkrɑːft/, **hovercrafts.** The form **hovercraft** can also be used for the plural. A **hovercraft** is a vehicle that can travel across land and water. It floats above the land or water on a cushion of air. — N COUNT

how /haʊ/. 1 You can use **how** in questions when you are asking about the method or way in which something is done, known, etc. EG *How did you know about this?... 'I knew you were landing today.'–'How?'... 'How are you related?'–'We're cousins.'* — WH : USED AS ADV

2 You can also use **how** at the beginning of a clause 2.1 to link clauses in which you are talking about the method or way in which something is done. EG *This is how I make a vegetable curry... Tell me how to get there... A lot depends on how the Americans handle the situation.* — WH : USED AS CONJ SUBORD; = the way 2.2 to introduce a statement of fact, often something that you remember or expect other people to know about. EG *Do you remember how you and I planned to live in Venice?... It's amazing how he survived to 94... You know how in Lesotho they have those very fine weavers... We are all aware of how an odour or a sound can bring back happy memories.* — WH : USED AS CONJ SUBORD

3 You can also use **how** 3.1 when you are asking about the way that something looks or is expressed, or the way that someone behaves. EG *Do you know how Schumann described Chopin's music?... It's a nice tune. Let me see now, how does it go?... How did they behave towards me? Very politely.* — WH : USED AS ADV 3.2 when you are asking someone to express their opinion on something, for example whether they think it is successful or enjoyable. EG *How do you think things are going?... How do you see the relationship between politics and sport developing?... 'How did school go?'–'It was all right.'... How was Paris?* — WH : USED AS ADV 3.3 when you are asking about or referring to someone's health or feelings, or asking for news about someone. EG *How's your head?... I'm going to see how Davis is... Jane wasn't sure how she felt about being married.* — WH : USED AS ADV

4 You can also use **how** in several expressions in informal spoken English when greeting people that you know. EG *'How are you?'–'Fine, thanks.' How are things?... How's it going?... How's everything?* — WH : USED AS ADV ● **'How do you do?'** is a polite way of greeting someone when you meet them for the first time. EG *I'm Nigel Jessop. How d'you do?* — ● CONVENTION

5 In informal English, you can also use **how** when you want to say that it does not matter which way something is done. EG *It's your garden–do it how you like.* — WH : USED AS ADV; = however

6 You can also use **how** 6.1 to emphasize a following adjective, adverb, or statement, for example in an exclamation in which you are emphasizing the quality or degree of something. EG *How pretty you look!... How terribly wrong you are... How I dislike that man!... He thought how agreeable it was that the house was so quiet... It rained–how it rained!* — WH : USED AS ADV 6.2 to ask or refer to a measurement, a quantity, or the degree of something, for example the size of an object, the distance of a journey, or the age of a person. EG *How old are you?... How far is Amity from here?... I asked how long the reserves of natural gas would last... I had forgotten how much David liked to talk... How many times have you been?* — WH : USED AS ADV ● If you ask **how much** something is, you are asking the price of something that you would like to buy. EG *I like that dress–how much is it?* — ● PHR

7 You can say **'How can** you...', **'How could** you...', 'I don't know **how** you **can** ...', etc to indicate that you disapprove of what someone has done or that you find it hard to believe what they have just said. EG *How could you be so stupid?... 'I'm bored.'–'How can you be bored?'... I don't know how anyone can play the bagpipes.* — PHR

8 In informal English, you can ask **'How come?'** or **'How so?'** when you are surprised by something and are asking why it happened or was said. EG *'I don't like him at all.'–'How come?'... How come you're up so early?... 'He seems to know the area pretty well.'–'Oh? How so?'* — PHR

9 If you say **'How do you mean?'** to someone, you are asking them to explain what they mean by what they have said. EG *'You are quite satisfied with Davis?'–'How do you mean satisfied?'* — PHR

10 If you say **'How about that?'**, **'How's that?'**, etc, you are drawing attention to something that has been said or done that you think is surprising or in some other way remarkable. EG *He called me an old fool. How's that for cheek!... How about this for a haul?... He turned out to be the guy's father. How about that?* — CONVENTION : IF +PREP THEN *for*; = what about that

11 You can say **how about** something, **how would you** like something, etc, or, in very informal English, **how's about** something, when you are making a suggestion or an offer. EG *If there isn't a playgroup locally, how about starting one?... How would you fancy a few months on the continent?... How's about some more drinks for the boys?* — PHR; = what about

12 You can also use **'How about...'** to introduce a new subject which you think might be worth considering because it is relevant to the conversation you have been having. EG *You've talked a bit about cars; how about trains?... How about natural gas? Is that an alternative?* — PHR; = what about

13 If you ask someone **'How about you?'**, you are asking them what they think or want, often after you have already stated your own opinion or choice. EG *I like that one best. How about you?... How about you Dorothy, what do you want?* — CONVENTION

14 If you say **'And how!'** when someone has asked you something, you are saying 'yes' in an emphatic way; used in informal English. EG *'Did you get into trouble?'–'And how!'* — CONVENTION; = you bet

15 **how's that.** 15.1 If you say **'How's that?'** to someone, you are asking whether something is acceptable or satisfactory. EG *I'll go up as high as fifteen pounds. How's that?... How's that for comfort?* — PHR : IF+PREP THEN *for* 15.2 If you say **'How's that?'** after someone has just said something, you are asking them to repeat what they have said; used in informal English. EG *'My name's Sijan.'–'How's that again?'* — CONVENTION; = pardon 15.3 In a game of cricket, a bowler or fielder shouts **'How's that!'** when they think that the batsman is out. — CONVENTION

howdah /haʊdə/, **howdahs.** A **howdah** is a seat that is put on an elephant's back for people to ride on it. — N COUNT

howdy /haʊdi[1]/ is an informal way of saying 'Hello'; used mainly in American English. EG *'Howdy, Jefferson,' he said.* — CONVENTION; ⇑ hello

however /haʊevə/. 1 You can use **however** 1.1 when you are adding a comment which is surprising or which seems to contradict what has just been said. EG *The more I talked, the more silent Eliot became. However, I left thinking that I had created quite an impression... That is one reason why their economic policies are unlikely to restore full employment. It is not, however, the only one... I had hoped that there might be a job for me. However, it was not to be.* — ADV SEN; = nevertheless 1.2 when you are adding a comment which contrasts with something that has just been said. EG *Losing at games doesn't seem to matter to some women. Most men, however, can't stand it at any price... Most people think David is really nice. Not me, however.* — ADV SEN; = though 1.3 before an adjective or adverb to say that it does not matter how big, good, deliberate, etc something is, because nothing will affect the result that you are describing. EG *She could not remember, however hard she tried, the first time they had met... However strong the temptation, don't stay in any job too long.* — WH : USED AS ADV; = no matter how 1.4 when you want to say that it makes no difference how something is done. EG *The important point is that, however the recording is done, the playback is high fidelity... However we add that up, it does not make a dozen... You can do it however you want.* — WH : USED AS CONJ SUBORD

2 If you add **or however many, or however much,** etc to a statement, you are indicating that you do not — PHR

know the exact quantity, size, or degree of something, and that this is not really important; an informal use. EG *...the twelve or eleven people on the jury or however many there are... ...a stick of 10cm, 12cm, or however long it is.*

3 You can also use **however** to ask in an emphatic way how something has happened which you are very surprised about. EG *However did you find me?* WH: USED AS ADV = how

howitzer /haʊɪtsə/, **howitzers**. A **howitzer** is a large gun with a short barrel, which fires shells high up into the air so that they will drop down onto the target. N COUNT

howl /haʊl/, **howls, howling, howled**. 1 If an animal such as a wolf or a dog **howls**, it utters a long, loud, crying sound. EG *The dog howled over his master's body.* ▸ used as a noun. EG *...the howls of the wolves.* ◊ **howling**. EG *He could hear the howling of hyenas.* V ⇑ cry ▸ N COUNT ◊ N UNCOUNT

2 If a person **howls,** they make a long, loud, cry expressing pain, anger, or unhappiness. EG *...howling babies... She heard the child howling at its mother.* ▸ used as a noun. EG *He gave a howl of pain.* ◊ **howling**. EG *...the constant howling of his children.* V ▸ N COUNT ◊ N UNCOUNT

3 When the wind **howls**, it blows hard and makes a loud noise. EG *The wind was howling through the smashed windowpanes.* ◊ **howling**. EG *He lay in bed listening to the howling of the wind.* V = wail ◊ N UNCOUNT

4 If you **howl** something, you say it in a very loud voice; an informal use. EG *'Be silent!' the judge howled.* V+O/REPORT-CL/QUOTE

5 If you **howl** with laughter, you laugh loudly. EG *They rolled around on the floor, clutching their stomachs and howling with laughter.* ▸ used as a noun. EG *...howls of laughter.* V: IF+PREP THEN *with* ▸ N COUNT: USU +*of*

6 See also **howling**.

howl down. If you **howl** someone **down,** you prevent them from speaking or giving their opinion, often by shouting angrily. EG *He was howled down by monarchists.* PHRASAL VB: V+O+ADV = shout down

howler /haʊlə/, **howlers**. A **howler** is 1 in informal English, a stupid mistake. EG *He made such awful howlers that even the teacher laughed.* 2 a person or animal that howls. N COUNT = blunder N COUNT

howling /haʊlɪŋ/. A **howling** success or mistake is an extremely great success or mistake. EG *Her new play was a howling success.* ADJ CLASSIF: ATTRIB = terrific

hp is an abbreviation for 'horsepower'. EG *...a 130 hp tractor.*

HP is an abbreviation for 'hire purchase'. EG *Buy an electric typewriter on HP as soon as you can afford it.*

HQ, HQs. **HQ** is an abbreviation for 'headquarters'. EG *...a journalist at the army HQ near Salisbury.*

hr, hrs are written abbreviations for 'hour' and 'hours'; used especially after a number which indicates the length of time an event takes, or after a time which is based on the 24 hour clock. EG *He won the Cardiff run in 2hrs 26mins 4secs... ...1600 hrs GMT.*

HRH is an abbreviation for 'His Royal Highness' or 'Her Royal Highness'; used as part of the title of a prince or princess. EG *...HRH Prince Charles... I suggested to HRH that we left immediately.*

hub /hʌb/, **hubs**. 1 The **hub** of a wheel is the part which is at the centre around the axle or to which the axle is joined. EG *...the hub of a bicycle wheel.* N COUNT: IF+PREP THEN *of*

2 The **hub** of a place or area is the centre or the most important part of it. EG *Amity would one day be the hub of commerce on Long Island... The village hall was the social hub of the district.* N COUNT+*of* = centre

hubbub /hʌbʌb/. A **hubbub** is 1 a noise made by a lot of people all talking or shouting at the same time. EG *There was an increasing hubbub from the great reception hall below... It was easy to talk on and on amid that hubbub of voices.* 2 great confusion or excitement that is created in a particular situation. EG *He would have been pardoned long ago if it had not been for the hubbub created by the newspapers.* N SING WITH DET = din N SING WITH DET = hullabaloo

hubby /hʌbi[1]/, **hubbies**. A woman can refer to her husband as her **hubby**; used in informal English. EG *I can't wait to get home and tell my hubby about it!* N COUNT: POSS+N

hubcap /hʌbkæp/, **hubcaps**; also spelled as two words. A **hubcap** is a metal disc that covers and protects the hub of a wheel, especially on a car. EG *Remove the hubcap and loosen the nuts with a spanner.* N COUNT ⇑ cap

hubris /hjuːbrɪs/ is arrogant pride; a formal or literary word. N UNCOUNT

huckster /hʌkstə/, **hucksters**. A **huckster** is a person who sells things in the street; an old-fashioned word. EG *...petty traders and hucksters.* N COUNT ⇑ salesman = hawker

huddle /hʌdə[0]l/, **huddles, huddling, huddled**. 1 If you **huddle** somewhere, you sit, stand, or lie there holding your arms and legs close to your body, usually because you are cold or frightened. ◊ **huddled**. EG *By the back door Dolly crouched, huddled and shaking... He imagined Piggy by himself, huddled in a silent shelter.* V+A = crouch, curl up ◊ ADJ CLASSIF = hunch up

2 If people **huddle** together or **huddle** round something, they stand, sit, or lie close to each other, usually because they all feel cold or frightened. EG *After their evening meal, the people huddled around their fires.* ◊ **huddled**. EG *We sat huddled together.* V OR V+A (*with*): RECIP = cluster ◊ ADJ CLASSIF

3 If people **huddle** in a group, they gather together to discuss something quietly or secretly. EG *The leaders huddled to discuss the matter... Ronald Reagan huddled with senior advisers at the White House.* V OR V+A (*with*): RECIP = meet

4 A **huddle** is a small, disorganized group of people or things that are standing very close together or lying on top of each other. EG *They flopped down in a huddle... ...the huddle of grubby, nervous faces.* N COUNT = mass

hue /hjuː/, **hues**. 1 A **hue** is a colour or a particular shade of a colour; a literary use. EG *Mrs Partridge's normally rosy face took on a deeper hue.* N COUNT

2 If people raise a **hue and cry** about something, they are very angry and protest about it. EG *When they discover what has happened there is bound to be a hue and cry.* PHR: USED AS O ⇑ fuss = outcry

huff /hʌf/, **huffs, huffing, huffed**; an informal word. 1 Someone who is **in a huff** is bad-tempered because they are annoyed or offended about something. EG *The people all left in a huff. 'We know when we're not wanted.'* PHR: USED AS AN A

2 If you **huff**, 2.1 you indicate that you are annoyed or offended about something, usually by the way that you say something. EG *'Completely irresponsible,' huffed a palace spokesman.* 2.2 you breathe out loudly and heavily, often onto a smooth surface in order to clean or polish it. EG *He held his glasses in one hand, rubbing them, huffing on them and settling them on his nose.* V OR V+QUOTE = snap V = puff

3 If you **huff and puff**, 3.1 you express your annoyance or dissatisfaction with something. EG *They had been huffing and puffing about the Marshall plan.* 3.2 you breathe loudly with your mouth open because you are tired, for example after running or doing hard work. EG *She was tired. She huffed and puffed in the heat.* PHR: VBS INFLECT PHR: VBS INFLECT = pant

huffy /hʌfi[1]/, **huffier, huffiest**. Someone who is **huffy** is obviously annoyed or offended about something; an informal word. EG *He became huffy and said he'd scrap the whole idea.* ◊ **huffily**. EG *Arthur rose huffily and left.* ADJ QUALIT = piqued ◊ ADV WITH VB = peevishly

hug /hʌg/, **hugs, hugging, hugged**. 1 When you **hug** someone, you put your arms around them and hold them tightly because you like them or are pleased to see them. EG *During our infancy, our parents cuddle and hug us... In an instant we were hugging and kissing.* ▸ used as a noun. EG *He greeted his mother with a hug.* ● See also **bear hug**. V OR V+O: RECIP = embrace ▸ N COUNT = squeeze

2 If you **hug** something, you hold it close to your body with your arms tightly round it. EG *...a basket of provisions which she hugged tight on her lap... He sat still, hugging his knees.* V+O = clutch

3 A vehicle that **hugs** the ground or a stretch of land or water stays very close to it while travelling. EG *Front wheel drive helps smaller cars hug the road... They had gone at high speed, hugging the ground at 60 metres over the mountains... Most of the boats hug the coastal inlets and will not fish further out.* V+O = grip

huge /hjuːdʒ/, **huger, hugest**. Something that is **huge** 1 is extremely large in size. EG *Huge wooden earrings dangled from her ears... The other man towered over him, huge and scowling.* 2 is extremely large in amount or degree. EG *They are pushing up the price and making a huge profit... Huge numbers of these children are leaving school... One more huge effort is needed.* ◊ **hugely**. EG *...a hugely expensive machine... Commercial use has increased hugely in recent years.* 3 exists or happens on a very large scale, and involves a lot of different people or things. EG *A huge industry has been built up... It's a huge subject and a complicated technical one.* ADJ QUALIT = gigantic ADJ QUALIT = enormous ◊ ADV = enormously ADJ QUALIT = vast

huh /hʌ, hə/. You say **'huh'**, in informal English, 1 at the end of a question to indicate that you are asking someone to agree with you or to reply in a particular way; used especially in American English. EG *'You been away, huh?'–'Yes,' I said.* 2 to indicate that you did not hear or understand what someone has just said to you and you want them to say it again. EG *'Let's go.'–'Huh?'–'Let's go,' I repeated.* 3 to indicate to someone that you are surprised by what they have said. EG *'We'll go and ask Parsons.'–'Huh? What can he do?'* 4 to indicate that you are not impressed by what someone has just said. EG *'I ran six miles today.'–'Huh, I do twice that much every weekend.'* = eh; CONVENTION = eh; CONVENTION; = big deal

hula hoop /hu:lə hu:p/, **hula hoops**; also spelled with a hyphen. A **hula hoop** is a large hoop that children play with by putting it around their waist and moving their waist and hips so that the hoop spins quickly around their waist. N COUNT ⇑ toy

hulk /hʌlk/, **hulks**. A **hulk** is 1 the main part of a large ship that has been wrecked or abandoned. EG *You can preserve some hulks by spraying them with chemicals.* 2 a large, heavy person, building, or object. EG *...raw-boned hulks with red hair and freckles... The Abbey is a great cross-shaped, blackish hulk... ...polishing the chrome of the shining hulks in the garage.* N COUNT ⇑ body = wreck; N COUNT

hulking /hʌlkɪŋ/. A **hulking** person or object is extremely large, heavy, or slow-moving. EG *...Henry, the hulking bodyguard... The path is channelled deep between hulking masonry on each side.* ADJ CLASSIF : ATTRIB = massive

hull /hʌl/, **hulls, hulling, hulled**. 1 A **hull** is 1.1 the main part of the body of a boat or tank. EG *Waves crashed on the hull.* 1.2 the stalk and ring of leaves at the base of some soft fruit such as strawberries. N COUNT; N COUNT

2 If you **hull** soft fruit such as strawberries, you remove the hulls from them. V+O

hullabaloo /hʌləbəlu:/, **hullabaloos**. A **hullabaloo** is a lot of noise or fuss, for example made by people who are upset or angry; an informal word. EG *It's too late to make a hullabaloo, now the poor man's dead.* N COUNT : USU SING = commotion

hullo /hə⁹ləʊ/. See **hello**.

hum /hʌm/, **hums, humming, hummed**. 1 To **hum** means to make a low continuous noise. EG *Cars honked and hummed in the road... Air conditioners are costly and tend to hum.* ▸ used as a noun. EG *The only sound she heard was the hum of a machine in the basement... ...the low hum of conversation.* 2 If you **hum**, you sing a tune by making a continuous noise with your lips closed. EG *I began to hum a bit and feel happy... She continued to hum the song over and over.* ● If you **hum and haw**, you express yourself badly and take a long time to say something because you are nervous or not sure what to say. EG *Spear hummed and hawed, trying to express his views.* V = drone; ▸ N COUNT = drone; V OR V+O; ● PHR : VBS INFLECT ⇑ speak

3 A place that is **humming** is very busy and full of activity. EG *...the endless documentation that keeps the community humming... The area is usually humming with shoppers.* ADJ CLASSIF : PRED, IF+PREP THEN *with* = bustling

4 **Hum** is sometimes used to represent the sound people make when they are not sure what to say. EG *'Hum...' He paused and thought a while.* CONVENTION = er

human /hju:mən/, **humans**. 1 **Human** means relating to or concerning people. EG *He had no regard for human life... ...the beauty of the human body... ...the purpose of human existence... This meat is not fit for human consumption.* ADJ CLASSIF : ATTRIB

2 An emotion, weakness, failure, etc that is **human** is typical of people. EG *...faults and weaknesses which are 'only human'... ...cars welded by machines to eliminate human error... There are no limits to human folly.* ADJ CLASSIF

3 A **human** is the same as a human being. EG *Could a computer ever beat a human at chess?* N COUNT

human being, human beings. A **human being** is a man, woman, or child. EG *This is a book on how to get on with your fellow human beings... He is a detestable human being.* N COUNT

humane /hju:meɪn/. 1 A person or group that is **humane** behaves with kindness, thoughtfulness, and sympathy towards other people. EG *Many of us are working for a more humane and civilized society.* ◊ **humaneness**. EG *...the moral necessity for humaneness towards all creatures.* ADJ QUALIT ⇑ considerate; ◊ N UNCOUNT = humanity

2 A **humane** action is one in which you cause as little pain or suffering as possible. EG *...the humane treatment of psychiatric patients.* ◊ **humanely**. EG *Animals must be killed humanely.* ADJ QUALIT ⇑ gentle; ◊ ADV WITH VB ≠ cruelly

3 A **humane** activity such as a type of study is one that is considered to have a civilizing and improving effect on people. EG *The study of literature is the pursuit of humane knowledge and understanding.* ADJ CLASSIF : ATTRIB

humanise /hju:mənaɪz/. See **humanize**.

humanism /hju:mənɪzə⁰m/ is a philosophy that believes in mankind's ability to achieve happiness and fulfilment without the need for religion. EG *...elements from Western Marxism and liberal humanism.* ◊ **humanist, humanists**. EG *...the humanist's belief in man... ...the socialist and humanist transformation of our society.* N UNCOUNT ⇑ philosophy; ◊ N COUNT ⇑ philosopher

humanistic /hju:mənɪstɪk/. A **humanistic** idea, condition, etc relates to humanism. EG *The vacuum left by religion has been filled by a kind of humanistic materialism... ...humanistic values.* ADJ CLASSIF

humanitarian /hju:mænɪtɛərɪən/, **humanitarians**. A **humanitarian** is a person who works for the welfare of mankind in the hope that life will be improved and there will be less suffering and pain. EG *...a humanitarian and pacifist called Godfrey Barber.* ▸ used as an adjective to describe people's ideas, attitudes, or behaviour. EG *They were influenced by the social and humanitarian arguments... ...liberal and humanitarian opinions.* N COUNT = philanthropist; ▸ ADJ CLASSIF : USU ATTRIB = altruistic

humanitarianism /hju:mænɪtɛərɪənɪzə⁰m/ is the concern that humanitarians have for the welfare of mankind. N UNCOUNT

humanity /hju:mænɪti¹/, **humanities**. 1 **Humanity** is 1.1 the same as mankind. EG *...a crime against humanity... ...a triumph for humanity.* 1.2 the condition of being a human being or the recognition that someone is a human being and not just a thing. EG *They degraded them and denied them their humanity.* 1.3 the quality of being kind, thoughtful, and sympathetic towards other people. EG *He has a sense of humour, a warm humanity, and a strong common sense.* N UNCOUNT; N UNCOUNT ⇑ status; N UNCOUNT = humaneness

2 The **humanities** are the subjects of study such as literature, philosophy, and history which are concerned with human beings, their ideas, actions, and relationships, rather than science subjects. EG *Is it in fact a Science rather than a Humanities subject?... She has a background in humanities and modern languages.* N PLURAL = arts

humanize /hju:mənaɪz/, **humanizes, humanizing, humanized**; also spelled **humanise**. 1 If you **humanize** a situation or condition, you improve it by changing it in a way which makes it more suitable and pleasant for people. EG *...the need to humanise the factory environment.* ◊ **humanization** /hju:mənaɪzeɪʃə⁰n/. EG *...promoting work humanisation in a number of key industries.* V+O = better; ◊ N UNCOUNT ⇑ improvement

2 If you **humanize** an animal or a machine, you give it human characteristics or qualities. V+O

humankind /hju:mənkaɪnd/ is the same as mankind. EG *This man was from the dregs of humankind.* N UNCOUNT

humanly /hju:mənli¹/ means relating to human beings. EG *What we are trying to achieve is a more humanly satisfying life for more people.* ● If you do something as much as or as fast as is **humanly possible**, you try very hard to do it as much as or as fast as you can in a particular situation. EG *An investigation will be made as quickly as is humanly possible... People were asked to reply within twenty-four hours whenever this was humanly possible.* ADV; ● PHR : USED AS C

human nature. 1 **Human nature** is the natural qualities and ways of behaviour that are shared by most people. EG *You can't change human nature.* N UNCOUNT

2 If you say that something such as a particular way of behaving is **human nature**, you mean that it is something natural that most people would do. N UNCOUNT

humanoid /hju:mənɔɪd/, **humanoids**. 1 Something that is **humanoid** has characteristics of a human being. EG *The doll has a twist-and-turn waist that makes her more humanoid than before.* ADJ QUALIT

2 A **humanoid** is a robot, or a creature in science fiction, that looks and acts like a human being. EG *...life-like computer-controlled humanoids capable of moving their arms and legs.* N COUNT ≠ human

human race. The **human race** is the same as mankind. EG *The very future of the human race might now be at stake.* N SING : *the*+N

human rights are basic rights which most nations agree that all people should have. EG *It would be a violation of human rights.* N PLURAL

humble /hʌmbəˀl/, **humbler, humblest; humbles, humbling, humbled.** 1 Someone who is **humble** 1.1 feels that they are not important or good enough to criticize other people or to have much attention paid to them by other people. EG *I think he is a very humble person... Jim bore this with humble patience.* ◇ **humbly.** EG *'You know much more about it, Sir, than I do,' said John humbly.* 1.2 is low in their social status or class. EG *...a humble curate in a small country region... ...men and women from very humble backgrounds.* ADJ QUALIT ⇑ modest = unassuming ≠ arrogant; ◇ ADV WITH VB; ADJ QUALIT = lowly

2 You use the word **humble** in a phrase such as **my humble opinion** as a polite way of gently emphasizing what you think. EG *My humble opinion is that an analysis would be very useful.* ◇ **humbly.** EG *They would do well, I humbly suggest, to stop now before it is too late.* ADJ QUALIT ⇑ personal = modest; ◇ ADV WITH VB = respectfully

3 You describe things or people as **humble** when you want to discuss them without making them seem more important than they really are. EG *My humble filing system started with two cardboard boxes... We only want one humble little room out of all those hundreds he's got available.* ADJ QUALIT ⇑ ordinary = insignificant

4 If you **eat humble pie**, you speak or behave in a way which tells people that you admit you were wrong about something. EG *Oh well, I'll have to eat humble pie, I'll have to go and see him.* PHR : VB INFLECTS = climb down

5 If you **humble** someone who is more important or powerful than you, you defeat them easily and humiliate them by doing so. EG *...the team that humbled British football pride.* V+O = crush

6 If you **are humbled**, you realize that you are not as important or valuable as you thought you were. EG *'It's a privilege to have met you.' I felt humbled that he should so express himself.* V+O : USU PASS ⇑ reduced

humbug /hʌmbʌg/, **humbugs.** 1 A **humbug** is a hard, black and white striped sweet that tastes of peppermint. N COUNT

2 **Humbug** is speech, behaviour, or ideas that are obviously dishonest and untrue, but which are intended to deceive you. EG *...parliamentary humbug... She was perfectly aware of the humbug.* N UNCOUNT ⇑ dishonesty = hocus-pocus

3 A **humbug** is also a person who you think is dishonest but who is trying to pretend they are not. EG *I called Lord John a lying humbug.* N COUNT = fraud

humdinger /hʌmdɪŋə/, **humdingers.** If you describe someone or something as a **humdinger**, you mean that they are marvellous; an informal word. EG *...a humdinger of a show.* N COUNT ⇑ marvel

humdrum /hʌmdrʌm/. Something that is **humdrum** is ordinary, dull, or boring with no excitement or interest in it. EG *Most men devote themselves to rather humdrum things: family weekends, holidays at the seaside... ...audiences, seeking diversion from their humdrum lives.* ADJ QUALIT = mundane

humerus /hjuːmərəs/, **humeruses** or **humeri.** Your **humerus** is the bone between your shoulder and your elbow; a technical term. N COUNT

humid /hjuːmɪd/. Places that are **humid** are very damp and usually very hot, so that the air feels wet all the time. EG *...humid jungles... Singapore was dank and humid... The air is so humid that your breath turns to mist in front of you.* ADJ QUALIT = clammy ≠ dry

humidify /hjuːmɪdɪfaɪ/, **humidifies, humidifying, humidified.** To **humidify** somewhere such as a room means to release more water into the air and thus make it more moist. EG *A small room is preferable as a sickroom because you can humidify it more easily.* V+O ⇑ wet

humidity /hjuːmɪdɪtiˡ/. 1 When there is **humidity,** the air or soil is moist. EG *...diseases and weeds, encouraged by heat and humidity.* N UNCOUNT ⇑ moisture = dampness

2 **Humidity** is also the amount of moisture in the air or soil, and how wet it feels. EG *The soil is exposed to sunlight and soil humidity declines.* N UNCOUNT

humiliate /hjuːmɪlieɪt/, **humiliates, humiliating, humiliated.** If you **humiliate** someone, you cause them to lose their pride and make them feel ashamed or stupid. EG *They didn't want to humiliate him... She had humiliated him in front of his friends.* ◇ **humiliated.** EG *I could die. I feel so humiliated.* V+O ⇑ humble = shame, disgrace; ◇ ADJ QUALIT

humiliating /hjuːmɪlieɪtɪŋ/. If something is **humiliating**, it embarrasses you and makes you feel ashamed and stupid. EG *He said it was humiliating for him that his wife should go out to work... ...the humiliating truth.* ◇ **humiliatingly.** EG *...the World Cup, which we lost so humiliatingly.* ADJ QUALIT = shaming; ◇ ADV WITH VB

humiliation /hjuːmɪlieɪʃəˀn/, **humiliations.** 1 **Humiliation** is the feeling of embarrassment caused by having lost your pride and so appearing to be helpless or stupid. EG *...an anger born of frustration and humiliation... ...suffering the humiliation of being screamed at if I made a mistake.* N UNCOUNT = indignity

2 A **humiliation** is an occasion or a situation in which you feel embarrassed and humiliated. EG *Taylor's humiliations had taken place in public.* N COUNT = affront

humility /hjuːmɪlɪtiˡ/ is the quality that someone has of being modest and not too proud, because they know that there are things about them which are not perfect. EG *The girl had the great virtues of humility and kindliness... ...the man who has sufficient humility to acknowledge his own imperfections.* N UNCOUNT = modesty ≠ pride

hummingbird /hʌmɪŋbɜːd/, **hummingbirds.** A **hummingbird** is a very small brightly coloured bird found mainly in America. It has a long thin beak and small powerful wings that make a humming sound as they vibrate. N COUNT ⇑ bird

humor /hjuːmə/. See **humour.**

humorist /hjuːmərɪst/, **humorists.** A **humorist** is a person, for example a writer or an entertainer, who makes jokes and uses humour in their writing or speech. EG *...Thurber, the supreme American humorist.* N COUNT = wit

humorous /hjuːmərəs/. 1 Something that is **humorous** is amusing, especially in a rather witty or clever way. EG *...humorous books... Otto was seeing the humorous side of it at that moment.* ◇ **humorously.** EG *He now frequently used the joke, humorously, against himself.* ADJ QUALIT ⇑ funny ≠ serious; ◇ ADV WITH VB = waggishly

2 Someone who is **humorous** is amusing and witty. EG *The men were humorous and made jokes about it all... ...a humorous child.* ▸ used of people's behaviour. EG *A faint, humorous smile came to her lips.* ◇ **humorously.** EG *'You're not that bad,' she said humorously.* ADJ QUALIT = merry; ◇ ADV WITH VB = jokingly

humour /hjuːmə/, **humours, humouring, humoured;** also spelled **humor** in American English. 1 **Humour** is 1.1 the ability that a person has to see when things are amusing, instead of being serious all the time. EG *All you needed was a keen sense of humour... She herself had no humour at all.* 1.2 the way that a particular person or group of people is amused by certain things but not by others. EG *I don't understand the English sense of humour.* 1.3 a quality in something that makes you laugh, for example in a situation, in someone's words or actions, or in a book or film. EG *She could appreciate the humour of the remark... In the radio play the humour of the original seems to have gone altogether.* N UNCOUNT ⇑ fun; N UNCOUNT ⇑ comedy; N UNCOUNT ⇑ amusement = comedy

2 Your **humour** is your mood and the way you feel about things at a particular time, for example how happy or unhappy you are. EG *I am in a bad humour... The work was proceeding with efficiency and good humour.* N UNCOUNT : MOD +N = temper

3 If you **humour** someone who is usually unreasonable or easily upset, you are very kind or nice to them, so that they will stay in a good mood. EG *He had bought it to humour Julie... Maybe if I humor him he'll go away.* V+O ⇑ indulge = play up to

humourless /hjuːməlɪˀs/. Someone who is **humourless** is very serious about everything and does not find things amusing even when other people do. EG *Always avoid the person who is cross, humourless, or full of theories.* ADJ CLASSIF = solemn

hump /hʌmp/, **humps, humping, humped.** 1 A **hump** is 1.1 a small hill or raised piece of ground. EG *...the humps and hollows of the old golf course.* 1.2 a large lump on the back of an animal such as a camel, which is used for storing fat and water. 1.3 a large lump on a person's back, usually caused by illness or old age. EG *Her hump was probably due to an injury that occurred when she was young.* N COUNT; N COUNT; N COUNT ⇑ deformity = hunchback

2 If you **hump** something, in informal English, 2.1 you carry something heavy from one place to another with great difficulty. EG *You will probably have to hump your own luggage, or push it on a trolley.* 2.2 you lift something very heavy, especially onto your back. EG *I tried to hump my bulging sack on to my shoulder.* V+O = lug; V+O : IF+PREP THEN *onto* = hoist

humpback /hʌmpbæk/, **humpbacks**. 1 A **humpback** is the same as a hunchback; an offensive word. N COUNT

2 A **humpback** bridge is the same as a humpbacked bridge. ADJ CLASSIF : ATTRIB

humpbacked /hʌmpbækt/; also spelled with a hyphen. 1 A **humpbacked** animal has a hump on its back. EG *They told us about the strange humpbacked animals they had seen on their travels.* ADJ CLASSIF : ATTRIB ⇑ humped

2 A **humpbacked** bridge is a small bridge which curves very steeply upwards. ADJ CLASSIF : ATTRIB

hunch /hʌntʃ/, **hunches, hunching, hunched**. 1 A **hunch** is an idea that you have which is accompanied by a strong feeling that it is correct or true, although you have not really thought about it carefully or got any proof for it; an informal use. EG *Morris had a hunch that she was a good cook... Watson frequently acted on a hunch.* N COUNT ⇑ guess = intuition

2 If you **hunch** or **hunch** down, you raise your shoulders, bring your head down, and lean forwards, usually because you are cold, ill, or unhappy. EG *She hunched down in her seat... I was cold as I hunched over my meagre fire.* V : USU+A = huddle, crouch

3 When you **hunch** your shoulders, you raise them and lean forwards slightly. EG *He hunched his shoulders and bent lower over his work.* V-ERG : USU+A = bend

hunchback /hʌntʃbæk/, **hunchbacks**. A **hunchback** is is an offensive word for a person who has a large lump on their back, either one which has always been there or one which has grown because of illness or old age. N COUNT ⇑ cripple

hunched /hʌntʃt/. If you are **hunched**, you are leaning forwards with your shoulders raised and your head down, usually because you are cold, ill, or unhappy. EG *His hunched posture looked painful... His eyes fell on Laing, hunched in a corner... He sat with his shoulders hunched up and his chin sunk into his neck.* ADJ CLASSIF ⇑ bent = stooped

hundred /hʌndrəd/, **hundreds**. 1 A **hundred** or one **hundred** is the number 100: see ☐ at NUMBER, AGE, MEASUREMENT, and MONEY. EG *There are more than two hundred languages spoken in Nigeria.* ▸ **Hundreds** is often used to mean a very large number. EG *He handed me hundreds of forms.* NUM : USU *a/NUM +hundred* ▸ NUM IN PL : USED AS N PART

2 You can use **a hundred per cent** or **one hundred per cent** to emphasize that you agree completely with something or that you think something is completely right or completely wrong; an informal expression. EG *I agree one hundred per cent with Carol... Your assessment of Otto is a hundred per cent wrong.* PHR : USED AS AN A

hundredth /hʌndrədθ/, **hundredths**. 1 The **hundredth** item in a series is the one that you count as number one hundred: see ☐ at NUMBER and AGE. EG *...the hundredth anniversary of tennis championships at Wimbledon... I had been wondering, for the hundredth time, whether Andy knew.* ORDINAL

2 A **hundredth** is one of a hundred equal parts of something. EG *...one hundredth of a second... These simple organisms are no more than one or two hundredths of a millimetre across.* N COUNT : USU+ *of* ⇑ fraction

hundredweight /hʌndrədweɪt/, **hundredweights**. **Hundredweight** is used as the plural form if it is preceded by a number or expression referring to a number. A **hundredweight** is a unit of weight that is equal to 112 pounds in Britain and to 100 pounds in the United States: see **pound**. EG *The tenor bell in St Paul's Cathedral weighs sixty-two hundredweight... ...half a hundredweight.* N COUNT/PART : USU NUM+N ⇑ weight

hung /hʌŋ/ is the past tense and past participle for some of the senses of **hang**: see **hang**.

Hungarian /hʌŋgɛərɪən/, **Hungarians**. 1 Something that is **Hungarian** belongs or relates to Hungary, or to its people or language. EG *She had acted as interpreter to a group of Hungarian judges.* ADJ CLASSIF

2 A **Hungarian** is a person who comes from Hungary. EG *She's met an awfully nice young Hungarian.* N COUNT

3 **Hungarian** is the language that is spoken by people who live in Hungary. EG *He spoke in his native Hungarian.* N UNCOUNT

hunger /hʌŋgə/, **hungers, hungering, hungered**. 1 **Hunger** is 1.1 the feeling of pain, weakness, or discomfort that you get when you need something to eat. EG *Babies show their hunger by waking up to be fed... His stomach started to growl with hunger.* N UNCOUNT ⇑ want

1.2 a lack of food which causes suffering or death. EG *There were families dying of hunger and disease.* N UNCOUNT = starvation

2 If you have a **hunger** for something, you want or need it very much; a rather formal or literary use. EG *What gives people the hunger for power?* N SING : IF+PREP THEN *for* = craving

3 If you **hunger** for something or **hunger** after something, you want it very much, often because it has been unavailable for some time EG *...a meeting place for Spaniards who hunger for Flamenco music.* V+A *(for/after)* = hanker

hung over; also spelled with a hyphen and as one word. Someone who is **hung over** has a headache and feels sick because they drank too much alcohol on the previous day; used in informal English. EG *We're all really hung over this morning.* ADJ QUALIT ⇑ unwell

hungry /hʌŋgri/, **hungrier, hungriest**. 1 When you are **hungry**, you want to eat because you have not eaten for some time and have an uncomfortable or painful feeling in your stomach. EG *I'm tired and hungry and I want some supper... ...a hungry baby.* ADJ QUALIT ≠ full
◊ **hungrily**. EG *I ate hungrily... They sat down hungrily to eat.* ◊ ADV WITH VB = greedily

2 If people **go hungry**, they suffer from hunger, either for a long period because they are poor or for a short period because they miss a meal. EG *...sad reports of children going hungry.* PHR : VB INFLECTS = starve

3 If something is **hungry work**, it makes the person who is doing it feel hungry. EG *Digging up the road is hungry work.* PHR : USED AS C

4 If you are **hungry** for something, you want to have it very much; a rather formal or literary use. EG *They were hungry for news.* ◊ **hungrily**. EG *The journalists fell hungrily on the story.* ADJ QUALIT : IF+ PREP THEN *for* ◊ ADV WITH VB = avidly

hung up. Someone who is **hung up** finds it difficult to deal with certain situations and ideas and so becomes nervous or worried about them; used in informal English showing disapproval. EG *I think you're just a little hung up, George... You're hung up about your father.* ADJ QUALIT ⇑ troubled = uptight

hunk /hʌŋk/, **hunks**. 1 A **hunk** of something is a large piece of it. EG *...a hunk of brown bread and some cheese.* N PART+N UNCOUNT = chunk

2 If you refer to a man as a **hunk**, you mean that he is big and strong and that people find him sexually attractive; a very informal use. EG *...a great big handsome hunk.* N COUNT = he-man

hunt /hʌnt/, **hunts, hunting, hunted**. 1 When people or animals **hunt**, they chase wild animals in order to kill them, either for food or as a form of sport. EG *Hyenas usually hunt at night... The men had gone to the forest to hunt wild game... ...communities who live by hunting... ...a hunted animal.* ▸ used as a noun. EG *At last they sight a zebra and the hunt begins... ...a tiger hunt.* V OR V+O ▸ N COUNT

2 In Britain, when people **hunt**, they chase and kill foxes as a form of sport, riding on horseback and using dogs called hounds. EG *They hunt every weekend.* V OR V+O : USU V

3 In Britain, a **hunt** is a group of people who meet together regularly in order to hunt foxes. EG *...a member of the local hunt.* N COUNT

4 If you **hunt** a criminal or an enemy or **hunt** them **down**, you search for them, with the intention of catching or defeating them. EG *The customs department devotes a lot of its time to hunting drug smugglers... Both the submarines were being hunted, and one of them was soon sunk.* V+O, OR PHRASAL VB : V+ O+ADV ⇑ pursue = track

5 If you **hunt** for something, you try to find it by searching carefully or thoroughly. EG *She began hunting frantically in the back of the car, but couldn't find the keys... She hunted for the right word... Their sharp eyes hunted for any signs of his mission or profession.* ▸ used as a noun. EG *...the hunt for new sources of energy... ...the hunt for the missing child.* V : USU+*for* ⇑ look for = search ▸ N COUNT : USU SING+*for* = search

hunt out. If you **hunt out** or **hunt up** something, you search for it and eventually find it, especially when it is hidden or difficult to find. EG *I'll try and hunt out the information you need... I trusted he wasn't likely to hunt up that particular page again.* PHRASAL VB : V+ O+ADV = ferret out

hunter /hʌntə/, **hunters**. A **hunter** is 1 a person or animal that hunts wild animals for food or as a sport. EG *...a big game hunter... The tiger is a very efficient hunter.* 2 someone who searches carefully or thoroughly for a particular thing. EG *...bargain hunters... ...before they are discovered by fossil hunters.* 3 a type of fast, strong horse that is used by people in Britain who hunt foxes. N COUNT ⇑ pursuer; N COUNT : AFTER N; N COUNT

hunting /hʌntɪŋ/ is 1 the chasing of wild animals by people or other animals, as a sport or for food. EG *They had gone hunting. ...hunting dogs... ...a hunting* N UNCOUNT

expedition. **2** in Britain, the sport of hunting foxes while riding on horseback and using dogs. EG *...her prowess in the hunting field.* **3** the activity of searching for a particular thing; an informal use. EG *...job hunting... ...house hunting.*
N UNCOUNT
N UNCOUNT + SUPP = seeking

hunting ground, hunting grounds. A **hunting ground** is a place where people who have a particular interest or hobby are likely to find something that they are looking for or something that will interest them. EG *This street has always been a happy hunting ground for antique collectors.*
N COUNT : IF + PREP THEN *for*

huntsman /hʌntsmən/, **huntsmen.** A **huntsman** is a person who hunts wild animals, especially one who hunts foxes using dogs.
N COUNT ⇑ hunter

hurdle /hɜːdəl/, **hurdles, hurdling, hurdled.** **1** A **hurdle** is a frame or fence that you have to jump over in some races. EG *The recreation ground had a proper cinder track, hurdles, and finishing tape.*
N COUNT ⇑ obstacle

2 Hurdles is a race in which you have to jump over a number of hurdles. EG *He was top man in one event, the 400 metre hurdles.*
N PLURAL

3 If you **hurdle** something, you jump over it while you are running. EG *They sit on these logs and small boys hurdle them.*
V+O

4 A **hurdle** is also a problem or difficulty that you have to overcome in order to be able to do something. EG *In a sense, that's the main hurdle... ...the hurdles presented by my new environment.*
N COUNT = obstacle

hurl /hɜːl/, **hurls, hurling, hurled.** **1** If you **hurl** something, you throw it violently and with a lot of force. EG *I went to his desk, took all his books, and hurled them out of the window.*
V+O : USU+A = fling

2 If you **hurl** abuse or insults at someone, you shout insults at them in a violent or aggressive way. EG *Abuse was hurled at the police.*
V+O : USU+A

hurly-burly /hɜːli bɜːli/. The **hurly-burly** of a place is the noise and activity created by the people and things that are there. EG *...the hurly-burly of excited children... He found all the noise and hurly-burly tiresome.*
N SING : *the*+N, IF + PREP THEN *of* = commotion

hurray /hərei/ and **hurrah** mean the same as hooray.
CONVENTION

hurricane /hʌrɪkən, -keɪn/, **hurricanes.** A **hurricane** is **1** an extremely violent wind or storm, especially one in the western Atlantic. EG *The island is in the path of the hurricanes in the Caribbean.* **2** a violent situation or event. EG *...a political hurricane which roamed for a year... ...the hurricane force of revolution.*
N COUNT = cyclone
N COUNT = storm

hurricane lamp, hurricane lamps. A **hurricane lamp** is a paraffin lamp in which the flame is specially protected by glass. EG *A few people ran about swinging hurricane lamps.*
N COUNT = storm lantern

hurried /hʌrɪd/. **1** Something that is **hurried** is **1.1** too quick; used especially of something that you would do more slowly if you had the time. EG *...an inadequate and hurried lunch... ...a hurried glance.* ◊ **hurriedly.** EG *We ate hurriedly... He kissed his wife hurriedly and rushed out of the door.* **1.2** sudden and perhaps unexpected; used especially of an action caused by something which has just happened. EG *He observed their hurried departure from the scene of the accident.* ◊ **hurriedly.** EG *He turned the light out hurriedly... He left very hurriedly as soon as I entered.*
ADJ QUALIT = hasty ≠ leisurely
◊ ADV WITH VB
ADJ QUALIT ⇑ quick = hasty
◊ ADV WITH VB

2 Someone who is **hurried** does things more quickly than they should because they do not have much time to do them. EG *He never seemed hurried or excited.*
ADJ QUALIT : PRED = rushed

hurry /hʌri/, **hurries, hurrying, hurried.** **1** If you **hurry** somewhere, you go there as quickly as you can. EG *He hurried off down the street... The people hurried home.*
V : USU+A ⇑ move = rush

2 If you **hurry** to do something, you do it more quickly than you would normally or than you have been doing. EG *We'll have to hurry... They hurried to finish the work.*
V : IF + VB THEN *to*-INF ⇑ hasten = rush

3 If you **hurry** something or **hurry it up**, you make it happen faster or sooner than it would have done. EG *If you want the ice in a fridge to melt more quickly, you can hurry it up by leaving the door open... He did not want to lose any of the day by hurrying its end.*
V+O, OR PHRASAL VB : V+O+ADV ⇑ quicken = speed

4 Hurry means doing something quickly or needing to do it quickly. EG *Otto had to leave in a great hurry... In the middle of all this hurry to turn the key, he dropped the bag.*
N UNCOUNT, OR N SING WITH DET = rush

5 The word **hurry** is also used in the following expressions. **5.1** If you say to someone **'There's no hurry'** or **'No great hurry'**, you are telling them that there is no need to do something immediately. EG *'There's no hurry,' says Flora, 'you've got until nine o'clock.'* **5.2** If you ask **'What's the hurry?'**, you want to know why you or other people need to do something quickly, because you think you have plenty of time. EG *'Drink up, Sarah!'–'What's the hurry?'* **5.3** If you are **in no hurry** or **not in any hurry**, you are able to wait before you do something or you can do it slowly because you have plenty of time. EG *Take your time–I'm in no hurry.* **5.4** If you are **in no hurry** to do something, you are very unwilling to do it. EG *He was in no hurry to confront Abraham Chase.*
CONVENTION
CONVENTION
PHR : USED AS AN A
PHR : USED AS AN A = reluctant

hurry on. If you **hurry on** to say something, you quickly continue speaking and do not allow anyone else to stop you. EG *Having admitted this, Robertson hurried on to say that it was not intentional.*
PHRASAL VB : V+ADV, USU + *to*+-INF

hurry up. **1** If you tell someone to **hurry up** or if you **hurry** them **up**, you make them do something more quickly than they were doing. EG *Hurry up, Bill... Try to hurry them up a bit.*
PHRASAL VB : V+ADV, OR V+O+ADV, USU IMPER

2 See also paragraph **3** of **hurry**.

hurt /hɜːt/, **hurts, hurting.** The form **hurt** is used in the present tense and is also the past tense and past participle of the verb. **1** When something **hurts** or when you **hurt** it, you feel pain because you have been injured. EG *My leg was beginning to hurt... How did you hurt your finger?... Did you hurt yourself?*
V-ERG

2 If you **hurt** someone, **2.1** you cause them to feel pain. EG *Did I hurt you?... Stop it! You're hurting!* **2.2** you cause them to feel emotional pain or unhappiness, often by being unkind to them. EG *I've never deliberately hurt anyone... He didn't want to hurt her feelings... She was easily hurt by an unkindness.*
V+O
V OR V+O = upset

3 If you are **hurt**, **3.1** you have been injured. EG *Margaret, are you hurt?... The soldier was obviously badly hurt.* **3.2** you are emotionally upset because of something that someone has said or done. EG *His mother was deeply hurt... ...a tone of hurt surprise.*
ADJ QUALIT
ADJ QUALIT = offended

4 Hurt is the damage to a person's feelings which is caused when they think that they have been treated badly or judged unfairly. EG *...feelings of anger and hurt... ...a glare of uncomprehending hurt... ...an accumulation of resentment and old hurts.*
N UNCOUNT/COUNT = injury

5 If something **hurts** someone or something else, it has a bad effect on them or prevents them from succeeding. EG *High interest rates hurt most of the governments of poor countries... The baseball strike is hurting Pete Rose's chances of ever beating Ty Cobb's record.*
V+O ⇑ affect = damage

6 If you say **'It won't hurt** you to do something' or **'It never hurts** to do something', etc, you are recommending something which you think is worth doing or is helpful or useful; used in informal English. EG *I don't think it hurts anybody to get up early... Just a little drink won't hurt... It wouldn't hurt most politicians if they tried using their brains.*
PHR + *to*-INF, OR PHR + NG + *to*-INF

hurtful /hɜːtful/. Something that is **hurtful** is unkind and causes you to feel unhappy and upset; used especially of things that are said or written about you. EG *Some of the things they say are hurtful... She had a sharp and a hurtful tongue.*
ADJ QUALIT ⇑ upsetting = cutting

hurtle /hɜːtəl/, **hurtles, hurtling, hurtled.** To **hurtle** means to move or travel very fast, especially in a way that seems dangerous or violent. EG *He didn't like hurtling along rough dirt roads in trucks at fifty miles an hour... He watched the airplane as it hurtled down the runway.*
V : USU+A = thunder

husband /hʌzbənd/, **husbands, husbanding, husbanded.** **1** A **husband** is the man that a woman is married to. EG *She wrote a letter to her husband... ...the relationship between husband and wife.*
N COUNT : USU POSS+N ⇑ spouse

2 If you **husband** something that you value, you use it very carefully and do not waste it, often because you do not have a lot of it. EG *The US were all the time concerned to husband their limited number of launchers... ...husbanding the nation's fuel resources.*
V+O ⇑ manage = conserve

husbandry /hʌzbəndri/ is farming, especially when it is done carefully and well. EG *...animal husbandry... Good husbandry keeps pests and diseases in check.*
N UNCOUNT

hush /hʌʃ/, **hushes, hushing, hushed.** **1** If you say **'Hush!'** to someone or you tell them to **hush**, you ask them to be quiet. EG *Hush, you'll wake the children!... 'Hush!' she insisted, and Marcella hushed.*
EXCLAM OR V = shush

2 If there is **hush** or a **hush** in a place it is quiet, still,
N UNCOUNT, OR N

and peaceful; used especially when there has previously been a lot of noise or excitement. You often use the word **hush** when people are suddenly quiet because they are waiting eagerly for something to happen. EG *An expectant hush fell on the gathering... The square offers immediate hush after the Knightsbridge traffic.* — SING WITH DET = stillness ≠ noise

hush up. If someone **hushes** something **up**, they manage to keep secret something that would normally become known to the public; used showing disapproval. EG *The police had hushed the matter up.* — PHRASAL VB : V+O+ADV ⇑ suppress = cover up

hushed /hʌʃt/. Somewhere that is **hushed** is much quieter and calmer than usual with almost no noise at all, giving a feeling of peace and stillness, or the feeling that people are waiting eagerly for something to happen. EG *The house was hushed... In the hotel lobby, people were talking in hushed tones.* — ADJ QUALIT ⇑ quiet = subdued

hush-hush. In informal English, something that is **hush-hush** is secret and not to be discussed with other people; used especially of official work or plans. EG *'We work in the same office.'-'One of those hush-hush jobs, isn't it?'* — ADJ QUALIT = confidential

hush money is money that is given to someone to persuade them to keep secret something that they know. — N UNCOUNT = bribe

husk /hʌsk/, **husks, husking, husked**. 1 A **husk** is the outer covering of grains or seeds. EG *While the grains were being pounded, the girls brushed away the husks and chaff.* — N COUNT ⇑ outside = shell

2 When you **husk** grains or seeds, you remove their husks. EG *He would roll the grains between his heavy palms to husk them.* — V+O = shell

husky /hʌski¹/, **huskier, huskiest**. 1 If someone's voice is **husky**, it sounds rough or hoarse, often because they are upset. EG *She had a curiously husky voice.* ◊ **huskily**. EG *'To my son Rudolph, on his birthday,' he said huskily.* — ADJ QUALIT = throaty; ◊ ADV WITH VB = hoarsely

2 A **husky** is a strong, furry dog, teams of which are used to pull sledges across snow. — N COUNT

3 If you describe a man as **husky**, you mean that he is tall, strong, and attractive; an informal use. — ADJ QUALIT ⇑ manly

hussy /hʌsi¹, hʌzi¹/, **hussies**. If you refer to a girl or woman as a **hussy**, you think that her behaviour is shocking or immoral, especially in a sexual way; an old-fashioned word, often used offensively. — N COUNT : USU MOD+N, ALSO VOC

hustings /hʌstɪŋz/. The **hustings** refer to the political activities such as speeches that take place in the period just before an election; a rather formal word. EG *...her presence at the hustings in December... I heard nothing about it anywhere on the hustings.* — N PLURAL

hustle /hʌsə⁰l/, **hustles, hustling, hustled**; an informal word. 1 If you **hustle** someone, you make them move quickly, often by bumping them and pulling or pushing them along. EG *Anyone who protested would be hustled out by a couple of cops... He hustled Fanny through the door.* — V+O : USU+A ⇑ propel = bundle

2 **Hustle** is a situation or feeling of excitement, activity, or confusion. EG *I loved the hustle and the feeling that you were among friends... ...the hustle and bustle of Marseilles.* — N UNCOUNT ⇑ liveliness = bustle

hustler /hʌslə/, **hustlers**. A **hustler** is a person who tries to earn money or gain an advantage from any situation they are in, often by using dishonest or illegal methods; used mainly in informal American English. EG *...a haunt of pimps and bookies and hustlers and dope peddlers.* — N COUNT

hut /hʌt/, **huts**. A **hut** is 1 a small house with only one or two rooms which is usually made of wood, mud, or grass. EG *The village consists of several small, mud-walled huts... He walked towards her hut with the baby in his arms.* 2 a small shed or shelter in someone's garden, or often a temporary one used, for example, by building or repair workers. — N COUNT ⇑ building; N COUNT

hutch /hʌtʃ/, **hutches**. A **hutch** is a cage that rabbits or other small pet animals are kept in. It is usually made of wood. — N COUNT

hyacinth /haɪəsɪnθ/, **hyacinths**. A **hyacinth** is a plant with a lot of small, sweet-smelling flowers growing closely around a single stem. It grows from a bulb and the flowers are usually blue, pink, or white. — N COUNT

hyaena /haɪiːnə/, **hyaenas**. See **hyena**.

hybrid /haɪbrɪd/, **hybrids**. 1 A **hybrid** is an animal or plant that has been bred from two different types of animal or plant; a technical term. EG *The new variety is a hybrid between a dessert apple and a small crab apple.* ▸ used as an adjective. EG *...a hybrid rice.* — N COUNT = cross; ▸ ADJ CLASSIF : ATTRIB

2 You can use **hybrid** to refer to anything that is a mixture of other things, especially two other things; a formal or literary use. EG *He looks uncannily like a hybrid of Tintin and Harry S. Truman.* ▸ used as an adjective. EG *...hybrid systems... ...a hybrid electric car.* — N COUNT = combination, composite; ▸ ADJ CLASSIF

hydrant /haɪdrənt/, **hydrants**. A **hydrant** is a pipe that is connected to the main water system of a town or city and from which water can be obtained, often one that is used only in emergencies, for example by the fire brigade. EG *...a cold-water hydrant at the end of the corridor.* — N COUNT

hydrate /haɪdreɪt/, **hydrates**. A **hydrate** is a chemical that contains water; a technical term used especially as the second part of the name of chemical compounds. EG *...chloral hydrate.* — N COUNT

hydraulic /haɪdrɒlɪk/, **hydraulics**. 1 Something that is **hydraulic** involves or is operated by water, oil, or another fluid that is under pressure. EG *...a leakage in the hydraulic system... ...hydraulic excavators and steam engines.* — ADJ CLASSIF

2 **Hydraulics** is the study and use of systems that work using hydraulic pressure. — N UNCOUNT

hydrocarbon /haɪdrəʊkɑːbə⁰n/, **hydrocarbons**. A **hydrocarbon** is a chemical compound that is a mixture of hydrogen and carbon. — N COUNT

hydro-electric /haɪdrəʊ ɪ¹lektrɪk/; also spelled without a hyphen. **Hydro-electric** means relating to or involving electricity made from the energy of running water such as rivers or waterfalls. EG *...hydro-electric power... ...the hydro-electric project a few miles from the city.* — ADJ CLASSIF : ATTRIB ⇑ electric

hydro-electricity /haɪdrəʊ ɪ¹lektrɪsɪti¹/ is electricity made from the energy of running water. — N UNCOUNT

hydrofoil /haɪdrəfɔɪl/, **hydrofoils**. A **hydrofoil** is a boat which can travel above the surface of the water by resting on a pair of special fins; used also to refer to the fins themselves. — N COUNT

hydrogen /haɪdrədʒə²n/ is the lightest gas and the simplest chemical element in nature. It is colourless, burns easily, and combines with oxygen to form water. EG *We could produce hydrogen from water... They use liquid hydrogen now to drive some rockets.* — N UNCOUNT

hydrogen bomb, hydrogen bombs. A **hydrogen bomb** is a bomb in which energy is released from hydrogen atoms. EG *They had just exploded a powerful hydrogen bomb.* — N COUNT

hydrogen peroxide is a chemical often used as a bleach for hair and as an antiseptic. — N UNCOUNT

hydrophobia /haɪdrəfəʊbɪə/ is the same as rabies; a formal or technical term. — N UNCOUNT

hydroplane /haɪdrəʊpleɪn/, **hydroplanes, hydroplaning, hydroplaned**. 1 A **hydroplane** is a speedboat which rises out of the water when it is travelling fast. — N COUNT

2 When a boat **hydroplanes**, its speed causes it to rise out of the water. — V

hydroponics /haɪdrəʊpɒnɪks/ is a method of growing plants in water rather than in soil. — N UNCOUNT ⇑ cultivation

hydrotherapy /haɪdrəʊθerəpi¹/ is a method of treating people with some diseases or injuries by making them swim or do exercises in water. — N UNCOUNT ⇑ treatment

hyena /haɪiːnə/, **hyenas**; also spelled **hyaena**. A **hyena** is an African animal that looks like a wolf and often hunts in groups. It utters a sound which is similar to a human laugh. EG *...the howling of the hyenas.* — N COUNT

hygiene /haɪdʒiːn/ is the practice of keeping yourself and your surroundings clean, especially in order to prevent illness or the spread of diseases. EG *They don't have the same standard of hygiene as we have... ...personal hygiene.* — N UNCOUNT ⇑ cleanliness

hygienic /haɪdʒiːnɪk/. Something that is **hygienic** is clean and unlikely to cause illness. EG *It's more hygienic to use disposable paper tissues... Slums have been cleared to make way for new, hygienic high-rise apartments.* — ADJ QUALIT

hymen /haɪmen/, **hymens**. A **hymen** is a piece of skin that often covers part of a girl's or woman's vagina and breaks before puberty or sometimes when she has sex for the first time; a technical term. — N COUNT

hymn /hɪm/, **hymns**. A **hymn** is a song that Christians sing in order to praise God or the saints. EG *...singing a hymn or a psalm... ...the pile of hymn books.* — N COUNT

hymnal /hɪmnə⁰l/, **hymnals**. A **hymnal** is a book of hymns; a formal word. N COUNT

hyper- is added to adjectives in order to form other adjectives that describe people or their behaviour as having too much of the particular quality mentioned. EG *...cautious→hyper-cautious... ...critical→hypercritical.* PREFIX

hyperactive /haɪpəræktɪv/. Someone who is **hyperactive** is unable to relax, and is always in a state of great agitation or activity. EG *The child was more active than I expected, almost hyperactive.* ADJ CLASSIF ⇑ lively

hyperbola /haɪpɜːbələ/, **hyperbolas**. A **hyperbola** is a smooth curve that gets steeper or flatter at a constant rate; a technical term in mathematics. N COUNT

hyperbole /haɪpɜːbəli¹/ is a style of speech and writing which uses exaggeration in order to achieve a particular effect. An example of hyperbole is 'I've told you a million times not to use that word!' because the actual number of times is usually much less than a million. N UNCOUNT

hypermarket /haɪpəmɑːkɪt/, **hypermarkets**. A **hypermarket** is an extremely large supermarket where you can buy a very wide range of products. N COUNT ⇑ store

hypersensitive /haɪpəsensɪtɪv/. Someone who is **hypersensitive** is 1 extremely sensitive to certain drugs, chemicals, changes in temperature, etc. ADJ CLASSIF 2 very easily annoyed or offended; used showing disapproval. EG *He was hypersensitive on this issue.* ADJ CLASSIF ⇑ sensitive = touchy

hypertension /haɪpətenʃə⁰n/ is a medical condition in which a person has very high blood pressure. EG *...overwork and hypertension.* N UNCOUNT

hyphen /haɪfə⁰n/, **hyphens**. A **hyphen** is a sign used to join words together to make a compound, or to indicate that the first part of a word has been written at the end of one line and the second part of it at the start of the next line. The word 'left-handed' has a hyphen in the middle of it. N COUNT = dash

hyphenated /haɪfə²naɪtɪ²d/. A word that is **hyphenated** is written with a hyphen between two or more of its parts. EG *The surname Gregor-Smith is hyphenated.* ADJ CLASSIF

hypnosis /hɪpnəʊsɪs/ is a state of unconsciousness in which a person seems to be asleep but can see or hear some things or can respond to things said by the person who put them into this state. EG *He has a method of hypnotizing pregnant women and delivering babies under hypnosis.* N UNCOUNT

hypnotic /hɪpnɒtɪk/. Something that is **hypnotic** has the effect of making a person feel as if they are hypnotized. EG *The effect of the rhythmic music can be hypnotic... Laing was a tall man with a silvery, hypnotic voice... Haldane was holding the Foreign Secretary under a hypnotic influence.* ADJ QUALIT = mesmerizing

hypnotise /hɪpnətaɪz/. See **hypnotize**.

hypnotism /hɪpnətɪzə⁰m/ is the practice of hypnotizing people or the skill and techniques involved. EG *...a book of hypnotism.* N UNCOUNT ◇ **hypnotist, hypnotists**. EG *Some hypnotists can help smokers to stop smoking.* ◇ N COUNT

hypnotize /hɪpnətaɪz/, **hypnotizes, hypnotizing, hypnotized**; also spelled **hypnotise**. To **hypnotize** someone means 1 to put them into a state of unconsciousness in which they seem to be asleep but can see or hear some things or respond to things said to them. EG *While in a trance a hypnotized person can be instructed to carry out some bizarre actions.* V+O ⇑ influence 2 to fascinate them so much that they cannot think of anything else or look at anything else. EG *The child was hypnotized by the machine... ...gazing at the sight, completely hypnotized.* V+O ⇑ interest = mesmerize

hypochondria /haɪpəkɒndrɪə/ is a state in which you continually worry about your health, usually when there is really nothing wrong with you. N UNCOUNT ⇑ obsession

hypochondriac /haɪpəkɒndrɪæk/, **hypochondriacs**. A **hypochondriac** is a person who continually worries about their health, usually when there is really nothing wrong with them. EG *They were so pampered that they had turned into hypochondriacs.* N COUNT

hypocrisy /hɪpɒkrəsi¹/, **hypocrisies**. **Hypocrisy** is the practice of pretending to have qualities, beliefs, or feelings that you do not really have; used showing disapproval. EG *What I can't stand is all that hypocrisy about the simple life... Many people have dismissed his criticism as hypocrisy.* N UNCOUNT ⇑ falseness ≠ sincerity ▸ used as a count noun. EG *...dissociating himself from all the prohibitions, crimes, and hypocrisies of the system.* ▸ N COUNT

hypocrite /hɪpəkrɪt/, **hypocrites**. A **hypocrite** is someone who pretends to have qualities, beliefs, or feelings that they do not really have; used showing disapproval. EG *And he, the hypocrite, was sitting there with tears in his eyes... They were nothing but a lot of hypocrites, pretending they had done everything they could to prevent this disaster.* N COUNT : USU USED AS C ⇑ person = phoney

hypocritical /hɪpəkrɪtɪkə⁰l/. Someone who is **hypocritical** pretends to have qualities, beliefs, or feelings that they do not really have; used showing disapproval. EG *They send you their love. It would be hypocritical of me to do the same... They're fighting for freedom while our hypocritical government stands by.* ADJ QUALIT ⇑ deceitful = two-faced ≠ sincere

hypodermic /haɪpədɜːmɪk/, **hypodermics**; a technical term. A **hypodermic**, or a **hypodermic needle** or **hypodermic syringe**, is a medical instrument consisting of a hollow needle attached to a cylinder and plunger. The needle is filled with a drug and used to inject the drug under a person's skin. N COUNT

hypotenuse /haɪpɒtɪ²njuːz/, **hypotenuses**. The **hypotenuse** of a right-angled triangle is the longest side and is opposite the right angle; a technical term in geometry. N COUNT : USU *the*+N

hypothermia /haɪpəθɜːmɪə/ is a condition in which a person is ill because their body temperature has become unusually low as a result of being in severe cold for a long time; a technical term. EG *Hypothermia is one of the main causes of death among the elderly.* N UNCOUNT ⇑ illness = exposure

hypothesis /haɪpɒθɪ²sɪs/, **hypotheses**; a formal word. 1 A **hypothesis** is an idea which is suggested as a possible explanation for a particular situation or condition, but which has not yet been proved to be correct. EG *People have proposed all kinds of hypotheses about what these things are.* N COUNT = theory

2 **Hypothesis** is the act of suggesting such an idea. EG *a world of hypothesis and speculation.* N UNCOUNT ⇑ suggestion

hypothetical /haɪpəθetɪkə⁰l/. Something that is **hypothetical** is based on ideas or situations that have been assumed or invented rather than on reality or facts. EG *Let me put a hypothetical question to you... ...speculating about hypothetical Martian life forms.* ADJ CLASSIF = theoretical, imaginary ◇ **hypothetically**. EG *What they do know, empirically and not hypothetically, is that this part does work.* ◇ ADV

hysterectomy /hɪstərektəmi¹/, **hysterectomies**. A **hysterectomy** is a surgical operation to remove a woman's womb; a technical term. N COUNT

hysteria /hɪstɪərɪə/ is 1 a state of uncontrolled excitement, anger, or panic among people; a formal or literary use. EG *...a growing climate of hysteria and racialism... ...this current hysteria about shortage of petrol.* N UNCOUNT 2 a state of violent and disturbed emotion that a person is in usually as a result of shock; a medical term. EG *...her thin shoulders shaking convulsively in hysteria... ...a bucket of iced water thrown over someone in hysteria.* N UNCOUNT = hysterics 3 loud uncontrolled laughter; an informal use. EG *We fell into fits of hysteria at each other's antics.* N UNCOUNT ⇑ amusement

hysterical /hɪsterɪkə⁰l/. 1 Someone who is **hysterical** 1.1 is in a state of uncontrolled excitement, anger, or panic. EG *...a mob of hysterical vigilantes.* ADJ QUALIT = crazed ▸ used of people's behaviour or actions. EG *...Farlow's hysterical letter... I waited until the political climate became less hysterical.* ▸ = frantic 1.2 is in a state of violent and disturbed emotion that is usually a result of shock. ADJ CLASSIF = demented ▸ used of a person's behaviour or actions. EG *...stress leading to irrational and hysterical behaviour.* ◇ **hysterically**. EG *A man was screaming hysterically.* ◇ ADV WITH VB

2 **Hysterical** laughter is loud and uncontrolled; an informal use. EG *...the helpless, hysterical laughter of children.* ADJ CLASSIF : USU ATTRIB ◇ **hysterically**. EG *We would laugh hysterically at the startled expressions on their faces.* ◇ ADV WITH VB

3 Something that you find **hysterical** is very funny and makes you laugh a lot; an informal use. ADJ QUALIT ◇ **hysterically**. EG *...one-liners which people find hysterically funny.* ◇ ADV+ADJ = hilariously

hysterics /hɪsterɪks/. If you are in **hysterics**, having **hysterics**, etc, 1 you are in a state of uncontrolled excitement, anger, or panic; an informal use. EG *If she didn't get home early, there would probably be hysterics from her mother.* N PLURAL 2 you are in a state of violent and disturbed emotion that is usually a result of shock; a medical term. EG *She went into sobbing hysterics... She was having a fit of hysterics.* N PLURAL = hysteria 3 you are laughing loudly in an uncontrolled way; an informal use. EG *The audience were in hysterics.* N PLURAL

Ii

I, i /aɪ/, **I's, i's**. 1 **I** is the ninth letter of the English alphabet. N COUNT

2 **I.** is an abbreviation for 'Island' or 'Isle', especially when it is written on maps. EG *...Banks I.*

3 **I** or **i** is the Roman numeral for 1.

I /aɪ/ is used as the subject of a verb. A speaker or writer uses **I** to refer to himself or herself. EG *I like your dress... I wanted to put my arm around her... I see what you mean... I shall be leaving soon... He and I were at school together... I'll come down to New York soon, I promise.* PRON : SING, USED AS S

-ian. See **-an**.

IBA /aɪ biː eɪ/. The **IBA** is an organization which controls all the broadcasting companies in the United Kingdom except the BBC; an abbreviation for 'Independent Broadcasting Authority'. EG *Religious advisers are appointed jointly by the BBC and the IBA.* N PROPER : *the*+N

-ibility, -ibilities. **-ibility** is added in place of -ible at the end of some adjectives in order to form nouns. Uncount nouns formed in this way often refer to a state: for example, 'accessibility' refers to the state of being accessible. Uncount nouns like these are not defined in this dictionary, but are treated with the related adjectives. EG *...responsible→responsibility... ...possible→possibility... ...flexible→flexibility... ...credible→credibility.* SUFFIX : FORMS NOUNS

ice /aɪs/, **ices, icing, iced**. 1 **Ice** is 1.1 water that has frozen and become solid. EG *We had to climb over smooth mounds of ice a hundred metres high... The river was freed now of ice... Defrost your refrigerator regularly to avoid a build-up of ice.* N UNCOUNT 1.2 pieces of ice that you use to keep food or drink cool. EG *Could I have a gin and tonic with ice and lemon please... We keep our meat on ice in hot weather.* N UNCOUNT

2 If you **ice** cakes, buns, etc, you cover them with icing. EG *Have you iced your Christmas cake yet?* V+O ⇑ decorate

3 An **ice** is a portion of ice cream. EG *He went over and bought ices and lollipops for the children.* N COUNT

4 If you are **on thin ice**, you are acting unwisely, because you are doing or saying something without proper knowledge or information. EG *You don't seem to realize what thin ice you are on... I can't forget how thin the ice is under me.* PHR : USED AS AN A ⇑ vulnerable

5 Someone or something that **breaks the ice** makes people feel relaxed and comfortable, for example at the beginning of a party. PHR : VB INFLECTS

6 If something **cuts no ice** with someone, it fails to impress or influence them. EG *This sort of thing will cut no ice on the international market... His ideas appear to have cut little ice with film producers.* PHR : VB INFLECTS

7 If you **put** a plan or project **on ice**, you take no action on it for a period of time. EG *We wanted the Government to put on ice the Industrial Relations Act.* PHR : VB INFLECTS = hold

8 See also **iced, icing, black ice**.

ice over. If something **ices over** or **ices up**, it becomes covered with a layer of ice. EG *The road becomes treacherous when it is iced over... ...iced-over puddles... My windscreen started to ice up again.* PHRASAL VB : V+ADV ⇑ freeze

Ice Age. The **Ice Age** was a period of time lasting many thousands of years, during which a lot of the earth's surface was covered with ice. N PROPER : *the*+N

iceberg /aɪsbɜːg/, **icebergs**. An **iceberg** is a large tall mass of ice floating in the sea. ● **tip of the iceberg**: see **tip**. N COUNT

ice-blue is a very pale blue colour. EG *...ice-blue eyes.* ADJ COLOUR

ice-box, ice-boxes; also spelled without a hyphen. An **ice-box** is a refrigerator; used in American English. EG *She fixed herself a plate of food out of the icebox.* N COUNT

ice-bucket, ice-buckets; also spelled without a hyphen. An **ice-bucket** is a container which holds ice cubes or cold water and ice. You can use it to provide ice cubes to put in drinks, or to put bottles of wine in and keep the wine cool. N COUNT

ice-cap, ice-caps; also spelled without a hyphen. An **ice-cap** is a layer of thick ice and snow that permanently covers a particular area of land. EG *The penguin can survive on the Antarctic ice-cap in winter... ...the polar ice caps.* N COUNT : USU *the*+N

ice-cold. Something that is **ice-cold** is very cold indeed. EG *The water was ice-cold... ...ice-cold beer.* ADJ CLASSIF = freezing

ice cream, ice creams; also spelled with a hyphen or as one word. 1 **Ice cream** is a very cold, sweet-tasting food made from frozen cream or an artificial substitute for cream, with a vanilla, chocolate, strawberry, or other flavouring. EG *For dessert there was vanilla ice cream.* N UNCOUNT ⇑ dessert

2 An **ice cream** is a portion of ice cream that you buy from a shop or van or in a cinema, theatre, etc. You usually buy it wrapped in paper, in a container, or placed between two pieces of thin biscuit. EG *They spent all their pocket money on sweets and ice-creams... ...an ice-cream van.* N COUNT

ice-cream soda, ice-cream sodas. **Ice-cream soda** is a dessert made from ice cream, fruit-flavoured syrup, and soda water. It is usually served in a tall glass. EG *...a glass of ice-cream soda... Karen gobbled an ice-cream soda.* N UNCOUNT/COUNT

ice cube, ice cubes; also spelled with a hyphen. An **ice cube** is a small square block of ice that you put into a drink in order to make it cold. EG *He dropped in a few ice cubes.* N COUNT

iced /aɪst/. 1 An **iced** drink has been made very cold by putting ice into it, or by putting it into a special machine. EG *She sat in the sun and sipped iced coffee... ...an iced beer.* ADJ CLASSIF : ATTRIB ⇑ cooled

2 An **iced** cake is covered with a layer of icing. EG *There were trays of tea and sandwiches and little iced cakes.* ADJ CLASSIF : ATTRIB ⇑ decorated

ice floe, ice floes; also spelled with a hyphen. An **ice floe** is a large area of ice floating in the sea. N COUNT

ice hockey ; also spelled with a hyphen. **Ice hockey** is a game played on ice by two teams. Each team tries to score goals by using long sticks to hit a small flat object called the puck into the opponents' net. N UNCOUNT ⇑ sport

Icelander /aɪsləndə/, **Icelanders**. An **Icelander** is a person who comes from Iceland. N COUNT

Icelandic /aɪslændɪk/. 1 Something that is **Icelandic** belongs or relates to Iceland, to its people, or to its language. ADJ CLASSIF

2 **Icelandic** is the official language of Iceland. N UNCOUNT

ice lolly, ice lollies; also spelled with a hyphen. An **ice lolly** is a piece of ice flavoured with fruit which is frozen onto a stick and eaten as a sweet. N COUNT

ice rink, ice rinks; also spelled with a hyphen. An **ice rink** is a level area of ice, usually inside a building, that has been made artificially and kept frozen so that people can skate on it. EG *Everybody goes down to Birmingham ice rink.* N COUNT

ice-skate, ice-skates, ice-skating, ice-skated. The noun is also spelled as two words. 1 An **ice-skate** is a shoe or boot with a metal bar attached to it that you wear when you skate on ice. N COUNT

2 If you **ice-skate**, you move about on ice wearing ice-skates. EG *I can't ice-skate to save my life... Two small children were ice-skating on the pond.* V ◊ **ice-skating**. EG *I like to watch soccer and ice-skating... Could parts of the playground be flooded for ice-skating during the winter?* ◊ N UNCOUNT = skating

icicle /aɪsɪkəl/, **icicles**. An **icicle** is a piece of ice shaped like a pointed stick that hangs down from a surface. It forms when water drips slowly off the surface, freezing as it falls. EG *Huge gleaming icicles hung halfway down her windows.* N COUNT

icing /aɪsɪŋ/. 1 **Icing** is a sweet substance made from powdered sugar and water or egg whites. It is used to cover cakes as a decoration. EG *A mixer is a great asset for preparing icing... ...sweet cakes covered in chocolate icing.* N UNCOUNT

2 If you describe something as **the icing on the cake**, you mean that it is an extra and unnecessary detail that has been added to something which is already satisfactory; used showing disapproval. EG *These were fripperies–the icing on the cake... All further changes are icing on a perfectly palatable cake.* PHR : USED AS C ⇑ addition

icing sugar is white sugar that has been ground to a very fine powder. It is used for making icing and sweets. EG *Add half the quantity of icing sugar gradually.* N UNCOUNT

-icity, -icities. -icity is added in place of -ic at the end of adjectives in order to form nouns. Uncount nouns formed in this way often refer to a state: for example, 'authenticity' refers to the state of being authentic. Uncount nouns like these are not defined in this dictionary, but are treated with the related adjectives. EG *...domestic→domesticity... ...eccentric→eccentricity... ...electric→electricity.* SUFFIX : FORMS NOUNS

icon /aɪkɒn/, **icons**; also spelled **ikon**. An **icon** is a picture of Christ, of the Virgin Mary, or of a saint painted in a traditional way on a wooden panel. Icons are regarded as holy by many Orthodox Christians. EG *...a silver-covered icon of the virgin... ...an icon found in the monastery of St Catherine.* N COUNT ↑ painting

iconoclast /aɪkɒnə⁶klæst/, **iconoclasts**. An **iconoclast** is a person who criticizes beliefs that are generally accepted in a society; a formal word. EG *The image presented of him is of a mindless iconoclast... ...one of the country's iconoclasts.* N COUNT ↑ critic

iconoclastic /aɪkɒnə⁶klæstɪk/. **Iconoclastic** ideas, theories, etc contradict established beliefs; a formal word. EG *...new iconoclastic ideas in medicine... ...his iconoclastic theories about language.* ADJ QUALIT ↑ critical

icy /aɪsi¹/, **icier, iciest. 1 Icy** air, water, etc is extremely cold. EG *As I opened the door a gust of icy air struck me... He scooped up some of the icy cold water.* ◇ **icily.** EG *Her skin was icily cold.* ADJ QUALIT = freezing ◇ ADV+ADJ

2 An **icy** road has ice on it. EG *Be careful, the roads are icy this morning... We made our way along the icy, muddy lanes... When it's icy, my husband worries.* ADJ QUALIT ↑ frozen

3 When someone's manner or way of speaking is **icy**, they indicate their dislike or anger in a quiet, controlled way. EG *Bowman spoke with an icy calm... Her tone was icy... The reception we got was icy.* ◇ **icily.** EG *'That is quite out of the question,' said Thomas icily.* ◇ **iciness.** EG *'Good,' I said with equal iciness.* ADJ QUALIT ↑ cold = glacial ◇ ADV WITH VB ◇ N UNCOUNT = coolness

I'd /aɪd/ is **1** the usual spoken form of 'I had', especially when 'had' is an auxiliary verb. EG *I couldn't believe it, because I'd just had a letter from her... ...something I'd never seen before.* **2** the usual spoken form of 'I would'. EG *I'd be terrified to try anything like that... I'd like to make my views clear.*

idea /aɪdɪə/, **ideas. 1** An **idea** is **1.1** a plan, proposal, or suggestion. EG *If you agree to the idea, we'll start straight away... I think that's a good idea... What a stupid idea... It was your idea.* N COUNT = scheme **1.2** an opinion or belief. EG *They had many ideas on how films should be made... People had some odd ideas about village children... He wound up with the idea that charity was better than chastity.* N COUNT : USU+ on/about/ REPORT-CL = notion, view

2 If you have an **idea**, or if something gives you an **idea**, you are suddenly aware of a possible way of doing something. EG *This has given me an idea... I suddenly had the idea of cutting a hole in the door... He had an idea for a play.* N COUNT : IF+ PREP THEN of/ for ↑ inspiration

3 The **idea** of a particular policy, course of action, etc is its aim or purpose. EG *The idea is to try and avoid further expense... The idea is to cut you down to size.* N SING = objective

4 Your **idea** of something is **4.1** your impression of what it is like, or should be like. EG *We can get a fairly clear idea of what they were like... Lying in bed all day is not my idea of a holiday.* N SING WITH DET : IF+PREP THEN of **4.2** what you know about it. EG *He has a very good idea of how the Civil Service functions... We have little idea about its original meaning... Have you any idea how much it would cost?... You must have some idea... He didn't have the faintest idea what to do... She had no idea of the time.* N UNCOUNT+of/ about/WH ↑ knowledge = notion

5 If you have an **idea** that something is true, you suspect that it is true, but are not certain about it. EG *I have an idea that Shaw wrote it as a skit... I was beginning to get the idea that they didn't like me... Not even my closest friends had any idea that something was wrong... They'd no idea it was there... What gave you that idea?* N SING WITH DET : USU+ REPORT-CL ↑ suspicion = notion

6 If you have the **idea** of doing something, you intend to do it. EG *I had little idea at that time of buying my own house... She had tried two doctors with the idea of having an abortion.* N COUNT+of/ REPORT-CL = intention

7 If someone **gives** you **an idea** of the cost of something or **an idea** of how long something will take to do, they tell you approximately how much it will cost or how long it will take. EG *Can you give us an idea of how much it will cost?* PHR : VB INFLECTS, IF+ PREP THEN of ↑ estimate

8 If someone **gets the idea**, they understand how to do something or understand what you are telling them; an informal expression. EG *You get the idea?... I'm sure he'll get the general idea.* PHR : VB INFLECTS ↑ comprehend

9 You say that doing something, having something, etc is **a good idea, a wonderful idea**, etc when you approve of it or think that it is worthwhile. EG *It's a good idea to get some instruction... Pets are a wonderful idea if you have time on your hands... I was beginning to think marriage was a good idea.* PHR : USED AS C

10 If you **put ideas into** someone's **head**, you make them think that certain things are possible for them which they had not thought about before, and you make them want to change their lives; used showing disapproval. EG *Don't start putting ideas into the boy's head... It was Percival who put ideas in my head.* PHR : VB INFLECTS ↑ suggest

11 An **idea** is also **11.1** the possibility that something will happen to you, especially when you are pleased or displeased about it. EG *He had liked the idea of his daughter marrying an Oxford man... I loved the idea of going to Parliament.* N SING : the+N+ of/REPORT-CL = thought **11.2** one of the basic units of thought by which we are able to understand the world. EG *...the idea of happiness... ...the idea of time.* N COUNT : IF+ PREP THEN of = concept

12 Idea is also used in the following expressions. **12.1** People say **'I've no idea'** to emphasize that they don't know something, sometimes when they are annoyed at being asked a question. EG *'How much does he earn?'–'I've no idea.'* CONVENTION = search me **12.2** Someone might say **'What's the idea?'** when they are angry with you because you are doing something that you are not allowed to do; an informal expression. EG *Hey! What's the idea?* EXCLAM **12.3** People say **'That's the idea'** to indicate that they approve of something that you have said or done. EG *'Shall I look and see?'–'That's the idea.'* CONVENTION **12.4** People say **'you've no idea'** when they are trying to describe how exciting or upsetting an experience was. EG *It's terrific when you're up there. You've no idea... It was a revelation, you've no idea... Oh, it was terrible, you've no idea.* PHR : USED AS ADV SEN

ideal /aɪdɪəl/, **ideals. 1** An **ideal** is a principle, idea, or standard that seems perfect to you so that you try to achieve it. For example, absolute honesty might be an ideal that you try to follow, or your religion or political beliefs might provide you with ideals. EG *He believed in parliamentary democracy as an ideal... She's committed to liberal ideals and civil liberties... Life does not always reflect our ideals... In the past, permanence was the ideal... There is no single path to the ideal of a disarmed world.* N COUNT : IF+ PREP THEN of ↑ concept

2 Your **ideal** of something is the person or thing that seems to you to be the best possible example of it. EG *In Ancient Greece an egg-shaped face was the ideal of female beauty... He idolizes her as his feminine ideal... She fails to conform to the supposed ideal.* N SING : IF+PREP THEN of ↑ model

3 The **ideal** person or thing for a particular task or purpose is the best possible person or thing for it. EG *He is the ideal person for the job... She may hardly be an ideal companion for young children... All-day playgroups are not an ideal answer when a woman works full time.* ADJ CLASSIF : IF+ PREP THEN for = perfect

4 An **ideal** society, **ideal** world, etc is the best possible kind of society, world, etc that you can imagine. EG *He wrote about his ideal society most eloquently.* ADJ CLASSIF : ATTRIB = model

idealise /aɪdɪəlaɪz/. See **idealize.**

idealism /aɪdɪəlɪzə⁰m/ is the beliefs and behaviour of someone who has ideals and who tries to base their behaviour on these ideals; usually used showing approval. EG *I came here out of conviction and idealism... ...a fever of romantic idealism... They're channelling the natural resources of youthful idealism into political action.* ◇ **idealist, idealists.** EG *Frank Elder was a lifelong socialist and idealist... You don't have to be an idealist to realize that there's something wrong with this society.* N UNCOUNT ↑ principles ◇ N COUNT = visionary

idealistic /aɪdɪəlɪstɪk/. An **idealistic** person has ideals, and bases their behaviour on these ideals. EG *He's too idealistic to be corrupted... We need to attract idealistic young people into politics.* ▸ used of people's ideas and attitudes. EG *It seemed an idealistic and illusory dream.* ADJ QUALIT ▸ = utopian

idealize /aɪdɪəlaɪz/, **idealizes, idealizing, idealized**; also spelled **idealise**. If you **idealize** something or someone, you think of them, or represent them to other people, as being perfect or much better than they really are. EG *Absent from home, he idealizes it... Romantic love and motherhood are sentimentally idealized... She has a tendency to idealise.* ◊ **idealized**. EG *The boy yearned to be like his idealized father... Man is tempted to live up to woman's idealized conception of himself.* ◊ **idealization** /aɪdɪəlaɪzeɪʃə⁰n/. EG *They're too prone to idealization of the opposite sex.*
V OR V+O = romanticize
◊ ADJ CLASSIF : USU ATTRIB = romanticized
◊ N UNCOUNT

ideally /aɪdɪəli¹/. 1 If you say that **ideally** something should happen, should be done, etc, you mean that this is the way you would like it to happen, like it to be done, etc, but you know that this is not possible or practical. EG *The government should ideally be run by the people... They can either help or stop criticizing or, ideally, both... Ideally, we would like to start at the beginning.*
ADV SEN = preferably

2 If you say that someone or something is **ideally** suited, **ideally** located, etc, you mean that they are as well suited, as well located, etc as they could possibly be; used showing approval. EG *He considered himself ideally suited for the job of Prime Minister... The Airbus proved ideally adapted to an era of high fuel costs... ...a superbly appointed holiday complex ideally located on wooded cliffs.*
ADV+PAST PART = perfectly

identical /aɪdentɪkə⁰l/. Two or more things that are **identical** are 1 exactly the same in every detail. EG *All individuals of the same species are not identical... ...two young women in identical pinafores... Chemically, it is almost identical to limestone... India's internal structure can never be identical with Europe's.* ◊ **identically**. EG *All nineteen wives were dressed identically and lined up in a row.* 2 very similar indeed. EG *The houses in this colony were all identical and stretched row upon row... They share identical attitudes to the subjects being discussed.*
ADJ CLASSIF
◊ ADV WITH VB
ADJ CLASSIF

identical twin, identical twins. **Identical twins** are two children or animals that are born from a single ovum in the mother, which divides into two after being fertilized by a single sperm. Identical twins are the same sex and look very much like each other.
N COUNT : USU PL

identifiable /aɪdentɪfaɪəbə⁰l/. Something that is **identifiable** is 1 able to be recognized because it has a particular known quality or because it is like something or someone else. EG *More and more serious fiction will be immediately identifiable in the coming years... ...a much more easily identifiable hand signal.* 2 able to be named because it can easily be recognized. EG *The figure of Mao Tse Tung is the immediately identifiable symbol of the revolution... They were convinced that certain identifiable groups were threatening them.*
ADJ CLASSIF ⇑ apparent
ADJ QUALIT ⇑ obvious

identification /aɪdentɪfɪkeɪʃə⁰n/, **identifications**. 1 The **identification** of people and things is the process of recognizing them because they are like other people or things, or because they have a particular quality. EG *...the identification of people who share the same interests... ...the identification of requirements and resources.*
N COUNT/ UNCOUNT ⇑ recognition

2 Your **identification** of a particular person or thing is your ability to name them because you know them or recognize them. EG *...the identification, examination, and disposal of a dead body.*
N COUNT/ UNCOUNT ⇑ process

3 If you have some **identification**, you have something such as a driving licence or a passport, that has your name, address, age, etc, printed on it, so that it proves or shows who you are. EG *Could I ask you to show me some identification?... ...the identification tags sewn on my school clothes.*
N UNCOUNT ⇑ documentation

4 **Identification** with a particular person, group, idea, or situation is the feeling of sympathy and support for them that you have. EG *...identification with football teams... ...a strong identification with our people and our history.*
N UNCOUNT+ with ⇑ relationship = empathy

identify /aɪdentɪfaɪ/, **identifies, identifying, identified**. 1 If you can **identify** someone or something, 1.1 you are able to recognize them because they are like other people or things or because they have a particular quality. EG *An individual bird can identify the call of its own species... ...a device which identifies its owner through his fingerprint pattern.*
V+O ⇑ select = notice

1.2 you are able to name them. EG *...schoolboys who could identify every car as it passed by... ...officials, who asked not to be identified... The guard had been identified as Victor Kowalski.*
V+O = specify

2 If something **identifies** someone or something else, it makes them easy to recognize, because it makes them different in some way. EG *Wear on your third finger an iron ring, which will identify you... This nickname was for several years enough to identify her in a headline.*
V+O ⇑ distinguish

3 If you **identify** facts, you notice them and realize that they are important. EG *We have identified three major issues... What the report does quite clearly is identify the fact that there is racial inequality.*
V+O = acknowledge

4 If you **identify** with someone or something, you feel that you understand them or their feelings and ideas. EG *He couldn't identify with other people's troubles... ...people with whom English-speaking readers could identify.*
V+O : IF+PREP THEN with = sympathize with

5 If you **are identified** with someone or something, you are very closely involved or associated with them. EG *During the 1950's he was identified with certain radical causes... Of the 34 candidates nearly a third were identified with revolutionary groups.*
V+O+A (with) = align with, involve with

6 If you **identify** one person or thing with another, you make them appear to be similar to each other because you think they both have a particular quality. EG *I knew that if I protested he would at once identify me with his father... ...a lecture in which he tried to identify realism with totalitarianism.*
V+O+A (with) = equate with, associate with

identikit /aɪdentɪkɪt/, **identikits**. An **identikit** or an **identikit picture** is a drawing of a person's face, which is made from descriptions of the person given to the police by people who saw him or her. The person in the drawing has not been identified and is wanted for some reason, usually because they are thought to have committed a crime.
N COUNT

identity /aɪdentɪti¹/, **identities**. 1 Your **identity** is 1.1 who you are. EG *I had guessed the identity of her lover... The clues he left did not establish his identity... Glenn whipped off the mask to reveal his identity.* 1.2 all the qualities, beliefs, and ideas which make you feel that you are different from everyone else or that you belong to a particular group. EG *...our identity as black people.... ...your sense of identity, of who you are and what you are... ...a region with its own cultural identity.*
N COUNT : WITH POSS
N COUNT/ UNCOUNT ⇑ self

2 If there is an **identity** between things, they are very similar or are exactly the same as each other. EG *There is a peculiar identity between his known political views and the mood of many of his pictures.*
N UNCOUNT = likeness

identity card, identity cards. Your **identity card** is a card that has your name, photograph, age, address, and other information on it. In some countries you have to carry an identity card in order to prove who you are. EG *The police were demanding to see the identity cards of all visitors.*
N COUNT ⇑ document

ideological /aɪdɪəlɒdʒɪkə⁰l/. Something that is **ideological** relates to principles, beliefs, or philosophy, especially to a particular set of political beliefs held by a person, party, or country. EG *...the ideological aspects of the dispute... They are going to examine all the candidates to see if their ideological credentials are right.* ◊ **ideologically**. EG *...the genuine martyr, the man who really is ideologically committed... She is one of the President's more ideologically sound allies in Europe at present.*
ADJ CLASSIF ⇑ philosophical
◊ ADV

ideology /aɪdi¹ɒlədʒi¹/, **ideologies**. An **ideology** is a belief or a set of beliefs, especially the political beliefs on which people, parties, or countries base their actions. EG *...the capitalist ideology of the West... ...comrades with whom I could share a common ideology... ...the conflict between ideology and practice.*
N COUNT+SUPP, OR N UNCOUNT = philosophy, creed

idiocy /ɪdɪəsi¹/, **idiocies**. The **idiocy** of something is the utter stupidity of it. EG *...the dreadful idiocy of the Battle of Balaclava... ...the idiocies of Freud.*
N UNCOUNT/ COUNT = lunacy

idiom /ɪdɪəm/, **idioms**. 1 The **idiom** of something such as speech, writing, music, or architecture is its particular style, especially when this style belongs to a certain country or period of history. EG *The Beatles changed for ever the idiom of popular music... ...a church in the idiom of the thirteenth century... ...his command of the American idiom.*
N COUNT+SUPP : USU SING

2 An **idiom** is a group of words which, when they are used together in a particular combination, have a different meaning from the one they would have if you took the meaning of all the individual words in the group. EG *...a knowledge of English idioms... ...the*
N COUNT = expression, phrase

idiom 'ladies' man' being untranslatable into Japanese.

idiomatic /ɪdɪ¹əʊmætɪk/. Language that is **idiomatic** uses words in a way that sounds natural and grammatically correct to native speakers of the language. EG *Her English was fluent and idiomatic... ...good idiomatic language in the form of connected passages.* ADJ QUALIT

idiosyncrasy /ɪdi¹ə⁶sɪnkrəsi¹/, **idiosyncrasies**. 1 Someone's **idiosyncrasies** are their own rather peculiar or unusual habits, likes, dislikes, etc. EG *She adjusted magnificently to her husband's many idiosyncrasies.* N COUNT = peculiarity, foible

2 An **idiosyncrasy** is a strange or unusual piece of behaviour. EG *...a machine whose idiosyncrasies are well known.* N COUNT = peculiarity

idiosyncratic /ɪdi¹ə⁶sɪnkrætɪk/. If someone's behaviour, habits, likes, etc are **idiosyncratic**, they are personal to them, and are often rather strange or unusual. EG *We all have our own idiosyncratic ways of coping with grief... ...Michelangelo's highly idiosyncratic style of painting.* ADJ QUALIT ⇑ individual = peculiar

idiot /ɪdɪət/, **idiots**. 1 If you call someone an **idiot**, you are saying that you think they have done something very stupid. EG *That idiot Antonio has gone and locked our cabin door... What an idiot I am!... You're behaving like a perfect idiot!* N COUNT: ALSO VOC = fool

2 An **idiot** is a person who is mentally ill or mentally handicapped and who therefore cannot behave or think in the same way as other people; a rather old-fashioned or offensive use. N COUNT

idiotic /ɪdi¹ɒtɪk/. Someone or something that is **idiotic** is very stupid indeed. EG *Of course it was an idiotic question to ask... They talked about how idiotic critics were.* ◊ **idiotically**. EG *I grinned idiotically as the tale began to appeal to me.* ADJ QUALIT = ridiculous, dumb ◊ ADV WITH VB = foolishly

idle /aɪdə⁰l/. 1 If you are **idle**, 1.1 you are not doing anything, especially when you could be doing something. EG *A healthy child cannot be idle; he has to be doing something all day long... What rather frustrated me was that you were kept idle all the time... He applied in an idle moment for a Fellowship to America.* ◊ **idleness**. EG *No one can afford to pay troops to sit about in idleness.* 1.2 you are lazy and do not do things you should do, because you think someone else will do them for you. EG *Women thought men idle good-for-nothings... Only the idle rich can contemplate such matters.* ◊ **idly**. EG *...those who sit idly by while you slave over a hot stove.* ◊ **idleness**. EG *He seems to think that poverty is a punishment for idleness.* 1.3 you do not have a job. EG *Whole streets of men were idle... There are 13,000 idle in a workforce of 170,000.* ◊ **idleness**. EG *They threatened employed workers with idleness and thus brought down wages.* ADJ CLASSIF ⇑ inactive ◊ N UNCOUNT ADJ QUALIT ◊ ADV WITH VB ◊ N UNCOUNT ADJ CLASSIF: PRED ◊ N UNCOUNT

2 Machines or factories that are **idle** are not working or being used. EG *The machinery could not be converted, and so stood idle... ...the £2 million date-processing plant that lay idle for two years because no one knew how to repair it.* ADJ CLASSIF: PRED = inoperative

3 If it is **idle** to do something, it is not worth doing it or spending time or energy on it, because no useful result would be achieved. EG *It would be idle to look for a solution at this stage... Speculation would be idle on how long any offensive could be sustained.* ADJ CLASSIF ⇑ worthless = futile

4 **Idle** is also used to describe 4.1 something that has no purpose or motive but just happens, exists, or is done because the opportunity arises, and you have nothing better to do. EG *Idle curiosity is certainly a vice... Sudhir and Judy carried on long, idle conversations... ...idle pleasure.* ◊ **idly**. EG *She glanced idly down the list of contents... He wondered idly whether he would get back his old job.* 4.2 something that someone has said or done that you do not treat seriously because you think it was said or done only to frighten, impress, or trick you. EG *This is no idle bluff... That we have the most musical workers in Birmingham is no idle boast... It's just an idle threat. They'd never dare sack us.* ADJ CLASSIF: ATTRIB = casual ◊ ADV AFTER VB = abstractedly ADJ CLASSIF: ATTRIB = empty, vain

5 If an engine is **idling**, it is running slowly and quietly because it is not in gear. EG *I let it idle while I packed the tools away.* ◊ **idling**. EG *The 604 Turbo D makes only a subdued mutter at idling speed... Adjust the carburettors until the idling sound changes.* V = tick over ◊ ADJ CLASSIF: ATTRIB

idle away. If you **idle away** a period of time, you spend it doing very little. EG *...three old men, idling away the summer afternoon under the trees.* PHRASAL VB: V+O+ADV

idler /aɪdlə/, **idlers**. An **idler** is a person who does nothing, especially one who you think should be working or doing something; used showing disapproval. EG *...a state full of idlers... ...the crowd of idlers who had assembled to watch the goings-on.* N COUNT = loafer

idol /aɪdə⁰l/, **idols**. An **idol** is 1 someone, such as a film, pop, or sports star, who is greatly admired or loved, especially by people who do not know them personally. EG *...the nonsense talked by the young pop idols... Django Reinhardt is evidently Chris Goddard's idol... ...Lewis Waller, the famous Edwardian matinee idol.* 2 a statue or other object that is worshipped by people who believe that it is a god. EG *Carved drums, ornate spears and idols were traded for firearms... Jack, painted and garlanded, sat there like an idol.* N COUNT = hero N COUNT ⇑ image

idolatrous /aɪdɒlətrəs/. Something that is **idolatrous** treats a particular person or group of people as an idol; used showing disapproval. EG *No newspaper was more idolatrous of the generals who commanded the campaign than the Express was.* ADJ QUALIT ⇑ worshipful

idolatry /aɪdɒlətri¹/; an old-fashioned word. Someone who practises **idolatry** worships idols; used showing disapproval by people whose religions teach that it is wrong to worship idols. EG *...the descent into idolatry... ...superstitious idolatry.* N UNCOUNT = paganism

idolize /aɪdəlaɪz/, **idolizes, idolizing, idolized**; also spelled **idolise**. If you **idolize** someone such as a film, pop, or sports star, you admire them very much and think that you are in love with them. EG *They somehow identify themselves with this person they idolize... He will want to protect, please and idolize her... Mothers are more likely to be idolized if the nanny is strict.* V+O = worship

idyll /ɪdɪl/, **idylls**. An **idyll** is a situation which is idyllic. EG *...the myth of an unchanging idyll of rural England... As the sailors came more often into conflict with the islanders, the idyll became harder to believe in.* N COUNT = paradise

idyllic /ɪ⁵dɪlɪk/. Something that is **idyllic** is extremely pleasant, simple, and peaceful without any difficulties or dangers. EG *...the idyllic calm of the South Seas... ...books and films which have portrayed an idyllic life with your new baby... They've retired to a cottage in Wales. Don't you think that sounds idyllic?* ADJ QUALIT ⇑ perfect

i.e. is used to introduce a word or sentence which gives more information about, or makes clearer, the meaning of something you have said; i.e. actually means 'that is to say'. EG *You should start to run down any freezer supplies (i.e. eat the stuff) as soon as you know you're moving... To keep a dog costs twice as much, i.e. £110 a year.*

-ied. See **-ed**.

-ier. See **-er 1**.

-iest. See **-est 1**.

if /ɪf/. 1 You use **if** in conditional sentences in which you say that one thing must happen first or be true first before it is possible for something else to happen or be true. In such sentences the present tense is used in the 'if'-clause; the present or future tense is used in the main clause. EG *He qualifies this year if he gets through his exams... If you can thread a needle you can mend a fuse... If all goes well, Voyager 2 will head on to Uranus... I'd like to book a table for tomorrow night, if possible... 'She's quite sweet, Sheila.'–'If you like the type.'* CONJ SUBORD = provided that

2 You use **if** in conditional sentences in which you talk about an event or situation which might happen, in order to consider or explain what the likely consequences might be. In such sentences the present tense or the modal 'should' is used in the 'if'-clause; the present or future tense, or a modal, is used in the main clause. EG *If any questions occur to you, then don't hesitate to write... If unemployment remains at present levels for a few more years, democracy could become unworkable... Check that you are on the correct tariff. If in doubt ask your local showroom... Perhaps she wanted to leave London. If so, she didn't tell James... Even if people just pop in for five minutes, it makes all the difference to someone who is elderly or bedridden.* CONJ SUBORD = given that

3 You use **if** in conditional sentences to explain the meaning or implication of a word or expression. In such sentences the present tense is used both in the 'if'-clause and in the main clause. EG *If you are accountable for something, you are responsible for* CONJ SUBORD

it... If I say that someone is just being nice about my work, I probably suspect that they don't really like it.

4 You use **if** in conditional sentences in which you talk about an event or situation in the future which is not very likely to happen, or when you imagine circumstances that are different from the actual state of affairs. In such sentences the past tense or the modal 'could' is used in the 'if'-clause; the modal 'would' is used in the main clause. EG *It would be funny if it wasn't so sad... If I could afford it I would buy a boat... If I were to ask you to scrub my back, what would you say?... If asked for an explanation of a video recorder I would definitely find it difficult.* CONJ SUBORD

5 You use **if** in conditional sentences in which you are talking about an event or situation which might have occurred in the past, in contrast to what you know actually occurred. In such sentences the past perfect tense is used in the 'if'-clause; the modals 'would have', 'could have', or 'might have' are used in the main clause. EG *If I'd known that you hadn't heard I wouldn't have told you... It would have been better if you had explained more clearly what you meant... If he hadn't been in such a hurry to find a place he might have found somewhere nicer.* CONJ SUBORD

6 You use **if** in indirect questions where the answer is either 'yes' or 'no'. EG *I asked her if I could help her... I rang up to see if I could get seats... I wonder if you'd give the children a bath?* CONJ SUBORD = whether

7 You can use **if** in sentences in which you compare two similar statements. If the person you are speaking to accepts or agrees with the first statement, then they ought to accept or agree with the second statement. EG *If the Romans brought civilization, the German tribes brought ritual codes... If he had his reasons for being alone, then so had I... If fear and love are indivisible, so too are fear and hate.* CONJ SUBORD = given that

8 You can use **if** in sentences in which you identify a possible exception to a general statement you have already made. EG *It was an excellent concert. If I had any disappointment at all it was the end... Few, if any, buyers were found.* CONJ SUBORD

9 You use **if** to introduce a comment on what you are saying, for example to apologize for it or to say that you are giving your own opinion. EG *If you don't mind my saying so, I think you are partly responsible... A machine's intelligence, if you must use the word, is purely automatic... If you want my opinion, she is a very lonely woman.* CONJ SUBORD

10 You can also use **if**, usually followed by a modal such as 'can', 'could', 'may' or 'might', at a point in a conversation when you are politely trying to change the subject or to interrupt another speaker. EG *If I could just come in there, Brian, I think I have a good example of what you mean... Let's leave it there, if we may, and move on to another question.* CONJ SUBORD : USU+MODAL

11 You can use a clause introduced by **if** to direct someone's attention to a particular topic, so that you can make some point about it. EG *If you read any of the Scottish papers they are always condemning the people who govern Scotland from Westminster... If anybody wants me, I'm downstairs.* CONJ SUBORD = when

12 You can also use a clause introduced by **if** as a polite way of asking someone to do something. EG *If you can sign that for me. Thank you... If you will just wait here, I'll be with you in a minute...* CONJ SUBORD

13 You use **if not** **13.1** to say that an amount, degree, time, etc might be even bigger, better, sooner, etc than the one you have mentioned. EG *The first microchip can represent hundreds of thousands if not millions of pounds of investment... He's earning £50,000 a year, if not £60,000... I'd like to see you tonight, if not sooner.* **13.2** to suggest that the real state of affairs might be even more remarkable, surprising, changed, etc, than you have stated. EG *She learned to accept him if not actually to like him... Her voice was, if not perfect, at least nearly so... It'll be exciting if nothing else.* CONJ SUBORD = perhaps

14 You say **'if I were you'** to someone when you are giving them advice. EG *If I were you I'd take the money.* PHR : USED AS ADV SEN

15 You use the expression **'if you like'** to indicate that you realize you are expressing something in a new or unusual way. EG *It's a great opportunity, a paid holiday if you like... ...the intentions, the needs, if you like, of the participants.* PHR : USED AS ADV SEN

16 You use **'if anything'**, especially after a negative statement, to say that something different from what you have just said is actually the case. EG *He didn't look nervous. If anything, he looked slightly perplexed... It certainly wasn't an improvement. We were, if anything, worse off than before.* PHR : USED AS ADV SEN

17 You use **if ever**, when you are giving a description of a person or thing, to emphasize how appropriate it is. EG *If ever I saw a girl who was due to rise in the world, it's you... She was a hopeless figure if ever I saw one.* CONJ SUBORD

18 You use **if only** **18.1** to introduce what you think is a fairly good reason for doing something, although you realize it may not be a very good one. EG *I'll have a glass myself, if only to stop you from drinking it all... If only for your own piece of mind you should know where the money came from.* CONJ SUBORD **18.2** to express a wish or desire, for example your wish that something in the past had happened differently. With this use, there is often no main clause to go with the 'if'-clause. EG *If only she could have lived a little longer... If only there were forty-eight hours in every day.* CONJ SUBORD = would that

19 You use **as if** **19.1** in comparisons, when you are describing something that is done in a way that suggests that something else is the case. EG *She folded her arms as if she were cold... He laid both his hands on his chest as if to demonstrate his sincerity... He cried out as if in pain.* CONJ SUBORD = as though **19.2** to emphasize that something is not the case, for example that something is not important. EG *He keeps worrying about what wine to buy. As if it mattered!* CONJ SUBORD = as though

20 You use **'It isn't as if'** or **'It's not as if'** to introduce a statement which might explain something puzzling if it were true, although in fact it is not true. EG *I can't understand why she likes him so much. It isn't as if he's good-looking at all... Why was James at the party? It was not as if he were a relative.* PHR : VB INFLECTS

21 **Ifs** or **ifs and buts** are doubts about whether or not something is going to happen, especially when this causes a delay. EG *The proposal was so full of 'ifs' and 'buts' that I seriously doubted whether the stadium would ever be built.* N COUNT : USU PL = uncertainty

iffy /ɪfi¹/. If you are **iffy** about something, you are uncertain about whether you are going to do it or not; an informal word. EG *'Are you going to the party?'–'I'm a bit iffy about it at the moment.'* ADJ QUALIT : PRED, IF+PREP THEN *about* = doubtful

-ify is used at the end of verbs that refer to the putting of something or someone into a particular state or condition. EG *...simplify... ...purify... ...mystify... ...terrify.* SUFFIX : FORMS VERBS

igloo /ɪglu:/, **igloos**. An **igloo** is a dome-shaped house that eskimos make out of blocks of hard snow. N COUNT

igneous /ɪgni¹əs/. **Igneous** rocks are formed by volcanic action; a technical geological term. ADJ CLASSIF

ignite /ɪgnaɪt/, **ignites, igniting, ignited**. When you **ignite** something or when it **ignites**, it starts burning or it explodes. EG *The device was supposed to ignite the fireworks... Fuel is ignited by the spark plug.* V-ERG

ignition /ɪgnɪʃə⁰n/. **1** The **ignition** in a car is the part of the engine where the fuel is ignited, and which starts the whole engine running when you start the car. EG *Have you switched the ignition on?... He turned the ignition key.* N COUNT : USU SING ⇑ device

2 **Ignition** is **2.1** the process by which a car engine is started. EG *...electronic ignition.* N UNCOUNT **2.2** the act or process of something starting to burn. EG *Burns amongst survivors resulted from ignition of clothing due to the great heat.* N UNCOUNT

ignoble /ɪgnəʊbə⁰l/. An **ignoble** person behaves in a way that is considered dishonourable or morally unacceptable. EG *There's something cowardly and ignoble about such an attitude.* ADJ QUALIT

ignominious /ɪgnə⁶mɪnɪəs/. Ignominious behaviour is considered shameful or morally unacceptable. EG *The marriage was considered especially ignominious since she was of royal descent.* ADJ QUALIT
◇ **ignominously**. EG *They were ignominiously defeated in the general election.* ◇ ADV

ignominy /ɪgnəmə¹ni¹/ is shame or public disgrace; a formal word. EG *...a life of prostitution and ignominy.* N UNCOUNT = disrepute

ignoramus /ɪgnəreɪməs/, **ignoramuses**. If you call someone an **ignoramus**, you mean that they have very little knowledge; a slightly offensive word. N COUNT

ignorance /ɪgnərəns/. **Ignorance** of something is lack of knowledge about it. EG *Her ignorance of* N UNCOUNT : IF+ PREP THEN *of*/

foreign policy was alarming... Forgive my ignorance, but what is Arista? about

ignorant /ɪgnərənt/. Someone who is **ignorant** has no knowledge either about a particular subject mentioned or about things in general. EG *Prime ministers are notoriously ignorant about foreign affairs... The masses were largely ignorant of the options open to them... How can they be so ignorant at that age?* ADJ QUALIT: IF+PREP THEN of/about = uninformed

ignore /ɪgnɔː/, **ignores, ignoring, ignored.** 1 If you **ignore** someone or something that you have seen, heard, or experienced, you act as if they are not there or do not exist, or as if the event has not happened. EG *Ralph ignored Jack's question... I went on talking and ignored his tears... It butted its way through the reeds, ignoring the other animals... The President cannot rudely ignore any head of state who chooses to come here.* V+O = disregard

2 If you **ignore** something that you have been advised, asked, or told to do, you deliberately do not do it. EG *The Government ignored his advice... Settlers in Africa may ignore state laws, but they always respect custom.* V+O ⇑ contravene = disregard

3 Something that **ignores** an important aspect of a situation fails to include it or take it into account. EG *These proposals tend to ignore the court's existing power... Such an education almost entirely ignores the emotions of life.* V+O = overlook

ikon /aɪkɒn/. See **icon**.

il- is added to adjectives, adverbs, and nouns that begin with the letter 'l', in order to form other adjectives, adverbs, and nouns with the opposite meaning. EG *...legal→illegal... ...legitimacy→illegitimacy.* PREFIX

ilk /ɪlk/. Something of a particular **ilk** is something of a particular type mentioned. EG *...Joan Baez and vocalists of that ilk... ...blueberries and many small berries of that ilk.* N SING: of+DET+N

ill /ɪl/, **ills.** 1 Someone who is **ill** is suffering from a disease or health problem which makes them unable to work or to live normally. EG *I feel ill... He was looking ill... Don't refreeze food. It could make you ill... ...a hospital for the mentally ill... She is ill with cancer.* ● If you **fall ill** or **are taken ill**, you become ill suddenly. EG *She was taken ill on holiday and had to find a doctor.* ● If you say that something **makes you ill**, you mean that it annoys or disgusts you; an informal expression. EG *It makes me quite ill, when one opens a newspaper and sees the cause of all this nuclear pollution.* ADJ QUALIT: USU PRED ⇑ unhealthy = sick, unwell ● PHR: VB INFLECTS ● PHR: VB INFLECTS

2 In formal or old-fashioned English, you might refer to difficulties or harmful influences as **ills**. EG *...the necessary ills of old age... No ill had yet come to Sarah's child.* N COUNT: USU PL ⇑ problem = evil, harm

3 **Ill** is evil or harm; an old-fashioned use. EG *Good is inextricably mixed with ill... Some feel guilty over the ill they have done.* ● If you say you are doing something **for good or ill**, you mean that you are doing it whether the effect of the situation will be good or harmful. EG *We must examine the effect this decision may have on other persons, for good or for ill... Those who have power will always take the opportunity to exercise it, for good or ill.* ● Something that **bodes ill, augurs ill**, etc for you gives you a reason to fear that something harmful might happen soon; used in literary English. EG *She was wearing a sullen expression which might bode ill... The sound of gasps and moans boded ill for what we would see when we opened the door... The doubts she had felt augured ill for the enterprise.* N UNCOUNT ● PHR: USED AS AN A ● PHR: VB INFLECTS

4 Something that is **ill** done is done badly; an old-fashioned or formal use. EG *The programme was ill researched... Some people think that red wine and fish fit ill together... The notion was ill received at Downing Street.* ● Something that **serves** you **ill** does you harm. EG *As a judge he was commended for his compassion, the very quality which had served him so ill at the Bar... The medical profession has been ill served by the cuts in health services.* ● If you **speak ill of** someone, you criticize them, usually when they are not there. EG *You can't expect me to speak ill of my employer.* ADV WITH VB = poorly ● PHR: VB INFLECTS = handicap ● PHR: VB INFLECTS = put down

5 You can use **ill** in front of some nouns to indicate that they are harmful or unpleasant. EG *Did you get any ill effects when you had your blood transfusion?... Protection against ill fortune and disaster... It happened by ill luck that she was out.* ADJ CLASSIF: ATTRIB = adverse

I'll /aɪl/ is the usual spoken form of 'I will' or 'I shall'. EG *I'll ring you tomorrow morning... I'll give it to you now.*

ill- is added to words, especially adjectives and past participles, to add the meaning 'badly' or 'inadequately'. For example, 'ill-written' means badly written, 'ill-judged' means judged with insufficient care or judgment. These compounds can also be written as two words. COMB: FORMS ADJS

ill-advised. An action that is **ill-advised** is not sensible or wise. ▸ used of people. EG *I think he may have been ill-advised to put his suggestions down on paper.* ADJ QUALIT ▸ ADJ QUALIT: IF+VB THEN to-INF

ill-assorted. Things that are in an **ill-assorted** group do not suit or match each other. EG *...an ill-assorted collection of books.* ADJ QUALIT ⇑ odd

ill at ease. Someone who is **ill at ease** feels uncomfortable, embarrassed, or unwelcome. EG *He was ill at ease with people whom he didn't understand... There was something about Dolly that made Madeleine a little ill at ease.* ADJ QUALIT: PRED = awkward

ill-bred. Someone who is **ill-bred** has bad manners. EG *He's just an ill-bred lout.* ADJ QUALIT ⇑ rude = coarse

ill-disposed. A person who is **ill-disposed** towards someone is unwilling to support them or to be sympathetic towards them. EG *The defence might be undone by ill-disposed judges.* ADJ CLASSIF: IF+PREP THEN to/towards = unsympathetic

illegal /ɪliːgəºl/. 1 An activity or action that is **illegal** is one that you are not allowed to do because of a law or official rule of the country you are in. EG *It is illegal in many countries for women to work on night shifts... He got a fourteen-year sentence for illegal possession of firearms.* ▸ used of things which you must not possess according to the law of the country you are in. EG *Marijuana is illegal in the United States.* ◇ **illegally.** EG *...illegally parked cars.* ◇ **illegality** /ɪlə'gælɪti'/, **illegalities.** EG *I spoke of the illegality of my arrest by the military... ...the illegality of abortion.* ADJ CLASSIF ⇑ wrong ▸ = prohibited ◇ ADV WITH VB ◇ N UNCOUNT/COUNT

2 An **illegal** organization is one which a government says must not exist. EG *...the Haganah, the illegal Jewish defence force... The Trotskyists were among a dozen organizations declared illegal.* ADJ CLASSIF = outlawed

3 An **illegal** action or system is one which breaks an international law or agreement, for example by taking control of a country without using the methods such as elections allowed by that country's constitution. EG *...the illegal colonial regime.* ◇ **illegally.** EG *Their country had been illegally occupied for many years.* ADJ CLASSIF ◇ ADV WITH VB

4 An **illegal** immigrant is a person who has entered a country without an official permit. EG *Employers must be held accountable for hiring illegal aliens.* ADJ CLASSIF: ATTRIB

illegible /ɪlɛdʒɪbəºl/. Writing that is **illegible** is so unclear that you cannot see what the letters or numbers are. ADJ QUALIT

illegitimacy /ɪlɪdʒɪtɪməsi'/ is the state of being born of parents who were not legally married at the time. EG *Victoria was not told of her illegitimacy until she moved from Paris.* N UNCOUNT

illegitimate /ɪlɪdʒɪtɪmə't/. 1 A person who is **illegitimate** was born of parents who were not legally married at the time. EG *...an illegitimate child.* ADJ CLASSIF = bastard

2 An **illegitimate** activity is not allowed or approved of by law or social customs. EG *...illegitimate friendships... ...the illegitimate gain of a considerable empire.* ADJ CLASSIF

ill-equipped. Someone who is **ill-equipped** to do something does not have the ability, the qualities, or the equipment necessary to do it. EG *The police were plainly ill-equipped to deal with the riot... They were ill-equipped for the part.* ADJ QUALIT: USU PRED ⇑ unable

ill-fated. If you describe something as **ill-fated**, you mean that you know that it is going to have a tragic or unlucky outcome. EG *Alice recounted the story of her ill-fated boating expedition.* ADJ CLASSIF: USU ATTRIB = doomed

ill-founded. Something that is **ill-founded** is not based on any proper proof or evidence. EG *He warned that their confidence was ill-founded.* ADJ CLASSIF ⇑ false

ill-gotten gains /ɪl gɒtəºn geɪnz/ are things that you have gained, received, or achieved by means of dishonesty or deceit; a formal expression. N PLURAL

ill health; also spelled with a hyphen. If you are in a state of **ill health**, you have an illness or keep feeling unwell for long periods of time. EG *Throughout his career he had suffered from ill-health.* N UNCOUNT

illiberal /ɪlɪbᵒərəl/. A law or system that is **illiberal** allows people very little freedom or choice of action. EG *...the very illiberal laws on divorce... The government was overthrown by an even more illiberal regime.*
ADJ QUALIT ⇑ strict = repressive

illicit /ɪlɪsɪt/. An **illicit** activity or substance is not allowed or not approved of by the laws and social customs of a country. EG *He had had an illicit association with Christine Bradshaw... They were all prosecuted for illicit liquor selling.*
ADJ CLASSIF : USU ATTRIB ⇑ wrong = illegal

illiteracy /ɪlɪtəᵒrəsi¹/ is the state of not knowing how to read or write. EG *...adult illiteracy... ...a country with 90 per cent illiteracy.*
N UNCOUNT

illiterate /ɪlɪtərə¹t/, **illiterates**. Someone who is **illiterate** does not know how to read or write. This word is also sometimes used as an insult to someone who seems very uneducated. EG *40 per cent of the country is reckoned to be illiterate... Some of them are so illiterate, it's unbelievable.* ▸ used as a noun. EG *...the teaching of adult illiterates.*
ADJ CLASSIF ▸ N COUNT

illness /ɪlnɪ²s/, **illnesses**. **1 Illness** is the experience of being ill for a period of time. EG *During his last illness we only saw him twice... People can recover from the symptoms of mental illness.*
N UNCOUNT/COUNT

2 An **illness** is a particular disease that people can suffer from, such as a cold, measles, or pneumonia. EG *She died of a mysterious illness... Finally a doctor diagnosed the illness... ...cures for various illnesses.*
N COUNT = ailment, complaint

illogical /ɪlɒdʒɪkəᵒl/. Something such as a feeling or action that is **illogical 1** is not reasonable or sensible, because you are not considering properly all the aspects of a particular situation. EG *...the illogical envy of a career she did not really want.* ◊ **illogically**. EG *I felt illogically that my own years there counted for nothing.* **2** does not follow a logical, rational, or ordered way of thinking. EG *It is clearly illogical to maintain such a proposition.*
ADJ QUALIT ⇑ irrational; ◊ ADV WITH VB; ADJ QUALIT = unreasonable

ill-omened means the same as ill-starred.
ADJ CLASSIF

ill-starred. If you describe someone or something as **ill-starred**, you mean that you know that they are going to be unlucky or ill-fated; a literary word. EG *...Prince Henry, the ill-starred brother of Charles I.*
ADJ CLASSIF : USU ATTRIB

ill-tempered. Someone who is **ill-tempered** has a bad temper; a fairly formal word. EG *Victoria Station was full of anxious ill-tempered travellers.*
ADJ QUALIT ⇑ cross = crotchety

ill-timed. Something that is **ill-timed** happens or is done at the wrong time, so that it is inappropriate or rude. EG *Her comments were ill-timed.*
ADJ QUALIT = tactless

ill-treat, ill-treats, ill-treating, ill-treated; also spelled as one word. If you **ill-treat** someone, you treat them badly or cruelly. EG *They claimed that they were being ill-treated by him.*
V+O = abuse, mistreat

ill-treatment is harsh or cruel treatment. EG *...creatures who are the victims of man's ill-treatment.*
N UNCOUNT = abuse

illuminate /ɪluːmɪneɪt/, **illuminates, illuminating, illuminated**. **1** If you **illuminate** something, you shine light on it and make it brighter and more visible. EG *They would illuminate the streets more brightly... The flames illuminated billows of smoke.*
V+O = light up

2 If you **illuminate** something that is unclear or difficult to understand, you make it easier to understand by explaining it carefully or giving examples. EG *Their doctrine illuminates much that might seem obscure in the Muslim teaching... This is a point which may illuminate other elements.* ◊ **illuminating**. EG *...Basil Spence, in his illuminating book on the subject... She found the two-year experience difficult but illuminating... He's very illuminating on many things.*
V+O = clarify; ◊ ADJ QUALIT = enlightening

illuminated /ɪluːmɪneɪtɪ²d/. **1** Something that is **illuminated** is lit up, usually from inside by electric lighting. EG *The instruction to fasten safety belts is illuminated at the front of the cabin... ...illuminated advertising.*
ADJ CLASSIF

2 Illuminated old books, manuscripts, and official documents have brightly coloured drawings and designs, often using gold paint.
ADJ CLASSIF = illustrated, decorated

illumination /ɪluːmɪneɪʃəᵒn/, **illuminations**. **1 Illumination** is **1.1** the lighting that a place has. EG *The dusty bulb gave barely adequate illumination... Daylight came in through its glass roof; this was now the only illumination.* **1.2** the art of painting pictures and designs in manuscripts, books, or official documents, done especially in former times. EG *...the great medieval tradition of manuscript illumination.*
N UNCOUNT; N UNCOUNT = decoration, illustration

2 Illuminations are coloured lights which are put up in towns, especially at Christmas, in order to make them look more attractive at night; used in British English. EG *...the illuminations in Regent Street at Christmas.*
N PLURAL

illumine /ɪluːmɪn/, **illumines, illumining, illumined**. To **illumine** something means the same as to illuminate it; a literary word.
V+O

illusion /ɪluːʒəᵒn/, **illusions**. An **illusion** is **1** an idea or belief which you think is true but is in fact false. EG *We have an illusion of freedom... Lord Mountbatten has warned against the illusion that tactical nuclear weapons could be used... I no longer had any illusions about what an education could do for me.* **2** something that looks like one thing in appearance but is another thing in reality, or is not really there at all. EG *The garden through the windows was merely a clever optical illusion.* **3** a magic trick in which the audience is fooled by the skill of the magician's actions and not by any special mechanical devices.
N COUNT/UNCOUNT ⇑ error = delusion; N COUNT = false impression; N COUNT

illusory /ɪluːsəri¹/. Something that is **illusory** seems to be true or possible, but is false or impossible in reality. EG *...illusory hopes that he would soon find a new job... We now see how fruitless and illusory these missions were.*
ADJ CLASSIF = vain

illustrate /ɪləstreɪt/, **illustrates, illustrating, illustrated**. **1** If you **illustrate** a point that you are making, you explain it and make it clear by using examples, stories or diagrams. EG *The Muslims tell a story to illustrate the fact that power changes people... Nothing illustrates his selfishness more clearly than his behaviour to his wife.*
V+O = exemplify

2 If you **illustrate** a book or lecture, you put pictures, photographs or diagrams into it. EG *Children's books are often beautifully illustrated... He illustrated his lecture with photographs of Rome... ...an illustrated copy of 'Alice in Wonderland'.*
V+O : USU PASS ⇑ decorate

illustration /ɪləstreɪʃəᵒn/, **illustrations**. **1** An **illustration** of a point is something such as an example or a story which is used to explain the point or make it clear. EG *It's a good illustration of the extent to which our education system has changed recently... I've included a few specific examples as illustrations of the difficulty of our work.* ● If you do something **by way of illustration**, you give an example to explain a point you are making. EG *I tell you this story by way of illustration.*
N COUNT : IF+PREP THEN *of* ⇑ instance; ● PHR : USED AS AN A

2 An **illustration** in a book is a picture, design or diagram which is used to decorate or explain parts of the writing in it. EG *...a cookery book with many illustrations.*
N COUNT

3 Illustration is the act of illustrating. EG *Illustration of a difficult idea is often effective in lectures.*
N UNCOUNT

illustrative /ɪləstrətɪv/. An **illustrative** picture, action, etc is an example or explanation of something. EG *These incidents are illustrative of the range of political actions being undertaken.*
ADJ CLASSIF : IF+PREP THEN *of* ⇑ explanatory

illustrator /ɪləstreɪtə/, **illustrators**. An **illustrator** is an artist who draws pictures and diagrams for books and magazines. EG *He is well known as an illustrator of children's books.*
N COUNT

illustrious /ɪlʌstrɪəs/. An **illustrious** person is extremely well known because they have a high position in society or they have done something impressive. EG *He was determined not to be outdone by his more illustrious partner.* ▸ used of a person's activities. EG *He enjoyed a long and illustrious career as a radio producer.*
ADJ QUALIT : USU ATTRIB ⇑ famous; ▸ ⇑ famous

ill will ; also spelled with a hyphen. **Ill will** is a feeling of hostility or spite that you have towards someone. EG *He assured me he felt no ill-will toward me.*
N UNCOUNT

ill wind. An **ill wind** is an event which you expect to be unpleasant, but which in fact has a good result. The expression occurs in the proverb 'It's an ill wind that blows nobody any good', meaning that however bad something is, it usually has one or two good aspects at least. EG *I counted on the ill wind at Oxford that blew me home to help us together.*
N SING WITH DET ⇑ luck

I'm /aɪm/ is the usual spoken form of 'I am'. EG *I'm not blaming you... I'm afraid I can't come.*

im- is added to adjectives, adverbs, and nouns that begin with the letter 'm', 'p', or 'b', in order to form other adjectives, adverbs, and nouns with the opposite meaning. EG *...mature→immature... ...balance→imbalance... ...politely→impolitely.*
PREFIX

image /ɪmɪdʒ/, **images**. 1 If you have an **image** of something or someone, 1.1 you have a mental picture of them, especially one that is created by words or music. EG *To most people, the term 'industrial revolution' conjures up images of smoky steel mills or clanking machines.* 1.2 you have an idea of what they are like; used especially of an idea that is wrong or inaccurate. EG *It's a bit like this image we have that only they have spies. They feel under pressure to conform to our image of them.*
N COUNT: USU+SUPP ⇑ idea
N COUNT: USU+SUPP = notion

2 The **image** of a person, group, or organization is the way that they appear to other people. EG *His attempts to improve the Post Office's image were criticised as 'gimmicks'... He projected the image of a thoughtful statesman.*
N COUNT: USU WITH POSS IN SING ⇑ appearance

3 An **image** is also 3.1 a picture or theme that features in a work of art such as a painting or a piece of writing, especially one that is considered to represent a particular idea or to have a special meaning. EG *He was one of the few painters who produced convincing, accessible images of life in contemporary America... We can illustrate this by tracing a particular image, that of death, through his plays.* 3.2 a picture that is formed by light which passes through a lens, for example the lens in your eye or in a camera. EG *An image of the target area seen by the television camera is displayed on a monitor screen.* 3.3 the picture that you see on a television or cinema screen or in a photograph. EG *...a musical sound track accompanying the visual image.* 3.4 the picture of yourself that you see in a mirror or a shiny surface. EG *He began to dress, never taking his eyes off his image in the mirror.*
N COUNT
N COUNT
N COUNT
N COUNT: USU WITH POSS = reflection

4 If you are **the image of** or **the living image of** someone else, you look very much like them. EG *She is the image of her mother.* • **mirror image**: see **mirror**.
N COUNT

imagery /ɪmɪdʒri¹/. **Imagery** is 1 the mental pictures that are created in your mind by poetic language; used also of the words which create these pictures. EG *He argued that Shakespeare's plays were patterns of imagery.* 2 pictures, statues, etc which represent ideas or situations. EG *Picasso's 'Guernica' is full of the imagery of terror, death, and destruction.*
N UNCOUNT ⇑ ideas
N UNCOUNT

imaginable /ɪmædʒɪnəbə⁰l/ is used, usually with a superlative such as 'best' or 'worst', to mean the most extreme example of a particular thing that you can possibly think of. EG *She wore her curly blonde hair in the prettiest fashion imaginable... ...the narrowest imaginable range of interests... We have been inundated with every bit of information imaginable.*
ADJ CLASSIF: ATTRIB, OR ADJ AFTER N

imaginary /ɪmædʒɪnə⁰ri¹/. Something that is **imaginary** exists only in your mind and not in real life. EG *Many children develop fears of imaginary dangers... ...a fantastic imaginary figure.*
ADJ CLASSIF ⇑ hypothetical

imagination /ɪmædʒɪneɪʃə⁰n/, **imaginations**. 1 Your **imagination** is 1.1 the ability that you have to think of and form pictures or ideas in your mind of things that are different, interesting, or exciting. EG *He has very good taste and a marvellous imagination... These plans reveal a complete failure of imagination.* 1.2 the part of your mind which allows you to form pictures or ideas of things that do not necessarily exist in real life. EG *I can still see her in my imagination.*
N COUNT/UNCOUNT ⇑ inventiveness
N COUNT: USU POSS+N = mind's eye

2 **Imagination** is 2.1 something that you think of that does not exist in real life or that never happened. EG *Of course nobody was trying to kill him.-It was all imagination.* 2.2 the ability to deal successfully with new or unexpected situations or problems. EG *Due to his lack of imagination, he just didn't know what to do.*
N UNCOUNT = illusion
N UNCOUNT = wit

imaginative /ɪmædʒɪnətɪv/. 1 Someone who is **imaginative** is easily able to think of and form pictures or ideas of things that are different, interesting, or exciting, especially things that do not exist in real life. EG *She is one of the more imaginative members of the class.*
ADJ QUALIT ⇑ inventive

2 **Imaginative** is used to describe things that are produced by people who have this ability. EG *The examiner was looking for more imaginative answers.* ◇ **imaginatively**. EG *...an imaginatively designed bathroom.*
ADJ QUALIT = original
◇ ADV WITH VB

imagine /ɪmædʒɪn/, **imagines, imagining, imagined**. 1 If you **imagine** something, 1.1 you think about it and your mind forms a picture or idea of it. EG *It is hard to imagine a greater threat to world peace... Try to imagine you're sitting on a cloud... Not one of us could imagine what he'd meant... I can't imagine asking him for money.* 1.2 you think that you have seen or heard something, although actually you haven't. EG *'Was that a ring at the door?'-'No. You must have imagined it.'... He imagined he saw things.*
V+O/REPORT-CL/-ING, OR V+O (NG/REFL)+A/-ING = visualize
V+O/REPORT-CL/-ING = dream

2 If you **imagine** that something is the case, you think that it is the case. EG *I should imagine he wants you to hold his hand... He was much more generous than people imagined.*
V+REPORT-CL: NO CONT = suppose

imaginings /ɪmædʒɪ¹nɪŋz/ are things that you think you have seen or heard, although actually you have not; a literary word.
N PLURAL

imbalance /ɪmbæləns/, **imbalances**. If there is an **imbalance** in a situation, things are not evenly or fairly arranged. EG *...the imbalance between the rich and poor countries... ...imbalances of social and economic development.*
N COUNT/UNCOUNT ⇑ inequality

imbecile /ɪmbɪsiːl, -saɪl/, **imbeciles**. 1 If you call someone an **imbecile**, you are saying that you think that they are stupid or have done something stupid; an offensive use. EG *For two years that imbecile threw his money away like this... You imbecile!* ▸ used as an adjective. EG *...a timid and imbecile smile... Her face wore an expression of imbecile happiness.* ◇ **imbecility** /ɪmbɪsɪlɪti¹/. EG *...at the height of his political imbecility... ...a monument to imbecility and perversity in scholarship.*
N COUNT: ALSO VOC = idiot
▸ ADJ CLASSIF
◇ N UNCOUNT = idiocy

2 An **imbecile** is a person who is mentally handicapped or is much less intelligent than most ordinary people; a rather old-fashioned or offensive use.
N COUNT = mental defective

imbibe /ɪmbaɪb/, **imbibes, imbibing, imbibed**; a formal word. 1 If you **imbibe** or if you **imbibe** alcohol, you drink it; often used in a humorous way. EG *'Whisky?'-'Thank you,' I said, 'but I never imbibe.'... They imbibed the local cider before walking home to dinner.*
V OR V+O

2 If you **imbibe** something such as ideas or arguments, you listen to them, accept them, and believe that they are right or true. EG *Readers began to show themselves ready to imbibe the propaganda... All students should not study the same course or imbibe the same facts.*
V+O ⇑ absorb = drink in

imbroglio /ɪmbrəʊlɪəʊ/, **imbroglios**. An **imbroglio** is a very confusing or complicated situation; a literary word. EG *His solution had from the start of the whole imbroglio been to put down the rebellion by force.*
N COUNT = mess

imbue /ɪmbjuː/, **imbues, imbuing, imbued**. If someone **is imbued** with something such as an idea or a feeling, they absorb it and become filled with it; a fairly formal word. EG *These cultivated individuals have been imbued with a sense of social purpose... He was able to imbue even the friendliest words with a tone of biting criticism.* ◇ **imbued**. EG *...a unified society deeply imbued with Marxist convictions.*
V+O: USU PASS+*with* ⇑ permeate
◇ ADJ CLASSIF: PRED

IMF /aɪ ɛm ɛf/ is an abbreviation for 'International Monetary Fund'; an international agency which is part of the United Nations and which tries to promote trade and improve economic conditions in the countries which belong to it. The IMF also lends money to its members to help them to develop industries, etc.
N SING: *the*+N

imitate /ɪmɪteɪt/, **imitates, imitating, imitated**. 1 If you **imitate** a person, group, society, etc, you behave in the same way as they do. EG *The party will lose its identity if it tries to imitate the Socialists... Other societies have begun to imitate the wastefulness of the West... He wanted to imitate a leading journal such as the New Yorker.*
V+O ⇑ copy = ape

2 If you **imitate** a person or animal, you copy the way they speak or behave, usually because you are trying to be funny. EG *'Sidney, you'll kill him,' he said, trying to imitate the girl's voice... He could imitate her brilliantly... Sam answered the owl's cry, imitating it exactly.*
V+O = mimic

imitation /ɪmɪteɪʃə⁰n/, **imitations**. 1 An **imitation** is 1.1 something which is supposed to be like something else, although it is usually not as good as the original. EG *Computers so far are just bad imitations of our brains... Indonesian crooners sing perfect imitations of American songs... Beware of cheap imitations.* 1.2 something that you do in order to copy the way someone else speaks or behaves. EG
N COUNT = copy
N COUNT ⇑ act

'Come here, my dear,' she said, giving a reasonable imitation of Isabel Travers... I thought he was giving a bad imitation of Olivier, but it was hardly my place to say so.

2 **Imitation** is behaviour which is modelled on someone else's behaviour. EG *You can learn by imitation... Boys can be seen to pat one another on the head in imitation of what their fathers do.* N UNCOUNT

3 Something that is **imitation** is specially made to look like a particular material or object, although it is usually much cheaper than the original would be. EG *...a pocket diary bound in black imitation leather... There was an awful orchestra playing away under a lot of imitation palm leaves.* ADJ CLASSIF = artificial, fake

imitative /ɪmɪtətɪv/. Behaviour that is **imitative** copies someone else's behaviour. EG *...an imitative process.* ▸ used of people. EG *This disproves the theory that children are purely imitative.* ADJ QUALIT

imitator /ɪmɪteɪtə/, **imitators**. An **imitator** is someone who copies or behaves in the same way as someone else. EG *The qualities which differentiate you from your many imitators can be seen in your sculptures.* N COUNT ⇑ person

immaculate /ɪmækjə⁴lə¹t/. Something that is **immaculate** is 1 absolutely clean, tidy, or neat; used showing approval. EG *Her apartment was immaculate... ...Florrie in her immaculate uniform.* ◇ **immaculately**. EG *Sir Oswald was immaculately dressed.* 2 perfect, without any mistakes at all. EG *Your timing and technique will have to be immaculate.* ADJ CLASSIF = spotless; ◇ ADV; ADJ CLASSIF = flawless

immaterial /ɪmətɪərɪəl/. Something that is **immaterial** is not important or not relevant to what you are talking about. EG *The price was immaterial... Some people think it immaterial what happens to a body after death.* ADJ CLASSIF = irrelevant

immature /ɪmətjʊə, -tʃʊə/. 1 Something that is **immature** is not yet completely grown or fully developed. EG *...a small, greenish-coloured, immature pike... ...an immature organism.* ◇ **immaturity** /ɪmətjʊərɪti¹/. ADJ CLASSIF ⇑ young; ◇ N UNCOUNT ⇑ youth

2 Someone who is **immature** is not sensible enough or old enough to behave properly; used showing disapproval. EG *Lord Kierton's going to say I'm being immature again.* ◇ **immaturity**. EG *There were complaints about my immaturity and lack of judgement.* ADJ QUALIT; ◇ N UNCOUNT

immeasurable /ɪmɛʒə⁰rəbə⁰l/. If an amount, distance, or quantity is **immeasurable**, it is too large or extreme to be measured or counted. EG *The gap between them was growing wide then, and now seems immeasurable.* ADJ CLASSIF ⇑ infinite

immeasurably /ɪmɛʒə⁰rəbli¹/ is used to emphasize adjectives in order to indicate that something has the quality mentioned to a very great extent. EG *Paul Getty had always been immeasurably wealthy... Their faces are lined, immeasurably sad.* ADV ⇑ extremely

immediacy /ɪmiːdɪəsi¹/ is the quality that something has of seeming to be happening at the present time or of being directly involved in things. EG *It is the immediacy of events which makes television so popular... ...the lack of immediacy, the lack of relevance of literature to young people.* N UNCOUNT ⇑ directness

immediate /ɪmiːdɪət/. 1 Something that is **immediate 1.1** happens or is done without any delay or hesitation. EG *They called for an immediate meeting of the Security Council... The matter deserves your immediate attention... My immediate reaction after he had gone was one of relief.* **1.2** actually exists at the present time, and needs to be considered or dealt with quickly. EG *...the immediate needs of people in western society... His attention was occupied with more immediate and pressing matters.* ADJ CLASSIF = instant; ADJ CLASSIF : USU ATTRIB

2 You use **immediate 2.1** to describe a time just before or just after a particular event. EG *The problems in the immediate aftermath of the war were immense.* **2.2** to describe a thing or person in a sequence just before or just after one that is mentioned. EG *Charlie was more honest than his immediate predecessor.* **2.3** to describe an area or direction that is next to or near to a particular place or person. EG *To the immediate south we can see the mountains... There are no solicitors who practise in his immediate neighbourhood.* ADJ CLASSIF : ATTRIB ⇑ near; ADJ CLASSIF : ATTRIB; ADJ CLASSIF : ATTRIB

3 If you talk about your **immediate** family, you are referring to the people who are very closely related to you, such as your parents, children, brothers, and sisters. EG *They rarely attended except when someone in their immediate family was involved.* ADJ CLASSIF : ATTRIB ⇑ near = close

immediately /ɪmiːdɪətli¹/. 1 If something happens **immediately**, it happens without any delay or hesitation. EG *I have to go down to Brighton immediately. It's very urgent... She finished her cigarette, then lit another one immediately.* ADV WITH VB ⇑ now = at once

2 You use **immediately 2.1** to refer to something that can be seen, understood, used, etc without any delay. EG *The connection was not immediately apparent... He was forced to improvise his art from the materials immediately at hand.* **2.2** to refer to something that is closely and directly involved in a situation. EG *The countries most immediately threatened are those to the south... Aircraft were diverted from Europe to other areas more immediately at risk.* **2.3** to refer to something that happens just before or just after a particular event. EG *The sequence of events immediately preceding the tragedy is uncertain... The school at Akenfield was built immediately after the passing of the 1870 Education Act.* **2.4** to refer to something that is next to or very close to a particular thing or place. EG *The name plate was screwed into the door frame immediately below the bell... The church is immediately on your right, behind the shops.* ADV ⇑ quickly = instantly; ADV; ADV+PREP; ADV+PREP

3 You also use **immediately** as a conjunction when you are saying what will happen or be done as soon as something else has happened. EG *Immediately I finish the show I get changed and go home... Contact can be made almost immediately the door is opened.* CONJ SUBORD ⇑ when

immemorial /ɪmɪ²mɔːrɪəl/. 1 If something has been happening **from time immemorial**, it has been happening for longer than anyone can remember. EG *Indian villages have governed themselves from time immemorial... Farmers since time immemorial have started with untamed land.* PHR : USED AS AN A

2 You use **immemorial** to describe something that is so old that nobody can remember a time when it did not exist. EG *The northern climate had been temperate for immemorial ages... ...the immemorial custom of all Western societies.* ADJ CLASSIF : USU ATTRIB ⇑ ancient

immense /ɪmɛns/. Something that is **immense** is extremely large. EG *Squids grow to an immense size... Gillian gave an immense sigh... This development has been of immense importance... Once progress has been made, the gains are likely to be immense.* ADJ QUALIT = enormous

immensely /ɪmɛnsli¹/ means to a very great extent or degree. EG *The issue is an immensely complex one... He was immensely generous... I enjoyed the course immensely.* ADV = enormously

immensity /ɪmɛnsɪti¹/. The **immensity** of something is the very large size or extent of it. EG *...the immensity of the building... ...serious issues, made more profound by the immensity of the possibilities.* N UNCOUNT = vastness

immerse /ɪmɜːs/, **immerses, immersing, immersed**. 1 If you **immerse** yourself in something that you are doing, you become completely involved in it. EG *That year I immersed myself totally in my work.* ◇ **immersed**. EG *He became immersed in the activities of the Oxford Union of Students.* V+O (REFL)+*in* = absorb; ◇ ADJ QUALIT : PRED+*in*

2 If you **immerse** something in a liquid, you put it into the liquid so that it is completely covered. EG *Ebony hairbrushes shouldn't be immersed in water... I crossed the Todd River and immersed my boiling body in a cool pool.* V+O : USU+*in* ⇑ sink

immersion /ɪmɜːʃə⁰n/. 1 Someone's **immersion** in a subject is their complete involvement in it. EG *Immersion in the world of uncertainty and political violence lay ahead... ...her years of immersion in the family.* N UNCOUNT

2 **Immersion** of something in a liquid means putting it into the liquid so that it is completely covered. EG *Treat sprained ankles by immersion in cold water... The dirt on the bottom of the bath didn't encourage total immersion.* N UNCOUNT = submerging

immersion heater, immersion heaters; also spelled with a hyphen. An **immersion heater** is an electric heater which people often have in their homes to provide them with hot water. N COUNT

immigrant /ɪmɪgrənt/, **immigrants**. An **immigrant** is a person who has officially come to live in a country from some other country. EG *...a Russian immigrant... ...an illegal immigrant... ...immigrant children.* N COUNT ⇑ foreigner = settler

immigration /ɪmɪgreɪʃə⁰n/, **immigrations**. 1 **Immigration** is the coming of people into a country N UNCOUNT/COUNT in order to live and work there. EG *The government decided to put stricter controls on immigration... I don't think immigration is a problem... ...immigration laws.*

2 **Immigration** or **immigration control** is the control section at a port, airport or international border, where officials check the passports of people who wish to come into the country. N UNCOUNT

imminence /ɪmɪnəns/. The **imminence** of an event is the near certainty that it will happen very soon. EG *Does your prediction of the imminence of very intelligent machines still hold?... ...the imminence of world revolution.* N UNCOUNT

imminent /ɪmɪnənt/. Something that is **imminent** is almost certain to happen very soon; usually used of things that are unpleasant or that you think will prove to be unpleasant. EG *I believed that war was imminent... There does not seem to be an imminent danger of famine on a world scale.* ADJ CLASSIF

immobile /ɪməʊbaɪl/. Someone or something that is **immobile** is 1 completely still. EG *Boylan sat immobile at the wheel, staring straight ahead... The dog lay at rest, its four feet stretched out, absolutely immobile.* ◊ **immobility** /ɪməʊbɪlɪti[1]/. EG *He froze once more into immobility.* 2 unable to move or unable to be moved. EG *Sea-snakes have fangs that are short and immobile.* ADJ CLASSIF : USU PRED = motionless; ◊ N UNCOUNT; ADJ CLASSIF = fixed, rigid

immobilize /ɪməʊbɪlaɪz/, **immobilizes, immobilizing, immobilized**; also spelled **immobilise**. 1 If you **immobilize** something, you completely stop it from working. EG *The machine was completely immobilized for ten minutes... When you ring the alarm it immobilizes the lift.* V+O

2 Something that **immobilizes** someone stops them from working efficiently or effectively. EG *They simply must cast off those bureaucratic practices that immobilize them... He was immobilized by concern for economic security.* V+O ⇑ prevent

immoderate /ɪmɒdə⁰rə¹t/ is used to describe people, behaviour, or beliefs that are considered to be too extreme; used showing disapproval. EG *We were taught by Brother Byrne, who was so immoderate in using the strap that the class started a campaign against him... It was a Left Wing, but not an immoderate Left Wing Social Democratic Alliance.* ◊ **immoderately**. EG *She laughed immoderately, and spilled some vodka on her frock.* ADJ QUALIT = excessive; ◊ ADV WITH VB = excessively

immodest /ɪmɒdɪst/. 1 Behaviour that is **immodest** shocks or embarrasses some people because they think that it is rude. EG *Breast feeding may seem immodest to some people... Her arms and legs were bare but Posy did not look immodest.* ◊ **immodesty**. ADJ QUALIT ⇑ improper = indecent; ◊ N UNCOUNT

2 Someone who is **immodest** is prepared to tell people how good, important, or clever they are. EG *He said it might be immodest for him to quote the next two lines of the review.* ◊ **immodestly**. EG *These claims are made, somewhat immodestly, for all modern civilizations.* ◊ **immodesty**. EG *...and the muddle, you may claim without immodesty, will be complete.* ADJ QUALIT ⇑ bold = big-headed; ◊ ADV WITH VB = vainly; ◊ N UNCOUNT = vanity

immoral /ɪmɒrəl/. If you believe that an activity, idea, etc is **immoral**, you believe that it is morally wrong. EG *He considered colonialism immoral... Nuclear energy is dangerous and immoral... It's immoral to sleep with someone if you're not in love.* ▸ used of people. EG *The guy thought I was immoral for changing my job for more money... ...an immoral seducer of youth.* ◊ **immorality** /ɪmə⁷rælɪti¹/. EG *...the immorality of apartheid.* ADJ QUALIT; ◊ N UNCOUNT

immortal /ɪmɔːtə⁰l/, **immortals**. 1 Someone or something that is **immortal** 1.1 is famous and likely to be remembered for a long time. EG *The play contained one immortal line.* ◊ **immortality** /ɪmɔ⁸tælɪti¹/. EG *He achieved a very late badge of immortality by having a street named after him.* 1.2 will live or last for ever and never die or be destroyed. EG *...old legends of immortal creatures... ...the immortal and unresting sea.* ◊ **immortality**. EG *We may trust in immortality in the face of incomprehensible death.* ADJ CLASSIF; ◊ N UNCOUNT = renown; ADJ CLASSIF ⇑ eternal = abiding; ◊ N UNCOUNT

2 An **immortal** is 2.1 a person who is famous for something they have achieved, and likely to be remembered for a long time. EG *W.G.Grace will be numbered among the immortals of cricket.* 2.2 a god or goddess who lives for ever. EG *They were as invulnerable as the immortals of Olympus.* N COUNT : USU PL = hero; N COUNT : USU PL = deity

immortalize /ɪmɔːtə⁰laɪz/, **immortalizes, immortalizing, immortalized**; also spelled **immortalise**. If you **immortalize** someone or something, you cause them to be remembered for a very long time, for example by writing about them or making a film. EG *She is immortalised by a very distinguished statue... ...a wondrous event which he had immortalised in verse.* V+O : USU+A ⇑ commemorate = celebrate

immovable /ɪmuːvəbə⁰l/. 1 Something that is **immovable** is fixed and cannot be moved from its position. EG *...an immovable pillar.* ◊ **immovably**. EG *Each picture was nailed immovably in place.* ADJ CLASSIF; ◊ ADV

2 If you have a feeling or opinion that is **immovable**, you are firm about it and will not change. EG *...fossilised ways and immovable conservatism... The foundations of personality were immovable.* ADJ CLASSIF

immune /ɪmjuːn/. 1 If you are **immune** to a particular disease, you cannot be affected by it. EG *We are virtually immune to certain diseases.* ◊ **immunity** /ɪmjuːnɪti¹/. EG *Babies receive immunity to a variety of infections.* ADJ CLASSIF : USU PRED; ◊ N UNCOUNT : IF+PREP THEN *to/against*

2 If you are **immune** to something that happens or is done, you are not affected by it. EG *He was immune to the flattery of political leaders... The American economy is proving surprisingly immune to big fluctuations in interest rates.* ◊ **immunity**. EG *This immunity to criticism is built into their whole system nowadays.* ADJ QUALIT : PRED, IF+PREP THEN *to*; ◊ N UNCOUNT : IF+PREP THEN *to*

3 Someone or something that is **immune** from a particular process or situation is able to escape it or avoid being affected by it. EG *...targets that the West had considered immune from air attack... The fabric of modern society is not immune from decay.* ◊ **immunity, immunities**. EG *He had been granted immunity from prosecution... ...an income tax immunity form... ...the privileges or immunities of citizens of the United States.* • See also **diplomatic immunity**. ADJ QUALIT : PRED, IF+PREP THEN ⇑ safe = exempt; ◊ N UNCOUNT/COUNT : IF+PREP THEN *from/against* = exemption

immunize /ɪmjə⁴naɪz/, **immunizes, immunizing, immunized**; also spelled **immunise**. If people or animals **are immunized**, they are made immune to a particular disease, often by being given an injection. EG *Everyone who is going abroad will need to be immunized against typhoid.* ◊ **immunization** /ɪmjə⁴naɪzeɪʃə⁰n/. EG *...a government programme of immunization.* V+O : IF+PREP THEN *against* = inoculate; ◊ N UNCOUNT/COUNT

immutable /ɪmjuːtəbə⁰l/. Something that is **immutable** will never change; a formal word. EG *Values and attitudes are not immutable, but are likely to change... The view of his time was that all species were immutable, created by God.* ADJ CLASSIF ⇑ permanent

imp /ɪmp/, **imps**. 1 An **imp** is a small creature in a fairy story that has magical powers and often causes trouble in a playful way. N COUNT

2 If you call a child an **imp**, you mean that they are naughty, but in a playful way that does not cause any serious harm. N COUNT = rascal

imp. is 1 an abbreviation for 'imperfect'. 2 an abbreviation for 'imperative'.

impact, impacts, impacting, impacted. The word **impact** is pronounced /ɪmpækt/ when it is a noun, and /ɪmpækt/ when it is a verb. 1 The **impact** that something has on a situation, process, person, etc is the effect that it has on it. EG *The new seeds had an immediate impact on food production... ...the impact of computing on routine office work... British authors make relatively little impact abroad.* N COUNT : USU SING, IF+PREP THEN *on/upon*

2 **Impact** is 2.1 the action of one object hitting another, usually with a lot of force. EG *Many modern bullets produce an explosive effect upon impact... The estimated point of impact of each missile was worked out by computer.* 2.2 the force with which one object hits another. EG *Hill 402 seemed to crumble with the impact of enemy artillery fire.* N UNCOUNT ⇑ contact; N UNCOUNT

3 If you **impact** an object into something, you drive it or press it there firmly with a lot of force. EG *An unexploded bomb has been impacted into the bank of the river.* V-ERG

impacted /ɪmpæktɪ²d/. An **impacted** tooth is unable to grow through your gum properly. EG *...an impacted wisdom tooth that had to be taken out.* ADJ CLASSIF : USU ATTRIB ⇑ embedded

impair /ɪmpeə/, **impairs, impairing, impaired**. If you **impair** something, you damage it or weaken it so that it stops being effective or working properly. EG *Continued criticism of the leaders could impair efforts to ease tensions in the area... His* V+O *digestion had been impaired by his recent illness.* ◇ **impaired**. EG ...*impaired vision or hearing.* ◇ ADJ CLASSIF

impale /ɪmpeɪl/, **impales, impaling, impaled**. If you **impale** something, you pierce through it with a sharp pointed object. EG *He cut off a piece of the meat and impaled it on his fork... He was holding a branch, and impaled upon it was the bloody head of a leopard.* V+O (NG/REFL): IF+PREP THEN *on/upon* = skewer

impart /ɪmpɑːt/, **imparts, imparting, imparted**; a formal word. **1** If you **impart** information or knowledge to people, you tell it or give it to them. EG *He told them that he had a terrible piece of news to impart... ...setting up schools to impart skills and knowledge.* V+O: IF+PREP THEN *to* ⇑ inform

2 If something **imparts** a particular quality, the quality comes out of it. EG *Peas and carrots during cooking impart a delicious flavour.* V+O: IF+PREP THEN *to* ⇑ give = exude

impartial /ɪmpɑːʃəˡl/. Someone who is **impartial** is not involved directly in a particular situation, and is therefore able to consider it and give an opinion about it fairly. EG ...*an impartial distant observer.* ▸ used of people's attitudes and opinions. EG *He gave an impartial view of the state of affairs in Northern Ireland.* ◇ **impartially**. EG *These men are to judge the people impartially.* ◇ **impartiality** /ɪmpɑːʃɪælɪti¹/. EG *His impartiality was highly suspect.* ADJ CLASSIF = neutral; ▸ ADJ CLASSIF; ◇ ADV; ◇ N UNCOUNT = neutrality

impassable /ɪmpɑːsəbəˡl/. A road, path, route, etc that is **impassable** is impossible to travel over because it is blocked or in bad condition. ADJ CLASSIF

impasse /ɒmpæs/. An **impasse** is a difficult situation in which it is impossible to make any progress. EG *The government had reached an impasse... I see no way out of this impasse.* N SING WITH DET ⇑ obstacle

impassioned /ɪmpæʃənd/. When you speak in an **impassioned** way, you express powerful emotion because you feel very strongly about something. EG *After three hours of impassioned debate the motion was defeated.* ADJ QUALIT ⇑ emotional

impassive /ɪmpæsɪv/. If your face is **impassive**, it does not show any emotion. EG *Her face remained impassive, studying the Belgian as he completed the form.* ◇ **impassively**. EG *He looked at me impassively.* ADJ CLASSIF ⇑ calm = expressionless; ◇ ADV: USU WITH VB

impatience /ɪmpeɪʃəns/. **1** Someone's **impatience** is **1.1** their annoyance at having to wait for something to happen. EG *Chris watched me with some impatience.* **1.2** their feeling of irritation about something; also used of someone's personal quality of becoming easily irritated by things. EG *There was increasing impatience with the reluctance of the party to grant these reforms... 'Well, obviously,' says Myra, with a little impatience.* N UNCOUNT ⇑ irritation; N UNCOUNT ⇑ annoyance

2 If you show **impatience** to do something or **impatience** for something to happen, you are eager to do it or for it to happen and do not want to wait. EG *There is always a certain impatience to try out an idea to see if it works... Rothermere was awaiting the outcome with impatience.* N UNCOUNT ⇑ restlessness

impatient /ɪmpeɪʃənt/. **1** Someone who is **impatient** is **1.1** annoyed because they have had to wait too long for something, or because they are not getting what they want. EG *Some ministers are growing impatient as the economy continues to flounder... The Englishman became impatient. 'Well, can you do it?'* ▸ used of people's actions and behaviour. EG *He swept all she said aside with a grand, impatient swing of his arm.* ◇ **impatiently**. EG *Omoro stood waiting impatiently.* **1.2** easily irritated by people or situations. EG *He was very impatient with students who could not follow him.* ◇ **impatiently**. EG *'I know, I know,' Vaughan said impatiently.* ADJ QUALIT ⇑ restless; ▸ ⇑ agitated ADJ QUALIT; ◇ ADV WITH VB; ADJ QUALIT: IF+PREP THEN *with* ⇑ intolerant; ◇ ADV WITH VB

2 If you are **impatient** to do something or **impatient** for something to happen, you are eager to do it or for it to happen and do not want to wait. EG *Philip was impatient to inspect his place of work... British troops were impatient for demobilization.* ◇ **impatiently**. EG *He looked forward impatiently to Kumar's next visit.* ADJ QUALIT: USU +*to*-INF/*for*; ◇ ADV WITH VB

impeach /ɪmpiːtʃ/, **impeaches, impeaching, impeached**. If someone **is impeached**, they are charged with committing a serious crime; used especially in the United States when a senior government official or politician is charged with a crime in connection with their job. EG *Elected officials can be impeached.* V+O ⇑ prosecute

impeachable /ɪmpiːtʃəbəˡl/. An **impeachable** crime or offence is one for which a public official can be impeached. ADJ CLASSIF ⇑ indictable

impeachment /ɪmpiːtʃməˀnt/. The **impeachment** of a public official, especially in the United States, is their trial for a serious crime committed in office. EG *They were deciding on the crimes that would justify impeachment.* N UNCOUNT

impeccable /ɪmpekəbəˡl/. If a person's behaviour or appearance is **impeccable**, it is excellent and cannot be faulted. EG *He had impeccable manners... He stood before them, impeccable as ever in his elegant suit.* ◇ **impeccably**. EG *As usual, he was impeccably dressed.* ADJ CLASSIF = faultless; ◇ ADV = faultlessly

impecunious /ɪmpɪ²kjuːniˡəs/. Someone who is **impecunious** has very little money; a formal word. ADJ CLASSIF ⇑ poor

impede /ɪmpiːd/, **impedes, impeding, impeded**. If you **impede** someone or something, you make their movement, development, or progress difficult. EG *Their advance was seriously impeded by the bad weather.* V+O = hamper, hinder

impediment /ɪmpedɪməˀnt/, **impediments**. **1** Something that is an **impediment** to a person or thing makes their movement, development, or progress difficult. EG *The new taxes were a major impediment to economic growth.* N COUNT: IF+PREP THEN *to* = obstacle, obstruction

2 Someone who has an **impediment** of a particular kind has a physical disability which makes something such as speaking or walking difficult. EG *The child suffers from a serious speech impediment.* N COUNT = defect

impedimenta /ɪmpedɪmentə/. A person's **impedimenta** are the bags and other things that slow them down on a journey; often used of the equipment carried by an army; a formal word. EG *He included among his impedimenta a wife and three children.* N PLURAL = paraphernalia

impel /ɪmpel/, **impels, impelling, impelled**. When something such as an emotion **impels** you to do something, it affects you so strongly that you feel forced to do it. EG *The administration was impelled by fear to transfer me to the maximum security wing... I feel impelled to express grave doubts about the project.* V+O: USU+*to*-INF, OR +*to*-*wards* = compel

impending /ɪmpendɪŋ/. An **impending** danger, arrival, etc is going to happen or appear very soon; a formal word. EG *We were well aware of impending disaster... ...signals of an impending split in the Labour Party.* ADJ CLASSIF: ATTRIB ⇑ imminent

impenetrable /ɪmpenɪtrəbəˡl/. Something that is **impenetrable** is **1** impossible to get through. EG ...*an impenetrable wall.* ◇ **impenetrably**. EG *Winter brought the fogs, impenetrably thick.* **2** impossible or very difficult to get into. EG ...*immense tracts of impenetrable jungle.* ◇ **impenetrability** /ɪmpenətrəbɪlɪti¹/. EG ...*the impenetrability of this fortress.* **3** impossible or very difficult to understand. EG *The law seems even more mysterious and impenetrable... ...those aspects of nature which are most impenetrable to intelligence.* ADJ QUALIT; ◇ ADV; ADJ QUALIT = inaccessible; ◇ N UNCOUNT; ADJ QUALIT: IF+PREP THEN *to* = unfathomable

IMPER □ In this dictionary IMPER is used in the grammar notes beside entries to describe the imperative form of verbs in which the verb is used in its infinitive form without 'to'. The imperative is used when you are giving commands to someone, telling them what to do or what not to do. An imperative verb does not normally have a subject. Examples of imperative verbs are **keep, do**, and **start** in ***Keep off the grass...Don't do that!...Start when you hear the bell.*** IMPER is used in the grammar notes to comment on the typical use of the imperative, so that NO IMPER is used to indicate that a verb is not normally used in the imperative. An example of a verb that is not normally used in the imperative is **hear 1.** You do not say as a command 'Hear me', although you can say 'Listen to me'.

imperative /ɪmperətɪv/, **imperatives**. **1** Something that is **imperative** is extremely important or urgent, and needs to be considered or dealt with before anything else; a fairly formal use. EG *I think it's imperative that we take care of Liebermann immediately... It was imperative to secure a position of strength without delay.* ▸ used as a noun. EG *Any species' first imperative is to survive... Hamid had his own moral imperatives to pursue.* ADJ QUALIT: USU PRED = vital; ▸ N COUNT ⇑ priority = duty

2 If you say something in an **imperative** tone of voice, you speak firmly so that you are likely to be obeyed; a fairly formal use. ADJ QUALIT = authoritative

3 In grammar, an **imperative** is a verb in the form that is typically used for giving orders. In this N COUNT dictionary verbs which are rarely used in the imperative have NO IMPER in the grammar notes beside the entry. See □ at IMPER.

imperceptible /ɪmpəsɛptɪbəºl/. Something that is **imperceptible** happens or exists without you feeling or noticing it. EG *...an almost imperceptible sensation... The transition is almost imperceptible.* — ADJ CLASSIF
◇ **imperceptibly**. EG *The days flowed imperceptibly into one another... Gradually, almost imperceptibly, the sun warms us up.* — ◇ ADV

imperfect /ɪmpɜːfɪ²kt/. 1 Something that is **imperfect** has faults or problems. EG *The copy is imperfect... The Party was only an imperfect tool for the workers' use.* — ADJ QUALIT ⇑ bad = flawed
2 In grammar, the **imperfect** or the **imperfect** tense is used in describing continuous or repeated actions in the past. — N SING : *the*+N, OR ADJ CLASSIF : ATTRIB

imperfection /ɪmpə⁵fɛkʃəºn/, **imperfections**. 1 **Imperfection** or an **imperfection** in someone or something is a fault or weakness that they have. EG *She has already noticed my imperfections... This world is riddled with imperfection.* — N COUNT/ UNCOUNT = failing, shortcoming
2 An **imperfection** in something is a small mark or piece of damage which may spoil its appearance. EG *There are no imperfections in this china.* — N COUNT = blemish, flaw

imperfectly /ɪmpɜːfɪ²ktli¹/. If you do something **imperfectly**, you do not do it completely or perfectly. EG *...a world which we only imperfectly understand... This society is imperfectly integrated.* — ADV ⇑ badly = incompletely

imperial /ɪmpɪərɪəl/. 1 **Imperial** is used 1.1 to refer to a country that is or was an empire. EG *...the Mandarins of Imperial China... ...the decline of Britain as an imperial power... ...Germany's imperial past.* — ADJ CLASSIF : USU ATTRIB
1.2 to describe something that belongs or relates to an emperor or empress. EG *...the Imperial Palace... ...His Imperial Highness the Prince Michael Alexandrovich.* — ADJ CLASSIF : ATTRIB ⇑ royal
2 The **imperial** system of units is the system of measurement, originally used in Britain, where length is measured in inches, feet, and yards, weight is measured in ounces and pounds, and volume is measured in pints and gallons. — ADJ CLASSIF : ATTRIB

imperialism /ɪmpɪərɪəlɪzəºm/ is a system of rule, or a belief in a system of rule, in which a rich and powerful country controls other countries in order to become richer and more powerful. EG *...British imperialism in India.* ◇ **imperialist, imperialists**. EG *...the imperialist, war-mongering ruling classes.* — N UNCOUNT; ◇ N COUNT, OR ADJ CLASSIF
◇ **imperialistic**. EG *...imperialistic patriotism.* — ◇ ADJ CLASSIF

imperil /ɪmpɛrɪºl/, **imperils, imperilling, imperilled**; also spelled **imperiling** and **imperiled** in American English. Something that **imperils** you puts you in danger; a formal word. EG *...a political crisis which had imperilled the future of the party.* — V+O = endanger

imperious /ɪmpɪərɪəs/. An **imperious** person is proud and domineering. EG *...the imperious overseer.* ▸ used of a person's actions or behaviour. EG *All his imperious orders were obeyed.* ◇ **imperiously**. EG *He began softly and yet imperiously to issue his commands.* — ADJ QUALIT ⇑ authoritative; ADV

imperishable /ɪmpɛrɪʃəbəºl/. Something that is **imperishable** cannot disappear or be destroyed. EG *There was a certain quality which was imperishable... ...imperishable plastics.* — ADJ CLASSIF

impermanence /ɪmpɜːmənəns/ is a quality of not being permanent; a formal word. EG *...a sense of fragile impermanence.* — N UNCOUNT

impermanent /ɪmpɜːmənənt/. Something that is **impermanent** is not permanent; a formal word. EG *Changes come slowly and are generally impermanent.* — ADJ CLASSIF ⇑ transient

impermeable /ɪmpɜːmjəbəºl/. Something that is **impermeable** will not allow fluid to pass through it; a formal word. EG *...impermeable membranes.* — ADJ CLASSIF ⇑ impervious

impers. is an abbreviation for 'impersonal': see **impersonal 3, 4**.

impersonal /ɪmpɜːsənəºl/. 1 Something such as a place or an activity that is **impersonal** makes you feel that you are not important or that your personality, feelings, and opinions do not matter; used showing disapproval. EG *...the rules and regulations of a vast, impersonal organization... ...dull, repetitive, impersonal work... The town of Elliotdale, being smaller, seemed less impersonal.* — ADJ QUALIT ⇑ distant
2 An **impersonal** feeling or action does not involve or relate to any particular person. EG *She mentioned no names in her impersonal criticism of the staff.* — ADJ CLASSIF ⇑ objective
◇ **impersonally**. EG *...written examinations marked impersonally and with no knowledge of the candidate.* — ◇ ADV
3 In grammar, an **impersonal** verb does not have a subject and is only used after 'it' or 'there', as in 'It is raining'. — ADJ CLASSIF : ATTRIB
4 In grammar, an **impersonal** pronoun is one that does not refer to a person, for example 'it'. — ADJ CLASSIF : ATTRIB

impersonate /ɪmpɜːsəneɪt/, **impersonates, impersonating, impersonated**. 1 If you **impersonate** a person, 1.1 you pretend that you are that person, usually by disguising yourself. EG *I ought to be arrested for impersonating an officer.* — V+O ⇑ imitate
◇ **impersonation** /ɪmpɜːsəneɪʃəºn/. EG *Some orchids attract insects by sexual impersonation.* — ◇ N UNCOUNT
1.2 you imitate the person's expressions, speech, or behaviour, especially when this is meant to be funny. EG *He can impersonate most well-known politicians on demand.* ◇ **impersonation, impersonations**. EG *...Harry's impersonation of a Russian prince... I was showing off madly, doing bad impersonations and cracking jokes.* — V+O ⇑ copy; ◇ N COUNT/ UNCOUNT = impression
2 If you **impersonate** a particular feeling or condition, you pretend that you have it; a formal use. EG *She stands waiting for me while I impersonate heat exhaustion.* — V+O = feign, sham

impersonator /ɪmpɜːsəneɪtə/, **impersonators**. An **impersonator** is someone who impersonates people, especially a comedian or comedienne. — N COUNT ⇑ mimic = impressionist

impertinence /ɪmpɜːtɪnəns/, **impertinences**. **Impertinence** or an **impertinence** is speech or behaviour that is impertinent. EG *He charitably chose to ignore her impertinence... A lot of businessmen consider it an impertinence for anyone to mention retirement to them.* — N UNCOUNT/ COUNT ⇑ rudeness

impertinent /ɪmpɜːtɪnənt/. Someone who is **impertinent** is rude rather than polite or respectful. EG *She is too free with her tongue and is rather impertinent to people.* ▸ used of people's actions or behaviour. EG *...impertinent questions.* — ADJ QUALIT = cheeky; ▸ = impudent

imperturbable /ɪmpətɜːbəbəºl/. Someone who is **imperturbable** remains calm and untroubled, even in a situation that is disturbing. EG *She had been admirably calm, imperturbable, and reasoning over the death of the cat.* — ADJ QUALIT = composed, collected

impervious /ɪmpɜːvɪəs/. 1 If you are **impervious** to someone's actions or attempts to try and make you do something, you are not affected or influenced by them. EG *He was impervious to the charm and eloquence of Fletcher... He did as he pleased and was impervious to punishment.* — ADJ QUALIT : USU PRED+*to*
2 Something that is **impervious** to water, heat, or a particular object, is able to resist it or stop it passing through it. EG *The tanks kept up a steady fire and seemed quite impervious to machine guns.* — ADJ CLASSIF : IF+ PREP THEN *to*

impetuous /ɪmpɛtjʊəs/. Someone who is **impetuous** is likely to act quickly and suddenly without thinking or being careful. EG *...a young, impetuous, highly-strung boy.* ▸ used of people's actions or behaviour. EG *She revealed her feelings in impetuous displays of spending and gambling.* ◇ **impetuosity** /ɪmpɛtjʊɒsɪti¹/. EG *Blind faith and impetuosity have led them into their present difficulties.* — ADJ QUALIT = impulsive, rash; ▸ = impulsive, rash; ◇ N UNCOUNT = rashness

impetus /ɪmpɪ²təs/. 1 **Impetus** or an **impetus** is an important effect that something has on a situation, which causes a process to develop more quickly. EG *Once a commercial impetus is given to their development, the products should improve rapidly... ...the social and cultural impetus that propelled university graduates into careers in management... The present conflict might provide fresh impetus for peace talks.* — N SING WITH DET, OR N UNCOUNT ⇑ force = drive
2 **Impetus** is the force that starts an object moving and resists changes in speed or direction once it is moving. EG *They raise their wings and beat a further few strokes, renewing their impetus and extending their flight.* — N UNCOUNT = momentum

impiety /ɪmpaɪɪti¹/ is a lack of respect or religious reverence that a person shows; a formal word used showing disapproval. — N UNCOUNT = irreverence

impinge /ɪmpɪndºʒ/, **impinges, impinging, impinged**. Something that **impinges** on you has an effect on you, often by restricting the way that you can behave; a formal word. EG *Your political opinions will necessarily impinge on your public life.* — V+A (*on/upon*) = encroach

impious /ɪmpi¹əs/. Someone who is **impious** shows a lack of respect or religious reverence; used showing disapproval. — ADJ QUALIT = irreverent

impish /ɪmpɪʃ/. Someone who has an **impish** quality appears cheeky or naughty in a playful way. EG *He had an impish, rather wicked humour.*
ADJ QUALIT ⇑ mischievous

implacable /ɪmplækəbəˀl/. Someone who is **implacable** has a strong feeling of anger, disapproval, resentment, etc that you are unable to change. EG *...the chief and most implacable opponent of the measure.* ▸ used of people's attitudes or behaviour. EG *...the implacable hatred that workers feel for their employers.* ◊ **implacably**. EG *They are implacably hostile.*
ADJ QUALIT = relentless; ▸ = merciless; ◊ ADV = mercilessly

implant, implants, implanting, implanted. The word **implant** is pronounced /ɪmplɑːnt/ when it is a verb, and /ɪmplɑːnt/ when it is a noun. **1** If someone **implants** something into a person's body, they put it there, usually by operating on them. EG *The operation to implant the artificial heart took 2 hours... ...experiments in which they implanted electrodes in the skull of a bull.*
V+O : IF+PREP THEN *in/into* ⇑ insert

2 An **implant** is something that is implanted into a person's body. EG *Hormone implants are often used as growth boosters.*
N COUNT ⇑ object

3 If you **implant** an idea, you make it become widely accepted or believed. EG *The CDR successfully implanted the ideas of Chinese communism in Britain.*
V+O : IF+PREP THEN *in/into* ⇑ establish

4 If you **implant** a feeling or an idea in someone's mind, you make it a strong part of the way that they think or behave. EG *...parents requiring teachers to implant religious attitudes in their children... Early experiences can implant strong fears in the subconscious.*
V+O : IF+PREP THEN *in/into* = instil

implausible /ɪmplɔːzəˡbəˀl/. Something that is **implausible** is not easy to believe, and therefore unlikely to be true or genuine. EG *This story sounded so implausible that I wondered whether he could possibly be telling the truth... It's an extremely likeable but very implausible romantic thriller... ...the implausible Latin name of the airline.*
ADJ QUALIT = improbable

implement, implements, implementing, implemented. The word **implement** is pronounced /ɪmplɪˡməˀnt/ when it is a verb, and /ɪmplɪˡmənt/ when it is a noun. **1** If you **implement** the ideas of a plan, system, law, etc, you carry them out in order to change or control a situation. EG *These are policies that they would like to see implemented in the next parliament.* ◊ **implementation** /ɪmplɪˡməˀnteɪʃəˀn/. EG *He did not do enough to secure the implementation of the desired reforms.*
V+O = effect; ◊ N UNCOUNT = enforcement

2 An **implement** is a tool or other piece of equipment. EG *The plough was unknown, the hoe being the most advanced implement in use... ...a household implement.*
N COUNT ⇑ utensil

implicate /ɪmplɪkeɪt/, **implicates, implicating, implicated**. If you **implicate** someone in a wrong or unpleasant event or situation, you show that they have been involved in it. EG *He was interned but, as he was in no way implicated in war crimes, was released.*
V+O : IF+PREP THEN *in* ⇑ involve

implication /ɪmplɪkeɪʃəˀn/, **implications**. **1** An **implication** is something that is suggested or implied by a particular situation, event, or statement. EG *Spencer began to query the political implications of Macaulay's statement... These principles have a number of implications for the future ordering of society... Many MPs are saying her policies have failed and, by implication, so has she.*
N COUNT, OR *by*+N ⇑ inference

2 The **implication** of someone in a wrong or unpleasant event or situation is the act of showing that they have been involved in it. EG *The implication of the government in the scandal would have been highly embarrassing.*
N UNCOUNT ⇑ suggestion

implicit /ɪmplɪsɪt/. **1** Something that is **implicit** is expressed in an indirect way, and is therefore not immediately noticeable or understandable. EG *...its implicit as opposed to its surface meaning... His statement contained an implicit acknowledgement that he had made a mistake.* ◊ **implicitly**. EG *The national security adviser implicitly condoned their retaliation.*
ADJ CLASSIF ⇑ inferred; ◊ ADV WITH VB

2 Something that is **implicit** in a statement, attitude, or system is contained in it as an essential element but not actually stated openly. EG *One can readily imagine the despair implicit in such a philosophy... Although it wasn't spoken, it was implicit in her attitude that she thought I had failed.*
ADJ QUALIT : PRED+*in* = inherent

3 If you have an **implicit** belief or faith in something, you have complete faith and no doubts about it at all. EG *I declare that I have implicit faith in Marxism.* ◊ **implicitly**. EG *I believe implicitly in the concept of Europe... They trust each other implicitly.*
ADJ QUALIT; ◊ ADV WITH VB ⇑ totally

implore /ɪmplɔː/, **implores, imploring, implored**. If you **implore** someone to do something, you desperately beg them to do it. EG *Some of the captives were afraid and implored the others to do as they were told... She implored forgiveness for what she had done.* ◊ **imploring**. EG *She gave him an imploring look.* ◊ **imploringly**. EG *'You will help me, won't you?' he said imploringly.*
V+O : USU+*to*-INF/QUOTE, OR V+QUOTE = beseech; ◊ ADJ QUALIT; ◊ ADV WITH VB

imply /ɪmplaɪ/, **implies, implying, implied**. **1** If you **imply** that something is the case, you suggest that it is the case without actually saying so. EG *Somehow he implied that he was the one who had done all the work... I don't wish to imply that you are stupid, but I do think you made a mistake.* ◊ **implied**. EG *I feel there is some implied criticism about the present you have chosen.*
V+O/REPORT-CL = hint; ◊ ADJ CLASSIF = hinted

2 When one situation or condition **implies** another, it suggests that the second situation is true as a necessary consequence of the first one being true. EG *To join a union does not also imply a freedom not to join.*
V+O ⇑ mean

impolite /ɪmpəlaɪt/. Someone who is **impolite** is rather rude and offends people. EG *It was very impolite of him to ask.* ▸ used of people's actions and behaviour. EG *Such an action is considered rather impolite.* ◊ **impolitely**.
ADJ QUALIT = discourteous; ▸ = discourteous; ◊ ADV WITH VB

impolitic /ɪmpɒlɪtɪk/. An **impolitic** action is unwise and likely to cause difficulty or embarrassment; a formal word. EG *It seemed impolitic to draw too much attention to this.*
ADJ QUALIT

imponderable /ɪmpɒndəˀrəbəˀl/, **imponderables**. **Imponderable** is used to describe something that is impossible or very difficult to assess or estimate. EG *...the great imponderable forces of nature.* ▸ used as a noun. EG *...such imponderables as power and knowledge.*
ADJ CLASSIF : ATTRIB ⇑ inestimable; ▸ N COUNT ⇑ incalculable

import, imports, importing, imported. The word **import** is pronounced /ɪmpɔːt/ when it is a verb, and /ɪmpɔːt/ when it is a noun. **1** If you **import** goods or services, you buy them from another country and have them sent to you for use in your own country. EG *Even the smallest piece of their machinery is imported... The government had an interest in importing scientific equipment of this kind... ...imported sugar.* ▸ used as a noun. EG *The import of cotton goods went up sharply in 1859... They are being asked to register all imports and exports of conventional weapons... ...a system of import controls.* ◊ **importation** /ɪmpɔːteɪʃəˀn/. EG *...the illegal importation of drugs into Britain.*
V OR V+O ≠ export; ▸ N SING WITH DET, OR N COUNT ⇑ purchase; ◊ N UNCOUNT = bringing in

2 If you **import** ideas, values, etc from a place, you introduce them in another place where they did not previously exist. EG *It's the latest dance craze imported from America... They also import rural social relationships into the towns.* ◊ **importation**. EG *A modern English ballet is to be danced in China, and its importation is another sign of China's strengthening links with the West.*
V+O ⇑ transfer; ◊ N UNCOUNT+SUPP

3 An **import** is **3.1** a product or raw material which you buy from another country for use in your own country. EG *They blamed the closure on cheap imports and the recession... Young professionals have been opting for imports such as the German Audi.*
N COUNT ≠ export

3.2 something such as an idea which has been introduced from one place or culture to another where it did not previously exist. EG *Some of the long words in our dictionaries are imports from other languages... It cannot be explained as a recent colonial or tourist import.*
N COUNT ⇑ transference

4 In formal English, the **import** of something is **4.1** the importance that it has because of the way it is likely to affect people or influence future events. EG *The future of the school may be of little import... He failed to comprehend the import of village scandals and tragedies.* **4.2** its meaning; used especially when the meaning is not clearly expressed. EG *He used poetic imagery to conceal the work's actual import.*
N SING WITH DET = consequence, significance; N SING WITH DET

5 A thing that **imports** something to you has a particular meaning for you and an effect on you; a formal use. EG *It is a means of capturing something beautiful, it is meant to import something to them.*
V+O : IF+PREP THEN *to* = convey, signify

importance /ɪmpɔːtəns/. **1** The **importance** of something is its quality of being important, neces-
N UNCOUNT

sary, or significant in a particular situation. EG *Here I would stress the importance of mathematics to the whole of science... These would be of vital importance to the assassin... ...an attempt to assess Stonehenge's historic importance.*

2 The **importance** of a person is the social influence, power, or status that they have. EG *Was he related to anyone of importance?... This idiot is in a position of importance.* — N UNCOUNT = significance

important /ɪmpɔːtənt/. 1 Something that is **important** is very significant, valuable, or necessary and should be considered when dealing with a particular topic. EG *This is the most important part of the job... That is a very important point that you've raised... She is highly skilled at her work; and, more important, she is happy in it... Whatever your crisis, it is important to realize that it has happened before... Your child's health is more important than the doctor's feelings.* — ADJ QUALIT = vital, essential
◊ **importantly**. EG *The problems the Chinese face differ importantly from those facing Africa.* — ◊ ADV WITH VB = essentially

2 Ideas, beliefs, etc that are **important** to you are ones that have great significance for you and that you consider very seriously. EG *I realize how important it is for me to have a job... It was important to me to know... Why isn't the existence of God important to you?* — ADJ QUALIT = essential

3 Someone who is **important** has influence or power within a society or particular group. EG *It wasn't as though Davis was anyone important in the firm... I'm going to notify all the important living composers everywhere... ...the list of important people who are coming on state visits... He's apt to feel less important than usual.* — ADJ QUALIT = influential

importer /ɪmpɔːtə/, **importers**. An **importer** is a person, country, or firm which buys goods or services from another country for use in his or its own country. EG *Many western countries have ceased to be major pet food importers.* — N COUNT ⇑ purchaser

importunate /ɪmpɔːtjəⁱnət/. Someone who is **importunate** is persistent in trying to get something that they want; a formal word. EG *She holds out her hand for money, importunate, insistent, desperate.* — ADJ CLASSIF = insistent

importune /ɪmpɔːtjuːn, -tʃuː-/, **importunes, importuning, importuned**. If you **importune** someone, you persistently ask them for something or urge them to do something; a formal word. EG *He began to importune her with offers of marriage.* — V+O ⇑ harass

importunity /ɪmpɔːtjuːnɪti[1], -tʃuː-/, **importunities**. **Importunity** or an **importunity** is an example of importunate behaviour; a formal word. EG *I was there to protect her from the importunities of unscrupulous and lascivious men.* — N UNCOUNT/COUNT

impose /ɪmpəʊz/, **imposes, imposing, imposed**. 1 If you **impose** something such as a condition or rule on people, you use your authority to force the condition or rule to be kept. EG *She was a harsh mother and imposed severe discipline on her children... What was the length of sentence imposed?... ...the four-fold increase in oil prices imposed by OPEC... ...the proposal to impose a 20p admission charge for museums and art galleries.* — V+O : IF+PREP THEN *on/upon* ⇑ enforce
◊ **imposition** /ɪmpəzɪʃəⁿn/. EG *...the imposition of a wages freeze.* — ◊ N UNCOUNT+SUPP

2 If you **impose** your opinions, beliefs, etc on other people, you try and make people accept them as a rule or a model to copy. EG *He is tempted to impose his own acting style on the class... ...parents who impose authoritative religion on their children... The more society imposes conformity upon its members, the more people want to rebel.* ◊ **imposition**. EG *...the external imposition on children of adult conceptions.* — V+O : IF+PREP THEN *on/upon* ⇑ inflict; ◊ N UNCOUNT+SUPP

3 Something that **imposes** an unwanted or unpleasant effect causes such an effect, usually because it prevents people from acting freely. EG *...the physical limitations imposed by the infant school and its building... ...the restraint imposed on them by the previous government... Overcrowding imposes mental strains.* — V+O : IF+PREP THEN *on/upon* ⇑ inflict

4 If someone **imposes** on you, they unreasonably expect you to do something for them or to spend time with them when you do not really want to. EG *Clarissa was like that, she imposed on people... Perhaps you won't like the idea of imposing on them, but plenty of people don't mind.* ◊ **imposition, impositions**. EG *It really did seem rather an imposition to ask him to go miles out of his way.* — V OR V+O (NG/REFL) : IF+PREP THEN *on* = obtrude; ◊ N COUNT ⇑ demand

5 If something **imposes** itself on a situation or activity, it becomes noticeable as a strong or important factor in the situation. EG *The jail routine began to inexorably impose itself... They make up for their lack of physical stature by imposing themselves on the situation around them.* — V+O (REFL) : IF +PREP THEN *on* ⇑ inflict

imposing /ɪmpəʊzɪŋ/. Someone or something that is **imposing** has an impressive appearance or manner. EG *Mrs Sabawala's house was large and imposing... Tall and imposing, they moved with graceful ease.* — ADJ QUALIT = grand

impossible /ɪmpɒsəˈbəⁿl/. 1 Something that is **impossible** is unable to be done, to happen, or to be believed. EG *They continued to struggle with it, even though it was an impossible task... Since staying awake all night was virtually impossible, they had both gone to sleep... 'Impossible. I don't believe it.'* — ADJ QUALIT ⇑ difficult = ridiculous
◊ **impossibly**. EG *He had impossibly thin legs.* — ◊ ADV
◊ **impossibility** /ɪmpɒsəbɪlɪti[1]/, **impossibilities**. EG *...the impossibility of change... They found a dozen reasons for its impossibility... That's a logical impossibility.* — ◊ N UNCOUNT/COUNT = inconceivability
● If you are **asking for the impossible** or if you **want the impossible**, you want something that is not able to be done or to happen in any way. EG *Don't you think that perhaps you want the impossible?* — ● PHR : VB INFLECTS

2 A situation that is **impossible** is one that you find very difficult and are unable to decide on or improve. EG *We are faced with impossible alternatives... They are in an impossible position on this matter.* — ADJ QUALIT = hopeless
◊ **impossibly**. EG *Flats make life impossibly restrictive for energetic young children... Parents may find their child's behaviour problems impossibly difficult.* — ◊ ADV = hopelessly

3 Someone who is **impossible** is very difficult to deal with, usually because of their bad behaviour or strong views. EG *My daughter is impossible!–She always says the wrong thing at the wrong time.* — ADJ QUALIT ⇑ intolerable
◊ **impossibly**. EG *She was impossibly rude to Miss Cormorant.* — ◊ ADV ⇑ intolerably

impostor /ɪmpɒstə/, **impostors**; also spelled **imposter**. An **impostor** is a person who dishonestly pretends to be someone else in order to get something that they want. EG *This is not Doctor Malcolm, he is an impostor.* — N COUNT

imposture /ɪmpɒstʃə/ is the behaviour of someone who is being an impostor; a very formal word. EG *If they knew, they would see through his imposture straight away.* — N UNCOUNT ⇑ deception

impotence /ɪmpətəns/ is 1 a lack of power to influence people or events; a formal word. EG *...the impotence and inactivity of the left-wing parties in Europe.* 2 a man's sexual problem in which his penis becomes soft before he can reach an orgasm. EG *His fear of impotence had affected him physically.* — N UNCOUNT ⇑ powerlessness = inability; N UNCOUNT

impotent /ɪmpətənt/. 1 Someone who is **impotent** has no power to influence people or events. EG *Those who do not conform must be rendered impotent.* — ADJ QUALIT : USU PRED ⇑ powerless = helpless

2 If a man is **impotent**, he is unable to reach an orgasm when having sex because his penis goes soft. — ADJ CLASSIF : USU PRED

impound /ɪmpaʊnd/, **impounds, impounding, impounded**. If policemen or other officials **impound** something that you own, they take legal possession of it. EG *Security Police had come to our house and impounded all our belongings... Their passports continued to be impounded and their bans maintained.* — V+O

impoverish /ɪmpɒvəⁿrɪʃ/, **impoverishes, impoverishing, impoverished**. 1 Something that **impoverishes** a person makes them poor. EG *They were impoverished by a prolonged spell of unemployment.* ◊ **impoverished**. EG *...an impoverished Third World country.* — V+O; ◊ ADJ QUALIT

2 A person or thing that **impoverishes** something makes it worse in quality. EG *Its use spreads disease and impoverishes the land.* ◊ **impoverished**. EG *A world without Shakespeare in it would be a world substantially impoverished.* — V+O; ◊ ADJ QUALIT

impoverishment /ɪmpɒvəⁿrɪʃməⁿnt/ is the state or process of being impoverished. EG *They managed to get through a period of very severe impoverishment... It leads to permanent impoverishment of huge land areas.* — N UNCOUNT = poverty

impracticable /ɪmpræktɪkəbəⁿl/. Something such as a course of action that is **impracticable** is impossible to do. EG *I believe that such a policy is both wrong and impracticable... It would be impracticable to ban all food additives.* — ADJ CLASSIF

impractical /ımpr<u>æ</u>ktıkəᵒl/. 1 An idea or course of action that is **impractical** is not sensible, realistic, or practical. EG *...a totally impractical view... To expect automatic protection from the police is impractical.* ADJ QUALIT ⇑ useless

2 Someone who is **impractical** does not have the abilities or skills to do practical work such as making, repairing, or organizing things. EG *He may well be brilliant, but he's completely impractical.* ADJ QUALIT ⇑ useless

imprecation /ımprı²k<u>eı</u>ʃəᵒn/, **imprecations**. An **imprecation** is something insulting that someone says to a person they are very angry with; a formal word. EG *He was exposed to the sleeve-tugging and imprecations of the crowd.* N COUNT = curse

imprecise /ımprıs<u>aı</u>s/. Something that is **imprecise** is not clear, accurate, or precise. EG *My ideas about it were imprecise... The terms he used were imprecise and emotional.* ◇ **imprecision** /ımprıs<u>ı</u>ʒəᵒn/. EG *He uses political language with an imprecision that I find worrying.* ADJ QUALIT ⇑ loose = inexact ◇ N UNCOUNT ⇑ looseness

impregnable /ımpr<u>e</u>gnəbəᵒl/5. 1 A building or other object that is **impregnable** is so strong or solid that it cannot be broken into or captured. EG *They will establish impregnable fortresses to defend themselves... ...an impregnable security truck, wired with explosives.* ADJ CLASSIF = impenetrable

2 A person or group that is **impregnable** cannot be affected or overcome by anyone. EG *They are virtually impregnable to attack from any other party... I was quite relieved to see that the impregnable Miss Crabbe could feel emotion.* ADJ CLASSIF

impregnate /ımpr<u>e</u>gneıt/, **impregnates, impregnating, impregnated**. 1 If someone or something **impregnates** a thing with a substance, they make the substance pass into it and spread through it. EG *The purpose of the marinade is to impregnate foods with the flavour of the ingredients... ...ordinary paper that has been impregnated with chemicals.* V+O : IF+PREP THEN *with* ⇑ soak

2 When a male animal **impregnates** a female, he makes her pregnant; a formal use. EG *The female presented herself for mating and, once impregnated, retired to the company of other females.* V+O ⇑ fertilize

impresario /ımprı²s<u>eə</u>ri¹əʊ/, **impresarios**. An **impresario** is a person whose job is to manage a theatre or music company. EG *...a show business and theatre impresario.* N COUNT

impress /ımpr<u>e</u>s/, **impresses, impressing, impressed**. 1 If you do something that **impresses** someone, you make them admire you and respect you. EG *I was hoping to impress my new boss with my diligence... I was greatly impressed by the pianist... My lame excuse that I had so much else to do did not impress the children.* V+O ⇑ please

2 If you **impress** something on someone, you make them understand the importance of it. EG *He was trying to impress something on their minds... She impressed on the Government the danger of making too many cuts.* V+O+A *(on/upon)* ⇑ emphasize

3 When an object **is impressed** onto a surface, it is pressed hard onto the surface so that it leaves a mark or outline. EG *This fossilized feather was found impressed in a slab of limestone.* V+O : USU PASS+A = imprint

impression /ımpr<u>e</u>ʃəᵒn/, **impressions**. 1 An **impression** that you have of a person or thing is the way that they look or seem to you. EG *All knowledge comes from sensory impressions... The immediate impression of the bedroom is one of sheer 1950s Hollywood.* N COUNT : USU+SUPP = appearance

2 Your **impression** of a situation, a place, or a person is the feelings, reactions, or opinions that you have about it. EG *My impression is that contemporary British authors have a lot to learn from American writing.... What's your general impression?... Reporters wanted my personal impressions of China... Vita's first impressions of my father are given in her autobiography.* N COUNT : USU WITH POSS+SUPP ⇑ idea

3 When something gives, creates, or conveys a particular **impression**, it causes people to believe that something is the case, often when it is not actually the case. EG *Whatever gave you that impression?... He gives the impression of a recluse... They give the impression of not working... No doubt that was the impression my host wanted to leave me with.* N SING WITH DET : USU+SUPP = idea, illusion

4 If you have, gain, or form a particular **impression**, you believe that something is the case, often when it is not actually the case. EG *I had the impression that he didn't trust me... I don't want anybody to get the wrong impression.* ● If you are **under the impression** that something is the case, you believe that it is the case, usually when it is not actually the case. EG *They were under the impression I had come to stay.* N SING WITH DET : USU+SUPP ⇑ idea ● PHR : USED AS A/C, USU+REPORT-CL

5 A particular **impression** that something makes on people is the particular effect that it has on them, especially on their ideas or attitudes. EG *What impression did she make on you?... It makes a bad impression to miss days at the office... I left thinking that I had created quite a good impression.* ● If you **make an impression**, you have a strong effect on people when you meet them, causing them to notice you, often admire you, and remember you later. EG *She did not fail to make an impression.* N COUNT : USU+SUPP ● PHR : VB INFLECTS = impress

6 An **impression** of an object is a mark or outline that it has left by being pressed hard onto a surface. EG *It made absolutely no impression on the rock-hard earth... We discovered what might be the impression of a hoof.* N COUNT : USU+*of* = imprint

7 An **impression** by a person is a funny imitation that they make of someone's behaviour or way of talking, usually of a well-known person. EG *Have you seen her impressions of the TV newscasters?* N COUNT ⇑ act

impressionable /ımpr<u>e</u>ʃəᵒnəbəᵒl/. Someone who is **impressionable**, usually a young person, is not very critical and therefore easy to influence. EG *Perhaps I was unduly impressionable.* ADJ QUALIT ⇑ open = gullible

Impressionism /ımpr<u>e</u>ʃənızəᵒm/ is a style of painting developed in France between 1870 and 1900. Artists who used this style often concentrated on showing the effects of moving light on their subjects, and painted vague shapes with blurred edges rather than neat realistic details of a scene. N UNCOUNT

impressionist /ımpr<u>e</u>ʃənıst/, **impressionists**. 1 An **Impressionist** is an artist who painted in the style of Impressionism. EG *When I was young, I liked the Impressionists.* ▸ used as an adjective to refer to the style of Impressionism. EG *The farm is like an impressionist painting, splashed with colour in the early morning light.* N COUNT ⇑ painter ▸ ADJ CLASSIF

2 An **impressionist** is a person who entertains by means of funny imitations of people's behaviour and ways of talking, usually of well-known people. N COUNT ⇑ comic = mimic

impressionistic /ımpr<u>e</u>ʃəᵒn<u>ı</u>stık/. A view of something that is **impressionistic** relies on general aspects of the thing rather than dealing with the real facts or details. EG *Are these notes properly finished or are they simply meant to be impressionistic?* ADJ QUALIT ⇑ vague = rough, sketchy

impressive /ımpr<u>e</u>sıv/. Something that is **impressive** impresses you, usually because it is large or important. EG *She is building up an impressive international reputation... The list of speakers was impressive.* ◇ **impressively**. EG *The Mysore Palace was impressively elegant and massive.* ◇ **impressiveness**. EG *The light served to enhance the impressiveness of the place.* ADJ QUALIT ⇑ great = imposing ◇ ADV = grandly ◇ N UNCOUNT = magnificence

imprint, imprints, imprinting, imprinted. The word **imprint** is pronounced /<u>ı</u>mprınt/ when it is a noun, and /ımpr<u>ı</u>nt/ when it is a verb. 1 An **imprint** that something in the past has on a place or on your mind is a strong and lasting effect that it has on it. EG *The past decades have left their imprint on all of us... These things have left a deep imprint on our thinking... The town still bears the simple imprint of its industrial origins.* N COUNT : USU SING ⇑ mark

2 If something **is imprinted** on your memory, it is firmly fixed in your memory so that you will not forget it. EG *The face of every one of you is imprinted on the memory of every cop in France... This is a sunset that will be forever imprinted in the mind... That strange, cruel look had imprinted itself on her mind.* V+O+A : USU PASS = stamp

3 An **imprint** is a mark or outline made by pressure of one object on another. EG *Right in its centre there was the imprint of his hand.* N COUNT = impression

4 If an object **is imprinted** onto a surface, it is pressed hard onto the surface so that it leaves a mark or an outline. EG *...the hand imprinted in the sand.* V+O+A : USU PASS

imprison /ımpr<u>ı</u>zəᵒn/, **imprisons, imprisoning, imprisoned**. 1 If someone **imprisons** you, they lock you up in prison, usually as a punishment for a crime. EG *They used to imprison many of those they caught... They probably wouldn't imprison me but they would fine me.* V+O = incarcerate

2 A condition or situation that **imprisons** you re- V+O

stricts your freedom or restrains you in some other way. EG *...the conditions that imprison the industrial worker today... They could enjoy the country without feeling imprisoned by it.*

imprisonment /ɪmprɪzəᵒnməˀnt/ is the state of being imprisoned. EG *They were sentenced to life imprisonment... Its members were threatened with imprisonment.* — N UNCOUNT ⇑ detention

improbable /ɪmprɒbəbəᵒl/. **1** Something that is **improbable** is unlikely to be true or to happen. EG *I speculated on the very improbable fact that she might be going to have a baby... His explanation seems highly improbable.* ◊ **improbability** /ɪmprɒbəbɪlɪti¹/, **improbabilities**. EG *We stood giggling at such an improbability.* — ADJ QUALIT = implausible; ◊ N COUNT/UNCOUNT

2 If something is **improbable**, you find it strange, unusual, or ridiculous. EG *...the gaudiest and most improbable water wheel the world has ever seen... The animal, however improbable it might seem, was a real one.* ◊ **improbably**. EG *...a statue of George IV, improbably bareback and barefoot in a toga.* — ADJ QUALIT ⇑ unlikely = fantastic; ◊ ADV

impromptu /ɪmprɒmptju:/. An **impromptu** action is one that you do without planning or organizing it in advance. EG *I quite by chance got drawn into a kind of impromptu party downstairs... ...the switch from planned to impromptu tactics.* — ADJ CLASSIF ⇑ spontaneous

improper /ɪmprɒpə/. **1** If a person's behaviour is **improper**, it is rude or shocking because they ignore people's ideas about the correct way to behave. EG *Charlotte thought my mirth improper.* ◊ **improperly**. EG *None of the customers dared to speak improperly to her in the restaurant.* — ADJ QUALIT ⇑ wrong = unseemly; ◊ ADV WITH VB

2 Improper activities are illegal or dishonest. EG *...allegations of improper business dealings.* ◊ **improperly**. EG *There were charges that Hugel had improperly provided them with cash.* — ADJ CLASSIF = irregular; ◊ ADV WITH VB

3 Improper conditions or methods of treatment are not suitable or adequate for a particular purpose. EG *I would not work in improper conditions: I meant to have a model farm with everything as it should be.* ◊ **improperly**. EG *Bottled milk, improperly handled, is a lethal carrier of disease.* — ADJ CLASSIF ⇑ incorrect; ◊ ADV WITH VB ⇑ incorrectly

impropriety /ɪmprəᵉpraɪɪ¹ti¹/ is improper behaviour; a formal word. EG *...the impropriety of publicly reading private letters.* — N UNCOUNT

improve /ɪmpru:v/, **improves, improving, improved**. **1** If something **improves** or if you **improve** it, it gets better. EG *The weather improved later in the day... ...soup, heavily spiced to improve the taste... These houses have been improved by the addition of bathrooms... ...technical advances that improve the productivity of the land.* ◊ **improved**. EG *In underdeveloped countries, improved health and education are urgently needed.* — V-ERG ⇑ change = ameliorate; ◊ ADJ CLASSIF

2 If you **improve** at a skill or in an area of knowledge, you get better at it by practising or studying. EG *Alf made strenuous efforts to improve, especially in his reading... She went to the club to improve her tennis... His French was improving.* — V OR V+O ⇑ change

3 If you **improve** after an illness or an injury, your health gets better or you get stronger. EG *She may improve with medical treatment... My health improved wonderfully.* — V ⇑ recover

4 Something that **improves** a person changes them so that they have a better character or a better social status. EG *He is enjoying his job, getting on and improving himself... It most certainly wouldn't improve me, I'd be the same person I was before.* — V+O (NG/REFL)

5 If you **improve** on a previous achievement of your own or of someone else, you achieve a better standard or result than the previous one. EG *He certainly thinks he's improving on my work... I found that the film improved on the book... Our techniques are already far advanced and being improved on daily.* — V+A *(on/upon)*

improvement /ɪmpru:vməˀnt/, **improvements**. **1 Improvement** or an **improvement** in a person or thing is an act or effect of improving the quality or condition of the person or thing. EG *The Company made a significant improvement in the wages and living conditions of its employees... ...the gradual improvement of relations between East and West... My supervisor had written 'This is a great improvement.'... There was no improvement immediately after the operation.* — N UNCOUNT/COUNT ⇑ change = amelioration

2 An **improvement** is a change made to something which improves it. EG *The locals view these road improvements with alarm... Life there would be such an improvement on dull dingy Paris.* — N COUNT

improvidence /ɪmprɒvɪdəns/ is improvident behaviour; a formal word. — N UNCOUNT

improvident /ɪmprɒvɪdənt/. Someone who is **improvident** is wasteful and does not think about the future; a formal word. EG *...a childhood that had caused him to turn out feckless and improvident... They have lived improvident lives.* — ADJ QUALIT = negligent

improvise /ɪmprəvaɪz/, **improvises, improvising, improvised**. **1** If you **improvise** or if you **improvise** something, you make or do something using whatever you have or without arranging it or planning it in advance. EG *We had to improvise as we went along... The sisters helped me improvise a curtain in front of the toilet.* ◊ **improvisation** /ɪmprəvaɪzeɪʃəᵒn/, **improvisations**. EG *...a classic case of British improvisation.* ◊ **improvised**. EG *Tanks were crossing the river on improvised bridges.* — V OR V+O; ◊ N UNCOUNT/COUNT; ◊ ADJ CLASSIF = makeshift

2 When musicians or actors **improvise**, they play music, speak, or act without set music or words, using their imagination instead. EG *He had a gift of playing by ear and could improvise quite ambitiously on classical themes.* ◊ **improvisation, improvisations**. EG *Jazz is always improvisation... He would make huge, fascinating leaps in his improvisations.* — V OR V+O ⇑ perform = ad-lib; ◊ N UNCOUNT/COUNT = ad-lib

imprudent /ɪmpru:dənt/. **Imprudent** behaviour is not sensible or carefully thought out. EG *It would be imprudent of you to make enemies of those who can help you.* — ADJ QUALIT ⇑ careless = unwise

impudence /ɪmpjəᵈdəns/ is impudent behaviour or speech. — N UNCOUNT

impudent /ɪmpjəᵈdənt/. Someone who is **impudent** behaves or speaks rudely or disrespectfully. EG *The impudent child extended her legs across my lap.* ▸ used of a person's actions or behaviour. EG *Your letter is impudent and it has angered me.* ◊ **impudently**. EG *'So you've changed your mind?' the gossip writer impudently asked.* — ADJ QUALIT; ◊ ADV WITH VB

impugn /ɪmpju:n/, **impugns, impugning, impugned**. Someone who **impugns** something such as a quality criticizes it, especially by expressing doubt about it; a formal word. EG *They were daring to impugn the profession of medicine... There is no ground to impugn the sincerity of his belief... He may attempt to impugn the reputation of his victim.* — V+O ⇑ challenge = question

impulse /ɪmpʌls/, **impulses**. **1** If you have an **impulse** to do something, often something that is wrong or irrational, you have a sudden desire to do it. EG *I had a sudden impulse to turn around and walk out... He had to fight down the impulse to hit the man.* ● If you do something **on impulse**, you decide to do it suddenly without planning. EG *On impulse he crouched down behind the wall... On a sudden impulse, he stopped and went into the library.* — N COUNT : IF+VB THEN *to*-INF = urge; ● PHR : USED AS AN A

2 An **impulse** to do or achieve something is a strong and constant feeling that you must do it, which affects your actions. EG *...the impulse towards democracy.... Survival depends upon an animal's impulse to fight for territory.* — N COUNT+A/*to*-INF = drive, urge

3 An **impulse** is a short electrical signal that is sent along a wire or nerve or through the air, usually as one of a series. EG *Some are modified to transmit electric impulses... ...nerve impulses.* — N COUNT = pulse

impulse buy, impulse buys. An **impulse buy** is something that you buy because you see it and like it rather than because you planned to buy it. — N COUNT

impulsion /ɪmpʌlʃəᵒn/, **impulsions**. An **impulsion** to do something is a strong desire to do it, usually a desire that you cannot control. EG *We all felt the impulsion to act out our roles.* — N COUNT : IF+VB THEN *to*-INF = compulsion, urge

impulsive /ɪmpʌlsɪv/. Someone who is **impulsive** does things suddenly without thinking about them carefully first. ▸ used of people's actions and behaviour. EG *Alice's overdose was an impulsive act.* ◊ **impulsively**. EG *She kissed him impulsively on the mouth.* ◊ **impulsiveness**. — ADJ QUALIT = reckless; ▸ = hasty; ◊ ADV WITH VB; ◊ N UNCOUNT

impunity /ɪmpju:nɪti¹/. If you do something **with impunity**, you are not punished for doing it, although you should be punished. EG *Landlords were simply ignoring the law, and with impunity... The child cannot express his hatred of adults with impunity.* — PHR : USED AS AN A

impure /ɪmpjʊə/. **1** A substance that is **impure** has small amounts of other dirty or less valuable substances mixed with it and so is not regarded as being of good quality. — ADJ CLASSIF = adulterated

2 Impure thoughts and actions are concerned with sex and are regarded as sinful; an old-fashioned use. ADJ CLASSIF

impurity /ɪmpjʊərɪti[1]/, **impurities. 1** An **impurity** is a substance that is present in small quantities in another substance making it dirty or of an unacceptable quality. EG *There are traces of impurities in the gold.* N COUNT = contaminant

2 Impurity is the state of being no longer pure, especially sexually pure. EG *He felt contaminated by her impurity.* N UNCOUNT

impute /ɪmpjuːt/, **imputes, imputing, imputed.** If you **impute** something such as blame, a crime, or a change to a person or thing, you say that this person or thing is responsible for it or the cause of it; a formal word. EG *No blame can be imputed to him... It is hard to impute a rise in output to any one factor.* V+O+A *(to)* = ascribe, attribute

in /ɪn/. **1** You use **in** when you are talking about where something is. You use it **1.1** to describe the position of an object when it is surrounded and enclosed by something such as a box or bag. EG *We put them away in a big box... She opened her bag and put her diary in... He fumbled in a pocket for his eyeglass... A man was selling roses in cellophane.* PREP, OR ADV AFTER VB **1.2** to describe the position of someone when they are on a chair, bed, etc and are partly enclosed by it, for example because it has high sides: compare **on.** EG *Etta sat in an armchair with her legs crossed... She was at home in bed... Colin was in the bath.* PREP, OR ADV AFTER VB **1.3** to indicate movement of air, water, or food from the outside of a person, animal, or plant to the inside. EG *The girl went on breathing in and out... Trees take in water through their roots.* ADV AFTER VB ≠ out

2 Something that is **in** a machine is one of the parts inside it. EG *One of the pistons in the engine had jammed.* PREP

3 If something is **in** your hand, you are holding it. EG *She had a newspaper in her hand... They were in each other's arms.* PREP

4 You use **in** to indicate a general area where something is or where something happens. EG *Artichokes are the principal crop in the area... I wanted to play in the garden... A boy had kicked the ball high in the air... He found her standing in the middle of the room... He nodded in the direction of the door.* PREP

5 If something is **in** or happens **in** a town, city, country, etc, that is where it is or where it happens. EG *A swimming pool in England is a luxury thing. In California it's not... In Hamburg the girls split up... Perth is in Australia.* PREP

6 If someone or something is **in** a building, institution, room etc, that is where they are, or where they live, work, etc: compare **at.** EG *We don't know many of the people living in the cottages near here... He's in hospital... He taught in a boys' school. It was the first time I'd ever eaten in a restaurant... She locked herself in the bathroom... In the kitchen there was a message for him.* PREP

7 You use **in** in expressions like 'write in' and 'send in' to indicate that you send something, for example a letter, to the organization that has asked you for it. EG *Please write in with your ideas or views... All applications must be in by the end of the month.* ADV AFTER VB

8 If you are **in**, you are present at your home or place of work. EG *She seems to be in... He's never in when I phone... We're staying in this evening.* ADV AFTER VB ≠ out

9 If you come **in**, walk **in**, etc, you enter a room, building, car, etc. EG *There was a knock at Howard's door. 'Come in,' he shouted... He struggled in with the cases... The children run in and out all the time... Let me in... He had his meals brought in by Mrs Hochstadt.* ADV AFTER VB

10 If a train, boat, plane, etc is **in** or has come **in**, it has arrived at the station, harbour, airport, etc. EG *The train's not in yet... We'll have something to eat when the boat gets in.* ADV AFTER VB

11 Something that is **in** a window is just behind the window so that you can see it through the window from outside. EG *How much is the hat in the window?... There was a really nice dress in the shop window.* PREP

12 If you can see something **in** a mirror, lake, etc, it is a reflection from that surface. EG *He couldn't bear looking at his own face in the mirror.* PREP

13 If you are **in** a dress, suit, etc, you are wearing that piece of clothing. EG *She was cooking in a long black dress... Martin was in his pyjamas... The bar was full of men in cloth caps.* PREP

14 If something is **in** a liquid, it is under it or covered with it. EG *We've just found a body in the water... I love apricots in white wine.* PREP, OR ADV AFTER VB

15 If something is **in** a book, speech, picture, film, play, etc, it can be found there. EG *In chapter 7 I discuss the relationship between sport and politics... She dies in the last act... There was a very funny bit in the film last night.* PREP, OR ADV AFTER VB

16 If something is **in** a group, queue, collection, etc, it is one of the group, queue, collection, etc. EG *She waited in the queue... This is one of the finest beetles in the collection... A lot of insects live in colonies.* PREP

17 If you are **in** a play, race, etc, you are one of the actors, runners, etc who take part. EG *He's in a play at the Theatre Royal next month... I know that face–what has she been in?... She took part in a marathon.* PREP

18 You also use **in** when you are talking about time. **18.1** If something happens **in** a particular year, month, period, etc, it happens during that time: compare **on, at.** EG *In 1872, Chicago was burned to the ground... In April we prepared to make our first trip to Europe... He went to sleep at two o'clock in the morning... In recent years this view has been very strongly criticized... It'll be warmer in the spring... In the meantime there had been a change of government.* PREP **18.2** If you do something **in** a particular period of time, that is how long it takes you to do it; used especially when this is a shorter time than might be expected. EG *He learnt to drive in six months.* PREP **18.3** If something happens **in** the confusion, **in** someone's absence, etc, it happens during the time that this state of affairs lasts. EG *Many questions were asked in the immediate aftermath of the accident... In the commotion, a man had been trapped... In my absence Stanley had been running the shop.* PREP **18.4** If something happens **in** a particular length of time, it happens after that length of time. EG *In another five minutes it'll be pitch dark... In a matter of days the unrest spread to industry... He was dead in a few seconds.* PREP **18.5** If you have not done something **in** years, months, etc, you have not done it for that length of time; used especially when referring to long periods of time. EG *I haven't seen him in years.* PREP WITH BROAD NEG

19 You use **in** to indicate that something happens or is true when there is a particular situation or set of circumstances. EG *Women hold a very strong position in aboriginal society... In these circumstances prices and profits would remain stable... Competition is also found in nature... In a laboratory situation precision is extremely important.* PREP

20 If you are **in** a particular state or situation, that is your present state or situation. EG *We are in a position to advise our Indian friends... We might be in a state of near chaos again... We are now in a very awkward situation.* PREP

21 You use **in** to indicate that something happens while there is a particular kind of weather or light. EG *You can't go home in all this rain... Did you go out in the sun?... Why are you sitting in the dark?... He looked around in the dim light.* PREP

22 If a particular characteristic or quality is **in** you, you have it. EG *There was always in Nell a hint of shallowness... She hated the bully in him... I'm not a hypocrite. It's not in my temperament... There was a certain dryness in her voice.* PREP

23 If you are **in** love, distress, agreement, etc, you are feeling the emotion mentioned, or you have the state of mind or attitude mentioned. EG *She was very much in love with him... We are all in a state of profound shock... I found her in low spirits... Brian left in a temper... He declared himself strongly in favour of free speech.* PREP

24 If you do something **in** surprise, **in** admiration, **in** your excitement, etc, you do it because of the way you are feeling or the attitude you have. EG *Mrs Kaul looked up in surprise... Clarissa cried out in pain... He shook his head in admiration... In his excitement, Billy had nearly forgotten the letter.* PREP

25 You use **in** in expressions like 'in an effort to' and 'in response to' when you are explaining the purpose or cause of something that you have done. EG *In an effort to conceal my thinness, I had worn two layers of clothing... She wrote off letters in answer to the advertisements... In response to pressure from bankers and jewellers the government has introduced new legislation.* PREP

26 You use **in** to indicate that a particular feeling is directed towards someone or something. EG *I have confidence in myself... No one took any interest in the exhibition.* PREP

27 You use **in** to specify a general subject or field of activity. EG *...recent advances in mathematics... She's an expert in children's literature... In British journalism no single figure exercised such tremendous power... I'm taking a course in Chinese.* PREP

28 If you are **in** business, computing, television, etc, that is the field in which you work. EG *She's in television... There is a sound future in farming... He plans to make his career in music... His father had made a lot of money in business.* PREP

29 You use **in** to indicate an approximate amount or number. EG *New firms take on workers in dozens rather than in hundreds... People arrived in dribs and drabs... The rain came down in buckets.* PREP

30 You say that someone is **in** their teens, twenties, eighties, etc, when you are giving their age approximately, or referring to a period of their life. EG *...an old man in his seventies... In her twenties and thirties she had had no difficulty getting jobs... In his old age Mr Starke has become much more tolerant.* PREP

31 You use **in** with words like 'view', 'opinion', and 'experience' to indicate that what you are saying is based on your own opinion or experience. EG *In Jenkin's view the movement will survive in Britain only if it is able to win the support of the younger generation... In my experience business lunches can be very useful... In his own eyes he was a patriot.* PREP+POSS+N

32 **In** is used to indicate how you communicate with someone, for example whether you speak or write, or what language or tone of voice you use. EG *They were speaking in Italian... I shall need your complaints in writing... I can't wait to see it in print... They sent messages to each other in code... She spoke in a calm, friendly voice.* PREP

33 If something is **in** a ring, line, block, etc, it is arranged like that or has that shape. EG *The students sit in a circle on the floor... They parked their cars in neat rows... You buy it in a block and cut it up yourself... He carried a damp cloth rolled in a ball.* ▸ used to say how someone's hair is worn. EG *She wore her hair in a bun... She's got her hair in pigtails.* PREP

34 You use **in** to specify the form of something such as an amount of money, for example the units it is made of. EG *He walked off with £300 million in cash... 'How would you like the money?'–'In tens, please.'... It's a lot cheaper if you buy it in kit form.* PREP

35 If something is **in** a particular colour, it has that colour. EG *We put up curtains in yellow and orange... He was dressed entirely in black.* PREP

36 You use **in** to say that there is a particular state which you are experiencing for a period of time. EG *He sits in silence for a few seconds... The company is in financial difficulty... I was not in any real danger... The project is still in the planning stage.* PREP

37 You use **in** to say that you are having a particular kind of medical treatment: compare **on**, **under**. EG *He's in traction at the moment... Claude will be in bandages for at least three more weeks.* PREP

38 When a plant or tree is **in** flower, blossom, leaf, etc, it has flowers, blossom, leaves, etc on it. EG *My geranium's in flower... The hedgerows were all in blossom.* PREP

39 You use **in** when you are saying that you divide something so that it becomes two or more separate parts. EG *He cut it in two... One of those kicks could snap you in half.* PREP = into

40 You use **in** to specify the aspect of a situation or subject that you are talking about. EG *Computers have recently shrunk in size... It grew to eight metres in length... We need a change in direction... We have a surplus in the number of probation officers... She was dismissed for slackness in her duties as secretary.* PREP

41 You use **in** in expressions like 'join in' and 'add in' to indicate that you join other people doing something or that you add one thing to another. EG *Can I join in?... New information can be typed in... First put the flour into a bowl then rub in the fat.* ADV AFTER VB

42 You use **in** to express a ratio, proportion, or probability. EG *You can save up to 10 pence in the pound... ...a slope of 1 in 3... You have a one in five chance of success.* PREP : USU NUM +PREP+NUM

43 If a ball or shuttlecock is **in** during a game of tennis, squash, badminton, etc, it lands on the playing area of the court and is not outside the white lines which mark the edge of the court. EG *I'm sure it was in!* ADV AFTER VB

44 If a cricket team or batsman is **in**, they are taking their turn at batting. ADV AFTER VB ≠ out

45 You use **in** when you are saying where pain, injury, or damage is. EG *I could not sleep because of the pain in my feet... Barnes has been shot in the leg... There were several deep incisions in the bark... He was examining the hole in his sock.* PREP

46 Something that is **in** is fashionable to wear, do, say, etc; an informal use. EG *Purple socks are the in thing at the moment. Bright colours are in this year... Is it still in fashion to go there?...* ADJ CLASSIF, OR PREP

47 When the sea or tide comes **in**, the sea moves closer towards the shore rather than farther away from it. EG *The tide's coming in very fast.* ADV AFTER VB ≠ out

48 You use **in** with a present participle of a verb to indicate that when you do something, something else happens as a consequence. EG *Babbage rejected the obvious, and in doing so achieved his magnificent insight... In accepting this view he was admitting the possibility that he was mistaken earlier.* PREP+-ING = by

49 If you spend time, waste time, etc **in** a particular activity, you spend time, waste time, etc doing it. EG *Most of this time was spent in heated arguments... She took her time in coming.* PREP+-ING/NG

50 You use **in** with certain verbs to indicate that a following noun or verb is related to them as an object. EG *She had succeeded in making him respond... The operation could result in her death... We believe in dividing all tasks equally down the middle.* PREP+-ING/NG

51 If something has a particular quality or worth **in itself**, it has this quality or worth because of its nature and it does not matter what the circumstances or other factors are. EG *It is foolish to believe that punishment in itself can induce a sense of responsibility... This was an achievement in itself... A picnic, always a delightful social event in itself, can also be an opportunity for an imaginative meal.* PHR : USED AS AN A = on its own

52 If someone **is in for** a shock, surprise, beating, etc, they are going to experience it and cannot avoid it. EG *He's in for a terrible shock, I'm afraid.* PHR : VB INFLECTS ● If someone **is in for it**, they are in trouble and are likely to be punished; an informal expression. EG *I'm really in for it now.* ● PHR : VB INFLECTS ● If you **have it in for** someone, you dislike them and try to cause problems for them or hurt them; an informal expression. EG *She's really got it in for me.* ● PHR : VB INFLECTS

53 If you are **in on** something, you are involved or take part in it. EG *I'd like to be in on the scheme... I think you should be in on this conversation.* PHR+NG

54 You use **in that** to introduce the reason for a statement you have just made. EG *I'm in a very difficult position, in that I've been offered three jobs and they all sound pretty good.* CONJ SUBORD

55 If you are **in with** someone, you are very friendly with them; an informal expression, used especially when you become friendly with someone because they are powerful or will be useful to you, rather than because you like them. EG *I was furious that she should try behind my back to get herself in with him... This is a good excuse to worm her way in with people.* PHR+NG

56 The **ins and outs** of a situation are all the detailed points and facts about it. EG *We had to discuss all the ins and outs of the proposals.* ● **in all**: see **all.** ● **in between**: see **between**. PHR : USED AS O OR S, IF+PREP THEN *of*

in. and **ins.** are written abbreviations for 'inch' and 'inches'. EG *...6 x 4 ins.*

in- is added to adjectives, adverbs, and nouns in order to form other adjectives, adverbs, and nouns with the opposite meaning. EG *...advisable→ inadvisable... ...audibly→inaudibly.* PREFIX

inability /ɪnəbɪlɪti^1/. If you refer to someone's **inability** to do something, you are referring to the fact that they are unable to do it. EG *We were frustrated by our inability to help her... The war was fought because of the inability of statesmen to stop its escalation.* N UNCOUNT : WITH POSS+ *to*-INF = powerlessness

inaccessible /ɪnə^{3}ksesə^{1}bə^{0}l/. If something is **inaccessible**, **1** it is impossible to reach or very difficult to reach. EG *...the most inaccessible reaches of the jungle.* ADJ QUALIT = remote ◊ **inaccessibility** /ɪnə^{3}ksesə^{1}bɪlɪti^1/. EG *The hilltop church attracted good congregations, in spite of its inaccessibility.* ◊ N UNCOUNT = remoteness **2** you are unable to see, use, or ADJ CLASSIF buy it. EG *Most of the data is inaccessible at the moment.* **3** you are unable to understand or appreciate it. EG *The music of Bartok is considered inaccessible by many people.* ADJ QUALIT = obscure

inaccuracy /ɪnæ̲kjəʳrəsiˡ/, **inaccuracies**. **1** If you refer to the **inaccuracy** of something, you are referring to the fact that it is inaccurate. EG *...the inaccuracy of my estimates.* N UNCOUNT

2 An **inaccuracy** is a statement or description that is inaccurate. EG *There are many inaccuracies in details.* N COUNT ⇑ error

inaccurate /ɪnæ̲kjəʳrət/. Something that is **inaccurate** is not accurate or correct. EG *...a wildly inaccurate editorial... To call their relationship 'love' is inaccurate.* ADJ QUALIT ⇑ wrong = incorrect

inaction /ɪnæ̲kʃəⁿn/. If you refer to someone's **inaction**, you are referring to the fact that they are doing nothing. EG *We do not accept this as an excuse for government inaction.* N UNCOUNT = inertia

inactive /ɪnæ̲ktɪv/. A person, animal, or thing that is **inactive** is not doing anything or not working. EG *Crocodiles are inactive for long periods.* ◇ **inactivity** /ɪnæktɪ̲vɪtiˡ/. EG *The dry season was traditionally a time of inactivity, devoted to feasts and festivals.* ADJ CLASSIF = inert; ◇ N UNCOUNT

inadequacy /ɪnæ̲dɪˡkwəsiˡ/, **inadequacies**. **1** If you refer to the **inadequacy** of something, you are referring to the fact that there is not enough of it or it is not good enough in quality for a particular purpose. EG *The defeat was laid down to the inadequacy of defence preparations... Parents are complaining at the inadequacy of education facilities in Britain.* N UNCOUNT/COUNT ⇑ lack = insufficiency

2 If someone has feelings of **inadequacy**, they feel that they do not have the qualities and abilities necessary to do something, to deal with something, or to cope with life in general. N UNCOUNT

3 An **inadequacy** is a weakness or fault in a person. EG *People are much too obsessed with their own inadequacies to be really concerned about yours.* N COUNT = failing

inadequate /ɪnæ̲dɪˡkwət/. **1** If something is **inadequate**, there is not enough of it or it is not good enough in quality for a particular purpose. EG *His income is inadequate to meet his basic needs... He had eaten an inadequate and hurried lunch... Their evidence was inadequate and confusing.* ◇ **inadequately**. EG *Many elderly people live in grossly inadequately heated accommodation.* ADJ QUALIT ⇑ unsatisfactory = insufficient; ◇ ADV WITH VB

2 If you say that someone is **inadequate**, you mean that they do not have the qualities or abilities necessary to do a particular thing or to cope with life in general. EG *We were apparently too inadequate to join his exclusive club... He makes me feel totally inadequate.* ADJ QUALIT ⇑ inferior = incompetent

inadmissible /ɪ̲nəˢdmɪ̲səˡbəⁿl/. **Inadmissible** evidence cannot be used as evidence in a court of law. EG *They told him his evidence would be inadmissible on the basis of hearsay testimony.* ADJ CLASSIF

inadvertent /ɪ̲nəˢdvɜ̲:tənt/. An **inadvertent** action is one that you do unintentionally without thinking or without realizing. EG *The suffering is inadvertent and unwanted.* ◇ **inadvertently**. EG *This confidence just slipped out inadvertently... In Ashanti he had inadvertently eaten human flesh.* ADJ CLASSIF ⇑ careless = heedless; ◇ ADV WITH VB = unconsciously

inadvisable /ɪnəˢdva̲ɪzəbəⁿl/. A course of action that is **inadvisable** should not be carried out because it is not wise or sensible. EG *It is inadvisable to plant lettuces too early.* ADJ QUALIT : USU PRED

inalienable /ɪne̲ɪljənəbəⁿl/. An **inalienable** right to something is a firm one that cannot be taken away; a formal word. EG *...personal freedom, the inalienable right to do anything you want.* ADJ CLASSIF : USU ATTRIB

inane /ɪne̲ɪn/. **Inane** behaviour or actions are silly or stupid. EG *...inane questions... ...inane chatter.* ◇ **inanely**. EG *He smiled rather inanely... EG ...chattering inanely* ◇ **inanity** /ɪnæ̲nɪtiˡ/. EG *...the mesmerizing inanity of television.* ADJ CLASSIF = idiotic; ◇ ADV WITH VB; ◇ N UNCOUNT

inanimate /ɪnæ̲nɪməˡt/. An **inanimate** object has no life. ADJ CLASSIF = lifeless

inapplicable /ɪ̲nəplɪ̲kəbəⁿl/. Something that is **inapplicable** to something that you are considering is not relevant or appropriate to it. EG *The phrase seemed inapplicable to the tall young man.* ADJ CLASSIF : IF + PREP THEN *to* = irrelevant

inappropriate /ɪ̲nəprə̲ʊpriəˡt/. **1** Something that is **inappropriate** is not useful or suitable for a particular occasion or purpose. EG *I arrived with a small suitcase full of inappropriate clothes... ...foreign ideas inappropriate to the Third World.* ◇ **inappropriately**. EG *Unable to cope, we respond inappropriately.* ADJ CLASSIF : IF + PREP THEN *to* ⇑ wrong = unsuitable; ◇ ADV WITH VB

2 If you say that someone's speech or behaviour in a particular situation is **inappropriate**, you disapprove of it. EG *He found it inappropriate for a former President to engage in conversation with a convicted criminal.* ADJ QUALIT ⇑ wrong = improper, unfitting

inapt /ɪnæ̲pt/. Something that is **inapt** is not useful or suitable for a particular occasion or purpose. EG *...an inapt term.* ADJ QUALIT = inappropriate

inarticulate /ɪ̲nɑ:tɪ̲kjəˡlət/. If you are **inarticulate**, you are unable to express yourself easily or well in speech. EG *His parents were dull and inarticulate... He became inarticulate in his anger.* ▸ used of a person's speech. EG *...inarticulate sounds.* ◇ **inarticulately**. EG *...mumbling inarticulately.* ADJ QUALIT ⇑ unintelligible = incoherent; ◇ ADV WITH VB

inasmuch /ɪnəˢzmʌ̲tʃ/; also spelled **in as much**. **Inasmuch as** is used to introduce a clause in which you say something that explains the preceding or following statement, or that limits it in some way; a formal expression. EG *The outcome of this was important inasmuch as it showed just what human beings were capable of... His duty is to assist the aggrieved person inasmuch as he is able.* CONJ SUBORD = insofar as

inattention /ɪ̲nəte̲nʃəⁿn/. A person's **inattention** is their lack of attention. EG *...scolding the maid for inattention.* N UNCOUNT : IF + PREP THEN *to*

inattentive /ɪ̲nəte̲ntɪv/. Someone who is **inattentive** is not paying enough attention to a person or thing. ADJ QUALIT

inaudible /ɪnɔ̲:dəˡbəl/. A sound that is **inaudible** is not loud enough to be heard. EG *Her voice became inaudible.* ADJ CLASSIF ⇑ quiet

inaugural /ɪnɔ̲:gjⁿərəl/. An **inaugural** meeting, speech, etc is one that takes place when a new organization has just been created or when someone has just become the leader of an organization. EG *...the President's inaugural speech... We held a number of successful inaugural meetings of the new party in the area.* ADJ CLASSIF : ATTRIB ⇑ initial = opening

inaugurate /ɪnɔ̲:gjⁿəreɪt/, **inaugurates, inaugurating, inaugurated**. **1** If you **inaugurate** an organization, festival, etc, you start it up or open it with an official ceremony. EG *She was invited over to inaugurate the first British women's temperance conference.* V+O ⇑ initiate

2 If you **inaugurate** an official or leader of an organization, you introduce them as a new official or leader with a special ceremony. ◇ **inauguration** /ɪnɔ̲:gjⁿəre̲ɪʃəⁿn/. EG *We are only a month away from the inauguration of a new President.* V+O; ◇ N UNCOUNT : USU + SUPP

3 If you **inaugurate** an idea, system, etc, you start it up and establish it firmly; a formal use. EG *They undertook to inaugurate measures to control and protect shipping... ...the tradition inaugurated by Machiavelli.* V+O

inauspicious /ɪ̲nɔ:spɪ̲ʃəs/. An **inauspicious** occasion seems unlucky and gives signs that success is unlikely. EG *The meeting was inauspicious.* ADJ CLASSIF ⇑ ominous

inborn /ɪ̲mˡbɔ̲:n/. **Inborn** qualities or ways of behaving are believed to be natural ones with which you are born, rather than ones which you need to learn. EG *...an inborn pattern such as crying... ...abilities that are alleged by men to be inborn in females... The nation had its problems, but the inborn good sense of its people had saved it.* ADJ CLASSIF = innate, inbred

inbred /ɪmˡbre̲d/. **1** An **inbred** quality is inborn. EG *This kind of fear is something that's inbred in us.* ADJ CLASSIF = innate

2 People who are **inbred** have ancestors who are all closely related to each other. EG *...the inbred royal family.* ADJ CLASSIF

inbreeding /ɪ̲mˡbri̲:dɪŋ/ is the repeated breeding of closely related animals or people. N UNCOUNT

inbuilt /ɪ̲mˡbɪ̲lt/. A quality that is **inbuilt** in a person or thing is one that they have from the time they were born or produced. EG *The child has got an inbuilt feeling of inferiority... This kind of thinking has inbuilt limitations.* ADJ CLASSIF

Inc. is an abbreviation for 'Incorporated'; used in the United States as part of the name of a company. EG *...the UK subsidiary of Safeway Stores Inc. of the USA.* N IN NAMES = Ltd., limited

inc. is **1** an abbreviation for 'including'; used especially in advertisements. EG *...Large gdn inc rockery.* PREP

2 an abbreviation for 'inclusive'; used especially in advertisements. EG *...Cost £250 inc. of VAT.* ADJ AFTER NUM

incalculable /ɪŋ¹kælkjələbəᵊl/. Something that is **incalculable** is too great to be calculated or estimated. EG *The loss to the race as a whole is incalculable... ...a hatred that could have incalculable consequences in the decades ahead.* — ADJ CLASSIF = inestimable

incandescence /ɪŋ¹kə³ndesəns/ is the quality that something has of giving out a lot of light when heated; a formal word. EG *The metal gleamed with a snowy incandescence.* — N UNCOUNT ⇑ luminosity

incandescent /ɪŋ¹kə³ndesənt/. Something that is **incandescent** gives out a lot of light when heated; a formal word. EG *...sparks of incandescent pink.* — ADJ CLASSIF ⇑ luminous

incantation /ɪŋ¹kænteɪʃəᵊn/, **incantations**. An **incantation** is a series of words that a person says or sings as a magic spell. EG *She would go into a trance and wail her incantations to the spirits.* — N COUNT = chant

incapable /ɪŋ¹keɪpəbəᵊl/. 1 Someone who is **incapable** of doing something is unable to do it. EG *He is incapable of understanding... The administration is incapable of putting any plan into effect.* — ADJ CLASSIF: PRED+of ⇑ incompetent

2 If you think that someone is **incapable** of doing something bad, you think that they would be unable to do such a thing because of their good character. EG *I had believed him to be incapable of lying... ...a woman incapable of murder.* — ADJ CLASSIF: PRED+of

3 An **incapable** person is weak and helpless or stupid. EG *...a lonely, incapable, fragile woman... He's both incapable and dishonest.* — ADJ CLASSIF

incapacitate /ɪŋ¹kə³pæsɪteɪt/, **incapacitates incapacitating, incapacitated**. If something **incapacitates** someone, it weakens them physically or in some other way, so that they become unable to do certain things; a formal word. EG *...tobacco and alcohol which kill or incapacitate tens of thousands each year.* — V+O ⇑ disable

incapacity /ɪŋ¹kə³pæsɪti¹/. The **incapacity** of a person, society, or system is their weakness or inability to do something. EG *Growing incapacity is expected with increasing age... ...her incapacity to forgive herself.* — N UNCOUNT

incarcerate /ɪŋ¹kɑːsəreɪt/, **incarcerates, incarcerating, incarcerated**. To **incarcerate** someone means to imprison them; a formal word. EG *She was to be incarcerated in a cell by herself.* — V+O

◊ **incarceration** /ɪŋ¹kɑːsəreɪʃəᵊn/. EG *...the incarceration of political dissenters.* — ◊ N UNCOUNT = internment

incarnate /ɪŋ¹kɑːneɪt/. Someone who is a thing or quality **incarnate** represents the thing or quality in human form; often used to emphasize how strongly someone has a particular quality. EG *...evil incarnate... They made me out to be that hideous reality incarnate.* — ADJ AFTER N = embodied

incarnation /ɪŋ¹kɑːneɪʃəᵊn/, **incarnations**. 1 Someone who is an **incarnation** of a particular quality represents that quality in human form in a very strong way. EG *...Miss Lenaut, that incarnation of feminine beauty... He became the incarnation of evil.* — N COUNT+of = embodiment

2 An **incarnation** is an instance of being alive on earth in a particular form. Some religions believe that people have several incarnations in different forms. EG *Perhaps they were lovers in a previous incarnation... Christians insist upon only one incarnation.* — N COUNT ⇑ life

incautious /ɪŋ¹kɔːʃəs/. Someone who is **incautious** does not take enough care over what they say or do. — ADJ QUALIT ⇑ unwise

▸ used of a person's actions or behaviour. EG *...an incautious remark.* — ▸ = rash

incendiary /ɪnsendjəri¹/, **incendiaries**. 1 **Incendiary** is used to describe weapons or attacks that involve setting fire to something. EG *The soldiers were trained to deal with incendiary attacks... ...incendiary bombs.* — ADJ CLASSIF: ATTRIB

2 An **incendiary** is an incendiary bomb. EG *...home-made incendiaries.* — N COUNT

incense, incenses, incensing, incensed. The word **incense** is pronounced /ɪnsens/ when it is a noun and /ɪnsens/ when it is a verb. 1 **Incense** is a substance that is burned for its sweet smell, often as part of a religious ceremony. EG *...a low table with a Buddha and lighted incense on it.* — N UNCOUNT ⇑ scent

2 Something that **incenses** you makes you extremely angry. EG *The proposed pay freeze has incensed the men.* — V+O = enrage

◊ **incensed**. EG *So incensed did I become at this that I slammed the door in his face.* — ◊ ADJ QUALIT: USU PRED

incentive /ɪnsentɪv/, **incentives**. An **incentive** is something that encourages you to do something. EG *Money is being used as an incentive... He had no necessity to write, and therefore no incentive to go on practising his spelling... At present there are few incentives for landowners to improve these woodlands.* — N COUNT = inducement

▸ used as an uncount noun. EG *Profit restriction can destroy incentive and motivation.* — ▸ N UNCOUNT = drive

inception /ɪnsepʃəᵊn/. The **inception** of an institution, activity, etc is the start of it; a formal word. EG *He has been associated with Everyman Opera since its inception in 1952.* — N UNCOUNT: WITH POSS

incessant /ɪnsesənt/. An activity that is **incessant** continues without stopping. EG *...long centuries of almost incessant warfare... ...the incessant demand for change.* — ADJ QUALIT = ceaseless

◊ **incessantly**. EG *She drank tea incessantly and chain-smoked... His telephone rang incessantly.* — ◊ ADV WITH VB = continually

incest /ɪnsest/ is the crime of someone having sex with a person in their own family; used for example of sex between a father and daughter or a brother and sister. EG *...incest victims.* — N UNCOUNT

incestuous /ɪnsestjuəs/. 1 An **incestuous** relationship or activity is one involving sexual intercourse between two people who are in the same family. EG *...incestuous assault.* — ADJ CLASSIF

2 An **incestuous** group of people is a small group of people who all know each other well and give each other benefits that they will not share with people who do not belong to the group; used showing disapproval. EG *It's a rather boring set of incestuous people.* — ADJ QUALIT = cliquey

inch /ɪntʃ/, **inches, inching, inched**. 1 An **inch** is an imperial unit of length, approximately equal to 2.54 centimetres. There are twelve inches in a foot. EG *A standard bed is 6 feet 3 inches long... Five inches of snow had fallen... The car moved forward inch by inch.* — N COUNT: USU an/NUM+N

● You use **every inch** to emphasize that you mean the whole of something, usually the whole of an area. EG *...searching every inch of the car... There were distractions every inch of the way.* — ● PHR+of+NG ⇑ all

2 If you **inch** in a particular direction, you move there very slowly and carefully. EG *You can only enter the caves by inching through a narrow tunnel on your stomach... Howard inched the van forward.* — V-ERG+A

inchoate /ɪŋ¹kəʊeɪt/. **Inchoate** ideas or attitudes are newly formed and therefore not yet properly developed or organized; an extremely formal word. EG *...the student's inchoate political awareness.* — ADJ CLASSIF: ATTRIB ⇑ amorphous

incidence /ɪnsɪdəns/. The **incidence** of something is the extent to which it happens or the frequency with which it happens. EG *There is a high incidence of heart disease among middle-aged men.* — N SING WITH DET +of ⇑ rate = occurrence

incident /ɪnsɪdənt/, **incidents**. An **incident** is 1 a single event or instance of something happening, often one that is not very important or that forms part of a larger event. EG *She told us about some of the amusing incidents of her holiday.* — N COUNT

2 a situation that involves or is likely to cause violence. EG *A serious incident along the border increased our fears of war.* — N COUNT = episode

● Something that takes place **without incident** takes place without anything unusual or troublesome happening. EG *The rest of the weekend passed without incident.* — ● PHR: USED AS AN A = uneventfully

incidental /ɪnsɪdentəᵊl/. Something that is **incidental** happens or exists in connection with something else that is more important. EG *As well as helping drivers, the new road will bring other incidental advantages... These extra duties are incidental to the job... ...incidental music for a film.* — ADJ CLASSIF ⇑ additional = supplementary

incidentally /ɪnsɪdentəᵊli¹/. You use **incidentally** to add something to what you are saying, often a question or an additional piece of information that you have just thought of. EG *So I agreed to lend him the money, which incidentally he still hasn't paid me back... The system is designed to prevent loss of heat, and it will also incidentally save you money.* — ADV SEN = by the way

incinerate /ɪnsɪnəreɪt/, **incinerates, incinerating, incinerated**. If you **incinerate** something, you burn it completely. — V+O

◊ **incineration** /ɪnsɪnəreɪʃəᵊn/. EG *...refuse incineration.* — ◊ N UNCOUNT

incinerator /ɪnsɪnəreɪtə/, **incinerators**. An **incinerator** is a furnace for burning rubbish. — N COUNT

incipient /ɪnsɪpɪənt/. An **incipient** condition or quality is one that is starting to happen or appear; a formal word. EG *...a good way of curing incipient baldness... ...the first signs of incipient malnutrition.* — ADJ CLASSIF: ATTRIB ⇑ apparent

incise /ɪnsaɪz/, **incises, incising, incised**. If you **incise** something, you cut into it carefully with a — V+O sharp instrument; a formal word. EG *We learn how to lance, incise and stitch the wound... His name was incised on the stone.*

incision /ɪnsɪʒəⁿn/, **incisions**. An **incision** is a sharp cut made in something, often by a surgeon who is operating on a patient. EG *Make the first incision here.* N COUNT

incisive /ɪnsaɪsɪv/. Speech or writing that is **incisive** is expressed in a clear and forceful way without using more words than necessary. EG *His presentation was clear and incisive... ...an intelligent and incisive critique of our society.* ADJ QUALIT = trenchant

incisor /ɪnsaɪzə/, **incisors**. An **incisor** is one of the teeth at the front of your mouth which you use for biting into food. N COUNT

incite /ɪnsaɪt/, **incites, inciting, incited**. 1 If you **incite** someone to do something, you encourage them to do it by making them excited or angry. EG *How free can free speech get before it threatens society by inciting it to riot?... They claimed we were inciting people against the Government.* V+O : USU+ to-INF, OR A ⇑ drive

2 If you **incite** particular feelings or behaviour, you cause people to begin having such feelings or behaving in such a way. EG *He was accused of inciting violence as well as undermining the Government.* V+O ⇑ instigate

incitement /ɪnsaɪtməⁿnt/ is the activity of inciting particular behaviour or feelings. EG *He made his reputation as a newspaper tycoon, specializing in the incitement of hatred... ...his incitement to the public to revolt.* N UNCOUNT : USU +of/to ⇑ encouragement

incl. is 1 an abbreviation for 'including'; used especially in advertisements. EG *...Fully fitted kitchen incl. washing machine and freezer.* 2 an abbreviation for 'inclusive'; used especially in advertisements. EG *...£150 pcm incl. of gas and elec.*

inclement /ɪŋˈklɛməⁿnt/. **Inclement** weather is unpleasantly cold or stormy; a formal word. ADJ CLASSIF ⇑ bad

inclination /ɪŋˈklɪneɪʃəⁿn/, **inclinations**. 1 An **inclination** that you have is a feeling that makes you act or want to act in a particular way without thinking or reasoning. EG *People decide on their aims in life according to their inclinations... There was a natural inclination to identify them as the enemy.* N COUNT = disposition, tendency
▸ used as an uncount noun. EG *She says her large family happened partly from inclination and partly from chance.* ▸ N UNCOUNT

2 The **inclination** of a surface is the angle by which it slopes from a flat horizontal or vertical position. N UNCOUNT

3 An **inclination** is also land that slopes at an angle. N COUNT ⇑ slope = incline

incline, inclines, inclining, inclined. The word **incline** is pronounced /ɪŋˈklaɪn/ when it is a noun and /ɪŋklaɪn/ when it is a verb. 1 A surface that **inclines** slopes in a certain direction at an angle to the flat horizontal or vertical position. EG *The table inclined at an angle of 30 degrees.* V = lean, slant

2 Something that **inclines** you to act in a certain way or **inclines** you towards a particular opinion makes you more likely to act in that way or to accept that opinion. EG *What I read in these books inclined me towards the nationalists... A bad day at work may incline you to be even more stubborn.* V+O+to-INF/ towards

3 An **incline** is land that slopes at an angle. EG *Houses stood in a row down the steep incline.* N COUNT

inclined /ɪŋˈklaɪnd/. 1 A line that is **inclined** in a particular direction is sloping in this direction at an angle to the horizontal or vertical position. EG *The southern hemisphere is inclined towards the sun.* ADJ CLASSIF+A = leaning

2 If you are **inclined** to behave in a particular way, **2.1** you tend to behave like this quite often because of your character. EG *He was inclined to be moody... ...she was inclined to fuss.* **2.2** you feel that you want to behave like this. EG *Some housewives only do the occasional dusting when they feel inclined... David was much less inclined to leave them out.* ADJ QUALIT : PRED+to-INF; ADJ QUALIT : PRED = disposed

3 If you say that you **are inclined** to have a particular opinion, you say that you have this opinion, but in a rather tentative way. EG *I'm inclined to agree with you... On the whole, I'm inclined to think I like people who retain their own customs.* PHR : VB INFLECTS+to-INF = tend

4 Someone who is mathematically **inclined**, artistically **inclined**, etc has a natural talent for mathematics, art, etc. ADJ CLASSIF : PRED ⇑ gifted

5 If you are **inclined** towards someone, you like them or support them; a fairly formal use. EG *...the leader towards whom Kunta was most inclined.* ADJ QUALIT : PRED+towards = disposed

include /ɪŋˈkluːd/, **includes, including, included**. 1 Something that **includes** a smaller thing has it as one of the parts that make up the whole thing. EG *The four-man crew included one Briton... The proposals included the nationalization of major industries... ...a booklet including advice on play materials, books, and toys.* V+O

2 If you **include** something in a whole thing, you make it a part of the whole thing. EG *Carpets and curtains are to be included in the purchase price... He asked the hotel staff to include the jar of marmalade on his tray each morning.* V+O+A ⇑ add

included /ɪŋˈkluːdɪᵈd/ is used to emphasize that the person or thing mentioned is part of the group of people or things that you are referring to. EG *All of us, myself included, had been totally committed to the party.* ADJ AFTER N

including /ɪŋˈkluːdɪŋ/ is used to say that one or more people or things mentioned are part of the larger group of people or things that you are referring to. EG *Costs can be from £5 per child per week including food... Nine persons were injured, including two wounded by gunfire... ...a home with 5 rooms (not including the bathroom)... ...education up to and including university level.* PREP ⇑ with = counting

inclusion /ɪŋˈkluːʒəⁿn/. The **inclusion** of someone or something in a larger thing is the act of making them a part of the larger thing. EG *He criticized my inclusion of courses involving radical ideas... ...the inclusion of the Old Testament in the Christian Bible.* N UNCOUNT : USU WITH POSS

inclusive /ɪŋˈkluːsɪv/. 1 A price that is **inclusive** includes all the charges and all the services offered. EG *It's a fully inclusive price... ...£168 (inclusive of tax).* ADJ CLASSIF ⇑ comprehensive

2 **Inclusive** is used to say that you are including the things mentioned when you refer to a series of things. EG *...Monday to Friday inclusive... ...ages 11 to 16 inclusive.* ADJ AFTER N

incognito /ɪŋˈkɒgniːtəʊ/. Someone who is travelling **incognito** is travelling in disguise, trying to hide their real identity. EG *...the disguise he wore when he escaped incognito to Wittenberg.* ADV AFTER VB
▸ used as a noun. EG *Could he hope to preserve his incognito?* ▸ N UNCOUNT

incoherence /ɪŋˈkəʊhɪərəns/. If you refer to the **incoherence** of something, you are referring to the fact that it is unclear and difficult to understand. EG *...the incoherence of his talk.* N UNCOUNT

incoherent /ɪŋˈkəʊhɪərənt/. 1 If something is **incoherent**, it is unclear and difficult to understand. EG *The aims were incoherent.* ADJ QUALIT

2 If someone is **incoherent**, they are talking in an unclear way. EG *...stammering incoherent apologies.* ADJ QUALIT = unintelligible
◊ **incoherently**. EG *Marcus stood up, muttering incoherently.* ◊ ADV WITH VB

income /ɪŋˈkəᵊm/, **incomes**. A person's **income** is the amount of money that they earn from their work or business, or the money that they get from other sources such as pension or investments. EG *My monthly income was over two hundred pounds... How does a pensioner on a low income manage to live?* N COUNT

income tax is the tax that you have to pay regularly to the government and which is a certain percentage of your income. EG *The Government has increased the standard rate of income tax.* N UNCOUNT

incoming /ɪŋˈkʌmɪŋ/. 1 An **incoming** tide, wave, etc is coming towards you. ADJ CLASSIF : ATTRIB

2 An **incoming** plane, passenger, etc is travelling towards a place and about to arrive. EG *...the incoming passengers at London Airport... ...incoming attack missiles.* ADJ CLASSIF : ATTRIB ⇑ arriving

3 An **incoming** message, piece of information, etc has been sent to you. EG *I throw incoming mail in a wicker basket.* ADJ CLASSIF : ATTRIB ⇑ arriving

4 An **incoming** official, administration, etc is one that has just been newly appointed or elected. EG *They gave their loyalty to the incoming Government... The outgoing and incoming Administrations will not agree.* ADJ CLASSIF : ATTRIB = new, succeeding

incommunicado /ɪŋˈkəmjuːnɪkɑːdəʊ/. If you are being kept **incommunicado**, you are not allowed to talk to anyone outside the place where you are. EG *They returned to their cabins, where they would remain incommunicado for the next ten hours.* ADV AFTER VB ⇑ imprisoned

incomparable /ɪŋˈkɒmpᵊərəbᵊl/. Something that is **incomparable** is so good or extreme that nothing else can be compared with it. EG *The computer proceeds with its incomparable logic and efficiency... ...a writer of incomparable prose.* ADJ CLASSIF = unequalled

◇ **incomparably**. EG *They are incomparably superior to those who imitate them.* ◇ ADV+ADJ/ADV

incompatible /ɪŋ'kəmpætə'bə°l/. Two things that are **incompatible** are unable to exist together or be considered together because they are completely different or opposite. EG *Their styles of life were incompatible... ...a man whose actions are totally incompatible with the group's well-being and safety. Businesses and unions are making incompatible demands.* ◇ **incompatibility** /ɪŋ'kəmpætə'bɪlɪti'/. EG *There is a fundamental incompatibility between the management and the unions.* ADJ CLASSIF ◇ N UNCOUNT

incompetence /ɪŋ'kɒmpɪtəns/. If you refer to someone's **incompetence**, you are referring to their inability to do a particular job or activity successfully. EG *...the incompetence and corruption of senior ministers... Graffman fired him for incompetence.* N UNCOUNT

incompetent /ɪŋ'kɒmpɪtənt/, **incompetents**. Someone who is **incompetent** does not have the skills that are needed in order to do something, especially a job successfully; used when they have shown this by doing it badly. EG *Our secret services and our navy are completely incompetent.* ▸ used of a person's work or actions. EG *...incompetent filming.* ▸ used as a noun. EG *My father was a hopeless incompetent on the domestic side.* ADJ QUALIT ⇑ unable ▸ ⇑ useless ▸ N COUNT

incomplete /ɪŋ'kəmpli:t/. Something that is **incomplete** 1 does not have all the parts that it should have. EG *...the problems of living in an incomplete family... ...a short and incomplete account of my life.* ADJ QUALIT ⇑ lacking

2 is not as great in extent, degree, or amount as it could be. EG *...the political consequences of incomplete military success.* ◇ **incompletely**. EG *The operation was done incompletely.* ADJ CLASSIF = partial ◇ ADV WITH VB

incomprehensible /ɪŋ'kɒmprɪhɛnsə'bə°l/. Something that is **incomprehensible** is impossible to understand. EG *...a long speech full of incomprehensible words like 'polemics' and 'dialectics'.* ADJ CLASSIF = unintelligible

incomprehension /ɪŋ'kɒmprɪhɛnʃə°n, ɪŋ'kɒm-/ is the state of being unable to understand something. EG *He went on staring in incomprehension.* N UNCOUNT ⇑ ignorance

inconceivable /ɪŋ'kənsi:vəbə°l/. If you describe something as **inconceivable**, you cannot believe that it could possibly happen or be true. EG *This is totally inconceivable... He found it inconceivable that Belov was insane... There is nothing inconceivable about a flying squirrel.* ADJ QUALIT = unthinkable, unimaginable

inconclusive /ɪŋ'kənklu:sɪv/. 1 If an argument, discussion, etc is **inconclusive**, it does not lead to any final decision being taken. EG *...an inconclusive debate... ...the inconclusive Conference vote.* ADJ QUALIT = indecisive

2 If evidence, an experiment, or a result is **inconclusive**, it has not proved anything. ADJ CLASSIF

incongruity /ɪŋ'kɒŋgru:ɪti'/, **incongruities**. The **incongruity** of something is the strangeness of it, usually because it does not fit properly into the rest of the event or situation. EG *I was struck by the glaring incongruity of the scene. There I was, my face dirty, my clothes torn; and there he was, immaculate as usual.* ▸ used as a count noun. EG *It is clear that tensions arise from incongruities between cultural elements in a society.* N UNCOUNT ⇑ discord ▸ N COUNT = discrepancy

incongruous /ɪŋ'kɒŋgru:əs/. Someone or something that is **incongruous** is strange because they do not fit properly into the rest of the event or situation. EG *He was an incongruous figure among the tourists... The sound of the horn hung in the air, lonely and incongruous.* ◇ **incongruously**. EG *I could smell the chlorine in the water mixed incongruously with the scent of the flowers.* ADJ QUALIT ⇑ discordant ◇ ADV WITH VB

inconsequential /ɪŋ'kɒnsi'kwɛnʃə°l/. Something that is **inconsequential** is not very important. EG *...some inconsequential conversation... His work, which seemed bold and innovative then, now seems trivial and inconsequential.* ◇ **inconsequentially**. EG *Nowadays he talks inconsequentially and doesn't seem interested in what other people say.* ADJ QUALIT = unimportant ◇ ADV WITH VB

inconsiderable /ɪŋ'kənsɪdə°rəbə°l/. If you describe something as not **inconsiderable**, you mean that it is large and well worth having. EG *£10,000 for a new and young author is not inconsiderable, is it?... The country's not inconsiderable army was mobilized.* ADJ CLASSIF : USU WITH BROAD NEG ⇑ small

inconsiderate /ɪŋ'kənsɪdə°rə't/. People who are **inconsiderate** do not care how their words or actions will affect other people. EG *He had behaved badly; he had been inconsiderate. ...the inconsiderate and single-minded nature of her pursuit of power.* ADJ QUALIT ⇑ unthinking

inconsistency /ɪŋ'kə'nsɪstənsi'/, **inconsistencies**. **Inconsistency** is behaviour which is unpredictable because it changes from one occasion to another; used showing disapproval. EG *He had noticed the president's inconsistency on abortion and marijuana... There is less security for children when they sense inconsistency.* ▸ used as a count noun. EG *The girls adopted a fairly cynical attitude to their mother's inconsistencies.* N UNCOUNT = irregularity ▸ N COUNT

inconsistent /ɪŋ'kənsɪstənt/. 1 Someone who is **inconsistent** is unpredictable and behaves differently in a particular situation each time it happens, rather than doing or saying the same thing each time; used showing disapproval. EG *The blame was laid on an inconsistent government.* ADJ QUALIT = fickle, irregular

2 Something that is **inconsistent** does not stay the same, being sometimes good and sometimes bad. EG *They play very inconsistent football.* ADJ QUALIT = unpredictable

3 Something that is **inconsistent** with a particular set of ideas, beliefs, or values cannot be considered right or proper according to those ideas, beliefs, or values. EG *He was a monarch whose behaviour they judged to be inconsistent with Hindu religious values.* ADJ QUALIT : PRED+*with* = incompatible

inconsolable /ɪŋ'kənsəʊləbə°l/. Someone who is **inconsolable** is very sad and cannot be comforted. EG *When his daughter was murdered Adam was inconsolable.* ▸ used also of someone's appearance or behaviour. EG *...looking up at me with her inconsolable face.* ◇ **inconsolably**. EG *Iris was inconsolably distressed.* ADJ CLASSIF ▸ ADJ CLASSIF ◇ ADV

inconspicuous /ɪŋ'kənspɪkju:əs/. 1 Something that is **inconspicuous** is 1.1 not easily seen because it is small or is hidden away. EG *There are no signs in the town, or only very inconspicuous ones... The other end of the string he pushed through an inconspicuous hole.* 1.2 does not attract much attention because it is not very large or unusual. EG *...an inconspicuous vehicle such as a transit van... ...the inconspicuous cul-de-sac that contains the residence of the Ambassador.* ADJ QUALIT ≠ conspicuous ADJ QUALIT ⇑ discrete

2 Someone who is **inconspicuous** does not attract much attention, often because they deliberately try not to let other people notice them. EG *I have asked the children to make themselves as inconspicuous as possible.* ◇ **inconspicuously**. EG *He slipped into the nearest bar as inconspicuously as he could.* ADJ QUALIT = unobtrusive ◇ ADV WITH VB

incontinence /ɪŋ'kɒntɪnəns/ is 1 the inability to control your bladder and bowels. EG *My father was on the verge of senility and incontinence.* 2 the inability to control your physical desires, especially your desire for sex. EG *He was renowned for his incontinence and profligacy.* N UNCOUNT N UNCOUNT ⇑ indulgence

incontinent /ɪŋ'kɒntɪnənt/. Someone who is **incontinent** is unable to control their bladder and bowels. EG *The stroke had made him incontinent.* ADJ CLASSIF

incontrovertible /ɪŋ'kɒntrəvɜ:tə'bə°l/. Something such as evidence that is **incontrovertible** is absolutely certain and no one can deny it or disprove it. EG *His picture collection was incontrovertible evidence of his wealth... ...a cold, wet nose, the incontrovertible sign of good health in any dog.* ◇ **incontrovertibly**. EG *It seemed to me to be obviously and incontrovertibly true.* ADJ CLASSIF = indisputable ◇ ADV WITH VB = indisputably

inconvenience /ɪŋ'kənvi:njəns, -vi:nɪəns/, **inconveniences, inconveniencing, inconvenienced**. 1 If someone or something causes **inconvenience**, they cause problems or difficulties. EG *She hated causing inconvenience... Alterations in our schedule meant a lot of inconvenience to the journalists.* ▸ used as a count noun. EG *He remained committed to an anti-nuclear posture, with all its inconveniences.* N UNCOUNT ⇑ trouble ▸ N COUNT ⇑ problem

2 If you **inconvenience** someone, you cause problems or difficulties for them. EG *All the residents have been inconvenienced by the road works.* V+O ⇑ put out

inconvenient /ɪŋ'kənvi:njənt, -vi:nɪənt/. 1 Something that is **inconvenient** makes problems or difficulties for you, rather than being efficient, effective, or simple. EG *You live quite a long way out. Don't you find it a bit inconvenient?... Although improved, the device was still inconvenient to prepare for each test... 'Could I have a word with you?'–'Well, it's a bit inconvenient at the moment.'* ADJ QUALIT = awkward

2 You can also describe things as **inconvenient** if they cause embarrassment or annoyance because they cannot be dealt with in the same way as ADJ QUALIT ⇑ difficult = awkward

everything else. EG *All inconvenient facts have been overlooked.* ◊ **inconveniently**. ◊ ADV WITH VB

incorporate /ɪŋˈkɔːpəreɪt/, **incorporates, incorporating, incorporated**. 1 If a thing **incorporates** something else, it includes it as one of the parts that make up the whole thing. EG *His coat of arms incorporates three apple trees.* V+O ⇑ contain

2 If someone or something **is incorporated** into a large group, system, or area, they become a part of it. EG *His picture had been incorporated without his permission into an advertisement for a new brand of soap.* V+O+A *(into/in)* = include

incorrect /ɪŋˈkərekt/. 1 Something that is **incorrect** is 1.1 wrong or untrue. EG *The predictions were proved again and again to be incorrect... ...incorrect information.* ◊ **incorrectly**. EG *The problem has been incorrectly defined.* 1.2 not completely correct or accurate. EG *...spelling mistakes and incorrect English.* ADJ CLASSIF; ◊ ADV WITH VB; ADJ CLASSIF ⇑ wrong

2 If you say that someone's behaviour is **incorrect**, you mean that it annoys or offends you because you do not believe that it is right for a particular situation, usually because it is rude or too informal. EG *He would not have consented to anything so incorrect.* ADJ QUALIT = improper

incorrigible /ɪŋˈkɒrɪdʒəˈbəᵊl/. Someone who is **incorrigible** has faults or bad habits that will never change or be corrected; sometimes used in a slightly humorous way about something stupid that someone has done. EG *...incorrigible criminals... 'Oh, James, you are incorrigible!' she said.* ◊ **incorrigibly**. EG *...a nation incorrigibly set upon world domination... I am incorrigibly hopeful.* ▸ used also of a person's behaviour. EG *...a victim of his own incorrigible lying.* ADJ CLASSIF = hopeless; ◊ ADV WITH VB; ▸ ADJ CLASSIF

incorruptible /ɪŋˈkərʌptəˈbəᵊl/. 1 Someone who is **incorruptible** cannot be bribed or corrupted in any other way. EG *They were both wise and incorruptible men.* ADJ CLASSIF

2 Something that is **incorruptible** does not decay and so can not be destroyed. EG *All over the world gold was precious because it was incorruptible.* ADJ CLASSIF = indestructible

increase, increases, increasing, increased. The word **increase** is pronounced /ɪŋˈkriːs/ when it is a noun and /ɪŋˈkriːs/ when it is a verb. 1 If something **increases** or you **increase** it, it becomes bigger in number, size, or amount. EG *World energy demand is increasing at a rate of about 3% per year... Crime has increased by three per cent in the past year... Police checks on banks were increased in frequency.* ◊ **increased**. EG *Industrial investment has not led to increased output.* ◊ **increasing**. EG *Japanese industry is making increasing use of robots... This idea crops up with increasing frequency.* V-ERG ⇑ grow; ◊ ADJ CLASSIF; ◊ ADJ CLASSIF : PREP ⇑ greater

2 An **increase** is a rise in the number, level, or amount of something such as prices or the population of a country. EG *At the meeting they demanded a sharp increase in wages... The report called for massive increases in defense spending... There will be a 20% increase in the number of over-75's by 1990.* N COUNT ⇑ growth

3 If something is **on the increase**, it is becoming more frequent than it was. EG *Crime seems to be on the increase.* PHR : USED AS AN A = rising

increasingly /ɪŋˈkriːsɪŋliˈ/. 1 If something is **increasingly** difficult, **increasingly** clear, etc, it is becoming more and more difficult, more and more clear, etc. EG *The numbers were so great that it was becoming increasingly difficult to find suitable jobs for everyone. ... There is an increasingly strong and well-organized lobby dealing with this issue.* ADV+ADJ/ADV

2 If something **increasingly** distresses you, **increasingly** pleases you, etc, it distresses or pleases you more and more as time passes. EG *As a lawyer the cases he was concerned with increasingly repelled him.* ADV WITH VB

3 If something occurs **increasingly**, it occurs more and more often or in more and more places. EG *Men increasingly find that women are taking their jobs... Increasingly, inner cities and suburbs are separate.* ADV WITH VB, OR ADV SEN

incredible /ɪŋˈkredəˈbəᵊl/. 1 Something that is **incredible** is 1.1 so amazing that you find it hard to believe or imagine. EG *They were wearing incredible uniforms... Their technical standard is incredible.* ◊ **incredibly**. EG *Upstairs, incredibly, the beds were already made.* EG *...I'm in an incredibly privileged position.* 1.2 greater in amount or degree than you expected or thought was possible. EG *They get an incredible amount of money.* ◊ **incredibly**. EG *The water was incredibly hot... They try incredibly hard.* ADJ CLASSIF = unbelievable; ◊ ADV+ADJ/ADV, OR ADV SEN; ADJ CLASSIF; ◊ ADV+ADJ/ADV

2 If you describe something you have experienced or seen as **incredible**, you mean that it was exceptionally good; used showing approval. EG *It was an incredible experience... ...gardens of incredible perfection.* ADJ QUALIT ⇑ wonderful = fantastic

3 You can also use **incredible** to describe something that you believe cannot possibly be true. EG *You've no basis for this incredible suggestion... The account cannot be dismissed as incredible.* ADJ CLASSIF ⇑ untrue = unbelievable

incredulity /ɪŋˈkrɪˈdjuːlɪtiˈ/ is total disbelief of something that is said or done. EG *...an expression of sheer incredulity... His decision produced shock and incredulity.* N UNCOUNT ⇑ surprise

incredulous /ɪŋˈkredəˈləs/. If someone is **incredulous**, they are unable to believe something because it is very surprising or shocking. EG *'You left her all alone?' He sounded incredulous.* ▸ used of people's expressions or behaviour. EG *My first reaction was an incredulous repetition of his name.* ◊ **incredulously**. EG *I stared at him incredulously.* ADJ QUALIT = disbelieving; ◊ ADV WITH VB

increment /ɪŋˈkrəməˈnt/, **increments**. 1 The **increment** in the value of something is the amount by which it increases. EG *Divorce appears to bring with it a sudden increment in mortality rates...* N COUNT

● **Unearned increment** is an increase in the value of something which a person gets, not because he or she has worked to get it, but because of other causes, such as a rise in the cost of land or in the price of shares. EG *The rents she receives are a pure unearned increment, not the product of any efforts on her part.* ● PHR : USED AS C OR O

2 An **increment** is the amount by which your salary automatically increases every year, every six months, etc. EG *...a salary of £15,000 a year with annual increments of £550 for six years... The University had tempted him with two additional increments.* N COUNT

incremental /ɪŋˈkrəmentəᵊl/. Something that is **incremental** increases in value, often by a regular amount. EG *Lecturers enjoy job security, steady incremental increases in salary, and more or less regular working hours.* ADJ CLASSIF

incriminate /ɪŋˈkrɪmɪneɪt/, **incriminates, incriminating, incriminated**. If something **incriminates** you, it suggests that you are the person responsible for a crime. EG *Williams had been forced to incriminate himself in cross-examinations.* ◊ **incriminating**. EG *...incriminating evidence.* V+O (NG/REFL) ⇑ implicate; ◊ ADJ QUALIT

incubate /ɪŋˈkjəˈbeɪt/, **incubates, incubating, incubated**. 1 When eggs **incubate** or when birds **incubate** them, they get ready to hatch. EG *The time needed for the eggs to incubate is nine or ten days... ...the female who is incubating the eggs.* ◊ **incubation** /ɪŋˈkjəˈbeɪʃəᵊn/. EG *The incubation period is a short one: three or four days at the most.* V-ERG; ◊ N UNCOUNT

2 When something such as bacteria **incubates** or when you **incubate** it, it changes or develops in some way due to the application of heat. EG *It took four days for the plague to incubate... We've incubated some of her serum with your blood.* ◊ **incubation**. EG *...incubation tanks.* V-ERG; ◊ N UNCOUNT

3 If you say that plans or ideas **incubate**, you mean that they slowly develop after a lot of thought and discussion. EG *...social revolution, long incubating in this country.* V = generate

incubator /ɪŋˈkjəˈbeɪtə/, **incubators**. An **incubator** is 1 a device which helps babies who are very small or weak to survive by keeping them in an environment in which the temperature, humidity, and flow of oxygen are carefully controlled. EG *She was taken to a hospital, where an incubator and expert care were available.* N COUNT

2 a device which keeps eggs or bacteria at the correct temperature for them to hatch or develop. N COUNT ⇑ breeder

inculcate /ɪŋˈkʌlkeɪt, ɪŋˈkʌlkeɪt/, **inculcates, inculcating, inculcated**. If you **inculcate** something such as an idea or an opinion in someone's mind, you fix it in their mind by repeating it again and again; a formal word. V+O : USU+A *(in/into)* = drum in

incumbent /ɪŋˈkʌmbənt/, **incumbents**; a formal word. 1 If it is **incumbent** on you to do something, you must do it. EG *It was incumbent on editors in these times to exercise discretion.* ADJ CLASSIF : IF+PREP THEN *on/upon* ⇑ necessary

2 An **incumbent** is someone who officially holds a particular post at a particular time. EG *...points of* N COUNT

policy on which he, as the incumbent, is vulnerable... The incumbent in 1905 was George B McClellan. ▸ used as an adjective. EG *...the incumbent President of the United States.*

incur /ɪŋˈkɜː/, **incurs, incurring, incurred.** If you **incur** something unpleasant such as a loss, the way in which you act or behave causes it to happen. EG *The final rewards will more than compensate for any loss you may incur.* — V+O = sustain, contract

incurable /ɪŋˈkjʊərəbəˀl/. 1 If someone has an **incurable** disease, they cannot be cured of it. EG *Jane, aged 24, developed incurable cancer.* — ADJ CLASSIF
◇ **incurably.** EG *He heard himself declared 'incurably insane'.* — ◇ ADV+ADJ/ADV
2 You can also use **incurable** to describe someone's habits, beliefs, or attitudes that they cannot or will not change. EG *...an incurable bigot... ...incurable optimists... What my mother has left me is an incurable gaiety which she had herself.* — ADJ CLASSIF: ATTRIB = incorrigible ◇ **incurably.** EG *...the incurably treacherous character of the regime.* — ◇ ADV = incorrigibly

incurious /ɪŋˈkjʊərɪəs/. Someone who is **incurious** does not pay very much attention to what is happening, either near them or in the world in general. EG *Ordinary country people are incurious–and proud of it.* — ADJ CLASSIF = indifferent ▸ used also of people's expressions and behaviour. EG *She gave the travellers a swift, incurious glance.* — ▸ ADJ CLASSIF: ATTRIB ◇ **incuriously.** EG *The girl raised her eyes and looked, briefly and incuriously, at them.* — ◇ ADV WITH VB = indifferently

incursion /ɪŋˈkɜːʃəˀn/, **incursion.** 1 An **incursion** into a country is a sudden and often unexpected invasion of it. EG *...their incursion into Yugoslavia... They strengthened their northern border against any possible incursions by guerrillas.* — N COUNT: USU+*from/into*
2 An **incursion** of something into a place is its entry into it, often in large and rather surprising numbers. EG *...the impressive incursion of the computer into the home and office.* — N COUNT+SUPP: IF+PREP THEN *into*

indebted /ɪndetɪˀd/. If you are **indebted** to someone for something, 1 you are grateful to them for something they have given you. EG *I am indebted to Bob Waller for many of the ideas expressed here... Most of his colleagues have been indebted to him for his assistance.* — ADJ QUALIT: PRED ◇ **indebtedness.** EG *I readily acknowledge my indebtedness to my friends for all they have done.* — ◇ N UNCOUNT 2 you owe them money. EG *It is one of the most indebted nations in the world.* — ADJ CLASSIF ◇ **indebtedness.** EG *Home ownership involves higher indebtedness than renting a house does... High prices have increased agriculture's burden of indebtedness.* — ◇ N UNCOUNT

indecency /ɪndiːsənsiˈ/. If you refer to the **indecency** of something or someone, you are referring to the fact that they are morally or sexually offensive. EG *...laws concerning obscenity, indecency, and violence.* — N UNCOUNT = lewdness

indecent /ɪndiːsənt/. 1 If you describe words, pictures, films, etc as **indecent**, you mean that they are shocking and offend you because they refer to, show, or suggest naked people or sexual acts. EG *...obscene and indecent advertising... ...indecent jokes.* — ADJ QUALIT = obscene ◇ **indecently.** EG *...an indecently short dress.* — ◇ ADV
2 If you describe something that happens as **indecent**, you mean that it breaks the established rules of good behaviour or morality. EG *The rush to become a White House correspondent was indecent.* — ADJ CLASSIF ↑ unacceptable = shocking ◇ **indecently.** EG *They got married indecently soon after his first wife's funeral... His voice sounded indecently loud.* — ◇ ADV

indecipherable /ɪndɪsaɪfəˀrəbəˀl/; a formal word. 1 If writing is **indecipherable**, you cannot read it. EG *...thin sheets, scribbled all over with indecipherable writing... His signature on the contract was indecipherable.* — ADJ QUALIT = illegible
2 If something such as the expression on a person's face is **indecipherable**, you cannot understand or interpret it. EG *An almost imperceptible and quite indecipherable glance passed between them.* — ADJ QUALIT

indecision /ɪndɪsɪʒəˀn/ is uncertainty about what you should do, where you should go, how you should behave, etc. EG *She felt ill with anxiety and indecision... After five minutes of indecision, I put the knife away.* — N UNCOUNT

indecisive /ɪndɪsaɪsɪv/. 1 If you are **indecisive**, you do not find it easy to make decisions about what you should do, where you should go, how you should behave, etc. EG *It was unlike him to be so indecisive.* — ADJ QUALIT: USU PRED ↑ hesitant ◇ **indecisiveness.** EG *He behaved with all his usual indecisiveness.* — ◇ N UNCOUNT ↑ hesitancy
2 **Indecisive** arguments, beliefs, etc cannot be proved one way or another. EG *The police had to investigate it. It was one of those indecisive things, in that the death was so unexpected that it could have been murder.* — ADJ CLASSIF = inconclusive

indeed /ɪndiːd/. 1 You use **indeed 1.1** to confirm or agree with something that has just been said. EG *'I think you knew him when you were in Pretoria.'–'I did indeed.'... 'I really think Charles Boon is here at last.' Boon had indeed arrived.* — ADV SEN = certainly **1.2** to add a further comment or statement which strengthens the point you have already made. EG *This act has failed to bring women's earnings up to the same level. Indeed the gulf is widening... I'm very happy, indeed anxious, that students' views should be expressed... Luckily, most of Julie's friends (and indeed Julie herself) had no conception of what was about to happen.* — ADV SEN = in fact
2 You also use **indeed** at the end of a clause to give extra force to the word 'very'. EG *We have very little information indeed... Thank you very much indeed.* — ADV AFTER N
3 You also use **indeed** after a word that you want to emphasize so that you can give extra force to the point that you are making. EG *The possibility of rescue now seemed remote indeed... That's praise indeed.* — ADV AFTER N/ADV/ADJ = truly
4 In spoken English, you can also use **indeed** to draw attention to a word or expression that someone has just used, especially when that word or expression is old-fashioned, inaccurate, or insulting. EG *'I heard it on the wireless.'–'Wireless, indeed! They're called radios now, you know.'* — EXCLAM

indefatigable /ɪndiˈfætɪgəbəˀl/; a formal word. 1 You use **indefatigable** to describe people who never get tired of doing something. EG *All through her life she was an indefatigable traveller... ...an indefatigable writer to the local papers.* — ADJ CLASSIF = untiring ◇ **indefatigably.** EG *He worked indefatigably for the conservation of wild animals.* — ◇ ADV WITH VB = untiringly
2 You also use **indefatigable** to describe something that continues for a long time without showing signs of weakening. EG *They beat out the indefatigable rhythm... ...her soft, indefatigable voice.* — ADJ CLASSIF = ceaseless

indefensible /ɪndiˈfensəbəˀl/. 1 Statements or ideas that are **indefensible** cannot be justified or supported because they are completely wrong, unacceptable, or untrue. EG *We spoke out, denouncing the judge's savage attack as totally indefensible... His views were condemned as utterly ridiculous and indefensible.* — ADJ QUALIT
2 Places or buildings that are **indefensible** cannot be defended if they are attacked. EG *...the massacre of brave men, who won just four miles of indefensible mud.* — ADJ CLASSIF ↑ vulnerable

indefinable /ɪndiˈfaɪnəbəˀl/. Qualities or attitudes that are **indefinable** cannot easily be described or fully explained. EG *...the indefinable pleasures that a bookshop supplies... ...the indefinable quality of leadership.* — ADJ CLASSIF ↑ indescribable ◇ **indefinably.** EG *My first impression was indefinably unpleasant... ...the signs of something indefinably but seriously wrong.* — ◇ ADV

indefinite /ɪndefɪnɪˈt/. 1 If something is **indefinite**, it has not been decided when it will stop or finish. EG *The union gave notice of indefinite strike... We are embarking on an adventure indefinite in length.* — ADJ CLASSIF
2 Actions, events, or situations that are **indefinite** are not exact, clear, or obvious. EG *Many of his hand movements are indefinite and vague. Milner advised him not to answer so indefinite a proposal.* — ADJ QUALIT = vague

indefinite article, indefinite articles. The **indefinite article** is a term used in grammar for the words *a* and *an*. In this dictionary *a* and *an* are described as DET. See **a, an** and ☐ at DET. — N SING: DET+N ↑ determiner

indefinitely /ɪndefɪnɪtˈliˈ/. If something is continuing **indefinitely**, it has not been decided when it will stop or finish. EG *The Regency Hotel was closed indefinitely... His policy could not be sustained indefinitely.* — ADV WITH VB

indelible /ɪndelɪbəˀl/. 1 If a mark or stain is **indelible**, it cannot be removed, erased, or washed out. EG *His fingertips had turned an indelible black... ...indelible writing.* — ADJ CLASSIF ↑ permanent ◇ **indelibly.** EG *Her dresses and pants were clearly and indelibly marked with her name.* — ◇ ADV WITH VB ↑ permanently ▸ **Indelible** pens, pencils, and ink make marks that cannot be removed, erased, or washed out. — ▸ ADJ CLASSIF ↑ permanent

2 Memories, impressions, etc that are **indelible** are not likely to be forgotten. EG *...all the indelible memories of childhood.* ◇ **indelibly**. EG *The number was indelibly printed on her brain.* ADJ CLASSIF ◇ ADV WITH VB

indelicate /ɪndelɪkɪ¹t/. You describe what someone says as **indelicate** when it is offensive, shocking, or embarrassing. EG *...a rather indelicate remark... Simon was hungry, but felt it would be indelicate to make too much fuss about it.* ADJ QUALIT

indemnity /ɪndemnɪti¹/, **indemnities**. 1 If something provides **indemnity**, it provides insurance or protection against damage or loss, especially in the form of financial compensation. EG *...the Engineering Employers' Indemnity Fund.* N UNCOUNT

2 An **indemnity** is an amount of money or goods that are received by someone as compensation for some damage or loss they have suffered. EG *The families of the two young men paid an indemnity to the victim after the accident.* N COUNT

indent /ɪndent/, **indents, indenting, indented**.
1 When you **indent** a word or a line, you start it further in from the margin than you start the other lines. V+O

2 If you **indent** for goods, you order them by filling in a special form; used in British English. EG *He indented for 5,000 miles of rubber tubing.* V+A *(for)*

indentation /ɪndenteɪʃə⁰n/, **indentations**. An **indentation** is 1 a space at the beginning of a line of writing, between the margin and the beginning of the writing. N COUNT 2 a notch or cut in the surface or on the edge of something. EG *...the indentations of the coastline... The high heels of her boots made little indentations in the sitting room carpet.* N COUNT

indented /ɪndentɪ²d/. If something is **indented**, it has notches or marks on its edge or its surface. EG *...the wooden block, indented by chopper and saw.* ADJ CLASSIF

independence /ɪndɪpendəns/. 1 If a country has **independence**, it has its own government and is not ruled by any other country. EG *It accepted the UN plan for independence... African territories eventually obtained their independence.* N UNCOUNT ⇑ freedom

2 If you refer to someone's **independence**, you are referring to the fact that they are independent. EG *They had no tradition of individualism and independence... She shows great independence of mind.* N UNCOUNT ⇑ freedom

Independence Day is a holiday in the United States when people celebrate the Declaration of Independence in 1776. N UNCOUNT = the Fourth of July

independent /ɪndɪpendənt/, **independents**. 1 Something that is **independent** exists, happens, or acts separately from other people, groups, or things. EG *Two independent studies each came to exactly the same conclusions... After 1963 they began to build an independent organisation outside the Labour Party.* ◇ **independently**. EG *Each signal can operate quite independently of the others... Similar customs have developed independently in different places at various times.* ADJ CLASSIF : IF + PREP THEN *of* ⇑ separate ≠ connected ◇ ADV WITH VB

2 If you are **independent**, you 2.1 have a lot of confidence and can develop your own opinions and can work alone without needing other people's help. EG *Their children are quite independent.* ▸ used of behaviour, attitudes, etc. EG *...fiercely independent individualism... They wanted to encourage independent thought.* 2.2 have your own money, food, housing, resources, etc so that you do not need to get help from other people in order to survive. EG *I became financially independent... I am resented because I'm absolutely independent of them all.* ● If you are **of independent means**, you have your own private income which enables you to survive without having to ask for money or earn it from other people. EG *She was a woman of independent means.* ADJ QUALIT ⇑ strong = self-reliant ≠ clinging ▸ = individual; ADJ QUALIT : IF + PREP THEN *of* ≠ reliant; ● PHR AFTER NG ⇑ self-supporting

3 An **independent** school, broadcasting company, etc does not receive money from the government. EG *The staff of many independent schools earn much higher salaries... ...the Independent Broadcasting Authority.* ADJ CLASSIF ⇑ private

4 **Independent** countries and states used to be ruled by other countries but now have their own government. EG *It became an independent republic.* ADJ CLASSIF ⇑ free

5 An **independent** inquiry, opinion, etc is one which is held by people who are not involved in a dispute or other situation and so are considered most likely to make a fair and honest judgement. EG *He backs the need for an independent inquiry into charity law... It might be helpful to get an independent opinion... ...an independent body.* ADJ CLASSIF : ATTRIB = impartial, outside

6 An **independent** is a politician who does not represent any political party. EG *She was standing as an independent.* N COUNT

indescribable /ɪndɪ²skraɪbəbə⁰l/. Something that is **indescribable** is too intense or extreme to be described properly; used especially of things which are unpleasant. EG *...the indescribable sadness of those final pages... The smell was indescribable... ...a feeling of indescribable pleasure.* ◇ **indescribably**. EG *The tasks of testing and quality control would be indescribably difficult.* ADJ CLASSIF = unbelievable ◇ ADV + ADJ/ADV = incredibly

indestructible /ɪndɪ²strʌktə¹bə⁰l/. Something that is **indestructible** cannot be destroyed. EG *Our friendship is indestructible... ...indestructible plants.* ◇ **indestructibility** /ɪndɪ²strʌktə¹bɪlɪti¹/. EG *...the indestructibility of their love.* ADJ CLASSIF ⇑ durable ◇ N UNCOUNT

indeterminable /ɪndi¹tɜːmɪnəbə⁰l/. An **indeterminable** number, amount, etc is unable to be counted or measured exactly. EG *There is an indeterminable number of factors.* ADJ CLASSIF ⇑ unknown ≠ exact

indeterminacy /ɪndi¹tɜːmɪnəsi¹/ is the quality of being uncertain or vague. EG *...the indeterminacy of thought and values that characterizes contemporary life.* N UNCOUNT ⇑ uncertainty

indeterminate /ɪndi¹tɜːmɪnət/. If something is **indeterminate**, you are not able to say exactly how much it is, where it is, what it is, etc. EG *The middle classes are indeterminate groups of occupations which defy exact description... He will be sent to prison for an indeterminate period... Marcus made an indeterminate gesture with his head.* ADJ QUALIT ⇑ uncertain ≠ exact, known

index /ɪndeks/, **indexes, indexing, indexed; indices**. **Indexes** is the usual form of the plural, but in technical senses such as 1.3 and 5 the plural form is usually **indices**. 1 An **index** is 1.1 an alphabetical list that is sometimes printed at the back of a book to tell you where particular subjects, people, places, events, etc are referred to in the book. EG *Is Arbuthnot in the index?* N COUNT 1.2 a collection of cards with information on them, arranged in alphabetical order. In a library the index lists the titles of books, names of authors, subjects, etc. EG *The headmaster kept a card index on each child... There were index cards in wooden boxes... To trace articles in periodicals, you can use the indexes available in the Reading Rooms.* N COUNT ⇑ system 1.3 a system by which changes in the value of something and the rate at which it changes can be compared or measured. EG *...a 0.3 percent rise in the wholesale prices index... We must carefully watch economic indices.* N COUNT + SUPP

2 If you **index** a book or collection of information, you provide an index for it. EG *...an indexed book bound in blue leather... Millions of names are indexed for easy electronic processing... I had the job of indexing everything published in the physical sciences.* V+O : USU PASS ⇑ order

3 If you **index** one thing to something else, you arrange it so that when one thing increases or decreases, the other thing also increases or decreases. EG *The report asks for the indexing of wages to inflation.* V+O+A *(to)* ⇑ relate

4 If one thing is an **index** of another thing, it is a sign of the changes that are taking place in the other thing. EG *The age of those who supported it could well be an index of the party's own obsolescence... Coal was the perfect index to Britain's situation.* N COUNT : USU + *of/to* ⇑ symbol = indication

5 In mathematics, **indices** are the little numbers that show how many times you must multiply a number by itself. In the equation $3^2 = 9$, the number 2 is an index. N COUNT

index finger, index fingers. Your **index finger** is the finger that is next to your thumb. N COUNT = forefinger

index-linked. **Index-linked** pensions, payments, etc are linked to the index measuring inflation or the cost of living. The value therefore changes every time inflation or the cost of living changes. ADJ CLASSIF

Indian /ɪndɪən/, **Indians**. 1 An **Indian** is 1.1 a person who comes from India, or whose family originally came from India. N COUNT 1.2 the same as an American Indian. ● **too many chiefs and not enough Indians**: see **chief**. N COUNT

2 Something that is **Indian** 2.1 belongs or relates to India, or to its people or languages. EG *My parents worked for the Indian independence movement.* ADJ CLASSIF 2.2 ADJ CLASSIF

belongs or relates to the American Indians or their languages. EG *...an Indian squaw.*
3 If a number of people walk **in Indian file**, they walk in a line, one behind the other. PHR : USED AS AN A
4 See also **West Indian**.

Indian ink is black ink which is used especially for drawing. N UNCOUNT

Indian summer, Indian summers. A **Indian summer** is a period of warm weather during the autumn. N COUNT

india rubber, india rubbers. **India rubber** is rubber used for erasing pencil marks and making balls, toys, etc. N UNCOUNT/COUNT

indicate /ɪndɪkeɪt/, **indicates, indicating, indicated**. **1** If something **indicates** that something is true, it gives you information which makes you come to that conclusion. EG *Evidence indicates that the experiments were unsuccessful... The studies that have been done indicate that it's best to change your car every two years.* V+O/REPORT-CL = suggest
2 If you **indicate** something to someone, you show them where it is, or which one it is, especially by pointing to it. EG *She sat down in the armchair that Mrs Jones indicated... 'The car's just down there' she said, indicating it with a nod of her head... The reader has to indicate the correct answer with a tick.* V+O/REPORT-CL = designate
3 If you **indicate** a particular opinion, plan, etc, you mention it in a brief, often general, way. EG *As I have already indicated, there is now more competition for jobs than there used to be... He has already indicated the outlines of his plan to the police.* V+O/REPORT-CL/QUOTE ⇑ communicate
4 If one thing **indicates** something else, it is a sign of that thing. EG *An erect tail on a cat indicates aggression... He spread his arms wide in a gesture which indicated total submission.* V+O/REPORT-CL ⇑ signify = express
5 If something such as a scientific instrument **indicates** something, it shows or gives a reading. EG *The light above the lift indicated that the lift was now at the fifteenth floor... The thermometer indicates that his temperature is 38.2.* V+O/REPORT-CL ⇑ register
6 If you **indicate** or if your car **indicates**, you show which way your car is going to turn by signalling with your hand or by using lights which flash at the front and back of the car. EG *He indicated that he was turning left... The car in front of me was indicating to turn right.* V+O/REPORT-CL

indication /ɪndɪkeɪʃəⁿn/, **indications**. An **indication** is a sign which gives you an idea of, for example, what people are thinking or feeling. EG *The President gave a clear indication yesterday of his willingness to meet the visitors... All the indications are that both sides will reach an agreement later in the week.* N COUNT/UNCOUNT

indicative /ɪndɪkətɪv/. **1** If something is **indicative** of something else, it is a sign of that thing. EG *It's indicative of the change in Rachel that this year she is having a big birthday party... Indicative of the confusion was the fact that no-one knew where the meeting point was.* ADJ CLASSIF : PRED+*of* = symptomatic
2 If a verb is in the **indicative**, it is in the form used for making statements. N SING : *the*+N

indicator /ɪndɪkeɪtə/, **indicators**. **1** An **indicator** is **1.1** something which acts as a sign and which tells you, for example, the way that people think or feel. EG *The union's attitude to the press is always seen as a critical indicator of how negotiations are progressing.* N COUNT = gauge **1.2** an instrument or a device which gives you information. Some cars have an indicator which shows that you have very little petrol left. N COUNT = gauge
2 A car's **indicators** are the flashing lights at the front and back which show that it is going to turn left or right. N COUNT

indices /ɪndɪsiːz/ is a plural form of **index**.

indict /ɪndaɪt/, **indicts, indicting, indicted**. To **indict** someone for a crime means to charge them with it officially. EG *whether or not to indict the government's chief witness... The five men were caught and indicted... He was indicted for manslaughter.* V+O : IF+PREP THEN *for* ⇑ accuse

indictable /ɪndaɪtəbəⁿl/. An **indictable** offence is one for which you can be indicted. ADJ CLASSIF

indictment /ɪndaɪtmənt/, **indictments**. **1** If you say that something is an **indictment** of something else, you mean that it shows how bad that thing is. EG *He sees the present level of unemployment as an indictment of Government policies... It is a striking indictment of our educational system that so many children cannot read or write.* N COUNT : IF+PREP THEN *of* = denunciation
2 An **indictment** is an official charge made to a person. EG *Robbins is under indictment for fraud... There was little likelihood of an indictment, and no likelihood of a prosecution.* N COUNT/UNCOUNT ⇑ accusation

indifference /ɪndɪfəⁿrəns/ is a complete lack of interest in something or someone. EG *Halliday's presence or absence was a matter of total indifference to him... After years of official indifference, the state nursery school campaign seems at last to be making progress.* N UNCOUNT ≠ attention, concern

indifferent /ɪndɪfəⁿrənt/. **1** If you are **indifferent** to something, you have no interest in it and show that you do not care at all. EG *Children fail to progress if their parents seem indifferent to their success... Her eyes assumed a strange, weary, indifferent look.* ADJ QUALIT = uninterested ≠ caring, responsive
◊ **indifferently**. EG *Mark smiled at me briefly, indifferently, and hurried away.* ◊ ADV WITH VB = distantly
2 Something that is **indifferent** is not of a very good standard or quality. EG *She was a gifted painter but an indifferent actor.* ADJ QUALIT = mediocre

indigenous /ɪndɪdʒɪnəs/. Something that is **indigenous** is originally from the country in which it is found, rather than coming or being brought there from some other country. EG *...the indigenous population... The elephant is indigenous to India... ...countries with rich indigenous cultural traditions.* ADJ CLASSIF : IF+PREP THEN *to* = native

indigent /ɪndɪdʒənt/. Someone who is **indigent** is very poor; a formal word. ADJ QUALIT = destitute

indigestible /ɪndɪdʒɛstəbəⁿl/. **1** Food that is **indigestible** cannot be digested easily. EG *The steak was tough and indigestible.* ADJ QUALIT
2 **Indigestible** facts, ideas, etc are difficult for you understand because they are very complicated. EG *...the indigestible language of lawyers.* ADJ QUALIT = impenetrable

indigestion /ɪndɪdʒestʃəⁿn/ is pain that you get when you find it difficult to digest food. EG *A food that is too fatty may cause indigestion.* N UNCOUNT

indignant /ɪndɪgnənt/. If you are **indignant**, you feel shock and anger when you think that other people have done something unjust or unfair, and that you have a right to be angry. EG *She looked like an indignant child... The more she talked, the more indignant she became... Many taxpayers are indignant at what they regard as an illegal use of public funds.* ▸ used to describe your voice, appearance, etc. EG *The man turned and gave him a strange, indignant glance.* ADJ QUALIT = outraged, incensed ◊ **indignantly**. EG *'Are you talking to me?' he asked indignantly.* ◊ ADV WITH VB

indignation /ɪndɪgneɪʃəⁿn/ is the feeling of shock and anger which you have when you think that other people have done something unjust or unfair, and that you have a right to be angry. EG *She seethed with indignation... He sat bolt upright in indignation... By the end of the week public indignation was running high.* N UNCOUNT = outrage, resentment

indignity /ɪndɪgnɪti¹/, **indignities**. An **indignity** is something that makes you feel embarrassed or humiliated. EG *He recalled the indignity of being handcuffed and searched... He hated the rules and the petty indignities of prison life.* N COUNT/UNCOUNT = humiliation

indigo /ɪndɪgəʊ/. **1** **Indigo** is a dark colour between blue and violet. ▸ used as an adjective. EG *...an indigo sky.* **2** a dye that is this colour. N UNCOUNT ▸ ADJ COLOUR N UNCOUNT

indirect /ɪndaɪrɛkt/. **1** Something that is **indirect** is not done or caused directly, but by means of something or someone else. EG *A sudden increase in oil prices would have serious indirect effects... Smoking is likely to lead in many indirect ways to a variety of cancers... People who live together often have indirect ways of communicating with each other.* ADJ CLASSIF : USU ATTRIB ≠ direct
◊ **indirectly**. EG *I suppose I was indirectly responsible for the whole thing.* ◊ ADV ≠ directly
2 An **indirect** route, flight, etc does not go in a straight line between two places and so takes a longer time. EG *An indirect flight from Rome to Marseilles would be cheaper.* ADJ CLASSIF ⇑ long
3 An **indirect** answer, reference, etc is one that does not directly mention the thing that is actually meant. EG *Joan's answer was typically indirect.* ADJ QUALIT = roundabout

indirect object, indirect objects. See **object**.

indirect tax, indirect taxes. An **indirect tax** is a tax on goods and services which is added to the price of these goods and services. VAT and import duty are indirect taxes: compare **direct tax**. N COUNT

indirect taxation is the raising of money by a government by means of indirect taxes. N UNCOUNT

indiscernible /ɪndɪsɜːnəbəˡl/. Something that is **indiscernible** cannot be seen clearly. EG *For some indiscernible reason she wants to marry him.* ADJ QUALIT = unfathomable

indiscipline /ɪndɪsɪplɪn/ is a lack of discipline. EG *Murphy was found guilty of indiscipline on the field.* N UNCOUNT

indiscreet /ɪndɪskriːt/. If you are **indiscreet**, you talk about things or do things openly when perhaps you should have kept them secret. EG *It's amazing how indiscreet and unprofessional top executives can be. If you can give me some news without being indiscreet, do not hesitate.* ▸ used of something you do or say. EG *...an indiscreet comment... She would not say anything indiscreet... ...a brief and extremely indiscreet affair.* ADJ QUALIT ⇑ unwise ≠ cautious ▸ = incautious

indiscretion /ɪndɪskrɛʃəⁿn/, **indiscretions**. **Indiscretion** is behaviour that shows that someone has not thought carefully or been cautious about their actions. EG *...an act of reckless indiscretion... How could she commit such an indiscretion?... Forgive me if any indiscretion on my part has embarrassed you.* N UNCOUNT/COUNT

indiscriminate /ɪndɪskrɪmɪnɪˡt/. Something that is **indiscriminate** does not involve any careful thought or choice. EG *Television watchers tend to be indiscriminate and casual in their viewing habits... There seemed to be indiscriminate slaughter of men, women , and children.* ◇ **indiscriminately**. EG *He reads widely and indiscriminately... In the article the words 'beer' and 'ale' are used indiscriminately.* ADJ QUALIT ⇑ general ≠ precise, specific ◇ ADV WITH VB

indispensable /ɪndɪspɛnsəbəˡl/. If something is **indispensable**, it is absolutely essential and you cannot do without it. EG *In my job, a telephone is indispensable... I was trying to make myself indispensable... His cap was as indispensable to him as the nose on his face.* ADJ CLASSIF : IF + PREP THEN *to* ⇑ necessary

indisposed /ɪndɪspəʊzd/. If someone, especially a performer or important person, is **indisposed**, they are ill; a formal word. EG *His Excellency is indisposed.* ADJ CLASSIF : PRED = unwell

indisposition /ɪndɪspəzɪʃəⁿn/, **indispositions**. **Indisposition** is slight illness which prevents you from doing something you had planned to do; a formal word. EG *He was prevented from finishing his lecture through sudden indisposition.* N UNCOUNT/COUNT

indisputable /ɪndɪspjuːtəbəˡl/. If something is **indisputable**, it cannot be denied or questioned. EG *We're going to have a very hard time. That's indisputable... This is a work of indisputable genius... ...an indisputable fact... It's indisputable that we are losing a lot of money.* ◇ **indisputably**. EG *...a man of indisputably high intelligence... The book is indisputably a masterpiece.* ADJ CLASSIF = undeniable ◇ ADV + ADJ/ADV/N = unquestionably

indissoluble /ɪndɪsɒljəbəˡl/. If a relationship, marriage, etc is **indissoluble**, it can never be broken up; a formal word. EG *...the indissoluble ties of mother to child.* ADJ CLASSIF

indistinct /ɪndɪstɪŋkt/. Something that is **indistinct** is difficult to see, hear, or recognize, because it is not clear. EG *Mary Stuart said something, her voice so muffled and indistinct that I couldn't make it out... The shadow made her features indistinct... ...an indistinct footpath.* ◇ **indistinctly**. EG *I mumbled indistinctly through a mouthful of food.* ADJ QUALIT = unclear, vague ◇ ADV WITH VB

indistinguishable /ɪndɪstɪŋgwɪʃəbəˡl/. If two things are **indistinguishable**, they are so similar that it is difficult to tell which is which. EG *The two brothers are almost indistinguishable... Some synthetic meat is indistinguishable from the natural product in taste.* ADJ CLASSIF : IF + PREP THEN *from*

individual /ɪndɪvɪdjʊˡəl/, **individuals**. **1 Individual** means relating to one particular person, rather than to a large group. EG *The preservation of individual liberty... Everyone's individual filing system is different... ...individual tuition.* ◇ **individually**. EG *The children can work individually or in small groups.* ADJ CLASSIF : ATTRIB = personal ≠ shared, collective ◇ ADV WITH VB = separately

2 You also use **individual** to indicate that you are considering each member of a group of people or things separately. EG *We can identify each individual whale by its song... Review committees consider the cases of individual prisoners.* ◇ **individually**. EG *I will speak individually to you later... Each fruit should be wrapped individually in paper.* ADJ CLASSIF : ATTRIB ⇑ single = specific ◇ ADV WITH VB ≠ collectively

3 An **individual** is **3.1** a person, different from any other person; used especially when you are saying that everyone is different, or that each person should be allowed to believe or do whatever they think is right. EG *...the freedom of the individual... Handwriting varies from individual to individual... I treat the girls as individuals.* **3.2** a person, especially someone who is interesting or unusual in some way. EG *Fourier seems to be a somewhat eccentric individual... My boss was a large, fat, red-faced individual called Frederick Pratt.* N COUNT; N COUNT = character

4 Someone who is **individual** behaves in a way that is quite different from the way other people behave. EG *She has something in her, something peculiar and individual.* ADJ QUALIT = unique

individualise /ɪndɪvɪdjəˡlaɪz/. See **individualize**.

individualism /ɪndɪvɪdjəˡlɪzəˡm/ is **1** behaviour that is quite different from anyone else's behaviour. EG *Why should we put such emphasis on individualism?* **2** the belief that economics and politics should not be controlled by the state. EG *The decentralization of power appeals to individualism and libertarian humanism.* N UNCOUNT; N UNCOUNT

individualist /ɪndɪvɪdjəˡlɪst/, **individualists**. **1** If you are an **individualist**, you like to do things by yourself and in your own way. EG *Aggressive people tend to be individualists.* ▸ used as an adjective. EG *They were rather individualist, and tended to live their own lives.* N COUNT = maverick, loner ▸ ADJ QUALIT = independent

2 An **individualist** is also someone who believes that economics and politics should not be controlled by the state. N COUNT

individualistic /ɪndɪvɪdjəˡlɪstɪk/. If you are **individualistic**, you like to do things by yourself and in your own way. EG *Group communication reduced the need for individualistic artistic expression.* ADJ CLASSIF = individualist

individuality /ɪndɪvɪdjuːælɪtiˡ/. If something has **individuality**, it is different from all other things. EG *The advertisement lacks any individuality... The thing that makes us so interesting is our individuality.* N UNCOUNT = uniqueness

individualize /ɪndɪvɪdjəˡlaɪz/, **individualizes, individualizing, individualized**. If you **individualize** something, you make it different from other things, and able to be recognized or identified; a formal word. EG *...all the subtle smells and textures that individualize any situation.* V+O ⇑ represent = characterize

indivisible /ɪndɪvɪzɪˡbəˡl/. If something is **indivisible**, it cannot be divided into different parts. EG *It used to be thought that an atom is the smallest indivisible particle of matter.* ADJ CLASSIF

Indo- is added to adjectives that describe nationalities in order to form other adjectives which describe something connected both with India and with another country or continent. EG *She has an Indo-Portuguese background.* PREFIX

indoctrinate /ɪndɒktrɪneɪt/, **indoctrinates, indoctrinating, indoctrinated**. If you **indoctrinate** someone, you teach them a particular belief or attitude with the aim that they will not accept any other belief or attitude; used showing disapproval. EG *He has managed to indoctrinate me with his prejudices... You've been indoctrinated from the day you were born.* ◇ **indoctrination** /ɪndɒktrɪneɪʃəⁿn/. EG *It is difficult to overcome the early indoctrination of children.* V+O = brainwash ◇ N UNCOUNT ⇑ instruction = brainwashing

indolence /ɪndələns/ means the same as laziness; a formal word. EG *He thinks that poverty is a punishment for idleness and indolence.* N UNCOUNT

indolent /ɪndələnt/. Someone who is **indolent** is lazy. EG *Her house is full of indolent cats.* ▸ used to describe an expression, gesture, etc. EG *...an indolent smile.* ADJ QUALIT

indomitable /ɪndɒmɪtəbəˡl/; a formal word. **1** You use **indomitable** to describe a quality that is so strong that it is impossible for anything to defeat or discourage it. EG *He was a symbol of indomitable courage... My mother had an indomitable spirit.* ADJ CLASSIF = invincible

2 Someone who is **indomitable** never gives up or admits that they have been defeated. EG *Miller was a small, indomitable figure.* ADJ QUALIT

Indonesian /ɪndəˡniːzɪən/, **Indonesians**. **1** Something that is **Indonesian** belongs or relates to Indonesia, or to its people or language. EG *...Indonesian TV.* ADJ CLASSIF

2 An **Indonesian** is a person who comes from Indonesia. N COUNT

3 Indonesian is the language that is spoken by people who live in Indonesia. N UNCOUNT

indoor /ɪndɔː/, **indoors**. **Indoor** is an adjective and **indoors** is an adverb. 1 You use **indoor** to describe things which are situated, happen, or are used inside a building rather than outside. EG *Our indoor games are table tennis, chess, cards... The Housing Commission has installed indoor bathrooms now.* ADJ CLASSIF: ATTRIB ≠ outdoor

2 If something happens **indoors**, it happens inside a building. EG *The concert is held indoors when it rains... We'd better go indoors.* ADV AFTER VB

indrawn /ɪndrɔːn/. An **indrawn** breath is one in which you breathe in suddenly, especially when you are shocked or waiting for something to happen. EG *There were one or two indrawn breaths from around the table.* ADJ CLASSIF: ATTRIB

indubitable /ɪndjuːbɪtəbəᵒl/. Something that is **indubitable** is definite and cannot be doubted; a formal word. EG *There have been indubitable signs already.* ADJ CLASSIF = undoubted

◊ **indubitably**. EG *There was Thomas, dirty and muddy but indubitably alive.* ◊ ADV = undoubtedly

induce /ɪndjuːs/, **induces, inducing, induced**.

1 To **induce** a particular state or condition means to cause it. EG *One of these pills is guaranteed to induce sleep... Failure induces a total sense of inferiority... The actor's demonstration of emotion induces similar emotions in his audience.* V+O: IF+PREP THEN *in*

2 If you **induce** someone to do something, you persuade or influence them to do it. EG *Nothing would induce me to see that play... What on earth had induced her to marry a man like that?* V+O+*to*-INF ⇑ make

3 If doctors **induce** labour or birth or **induce** a pregnant woman, they cause labour to begin in her by the use of drugs or other medical means. EG *They induced labour for her second pregnancy.* V+O ⇑ initiate

-induced combines with nouns to forms adjectives to indicate that a state, condition, illness, etc is caused by the effects of a particular thing. EG *...work-induced diseases... ...self-induced hypnosis.* COMB: FORMS ADJ CLASSIFS

inducement /ɪndjuːsməᶻnt/, **inducements**. An **inducement** is something that is used in order to persuade someone to do something, especially a gift or bribe or something pleasant. EG *This measure is a significant inducement to business growth... He was, like most human beings, susceptible to material inducements.* N COUNT = incentive

induct /ɪndʌkt/, **inducts, inducting, inducted**.

1 If you **induct** someone, you officially place them in a particular job, rank, position, etc in a formal ceremony; a formal word. V+O ⇑ install

2 In American English, if someone **is inducted** into the army, they are required by law to start military service. EG *Her son had refused to be inducted into the U.S. Army.* V+O: IF+PREP THEN *into* = draft

induction /ɪndʌkʃəᵒn/, **inductions**. **Induction** is 1 a way of reasoning in which you use individual ideas or facts to give you a general rule or conclusion. EG *My argument follows the rules of logical induction.* 2 the process of inducing a pregnant woman. 3 the process by which electricity or magnetism is passed between two objects or circuits without them touching each other. 4 a formal introduction to a new job or way of life. EG *Next month there will be the ceremony of induction of the new chancellor.* N UNCOUNT ⇑ process; N UNCOUNT; N UNCOUNT; N UNCOUNT/COUNT

induction coil, induction coils. An **induction coil** is a transformer that is used to produce a high voltage from a low voltage. N COUNT

induction course, induction courses. An **induction course** is a course arranged for new students at a college or university or for people who have just started a job. An induction course helps the students or new employees to become familiar with their surroundings and with the work that they will be doing. N COUNT

inductive /ɪndʌktɪv/. **Inductive** reasoning, logic, etc is based on induction. ADJ CLASSIF ≠ deductive

indulge /ɪndʌldʒ/, **indulges, indulging, indulged**. 1 If you **indulge** in something or **indulge** a particular vice, appetite, passion, etc, you allow yourself to have or do something that you know you will enjoy. EG *He indulged heavily in conversation and drink... Let us indulge in a little daydreaming... Jack had spent the previous three weeks indulging his passion for climbing.* V+A *(in)*, OR V+O (NG/REFL)

2 If you **indulge** someone or their wishes, you let them have or do what they want and treat them with special kindness, often in a way that is not good for them. EG *His mother indulged him in material possessions... I'd love an ice-cream. Will you indulge me?... It pleased me to indulge her wishes.* V+O = pamper, spoil

3 If you say that you **indulge**, you mean that you sometimes drink alcohol; an informal use. EG *I occasionally allow myself to indulge at parties.* V

indulgence /ɪndʌldʒəns/, **indulgences**. 1 An **indulgence** is something that you allow yourself to do or have because it gives you pleasure. EG *Smoking was his one indulgence... Madame Pennington allowed herself small indulgences.* N COUNT

2 **Indulgence** is the act of indulging yourself or another person. N UNCOUNT

indulgent /ɪndʌldʒənt/. If you are **indulgent**, you treat a person with special kindness, often in a way that is not good for them. EG *He was an indulgent father, ever ready to provide new clothes.* ADJ QUALIT ⇑ kind

◊ **indulgently**. EG *You were treated more indulgently... He smiled indulgently at her.* ◊ ADV WITH VB ⇑ benevolently

industrial /ɪndʌstrɪəl/. 1 You use **industrial** to describe things which relate to or are used in industry. EG *By the end of the next decade industrial robots will be in widespread use... ...industrial and technical change.* ADJ CLASSIF: USU ATTRIB

2 An **industrial** city, country, etc is one in which industry is important or highly developed. EG *...Europe's big industrial cities.* ADJ CLASSIF: USU ATTRIB

industrial action consists of strikes and all the other ways in which workers are able to protest about pay, working conditions, etc. EG *The number of days lost through industrial action is the lowest for many years.* N UNCOUNT ⇑ action

industrial estate, industrial estates. An **industrial estate** is an area that has been specially designed so that factories can be built there. N COUNT

industrialise /ɪndʌstrɪəlaɪz/. See **industrialize**.

industrialism /ɪndʌstrɪəlɪzəᵒm/ is the system that is used to organize society when it is controlled by industry or depends on it. N UNCOUNT

industrialist /ɪndʌstrɪəlɪst/, **industrialists**. An **industrialist** is a person who owns or controls large amounts of money or property in industry. EG *...a leading industrialist with business interests in Germany.* N COUNT = capitalist

industrialize /ɪndʌstrɪəlaɪz/, **industrializes, industrializing, industrialized**; also spelled **industrialise**. When a country **industrializes**, or when people **industrialize** it, it develops a lot of industries. EG *The only way we're going to compete with the west is to industrialise.* ◊ **industrialization** /ɪndʌstrɪəlaɪzeɪʃəᵒn/. EG *We are vitally interested in industrialization.* V-ERG; ◊ N UNCOUNT

industrialized /ɪndʌstrɪəlaɪzd/. An **industrialized** area or place is one in which society depends heavily on industry. EG *...the industrialised world.* ADJ CLASSIF: ATTRIB

industrial relations consist of the relationship between employers and employees in industry that is established and maintained by a system of agreements and laws. EG *...the future of industrial relations in Britain... We agreed to higher productivity at a time when industrial relations were poor... ...industrial relations reform.* N PLURAL: PL FORM WHEN MOD

industrious /ɪndʌstrɪəs/. Someone who is **industrious** works very hard. EG *Rosa was an industrious and brilliant student.* ADJ QUALIT = diligent

industry /ɪndəstri¹/, **industries**. 1 **Industry** is the work and processes involved in manufacturing things in factories. EG *Japanese industry is making increasing use of robots... ...the kind of bargaining which goes on in industry between the workers and their employers.* N UNCOUNT

2 An **industry** consists of all the people and the processes that are involved in manufacturing or producing a particular thing. EG *...the oil industry... India has always had one of the largest film industries in the world.* N COUNT ⇑ business

3 **Industry** is also the quality of working very hard; a formal use. EG *...the old virtues of self-reliance, industry, and frugality.* N UNCOUNT = hard work, labour

inebriate /ɪniːbri¹eɪt/, **inebriates**. Someone who is **inebriate** drinks alcohol a lot and is regularly drunk; a formal word. EG *...his inebriate father.* ▸ used as a noun. EG *He had died in a home for inebriates.* ADJ CLASSIF; ▸ N COUNT

inebriated /ɪniːbri¹eɪtɪᶻd/. Someone who is **inebriated** is drunk; a formal word. EG *I was part of a hopelessly inebriated audience.* ADJ CLASSIF = intoxicated

inedible /ɪnedɪbə⁰l/. Something that is **inedible** is too nasty or poisonous to eat. EG *The food was mostly inedible... ...inedible plants.* ADJ CLASSIF

ineffable /ɪnefəbə⁰l/. Something that is **ineffable** is so wonderful or great that it cannot be described in words; a formal word. EG *Sometimes music can produce an ineffable joy... ...the ineffable story-teller, P.G. Wodehouse.* ◊ **ineffably**. EG *They were ineffably sad.* ADJ CLASSIF : USU ATTRIB = indescribable ◊ ADV

ineffective /ɪnɪfektɪv/. Something that is **ineffective** has no effect on a process or situation. EG *The therapy was obviously ineffective... This kind of thinking is ineffective in generating new ideas... He has been an ineffective minister.* ◊ **ineffectiveness**. EG *He was disgusted by the ineffectiveness of governments between the wars.* ADJ CLASSIF ⇑ useless = ineffectual ◊ N UNCOUNT

ineffectual /ɪnɪfektʃʊ⁰əl/. Something that is **ineffectual** fails to do what it is supposed to do. EG *...a genial but ineffectual man... ...ineffectual policies.* ◊ **ineffectually**. EG *She fell on her knees and ineffectually tried to pick up the broken fragments of the vase.* ADJ QUALIT ⇑ useless = unsuccessful ◊ ADV WITH VB

inefficiency /ɪnɪfɪʃənsi¹/. If you refer to the **inefficiency** of a person, organization, or system , you are referring to the fact that they are badly organized and do not use resources, equipment, or time in the best possible way. EG *He criticised the inefficiency of public authorities.* N UNCOUNT = incompetence

inefficient /ɪnɪfɪʃənt/. **1** A person, organization or system that is **inefficient** is badly organized and does not use resources, equipment, or time in the best possible way. EG *She says that schools are inefficient and operate at a very low standard... They saw the need to end wasteful competition, inefficient farming and processing.* ◊ **inefficiently**. EG *She works slowly and inefficiently.* ADJ QUALIT ⇑ bad ◊ ADV

2 An **inefficient** machine or piece of equipment does not work effectively and is wasteful. EG *You should consider replacing old, inefficient or broken appliances with efficient new ones.* ADJ QUALIT ⇑ bad

inelegant /ɪnelɪgənt/. Something that is **inelegant** is not attractive or graceful. EG *Glass chandeliers have been replaced by inelegant plastic ones.* ADJ QUALIT ⇑ ugly

ineligible /ɪnelɪgə¹bə⁰l/. If you are **ineligible** for something, you are not qualified for it or entitled to it. EG *I am ineligible for unemployment benefit.* ADJ CLASSIF : IF + PREP THEN *for*

ineluctable /ɪnɪlʌktəbə⁰l/ describes something that nobody can escape from; a formal word. EG *...a world of ineluctable corruption.* ADJ CLASSIF : ATTRIB = inescapable

inept /ɪnept/. Someone who is **inept** does something with a complete lack of skill. EG *He was an inept politician.* ▸ used of something that is done. EG *...the government's inept handling of the crisis.* ADJ QUALIT = bungling ▸ = clumsy

ineptitude /ɪneptɪtju:d/. If you refer to someone's **ineptitude**, you are referring to the fact that they do something with a complete lack of skill. EG *...his record of political ineptitude.* N UNCOUNT = incompetence

inequality /ɪnɪkwɒlɪti¹/, **inequalities**. **1 Inequality** is **1** the difference in social status, wealth, opportunity, etc between two or more people or groups in a society. EG *Poverty and growing inequality are the inevitable outcome of population expansion.* ▸ used to refer to an example of this. EG *We found great inequalities of opportunity... ...the cultural inequalities between different social classes.* N UNCOUNT ▸ N COUNT

2 An **inequality** is also a difference in the size or amount of two or more things. N COUNT/UNCOUNT

inequitable /ɪnekwɪtəbə⁰l/. Something that is **inequitable** is unfair or unjust; a formal word. EG *...the inequitable division of wealth... ...inequitable taxation.* ADJ CLASSIF

inequity /ɪnekwɪti¹/, **inequities**. If you refer to the **inequity** of something, you are referring to the fact that it is unfair; a formal word. EG *It is time to review the inequity of the budgetary system.* ▸ used to refer to an example of this. EG *...the inequities in our economy.* N UNCOUNT ⇑ unfairness ▸ N COUNT : USU PL

ineradicable /ɪnɪ²rædɪkəbə⁰l/. Something that is **ineradicable** cannot be removed; a formal word. EG *...an ineradicable tendency to be frivolous.* ADJ CLASSIF ⇑ fixed

inert /ɪnɜ:t/. **1** Something that is **inert** **1.1** does not move at all and appears to be lifeless. EG *Posy lay inert... I carried her, still inert, up the stairs to my room.* **1.2** has no liveliness or interest. EG *...an inert, undemanding marriage.* ADJ CLASSIF ⇑ immobile ADJ CLASSIF ⇑ inactive

2 An **inert** gas is one which does not react with other chemical substances. ADJ CLASSIF

inertia /ɪnɜ:ʃɪ⁰ə/. **1** If you have a feeling of **inertia**, you feel very lazy and unwilling to move or be active. EG *Love brought me to Liverpool and inertia kept me there... I remained there from sheer inertia, while she smoked her tenth cigarette of the morning.* N UNCOUNT = apathy

2 Inertia is also the tendency of a physical object to remain still, or to continue moving if it is already moving, unless a force is applied to it; a technical term in physics. N UNCOUNT

inescapable /ɪnɪ²skeɪpəbə⁰l/. If something is **inescapable**, it cannot be avoided. EG *...an inescapable conclusion... The impression of villainy was inescapable.* ADJ CLASSIF = unavoidable

inessential /ɪnɪsenʃə⁰l/, **inessentials**. **1** If something is **inessential**, you do not need it. EG *She thought she would sell any inessential furniture.* ADJ CLASSIF

2 The **inessentials** are the things that you do not really need. EG *I felt that my life was suddenly stripped of inessentials such as worries about money.* N PLURAL

inestimable /ɪnestɪməbə⁰l/. Something that is **inestimable** is too great to be calculated. EG *Maria's advice proved of inestimable value... The cost of damage repair is inestimable.* ADJ CLASSIF = incalculable

inevitability /ɪnevɪtəbɪlɪti¹/, **inevitabilities**. **1** If you refer to the **inevitability** of something, you are referring to the fact that it is predictable and unavoidable. EG *You must recognize the inevitability of change... The task has an almost religious inevitability about it.* N UNCOUNT ⇑ certainty = predictability

2 An **inevitability** is something that is predictable or unavoidable. EG *Instead of being an inevitability of marriage, babies are now a choice.* N COUNT : USU SING ⇑ certainty

inevitable /ɪnevɪtəbə⁰l/. **1** If something is **inevitable**, it is certain to happen and cannot be prevented or avoided. EG *If this policy continues, then violence is inevitable... It's inevitable that you should feel indignant.* ADJ CLASSIF = definite, unavoidable

2 The **inevitable** is a thing or situation that is certain to happen and cannot be prevented or avoided. EG *How could she possibly have attempted to change the inevitable?... I suddenly became fatalistic, resigning myself to the inevitable.* N SING : *the*+N ⇑ certainty

3 You can also use **inevitable** humorously to describe something that happens so regularly that you are able to predict it. EG *We went inside for the inevitable cup of tea.* ADJ CLASSIF : ATTRIB ⇑ usual = predictable

inevitably /ɪnevɪtəbli¹/. If something happens **inevitably**, it is the only possible result. EG *Those who are created by publicity will inevitably be destroyed by it... Inevitably, a shouting match ensued between us... Great armaments lead inevitably to war.* ADV WITH VB ⇑ surely = undoubtedly

inexact /ɪnɪ²gzækt/. Something that is **inexact** is not precise or accurate. EG *Lip reading is an incomplete, inexact form of comprehending for the deaf.* ADJ CLASSIF ≠ exact

inexcusable /ɪnɪ²ksku:zəbə⁰l/. Something that is **inexcusable** is too bad to be justified or tolerated. EG *The local paper declared such waste inexcusable... Animal experiments are inexcusable.* ◊ **inexcusably**. EG *Amanda had inexcusably left the gate open.* ADJ QUALIT ⇑ wrong ◊ ADV WITH VB

inexhaustible /ɪnɪ²gzɔ:stəbə⁰l/. If something is **inexhaustible**, there is so much of it that it cannot all be used up. EG *His patience must be inexhaustible... The sun is an inexhaustible source of energy.* ADJ CLASSIF = infinite

inexorable /ɪneksə⁰rəbə⁰l/. Something that is **inexorable** cannot be prevented from continuing or progressing in a particular direction; a formal word. EG *This trend is inexorable... ...the inexorable rise in the cost of living.* ◊ **inexorably**. EG *The water rose inexorably... These facts led inexorably to one conclusion.* ADJ CLASSIF = relentless ◊ ADV WITH VB = relentlessly

inexpensive /ɪnɪ²kspensɪv/. Something that is **inexpensive** does not cost very much. EG *...an inexpensive wine.* ADJ QUALIT = cheap, reasonable

inexperience /ɪnɪ²kspɪərɪəns/. If you refer to someone's **inexperience**, you are referring to the fact that they are inexperienced. EG *In later months I could laugh at my inexperience... You're bound to make a few mistakes through inexperience.* N UNCOUNT = ignorance

inexperienced /ɪnɪ²kspɪərɪənst/. If you are **inexperienced**, you have no knowledge or experience of a particular situation, activity, etc. EG *I was a totally inexperienced girl of nineteen... ...an inexperienced swimmer.* ADJ QUALIT ⇑ innocent

inexpert /ɪnekspɜːt/. Something that is **inexpert** shows a lack of skill. EG *...Harris's inexpert but conscientious gardening.* — ADJ CLASSIF = unskilful

inexplicable /ɪnɪ[2]ksplɪkəbə[0]l/. If something is **inexplicable**, you cannot explain why it happened or why it is true. EG *I still find this incident inexplicable... For some inexplicable reason I was not allowed to go.* — ADJ QUALIT = incomprehensible
◊ **inexplicably**. EG *Anita had inexplicably disappeared... Inexplicably, I was shaking all over.* — ◊ ADV WITH VB

inexpressible /ɪnɪ[2]kspresə[1]bə[0]l/. An **inexpressible** feeling is too strong to be expressed in words. EG *It was an inexpressible relief.* — ADJ CLASSIF = indescribable

inexpressive /ɪnɪ[2]kspresɪv/. If someone's face or eyes are **inexpressive**, you cannot tell what the person is thinking. EG *...his inexpressive eyes.* — ADJ CLASSIF

in extremis; a formal expression. If someone is **in extremis**, 1 they are about to die. EG *He is in extremis and unlikely to see the night out.* 2 they are in a very difficult situation and have to use extreme methods in order to solve their problems. — PHR : USED AS AN A; PHR : USED AS AN A

inextricable /ɪnekstrɪkəbə[0]l/. You use **inextricable** to describe things that cannot be separated or easily understood. EG *Art and history fuse in inextricable magic.* — ADJ CLASSIF = inseparable

inextricably /ɪnekstrɪkəbə[0]li[1]/. If two or more things are **inextricably** mixed, linked, etc, they cannot be separated. EG *The fate of authors is to become inextricably confused with their characters... Social and economic factors are inextricably linked.* — ADV WITH VB = inseparably

> **INF** □ In this dictionary INF is used in the grammar notes beside the entries to refer to the infinitive form of a verb. The infinitive form is the form without inflections, for example *do, take, make,* and *eat*. The infinitive can also be used with 'to' in front of it. In this dictionary the abbreviation *to*-INF is used to refer to the infinitive with *to*. See □ at ***to*-INF**. INF is used in the grammar notes beside meanings of words which are used with an infinitive form after them. An example is **make 8** described as V+O+INF. EG *They used to make me **feel** guilty... Absence makes the heart **grow** fonder... Make him **listen...** I couldn't make her **change** her mind.*

infallible /ɪnfælɪbə[0]l/. If a person or thing is **infallible**, they are never wrong. EG *Doctors aren't infallible... Her instincts were infallible.* — ADJ CLASSIF faultless
◊ **infallibility** /ɪnfælɪ[1]bɪlɪti[1]/. EG *...the infallibility of their argument.* — ◊ N UNCOUNT ≠ fallibility

infamous /ɪnfəməs/. A person, time, action, etc that is **infamous** is well known because of something bad or evil. EG *How well I remember that infamous night.* — ADJ CLASSIF = notorious, disreputable

infamy /ɪnfəmi[1]/ is the state of being infamous. EG *This is a day that will live in infamy.* — N UNCOUNT = ignominy

infancy /ɪnfənsi[1]/. 1 Your **infancy** is the period in your life when you are a very young child. EG *The child died in infancy... He came to England in his infancy... They stayed together throughout the infancy of their offspring.* — N UNCOUNT : USU PREP/POSS+N

2 If something is in its **infancy**, it has only just started and so is in its earliest stages. EG *This research is only in its infancy.* — N UNCOUNT : USU PREP/POSS+N ⇑ beginning

infant /ɪnfənt/, **infants**. 1 An **infant** is a very young child or baby. EG *My infant for once lay quiet in his cot.* ▸ used of very young animals. EG *With goats, mother and infant form a close bond in the first five minutes.* — N COUNT

2 **Infant** means designed or made especially for very young children. EG *...infant foods... ...infant seats.* — ADJ CLASSIF : ATTRIB ⇑ baby

3 An **infant** organization, movement, etc is new and so has not developed very much. — ADJ CLASSIF : ATTRIB

infanticide /ɪnfæntɪsaɪd/ is the crime of killing a young child. — N UNCOUNT ⇑ murder

infantile /ɪnfəntaɪl/. 1 You use **infantile** to describe behaviour, disease, etc which is typical of very young children. EG *Some infantile actions survive into adulthood... ...infantile paralysis.* — ADJ QUALIT

2 If someone is **infantile**, they are behaving in a foolish and childish way. EG *He was destructive, sullen, infantile.* — ADJ QUALIT = babyish

infantry /ɪnfəntri[1]/. The **infantry** are the soldiers in an army who fight on foot or in small vehicles rather than in tanks or on horses. EG *...a platoon of infantry... The infantry did splendidly... ...an infantry regiment.* — N SING : *the*+N, OR N UNCOUNT

infantryman /ɪnfəntrɪmə[3]n/, **infantrymen**. An **infantryman** is a soldier in an infantry regiment. — N COUNT

infant school, infant schools. An **infant school** is a school for children between the ages of five and seven; used mainly in British English. — N COUNT

infatuated /ɪnfætjʊeɪtɪ[2]d/. If you are **infatuated** with someone, you have a strong feeling of love or passion for them that you cannot think clearly or sensibly about the relationship. EG *He was infatuated with her and could refuse her nothing.* — ADJ QUALIT : USU PRED+*with* = besotted

infatuation /ɪnfætjʊeɪʃə[0]n/. If you have an **infatuation** for someone, you have such a strong feeling of love or passion for them that you cannot think clearly or sensibly about the relationship. EG *She realized that she felt fear as well as infatuation for this man... This is not love but a foolish infatuation.* — N UNCOUNT : IF+ PREP THEN *for/with*

infect /ɪnfekt/, **infects, infecting, infected**. 1 Someone or something that **infects** a person or an animal causes that person or animal to catch a disease or infection. EG *The worms bury themselves in his skin and infect him with all kinds of serious diseases... Her younger daughter was infected and became an invalid for some years.* — V+O : IF+PREP THEN *with* ⇑ affect

2 Something that **infects** food or some other substance causes it to become poisoned by germs or dirt. EG *You can catch cholera and typhoid from food infected by handling.* — V+O ⇑ spoil = contaminate

3 When a damaging influence **infects** people, places, or things, it spreads to them and affects them as if it were a disease. EG *Pessimism had a way of infecting everyone... Whole societies become infected by these vices.* — V+O : IF+PREP THEN *with/by* = poison

4 If a pleasant or exciting feeling that you have **infects** other people or places, it spreads to them so that they feel it too. EG *The mounting foreign enthusiasm is now infecting Japanese investors... Your excitement fails to infect me.* — V+O ⇑ influence

infected /ɪnfektɪ[2]d/. 1 An **infected** wound or part of your body is unable to heal properly because of germs. EG *She had a large infected gash in her head... Their arms and legs are covered with infected bites.* — ADJ CLASSIF : IF+ PREP THEN *with/by*

2 An **infected** place is one where an infection or disease is present and spreading amongst people or animals. EG *Keep outside the infected area.* — ADJ CLASSIF : IF+ PREP THEN *with/by*

infection /ɪnfekʃə[0]n/, **infections**. 1 **Infection** or an **infection** is 1.1 a disease that you catch, especially by breathing in germs which your body cannot fight off. EG *Her infections could be cleared up easily with antibiotics... I had an ear infection that made me stone deaf... White blood cells fight infection... Radiation lessened bodily resistance to infection.* 1.2 germs or dirt that have got into a cut or wound, causing it to produce pus and preventing it from healing properly. EG *The soldiers were coming back with infections in their wounds... Healing is delayed by infection.* — N COUNT/ UNCOUNT; N COUNT/ UNCOUNT = poisoning

2 **Infection** is the action or result of someone or something being infected. EG *In a family group there is little risk of infection unless some member has a fresh cold.* — N UNCOUNT

infectious /ɪnfekʃəs/. 1 If you have a disease that is **infectious**, other people can catch it from you, especially by breathing close to you: compare **contagious**. — ADJ QUALIT

2 Something that is **infectious**, for example a feeling that you have, spreads to other people and makes them share it or copy it. EG *Don't you find her enthusiasm infectious?... Misery is infectious... I think the Glasgow accent is very infectious.* — ADJ QUALIT = catching

infer /ɪnfɜː/, **infers, inferring, inferred**. If you **infer** that something is the case, 1 you decide that it is true on the basis of information that you already have. EG *He can logically infer that if the battery is dead then the horn will not sound... Eternal historical tendencies cannot be inferred from data covering a mere century or so.* 2 you say something to suggest that it is the case without actually saying so directly; an informal use. Many people consider that this second use is wrong, and that the right word to use is **imply**. EG *I do not want to infer by this criticism that there is something fundamentally wrong with your argument.* — V+REPORT-CL, OR V+O : IF+ PREP THEN *from* ⇑ conclude = deduce; V+REPORT-CL, OR V+O : IF+ PREP THEN *from*

inference /ɪnfərəns/, **inferences**. 1 An **inference** is a conclusion that you make about something by using information that you already have about it. EG *The inferences drawn from data have led to some major changes in our policy... The clear inference was that they were searching for someone to blame.* — N COUNT ⇑ assumption

2 **Inference** is the act of making conclusions about something on the basis of information that you already have. EG *But inference was not enough...* — N UNCOUNT ⇑ guesswork = deduction

They wanted information on the relative closeness and, by inference, the availability of the task force.

inferior /ɪnfɪərɪə/, **inferiors**. 1 Someone who is **inferior** or who has an **inferior** position is of less worth than other people or has a lower position in society. EG *Charlie, aged sixteen, felt much inferior to boys of his own age... Mary does not rebel against her inferior status.* ▸ used as a noun to refer to people. EG *She is never looked down upon and never considered an inferior.* ◊ **inferiority** /ɪnfɪərɪɒrɪti¹/. EG *The system is based upon an enforced inferiority of other human beings... She has imagined feelings of inferiority.* — ADJ QUALIT : IF+PREP THEN *to/in* = subordinate; ▸ N COUNT = subordinate; ◊ N UNCOUNT = subservience

2 A person who is your **inferior** has a lower position or status in an organization or company than your own position. EG *He complained of the slackness and stupidity of his inferiors.* — N COUNT : USU POSS+N = junior

3 Something that is **inferior 3.1** is of worse quality than something else of a similar type. EG *It was a cheap and inferior product... Their air combat skills were shown up as inferior to those of our pilots.* ◊ **inferiority**. EG *They would have to do a great deal to offset a heavy numerical inferiority.* **3.2** has a lower status or position in a system than something else of a similar type. EG *The case went to an inferior court.* — ADJ QUALIT : IF+PREP THEN *to/in* = second-rate; ◊ N UNCOUNT; ADJ QUALIT

inferiority complex, inferiority complexes. Someone who has an **inferiority complex** feels that they are of less worth or importance than other people. An inferiority complex causes some people to be very shy, and others to be aggressive and to try to attract attention. EG *...a boy who had an inferiority complex about his size.* — N COUNT

infernal /ɪnfɜːnə⁰l/. 1 An **infernal** emotion, situation, etc is very unpleasant or cruel. EG *I'm sorry I shouted at you. It's my infernal temper... Will you stop that infernal noise?* — ADJ CLASSIF : ATTRIB ⇑ awful = hellish

2 You also use **infernal** to describe things that relate to hell. EG *...the infernal depths beneath.* — ADJ CLASSIF : ATTRIB

inferno /ɪnfɜːnəʊ/, **infernos**; a literary word. 1 If you refer to a situation or place as an **inferno**, you mean that it is very unpleasant, usually because there are too many people and too much noise in it. EG *Parsons, at the centre of an inferno of sound, is going mad... ...the dust-filled sweaty inferno that central London had become.* — N COUNT

2 If you refer to a fire as an **inferno**, you mean that it is very large and powerful, so as to burn up all the buildings, trees, etc, in a particular place. EG *It had become white-hot everywhere. A real inferno.* — N COUNT : USU SING

infertile /ɪnfɜːtaɪl/. 1 **Infertile** soil is of poor quality so that plants cannot grow in it. EG *The soil proved too infertile to sustain real pasture or arable crops.* ◊ **infertility** /ɪnfɜːtɪlɪti¹/. EG *...the infertility of the soil.* — ADJ QUALIT = barren; ◊ N UNCOUNT = aridity

2 A person or animal that is **infertile** is unable to have or produce babies. EG *She learned that she was now infertile.* ◊ **infertility**. — ADJ CLASSIF; ◊ N UNCOUNT

infest /ɪnfɛst/, **infests, infesting, infested**. When insects, rats, or other animals **infest** a plant, area, etc, they spread in large numbers and cover the plant or area, usually causing damage. EG *...the vermin that infest the crops... ...roses which are now infested with greenfly... The back yard was infested by rats.* ◊ **infestation** /ɪfɛsteɪʃə⁰n/, **infestations**. EG *...a bad infestation of woodworm.* — V+O : USU PASS = overrun; ◊ N UNCOUNT/COUNT

infidel /ɪnfɪdə⁰l/, **infidels**; a literary word used showing disapproval. An **infidel** is a person who has no religion, or a person whose religion is different from that of the speaker. EG *...the spiritual duty of liberating the infidels.* ▸ used as an adjective. EG *...the wicked opinions of her infidel son.* — N COUNT = heathen, unbeliever; ▸ ADJ CLASSIF : ATTRIB

infidelity /ɪnfɪdɛlɪti¹/, **infidelities**. 1 **Infidelity** is the act of being unfaithful to the person to whom you are married or with whom you are having a relationship. EG *...relationships free of jealousy and infidelity.* — N UNCOUNT ⇑ betrayal

2 An **infidelity** is an occasion on which someone is unfaithful to the person to whom they are married or with whom they are having a relationship. EG *It distressed me when I returned after long infidelities to see her suffering.* — N COUNT = affair

in-fighting is rivalry or quarrelling between members of the same group or organization. EG *...bureaucratic in-fighting... The in-fighting among the six parties is ferocious.* — N UNCOUNT

infiltrate /ɪnfɪltreɪt/, **infiltrates, infiltrating, infiltrated**. If people **infiltrate** an organization, they gradually enter it in secret in order to spy on its activities or to influence its decisions. EG *Members have been active in attempts to infiltrate and disrupt meetings organized by opponents... The organization was infiltrated by the police.* ◊ **infiltration** /ɪnfɪltreɪʃə⁰n/. EG *...a report on the infiltration of the party by extreme left-wing groups.* — V+O, OR V : USU +A; ◊ N UNCOUNT ⇑ penetration

infiltrator /ɪnfɪltreɪtə/, **infiltrators**. An **infiltrator** of an organization is a person who infiltrates it. EG *Numbers of police agents had been discovered to be infiltrators inside the party.* — N COUNT

infin. is an abbreviation for 'infinitive'.

infinite /ɪnfɪnɪt/. Something that is **infinite 1** is extremely large in amount or degree. EG *Medically qualified doctors are found in an infinite variety of careers.* ◊ **infinitely**. EG *The process of unloading had been infinitely more strightforward than putting the stuff on.* **2** has no limit, end, or edge. EG *...in any other universe in the infinite reaches of space... He will have to do it all again and again in an infinite regress.* — ADJ CLASSIF ⇑ great = unlimited; ◊ ADV+ADJ/ADV; ADJ CLASSIF = boundless, limitless

infinitesimal /ɪnfɪnɪtɛsɪmə⁰l/. Something that is **infinitesimal** is extremely small or so small that it is not important. EG *The chances that that company will have any problems are infinitesimal.* — ADJ CLASSIF = minute, tiny

infinitive /ɪnfɪnɪtɪv/, **infinitives**. The **infinitive** or the **infinitive** form of a verb is the form which does not have inflections, such as *do, take, make,* and *eat*. The infinitive can either be used on its own or with *to* in front of it. The infinitive is abbreviated to INF in the grammar notes in this dictionary. See ☐ at INF and *to*-INF for an explanation of how it is used. — N COUNT

infinity /ɪnfɪnɪti/ is 1 a number that is larger than any other number and can never be counted or given an exact value. EG *It is impossible to count up to infinity... Out there is an infinity of worlds.* **2** a point that is further away than any other point and can never be reached. EG *A distance of countless light-years still comes no closer to infinity than does a single centimetre.* **3** a point that is far enough away from a lens or mirror for the light from it to reach the lens or mirror as parallel rays; a technical term in physics. EG *The camera is focused at infinity.* — N UNCOUNT : ALSO N+*of*+N IN PL/N UNCOUNT; N UNCOUNT; N UNCOUNT

4 an area with no limit, end, or edge. EG *The spacecraft is now speeding away into infinity.* — N UNCOUNT

infirm /ɪnfɜːm/. A person who is **infirm** is weak or ill, usually because they are old. EG *...his great grandfather, over eighty years of age, infirm and totally blind.* ▸ The **infirm** is used to refer to people who are infirm. EG *...the needs of the old and infirm.* ◊ **infirmity** /ɪnfɜːmɪti¹/, **infirmities**. EG *Rheumatism was an old infirmity in his family... ...old age and infirmity.* — ADJ QUALIT; ▸ N PLURAL : the +N; ◊ N COUNT/UNCOUNT

infirmary /ɪnfɜːmə⁰ri¹/, **infirmaries**. Some hospitals are called **infirmaries**. EG *My little brother was taken to the infirmary... ...Manchester Royal Infirmary.* — N COUNT : ALSO IN NAMES AFTER N

inflame /ɪnfleɪm/, **inflames, imflaming, inflamed**. Something that **inflames** a person makes them very angry or agitated. EG *Her question seemed to inflame him all the more... His remarks inflamed the crowd.* — V+O : USU PASS ⇑ rouse

inflamed /ɪnfleɪmd/. If part of your body is **inflamed**, it is red and often hot and swollen, usually as a result of an infection or an injury. EG *The ointment soothes the inflamed nose and throat... The worst danger is that the inflamed appendix will burst.* — ADJ QUALIT ⇑ aggravate

inflammable /ɪnflæməbə⁰l/. A material or chemical that is **inflammable** catches fire and burns easily. EG *...highly inflammable aircraft fuel.* — ADJ QUALIT

inflammation /ɪnfləmeɪʃə⁰n/, **inflammations**. An **inflammation** is a painful redness or swelling of the skin that results from an infection or an injury. EG *Many babies develop a mild inflammation in the eyes a few days after birth.* — N COUNT

inflammatory /ɪnflæmətə⁰ri¹/. An **inflammatory** action is likely to make people very angry or agitated. EG *...the wave of inflammatory speeches attacking him.* — ADJ QUALIT = fiery

inflatable /ɪnfleɪtəbə⁰l/. An **inflatable** object can be filled with air. EG *Everyone wore inflatable life-jackets... ...an inflatable doll.* — ADJ CLASSIF

inflate /ɪnfleɪt/, **inflates, inflating, inflated**. 1 When you **inflate** something or when it **inflates**, it becomes bigger by being filled with air or other gas. EG *The toad, when it meets a snake, inflates its body and stands on tip-toe... ...chairs that inflated or folded* — V-ERG ⇑ expand = enlarge *up.* ◊ **inflated.** EG *...the large inflated tyre they used as a raft.* ◊ ADJ CLASSIF

2 If you **inflate** an idea or opinion, often one about yourself, you try to make it appear better or more important than it really is. EG *The father inflated his son's position to friends... Expectations need not be unduly inflated.* ◊ **inflated.** EG *...his inflated self-image... They all seem to take an inflated view of their collective identity.* V+O = puff up; ◊ ADJ QUALIT = swollen

3 When someone **inflates** the price of something or when the price **inflates**, it increases, usually so that someone can make a profit. EG *Land prices have been inflated... The prices of all houses inflate at approximately the same rate.* ◊ **inflated.** EG *...food and clothing which had to be bought at inflated prices.* V-ERG; ◊ ADJ QUALIT

inflation /ɪnfleɪʃəⁿn/ is a general increase in the prices of goods and services in a country. EG *The present economic situation combines a high rate of inflation with a high level of unemployment... Chile has reduced its inflation in the past year from a hundred per cent to fifty.* N UNCOUNT

inflationary /ɪnfleɪʃənəⁿri[1]/. Something that is **inflationary** is connected with inflation or causes inflation. EG *Inflationary pressures have tended to come from wages and salaries... Tax cuts need not be inflationary.* ADJ QUALIT : USU ATTRIB

inflect /ɪnflɛkt/, **inflects, inflecting, inflected. 1** If you **inflect** your voice, you change the sound of it when you speak, for example when you emphasize particular words. EG *He spoke in a southern Yorkshire voice, less inflected and singing than Winifred's northern one.* V+O

2 If a word **inflects**, its ending or form changes in order to show its grammatical function. If a language **inflects**, it has words in it that change their endings or forms in order to show their grammatical functions. ◊ **inflected.** EG *German is an inflected language.* V; ◊ ADJ CLASSIF

inflection /ɪnflɛkʃəⁿn/, **inflections**; also spelled **inflexion. Inflection** or an **inflection** is **1** the way that you change the sound of your voice when you speak, for example when you emphasize particular words. EG *She spoke in a low voice, always without inflection... ...the typical French inflection, rising slightly at the end.* **2** a change in the form of a word that shows its grammatical function, for example a change that makes a noun plural or makes a verb into the past tense. N COUNT/UNCOUNT; N COUNT/UNCOUNT

inflexible /ɪnflɛksɪbəⁿl/. **1** An **inflexible** rule, system, etc is firmly fixed and cannot be altered in any way. EG *Nursery schools have inflexible hours... ...building regulations which are inflexible and often discourage architectural innovation.* ◊ **inflexibility** /ɪnflɛksɪbɪlɪti[1]/. EG *...dogmatic inflexibility in the face of change.* ADJ QUALIT = rigid ≠ flexible; ◊ N UNCOUNT = rigidity

2 If an object or part of your body is **inflexible**, it is stiff and will not bend. EG *...the heavy inflexible armour of the beetles.* ADJ QUALIT = rigid ≠ flexible

inflexion /ɪnflɛkʃəⁿn/, **inflexions**. See **inflection**.

inflict /ɪnflɪkt/, **inflicts, inflicting, inflicted.** If you **inflict** something unpleasant on someone, you make them suffer it. EG *...the suffering inflicted by the bombing... People were accusing her of inflicting bad fortune on them through evil magic.* ◊ **infliction** /ɪnflɪkʃəⁿn/. EG *...the infliction of pain.* V+O : IF+PREP THEN *on/upon* ⇑ impose; ◊ N UNCOUNT ⇑ imposition

inflow /ɪnfləʊ/. You might refer to a steady movement of things arriving in a place as an **inflow** of things. EG *...the inflow of cheap raw materials... Money supply has been swollen by a large capital inflow from abroad.* N SING WITH DET +SUPP

influence /ɪnfluəns/, **influences, influencing, influenced. 1 Influence** is power which enables you to make other people agree with your opinions, do what you want, etc. EG *His wife had a lot of influence... The government would use its influence to try to make the negotiations successful... People in positions of power and influence have not always got there easily.* N UNCOUNT

2 Influence that one group or country has within another group or country is political power or popularity that they have there. EG *Moscow retains some influence over their affairs... The old regime was no longer able to exert its influence in those areas... The French colonial influence in Tunisia has left its imperial mark.* N UNCOUNT

3 An **influence** that someone or something has on people or situations is an effect that they have on the way people think or act or on what happens. EG *She had a great influence on the family... His teachings still exert a strong influence... We shall be looking at the influence of religion on society... We are all subject to influences from the mass media.* ● If you are **under the influence** of someone or something, you are being affected or controlled by them. EG *The exact form it takes will soon come under the influence of unwritten social rules... Some border areas were now under enemy influence.* ● Someone who is **under the influence** is drunk; a polite or formal expression. EG *He was caught driving under the influence... He was under the influence of a whisky too many.* N COUNT; ● PHR : USED AS A/C; ● PHR : USED AS A/C

4 An **influence** in art, music, writing, etc is a particular style which becomes popular and is later used or adapted in other styles. EG *Modern buildings still display the mark of early Greek influence... The beat still shows strong reggae influences... ...influences in drama and literature.* N COUNT

5 Someone or something that is a particular kind of **influence** on people has an effect on them of the kind mentioned. EG *He was a bad influence on the children... She was expelled from her grammar school as 'a disruptive influence'... It's still the most important influence in our lives.* N COUNT+SUPP : USU SING

6 If you **influence** a person or a situation, you have an effect on the way they act or on what happens. EG *There was little opportunity to influence foreign policy... How does politics influence the university?... Is British art influenced at all by American painting?.* V+O ⇑ affect

7 If you **influence** someone, you cause them to act in a particular way by making suggestions or by controlling the situation so that they believe that they are making their own choices. EG *I didn't want him to influence me in my choice... It's all too easy to be influenced by your parents.* V+O = manipulate, persuade

influential /ɪnfluɛnʃəⁿl/. Someone who is **influential** has a lot of influence over people and often affects their actions and behaviour. EG *She is a respected and influential woman... He had the support of a powerful and influential politician... She was influential in persuading Government to enact the new law... Moore was enormously influential to me as a very young sculptor.* ADJ QUALIT ⇑ powerful

influenza /ɪnfluɛnzə/ is the same as flu; a formal word. EG *I had ten days ill in bed with influenza.* N UNCOUNT ⇑ illness

influx /ɪnflʌks/. An **influx** of people or things into a place is their steady arrival there, usually in large numbers. EG *Foreign aid helped Chad cope with a massive influx of refugees from neighbouring countries.* N SING WITH DET : USU+*of* ⇑ movement

info. /ɪnfəʊ/ is the same as information; an informal word. EG *...the info. on where the meeting was.* N UNCOUNT

inform /ɪnfɔːm/, **informs, informing, informed. 1** If you **inform** someone of something or **inform** them that something is the case, you tell them about it. EG *He intended to see Barbara to inform her of his objections... I informed her that I was unwell and could not come to her party... The news had arrived too late for Bradley to inform us... It is helpful if students inform their landladies when they are going away.* V+O, USU+*of*/REPORT-CL

2 If you **inform** on or against a person, you give information about that person, for example to the police, with the result that he or she is accused of committing a crime or is shown to be guilty by your evidence. EG *It can be difficult for a child to inform on someone he knows.* V+A *(on/against)* ⇑ tell

informal /ɪnfɔːməⁿl/. **1** You use **informal** to describe a way of behaving or speaking that is relaxed and casual rather than correct and serious. You usually behave or speak like this when you are with people you know well. In this dictionary language of this kind is indicated by the use of the word 'informal' in definitions. EG *...an informal interview... ...a relaxed and quite informal discussion.* ◊ **informally.** EG *...people talking informally together... ...diners sitting informally around a long table.* ◊ **informality** /ɪnfɔːmælɪti[1]/. EG *...an atmosphere of informality in the relationship between staff and pupils.* ADJ QUALIT; ◊ ADV WITH VB; ◊ N UNCOUNT

2 You also use **informal** to describe **2.1** social occasions which are relaxed and friendly, where you do not have to wear smart clothes or behave in accordance with particular conventions. EG *...an in-* ADJ QUALIT = casual *formal party.* **2.2** clothes that are suitable for wearing when you are relaxing, but not for wearing on formal occasions. EG *They are conservative people unaccustomed to informal dress.* ◊ **informally**. EG *The producer was informally dressed in a blue silk shirt open at the neck.* **2.3** something that is not officially organized or established but is done casually without planning. EG *We often hold informal policy meetings on the seafront... We have informal contacts with over 500 firms.* ◊ **informally**. EG *Germany and Russia agreed informally to abide by the agreement.*

ADJ QUALIT = casual; ◊ ADV WITH VB; ADJ CLASSIF = unofficial; ◊ ADV WITH VB = unofficially

informant /ɪnfɔːmənt/, **informants**. An **informant** is 1 someone who can provide another person, for example a researcher, with useful information about something. 2 the same as an informer. — N COUNT; N COUNT

information /ɪnfəmeɪʃəⁿn/. If you have **information** on or about something, you know something about it. EG *I'm afraid I have no information on that... I'd like some information about trains, please... For further information please contact your local library... She provided me with a very interesting piece of information about his past... We arranged to meet at the information desk of the hotel.* — N UNCOUNT ⇑ fact

informative /ɪnfɔːmətɪv/. Something that is **informative** gives you useful information. EG *...informative comments... Man's sense of smell is much less informative than his sight.* — ADJ QUALIT

informed /ɪnfɔːmd/. 1 Someone who is well **informed**, or badly **informed**, knows a lot about, or not much about, what is happening in the world. EG *She's an extremely well informed woman... Television has made people better informed.* — ADJ QUALIT : ADV + ADJ = knowledgeable

2 If you make an **informed** guess about something, you use the knowledge that you have to decide what you think the answer should be. — ADJ CLASSIF : ATTRIB

informer /ɪnfɔːmə/, **informers**. An **informer** is somebody who gives information about a person, for example to the police, with the result that the person is accused of committing a crime or is shown to be guilty by the informer's evidence. EG *The group claimed that he was an informer to the secret police... The service had planted its agents and informers in some key positions in industry.* — N COUNT = grass

infra dig /ɪnfrə dɪg/. If you feel that it is **infra dig** to do something, you feel that you are too good or too important to do it. EG *It is very infra dig to do housework.* — ADJ QUALIT : PRED = demeaning

infra-red /ɪnfrə red/. **Infra-red** rays of light are rays which are invisible because they are below the colour red in the spectrum. EG *...infra-red radiation... ...infra-red photography.* — ADJ CLASSIF

infrastructure /ɪfrəstrʌktʃə/. The **infrastructure** of something such as a country, society, or organization is the basic structure on which it is built, such as the facilities, services and equipment that are needed for it to function properly. EG *Western technology needs a reliable infrastructure which is sometimes lacking in developing countries.* — N COUNT = base

infrequent /ɪnfriːkwənt/. If something is **infrequent**, it does not happen often. EG *The buses are so infrequent that it's hardly worth waiting for them... ...her sister's infrequent letters.* ◊ **infrequently**. EG *Communication was difficult because she could go to London only infrequently and Bill lacked the time to go to her... A doctor not infrequently has the task of telling people distressing news.* — ADJ QUALIT ⇑ rare; ◊ ADV WITH VB

infringe /ɪnfrɪndʒ/, **infringes, infringing, infringed**. 1 If you **infringe** a law or an agreement, you break it. EG *They occasionally infringe the law by parking near a junction.* — V+O

2 If you **infringe** people's rights, you interfere with them and do not allow them the freedom they are entitled to. EG *They were citizens with legal rights, which were being infringed.* — V+O

3 If something **infringes** on or upon you, it affects your behaviour by making it difficult for you to do what you want to do. EG *No man was allowed to infringe on the livelihood of his neighbour... I found that constant surveillance was infringing on my private life.* — V+O+A *(on/upon)* = trespass, encroach

infringement /ɪnfrɪndᵊʒməᵊnt/, **infringements**. 1 An **infringement** is something that affects you by interfering with your rights and your freedom to behave as you want to behave. EG *His arrest and detention was an infringement of his civil liberties... The new law is inflexible, an infringement on free speech.* ▸ used as an uncount noun. EG *I refuse to tolerate infringement of my privacy in this way.* — N COUNT : USU + *of/on*; ▸ N UNCOUNT : USU + *of/on*

2 An **infringement** of a law, rule, or agreement is the breaking of it. EG *...small infringements of prison discipline... Their job is to check these establishments and report on any infringements of the 1976 Act.* ▸ used as an uncount noun. EG *The strikers were soon in infringement of the law.* — N COUNT : USU + *of* = violation; ▸ N UNCOUNT : USU + *of*

infuriate /ɪnfjʊəriˡeɪt/, **infuriates, infuriating, infuriated**. If something or someone **infuriates** you, they make you extremely angry. EG *His speech really infuriated me... As well as infuriating the Prince, Cliff ruined his chances of promotion by getting drunk... Local people are infuriated by the way the traffic has increased through the village.* ◊ **infuriated**. EG *...a small group of infuriated little boys.* — V+O = outrage; ◊ ADJ QUALIT = outraged

infuriating /ɪnfjʊəriˡeɪtɪŋ/. Something that is **infuriating** annoys you very much. EG *...her infuriating habit of criticizing people all the time... Daniel found such incompetence infuriating.* ◊ **infuriatingly**. EG *John remained infuriatingly calm and placid throughout the dispute.* — ADJ QUALIT = maddening; ◊ ADV

infuse /ɪnfjuːz/, **infuses, infusing, infused**. 1 If you **infuse** something into someone or you **infuse** someone with something, you fill them with it; a formal use. EG *The appearance of young soldiers infused new hope and morale into the army... The morning air was infused with something very nice.* — V+O+A *(with/into)*

2 If you **infuse** something such as a drink or medicine, you pour hot water onto herbs or leaves and you leave it for a few minutes for the liquid to absorb the flavour. EG *Add the tea leaves and leave to infuse for five minutes.* — V-ERG = brew

infusion /ɪnfjuːʒəⁿn/, **infusions**. 1 If there is an **infusion** of one thing into another, the first thing is added to or incorporated into the second and gives it new life and vigour; a formal use. EG *...an infusion of new capital of £1 billion... Old families need an infusion of new blood from time to time.* — N COUNT/UNCOUNT : USU + *of* = input

2 An **infusion** is also a liquid made by leaving herbs in hot water until the flavour is strong; often used as a kind of medicine. EG *...infusions of camomile tea... The syrup contained an infusion of cocaine.* — N COUNT/UNCOUNT : IF + PREP THEN *of* ⇑ brew

> **-ING** □ In this dictionary -ING is used in the grammar notes beside entries to refer to the form of a verb which ends with '-ing', for example *laughing, doing,* and *hoping*. It is used beside meanings of words which need an '-ing' form after them. Examples of meanings that are followed by an '-ing' form are **finish** 1 and **for fear of** in **fear**. EG *Can I just finish* ***doing*** *this?... We'd finished* ***talking****... He didn't want to go for fear of* ***getting*** *lost... They won't use plastic bullets for fear of* ***increasing the violence.***

-ing. 1 **-ing** is added to verbs **1.1** in order to form present participles. EG *fight→fighting... take→taking... stop→stopping.* **1.2** in order to form uncountable nouns that refer to activities. EG *farm→farming... ski→skiing... advertise→advertising.* — SUFFIX; SUFFIX

2 In this dictionary adjectives and nouns ending in **-ing** are often not defined, but are included with their appropriate verbs when their meaning is obvious. For example, 'a sitting boy' is a boy who is sitting; 'the taking of life' means the same as 'when life is taken'. Most present participles can be used in this way. They are only included in the dictionary when there is evidence that it is a typical structure for the word, or the sense of the word, being explained.

ingenious /ɪndʒiːnjəs, -nɪəs/. Something that is **ingenious** is very clever, involving new ideas, methods, or equipment. EG *They competed with each other to find the most ingenious and original punishments... The idea was an ingenious one.* ◊ **ingeniously**. EG *The hangers were ingeniously fixed to the wardrobe by pieces of wire... ...his ingeniously cynical novel, The Spy who Came in from the Cold.* — ADJ QUALIT = imaginative; ◊ ADV

ingenue /æn ʒeɪnjuː/, **ingenues**. You use the word **ingenue** to describe a young, innocent woman, especially when this is actually a role being played by an actress; a formal word. EG *I played the poor, innocent little ingenue... ...ingenue roles.* — N COUNT : USU SING

ingenuity /ɪndʒɪnjuːɪtiˡ/ is cleverness and skill at inventing new equipment or new ways of doing something, or at working things out. EG *With a bit of* — N UNCOUNT = inventiveness *ingenuity you can do almost anything... He uses his ingenuity as best he can to make ends meet.*

ingenuous /ɪndʒenju:əs/. If you describe someone as **ingenuous**, you mean that they are innocent, trusting, and incapable of deceiving anyone; sometimes used in a disapproving way. EG *He was soft-spoken and ingenuous... ...an ingenuous student.* ▸ used also of people's behaviour and expressions. EG *His expression was frank, ingenuous, and engaging... His apology was so obviously sincere and ingenuous that his opponent was disconcerted.* ◇ **ingenuously**. EG *He smiled at her ingenuously.*

ADJ QUALIT ⇑ honest; ◇ ADV WITH VB ⇑ honestly

inglorious /ɪŋ¹glɔ:rɪəs/. Something that is **inglorious** is shameful and brings dishonour to the person involved. EG *Rudolph's choice was inglorious.* ◇ **ingloriously**. EG *In the nineteen fifties he had briefly and ingloriously been Prime Minister.*

ADJ CLASSIF; ◇ ADV WITH VB

ingot /ɪŋ¹gɒt/, **ingots**. An **ingot** is a lump of metal, usually shaped like a brick. EG *...an ingot of genuine gold... ...cast iron ingots.*

N COUNT : USU+SUPP

ingrained /ɪŋ¹greɪnd/. If habits and beliefs are **ingrained**, they are so fixed that they are difficult to change or to destroy. EG *The belief that one should work hard is ingrained in our culture... ...their ingrained assumption of social superiority... ...the deeply ingrained belief that the pursuit of material wealth is good.*

ADJ QUALIT : IF+PREP THEN *in*

ingratiate /ɪŋ¹greɪʃi¹eɪt/, **ingratiates, ingratiating, ingratiated**. If you **ingratiate** yourself with other people, you try to make yourself popular or liked by them; used showing disapproval. EG *The other men resented his knack for ingratiating himself with officers.*

V+O (REFL) : USU+*with*

ingratiating /ɪŋ¹greɪʃi¹eɪtɪŋ/. If you are **ingratiating**, you try to make yourself popular or liked by other people; used showing disapproval. EG *He was ingratiating in the extreme... ...an ingratiating employee of fifty-five.* ▸ used also of people's behaviour. EG *Stroop went to him with open arms and an ingratiating smile.*

ADJ QUALIT ⇑ friendly; ▸ ⇑ friendly

ingratitude /ɪŋ¹grætɪtju:d/ is the absence of gratitude or thanks for something that has been done for you. EG *I was shocked and enraged at such ingratitude... ...distressed by the ingratitude of a son whom she had loved above all things.*

N UNCOUNT

ingredient /ɪŋ¹gri:dɪənt/, **ingredients**. 1 **Ingredients** are the things that are used to make something, for example all the different foods you use when you are cooking a particular dish. EG *Mix all the ingredients together in a large saucepan... Ingredients: tomatoes, sugar, spirit vinegar, salt, spices. ... This process is called photosynthesis and one of the ingredients it requires is hydrogen.*

N COUNT ⇑ component

2 An **ingredient** of a situation or in a situation is something that helps to cause that particular situation or to make it successful. EG *Mental illness and detachment from society are the ingredients of suicide... Travelling abroad is an essential ingredient in your business career.*

N COUNT : IF+PREP THEN *of/in* = factor

ingrowing /ɪngrəʊɪŋ/. An **ingrowing** toenail is one which is growing into someone's toe, causing them pain.

ADJ CLASSIF

inhabit /ɪnhæbɪt/, **inhabits, inhabiting, inhabited**. If a place or region **is inhabited**, people live there. EG *The town was a lazy winter seaside resort, inhabited by fishermen and hoteliers... ...an inhabited house.*

V+O : USU PASS = dwell in

inhabitant /ɪnhæbɪtənt/, **inhabitants**. The **inhabitants** of a place are the people or animals that live there. EG *Years ago the inhabitants of the town fought for their right to collect their own taxes.*

N COUNT ⇑ resident

inhale /ɪnheɪl/, **inhales, inhaling, inhaled**. When you **inhale** or when you **inhale** something such as smoke, you breathe it in. EG *She put the cigarette between her lips and inhaled deeply... They pushed open the door and inhaled the familiar smell.*

V OR V+O

inherent /ɪnhɪərənt, -her-/. Qualities or characteristics that are **inherent** in something or someone exist as a necessary and natural part of that person or thing. EG *We have pointed to the dangers inherent in this kind of political system... ...my inherent laziness.* ◇ **inherently**. EG *Power stations are themselves inherently inefficient.*

ADJ CLASSIF : IF+PREP THEN *in* = innate; ◇ ADV = intrinsically

inherit /ɪnherɪt/, **inherits, inheriting, inherited**. 1 If you **inherit** something such as a position, situation, or attitude, you take it over from someone else and use it or deal with it yourself. EG *They inherited a weak economy... ...traditions inherited from the past.*

V+O

2 If you **inherit** money or property, you receive it from someone who has died. EG *He will inherit this money at the age of twenty-five... ...a man of considerable inherited wealth.*

V OR V+O ⇑ acquire = come into

3 If you **inherit** a characteristic or quality, you are born with it, because your parents or ancestors also had it. EG *Differences in intelligence were largely inherited... This kind of brain damage may be inherited.*

V+O

inheritance /ɪnherɪtə⁰ns/, **inheritances**. 1 An **inheritance** is money or property which you receive from someone who is dead. EG *He had no other motive for depriving his son of the inheritance.* ▸ used as an uncount noun. EG *...the customs of inheritance in Asia... There may be restrictions on the inheritance of wealth.*

N COUNT : USU SING = bequest, legacy; ▸ N UNCOUNT : USU+SUPP

2 **Inheritance** is also 2.1 the fact of being born with particular characteristics or qualities which your family or ancestors had. EG *To what extent does human nature depend on genetic inheritance as opposed to environment?* 2.2 a situation or state of affairs which has been influenced by a particular event, person, book, etc. EG *This is the cultural inheritance of independence... ...our alphabet, an inheritance from the Greeks.*

N UNCOUNT : USU ⇑ transfer; N SING WITH DET +SUPP ⇑ heritage = bequest

inheritor /ɪnherɪtə/, **inheritors**. An **inheritor** is 1 someone who inherits money or property from someone who is dead. EG *...the inheritors of multi-million dollar estates.* 2 someone who inherits something such as culture and tradition from the past. EG *...the inheritors of a literary tradition.*

N COUNT = legatee; N COUNT+SUPP

inhibit /ɪnhɪbɪt/, **inhibits, inhibiting, inhibited**. 1 If you **inhibit** someone from doing something, you prevent them from doing it, although they want to do it or should be able to do it. EG *This feature of the book would be enough to inhibit a lot of people from reading it... He seems to have been held back and inhibited in his work.*

V+O ⇑ restrain

2 If something **inhibits** the growth or development of something else, it prevents or slows down its growth. EG *The drugs with which the animals are fed inhibit their development and they remain sterile... It has sometimes helped to inhibit progress, not promote it.*

V+O ≠ encourage

inhibited /ɪnhɪbɪtɪ²d/. If you are **inhibited**, you find it difficult to behave naturally and show your real feelings because you worry too much about what you say or do or about what other people will think of you. EG *Her severe upbringing had left her inhibited... I felt inhibited from joining the others... ...a very inhibited young man.*

ADJ QUALIT ⇑ reserved = repressed

inhibition /ɪnh⁰ɪbɪʃə⁰n/, **inhibitions**. **Inhibitions** are feelings of fear or embarrassment that make it difficult for you to behave naturally because you worry too much about what you say or do or about what other people think of you. EG *The child is free from inhibitions... The intended effect of the wine was to take away people's inhibitions.* ▸ used as an uncount noun. EG *She's prepared to argue without inhibition.*

N COUNT ⇑ anxiety = hang-up; ▸ N UNCOUNT ⇑ restraint

inhospitable /ɪnhɒspɪtəbə⁰l/. 1 If you are **inhospitable**, you do not like having guests and do not make people feel welcome when they visit you. EG *They're extremely inhospitable these days... I don't like to be inhospitable, but I've got an awful lot to do.*

ADJ QUALIT : USU PRED ⇑ unfriendly

2 If a place is **inhospitable**, it is not easy for people to live in it or even to find shelter there. EG *...the inhospitable monsoon areas of the tropics... During the last decades men have invaded the once inhospitable deserts.* ▸ also used of the weather. EG *The weather was about as inhospitable as it could be.*

ADJ QUALIT : USU ATTRIB; ▸ ADJ QUALIT

inhuman /ɪnh⁰ju:mən/. 1 Behaviour that is **inhuman** is so cruel or brutal that you cannot imagine people behaving in such a way. EG *The violence of the gunman was inhuman, barbaric, impossible to justify... ...barbarous and inhuman atrocities.*

ADJ QUALIT : USU PRED ⇑ harmful

2 Something that is **inhuman** is not human, and therefore often seems strange or frightening to people. EG *...their faces looked inhuman, covered with scarlet and black paint... They are technologists, and they speak an inhuman language when describing what they do.*

ADJ CLASSIF

inhumane /ɪnhju:meɪn/. Something that is **inhumane** is so cruel that you can hardly believe that people can use or accept it. EG *The new weapon was considered to be too inhumane to be used.* ▸ used

ADJ QUALIT : USU PRED; ▸ ADJ QUALIT :

also of people and their behaviour. EG *Humans are innately inhumane, and this explains much of the misery and suffering in the world.* USU PRED

inhumanity /ɪnhju:mænɪti¹/ is extreme cruelty of a kind which shows total lack of feeling towards other people. EG *...callous inhumanity and sadistic bullying... ...man's inhumanity to man.* ▸ used as a count noun. EG *...speeches on the inhumanities of the system.* N UNCOUNT = barbarity ▸ N COUNT

inimical /ɪnɪmɪkə⁰l/. 1 Conditions that are **inimical** to someone or something are hostile and harmful rather than being friendly and favourable. EG *At first sight the area seems arid, inimical to man... His methods are inimical to radical change.* ADJ CLASSIF : USU PRED+*to*

2 People or animals that are **inimical** are hostile and unfriendly. EG *...inimical species... ...an inimical critic.* ADJ QUALIT

inimitable /ɪnɪmɪtəbə⁰l/. If someone has a quality or a characteristic that is **inimitable**, it is impossible for other people to copy it, either because it is very good or because it is very typical of that person. EG *He cried 'Oh Death, Death, Death!' in an inimitable tone which struck me with horror... The Welsh Rugby team have their own inimitable, almost arrogant, style.* ADJ QUALIT ⇑ unique

iniquitous /ɪnɪkwɪtəs/. Something that is **iniquitous** is bad and very unfair; a formal word showing disapproval. EG *...the long-established and iniquitous system of rewarding politicians... Many historians, of course, regard this as iniquitous.* ADJ CLASSIF ⇑ wicked

iniquity /ɪnɪkwɪti¹/, **iniquities**. Iniquity is wickedness or injustice; a formal word showing disapproval. EG *...their attempt to cleanse society of this iniquity.* ▸ used as a count noun. EG *We fought a revolution to put an end to such iniquities... ...the iniquities of a two-party system.* N UNCOUNT ▸ N COUNT

initial /ɪnɪʃə⁰l/, **initials, initialling, initialled**.
1 **Initial** describes something that happens at first or at the beginning of a process, in contrast to what happens later. EG *We are not at the initial stage of learning English... After the initial shock I began to accept the situation... My initial reaction was one of great relief... Despite these initial handicaps, she intends to make a success of it.* ADJ CLASSIF : ATTRIB ⇑ early = original

2 An **initial** or an **initial letter** is the first letter of a word, especially a person's name, and is often used to represent that name as part of a title. EG *Now can I have your initial, Mrs Jones?... She was updating the file cards and sorting them by surname, according to initial letter.* N COUNT

3 Your **initials** are the set of capital letters which represent each of your names. For example, if your full name is Karen Anne Fox, your initials will be K.A.F. EG *His initials are in his hat... He began to carve his initials on the tree.* N PLURAL

4 When you **initial** something, you write your initials on it as a signature, in order to show that you own, authorize, or agree with it. EG *He picked up his pen and initialled the papers.* V+O ⇑ sign

initially /ɪnɪʃə⁰li¹/ means in the first, early, or original stages of a process, in contrast to later stages. EG *Feathers initially developed from insect scales... George's response was initially adamant... I don't remember who initially conceived the idea.* ADV WITH VB

initiate, initiates, initiating, initiated. The word **initiate** is pronounced /ɪnɪʃi¹eɪt/ when it is a verb, and /ɪnɪʃi¹ət/ when it is a noun. 1 If you **initiate** something, you start it or cause it to happen. EG *We should initiate direct talks with the trades unions... These countries have recently initiated some improvements in their defence systems... This initiated a further reorganization of the company.* V+O

2 If you **initiate** someone into something, **2.1** you introduce them to a particular skill, type of knowledge, etc and you teach them about it. EG *Pat wanted to initiate his son into fishing... Harland and I were initiated with elaborate care into the handling of the lizards in the Reptile House.* **2.2** you allow them to enter a particular social group, club, status, etc, usually by having special ceremonies or by teaching them particular secrets and skills. EG *Once a youth was initiated into manhood, a six-month ceremonial process began.* V+O+A *(into)* V+O : IF+PREP THEN *into*

3 An **initiate** is **3.1** a person in some societies who is in the process of officially becoming an adult, especially by being involved in social or religious ceremonies and by learning particular skills and secrets. **3.2** a person who has recently been allowed to join a particular group, club, etc, and who has been taught particular secrets and skills. EG *...a circle of knowledgeable intellectual initiates and professionals... ...an initiate into the world of politics.* N COUNT N COUNT

initiation /ɪnɪʃieɪʃə⁰n/. 1 The **initiation** of something is the start of it or the process of causing it to happen. EG *...the termination of old, and the initiation of new, human relationships... ...the initiation of a new revolutionary practice.* N UNCOUNT+*of*

2 Your **initiation** into adulthood is the act or process of officially becoming an adult in some societies, especially by being involved in social and religious ceremonies and being taught particular skills and secrets. EG *...an initiation ceremony.* N UNCOUNT

initiative /ɪnɪʃi⁰ətɪv/, **initiatives**. 1 An **initiative** is an important act, action, or statement, which is seen as an attempt to solve a problem or to get something done. EG *The headmaster welcomed the initiative and paid tribute to the teacher's single-mindedness... You seem to be critical of the chairman's political initiatives... ...various left-wing initiatives.* N COUNT : USU PL ⇑ move

2 If you have the **initiative**, you are in a position of superiority or advantage over another person or group, and so you have the power to make decisions or to control how or when something happens. EG *It was evident that he had recovered the initiative... They had lost the initiative.* N SING : *the*+N

3 If you **take the initiative** in a situation, you are the first person to do something important or to make the first move. EG *In Sweden employers have taken the initiative, with union support, in promoting health insurance schemes... The Prime Minister was aware of this and in the autumn took the initiative by promising legislation to introduce better housing.* PHR : VB INFLECTS ⇑ lead

4 If you have **initiative**, you are able to see what needs to be done and can then do it in an intelligent and efficient way, without needing other people to give you orders or instructions. EG *You will be working in a changing situation, where initiative, inventiveness and a bold independence are important... If you act responsibly and show that you have initiative, you will sooner or later be promoted.* N UNCOUNT = drive, enterprise

5 If you **use** your **initiative** or if you do something **on** your **own initiative**, you think about it and do it using your own judgement rather than relying on other people to tell you what to do. EG *In special circumstances we have to use our initiative... In 1912 he had gone to Berlin on his own initiative.* PHR : VB INFLECTS, OR PHR : USED AS AN A ⇑ independently

inject /ɪndʒɛkt/, **injects, injecting, injected**. 1 If you **inject** someone with a liquid such as medicine or poison, you use a needle and syringe to get it into their body through their blood. EG *She had enough mercy to inject a sleeping drug into my arm... We must for our protection be injected with antibiotics.* V+O : IF+PREP THEN *into/with*

2 If you **inject** someone **against** a particular disease or infection, you inject them with drugs that will prevent it. EG *She was injected against tetanus.* PHR : VB INFLECTS = vaccinate, inoculate

3 If you **inject** something new, such as excitement or interest, into a situation, you add it. EG *She was trying to inject some fun into the grim proceedings... It has injected a new spark of life into the city.* V+O : IF+PREP THEN *into* ⇑ introduce = bring

4 If you **inject** money or resources into a business or organization, you provide more money or resources for it. EG *Enormous sums of money are injected each year into teaching.* V+O : IF+PREP THEN *into* = pump

injection /ɪndʒɛkʃə⁰n/, **injections**. 1 If you have an **injection**, someone, usually a doctor or nurse, pricks your skin with the needle of a syringe and puts drugs or other liquids into your blood. Injections are usually used to prevent illnesses or infection. EG *You had a smallpox injection when you were five... She gave me some injections for tetanus... Another course of injections was prescribed.* ▸ used as an uncount noun. EG *This hormone could be supplied by injection.* N COUNT ⇑ treatment = jab ▸ N UNCOUNT

2 An **injection** of money or resources into a business, project, or organization is the putting of extra money or resources into it in order to help it become efficient or profitable. EG *A slightly larger injection of money from local authorities would be helpful now... They only survived because of massive injections of commercial funds.* N COUNT+*of* = infusion

injudicious /ɪndʒu:dɪʃəs/. Something or someone that is **injudicious** shows very poor judgement; a formal word. EG *He thought it would be injudicious to question her.* ADJ QUALIT = imprudent

injunction /ɪndʒʌŋkʃəⁿn/, **injunctions**. An **injunction** is 1 an instruction or order that is given officially and formally by a court of law. EG *We will apply to the courts for an injunction against the march... The court should issue an injunction.* N COUNT 2 an instruction or order. EG *The sermon was full of injunctions to refrain from sin... The usual last minute injunctions were given me by my mother.* N COUNT : IF+VB THEN to-INF = warning

injure /ɪndʒə/, **injures, injuring, injured**. 1 If you **injure** a person or animal, you damage some part of their body. EG *He's going to injure himself if he isn't careful... Peter recently injured his right hand in a training accident... The earthquake killed 24,000 people and injured 77,000.* V+O (NG/REFL) = hurt

2 If you **injure** someone's feelings, you offend the person or damage their confidence. EG *You've injured my self-esteem once too often.* V+O ⇑ hurt

injured /ɪndʒəd/. 1 A person or animal that is **injured** is damaged in some part of the body, usually as a result of an accident or fighting. EG *She was not badly injured but she couldn't speak... The soldiers were dragging their injured comrades with them.* ADJ QUALIT = hurt, wounded

▸ The **injured** is used to refer to people who are injured. EG *We must provide medical attention to the injured.* ▸ N PLURAL : the +N = wounded

2 If you feel **injured**, you feel upset because something unjust or unfair has happened to you. EG *One feels faintly injured if the buses don't come on time.* ADJ QUALIT : PRED = put out, offended ▸ used to describe your feelings. EG *Haggerty's injured professional pride quite overcame any desire for reconciliation.* ▸ ADJ QUALIT = hurt

injured party, injured parties. If you describe someone as the **injured party**, you mean that they have been treated unfairly, especially when they are involved in a court case to try and get justice; a legal term. N COUNT : USU the+N ⇑ victim

injurious /ɪndʒʊərɪəs/ means harmful or damaging. EG *A strike could be gravely injurious to the national economy... ...an injurious effect.* ADJ QUALIT : IF+ PREP THEN to = deleterious

injury /ɪndʒəri¹/, **injuries**. An **injury** is 1 damage or harm done to a person's or an animal's body. EG *The earthquake caused many deaths and severe injuries... After an injury an X-ray is often desirable... Building workers risk injury by not wearing helmets... Injury to the eye should be reported promptly.* N COUNT/ UNCOUNT 2 damage or harm done to your feelings. EG *Most people protect themselves from injury to their self-esteem.* N UNCOUNT/ COUNT • to **add insult to injury**: see **insult**.

injury time is the period of time added at the end of a football match because play was interrupted during the match when players were injured. N UNCOUNT

injustice /ɪndʒʌstɪs/, **injustices**. 1 **Injustice** is unfairness and lack of justice in a situation. EG *There's repression and social injustice everywhere... A vast sense of injustice haunted me.* N UNCOUNT ⇑ wrong ▸ used to refer to an example of this. EG *He contemplated the injustices of life.* ▸ N COUNT

2 If you **do** someone **an injustice**, you are unfair in the way that you deal with them, for example judging their character too harshly without considering all their good qualities. EG *I feel I've done him rather an injustice.* PHR : VB INFLECTS = misjudge

ink /ɪŋk/, **inks, inking, inked**. 1 **Ink** is 1.1 the coloured liquid used for writing or printing. EG *Please write in ink... ...ink stains... ...an ink bottle.* N MASS 1.2 the black liquid that a squid, octopus, etc produces. N UNCOUNT

2 If you **ink** something, you put ink on it. EG *They inked their thumbs on an inking pad.* V+O

ink in. If you **ink** something **in**, you write or mark it in ink, usually after it has already been written or marked in pencil. EG *The revisions can now be inked in.* PHRASAL VB : V+ O+ADV

inkling /ɪŋklɪŋ/, **inklings**. If you **have an inkling** of something, you have a vague idea about it. EG *He had no inkling of the cause of the delay... 'Does she know?'–'I think she must have an inkling'.* PHR : VB INFLECTS, USU+ of/REPORT-CL

inkstand /ɪŋkstænd/, **inkstands**. An **inkstand** is a container for ink bottles and pens. N COUNT

inkwell /ɪŋkwɛl/, **inkwells**. An **inkwell** is a container for ink in a desk. N COUNT

inky /ɪŋki¹/. Something that is **inky** is 1 very black, like ink. EG *There isn't even a farmhouse light showing, to break the inky blackness... Several times ash rained from an inky sky.* ADJ COLOUR : ATTRIB 2 covered in ink. EG *...an inky handkerchief... ...inky fingers.* ADJ QUALIT : ATTRIB

inlaid /ɪnleɪd/. 1 An object that is **inlaid** has a design on it which is made by putting wood, gold, silver, etc into the surface of the object. The surface which results from this is completely smooth and flat. EG *...a lavishly inlaid table... The box was inlaid with gold monograms.* ADJ CLASSIF : IF+ PREP THEN with

2 **Inlaid** is the past tense and past participle of **inlay**.

inland /ɪnlə³nd/. 1 If you go **inland**, you go away from the coast, towards or near the middle of a country. EG *If I get more than ten miles inland, I begin to feel claustrophobic... It was hard to believe we were in Central Africa, deep inland, rather than on the shores of the ocean... Donkeys bear goods inland to the towns and villages.* ADV

2 **Inland** areas, lakes, etc are not on the coast, but in or near the middle of a country. EG *Manchester has an inland harbour... The captives were beaten and driven across the hot, hard inland country for many days.* ADJ CLASSIF : ATTRIB ≠ coastal

in-laws. Your **in-laws** are the members of your husband's or wife's family. N PLURAL : USU POSS+N

inlay /ɪnleɪ/, **inlays, inlaying, inlaid**. 1 An **inlay** is 1.1 a design or pattern on an object which is made by putting wood, gold, silver, etc into the surface of the object. The surface which results from this is completely smooth and flat. EG *...a writing desk of rosewood with ebony inlay.* N COUNT/ UNCOUNT ⇑ decoration 1.2 a substance such as gold or porcelain which is used by dentists to fill a damaged tooth. EG *Biting on an apple, I pulled an inlay out of my tooth.* N COUNT/ UNCOUNT = filling

2 To **inlay** something means to put an inlay into it. EG *The box must have been inlaid with lead.* V+O : USU PASS+ with

inlet /ɪnlɛt/, **inlets**. An **inlet** is 1 a narrow strip of water which goes from a sea or lake into the land or between two islands. EG *The inlet was a cleft in the gorge, open on both sides.* N COUNT = creek 2 the part of a machine through which a flow of liquid enters. EG *You must unscrew the valve at the inlet end.* N COUNT ⇑ entrance

in loco parentis /ɪn ləʊkəʊ pərɛntɪs/. If you are **in loco parentis**, you are, for a short time, in the position of a parent towards someone else's children. Teachers are often regarded as being in loco parentis; a Latin expression. PHR : USED AS AN A

inmate /ɪnmeɪt/, **inmates**. An **inmate** is one of the people living in a prison, hospital, or other institution. EG *In prison you learned about other inmates and their crimes.* N COUNT ⇑ resident

inmost /ɪnməʊst/ means deepest and most secret. EG *You read my inmost thoughts... ...the inmost core of his being.* ADJ CLASSIF : ATTRIB = innermost

inn /ɪn/, **inns**. An **inn** is a small, old hotel, usually in the country, especially one which is also a pub. EG *We stopped at an inn for lemonade and chips.* N COUNT : ALSO IN NAMES AFTER N

innards /ɪnədz/. 1 The **innards** of a person or animal are the organs inside the body. N PLURAL : USU WITH POSS

2 A machine's **innards** are the parts inside it. N PLURAL

innate /ɪneɪt/. An **innate** quality or ability is one which a person is born with, rather than those that they learn or obtain during life. EG *They believed intelligence was innate, and unlikely to change... You obviously have an innate talent for music... ...the innate dignity of every human being.* ADJ CLASSIF ⇑ inborn ≠ learnt ◊ **innately**. EG *I don't think that anybody is innately good.* ◊ ADV = naturally

inner /ɪnə/ is 1 used to describe something which is contained or enclosed inside something else. EG *There were several flats overlooking the inner courtyard... The door to the inner office opened and Miss Saunders came out... ...the inner wrapping.* ADJ CLASSIF : ATTRIB 2 used to describe feelings or emotions which you have but which you do not express or show to other people. EG *...his inner feelings of failure... She longed for inner calm.* ADJ CLASSIF : ATTRIB = inward 3 used to describe the group of people in an organization who have the most power and control in the organization and who work in secret. EG *...the inner circle.* ADJ CLASSIF : ATTRIB 4 used when you refer to the central part of a large city. EG *...a comprehensive school in Inner London.* ADJ CLASSIF : ATTRIB

inner city, inner cities; also spelled with a hyphen, especially when used before another noun. An **inner city** consists of the parts in the centre of a large city where people live and where there are often social and economic problems. EG *This is one of the most serious problems in the Inner Cities... ...an inner-city area... ...the problems for inner-city children.* N COUNT

innermost /ɪnəməʊst/. 1 Your **innermost** feelings or thoughts are the very private feelings or thoughts which you are unlikely to express or show to other ADJ CLASSIF : ATTRIB = intimate people. EG *He wrote in his diary his innermost thoughts... ...his innermost being.*

2 The **innermost** thing is the one nearest to the centre. EG *...the innermost room of the castle.* ADJ CLASSIF

3 **Innermost** is used to describe the group of people in an organization who have the most power and control in the organization and whose work is very secret. EG *...the party's innermost council.* ADJ CLASSIF: ATTRIB

inner tube, inner tubes; also spelled with a hyphen. An **inner tube** is a rubber tube inside a car tyre or bicycle tyre, containing air. N COUNT

inning /ɪnɪŋ/, **innings**. **Innings** is both the singular and the plural form for paragraph 2. 1 An **inning** is a period in a game of baseball during which each team has a turn at bat. N COUNT 2 An **innings** is a period in a game of cricket during which a particular player or team is batting. EG *...an innings of 84 from Gower... He took five wickets in the New Zealand innings.* N COUNT

3 In British English, if you say that someone **has had a good innings**, you mean that they have had a long and successful life; an informal expression, used especially about someone who is old or who has just died. PHR: VB INFLECTS

innkeeper /ɪŋ¹ki:pə/, **innkeepers**. An **innkeeper** is someone who looks after an inn. N COUNT = landlord

innocence /ɪnəsəns/ is 1 the quality of having no experience or knowledge of the more complex, evil, or unpleasant aspects of life; often used of children. EG *He had a peculiar air of childlike innocence... We have lost our innocence.* N UNCOUNT = naivety 2 the quality of not being guilty of a crime. EG *He desperately protested his innocence.* N UNCOUNT ≠ guilt

innocent /ɪnəsənt/, **innocents**. 1 If someone is **innocent**, 1.1 they are not guilty of a crime which they have been accused of. EG *He was accused of a crime of violence of which he was innocent... ...the principle that a person is innocent until found guilty.* ADJ CLASSIF ≠ guilty

1.2 have no experience or knowledge of the more complex, evil, or unpleasant aspects of life. EG *I was very young, and very innocent... Claud turned his head and looked at me with large innocent eyes.* ADJ QUALIT = naive

2 **Innocent** people are those who are not involved in a crime, conflict, or other situation, but who nevertheless get injured or killed. EG *Terrorism kills innocent people.* ADJ CLASSIF = blameless

3 An **innocent** is a person who is inexperienced and ignorant about the more complex, evil, or unpleasant aspects of life. EG *I'm not a total innocent... He was a financial genius but a political innocent.* N COUNT = ignoramus

4 If something that you do or say is **innocent**, you do not realize that it may offend people or be tactless. EG *It was an innocent question.* ◊ **innocently**. EG *'What did I do?' asked Howard, innocently... 'How's Jimmie?' Mrs Burns asked, innocently enough.* ADJ QUALIT = innocuous ◊ ADV

innocuous /ɪnɒkju:əs/. Something that is **innocuous** is not at all harmful or controversial. EG *...innocuous substances... I made my opening words as innocuous as possible.* ADJ QUALIT = harmless

innovate /ɪnə⁶veɪt/, **innovates, innovating, innovated**. 1 If you **innovate**, you introduce changes and new ideas in the way something is done or made. EG *Businesses had to plan in order to meet demand and innovate.* V

innovation /ɪnə⁶veɪʃə⁰n/, **innovations**. 1 An **innovation** is a new idea or method that is introduced in the way that something is done or made. EG *Farmers are introducing innovations that increase the productivity per worker... ...major innovations such as frozen food and antibiotics.* N COUNT ⇑ change

2 **Innovation** is EG *the introduction of new ideas or methods in the way that something is done or made. ...a period of technological innovation.* N UNCOUNT ⇑ change

innovative /ɪnəvətɪv/. Something that is **innovative** introduces changes and new ideas in the way things are done or made. EG *He produced stylistically innovative works... How innovative is British industry?* ADJ QUALIT = progressive

innovator /ɪnə⁶veɪtə/, **innovators**. An **innovator** is someone who introduces changes and new ideas in the way something is done or made. EG *D G Bridson was one of the innovators of radio feature writing.* N COUNT = pioneer

innovatory /ɪnəvətə⁰ri¹, ɪnəveɪtə⁰ri¹/ means the same as innovative. EG *His music was innovatory in its time.* ADJ QUALIT

innuendo /ɪnju:ɛndəʊ/, **innuendoes**. The plural can also be spelled **innuendos**. 1 **Innuendo** is indirect reference to something rude or unpleasant. EG *...a campaign of innuendo and gossip.* N UNCOUNT

2 An **innuendo** is a remark which indirectly refers to something rude or unpleasant. EG *He became a target for sexual innuendoes.* N COUNT = insinuation

innumerable /ɪnju:mə⁰rəbə⁰l/ means too many to be counted. EG *The industrial age has brought innumerable benefits.* ADJ CLASSIF: USU ATTRIB = countless

inoculate /ɪnɒkjə⁴leɪt/, **inoculates, inoculating, inoculated**. To **inoculate** a person or animal means to inject a weak form of a disease into the body as a way of protecting them from the disease. EG *A pedigree pup should have been inoculated against serious diseases before it's sold.* V+O: IF+PREP THEN against/with = vaccinate

inoculation /ɪnɒkjə⁴leɪʃə⁰n/, **inoculations**. 1 **Inoculation** is the practice of inoculating people or animals. N UNCOUNT

2 An **inoculation** is an instance of this. EG *...inoculations against tetanus.* N COUNT

inoffensive /ɪnəfɛnsɪv/. Someone or something that is **inoffensive** is harmless and does not give offence to people. EG *He's an inoffensive little fellow.* ADJ QUALIT = innocuous

inoperable /ɪnɒpə⁰rəbə⁰l/. An **inoperable** tumour, cancer, etc, is one that cannot be removed by a surgical operation. ADJ CLASSIF

inoperative /ɪnɒpə⁰rətɪv/. An **inoperative** rule, principle, tax, etc is one that does not work any more or that cannot be made to work. ADJ CLASSIF = unworkable

inopportune /ɪnɒpətju:n/. 1 Something that is **inopportune** is done or happens at an unsuitable time, and causes trouble or embarrassment because of this. EG *...an inopportune remark.* ADJ QUALIT = unfortunate

2 An **inopportune** moment, time, etc is one that is unsuitable for a particular thing to happen. EG *You've called at a rather inopportune moment.* ADJ QUALIT = inconvenient

inordinate /ɪnɔ:dɪnɪ¹t/. 1 Something that is **inordinate** is extreme and not limited in any way. EG *The idea of this gave me inordinate pleasure... He has an inordinate thirst.* ◊ **inordinately**. EG *We were inordinately attached to each other.* ADJ CLASSIF: USU ATTRIB = great, immense ◊ ADV+ADJ/ADV

2 An **inordinate** amount of something is much greater than you would normally expect. EG *Colin always spent an inordinate length of time in the bathroom.* ◊ **inordinately**. EG *In America old people account for an inordinately high proportion of suicides.* ADJ CLASSIF = excessive, surprising ◊ ADV+ADJ/ADV

inorganic /ɪnɔ:gænɪk/ describes or refers to things which are not living or which never have life of their own, for example stone, metal, liquids, gases, or man-made chemical compounds. EG *...inorganic materials... ...inorganic fertilizers... ...inorganic chemistry.* ADJ CLASSIF = artificial ≠ organic

in-patient, in-patients. An **in-patient** is someone who stays in hospital while they receive their treatment. N COUNT

input /ɪnpʊt/, **inputs, inputting, input**. 1 **Input** or an **input** consists of resources such as money, workers, or power that are given to something such as a machine or a project to make it work. EG *The project requires the input of more labour... ...high-cost inputs such as energy.* N UNCOUNT/COUNT

2 **Input** is also information that is fed into an information-processing device such as a computer or the brain of a person or animal. EG *We are unlikely to generate new ideas if the information input is strictly limited to relevant information.* N UNCOUNT

3 If you **input** information into a computer, you feed it in, for example by typing it on a keyboard. EG *Now we'll input the numbers.* V+O

inquest /ɪŋ¹kwɛst/, **inquests**. An **inquest** is an official inquiry to find out the facts about something, especially about a death which may not be from natural causes. EG *There have been demands for an inquest.* N COUNT ⇑ investigation

inquire /ɪŋ¹kwaɪə/, **inquires, inquiring, inquired**; also spelled **enquire**. **Inquire** is a more formal word than 'ask'. 1 If you **inquire** something, you ask someone to tell you something. EG *'Tell me, Jennifer,' I inquired. 'What do you think of pop music?'... He inquired whether it was possible to leave his case in the Left Luggage Office... I enquired the way to the bus station... She inquired of me how I had enjoyed the play.* V+O/REPORT-CL/QUOTE

2 If you **inquire** about something, you ask for information about it. EG *He went to the station to enquire about the times of trains to Edinburgh... There was no-one who was sufficiently concerned to inquire as to his whereabouts.* V: USU+about/as to

inquire after. If you **inquire after** someone, you ask for information about them, for example about how they are or what they are doing. EG *She enquired after Mrs Carstair's daughter, who had just had a baby.* PHRASAL VB : V+PREP, HAS PASS = ask after

inquire into. If you **inquire into** something such as a person's death, you investigate it carefully. EG *The police inquired into the deaths of two young girls.* PHRASAL VB : V+PREP, HAS PASS = look into

inquirer /ɪŋ¹kwaɪərə/, **inquirers**. An **inquirer** is a person who asks for information about something or someone; a fairly formal word. EG *We told all inquirers to phone again later.* N COUNT

inquiring /ɪŋ¹kwaɪərɪŋ/. 1 If you have an **inquiring** mind, you have a great interest in learning new things. EG *All her children seem to have very inquiring minds.* ADJ QUALIT : ATTRIB = inquisitive

2 An **inquiring** expression, look, etc shows that you are asking something or want to know something. EG *He raised an inquiring eyebrow.* ◊ **inquiringly**. EG *Her husband looked at her inquiringly and she shook her head.* ADJ QUALIT = questioning ◊ ADV WITH VB

inquiry /ɪ¹nkwaɪəri¹/, **inquiries**; also spelled **enquiry**. **Inquiry** and **enquiry** can both be used in the meanings given below. However, **enquiry** is more common in sense 1.1 and **inquiry** is more common in sense 1.2. Both spellings are common for paragraph 2. 1 An **inquiry** is 1.1 a question which you ask someone in order to get some information from them. EG *This is what I have been able to learn in my enquiries... We had 500 enquiries about our advertisement... He sent an urgent inquiry to his staff: 'What do you know about the new Japanese computer?'* ▸ **Enquiries** is often used as the name of the department in a shop or organization that you can go to or phone up for information. EG *Get me international enquiries please.* ● If you **make inquiries** about something, you ask questions about it. EG *I shall make some enquiries.* 1.2 an investigation, especially an official one, into something that has happened or something that people feel needs to be examined. EG *Opposition MPs have called for an inquiry... There will be an official inquiry into conditions at the plant... ...a public enquiry.* N COUNT ▸ N PLURAL ● PHR : VB INFLECTS N COUNT

2 **Inquiry** is the process of asking about or investigating something in order to find out more about it. EG *He looked round in inquiry to make sure that everyone understood... On further enquiry, however, I discovered that there had been nobody at home that evening... It seemed a possible line of enquiry... ...a court of inquiry.* N UNCOUNT ⇑ investigation

inquisition /ɪŋ¹kwɪzɪʃə⁰n/, **inquisitions**. An **inquisition** is an official investigation, especially one which is very thorough and uses harsh methods of questioning. N COUNT = interrogation

inquisitive /ɪŋ¹kwɪzɪ¹tɪv/. If you are **inquisitive**, you like asking a lot of questions and finding out about things, especially about other people. EG *...an inquisitive old man... He tried not to sound inquisitive.* ◊ **inquisitively**. EG *I glanced inquisitively through the open doorway.* ◊ **inquisitiveness**. EG *Her inquisitiveness surprised him.* ADJ QUALIT ⇑ curious = nosy, prying ◊ ADV WITH VB ◊ N UNCOUNT

inquisitor /ɪŋ¹kwɪzɪ¹tə/, **inquisitors**. An **inquisitor** is someone who asks questions in an inquisition. EG *The old man glared at him like an inquisitor.* N COUNT = interrogator

inquisitorial /ɪŋ¹kwɪzɪ¹tɔːrɪəl/. Someone or something that is **inquisitorial** asks questions, as if in an inquisition. EG *...an inquisitorial voice.* ADJ QUALIT ⇑ questioning

inroads /ɪnrəudz/. If something **makes inroads** into something or on something, it spreads and successfully takes time, money, votes, etc for itself and away from something else. EG *Computers will make significant inroads into these areas... My gambling has made great inroads on my savings.* PHR + A : VB INFLECTS

insalubrious /ɪnsəluːbrɪəs/. A place or climate that is **insalubrious** is likely to make you unhealthy; a formal word. EG *The site was surrounded by insalubrious swamps.* ADJ QUALIT = unwholesome

insane /ɪnseɪn/. 1 Someone who is **insane** has a mind that does not work in a normal way. This makes their behaviour very strange, so that often such people need to be cared for in an institution. **Insane** is a more formal word than 'mad'. EG *Pugin died insane at the age of forty... He was committed as insane.* ▸ The **insane** is used to refer to people who are insane. EG *...the criminally insane.* ADJ CLASSIF ⇑ ill = mad ▸ N PLURAL : *the* + N

2 **Insane** also means very foolish; an informal use. EG *This idea is totally insane... You'd be insane to let him have the final say.* ◊ **insanely**. EG *I was insanely jealous.* ADJ QUALIT ◊ ADV = madly

insanitary /ɪnsænɪtə⁰ri¹/. Something that is **insanitary** is so dirty that it is likely to have a bad effect on people's health. EG *They are living in insanitary conditions.* ADJ QUALIT = unhygienic

insanity /ɪnsænɪti¹/ is 1 the state of being insane. EG *...insanity due to disorders in the nervous system... He saw the beginnings of insanity in her.* 2 stupidity. EG *I had to laugh at the insanity of it all.* N UNCOUNT = madness N UNCOUNT = craziness

insatiable /ɪnseɪʃɪ⁰əbə⁰l/. A desire, greed, etc that is **insatiable** is unable to be satisfied. EG *...an insatiable curiosity... The desire for justice can be as insatiable as any other lust.* ▸ used of people. EG *The kids are insatiable.* ◊ **insatiably**. EG *She was insatiably curious.* ADJ CLASSIF ◊ ADV

inscribe /ɪnskraɪb/, **inscribes, inscribing, inscribed**. 1 If you **inscribe** words on an object or if you **inscribe** an object with words, you write or carve the words on the object. EG *The names of the dead were inscribed on the wall... ...a banner inscribed with verses from Isaiah... I found a silver wedding ring inscribed 'To My Darling'.* V+O, V+O+A (*with*), OR V+O+C : USU PASS

2 If you **inscribe** a book or **inscribe** something such as your name in a book, you write your name and perhaps a short message at the front of the book, especially when you are giving the book as a present. EG *I inscribed the book in Latin... Will you inscribe your names in it?* V+O : IF+PREP THEN *in*

inscription /ɪnskrɪpʃə⁰n/, **inscriptions**. An **inscription** is 1 something written by hand in the front of a book, especially when the book is a present. EG *Inside the front cover was an inscription: 'To Virginia from Helena'.* 2 writing carved into something made of stone or metal, such as a gravestone, monument, coin, or ring. EG *The inscription above the door was in English.* N COUNT = dedication N COUNT ⇑ carving

inscrutable /ɪnskruːtəbə⁰l/. Someone who is **inscrutable** is mysterious about what they are really thinking. EG *The candidates are pretty inscrutable.* ▸ used to describe expressions, remarks, etc. EG *...an inscrutable expression.* ADJ QUALIT

insect /ɪnsɛkt/, **insects**. An **insect** is a small animal that has six legs. Most insects have wings. Ants, flies, butterflies, and beetles are all insects. EG *Most frogs feed on insects... ...insect bites.* N COUNT

insecticide /ɪnsɛktɪsaɪd/, **insecticides**. **Insecticide** is a chemical substance that is used to kill insects that are a nuisance, for example because they eat crops. EG *...a cargo of insecticide... Many pests are resistant to the commoner insecticides.* N MASS ⇑ poison

insecure /ɪnsɪkjʊə/. 1 If you are **insecure**, you feel unsure of yourself and your abilities and doubt that other people still like or respect you. EG *We often feel insecure... They felt helpless, insecure, and incapable of handling the job.* ◊ **insecurity** /ɪnsɪ²kjʊərɪti¹/. EG *...feelings of insecurity.* ADJ QUALIT ⇑ uncertain ≠ confident, self-assured ◊ N UNCOUNT ⇑ uncertainty

2 Something that is **insecure** is not safe or well-protected and may be lost or taken over. EG *Her tenancy is insecure... The country was made insecure by border invasion...* ◊ **insecurity**. EG *She's faced with a high degree of job insecurity... ...financial insecurity.* ADJ QUALIT ⇑ unsafe ≠ secure ◊ N UNCOUNT : USU + SUPP = uncertainty

inseminate /ɪnsɛmɪneɪt/, **inseminates, inseminating, inseminated**. To **inseminate** a female animal means to put a male's sperm into her in order to make her pregnant. ◊ **insemination** /ɪnsɛmɪneɪʃə⁰n/. EG *...the artificial insemination of cows.* V+O ⇑ impregnate ◊ N UNCOUNT

insensible /ɪnsɛnsɪ¹bə⁰l/. 1 A person or animal that is **insensible** to a physical sensation is unable to feel it. EG *We believe that all animals should be rendered insensible to pain before slaughter.* ADJ CLASSIF : PRED, IF+PREP THEN *to*

2 Someone who is **insensible** to something that has happened is unaffected by it. ADJ QUALIT : PRED

3 Someone who is **insensible** of something that has happened is unaware of it. EG *She seemed wholly insensible of the honour done to her... ...children that lived and died insensible of their misery.* ADJ QUALIT : PRED, IF+PREP THEN *of*

insensitive /ɪnsɛnsɪtɪv/. 1 Someone who is **insensitive** is unaware of other people's feelings, and unable to see when they have upset or annoyed them; used showing disapproval. EG *...bad-mannered, loud, insensitive oafs... ...the insensitive attitude of the government.* ▸ used of people's behaviour and actions. EG *The population has grown restive over his often* ADJ QUALIT = uncaring ▸ = callous *insensitive policies.* ◊ **insensitivity** /ɪnsensɪtɪvɪti[1]/. EG *There were times when he showed a curious insensitivity and lack of tact.* ◊ N UNCOUNT = indifference

2 Someone who is **insensitive** to a situation or requirement is unaware of its importance and does not react to it. EG *People became insensitive to their own needs... He was insensitive to public opinion.* ADJ QUALIT+to

3 Someone who is **insensitive** to a physical sensation is unable to feel it. ◊ **insensitivity.** EG *...muscular insensitivity.* ADJ CLASSIF ◊ N UNCOUNT

inseparable /ɪnsepə⁰rəbə⁰l/. 1 People who are **inseparable** feel so close to each other that they always stay together. EG *They have struck up a strong friendship and are quite inseparable... The three were now an inseparable team.* ◊ **inseparably.** EG *Karen and Kitty had grown inseparably close.* ADJ QUALIT ◊ ADV

2 If one thing is **inseparable** from another, the things are so closely connected that they cannot be considered separately. EG *Culture is inseparable from class... The social and ecological costs are inseparable.* ◊ **inseparably.** EG *Their mode and place of residence is inseparably linked to their income and livelihood.* ADJ CLASSIF: IF+ PREP THEN *from* = indivisible ◊ ADV WITH VB

insert, inserts, inserting, inserted. The word **insert** is pronounced /ɪnsɜːt/ when it is a verb, and /ɪnsɜːt/ when it is a noun. 1 If you **insert** an object into something, you put the object inside it, usually in a place where it fits tightly. EG *He inserted the wooden peg into the hole... She removed the sheet of paper on which she had been typing and inserted a new one... Always insert plugs at right angles to the wall.* ◊ **insertion** /ɪnsɜːʃə⁰n/. EG *...the insertion of the peg.* V+O: USU+A ◊ N UNCOUNT/ COUNT

2 If you **insert** a comment in a piece of writing, speech, etc, you include it or add it as an extra comment. EG *The President inserted one unscripted item in his speech... He did not insert a penalty clause.* V+O = put in, add

3 An **insert** is something that is inserted somewhere, especially an advertisement on a piece of paper that is included loose between the pages of a book or magazine. EG *We have here some prescription inserts to help people to use medicine properly... ...supportive shoes with special inserts.* N COUNT

inset /ɪnset/. Something that is **inset** with a decoration, piece of material, etc has the decoration or material set inside it. EG *...gold or silver inset with gems... The eyes are alabaster ovals with inset pupils of ivory.* ADJ CLASSIF: IF+ PREP THEN *with*

inshore /ɪnʃɔː/. Something that is **inshore** is situated near a sea shore. EG *These fish are not found close inshore... We moved the bait inshore... ...the shallow waters of flat inshore areas.* ADV AFTER VB, OR ADJ CLASSIF: ATTRIB ≠ offshore

inside /ɪnsaɪd/, **insides.** 1 **Inside** is used to refer to 1.1 the part of something which is surrounded and often enclosed or hidden by the main part that you usually see. EG *It is a fruit with a seed inside... Dry the cup inside and out with a cloth... Two minutes later we were safely inside the taxi.* ▸ used as an adjective or noun. EG *He reached into his inside jacket pocket... The inside of my mouth was dry... The insides of aluminium pans often discolour.* 1.2 the part of a building which is surrounded by the walls of the building and covered by its roof. EG *'I have expected you,' she said, inviting him inside... Hey, you left your lighter inside... Fires were started inside and outside buildings.* ▸ used as an adjective or noun. EG *We haven't got an inside loo... He didn't lock the door from the inside.* ADV/PREP ≠ outside ▸ ADJ CLASSIF: ATTRIB, OR N COUNT ADV/PREP ≠ outside ▸ ADJ CLASSIF: ATTRIB, OR N COUNT

2 In informal English, someone who is **inside** is in prison. EG *After half a day inside, I felt as if I'd been there weeks... She runs an organization to provide bail for women inside.* ADV, OR ADJ CLASSIF: PRED ≠ outside

3 If you have food, drink, or something else **inside** you, it is present in your body, especially in your stomach. EG *He had to keep the food inside him if he was going to live... He left with several more glasses of brandy inside him... She inhaled deeply, and held the smoke inside her lungs for three or four seconds.* PREP/ADV

4 If you say that someone or something is **inside** a town, country, etc, you emphasize that they are situated or happening actually in the town or country and not outside it. EG *There are several thousand of these people now living inside France... There have been bombing raids up to 200 kilometres inside the country.* PREP ⇑ in ≠ outside

5 The **inside** of your arm or leg is the part of your arm which is closest to your body when your arms are by your sides, or the part of your leg which is closest to your other leg. EG *She shook a few drops of milk onto the inside of her wrist... The insides of his forearms are sore.* ▸ used as an adjective. EG *What's your inside leg measurement?* N COUNT: the+N +of ≠ outside ▸ ADJ CLASSIF: ATTRIB

6 An **inside** lane is 6.1 the lane on a large road which is nearest to the left in a country where you drive on the left, and nearest to the right in a country where you drive on the right. EG *All the lorries were in the inside lane.* ▸ used as a noun. EG *He overtook me on the inside.* 6.2 the lane on a circular racetrack which is nearest to the centre of the circle and therefore shorter in distance than the lanes next to it. EG *He had the inside lane.* ▸ used as a noun. EG *And now Ovett is coming up on the inside.* ADJ CLASSIF: ATTRIB = nearside ▸ N SING: the+N ADJ CLASSIF: ATTRIB ≠ outside ▸ N SING: the+N ≠ outside

7 **Inside** information is information which you gain because you are actually involved in a situation and therefore know more about it. EG *He was in a position to give valuable inside information... My journalist friends would tell me all the inside news that wasn't fit to print.* ADJ CLASSIF: ATTRIB ≠ outside

8 People who are **inside** a particular group or organization belong to the group or organization. EG *It was always safer, he explained, to have an affair inside the department... Do we want to stay inside the EEC?* PREP = within

9 If you do something **inside** a particular time or limit that is allowed, you do it without using more time, money, speed, etc than is allowed. EG *I was just inside the speed limit.* PREP = within

10 If you do something **inside** an amount of time specified, you do it before that amount of time has passed. EG *Inside three hours, we were back again.* ▸ **Inside of** is sometimes used in informal English. EG *We should be finished inside of three weeks.* PREP = in, within

11 If you have a particular feeling **inside** you, you have the feeling but do not express it to other people. EG *His true feelings keep surging up inside him... Fury continually rose inside me. I always felt inside that I wanted to write.* PREP/ADV

12 If you have an idea or thought **inside** your head, you are thinking it or remembering it. EG *They have a map of the game inside their heads.* PREP

13 When something such as a piece of clothing is **inside out**, it has the inside part of the clothing turned outside and the outside part turned inside, for example closest to your body if you are wearing it. EG *You're wearing that jumper inside out.* ● In informal English, if you say that you **know** someone or something **inside out**, you mean that you know them extremely well. PHR: USED AS C/ ● PHR: VB INFLECTS

14 The **insides** of a person or an animal are their internal organs, especially their stomach; an informal use. EG *We went to Danny's farm to collect the pig's insides... We all need a bit of something nice in our insides and then we'll feel much better.* N PLURAL: USU WITH POSS = innards

insider /ɪnsaɪdə/, **insiders.** An **insider** is someone who belongs to a particular organization or is involved in a particular situation and therefore knows more about it than other people. EG *According to one insider, the government is getting very worried.* N COUNT ≠ outsider

insidious /ɪnsɪdi¹əs/. A quality or activity that is **insidious** is unpleasant and develops gradually without being noticed. EG *The leaflets were a more insidious form of propaganda... ...this insidious kind of suppression.* ◊ **insidiously.** EG *I feel he might have an insidiously corrupting influence... The revolution is spreading insidiously throughout the land.* ADJ QUALIT = cunning ◊ ADV WITH VB

insight /ɪnsaɪt/, **insights.** If you gain **insight** or an **insight** into a complex situation or problem, you gain accurate and deep understanding of it. EG *The idea itself may arrive in a flash of insight... He has given me an insight into Russian literature... ...a number of interesting psychological insights.* N UNCOUNT/ COUNT

insignia /ɪnsɪgnɪə/. **Insignia** is both the singular and the plural form. An **insignia** is a badge or sign which officially shows that a person or object belongs to a particular group or organization. EG *...military insignia... ...a plane bearing the insignia of the Condor Legion.* N COUNT

insignificance /ɪnsɪgnɪfɪkəns/ is the quality of being insignificant. EG *The influence of the party was all but gone, and it dwindled into insignificance.* N UNCOUNT ≠ importance, significance

insignificant /ɪnsɪgnɪfɪkənt/. Something that is **insignificant** is unimportant, usually because it is very small in size, degree, or amount. EG *Even the* ADJ QUALIT *most insignificant part of the problem ought to be carefully considered... The proportion of Indian capital in the project was relatively insignificant... Who were these nationalists? Merely an insignificant minority.*

insincere /ɪnsɪnsɪə/. Someone who is **insincere** is not sincere; used showing disapproval. ▸ used of actions and behaviour. EG *...people whose admiration is extravagant and often insincere.* ◇ **insincerely**. EG *...bereaved women who exhibit their widowhood insincerely.* ◇ **insincerity** /ɪnsɪnsɛrɪti¹/, **insincerities**. EG *He does not have to go through all this insincerity and acting... ...the insincerities of diplomacy.* — ADJ QUALIT = hypocritical, deceitful; ◇ ADV; ◇ N UNCOUNT/COUNT = hypocrisy

insinuate /ɪnsɪnjuːeɪt/, **insinuates, insinuating, insinuated**. 1 If you **insinuate** that something is the case, you hint that it is the case in a very unpleasant way; used showing disapproval. EG *He insinuated that my wife had betrayed my trust in her... He destroyed the witness's character by insinuating base motives to his actions.* ◇ **insinuation** /ɪnsɪnjʊeɪʃ⁰n/, **insinuations**. EG *I decided to ignore his insinuations about my behaviour... Their years in Parliament had sharpened their wits and made them adept at insinuation.* — V+O/REPORT-CL = imply; ◇ N COUNT/UNCOUNT

2 If you **insinuate** yourself or something into a particular position, you manage slowly and cleverly to get yourself or the thing into that position; used showing disapproval. EG *He eventually insinuated himself into a key position in the Party... The past invariably insinuates itself into our present life... He wishes to insinuate suspicion and hatred into the mind of the people.* — V+O (REFL/NG) +A *(into)* = worm, install

insipid /ɪnsɪpɪd/. 1 Food or drink that is **insipid** has very little taste; used showing disapproval. EG *It may seem insipid and flavourless to an adult's tastes... ...gigantic insipid tomatoes, huge flavourless lettuces.* — ADJ QUALIT ⇑ tasteless

2 An **insipid** person or activity is dull and boring. EG *I used to find him insipid... ...boring insipid recorder-playing.* — ADJ QUALIT

insist /ɪnsɪst/, **insists, insisting, insisted**. 1 If you **insist** that something must be done or that something is the case, you say this very firmly and refuse to give in, even though other people disagree with you. EG *She insisted that Jim must leave or she would call the police... 'But you know that she's innocent,' the girl insisted. 'You must help her.'... What have you been doing? I insist you tell me.* — V+REPORT-CL/QUOTE, OR V+A *(on)*

2 If you **insist** on doing something or receiving something, you firmly ask for it or ask to do it and refuse to give in or accept anything else. EG *He insisted on paying for the meal... Most universities insist on an interview before they accept a student... I insisted on a contract that gave me some sort of security.* — V+A *(on)* ⇑ demand

insistence /ɪnsɪstəns/ is a person's act of insisting that something must be done. EG *He went inside the house at Jean's insistence... He has long angered the Government with his insistence on minority rights.* — N UNCOUNT : IF+PREP THEN *on* ⇑ resolution

insistent /ɪnsɪstənt/. 1 Someone who is **insistent** keeps insisting that something must be done. EG *He was insistent that we should have a drink.* ▸ used of people's actions and behaviour. EG *There have been insistent demands that more should be done to provide for poor families.* ◇ **insistently**. EG *No-one has spoken more insistently on the subject of education than her.* — ADJ QUALIT ⇑ resolute; ▸ ⇑ resolute; ◇ ADV WITH VB ⇑ resolutely

2 An **insistent** noise keeps going on for a long time and demanding attention. EG *She was startled by the unexpected and insistent ringing of the telephone.* — ADJ QUALIT ⇑ constant

in situ /ɪn sɪtjuː/ is used to describe something that remains in its original or appropriate place while work is done on it; a formal expression. EG *They will carry out further analysis in situ... ...an in situ investigator.* — ADV AFTER VB, OR ADJ CLASSIF

insofar as /ɪnsə⁶fɑːr ə³z/ is used to introduce a clause in which you mention something that is relevant to the truth of the preceding or following statement, for example something that gives its extent or that gives a reason for it. EG *I wanted to see where Miss Head's line of thought–and mine insofar as I had taken her as my mentor–was leading... ...contemptuous of the traditional culture, except insofar as it provided precious metals.* — CONJ SUBORD

insole /ɪnsəʊl/, **insoles**. The **insole** of a shoe is the soft layer of material inside it, which the sole of your foot rests on. — N COUNT

insolence /ɪnsələns/ is behaviour that is insolent. EG *I was taken to Mother Superior for my insolence.* — N UNCOUNT ⇑ rudeness

insolent /ɪnsələnt/. Someone who is **insolent** is very rude or impolite. EG *...a nasty common little man, obsequious but also insolent.* ▸ used of a person's actions or behaviour. EG *...an insolent remark.* — ADJ QUALIT impudent

insoluble /ɪnsɒljə⁴bə⁰l/. An **insoluble** problem is so difficult that it is impossible to solve. EG *The problems confronting this country are insoluble within the framework of the parliamentary system.* — ADJ CLASSIF

insolvency /ɪnsɒlvənsi¹/ is the state of a person or organization that does not have enough money to pay their debts. EG *The bank had forced him into insolvency.* — N UNCOUNT = bankruptcy

insolvent /ɪnsɒlvənt/. A person or organization that is **insolvent** does not have enough money to pay their debts. EG *He revealed that he was insolvent by 1.2m pounds.* — ADJ CLASSIF = bankrupt

insomnia /ɪnsɒmnɪə/. Someone who suffers from **insomnia** finds it difficult to sleep. — N UNCOUNT

insomniac /ɪnsɒmnɪ¹æk/, **insomniacs**. An **insomniac** is a person who finds it difficult to sleep. — N COUNT

insouciance /ɪnsuːsɪəns/ is lack of concern shown by a person; a literary word. EG *She smiled and shook her head with pert insouciance.* — N UNCOUNT = unconcern

insouciant /ɪnsuːsɪənt/. An **insouciant** action or quality shows a lack of concern; a literary word. EG *...sitting side-saddle in the most dashing and insouciant style.* — ADJ QUALIT = careless

Insp. is an abbreviation for 'Inspector'. EG *...Det. Chief Insp. Wallace.* — N IN TITLES

inspect /ɪnspɛkt/, **inspects, inspecting, inspected**. 1 If you **inspect** something, you look at every part of it carefully in order to find out about it or check that it is all right. EG *She inspected his scalp for ticks... She mended the wire, and then held it up to the light to inspect the results.* ◇ **inspection** /ɪnspɛkʃ⁰n/, **inspections**. EG *Closer inspection revealed sea cucumbers among the rocks.* — V+O = examine; ◇ N UNCOUNT/COUNT = investigation

2 When an official **inspects** a place or a group of people, they visit it and look at it carefully in order to find out whether regulations are being obeyed. EG *The fire prevention branch of the Fire Brigade inspects factories and all sorts of public buildings.* ◇ **inspection**. EG *...carrying out a medical inspection of the kitchen.* — V+O = survey; ◇ N COUNT/UNCOUNT = examination

inspector /ɪnspɛktə/, **inspectors**. An **inspector** is 1 a person, usually employed by a government agency, who finds out whether individuals or organizations are obeying official regulations, for example health and safety regulations in a work place. EG *...the factory inspector... The inspector's report was released to the public.* 2 an officer in the police force who is higher in rank than a sergeant and lower in rank than a superintendent; also used as a title before their surname. EG *...Inspector Flint.* — N COUNT; N COUNT : ALSO IN TITLES

inspectorate /ɪnspɛktə⁰rə¹t/, **inspectorates**. An **inspectorate** is a group of inspectors who are employed to work on the same issue or area. EG *...the Nuclear Inspectorate's report on a leak of radioactive waste...* — N COUNT : ALSO IN NAMES AFTER N

inspector of taxes, inspectors of taxes. An **inspector of taxes** is a person who is employed by the government to calculate the amount of tax that people should pay. — N COUNT = tax collector

inspiration /ɪnspɪreɪʃ⁰n/, **inspirations**. 1 If you get **inspiration** from someone or something, you get new ideas from them which make you enthusiastic and encourage you to do something. EG *I have derived inspiration from Freud... Nationalists in the colonial countries drew inspiration from outside.* — N UNCOUNT

2 Someone or something that is the **inspiration** for a particular piece of work, theory, etc is the thing that provides new ideas and acts as a model for the work. EG *China has been the inspiration for a new and distinct ideological growth in the West... He was later to become the inspiration for the American comic strip character, Superman.* — N SING : *the*+N, USU+*for* ⇑ influence

3 If you suddenly get **inspiration** or an **inspiration,** you suddenly think of an idea of what to do or say. EG *I had an inspiration–why not take them all to the beach?... He paused, searching for inspiration.* — N UNCOUNT/COUNT

inspirational /ɪnspɪreɪʃə⁰nəl, -ʃənə⁰l/. Something that is **inspirational** provides you with inspiration. EG *The book was of the greatest inspirational value.* — ADJ CLASSIF

inspire /ɪnspaɪə/, **inspires, inspiring, inspired**. 1 If someone or something **inspires** you to — V+O, OR V+O+

do something, they make you want to do it by giving you new ideas and the enthusiasm to carry them out. EG *Not even Churchill's vision could inspire the Party to reform... They were in too gloomy a mood to be inspired by his enthusiasm... The strikes appear to be politically inspired... Pizzaro had the example of Cortes to inspire and guide him.* — TO-INF = fire, encourage

2 Someone or something that **inspires** a particular emotion or reaction in people makes them feel this emotion or reaction. EG *He had the assured voice of a man who inspired confidence in women... Successful officers have the capacity to lead others, to inspire respect in their followers.* — V+O : IF+PREP THEN *in*

inspired /ɪnspaɪəd/. 1 Someone who is **inspired** is influenced by inspiration. EG *As an architect, he was an inspired amateur.* — ADJ QUALIT ⇑ brilliant

2 Something that is **inspired** is produced or caused by inspiration. EG *...works of inspired beauty.* — ADJ QUALIT

3 An **inspired** guess or idea is very clever and accurate. EG *I think I can make an inspired guess... Many people prefer mathematical probabilities to inspired guess-work.* — ADJ QUALIT

inspiring /ɪnspaɪərɪŋ/. Something or someone that is **inspiring** is exciting and makes you feel enthusiastic and interested. EG *It was an inspiring occasion... Every line on their face tells a story. It's so inspiring for an artist.* — ADJ QUALIT

inst. 1 You write **inst.** as an abbreviation for 'instant' in formal letters to refer to the current month. EG *Thank you for your letter of 28th inst.*

2 **Inst.** is an abbreviation for 'Institute'; used as part of the name of a particular institute. EG *...Inst. of Archaeology.*

instability /ɪnstəbɪlɪti[1]/, **instabilities**. **Instability** or an **instability** is a lack of stability in a place or situation. EG *Various signs of political instability began to appear.* — N UNCOUNT/COUNT ⇑ vulnerability

install /ɪnstɔːl/, **installs, installing, installed**.
1 If you **install** a machine or other large object in a particular place, you put it there so that it is ready to be used. EG *We have just installed central heating... They had installed hidden microphones in the house.* — V+O, OR V+O+A ⇑ fit

2 If you **install** someone in an important job or position, you officially give them the job or position. EG *As head of the department he installed a young man named Briceland... ...the ceremony which installed a new Vice-President.* — V+O, OR V+O+A ⇑ appoint

3 If you **install** yourself in a particular place, you settle there and make yourself comfortable; a formal use. EG *He installed himself in an armchair and spent the afternoon watching the snooker on TV... By now he was installed at number 7 New King Street.* — V+O (REFL): USU+A

installation /ɪnstəleɪʃə⁰n/, **installations**. 1 An **installation** is 1.1 a place that has been specially built by the army, navy, or air force to contain people or equipment. EG *...missile installations... ...installations as big as cities.* — N COUNT ⇑ base = depot. 1.2 a place that contains equipment and machinery which are being used for a particular purpose. EG *...North Sea oil and gas installations... ...hydro-electric installations.* — N COUNT ⇑ plant

2 The **installation** of a piece of equipment is the act of putting it into place and making it ready for use. EG *...the installation of the colour TV.* — N UNCOUNT : USU +SUPP

3 The **installation** of a person in an important job or position is the event or ceremony in which they officially start their new job. EG *Not long after his installation as rector at Edinburgh, he appeared on TV.* — N UNCOUNT : USU +SUPP

instalment /ɪnstɔːlmə²nt/, **instalments**; also spelled **installment** in American English. 1 If you pay for something in **instalments**, you pay small sums of money at regular intervals over a period of time, rather than paying the whole amount at once. EG *I paid one hundred dollars in four monthly instalments of twenty-five dollars.* — N COUNT = payment

2 An **instalment** of a story, plan, etc is one of its parts that are published or carried out separately one after the other. EG *...the first instalment of a plan.* — N COUNT

instance /ɪnstəns/, **instances**. 1 You use **for instance** when you want to mention a particular event, situation, person, etc that illustrates the subject that you are discussing or the point that you are making. EG *I mean for instance a man like Tom... Take advertising for instance... For instance, an electric fire is a relatively expensive method of heating a room.* — PHR : USED AS ADV SEN = for example, say

2 An **instance** is a particular example or occurrence of an event, situation, person, etc. EG *There are numerous instances of family rifts and angry scenes... I do not think that in this instance the doctor was right... Pollock was an extreme instance, but his failure epitomizes that of many.* — N COUNT = case
● You say **in the first instance** to mention something that is the first step in a series of actions. EG *The library will supply a list of addresses to which you should apply in the first instance... They have to help themselves at least in the first instance.* — ● PHR : USED AS AN A ⇑ initially
● If you do something **at someone's instance**, you do it because they have ordered or requested you to do it; a formal expression. EG *They switched to this location at the urgent instance of the Commander in Chief.* — ● PHR : USED AS AN A

instant /ɪnstənt/, **instants**. 1 If you do something for an **instant**, you do it for an extremely short period of time, for example a second. EG *Bal hesitated for an instant... It was all gone in a single instant... An instant later his body was banging against the side of the boat.* — N COUNT : USU SING ⇑ moment
● If you say that something must be done **this instant**, you mean that it must be done immediately. EG *Take it out this instant.* — ● PHR : USED AS AN A = at once
● In a story, **'the next instant'** is used to say that one event happens immediately after another. EG *The next instant I heard her.* — ● PHR : USED AS AN A

2 If you say that something happened at a particular **instant**, you refer to the actual moment at which it happened. EG *They saw a man who caught sight of them at the same instant... At that instant, an angry buzzing began... ...at the very instant of triumph.* — N SING+SUPP : WITH DET
● If you do something **the instant** something else happens, you do it as soon as it happens. EG *She must have dashed out the instant I grabbed the phone.* — ● CONJ SUBORD ⇑ when

3 **Instant** is used 3.1 to describe a result, situation, or event that happens immediately without any delay. EG *Herschel did not have instant success... This will allow instant access to relevant data.* — ADJ CLASSIF = immediate ◊ **instantly**. EG *He was killed instantly... 'I think it stinks,' I replied and instantly regretted it.* — ◊ ADV = at once 3.2 to describe food or some other product that is manufactured in such a way that you can make it ready for eating or using with very little time or effort, for example by just adding water. EG *...instant coffee that tasted like hot disinfectant... ...instant curries or chop suey.* — ADJ CLASSIF

instantaneous /ɪnstənteɪnɪəs/. Something that is **instantaneous** happens immediately and very quickly. EG *She had the instantaneous certainty that it must be Boylan downstairs.* — ADJ CLASSIF ◊ **instantaneously**. EG *We recognize whole groups of words instantaneously.* — ◊ ADV

instead /ɪnsted/. 1 You use **instead** to say that something is done in place of something else that you have mentioned, or that one thing is true rather than something else that you have mentioned. EG *Judy did not answer. Instead she looked out of the taxi window... Robert had a great desire to turn away from her but instead he took her and led her towards the house... We must abandon our dependence on conventional fossil fuels and instead move over to a hydrogen-based economy.* — ADV SEN

2 You use **instead of** to introduce something which is not done or not true when you contrast this with something else which is done or is true. EG *I'm tired of sleeping in the mud instead of a nice, warm bed... If you want to have your meal at seven o'clock instead of five o'clock, you can... Instead of putting it down here we'll put it up there.* — PREP = as opposed to

instep /ɪnstep/, **insteps**. Your **instep** is the middle part of your foot, where it curves upwards. ▸ also used of the part of a shoe which covers this part of your foot. EG *She took off her shoe and looked at the name in the instep.* — N COUNT

instigate /ɪnstɪgeɪt/, **instigates, instigating, instigated**. Someone who **instigates** an event or situation causes it to happen by their own effort or work. EG *Sir Ernest Cassel instigated the Anglo-German talks of 1912... It would not prove worthwhile to instigate a nuclear attack.* — V+O = initiate ◊ **instigation** /ɪnstɪgeɪʃə⁰n/. EG *A series of court cases have been brought at the instigation of a former MP, Raymond Blackburn.* — ◊ N UNCOUNT

instigator /ɪnstɪgeɪtə/, **instigators**. The **instigator** of an event or situation is the person who instigates it. EG *The instigator of the plot was Colonel Fletcher... The instigators of the monstrous violence we see all around us must be found.* — N COUNT ⇑ cause = author, agent

instil /ɪnstɪl/, **instils, instilling, instilled**. American English also uses the spellings **instill, instills**. If you **instil** an idea or feeling into someone, you make them feel it or think it, usually gradually. EG *I consider it important to instil a pride in the players... The presence of the guard was supposed to instil awe and fear in us.* — V+O: USU+*in/into* = inculcate

instinct /ɪnstɪŋkt/, **instincts**. 1 The **instinct** of a person or an animal is a natural tendency that they have to behave or react in a particular way without the need for thought or planning. EG *Some fundamental instinct for survival welded them together... In a game like ours one begins to trust one's instincts... The infant starts to learn rather than merely act out of instinct... ...the maternal instinct.* ● See also **killer instinct**. — N COUNT/UNCOUNT ↑ feeling = impulse, urge

2 If it is your **instinct** to do something, this is the course of action that naturally occurs to you to take in reaction to a particular event or situation. EG *My first instinct was to resign... Your instinct may be to smack him on the wrist... It's my natural instinct not to inquire too closely into the matter.* — N SING: USU POSS +N+*to*-INF ↑ inclination

3 **Instinct** is a feeling that you have that something is the case, rather than an opinion or idea based on facts. EG *She knew, by instinct, that he wouldn't come back... Your instinct is correct.* — N UNCOUNT = intuition

instinctive /ɪnstɪŋk⁰tɪv/. An **instinctive** feeling, action, or idea is one that someone has or does naturally rather than one which is based on reasons or facts. EG *Brody took an instant instinctive dislike to the man... My instinctive reaction was to take a couple of rapid steps backwards.* ◇ **instinctively**. EG *Charles instinctively understood I wanted to be alone.* — ADJ CLASSIF ↑ irrational; ◇ ADV WITH VB = intuitively

instinctual /ɪnstɪŋk⁰tjʊ⁰əl/. An **instinctual** feeling, action, or idea is an **instinctive** one. EG *...instinctual impulses.* — ADJ CLASSIF

institute /ɪnstɪtju:t/, **institutes, instituting, instituted**. 1 An **institute** is an organization set up to do a particular type of work, especially research or teaching. EG *I visited a number of research institutes in Asia... ...John Edmond of the Massachusetts Institute of Technology... ...the British Film Institute.* ▸ used of the building where the work of such an organization is done. EG *...standing outside the Institute for Contemporary Studies.* — N COUNT: ALSO IN NAMES

2 If you **institute** a system, rule, or course of action, you start it or bring it in; a formal use. EG *The Director of Public Prosecutions may institute proceedings against them... Mr Wilson was in Opposition when the scheme was instituted.* — V+O = take up

institution /ɪnstɪtju:ʃə⁰n/, **institutions**. 1 An **institution** is 1.1 something such as a custom or a system that is considered an important or typical feature of a particular society or group, usually because it has existed for a long time. EG *She had no objections to the institution of marriage as such... They adopted western culture, institutions, and even clothing.* — N COUNT ↑ practice 1.2 a large important organization of a particular type mentioned, for example a university, bank, or church. EG *These universities accept lower grades than the more prestigious institutions... ...financial institutions... ...institutions (typically trade unions) which control the supply of labour.* — N COUNT: ALSO IN NAMES 1.3 a building where certain people are kept or looked after, for example people who are mentally ill or children who have no parents. EG *He may end up in a mental institution... This has given children in institutions a better chance of being adopted.* — N COUNT ↑ place = home

2 The **institution** of a new system is the act of starting it or bringing it in. EG *The institution of life peerages has quickened proceedings in the House of Lords considerably.* — N UNCOUNT: USU WITH POSS = establishment

institutional /ɪnstɪtju:ʃə⁰nəl, -ʃnə⁰l/. 1 **Institutional** means 1.1 relating to a large organization, for example a university, bank, or church. EG *He had no institutional education beyond high school.* — ADJ CLASSIF: ATTRIB 1.2 relating to a building where people are kept or looked after. EG *The child has been in institutional care for many years.* — ADJ CLASSIF: ATTRIB

2 An **institutional** value, quality, etc is considered an important and typical feature of a particular society or group, usually because it has existed for a long time. — ADJ CLASSIF: ATTRIB

institutionalize /ɪnstɪtju:ʃə⁰nəlaɪz/, **institutionalizes, institutionalizing, institutionalized**; also spelled **institutionalise** . 1 If you **institutionalize** someone, you put them in an institution, for example a hospital for people who are mentally ill or a home for children with no parents. Being institutionalized can affect a person's personality, so that they are not very good at looking after themselves. EG *His wife persuaded him to institutionalize his ageing mother.* ◇ **institutionalized**. EG *Philip has been institutionalized since birth... ...institutionalized children.* — V+O; ◇ ADJ CLASSIF

2 To **institutionalize** something means to establish it as part of a social system or other organization. EG *What is required is a means of institutionalizing the new power of labour.* ◇ **institutionalized**. EG *...institutionalized religion.* — V+O ↑ organize; ◇ ADJ CLASSIF ↑ organized

3 If a custom or a system becomes **institutionalized**, it becomes an important and typical feature of a society or group, usually because it has existed for a long time. EG *Disco is becoming an institutionalized part of contemporary youth culture.* — ADJ CLASSIF ↑ establish

instruct /ɪnstrʌkt/, **instructs, instructing, instructed**. 1 If you **instruct** someone to do something, you tell them to do it in a formal or severe way. EG *'Breathe in,' he instructed her... I've been instructed to take you to London.* — V+O+QUOTE/*to*-INF/REPORT-CL = direct, order

2 Someone who **instructs** people in a subject or skill teaches them about it by giving factual information or by explaining how to do something. — V OR V+O

instruction /ɪnstrʌkʃə⁰n/, **instructions**. 1 An **instruction** is something that someone tells you or orders you to do. EG *I disagree with what I am doing but it is an instruction, so I will carry it out.* — N COUNT = directive, order

2 **Instruction** in a subject or skill is teaching that someone gives you in it. — N UNCOUNT

3 **Instructions** are clear and detailed information on how to do something, especially in written form. EG *Read the instructions before you switch on the engine... ...the manufacturers' instruction book.* — N PLURAL

instructive /ɪnstrʌktɪv/. Something that is **instructive** gives useful information. EG *His seminars were instructive and illuminating occasions.* — ADJ QUALIT = informative

instructor /ɪnstrʌktə/, **instructors**. An **instructor** is a person who teaches you, especially in a practical activity such as driving or skiing. EG *...a Swiss ski instructor.* — N COUNT ↑ teacher

instrument /ɪnstrə⁴mə²nt/, **instruments**. 1 An **instrument** is 1.1 a tool or device that is used to do a particular task. EG *...surgical instruments... ...instruments of torture.* — N COUNT 1.2 an object such as a piano, guitar, or violin, which you play in order to produce music. EG *Do you play any other instrument besides the trumpet?* ● See also **stringed instrument, wind instrument**. — N COUNT = musical instrument 1.3 a device that is used for making measurements of something such as speed, air pressure, height, or sound. Cars and aircraft have instruments which display measurements of the speed, fuel available, engine temperature, etc, to the driver or pilot. EG *...precision measuring instruments... ...the co-pilot watching a panel of instruments.* — N COUNT

2 A person, system, or organization that is an **instrument** for achieving a particular aim is used by people as a way of achieving that aim. EG *The Labour Party is the only instrument of change open to them... Incomes policy is a weak instrument for reducing inflation in the long term... The schools have been patent instruments of westernization among the young.* — N COUNT+SUPP ↑ method = means

instrumental /ɪnstrə⁴mentə⁰l/. 1 Someone or something that is **instrumental** in a process or development has a very important function in it. EG *As financial director he was instrumental in supervising several takeover bids... Being very instrumental in post-war political affairs, they had their way... They took an instrumental role in the formation of Britain's first such organization.* — ADJ QUALIT = significant

2 **Instrumental** music is performed by instruments and not by voices. EG *Thereafter, he played only instrumental music... ...instrumental patterns very similar to the late sixties Stones material.* — ADJ CLASSIF ≠ vocal

instrumentalist /ɪnstrə⁴mentə⁰lɪst/, **instrumentalists**. An **instrumentalist** is a person who plays a musical instrument. — N COUNT ↑ performer

instrumentation /ɪnstrə⁴mə²nteɪʃə⁰n/ is 1 a group or collection of instruments, usually ones that are part of the same machine. EG *...car radios, instrumentation, and various types of ornamentation.* — N UNCOUNT ↑ devices 2 a list of the musical instruments that are required to perform a particular piece of music. — N UNCOUNT = orchestration

instrument panel, instrument panels. An **instrument panel** is the panel in a car, aircraft, or motor boat that holds the dials and switches. N COUNT = dashboard

insubordinate /ɪnsəbɔːdɪnət/. Someone who is **insubordinate** is disobedient; a formal word. ▸ used of a person's behaviour or actions. EG *...to punish insubordinate behaviour.* ◇ **insubordination** /ɪnsəbɔːdɪneɪʃəⁿn/. EG *Failure to work overtime was punishable as insubordination.* ADJ QUALIT = rebellious ◇ N UNCOUNT = rebellion

insubstantial /ɪnsəbstænʃəⁿl/. Something that is **insubstantial** is not very large, solid, or strong. EG *Lynn's shoulders were bony and insubstantial... ...a feathery, insubstantial plant... ...slender and insubstantial structures.* ADJ QUALIT ⇑ small = frail, fragile

insufferable /ɪnsʌʃəⁿrəbəⁿl/. If you find someone or something **insufferable**, they are so unpleasant or annoying that you cannot bear them or accept them. EG *He was becoming an insufferable pest with his stealing... Housework was insufferable.* ◇ **insufferably**. EG *We've all behaved insufferably.* ADJ CLASSIF = unbearable ◇ ADV WITH VB

insufficiency /ɪnsəfɪʃənsi¹/ is the state of something not being large enough in amount for a particular purpose. EG *...fighting against economic insufficiency... ...an insufficiency of Vitamin C in the diet.* N UNCOUNT = dearth, paucity

insufficient /ɪnsəfɪʃənt/. Something that is **insufficient** is not large enough in amount for a particular purpose. EG *Insufficient research has been done... Our information is insufficient for us to make judgements.* ◇ **insufficiently**. EG *He felt insufficiently supported in his aim and resigned.* ADJ CLASSIF : IF + PREP/VB THEN *for/to*-INF = inadequate ◇ ADV

insular /ɪnsjə⁴lə/. Someone who is **insular** is unwilling to meet new people or to consider new ideas; used showing disapproval. EG *He lived a rather insular life.... People who stay in one place all their lives are not necessarily insular or bigoted.* ◇ **insularity** /ɪnsjə⁴lærɪti¹/. EG *Cynicism and insularity had long been major barriers to my lasting peace.* ADJ QUALIT ⇑ isolated = withdrawn ◇ N UNCOUNT = detachment

insulate /ɪnsjə⁴leɪt/, **insulates, insulating, insulated.** 1 If you **insulate** a person or group from the rest of society or from outside influences, you separate them from the society or influences, either in order to protect them or in order to prevent them from communicating with others. EG *The leaders were able to insulate the local population from these dangerous influences... No country can insulate itself from the affairs of others.* V+O (NG/REFL): IF + PREP THEN *from/against* = shelter, segregate

2 If material such as feathers, fur, or foam **insulates** a place or body, it keeps it warm by covering it or surrounding it in a thick layer. EG *The function of a mammal's hair coat is to insulate the body... Duck down is used in sleeping bags and has good insulating quality... ...foam ceiling tiles to insulate a room... They moved to better insulated accommodation.* V+O ⇑ protect

3 If you **insulate** a tool or other object, you cover it with rubber, plastic, etc in order to prevent electricity passing through it and giving the person using it an electric shock. EG *Insulate the copper so that there can be no flow of electricity... ...two small electrical screwdrivers with insulated handles.* ◇ **insulating**. EG *She closed the slit with a strip of black insulating tape.* V+O ◇ ADJ CLASSIF : ATTRIB

insulation /ɪnsjə⁴leɪʃəⁿn/ is 1 separation of a person or group from the rest of society or from outside influences. EG *...an era of increasing insulation of elites from other people.* 2 a thick warm layer of something such as feathers, fur, or foam, which keeps a place or an animal's body warm. EG *Birds' feathers originally developed from reptilian scales to provide insulation. ...a long roll of roof insulation.* N UNCOUNT = segregation; N UNCOUNT ⇑ protection

insulator /ɪnsjə⁴leɪtə/, **insulators.** An **insulator** is material that insulates something. EG *Few substances can equal fur as an insulator.* N COUNT : USU SING

insulin /ɪnsjə⁴lɪn/ is a substance that most people produce naturally in their body and which controls the level of sugar in their blood. People with diabetes cannot produce insulin and have to take regular doses of it. N UNCOUNT

insult, insults, insulting, insulted. The word **insult** is pronounced /ɪnsʌlt/ when it is a verb, and /ɪnsʌlt/ when it is a noun. 1 If you **insult** someone, you offend them by doing something rude, usually by speaking rudely to them. EG *You don't have to apologize to me. You didn't insult me... He feels deeply insulted.* ◇ **insulting**. EG *He did use insulting language.* ◇ **insultingly**. EG *Men talked insultingly to women telephonists.* V+O = affront ◇ ADJ QUALIT ◇ ADV = offensively

2 An **insult** is something that a person does to you that offends you, usually something rude that they say to you. EG *He made the usual insults about her cooking... The older boys yelled out insults... I would take it as an insult if you left... It was an insult to the audience's intelligence.* ● You say **'to add insult to injury'** to mention something that adds to the damage that has already been done to a situation or to your feelings. EG *To add insult to injury, the penalty was awarded to the other side... It's bad enough being told that you're wrong. But when the upstart is a child it simply adds insult to injury.* N COUNT = affront ● PHR : VB INFLECTS

insuperable /ɪnsjⁿuːpəⁿrəbəⁿl/. A problem that is **insuperable** cannot be dealt with successfully. EG *He was forced to admit that the problems were insuperable.* ADJ CLASSIF = insurmountable

insupportable /ɪnsəpɔːtəbəⁿl/. If you find someone or something **insupportable**, they are so unpleasant that you cannot bear them or accept them. EG *Accusations of that kind are quite insupportable... The strain would be insupportable.* ADJ CLASSIF ⇑ unbearable = intolerable

insurance /ɪnʃʊərəns, -ʃɔː-/, **insurances.** 1 **Insurance** is 1.1 an agreement in which you pay a fixed amount of money each year to a special company as a means of protection for something, for example your house, car, or health. If something happens to your house or car, or if you become ill, the company pays you a sum of money. EG *You will need your driving licence and car insurance certificate... ...private health insurance... ...insurance companies.* ● See also **national insurance.** 1.2 the amount of money which you pay to a company in order to obtain insurance, or the amount of money which a company pays to you if you have an accident, become ill, etc. EG *He gave me £65 a year towards car repairs and insurance... The holiday costs fifty nine pounds plus insurance and airport taxes.* N UNCOUNT; N UNCOUNT = premium

2 If you do something as an **insurance** against something unpleasant happening, you do it in order to protect yourself in case it happens, or in order to prevent it from happening. EG *Nomads overstock their land as an insurance against drought... These measures are believed to be a good insurance against disorder.* N COUNT + *against*

insurance policy, insurance policies. An **insurance policy** is a written agreement which you sign in order to insure someone or something. EG *We must find out if there is any insurance policy covering the mortgage.* N COUNT

insure /ɪnʃʊə, -ʃɔː/, **insures, insuring, insured.** 1 If you **insure** someone or something, you protect them by having an agreement with an insurance company to pay them money regularly so that, if there is an accident or if someone is ill, the company will pay the amount of money necessary for repairs, medical treatment, etc. EG *Insure your baggage before you leave home.* ◇ **insured**. EG *The house is not insured against fire... All members of the film cast and crew are insured.* V+O (NG/REFL) ◇ ADJ CLASSIF : PRED

2 If you do something to **insure** against something unpleasant happening, you do it in order to protect yourself in case it happens, or in order to prevent it from happening. EG *During years of good rainfall the people expand their stocks to insure against drought.* V+A *(against)*

3 To **insure** that something will happen means the same as to ensure that it will happen; used in American English. EG *The long-term consolidation of party power is further insured by the building of a youth movement.* V+O/REPORT-CL

insurer /ɪnʃʊərə, -ʃɔː-/, **insurers.** An **insurer** is a company that sells insurance. N COUNT

insurgent /ɪnsɜːdʒənt/, **insurgents.** An **insurgent** group of people is a group who are fighting against the government or army of their own country, usually because they want a different system of government. EG *...propaganda campaigns by politically insurgent groups.* ▸ used as a noun to refer to a member of such a group. EG *...insurgents partially damaged the embassy.* ADJ CLASSIF : ATTRIB ⇑ rebellious = mutinous ▸ N COUNT : USU PL = rebel

insurmountable /ɪnsəmaʊntəbəⁿl/. A problem that is **insurmountable** is so great that it cannot be dealt with successfully. EG *One problem emerged as virtually insurmountable... ...adults for whom learning to read and write seemed an insurmountable barrier.* ADJ CLASSIF = insuperable

insurrection /ɪnsərɛkʃəⁿn/, **insurrections.** An **insurrection** is violent action that is taken by a large N COUNT/ UNCOUNT group of people against the rulers of their country, usually in order to change the system of government. EG *We are not prepared for an armed insurrection.*

int. is an abbreviation for 'internal' or for 'international'.

intact /ɪntækt/. Something that is **intact** is complete and has not been damaged or changed. EG *We found fossils of lobsters with even their finest antennae intact... They are fighting to keep village life intact.* ADJ QUALIT : USU PRED ⇑ whole = undamaged

intake /ɪnteɪk/, **intakes**. 1 A person's **intake** of food, drink, air etc is the process of taking the substance into their body, usually through their mouth or nose; often used to talk about the amount that they take in. EG *High sugar intake was not the only villain... ...oxygen intake.* N UNCOUNT + SUPP ● If you have an **intake of breath**, you breathe in quickly and deeply, often when you are shocked at something. EG *There is an intake of breath and some of us look at each other.* ● PHR : USED AS O

2 The **intake** of an institution or organization is the number of people or things that are accepted into it at a particular time. EG *...the army's huge emergency intake of soldiers... We will have to reduce this year's intake of trainees.* N COUNT : USU SING + SUPP

intangible /ɪntændʒɪbəˡl/. A quality or idea that is **intangible** is not clear enough or definite enough for you to see, feel, or notice easily. EG *...a vast and intangible subject.* ADJ QUALIT = imponderable

integer /ɪntɪdʒə/, **integers**. An **integer** is an exact whole number such as 1, 7, 24, etc as opposed to a number with fractions or decimals; a technical term in mathematics. N COUNT ≠ fraction

integral /ɪntɪ²grəl/. Something that is an **integral** part of a whole thing is an essential part of the whole thing. EG *It is a democratic party and an integral part of British politics and society... The Young Socialists were to be an integral feature of the Labour movement... Bus and underground are integral to experience of London.* ADJ CLASSIF : IF + PREP THEN *to* = intrinsic

integrate /ɪntɪ²greɪt/, **integrates, integrating, integrated**. 1 If you **integrate** someone into a social group, or if they **integrate** into it, they become part of the whole group. EG *He took pains to integrate me into the group... Local organizations play an important part in helping the individual integrate quickly into the community.* V-ERG + A *(into)* ⇑ incorporate ◇ **integration** /ɪntɪ²greɪʃəⁿn/. EG *He campaigned for the integration of immigrants into British society.* ◇ N UNCOUNT + *into*

2 If a person or group **integrates** with other people or groups in society, they mix with them and join in the life of the community. EG *A good citizen is one who is willing to integrate with workers, peasants, and soldiers... I would think that when immigrants have been here for some years they would begin to integrate somewhat.* V-ERG : ALSO V OR V + A *(with)* : RECIP ⇑ associate ◇ **integration**. EG *...the forcible integration of the races in schools... All members of the party were committed to the idea of European integration.* ◇ N UNCOUNT

3 If you **integrate** things, you combine them so that they are closely linked or they form part of a whole idea or system. EG *...a good teacher of juniors who can supervise and integrate their work and activities... The two regional railway systems were integrated... In Europe, arable and livestock farming were integrated.* V + O

integrated /ɪntɪ²greɪtɪ²d/. An **integrated** institution is intended for use by all races or groups. EG *...an integrated school for Protestants and Catholics... The Coram Children's Centre in London is a revolutionary integrated centre.* ADJ CLASSIF : ATTRIB

integrity /ɪntegrɪtiˡ/. 1 **Integrity** is the quality of being honest and firm in your moral principles; used showing approval. EG *He was particularly respected for his integrity... My husband was a man of the highest integrity.* N UNCOUNT ⇑ virtue

2 The **integrity** of something such as a group of people or a text is its state of being united as one whole. EG *They were totally committed to the survival and integrity of the nation... On the whole they have managed to keep their cultural integrity intact... Relatives of victims have expressed concern that the integrity of the physical evidence might not be maintained.* N UNCOUNT : WITH POSS ⇑ wholeness = unity

intellect /ɪntə²lekt/, **intellects**. 1 **Intellect** is 1.1 the ability to understand or deal with ideas and information. EG *My own opinion is that the intellect of modern man isn't superior... ...the idea of computers with intellects.* N UNCOUNT/ COUNT ⇑ mind = intelligence 1.2 the quality of being very intelligent or clever. EG *He was born into a family noted for its intellect.* N UNCOUNT ⇑ cleverness

2 An **intellect** is a very intelligent person. EG *They were both intellects whose work was widely respected.* N COUNT

intellectual /ɪntə²lektʃʊᵒəl/, **intellectuals**. 1 An **intellectual** activity, quality, etc involves a person's ability to understand or deal with ideas and information. EG *...children in need of extra emotional or intellectual stimulation... ...intellectual pursuits like studying French... ...his tremendous intellectual powers.* ADJ CLASSIF ⇑ mental ◇ **intellectually**. EG *Intellectually, they knew a great deal. Practically, they were useless.* ◇ ADV ⇑ theoretically

2 An **intellectual** is someone who spends a lot of time studying and thinking about complicated ideas. EG *...the failure of the intellectuals to communicate their ideas to a wider audience... ...scholars and intellectuals.* N COUNT = highbrow

intelligence /ɪntelɪdʒəns/. 1 The **intelligence** of a person or animal is their ability to understand, learn, and think things out quickly, especially compared with other people or other animals of the same kind. EG *...a person of average intelligence... She prided herself on her intelligence.* ▸ used of actions and behaviour. EG *She complimented her opponents on the intelligence of their remarks.* N UNCOUNT = wit

2 **Intelligence** is 2.1 the ability to think and understand instead of doing things automatically or by instinct. EG *Do hedgehogs have intelligence?... ...computer intelligence.* ● See also **artificial intelligence**. N UNCOUNT 2.2 information that is gathered by the government or the army about their country's enemies and their activities. EG *...the acquisition and dissemination of radiation intelligence.* ▸ used of the people who gather this information. EG *He was recruited as a translator for U.S. military intelligence.* N UNCOUNT

intelligent /ɪntelɪdʒənt/. 1 A person or animal that is **intelligent** has the ability to understand, learn, and think things out quickly and well. EG *Jo is an intelligent student... ...an intelligent dog.* ▸ used of actions and behaviour. EG *...a very intelligent question.* ADJ QUALIT = clever ◇ **intelligently**. EG *They dealt with that problem intelligently.* ◇ ADV WITH VB = sensibly

2 An animal or computer that is **intelligent** has the ability to think and understand instead of doing things automatically or by instinct. EG *Are there intelligent life forms on other planets?... We have shown that computers can be intelligent.* ADJ CLASSIF = rational

intelligentsia /ɪntelɪdʒentsɪə/. The **intelligentsia** in a country or community are the most educated people there, especially those interested in the arts, philosophy, and politics. EG *...illiterate peasants with whom the intelligentsia had nothing in common.* N SING : *the* + N = literati

intelligible /ɪntelɪdʒəbəˡl/. Something that is **intelligible** is able to be understood. EG *They tried to describe it in such a way that it would be intelligible to an outsider... Make sure that your memos and letters are intelligible.* ADJ QUALIT ⇑ clear

intemperate /ɪntempəʳrət/. **Intemperate** behaviour or opinions are unreasonably strong and uncontrolled; a formal word. EG *...an organization about which Charles had made several intemperate and highly publicized remarks.* ADJ QUALIT

intend /ɪntend/, **intends, intending, intended**.
1 If you **intend** to do something, you have decided or planned to do it. EG *This is my job and I intend to do it... He had really intended staying longer... He woke later than he had intended.* V + *to*-INF/-ING, OR V + O = mean

2 If you **intend** something to have a particular purpose, quality, or effect, you have planned that it should have this purpose, quality, or effect. EG *Everything they do and say is intended to promote sales... We never intended the guarantee scheme to be permanent... It is intended as a handbook, for frequent reference.* V + O : USU + *to*-INF/*as*/ REPORT-CL = mean

3 When you **intend** a particular idea or feeling to be understood in something that you say or do, this is the idea or feeling that you are trying to express; often used with a negative to say what you did not mean to express. EG *She took a lot of convincing that no criticism was intended... I don't think he intended any disrespect.* V + O

4 Something that **is intended** for a particular person or purpose has been planned or made for that person or purpose. EG *The man had drunk what had been* V + O + *for* : USU PASS = be destined for

intended for me... ...the budget intended for the higher education of mature students... They are not yet intended for use.

intended /ɪntɛndɪ²d/. 1 **Intended 1.1** is used of the particular thing you are trying to achieve or person you are trying to affect. EG *What is the intended result?... ...his intended victim.* **1.2** is used of something that is planned to happen in the future. EG *...your intended trip abroad.*
ADJ CLASSIF : ATTRIB = desired; ADJ CLASSIF : ATTRIB

2 Someone's **intended** is the person they are planning to marry; an old-fashioned word, often used humorously.
N SING : POSS+N = betrothed

intense /ɪntɛns/. 1 Something that is **intense** is very great in strength, amount, or degree. EG *The effects of the drug are intense and brief... Because of the intense heat, I slept very little that night... ...a period of hard work and intense effort.* ◊ **intensely**. EG *...an intensely active, excited gathering of friends.* ◊ **intensity** /ɪntɛnsɪti¹/. EG *The debates are renewed with great intensity.*
ADJ QUALIT = acute, severe; ◊ ADV = extremely; ◊ N UNCOUNT ⇑ force

2 **Intense** emotions or experiences are very strongly and deeply felt. EG *...an intense resentment of privilege in any form... The row caused her intense unhappiness and anguish.* ◊ **intensely**. EG *I dislike him intensely... She had suffered intensely.* ◊ **intensity**. EG *The intensity of feeling against the regime was apparent.*
ADJ QUALIT ⇑ extreme = deep; ◊ ADV WITH VB ⇑ extremely; ◊ N UNCOUNT

3 If you describe a person as **intense**, you mean that they appear to concentrate very hard on everything that they do and they feel and show their emotions in a very extreme way. EG *It was like Jane to be so intense and dramatic about the future.*
ADJ QUALIT = deep, serious

4 An **intense** colour or light is extremely bright or deep. EG *...the intense hot dark blue of a cloudless sky... Everything is so intense in this sunlight.*
ADJ QUALIT ⇑ strong

5 An activity that is **intense** is very serious and concentrated, often involving doing a great deal in a short time. EG *It was a very intense lecture... My studies were meticulous and intense, although not particularly fruitful... This prompted an intense discussion.*
ADJ QUALIT

intensifier /ɪntɛnsɪfaɪə/, **intensifiers**. An **intensifier** is a word such as 'very' or 'extremely', which you can put in front of an adjective or adverb in order to make its meaning stronger; a grammatical term.
N COUNT

intensify /ɪntɛnsɪfaɪ/, **intensifies, intensifying, intensified**. If you **intensify** something or if it **intensifies**, it becomes greater in strength, amount, or degree. EG *That process has been greatly intensified by the breakdown of the Keynesian world-view... In the late 1960s the pressures suddenly intensified.* ◊ **intensified**. EG *...intensified international competition.* ◊ **intensification** /ɪntɛnsɪfɪkeɪʃə⁰n/. EG *They dramatised the intensification of the crisis.*
V-ERG ⇑ increase; ◊ ADJ CLASSIF; ◊ N UNCOUNT

intensive /ɪntɛnsɪv/. An **intensive** activity involves concentrating energy, people, tools, etc on to one particular task in order to try to achieve a great deal in a short time. EG *...the last intensive preparation for my exams... ...an intensive course... What are the ecological effects of intensive agricultural production?... ...a call for a renewed, intensive struggle against racism.* ◊ **intensively**. EG *The land was developed very intensively in the mid 1930s.*
ADJ QUALIT ⇑ concentrated; ◊ ADV WITH VB ⇑ heavily

intensive care is extremely thorough treatment provided by hospitals for people who are so ill that they would die quickly if they were not being looked after. EG *He spent nearly two weeks in intensive care.*
N UNCOUNT : USU *in*+N

intent /ɪntɛnt/, **intents**. 1 A person's **intent** is their intention to do something; a formal word. EG *The conference declared its intent to organize a national movement... They signed a declaration of intent.*
N UNCOUNT

● **Loitering with intent** is the offence of staying for an unnecessarily long time somewhere, for example outside a building, so that you look as if you are intending to commit a crime; a legal term.
● PHR : USED AS S/O

2 When you look **intent**, you show that you are paying great attention to someone or something, especially when you are watching them or listening to them. EG *He gazed at their intent faces... She was brushing her hair, intent on her face in the mirror.* ◊ **intently**. EG *I stood behind a parked van, watching intently... The woman listened intently.* ◊ **intentness**. EG *The intentness of his gaze drew all eyes that way.*
ADJ QUALIT = fixed, absorbed; ◊ ADV WITH VB = closely; ◊ N UNCOUNT = depth

3 If you are **intent** on doing something, you are eager and determined to do it. EG *They were intent on keeping what they had... They were intent on my downfall.*
ADJ QUALIT : PRED+*on/upon* = bent

4 You use the expression **to all intents and purposes** to suggest that a situation is not exactly as you describe it but the effect is the same as if it were. EG *She was to all intents and purposes the infant's mother... The forces that had opposed the change to all intents and purposes collapsed.*
PHR : USED AS ADV SEN

intention /ɪntɛnʃə⁰n/, **intentions**. An **intention** that you have is an idea or plan of what you are going to do. EG *My opponent has declared his intention to petition the Election Court... She had no intention of spending the rest of her life working as a waitress... She is motivated by good intentions.*
N COUNT/UNCOUNT = aim, purpose

intentional /ɪntɛnʃə⁰nəl, -ʃənə⁰l/. Something that is **intentional** is deliberate and intended to happen or be done. EG *...intentional misrepresentation.* ◊ **intentionally**. EG *I was convinced that she had been placed there intentionally.*
ADJ CLASSIF; ◊ ADV WITH VB = on purpose

inter- is added to adjectives and nouns in order to form other adjectives and nouns that refer to something existing or happening between similar things or groups of people. EG *...continental→intercontinental... ...racial→interracial... ...marriage→intermarriage.*
PREFIX

inter /ɪntɜː/, **inters, interring, interred**. To **inter** someone means to bury them; a formal word. EG *Thomas was interred next to his grandmother.*
V+O

interact /ɪntəræktl/, **interacts, interacting, interacted**. 1 When people **interact** with each other, they communicate or work together in a situation. EG *Mothers and babies interact in a very complex way... The creature begins to interact with the world around it.* ◊ **interaction** /ɪntərækʃə⁰n/. EG *There is a need for more interaction between staff and children... ...social interactions... ...the interaction of experts and laymen.*
V OR V+A (*with*) : RECIP; ◊ N UNCOUNT/COUNT

2 When one thing **interacts** with another, the two things react together in the same situation, so that they affect each other's development or condition. EG *Some bacteria's genes interact with those of many plants.* ◊ **interaction**. EG *...a method of encouraging the chance interaction of ideas... ...the interaction between sea-water and molten lava.*
V OR V+A (*with*) : RECIP; ◊ N UNCOUNT/COUNT = interplay

interactive /ɪntəræktɪv/. 1 An **interactive** group of people is one in which the people interact with each other. EG *...a small teacher-student ratio, a mutually interactive group.*
ADJ CLASSIF ⇑ communicating

2 **Interactive** use of a computer is use in which the user and the computer communicate directly with each other via a keyboard and a screen, rather than the user just putting in programs to be run. EG *...powerful interactive computers... ...interactive graphic systems... ...a technology capable of providing interactive personal tuition.*
ADJ CLASSIF

inter alia /ɪntər eɪlɪə/ means 'among other things'; a formal expression used to say that there are other things or aspects apart from the one you are mentioning. EG *Buckingham Palace houses, inter alia, a fine collection of paintings.*
PHR : USED AS ADV SEN

intercede /ɪntəsiːd/, **intercedes, interceding, interceded**. If you **intercede** with a person or group, you talk to them in order to try to put an end to a disagreement that they have with another person or group, or to persuade them to be merciful or fair to a person who is in their power. EG *He came to beg him to intercede with the revolutionaries... I interceded for him with his employer.*
V : IF+PREP THEN *with* ⇑ intervene = mediate

intercept /ɪntəsɛpt/, **intercepts, intercepting, intercepted**. If you **intercept** someone or something that is travelling from one place to another, you stop them before they get to their destination. EG *The car was intercepted and stopped by a policeman... Missiles were mounted at various points to intercept aircraft coming from the north.* ◊ **interception** /ɪntəsɛpʃə⁰n/. EG *Messages were not transmitted by radio for fear of interception by enemy monitoring services.*
V+O ⇑ meet; ◊ N UNCOUNT = interference

interceptor /ɪntəsɛptə/, **interceptors**. An **interceptor** is a fighter aircraft designed to intercept and attack enemy planes.
N COUNT

intercession /ɪntəsɛʃə⁰n/, **intercessions**. **Intercession** or an **intercession** is an act of interceding to try to put an end to a disagreement or to try to persuade someone powerful to be merciful or fair to a weaker person. EG *Through the intercession of a*
N UNCOUNT/COUNT

friend, my request was granted... ...through the miraculous intercession of God himself.

interchange /ɪntətʃeɪnd°ʒ/, **interchanges, interchanging, interchanged.** 1 The **interchange** of things, people, or ideas is the act or process of exchanging them. EG *...a regular forum for the interchange of information and ideas... We need more interchange of staff between prison hospitals and NHS hospitals.* — N COUNT+SUPP : USU SING ⇑ exchange

2 When things, people, or ideas **interchange** or when you **interchange** them, they change places or are exchanged with each other. EG *In nature we know that genes interchange with each other.* — V-ERG ⇑ exchange

3 An **interchange** on a motorway is a junction where it meets a main road or another motorway. — N COUNT

interchangeable /ɪntətʃeɪnd°ʒəbə°l/ Things that are **interchangeable** can be exchanged with each other without making any difference to a particular process or situation. EG *We tend to use these terms as if they were freely interchangeable... ...interchangeable forms of energy.* — ADJ CLASSIF ◊ **interchangeably.** EG *In many of the speeches, the word 'fascism' was used interchangeably with the word 'racism'.* — ◊ ADV WITH VB

intercom /ɪntəkɒm/, **intercoms.** An **intercom** is a device which people use to communicate with each other when they are in different rooms or vehicles. It is usually like a box with a microphone for talking into and a loudspeaker to hear the reply. EG *A voice on the intercom said, 'It's Mr Vaughan.'* — N COUNT

interconnect /ɪntəkənɛkt/, **interconnects, interconnecting, interconnected.** Things that **interconnect** are connected to each other. EG *The nervous system is a complicated network of interconnecting parts.* — V OR V+A (with) : RECIP ⇑ connect = interact ◊ **interconnected.** EG *Monarch, court and government were all interconnected.* — ◊ ADJ CLASSIF = interrelated ◊ **interconnecting.** EG *The interconnecting wall had been recently replastered.* — ◊ ADJ CLASSIF

intercontinental /ɪntəkɒntɪnɛntə°l/ is used to describe something that exists or happens between continents. EG *...an intercontinental flight.* — ADJ CLASSIF

intercourse /ɪntəkɔːs/ is 1 the act of having sex; a rather formal use. EG *Intercourse may mean a baby in nine months' time.* — N UNCOUNT 2 communication between two people or two groups; a rather old-fashioned use. EG *There is increasing intercourse between the scientific community and the ordinary people... During ordinary social intercourse it is considered rude to interrupt other people.* — N UNCOUNT = exchange

interdependence /ɪntədɪ¹pɛndəns/ is the condition of a group of people or things all depending on each other. EG *World trade, and the interdependence of economies, developed as never before.* — N UNCOUNT

interdependent /ɪntədɪ¹pɛndənt/. People or things that are **interdependent** all depend on each other. EG *Some nations must remain interdependent.* — ADJ CLASSIF

interdisciplinary /ɪntədɪsɪplɪnəri¹/ means involving more than one academic subject. EG *...an interdisciplinary course in African studies.* — ADJ CLASSIF

interest /ɪntə°rɛst/, **interests, interesting, interested.** 1 If you have an **interest** in something, you are keen to learn or hear more about it. EG *None of them had the slightest interest in music... ...people who have taken an active interest in the project... The girl in the next seat is studying him with interest... Brody was beginning to lose interest.* — N SING WITH DET, OR N UNCOUNT

2 Something that is of **interest** attracts your attention because it is rather exciting or unusual. EG *There was nothing of any great interest in the paper today... Striped wallpaper can add interest to a long narrow hall.* — N UNCOUNT

3 Something that **interests** you attracts your attention so that you want to learn or hear more about it or continue doing it. EG *Young men should always look for work which interests them... It may interest you to learn that he died last year.* — V+O

4 If you **interest** someone in something, you persuade them to do it or buy it because it attracts them. EG *Can I interest you in yet another horror movie?... He's been trying to interest film producers in an idea for a musical.* — V+O : USU+in

5 An **interest** that you have is something that you spend time on because you enjoy doing it or learning about it. EG *Throughout his youth he had two consuming interests: rowing and polo... ...people of the same age, background and interests... For me, music is more a way of life than an interest.* — N COUNT = hobby

6 If you have an **interest** in something being done, you want it to be done because it will benefit you, for example because it will protect your money, power, or position. EG *Governments have an interest in seeing minimum wages kept above subsistence level... They had no interest in the overthrow of the established order... They would protect the interests of their members... I have to declare an interest here.* — N COUNT : IF+PREP THEN in ⇑ reason ● See also **vested interest.** ● Something that is **in the interests** or **in the interest** of a person or group will benefit them in some way. EG *It is not in the interests of any of us to have a weak government... They decided to withhold the information in the public interest.* — ● PHR : USED AS AN A ● If you do something **in the interests** or **in the interest** of a particular condition, you do it in order to bring about or maintain this condition. EG *She was prepared to sacrifice this principle in the interests of domestic harmony... ...in the interest of safety and hygiene.* — ● PHR : USED AS AN A ⇑ for ● If you **have** someone's **interests at heart**, you care about them and try to help them. EG *She thought he would have her interests at heart.* — ● PHR : VB INFLECTS

7 An **interest** is a group of people who use their power to protect their own money, position, etc. EG *...the threats of the Big Business interests... Their leaders had become the tools of foreign interests... ...rather powerful lobbies of scientific interest groups.* — N COUNT+SUPP : USU PL

8 Someone who has an **interest** in a company has a share in the ownership of the company. EG *The family bought a controlling interest in a paper mill.* — N COUNT : IF+PREP THEN in

9 A person or organization that has **interests** in a particular type of business owns companies or branches in the business. EG *...Pirelli's cable manufacturing interests... ...an industrialist with business interests in Germany.* — N PLURAL

10 **Interest** is a sum of money that is paid as a percentage of a larger sum of money which has been borrowed or invested. You receive interest on money that you invest and pay interest on money that you borrow. EG *...the interest you pay on your mortgage... ...a prolonged period of high interest rates... He borrowed a large sum of money at 25 per cent interest.* — N UNCOUNT ● See also **compound interest, simple interest.**

interested /ɪntə°rɛstɪ²d/. 1 Someone who is **interested** in something 1.1 is keen to know or hear more about it or to spend time doing it. EG *I'm very interested in birds... We're interested in what kind of language they use... I'm not really interested in sport.* — ADJ QUALIT : USU PRED+in 1.2 thinks that it is important and worth giving attention to; used especially to indicate a specific area of a subject. EG *We are interested only in the efficiency of the company as a whole... I'm only interested in productions which test the limits of my capabilities.* — ADJ QUALIT : PRED+in = concerned

2 Someone who is **interested** in doing something is keen to do it. EG *My sister is interested in becoming a nurse... Will you buy them? Are you interested?* — ADJ QUALIT : USU PRED, IF+PREP THEN in

3 An **interested** party or group of people is a group that is affected by or involved in a particular event or situation. EG *We talked to a group of scientists who know about this work, and other interested parties... We shall be consulting 180 interested bodies.* — ADJ CLASSIF : ATTRIB = concerned

interest-free. An **interest-free** loan has no interest charged on it: see **interest.** ▸ used as an adverb. EG *...if you lent someone money interest free.* — ADJ CLASSIF ▸ ADV WITH VB

interesting /ɪntə°rɛstɪŋ/. If you find something **interesting**, it attracts your attention, for example because you think it is rather exciting or unusual; used showing approval. EG *That's a very interesting question... The interesting thing is that this is exactly the answer we got before... He was not very interesting to talk to... It must be quite interesting for you.* — ADJ QUALIT = intriguing

interestingly /ɪntə°rɛstɪŋli¹/. You use **interestingly** to introduce a piece of information that you think is interesting and unexpected. EG *Interestingly enough, America is now dependent on Africa for 40% of its oil imports.* — ADV SEN = curiously

interface /ɪntəfeɪs/, **interfaces.** The **interface** between two subjects, systems, etc is the area in which they affect each other or have links with each other; a formal word. EG *...new ways of involving young people with the interface between technology and design.* — N COUNT : IF+PREP THEN between ⇑ overlap

interfere /ɪntəfɪə/, **interferes, interfering, interfered.** 1 If you **interfere** in a relationship or situation between people, you try to influence it. — V : IF+PREP THEN in with especially when there is a dispute and you aim to solve the problem; often used showing disapproval. EG *He has instructed his family not to interfere... My mother interferes in things... They didn't interfere with us and we didn't interfere with them... It is sometimes dangerous to interfere between parents and children.* — between = meddle

2 If you **interfere** in a conversation between other people, you interrupt them when their conversation does not concern you; used showing disapproval. EG *Please don't interfere, Boris. This is very important... Don't let me interfere.* — V: IF+PREP THEN *in* = butt in

3 Something that **interferes** with a situation or activity has a damaging effect on it, often preventing something from happening or succeeding; used showing disapproval. EG *Child-bearing will not interfere with a career... She has done nothing that directly interfered with the actions of the others... The clock was stopped from striking because it interfered with the performances.* — V: IF+PREP THEN *with* = conflict, clash

4 When sounds or radio waves **interfere** with each other, they get too close to each other and become mixed up, so that people cannot hear them or receive them properly. EG *Why did their calls not interfere with one another, jamming the signals?... There was evidence of pirate radios interfering with shipping.* — V+A *(with)*

5 Someone who **interferes** with a child behaves in a sexual way towards him or her; used showing disapproval. EG *They were interfered with by their babysitter.* — V+A *(with)*

interference /ɪntəfɪərəns/ is 1 the act of interfering in something; used showing disapproval. EG *Bureaucracy resulted in more official interference in peoples' lives... I wanted to do the thing on my own without outside interference or help... They didn't want any interference from their national government.* 2 a situation in which radio waves get too close to each other and become mixed up, so that a radio receiver cannot receive them properly. When a radio makes a crackling sound, this is caused by interference. EG *Reception has been affected by electronic interference.* — N UNCOUNT ⇑ involvement = intervention; N UNCOUNT

interfering /ɪntəfɪərɪŋ/. An **interfering** person tries to get involved in other people's affairs or to give them advice, especially when the advice is not wanted; used showing disapproval. EG *I'm sick of all those men who claim they have interfering wives and girl friends.* — ADJ CLASSIF: ATTRIB = meddling, nosy

interim /ɪntərɪm/. 1 **Interim** describes something that is intended to be temporary until something more permanent is established. EG *They hope to create an interim company... It is recognized as a temporary or interim arrangement.* — ADJ CLASSIF: ATTRIB = provisional

2 You say **in the interim** to refer to something that has happened in the time between two events or between the present and an event in the past which has just been mentioned; a formal expression. EG *Little seems to have happened in the interim.* — PHR: USED AS AN A = meanwhile

interior /ɪntɪərɪə/, **interiors**. 1 The **interior** of something such as a container is the inside part of it which is surrounded by the main part that you usually see. EG *Flora picked up her handbag and felt into its interior... ...ovens with see-through doors and light-up interiors... Very little is known about the deep interior of the earth.* — N COUNT: IF+PREP THEN *of* ≠ exterior, outside

2 The **interior** of a building or a room is the inside of it; used when you are considering its design and appearance. EG *...different people's ideas of what a domestic interior should look like... The building has its interior well preserved... ...a landmark in the history of interior design.* — N COUNT: IF+PREP THEN *of* ≠ exterior, outside

3 **Interior** is used to describe **3.1** the situation of something that is inside a building, vehicle, etc. EG *It has 104 cubic feet of interior space... ...an interior room without windows... ...fixing plastic foam strips around interior doors and windows.* — ADJ CLASSIF: ATTRIB ≠ exterior, outside **3.2** a scene in a film in which the action takes place indoors. EG *There are as many helicopter shots as interior shots.* — ADJ CLASSIF: ATTRIB ⇑ inside

4 The **interior** of a country or continent is the central area which is the furthest from the sea. EG *The interior of the island consists largely of swamps... It was to be a journey to the interior.* — N SING: *the*+N ⇑ centre = heartland

5 An **interior** minister or political department deals with affairs and organizations within their own country. EG *The Interior Department framed a criminal code forbidding church services.* ▸ used as a noun in the title of a minister's post. EG *...the Minister of the Interior.* — ADJ CLASSIF: ATTRIB ⇑ domestic ≠ foreign; ▸ N IN TITLE: *the*+N

6 **Interior** thoughts, ideas, and processes happen in your head and are not expressed out loud; a formal use. EG *His great head seemed to obey an interior command... ...psychic diagrams of the artist's interior development.* — ADJ CLASSIF: ATTRIB = inner

interior decorator, interior decorators. An **interior decorator** is a person whose job is to plan the way that the inside of a house is decorated by choosing the colours and designs of wallpaper, carpets, furniture, etc. — N COUNT ⇑ designer

interject /ɪntədʒɛkt/, **interjects, interjecting, interjected**. If you **interject** something, you say it and interrupt someone else who is speaking. EG *If I may interject a word here... 'No, no,' interjected Schmidt.* — V+O/QUOTE/REPORT-CL = interpose

interjection /ɪntədʒɛkʃə⁰n/, **interjection**. 1 An **interjection** is something you say which interrupts someone else who is speaking. EG *The bishop was prepared for this interjection.* — N COUNT ⇑ interruption

2 In grammar, an **interjection** is a word or expression which you use to express a strong feeling such as surprise, pain, or horror, and which you often say loudly and emphatically. In this dictionary words like this are described as EXCLAM in the grammar notes beside the entries. See □ at EXCLAM. — N COUNT ⇑ exclamation

interlaced /ɪntəleɪst/. Things that are **interlaced** are joined closely together as if they are woven. EG *...interlaced branches... She sat cupping a knee with interlaced fingers.* — ADJ CLASSIF: IF+PREP THEN *with* = intertwined

interlink /ɪntəlɪŋk/, **interlinks, interlinking, interlinked**. Things that **interlink** are linked with each other in some way. EG *...the interlinking of good and evil.* ◊ **interlinked**. EG *The social and economic factors are inextricably interlinked.* — V OR V+A *(with)*: RECIP = interconnect; ◊ ADJ CLASSIF

interlock /ɪntəlɒk/, **interlocks, interlocking, interlocked**. Things that **interlock** with each other are firmly joined together. EG *All the units interlock with one another rigidly... He interlocked his fingers... ...making a cross from strong rods interlocked at right angles.* — V-ERG: ALSO V OR V+A *(with)*: RECIP ⇑ connect

interlocutor /ɪntəlɒkjə⁴tə/, **interlocutors**. Your **interlocutor** is the person with whom you are having a conversation; a formal word. EG *He looked at his interlocutor across the table.* — N COUNT: USU POSS+N

interloper /ɪntələʊpə/, **interlopers**. An **interloper** is a person who interferes in something, usually when they are not supposed to. EG *Any interloper who got up and heckled would be removed from the meeting.* — N COUNT ⇑ intruder

interlude /ɪntəlu:d/, **interludes**. An **interlude** is a short period of time when an activity or event stops for a break and something else happens or you have a rest. EG *After this interlude, the band started up again... ...a pleasant interlude between crises at home.* — N COUNT ⇑ pause = respite

intermarriage /ɪntəmærɪdʒ/ is marriage between people from different social, racial, or religious groups. EG *There will be intermarriage between our people and yours.* — N UNCOUNT: IF+PREP THEN *between* ⇑ union

intermarry /ɪntəmæri¹/, **intermarries, intermarrying, intermarried**. When people from different social, racial, or religious groups **intermarry**, they marry each other. — V OR V+A *(with)*: RECIP ⇑ unite

intermediary /ɪntəmi:djəri¹/, **intermediaries**. An **intermediary** is a person who tries to create agreement or pass information between two groups of people by talking to both groups. EG *The girls' plea for mercy through an intermediary resulted in the reduction of his death sentence... A spirit figure serves as an intermediary between men and the gods.* — N COUNT ⇑ representative = go-between

intermediate /ɪntəmi:dɪət/, **intermediates**. 1 An **intermediate** stage, position, etc is one that occurs between two other stages, positions, etc. EG *There are many intermediate stages in this degenerative process... One group of animals developed into another by way of intermediate forms.* — ADJ CLASSIF: USU ATTRIB ⇑ halfway = transitional

2 **Intermediate** is used to refer to students and their level of work in a subject when they are not beginners, but are not yet advanced. EG *...an English course, intermediate level, for adult students... ...the intermediate group.* — ADJ CLASSIF

3 An **intermediate** is a student of a subject who is not a beginner but who is not yet advanced. EG *...the* — N COUNT

youngest range from five to seven, the intermediates from eight to ten.

interment /ɪntɜːməˀnt/. The **interment** of a dead person is their burial; a formal word. EG *They brought back their lamented comrade's remains for interment on the farm.* N UNCOUNT

interminable /ɪntɜːmɪnəbəˀl/. Something that is **interminable** continues for such a long time that it seems as if it will never end; used showing disapproval. EG *I was glad of company for the last, long hours of this interminable flight... The list is interminable.* ◇ **interminably**. EG *MPs argued each point interminably.* ADJ CLASSIF = never-ending; ◇ ADV WITH VB = endlessly

intermingle /ɪntəmɪŋgəˀl/, **intermingles, intermingling, intermingled**. When people **intermingle**, they move around and mix with each other. EG *They should intermingle more freely... Different tribes and languages all intermingled in his uncle's village... The police intermingled with the crowds.* V OR V+A (with): RECIP

intermission /ɪntəmɪʃəˀn/, **intermissions**. An **intermission** is a short interval between two parts of a film, play, opera, etc. EG *...a ballet in three acts with two intermissions.* N COUNT ⇑ break

intermittent /ɪntəmɪtənt/. Something that is **intermittent** happens or appears occasionally or at regular intervals rather than constantly or continuously. EG *The masthead light was no more than an intermittent glow in the gloom... The milk-float is a vehicle suitable for intermittent use.* ◇ **intermittently**. EG *The magazine had been published intermittently since the war.* ADJ QUALIT = occasional ≠ constant; ◇ ADV WITH VB = irregularly

intern, interns, interning, interned. The word **intern** is pronounced /ɪntɜːn/ when it is a verb, and /ɪntɜːn/ when it is a noun. 1 To **intern** someone means to imprison them or keep them in a place. EG *They were interned for subversive activities... ...the practice of interning dissenters in mental hospitals.* V+O ⇑ confine

2 In American English, an **intern** is someone who has completed or is about to complete their studies as a medical student and who is being trained as a doctor in a hospital under supervision. EG *...four years in medical school, and two more as an intern.* N COUNT = houseman

internal /ɪntɜːnəˀl/. 1 **Internal** is used 1.1 to describe things that exist or happen inside a particular place, person, or object. EG *You should lag internal pipes to prevent them from freezing... Our internal human system uses about 100 watts of energy.* ◇ **internally**. EG *The house has been rebuilt internally.* 1.2 to describe the political and commercial activities that take place inside a country. EG *...the internal politics of France... ...internal and international tensions... This left fewer troops for internal security in Poland.* 1.3 to describe a situation, activity, system, etc that exists or happens within a particular organization and is not intended to be connected with anything outside the organization. EG *The large organizations were forced to change their internal structure... An authoritarian leadership stifled internal debate... ...an internal bank memorandum.* ◇ **internally**. EG *...legal advice, which the Department says was given internally long ago but never enforced.* ADJ CLASSIF: ATTRIB = interior ≠ external, outside; ◇ ADV WITH VB; ADJ CLASSIF: ATTRIB ⇑ domestic; ADJ CLASSIF: ATTRIB ⇑ inside; ◇ ADV WITH VB

2 **Internal** ideas or images exist in your thoughts or in your mind. EG *Music sets the internal image machinery working... We may think of this mental model as a fantastic internal warehouse... ...the Hamlet in which the Ghost is some internal, sepulchral demon.* ◇ **internally**. EG *Internally, it is the conflict between fear and security which creates the problem.* ADJ CLASSIF = inner, mental; ◇ ADV = subconsciously

internal combustion engine, internal combustion engines. An **internal combustion engine** is an engine that creates its energy by burning fuel inside itself. Most cars have an internal combustion engine. N COUNT

internalize /ɪntɜːnəlaɪz/, **internalizes, internalizing, internalized**; also spelled **internalise**. If you **internalize** something such as a belief or a set of values, you make it become a part of your attitude or way of thinking; a formal word. EG *He has not yet internalized that knowledge... They are constrained by an internalized ideology.* ◇ **internalization** /ɪntɜːnəlaɪzeɪʃəˀn/. EG *They were weighed down by this internalization of the belief in their own superiority.* V+O ⇑ incorporate; ◇ N UNCOUNT: USU WITH POSS ⇑ incorporation

international /ɪntənæʃənəˀl/, **internationals**. 1 **International** means between or involving different countries. EG *...international affairs... They signed an international agreement on nuclear waste... International tension mounted throughout the 1970's.* ◇ **internationally**. EG *She's an internationally famous historian... Internationally, the situation is even worse.* ADJ CLASSIF; ◇ ADV

2 An **international** is 2.1 a football match, rugby match, etc between teams from two countries. 2.2 a player who plays in one of these matches. EG *She's an England international.* N COUNT; N COUNT

internationalism /ɪntənæʃəˀnəlɪzəˀm/ is the belief that countries should co-operate with one another and try to understand one another. EG *This is an age of internationalism.* N UNCOUNT

international relations consist of the political relationship between different countries. EG *What effect will this incident have on international relations?* N PLURAL

internecine /ɪntəniːsaɪn/. An **internecine** conflict, war, quarrel, etc is one which causes destruction to both sides. EG *...internecine struggles... ...internecine warfare.* ADJ CLASSIF: ATTRIB ⇑ destructive

internee /ɪntɜːniː/, **internees**. An **internee** is a person who has been imprisoned. EG *We try to help the families of internees.* N COUNT ⇑ prisoner

internment /ɪntɜːnməˀnt/, **internments**. 1 **Internment** is the state of being imprisoned. EG *...two years of internment... ...an internment camp.* N UNCOUNT = imprisonment

2 An **internment** is a period of imprisonment. EG *Their internments are well documented.* N COUNT

interpersonal /ɪntəpɜːsəˀnəl/ means relating to the relationship between people. EG *...interpersonal relationships... ...interpersonal skills.* ADJ CLASSIF: ATTRIB ⇑ social

interplay /ɪntəpleɪ/. The **interplay** between two or more things is the way that they react with one another and have an effect on one another. EG *I am interested in the interplay between practical and theoretical linguistics... ...the interplay of many factors.* N UNCOUNT: USU +of/between = interaction

interpolate /ɪntɜːpəleɪt/, **interpolates, interpolating, interpolated**. If you **interpolate** a comment, passage, etc into a conversation or piece of writing, you put it in as an addition; a formal word. EG *'It was last Friday', interpolated Sheila... A later edition interpolated the following passage.* V+O/QUOTE/REPORT-CL = add, insert

interpolation /ɪntɜːpəleɪʃəˀn/, **interpolations**. An **interpolation** is an addition to a piece of writing. EG *Interpolations in brackets are the author's.* N COUNT = insertion

interpose /ɪntəpəuz/, **interposes, interposing, interposed**. 1 If you **interpose** something between two people or things, you place it between them. EG *Amelia interposed herself between Luciana and the door.* V+O (NG/REFL): USU+between = put

2 If you **interpose** something, you interrupt with a comment or question. EG *'Enough of this!' interposed Miss Musson.* V+O/QUOTE/REPORT-CL = interject

interpret /ɪntɜːprɪt/, **interprets, interpreting, interpreted**. 1 If you **interpret** what someone says or does in a particular way, you decide that this is its meaning or significance. EG *My parents insist on interpreting my visits as some sort of criticism... I'm not quite sure how to interpret that question... The election result is being interpreted as a serious setback for the government.* V+O: IF+PREP THEN as ⇑ understand = take

2 If you **interpret** a novel, dream, result, etc, you give an explanation of what it means. EG *We have to interpret our findings... Can you interpret the meaning of these passages?... I'm not much good at interpreting dreams.* V+O = make sense of

3 If you **interpret** a work of art such as a piece of music, a play, a dance, etc, you perform it in a particular way, especially a way that shows your feelings about it. EG *I wrote the story and the girls interpreted it in dance... I have never heard the song interpreted better than that.* V+O: USU+A

4 If you **interpret** what someone is saying, you translate it immediately into another language, so that speakers of that language can understand. EG *Paul had to interpret for us.* V OR V+O: IF+PREP THEN for

interpretation /ɪntɜːprɪteɪʃəˀn/, **interpretations**. 1 The **interpretation** of a particular situation, law, statement, etc is the explanation of what it means. Different people may have different interpretations of the same thing. EG *I hope this is a justifiable interpretation... This passage is open to a* N UNCOUNT/COUNT ⇑ understanding *variety of interpretations... The current law has many problems of interpretation... She referred the matter for interpretation to the European Court of Justice.*

2 A performer's **interpretation** of a piece of music, a play, a dance, or some other work of art is the particular way in which they choose to perform it, which shows their feelings about it. EG *Do you find his interpretation of Chopin satisfactory?* — N UNCOUNT/COUNT ⇑ performance = rendition

interpretative /ɪntɜːprɪtətɪv/. Something that is **interpretative** provides an interpretation. EG *...an interpretative article.* — ADJ CLASSIF ⇑ explanatory

interpreter /ɪntɜːprɪtə/, **interpreters**. An **interpreter** is 1 a person who repeats what someone else is saying by translating it immediately into another language so that other people can understand it. EG *He spoke very little English, so I talked to him through an interpreter... Sometimes Chang was with me and acted as interpreter.* — N COUNT = translator 2 a person who explains the meaning or significance of something. EG *A foreign correspondent is both an interpreter and a victim of his subject matter.* — N COUNT = exponent 3 a person who performs a work of art in a particular way, especially a way that shows the performer's feelings about it. EG *Max Wall is a marvellous interpreter of Beckett's work.* — N COUNT

interregnum /ɪntərɛgnəm/, **interregnums, interregna**. The plural can be either **interregnums** or **interregna**. An **interregnum** is the period between the end of one ruler's reign and the beginning of the next ruler's reign. — N COUNT ⇑ interval

interrelate /ɪntəriˈleɪt/, **interrelates, interrelating, interrelated**. If two or more things **interrelate** or **are interrelated**, there is some kind of connection between them, so that they have an effect on one another. EG *These courses interrelate in a variety of ways... All three factors are interrelated... ...a system of interrelated parts.* — V-ERG : USU PASS ⇑ connect = interconnect

interrelationship /ɪntəriˈleɪʃəⁿnʃɪp/, **interrelationships**. An **interrelationship** is a close relationship between two or more things. — N COUNT : IF + PREP THEN *between/of*

interrogate /ɪntɛrəgeɪt/, **interrogates, interrogating, interrogated**. If you **interrogate** someone, you question them thoroughly and for a long time, in order to get some information from them. EG *They said they had been interrogated for 20 hours about political demonstrations... Julie was waiting to interrogate him, when he got downstairs.* — V+O ⇑ examine = grill

interrogation /ɪntɛrəgeɪʃəⁿn/, **interrogations**. 1 An **interrogation** is a period of time spent questioning someone thoroughly, for example a prisoner or someone charged with a crime. EG *Despite interrogations at police headquarters, no evidence against him could be found.* — N COUNT ⇑ examination

2 **Interrogation** is the act of questioning someone thoroughly in order to get some information from them. EG *We've had him under interrogation for 36 hours now... ...modern methods of interrogation.* — N UNCOUNT ⇑ examination

interrogative /ɪntərɒgətɪv/, **interrogatives**; a grammatical term. 1 An **interrogative** pronoun, sentence, etc asks a question or has the form of a question. For example, 'who' is an interrogative pronoun. — ADJ CLASSIF

2 An **interrogative** is a word such as 'who', 'how', or 'why', which can be used to ask a question. — N COUNT

interrogator /ɪntɛrəgeɪtə/, **interrogators**. An **interrogator** is a person who questions someone thoroughly and for a long time. EG *'What do you mean by that?' Dicky asked sharply like an interrogator.* — N COUNT ⇑ questioner

interrupt /ɪntərʌpt/, **interrupts, interrupting, interrupted**. 1 If you **interrupt** someone or if you **interrupt**, you start talking so that they cannot continue with what they were saying. EG *Don't interrupt, William... Sorry to interrupt but I have an urgent message for you... I knew better than to interrupt him when he was on the phone.* — V OR V+O/QUOTE = butt in, barge in

2 If you **interrupt** a process or activity, you stop it continuing for a time. EG *I allowed nothing to interrupt my studying... Work on the project was begun in 1941, interrupted by the war in 1942, and resumed in 1945.* — V+O = disrupt, disturb

3 If something **interrupts** a continuous or uniform line, surface, etc, it breaks it by making it uneven. EG *The normally bleak landscape was interrupted by a long row of trees.* — V+O : USU PASS

interruption /ɪntərʌpʃəⁿn/, **interruptions**. 1 An **interruption** is something which breaks the continuity of an action or process. EG *She hates interruptions when she's working.* — N COUNT = disruption

2 **Interruption** is the act of interrupting something or the state of being interrupted. EG *We should be safe from interruption.* — N UNCOUNT = disturbance

intersect /ɪntəsɛkt/, **intersects, intersecting, intersected**. 1 If two or more lines, roads, etc **intersect**, they meet or cross each other. EG *Somewhere all the tracks intersected... The satellite is on a course which should intersect that of the asteroid.* — V, V+O, OR V+A *(with)* : RECIP

2 If you **intersect** a place, area, or surface, you divide it by crossing it or marking it. EG *The marshes were intersected by a maze of ditches.* — V+O : USU PASS

intersection /ɪntəsɛkʃəⁿn/, **intersections**. An **intersection** is a place where roads or other lines meet or cross. EG *The city lies at the intersection of three motorways... The car surged forward towards the intersection with the Avenue du Bois.* ▸ used as an uncount noun. EG *...the point of intersection.* — N COUNT : IF + PREP THEN *of/with* ⇑ junction ▸ N UNCOUNT

intersperse /ɪntəspɜːs/, **intersperses, interspersing, interspersed**. If something **is interspersed** with a number of other things, these things are put in here and there. EG *...a street of old shops and houses interspersed with modern offices and banks... The days pass with trips to the pool, interspersed with long naps in a deckchair.* — V+O : USU PASS *with/by*

interstate /ɪntəsteɪt/ means between states, especially the states of the USA. EG *...the interstate highway.* — ADJ CLASSIF : ATTRIB

interstellar /ɪntəstɛlə/ means between the stars; a formal word. EG *...interstellar travel... ...the nature of interstellar space.* — ADJ CLASSIF : ATTRIB

interstice /ɪntɜːstɪs/, **interstices**. **Interstices** are small gaps or cracks between things that are placed very close together; a formal word. EG *...pieces of limestone and granite, the interstices padded with wet earth.* — N COUNT : USU PL ⇑ space

intertwine /ɪntətwaɪn/, **intertwines, intertwining, intertwined**. If two things **intertwine** or **are intertwined**, they are twisted together. EG *...a bowl with intertwined serpents for handles... Their arms intertwined... History and ideology intertwined... Gold was intertwined with silver round the handle of the goblet.* — V-ERG : IF V+O THEN USU PASS, ALSO V OR V+A *(with)* : RECIP = interweave

interval /ɪntəvəl/, **intervals**. 1 An **interval** is 1.1 the period of time that passes between two particular moments or dates. EG *Much had changed in the interval... The interval between these two dates is about six months... The baby had woken up for another feed after an interval of 3 or 4 hours... Some insects are able to distinguish intervals of one hundredth of a second.* — N COUNT : IF + PREP THEN *of/between* 1.2 a short break during a play, concert, etc, during which the performers leave the stage. EG *During the interval, we were taken to the coffee bar.* — N COUNT = intermission 1.3 the difference in pitch between two musical notes; a technical term in music. — N COUNT

2 If something happens **at intervals**, it happens again and again, though not necessarily regularly. EG *The monotonous noise would stop at intervals, then resume after a while.* — PHR : USED AS AN A = occasionally

3 If something happens **at regular intervals**, **at weekly intervals**, etc, it happens again and again, with a particular amount of time or space between each time it happens. EG *They kept coming back to him at six-month intervals... They saw each other at intervals of a year or two.* — PHR : USED AS AN A ⇑ regularly

4 If people or objects are positioned **at** particular **intervals**, there is a certain amount of space between them. EG *Look-out posts were scattered through the forest, at widely varying intervals.* — PHR : USED AS AN A

intervene /ɪntəviːn/, **intervenes, intervening, intervened**. 1 If you **intervene**, 1.1 you take action in a situation that did not originally involve you, especially in order to prevent conflict between two people or groups, or to help someone. EG *There were many other occasions when we were forced to intervene in order to ensure medical help for one of the prisoners... Lord Beaverbrook intervened on behalf of his Canadian friend... The Bank of England had been intervening in foreign exchange markets.* — V : IF + PREP THEN *in* = step in 1.2 you interrupt a conversation in order to add something to it. EG *'It won't do, George,' said Howard, intervening... Can I just intervene for one moment?* — V OR V+QUOTE = interject

2 If an event **intervenes**, it happens suddenly in a way that stops, delays, or prevents something. EG *They wish to end the fight before death intervenes...* — V ⇑ occur

Neither Bill became law because the General Election intervened.
3 If a period of time **has intervened**, it has come between a particular event or time and the present. EG *Ten years had intervened since she had last seen Joe.* V ⇑ pass = elapse

intervening /ɪntəvi:nɪŋ/. **1** The **intervening** period of time is the period between two points in time. EG *The Labour Party had altered considerably during the intervening period... Over those intervening years our lives had drifted apart.* ADJ CLASSIF : ATTRIB = interim
2 An **intervening** object or area comes between two other objects or areas. EG *The distant wooded hills to the west and the intervening meadows are bathed in the autumn moonlight.* ADJ CLASSIF : ATTRIB

intervention /ɪntəvenʃə⁰n/, **interventions**. **Intervention** is the act of intervening, especially in order to influence a situation in some way. EG *They want to avoid armed intervention at all costs... He believes in state intervention in the economy.* N UNCOUNT/ COUNT : IF+ PREP THEN *in* ⇑ interference

interview /ɪntəvju:/, **interviews, interviewing, interviewed**. **1** An **interview** is **1.1** a meeting at which someone asks you questions about yourself, your abilities, your experience, etc, especially in order to find out if you are suitable for a particular job. EG *I had an interview for a job on a newspaper... Big industrial companies hold interviews all over the country... He was invited for interview at three universities.* N COUNT/ UNCOUNT **1.2** a conversation in which a well-known person talks to a reporter about the interesting or important things that they do. Interviews are published in newspapers and magazines, and are broadcast on television and radio. EG *After he had won the world championship he gave a series of interviews to newspapers and television... The President explained the United States strategy in an interview in the New York Times.* N COUNT = audience, press conference
2 If you **interview** someone, you ask them questions, for example about their suitability for a job or about their interests, ideas or beliefs. EG *I was once interviewed for a part in a film... They interviewed me very hard.* V+O : USU PASS ⇑ question

interviewee /ɪntəvju:i:/, **interviewees**. An **interviewee** is a person who is being interviewed. N COUNT

interviewer /ɪntəvju:ə/, **interviewers**. An **interviewer** is the person who asks you questions in an interview. N COUNT ⇑ questioner

interweave /ɪntəwi:v/, **interweaves, interweaving, interwove, interwoven**. If two or more things **interweave** or **are interwoven**, they are very closely connected and appear to wrap themselves around each other. EG *This is only one of the many interwoven trends... You could see the columns of smoke interweaving... The four voices were interwoven in a beautifully sung quartet.* V-ERG : IF V+O THEN USU PASS, ALSO V OR V+A (*with*) : RECIP = intermingle, intertwine

intestate /ɪntesteɪt/. If someone dies **intestate**, they die without making a will. ADV AFTER VB

intestinal /ɪntestɪnə⁰l/ means relating to the intestines. EG *...an intestinal infection.* ADJ CLASSIF : ATTRIB

intestine /ɪntestɪn/, **intestines**. Your **intestine** is the tube in your body that carries food from your stomach. EG *...obstruction of the intestines... ...sharp pains in the intestine.* N COUNT : SING=PL = gut

intimacy /ɪntɪməsi¹/, **intimacies**. **1 Intimacy** between two people is a very close personal relationship between them. EG *...the intimacy between mother and child... Never before had he known such intimacy with another person.* N UNCOUNT : IF+ PREP THEN *with/between* = closeness
2 Intimacies are things that you say or do to someone you have a very close personal relationship with. EG *There have even been closer intimacies between them... I like sharing these little intimacies.* N COUNT : USU PL

intimate, intimates, intimating, intimated. The word **intimate** is pronounced /ɪntɪmət/ when it is an adjective or noun, and /ɪntɪmeɪt/ when it is a verb. **1** If two people are **intimate** or if they have an **intimate** relationship, they know and like each other very well. EG *Jean was her dearest and most intimate friend... I wanted to establish more personal and intimate contact with Chang.* ADJ QUALIT ≠ distant ▸ used as a noun. EG *There were no women among her intimates.* ▸ N COUNT ⇑ friend ◊ **intimately**. EG *We were intimately acquainted.* ◊ ADV WITH VB
2 If you are **intimate** with someone, you have a sexual relationship with them; a formal use. EG *I will not stand for it if you propose to be intimate with anyone other than myself... He had been having intimate relations with her quite unknown to his wife.* ADJ CLASSIF ◊ **intimately**. ◊ ADV WITH VB
3 An **intimate** conversation, detail, matter, etc is one that concerns something which is very personal and private. EG *It was the first really intimate conversation we had had... They had already exchanged the most intimate details of their personal lives.* ADJ QUALIT : USU ATTRIB ◊ **intimately**. EG *Sylvia and Chris talked intimately about their hopes and fears.* ◊ ADV WITH VB = confidingly
4 An **intimate** restaurant, theatre, etc is small and has a pleasant, quiet atmosphere. EG *...an intimate little restaurant.* ADJ QUALIT = cosy ▸ used of a meal, evening, etc that two, or sometimes more, people have in a place like this. EG *We enjoyed an intimate meal together.* ▸ = cosy
5 An **intimate** link or connection between ideas, organizations, etc is a very strong link between them. EG *...proud of their intimate bonds with crown and government.* ADJ QUALIT : USU ATTRIB ◊ **intimately**. EG *These two questions are intimately linked in practice... The sounds of language are intimately bound up with meaning... The argument for equality was intimately connected with the case for public ownership.* ◊ ADV WITH VB = closely
6 An **intimate** knowledge of something is a deep and detailed knowledge of it. EG *It must have been someone with an intimate knowledge of the station.* ADJ QUALIT : USU ATTRIB = thorough ◊ **intimately**. EG *He knew the contents of all three files intimately.* ◊ ADV WITH VB = inside out
7 If you **intimate** something, you make it known to someone else by expressing it in an indirect way. EG *Miller intimated that he had a few words to say... She had earlier intimated her disapproval.* V+O/REPORT-CL ⇑ suggest = hint

intimation /ɪntɪmeɪʃə⁰n/, **intimations**. An **intimation** is an indirect suggestion or sign that something is likely to happen or be true; a fairly formal word. EG *For the first time I felt some intimation of danger... He had no intimation that he was on the point of another disaster... It fills me with intimations of mortality.* N COUNT : USU+ *of*/REPORT-CL ⇑ indication = inkling

intimidate /ɪntɪmɪdeɪt/, **intimidates, intimidating, intimidated**. If you **intimidate** someone, you make them frightened enough to do what you want them to do, especially by behaving in a threatening way. EG *In 1972 his neighbours intimidated his family into leaving... He too could be intimidated by Mrs Burns.* V+O = scare, browbeat ◊ **intimidation** /ɪntɪmɪdeɪʃə⁰n/. EG *An official warned them of possible intimidation by local gangs.* ◊ N UNCOUNT

intimidated /ɪntɪmɪdeɪtɪ²d/. Someone who is **intimidated** feels frightened and so loses confidence. EG *I was intimidated by so many strangers.* ADJ QUALIT : USU PRED = overawed

intimidating /ɪntɪmɪdeɪtɪŋ/. Someone or someone that is **intimidating** is frightening and makes you lose confidence. EG *In old age loneliness can be very intimidating... ...a realistic but not intimidating view of the task ahead.* ADJ QUALIT

into /ɪntu:/. **1** If you put one thing **into** something else such as a container, you put it in that other thing, so that it is enclosed or surrounded by it. EG *If you pour hot water into a glass, it may crack... She put a cigarette into her mouth... I finally got into bed... She fell into a ditch.* PREP
2 If one thing goes **into** something else, it moves from the outside to the inside, by breaking or damaging the surface of it. EG *She stuck her knitting needles into a ball of wool... Jack slammed his knife into a trunk... She bit into her apple.* PREP ▸ used to indicate that a substance dissolves or is absorbed in another substance or material. EG *The oil will soak into the wood... Some drugs may get into the milk.*
3 If you go **into** a room, building, town, country, etc, you move from being outside it to being inside it. EG *He followed Boris into the room... He walked into a police station... She had to go into hospital... We were coming into London... They dived into the water.* PREP
4 If you bump, crash, knock, etc **into** something, you hit it because it is in your way and you do not slow down or avoid it. EG *The man bumped into me as he came out of the shop... A car had gone into the truck... We crashed into a wall.* PREP
5 If you get, change, etc **into** clothing, you put it on. EG *She changed into her best dress... You can always wriggle into a sweater if you're not warm enough.* PREP
6 If you put money or information **into** a place, you put it there so that it can be stored. EG *The information goes into a computer... The money will be paid into a bank account.* PREP
7 If you look, speak, etc **into** something, you look or PREP

speak towards it. EG *She looked into Deidre's eyes... 'I'm terribly sorry,' she said into the phone.*

8 If you move **into** a particular kind of weather or an activity, you move to a place which has that weather or where that activity is going on. EG *He moved back into the darkness... We rushed out of the house into a whirling snowstorm.* PREP

9 If you go **into** the wind or the sun, you move towards the direction the wind is blowing from or towards the direction from where the sun is shining. EG *She turned the plane into the wind to take off... We began walking into the afternoon sun.* PREP

10 If someone or something gets **into** a particular state, activity, or way of life, they enter or begin it. EG *She fell into a dreamless sleep... He was worrying himself into a state of depression... The Labour Government came into power in March 1974... Robert was trying to provoke them into fighting... The assembly was shocked into silence... ...Britain's entry into the Common Market.* PREP

11 If something changes or develops **into** something else, it becomes this new thing. EG *The bud develops into a flower... The book has been made into a movie... Dusk deepened into night... This should help to turn the nation's assets into cash... Is it difficult translating from Arabic into English?* PREP

12 If you make, fold, etc something **into** a particular shape or consistency, you change it to that shape or consistency. EG *He folded his newspaper into a neat rectangle... The beeswax should be made into a stiff paste with turpentine... Ian curved his mouth into a friendly smile.* PREP

13 If you are **into** your thirties, forties, middle age, etc, you are already in that period of your life. EG *She must be into her thirties by now... He remained a bank clerk until well into middle age.* PREP

14 If something continues **into** the evening, the following day, etc, it continues until the approximate time mentioned. EG *We used to talk into the small hours... The meeting carried on into the afternoon.* PREP = till

15 If you look **into** the future or the past, you consider what is likely to happen or examine what did happen. EG *I wish I could see into the future... We can look into his past to find out why.* PREP

16 If you are **into** something, you are very interested in it and like it very much; used in very informal English. EG *Teenagers are into those old, romantic novels... I'm really into jazz these days.* PREP = hooked on

17 A study, investigation, etc **into** a particular subject or event is concerned with that subject or event. EG *...an investigation into sky brightness in Southern Ontario... Some MPs demanded a full enquiry into the incident... Are you still doing research into Linguistics?* PREP

18 If you move or go **into** a particular career, field, profession, etc, you start working in it, or change to it from something else. EG *I'd like to move into marketing.* PREP

19 You use **into** **19.1** when you are describing the smaller parts that something has when it is divided or separated. EG *The houses are all divided into flats... I carefully tore it into two, four, eight pieces.* PREP
19.2 to indicate the amount of time which has already passed during a particular period. EG *Eight months into his stay he suddenly started to feel home-sick... We're well into May and I still haven't done half the things I should have done in April.* PREP **19.3** to indicate that a number increases or decreases until it reaches the approximate level mentioned. EG *A loss that would run into millions... We want to get inflation down into single figures.* PREP **19.4** to express a division sum; for example 'four into eight' means the same as 'eight divided by four'. An informal use. EG *What's five into forty?... Five into seven won't go.* PREP : NUM + *into* + NUM

intolerable /ɪntɒlərəbəºl/. If something is **intolerable**, it is so bad or extreme that no one can bear it or tolerate it. EG *They find this situation intolerable... ...the things that made his life intolerable... It was intolerable that they should order her around... Their methods are intolerable to those who care for liberty.* ◊ **intolerably**. EG *She had become intolerably possessive.* ADJ QUALIT ↑ unbearable = insufferable ≠ tolerable; ◊ ADV = impossibly

intolerance /ɪntɒlərəns/ is unwillingness to let other people act in a different way or hold different opinions from you; used showing disapproval. EG *She accused the men of ignorance and intolerance... He complained about the intolerance of the party... ...a world engulfed in hatred and intolerance.* N UNCOUNT = narrow-mindedness

intolerant /ɪntɒlərənt/. If you are **intolerant**, you try to prevent other people from acting in a different way or holding different opinions from you; used showing disapproval. EG *She is intolerant by nature... They tend to be intolerant of anything strange... ...intolerant regimes.* ADJ QUALIT : IF + PREP THEN *of/to/towards* ≠ liberal, open-minded

intonation /ɪntəºneɪʃəºn/, **intonations**. Your **intonation** is the way that the sound of your voice rises and falls when you speak. Intonation can help you to understand what people are saying. EG *The dialect of the area has a gentle sing-song intonation... It is impossible, in print, to reproduce Sarah's intonation.* N UNCOUNT/COUNT

intone /ɪntəʊn/, **intones, intoning, intoned**. If you **intone** something, you speak or recite it slowly and clearly, keeping most of the words on one musical note. EG *They stood and intoned their afternoon prayers... A dark voice intoned: 'Except a man die and be born again.'* V+O/QUOTE ↑ say = chant

intoxicant /ɪntɒksɪkənt/, **intoxicants**. An **intoxicant** is something such as an alcoholic drink, which can cause you to become drunk; a formal word. N COUNT

intoxicated /ɪntɒksɪkeɪtɪ²d/. **1** If you are **intoxicated**, you are drunk; a formal word, sometimes used humorously. EG *One in four admitted being intoxicated... Thompson and I went into town and got thoroughly intoxicated.* ADJ QUALIT = inebriated

2 If you are **intoxicated** with something such as a feeling or **intoxicated** by it, it makes you behave in a wild or excited way. EG *They became intoxicated with chauvinist pride... She was intoxicated by her position as manager of the company... Intoxicated by victory, they sang and danced all night.* ADJ QUALIT : PRED + *by/with* = carried away

intoxicating /ɪntɒksɪkeɪtɪŋ/. **1 Intoxicating** drink contains alcohol and can make you drunk. EG *He burst into the room, frenzied with passion and intoxicating drink... ...a fruity, intoxicating wine.* ADJ QUALIT ↑ alcoholic

2 Something that is **intoxicating** makes you very excited, so that you lose your self-control and act in a foolish way. EG *This realization had an intoxicating effect... She had an intoxicating delusion of being intensely active.* ADJ QUALIT = exhilarating

intoxication /ɪntɒksɪkeɪʃəºn/ is **1** the state of being drunk. EG *They were in an advanced state of intoxication.* **2** a state in which you are very excited, and likely to lose your self-control and act in a foolish way. EG *...the intoxication of success... I lived in a state of intoxication with my own existence.* N UNCOUNT; N UNCOUNT = exhilaration

intractable /ɪntræktəbəºl/; a formal word. **1 Intractable** people are difficult to control or influence. EG *Her father had to deal with intractable people occasionally... On one issue Luce was intractable.* ADJ QUALIT = awkward, obdurate

2 Intractable problems or situations are difficult to deal with. EG *Labour problems tend to be more intractable... It emerged as the most intractable issue of our era.* ADJ QUALIT = problematic

intransigence /ɪntrænsɪdʒəns/ is refusal to behave differently or to change your attitude to something; used showing disapproval. EG *...the intransigence of the landowners... ...the Government's intransigence over price-controls.* N UNCOUNT : WITH POSS = obstinacy ≠ flexibility

intransigent /ɪntrænsɪdʒənt/. When someone is **intransigent**, they refuse to behave differently or to change their attitude to something; used showing disapproval. EG *He can be intransigent and pigheaded at times.* ▸ used of behaviour. EG *...an intransigent and unrealistic approach.* ADJ QUALIT = obstinate, stubborn

intransitive /ɪntrænsɪtɪv/. An **intransitive** verb is a verb which does not have an object. In this dictionary v is used in the grammar notes beside entries to mean 'intransitive'. See ☐ at v. ADJ CLASSIF ≠ transitive

intravenous /ɪntrəviːnəs/. **Intravenous** foods or drugs are given to sick people through their veins, rather than their mouths; a technical word. EG *We fed them an intravenous sugar solution... The intravenous fluids kept him alive.* ◊ **intravenously**. EG *Steve had been fed intravenously.* ADJ CLASSIF : ATTRIB; ◊ ADV WITH VB

in tray, in trays; also spelled with a hyphen. An **in tray** is a tray or shallow basket used in offices to put letters and documents in when they arrive or when they are waiting to be dealt with: compare **out tray**. N COUNT

intrepid /ɪntrepɪd/. An **intrepid** person acts in a brave way; an old-fashioned word, often used humorously. EG *Some intrepid individuals were still prepared to make the journey... Wasn't I on the route of those intrepid explorers, Lewis and Clark?* ADJ QUALIT = fearless, plucky

◊ **intrepidly** EG *Intrepidly, Fanny ventured out into the snow.* ◊ **intrepidity** /ɪntrə²pɪdɪti¹/. EG *...these perils they had overcome by sheer intrepidity.*
◊ ADV WITH VB
◊ N UNCOUNT

intricacy /ɪntrɪkəsi¹/, **intricacies**. **1 Intricacies** are fine and often complicated details. EG *We became aware of the intricacies of these processes... The intricacies of American politics bored me.*
N COUNT : USU PL +of

2 Intricacy is the state of being made up of many small parts or details. EG *...the complexity and technical intricacy of modern industry... This anthology shows the intricacy and range of women's experience.*
N UNCOUNT = complexity

intricate /ɪntrɪkət/. Something that is **intricate** has many small parts or details, often as a result of very skilful artistic work. EG *The women and children did intricate carvings... They were painted all over in intricate patterns... ...the country's vast, intricate social ills.* ◊ **intricately**. EG *...intricately patterned bead necklaces... ...an intricately carved door.*
ADJ QUALIT ⇑ complicated ≠ simple
◊ ADV = elaborately

intrigue /ɪntri:g/, **intrigues, intriguing, intrigued**. **1 Intrigue** is the making of secret plans that are intended to harm people's reputations, careers, friendships, etc; used showing disapproval. EG *The staff room was full of intrigue, hate, and jealousy... She's accustomed to intrigue and deception.* ▸ used as a count noun. EG *...the intrigues and jealousies of his colleagues.* ▸ used as a verb. EG *He had intrigued with his brother against the king... In a good cause, even I will intrigue.*
N UNCOUNT = plotting, trickery
▸ N COUNT
▸ V OR V+A (with) : RECIP = scheme

2 If something **intrigues** you, you are fascinated by it and curious about it. EG *Anything colourful intrigued the little boy... The idea seemed to intrigue him.*
V+O ⇑ interest

intrigued /ɪntri:gd/. If you are **intrigued** by something, you are fascinated by it and curious about it. EG *She seemed intrigued by all the smaller birds... Intrigued, I followed the instructions.*
ADJ QUALIT : USU PRED ⇑ interested

intriguing /ɪntri:gɪŋ/. If you describe someone or something as **intriguing**, you mean that you are fascinated by them and curious about them; used showing approval. EG *She had an unusual and intriguing face... Our team came up with some intriguing finds... What you said just now sounds most intriguing.* ◊ **intriguingly**. EG *Libby's questions were always intriguingly different... Most intriguingly, no fingerprints were to be found.*
ADJ QUALIT ⇑ interesting = fascinating
◊ ADV, OR ADV SEN ⇑ interestingly

intrinsic /ɪntrɪnsɪk/; a formal word. **1** The **intrinsic** qualities that something has are part of its basic nature or character. EG *He believed in the intrinsic superiority of his people... Dependency is an intrinsic part of love.* ◊ **intrinsically**. EG *Children are not intrinsically lovable.*
ADJ CLASSIF : ATTRIB = inherent
◊ ADV

2 If something has **intrinsic** value, **intrinsic** interest, etc, it is valuable, interesting, etc because of what it is, and not because of its connection with other things. EG *These objects have no intrinsic value... The problem of machine intelligence is one of great intrinsic interest.* ◊ **intrinsically**. EG *His material was so intrinsically interesting that we invited him round to discuss it.*
ADJ CLASSIF : ATTRIB
◊ ADV

introduce /ɪntrədju:s/, **introduces, introducing, introduced**. **1** If you **introduce** someone to someone else, you formally tell them each other's names, so that they can get to know each other. EG *The stranger asked Hogan to introduce him to Karl... At a cocktail party in Hollywood, I was introduced to Charlie Chaplin.*
V+O : IF+PREP THEN to ⇑ present

2 If you **introduce** yourself to someone, you formally tell them your name, so that you can get to know them. EG *I had better introduce myself. I am Colonel Marc Rodin.*
V+O (REFL) : IF +PREP THEN to ⇑ present

3 If you **introduce** a speaker or lecturer to an audience, you tell the audience what the speaker's name is and usually say a few things to describe them or their work. EG *It's my great pleasure to introduce tonight's speaker, Professor Lewis.*
V+O ⇑ present

4 When someone **introduces** a television or radio programme, they say a few words st the beginning of it to tell you what it will be about. EG *Tonight's edition was introduced by Paul Allen.*
V+O = host

5 If you **introduce** something to a place, you start using it there for the first time or cause it to exist there for the first time. EG *Rabbits had been introduced into Australia by Europeans... They intended to introduce investment and technology into the region... Nobody expected a Republican president to introduce compulsory price and wage control... Farmers are introducing innovations that increase productivity.*
V+O : IF+PREP THEN to/into/in = bring in

6 If you **introduce** someone to something, you cause them to learn about it or experience it for the first time. EG *Born in the middle of London, he was first introduced to politics as a child... This leaflet introduces you to social security... It was my wife who introduced Dicky to yoga.*
V+O+A (to)

7 If you **introduce** a new subject during a talk, lecture, etc, you talk about it for the first time, usually in a general way. EG *This afternoon, I want to introduce the concept of metaphor.*
V+O = present

8 When the government **introduces** a Bill in the House of Commons, they present it formally, so that it can be discussed and voted upon; a formal use. EG *In February 1967 he introduced the Shipbuilding Industry Bill... The Conservatives introduced a Bill to tighten national security.*
V+O = propose

introduction /ɪntrədʌkʃə⁰n/, **introductions**. **1** The **introduction** of something into a place or system is the act of causing it to exist or be used there for the first time. EG *...the introduction of computerized credit cards in Britain... The Government saw the introduction of new technology as vital.*
N UNCOUNT : USU +of = institution

2 Your **introduction** to something is the occasion when you experience it for the first time. EG *This was my first real introduction to agriculture... China's introduction to modern British ballet.*
N SING : USU POSS +N+to-INF = initiation

3 An **introduction** is **3.1** the first part of a book or talk, in which the writer or speaker tells you what the rest of the book or talk is about. EG *Brian Johnston contributes a delightful introduction to Anthony Smith's book... ...the passage I quoted at the beginning of this introduction.* **3.2** a book that explains the basic facts about a particular subject. EG *An Introduction to English Literature.* **3.3** the act of formally telling people each other's names so that they can get to know each other. EG *He was shaking her hand before I could finish the introduction... With a smile, William makes introductions all round.*
N COUNT = foreword
N COUNT : ALSO IN NAMES
N UNCOUNT/COUNT ⇑ presentation

introductory /ɪntrədʌktə⁰ri¹/. An **introductory** remark, talk, book, etc tells you a little about a particular subject, often at the beginning of a more detailed explanation. EG *...his introductory remarks at the opening of the exhibition... After the introductory speeches Hughes rose to begin his talk... It includes a good introductory chapter on forests.*
ADJ CLASSIF : ATTRIB ⇑ first = preliminary

introspection /ɪntrə⁶spekʃə⁰n/ is the examining of your own thoughts, ideas, and feelings, often over a long period of time. EG *He rode along in a mood of melancholy introspection... We learn by practice, rather than through introspection... I simply hadn't time for introspection.*
N UNCOUNT

introspective /ɪntrə⁶spektɪv/. **Introspective** people spend a lot of time examining their own thoughts, ideas, and feelings. EG *The boy was downcast and introspective... ...a withdrawn, introspective man.* ▸ used of behaviour. EG *...a talent for introspective observation.*
ADJ QUALIT = contemplative, inward-looking

introvert /ɪntrə⁶vɜ:t/, **introverts**. An **introvert** is someone who spends more time thinking about themselves and their private feelings than about the world around them, and who often finds it difficult to talk to other people and make friends. EG *The introvert sits in a corner and dreams... ...a bashful, softly-spoken introvert.*
N COUNT

introverted /ɪntrə⁶vɜ:tɪ²d/. **Introverted** people spend more time thinking about themselves and their private feelings than about the world around them, and often find it difficult to talk to other people and make friends. EG *Rosa was quiet and introverted... During pregnancy a woman often becomes introverted.* ▸ used of feelings and activities. EG *He was now in a slightly introverted mood... Creation is a lonely and introverted activity.*
ADJ QUALIT = withdrawn, introspective

intrude /ɪntru:d/, **intrudes, intruding, intruded**. **1** If you **intrude** on someone or **intrude** upon them, you disturb them when they are in a private place or having a private conversation. EG *I don't want to intrude on your family... In large cities neighbours are unwilling to intrude... Some women would feel intruded upon.*
V : IF+PREP THEN on/upon = encroach

2 If something **intrudes** on your mood, your way of life, etc, it has an unwelcome or unpleasant effect on it. EG *The pessimism did not visibly intrude on the President's holiday mood... Nothing was allowed to*
V+A (on) ⇑ influence = interfere with

intrude on their evening ritual... A park would intrude on the region's way of life.

3 If you **intrude**, you go into a place where you are not supposed to be. EG *I heard peals of laughter from the intruding children.* V : IF+PREP THEN *on/upon* = trespass

intruder /ɪntruːdə/, **intruders**. An **intruder** is a person who goes into a place where they are not supposed to be, often in order to steal things. EG *He felt threatened, as if an intruder had come into his home... They make useful hedges to keep out intruders.* N COUNT = interloper, trespasser

intrusion /ɪntruːʒəⁿn/, **intrusions**. An **intrusion** is **1** an act in which you disturb someone when they are in a private place or having a private conversation. EG *I must ask your pardon for this intrusion... It was an unthinkable intrusion into a man's house... I did not blame her for resenting my intrusion into her private affairs.* N COUNT/UNCOUNT = incursion **2** something that affects your mood, your way of life, etc in an unwelcome way. EG *I resent the intrusion of the outside world... A half-century of Western intrusion had seriously unbalanced the traditional culture.* N COUNT/UNCOUNT

intrusive /ɪntruːsɪv/. Something that is **intrusive** spoils or harms your mood, your way of life, etc. EG *He tried to render himself oblivious to these intrusive sounds... I can only see my presence here as intrusive.* ADJ QUALIT = unwelcome

intuit /ɪntjuːɪt/, **intuits, intuiting, intuited**. If you **intuit** something, you discover what it is, or decide that it is true, by using your intuition. EG *I was trying to intuit what you wanted... Anne intuited that he regarded them as snobbish.* V+O/REPORT-CL ⇑ guess

intuition /ɪntjuːɪʃəⁿn/, **intuitions**. Your **intuition** or your **intuitions** are unexplained feelings within you that something is true or exists even when you have no evidence or proof of it. EG *She refused to listen, trusting what she called her intuition... My intuition told me to stay away... These intuitions were quite correct.* N UNCOUNT/COUNT = instinct

intuitive /ɪntjuːɪtɪv/. If you have an **intuitive** idea or feeling, you feel that something is true or exists although you have no evidence or proof of it, and you cannot explain why you have this idea or feeling. EG *I got a strong intuitive feeling that he was trying to deceive me... He never lost his intuitive understanding of nature... He must have known in his intuitive way that we were there.* ◇ **intuitively**. EG *They intuitively feel that this is the safest way.* ADJ QUALIT : USU ATTRIB = instinctive ◇ ADV WITH VB

inundate /ɪnʌndeɪt/, **inundates, inundating, inundated**. **1** If you **are inundated** with letters, demands, requests, etc, you receive so many of them that you cannot deal with them all. EG *She was inundated with telephone calls and begging letters... Hospitals were being inundated with requests for help.* V+O : USU PASS+*with* = swamp

2 If an area of land **is inundated**, it becomes covered with water. EG *The valley was completely inundated within half an hour... In autumn 1978, a flash flood inundated 66,000 villages... ...the area the enemy had inundated as part of their defences.* V+O : USU PASS = be flooded

inure /ɪnjʊə/, **inures, inuring, inured**. If you **inure** yourself to something unpleasant, you accustom yourself to it and accept it; a formal word. EG *They inure themselves to a lifetime of self-restraint.* ◇ **inured**. EG *They were even inured to the economic instability that had followed the change of government.* V+O (REFL)+A *(to)* = habituate, harden ◇ ADJ QUALIT : PRED+*to* = habituated

invade /ɪnveɪd/, **invades, invading, invaded**. **1** To **invade** a country means to enter it by force with an army. EG *While King Harold was in the North, William thought this would be a good chance to invade England... If his country was invaded by a foreign enemy, he would return at once.* ◇ **invading**. EG *...the invading forces.* V OR V+O = overrun, attack ◇ ADJ CLASSIF : ATTRIB

2 If people, animals, or insects **invade** a place or a building, they enter it in large numbers; sometimes used humorously. EG *On Saturday they invaded the shopping area... The town was being invaded by reporters offering money to anyone who had seen the plane crash... ...the small, crawling pests that invade the home.* V+O = overrun

3 If someone or something **invades** your privacy, they disturb you when you are peaceful or when you want to be alone. EG *People invade your privacy in a way they wouldn't with senior managers.* V+O

invader /ɪnveɪdə/, **invaders**. **1 Invaders** are soldiers who are invading a country. EG *Heavy fire greeted the invaders... They were cruel and sadistic invaders.* ● See also **Space Invaders**. N COUNT : USU PL

2 An **invader** is a country or army that has invaded or is about to invade another country. EG *It will be no easy task to repel an invader... We may have to make peace with the invader.* N COUNT : USU SING

invalid, invalids. The word **invalid** is pronounced /ɪnvəlɪd/ when it is a noun, and /ɪnvælɪd/ when it is an adjective. **1** An **invalid** is someone who is so ill or disabled that they need to be cared for by someone else. EG *He's got a wife who's an invalid... The family had treated her like an invalid... She looked after her invalid mother... ...a Home for Invalids.* ◇ **invalidity** /ɪnvəlɪdɪti¹/. EG *You may be entitled to an invalidity pension.* N COUNT ◇ N BEFORE N

2 If an argument, conclusion, result, etc is **invalid**, it is not acceptable, because it is based on a mistake. EG *The comparison is invalid... The conclusions drawn from Glass's work are equally invalid... The distinction, therefore, might be considered invalid.* ◇ **invalidity**. EG *My experiments show the invalidity of his argument.* ADJ CLASSIF : USU PRED = unsound ◇ N UNCOUNT

3 If a law, marriage, or election is **invalid**, it is illegal, because it has not been made or carried out in the officially correct way. EG *In the Supreme Court the judges ruled the law invalid... The marriage would have been invalid because she was already married to Oliver... The court ruled his election invalid.* ◇ **invalidity**. ADJ CLASSIF : USU PRED ≠ legal, lawful ◇ N UNCOUNT

invalidate /ɪnvælɪdeɪt/, **invalidates, invalidating, invalidated**. **1** If you **invalidate** an argument, conclusion, result, etc, you prove that it is wrong. EG *It certainly invalidates any argument that the murderer is left-handed.* V+O = negate

2 If something **invalidates** a law, marriage, election, etc it causes it to be considered illegal. EG *Such exceptions do not invalidate the rule... The judgement would invalidate any earlier will.* V+O = cancel, negate

invaluable /ɪnvæljuᵒəbəᵒl/. If someone or something is **invaluable**, they are extremely useful; used showing approval. EG *The preservation of good relations with the police is invaluable... Interested parents are invaluable to any child... ...his invaluable manservant.* ADJ CLASSIF ⇑ valuable

invariable /ɪnveərɪəbəᵒl/. Something that is **invariable** never changes. EG *It became their invariable practice to allow immediate entry... The invariable comment was that it was all costing too much... This process, however, was not invariable.* ADJ CLASSIF : USU ATTRIB = habitual, unchanging

invariably /ɪnveərɪəbli¹/. If something **invariably** happens or is **invariably** true, it always happens or is always true. EG *The awards invariably go to someone other than myself... He was invariably courteous and considerate... Our receptionists are almost invariably female.* ADV, OR ADV SEN ≠ never

invasion /ɪnveɪʒəⁿn/, **invasions**. **1** An **invasion** is the action of an army entering a country by force. EG *...the Roman invasion of England... He condemned the invasion in the most forthright terms... The country remained free from invasion for three hundred years.* N COUNT/UNCOUNT ⇑ entry

2 An **invasion** is also **2.1** the arrival of someone or something in a place where they are not wanted. EG *The girl was annoyed at my invasion... ...an invasion of privacy.* N COUNT/UNCOUNT : IF+PREP THEN *of* **2.2** the arrival in a place of large numbers of people or things; often used humorously. EG *The local merchants regard this annual invasion as a blessing... ...the invasion of Italian movies that hit the United States in the fifties.* N COUNT/UNCOUNT : IF+PREP THEN *of* = influx

invective /ɪnvektɪv/ is rude and unpleasant things that people shout at others when they are very angry with them; a fairly formal word. EG *She struggled like a wildcat, screaming invective at Allen... He began to assail them with every kind of invective he could think of.* N UNCOUNT = abuse ≠ pleasantries

inveigh /ɪnveɪ/, **inveighs, inveighing, inveighed**. If you **inveigh** against something, you strongly criticize it; a formal word. EG *It is fashionable in some quarters to inveigh against a 'competitive ladder' society.* V+A *(against)* ⇑ attack = rail

inveigle /ɪnveɪgəᵒl/, **inveigles, inveigling, inveigled**. If you **inveigle** someone into doing something, you cleverly persuade them to do it when they do not really want to; a formal word. EG *The Duke tried to inveigle him into his service... He was inveigled into meeting a few more people... He could not inveigle Benny as he had the others.* V+O : IF+PREP THEN *into* = cajole

invent /ɪnvent/, **invents, inventing, invented.** 1 If you **invent** a machine, process, game, etc, you are the first person to think of it, and usually the first person to make or use it. EG *...the man who invented the combine harvester... He invented the popular national daily newspaper... He taught them a game he had invented.* — V+O ⇑ create = originate

2 If you **invent** a story, excuse, etc, you try to make other people believe that it is true when in fact it is not, usually for a bad or dishonest reason. EG *You may invent a few stories against your opponents... He would have to invent some alibi... If you want to make me jealous, why not invent something more probable?* — V+O = concoct, fabricate

invention /ɪnvenʃəⁿn/, **inventions.** 1 An **invention** is 1.1 a machine, device, or system that has been invented by someone, or that is just being invented. EG *He was working on his invention... ...an invention of the Frenchman Joseph Jacquard... Writing was the most revolutionary of all human inventions.* — N COUNT ⇑ creation 1.2 something untrue that someone wants you to believe; used showing disapproval. EG *The account is a deliberate and malicious invention... The whole thing was an invention of a New York newspaper.* — N COUNT/UNCOUNT = fabrication

2 **Invention** is 2.1 the act of inventing something that has never been made or used before. EG *Mass literacy was only possible after the invention of printing... ...the invention of the transistor.* — N UNCOUNT: IF+PREP THEN *of* ⇑ creation 2.2 the ability to invent things or to have clever and original ideas. EG *...powers of invention... ...the reservoir of invention that exists in developing countries.* — N UNCOUNT ⇑ talent

inventive /ɪnventɪv/. An **inventive** person is good at inventing things or at having clever and original ideas. EG *He was highly inventive... ...a very inventive child.* — ADJ QUALIT = creative ◊ **inventiveness.** EG *His inventiveness was amazing.* — ◊ N UNCOUNT ⇑ talent

inventor /ɪnventə/, **inventors.** An **inventor** is a person who has invented something, or whose job is to invent things. EG *She was the inventor of modern ballet... ...a novel wind turbine devised by a British inventor.* — N COUNT ⇑ creator

inventory /ɪnvəʳntri¹/, **inventories.** An **inventory** is a written list of all the objects in a particular place. EG *An inventory of 1556 lists the contents of the earlier building... She was taking an inventory of the committee's files.* — N COUNT

inverse /ɪnvɜːs/; a formal or technical word. 1 If there is an **inverse** relationship between two things, one of them becomes smaller as the other becomes larger. EG *There seems to be an inverse relationship between audience size and audience response... The amount of time spent on my work varies in inverse proportion to the amount I get done.* — ADJ CLASSIF: USU ATTRIB ≠ direct

2 The **inverse** of something is its exact opposite. EG *It represents the inverse of everything I find worth preserving.* — N SING: *the/POSS*+N ▸ used as an adjective. EG *The inverse case is also worth considering.* — ▸ ADJ CLASSIF: ATTRIB

inversion /ɪnvɜːʃəⁿn/, **inversions. Inversion** is the changing of something by turning it round to make it into its opposite. EG *...this curious inversion of facts... ...this apparent inversion of the rules.* — N UNCOUNT: IF+PREP THEN *of* ⇑ reversal ▸ An **inversion** is the result of this. EG *The term materialism emerges as the exact inversion of what it meant in earlier times.* — ▸ N COUNT: USU SING+*of*

invert /ɪnvɜːt/, **inverts, inverting, inverted.** If you **invert** something, you turn it upside down or back to front. EG *The spikes break up the ground but do not invert the soil... Remove the seeds by inverting the flower heads.* — V+O ⇑ reverse ◊ **inverted.** EG *It was shaped like an inverted cone... ...an inverted sentence.* — ◊ ADJ CLASSIF ● See also **inverted commas.**

invertebrate /ɪnvɜːtɪbrɪ³t/, **invertebrates.** An **invertebrate** is a creature that does not have a spine, for example an insect, a worm, or an octopus; a technical term. EG *Other descendants of marine invertebrates have also left the water.* — N COUNT ⇑ vertebrate ▸ used as an adjective. EG *...invertebrate animal life.* — ▸ ADJ CLASSIF

inverted commas are the punctuation marks (' and' or "and") that are used in writing to indicate where speech or a quotation begins and ends, Inverted commas are also sometimes used round the titles of books, songs, etc or round a word or phrase that is being discussed. — N PLURAL = quotation marks, quotes ● If you say **in inverted commas** after a word or phrase, you mean that, although it is the word or phrase that is normally used, you think that it is very unsuitable. EG *We'd survived, in inverted commas... A lot of the technology, in inverted commas, is virtually useless.* — ● PHR: USED AS ADV SEN

invest /ɪnvest/, **invests, investing, invested.** 1 If you **invest** an amount of money, you pay it into a bank or buy shares with it, so that you will receive a profit. EG *I invested in a few shares in the same company... Many businessmen are investing in farming... £20 million of public money had been invested.* — V OR V+O: IF+PREP THEN *in* ⇑ lay out

2 If you **invest** money, time, or energy in something, you use your money, time, or energy in trying to make it a success. EG *They were reluctant to invest money in new ideas... They have failed to invest in job creation in the cities... They are willing to invest energy and ingenuity in a European disarmament programme.* — V+A *(in)*, OR V+O: IF+PREP THEN *in* ⇑ spend

3 If you **invest** in something useful, you buy it, because it will help you to do something more efficiently or more cheaply. EG *A number of people have invested in night storage heaters... General Motors had invested in new machinery.* — V+A *(in)*, OR V+O+A *(in)* ⇑ purchase ≠ sell

4 If you **invest** somebody with rights or responsibilities, you give them those rights or responsibilities legally or officially; a formal use. EG *The law invests the shareholders alone with legal rights... The Welfare State has invested the artist with no official 'social duty'.* — V+O+A *(with)* ⇑ confer

investigate /ɪnvestɪgeɪt/, **investigates, investigating, investigated.** If you **investigate** an event or situation, you examine all the details, in order to find out what happened or what is happening. EG *The inspector had come to investigate a murder... We set out to investigate the mood of the community... He has carefully investigated the allegations... If you hear such a rumour, investigate it thoroughly.* — V OR V+O = look into ◊ **investigation** /ɪnvestɪgeɪʃəⁿn/, **investigations.** EG *The FBI is conducting an investigation into the affair... His bureau will become more involved in drug investigations.* — ◊ N COUNT/UNCOUNT ⇑ examination

investigative /ɪnvestɪgətɪv/. **Investigative** activities involve or are concerned with investigations. EG *He was doing investigative work... ...investigative journalism.* — ADJ CLASSIF: USU ATTRIB ▸ used of people. EG *...investigative reporters.*

investigator /ɪnvestɪgeɪtə/, **investigators.** An **investigator** is someone who carries out investigations, especially as part of their job. EG *He was a special investigator for the FBI.* — N COUNT

investigatory /ɪnvestɪgətri¹/ means the same as investigative. EG *The CIR should be retained, but with its investigatory role only.* — ADJ CLASSIF: ATTRIB

investiture /ɪnvestɪtʃə/, **investitures.** An **investiture** is a ceremony in which someone is given an official title. EG *...plans for the Investiture of Prince Charles as Prince of Wales.* — N COUNT: ALSO IN NAMES

investment /ɪnvestməʳnt/, **investments.** 1 **Investment** is the paying of money into a bank or the buying of shares, in order to receive a profit. EG *We aim to encourage investment.* — N UNCOUNT/COUNT = outlay ▸ An **investment** is the sum of money that you have paid. EG *...a better return on the investment.* — ▸ N COUNT = outlay

2 An **investment** is also something that you buy because it will help you to do a task more cheaply or efficiently, or because it will become more valuable. EG *A deep freeze is a major housekeeping investment... The tractors proved a superb investment... I bought it as an investment, really.* — N COUNT = acquisition

3 **Investment** of time or effort is the spending of time or effort on something in order to make it a success. EG *It might be a better investment of time to teach the children to cook.* — N UNCOUNT+SUPP

investor /ɪnvestə/, **investors.** An **investor** is a person who buys shares or who pays money into a bank in order to receive a profit. EG *The investor is entitled to a reasonable return on his money... Investors sought to recover losses sustained earlier in the week.* — N COUNT

inveterate /ɪnvetərət/. An **inveterate** liar, smoker, etc has lied, smoked, etc for a long time and is not likely to stop doing it. EG *The two boys were inveterate liars... Hubert had been an inveterate hunter.* — ADJ CLASSIF: ATTRIB ▸ used also of behaviour and attitudes. EG *...their inveterate distrust and hatred of strangers.*

invidious /ɪnvɪdɪəs/. 1 An **invidious** task, job, etc is unpleasant to do, because it is likely to make you unpopular. EG *The role of a reviewer can be an invidious one... The deputies were placed in an invidious position.* — ADJ QUALIT

2 An **invidious** comparison, choice, etc between two things is an unfair one because because the two things are not comparable or because there is only thing that you can choose. EG *We should guard against invidious comparisons with Scotland Yard... For reasons of space, this involves an invidious choice.* ADJ CLASSIF = impossible

invigilate /ɪnvɪdʒɪleɪt/, **invigilates, invigilating, invigilated**. If you **invigilate** an examination, you supervise the people who are taking it in order to ensure that it starts and finishes at the correct time, and also to prevent cheating. EG *He wrote this whilst invigilating a biology examination.* V: IF + PREP THEN *at*, OR V+O ⇑ oversee

invigilator /ɪnvɪdʒɪleɪtə/, **invigilators**. An **invigilator** supervises the people who are taking an examination in order to ensure that it starts and finishes at the correct time, and also to prevent cheating. EG *Most invigilators will not allow this.* N COUNT ⇑ supervisor

invigorated /ɪnvɪgəreɪtɪ²d/. If you feel **invigorated**, you feel more energetic than you did because you have just been involved in something that has refreshed you. EG *He felt invigorated... The audience left fresh and invigorated.* ADJ QUALIT

invigorating /ɪnvɪgəreɪtɪŋ/. Something that is **invigorating** makes you feel more energetic. EG *The air here is invigorating... I had an invigorating bath.* ADJ QUALIT: USU PRED = refreshing

invincible /ɪnvɪnsə¹bə⁰l/. **1** An **invincible** army or sports team cannot be defeated. EG *They are invincible in battle and wise in peace... ...an army of invincible strength... ...the invincible Real Madrid side of the early sixties.* ◊ **invincibility** /ɪnvɪnsə¹bɪlɪti¹/. EG *They were convinced of the invincibility of their aircraft and tanks.* ADJ CLASSIF = unbeatable; ◊ N UNCOUNT

2 If someone has an **invincible** belief or attitude, it cannot be changed. EG *...his invincible belief in himself... ...their invincible contempt for foreigners.* ◊ **invincibly**. EG *My father remained invincibly ignorant... For once in his life he knew himself to be invincibly right and everyone else totally wrong.* ADJ CLASSIF: USU ATTRIB = unshakeable; ◊ ADV = unshakeably

inviolable /ɪnvaɪələbə⁰l/. If a law, principle, etc is **inviolable**, you cannot or must not break it; a formal word. EG *Basic law or tradition was considered inviolable... The company made one inviolable condition.* ◊ **inviolability** /ɪnvaɪələbɪlɪti¹/. EG *...the inviolability of the principle of democracy.* ADJ CLASSIF ⇑ strict; ◊ N UNCOUNT

inviolate /ɪnvaɪələt/. If something is **inviolate**, it cannot be harmed or affected by something that is happening; a formal word. EG *The medical profession is by no means inviolate from automation.* ADJ CLASSIF: IF + PREP THEN *from* = safe

invisible /ɪnvɪzə¹bə⁰l/. **1** If something is **invisible**, **1.1** it cannot be seen because it is hidden, disguised, or too small. EG *From here Collindeane Tower was invisible... Her legs were invisible beneath the table... They are almost invisible, crouching among the leaves... ...microscopic hairs, invisible to the naked eye.* ◊ **invisibly**. EG *Millions of tiny specks fall invisibly every second.* ◊ **invisibility** /ɪnvɪzə¹bɪlɪti¹/. EG *The main advantage is the submarine's invisibility.* **1.2** it is imaginary. EG *She was having a violent argument with some invisible figure in her cell... The bird made snapping motions at invisible flies in the air.* ◊ **invisibly**. EG *Between the typed lines was written, invisibly, my future.* ADJ CLASSIF: IF + PREP THEN *to* = hidden ≠ visible; ◊ ADV; ◊ N UNCOUNT; ADJ CLASSIF: ATTRIB = non-existent; ◊ ADV

2 In stories, **invisible** people or things cannot be seen by anybody. EG *...the Invisible Man... He waves his magic wand and turns himself invisible... Perhaps my new glasses made me invisible.* ADJ CLASSIF

invitation /ɪnvɪteɪʃə⁰n/, **invitations**. **1** An **invitation** is **1.1** a written or spoken request to come to a party, meal, etc. EG *His invitations to dinner were famous... I accepted the invitation... Wives are included in the invitation.* **1.2** the card or paper on which an invitation is written or printed. EG *The invitation is addressed to your husband.* **1.3** a request to do something or to take part in something, for example to give a talk or attend a meeting. EG *We've come to South Wales this week at the invitation of the Gwent Federation of Women's Institutes... A year or two ago, I had an invitation to go and talk to the cadets at West Point.* N COUNT; N COUNT; N COUNT

2 An **invitation** is also an encouragement to someone to do something. EG *It was an invitation to love... She declined the invitation to address him as 'Charles'.* ● An **open invitation** is a careless or foolish action that makes it easier for someone to do something criminal. EG *Houses left unlocked are an open invitation to burglary.* N SING WITH DET + *to*-INF/*to*; ● PHR + *to*-INF/*to*: USED AS C

invite, invites, inviting, invited. The word **invite** is pronounced /ɪnvaɪt/ when it is a verb, and /ɪnvaɪt/ when it is a noun. **1** If you **invite** someone to a party, meal, etc, you ask them to come to it. EG *I asked my director to invite her to the party... He had been invited for dinner at Julie's house... It's very kind of you to invite me.* V+O: USU + *to/for/to*-INF ⇑ request

2 If someone **invites** you to attend something or to take part in something, they ask you to do it. EG *I was invited by a friend to attend meetings of a youth organization... He was invited for interview at Leeds... We were invited to sit on committees... I was invited to become the first woman Chancellor.* V+O: USU + *to/for/to*-INF ⇑ request

3 If someone **invites** discussion, criticism, etc, they encourage you to discuss something, criticize it, etc. EG *He stopped speaking and invited discussion... Intellectuals were invited to criticise the revolution.* V+O, OR V+O+*to*-INF

4 If someone or something **invites** confidence, disbelief, etc, they make you feel confident in them, or disbelieve them, etc. EG *He was too discreet to invite real confidence... This kind of statement invites disbelief.* V+O = inspire

5 If a situation or action **invites** danger, trouble, etc, it makes danger or trouble more likely. EG *To speak of it to others would invite danger... This 'appeasement policy' invites disaster... A premature general strike would invite total defeat.* V+O

6 An **invite** is a written invitation to a party, meal, etc; an informal use. EG *We need to photocopy another twenty invites.* N COUNT

inviting /ɪnvaɪtɪŋ/. If something looks, sounds, or smells **inviting**, it is attractive to you and makes you think that it would give you pleasure or enjoyment. EG *The place where they landed was green and inviting... She had large dark eyes, shy but inviting... This was an inviting idea... He could smell their inviting aroma.* ◊ **invitingly**. EG *The packet of cigarettes lay invitingly open... The soup steamed invitingly.* ADJ QUALIT = attractive, appealing; ◊ ADV = appealingly

invocation /ɪnvə⁷keɪʃə⁰n/, **invocations**. An **invocation** is an appeal to a god for help, forgiveness, etc. EG *He chanted continuous invocations... They murmured invocations to the gods.* N COUNT/UNCOUNT ⇑ plea

invoice /ɪnvɔɪs/, **invoices, invoicing, invoiced**. **1** An **invoice** is a document that lists goods that have been supplied or services that have been done, and says how much money you owe for them. EG *All they did was file the odd document and invoice... No invoices had been found for any of the goods.* N COUNT: IF + PREP THEN *for* = bill

2 If you **invoice** someone, you send them a bill for goods or services you have provided them with. EG *Have they invoiced us for the stationery yet?* V+O

invoke /ɪnvəʊk/, **invokes, invoking, invoked**; a fairly formal word. **1** If you **invoke** a law, you use it to justify what you are doing. EG *She had invoked the law in her own defence... The Government invoked the Emergency Powers Act... Most people assumed that I would invoke the Fifth Amendment.* V+O ⇑ cite

2 If you **invoke** a principle, wise saying, etc, you refer to it in order to persuade people to do something. EG *These principles were invoked in opposition to proposals for financial reform.* V+O ⇑ use = quote

3 If you **invoke** feelings of a particular kind, you cause someone to have these feelings. EG *They did their best to invoke popular enthusiasm for the war... ...nursery rhymes that invoke memories of my childhood... In his new work, he invokes an atmosphere of careless rapture.* V+O ⇑ raise = conjure

4 If you **invoke** a god, you appeal to the god for help, forgiveness, etc. EG *Gods will be invoked, spirits raised, rituals carried out.* V+O ⇑ call = raise

involuntary /ɪnvɒləntə⁰ri¹/. If you make an **involuntary** movement, exclamation, etc, you make it suddenly and without intending to because you are unable to control or prevent it. EG *She took an involuntary step towards him... 'Ugh!' he exclaimed with an involuntary shudder... There were one or two involuntary exclamations.* ◊ **involuntarily**. EG *I shivered involuntarily.* ADJ CLASSIF ≠ deliberate; ◊ ADV WITH VB

involve /ɪnvɒlv/, **involves, involving, involved**. **1** If a situation or activity **involves** someone or something, **1.1** it includes them as a necessary part or it uses them in some way. EG *The business seemed to involve an enormous amount of sales...* V+O/-ING = entail ≠ exclude

Caring for a one-year-old involves changing nappies and making special meals... 'I'm doing European Studies.'–'What does that involve?' I only want this job if the work involves young children... There's a lot of confusion about what this notion involves... Some of the experiments I've done involve the equipment you've seen... There are a tremendous number of accidents involving lorries. **1.2** it concerns or affects them. EG *Workers are never told about things which involve them. ...a project involving 206 families.* V+O

2 If you **involve** yourself in something, you take part in it. EG *I was reluctant to involve myself in this private fight... They continue to involve themselves deeply in community affairs.* V+O (REFL) : IF +PREP THEN *in/with* ⇑ participate

3 If you **involve** someone else in something, you get them to take part in it. EG *His real achievement was to involve the trade unions in plans for modernisation... I told her to get in touch with you, but she didn't want to involve you... Did you have to involve me in this?* V+O : IF+PREP THEN *in* = bring in ≠ exclude

4 If a book, film, etc **involves** you, it makes you feel that you are taking part in the events it describes or shows. EG *...the ability of the film to involve you imaginatively.* V+O (NG/REFL) : IF+PREP THEN *in* = absorb, engage

involved /ɪnvɒlvd/. **1** If someone or something is **involved** in a situation or activity, or if they are **involved** with it, they are taking part in it. EG *More women should be involved in decision-making... The nation is involved with building socialism... In all, 6,000 companies are involved in producing the parts that are needed for these aircraft... We never managed to get anything done, simply because of the large number of people involved... Should religious leaders get involved in politics?... The police are heavily involved.* ADJ QUALIT : PRED IF+PREP THEN *in/with*

2 If you are deeply **involved** in something, intensely **involved** in it, etc, you feel very strongly about it, usually enthusiastically. EG *I was deeply involved in my work... He is intensely and emotionally involved with his wife's public appearances... You're too much involved to have an objective view.* ADJ QUALIT : PRED, IF+PREP THEN *with/in* ⇑ interested = absorbed

3 The work, money, etc **involved** in something is the work that must be done, the money that must be spent, etc in order to achieve it. EG *There is quite a lot of work involved... Large amounts of money are involved... People have some idea of what is involved in making a television programme... Let me explain some of the principles involved... She had no real understanding of the problems involved.* ADJ CLASSIF : PRED, IF+PREP THEN *in* = in question

4 If you describe a situation or activity as **involved**, you mean that it is very complicated;. EG *We had long, involved discussions... It's terribly involved–I can't follow it... The problem's a little bit more involved than I suggested.* ADJ QUALIT = complex ≠ straightforward

5 If you are **involved** with another person, you are having a close relationship with them. EG *She got involved with lots of lovers... He had become involved with her when they were in Brussels.* ADJ CLASSIF : PRED, IF+PREP THEN *with*

involvement /ɪnvɒlvməⁱnt/, **involvements**. **1** Your **involvement** in something is the fact that you are taking part in it. EG *...parental involvement in primary schools... He avoids involvement in the political life of his community... It's not unfair to question the Americans' involvement... ...the active involvement of thousands of people in the election campaign.* N UNCOUNT : IF+ PREP THEN *in/of/with* = participation

2 Involvement is also the enthusiasm that you feel when you are taking part in something that you care deeply about. EG *Science lacks emotional involvement and universal appeal... Millions of young people go about seeking 'total' involvement.* N UNCOUNT : IF+ PREP THEN *in/with* ≠ distance

3 An **involvement** is a close relationship between two people, especially if they are not married to each other; used in informal English. EG *Both agreed that it was not to be a lasting involvement.* N UNCOUNT/ COUNT : IF+ PREP THEN *with* = intimacy, liaison

invulnerable /ɪnvʌlnəᵒrəbəᵒl/. If someone or something is **invulnerable**, they cannot be harmed or damaged. EG *The Count had come to think himself invulnerable... The strategic nuclear submarine is almost invulnerable.* ◊ **invulnerability** /ɪnvʌlnəᵒrəbɪlɪtiⁱ/. EG *Parents have a feeling of invulnerability.* ADJ CLASSIF : IF+ PREP THEN *to* ⇑ safe; ◊ N UNCOUNT

inward /ɪnwəd/. **1** Your **inward** thoughts or feelings are the thoughts and feelings that you do not express or show to other people. EG *He was constantly preoccupied with his inward thoughts... ...an expression of pain and inward concentration.* ◊ **inwardly**. EG *Floyd groaned inwardly... I remained inwardly unconvinced by what she had said.* ADJ CLASSIF : ATTRIB = inner; ◊ ADV = privately

2 If something moves **inward**, it moves towards the inside or centre of something. EG *The door swung inward... The soil must have subsided, pushing the walls inward.* ▸ used as an adjective. EG *...the inward flood of foreign capital.* ADV AFTER VB = inwards ≠ outward; ▸ ADJ CLASSIF : ATTRIB

inward-looking. **Inward-looking** people and societies are more interested in themselves than in other people or societies. EG *...an inward-looking visionary.* ▸ used of feelings and behaviour. EG *...an inward-looking nostalgia.* ADJ QUALIT = introspective

inwards /ɪnwədz/. If something moves or faces **inwards**, it moves or faces towards the inside or centre of something. EG *The doors opened inwards... His cell faced inwards over the garden.* ADV AFTER VB = inward

iodine /aɪədi:n/ is a dark blue or black liquid substance that is used especially in medicine and photography. N UNCOUNT

ion /aɪəⁱn/, **ions**. **Ions** are electrically charged atoms; a technical term. N COUNT : USU PL

-ion. See **-ation**.

iota /aɪəʊtə/. An **iota** of something is an extremely small amount of it. EG *I don't feel one iota of guilt... The buyer would not go one iota higher... You know, I don't think you've changed an iota.* N PART : SING+N UNCOUNT, USU WITH BROAD NEG ⇑ bit = jot

IOU /aɪ əʊ ju:/, **IOUs**. An **IOU** is a written promise that you will pay back some money that you have borrowed; an abbreviation for 'I owe you'. EG *He wrote out an IOU for five thousand dollars... We found a large number of unpaid bills and IOUs.* N COUNT ⇑ note

-ious. See **-ous**.

IQ /aɪ kju:/, **IQs**. Your **IQ** is your level of intelligence, which is calculated from the results of a special test that you do; an abbreviation for 'intelligence quotient'. EG *He had an IQ of 50... The IQ of our students is quite low.* N COUNT/ UNCOUNT : USU WITH POSS/SUPP

ir- is added to adjectives, adverbs, and nouns in order to form other adjectives, adverbs, and nouns with the opposite meaning. EG *...replaceable→irreplaceable.* PREFIX

IRA /aɪ ɑ:r eɪ/. The **IRA** is an organization that wants Northern Ireland to become independent of the United Kingdom and to be united politically with the Irish Republic. The IRA sometimes use violence to try to achieve this. IRA is an abbreviation for 'Irish Republican Army'. EG *The prison hunger strike increased support for the IRA.* N PROPER : *the*+ N

Iranian /ɪreɪniən/, **Iranians**. **1** Something that is **Iranian** belongs or relates to Iran, to its people, or to its language. EG *...Iranian oil refineries.* ADJ CLASSIF

2 An **Iranian** is a person who comes from Iran. N COUNT

3 Iranian is the language that is spoken by people who live in Iran, and in parts of some other countries, including Afghanistan and Pakistan. N UNCOUNT

Iraqi /ɪrɑ:ki:/, **Iraqis**. **1** Something that is **Iraqi** belongs or relates to Iraq, to its people, or to its language. ADJ CLASSIF

2 An **Iraqi** is a person who comes from Iraq. N COUNT

3 Iraqi is an Arabic language that is spoken in Iraq. N UNCOUNT

irascible /ɪræsɪⁱbəᵒl/. An **irascible** person becomes angry very easily; a formal word. EG *They were fractious and irascible... ...an irascible, difficult man.* ▸ used of behaviour. EG *...irascible outbursts.* ADJ QUALIT = short-tempered

irate /aɪreɪt/. If you are **irate**, you are very angry about something. EG *Next to him was the irate manager... The Bishop now looked distinctly irate.* ▸ used of things people say or write. EG *...irate complaints from car owners... ...an irate letter.* ADJ QUALIT = infuriated; ▸ = furious

ire /aɪə/ means the same as anger; an old-fashioned literary word. EG *He incurred the ire of the authorities.* N UNCOUNT = wrath

iridescent /ɪrɪdesənt/. Something that is **iridescent** has many bright colours that seem to keep changing; a formal word. EG *A dragon-fly hovered, vibrating and iridescent over the water... ...two gloriously iridescent small birds.* ADJ CLASSIF

iris /aɪrɪs/, **irises**. An **iris** is **1** the round coloured part of a person's eye. EG *The irises were of flecked grey... ...inflammation of the irises.* **2** a tall plant with long leaves and large purple, yellow, or white flowers. EG *The cottage gardens blaze with irises, lilies and peonies.* N COUNT; N COUNT

Irish /aɪrɪʃ/. **1** Something that is **Irish 1.1** belongs or relates to the whole of Ireland, to its people, or to its language. EG *She spoke with an Irish accent... ...Americans of Irish descent... ...an Irish doctor.* **1.2** ADJ CLASSIF; ADJ CLASSIF

belongs or relates to the Republic of Ireland. EG *...the Irish Prime Minister... ...a car bearing Irish licence plates.*

2 The **Irish** are the people who come from Ireland. EG *The Irish have a unique sence of humour.* [N PLURAL: the+N]

3 Irish is a language that some people speak in Ireland, especially in the South. [N UNCOUNT]

Irishman /aɪrɪʃmə^{3}n/, **Irishmen**. An **Irishman** is a man who comes from Ireland. EG *...a magazine edited by an Irishman living in London.* [N COUNT]

Irishwoman /aɪrɪʃwʊ^{1}mə^{0}n/, **Irishwomen**. An **Irishwoman** is a woman who comes from Ireland. EG *The Mother Superior was an Irishwoman.* [N COUNT]

irk /ɜːk/, **irks, irking, irked**. If something **irks** you, you do not like it, and it makes you annoyed because you cannot do anything about it. EG *His evident superiority must have irked them... British diplomatic tactics clearly irked the President.* [V+O: NO IMPER = irritate, vex]

irksome /ɜːksəm/. If something is **irksome**, it makes you annoyed because you do not like it and you know that you cannot do anything about it; used showing disapproval. EG *The intensity of his stare grew irksome... He thought of her as an irksome responsibility.* [ADJ QUALIT = irritating, tiresome]

iron /aɪən/, **irons, ironing, ironed**. **1 Iron** is a strong hard metallic element that is found in rocks. It is used for making many things, especially gates and fences. Your body also needs tiny quantities of iron in order to help your blood carry oxygen from your lungs to the other parts of your body. EG *...a soil high in iron and aluminium... The heavy iron gates closed behind her... He grasped the iron railing with both hands... No other food has so high an iron content.* ● See also **cast iron**. [N UNCOUNT ⇑ mineral]

2 An **iron** is a device for removing creases from clothes, sheets, towels, etc. An iron has a handle and a flat metal base. You heat it until the base is hot, then rub it over the clothes, etc. EG *If you know it's cotton or linen, use a hot iron.* [N COUNT ⇑ appliance]

3 If you **iron** clothes, etc, you remove the creases from them using an iron. EG *I can't iron shirts... My husband tries his best to wash and iron.* ● See also **ironing, ironing board**. [V OR V+O = press]

4 If you say that you must **strike while the iron is hot**, you mean that you must act quickly in order to benefit from a situation that is advantageous to you, because it may change soon. [PHR: VBS INFLECT]

5 If you **have** many **irons in the fire**, you are involved in several different activities or have several different plans. EG *I've got plenty of irons in the fire... Too many irons in the fire, that's your trouble.* [PHR: VB INFLECTS]

6 You use the word **iron** when you are describing a person's character, in order to say that they are very determined, and that they have great control over other people or over their own feelings. EG *He was able to enforce his iron will... ...the iron discipline of the Marines.* ▸ used as a noun. EG *That must require nerves of iron...* [ADJ CLASSIF: ATTRIB; ▸ N UNCOUNT]

iron out. If you **iron out** small problems, difficulties, etc, you get rid of them by successfully dealing with them. EG *I thought most of our problems were ironed out.* [PHRASAL VB: V+O+ADV ⇑ resolve]

Iron Age. The **Iron Age** was a period of time which began when people started making things from iron about three thousand years ago. [N PROPER: the+N]

Iron Curtain. **1** Some people refer to the **Iron Curtain** when they are talking about the border that separates the Soviet Union and its European allies from the other European countries. ● If someone says that something happens **behind the Iron Curtain**, they mean that it happens in the Soviet Union or in one of the countries allied to it. EG *Sales of his novels were most brisk behind the Iron Curtain.* [N PROPER: the+N; ● PHR: USED AS AN A]

2 Some people refer to the **Iron Curtain** countries when they are talking about the Soviet Union and the countries allied to it. EG *I have been to a number of Iron Curtain countries.* [N BEFORE N]

iron-grey; also spelled **iron-gray** in American English. **Iron-grey** hair is a dark grey colour. EG *He had iron-grey hair cut at medium length... He looked down at the iron-grey head.* [ADJ COLOUR]

ironic /aɪrɒnɪk/. **1** When you make an **ironic** or **ironical** remark, you say something in such a way that people realize that you are joking or that you really mean the opposite of what you say. EG *'Oh dear.' This comment was meant to be ironic... It was possible that his thanks were ironic... He wrote a characteristically ironical article.* ▸ used of people. EG *My father was ironical at first.* [ADJ QUALIT = sardonic]

2 An **ironic** or **ironical** situation is odd or amusing because it involves two factors that you would not normally expect to be connected or related. EG *It is ironic that the people who complain most loudly are the ones who do least to help... You know, there's something really ironical about all this.* [ADJ QUALIT]

ironically /aɪrɒnɪkə^{0}li^{1}/. **1** You add **ironically** to a sentence when you want to draw attention to an unexpected connection between things that is odd or amusing. EG *Many buildings in London (including, ironically, the Treasury) need a great deal of money spending on them... Ironically, the intelligence chief was the last person to hear the news.* [ADV SEN]

2 When you say something **ironically**, you say it in such a way that people realize that you are joking or that you really mean the opposite of what you say. EG *'How do you manage to get to work so early?' he said ironically.* [ADV WITH VB = sarcastically]

ironing /aɪənɪŋ/ is **1** the task or activity of ironing clothes in order to get rid of the creases. EG *I've got my ironing to do... Aren't you ever going to finish the ironing?* **2** all the clothes you have that need ironing. EG *She took up the pile of ironing and set it on the dresser.* [N UNCOUNT; N UNCOUNT]

ironing board, ironing boards; also spelled with a hyphen. An **ironing board** is a long narrow board usually covered by cloth and supported by folding legs, on which you iron clothes, etc. [N COUNT]

ironmonger /aɪənmʌŋgə/, **ironmongers**. An **ironmonger** or an **ironmonger's** is a shop which sells tools, nails, pans, and many other things that you need for doing jobs in your house or garden. EG *Insecticides should be available from big stores or ironmongers.* ▸ An **ironmonger** is also a person who runs an ironmonger's shop. [N COUNT]

ironmongery /aɪənmʌŋgri^{1}/ is the metal things that an ironmonger sells. EG *I was surprised to find ironmongery all over the place.* [N UNCOUNT = hardware]

ironstone /aɪənstəʊn/ is rock that contains a lot of iron. EG *...great ironstone boulders... ...an outcrop of ironstone.* [N UNCOUNT]

ironwork /aɪənwɜːk/. Gates, balconies, etc that are made of iron in a skilful and attractive way are called **ironwork**. EG *The staircase has fine ironwork... ...ironwork gates... ...brick houses with painted ironwork.* [N UNCOUNT]

irony /aɪrəni^{1}/, **ironies**. **1 Irony** is a form of humour, or an indirect way of conveying meaning, in which you say something in such a way that people realize that you are joking or that you really mean the opposite of what you say. EG *She said with slight irony, 'Bravo'... 'In theory,' continued Bouvier with heavy irony, 'we shall all be available.'... She spoke simply, without irony... In his voice she could detect a certain tinge of irony.* [N UNCOUNT = sarcasm, mockery]

2 The **irony** of a situation is the way in which it is odd or amusing because it involves factors which are not usually connected or related. EG *His reputation as a left-wing sympathizer added to the irony of the situation... By a curious irony, both of her husbands died of the same rare illness... The irony is that many politicians agree with what he says... History has many ironies.* [N COUNT/UNCOUNT]

irradiate /ɪreɪdi^{1}eɪt/, **irradiates, irradiating, irradiated**. If you **are irradiated**, you are exposed to a large amount of radioactivity; a technical term. EG *People in the area could be blinded or irradiated.* [V+O: USU PASS ⇑ contaminate]

◊ **irradiation** /ɪreɪdi^{1}eɪʃə^{0}n/. EG *...nuclear irradiation studies.* [◊ N UNCOUNT]

irrational /ɪræʃə^{0}nəl, -ʃənə^{0}l/. **Irrational** feelings and behaviour are not based on logical reasons or clear thinking. EG *His anxiety was irrational... ...a deep and irrational fear of change... ...great bursts of irrational hostility.* ▸ used of people. EG *She was irrational, bigoted and cold... ...an irrational child.* [ADJ QUALIT = illogical, unreasonable ≠ rational]

◊ **irrationally**. EG *They were accused of acting irrationally... I remained irrationally convinced that I could escape.* [◊ ADV] ◊ **irrationality** /ɪræʃə^{0}nælɪti^{1}/. EG *She saw Guy's irrationality as something terrifying and almost disgusting.* [◊ N UNCOUNT]

irreconcilable /ɪrekənsaɪləbə^{0}l/. **1** If two opinions, proposals, etc are **irreconcilable**, they are so strongly opposed to each other that it is not possible to believe both of them or to carry both of them out; a formal word. EG *Their views had been irreconcilable* [ADJ CLASSIF = conflicting, incompatible] *from the beginning... The two sides had irreconcilable objectives.*

2 An **irreconcilable** disagreement is so serious that it cannot be settled. EG *...an irreconcilable conflict between capital and labour... ...an irreconcilable clash of interests.* ADJ CLASSIF

irredeemable /ɪrɪdiːməbəˀl/. If someone has an **irredeemable** fault in their character or personality, it cannot ever be corrected; a rather literary word. EG *...a complete and irredeemable selfishness.* ◇ **irredeemably**. EG *I saw him as old, corrupt and irredeemably evil.* ADJ CLASSIF ⇑ hopeless = incurable ◇ ADV+ADJ/ADV

irreducible /ɪrɪdjuːsɪˈbəˀl/. Something that is **irreducible** cannot be explained in terms of simpler things; a very formal word. EG *...the irreducible essence of art... The fifth theory is irreducible to simpler terms.* ADJ CLASSIF : IF+ PREP THEN *to*

irrefutable /ɪrɪfjuːtəbəˀl/. A statement that is **irrefutable** cannot be denied or shown to be incorrect; a formal word. EG *What you are saying is an opinion, not an irrefutable fact... His argument is virtually irrefutable.* ADJ CLASSIF = indisputable

irregular /ɪrɛgjəˀlə/, **irregulars**. **1** Something that is **irregular** is not even, regular, or perfectly balanced. For example, an irregular surface is not flat or level, an irregular pattern does not repeat itself exactly, and an irregular face is not symmetrical. EG *She touched its rough irregular surface... ...a dress with fraying sleeves and an irregular hem line... John had a sharp, irregular face.* ◇ **irregularity** /ɪrɛgjəˀlærɪti¹/, **irregularities**. EG *Minor irregularities in the components might lead to machine failure.* ADJ QUALIT = uneven ≠ smooth, symmetrical ◇ N COUNT/ UNCOUNT

2 Irregular actions happen at intervals which are not regular. EG *I breathed in deep irregular gasps... The newspaper's appearance became increasingly irregular.* ◇ **irregularly**. EG *He went home, irregularly, at weekends... Our research seminar meets rather irregularly.* ◇ **irregularity**. EG *This is likely to produce irregularities of heart rate.* ADJ QUALIT = spasmodic ◇ ADV WITH VB ◇ N COUNT/ UNCOUNT

3 Irregular behaviour and actions do not conform to accepted rules or procedures; used showing disapproval. EG *She led a somewhat irregular private life... He accepted the mutilated document, muttering: 'Most irregular. Most irregular.'* ◇ **irregularity**. EG *There was some irregularity in the man's papers... The report revealed a large number of irregularities.* ADJ QUALIT ⇑ unusual = unorthodox ◇ N COUNT/ UNCOUNT = anomaly

4 An **irregular** verb, noun, or adjective does not inflect in the same way as most other verbs, nouns, or adjectives in the language. ADJ CLASSIF

5 Irregulars are soldiers who do not belong to an official national army. EG *...a winter campaign against armed irregulars... Hundreds of the irregulars deserted.* ▸ used as an adjective. EG *...irregular forces.* N COUNT : USU PL ▸ ADJ CLASSIF : ATTRIB

irrelevance /ɪrɛləvəns/, **irrelevances**. **1** The **irrelevance** of something is the fact that it is not at all connected with what you are discussing or dealing with. EG *The irrelevance of nationalism was clear... She made long involved remarks of obvious irrelevance.* N UNCOUNT : IF+ PREP THEN *of/to*

2 An **irrelevance** is a fact, activity, institution, etc that has no useful purpose; used showing disapproval. EG *The Commonwealth is an irrelevance: we are a Pacific country... ...an education made up of academic irrelevances.* N COUNT = irrelevancy

irrelevancy /ɪrɛləvənsi¹/, **irrelevancies**. An **irrelevancy** is a fact, activity, institution, etc that has no useful purpose; used showing disapproval. EG *The committee was looked upon as an irrelevancy... A professional should not waste his time with irrelevancies.* N COUNT/ UNCOUNT = irrelevance

irrelevant /ɪrɛləvənt/. **1** An **irrelevant fact, remark, etc is** not at all connected with what you are discussing or dealing with, and is therefore not important; used showing disapproval. EG *The book was full of irrelevant information... He blandly dismissed what she said as irrelevant... He felt that right and wrong were irrelevant to the situation.* ◇ **irrelevantly**. EG *'How old are you?' he asked irrelevantly.* ADJ QUALIT : IF+ PREP THEN *to* ⇑ inappropriate ≠ relevant ◇ ADV

2 If you describe an activity, institution, etc as **irrelevant**, you mean that you think it has no useful purpose; used showing disapproval. EG *The courses I was compelled to take were irrelevant... Populist solidarity will become increasingly irrelevant.* ADJ QUALIT : USU PRED ⇑ useless = obsolete

irreligious /ɪrɪlɪdʒəs/. An **irreligious** person does not accept the beliefs of any religion or opposes all religions. EG *My family were completely irreligious... I may marry an irreligious person.* ▸ used of beliefs, attitudes, and statements. EG *Belief in evolution is irreligious.* ADJ QUALIT ⇑ unbelieving

irremediable /ɪrəˈmiːdjəbəˀl/. If a situation or state is **irremediable**, it is bad and cannot be improved; a formal word. EG *...no irremediable damage arises.* ADJ CLASSIF

irreparable /ɪrɛpəˀrəbəˀl/. **Irreparable** damage, harm, etc is so bad that it cannot be put right again; a formal word. EG *To accelerate this stage does the child irreparable damage... She may have done irreparable harm to her reputation.* ADJ CLASSIF = irretrievable

irreplaceable /ɪrɪpleɪsəbəˀl/. **Irreplaceable** things are so special that they cannot be replaced if they are lost or destroyed. EG *My jewellery is totally irreplaceable... Irreplaceable woodland is being destroyed.* ADJ CLASSIF

irrepressible /ɪrɪprɛsɪˈbəˀl/. An **irrepressible** person is lively and energetic and never seems to be depressed; often used showing approval. EG *Basil is irrepressible, funny, and affectionate... ...the irrepressible Frederica.* ▸ used of behaviour and attitudes. EG *...their irrepressible good humour.* ◇ **irrepressibly**. EG *A howl of laughter went up irrepressibly.* ADJ QUALIT = buoyant ◇ ADV

irreproachable /ɪrɪprəʊtʃəbəˀl/. You say that someone's character or behaviour is **irreproachable** when you consider that they behave so well that you cannot criticize them; used showing approval. EG *They praised his irreproachable character.* ADJ CLASSIF = impeccable

irresistible /ɪrɪzɪstəbəˀl/. **1** You describe your wish to do something as **irresistible** when you want to do it so much that you cannot prevent yourself doing it. EG *For me the urge to perform is irresistible... I was overcome by an almost irresistible desire to break into song.* ADJ QUALIT = overwhelming

2 You describe someone or something as **irresistible** when you find them very attractive or entertaining; used showing approval. EG *Jim Lithgow was irresistible... He found her wit irresistible.* ◇ **irresistibly**. EG *The songs are irresistibly catchy.* ADJ QUALIT ⇑ appealing = fascinating ◇ ADV

3 You also describe something as **irresistible** when it cannot be stopped or prevented. EG *...an irresistible political force... The pressure for development is almost irresistible.* ◇ **irresistibly**. EG *It forces itself irresistibly upon our attention.* ADJ CLASSIF = inexorable ◇ ADV WITH VB = inexorably

irresolute /ɪrɛzəluːt/. If you are **irresolute**, you cannot decide what to do; a formal word. EG *I stopped, irresolute... The councillors were timid, mediocre and irresolute.* ADJ QUALIT = indecisive

irrespective /ɪrɪspɛktɪv/. If you say that something will be done **irrespective of** certain things, you mean that it will be done without taking those things into consideration. EG *They will close the premises irrespective of who is running them... Everyone, irrespective of means or occupation, shall have an equal opportunity.* PREP = regardless of

irresponsible /ɪrɪspɒnsɪˈbəˀl/. An **irresponsible** action is one in which you do not properly consider the possible consequences of what you are doing; used showing disapproval. EG *...hasty and irresponsible action... ...the irresponsible application of technology... It would be irresponsible of me to encourage you.* ▸ used of people. EG *You've behaved like an irresponsible idiot... She wrote that he was irresponsible and selfish.* ◇ **irresponsibly**. EG *They irresponsibly allowed wages to rise.* ◇ **irresponsibility** /ɪrɪspɒnsɪbɪlɪti¹/. EG *...the consequences of their irresponsibility.* ADJ QUALIT = reckless ▸ = thoughtless ◇ ADV WITH VB ◇ N UNCOUNT

irretrievable /ɪrɪtriːvəbəˀl/. **Irretrievable** harm, damage, etc has gone so far that it cannot be put right again. EG *They have done irretrievable damage to the physical environment... The Party is showing all the signs of irretrievable breakdown.* ◇ **irretrievably**. EG *The war was irretrievably lost.* ADJ CLASSIF = irreparable ◇ ADV

irreverence /ɪrɛvəˀrəns/ is behaviour in which you talk to someone, or talk about them, without showing the respect for them that people would expect. EG *His irreverence has frequently landed him in trouble.* N UNCOUNT : IF+ PREP THEN *to/towards* = disrespect

irreverent /ɪrɛvəˀrənt/. When you are **irreverent**, you talk to someone, or talk about them, without showing the respect for them that people would expect. EG *I do not mean to be irreverent... Some of those leaving were making rude and irreverent* ADJ QUALIT : IF+ PREP THEN *to/towards* = disrespectful, impertinent *comments.* ◊ **irreverently**. EG *...the KSLI, known irreverently as the King's Silly Little Idiots.* ◊ ADV WITH VB

irreversible /ɪrɪvɜːsɪˈbəºl/. If you do **irreversible** harm or damage to something, you cannot undo it or put it back to its original state. EG *The damage may be irreversible... ...irreversible changes to the climate... We've done something irreversible.* ◊ **irreversibly**. EG *The ozone layer would be irreversibly damaged.* ADJ CLASSIF = irrevocable; ◊ ADV

irrevocable /ɪrevəkəbəºl/. If something is **irrevocable**, it cannot be stopped or changed. EG *The surrender of liberties is irrevocable... His life was set on an irrevocable course.* ◊ **irrevocably**. EG *He was in danger of irrevocably losing his son.* ADJ CLASSIF = unalterable; ◊ ADV

irrigate /ɪrɪgeɪt/, **irrigates, irrigating, irrigated.** If you **irrigate** land, you supply all of it with water through ditches or pipes that are specially put there in order to help crops to grow. EG *You had to work hard to irrigate the fields... A windmill will power a small pump and irrigate about an acre of land.* ◊ **irrigated**. EG *...the irrigated areas of the Ganges plain.* ◊ **irrigation** /ɪrɪgeɪʃəºn/. EG *They had a complex irrigation system... Only 1 per cent of the area was under irrigation.* V+O; ◊ ADJ CLASSIF; ◊ N UNCOUNT

irritable /ɪrɪtəbəºl/. If you are **irritable**, you are in a mood in which you easily become annoyed. EG *Judy was feeling hot, tired, and irritable... The cold was making Posy irritable.* ◊ **irritably**. EG *'What do you want me to do?' she said irritably... He shrugged irritably and said: 'He's out'.* ◊ **irritability** /ɪrɪtəbɪlɪti¹/. EG *Signs of overwork are nervous tension, irritability and indigestion.* ADJ QUALIT = peevish, snappy; ◊ ADV WITH VB = peevishly; ◊ N UNCOUNT

irritant /ɪrɪtənt/, **irritants**; a formal word. An **irritant** is 1 something that annoys you because you do not like it and because you know that you cannot stop it continuing. EG *Their persistence acts as a constant irritant... Lack of national independence continued to be an irritant.* 2 a substance which causes a part of your body to become tender or sore. EG *...a dangerous internal irritant. ...irritant gases.* N COUNT = irritation; N COUNT

irritate /ɪrɪteɪt/, **irritates, irritating, irritated.** 1 If something **irritates** you, it annoys you because you do not like it and because you know that you cannot stop it continuing. EG *His style irritated some senior officials... The way he ate irritated her so much that she could have screamed.* ◊ **irritated**. EG *My sister got a bit irritated... He made an irritated gesture.* ◊ **irritating**. EG *I find the people here very irritating... ...his irritating habits.* ◊ **irritatingly**. EG *She found him irritatingly slow.* V+O = irk; ◊ ADJ QUALIT; ◊ ADJ QUALIT; ◊ ADV

2 If something **irritates** a part of your body, it causes it to become tender or sore and often makes you want to scratch. EG *Cream should be used to avoid irritating the skin.* ◊ **irritating**. EG *Their irritating bites leave large red patches.* V+O ⇑ inflame; ◊ ADJ QUALIT

irritation /ɪrɪteɪʃəºn/, **irritations**. 1 **Irritation** is 1.1 a feeling of annoyance, often one that you get when something that you do not like continues to happen. EG *He felt a sudden irritation against Percival... Dennis knew better than to show his irritation... They remain a constant source of irritation.* 1.2 the painful feeling that you get when something causes a part of your body to become tender or sore. EG *...eye irritation.* N UNCOUNT = vexation; N UNCOUNT

2 An **irritation** is something that annoys you because you do not like it and because you know that you cannot stop it continuing. EG *...the irritations of everyday life.* N COUNT = irritant

Is. is a written abbreviation for 'Island', 'Islands', 'Isle', or 'Isles'. EG *...Tokelau Is... ...Western Is.* N IN NAMES

is /ɪz/ is the third person singular of the present tense of **be**.

-ise. See **-ize**.

-ish. 1 **-ish** is added to many adjectives in order to form other adjectives. Adjectives formed like this describe something as having a particular property, quality, or colour, but only to a limited extent. For example, 'reddish' means slightly red, and 'smallish' means slightly smaller than average, but not very small. EG *...dark→darkish... ...young→youngish... ...big→biggish... ...yellow→yellowish.* SUFFIX : FORMS ADJS

2 **-ish** is also added to some nouns in order to form adjectives. Adjectives formed like this describe someone or something as being like a particular kind of person or thing. For example, 'childish' means like a child, or typical of a child. EG *...girl→girlish... ...monk→monkish... ...kitten→kittenish.* SUFFIX : FORMS ADJS

Islam /ɪzlaːm/. 1 **Islam** is the religion of the Muslims, which teaches that there is only one God and that Mohammed is His prophet. The sacred book of Islam is the Koran. EG *The Berbers adopted Islam... ...the religious ethics of Islam.* N UNCOUNT

2 Some people refer to **Islam** when they are talking about all the countries where Islam is the main religion. EG *...a practice still carried out in parts of Islam.* N UNCOUNT

Islamic /ɪzlæmɪk/ means belonging or relating to Islam. EG *...the Islamic civilization... ...Islamic laws... ...other Islamic countries.* ADJ CLASSIF : ATTRIB = Muslim

island /aɪlənd/, **islands**. An **island** is a piece of land that is completely surrounded by water. EG *There aren't any beasts to be afraid of on this island... ...the Mediterranean island of Cyprus... ...the Channel Islands.* N COUNT : ALSO IN NAMES

islander /aɪləndə/, **islanders**. **Islanders** are people who live on an island, especially a small one. EG *...the spartan lives of the islanders... ...the Channel Islanders.* N COUNT : USU PL ⇑ inhabitant

isle /aɪl/, **isles**. An **isle** is an island; a literary word, sometimes used as part of a name. EG *...a desert isle... ...the Isle of Man... ...Fair Isle... ...the British Isles.* N COUNT : ALSO IN NAMES

islet /aɪlɪ²t/, **islets**. An **islet** is a small island; a rather literary word. EG *They live on a small islet... There is one taverna on this tiny islet.* N COUNT

-ism, -isms. 1 **-ism** is used at the end of uncount nouns that refer to beliefs or to political or religious movements. EG *...radicalism... ...nationalism... ...feminism... ...Hinduism... ...Judaism.* SUFFIX : FORMS N UNCOUNTS

2 **-ism** is also added to some nouns in order to form uncount nouns that refer to attitudes and behaviour. EG *...stoic→stoicism... ...cynic→cynicism... ...hero→heroism... ...fanatic→fanaticism.* SUFFIX : FORMS N UNCOUNTS

3 **-ism** is also added in place of -ize or -ise at the end of many verbs in order to form nouns. Nouns formed in this way refer to behaviour, to particular actions, and to ceremonies. EG *...criticize→criticism... ...ostracize→ostracism... ...baptize→baptism... ...exorcise→exorcism.* SUFFIX : FORMS NOUNS

isn't /ɪzəºnt/ is the usual spoken form of 'is not'. EG *It isn't the children who worry about exams... That's all we want, isn't it?*

isolate /aɪsəleɪt/, **isolates, isolating, isolated.**
1 If something **isolates** you or if you **isolate** yourself, you are physically or socially set apart from other people. EG *His wealth isolated him... They resolved to isolate themselves entirely in order to build a new society... Under capitalism, people are isolated from each other.* V+O (NG/REFL) ⇑ separate = cut off

2 If you **isolate** an idea, word, etc, you set it apart and treat it separately from all the other ideas, words, etc that are connected with it or close to it. EG *Concentration on an idea isolates it from its surroundings... I isolated that simple sentence from the huge transcription.* V+O : IF+PREP THEN *from* ⇑ separate

3 If you **isolate** a substance, chemical element, etc, you separate it from other substances so that you can examine it or deal with it on its own; a technical term. EG *You can isolate genes and study how they work... They isolated the acid from the fungus.* V+O : IF+PREP THEN *from* ⇑ extract

4 If you **isolate** a sick person or animal, you keep them apart from other people or animals, so that their illness does not spread. EG *David had to be isolated for whooping cough.* V+O = quarantine

5 If you **isolate** people, 5.1 you cause them to lose their friends, contacts, or supporters within a group or an organization, often because you are opposed to them and want to weaken them. EG *Could we isolate the administration, and thus force it to accept our demands?* 5.2 you cause them to stop liking you or supporting you because you do things that they do not approve of. EG *One by one, this chairman effectively isolated all the good people in the company.* V+O ⇑ separate = alienate; V+O = alienate

isolated /aɪsəleɪtɪ²d/. 1 An **isolated** house, village, etc is set apart, usually by a long distance, from other houses or villages. EG *His house was very isolated and it must have been lonely there.* ▸ used of people, and of their way of life. EG *The islanders were very isolated... She lived a strange, isolated life, alone in a tiny cottage.* ADJ QUALIT = cut-off, remote

2 If you feel **isolated**, you feel lonely and without friends or help. EG *I felt more and more isolated... I had become isolated, defensive, and humourless.* ADJ QUALIT : USU PRED ⇑ alone

3 An **isolated** example, incident, etc is a single example, incident, etc that is not part of a general ADJ CLASSIF : ATTRIB

pattern or sequence. EG *I didn't know enough Czech to understand the poem, but I could pick out a few isolated words... ...a series of isolated episodes... This is what happened in several isolated cases.*

isolation /aɪsəleɪʃəⁿn/. 1 **Isolation** is 1.1 the state of being set apart physically, socially, or politically from other people, places, or organizations. EG *...cultural isolation followed quickly... ...the isolation and alienation of city life.* 1.2 the process of isolating someone from a group that they belonged to. EG *...the isolation of a relatively small number of activists.* 1.3 the state of being alone and without friends or help. EG *I had to find some way of escaping this terrible isolation... Thousands of single mothers live in isolation and poverty.* — N UNCOUNT; N UNCOUNT = alienation; N UNCOUNT ⇑ loneliness

2 If something exists, happens, or is done **in isolation**, it exists, happens, or is done separately from other things that are similar to it. EG *No class can exist in isolation... Do governments act in isolation from the other forces of society?... We had to decide whether food supplies should be dealt with in isolation... These varied questions can't be answered in isolation from each other.* — PHR : USED AS AN A ⇑ apart = independently

isolationism /aɪsəleɪʃənɪzəⁿm/ is the policy of a country when it avoids becoming involved in disputes between other countries; usually used showing disapproval. EG *The report blames British isolationism.* ◊ **isolationist.** EG *He was still an isolationist... ...isolationist attitudes.* — N UNCOUNT

isometric /aɪsəⁿmetrɪk/, **isometrics. Isometrics** or **isometric exercises** are exercises in which you make your muscles work against each other or against something else, for example by pressing your hands together. EG *Isometrics may increase muscle bulk.* — N PLURAL

isosceles triangle /aɪsɒsəliːz traɪæŋgəⁿl/, **isosceles triangles.** An **isosceles triangle** is a triangle which has two sides that are the same length; a technical term in geometry. — N COUNT

isotope /aɪsəⁿtəʊp/, **isotopes. Isotopes** are atoms which have the same atomic number but which have different physical properties because they do not have the same number of neutrons; a technical term in science. EG *Tritium is one of the mildest radioactive isotopes.* — N COUNT

Israeli /ɪzreɪliⁱ/, **Israelis.** 1 Something that is **Israeli** belongs or relates to Israel or to its people. EG *...Israeli oranges... ...the Israeli Prime Minister.* — ADJ CLASSIF

2 An **Israeli** is a person who comes from Israel. EG *The Israelis worked their land close up to the border.* — N COUNT

issue /ɪʃjuː/, **issues, issuing, issued.** 1 An **issue** is an important subject that people are discussing or arguing about. EG *People should let their MPs know where they stand on this issue... This has not been raised as an issue by the West... ...the issues at stake... ...an important and serious issue... ...social issues.* — N COUNT : USU + SUPP = matter

2 When you talk about **the issue**, you are referring to the really important part of the thing that you are considering or discussing. EG *That's just not the issue... What I think of you simply isn't the issue.* — N SING : *the*+N = the point

3 The point **at issue**, question **at issue**, etc is the most important part of something that you are considering or discussing. EG *The point at issue is this... It was the content of literacy studies that was at issue... What is at issue is the extent to which inflation causes unemployment.* — PHR : USED AS AN A, OR NG+PHR = in question

4 If you **evade the issue, duck the issue**, etc, you refuse to accept or deal with an important problem or a difficult subject; used showing disapproval. EG *You can no longer go on evading the issue... Congress ducked the issue... He was skirting the issue.* — PHR : VB INFLECTS = prevaricate

5 If you **cloud the issue, confuse the issue**, etc, you introduce unimportant matters into a discussion or conversation, preventing people from paying attention to the main subject; used showing disapproval. EG *Her explanations usually just clouded the issue... Let's not confuse the issue.* — PHR : VB INFLECTS

6 An **issue** is also a reason for quarrelling or disagreement. EG *If you'd stayed at home, we wouldn't have had an issue... He stood up, determined to settle the issue between them finally and at once.* — N COUNT : USU SING ⇑ difference = argument

7 If you **make an issue of something**, you make an unnecessary fuss about it; used showing disapproval. EG *She didn't want to make an issue of it... Some parents make such an issue of adoption.* — PHR : VB INFLECTS

8 If you **take issue with** someone or **take issue with** something that they have said, you disagree with what they have said, and start arguing about it. EG *I was bold enough to take issue with the director... I want to take issue with John Taylor about his ideas on illegitimacy... I would take issue with that.* — PHR : VB INFLECTS ⇑ contradict

9 An **issue** is also 9.1 a particular edition of a magazine, newspaper, etc. EG *We sell 2,000 copies per issue... The article had appeared in the previous day's issue.* 9.2 the result or outcome of something; a formal or literary use. EG *He wants his prayers to have a prosperous issue... He was on the way to insure a happy issue for their love.* — N COUNT; N SING : a+ADJ+N

10 Your child or children can be referred to as your **issue**; a legal or old-fashioned use. EG *He died without issue.* — N UNCOUNT = progeny

11 If you **issue** a statement, warning, etc, you make it formally or publicly. EG *We considered issuing some sort of statement or press release... They issued a serious warning... We issued a formal invitation from this department.* — V+O = send out

12 If you **issue** something or if you issue someone with it, you officially provide or equip them with it. EG *We were issued with a set of instructions... Who issued the travel documents?... I was issued with a new rifle.* ▸ used as a noun. EG *The issue of firearms... It is illegal for a soldier to retain any piece of war issue.* — V+O : IF+PREP THEN *with* ⇑ supply; ▸ N UNCOUNT ⇑ provision

13 If you **issue** a document, you officially produce it and make it available. EG *The Ministry had to cancel plans to issue government bonds.* ▸ used as a noun. EG *...the issue of commemorative stamps.* — V+O : IF+PREP THEN *to*; ▸ N UNCOUNT/COUNT

14 When a liquid, sound, smell, etc **issues** from something, it comes out of it. EG *There were caves, with streams issuing from them... ...the smells issuing from the back kitchen... Mr Hughes's voice, issuing from the darkness, sounded loud and frightening.* — V+A *(from)* = emerge

-ist, -ists. 1 **-ist** is added in place of -ism at the end of uncount nouns in order to form count nouns and adjectives. Count nouns formed in this way refer to people who have particular opinions or do a particular kind of work. For example, a pacifist believes in pacifism, and a journalist works in journalism. Nouns and adjectives formed in this way are not defined in this dictionary, but are treated with the related uncount nouns. EG *...socialism→socialist... ...nationalism→nationalist... ...journalism→journalist.* — SUFFIX : FORMS N COUNTS AND ADJS

2 **-ist** is also added, especially in place of -y and -s, at the end of uncount nouns in order to form count nouns referring to people who do a particular kind of work. EG *...botany→botanist... ...metallurgy→metallurgist... ...physics→physicist... ...propaganda→propagandist.* — SUFFIX : FORMS N COUNTS

3 **-ist** is also added at the end of nouns referring to musical instruments, in order to form nouns that refer to people who play these instruments. EG *...piano→pianist... ...guitar→guitarist... ...bassoon→bassoonist.* — SUFFIX : FORMS N COUNTS

isthmus /ɪsθəⁿməs/, **isthmuses.** An **isthmus** is a narrow area of land connecting two very large areas. EG *...the Isthmus of Panama.* — N COUNT : USED IN NAMES

it /ɪt/ is used as the subject of a verb or as the object of a verb or preposition. 1 You use **it** 1.1 to refer to something that has already been mentioned, or to something in the situation around you. **It** can refer to an object, place, or animal, to something abstract, or to a group of things or people. EG *...a tray with glasses on it... The man went up to the cat and started stroking it... The Council said it would close the flats and pull them down... They learn to speak English before they learn to read it... The strike went on for over a year before it was finally settled... Everyone is asking for love but few seem able to provide it.* 1.2 to refer to a child or baby whose sex you do not know or whose sex is not considered to be important for what you are saying. EG *...the processes that every child must learn as it grows up... What would happen to the infant once it was born?* 1.3 to refer to the subject matter of what you have just said or of what you are going to say. EG *She was frightened, but tried not to feel it or show it... Maybe he changed his mind, but I doubt it... I would get new socks. It seemed like a good idea... The government has let it be known that food prices will be vastly increased.* 1.4 to refer to a situation, activity, or event that you — PRON : SING; PRON : SING; PRON : SING; PRON : SING are involved in or have been involved in. EG *It was very pleasant at the Hochstadts... They waited for it all to end... I like it here... We had better get down to it... It doesn't matter.*

2 You also use **it** 2.1 usually as the subject of a verb, in sentences where you describe something that has happened or is happening. EG *It happened that I was offered this job... As it turned out, we still had dozens of offers... It took Simon some time to work out what she meant... It is impossible to make any decision... It occurred to him that he hadn't eaten anything since the night before... The United States should, it was argued, attempt to ride the storm... He found it hard to make friends.* 2.2 in expressions such as 'if it wasn't for...', where you mention a particular person or thing that is responsible for something happening or not happening. EG *If it hadn't been for Carson, Sam would never have got here... If it weren't so damn cold this would be just gorgeous... Were it not for Helen's nagging, he would have given up.* — PRON : SING, USU USED AS S / PRON : SING, USED AS S

3 You also use **it** mainly as the subject of a verb such as 'be' or 'seem' in sentences where you give your opinion or express your attitude towards something. EG *It was a pity that her spelling was so bad... It's necessary to have a good grasp of the laws of logic... It is madness for Great Britain to remain opposed to the deal... Is it really worth double glazing a house?... We believe it right that the unions should have greater power.... It doesn't matter what you do at this point.* — PRON : SING, USU USED AS S

4 You also use **it**, mainly as the subject of the verb 'be', 4.1 when you are making statements about the weather, time, date, or day of the week. EG *It's raining here at the moment... It's hot. Must be in the eighties already... Early this morning it snowed... It is nearly one o'clock... It's the 6th of April today... It's Saturday afternoon and all my friends are out.* 4.2 when you are telling someone who you are, or asking them who they are, especially at the beginning of a phone call. You also use **it** in statements and questions about the identity of other people. EG *Hello?–Good morning, it's Yakov Liebermann again... It's me–Mary... 'Grandmother!' he called at the door. 'Who is it?' came the reply... Who was that you were speaking to?–It was only the postman... Who's there? Oh, it's you.* 4.3 when you are emphasizing or drawing attention to something. EG *She still lives in London. Or perhaps it's Cambridge she lives in... It's my mother I'm worried about... He kept looking at me as if it was I who was going to give him the money.* — PRON : SING, USED AS S (4.1, 4.2, 4.3)

5 **It** is also used without any meaning, or with very little meaning, in many common expressions. EG *He'd asked for it and he was going to get it... We are just going to have to run for it... Look, Rick, he doesn't like being photographed, so quit it... Gossip had it that she would marry Granby... You wouldn't want to be like me, I take it?* — PRON : SING, USU USED AS O

6 In informal English, **it** means sex, especially in such expressions as 'have it', 'do it', and 'get it'. — N UNCOUNT : USU USED AS O

7 When you say that someone **thinks** that they **are it**, you mean that they think that they are very important; used showing disapproval. EG *She really thinks she's it.* — PHR : VBS INFLECT

Italian /ɪtæljən/, **Italians**. 1 Something that is **Italian** belongs or relates to Italy, to its people, or to its language. EG *...Italian music... ...the Italian news agency AGI.* — ADJ CLASSIF

2 An **Italian** is a person who comes from Italy. EG *His first and second officers were Italians.* — N COUNT

3 **Italian** is the language spoken by people who live in Italy. EG *I don't know any Italian.* — N UNCOUNT

italic /ɪtælɪk/, **italics**. **Italics** are letters which have been printed in a special way so that they slope to the right, often in order to emphasize a particular word or sentence. The examples in this dictionary are printed in italics. EG *The differences between the two are given in italics... ...italic lettering.* — N PLURAL

itch /ɪtʃ/, **itches, itching, itched**. 1 When you **itch** or when a part of your body **itches**, you have an unpleasant feeling on your skin that makes you want to scratch. EG *We are scratching like this because we itch... My toes are itching like mad.* ▸ used as a noun. EG *...an itch that must be scratched.* — V; ▸ N COUNT

2 If you **itch** to do something or if you **are itching** to do it, you are very eager or impatient to do it; an informal use. EG *He itched to tell them... I was itching to get away.* — V+to-INF/for; ⇑ want

3 If you have an **itch** to do something or to have something, you have a strong desire to do it or have it. EG *The itch to travel begins long before the teenage years... We have to cure ourselves of the itch for absolute knowledge and power.* — N SING WITH DET +to-INF/for; ⇑ wish; = hankering

itchy /ɪtʃi¹/; an informal word. 1 If you are **itchy** or if a part of your body is **itchy**, you have an unpleasant feeling on your skin that makes you want to scratch. EG *Don't you feel all itchy?... Their skin becomes dry and itchy.* — ADJ QUALIT

2 If you **have itchy feet**, you have a strong desire to leave a place and to travel. — PHR : VB INFLECTS

it'd /ɪtə⁰d/ is 1 a spoken form of 'it would'. EG *If I went on the train it'd be cheaper... It'd be warm enough to sunbathe.* 2 a spoken form of 'it had', especially when 'had' is an auxiliary verb. EG *It'd rained all day.*

item /aɪtəm/, **items**. An **item** is 1 one of a collection or list of objects, especially objects that you are buying or selling. EG *The first item he bought was an alarm clock... ...a list of household items... ...items of clothing... The shop window was filled with hundreds of items.* 2 one of a number of matters that you are dealing with. EG *I had two items of business to attend to before lunch... This tax cut is the most crucial item left on our agenda... Item 17 is concerned with the chairman's expenses.* 3 a report or article in a newspaper or magazine. EG *...an item in the Sacramento Reporter... She cuts out items from the newspaper.* — N COUNT/PART; = thing / N COUNT/PART / N COUNT

itemize /aɪtəmaɪz/, **itemizes, itemizing, itemized**; also spelled **itemise**. If you **itemize** a number of things, you make a list of them. EG *The contents of his pockets were itemized and confiscated.* — V+O; ⇑ record

itinerant /ɪ⁵tɪnərənt/, **itinerants**; a fairly formal word. 1 An **itinerant** preacher, judge, etc travels around a region, working for short periods in different places. EG *Two of his six sons had become itinerant preachers... ...itinerant vegetable sellers.* — ADJ CLASSIF : ATTRIB; ⇑ travelling; = roving

2 An **itinerant** is a person who travels regularly as his or her way of life. EG *Some itinerant had stopped at her place a few weeks before.* — N COUNT; ⇑ traveller

itinerary /ɪ⁵tɪnərəri¹/, **itineraries**. An **itinerary** is a plan of a journey showing the route and the places that you will visit. EG *I had planned a luxurious itinerary in my head... A visit to Rome must be included in the itinerary.* — N COUNT; = programme

it'll /ɪtə⁰l/ is a spoken form of 'it will'. EG *It'll be quite interesting... It happened before and it'll happen again... It'll never work.*

its /ɪts/. You use **its** to indicate that something belongs or relates to a thing, place, animal, child, etc that has just been mentioned or whose identity is clear. See **it**. EG *The creature lifted its head... He liked London for its exotic quality... The baby lay in its carrycot in its room... The group held its first meeting last week... The film must be judged in its own right.* — DET POSS

it's /ɪts/ is the usual spoken form of 'it is' or 'it has', especially when 'has' is an auxiliary verb. EG *It's a complete waste of time... Just tell me one thing please. It's very important... It's snowing out there... It is a very nice town; it's got very nice shops for instance... Well, it's been very nice talking to you.*

itself /ɪtself/. 1 You use **itself** as the object of a verb or preposition in order to refer to the same thing, place, animal, child, etc that is mentioned as the subject of the clause or as a previous object in the clause. See **it**. EG *A particularly knotty problem presented itself... Britain must bring itself up to date... Greenwich gained itself a permanent place in history... It wraps its furry tail around itself.* ▸ You also use **itself** to emphasize the subject or object of a clause and to make it clear what you are referring to. **Itself** is usually used in addition to a subject or object, although it is sometimes used instead of 'it' as an object. EG *The town itself was so small that it didn't have a priest.... Growing up in the heart of London was itself exciting... The lane ran right up to the wood itself.* • **an end in itself**: see **end**. — PRON REFL : SING, USED AS O; ▸ PRON REFL : SING

2 If you say that someone **is** politeness **itself**, **is** kindness **itself**, etc, you mean that they are extremely polite, extremely kind, etc. EG *He is always politeness itself whenever he meets us.* — PHR : VB INFLECTS

ITV /aɪ ti: vi:/ refers to a group of several British commercial television channels; an abbreviation for Independent Television. EG *Subsequent episodes will be broadcast on Tuesdays on ITV.* N PROPER

-ity, -ities. **-ity** is added to adjectives, sometimes in place of -ious, in order to form nouns. Uncount nouns formed in this way often refer to a state or quality; for example, 'tranquillity' refers to the state of being tranquil. These uncount nouns are not defined in this dictionary, but are treated with the related adjectives. EG *...rigid→rigidity... ...legal→legality... ...scarce→scarcity... ...audacious→audacity... ...ferocious→ferocity.* SUFFIX : FORMS NOUNS

IUD /aɪ ju: di:/, **IUDs**. An **IUD** is a piece of plastic or metal which is put inside a woman's womb in order to prevent her from becoming pregnant; an abbreviation for 'intra-uterine device'. N COUNT ⇑ contraceptive

I've /aɪv/ is the usual spoken form of 'I have,' especially when 'have' is an auxiliary verb. EG *I've never met her... ...as I've said before... I've got a question.*

ivory /aɪvəᵒri¹/, **ivories**. 1 **Ivory** is a hard smooth creamy-white type of bone, which forms most of the tusks of an elephant. It is valuable, and is often used for making carved ornaments. EG *Gold, slaves and ivory were sent north... ...an ivory dealer.* N UNCOUNT ▸ used of things that are made from ivory. EG *...ivory chess sets.* ▸ ADJ CLASSIF : ATTRIB

2 **Ivory** is also a creamy-white colour. EG *...her ivory legs... The linen was ivory-coloured with age.* ADJ COLOUR

3 If you talk about the **ivories**, you are referring to the keys of a piano; an informal or humorous use. EG *...his hands flashing over the ivories.* N PLURAL

ivory tower, ivory towers If you describe someone as living in an **ivory tower**, you mean that they deliberately keep themselves away from practical matters or from the problems of everyday life; used showing disapproval. EG *We hope that people here don't just live in an ivory tower... He urged them to get out of their ivory tower.* N COUNT : USU PREP+N

ivy /aɪvi¹/ is a plant that grows up walls or along the ground. Ivy does not lose its leaves in winter. EG *...a clump of ivy.* N UNCOUNT

Ivy League. The **Ivy League** is a group of eight important universities in the eastern part of the United States. EG *...Ivy League colleges... I very much doubt his being the genuine Ivy League article.* N PROPER

-ize, -izes, -izing, -ized; also spelled **-ise, -ises, -ising, -ised**. Where verbs can end in either '-ize' or '-ise', they are dealt with in this dictionary as ending in '-ize'. 1 **-ize** is added to some nouns, often in place of -y, in order to form verbs. EG *...apology→apologize... ...sympathy→sympathize... ...terror→terrorize... ...synthesis→synthesize.* SUFFIX : FORMS VERBS 2 **-ize** is also added to some adjectives in order to form verbs. Verbs formed in this way describe the processes by which things or people are changed to a particular state or condition. EG *...human→humanize... ...popular→popularize... ...industrial→industrialize.* SUFFIX : FORMS VERBS

Jj

J, j /dʒeɪ/, **Js, j's**. 1 **J** is the tenth letter of the English alphabet. N COUNT

2 **J** or **j** is also an abbreviation for various words beginning with J or j, such as 'joule' and 'journal'.

jab /dʒæb/, **jabs, jabbing, jabbed**. 1 If you **jab** something somewhere, you push it there with a quick, sudden movement and with a lot of force. EG *She jabbed her knitting needles into a ball of wool... He raised his voice and jabbed his finger at me.* V+O+A ⇑ push = stab ▸ used as a noun. EG *He gave it a sharp jab.* ▸ N COUNT

2 In informal British English, a **jab** is an injection of something into your blood to prevent illness. EG *Everyone was queueing up together to have the jabs.* N COUNT = injection

jab at. If you **jab at** something, you hit it repeatedly with quick, sharp strokes using your finger or something long and thin. EG *She could hear him jabbing viciously at the keys of the typewriter.* PHRASAL VB : V+PREP ⇑ hit

jabber /dʒæbə/, **jabbers, jabbering, jabbered**. Someone who is **jabbering** is talking very quickly and excitedly; an informal word. EG *There were about a dozen of them jabbering away in the kitchen... The children began to jabber among themselves.* V : USU+A, OR V+O ⇑ talk = yak

jack /dʒæk/, **jacks**. 1 A **jack** is 1.1 a mechanical device that you use to lift a heavy object off the ground, for example a car when you want to change a wheel. N COUNT ⇑ device 1.2 a playing card that has a picture of a young man on it. There are four jacks in a pack of cards, and they rank in order between the ten and the queen. EG *Why didn't you play the jack of clubs?* N COUNT : IF+PREP THEN *of* = knave

3 **Every man jack** means every single person; an old-fashioned expression. EG *It turned out that every man jack of them had a criminal record.* PHR : USED AS S OR O ⇑ everyone

4 If you say that someone has the attitude of **I'm all right Jack**, you mean that they are selfish and do not care that other people are suffering or in trouble; an informal expression. CONVENTION

5 See also **Union Jack, blackjack**.

jack in. If you **jack in** something such as an activity or a job, you stop doing it; used in informal British English. EG *There is simply no answer. You might as well jack it in then and there... One of these days I'm going to jack this job in and sail round the world.* PHRASAL VB : V+O+ADV ⇑ abandon = pack in

jack up. If you **jack up** a heavy object such as a car, you raise it off the ground using a jack. EG *Make sure you've got the tools ready before you jack up the car.* PHRASAL VB : V+O+ADV ⇑ raise

jackal /dʒækəᵒl/, **jackals**. A **jackal** is a wild animal that looks like a dog, has long legs and pointed ears, and lives in Africa and Southern Asia. EG *Now and again the jackals howled.* N COUNT ⇑ canine

jackass /dʒækæs/, **jackasses**. A **jackass** is a stupid and foolish person; an old-fashioned word. EG *He's the biggest jackass we have ever had as president.* N COUNT/VOC = imbecile

jackboot /dʒækbu:t/, **jackboots**. 1 **Jackboots** are heavy, long boots that come up to the knee. They used to be worn by soldiers, especially in the cavalry. N PLURAL : ALSO *a pair of*+N ⇑ boot

2 If you say that a country, group, etc is **under the jackboot** of someone such as a dictator or military ruler, you mean that it is suffering from harsh and unjust government by them; an informal expression. EG *National culture was crushed under the invader's jackboot.* PHR : USED AS AN A ⇑ rule = repression

jackdaw /dʒækdɔ:/, **jackdaws**. A **jackdaw** is a large black-and-grey bird that looks like a crow. Jackdaws live in Europe and Asia. N COUNT ⇑ bird

jacket /dʒækɪt/, **jackets**. 1 A **jacket** is a short coat that has long sleeves and an opening at the front. EG *He wore a tweed sports jacket of a greenish colour... From his jacket pocket he took out a small screwdriver... Waiters in white jackets arrived with drinks.* N COUNT ⇑ coat
● See also **life-jacket, dinner jacket**.

2 The **jacket** of a baked potato is its skin. EG *...potatoes in their jackets... ...jacket potatoes.* N COUNT ⇑ covering

3 The **jacket** of a book is the paper cover that is used to protect the book. N COUNT : USU+SUPP

4 In American English, a **jacket** is the sleeve of a record: see **sleeve**. N COUNT

jack-in-the-box, jack-in-the-boxes. A **jack-in-the-box** is a child's toy that consists of a box with a doll inside it. When you open the lid, the doll springs out. N COUNT ⇑ toy

jack-knife /dʒæknaɪf/, **jack-knifes, jack-knifing, jack-knifed; jack-knives**; also spelled without a hyphen. **Jack-knives** is the plural of the noun. 1 If an articulated truck **jack-knifes**, the trailer swings round at a sharp angle to the cab in an uncontrolled way as the truck is moving. EG *Traffic was stopped after a lorry jack-knifed in heavy rain.* V ⇑ bend

2 A **jack-knife** is a large knife that has a blade that can be folded away into the handle. N COUNT ⇑ knife

jack of all trades, jacks of all trades. Someone who is a **jack of all trades** is able to do a variety of different jobs; often used to suggest that they are not expert at any of the jobs. N COUNT : USU USED AS C = handyman

jackpot /dʒækpɒt/, **jackpots**. 1 A **jackpot** is the most valuable prize in a game or lottery, especially when the game involves increasing the value of the prize until someone wins it. EG *The jackpot now stands at £500.* N COUNT : USU SING ⇑ prize

2 If you **hit the jackpot**, you win a lot of money or have a piece of great good luck; an informal expression. PHR : VB INFLECTS

Jacobean /dʒækəbɪən/. A building, piece of furniture, or work of art that is **Jacobean** was built or produced in the style of the period between 1603 and 1625. EG *...a Jacobean house on a great estate.* ADJ CLASSIF ⇑ period

Jacuzzi /dʒəkuːzi[1]/, **Jacuzzis**. A **Jacuzzi** is a trademark for a large circular bath which is fitted with a device that makes the water swirl around. N COUNT ⇑ bath

jade /dʒeɪd/. is a hard stone, usually green in colour, that is used for making jewellery and ornaments. EG *...jewels made from jade, sapphires and rubies.* N UNCOUNT ⇑ gem

jaded /dʒeɪdɪ[2]d/. If you are **jaded**, you have no enthusiasm because you are tired of something or because you have had too much of the same thing. EG *If you don't vary the diet, you risk the whole family getting jaded within a week... ...jaded housewives who'd like to try something exciting.* ADJ QUALIT ⇑ bored = tired

jaffa /dʒæfə, dʒɑː-/, **jaffas**. A **jaffa** is a large orange that is grown especially in Israel. N COUNT ⇑ orange

jagged /dʒægɪ[2]d/. Something that is **jagged** has a rough, uneven shape or edge with lots of sharp points. EG *...the jagged outline of the crags... ...small pieces of jagged metal... ...a jagged hole.* ADJ QUALIT ⇑ rough = ragged

jaguar /dʒægju[4]ə/, **jaguars**. A **jaguar** is a large animal with spots on its back, rather like a leopard, that lives in south and central America. Jaguars are members of the cat family. N COUNT ⇑ animal

jail /dʒeɪl/, **jails, jailing, jailed**; also spelled **gaol** in British English. 1 A **jail** is a place where people are kept locked up, either because they have been found guilty of committing a crime or because they are waiting to be tried for a crime. EG *...women who spent years in jail... He went to jail for dangerous driving... I went into the jail and visited him.* N COUNT/ UNCOUNT = prison

2 If someone **is jailed**, they are put into jail. EG *He was jailed for five years.* V+O : USU PASS = put away

jailbird /dʒeɪlbɜːd/, **jailbirds**; also spelled **gaolbird** in British English. A **jailbird** is a person who is in prison or who has been to prison; an old-fashioned informal word. N COUNT = convict

jailbreak /dʒeɪlbreɪk/, **jailbreaks**. A **jailbreak** is an escape from jail. N COUNT = escape

jailer /dʒeɪlə/, **jailers**; also spelled **gaoler** in British English. A **jailer** is a person who is in charge of a jail and the prisoners in it; an old-fashioned word. EG *They had already been searched by the police and the jailers.* N COUNT ⇑ warden = gaoler

jalopy /dʒəlɒpi[1]/, **jalopies**. A **jalopy** is a car; an informal, rather old-fashioned word. N COUNT = car

jam /dʒæm/, **jams, jamming, jammed**. 1 **Jam** is a food that is made by cooking fruit with a large amount of sugar. Usually you spread jam on bread. EG *...pots of raspberry and blackcurrant jam... They were hungry and got bread and jam.* N MASS = preserve

2 If you **jam** something somewhere, you push it there roughly, using a lot of force. EG *Then he jammed his hat back on... Reporters jammed microphones in our faces.* V+O+A ⇑ push = ram

3 If something such as a part of a machine **jams** or if you **jam** it, it becomes fixed in position and is unable to move freely or work properly. EG *Grit has jammed the lever arm... The machines jammed and broke down.* V-ERG ⇑ stick

4 If you **jam** something in a particular position, you fix it firmly in that position by wedging it with another object. EG *I jammed the window shut.* V+O+A ⇑ wedge

5 If a road **is jammed** with vehicles, it is filled completely with them, so that the traffic cannot move. ◊ **jammed**. EG *Some side roads soon became jammed.* V+O ⇑ block ◊ ADJ QUALIT = congested

6 If a lot of people **jam** into a place or if you **jam** a lot of people or things into a place, they are pressed tightly together so that they can hardly move. EG *Fridges will not work properly if you jam in so much food that the cold air can't circulate... More than seventeen thousand people jam into the stadium for the final. The others sat jammed together on the sofa.* V-ERG+A ⇑ crowd = squash, squeeze

7 A **jam** is 7.1 a situation where there are so many people or things in a place that it is impossible for them to move. EG *There's such a jam of people in there, I didn't try to go in.* 7.2 a situation where there are so many vehicles on a road that none of them can move. EG *There were traffic jams, and police clearing people away... ...these terrific jams half a mile long.* 7.3 a very difficult situation that someone is in; used in informal English. EG *He finds himself in exactly the same jam as his brother was in ten years before... ...a man who he had helped out of a financial jam.* N COUNT = swarm; N COUNT : USU traffic+N = queue; N COUNT : USU in/out of+a+N ⇑ trouble = predicament

8 To **jam** a radio, radar, or electronic signal means to prevent it from being received or heard clearly. This happens because noise or other signals are being transmitted on the same wavelength, usually deliberately. EG *The authorities were able to jam this wavelength.* ◊ **jamming**. EG *One of its strong points is its resistance to electronic jamming.* V+O ⇑ block; ◊ N UNCOUNT ⇑ interference

9 When musicians are **jamming**, they are playing jazz or rock music informally without playing parts that have been written down or planned in advance; an informal use. EG *...while Paul, George, and Ringo jammed on piano, guitar, and a champagne bucket.* V ⇑ improvise

jam on. If you **jam on** the brakes while you are driving, you use them suddenly and with a lot of force so that the vehicle stops quickly; an informal expression. PHRASAL VB : V+O+ADV = slam on

Jamaican /dʒəmeɪkə[0]n/. 1 **Jamaican** means belonging or relating to Jamaica, or to its people. EG *...a Jamaican housewife.* ADJ CLASSIF

2 A **Jamaican** is a person who comes from Jamaica. N COUNT

jamb /dʒæm/, **jambs**. A **jamb** is a post that forms the side part or upright of a door frame or window frame. EG *...a bell on the jamb of the door.* N COUNT ⇑ post

jamboree /dʒæmbəriː/, **jamborees**. A **jamboree** is a party, celebration, or other gathering where there is a large number of people and lots of excitement, fun, and enjoyment. EG *...an open-air jamboree that attracted 250,000 people.* N COUNT ⇑ gathering = carnival

jam-jar, jam-jars; also spelled as two words. A **jam-jar** is a glass jar which is used for keeping jam in; used in American English. N COUNT ⇑ container

jammy /dʒæmi[1]/, **jammier, jammiest**. 1 Something that is **jammy** is dirty and sticky because it is covered with jam; used mainly in spoken English. EG *Be careful where you put those jammy fingers.* ADJ QUALIT ⇑ sticky

2 If you say that a person or something that a person does is **jammy**, you mean that they are very lucky because something good has happened by chance and they did not have to do anything extra or difficult to make it happen; an informal use. EG *You jammy so-and-so!... He'll get a jammy job somewhere.* ADJ QUALIT ⇑ lucky

jam-packed. A place that is **jam-packed** is so full of people or things that there is no room for any more; an informal expression. EG *The streets might be jam-packed... The drawers were all jam-packed with old notes and letters.* ADJ CLASSIF ⇑ crowded

Jan. is an abbreviation for January.

jangle /dʒæŋgə[0]l/, **jangles, jangling, jangled**. To **jangle** means to make an unpleasant ringing noise; used for example of metal objects striking against each other. EG *...enamel mugs and saucepans which jangled in the wind... I rejoined him upstairs, the keys jangling in my pockets like gold.* ▸ used as a noun. EG *She would wake up every morning to the jangle of the alarm clock.* V-ERG = clank, rattle; ▸ N SING WITH DET : IF+PREP THEN of ⇑ noise

janitor /dʒænɪtə/, **janitors**. A **janitor** is a person whose job is to look after a building; used especially in American English. EG *He spent four summers being a janitor in a large office building.* N COUNT = caretaker

January /dʒænju[0]əri[1]/ is the first month of the year in the Western calendar. EG *On 24 January Harold left for Constantinople.* N UNCOUNT

Japanese /dʒæpəniːz/. **Japanese** is both the singular and the plural form of the noun. 1 **Japanese** means belonging or relating to Japan, its people, or their language. ADJ CLASSIF

2 The **Japanese** are the people who come from Japan. EG *A group of Japanese, dressed in business suits and ties, was standing by the door.* N COUNT ⇑ person

3 **Japanese** is the language that is spoken by people who live in Japan. N UNCOUNT ⇑ language

jar /dʒɑː/, **jars, jarring, jarred.** 1 A **jar** is a container, usually made of glass, that has a wide top and is used for storing food such as jam and preserved fruit. EG *I was having trouble unscrewing the tops of fruit jars, jam jars and so on.* ▸ used to refer to the food inside a jar or the amount of food that a jar contains. EG *He bought a jar of English marmalade... Make a note to buy more marmalade before you finish the jar.*
N COUNT ⇑ container = pot
▸ N PART ⇑ amount

2 If something **jars** or **jars** on you, you find it unpleasant or annoying. EG *The harsh, metallic sound jarred on her.... He had a way of speaking that jarred.* ◊ **jarring.** EG *...a jarring contradiction... This will not take the form of a jarring office block, according to the planners.*
V: IF+PREP THEN *on* ⇑ irritate = grate
◊ ADJ QUALIT = irritating

3 If something **jars** you, it gives you an unpleasant shock or causes you discomfort. EG *This thought jarred me... The policeman in charge was evidently jarred by my appearance.* ◊ **jarring.** EG *...the thudding jarring vibration... ...a jarring experience.*
V+O ⇑ shock = shake
◊ ADJ QUALIT = jolting

4 If things **jar** or if something **jars** them, they strike against each other with quite a lot of force. EG *The house shook and his bones were jarred.*
V-ERG = jolt

5 A **jar** is also a jolt or shock. EG *Knocks and jars can cause weakness in the spine.*
N COUNT = jolt

jargon /dʒɑːgəⁿn/ is language containing words that are used in special or technical ways. Jargon is used to talk about particular subjects or by particular groups of people. EG *She could explain it without recourse to the jargon of psychoanalysis... I have endeavoured to avoid boring legal jargon in this book.*
N UNCOUNT: USU +SUPP ⇑ words = language, parlance

jasmine /dʒæzmiⁱn/. is a climbing plant which has small white or yellow flowers with a pleasant smell.
N UNCOUNT ⇑ plant

jaundice /dʒɔːndɪs/ is an illness that makes your skin and eyes become yellow. EG *Fortunately, Kate did not have jaundice.*
N UNCOUNT ⇑ illness

jaundiced /dʒɔːndɪst/. A **jaundiced** attitude or view is unenthusiastic or pessimistic. EG *The well-placed executive will view your progress with a jaundiced eye... He takes a rather jaundiced view of societies and clubs.*
ADJ QUALIT ⇑ gloomy = cynical

jaunt /dʒɔːnt/, **jaunts, jaunting, jaunted.** 1 A **jaunt** is a journey which you go on for pleasure or enjoyment. EG *We got lost on a motor jaunt to Marrakesh.*
N COUNT ⇑ journey = trip

2 If you **jaunt** somewhere, you go on a journey, usually for pleasure or enjoyment. EG *I jaunted daily back and forth to school on a bus... I suppose Manfred's jaunting off to Zurich as usual.*
V: NO IMPER ⇑ travel

jaunty /dʒɔːntiⁱ/. Something that you do or wear that is **jaunty** shows that you are cheerful, full of confidence, and energetic. EG *She adjusted her hat to a more jaunty angle... He spoke suddenly in a jaunty tone.* ▸ used also of people. EG *...a small jaunty soldier.* ◊ **jauntily.** EG *He greeted them jauntily... ...whistling jauntily.*
ADJ QUALIT ⇑ bright = sprightly
◊ ADV WITH VB = buoyantly

javelin /dʒævəⁿlɪn/, **javelins.** A **javelin** is a long spear that is used in sports competitions. Competitors try to throw the javelin as far as possible. ▸ used of the competition in which the javelin is thrown. EG *She came second in the javelin.*
N COUNT ⇑ spear
▸ N SING: *the*+N ⇑ competition

jaw /dʒɔː/, **jaws, jawing, jawed.** 1 Your **jaw** is the lower part of your face below your mouth which moves down, for example when you yawn. EG *His jaw dropped in surprise.*
N COUNT

2 A person's or animal's **jaw** is also one of the two bones in their head which their teeth are attached to. EG *Its biggest teeth are at the back of the upper jaw.*
N COUNT ⇑ bone = jawbone

3 A person's or animal's **jaws** are their mouth and teeth. EG *The panther held a snake in its jaws... He clamped his jaws shut rather than be forced to eat.*
N PLURAL ⇑ mouth

4 The **jaws** of a machine or tool such as a vice are the two parts which open and close and which can grip something tightly between them.
N PLURAL ⇑ clamp

5 If you talk about the **jaws** of something, you are referring to the possible beginning of a dangerous or unpleasant situation. EG *The nation has been snatched out of the jaws of war.*
N PLURAL: USU *the*+N+*of*+N UNCOUNT = clutches

6 If people are **jawing,** they are talking to each other, often for a long time, without saying anything important; used in informal English. EG *I can't spend all day jawing with you.* ▸ used as a noun. EG *I had a good jaw with Sally yesterday afternoon.*
V OR V+A (*with*): RECIP ⇑ talk = natter
▸ N COUNT = natter

jawbone /dʒɔːbəun/, **jawbones;** also spelled with a hyphen. A **jawbone** is the bone in the lower jaw of a person or animal.
N COUNT

jay /dʒeɪ/, **jays.** A **jay** is a brownish-pink bird with blue and black wings. Jays live in Europe and Asia.
N COUNT ⇑ bird

jaywalker /dʒeɪwɔːkə/, **jaywalkers** also spelled with a hyphen. A **jaywalker** is a person who crosses roads in a careless and dangerous way. EG *The trouble with driving in the city is that there are so many jaywalkers.*
N COUNT ⇑ pedestrian

jaywalking /dʒeɪwɔːkɪŋ/; also spelled with a hyphen. **Jaywalking** is the act of crossing a road or walking in a road in a careless and dangerous way. EG *In some countries you can be arrested for jaywalking.*
N UNCOUNT

jazz /dʒæz/. 1 **Jazz** is a style of popular music that has an exciting rhythm and is usually played by groups of musicians using drums, saxophones, trumpets, etc. EG *I tried to interest them in going to a jazz concert that evening... They call themselves The Original Dixieland Jazz Band.*
N UNCOUNT ⇑ music

2 In very informal spoken English, you can add **'and all that jazz'** to suggest that there are wider aspects to the topic or topics which you have just mentioned, but that you do not think that it is worth explaining them in detail. EG *I suppose you saw Versailles and the Eiffel Tower and all that jazz... ...psychotherapy and all that jazz.*
PHR

jazz up, jazzes up, jazzing up, jazzed up. If you **jazz** something **up**, you make it look or seem more interesting, colourful, or exciting; a rather old-fashioned informal expression. EG *They've certainly jazzed this place up since the last time I was here.*
PHRASAL VB: V+O+ADV ⇑ enliven

jazzed-up. Music that is **jazzed-up** has been changed in order to make it sound more like popular music or jazz; an informal use. EG *...a jazzed-up version of one of the Brandenburg Concertos.*
ADJ QUALIT ⇑ enlivened

jazzy /dʒæziⁱ/, **jazzier, jazziest.** 1 If you say that something is **jazzy**, you mean that it is colourful or modern in appearance, but that you consider it has no taste or style. EG *The fat, jazzy steering wheel was padded with real leather.*
ADJ QUALIT = flashy

2 Music that is **jazzy** is in the style of jazz. EG *...that large unseen orchestra playing jazzy rhythms.*
ADJ CLASSIF

jct is a written abbreviation for 'junction'; used on maps and signs to refer to junctions on roads, railways, and motorways.

jealous /dʒeləs/. If you are **jealous,** 1 you feel that it is unfair that someone else has achieved something that you wanted, or that they have possessions or qualities that you would like to have and you feel anger or bitterness towards that person. EG *I often felt jealous because David could go out when he wished... They may feel jealous of your success.* ▸ used of attitudes and behaviour. EG *...the jealous whinings of those who had not fared so well.* ◊ **jealously.** EG *He sat high up in the stand, jealously watching the skaters.* 2 you feel that you must try to keep something you have got, for example a partner or a possession, because you think somebody else might take them away from you. EG *She was a very jealous woman... He was jealous of his wife and suspected her of adultery.* ◊ **jealously.** EG *They become people again, jealously guarding their independence.*
ADJ QUALIT = envious, resentful
◊ ADV WITH VB
ADJ QUALIT = possessive
◊ ADV WITH VB

jealousy /dʒeləsiⁱ/, **jealousies. Jealousy** is 1 the feeling of resentment and bitterness that you have when you think someone is trying to take away something that you feel belongs to you, for example a partner or a possession. EG *Hate, jealousy, the desire to kill all rose to the surface... He was very good at talking me out of things, suspicions and jealousies and so on.* 2 the feeling you have when you wish that you could have the qualities or possessions that someone else has. EG *...the notion of sibling rivalry: jealousy of our brothers and sisters.*
N UNCOUNT/COUNT ⇑ emotion = resentment
N UNCOUNT/COUNT ⇑ emotion = envy

jeans /dʒiːnz/ are casual trousers that are usually made of strong blue denim. Sometimes, trousers made of other cloth such as corduroy or thick cotton are also referred to as jeans. EG *Three young men came out, all in jeans... It's in my jeans pocket.*
N PLURAL: ALSO *a pair of*+N ⇑ trousers = denims

jeep /dʒiːp/, **jeeps.** A **jeep** is a small, four-wheeled vehicle that can travel over rough ground and is often used by the American army: compare **Land Rover.** EG *A jeep pulled up to the dump and a marine jumped out.*
N COUNT

jeer /dʒɪə/, **jeers, jeering, jeered**. 1 If you **jeer** at someone, you show that you think that they are stupid and not worthy of respect by saying rude and insulting things to them. EG *They jeered at him for mollycoddling his little brother... Only one man stood up for me and he was jeered.* ◊ **jeering**. EG *...strangers who never glanced at the jeering crowd.* ◊ **jeeringly**. EG *He smiled jeeringly.* — V, V+O/QUOTE, OR V+A (at) = scoff, mock; ◊ ADJ CLASSIF; ◊ ADV WITH VB

2 **Jeers** are rude or insulting things that you shout in order to show that you think someone is stupid and not worthy of respect. EG *There were as many jeers as cheers at the meeting.* — N COUNT : USU PL ⇑ insult = jibe

Jehovah /dʒɪhəʊvə/ is the name given to God in the Old Testament. — N PROPER

Jehovah's Witness, Jehovah's Witnesses. A **Jehovah's Witness** is a member of a religious organization which accepts some Christian ideas and believes that the world is going to end very soon. — N COUNT ⇑ believer

jejune /dʒɪdʒuːn/; a formal or literary word. Something that is **jejune** is 1 considered to be very simple and unsophisticated. EG *...a jejune notion that she'd seen it all.* 2 dull and boring; an old-fashioned use. However, some people consider that this is the 'correct' sense and that sense 1 is incorrect. — ADJ QUALIT = naive; ADJ QUALIT

jell /dʒel/. See **gel**.

jellied /dʒelɪd/. **Jellied** food is prepared and eaten in a jelly. EG *If you don't like oysters, you probably won't like jellied eels.* — ADJ CLASSIF : USU ATTRIB ⇑ coated

Jello /dʒeləʊ/, **Jellos**. **Jello** is is an American trademark for **jelly**. — N UNCOUNT

jelly /dʒeli¹/, **jellies**. 1 **Jelly** is 1.1 a clear food made from gelatine, which wobbles when you move it. It is usually sweetened, flavoured with fruit juices, and eaten as dessert. fruit juice. EG *Would you like some jelly?* 1.2 a sweet food made by boiling fruit juice and sugar, which becomes firm when it gets cold, and which you eat like jam. EG *...slices of bread, smeared with butter and jelly.* 1.3 a firm substance that forms when the juices from cooked meat become cold. EG *Don't shake the pan or you'll mix the fat with the jelly.* — N MASS ⇑ dessert; N MASS ⇑ preserve; N UNCOUNT ⇑ substance

2 If your legs or arms feel like **jelly**, they feel very weak, usually because you are nervous or afraid. EG *His legs turned to jelly... 'It's my legs, my arms–they feel like jelly.'* — N UNCOUNT = putty

jellyfish /dʒeli¹fɪʃ/; **jellyfish** is both the singular and the plural form. A **jellyfish** is a creature that lives in the sea and has a body that looks like clear jelly. Some jellyfish can sting you. — N COUNT ⇑ invertebrate

jemmy /dʒemi¹/, **jemmies**. A **jemmy** is a heavy metal bar which is curved at one end and which is used as a tool especially by criminals for forcing things open; used in British English. EG *Any filing cabinet will yield to a jemmy and a bit of brute force.* — N COUNT ⇑ tool = crowbar

jeopardize /dʒepədaɪz/, **jeopardizes, jeopardizing, jeopardized**; also spelled **jeopardise**. If you **jeopardize** something, you do something that may destroy it, damage it, or cause it to be lost. EG *This judgment may jeopardize his job... I didn't want to jeopardize my relationship with my new friend.* — V+O ⇑ threaten = endanger

jeopardy /dʒepədi¹/. If someone or something is **in jeopardy**, they are in a dangerous situation, where they might fail, be lost, or be destroyed. EG *Their hasty action puts the plan into grave jeopardy... She had placed herself in jeopardy in order to save my life.* — PHR : USED AS AN A ⇑ endangered = at risk

jerk /dʒɜːk/, **jerks, jerking, jerked**. 1 If you **jerk** something, you pull it suddenly and forcefully, for example to release it when it is caught. EG *He jerked the boy savagely to his feet... The door of the van was jerked open... I jerked the fishing rod back and lost the fish.* ▸ used as a noun. EG *The man pulled the girl back from the road with a jerk... He gave the root a mighty jerk and pulled it free.* — V+O+A ⇑ pull = yank; ▸ N COUNT = wrench

2 When something **jerks** or when you **jerk** it, it moves a short distance very suddenly and forcefully. EG *He jerked his head around to stare at the man... His hand jerked up to push him away.* — V-ERG ⇑ move

3 If you **jerk** in a particular direction or in a particular way, you move or do something with a very sudden and quick movement. EG *She jerked away from him. 'Leave me alone!' she screamed... Jerking suddenly awake, he lay very still and listened... He jerked and cried out, 'Who's there?'* ▸ used as a noun. EG *He asked her to join him with a jerk of his head... The traffic moved along in jerks.* — V : USU+A ⇑ move = start; ▸ N COUNT ⇑ movement

4 A **jerk** is a person who you think is stupid and ignorant; an offensive word used in informal English. EG *'Listen, you jerk,' Brody said. 'A boy almost got killed just now.'* — N COUNT/VOC ⇑ person

jerk off. To **jerk off** means to masturbate; a rude expression. — PHRASAL VB : V+ADV

jerk out. If you **jerk out** a remark or comment, you say it in a very abrupt and nervous way. EG *'I can't argue with you, but you're wrong,' he jerked out... She jerked out an apology.* — PHRASAL VB : V+ADV+QUOTE/O ⇑ say = blurt out

jerkin /dʒɜːkɪn/, **jerkins**. A **jerkin** is a sleeveless jacket worn by men and women, especially in former times. — N COUNT ⇑ garment

jerky /dʒɜːki¹/, **jerkier, jerkiest**. Movements that are **jerky** are very sudden and abrupt and do not flow smoothly. EG *She lit a cigarette with quick, jerky movements... She swam with the jerky stroke of a beginner.* ◊ **jerkily**. EG *Now I saw him at last, striding jerkily down the street.* ◊ **jerkiness**. — ADJ QUALIT ⇑ uneven = staccato; ◊ ADV WITH VB; ◊ N UNCOUNT

jerry-build /dʒeri¹ bɪld/, **jerry-builds, jerry-building, jerry-built**. If houses or blocks of flats are **jerry-built**, they have been built very quickly and cheaply, without much care for safety or quality. EG *...the speculators who jerry-build city slums without light, roads, or water supply.* ◊ **jerry-built**. EG *Everybody was out of work and the jerry-built houses had been neglected.* — V+O ⇑ build = throw together; ◊ ADJ CLASSIF : ATTRIB = cheap, flimsy

jersey /dʒɜːzi¹/, **jerseys**. 1 A **jersey** is 1.1 a piece of clothing usually worn over a shirt or blouse and made of knitted wool. EG *She pulled on her striped jersey and her jeans.* — N COUNT ⇑ clothing = pullover, sweater

2 **Jersey** is a knitted woollen fabric used especially to make women's clothing. — N UNCOUNT ⇑ cloth

3 A **Jersey** is also a cow that is light brown in colour and produces good quality milk. — N COUNT ⇑ cow

jest /dʒest/, **jests, jesting, jested**. 1 A **jest** is something that you say which is intended to be amusing in a rather clever way. EG *His Lordship hoped that a jest would be excused.* ● If you say something **in jest**, you do not mean it seriously, but want to be amusing. EG *An official told me this, not quite in jest... It was said half in jest.* — N COUNT ⇑ joke = witticism; ● PHR : USED AS AN A = jokingly

2 If you **jest**, you tell jokes or say amusing things; a formal word. EG *'Do rabbits eat buns?' Philip jested weakly.* — V OR V+QUOTE/REPORT-CL = joke

jester /dʒestə/, **jesters**. A **jester** is a man in former times whose job it was to amuse the king or queen, for example by telling jokes or performing tricks. EG *...the medieval Court Jester.* — N COUNT ⇑ entertainer = fool

Jesuit /dʒezjʊɪt/, **Jesuits**. 1 A **Jesuit** is a Catholic priest who belongs to the Society of Jesus, which does a lot of missionary work and is especially loyal to the Pope. — N COUNT ⇑ priest

2 In informal English, if you call someone a **Jesuit**, you mean that they use clever and cunning arguments to prove that they are correct in what they say; used showing disapproval. — N COUNT

Jesuitical /dʒezjʊɪtɪkə⁰l/ behaviour is intended to achieve a particular result by using very clever and cunning arguments; used showing disapproval. EG *The emphasis is once more on Jesuitical methods within the organisation.* — ADJ QUALIT = devious

Jesus /dʒiːzəs/. **Jesus** or **Jesus Christ** is 1 the name of the man who Christians believe was the son of God, and whose teachings are the basis of Christianity. 2 a swear word used to express surprise, shock, annoyance, etc, or to emphasize what you are saying. — N PROPER; EXCLAM

jet /dʒet/, **jets, jetting, jetted**. 1 A **jet** is 1.1 a modern aeroplane which has jet engines which enable it to fly very fast and high up. EG *She woke just as the big jet from Hong Kong touched down... They could be transported home by jet... Jet fighters fly overhead.* ● See also **jump jet, jumbo**. — N COUNT, OR *by*+N ⇑ aeroplane

2 If you **jet** somewhere, you travel in a modern aeroplane from one place to another; an informal use. EG *A Pennsylvania teenager jets regularly to a dentist in Frankfurt, Germany... ...as the heads of government jetted in for the latest EEC summit meeting.* — V+A ⇑ travel = fly

3 A **jet** is also 3.1 a hole in a piece of equipment such as an engine or gas cooker through which the petrol or gas is forced before it burns. EG *The engine just had a single high velocity jet... The jets must be clogged up: try poking them with a pin.* 3.2 a thin and forceful stream of water, gas, etc. EG *He immersed his mouth and blew a jet of water into the* — N COUNT ⇑ hole = nozzle; N COUNT : IF+PREP THEN *of* ⇑ stream = spout

air... *It'll be boiling hot and the water may be a scalding jet.*

4 Jet is a hard black stone that is polished so that it shines, and is used for ornaments in jewellery. N UNCOUNT/COUNT

jet-black; also spelled as two words. **jet-black** means very dark black in colour. EG *...yellow eyes that had small jet-black bars lying vertically in their centres... His hair was jet black and well combed around the ears.* ADJ COLOUR

jet engine, jet engines. A **jet engine** is an engine in which hot air and gases are pushed out at the back. Jet engines are used for most modern airliners. N COUNT ⇑ engine

jetlag /dʒetlæg/; also spelled with a hyphen. **Jetlag** is a slight sense of confusion and tiredness that people experience after a long journey in an aeroplane, especially after arriving in a place where the time is several hours different from the place that they left. EG *With jet-lag still a problem, I almost fell asleep during the meeting.* N UNCOUNT ⇑ fatigue

jet-propelled. An aeroplane that is **jet-propelled** uses jet engines to provide its power. ADJ CLASSIF ⇑ powered

jetsam /dʒetsəm/ is rubbish that is floating on the sea or that has been left by the sea on the shore: compare **flotsam**. N UNCOUNT

jet set; also spelled with a hyphen. The **jet set** are rich and successful people, especially young people, who live in a luxurious way. EG *...a satire on the whole French and Italian jet set... This was once a popular place for jet-set travellers.* N SING : *the*+N, USU BEFORE N ⇑ people = high society

jettison /dʒetɪsəⁿn, -zəⁿn/, **jettisons, jettisoning, jettisoned**. **1** If you **jettison** something such as an idea or chance, you deliberately reject it or decide not to use it. EG *...ideas too valuable, too sacred, too deeply believed to jettison... They were willing to jettison the chance of earning £10,000... Those artists have jettisoned so much of the theory and practice of cubism.* V+O ⇑ reject = abandon, toss away

2 If you **jettison** something that you no longer need, you throw it away. EG *I also thought it was time to jettison the blue overcoat.* V+O = discard

jetty /dʒetiˡ/, **jetties**. A **jetty** is a wide stone wall or wooden platform at the edge of the sea or a river, where boats can wait while people get on and off or while goods are loaded and unloaded. EG *The boat was tied up alongside a crumbling limestone jetty.* N COUNT ⇑ wall = pier

Jew /dʒuː/, **Jews**. A **Jew** is a person who believes in and practices the religion of Judaism. Jews are considered to be the descendants of the ancient Hebrew people. Many Jews now live in Israel. EG *He was a journalist, a brilliant intellectual, and a Jew... ...American Jews.* N COUNT ⇑ person

jewel /dʒuːəⁿl/, **jewels**. **1** A **jewel** is **1.1** a precious stone such as a diamond or ruby that is used to decorate valuable ornaments or other special objects such as rings or necklaces. EG *She was wearing even more jewels than the Queen Mother!... ...a jewel box.* • See also **crown jewels**. N COUNT ⇑ stone = jewellery **1.2** a very small precious stone or piece of specially cut glass that is used as part of the machinery of a watch. N COUNT ⇑ stone

2 If you say that someone or something is a **jewel**, you mean that they are more special, beautiful, or better than the other things or people around them. EG *...the great gaudy jewel of the Gardens, the Albert Memorial... ...the girl who announces brightly that her husband is a jewel.* N COUNT = treasure

jewelled /dʒuːəⁿld/; also spelled **jeweled** in American English. **Jewelled** items and ornaments are decorated with precious stones. EG *...a jewelled brooch.* ADJ CLASSIF ⇑ decorated

jeweller /dʒuːəⁿlə/, **jewellers**; also spelled **jeweler** in American English. A **jeweller** is a person who buys, sells, and often repairs jewellery and watches. N COUNT ⇑ craftsman

jewellery /dʒuːəⁿlriˡ/; also spelled **jewelry** in American English. **Jewellery** is ornaments such as rings, bracelets, or necklaces which are often made of valuable metal such as gold, and which are sometimes decorated with precious stones. EG *She thought some of her jewellery was missing... ...a jewellery box.* N UNCOUNT ⇑ ornaments

Jewess /dʒuːɪˢs/, **Jewesses**. A **Jewess** is a woman or girl who is Jewish. Many people consider this to be an offensive word. N COUNT ⇑ Jew

Jewish /dʒuːɪʃ/. A person or thing that is **Jewish 1** belongs or relates to the religion of Judaism or to the people who are considered to be the descendants of the ancient Hebrew people. EG *Jewish scholars... ...a beautiful Jewish woman... ...a Jewish wedding.* ADJ CLASSIF **2** has qualities or characteristics typical of someone or something which belongs to the Jewish religion or to Jewish people. EG *I feel more Jewish in Israel than I do here.* ADJ QUALIT

Jewishness /dʒuːɪʃnɪˢs/ is the quality or state of being a Jewish person. EG *Sooner or later we'd have to talk about my Jewishness.* N UNCOUNT

Jewry /dʒuːriˡ/ is all the people who believe in and practise the religion of Judaism; a formal word. EG *...it shook world Jewry to its depths.* N UNCOUNT = Judaism

jib /dʒɪb/, **jibs, jibbing, jibbed**. If a horse or donkey **jibs**, it stops suddenly and refuses to continue. EG *Once again the donkey jibbed and would not pass it.* V ⇑ stop

jib at. If you **jib at** something, you are unwilling to do it or to accept a new situation; a rather old-fashioned expression. EG *He had begun to jib at carrying out the orders of his masters.* PHRASAL VB : V+PREP, HAS PASS = balk at

jibe /dʒaɪb/, **jibes**; also spelled **gibe**. A **jibe** is a rude or insulting remark about someone that is intended to make them look foolish. EG *Freddie smiled politely at the jibe and cleared his throat.* N COUNT ⇑ remark = insult

jiffy /dʒɪfiˡ/. In informal spoken English, if you say that you will do something **in a jiffy**, you mean that you will do it quickly and very soon. EG *I'll be back in a jiffy.* PHR : USED AS AN A ⇑ quickly

jig /dʒɪg/, **jigs, jigging, jigged**. **1** A **jig** is **1.1** a lively folk dance, popular in the past among country people, and the music that accompanied it. N COUNT ⇑ dance **1.2** a particular sort of behaviour or activity which varies according to the situation that someone is in. EG *The Prime Minister was dancing yet another jig.* N COUNT ⇑ role **1.3** a device that holds something in position and guides a mechanical tool which works on that thing. EG *You can buy a guide, or jig, to help set the angle.* N COUNT ⇑ device

2 To **jig** means **2.1** to dance, especially in the style of a lively folk dance. V **2.2** to move in an uneven way, especially bouncing up and down. EG *...others began to jig and stamp and shuffle.* V : USU+A ⇑ move = bob

jiggery-pokery /dʒɪgəⁿrɪpəukəⁿriˡ/ is behaviour or activity that involves mischief, trickery, or dishonesty, and is often done in secret; used in informal British English. EG *...he thought there was jiggery-pokery going on in the stables.* N UNCOUNT = mischief

jiggle /dʒɪgəⁿl/, **jiggles, jiggling, jiggled**. **1** If you **jiggle** something, you move it quickly from side to side. EG *...it worked intermittently when I jiggled the switch... Ginny jiggled the front door handle.* V+O ⇑ move = wiggle

2 If you **jiggle** about, you move up and down or from side to side in a nervous and jerky way. V ⇑ move

jigsaw /dʒɪgsɔː/, **jigsaws**. A **jigsaw** or **jigsaw puzzle** is **1** a game, especially for children, using a picture on cardboard or wood that has been cut up into odd shapes. You have to make the picture again by putting the pieces together correctly again. EG *...watching pieces of a jigsaw puzzle fit into place and a picture emerge... I still had a part-constructed jigsaw on my table... ...trying to piece together like a jigsaw the various bits of information.* N COUNT ⇑ game = puzzle **2** a complicated situation. EG *Local government was re-organized in 1974 into a three tier jigsaw... ...an insight that could somehow complete this human jigsaw puzzle.* N COUNT : USU SING ⇑ situation

jihad /dʒɪhæd/. A **jihad** is a holy war which Islam allows Muslims to fight against those who reject its teachings. N SING WITH DET ⇑ war

jilt /dʒɪlt/, **jilts, jilting, jilted**. If you **jilt** someone who you have promised to marry, you end your relationship with them suddenly in a way that surprises and upsets them; used showing disapproval. EG *He had jilted her to marry a maidservant... ...a song about a girl who has been jilted.* V+O ⇑ reject = abandon ◊ **jilted**. EG *...the last few leaves hanging on the trees like jilted lovers.* ◊ ADJ CLASSIF : ATTRIB

jimmy /dʒɪmiˡ/, **jimmies**. A **jimmy** is the same as a jemmy; an American word. N COUNT

jingle /dʒɪŋgəⁿl/, **jingles, jingling, jingled**. **1** When something **jingles** or when you **jingle** it, it makes a gentle ringing noise, like small bells. EG *...waving her arms in the air so that her charm bracelet jingled... Don't jingle that bunch of keys in your pocket!* V-ERG ⇑ ring ◊ **jingling**. EG *The groom buckled his jingling straps.* ◊ ADJ CLASSIF ⇑ ringing

2 A **jingle** is **2.1** a gentle ringing noise, that sounds like small bells. EG *I can hear the jingle of bracelets coming up behind me in the dark.* N SING WITH DET **2.2** a short and simple tune, often with words, used to advertise a N COUNT ⇑ tune product on radio, television, or in a cinema. EG ... *an advertisement jingle.*

jingoism /dʒɪŋgəʊɪzə⁰m/. **Jingoism** is enthusiastic and unreasonable belief in the superiority of your country, especially when it involves support for a war against another country. EG *In the United States there was a rift between jingoism and calm counsel.* N UNCOUNT ⇑ nationalism = bigotry

jingoistic /dʒɪŋgəʊɪstɪk/. Something that is **jingoistic** shows enthusiastic and unreasonable belief in the superiority of a particular country, especially in support of a war against another country. EG ...*jingoistic songs, flag-waving, and patriotic orations.* ADJ CLASSIF ⇑ nationalistic = bigoted

jink /dʒɪŋk/, **jinks, jinking, jinked.** 1 To **jink** means to move forward quickly in an irregular way, and not in a straight line, usually to avoid being caught or shot at; an informal word. EG *They scampered forward to the ridge, jinking from side to side as they went.* V+A = zigzag

2 See **high jinks**.

jinx /dʒɪŋks/, **jinxes.** A **jinx** is bad luck, or something or someone that is thought to bring bad luck. EG ...*Muck Hall: the farm with the jinx, with the legend of ruin and defeat... There's a jinx on it, mark my words.* N COUNT : USU SING = curse

jinxed /dʒɪŋk⁰st/. Something that is **jinxed** is considered to be unlucky or to bring bad luck. ADJ CLASSIF = cursed

jitters /dʒɪtəz/. The **jitters** are feelings of extreme nervousness that you get just before you have to do something important or when you are expecting important news; an informal expression. EG *To keep her from getting the jitters, I pretended to know what I was doing.* N PLURAL : USU *the*+N ⇑ nervousness = willies

jittery /dʒɪtə⁰ri¹/. Someone who is **jittery** feels nervous or shows feelings of nervousness; an informal word. EG *'You're pretty jittery,' Boylan said gravely, 'for a nature lover. It's only a snake.'* ▸ used of situations which make you feel nervous or worried. EG *It was probably at this jittery stage of his life that he started gambling.* ADJ QUALIT ⇑ nervous = jumpy ▸ ADJ QUALIT = shaky

jive /dʒaɪv/, **jives, jiving, jived.** 1 The **jive** is a dance which became popular in the 1940s and 1950s, at first performed to jazz music and later to rock and roll music. N SING : USU *the*+N ⇑ dance

2 To **jive** means to dance the jive. EG *You don't have to know how to twist and jive.* V ⇑ dance

Jnr is a written abbreviation for 'Junior'; used especially in American English after someone's name to distinguish them from an older member of the family who has the same name. EG ...*Fred A. Hartley Jnr.*

job /dʒɒb/, **jobs.** 1 A **job** is **1.1** the work that a person does regularly in order to earn money. EG *Gladys finally got a good job as a secretary... He considered himself ideally suited for the job of Prime Minister... ...teaching jobs... ...an unusually good job offer.* N COUNT ⇑ employment = post **1.2** something that you do as part of your regular work which may consist of many smaller tasks. EG *We managed to finish the entire job in under three months... The man who did the design job had ten years' training behind him.* N COUNT ⇑ work = assignment **1.3** a particular task that you have to do, especially something that you do with your hands or with special tools. EG *There are always plenty of jobs to be done round here... ...a repair job... I think he did a great job of work.* ● See also **odd job**. N COUNT ⇑ work = task **1.4** especially in spoken English, an object or a finished piece of work that is of good quality and that has been made or done skilfully and carefully. EG *Today, a job like that would cost £30... 'Damn good paint job,' he says out loud.* N COUNT : USU+SUPP **1.5** especially in informal spoken English, an action or activity that is dishonest, unfair, or unpleasant. EG *I mean, it was a put-up job, if ever there was one... The press did a hatchet job on him.* N COUNT : USU MOD+N **1.6** in informal English, a crime, especially a burglary. EG *They caught him after that job in Brixton.* N COUNT ⇑ crime

2 The **job** of a particular thing or kind of person is **2.1** a duty, responsibility, or function that they have or are considered to have. EG *It's the job of journalism to remain detached... ...complex facial muscles whose sole job it is to make expressions.* N COUNT : USU POSS+N IN SING ⇑ role = function **2.2** the kind of work and duties that they do or are expected to do. EG *She was criticized for doing 'a man's job'.* N COUNT : USU POSS+N IN SING = work

3 If you say that you had a difficult **job**, a hard **job**, etc to do something, you are emphasizing how difficult that situation or activity was. EG *I had a difficult job sneaking into the house and changing my filthy clothes... It was going to be a bit of a job to find George.* N SING : USU *a*+MOD+N+-ING/*to*-INF ⇑ problem = task

4 The word **job** is also used in the following expressions relating to work. **4.1** If you say that someone **did** or **made a good** or **bad job** of a particular task, you are describing how well or badly they have done it. EG *Daddy thought we'd made a very good job of the bathroom... He had done an irreproachable job of presiding over the tribunal.* PHR : VB INFLECTS **4.2** If you say that someone **is doing a good job**, you mean that they are doing their work well and are carrying out all the duties expected of them. PHR : VB INFLECTS

4.3 The job in hand is the piece of work which you are doing at the present time. EG *Let's get on with the job in hand.* PHR : USED AS O/S

4.4 If someone is **on the job**, they are actually doing a particular piece of work. EG *Find out how many men there will be on the job.* PHR : USED AS A/C ⇑ working **4.5** If you refer to work as **jobs for the boys**, you mean that it is not necessary and has been provided by someone for their friends or relations; used in British English. EG *The whole project's unnecessary. It's just jobs for the boys.* PHR ⇑ favouritism

5 If you say **it's a good job** something is true or has happened, you mean that the event or situation you are describing was a good thing for someone and has helped them in some way; an informal use. EG *It's a good job you brought your brolly, it's starting to rain.* PHR+REPORT-CL ⇑ fortunately

6 In informal spoken English, if you say that something is **just the job**, you mean that it is exactly what you wanted or needed at that moment. EG *Thank you–that's just the job.* PHR : USED AS C ⇑ suitable

7 In informal English, if something **does the job**, it succeeds in achieving the result that was desired. EG *I don't care what you use, as long as it does the job.* PHR : VB INFLECTS ⇑ succeed

8 If you **make the best of a bad job**, you accept an unsatisfactory situation that you cannot change and do the best that you can in the circumstances. EG *They may as well make the best of a bad job.* PHR : VB INFLECTS

9 If you **give** someone or something **up as a bad job**, you decide that you can no longer continue having anything to do with them because you will not be able to change or improve them. EG *I gave it up as a bad job in the end.* PHR : VB INFLECTS ⇑ abandon

Job /dʒəʊb/ 1 If you say that someone has **the patience of Job**, you mean that they are extremely patient; a rather old-fashioned expression. PHR : USED AS O ⇑ patience

2 If you call someone a **Job's comforter**, you mean that they make someone who is unhappy or in trouble even more unhappy by talking about his or her troubles. PHR

jobbing /dʒɒbɪŋ/. A **jobbing worker** does not work for someone on a regular basis, but does particular jobs when they are asked to. EG ...*a jobbing builder.* ADJ CLASSIF : ATTRIB ⇑ occasional

jobless /dʒɒblɪ²s/. Someone who is **jobless** does not have a job, even though they would like one. EG *During the depression millions were jobless and homeless.* ▸ The **jobless** is used to refer to people who are jobless. EG *We have to do more for the poor and the jobless.* ADJ CLASSIF = unemployed ▸ N PLURAL : *the*+N = unemployed

job lot, job lots. A **job lot** is a number of cheap things of low quality which are sold together, for example in auctions or second-hand shops. EG *Nearly 20 years ago he bought his first job lot of 50 books for £3.* N COUNT ⇑ assortment

job sharing is the arrangement by which two people work part-time at the same job, for example one person working in the morning and the other in the afternoon. EG *We must begin to look seriously at the whole question of job sharing.* N UNCOUNT ⇑ arrangement

jockey /dʒɒki¹/, **jockeys, jockeying, jockeyed.** 1 A **jockey** is someone who rides a horse in a horse race, especially when this is their job. EG ...*legends about his prowess as a jockey... I think he was Champion Jockey or something one year as well, wasn't he?* N COUNT ⇑ rider

2 If someone is **jockeying for position**, they are using whatever methods they can in order to try and get into a better position than their rivals. EG *They must devote a precious amount of energy simply to jockeying for position... ...rival trade union organizations continuously jockey for position.* PHR : VB INFLECTS ⇑ compete

Jockey Shorts is a trademark for men's underpants that are shaped like the shorts worn for playing sports, and cover the top part of the thighs. N PLURAL : ALSO *a pair of*+N ⇑ underpants

jockstrap /dʒɒkstræp/, **jockstraps.** A **jockstrap** is a piece of clothing worn by sportsmen under their shorts or trousers to support their genitals. N COUNT ⇑ garment

jocose /dʒəkəʊs/ means amusing or humorous; an old-fashioned word. EG *He said this in a tone of jocose raillery.* ◊ **jocosely**. EG *...after twenty months of cold labour, as one of them jocosely put it.* — ADJ QUALIT : USU ATTRIB; ◊ ADV WITH VB

jocular /dʒɒkjə⁴lə/. 1 Someone who is **jocular** is cheerful and often makes jokes or tries to make people laugh. EG *The resemblance had once been noted by some jocular English visitor.* — ADJ QUALIT ⇑ cheerful = humorous

2 Something that is **jocular** is intended to make people laugh. EG *...a jocular remark... I only mentioned it in passing, in a jocular fashion.* ◊ **jocularity** /dʒɒkju⁴lærɪti¹/. EG *He didn't appreciate the jocularity of these letters.* ◊ **jocularly**. EG *'We'll probably all die with you,' Eddie said jocularly.* — ADJ QUALIT = humorous; ◊ N UNCOUNT + SUPP; ◊ ADV WITH VB

jodhpurs /dʒɒdpəz/ are trousers that you wear when you are riding a horse. Jodhpurs are loose from the thigh to the knee and tight below the knee. — N PLURAL : ALSO *a pair of*+N ⇑ trousers

jog /dʒɒg/, **jogs, jogging, jogged**. 1 To **jog** means 1.1 to run slowly. EG *He jogged out to see what was happening.* ▸ used as a noun. EG *I speeded up to a jog and moved up the road briskly.* 1.2 to run slowly for a period of time as a form of exercise. EG *...people who jog or play squash.* ▸ used as a noun. EG *Coming for a jog?* ◊ **jogging**. EG *...the current enthusiasm for jogging.* — V+A; ▸ N SING; V; ▸ N SING; ◊ N UNCOUNT

2 If you **jog** something, you push or bump it slightly and cause it to shake or move. EG *She had jogged her cup of chocolate.* — V+O ⇑ push = nudge

3 If something or someone **jogs** your **memory**, they remind you of something. EG *He had demonstrated the sound to jog my memory.* — PHR : VB INFLECTS ⇑ remind

jogger /dʒɒgə/, **joggers**. A **jogger** is a person who runs slowly as a form of exercise. — N COUNT

joggle /dʒɒgə⁰l/, **joggles, joggling, joggled**. If you **joggle** something, you move or shake it gently and repeatedly, especially up and down. EG *She joggled the baby on her arm.* — V+O = bounce

joie de vivre /ʒwɑː də viːvrə⁰/. is a feeling of happiness and enjoyment of life; a literary expression. EG *They were filled with joie de vivre.* — N UNCOUNT

join /dʒɔɪn/, **joins, joining, joined**. 1 If someone or something **joins** another, they move so that the two people or things come together in the same place, for example so that both of them can do something together. EG *He went for a walk before joining his brother for tea... She flew out to join him on the first available plane... The helicopter was quickly joined by a second.* — V+O ⇑ go = meet

2 If you **join** a queue, you stand at the end of it so that you are part of it. EG *They went off to join the queue for coffee. The van joined the row of cars... They joined a moving line of marchers.* — V+O ⇑ move = tag on

3 If you **join** a club, society, or organization, you become a member of it or to start work as an employee of it. EG *We both joined the Labour Party... I joined the bank as a graduate trainee in 1976... He's joined the army.* — V OR V+O : USU V+O = enter

4 If you **join** an activity that other people are doing, you take part in it or become involved with it. EG *They were invited to join the feasting... After a little while she joined the dancing.* ● to **join forces**: see **force**. — V+O ⇑ participate in

5 If two roads or rivers **join** or if one road or river **joins** another, the two meet or come together at a particular point. EG *This road joins the motorway at junction 16... The Missouri joins the Mississippi at St Louis.* — V OR V+O : RECIP ⇑ meet

6 If you **join** two things, you fasten, fix, or put them together. EG *Cut them down the middle and join the two outside edges together... The house was actually two cottages joined together.* — V+O : USU+A ⇑ fasten = combine

7 If something such as a line, a path, or a bridge **joins** two other things, it connects or links them together. EG *Draw a straight line joining these two points... The High Street is joined to Market Street by an arcade... The cities are joined by close telecommunication links.* — V+O : USU+A = connect, link

8 A **join** is a place where two things are fastened or fixed together. EG *The repair was done so well, you could hardly see the join.* — N COUNT = joint

9 When an army **joins** battle, it starts to fight; a formal use. — V+O

join in. If you **join in** an activity, you take part in it or become involved in it. EG *He took his coat off and joined in the work... Parents should join in these discussions... When other games are played, he tries to join in.* — PHRASAL VB : V+ADV/PREP ⇑ take part in

join up. 1 If someone **joins up**, they become a member of the army, the navy, or the air force; used in British English. — PHRASAL VB : V+ADV = enlist

2 If you **join up** two things, you fasten, fix, or put them together. EG *I used to join up all his paper clips in a long chain.* — PHRASAL VB : V+O+ADV ⇑ fasten

3 If one person or thing **joins up** with another or if two people or things **join up**, they move so that they come together in the same place. EG *The two families joined up for the rest of the holiday... They are moving out to join up with the headquarters.* — PHRASAL VB : V+ADV, OR V+ADV+A *(with)*: RECIP ⇑ combine

joiner /dʒɔɪnə/, **joiners**. In British English, a **joiner** is a person who makes wooden window frames, door frames, and doors: compare **carpenter**. — N COUNT ⇑ craftsman

joinery /dʒɔɪnə⁰ri¹/ is the skill and work of a joiner. — N UNCOUNT

joint /dʒɔɪnt/, **joints**. 1 **Joint** means shared by or belonging to two or more people. EG *We have opened a joint account at the bank. The presentation was a joint effort.* ◊ **jointly**. EG *It was built jointly by France and Germany... They had a huge argument about their jointly owned car.* — ADJ CLASSIF : ATTRIB ⇑ shared = combined; ◊ ADV WITH VB

2 A **joint** is 2.1 a part of your body such as your elbow or knee where two bones meet and are able to move together. EG *He can feel the rheumatism in his joints... ...the joints of the fingers.* 2.2 the place where two things are fastened or fixed together. EG *Cracks appeared at the joints between the new plaster and the old... Check the pipes for leaks at the joints.* 2.3 a way of joining two pieces of wood together. EG *...a neat dovetail joint.* 2.4 a fairly large piece of meat which is suitable for roasting. EG *...a joint of roast beef... The joint was overcooked.* 2.5 a small piece of a chicken or other bird which has been cut up so that you can cook and eat it. EG *This sauce goes well with gammon steaks or chicken joints.* 2.6 a building or place, especially somewhere where people go for some form of entertainment, for example a gambling club, a night club or a cafe; used in informal English. EG *He was employed in a poky little jazz joint in San Francisco.* 2.7 a cigarette which contains cannabis; an informal term. — N COUNT ⇑ junction; N COUNT = join; N COUNT; N COUNT ⇑ meat; N COUNT ⇑ piece; N COUNT ⇑ building; N COUNT

3 If you put a part of your body such as your elbow or knee **out of joint** or if it is **out of joint**, it is injured and the bones are not in their correct position. EG *He's put his shoulder out of joint.* — PHR : USED AS A C

4 If you **put** or **throw** something **out of joint**, you disturb or upset it so that it can no longer operate correctly; an informal use. EG *It's possible to throw the computer program out of joint by typing in nonsense.* — PHR : VB INFLECTS = upset

5 If something **puts** someone's **nose out of joint**, it makes them feel upset because they are no longer receiving as much attention or having as much success as they did in the past; used in informal English. EG *I think it put his nose out of joint when she was promoted.* — PHR : VB+*nose* INFLECT ⇑ upset

jointed /dʒɔɪntɪ²d/. 1 Something that is **jointed** has joints that move. EG *The doll had jointed legs and arms.* — ADJ CLASSIF ⇑ moveable

2 A chicken or other bird that is **jointed** has been cut into pieces so that it is ready to cook. — ADJ CLASSIF ⇑ cut

joint-stock company, joint-stock companies. A **joint-stock company** is a business company that is owned by the people who have bought shares in that company; a technical term in business. — N COUNT ⇑ company

joist /dʒɔɪst/, **joists**. A **joist** is a long thick piece of wood, metal, or concrete that is used in buildings or other structures, especially to support a floor or ceiling. — N COUNT ⇑ support = beam

joke /dʒəʊk/, **jokes, joking, joked**. 1 A **joke** is 1.1 something that is said or done to make you laugh, for example a funny story. EG *Did you hear the joke about the giraffe with a sore throat?... They were all shouting at the tops of their voices and cracking jokes and screaming with laughter... When she stood up, the father made his usual joke... I tried to tell somebody that joke and they didn't get it.* ● If you say that someone **can't take a joke**, you mean that they do not laugh when you play a trick on them, but instead become upset or angry. 1.2 something untrue that you tell another person in order to amuse yourself or them. EG *She ignored what he said. Obviously it was a joke.* — N COUNT = gag; ● PHR : VB INFLECTS; N COUNT = prank

2 If you **joke**, 2.1 you tell funny stories or say amusing things. EG *They never joked about sex in front of the children... They were in the presence of a cheerful companion who joked with them.* 2.2 you tell some- — V : IF+PREP THEN *about/with* = jest; V

one something that is not true, so that you can laugh, either because they have believed you, or later, when you tell them the truth. EG *Don't worry, I was only joking... She started to get very angry, before she realized he was joking.*

3 If you say that someone or something is a **joke**, you mean that they are ridiculous and not worthy of respect; used in informal English. EG *His colleagues regard him as a joke... Everyone knows the election was a joke.* N SING : a+N = farce

4 If you **make a joke of** something, you laugh at it even though it is in fact rather serious or sad. EG *Davis made a joke of his own melancholy.* PHR : VB INFLECTS = laugh at

5 If you say that a situation **is going** or **has gone beyond a joke**, you mean that it has become or is becoming rather annoying or worrying. EG *The whole thing is getting beyond a joke.* PHR : VB INFLECTS

6 If you say that **the joke is on** a particular person, you mean that they have been made to look very foolish although they have been trying to make someone else look foolish; an informal expression. EG *The joke was on her.* PHR : VB INFLECTS

7 If you say that something is **no joke**, you mean that it is very difficult and unpleasant; an informal expression. EG *It's no joke running up mountains at the age of forty six!... My financial situation is no joke!* PHR : USED AS C = no laughing matter

8 You say **joking apart** when you have been laughing or joking about something and now you want people to listen seriously to what you are going to say. EG *After he had taken another whisky, she said, 'Joking apart, you are drinking too much.'* ADV SEN = seriously

9 You say **you're joking** when you have just been told something that is so surprising that you find it difficult to believe. EG *The silence was broken eventually by Ingrid. 'You're joking,' she said, in a horrified voice.* CONVENTION = you're kidding

10 You say things such as **'you must be joking'** or **'she has got to be joking'** 10.1 when you think that what that person has said is ridiculous, or completely untrue. EG *'He's very good at his job, isn't he?'-'You must be joking! He's absolutely useless!'* CONVENTION **10.2** to say that you are not going to do something that has been suggested, because you think it is completely ridiculous. EG *He's got to be joking if he thinks we're going to stay here until seven o'clock tonight!* CONVENTION

joker /dʒəʊkə/, **jokers**. A **joker** is 1 someone who likes making jokes or saying things that are not true in order to provide amusement. EG *I enjoyed working with Hitchcock. He was a great joker.* N COUNT = jester 2 someone who you think is not worthy of respect. EG *They're just a couple of jokers.* N COUNT 3 one of the playing cards in a pack of cards, which does not belong to any of the four suits. In many card games it can be used in place of any card. N COUNT ⇑ playing card = wild card

jokey /dʒəʊki¹/. Something that is **jokey** is amusing and does not have any serious meaning or intentions; an informal word. EG *They all had jokey nicknames.* ADJ QUALIT = amusing

jokingly /dʒəʊkɪŋli¹/. If you say or do something **jokingly**, you do it with the intention of amusing someone or without seriously meaning it. EG *My friend said jokingly that George had lost around two hundred pounds.* ADV WITH VB

jollity /dʒɒlɪti¹/ is behaviour which expresses cheerfulness and happiness. EG *He admired her high spirits, her jollity, and her very unusual beauty.* N UNCOUNT ⇑ happiness = gaiety

jolly /dʒɒli¹/, **jollier, jolliest**. 1 Someone who is **jolly** is happy and cheerful in their appearance or behaviour. EG *Buddy's mother was a jolly, easy-going woman... The little fellow was always jolly and smiling.* ADJ QUALIT ⇑ happy = cheerful

2 Something that is **jolly** is amusing in a lively and enjoyable way; used in rather old-fashioned English. EG *At Christmas we have an awfully jolly time: tree, carols and all that stuff.* ADJ QUALIT ⇑ amusing = enjoyable

3 **Jolly** is also used in informal British English to emphasize something, especially when you want to show approval of it. EG *We provide a jolly good service, I think... It was jolly decent of him to think of me, I must say... He's going to be a jolly tough candidate to beat when the election comes along.* ADV+ADJ/ADV = extremely, very

4 **Jolly well** is used in informal British English to emphasize what you are saying, especially when you are annoyed or irritated. EG *I had no sympathy for them, it jolly well served them right... I'm jolly well not going to ring her up and be told to get lost!* ADV WITH VB ⇑ really

jolt /dʒəʊlt/, **jolts, jolting, jolted**. 1 If something **jolts** or if someone **jolts** it, it moves suddenly and quite violently. EG *She jolted his arm... The bus moved off, sending up a trail of dust and jolting them unmercifully... ...enormous loads that jolted and swayed.* V-ERG = shake

2 A **jolt** is a sudden and rather violent movement. EG *I came down slowly at first, but then with a jolt.* N COUNT = jerk

3 If someone **is jolted** by something, it gives them a sudden and often unpleasant surprise or shock. EG *You cannot help but be jolted by the sight... I was jolted into wakefulness by a bright light... I was jolted out of my exhaustion by piercing screams in the next room... It jolted me seeing them just then.* V+O : USU PASS = shake

4 A **jolt** is also a sudden and unpleasant surprise that shocks you or makes you change. EG *I had two nasty jolts... The aim of Detention Centres is to give kids a jolt.* N COUNT ⇑ shock

Jordanian /dʒɔːdeɪnɪən/, **Jordanians**. 1 **Jordanian** means belonging or relating to Jordan, or to its people. ADJ CLASSIF

2 A **Jordanian** is a person who comes from Jordan. N COUNT

joss stick /dʒɒs stɪk/, **joss sticks**. A **joss stick** is a thin stick covered with a substance that burns very slowly and fills the air with a perfumed smell. N COUNT ⇑ incense

jostle /dʒɒsə⁰l/, **jostles, jostling, jostled**. If you **jostle** other people or **jostle**, 1 you bump against them or push them in a way that annoys them, usually because you are in a crowd and you are trying to get past them. EG *Pedestrians jostled them on the pavement... Flocks of sheep jostled and bleated in the street.* V+O OR V ⇑ bump 2 you compete with other people in a selfish way for attention or for a reward. EG *Barbers, photographers, models, and singers all jostled for money and fame.* V OR V+O ⇑ compete

jot /dʒɒt/, **jots, jotting, jotted**. 1 If you **jot** something somewhere, you write it down in the form of a short informal note, usually so that you will not forget about it. EG *I jot odd notes in the back of the diary.* V+O+A ⇑ write = scribble

2 A **jot** is a very small amount. EG *His sympathy for causes that could not benefit him one jot was easily roused... In the long run it does not matter a jot that Dolores had been deprived of her childhood.* N SING : a/one+N, USU WITH BROAD NEG ⇑ amount = bit

jot down. If you **jot** something **down**, you write it down briefly in the form of a short informal note. EG *Renshaw jotted down a few particulars in his notebook... I asked you to jot down a few ideas when I was here last time.* PHRASAL VB : V+O+ADV ⇑ write = note down

jotter /dʒɒtə/, **jotters**. A **jotter** is a pad or notebook that you write things, usually in the form of short informal notes; used in British English. EG *I looked up a scribbled formula I had in a jotter.* N COUNT = note pad

jotting /dʒɒtɪŋ/, **jottings**. A **jotting** is a brief note that you make about something. EG *For the purpose of writing my statement, I looked up some old jottings.* N COUNT : USU PL ⇑ note

joule /dʒuːl/, **joules**. A **joule** is a unit of energy or work; a technical term in physics. N COUNT

journal /dʒɜːnə⁰l/, **journals**. A **journal** is 1 a magazine which is published regularly and which is devoted to a particular profession, trade or subject. The word journal is often used in the title of the magazine. EG *I picked up a journal from the shelf... I got a job as editor of a trade journal.* N COUNT : ALSO IN NAMES ⇑ magazine 2 a daily or weekly newspaper. The word journal is often used in the name of the paper. EG *The Wall Street Journal carried a long report on the situation... ...an Evening Journal cameraman.* N COUNT : ALSO IN NAMES ⇑ newspaper 3 an account which you write of your daily activities. EG *For nearly three months he had been keeping a journal of his travels around Europe.* N COUNT ⇑ diary

journalese /dʒɜːnə⁰liːz/ is a style of writing which is often found in newspapers or magazines and is characterised by the frequent use of clichés, usually in order to exaggerate the seriousness or importance of something. N UNCOUNT ⇑ style

journalism /dʒɜːnə⁰lɪzə⁰m/ is 1 the job of collecting, writing and publishing news in newspapers and magazines and on television and radio. EG *I have already mentioned journalism as a career... Have you ever thought of going into journalism?* N UNCOUNT ⇑ profession 2 the material which is published in newspapers and magazines. EG *The article was an example of journalism at its best.* N UNCOUNT = reporting

journalist /dʒɜːnə⁰lɪst/, **journalists**. A **journalist** is a person who works on a newspaper or magazine and writes articles for it. EG *She worked as a journalist on The Times.* N COUNT = newspaperman

journalistic /dʒɜːnəˀlɪstɪk/. **Journalistic** means relating to the work of a journalist. EG *I had no journalistic experience in Britain... ...good or bad journalistic practices.*
ADJ CLASSIF: ATTRIB = reporting

journey /dʒɜːniˈ/, **journeys, journeying, journeyed.** 1 A **journey** is 1.1 the act or process of travelling from one place to another. EG *He went on a journey to London... She'll want her supper straightaway after that long journey.* ● If you **break** your **journey** somewhere, you stop there for a short time so that you can have a rest. EG *He is staying in Singapore, where he is breaking his journey home to Australia.* 1.2 an experience of changing or developing from one state of mind to another; a literary use. EG *...people who are on the brink of a spiritual journey.*
N COUNT = trip; ● PHR : VB INFLECTS ⇑ stop; N COUNT+SUPP ⇑ experience

2 To **journey** means to travel somewhere; a formal word. EG *He landed on the west coast and journeyed for several weeks over rough roads... The nights became colder as they journeyed north.*
V+A ⇑ travel

journeyman /dʒɜːnɪməˀn/, **journeymen.** A **journeyman** is a worker who has finished learning a trade but who is employed by someone else rather than working on his or her own; a rather old-fashioned expression. EG *The printing press employed a small number of journeymen and apprentices.*
N COUNT ⇑ worker = artisan

joust /dʒaʊst/, **jousts, jousting, jousted.** When two knights on horseback **jousted** in medieval times, they fought against each other, using lances.
V ⇑ fight = tilt

Jove /dʒəʊv/. **By Jove** is used to emphasize that you are surprised; a rather old-fashioned informal term. EG *By Jove, he's got a talent.*
EXCLAM

jovial /dʒəʊvɪəl/. Someone who is **jovial** seems happy and behaves in a cheerful way. EG *Uncle Duff was quite jovial at tea that evening... He was a big, heavy, jovial man.* ◊ **joviality** /dʒəʊvɪælɪtiˈ/. EG *She welcomed me with uncharacteristic joviality.* ◊ **jovially.** EG *'Come out here any time you like,' said the man jovially.*
ADJ QUALIT ⇑ happy = jolly; ◊ N UNCOUNT = merriment; ◊ ADV WITH VB ⇑ happily

jowl /dʒaʊl/, **jowls.** Your **jowls** are the lower parts of your cheeks, covering your jawbones. EG *...an old woman with heavy jowls and a double chin.* ● **Cheek by jowl** means very close together. EG *For two years we lived cheek by jowl with them.*
N COUNT : USU PL; ● PHR : USED AS AN A ⇑ close

joy /dʒɔɪ/, **joys.** 1 **Joy** is 1.1 a feeling of great happiness and contentment. EG *She hated all subjects and shouted with joy when I told her she was free... They find joy in geography and in history... You could jump for joy or break your heart... As soon as Judy said that, her look of joy gave way to one of misery.* 1.2 in informal British English, success or luck in achieving what you are trying to do. EG *'You won't get any joy out of that. The battery's completely dead'... 'Any joy at the Job Centre?'–'No, usual story'.*
N UNCOUNT ⇑ happiness = delight; N SING WITH DET ⇑ luck

2 A **joy** is something that makes you feel happy or gives you great pleasure. EG *She discovered the joy of writing... His one joy is playing squash... Her sheer professionalism made her a joy to watch.*
N COUNT+SUPP ⇑ pleasure

joyful /dʒɔɪful/. 1 Something that is **joyful** causes happiness and pleasure. EG *The total effect is so intensely joyful that it comes across like dance therapy... I still felt sad even after you'd announced the joyful tidings... I think she has got something serious as well as joyful to offer young people.*
ADJ QUALIT ⇑ pleasing = happy

2 Someone who is **joyful** is extremely happy. EG *The joyful parents named him Lexington... A deliriously joyful boy came running into the village.* ◊ **joyfully.** EG *Then everyone comes on and sings joyfully... Their own criterion of success is the ability to work joyfully and to live positively.*
ADJ QUALIT = delighted; ◊ ADV WITH VB ⇑ happily

joyless /dʒɔɪlɪˀs/. Something or someone that is **joyless** produces or experiences no pleasure. EG *...years and years of joyless married life... I hope I never become as joyless as they have become.*
ADJ QUALIT = miserable

joyous /dʒɔɪəs/ means extremely happy and enthusiastic; a literary word. EG *I spread my arms wide and felt joyous and exalted and free... What meagre surplus there was would be consumed with joyous abandon.* ◊ **joyously.** EG *He flung back the curtains joyously and let the sunlight pour in... He spoke out joyously.*
ADJ QUALIT ⇑ happy = joyful; ◊ ADV WITH VB ⇑ happily = gaily

joyride /dʒɔɪraɪd/, **joyrides, joyriding, joyrode, joyridden;** an informal word. 1 A **joyride** is the activity of driving around for pleasure in a car that you have just stolen. EG *That joyride, I grant you, was a silly stunt... ...a bunch of kids out for a joyride.*
N COUNT ⇑ drive

2 If someone goes **joyriding**, they drive around for pleasure in a car that they have just stolen.
V ⇑ drive

joystick /dʒɔɪstɪk/, **joysticks.** The **joystick** is, a lever in an aeroplane which the pilot uses in order to control the direction or height of the aeroplane. EG *Easing the joystick back she brought the plane in to land.*
N COUNT ⇑ lever

JP /dʒeɪ piː/, **JPs.** A **JP** is a local magistrate in Britain; an abbreviation for 'Justice of the Peace'. EG *At first the new JP attends court as an observer.*
N COUNT

Jr is an American abbreviation for 'Junior'; used especially after a man's name when he has the same name as his father. EG *...Alfred P. Sloan Jr.*

jubilant /dʒuːbɪlənt/ means feeling extremely happy and successful. EG *He was jubilant... ...a jubilant Labour Party Conference.*
ADJ QUALIT = gleeful

jubilation /dʒuːbɪleɪʃəˀn/ is a feeling of great happiness and success. EG *I felt not jubilation but sadness for the family... There was a general air of jubilation.*
N UNCOUNT = glee

jubilee /dʒuːbɪliː, dʒuːbɪliˈ/, **jubilees.** A **jubilee** is a special anniversary of an event, especially the 25th or 50th anniversary. EG *...the college's silver jubilee year.* ● See also **diamond jubilee, golden jubilee,** and **silver jubilee.**
N COUNT ⇑ anniversary

Judaic /dʒuːdeɪɪk/ means belonging or relating to Judaism; a formal word. EG *Christianity was able to maintain a close link with the Judaic tradition.*
ADJ CLASSIF: ATTRIB = Jewish

Judaism /dʒuːdeɪɪzəˀm/ is the religion of the Jewish people, which is based on the Old Testament of the Bible and the Talmud or book of laws and traditions. EG *...the religious ethics of Judaism.*
N UNCOUNT ⇑ religion

Judas /dʒuːdəs/, **Judases.** A **Judas** is someone who betrays a friend. EG *You're a traitor, a liar, a phony, and a Judas.*
N COUNT ⇑ traitor

judder /dʒʌdə/, **judders, juddering, juddered.** If something **judders**, it shakes and vibrates violently. EG *Lorries judder along beneath my window.*
V ⇑ vibrate

judge /dʒʌdʒ/, **judges, judging, judged.** 1 A **judge** is 1.1 the person in a court of law who has the power to make decisions about how the law should be applied to people, for example how a person who has been found guilty of a crime should be punished. EG *Last week she appeared before a judge... Judge Arnason set Miss Davis free on bail... The judge ruled that those statements could not be allowed as evidence.* 1.2 a person who has been chosen to give his or her opinions in a competition and to decide who or what will be the winner. EG *The panel of judges consisted of a variety of famous people... The judges' decision is final and no correspondence will be entered into.*
N COUNT : ALSO IN TITLES ⇑ official; N COUNT : USU PL = adjudicator, referee

2 If you say that someone is a good or a bad **judge** of something, you mean that they are a person whose opinions about that thing are valuable and useful because they are based on a lot of experience or knowledge. EG *He knew Muller would be a good judge of character... Nick, a perfect judge of such matters, had ordered a light French wine.* ● If you say **'I'll be the judge of that'** or **'Let me be the judge of that',** you mean that you will decide for yourself about something; used as a reply when someone has just suggested what you should or should not do. EG *'Don't you think you've had a bit too much to drink, dear?'–'I'll be the judge of that.'*
N COUNT : ADJ QUALIT+N, USU SING, IF+PREP THEN *of* = expert; ● CONVENTION ⇑ decide

3 If you **judge** something such as a competition, you decide who or what is the winner. EG *I have been judging village flower shows and gardens for nearly thirty years... The competition was judged by the local mayor.*
V+O = adjudicate

4 If you **judge** something, 4.1 you guess the amount or value of it by thinking carefully about it. EG *It's impossible to judge her age... It was difficult to judge the seriousness and depth of their commitment... I'd judge that there are fifteen rooms in that house... How will they judge which is likely to be the most reliable?* 4.2 you come to an opinion about how good, useful, or successful it is, after you have carefully examined the evidence. EG *You need to be able to judge your own progress... This sleeping accommodation is somewhat primitive when judged by normal standards... I don't mind my personality being judged on my performance... I'm not in a position to judge.* 4.3 you decide that something or someone has particular qualities. EG *I saw him on his bed in pain and judged him unfit to move around... A person is*
V+O/REPORT-CL = assess, estimate; V OR V+O : IF+PREP THEN *by/from/on* = assess, evaluate; V+O+C, OR V+O+*to*-INF ⇑ consider = deem

judged to be clever if they answer the questions in the right way... The operation must so far be judged a failure... He judged it wiser to put a stop to this quarrel.

5 If you **judge** someone, you decide whether they are a good person or not after you have thought about the good points and the faults in their character, behaviour, and life style. EG *She seemed to be watching him, judging him... Social workers declare that they are not out to judge people, but simply want to help.* — V OR V+O (NG/REFL) : IF+PREP THEN *by* ⇑ criticize

6 The informal expressions **judging from** something, or **to judge by** something are used to mention the reasons that cause you to believe something or to make a particular comment. EG *Judging from the findings of the research, this animal is immune to many diseases... There was some great national celebration in town, judging by the firework displays everywhere... The new king was attractive, to judge from the newspaper photographs.* — PREP ⇑ considering = given

7 If you say that something is true **as far as can be judged**, or **as far as** you **can judge**, you mean that you are assuming or guessing that it is true, although you do not know all the details and facts about it. EG *Their teaching of politics is, as far as can be judged, enlightened and effective... No one, as far as I could judge, was paying any attention to the lesson.* — ADV SEN

judgement /dʒʌdʒməⁿt/, **judgements**; also spelled **judgment**. 1 A **judgement** is 1.1 an opinion that you have or give after thinking carefully about something. EG *I felt completely unable to come to any judgement about it at all... I shall make my own judgement on this matter when I see the results.... My personal judgement is that it will be absolutely essential to sell the business.... In our judgment, her plan has definitely succeeded.* — N COUNT : IF+PREP THEN *about/of/on* ⇑ opinion = verdict 1.2 a decision made by a judge or by a court of law. EG *The final judgment will probably be made in court... Mr Justice Dillon gave his judgement the week before.* — N COUNT/UNCOUNT ⇑ decision = ruling, verdict

2 **Judgement** is 2.1 the ability to make sensible guesses about a situation or sensible decisions about what to do. EG *This is a delicate case that calls for judgement rather than expert knowledge... Decision-making is an art based on good judgement and experience... My father did not permit me to question his judgement... Telling the truth this time was an error of judgement.* — N UNCOUNT ⇑ sense = discernment 2.2 the act or process of deciding how good or worthwhile something or someone is. EG *I have a great fear of judgment... During her career a scientist must survive many judgments.* — N UNCOUNT/COUNT ⇑ criticism

3 If you **pass judgement** on or about something, you give your opinion about it, especially if you are making a criticism. EG *I can't pass judgement until I know all the facts.* — PHR : VB INFLECTS, IF+PREP THEN *about/on* ⇑ comment

4 If you **reserve judgement** about something, you refuse to give an opinion about it until you know more about it. EG *Jenny was still reserving judgment until she could check out the details.* — PHR : VB INFLECTS, IF+PREP THEN *about* ⇑ wait

5 To **sit in judgement** over someone or on someone means to decide whether or not they are guilty of doing something wrong; used showing disapproval. EG *How can we sit in judgment over them when we are equally guilty ourselves?* — PHR : VB INFLECTS, IF+PREP THEN *on/over* ⇑ judge

6 If something is **against** your **better judgement** or if you do something **against** your **better judgement**, you believe that it would be more sensible or better not to do it. EG *It's against my better judgement, but I'll let you go.* — PHR : USED AS A/C

7 A **judgement** is also something unpleasant that happens to you and that is considered to be a punishment from God for something you have done wrong. EG *War is a judgement on us all for our sins.* — N COUNT ⇑ punishment

judicial /dʒuːdɪʃəⁿl/ means 1 relating to judgement in a court of law. EG *The two territories had differing political, judicial, and educational systems... Lord Denning was appointed to conduct a judicial inquiry... I would like to go through proper judicial procedures.* — ADJ CLASSIF : ATTRIB ⇑ legal 1.2 showing or using judgement in thinking about something. EG *Lodge began his judicial summing-up.* — ADJ CLASSIF : ATTRIB ◊ **judicially**. EG *'He shows considerable talent,' replied Sheila judicially.* — ◊ ADV WITH VB

judiciary /dʒuːdɪʃəri¹/. The **judiciary** is the branch of authority in a country which is concerned with justice and the legal system; a formal word. EG *...members of the judiciary.* — N SING : *the*+N ⇑ authority

judicious /dʒuːdɪʃəs/. An action or decision that is **judicious** shows good judgement and sense; a formal word. EG *They made judicious use of government incentives.* — ADJ QUALIT ⇑ sensible ◊ **judiciously**. EG *You put your case most judiciously.* — ◊ ADV WITH VB ⇑ sensibly

judo /dʒuːdəʊ/ is a sport in which two people fight each other and each tries to throw or force the other one to the ground. EG *Courses are offered in unarmed combat, karate, and judo.* — N UNCOUNT ⇑ sport

jug /dʒʌg/, **jugs**. A **jug** is a cylindrical container with a handle and a lip or spout, used for holding and pouring liquids; used in British English. EG *...a big white jug full of beer... He poured milk into a jug from a carton.* — N COUNT ⇑ container ▸ used to refer to the liquid inside a jug or the amount of liquid that a jug contains. EG *...sharing a jug of wine... Stand the flowers in half a jug of water.* — ▸ N PART

jugged hare /dʒʌgd hɛə/ is a stew of hare cooked in a casserole. — N UNCOUNT ⇑ stew

juggernaut /dʒʌgənɔːt/, **juggernauts**. A **juggernaut** is a very large lorry; used in British English. EG *...a million other motor vehicles, from motor cycles to juggernauts.* — N COUNT ⇑ lorry

juggle /dʒʌgəⁿl/, **juggles, juggling, juggled**. 1 Someone who is **juggling** is throwing balls or other things up into the air, repeatedly catching each one and throwing it up again so that there are several of them in the air at the same time. Juggling is usually done as a form of entertainment. EG *They learn to juggle and to walk the tight-rope.* — V ⇑ perform

2 If you **juggle** things such as numbers or ideas, or **juggle with** them, you change or rearrange them repeatedly in order to make them fit the pattern that you want them to fit. EG *Both of them juggle their working hours to be with the children... He was still juggling with figures and possibilities.* — V+O, OR V+A *(with)* ⇑ rearrange

3 If you **juggle with** something or if you **juggle** it, you move it about with short quick movements. EG *He juggled with the controls.* — V+O, OR V+A *(with)* ⇑ move = fiddle

juggler /dʒʌglə/, **jugglers**. A **juggler** is someone who juggles in order to entertain people. EG *I had watched a juggler practising his act.* — N COUNT ⇑ performer

jugular /dʒʌgjə⁴lə/, **jugulars**. Your **jugular** or your **jugular vein** is a very important vein in your neck that carries blood from your head back to your heart. EG *I felt like sliding my pointed nail file into her jugular vein.* — N COUNT ⇑ vein ● If you say that someone **goes for the jugular**, you mean that they ruthlessly attack another person's weakest points, for example a major error in their argument or a subject that they feel very ashamed of or embarrassed about; used in informal English. — ● PHR : VB INFLECTS ⇑ attack

juice /dʒuːs/, **juices**. 1 **Juice** is 1.1 a drink that is made from the liquid part of a fruit. EG *He came back with two tall glasses of pineapple juice... She was standing by the refrigerator with a juice carton in her hand.* — N MASS ⇑ drink 1.2 the liquid that can be obtained from a fruit or a plant. EG *Try squeezing a little lemon juice and garlic into it.* — N UNCOUNT ⇑ liquid

2 The **juices** of a joint of meat are the liquid that comes out of it when you cook it. EG *...spooning the juices over the top of a leg of lamb.* ● to **stew in** your **own juice**: see **stew**. — N COUNT/UNCOUNT ⇑ liquid

3 The **juices** in your stomach are the fluids that help you to digest food. EG *They photographed his arteries and lungs and chemically analyzed all his juices... ...digestive juices.* — N PLURAL ⇑ fluid

4 In informal English, **juice** also means 4.1 petrol. EG *If we're not careful, we're going to run out of juice.* — N UNCOUNT = petrol 4.2 electricity. EG *Just turn on the juice, and we'll see if it works.* — N UNCOUNT = electricity

juicy /dʒuːsi¹/, **juicier, juiciest**. Something that is **juicy** 1 has a lot of juice in it and is very enjoyable to eat. EG *He had a longing for some juicy, red-ripe tomatoes.* — ADJ QUALIT = succulent 2 is very interesting and full of good things; an informal use. EG *The title part of the play is the juiciest for an actor.* — ADJ QUALIT ⇑ desirable 3 describes or represents sexual behaviour in a way that the speaker or writer considers to be pleasing or exciting, although other people might consider it to be offensive; a very informal use. EG *He describes some juicy scenes in the 'Priest of Love'.* — ADJ QUALIT ⇑ revealing = spicy

juju /dʒuːdʒuː/ is a kind of magic, used especially in parts of West Africa, in which people use charms and fetishes in order to try to harm other people. — N UNCOUNT ⇑ magic

jukebox /dʒuːkbɒks/, **jukeboxes**; also spelled with a hyphen and as one word. A **jukebox** is a large — N COUNT ⇑ gramophone record player in cafes, bars, etc which you put coins into and press buttons to choose the records you want to hear. EG *...the noise of reggae music from the jukebox... The cafeteria had the best jukebox in Malaysia.*

Jul. is an abbreviation for July.

julep. See **mint julep**.

July /dʒə⁴laɪ/ is the seventh month of the year in the Western calendar. EG *On leaving school in July 1942, Tony very much wanted to join the RAF.* N UNCOUNT

jumble /dʒʌmbə⁰l/, **jumbles, jumbling, jumbled**. 1 A **jumble** is 1.1 a lot of different things that are found in the same place but look very untidy or have not been neatly arranged. EG *...the jumble which covers the surface of my desk... ...a chaotic jumble of motor vehicles of every description.* N SING WITH DET : USU+*of* ⇑ group = muddle 1.2 a group of things, for example feelings or sensations, that seem to be confused and unorganized, so that it is hard to understand them. EG *...a kaleidoscopic jumble of colours and patterns and noises and smells.* N PART = muddle

2 If you **jumble** things, or **jumble** them **up**, you mix them together so that they are untidy or not in the correct order. EG *The bits and pieces were jumbled up with a lot of stuff that would never be needed again... If a sentence is jumbled, a child can be asked to arrange it correctly.* V+O, OR V+O+A *(up)* : USU PASS ⇑ mix = muddle

jumble sale, jumble sales. A **jumble sale** is an event that is held to raise money, usually for a charity. People bring old things that they do not want any longer, and other people buy them for small amounts of money. EG *...furniture acquired from junk shops and jumble sales.* N COUNT ⇑ sale = rummage sale

jumbo /dʒʌmbəʊ/, **jumbos**. 1 **Jumbo** means very large; used especially in advertising. EG *...a jumbo packet of soap powder.* ADJ CLASSIF : ATTRIB ⇑ large = enormous

2 A **jumbo** or a **jumbo jet** is a very large jet aeroplane that can carry several hundred passengers. N COUNT ⇑ aeroplane

jump /dʒʌmp/, **jumps, jumping, jumped**. 1 If you **jump**, 1.1 you move quickly and suddenly up into the air, using your own strength. EG *He jumped down from the terrace. The horse jumps over a small stream... ...a frog that is able to jump three metres.* V : USU+A ⇑ move = leap ▸ used as a noun. EG *It was a spectacular jump.* ▸ N COUNT ● *See also* **high jump, long jump, triple jump**. 1.2 you move quickly and suddenly. EG *Ralph jumped to his feet... He jumped up and went across to the large bookcase... Crowds of photographers jumped out of the shadows.* V+A = leap, spring 1.3 you suddenly move because you have just been badly frightened or surprised by something. EG *A sudden noise made Brody jump.* V = start ● to **jump out of** your **skin**: see **skin**.

2 If someone **jumps** from one subject to another, they suddenly change the subject of a discussion or conversation and start talking about something else. EG *What annoys me is the way you jumped from one thing to another.* V+A *(from/to)* ⇑ change = switch ▸ used as a noun. EG *...sudden conversational jumps in either direction.* ▸ N COUNT ⇑ leap ● to **jump to conclusions**: see **conclusion**.

3 If you **jump** something such as a fence, you move quickly up and through the air over or across it. EG *The horses are on the race course and the fence is there so they've got to jump it.* V+O ⇑ move = clear

4 If an object **jumps**, it moves suddenly, especially when you did not expect it to do so and cannot prevent it. EG *They hold a pencil as if it might jump out of their hand... His body jumped and twitched.* V : USU+A ⇑ move = spring

5 If an amount or level **jumps**, it suddenly increases or rises by a large amount in a short time. EG *The population jumped to nearly 10,000... The rate of price increase throughout the western world jumped dramatically.* V ⇑ increase = shoot ▸ used as a noun. EG *...a massive jump in expenditure.* ▸ N COUNT : USU +SUPP

6 If you **jump** something such as a question or a step in an argument, you miss it out, either deliberately or accidentally. EG *Oh sorry, have I jumped some questions?* V+O ⇑ omit = skip ● to **jump bail**: see **bail**. ● to **jump the gun**: see **gun**.

7 If you **jump** a queue, you move nearer to the front of it so that you reach the front before it is your turn to do so; used showing disapproval; used in British English. EG *I thought you were good at jumping queues.* V+O ⇑ cheat

8 If someone **jumps** you, they attack you suddenly; used in informal English. EG *He jumped me in the street... The Crime Squad says four guys jumped you.* V+O ⇑ attack

9 A **jump** is also 9.1 a sudden large change, especially one which improves the quality of something. EG *...what a mighty jump forward... Eventually however, a further huge jump was made.* N COUNT : USU MOD+N ⇑ change = leap 9.2 one of a series of events or actions that need to be done in order to achieve something. EG *You are only one jump away from your goal... Her need was to keep one jump ahead of her opponent's moves.* N COUNT ⇑ stage = step

10 If you say that someone **jumps for joy**, you mean that they are very pleased or happy about something. PHR : VB INFLECTS

11 If you are **jumping up and down**, you are behaving in a way that shows that you are very excited, happy, or angry about something. EG *If you had, you'd be jumping up and down with indignation... I felt very angry, jumped up and down in my room and yelled abuse at everyone.* PHR : VB INFLECTS ⇑ excited

12 If you **jump down** someone's **throat**, you speak suddenly and angrily to them; used in informal English. EG *There was no need to jump down his throat like that.* PHR : VB INFLECTS ⇑ retort

13 If you say that something **jumps** out **at** you, you mean that it is very obvious or easy to notice because it is different in some way; an informal expression. EG *If there is any change, it simply jumps at you.* PHR : VB INFLECTS = hit you

14 You say **'Jump to it'** to tell someone to act quickly, immediately, and efficiently; used in informal English to people who you are in charge of. PHR : VB INFLECTS, USU IMPER

jump at. If you **jump at** something such as an offer or opportunity, you accept it eagerly as soon as it has been offered to you. EG *I suggested it to him, and he jumped at the idea... We decided to turn it over to the Argus Company, which jumped at the chance.* PHRASAL VB : V+PREP, HAS PASS ⇑ accept = leap at

jump in. If you **jump in**, you suddenly join in a conversation or discussion, usually by interrupting other people or saying something that they do not want you to say. EG *Neil jumped in to contradict me.* PHRASAL VB : V+ADV ⇑ interrupt = butt in

jump on. If you **jump on** something or someone, you quickly criticize them if they do something that you do not approve of. EG *I always jump on this sort of thing very hard.* PHRASAL VB : V+PREP, HAS PASS ⇑ criticize

jumped-up. **Jumped-up** people consider themselves to be more important than they really are; an informal expression in British English, used showing disapproval. EG *...a jumped-up office boy.* ADJ QUALIT : ATTRIB ⇑ aspiring

jumper /dʒʌmpə/, **jumpers**. A **jumper** is 1 in British English, a piece of clothing, usually made of wool, that covers the upper part of your body and your arms and that does not open at the front. N COUNT = pullover, sweater 2 an American word for a **pinafore**. N COUNT 3 a person or animal that is good at jumping or that jumps in a particular way. EG *This particular monkey is the most magnificent jumper of all.* N COUNT : USU+SUPP ⇑ mover

jumping-off point. A **jumping-off point** or a **jumping-off place** is a situation, occasion, or place which you use as the starting point for something new and important. EG *This could be a jumping-off point for naval and air operations elsewhere.* N COUNT = springboard

jump jet, jump jets. A **jump jet** is a jet aircraft that can take off and land vertically. EG *...the Harrier, Britain's revolutionary jump jet.* N COUNT ⇑ aircraft

jump leads are two thick wires that can be used when a car will not start because its battery does not have enough power. The jump leads are used to connect the battery to the battery of another car to give enough power to start the engine. N PLURAL ⇑ wires

jump suit, jump suits; also spelled with a hyphen. A **jump suit** is a piece of clothing in the form of a top and trousers in one continuous piece. EG *She had blonde hair and wore a green jump suit.* N COUNT = flying suit

jumpy /dʒʌmpi¹/, **jumpier, jumpiest**. If you are **jumpy**, you are nervous or worried about something; an informal word. EG *She seemed very jumpy.* ADJ QUALIT = nervous, edgy

Jun. is an abbreviation for 'June' or 'Junior'.

junction /dʒʌŋkʃə⁰n/, **junctions**. A **junction** is a place where roads or railway lines join. EG *We met up at the junction of Pall Mall and St James's Street... ...the abandoned building at a road junction just south of the Thames... Leave the M5 at junction 4... It's near Clapham Junction.* N COUNT : ALSO IN NAMES AFTER N ⇑ connection

juncture /dʒʌŋktʃə/, **junctures**. At a particular **juncture** means at a particular point in time, especially when it is a very important time in a process or series of events. EG *The shadow cabinet decided to support Benn at a crucial juncture in the entire* PHR : USED AS AN A ⇑ point = now *story... She knew that any move on her part at this juncture would be interpreted as a sign of weakness.*

June /dʒuːn/ is the sixth month of the year in the Western calendar. EG *Labour was defeated in the General Election of 19 June 1970.* N UNCOUNT

jungle /dʒʌŋgəl/, **jungles**. A **jungle** is 1 a forest in a hot country where there is a very large number of tall trees and other plants growing very closely together. EG *The vegetation thickens into jungle woven with creepers and vines... ...warlike tribes from the Amazon jungle... ...a soldier standing by himself in a small jungle clearing.* N COUNT/UNCOUNT ↑ forest = rain forest 2 a place full of things that are close together and untidily arranged, so that it is hard to get through them to where you want to be. EG *She turned and made her way through the jungle of tables towards the back of the room.* N SING WITH DET +SUPP ↑ muddle = forest 3 a situation where it is very hard to get what you want, because everything is very complicated and there are a lot of other people who are also trying to get what they want. EG *Here, for instance, it's a jungle in which the weakest go to the wall... He'd never have got anywhere in the jungle of real politics.* N SING WITH DET +SUPP ↑ situation

junior /dʒuːnjə/, **juniors**. 1 Someone who is **junior** holds a relatively unimportant position in an organization or profession. EG *She's a junior minister at the Home Office... At that time I was one of the most junior members of the school staff... We could give the job to somebody more junior... He's been given a company car, even though he's junior to me.* ADJ QUALIT : IF + PREP THEN *to* ≠ senior

2 A **junior** is 2.1 someone who holds a relatively low or unimportant position in an organization or profession. EG *Police officers later chided their juniors for not spotting these clues.* N COUNT = subordinate 2.2 in British English, a child who goes to a junior school. EG *The juniors have a different uniform from the infants.* N COUNT ↑ pupil

3 If you are a particular number of years someone's **junior**, you are that number of years younger than they are. EG *She was married at the age of seventy-seven to a man seventeen years her junior.* N SING : POSS + N

4 **Junior** means younger; used after a person's name to refer to the younger of two people in a family, especially a father and son, who both have the same surname. EG *Do you mean Douglas Fairbanks Senior or Douglas Fairbanks Junior?* ADJ IN NAMES AFTER N

junior school, junior schools. A **junior school** in England or Wales is a school for children between the ages of about seven and eleven, or the part of a primary school that teaches children of this age. EG *When will she be going to junior school?... My parents were always moving and I went to seven different junior schools.* N COUNT/UNCOUNT ↑ school

juniper /dʒuːnɪpə/, **junipers**. A **juniper** is an evergreen bush with purple berries which can be used in cooking and medicine. N COUNT/UNCOUNT ↑ bush

junk /dʒʌŋk/; a fairly informal word. 1 **Junk** is 1.1 a group of things together that you think are old or useless. EG *'Look, get that junk off the table, will you!'... He filled up that passageway with so much junk that nobody can get past.* N UNCOUNT = rubbish 1.2 old and second-hand goods that are being sold cheaply. EG *We got most of our furniture from junk shops and jumble sales... She looked like the wife of the local junk dealer.* N BEFORE N

2 A **junk** is a Chinese sailing boat that has a flat bottom and square sails. N COUNT ↑ boat

junket /dʒʌŋkɪt/, **junkets**. 1 A **junket** is a trip or visit made by an official or a group of officials and paid for with public money; used in informal English showing disapproval. EG *It's over £500 per person for fares and lodging, but a comparable junket to Hawaii costs only £389.* N COUNT ↑ visit

2 **Junket** is a sweet dessert food made with milk and rennet. N UNCOUNT/COUNT

junketing /dʒʌŋkɪtɪŋ/ is entertainment arranged for visiting officials and usually paid for with public money; used in informal English showing disapproval. N UNCOUNT = beano

junk food, junk foods. **Junk food** is food that is not very good for your health, but which you eat because it is easy and quick to prepare. EG *What their relatives yearn for is real junk food.* N UNCOUNT/COUNT ↑ food

junkie /dʒʌŋki/, **junkies**. A **junkie** is a person who injects a drug, especially heroin, into their body because they are addicted to it; a very informal word. EG *Of course I'm worried. You're turning into a junkie!* N COUNT ↑ addict = drug addict

junk mail is advertising and publicity materials that you receive through the post, even though you have not asked for them; used showing disapproval. EG *...the deluge of newspapers, magazines, reports, letters, junk mail and bulletins that hits us daily.* N UNCOUNT ↑ mail = circulars

junta /dʒuntə, dʒʌn-/, **juntas**. A **junta** is a military government that has taken power by force, and not through elections; usually used showing disapproval. N COUNT ↑ government

jurisdiction /dʒuərɪsdɪkʃən/ is the power that a court of law or an official person has to carry out legal judgements or enforce laws; a formal word. EG *The Governor had no jurisdiction over commodity prices... These offenders have been removed altogether from the jurisdiction of the juvenile courts.* N UNCOUNT ↑ power = authority

jurisprudence /dʒuərɪspruːdəns/ is the study of law and the principles on which laws are based; a formal word. N UNCOUNT = law

jurist /dʒuərɪst/, **jurists**. A **jurist** is a person who is an expert on law. EG *Their decision was based on the authority of leading jurists.* N COUNT ↑ expert

juror /dʒuərə/, **jurors**. A **juror** is a member of a jury. EG *She was sworn in, along with eleven other jurors.* N COUNT ↑ person

jury /dʒuəri/, **juries**. A **jury** is 1 a group of people in a court of law who have been chosen to listen to the facts about a crime and to decide whether the person accused is guilty or not. EG *A jury would never convict on that evidence... ...the twelve people on the jury... Demands that the right to trial by jury be abolished brought vigorous protests.* N COUNT : IF SING, VB CAN BE SING OR PL, OR *by* +N ↑ panel 2 a group of people chosen by the people organizing a competition to decide who the winner is. EG *We'd like to test the opinion of our jury in Broadcasting House.* N COUNT : IF SING, VB CAN BE SING OR PL = panel

jury box, jury boxes. A **jury box** is the place in a court where the jury sits. N COUNT ↑ courtroom

just /dʒʌst/. 1 If you say that something has **just** happened, you mean that it happened a very short time ago. In this sense, **just** is usually used with verbs in perfect tenses. However, it is also possible in informal English to use **just** in this way with verbs in the simple past tense. EG *I've just sold my car... She had only just moved in... Yes, I just heard yesterday... I thought of you just a second ago.* ADV ↑ recently

2 If you say that you are **just** doing something or that you are **just** going to do it, you mean that you will finish doing it or that you will do it in a very short time after the time of speaking. In this sense, **just** is used with verbs in continuous tenses and with the expressions 'about to' and 'going to'. EG *I'm just coming... I'm just making us some coffee, Chris... They were just about to leave when there was a knock on the door.* ADV WITH VB ↑ soon = directly

3 You can also use **just** to say that something is happening at exactly the moment of speaking or at exactly the moment that you are talking about. EG *I don't want you to ask any questions just at the moment.* ADV ● The expression **just as** is used to say that one thing happened at exactly the same time as something else. EG *The telephone rang just as I was about to serve up the dinner... Just as she took it, Soames spotted her.* ● CONJ SUBORD

4 **Just now** means 4.1 a very short time ago. EG *She was here just now. ...I apologize for my outburst just now.* PHR : USED AS AN A 4.2 at the present time. EG *...nasty weather we're having just now... She's in Greece just now.* PHR : USED AS AN A ↑ now

5 The expressions **just a minute**, **just a moment**, or **just a second** are used in spoken English 5.1 to ask someone to wait for a short time. EG *'I'm looking for Mr Hooper's room.'–'Just a minute, please–er, Hooper–ah, here it is. Number 357.'* CONVENTION 5.2 to indicate that you want to interrupt someone, for example in order to disagree with them, explain something, or calm them down. EG *'You're wasting your time.'–'Now, just a minute, sir.'... Just a moment! Hold it right there!... Now, just a minute, Louisa. What's the matter?* CONVENTION ↑ wait = hold on

6 **Just then** means at a particular time in the past. EG *Judy didn't like to tell him just then... Just then, Ellen heard footsteps on the stairs.* PHR : USED AS AN A ↑ then

7 You also use **just** 7.1 to indicate that something is no more important, interesting, difficult, etc than you say it is. You use **just** in this way when you want to correct a wrong idea that someone may get or has already got. EG *It's just a story. One that we made up... Is it derived from authentic data or is it just another theory?... It is not just a children's film... I just want some information on ferries please... Just* ADV = merely, only

add boiling water... It's just that it's gone on so long... He can tell thirty-two things just by taking your pulse... Stop feeling obliged to do things just because others expect them from you. **7.2** to indicate that you are talking about a small part or sample, not the whole of an amount. EG *These are just a few of the enquiries which may come in... That's just one aspect of my work.* **7.3** to draw attention to how small an amount is or how short a length of time is. EG *They were just thirty yards away... Brandt was just eighteen when Hitler came to power... If only I could see it once–just once.* **7.4** to indicate that what you are saying is the case, but only by a very small degree or amount. EG *It is just possible... The heat was just bearable... He could only just hear them... We're just in time... ...a net profit of just over 23%... It struck me just above the elbow.* **7.5** with 'might,' 'may,' and 'could', when you mean that there is a small chance of something happening, despite the fact that it is not very likely. EG *It might just help... It may just be true.* **7.6** to give emphasis to what you are saying. The word following 'just' is usually stressed. EG *He won't listen! He just won't!... There's just no reason for him to be here... I just know there's something wrong... I just can't remember... We've just got to wait... The idea of a woman general is just absurd.* • it **just goes to show**: see **show**. • **just as well**: see **well**. **7.7** to emphasize an imperative, especially when you want another person to share an experience with you or when you are giving advice or an order; used mainly in spoken English. EG *Just listen to that noise... Albert! Just look at the time!... Judy, just think, what an opportunity!* **7.8** to say that you agree completely with what another person has said; used in negative question tags in spoken English. EG *'I think we all look very smart.'–'Don't we just!'... 'He's a good talker, isn't he?'–'Isn't he just.'* **7.9** to say that something which has already been referred to or is known about is exactly what you want to talk about now. EG *We were prepared for just this eventuality... I've been waiting for just such an occasion... That's just what I wanted to hear.*

ADV = but, merely; ADV = a mere, only; ADV : ALSO *only*+ADV = barely; ADV : MODAL+ADV; ADV = simply; ADV : VB (IMPER)+ADV; ADV = indeed; ADV = exactly, precisely

8 If you say that you can **just** do something such as see or hear something, you mean that it is easy for you to imagine seeing or hearing it. EG *Ah yes, I can just see him as a dentist... What a wonderful description. I can just smell the sea air... Oh, I can just taste that gorgeous cheese.* — ADV : *can/could*+ADV = easily

9 You also use **just** in spoken English to be polite when you are making a request, interrupting someone, or changing the subject. EG *I wonder if we can just turn our attention to something you mentioned earlier... Can I just use your lighter, I've run out of matches... If you can just sign there please.* — ADV : MODAL/AUX+ADV

10 You use **just** to indicate that you want to be precise or exact, **10.1** with words like 'what', 'why', or 'how', when you want precise information. EG *It is worth knowing just why this is so... The real debate is about just how much money you should spend.* **10.2** to indicate that a particular thing is exactly what is needed. EG *I believe my Sam here would be just the person!... He knew just the place.* **10.3** to specify a number or amount exactly. EG *That will be just forty pounds.* **10.4** when you specify exactly what place you mean. EG *He stuck the knife right in, just here... ...just opposite St George's Square.* — ADV+WH = exactly; ADV+NG; ADV+NUM = exactly; ADV+A = right

11 Expressions such as **just the same**, **just like**, and **just as...as** are used to emphasize the similarity between two things or two people. EG *Rattlesnake is just like chicken, only tougher... I've received just the same orders as you have... She was just as fat as he was and just as unattractive.* — ADV+*like/the same/as* = equally, exactly

12 Just on is used, in informal English, to specify an exact number or amount. EG *It was just on seven when he reached the farmhouse... The oldest and the youngest people in the village, just on a century of children, have sat in these desks.* — PHR+NUM : USED AS AN A = exactly

13 Just about is used **13.1** to say that something is so close to a particular level or state that it can be regarded as having reached it. EG *She was just about his age... Everything is just about ready.* **13.2** to say that something is in fact possible, although it is very nearly not possible. EG *It is I suppose just about possible... 'Can we get to the airport in an hour?'–'Just about.'* — PHR : USED AS AN A ⇑ about = roughly; PHR : USED AS AN A = barely

14 If you say that a piece of clothing, a style, or a colour is **just** someone, you mean that it suits them perfectly; used in informal spoken English. EG *Don't you think this hat is just me?... That colour is just you.* — PHR : USED AS C

15 Just so 15.1 is used to express agreement with or support for a statement that has been made; used mainly in spoken English. EG *'You are a mathematician, aren't you?'–'Just so.'* **15.2** means arranged very neatly so that everything is in its proper place. EG *When the Japanese make tea, everything has to be just so... He laid out his clothes, just so, by the fire.* — CONVENTION ⇑ yes = indeed; PHR : USED AS C/A

16 You say that something is **just** your **luck** when you have learned that something unpleasant is going to happen to you, to suggest that such bad luck is typical for you. EG *'So she caught you then?'–'Yes, it was just my luck that she decided to come back.'* — PHR : USU USED AS C

17 A person or organization that is **just** is completely fair and impartial in the way that they treat people; a fairly formal word. EG *Let us be cautious in our actions, cautious but just... ...an orderly, just, and civilised society.* ◊ **justly**. EG *I believe that I have acted justly.* — ADJ QUALIT = fair; ◊ ADV WITH VB = fairly

18 An argument, idea, or action that is **just** is reasonable and morally justifiable in the circumstances; a fairly formal word. EG *...the difference between a just and an unjust cause... ...a just war.* ◊ **justly**. EG *Elvis Presley can justly be called the King of Rock and Roll.* — ADJ QUALIT ⇑ reasonable; ◊ ADV WITH VB ⇑ reasonably

19 A punishment or reward that is **just** is reasonable and fully deserved by the person who has received it. EG *It would be much more satisfactory if new ideas were the just reward for hard work and persistent effort... Do you think that imprisonment represents a just or an unjust punishment?* ◊ **justly**. EG *...this justly popular show.* • *to get one's* **just deserts**: see **desert**. — ADJ CLASSIF ⇑ deserved; ◊ ADV ⇑ deservedly

justice /dʒʌstɪs/. **1 Justice** is **1.1** fairness in your behaviour or in the way that people are treated. EG *The concept of justice is very basic in human thought... Tom has a strong sense of justice... They formed themselves into trade unions to achieve economic justice.* **1.2** the quality of being reasonable and justifiable; used of claims, arguments, causes, etc. EG *They believe in the justice of their cause... Do you feel that there is justice in the British claim?... We were the only two there who might with any justice be called working-class.* **1.3** the system that a country or other group of people uses in order to make sure that people obey laws and that punishment is given to those people who break the law. EG *The courts are a very important part of our British system of justice... ...the administration of justice.* **1.4** punishment that someone gets for doing something bad, especially when this is regarded as being fully deserved. EG *Justice will come your way, you mark my words.* — N UNCOUNT = fairness ≠ injustice; N UNCOUNT = legitimacy; N UNCOUNT ⇑ system; N UNCOUNT ⇑ punishment = retribution

2 If a criminal is **brought to justice**, he or she is punished for a crime by being arrested and tried in a court of law. EG *The murderer will in time be brought to justice.* — PHR : VB INFLECTS

3 If you **do justice to** someone or something, **3.1** you describe or reproduce them in a way that shows fairly how good or valuable they are. EG *The radio can't do justice to the full quality of her voice–you have to hear her live to appreciate it.* **3.2** you deal with them properly and completely. EG *They did justice to the huge plates of food that they'd been served... I am the only man in Europe capable of doing it justice, of making a perfect job of it.* — PHR : VB INFLECTS ⇑ represent = capture; PHR : VB INFLECTS

4 If you **do yourself justice**, you do something as well as you are capable of doing it. EG *She didn't do justice to herself in the exam.* — PHR : VB INFLECTS

5 In American English, a **justice** is a judge. EG *...a Supreme Court justice.* — N COUNT = judge

6 Justice is used in British English as part of the title of a judge. EG *The Courts of Appeal upheld the decision of the Lord Chief Justice... Mr Justice Dillon gave his judgement the week before.* — N UNCOUNT : USED IN TITLES = Judge

Justice of the Peace, Justices of the Peace. In Britain and elsewhere, a **Justice of the Peace** is a person who is not a lawyer but who is authorized to act as a judge in a local law court. A Justice of the Peace can deal with less serious crimes, but must pass cases involving more serious crimes on to a higher court. — N COUNT = JP, magistrate

justifiable /dʒʌstɪfaɪəbəl/. A statement, opinion, or fact that is **justifiable** is one that you think is acceptable or correct because you are able to see a — ADJ QUALIT ⇑ reasonable = legitimate, valid good reason for it. EG *I hope this is a justifiable interpretation... I couldn't even call it a justifiable Women's Lib attitude.* ◇ **justifiably**. EG *The Government is understandably, if not justifiably, unpopular.* ◇ ADV = fairly

justifiable homicide, justifiable homicides. **Justifiable homicide** is an act of killing someone which is considered to be excusable or lawful, for example if you kill someone in self-defence; a legal term. EG *They claimed that the killing of Gregory Clark was a 'justifiable homicide.'* N UNCOUNT/COUNT ⇑ killing

justification /dʒʌstɪfɪkeɪʃəºn/, **justifications.** 1 A **justification** for a particular action, process, or situation is an acceptable reason or explanation for it. EG *What is the social justification of University Education?... We all have sound justifications for what we do... There was no justification for higher interest rates... It could be said, with some justification, that the choice has already been made.* N COUNT/UNCOUNT : IF + PREP, THEN *for/of* ⇑ reason = defence, excuse ● If something is said **in justification of** a particular idea or action, it is said in order to show that the idea or action is reasonable. ● PHR : USED AS AN A = in defence of

2 **Justification** is the arrangement of pages of print or typing so that both the left hand and right hand edges are straight; a technical term in printing. EG *They were having terrible problems with the hyphenation and justification.* N UNCOUNT

justified /dʒʌstɪfaɪd/. 1 If you think that someone is **justified** in doing something, you think that their reasons for doing it are good and valid. EG *I think he was quite justified in refusing to help her.*

2 An action that is **justified** is reasonable and acceptable. EG *In these circumstances, massive industrial action is justified and necessary.* ADJ QUALIT ⇑ reasonable = right

2 A page of print or of typing that is **justified** is arranged so that both the left hand and right hand edges are straight; a technical term in printing. EG *Our latest model offers a facility for justified margins.* ADJ CLASSIF ⇑ arranged = aligned

justify /dʒʌstɪfaɪ/, **justifies, justifying, justified.** 1 If someone **justifies** a particular action or idea, 1.1 they show or prove that it is reasonable or necessary, especially when people have said that it was not. EG *The decision has therefore been fully justified... Research programmes almost always justify themselves by producing some pattern or other... Such measures are easily justified and meet with approval.* V+O (NG/REFL), OR V+REPORT-CL/-ING ⇑ demonstrate = explain, substantiate 1.2 they explain why they think it is reasonable or necessary. EG *So how did they justify putting the thing on a gallery wall?... 'I'm not going to try and justify or excuse myself...' She had no need to justify herself.* V+O (NG/REFL), OR V+REPORT-CL/-ING ⇑ explain = defend

2 To **justify** a text when typing it or printing it to arrange it so that both the left-hand and right-hand margins are straight. V+O ⇑ arrange

jut /dʒʌt/, **juts, jutting, jutted.** If something **juts** out, it sticks out above or beyond a surface or edge. EG *The bit where the living room window juts out... There, too, jutting into the lagoon, was the platform.* V+A ⇑ project = protrude, stick out ◇ **jutting**. EG *The tent was lashed to the jutting limb of a tree.* ◇ ADJ CLASSIF : ATTRIB

jute /dʒuːt/ is a substance that is used to make cloth and rope. It comes from a plant which grows mainly in South-East Asia. N UNCOUNT ⇑ fibre

juvenile /dʒuːvəˡnaɪl/, **juveniles.** 1 **Juvenile** activity or behaviour 1.1 involves young people who are not yet old enough to be considered as adults; a fairly formal word. EG *...the increase in juvenile crime.* ▸ used of people. EG *...juvenile offenders.* ADJ CLASSIF : ATTRIB ⇑ young 1.2 is immature and rather silly. EG *Don't be so juvenile!... He made a few ridiculously feeble and juvenile jokes.* ADJ QUALIT ⇑ immature = childish

2 A **juvenile** is a child or young person who is not yet old enough to be regarded as an adult; a formal or legal term. EG *17% of all crime in 1983 was committed by juveniles.* N COUNT ⇑ child

juvenile court, juvenile courts. A **juvenile court** is a court which deals with crimes committed by young people who are not yet old enough to be considered as adults. N COUNT ⇑ court

juvenile delinquency is vandalism and other criminal behaviour that is committed by young people who are not yet old enough to be legally considered as adults. EG *High unemployment has produced a growing problem of juvenile delinquency.* N UNCOUNT ⇑ crime

juvenile delinquent, juvenile delinquents. A **juvenile delinquent** is a young person who is guilty of a crime, especially vandalism or some form of violence. N COUNT ⇑ offender

juxtapose /dʒʌkstəpəʊz/, **juxtaposes, juxtaposing, juxtaposed.** If you **juxtapose** two things or ideas, you put them close together or next to each other, often in order to emphasize the difference between them; a fairly formal word. EG *She juxtaposes these photographs with illustrations of flowers.* V+O ⇑ place = contrast

juxtaposition /dʒʌkstəpəzɪʃəºn/. **Juxtaposition** is the state of being placed next to or very close to something else, especially something that is very different; a fairly formal word. EG *...the juxtaposition of extreme wealth and poverty... Inside me there is also this juxtaposition of cultures.* N COUNT/UNCOUNT ⇑ position

Kk

K, k /keɪ/, **Ks, k's.** 1 **K** is the eleventh letter of the English alphabet. N COUNT

2 **K** is an abbreviation for 'king'. = king

3 **K** is also used in informal English to represent the number 1000; an abbreviation for 'kilo-'. N SING : NUM+N = 1000

kaftan /kæftæn, -tɑːn/, **kaftans.** See **caftan**.

kale /keɪl/ is a vegetable that is similar to a cabbage. It has curly leaves which you can cook and eat. N COUNT/UNCOUNT ⇑ vegetable

kaleidoscope /kəlaɪdəºskəʊp/, **kaleidoscopes.** 1 A **kaleidoscope** is a toy in the shape of a tube with a small hole at one end. If you look through the hole and turn the other end of the tube, you can see a pattern of colours which changes as you turn the tube round. N COUNT ⇑ toy

2 A **kaleidoscope** of different colours, images, etc is a pattern of them that is rapidly changing. EG *Alongside the railway line, in a kaleidoscope of colours, cars and lorries waited patiently.* N SING WITH DET : USU+SUPP

kaleidoscopic /kəlaɪdəºskɒpɪk/. **Kaleidoscopic** patterns and images are made up of rapidly changing colours and shapes. ADJ CLASSIF : ATTRIB ⇑ patterned

kamikaze /kæmɪˡkɑːziˡ/. If you perform a **kamikaze** act, you attack the enemy knowing that you will be hurt or killed doing it. EG *It was a kamikaze mission.* ADJ CLASSIF : ATTRIB

kangaroo /kæŋgəruː/, **kangaroos.** A **kangaroo** is a large Australian animal which moves forward by jumping on its back legs. Female kangaroos carry their babies in a special pouch on their stomachs. N COUNT ⇑ animal

kangaroo court, kangaroo courts. A **kangaroo court** is an unofficial trial of a member of an organization who is accused of having seriously broken the rules of that organization. N COUNT ⇑ trial

kapok /keɪpɒk/ is a soft white fluffy material that is used for stuffing cushions or is put inside sleeping bags, jackets, etc, to provide warmth. N UNCOUNT ⇑ fibre = stuffing

kaput /kæpʊt/. If you say that something is **kaput**, you mean that it is broken; used in informal spoken English. EG *The record player seems to be kaput.* ADJ CLASSIF : PRED

karate /kərɑːtiˡ/ is a sport in which people fight without weapons, using only their hands, elbows, feet, and legs. Karate was originally a method of self-defence in Japan. EG *She knew a little karate... ...a karate chop.* N UNCOUNT ⇑ sport

karma /kɑːmə/ is the belief, in the Buddhist religion, that your actions in one life affect all your other lives after that one. N UNCOUNT = destiny, fate

kayak /kaɪæk/, **kayaks.** A **kayak** is a small boat, like a canoe, used by Eskimos. N COUNT

kebab /kəˈbæb/, **kebabs**. A **kebab** is a dish consisting of small pieces of meat and sometimes vegetables that are put on a long thin metal rod and grilled. [N COUNT ⇑ dish]

kedgeree /kedʒəriː/ is a cooked dish consisting of rice, fish, and eggs. [N UNCOUNT ⇑ dish]

keel /kiːl/, **keels, keeling, keeled**. 1 The **keel** of a boat is the long, specially shaped piece of wood or steel along the bottom of a boat. The sides of the boat are fixed to it and it helps to keep the boat steady. [N COUNT ⇑ base]

2 If you say that someone or something is **on an even keel**, you mean that they are working or progressing smoothly, without any sudden changes. EG *He took lots of different medicines which kept him on an even keel... Most governments are able to keep their economies on an even keel.* [PHR : USED AS AN A ⇑ stable]

keel over. If something **keels over**, it falls over sideways. EG *The pillar was liable to keel over at any moment... The others had either keeled over or were laughing hysterically.* [PHRASAL VB : V+ADV ⇑ fall]

keen /kiːn/, **keener, keenest; keens, keening, keened**. 1 Someone who is **keen** 1.1 wants to do something very much or wants something to happen very much. EG *Her solicitor was much keener to talk to her than she was to talk to him... He's not at all keen for Charlotte or anybody else to know that... I'm never very keen on keeping a car for more than a year.* ◊ **keenness**. EG *The only thing I could see in him was a certain keenness for action.* [ADJ QUALIT : PRED, USU+to-INF/on = anxious] [◊ N UNCOUNT] 1.2 has a great deal of enthusiasm for a particular activity, for example a sport or a hobby, and spends a lot of time doing it. EG *He was not a keen gardener... Boys are just as keen on cooking as girls are.* [ADJ QUALIT : IF+PREP THEN on = enthusiastic] 1.3 has an enthusiastic nature and is interested in everything they do. EG *...a keen, enthusiastic lad... We should be looking for an abler, keener, more resourceful President.* [ADJ QUALIT]

2 A **keen** desire, emotion, or interest is one that is extreme and intense. EG *He took a keen interest in domestic affairs... ...a keen desire to see the union brought under the rule of law.* ◊ **keenly**. EG *I was still keenly interested in outdoor activities... He felt the pain in his side keenly.* [ADJ QUALIT : USU ATTRIB = deep, intense] [◊ ADV WITH VB]

3 If you are **keen** on someone, you feel attracted to them and would like to get to know them better; an informal use. EG *Molly was very keen on the music master.* [ADJ QUALIT : PRED+on]

4 If someone's expression is **keen**, it shows eagerness, intelligence, and concentration. EG *His face was, like a soldier's or an explorer's, stern and keen in its expression.* ◊ **keenly**. EG *She was watching keenly.* [ADJ QUALIT = alert] [◊ ADV]

5 If you have **keen** senses, you are able to see, hear, etc, very well. EG *They blend so well into foliage that it takes a keen eye to spot them if they keep still... ...people of extraordinary intelligence and with very keen powers of observation.* ◊ **keenness**. EG *...because of their keenness of eye and steadiness of hand.* [ADJ QUALIT = acute] [◊ N UNCOUNT = sharpness]

6 If you say that someone's mind is **keen**, you mean that they are very clever and aware of what is happening around them. EG *He had a keen appreciation of the power and dangers of the mass media... The Emperor had a keen sense of humour.* [ADJ QUALIT = sensitive, sharp]

7 A **keen** contest is one in which the competitors are all trying very hard to win, and the outcome is not clear. EG *The competition for the first prize was keen.* ◊ **keenly**. EG *Companies competing against each other in keenly contested world markets.* [ADJ QUALIT = fierce] [◊ ADV = fiercely]

8 A **keen** wind is very cold and unpleasant. [ADJ QUALIT]

9 Knives and blades that are **keen** are very sharp. [ADJ QUALIT]

10 If you **keen**, you make a wailing sound, usually as a sign of grief because someone has died; a rather old-fashioned word. [V = wail]

keep /kiːp/, **keeps, keeping, kept**. 1 To **keep** someone or something in a particular way means to cause them to stay in the particular state, condition, or position that is mentioned. EG *I'm holding my arms like this because it keeps me warm... At night they had been kept awake by nightingales... The doors were kept permanently locked... Sorry to keep you waiting... They've got to hunt for food to keep alive... We ask people to keep in touch with us... She kept her arm around her husband as she spoke.* [V+O+C (ADJ), V+O+-ING, V+O+A, OR V+C (ADJ)]

2 If someone or something **keeps** you somewhere, they make you stay there. EG *They kept her there in hospital and then they said she was all right... The weather had kept us indoors that day.* [V+O+A = detain]

3 If you **keep** something, 3.1 you have it in your possession and do not throw it away, give it away, or sell it. EG *I'm never very keen on keeping a car for more than a year... ...a gun that he kept for his private use.* [V+O ⇑ have = retain] 3.2 you continue to have it and do not lose it or allow it to disappear. EG *She would probably not be able to keep her job... We should try and keep a broad mix of subjects in the course.* [V+O ⇑ have = preserve] 3.3 you have it and look after it for someone for a fairly short time. EG *We'll keep your tickets for you until Wednesday... Can you keep me two loaves of bread?* [V+O, V+O+O, OR V+O+A (for) = hold] 3.4 you always have it in a particular place so that you can use it whenever you need it. EG *Keep a notebook in the kitchen for shopping lists.* [V+O : USU+A ⇑ have] 3.5 you put it in a particular place and store it there. EG *...the basement of the building, where the rubbish is kept... Keep your card in a safe place.* [V+O+A ⇑ have = store]

4 If you **keep** to a particular direction, you continue to move in that direction. EG *We kept to the left... We'll keep along by the sands... Keep to the path.* [V+A ⇑ continue]

5 If a shopkeeper **keeps** something, he or she regularly has it for sale in their shop. EG *She keeps a very fine range of cheeses.* [V+O ⇑ have = stock]

6 If you **keep** doing something, you do it over and over again, often without being able to prevent yourself doing it. EG *I keep making the same mistake... Since I read it, I keep thinking about it... They kept coming back to him at six-month intervals.* [V+-ING : NO CONT = continue] ● If you say to someone **'Keep going'**, you are encouraging them to continue in what they are doing, especially when it is something difficult and they want to give up. [● CONVENTION]

7 You use **keep** with individual nouns to indicate that you do the activity which the noun refers to, usually over a period of time. EG *They would keep a look-out for him... A woman kept watch at the gate... I didn't agree but I kept silence.* [V+O : NO PASS = maintain]

8 If someone **keeps** you, they delay you and make you arrive somewhere later than expected. EG *What kept you ?... Am I keeping you from your party?* [V+O : IF+PREP THEN from = detain]

9 If you **keep** yourself or **keep** someone else, you support yourself or the other person by earning enough money to provide food, clothing, money, and other necessary things. EG *He gets four pounds a week to keep himself... I want to keep you all in luxury.* [V+O (NG/REFL) = maintain]

10 Someone's **keep** is the cost of food and other things that they need in their daily life. EG *The grant includes £19 for your keep during the short vacations.* [N SING : POSS+N ⇑ cost = board]

11 When you **keep** something such as a promise or an appointment, you do what you said you would do. EG *I always keep my promises... I'm afraid I won't be able to keep my appointment for this afternoon.* [V+O = fulfil]

12 If you **keep** a religious festival or if you **keep** the sabbath, you treat those days in the special way that is traditional in a particular religion. EG *The sabbath should be kept in order to bring the family together.* [V+O = observe]

13 If you **keep** something from someone, you do not tell them about it. EG *He seemed to be keeping something from me.* [V+O : IF+PREP THEN from] ● If you **keep** a piece of information to yourself, you do not let anybody else know about it. EG *They keep their discoveries to themselves.* [● PHR : VB INFLECTS ≠ share]

14 If you **keep** yourself **to** yourself, you stay on your own a great deal and not mix socially with other people. [PHR : VB INFLECTS ≠ mix, socialize]

15 If you **keep** a diary, list, or some other kind of record, you regularly write down an account of something or you make a written record of an event so that you will be able to refer to it at a later date. EG *We keep a record of the noise-levels produced by the machines... I did not keep any notes.* [V+O = maintain]

16 If you **keep** animals, you own and take care of them, either as a hobby or so that you can use them or make money from them in some way. EG *...a man who kept 160 pigs... It would be nice to keep bees.* [V+O]

17 If you **keep** a business such as a small shop or hotel, you own it and manage it. EG *I used to live with my auntie. She kept a sweet-shop.* [V+O = run]

18 If food **keeps**, it stays fresh and in good condition for a certain length of time. EG *Fish doesn't keep very well, not even in a fridge.* [V : NO CONT ⇑ last]

19 If you ask how someone **is keeping**, you are [V+A : ONLY CONT]

asking if they are well. EG *How is your mother keeping?... I hope you're keeping well.*

20 If you **keep at it**, you continue doing something that you have started, even if you are tired and would prefer to stop. — PHR : VB INFLECTS = persevere, stick at it

21 If you **keep** someone **at it**, you make them work hard and continuously, even if they are tired. EG *The teachers kept us at it all afternoon.* — PHR : VB INFLECTS ⇑ work

22 If you say that something happens **for keeps**, you mean that it will never change again but will remain the same; an informal expression. EG *I came back to the United States for keeps.* — PHR : USED AS AN A = forever

23 A **keep** is the main tower of a medieval castle, in which people lived. EG *...a four-sided medieval keep.* — N COUNT

24 The word **keep** is also used in the following expressions, which are explained at other places in this dictionary. • to **keep** someone **company**: see **company**. • to **keep** your **end up**: see **end.** • **to keep a straight face**: see **face.** • to **keep** your **hand in**: see **hand.** • to **keep** your **head**: see **head.** • to **keep house**: see **house.** • to **keep pace**: see **pace.** • **to keep the peace**: see **peace.** • **to keep a secret**: see **secret.** • **to keep track of**: see **track.**

25 See also **keeping, kept.**

keep away. 1 If you **keep away** from somewhere, you avoid going there. EG *They kept away from the forest... He lacked the power to keep away.* — PHRASAL VB : V+ ADV, IF+PREP THEN *from*

2 If you **keep** someone or something **away** from somewhere, you prevent them from going there. EG *Keep animals away from the kitchen... If you don't keep them away, they'll take over.* — PHRASAL VB : V+ O+ADV, IF+ PREP THEN *from*

keep back. 1 If you **keep** part of something **back**, you make sure that you do not use or give away all of it, so that you still have some to use at a later time. EG *Remember to keep back enough cream to make the topping.* — PHRASAL VB : V+ O+ADV

2 If you **keep** some information **back**, you do not tell all that you know about something. EG *You can't write an autobiography without keeping something back.* — PHRASAL VB : V+ O+ADV = withhold

keep down. 1 If you **keep** the number, size, or amount of something **down**, you do not let it get bigger or go higher. EG *The French too are very concerned to try and keep costs down... This keeps prices down.* — PHRASAL VB : ORDER V+O+ ADV ⇑ limit

2 If you **keep down** or you **keep** your head **down**, you stay in a lying or low position in order to avoid being seen or attacked. EG *Keep down!... They kept their heads down.* — PHRASAL VB : V+ ADV OR V+O+ ADV = duck

3 If someone **keeps** a group of people or a nation **down**, they keep them in a state of powerlessness, and prevent them from being completely free. EG *For centuries men have been trying to keep women down.* — PHRASAL VB : ORDER V+O+ ADV = suppress

4 If you **keep** food or drink **down**, you succeed in not vomiting when you feel sick. EG *I can't keep anything down, not even water.* — PHRASAL VB : ORDER V+O+ ADV

keep in. 1 If you **keep** someone **in**, you make them stay indoors or you make them stay late at school, as a punishment. EG *John was kept in at school one day last week.* — PHRASAL VB : V+ O+ADV ⇑ detain

2 If you **keep in**, you stay near the edge of a road or path when you are walking, cycling, or driving along it, instead of being in the middle of it. EG *Keep in! You'll be run over if you don't watch it!* — PHRASAL VB : V+ ADV

keep in with. If you **keep in with** someone, you stay friendly with them, often in order to gain some advantage for yourself because they have power or influence. EG *You really ought to try and keep in with George... Now he is getting old he wishes he had kept in with his family.* — PHRASAL VB : V+ ADV+PREP

keep off. 1 If you **keep** someone or something **off** a particular place, you prevent them from going there. EG *In Scotland you have no right to keep people off your land.* — PHRASAL VB : V+ O+ADV/PREP = bar from

2 If you **keep** something **off** someone, you prevent it from touching or attacking them. EG *Keep those dogs off her!... ...a bamboo shelter to keep the rain off.* — PHRASAL VB : V+ O+ADV/PREP ⇑ prevent

3 If unpleasant weather **keeps off**, it does not begin. EG *Luckily the rain kept off.* — PHRASAL VB : V+ ADV

4 If you **keep off** a particular kind of food or drink, you avoid eating or drinking it, usually because it is something that you know will make you feel ill. EG *She can drink skimmed milk, but she has to keep off butter.* — PHRASAL VB : V+ PREP, HAS PASS

5 If you **keep off** a particular subject, you deliberately do not talk about it during a discussion or conversation. EG *He kept off the question of whose fault it was.* — PHRASAL VB : V+ PREP

keep on. 1 If you **keep on** doing something, you continue to do it and do not stop. EG *They kept on walking for a while in silence... I'm so sorry to keep on coughing.* — PHRASAL VB : V+ ADV+-ING, NO CONT

2 If you **keep** someone **on**, you continue to employ them or to educate them at school, although, for example, their contract has ended or they are old enough to retire or leave school. EG *Only half the workforce will be kept on after this order has been completed... Some councils make a grant to keep a pupil over 16 on at school.* — PHRASAL VB : V+ O+ADV

3 If you **keep on** about something, you continue to talk about it in a boring or repetitive way. EG *She kept on about the stupid car.* — PHRASAL VB : V+ ADV, IF+PREP THEN *about*

keep on at. If you **keep on at** someone, you repeatedly ask them something or tell them something in a way that annoys them. EG *I made no reply, but he kept on at me.* — PHRASAL VB : V+ ADV+PREP, NO CONT = nag

keep out. 1 To **keep** someone or something **out** means to prevent them from entering or being in a particular place. EG *...a guard dog to keep out intruders... This should keep them out.* — PHRASAL VB : V+ O+ADV

2 If a sign says **'Keep Out'**, it is warning you not to go onto that piece of land. EG *'Private property. Keep out.'* — PHRASAL VB : V+ ADV

keep out of. 1 If you **keep** someone **out of** a particular situation, you avoid involving them in it because you think it would be unpleasant for them. EG *You should try and keep him out of it, or it will only complicate things further.* — PHRASAL VB : V+ O+ADV+PREP ⇑ exclude

2 If you **keep out of** a situation, you avoid becoming involved in it. EG *You keep out of this. It's got nothing to do with you.* — PHRASAL VB : V+ ADV+PREP

keep to. 1 If you **keep to** a regulation or agreement, you do exactly what you are expected or supposed to do. EG *We must keep to the deadlines... Keep to the letter of the law.* — PHRASAL VB : V+ PREP, HAS PASS = observe

2 If you **keep to** a particular subject, you talk only about that subject, and do not talk about anything else. EG *I wish you'd keep to the point.* — PHRASAL VB : V+ PREP, HAS PASS ≠ deviate

3 If you **keep** something **to** a particular number or quantity, you limit it to that number or quantity. EG *Keep it to a minimum.* — PHRASAL VB : V+ O+PREP, OR V+ PREP

4 If you **keep to** somewhere such as your bed or a room in your home, you stay there for a period of time, for example if you are ill or if the weather is bad. EG *He kept to his bed when he had flu.* — PHRASAL VB : V+ PREP

keep under. If you **keep** someone **under**, 1 you control them so that they only behave in the way you want them to. — PHRASAL VB : V+ O+ADV = repress 2 you keep them in a state of unconsciousness by giving them drugs. EG *She was kept under with a mixture of morphine and chloroform.* — PHRASAL VB : V+ O+ADV ⇑ drug

keep up. 1 If someone or something **keeps up**, **1.1** they move at the same speed as someone or something else. EG *I started to run a bit so that she had to hurry to keep up with me... They will have to get off the highway because they can't keep up.* — PHRASAL VB : V+ ADV, IF+PREP THEN *with* **1.2** they increase at the same speed and in the same way as something else is increasing. EG *Supply could never have kept up with consumption... Pensions were increased to keep up with the rise in prices.* — PHRASAL VB : V+ ADV, USU+ *with*

2 If someone **keeps up**, **2.1** they learn all the most recent facts about something. EG *They kept up with what was happening in their work... Even friends have trouble keeping up with each other's whereabouts.* — PHRASAL VB : V+ ADV, USU+ *with* ⇑ know **2.2** they work at the speed that is necessary for them to perform as well as other people in their group or to get all their work done in the required time. EG *They appear to be able to keep up with the class... I shall be taking work home every night, you know, to keep up.* — PHRASAL VB : V+ ADV, IF+PREP THEN *with* ≠ fall behind **2.3** they deal successfully with a situation in which things are changing quickly or to a great extent. EG *...the struggle to keep up with inflation... It has increased so much that our imagination can't keep up.* — PHRASAL VB : V+ ADV, USU+ *with* ⇑ adjust

3 If you **keep** something **up**, **3.1** you continue to do it and do not let it stop or end. EG *It is very important for me to keep up my contacts... He was unable to keep up the payments... The tanks kept up a steady fire.* — PHRASAL VB : ORDER V+ADV+ O ⇑ maintain **3.2** you prevent it from growing less in amount, size, or degree. EG *I can't see how we can keep this pace up for more than a day or two... It's important to keep up the standard.* — PHRASAL VB : V+ O+ADV ⇑ maintain **3.3** you continue to study, practise, or use a particular subject or skill. EG *We* — PHRASAL VB : V+ O+ADV

have to keep up some mathematics at university... He's managed to keep his Spanish up quite well.

4 If you **keep it up**, you continue working or trying as hard as you have been in the past. EG *Being human, he can only keep it up for eight hours a day, five days a week.* PHR : VB INFLECTS ⇑ continue

5 If you **keep** someone **up**, you stop them from going to bed, usually by talking to them. EG *I ought never to have kept you up so late.* PHRASAL VB : ORDER V+O+ADV

keep up with. 1 If you **keep up with** a friend, you stay in contact with them by writing, telephoning, or seeing them regularly. EG *We've kept up with each other ever since we left school.* PHRASAL VB : V+ADV+PREP = stay in touch

2 If you **are keeping up with the Joneses**, you are trying to have all the same possessions as your friends and neighbours and to do all the same things as them, because you do not want to seem inferior to them. PHR : VB INFLECTS ⇑ copy

keeper /kiːpə/, **keepers**. 1 A **keeper** is 1.1 a person who takes care of the animals in a place such as a game reserve or a zoo. EG *I began to interview retired zoo keepers.* N COUNT = warden 1.2 a person in a museum or art gallery who is in charge of the exhibits or works of art. EG *...the former Principal Keeper of Printed Books at the British Museum.* N COUNT ⇑ custodian 1.3 a goal-keeper; an informal use. N COUNT 1.4 a wicket-keeper; an informal use. N COUNT

2 If you say that you **are not** someone's **keeper**, you mean that you are not willing to accept responsibility for anything unpleasant that might happen to them or any trouble they might cause. EG *I am not my brother's keeper.* PHR : VB INFLECTS

3 **finders keepers**: see **finder**.

-keeper, **-keepers**. **-keeper** is added to some nouns to form a noun which means a person who is in charge of the particular thing referred to. EG *...shop-keepers... ...bee-keepers... ...hotel keepers.* COMB : FORMS N COUNTS

keep-fit is the activity of keeping your body in good condition by doing special exercises, usually in organized classes. N UNCOUNT : USU BEFORE N ⇑ exercises

keeping /kiːpɪŋ/. 1 If you say that something is **in keeping** with a particular situation or activity, you mean that it seems to be suitable and appropriate. EG *White socks and brown shoes were not quite in keeping with her beautiful satin evening dress... In keeping with the government policy of non-interference, they refused to take any action.* PHR : USU+*with*, USED AS AN A

2 If something is **out of keeping** with a particular situation or activity, it is not considered to be suitable or appropriate. EG *Her costume was quite out of keeping with the character she was supposed to be playing.* PHR : USU+*with*, USED AS AN A = out of line

3 If something is in your **keeping**, you are looking after it and are responsible for it. EG *He entrusted the book to my keeping.* N SING : POSS+N = charge

keepsake /kiːpseɪk/, **keepsakes**. A **keepsake** is a small present that someone gives you so that you will not forget them. N COUNT = memento

keg /kɛg/, **kegs**. 1 A **keg** is a small barrel used for storing something such as beer or other alcoholic drinks. N COUNT

2 **Keg** is a kind of beer which is kept under pressure in a metal barrel. N UNCOUNT ⇑ draught beer

ken /kɛn/. If something is **beyond** your **ken**, you do not have enough knowledge to be able to understand it; an old-fashioned expression. EG *The reason for such strange behaviour is beyond my ken.* PHR : USED AS AN A

kennel /kɛnəˡl/, **kennels**. The form **kennels** can also be used as the singular for paragraph 2. 1 A **kennel** is a small building made especially for a dog to sleep in. EG *Sporting dogs should be kept out of doors in a kennel.* N COUNT ⇑ building

2 A **kennels** or a **kennel** is an establishment where people can leave their pet dogs when they go away, for example on holiday, or where dogs are bred and trained. EG *He had arranged to leave Towser at a kennels.* N COUNT

Kenyan /kiːnjən, -kɛn/, **Kenyans**. 1 Someone or something that is **Kenyan** belongs or relates to Kenya or to its people. EG *He is a Kenyan citizen.* ADJ CLASSIF

2 A **Kenyan** is a person who comes from Kenya. N COUNT ⇑ person

kept /kɛpt/. 1 **Kept** is the past tense and past participle of **keep**.

2 A **kept** woman or man is financially supported by someone who is not married to them in return for having a sexual relationship with them. EG *I could be a kept woman with nothing to do all day but paint.* ADJ CLASSIF : ATTRIB ⇑ maintained

kerb /kɜːb/, **kerbs**. A **kerb** is the raised edge between a pavement and a road. EG *The taxi pulled into the kerb... She stepped off the kerb.* N COUNT ⇑ edge

kerb-crawling is the activity of driving slowly along a kerb in order to speak to and hire a prostitute. N UNCOUNT

kerchief /kɜːtʃiˡf/, **kerchiefs**. A **kerchief** is a piece of cloth that you can wear on your head or round your neck; an old-fashioned word. EG *He was dressed in a black silk shirt with a red kerchief knotted round his throat.* N COUNT ⇑ scarf

kerfuffle /kəfʌfəˡl/, **kerfuffles**. A **kerfuffle** is a noisy and disorderly incident often resulting from an argument; used in informal British English. EG *Fletcher enjoyed the resulting kerfuffle.* N COUNT : USU SING ⇑ activity = commotion

kernel /kɜːnəˡl/, **kernels**. 1 The **kernel** of a nut is the part that is inside the shell. EG *Its wings are wrinkled like the kernel of a walnut.* N COUNT ⇑ seed

2 The **kernel** of something is the central and most important part of it. EG *He gave these paintings to the nation as the kernel of the Tate Gallery... There is a kernel of truth in what you say.* N COUNT+*of* ⇑ essence = core, heart

kerosene /kɛrəsiːn/ is a clear, strong-smelling liquid which is used as a fuel, for example in heaters and lamps; used especially in American English. EG *Instead of electricity, there were kerosene lanterns.* N UNCOUNT = paraffin

kestrel /kɛstrəl/, **kestrels**. A **kestrel** is a type of small hawk that kills and eats other birds and small animals such as mice. N COUNT ⇑ bird

ketch /kɛtʃ/, **ketches**. A **ketch** is a type of sailing ship that has two masts. N COUNT ⇑ ship

ketchup /kɛtʃəp/, **ketchups**. **Ketchup** is a thick, cold sauce usually made from tomatoes. EG *I think there's a spot of tomato ketchup on the tablecloth.* N UNCOUNT ⇑ sauce

kettle /kɛtəˡl/, **kettles**. 1 A **kettle** is a covered round container with a handle on the top and a spout on the side, that is used for boiling water. EG *They put the kettle on to make a cup of tea... ...an electric kettle.* N COUNT ⇑ container ▸ also used to refer to the water inside a kettle. EG *The kettle's boiling.* ▸ N SING : *the*+N

2 **kettle of fish**. 2.1 If you say that something is **another kettle of fish** or **a different kettle of fish**, you are emphasizing that it is very different from something else that you were just talking about; used in informal English. EG *A relationship with an artist is a very different kettle of fish from a relationship with an ordinary person.* PHR : USED AS C 2.2 If you describe a situation as **a fine** or **pretty kettle of fish**, you mean that it is very awkward and will cause difficulties. PHR : USED AS C

kettledrum /kɛtəˡldrʌm/, **kettledrums**. A **kettledrum** is a large drum with a curved bottom, which usually stands on a tripod. N COUNT

key /kiː/, **keys, keying, keyed**. 1 A **key** is 1.1 a specially shaped piece of metal which you place in a lock and turn, in order to open a door, a suitcase, a cupboard, etc, or to close it so that it stays closed. EG *He locked the bag and put the key in his pocket... Keep a list of anyone who has a front door key... I'm afraid I've lost the key to the filing cabinet... ...the sound of the key turning in the lock.* N COUNT 1.2 a specially shaped piece of metal or plastic that you use to wind up clocks, clockwork toys, etc. N COUNT 1.3 a button on a typewriter, computer keyboard, cash register, etc which you press in order to type a letter or number, or to make the machine perform a particular task. EG *...jabbing viciously at the keys of the typewriter... He rang the 'No Sale' key and looked into the till... Hit the keys and the appropriate number or letter appears on the screen.* N COUNT ⇑ button 1.4 a list of explanations of symbols or abbreviations used on a map or diagram, in a book, etc. EG *You will find a key at the front of book.* N COUNT

2 In music, a **key** is 2.1 a long narrow piece of wood, plastic, etc, on a musical instrument such as a piano, which you press in order to produce a particular musical note. N COUNT 2.2 a scale of musical notes that starts at one specific note. EG *...a startling change of key... A bell can be in the key of D but it will still contain many other tones.* N UNCOUNT/COUNT

3 **Key** people, ideas, or things are very important and often control or influence other people, ideas, or things. EG *The country's key industries are coal, engineering, and transport... Unemployment was a key issue during the last election campaign... Confidence, we know, is the key factor in any successful career.* ADJ CLASSIF : ATTRIB ⇑ important = crucial, vital

4 The **key** to a situation is the most important thing N COUNT : IF SING

in it, for example the solution to a problem, the means to achieve a particular goal, or the explanation of something which has been a puzzle. EG *Education became the key to progress... Planning is the key.* — the+N, USU+to

5 • **under lock and key**: see **lock**. • See also **low key, master key**. — PHR

key in. If you **key** something **in**, you put information into a computer or you tell the computer to do a particular task by typing the information or instruction on a keyboard. EG *To extract information you key in the word you require.* — PHRASAL VB : V+O+ADV ⇑ input = enter, type in

keyboard /kiːbɔːd/, **keyboards**. A **keyboard** is 1 a set of keys on a typewriter or computer terminal which includes keys for all the letters of the alphabet, numbers, symbols, and other keys for making the machine perform particular tasks. EG *Type L I S T on the keyboard and the instructions are displayed.* — N COUNT ⇑ set 2 a row of keys on a piano, organ, or synthesizer, which are usually arranged in a particular sequence of black and white keys. EG *She reached out her hands to the keyboard and began to play.* — N COUNT ⇑ row 3 a musical instrument with a keyboard; used mainly in pop music. EG *...and Colin Browne (keyboards and guitar).* — N COUNT : USU PL ⇑ instrument

keyed up. If you are **keyed up**, you are very excited or nervous before an important or dangerous event. EG *Surely he should be feeling not just keyed up but different in some way.* — ADJ QUALIT : PRED ⇑ excited = tense

keyhole /kiːhəʊl/, **keyholes**. A **keyhole** is a hole in a lock into which you put the key in order to open the door, suitcase, cupboard, etc. EG *She slid the key into the keyhole and was about to turn it.* — N COUNT ⇑ hole

keynote /kiːnəʊt/, **keynotes**. The **keynote** of an idea or speech is the part of it that is emphasized or given great importance. EG *The keynote for Labour policy, he saw, was planning.* — N COUNT : USU SING

keyring /kiːrɪŋ/, **keyrings**; also spelled with a hyphen. A **keyring** is a ring of metal, plastic, etc, which you can use to keep your keys together. — N COUNT ⇑ ring

keystone /kiːstəʊn/, **keystones**. A **keystone** is 1 a stone at the top of an arch, which keeps the other stones in place by its weight and position. — N COUNT ⇑ slab 2 an important part of a process, which is the basis for later developments. EG *The first National Insurance Bill in 1911 was the keystone of the future Welfare State.* — N COUNT+SUPP : USU SING ⇑ basis

kg is an abbreviation for 'kilogram'; used especially after a number to indicate a measurement of weight. — N COUNT/COUNT : USU NUM+N

khaki /kɑːki[1]/. 1 **Khaki** is a strong material of a yellowish-brown colour, used especially to make uniforms for soldiers. EG *The boys looked smart in khaki and polished brass.* — N UNCOUNT ⇑ fabric

2 Something that is **khaki** is yellowish-brown in colour. EG *...a tiny shelter of torn khaki canvas.* — ADJ COLOUR

kHz is a written abbreviation for 'kilohertz'; written on radios beside a range of numbers to help you find a particular radio station. — N COUNT : USU NUM+N = kilohertz

kibbutz /kɪbʊts/, **kibbutzes, kibbutzim**. The plural can be either **kibbutzes** or **kibbutzim**. A **kibbutz** is a farm, factory, or other workplace in Israel, where the workers live together and share all the duties and income. EG *He wrote to the Jewish agency asking to visit a kibbutz.* — N COUNT ⇑ commune

kibosh /kaɪbɒʃ/. If something **puts the kibosh on** something else, it completely ruins an event, a situation, or someone's plans; an informal expression. EG *It would certainly put the kibosh on any lingering hopes they might have had.* — PHR : VB INFLECTS ⇑ ruin = halt

kick /kɪk/, **kicks, kicking, kicked**. 1 If you **kick** someone or something, you hit them forcefully with your foot. EG *He protested violently, and threatened to kick me.* — V+O ⇑ hit • If you **kick** someone **when** or **while they are down**, you unfairly attack them or criticize them while they are unable to protect themselves, for example after they have already been attacked or criticized. EG *They're kicking us while we're down because none of us belong to their union.* — • PHR : VB INFLECTS ⇑ attack

2 If you **kick**, 2.1 you move your feet about violently or suddenly. EG *I fought and clawed and bit and kicked... Simon was floating in the water and kicking with his feet.* — V ⇑ move 2.2 you lift your leg up very high, for example when you are dancing. EG *The audience began to applaud and we kicked higher... Together we kicked our legs high in the air.* — V OR V+O : USU+A ⇑ lift

3 When you **kick** a ball or other object, you hit it with your foot, so that it moves through the air. EG *We caught sight of Christopher, kicking a tin can down Camden High Street... Nobody could kick a ball as hard as Charlton could.* — V OR V+O ⇑ strike

4 A **kick** is 4.1 a sudden movement or blow with your foot. EG *A heavy kick in the ribs left him gasping for breath... He gave him a good kick... One of those kicks could snap you in half.* — N COUNT ⇑ blow 4.2 the occasion when a player kicks the ball from a particular place on the pitch, for example as a penalty, in a game such as football or rugby. EG *Seffin put the kick over and won the match... Robson headed in from Hoddle's kick.* • See also **free kick**. — N COUNT ⇑ occasion 4.3 the sudden movement that a gun makes when you have fired it. EG *A .303 has quite a kick.* — N COUNT ⇑ movement = recoil

5 If an alcoholic drink has a **kick**, it is surprisingly strong; an informal use. — N SING WITH DET

6 If you get **a kick in the teeth**, you experience an embarrassing refusal or failure; an informal expression. EG *The cause had received a strong kick in the teeth.* — PHR : *kick* INFLECTS ⇑ setback

7 If you say that someone **gets a kick** from something, you mean that they get a feeling of intense pleasure or excitement from it; an informal expression. EG *They loved argument, and got a kick out of court proceedings... He's in the next room pressing his ear to the wall and getting his kicks listening to us.* — PHR : VB INFLECTS, IF+PREP THEN *from/out of* • If you say that someone does something **for kicks**, you mean that they do it because they think it will be exciting; an informal expression. EG *This isn't for kicks. This is for a specific purpose.* — • PHR : USED AS AN A

8 If you say that you **kicked** yourself or that you could have **kicked** yourself, you mean that you were very annoyed with yourself because of something you did wrong, or because you missed an opportunity to do something well. EG *I kicked myself for not having thought of it earlier... I called her Mary instead of Margaret. I could have kicked myself.* — V+O (REFL)

9 If you **kick** a habit, such as smoking, that you have had for a long time, you give it up; an informal use. — V+O ⇑ stop

10 • **to kick the bucket**: see **bucket**.

kick about. If something **is kicking about** somewhere, it is lying there and has usually been forgotten; an informal expression. EG *His old bike has been kicking about among the bushes for days.* — PHRASAL VB : V+ADV

kick against. If you **kick against** a situation you dislike but cannot control, you react against it in a violent, sudden, or extreme way. EG *He's always kicking against the system.* — PHRASAL VB : V+PREP ⇑ react

kick around. 1 If you **kick around** ideas or suggestions, you discuss them informally; an informal expression. EG *The first step was to call in some writers and kick around ideas.* — PHRASAL VB : V+O+ADV ⇑ consider

2 To **kick around** also means the same as to kick about. — PHRASAL VB : V+ADV

kick down. If you **kick** something **down**, you hit it violently with your foot so that it falls over. EG *They tried to kick down the front door.* — PHRASAL VB : V+O+ADV

kick in. If you **kick** something **in**, you hit it violently with your foot so that it breaks into pieces. EG *The fireman kicked in one of the windows.* — PHRASAL VB : V+O+ADV ⇑ break

kick off. 1 When you **kick off**, 1.1 you start a game of football by kicking the ball from the centre of the pitch. — PHRASAL VB : V+ADV 1.2 you start an event, discussion, conversation, etc; an informal expression. EG *At 10 p.m. Prince Charles kicks off 45 minutes of fireworks... They kicked off a two-month tour of the U.S. with a party in Washington.* — PHRASAL VB : V+ADV, OR V+O+ADV ⇑ start

2 If you **kick off** your shoes, you shake your feet so that your shoes come off. — PHRASAL VB : V+O+ADV ⇑ remove

3 See also **kick-off**.

kick out. If you **kick** someone **out**, you force them to leave a particular place, either by using your authority or by using physical strength; an informal expression. EG *I'm afraid I'm going to have to kick you out... They took a dog away from this woman and they kicked her out of her house.* — PHRASAL VB : V+O+ADV ⇑ eject = throw out

kick out against. To **kick out against** something means the same as to kick against it. EG *...a lorry-driver called John who suddenly kicked out against the daily grind of his life.* — PHRASAL VB : V+ADV+PREP ⇑ react

kick up. 1 If you **kick up** a fuss or a row, you get very annoyed or upset about something, especially when this does not seem necessary; an informal expression. EG *He kicked up a great fuss and swore our friendship was at an end.* — PHRASAL VB : ORDER V+ADV+O

2 If you **kick up** dust, dirt, etc, you create a cloud of — PHRASAL VB : V+

dust or dirt as you move along a dusty road. EG *...the dust clouds their feet kicked up.* — O+ADV = raise

kickback /kɪkbæk/, **kickbacks**; also spelled with a hyphen. A **kickback** is a sum of money that is paid to someone illegally, for example by a company that wants to be chosen to do an important job. EG *He has always denied that he received any kickbacks from contractors.* — N COUNT ⇑ bribe

kick-off, **kick-offs**. A **kick-off** is 1 the kick that officially starts a game of football. — N COUNT 2 the time at which a particular game of football starts. EG *The kick-off's at 3 o'clock... ...a 3 o'clock kick-off.* — N COUNT 3 the time at which something such as a party or concert starts; used in informal British English. — N COUNT ● You can say **for a kick-off** at the beginning of a question or list to emphasize that you are only beginning what you want to ask or say; an informal expression. EG *Well, for a kick-off, he can't act.* — ● PHR : USED AS AN A = for starters

kick-start, **kick-starts**. A **kick-start** or a **kick-starter** is the lever that you press with your foot to start a motorbike; used in British English. — N COUNT ⇑ lever

kid /kɪd/, **kids, kidding, kidded**. 1 A **kid** is 1.1 a child; an informal use. EG *I can remember the strange feelings I had when I was a kid looking at those photographs... ...five-year-old kids.* — N COUNT ● If you describe something as **kids' stuff**, you mean that it is only suitable for children, for example because it is so easy; used showing disapproval. EG *These questions are kids' stuff.* — ● PHR : USED AS C 1.2 a child or older person who is being referred to as someone's son or daughter; an informal use. EG *It was good to see Lennie and Helen and the kids again.... Every night his wife and three kids would move the kitchen table.* — N COUNT : USU PL ⇑ child 1.3 a young person who is no longer considered to be a child; used in American English. EG *'All right,' Mayhew said. 'Don't believe me. This kid was a clerk'... GM's college kids pay only $1,200 tuition.* — N COUNT ⇑ person

2 You can use **kid** to address someone who is younger than you, especially if you are trying to tell them something or give them some advice; an informal use. EG *Keep your hands to yourself, kid, or you'll get hurt... Listen, kid, let me give some fatherly advice. Don't do it.* — N USED AS VOC = mate, chum

3 Someone's **kid** brother or sister is their younger brother or sister; an informal use. — ADJ CLASSIF : ATTRIB

4 If you **kid** someone, you tease them or try and make them believe something that is not true in order to make fun of them. EG *Tim's friends kidded him about his odd clothes... 'I'm not kidding, Jill. He could have taken it if he'd wanted.'* — V OR V+O

5 If you say to someone **'you're kidding'**, you are telling them that you do not believe what they are saying. EG *'I passed the exam.'–'You're kidding.'* — CONVENTION = you're joking

6 You can say **'I kid you not'** to emphasize that what you are saying is true, even though it sounds unlikely or impossible; an informal expression. EG *It was on the tenth floor in Collindeane Tower, I kid you not.* — CONVENTION = honestly

7 You can say **'no kidding'** to emphasize that what you are saying is true and that you are not trying to deceive anyone; an informal expression. EG *'I really like your friends. No kidding. I'll prove it to you.'* — CONVENTION = honest ≠ fooled you

8 If you **kid** yourself, you allow yourself to believe something that is not true because it is something that you wish was true. EG *'Oh, don't kid yourself, he's about thirty-eight now.'... They like to kid themselves they're keeping fit.* — V+O (REFL)/ REPORT-CL = fool

9 A **kid** is also a young goat. — N COUNT

10 **Kid** is very soft leather that is made from the skin of a young goat. EG *...a pair of kid gloves.* — N UNCOUNT ⇑ leather

kiddie /kɪdi[1]/, **kiddies**. A **kiddie** is, a very young child; an informal word. EG *His young kiddie was in hospital.* — N COUNT ⇑ child = infant, toddler

kid gloves. If you **treat** or **handle** someone **with kid gloves**, you are very careful in the way you deal with them because you do not want to make them angry or upset. EG *Treat him with kid gloves and you won't get your head bitten off.* — PHR : VB INFLECTS ≠ bully

kidnap /kɪdnæp/, **kidnaps, kidnapping, kidnapped**. 1 If someone **kidnaps** another person, they take them away by force, usually in order to demand money from their family, employers, government, etc. EG *His plan is to kidnap the President of the United States... He was kidnapped by terrorists just over a month ago.* — V+O ⇑ abduct ◇ **kidnapping, kidnappings**. EG *She is charged with murder, kidnapping, and criminal conspiracy... ...a thriller based on the kidnapping of a royal child... ...an effective policy that will break up kidnappings of this sort.* — ◇ N UNCOUNT/ COUNT = abduction ◇ **kidnapped**. EG *It is not only likely to get the kidnapped people out, but it's a deterrent as well.* — ◇ ADJ CLASSIF : ATTRIB = abducted

2 **Kidnap** is the crime of taking someone away by force and demanding money from their family, employers, or government. EG *...the threat of kidnap or assassination... ...a kidnap victim.* — N UNCOUNT ⇑ crime = abduction

kidnapper /kɪdnə[3]pə/, **kidnappers**. A **kidnapper** is a person who has taken someone away by force and is demanding money from their family, employers, or government. EG *I had given up all hope of tracing her kidnapper.* — N COUNT ⇑ criminal

kidney /kɪdni[1]/, **kidneys**. 1 **Kidneys** are the organs in your body that produce urine from the waste matter in your blood. You have two kidneys, which are shaped like a semicircle with a piece taken out of the straight side. EG *...permanent damage to the liver and kidneys... He thought he had kidney trouble... ...cancer of the kidney.* — N COUNT ⇑ organ

2 **Kidneys** are also the kidneys of an animal, such as a lamb, calf, or pig, that are eaten as meat. EG *There were grilled kidneys for Sunday breakfast... ...steak and kidney pie.* — N COUNT/ UNCOUNT ⇑ offal

3 Your **kidneys** are the area of your back that covers your kidneys. EG *He was kicked so severely in the kidneys that he never fully regained his health... He wrenched his right hand free and clubbed at the soldier's kidneys.* — N PLURAL : USU POSS+N ⇑ back

kidney bean, kidney beans; also spelled with a hyphen. **Kidney beans** are beans that have the same shape as a kidney, and which are eaten as a vegetable. — N COUNT : USU PL ⇑ pulse

kidney machine, kidney machines. A **kidney machine** is a machine that is used to do the work of a kidney for people whose own kidneys are diseased or do not work properly. — N COUNT

kill /kɪl/, **kills, killing, killed**. 1 To **kill** a person, animal, plant, or other living thing means to cause the person or thing to die. EG *She killed him with a hammer... ...a desire to kill... The sun had killed most of the plants... Her mother was killed in a car crash... He had tried to kill himself five times.* — V+O (NG/REFL) OR V

2 A **kill** is an act of killing an animal, or the moment when an animal is killed, after a hunt, bullfight, etc. EG *The female lions make the majority of kills.* — N COUNT

3 If something **is killing** you, it is causing you great physical or mental pain; an informal use. EG *My back's killing me.* — V+O ⇑ hurt = torture

4 If you **kill** yourself to do something, you make a great effort to do it, even though it causes you a lot of trouble or suffering; an informal use. EG *I'm killing myself to get this finished tonight... He didn't exactly kill himself to get here on time.* — V+O (REFL)+ to-INF ● If you say that you will do something, even **if it kills you**, you mean that you are determined to do it even though it is extremely difficult or painful. EG *I was determined to finish even if it killed me.* — ● PHR : VB INFLECTS

5 If you say that you will **kill** someone, you mean that you are extremely angry with them or with something that they have done; an informal use. EG *If I ever find out that you gave me away I'll kill you... I could have killed them.* — V+O : MODAL+V = murder

6 If you say that something won't **kill** you, you mean that it is not really as difficult or as dangerous as it might seem; an informal use. EG *I'm not supposed to, but it won't kill me... It wouldn't kill him to do a bit more work.* — V+O : *will/would* +V, WITH BROAD NEG = hurt

7 If you **kill** an activity or process, you completely destroy or end it. EG *With this remark he killed further conversation dead.* — V+O ⇑ end = stop

8 To **kill** a sensation that is unpleasant means to weaken it so that it is no longer as strong as it was. EG *I'll give you something to kill the pain... They put in insulating panels to kill the sound.* — V+O ⇑ weaken = deaden

9 If you **kill** an engine, machine, light, etc, you stop it working by switching it off; an informal use. EG *He stopped the car suddenly, killing the motor.* — V+O ⇑ stop

10 If you **kill** time, you occupy yourself while you are waiting for something to happen by doing something that is not very interesting or useful. EG *He spent long hours keeping out of the way, killing time.* — V+O ⇑ pass time

11 If you **kill** yourself **laughing** or you **kill** yourself **with laughter**, you laugh a lot because you think something is extremely funny; an informal expression. EG *They're sitting killing themselves with laughter.* — PHR : VB INFLECTS = fall about

12 If you say that something will **kill or cure**, you — PHR : VB

mean that it is a very extreme course of action which will either succeed completely or fail completely. EG *...a measure designed to kill or cure.* INFLECTS

13 If you **come, move**, or **close in for the kill**, you prepare to completely destroy someone's arguments that you have already partly destroyed. EG *The interviewer came in for the kill with his next question.* PHR : VB INFLECTS ≠ back off

14 If you **are in at the kill**, you are present when something happens that is dramatic and unpleasant for someone else. EG *I got the story from Fred, who was apparently in at the kill.* PHR : VB INFLECTS ⇑ witness

15 • to **kill two birds with one stone**: see **bird**. • **dressed to kill**: see **dress**. • to **kill the goose that lays the golden eggs**: see **goose**.

16 See also **killing**.

kill off. If you **kill** something **off**, you completely end it and prevent it from returning again. EG *This discovery killed off one of the last surviving romances about the place... The bacteria had been killed off.* PHRASAL VB : V+O+ADV

killer /kɪlə/, **killers**. A **killer** is 1 a person who has killed someone, or who intends to kill someone. EG *He became a ruthless killer.* N COUNT = murderer 2 something such as an animal, substance, or situation that is dangerous and that may cause the death of people or other living things. EG *The lion is one of the most efficient killers in the animal world... Heart disease is the major killer of our time.* N COUNT ⇑ destroyer

killer instinct. A **killer instinct** is a great determination to get what you want, even though getting it might involve causing harm to other people. EG *He has a competitive killer instinct that makes everything he does a challenge.* N SING WITH DET ⇑ drive = ruthlessness

killer whale, killer whales. A **killer whale** is a fierce black and white whale. N COUNT

killing /kɪlɪŋ/, **killings**. 1 A **killing** is an act of deliberately killing a person. EG *We learned about a brutal killing which had occurred in the neighbourhood... The killings were random, gruesome, and baffling.* N COUNT = murder

2 If you **make a killing**, you make a large profit very quickly and easily; an informal expression. EG *Atkins was able to make a killing by buying up all the shares.* PHR : VB INFLECTS

3 Something that is **killing** is extremely funny; a rather old-fashioned use. EG *The last sketch was absolutely killing.* ADJ CLASSIF ⇑ funny = hilarious

killjoy /kɪldʒɔɪ/, **killjoys**. A **killjoy** is someone who stops other people from enjoying themselves, often by reminding them of something unpleasant. EG *Don't be such a killjoy!* N COUNT = spoilsport

kiln /kɪln/, **kilns**. A **kiln** is an oven that is used to bake pottery, bricks, etc, in order to make them become hard. EG *The house had been built with bricks from his own kilns.* N COUNT = furnace, oven

kilo /kiːləʊ/, **kilos**. A **kilo** is the same as a kilogram. EG *...a kilo of fresh strawberries.* N COUNT/PART = kilogram

kilo- is added to nouns that refer to units of measurement in order to form other nouns referring to units that are a thousand times bigger. EG *...metre→kilometre... ...gram→kilogram... ...hertz→kilohertz.* PREFIX ≠ milli-

kilogram /kɪlə⁶græm/, **kilograms**; also spelled **kilogramme**. A **kilogram** is a metric unit of weight that is a thousand grams, or a thousandth of a metric ton, and is equal to 2.2 pounds. Its abbreviation is 'kg'. EG *The largest brain possessed by any dinosaur weighed about a kilogram... The government had to reduce monthly meat rations to 3 kilograms a person... ...the 815 kilogram spacecraft.* N COUNT/PART

kilohertz /kɪlə⁶hɜːts/. **Kilohertz** is both the singular and the plural form. A **kilohertz** is a unit of measurement of radio waves that is equal to one thousand hertz. It is used especially to indicate how you can find a radio station on your radio, and its abbreviation is 'kHz'. EG *...a ten kilohertz sound, which is very high pitched.* N COUNT

kilometre /kɪlə⁶miːtə, kɪlɒmɪtə/, **kilometres**; also spelled **kilometer** in American English. A **kilometre** is a metric unit of distance or length that is a thousand metres. Its abbreviation is 'km'. EG *The platoon retreated a few kilometres... We could see rain falling about a kilometre away... Their plan calls for a 75 kilometre tunnel.* N COUNT/PART

kilowatt /kɪlə⁶wɒt/, **kilowatts**. A **kilowatt** is a unit of power that is one thousand watts. Its abbreviation is 'kW'. EG *...the amount of electricity needed to produce one kilowatt of power for one hour... A one kilowatt fire uses one unit in one hour.* N COUNT

kilowatt hour, kilowatt hours. A **kilowatt hour** is a unit of energy that is equal to the power provided by a thousand watts in one hour. N COUNT ⇑ unit

kilt /kɪlt/, **kilts**. A **kilt** is a short, full, pleated tartan skirt that is traditionally worn by Scotsmen. Kilts can also be worn by women and girls. N COUNT

kimono /kɪməʊnəʊ/, **kimonos**. A **kimono** is a Japanese item of clothing that is long, with wide sleeves, and shaped like a coat. N COUNT ⇑ garment

kin /kɪn/. Your **kin** are your relatives; a rather old-fashioned word. EG *He needs to identify perhaps with kin or family or peer group of some kind.* • See also **kith and kin, next of kin**. N UNCOUNT ⇑ relatives

kind /kaɪnd/, **kinds; kinder, kindest**. 1 If you talk about a particular **kind** of something, 1.1 you are referring to the class or sort of thing that it belongs to. EG *Was he carrying a weapon and, if so, what kind of weapon?... ...hundreds of different kinds of small creatures... ...processes of an entirely new kind... He had a fit or a seizure of some kind and then drowned... Atomic power is different in kind from that generated by oil- and coal-fired stations.* N COUNT+SUPP, OR *in*+N = sort, type, variety 1.2 you are referring to a particular thing or person in relation to other things and people that have similar natures or qualities, or in relation to something else that has just been mentioned. EG *She makes the same kind of point in another essay... These thoughts weren't the kind he could ever share with anyone... Obviously there's a connection of some kind between them... ...relief work, emergency, floods, that kind of thing.* N COUNT+SUPP = sort, type

2 **All kinds** of things or people means a great variety of different things or people. EG *She was offered all kinds of things... It will give you an opportunity to meet all kinds of people... The trees were filled with birds of all kinds.* PHR : USU+*of*+N IN PL ⇑ many

3 You use **kind of** 3.1 to describe or refer to something that you are uncertain about but that is roughly like the thing mentioned or has the qualities mentioned; used in very informal English. EG *I'm a kind of anarchist, I suppose... It looks like a bowl with a kind of a stirrer thing.* PHR : DET+PHR +N IN SING = sort of 3.2 to say that something is partly true or partly the case, but does not fully describe the actual situation; a very informal use, especially in American English. EG *Actually, I felt kind of sorry for him... I guess they're kind of mad at me for getting them up so early... 'You had an argument then with him?'–'Well, kind of.'... She was very ill. Kind of a funny green colour and sick all over the place.* PHR : N+*of* = somewhat 3.3 if you are uncertain about what you are saying and wondering if you are using the right word; used in very informal English. EG *I just kind of went for walks and things... It's just a kind of haphazard, er, conglomeration.* PHR : USED AS ADV SEN

4 If you describe something as **of a kind**, you mean that it is of a poorer quality or standard than you wanted or expected, but that it is the best that is possible in the circumstances. EG *A solution of a kind has been found to this problem... ...as life of a kind revives in the war-torn countryside.* PHR : USU AFTER N = of a sort

5 Someone's or something's **kind** are all the other people or things that are like them or that belong to the same class or set. EG *Eddie and his kind were not civilized... Their kind are all alike... They feel that he is a traitor to their own kind... ...a Victorian lamp-post, perhaps the finest of its kind left in London.* N COUNT : POSS+N

6 A particular **kind** of person has the character or behaviour that is mentioned or implied. EG *Her name was Ivy but she was not the clinging kind... She's that kind of person. She gets around, if you know what I mean.* N SING WITH DET : USU+SUPP ⇑ person = sort, type

7 Payment **in kind** is in the form of goods or services and not money. EG *I'll be getting paid in kind–she's giving me bed and breakfast.* PHR : USED AS AN A

8 If you do something **in kind**, you react to someone's action by doing the same thing as they have just done. EG *Our troops would retaliate in kind if attacked with chemical agents... I gave him an acknowledging wave of my hand and he answered in kind.* PHR USED AS AN A

9 Someone who is **kind** behaves in a gentle, caring, and helpful way towards other people. EG *We were much kinder to one another after that night... I find them all very pleasant and extremely kind and helpful... She was smiling a little and looked quite* ADJ QUALIT

kind... His voice was very kind. ◊ **kindly**. EG *'You're not to blame yourself, Smithy,' Rick said kindly... It gives people pain if they are not treated very kindly and thoughtfully.* ◊ **kindness**. EG *He treated his labourers with kindness and understanding.*
◊ ADV WITH VB
◊ N UNCOUNT

10 You tell someone that they have been **kind** when you are thanking them for something that they have done for you. EG *Thank you, Mrs Oliver. You've been very kind and you've put in a lot of work... It was kind of you to come.* ◊ **kindness**. EG *Thank you very much indeed for coming to see me. I appreciate your kindness very much.*
ADJ QUALIT : USU PRED = good
◊ N UNCOUNT = thoughtfulness

11 Kind is also used in spoken English to show politeness or firmness when you are asking someone to do something. EG *Before you go to bed, would you be kind enough to pop into the sitting-room and close the window.... I wonder if you'd be so kind as to remove your cap.*
ADJ QUALIT : PRED ⇑ please = good

12 Something that is **kind 12.1** emphasizes the good qualities in something or someone, and perhaps makes them appear better than they really are. EG *The reviews were interesting and reasonably kind... Candlelight or soft lamplight is kind to your face.*
ADJ QUALIT : USU PRED, IF + PREP THEN *to* = charitable

12.2 does not have a harmful effect. EG *...a washing-up liquid that is truly kind to your hands.*
ADJ QUALIT : USU PRED, IF + PREP THEN *to*

13 See also **kindly, kindness.**

kindergarten /kɪndəgɑːtə^{ə}n/, **kindergartens**. A **kindergarten** is a school for young children who are not yet old enough to go to primary school. EG *We need more nursery schools, creches and kindergartens... ...children of kindergarten age.*
N COUNT = nursery school, playgroup

kind-hearted. Someone who is **kind-hearted** is kind, loving, and gentle. EG *...one of the most kind-hearted men that the world ever produced.*
ADJ QUALIT ⇑ kind

kindle /kɪndə^{ə}l/, **kindles, kindling, kindled**. **1** If you **kindle** a fire, you light wood, coal, paper, etc, in order to start it. EG *A great fire was kindled and everyone rejoiced.*
V + O, OR V

2 If something **kindles** a particular emotion in someone, it makes them start to feel it. EG *Every word she uttered kindled his jealousy... ...the aspirations kindled in us in early childhood.*
V + O ⇑ arouse = inspire

kindliness /kaɪndlɪnɪ^{2}s/. See **kindly**.

kindling /kɪndlɪŋ/ is small pieces of dry wood and other materials that you use to start a fire. EG *The trick is to get lots of air into the paper and kindling... Lay a lattice of kindling on top and around the sides.*
N UNCOUNT ⇑ tinder

kindly /kaɪndli^{1}/. **1** Someone who is **kindly** is kind, caring, and sympathetic. EG *Being a kindly and reasonable man, he at once apologized.* ▸ used of people's attitudes and behaviour. EG *The students were watching her with kindly interest.* ◊ **kindliness**. EG *...the great virtues of humility and kindliness.*
ADJ QUALIT : USU ATTRIB
▸ ADJ QUALIT : USU ATTRIB
◊ N UNCOUNT ⇑ benevolence

2 If you ask someone to **kindly** do something, you are showing that you are angry with them, or that you have a feeling of superiority over them. EG *Kindly take your hand off my knee... Can you kindly tell me how this situation has got this far?*
ADV + INF = please

3 The word **kindly** is also used in the following expressions. **3.1** If you **look kindly on** or **upon** something or someone, you approve of them. EG *The White House will look more kindly on a robust economy.* **3.2** If you **think kindly of** someone or something, you like them and have a good opinion of them. EG *I began to think more kindly of Mr Zapp.*
PHR : VB INFLECTS ⇑ approve
PHR : VB INFLECTS ⇑ like

3.3 If you do not **take kindly to** something or someone, you do not react favourably towards them and you do not accept them willingly. EG *They are unlikely to take kindly to this suggestion... He won't take kindly to having a dog in the house.*
PHR : VB INFLECTS, USU WITH BROAD NEG ⇑ like

4 See also **kind**.

kindness /kaɪndnɪ^{2}s/, **kindnesses**. A **kindness** is a helpful or considerate act. EG *She thanked them both many times for all their kindnesses.* ● See also **kind**.
N COUNT

kindred /kɪndrɪ^{2}d/; a rather old-fashioned word. **1 Kindred** things or ideas are similar to other things or ideas. EG *It produced upon the ear a kindred effect to that produced by a cello.*
ADJ CLASSIF : ATTRIB ⇑ similar

2 Your **kindred** are your family, and all the people who are related to you. EG *We would like to thank you on behalf of our kindred and our neighbours.*
N UNCOUNT : USU POSS + N ⇑ family

kindred spirit, kindred spirits. A **kindred spirit** is a person who has the same view of life or the same interests as you. EG *When I saw his work for the first time I recognized a kindred spirit... They have found many kindred spirits in the Labour Party.*
N COUNT ⇑ person = soul mate

kinetic /kɪ^{5}nɛtɪk/, **kinetics**. **1 Kinetic** is used to describe something that is concerned with movement; a technical term in physics.
ADJ CLASSIF : USU ATTRIB

2 Kinetics is the scientific study of the way energy behaves when something moves; a technical term in physics.
N UNCOUNT

kinetic art is visual art, especially sculpture, which has parts that move. EG *...a work of kinetic art.*
N UNCOUNT ⇑ art

kinetic energy is the energy that is produced when something moves; a technical term in physics. EG *This energy is turned into kinetic energy.*
N UNCOUNT ⇑ energy

king /kɪŋ/, **kings**. **1** A **king** is a man who rules a country as its monarch. Kings are not elected, but are born into a royal family. EG *Three famous Saxon kings are buried here... The King knighted him... ...the legend of King Arthur... ...Napoleon's brother Joseph, King of Spain.*
N COUNT : ALSO IN TITLES ⇑ sovereign

2 If you say that someone **lives like a king**, you mean that they are able to live in a very comfortable or luxurious way. EG *We'll live like kings on my pension.*
PHR : VB INFLECTS

3 The **king** of a particular group is the most important or most powerful male in that group. EG *The lion is the king of the jungle.*
N COUNT : USU SING, IF + PREP THEN *of* = lord

4 If you describe a man as the **king** of something, you mean that he is particularly famous or outstanding. EG *Elvis Presley is the king of Rock and Roll.*
N COUNT : USU SING, IF + PREP THEN *of*

5 In chess, the **king** is the most important piece, which can only travel one square at a time. When you are in a position to capture your opponent's king, you win the game.
N COUNT : USU SING

6 A **king** is also a playing card with a picture of a king on it. EG *Is that a king or a jack she's just played?*
N COUNT : IF + PREP THEN *of* ⇑ playing card

kingdom /kɪŋdəm/, **kingdoms**. **1** A **kingdom** is **1.1** a country or region that is ruled by a king or queen. EG *The village of Kootacunda is in the kingdom of Wooli... They have no real kingdoms to rule, or lands to conquer.* ▸ used as part of the name of a country. EG *...the United Kingdom.* **1.2** a place or area that is considered to be under the total power and control of a person, organization, or thing. EG *...the far-flung kingdoms of the Church of England... The slave states of the American South used to be called the Cotton Kingdom... ...the Kingdom of God.*
N COUNT = monarchy
▸ N IN NAMES
N COUNT : USU + SUPP = dominion

2 The animal **kingdom**, the plant **kingdom**, and the mineral **kingdom** are the three main divisions which are used to describe the natural world. EG *This creature has the largest eyes in the whole animal kingdom.*
N COUNT : MOD + N, IF SING *the* + N ⇑ class = world

kingfisher /kɪŋfɪʃə/, **kingfishers**. A **kingfisher** is a brightly-coloured, fast-moving bird which lives on the banks of rivers and lakes, and which catches fish.
N COUNT

kingship /kɪŋʃɪp/ is the fact or position of being a king. EG *...an emblem of kingship.*
N UNCOUNT = leadership

king-size. Something that is **king-size** or **king-sized** is the largest size of it that you can get. EG *She stayed in a luxury hotel suite with a king-size bed... She lit another king-size filter cigarette.*
ADJ CLASSIF : USU ATTRIB

kink /kɪŋk/, **kinks, kinking, kinked**. **1** A **kink** is a curve or twist in something such as a piece of wire which is otherwise straight. EG *I'm trying to get the kinks out of my hair.*
N COUNT

2 If you **kink** something or if it **kinks**, it has, or it develops, a curve or twist in it. EG *Don't press the cable too much or it will kink.*
V-ERG ⇑ bend

3 A **kink** is also a particular quality or feature of a person's mind or character, especially one which is thought to be unusual or abnormal; an informal use. EG *He got to know their individual habits, kinks, and procedures.*
N COUNT ⇑ trait = foible

kinky /kɪŋki^{1}/, **kinkier, kinkiest**. **1** Something that is **kinky** has a lot of curves or twists. EG *...bits of kinky green string... ...kinky hair.*
ADJ QUALIT

2 Behaviour that is **kinky** is considered to be strange, for example because it involves unusual sexual practices; an informal use. EG *There must be something very kinky going on.*
ADJ QUALIT

kinship /kɪnʃɪp/ is **1** the relationship that exists between members of the same family. EG *Their ties of kinship mean a lot to them.* **2** a relationship or close feeling that exists between people who share similar characteristics, origins, ideas, etc. EG *He felt a deep kinship with the other students.*
N UNCOUNT = blood
N UNCOUNT + SUPP ⇑ relationship = tie

kinsman /kɪnzmə^{3}n/, **kinsmen**. A **kinsman** is a male relative; an old-fashioned word. EG *...the descendants of a distant kinsman named McCaslin.* N COUNT ⇑ relative

kinswoman /kɪnswʌ^{1}mə^{0}n/, **kinswomen**. A **kinswoman** is a female relative; an old-fashioned word. N COUNT ⇑ relative

kiosk /kiːɒsk/, **kiosks**. A **kiosk** is 1 a small shop in the street where you can buy things such as sandwiches or newspapers through an open window. EG *We were eating hamburgers at an all-night kiosk.* N COUNT ⇑ shop = booth, stall 2 a public telephone box; used mainly in British English. EG *I went into a kiosk to call Helen.* N COUNT

kip /kɪp/, **kips, kipping, kipped**; an informal word. 1 If you **kip**, you sleep, usually when you are away from your home. EG *Why don't you go up and kip on my bed?* V

2 A **kip** is a period of sleep. EG *I might leave David at your place and get some kip... I feel like a kip.* N SING WITH DET = sleep

kip down. If you **kip down** somewhere, you go to sleep there for the night. EG *Why don't you kip down here?* PHRASAL VB : V+ADV = bed down

kipper /kɪpə/, **kippers**. A **kipper** is a herring which has been preserved by being hung in smoke. EG *I had kippers for breakfast.* N COUNT : USU PL

kirsch /kɪəʃ/ is a strong, colourless, alcoholic drink made from cherries which is usually drunk after a meal. EG *...a glass of kirsch... ...pineapples in kirsch.* N UNCOUNT ⇑ liqueur

kiss /kɪs/, **kisses, kissing, kissed**. 1 If you **kiss** someone, 1.1 you touch them lightly with your lips to show affection or to greet them. EG *She kissed her sister on both cheeks... I kissed her goodbye and drove away... He bent down and kissed his wife lightly on the cheek.* V+O, OR V+O+A ⇑ touch 1.2 you press your mouth onto their mouth in order to show affection or sexual desire. EG *He tried to kiss her but she turned her head away... They stopped under the tree and kissed... She leant forward and kissed him impulsively on the mouth.* V OR V+O : RECIP

2 If you **kiss** something, you touch it lightly with your lips, usually as a sign of reverence. EG *She had always wanted to kiss the Pope's ring... Teddy kissed her hand.* V+O ⇑ touch

3 If you **kiss** something **goodbye**, you accept the fact that you are going to lose it and you give up hope of getting it back, especially when it is something that you like or want; an informal use. EG *You can kiss your degree goodbye, if you don't work harder.* PHR : VB INFLECTS ⇑ relinquish

4 A **kiss** is an act of touching someone or something with your lips as a sign of affection, greeting, or reverence. EG *Give me a kiss... They long for a mother's goodnight kiss.* N COUNT ⇑ touch

5 If you **blow** someone **a kiss**, you touch your hand lightly with your lips, and then blow on your hand towards the person. EG *I blew him a kiss as he drove off.* PHR : VB INFLECTS

6 If something such as the wind or sunlight **kisses** something, it touches it very gently; a literary use. EG *The sunlight kissed his cheek.* V+O ⇑ caress

kiss of death. If you say that something is the **kiss of death**, you mean that it is certain to make something fail or be a disaster. EG *It's the kiss of death whenever Paul says he'll help with the cooking.* N SING : *the*+N

kiss of life. 1 If you give someone the **kiss of life**, you put your mouth onto their mouth and breathe into their lungs to make them start breathing again, for example because they have nearly drowned. EG *She pulled him out of the lake and gave him the kiss of life.* N SING : *the*+N

2 The **kiss of life** is something which gives new life or energy to something else which is failing. EG *Government investment would be the kiss of life to the coal industry.* N SING : *the*+N

kit /kɪt/, **kits, kitting, kitted**. 1 A **kit** is 1.1 a group of items that are kept together, often in the same container, because they are all used for similar purposes. EG *Make use of the small tool kits and instruction booklets supplied with each machine... ...my first-aid kit... ...car body repair kits.* N COUNT : MOD+N ⇑ equipment 1.2 special clothing and equipment that you use when you take part in a particular activity, especially a sport. EG *Have you brought your squash kit?... I looked around before leaving the track to ensure that no clothing or kit had been left behind.* N COUNT : USU MOD+N = gear 1.3 the special clothing or equipment used by people in the army, navy, or air force. N COUNT : USU MOD+N

2 A **kit** is also a set of parts that can be put together in order to make something. EG *...a do-it-yourself kit... They assemble kits of components shipped in from industrialized nations... ...people who build their cars from kits.* N COUNT ⇑ set

kit out. If you **kit** someone or something **out**, you provide them with everything they need at a particular time, such as clothing, equipment, furniture, etc; an informal expression. EG *I was supposed to get kitted out on Tuesday... Their interiors are kitted out more like submarines than spaceships.* PHRASAL VB : V+O+ADV, USU PASS ⇑ provide = equip

kitbag /kɪtbæg/, **kitbags**. A **kitbag** is a long narrow bag usually made of canvas in which soldiers or sailors keep clothing and personal belongings. N COUNT

kitchen /kɪtʃɪn/, **kitchens**. A **kitchen** is a room that is used for cooking and for household jobs such as washing dishes. EG *Brody went into the kitchen and opened the refrigerator... She left the cheese on the kitchen table.* • See also **soup kitchen**. N COUNT

kitchenette /kɪtʃɪnɛt/, **kitchenettes**. A **kitchenette** is a small kitchen, or a part of a larger room that is used for cooking. EG *...two small rooms, with a kitchenette and a tiny bathroom.* N COUNT ⇑ kitchen

kitchen garden, kitchen gardens. A **kitchen garden** is a part of a garden in which vegetables, herbs, and fruit are grown. N COUNT

kitchen sink, kitchen sinks. 1 A **kitchen sink** is a sink in a kitchen. N COUNT

2 If you go somewhere and take **everything but the kitchen sink** or **everything except the kitchen sink**, you take a very large amount of luggage or belongings, perhaps including many unnecessary things; a humorous use. PHR : USED AS O

kite /kaɪt/, **kites**. 1 A **kite** is 1.1 an object consisting of a light frame covered with paper or cloth and with a long string attached. You hold the string and the kite flies in the air. Many kites are shaped like a diamond, with the two lower sides longer than the two higher sides. EG *She had never learned to fly a kite.* N COUNT ⇑ toy 1.2 a type of hawk which hunts and kills small animals for food. N COUNT ⇑ bird

2 If you **fly a kite**, you put forward new or different ideas to several people in an informal way, so that you can find out how they react to the ideas. EG *...the first modern politician to fly the centre party kite.* PHR : VB INFLECTS ⇑ test

3 If you say that someone is **as high as a kite**, you mean that they are heavily affected by drink, drugs, or excitement. PHR : USED AS C

kith and kin /kɪθ ənd^0 kɪn/. Your **kith and kin** are your friends and relatives; an old-fashioned expression. N UNCOUNT

kitsch /kɪtʃ/ is used to refer to objects or works of art which people think are silly or unattractive because they are made in a sentimental style. EG *He dismissed the exhibition as commercial kitsch.* N UNCOUNT ⇑ art ▸ used as an adjective. EG *...a kitsch design.* ▸ ADJ QUALIT

kitten /kɪtə^{0}n/, **kittens**. 1 A **kitten** is a very young cat. N COUNT ⇑ cat

2 If you say that someone **is having kittens**, you mean that they are behaving in a way that shows they are very worried or upset about something; used in informal English. EG *Your father is having kittens.* PHR : VB INFLECTS ⇑ worry = go spare

kittenish /kɪtə^{0}nɪʃ/. A woman who is **kittenish** flirts with men by behaving in a playful and affectionate way. EG *She was feminine, sprightly, spoiled and kittenish.* ADJ QUALIT

kitty /kɪti^1/, **kitties**. 1 A **kitty** is 1.1 an amount of money consisting of contributions from several people, which is meant to be spent on things that these people will share or use together. EG *After we paid the phone bill there was nothing left in the kitty... I owe the food kitty three pounds.* N COUNT : USU SING ⇑ money = funds 1.2 the total amount of money which is bet by all the players in a card game, and which is taken by the winner. EG *It was hardly worth the effort. There was only fifty pence in the kitty.* N COUNT : USU SING ⇑ money = pool

2 **Kitty** is sometimes used as an affectionate way of addressing a cat or kitten; often used by children. EG *Here, kitty!* N VOC

kiwi /kiːwi^1/, **kiwis**. 1 A **kiwi** is a type of bird that lives in New Zealand and that cannot fly. N COUNT

2 A person who comes from New Zealand can be referred to as a **Kiwi**; an informal use. N COUNT

klaxon /klæksə^{0}n/, **klaxons**. A **klaxon** is a loud horn that is used on some police cars, fire engines, and ambulances in emergency situations to warn people and other traffic. N COUNT = siren

Kleenex /kli:nɛks/. **Kleenex** is both the singular and the plural form. **Kleenex** is a trademark for soft tissue paper that is used as a handkerchief. EG *...a packet of Kleenex... Have you got a Kleenex?* — N UNCOUNT/COUNT ⇑ handkerchief = tissue

kleptomania /klɛptə⁶meɪnɪə/ is a strong and uncontrollable desire to steal things, often occurring as a mental illness; a technical term in psychiatry. — N UNCOUNT ⇑ mental illness

kleptomaniac /klɛptə⁶meɪnɪæk/, **kleptomaniacs**. A **kleptomaniac** is a person who cannot control the desire to steal things, often because of a mental illness. — N COUNT ⇑ thief

km, kms. The plural form is either **kms** or **km**. **km** is a written abbreviation for 'kilometre'; used especially after a number to indicate a measurement of length. — N COUNT/PART ⇑ measurement = kilometre

knack /næk/. A **knack** is a particularly clever or skilful way of doing something successfully, especially something which most people find difficult. EG *Some of the village boys had the knack of imitating her voice.... His fellow soldiers resented his knack for ingratiating himself with officers.* — N SING WITH DET : USU + *of/for* ⇑ technique = talent, skill

knackered /nækəd/. If you are **knackered**, you are extremely tired; an informal word. EG *Is it much further? I'm knackered.* — ADJ QUALIT : PRED = exhausted

knapsack /næpsæk/, **knapsacks**. A **knapsack** is a canvas or leather bag that you carry strapped over your back or slung over your shoulder, used for example by walkers for carrying food and personal belongings. — N COUNT

knave /neɪv/, **knaves**. A **knave** is a dishonest man; an old-fashioned word. EG *You take me for a fool as well as a knave.* — N COUNT = rogue

knavery /neɪvə⁰ri¹/ is dishonesty; an old-fashioned word. EG *It really upsets me to contemplate such knavery.* — N UNCOUNT = dishonesty

knead /ni:d/, **kneads, kneading, kneaded**. 1 When you **knead** dough or other food, you press and squeeze it with your hands so that it becomes smooth and ready to cook. EG *Knead dough on a well-floured surface.* — V+O ⇑ press

2 If you **knead** a part of someone's body, you press or squeeze it with your fingers. EG *He started to knead my aching shoulders.* — V+O ⇑ press = massage

knee /ni:/, **knees, kneeing, kneed**. 1 Your **knee** is 1.1 the place where your leg bends. EG *He leaned forward, his elbows on his knees... He started to get up but his knees gave under him.* — N COUNT : USU POSS+N. 1.2 the area around or above your knee when you are sitting down. EG *She sat with Marcus by her side and Maria on her knee... Kindly take your hand off my knee.* — N COUNT : USU POSS+N ⇑ area

2 The **knee** on a piece of clothing is the part that covers or protects your knee. EG *He had his waders on, and there was a triangular tear at the knee of one of them.* — N COUNT ⇑ part

3 If you are on your **knees**, you are kneeling. EG *He staggered back, and fell to his knees... The woman got up off her knees and went over to him... Kurt threw himself on his knees.* — N PLURAL : PREP + DETPOSS+N

4 To **bring** or **force** a person or country **to** their **knees** means to completely defeat and almost destroy them. EG *The cost of such a war would have brought the kingdom to its knees.* — PHR : VB INFLECTS ⇑ defeat

5 If you **knee** someone, you hit them using your knee. — V+O ⇑ hit

kneecap /ni:kæp/, **kneecaps, kneecapping, kneecapped**; also spelled with a hyphen when used as a noun. 1 A **kneecap** is the bone that covers and protects the front of your knee. — N COUNT

2 To **kneecap** someone means to shoot them in their kneecaps so as to cripple them. Kneecapping is a punishment used by some groups of terrorists. — V+O ⇑ shoot

knee-deep. 1 Something that is **knee-deep** is as high as your knees. EG *We climbed into the knee-deep water.* — ADJ CLASSIF = shallow

2 If you are **knee-deep** in something, you are standing in something that comes up to your knees. EG *He stood there knee-deep in the grass for several minutes.* — ADJ CLASSIF : PRED + *in*

knee-high. Something that is **knee-high** is as tall or high as an adult's knees. EG *...the knee-high, fresh snow that covered the fields... She could swim before she was knee-high.* — ADJ CLASSIF ⇑ tall

kneel /ni:l/, **kneels, kneeling, kneeled, knelt**. **Kneeled** and **knelt** can both be used as the past tense and past participle. When you **kneel** or you **kneel down**, you sit down with your weight on your knees and your legs bent underneath you. EG *He kneels beside the girl... Lottie knelt down to pray.* — V OR V+A (*down*) ⇑ sit

◇ **kneeling**. EG *The kneeling figure was Mary Darling.* — ◇ ADJ CLASSIF : ATTRIB

knees-up, knees-ups. A **knees-up** is a party or celebration; used in informal British English. EG *We'll be having a bit of a knees-up on Thursday evening after work.* — N COUNT = shindig

knell /nɛl/. If you say that the **knell** of something sounds or tolls, you mean that it is going to end soon; a literary word. EG *The knell of her carefree childhood was sounding.* ● See also **death knell**. — N SING : *the*+N+*of* ⇑ end

knelt /nɛlt/ is a past tense and past participle of **kneel**.

knew /nju:/ is the past tense of **know**.

knickerbockers /nɪkəbɒkəz/ are loose trousers which reach as far as the knees, usually worn by women or children. EG *She wore knickerbockers, a white frilled blouse and a velvet jacket.* — N PLURAL : ALSO *a pair of*+N ⇑ trousers = breeches

knickers /nɪkəz/. 1 **Knickers** are women's underpants. EG *She bought herself a nice pair of knickers... ...knicker elastic.* — N PLURAL : ALSO *a pair of*+N = pants

2 If you say that someone **is getting** their **knickers in a twist**, you mean that they are getting angry, annoyed, or upset; an informal expression. — PHR : VB INFLECTS

3 People sometimes say **'knickers'** to show that they disagree with what someone has just said; a very informal use. — EXCLAM

knick-knacks /nɪk næks/ are small objects which people enjoy looking at or playing with, rather than having a use for them. EG *Their house was spotless and smart, full of plants and attractive little knick-knacks.* — N PLURAL

knife /naɪf/, **knives; knifes, knifing, knifed**. **Knives** is the plural form of the noun and **knifes** is the third person singular of the verb. 1 A **knife** is an object that you hold in your hand and use to cut things or as a weapon. It usually consists of a sharp, flat piece of metal attached to a handle. EG *The knives and forks were kept in a large jam jar... Each man had a huge long knife stuck into his belt... ...a knife blade.* — N COUNT ⇑ implement

2 If you say that **the knives are out**, you mean that a disagreement is becoming unpleasant because people dislike each other so much and are trying to upset each other. EG *It won't be easy, I know that. The knives are out on both sides.* — PHR : VB INFLECTS

3 If you **twist** or **turn the knife in the wound**, you remind someone about something very unpleasant or embarrassing in order to make them feel even more upset or worried about it. EG *He had been twisting the knife harder and harder lately, in the hope that I would give in.* — PHR : VB INFLECTS ⇑ remind

4 To **knife** someone means to attack and injure them with a knife. EG *Rausenberger had been knifed and robbed near his home.* — V+O = stab ◇ **knifing, knifings**. EG *There were often knifings or brawls.* — ◇ N COUNT = stabbing

5 See also **carving knife, flick-knife, jack-knife, penknife, palette knife, paper knife, pocket knife.**

knife-edge, knife-edges. A **knife-edge** is a situation that is extremely difficult, because you are not sure what is going to happen or what you should decide. EG *He seemed perpetually balanced on the knife-edge of agonizing decisions.* — N COUNT : USU SING ⇑ situation = tightrope

knight /naɪt/, **knights, knighting, knighted**. 1 In medieval times, a **knight** was a man, usually of noble birth, who served his king or lord in battle, riding a horse and wearing armour. EG *...tales of chivalrous knights and their brave deeds.* — N COUNT

2 In modern times, a **knight** is a man who has been given a knighthood. — N COUNT

3 In chess, a **knight** is a piece which is shaped like a horse's head. — N COUNT ⇑ chess piece

4 If someone **is knighted**, they are given a knighthood. EG *He was knighted by Queen Anne in 1705.* — V+O : USU PASS

knighthood /naɪthʊd/, **knighthoods**. A **knighthood** is a title that is given to a man by a British king or queen for his outstanding achievements or his service to his country. A man who has been given a knighthood can put 'Sir' in front of his name. EG *Whatever happens, he deserves a knighthood.* — N COUNT

knightly /naɪtli¹/ means characteristic of a knight, especially by showing chivalry, bravery and fairness; an old-fashioned word. EG *...the pursuit of the knightly ideal.* — ADJ CLASSIF : ATTRIB = chivalrous

knit /nɪt/, **knits, knitting, knitted**. 1 If you **knit** or you **knit** something, you make something from wool or a similar thread by using two knitting needles to make loops of wool and join the loops — V, V+O, V+O (NG/REFL)+O, OR V+O+A (*for*) ⇑ make together. EG *The old lady sat in her doorway and knitted... She wore a scarf that she had knitted for herself... I'm knitting myself a jumper.* ◊ **knitted**. EG *...a knitted shawl.* ◊ ADJ CLASSIF

2 If you **knit**, you do the most basic kind of stitch when you are knitting. V+O

3 If someone or something **knits** things or people together, they make them fit or work together closely and successfully. EG *It needed an outsider to knit our ideas together.* V+O+A : USU A (together) ⇑ join = unify

4 When broken bones **knit**, the broken pieces grow together again. V = mend

5 If you **knit** your **brows** or your **eyebrows**, you frown because you are angry or worried. EG *He sat there knitting his brows and twisting his napkin.* PHR : VB INFLECTS ⇑ frown

knit up. 1 If you **knit up** something such as a jumper, you knit the whole of it. EG *I'm going to knit up this scarf tomorrow.* PHRASAL VB : V+O+ADV

2 If you say that wool **knits up** quickly or well, you mean that you can knit it quickly or well. EG *This wool knits up beautifully.* PHRASAL VB : V+ADV+A

-knit is used 1 after adjectives to show what kind of wool has been used to knit something. EG *...a chunky-knit sweater.* 2 after adverbs to show how close and united a particular group of people is. EG *They lived in tightly-knit families.* COMB : FORMS ADJS; COMB : FORMS ADJS ⇑ united

knitter /nɪtə/, **knitters**. A **knitter** is a person who knits. EG *She was a great knitter.* N COUNT ⇑ person

knitting /nɪtɪŋ/ is 1 something such as a garment that is being knitted. EG *The bundle of knitting lay on the chair... She picked up her knitting.* 2 the action or process of knitting. EG *I hate knitting!* N UNCOUNT, OR N SING : POSS+N; N UNCOUNT

knitting machine, knitting machines. A **knitting machine** is a machine that you can use at home for knitting things. N COUNT ⇑ machine

knitting needle, knitting needles. A **knitting needle** is a thin stick that is usually made of plastic or metal and has a point at one end. Knitting needles are used for knitting. N COUNT

knitwear /nɪtweə/ is clothing that has been knitted, for example jumpers, cardigans, scarves, and gloves. EG *The shop in the High Street is having a sale of knitwear next week.* N UNCOUNT

knives /naɪvz/ is the plural of **knife**.

knob /nɒb/, **knobs**. A **knob** is 1 a round handle on a door or drawer which you use in order to open or close it. EG *He turned the knob and the door burst open.... There were also mahogany cabinets with polished brass knobs.* 2 a rounded lump or ball which sticks out above a flat surface or on top of a stick or post. EG *Her umbrella is elegantly capped with a glass knob... The bed, with the one gilt knob missing, attracted his attention.* 3 a round switch on a piece of machinery or equipment, for example a television, which you press or turn in order to adjust the way it is operating. EG *You adjust the contrast by turning the knob at the bottom.* 4 a small amount of butter, lard, etc. EG *...mashed potatoes with a knob of butter on top.* N COUNT ⇑ handle; N COUNT; N COUNT ⇑ control = button, switch; N PART+N UNCOUNT

knobbly /nɒbli¹/. Something that is **knobbly** has lumps on it which stick out above a flat surface so that it feels rough and uneven. EG *Her knobbly old hand was outstretched... He's got such knobbly knees.* ADJ QUALIT ⇑ lumpy

knobby /nɒbi¹/ means the same as knobbly; used in American English. EG *He caught her by her thin knobby wrist.* ADJ QUALIT = knobbly

knock /nɒk/, **knocks, knocking, knocked**. 1 If you **knock** on or at a door or window, you hit it in order to make a noise and attract someone's attention. EG *He was carrying a lantern and knocking at the door of a cottage... At quarter to four someone knocked on the window... He didn't even knock as he burst inside.* V : IF+PREP THEN at/on

2 A **knock** is a sharp blow on a door or window which you give in order to make a noise and attract someone's attention. EG *There was a knock at the door... No one answered our knocks when we returned to the office after the Christmas holidays.* N COUNT : IF+PREP THEN at/on ⇑ blow = rap

3 If you **knock** something, you touch or hit it roughly, especially so that it falls over or moves out of its original position. EG *He managed to knock over a box on the low table near him... There were gaping holes where the glass had been knocked out from windows.* ▸ used as a noun. EG *Knocks and jars can cause weaknesses in the spine.* V+O : USU+A ⇑ hit = bang; ▸ N COUNT = bang

4 To **knock** a hole or gap in something means to make it by hitting the thing and removing part of it. EG *We knocked holes in the tin with a hammer... A lorry had careered off the road and knocked a gaping hole in their living room.* V+O+A

5 If you **knock** someone in the way stated or with the result stated, you hit them very hard with your hand or with a weapon, especially so that they fall over or become unconscious. EG *Rudolph had seen him knock Thomas unconscious with one blow of his fist... Dad knocked him to the floor.* ● If something **knocks** you **flat** or **knocks** you **sideways** or **knocks** you **for six**, it surprises you so much that you do not know how to react. V+O+C (ADJ), OR V+O+A ⇑ hit = strike; ● PHR : VB INFLECTS ⇑ surprise

6 If you **knock some sense into** someone, you teach them in a rough and uncaring way to be wiser or more sensible; used in informal English. EG *I hope they'll knock some sense into him at this new school of his.* PHR : VB INFLECTS ⇑ teach

7 To **knock** a quality or characteristic **out of** someone means to cause them to lose it, especially when it is an undesirable or unpleasant quality; an informal expression. EG *All this training might knock the enthusiasm out of him a bit... He was to knock the foolishness out of me eventually.* PHR : VB INFLECTS

8 If something **knocks**, it makes a repeated sharp banging noise. EG *A pipe beside the wardrobe started to knock.* V

9 If an engine **knocks**, it makes a regular beating noise because it is damaged or not working properly. EG *You can use a low grade oil if your engine doesn't knock.* V

10 If your heart is **knocking**, it is beating very fast and strongly, which happens when you are very nervous or excited. EG *My heart was knocking with fright.* V : USU+A ⇑ beat = throb

11 If you **knock** something or someone, you criticize them and say unpleasant things about them; used in informal English. EG *I'm not really interested in knocking Sandra Blair, because I think she is a brilliant writer.* V+O : USU CONT

12 If someone receives a **knock**, they have an unpleasant experience which prevents them from achieving something or which causes them to change their attitudes or plans. EG *We're going to give the government a knock... His time in Africa may have given him a few knocks.* N COUNT ⇑ setback = jolt

13 You use **knocking on** when you are saying that something or someone has almost reached a particular number or age; an informal expression. EG *He must be knocking on 80... It's knocking on twenty years since I saw him.* PREP = nearly

14 The word **knock** is also used in the following expressions, which are explained at other places in this dictionary. ● to **knock the living daylights out of** someone: see **daylight**. ● to **knock** someone or something **into shape**: see **shape**. ● to **knock the stuffing out of** someone or something: see **stuffing**.

knock about or **knock around**; used in informal English. 1 If someone **is knocked about** or **is knocked around**, they are hit or kicked several times. EG *He did not like the thought of a woman being knocked about or locked up in her bedroom.* PHRASAL VB : ORDER V+O+ADV, USU PASS

2 If someone **knocks about** or **knocks around**, they get experience in a lot of different situations, especially by travelling to different places and meeting people with different customs and attitudes. EG *I'm a bachelor, I've knocked about the world a bit, known a few women... I knocked around for a few years after university.* PHRASAL VB : V+ADV/PREP

3 If someone or something is **knocking about** or **knocking around**, they are present in a particular place. EG *There's the odd Scotsman knocking about... My brothers should be knocking around somewhere.* PHRASAL VB : V+ADV

4 If you **knock about** or **knock around** with someone, you spend your spare time with them, either because you are one of their friends or because you are their special boyfriend or girlfriend. EG *He's knocking about with a gang from the next village... Who's she knocking around with now?* PHRASAL VB : V+ADV, USU+with = associate

5 If you **knock** an idea **about** or **around**, you discuss it with other people so that they can suggest ways of improving it. EG *The document was then knocked about and redrafted by a dozen hands.* PHRASAL VB : V+O+ADV

knock back. 1 If you **knock back** a drink, you drink it; an informal expression. EG *He won't be too happy when he comes up here and finds me knocking back his favourite whisky.* PHRASAL VB : V+O+ADV

2 If something **knocks** you **back** a particular amount of money, it costs you that amount of money; an informal expression. EG *How much did that car knock you back?* PHRASAL VB : V+O+ADV+O = set back

knock down. **1** If a car or other vehicle **knocks** someone **down**, it hits them so that they fall to the ground and may be injured or killed. EG *A bus came screeching to a stop, practically knocking him down.* PHRASAL VB : V+O+ADV = knock over

2 If you **knock** someone **down**, **2.1** you hit them or push them, deliberately or accidentally, so that they fall to the ground. • See also **knockdown**. PHRASAL VB : V+O+ADV **2.2** you hit them with a car or other vehicle that you are driving, so that they fall to the ground and may be injured or killed. PHRASAL VB : V+O+ADV

3 If you **knock down** an idea or opinion, you argue successfully against it, so that it is no longer considered valid. EG *Jane has systematically knocked down every one of her friend's suggestions... The argument is in a form in which you can easily knock it down.* PHRASAL VB : V+O+ADV = demolish

4 To **knock down** a building or part of a building means to demolish it. EG *I'd knock the wall down between the front room and dining room.* PHRASAL VB : V+O+ADV = demolish

5 If you **knock** someone **down** when they are selling you something, or if you get a price **knocked down**, you persuade the seller to reduce the price; used in informal English. EG *I tried to knock him down a few pounds but he wouldn't have it... We managed to knock the price down quite a lot because it was torn.* PHRASAL VB : V+O+ADV, OR V+O+ADV+O ⇑ reduce

knock off. **1** If a seller **knocks off** an amount from the price or cost of something, he or she reduces the price or cost by that amount. EG *Liz helped me with the estimates, and managed to knock pounds off the lowest one... He said he'd knock £50 off the price.* PHRASAL VB : V+O+ADV/PREP

2 If you **knock** something **off** a list or document, you remove it. EG *You'll have to knock sugar off your shopping list.* PHRASAL VB : V+O+ADV/PREP

3 In informal English, if someone **knocks** something **off**, **3.1** they steal it. EG *He was planning to knock off a few videos.* PHRASAL VB : V+O+ADV **3.2** they finish it very quickly and easily. EG *I thought I could knock off a couple of essays in no time.* PHRASAL VB : V+O+ADV

4 When you **knock off**, you finish work at the end of the day or before a break; an informal use in British English. EG *We knock off at 5.* PHRASAL VB : V+ADV

5 In very informal English, if you **knock** someone **off**, **5.1** you murder them. EG *I think he had one of his elderly relatives knocked off so that he could inherit the fortune.* PHRASAL VB : V+O+ADV **5.2** you have sex with them; a rude expression used in British English. PHRASAL VB : V+O+ADV

6 If you say **'knock it off'**, you are telling someone to stop doing something which is annoying you; an informal expression. EG *'Knock it off, Billy,' said the boy.* CONVENTION

7 to **knock** someone's **block off**: see **block**.

knock out. **1** To **knock** someone **out** means to cause them to become unconscious or to go to sleep. EG *The old man hit him so hard that he knocked him out... The explosion hurt no one, except that it knocked out Colonel Lacour... The tablet had knocked her out for four solid hours.* • See also **knockout**. PHRASAL VB : V+O+ADV

2 In informal English, if something **knocks** you **out**, **2.1** it shocks you so much that you cannot think clearly or react immediately. EG *I didn't mean to be rude. I was sort of knocked out... The news absolutely knocked me out.* PHRASAL VB : V+O+ADV ⇑ surprise = overcome **2.2** it impresses you greatly by being better than you had expected. EG *Her performance completely knocked me out.* PHRASAL VB : V+O+ADV

3 If a person or team **is knocked out** of a competition, they are defeated in a game, so that they take no more part in the competition. EG *Connors just avoided being knocked out in the second round.* PHRASAL VB : V+O+ADV : USU PASS, IF+PREP THEN *of* = eliminate

4 In war, if something **is knocked out** by enemy action, it is destroyed. EG *Radars were knocked out, aircraft were shot down... Almost 2000 tanks had been knocked out of action by missiles.* PHRASAL VB : V+O+ADV : USU PASS

knock over. To **knock** someone **over** means the same as to knock them down. EG *I got knocked over by a car when I was six.* PHRASAL VB : V+O+ADV

knock together. To **knock** something **together** means the same as to knock it up. EG *The residents here pay rents to the landlords who knocked the shacks together.* PHRASAL VB : V+O+ADV

knock up. **1** If you **knock** something **up**, you make it or build it very quickly, using whatever materials are available. EG *They do not ask official permission to knock up a ramshackle home to live in... Do you want me to knock up a meal for you?* PHRASAL VB : V+O+ADV

2 In British English, if you **knock** someone **up**, you knock on the door of their bedroom or of their house during the night in order to wake them. EG *He knocked me up at 4 to ring for an ambulance.* PHRASAL VB : V+O+ADV = rouse

3 In very informal American English, if a man **knocks** a woman **up**, he makes her pregnant. PHRASAL VB : V+O+ADV

4 In a game such as tennis, squash, or badminton, when the players **are knocking up**, they are practising hitting the ball or shuttlecock to each other before they begin a game. • See also **knock-up**. PHRASAL VB : V+ADV

knockdown /nɒkdaʊn/; also spelled with a hyphen. **1** A **knockdown** price is one that is a lot lower than it would be normally; an informal use. EG *I got it for a knockdown price.* ADJ CLASSIF : ATTRIB

2 A **knockdown** argument or piece of reasoning is very strong and powerful and difficult to argue against; an informal use. EG *Opponents of expansion believe they have a knockdown argument.* ADJ CLASSIF : ATTRIB

knocker /nɒkə/, **knockers**. **1** A **knocker** is a piece of metal on the front door of a building, which you use to hit the door in order to attract the attention of the people inside. EG *He rapped gently with the knocker... It was an attractive knocker, a new one, a shining brass lion's head.* N COUNT

2 In rude and very informal English, a woman's **knockers** are her breasts. N PLURAL

knock-kneed. Someone who is **knock-kneed** has legs which turn inwards at the knees. ADJ CLASSIF

knock knees. Someone who has **knock knees** has legs which turn inwards at the knees. EG *They all had the same golden hair, knock knees, and upturned noses.* N PLURAL

knock-on. A **knock-on** effect or process is one in which one initial action or event causes several other events to happen one after the other. EG *We need to find a solution that doesn't have so many knock-on effects.* ADJ CLASSIF : ATTRIB

knockout /nɒkaʊt/, **knockouts**; also spelled with a hyphen for paragraphs 2 and 3. **1** In boxing, wrestling, etc, a **knockout** is a blow that makes your opponent fall to the ground and unable to stand up before the referee has counted to ten. EG *Davies won by a knockout.* N COUNT ⇑ blow

2 A **knockout** blow or victory is one that completely destroys an opponent. ADJ CLASSIF : ATTRIB

3 A **knockout** competition is one in which several competitors or teams take part, and the winner of each match goes on to the next round while the loser drops out, until one competitor or team is the winner. EG *Last year we won the knock-out cup.* ADJ CLASSIF : ATTRIB

4 If you say that someone is a **knockout**, you mean that they are extremely attractive or clever. EG *Sandra looked a knockout in her new dress.* N SING : *a*+N

knock-up, knock-ups. A **knock-up** is a period of time in which the players practise hitting a ball or shuttlecock to each other before beginning a game of tennis, squash, or badminton. EG *Let's have a knock-up before we start.* N COUNT : USU SING

knoll /nəʊl/, **knolls**. A **knoll** is a low hill with gentle slopes and a rounded top; a literary word. EG *Jess wandered down through some trees beyond a grassy knoll to a small stream.* N COUNT ⇑ hill

knot /nɒt/, **knots, knotting, knotted**. **1** A **knot** is **1.1** a place in a piece of string, rope, cloth, or other material where one end or part has passed through a loop and been pulled tight. You tie a knot in order to join two things together or to keep something firmly in place. EG *He had tied a crude knot... The knot of her headscarf hung beneath her chin... She did her hair up in a knot on top of her head.* N COUNT **1.2** a small tight lump of something. EG *The smoke was a tight little knot on the horizon... She managed to swallow down the last knot of half-chewed bread.* N COUNT+SUPP ⇑ lump

2 A **knot** of people is a group of people who are standing very close together. EG *They were huddled into a tight knot of bodies... ...watched by a constant knot of sightseers.* N PART+N PLURAL

3 A **knot** in a piece of wood is a small hard area where a branch grew. EG *Look for knots in the planks.* N COUNT

4 If you **tie** yourself **in knots** or if you **are tied up in knots**, you get very confused and anxious. EG *I could see he was really tied up in knots inside... He could tie himself in knots over the simplest thing.* PHR : VB INFLECTS ⇑ be confused

5 If you **knot** a piece of string, rope, etc, you pass one V+O end of it through a loop and pull it tight. EG *She knotted the handkerchief corners and tied it tight... Kitty knotted the girl's hair.* ◇ **knotted.** EG *...a knotted handkerchief.* ◇ ADJ CLASSIF

6 If you **knot** something somewhere, you fasten it there by tying a knot. EG *He knotted a towel about Sharon's neck... ...with the rope knotted round my waist.* V+O+A ⇑ tie

7 If your muscles **knot** or if something **knots** them, they become tense, for example because you are worried or angry. EG *Harry's muscles were knotted with rage.* ▸ used as a noun. EG *I've got little knots of tension.* V-ERG ⇑ tense ▸ N COUNT

8 If your stomach **knots** or if something **knots** it, it feels tight because you are afraid or excited. EG *My shoulders tightened and my stomach knotted as I searched for the right path... ...the fear that knotted the pit of his stomach.* V-ERG = tighten

9 A **knot** in your stomach is an uncomfortable tight feeling in your stomach, usually because you are afraid or excited. N COUNT ⇑ feeling

10 A **knot** is also a unit of speed used to measure the movement of ships and ocean currents. EG *Our speed is fifteen knots.* N COUNT : USU NUM+N IN PL ⇑ unit of speed

11 If you travel, move, etc **at a rate of knots**, you do so very quickly indeed. EG *They went off at a rate of knots.* PHR : USED AS AN A

knotty /nɒti[1]/, **knottier, knottiest. 1** A **knotty** problem is complicated and difficult to solve. EG *I now face the knotty question of what to have for breakfast.* ADJ QUALIT : USU ATTRIB ⇑ awkward = thorny

2 Knotty is used to describe something that has hard lumps or knots. EG *...knotty fingers... ...a knotty whip.* ADJ QUALIT : ATTRIB

3 Knotty wood has a lot of small hard areas on it where branches once grew. EG *...knotty pine.* ADJ QUALIT : USU ATTRIB

know /nəʊ/, **knows, knowing, knew, known.**

1 If you **know** a fact, a piece of information, or an answer, you have it in your mind and are certain that it is correct. EG *I don't know her address... I knew that she had recently graduated from law school... We had been there before so we knew what to expect... I know for a fact that what he said is untrue... Claud knew about the killing... We don't know how children acquire language.* V+O/REPORT-CL, OR V+A *(about/ of)* : NO CONT, NO IMPER ● If you **let** someone **know** about something, you give them information or tell them about it. EG *Can you let her know about the meeting?... I'll find out tomorrow about the car and let you know what happened.* ● PHR : VB INFLECTS, IF + PREP THEN *about/of* = inform

2 If you **know** of something, you have heard of it but you do not necessarily have a lot of information about it. EG *I know of one girl who moved into a flat with two others... Many people did not even know of their existence.* V+A *(of)* : NO CONT, NO IMPER

3 If you are **in the know** about something, you have information about it, especially when it is something that is secret and not many people know about it. EG *I heard this from someone who is in the know.* PHR : USED AS AN A

4 If you **know** a language, you have learnt it and can speak it. EG *Shanti knew a few words of English... I didn't know Czech well enough.* V+O : NO CONT, NO IMPER

5 If you **know** about a subject, you have studied it and understand part or all of it. EG *I want to know about sharks... She knew a bit about acoustics.* V+A *(about)* : NO CONT, NO IMPER

6 If you **know** a place, a work of art, an idea, etc, you are familiar with it. EG *He knew London well... Do you know the poem 'Kubla Khan'?* V+O : NO CONT, NO IMPER ● If you refer to something **as we know it**, you are referring to the form in which it exists now and which is familiar to you. EG *The survival of civilization as we know it is under threat.* ● PHR AFTER N

7 If you **know** someone, you are familiar with them because you have met them and talked to them before. EG *'Do you know David?'–'Yes, I do.'... He hardly knew Andrew at college... She knew old Willie very well.* V+O : NO CONT, NO IMPER ● If you **get to know** someone, you meet them and find out what they are like. EG *I'd like the chance to get to know him.* ● PHR : FIRST VB INFLECTS ● If you say that you do **not know** someone **from Adam**, you mean that you do not know them at all. ● PHR : FIRST VB INFLECTS

8 If you **know** how to do something, you have the necessary skills and knowledge to do it. EG *No one knew how to repair it... Do you know how to drive?... I don't know how to explain it.* V+REPORT-CL, OR V+A *(about)* : NO CONT, NO IMPER ● If you say that someone **knows how** to do something, you mean that they are very skilful at doing it. EG *They knew how to make cloth in those days.* ● PHR + *to*-INF : VB INFLECTS

9 know better. 9.1 If you **know better** than someone else, you have more information and experience than them, so that your ideas are more sensible or acceptable. EG *The experts who knew better laughed at the idea... His son couldn't possibly know better than his commanding officer.* PHR : VB INFLECTS, NO CONT **9.2** If you say that someone **knows better** or **ought to know better**, you mean that they have, or ought to have, the experience and maturity to be able to behave sensibly and acceptably. EG *Brian is old enough to know better... He doesn't know any better... ...liberals who ought to know better.* PHR : VB INFLECTS, NO CONT

10 If you say that a particular person **knows best**, you mean that they have a lot of experience and should therefore be trusted to make decisions for other people. EG *Parents always know best... He generally took the view that the experts knew best.* PHR : VB INFLECTS, NO CONT

11 If you **know** that something is happening, you become aware of it. EG *I knew at once that something was wrong... He knew as he spoke that he had just made a mistake.* V+REPORT-CL : NO CONT, NO IMPER = realize

12 If you **know** something or someone, you recognize them when you see them or hear them. EG *I knew Glenda's caravan immediately... He knew a good bargain when he saw one.* V+O : NO CONT, NO IMPER = recognize

13 If someone or something **is known** as a particular name, they are called by that name. EG *...Lev Davidovitch Bronstein, otherwise known as Leon Trotsky... ...William Kent, known to his friends and family as Will... In South America they are known as army ants, in Africa as drivers.* V+O+A *(as)* : ONLY PASS

14 If you say that something is true **as far as** you **know**, you mean that you think it is true but you are not sure. EG *He was working in the bank, as far as I know.* PHR : USED AS ADV SEN

15 You say **'you know' 15.1** to emphasize or to draw attention to what you are saying. EG *It's true, you know. It's true.... You were very naughty, you know... You know, most of the time he seems like such a fool.* **15.2** to fill a gap in a conversation, for example when you are uncertain about what you are saying or what you are going to say next. EG *She thought a lot about her appearance, you know, and spent a lot of her money on clothes... If you found a dead cockroach, you know, in the soup, you wouldn't go to that restaurant again.* **15.3** when you are trying to explain more clearly what you mean, by referring to something that the person you are talking to knows about. EG *...the old desk. You know, the one that's broken... I can never remember dates. You know, I get mixed up.*

16 If you say **'You know what I mean'**, you are suggesting that the person listening to you understands what you are trying to say, and so you do not have to explain any more. EG *She's a bit bossy. You know what I mean.* CONVENTION

17 People sometimes say **'What do you know'** when they are very surprised about something; an informal expression. EG *Well, what do you know!* EXCLAM

18 'You don't know' is used in spoken English to introduce an opinion or remark, in order to emphasize it because the speaker feels strongly about it. EG *I'm so glad you came. You don't know how glad I am to see you... You don't know what I've been going through for four years.* PHR + WH

19 You say **'I know' 19.1** to show that you agree with what has just been said. EG *'It's quite extraordinary.'–'I know'... 'There is nothing you can do to help them.'–'I know'.* CONVENTION ⇑ yes **19.2** to show that you accept that something is true, but think that it is only partly true or or not very important. EG *You can't generalize, I know, but it's quite important really... And long ago, I know, people had to work far too hard... 'I know, I know,' Vaughan said impatiently.* CONVENTION

20 You say **'I don't know' 20.1** when you do not have enough knowledge or information to answer the question you have been asked. EG *'Will they come back?'–'I don't know'... I don't know exactly where it is.* CONVENTION, OR PHR + WH **20.2** to express uncertainty or hesitation when you are making a statement or answering a question. EG *The girl is nine or ten, but perhaps older, I don't know... I don't know, but I think I would be a good teacher.* PHR **20.3** to say that you are unable to explain or decide about something and to emphasize how angry, unhappy, puzzled, etc you feel. EG *I just don't know where to go... I don't know why they did it.* PHR, OR PHR + WH = I'm not sure **20.4** as an introduction to a critical opinion or PHR + WH remark in order to emphasize it. EG *I don't know how you can walk on those high heels.*

21 If you say **'I don't know about you'**, you are going to give your own opinion about something and are suggesting that the person listening to you may want to disagree with you. EG *I don't know about you, but I love roses.* — PHR : USU + *but*

22 You say **'Not that I know of'** when someone has asked you whether or not something is true and you think the answer is 'no' but you cannot be sure because you do not know all the facts. EG *'Was nobody else there?'–'Not that I know of'.* — CONVENTION

23 You say **'I'm blessed if I know'** or **'I'm damned if I know'** to emphasize the fact that you do not know something; a very informal expression which some people consider rude. — CONVENTION

24 You say **'You never know'** or **'One never knows'** to say that it is not definite or certain what will happen in the future, and to suggest that there is some hope that things will turn out well. EG *Well, I can't promise anything, but you never know.* — CONVENTION

25 You say **'How was I to know'** as an excuse to say that you could not have acted differently or more effectively because you did not have enough information. EG *But how was I to know that there was going to be trouble like this?* — CONVENTION, OR PHR + REPORT-CL

26 In very informal English, some people say **'Heaven knows'** or **'God knows'** or **'Christ knows'** when they do not know something and want to suggest that nobody could possibly know it. Many people avoid using these expressions because they consider them to be offensive or blasphemous. EG *God knows how they knew I was coming... What would he do with them? Heaven only knows.* — CONVENTION, OR PHR + WH

27 See also **knowing, known.**

knowable /nəʊəbəºl/. Things that are **knowable** can be known about. EG *The answers are knowable in advance.* — ADJ CLASSIF

know-all, know-alls. A **know-all** is someone who thinks that they know a lot more than other people; an informal word. — N COUNT

know-how; also spelled as one word. **Know-how** is the knowledge of the methods or techniques of doing something, especially something scientific or technical; an informal word. EG *They are almost totally dependent on Western knowhow.* — N UNCOUNT

knowing /nəʊɪŋ/. A **knowing** gesture or remark is one that shows that you understand something, for example the way that someone is feeling or what they really mean, even though it has not actually been mentioned directly. EG *This is usually greeted with deep sighs and knowing looks... The knowing shouts and bellows of laughter made me sick.* — ADJ CLASSIF : ATTRIB

knowingly /nəʊɪŋli¹/. 1 If you do something wrong **knowingly**, you know that it is wrong but you do it anyway. EG *All of them knowingly broke laws that ban trade in rare reptiles.* — ADV WITH VB

2 If you look, smile, wink, etc **knowingly**, you do it in a way that shows that you understand something, even though it has not actually been mentioned directly. EG *The girls laughed at the joke and looked knowingly at each other.* — ADV WITH VB

know-it-all, know-it-alls. A **know-it-all** is the same as a know-all; used in informal American English. EG *He's a bit of a know-it-all, but that's not surprising.* — N COUNT

knowledge /nɒlɪdʒ/. 1 **Knowledge** is information and understanding about a subject which a person has in his or her mind or which is shared by all human beings. EG *...advances in scientific knowledge... All knowledge comes to us through our senses... He is the only person I know with a real knowledge of income-tax legislation.* — N UNCOUNT : USU + SUPP ≠ ignorance

2 If you say that something is true **to your knowledge**, you mean that you are fairly certain that it is true. EG *Of these thirty-seven couples, thirty-five, to my knowledge, are still married, two divorced.* — PHR : USED AS ADV SEN ● If you say that something is true **to the best of** your **knowledge**, you mean that you believe that it is true but you do not know all the facts so you cannot be sure. EG *This is a play which to the best of my knowledge has never been performed in Britain.* — ● PHR : USED AS ADV SEN

knowledgeable /nɒlɪdʒəbəºl/. Someone who is **knowledgeable** has or shows a clear understanding of many different facts about the world or about a particular subject. EG *He was surprisingly knowledgeable about what was going on in the theatre.* — ADJ QUALIT = well-informed

◇ **knowledgeably.** EG *They use the service regularly and are able to speak knowledgeably on behalf of other users.* — ◇ ADV

known /nəʊn/. 1 **Known** is the past participle of **know**.

2 Something that is **known** is clearly recognized and understood by all human beings or by a particular group of people. EG *There's no known cure for a cold... He was a known criminal... ...the most dangerous substance known to man... Politicians are known for making vague promises.* — ADJ CLASSIF

3 If you **let it be known** that something is the case, you make sure that people know it or can find out about it, without telling them directly. EG *She let it be known that she wanted to leave China... He let it be known that he would have great difficulty in finishing the work on time.* — PHR + REPORT-CL ⇑ indicate

4 **Known** is also used to mention how famous or popular someone or something is. EG *The outcome of this process is well known... She had become widely known as a dispenser of large sums of money... ...a little known holiday resort.* — ADJ CLASSIF : ADV + ADJ

knuckle /nʌkəºl/, **knuckles, knuckling, knuckled.** 1 Your **knuckles** are the rounded pieces of bone on your hands where your fingers join your hands, sometimes also including the parts on the back of your fingers where they bend. EG *Her thin hands were twisted by swollen knuckles... Ralph scraped the skin off his knuckles... Her hands were clasped so violently that the knuckles showed white.* — N COUNT : USU PL ⇑ joint

● a **rap on the knuckles**: see **rap**.

2 If a person's words or actions are **near the knuckle**, they are likely to offend people, for example because they are rude or very outspoken. EG *His last remark was a bit near the knuckle.* — PHR : USED AS AN A = rude, outspoken

knuckle down. If someone **knuckles down**, they begin to work or study very hard, especially after a period when they have done very little work; an informal expression. EG *It's high time you knuckled down to some hard study... Don't you think you ought to knuckle down a bit?* — PHRASAL VB : V + ADV, IF + PREP THEN *to* ⇑ work

knuckle under. If you **knuckle under**, you do what someone else tells you to do or what a situation forces you to do, because you realize that you have no choice; an informal expression. EG *He refused to knuckle under and was asked to leave.* — PHRASAL VB : V + ADV, IF + PREP THEN *to*

knuckle-duster, knuckle-dusters. A **knuckle-duster** is a piece of metal which can be worn on the back of a someone's fingers as a weapon, so that if they punch someone they can hurt them badly. — N COUNT : USU PL

KO /keɪ əʊ/, **KO's, KO'd**; also written **k.o.** 1 **KO** is an abbreviation for 'knockout'. EG *Davis won by a k.o. in the 4th round.* — N COUNT = knockout

2 To **KO** someone means to hit them so hard that they become unconscious; an informal expression. — V + O : NO CONT

koala /kəʊɑːlə/, **koalas.** A **koala** or a **koala bear** is an Australian animal which looks like a small bear with grey fur and small tufted ears. Koalas live in trees and eat leaves. — N COUNT ⇑ animal = koala bear

kohl /kəʊl/ is a cosmetic used to darken the edge of a person's eyelids. — N UNCOUNT

Koran /kɔːrɑːn/. The **Koran** is the sacred book on which the religion of Islam is based. — N PROPER : *the* + N

Koranic /kə⁷rænɪk/ is used to describe something which belongs or relates to the Koran. EG *...Koranic verses.* — ADJ CLASSIF : ATTRIB

Korean /kə⁸riːən/, **Koreans.** 1 Something that is **Korean** belongs or relates to North or South Korea, or to their people or language. EG *...the Korean war.* — ADJ CLASSIF

2 **Korean** is the language that is spoken by people who live in North and South Korea. EG *In China I saw street signs in Korean.* — N UNCOUNT

3 A **Korean** is a person who comes from North or South Korea. — N COUNT

kosher /kəʊʃə/. Something that is **kosher** is 1 approved of by the laws of Judaism; used especially of foods which Jews are permitted by their laws to eat. EG *It's not a true kosher home, but they all buy kosher meat.* — ADJ CLASSIF 2 right and honest, and behaving or happening in the way which is approved of or expected; an informal use. EG *There's something not quite kosher about it, if you know what I mean.* — ADJ QUALIT = proper

kow-tow /kaʊ taʊ/, **kow-tows, kow-towing, kow-towed**; also spelled as one word. If you **kow-tow**, you behave very humbly towards someone and try to please them, especially because you hope to get something for yourself from them; an informal — V : IF + PREP THEN *to* = ingratiate word. EG *Murphy would always kow-tow to gain the support of the newspapers... You see the descendants of genuine noble houses kow-tow and haggle for a good table in the restaurant.*

kph is an abbreviation for 'kilometres per hour'; used after a number to indicate the speed at which something is moving. EG *Airships can travel in excess of 240 kph.* — N COUNT : USU NUM+N

kraal /krɑːl/, **kraals**. A **kraal** is a type of village in southern Africa, which contains huts and which is surrounded by a wooden fence. EG *He had to learn always to be truthful to the people of his own tribe and kraal.* — N COUNT ⇑ village ▸ used to refer to all the people who live in a kraal. EG *Young girls walked by to buy food for the kraal.* — N SING : *the*+N

Kremlin /kremlɪn/. The **Kremlin** is used to refer to the central government of the Soviet Union. EG *This change was welcomed by the Kremlin... There was a chance that Kremlin leaders would give their approval.* — N SING : *the*+N, VB CAN BE SING OR PL ⇑ government

krugerrand /kruːgərænd/, **krugerrands**. A **krugerrand** is a South African gold coin which some people buy as an investment. — N COUNT ⇑ coin

kudos /kjuːdɒs/ is fame, glory, or admiration that someone gets as a result of a particular action or achievement. EG *He enjoys all the kudos that goes with being a successful doctor.* — N UNCOUNT = glory, prestige

Kung Fu /kʌŋ fuː/ is a Chinese style of fighting which involves using only your hands and feet. EG *...Kung Fu classes.* — N UNCOUNT ⇑ martial art

Kuwaiti /kʊweɪti¹/, **Kuwaitis**. 1 Something that is **Kuwaiti** belongs or relates to Kuwait or to its people. EG *...the Kuwaiti ruling council.* — ADJ CLASSIF

2 A **Kuwaiti** is a person who comes from Kuwait. — N COUNT

kW is a written abbreviation for 'kilowatt'; used especially after a number to indicate a measurement of electrical power. EG *...a 1kW electric fire.* — N COUNT : USU NUM+N = kilowatt

kwashiorkor /kwæʃɪ¹ɔːkə/ is a serious illness that affects some young children when they have not had enough protein in their diet. — N UNCOUNT ⇑ malnutrition

Ll

L, l /el/, **Ls, l's**. 1 L is the twelfth letter of the English alphabet. — N COUNT

2 L is also the symbol for 'learner driver'. In Britain, a large red 'L' on a white background is attached to cars in which people are learning to drive. — N COUNT

3 L or l is also an abbreviation for various words beginning with L or l, such as 'litre', 'lire', 'lake', and 'left'.

4 L or l is the Roman numeral for 50.

La is a written abbreviation for 'lane', and is used especially in addresses and on maps or signs. EG *...Petticoat La.* — N IN NAMES AFTER N

lab /læb/, **labs**. A **lab** is a laboratory; an informal word. — N COUNT

label /leɪbə⁰l/, **labels, labelling, labelled**; also spelled **labeling** and **labeled in American English. 1** A **label** is a piece of paper or plastic that is attached to an object in order to give information about the object. A label can tell you what the object is, who owns it, how you should use it, etc. EG *The bottles got wet and all the labels came off.* — N COUNT = tag

2 If you **label** something, you attach a label to it. EG *I've just spent a whole day labelling all the items... ...the dark brown pot labelled 'Salt'.* — V+O, OR V+O+C = mark

3 A **label** is also **3.1** a word or a short phrase that describes one part of a person's character, but which you use as a general description of that person's character. EG *He was not one of those who would accept the label of anarchist.* — N COUNT **3.2** the identifying name or trademark of a company that produces gramophone records, especially pop records. EG *Joan Armatrading's 'Walk Under Ladders' is on the A and M label.* — N COUNT : USU MOD+N

4 When you **label** someone or something, you use a word or a short phrase in order to briefly describe them, and to show what you really think about them. EG *Nothing can of itself always be labelled as 'wrong'... Men who do this are often labelled as 'work-shy'.* — V+O+A *(as)*, V+O+C, OR V+O ⇑ categorize = brand

labial /leɪbɪəl/. A **labial** sound is produced with your lips; a technical term in phonetics. — ADJ CLASSIF

labor /leɪbə/. See **labour**.

laboratory, laboratories. **Laboratory** is pronounced /lə³bɒrətə⁰ri¹/ in British English, and /læbə⁰rətɔːri¹/ in American English. A **laboratory** is 1 a building or a room that contains special scientific equipment. Scientists use laboratories to do experiments or to do research. EG *The geologists took the samples back to the laboratory.* — N COUNT ⇑ place = lab **2** a room in a school, university, etc, which contains some scientific equipment, and where students are taught about science subjects such as chemistry. ● See also **language laboratory**. — N COUNT = lab

laborious /lə³bɔːrɪəs/. Something that is **laborious** needs a lot of effort, especially because it is hard work, difficult, or complicated. EG *Clearing the forest is a laborious business.* — ADJ QUALIT = arduous ◇ **laboriously**. EG *...a few laboriously hand-written books.* — ◇ ADV

labor union, labor unions. A **labor union** is an organization that has been formed by workers in order to represent their rights and interests to their employers, for example in order to improve working conditions or wages; used in American English. — N COUNT = trade union

labour /leɪbə/, **labours, labouring, laboured**; also spelled **labor** in American English. **1 Labour** is **1.1** very hard work, often work that does not need a lot of skill. EG *I really enjoy manual labour... ...the culmination of fifteen months' incessant labour... I was much occupied at the time with my own literary labours.* — N UNCOUNT/ COUNT : SING=PL = effort, toil **1.2** the last stage of pregnancy, in which the baby is gradually pushed out of the womb by the mother. EG *She was in labour for seven hours... Mrs Macintosh was having labour pains.* — N UNCOUNT

2 A **labour of love** is something which you do because you really want to do it, even though it involves a lot of hard work and you will get no pay or reward for it. EG *It was a very amateurish effort but it was a labour of love and took many months.* — PHR : USED AS C, FIRST N INFLECTS

3 If you **labour** at something, **3.1** you work very hard, for example doing physical work such as digging. EG *He was sent to labour as a peasant in a corrective commune.* — V : USU+A = toil **3.2** you do it with difficulty, for example because you are not strong enough or clever enough. EG *He was labouring under the strain of a political crisis which was worsening daily... His classmates were labouring with elementary algebra.* — V+A = struggle ◇ **laboured**. EG *McKellen's breathing was laboured... ...the laboured writing of a seven-year-old.* — ◇ ADJ QUALIT

4 **Labour** is used to refer to **4.1** the workers of a country or industry, considered as a group, either as a political force or as one of the resources that are needed to produce goods and services. EG *...a shortage of skilled labour in some industries... ...the forces of outside capital and organized labour... Labour costs are increasing.* — N UNCOUNT **4.2** the work that people do, when it is considered as their contribution to a project, an industry, or an economic system. EG *They are threatening a withdrawal of labour in support of their claims.* — N UNCOUNT

5 You can use **Labour** to refer to the Labour Party. EG *What would Labour do if they got in, then?... ...the Labour MP for Ormskirk.* — N PROPER

6 If you **labour** under a delusion, misapprehension, etc, you continue to think or believe something which other people know to be wrong or false. EG *I still laboured under the delusion that policemen never told lies... He was a very timid man who laboured under the constant misapprehension that nobody liked him.* — V+A *(under)*

7 If you **labour** a point or an argument, you talk about something for a long time, in great detail, or with great emphasis, because you want to persuade people of its importance, even though they might — V+O = stress, dwell on

think you are talking about it too much. EG *This may seem to be labouring the obvious, but it is necessary to do so... There is no need to labour the point.*

labourer /leɪbəʳrə/, **labourers**. A **labourer** is a person who does a job which involves a lot of hard physical work, for example digging or carrying bricks. EG *Larry went to work as a labourer at a sawmill... ...an old farm labourer.*
N COUNT ⇑ worker

labour force. The **labour force** consists of all the people who are able to work in the country or all the people who work for a particular company. EG *...twenty per cent of the total labour force.*
N SING WITH DET : USU *the*+N = work force

labour-intensive. Industries or techniques that are **labour-intensive** need or use a lot of workers. EG *...the traditional labour-intensive manufacturing industries.*
ADJ QUALIT

labour market. The **labour market** consists of all the people who want work at a particular time, or the demand for work, especially in relation to the amount of work available; a technical term in economics. EG *...women wanting to break into the labour market.*
N SING WITH DET : USU *the*+N

Labour Party; spelled **Labor Party** in Australian English. The **Labour Party** in Britain and Australia is the political party which believes particularly in the importance of a socialist economy with state ownership and control rather than private ownership. EG *Half our unions are affiliated to the Labour Party... He declined to speak at the Labour Party rally in Hyde Park last month.*
N PROPER : *the*+N

labour-saving. A machine or method that is **labour-saving** saves you a lot of hard work or effort. EG *...labour-saving appliances... ...a new labour-saving technique.*
ADJ QUALIT

laburnum /ləbɜːnəm/, **laburnums**. A **laburnum** is a small tree which has long stems of yellow flowers, and which is often planted in gardens.
N COUNT

labyrinth /læbəʳrɪnθ/, **labyrinths**. A **labyrinth** is a complicated series of narrow corridors or streets, where it is difficult to find your way and easy to get lost. EG *He wandered through the labyrinths of the Old Town.*
N COUNT = maze

labyrinthine /læbəˈrɪnθaɪn/. Something that is **labyrinthine** is **1** like a labyrinth. EG *The castle is labyrinthine, dark, and mysterious.* **2** very complicated and difficult to understand; a formal use. EG *...a nightmare of labyrinthine bureaucratic procedures.*
ADJ QUALIT; ADJ QUALIT : USU ATTRIB = tortuous

lace /leɪs/, **laces, lacing, laced**. **1 Lace** is a very delicate cloth which is made with a lot of holes in it. It is made by twisting together very fine threads of cotton to form patterns. EG *The tablecloth was edged with lace... ...a white lace handkerchief.*
N UNCOUNT ⇑ fabric

2 Laces are pieces of cord or string that are put through the holes along the two edges of something, pulled tight, and tied, in order to fasten the two edges together. EG *He spent ten minutes tying the laces of his shoes.*
N COUNT : USU PL

3 If you **lace** something, you thread a cord or string through holes in the two edges of it. EG *Her fingers were too cold to lace the tent flap.*
V+O

4 If you **lace** food or drink with a substance such as alcohol or a drug, you put a small amount of the substance into the food or drink. EG *She laced her coffee with brandy.*
V+O : IF+PREP THEN *with* ⇑ mix = spike

lace up. If you **lace** something **up**, you pull the two ends of a lace tight and tie them together, in order to fasten something. EG *He bent and laced up his shoes.*
PHRASAL VB : V+O+ADV = do up

lacerate /læsəreɪt/, **lacerates, lacerating, lacerated**. If something **lacerates** your skin, it cuts it badly and deeply. EG *The barbed wire had lacerated her arm.*
V+O = gash

laceration /læsəʳreɪʃəʳn/, **lacerations**. A **laceration** is a bad cut on your skin. EG *She had terrible lacerations on her legs and arms.*
N COUNT = gash

lace-up, lace-ups. **Lace-ups** or **lace-up** shoes are shoes which are fastened with laces. EG *Maria's lace-ups had got holes in the toes... ...black lace-up shoes.*
N COUNT : USU PL

lachrymose /lækrɪməʊs, -məʊz/. Someone who is **lachrymose** cries very easily and very often; a formal word. EG *She was irritable and lachrymose.*
ADJ QUALIT = tearful

lack /læk/, **lacks, lacking, lacked**. **1** If there is a **lack** of something, there is not enough of it or it does not exist at all. EG *I hated the lack of privacy in the dormitory... He wasn't a stern man at all, in spite of his lack of humour... Lack of proper funding is making our job more difficult.*
N SING WITH DET, OR N UNCOUNT : N+*of* = shortage, absence

2 If something happens **for** or **through lack of** a particular thing, it happens because there is not enough of that thing for a particular purpose. EG *His department was shut down for lack of funds... The officials were acquitted for lack of evidence.*
PHR : USED AS AN A

3 If there is **no lack of** something, there is a great deal of it and often more than you need. EG *There was certainly no lack of excitement in the Sixties... There was no lack of schools to choose from.*
PHR+N IN PLURAL ⇑ plenty

4 If something **is lacking** or if you **lack** something, it does not exist at all or there is not enough of it. EG *The advertisement lacks any stamp of individuality... 'What is lacking in this case,' he concluded, 'is a corpse.'... It is lacking a signature... They live in a shadowy, secret world, lacking the confidence to socialize... Whatever New England may lack in materials it makes up in bright ideas.*
V-ERG : IF V, THEN USU CONT : ALSO V+A *(in)* ⇑ miss ≠ have

5 See also **lacking**.

lackadaisical /lækədeɪzɪkəʳl/. Someone who is **lackadaisical** does not show any interest or enthusiasm and acts as if they are daydreaming. EG *She was annoyingly lackadaisical and impractical.*
ADJ QUALIT = dreamy

lackey /lækiʳ/, **lackeys**. A **lackey** is someone who follows another person's orders completely, without ever questioning them or thinking about the situation themselves; used showing disapproval. EG *They believed that the police were lackeys of the Establishment.*
N COUNT

lacking /lækɪŋ/. **1** If someone or something is **lacking** in a particular quality, they do not have enough of it or have none of it at all. EG *Philip was not lacking in intelligence or ability... Its ideology is sterile and lacking in originality... But he was also lacking in charity.*
ADJ CLASSIF : PRED+*in* = wanting

2 If a quality is **lacking**, it is not there, although you would expect it to be there. EG *But once in power, political confidence appeared lacking... Innovation has been sadly lacking.*
ADJ CLASSIF : PRED = absent

3 Someone who is **lacking** is not very clever or intelligent; a rather old-fashioned use. EG *If you ask me, he's a bit lacking.*
ADJ QUALIT = dim, slow

lacklustre /læklʌstə/; also spelled **lackluster** in American English. Something or someone that is **lacklustre** has no brightness or liveliness. EG *The pianist gave a lacklustre performance.*
ADJ QUALIT = lifeless

laconic /ləʳkɒnɪk/. If you are **laconic**, you use very few words to say something, so that you sometimes seem rude and unfriendly. EG *'How many are there?' enquired Mary in a low voice. 'Two,' was Philip's laconic answer... The story displays the somewhat laconic wit of these people.* ◊ **laconically**. EG *Sam was laconically directed to an office in a nearby street.*
ADJ QUALIT ⇑ brief ≠ verbose; ◊ ADV WITH VB = tersely

lacquer /lækə/, **lacquers, lacquering, lacquered**. **1 Lacquer** is **1.1** a special liquid which is painted on wood or metal in order to protect it and to make it shiny. When lacquer dries it becomes very hard. EG *Why don't you spray it with lacquer?... The red lacquer work on the upper walls was badly chipped.* **1.2** a clear, sticky liquid, usually in the form of a spray, which some women put on their hair to hold their hairstyle neatly in place; an old-fashioned use. EG *...hair lacquer.*
N UNCOUNT ⇑ substance; N UNCOUNT

2 If you **lacquer** something such as wood or metal, you cover it with lacquer paint in order to protect it and to make it shiny. EG *If brass and bronze is lacquered it doesn't need cleaning, only dusting.* ◊ **lacquered**. EG *He opened a lacquered box and took out a cigarette.*
V+O; ◊ ADJ CLASSIF

lacrosse /ləʳkrɒs/ is an outdoor game played between two teams of players. They use long sticks with nets at the end to catch and throw a small ball, in order to try and score goals.
N UNCOUNT

lactation /lækteɪʃəʳn/ is the production of milk by women and female mammals during the period before and after they give birth; a formal word.
N UNCOUNT

lactic acid is a type of acid which is found in sour milk and is also produced by your muscles when you have been exercising a lot.
N UNCOUNT

lactose /læktəʊs, -təʊz/ is a type of sugar which is found in milk and which is sometimes added to food.
N UNCOUNT

lacy /leɪsiʳ/, **lacier, laciest**. **1** Something that is **lacy** is made from lace or has a lot of pieces of lace attached to it. EG *...a pretty, black, lacy dress.*
ADJ CLASSIF

2 Lacy is also used to describe something that looks like lace, especially because it is very delicate. EG *...lacy white flowers.*
ADJ QUALIT

lad /læd/, **lads**. 1 A **lad** is a young man or boy. EG *He was an intelligent lad but easily bored... He used to collect stamps when he was a lad.* N COUNT: ALSO VOC

2 People sometimes use the **lads** to refer to a group of young men who do a lot of things together, like going to pubs and playing football, and who share the same attitudes and interests; an informal use. EG *He just wants to be one of the lads.* N PLURAL: USU the+N

ladder /lædə/, **ladders, laddering, laddered**. 1 A **ladder** is a piece of equipment used for climbing up or down from a wall, ship, tree, etc. A ladder consists of two long pieces of wood, metal, or rope with steps fixed between them. EG *They walked along the wooden pier and climbed down the short ladder into the boat.* N COUNT

2 You can use **ladder** to refer to 2.1 the different stages and levels of a society, organization, etc. EG *Joining the golf club takes you up the social ladder a little bit more... ...younger people working their way up the ladder.* N SING: the+N ⇑ scale 2.2 any system that has several different stages and levels. EG *These animals are lower on the evolutionary ladder than the primates.* N SING WITH DET +SUPP ⇑ scale

3 A **ladder** in a woman's stockings or tights is a torn part where some of the vertical threads have broken, leaving only the horizontal threads across it. EG *...the ladder in her only pair of silk tights.* N COUNT ⇑ tear ▸ used as a verb. EG *Damn! I've laddered the only pair of tights I've got left.* ▸ V-ERG ⇑ damage

laddie /lædi¹/, **laddies**. A **laddie** is a young man or boy; used especially in Scottish English. EG *You've been in a fight, laddie.* N COUNT: ALSO VOC = lad

laden /leɪdə⁰n/. If you are **laden** with something, you are holding or weighed down with a lot of heavy things; a rather literary word. EG *The trees were laden with fruit... Ken arrived laden with presents for the children... ...heavily laden ships.* ADJ CLASSIF: IF+ PREP THEN+ with = loaded

la-di-da /lɑː di¹d ɑː/; also spelled **lah-di-dah**. Someone who is **la-di-da** has an upper-class way of behaving or speaking, which seems very affected; an old-fashioned word used showing disapproval. EG *...his la-di-da family, as she called them... ...a posh twit, talking so la-di-da I had to leave the room.* ADJ QUALIT, OR ADV WITH VB = posh

ladies' man, ladies' men. A **ladies' man** is a man who enjoys flirting with women in a way that they also enjoy; often used showing approval. EG *Mr Spencer was a great ladies' man.* N COUNT: USU SING = flirt

ladies' room. The **ladies' room** is a public toilet for women, especially in a large public building. EG *Can you tell me where the ladies' room is?* N SING: the+N

ladle /leɪdə⁰l/, **ladles, ladling, ladled**. 1 A **ladle** is a large, round, deep spoon with a long handle, used for putting soup, stew, sauce, etc into bowls. N COUNT

2 If you **ladle** soup, stew, etc, you serve it, especially with a ladle. EG *'Plenty here,' said the man, ladling the soup into bowls.* V+O: USU+A = dish out

ladle out. If you **ladle out** something such as money, information, advice, etc, you give it freely and in large quantities. EG *...the knowledge that is ladled out daily in high schools.* PHRASAL VB: V+O+ADV = dole out

lady /leɪdi¹/, **ladies**. 1 You use the word **lady** when you are referring to a woman, especially when you are showing politeness or respect. EG *He had fallen in love with a rich American lady... A little old lady came out... Ladies first, John... The lady at the library said it was a good book.* N COUNT ▸ used as an adjective. EG *...a lady novelist... The two most important lady guests were Karen Blixen and Edith Sitwell.* ● See also **young lady**. ▸ ADJ CLASSIF: ATTRIB

2 You use **lady** to express formality and respect when you are addressing women, for example when you start a public speech by saying Ladies and gentlemen'. This use is more formal and old-fashioned in the singular than in the plural. EG *Ladies and gentlemen of the jury, exhibit number one is this notebook... 'Ladies,' Henry appealed in a calm and reasonable voice... He bowed deeply and said, 'After you, dear lady.'... Now you come and sit next to me, young lady.* N COUNT: USED AS VOC

3 **Lady** is sometimes used by men as a form of address when they are talking to a woman that they do not know, especially in shops, in the street, etc ; an informal expression used especially in American English. EG *Well, lady, I can't do anything about this... 'Hey, lady,' he said to the waitress... Pay your bill, lady.* N VOC = miss

4 A **lady** is 4.1 a woman who behaves in a polite, dignified and graceful way, especially if she comes from the upper classes. EG *I am not a lady, and never will be... Many of the farmers' wives were trying to be ladies... A lady never crosses her legs.* N COUNT: USU SING 4.2 a noblewoman or a woman from the upper classes, especially in former times. EG *I rode in her carriage like a lady... D H Lawrence's most famous book is about a gamekeeper and a lady... The lords and ladies are all gathered at the palace.* ● See also **First Lady**. N COUNT

5 **Lady** is a title used in front of the name of some female members of the nobility, wives of knights and peers, etc. EG *She was one of Lady Keeble's greatest friends... ...Lady Diana Cooper... I talked to his wife (Lady Clarissa, the daughter of Lord Elasson).* N IN TITLES

6 Christians, especially Catholics, use **Our Lady** as a title to refer to the Virgin Mary. EG *Our Lady was crowned heavenly queen.* N PROPER

7 A **ladies** is a public toilet for women. EG *Make for the ladies and check that your hair and make-up are all right.* N SING WITH DET: USU the+N

8 **Ladies'** or **lady's** is used to describe something that belongs to girls or women, or something that is done or used by them. EG *She sang in a ladies' choir... ...Mellifont Ladies' College... ...an exhibition of firearms, from the tiniest lady's automatic to the heaviest of machine guns.* ADJ CLASSIF: ATTRIB

ladybird /leɪdi¹bɜːd/, **ladybirds**. A **ladybird** is a small, round, red beetle with black spots. N COUNT

lady friend, lady friends. A man's **lady friend** is his girlfriend; an old-fashioned expression. EG *I overheard the servants discuss his various lady friends.* N COUNT: USU SING

lady-in-waiting, ladies-in-waiting. A **lady-in-waiting** is a woman from the aristocracy or upper classes, who acts as a companion to a female member of the royal family. EG *The Queen was accompanied by three ladies-in-waiting.* N COUNT ⇑ attendant

lady-killer, lady-killers. A **lady-killer** is an attractive man who enjoys flirting with or seducing women, but who soon leaves each woman to search for someone new. N COUNT: USU SING

ladylike /leɪdi¹laɪk/. If a woman or girl is **ladylike**, she behaves in a way that suits a lady and seems polite, restrained, dignified, and graceful. EG *Alice's mother had always considered Jill to be ladylike and discreet... She took little ladylike sips of the cold drink.* ADJ QUALIT = genteel

Lady Muck. If you refer to a woman or girl as **Lady Muck**, you are showing that you think she is too bossy and has too high an opinion of herself; an offensive expression. EG *Who the hell does she think she is? Lady Muck?* N PROPER

ladyship /leɪdi¹ʃɪp/, **ladyships**. **Ladyship** is used in the expressions 'your ladyship', 'her ladyship', and 'their ladyships' as a respectful way of addressing or talking about a female member of the nobility, the wife of a knight or peer, etc. EG *Her Ladyship will see you in the library, sir.* N COUNT: DETPOSS+N, USED IN TITLES

lady's maid, lady's maids. A **lady's maid** was a female servant, especially in 18th or 19th century Britain, who worked for a rich woman, looking after her clothes, helping her to dress, doing her hair, etc. N COUNT

lag /læg/, **lags, lagging, lagged**. 1 If you **lag** behind someone or something, you move or progress more slowly than them. EG *Britain's economic development must lag behind that of almost every other industrial nation... He set off at a brisk walk, Kate lagging behind... The boys crept forward, Roger lagging a little.* V: IF+ADV/PREP THEN behind = trail, drag

2 If something such as trade or investment **lags**, it does not do as well as it has done in the past. EG *Trade has lagged since the embargo... Production lagged and unemployment rose.* V: IF+ADV/PREP THEN behind = drop

3 A time **lag** or a **lag** of a particular length of time is a period of time between one event and another related event, usually when this period is considered as a delay. EG *There will be a one-year lag between the time I write the book and its publication... There is a time lag of about fifteen years.* N COUNT+SUPP ⇑ = gap

4 When you **lag** pipes, hot water tanks, or the inside of a roof, you cover them with a special material to prevent heat escaping from them and to prevent them from freezing. EG *If you lag your hot water tank, you'll save money on your fuel bills.* V+O ⇑ insulate

5 A **lag** is someone who is in prison or has been in prison for a long time because they have committed a crime; used in informal English. EG *He felt the* N COUNT ⇑ convict

security that an old lag feels when he goes back to the prison he knows.
6 See also **lagging**.

lager /lɑ:gə/, **lagers**. **Lager** is a type of light beer that has a lot of bubbles. EG *Two lagers, please.* N MASS

laggard /læɡəd/, **laggards**. A **laggard** is someone who is slower than everyone else, especially in their work; an old-fashioned word showing disapproval. N COUNT

lagging /læɡɪŋ/ is special material which is used to lag pipes, water tanks or the inside of a roof. N UNCOUNT ⇑ insulation

lagoon /lə³gu:n/, **lagoons**. A **lagoon** is an area of calm sea water that is separated from the ocean by reefs or sandbanks. EG *...the hot, white sands and limpid, blue lagoons of the Indian Ocean.* N COUNT

lah-di-dah /lɑ: di¹ dɑ:/. See **la-di-da**.

laid /leɪd/ is the past tense and past participle of **lay**.

laid-back. Someone who is **laid-back** behaves in a calm, relaxed way as if nothing will ever worry them; an informal expression. EG *James believed in a laid-back approach.* ADJ QUALIT = easy-going

lain /leɪn/ is the past participle of **lie**.

lair /lɛə/, **lairs**. A **lair** is 1 a place where a wild animal lives, usually one which is underground or well-hidden. EG *We spent the morning tracking the beast to its lair.* N COUNT = den 2 a room or hiding place that someone goes to in order to get away from other people; an informal use. EG *I retired to my lair, and wrote letters.* N COUNT = hideout

laird /lɛəd/, **lairds**. A **laird** is a landowner in Scotland who owns a large area of land. N COUNT

laissez-faire /leɪseɪ fɛə/ is the policy which is based on the idea that governments and the law should not interfere with business, finance, or the conditions of people's working lives. N UNCOUNT ▸ used as an adjective. EG *It is therefore unlikely that a laissez-faire policy will succeed.* ▸ ADJ QUALIT

laity /leɪə¹ti¹/. The **laity** are 1 all the people involved in the work of a church who are not clergymen, monks, nuns, etc. EG *...the Catholic laity... ...all the bodies in which the laity help to manage the affairs of their church.* N PLURAL : the+N 2 all the people who do not belong to a particular profession. N PLURAL : the+N

lake /leɪk/, **lakes**. A **lake** is a large area of fresh water, surrounded by land. EG *On the edge of the lake was a pavilion.* N COUNT ▸ used as part of a name. EG *...the calm waters of Lake Michigan... ...the Great Lakes separating Canada and America.* ▸ N IN NAMES

lakeside /leɪksaɪd/. The **lakeside** is the area of land around the edge of a lake. EG *We got up to walk along the lakeside at an early hour... He had lunch at a lakeside restaurant.* N SING : the+N ⇑ shore

lam /læm/, **lams, lamming, lammed**. To **lam** someone or something or to **lam** into someone or something means to hit them very hard; an informal word. EG *If he says it again, lam him.* V+O, OR V+A *(into)* = thump

lama /lɑ:mə/, **lamas**. A **lama** is a Buddhist priest or monk in Tibet and Mongolia. N COUNT

lamb /læm/, **lambs**. 1 A **lamb** is a young sheep. EG *The farm had sold the pigs and the lambs at the fair.* N COUNT
● If you say that a person or animal does something **like a lamb**, you mean that they do it gently and obediently, without causing any trouble. EG *The camels were going well and behaving like lambs.* ● PHR : USED AS AN A = docilely
● **mutton dressed as lamb**: see **mutton**.
2 **Lamb** is the flesh of a lamb eaten as food. EG *...roast lamb.* N UNCOUNT ⇑ meat
3 People sometimes use **lamb** when they are talking about someone they are fond of and who is gentle and lovable, for example a young child. EG *And what does he do? He drops off to sleep, the lamb.* N COUNT = darling
4 In the Christian religion, the **Lamb** is sometimes used to refer to Jesus Christ; a formal use. EG *And the blood of the Lamb had cleansed me.* N PROPER : the+N

lambing /læmɪŋ/ is the time in the spring when female sheep give birth to lambs. EG *...the lambing season.* N UNCOUNT

lambskin /læmskɪn/, **lambskins**. **Lambskin** is the skin of a lamb, usually with the wool still on it, used for making slippers, coats, rugs, etc. EG *...a lambskin hat... ...lambskin slippers.* N UNCOUNT/COUNT ⇑ leather

lame /leɪm/, **lamer, lamest**. 1 If you are **lame**, you are unable to walk properly because an injury or illness has damaged one or both of your legs. EG *She's lame–she nearly died of polio... You are too lame to be walking like this... ...a lame horse.* ADJ QUALIT ⇑ disabled ⇑ crippled ≠ able-bodied ▸ The **lame** is used to refer to people who are lame. EG *...bringing hope to the old and the lame.* ▸ N PLURAL : the+N ◊ **lameness**. EG *He was prevented by lameness from taking part in the games of the other children.* ◊ N UNCOUNT
2 If you describe an excuse, proposal, argument, etc as **lame**, you mean that it is poor or weak. EG *At best, the proposal was a lame compromise... My lame excuse was that I had too much else to do.* ADJ QUALIT = inadequate, feeble ◊ **lamely**. EG *'I'm a nature lover,' she said lamely. What a clod he must think I am, she thought.* ◊ ADV ◊ **lameness**. EG *Even he was ashamed of the lameness of his suggestions.* ◊ N UNCOUNT+SUPP

lamé /lɑ:meɪ/ is cloth that has threads of gold or silver woven into it, which make it sparkle. EG *The band-leaders got themselves up in gold lamé and sequins.* N UNCOUNT ⇑ fabric

lame duck, lame ducks. A **lame duck** is someone who is not successful and who needs to be helped by other people. EG *He was yet another of my sister's lame ducks.* N COUNT ⇑ failure

lament /ləment/, **laments, lamenting, lamented**. 1 If you **lament** something, you express your sadness, regret, or disappointment about it. EG *He laments the changing pattern of life in the countryside... 'All the flour is wet!' lamented Miss Musson.* V+O/QUOTE/REPORT-CL, OR V = bemoan, mourn
2 A **lament** is 2.1 something that is said that expresses a person's sadness, regret, or disappointment about something. EG *'It's a dying industry,' is his lament... ...a general lament about humanity.* N COUNT = lamentation 2.2 a poem, song, or piece of music which expresses sorrow that someone has died. EG *He composed a lament to the dead soldier.* N COUNT = elegy

lamentable /ləmentəbə⁰l, læməntəbə⁰l/. If you describe something as **lamentable**, you mean that you think it is very unfortunate or disappointing. EG *...the lamentable state of the industry in the Sixties... Three years after this lamentable affair, Colonel Burr was arrested.* ADJ CLASSIF : USU ATTRIB = regrettable ◊ **lamentably**. EG *...the lamentably inadequate plans for retraining officers.* ◊ ADV, OR ADV SEN

lamentation /læmenteɪʃə⁰n/, **lamentations**. A **lamentation** is an expression of grief or great sorrow; a formal word. EG *She accused herself, with tears and lamentations, of giving him bad food... ...a cry of lamentation went up.* N COUNT/UNCOUNT = lament

laminated /læmɪneɪtɪ²d/. 1 Material such as wood or plastic that is **laminated** consists of several thin sheets or layers that are stuck together. EG *...windscreens made of laminated glass.* ADJ CLASSIF ⇑ layered
2 A product that is **laminated** is covered with a thin sheet of clear plastic in order to protect it. EG *...an advertisement, glossy and laminated.* ADJ CLASSIF

lamp /læmp/, **lamps**. A **lamp** is 1 a device which produces light by burning oil or gas or by using electricity. EG *...reading his paper by the light of his gas lamp... She turned on the bedside lamp... ...the street lamp outside Mrs Flanagan's house.* N COUNT 2 an electrical device which produces a special type of light or heat, used especially in medical or beauty treatment. EG *...an infra-red lamp... ...glowing and tanned after sunlamp sessions.* N COUNT

lamplight /læmplaɪt/ is the light produced by a lamp. EG *...her hair gleaming in the lamplight.* N UNCOUNT

lamplit /læmplɪt/. If something is **lamplit**, it can be seen because there is light from a lamp. EG *We saw the lamplit windows ahead.* ADJ CLASSIF ⇑ illuminated

lampoon /læmpu:n/, **lampoons, lampooning, lampooned**. 1 If you **lampoon** someone or something, you criticize them very strongly, but using humorous means. EG *The governor was lampooned by the Journal's cartoonists... The Premier was lampooned as Bumbling Baldwin in the Express.* V+O : USU PASS ⇑ satirize
2 A **lampoon** is a piece of writing or speech which criticizes someone or something very strongly, but using humorous means. EG *Lampoons were written and passed from hand to hand.* N COUNT ⇑ satire

lamp-post, lamp-posts. A **lamp-post** is a tall metal or concrete pole that is fixed beside a road and has a light at the top. EG *He leaned against the lamp-post.* N COUNT

lampshade /læmpʃeɪd/, **lampshades**. A **lampshade** is a covering that is fitted round or over an electric light bulb in order to protect it, decorate it, or to make the light less harsh. EG *The silk lampshades matched the curtains.* N COUNT

lance /lɑ:ns/, **lances, lancing, lanced**. 1 If you **lance** a boil on someone's body, you pierce it with a sharp instrument in order to let the pus drain out; a V+O

technical term in medicine. EG *The doctor lanced the abscess.*
2 A **lance** is a long spear used in former times, especially by soldiers on horseback. N COUNT ⇑ weapon

lancet /lɑːnsɪ²t/, **lancets**. A **lancet** is a small knife with a sharp point and two sharp edges. It is used by doctors for cutting people's skin. N COUNT

land /lænd/, **lands, landing, landed**. 1 **Land** is an area of ground, especially one that is used for a particular purpose such as farming or building. EG *...five acres of land... It's good agricultural land... I'm looking for a piece of land to build on.* N UNCOUNT
2 If you refer to someone's **land** or **lands**, you mean an area of land which they own. EG *The wife lost her dowry and her lands.* N COUNT : WITH POSS, SING = PL
3 **Lands** of a particular type are large areas of land which are similar to one another because they have important geographical or climatic features in common. EG *Too much rain is the problem of the equatorial lands... In this zone lie the dry lands.* N PLURAL + SUPP = regions
4 If you talk about **the land**, you are referring to farming and the way of life in farming areas, as opposed to in the cities. EG *There is no work to be had on the land.* N SING : *the*+N
5 **Land** or **the land** refers to the part of the world that is solid, dry ground rather than sea or air. EG *We turned away from land and headed out to sea... ...a river that has cut deep into the land... Our armies have triumphed on land.* N UNCOUNT, OR N SING : *the*+N
6 You use **land** to refer generally to a country, for example when you do not mean any particular country, when you are talking about an imaginary or ideal country, or when you are talking about your own country in an emotional or patriotic way; a rather literary use. EG *We were lost in a foreign land... ...a land where there is never any rain... Australia is the land of opportunities... ...throughout the length and breadth of the land.* N COUNT : USU + SUPP
7 You sometimes use **land** when you want to refer to all the ideas and attitudes that are associated with a particular subject or view of the world; a literary use. EG *We seem to be in fantasy land... ...the land of true love.* N UNCOUNT + SUPP = world
8 If someone or something **lands** somewhere, 8.1 they come down to the ground after moving through the air or falling. EG *...bombs landing further down the strip... The last man slipped and landed in the water.* 8.2 they arrive there after a journey by air, or sometimes by sea. EG *His plane lands at six-thirty... They would land at the airfield in Wiltshire.* V : USU + A ⇑ arrive; V : USU + A = touch down
9 To **land** people or goods somewhere means to successfully unload them there at the end of a journey, especially by ship. EG *...small ships sailing from Florida to land arms and combatants... The catch had been landed at Grimsby... ...the goal of landing a man on the moon.* V + O : USU + A
10 If you **land** in an unpleasant situation or place or something **lands** you in it, you are placed in it, often through no fault of your own; an informal use. EG *That would have landed him in jail... We have landed ourselves in this primitive society.* V-ERG + A
11 If something **lands** somewhere, it arrives there unexpectedly and causes problems; an informal use. EG *The report landed on the desk of General Guibaud... They must stop the expected surplus from landing on the market.* V + A
12 If you **land** someone with a difficult situation or person, you cause them to have to deal with the difficulties involved; an informal use. EG *You landed us with that awful Hector... ...a clergyman landed with a rectory the size of a mansion.* V + O + A *(with)* = saddle
13 If you **land** a fish, you succeed in catching it and getting it out of the water. EG *After you've landed your fish remove the hook very carefully.* V + O
14 If you **land** something that is difficult to get and that many people want, you are successful in getting it; an informal use. EG *She has just landed herself a job... A friend of mine landed a three-roomed flat.* V + O, OR V + O (NG/REFL) + O ⇑ obtain
15 If you **land** a blow or punch, you succeed in hitting someone. EG *The Cuban boxer is landing many more blows than his opponent.* V + O
16 If someone **lands on** their **feet**, they are lucky and successful after being in a difficult situation. PHR : VB INFLECTS
17 See also **landed, landing**. • **the lie of the land**: see **lie**. • to **see how the land lies**: see **lie**.

land up. If you **land up** in a place or situation, you arrive in it after a long journey or at the end of a long series of events; an informal expression. EG *She landed up in Rome... ...social misfits who landed up teaching English.* PHRASAL VB : V + ADV, USU + A/-ING

landau /lændɔː/, **landaus**. A **landau** is a covered four-wheeled carriage pulled by four horses and used especially in the nineteenth century. N COUNT

landed /lændɪ²d/ means possessing or including a large amount of land, especially when it has belonged to the same family for several generations. EG *...a family of landed gentry... ...the huge landed estate.* ADJ CLASSIF : ATTRIB

landfall /lændfɔːl/, **landfalls**. **Landfall** is the first bit of land which you see or arrive at after a voyage at sea. EG *...four more days without landfall, water running short, no fresh meat... We shouted like seamen making landfall.* N UNCOUNT/ COUNT

landing /lændɪŋ/, **landings**. A **landing** is 1 an area in a house or other building which is at the top of a staircase and has rooms leading off it. EG *I switched on the light on the landing... ...the first-floor landing.* N COUNT
2 the act of bringing an aircraft or spacecraft down to the ground. EG *We had to make an emergency landing... ...a plane coming in for a landing... ...a landing on the moon.* N COUNT/ UNCOUNT 3 the act of unloading troops in a place as part of a military invasion or operation. EG *...paratroop landings... They made a landing at Suvla Bay... ...the Allied landings in France.* N COUNT/ UNCOUNT 4 a place with a wooden platform where boats stop to let people get on or off or to load or unload goods. EG *You take the bus up to the landing at twelve-thirty... Too bad you didn't come down to the landing that Saturday.* N COUNT = jetty

landing craft; also spelled with a hyphen. **Landing craft** is both the singular and the plural form. A **landing craft** is a small boat designed for the landing of troops and equipment on the shore; a technical term. EG *...slow-moving landing-craft, heavily loaded with troops and supplies.* N COUNT

landing stage, landing stages; also spelled with a hyphen. A **landing stage** is a wooden platform used for landing goods and passengers from a boat. EG *...holiday houses, each with its own landing stage.* N COUNT

landing strip, landing strips; also spelled with a hyphen. A **landing strip** is a long flat piece of land from which aircraft can take off and land, especially one used only by private or military aircraft. N COUNT = airstrip

landlady /lændleɪdi¹/, **landladies**. A **landlady** is 1 a woman who allows you to live or stay in a room in her house, or in a house or flat that she owns, in return for payment of rent; also used of the wife of a landlord. EG *Ellen gave the landlady a cheque... His landlady wasn't there.* N COUNT 2 a woman who owns or runs a pub, or the wife of a man who owns or runs it. EG *The landlady refused to serve him.* N COUNT ⇑ licensee

landless /lændlɪ²s/. Someone who is **landless** is prevented from owning the land that they farm, usually by large landowners or by the economic system. EG *...landless agricultural labourers...* ▸ The **landless** is used to refer to people who are landless. EG *It raised expectations among the landless.* ◊ **landlessness**. EG *...an increase in landlessness and poverty.* ADJ CLASSIF ≠ landowning; ▸ N PLURAL : *the*+N; ◊ N UNCOUNT

landlocked /lændlɒkt/; also spelled with a hyphen. A country that is **landlocked** is surrounded by other countries and does not have its own ports or sea coast. EG *Paraguay is landlocked.* ADJ CLASSIF

landlord /lændlɔːd/, **landlords**. 1 A **landlord** is 1 a man who allows you to live or stay in a room in his house, or in a flat or house that he owns, in return for payment of rent; also used of the husband of a landlady. EG *Do you pay your landlord a fixed charge for heating and lighting?* N COUNT ⇑ householder 2 a person who owns a lot of land and allows other people to use parts of it for farming, in return for money or a share of the crops which are grown. EG *They do fifteen days' free labour a year on the landlords' fields, over and above their rents... Local landlords drove them off their plots.* N COUNT ⇑ owner • See also **absentee landlord**. 3 a man who owns or runs a pub, or the husband of a woman who owns or runs it. EG *The landlord himself was behind the bar.* N COUNT ⇑ licensee

landlubber /lændlʌbə/, **landlubbers**. A **landlubber** is a person who does not like travelling by boat or ship, and is not knowledgeable about the sea; a rather old-fashioned word. N COUNT

landmark /lændmɑːk/, **landmarks**. A **landmark** is 1 a building or feature of the land which is easily noticed and can be used to judge your position or the position of other buildings or features. EG *...a little fig* N COUNT *tree which offered a rare landmark... The Chamberlain tower is a landmark visible for miles... ...this well known Australian landmark.* **2** an event, idea, or stage in a process which people think is very important and different and will be remembered for a long time in the future. EG *The discovery of penicillin was a landmark in medicine... ...landmarks on the road to democratic self-government.* N COUNT = milestone

land mass, land masses. A **land mass** is a very large area of land such as a continent. EG *The air over the great land mass heats up and rises... ...the Eurasian land mass.* N COUNT

landmine /lændmaɪn/, **landmines.** A **landmine** is an explosive device which is placed on or under the ground and explodes when a person or vehicle touches it. N COUNT

landowner /lændəʊnə/, **landowners.** A **landowner** is a person who owns land, especially a large amount of land. EG *...a rich landowner who had a house near the temple... Banks lend to the big landowners at much lower rates... ...conflicts between peasants and landowners.* N COUNT

landowning /lændəʊnɪŋ/ is used to describe people who own a lot of land, especially when they are considered as a group within society. EG *The landowning class opposed the spread of education... ...political, bureaucratic, and landowning elements.* ADJ CLASSIF : ATTRIB

land reform is a change in the system of land ownership, especially when it involves giving land to the people who actually farm it and taking it away from people who own large areas for profit. EG *They formed themselves into trade-union style associations to press for land reform... ...land reform laws.* N UNCOUNT

land registry, land registries. A **land registry** is a government office where records are kept about each area of land in a country or region, its exact size and location, its owner, etc. N COUNT

Land-Rover, Land-Rovers. **Land-Rover** is a trademark for a strong four-wheeled motor vehicle which can travel over rough or steep ground, and is used especially by farmers and other people who work in rural areas. N COUNT

landscape /lændskeɪp/, **landscapes, landscaping, landscaped.** **1** A **landscape** is **1.1** everything you can see when you look across an area of land, including hills, rivers, buildings, trees, and plants. EG *...the beauty of the Welsh landscape... ...an industrial landscape... ...a landscape of lush green meadows... Small bushes dot the landscape.* N COUNT ⇑ scenery

1.2 all the features that are important in a particular subject or situation, and which give it a unique character. EG *They seemed a permanent part of the pop landscape... ...the landscape of love... ...the landscape of Marcel's mind.* N COUNT+SUPP ⇑ environment **1.3** a painting which shows a scene in the countryside. EG *...a beautiful moonlit landscape by Atkinson Grimshaw... She painted landscapes and portraits.* N COUNT

2 If someone **landscapes** an area of land, they design and alter it in order to produce a pleasing, artistic effect, for example by creating different levels, adding streams or ponds, and planting trees and bushes. EG *He landscaped the park forty-five years ago... There are a few carefully landscaped gardens.* V+O ⇑ plan

◇ **landscaping.** EG *No London park has more beautiful flowerbeds or landscaping.* ◇ N UNCOUNT

landscape architect, landscape architects. A **landscape architect** is a person who designs gardens or parks so that they look more attractive. N COUNT

landscape gardener, landscape gardeners. A **landscape gardener** is the same as a landscape architect. N COUNT

landslide /lændslaɪd/, **landslides.** A **landslide** is **1** a victory in an election in which a person or political party gets far more votes or seats than their opponents. EG *Benn lost his seat in the landslide of 1931... Taylor should win by a landslide... ...a landslide victory.* N COUNT ⇑ win **2** a large amount of earth and rocks falling down a cliff or the side of a mountain. EG *...clinging to the walls like a climber in a landslide... The slightest noise might set off a landslide.* N COUNT = avalanche

landslip /lændslɪp/, **landslips.** A **landslip** is a small movement of soil and rocks down a slope. EG *A landslip had made the house unsafe.* N COUNT

landward /lændwəd/ means nearest to the land or facing the land, in contrast to the sea. EG *...the cottage with its recent additions on the landward side.* ADJ CLASSIF : ATTRIB

lane /leɪn/, **lanes.** A **lane** is **1** a narrow road, especially in the country; also used in the names of streets in towns and cities. EG *She turned and went back down the lane... ...over the small bridges, down narrow lanes... ...Park Lane.* N COUNT : ALSO IN NAMES AFTER N **2** a part of a main road that is marked by the edge of the road and a painted line, or two rows of painted lines, which tell drivers where to drive. EG *He was in the wrong lane... He changed lanes to make a left turn... ...bus lanes.* N COUNT ▸ used of the cars in a particular lane. EG *The other lane seemed to be rather held up.* **3** a part of a race course or a swimming pool that is marked by two lines or ropes. Competitors must run or swim in the particular lanes that they have been told to. EG *The first 400 metres is run in lanes.* N COUNT = track **4** a route that is frequently used by aircraft or ships and which private or small vehicles must not use. EG *The pilot was way outside any safe lane... That will help to keep the sea lanes open.* N COUNT

lang. is an abbreviation for 'language'; used especially as a part of the name of subjects at school and university. EG *Eng. Lang. and Lit.*

language /læŋgwɪdʒ/, **languages.** **1** A **language** is **1.1** a system of communication which consists of a set of sounds and written symbols which are used by the people of a particular country or region for talking or writing in. EG *...the history of the English language... ...a foreign language... I can speak six languages... They often work with women who speak their own language.* N COUNT = tongue **1.2** a particular set of words or symbols that a computer will accept and which can therefore be used in writing computer programs or giving instructions to the computer. EG *...higher level languages such as Fortran and Basic.* N COUNT ⇑ code

2 If you talk about **the language**, you mean all the words which are used in a particular language at a particular time. EG *New words stream rapidly into the language... Within a month the phrase would be part of the language.* N SING : *the*+N

3 Language is **3.1** the study of the words and grammar of a particular language; used especially in schools and universities. EG *The first part of the course is language... ...one literature and one language paper.* N UNCOUNT **3.2** the words or the type of words used by a particular group of people, for example scientists or politicians, or in a particular type of activity. EG *...the language of sociology... ...the formal prose of official language.* N UNCOUNT+SUPP ⇑ vocabulary = jargon **3.3** rude words and swearing; used when you are telling someone not to be rude. EG *'Albert,' she said. 'Your language!'... There's too much bad language on TV... 'Watch your language,' the soldier said.* N UNCOUNT : USU DETPOSS/MOD+N **3.4** the ability to use words in order to communicate, which human beings have and animals do not. EG *...help teachers to understand how children acquire language... Gestures are more basic, are deeper than language.* N UNCOUNT **3.5** the style in which something is written or spoken. EG *Congreve's language is wonderful... I admire the directness of the language.* N UNCOUNT **3.6** signs, actions, or movements which have special meanings in particular situations, or for particular groups such as deaf people. EG *...the language of love-making.* ● See also **body language, sign language.** N UNCOUNT+SUPP

4 If you say that someone **talks** or **speaks the same language, talks** your **language**, etc, you mean that they have similar ideas or opinions to you and you can understand the way they think and behave; used in informal English. EG *They both talked the same language.* PHR : VB INFLECTS

language laboratory, language laboratories; also referred to as a **language lab** in informal English. A **language laboratory** is a room in a college or school in which people can learn to speak languages or improve their knowledge of languages by listening to tape recordings, recording their own voices, and having their mistakes corrected. EG *Our institution had no language laboratory of its own... Do you encourage language lab work?* N COUNT

languid /læŋgwɪd/. Someone who is **languid** shows little energy or interest and is very slow and casual in their movements, often in a rather attractive or affected way; a literary word. EG *She lay on the rug, making every effort to look languid and bored... ...a languid wave of the hand.* ADJ QUALIT = languorous, lazy ◇ **languidly.** EG *The waitress looked up languidly.* ◇ ADV = lazily

languish /læŋgwɪʃ/, **languishes, languishing, languished.** **1** If someone **languishes**, they are V : USU+A forced to remain and suffer in an unpleasant place or situation. EG *These men have never been convicted of anything, yet they languish in these cells... A few rich people enjoyed western consumer lifestyles while the majority languished in poverty.*

2 If something **languishes**, it is not successful, often because of a lack of effort or because of a large number of difficulties. EG *The project languished and never rose above its foundations... The case languished for four years... Meanwhile, more conventional fashions languished on the racks.* V ⇑ fail

languishing /læŋgwɪʃɪŋ/. Someone who is **languishing** is relaxed and lazy, often in a rather attractive way. EG *...pictures of actors and actresses in languishing attitudes.* ADJ CLASSIF = languid

languor /læŋgə/ is a feeling of not having any energy or interest, often a pleasant feeling; a literary word. EG *As he watched her doing this, a most delicious languor rippled through him like a warm tide... Dizziness, headaches, and languor afflicted her all day... ...the humid languor of that Manhattan evening.* N UNCOUNT = indolence

languorous /læŋgərəs/. If you describe something as **languorous**, you mean that it is lazy, relaxed, and not energetic, usually in a pleasant way. EG *...Helen's languorous waves of the hand... ...the perfect, languorous, endless hot summer.* ADJ CLASSIF

lank /læŋk/. If someone's hair is **lank**, it is long and perhaps rather greasy and it lies or hangs in a dull and unattractive way. EG *Her lank, sandy locks dangled limply about her neck.* ADJ QUALIT

lanky /læŋki[1]/, **lankier, lankiest**. Someone who is **lanky** is tall and thin and moves rather awkwardly. EG *He shifted his lanky frame in the chair... She was transformed from a lanky kid into a voluptuous young woman.* ADJ QUALIT = gangling

lantern /læntən/, **lanterns**. A **lantern** is a lamp used in former times. It consists of a metal frame with glass sides, an oil lamp or candle inside, and a handle on top for carrying it. • See also **magic lantern**. N COUNT ⇑ light

lanyard /lænjəd/, **lanyards**. A **lanyard** is a piece of thick string, usually with a whistle or knife attached to it and worn around someone's neck as part of a uniform. EG *...sailor dress complete with a lanyard.* N COUNT

Laotian /laʊʃɪən/, **Laotians**. 1 Something that is **Laotian** comes from or concerns Laos or its people, culture, or language. EG *The track ran along the Laotian border.* ADJ CLASSIF

2 A **Laotian** is a person who comes from Laos. N COUNT

lap /læp/, **laps, lapping, lapped**. 1 Your **lap** is the flat, slightly hollow area that is formed by your thighs when you are sitting down. EG *Their youngest child was asleep in her lap... The man was sitting in a chair with his hat on his lap... They folded their hands in their laps.* N COUNT : POSS+N

2 If you say that someone lives **in the lap of luxury**, you mean that they are living in conditions of great comfort and wealth. PHR : USED AS AN A

3 If you say that a situation is **in the lap of the gods**, you mean that its success or failure depends entirely on luck or on things that are outside your control. PHR : USED AS AN A

4 In a race, a **lap** is when a competitor goes once round a course or track. EG *The race consists of six laps of the track... He put in a spurt at the beginning of the eighth lap... Russell Spence has just set a new lap record.* • See also **lap of honour**. N COUNT = circuit

5 If you **lap** another competitor in a race, you go past them while they are still on the previous lap. EG *We used to go at a cracking pace, lapping all the others several times.* V+O ⇑ overtake

6 A **lap** of a long journey is a particular part of it, between one place where you stop and the next. EG *She had been silent during the last lap–two hundred miles of mountain roads.* N COUNT+SUPP = stage

7 When water **laps** against the shore, the side of a boat, or something else, it touches it gently and makes a soft sound; a rather literary use. EG *Waves lapped against the side of the boat... ...water lapping at the bridge.* ◇ **lapping**. EG *...the gentle, rhythmic lapping of the sea.* V+A, OR V+O = wash ◇ N UNCOUNT

8 When a cat or other animal **laps** a drink, it uses short, quick movements of the tongue to flick liquid up into its mouth. EG *The little cat was lapping at a saucer of milk on the path.* V+A, OR V+O

lap up. 1 When a cat or other animal **laps up** a drink, it drinks it up very eagerly. EG *The cat was lapping up the milk as if it had not been fed for days.* PHRASAL VB : V+O+ADV

2 If someone **laps up** information or attention, they accept it eagerly, often when it is not really true or sincere. EG *He continued to eat, lapping up the attention... It was a lie, but millions of newspaper readers lapped it up.* PHRASAL VB : V+O+ADV = soak up

lapel /lə[3]pel/, **lapels**. The **lapels** of a jacket or coat are the two top parts at the front that are folded back on each side and join on to the collar. EG *There were gravy stains on his lapel... He held him by the lapels and shook him... ...a lapel badge.* N COUNT

lapis lazuli /læpɪs læzjə[4]laɪ/ is a bright blue semi-precious stone, used especially in making jewellery. N UNCOUNT ⇑ gem

lap of honour, laps of honour. A **lap of honour** is a slow run or drive around a race track by the winner of a race in order to receive the applause of the crowd. N COUNT

lapse /læps/, **lapses, lapsing, lapsed**. 1 A **lapse** is 1.1 a moment or instance of bad behaviour, especially by somebody who usually behaves well. EG *...the unfortunate lapses of your male colleagues... I intended to make up for this lapse in manners at the next party.* N COUNT = slip 1.2 a moment of forgetfulness or lack of concentration which can cause you to make a mistake. EG *The actors had skilful ways of covering their lapses of memory... ...a lapse of attention by the spectator.* N COUNT+SUPP = slip

2 If you **lapse** into a quiet or inactive state, you stop talking or being active. EG *He sat down and lapsed into an unhappy silence... She lapsed into thought... She lapsed back into sleep.* V+A *(into)* = fall

3 If you **lapse** into a particular way of speaking or behaving, you start speaking or behaving in a way that other people find unacceptable; used showing disapproval. EG *He keeps lapsing into jargon... Students tend to lapse into technical discussions... He will lapse into a state of despair.* V+A *(into)* = slip

4 A **lapse** is also a period of time that is long enough for a situation to change or for people to have a different opinion about it. EG *He was not conscious of the time lapse... The law required a twenty-year lapse before immunity from prosecution... After a certain lapse of time it would be safe for Daisy to return.* ▸ used as a verb. EG *Hours lapsed between each phone call.* N SING WITH DET = interval ▸ V = pass

5 If a situation, relationship, or legal contract **lapses**, it is allowed to end or to become invalid rather than being continued, renewed, or extended. EG *...traditions which had never lapsed... He allowed his membership of the union to lapse... American goodwill has not lapsed in two hundred years.* V ⇑ stop ≠ continue

6 If a member of a particular religion **lapses**, he or she no longer believes in it or follow its rules and practices. EG *I lapsed many years ago, I'm afraid.* ◇ **lapsed**. EG *...a lapsed Catholic.* V = lose faith ◇ ADJ CLASSIF

lapwing /læpwɪŋ/, **lapwings**. A **lapwing** is a small bird with dark green feathers, a white breast, and a tuft of feathers on its head. Lapwings live mainly in fields and on moorland. N COUNT = peewit

larceny /lɑːsɪni[1]/ is the crime of theft; a technical term in law, formerly used in British English and still used in American English. EG *The youth was charged with larceny... ...petty larceny.* N UNCOUNT = burglary

larch /lɑːtʃ/, **larches**. The form **larch** can also be used as the plural. A **larch** is a coniferous tree with needle-shaped leaves which it loses in winter. N COUNT

lard /lɑːd/, **lards, larding, larded**. 1 **Lard** is soft white fat obtained from pigs and used in cooking. EG *...half a pound of lard... ...chips fried in lard.* ▸ used as a verb. EG *Lard it well or marinate it in oil and vinegar.* N UNCOUNT = dripping ▸ V+O ⇑ cover

2 If you **lard** your speech or writing with particular types of words, you put them in excessively or unnecessarily; used showing disapproval. EG *Why do you lard your conversation with bits of slang?... His writings were still liberally larded with brand names.* V+O+A *(with)* = pepper

larder /lɑːdə/, **larders**. A **larder** is a room or cupboard in a house in which food is kept. EG *...a well-stocked larder... ...an old-fashioned larder with marble shelves.* • If someone **raids the larder**, they take food from it and eat it without permission; an informal expression. EG *They promised never to raid the larder again.* N COUNT • PHR : VB INFLECTS

large /lɑːdʒ/, **larger, largest**. 1 Something that is **large** is greater in size than usual or average. EG *He* ADJ QUALIT *had large black eyes... ...large areas of Asia... ...a large house overgrown with brambles... ...a large and well equipped army... How large is it?*

2 If you describe someone as **large**, you mean that they are tall, with broad shoulders and a wide chest, and often fatter than average. EG *...the electrician, a large, red-faced individual... ...one of those large, bossy women.* ADJ QUALIT

3 A **large** amount is more than the average amount. EG *She made a very large amount of money... ...drugs taken in large quantities... He claimed a large share of the credit.* ADJ QUALIT = considerable

4 A **large** group of people or things contains many of them. EG *...a large number of people... ...large families with four or more children... ...a large wine list.* ADJ QUALIT

5 A **large** organization or business does a lot of work or commercial activity and employs a lot of people. EG *...a large advertising company... ...British Rail and other large organizations... ...the largest employer of industrial labour.* ADJ QUALIT = big

6 **Large** is used to describe a particular size of a product, such as an item of food or clothing, which is sold in several sizes; used especially on labels and in advertising. EG *Get the large size... ...half a dozen large envelopes... I bought her a large-sized bottle.* ADJ CLASSIF : ATTRIB ⇑ big

7 **Large** is also used to describe something that is important or serious because it concerns or affects a lot of different people or situations. EG *...the world's problems, large and small... The changes will not be very large... That's such a large question.* ADJ QUALIT = vast

8 **By and large** is used to indicate that a statement is not completely true, but is mostly true. EG *Full employment was by and large achieved... By and large, the broadcasters were free to treat this material as they saw fit.* PHR : USED AS ADV SEN = on the whole

9 **at large. 9.1** You use **at large** to indicate that you are talking about most or all of the people in a group. EG *...their attitude to the world at large... There has been unrest in the country at large, and in particular in five major cities.* PHR AFTER N = in general **9.2** If you say that someone or something that is dangerous is **at large**, you mean that they are moving about freely or are not under control and may cause harm. EG *There were three convicts still at large... The virus is still at large... Was that evil influence still at large?* PHR : USED AS AN A = on the loose

10 If you say that someone or something is present or suddenly appears **as large as life**, you are indicating that their presence or sudden appearance is unexpected and surprising; an informal expression. EG *There he was, as large as life.* PHR : USED AS AN A

11 If you say that someone or something is **larger than life**, you mean that they appear or behave in a way that seems more important or exaggerated than usual. EG *The central character is a larger than life, cantankerous New Englander... ...a larger-than-life version of our present society.* ADJ CLASSIF ⇑ extreme

12 ● **to a large extent**: see **extent**. ● **to loom large**: see **loom**. ● **in large measure**: see **measure**. ● **in large part**: see **part**.

largely /lɑːdʒli¹/ is used **1** to say that a statement is not completely true but is mostly true. EG *The evidence shows them to be largely correct... Her work is largely confined to the cinema... His support came largely from outside the Party.* ADV = mainly **2** to introduce the main reason for a particular event or situation. EG *We were there largely because of the girls... He was acquitted, largely on the evidence of a tape recording... The Prime Minister's mind was largely made up for him by the persistence of the Lords.* ADV, OR ADV SEN = chiefly

large-scale. 1 A **large-scale** action or event happens over a very wide area or involves a lot of people or things. EG *...large-scale forest fires... ...the end of large-scale hostilities in Europe... The large-scale producer can usually undercut his smaller competitors.* ● **on a large scale**: see **scale**. ADJ QUALIT : ATTRIB

2 A **large-scale** map or diagram represents a small area of land, a house, etc on a scale that is large enough to enable small details to be shown. ADJ QUALIT : ATTRIB

largesse /lɑːdʒes/; also spelled **largess. Largesse** is kindness or generosity, especially when this involves giving more money than was expected or asked for; a formal word. EG *Harold's largesse did not equal Lord Nuffield's £50,000... I was going to give him five dollars, but thought the largesse might be misconstrued.* N UNCOUNT

largish /lɑːdʒɪʃ/ means fairly large. EG *...a largish man... ...a largish town.* ADJ CLASSIF

lark /lɑːk/, **larks, larking, larked. 1** A **lark** is a small brown bird that has a pleasant song, which it usually sings while it is hovering high above the ground. N COUNT = skylark

2 If you say that someone is **up with the lark**, you mean that they get out of bed very early in the morning. PHR : USED AS AN A

3 In informal British English, a **lark** is also **3.1** an action that is naughty, unconventional, or daring, but also amusing or funny. EG *For a lark, she walked in and asked his name... She was treating it all as a great lark... ...boyish larks... What a lark!* N COUNT = joke **3.2** an activity or job that you think is foolish or unnecessary. EG *What do you think of this Civil Defence lark?... How long have you been doing this teaching lark, then?* N COUNT : USU MOD+N

lark about. If you **lark about**, you enjoy yourself by doing silly or naughty things; used in informal British English. EG *...a lovely holiday, sunbathing and larking about... ...their favourite activity, larking about at the Club.* PHRASAL VB : V+ADV = muck about

larva /lɑːvə/, **larvae** /lɑːviː/. A **larva** is an insect at the stage of its life when it looks like a short, fat worm. This is the stage after it has developed from an egg and before it changes into its adult form as a fly, ant, beetle, etc. EG *The larva hatches out and lives in the soil... ...dragonfly larvae.* N COUNT = grub

larval /lɑːvəˡl/ means concerning insect larvae or in the state of being an insect larva. ADJ CLASSIF

laryngitis /lærɪndʒaɪtɪs/ is an infection of the throat in which your larynx becomes swollen and painful, making it difficult for you to speak. N UNCOUNT ⇑ illness

larynx /lærɪŋks/, **larynxes**. The form **larynges** is also used for the plural in more formal or technical English. Your **larynx** is the top part of the passage that leads from your throat to your lungs and contains your vocal cords; a technical term in anatomy and medicine. N COUNT = voice box

lascivious /ləsɪvɪəs/. If you describe someone or something as **lascivious**, you mean that they express a strong desire for sex or show a strong interest in it; used showing disapproval. EG *He wanted to protect Frances from unscrupulous or lascivious men... There was nothing lascivious in his caresses... ...books of lascivious poetry.* ◇ **lasciviously**. EG *She grinned back lasciviously.* ADJ QUALIT = lewd ◇ ADV WITH VB

laser /leɪzə/, **lasers**. A **laser** is **1** a narrow beam of concentrated light produced by a special machine. It is used for cutting very hard materials, in surgery, for telecommunications, etc. EG *...experiments with laser weapons... ...a laser beam would cut into it... ...to trap solar energy using laser technology.* N COUNT **2** a machine that produces a laser beam. EG *...from machine tools to lasers.* N COUNT ⇑ device

lash /læʃ/, **lashes, lashing, lashed. 1** Your **lashes** are the hairs that grow on the edge of your upper and lower eyelids. EG *He had nice sad eyes with beautiful lashes... Tear drops fell from her long lashes.* N PLURAL = eyelashes

2 A **lash** is **2.1** the thin strip of leather at the end of a whip. EG *He gasped as the lash hit him... ...cracking the lash of his long whip expertly over their horns.* N COUNT **2.2** a blow with a whip, especially a blow on someone's back as a punishment. EG *...a public flogging of thirty-nine lashes across his bare back.* N COUNT = stroke **2.3** a cruel or unpleasant way of speaking. EG *...the lash of Sally's tongue... Stryker's voice was a lash.* N SING WITH DET

3 If someone **lashes** another person, they hit that person with a whip. EG *They snatched up whips and lashed the backs of those who had fallen.* V+O = flog

4 If someone **lashes** someone else or **lashes** into them, they speak very angrily to them, criticizing them or scolding them. EG *They listened to Jimmie lashing into the extremists... I lashed the amazed trio with my tongue.* V+O, OR V+A *(into)* = lay into

5 If something such as an animal's tail **lashes** or if the animal **lashes** it, it moves very fast and violently. EG *The tail lashed briefly... His foot lashed up and caught the man in the belly... It lashes its tail in frenzy.* V-ERG

6 If wind, rain, or water **lashes** someone or something, it hits them violently; a literary use. EG *High winds lashed the branches of the elm... The waves lashed its base... The rain lashed down, so we went into the pub.* V+O, OR V+A

7 If you **lash** one thing to another, you tie them firmly together. EG *We lashed our boats together... A* V+O+A *(to/together)*

fisherman brought one in, lashed to the side of his canoe.

lash out. 1 If you **lash out**, you attempt to hit someone quickly and violently with a weapon or with your hands or feet. EG *When cornered, they lash out with savage kicks.* PHRASAL VB : V+ADV = hit out

2 If you **lash out** at or against someone, you suddenly speak to them very angrily or cruelly, criticizing or scolding them. EG *I lashed out at Kurt, calling him every name under the sun... Harris lashed out against the Committee.* PHRASAL VB : V+ADV, USU+A *(at/against)* ⇑ attack

lashing /læʃɪŋ/, **lashings**. 1 A **lashing** is 1.1 a rope or cable used to tie something firmly to something else. EG *They began to remove the lashings from the deck cargo.* N COUNT : USU PL ⇑ fastening 1.2 a punishment in which a person is hit with a whip. EG *Some of them never recovered from the shock of these lashings.* N COUNT = flogging 1.3 a cruel and angry speech, criticizing or scolding someone or something. EG *She was determined to give him a lashing with her tongue.* N COUNT

2 **Lashings** of something means a large quantity or amount of it; used in informal English. EG *We had scones, and lashings of cream.* N PART : PLURAL = masses

lass /læs/, **lasses**. A **lass** is a young woman or girl; used mainly in Scottish and Northern English. EG *She'd worked on the farm as a lass... ...lads and lasses.* N COUNT : ALSO VOC = lassie

lassie /læsi[1]/, **lassies**. A **lassie** is a young woman or girl; an informal or affectionate word used mainly in Scottish English. N COUNT : ALSO VOC

lassitude /læsɪtju:d/ is a state of tiredness, laziness, or lack of interest; a formal word. EG *...a lassitude that Simon had felt for some time... ...symptoms of irritability and profound lassitude.* N UNCOUNT = lethargy

lasso /læsəʊ, læsu:/, **lassoes, lassoing, lassoed**; also spelled **lassoo**. 1 A **lasso** is a long rope with a noose at one end, used especially by cowboys for catching cattle and horses. N COUNT

2 If you **lasso** an animal such as a cow or horse, you catch it by throwing the noose of a lasso round its neck and pulling it tight. V+O

last /lɑ:st/, **lasts, lasting, lasted**. 1 The **last** event, person, or thing is 1.1 the most recent one. EG *I went to a party last night... ...the last four years... ...last Saturday's edition of 'The Times'... The grain from the last harvest was gone... Thanks for your last letter... We must act more effectively in the next decade than we have in the last.* ORDINAL ⇑ previous 1.2 the item on a list or the person or thing in a group that was mentioned most recently. EG *This last group poses a serious threat... This last, it must be said, was a reasonable point... That is a very difficult question, that last one.* ORDINAL 1.3 the final part of something. EG *I saw the last five minutes of it.* ORDINAL 1.4 the one that comes after all the others in a list or set of things in a fixed order. EG *He missed the last bus... The last volume was dated 1915... The last on the list was Potter... How did Mary do in the high jump?-She came last.* ORDINAL 1.5 the one that is at the end of a row of similar things or people. EG *...the last rungs of the fire-escape... ...the last classroom along that passage... Key West is the last of a 100-mile string of islands.* ORDINAL 1.6 the only one that remains out of a group of things or people or the only part of something that remains. EG *She wanted to get rid of the last traces of make-up... Otto drank the last of the brandy... 'Are there any more apples?'-'No, that was the last'.* ORDINAL

2 You can use **last** to emphasize that you definitely do not want to do something or that something is very unlikely to happen or be true. EG *The last thing I want to do is offend you... You're the last person I'd want to talk to about this... I would be the last to suggest that businessmen are always right.* ORDINAL

3 If something **last** happened on a particular occasion, it has not happened since then. EG *They last saw their homeland nine years ago... It's a long time since we met last.* ADV WITH VB

4 If something is done, dealt with, or happens **last**, it is done, dealt with, or happens after everything else has been done or after everyone else has done it. EG *He added the milk last... The grey-haired man went after him, and I went last.* ADV WITH VB

5 You use **the last** to indicate that something never happened again or no longer existed after a particular time in the past, or will never happen or exist again in the future. EG *That was the last I ever saw of Northcliffe... I hope we've heard the last of that idea... That was the last of the affair.* PHR : USU USED AS C

6 If you are the **last** to do something, nobody does it after you. EG *Hooper was the last to leave... Last to leave was Prince Andrew.* ORDINAL + *to*-INF

7 If something **lasts** or **lasts** for a particular length of time, 7.1 it continues to exist or happen for the length of time indicated. EG *His speech lasted for exactly fourteen minutes... Her fifth marriage lasted only a month... The alliance did not last long... Profits are as high as ever. It won't last.* V : USU+A 7.2 it continues to be in good condition, to work, or to survive for the length of time indicated. EG *A fresh pepper lasts about three weeks... Those components are kept cool so that they last... You wouldn't last two rounds against him.* V : USU+A

8 If a quantity of something **lasts** for a particular period of time, there is enough of it for someone to use. EG *A cheap box of toothpowder lasts two years... The curry lasted me for two nights... He had only £8 left to last him till he reached Bury.* V+A, OR V+O+A

9 See also **lasting**.

10 The word **last** is also used in the following expressions. 10.1 When you talk about **the year before last, the election before last, the leader before last**, etc, you are referring to the period of time, event, person, or thing that happened or came immediately before the most recent one in a series. EG *He had pleurisy the winter before last... The President before last had started the reforms.* PHR 10.2 If you add **'the last I heard', 'the last she heard', etc** before or after a statement, you are indicating that it is the most recent piece of information available. EG *The last I heard they were having difficulty in programming it... The last I heard of you, you were still living in Philadelphia.* PHR 10.3 If you tell someone that they **haven't heard the last of** someone or something, you are suggesting that a situation has not ended and that further related events are likely to occur; often used as a warning or threat. EG *We haven't heard the last of Newby... You haven't heard the last of this, I can tell you!* PHR : VB INFLECTS 10.4 If you **see the last of** someone or something, you do not expect to see or deal with them again. EG *You'll be glad to see the last of me.* PHR : VB INFLECTS 10.5 If you say that you will do something **if it is the last thing** you **do**, you are emphasizing your intention to do it, even though it may be difficult or have serious consequences for you. EG *Kurt said he would get me a dog if it was the last thing he did... I'll kill you, J.R., if it's the last thing I do!* PHR : USED AS ADV SEN ⇑ definitely 10.6 If you say that something happens **last thing**, you mean that it happens at the end of the day or at the end of a particular period of time. EG *...the sink where we all had to wash in the mornings and last thing at night... Some people are more energetic on Monday morning than they are last thing Friday afternoon.* PHR : USED AS AN A 10.7 If you say that something goes on happening **to the last**, you mean that it happens throughout an event or someone's lifetime. EG *Judy gave birth to a son (insisting to the last 'there isn't a baby').* PHR : USED AS AN A 10.8 If you say that something happens **at the last**, you mean that it happens at the end of an event or activity; a formal expression. EG *The judges had chosen Rushdie at the last... At the last the government thwarted him.* PHR : USED AS AN A ⇑ finally 10.9 If you say that someone **looks** their **last** on something, you mean that they look at it for the final time, for example before leaving a place or before dying; a literary and old-fashioned expression. EG *People had come on deck to look their last on their country.* PHR : VB INFLECTS, USU+A 10.10 If someone **breathes** their **last** they die; a literary expression. EG *He gave a loud cry and breathed his last.* PHR : VB INFLECTS 10.11 If you **leave** someone or something **till last**, you delay dealing with them until you have dealt with everyone or everything else. EG *I left her till last.* PHR : VB INFLECTS ⇑ put aside 10.12 The expression **'Last in, first out'** is used to say that the last person who started work in an organization should be the first person to leave it, if fewer people are needed. EG *Enforced redundancies operate on a last-in first-out basis.* PHR 10.13 You use expressions such as **to the last detail, to the last man, etc** to emphasize that a plan, situation, or action includes every single person, thing, or part involved. EG *The robbery was planned down to the last detail... We are ready to fight to the last man... State the actual amount down to the last 10p... ...finishing the bottle to the last drop.* PHR : USED AS AN A 10.14 If you say that someone or something has PHR : USED AS AN

a quality **to the last degree**, you mean that they have a great deal of it; a formal expression. EG *He was stubborn to the last degree.* A ⇑ extremely **10.15** You say **every last** person, thing, or part to emphasize that you are talking about all the people or things in a group without exception or all the parts of something. EG *He told us to clear every last one of them out of the area... ...squeezing from it every last drop of nourishment it can provide.* PHR+N IN SING = each and every **10.16** If you refer to the **last but one, last but two, last but three**, etc in a series or group, you are referring to the thing or person that is one, two, three, etc before the final one. EG *...during the last day but one of the trial.* PHR

11 at last. 11.1 If you say that something has happened **at last** or **at long last**, you mean it has happened after you have been waiting for it for a long time. EG *I'm free at last... At long last I've found a girl that really loves me.* PHR : USED AS AN A ⇑ finally **11.2** If something happened **at last**, it happened at the end of a long period of time; used especially in literary English. EG *At last Ralph stopped work and stood up... 'Are you all right, John?' she whispered at last.* PHR : USED AS AN A = eventually

last out. 1 If someone **lasts out** or **lasts out** a period of time, they manage to stay alive or to reach the end of a difficult experience. EG *I'm afraid she might not last out the winter... I don't think I can last out without any cigarettes.* PHRASAL VB : V+ADV, OR V+O+ADV = survive

2 If something **lasts out** or **lasts out** a period of time, there is enough of it for someone to use as long as it is needed or for that period of time. EG *The heater needed two bottles of fuel to last out a full meeting... How long will our gas reserves last out?* PHRASAL VB : V+ADV, OR V+O+ADV = hold out

last-ditch. A **last-ditch** action is done only because there are no other ways left to achieve something or to prevent something happening. It is often done without much hope that it will succeed. EG *...a last-ditch fight with clubs and bare hands... The Treasury made a last-ditch attempt to intervene.* ADJ CLASSIF : ATTRIB ⇑ final

lasting /lɑːstɪŋ/. Something that is **lasting** continues to exist or have an effect for a very long time. EG *This may provide a lasting solution to our problems... ...lasting friendships.* ADJ CLASSIF : USU ATTRIB = enduring, long-term

Last Judgement; also spelled **Last Judgment**. The **Last Judgement** is, in the Christian religion, the last day of the world, on which God will judge everyone. N PROPER : *the*+N

lastly /lɑːstli¹/. You use **lastly 1** when you want to make a final point, ask a final question, or mention a final item that is connected with the other ones you have already asked or mentioned. EG *Lastly, I would like to ask you about your future plans... And lastly, what do we mean by acceptable technology?* ADV SEN = finally **2** when you are saying what happens after everything else in a series of actions or events. EG *Lastly he jabbed the knife hard into the trunk of the tree.* ADV WITH VB

last-minute is used to describe actions, events, decisions, etc that happen just before something else happens, usually something important which is planned to happen at a fixed time. EG *...a last-minute attempt to stop the school being closed... We have some last-minute details to talk over... ...last-minute packing.* ADJ CLASSIF : ATTRIB ⇑ late

last rites. The **last rites** are a religious ceremony performed by a Christian priest for someone who is about to die, and performed in the presence of the dying person. It consists of prayers, readings, etc, and sometimes a short service of Holy Communion. EG *A priest gave her the last rites.* N PLURAL : *the*+N

latch /læʧ/, **latches, latching, latched**. **1** A **latch** is a fastening on a door or gate. It consists of a metal bar which is held in place to lock the door and which you lift in order to open the door. EG *...a broken door latch... She dropped the latch of the little gate.* N COUNT

2 To **latch** a door or gate means to fasten it by means of a latch. EG *Both glass doors were open and latched in position.* V+O

3 A **latch** is also a lock on a door which locks automatically when you shut the door, so that you need a key in order to open it from the outside. N COUNT ● If a door is **on the latch** or **off the latch**, it is shut but not locked, because the latch has been set in a position so that it will not lock automatically when you shut the door. EG *She went out, leaving the door on the latch... You can go in. The door's off the latch.* ● PHR : USED AS A C

latch onto. If you **latch onto** a person or an idea, you become so interested in them or find them so useful that you do not want to abandon them; an informal expression. EG *She latched onto someone with a family business.* PHRASAL VB : V+PREP, HAS PASS

latchkey /læʧkiː/, **latchkeys**. A **latchkey** is a key for a latch. N COUNT

latchkey child, latchkey children. A **latchkey child** is a child whose parents both work during the day and who has a key to the house so that he or she can get into the house after school; a rather old-fashioned expression. EG *...the problem of latchkey children.* N COUNT

late /leɪt/, **later, latest**. **1** **Late** is used to describe things that happen or are done near the end of a particular evening, day, year, etc. EG *She had stayed up late drinking vodka... ...in the late afternoon... Very late at night, I got a phone call... ...late last week... Decker arrived in late September... ...late in 1952.* ADV, OR ADJ QUALIT ≠ early

2 If you are **late** for something, arrive **late**, get up **late**, etc, you arrive, get up, etc after the time that was arranged or expected. EG *Your train was late... Etta arrived late... He woke later than he had intended... I was ten minutes late for my appointment... I apologize for my late arrival.* ADV WITH VB, OR ADJ QUALIT = tardy

3 If an action or event is **too late** or happens **too late**, it is useless or ineffective because it occurs at a time after the proper or best time for it. EG *It's too late to change that now... They operated but it was too late... I realized my mistake too late.* PHR : USED AS C/A

4 You use **late in the day** to say **4.1** that someone's action or behaviour may not be fully effective because they have waited too long before doing it. EG *It's a little late in the day to start talking about policy changes.* PHR : USED AS C/A **4.2** that something happens in the final stages of an event or situation, at almost the last possible time. EG *It was the pensioners' vote late in the day which influenced the election of Mr Simmons.* PHR : USED AS C/A

5 **Late** is used to describe things that happen **5.1** after the usual or normal time, or that happen when someone is older than usual. EG *We had a late lunch at the hotel... He was a late developer... Liz had started learning German quite late in life.* ADV WITH VB, OR ADJ QUALIT ≠ early **5.2** near the end of a period in history or someone's life or career. EG *...in the late 1970s... ...a late Georgian house... He was in his late thirties... ...Picasso's late work.* ADJ CLASSIF : ATTRIB ≠ early **5.3** in the final stages of something, or at one of the last possible times. EG *It's a late booking... ...reports that there had been a late swing to the Conservatives.* ADJ QUALIT : ATTRIB ≠ early ● **late night**: see **night**.

6 **As late as** means at a particular time or period that you think is surprisingly late. EG *Even as late as 1950 coal provided over 90% of our energy.* PREP

7 If flowers or crops are **late**, they begin to grow or get ripe after the normal time in the main season. EG *Everything's terribly late this year.* ADV WITH VB, OR ADJ QUALIT : ATTRIB

8 You use **late** when you are talking about someone who is dead, especially someone who has died recently. EG *...the late Harry Truman... I'd like to talk with you about your late husband.* ADJ CLASSIF : ATTRIB ⇑ deceased

9 Something that has happened **of late** has happened recently; used in fairly formal English. EG *My wife has been rather tired of late.* PHR : USED AS AN A = lately

10 Someone who is **late of** a particular place lived in that place until fairly recently; a formal expression. EG *...Jane Smith, late of Bristol.* PREP

11 See also **later, latest**.

latecomer /leɪtkʌmə/, **latecomers**. A **latecomer** is someone who arrives after the time that they should have done. EG *We were disturbed by latecomers at the theatre.* N COUNT

lately /leɪtli¹/. If something has happened **lately**, it has happened recently. EG *John has seemed worried lately... I have lately received a number of letters about this.* ADV WITH VB = of late

late-night is used to describe **1** events, especially entertainments, that happen late in the evening or late at night. EG *...an absurd late-night movie.* ADJ CLASSIF : ATTRIB **2** shops that stay open late in the evening, either every evening or on particular evenings in the week. EG *Late-night shopping is on Thursdays in the city centre.* ADJ CLASSIF : ATTRIB

latent /leɪtənt/ is used to describe something which is hidden and not obvious at the moment, but which may develop further in the future. EG *He must have seen in his eldest daughter latent qualities which convinced him that she would succeed in life... These recent price increases have added to the latent* ADJ CLASSIF ⇑ potential = dormant *tensions between the richer North and the poorer South.*

later /leɪtə/. 1 **Later** is the comparative of **late**.
2 You use **later** 2.1 to refer to a time or situation that is after the one that you have been talking about or after the present one. EG *Later she went up to the office... I returned some three or four weeks later... Later on this evening, we shall have some more music... See you later... We will discuss this in more detail in a later chapter.* • **sooner or later**: see **sooner**. 2.2 to refer to the second half or last part of a period of history or someone's life or career, rather than the beginning or the middle. EG *This may cause psychological distress and illness in later life... ...the later eighteenth century.* ADV AFTER VB, OR ADJ QUALIT: COMPAR ≠ earlier; ADJ QUALIT: COMPAR ⇑ latter

lateral /lætəʳrəl/ is used to describe something which relates to the sides of something, rather than to the top or bottom, or to describe a sideways movement. EG *All of these primitive sea creatures had well developed lateral fins.* ◊ **laterally**. EG *He used to fold the newspaper laterally into one column-width at a time.* ADJ CLASSIF: ATTRIB; ◊ ADV WITH VB

lateral thinking is a method of solving problems by using your imagination to help you think of solutions that are not at first obvious, rather than by using logic or other conventional ways of thinking. EG *When a new idea is required, then lateral thinking should be used.* N UNCOUNT

latest /leɪtɪʳst/. 1 **Latest** is the superlative of **late**.
2 **Latest** is used to describe 2.1 something that is the most recent thing of its kind or in a series of similar things. EG *...the latest figures for wholesale prices... ...the latest news... Her latest book is called 'Second Class Citizen'.* 2.2 clothes that are extremely fashionable because they are the most recent designs. EG *...the latest fashions from Paris.* ADJ QUALIT: SUPERL: the/POSS+ADJ+N = newest; ADJ QUALIT: SUPERL: the/POSS+ADJ+N
3 **At the latest** is used to emphasize that something must happen at or before a particular time and not after that time. EG *I'll see you at six o'clock at the latest... Changes will become necessary by the autumn at the latest.* PHR: USED AS AN A

latex /leɪtɛks/ is a substance obtained from some kinds of trees, which is used to make products like rubber and glue. EG *Latex adhesive can be removed with special remover.* N UNCOUNT

lath /lɑːθ/ consists of strips of thin wood which are put onto the inside walls of houses or other buildings and are then covered with plaster; a technical term in the building industry. EG *The narrow corridor had walls of plastered lath.* N UNCOUNT

lathe /leɪð/, **lathes**. A **lathe** is a machine which is used for shaping wood or metal. It works by turning the wood or metal continually against a tool which cuts it. EG *From the garage there came the sound of Derek working a lathe.* N COUNT ⇑ device

lather /lɑːðə/, **lathers, lathering, lathered**. 1 A **lather** is a white mass of bubbles which is produced by mixing soap, washing powder, etc with water. EG *It is important when washing clothes to maintain a good lather throughout the wash.* 1.2 the frothy sweat that appears on a horse when it has been exercising a lot. N COUNT: USU a+N, OR N UNCOUNT ⇑ suds; N COUNT: USU a+N, OR N UNCOUNT ⇑ foam
2 When soap, washing powder, etc **lathers**, it produces a white mass of bubbles because it has been mixed with water. EG *You can't use this powder, it lathers far too much.* V ⇑ froth
3 If you **lather** something, you rub soap, washing powder, etc, into it or on it until a lather is produced, in order to clean it. EG *Lather the carpet with a sponge and rub gently until the stain has gone.* V+O
4 If you describe someone as being **in a lather**, you mean that they are very upset, confused, or angry, and do not know what to do. EG *You expected to find me in a lather, didn't you?* PHR: USED AS AN A ⇑ het up

Latin /lætɪn/, **Latins**. 1 **Latin** is the language which the ancient Romans used to speak. EG *I learned enough Latin to pass the entrance exam.* N UNCOUNT
2 Something that is **Latin** relates to the languages or the people from countries like Spain, Italy, and France, whose languages have developed from Latin. EG *He had Latin blood... ...the Latin nations.* ADJ CLASSIF
3 A **Latin** is someone who comes from the Mediterranean area, especially Spain, Italy, or southern France. EG *During the Dark Ages, the German tribes regularly made raids on the Latins.* N COUNT ⇑ person

Latin American, Latin Americans. 1 **Latin American** means relating or belonging to the countries of South America, Central America, and Mexico. EG *...Latin American countries... ...Latin American politics.* ADJ CLASSIF
2 A **Latin American** is someone who lives in or comes from South America, Central America, and Mexico. N COUNT ⇑ person

latitude /lætɪtjuːd/, **latitudes**. 1 A **latitude** is a position on a map of the world measured as the distance to the North or South of the equator; compare **longitude**. EG *We are at the precise latitude of Corfu... A submarine reported seeing enemy ships in about the latitude of Trondheim.* N COUNT: USU+SUPP = parallel
2 You use the word **latitudes** to refer to parts of the world when you are thinking about how far away they are from the equator. High latitudes are further away from the equator and so have a colder climate than low latitudes. EG *The sun rises up further and faster at lower latitudes than at higher latitudes... Many birds migrate to warmer latitudes.* N PLURAL+SUPP ⇑ area
3 **Latitude** is a degree of freedom to choose the way in which you do something. EG *He was always prepared to give an actor a certain amount of latitude... She was given considerable latitude in how she spent the money.* N UNCOUNT = scope

latrine /lətriːn/, **latrines**. A **latrine** is a hole in the ground which you dig to use as a toilet, for example when you are camping. EG *The showers and latrines were several fields away.* N COUNT

latter /lætə/. 1 When two people, things, or groups have just been mentioned, you refer to the one that was mentioned second as the **latter**. EG *There were three young men in the room, and two young women. The latter were Melanie's flat-mates... They were eating sandwiches and little iced cakes, (the latter obtained from Mrs Kaul's bakery).* ▸ used as an adjective. EG *The novel was made into a film in 1943 and again in 1967: I prefer the latter version to the former.* N SING/PLURAL: the+N ≠ former; ▸ ADJ CLASSIF: the+ADJ+N ≠ former
2 **Latter** is also used to describe the second part of a period of time, or the part which is nearer to the end than the beginning. EG *By the latter half of July the total was well over two million... He spent the latter part of his life in Birmingham.* ADJ CLASSIF: the+ADJ+N
3 **Latter** also means the same as recent; a formal use. EG *He was the sort of admirer she had been having in these latter years.* ◊ **latterly**. EG *She was wearing the very special French perfume I had latterly allowed her to use.* ADJ CLASSIF: ATTRIB; ◊ ADV WITH VB

latter-day is used to describe something or someone that is a modern equivalent of something or someone in the past. EG *...latter-day troubadours.* ADJ CLASSIF: ATTRIB

lattice /lætɪs/, **lattices**. A **lattice** is a pattern or structure made of strips of wood or another material which cross over each other diagonally leaving holes in between. A lattice can be used as a framework or as a decoration. EG *Their houses are in traditional style of clay over a lattice of bamboo.* N COUNT: USU SING ⇑ network

latticed /lætɪst/. Something that is **latticed** is decorated with or in the form of a lattice. EG *Mrs Halliday was wearing a hat with a latticed brim.* ADJ CLASSIF: ATTRIB ⇑ woven

lattice window, lattice windows. A **lattice window** or a **latticed window** is a window which is decorated with a pattern of strips of lead which cross over each other diagonally. EG *The houses had little arches and pillars and latticed windows.* N COUNT

latticework /lætɪswɜːk/ is any structure that is made in the form of a lattice. EG *...a latticework of silver.* N UNCOUNT

laud /lɔːd/, **lauds, lauding, lauded**. If you **laud** someone, you praise and admire them; a fairly old-fashioned and formal word. V+O

laudable /lɔːdəbəʳl/. Something that is **laudable** is worthy of praise or admiration; a formal word. EG *The vigorous demolition programme was inspired by laudable motives of improving housing conditions.* ◊ **laudably**. EG *He has behaved laudably in the circumstances.* ADJ QUALIT; ◊ ADV WITH VB

laudanum /lɔːdəʳnəm/ is a drug containing opium, which was popular in Victorian times and was used to help people sleep. N UNCOUNT

laudatory /lɔːdətəʳriˡ/. If a piece of writing or speech is **laudatory**, it expresses praise or admiration of someone; a formal word. EG *She has a way of disparaging me even while uttering laudatory phrases.* ADJ QUALIT = complimentary

laugh /lɑːf/, **laughs, laughing, laughed**. 1 When you **laugh**, you make the sound by which V people show that they are happy or amused. People sometimes also laugh when they feel unhappy, nervous, or unfriendly. EG *He grinned, then started to laugh... All the young men laughed at the jokes Lenny told... He laughed nervously and asked me what I meant.* ▸ used as a noun. EG *'Hurry up,' said Tony with a laugh... He patted her on the head and gave a laugh... It was a terrible laugh, very quiet and intense.* ▸ N COUNT

2 The word **laugh** is used as a verb in the following expressions. **2.1** If you **laugh** your **head off**, you laugh very loudly for a long time because you are amused; an informal expression. EG *The fishermen were laughing their heads off.* PHR : VB AND N INFLECT **2.2** When you **laugh out loud** or **laugh aloud**, you laugh loudly at something because it is so funny, especially in a situation in which this is an unusual thing to do, for example when you are on your own. EG *It's rare to come across any book which makes you laugh out loud... It all sounded so crazy that I laughed out loud.* PHR : VB INFLECTS **2.3** If you say that someone **is laughing**, you mean that they are able to safely or successfully control a particular situation; an informal expression. EG *If the gas bill is as low as the electricity bill, we're laughing.* PHR : AUX INFLECTS **2.4** If someone **does not know whether to laugh or cry**, they are so surprised or shocked that they are not sure how to react in a particular situation. EG *My poor husband doesn't know whether to laugh or cry.* PHR : AUX INFLECTS **2.5** If you say that someone or something **makes** you **laugh**, you mean that you think that they are stupid or foolish, especially because you disagree with them or disapprove of them. EG *'I intend to deal with him myself.'-'You! Don't make me laugh'.* PHR : VB INFLECTS **2.6** If you say **'you've got to laugh'** or **'you have to laugh'**, you are saying that you can see the amusing side of a difficult or disappointing situation rather than being sad or angry about it; an informal expression. EG *It's very serious I agree, but you have to laugh, really, don't you?* CONVENTION **2.7** If you say that someone **is laughing all the way to the bank**, you mean that they are making a lot of money easily and feel very confident. PHR : VB INFLECTS ⇑ profit **2.8** If you say that someone **is laughing on the other side of** their **face**, you mean that they are now suddenly upset or annoyed after being pleased or happy about something. You use this expression especially when you think that they deserve to be disappointed. PHR : VB + INFLECTS **2.9** If you say **'He who laughs last laughs longest'**, you mean that the most successful person in a situation is the one who finally ends up in control, even if it takes them a long time to achieve this. PHR : VB INFLECTS

3 The word **laugh** is used as a noun in the following expressions. **3.1** If comedians or entertainers **get** or **raise a laugh**, they make their audience laugh. EG *He walked slowly off the stage, turning back at the door to get a laugh... His act would always get a huge laugh.* PHR : VB + N INFLECT ⇑ amuse **3.2** If you do or say something **for a laugh** or **for laughs**, you do or say it as a joke or for fun rather than for any other reason. EG *People in the crowd seemed bent on heckling the speakers for a laugh... I gave him the wrong address just for a laugh.* PHR : USED AS AN A **3.3** If you describe a situation as **a laugh, a good laugh**, or **a bit of a laugh**, you mean that you do not take it seriously but find it amusing or trivial. EG *Most of the school regarded games lessons as a bit of a laugh.* PHR : USED AS C ⇑ joke
3.4 If you describe someone as **a laugh, a good laugh**, or a **bit of a laugh**, you mean that they are amusing and fun to be with. EG *He's alright, he's a good laugh.* PHR : USED AS C
3.5 If you **have a laugh** about something, you find it amusing and see the funny side of it, especially if it is a situation that was at first rather upsetting. EG *Debbie and I had a good laugh about it all.* PHR : VB INFLECTS **3.6** If someone **has the last laugh**, they are at last successful after appearing to have been defeated, or eventually get their revenge. EG *The establishment had the last laugh as far as the Sixties were concerned... Henry had outlived all the others to have the last laugh.* PHR : VB INFLECTS ⇑ triumph

laugh at. If you **laugh at** someone or something, you mock them or make jokes about them. EG *I don't think it's nice to laugh at people's disabilities... He seldom laughed at himself.* PHRASAL VB : V + PREP, HAS PASS ⇑ ridicule = deride

laugh off. If you **laugh off** a difficult or serious situation, you try to suggest that it is amusing and unimportant, for example by making a joke about it. EG *Despite being in trouble with the Government, Northcliffe attempted to laugh the matter off.* PHRASAL VB : V + O + ADV ⇑ dismiss = shrug off

laughable /lɑːfəbəᵒl/. Something that is **laughable 1** seems amusing and stupid because it is so obviously unsuccessful, foolish, or poor in quality. EG *...a laughable piece of inefficiency and bureaucracy.* ADJ QUALIT = absurd, ridiculous **2** is very amusing. EG *...Groucho's laughable view of human pomp.* ADJ QUALIT

laughing gas is a type of anaesthetic gas. It sometimes has the effect of making people laugh uncontrollably if it is sniffed in small quantities. N UNCOUNT

laughingly /lɑːfɪŋli¹/. **1** You use **laughingly** to indicate that you think that something is very badly done or are of very poor quality, especially when this annoys you. EG *...a recent example of what is laughingly defined as classical singing... These drunken discussions are laughingly called the planning process.* ADV WITH VB
2 If something is **laughingly** done, it is done while someone is laughing. EG *We called at the information desk, and the misunderstanding was laughingly explained.* ADV WITH VB ⇑ cheerfully

laughing stock, laughing stocks; also spelled with a hyphen. A **laughing stock** is something that is supposed to be important or serious but that has been made to seem stupid and funny. EG *Arthur's garden was the laughing stock of the neighbourhood... We're an international laughing-stock, a nation brought to its knees.* N COUNT ⇑ joke

laughter /lɑːftə/ is the act of laughing, or the sound of people laughing, especially because they are very amused or happy. EG *Mr Evans heard laughter and applause as the speaker ceased... Bill and Fay were both weak with laughter... Sponge roared with laughter... She let out a shriek of laughter.* N UNCOUNT

launch /lɔːntʃ/, **launches, launching, launched**. **1** To **launch** a ship or boat means to put it into water for the first time after it has been built. EG *This ship was launched two years ago.* ▸ used as a noun. EG *When is the launch?* V+O ▸ N COUNT
2 To **launch** a rocket, missile, or satellite means to send it into the air or into space. EG *Soviet rockets launched more satellites into orbit... The first missiles have been launched.* ▸ used as a noun. EG *The launch was a complete success.* V+O ▸ N COUNT
3 To **launch** a large and important activity, for example a political movement or a military attack, means to start it. EG *The government has launched a massive literacy campaign... Guerrilla attacks were launched against the police and military barracks... A Union official said that strikes should be launched on a limited scale only.* V+O ⇑ begin
4 If a company **launches** a new product, it makes it available to the public. EG *The new range of products launched last autumn is already selling well... A magazine called 'The Week' was launched in January 1964.* ▸ used as a noun. EG *The newspaper was already selling millions of copies just one year after the launch.* V+O = introduce ▸ N COUNT
5 A **launch** is a large motor-boat that is used for carrying people on rivers and lakes and in harbours. EG *He led me out to his launch.* N COUNT

launch into. If you **launch into** something such as a speech, task, or fight, you enthusiastically start it. EG *He launched into a long speech about the dangers of taking drugs... She launched into an interminable battle with the school governors.* PHRASAL VB : V + PREP, HAS PASS = embark on

launch out. If you **launch out** on or into something, you start something that is new to you, such as an activity or job. PHRASAL VB : V + ADV, IF + PREP THEN *into/on*

launching pad, launching pads. **1** A **launching pad** is a platform from which rockets, missiles, or satellites are launched. N COUNT **2** a situation, for example a job, which you can use in order to go forward to something better. EG *Sometimes a first job can act as a launching pad into something else.* N COUNT

launder /lɔːndə/, **launders, laundering, laundered**. **1** When you **launder** clothes, bed linen, etc, you wash and iron them; an old-fashioned word. EG *I was supposed to launder the old socks.* V+O ⇑ clean
2 To **launder** money that has been illegally obtained means to send it abroad to a foreign bank, so that when it is brought back into the country nobody knows that it was illegally obtained; used showing disapproval. EG *Someone was laundering secret campaign money in Mexico... ...modern drug traffickers who can launder their money offshore.* V+O

launderette /lɔːndəᵒret/, **launderettes**; also spelled **laundrette**. A **launderette** is a shop in which N COUNT = Laundromat there are coin-operated washing machines and driers which people can use to wash and dry their clothes. EG *I found him washing his shirts in the campus launderette.*

Laundromat /lɔːndrəˢmæt/, **Laundromats**. A **Laundromat** is an American trademark for a launderette. EG *Sylvia is with Chris at a Laundromat doing the laundry.* — N COUNT

laundry /lɔːndri¹/, **laundries**. 1 The **laundry** is 1.1 the dirty clothes, sheets, towels, etc that are being washed or are about to be washed. EG *The washing machine takes about two hours to do my family laundry... ...the laundry basket.* — N UNCOUNT : USU the/POSS+N = washing
1.2 the clean clothes, sheets, towels, etc that have been washed. EG *I loved the clean laundry hung from bamboo poles on all the balconies.* — N UNCOUNT : USU the+N = washing

2 A **laundry** is 2.1 a firm or business that washes and irons clothes, sheets, towels, etc for people. EG *Send it to the laundry. Don't dry clean it.* — N COUNT
2.2 a room in a large house or in a hotel where clothes and linen are washed. EG *They're making the other kitchen into a laundry.* — N COUNT : USU SING

laurel /lɒrəˢl/, **laurels**. 1 A **laurel** is a small evergreen tree with shiny leaves. EG *The path was lined with laurels.* — N COUNT

2 **Laurel** is used to describe something that is made of laurel leaves, sometimes as a sign of victory. EG *He was wearing a Roman kilt and laurel wreath.* — ADJ CLASSIF : ATTRIB

3 If you say that someone **is resting on** their **laurels**, you mean that they feel so satisfied with what they have already achieved that they are not bothering to make any more effort. EG *We have no cause to rest on our laurels.* — PHR : VB INFLECTS = sit back

lava /lɑːvə/ is a kind of rock which comes out of a volcano in the form of a very hot liquid, and gradually cools and becomes solid. EG *Black tides of lava flowed down the sides of the volcano.* — N UNCOUNT

lavatory /lævətəˢri¹/, **lavatories**. A **lavatory** is the same as a toilet. EG *If your lavatory gets blocked call for a plumber... ...public lavatories.* — N COUNT

lavatory paper is the same as toilet paper. — N UNCOUNT

lavender /lævɪ¹ndə/. 1 **Lavender** is a garden plant that has spiky greyish-green leaves and sweet-smelling, bluish-purple flowers on long stalks; used also of the flowers themselves, which are often used to make things smell pleasant. — N UNCOUNT

2 Something that is **lavender** is of a pale bluish-purple colour. — ADJ COLOUR

lavender water is a light perfume that is made from and smells of lavender. — N UNCOUNT ⇑ scent

lavish /lævɪʃ/, **lavishes, lavishing, lavished**. 1 If you are **lavish**, you are very generous in the way that you spend your money on other people or give your time and attention to a particular activity. EG *He was affectionate with his two daughters and lavish with gifts for his wife... The whole building was given the lavish attention of craftsmen.* — ADJ QUALIT : IF+PREP THEN *with* = liberal, unstinting
◇ **lavishly**. EG *Rich merchants lavishly entertained travelling tradesmen.* — ◇ ADV ⇑ generously

2 If you **lavish** something such as money, affection, or time on someone or something, you spend a lot of money on them or give them a lot of affection or attention. EG *Everything was lavished on her one and only child... The media lavish a lot of attention on people like Hinckley.* — V+O+A *(on/upon)* = heap

3 Something that is **lavish** 3.1 is very large in quantity or amount. EG *The meal, he said, would be nothing fancy, but the portions would be lavish.* — ADJ QUALIT = generous
◇ **lavishly**. EG *They were trained severely but lavishly paid.* — ◇ ADV
3.2 has an appearance of great wealth and extravagance. EG *He controlled a corporation that owned a chain of nine lavish funeral parlours in the city.* — ADJ QUALIT = sumptuous
◇ **lavishly**. EG *The building has been lavishly restored to a fresh brilliance.* — ◇ ADV = splendidly

law /lɔː/, **laws**. 1 The **law** is a system of rules that a society or government develops over time in order to deal with business agreements, social relationships, and crimes such as theft, murder, or violence. EG *You can't hold your demonstration here–it's against the law... She was caught in the act of breaking the law... Respect for the law is the foundation of civilized living... Every company must by law submit accounts annually... On 31 July the Peerage Bill became law... It is important for pressure groups to remain within the law... She seems to think she is above the law.* — N SING : *the*+N, OR N UNCOUNT

2 A particular type of **law**, for example company **law**, criminal **law**, etc, is the group of rules in a system of law which deals with a particular set of agreements, relationships, or crimes. EG *I don't understand all the intricacies of company law... She's the Senate's expert on constitutional law... ...divorce law... The soldiers faced charges under military law.* — N UNCOUNT : MOD +N = legislation

3 A **law** is 3.1 one of the rules in a system of law which deals with a particular type of agreement, relationship, or crime. EG *We hope that this will become a national law... Many of the laws passed by Parliament are never enforced... We must protest against racialism and immigration laws.* — N COUNT
3.2 a rule or set of rules for good behaviour which is not necessarily part of a system of government, but which seems right and important for moral, religious, or emotional reasons. EG *Children soon accept social laws... There was one law for men, and another law for women, so far as love was concerned... The clergy were having an argument about God's law.* — N COUNT/UNCOUNT ⇑ standard
3.3 any rule or system of rules, such as those used in sport or art. EG *This painting doesn't obey the laws of perspective... ...the laws of football... It's necessary to have a good grasp of the laws of logic.* — N COUNT+SUPP = principle
3.4 a natural process or pattern that seems completely necessary and impossible to change, in which a particular cause always leads to a particular effect and nothing can stop it happening. EG *What's born has to die–that's a law of nature... The laws that govern the behaviour of light are universal.* — N COUNT+SUPP ⇑ rule = principle
3.5 a scientific rule that people have invented to describe and explain the way that nature works. EG *...the second law of thermodynamics... We need to have a good understanding of Newton's Laws before we study Einstein.* — N COUNT+SUPP = principle

4 **Law** or **the law** is all the professions which deal with advising people about the law, representing people in court, or giving decisions and punishments. EG *There are curious parallels between medicine and the law... I was planning a career in law... ...a New York law firm.* — N UNCOUNT, OR N SING : *the*+N

5 **Law** is the study of systems of law and how laws work, or a course of study that trains you for a profession in law. EG *A degree in law would be an advantage in the job market... She had recently graduated from law school.* — N UNCOUNT ⇑ subject

6 In informal English, **the law** is the government authorities, especially the police. EG *Don't open the door–it might be the law!... He found himself in trouble with the law once again.* — N SING : *the*+N

7 The word **law** is also used in the following expressions. 7.1 If you **go to law**, you go to court in order to deal with a dispute, or arrange to do this. EG *If they won't agree to our terms, we'll have to go to law.* — PHR : VB INFLECTS
7.2 If you say that you will **have the law on** someone, you mean that you will call the police in order to arrest that person; an informal expression. EG *If I catch you stealing again, I'll have the law on you!* — PHR : VB INFLECTS
7.3 If you say that someone is **a law unto** himself or herself, you mean that they behave in an independent way, often ignoring rules of good behaviour and not accepting conventional beliefs and attitudes. — PHR+PRON REFL : USED AS C
7.4 If someone **lays down the law**, they give other people orders in a bossy way, because they think that they are right and that the other people are wrong; used showing disapproval. — PHR : VB INFLECTS
7.5 If someone's **word is law**, they are so powerful and important that everyone in a particular group respects and obeys what they say. EG *Mum's word is law in this house.* — PHR
7.6 If you **take the law into** your **own hands**, you deliberately break the law, usually when you want to punish someone according to your own ideas of justice. EG *One farmer dared to take the law into his own hands by shooting one of the trespassers.* — PHR : VB INFLECTS

law-abiding. Someone who is **law-abiding** always obeys the law; used showing approval. EG *The first duty of the state is to ensure that law-abiding people are protected... ...a law-abiding citizen.* — ADJ QUALIT : USU ATTRIB

law and order. When people talk about **law and order**, they are referring to 1 the peace and co-operation that exists amongst law-abiding people; used showing approval. EG *They wanted to get law and order by consent of the majority... There were periods of civil war, unrest, and breakdown of law and order.* — N UNCOUNT ⇑ harmony
2 the use of strict laws as a way of controlling a society, especially when the police or the army are used to force people to obey their government. EG *She had no respect for the forces of law and order.* — N UNCOUNT ⇑ control

law-breaker, law-breakers; also spelled as one word. A **law-breaker** is someone who breaks the law, especially regularly. EG *She is not a law-breaker by nature.* — N COUNT ⇑ criminal

law-breaking is used to describe a person or an action involved in doing something that is illegal. EG *...policies to keep law-breaking youngsters off the streets.* — ADJ CLASSIF : ATTRIB ⇑ criminal = delinquent

law court, law courts. A **law court** is a place where legal matters are decided by a judge and jury or by a magistrate. EG *He took his pupils to see the law courts.* — N COUNT

law-enforcement agencies or officials are those such as the police and government legal departments that are responsible for making sure that people do not break the laws of a country or state; used especially in American English. EG *The bank's transaction was criticized by law-enforcement officials... ...indiscriminate use of gas by law-enforcement agencies.* — N UNCOUNT ⇑ control

lawful /lɔːful/ is used to describe an activity, organization, etc which is allowed by law or acceptable to the law; a formal word. EG *...lawful publications... ...use all lawful means to persuade employers.* — ADJ CLASSIF ⇑ legal = legitimate
◊ **lawfully**. EG *The tenant cannot be lawfully evicted.* — ◊ ADV

lawless /lɔːlɪ²s/. **1 Lawless** actions break the laws of a country or state, especially in a wild and violent way. EG *...the lawless activities of these gangs... ...provoke them into further lawless violence.* — ADJ CLASSIF
◊ **lawlessness**. EG *...our disapproval of lawlessness and violence in television programmes.* — ◊ N UNCOUNT
2 A **lawless** place or time is not governed by laws. EG *...a lawless community... ...the lawless days of the West.* — ADJ CLASSIF

lawn /lɔːn/, **lawns**. **1** A **lawn** is an area of grass that is kept carefully cut short and is usually part of someone's garden or a park. EG *Tom strode across the lawn away from the house... When are you going to mow the lawn?... ...several acres of lawns and flowerbeds.* — N COUNT/UNCOUNT
2 Lawn is a type of thin cotton or linen, used especially for making shirts, dresses, etc. EG *...dressed in fine white lawn... ...a summer dress made of pink lawn.* — N UNCOUNT ⇑ fabric

lawnmower /lɔːnməʊə/, **lawnmowers**; also spelled with a hyphen. A **lawnmower** is a machine for cutting grass on lawns. — N COUNT

lawn tennis is **1** the same as tennis; a formal term. — N UNCOUNT
2 tennis played on grass, rather than on a hard court. — N UNCOUNT

lawsuit /lɔːsuːt/, **lawsuits**. A **lawsuit** is a case in a court of law which concerns a dispute between two people or organizations rather than the prosecution of a criminal by the police; a formal word. EG *He had sought to bring a lawsuit against the airline... The newspaper's lawyers advised against lawsuits.* — N COUNT = suit, action

lawyer /lɔːjə, lɔɪə/, **lawyers**. A **lawyer** is a person who is qualified to advise people about the law and represent them in court. EG *I sought the advice of his lawyer, who practised in Leeds... The case cost £40,000 in lawyers' fees alone.* — N COUNT

lax /læks/, **laxer, laxest**. If you say that a person, their behaviour, or a system is **lax**, you mean that they are not careful or strict in making or obeying rules or maintaining high standards; a formal word used showing disapproval. EG *Standards are regarded by some experts as being far too lax... 'I have been lax,' he thought. 'This conversation should have been avoided'... ...procedures are lax, discipline is weak.* — ADJ QUALIT ⇑ careless = slack
◊ **laxity**. EG *...the moral laxity of the people.* — ◊ N UNCOUNT

laxative /læksətɪv/, **laxatives**. A **laxative** is something which you eat or drink that relieves constipation by making you defecate. EG *There are some stomach aches for which a laxative is dangerous.* — N COUNT
▸ used as an adjective. EG *Prunes are mildly laxative.* — ▸ ADJ QUALIT

lay /leɪ/, **lays, laying, laid**. In standard English, the form **lay** is also the past tense of the verb **lie** in some meanings. In informal English, people sometimes use the word **lay** instead of **lie** in those meanings. **1** The word **lay** is used in this paragraph with the general meaning of putting something carefully in a particular place or position. **1.1** If you **lay** something somewhere, you put or place it there in a careful, gentle, or neat way. EG *She laid the baby gently down on its bed... The cards are laid face up on the table... There were two or three pictures laid flat on top... He laid the rifle against the tree... Take the top sheet and lay it in the centre of the bed... She laid a hand on his shoulder... She looked at him with her head laid to one side.* — V+O+A
1.2 If you **lay** the table or **lay** the places at a table, you arrange the knives, forks, plates, etc on a table before a meal. EG *Lay the table... The table was all laid for lunch... I'm not laying a place at table for him.* — V+O = set
1.3 If you **lay** a carpet or other covering, you spread it over the floor of a room or other area and often fix it in position. EG *The carpets had been laid by a fitter from the shop... She was busy laying turf.* — V+O = put down
1.4 If you **lay** things such as pipes, drains, or cables, you put them in or on the ground so that they can carry water, oil, sewage, or electricity from one place to another. EG *They're laying water pipes and electricity cables... We'll need help to lay these drains.* — V+O = put in
1.5 If someone **lays** bombs or explosives, they put them in a place, especially in or on the ground, where they will cause damage. EG *The terrorists laid mines near the pipelines.* — V+O = plant
1.6 If you **lay** a fire, you arrange sticks, paper, etc on the ground or in a fireplace before lighting the fire. — V+O ⇑ prepare
1.7 If you **lay** a trail, you put little signs, pieces of food, etc on the ground in a long line because you want people or animals to follow them. — V+O = leave
2 If you **lay** a trap, **2.1** you hide the trap carefully and set it so that if an animal goes near it, the trap will operate and catch the animal. EG *She knows how to lay a trap.* — V+O
2.2 you deceive someone by creating a situation in which they feel safe so that they do something that you wanted them to. EG *He walked right into the trap I had laid for him... If there is any attempt to contact the police or lay a trap, you will die.* — V+O
3 When a bird or female animal **lays** an egg, it pushes the egg out of its body. EG *All birds lay eggs... A female toad may lay 20,000 eggs each season... She lays at night, producing 40 eggs in several batches.* — V OR V+O ⇑ produce
4 The word **lay** is used with words referring to parts of your body in the following expressions. **4.1** If you say that you did not **lay a finger on** someone or if you warn someone else not to, you mean that you did not or they should not touch or harm the person in the slightest way; an informal expression. EG *He didn't lay a finger on you... I never so much as laid a finger on them.* — PHR : VB INFLECTS
4.2 If you **lay** your **hands on** someone or something, you manage to discover or obtain them when they are rare or hard to find; an informal expression. EG *She read anything she could lay her hands on... I wondered how I could lay my hands on the money.* — PHR : VB INFLECTS
4.3 If you **lay eyes on** someone or something, you see them, especially suddenly or for the first time; an informal expression. EG *Ever since I first laid eyes on you I can't think about anybody else... ...the most extraordinary individual I had ever laid eyes on.* — PHR : VB INFLECTS = set eyes on
5 If you **lay hold of** someone or something, you catch or grab them quickly and hold them tight. EG *He laid hold of the creepers to pull himself up.* — PHR : VB INFLECTS = grasp
6 The word **lay** is used with various nouns in expressions which relate to making official plans, statements, or claims, giving people duties or responsibilities, or blaming people. **6.1** If you **lay** the basis for something or **lay** plans for it, you prepare it carefully so that you can continue with it, develop it, or benefit from it later. EG *The conference laid the basis for a series of annual gatherings... Her new policy helped to lay the foundations of electoral success... Next day, they laid their plans to increase cigarette advertising.* — V+O = establish
6.2 If you **lay claim to** something, you say that it belongs to you. EG *We should lay claim to our inheritance... Both countries had laid claim to the territory.* — PHR : VB INFLECTS
6.3 If you **lay emphasis on** something, you emphasize it or consider it to be very important. EG *The Army laid great emphasis on the use of helicopters... Their lawyer will lay great emphasis on his state of mind at the time.* — PHR : VB INFLECTS
6.4 If you **lay** a duty or responsibility upon a person or organization, you officially state that they must do it or be responsible for it. EG *...administrative duties laid upon them by Acts of Parliament... That lays upon us an awesome burden of responsibility.* — V+O+A *(upon/on)* = impose
6.5 If you **lay the blame** on someone or something, you say or show that they are responsible for a mistake, or for harm or damage that has occurred. EG *Everyone looked for a place to lay the blame... Women lay most of the blame on men... Now the government has the chance to lay part of the blame outside the country.* — PHR : VB INFLECTS
6.6 If you **lay** something **at the door** of a particular — PHR : VB

person or group, you are emphasizing that it is their responsibility or their fault. EG *The pressure to defend teaching methods was laid at the door of the paid staff... There is a mass of charges that could be laid at the President's door.* **6.7** If you **lay** a charge or charges against someone, you officially complain about them or accuse them of something. EG *Criminal charges were laid against him.* **6.8** If someone **lays a curse** on a person or thing, they state that that person or anyone interfering with that thing will be harmed in some way. EG *A curse has been laid on those who violated the tomb of the King.* INFLECTS / PHR : VB INFLECTS = lodge / PHR : VB INFLECTS

7 If you **lay** yourself, someone else, or something **open to** criticism, attack, etc, you do something which is likely to make other people criticize or attack you or them. EG *That kind of behaviour can lay you open to the charge of wasting the company's time... Social democracy thereby laid itself open to the charge of hypocrisy.* PHR : VB INFLECTS

8 If you **lay a ghost**, you finally deal with and get rid of an unpleasant feeling or memory that you have had for a long time. EG *I had the need to lay a ghost, I suppose, before it was too late.* PHR : VB INFLECTS

9 If you **lay** a bet, **lay** an amount of money, or **lay** particular odds on the result of a game or race, you risk your money by saying that you will win or that a particular result will occur. V+O : IF+PREP THEN *on* = stake

10 To **lay** someone means to have sex with them; a very informal and offensive use. V+O

11 A **lay** is **11.1** an act of having sex; a very informal and offensive use. N COUNT **11.2** a person that you have sex with; a very informal and offensive use. N COUNT

12 You use **lay** to describe people who are **12.1** involved with a Christian church but are not members of the clergy, monks, or nuns, etc. EG *...lay members of the Church... Dad became a lay preacher of some renown.* ADJ CLASSIF : ATTRIB **12.2** not trained, qualified, or experienced in a particular subject or activity. EG *The computer has become much more accessible to the lay person... Most of the objections to the nuclear power programme came from the lay public.* ADJ CLASSIF : ATTRIB

13 A **lay** is also a poem or song; an old-fashioned use. N COUNT

14 The word **lay** is also used in following expressions, which are explained at other places in this dictionary. • to **lay** something **bare**: see **bare**. • to **lay** something **on the line**: see **line**. • to **lay** someone or something **to rest**: see **rest**. • to **lay siege to**: see **siege**. • to **lay waste**: see **waste**.

lay about. **1** If you **lay about** someone, often with a weapon of some kind, you hit them with it very hard and in an uncontrolled way; an old-fashioned or formal expression. EG *They began laying about with whips... Two assistants sprang forward and began to lay about the boys with sticks.* PHRASAL VB : V+ ADV/PREP

2 See also **layabout**.

lay aside. **1** If you **lay** something **aside**, **1.1** you put it down, usually because you have finished using it. EG *She laid aside her magazine while she ate her tea.* PHRASAL VB : V+ O+ADV **1.2** you separate it from a group of similar things, usually in order to save it for future use. EG *I'll lay that one aside for later.* PHRASAL VB : V+ O+ADV

2 If you **lay aside** a particular feeling, belief, or activity, you reject it or give it up. EG *They should try to lay aside their usual inhibitions and join in the fun.* PHRASAL VB : V+ O+ADV

lay before. If you **lay** an idea, problem, or argument **before** someone, you present it to them in detail, usually in order to obtain their approval, permission, or advice; a formal expression. EG *What exactly was the scheme he intended to lay before them?... If you have any proof of that allegation, I advise you to lay it before the police.* PHRASAL VB : V+ O+PREP = put before

lay by. **1** If you **lay** something such as money **by**, you save it for future use. EG *I've got something laid by.* PHRASAL VB : ORDER V+O+ ADV

2 See also **lay-by**.

lay down. **1** If you **lay** something **down**, you put it down, usually because you have finished using it. EG *I laid down the pen and shut the book.* PHRASAL VB : V+ O+ADV

2 If you **lay down** an idea, attitude, rank, etc, you give up, reject, or renounce it; a formal use. EG *In those days, a peer could not lay down his title... Her smile encouraged him to lay down the burden of secrecy.* PHRASAL VB : ORDER V+ADV+ O

3 If someone **lays down** their arms or weapons, they stop fighting a battle or war and make peace; a literary use. EG *I will not rest until my country has laid down its arms.* PHRASAL VB : V+ ADV+O

4 If someone **lays down** their **life** in a war or for a particular cause, they are killed because they are involved in it or support it; a literary use. PHR : VB INFLECTS

5 If someone **lays down** a plan, they carefully prepare it, so that they can continue with it, develop it, or benefit from it later. EG *But do you lay down a plan beforehand?* PHRASAL VB : V+ O+ADV = formulate

6 If a person or organization **lays down** rules, ideas, etc, or if the rules **lay down** what people should do, they state them with official authority, and other people are expected to obey them or agree with them. EG *...the conditions laid down by the Department of Health... ...rules laying down what is allowable... The policy has been laid down and agreed for years.* • *to* **lay down the law**: see **law**. PHRASAL VB : V+ O+ADV = set out

lay in. If you **lay in** an amount of something, you buy it and store it to be used later. EG *The Governor has laid in a plentiful supply of champagne.* PHRASAL VB : V+ O+ADV

lay into. **1** If you **lay into** someone or something, you start attacking them with physical violence or by severe criticism; an informal use. EG *She really laid into the management.* PHRASAL VB : V+ PREP, HAS PASS

2 If you **lay into** food or drink, you eat or drink it very eagerly and in large quantities; an informal use. PHRASAL VB : V+ PREP, HAS PASS

lay off. **1** If someone **is laid off** by their employers, they have been told to leave their job, usually because there is no more work for them to do. EG *The directors made plans to lay off 3,000 workers... Workers are being laid off at the rate of 100 a week.* PHRASAL VB : V+ O+ADV, USU PASS = sack

2 If you tell someone to **lay off**, you mean that they should leave you alone or stop touching something of yours; an informal use. EG *Lay off, will you... Lay off that book–it's mine!* PHRASAL VB : V+ ADV/PREP, USU IMPER

3 If you **lay off** doing something, you give up or stop doing it; an informal use. EG *I had to lay off for a couple of years... He never lays off.* PHRASAL VB : V+ ADV

4 See also **layoff**.

lay on. **1** If you **lay on** something such as food, entertainment, or a service, etc, you provide or supply it, especially in a generous or lavish way. EG *The first tram service was laid on from the Abbey to the Station... We laid on a great show for them... Mrs Kaul had laid on tea.* PHRASAL VB : V+ O+ADV

2 If someone **lays it on, lays it on thick**, etc, they exaggerate a statement, experience, or emotion in order to try to impress people; an informal expression. EG *I used grander expressions and laid it on much more thickly than I should have done.* PHR : VB INFLECTS

3 If you **lay one on** someone, in very informal British English, **3.1** you trick them or cause them to appear foolish. EG *They managed to lay one on the old man.* PHR : VB INFLECTS **3.2** you hit or punch them; often used in threatening people. EG *Shut up, or I'll lay one on you!* PHR : VB INFLECTS

lay out. **1** If you **lay out** a group of things, you spread them out and arrange them neatly, usually so that they can all be seen clearly. EG *Clothes, jewels, and ornaments were laid out on the ground or piled on stalls... We found a huge buffet laid out.* PHRASAL VB : V+ O+ADV

2 If you **lay out** ideas or information, you express or present them clearly and thoroughly. EG *This pamphlet lays out all the facts... The subject of the debate must be laid out clearly.* PHRASAL VB : V+ O+ADV

3 If you **lay out** a garden, building, town, etc, you plan and design how it should appear. EG *Olmsted went on to lay out three more parks in New York... The whole plan of the place is laid out in my head... Their settlement is laid out traditionally as a small village.* PHRASAL VB : V+ O+ADV ↑ arrange

4 If you **lay out** a dead person, you clean their body and dress them for people to see before the funeral. EG *We laid him out in his old military uniform.* PHRASAL VB : V+ O+ADV

5 If you **lay out** money on something, you spend a large amount of money on it; an informal use. EG *I laid out hundreds on the new house.* PHRASAL VB : V+ O+ADV = shell out

6 If someone or something **lays** a person **out**, they cause that person to lie down or fall over, especially by hitting them hard or making them feel very ill. EG *He's laid out in the hospital, on oxygen.* PHRASAL VB : V+ O+ADV

7 See also **layout**.

lay over. If you **lay over** in a place, you stop there for the night before continuing your journey; used mainly in American English. PHRASAL VB : V+ ADV, USU+A = stop over

lay up. **1** If an illness **lays** someone **up**, it causes them to stay in bed; an informal use. EG *The gentleman had been laid up for five days with a bad cold.* PHRASAL VB : V+ O+ADV

2 If you **lay up** something, you gradually save quantities of it for future use; an old-fashioned use. PHRASAL VB : V+ O+ADV

layabout /leɪəbaut/, **layabouts**. If you say that someone is a **layabout**, you mean they are idle and lazy. EG *He's just a drunken layabout.*
N COUNT = loafer

lay-by, lay-bys. A **lay-by** is a short strip of road by the side of a main road, where cars can stop for a while. EG *Pull into the next lay-by.*
N COUNT ⇑ area

layer /leɪə/, **layers**. 1 A **layer** of a material or substance is a quantity or piece of it that covers something or that exists in a flat, thin strip underneath or on top of other similar strips. EG *Rocks lie in layers... A fine layer of dust covers everything... He wrapped each component in several layers of foam rubber... ...the electrically charged layer in the atmosphere.*
N COUNT : USU + SUPP

2 If you refer to **layers** when you are talking about ideas, systems, people's personalities, etc, you are referring to the different parts of them and the way that they are added together or hide each other. EG *There are many layers of meaning... The ritual was buried beneath layer after layer of civilization... ...another layer of government.*
N COUNT : USU N IN PL + SUPP ⇑ level

layered /leɪəd/. Something that is **layered** is made or exists in layers. EG *Put the potatoes in the dish layered with the onion and parsley mixture... ...the layered nature of certain rocks.*
ADJ CLASSIF

layette /leɪet/, **layettes**. A **layette** is a set of the things that you need for a baby, such as clothes and nappies. People usually buy a layette before the baby is born; a formal word.
N COUNT : USU SING ⇑ equipment

layman /leɪmə[3]n/, **laymen**. A **layman** is 1 a person who is not trained, qualified, or experienced in a particular subject or activity. EG *To the layman, the questions which a doctor puts to the patient may seem irrelevant... ...a task for industrial experts rather than for laymen.* 2 a man who is involved with the Christian church but is not a member of the clergy or a monk. EG *...a prominent Catholic layman.*
N COUNT; N COUNT

layoff /leɪ[0]ɒf/, **layoffs**; also spelled with a hyphen. A **layoff** is 1 the act of an employer telling people to leave their jobs, usually because there is no more work for them to do. EG *Is a layoff in prospect?... In defense industries, sudden layoffs are common... Textile companies announced 2,000 fresh layoffs last week.* 2 a period of time in which people do not work or take part in their normal activities, often because they are resting or are injured. EG *He was bowling badly after his long lay-off.*
N COUNT = redundancy; N COUNT = break

layout /leɪ[0]aʊt/, **layouts**. The **layout** of a garden, building, piece of writing, etc is the way in which the parts of it are arranged. EG *...the general layout of the farm... He knew the airport layout intimately... ...a full-page layout in tomorrow's paper... ...the poor layout and organization of the report.*
N UNCOUNT + SUPP ⇑ design = arrangement

laze /leɪz/, **lazes, lazing, lazed**. If you **laze** or **laze about** in a place or for a period of time, you relax and enjoy yourself, not doing any work or anything else that requires effort. EG *They can laze in the sun without a care... ...cleaning and washing up while the other women laze about... ...lazing by the hotel pool.*
V, OR PHRASAL VB : V + ADV ⇑ rest = lounge

lazy /leɪzi[1]/, **lazier, laziest**. 1 Someone who is **lazy** does not want to work or make any effort to do anything; used showing disapproval. EG *He became remarkably lazy... ...a lazy fellow... His teacher thought he was lazy.* ◇ **laziness**. EG *Only laziness prevented him from doing it.*
ADJ QUALIT = idle; ◇ N UNCOUNT = idleness

2 **Lazy** actions or ways of behaving are done gently or easily without making very much effort. EG *She gave a lazy smile... He had a lazy, drawling way of talking.* ◇ **lazily**. EG *Thomas looked at it lazily... ...lazily combing his hair.*
ADJ QUALIT : ATTRIB ⇑ casual; ◇ ADV WITH VB ⇑ casually

3 If you describe the movement of something as **lazy**, you mean that it moves slowly and gently. EG *The current is lazy and meandering... ...going at the same lazy pace.* ◇ **lazily**. EG *The clouds passed lazily across the sky... The Mercedes drove lazily past.*
ADJ QUALIT; ◇ ADV WITH VB

4 **Lazy** ideas, excuses, etc are unsatisfactory because they have not been thought about carefully enough; used showing disapproval. EG *The generation gap is a lazy excuse for the age-old problems between parents and children... ...the lazy assumption that he was past the worst of his problems.*
ADJ QUALIT : ATTRIB

lazybones /leɪzi[1]bəʊnz/. If you say that someone is a **lazybones**, you mean that they are very lazy indeed.

lb, lbs. **lb** is an abbreviation for a pound in weight; used in written English, usually after a number. EG *...a 2lb bag of sugar... ...from 1000 lbs to 11 tons... I even gained 3lb.*

lead, leads, leading, led. The word is pronounced /liːd/ in all paragraphs except paragraphs 26 to 28, where it is pronounced /led/. 1 If a person or vehicle **is leading** a moving group, they are in front of the other people or vehicles. EG *Jenny was leading and I was at the back... ...two tanks leading, the remainder of the force in two parties behind.* ● If you are **in the lead**, you are in front of a moving group. EG *I now had Sheila in the lead and Bob at the rear.*
V OR V + O ⇑ head; ● PHR : USED AS AN A

2 If you **lead** a group of moving people, you walk or ride in front of them, because you are in charge of them. EG *...a general leading an army into battle... He led a demonstration through the City.*
V + O : USU + A ⇑ head

3 If you **lead** someone to a particular place or object, you go with them to show them where it is. EG *'This way.' Morris led Ellen to a cabinet in the store... Mrs Kaul was leading him to his seat... Captain Imrie led me round the crew's quarters.* ● If you **lead the way** along a particular route, you go along it in front of someone in order to show them where to go. EG *Jack led the way down the rock... I led the way to Andrew's cabin.*
V + O + A ⇑ take = escort, guide; ● PHR : VB INFLECTS

4 If you **lead** a person or animal, you hold the person's arm, hold the animal by a rope, etc in order to keep control over them, in case they fall or try to run away. EG *My mother takes me by the hand and leads me downstairs... I was led into the prisoner's dock... I let them lead the camels.*
V + O ⇑ take

5 If something such as a road, pipe, or wire **leads** to a particular place or in a particular direction, it goes to that place or follows that direction. EG *...a path leading straight to Stonehenge... The steps lead down to his basement... ...a road leading away from the town... ...two wires leading to an amplifier.* ● If a road or route **leads** someone to a particular place or in a particular direction, they get to that place or go in that direction by using it. EG *He went where the path led him.*
V + A; ● V + O + A ⇑ send = direct

6 If a door or other entrance **leads** to or into a place, you can get to that place by going through it. EG *There was a gate on our left leading into a field... ...the entrance that leads to the House of Commons.*
V + A *(to/into)*

7 If you **lead** at a particular point in a race or competition, you are winning at that point. EG *Who is leading?... Becker leads by five games to four.* ● If you have **the lead** at a particular point in a race or competition, you are winning at that point, for example by being in front of your opponents, or by having more points or goals than they have. EG *They share the first round lead... This win gave him the overall lead... New Zealand went into an early lead.*
V; ● N SING WITH DET ⇑ position

8 The **lead** that someone has at a particular point in a race or competition is the distance, amount of time, etc by which they are winning. EG *A recount gave McClellan a lead of only 3,472 over Hearst... The Australian yacht's lead looked unbeatable.*
N SING WITH DET : USU + SUPP

9 If one company or country **leads** others in a particular activity such as scientific research or business, it is more successful or advanced than they are in that activity. EG *Britain briefly led the world in computing science... In 1950-73 Japan led the industrial growth league.*
V + O, OR V : USU + A

10 If you **lead** a group of people, organization, or activity, you are officially in control or in charge of them. EG *The Labour Party was led by Wilson... His brother was about to lead an expedition into Arctic Canada... He lacked any desire to lead.*
V OR V + O

11 If you **lead** an activity such as a political campaign or a riot, you start it or are very involved or active in it. EG *The rioting was led by students... The educated middle class led the move towards independence.*
V + O ⇑ initiate

12 If you **take the lead** or **take a lead** in a particular situation or group, 12.1 you put yourself in a position of authority in it and start making decisions and organizing people. EG *He always takes the lead in any group... Other feminists won't mind us taking a lead.*
PHR : VB INFLECTS

12.2 you develop new ideas or methods that other people consider to be a good example or model to follow; used showing approval. EG *Other firms are now following the company's lead in the integration of research and development... The European Community should give a lead in respect of disarmament*
N COUNT

talks... The men will support us if we take a strong, clear lead.

13 If you **lead** a particular kind of life, you do things or experience things that give it that particular quality. EG *My friends seemed to be leading a much more exciting life... ...the difficult life she had led as a child.* [V+O ⇑ have]

14 If an action, idea, or problem **leads** to an unpleasant situation, it begins a process which ends in that situation, but may not directly cause it. EG *...a drinking spree which had led to his court appearance... It was his incomes policy which finally led to his downfall... Worn bearings will lead to a gradual wearing down of the engine.* [V+A *(to)* = result in]

15 If something **leads** you to do, experience, or feel something, it influences or affects you in such a way that you do, experience, or feel it. EG *Recent evidence is leading historians to reassess that event... Julie's work has led her into some peculiar situations... My thoughts led me further in the direction of self pity.* [V+O+*to*-INF, OR V+O+A ⇑ motivate]

16 If someone or something **leads** you to think or believe something, they cause you to think or believe it, sometimes when it is incorrect or foolish. EG *What leads you to expect that you will be chosen?... Their doctrines led them to believe in their ultimate victory... The house is not as grand as the porch in front led one to believe.* • to **lead** someone **astray**: see **astray**. [V+O+*to*-INF]

17 If you **lead** a conversation or story, you control the way that it develops so that you can introduce a particular subject. EG *He tried to lead the conversation to a point where he could ask about Jimmy.* [V+O, OR V : USU +A]

18 In formal conversations, discussions, or lectures, people say **'This leads me to'** in order to introduce a new topic by indicating its connection with the previous one. EG *This leads me to an important point about Hoyland's experiments... This leads us naturally to ask what careers advisers should aim at.* [PHR ⇑ connect]

19 You say **one thing led to another** when you want to emphasize the end of a story and reach it quickly without discussing the details of what happened, for example because they are boring, embarrassing, or can be easily imagined. EG *Well, one thing led to another and we ended up at the police station!... Supposing they have lunch; and supposing one thing leads to another?* [PHR : VB INFLECTS]

20 A dog's **lead** is a long, thin piece of leather or a chain. You attach one end of it to the dog's collar and hold the other end in your hand so that you can control the dog. [N COUNT = leash]

21 A **lead** in a piece of equipment is a piece of wire covered in plastic which supplies electricity to the equipment or carries it from one part of the equipment to another. EG *Check that the leads to the battery are in good condition.* [N COUNT]

22 The **lead** in a play, film, or artistic group is the most important part in it. EG *Richard was signed up to play the lead in their new film... ...the lead part.* ▸ also used of the person who plays this part. EG *...the lead singer of the group.* [N COUNT ⇑ star]

23 The **lead** in a newspaper is the most important story in it. EG *...the front page lead... ...the lead story.* [N SING WITH DET]

24 **Lead** is used in the following ways when talking about card games. **24.1** If you **lead** a particular card, you play it as the first card in one part of the game. EG *She led the king of diamonds.* [V OR V+O ⇑ start] **24.2** When it is your **lead**, it is your turn to play the first card. [N SING : POSS+N] **24.3** A **lead** is the card that is played first in one part of the game. EG *The queen would be a good lead in that situation.* [N COUNT]

25 A **lead** in a situation where many facts are not known, for example in the investigation of a crime or in a scientific experiment, is a piece of information or an idea which may help people to discover those facts. EG *The police were following up several leads.* [N COUNT = clue]

26 **Lead** is a soft, grey, heavy metal. It is mixed with other metals to form alloys. Lead is used to protect people from X-rays, and is also sometimes added to petrol. If taken into the body, lead can be poisonous. EG *...the dark lead spire of the church... ...a box of lead soldiers... ...lead levels in petrol.* [N UNCOUNT]

27 The **lead** in a pencil is the centre part of it which makes a mark on paper. EG *...a soft lead pencil.* [N COUNT = graphite]

28 In informal English, **lead** is also used to refer to bullets. EG *He walked on despite all the lead in his body.* [N UNCOUNT]

29 See also **leading**.

lead off. 1 If a road, corridor, etc **leads off** from a place, it starts at that place and goes away from it. EG *From the lift shaft four straight corridors lead off at right angles... ...a side street leading off from a road of shops.* [PHRASAL VB : V+ADV+A]

2 If a door or room **leads off** a place, it is or has an entrance which connects it directly with that place. EG *...two doors leading off the hallway... ...rooms leading off the courtyard.* [PHRASAL VB : V+PREP]

3 If someone **leads off** in a meeting, conversation, or performance, they start it. EG *She led off with a few of her old hit songs... The chairman led off with a financial statement.* [PHRASAL VB : V+ADV, USU+*with* = kick off]

lead on. If someone **leads** you **on**, they deceive you by giving you false information or by behaving in a misleading way. EG *Sheila seemed to be leading them both on.* [PHRASAL VB : ORDER V+O+ADV]

lead up to. 1 If events **lead up to** a final event or situation, they happen one after the other until that final event or situation is reached, and often provide the reasons for it. EG *...the chain of events that led up to her death.* [PHRASAL VB : V+ADV+PREP ⇑ precede]

2 If someone **leads up to** a particular subject, they gradually guide a conversation to a point where they feel that they can introduce the subject, often because they are embarrassed about it or think that the other person might be offended or upset by it. EG *Ever since you came in you've been leading up to this one question.* [PHRASAL VB : V+ADV+PREP]

leaded /lɛdɪd/ windows are made of small pieces of glass held together in a pattern by strips of lead placed between each piece. [ADJ CLASSIF : USU ATTRIB]

leaden /lɛdən/; a literary word. **1** A **leaden** sky or sea is dark grey in colour with no movement of clouds or waves, usually indicating that there will soon be bad weather. EG *The sky was leaden and thick... They prayed for a slight breeze from the leaden sea.* [ADJ CLASSIF]

2 If you describe people's movements or conversation as **leaden**, you mean that they are moving or talking with great difficulty, often because they are tired or embarrassed. EG *My steps felt slow and leaden... The conversation seemed leaden and awkward.* [ADJ QUALIT ⇑ heavy = tedious]

3 If you describe food as **leaden**, you mean that it is very heavy, solid, and difficult to eat and digest; used showing disapproval. EG *...a leaden piece of Christmas cake.* [ADJ QUALIT = stodgy]

4 A **leaden** object is made of lead; an old-fashioned use. EG *Hunting bullets have a dull leaden head.* [ADJ CLASSIF : ATTRIB ⇑ metal]

leader /liːdə/, **leaders. 1** The **leader** of a group of people or an organization is the person who is in control of it or in charge of it. EG *...the leader of the Labour Party... The group's leader died of exposure... He didn't know how to be a decisive leader.* [N COUNT = chief, head]

2 The **leader** at a particular point in a race or competition is the person who is winning at that point. EG *The leader after the first lap was a girl from New Zealand... The Liberal candidate is the current leader in the polls.* [N COUNT]

3 The **leader** among a range of products or companies is the one that is most successful. EG *It is the market leader in both countries and has 40 per cent of the total sales.* [N COUNT]

4 The **leader** of a group of moving people or vehicles is the person or vehicle that is in front of the others. EG *Thousands of people went on the walk and Sandy and Sue were among the leaders for most of the way.* [N COUNT]

5 The **leader** of an orchestra is **5.1** in British English, the most senior violin player, who acts as a deputy to the conductor. [N COUNT] **5.2** in American English, the conductor. [N COUNT]

6 The **leader** in a newspaper is the main article in it, usually expressing the editor's opinion on the most important news items of the day. [N COUNT = editorial]

leadership /liːdəʃɪp/. **1** The **leadership** is **1.1** the people who are in control of a group or organization. EG *Despite pressure from the leadership, the conference rejected official policy... ...the gap between the leadership and the men they represent.* [N SING : *the*+N] **1.2** the position or state of being in control of a group of people. EG *...the election of Wilson to the leadership... ...an independent group under the leadership of Jones.* [N SING : *the*+N, OR N UNCOUNT]

2 **Leadership** refers to 2.1 the qualities that make someone a good leader, for example the ability to make decisions, give orders, and gain people's respect and trust. EG *They count on their parents for leadership, love, and security... The community would be looking to us for leadership... ...a task calling for energy and leadership.* 2.2 the particular methods that a leader chooses to use in doing his or her job. EG *He was determined to establish a new style of leadership.* N UNCOUNT; N UNCOUNT ⇑ control

lead-free /lɛdfriː/. **Lead-free** petrol has no lead in it. ADJ CLASSIF

lead-in /liːdɪn/, **lead-ins**. A **lead-in** is what is said or done as an introduction before the main subject or event, especially the introduction to a radio or television programme. EG *...a typical lead-in to a news report... ...a good lead-in to the final phase.* N COUNT

leading /liːdɪŋ/. 1 **Leading** people or things are the ones that are in the most important, responsible, or successful positions. EG *A demand for change came from leading politicians... ...some of the leading women's organizations... Among ten leading American cigarettes, only one has a low tar rating.* ADJ CLASSIF: ATTRIB ⇑ main = chief

2 The **leading** part or role in a play or film is the main part or role. EG *She played the leading role in The Winter's Tale.* ▸ used to describe people who play the leading role. EG *...their enchanting leading lady, Yvonne Printemps.* ADJ CLASSIF: ATTRIB = principal

3 People or things that are **leading** are at the front of a line of moving people or things. EG *The leading battalions were forced back several kilometres... The leading car was full of security men.* ADJ CLASSIF = first

leading article, leading articles. A **leading article** is an article in a newspaper which comments on an item of news and which explains the opinion of the editor or publisher. EG *He was able to continue his attack in a leading article of 30th October.* N COUNT

leading light, leading lights. If someone is a **leading light** in an organization or campaign, they are one of the most important, active, enthusiastic, and successful people in it; used showing approval. N COUNT ⇑ person

leading question, leading questions. A **leading question** is a question that is asked in such a way that it seems that a particular answer is expected; used showing disapproval. N COUNT ⇑ hint

leaf /liːf/, **leaves**; **leafs, leafing, leafed**. 1 A **leaf** is one of the flat, thin, and usually green parts of a tree or plant. Leaves have various shapes depending on the type of plant. EG *The plant's red berries remain long after the leaves have fallen.* N COUNT
● When trees **come into leaf**, they produce leaves; used of trees which lose their leaves in winter. EG *I love this time of year when all the trees are coming into leaf.* ● PHR : VB INFLECTS
● When trees are **in leaf**, they have leaves on their branches; used of trees which lose their leaves in winter. EG *The trees and shrubs were in full leaf.* ● PHR : USED AS AN A

2 A **leaf** is also 2.1 one of the pieces of paper of which a book is made. EG *Slowly, she turned the leaves of the beautiful old book.* 2.2 the part of the top of a table that can be folded down or away when it is not needed. EG *Could you put the leaf up and set the table for breakfast please?* N COUNT = page; N COUNT ⇑ extension

3 If you say that are going to **turn over a new leaf**, you mean that you are going to start to behave in a better and more acceptable way. EG *Right! I'm going to turn over a new leaf. I'm going to get to work on time in future.* PHR : VB INFLECTS ⇑ improve

4 If you **take a leaf from** someone's **book**, you behave or act in the same way as that person because their behaviour is considered to be especially good, or because they have been successful. EG *They believe that we should take another leaf from the Japanese book and invest heavily in new technology.* PHR : VB INFLECTS ⇑ imitate

leaf through. If you **leaf through** a book or magazine, you turn the pages quickly without reading or looking at them carefully. EG *While he is waiting he leafs through a magazine.* PHRASAL VB : V+PREP+O = flip through, thumb through

leafless /liːflɪ²s/. If a tree is **leafless**, it has no leaves; used to describe trees which lose their leaves in winter. EG *The trees stand dead, white, and leafless.* ADJ CLASSIF = bare

leaflet /liːflɪ²t/, **leaflets, leafleting, leafleted**. 1 A **leaflet** is a little book or a piece of paper containing information about a particular subject. Usually leaflets are given free to the public by organizations. EG *If you want to know more about this scheme, get leaflet RPL.6 from the employment office... The company produces a little leaflet called 'Protect your Pipes from Frost'.* N COUNT = booklet, pamphlet

2 If you **leaflet** a place, you distribute leaflets there, for example by handing them to people, or by putting them through letter boxes. EG *The committee decided to leaflet housing estates to publicize its campaign.* V+O

leafy /liːfi¹/. 1 Trees and branches that are **leafy** have lots of leaves on them. EG *The children shouted, waving leafy branches above their heads.* ADJ QUALIT

2 A place that is **leafy** has lots of trees and plants; used showing approval. EG *...a leafy suburb... ...the leafy shade of the avenue.* ADJ QUALIT ⇑ green = verdant

league /liːg/, **leagues**. 1 A **league** is 1.1 a group of people, clubs, or countries that have joined together for a particular purpose, or because they share a common interest. EG *...the League of Nations... ...the National Book League.* 1.2 a group of sports clubs which play the same sport in competition with each other to see which club is the best. EG *...the football league... How's Sussex doing in the league?... ...league cricket.* N COUNT : ALSO IN NAMES; N COUNT

2 If you are **in league** with someone, you are working together with them for a particular purpose, often secretly; sometimes used showing disapproval. EG *They found out that he was really in league with the police... They're in league, you know.* PHR : USED AS AN A, IF+PREP THEN *with* ⇑ cooperate

3 People often use the word **league** when they are making comparisons between different people or things, especially in terms of their quality. EG *She was very elegant but he seemed to be in a different league altogether... Teeside shot towards the top of the unemployment league 18 months ago.* N COUNT+SUPP ⇑ scale

4 A **league** is also an old-fashioned measurement of distance, which was equal to about three miles or five kilometres. People now sometimes say 'leagues' when they mean a very long way. EG *...the great towers of Ely cathedral, visible across leagues of flat marshland.* N COUNT

leak /liːk/, **leaks, leaking, leaked**. 1 If a solid object **leaks**, it lets a substance such as liquid or gas pass through a hole or crack in it. EG *The roof leaks... Do you remember the way the boat leaked?... ...faulty, leaking drain pipes.* V ⇑ seep

2 If a liquid, gas, etc **leaks**, it passes through a hole or crack in an object that is supposed to be solid. EG *The water was still slowly leaking out... ...a really damp, wet place where you get leaking water, such as a cellar.* V : USU+A ⇑ escape = seep

3 A **leak** is 3.1 a crack, hole, or other fault that liquid, gas, etc can pass through. EG *The pipe's got a leak.* N COUNT
3.2 an amount of liquid, gas, etc that is escaping from an object by means of a crack, hole, or other fault. EG *Never look for a gas leak with a naked flame... ...a large leak of radioactivity at Windscale.* N COUNT ⇑ seepage

4 If someone **leaks** a piece of information, especially one that is secret, they let the public know about it, for example by showing a document to the newspapers. EG *He made sure the story was leaked to the media.* ▸ used as a noun. EG *...the possibility of a security leak... No-one outside would know how small and unimportant the leaks were.* V+O : IF+PREP THEN *to* ⇑ divulge, disclose; ▸ N COUNT ⇑ disclosure

5 If you **take a leak** or **go for a leak**, you urinate; a very informal expression. PHR : VB INFLECTS

leak out. If information or news that you want to keep secret **leaks out**, it becomes generally known, often because people have been gossiping or talking carelessly. EG *News of their engagement leaked out just before Christmas... Tales of this kind leak out from time to time.* PHRASAL VB : V+ADV ⇑ divulge

leakage /liːkɪdʒ/, **leakages**. A **leakage** is an amount of liquid, gas, etc that is escaping from an object by means of a crack, hole, or other fault. EG *A leakage in the hydraulic system was diagnosed.* N COUNT

leaky /liːki¹/, **leakier, leakiest**. Something that is **leaky** has holes, cracks, or other faults which allow liquids and gases to pass through. EG *It has a leaky roof and many other problems.* ADJ QUALIT ⇑ damaged

lean /liːn/, **leans, leaning, leaned, leant**. The forms **leaned** and **leant** are both used as the past tense and past participle of the verb. 1 When you **lean** in a particular direction, you bend or move your body in that direction. EG *He was sitting on the edge of his chair and leaning eagerly forwards... If I hold your legs, you can lean over and take a look at those holes down there... I leaned out of the window... She* V+A ⇑ incline *leaned back on the sofa.* ◇ **leaning.** EG *...the Leaning Tower of Pisa.* ● If you say that you are **leaning over backwards** for someone, you mean that you are doing everything that you possibly can to help them. EG *I've leant over backwards to help her.* ◇ ADJ CLASSIF ● PHR : VB INFLECTS

2 If you **lean** on or against something or **lean** an object on or against something, you place your body or the object so that it is partly supported by something such as a wall or table. EG *He leaned against a tree... He leaned the bike against a railing... It was so crowded I couldn't help leaning on him a little.* V-ERG+A

3 If you **lean** towards a particular idea, belief, or type of behaviour, you have a tendency to think or act in a particular way. EG *I think that good parents who naturally lean towards strictness should stick to their beliefs... They lean towards the politics of the International communists.* V+PREP *(towards)*

4 Someone who is **lean** is very thin but looks strong and healthy; used showing approval. EG *He was forty years old, a lean, handsome man... He was in his early thirties and had a lean, athletic build... Their bodies were lean, their muscles toned by boxing lessons.* ADJ QUALIT ⇑ slim

5 **Lean** is used to describe **5.1** meat which does not have very much fat. EG *I only eat lean meat.* **5.2** periods of time when people do not have very much food or money. EG *In the lean years, crop failures are common... ...a lean winter.* ADJ QUALIT; ADJ QUALIT : ATTRIB ⇑ difficult

lean on. If you **lean on** or **lean upon** someone, **1** you try to influence them by threatening them. EG *They can lean on the administration by threatening to withhold their subscriptions.* **2** you depend on them for support and encouragement. EG *He leant on the calm and steadfast Kathy... They lean heavily upon each other for support.* PHRASAL VB : V+PREP, HAS PASS ⇑ pressurize; PHRASAL VB : V+PREP ⇑ rely on

leaning /liːnɪŋ/, **leanings.** A **leaning** towards particular beliefs, ideas, or aims is a tendency to have these beliefs, ideas, or aims. EG *She had occasionally shown a leaning towards communism.* N COUNT+SUPP = inclination, proclivity

leant /lɛnt/ is one of the forms of the past tense and past participle of **lean**.

lean-to, lean-tos. A **lean-to** is a shed which is attached to one wall of a house, garage, or other building. N COUNT

leap /liːp/, **leaps, leaping, leaped, leapt.** The forms **leaped** and **leapt** are both used as the past tense and past participle of the verb. **1** If you **leap** or **leap** somewhere, you jump high in the air or jump a long distance. EG *Some monkeys can leap four or five metres from one tree to another... They took off their clothes and leaped into the water.* ▸ used as a noun. EG *She made a leap for the sofa and nearly went through the springs.* V OR V+O : USU+A ⇑ spring; ▸ N COUNT ⇑ bound

2 If you **leap** somewhere, you move there suddenly and quickly. EG *She leapt into a taxi and headed for the Bronx... We had to leap across the road to the car... She leaped up and ran off.* V+A ⇑ bound

3 If you say that someone should **look before** they **leap**, you mean that before they take any action they should think about what problems their actions might create or what consequences there might be. PHR : VBS INFLECT

4 If flames, shadows, etc, **are leaping**, they are moving quickly and in an irregular way backwards and forwards or up and down. ◇ **leaping.** EG *The shed was filled with leaping shadows... They sat against a background of leaping flames.* V : USU+A; ◇ ADJ CLASSIF : ATTRIB

5 A **leap** forward or a **leap** ahead is a large and important change, increase, or advance. EG *We need a new economic leap forward into an age of high technology... He blamed the leap in oil prices for our present economic problems.* ● **quantum leap**: see **quantum.** ● **by leaps and bounds**: see **bound.** N COUNT : USU SING

6 If you **leap** to a particular place or position, you make a large and important change, increase, or advance. EG *The US leapt from sixth place to second.* V+A ⇑ move

7 If your **heart leaps**, you experience a sudden, very strong feeling of surprise, fear or happiness; a fairly literary expression. EG *My heart leapt at the thought of seeing her again... A noise behind Castle made his heart leap.* PHR : VB AND N INFLECT

8 If something that you are reading **leaps out at** you or **leaps off the page at** you, it suddenly seems extremely obvious to you. EG *The answer leapt out at me.* PHR : VB INFLECTS

9 If something **leaps to** your **mind** or **leaps into** your **mind**, you suddenly think of it. EG *The name of Otto Gerran was not one that would leap automatically to my mind.* PHR : VB AND N INFLECT

leap at. If you **leap at** a chance, opportunity, etc, you accept it quickly and eagerly. EG *David would have leaped at the chance.* PHRASAL VB : V+PREP, HAS PASS = seize

leapfrog /liːpfrɒg/, **leapfrogs, leapfrogging, leapfrogged**; also spelled with a hyphen. **1 Leapfrog** is a game which children play, in which one group of children bend over, while others jump over their backs. N UNCOUNT

2 If one group of people **leapfrogs** into a particular position or **leapfrogs** someone else, they use the technical or other achievements of another person or group in order to make advances of their own. EG *It gives the third world a chance to leapfrog into the space age.* V+A, OR V+O

leapt /lɛpt/ is one of the forms of the past tense and past participle of **leap**.

leap year, leap years. A **leap year** is a year which has 366 days. There is a leap year every four years. N COUNT

learn /lɜːn/, **learns, learning, learned, learnt.** The forms **learned** and **learnt** are both the past tense and past participle of the verb. **1** If you **learn** something or **learn** to do something, you get knowledge of it or skill in doing it by your own efforts and hard work, for example by studying a subject at school. EG *Children learn foreign languages very easily... He had never learnt to read and write.* ◇ **learned.** EG *The rat's response was clearly learned behaviour.* ◇ **learning.** EG *He found learning very difficult... Our aim was to design an entirely new learning programme.* V OR V+O/*to*-INF; ◇ ADJ CLASSIF; ◇ N UNCOUNT

2 If you **learn** something such as a poem or the script of a play, you get to know the words so well that you can remember them without looking at them. EG *We have to learn the whole poem by heart.* V+O = memorize

3 If people **learn** to do something, they gradually become able to do something or to accept something, especially by changing their attitudes. EG *We still have to learn how to live peacefully... You will have to learn to accept my authority... Inflation is something that people have learned to live with.* ● If you **learn from** your **mistakes**, you improve the way that you behave or that you do things because of the mistakes that you have made in the past. EG *He never seems to learn from his mistakes.* ● If you **learn** something **the hard way**, you have to make mistakes or face difficulties and hardships before you can improve your behaviour or the way that you do things. EG *They learned the lesson the hard way.* V+*to*-INF; ● PHR : VB AND N INFLECT; ● PHR : VB INFLECTS

4 If you **learn** of something, you find out about it, especially by being told about it by other people; a fairly formal use. EG *They offered help as soon as they learnt of the accident... She was extremely upset to learn that he had died...* V+A *(of)*, OR V+O/REPORT-CL ⇑ discover

5 In very informal English, people sometimes use the word **learn** instead of the word 'teach'. Most speakers of English dislike this use. EG *That'll learn you.* V+O

6 See also **learning.**

learned /lɜːnɪ²d/. **1** Someone who is **learned** has gained a lot of knowledge, especially by studying, and is thought of as being very wise. EG *He was one of that rare breed of wise and learned men.* ADJ QUALIT : USU ATTRIB = erudite

2 Books, papers, etc, that are **learned** have been written by somebody with a lot of knowledge, especially about an academic subject. EG *He thought little of experts and their learned text books.* ADJ QUALIT : USU ATTRIB = scholarly

learner /lɜːnə/, **learners.** A **learner** is someone who is learning about a particular subject or how to do something. EG *She is a very slow learner... ...learners of English... ...a learner driver.* N COUNT

learning /lɜːnɪŋ/ is knowledge or skill that has been gained through studying. EG *He's clearly a man of learning.* ● See also **learn.** N UNCOUNT

learnt /lɜːnt/ is one of the forms of the past tense and past participle of **learn**.

lease /liːs/, **leases, leasing, leased. 1** A **lease** is an official written agreement by which the owner of a piece of property allows someone else to use that property for a period of time in return for agreed amounts of money. EG *She took a lease on the house in 1916... The lease had expired and would not be renewed... The house was let on a 99-year lease.* N COUNT ⇑ contract

2 If you **lease** property, **2.1** you allow someone else to use it in return for regular payments according to an V+O, V+O+O, OR V+O+A *(to)*

official agreement. EG *He had persuaded the local council to lease him a house.* **2.2** you have the use of it in return for regular payments of money to the owner, according to an official agreement. EG *They leased a Turkish house at Cospoli.* V+O ⇑ rent

3 If you say that someone or something has **a new lease of life**, you mean that there is some improvement in the general situation or that something has been done which allows them to last longer or to be more successful. EG *That service has given my car a new lease of life!* PHR : USU USED AS O

leasehold /liːshəuld/. If a building or land is described as **leasehold**, it is allowed to be used in return for payment of money as arranged according to a lease. EG *...a leasehold property.* ADJ CLASSIF ≠ freehold

leaseholder /liːshəuldə/, **leaseholders**. A **leaseholder** is a person who is allowed to use a property according to the terms of a lease. N COUNT ⇑ tenant

leash /liːʃ/, **leashes**. A dog's **leash** is a long thin piece of leather or a chain, which you attach to the dog's collar so that you can keep the dog under control. EG *I kept Sandy on the leash.* N COUNT = lead

least /liːst/. **1** You use **at least** **1.1** to say that the number or amount mentioned is a minimum and that the actual number or amount is greater. EG *At least a dozen ideas were considered and rejected... I must have slept twelve hours at least... He drank at least half a bottle of whisky a day... Women have at least as much intellectual ability as men.* PHR : USED AS AN A ⇑ more than **1.2** to indicate that something is the minimum which can be done, even if nothing else is done. EG *We've got to change the law in that direction at least... They took steps to ensure that whoever else suffered, they at least did not lose out in the struggle... Go to see the administrator or at least write a letter.* PHR : USED AS AN A **1.3** to indicate an advantage that exists in spite of the disadvantage or bad situation that was previously mentioned. EG *The process looks rather laborious but at least it is not dangerous... At least you and he have something in common... It made a change at least.* PHR : USED AS ADV SEN = still

2 You can also use **at least** when you want to modify or correct something that you have just said. EG *A couple of days ago I spotted my ex-wife; at least I thought I did, I wasn't sure... In his face I sometimes see a look of worry, or at least anxiety... He didn't expect to be so busy, at least not initially... Etta appeared to be asleep; at least her eyes were shut.* PHR : USED AS ADV SEN

3 You use **least** **3.1** to indicate that an amount of something is as small as it can be. EG *...the thinner animals, who had the least muscle over their bones... ...the area where there is the least success... ...doing the things that cost the least.* QUANTIF+N UNCOUNT : SUPERL ≠ most **3.2** to indicate that something happens to as small a degree or extent as is possible. EG *He came out when I least expected it... They're the ones who need it the least.* ADV SUPERL : WITH VB ≠ most **3.3** to indicate that someone or something has less of a particular quality than most other people or things. EG *One of the smallest and least powerful of the African states... He was certainly the least technically proficient of all the finalists.* ADV SUPERL + ADJ/ADV ≠ most **3.4** to emphasize the smallness of a particular quality, especially when it hardly exists at all. EG *I don't believe that any of you find the least difficulty in making decisions... He stood there staring into the sky and without the least idea as to why he did so... The least pressure would suffice to crack the tube.* ADJ QUALIT : ATTRIB, SUPERL = tiniest, faintest **3.5** to emphasize that a particular situation or event is much less important or serious than other possible or actual situations or events. EG *The sack was the least you'd get if you failed to get your work done in time... That was the least of her worries.* ADJ QUALIT : SUPERL, IF + PREP THEN *of* ≠ the most

4 The word **least** is also used in the following expressions. **4.1** You can use **in the least** and **the least bit** to emphasize a negative. EG *I don't mind in the least, I really don't... She wasn't the least bit jealous... It was changing me in a way that I had not in the least expected.* PHR : USED AS AN A OR + ADJ, WITH BROAD NEG = at all **4.2** If you say **'that's the least of it'**, you are suggesting that what you are about to say is much more surprising or serious than what you have just said. EG *That's the least of it. You wait till I tell you what happened next.* CONVENTION **4.3** If you say that something is **the least that** someone **can do**, you are referring to the one thing that you think must be done by someone in a particular situation, even if nothing else can be done. EG *It was the least he could do for her... And if I can't protect them from something, the least I can do is warn them that there is a danger.* PHR : USED AS C/S **4.4** If you say **'it was the least I could do'**, you are politely acknowledging someone's thanks for something that you have done for them and are implying that you owe them something. EG *'Thank you very much.'–'It was the least I could do.'* CONVENTION **4.5** You can use **to say the least** or **to say the least of it** to suggest that a situation is actually much more serious, shocking, or extreme than it seems. EG *She lacked tact (to say the least) in expressing herself... They're unusual to say the least of it... ...a development which will have, to say the least, intriguing effects.* PHR : USED AS ADV SEN **4.6** You can use **not least** to emphasize a particularly important example or reason. EG *...all western countries, not least the USA... ...for a whole variety of reasons, not least because people have begun to find that it is too expensive.* PHR : USED AS AN A ⇑ especially ⇑ in particular **4.7** You can use **least of all** after a negative statement to emphasize that there is one person or thing that is certainly not involved in what you are talking about. EG *Nobody seemed amused, least of all Jenny... We are not psychologists or doctors, least of all social workers.* PHR : USED AS AN A, WITH BROAD NEG = especially not

5 You can also use **least** to describe someone or something that is considered to be less important than anyone or anything else; a formal use. EG *The last and least of the line was his son Edward... ...the museums of South Kensington, the least of which demands a day for a visit.* ADJ QUALIT : SUPERL, IF + PREP THEN *of*

6 You use **last but not least** or **last but by no means least** to say that the last person or thing to be mentioned is definitely not unimportant, but is in fact considered to be rather important. EG *Oh yes, last but not least, as Mother says, is my sister Sarah.* PHR : USED AS ADV SEN

leather /leðə/ is the specially treated skin of animals. It is used for making shoes, clothes, bags, furniture, etc. EG *...a black leather chair... ...leather jackets.* N UNCOUNT ⇑ material

leathery /leðəri[1]/. If the texture of something, for example someone's skin, is **leathery**, it is tough and hard, like leather. EG *The skin of both women was tanned deep brown and leathery by their years of travel.* ADJ QUALIT

leave /liːv/, **leaves, leaving, left**. **1** If you **leave** a place or person, you go away from that place or person. EG *My plan now was to leave for the seaside... My train leaves Euston at 11.30... They left the house to go for a walk after tea... He stood up to leave... I left Conrad and joined the Count at his table.* V OR V+O ⇑ depart

2 If you leave a place or institution, you go away permanently from that place or no longer attend that institution. EG *Many of the children I met had left home after a savage beating... What do you want to do when you leave school?... She told him she was going to leave her job and move to London... All they want to do is leave at 16 and get a job.* ◊ **leaving**. EG *...a leaving present.* V OR V+O ⇑ quit ◊ ADJ CLASSIF : ATTRIB

3 If you **leave** someone that you have had a close relationship with, for example your husband or wife, you stop living with them or you finish the relationship. EG *Look, you mustn't tell Henry I'm leaving him... My husband had left me for another woman.* V OR V+O ⇑ desert = abandon

4 If you **leave** someone or something in a particular place, you let them remain there when you go away. EG *Leaving Rita in a bar, I made for the town library... I left my pack behind and took only my water bottle... If you leave things on the floor, they get trodden on.* V+O+A

5 If you **leave** something somewhere, **5.1** you forget to take it with you when you go away from a place. EG *I had left my raincoat in the restaurant... Millie had left her watch behind.* V+O+A **5.2** you put it where someone can find it and use it or you put it where it will be safe while you are away. EG *Leave your phone number with the secretary... Castle left his bicycle with the ticket collector at Berkhamsted station.* V+O, V+O+O, OR V+O+A *(for/with)*

6 If you **leave** someone doing something or **leave** them to an activity, you allow them to carry on with what they are doing when you go away from them. EG *We left him snoring in the front room... He left them making their calculations... I left her to her knitting.* V+O+-ING, OR V+O+A

7 If you **leave** someone to himself or to herself, you go away from them so that they are alone. V+O+A *(to)*+O (REFL)

8 If you **leave** a certain amount of something or if something is **left**, it remains when the rest has been taken away or used. EG *Nine from sixteen leaves seven... He drained what was left of his drink... Leave* V+O *some of the stew for the boys... There was only about ten minutes left of the lecture.* ● If you **have** something **left**, you have it after the rest has gone or been taken away or used. EG *I only had two pounds left... How many pills have you got left?... You have seventeen minutes left.* ● PHR : FIRST VB INFLECTS

9 If you **are left with** something, you have it in your possession, care, or responsibility after the rest has gone or been taken away or used. EG *You're left with a whole lot of stock that you can't get rid of... They were left with nothing.* PHR : AUX INFLECTS

10 If you **leave** food or drink, you do not eat or drink it, often because you do not like it. EG *If you don't like the potatoes, just leave them... Leave your drink, darling.* V+O

11 If you **leave** yourself something or **leave** yourself with something, you deliberately keep it because you know you will want to use it. EG *I meant to leave myself with fifteen pounds a week... I must leave myself half an hour extra to get into town.* V+O (REFL)+O, OR V+O (REFL)+A *(with)* ⇑ put aside

12 If something **leaves** a mark, effect, or sign, it causes that mark, effect, or sign to remain as a result. EG *I didn't want him to leave a trail of wet footprints... You shouldn't use detergent because it can leave a soapy smell... Coffee leaves a stain.* V+O

13 If you **leave** something in a particular state, position, or condition, you let it remain in that state, position or condition. EG *Leave the television on, I'm watching... Who left the gates open?... The result has left everybody dissatisfied... This new legislation would leave taxpayers worse off.* V+O+A/C

14 If you **leave** a space or gap in something, you deliberately make that space or gap, usually as part of another process or action. EG *Remember to leave a space between the fridge and the wall... He had the tact to leave a moment's respectful silence.* V+O

15 If you **leave it** to someone to do something or you **leave it** with someone, you give that person the responsibility for doing something or for dealing with a situation. EG *Leave it to me, I'll fix it... He left it to us to try and sort it out... It was left to the tenants to clean the lifts... Well, leave it with me and I'll see what I can do.* PHR : VB INFLECTS, USU+A ⇑ entrust

16 If you **leave** someone to do something, you allow them to do it without interfering or trying to influence them. EG *You really must leave me to decide what is possible and what isn't... I'll leave him to find that out for himself.* V+O+*to*-INF ⇑ let

17 If you **leave** something such as a decision or choice to someone, you allow them to do it or deal with it without interfering or trying to influence them. EG *My father left the choice to me, and I opted for the law... He said the whole business should be left to the courts.* V+O+A *(to)*

18 If you **leave** someone a particular course of action or the opportunity to do something, you make it available to them. EG *We must leave him some escape... You leave me no choice... You are therefore left with two alternatives.* V+O+O, OR V+O+A *(for/with)*

19 If you **leave** something until a particular time, you delay doing it or dealing with it until then. EG *Why do you always leave things to the last minute?... We decided to leave the opening of presents until morning.* V+O+A = put off

20 If you **leave** something that you ought to do, you do not do it or deal with it. EG *I couldn't be bothered to do my homework so I left it.* V+O ⇑ neglect

21 If you **leave** a particular subject, you stop talking about it and start discussing something else. EG *All right, let's leave it at that for today... Let's leave the budget and go on to another question... He would not make difficulties. Thus it was left.* V+O ⇑ put aside

22 You can use **leaving aside** to indicate that you do not want to discuss or take into account a particular subject or aspect of something. EG *Leaving aside for a moment a discussion of the disadvantages, let's turn to the advantages.* PREP

23 If you **leave** property or money to someone, you arrange for it to be given to them after you have died. EG *He left all his property to his wife... The money was left in trust for him to acquire at the age of twenty-one.* V+O, V+O+O, OR V+O+A *(to)* ⇑ give = bequeath

24 If someone **leaves** a wife, husband, children, etc, the wife, husband, or children remain alive after that person has died. EG *He leaves two sons and a daughter.* V+O ⇑ die

25 Take it or leave it. 25.1 If you say to someone **'take it or leave it'**, you are telling them that they can either accept something or not accept it, and that there must be no more discussion about the subject. EG *It's 65 pounds, take it or leave it.* PHR : USED AS ADV SEN **25.2** If you say about something that you can **take it or leave it**, you mean that you do not particularly like it but nor do you strongly dislike it. EG *'What about this for the front room?' 'I can take it or leave it.'* PHR

26 Leave is **26.1** a period of time when you do not have to do your usual job, but which is not a holiday. People have leave, for example, when they are ill or when they are having a baby. EG *She was granted a year's maternity leave... Paid holidays do not affect your entitlement to sick leave... She's on study leave until the end of September.* N UNCOUNT+SUPP ⇑ absence **26.2** a period of time when you are on holiday from your job; used especially for people who are in the army or employed by the government. EG *He'd come over on leave from Northern Ireland... He asked for forty-eight hours' leave.* N UNCOUNT = time off **26.3** permission to do something; a formal use. EG *He has asked leave to address the House.* N UNCOUNT : USU + *to*-INF

27 If you **take your leave** or **take leave of** someone, you say goodbye and go; a formal expression. EG *I think we had best take our leave... It's time for us to take our leave of you.* PHR : VB INFLECTS ⇑ depart = go

28 Leaves is also the plural form of **leaf**.

29 The word **leave** is also used in the following expressions, which are explained at other places in this dictionary. ● to **leave** someone **to their own devices**: see **device**. ● to **leave a lot to be desired**: see **desire**. ● to **take leave of** your **senses**: see **sense**.

leave behind. **1** If you **leave** someone or something **behind**, you go away permanently from them. EG *I hated having to leave behind all my friends... We must leave our childhood behind.* PHRASAL VB : V+O+ADV ⇑ desert, abandon

2 If you **leave** an object or a situation **behind**, it remains after you have left a place. EG *...leaving behind an unsolved mystery... These little details I leave behind for you to settle.* PHRASAL VB : V+O+ADV

3 If someone has been **left behind**, for example in their work or studies, they have not been as quick as other people at understanding things, so that they are at a lower level of progress or development. EG *You had to follow closely if you wanted to avoid being left behind... If you don't know your technical jargon, you're going to be left behind.* PHRASAL VB : V+O+ADV, USU PASS

leave off. **1** If you **leave** someone or something **off** a list, you do not include them in that list. EG *Hopper was too important to be left off the guest list.* PHRASAL VB : V+O+PREP ⇑ omit

2 If you continue doing something **from where** you **left off**, you start doing it again at the point where you had previously stopped doing it. EG *He sat down at the piano again and started playing from where he left off... She carried on from where she had left off.* PHR : USED AS AN A

3 If you tell someone to **leave off**, you are telling them to stop annoying you; an informal use. EG *Just leave off, will you!* PHRASAL VB : V+ADV, USU IMPER

leave out. **1** If you **leave** someone or something **out**, you do not include them in an activity, collection, discussion, group, etc. EG *One or two scenes in the play were left out... I'm aware that we've had to leave out much interesting and important work.* PHRASAL VB : V+O+ADV ⇑ omit = exclude

2 If someone is **left out** or feels **left out**, they are not included in a group or activity that they want to be a part of. EG *He never liked anyone to be left out of anything... He had no one to talk to and was feeling left out.* PHRASAL VB : V+O+ADV ⇑ ignore = exclude

leaven /lɛvən/. **1 Leaven** is something that is introduced to a very dull or boring activity or situation in order to make it more interesting or lively. EG *...a dangerous revolutionary leaven.* N UNCOUNT ⇑ agent

2 Leaven is also yeast; an old-fashioned use. N UNCOUNT

leavened /lɛvənd/. **Leavened** bread or dough has had yeast added to it. EG *Leavened bread stays fresh longer than unleavened bread.* ADJ CLASSIF : USU ATTRIB

leave of absence. If you have **leave of absence**, you have permission to be away from work for a certain period. N UNCOUNT = time off

leaves /li:vz/ is **1** the plural of **leaf**. **2** the third person singular form of **leave**.

leavings /li:vɪŋz/ are the things that remain after something has been finished, for example food on a plate, rubbish, etc. EG *We had littered the tables with our messy leavings of cake-crumbs and broken meat.* N PLURAL : USU WITH POSS ⇑ waste = leftovers

Lebanese /lɛbəniːz/. **1** Something that is **Lebanese** belongs or relates to Lebanon or to its people. EG *...the Lebanese coast south of Beirut.* — ADJ CLASSIF

2 A **Lebanese** is someone who comes from Lebanon. — N COUNT

lecher /lɛtʃə/, **lechers**. A **lecher** is a man who is continually thinking about sex, or continually wanting to have sex with different women; used showing disapproval. — N COUNT = philanderer, womanizer

lecherous /lɛtʃərəs/ means showing or expressing lechery; used showing disapproval. EG *He had a lecherous expression on his face.* — ADJ QUALIT ⇑ lustful = salacious

lechery /lɛtʃəri¹/ is the behaviour or feelings of people, especially men, who are continually thinking about sex, especially when they behave towards other people in a sexual way; used showing disapproval. EG *...a shameless glance of lechery... ...cold-blooded lechery.* — N UNCOUNT ⇑ lust = salaciousness

lectern /lɛktəˢn/, **lecterns**. A **lectern** is a high sloping desk on which you put your notes when you are standing up and giving a lecture. EG *He turned over one of his note cards on the lectern.* — N COUNT

lecture /lɛktʃə/, **lectures, lecturing, lectured**. **1** A **lecture** is a talk on a particular subject that is given in order to teach people about that subject, for example by a university or college teacher. EG *...a series of lectures on literature... I went to a lecture he gave at the African Institute... ...lecture notes.* — N COUNT ⇑ address

2 If you **lecture**, you give a lecture or a series of lectures. EG *He had subsequently lectured in America... He lectured on Colonial Economic History at the University of Exeter.* — V

3 If someone **lectures** you about something, they scold you for something that you have done wrong, especially because they feel that you have behaved badly. EG *I had always been lectured about not talking with my mouth full... Peter was severely lectured for lack of consideration to his mother.* — V OR V+O, USU+A ⇑ criticize = reprove

4 A **lecture** is also strong criticism that someone makes about something that they do not like. EG *He will almost certainly launch into a little lecture about how bad times are.* — N COUNT = reprimand, reproof

lecturer /lɛktʃərə/, **lecturers**. A **lecturer** is someone who teaches at a university or college. EG *...a lecturer in sociology.* — N COUNT ⇑ teacher

lectureship /lɛktʃəʃɪp/, **lectureships**. A **lectureship** is the position of a lecturer at a university or college. EG *She was offered a lectureship at Birmingham University.* — N COUNT ⇑ post

led /lɛd/ is the past tense and past participle of **lead**.

ledge /lɛdʒ/, **ledges**. A **ledge** is **1** a piece of rock on the side of a cliff or mountain, which is in the shape of a narrow shelf. EG *Only a bird could get to that ledge.* — N COUNT **2** a small narrow shelf attached to a wall. EG *Could you leave it on the ledge by the cooker?* — N COUNT

ledger /lɛdʒə/, **ledgers**. A **ledger** is a book in which a company or organization writes down the amounts of money it spends and the amounts of money it receives. EG *The ledgers and account books had all been destroyed... ...the sales ledger.* — N COUNT

lee /liː/, **lees**; a formal word. **1** The **lee** of a place is the shelter that it gives from the wind or bad weather. EG *...in the lee of a rock.* — N SING: the+N+of

2 **Lee** means on the side of a ship which is away from the wind; a technical term in sailing. EG *I stepped out onto the starboard ladder on the lee side.* — ADJ CLASSIF: ATTRIB

3 The **lees** are the sediment that collects at the bottom of a bottle of wine, barrel of beer, etc. — N PLURAL

leech /liːtʃ/, **leeches**. **1** A **leech** is a small animal which looks rather like a worm and lives in water. Leeches feed by attaching themselves to other animals and sucking their blood. EG *The pond was full of leeches.* — N COUNT

2 If you call someone a **leech**, you mean that they live off other people, often making money out of them; used showing disapproval. EG *He's nothing but a leech.* — N COUNT = parasite

leek /liːk/, **leeks**. A **leek** is a long thin vegetable which is white at one end and has long green leaves. It is used in cooking and tastes rather like an onion. EG *...a casserole of fresh leeks and whole wild mushrooms.* — N COUNT

leer /lɪə/, **leers, leering, leered**. If someone **leers** at you, they smile in an unpleasant way, usually because they are sexually interested in you; used showing disapproval. EG *He leaned over and leered at them, saying, 'Good morning, little girls.'* ▸ used as a noun. EG *...a kind of bored leer.* — V: IF+PREP THEN at; N COUNT

leery /lɪəri¹/. If you are **leery** of something, you are cautious and suspicious about it and try to avoid it; an informal word. EG *I am always leery of sentences that contain the phrase 'My dear fellow'.* — ADJ QUALIT: PRED+of = wary

leeway /liːweɪ/; also spelled with a hyphen. **1** **Leeway** is the flexibility that someone has to change their plans, for example by taking more time or spending more money than they had originally intended to. EG *It doesn't give you much lee-way, does it?* — N UNCOUNT

2 If you have **leeway** to make up, you have to work very fast or hard because you do not have much time to reach a particular goal or because you have not made much progress. — N UNCOUNT = slack

left /lɛft/. **1** **Left** is the past tense and past participle of **leave**.

2 **Left** means **2.1** on or towards the side which, in English writing, has the first letter of a word, or the side of the body which for most people has the hand they do not write with. EG *He wore a black patch over the left eye... She came forward looking neither right nor left... He turned left and began strolling slowly down the street.* — ADV, OR ADJ CLASSIF: ATTRIB ≠ right **2.2** worn, or intended to be worn, on the left foot, hand, etc. EG *He was putting on his left glove.* — ADJ CLASSIF: ATTRIB ≠ right

3 The **left** is the left side, direction, or position. EG *There was a gate on our left leading into a field... His was the third door to the left... Her office is down the corridor on the left... In this row of statues, the third from the left is the Black Prince... He sat on the stage with Stroop at his left... Take the first left after the church... There was a strong light coming from the left.* — N SING: WITH the/POSS ≠ right

4 A **left** is your left hand when you punch someone with it or a punch given with your left hand; a boxing term. EG *'With your left now!' she cried. 'Your left! Your left!'... Ali felled him with a left to the jaw.* — N COUNT: USU a/POSS+N IN SING ≠ right

5 The **Left** or **the left** is **5.1** the people or groups of people who support the political ideals of socialism rather than capitalism. EG *While the Right is holding its ground, the Left is shifting its ground... This fear is by no means confined to the extreme left.* — N SING: the+N, VB CAN BE SING OR PL ≠ right **5.2** the political ideals, groups, and activities which are closer to socialism or communism than conservatism. Some people think of political ideals as being like a line with communism on the left and fascism on the right. EG *I gather that politically he's a bit on the left... ...numerous other organisations on the Marxist left... ...the far left.* — N SING: the+N ≠ right

left-hand describes the position of something when it is on the left side. EG *She noted it down on the left-hand side of the page... The left-hand wall was lined with shelves.* — ADJ CLASSIF: ATTRIB ≠ right-hand

left-hand drive. A **left-hand drive** car, van, or lorry has the steering wheel on the left side, and is designed to be used in countries where people drive on the right-hand side of the road. EG *She has a left-hand drive mini that she got in France.* — ADJ CLASSIF: ATTRIB

left-handed. Someone who is **left-handed** uses their left hand rather than their right hand for activities such as writing, painting, and eating. EG *Virtually nothing is specifically designed for left-handed people... She writes right-handed but plays tennis left-handed.* — ADJ CLASSIF, OR ADV ≠ right-handed

left-hander, left-handers. A **left-hander** is someone who uses their left hand rather than their right hand for activities such as writing and painting. EG *Da Vinci, Michelangelo, Raphael, and Picasso were all left-handers.* — N COUNT ⇑ person

leftie /lɛfti¹/, **lefties**; also spelled **lefty**. **1** If you refer to someone as a **leftie**, you mean that they have socialist beliefs; used mainly in informal British English showing disapproval. EG *...troublemakers and lefties.* — N COUNT: ALSO VOC ⇑ person

2 A **leftie** is someone, especially a sports player, who is left-handed; used mainly in informal American English. — N COUNT ⇑ person

leftism /lɛftɪzm/ refers to the beliefs and behaviour of people who support socialist or communist ideals. EG *...the fashionable leftism of students.* — N UNCOUNT ≠ rightism

leftist /lɛftɪst/, **leftists**. **1** A **leftist** is a person who supports the ideals of socialism or communism. EG *A band of leftists took over the consulate.* — N COUNT = left-winger

2 **Leftist** ideals, activities, and people support or believe in the ideas of socialism or communism. EG — ADJ CLASSIF: ATTRIB

...extreme leftist activities... ...the first leftist President.

left-luggage office, left-luggage offices. A **left-luggage office** is a place in a railway station or airport where you can pay to leave your luggage for a short period of time; used in British English. N COUNT = repository

left-of-centre people or political parties support political ideas which are closer to socialism than to capitalism. EG *...left-of-centre MPs... ...a mildly left-of-centre government.* ADJ CLASSIF

leftover /lɛftəʊvə/, **leftovers**; also spelled with a hyphen. 1 A **leftover** is something that belongs to a past period of time and surprisingly still exists, although most other things of that period no longer do. EG *...a leftover from our hunting past... ...the dynamite, a leftover from his days as a mining contractor... ...another charming left-over, the Opera Arcade.* N COUNT = throwback

2 **Leftover** is used to describe an amount of something that remains after you have finished using it. EG *...a bottle of left-over perfume... Put leftover soap in the dish.* ADJ CLASSIF: ATTRIB

3 **Leftovers** are the food that remains uneaten after a meal. EG *The leftovers were thrown to the village dogs... ...warming up the leftovers.* N PLURAL = scraps

leftward /lɛftwəd/. The form **leftwards** is also used, mainly in British English. **Leftward** or **leftwards** means on or towards a political position that is closer to socialism than to capitalism. EG *...the leftward shifts in his party since 1945... The Labour Party moved in a leftwards direction.* ▸ used as an adverb. EG *...a more leftward looking Democratic Party... The party has moved leftwards while in opposition.* ADJ CLASSIF: ATTRIB ▸ ADV AFTER VB

left-wing; also spelled without a hyphen. 1 **Left-wing** means having or supporting political ideas that are close to socialism or communism. EG *They were very left wing, perhaps all students are... ...left-wing policies... ...a well-known left-wing publisher.* ADJ QUALIT = radical

2 The **left wing** of a group of people, especially a political party, consists of the members of it whose beliefs are closer to socialism or communism than are those of its other members. EG *He was on the left wing of the Labour Party... ...the emergence of a strong left wing... ...left-wing disapproval.* N COUNT: IF SING the+N ≠ right-wing

left-winger, left-wingers. A **left-winger** is a person whose political beliefs are close to socialism or communism, or closer to them than most of the other people in the same group or party. EG *...the veteran left-winger Michael Foot... ...left-wingers in his own union.* N COUNT ≠ right-winger

leg /lɛg/, **legs, legging, legged.** 1 Your **legs** are the long parts of your body that are attached to your hips and have your feet at the end of them. EG *She broke a leg about a year ago... Etta sat with her legs crossed... Gita had long, thin, brown legs... She had rheumatism in her bad leg.* N COUNT ⇑ limb

2 The **legs** of an animal, bird, or insect are the thin parts of its body that it uses to stand on or to move across the ground. EG *...the legs of a spider... Their hind legs are enormously powerful.* N COUNT

3 The **legs** of a pair of trousers are the parts that cover your legs. EG *His briefcase moved against his trouser leg... The wind flapped at the legs of my shorts.* N COUNT: USU the/MOD+N

4 A **leg** of lamb, pork, or chicken is a piece of meat that consists of the animal's or bird's leg, especially the thigh. EG *She was roasting a leg of lamb in the oven... ...a chicken leg.* N COUNT+SUPP ⇑ joint

5 A **leg** of a piece of furniture such as a table or chair is one of the parts of it that rests on the floor and helps to support its weight. EG *...a chair leg... ...tables with metal legs and yellow tops.* N COUNT+SUPP

6 A **leg** of a long journey is one part of it, usually between two points where you stop. EG *They set off on the first leg of their 12,000 mile journey.* N COUNT: USU ORDINAL+N+of = stage

7 In some sports, for example in darts matches, relay races, and some football competitions, a **leg** is a part of a game, a part of a race, or one game of a pair or series of games. EG *Leeds United got through to the second leg of the European Cup.* N COUNT

8 If you **leg it**, you run away very quickly, usually in order to escape from someone or something; an informal use. EG *He'd probably take fright and leg it.* PHR: VB INFLECTS = flee, scarper

9 The word **leg** is also used in the following expressions in informal English. **9.1** If you **give** someone a **leg up**, you help them to climb something such as a wall by supporting or pushing their leg. ▸ also used to mean that you help them in something such as their career. PHR: VB INFLECTS **9.2** If you **pull** someone's **leg**, you tell them something untrue for a joke which will shock or worry them, but which they will find amusing when they realize it is not true. EG *Don't take any notice of what he says–he's pulling your leg.* PHR: VB AND N INFLECTS = tease **9.3** If you say that someone **does not have a leg to stand on**, you mean that a statement or claim that they have made cannot be justified or proved at all. PHR: FIRST VB INFLECT **9.4** If you say that someone or something is **on** their **last legs**, you mean that they are in a very bad or weak condition and will probably collapse or die soon. EG *Most of the houses were on their last legs.* PHR: USED AS AN A **9.5** **to shake a leg**: see **shake**. • **with** your **tail between** your **legs**: see **tail**.

legacy /lɛgəsi[1]/, **legacies.** 1 A **legacy** is money or property which you receive after someone has died, because they said in their will that you should have it. EG *All I've got is that little legacy my Aunt left.* N COUNT ⇑ gift = bequest

2 The **legacy** of a person, event, or period of history is the situation or attitudes that they leave behind them, and the influence that they have on the future. EG *...the legacy of Colonialism... There was no bitter struggle, no legacy of animosity.* N COUNT+SUPP ⇑ consequence

legal /liːgəᵊl/. 1 **Legal** is used to describe things that involve the law, knowledge of the law, or the use of the law. EG *...the British legal system... I'm taking legal action... ...legal advice... ...legal fees.* ◇ **legally.** EG *Divorce could be made less legally complicated.* ADJ CLASSIF: ATTRIB ◇ ADV WITH VB

2 An action or situation that is **legal** is allowed or approved by law. EG *Capital punishment is legal in many countries... Wendy is below the legal age of consent.* ◇ **legally.** EG *We are not legally married... ...to make the contracts legally binding.* ADJ CLASSIF = lawful ◇ ADV WITH VB = lawfully

legal aid is financial assistance given by the government or another organization to people who cannot afford to pay for a lawyer at a time when they need advice or to be represented in court; a technical term. EG *She has applied for legal aid.* N UNCOUNT ⇑ welfare

legalise /liːgəlaɪz/. See **legalize**.

legalistic /liːgəlɪstɪk/ means using, expressing, or understanding the law in a very precise and careful way, often showing excessive attention to its details. EG *Daintry's got a very legalistic mind.* ◇ **legalistically.** EG *It is a lengthy document, legalistically expressed.* ADJ QUALIT ◇ ADV

legality /li[1]gælɪti[1]/. If you talk about the **legality** of an action or situation, you are talking about whether it is legal or not. EG *He disputed the legality of the invasion... The Supreme Court confirmed the bill's legality.* N UNCOUNT+SUPP = legitimacy

legalize /liːgəlaɪz/, **legalizes, legalizing, legalized**; also spelled **legalise**. If an action or situation **is legalized**, a law is passed that makes it allowed or acceptable. EG *Citizens' band radio has now been legalized.* ◇ **legalization** /liːgəlaɪzeɪʃəᵊn/. EG *She argued for the legalization of marijuana.* V+O: USU PASS ⇑ permit ◇ N UNCOUNT+SUPP

legal tender is money, especially a particular coin or banknote, which is officially part of a country's currency at a particular time. For example, the halfpenny coin is no longer legal tender in Britain. N UNCOUNT

legate /lɛgət/, **legates.** A **legate** is a person who is the official representative of another person, especially the Pope's official representative in a particular country; a formal word. EG *...the Pope's legate in France... ...the papal legate.* N COUNT

legation /lɪ[2]geɪʃəᵊn/, **legations.** A **legation** is a group of government officials and diplomats who work in a foreign country and represent their government in that country; a technical term. EG *...the large staff of the legation.* ▸ used also of the building in which they work. EG *...the huge front windows of the Legation.* N COUNT: ALSO IN NAMES AFTER N ⇑ mission

legend /lɛdʒənd/, **legends.** 1 A **legend** is a very old and popular story that may or may not be true. EG *...fairy tales, folk tales, legends and myths... Christian and Jewish legends tell of these mysterious strangers... ...the legend of King Arthur.* N COUNT = myth, saga

2 **Legend** is used to refer to all the stories of this kind considered as a group or type. EG *The original inhabitants are supposed, according to legend, to have been blacksmiths... Legend has it that the sun sent down two of his sons to help them.* N UNCOUNT

3 A **legend** is also a story that many people are talking about, which concerns people, places, or events that are famous at the present time. EG *The newspapers were describing it as 'the end of the* N COUNT

Gdansk legend'... ...legends about Piggott's skill as a jockey.

4 If you refer to someone as being a **legend**, you mean that they are so famous in a particular field that their actions and achievements are often talked about. EG *Brook has become something of a legend... Both men were legends in their own time.* — N COUNT

5 The **legend** on a picture, coin, map, etc consists of the words which are written on it or next to it that state its title or purpose or explain something about it. EG *'Picture of the week,' said the legend... ...a banner inscribed with the legend, 'Twenty Years of Treason'.* — N COUNT = inscription

legendary /lɛdʒəndə^{0}ri^1/. A **legendary** person, place, or event is 1 very famous and many stories are told about it. EG *...one of his many legendary acts of courage... ...the legendary beauty of the Caribbean... Her enormous appetite is legendary in our family.* — ADJ CLASSIF = renowned 2 mentioned or described in an old legend. EG *...the legendary king who turned back the Danes... ...the legendary past of myths and history.* — ADJ CLASSIF : USU ATTRIB

-legged /lɛgɪd, lɛgd/ is used after numbers or adjectives to indicate how many legs someone or something has or to describe the legs. EG *...a three-legged stool... ...a square-legged table... Jimmy is a bandy-legged 71-year old... She was sitting cross-legged.* — COMB : FORMS ADJS

leggings /lɛgɪŋz/ are an outer covering of leather or other strong material, often in the form of trousers, that you wear over your normal trousers in order to protect them. EG *...farmers in leather breeches and leggings.* — N PLURAL : ALSO *a pair of*+N

leggy /lɛgi^1/, **leggier, leggiest**. If you describe someone as **leggy**, you mean that they have very long legs. EG *...the sultry, leggy Marlene Dietrich... ...a beautiful girl: leggy, Italian-looking.* — ADJ QUALIT

legibility /lɛdʒɪbɪlɪti^1/. If you talk about the **legibility** of a piece of writing, you are talking about how easy or difficult it is to read, for example how large or small, clear or faint the letters written or printed in it are. — N UNCOUNT

legible /lɛdʒə^{1}bə^{0}l/. A piece of writing that is **legible** is written or printed clearly and can be read easily. EG *...a crumpled but still legible document... It is clearly legible to the student.* — ADJ QUALIT ◇ **legibly**. EG *Please add your name. Legibly.* — ◇ ADV WITH VB

legion /liːdʒə^{0}n/, **legions**. 1 A **legion** is 1.1 a large group of soldiers who form one section of an army. EG *He was buried by the legion patrol who took the village... ...the Condor legion.* — N COUNT : ALSO IN NAMES AFTER N ⇑ unit 1.2 a large number of people who do the same thing. EG *...legions of foreign visitors to New York... Cameron had seen a legion of fortune-tellers in his time.* — N COUNT/PART ⇑ group = hoards, masses

2 If you say that things of a particular kind are **legion**, you mean that there are a great number of them; a formal use. EG *Their own internal problems were legion... Stories about him are legion.* — ADJ CLASSIF : PRED = numerous

legionnaires' disease is a serious lung infection that can kill people. — N UNCOUNT

legislate /lɛdʒɪsleɪt/, **legislates, legislating, legislated**. When a government or state **legislates**, it officially passes a new law; a formal word. EG *...the Government's intention to legislate... Parliament must legislate against fox-hunting.* — V : IF+PREP THEN *for/against*

legislation /lɛdʒɪsleɪʃə^{0}n/; a formal word. **Legislation** refers to 1 the laws that are passed by a government or state concerning a particular situation or thing. EG *...tax legislation... ...the introduction of legislation to govern industrial relations... ...legislation on prices and incomes.* — N UNCOUNT+SUPP 2 the act or process of passing a law. EG *The Government rejected any idea of legislation.* — N UNCOUNT

legislative /lɛdʒɪslətɪv/; a formal word. **Legislative** means 1 involving or relating to the process of making and passing laws. EG *The Government should consider further legislative reforms... Education is low on the Government's legislative priorities.* — ADJ CLASSIF : ATTRIB ⇑ legal 2 having the power or ability to make and pass laws. EG *...the Bengal Legislative Council.* — ADJ CLASSIF : ATTRIB

legislator /lɛdʒɪsleɪtə/, **legislators**; a formal word. A **legislator** is a person who is involved with making or passing laws, especially a member of a government or parliament. EG *Many of the legislators who drafted the bill are landowners... ...some state legislator makes a speech, forms a committee.* — N COUNT

legislature /lɛdʒɪslətʃə/, **legislatures**; a formal word. The **legislature** of a particular state or country is the group of people in it who have the power to make and pass laws. EG *...the New York legislature... The legislature approved a loan... ...a state legislature committee.* — N COUNT : USU *the*+N ⇑ body

legitimacy /lɪ^{2}dʒɪtɪmɪ^{1}si^1/; a formal word. 1 The **legitimacy** of something is 1.1 its right to be officially accepted because it is based on a law or a lawful process such as an election or an international agreement. EG *They challenge the very legitimacy of the government... ...the new frontiers had no legitimacy.* — N UNCOUNT : IF+PREP THEN *of* = legality, validity 1.2 its correctness according to the facts of a situation, the logic of an argument, or the opinions of most people. EG *...the legitimacy of our complaint... ...opinions about the degree of legitimacy of these reports... ...the legitimacy of scientific experiments on animals.* — N UNCOUNT : IF+PREP THEN *of* = validity

2 The **legitimacy** of a child is the fact that their parents were legally married at the time when the child was born, which is especially important in legal matters such as inheritance. EG *If Henry could prove his legitimacy, she and her husband would be dispossessed.* — N UNCOUNT : USU WITH POSS

legitimate, legitimates, legitimating, legitimated; a formal word. The word **legitimate** is pronounced /lɪ^{2}dʒɪtɪmɪ^{1}t/ when it is an adjective and /lɪ^{2}dɪtɪmeɪt/ when it is a verb. 1 Something that is **legitimate** can be proved to be correct or reasonable according to a law, the facts of a situation, the logic of an argument, or the opinions of most people. EG *Religious leaders have a legitimate reason to be concerned... ...a legitimate business transaction... You have a legitimate excuse.* — ADJ CLASSIF = valid, acceptable ◇ **legitimately**. EG *This material is legitimately owned by our Swiss associates... He apologized, quite legitimately blaming his assistant for the mistake.* — ◇ ADV WITH VB = justifiably

2 Someone who is **legitimate** was born of parents who were legally married at the time, and can claim a share of their wealth or possessions when they die. EG *...evidence that he was his father's legitimate son, the rightful heir to Knole.* — ADJ CLASSIF ⇑ lawful

3 To **legitimate** something means the same as to **legitimize** it. EG *Their reputation must be legitimated by actual achievements... This policy legitimates home ownership.* — V+O = validate ◇ **legitimation** /lɪ^{2}dʒɪtɪmeɪʃə^{0}n/. EG *These institutions depend on the state for their legitimation.* — ◇ N UNCOUNT

legitimize /lɪ^{2}dʒɪtɪmaɪz/, **legitimizes, legitimizing, legitimized**; also spelled **legitimise**. **Legitimize** is a formal word. To **legitimize** something means to officially allow it, accept it, or approve of it. EG *...the process was legitimized in the Enclosure Acts... If a group is not legitimized, their meetings can be forbidden.* — V+O = sanction ◇ **legitimization** /lɪ^{2}dʒɪtɪmaɪzeɪʃə^{0}n/. EG *...the need for legitimization by elections.* — ◇ N UNCOUNT

legless /lɛglɪ^{2}s/. If someone is **legless**, 1 they have no legs, for example as the result of an accident. EG *...the legless beggars who pull themselves along the pavement.* — ADJ CLASSIF : ATTRIB 2 they are extremely drunk; used mainly in very informal British English. EG *He was more or less legless already and we were only on our third pint.* — ADJ QUALIT ⇑ incapable

leg room; also spelled with a hyphen. **Leg room** is the amount of space, especially in a car or other vehicle, that is left in front of your seat and in which you can stretch or move your legs. EG *...the lack of leg-room in a modern jet.* — N UNCOUNT

leisure /lɛʒə/. 1 **Leisure** is the time when you are not working and you can relax and do things that you enjoy doing. EG *Not everybody wants more leisure... ...leaving families with little leisure time to spend together.* — N UNCOUNT = relaxation

2 If someone does something **at leisure** or **at** their **leisure**, they do it slowly, taking as much time as they want and doing it when they want to. EG *Now I can read at leisure... ...thinking about things at great leisure... He accumulates the necessary materials at his leisure.* — PHR : USED AS AN A

leisured /lɛʒəd/. 1 **Leisured** people are people who do not work, usually because they are rich. EG *Culture was for the leisured classes.* — ADJ CLASSIF : ATTRIB

2 **Leisured** activities are done in a relaxed way or do not involve work. EG *...a leisured life in the suburbs... He ate a leisured luncheon.* — ADJ QUALIT : ATTRIB = easy-going

leisurely /lɛʒəli^1/. A **leisurely** action or one that is done at a **leisurely** pace is done in a relaxed way without hurrying. EG *My wife went off for a leisurely* — ADJ QUALIT = unhurried *walk round the gardens... I explained in a leisurely way what was going on... ...the leisurely tempo of progress.* ▸ used as an adverb. EG *He strolled leisurely away from the bar.* ▸ ADV WITH VB = calmly

lemming /lemɪŋ/, **lemmings**. A **lemming** is an animal that looks like a large rat with thick fur. Lemmings lives in cold northern regions. Many people believe that lemmings rush over the edge of cliffs in large numbers and die. ▸ used to describe people who follow leaders or ideas without thinking what they are doing. EG *Everybody's following her like lemmings over the precipice... ...our acceptance of everything and lemming-like blindness to any disagreeable aspect.* N COUNT ⇑ rodent

lemon /lemənn/, **lemons**. 1 A **lemon** is an oval-shaped fruit with a thick bright yellow skin. Lemons are juicy but sour, and lemon juice or slices of lemon are often used to flavour food or drinks. EG *Try squeezing a little lemon juice into it... ...a slice of lemon... ...lemon peel.* ▸ used of the tree on which lemons grow. EG *...a lemon grove.* N COUNT/UNCOUNT ▸ N COUNT

2 **Lemon** is a drink that is made from or that tastes of lemons. EG *...a glass of lemon.* N UNCOUNT

3 Something that is **lemon** is bright yellow in colour. EG *...her lemon pyjamas... ...lemon yellow.* ▸ used as a noun. EG *She was dressed head to toe in lemon.* ADJ COLOUR ▸ N UNCOUNT

4 In informal English, a **lemon** is also **4.1** something that is a failure, or that is not as good or useful as you expected it to be. EG *This car has been something of a lemon as far as reliability is concerned.* **4.2** someone who is made to appear or feel foolish in a particular situation. EG *I felt a bit of a lemon, just standing there... I'm going to look a lemon, aren't I?* N COUNT = loser; N COUNT ⇑ fool = twit

lemonade /lemәneɪd/. **Lemonade** is 1 a colourless, sweet, fizzy drink. EG *...bottles of lemonade.* 2 a drink that is made from lemons, sugar, and water. N UNCOUNT; N UNCOUNT

lemon curd. **Lemon curd** or **lemon cheese** is a thick yellow substance made of lemons which you can spread on bread or put in tarts. N UNCOUNT ⇑ preserve

lemon sole, lemon soles. A **lemon sole** is a flat fish that can be cooked and eaten. N COUNT/UNCOUNT

lemur /liːmə/, **lemurs**. A **lemur** is an animal that looks like a small monkey and has thick fur, a long snout and a long tail. Lemurs live mainly in Madagascar and are active at night. N COUNT ⇑ primate

lend /lend/, **lends, lending, lent**. 1 If you **lend** something to someone, you allow them to have or to use something of yours for a period of time. EG *Will Bob lend you his car?... She was reading a book I had lent her.* V+O+O, OR V+O +A *(to)* ⇑ loan

2 When people or organizations such as banks **lend** you money, they give it to you and you agree to pay it back at a future date, often with an extra amount as interest. EG *I often lend her money... The treasurer has authority to lend up to half a million dollars... The banks are lending to the big landowners at much lower rates.* V+O, V+O+O, OR V+O+A *(to)* = loan

3 If you **lend** support or **lend** your support to someone or something, you support them. EG *They refused to lend their support to the North... This material lends support to the assumption that we will win.* V+O+A *(to)*, V+O+O, OR V+O ⇑ give

4 If something **lends** a particular quality to something else, it adds that quality to it. EG *Tradition lends order to the world... ...lending the place a festive look... It would lend credibility to her arguments.* V+O+A *(to)*, V+O+O, OR V+O

5 If people or things **lend** themselves **to** being dealt with or considered in a particular way, it is easy to deal with them or consider them in that way. EG *...problems which do not lend themselves to simple solutions.* PHR : VB INFLECTS

6 If you **lend** someone **a hand**, you help them. EG *I was hoping you'd lend a hand... You'd probably have to lend a hand with the training.* PHR : VB INFLECTS ⇑ assist

7 If you **lend an ear** to someone or their problems, you listen to them carefully and sympathetically. PHR : VB INFLECTS

8 If you **lend** your **name** to a cause or project, you support it. EG *Famous personalities were willing to lend their names to the enterprise.* PHR : VB INFLECTS

lender /lendə/, **lenders**. A **lender** is a person or an institution that lends money to people. EG *They were considered a good risk by lenders... ...loans made by banks and other lenders.* N COUNT

lending library, lending libraries. A **lending library** is a library which allows people to take books away with them for a period of time, rather than reading them inside the library. N COUNT

lending rate, lending rates. The **lending rate** is the rate of interest that you have to pay when you are repaying a loan. EG *...the 12 per cent minimum lending rate... Bank lending rates have to rise.* N COUNT

length /leŋkθ/, **lengths**. 1 The **length** of something is the amount that it measures from one end to the other along the longest side. EG *It grows to a length of three or four metres... ...a metre and a half in length and as thick as a man's arm... Your own hair cut to this length could look very nice.* N UNCOUNT : USU +SUPP ⇑ measurement

2 If something happens or exists **the length of** something, **along the length of** it, etc, it happens or exists for the whole distance or way along it. EG *They travelled the length of the island... ...the sea which roared along the length of the shore... ...standing on the corner looking down the length of the street.* PREP

3 If you say that something happens throughout or across **the length and breadth** of a place, you are emphasizing that it happens everywhere in it; a literary expression. EG *Their protest will be echoed throughout the length and breadth of the land.* PHR

4 If you swim a **length** in a swimming pool, you swim the distance between the ends that are furthest from each other. N COUNT : USU NUM/QUANTIF+N

5 A **length** is the length of a thing that is involved in a particular situation such as a race and is therefore used as a unit of distance in that situation. EG *Her horse finished six lengths ahead... The Cambridge boat won by two clear lengths.* N COUNT : USU NUM/QUANTIF+N

6 A **length** of wood, string, cloth or other material is a piece of it that is intended to be used for a particular purpose or that exists in a particular situation. EG *...a short length of steel chain... Cut it up into half-inch lengths.* N COUNT+SUPP

7 The **length** of a book, film, or speech is the amount of writing or material that is contained in it. EG *A comprehensive dictionary would involve many more years' work and a length of text beyond the scope of a single volume... Make sure that it is of sufficient length for it to be divided into chapters.* N COUNT+SUPP, OR N UNCOUNT ⇑ size

8 The **length** of an event, activity, or situation is the period of time from beginning to end for which something lasts or during which something happens. EG *The length of the visit depends on you... ...an adventure indefinite in length. A month, a year, a decade... The children are excluded for certain lengths of time... It is extremely difficult to keep going for any length of time.* N UNCOUNT, OR N COUNT+SUPP ⇑ amount

9 The **length** of something is also its quality of being long, especially when it is longer than usual. EG *I hope the length of this letter will make up for my not having written earlier.* N UNCOUNT ⇑ size

10 If someone does something **at length, 10.1** they do it eventually, after a long interval or period of time. EG *'What kind of thing?' asked Basson at length... There was another silence. At length Claire said, 'You mean you're not going?'* **10.2** they do it in great detail or for a long time. EG *This will be discussed at length in the next chapter... He spoke at some length about the press.* PHR : USED AS AN A ⇑ then = at last; PHR : USED AS AN A ⇑ fully

11 If someone **goes to** great **lengths** to achieve something, they spend a great deal of time and effort and are willing to do whatever is necessary to achieve it, even if other people think they are being unreasonable. EG *He was willing to go to great lengths to avoid admitting his error... If they were prepared to go to these lengths, there was a good chance of a deal.* PHR : VB INFLECTS ⇑ try

12 See also **full-length**. ● **at arm's length**: see **arm**.

-length is added to nouns to form adjectives that describe something that is long enough to reach the point indicated by the noun. EG *...shoulder-length hair... ...a knee-length skirt.* COMB : FORMS ADJ CLASSIFS

lengthen /leŋkθən/, **lengthens, lengthening, lengthened**. When something **lengthens** or when you **lengthen** it, 1 it increases in length. EG *The waiting lists are lengthening... ...the lengthening dole queues... ...an adjustable handle that lengthens your reach by two feet.* 2 it lasts for a longer time than it did previously. EG *The silence lengthened... Babies gradually lengthen the interval between feeds.* V-ERG; V-ERG ⇑ increase

lengthways /leŋkθweɪz/. **Lengthways** or **lengthwise** means in a direction or position along the length of something. EG *The marrow is sliced in half lengthways... The blanket had to be folded lengthways.* ADV AFTER VB

lengthy /lɛŋk⁰θi¹/, **lengthier, lengthiest**. Something that is **lengthy 1** lasts for a long time. EG *It turned out to be a lengthy stay, from 1948 to 1952... This is a lengthy process for the patient.* ADJ QUALIT **2** contains a lot of writing, speech, or other material. EG *Howard found himself detained in lengthy conversation by a middle-aged man... It is a lengthy document... ...lengthy explanations.* ADJ QUALIT = extensive, long **3** is longer from one end to the other than usual. EG *...a lengthy creature like an eel.* ADJ QUALIT ⇑ big

leniency /liːnɪənsi¹/ is a lenient attitude or lenient behaviour. EG *...pleading for leniency... She was grateful for his leniency.* N UNCOUNT = clemency, mildness

lenient /liːnɪənt/. When a person is **lenient**, they are not as strict or severe as expected, especially when they are involved in punishing someone or supervising them. EG *Fines were low and magistrates often too lenient... If you weren't so lenient with her, she wouldn't be so badly behaved.* ADJ QUALIT ⇑ lax = mild, soft ▸ used also of people's attitudes and behaviour. EG *I had been too lenient in my criticism.* ◊ **leniently**. EG *Offenders had been treated leniently by the judge.* ◊ ADV WITH VB = mildly

lens /lɛnz/, **lenses**. A **lens** is **1** a thin piece of transparent material such as glass with a curved surface or surfaces, which makes things appear clearer, larger, or smaller when you look through it. Lenses are used in cameras, telescopes, and people's glasses. EG *It was barely visible even through a strong lens... Have your glasses got plastic lenses?... ...the camera lens.* N COUNT **2** the part of your eye behind the pupil that focuses light and helps you to see clearly. N COUNT
3 See also **contact lens, zoom lens**.

lent /lɛnt/. **1** The form **lent** is the past tense and past participle of **lend**.
2 In the Christian calendar, **Lent** is the period of forty days before Easter, during which some Christians eat less or give up something that they enjoy. N UNCOUNT

lentil /lɛntɪ¹l/, **lentils**. **Lentils** are the small seeds from the pods of a particular plant. Lentils are usually dried and used in cooking, especially to make soups and stews. N COUNT : USU PL ⇑ pulse

leonine /liːənaɪn/ means like a lion, and is used especially to describe men with a lot of hair on their head or big beards; a literary word. EG *...her husband's leonine head... ...his leonine beard.* ADJ CLASSIF : ATTRIB

leopard /lɛpəd/, **leopards**. A **leopard** is an animal that looks like a large cat and has yellow fur with black spots and a long tail. Leopards kill and eat other animals. EG *...a wounded leopard... ...a man in a leopard skin.* N COUNT

leotard /lɪətɑːd/, **leotards**. A **leotard** is an item of clothing that fits tightly over your body except for your legs. People, especially women, wear leotards when they are doing physical exercises or practising dancing. EG *The class was full of middle-aged women, stripped to their leotards.* N COUNT

leper /lɛpə/, **lepers**. A **leper** is **1** a person who has leprosy. N COUNT **2** a person who is avoided by other people because they have done something that has shocked or offended other people. EG *They've made you a leper in your own community.* N COUNT = outcast, pariah

leprosy /lɛprəsi¹/ is an infectious disease that causes painful white areas on people's skin, kills the nerves, and can cause fingers and toes to drop off. N UNCOUNT

lesbian /lɛzbɪən/, **lesbians**. **1** A **lesbian** is a homosexual woman. N COUNT ⇑ gay
2 Lesbian is used to describe homosexual women, their relationships and activities, and organizations or publications intended for them or created by them. EG *Many of the women were openly lesbian... She had a lesbian love affair with her secretary.* ADJ CLASSIF ⇑ gay

lesbianism /lɛzbɪənɪzə⁰m/ refers to homosexual relationships between women or the preference that a woman shows for sexual relationships with women. EG *Lesbianism is still seen as a problem in many societies.* N UNCOUNT ⇑ homosexuality

lesion /liːʒən/, **lesions**. A **lesion** is an injury or wound to someone's body; a medical term. EG *Most of the lesions were superficial.* N COUNT

less /lɛs/. **1 Less** means **1.1** not as much as before or not as much as something else. EG *A shower uses less water than a bath... I know I'm taking a chance, but less of one than I thought at first... It gets less attention than it deserves... We had less than three miles to go... Sixty per cent of them are aged 20 or less.* QUANTIF : USU + N UNCOUNT, COMPAR ≠ more **1.2** to a smaller extent than before or than is usual. EG *I liked it considerably less than before... You probably use them less than I do... Frankly, the more I hear about him, the less I like him.* ADV COMPAR : WITH VB **1.3** having a smaller amount of a particular quality than something or someone else, or than it had before. EG *Most of the other plays were less successful... From this time on, I felt less guilty... Fires occurred less frequently outside this area... The oil supplies were much less important than anybody had forecast.* ADV COMPAR + ADJ/ADV ≠ more **1.4** having a particular quality to a smaller degree or extent than the average. EG *...the less developed countries... The less educated may have difficulty in finding work.* ADV COMPAR + ADJ ≠ more
2 In sums, **less** means the same as minus. EG *Five less three is two.* = take away
3 Less is used to introduce something and to say that it is not as true, serious, good, bad, etc as something else which you mention later. EG *We regarded the newspapers there less as newspapers than as political statements... The group is really less of a threat than a nuisance.* ADV COMPAR + as/of
4 You use **less and less** to say that something is becoming smaller all the time in extent, degree, or amount. EG *He found them less and less interesting... There is less and less freedom for children... They had less and less to talk about.* PHR
5 You use the expressions **still less, much less, even less** after a negative statement in order to emphasize that the second statement which they are introducing is also negative; a formal use. EG *It was not a merely scientific interest; still less was it a political one... I did what I had never done in his presence, much less in his arms. I cried.* CONJ SUBORD ⇑ nor
6 Less than is used in front of an adjective or adverb in order to add a negative quality to the statement that is being made. EG *It would have been less than fair... ...a good deal less than perfect... ...the one thing that I was less than totally happy about.* PHR + ADJ ≠ more than
7 You can use **no less** as an emphatic way of expressing surprise, admiration, or sometimes sarcasm. EG *...the President of the United States, no less.... She spoke on no less a subject than the future of the human race... He was brooding about the meaning of his life, no less.* PHR : USED AS ADV SEN
8 You can use **no less than** when you are giving a number to indicate that you think that it is surprisingly large. EG *By 1880, there were no less than fifty-six coal mines... ...no less than 40 per cent of the material.* PHR + NUM = as many as
9 You say **'less of that'** or **'less of it'** to tell someone, especially children, to stop doing something annoying or naughty, when you are in a position of authority over them. CONVENTION
10 See also **lesser, nonetheless**.
11 more or less: see **more**. ● **nothing less than**: see **nothing**.

-less is added to nouns in order to form adjectives that describe something or someone as not having the thing indicated by the noun. EG *...meaning→meaningless... ...land→landless... ...power→powerless.* SUFFIX : FORMS ADJS ≠ -ful

lessen /lɛsən/, **lessens, lessening, lessened**. If something **lessens** or you **lessen** it, it becomes smaller in size, amount, degree, or importance. EG *Separating the sick from the healthy lessens the risk of infection... Their financial hardship has lessened as Rosemary has succeeded as a writer.* V-ERG = decrease ◊ **lessening**. EG *...a lessening of his power.* ◊ N UNCOUNT

lesser /lɛsə/. **1 Lesser** is used to indicate **1.1** that something is smaller in extent, degree, importance, or amount than something else that is mentioned. EG *These customs are common in Czechoslovakia and to a lesser extent in Hungary and Romania... ...charges of attempted murder and lesser counts.* ADJ QUALIT : ATTRIB, COMPAR ≠ greater **1.2** that something is fairly unimportant if considered in relation to other things of the same kind or to the average. EG *...all those lesser powers in Europe.* ADJ QUALIT : ATTRIB, COMPAR ⇑ smaller
2 Lesser is also used as part of the name of a plant, bird, or animal when that plant, bird, or animal is a sub-species, often smaller in size and with minor different characteristics, of the main group to which it belongs. EG *...the lesser celandine.* ADJ IN NAMES BEFORE N

lesson /lɛsən/, **lessons**. **1** A **lesson** is **1.1** a short period of time when people are taught about a particular subject or taught how to do a particular activity. EG *...tennis lessons... ...a history lesson.* N COUNT = class **1.2** one of the periods of time during a school day in which a pupil or class is taught. EG *Lessons begin at* N COUNT

9.30. **1.3** a section in a textbook which deals with one particular aspect of a subject. EG *See your notes in lesson 34.* N COUNT = chapter

2 In a church service, a **lesson is** a short piece of text which is read aloud from the Bible. EG *The vicar read the lesson from the first epistle of the Corinthians.* N COUNT

3 You can also use the word **lesson** to mean an experience which acts as a warning to you or an example from which you should learn. EG *I had learned the first lesson of doing somebody else's job: it's always more difficult than it looks.* N COUNT : USU SING

4 If you **teach** someone **a lesson**, you punish or scold them for something that they have done in order to make sure that they do not make the same mistake again. PHR : VB INFLECTS

lest /lest/; a formal word. You use **lest 1** to introduce the reason for an action, when the reason is that something unpleasant or undesirable may happen if the action does not take place. EG *He was extra polite to his superiors lest something adverse might be written into his records... I had to grab the iron rail at my side lest I slipped off.* CONJ SUBORD = in case **2** to introduce the reason for an extra piece of information that you are giving. EG *Glenn, lest the reader has forgotten, was the first American astronaut to orbit in space.* CONJ SUBORD = in case

let /let/, **lets, letting**. The form **let** is used in the present tense and is the past tense and past participle of the verb. **1** If you **let** something happen, you allow it to happen without doing anything to stop or prevent it. EG *He let Jack lead the way... She kept lifting handfuls of fine sand and letting it pour through her fingers... Don't let me put you off... People here sit back and let everyone else do the work... She had let him go off with her papers.* V+O : USU+INF, NO PASS

2 If you **let** someone do something, you allow them to do it by giving them your permission. EG *My parents wouldn't let me go out with boys... Let me go to the party on Saturday. I won't be late... You will let me stay here, won't you?... Please let me read the paper... Goodbye, I hope you'll let me see you again.* V+O : USU+INF, NO PASS ⇑ permit

3 You can use **let me** in conversations and discussions to show politeness, for example before you ask a question, express an opinion, or give an instruction. EG *Richard, let me start by asking you, what is the Institute's main aim?... Let me just go through the process... Let me try and explain: Melanie is Paul's daughter.* PHR+INF

4 You can also use **let me** to introduce a threat. EG *Just let me see you doing that again, and you'll not go out for a week!* PHR+INF

5 People often say **let me see, let's see**, or **let me think** when they are hesitating or working out what to say next. EG *His address was, let me see, 10 Killer Street... Your husband is–let's see–a lawyer... She's–now let me think a second–she is about twenty eight.* PHR : USED AS ADV SEN

6 You can use **let's say** or **let us say** to show that you are giving only one of several possible examples that you could use to illustrate the point that you are making. EG *More Italians express themselves in music compared, let's say, to the Germans.* PHR : USED AS ADV SEN

7 You say **let us** or, in less formal English, **let's 7.1** to direct the attention of the people you are talking to towards the subject that you want to consider next. EG *Let's talk about bees in general first of all... Things are bound to go wrong. Let us look at them one by one.* PHR+INF **7.2** when you are making a suggestion that you hope the person you are talking to will agree to. When used in this way, **let's** is much more common than **let us**. EG *'Let's take Angela up to Red Barn Hill.'–'Oh, let's!' said my sister... Let's give her another five minutes, should we?... Hurry up Bill, and let's get out of here.* PHR+INF **7.3** when you are suggesting tactfully or politely that you want to do something, and want the other person to agree or co-operate with you. Teachers often say 'let us' rather than 'let me.' EG *Let's have a look at what we've got here... It gets even more complicated now, let's see if Philip can work this one out.* PHR+INF

8 You can use **let 8.1** when you are expressing criticism for an unreasonable action or attitude, and to introduce what you think should be done because you feel that it is necessary or important. EG *If a man wants the status of breadwinner, let him earn it... But let those who are inclined to condemn me look at their own behaviour before they speak out... If she insists on going so early, let her take a taxi.* V (IMPER)+O+INF **8.2** to say that even though you cannot prevent something unpleasant from happening, you feel able to cope with it or deal with it. EG *Let him come if he insists. Let them look, she felt; she didn't care.* V (IMPER)+O+INF **8.3** when people are praying and asking for something to happen that they want desperately. EG *Let her come soon, I prayed... Please God, don't let there be a train crash.* V (IMPER)+O+INF

9 You can also use **let** to introduce a theory or assumption that you are making. EG *Let's suppose that time is not important... Let me assume, for the sake of argument, that inflation will continue indefinitely.* ▸ also used to introduce mathematical formulae. EG *Let x = 2, y = 3.* V (IMPER)+O (US/ME)+INF+REPORT-CL ▸ V (IMPER)+O

10 If you **let** your house or land to someone, you allow them to use it in exchange for regular weekly, monthly, or yearly payments from them. EG *Canaletto's old lodging house was to let... 'To Let' signs hung at every window.* V+O ⇑ hire = rent, lease

11 A **let** is an agreement to rent a house or land in exchange for regular payments. EG *I decided to take a two year let on a flat in Birmingham.* N SING WITH DET = lease

12 In tennis or badminton, if you serve a **let**, the ball or shuttlecock touches the net but is in the correct part of the court. You then serve again. N COUNT : USU SING

13 Let go. 13.1 If you **let go of** someone or something, you stop holding them. EG *He let go of Beynon's hand... Arnold didn't let go of her arm... 'Let go of me,' she said.* PHR : *let* INFLECTS **13.2** If you **let** a person or animal **go**, you allow them to leave or to escape. EG *Eventually I let the frog go.* PHR : *let* INFLECTS **13.3** If you **let go** something that someone says or does, you say no more about it. EG *It was stupid of you, but we'll let it go at that.* PHR : *let* INFLECTS

14 If you **let** yourself **go, 14.1** you behave much more freely than usual, allowing yourself to show your feelings and to follow your impulses. EG *I let myself go with her more completely than I've ever done before.* PHR : *let* INFLECTS **14.2** you pay much less attention to yourself or your appearance than you used to so that you look untidy and messy. EG *You look awful. You've let yourself go since Jean died.* PHR : *let* INFLECTS

15 If you **let drop** or **let fall** information, you tell people something casually or by accident, because it is not the main thing being talked about in the conversation. EG *She let fall the fact that she came from Seyer Street.* PHR : *let* INFLECTS ⇑ reveal

16 To **let** someone **be** means to leave them alone and not interfere in what they are doing. EG *'No, no,' said John, 'let them be.'* PHR : *let* INFLECTS

17 Let alone is used after a negative statement to indicate that a particular situation is extremely unlikely or impossible, because something much less difficult or unusual has never happened. EG *No one was sure exactly what had happened, let alone how... She had scarcely ever talked to a policeman, let alone gone out with one.* PHR = never mind, still less

18 If you say that something should happen **without let or hindrance**, you mean that it should happen without anything stopping or preventing it; a formal expression. EG *All people must be allowed to pass freely through the West End without let or hindrance.* PHR : USED AS AN A

19 The word **let** is used in the following expressions, which are explained at other places in this dictionary. • to **let fly**: see **fly**. • to **let** someone **know** something: see **know**. • to **let it be known**: see **known**. • to **live and let live**: see **live**.

let down. **1** If you **let** someone **down**, you disappoint them, usually by not doing something that you have said you will do. EG *They felt strongly that the school system had let them down... Charlie's never let me down yet.* ◊ **let down**. EG *I felt let down and depressed when he didn't phone me.* • See also **letdown**. PHRASAL VB : V+O+ADV ◊ ADJ QUALIT : PRED

2 If you say that someone **has let the side down**, you mean that they have done something which you feel reflects badly on the group of people that they and you belong to. PHR : VB INFLECTS

3 If you **let down** something such as a tyre, hot-air balloon, or rubber dinghy, you allow air to escape from it. EG *When I came out this morning, all my tyres had been let down.* PHRASAL VB : V+O+ADV = deflate

4 If you **let down** the hem of a garment such as a dress or skirt, you make the garment longer by making the hem at the bottom of it shorter than it was. PHRASAL VB : V+O+ADV = lengthen

5 If you **let** your **hair down**, you relax completely and thoroughly enjoy yourself. PHR : VB INFLECTS

let in. **1** If you **let** a person or animal **in**, you allow them to come into a place, especially by opening the door for them. EG *Go and let them in, Howard... Let the cat in, will you?... 'I rang the bell,' Rudolph said, 'and your friend let me in.'* PHRASAL VB : V+O+ADV ⇑ admit

2 If something **lets in** water, mud, air, etc, it allows the water, mud, or air to get into it, usually because there is a hole or crack. EG *My old boots had been letting in water on even slightly damp ground.* PHRASAL VB : V+O+ADV = leak

let in for. If you **let** someone **in for** something, you involve them in something that causes them difficulty, unpleasantness, or unnecessary expense; an informal expression. EG *What have we let ourselves in for?... People who voted Tory in 1979 did not know what they were letting themselves in for.* PHRASAL VB : V+O+ADV+PREP

let in on. If you **let** someone **in on** something, you allow them to know about it or to join in something which is kept a secret from most people; an informal expression. EG *He didn't let Uncle Harold in on the news.* PHRASAL VB : V+O+ADV+PREP = let into

let into. **1** If something **has been let into** a flat object such as a wall, it has been placed in that object so that it does not stick out beyond the surface of the object. EG *...a rather agreeable statue let into the embankment wall.* PHRASAL VB : V+PREP, ONLY PASS = inset

2 If you **let** someone **into** something such as a secret or your confidence, you allow them to know things that you have not told anyone else. EG *They agreed to let him into their secret.* PHRASAL VB : V+O+PREP = let in on

3 If you **let** a person or animal into a house or room, you allow them to come into that house or room. PHRASAL VB : V+O+PREP

let off. **1** If you **let** someone **off** something such as a duty or chore, you say that they need not do it. EG *We have been let off our homework because of the concert... He believes that if he works all day he should be let off domestic chores.* PHRASAL VB : V+O+ADV/PREP = excuse

2 If you **let** someone **off**, you give them a lighter punishment than they expect or no punishment at all. EG *He let me off with a reprimand.* PHRASAL VB : V+O+ADV ⇑ acquit

3 If you **let off** a gun or a bomb, you fire the gun or cause the bomb to explode. EG *His hearing is so poor that you could let off a gun within inches of him and he wouldn't flinch.* ● to **let off steam**: see **steam**. PHRASAL VB : V+O+ADV

let on. If you **let on** about something, you tell someone something that was intended to be kept secret; an informal expression. EG *Don't let on we went to that dance... I was furious when she let on to everyone about my new boyfriend.* PHRASAL VB : V+ADV, USU+REPORT-CL/*about* = reveal

let out. **1** If you **let** a person or animal **out**, you allow them to leave a place, especially by opening or unlocking a door. EG *The other prisoners were locked into their cells before I was let out of mine... I began to long to be released. 'Please let me out,' I kept pleading with the doctors... If I'm still asleep in the morning, just let yourself out.* PHRASAL VB : V+O+ADV ⇑ free

2 If you **let** water, air, or breath **out**, you allow it to flow out freely. EG *He let the water out and refilled the bath with cold water... Piggy let out his breath with a gasp... She let air out of her lungs and felt better.* PHRASAL VB : V+O+ADV = let escape

3 If you **let out** a particular sound, you make that sound; used in formal or literary English. EG *She let out a terrible shriek... Montclair let out a low whistle.* PHRASAL VB : V+O+ADV = emit

4 If you **let out** houses, rooms, etc, you make them available for people to rent. EG *My father owned two houses which he let out as rooms to his friends.* PHRASAL VB : V+O+ADV

5 If you **let out** a garment such as a dress or pair of trousers, you make it larger, usually by unpicking the seams and sewing nearer the edge of the material. EG *I'll have to let this dress out a bit before the wedding next week.* PHRASAL VB : V+O+ADV ⇑ alter

let up. If something **lets up**, it stops or becomes less. EG *Day followed day and still the heat did not let up... We thought that if we went out the rain would probably let up after a while.* PHRASAL VB : V+ADV

letdown /lɛtdaun, lɛtdaun/, **letdowns**; also spelled with a hyphen. A **letdown** is a disappointment that you suffer, usually because something has not happened in the way in which you expected it to happen; an informal word. EG *Everybody told us we were in for a letdown when we came here... There tends to be a sameness about the job, which can be a bit of a let-down.* N COUNT : USU a+N

lethal /li:θəᵒl/. Something that is **lethal** is **1** easily able to kill people or animals. EG *The mine exploded, sending lethal fragments flying in all directions... The chemical is lethal to rats but safe for cattle.* ADJ QUALIT ⇑ harmful **2** dangerous or harmful. EG *Milk, improperly handled, is a lethal carrier of bacteria... ...a wily and politically lethal opponent.* ADJ QUALIT = deadly

lethargic /lɪ²θa:dʒɪk/. Someone who is **lethargic** does not have enough energy or enthusiasm to do anything. EG *His display of energy only made Julia more lethargic.* ADJ QUALIT ⇑ tired

lethargy /lɛθədʒi¹/ is the condition or state of being lethargic. EG *He was determined to shake them out of their lethargy... ...a paralysing feeling of lethargy.* N UNCOUNT ⇑ tiredness

let's /lɛts/ is a less formal form of the expression 'let us': see **let**.

letter /lɛtə/, **letters**. **1** A **letter** is **1.1** a message which is written down on paper and which you send to someone, usually in an envelope and by post. EG *She wrote a letter to Harold... Did you get my last letter?... Fifty-five priests had signed the letter of protest... Peter received a letter from his wife... They informed Victor by letter.* N COUNT, OR *by*+N **1.2** a written symbol which represents one of the sounds in a language. EG *On the wall was a board covered with the letters of the alphabet... The shop bore the sign 'Books' in scarlet letters.* N COUNT

2 If you **keep** or **stick to the letter of** an agreement or law, you do not do anything that is directly against what is actually written in the agreement or law, even if you act against the general principles of it. EG *They stuck to the letter of the agreement... Congress will keep to the letter of the Twenty-fifth Amendment.* PHR : VB INFLECTS

3 See also **covering letter, love letter, newsletter, poison-pen letter.**

letter-bomb, letter-bombs. A **letter-bomb** is a small bomb which is disguised as a letter or parcel and sent to someone through the post. It is designed to explode when it is opened. EG *Offices are asked to be on the look-out for letter-bombs in the weeks before Christmas.* N COUNT ⇑ device

letterbox /lɛtəbɒks/, **letterboxes**; also spelled with a hyphen. A **letterbox** is **1** a rectangular hole in a door or a small box at the entrance to a building into which letters and small parcels are delivered. EG *The firm sought business by pushing leaflets through letter boxes.* N COUNT **2** a large metal container in the street or at a post office into which you post letters. EG *I put the letter into the letterbox.* N COUNT = mailbox

lettered /lɛtəd/. Something that is **lettered** is covered or decorated with letters or words. EG *...a crudely lettered banner.* ADJ CLASSIF : USU ADV+ADJ

letterhead /lɛtəhɛd/, **letterheads**. A **letterhead** is the name and address of a person, company, or organization which is printed at the top of their own writing paper. EG *When he gave her the envelope, she immediately recognized the letterhead.* N COUNT

lettering /lɛtəᵒrɪŋ/ is writing, especially when you are describing the type of letters that are being used. EG *I love the graceful curves that characterize this type of lettering... Underneath it, in smaller lettering, was a name.* N UNCOUNT : USU MOD+N

lettuce /lɛtɪs/, **lettuces**. A **lettuce** is a plant with large green leaves that you eat in salads. There are many different kinds of lettuce. N COUNT/UNCOUNT

let-up, let-ups. A **let-up** in something is a reduction in the intensity of an activity, especially in the effort that you have been putting into work. EG *There is no sign yet of any let-up.* N UNCOUNT/COUNT = lull

leukaemia /lu:ki:mɪə/; also spelled **leukemia**, especially in American English. **Leukaemia** is a disease in which your body produces too many white blood cells. EG *He was dying of leukaemia.* N UNCOUNT

level /lɛvəᵒl/, **levels, levelling, levelled**; also spelled **leveling** and **leveled** in American English. **1** Something that is **level** is completely flat and with no part higher than any other. EG *The floor is quite level... He looked across absolutely level fields.* ADJ QUALIT = even, flush

2 A **level** is a flat part of land that is parallel with the earth's surface. EG *There were little houses built on ascending levels on the slopes of hills.* N COUNT

3 If you **level** something, for example a building or area of land, you make it flat or level with the ground, for example by demolishing the building. EG *Specially built tractors levelled more than 1,000 acres of forest.* V+O ⇑ flatten = raze

4 The **level** of a liquid in a container or of the water in a lake, river, etc, is the height of its surface, N SING : *the*+N especially when you are comparing it with the height that it used to be or the height of its surroundings. EG *Check the oil level and tyre pressure of your car regularly... The level of the lake continues to rise.* • See also **sea level**.

5 In cookery, a **level** teaspoonful or cup of flour, sugar, etc, is an amount of flour or sugar that fills the spoon or cup exactly and does not go above the top edge of the spoon or cup. EG *Add three level tablespoons of sugar.* — ADJ CLASSIF : *a*/NUM+ADJ+N ≠ heaped

6 You use **level** to refer to how high something is in relation to the things around it. EG *He had a large pile of books which reached to the level of his chin... This cooker has an eye level grill.* — N SING WITH DET +SUPP = height

7 If one thing is **level** with another thing, it is at the same height as it. EG *He had his hands in front of him, level with his chest.* — ADJ CLASSIF : PRED, IF+PREP THEN *with* = even

8 If two things are **on a level**, they are both the same height. EG *The tables were on a level with each other.* — PHR : USED AS AN A

9 If one thing is **level** with another, it is neither in front nor behind in position, quality, or quantity. EG *Food production is going to keep level with population growth... Coming towards me was a man and when we drew level, I smiled.* — ADJ CLASSIF : PRED, IF+PREP THEN *with* = abreast

10 Level is used to describe **10.1** the degree of strength or concentration of something. EG *Mammals maintain their body temperature at a constant level... The noise levels were too high.* — N COUNT+SUPP **10.2** the amount of something at a particular time. EG *We now have a high level of unemployment... Appropriate levels of defence spending were discussed.* — N COUNT+SUPP **10.3** a particular stage or situation in a political or business organization. EG *It's important to have good organization, particularly at a local level... These decisions are made well below the level of top management... Women must have a voice at all levels in the union.* — N COUNT+SUPP, OR *at*+MOD+N = stratum **10.4** the good or bad quality of something. EG *The general level of troop training was not high... The level of the political debate is very poor.* — N COUNT+SUPP = standard **10.5** the particular point of view that you are using to look at or examine something. EG *On a purely practical level there will be an awful lot of work to do.* — N COUNT : *on/at* +N+SUPP = plain **10.6** a particular stage or standard of work, for example educational work. EG *We're writing an English course, intermediate level, for students studying science... They were talking at a fairly high level about their research.* • See also **A level, O level**. — N COUNT+SUPP

11 People or things that are **on the level** are sincere or genuine, and not dishonest or attempting to deceive people; an informal expression. EG *Honestly this plan is on the level... Is this guy really on the level?* — PHR : USED AS AN A = honest

12 If you **do** your **level best**, you do the best that you can, usually in a difficult situation. EG *He promised he would do his best to help.* — PHR : VB INFLECTS

13 If the expression on someone's face is **level**, it is calm and steady. EG *He gave her a level look.* — ADJ QUALIT
◇ **levelly**. EG *He gazed at her levelly.* — ◇ ADV WITH VB

14 If your voice is **level** or you speak in a **level** way, you are speaking in a deliberately calm way in order to prevent the conversation from becoming too emotional. EG *She spoke in a level voice.* — ADJ QUALIT = restrained ◇ **levelly**. EG *'I don't know what the enemy is thinking,' he said levelly.* — ◇ ADV WITH VB = flatly

15 If you **level** something such as a criticism or accusation at or against someone, you criticize or accuse them. EG *This criticism has been levelled at the USA... ...charges levelled against gangsters and the police.* — V+O+A *(at/against)* = lay, direct, aim

16 If you **level** an object at someone or something, you lift it and point it in their direction. EG *Someone came in; I turned and levelled the gun... Lady Mountague levelled her lorgnette at him.* — V+O : IF+PREP THEN *at* ⇑ direct

level off. 1 If something that is progressing or developing **levels off** or **levels out**, it stops growing or diminishing at such a fast speed. EG *Economic growth was almost certainly starting to level off... ...the levelling out of energy demand.* — PHRASAL VB : V+ADV ⇑ slow = stabilize

2 If you **level** a surface **off** or **out**, you make it flat, for example at the end of a job such as building or gardening. EG *The surface had been smoothed over and levelled out.* — PHRASAL VB : V+O+ADV ⇑ plane

3 If an aircraft **levels off** or **levels out**, it travels horizontally after having been travelling in an upwards or downwards direction. EG *The plane levelled off at 35,000 feet.* — PHRASAL VB : V+ADV ⇑ straighten

level with. If you **level with** someone, you tell them the truth and do not keep anything secret. EG *I don't think you're levelling with me... I've always levelled with you, haven't I, Sam?* — PHRASAL VB : V+PREP = be frank

level crossing, level crossings; also spelled with a hyphen. A **level crossing** is a place where a railway line crosses a road; used in British English. — N COUNT ⇑ junction

level-headed. Someone who is **level-headed** is able to act calmly and to make sensible decisions in difficult situations and in emergencies. EG *She was probably the most level-headed teacher in the school.* — ADJ QUALIT

lever /liːvə/, **levers, levering, levered. 1** A **lever** is **1.1** a handle or bar that is attached to a piece of machinery, and that you pull or push in order to operate the machinery. EG *Howard pushes the gear lever in.* — N COUNT **1.2** a long bar, one end of which is placed under a heavy object, so that when you press down on the other end of the bar you can move the object. EG *Robert leaned lightly on the lever and the rock groaned.* — N COUNT

2 If you **lever** something in a particular direction, you move it there, especially by using a lot of effort. EG *Mrs Burns levered herself up by using Lionel's shoulder.* — V+O+A ⇑ prise = force

3 A **lever** is also an idea or action that you can use to make people do what you want them to do, rather than what they want to do. EG *Industrial action may be threatened as a political lever.* — N COUNT : USU+SUPP ⇑ tactic = stratagem

leverage /liːvərɪdʒ/ is **1** the amount of force that can be applied by a lever onto an object. EG *You're going to have so much leverage it's going to pull the screw out.* — N UNCOUNT **2** the ability to influence people to do what you want them to do. EG *Relatively small groups can exert immense political leverage... I'm afraid I have no leverage with the committee.* — N UNCOUNT : USU +SUPP ⇑ power = hold

leveret /lɛvərɪt/, **leverets**. A **leveret** is a young hare, especially when it is less than one year old. — N COUNT ⇑ animal

leviathan /lɪvaɪəθən/, **leviathans**. A **leviathan** is something which is extremely large and difficult to control, and which you find rather frightening; a word used especially in sociological texts. EG *...the leviathan of the nation-state.* — N COUNT : USU SING ⇑ giant

Levi's /liːvaɪz/ is a trademark for a brand of denim jeans. People often talk about 'levi's' when they mean any brand of jeans. — N PLURAL : ALSO *a pair of*+N

levitate /lɛvɪteɪt/, **levitates, levitating, levitated.** To **levitate** means to rise and float in the air without any support from other people or objects. Some people believe that meditation or magic will help them to levitate. — V-O ◇ **levitation** /lɛvɪteɪʃən/. EG *The huge form in the chair rose as if by levitation.* — ◇ N UNCOUNT

levity /lɛvɪti/ is behaviour that shows a tendency to treat serious matters in a non-serious way; a fairly literary word. EG *She was trying to inject some levity into the grim proceedings... I've been a little bit appalled by the levity with which some of our politicians discuss this issue.* — N UNCOUNT = flippancy, frivolity

levy /lɛvi/, **levies, levying, levied. 1** A **levy** is a sum of money that you have to pay, for example as a tax to the government. — N COUNT ⇑ duty

2 If a government or organization **levies** a tax or other sum of money, it demands that sum from ordinary people or from smaller organizations. EG *...the outrageous new taxes that were levied to pay for the war.* — V+O ⇑ impose = charge

lewd /ljuːd/ means behaving or speaking about sex in a crude way that indicates that you are very interested in it; used showing disapproval. EG *...a lewd joke... She had a look almost of lewd abandon.* — ADJ QUALIT = wanton ◇ **lewdness**. EG *She winked with a lewdness that would have shocked Mrs Townsend.* — ◇ N UNCOUNT ⇑ lechery

lexical /lɛksɪkəl/ means concerning the words or vocabulary of a language; a technical term in linguistics. — ADJ CLASSIF

lexicography /lɛksɪkɒgrəfi/ is the activity or profession of writing and editing dictionaries; a formal word. EG *...the long history of lexicography.* — N UNCOUNT ◇ **lexicographer, lexicographers**. EG *Lexicographers are daily discovering new facts about words.* — ◇ N COUNT

lexicon /lɛksɪkən/, **lexicons**. A **lexicon** is **1** an alphabetical list of words of a language or of a particular subject. — N COUNT **2** a dictionary, especially of a very old language such as Greek or Hebrew; an old-fashioned use. — N COUNT ⇑ book

liability /laɪəbɪlɪti/, **liabilities. 1** A **liability** is someone or something that causes you a lot of problems or embarrassment; often used humorously. — N COUNT : USU SING

EG *Colley was an asset in the drawing room but a liability on any battlefield... My car's a real liability.*

2 A company or organization's **liabilities** are the sums of money which it owes, for example because it has made promises or signed agreements; a technical term in law and finance. EG *...assets and liabilities.* N COUNT : USU PL ⇑ costs

3 **Liability** for something such as a debt or crime is the legal responsibilty for it; a technical term in law. EG *Parents or guardians may avoid liability for their children's crimes if they satisfy the court that they have done everything they can to prevent it... There are limitations to the contractors' liability.* N UNCOUNT

liable /laɪəbə⁰l/. 1 Something that is **liable** to happen will probably happen or is very likely to happen. EG *The houses are made of wood, mud, and straw, and liable to collapse in a heavy storm... We are all liable to make mistakes... My own feeling is that the play is liable to give offence to many people.* ADJ QUALIT : PRED + *to*-INF = prone

2 If people or things are **liable** to a particular state or situation, that state or situation happens to them fairly frequently. EG *We now have an improved design which is simpler to make and less liable to faulty assembly... Was he liable to sea-sickness?* ADJ QUALIT : PRED + *to* = prone

3 If you are **liable** for something such as a debt or a crime, you are legally responsible for it; a legal term. EG *If he's not careful he will become liable for the debts.* ADJ CLASSIF : PRED : IF + PREP THEN *for*

4 If you are **liable** to a particular type of legal action, you are in a situation where that legal action can be taken against you; a legal term. EG *The husband is liable to arrest and, quite likely, a prison sentence... Technically you would be in breach of contract and so would be legally liable to the loss of the whole contract fee.* ADJ CLASSIF : PRED + *to* ⇑ susceptible

liaise /li'eɪz/, **liaises, liaising, liaised**. When organizations or people **liaise**, they work together and keep each other fully informed about what is happening. EG *We're liaising very closely with them.* V + A (*with/between*) ⇑ co-operate = mediate

liaison /li'eɪzɒn/. 1 **Liaison** is cooperation and the exchange of information between different organizations or between different sections of an organization. EG *Liaison with academic staff is also very important... ...better liaison between the health and social services... ...a liaison officer.* N UNCOUNT ⇑ contact

2 You can use the word **liaison** to refer to a relationship between two people which is regarded as immoral, for example a sexual relationship between a man and a woman who are not married to each other, or to refer to a relationship which is illegal or criminal, such as one between a spy and a government official. EG *The security services had discovered his liaison with Miss Keeler.* N COUNT = affair, intrigue

liar /laɪə/, **liars**. A **liar** is someone who tells lies. EG *You're a liar... He called the Minister a liar... I was a convincing liar, I thought.* N COUNT ⇑ person

lib /lɪb/. 1 **Lib** is an abbreviation for 'liberation'. It is used in the names of some movements that are concerned with freeing people from systems of government or traditional ideas, which the members of the movements believe to be the cause of people's problems or unhappiness. EG *...women's lib.* • See also **gay lib.** N UNCOUNT : POSS + N

2 See **ad-lib.**

libation /laɪbeɪʃə⁰n/, **libations**. A **libation** was an alcoholic drink which was offered to the gods in ancient Greece and Rome; a literary word. EG *...a libation to the gods.* N COUNT

libel /laɪbə⁰l/, **libels, libelling, libelled**; also spelled **libeled, libeling** in American English. 1 **Libel** is something written in a book or a newspaper which wrongly damages someone's reputation, and which is therefore against the law: compare **slander.** EG *Hinds brought an action for libel against him... He appeared in court in the libel case against the Daily Mail... This was a gigantic libel.* N UNCOUNT/COUNT ⇑ defamation

2 If you **libel** someone, you write or print something in a book or a newspaper which wrongly damages that person's reputation and which is therefore against the law. V + O ⇑ defame

libellous /laɪbə⁰ləs/; also spelled **libelous** in American English. If something in a book or newspaper is **libellous**, it wrongly damages someone's reputation and is therefore against the law. EG *...libellous comments... We must be careful not to say anything libellous.* ADJ QUALIT ⇑ defamatory

liberal /lɪbə⁰rəl/, **liberals**. 1 **Liberal** is used to describe 1.1 a person or institution that is tolerant of different kinds of behaviour or opinions. EG *I hope I'm as liberal as your father was... My school was traditional, but more liberal than other public schools.* ▸ used as a noun. EG *...a pair of enlightened liberals.* ADJ QUALIT = lenient ▸ N COUNT 1.2 a person who is moderate in their political beliefs, favouring gradual social progress by the changing of laws, rather than by revolution. EG *...liberal and radical groups... ...a liberal Democrat.* ▸ used as a noun. EG *He warned liberals against mimicking Republican policies.* ADJ QUALIT = progressive ▸ N COUNT 1.3 a person who is in favour of people having a lot of political freedom or a system which allows a lot of it. EG *...a liberal democracy... ...liberal distaste for European domination.* ▸ used as a noun. ADJ QUALIT ⇑ democratic ▸ N COUNT

2 A **Liberal** is a person who belongs to the Liberal Party in Britain, or to the Liberal Party of another country. EG *The Liberals will support the motion... ...a Liberal MP... ...the 1906-10 Liberal Government.* N COUNT

3 **Liberal** also means 3.1 giving, using, or taking a lot of something, or existing in large quantities. EG *Could any man make a more liberal offer?... ...a more liberal use of parliamentary committees... ...a liberal provision of guns.* ◊ **liberally**. EG *He cut four slices of bread and buttered them liberally... Tim helped himself liberally to some more wine.* ADJ QUALIT = generous ◊ ADV WITH VB = generously 3.2 allowing and encouraging people to study a lot of different academic subjects, especially arts subjects. EG *...a liberal education... ...a liberal studies course.* ADJ QUALIT ⇑ general

liberalism /lɪbə⁰rəlɪzə⁰m/ is 1 the belief in gradual social progress by reform and by changing laws, rather than by revolution. EG *...the debate about the future of liberalism... Radical black students saw liberalism as an inadequate response.* N UNCOUNT 2 the belief in people having a lot of political freedom. EG *...a general atmosphere of repression or liberalism.* N UNCOUNT

liberalize /lɪbə⁰rəlaɪz/, **liberalizes, liberalizing, liberalized**; also spelled **liberalise**. When a country or government **liberalizes** its laws or its attitudes, it makes them less strict and allows people more freedom in their actions. EG *...a move to liberalize the state abortion laws... His solution lay in a liberalised Official Secrets Act.* ◊ **liberalization** /lɪbə⁰rəlaɪzeɪʃə⁰n/. EG *He called for the liberalization of the laws relating to immigration.* V OR V + O = relax ◊ N UNCOUNT ⇑ change = relaxation

Liberal Party. The **Liberal Party** in Britain is a political party which believes that the government should have some control of industry, provide welfare services, and allow more local government and individual freedom; used also of similar parties in some other countries. N PROPER : *the* + N

liberate /lɪbəreɪt/, **liberates, liberating, liberated**; a formal word. 1 If someone or something **liberates** a person, 1.1 they help that person to overcome a problem or to change their way of thinking so that they become happier or improve their position in society. EG *He demonstrated that socialism alone could liberate black people... ...liberating people from poverty.* ◊ **liberation** /lɪbəreɪʃə⁰n/. EG *...the women's liberation movement.* V + O : IF + PREP THEN *from* ⇑ free ◊ N UNCOUNT ⇑ freedom 1.2 they set that person free after he or she had been captured or imprisoned. EG *Decker liberated the captive... I went out and liberated a prisoner.* V + O = release

2 If someone or something **liberates** a place or the people in it, the place or the people are made free from being under the political or military control of another country, area, or group of people. EG *...the hero who liberated Cuba... ...the rebel commanders in the liberated area of the province.* ◊ **liberation**. EG *...wars of national liberation... ...the industrial surge of the country since liberation.* V + O ◊ N UNCOUNT

liberated /lɪbəreɪtɪ²d/. Someone who is **liberated** is free from traditional ideas which had previously forced them to behave in a fixed way, often according to their sex or social position; used showing approval. EG *...a liberated woman–intelligent, creative, active... ...liberated couples... ...a liberated lifestyle.* ADJ QUALIT = emancipated

liberator /lɪbəreɪtə/, **liberators**. A **liberator** is someone who sets people free from captivity or from behaving in a fixed way because of traditional ideas; a formal word. EG *...Joan of Arc, the liberator of her people... Flags were being prepared to welcome the liberators.* N COUNT

Liberian /laɪbɪərɪən/, **Liberians**. 1 Something that is **Liberian** belongs or relates to Liberia or to its people. ADJ CLASSIF ⇑ African

2 A **Liberian** is a person who comes from Liberia. N COUNT

libertarian /lɪbəteərɪən/, **libertarians**. If someone is **libertarian** or has **libertarian** attitudes, they believe in or support the idea of people being free to think and behave in the way that they want; a formal word. EG *...the libertarian pursuit of individual wealth... European nationalism was by no means always libertarian and democratic... ...the libertarian attitude, its rejection of dogma.* ▸ used as a noun. EG *Education is a topic in which libertarians have taken a close interest.* ADJ CLASSIF ≠ authoritarian ▸ N COUNT

libertine /lɪbəti:n/, **libertines**. A **libertine** is a person who is immoral and unscrupulous in their sexual activities and who does not care about the offence or harm they may cause; a formal word, used showing disapproval. EG *I had convinced her that he was a notorious libertine... ...libertine playboys.* N COUNT

liberty /lɪbəti[1]/, **liberties**; a formal word except in paragraph 4. 1 **Liberty** is 1.1 the freedom to live your life in the way that you want, especially without a lot of interference from the government. EG *The emphasis was more on social conformity than on individual liberty.* ▸ The word **liberties** is also used with this meaning. EG *...increasing attacks on their liberties and living standards.* • See also **civil liberty**. 1.2 the freedom to go wherever you want, which you lose when you are a criminal in jail, a prisoner of war, etc. EG *...that fundamental aspect of imprisonment, the loss of liberty.* N UNCOUNT ▸ N PLURAL N UNCOUNT

2 If you say that a criminal or animal is **at liberty**, you mean that they have not yet been caught, or that they have escaped from a prison, zoo, etc. EG *Only one important figure remains at liberty.* PHR : USED AS AN A = at large, free

3 If someone is not **at liberty** to do something, especially to reveal information, they have not been given permission or authority to do it, for example by their employer or the government. EG *I'm not at liberty to say who it was.* PHR : USED AS AN A + *to*-INF ⇑ allowed = authorized

4 A **liberty** is something that you do or say without someone's permission and which they might get upset about, for example because they wanted to do it themselves or to keep it secret; a fairly informal use. EG *Using them without asking permission is a bit of a liberty, to put it mildly... I took the liberty of looking you up in the phone book.* • If you **take a liberty** or **take liberties** with someone, you behave in a bold or impolite way towards them, for example because you think that you know them well and that they will not mind. EG *She would never have taken a liberty with anyone... He was not the sort of man with whom one took liberties.* N COUNT ⇑ impertinence = cheek • PHR : VB AND N INFLECT = be forward

libidinous /lɪbɪdɪnəˢs/. People who are **libidinous** have strong sexual feelings and express them in their behaviour; a formal or literary word. EG *She behaved in a libidinous way with the men... ...the libidinous spark in Willie's eye.* ADJ QUALIT = lustful

libido /lɪbi:dəʊ/, **libidos**. A person's **libido** is the part of their personality that is considered to cause their emotional, especially sexual, desires; a technical term in psychology. EG *...a reaction against repression of the libido.* N COUNT : USU SING, OR N UNCOUNT

librarian /laɪbreərɪən/, **librarians**. A **librarian** is a person who is in charge of a library or who has been specially trained to do responsible work in a library. EG *...qualified librarians... ...the local librarian.* N COUNT ⇑ worker

library /laɪbrəri[1]/, **libraries**. 1 A **library** is an institution or a part of an institution that keeps books, newspapers, gramophone records, etc for people to read, study, or use. Most libraries allow their members to borrow items for certain periods of time. EG *Some public libraries have good reference sections... These libraries are open to all members of the University... ...my library book... ...the Library of Congress.* ▸ used of the building where the items are kept. EG *...the display shelf at the entrance to the library... ...a new extension to the library.* N COUNT : ALSO IN NAMES ▸ N COUNT

2 A **library** is also 2.1 a private collection of books or gramophone records. EG *...libraries in country houses... He has built up a splendid library of recorded music.* 2.2 a set of books that is published as a series, usually with the same style of cover and contents. EG *...published in the Library of Knowledge series.* 2.3 a collection of standard computer programs that is stored on disk or tape; a technical term. N COUNT : USU + SUPP N COUNT : ALSO IN NAMES ⇑ collection N COUNT

librettist /lɪbretɪst/, **librettists**. A **librettist** is a person who writes the words that are used in an opera or musical play. EG *...a fine poet and librettist.* N COUNT ⇑ lyricist

libretto /lɪbretəʊ/, **librettos, libretti**. The plural can be either **librettos** or **libretti**. The **libretto** of an opera or musical play is the words that are sung and spoken in it. EG *...librettos published in translation... He knew the libretto well.* N COUNT = text

Libyan /lɪbɪən/, **Libyans**. 1 Something that is **Libyan** belongs or relates to Libya or to its people. EG *...60 miles off the Libyan coast.* ADJ CLASSIF

2 A **Libyan** is a person who comes from Libya. N COUNT

lice /laɪs/ is the plural of **louse**.

licence /laɪsəns/, **licences**; also spelled **license** in American English. 1 A **licence** is an official document which gives you permission to do, use, or own something. EG *The first page carried the licence number and the full name of the holder... ...a driving licence... ...the television licence form... ...import licences.* • See also **off-licence**. N COUNT = permit

2 If someone does something **under licence**, they do it by special permission from a government or other authority. EG *They decided to have it built under licence in Switzerland... Badgers can be killed under licence in those areas.* PHR : USED AS AN A

3 **Licence** is 3.1 immoral or offensive behaviour that involves using the freedom that you have in a wrong or irresponsible way. EG *...a world of licence and corruption... It is this distinction between freedom and licence that many parents cannot grasp.* 3.2 permission to do something, which you use as an excuse to behave in an irresponsible or excessive way. EG *We must not see it as a licence to trap people into an arrangement.* 3.3 the way that an artist, poet, etc uses words and images in an exaggerated or unusual way. EG *...artistic licence.* • See also **poetic licence**. N UNCOUNT = latitude N UNCOUNT + SUPP = authorization N UNCOUNT : USU MOD + N ⇑ freedom

license /laɪsəns/, **licenses, licensing, licensed**. If a government or other authority **licenses** a person, organization, or activity, they officially give permission for the person or organization to do something, or for the activity to take place. EG *The Royal College examines and licenses surgeons... ...a licensing authority.* V + O : USU + *to*-INF ⇑ permit = authorize

licensed /laɪsənst/. 1 If you are **licensed** to do something, you have official permission from a government or other authority to do it. EG *These men are licensed to carry firearms... She is licensed to drive motor vehicles... ...a licensed pilot.* ADJ CLASSIF = authorized

2 If something that you own or use is **licensed**, you have official permission to own it or use it. EG *Dogs have to be licensed... The car is licensed and insured... ...a licensed pistol.* ADJ CLASSIF

3 If a place such as a restaurant or hotel is **licensed**, it has a licence to sell alcoholic drinks. EG *He won't stay at a hotel unless it's licensed... ...licensed premises.* V + O : ONLY PASS

licensee /laɪsənsi:/, **licensees**. A **licensee** is a person who has been given a licence, especially a licence to sell alcoholic drinks; a formal word. N COUNT ⇑ retailer

licensing hours are the particular times of the day when a pub is allowed to sell alcoholic drinks; used mainly in British English. N PLURAL

licensing laws are the laws which control the selling of alcoholic drinks; used mainly in British English. N PLURAL

licentious /laɪsenʃəs/. If you describe a person as **licentious**, you mean that they are very immoral, especially in their sexual behaviour; used in formal English showing disapproval. EG *There was something licentious in her smile... ...coarse, brutal and licentious men.* ◊ **licentiousness**. EG *He was shocked by my licentiousness.* ADJ QUALIT ◊ N UNCOUNT

lichee /laɪtʃi:/. See **lychee**.

lichen /laɪkən, lɪtʃən/, **lichens**. **Lichen** is a cluster of tiny plants that looks like moss and grows on rocks, trees, walls, etc. EG *...a stone stairway covered with lichen... ...mosses and lichens.* N MASS

lick /lɪk/, **licks, licking, licked**. 1 When people or animals **lick** something, they move their tongue across its surface, as a way of eating it or making it wet or clean. EG *He licked the last of the egg off his knife... The cat was licking its paw... All I do is lick stamps and address envelopes.* V + O

2 If you say that someone **licks** their **lips**, you mean that **2.1** they move their tongue across their lips, in order to wet or clean them. EG *She drank, lowered the glass, licked her lips.* **2.2** they are experiencing a strong emotion because they are eagerly looking forward to something that they like; an informal use. PHR : VB INFLECTS / PHR : VB INFLECTS, USU+A ⇑ anticipate

3 If you **lick** someone, **3.1** you easily defeat them in a fight or competition; an informal use. EG *I'm sure you could lick both of them... Why go to Athens to watch the Wanderers get licked?* **3.2** you punish them by hitting them repeatedly; an informal use. V+O ⇑ beat = thrash / V+O ⇑ beat

4 When flames, waves, etc **lick** something, they touch it very lightly and briefly; a literary use. EG *There were a few last flames licking the city... Long shadows licked the curves of the fields.* V+O

5 A **lick** is **5.1** a single movement of a person's or animal's tongue across the surface of something. EG *...a few licks and nibbles... That ice cream costs a dollar a lick.* **5.2** a small amount of something; an informal use. EG *The door could do with a lick of paint... For twenty years I haven't done a lick of work.* **5.3** a punch or blow; an informal use. EG *One good lick knocked him down... I had given him a few good licks in return.* N COUNT / N PART+N UNCOUNT = a spot of / N COUNT

6 If something happens **at a great lick, at a tremendous lick**, etc, it happens extremely fast; an informal use. EG *It came out of the bag at a hell of a lick... Both teams set off at a tremendous lick.* PHR : USED AS AN A ⇑ quickly

7 Lick is also used in the following phrases: **7.1** If you say that someone is **licking** their **wounds**, you mean that they are recovering after being thoroughly defeated or humiliated. EG *She'd rather be left alone to lick her wounds in solitude.* **7.2** If you **lick** something **into shape**, you improve it so that it is ready to be used. EG *The house was a complete mess, but we soon licked it into shape.* **7.3** If you say that someone wants you to **lick** their **boots**, you mean that they want you to obey them completely, like a slave. EG *You expect me to kneel down and lick your boots.* PHR : VB INFLECTS / PHR : VB INFLECTS / PHR : VB INFLECTS = grovel

licking /lɪkɪŋ/, **lickings**; an informal word. A **licking** is **1** a severe defeat by someone in a fight, battle, or competition. EG *The team got another licking on Saturday... The general took a sound licking and lost Nazareth.* **2** a punishment which involves beating someone several times, especially a child. EG *You'll get a good licking if your father catches you.* N COUNT = hiding, thrashing / N COUNT = hiding

licorice /lɪkərɪs, -ɪʃ/. See **liquorice**.

lid /lɪd/, **lids**. **1** A **lid** is the top of a box or other container which can be removed or raised when you want to open the container. EG *I went over to the box and lifted the lid... She was opening and closing the lid of her tin... I'll take the lid off... Put the lid on loosely.* N COUNT

2 Your **lids** are the pieces of skin which cover your eyes when you close them. EG *She looked round from under half-closed lids to see if there was anyone interesting... When she closed her eyes tears came from beneath the lids.* N COUNT : USU PL = eyelid

3 If you say that someone has put the **lid** on an activity or a piece of information, you mean that they are preventing or restricting the activity or are not allowing the information to become known by other people; an informal use. EG *The Federal Reserve keeps a tight lid on monetary growth... The government managed to clamp the lid on before the actual details became public.* N SING WITH DET

lidded /lɪdɪ²d/ is used to describe **1** a container that has a lid. EG *...lidded jars containing ointments.* **2** a person's eyelids. EG *...a large man with heavily lidded eyes.* ADJ CLASSIF / ADJ CLASSIF : USU ATTRIB

lido /liːdəʊ/, **lidos**. A **lido** is an open-air swimming pool, or a part of a beach, which is used by the public for swimming, sunbathing, or water sports. N COUNT

lie /laɪ/, **lies, lying, lay, lain; lied**. The forms **lie, lies, lying, lay, lain** are used for the verb in paragraphs 1 to 13 and in the phrasal verbs. In informal English, people sometimes use the word **lay** instead of **lie** in these meanings: see **lay**. The forms **lie, lies, lying, lied** are used for the verb in paragraphs 19 and 20. The form **lies** is the plural form of the noun in paragraphs 14 to 16. **1** If a person or animal **lies** in a particular position or place, they are in or move into a flat or horizontal position and are not standing or sitting. EG *Judy was lying flat on the bed... He lay sprawled on his back... I lay there trying to remember what he looked like... She lay in the sun.* V+A ⇑ be

2 If a person or animal **lies** in a particular state or condition, they are in a horizontal position and in that state or condition, or remain in it for a period of time. EG *Just lie still... The girl was lying fast asleep... I used to lie awake at night watching the rain... She lay ill for days.* V+C ⇑ be

3 If you say that a dead person **lies** in a particular place, you mean that they are buried there; used in formal English, especially in the writing on gravestones, memorials etc. EG *Her grandparents lie there... Here lies William Shakespeare.* ● to **lie in state**: see **state**. V+A ⇑ be

4 If a person, team, country, etc **lies** in a particular position in a competition or in a situation where several of them are being compared, they occupy or hold that position. EG *France and Britain lie third and fourth respectively.* V+A = stand, rank

5 If you are in a difficult or embarrassing situation and **let it lie, let things lie**, etc, you do not do anything to interfere with the situation because you may cause more problems or offend someone. EG *Should I try to correct it, or let it lie?* ● to **let sleeping dogs lie**: see **dog**. PHR : FIRST VB INFLECTS

6 If an object **lies** in a particular place, it is in a flat position on a horizontal surface in that place. EG *Several dictionaries lay on a shelf... The weapon was found lying in a ditch... There were lumps of dirty snow lying everywhere... She let her embroidery lie where it fell.* V+A ⇑ be

7 If something **lies** in a particular state or condition, it is in that state or condition. EG *Another boat lies moored there... ...the folder lying open before him... A pile of fuel lay ready... The snow lay thick on the ground.* V+C ⇑ be

8 If you say that light, clouds, fog, etc **lie** somewhere, you mean that they exist there or are spread over the area mentioned; a literary use. EG *The sun lay over the platform... A cold October mist was lying around the castle.* V+A ⇑ be

9 If you say that a place **lies** around you, below you, etc, you mean that it covers a large area around you or below you; a literary use. EG *London lay beneath us... The sea lay on every side... The dark garden lay out there beyond the glass.* V+A = spread, stretch

10 If you say that a place **lies** in a particular position or direction, you mean that it is situated there. EG *The bridge lies beyond the docks... All the richer countries lie outside this danger zone... Frankfurt lay only 100 kilometres from the demarcation line.* V+A ⇑ be = be found

11 You use **lie** to indicate where you think the cause of a problem, the solution to a problem, the source of a feeling, etc may be found; a formal use. EG *The causes of this lie deep in the history of society... The solution must lie in giving parents more choice... The party had to decide where its future lay... Its attraction lay in its simplicity... Their real interests lie somewhere quite different.* V+A = occur, be located

12 Lie is used in formal or literary English with some adjectives and noun phrases to indicate that **12.1** objects are left somewhere or are not used. EG *Her white Sunday purse lay discarded near the phone... It has lain for years in a cupboard... The stone coffin lay undisturbed... The machine lay idle for two years.* **12.2** ideas, hopes, relationships, etc are not developed or do not succeed. EG *Many new ideas are lying dormant in already collected information... The Alliance would have lain in ruins... There lay Julie's hopes, shattered.* V+C/A ⇑ be = remain, stay / V+C/A ⇑ be = remain, stay

13 You use **lie** in expressions such as 'lie ahead', 'lie before', 'lie beyond', 'lie in store', and 'lie in wait' when you are talking about an event that is going to happen to someone in the future, especially when they do not know about it yet. EG *...the horrors lying in wait for them round every corner... ...an unwelcome foretaste of what lay in store... What lay ahead of them?... Endless hours of pleasure lie before you.* V+A ⇑ await

14 The **lie** of an object is the position in which it lies; a technical use in sport. EG *Have you thought of moving the ball into a better lie?* N SING WITH DET +SUPP

15 If you talk about **the lie of the land**, or **how the land lies**, you are referring to what is happening or to what a situation really is. EG *He said he was not committing himself until he had seen how the land lay.* PHR : VB INFLECTS = circumstances

16 A **lie** is something that someone says or writes N COUNT which they know is untrue. EG *You're telling lies now... It is all a pack of lies.* ● See also **white lie**.

17 Some people say **'I tell a lie'** when they have just made a mistake in something that they are saying and immediately correct it; a rather old-fashioned expression. EG *It was in 1980–no, I tell a lie, it was 1981.*
CONVENTION ⇑ sorry

18 If something **gives the lie to a statement, claim, or theory,** it proves that it is not true; a fairly formal expression. EG *That gives the lie to all her theories.*
PHR : VB INFLECTS ⇑ disprove

19 If someone **lies** or **is lying**, they are telling a lie on a particular occasion. You also say that someone **lies** when they tell lies often or habitually. EG *Rudolph was sure that Thomas was lying... It's no good lying, Doctor... 'Certainly not,' I lied... You lied to me... Age is one thing, but how do you lie about your height?... I don't like her–she swears and she lies.*
V : IF+PREP THEN *about*, OR V +QUOTE = fib

20 If you say that something **lies**, you mean that it does not indicate or express the truth, or the whole truth. EG *The camera does not lie... Mirrors can only lie... History will lie... To a trained expert, even the face cannot lie.*
V ⇑ deceive = misrepresent

21 See also **lying**.

lie about. 1 If you **lies about** or **lies around**, you spend your time relaxing and being lazy; used in informal English. EG *They were lying about in the doorways... We lay around smoking.*
PHRASAL VB : V+ADV = loiter, laze

2 If things are left **lying about** or **lying around**, they are left somewhere in an untidy way. EG *...an old boot which some fool had carelessly left lying about... The bottles and knives were left lying around overnight.*
PHRASAL VB : V+ADV

lie back. If you **lie back**, 1 you move from a sitting position into a horizontal position by lowering your head and shoulders backwards until you are lying on your back. EG *Now lie back and relax.* 2 you accept a situation without making any attempt to change it or prevent it happening; an informal use. EG *When it's inevitable, lie back and enjoy it.*
PHRASAL VB : V+ADV; PHRASAL VB : V+ADV = acquiesce

lie behind. If you say that something **lies behind** a situation or event, you mean that it is the reason for the situation or event, often when this fact is not easy to see or understand. EG *It's this kind of irresponsibility that lay behind the crisis... ...the real cause that lay behind the rise in divorce.*
PHRASAL VB : V+PREP

lie down. 1 When you **lie down**, you move into a horizontal position, usually in order to rest or sleep. EG *I helped her to lie down again... We lay down side by side.* ● See also **lie-down**.
PHRASAL VB : V+ADV

2 To **take** something **lying down** means to accept an unfair decision or unfair treatment from someone without complaining or resisting; used in informal English. EG *She was never one to take bureaucratic bullying lying down.*
PHR : FIRST VB INFLECTS

lie in. If you **lie in**, you stay in bed later than usual in the morning; a fairly informal expression. EG *I think I'll lie in tomorrow.* ● See also **lie-in**.
PHRASAL VB : V+ADV

lie up. If you **lie up**, you stay in bed for a long time, usually because you are ill or injured; an informal expression. EG *They'd take pills and lie up a bit from time to time.*
PHRASAL VB : V+ADV ⇑ rest

lie with. When a duty, fault, choice, etc **lies with** someone, it is their responsibility, or their choice; a formal expression. EG *The burden of proof lies with the accuser... Are you saying that the fault generally lies with the management?*
PHRASAL VB : V+PREP = depend on

lie-down. A **lie-down** is a short rest, usually in bed; an informal word. EG *Have an aspirin and a cup of tea and a good lie-down.*
N SING : USU *a*+N = nap, snooze

lie-in. A **lie-in** is a rest that you have by staying in bed later than usual in the morning; an informal word. EG *The meeting's not until ten o'clock, so I can have a lie-in.*
N SING : USU *a*+N

lieu /ljᵊuː/. If you do, get, or give one thing **in lieu of** another, you do, get, or give it instead of the other thing, because the two things are considered equally acceptable, or of the same value or importance; a formal expression. EG *You may offer a dissertation in lieu of part of the final examination... ...an annual payment in lieu of the property tax.*
PREP = in place of

Lieut. is a written abbreviation for **lieutenant** when it is a person's title. EG *...Lieut. Collings.*
= Lt

lieutenant, lieutenants. The word **lieutenant** is pronounced /lɛftɛnənt/ in British English and /luːtɛnənt/ in American English. 1 A **lieutenant** is a person who holds a junior officer's rank in the army, navy, or air force, or in the American police force. EG *...a young infantry lieutenant... ...Lieutenant Lawton.*
N COUNT : ALSO IN TITLES

2 **Lieutenant** is used in combination with other titles to describe a rank, especially an officer's rank in the army, navy, or air force. EG *...a Lieutenant Colonel... ...the Lieutenant Governor of South Dakota... ...First Lieutenant Bullon.*
N IN TITLES

3 You refer to someone as a person's **lieutenant** when they are that person's assistant, especially their main assistant, in an organization, activity, etc.
N COUNT : USU POSS+N IN SING

life /laɪf/, **lives** /laɪvz/. The form **lives** is also the third person singular of the present tense of the verb 'live' and is pronounced /lɪvz/. 1 **Life** is 1.1 the quality which people, animals, and plants have when they are not dead and which objects and substances do not have. EG *...her last hours of life... ...the life-giving rain... How far do we allow a doctor to have power over life and death?* 1.2 everything which has the quality of being alive. EG *...evidence for the very beginnings of life... Is there life on Jupiter?* 1.3 a particular group of living things. EG *...a zoologist who specializes in fish life... ...plant life.* 1.4 the ability to feel or move which living things have; used especially when a living thing has lost this ability because of illness or injury. EG *He tried to rub life back into his foot.*
N UNCOUNT ⇑ existence; N UNCOUNT; N UNCOUNT : MOD+N; N UNCOUNT ⇑ activity

2 Someone's **life**, or the **life** of an animal or plant, is 2.1 their state of being alive; used especially when there is a risk or danger of them dying. EG *She had risked her life to save mine... ...the attempt on the President's life... He nearly lost his life... I was fighting for my life.* 2.2 the period of time during which they are alive. EG *People spend their lives worrying about money... I've never boiled a potato in my life... He was made a life member of the club.*
N COUNT : POSS+N ⇑ existence; N COUNT : POSS+N = days, lifetime

3 When you are talking only about people, **life** is also 3.1 the events and experiences that happen to them while they are alive. EG *Life had not been kind to her... Life is probably harder for women... I don't know what you want out of life... I prefer books that are true to life.* 3.2 the varied experience that they get by travelling a lot, meeting different kinds of people, etc. EG *I'm interested in life, not books.* 3.3 the things that they do and experience that are characteristic of a particular place, group of people, or activity. EG *Sport has always been a part of university life... ...the speed of city life... ...people from all sections of public life.* 3.4 the activity or interest which they consider to be the most important or enjoyable thing in their life and which they spend most of their time on. EG *Their life is the school... Fishing was their entire life.* 3.5 the things they do or experience that form all or part of their life. EG *...my life in medicine... I've had such a fascinating life... ...the life of a hermit... Walter's life is one of organised chaos.* 3.6 the excitement, energy, or cheerfulness in the way that they behave or speak. EG *...a quiet street where there's not much life... Anne is so full of life... They have no life in their voices at all.*
N UNCOUNT = living; N UNCOUNT = world; N UNCOUNT : USU MOD+N ⇑ existence = life style; N SING : POSS+N = obsession; N COUNT : USU SING+POSS = way of life; N UNCOUNT = vitality, liveliness

4 A **life** is 4.1 a person who has died or been rescued in an accident or disaster; used mainly in newspapers and on radio and television. EG *Eight lives were lost. ...Five lives were saved.* 4.2 a book, film, etc which tells the story of a real person's life. EG *He was trying to write a life of Wilde... ...The Life and Times of Charles Dickens.*
N COUNT; N COUNT : IF+PREP THEN *of* ⇑ account = biography

5 In art, **life** means the producing of drawings, paintings, or sculptures that represent actual people, objects, or landscapes rather than images from the artist's imagination; a technical term. EG *I like to draw from life... ...life classes.*
N UNCOUNT

6 **Life** is also the same as life imprisonment; an informal use. EG *Williams got life.*
N UNCOUNT

7 The **life** of a machine, material, or substance is the period of time that it lasts for or the period during which it is useful, edible, etc. EG *Underlays double the life of a carpet.*
N SING : USU+*of* = durability

8 The **life** of a government, job, agreement, etc is the period of time during which it exists or is valid. EG *...during the life of our last Labour government... The average life of a mortgage is eight to nine years.*
N SING : USU+*of* = duration

9 In children's games, a **life** is one of the fixed number of times when you can lose but still continue to play. If you lose all the lives that are allowed, you can no longer take part in the game. EG *How many lives have you lost?*
N COUNT ⇑ chance = forfeit

10 If you **bring** something **to life**, 10.1 you make it lively and interesting. EG *His arrival brought the party to life.* 10.2 you represent it in a work of art in an extremely realistic and lifelike way. EG *The play succeeds in bringing Churchill and his family to life.* PHR : VB INFLECTS

11 To **come to life** means 11.1 to wake up, become active, or start growing. EG *I love to watch everything coming to life again in the spring.* 11.2 to become lively and interesting. EG *The party never really came to life, did it?... He came to life only at the last rehearsal.* 11.3 to be represented in a work of art in an extremely realistic and lifelike way. EG *Venice comes to life in this delightful book... I wanted to make the character come to life.* PHR : VB INFLECTS = liven up, perk up

12 The word **life** is also used in the following expressions. 12.1 If you do something **for** your **life** or **for dear life**, you do it with great strength and effort because you are in a dangerous or urgent situation; an informal expression. EG *I held on to the ledge for dear life.* PHR : USED AS AN A = tenaciously 12.2 **For life** means for the rest of a person's life. EG *If you help me, I'll be your friend for life... They will be badly scarred for life.* PHR : USED AS AN A = lifelong 12.3 If you say that you cannot understand or remember something **for the life of** you, you mean that you cannot understand or remember it, however hard you try; a fairly informal expression. EG *I can't for the life of me see why you want them... For the life of me I couldn't remember it.* PHR : USED AS AN A, WITH NEG 12.4 Some people say **'How's life?'** as an informal greeting, instead of 'How are you?'. CONVENTION 12.5 If you talk about the man or woman **in** someone's **life**, you mean the person that they are having a close relationship with, especially a sexual relationship. EG *Is there a man in Jane's life?... He needs a woman in his life.* PHR : USED AS AN A 12.6 If you talk about machines, vehicles, etc coming **to life**, roaring **into life**, etc, you mean that they suddenly start working or moving; a rather literary use. EG *The tanks lurched once again into life.* PHR : USED AS AN A 12.7 If you talk about **life after death** or **a life after death**, you are discussing the possibility that people may continue to exist in some form after they die. PHR : USED AS S/O ⇑ existence = after life 12.8 If you refer to someone as **the life and soul of the party**, you mean that they are very lively and entertaining at social occasions, and are good at mixing with people. PHR : USU USED AS C

12.9 If you say that **life isn't worth living without** someone or something, or that someone or something **makes life worth living**, you mean that you cannot enjoy life without them; often used in an exaggerated way. PHR : AUX INFLECTS 12.10 If you say that someone **lives life to the full**, you mean that they are always busy and enjoy trying new activities. PHR : VB INFLECTS 12.11 If you say that someone is living **the life of Riley**, you mean that they are enjoying themselves, doing very little work, and living in comfortable surroundings; an informal expression. PHR : USED AS O 12.12 If you **live** your **own life**, you live in the way that you want to and accept responsibility for your actions and decisions, without other people's advice or interference. EG *She was 18 after all, entitled to live her own life.* PHR : VB AND N INFLECT 12.13 If you make **a new life** for yourself, start **a new life**, etc, you move to another place or country, or change your career, usually to try and recover from an unpleasant experience. EG *After the divorce she moved to Buckingham to make a new life for herself.* PHR : USED AS O = a fresh start 12.14 If you describe a situation as **a matter of life and death**, you mean that it is extremely dangerous and urgent, and that someone may die if people do not act immediately. EG *Phone an ambulance. It's a matter of life and death.* • See also **life-and-death**. PHR : USED AS C = critical 12.15 If someone says **'Not on your life'**, they are totally rejecting a suggestion that has been made; an informal expression. EG *What? And leave you here? Not on your life!* CONVENTION = no chance 12.16 If you say that you have received **the fright of** your **life**, run **the race of** your **life**, etc, you mean that something has made you more frightened than you have ever been before, that you have run faster than you have ever run before, etc. EG *You gave me the fright of my life just then.* PHR : USED AS O 12.17 **Real life** means the actual experiences that people have, rather than what happens in stories or in people's imaginations. EG *They are not only married in the play but in real life as well.* ▸ used as an adjective. EG *...real-life situations.* PHR : USED AS S/O/C = reality 12.18 If someone **risks life and limb**, they do something very dangerous that may cause them to die or be seriously injured. PHR : VB INFLECTS 12.19 To **see life** means to experience a wide variety of things, especially by travelling a lot. EG *You should see life before you settle down.* PHR : VB INFLECTS 12.20 If someone **takes** another person's **life**, they kill them; a formal expression. EG *He sat there appalled that he had taken a freind's life.* PHR : VB AND N INFLECT 12.21 If someone **takes** their own **life**, they deliberately kill themselves; a formal expression. EG *What could have made him take his own life?* PHR : VB AND N INFLECT = commit suicide 12.22 If you **take** your **life in** your **hands**, you do something very dangerous that may kill you. EG *Anyone who tries to cross the Bristol Road is taking their life in their hands.* PHR : VB INFLECTS 12.23 People say **'That's life'**, especially after an unlucky, unpleasant, or surprising event, to show that they are not going to complain, protest, or react in any strong way, because they feel that such events will happen occasionally and must be accepted. CONVENTION 12.24 If you say **'This is the life'**, you mean that you are really enjoying the situation that you are in. EG *Sun, sea, and sand. This is the life!* CONVENTION 12.25 If you say that someone has been drawn or painted **to the life**, you mean that the drawing or painting looks exactly like them. EG *The artist has succeeded in portraying my father to the life.* PHR : USED AS AN A ⇑ realistically = faithfully 12.26 If you say that someone cannot do something **to save** their **life**, you mean that they cannot do it very well at all; an informal expression. EG *He couldn't spell to save his life.* PHR : USED AS AN A = for toffee 12.27 People say **'What a life'** to indicate that they are very dissatisfied or are having great difficulties. CONVENTION

13 **Life** is also used in the following phrases which are dealt with at other entries in this dictionary. • **it's a dog's life**: see **dog**. • **as large as life**: see **large**. • **larger than life**: see **large**. • **the time of** your **life**: see **time**. • See also **way of life**.

life-and-death. A **life-and-death** situation or problem is an extremely serious or dangerous one. EG *Such courts are far less qualified to make life-and-death decisions... ...creatures engaged in a life-and-death struggle.* ADJ CLASSIF : ATTRIB = critical

life assurance is the same as life insurance. EG *...a life assurance policy.* N UNCOUNT

lifebelt /laɪfbɛlt/, **lifebelts**. A **lifebelt** is a large ring used to keep a person afloat and prevent them from drowning when they fall into the sea or other area of water. Lifebelts are usually made of light material or filled with air. EG *...inflating their lifebelts and plunging into the sea... Throw her a lifebelt!* N COUNT ⇑ safety equipment

lifeblood /laɪfblʌd/; also spelled with a hyphen. 1 A person's **lifeblood** is their blood when it is being considered as the power that keeps them alive; a formal or literary use. EG *She felt her lifeblood ebb away.* N SING : USU POSS +N

2 The **lifeblood** of something is the most important thing that it needs in order to exist, develop, or be successful. EG *Fast communications are the lifeblood of any successful business... Self-confidence is the lifeblood of real democracy.* N SING : USU POSS +N

lifeboat /laɪfbəʊt/, **lifeboats**. A **lifeboat** is 1 a medium-sized boat which is sent out from a port or harbour in order to rescue people who are in danger at sea. EG *The lifeboat was called out again during the night.* N COUNT ⇑ rescue vessel 2 a small boat which is carried on a ship and which people on the ship use to escape when the ship is in danger of sinking. EG *The ship's cargo was intact and the lifeboats in place.* N COUNT ⇑ emergency craft

lifebuoy /laɪfbɔɪ/, **lifebuoys**. A **lifebuoy** is the same as a lifebelt. N COUNT

life-cycle, life-cycles; also spelled as two words. 1 The **life-cycle** of an animal or plant is the particular series of changes and developments that it passes through from the beginning of its life until its death. EG *...the life-cycle of the salmon... They complete their life-cycle in a single growing season.* N COUNT : USU WITH POSS

2 The **life-cycle** of something such as an idea or organization is the series of developments that take place in it from its beginning until the end of its usefulness. EG *...the life-cycle of every scientific theory.* N COUNT : USU WITH POSS

life expectancy, life expectancies. 1 The **life expectancy** of a person, animal, or plant is the length of time that they are normally likely to live. EG *Women have a longer life expectancy than men... Bats have a life expectancy of around twenty years.* N COUNT/UNCOUNT = life-span

2 The **life expectancy** of an idea, a machine, or an organization is the length of time that it is likely to remain in use. EG *...the life expectancy of any scientific truth.* N COUNT/UNCOUNT

life form, life forms. A **life form** is any living thing such as an animal or plant. EG *...life forms* N COUNT+SUPP = creature *hostile to man... Many of the deep-sea life forms feed directly on bacteria.*

lifeguard /laɪfgɑːd/, **lifeguards**. A **lifeguard** is a person at a beach or swimming pool whose job is to rescue people when they are in danger of drowning. N COUNT ↑ attendant

life imprisonment is a punishment given to a criminal which means that the criminal must spend the rest of his or her life in prison. EG *They were sentenced to life imprisonment.* N UNCOUNT

life insurance; also spelled with a hyphen. **Life insurance** is a form of insurance in which a person makes regular payments to an insurance company. In return, a sum of money is paid to them when they reach a certain age or to their wife, husband, or children when they die. EG *I always keep my life insurance payments up to date.* N UNCOUNT = life assurance

lifejacket /laɪfdʒækəˈt/, **lifejackets**; also spelled with a hyphen. A **lifejacket** is a sleeveless jacket which you wear in order to stay afloat in the water when you are in danger of drowning. Lifejackets are made of light material or filled with air. EG *She opened the locker and took out the lifejackets and threw them over the side... They were without radios, life-jackets, or even compasses.* N COUNT ↑ garment

lifeless /laɪflɪˀs/. **1** If a person or animal is **lifeless**, they are dead, or are so still that they appear to be dead. EG *...the lifeless body of Lieutenant Dowling.* ADJ CLASSIF

2 Lifeless is used to describe machines and objects, when you want to emphasize that they are not living things. EG *...something inhuman, mechanical, lifeless... ...a lifeless chunk of rock.* ADJ CLASSIF = inanimate

3 A **lifeless** place or area does not have anything living or growing there at all. EG *...a time when the earth was completely lifeless... ...a barren and lifeless land.* ADJ CLASSIF ↑ infertile

4 If you describe people, artistic performances, or works of art as **lifeless**, you mean they are dull and not lively or exciting; used showing disapproval. EG *The characters in the novel are lifeless... ...a lifeless voice.* ADJ QUALIT

lifelike /laɪflaɪk/. **1** Something that is **lifelike** has the appearance of being alive. EG *...extremely lifelike computer-controlled robots.* ADJ QUALIT = realistic

2 A **lifelike** painting, acting performance, etc is so skilfully done that it appears very like the person or thing that it is supposed to represent. ADJ QUALIT = vivid

lifeline /laɪflaɪn/, **lifelines**. A **lifeline** is **1** something that is considered to be very important in helping people to survive or to continue with an activity. EG *The Mackinnon household became my lifeline, my only link with the outside world... ...the oil lifeline of Western Europe... ...the river lifeline to Pnomh Penh.* N COUNT : USU+SUPP ↑ link **2** a rope which you throw to someone when they are in danger of drowning in the sea, a river, etc. N COUNT

lifelong /laɪflɒŋ/ means existing or happening for the whole of a person's life. EG *...her friend and lifelong companion... From lifelong habit, I called him 'Sir'... ...my lifelong admiration for men of action.* ADJ CLASSIF : ATTRIB

life peer, life peers. In Great Britain, a **life peer** is a man who is given a title such as 'Lord' which he can use for the rest of his life but which he cannot pass on to his eldest son when he dies. EG *...an amendment to allow hereditary peers to become life peers.* N COUNT

lifer /laɪfə/, **lifers**. A **lifer** is a criminal who has been sent to prison for the rest of his or her life; an informal word. N COUNT ↑ convict

life science, life sciences. The **life sciences** are the group of academic subjects such as zoology, botany, and anthropology, which are concerned with human beings, animals, and plants and their physical structure and behaviour. N COUNT : USU PL ↑ science

life sentence, life sentences. A **life sentence** is a legal punishment in which a criminal is sent to prison for the rest of his or her life. EG *He is at present serving a life sentence for murder.* N COUNT

life-size. A **life-size** painting, sculpture, etc represents a person or thing in their real size. EG *...a life-size statue of Christ... They arranged to have a life-size inflatable whale float down the Thames.* ADJ CLASSIF = full-size

life-sized means the same as life-size. ADJ CLASSIF

lifespan /laɪfspæn/, **lifespans**; also spelled with a hyphen. **1** The **lifespan** of a person, animal, or plant is the period of time for which they live or are normally expected to live. EG *In our brief life-span we normally experience only a few of these problems... A fox's natural lifespan could be ten years.* N COUNT : USU WITH POSS

2 The **lifespan** of a product, organization, or idea is the period of time for which it is expected to work properly or to last. EG *This job had a planned life-span of five years... ...shortening the lifespan of its components.* N COUNT+SUPP = duration

life style, life styles; also spelled with a hyphen and as one word. The **life style** of a particular person or group of people is the conditions, behaviour, and habits that are typical of them or are chosen by them. EG *They couldn't see that it was their life style that was wrong... ...this highly urban lifestyle... This is going to affect the life-styles of a great many people.* N COUNT+SUPP = way of life

life-support system, life-support systems. A **life-support system** is **1** the combination of all the things that living things, especially human beings, need to survive. EG *...the destruction of our environment and life-support systems... ...the Earth's basic life-support systems.* N COUNT **2** the equipment that is used to keep a person alive, for example when they are very ill or in a dangerous environment such as under the sea or in space. EG *His task was to monitor the life-support systems, checking oxygen levels.* N COUNT

life's work. Someone's **life's work** is the main activity that they have been involved in during their life, or their most important achievement. EG *...a scholar whose life's work had been devoted to the mystics... The French settlers sold their life's work and fled.* N SING : POSS+N = lifework

lifetime /laɪftaɪm/, **lifetimes**. **1** A **lifetime** is **1.1** the length of time that someone is alive. EG *I have spent a lifetime in politics... I've seen a lot of changes in my lifetime.* N COUNT : USU SING ↑ period = life **1.2** the period of time that something lasts. EG *...during the lifetime of this parliament.* N SING : WITH POSS

2 If you describe an experience as the experience **of a lifetime**, you mean that it is the most memorable or important experience of a particular type that you are ever likely to have; used showing approval. EG *You may be able to win the holiday of a lifetime.* PHR AFTER N = in a million

lift /lɪft/, **lifts, lifting, lifted**. **1** If you **lift** something, **1.1** you take it in your hand or hands and move it, especially upwards, to another position. EG *The man lifted a pile of books from the bedside table... He lifted the glass to his mouth... One by one, she lifted down the wooden boxes in which the eggs were packed... Reaching inside, he lifted the baby out with both hands.* V+O : USU+A ≠ lower, put down

2 If you **lift** a part of your body, you move it to a higher position. EG *He lifted his hand to ring the doorbell... He lifts his foot from the accelerator... Hargreaves lifted his bad leg and eased it to a better position.* V+O = raise ● If someone does not **lift a finger** to do something, they do not make the slightest effort to do it. EG *I won't lift a finger to stop you.* ● PHR : VB INFLECTS

3 If you **lift** your eyes or your head, you look up, for example when you have been reading a book and someone comes into the room; a fairly formal use. EG *He lifted his eyes from the table... After a while she lifted her head and stared out of the window.* V+O ≠ look down, lower

4 If you **lift** your voice or if your voice **lifts**, you speak or sing more loudly; a fairly formal use. EG *She lifted her voice for the children to hear.* V-ERG ↑ increase = raise

5 A **lift** is a device that moves up and down inside a vertical shaft in a tall building. You can travel in it or take goods from one floor to another in it. Lifts are usually shaped like small rooms; used in British English. EG *I took the lift to the eighth floor... There was a man in the lift as we went down... The lift doors opened, and they stepped out into the empty corridor.* ● See also **ski lift**. N COUNT = elevator

6 If you give someone a **lift**, you take them in your car from one place to another in order to help them and not in return for money. EG *He gave her a lift back to London that night... Try and get a lift with them.* N COUNT : USU a+N = ride

7 If a government or organization **lifts** goods or people in or out of a country or area, it transports them by aeroplane into or out of that country or area, especially in special circumstances such as a war or a famine. EG *There is a restriction on the number of passengers foreign airlines can lift from the island.* V+O : USU+A

8 If a government, official, or committee **lifts** a law or rule that prevents people from doing something, they end it. EG *They urged the United States to lift all* V+O = rescind, revoke controls on textile imports... He lifted the ban on the People's Party.

9 If something such as a difficulty or problem **lifts** or **is lifted** from you, it is removed so that you no longer feel worried or depressed by it. EG *A great burden seems to have been lifted off me... ...an age in which so much responsibility is lifted from individual shoulders and transferred to the state.* V-ERG+A

10 To **lift** a group of people means to improve their situation; a formal word. EG *Their task was not easy: to lift a whole people weighed down by a past of slavery and oppression.* V+O = raise, uplift

11 If something **lifts** your spirits or your heart, or if they **lift**, you start feeling more cheerful. EG *These delightful children lifted my spirits with their laughter... Such a meal did nothing to lift her spirits... He will be here in a few days, Fanny thought, her heart lifting.* V-ERG ⇑ cheer up

12 If a depression or bad mood **lifts**, you stop feeling depressed or sad and become more cheerful. EG *If the depression does not lift in a few days, come back and see me again... His moodiness seemed to have lifted.* V ⇑ go

13 If something gives you a **lift**, it gives you a feeling of greater confidence, energy, or enthusiasm; an informal use. EG *It gives the worker an extraordinary psychological lift... Drink this. It's supposed to give you a lift.* N SING: USU *a*+N = boost

14 If you **lift** something from a place, you steal it; an informal use. EG *Uncle Harold had lifted the morning's receipts... They break into steel filing cabinets, open cupboards, or lift a briefcase from a locked car or office.* V+O = pinch, swipe

15 If you **lift** a piece of writing or music that has been written by someone else, you copy it and use it so that people think that you wrote it. EG *Most of the article was lifted from a woman's magazine.* V+O: IF+PREP THEN *from* ⇑ plagiarize = pinch

16 To **lift** something also means to increase the amount of something or to increase its level or the rate at which it happens. EG *They expect that this will lift the rate of inflation back to 13 per cent... They want to lift the threshold at which extra interest is charged.* V+O ⇑ raise

17 If fog or mist **lifts**, it becomes less, for example by moving upwards or by becoming less thick. EG *The morning mist is lifting... Around midday, the fog lifted.* V ⇑ lessen

18 If you **lift** root vegetables or bulbs, you dig them out of the ground; a technical term in gardening. V+O = dig up

lift off. When an aircraft or rocket **lifts off**, it leaves the ground and rises into the air. EG *The plane lifted off just as the ground seemed to open beneath them.* • See also **lift-off**. PHRASAL VB: V+ADV = take off

lift up. **1** If you **lift** something **up**, you take it in your hand or hands and move it upwards to another position. EG *Stephen was attempting to lift up the two pint tankards from the bar.* PHRASAL VB: V+O+ADV

2 If you **lift up** a part of your body, you move it to a higher position. EG *She lifted up her head to smile at him.* PHRASAL VB: V+O+ADV

3 If you **lift up** your voice, you speak or sing more loudly; a fairly formal use. EG *It was John who lifted up his voice in answer.* PHRASAL VB: ORDER V+ADV+O = raise

lift-off, lift-offs. **Lift-off** or **a lift-off** is the act of launching a rocket into space, when it leaves the ground and rises into the air. EG *...lift-off from a floating launching pad... We have lift-off.* N COUNT/UNCOUNT = blast-off

ligament /lɪgəməˀnt/, **ligaments**. A **ligament** is a band of strong tissue in a person or animal's body, which connects bones. EG *...a torn ligament.* N COUNT

light /laɪt/, **lights, lighting, lighted, lit; lighter, lightest**. The forms **lighted** and **lit** are both used as the past tense and past participle of the verb, although **lit** is more usual. **1 Light** is **1.1** the thing that lets you see things, and that comes from the sun, moon, lamps, fire, etc. EG *Suddenly there was a flash of white light in the sky... By the light of a torch, she began to read... He looked around in the dim light... The house blazed with light... We are dependent on the sun for heat and light... ...artificial light.* N UNCOUNT ⇑ radiation **1.2** the quality of light that there is in a particular place or at a particular time. EG *She loved the intense light of the African plains... ...hair that is almost black in certain lights.* N MASS+SUPP **1.3** the light that you need in order to be able to do an activity such as painting, reading, writing, etc. EG *Move! You're standing in my light. Stand out of the light... He moved aside to allow him more light.* N UNCOUNT **1.4** the natural light that occurs during the daytime and that is produced by the sun. EG *At four o'clock the light was going fast... We wanted to get home during the light.* N SING: *the*+N = daylight

2 A **light** is **2.1** anything that produces or reflects light, or that seems to shine. EG *There were other lights in the sky that moved fast or flashed... Up ahead I see the lights of a town.* N COUNT **2.2** an electric light in a house or other building. EG *He undressed and put out the light... She went into her daughter's room and turned on the light... I turned off the lights and got into bed.* N COUNT = lamp **2.3** a traffic light. EG *I had to apply the brakes rather abruptly at a red light... The lights were against us all the way. ...Turn left at the next set of lights.* N COUNT: IF SING THEN ADJ COLOUR+N **2.4** one of the lights on a car or other vehicle. EG *Very few cars had reversing lights... The driver turned off his lights... People drove under the speed limit, with their lights on.* N COUNT: USU PL

3 To **light** something means to cause light to shine on it or in it. EG *The flames lit their faces... The room was lighted by a very small, dim bulb... The corridors are lit only by artificial light.* V+O = illuminate ◊ **lighted**. EG *He looked up at the lighted windows.* ◊ ADJ CLASSIF: ATTRIB

4 If a place is described as **light**, it has a lot of natural light in it, for example because it has large windows. EG *The house was airy and light inside.* ADJ QUALIT ◊ **lightness**. EG *There was a curious lightness, a luminescence in the atmosphere.* ◊ N SING WITH DET ⇑ brightness

5 If it is **light**, there is enough natural day light to see because the day has begun. EG *It's getting light.* ADJ QUALIT: PRED

6 If someone **sees the light**, **6.1** they finally understand something after having thought about it for some time. EG *We finally made him see the light.* PHR: VB INFLECTS **6.2** they become converted to a particular religion. EG *He says he's seen the light–he's going to become a Buddhist.* PHR: VB INFLECTS

7 If something **sees the light of day** at a particular time, it comes into existence or is made known to the public at that time. EG *The report saw the light of day last month.* PHR: VB INFLECTS

8 If there is a **light** in someone's eyes, there is an expression in them that shows you the mood that person is in or what they are thinking about; a literary use. EG *The murderous light never left his eyes during those weeks... I could see a questioning and reproachful light in Jane's eyes... From the light in his eye she recognized why his battalion called him 'Tiger Hanks'.* N SING WITH DET = look, glint, gleam

9 If you **light** something, you make it start burning. EG *She stopped and lit a match... Lizzie lighted a cigarette... The fire took a long time to light.* V OR V+O: USU V+O ◊ **lighted**. EG *A lighted candle burned in a saucer.* ◊ ADJ CLASSIF

10 A **light** is also a match or cigarette lighter that you can use to make a cigarette start burning; a fairly informal use. EG *Have you got a light?* N SING: *a*+N

11 If you **set light to** something, you make it start burning. EG *She set light to the photographs.* PHR: VB INFLECTS ⇑ ignite = set fire

12 Light is also used in the following expressions: **12.1** If something **throws** or **casts light on** something else, it makes it easier to understand, because more information has been added to what was previously known. EG *This casts light on a problem which I mentioned last year... His diaries throw a new light upon certain incidents.* PHR: VB INFLECTS = clarify, make clear **12.2** If something **comes to light**, it becomes obvious or is made known to a lot of people. EG *It has come to light that he was lying... No immediate suspect came to light.* PHR: VB INFLECTS = be disclosed **12.3** If something **is brought to light**, it is revealed or made known to a lot of people. EG *I will bring to light the truth.* PHR: VB INFLECTS **12.4** If **light dawns** on you, you at last begin to understand something. EG *Light dawned on her at last.* PHR: VB INFLECTS **12.5** When you talk about **the light at the end of the tunnel**, you are referring to a pleasant situation in the future which gives you a lot of hope and optimism, especially because you are in a difficult or unpleasant situation at the moment. EG *She thought of her retirement day as the light at the end of the tunnel... There was no victory in sight, no light at the end of the tunnel.* PHR: USU USED AS C/O **12.6 First light** is the time in the early morning when light first appears and before the sun rises; a formal or old-fashioned expression. EG *They attacked at first light... We should get there by first light.* PHR: USED AS O = daybreak **12.7** If someone **goes out like a light**, they fall asleep or become unconscious very quickly or immediately; an informal expression. EG *He went out like a light.* PHR: VB INFLECTS **12.8** • **green light**: see **green**. • **sweetness and light**: see **sweetness**. • See also

bright lights, leading light, night-light, pilot light, red light. ● See also **lighting, lit.**

13 Light is also used to refer to **13.1** a particular way of thinking about something or the way it appears in a particular situation. EG *We were now seeing things in a different light... He appeared that day in the worst possible light.* **13.2** the type of influence that something has on situations, people or things. EG *...the fierce light of publicity... ...the cold clear light of reason.* N SING WITH DET +SUPP = aspect, facet; N SING : the+N+ SUPP

14 In the light of particular information, knowledge, etc means considering or using this information, knowledge, etc in order to make a decision or understand something. EG *The doctor should do what in the light of his experience is best for that patient... This development is significant in the light of what happened later... This should be discussed more fully, particularly in light of the developments in the University.* PREP = in view of

15 Something that is **light 15.1** does not weigh very much, or weighs less than you would expect it to. EG *The bag was very light, as though there were nothing in it... We need a light metal, like aluminium.* ◊ **lightness.** EG *...the extreme lightness of this particular shoe.* **15.2** is not very great in amount or degree or intensity. EG *A light rain was falling... My tomatoes produced only a light crop this year... The traffic on the highway was light that day... ...a light mist.* ● If someone or something is **as light as a feather**, they weigh very little indeed. EG *You're as light as a feather!* ADJ QUALIT ≠ heavy; ◊ N UNCOUNT; ADJ QUALIT ≠ heavy; ● PHR : USED AS C

16 Clothes that are **light** are made of thin fabric that does not weigh very much, and are worn in the summer or in hot weather. EG *She wore only a light cotton frock and sandals.* ◊ **lightly.** EG *Many people were lightly dressed.* ADJ QUALIT; ◊ ADV WITH VB

17 Light equipment and machines are small and easily moved, especially because they are not heavy. EG *...a light railway engine... ...light modern weapons.* ADJ CLASSIF : ATTRIB = portable

18 Soil that is **light** is easy to dig, because it has a loose texture and is not sticky or solid. ADJ QUALIT = friable

19 Light colours are very pale. EG *He was wearing a light blue shirt... Her skin is lighter than the rest of her family.* ADJ QUALIT

20 Light winds and breezes blow gently. EG *A light breeze got up.* ADJ QUALIT ⇑ gentle

21 A **light** sleep is one that is easily disturbed and in which you are often aware of the things around you. ▸ used to describe people who sleep lightly. EG *Actually, I'm a very light sleeper.* ◊ **lightly.** EG *...lightly dozing in front of the fire.* ADJ QUALIT : ATTRIB = shallow; ◊ ADV WITH VB

22 A **light** sound is one that is not loud. EG *A light rap sounded at the door.* ◊ **lightly.** EG *She tapped lightly at the door.* ADJ QUALIT; ◊ ADV WITH VB

23 A **light** meal is small in quantity. EG *...a light lunch.* ◊ **lightly.** EG *After lunching lightly at Queenie's he slipped into the National Gallery.* ADJ QUALIT; ◊ ADV WITH VB

24 If food is described as **light, 24.1** it contains a lot of air. EG *Your cakes are always so wonderfully light.* **24.2** it has a delicate flavour and is easy to digest. EG *She had made a very light tomato soup.* ADJ QUALIT; ADJ QUALIT

25 Light work does not involve much physical effort. EG *The children help with light housework.* ADJ QUALIT

26 Movements and actions that are **light** are graceful or gentle and are done with very little force or effort. EG *She runs up the stairs two at a time with her light graceful step... Andrew blows a light kiss to Jane... ...a light clasp on her arm.* ◊ **lightly.** EG *He kissed his wife lightly on the cheek... He moved lightly, he was never clumsy.* ◊ **lightness.** EG *For a heavy man he moves with surprising lightness and speed.* ADJ QUALIT; ◊ ADV WITH VB; ◊ N UNCOUNT

27 If you describe books, plays, music, etc as light, they entertain you without making you think very deeply. EG *She was engrossed in the lighter sections of a newspaper... ...light entertainment and comedy.* ADJ QUALIT ⇑ entertaining

28 If you say something in a **light** way, you sound as if you think that something is not important or serious. EG *She said, 'How d'you do,' in a cool, light, insolent voice.* ◊ **lightly.** EG *He said sorry as lightly as possible.* ADJ QUALIT; ◊ ADV WITH VB

29 Something that is **light** is treated or considered as being unimportant and not serious. EG *This is no light matter: I am extremely worried about it.* ◊ **lightly.** EG *This is not a charge to make lightly against the government.* ADJ QUALIT : USU WITH BROAD NEG; ◊ ADV WITH VB

30 If you **make light of** something, you indicate by your behaviour that you think that it is not important or serious. EG *They make light of their handicaps... He laughed and made light of it all.* PHR : VB INFLECTS

31 Lights are the lungs of sheep, pigs, etc, used as food; an old-fashioned use. N PLURAL

light up. 1 If something **lights up** something else, it shines light on all of it or in all of it. EG *Above the town the fire was still blazing, lighting up the sky... For some reason her car was lighted up inside.* PHRASAL VB : V+O+ADV ⇑ illuminate

2 If your face or your eyes **light up**, you suddenly look very happy. EG *His face lit up at the sight of Cynthia... His eyes lighted up when he saw me.* PHRASAL VB : V+ADV ⇑ brighten

3 If you **light up**, you make a cigarette, cigar, or pipe start burning and you start smoking it; a fairly informal expression. EG *George lit up and puffed away for a while.* PHRASAL VB : V+ADV ⇑ smoke

light upon. If you **light upon** something or **light on** it, or if your eyes **light upon** it or **on** it, you suddenly notice it or find it. EG *Her eyes then lit upon the piece of paper in the corner.* PHRASAL VB : V+PREP, HAS PASS = chance upon

light aircraft. Light aircraft is both the singular and the plural form. A **light aircraft** is a type of small aeroplane that is designed to carry a small number of passengers or a small amount of goods. EG *We ought to be able to produce light aircraft in this country.* N COUNT/UNCOUNT

light bulb, light bulbs; also spelled with a hyphen and as one word. A **light bulb** is the round glass part of an electric light or lamp from which light shines when the lamp or light is switched on. N COUNT

lighten /laɪtəⁿn/, **lightens, lightening, lightened. 1** When something **lightens** or when you **lighten** it, it becomes brighter or less dark in colour. EG *After the rain stops, the sky lightens a little... Constant exposure to the sun had lightened my hair.* V-ERG

2 If you **lighten** something such as a load or burden, you make it lighter by removing some of it. EG *By doing this you are lightening the load of hospital doctors.* V+O ⇑ ease = alleviate

3 If someone's face or expression **lightens**, it becomes more cheerful, happy, and relaxed. EG *Her whole expression lightened.* V = lift

4 If you **lighten** an object, you make it less heavy. EG *Almost immediately they began to lighten their products in an effort to increase sales.* V+O

lighter /laɪtə/, **lighters. 1 Lighter** is the comparative of **light.**

2 A **lighter** is a small device that produces a flame which you can use to light cigarettes, cigars, pipes, etc. EG *Can I just use your lighter? I've run out of matches.* ● See also **fire lighter.** N COUNT = cigarette lighter

light-fingered. Someone who is **light-fingered** steals things, for example out of people's pockets; a rather old-fashioned word. ADJ CLASSIF

light-headed. If you are **light-headed**, you feel rather dizzy and faint, for example because you are ill or because you have drunk too much alcohol. EG *I was light-headed; I had not slept and I was very hungry.* ADJ QUALIT ⇑ unwell = giddy

light-hearted. 1 Someone who is **light-hearted** is cheerful and happy. EG *He was in a light-hearted mood.* ◊ **light-heartedly.** EG *She flirted with them light-heartedly and enjoyed herself enormously.* ADJ QUALIT = carefree; ◊ ADV WITH VB = gaily

2 Something that is **light-hearted** is entertaining or amusing, and not at all serious. EG *Let me finish with a slightly more light-hearted question... ...a light-hearted remark.* ADJ QUALIT

lighthouse /laɪthaus/, **lighthouses.** A **lighthouse** is a tower containing a powerful flashing lamp that is built on the coast or on a small island or rock in the sea. Lighthouses are used to guide ships or to warn them of danger. EG *She walked down the quay towards the lighthouse.* N COUNT

light industry, light industries. Light industry is industry in which only small items are made, for example household goods and clothes, and in which large heavy machinery is not used. N COUNT/UNCOUNT

lighting /laɪtɪŋ/. **1** The **lighting** in a place is the way that it is lit, for example by electric lights, by candles, by windows, etc, or the quality of the light in it. EG *They walked along the corridor, with its artificial lighting, towards the department office... ...poorly designed street lighting... The lighting was restful.* N UNCOUNT ⇑ system

2 The **lighting** in a film or play is the arrangement of electric lights that are used to light the film or play. N UNCOUNT

lightning /laɪtnɪŋ/. **1 Lightning** is the very bright flashes of light in the sky that happen during thunderstorms. EG *...a flash of lightning... He was struck by lightning, and nearly died.* ● See also **forked lightning, sheet lightning.** N UNCOUNT

2 Lightning describes things that happen very quickly or last for only a short time. EG *Terry and I exchanged lightning sidelong glances... He drew his gun with lightning speed.* ADJ CLASSIF : ATTRIB

lightning conductor, lightning conductors. A **lightning conductor** is a long thin piece of metal that is placed on top of a building and that goes as far as the ground. It allows lightning to reach the ground safely without damaging the building; used in British English. N COUNT = lightning rod

lightning rod, lightning rods. A **lightning rod** is the same as a lightning conductor; used in American English. N COUNT

lightning strike, lightning strikes. A **lightning strike** is a strike in which workers stop work suddenly and without any warning, in order to protest about something. N COUNT ⇑ action

lightship /laɪtʃɪp/, **lightships.** A **lightship** is a small ship that stays in one place and that has a powerful flashing lamp like a lighthouse. It is used to guide ships or to warn them of danger. N COUNT

lightweight /laɪtweɪt/, **lightweights**; also spelled with a hyphen. **1** Something that is **lightweight** weighs less than most other things of the same type. EG *...a grey lightweight suit... ...lightweight electronic equipment.* ADJ QUALIT ⇑ light

2 A **lightweight** is a boxer weighing between 130 and 135 pounds; a technical term in boxing. EG *He had fought some good lightweights in the late twenties and thirties.* N COUNT

3 You also describe someone as a **lightweight** when you think that he or she is not very important in a particular area of activity, or is not very skilful or clever at it; used showing disapproval. EG *Most of them have been political lightweights.* ▸ used as an adjective. EG *...one of those ever-youthful lightweight intellectuals.* N COUNT ⇑ nonentity ▸ ADJ QUALIT

light-year, light-years. 1 A **light-year** is the distance that light travels in a year; a technical term in astronomy. N COUNT

2 You can use **light-years** to mean a very long time; an informal use. EG *Last Tuesday week seemed several light-years away already... Neither of them stirred for several light-years.* N COUNT : USU PL = ages

likable /laɪkəbə[0]l/. See **likeable.**

like /laɪk/, **likes, liking, liked.** In this entry, categories 1 to 23 deal with 'like' mainly as a preposition or conjunction expressing ideas of similarity and comparison. Categories 24 to 32 deal with 'like' as a verb expressing ideas of enjoyment, wanting, or preference. **1** If you say that one person or thing is **like** another, you mean that the two people or things have similar qualities, features, or characteristics. EG *He looked like Clark Gable... She sounded just like Nell... I saw a dog like ours on the beach... She's very like her sister.* PREP ⇑ similar to

2 You can use **like** to say that someone or something has particular qualities that remind you of another type of person or thing, or that make them behave as if they were that person or thing. EG *These boys weren't twins; they only looked like twins... Keith and I, we were so close, like brothers... After what seemed like hours, he came out... 'I'm glad you came.'-'Yes. It was like old times.'... My watch said four o'clock but it looked like early evening outside... It tastes like a mango... She's nothing like I imagined.* ▸ used informally as a conjunction. EG *You look like you'd seen a ghost... He felt like he'd won the pools.* PREP ▸ CONJ SUBORD

3 Like is used to introduce a simile, describing something or expressing an idea in a more effective, imaginative, or vivid way by comparing it with something else. EG *He's like a little baby... ...one of those small pocket flashlights shaped like a fountain pen... The lake was like a bright blue mirror... ...toothbrushes huddled together in a tumbler like old men at a wedding... ...a scream of pain, like a tiny child's.* PREP ⇑ similar to

4 If you ask someone what something is **like**, you are asking them to describe it or to give their opinion of it. EG *What was Essex like as a place?... What was it like; was it interesting?... What did they taste like?* PREP : *what*+VB +S+PREP

5 You can use **like** to say that something or someone belongs to or appears to belong to a particular group or set of things or people. EG *You only get them in big countries, like Africa or India... Frank doesn't sound like the kind of person who'd get on with you... It's not just an isolated request, I get lots like it... They knew little about everyday home activities like cooking.* PREP

6 You can use **like** to draw attention to a particular thing about which you want to say something. EG *In a game like ours, one begins to trust one's instincts... There's no point in stirring up a lot of publicity about a foolish thing like this.* PREP

7 You can use **like** to say that someone or something is in the same situation as another person or thing. EG *His visas, like his passport, had been issued in December... Like all creative industries, it's short of talent... She, like everybody else, had worried about it.* ▸ used as an adjective. EG *We must strive for greater uniformity so that like offenders should be treated in similar fashion.* PREP ▸ ADJ CLASSIF : ATTRIB = similar

8 If you say that something is happening **like** something else, you are emphasizing the way that it is happening by mentioning something that is well-known for behaving in that way. There are many set phrases that use **like** in this way, for example 'to watch someone like a hawk' and 'to work like Trojans'. EG *During the war we worked like slaves to produce good food for the country... They were dropping like flies... The boys lay, panting like dogs.* PREP

● In informal English, if you say that something happens or is done **like anything, like crazy,** or **like mad,** you mean that it happens or is done in a particularly intense or noticeable way. EG *He waved to us and we waved back like anything... She patronized me like mad, of course!* ● **like hell**: see **hell.** ● **like nothing on earth**: see **earth.** ● PHR : USED AS AN A

9 If you say that someone is behaving **like** something or someone else, you mean that they are behaving in a way that is typical of that kind of thing or person. EG *Oh, don't be so stuffy. You're behaving like a perfect idiot... People expect rulers to live like rulers.* PREP

10 You can use **like** in expressions such as 'That's just like Jane' and 'She was not like herself' when you mean that the person's behaviour is or is not typical of their character. EG *Julie seemed subdued, not like herself... It was so like Jane to be so intense and dramatic about things.* PREP+PRON/N PROPER ⇑ characteristic

11 If you talk about things or people **and the like,** you are indicating that there are other similar things or people that can be included in what you are saying. EG *...the activities of ruthless mine owners and the like... ...job creation schemes and the like.* PHR : USED AS AN A ⇑ etc = and such

12 You say **'like this', 'like that',** or **'like so'** when you are showing someone how something is done. EG *Twist it round and put it on here, like that... Keep them moving right to left about their centre, like so.* PHR : USED AS ADV SEN

13 You also use **'like this'** or **'like that'** when you are drawing attention to something that you are doing or that someone else is doing. EG *Ralph! Stop laughing like that... Sorry to break in on you like this, Dr Marlowe.* PHR : USED AS AN A

14 You use **the like of which** or **the likes of which** when you are saying that an experience or event that you have mentioned is very important, intense, or noticeable; a literary use. EG *It had stirred up in him an excitement the like of which he had never felt in all his life before... ...a carnage the likes of which has been unknown to man.* PHR

15 The likes of someone or something is an expression used to indicate that you disapprove of that type of person or thing; an informal, rather old-fashioned use. EG *He wasn't going to move for the likes of them.* PHR : USU USED AS O

16 Like is sometimes used as a conjunction when you are making a comparison between two things. This is an informal use, which many speakers of English consider to be incorrect. EG *Is it like you remembered it?... It didn't work out quite like I intended it to... Instructions are displayed on a monitor, rather like on a television set... 'You want a pig,' said Roger, 'like in a real hunt.'* CONJ SUBORD = as

17 You can use **like 17.1** in negative expressions such as **nothing like it** and **no place like it** to suggest that there is nothing as good as the situation, thing, or person mentioned. EG *There is nothing like education for breaking down class barriers... He had never heard woodwind like it... 'I've never seen anything* *like it,' he said with admiration... There's no place like home.* **17.2** to emphasize a negative statement. EG *The cast is large, though nothing like as numerous as one might suppose... Their relationship is certainly not anything like as close as ours... There is nothing like enough practice given in solving problems.*

18 You use the expression **something like** to say that a number, quantity, time, etc is an estimate, not an exact figure. EG *They get a basic wage, something like £5,000 and a car as well... Something like ninety per cent of the crop was destroyed... ...something like ten years ago... The first train wasn't until something like 7 o'clock.* [PHR : USU+NUM = about, around, roughly]

19 You use the expression **more like** to mention an amount or number that in your opinion is closer to the actual figure than one that has already been mentioned. EG *'You mean it'll be worth fifty dollars?'–'More like five hundred.'... I budgeted for fifteen pounds a week and in fact left myself with more like eighteen pounds ten.* [PHR : USU+NUM = nearer]

20 If you say **'That's more like it'**, you mean that the thing that you are referring to is more satisfactory than it was on earlier occasions. EG *Fifteen miles a day, that's more like it.* [CONVENTION ⇑ better]

21 Like as not is used to say that something will probably happen. EG *Like as not, he won't be back until five... The nearby Abbey in which, like as not, he would be buried.* [PHR : USED AS ADV SEN]

22 Like enough is used to say that something will probably happen or has probably happened; an informal and old-fashioned expression. EG *I bet he's done something terrible, eaten his own offspring like enough.* [PHR : USED AS ADV SEN]

23 In spoken English, people sometimes say **like** when they are hesitating or when they are thinking about what to say next. This is a very informal use, which many speakers of English consider to be incorrect. EG *I was feeling peckish, like... He didn't identify himself, like deliberately, and we all sat there for an hour.*

24 If you **like** something, you enjoy it or find it pleasant or attractive. EG *Which did you like best–the Vivaldi or the Schumann?... There's nothing I like about town life... I like reading... Look, Rick, he doesn't like being photographed, so stop it.* [V+O/-ING/to-INF]

25 If you **like** someone, you enjoy being with them because they are interesting and pleasant. EG *She's a nice girl, I like her... He had always been well liked and admired.* [V+O]

26 If you ask someone how they **like** something, you are asking them for their opinion or judgement about it and whether they enjoy it. EG *How do you like it here?... How do you like the apples?* [V+O/-ING = find]

27 If you **like** something such as a particular course of action or way of behaving, you approve of it. EG *Most students don't like the way colleges and universities are run... He liked precision... I do not like people turning their backs on me when I am talking... I wasn't sure I liked what I faced.* ● If you say that something will happen **like it or not** or **whether** someone **likes it or not**, you mean that although a situation may be unpleasant or difficult, it has to be faced and accepted because it cannot be changed. EG *Most of us actually do come in to work at weekends, like it or not... A strike is going to take place whether we like it or not.* [V+O/WH, OR V+O+-ING/to-INF] [● PHR : USED AS ADV SEN]

28 If you say that you would **like** something or would **like** to do something, you are indicating a wish or desire that you have. EG *I'd like to change my room and go somewhere else but it's so cheap where I am... He would have liked a pint of beer before he started... Do what you like... Let's go away somewhere, France, Italy, anywhere you like... He can stay here if he likes... The children are free to spend as long as they like at any one activity.* [V+O/to-INF ⇑ want, prefer]

29 If you ask someone if they would **like** something or would **like to do something**, you are politely offering them something. EG *'Would you like some coffee?'–'No thank you.'... Would you like me to get something for you?* [V+O/to-INF, OR V+O+to-INF ⇑ want]

30 If you say to someone that you would **like** something or would **like** them to do something, you are politely asking them for something or to do something. EG *I'd rather like your views on that... Well look, Ian, what I would like you to do is to try.* [V+O, OR V+O+to-INF ⇑ want]

31 You say **if you like 31.1** when you are offering to do something for someone. EG *I'll drive, if you like.* [PHR : USED AS ADV SEN] **31.2** when you are agreeing to something in a rather reluctant and grudging way; an informal and slightly rude use. EG *'Shall I put the fire on?'–'If you like.'* [CONVENTION ⇑ yes] **31.3** when you have just expressed something in a different way. EG *It's a great opportunity, a paid holiday if you like... ...changes in their way of life, enormous changes, if you like.* [PHR : USED AS AN A ⇑ really]

32 If you say that you **like** to do something or that you **like** something to be done, you mean that you prefer to do it or prefer it to be done as part of your normal life or routine. EG *In the evening I like to lay breakfast for the morning... Her folks like her to get in early... One doesn't like to ask questions.* [V+to-INF, OR V+O+to-INF]

33 Someone's **likes** are the things that they enjoy or find pleasant. EG *Try to discover your guests' various likes and dislikes with regard to food.* [N PLURAL : USU POSS+N = preferences]

34 If you talk about **like** and **like**, you are referring to two or more people or things that have the same or similar characteristics; a formal use. EG *We don't have any studies comparing like for like of people who were in prison and people doing community service... Basically, like breeds like.* [N UNCOUNT : N+PREP/VB+N]

35 See also **liking**.

-like. You can add **-like** to the end of nouns in order to form adjectives. Adjectives formed in this way describe things as similar in appearance or nature to the thing referred to by the noun. EG *The landscape has a dream-like air... ...a rock-like hump.* [COMB : FORMS ADJS]

likeable /laɪkəbəl/; also spelled **likable**. You say that someone or something is **likeable** when they are pleasant and therefore easy to like. EG *...a very attractive and likeable young man... It's an extremely likeable but very implausible romantic thriller.* [ADJ QUALIT ⇑ nice = agreeable]

likelihood /laɪklihʊd/. The **likelihood** of something happening is the probability of it happening. EG *There is every likelihood that she will succeed... We shall find in all likelihood that we have lost out.* [N SING WITH DET : USU+of/REPORT-CL]

likely /laɪkli/, **likelier, likeliest**. **1** You use **likely** to indicate that something is probably the case or will probably happen in a particular situation. EG *What kind of change is likely?... ...the likely consequences of going ahead with the scheme... It seemed hardly likely that they would agree... I don't think it likely that she'd have gone out for a walk... Very likely none of them would know the name.* [ADJ QUALIT, OR ADV WITH VB]

2 If someone or something is **likely** to do something, they will very probably do it. EG *They were not likely to forget it... A butcher will not be likely to preach vegetarianism... These services are likely to be available to us all before long.* [ADJ QUALIT : PRED+to-INF]

3 Not likely is an emphatic way of saying 'no', especially when someone asks you whether you are going to do something; an informal expression. EG *'Will you come back when he recovers?'–'Not likely!'* [CONVENTION]

4 If you say to someone that what they have just told you is **a likely story, a likely tale**, etc, you are saying in a humorous way that you don't believe it. EG *'The teacher said I could come home early.'–'A likely story!'.* [PHR : USED AS C, OR CONVENTION]

5 You describe people or things as **likely** when it is probable that they will be suitable for a particular purpose. EG *The local committee is always looking out for likely recruits... I searched a likely looking tree with my binoculars.* [ADJ CLASSIF : ATTRIB = prospective]

like-minded. People who are **like-minded** have similar opinions, ideas, attitudes, or interests. EG *Hubbard and his like-minded colleagues formed a new group within the party.* [ADJ CLASSIF]

liken /laɪkən/, **likens, likening, likened**. If you **liken** one thing or person **to** another, you compare them in words by showing how similar they are. EG *It has a mildly nutty taste which has been likened to new potatoes... Life on this planet has been likened to a pyramid.* [PHRASAL VB : V+O+PREP]

likeness /laɪknɪs/, **likenesses**. **1** If two things have a **likeness** to each other, they are similar in appearance. EG *...two china dogs that bore a likeness to his aunt.* [N SING WITH DET : IF+PREP THEN to = resemblance]

2 A **likeness** is a picture of someone, considered from the point of view of how accurately it represents that person. EG *The portrait shows a lot of talent. A very good likeness.* [N COUNT : USU SING, IF+PREP THEN of]

likewise /laɪkwaɪz/. **1** You use **likewise** when you are comparing two methods, states, situations, etc and saying that they are similar. EG *In Yugoslavia there was a special local way of doing it, likewise in* [ADV SEN = similarly]

Italy... You can't teach navigation in the middle of a storm. Likewise, you can't build a system of values in the current educational climate.

2 If you do one thing, and someone else **does likewise**, they do the same or a similar thing. EG *She had learned to look after herself at an early age and encouraged her children to do likewise.* PHR : VB INFLECTS ⇑ copy

liking /laɪkɪŋ/. **1** If you have a **liking** for something or someone, you like them. EG *She was developing a liking for Scotch... I took an enormous liking to Davies the moment I met him.* N SING WITH DET ⇑ feeling

2 If something is **to** your **liking**, it is pleasant and suited to your interests, needs, or wishes. EG *Organising Christmas relief funds was more to his liking than the routine work on Capitol Hill... Did they find the temperature to their liking?* PHR : USED AS AN A ⇑ suitable

3 If something is too big, too fast, etc **for** your **liking**, you would prefer it to be smaller, slower, etc. EG *You are progressing too fast for his liking.* PHR : USED AS AN A

lilac /laɪlək/, **lilacs**. **Lilac** can also be used as the plural form. **1** A **lilac** is a small tree which has pleasant-smelling purple, pink, or white flowers in large, cone-shaped clusters. EG *...houses with lilac bushes in their gardens.* ▸ also used to refer to the flowers. EG *It would be nice to have some lilac for the drawing-room.* N COUNT/UNCOUNT ⇑ shrub

2 Something that is **lilac** is pale pinkish-purple in colour. EG *...her plain lilac dress... ...the lilac of the autumn sky.* ADJ COLOUR = mauve

Lilliputian /lɪlɪpjuːʃɪən/. If you describe something as **Lilliputian**, you mean that it is very small or is intended for very small people; a literary word. EG *...a Lilliputian chest of drawers.* ADJ CLASSIF = miniature, diminutive

Lilo /laɪləʊ/, **Lilos**. **Lilo** is a trademark for a long, flat, plastic mattress that you fill with air and use for lying on, for example when you are camping or at the seaside. N COUNT ⇑ mattress

lilt /lɪlt/, **lilts**. A **lilt** is **1** a way of speaking in which your voice rises and falls in a pleasant way as if you were singing. EG *There was something familiar in the lilt of the voice... ...his Irish lilt.* N COUNT : USU SING ⇑ intonation **2** a graceful, rhythmic way of moving. EG *The woman was small and plump, with a lilt in her walk.* N COUNT : USU SING

lilting /lɪltɪŋ/. **1** A **lilting** voice or song rises and falls in tone in a pleasant way. EG *The lark sings its lilting song... She spoke to him in her lilting Arabic.* ADJ CLASSIF ⇑ musical = melodious

2 A **lilting** movement is graceful and rhythmic. EG *...a lilting trot on the soft soil.* ADJ CLASSIF ⇑ elegant

lily /lɪli¹/, **lilies**. **1** A **lily** is **1.1** a plant that grows from a bulb and that has large flowers, often white ones. EG *Plant lily bulbs in autumn.* ▸ also used to refer to the flowers. EG *She added a wild lily to her bouquet.* N COUNT **1.2** a water-lily. EG *...a lake full of lilies and goldfish... ...lawns, walks, and lily ponds.* N COUNT

2 If you say that someone is **gilding the lily**, you mean that they are trying to improve something that is already perfect or very beautiful; an old-fashioned expression. PHR : VB INFLECTS

lily-livered. If you describe someone as **lily-livered**, you mean that they are cowardly; an old-fashioned word. ADJ QUALIT

lily of the valley, lilies of the valley. **Lily of the valley** can also be used as the plural form. **Lily of the valley** is a small plant which often grows wild and which has large leaves and many small, white, bell-shaped flowers. ▸ also used to refer to the flowers. N UNCOUNT/COUNT

limb /lɪm/, **limbs**. **1** Your **limbs** are your arms and legs. EG *He was very tall with long limbs... We cough, yawn, and stretch our limbs... Don't move the injured limb.* ▸ used also to refer to the legs of animals such as horses, dogs, tigers, etc. EG *Its limbs were not particularly well suited to running.* N COUNT : USU PL = member

2 The **limbs** of a tree are its branches; a rather literary use. EG *Thick, choking smoke rose into the tree's upper limbs... ...fallen limbs that had become dry enough to burn well.* N COUNT ⇑ member = bough

3 Limb is also used in the following expressions. **3.1** If someone is or has gone **out on a limb**, they have done or said something that is risky or extreme, and are likely to fail or be criticized by other people; an informal expression. EG *I never heard him go out on a limb like that before.* PHR : USED AS AN A **3.2** If you threaten to **tear** someone **limb from limb**, you mean that you are extremely angry with them, and may use violence against them. EG *If I ever get my hands on him, I'll tear him limb from limb!* PHR : VB INFLECTS ⇑ attack **3.3** If someone **risks life and limb**, they do something very dangerous that may cause them to die or be seriously injured. PHR : VB INFLECTS

-limbed is used after an adjective to indicate that a person or animal has limbs of a particular type or appearance. EG *The female athlete tends to be longer limbed... ...loose-limbed, well-built kids.* COMB : FORMS ADJS

limber /lɪmbə/, **limbers, limbering, limbered**. Someone who is **limber** is able to move and bend easily; a rather literary word. EG *His leg felt comparatively limber.* ADJ QUALIT = lithe, supple

limber up. If you **limber up**, you prepare for an activity, especially a sport of some kind, by doing some exercises or practice. EG *I had no time to limber up on the practice range... They were just limbering up.* PHRASAL VB : V+ADV, OR V+O (NG/REFL)+ADV = loosen up

limbo /lɪmbəʊ/. **1** If you are in **limbo**, you are in a situation where you do not know what will happen next and where you have no control over things. EG *Refugees may remain in limbo for years... I waited in a state of limbo until another officer appeared to escort me to the cell.* N UNCOUNT ⇑ uncertainty

2 Limbo or the **limbo** is a West Indian dance in which you have to pass under a low bar while leaning backwards. The bar is moved nearer to the floor each time you go under it. N SING : *the*+N

lime /laɪm/, **limes**. **1** A **lime** is **1.1** a small round fruit that has a dark green skin and tastes like a lemon. EG *She watched Bernard squeeze the limes.* ▸ also used to refer to the tree on which this fruit grows. N COUNT ⇑ citrus fruit **1.2** a large tree with pale green leaves which is often planted in parks in towns and cities. EG *...the long avenue of limes... ...the yellow flowers of mature lime trees.* N COUNT = linden

2 Lime or **lime juice** is a non-alcoholic drink that is made from the juice of limes or that tastes like this juice. EG *She was drinking vodka and lime.* N UNCOUNT

3 Lime is also **3.1** a chemical substance which you spread onto soil in order to improve it by making it less acid. EG *...expenditure on fertilizers and lime.* N UNCOUNT **3.2** a white-coloured rock used for building or for making cement. EG *...a lime quarry.* N UNCOUNT = limestone **3.3** a white substance made by heating limestone and used for making cement or painting walls. EG *...bricks, sand, and lime for the schoolroom.* N UNCOUNT = quicklime

lime-green. Something that is **lime-green** is pale yellowish-green in colour. EG *...the faded bit of lime-green silk.* ADJ COLOUR

limelight /laɪmlaɪt/. If someone is in the **limelight**, they are in a situation in which everyone's attention is fixed on them, for example because they are famous or have done something unusual or exciting. EG *He was only happy when he was in the limelight... They tried to keep the women out of the limelight... I hated the limelight and found it unbearable.* N SING : *the*+N

limerick /lɪmərɪk/, **limericks**. A **limerick** is a humorous poem which has five lines and a special rhythm and way of rhyming. N COUNT

limestone /laɪmstəʊn/ is a white-coloured rock which is used for building and making cement. EG *...the extensive systems of limestone caves... ...pieces of local limestone and granite.* N UNCOUNT

limey /laɪmi¹/, **limeys**. Some Americans refer to British people as **limeys** in a disapproving or humorous way; an offensive word. EG *You're what the limeys call a nanny... I told those limey bastards to take you to a hospital... ...the guy's limey accent.* N COUNT = British

limit /lɪmɪt/, **limits, limiting, limited**. **1** The **limit** of something is its greatest possible extent or degree. EG *Marsha's tolerance reached its limit... There is no limit to the risks they are prepared to take... The powers of the human brain are stretched to the limit... She was trying her mother's patience to its limits.* N COUNT : USU SING=PL

2 A **limit** of a particular kind is the largest or smallest amount of money, period of time, etc that is allowed because of a law, rule, or decision. EG *...a motorist exceeding the speed limit... ...a time limit of two years... There was a limit on what we could buy.* N COUNT+SUPP

3 The **limit** of an area is its boundary or edge. EG *...the southern limit of the affected area... ...outside the country's own territorial limits.* N COUNT+SUPP

4 The **limits** of a situation are the facts involved in it which allow only some actions, decisions, or results and make others impossible or unlikely. EG *...the problems of applying that system within the limits of a weekly, two-hour meeting... We assume a set of limits within which the solution must lie.* N PLURAL

5 If you **limit** something, you decide that it will not become greater than a particular amount or degree. EG *The government plans to limit military expenditure... Japanese exports would be limited to 1.68m vehicles... Measures had been taken to limit the effectiveness of their navy.* V+O = restrict

6 If someone or something **limits** you, they control or reduce the number of things that you can have or do. EG *Why should this country limit me that way?* V+O = restrict

◇ **limiting**. EG *Many of these customs were narrow, limiting and bad.* ◇ ADJ QUALIT = restrictive

7 If you **limit** yourself or **limit** your actions, you deal only with particular things or people. EG *His enjoyments in life are limited to fighting and drinking... Will he limit himself to seeing that the enterprise is approved?... I am limiting my observations to the Christian faith.* V+O (NG/REFL.): USU+A *(to)* = confine, restrict

8 If something **is limited** to a particular place or group of people, it exists only in that place, or is had or done only by that group. EG *Nor is the problem limited to Sweden... Many slang expressions are limited to certain small areas.* V+O: USU PASS+ *to* = be confined, be restricted

9 See also **limited**.

10 The word **limit** is also used in the following phrases. **10.1** If you add **within limits** to a statement, you mean that it is true or applies only when talking about reasonable or normal situations. EG *Within limits, the higher the temperature, the quicker the chemical reaction... I'd do anything for him; well, within limits!* PHR: USED AS ADV SEN **10.2** If you describe a place as **off limits**, you mean that particular people, usually soldiers or sailors, are not allowed to go there; used mainly in American English. EG *The area would be off limits during the interrogation... Mayhew had gone off limits.* PHR: USED AS AN A ⇑ forbidden **10.3** You say that someone **is the limit** when you are very annoyed with them because of something that they have just done or said; an informal expression. EG *Really, Sheila, you are the limit!* PHR: VB INFLECTS = be the end **10.4** If you say **the sky's the limit**, you mean that there is nothing to prevent someone or something from being very successful. CONVENTION

limitation /lɪmɪteɪʃəⁿn/, **limitations**. **1 Limitation** is the act or process of controlling or reducing the amount or degree of something or the number of things that a person can have or do. EG *...the limitation of trade union power... ...arms limitation talks.* N UNCOUNT ⇑ control = restriction

2 If you talk about a person's **limitations** or the **limitations** of a particular method, system, or thing, you mean that they are only able to do some things and not others, or only able to achieve a relatively low degree of success or excellence. EG *It's important to know your own limitations... ...her limitations as an actress... ...the limitations of traditional methods of coding... Sonar has its limitations.* N PLURAL: USU WITH POSS = shortcomings

3 A **limitation** is also **3.1** a fact or situation that allows only some actions or decisions and makes others impossible. EG *I am willing to accept certain limitations on my freedom.* N COUNT: USU PL = restriction **3.2** the greatest amount or extent of something that is allowed or possible. EG *All limitations on earnings after retirement must cease... There are limitations to the contractors' liability.* N COUNT: USU PL = limit

limited /lɪmɪtɪ²d/. **1** Something that is **limited** is not very great in amount, range, or degree, or not great enough. EG *...the limited resources that the West were prepared to invest in the project... The choice was very limited... ...a painter of limited abilities.* ADJ QUALIT ⇑ small

2 A **limited** company is one in which the shareholders are legally responsible for only a part of any money that it may owe to other people or companies, for example if it goes bankrupt; a technical term, used mainly in British English, especially after the name of a company. EG *...Hourmont Travel Limited... The Foundation had become a limited company.* ADJ CLASSIF: ATTRIB, ALSO IN NAMES: NAME+ ADJ

limited edition, limited editions. A **limited edition** of a work of art, especially a book, is one in which only a small number of copies are produced, so that they will be very valuable in the future. N COUNT

limitless /lɪmɪtlɪ²s/. Something that is **limitless** is extremely great in amount or number; a rather literary word. EG *...the computer's limitless memory... ...our limitless fascination with toys and games... ...the seemingly limitless resources of the United States.* ADJ CLASSIF = boundless, endless, infinite

limousine /lɪməzi:n/, **limousines**. A **limousine** is a large and very comfortable car, especially one with a glass screen between the front and back seats. Limousines are usually driven by a chauffeur and are used by very rich or important people. N COUNT

limp /lɪmp/, **limps, limping, limped; limper, limpest**. **1** If a person or animal **limps**, they walk with difficulty or in an uneven way because one of their legs or feet is hurt or because they cannot bend one of their legs easily. EG *He picked up his bag and limped back to the road... Two of the dogs were limping badly.* V = hobble ▸ used as a noun. EG *He walks with a limp... She had a slight limp.* ▸ N COUNT: USU a+N IN SING

2 If someone is **limp**, they have no strength or energy, for example because they are asleep or unconscious. EG *Her hand felt limp and damp... Karen moaned, went limp, and rolled into the water.* ADJ QUALIT = floppy

◇ **limply**. EG *The tiny baby lay limply on her arm.* ◇ ADV WITH VB

3 Something that is **limp** is soft and not stiff or firm. EG *The leaves of the bamboo were hanging limp in the dry air... ...his pale, limp hair... ...a dressing-gown of limp, shiny fabric.* ADJ QUALIT ◇ **limply**. EG *The rope fell limply to the ground.* ◇ ADV WITH VB

limpet /lɪmpɪt/, **limpets**. A **limpet** is a small sea animal that has a conical shell and that attaches itself tightly to rocks. N COUNT ⇑ mollusc

limpid /lɪmpɪd/; a literary word. Something that is **limpid** is **1** so clear that you can see through it easily. EG *...a pool of limpid water... ...the limpid October air... ...a limpid and cloudless sky.* ADJ QUALIT ⇑ transparent = translucent, pellucid

2 Limpid speech or writing is clear and easy to understand. EG *...Heissman's limpid prose... He spoke exquisite, limpid Castilian.* ADJ CLASSIF: ATTRIB = lucid

linchpin /lɪntⁿʃpɪn/, **linchpins**; also spelled **lynchpin**. The **linchpin** of something is the most important person or thing involved in it; a formal word. EG *Gold was, until quite recently, the linchpin of major currencies... As the linchpin of Mr Callaghan's government, Mr Foot was the obvious candidate.* N COUNT: USU SING+SUPP = mainstay

linctus /lɪŋktəs/, **linctuses**. A **linctus** is a fairly thick liquid medicine that you take when you have a sore throat or a cough; a technical term, usually written on the label of medicine bottles. N MASS = cough mixture

linden /lɪndəⁿn/, **lindens**. A **linden** or **linden tree** is a large tree with pale green leaves which is often planted in parks in towns and cities. EG *...the linden trees along the driveway.* N COUNT: USU BEFORE N = lime

line /laɪn/, **lines, lining, lined**. **1 Line** is used in the following ways to refer to markings on a surface.

1.1 A **line** is a long thin mark which is drawn, painted, or printed on a surface. EG *...a diagonal red line on the label... ...a straight line joining those two points... The lines are slightly curved... ...parallel lines.* N COUNT ⇑ marking **1.2** The **lines** on a piece of paper are straight lines printed on it in order to show you where to write. EG *The pen moved on down to the next line.* N COUNT ⇑ marking

1.3 A **line** is also a white or yellow line painted on a road in order to show you where you can drive, overtake, park your car, etc. EG *She was fined for parking on a single yellow line.* N COUNT ⇑ marking **1.4** In sports, a **line** on a court, pitch, or track is one that is painted on it in order to indicate the boundary of the playing area, or to indicate areas used for particular purposes during a game, or where athletes must stand, run, start or finish. EG *...on the fifty-yard line... ...the goal line... ...and first over the line is Cram.* N COUNT: USU *the*+N IN SING ⇑ marking **1.5** The **lines** on someone's skin, especially on their face, are long, thin marks that appear there as they grow older. EG *...the lines of late middle age in his face... ...a hand covered with fine dry lines.* N COUNT: USU PL ⇑ groove = wrinkle

2 Line is used in the following ways to refer to people or things that are next to each other in a row.

2.1 A **line** of people or things is a number of them arranged or standing one behind another or side by side and forming a continuous row. EG *...the line of mountains at the edge of town... ...long lines of poplar trees on the avenue... The men formed themselves into a line... ...the first pump in the line.* N COUNT/PART **2.2** A **line** of people or cars is a number of them that are waiting one behind another, for example in order to buy something or to go in a particular direction. EG *At the Church, I joined the line and filed inside... There were two lines at the ticket counter.* N COUNT = queue **2.3** A **line** of people such as police, workers on strike, etc is a group of them who are organized into a row in order to prevent other people from going past them, for example demonstrators or workers who do not want to strike. ● See also **picket line**. N COUNT: USU MOD+N ⇑ grouping **2.4** A **line** in a game N COUNT: USU such as rugby or American football is the row formed by the players of each team when the game begins or is started again, for example after the ball has gone out of the playing area. the+N IN SING ⇑ group

3 Line is used in the following ways to refer to groups of words, numbers, etc in a piece of work such as a book, speech, song, or film. **3.1** A **line** in a piece of writing is one of the rows of words, numbers, or other symbols in it. EG *I have read every line... The article was cut down to two or three lines.* N COUNT

3.2 A **line** of a poem, song, or play is a group of words in it that are usually printed in one row, or spoken or sung together, for example the words between one rhyming word and the next in a poem. EG *They sang the next line of the song... She quoted a line from Shakespeare.* N COUNT **3.3** When you are acting in a play or film, a **line** is a sentence or remark that you have to say at a particular point in it. EG *In the last act, I had four lines... She found it impossible to remember her lines.* N COUNT ⇑ utterance **3.4** A particular type of **line** in a conversation is a remark that is intended to have a particular effect. EG *You can make your point in a throwaway line at the end of a casual conversation... He began with the memorable line: 'Let's have an end of all this.'* N COUNT+SUPP **3.5** A **line** is a letter, often a short one; an informal use. EG *Ask them to write a line to their old Dad.* N SING : a+N = note **3.6** In school, if a child is given **lines**, he or she is punished by being made to write out a sentence many times or to write out a passage from a book. EG *He was given a hundred lines.* N PLURAL ⇑ punishment

4 Line is used to refer to long narrow pieces of string, wire, or pipe, such as: **4.1** a rope or wire on which you hang clothes after washing them so that they will become dry. EG *...washing hanging on a line... ...a clothes line.* N COUNT/UNCOUNT : USU+SUPP **4.2** a long piece of string, wire, nylon, etc that is used in catching fish. EG *The fish was heavy at the end of my line... The boat drifted slowly, with two wire lines trailing behind... ...a harpoon line.* N COUNT/UNCOUNT : USU+SUPP **4.3** a wire or cable along which electricity or telephone signals are transmitted, especially over long distances. EG *High winds had brought the lines down... ...a fallen power line.* N COUNT/UNCOUNT : USU+SUPP **4.4** a pipe along which gas, oil, or other liquid flows, for example from an oilwell or in an engine. EG *...a clogged fuel line... ...oil and natural gas pipe lines.* N COUNT/UNCOUNT : USU+SUPP **4.5** one of the metal rails on which trains run. N COUNT/UNCOUNT : USU+SUPP

5 Line is used to refer to specific routes used in communications, when they connect places or people, for example: **5.1** a route along which electronic signals pass, for example in broadcasting or between a computer and a terminal. EG *...linked to other word-processors by a direct line.* N COUNT : USU MOD+N ⇑ link **5.2** a connection to a telephone system which makes it possible for you to make telephone calls. EG *Knowing that the lines were tapped, I risked a call... The line had gone dead.* ● See also **party line**. N COUNT ⇑ link **5.3** a connection that exists when two people are talking to each other on the telephone. EG *There was silence on the other end of the line... Then Sally came back on the line.* N COUNT : USU the+N IN SING **5.4** a route along which people move or send messages or supplies, often a dangerous or secret route. EG *After his final report all lines of communication had been cut... It was essential to have their escape lines clear... ...the supply lines to enemy formations.* N COUNT : USU N IN PL+SUPP **5.5** a particular route along which something exists or moves. EG *...along the line of the motorways... ...a system of canals in a line parallel to the coast... Wireless waves travel in straight lines.* N COUNT : USU PREP+N+SUPP ⇑ direction = course **5.6** a railway line. EG *...repairs to the line beyond Tring.* N COUNT **5.7** a particular route, involving the same stations, roads, or stops along which a train, coach, or bus service regularly operates. EG *They had taken the wrong line on the London Tube... ...a conductor on the New Haven commuter line... ...the last stop on the local bus line.* N COUNT : USU+SUPP **5.8** a company which provides services for transporting people or goods by sea, air, bus, or rail. EG *...air and shipping lines... ...a former employee of the Hamburg-Amerika Line.* N COUNT : USU MOD+N

6 Line is used to refer to the edge of a physical object or area, for example: **6.1** the edge, outline, or shape of an object or a person's body, especially when you are commenting on the effect that it has on the person looking at it; a slightly literary use. EG *...the firm, delicate lines of Paxton's buildings... ...a superb line from nose to brow, a real conqueror's face... ...the hard thin line of Lynn's mouth.* N COUNT+SUPP ⇑ form **6.2** the edge of an area or place, especially a long, thin division between two areas that are next to each other. EG *...the sun-bleached shoreline... ...the taut blue line of the horizon.* N COUNT+SUPP : USU SING **6.3** a boundary between two states, counties, etc; used mainly in American English. EG *...crowding across the state line to escape taxes.* N COUNT+SUPP : USU SING = border **6.4** the boundary between areas occupied by enemy armies during a war. EG *...Allied forces struggling to hold the line at Trondheim.* ● See also **front line**. N COUNT : USU SING+SUPP ⇑ limit

7 The **lines** are the set of physical defences, the patrols, etc that have been established along the boundary of an area occupied by an army. EG *They were dropped by parachute behind enemy lines... ...a sentry moving slowly down one of the lines... The letters just aren't getting through the lines.* N PLURAL

8 Battle lines are **8.1** the positions taken by the different units of an army just before a battle. EG *...when the battle lines are drawn up... The lines had been drawn for the battle.* PHR : USED AS O/S ⇑ formation **8.2** the attitudes that people have or the policies that they decide to support before the beginning of an argument, meeting, or political campaign. EG *By now these battle lines should sound a little familiar.* PHR : USED AS O/S ⇑ position = stances

9 The **line** or **dividing line** between similar things, people, actions, etc is the point at which you judge them to belong to different classes or types. EG *The traditional social dividing lines are becoming blurred... It is not easy to draw the line between carefulness and anxiety.* N COUNT+SUPP ⇑ division

10 A **line** on a scale of measurement is an important point on it or a division between two sections of it. EG *She will be living below the poverty line... ...the 400-mph line.* N COUNT+SUPP ⇑ limit

11 A **line** in an activity is the way in which the activity develops or the method that you use in doing it. EG *...his particular line of research... ...an unprofitable line of thinking... ...future lines of development... A third possible line of attack would be to restrict wage increases.* N COUNT+SUPP ⇑ type = course

12 The particular **line** that a person or group has towards a problem or topic is the attitude or policy that they have towards it. EG *...the official line of the Labour Party... ...committed to a certain political line... The President takes a much harder line.* ● See also **party line**. N COUNT+SUPP : USU SING = position, stance

13 Your **line** of business or work is the kind of work that you do. EG *The best job you can get in our line is in a nationalized industry... A man in my line of business has to take precautions.* N COUNT : USU POSS/MOD+N IN SING

14 A **line** is also a particular type of product that a company makes or sells. EG *...a new line of computer printers they were developing... ...a special line in English-style cooking... Unprofitable lines will be discontinued.* N COUNT

15 A **line** in a factory is an assembly line or production line. EG *A new model will be rolling off the lines at British Leyland.* N COUNT

16 A person's **line** is the series of individuals that he or she is descended from, which affects his or her physical characteristics, social status, etc. EG *...the royal line of ancient Chaldea... The inheritance would go in the female line.* ▸ used of animals and plants. EG *Their line had died out many millions of years earlier... ...the significance of pure lines in plant breeding.* N COUNT : USU POSS/MOD+N IN SING ⇑ family = lineage

17 A particular **line** of people or things is also a series of them that has existed over a period of time, when they have all been similar in some way, or done similar things. EG *...a prestigious line of authors from Kafka to Marcuse... ...the long line of American Presidents.* N COUNT : USU SING+SUPP ⇑ group = tradition

18 The main **lines** of a story, situation, plan, etc are the main ideas or facts that are involved in it. EG *In spite of these gaps, the broad lines of the story remain clear... ...the main lines of the Five-Year Plan.* N PLURAL : USU ADJ+N+of = outline, themes

19 If people or things **line** a road, a room, etc, they are present in large numbers along its edges or sides. EG *The streets were lined with cars... Crowds lined the processional route... ...the shelves lining the walls.* V+O ⇑ fill

20 If you **line** a container, a piece of clothing, etc, you put a layer of something such as cloth or paper on the inside surface of it in order to make it stronger, warmer, or cleaner. EG *Line the cupboards and drawers with paper... ...a beautiful cot, lined with silk... ...a pair of thick fur-lined boots.* V+O : IF+PREP THEN with ⇑ fit

21 If something **lines** a container or area, especially an area inside a person, animal, or plant, it forms a layer on the inside surface. EG *...the moist membranes lining their mouths... ...bacteria lining the digestive system... ...tiny, invisible hairs in the cells lining the nose.*
V+O ⇑ coat

22 See also **lined, lining.**

23 Line is used after the preposition 'in' in the following expressions. **23.1** When people or cars are **in line** or wait or stand **in line**, they are in a row one behind another and waiting for something. EG *We had to wait in line at the counter... Everyone was pushing to get first in line.*
PHR : USED AS AN A = in a queue

23.2 If you are first **in line**, second **in line**, etc for something, you are ranked first, second, etc in an order of preference or superiority. EG *You are next in line for promotion... He is fifth in line of precedence after the King.*
PHR : USED AS AN A

23.3 If you are **in line for** something, you are likely to have it happen to you. EG *I was in line for more promotion... If anyone's in line for a knighthood, he is.*
PHR+NG : USED AS AN A = due

23.4 If one thing is **in line** with another or moves **into line** with it, the two things are next to each other, parallel with each other, or form part of a straight row of several things. EG *He swung his car into line with the presidential convoy... The target is in line with the sun... The choir huddled into line.*
PHR : USED AS AN A, IF+PREP THEN *with*

23.5 If people do something **in line** with others or come **into line** with them, they do it so that everyone involved is doing the same thing or following the same plan. EG *The Society has finally come into line on mortgages... He was expelling Franklin in line with the policy of the national organization.*
PHR : USED AS AN A

23.6 If two amounts or rates are **in line** with each other or if you bring them **into line**, they remain or change at the same rate or in proportion to each other. EG *He must bring prices into line with supply... ...increasing their incomes in line with rising prices.*
PHR : USED AS AN A, IF+PREP THEN *with*

23.7 If you keep **in line** or step **into line** , you behave or start to behave in the way that you are supposed to. EG *You need a very strict director to keep you in line... He felt certain that the women would step into line.*
PHR : USED AS AN A ⇑ down

23.8 In the electrical **line, in the** sports **line**, etc means connected with electricity, sports, etc. EG *Send for Lane if anything in the electrical line has to be done... I was thinking more in the arts line.*
PHR : USED AS AN A

23.9 If something is **in** someone's **line** or is their **line**, it is the sort of thing that they often do, or enjoy doing; an informal use. EG *Well, it's not my line, really, is it?... This is rather a new thing for us, more in your line I'd say.*
PHR : USED AS AN A, OR N SING : POSS+N

23.10 If you do something or if it happens to you **in the line of duty** or **in the line of service**, you do it or it happens as part of your regular work or as a result of it. EG *...the violence that he encounters in the line of duty.*
PHR : USED AS AN A

24 Line is used after the preposition 'on' in the following expressions. **24.1** If something such as a machine, power station, defence system is **on line**, or if you bring it **on line**, it is operating or you make it start operating; a technical expression. EG *A mobile radar could be brought on line... The improved system had not come on line as intended.*
PHR : USED AS AN A

24.2 When you use a large computer, if you are **on line** or do something **on line**, you communicate directly with the computer and do your work immediately, so that you can control and check every operation as you do it; a technical expression. EG *We are editing the dictionary on line.*
PHR : USED AS AN A

24.3 If something such as your job, career, or reputation is **on the line**, or if you put it **on the line**, you may lose or harm it as a result of doing something brave or foolish. EG *I didn't dare fight and put my job on the line, so I went along with them... His future is on the line.*
PHR : USED AS AN A = at risk, at stake

24.4 If you **lay it on the line**, you say something frankly and directly; an informal expression.
PHR : VB INFLECTS

25 Line is used after the preposition 'out of' in the following expressions. **25.1** If something is **out of line** or moves **out of line**, it is not next to or not parallel with other things, does not form a straight row with them, or is not in its correct position. EG *One of them dropped out of line... It is tucked away out of line of the main entrance.*
PHR : USED AS AN A

25.2 If people or things are **out of line** with other people or things, they are not acting in the same way or not following the same plan. EG *Some of us seem to be getting out of line... Higher interest rates would not be out of line.*
PHR : USED AS AN A

25.3 If someone is **out of line** or steps **out of line**, they are not behaving in the way that they are supposed to, or are behaving badly. EG *They were severely punished for stepping out of line.*
PHR : USED AS AN A

26 Line is used in the singular in the following expressions. **26.1** If something happens **along the line**, it happens during the course of a situation or activity, often at a point that cannot be exactly identified. EG *We slipped up somewhere along the line... Somewhere along the line your strategy has gone badly wrong... Along the line she discovered a talent for improvisation... He had fought us all along the line.*
PHR : USED AS AN A

26.2 If something happens **down the line**, it happens to all the people or things involved in a situation or activity, or all the time that the situation or activity happens or exists. EG *This condescending approach continues down the line... I voted the liberal ticket straight down the line.*
PHR : USED AS AN A ⇑ throughout

26.3 If you **draw the line** at a particular activity, you refuse to do it, because it is more than you are prepared to do. EG *She drew the line at cleaning his shoes... A line has to be drawn somewhere.*
PHR : VB INFLECTS ⇑ stop

26.4 If you **get a line on** someone or something, you find out some information about them; an informal expression.
PHR : VB INFLECTS

26.5 If you say that someone **is shooting a line**, you mean that they are exaggerating, boasting, or lying, in order to impress other people or gain some advantage.
PHR : VB INFLECTS

27 Lines is used in the following expressions. **27.1** If something happens or is done **on** or **along** particular **lines**, it happens or is done in that way. EG *The population is split along religious lines... ...societies organised along private enterprise lines... They formed District Committees on the lines suggested... He thinks along the same lines as you.*
PHR : USED AS AN A

27.2 You use the expressions **on the lines of** and **along the lines of** in order to indicate that you are only giving a general summary or approximate account of what someone has said, and are not quoting their exact words. EG *Driberg opened with a question on the lines of: 'What do you think about the present political situation?'... ...some thoughts along those lines.*
PHR ⇑ roughly

27.3 If someone is **on the right lines** or if their proposals or actions are **on the right lines**, they are thinking or acting in a way that is sensible or likely to produce useful results; used showing approval. EG *Do his policies strike you as being on the right lines?... I still think I'm on the right lines.*
PHR : USED AS AN A

28 Line is also used in the following expressions which are dealt with at other entries in this dictionary. • to **sign on the dotted line**: see **dotted.** • to **drop** someone **a line** or **note**: see **drop.** • to **line** your **pockets**: see **pocket.** • to **read between the lines**: see **read.** • **the line of least resistance**: see **resistance.** • to **toe the line**: see **toe.** • See also **branch line, hard-line, hot line.**

line up. 1 If people **line up** or you **line** them **up**, they stand in a row or form a queue. EG *The children line up under the shade of a thatch roof... Find partners and line up as quickly as you can... They lined us up and marched us off.*
PHRASAL VB : V-ERG+ADV

2 If you **line** something **up**, you arrange it neatly or move it into a straight row or into its correct position in relation to something else. EG *Adjust them so that the two are exactly lined up.*
PHRASAL VB : V+O+ADV, USU+A = align

3 If you **line up** something or someone in preparation for an event or activity, you arrange for them to be available for that event or activity. EG *I had lined up a wonderful cast... ...a formal greeting party was lined up.*
PHRASAL VB : ORDER V+ADV+O

4 If you **line up** with, behind, or alongside a person or group, you support them. If you **line up** against a person or group, you oppose them.
PHRASAL VB : V+ADV+A

5 See also **line-up**.

lineage /lɪni¹ɪdʒ/, **lineages**. Someone's **lineage** is the series of families from which they are directly descended; a formal word. EG *...the names and lineage of the women.*
N COUNT/UNCOUNT = descent line

lineal /lɪni¹əl/. If someone is described as being a **lineal** descendant of a particular person or family, they are directly descended from that person or family; a formal word. EG *...in direct lineal descent of a soldier of the period.*
ADJ CLASSIF : ATTRIB = direct

lineament /lɪni¹əmə²nt/, **lineaments**. If you talk about someone's **lineaments**, you are referring to the outlines and features of their face; a literary word. EG *...the exquisite lineaments of his face.*
N COUNT : USU PL +SUPP

linear /lɪni¹ə/; a formal or technical word. **1** A process or development that is **linear** changes or progresses from one stage to another in a simple
ADJ CLASSIF : USU ATTRIB

way, for example at a constant rate, or never varying in sequence or direction. EG *In our brief life-span we normally experience only linear change... ...functions occurring simultaneously rather than in a linear sequence.*

2 A shape or form that is **linear** consists of straight lines. ADJ CLASSIF : USU ATTRIB

3 If a movement, force, or mathematical relationship is **linear**, it occurs in a straight line rather than in a curve. ADJ CLASSIF : USU ATTRIB

4 **Linear** measures refer to the length of something. EG *...linear measurement.* ADJ CLASSIF : USU ATTRIB

lined /laɪnd/. 1 If someone's face or skin is **lined**, it has wrinkles or lines on it as a result of old age, tiredness, worry, or illness. EG *Her skin was more grey and lined than before... Their faces are lined, immeasurably sad.* ADJ QUALIT = wrinkled

2 **Lined** paper has lines printed across it to help you write neatly. EG *He was sitting there, writing grimly on a lined pad.* ADJ CLASSIF ↑ marked = ruled

line drawing, line drawings. A **line drawing** is a drawing which consists only of lines, in which darker or lighter areas are shown by the spacing and thickness of the lines. N COUNT

linen /lɪnɪn/, **linens**. 1 **Linen** is 1.1 a kind of cloth that is made from a plant called flax. It is used especially for making tea-towels, tablecloths, and sheets. EG *...a white linen towel... ...grey flannel slacks and a crisp linen jacket.* 1.2 tablecloths, napkins, sheets, pillowcases, and similar things made of cloth that are used in the house. EG *...bed linen... Matron stood by the open linen cupboard.* N MASS; N UNCOUNT/COUNT

2 If someone **washes** their **dirty linen in public**, they discuss or argue about unpleasant personal or private things in front of other people. PHR : VB INFLECTS ↑ talk

line of sight. Your **line of sight** is an imaginary line that stretches between your eye and the object that you are looking at. EG *The laser crossed his line of sight.* N SING WITH DET : USU WITH POSS

line of vision. Your **line of vision** is the same as your line of sight. N SING WITH DET : USU WITH POSS

line printer, line printers. A **line printer** is a printer that prints a line at a time rather than a single character, and so can operate very quickly. It is usually part of a computer system. N COUNT

liner /laɪnə/, **liners**. A **liner** is 1 a large ship in which people travel long distances or go on holiday cruises. EG *She stood on the deck of a liner bound from Southampton to New York... ...Atlantic ocean liners.* 2 a plastic bag that you put inside a waste bin or dustbin so that you can get rid of your rubbish more easily. EG *...black polythene bin liners.* N COUNT; N COUNT : MOD + N

linesman /laɪnzmə³n/, **linesmen**. A **linesman** is 1 someone whose job involves maintaining and repairing telephone or power lines. EG *...an electrical linesman trying to repair a sabotaged main pylon.* 2 an official who assists the referee or umpire in a game of football, tennis, etc by watching to see where the ball goes outside the boundary line of the field, court, etc. N COUNT ↑ worker; N COUNT

line-up, line-ups. A **line-up** is 1 a row or queue of people who are waiting for something; used especially in American English. EG *He was clearly unhappy about the length of the line-up ahead of him.* 2 a row of people who have been assembled in a police station. One of the people is a suspected criminal, and victims or witnesses of a crime try to identify that person. 3 a series of things or a group of people that are assembled for a particular activity or event. EG *The England line-up for their match against Poland was announced this morning.* N COUNT = line; N COUNT ↑ parade; N COUNT ↑ programme

linger /lɪŋgə/, **lingers, lingering, lingered**. 1 If ideas or feelings **linger**, they continue to exist for a longer time than people expect before they finally disappear. EG *This tradition apparently manages to linger on... The resentments and the longings lingered.* ◇ **lingering**. EG *There was no lingering sense of guilt.* V, IF + ADV THEN *on* = last, remain; ◇ ADJ CLASSIF : ATTRIB

2 If you **linger** somewhere, you stay there for a longer time than is necessary, for example because you are enjoying yourself or because you want to talk to someone. EG *Davis lingered for a moment in the bar... He will linger behind occasionally to chat.* V + A ↑ remain = tarry

3 If you **linger** on something or over something, you spend a long time doing it or thinking about it. EG *I have lingered longer on some smaller, relatively less well-known poems... She lingered over coffee.* V + A *(on/over)* = dwell

4 When someone who is dying **lingers**, they stay alive for longer than people expect, even though they are very weak. EG *There's no way of knowing how long she'll linger.* V, IF + ADV THEN *on* ↑ live = last

lingerie /lɒnʒəri¹/ is women's underwear and nightclothes; a formal word. EG *...lacy white lingerie.* N UNCOUNT ↑ clothes

lingo /lɪŋgəʊ/, **lingoes**; an informal word. A **lingo** is 1 a foreign language, especially one which you cannot speak or understand. EG *It has its own local lingo for its different districts.* 2 a range of vocabulary which is normally used in a special context or by a small group of people. EG *I had mastered the commercial lingo at least.* N COUNT : USU SING; N COUNT : USU SING + SUPP = argot, jargon

lingua franca /lɪŋgwə fræŋkə/, **lingua francas, lingua francae**. The plural can be either **lingua francas** or **lingua francae**; a formal term. A **lingua franca** is a language or way of communicating which is used by people who do not speak the same native language. EG *The course was taught in German, which was the lingua franca of Basel university.* N COUNT

linguist /lɪŋgwɪst/, **linguists**. A **linguist** is 1 someone who is learning or is good at learning foreign languages. EG *I was now officially a fifth form modern linguist.* 2 someone who studies or teaches linguistics. EG *He sees the role of the linguist as being useful.* N COUNT; N COUNT ↑ specialist

linguistic /lɪŋgwɪstɪk/, **linguistics**. **Linguistic** is an adjective and **linguistics** is an uncount noun. 1 **Linguistics** is the study of the way in which language works. EG *Are you still doing research into linguistics?.* N UNCOUNT ↑ discipline

2 **Linguistic** studies, developments, ideas, etc are involved with language or linguistics. EG *...linguistic development between the ages of nought and four.* ◇ **linguistically**. EG *...conversations which are linguistically perfect.* ADJ CLASSIF ≠ visual; ◇ ADV WITH VB ↑ verbally

liniment /lɪnɪmə³nt/, **liniments**. **Liniment** is a liquid that you rub into your skin in order to reduce pain or stiffness. N MASS ↑ ointment = embrocation

lining /laɪnɪŋ/, **linings**. A **lining** is 1 a layer of cloth attached to the inside of a piece of clothing, curtain, etc in order to make it thicker or warmer, or in order to make it hang better. EG *...a dark blue raincoat with a scarlet lining.* 2 a layer of paper, plastic, metal, etc that is attached to the inside of something in order to insulate or protect it. EG *...a new suitcase with a shiny lining.* 3 a layer of tissue on the inside of something such as your stomach. EG *Carbon dioxide attacks the lining of your stomach.* N COUNT/UNCOUNT; N COUNT/UNCOUNT ↑ insulation; N COUNT : USU + SUPP = coating

link /lɪŋk/, **links, linking, linked**. 1 A **link** is 1.1 something that forms an emotional or logical connection between two things. EG *He felt a link of trust between them... ...the close link between love and fear.* 1.2 an organization or relationship that connects two things and makes them able to mix or work together. EG *The arts centre is probably the most obvious link between the university and the wider community... We now have closer links with overseas universities.* 1.3 a relationship between two things or situations in which one causes the other to exist or happen. EG *He talked about new technology and its link with the unemployment problem.* 1.4 something that forms a connection between two things or places, often so that you can travel between them or communicate between them. EG *They are opening a twenty mile rail link between the two towns... A telephone link between Washington and Moscow was established... ...a link road between the town and the motorway.* 1.5 one of the rings in a chain. N COUNT : IF + PREP THEN *between* ↑ bond; N COUNT : IF + PREP THEN *between/with* ↑ connection = tie; N COUNT : IF + PREP THEN *between/with* = connection; N COUNT : IF + PREP THEN *between*; N COUNT

2 If something **links** two things or if the two things **are linked** with each other, there is a relationship between them, for example because one causes the other. EG *There is evidence that some kinds of cancers are linked with the contraceptive pill... Evidence has been offered linking the group to a series of fire-bomb attacks... The evidence for linking cause and effect seems rather strong.* ◇ **linked**. EG *These linked problems must be tackled at the same time.* V + O : IF + PREP THEN *with/to*; ◇ ADJ CLASSIF

3 If one place or object **is linked** to another or if something **links** them, there is a physical connection between them so that you can travel between them or communicate between them. EG *...the television camera had been linked to a computer... ...a canal linking the Pacific and Atlantic oceans.* V + O, OR V + A *(to)* ↑ connect

4 If you **link** together two things such as pieces of metal or rope or two people's arms, you join them by putting one part through the other, or by knotting them together. EG *She took his arm, linking her hand through the crook of his elbow.* ◊ **linked**. EG *They walked along arms linked.* V+O ◊ ADJ CLASSIF

5 A **links** is a golf course, especially one that is near the sea. N SING WITH DET

link up. 1 If you **link up** with someone, you meet them somewhere, usually before travelling on to another place with them. EG *We drove on from Florence and linked up with them in Rome.* PHRASAL VB : V+ADV, OR V+ADV +with : RECIP

2 If you **link up** two items or places, you connect them to each other in some way. EG *This computer can be linked up to other computers.* PHRASAL VB : V+ADV

4 See also **link-up**.

linkage /lɪŋkɪdʒ/, **linkages**. **Linkage** is 1 the act or process of joining two things or ideas so that they become connected in some way. EG *...the linkage between causes and effects.* N UNCOUNT/COUNT 2 a process in international diplomacy where one country agrees to do something only if another country agrees to do something in return. EG *The Administration's commitment to linkage as a 'fact of life' was stressed.* N UNCOUNT

linkman /lɪŋkmə³n/, **linkmen**; also spelled with a hyphen. A **linkman** is a person who appears on television or radio between items or programmes to tell you what is coming next and to make other announcements. N COUNT ↑ broadcaster

link-up, link-ups. A **link-up** is a connection or meeting between two systems or machines. EG *...the link-up of the US Apollo and Soviet Soyuz spacecraft.* N COUNT

lino /laɪnəʊ/. **Lino** is the same as linoleum; an informal word. EG *...yellow lino worn into holes.* N UNCOUNT ↑ flooring

linoleum /lɪnəʊlɪəm/. **Linoleum** is a floor covering which is made of cloth covered with a hard shiny substance. EG *...shiny linoleum floors... I could hear the click of my own heels on the linoleum.* N UNCOUNT ↑ flooring = lino

Linotype /laɪnə⁶taɪp/is a trademark for a printing machine that is operated by a keyboard like a typewriter, and that holds each line it types on one piece of metal. N SING : USU BEFORE N

linseed oil /lɪnsi:d ɔɪl/ is an oil made from seeds of the flax plant. It is used to make paints and inks, or to rub into wooden surfaces to protect them. N UNCOUNT

lint /lɪnt/ is cotton or linen fabric which you can put on your skin if you have a cut. EG *...several rolls of lint bandages.* N UNCOUNT

lintel /lɪntə⁰l/, **lintels**. A **lintel** is a piece of stone or wood over a door or window. The lintel supports the bricks above the door or window; a technical term in architecture. N COUNT

lion /laɪən/, **lions**. 1 A **lion** is 1.1 an animal with brownish yellow fur which looks like a big cat and kills and eats other animals. A female lion is often called a lioness. EG *...lions and tigers... ...lion cubs.* N COUNT ↑ mammal 1.2 a person or a country that is considered to be strong and powerful, and which other people respect or fear; a rather literary word. N COUNT+SUPP

2 If you say that someone **fought like a lion**, you mean that they fought very hard and were extremely brave in their actions. PHR : VB AND N INFLECT

lioness /laɪənɪ²s/, **lionesses**. A **lioness** is a female lion. N COUNT ↑ animal

lion's share. If a person or group gets the **lion's share** of something, they get the largest part of it, leaving very little for other people. EG *The lion's share of investment has gone to a few favoured companies.* N SING WITH DET

lip /lɪp/, **lips**. 1 A person's or animal's **lips** are the two outer parts of the edge of their mouth. EG *...the cigarette hanging carelessly from her lower lip... He had the freshly lit cigarette between his lips.* N COUNT : USU PL

2 If someone **bites** their **lip**, they try very hard not to show the anger or distress that they are feeling. EG *She held the chair and bit her lip and looked round.* PHR : VB INFLECTS

3 If you say that something is **on everyone's lips** or **on every lip**, you mean that it is a subject which everyone seems to be interested in and is talking about. EG *But now, the word is on every lip... Whether she will get the job is the question on everybody's lips.* PHR : USED AS AN A

4 If you say **'my lips are sealed'**, you are telling someone that you will keep a secret that they have just told you. CONVENTION

5 If you say that someone is **keeping a stiff upper lip**, you mean that they are behaving in a firm way and are not showing any emotion even though it is difficult for them not to. EG *We must be firm in our resolve to keep a stiff upper lip.* PHR : VB INFLECTS

6 A **lip** is the edge of a container such as a jug, which hangs over slightly and from which a liquid is poured. EG *A single drop of cream hung temptingly from the lip of the jug.* N COUNT : USU+SUPP ↑ spout

7 You can also use **lip** to refer to rude or cheeky remarks that someone makes; a very informal use. EG *I don't want to hear any more lip from you, young man!* N UNCOUNT = impertinence, cheek

-lipped is used after adjectives to form other adjectives which describe the sort of lips that someone has. EG *There was a look of surprise on his thin-lipped weather-beaten face.* See also **tight-lipped**. COMB : FORMS ADJS

lip-read, lip-reads, lip-reading. The form **lip-read** is used in the present tense and is the past tense and past participle. It is pronounced /lɪp ri:d/ when it is the present tense, and /lɪp rɛd/ when it is the past tense and past participle. If someone can **lip-read**, they are able to understand what someone else is saying by looking at the way the other person's lips move as they speak. People who are deaf often do this. EG *Papa lip-reads; you must face him when you speak.* V ↑ interpret

lip-service; also spelled without a hyphen. If you pay **lip-service** to an idea, you say that you are in favour of it, although really you have no intention of supporting it properly; used showing disapproval. EG *Our major political parties pay lip-service to the ideal of community participation.* N UNCOUNT

lipstick /lɪpstɪk/, **lipsticks**. **Lipstick** is a coloured substance which women put on their lips. It comes in the form of a small stick. EG *She was wearing lipstick and mascara.* N COUNT/MASS ↑ make up

liquefy /lɪkwɪfaɪ/, **liquefies, liquefying, liquefied**. When a gas or solid substance **liquefies** or when someone **liquefies** it, it changes its form and becomes liquid. EG *Under these conditions hydrogen liquefies.* V-ERG

liqueur /lɪkjʊə/, **liqueurs**. A **liqueur** is a strong alcoholic drink which usually has quite a sweet taste and is often drunk after a meal. N MASS

liquid /lɪkwɪd/, **liquids**. 1 A **liquid** is a substance such as water which is not solid or rigid, but which flows and can be poured. EG *She poured out a large quantity of liquid from a bottle... The liquid was thin and greyish brown.* N MASS

2 Something that is **liquid** is in the form of a liquid rather than being solid or a gas. EG *...liquid polish... It does the same job as a washing powder: it is liquid for convenience.* ADJ CLASSIF

3 If someone is described as having **liquid** eyes, their eyes are clear, soft, and slightly shiny; used showing approval. ADJ CLASSIF : ATTRIB

4 **Liquid** assets are the things that a person or company owns, which can be quickly turned into cash if necessary; a technical term in finance. ADJ CLASSIF

liquidate /lɪkwɪdeɪt/, **liquidates, liquidating, liquidated**. 1 If someone **liquidates** people or groups who are causing problems, they get rid of them, usually by killing them; an informal use. EG *All his supporters were expelled, exiled, or liquidated.* V+O = exterminate ◊ **liquidation** /lɪkwɪdeɪʃə⁰n/. EG *They pressed ahead with the liquidation of hostile elements among the people.* ◊ N UNCOUNT ↑ removal = extermination

2 When someone **liquidates** a company, they close it down, usually because it has large debts that it cannot pay; a technical term in finance. EG *You're talking airily of liquidating our company and putting dozens of technicians on the dole.* ◊ **liquidation, liquidations**. EG *By April 1969, the group faced liquidation.* V+O = wind up ◊ N UNCOUNT/COUNT

3 If someone **liquidates** their assets, they sell their property such as buildings or machinery, in order to get money; a technical term in finance. V+O

liquidator /lɪkwɪdeɪtə/, **liquidators**. A **liquidator** is a person who is responsible for settling the affairs of a company that is being liquidated. N COUNT

liquidity /lɪkwɪdɪti¹/. A company's **liquidity** is its ability to pay its debts by having enough cash or liquid assets easily available; a technical term in finance. EG *It was evident that it had created liquidity problems.* N UNCOUNT

liquidize /lɪkwɪdaɪz/, **liquidizes, liquidizing, liquidized**; also spelled **liquidise**. If you **liquidize** food, you process it in an liquidizer in order to make V+O = puree it liquid. EG *...either liquidize the vegetables or pass them through a sieve.*

liquidizer /lɪkwɪdaɪzə/, **liquidizers**. A **liquidizer** is an electric machine that you use to liquidize food. N COUNT = blender

liquid lunch, liquid lunches. A **liquid lunch** is a lunch that consists mostly of alcoholic drinks; a humorous usage. N COUNT

liquor /lɪkə/, **liquors**. **Liquor** is a drink that contains alcohol, usually a lot of alcohol; used especially in American English. EG *They spent their evenings drinking cheap liquor that made their heads ache... I never touch hard liquor.* N MASS

liquorice /lɪkərɪs, ərɪʃ/; also spelled **licorice**. **Liquorice** is a firm black substance with a strong taste which is used for making sweets. N UNCOUNT

lira /lɪərə/, **lire, liras**. The plural can be either **lire** or **liras**. A **lira** is 1 the unit of money that is used in Italy. EG *The hire charge for two days was ten thousand lire.* 2 the unit of money that is used in Turkey and in Syria. N COUNT : USU NUM+N; N COUNT : USU NUM+N

lisp /lɪsp/, **lisps, lisping, lisped**. 1 If someone has a **lisp**, they pronounce the sounds 's' and 'z' as if they were 'th'. For example, they say 'thing' instead of 'sing'. N COUNT : USU SING

2 If someone **lisps** or if they **lisp** something, they speak with a lisp. EG *When people asked him what he wanted to be when he grew up, he would lisp childishly, 'A policeman.'* V OR V+QUOTE

lissom /lɪsə⁰m/; also spelled **lissome**. Someone who is **lissom** is slim and graceful; a literary word. ADJ QUALIT = lithe

list /lɪst/, **lists, listing, listed**. 1 A **list** is 1.1 a set of things which are written down one below the other, often in a particular order, for example so that you can remember them or check them easily. EG *Look at your list of things to be mended... Find out all their names and make a list... She saw the list up on the board when she came in... Doctors are the first to deplore long waiting lists... ...the other people on his mailing list.* • See also **short-list**. 1.2 a set of things that you think of as being in a particular order or mention in a particular order. EG *They put this higher on their list of priorities.* N COUNT : IF+PREP THEN *of* = catalogue, schedule, table; N COUNT

2 If a person or a piece of writing **lists** a particular set of things, they mention them all one after the other, in writing or when speaking. EG *There was a label on each case listing its contents... Let's just list these factors: we have temperature, speed, pressure–what else?* V+O = catalogue, index

3 If a person or a piece of writing **lists** a particular thing, they include it as an item on a list, and perhaps give some information about it too. EG *He is still listed in the files by his code name, the Jackal... The death was officially listed as drowning.* V+O

4 If something, especially a ship, **lists**, it leans over to one side; a technical term used mainly by sailors. EG *The old ship was listing badly.* ▸ used as a noun. EG *...a list to starboard.* V = tilt; ▸ N SING WITH DET

5 If someone **enters the lists**, they start taking part in a competition or argument; a fairly formal expression. EG *Foreign companies may be allowed to enter the lists for the first time.* PHR : VB INFLECTS ⇑ participate = compete

6 See also **listed, listing**.

listed /lɪstɪ²d/. A **listed** building is on a list of buildings which are protected by law against being demolished or altered because they are old and important; used in British English. EG *...a Grade One listed building.* ADJ CLASSIF : USU ATTRIB ⇑ historical

listen /lɪsə⁰n/, **listens, listening, listened**. 1 If you **listen** to someone who is talking or to a sound that you can hear, you give your attention to them or it. EG *Paul, are you listening?... Listen carefully to what he says... I do my ironing while listening to the radio... He would listen to some music or read until I came in.* V : IF+PREP THEN *to*

2 If you **listen** for something that you are expecting to hear or **listen out** for it, you keep alert and make an effort to be ready to hear it if it occurs. EG *He listened for the slightest sound... She sat quite still, listening for her baby's cry... Listen out for the signal to start.* V+A *(for)*, OR PHRASAL VB : V+ADV+A *(for)*

3 You say **listen** when you want someone to pay attention to you because you are going to say something important. EG *Hey, listen, I've got a great idea!... Listen Carol, I don't think you're going about this the right way.* V : ONLY IMPER

4 If you **listen** to someone, you do what they advise you to do, or you believe them. EG *I told you what would happen but you wouldn't listen... No one here will listen to you, not without proof... He refused to listen to reason.* V : IF+PREP THEN *to*

listen in. If you **listen in** to a private conversation, usually a telephone conversation, you secretly listen to it. EG *Do you really think they bother to listen in to us?* PHRASAL VB : V+ADV = eavesdrop

listener /lɪsə⁰nə/, **listeners**. A **listener** is 1 a person who is listening to someone who is talking. EG *She told the tale with so much spirit that both her listeners were quite enchanted... The best one can do at such a time is to be a good listener.* 2 a person who listens to the radio or to a particular radio programme. EG *We've had a number of letters from listeners about the future of British industry.* N COUNT; N COUNT

listing /lɪstɪŋ/, **listings**. A **listing** is a list, or an item in a list. EG *She checked the telephone directory and found a listing for E. Howard Hunt, Jr., in Potomac, Maryland... Grechko was shown in the listings as a naval captain, third rank.* N COUNT = entry

listless /lɪstlɪ²s/. Someone who is **listless** has no energy or enthusiasm.. EG *She became listless and bored.* ◇ **listlessly**. EG *Rose followed him and watched him, listlessly, as he fried a couple of eggs.* ◇ **listlessness**. ADJ QUALIT ⇑ tired; ◇ ADV WITH VB; ◇ N UNCOUNT

list price, list prices. The **list price** of an item is the price which the manufacturer suggests that a shopkeeper should charge for it. N COUNT = recommended retail price

lit /lɪt/. is a past tense and past participle of **light**.

Lit. is an informal abbreviation for 'Literature'; used when referring to the study of literature, especially the literature of a particular country.

litany /lɪtə⁰ni¹/, **litanies**. A **litany** is 1 part of a church service in which the priest says a set group of words and the people reply, also using a set group of words. 2 something, especially a list, that is often said using the same words or that is said in a boring or insincere way. EG *She will then reel off a litany of bills and responsibilities... The officer on the door chanted the litany 'Who are you and where are you going?'* N COUNT; N COUNT : USU+SUPP

liter /liːtə/, **liters**. See **litre**.

literacy /lɪtə⁰rəsi¹/ is the ability to read and write. EG *Mass literacy was only possible after the invention of printing... ...the adult literacy campaign in the UK.* N UNCOUNT

literal /lɪtə⁰rəl/. 1 If you use a word or expression in its **literal** sense, you use it with its most basic meaning or its main meaning. EG *She was older than I was, and not only in the literal sense.* ADJ CLASSIF : USU ATTRIB ⇑ exact = true

2 A **literal** translation is one in which you translate each word of the original work rather than giving the meaning of each expression or sentence using words that sound natural. EG *...a literal translation from the German.* ADJ CLASSIF : USU ATTRIB ⇑ direct = verbatim

3 You can also use **literal** to describe someone who uses or understands words in a plain and simple way. EG *He is very literal minded.* ADJ CLASSIF = prosaic

4 If you describe something as a **literal** fact or the **literal** truth, you are emphasizing that it is true. EG *This is a literal fact that applies to every married person.* ADJ CLASSIF : USU ATTRIB ⇑ real = accurate, genuine

literally /lɪtə⁰rəli¹/. 1 You use **literally** 1.1 to emphasize that what you are saying is actually true, even though it seems surprising or exaggerated. EG *I have literally begged my son for help... To change a program, one literally had to rewire part of the machine... They were literally starving to death.* 1.2 to indicate that a word or expression which has more than one meaning is being used in its most concrete or basic sense, rather than in a more abstract, figurative sense. EG *They are people who have literally and spiritually left home... At the last minute, literally overnight, they changed their minds.* 1.3 to make a statement even more exaggerated than it already is. EG *We've had letters from all over the world, literally thousands of them... They are literally willing to sell you the shirt off their backs.* ADV ⇑ in fact; ADV ⇑ actually; ADV

2 If a word or expression is translated **literally**, its most simple or basic meaning is translated. EG *...an old man, an elder, a wati-pulka (literally 'big man').* ADV ⇑ actually = really

3 If you **take** something **literally**, you think that a word or expression is being used with its most simple or basic meaning. EG *Don't misunderstand or take that too literally.* PHR : VB INFLECTS

literary /lɪtə⁰rəri¹/. 1 **Literary** means concerned with or connected with the writing, study, or appre- ADJ CLASSIF : ATTRIB ciation of literature. EG *...his genuine pleasure at her literary success... The text has some literary merit... Cyril Connolly was an English literary critic.*

2 **Literary** words and expressions are often unusual in some way and are used to create a special effect in a poem, speech, novel, etc. In this dictionary, words and expressions of this kind are indicated by the use of the word 'literary' in definitions. ADJ QUALIT

literate /lɪtəºrəˡt/. Someone who is **literate** is **1** able to read and write. EG *Only half the children in this class are literate.* **2** well educated and intelligent. EG *...the children of highly literate parents.* ADJ CLASSIF; ADJ QUALIT = well-read

literati /lɪtərɑːtiˡ/ are well-educated people who are interested in literature; a formal word. EG *...legendary gatherings of literati.* N PLURAL

literature /lɪtəºrətʃə/. **1** Novels, plays, poetry, and other creative written works are referred to as **literature**, especially when they are considered to have artistic qualities. EG *I envy you having a friend with whom you can discuss art and literature... Nobody would consider it great literature... ...a postgraduate degree in English Literature.* N UNCOUNT ⇑ writing

2 The books and articles about a particular subject of study are referred to as the **literature** relating to it. EG *The recent literature on animal behaviour is extensive... Scientific and technical literature mounts at a rate of some 60,000,000 pages a year.* N UNCOUNT+SUPP ⇑ information

3 **Literature** is also written information, usually in the form of leaflets, that is produced by people who want to sell you something or help you by giving this information. EG *All major political parties print helpful literature for hopeful candidates... The party spent a fortune on campaign literature... Don't forget to pick up the literature about the ovens, will you?* N UNCOUNT: USU +SUPP = circulars

lithe /laɪð/. A person or animal who is **lithe** or who has a **lithe** body, is able to move and bend their body easily and gracefully; a formal word. EG *He looked out at the jewelled sea and the lithe brown girls walking along the beach.* ADJ QUALIT = lissom, supple

lithograph /lɪθə⁶grɑ³f/, **lithographs**. A **lithograph** is a printed picture made by the method of lithography. EG *...the lithograph of Queen Victoria over the mantlepiece.* N COUNT

lithography /lɪθɒgrəfiˡ/ is a method of printing in which a piece of stone or metal is specially treated so that ink sticks to some parts of it and not to others. ◇ **lithographic**. EG *...a type of stone ideal for use in lithographic printing.* N UNCOUNT; ◇ ADJ CLASSIF: ATTRIB

Lithuanian /lɪθjuːeɪnɪən/, **Lithuanians**. **1** A **Lithuanian** person or thing comes from or relates to Lithuania. EG *...Lithuanian peasants.* ADJ CLASSIF

2 A **Lithuanian** is a person from Lithuania. N COUNT

litigant /lɪtɪgənt/, **litigants**. A **litigant** is a person who makes a formal complaint about someone to a civil court of law, or the person that the complaint is made about. EG *In my experience litigants nearly always deceive their solicitors.* N COUNT = accused, plaintiff

litigation /lɪtɪgeɪʃəºn/ is the process of fighting or defending a case in a civil court of law. EG *It was not unusual for the bank to be involved in litigation over failed companies.* N UNCOUNT ⇑ action

litigious /lɪtɪdʒəs/. Someone who is **litigious** often makes formal complaints about people to a civil court of law; a formal word. ADJ CLASSIF

litmus paper /lɪtməs peɪpə/ is paper which has a chemical in it that makes it turn red when it touches an acid and blue when it touches an alkali. N UNCOUNT

litmus test /lɪtməs test/. If you say that something is a **litmus test** of something else, for example of someone's attitude to a particular thing, you mean that it is a simple and effective test of it. EG *This may be a litmus test of their commitment to serious limitations on the use of such devices.* N SING WITH DET: USU+SUPP

litre /liːtə/, **litres**; also spelled **liter** in American English. **1** A **litre** is a metric unit of volume that is a thousand cubic centimetres, and is equal to 1.76 pints. Its abbreviation is 'l'. EG *...a litre of wine.* N COUNT, OR N PART+N UNCOUNT

2 If a vehicle has, for example, a 1.3 **litre** engine, the engine's cylinders have that capacity; also used to refer to the vehicle. EG *The new model has a 2.2 litre engine and power steering... ...a 1.3 litre Vauxhall Astra.* N COUNT: USU NUM+N ⇑ capacity

litter /lɪtə/, **litters, littering, littered**. **1 Litter** is rubbish, for example bits of paper and old bottles, that is left untidily lying around outside. EG *There were piles of litter in the streets... People have always dropped litter.* N UNCOUNT

2 A **litter** of things is a quantity of them that are lying on the floor or ground in a disorganized way. EG *Kate sat on the floor surrounded by a litter of magazines... There was the usual litter of rubble and fallen stones underfoot... They are almost invisible, crouching among the leaf litter on the forest floor.* N UNCOUNT+SUPP = jumble, confusion

3 If a number of things **litter** a surface or a place, they are scattered around on it or in it in a disorganized and untidy way. EG *She drove away, bumping over sticks and debris littering the drive... His desk was littered with papers... The living-room was dark and empty, littered with empty glasses and ashtrays.* V+O = clutter

4 If something **is littered** with things, it is full of them. EG *The manuscripts of the Dark Ages are littered with accounts of miraculous happenings... The history of science is littered with 'original' ideas that turned out not to be original after all.* V+O: USU PASS+*with*

5 If you **litter** a place, you leave unwanted things there so that it is untidy. EG *We had littered the table with our messy leavings of cake crumbs.* V+O ⇑ dirty

6 **Litter** is also **6.1** straw, hay, etc which animals are given to sleep on. **6.2** a dry substance that you put in the container where you want your cat to defecate. N UNCOUNT; N UNCOUNT

7 A **litter** is **7.1** a group of animals born to the same mother at the same time. EG *It was the finest puppy in a litter of six born to my father's bitch, Mollie.* **7.2** a bed or seat on which someone can be carried, for example someone who is injured. Rich people were sometimes carried in litters in former times. EG *The Colonel winced as the porters jolted the litter... She had been brought in a litter from the city.* N COUNT; N COUNT ⇑ transport

litter bin, litter bins. A **litter bin** is a container, usually outside or in a public building, into which people can put rubbish. N COUNT

litterbug /lɪtəbʌg/, **litterbugs**. A **litterbug** is a person who drops or leaves rubbish in public places. N COUNT

litter lout, litter louts. A **litter lout** is a person who drops or leaves rubbish in public places. N COUNT = litterbug

little /lɪtəºl/. The comparative **littler** and the superlative **littlest** are sometimes used in non-standard, spoken English for paragraphs 1, 2, and 3, but otherwise the adjective **little** is not used in a comparative or superlative form. The comparative for the quantifier explained in paragraph 8 and the adverb in paragraph 10 is **less** and the superlative is **least**: these words are dealt with separately in this dictionary. **1** You use **little** to describe something that is small in physical size. The word 'little' is slightly more informal than 'small'. EG *...a little table with a glass top... ...those little dark villages... ...a little piece of rock... He rose and crossed to the desk, towering over the little Belgian.* ADJ QUALIT: USU ATTRIB ≠ big

2 A **little** child is young and therefore quite small in size. EG *...two little girls, Marion and Mabel... The little children played in the sand at the water's edge... I've heard him do that often when I was little.* ADJ QUALIT

3 Your **little** sister or brother is younger than you are. EG *She was bringing her little brother Kevin with her.* ADJ QUALIT: ATTRIB

4 A **little** distance or period of time is short in length. EG *...after he had walked for a little way... She lay awake a little while longer.* ADJ QUALIT: ATTRIB ≠ long

5 A **little** group of things or people or a **little** quantity of something is small and does not contain many things or people or does not consist of much of something. EG *...little groups of people in black... 'Have a drink. Scotch or Bourbon?'–'A little drop of Scotch would be very welcome.'* ADJ QUALIT: ATTRIB+N COUNT/PART ≠ large

6 A **little** smile, grin, cry, etc is one where emotion is expressed to only a limited extent. EG *...a little smile... Mrs Jane gave a little cry and hurried on.* ADJ QUALIT: ATTRIB ≠ great

7 You use **little** **7.1** to indicate or emphasize your attitude towards someone or something, usually when they are quite small in size, but sometimes when you just want to make them seem unimportant. EG *We had a nice little house with three bedrooms... A little old lady came out very quietly.... ...the selfish little beast!* **7.2** to indicate that something is not serious or significant, or is not done on a large scale, and when you want to make it seem unimportant. EG *They had a little discussion on it... Can I have a little look?... I've just brought out a little book on Dostoyevski... Don't bother me with little things like that.* ADJ CLASSIF: ATTRIB ≠ big; ADJ CLASSIF: ATTRIB ⇑ slight

8 **Little** is used to indicate that there is only a small amount of something or almost none at all, often when this is not enough. EG *We had little chance of* QUANTIF+N UNCOUNT ≠ much

success... John and I had very little money left... Little of the equipment was standardized... She ate little. Food sickened her... There is little to worry about... He should say as little as possible.

9 If something happens **little by little**, it happens very gradually, or only a small amount at a time. EG *Then I learnt little by little the early history of her and her family... Little by little, over the next hour or so, they grew more hopeful.* — PHR : USED AS AN A; = bit by bit

10 Little also means almost not at all, or to only a very limited extent. EG *Richardson interrupted very little... We tried to influence their play as little as possible... ...a city that is so far very little damaged.* — ADV BRD NEG; ⇑ barely, hardly

11 If you say **little** does someone know or care about something, you are saying and emphasizing that they do not know or care about it; a fairly formal use. EG *Little did I know when I embarked on this quest where it would lead me... She little thought that everything was about to change.* — ADV WITH VB

12 A little of something is a small amount of it, but not very much. EG *He spoke a little French... ...a little bit of French... Don't worry, everything will be OK, it just needs a little time, that's all... The head waiter ceremoniously poured a little of the wine into a huge, deep glass... Try to persuade her to eat a little.* — QUANTIF+N UNCOUNT; ⇑ some

13 A little or **a little bit** means **13.1** to a small extent or degree. EG *He frowned a little and then closed his eyes... ...something that's always worried me a little bit... It was, however, a little disappointing... I thought he was a little bit afraid... ...a little later that evening... He sometimes gets a little carried away.* — PHR : USED AS AN A; = a bit

13.2 for a short time or distance. EG *We went on a little, and then stopped again... He sits there for a little... ...moving a little bit to the left.* — PHR : USED AS AN A

little finger, little fingers. 1 Your **little finger** is the smallest finger on your hand. — N COUNT

2 If you can **twist someone round your little finger**, they will do anything that you ask them to. EG *She can twist the old boy round her little finger.* — PHR : VB INFLECTS; = manipulate

littoral /lɪtərəᵊl/ means near the coast; a technical term in geography. EG *...the littoral hills.* — ADJ CLASSIF : ATTRIB

liturgical /lɪtɜːdʒɪkəᵊl/. **Liturgical** things are used in or relate to church services. — ADJ CLASSIF : USU ATTRIB

liturgy /lɪtədʒiˡ/, **liturgies. 1** The religious services that are carried out in a set way in the Christian Church are referred to as **liturgy**. EG *...the business of revising the liturgy.* — N UNCOUNT

2 A **liturgy** is a particular form of religious service. EG *She would have preferred a simpler liturgy.* — N COUNT

live, lives, living, lived. The word **live** is pronounced /lɪv/ when it is a verb and /laɪv/ when it is an adjective. The word **lives** is pronounced /lɪvz/ when it is a verb and /laɪvz/ when it is the plural of **life. 1** If someone **lives** in a particular place, their home, where all their belongings are, is there. EG *Where do you live?... I used to live in Grange Road... My grandmother lived with us for 15 years.* — V+A; = dwell, reside

2 If a type of animal **lives** in a particular kind of area or part of the world, it can be found there. EG *Gorillas live in central Africa.* — V+A

3 If you **live** in particular circumstances or **live** a particular kind of life, you are in those circumstances or your life is of the kind indicated. EG *...people who live in poverty... We lived very simply... I began to live in an almost permanent state of fear... They are forced to live entirely artificial lives.* — V+A, OR V+O; ⇑ exist

4 If someone **lives** in a particular kind of society or period of history, they are in that kind of society or are alive during that period of history. EG *We live in a technological society... ...people who lived in the eighteenth century.* — V+A

5 To **live** means to be alive; used of people, animals, and plants. EG *We need water to live... People cannot live without air... Women seem to live longer than men.* — V : NO CONT; = exist

6 If a person, animal, or plant **lives** after a particular point in time or until a particular point in time, they stay alive. EG *I think the patient will live, nurse... She lost her will to live... I hope I shall live to see peace in my country.* — V : NO CONT; = survive

7 If you say that someone **has lived**, you mean that they have done exciting and interesting things, for example they have visited interesting places. EG *If you haven't seen Paris at night, you haven't lived... I've never lived really.* — V; = see life

8 If people **live** in a particular way, they get the things that they need in their daily life, for example food and clothing in that way. EG *Communities who live by hunting and gathering still exist.* — V

9 If something **lives** in someone's memory or in history, it is remembered for ever or for a long time by them because it is important to them. EG *Her voice will live with me until I die... ...a night that will surely live in American history.* — V+A; ⇑ stay; = endure, last

10 If you **live** a story that you are hearing or watching, you imagine that you are actually experiencing the events in it. EG *They lived every turn of the story as he related it.* — V+O; = experience

11 If you **live and breathe** a particular subject or activity, you are so enthusiastic about it that you hardly think about anything else; a fairly informal use. EG *My brother lives and breathes football.* — PHR : VB INFLECT

12 Live animals or plants are alive, rather than being dead or artificial. EG *There are many problems in transporting live animals.* — ADJ CLASSIF : ATTRIB; = living

13 A **live** television programme or radio programme is a programme in which an event or performance is broadcast at exactly the same time as it happens, rather than being recorded first. EG *...live pictures of a man walking on the moon... ...a live broadcast.* — ADJ CLASSIF
▸ used as an adverb. EG *The concert will be broadcast live on Radio Three.* — ▸ ADV AFTER VB

14 A **live** performance or a performance that is done **live** is done in front of an audience, rather than being recorded and then broadcast or shown in a film. EG *...live theatre... I would like to perform live as much as possible.* ▸ used of the audience at a live performance. EG *I love performing in front of a live audience.* — ADJ CLASSIF, OR ADV AFTER VB

15 A **live** wire or piece of electrical equipment is directly connected to a source of electricity. EG *Cut back the covers of the neutral and live wires... ...a microphone inadvertently left live.* — ADJ CLASSIF

16 Live bullets, bombs, or missiles have not yet exploded or been fired. EG *...live ammunition.* — ADJ CLASSIF

17 Live coals or pieces of wood are still gently burning after being on a fire. — ADJ CLASSIF : ATTRIB

18 Live yoghurt contains the living bacteria which you need to make milk into yogurt. — ADJ CLASSIF : ATTRIB

19 Lives is the plural of **life**.

20 The word **live** is also used in the following expressions. **20.1** You say **'you live and learn'** or **'we live and learn'** when you are surprised at a fact that you have just become aware of. EG *'Did you know that one in four animals is a beetle?'–'Well, you live and learn.'* — CONVENTION
20.2 You say **'live and let live'** as a way of saying that you should let other people behave in the way that they want to and not criticize them for behaving differently from you. EG *Well, I'm not going to stop them. 'Live and let live'–that's my motto.* — CONVENTION
20.3 If you **live a lie**, you continually act in a way that hides the kind of person that you really are or what you are really doing; a literary expression. EG *For years I've been living a lie.* — PHR : VB INFLECTS
20.4 If you **live it up**, you have a very enjoyable and exciting time, for example by going to lots of parties or going out drinking with friends; an informal expression. EG *We've been living it up in Amsterdam.* — PHR : VB INFLECTS
20.5 You refer to someone as a **real live** person to emphasize that they are actually present, when this is exciting and unusual or unexpected; used in informal English. EG *Wow! I've never met a real live cowboy before!* — PHR+N
20.6 • to **live beyond your means** or **within your means**: see **mean.** • to **live in sin**: see **sin.** • to **live by your wits**: see **wit.** • See also **living.**

live by. If you **live by** a particular rule, belief, or ideal, you behave in the way in which it says you should behave. EG *Many people proclaim adherence to a religious ethic but do not live by it.* — PHRASAL VB : V+PREP

live down. If you are unable to **live down** a mistake, failure, or foolish action, you are unable to make people forget that you did it. EG *If you were beaten by Jack, you'd never live it down.* — PHRASAL VB : V+O+ADV

live for. If you **live for** a particular thing, it is the most important thing in your life. EG *...a man who lived for pleasure.* — PHRASAL VB : V+PREP
• If you **live for the day** or **time** when a particular thing will happen, you look forward to it with great enthusiasm. EG *I live for the day when I retire.* — • PHR : VB INFLECTS

live in. If someone, especially a servant or a student, **lives in**, they sleep, have their meals, etc in the place where they work or study. EG *Would you be prepared to live in?... ...the present shortage of 'living in' nannies.* — PHRASAL VB : V+ADV; = be resident

live off. 1 If you **live off** someone else, you get from them the money that you need in order to buy necessary things, because you do not have any money of your own; often used showing disapproval. EG *I was living off my parents... The family was in such difficult straits they were living off welfare.* [PHRASAL VB : V+PREP = sponge off]

2 If you **live off** a particular kind of food, it is the only kind of food you eat; an informal use. EG *We lived off fruit for a week.* [PHRASAL VB : V+PREP = live on]

3 If you **live off the land**, you eat plants and fruit that you find or grow yourself and animals that you hunt or keep, rather than buying things. [PHR : VB INFLECTS]

live on. 1 If you **live on** a particular amount of money, you have that amount of money to spend and it is enough to buy food and other necessary things. EG *How do you expect me to live on £150 a year?... I don't have enough to live on.* [PHRASAL VB : V+PREP]

2 If you **live on** a particular kind of food, it is the only kind of food you eat. EG *She lived on berries and wild herbs.* [PHRASAL VB : V+PREP = live off]

3 If someone **lives on**, they continue to be alive for a long time after a particular point in time. EG *Charles de Gaulle lived on, to retire in peace.* [PHRASAL VB : V+ADV ⇑ last = survive]

4 If something such as a memory or historical event **lives on** , it is remembered for ever or for a long time because it is important. EG *The Marilyn Monroe legend lives on in Hollywood.* [PHRASAL VB : V+ADV, USU+A]

live out. 1 If you **live out** a particular set of things that you are fated or intended to do, you actually do them; a formal use. EG *Each of us lives out our destiny... She lived out to the extreme the teachings of our faith.* [PHRASAL VB : ORDER V+ADV+O = fulfil]

2 If someone, especially a servant or a student, **lives out**, do not they sleep, have their meals, etc in the place where they work or study. [PHRASAL VB : V+ADV]

3 If you **live out** your life in a particular place or in particular circumstances, you stay in that place or are in those circumstances until the end of your life or of a particular period of it. EG *We all lived out our lives entirely on the farm... He lived out the remaining 56 years of his life in London.* [PHRASAL VB : V+O+ADV, USU+A]

4 If you **live out of a suitcase** or **a trunk**, you spend all your time travelling and staying in hotels, usually because of your job; used in informal English. [PHR : VB AND N INFLECT]

5 If you **live out of tins, cans, dustbins, etc**, you get your food from the source mentioned because you cannot afford or cannot find anything else to eat. EG *Many people were so destitute they lived out of garbage cans.* [PHR : VB INFLECTS]

live through. If you **live through** a particular event or change, usually an unpleasant one, you experience it and survive it. EG *You've got to have courage to live through something like that.* [PHRASAL VB : V+PREP, HAS PASS ⇑ withstand]

live together. If two people **live together**, they live in the same house and have a sexual relationship but are not married to one another. EG *Increasing numbers of young people choose to live together rather than to marry.* [PHRASAL VB : V+ADV = cohabit]

live up to. If someone or something **lives up to** what they were expected or desired to be or do, they are as good as they were expected or desired to be. EG *The film didn't live up to my expectations... She succeeded, to my mind, in living up to her extraordinary reputation... They have no artificial standards of behaviour to live up to.* [PHRASAL VB : V+ADV+PREP ⇑ reach = fulfil, realise]

live with. 1 If you **live with** someone, you live in the same house as them and have a sexual relationship with them but are not married to them. EG *The social security people found out she was living with a man.* [PHRASAL VB : V+PREP = cohabit]

2 If you have to **live with** an unpleasant or unwelcome situation that is likely to continue, you have to accept it and carry on with your life or work. EG *They have to live with the consequences of their decision... The job involved a lot of stress and pressure, but you learnt to live with it.* [PHRASAL VB : V+PREP, HAS PASS = put up with]

live-in /lɪvɪn/. 1 A **live-in** partner is someone who lives in the same house as the person they are having a sexual relationship with, but is not married to them; a fairly informal use. EG *...his live-in girlfriend.* [ADJ CLASSIF : ATTRIB]

2 A **live-in** servant or other worker sleeps and eats in the place where they work. EG *Martha was the live-in maid.* [ADJ CLASSIF : ATTRIB = resident]

livelihood /laɪvlɪhʊd/, **livelihoods**. Your **livelihood** is the job or other source of income which gives you the money to buy the things that you need in your daily life. EG *...their fear of losing their livelihood... Their principle livelihood was in the sea.* [N COUNT/UNCOUNT = living]

livelong /lɪvlɒŋ/. You say that something happens **all the livelong day**, to emphasize that it happens over what seems a long and tedious time; an old-fashioned, literary expression. EG *All the livelong day, Father and Mother strove to please their darling child.* [PHR : USED AS AN A = entire]

lively /laɪvli[1]/, **livelier, liveliest**. 1 Someone who is **lively** speaks and behaves in an active, enthusiastic, and cheerful way; used showing approval. EG *Her parents were both lively, eccentric, and attractive individuals... Four lively youngsters suddenly burst into the room.* ◊ **liveliness**. EG *...his liveliness and good humour.* [ADJ QUALIT = bubbly, vivacious; ◊ N UNCOUNT = vivacity]

2 A **lively** event, place, book, etc has lots of interesting and exciting things happening or being said in it; used showing approval. EG *The debate should be lively... We had a lively conversation... Things are a little livelier in June and July.* ◊ **liveliness**. EG *He surprised Fanny by the liveliness of his questions.* [ADJ QUALIT = animated; ◊ N UNCOUNT = animation]

3 An animal that is **lively** moves about quickly all the time. EG *...some very lively fish.* ◊ **liveliness**. [ADJ QUALIT; ◊ N UNCOUNT]

4 Someone who has a **lively** mind is intelligent and interested in a lot of different things. ◊ **liveliness**. [ADJ QUALIT; ◊ N UNCOUNT]

5 A **lively** feeling or awareness is a great, enthusiastic, or intense one. EG *She took a lively interest in everything... ...an institution for which I normally have a lively admiration.* [ADJ QUALIT : ATTRIB = hearty]

6 If you say **'look lively'** to someone, you are telling them to hurry up or start doing something; an informal expression. EG *Come on, look lively!* [CONVENTION]

liven up /laɪvə[0]n ʌp/, **livens up, livening up, livened up**. 1 If something **livens up** a place or event, or if it **livens up**, it makes it more interesting and exciting. EG *There are lots of new shops and things. The place is really livening up.* [PHRASAL VB : V-ERG+ADV]

2 If something **livens up** a person or group, or if they **liven up**, they become more cheerful and energetic. EG *We should do things to help liven up the community... At least the incident had livened her up.* [PHRASAL VB : V-ERG+ADV = perk up]

liver /lɪvə/, **livers**. 1 Your **liver** is a large organ in your body which processes your blood and helps to clean unwanted substances out of it. EG *These chemicals can cause damage to the liver, heart, and kidneys.* [N COUNT]

2 **Liver** is the liver of some animals, especially lambs, pigs, and cows, which is cooked and eaten. EG *This wine should be drunk with liver, game, or tongue... ...chicken liver pate.* [N UNCOUNT ⇑ offal]

liveried /lɪvə[0]rɪd/. A **liveried** servant is a servant who wears a special uniform. EG *...a liveried footman.* [ADJ CLASSIF : ATTRIB]

liverish /lɪvə[0]rɪʃ/. Someone who is **liverish** feels slightly sick. [ADJ QUALIT ⇑ unwell]

livery /lɪvə[0]ri[1]/, **liveries**. 1 A servant's **livery** is the special uniform that he or she wears, especially a uniform that is worn only by the servants of a particular person. EG *Sixteen servants in rich livery waited on them... They wore his badge and livery.* [N UNCOUNT/COUNT]

2 The **livery** of a particular company is the special design or set of colours associated with it that is put on its products and possessions. EG *...the aircraft's sleek design and blue and grey livery.* [N COUNT : USU WITH POSS]

lives. See **life, live.**

livestock /laɪvstɒk/. Animals such as cattle and sheep which are kept on a farm are referred to as **livestock**. EG *They encourage farmers to keep more livestock.* [N PLURAL/N UNCOUNT]

live wire /laɪv waɪə/, **live wires**. If you describe someone as a **live wire**, you mean that they are lively and energetic; an informal expression. [N COUNT : USU USED AS C]

livid /lɪvɪd/. 1 Someone who is **livid** is extremely angry; an informal use. EG *I said, 'I'll have a beer.' He said, 'No, you won't.' I was absolutely livid.* [ADJ QUALIT = fuming, furious]

2 Something that is **livid** is an unpleasant dark purple or greyish blue colour. EG *...livid bruises... ...under a livid sky... ...a face livid with helpless rage.* [ADJ QUALIT]

living /lɪvɪŋ/, **livings**. 1 A **living** person or animal is alive. EG *I have no living relatives... ...Joe Namath, the greatest living American footballer... She had been in Amity for as long as anyone living could remember.* ▸ The **living** is used to refer to people who are alive. EG *There'll be plenty of money for the living, and a decent burial for the dead.* [ADJ CLASSIF : USU ATTRIB, OR ADJ AFTER N; ▸ N PLURAL : the +N]

2 **Living** creatures are able to be alive; used when contrasting these creatures with things which can [ADJ CLASSIF : ATTRIB]

never be alive. EG *...living organisms such as bacteria.*

3 If you refer to the way in which someone makes or earns their **living**, you mean the way in which they earn money in order to buy the things that they need in their daily life. EG *I never expected to earn my living as an artist... It is possible to make a very good living from modelling... What do you do for a living?* N SING WITH DET : USU *a/POSS* +N = livelihood

4 You can refer to the things that people do and experience that are characteristic of a particular place or way of life. as a particular kind of **living**. EG *The quality of urban living has been damaged by excessive noise levels.* N UNCOUNT : MOD +N

5 **Living** is also used of the place where someone sleeps, eats, relaxes, etc when they are not working, and of things relating to it. EG *I'll show you to the living quarters... The Merchant Shipping Bill which sought to improve living conditions at sea.* ADJ CLASSIF : ATTRIB

6 A **living** language is still spoken by people in the course of their everyday lives. EG *Gaelic is still a living language.* ADJ CLASSIF : ATTRIB = in use

7 A **living** is the job of being the member of the clergy responsible for a particular area; a technical term relating to the Church of England. N COUNT

8 If you describe a kind of life as a **living death**, you mean that it is so awful that it seems worse than being dead; a literary expression. EG *...sending a criminal to the living death we call prison.* PHR : USU USED AS C/O ↑ existence = hell

9 • **the living daylights**: see **daylight**. • **the living image of** someone: see **image**. • **within living memory**: see **memory**. • See also **cost of living, standard of living**.

living-room, living-rooms; also spelled without a hyphen. The **living-room** in a house is the room which people sit and relax in, but do not usually eat in. EG *She went back into the living-room... The cottage had a living-room and two bedrooms... ...the living-room window.* N COUNT = lounge, sitting room

living standards. When you refer to **living standards**, you are referring to the level of comfort in which people live, which usually depends on how much money they have. EG *...a fall in real living standards... ...the demand for better living standards.* N PLURAL

living wage. A **living wage** is a wage which is large enough to enable you to buy food, clothing, and other necessary things. EG *It's impossible to employ so many people and go on paying them a living wage.* N SING : *a*+N

lizard /lɪzəd/, **lizards**. A **lizard** is a small animal with four short legs, a long tail, and a rough dry skin. Lizards live in hot countries. N COUNT

-'ll is the shortened form of 'will' or 'shall' that is added in spoken English to the end of the pronoun or noun which is the subject of the verb. For example, 'you will' can be shortened to 'you'll'. EG *He'll come back... They'll spoil our picnic... That'll be all right.*

llama /lɑːmə/, **llamas**. A **llama** is a South American animal that is like a small camel without a hump. Llamas have thick hair on their bodies. N COUNT

lo /ləʊ/. You say **lo** or **lo and behold** to draw attention in a literary or humorous way to a surprising or interesting event that you are about to mention. EG *In the end they gave up and adopted a child, and lo and behold all her tensions disappeared and she became pregnant... Then men from the East stick needles in you and lo, you feel no pain and are healed.* PHR : USED AS ADV SEN, OR CONVENTION

load /ləʊd/, **loads, loading, loaded**. **1** If you **load** a vehicle, animal, or container or **load** things into or onto it, you put things into or onto it, especially so that they can be taken somewhere else. EG *They came to load the van... ...a truck loaded with sacks of flour... We started loading the pheasants into the sacks...* ◊ **loading**. EG *Foster was watching the loading.* V+O, OR V = pack ◊ N SING : *the*+N, USU+*of*

2 If you **load** someone with things, especially heavy things, you give them a large number of them to carry. EG *They loaded us with gifts.* V+O+A *(with)* = burden

3 A **load** is **3.1** something, or a quantity of things, which is being carried somewhere. EG *We took up our heavy load and trudged back... Its load of minerals was dumped at sea.* N COUNT **3.2** a quantity of clothes, sheets, etc which need washing and which are washed together in a washing machine. EG *I've got another load to do while that one's drying.* N COUNT

4 If you refer to **loads** of something or to a **load** of something, you are referring to a large amount of it and emphasizing that it is large; an informal use. EG *We've talked about loads of things... He had loads of charm... I got a load of tax back this month.* N PART+N UNCOUNT/N IN PLURAL

5 When someone **loads** a gun, they put a bullet or missile in it so that it is ready to use. EG *So I loaded the gun and slung it back on the saddle... ...the order to load, prepare for action and be on the alert.* V OR V+O ↑ fill = charge

6 When someone **loads** a camera, computer, or tape recorder or **loads** film or tape into it, they put film or tape into it so that it is ready to use. V+O

7 Someone's **load** is the amount of work which they have to do. EG *So in fact, you are lightening the load of the hospital doctors?... Spread the load by doing a little cleaning every day.* • See also **work-load**. N COUNT : USU+SUPP = burden

8 The **load** on a system or piece of equipment, especially a computer or a system supplying electricity, is the extent to which it is being used at a particular time. EG *...power cuts due to lack of maintenance, excess loads, or tropical storms.* N COUNT

9 The **load** on something, for example the wall of a building, is the amount of weight that is pressing down on it. N SING WITH DET

10 You say that something is **a load of rubbish, a load of junk**, etc or that a group of people are **a load of tramps, a load of has-beens**, etc, as a way of showing and emphasizing your disapproval of it or them; an informal use. EG *Their manifesto is a load of meaningless rubbish... Fancy him giving twenty pounds for a load of junk like this... They're nothing but a load of old has-beens.* PHR : USED AS O/C

11 You say **get a load of this** to make someone pay attention to something interesting; a very informal use. EG *Hey! Get a load of this! It says here that Trevor's been arrested.* CONVENTION

12 • **a load off** someone's **mind**: see **mind**.

load down. **1** If you **load** someone **down** with things, especially heavy things, you give them a large number of them or put a large number of them on them. EG *She loaded her daughter down with packages.* PHRASAL VB : V+O+ADV, USU+*with* ↑ encumber

2 If you **load** someone **down** with work, responsibilities, etc, you give them more work, responsibilities, etc than they can easily manage. PHRASAL VB : V+O+ADV, USU+*with*

load up. If you **load up** or if you **load up** a vehicle or animal, you put things into or onto it so that they can be taken somewhere. EG *They helped us load up the mule wagons with fresh meat and vegetables... I usually took off my coat while I was loading up.* PHRASAL VB : V+ADV, OR V+O+ADV

-load, -loads combines with nouns referring to a vehicle or container to form nouns that refer to the total amount of something that the vehicle or container mentioned can hold or carry. EG *...three lorryloads of tyres... Don't wash up unless you have a sink load.* COMB : FORMS N PARTS = full

loaded /ləʊdɪd/ **1** If something is **loaded** with things, it is very full and seems unable to hold any more. EG *The car seemed loaded with people... ...waitresses in muslin aprons hurrying with loaded trays.* ADJ QUALIT : IF+PREP THEN *with* = laden, brimming

2 If you are **loaded** with things or **loaded down** with them, you are carrying a large number of things, especially ones that are heavy or difficult to carry. EG *A man precedes him up the stairs, loaded with bundles... She was loaded down with parcels.* ADJ CLASSIF : PRED, IF+PREP THEN *with* = laden

3 If you say that someone is **loaded**, you mean that they have a lot of money; an informal use. EG *The twins' parents were loaded with money... All right, you're loaded. How's about lending us a buck?* ADJ QUALIT : PRED, IF+PREP THEN *with* = rich

4 If something such as a word, remark, or question is **loaded**, it has more significance than first appears, for example because it causes you to think of particular ideas or emotions, or because it causes you to admit something that you did not want to admit. EG *Love is a 'loaded' word... I hated him and all his loaded questions.* ADJ QUALIT : USU ATTRIB = charged

5 **Loaded** dice have been weighted so that they always fall with a particular side on top. • If you say that **the dice are loaded** against someone or something, you mean that they have very little chance of success. ADJ CLASSIF • PHR : VB INFLECTS

loaf /ləʊf/, **loaves** /ləʊvz/; **loafs, loafing, loafed**. **Loaves** is the plural of the noun. **Loafs** is the 3rd person singular present tense of the verb. **1** A **loaf** of bread is bread that has been shaped and baked as a large lump which you can slice. EG *He asked for a loaf of white bread... Bread would be increased from 21 pence to 26 pence a loaf.* N COUNT ↑ mass

2 If you say to someone **'Use your loaf!'**, you are CONVENTION telling them to use their common sense or to think harder because they are being slightly stupid; an informal expression.

3 If you **loaf** or if you **loaf** about or around, you spend your time not working or not doing the things that you ought to be doing; an informal use. EG *She loafed about for three years.*
V: USU+A *(about/around)* ⇑ idle = loiter

loafer /ləʊfə/, **loafers**. A **loafer** is someone who spends their time not working or not doing the things that they ought to be doing; an informal word. EG *...a pack of idle loafers.*
N COUNT ⇑ person = idler

loam /ləʊm/ is soil that is good for growing crops and plants in because it contains a lot of decayed vegetable matter and does not contain too much sand or clay.
N UNCOUNT

loan /ləʊn/, **loans, loaning, loaned**. **1** A **loan** is a sum of money that you borrow, for example from a bank, and which you have to pay back, usually in weekly or monthly payments. You usually have to pay interest on loans. EG *They found it impossible to get a bank loan... The government had to make a further loan of £3.3m to save the industry.*
N COUNT

2 If someone gives you a **loan** of something or if you have the **loan** of it, you borrow it from them. EG *Could I have the loan of your car for the weekend?*
N SING WITH DET *+of*

3 If something is **on loan**, it has been borrowed. EG *Most of his books are on loan from the London Library.*
PHR: USED AS AN A

4 If you **loan** something to someone, you lend it to them. EG *He never loaned his car to anybody.*
V+O, V+O+O, OR V+O+A *(to)*

5 If you **loan** money to someone, you lend them money which they have to pay back, usually in weekly or monthly payments and usually with interest on it. EG *I'll loan you fifty dollars.*
V+O, V+O+O, OR V+O+A *(to)*

loan shark, loan sharks. A **loan shark** is a person who lends money to people and then charges them extremely high rates of interest on the loan; an informal word used showing disapproval.
N COUNT

loath /ləʊθ/; also spelled **loth**. If you are **loath** to do something, you are unwilling to do it or do not like the thought of doing it. EG *...governments which have been loath to impose any sanctions... He was loath to see her go.*
ADJ QUALIT: PRED+*to*-INF = reluctant

loathe /ləʊð/, **loathes, loathing, loathed**. If you **loathe** something or someone, you dislike them very much. EG *I particularly loathed team games at school... She said she loathed me.*
V+O = hate

loathing /ləʊðɪŋ/ is a feeling of great dislike and disgust. EG *He remembered his school days with loathing... She had a loathing for the smell of meat cooking.*
N UNCOUNT ⇑ hatred = abhorrence

loathsome /ləʊðsəm/. If you say that someone or something is **loathsome**, you mean that they are horrible and you dislike them very much. EG *She thought he was a loathsome creature... What I hate about you most is the loathsome way you use other people.*
ADJ QUALIT ⇑ unpleasant = abominable

loaves /ləʊvz/ is the plural of **loaf**.

lob /lɒb/, **lobs, lobbing, lobbed**. **1** If you **lob** something, you throw it so that it goes quite high in the air. EG *She wrapped a piece of paper round a stone and lobbed it into the next garden.*
V+O: USU+A = toss

2 If you **lob** the ball in a game of tennis, you hit it high into the air so that it lands behind your opponent. EG *Miss Evert reached to lob a return of Miss Wade's.* ▸ used as a noun. EG *He played a couple of good lobs.*
V OR V+O ▸ N COUNT ⇑ stroke

lobby /lɒbi[1]/, **lobbies, lobbying, lobbied**. **1** A **lobby** is **1.1** the area that is behind the main door of a hotel or other large building and that has corridors and staircases etc leading off it. EG *I rushed into the hotel lobby, where our luggage was still piled high.*
N COUNT ⇑ entrance = vestibule

1.2 a group of people who try actively to persuade a government or council that a particular law should be changed or that a particular thing should be done. EG *...an increasingly strong and well organized lobby for the abolition of film censorship... The anti-nuclear lobby is far more powerful on the continent than in Britain.*
N COUNT: USU MOD+N, VB CAN BE SING OR PL ⇑ protesters

1.3 an attempt to persuade a government or council that a particular law should be changed or that a particular thing should be done. EG *The following New Year the lobby was repeated.*
N COUNT ⇑ campaign

2 If you **lobby** someone such as a member of a government or council, you actively try to persuade them that a particular law should be changed or that a particular thing should be done. EG *Unfortunately for the government, the ecologists lobbied powerfully on the anti-nuclear issue... He lobbied the Home Secretary, ministers, and other members of parliament.*
V+O, OR V+A ⇑ campaign

lobbyist /lɒbi[1]ɪst/, **lobbyists**. A **lobbyist** is someone who tries actively to persuade a government or council that a particular law should be changed or that a particular thing should be done.
N COUNT ⇑ campaigner

lobe /ləʊb/, **lobes**. **1** The **lobe** of your ear is the rounded fatty part at the base of the outside part of it.
N COUNT = ear lobe

2 A **lobe** is also a rounded part of something, for example one of the sections of your brain or lungs, or one of the rounded sections along the edges of some leaves. EG *The frontal lobe of the brain is responsible for controlling movement.*
N COUNT: USU+SUPP

lobotomy /lə[6]bɒtəmi[1]/, **lobotomies**. A **lobotomy** is a surgical operation in which some of the nerves in the brain are cut in order to treat severe mental illness; a technical term in medicine.
N COUNT/UNCOUNT

lobster /lɒbstə/, **lobsters**. A **lobster** is a sea creature that has a hard shell, two large claws, and eight legs. A lobster has a long body and a tail folded beneath it. You can cook lobsters and eat the flesh inside the shell.
N COUNT ⇑ crustacean, shellfish

lobster pot, lobster pots. A **lobster pot** is a trap in the shape of a basket that is used for catching lobsters.
N COUNT

local /ləʊk[ə]l/, **locals**. **1 Local** means **1.1** responsible for or concerned with a small area of a country, for example a county or city. EG *Some local councils give grants to parents with low incomes... Local government expenditure has come down by some ten per cent.* ◇ **locally**. EG *Should housing policy be decided nationally or locally?*
ADJ CLASSIF: ATTRIB ◇ ADV WITH VB

1.2 existing in or belonging to the area in which you live or work or the area which you are talking about. EG *Members are drawn from all sections of the local community... ...a picture in the local paper of him and the car... Local people know how severe the weather is here in the mountains.* ◇ **locally**. EG *Everything we used was bought locally.*
ADJ CLASSIF: USU ATTRIB ⇑ near by ◇ ADV WITH VB

1.3 limited to a specified part of your body; a medical use. EG *...local anesthetic.*
ADJ CLASSIF ≠ general

2 A **local** is **2.1** a person who lives near where you live or work, or in the area that you are talking about; a fairly informal use. EG *The locals view these road improvements with alarm.*
N COUNT = resident

2.2 a pub which is near where you live and where you often go for a drink; an informal British English use. EG *Why don't we go to my local?*
N COUNT: USU SING

local colour is experience or knowledge of a particular place or period of history and the way this is used in a book or a film in order to make it seem more realistic. EG *It all gives local colour to the book.*
N UNCOUNT = atmosphere, feel

locale /ləʊkɑːl/, **locales**. A **locale** is a small area, for example the place where something happens or where the action of a book or film is set; a fairly formal word. EG *They were born, grew up, and died in the same locale.*
N COUNT = environment, setting

locality /ləʊkælɪti[1]/, **localities**. A **locality** is a small area of a country or city; a fairly formal word. EG *...the anxiety of people living in the same locality... The plant grows on sheltered limestone cliffs in a few localities in the west.*
N COUNT = vicinity

localize /ləʊkəlaɪz/, **localizes, localizing, localized**; also spelled **localise**. **Localize** is a formal word. If you **localize** something, **1** you identify precisely where it is. EG *As I reported earlier, I can't localise the trouble.* **2** you limit the size of the area that it affects and prevent it from spreading. EG *...an attempt to localize the effect of these disturbances.*
1: V+O = locate; 2: V+O = contain

localized /ləʊkəlaɪzd/; also spelled **localised**. Something that is **localized** remains within a small area and does not spread; a fairly formal word. EG *It caused localized problems of erosion on sand dunes... There may be a localized haemorrhage under the skin.*
ADJ CLASSIF ⇑ limited

local time is the official time in a particular region or country. EG *The plane arrives in London at 17.50 local time.*
N UNCOUNT

locate /ləʊkeɪt/, **locates, locating, located**; a fairly formal word. **1** If you **locate** something or someone, you find out where they are. EG *They never managed to locate the main sections of the spacecraft... He located a better restaurant in the north of the city.*
V+O = pinpoint

2 If something **is located** in a particular place, it is present or has been built there. EG *The house was*
V+O: USU PASS+A

located in the heart of the city... ...one of the most prestigious and desirably located universities in America.

location /ləʊkeɪʃəⁿn/, **locations.** 1 A **location** is 1.1 a place, especially the place where something happens or where something is situated. EG *They set off to look for Dealer Hall, the location of the English Department... Election officials ran out of ballot papers at six locations... The new job involves a new employer, a new location, and a new set of colleagues.* 1.2 a place away from a studio where a film or part of a film is made. EG *It was too expensive to film in foreign locations.* • If a film or part of a film is made **on location**, it is made away from a studio. EG *She had just come back from doing a picture on location.*
N COUNT: USU+SUPP ⇑ situation = site
N COUNT: USU+SUPP
• PHR: USED AS AN A

2 **Location** is the act of finding the exact place where something is. EG *...the fascinating problem of radio location of aircraft.*
N UNCOUNT: USU+SUPP = pinpointing

loch /lɒx/, **lochs.** A **loch** is a lake; used in Scottish English or as part of the names of places in Scotland. EG *...Loch Lomond.*
N COUNT: ALSO IN NAMES BEFORE N

loci /ləʊkaɪ/ is the plural of **locus.**

lock /lɒk/, **locks, locking, locked.** 1 When you **lock** something such as a door, drawer, or case, you fasten it, usually by means of a key, so that other people cannot open it. EG *I tried the front door, and found that it was locked... Howard gets out of the van and locks it.*
V+O

2 If you **lock** something in a cupboard, drawer, room, etc or if you **lock** it up or away there, you put it in that place and fasten the key, so that nobody else can get it. EG *He had locked all his papers in the safe... He locked them away in a drawer... She should lock the money up in a safe.*
V+O: USU+A ⇑ secure

3 When you **lock** something or when it **locks** in a particular position or place, it is held or fitted firmly in that position. EG *John and Phyllis locked arms... Smoothly the battery locked into place.*
V-ERG: USU+A = clasp, click

4 If you **are locked** with someone in a fight, argument, or other conflict, you are in a situation where you are both try hard to win and are both equally strong. EG *Rebel groups and government forces are locked in a fierce battle for control of the country... He's locked in a test of wills with the Prime Minister.*
V+O, OR V+O+A *(with)*: RECIP, USU PASS+A ⇑ engage

5 A **lock** is 5.1 a device which is used to keep shut a door, drawer, case, etc, usually by means of a key, so that only a person with a key can open it. EG *At the sound of the key turning in the lock, her eyes brighten... He had to force the lock on the trunk.* • If something is **under lock and key**, it is in a room or container which has been locked. EG *She would keep any sensitive documents under lock and key.* 5.2 a particular way of holding someone in a position so that they cannot move or hit you. EG *He held my arm in a fierce lock.* 5.3 a place on a canal or river where walls have been built with gates at each end so that boats can move from one section of the canal or river to a higher or lower section, by gradually changing the water level inside the gates.
N COUNT ⇑ mechanism
• PHR: USED AS AN A ⇑ secure
N COUNT = grip, hold
N COUNT: ALSO IN NAMES AFTER N

6 A **lock** of hair is a small bunch of hairs on your head that grow together and curl or curve in the same direction. EG *A lock of hair had fallen down over her eyes.*
N COUNT = tress

7 Your **locks** are your hair; an old-fashioned, literary use. EG *He shook his black locks.*
N PLURAL: USU POSS+MOD+N

8 If you refer to the **lock** on a car, you are referring to the degree to which you can turn its steering wheel and so turn the car. EG *Our car's got a very good lock.*
N COUNT: USU SING

9 **Lock stock and barrel** means including every single part of something and without changing it at all. EG *I got it for £5000, lock, stock and barrel, a sixty-five-acre Suffolk farm... It's difficult to transport somebody else's experience, lock, stock and barrel onto the stage.*
PHR: USED AS AN A

lock in. If you **lock** someone **in**, you put them in a room, prison cell, or other place and lock the door so that they cannot get out. EG *The prisoners were not locked in... After they had locked me in, the officer in charge came to see me.*
PHRASAL VB: ORDER V+O+ADV ⇑ confine, imprison

lock out. 1 If you **lock** someone **out** of a place, you prevent them from entering it by locking the doors. EG *She had been locked out of the house in her nightdress.*
PHRASAL VB: ORDER V+O+ADV ⇑ exclude

2 If you **lock** yourself **out** of a place, such as your own house, you are outside it and cannot get in, for example because you have left your keys inside. EG *I went to empty the bins and found that I'd locked myself out.*
PHRASAL VB: V+O (REFL)+ADV

3 If the management of a factory or other place of work **locks out** the workers, it closes the factory and prevents the workers from coming in, because the workers refuse to accept the management's proposals or conditions of work. EG *Cigar workers were locked out in industrial disputes.* • See also **lockout.**
PHRASAL VB: V+O+ADV ⇑ exclude

lock up. 1 If you **lock** someone **up**, you put them in prison or a special psychiatric hospital. EG *The idea of being locked up in jail filled her with horror... They locked him up as a madman.* • See also **lockup.**
PHRASAL VB: V+O+ADV ⇑ incarcerate

2 When you **lock up**, you make sure that all the doors and windows of a building are properly closed or locked so that burglars cannot get in. EG *Don't forget to lock up when you leave.*
PHRASAL VB: V+ADV, OR V+O+ADV ⇑ secure

3 If something **is locked up** in a particular place or state, it is in that place or state and cannot easily be taken out, used, or changed. EG *So much water locked up in the ice caps caused a lowering of the sea level... The majority of the money required is locked up in the costs of raw materials.*
PHRASAL VB: V+O+ADV, USU PASS +A

locker /lɒkə/, **lockers.** A **locker** is a small cupboard, usually made of metal, which you can keep personal belongings in and lock with a key. Lockers are often provided in schools, colleges, and places of work for students or workers to use, or in railway stations for travellers.
N COUNT

locker room, locker rooms; also spelled with a hyphen. A **locker room** is a room in which there are a lot of lockers, especially a room in a school, place of work, or sports club where people keep their personal belongings.
N COUNT

locket /lɒkɪ²t/, **lockets.** A **locket** is a piece of jewellery which you wear on a chain round your neck and which you can open and keep small pictures or pieces of hair in, for example of a person you love.
N COUNT ⇑ pendant

lockout /lɒkaʊt/, **lockouts;** also spelled with a hyphen. A **lockout** is a situation in which the management of a factory or other place of work closes it and prevents the workers from coming in until the workers accept the management's proposals or conditions of work.
N COUNT

lockup /lɒkʌp/, **lockups;** also spelled with a hyphen. A **lockup** is the same as a jail; an informal word used in American English. EG *They hustled him off and put him in the lockup.*
N COUNT ⇑ room

locomotion /ləʊkəməʊʃəⁿn/ is the ability to move and the act of moving from one place to another; a formal word. EG *The child begins to experience the power of locomotion... ...the enormous variety of locomotion techniques of which the human frame is capable.*
N UNCOUNT ⇑ movement

locomotive /ləʊkəməʊtɪv/, **locomotives.** A **locomotive** is the same as a railway engine; a formal word. EG *The modern steam locomotives were superseded by diesel units.*
N COUNT ⇑ train

locum /ləʊkəm/, **locums.** A **locum** is a doctor or priest who does the work for another doctor or priest, for example while the second doctor or priest is on holiday or ill.
N COUNT ⇑ substitute, stand-in

locus /ləʊkəs/, **loci.** The **locus** of something is the place where it happens or the most important area or point with which it is associated; a very formal word. EG *The locus of the conflict has been shifting.*
N COUNT: USU SING+*of*

locust /ləʊkəst/, **locusts.** A **locust** is an insect with long legs and wings that lives mainly in hot countries and usually flies in very large groups. Locusts eat crops and can cause a lot of damage.
N COUNT ⇑ grasshopper

locution /ləᶿkjuːʃəⁿn/, **locutions.** A particular **locution** is a particular way of expressing something in words; a formal word. EG *...employing a locution characteristic of California.*
N COUNT+SUPP ⇑ manner = phrase

lodge /lɒdʒ/, **lodges, lodging, lodged.** 1 A **lodge** is 1.1 a small house at the entrance to the grounds of a large house. A lodge is often the home of a gatekeeper or other servant. 1.2 a hut or small house in the country or in the mountains which people stay in, especially when they go to shoot animals for sport or to fish. EG *They went to a shooting lodge in Scotland for the weekend.* 1.3 a local branch of a society, especially the Freemasons. EG *Several of the officials involved were named as members of a masonic lodge.* 1.4 the home which a beaver builds.
N COUNT
N COUNT: USU MOD+N
N COUNT: USU MOD+N
N COUNT

2 If you **lodge** in someone else's house or if you **are**
V-ERG+A

lodged there, you live there, often for only a short period of time. EG *He had arranged for me to lodge with his daughter and son-in-law... Wycherly lodged in Bow Street... They lodged old people there.*

3 If something **lodges** somewhere or **is lodged** there, it becomes stuck there so that it remains there. EG *The bullet had lodged a mere quarter of an inch from his spine... A dozen pellets had lodged themselves in his hind leg... I had somehow got the bone lodged in my throat.* V-ERG+A : IF V+O THEN USU PASS

4 If a fact or feeling **lodges** in your mind, heart, etc or **is lodged** there, you remember it for a long time afterwards. EG *Facts don't lodge easily in my mind... I'll tell you what I remember, while it is still lodged in my mind... But now, with her cruel words lodged in his soul forever, how could he carry on?* V-ERG+A : IF V+O THEN ONLY PASS ⇑ stay

5 If you **lodge** something somewhere where it will be safe, you put it there to be kept for a while; a formal use. EG *She said they would try to get at the documents lodged with my solicitor.* V+O+A ⇑ store

6 If you **lodge** a complaint, protest, accusation, or claim, you formally make it. EG *I was just going to ring you to lodge a formal complaint... ...the charges that had been lodged against them... More than 2000 claims have already been lodged.* V+O = bring

lodgement /lɒdʒmə²nt/, **lodgements**; also spelled **lodgment**. **Lodgement** or a **lodgement** is a place where something can stick or remain firmly; a formal word. EG *Roger found a lodgment for his knife and began to push.* N UNCOUNT/COUNT

lodger /lɒdʒə/, **lodgers**. A **lodger** is a person who lives in someone's else house and pays them money. EG *She allowed her student lodgers a lot of freedom.* N COUNT ⇑ tenant

lodging /lɒdʒɪŋ/, **lodgings**. 1 **Lodging** is a place to stay in for a period of time, which you usually pay for. EG *They were offered free lodging and food in first-class hotels... My friend Mr Bunce will be able to find you a night's lodging.* • See also **board and lodging**. N UNCOUNT ⇑ accommodation

2 If you live in **lodgings**, you live in a room or rooms in someone's house and you pay to live there. EG *The rest of the student population tends to live in lodgings.* N COUNT : USU PL = digs

lodging house, lodging houses; also spelled with a hyphen. A **lodging house** is a house where people can rent rooms to live in or stay in. N COUNT

lodgment /lɒdʒmə²nt/, **lodgments**. See **lodgement**.

loft /lɒft/, **lofts, lofting, lofted**. 1 A **loft** is 1.1 the space inside the sloping roof of a house or other building, where things are sometimes kept. EG *I consigned the wretched thing to the loft, where it languished, gathering dust, for many years.* N COUNT = attic 1.2 a gallery in a church. EG *I sat with him in the organ loft.* N COUNT

2 When someone, especially a cricketer or golfer, **lofts** something, especially a ball, they hit it or send it high into the air. EG *Kenny McEwan lofted one straight to me at deep midwicket.* V+O : USU+A = lob

lofty /lɒfti¹/, **loftier, loftiest**; a formal or literary word. 1 A **lofty** room, structure, mountain, etc is very high. EG *We explored lofty corridors... ...a lofty platform.* ADJ QUALIT

2 A **lofty** idea, aim, etc is noble and morally admirable. EG *...a noble and lofty concept... Such lofty goals were held to justify any means.* ADJ QUALIT ⇑ fine = exalted

3 Someone who is **lofty** is very proud in an unpleasant way and behaves as if they think that they are better than other people; used showing disapproval. EG *She hated his lofty manner.* ◊ **loftily**. EG *'You mean,' said Roddy loftily, 'houses for ordinary people.'* ADJ QUALIT = superior; ◊ ADV WITH VB = haughtily

4 A **lofty** style of writing or speaking is very grand and literary. EG *...the lofty style of its editorials.* ADJ QUALIT = elevated

log /lɒg/, **logs, logging, logged**. 1 A **log** is a piece of a thick branch or a piece of the trunk of a tree which has fallen to the ground or has been cut down. EG *He threw another log on the fire... ...the log cabin where Lincoln was born.* N COUNT ⇑ wood

2 A **log** is also an official written account which describes the important events that happen each day, for example on board a ship. EG *The Controller entered this in his log.* N COUNT = record

3 If you **log** an event or fact, you record it officially in writing. EG *The death must be logged.* V+O ⇑ write

4 In mathematics, the **log** of a number is a number that it can be represented by in order to make a difficult multiplication or division sum simpler. You can find out what the log of a number is by looking at a special list. EG *You have to convert the numbers to their appropriate logs... ...the compilation of log tables.* N COUNT = logarithm

5 If you say that you **slept like a log**, you mean that you slept very deeply and continuously. PHR : VB INFLECTS

log in. When someone **logs into** a computer system or **logs in**, they gain access to the system, usually by giving a special word or name so that the computer can check whether they are allowed to use it; a technical term. PHRASAL VB : V+PREP/ADV = enter

log out. When someone **logs out**, they finish using a computer system, usually by giving a special word which tells the computer that they do not need to use it any more. PHRASAL VB : V+ADV = exit

loganberry /ləʊgə⁰nbə²ri¹/, **loganberries**. A **loganberry** is a purplish red fruit that is similar to a raspberry. N COUNT ⇑ berry

logarithm /lɒgərɪðə⁰m/, **logarithms**. In mathematics, the **logarithm** of a number is a number that it can be represented by in order to make a difficult multiplication or division sum simpler. You can find out what the logarithm of a number is by looking at a special list. EG *Multiplication of any two numbers is achieved by adding their logarithms.* N COUNT = log

log book, log books; also spelled with a hyphen. A **log book** is a book in which someone records details and events relating to something, especially to their car. EG *Keep the test certificate, the log book, and the insurance certificate at home.* N COUNT

loggerheads /lɒgəhɛdz/. If two or more people or groups are **at loggerheads**, they disagree very strongly with each other. EG *He and Thomas were continually at loggerheads... She was at loggerheads with the Establishment over many matters.* PHR : USED AS AN A = at odds

loggia /lɒdʒɪ⁰ə/, **loggias**. A **loggia** is a roofed area attached to a house; a fairly formal word. N COUNT = porch

logging /lɒgɪŋ/ is the activity of cutting down trees in order to sell the wood. EG *...forests where illegal logging had been reported.* N UNCOUNT = felling

logic /lɒdʒɪk/. 1 **Logic** is 1.1 a method of reasoning that involves a series of statements, each of which must be true if the statement that comes before it is true. EG *It's necessary to have a good grasp of the laws of logic... The computer then proceeds with its incomparable logic and efficiency to work out the problem.* N UNCOUNT 1.2 the quality of being correctly worked out according to the laws of logic. EG *It is difficult to believe, and yet the logic of the deduction is undeniable... Their arguments for atheism do not have much logic or cogency.* N UNCOUNT ⇑ reasoning

2 You can refer to a way of thinking which you believe is typical of a particular person or group as a particular kind of **logic**. EG *Even the wilder excesses of Masculine Logic can hardly explain it... It was futile to try to understand the perverted logic of jailers.* N UNCOUNT+SUPP

3 A particular **logic** is the way of considering things, or the belief that particular things are sensible, that is characteristic of a particular field of activity. EG *Economic logic dictated the policy of centralization... The mergers he inspired had industrial logic behind them at least.* N UNCOUNT+SUPP ⇑ reasoning

logical /lɒdʒɪkə⁰l/. 1 A **logical** argument or analysis is one in which each step or point must be true if the step that came before it is true. EG *I made little attempt at logical argument... This is a masterly, logical analysis of the procedure.* ◊ **logically**. EG *Everything has to be logically analysed and synthesized.* ADJ CLASSIF ⇑ analytical = reasoned; ◊ ADV WITH VB = methodically

2 A **logical** conclusion, result, or series is one which results from or is part of a series of facts or events which, in your opinion, can lead to only one conclusion. EG *There is only one logical conclusion... To him violence was a logical inevitability... But development did follow a logical sequence.* ◊ **logically**. EG *The solution does seem logically obvious once it has been reached... It follows logically that one of them is lying.* ADJ CLASSIF ⇑ reasoned; ◊ ADV WITH VB ⇑ rationally = clearly

3 Something that is **logical** seems reasonable or sensible in the circumstances. EG *Wouldn't it have been more logical for them to make the arrest downstairs?... It seemed a logical idea to everyone but my mother.* ◊ **logically**. EG *Therefore, logically, he had to go.* ADJ QUALIT; ◊ ADV WITH VB, OR ADV SEN

-logical. See **-ological**.

logician /lə'dʒɪʃə⁰n/, **logicians**. A **logician** is a person who is a specialist in logic. N COUNT

-logist. See **-ologist**.

logistic /lə'dʒɪstɪk/, **logistics**. **Logistic** is an adjective, and **logistics** is a plural noun or an uncount noun. **Logistical** is another form of the adjective. **1** If you refer to the **logistics** of doing something complicated that involves a lot of people or equipment, you are referring to the skilful organization of it so that it can be done successfully and efficiently. EG *...the tiresome logistics of modern broadcasting... Logistics and transport remained a problem.* N PLURAL/N UNCOUNT ⇑ strategy

2 Logistic or **logistical** means relating to the organization of something complicated. EG *...faced with daunting logistic and administrative problems... I used to shudder at the logistical difficulties of getting the huge programme on the air.* ◊ **logistically**. ADJ CLASSIF: ATTRIB ⇑ tactical ◊ ADV WITH VB

logo /ləʊgəʊ/, **logos**. The **logo** of a company or organization is the special design or way of writing its name that it puts on all its products, notepaper, advertisements, etc. EG *You will be welcome at all hotels displaying our logo.* N COUNT ⇑ emblem, trademark

-logy. See **-ology**.

loin /lɔɪn/, **loins**. Someone's **loins** are the front part of their body between their waist and thighs, especially their sexual parts; a literary or old-fashioned word. EG *My loins still tingle when I think of her... ...Sam, the son of his loins.* N PLURAL ⇑ genitals

2 Loin or a **loin** is a piece of meat which comes from the back or sides of an animal, quite near the tail end. EG *...loin chops... ...loin of veal in cream and brandy.* N UNCOUNT/COUNT

3 If you **gird up** your **loins** or **gird** your **loins**, you prepare to do something difficult or dangerous; an old-fashioned expression. EG *It's time for them to leave their cushioned chairs, gird up their loins and stride out into the world.* PHR: VB INFLECTS

loincloth /lɔɪklɒθ/, **loincloths**. A **loincloth** is a piece of cloth that men sometimes wear in order to cover their sexual parts, especially in hot countries when it is too hot to wear any other form of clothing. EG *...an old man, bareheaded, barefoot and wearing only a loincloth.* N COUNT ⇑ clothing

loiter /lɔɪtə/, **loiters, loitering, loitered**. If you **loiter** somewhere, you remain there or walk up and down without any real purpose. EG *Remember not to loiter on the way.* • **loitering with intent**: see **intent**. V ⇑ wait = linger

loll /lɒl/, **lolls, lolling, lolled**. **1** If you **loll** somewhere or **loll about**, you sit or lie in a very relaxed position. EG *The students lolled in the grass... He kept saying he should be at home and not lolling about in the summer sun.* V+A, OR PHRASAL VB: V+ADV = lounge, sprawl

2 If something fairly heavy, especially someone's head or tongue, **lolls**, it hangs down in a loose, uncontrolled way. EG *Her tongue lolled out, her eyes were rolled back... ...feeling so sleepy, head lolling, eyes closing.* V: USU+A = flop

lollipop /lɒlipɒp/, **lollipops**. A **lollipop** is **1** a sweet consisting of a hard disc or ball of a sugary substance on the end of a stick. EG *She was sitting on the front step sucking a lollipop.* **2** a piece of ice flavoured with fruit that is frozen onto a stick and eaten as a sweet. N COUNT = lolly; N COUNT = lolly

lollipop lady, lollipop ladies; an informal expression in British English. A **lollipop lady** is a woman whose job is to help children cross a particular road safely. She carries a pole with a circular sign at the top that tells traffic to stop. N COUNT

lollipop man, lollipop men; an informal expression in British English. A **lollipop man** is a man who does the same job as a lollipop lady. N COUNT

lollop /lɒləp/, **lollops, lolloping, lolloped**. When an animal or perhaps a person **lollops** along, they run along awkwardly and not very fast; an informal word. EG *...a lolloping hound, eager for the chase.* V: USU+A ⇑ bound = lope

lolly /lɒli¹/, **lollies**; an informal word. **1** A **lolly** is **1.1** a sweet consisting of a hard disc or ball of a sugary substance on the end of a stick. **1.2** a piece of ice flavoured with fruit that is frozen onto a stick and eaten as a sweet. N COUNT; N COUNT = ice lolly

2 Lolly is money; a slightly old-fashioned informal use. EG *They took all his lolly and his clothes.* N UNCOUNT = dough

lone /ləʊn/. **1** A **lone** person or thing is alone or is the only one in a particular place or group. EG *They saw ahead a lone figure walking towards them on the trail... He was accompanied by a lone Secret Service man... They made a concerted attack on the area's lone hospital.* ADJ CLASSIF: ATTRIB = single, solitary

2 A **lone** parent is a parent who is looking after his or her child or children and who is not married or living with a partner. EG *Only seventeen per cent of lone mothers own their homes.* ADJ CLASSIF: ATTRIB = single

3 lone wolf: see **wolf**.

loneliness /ləʊnlinɪ²s/ is the unhappiness that is felt by someone because they do not have any friends or do not have anyone to talk to. EG *They suffer from isolation, poverty and loneliness.* N UNCOUNT

lonely /ləʊnli¹/, **lonelier, loneliest**. **1** Someone who is **lonely** is unhappy because they do not have any friends or do not have anyone to talk to. EG *He was rather sad and lonely. I believe his wife ran off with another man... I didn't feel lonely at all... ...lonely widows.* ▸ The **lonely** is used to refer to lonely people. EG *The old, the sick and the lonely are most at risk.* ADJ QUALIT = lonesome, desolate ▸ N PLURAL: *the*+N

2 A **lonely** situation or period of time is one in which you feel lonely and unhappy. EG *...a lonely childhood... Saturday still looms large as the loneliest day of the week... I've always heard it's lonely here at the top.* ADJ QUALIT = forsaken

3 A **lonely** place is one where very few people come and which is a long way from places where people live. EG *...lonely country roads... ...the loneliest and most desolate places on earth.* ADJ QUALIT ⇑ remote = deserted

4 A **lonely** sound is long and high-pitched and sounds rather sad or strange; a literary use. EG *Our ears were full of the high and lonely lament of the wind.* ADJ QUALIT = haunting, mournful

lonely hearts. A **lonely hearts** section in a newspaper or a **lonely hearts** club is used by people who are trying to find a lover or friend. N BEFORE N

loner /ləʊnə/, **loners**. A **loner** is a person who prefers to be alone rather than with a group of people, and who perhaps has opinions which are different from other people's. EG *He was aloof, a loner. He kept his distance.* N COUNT ⇑ individualist

lonesome /ləʊnsə⁰m/; an informal word used mainly in American English. **1** Someone who is **lonesome** is unhappy because they do not have any friends or do not have anyone to talk to. EG *Don't you know that boy is lonesome?* ADJ QUALIT = lonely, forsaken

2 A **lonesome** place is one where very few people come and which is a long way from places where people live. EG *...a lonesome valley.* ADJ QUALIT ⇑ remote = deserted

long /lɒŋ/, **longs, longing, longed**; **longer** /lɒŋgə/, **longest** /lɒŋgɪ²st/. **1** You use **long** to say that a great amount of time passes while something is happening or is in existence. EG *I haven't known her that long... Sorry it took so long... I won't be long. Stay right here... It was not long before they reached the village... Our oil won't last very much longer... ...Britain's longest surviving transplant patient... This is a difficulty that has long been recognized.* ADV WITH VB

2 A **long** period of time, event, task, etc lasts for a great amount of time or takes a great amount of time. EG *There was a long pause... I should think it would last quite a long time... They are demanding longer holidays... We sat there for a long while... ...the long hot dry season.* ◊ **longish**. EG *There was a longish pause.* ADJ QUALIT ≠ short ◊ ADJ CLASSIF: ATTRIB

3 Something that happened **long** before the present time or before a particular point in time, or happens **long** after it, happened a great amount of time before it or happens a great amount of time after it. EG *She thought I had guessed long ago... Not long after our arrival a curious thing happened... It was at this point, long before their marriage, that he began to feel doubtful... The shipbuilding industry on the Clyde had long been abandoned.* ADV, OR ADJ QUALIT: ATTRIB

4 If something does not happen or is not the case **for long** or **for much longer**, it happens or is the case for only a small period of time after a particular point in time. EG *Few of these organizations survive for long... It can't go on for much longer.* PHR: USED AS AN A, WITH BROAD NEG

5 The expressions **for long** and **for longer** are used when you are saying that something happens or is the case for a great amount of time, or for a greater amount of time than has already passed or than is mentioned. EG *Both men and women have been indoctrinated for too long... Can I keep it for a bit longer?... They have been involved for much longer than I have.* PHR: USED AS AN A

6 Long is used after 'how' to ask questions about amounts of time, and is sometimes also used when you are giving information about amounts of time. EG ADV: *how*+ADV, OR *as*+ADV+*as*, OR ADJ AFTER N

'How long have you been married?'–'Five years.'... How much longer can you stay?... How long is it since he died?... How long are you staying for?... She had taken care of them for as long as they could remember... The documentary is an hour and a half long.

7 Something that is **no longer** the case, or **no longer** happens, used to be the case but is not the case now, or happened in the past but does not happen now. EG *Maths is no longer a prime requirement for a career in accountancy... We can no longer afford to live there... Suddenly, I couldn't stand it any longer.* PHR : USED AS ADV SEN = no more

8 If you say that something will happen **before long**, you mean that it will happen soon. EG *They're bound to catch the poor devil before long.* PHR : USED AS ADV SEN

9 A **long** period of work or activity lasts for more hours or days than is usual. EG *I'm sorry. It's just been a long day... I work long, hard hours.* ADJ QUALIT ≠ short

10 **Long** is used in expressions such as 'all year long', 'the whole day long', and 'your whole life long' to say and emphasize that something happens for the whole of a particular period of time. EG *I don't think there was any rain all summer long.*

11 Something that is **long** measures a great distance from one end to the other. EG *She was slender and had long dark hair... ...a long line of cars... She pedalled up the long drive towards the house... ...long Russian names... ...an enormously long room... The women sat at long tables.* ADJ QUALIT ≠ short

12 **Long** dresses, trousers, sleeves, etc reach to the ankle or wrist rather than, for example, to the calf, knee, or elbow. EG *A tall lean woman in a long dress climbed into a Rolls Royce.* ADJ CLASSIF : ATTRIB = full length

13 A **long** distance, journey, route, etc is a great distance or covers a great distance. EG *It may look a long way on the map but it isn't... They run long distances at speed as a test of endurance... They took him on long hikes through the hills.* ADJ QUALIT : USU ATTRIB ≠ short

14 **Long** is used when giving information about the length of something or sometimes to ask questions about the length of something. EG *...an area up to 3,000 feet long and 900 feet wide... How long is that side of the triangle?* ADJ AFTER N, OR ADJ : *how*+ADJ

15 A **long** book, article, list, programme, film, etc contains a lot of information or a lot of items and takes a lot of time to read, watch, deal with, etc. EG *I sent you rather a long list of questions... It's the longest and most ambitious book she has produced so far... Romeo is a very long and arduous part... It's a long story, I won't bother you with it now.* ADJ QUALIT : USU ATTRIB ⇑ large
◊ **longish**. EG *...a longish novel.* ◊ ADJ CLASSIF

16 A **long** period of time or a **long** distance is also one that seems to take or last a much greater time than it actually does. EG *It was awful waiting for the phone to ring. Days spread into long months... That was a long two miles!* ADJ QUALIT : ATTRIB

17 If someone has a **long** memory, they are able to remember things that happened far back in the past. ADJ QUALIT : USU ATTRIB

18 If you **long** for something, especially something that you are unlikely to get or that is unlikely to happen, you want it very much. EG *They longed for green trees and open spaces... She was exhausted and longing for them to go... They're just longing to see you.* V+*to*-INF/*for* = yearn

19 The expressions **as long as** and **so long as** are used in the following ways. **19.1** If you say that something is the case **as long as** or **so long as** something else is the case, you mean that it is only the case if the second thing is the case. EG *We were all right as long as we kept our heads down... Detergent cannot harm a fabric, so long as it has been properly dissolved.* CONJ SUBORD **19.2** If you say **as long as** or **so long as** something is the case, you are indicating that you will only be satisfied if it is the case. EG *'I've got something for you that will make you feel better.'–'As long as it's not another medicine.'* CONJ SUBORD **19.3** If something happens or is the case **so long as** or **as long as** something else happens or is the case, it happens or is the case all the time that the second thing is happening or is the case. EG *You couldn't turn the heat off as long as the system was operating.* CONJ SUBORD = while, whilst

20 You say **long live** a particular person or thing as a way of indicating that you support them and want them to live or last for a long time. EG *Long live the Queen!... Long live television!* PHR+NG : USED AS CONVENTION

21 If you refer to **the long and the short of it**, you are referring to the basic facts of a situation that you are mentioning or summarizing. EG *The long and the short of it is that they are being made bankrupt.* PHR : USED AS S/ C/O

22 You say **so long** as an informal way of saying goodbye. EG *'Well. So long.' He turned and walked back to the car.* CONVENTION = bye, see you

23 • **as long as** your **arm**: see **arm**. • **not by a long chalk**: see **chalk**. • **a long face**: see **face**. • **at long last**: see **last**. • **in the long run**: see **run**. • **a long shot**: see **shot**. • **long since**: see **since**. • **long in the tooth**: see **tooth**. • to **take the long view**: see **view**. • to **go a long way**: see **way**. • See also **longing**.

long-awaited. A **long-awaited** event or thing is one that someone has been waiting for for a long time. EG *His long-awaited opportunity had now at last come.* ADJ CLASSIF : ATTRIB

longbow /lɒŋbəʊ/, **longbows**. A **longbow** is a weapon for firing arrows used especially by medieval archers. N COUNT ⇑ weapon

long-distance is used to describe **1** travel between places that are far apart. EG *...a long-distance runner... ...long-distance motor coaches... ...long-distance air travel.* ADJ CLASSIF : ATTRIB **2** communication that takes place between people who are far apart. EG *...long-distance phone calls.* ADJ CLASSIF : ATTRIB ▸ used as an adverb. EG *He called me long-distance from Miami.* ▸ ADV AFTER VB

long division, long divisions. Long division is a method of dividing one large number by another which involves writing out all the stages instead of doing some of them in your head. N UNCOUNT/ COUNT ⇑ calculation

long-drawn-out. A **long-drawn-out** process, conflict, etc lasts an unnecessarily long time or an unpleasantly long time. EG *...a long-drawn-out struggle.* ADJ CLASSIF : ATTRIB ⇑ lengthy = prolonged, tedious

long drink, long drinks. A **long drink** is a drink which consists of or contains a large amount of either a non-alcoholic drink or a weak alcoholic drink. N COUNT

longed-for. A **longed-for** thing or event is one that someone wants very much. EG *At last the longed-for refreshment arrived.* ADJ CLASSIF : ATTRIB ⇑ craved

longevity /lɒndʒe̲vɪti[1]/ is long life or existence. EG *...improved health care resulting in increased longevity... Many offer the longevity of their marriage as proof of enduring love.* N UNCOUNT

longhand /lɒ̲ŋhænd/. If you write something down in **longhand**, you write it by hand using complete words and normal letters rather than typing it or using shortened forms or special symbols. EG *The clerk had to write all the evidence down in longhand.* N UNCOUNT ⇑ writing

longing /lɒ̲ŋɪŋ/, **longings**. **Longing** or a **longing** is a rather sad feeling of wanting something very much, especially something that you are unlikely to get. EG *He gazed with longing and apprehension into the future... Soon several of them were divulging their secret longings... People have a longing for normality.* N COUNT/ UNCOUNT ⇑ desire = yearning

longingly /lɒ̲ŋɪŋli[1]/. If you look **longingly** at something you want or think **longingly** about it, you look at it or think about it with a feeling of desire. EG *I eyed the cold drinks longingly... I began to think longingly of bed.* ADV WITH VB

longitude /lɒ̲ŋɪtju:d/, **longitudes**. A **longitude** is a position on a map of the world measured as the distance to the East or West of a set line: compare **latitude**. N COUNT/ UNCOUNT

longitudinal /lɒndʒɪtju̲:dɪnə[0]l/. A **longitudinal** measurement, axis, cross-section, etc goes from one end of an object to the other rather than across it from side to side; a technical term. EG *It then falls, spinning rapidly about its longitudinal axis.* ADJ CLASSIF : ATTRIB
◊ **longitudinally**. EG *The fibres run longitudinally.* ◊ ADV WITH VB

long johns /lɒ̲ŋ dʒɒnz/ are warm underpants with long legs. N PLURAL : ALSO *a pair of*+N

long jump. The **long jump** is an athletics contest which involves jumping as far as you can from a marker which you run up to. N SING, *the*+N

long-lasting, longer-lasting. Something that is **long-lasting** lasts for a long time. EG *The failure of the dam is unlikely to have long-lasting environmental consequences... Solid rubber is longer-lasting.* ADJ QUALIT

long-life. **Long-life** milk, fruit juice, or batteries last a longer time than the ordinary sort. ADJ CLASSIF : ATTRIB

long-lived. Something that is **long-lived** lives or lasts for a long time. EG *Bats are, for their size, surprisingly long-lived creatures... ...an explosive and long-lived rebellion.* ADJ QUALIT

long-lost. **Long-lost** is used of someone or something that has not been seen for a long time by a particular person or by anyone. EG *She greeted me like a long-lost daughter... These pictures were based on a long-lost mosaic.* — ADJ CLASSIF : ATTRIB ⇑ missing

long-range. 1 A **long-range** piece of military equipment, vehicle, etc is able to hit or detect a target a long way away or to travel a long way in order to do something. EG *...a modern long-range strategic missile... ...a long-range assassin's rifle... ...long-range bombers.* — ADJ CLASSIF : ATTRIB

2 A **long-range** plan, aim, prediction, effect, etc affects, covers, or relates to a period extending a long time into the future. EG *At that time I was making no long-range plans... ...the long-range weather forecast.* — ADJ CLASSIF : ATTRIB

long-running, longest-running. A **long-running** play or television programme has been performed or in existence for a long time. EG *...a long-running soap opera.* — ADJ QUALIT : ATTRIB

longshoreman /lɒŋʃɔːmᵊn/, **longshoremen**. A **longshoreman** is a person who works in the docks, loading and unloading ships; used in American English. — N COUNT ⇑ worker = docker

long-sighted. If you are **long-sighted**, you can only see things clearly when they are quite far away. — ADJ QUALIT

long-standing. Something that is **long-standing** has existed for a long time. EG *...his long-standing reputation as a scholar... The British Government accepted a long-standing offer from the International Committee.* — ADJ QUALIT

long-suffering. Someone who is **long-suffering** patiently bears continual trouble or unhappiness, especially unhappiness caused by someone else. EG *...his noble, long-suffering wife.* — ADJ QUALIT

long-term, longer-term. 1 **Long-term** is used of things that will continue for a very long time or will be effective for a very long time in the future. EG *Regional Health Authorities are responsible for long-term planning in their regions... ...hopes for a long-term solution to the problem... ...long-term prisoners... I hesitated before making a long-term commitment of this importance.* — ADJ QUALIT : USU ATTRIB ≠ short-term

2 When you talk about what happens in the **long term**, you are talking about what happens over a long period of time, either in the future or after a particular event. EG *The results, in the long term, were academic success stories... Industry needs to compete effectively over the long term.* — N SING : *the*+N

long-time. **Long-time** is used of something that has existed or been a particular thing for a long time. EG *He set off, accompanied by his long-time friend and travelling companion Ralph Taylor... ...a wildlife photographer with a long-time interest in owls.* — ADJ CLASSIF : ATTRIB = long-standing

long vacation, long vacations. The **long vacation** is the period of time during the summer when universities, colleges, and schools are closed. — N COUNT : IF SING *the*+N = summer holidays

long wave is a range of radio waves used for broadcasting which are 1000 or more metres in length. EG *This programme will be broadcast on long wave only... You can get Radio 4 on 200 kHz long wave.* — N UNCOUNT ⇑ waveband = LW

long-winded. If something that is written or said is **long-winded**, it contains many more words than are necessary and is therefore boring. EG *When you get back, write a report–not too long-winded, you don't want to bore people.* ▸ used of people. EG *The speaker was young, ardent, and appallingly long-winded.* — ADJ QUALIT ≠ concise, neat, terse; ▸ ⇑ loquacious

loo /luː/, **loos**. A **loo** is a toilet; an informal word. EG *I think she's in the loo... David said he wanted to go to the loo.* — N COUNT : USU *the*+N IN SING

loofah /luːfə/, **loofahs**. A **loofah** is an object like a long, rough sponge, which you use to wash yourself in the bath. — N COUNT

look /lʊk/, **looks, looking, looked**. 1 If you **look** in a particular direction, you direct your eyes in that direction, especially so that you can see what is there or see what something is like. EG *She turned to look out of the back window... They looked across the room at each other... Their eyes met and he blushed and looked away... His father looked up and grunted, then went back to his work... When I look hard I can see stars overhead.* ▸ used as a noun. EG *Take a good look and tell me if you see anything different... Did you have a look at the shop when you were there?* — V : USU+A; ▸ N COUNT : USU SING

2 If you **look** at something that is moving or happening, or at the television, you watch it. EG *People like to look at animals and birds... You spend far too much of your time looking at the television.* — V+A *(at)*

3 If you **look** at a book, newspaper, etc, you read it fairly quickly or read part of it. EG *I've looked at your essay and I think it's very good.* ▸ used as a noun. EG *One look at a newspaper would show that this idea is absurd.* — V+A *(at)*; ▸ N SING WITH DET

4 If someone, especially an expert, **looks** at something, they examine it, and then deal with it or say how it should be dealt with. EG *That leg's a bit swollen. I'd like John Wells to look at it.* ▸ used as a noun. EG *Could you take a look at this please, John?* — V+A *(at)*; ▸ N SING WITH DET

5 If you give someone a **look**, you direct your eyes at them with an expression on your face that shows what you are feeling or thinking. EG *Don't give me such severe looks. What have I done?... She gave me a look and said, 'I don't suppose you like me much.'* — N COUNT : USU+SUPP

6 If you take a **look** at an interesting place or building, you visit it, especially informally or for a short time. EG *Since you're so close, you really ought to take a look at the canals of Venice... The interior of the building is well worth a look.* — N COUNT : USU SING

7 If you **look** for someone or something, for example something that you have lost or that you want or need, you try to find it or see it. EG *I've been looking for you all over... She took a pencil out of her pocket and looked around for some paper... I've looked everywhere!... There are a lot of people looking for houses in this area... There was a flood of people looking for work.* ▸ used as a noun. EG *Have another look. It must be there.* — V : IF+PREP THEN *for* = search; ▸ N COUNT : USU SING

8 If you are **looking** for something such as the solution to a problem or a new method, you want it and are trying to obtain it or think of it. EG *Britain is looking for a peaceful, diplomatic solution... What we are looking for is a firm commitment on the part of the government.* — V+A *(for)* ⇑ pursuing

9 If you **look** at something such as a particular subject, problem, or situation, you think about it or study it, so that you know all about it and can perhaps consider what should be done in relation to it. EG *Let's look at the implications of some of these changes... Bowlby looked at children in institutions and claimed that they suffered no deprivation at all.* ▸ used as a noun. EG *The figures indicate we have to take a hard look at the whole situation... Tonight we're going to have a look at some aspects of the social services.* — V+A *(at)*; ▸ N SING WITH DET ⇑ consideration

10 If you **look** at a particular situation or subject from a particular point of view, you judge it or consider it from that point of view. EG *If you're a Democrat, you look at things one way, and if you're a Republican you look at them in a very different way... Look at it my way.* — V+A *(at)* = see

11 You say **look** when you want someone to pay attention to you because you are going to say something important. EG *Bill? Look, I want to go to Europe for six months... Look, Paul, this is ridiculous... Now look, Mrs Kintner, you've got it wrong.* — CONVENTION

12 You say **look here** when you are going to say something important to someone, especially when you are angry or upset at something they have done; a slightly old-fashioned expression. EG *Now look here, old boy, there's no need for that sort of behaviour.* — CONVENTION

13 You say **look** at a particular situation, person, or thing when you want to draw attention to it, for example because you find it very surprising, annoying, or shocking. EG *My God, look at the time. I promised I'd be home at six... Now look what you've done... 'You just can't afford to make any mistakes. Look at Judy.'–'Yes, poor Judy.'* — V+A *(at)*, OR V+WH : ONLY IMPER

14 If a window, room, or building **looks** out onto a particular thing or area, it has a view of that thing. EG *The kitchen window looks out onto a yard... Our house looks out over the reservoir.* — V+A = give onto

15 You say that someone or something **looks** nice, ill, sad, etc when describing or commenting on their appearance or expression. EG *You look very pale... Doesn't she look lovely?... The place looked a bit bare without them... The animal looks like a large flattened hedgehog... He looked scared... He looked as if he hadn't slept very much... She looked English.* — V+C, OR V+A *(as/like)* ⇑ appear, seem

● When you talk about what someone or something **looks like**, you are talking about their appearance. EG *'What does he look like?'–'Pale, thin, dark-* — ● PHR : VB INFLECTS *haired.'... Try it on. Let's see what it looks like on you.*

16 If someone or something has a particular **look**, they have the appearance or expression indicated. EG *He didn't have a sick look about him any more... He didn't have the look of a man who was thinking... There is a nervous look in their eyes... Everything had a sad, faded look.* N SING WITH DET + SUPP = mien

17 When you refer to someone's **looks**, you are referring to how beautiful or ugly they are, especially how beautiful they are. EG *She had lost her looks... I don't think much of his looks!... She had everything: looks and youth and sophistication.* • See also **good looks**. N PLURAL

18 A particular **look** is a particular style of clothes, hairstyles, furniture, etc which is in fashion. EG *This year's look is short skirts and T-shirts... ...the punk look.* N COUNT + SUPP

19 You say that a situation or thing **looks** good, interesting, depressing, etc, or that it **looks** like something is the case or will happen, when you are saying how it seems to you or are expressing an opinion about it. EG *The plan looks impressive enough on paper... Things look black for the husband... It looks to me as if he wrote down some notes while he was listening... Looks like we're going to be late again... It looks like rain.* V + C, OR V + A *(as if/like)* = appear

20 You use **by the look of** and **by the looks of** something or someone when you are expressing an opinion about something or someone that seems to be true, judging by their appearance. EG *It's been there all summer by the look of it.* PHR : USED AS AN A = apparently

21 If you **don't like the look of** a situation or thing, you feel that it may be dangerous or result in something harmful or unpleasant. EG *I don't like the look of this at all.* PHR : AUX INFLECTS

22 If you **are not looking yourself**, you appear rather ill or tired. PHR : AUX INFLECTS

23 If someone **looks** you **up and down**, they direct their eyes over the whole length of your body, from your head to your feet, in a superior way, as though they are inspecting you; used showing disapproval. PHR : VB INFLECTS

24 If you **look** someone **in the face** or **look** someone **in the eye**, you look straight at their eyes in a bold and open way, for example in order to make them realize that you are not afraid of them or that you are telling the truth. EG *I stood my ground and looked her straight in the eye.* PHR : VB INFLECTS

25 The word **look** is also used in the following expressions, which are explained at other places in this dictionary. • to **look before you leap**: see **leap**. • **look lively**: see **lively**. • to **look down** your **nose at** someone: see **nose**. • **look sharp**: see **sharp**. • to **look small**: see **small**.

look after. 1 If you **look after** someone or something, you take care of them and do what is necessary for them to stay in good condition. EG *Does your husband accept that he ought to be looking after the baby?... Look after my garden... Look after your new car. Don't abuse it.* PHRASAL VB : V + PREP, HAS PASS = tend

2 If you **look after** something, you are responsible for it and deal with it or make sure it is all right, especially because it is your job to do so. EG *Do you think Walker should stay there all the time to look after things?... They look after the employment and finance of doctors... The duty of the local authority is to look after the interests of local people.* PHRASAL VB : V + PREP, HAS PASS = tend

3 If you **look after** something that belongs to someone else, you take charge of it for them so that you can prevent it from being lost or damaged. EG *Will you look after my money for me while I go swimming?* PHRASAL VB : V + PREP, HAS PASS

4 If you can **look after** yourself, you are able to make sure that you are not harmed or cheated by other people. PHR : VB INFLECTS

look ahead. If you **look ahead**, you think about what is going to happen in the future and perhaps make plans for the future. EG *We're trying to look ahead... You'll need to look ahead four or five years.* PHRASAL VB : V + ADV

look back. 1 If you **look back**, you think about things that happened in the past. EG *People can often look back and reflect on happy childhood memories... The past always seems better when you look back on it.* PHRASAL VB : V + ADV, IF + PREP THEN *on* ↑ remember

2 If you say that someone did something and **never looked back**, you mean that they then became very successful. EG *He borrowed $10,000 to start his Hollywood restaurant and never looked back.* PHR ↑ succeed

look down on. If you **look down on** someone or something, you think that they are inferior or unimportant. EG *The farm labourer used to be looked down on.* PHRASAL VB : V + ADV + PREP = despise

look forward to. If you **look forward** to something that is going to happen, you want it to happen because you think you will enjoy it. EG *I'm quite looking forward to it... I look forward to seeing you in Washington.* PHRASAL VB : V + ADV + PREP ↑ anticipate

look in. If you **look in** on a person or place, you visit them for a short time; used especially when your visit was not planned in advance. EG *Could I look in on Sam?* • See also **look-in**. PHRASAL VB : V + ADV, IF + PREP THEN *on* = drop in

look into. If you **look into** a particular problem, subject, situation, etc, you find out and examine the facts relating to it. EG *In 1959 a working party was set up to look into the problem... They wanted an independent financial controller to look into the city's accounts.* PHRASAL VB : V + PREP, HAS PASS = investigate

look on. 1 If you **look on** while something happens, you watch it happening without taking part yourself. EG *His parents looked on with a triumphant smile as he collected his prize.* PHRASAL VB : V + ADV

2 If you **look on** something as a particular thing or in a particular way, you think of it as that thing or in that way. EG *She looked on us as simpletons.* PHRASAL VB : V + PREP + A, HAS PASS = consider

look out. 1 You say or shout **'look out'** to warn someone that they are in danger. EG *'Look out,' I said. 'There's something coming.'* CONVENTION = watch out

2 If you **look out** for a particular problem or danger that you are aware of, you are careful and try to avoid it. EG *Just a word of warning: look out for union problems.* PHRASAL VB : V + ADV, IF + PREP THEN *for* = watch out

3 If you **look out** something that is stored away, you find it and take it out, for example because you want to show it to someone. EG *I'll look out that dress for you this evening.* PHRASAL VB : V + O + ADV

4 See also **lookout**.

look out for. 1 If you **look out for** a particular thing that you want to find or see, you pay attention to things around you so that you notice that thing. EG *If you are choosing a red wine, look out for Chianti... It's a film we shall look out for in the next couple of months.* PHRASAL VB : V + ADV + PREP

2 If you **look out for** yourself, you make sure that you have all the advantages that you can. EG *We all look out for number one.* PHRASAL VB : V + ADV + PREP

look over. If you **look** something **over**, you examine it quite quickly in order to get a general idea of what it is like. EG *Sometimes he used to look over the article I had written, shrug, and tear it up... He was called in to look over the bomb damage to the House of Commons.* PHRASAL VB : V + O + ADV

look round. If you **look round** a large building or place, you walk round it and look at the different parts of it. EG *Shall we look round the Cathedral this afternoon?* PHRASAL VB : V + PREP

look through. If you **look through** a group of things, you examine each one so that you can find or choose the one that you want. EG *He looked through the clothing on the bed... They will look through the applications and pick out the best.* PHRASAL VB : V + PREP, HAS PASS = sift through

2 If you **look through** something that has been written or printed, you read it carefully to check that there are no mistakes in it. EG *I always looked through my work carefully before I handed it in.* PHRASAL VB : V + PREP, HAS PASS

3 If you say that someone **looks through** another person, you mean that they look at that person without showing that they have seen them or recognized them, for example because they are angry with them or are thinking deeply about something else. EG *They looked straight through him.* PHRASAL VB : V + PREP ↑ ignore

look to. 1 If you **look to** someone or something for a particular thing that you want, for example help or advice, you expect or hope that they will provide it. EG *We should look to the economists for advice on how to overcome inflation... Many people in the community would be looking to us for leadership... They look to others to structure time for them... People look to education to bring this about.* PHRASAL VB : V + PREP, USU + *to-INF/for*, HAS PASS ↑ ask = turn to

2 If you **look to** something, you make sure that it is in good condition or you protect it, rather than neglecting it; a formal use. EG *They must look to their defences... Look to your health.* PHRASAL VB : V + PREP, HAS PASS = take care of

3 If you **look to** something that will happen in the PHRASAL VB : V +

future, you think about it, often with a particular emotion. EG *Some New Englanders look to the future with a certain anxiety.* PREP, HAS PASS

4 If you tell someone to **look to it** that something is done, you are telling them to make sure that it is done. EG *Look to it that you have got all this done by this evening.* PHR : USU IMPER +REPORT-CL

look up. 1 If you **look up** a fact or a piece of information, you find it out by looking in a reference book, a list, etc. EG *He consulted his dictionary to look up the meaning of the word 'apotheosis'.* PHRASAL VB : V+O+ADV

2 If you **look** someone **up**, you visit them after not having seen them for a long time. EG *Look me up when you're next in the area.* PHRASAL VB : V+O+ADV

3 If a situation **is looking up**, it is improving; a fairly informal use. EG *Things are looking up.* PHRASAL VB : V+ADV, USU CONT

look upon. If you **look upon** something as a particular thing or in a particular way, you think of it as that thing or in that way. EG *Houses are looked upon as investments... The nuclear powers would not look kindly upon such a development.* PHRASAL VB : V+PREP+A, HAS PASS = consider, regard, look on

look up to. If you **look up to** someone, you respect and admire them. EG *She looks up to her father.* PHRASAL VB : V+ADV+PREP

look-alike, look-alikes. A **look-alike** is someone who has a very similar appearance to another person, especially a well-known person. EG *It was only the Minister's look-alike.* N COUNT = double

looker-on, lookers-on. A **looker-on** is someone who watches an activity or event, often from a distance, without taking any part in it themselves. N COUNT = onlooker

look-in. If you are trying to do something or take part in an activity and you do not get a **look-in**, you are unable to do it or take part because other people are more successful than you or more forceful in their behaviour; an informal expression. EG *James talks so much that all the others barely get a look-in.* N SING : a+N, WITH BROAD NEG ⇑ chance

-looking is used after adjectives to form other adjectives which describe what someone or something looks like. EG *...a very bright-looking girl... He pretended interest in a dull-looking intellectual weekly.* COMB : FORMS ADJS

looking-glass, looking-glasses. A **looking-glass** is a mirror; an old-fashioned word. N COUNT

lookout /lu̲kaut/, **lookouts**; also spelled with a hyphen. 1 A **lookout** is 1.1 a place that is usually quite high up, for example in a building or on a ship, from which you can see clearly in all directions. N COUNT 1.2 someone who is watching for danger, for example from a ship or building. EG *Two of the burglars were tipped off by a lookout and escaped... ...a night's lookout duty.* N COUNT = sentry

2 If you are **on the lookout**, you are paying attention to things around you so that you know what is happening and are able to take opportunities as they arise. EG *Everyone here is on the lookout for extra work.* PHR : USED AS AN A

3 If you are **keeping a lookout** for something, you are paying attention carefully to things around you all the time so that you will notice it when it appears or happens. EG *Insects cannot keep a good lookout for predators all the time.* PHR : VB INFLECTS ⇑ watch

4 If someone tells you that something is **your lookout**, they mean that it is you who will suffer if you do not do anything about the situation you are in; an informal expression. EG *If he wants to throw his money away that's his lookout.* PHR : USED AS C

loom /lu̲:m/, **looms, looming, loomed**. 1 If something **looms**, 1.1 it appears as a tall, unclear shape, often in a frightening way. EG *As you get closer they loom above you like icebergs.* ◊ **looming**. EG *...the looming towers of Oxford Street.* V : USU+A = tower ◊ ADJ CLASSIF 1.2 it appears as a problem or event that is approaching, or that will soon happen; a rather literary use. EG *The shadow of euthanasia will loom ever closer... Strictness or permissiveness?–This looms as a big question for many new parents.* ◊ **looming**. EG *...industrial problems ranging from technology gaps to looming trade wars.* V ⇑ approach = threaten ◊ ADJ CLASSIF = impending

2 If a problem or event **looms large**, it appears in your mind as a frightening prospect that you feel you cannot avoid. EG *Saturday still looms large as the loneliest day of the week.* PHR : VB INFLECTS

3 A **loom** is a machine that is used for weaving thread into cloth. EG *A series of rods carry the threads into the loom.* N COUNT

loom up. If something **looms up**, it comes into sight as a tall, unclear shape, often in a frightening way. EG *...a huge Victorian edifice that loomed up.* PHRASAL VB : V+ADV ⇑ appear

loony /lu̲:ni[1]/, **loonier, looniest; loonies**. **Loony** is a very informal word. 1 **Loony** behaviour or ideas seem mad, strange, or eccentric. EG *There seems to be this loony idea that you have to be passionately in love.* ADJ QUALIT = barmy

2 A **loony** is a person who behaves in a way that seems mad, strange, or eccentric. EG *...some poor old loony repeating the same bit of nonsense.* N COUNT = weirdo

loony bin, loony bins. A **loony bin** is a psychiatric hospital; a very informal expression. N COUNT

loop /lu̲:p/, **loops, looping, looped**. 1 A **loop** is a curved or circular shape in something long. You can make a loop by taking a piece of string and crossing one end over the other. EG *With any luck the ring will have fallen in the loop of pipe under the sink... Her wavy hair fell in loose wisps and loops upon her shoulders.* N COUNT ⇑ circle

2 If you **loop** something such as a piece of rope around an object, you tie a length of it in a loop around the object, usually in order to fasten the object. EG *Ropes were being looped around him and he was helpless to resist.* V+O : USU+A = coil

3 If something **loops**, it goes in a circular direction that makes the shape of a loop. EG *Trails loop and weave through the tall trees.* V = curve ● When an aeroplane **loops the loop**, it flies in a vertical circle so that it goes upside down and then comes back to being the right way up again. EG *I saw the plane loop the loop right over the church.* ● PHR : VB INFLECTS

4 A **loop**, in a computer program, is a set of instructions that is arranged in such a way that the computer must return to a task and complete it before it can start the next task; a technical term. EG *I would need to add an extra loop involving fifty or so steps.* N COUNT ⇑ series

loophole /lu̲:phəʊl/, **loopholes**. A **loophole** is a small mistake or omission in the law, so that you can avoid doing something that the law intends you to do. For example, some people do not pay very much tax because of loopholes in the law. EG *The next Labour government intends to tighten the loopholes in those acts.* N COUNT : IF+PREP THEN *in* ⇑ error

loose /lu̲:s/, **looser, loosest; looses, loosing, loosed**. 1 Something that is **loose** is 1.1 not firmly held or fixed in place. EG *The doorknob is loose and rattles... Make sure that there are no loose strands of wire... One tooth was missing and another so loose that it was going to be missing very soon.* ◊ **loosely**. EG *Willie held the phone loosely.* ADJ QUALIT = wobbly ≠ firm ◊ ADV WITH VB 1.2 not attached to anything else. EG *...a few loose sheets of paper... They had time to rake up all the loose corn before the farmer came back... Green leaves had been beaten loose by the rain of the night before.* ● to **have a screw loose**: see **screw**. ADJ CLASSIF

2 Clothes that are **loose** are rather large and do not fit very closely to your body. EG *Mary wore loose clothes that did not show off her figure... He was hot beneath the loose cotton shirt.* ◊ **loosely**. EG *His black garments hung loosely from powerful shoulders.* ◊ **looseness**. EG *He noticed the conservative looseness of her dress.* ADJ QUALIT = baggy ≠ tight ◊ ADV WITH VB ≠ tightly ◊ N UNCOUNT+SUPP

3 If someone's skin is **loose**, it is not stretched tightly over their bones, for example because they are old or ill. EG *His mouth was slack, his cheeks loose and flabby... Her skin hung loose and grey.* ADJ QUALIT = slack ≠ taut

4 If your hair is **loose**, it hangs freely round your shoulders and is not tied back. EG *Her long brown hair was loose about her shoulders... ...her brittle blonde hair hung loose.* ADJ CLASSIF

5 If cloth has a **loose** weave, it is not closely woven or knitted. EG *Avoid loose weaves which will develop holes quickly.* ◊ **loosely**. EG *...a loosely woven mesh.* ADJ QUALIT ≠ close, tight ◊ ADV WITH VB

6 If you set people or animals **loose**, you allow them to move freely after you have restrained them or kept them confined. EG *He had taken a pair of white rats into the church and had let them loose on the floor... John's answer to this was to tear himself loose, and go down on his knees.* ADJ CLASSIF = free

7 If people cut **loose** or are set **loose**, they become free from the influence or authority of other people. EG *The younger generation in particular have tended to cut loose from the tentacles of class background... It might be better if the children were let loose a bit earlier.* ADJ CLASSIF : PRED

8 If a person is **on the loose**, they are free because PHR : USED AS AN

they have escaped from a person or place. EG *A bandit leader was on the loose in the hills.* — A = at large

9 Crowds or groups that are **loose** are not very densely grouped together. EG *There were men sitting in loose groups all around the square.* — ADJ QUALIT = straggling

10 If an organization, administration, etc is **loose**, it is not very strictly controlled. EG *They thought that loose organization was more democratic... A loose grouping of 'radicals' was formed which met once a week.* ◇ **loosely**. EG *The book is loosely organized around the theme of war.* ◇ **looseness**. EG *Because of the looseness of its structure, there were considerable problems.* — ADJ QUALIT ⇑ informal ≠ strict; ◇ ADV WITH VB; ◇ N UNCOUNT + SUPP ≠ strictness

11 Expressions, words, meanings, etc that are **loose** are rather vague and not clearly defined. EG *I'm sorry that I have to use this rather loose terminology but I hope you'll know what I mean.* ◇ **loosely**. EG *The term 'dyslexia' has been very loosely used in educational contexts.* — ADJ QUALIT = broad ≠ precise; ◇ ADV WITH VB ≠ precisely

12 If someone has a **loose** tongue, they talk about things that should really be kept secret. — ADJ QUALIT = careless

13 If someone tells you to **stay loose**, **hang loose**, etc, they are telling you to stay calm and relaxed; used in informal American English. EG *'It's all under control,' I replied. 'Stay loose.'* — CONVENTION = keep cool

14 If a woman is described as a **loose** woman, she is considered to be sexually promiscuous; an old-fashioned use showing disapproval. EG *He tried to keep away from loose women.* ▸ used of people's behaviour and attitudes. EG *...loose morals.* — ADJ QUALIT : USU ATTRIB = immoral; ▸ = lax

15 If someone's bowels are **loose**, they have diarrhoea; a rather old-fashioned use. ◇ **looseness**. — ADJ QUALIT; ◇ N UNCOUNT

16 If an unpleasant situation **breaks loose**, it begins or develops very suddenly and rather violently. EG *Chaos often breaks loose in our committee meetings.* — PHR : VB INFLECTS = break out

17 To **loose** something unpleasant means to cause it to begin; a literary use. EG *It remained to be seen whether the gambling-fever loosed by the earlier Act would be ended by the new law.* — V+O = unleash

18 If you **loose** a dangerous person or animal, you release them from where they are being kept; a literary use. EG *The wolves were loosed.* — V+O = let loose

loose cover, loose covers. A **loose cover** is a cover for something such as a chair or cushion, which you can remove when you want to clean it. — N COUNT

loose end, loose ends. **1** A **loose end** is a part of a story, situation, or crime that has not been explained even though the rest of it has been explained or is known. EG *There are too many loose ends in this case.* — N COUNT

2 If you are **at a loose end**, you are bored because you do not have anything to do and cannot think of anything that you want to do; an informal expression. — PHR : USED AS AN A ≠ busy

loose-fitting. Clothes that are **loose-fitting** are rather large and do not fit tightly on your body. — ADJ QUALIT = baggy

loose-leaf. A **loose-leaf** book or folder has pages in it which can be removed and replaced. — ADJ CLASSIF : ATTRIB

loosen /lu:sən/, **loosens, loosening, loosened**.
1 If you **loosen** something or if it **loosens**, it becomes less firm or less tightly held in place. EG *With the aid of a screwdriver, loosen the two screws at each end... The tyre on one of his wheels had loosened... The wind had loosened some leaves.* — V-ERG

2 If you **loosen** your clothing or something that is tied or fastened, you undo it slightly so that it is not tight. EG *He loosened his seat-belt... He took off his jacket and loosened his tie... She loosened her hair and began to unbutton her dress.* — V+O ⇑ unfasten

3 If something such as someone's skin **loosens**, it becomes less stretched or tight. — V = sag

4 If something **loosens** strong feelings of attachment between people or groups of people, it causes these feelings to become weaker. EG *The effect of boarding school is often to loosen ties between children and their parents... The organization has been able to loosen its dependence on existing political institutions.* — V+O ⇑ reduce = weaken

5 If you **loosen** laws, restrictions, etc, you make them less strict or severe. EG *They eventually loosened the strait-jacket policy of Republicanism.* — V+O = relax

loosen up. When you **loosen up**, **1** you prepare your muscles for a difficult physical activity, such as running, playing football, or playing a musical instrument, by doing simple exercises. **2** you become calmer and less worried. EG *Her second drink loosened her up.* — PHRASAL VB : V+ADV, OR V+O (NG/REFL)+ADV; PHRASAL VB : V+ADV, OR V+O (NG/REFL)+ADV

loot /lu:t/, **loots, looting, looted**. **1** If people **loot** shops, churches, houses, etc, they steal or take things from them by force, usually during a violent event such as a battle or a riot. EG *Shops were looted and wrecked in London.* ◇ **looting**. EG *There was widespread looting of stores and shops.* — V OR V+O = plunder; ◇ N UNCOUNT

2 If people **loot** valuable objects or money, they steal them during fighting in a war or riot. EG *It was Napoleon's greatest boast to have looted it from the Vatican.* — V+O = plunder

3 **Loot** is **3.1** money and valuable goods that soldiers or an army steal from an enemy after they have defeated them. EG *The original head was silver and irresistible as loot.* **3.2** money or goods that have been stolen or taken illegally; an informal use. EG *He told his wife where the loot was hidden.* **3.3** money; an old-fashioned, informal use. — N UNCOUNT = booty; N UNCOUNT; N UNCOUNT

looter /lu:tə/, **looters**. A **looter** is a person who steals things or takes things by force during a war, riot, etc. — N COUNT

lop /lɒp/, **lops, lopping, lopped**. If you **lop** a tree, you cut some of its branches off to make it neater or safer. EG *He borrowed it a fortnight ago to lop his plum tree.* — V+O = prune

lop off. If you **lop** something **off**, you cut it away from what it was attached to, usually with a quick, strong stroke. EG *The flash of a long knife lopped off his head cleanly at the shoulders.* — PHRASAL VB : V+O+ADV ⇑ sever

lope /ləʊp/, **lopes, loping, loped**. If a person or animal **lopes**, they run in an easy and relaxed way, taking long steps. EG *The keeper came loping softly up the lane... The dog started to lope alongside my car.* ▸ used as a noun. EG *She settled into the easy deceptive lope of the experienced athlete.* — V+A = bound; ▸ N SING WITH DET+SUPP = stride

lopsided /lɒpsaɪdɪ²d/; also spelled with a hyphen. Something that is **lopsided** is uneven because its two sides are different from each other, for example when one side is heavier or higher than the other side. EG *Gradually a lopsided smile settled on her face.* — ADJ QUALIT = crooked ≠ symmetrical

loquacious /lə⁶kweɪʃəs/. People who are **loquacious** talk a great deal; a formal word. EG *He is an easy, loquacious man... They soon formed a loquacious group around the car.* — ADJ QUALIT = talkative

loquacity /lə⁶kwæsɪti¹/ is the habit of talking a great deal; a formal word. EG *What he lacked in charm he could make up in loquacity.* — N UNCOUNT

lord /lɔ:d/, **lords, lording, lorded**. **1** **Lord** is the title used in front of the name of British earls, viscounts, marquesses, etc. EG *Lord Harewood is George V's grandson... ...Lord Alfred Douglas... ...Lords Hailsham and Home.* — N IN TITLES : WITH PL

2 In Britain, you address a man as '**my Lord**' when he is a judge or bishop, or if he is an earl, viscount, marquess, etc. EG *I can do nothing more, my Lord: I cannot defend myself any further.* — N VOC : DETPOSS +N

3 The word **Lord** is also used as part of the title of certain officials of very high rank in Britain. EG *...The Lord Mayor of London... His successor as Lord Chancellor was another Liberal.* — N IN TITLES

4 A **Lord** is a man who has a high rank in the British nobility. EG *How do you square being a Lord with being a Socialist?* — N COUNT

5 In former times, especially in medieval times, a **lord** was a man who owned land or property and who had power and authority over other people. EG *Serfs would provide their lord with labour and produce, and in exchange he would protect them.* — N COUNT

6 The word **lord** is often used in expressions such as 'lord and master' and 'lord of the manor' to refer to men who are in positions of authority. — N COUNT

7 The **Lords** is the House of Lords; used in slightly informal British English. EG *He announced the decision in the Lords this morning... The Lords debated the proposal on 10 April.* — N PLURAL : *the*+N

8 In the Christian church, **Lord** is used to refer to God and to Jesus Christ, especially as a form of address in prayers. EG *Lord, take my heart of stone and give me flesh, he prayed... It is right to worship the Lord... ...Lord Jesus Christ.* — N SING/PROPER : *the*+N, N IN TITLE, OR VOC

9 In informal English, you can say '**good Lord!**', '**oh Lord!**', etc when you are surprised, amused, shocked, or worried about something. EG *Oh Lord, I don't know what I'm talking about... 'Good Lord!' I said. 'You still here?'* — EXCLAM = heavens

10 If someone **lords it over** you, they act in a way — PHR : VB that shows that they think they are better than you, especially by giving lots of orders. INFLECTS

lordly /lɔːdli¹/. Someone who is **lordly** is proud and arrogant, showing that they think they are better than other people; used showing disapproval. EG *...the lordly elder brother.* ▸ used of people's behaviour. EG *His lordly manners were quite repulsive.* ADJ QUALIT = imperious ▸ = haughty

Lordship /lɔːdʃɪp/, **Lordships**. Your **Lordship** or his **Lordship** is a respectful way of addressing or talking about a judge, bishop, or male member of the nobility in Britain. EG *If your Lordship will give me time I will produce the evidence.... I'm sorry, sir, his Lordship is in his bath... Their Lordships were already late for dinner.* N COUNT: DETPOSS+N, USED IN TITLES

Lord's Prayer. The **Lord's Prayer** is a very important Christian prayer that was originally taught by Jesus Christ to his disciples. N SING: *the*+N = Our Father

lore /lɔː/ is the traditional stories and history of a particular culture or field of activity. EG *...the transmission of Jewish mystical lore through the Renaissance.* N UNCOUNT+SUPP ⇑ traditions

lorgnette /lɔːnjɛt/, **lorgnettes**. A **lorgnette** is a pair of glasses with a handle so that you can hold it to your eyes. Lorgnettes are very old-fashioned now. EG *Lady Montague looked through her lorgnette at him.* N COUNT

lorry /lɒri¹/, **lorries**. A **lorry** is a large vehicle that is used to transport goods by road; used in British English. EG *...a heavy lorry... He'd run across the road and the lorry couldn't possibly stop.* N COUNT = truck

lose /luːz/, **loses, losing, lost**. **1** If you **lose** something, **1.1** you do not know where it is, for example because you have forgotten where you put it. EG *I've lost the piece of paper with your address on it... I was afraid I'd lose my passport... She's always losing her cigarette lighter... I'm not broke, if that's what you mean: I simply lost my purse... You haven't lost the ticket, have you?* V+O = mislay ≠ find **1.2** you no longer have it because it has been taken away from you, for example in an accident. EG *...the people who lost their homes in the earthquake... I might even lose my job... If we did, we would lose our seat at the conference table.* V+O **1.3** it goes out of sight so that you can no longer see it. EG *...carpets so thick you could lose a cat in them.* V+O

2 If you **lose** an ability, you stop having that ability because of something such as an accident. EG *He lost the use of his legs after the illness... ...so shocked that she lost her powers of speech... Then he would lose his voice and be unable to work... He kept losing his balance and grabbing for the handrail.* V+O

3 If someone or something **loses** a quality, attitude, or belief that they had, they no longer have it. EG *You are beginning to lose confidence in your sense of direction... Brody was beginning to lose interest... Old occupations lose importance or vanish altogether... The trip was beginning to lose its simplicity... She began to lose patience with him... I felt I would lose all control over the car.* V+O

4 If someone or something **loses** weight, blood, heat, etc, some of it disappears so that they have less than they had before. EG *He has lost a lot of weight since his illness... How long does it take you to make up the blood you lose?... The body has to lose excess heat if it is to go on working efficiently... The engine's been losing a lot of oil.* V+O

5 If you **lose** a part of your body, it is cut off in an operation or in a violent accident. EG *He had lost a finger and part of a thumb in a fight.* V+O

6 If you **lose** a close relative or friend, they die. EG *I lost my father when I was nine... He had just lost his wife.* V+O: NO CONT

7 If something **was lost**, it was destroyed in an accident or disaster, often resulting in people being killed. EG *Crew and cargo were lost in the storm... ...a complete list of all the goods lost in the fire.* V+O: USU PASS = be wiped out

8 If you **lose** something useful or precious, you waste it by not using it properly. EG *He will lose his chances of promotion... ...you lose some of the major advantage... Bill lost no time in telling everyone about his idea.* V+O

9 If a business **loses** money, it earns less money than it spends, and is therefore in debt. EG *At one time the company was losing a million pounds a week... State-owned industries are losing millions of dollars.* V+O ≠ make

10 If you **have** something **to lose**, you are in a position where you might suffer if you carry out a particular action unsuccessfully. EG *I don't see what you've got to lose... The price was too high and he had too much to lose... They were tough and they had absolutely nothing to lose.* PHR: *have* INFLECTS

11 Lose sight of. 11.1 If you **lose sight of** something, it has moved into a position where you can no longer see it. PHR: VB INFLECTS **11.2** If you **lose sight of** an aim, objective, argument, etc, you become confused or distracted and forget the point of what you are doing, talking about, or thinking about. EG *And of course we lose sight of this certainty... We've lost sight of the moral values.* PHR: VB INFLECTS

12 If a clock or watch **loses** time, it goes slower than it is meant to, and therefore shows a time that is earlier than the correct time. EG *My watch loses about five minutes a day.* V+O

13 If you **lose** a competition, argument, etc, you do not succeed because someone does better than you and defeats you. EG *They expected to lose the election... They have lost six games and won ten... Nobody expected her to lose.* V OR V+O ⇑ fail ≠ win ◇ **losing**. EG *Seven years and he'd never played on a losing side.* ◇ ADJ CLASSIF: ATTRIB

14 If an event or action **loses** you a contest or **loses** you something that you had, it causes you to fail or to no longer have what you had. EG *That mistake lost us the game.* V+O+O = cost

15 If you **lose** your way, **15.1** you become lost when you are trying to go somewhere. V+O **15.2** you fail to understand something complicated such as an argument or explanation. EG *I couldn't help losing my way in the maze of their well-meaning instructions.* V+O

16 If you **are lost** in thought, in a book, etc, you are extremely interested in it and are giving it all your attention so that you do not notice what is happening around you. EG *Both men were again lost in reading... He lost himself in a maze of thoughts... She sat with her camera in her lap, lost in concentration.* V+O: ONLY PASS, OR V+O (REFL), USU+A (IN)

17 If a comment or joke **is lost** on someone, they do not understand it properly. EG *I'm afraid his humour is just lost on me.* V+O+A *(on)*: ONLY PASS

18 If you say that someone **is lost** without someone or something else, you mean that they are unhappy or unable to work properly without the other person or thing being present. EG *I am lost without him.* V+O+A *(without)*: ONLY PASS = be helpless

19 See also **lost**.

20 The word **lose** is also used in the following expressions, which are explained at other places in this dictionary. • to **fight a losing battle**: see **battle**. • to **lose contact**: see **contact**. • to **lose** your **cool**: see **cool**. • to **lose face**: see **face**. • to **lose** your **head**: see **head**. • to **lose** your **nerve**: see **nerve**. • to **lose** your **temper**: see **temper**. • to **lose touch**: see **touch**. • to **lose track** of: see **track**.

lose out. If you **lose out**, you suffer a loss or disadvantage because you have not succeeded in what you were doing. EG *They at least did not lose out in the struggle to keep up with inflation.* PHRASAL VB: V+ADV

loser /luːzə/, **losers**. **1** The **loser** of a game, contest, or struggle is the person who is defeated or beaten. EG *After one match, the loser actually sent him a present... ...the winners and losers in the development game.* N COUNT ≠ winner • Someone who is **a good loser** accepts the fact that they have lost a game or contest and does not complain. Someone who is **a bad loser** hates losing and complains or makes a fuss when they do. • PHR: USED AS C

2 A **loser** is a person or thing that is always unsuccessful or seems likely to be unsuccessful; a fairly informal use. EG *You're a loser, Bill... You told me about the magazine you were going to publish–a real loser, it sounded like.* N COUNT ⇑ failure

3 If someone is the **loser** as the result of an action or event, they are in a worse situation because of it or do not benefit from it. EG *She will probably conclude that she will be the loser if she fails to respond to your friendly overtures.* N COUNT: IF SING *the*+N

loss /lɒs/, **losses**. **1 Loss** is **1.1** the fact of no longer having something that you had before, especially something useful, valuable, or desirable. EG *The loss was registered at the consulate... ...temporary or permanent loss of vision... ...the loss of liberty... ...the fear of loss of jobs.* N UNCOUNT: IF+PREP THEN *of* **1.2** the feeling of sadness you experience when someone or something you like is taken away from you. EG *He felt a pang of loss as she left.* N UNCOUNT

2 The **loss** of something such as heat, blood, or fluid is the gradual reduction of it or of its level in a system or in someone's body. EG *...heat loss from the* N UNCOUNT+SUPP *radiator... Some patients worry unnecessarily about the initial weight loss... Death usually results from loss of fluids.*

3 Loss or **loss** of life occurs when many people die, for example in a battle or a disaster. EG *The aircraft was blown up with total loss of life... The loss of life was appalling... Allied artillery fire caused heavy losses.* N UNCOUNT/ COUNT

4 The **loss** of a close relative happens when they die. EG *In the past the loss of a baby was almost commonplace... That does not make up for the loss of my daughter and husband.* N UNCOUNT+ SUPP

5 A **loss** is the disadvantage you suffer when a valuable and useful person or thing leaves or is taken away. EG *He'll be no great loss when he goes... You must consider it rather a gain than a loss.* N COUNT : USU SING

6 If a business makes a **loss**, it earns less money than it spends and is therefore in debt. EG *...profit and loss... The company announced a huge loss for the first half of the year... ...their record $242 million loss for 1980 and the first quarter of 1981... The company's losses have worsened to $6.1 million.* N COUNT : SING=PL, OR N UNCOUNT = deficit

7 At a loss. 7.1 If a business or shop sells something **at a loss**, they sell it for a price which is less than it cost to produce or less than it cost them to buy it. PHR : USED AS AN A **7.2** If you are **at a loss**, you are very uncertain about what to do in a particular situation. EG *I was at a complete loss as to how I could lay my hands on the money... I'm at a loss to find anything wrong with them.* PHR : USED AS AN A = stuck

8 If you **cut** your **losses**, you stop doing an activity in order to prevent your situation becoming worse, even though you have already suffered some disadvantage or loss. PHR : VB INFLECTS

9 If you say that someone or something is a **dead loss**, you mean that they do not work properly or successfully; an informal expression. EG *He's a dead loss, that goalkeeper.* PHR : USED AS C = washout

lost /lɒst/. If you are **lost** or if you get **lost**, **1.1** you are unable to find your way or do not know where you are. EG *There was that time when we got lost out in Dennington... I think we're lost... That little boy looks lost.* ADJ CLASSIF : USU PRED **1.2** you feel very uncomfortable because you are surrounded by a lot of unfamiliar people or are in an unfamiliar situation. EG *...strolling down Eighth Avenue, lost in crowds of New Yorkers.* ADJ QUALIT : USU PRED = overwhelmed

2 If something is **lost** or gets **lost**, **2.1** you cannot find it, for example because you have forgotten where you put it. EG *I have no proof because the laundry list is in the lost box.* ADJ CLASSIF = mislaid **2.2** it is forgotten and not dealt with during a complicated process or period of time. EG *Dietary needs get lost in the savage demands of our inflationary economy.* ADJ CLASSIF = swamped

3 Someone or something that is **lost 3.1** is no longer possessed by the person, group, or thing that they once belonged to. EG *They need to win back their lost supporters.* ADJ CLASSIF : ATTRIB **3.2** has not been used properly and is therefore considered to be wasted. EG *By nine p.m. some would be in tears over lost opportunities... Time which had now been lost for twelve years had to be regained somehow.* ADJ CLASSIF

4 If advice is **lost** on someone, it has no influence on them because they do not pay any attention to it. EG *The lesson was lost on the committee, who re-elected him for a further year in office.* ADJ CLASSIF : USU PRED+*on* = wasted

5 If you tell someone to **get lost**, you are rudely telling them to go away; an informal expression. PHR : ONLY IMPER/*to*-INF

lost cause, lost causes. A **lost cause** is an attempt to achieve something that has no chance of succeeding; also used of the thing that you are trying to achieve. EG *...a champion of lost causes.* N COUNT

lost property is **1** things that people have lost or accidentally left in a public place, for example on a train or in a school. N UNCOUNT **2** a place where lost property is kept. EG *Go and see if it's in lost property.* N UNCOUNT

lost-property office, lost-property offices. A **lost-property office** is a place, for example at a railway station, where lost property is kept and where it can be claimed back by the owner. N COUNT

lot /lɒt/, **lots**. **1** A **lot** of something or **lots** of something is a large amount of it. **Lots** is used in informal English. EG *We owed a lot of money... This is a subject that worries a lot of people... I feel that we have a lot to offer... Though she was thin, she weighed quite a lot... He remembered a lot more about me than I did about him... ...a big house with lots of windows... There are lots and lots of antique shops in Australia now... Oh, you've got lots of time.* N PART : SING=PL, IF SING THEN *a*+N = masses

2 A lot or **lots** means to a great extent or degree. **Lots** is used in informal English. EG *There was a man in the photograph who looked a lot like Mr Williams... You like Ralph a lot, don't you?... 'Alright then?'–'Yes, thanks a lot.'... The weather's a lot warmer there... 'Feeling a bit better?'–'Lots, Doctor. Lots better.'* PHR USED AS AN A, OR ADV = very much

3 A lot also means very often or more often than you would expect. EG *She had a husband whose job took him away a lot... They talk a lot about equality... You get this a lot, don't you?* PHR : USED AS AN A = a great deal

4 When you refer to the **lot**, you are referring to the whole of a particular amount of something; used in fairly informal English. EG *Wilks bet his last ten pounds in a game of poker and lost the lot... She's taken the whole lot!* N SING : *the*+N ⇑ all

5 You can refer to a particular group of people as a particular **lot**; used in informal English. EG *They were a rather arrogant boring lot... Was he one of your lot?... Will you shut up and give some of us lot a chance.* N SING WITH DET +SUPP = crowd

6 You can refer to a set or group of things, usually one of several sets or groups, as a particular **lot**; used in fairly informal English. EG *...two sets of cards, one lot written in blue, the other in red... They are busy giving out two lots of pamphlets to people in the street.* N COUNT/PART = batch

7 Your **lot** is the kind of life you have or the things that you have or experience. EG *...attempts by the workers to improve their lot... She was quite content with her lot.* N COUNT : USU WITH POSS = fortune

8 A **lot** is **8.1** an area of land; used mainly in American English. EG *He had become the owner of a garage and a used car lot... Most of the forest that covers New England is in lots of 50-100 acres.* ● See also **parking lot**. N COUNT **8.2** a film studio and the land around it. EG *The lot and its buildings used to be owned by RKO Pictures.* N COUNT ⇑ place **8.3** an object or group of objects that are being sold as an item in an auction. EG *Lot No 359 was a folder of 11 original sketches.* N COUNT

9 If you describe someone as **a bad lot**, you mean that they do bad or unacceptable things; an informal expression. PHR : USED AS C

10 If a group of people **draw lots** or **cast lots** to decide which of them will do a particular thing, each of them takes one of a number of sticks, pieces of paper, etc from a container. The person who takes the one that is different from the others is chosen. EG *They drew lots to decide which of them should go first.* PHR : VB INFLECTS = draw straws

11 If the question of who will do a particular thing is decided **by lot**, the people involved draw lots. Alternatively, objects or pieces of paper representing each person involved are put in a container and the person represented by the first one taken out is chosen. PHR : USED AS AN A

12 If **the lot falls to** a particular person to do something or if **it falls to** their **lot** to do it, they are the person who happens to do it or who is chosen to do it. EG *The lot fell to me to make the attempt... Not long afterwards, it fell to his lot to rule on the case of a Russian seaman.* PHR : VB INFLECTS

13 If you **throw in** your **lot with** a particular person or group, you decide to work with them or support them from then on, whatever happens. PHR : VB INFLECTS ⇑ join

loth /ləʊθ/. See **loath**.

lotion /ləʊʃəⁿn/, **lotions**. A **lotion** is a liquid that you use to clean, improve, or protect your skin or hair. EG *...a bottle of suntan lotion.* N MASS

lottery /lɒtəⁿri¹/, **lotteries**. **1** When a **lottery** is held in order to make money for the state or for a charity, people buy tickets with different numbers on them. Several numbers are then chosen at random and the people whose tickets have these numbers on them win prizes. EG *She won a fortune in a state lottery... ...a lottery ticket.* N COUNT = raffle

2 If you describe a contest as a **lottery**, you mean that the result of it depends entirely on luck or chance, rather than being decided in a fairer way; used showing disapproval. EG *The British election system will become a lottery.* N SING : *a*+N = gamble

lotus /ləʊtəs/, **lotuses**. A **lotus** is a type of water-lily that grows in Africa and Asia. N COUNT ⇑ flower

lotus-eater, lotus-eaters. A **lotus-eater** is someone who lives an idle, comfortable life and does not think or care very much about anything. N COUNT

lotus position, lotus positions. Someone who is sitting in the **lotus position**, is sitting with their legs crossed and their feet resting on top of their thighs, usually when they are doing yoga or meditating. N COUNT : USU *the*+N IN SING

loud /laʊd/, **louder, loudest.** 1 A **loud** sound or producer of sound consists of or produces a large amount of sound. EG *She wore lipstick and had a loud voice... Don't you think the radio's a bit loud?... ...the loudest and longest standing ovation I have ever heard... The special effects get louder and louder.* ADJ QUALIT ⇑ noisy ▸ used as an adverb. EG *He spoke loud enough for most of the audience to hear him.* ▸ ADV WITH VB ◊ **loudly.** EG *He had spoken loudly and angrily.* ◊ ADV WITH VB ◊ **loudness.** EG *The drone of a plane came with increasing loudness through the curtains.* ◊ N UNCOUNT = volume

2 If someone is **loud** in their support for something, in their criticism of something, etc, they express their opinion very often and in a very strong way. EG *Northcliffe's newspapers were loud in their condemnation of British sentimentality.* ADJ QUALIT = clamorous ◊ **loudly.** EG *Most people rather loudly allege that all this is just another excuse.* ◊ ADV WITH VB = vehemently

3 Something that is **loud**, especially a piece of clothing, has very bright colours or a very large, bold pattern and looks unpleasant. EG *...white-faced young men in loud shirts and jackets.* ADJ QUALIT = garish

4 If you tell someone something **loud and clear**, you are very easily understood, either because your voice is very clear or because you express yourself very clearly. EG *The message goes out loud and clear.* PHR : USED AS A/C ⇑ comprehensibly

5 If you express a thought or feeling **out loud** or read **out loud**, you speak or make a noise rather than just thinking the words in your head or staying silent. EG *I laughed out loud at the thought... I guess I was thinking out loud.* PHR : USED AS AN A = aloud

loudhailer /laʊdheɪlə/, **loudhailers**; also spelled with a hyphen. A **loudhailer** is a piece of equipment that you can hold in your hand and use to make your voice heard over a long distance. EG *The colonel, using a loudhailer, tried to reassure the residents.* N COUNT = megaphone

loudmouth /laʊdmaʊθ/, **loudmouths** /laʊdmaʊðz/; also spelled with a hyphen. A **loudmouth** is someone who talks a lot, especially in an unpleasant, offensive, or stupid way; used showing disapproval. N COUNT

loud-mouthed. Someone who is **loud-mouthed** talks a lot, especially in an unpleasant, offensive, or stupid way; used showing disapproval. EG *...a loud-mouthed, hard-drinking actor.* ADJ QUALIT = blustering

loudspeaker /laʊdspiːkə/, **loudspeakers**; also spelled with a hyphen. A **loudspeaker** is a piece of equipment that turns electrical signals into sound. Loudspeakers are used so that words spoken into a microphone or sound from a radio or record player can be heard. N COUNT

lounge /laʊndʒ/, **lounges, lounging, lounged.**
1 A **lounge** is 1.1 a room in a house where people sit and relax; used in British English. EG *She went and sat in the lounge.* N COUNT 1.2 a room in a hotel, club, etc where people can sit and relax. EG *...the hotel lounge.* N COUNT 1.3 a very large room in an airport where people can sit and wait for aircraft to arrive or depart. EG *The passengers filed into the arrivals lounge.* N COUNT : AFTER N 1.4 a bar in a pub or hotel which is comfortably furnished and in which the drinks are more expensive than in the other bars; used in British English. EG *...a cocktail lounge.* N COUNT = lounge bar

2 If you **lounge** somewhere, you lean against something or lie somewhere in a way that looks very lazy. EG *It pained him to see Thomas lounging like that against the wall... She lounged on the rug.* V : USU+A = loll

lounge about. If you **lounge about** or **lounge around**, you do not do anything useful and you spend your time in a relaxed and lazy way; usually used showing disapproval. EG *...various persons who were lounging about, apparently with nothing to do.* PHRASAL VB : V+ADV/PREP = loaf

lounge bar, lounge bars. A **lounge bar** is a bar in a pub or hotel which is comfortably furnished and in which the drinks are more expensive than in the other bars; used in British English. N COUNT

lounge suit, lounge suits. A **lounge suit** is an ordinary suit that is worn by men for work in offices and businesses and on fairly formal occasions. N COUNT

louse /laʊs/, **lice; louses, lousing, loused.** Lice is the plural of the noun in paragraph 1. **Louses** is the plural of the noun in paragraph 2, and the third person singular, present tense, of the verb.
1 A **louse** is a small insect that lives on the bodies of people or animals and bites them in order to use their blood as food. EG *Worse even than the lice and rats was the pain in his shoulder.* N COUNT : USU PL ⇑ parasite

2 If you refer to someone as a **louse**, you mean that they are unpleasant and do nasty, dishonourable things; used in informal English. EG *He wouldn't even listen to me. What a louse.* N COUNT : USU USED AS C = swine

louse up. If someone or something **louses up** a plan, situation, etc, they cause it to fail or to be ruined; a very informal expression. EG *It could louse up your divorce petition.* PHRASAL VB : V+O+ADV ⇑ spoil = foul up

lousy /laʊzi¹/, **lousier, lousiest.** 1 If you say that something is **lousy**, you mean that it is of very low quality or that you do not like it at all; an informal use. EG *The food is execrable, the hotels are lousy, the people are rude... Why the hell should I come to a lousy hockey game?* ADJ QUALIT ⇑ bad = rotten

2 You use **lousy** when referring to a quantity that you think is too small or a level that you think is too low; an informal use. EG *You guys have five million books. We have a few lousy thousand... He gave me a lousy 'C' for this paper.* ADJ CLASSIF : ATTRIB ⇑ meagre = mingy

3 If you feel **lousy**, you feel very ill; an informal use. EG *He felt really lousy the next morning.* ADJ QUALIT : PRED

4 A person or animal that is **lousy** has lice on their body or in their hair. ADJ CLASSIF

lout /laʊt/, **louts.** A **lout** is a man or boy who behaves in an impolite or aggressive way. EG *...gangs of drunken louts.* N COUNT = yob

loutish /laʊtɪʃ/. **Loutish** behaviour is impolite and aggressive. EG *He had a scruffy appearance and loutish manners.* ADJ QUALIT = uncouth

louvre /luːvə/, **louvres**; also spelled **louver** in American English. A **louvre** or a **louvre** door or window is a door or window with flat, sloping pieces of wood or glass across its frame. N COUNT, OR N BEFORE N

louvred /luːvəd/; also spelled **louvered** in American English. A **louvred** door or window has flat, sloping pieces of wood or glass across its frame. ADJ CLASSIF ⇑ slatted

lovable /lʌvəbəˈl/. Someone who is **lovable** has attractive qualities, and is therefore easy to like very much. EG *...a mischievous but lovable child.* ADJ QUALIT ⇑ likeable = engaging

love /lʌv/, **loves, loving, loved.** 1 If you **love** someone, 1.1 you have very strong feelings of affection towards them and feel romantically or sexually attracted to them, and they are very important to you. EG *I do not think I love him enough to marry him... 'I love you, Albert.'–'I love you too, Mabel.'... They had not ceased to love each other... She could hate as passionately as she could love.* V+O, OR V ⇑ care for 1.2 you feel that their happiness is very important to you, and usually show this feeling in the way you behave towards them. EG *He gave us a little baby. A little baby to love... They make us feel safe and secure, loved and wanted.* V+O = cherish

2 If you **love** something, 2.1 you feel that it is important and want to protect it or help it. EG *They don't love their individual villages in the way that their parents did... ...people who love freedom and democracy.* V+O = prize 2.2 you like it very much; a slightly informal use. EG *We both love dancing... I love Haydn and Schubert... Oh, what a wonderful smell. I do love cigar smoke.* V+O = adore

3 **Love** is 3.1 very strong feelings of affection towards someone who you are romantically or sexually attracted to. EG *From that moment until her death fifty years later her love for him never wavered... You are not marrying for love... ...a Russian love song.* N UNCOUNT : IF+PREP THEN *for* 3.2 the feeling that a person's happiness is very important to you, and the way you show this feeling in your behaviour towards them. EG *...maternal love... Children do not need teachers as much as they need love and understanding... Only love can save the world.* N UNCOUNT = affection • See also **cupboard love, tug-of-love.** 3.3 a deep liking for something or enjoyment of it, or a belief that it is important. EG *...a man with a genuine love of literature in all its forms... ...his love for his country... ...people who compete for the love of the sport... It was designed and built with love... ...the love of destruction.* N UNCOUNT : IF+PREP THEN *of*

4 Your **love** is the person that you love and have romantic or sexual feelings for. EG *A man always* N COUNT : USU WITH POSS

remembers his first love... It was in my apartment that you met the great love of your life.

5 If you refer to a particular activity or thing as someone's great **love**, their first **love**, etc, you mean that they like it very much and are very interested in it. EG *His first love was painting but he later turned to sculpture.* N COUNT: USU POSS+N = passion

6 If you would **love** to have or do something, you very much want to have it or do it. EG *I would love a photograph of Edith Evans... Posy said she'd love to stay... I'd love to have seen the old man's face.* V: *would*+V+O/ *to*-INF ⇑ like

7 In informal spoken English, **love** is used as an affectionate or friendly way of addressing someone, either a relative or friend or someone you are talking to. Men usually address only women and children as **love**, not other men EG *'Come along, Jim.'–'Yes, Nora, my love.'... Thanks a lot, love.* N VOC = dear

8 In tennis, **love** is a score of zero; usually used when speaking rather than writing. EG *Lloyd won the first set six-love.* NUM

9 You can write **love**, **love from**, **all my love**, etc, followed by your name, as an informal way of ending a letter to a friend or relation. EG *Hope you are all well at home. Love, Dan... Hope you are being good. Love from Daddy and Mummy... ...All my love, Philip.* CONVENTION

10 If you **send** someone your **love** or say **'give them my love'**, you ask another person, who will soon be speaking or writing to them, to tell them that you are thinking about them with affection. EG *They send you their love... Aunt Maude sent you her love as usual.* PHR: VB INFLECTS

11 If you are **in love** with someone, you have very strong feelings of affection towards them and feel romantically or sexually attracted to them, and they are very important to you. EG *They are in love with each other and wish to marry... ...a woman in love.* PHR: USED AS AN A, IF+PREP THEN *with* = smitten ▸ also used of a very strong liking for something. EG *We are in love with everything this morning.* ▸ = enraptured

12 If you **fall in love** with someone, you start to be in love with them. EG *I fell madly in love with Ellen the first time I ever saw her... We like to think that falling in love is entirely irrational.* ▸ also used of starting to like something very much. EG *I had fallen in love with the city.* PHR: VB INFLECTS, IF+PREP THEN *with*

13 **Love at first sight** is the experience of starting to be in love with someone as soon as you see them for the first time. EG *It was love at first sight.* ▸ also used of starting to like something very much. PHR: USU USED AS C

14 When two people **make love**, especially two people who love or are attracted to each other, they have sex. EG *He made love to her early that evening.* PHR: VB INFLECTS, IF+PREP THEN *with/to*

15 In very old-fashioned English, if you **make love** to someone, you tell them that they are lovely, say that you love them, etc. EG *I can't make love in my own language for some strange reason.* PHR+*to*: VB INFLECTS

16 Some people refer to having sex as **the act of love**; a polite and rather old-fashioned expression. PHR: USED AS O/S

17 If you say that someone has **a love-hate relationship** with a particular person or thing or that it is **a love-hate situation**, you mean that they have strong feelings of both love and hate towards that person or thing. EG *They joked that Jim and I had a love-hate relationship.* PHR: USED AS O/C

18 If you say that **there is no love lost** between two people or groups or **there is little love lost** between them, you mean that the relationship between them is not a friendly one. PHR: AUX INFLECTS, USU+ *between*

19 If you **cannot do something for love or money** or **for love nor money**, you are completely unable to do it. EG *You can't find another room at this hour in this town for love or money.* PHR: VB INFLECTS

20 ● **a labour of love**: see **labour**. ● See also **loving**.

love affair, love affairs; also spelled with a hyphen. A **love affair** is a romantic and often sexual relationship, usually a short one, between two people who love each other but who are not married to each other. EG *I am not suggesting that you and he had a love-affair.* N COUNT

lovebirds /lʌvbɜːdz/; also spelled with a hyphen. You can refer in a humorous way to two people as **lovebirds** when they are obviously very much in love. EG *I shared a compartment with the lovebirds.* N PLURAL

love child, love children. A **love child** is someone whose parents have never been married to each other; a euphemistic expression. EG *...thirty-five infants, all the pathetic 'love-children' of women betrayed.* N COUNT = bastard

loveless /lʌvlɪ²s/. Something that is **loveless** is without love. EG *She was his first wife, his partner in a loveless marriage... ...a loveless home.* ADJ CLASSIF: USU ATTRIB ≠ loving

love letter, love letters; also spelled with a hyphen. A **love letter** is a letter that you write to someone in order to tell them that you love them or to describe your feelings of love for them. EG *It was the first love letter my husband wrote to me.* N COUNT

love life, love lives; also spelled with a hyphen. Someone's **love life** is the part of their life that consists of their romantic and sexual relationships. EG *He had a very emotional lovelife and was always changing partners.* N COUNT

lovely /lʌvli¹/, **lovelier, loveliest**. 1 Something that is **lovely** is very beautiful and therefore pleasing to look at or listen to. EG *They spent a few days at Coker, a lovely Elizabethan house in Somerset... 'Doesn't she look lovely, Albert?' she whispered. The setting couldn't have been lovelier... To me Hong Kong had always been one of the loveliest places in the world.* ◇ **loveliness**. EG *Coffee was being handed out by a girl of film-star loveliness.* ADJ QUALIT; ◇ N UNCOUNT = beauty

2 If you describe something as **lovely**, you are showing the pleasure that you have from it or your approval or appreciation of it. EG *'What a lovely surprise!' she said... ...Lovely day, isn't it?... Sit next to me and warm yourself in front of this lovely fire... It was lovely to hear from you again... They've got a lovely big party tomorrow for seventy of them.* ADJ QUALIT = marvellous, wonderful

3 A **lovely** person is one that you like very much because they are friendly, kind, generous, etc; used showing approval. EG *We've got lovely neighbours... I've made some lovely friends... She's really lovely... She's the sweetest, loveliest person.* ADJ QUALIT = smashing, charming

love-making refers to romantic activities, especially sexual activities, that take place between two people, often including sexual intercourse. EG *...ardent love-making... His love-making was odious to her.* N UNCOUNT

love potion, love potions. A **love potion** is a drink that is supposed to cause sexual desire in the person who drinks it. EG *They have no need of love potions.* N COUNT = aphrodisiac

lover /lʌvə/, **lovers**. 1 Your **lover** is 1.1 someone who you are having a sexual relationship with but are not married to. EG *I had guessed the identity of her lover... He went to Tewkesbury to see one of his son's lovers... I admitted that Jenny and I were lovers.* N COUNT 1.2 someone who you are in love with but not married to; an old-fashioned use. EG *She was talking to me like a lover... ...young lovers.* N COUNT

2 If you are a **lover** of art, nature, cats, etc, you enjoy them very much and take great pleasure in them. EG *He grew up a lover of open country... There's something here for lovers of every style of jazz... He is a music lover.* N COUNT+SUPP ⇑ fan

love story, love stories; also spelled with a hyphen. A **love story** is a novel, film, etc about a love affair. EG *It is a love-story of unbelievable austerity.* N COUNT = romance

loving /lʌvɪŋ/. 1 Someone who is **loving** feels or shows love to other people. EG *They began to feel more and more loving to each other... ...a loving, beautiful wife.* ▸ used of someone's behaviour. EG *Her look is loving... The natural loving care that kindly parents give their children.* ◇ **lovingly**. EG *For a moment she looked at her grandson lovingly.* ADJ QUALIT = devoted; ◇ ADV WITH VB = affectionate, fondly

2 **Loving** describes actions that are done with great enjoyment and care, especially by someone with special knowledge or understanding. EG *...a careful and loving Raymond Chandler parody... We moved it with loving care.* ◇ **lovingly**. EG *The Society of Antiquaries have lovingly restored the fabric, inside and out... My breakfast tray had been lovingly prepared by my landlady.* ADJ CLASSIF: ATTRIB; ◇ ADV WITH VB

low /ləʊ/, **lower, lowest; lows, lowing, lowed**.

1 Something that is **low** 1.1 measures only a short distance from the bottom to the top, or from the ground to the top. EG *On the other side of the road stood a low brick wall... She set the tea-tray down on the low table in front of the sofa... ...a horrid little low-ceilinged room... We came to some low hills... ...low doorways.* ADJ QUALIT ≠ high 1.2 is close to the ground. EG *She made a low curtsey... One of the bridges is six inches too low... ...low cloud... I asked him to fly low over the beach... The noise diminishes as we reach lower altitudes... In a series of quick jerky movements, he bent lower and lower.* ADJ QUALIT, OR ADV WITH VB ≠ high 1.3 is close to the bottom of ADJ QUALIT, OR

something. EG *She saw the long scar low on his spine... He pushed his glasses lower on his nose and looked at the men over them.* ADV WITH VB ≠ high

2 Low is used to describe the position of your head when you move it downwards or of your face when you look down. EG *She stood in the doorway, hands clasped, her head low... Judy bent her face low over the notebook... He wore a brown cloth cap with the peak pulled down low over his eyes.* ADJ QUALIT : PRED, OR ADV WITH VB

3 If the sun or moon is **low**, it is close to the horizon. EG *The low sun cast long shadows from the trees... The afternoon sun was low above the gorse bushes.* ADJ QUALIT ≠ high

4 A dress, blouse, etc that is described as **low** leaves a woman's neck, shoulders, and the top part of her chest bare. EG *...a low neckline... Her dress was cut low in front.* ADJ QUALIT, OR ADV WITH VB ≠ high

5 If a river is **low**, it contains much less water than usual. ADJ QUALIT

6 Low means **6.1** small in number, amount, or value, or near the bottom of a scale. EG *...workers on low incomes... Oil prices were as low as £5 a barrel... Temperatures are lower on the continent in winter than in Britain... Party membership was at its lowest figure for fourteen years... He had low grades in all his papers... The new fuel has a lower octane value.* ADJ QUALIT ≠ high
6.2 less than what is needed or less than the right amount. EG *Tropical soils are often low in nitrogen... We're pretty low on holiday brochures for Majorca... Her blood count is low.* ADJ QUALIT ⇑ short **6.3** poor in quality; used showing disapproval. EG *...a low standard of living... ...low-grade material... The standard of child care is very low in many homes.* ADJ QUALIT ≠ high

7 If something is **in the low twenties, thirties, forties,** etc, it is more than twenty, thirty, forty, etc, but not as much as twenty-five, thirty-five, forty-five, etc. EG *The temperature is in the low eighties.* PHR : USED AS AN A ⇑ about

8 Low is used in descriptions of goods to indicate that the goods contain only a small amount of a particular substance. EG *...a low tar cigarette... ...low fat yoghurt.* ADJ QUALIT ≠ high

9 If a battery is **low**, it has very little power or energy left. EG *When their batteries were low a switch would turn them off.* ADJ QUALIT : PRED ⇑ weak

10 Low describes people who are not considered to be very important because they are near the bottom of a particular scale or system. EG *...a junior executive of a fairly low grade... The lowest 85 per cent of the working population received just 9 per cent of the total income... The low status of the farm men was widely acknowledged.* ADJ QUALIT ≠ high

11 If you have a **low** opinion of someone, you disapprove of them or dislike them, usually because of their behaviour or attitudes. EG *They have a very low opinion of us.* ADJ QUALIT ⇑ bad = poor

12 Low also describes people whose behaviour you disapprove of, usually because they are less respectable than you and do not have the same social status as you do, or because they are not honest. EG *Well I'm not doing that. I haven't sunk that low... The idea that you are used to mixing with low company is not good for the image.* ADJ QUALIT, OR ADV WITH VB ⇑ bad

13 Low is used to describe qualities or attitudes that you normally expect to be good and positive, but which at the moment are not. EG *Expectations were low, they became accustomed to a life of poverty... His optimism contrasted sharply with the low morale of his colleagues.* ADJ QUALIT ⇑ poor

14 If a sound or noise is **low**, it is deep. EG *A whistle came from Janie, long and low... ...a long low note on the cor anglais... He had a voice in the low tenor range.* ADJ QUALIT, OR ADV WITH VB

15 If someone's voice is **low**, it is quiet or soft. EG *Smithy spoke to him in a low and urgent voice... There was a low murmur of conversation in the hall... He turned the radio on low, hoping it would send him to sleep.* ADJ QUALIT, OR ADV WITH VB

16 A light that is **low** is dim, rather than being bright or strong. EG *The lights in the entrance hall were low.* ADJ QUALIT ⇑ weak

17 Low is used to say that a stove, oven, etc has been adjusted to produce only a small amount of heat. EG *Frozen croissants can go straight into a low oven for ten minutes... I put the pan on a low heat... Turn the gas as low as possible.* ADJ QUALIT = warm

18 Someone who is **low** is depressed. EG *Your work is slipping because you are feeling so low... Finding her in low spirits, they had persuaded her to join them for lunch... He had recovered from his very low state of the previous evening.* ADJ QUALIT ⇑ bad

19 If you say that something is **at a record low** or **at an all-time low**, you are describing a situation in which things are much worse than they have ever been before. EG *Output was at a record low... Relations between Britain and America were at an all time low.* PHR : USED AS AN A

20 If a disease or illness **lays** you **low**, it makes you weak or ill. EG *Salmonella laid low about thirty people in Stoke-on-Trent... Weight-lifters are frequently laid low with muscle spasms and slipped discs.* PHR : VB INFLECTS

21 If you **are lying low**, you are in hiding or are avoiding being seen in public; an informal expression. EG *She'll have to lie low for a couple of years.* PHR : VB INFLECTS ⇑ hide

22 If a cow **lows**, it makes a deep, long sound; a rather old-fashioned word. EG *The cattle are lowing.* V = moo

lowbrow /ləʊbraʊ/. Something that is **lowbrow** is simple and easy to understand rather than being intellectual or complicated. EG *...lowbrow culture... ...lowbrow entertainment.* ADJ QUALIT ⇑ common

low-cut dresses and blouses leave a woman's neck, shoulders, and the top part of her chest bare. EG *...a low-cut lace nightgown.* ADJ QUALIT

low-down; also spelled as one word. **Low-down** is pronounced /ləʊdaʊn/ in paragraph 1 and /ləʊdaʊn/ in paragraph 2. **1** The **low-down** on something is all the important information that people want or need about it; used in informal English. EG *They are dying to get the low-down on what's going on in Birmingham.* N SING : *the*+N, IF+PREP THEN *on*

2 Low-down also means dishonest or unfair; an informal word used showing disapproval. EG *He's a low-down, rotten bum... What a nasty, low-down trick.* ADJ QUALIT : ATTRIB

lower, lowers, lowering, lowered. Lower is pronounced /ləʊə/ except in paragraph 8, when it is pronounced /laʊə/. **1 Lower** is the comparative of **low**.

2 Lower describes **2.1** something that is below something else, usually the bottom one of a pair of things. EG *Thomas was lying in the lower bunk... He slid the top bolt then bent down and slid the lower bolt... Jane sucked at her lower lip.* ADJ CLASSIF : ATTRIB **2.2** the second or less important one of two organizations, groups, or systems that work together, for example in law or government. EG *...the Speaker of the lower house... He could argue his case in the lower court.* ADJ CLASSIF : ATTRIB ≠ upper **2.3** the bottom part of something. EG *The bullet had penetrated the lower left corner of his back.* ADJ CLASSIF : ATTRIB

3 Lower also describes people or things that have less importance than other people or things, or that are near the bottom of a particular scale. EG *...the lower animals... ...a class of junior bureaucrats and lower military officers... There is stagnation at the lower levels of the party.* ADJ CLASSIF : ATTRIB ≠ higher

4 If you **lower** something, **4.1** you move it slowly downwards. EG *He lowered his glass as I sat down beside him... He put his arm round her and lowered her on to the chair... Lynn ran a bath and lowered herself into the water.* V+O (NG/REFL) ⇑ drop ≠ raise ◊ **lowering**. EG *The frozen water in the ice caps caused a lowering of the sea level.* ◊ N SING WITH DET ⇑ dropping **4.2** you make it less in amount, degree, value, or quality. EG *Poverty has lowered the quality of life in cities... The voting age was lowered to eighteen... Mexican hotels are lowering their rates sharply.* V+O ≠ raise ◊ **lowering**. EG *We have changed several courses without any lowering of examination standards.* ◊ N SING WITH DET

5 If you say that you would not **lower** yourself by doing something, you mean that you would not behave in a way that would make you or other people respect you less. EG *I wouldn't lower myself by answering such a question.* V+O (REFL) : USU WITH BROAD NEG = demean

6 If you **lower** your eyes, you look downwards. EG *She lowered her eyes and remained silent for a moment... The girl shot a look at Judy from under her lowered lids.* V+O ≠ raise

7 If you **lower** your voice, you speak more quietly. EG *She lowered her voice and leaned forward.* V+O ≠ raise

8 If the sky **is lowering**, it is very dark and unpleasant, and looks as if there will soon be rain, snow, etc. EG *...grey and lowering skies full of snow.* V : USU CONT

lower case; usually used before another noun and spelled with a hyphen. **Lower-case** letters are small letters, not capital letters. EG *...signs in lower-case lettering.* N UNCOUNT, OR ADJ CLASSIF ⇑ small

lower class, lower classes. The **lower class** or **lower classes** are the class in society that is below the middle class. EG *I'm one of the lower classes and I'm proud of it.* ▸ used as an adjective, usually spelled with a hyphen. EG *Many lower-class families are richer than upper-class ones.*
N COUNT : USU PL, SING=PL = working class ▸ ADJ CLASSIF = working class

lowest common denominator, lowest common denominators. 1 The **lowest common denominator** in a situation is the thing that interests or is understood by most people in a particular group; used especially to refer to something that is not considered to be attractive or valuable. EG *...debased arguments from populism, pandering to the lowest common denominator... Trade associations and employer groups tend to reflect the lowest common denominator among their members.*
N COUNT : USU SING

2 In mathematics, the **lowest common denominator** is the smallest number that all the numbers on the bottom of a particular group of fractions can be divided into; a technical term.
N COUNT

low-flying aircraft, birds, etc are flying very close to the ground, or lower than normal. EG *The new system could provide warning of low-flying aircraft or missile attack.*
ADJ CLASSIF : USU ATTRIB

low-key. Something that is **low-key** or **low-keyed** is not obvious or intense in the way that it is done or dealt with. EG *The organization lent us support in its own low-key way... ...quarrels so low-keyed as to be almost invisible.*
ADJ QUALIT ⇑ moderate

lowlands /ləʊlə³ndz/ are an area of land that is flat and close to sea level in height. EG *...the lowlands of Holland and Belgium.*
N PLURAL : the+N

lowly /ləʊli¹/, **lowlier, lowliest.** Something that is **lowly** is low in rank, status, or importance. EG *A number of trades, previously thought of as lowly ones, began to receive more attention... The magazine ranked a lowly 52nd among British publications.*
ADJ QUALIT = humble, inferior

low-lying land is at, near, or below sea level. EG *All the low-lying areas were affected by the recent floods.*
ADJ QUALIT

low-minded. If you describe someone as **low-minded**, you mean that you consider them to be crude and vulgar, especially because they think or talk about sex a lot. EG *Certain low-minded individuals would laugh every time sex was even mentioned.*
ADJ QUALIT = base

low-necked dresses, blouses, etc leave a woman's neck, shoulders, and the top part of her chest bare.
ADJ QUALIT

low-paid describes people and jobs that are only paid a small amount of money. EG *...low-paid workers... ...women in low paid jobs.* ▸ The **low-paid** is used to refer to people who are low-paid. EG *People like the low paid and the unemployed need special help.*
ADJ QUALIT ▸ N PLURAL : the+N

low-pitched. 1 A sound that is **low-pitched** is deep. EG *...a low-pitched whistle.*
ADJ QUALIT

2 A voice that is **low-pitched** is very soft and quiet.
ADJ QUALIT

low season. The **low season** is the time of year when a holiday resort, hotel, tourist attraction, etc receives the fewest visitors. EG *Going to Venice in the low season is bound to be a lot cheaper.*
N SING : the+N

low-spirited. If you are **low-spirited**, you are depressed.
ADJ QUALIT = low

low tide is the lowest point that the sea reaches at the coast twice each day; used also to refer to the time at which this happens. EG *We walked across to Hilbre Island at low tide... Anemones sticking to the rocks are exposed at low tide.*
N UNCOUNT ⇑ tide

low water is the same as **low tide**.
N UNCOUNT

loyal /lɔɪəl/. Someone who is **loyal** remains firm in their friendship or support for someone or something; used showing approval. EG *Most Tories remained loyal to the Government... ...a loyal supporter of Hughes... ...a loyal friend.* ◊ **loyally.** EG *For thirty years she had served him loyally.*
ADJ QUALIT = faithful, true ≠ fickle ◊ ADV WITH VB = faithfully

loyalist /lɔɪəlɪst/, **loyalists.** A **loyalist** is a person who remains firm in their support for a government or ruler. EG *Thatcher's loyalists are worried about the future... ...a loyalist Army unit.*
N COUNT ⇑ supporter

loyalty /lɔɪəlti¹/, **loyalties.** 1 **Loyalty** is the quality of being firm in your friendship or support for someone or something. EG *The loyalty of the Army was put to the test... I am convinced of your loyalty to the cause.*
N UNCOUNT = faithfulness

2 A **loyalty** is a feeling of friendship, support, or duty towards someone or something. EG *...a constitutional issue that transcended party loyalties... Children suffer from divided loyalties when their parents separate.*
N COUNT : USU PL = allegiance

lozenge /lɒzɪ²ndʒ/, **lozenges.** A **lozenge** is 1 a tablet which you can suck when you have a cough or sore throat. Lozenges contain medicine that helps to reduce the pain or irritation. EG *...throat lozenges.* 2 a shape like a square which usually has two corners pointing up and down that are further apart than the corners that point sideways.
N COUNT = pastille; N COUNT = diamond

LP, LPs. An **LP** is a record which usually has about 25 minutes of music, speech, etc on each side. EG *I put an Aretha Franklin LP on.*
N COUNT = album

L-plate /ɛl pleɪt/, **L-plates.** **L-plates** are attached to the front and back of a car in Britain when you are learning to drive. They are square white pieces of plastic or metal with a large, red letter 'L' on them.
N COUNT

LSD is a drug which has a very strong effect on your mind and often causes you to see things that do not really exist or to feel very confident or scared.
N UNCOUNT = acid

Lt (pronounced as 'lieutenant') is a written abbreviation for 'lieutenant'; used before a person's name as part of their title. EG *...Lt Horst... ...Lt. Col. Ferguson.*

Ltd (pronounced as 'limited') is a written abbreviation for 'limited'; used after the name of a company: compare **PLC**. EG *...Walker Computers Ltd.*

lubricant /luːbrɪkənt/, **lubricants.** A **lubricant** is a substance such as oil which you put on the surfaces or parts of something so that they move smoothly, for example in a machine; a formal word. EG *...a can of spray lubricant.*
N COUNT/UNCOUNT

lubricate /luːbrɪkeɪt/, **lubricates, lubricating, lubricated.** If you **lubricate** something such as a part of a machine, you put a substance such as oil on it so that it moves smoothly; a formal word. EG *The chain might need lubricating.* ◊ **lubrication** /luːbrɪkeɪʃə⁰n/. EG *...the lubrication system of the engine.*
V+O = grease ◊ N UNCOUNT

lubricious /luːbrɪʃəs/ means having or indicating a strong interest in sex; a literary word, often used showing disapproval. EG *...the landlady's lubricious daughter... He uttered a lubricious chuckle.*
ADJ QUALIT = lascivious

lucerne /luːsɜːn/ is a plant that is grown for animals to eat and in order to improve the soil. EG *...fodder crops like clover and lucerne.*
N UNCOUNT

lucid /luːsɪd/; a formal or literary word. 1 Writing or speech that is **lucid** is expressed in a way which is clear and easy to understand. EG *...a brief and lucid account of its growth and scale... His recent and very lucid biography of Marx.* ◊ **lucidly.** EG *Her ideas are very lucidly set out in his book.* ◊ **lucidity** /luːsɪdɪti¹/. EG *He expresses himself with quiet lucidity... The speech was a model of lucidity.*
ADJ QUALIT = comprehensible ◊ ADV WITH VB ◊ N UNCOUNT ⇑ clarity

2 If you say that someone is **lucid**, you are emphasizing that they are thinking clearly, especially if they have previously been unwell, confused, or mentally ill. EG *There was a ringing in my head, yet I was lucid.* ◊ **lucidity.** EG *In one of his moments of lucidity, he came upstairs to talk.*
ADJ QUALIT = clear-headed ≠ confused, dazed ◊ N UNCOUNT ⇑ clarity

3 Something that is **lucid** is very bright and clear. EG *...the lucid air... In the twilight everything is lucid but colourless... ...a lucid light.* ◊ **lucidity.** EG *Her eyes had a beautiful lucidity.*
ADJ QUALIT = limpid ◊ N UNCOUNT ⇑ clarity

luck /lʌk/. 1 **Luck** is 1.1 a force or quality that seems to cause good things to happen to some people but not to others, without any reason or purpose. EG *Of course it's all luck. You never know how many you are going to get... ...a stroke of luck... I couldn't believe my luck.* 1.2 the success that a person has, especially when it does not seem to result from their abilities, qualifications, or efforts. EG *I had some wonderful luck... All he did was shake hands and wish me luck... They didn't have much luck with government support.*
N UNCOUNT ⇑ chance; N UNCOUNT ⇑ fortune

2 The word **luck** is also used in the following expressions. 2.1 If you ask someone the question **'Any luck?'** or **'No luck?'**, you want to know whether they have been successful in finding something or doing something; an informal expression. EG *'Any luck?' Boylan asked. 'There are two in the basket,' I said.* 2.2 You say **'Bad luck'**, **'Hard luck'**, or **'Tough luck'** to someone in order to express sympathy for them, for example when they fail to do or get something. EG *Tough luck, Barrett. You played a great game... Oh, bad luck. I'm terribly sorry.* 2.3 If you say that it is **bad luck** or **good luck** to do something, you mean that you believe that anyone
CONVENTION; CONVENTION; PHR : USU USED AS C = unlucky

who does it is less likely or more likely to succeed or have pleasant experiences. EG *It's bad luck to tell... To touch a rooster's spur was even worse luck.* **2.4** If you say that something **brings** someone **luck**, **brings bad luck**, etc, you mean that you believe that it makes them more likely or less likely to succeed or to have pleasant experiences. EG *Silver brings good luck, they believe.* [PHR : VB INFLECTS] **2.5** If you say that someone **is down on** their **luck**, you mean that they have been unfortunate, and especially that they have very little money; an informal expression. [PHR : VB INFLECTS] **2.6** If you do something **for luck**, you do it without any real reason or purpose. EG *...adding an extra spoonful for luck.* [PHR : USED AS AN A] **2.7** If you say **'Good luck'** or **'Best of luck'** to someone, you are telling them that you hope they will be successful. EG *Good luck to you, my boy... Best of luck with the exams.* [CONVENTION] **2.8** If you say that someone is **in luck**, you mean that they are fortunate, especially when something they want is available and they can have it. EG *You're in luck. I even found a clean sheet... We were in luck, it was the last one I had.* [PHR : USED AS AN A = lucky] **2.9** If you say that **luck was with** someone or that **luck was on** their **side**, you mean that they won or succeeded unexpectedly and by chance, and not because of their abilities, qualifications, or efforts. EG *I only had the minimum qualifications, but luck was with me... The enemy commanders were even sillier than ours. Luck was on our side.* [PHR : VB INFLECTS] **2.10** If you say that someone is **out of luck**, you mean that they are unfortunate, especially when they cannot get or do something that is normally easy to get or do. [PHR : USED AS AN A] **2.11** You say **'No such luck'** to emphasize your disappointment when something you wanted to happen did not happen; an informal expression. EG *We had hoped the rain would let up. No such luck.* [CONVENTION/PHR = some hope] **2.12** If someone **pushes** their **luck**, they take a risk and try to achieve more than is reasonable in a particular situation. EG *Don't push your luck!... Pushing my luck, I asked why I was being sent... Aren't you pushing your luck at your age?* [PHR : VB INFLECTS] **2.13** If someone **tries** their **luck**, they try to succeed or to obtain something, especially something new or different, often after failing or when there is little hope of success. EG *He came to England to try his luck at a musical career... I tried my luck at another farm... Davis lingered in the bar to try his luck with a fruit machine.* [PHR : VB INFLECTS] **2.14** You say **with luck, with any luck**, etc, to indicate that you are not sure, but you hope that a particular thing will happen or be correct; an informal expression. EG *This one should work with a bit of luck... ...60, 80, or with luck a hundred hours... With any luck they might forget all about it.* [PHR : USED AS AN A ⇑ maybe] **2.15** If you add **worse luck** after a statement, you are expressing disappointment or annoyance about it; an informal expression. EG *I've got an aunt coming this afternoon, worse luck.* [PHR : USED AS ADV SEN = unfortunately] **2.16** • **luck of the draw**: see **draw**. See also **hard luck story, pot luck**.

luckily /lʌkɪli¹/. You can add **luckily** to a statement to say that it is very fortunate that something happened or is the case, because otherwise the situation would have been embarrassing, unpleasant, or dangerous. EG *Luckily, Saturday was a fine day... Luckily, Joly came to my rescue... Luckily for you, I happen to have the key.* [ADV SEN = fortunately]

luckless /lʌklɪ²s/. Someone or something that is **luckless** is unsuccessful or unfortunate; a formal or literary word. EG *Half the luckless troops that remained behind were dead or dying... This trip of ours, so far, has been singularly luckless... He had some luckless affairs at college.* [ADJ QUALIT : USU ATTRIB = ill-fated]

lucky /lʌki¹/, **luckier, luckiest**. **1** Someone who is **lucky** seems always to have good luck. EG *He hates me because I am younger and luckier... He was the luckiest man in the world... Are you lucky at cards?* [ADJ QUALIT = fortunate]
2 If you say that someone is **lucky** on a particular occasion or in a particular situation, you mean that they are more fortunate than on other occasions or than other people in the same situation. EG *The average peasant may be lucky enough to find eight months work a year... ...the lucky winners... I'm lucky in having an excellent teacher... Jim was one of the lucky ones... He's lucky I didn't kill him.* [ADJ QUALIT]
3 If you describe a situation or event as **lucky**, you mean that it was fortunate or successful, and you are emphasizing that it happened by chance and not as a result of planning or preparation. EG *It's lucky I'm here... It was lucky that I had cooked a big joint... ...a lucky guess... This was going to be one of his lucky days... They had a lucky escape.* [ADJ QUALIT]
4 A **lucky** object of some kind is one that you believe helps you to be successful or to have pleasant experiences. EG *...his lucky sweater... ...a lucky rabbit's foot. ...a lucky charm.* [ADJ CLASSIF : USU ATTRIB]
5 The word **lucky** is also used in the following expressions. **5.1** You say **'Lucky you', 'Lucky devil'**, etc when you are slightly jealous of someone else's good fortune or success, or surprised at it; an informal expression. EG *Some people have them, lucky devils!... Lucky old Thomson!* [CONVENTION] **5.2** If someone **thanks** their **lucky stars**, they are extremely pleased and grateful that something has happened; an informal expression. EG *...thanking my lucky stars that I got in.* [PHR : VB INFLECTS] **5.3** If you say that someone **will be lucky** to do or get something, or **is lucky** if they do or get it, you mean that they are very unlikely to be able to do or get it, and certainly will not do or get any more than that. EG *He's lucky if he can stay on for three months... We will be lucky to get five pounds for it.* [PHR : VB INFLECTS] **5.4** You say **'You'll be lucky'** or **'You should be so lucky'** to someone when you think they want more than is reasonable in a particular situation; used especially when you are refusing to do something that they have asked you to do. It is a very informal expression. [CONVENTION]

lucky dip, lucky dips. **Lucky dip** is a game in which you take an object out of a covered container full of different objects and then find out what you have chosen. The game is often played at fairs, where you pay a small amount of money first and keep the object as a sort of prize; used in British English. [N UNCOUNT/COUNT]

lucrative /lu:krətɪv/. An activity, job, or business deal that is **lucrative** is one that earns you a lot of money or makes large profits. EG *It had been an exciting and lucrative business... ...the lucrative spice trade... ...a lucrative arms deal.* [ADJ QUALIT = profitable]

lucre /lu:kə/ is money or profit, often when it is obtained by dishonest means or in a situation where money should not be the main concern; an informal or old-fashioned word. EG *...marketed for lucre in the name of liberty... ...a share of the lucre.* [N UNCOUNT = loot]

Luddite /lʌdaɪt/, **Luddites**. If you refer to someone as a **Luddite**, you mean that they strongly oppose changes in industrial methods, especially the introduction of new machines, because they think it will lead to people losing their jobs; a formal word, used showing disapproval. EG *...the nation's leading Luddite... ...fighting in a Luddite way against improvements and productivity.* [N COUNT ⇑ reactionary]

ludicrous /lu:dɪkrəs/. If you describe someone or something as **ludicrous**, you mean that they are extremely foolish, unreasonable, or unsuitable. EG *...one teacher for every 100 pupils, it was ludicrous... Men go on doing ludicrous and irresponsible things... ...at a cost which now seems ludicrous.* [ADJ QUALIT = absurd, ridiculous] ◊ **ludicrously**. EG *The farm was for sale at a ludicrously low price... ...ludicrously blond hair.* [◊ ADV = ridiculously]

lug /lʌg/, **lugs, lugging, lugged**. If you **lug** someone or something from one place to another, you carry or take them there with some difficulty, for example because they are heavy; an informal word. EG *She lugged the suitcase out into the hallway... ...bits of paper that I didn't want to lug along with me.* [V+O : USU+A = drag, cart]

luggage /lʌgɪdʒ/ consists of the suitcases, bags, etc that you have with you when you are travelling; used mainly in British English. EG *They did not have much luggage... We waited for our luggage... The car was overloaded with luggage... I'm just going to put the luggage in now.* • See also **left luggage**. [N UNCOUNT ⇑ belongings = baggage]

lughole /lʌghᵒəʊl/, **lugholes**. Your **lugholes** are your ears; used in very informal British English. [N COUNT : USU POSS+N]

lugubrious /lə⁴gu:brɪəs/. Someone or something that is **lugubrious** is sad and dull, not lively or cheerful; a literary word. EG *...a lugubrious face... ...the rather lugubrious facade of the big house... ...some lugubrious hymn.* [ADJ QUALIT = sombre, gloomy] ◊ **lugubriously**. EG *'Alas, we have indeed,' the little man muttered lugubriously.* [◊ ADV WITH VB = gloomily]

lukewarm /lu:kwɔ:m/. **1** Something, especially a liquid, that is **lukewarm** is only slightly warm. EG *Try using lukewarm water and ordinary soap... The coffee was still lukewarm, but untouched... ...a current of lukewarm air.* [ADJ QUALIT = tepid]

2 If you describe a person or their attitude as **lukewarm**, you mean that they are not showing much enthusiasm or interest. EG *...her parents' lukewarm response... They offered only lukewarm support... He was lukewarm about the committee.* — ADJ QUALIT = half-hearted ≠ enthusiastic

lull /lʌl/, **lulls, lulling, lulled.** 1 A **lull** is a period of quiet or of little activity in a longer period of greater activity or excitement. EG *...a momentary lull in the Watergate case... After a lull of several weeks, there has been a resumption of bombing... ...during one of those unfortunate lulls in the conversation.* — N COUNT ⇑ pause

2 If you describe a situation as the **lull before the storm**, you mean that you think something very unpleasant is going to happen soon. — PHR : USED AS C/O

3 If someone or something **lulls** you, 3.1 they cause you to feel calm or sleepy. EG *...lulling us into slumber... The motion of the bus lulled her.* — V+O 3.2 they cause you to feel safe, especially as a deliberate plan before they attack or cheat you. EG *This will lull them into a false sense of security... He had lulled me into thinking that I had won... We have been lulled by a generation of peace in Europe.* — V+O : USU+*into* ⇑ deceive

lullaby /lʌləbaɪ/, **lullabies.** A **lullaby** is a quiet song which you sing in order to help a child go to sleep. EG *When he was a little lad, I used to sing him lullabies.* — N COUNT

lumbago /lʌmbeɪgəʊ/ is a severe pain in the lower part of your back. It can be caused by an illness, an accident, old age, etc. EG *Many of the devices are aimed at people with lumbago.* — N UNCOUNT ⇑ backache

lumbar /lʌmbə/ means existing or occurring in the lower part of your back; a medical term. EG *...the five lumbar joints... ...the lumbar region of the spine.* — ADJ CLASSIF : ATTRIB

lumber /lʌmbə/, **lumbers, lumbering, lumbered.** 1 **Lumber** consists of 1.1 tree trunks, logs, or planks of wood that have been cut for use, but only roughly; used mainly in American English. EG *I followed the road down past the piles of lumber... ...a northern lumber company.* — N UNCOUNT = timber 1.2 old and unwanted things, especially large things such as old pieces of furniture; used mainly in British English. EG *The wheels had been consigned to the loft as useless lumber... ...the lumber room.* — N UNCOUNT = junk

2 If someone or something **lumbers** from one place to another, they move very slowly and often clumsily or with difficulty. EG *Donkeys lumbered by... The armoured vehicles started to lumber towards the tower... He lumbered upstairs looking for the bathroom.* ◊ **lumbering.** EG *...a heavy, lumbering trot.* — V+A = trundle; ◊ ADJ CLASSIF

lumber with. If someone **lumbers** you **with** something, they cause you to have or do something difficult that you don't really want; an informal expression. EG *New families were unwilling to lumber themselves with too much land... Women are still lumbered with the cooking and cleaning... I can see I'm going to get lumbered with it if I'm not careful.* — PHRASAL VB : V+O (NG/REFL.)+PREP, HAS PASS = saddle

lumberjack /lʌmbədʒæk/, **lumberjacks.** A **lumberjack** is a man whose job is to cut down trees. — N COUNT

lumberyard /lʌmbəjɑ:d/, **lumberyards.** A **lumberyard** is a place where roughly cut tree trunks, logs, or planks of wood are stored or sold. — N COUNT

luminary /lu:mɪnəʳri¹/, **luminaries.** A **luminary** is someone who is famous or who is an expert in a particular subject or activity; a literary word. EG *...visits by such luminaries as Elizabeth Taylor... ...a major luminary of British architecture... ...legal luminaries.* — N COUNT = notable

luminescence /lu:mɪnesəns/ is a soft, glowing light; a literary word. EG *...a dim room lit by a pinkish luminescence... The sky became suffused with a pale, milky luminescence.* — N UNCOUNT = glow

luminosity /lu:mɪnɒsɪti¹/ is bright light; a literary word. EG *...twinkling points of pale luminosity... Mysterious patterns of luminosity glowed in the night.* — N UNCOUNT = radiance

luminous /lu:mɪnəs/. Something that is **luminous** shines or glows with light, especially in the dark. EG *...the luminous hands of my watch... The sky was not black but luminous with stars... ...luminous beetles.* — ADJ QUALIT ⇑ shining

lump /lʌmp/, **lumps, lumping, lumped.** 1 A **lump** is a piece of a solid substance, of any shape or size. EG *...lumps of clay... ...raw lumps of meat... ...a lump of butter.* — N COUNT/PART = chunk, dollop

2 A **lump** on or in someone's body is a small, hard piece of flesh that is formed as a result of an injury or an illness. EG *...a report recommending women to examine their own breasts for lumps.* — N COUNT ⇑ swelling = growth

3 A **lump** of sugar is a small amount of sugar shaped like a cube, which is added to hot drinks. EG *'Black coffee, two lumps, please.'... She dropped several lumps of sugar into her tea.* — N PART

4 **Lump** is used to refer to an amount of something, especially money, that you use, give, or receive as one large amount on a single occasion rather than as smaller amounts on several separate occasions. EG *...a lump donation to an African charity... There's another lump due when I'm thirty-five.* ● See also **lump sum.** — N COUNT, OR N BEFORE N

5 If you say that someone has a **lump in** their **throat**, you mean that they have a tight feeling in their throat because of a strong emotion such as sorrow or gratitude; an informal expression. EG *I couldn't account for the lump in my throat as I told him the news.* — PHR : USED AS O/S, NOUNS INFLECT

6 If you say that someone will **lump it** or will **have to lump it**, you mean that they must accept a situation or decision whether they like it or not. EG *Otherwise I'll have both halves and you'll have to lump it... 'He won't like that.'–'Then he'll lump it.'* — PHR : VB INFLECTS = put up with

7 If you **lump** different people or things **together**, you consider or treat them in the same way or combine them into one large group, especially without thinking or caring about them very much. EG *'Don't lump me and Dave together,' he interrupted... The old rural counties were lumped together into new units... The budget for saving should not be lumped with the disaster fund.* — V+O+A *(with/together)*

lump sum, lump sums. A **lump sum** is an amount of money that is paid as a large amount on a single occasion rather than as smaller amounts on several separate occasions. EG *He has been offered a tax-free lump sum of $4,000... Under 20 per cent you get a lump sum, over 20 per cent you get a pension each week... ...lump sum payments for special needs.* — N COUNT

lumpy /lʌmpi¹/, **lumpier, lumpiest.** Something that is **lumpy** contains lumps or is covered with lumps. EG *...sitting on his lumpy mattress... Her face tends to be puffy and lumpy... ...a big bowl of lumpy porridge.* — ADJ QUALIT ⇑ uneven

lunacy /lu:nəsi¹/ is 1 behaviour which seems very strange, foolish, or annoying, because there is no reason or justification for it. EG *This comment would have seemed sheer lunacy to his ancestors... ...a demonstration of industrial lunacy... It would be lunacy to marry.* — N UNCOUNT ⇑ folly = madness 2 severe mental illness; an old-fashioned use. EG *His eyes were bright with lunacy.* — N UNCOUNT = insanity

lunar /lu:nə/ means concerning the moon, or its movement, or travel to the moon; a fairly formal word. EG *...a slanting descent to the lunar surface... ...floating in lunar orbit... ...the lunar spacecraft.* — ADJ CLASSIF : ATTRIB

lunar month, lunar months. A **lunar month** is twenty-nine and a half days, which is the time that the moon takes to go round the earth. — N COUNT ⇑ period

lunatic /lu:nətɪk/, **lunatics.** 1 A **lunatic** is 1.1 someone whose behaviour is very strange, foolish, or annoying; used showing disapproval in informal English. EG *The man's a bloody lunatic... ...cars filled with noisy lunatics.* — N COUNT = idiot 1.2 someone who is mentally ill; an old-fashioned use. EG *Out of more than a dozen patients, three or four were lunatics.* — N COUNT = madman

2 Behaviour, actions, or ideas that are **lunatic** are very foolish and likely to be dangerous; used showing disapproval. EG *This Government's policies are lunatic... The arms race is resuming on a scale more lunatic than ever.* — ADJ QUALIT = crazy

3 A **lunatic** situation is confused and seems out of control. EG *...the lunatic atmosphere... ...a lunatic cacophony of noises.* — ADJ QUALIT : ATTRIB = wild

lunatic asylum, lunatic asylums. A **lunatic asylum** is a place where people were locked up in former times if they were considered to be mad. EG *...hospitals, prisons and lunatic asylums... He ended his life in a lunatic asylum.* — N COUNT

lunatic fringe. If you refer to a group of people as the **lunatic fringe**, you mean that they are very extreme in their opinions or behaviour; used showing disapproval. EG *...a group on the lunatic fringe... ...the lunatic fringe of the movement... Who but the lunatic fringe thinks colour is the issue now?* — N SING : *the*+N

lunch /lʌntᵒʃ/, **lunches, lunching, lunched.** 1 **Lunch** is 1.1 a meal that you have in the middle of the day. EG *What did you have for lunch?... I'm going out to lunch... He quietly ate his lunch... ...long lunches with friends... We had a late lunch.* — N COUNT/UNCOUNT 1.2 the — N UNCOUNT

time around midday when you have a meal. EG *Next day, after lunch, I went to see our doctor... ...engaged in conversation from breakfast till lunch.*
2 A **lunch** is a formal meal around midday, usually in honour of a famous person or to celebrate an important event. EG *He had never been invited to a Palace lunch... Is the Prime Minister giving a lunch?* N COUNT = luncheon
3 When you **lunch**, you eat a meal in the middle of the day, especially at a restaurant; a fairly formal use. EG *Why don't you two lunch with me tomorrow?... ...lunching at the Savoy on smoked Salmon and grouse... ...lunching off beer and cheese rolls in a pub.* V: USU+A

luncheon /lʌntʃən/, **luncheons**. 1 A **luncheon** is a formal meal around midday, usually in honour of a famous person or to celebrate an important event. EG *...cocktail parties, women's luncheons, family reunions... ...a private luncheon at the Aldwych Club... She met her at a literary luncheon.* N COUNT ⇑ celebration
2 **Luncheon** is the meal that you eat around midday; a formal or old-fashioned use. EG *...as you sit down to luncheon... I bought a pie for luncheon.* N COUNT/UNCOUNT = lunch

luncheon meat is a mixture of meat, usually pork, and cereal. It is sold in tins. EG *...cheese, bread, luncheon meat, sausage.* N UNCOUNT

luncheon voucher, luncheon vouchers. **Luncheon vouchers** are vouchers that are given by a company to its employees. They can be used instead of cash to pay for food in some restaurants; used mainly in British English. N COUNT = meal ticket

lunch hour, lunch hours; also spelled with a hyphen. A **lunch hour** is the period in the middle of the day when most people stop work in order to have a meal. EG *It's simple, you can do it in a lunch hour... They spend their lunch hours in smoky pubs... The secretaries were just back from their lunch hour.* N COUNT

lunchtime /lʌntʃtaɪm/, **lunchtimes**; also spelled with a hyphen. **Lunchtime** is the time in the middle of the day when most people have lunch. EG *She's going to see him at lunchtime... By lunchtime the next day the whole school knew every detail... ...lunchtime meetings.* N COUNT/UNCOUNT ⇑ midday

lung /lʌŋ/, **lungs**. Your **lungs** are the two parts of your body inside your chest which fill with air when you breathe. EG *She filled her lungs with smoke... Her father died of lung cancer.* N COUNT: USU PL ⇑ organ

lunge /lʌndʒ/, **lunges, lunging, lunged**. If you **lunge** in a particular direction, you move in that direction suddenly and clumsily, usually in order to catch or hit someone or something. EG *He lunged toward me... ...lunging with a rolled-up newspaper at the dog.* ▸ used as a noun. EG *When he makes a lunge at you, run.* V: USU+A = dart ▸ N COUNT: USU SING

lurch /lɜːtʃ/, **lurches, lurching, lurched**. 1 To **lurch** means to make a sudden, jerky movement, especially when moving forward. EG *He lurched and fell... The boat lurched ahead... The young man lurched to his feet.* ▸ used as a noun. EG *With a tremendous lurch he fell over me.* V: USU+A = stumble, flounder ▸ N COUNT
2 If you **lurch** from one thing to another, you suddenly change your opinions, attitude, or behaviour. EG *After lurching away from Socialism in 1976, they now seem to be lurching back.* ▸ used as a noun. EG *...the Labour Party's unilateralist lurch.* V: USU+A = shift ▸ N COUNT = shift
3 If someone **leaves** you **in the lurch**, they go away or stop helping you at a very difficult or dangerous time; an informal expression used showing disapproval. EG *'He'll bolt now and leave me in the lurch,' he thought.* PHR: VB INFLECTS ⇑ abandon = desert

lure /lʊə/, **lures, luring, lured**. 1 To **lure** someone means to attract them and cause them to go to a particular place or to do something that they should not do. EG *The price also lures students... Why else had Halliday come up to the saloon, if not to lure me away?... You were lured away from your political commitment by an appeal to your patriotism.* V+O: USU+A = draw, entice, tempt
2 A **lure** is an attractive quality that something has, or something that you find attractive. EG *Many economists have succumbed to the fatal lure of mathematics... Keep him away from drink and the lure of other women.* N COUNT: USU SING+SUPP = attraction

lurgy /lɜːgi¹/. If you have the **lurgy**, you have an illness which is not serious, for example a cold; used humorously in informal British English. EG *Oh no, I think I've got the dreaded lurgy again.* N SING WITH DET

lurid /lʊərɪd/. Something that is **lurid** 1 involves violence, sex, or other immoral activities, or descriptions of these activities; used showing disapproval. EG *He'd tell them lurid stories about the war... ...lurid novels... ...his lurid sexual history.* 2 is very brightly coloured. EG *...lurid polyester skirts...* ◇ **luridly**. EG *The living-room was luridly lit by a large orange paper globe... ...a luridly coloured advertisement.* ADJ QUALIT ⇑ shocking; ADJ QUALIT; ◇ ADV = garishly

lurk /lɜːk/, **lurks, lurking, lurked**. 1 To **lurk** somewhere means to wait there secretly so that you cannot be seen, especially in order to attack someone or something or to spy on them. EG *Wild boars and wolves lurked near the isolated camp... I dared not open the door for fear of the photographer lurking outside.* V: USU+A = skulk
2 If something such as a memory, suspicion, or danger **lurks**, it exists, but you are only slightly aware of it. EG *...outdated prejudices and fancies lurking in the minds of individuals... But danger lurked in the atmosphere.* V: USU+A = hover

luscious /lʌʃəs/. 1 If you describe something as **luscious**, you mean that you find it extremely attractive. EG *...a luscious car... She was looking luscious in faded overalls and a flannel shirt.* ADJ QUALIT ⇑ pleasurable = desirable
2 **Luscious** food is juicy and delicious. EG *...a basket of luscious figs.* ADJ QUALIT

lush /lʌʃ/, **lusher, lushest**; used showing approval. **Lush** describes 1 plants, trees, gardens, etc that are healthy and growing well and thickly. EG *...a landscape of lush green meadows... ...lush tropical vegetation.* ◇ **lushness**. EG *...all the lushness of nature.* 2 places or ways of life that are very rich and full of luxury. EG *...lush restaurants in London and Paris... ...lush jobs in the UN.* ◇ **lushness**. EG *He began to feel he might soon be smothered in lushness.* 3 music that is very rich and pleasing. EG *The recording by the Philharmonic is very lush indeed, not at all what you expect of Sibelius.* ◇ **lushness**. ADJ QUALIT = rich, verdant; ◇ N UNCOUNT; ADJ QUALIT = plush; ◇ N UNCOUNT = opulence; ADJ QUALIT ⇑ pleasurable; ◇ N UNCOUNT

lust /lʌst/, **lusts, lusting, lusted**. 1 **Lust** is a feeling of strong sexual desire for someone; used showing disapproval. EG *He caught himself gazing with idle lust at one of the young, long-legged girls who served behind the bar.* N UNCOUNT ⇑ passion
2 A **lust** for something is a very strong and eager desire to possess or gain it; used showing disapproval. EG *...the lust for power... People sometimes go to extraordinary lengths to satisfy their lusts.* N COUNT: IF+PREP THEN *for* ⇑ greed

lust after. 1 If you **lust after** something or **lust for** it, you have a very strong desire to possess it. EG *They lusted after the gold of El Dorado... She is like a child lusting for toys.* PHRASAL VB: V+PREP, HAS PASS ⇑ want, crave
2 If you **lust after** someone or **lust for** them, you feel a very strong sexual desire for them. EG *She had lusted after other men... How I lusted for that girl!* PHRASAL VB: V+PREP, HAS PASS = hunger

lustful /lʌstfʊl/ means feeling or expressing strong sexual desire. EG *...lustful thoughts... ...lustful youths.* ADJ CLASSIF = lecherous

lustre /lʌstə/; also spelled **luster** in American English. 1 **Lustre** is 1.1 gentle shining light that is reflected from a surface, for example from polished metal. EG *...the extraordinary lustre and beauty of her eyes... ...the lustre of encrusted gold.* **1.2** the qualities that something has that make it interesting and exciting. EG *...the tarnished lustre of his name.* N UNCOUNT ⇑ shine = sheen; N UNCOUNT = prestige

lustrous /lʌstrəs/. Something that is **lustrous** shines brightly and gently, because it has a smooth or polished surface. EG *She had lustrous grey-green eyes... The feathers are so fine and lustrous that they look like rich black velvet.* ADJ QUALIT ⇑ shining = glossy

lusty /lʌsti¹/, **lustier, lustiest**. Something that is **lusty** is healthy and full of strength and energy. EG *...a strong and lusty boy of whom any father could be proud... ...her son's lusty cries.* ◇ **lustily**. EG *John Burton was pulling lustily at the bell-rope... They stood waving their Union Jacks and singing lustily.* ADJ QUALIT ⇑ vigorous = sturdy; ◇ ADV WITH VB ⇑ strenuously

lute /luːt/, **lutes**. A **lute** is an old-fashioned musical instrument with strings, which is played like a guitar. EG *He idly plucked the strings of the lute.* N COUNT

luv /lʌv/ is an informal written form of the word 'love', when it is being used as a way of addressing someone. EG *It's different with you, luv.* N VOC = dear, pet

luxuriance /lʌgzjʊərɪəns, lʌgʒ-/. You use **luxuriance** when you are talking about plants, gardens, etc which are healthy and growing well; used showing approval. EG *...the dark luxuriance of the forest.* N UNCOUNT = lushness

luxuriant /lʌgzjʊərɪənt, lʌgʒ-/ describes 1 plants, trees, and gardens which are large, healthy, and growing well. EG *...gardens full of luxuriant plants... ...luxuriant forests and greenery.* ◇ **luxuriantly**. EG *...the sub-tropical vegetation that grew luxuriantly in* ADJ QUALIT = lush; ◇ ADV WITH VB = profusely

the gardens. **2** someone's hair when it is very thick and healthy. EG *...his pale lined face and luxuriant, flowing hair.* ◇ **luxuriantly**. EG *...luxuriantly silky beards.* ADJ QUALIT = profuse ◇ ADV = abundant

luxuriate /lʌgzjʊ̲əriert, lʌgʒ-/, **luxuriates, luxuriating, luxuriated**. If you **luxuriate** in something, you relax in it and enjoy it very much, especially because you find it comfortable and luxurious. EG *...bath tubs in which you could lie back and luxuriate... I luxuriated in my retirement.* V : USU+A *(in)*

luxurious /lʌgzjʊ̲əriəs, lʌgʒ-/. **1** Something that is **luxurious** is very comfortable and expensive. EG *...big, luxurious cars.* ◇ **luxuriously**. EG *We lived luxuriously.* ADJ QUALIT ◇ ADV WITH VB

2 Luxurious means feeling or expressing great pleasure and comfort. EG *He felt comfortable and even luxurious... She took a deep luxurious breath.* ◇ **luxuriously**. EG *She stretched luxuriously.* ADJ QUALIT ⇑ comfortable ◇ ADV

luxury /lʌ̲kʃəri/, **luxuries**. **1 Luxury** is very great comfort, especially beautiful and expensive surroundings, possessions, clothes, etc. EG *We lived for a time in great luxury... ...a life of ease and luxury... This chair is the ultimate in luxury.* N UNCOUNT

2 A **luxury** is **2.1** something quite expensive to buy which is not necessary but which gives you pleasure. EG *...unavailable luxuries–cream, grapes, oranges and lemons... Her mother provided her with clothes and food and little luxuries.* **2.2** a pleasure which you do not often have the opportunity to enjoy, or which very few people are able to enjoy. EG *It's a luxury for me to be able to sleep late... Privacy was an unknown luxury.* N COUNT ⇑ treat; N SING WITH DET +SUPP ⇑ joy

3 Luxury describes things which are expensive, and usually very comfortable or of a special design; used especially in advertising. EG *...luxury hotels... ...a luxury car.* ADJ CLASSIF : ATTRIB

luxury goods are things which are not necessary, but which give you pleasure or make your life more comfortable. Record players, jewellery, and perfume are examples of luxury goods. EG *...a new tax on luxury goods.* N PLURAL ≠ necessities

LV, LV's. **LV** is an abbreviation for 'luncheon voucher'. EG *...salary £9,375 per annum, plus LV's.*

LW is an abbreviation for 'long wave', and is written on radios to help you tune into radio stations which broadcast on long wave. EG *...Radio 4: 1500 LW.*

-ly, -lier, -liest. **1 -ly** is added to adjectives to form adverbs. For example, 'loudly' means in a loud way, and 'rudely' means in a rude manner. Adverbs like these are often not defined in this dictionary but are treated with the related adjectives. EG *...bad→badly... ...quick→quickly... ...probable→probably... ...typical→typically... ...obedient→obediently... ...relentless→relentlessly.* SUFFIX : FORMS ADVS

2 -ly is also **2.1** added to nouns to form adjectives that describe someone or something as being like or typical of a particular kind of person or thing. EG *...friend→friendly... ...saint→saintly... ...coward→cowardly... ...god→godly... ...prince→princely.* **2.2** added to nouns referring to periods of time to form adjectives or adverbs that say how often something happens or is done. EG *...day→daily... ...week→weekly... ...month→monthly.* SUFFIX : FORMS ADJS; SUFFIX : FORMS ADJS/ADVS

lychee /laɪ̲tʃiː/, **lychees**; also spelled **lichee**. A **lychee** is a Chinese fruit which has white flesh and a large stone in the centre. N COUNT

lychgate /lɪ̲tʃgeɪt/, **lychgates**. A **lychgate** is a gate with a roof, which you sometimes see at the entrance to an old churchyard. EG *They were standing now under the arch of the lychgate.* N COUNT

lying /laɪ̲ɪŋ/. **1 Lying** is used to describe someone who is considered to be dishonest or deceitful; used showing disapproval. EG *I wasn't like those other lying journalists... Mr Jones called him a 'lying humbug'.* ADJ CLASSIF : ATTRIB ⇑ untruthful

2 Lying is the act of telling lies. EG *For all of these children, lying is a way of life... She's incapable of lying.* N UNCOUNT ⇑ deceit = dishonesty

lying-in. A woman's **lying-in** is the time that she needs to spend resting, usually in bed, when she gives birth to a child; a fairly old-fashioned expression. EG *Nowadays the lying-in period is usually less than a week.* N UNCOUNT ⇑ rest = confinement

lymph gland, lymph glands. A **lymph gland** is a small mass of tissue inside your body where special white blood cells are formed which help your body to fight infections; a medical term. N COUNT

lynch /lɪ̲ntʃ/, **lynchs, lynching, lynched**. If an angry crowd of people **lynch** someone, they kill that person by hanging them without letting them have a trial, because they believe that that person has committed a crime. EG *At one point he was in danger of being lynched.* V+O

lynchpin /lɪ̲ntʃpɪn/. See **linchpin**.

lynx /lɪ̲ŋks/, **lynxes**. A **lynx** is a wild animal rather like a cat, with a short tail and very good eyesight. N COUNT ⇑ mammal

lyre /laɪ̲ə/, **lyres**. A **lyre** is a musical instrument with strings, rather like a small harp. It was used in ancient Greece. EG *He was plucking at a lyre.* N COUNT

lyric /lɪ̲rɪk/, **lyrics**. **1 Lyric** poetry is written in a simple and direct style, and usually expresses personal emotions such as love. EG *He's almost the greatest lyric poet since Shakespeare... ...lyric poetry.* ADJ CLASSIF : ATTRIB

2 A **lyric** is a poem which is written in the lyric style; a formal or technical term. EG *...a medieval love lyric.* N COUNT

3 The **lyrics** of a modern song are its words. EG *The songs are irresistibly catchy, and the lyrics maddeningly memorable... New lyrics had been written for the song.* N PLURAL

lyrical /lɪ̲rɪkəl/. **1** Something that is **lyrical** is **1.1** poetic and musical. EG *He tries to bring into his plays a special lyrical quality.* ◇ **lyrically**. EG *Lyrical passages should be sung lyrically.* **1.2** very romantic. EG *...a dreamy, lyrical study of the Covent Garden flower market.* ADJ CLASSIF ◇ ADV WITH VB; ADJ QUALIT

2 If you are **lyrical** about something, you are very enthusiastic and eager about it. EG *Ned was growing lyrical.* ◇ **lyrically**. EG *It was Johnson, I remembered, who had written so lyrically about Woolley.* ADJ QUALIT : PRED ◇ ADV WITH VB

lyricism /lɪ̲rɪsɪzəm/ is gentle and romantic emotion, often expressed in writing, poetry, music, etc. EG *A new group of writers seem to revel in the sort of lyricism once regarded as sentimental.* N UNCOUNT

lyricist /lɪ̲rɪsɪst/, **lyricists**. A **lyricist** is someone who writes the words for modern songs or for musicals. EG *...the lyricist Alan Jay Lerner.* N COUNT

Mm

M, m /ɛ̲m/, **Ms, m's**. **1 M** is the thirteenth letter of the English alphabet. N COUNT

2 m is a written abbreviation for 'metres' or 'metre'. EG *...3.5m.*

3 m or **M** is a written abbreviation for the number million. EG *...£56m... ...1.2m barrels a day.*

4 M or **m** is also an abbreviation for other words beginning with M or m, such as 'minutes', 'married', 'male', and 'masculine'.

5 M or **m** is the Roman numeral for the number 1000.

-'m is a short form of 'am' that is used after the pronoun 'I' in spoken English, and in informal written English. EG *I'm happy here... I'm going to fetch the van.*

ma /mɑ̲ː/, **mas**. Your **ma** is your mother; an informal word. EG *I often think about the things Ma used to tell me.* N PROPER/VOC : ALSO N COUNT

MA /ɛm e̲ɪ/, **MAs**. **MA** is an abbreviation for 'Master of Arts'; a higher degree awarded by a university or polytechnic to people who have studied arts or social science subjects and have passed examinations or written a satisfactory thesis. In Scotland an MA is a first degree. EG *...an MA in Applied Linguistics.* ▸ also used to refer to a person N COUNT : USU SING, ALSO IN TITLES AFTER NAME ▸ ⇑ graduate with an MA degree. EG *My old headmaster was an M.A. from Durham... Hilda Stevens MA.*

ma'am /mɑːm/ is a spoken abbreviation for 'madam'. EG *A gentleman has called, ma'am.*

mac /mæk/, **macs**. A **mac** is the same as a mackintosh; an informal word, used in British English. EG *She was pulling on her old mac.* — N COUNT

macabre /məkɑːbrə⁰/. **Macabre** events, stories, etc are very strange and horrible, and usually involve death or injury. is one in which someone is hurt or killed in a horrible or strange way. EG *...macabre sacrifices... ...a macabre story.* — ADJ QUALIT = gruesome, horrific

macaroni /mækərəʊni¹/ is a kind of pasta made in the shape of short hollow tubes. EG *He sat down to a great dish of macaroni.* — N UNCOUNT

macaroon /mækəruːn/, **macaroons**. A **macaroon** is a sweet biscuit flavoured with almonds or coconut. — N COUNT

mace /meɪs/, **maces**. 1 A **mace** is an ornamental stick carried by an official or placed somewhere as a symbol of authority. EG *The Lord Chancellor presides over the House, with the mace behind him.* — N COUNT ⇑ rod

2 **Mace** is a spice, usually in the form of a powder, made from the shell of nutmegs and used in cooking. EG *Remove the onion and mace and add the breadcrumbs.* — N UNCOUNT

Mach /mɑːk/ is a unit of measurement for very high speeds. Mach 1 at a particular height above the ground is the speed of sound at that height; a technical term. EG *The missile can cruise at Mach 1.4.* — N UNCOUNT+NUM

machete /məʃeti¹/, **machetes**. A **machete** is a large knife with a broad blade. EG *I used the machete to hack up some of the larger pieces of wood.* — N COUNT

Machiavellian /mækɪ¹əveli¹ən/. **Machiavellian** behaviour is behaviour in which someone tries to get what they want by deceiving and cheating people in clever ways; a literary word. EG *You've got to be positively Machiavellian.* — ADJ QUALIT ⇑ cunning = devious

machinations /mæʃɪneɪʃə⁰nz/ are secret and complicated plans to gain power or harm someone; used showing disapproval. EG *He could no longer endure the machinations of his colleagues.* — N PLURAL ⇑ plots = intrigues

machine /məʃiːn/, **machines, machining, machined**. 1 A **machine** is a piece of equipment which does a particular type of work and which usually uses power from an engine or electricity. EG *She took the sheet of paper out of the roller and shut the machine... Unfortunately the machine is beyond repair... The wood can be sanded by machine.* • See also **fruit machine, sewing machine, slot machine, vending machine, washing machine**. — N COUNT, OR *by*+N

2 If you **machine** something, you make it, cut it, or change its shape using a machine; a technical term. EG *The work of machining a part is very slow... ...a person who does machining or foundry work.* — V OR V+O ⇑ manufacture

3 If you **machine** clothes, you make them or mend them using a sewing machine. EG *I machined the cuffs, but the collar was done by hand.* — V OR V+O

4 A **machine** is also a well-controlled system or organization for doing or making something. EG *...a squalid battle as to who controls the party machine... ...the might of the enemy war machine... They had perfected their own propaganda machine.* — N COUNT : USU MOD+N = machinery

5 If you refer to a person as a **machine**, you mean that they do a type of work without thinking about it, because they have done it for a long time, or because they do not need to think in order to do it; used showing disapproval. EG *He had dedicated himself to work and become just a writing machine... The judge is a machine, a deciding machine.* — N COUNT = automaton

machine code is a system for expressing information in a form that can be understood and used by a machine, especially a computer; a technical term. EG *...instructions for translating the program into machine code.* — N UNCOUNT ⇑ code

machine gun, machine guns; also spelled with a hyphen, especially when used before another noun. A **machine gun** is a gun which works automatically and which fires a lot of bullets one after the other very quickly. EG *Machine guns had been mounted on the roof of the building... Tucker set up his machine-gun behind a tree... We ran into machine-gun fire and had to fall flat on the ground.* — N COUNT

machinery /məʃiːnə⁰ri¹/. 1 If you talk about **machinery**, you are referring to machines in general, or to all the machines that are used in a factory or on a farm. EG *Machinery is being introduced to save labour... ...the export of textile machinery to India... ...a hut full of farm machinery.* — N UNCOUNT ⇑ equipment

2 The **machinery** of a piece of equipment such as a clock is the group of its parts that move when it is working. EG *Jeff seemed to hear the creaking of its machinery as it turned.* — N UNCOUNT : USU WITH POSS = works

3 **Machinery** is also the set of procedures that are used in a particular system in order to achieve things. EG *The party controls the state machinery... We need to discuss ways of improving the machinery of government... They haven't got the machinery to call a meeting.* — N UNCOUNT : USU +SUPP ⇑ organization

machine tool, machine tools; often used before another noun and spelled with a hyphen. A **machine tool** is a machine driven by power that cuts, shapes, or finishes metal or other materials; a technical term. EG *Four hundred of them worked busily making machine tools... ...the machine-tool industry.* — N COUNT

machinist /məʃiːnɪst/, **machinists**. A **machinist** is a person whose job is to operate a machine, especially in a factory. — N COUNT ⇑ worker

machismo /mækɪzməʊ, -tʃɪz-/ is aggressively masculine behaviour or attitudes; used showing disapproval. EG *...the powerful machismo of the Hollywood hero.* — N UNCOUNT

macho /mætʃəʊ/. You describe a man's behaviour, attitudes, or appearance as **macho** when you think that he behaves, thinks, or dresses in an aggressively masculine way; an informal word, usually used showing disapproval. EG *He emerged with a macho swagger... They were dressed in macho leather... We're not having a macho bloke around here.* — ADJ QUALIT

macintosh /mækɪntɒʃ/, **macintoshes**. See **mackintosh**.

mackerel /mækə⁰rəl/, **mackerels**; **mackerel** can also be used as the plural form. A **mackerel** is a sea fish with a greeny-blue skin, and is often caught and eaten. EG *...shoals of mackerel.* — N COUNT/UNCOUNT

mackintosh /mækɪntɒʃ/, **mackintoshes**; also spelled **macintosh**. A **mackintosh** is a raincoat, especially one made from a particular kind of waterproof cloth. EG *He took off his black mackintosh.* — N COUNT ⇑ coat = mac

▸ used of this type of cloth. EG *...a good pair of mackintosh trousers.* — ▸ N UNCOUNT

macro- is added to some words in order to form technical words that refer to things that are large in size or scope. EG *...economic→macro-economic... ...level→macrolevel.* — PREFIX

macrobiotic /mækrəʊbaɪɒtɪk/. **Macrobiotic** food consists of whole grains and vegetables grown without chemical additives; a technical term. EG *...the macrobiotic food store... ...macrobiotic cooking.* — ADJ CLASSIF ⇑ natural ≠ artificial, processed

macrocosm /mækrəʊkɒzə⁰m/. A **macrocosm** is an organized system such as the universe or a society, which is considered as a single unit. EG *...the microcosm of the human body and the macrocosm of nature.* — N COUNT : IF+PREP THEN *of*

mad /mæd/, **madder, maddest**. 1 Someone who is **mad** has a mind that does not work in a normal way, with the result that their behaviour is very strange. People who are mad often need to be cared for in an institution. EG *Rose was mad, there was no doubt about it... She was married to a man who'd gone mad... Her parents clearly considered her dangerously mad.* ◊ **madness**. EG *...the terrible madness that overtook the king... ...the most extraordinary study of madness that I have ever read.* • **as mad as a hatter**: see **hatter**. — ADJ CLASSIF ⇑ ill = insane, demented; ◊ N UNCOUNT = insanity

2 You also say that someone is **mad** 2.1 when they do or say something that you think is very foolish. EG *You must be mad!... They think I am mad to live in such a place... They are still mad enough to go to war.* ◊ **madness**. EG *It is madness for them to remain unarmed.* 2.2 when they are very angry. EG *I guess they're mad at me for getting them up so early... Jeannie gets mad when you talk like that.* — ADJ QUALIT = crazy, mental; ◊ N UNCOUNT; ADJ QUALIT : USU PRED = furious

3 If you describe something as **mad**, you mean that you think it is not logical or reasonable; used showing disapproval. EG *...a completely mad scheme to build a bridge between the two mountains.* — ADJ QUALIT : USU ATTRIB = madcap

4 If you are **mad** about something, you like it very much and spend a lot of time on it; an informal expression. EG *For years he's been mad about opera.* — ADJ QUALIT : PRED+*about* ⇑ keen = crazy

5 If you are **mad** about someone, you love or admire them so much that you think of them most of the time; an informal expression. EG *He's mad about my sister, but is too shy to tell her.* — ADJ QUALIT : PRED+*about* ⇑ keen = crazy

6 **Mad** is also used to describe wild, uncontrolled behaviour. EG *I was in the usual mad panic, dashing here and there... ...the mad whirl of pleasure.* ADJ CLASSIF : ATTRIB ⇑ excited = frantic

7 If you say that someone **will drive** you **mad** or **is driving** you **mad**, you mean that they are annoying you very much, and that you will not be able to tolerate their behaviour much longer. EG *These blinking kids will drive me mad.* PHR : VB INFLECTS ⇑ annoy

8 If you do something **like mad**, you do it very energetically or enthusiastically; an informal expression. EG *We rehearsed like mad and learned to sing the gypsy songs... They were still arguing like mad at six in the evening.* PHR : USED AS AN A = furiously ≠ casually

9 If someone **goes mad**, 9.1 their mind stops working in a normal way and their behaviour becomes very strange as a result. PHR : VB INFLECTS 9.2 they spend a great deal more energy or time on doing something than they normally would; an informal use. EG *I went really mad and worked seven days a week... My wife has been going mad cleaning everything.* PHR : VB INFLECTS

10 If an audience **goes mad**, they cheer and clap very enthusiastically; an informal expression. EG *Thousands of people are ready to go mad at the mere sight of him.* PHR : VB INFLECTS ⇑ applaud = go wild

madam /mædə⁰m/ **madams**. 1 People sometimes address a woman as **Madam** when they are being very formal and polite. 'Dear Madam' is often used at the beginning of official letters. 'Madam' is most commonly used in speech by shop assistants, hairdressers, and waiters. EG *Dear Madam, I am writing to acknowledge receipt of your letter dated 14.1.85... She likes being called Madam Chairman... Would Madam like to try the striped one?... It's ten minutes past nine, Madam.* N VOC : ALSO IN TITLES

2 A **madam** is a woman who is in charge of a brothel; a rather old-fashioned term. N COUNT ⇑ keeper

3 You refer to a little girl as a **madam** when she is very naughty and behaves as if she expects to get her own way. EG *The little madam!* N COUNT : USU MOD+N, ALSO VOC

madcap /mædkæp/. A **madcap** plan, scheme, etc is very foolish and not likely to succeed. EG *...some madcap scheme that he had devised.* ADJ QUALIT : ATTRIB = harebrained

madden /mædə⁰n/, **maddens, maddening, maddened**. If you **madden** a person or an animal, you make them very angry. EG *The colonel's calmness maddened Pluskat.* V+O ⇑ anger = infuriate ◇ **maddened**. EG *...a maddened buffalo.* ◇ ADJ CLASSIF = enraged

maddening /mædə⁰nɪŋ/. Something that is **maddening** makes you feel angry, irritated, or frustrated. EG *It makes a maddening clicking noise... How maddening it was to be so hot and not to be able to bathe.* ADJ QUALIT ⇑ irritating = infuriating, annoying ▸ used of people. EG *Lady Sackville was a maddening person to live with.* ◇ **maddeningly**. EG *The problem of nuclear arms is maddeningly complex.* ◇ ADV

made /meɪd/. 1 **Made** is the past tense and past participle of **make**.

2 If you **have it made**, you are certain to be rich or successful; an informal expression. EG *My colleagues had all had it made from birth.* PHR : VB INFLECTS ⇑ prosper

-made combines with words such as 'factory' to indicate that something has been made or produced in a particular way or at a particular place. EG *I bet you some of it's factory-made... It was a studio-made film... Locally-made goods had to pay internal customs duties.* ● See also **man-made, self-made**. COMB : FORMS ADJS

made-to-measure. A **made-to-measure** suit, shirt, etc is one that is made by a tailor to fit you exactly, rather than one that you buy in a shop. ADJ CLASSIF : USU ATTRIB ≠ off-the-peg

made-up. 1 If you or your face, lips, eyes, etc are **made-up**, you are wearing make-up such as lipstick and eyeshadow. EG *...freshly made-up lips... She had magnificent eyes, heavily made-up.* ADJ CLASSIF ⇑ painted

2 Something that is **made-up** 2.1 has already been prepared so that you do not have to make it yourself. EG *Add 1 teaspoonful white vinegar to 1 pint made-up carpet shampoo.* ADJ CLASSIF : ATTRIB ⇑ ready-made 2.2 is invented and not actually true. EG *...a made-up story.* ADJ CLASSIF

madhouse /mædhᵒaʊs/, **madhouses**; an informal word. A **madhouse** is 1 a mental hospital; an old-fashioned use. EG *They were put in the madhouse.* N COUNT 2 a place or situation which is full of confusion and noise. EG *This place will be a madhouse when all the kids arrive.* N COUNT : USU SING

madly /mædliˡ/. 1 If you do something **madly**, you do it very quickly, because you are eager, excited, or afraid. EG *We began rushing around madly in the dark.* ADV = frantically

2 Some people use **madly** in place of 'very' before adjectives such as 'gay' and 'exciting'. EG *I want to go somewhere madly exciting.* ADV+ADJ/ADV = wildly

3 If you are **madly in love** with someone, you are very much in love with them. EG *I fell madly in love with Ellen the first time I ever saw her.* PHR : USED AS C

madman /mædmə³n/, **madmen**. A **madman** is 1 a man who behaves in a strange and uncontrolled way, and perhaps violently. EG *Otto is a raving madman... MacDonald drove like a madman.* N COUNT = lunatic, nutter 2 a man who is insane. EG *They locked him up as a madman, of course.* N COUNT = lunatic

Madonna /mədɒnə/, **Madonnas**. 1 In Christianity, the **Madonna** is Mary, the mother of Christ. N PROPER

2 A **Madonna** is a painting or sculpture of Mary, the mother of Christ. EG *...Raphael's Madonna... ...little ivory madonnas.* N COUNT ⇑ representation

madras /mədræs, -drɑːs/ is a striped cotton cloth. EG *He was wearing a blue madras shirt.* N UNCOUNT : USU BEFORE N

madrigal /mædrɪgə⁰l/, **madrigals**. A **madrigal** is a song which is sung by several singers without any instruments. Madrigals were especially popular in England in the sixteenth century. EG *...a six-part madrigal.* N COUNT

madwoman /mædwuˡmə⁰n/, **madwomen**. A **madwoman** is a woman who is insane; an informal word. EG *Her mother's eyes were those of a madwoman.* N COUNT

maelstrom /meɪlstrəum, -ɒm/. A **maelstrom** is a situation which is extremely confused and violent, and usually destructive; a formal word. EG *Then we the country was plunged into the maelstrom of the First World War.* N SING WITH DET : IF+PREP THEN *of* = eddy, vortex

maestro /maɪstrəʊ/, **maestros**. A **maestro** is someone who is extremely skilful at something, especially conducting or playing music. EG *He was an absolute maestro on the piano.* N COUNT/VOC = master

Mafia /mæfɪə/. The **Mafia** is a secret criminal organization that was founded in Sicily and organizes many illegal activities in the U.S. N SING : *the*+N, VB CAN BE SING OR PL

mag /mæg/, **mags**. A **mag** is the same as a magazine; an informal word. EG *The most amusing parts of the mag are the ads.* N COUNT ⇑ periodical

magazine /mægəziːn/, **magazines**. A **magazine** is 1 a publication with a paper cover which is issued regularly, usually weekly or monthly, and which contains articles, stories, photographs and advertisements. EG *I got the recipe from a woman's magazine... ...a magazine article.* N COUNT ⇑ periodical 2 a topical news programme on radio or television, with a lot of short, interesting items. EG *A nightly news magazine on B.B.C. television.* N COUNT 3 a compartment in a gun for cartridges. EG *Push the magazine into the butt.* N COUNT 4 a building in which ammunition and explosives are kept. N COUNT ⇑ storeroom

magenta /mədʒentə/. Something that is **magenta** is of a dark, reddish-purple colour. EG *He was wearing a silk shirt and magenta slacks.* ADJ COLOUR ▸ used as a noun. EG *It's a kind of magenta.* ▸ N UNCOUNT

maggot /mægət/, **maggots**. A **maggot** is a tiny creature that looks like a very small worm. As maggots develop, they turn into flies. N COUNT ⇑ larva

Magi /meɪdʒaɪ/. The **Magi** were the three wise men who visited Jesus soon after he was born, bringing gifts for him. EG *...the Adoration of the Magi.* N PLURAL : *the*+N

magic /mædʒɪk/, **magics, magicking, magicked**. 1 **Magic** is 1.1 the power to use supernatural forces to make apparently impossible things happen, such as making people disappear or controlling events in nature. Magic is often used in fairy stories. EG *Do you believe in magic?... They claimed that he had inflicted bad fortune on them through evil magic... This spray is good but don't expect it to work magic.* ● **black magic**: see **black**. N UNCOUNT 1.2 the art and skill of performing mysterious tricks to entertain people, for example by making things appear and disappear. EG *We're trying to find someone to do some magic at the children's party... Uncle Jim did some magic tricks.* N UNCOUNT

2 If something happens **as if by magic** or **like magic**, it happens unexpectedly and without any apparent explanation so that it seems as if magic has been used. EG *As if by magic, his face turned green.* PHR : USED AS AN A ⇑ amazingly

3 You use **magic** to describe something that does things, or appears to do things, by magic. EG *...the magic forest... ...a magic potion... There is no magic formula.* ADJ CLASSIF : ATTRIB = enchanted

4 The **magic** of something is a special mysterious quality in it that makes it seem wonderful and exciting to you and that makes you feel happy. EG *...the magic of theatre... We need a bit of magic in our lives.* — N UNCOUNT = mystery

5 If you say that something is **magic**, you mean that it has a special mysterious quality that makes it seem wonderful and exciting. EG *That was a truly magic moment.* — ADJ QUALIT

6 **Magic** is also a mysterious quality or ability which a person has and which seems to be the reason that they can do something really well. EG *Some of the old magic crept back... There is magic in his feet.* — N UNCOUNT ↑ gift

7 The **magic** number, word, name, etc is the one that is really important in a particular situation. EG *'How many points do I need to win?'–'The magic figure is 63'... Let me ask you about this magic word 'tenure'.* — ADJ CLASSIF : ATTRIB ↑ special = key

8 If you refer to a suggestion, performance, etc as **magic**, you are saying enthusiastically that it is very good; a very informal use. EG *'Pint of bitter?'–'Magic!'... That was a magic goal!* — EXCLAM, OR ADJ QUALIT = ace, great

magic away. If you **magic** something **away**, you make it disappear suddenly and unexpectedly. EG *He can magic away a child's tears in no time at all.* — PHRASAL VB : V+O+ADV = spirit away

magic up. If you **magic** something **up** , you make it appear suddenly and unexpectedly. EG *An individual can force love to descend, can magic it up.* — PHRASAL VB : V+O+ADV = conjure up

magical /mædʒɪkə⁰l/. Something that is **magical** 1 uses, or is able to produce, magic. EG *I used to believe my mother had magical powers... ...magical rituals... ...a blood red stream of magical water.* ◊ **magically**. EG *It was a sort of magically released ancient force... The door opens magically as you walk up to it.* 2 has a special mysterious quality that makes it seem wonderful and exciting, and makes you feel happy. EG *It was a magical experience... The journey had lost all its magical inspiring quality.* — ADJ CLASSIF ↑ mysterious; ◊ ADV ↑ mysteriously; ADJ QUALIT = enchanting

magic carpet, magic carpets. In fairy stories, a **magic carpet** is a special carpet that can fly through the air carrying someone on top of it. — N COUNT ↑ transport

magician /mədʒɪʃə⁰n/, **magicians**. A **magician** is 1 a person who performs tricks that seem to involve the use of magic as a form of entertainment. EG *This process is very effectively used by stage magicians.* — N COUNT = conjurer
2 a person in a fairy story who has magic powers; usually used of a man. — N COUNT

magic lantern, magic lanterns. A **magic lantern** is an old-fashioned kind of projector in which large pieces of glass are used as slides to project a picture on to a screen. — N COUNT

magisterial /mædʒɪstɪərɪəl/. 1 If your behaviour or manner is **magisterial**, you act or speak as if you were in a position of authority. EG *...the colonel's somewhat magisterial manner... He began to address me in a magisterial voice.* ◊ **magisterially**. EG *'Supper,' announced Winifred magisterially.* — ADJ QUALIT : USU ATTRIB = authoritative; ◊ ADV WITH VB
2 **Magisterial** also means relating to a magistrate. EG *...the magisterial district of East London.* — ADJ CLASSIF : ATTRIB

magistrate /mædʒɪstreɪt/, **magistrates**. A **magistrate** is an official who acts as a judge in law courts which deal with less serious crimes or disputes, and decides whether cases are important enough to be passed on to higher courts. EG *You'll have to appear before the magistrate... ...the magistrate's court.* — N COUNT

magnanimity /mægnənɪmɪti¹/ is generosity towards someone else, especially after you have beaten them in a fight or contest; a fairly formal word. EG *He displayed extraordinary magnanimity towards his adversary.* — N UNCOUNT

magnanimous /mægnænɪməs/. If you are **magnanimous**, you are generous towards someone else, especially after you have beaten them in a fight or contest; a fairly formal word. EG *You can afford to be magnanimous.* ◊ **magnanimously**. EG *'I'll give it to you for Christmas,' Mrs Bixby said magnanimously.* — ADJ QUALIT; ◊ ADV WITH VB ↑ generously

magnate /mægneɪt/, **magnates**. A **magnate** is someone who has earned a lot of money from a particular business or industry. EG *...a rich shipping magnate... ...a press magnate.* — N COUNT : USU MOD+N ↑ person

magnesium /mægniːzɪəm/ is a metallic element which is used for making fireworks and flares because it burns very brightly. EG *The water contains high amounts of magnesium... ...magnesium flares.* — N UNCOUNT

magnet /mægnɪ²t/, **magnets**. 1 A **magnet** is a piece of iron or other material which attracts iron towards it. EG *The pin was extracted with a magnet... ...a bar magnet.* — N COUNT ↑ force
2 If you say that something is a **magnet** or is like a **magnet**, you mean that it is so interesting or exciting that it makes people go to it or look at it. EG *The river banks are a magnet for bird watchers... She was like a magnet. One couldn't look at anyone else.* — N COUNT : USU a+N IN SING ↑ attraction

magnetic /mægnetɪk/. 1 Something that is **magnetic** has the power of a magnet to attract iron or other metal towards it. EG *He took a carving knife from a magnetic board on the wall.* ▸ used of something that is caused by the power of magnetism. EG *...magnetic attraction.* ◊ **magnetically**. — ADJ CLASSIF : USU ATTRIB; ◊ ADV WITH VB
2 Something that is **magnetic** is very attractive to people because it has unusual and exciting qualities. EG *Without magnetic appeal, the politician is unlikely to succeed... ...a magnetic personality.* ◊ **magnetically**. EG *She was always magneticlly drawn to this colour.* — ADJ QUALIT : USU ATTRIB = compelling; ◊ ADV WITH VB

magnetic field, magnetic fields. A **magnetic field** is an area around a magnet, or something functioning as a magnet, in which its power to pull things towards it is felt. EG *There is a huge magnetic field around Jupiter.* — N COUNT ↑ force field

magnetic north is the direction that a compass needle points to. — N UNCOUNT

magnetic tape is narrow tape which is made of plastic covered with a magnetic substance and which is used for recording sounds, film, or computer information. — N UNCOUNT/COUNT

magnetism /mægnɪ²tɪzə⁰m/ is 1 the power of some substances, especially iron, to attract other substances towards them. EG *Gravity is a form of magnetism.* 2 the strong attractiveness that some people have because they have unusual and exciting qualities. EG *He had immense personal magnetism... ...sexual magnetism.* — N UNCOUNT ↑ force; N UNCOUNT : USU +SUPP ↑ quality = attraction

magnetize /mægnɪ²taɪz/, **magnetizes, magnetizing, magnetized**; also spelled **magnetise**. If you **magnetize** a substance or object, you give it the power to draw iron and other metals towards it. — V+O

magnification /mægnɪfɪkeɪʃə⁰n/, **magnifications**. **Magnification** is 1 the act of making something appear bigger in size than it actually is, for example by using a microscope. 2 the degree to which something can magnify things or the degree to which it has been magnified. EG *He stepped up the magnification of the telescope to thirty... All the images, even under the highest magnification, were simply points of light.* — N UNCOUNT ↑ enlarge; N UNCOUNT/COUNT

magnificence /mægnɪfɪsəns/ is the quality of being very beautiful or impressive. EG *...the magnificence of the forest... This was a spectacle of rare magnificence.* — N UNCOUNT = splendour

magnificent /mægnɪfɪsənt/. If you describe something as **magnificent**, you mean that it is extremely good, beautiful, or impressive. EG *It's a magnificent book... Her performance is magnificent... The town is renowned for its magnificent Abbey.* ◊ **magnificently**. EG *They performed magnificently... ...a great natural amphitheatre magnificently situated at the head of the valley.* — ADJ QUALIT = splendid, superb; ◊ ADV = superbly

magnify /mægnɪfaɪ/, **magnifies, magnifying, magnified**. 1 If you **magnify** an object, you make it appear bigger in size than it actually is, for example by using a microscope. EG *I want to magnify this picture... His glasses magnified his eyes to the size of dinner plates.* — V+O ↑ enlarge
2 If you **magnify** something, you make it seem more important than it actually is. EG *His fears have magnified the true dangers... Their problems are magnified by poverty.* — V+O ↑ exaggerate

magnifying glass, magnifying glasses. A **magnifying glass** is a piece of glass, usually in a frame, which makes objects appear to be bigger than they actually are. — N COUNT ↑ lens

magnitude /mægnɪtjuːd/ is the great size or great importance of something. EG *They do not recognize the magnitude of the problem... A decision of this magnitude had to have national support.* — N UNCOUNT ↑ importance = size

magnolia /mægnəʊlɪə/, **magnolias**. A **magnolia** is a kind of tree which produces white, pink, yellow, or purple flowers. — N COUNT

magnum /mægnəm/, **magnums**. A **magnum** is a wine bottle holding the equivalent of two normal bottles, approximately 1.5 litres. EG *...a magnum bottle of champagne.* — N COUNT

magnum opus /mægnəm əʊpəs/. A **magnum opus** is the greatest or most important single work done by a writer, painter, composer, or other artist. EG *Now she has completed what looks to me like her magnum opus.* N SING WITH DET = masterpiece

magpie /mægpaɪ/, **magpies**. A **magpie** is 1 a bird with black and white markings and a long tail. Magpies are attracted by shiny objects which they pick up and take to their nests. N COUNT 2 a person who likes collecting and keeping objects, often objects that have no use or value; an informal use. EG *Duncan is such a magpie.* N COUNT ⇑ collector

maharaja /mɑːhərɑːdʒə/, **maharajas**. A **maharaja** is the head of one of the royal families that used to rule parts of India. N COUNT: ALSO USED IN TITLES = prince

mah-jong /mɑː dʒɒŋ/ or **mah-jongg** is a very old Chinese game played with small tiles in which the players pick up and discard tiles until one of them has a winning combination. N UNCOUNT

mahogany /məhɒgəni¹/is a dark reddish-brown wood that is used to make furniture. EG *...a tall mahogany bookcase.* N UNCOUNT

maid /meɪd/, **maids**. A **maid** is 1 a woman who works as a servant in a hotel or private house. EG *The maid will bring you your wine in a moment... ...a laundry maid.* N COUNT ⇑ employee = girl 2 a young unmarried woman; a rather old-fashioned use. ● See also **old maid.** N COUNT ⇑ girl

maiden /meɪdəⁿn/, **maidens**. 1 A **maiden** is a young girl or woman, especially a beautiful one; a rather literary use. EG *She was a tender, watchful maiden... A procession of maidens bore the weight of the broken body.* N COUNT

2 The **maiden** voyage or flight is the first official journey that a ship or aeroplane makes with passengers. EG *Date after date for the maiden voyage was chosen and abandoned.* ADJ CLASSIF: ATTRIB

maiden aunt, maiden aunts. A **maiden aunt** is an aunt who is not married; used in old-fashioned English. N COUNT

maiden name, maiden names. A woman's **maiden name** is the surname she had before she got married and took her husband's surname. EG *My maiden name was Byers.* N COUNT

maiden over, maiden overs. In cricket a **maiden over** is an over in which no runs are scored by the batsman. N COUNT

maiden speech, maiden speeches. Someone's **maiden speech** is the first formal speech that they make as a Member of Parliament in the House of Commons or as a Peer in the House of Lords. EG *He broke with precedent by making his maiden speech on a controversial subject.* N COUNT

maid of honour, maids of honour. A **maid of honour** is the chief bridesmaid at a wedding; used in American English. N COUNT

mail /meɪl/, **mails, mailing, mailed**. 1 **Mail** is the letters, parcels, etc that the post office delivers to you at home or at your place of work. EG *If there's anything urgent in the mail, just give it to me and I'll deal with it... Minnie was alone in the post office, sorting mail, when Ellen arrived... The afternoon's mail brought the letter he was waiting for.* N UNCOUNT ⇑ correspondence

2 The **mail** is the system used by the post office for collecting and delivering letters, parcels, etc. EG *Your reply must have been lost in the mail... The books will be sent to you by mail.* N SING: *the*+N, OR *by*+N

3 If you **mail** something, you post it; used especially in American English. EG *The books had to be mailed directly from the publisher.* V+O = send

4 See also **chain mail.**

mailbag /meɪlbæg/, **mailbags**. A **mailbag** is a large bag that is used by the post office for carrying mail. N COUNT

mailbox /meɪlbɒks/, **mailboxes**. A **mailbox** is a box outside American houses where the mailman delivers letters. N COUNT ⇑ container = letterbox

mailing list, mailing lists. A **mailing list** is a list of names and addresses that a company or organization keeps so that they can send people information or advertising material. EG *If anyone wishes to be put on the mailing list they should write to us.* N COUNT = register

mailman /meɪlməⁿn/, **mailmen**. A **mailman** is the same as a postman; used in American English. N COUNT

mail order; often used before another noun and spelled with a hyphen. **Mail order** is a system of buying and selling goods where you choose what you want from a firm's catalogue and the firm sends you what you have ordered by post. EG *The record is available by mail order... ...a mail-order firm.* N UNCOUNT ⇑ trading

maim /meɪm/, **maims, maiming, maimed**. If you **maim** someone, you injure them so badly that they cannot use part of their body properly for the rest of their life. EG *These people kill and maim innocent civilians.* V+O

main /meɪn/, **mains**. 1 The **main** thing is the most important thing in a particular situation. EG *What are the main reasons for going to university?... The main point is that it lasts for a long time... Mrs Foster hurried through the main entrance into the building... He didn't finish his main course.* ADJ CLASSIF: ATTRIB = chief, major

2 You use **in the main** when you want to say that something is generally true, although there may be exceptions. EG *The Worthingtons are in the main decent, friendly folk... In the main, overseas students want to be on campus... They get good wages, too, in the main.* PHR: USED AS ADV SEN = in general

3 The **mains** are the pipes or wires which supply gas, water, or electricity to buildings, or which take sewage from them; used especially to refer to the place where these pipes or wires end inside the building. EG *First turn the water supply off at the mains... The radio we have at home plugs into the mains... ...a mains plug.* N PLURAL: *the*+N, PL FORM WHEN MOD

4 A **main** is a large pipe which carries gas, water, or sewage, and is connected to smaller pipes which link it to individual houses or buildings. EG *A bulldozer had severed a gas main.* N COUNT

5 If you **have an eye to the main chance**, you are always looking for an opportunity to make money for yourself or to improve your situation in some other way; usually used showing disapproval. PHR: VB INFLECTS

main clause, main clauses. In grammar, a **main clause** is a clause that can stand alone as a complete sentence. N COUNT

main drag, main drags. The **main drag** is the main street in a large town or city; an informal American use. N COUNT: IF SING *the*+N

mainframe /meɪnfreɪm/, **mainframes**. A **mainframe** is a large computer which can be used by many people at the same time, and can do very large or complicated tasks. N COUNT

mainland /meɪnləᵊnd/. The **mainland** is the large, principle part of a country or continent considered in contrast to the islands that form smaller parts of the country or continent. EG *The motorboat was waiting to ferry him back to the mainland.* N SING: *the*+N ⇑ land ▸ used as an adjective. EG *...the coast of mainland Greece.* ▸ ADJ CLASSIF: ATTRIB

main line, main lines. A **main line** is an important route on a railway system, usually linking one large city with another. EG *The advantage of Weybridge is that it's on the main line and you can get to London in twenty-five minutes.* N COUNT: USU SING

mainline /meɪnlaɪn/, **mainlines, mainlining, mainlined**. 1 A **mainline** station is one that lies on a main line. EG *He took a taxi straight to the mainline station.* ADJ CLASSIF: ATTRIB

2 If you **mainline** or if you **mainline** a drug, you inject a drug into yourself; used especially of drug addicts. EG *People either smoke or mainline the stuff.* V OR V+O

mainly /meɪnli¹/. You use **mainly** when you want to say that a statement is true in most cases or to a large extent. EG *The political groups will have more power, mainly because of their larger numbers... I'll be concentrating mainly on French and German... The union soon formed twenty branches, mainly in London... ...a queue of people, mainly children and old men.* ADV: ALSO+NG ⇑ mostly = chiefly

main road, main roads. A **main road** is an important road that leads from one town or city to another, and that is designed to carry a large amount of traffic. EG *We turned off the main road shortly after Alcester.* N COUNT

mainspring /meɪnsprɪŋ/. The **mainspring** of something is the most important reason for it or the thing that is essential to it. EG *Technology was the mainspring of economic growth.* N SING WITH DET +SUPP: USU *the*+N+*of*

mainstay /meɪnsteɪ/, **mainstays**. The **mainstay** of something is the part of it which is the most important source of its strength or effectiveness. EG *Homemade chocolate chip cookies were the mainstay of my diet along the campaign trail... The short story has been the mainstay of science fiction.* N COUNT+SUPP: USU *the*+N+*of* ⇑ prop = foundation

mainstream /meɪnstriːm/. The **mainstream** is the group of people or ideas that most people belong to N SING WITH DET: USU *the*+N

or agree with, and which is therefore regarded as being normal and conventional. EG *We feel isolated from the mainstream of social life in the community... He felt that the he was entering the American mainstream.* ▸ used as an adjective. EG *This brought even mainstream Democrats to their feet... ...the mainstream cinema.*
+of = core
▸ ADJ CLASSIF : ATTRIB ⇑ ordinary

maintain /meɪnteɪn/, **maintains, maintaining, maintained.** 1 If you **maintain** something, you continue to have it, and do not let it stop or grow weaker. EG *I wanted to maintain my friendship with her... ...their role in maintaining world peace... For twenty-five years they had failed to maintain law and order.*
V+O ⇑ keep = preserve

2 If you **maintain** something at a particular rate or level, you keep it at that rate or level, and do not let it grow less. EG *Busby maintained a cracking pace... One has to maintain the temperature at a very high level... The party maintains a constant output of pamphlets.*
V+O = keep up, sustain

3 If you **maintain** someone, you provide them with money and the things that they need. EG *I need the money to maintain me for at least the next month until I start a job.*
V+O = provide for

4 If you **maintain** something such as a building, road, or machine, you keep it in good condition by regularly checking it and doing necessary repairs. EG *...the ever-rising cost of maintaining the equipment.*
V+O ⇑ run

5 If you **maintain** that something is true, you state your opinion or belief very strongly, especially when other people disagree with you. EG *Mrs Camish always maintained that he had been a brilliant thinker... The police maintained he acted alone in the shooting.*
V+REPORT-CL/QUOTE = claim, believe

maintenance /meɪntɪ⁰nəns/. 1 **Maintenance** is 1.1 the activity of keeping something such as a building, vehicle, or machine in good condition by regularly checking it and doing necessary repairs. EG *He learnt tractor maintenance... Who's responsible for the maintenance and care of the buildings?... ...maintenance jobs.* 1.2 the money that someone gives to a person that they are legally responsible for but not living with, in order to pay for their food, clothes, and other necessary things. For example, a man may have to pay maintenance to his ex-wife after a divorce. Used in British English.
N UNCOUNT ⇑ care = running
N UNCOUNT ⇑ allowance = alimony

2 The **maintenance** of something is the act of continuing it, and of not letting it diminish, stop, or grow weaker. EG *...the maintenance of law and order... ...the maintenance of an effective incomes policy. ...the maintenance of the same rate of expansion.*
N SING WITH DET +of: the+N ⇑ preservation

maisonette /meɪzənet/, **maisonettes.** A **maisonette** is a small flat on two floors of a larger building; used in British English. EG *She shared an upper maisonette with two other girls.*
N COUNT

maize /meɪz/ is a tall plant which produces large cobs of sweet-corn. Maize is grown as the basic food crop in many parts of the world. EG *...a field planted with maize.*
N UNCOUNT = corn

Maj. is a written abbreviation for 'major'. EG *...Maj. James Johnson.*
N IN TITLES

majestic /mədʒestɪk/. Something or someone that is **majestic** is very beautiful, dignified, and impressive. EG *The majestic proportions of the great Pyramid... ...majestic scenery... She looked majestic in her white robes.* ◇ **majestically.** EG *Wet clouds, heavy with rain, moved majestically overhead... St Paul's rose majestically from the trees.*
ADJ QUALIT
◇ ADV ⇑ grandly

majesty /mædʒɪ²sti¹/, **majesties.** 1 You say **Your Majesty, Her Majesty,** etc when you address or refer to a King or Queen. EG *...Her Majesty the Queen... Thank you, Your Majesty.*
N COUNT : DETPOSS+N, USED IN TITLES

2 **Majesty** is 2.1 the quality of being beautiful, dignified and impressive. EG *...the majesty of floating icebergs.* 2.2 the state of being a King or Queen. EG *...the tradition of English majesty.*
N UNCOUNT ⇑ grandeur
N UNCOUNT ⇑ sovereignty

major /meɪdʒə/, **majors, majoring, majored.** 1 You use **major** when you want to describe something which is more important, serious, or significant than other things in a group or situation. EG *Jones was also to play a major part in the improvement of the paper... One major factor was the revolution in communications... ...major changes... Even finding a solicitor had been a major problem.*
ADJ QUALIT : ATTRIB ⇑ important = significant

2 A **major** is 2.1 an army officer of medium rank, just above captain. EG *...Major Burton-Cox... By the end of the Indo-China campaign he was a major.* 2.2 the most important of the subjects that a university student is studying. EG *My major's English; I get As and high Bs in that.* 2.3 a university student whose main subject is the one that is mentioned. EG *Steve Jandrell is a third year music major.*
N COUNT : ALSO IN TITLES
N COUNT ⇑ subject
N COUNT : MOD+N ⇑ person

3 A **major** key is one of the two types of key in which most European music is written. It is based on a scale of notes in which the third note is two tones higher than the first note. EG *They're both in D major.*
ADJ CLASSIF : ATTRIB, OR AFTER N ≠ minor

4 **Major** is used after a boy's name in some British schools in order to show that he is the elder of two boys with the same name. EG *...Jones Major.*
ADJ AFTER N ⇑ senior

major in. If you **major in** a particular subject, you study it as your main subject at university. EG *I decided to major in French.*
PHRASAL VB : V+PREP, HAS PASS

major-domo /meɪdʒə dəʊməʊ/, **major-domos;** also spelled as one word. A **major-domo** is the chief servant in charge of the other servants in a large house; a rather old-fashioned word.
N COUNT

majorette /meɪdʒəret/, **majorettes.** A **majorette** is a girl or young woman who marches at the front of a musical band in a procession. Majorettes wear a uniform and carry sticks which they sometimes throw into the air and catch.
N COUNT ⇑ person

major-general, major-generals; also spelled as two words. A **major-general** is a senior officer in the army, one rank above a brigadier.
N COUNT : ALSO IN TITLES

majority /mədʒɒrɪti¹/, **majorities.** 1 The **majority** of people or things in a larger group is a number of them that form more than half of the larger group. EG *The great majority of incomes consist of wages and salaries... ...mass movements involving the overwhelming majority of the people... ...the principle of government by the majority.* ● If a person or group is **in a majority** or **in the majority,** they belong to a number of people or things that form more than half of a larger group.
N SING WITH DET : USU+of ⇑ part ≠ minority
● PHR : USED AS AN A ≠ in a minority

2 A **majority** is the difference between the number of votes or parliamentary seats that the winner gets in an election or vote and the number of votes or parliamentary seats that the next person or party gets. EG *I was beaten by a large majority... Benn was returned by a majority of 15,479... He's rather better known than many MPs with bigger majorities.*
N COUNT : USU+SUPP, USU SING = margin

3 **Majority** is the state of legally being an adult. In Britain, people reach their majority at the age of eighteen. EG *I suppose she'll inherit the money when she reaches the age of majority.*
N UNCOUNT ⇑ adulthood

make /meɪk/, **makes, making, made.** 1 **Make** is one of the most common verbs in English. It is often used in expressions where it does not have a very distinct meaning of its own, but where most of the meaning is in the noun that follows it. So, for example, 'he made an enquiry' means almost the same as 'he enquired'. This structure is often chosen in order to suggest that the action is more deliberate, or in order to give more information about the noun. The following paragraph shows **make** used in this way: 1.1 with nouns that express speech actions. EG *He made the shortest speech I've ever heard... He made no comment... A number of points need to be made about this thesis... May I make a suggestion?... I shall make some enquiries and call you back.* 1.2 with nouns that refer to sounds. EG *Dolly, try not to make so much noise... She didn't make a sound... We made a terrible racket as we came out of the club.* 1.3 with nouns like 'change' and 'alteration'. EG *I managed to persuade Christopher to make a few minor changes in the play.* 1.4 with nouns that describe the result of an action or event. EG *She made a great success of Ophelia at Stratford last year... Let's not make a mess of this... Daddy thought we'd made a very good job of the bathroom.* 1.5 with many other nouns to form expressions which take most of their meaning from the noun. EG *We have got to make a really serious effort... She's always making a fuss about something or other... You should first make a claim for unemployment benefits... Mrs Atkins makes no charge for visitors... He made a bad impression on his first appearance... She speaks French well and is making good progress with her German... She was treated on penicillin for six weeks and made a very good recovery... In many areas, guerrilla forces are making gains.* 1.6 with adjectives like 'clear', 'certain' and 'sure' to form expres-
V+O
V+O
V+O
V+O
V+O
V : WITH ADJ, USU WITH O/REPORT-

sions which take most of their meaning from the adjective. If you **make** something clear, you explain or express it clearly. EG *I haven't made it clear what I'm going to do... I'd like to make my views clear... Children need to be seen regularly by a doctor to make sure that they are healthy.* CL

2 If you **make** a telephone call, you telephone someone. EG *He had two phone calls to make... I've got to go and make a telephone call.* V+O

3 If you **make** a decision, choice, or judgement, you decide what to do about something, usually after you have thought about it. EG *I think that I made the wrong decision... The final judgement will be made in court... You have to make a choice between us... It's important to help the students make choices.* V+O

4 If you **make** a visit, trip, or journey, you go or visit somewhere. EG *In 1978 he made the first of several extended visits to Australia... Stokely was about to make a trip to Cuba... I made a five-month tour of India and the Far East.* • to **make** your **way**: see **way**. V+O

5 **Make** is used in expressions like 'make a move' and 'make a start' to indicate that you are beginning to do something that requires movement or activity. EG *Hargreaves really ought to make a move, but he can't be bothered... You've got to make a start somewhere.* V+O

6 If you **make** a mistake or error, you do something wrong. EG *He felt I was making a terrible mistake... You're more likely to make mistakes in writing than you are in speech.* V+O

7 If something **makes** you do something, it causes you to do it. EG *What makes you ask that?... Don't make me laugh!... A sudden noise made Brody jump... The warm sun began to make me feel a little better...* V+O+INF : IF PASS V+*to*-INF

8 If you **make** someone do something, you force them to do it. EG *You've got to make him listen... They were made to sit and wait for two hours.* V+O+INF : IF PASS V+*to*-INF = compel

9 If something **makes** you a particular thing, or if it **makes** that particular thing of you, it causes you to be or become that thing. EG *He had a friendly, popular style that was to make him a star... Don't make a fool of me... He used to make her life hell... Visitors can make Luxembourg city, the capital, their base... I'd like to know that I had done something to make the world a better place.* V+O+C, OR V+O +A (*of*)

10 If something **makes** you late, happy, angry, etc, it causes you to have or acquire the quality or feeling mentioned. EG *She isn't ready: she'll make us late... The cold was making Posy irritable... Sit down and make yourself comfortable... The agenda of the discussions has not been made public... He feared the story had made things worse.* V+O (NG/REFL) +C (ADJ)

11 If you **make** yourself understood, heard, known, etc, you succeed in getting people to understand you, hear you, etc. EG *He managed to make himself understood... Jack was the first to make himself heard.* V+O (REFL)+ PAST PART

12 If you **make** something, you create or produce it by putting different things together or by some kind of effort; used especially when you are talking about activities such as cooking, sewing, or painting. EG *Chimpanzees not only use tools but make them... I like making cakes... Sheila makes all her own clothes... An electric blender makes soups, purees and puddings in a few seconds.* V+O ⇑ construct

13 If you **make** films, television programmes, etc, you organize and supervise the production. EG *...the greatest film ever made... 'The Outsider' was made with Dutch money.* V+O

14 If you **make** a meal or a drink, you prepare it so that it is ready for eating or drinking. EG *I'll make a fresh pot of tea... The coffee's made... I'll go and make dinner.* V+O = fix

15 If you **make** the bed, you prepare it so that it is neat and tidy and ready for someone to sleep in. EG *Here's your room. I'm afraid the bed's not made.* V+O

16 If a company **makes** something, it manufactures or produces it. EG *The firm makes a wide range of electrical goods.* V+O

17 The **make** of something such as a car or radio is the name of the particular company that made it. EG *She couldn't even tell what make of car he was driving... There are now over a hundred makes of micro-computers for sale in the United Kingdom.* N COUNT+SUPP : USU+*of* ⇑ type = brand

18 If something **is made** of a particular substance or material, that substance or material was used to build or construct it. EG *The houses were made of brick... What is it made of?* V+O+A : ONLY PASS ⇑ composed

19 If you **make** something from or out of a material, you manufacture or construct it using that material. EG *You can make petroleum out of coal... They used to make their own glass out of sand and silica... The Churchill Arch was made from stones damaged in the fire of 1941.* V+O+A (*from/ out of*) ⇑ produce

20 If you **make** one thing into something else, you change it in some way so that it becomes that other thing. EG *They're having two houses made into one... They're making the old kitchen into a little bedroom.* V+O+A (*into*) = turn

21 You can use **make** when you are saying that something adds up to a particular number or amount. EG *Two and two make four... Sixteen ounces make a pound... There are eight of us. And the dog makes nine.* V+C (NG/NUM) ⇑ be

22 If you **make** an answer, a distance, etc a particular amount or value, you calculate or guess that this is the amount or value. EG *I make the answer 144... I make it £7 each. How about you?* V+O+C (NG/ NUM) = reckon

23 If you **make** it a particular time, that is the time that your watch says. EG *What do you make the time?... I make it nearly 9.30.* V+O+C : USU O (*it*)

24 If you **make** a score or total a particular amount, you increase it to that amount, or score that number of points. EG *Hoddle's second goal makes it three nil to Spurs... I have already shot 12. Soon I will make it 13.* V+O, OR V+O+ C : USU O (*it*)

25 If you **make** money, you get it by working for it or winning it. EG *He's made quite a bit of money... He was making ninety dollars a week... She made a £200 profit on the deal.* V+O

26 If you **make** someone something, you appoint them to a particular job, role, or position. EG *John Wallaby has been made Foreign Secretary... She set up a company and made him managing director.* V+O+C (NG)

27 If you say that someone will **make** a soldier, writer, etc, you mean that they have the qualities or the talent which they need to become that thing. EG *I like the way you write, and I think you might make a journalist... She will make an extremely lively member of parliament.* V+C (NG) = amount to

28 If something **makes** a best seller, an interesting read, a good gift, etc, it has the right qualities or features to be that thing. EG *What makes a good read?... The ownership of some of the private Provident Societies makes interesting reading... Do chemistry sets make good gifts from a scientific point of view?* V+O = constitute

29 If you **make** someone a particular kind of husband, wife, etc, you fulfil that role or job for them in the way mentioned. EG *She would make him a good wife... I think he'll make them the best junior partner they've ever had.* V+O, OR V+O+C (NG) ⇑ be

30 If something **makes** something of you, or if you **make** something of yourself, you are changed into a better or more successful person. EG *The army made a man of me... If he could only be bothered, that man could make of himself whatever he wanted.* V+O+PREP : NO PASS ⇑ transform

31 If something **makes** something else, it is responsible for the success of the other thing. EG *It's Jack Nicholson's acting that really makes the film.* • to **make** your **day**: see **day**. V+O

32 If someone **makes** the team, they earn a place in it. EG *You'll never make the team if you don't turn up for training.* V+O ⇑ attain

33 If you **make** somewhere, you get there, often with some difficulty. EG *I might have made Ramsdale by dawn if the car had held out... Can we make the station in five minutes?* V+O : USU+A = reach

34 If you **make it**, **34.1** you succeed in getting somewhere, usually in time to do something such as catch a bus or a train. EG *We'll make it with a minute or two to spare.* PHR : VB INFLECTS = arrive **34.2** you are successful in doing or getting something that you want. EG *Blake failed to make it as a commercial airline pilot... After failing the exams three times, I realized I'd never make it in accountancy.* PHR : VB INFLECTS ⇑ succeed

35 If you can **make it**, you are able to attend something that you have been invited to. EG *Come round for drinks on Sunday, about 5. Can you make it?... The Baxters couldn't make it this evening, I'm afraid.* PHR : VB INFLECTS = come

36 You can also use **make** in expressions like 'make friends' when you are talking about the relationship V+O : USU+A someone has with other people. EG *Karen made friends with several children her own age... Roger made a number of enemies... I don't make friends very easily.*

37 If you **make** as if to do something or **make** to do it, you behave in such a way that it seems that you are just about to do it. EG *She made as if to speak... They saw me, hesitated, looked at each other and made to leave.* V+*as if*+*to*-INF, OR V+*to*-INF

38 If you **make like** something, you behave in a particular way, sometimes as if you are acting a part; an informal expression. EG *I ran down towards them, making like a messenger.* PHR : VB INFLECTS

39 If people **make** a line, a circle, a group, etc, they arrange themselves in this way. EG *Let's make a ring... New management would cooperate with the unions to make a viable company.* V+O = form

40 If you **make** a note, list, etc, you write something down in that form. EG *You should make a shopping list... I'll make a note so that I don't forget.* V+O

41 If you **make** an offer, arrangement, etc, you offer or agree to something which another person either accepts or rejects. EG *The government has made an offer, and that offer must now be considered... I'd like to make arrangements to stay for a week... It's advisable to ring up first to make an appointment.* V+O

42 If you **make** rules, laws, etc, you decide what these should be. EG *Don't blame me! I don't make the rules.* V+O ⇑ formulate

43 If you **make** a loan, grant, donation, etc, you give someone money that they need. EG *Some councils make a grant to keep a pupil over 16 on at school... The government had to make a further loan of £3.3m.* V+O

44 If someone **makes** a number of points in a game, they score that number. EG *He made 70 in just over an hour.* V+O ⇑ get

45 If someone **makes** another person, they persuade that person to have sex with them; an offensive use in very informal English. V+O

46 If you **make do** or **make do** with something, you use it instead of something else that you do not have. The thing you use is not as good as the thing that you would like to have used. EG *Nell had to make do with a cleaner only two days a week... We'll just have to make do with ten players.* PHR : *make* INFLECTS = get by

47 If you **make a day, evening, night,** etc **of it**, you spend the whole of that period of time doing something, usually something pleasant. EG *Why don't we get an early train and make a day of it?* PHR : VB INFLECTS

48 If you are **on the make**, you are trying to get a lot of money or power for yourself. The way you achieve this is often slightly illegal or immoral. EG *The morality of the decision was of no concern to businessmen on the make.* PHR : USED AS AN A, OR AFTER N

49 The word **make** is used in the following expressions, which are explained at other places in this dictionary. • to **make the best of** something: see **best**. • to **make good**: see **good**. • to **make a name for** yourself: see **name**. • to **make sense**: see **sense**. • to **make way**: see **way**.

make away with. 1 If you **make away with** something, you steal it and take it away with you. EG *He's afraid someone might make away with the takings.* PHRASAL VB : V+ADV+PREP

2 If you **make away with** someone or with yourself, you kill the other person or you kill yourself. PHRASAL VB : V+ADV+PREP

make for. 1 If you **make for** a place, you move towards it. EG *We joined the jostling crowd making for the only exit... The best thing now would be to make for the top of Brill Hill.* PHRASAL VB : V+PREP ⇑ go = head for

2 If something **makes for** another thing, it makes it likely that this other thing will happen. EG *I don't know if unilateral disarmament would make for peace or would make for war... What are the values that make for happy family life?* PHRASAL VB : V+PREP ⇑ result in = contribute to

make of. If you ask a person what they **make of** something, you want to know 1 what their impression or opinion is of it. EG *I wondered what they made of it all... What are we to make of Afghanistan?... It would have been fascinating to know what he made of Djeddah.* 2 if they understand what it means. EG *Sherlock Holmes might have made something of these clues... I don't know what to make of this at all.* PHRASAL VB : ORDER V+PREP +O, USU WITH BROAD NEG = think of; PHRASAL VB : V+O+PREP, USU WITH BROAD NEG

make off. If you **make off**, you leave somewhere as quickly as possible, often in order to escape. EG *The vehicle made off at once.* PHRASAL VB : V+ADV

make off with. If you **make off with** something, you steal it and take it away with you. EG *Otto made off with the last of the brandy.* PHRASAL VB : V+ADV+PREP

make out. 1 If you **make** something **out**, 1.1 you manage with difficulty to see or hear it. EG *He could just make out the number plate of the car... It's sometimes difficult to make out what is said over an airport loudspeaker.* PHRASAL VB : V+O+ADV = discern 1.2 you try to understand something or decide whether or not it is true. EG *I can't make out if Nell likes him or not... He tried to make out what they meant by the word 'scandal'... I can never make out whether Mac smokes or not.* PHRASAL VB : V+ADV+*if*/WH, OR V+O+ADV ⇑ comprehend

2 If you **make out** that something is the case, you try to cause people to believe that it is the case. EG *People tried to make out that the play was about Britain... He's not really as hard as people make out.* PHRASAL VB : V+ADV+REPORT-CL, OR V+O+ADV

3 If you **make** yourself **out** to be something, you give the impression that you are that sort of person. EG *He makes himself out to be a bit of a poet.* PHRASAL VB : V+O (NG/REFL)+ADV+*to*-INF

4 If you **make out** to do something, you pretend to do it. EG *He opened a drawer and made out to be looking for something in it.* PHRASAL VB : V+ADV+*to*-INF

5 If you **make out** a case for something, you try to establish or prove that it is the best thing to do. EG *I think you can make out a very strong case indeed for educating young people for as long as possible.* PHRASAL VB : V+O+ADV/PREP

6 When you **make out** a form, cheque, receipt, etc, you write on it all the necessary information. EG *I made a cheque out for £1200... Did you make out a receipt?* PHRASAL VB : V+O+ADV/PREP ⇑ write out

7 In informal English, if you **make out**, you are doing reasonably well in your work or in your life. EG *No matter what happens, he'll always make out... How are you making out these days?* PHRASAL VB : V+ADV = get by

make out with. If you **make out with** another person, you succeed in persuading them to have sex with you; a very informal use. EG *Did you make out with him, then?* PHRASAL VB : V+ADV+PREP = score

make over. If you **make** something **over**, you legally transfer the ownership of it from one person to another. EG *The land was made over to the Council for building purposes.* PHRASAL VB : V+O+ADV : USU+*to*

make up. 1 If you **make up**, or if you **make** yourself **up**, you put make-up such as powder or lipstick on your face. EG *It was time to start making up for the evening performance.* PHRASAL VB : V+ADV, OR V+O (REFL)+ADV

2 If you **make** someone **up**, you put make-up on their face. PHRASAL VB : V+O+ADV

3 If you **make up** something such as medicine or food, you prepare it by putting different things together. EG *I have had them made up especially for you... Let me make up a parcel for you.* PHRASAL VB : V+O+ADV

4 If you **make up** a bed or couch, etc, you put sheets and blankets onto a spare bed or onto something that is not usually used as a bed because you have a visitor who is going to stay the night. PHRASAL VB : V+O+ADV

5 If you **make up** a fire or boiler, you add coal or wood to it. EG *Eric watched Sam make up the fire.* PHRASAL VB : V+O+ADV

6 If a number of things **make up** something else, they join together to form the whole or a part of that thing. EG *Women now make up two-fifths of the British labour force... ...the various groups which make up society... All substances are made up of molecules... Nearly half the Congress is made up of lawyers.* PHRASAL VB : ORDER V+ADV+O, IF PASS THEN+*of* = comprise

7 If you **make** something **up**, 7.1 you invent it, sometimes in order to deceive people or to explain something you have done. EG *What I didn't know I had to find out or make up... He was very good at making up convincing excuses.* PHRASAL VB : V+O+ADV 7.2 you complete it by bringing it up to the required number or amount. EG *How long does it take you to make up blood you lose?... He went to the international markets in an effort to make up the difference... He had been invited to make up the numbers at dinner.* PHRASAL VB : V+O+ADV

8 If two people **make up** or **make it up**, they become friends again after they have had a quarrel or a disagreement. EG *They'd kissed and made up but Lynn stayed awake for a long time... Let's make it up, shall we?* PHRASAL VB : V+ADV OR V+O+ADV = become reconciled

9 If you **make up** for something, you do something to replace what is damaged, lost, or missing. EG *If babies put on very little weight at first, eventually they will gain rapidly to make up for it... Whatever New England may lack in materials it makes up in bright ideas.* PHRASAL VB : V+ADV : USU+*for*

10 If you **make it up to** someone **for** something, you PHR : VB

give them something or do something for them to show how sorry you are that you caused them a disappointment. EG *I'm sorry I've got to go away again. I promise I'll make it up next week.* INFLECTS

11 If you **make up** your **mind**, you make a decision about something or you decide to do something. EG *I can't make up my mind which book to have... I had made up my mind to apply for a scholarship... I had made up my mind that I was going to be a doctor... The Prime Minister's mind was largely made up for him by the persistence of Lord Northcliffe.* PHR : VB AND N INFLECT = decide

12 If you **make the time up**, you either work faster than usual, or you work at a time when you would normally not be working because you have had some time off to which you were not really entitled. PHR : VB INFLECTS = catch up ● If someone is **making up for lost time**, they are doing something intensively and with enthusiasm because they did not do it when they were younger. EG *Don't worry, she'll be all right. She's making up for lost time, that's all she's doing.* ● PHR : VB INFLECTS

13 See also **made-up**.

make up to. If you **make up to** someone, you try to get them to like you by being very friendly towards them and by paying them a lot of compliments. EG *I always believed he was making up to me because of my money.* PHRASAL VB : V + ADV + PREP ⇑ flatter

make-believe is pretending that things are better or more exciting than they really are. EG *His whole life these days was a game of make-believe... Hours were spent in make-believe and dressing up... He's got to learn the difference between what's real and what's make-believe.* N UNCOUNT ⇑ pretence

maker /meɪkə/, **makers**. 1 A **maker** is a person who makes the thing mentioned. EG *In the studio with me is film maker and critic, Iain Johnstone... ...dictionary makers... The makers of the programme seemed to lose confidence in it.* N COUNT + SUPP

2 The **maker** of something that is sold is the firm or company that manufactures it. EG *The maker's label was carefully removed.* N COUNT

makeshift /meɪkʃɪft/. Something that is **makeshift** is temporary and probably of rather poor quality, but is used because there is nothing better available at the time. EG *Youths erected makeshift barricades... The accommodation for the press was makeshift at best.* ADJ QUALIT

make-up; also spelled as one word. 1 **Make-up** is substances like lipstick, eyeshadow, mascara, powder, etc which women use to make themselves look more attractive, or which actors use to make themselves look like the characters they are playing. EG *...eye make-up... She had a lot of make-up on.* N UNCOUNT = cosmetics

2 Someone's **make-up** is their nature and the various qualities in their character. EG *There are things in my make-up which do not bear close examination.* N UNCOUNT + SUPP

3 The **make-up** of something is the combination of its various parts and the way these parts are arranged. EG *What is the make-up of a normal theatre audience?... My reactions to the news were a product of my own history and genetic make-up.* N UNCOUNT + SUPP = composition

make-weight, make-weights. A **make-weight** is something which is added to something else so that there is the right amount, or in order to compensate for something that is missing. EG *They are good added whole to apple pies, or added as a make-weight to blackberry jelly... I'm only in the team as a sort of make-weight.* N COUNT

making /meɪkɪŋ/, **makings**. 1 **Making** is the act or the process of doing or producing something. EG *At the end of his life he turned to the making of beautiful books... ...the making of resolutions... Pictures were made because picture making was a way of life... Pensioners should be involved in all decision-making which affects them.* N SING : *the* + N + *of*, OR N UNCOUNT : MOD + N

2 If something such as a problem is **of your own making**, it has been done or caused by you alone and not by anyone else. EG *The trouble here is of the President's own making.* PHR : USED AS AN A

3 When you describe a person as something **in the making**, you mean that they are gradually becoming that thing. EG *She's obviously a linguist in the making.* PHR : USED AS AN A

4 If something **is the making of** a person or thing, it is the reason that the person or thing is successful or is very much better than they used to be. EG *The passage across to Belfast is the making of the book... That speech was the making of him.* PHR : VB INFLECTS

5 If you say that a person or thing has **the makings** of something, you mean that they seem likely to develop in that way. EG *The group reputedly had all the makings of a modern new intelligentsia... She perceived that here might be the makings of the friendship that had so eluded her in the past.* PHR : USED AS O/C

mal- is added to words in order to form other words that refer to things being done badly or wrongly. EG *...nutrition→malnutrition... ...administration→maladministration... ...treat→maltreat... ...adjusted→maladjusted.* PREFIX = mis-

maladjusted /mæləd͟ʒʌstrᵊd/. When you describe a child as **maladjusted**, you mean that he or she has psychological problems and behaves in a way which is not acceptable to society. EG *...special schools for maladjusted children.* ADJ CLASSIF = disturbed

maladjustment /mæləd͟ʒʌstməᵊnt/, **maladjustments**. **Maladjustment** is the state of having psychological problems and behaving in a way which is not acceptable to society. EG *Over-eating is often a symptom of loneliness or maladjustment.* N UNCOUNT/COUNT

maladroit /mælədrɔɪt/. Something that is **maladroit** is done in a clumsy, awkward, or tactless way; a fairly formal word. EG *...maladroit public relations.* ADJ QUALIT ⇑ inept ◊ **maladroitness**. EG *It is from their very naivety and maladroitness that their appeal flows.* ◊ N UNCOUNT = clumsiness

malady /mælədiᴵ/, **maladies**. A **malady** is the same as an illness; an old-fashioned word. EG *Separation anxiety was a malady she was intimately acquainted with.* N COUNT

malaise /məᵌleɪz/ is a state in which there is something wrong with society and people feel dissatisfied or unhappy but do not know exactly what is wrong; a formal word. EG *The self-indulgent instropection which was so much the malaise of my generation... Malaise had set in with the coming of the twentieth century.* N UNCOUNT ⇑ disease

malaria /məleərɪə/ is a disease which you can get from some mosquitoes and which causes periods of fever and shivering. N UNCOUNT

malarial /məleərɪəl/ means suffering from or producing malaria. ADJ CLASSIF

Malay /məᵌleɪ/, **Malays**. 1 **Malay** means belonging or relating to Malaysia, its people, or its language. EG *...the Malay peninsula and the South East Asian Islands.* ADJ CLASSIF : US ATTRIB

2 A **Malay** is a person who comes from Malaysia. N COUNT

3 **Malay** is a language that is spoken in Malaysia and in parts of Indonesia. N UNCOUNT

Malaysian /məᵌleɪzɪən/. Something that is **Malaysian** belongs or relates to Malaysia or to its people. EG *...the Malaysian forest.* ADJ CLASSIF

malcontent /mælkəntent/, **malcontents**. A **malcontent** is a person who is unhappy with the way society is organized and who wants to try and change it; a formal word. EG *The rioters were not the usual run of urban malcontents but men of responsibility.* N COUNT : USU ⇑ rebel = agitator

male /meɪl/, **males**. 1 A **male** is 1.1 an animal that belongs to the sex that cannot have babies. EG *The males establish a breeding territory.* N COUNT ≠ female ▸ used as an adjective. EG *Male hamsters court females with cries like nestlings.* ▸ ADJ CLASSIF 1.2 a man or boy; used especially when you are thinking of a man as a type rather than as an individual. EG *...the average American male... ...a particularly attractive eligible male... We live in a male-dominated society.* N COUNT ≠ female ▸ used as an adjective. EG *Your boss is almost certainly there because he is male... We now have male nurses.* ▸ ADJ CLASSIF

2 Something that is **male** concerns, relates to, or affects men rather than women. EG *...the production of male hormones... Union leaders realise the importance of changing male attitudes in the home... ...male unemployment... Women want to share some of the traditional male roles outside the home.* ADJ CLASSIF : ATTRIB ≠ female ◊ **maleness**. EG *Baldness is a sign of both maleness and advancing age.* ◊ N UNCOUNT = masculini

3 **Male** is a group or category that represents males. EG *The old stereotypes of male and female are increasingly being questioned.* N UNCOUNT ≠ female ▸ used as an adjective. EG *...the male sex.* ▸ ADJ CLASSIF ATTRIB

4 A **male** plant or part of a plant fertilizes the part which will become the fruit. ADJ CLASSIF ≠ female

5 The **male** part of a device or piece of equipment is one of two parts which fit together. The male part is pressed into a hole in the female part; a technical term. ADJ CLASSIF ≠ female

male chauvinism is the belief which some men have that men are naturally better and more important than women. N UNCOUNT ⇑ sexism

male chauvinist, male chauvinists. 1 A **male chauvinist** is a man who believes that men are naturally better and more important than women. EG *The men in my office are all blatant male chauvinists.* ▸ used as an adjective. EG *I hope this won't be taken as a male chauvinist remark.* N COUNT ⇑ sexist; ▸ ADJ CLASSIF: USU ATTRIB

2 If you refer to someone as a **male chauvinist pig**, you mean that they treat women unfairly because they do not have enough respect for women in general; used showing disapproval. EG *Some waiters I've come across have been real male chauvinist pigs.* PHR: USED AS C/O/S ⇑ sexist = misogynist

malefactor /mælɪfæktə/, **malefactors**. A **malefactor** is someone, often a criminal, who does something bad; a formal word. EG *He prosecuted malefactors vigorously.* N COUNT

malevolence /mə³lɛvələns/ is the act of deliberately causing harm or evil, or the feeling of wanting to do this; a fairly formal word. EG *...a look of malevolence.* N UNCOUNT

malevolent /mə³lɛvələnt/. Someone who is **malevolent** wants to deliberately cause harm or evil; a fairly formal word. EG *These people seemed hard and malevolent... The world is neither good nor malevolent.* ▸ used of a person's appearance or behaviour. EG *His face was malevolent... There was malevolent criticism of Government policies... The men peered at us with malevolent curiosity.* ◇ **malevolently**. EG *Billy looked at him malevolently.* ADJ QUALIT = spiteful, malicious; ◇ ADV ⇑ spitefully

malformation /mælfɔːmeɪʃə⁰n/, **malformations**. 1 **Malformation** of something such as a part of a person's body is the state of having the wrong shape or form. EG *Taking these drugs can lead to malformation of the baby's limbs.* N UNCOUNT ⇑ distortion = deformity

2 A **malformation** is a part of something, especially a person's body, which does not have the proper shape or structure. EG *What you have is a pelvic malformation.* N COUNT = deformity

malformed /mælfɔːmd/. Something that is **malformed** does not have the shape that it is supposed to have. EG *...a malformed leg.* ADJ QUALIT = deformed

malfunction /mælfʌnkʃə⁰n/, **malfunctions, malfunctioning, malfunctioned**. If a machine or a computer **malfunctions**, it fails to work properly. EG *This would cause the rest of the machine to malfunction.* ▸ used as a noun. EG *...a malfunction of the generator.* V ⇑ go wrong; ▸ N COUNT ⇑ fault

malice /mælɪs/ is a desire to cause harm to other people. EG *The librarian had spoken through ignorance or malice... 'So I notice,' he added with a touch of malice.* N UNCOUNT ⇑ cruelty = spite

malicious /məlɪʃəs/. **Malicious** talk or behaviour is intended to harm a person or their reputation. EG *Their talk was slightly malicious and gossipy... ...cold-blooded malicious cruelty.* ◇ **maliciously**. EG *Christopher remarked maliciously that this was an unprecedented development.* ADJ QUALIT = spiteful; ◇ ADV = spitefully

malign /məlaɪn/, **maligns, maligning, maligned**; a fairly formal word. 1 If you **malign** someone, you say unpleasant and untrue things about them. EG *He had maligned both women... ...the countries maligned by his newspapers.* V+O = slander

2 **Malign** behaviour is behaviour that is intended to harm someone. EG *Malign intervention can pollute and kill... This leaves his speeches open to all sorts of malign interpretation.* ▸ used of people and groups. EG *Your uncle is malign and treacherous.* ◇ **malignity** /məlɪgnɪti¹/. EG *...a look of concentrated malignity.* ADJ QUALIT ⇑ evil; ◇ N UNCOUNT ⇑ evil

malignancy /məlɪgnənsi¹/ is 1 the desire or intention to harm people. N UNCOUNT

2 the uncontrolled state of a disease, tumour, etc which is likely to cause death. EG *The next step depends on the malignancy of the patient's condition.* N UNCOUNT

malignant /məlɪgnənt/. 1 **Malignant** behaviour, intentions, etc are behaviour, intentions, etc which are harmful and cruel. EG *...the consequence of a malignant plot... A sense of humour that is malicious but not malignant... Childish high spirits turned malignant.* ▸ used of people and groups. EG *...some malignant enemy.* ◇ **malignantly**. EG *Had any country ever been so malignantly destroyed?* ADJ QUALIT ⇑ evil = malevolent; ◇ ADV WITH VB

2 A **malignant** disease, tumour, etc is uncontrollable and likely to cause death. EG *The tumours were found to be malignant... I was certain that you had a malignant growth in your larynx.* ADJ CLASSIF

malinger /məlɪŋgə/, **malingers, malingering, malingered**. If you **malinger**, you pretend to be ill in order to avoid working. EG *I'm not malingering, really I'm not.* V: USU CONT ⇑ feign

malingerer /məlɪŋgə⁰rə/, **malingerers**. A **malingerer** is a person who pretends to be ill in order to avoid doing work. N COUNT

mall /mɔːl, mæl/, **malls**. A **mall** is a shopping area where cars are not allowed. N COUNT = precinct

mallard /mælɑːd/, **mallards**; **mallard** can also be used as the plural form. A **mallard** is a very common kind of wild duck. N COUNT

malleable /mælɪəbə⁰l/; a fairly formal word. 1 Someone who is **malleable** is easily influenced or controlled by other people. EG *He was kind and malleable... ...a cheap and malleable labour force.* ADJ QUALIT = impressionable, tractable

2 A substance that is **malleable** can easily be changed into a new shape. EG *The clay is of the right consistency, solid but malleable.* ADJ QUALIT = pliable, soft

mallet /mælɪt/, **mallets**. A **mallet** is a wooden hammer with a square head. N COUNT

malnourished /mælnʌrɪʃt/. Someone who is **malnourished** is physically weak because they have not eaten enough food or because they have been eating unhealthy food; a formal word. EG *The majority of the population is malnourished.* ADJ QUALIT

malnutrition /mælnjuːtrɪʃə⁰n/ is physical weakness caused by not eating enough good food or by eating unhealthy food; a formal word. EG *He is showing the first signs of malnutrition... Twenty-five per cent of the population suffers from malnutrition.* N UNCOUNT

malodorous /mæləʊdə⁰rəs/. Something that is **malodorous** has an unpleasant smell; a literary word. EG *The air outside was almost as dank and malodorous as inside.* ADJ QUALIT = smelly

malpractice /mælpræktɪs/, **malpractices**. **Malpractice** is behaviour in which someone breaks the law or the rules of their profession in order to gain some personal advantage; a legal term. EG *A doctor who refused to give treatment is on trial for medical malpractice... ...fury over allegations of electoral malpractice.* N UNCOUNT/COUNT = impropriety

malt /mɒlt/ is grain, especially barley, that is put in water and then dried in a hot oven. Malt is used in the making of whisky, beer, and other alcoholic drinks. EG *...a bottle of malt whisky.* N UNCOUNT

malted milk, malted milks. **Malted milk** is a drink made from a special powder that contains malt. EG *He ordered a malted milk.* N MASS

Maltese /mɒltiːz/; **Maltese** is both the singular and the plural form. 1 Something that is **Maltese** belongs or relates to Malta, to its people, or to its language. ADJ CLASSIF

2 A **Maltese** is a person who comes from Malta. N COUNT

3 **Maltese** is a language that is spoken by people who come from Malta. N UNCOUNT

maltreat /mæltriːt/, **maltreats, maltreating, maltreated**. If you **maltreat** a person or an animal, you treat them badly, especially by hurting them. EG *We do not intervene unless the children are being physically maltreated... One litter was consistently maltreated by their owner.* V+O: USU PASS = abuse, ill-treat

maltreatment /mæltriːtmənt/ involves treating someone or something cruelly, or in a way that will damage or hurt them. EG *In these circumstances, you are more vulnerable to maltreatment.* N UNCOUNT

mam /mæm/, **mams**. **Mam** means the same as mother; a word used in some regions of Britain. EG *Mam had beaten the fear of God into me... Mam, when did Dad die?* N PROPER/VOC: ALSO N COUNT = mum

mama /məmɑː/, **mamas**. **Mama** means the same as mother; an old-fashioned word. EG *He told Mama he would like to live there... Oh mama, I am so unhappy.* N PROPER/VOC: ALSO N COUNT = mummy

mamba /mæmbə/, **mambas**. A **mamba** is a poisonous snake that lives in central Africa. EG *He had been bitten on the ankle by a black mamba.* N COUNT

mamma /mæmə/, **mammas**. **Mamma** means the same as mother; an informal word. EG *Mamma used to scold us... I shall tell your mamma what you did.* N PROPER/VOC: ALSO N COUNT = mummy

mammal /mæmə⁰l/, **mammals**. A **mammal** is an animal, the female of which gives birth to babies not eggs and feeds them with milk from her body. Human beings, dogs, lions, and whales are all mam- N COUNT mals. EG *Reptiles can live in deserts where a mammal would starve.*

mammalian /mæmeɪlɪən/ means relating to mammals; a technical term in biology. EG *...the earliest mammalian fossils that have been identified.* ADJ CLASSIF : ATTRIB ⇑ animal

mammary /mæmə⁰ri¹/ means relating to the breasts; a technical term in biology. EG *...the mammary gland.* ADJ CLASSIF : USU ATTRIB

mammon /mæmən/ is the acquiring of wealth, and the belief that this is the most important thing in life; used showing disapproval. EG *New York was built to the glory of mammon.* N UNCOUNT

mammoth /mæməθ/, **mammoths.** **1 Mammoth** means very large indeed. EG *...the immense foyer with its mammoth gold-backed mirrors... ...a mammoth task.* ADJ CLASSIF : ATTRIB = enormous

2 A **mammoth** was an animal like an elephant, but with very long tusks and long hair. Mammoths no longer exist. N COUNT

mammy /mæmi¹/, **mammies. Mammy** means the same as mother; a word used in some regions of Britain. EG *What did your Mammy say?* N PROPER/VOC : ALSO N COUNT = mummy

man /mæn/, **men; mans, manning, manned.** **Men** is the plural of the noun. **Mans** is the 3rd person singular, present tense, of the verb. **1** A **man** is **1.1** an adult male human being. EG *Larry was a handsome man in his early fifties... He's a great President but a remarkably boring man... Every man, woman, and child will be taken care of... ...the first man on the moon, Armstrong wasn't it?* N COUNT ⇑ person ≠ woman **1.2** a human being of either sex. EG *All men are born equal... Darwin concluded that men were descended from apes... ...a deserted island where no man could live.* N COUNT ⇑ person

2 The word **man** is used in the following expressions.

2.1 The **man in the street** is an ordinary person who is not especially rich or educated or famous, and who is therefore considered to be a typical representative of public taste and opinion. EG *How will these changes affect the man in the street?* PHR **2.2** If a group of people do something **as one man**, they do it at exactly the same time. EG *The whole crowd rose to its feet as one man.* PHR : USED AS AN A **2.3** If a group of people think something, believe something, etc **to a man**, every one of them thinks or believes it. EG *Congress almost to a man thought that abstract art was undesirable.* PHR : USED AS AN A ⇑ all

2.4 If people talk to each other **man to man**, they talk honestly and openly, treating each other as equals. EG *Few people are prepared to talk 'man to man' with the boss... She wanted to speak to her father 'man to man'.* ● See also **man-to-man.** PHR : USED AS AN A

3 You can refer to human beings in general as **man.** EG *Why does man seem to have more diseases than animals?... ...the most dangerous substance known to man.* N UNCOUNT ⇑ people = humanity

4 Modern **man**, primitive **man**, etc means all modern people, primitive people, etc considered as a group. EG *Modern man refuses to acknowledge his need for mercy... ...neolithic man.* N UNCOUNT : ADJ +N

5 People sometimes refer to a man as the **man** instead of 'he' or 'him', especially when they do not like him; an informal use. EG *The man must be mad!... I won't see him anyway. I don't like the man.* N SING : *the*+N = chap, fellow

6 People sometimes talk about a **man** when they want to make a statement about people in general; a fairly informal use. EG *How much can a man stand?... What else can a man do at a time like that?... You'd think they would at least leave a man in peace on a Sunday afternoon.* N SING : *a*+N ⇑ one = you

7 In informal English, a woman's **man** is her husband, lover, or boyfriend. EG *The two women have abandoned their men and are going to spend the evening in town.* N COUNT : USU POSS+N ⇑ partner = fellow

8 A sporting **man**, outdoor **man**, etc is a man who likes sport, outdoor activities, etc. EG *I gather you're a sporting man... I'm an outdoor man.* N SING+SUPP : *a* +N ● A **man about town** is a smart young man who goes to a lot of parties and is well-known in fashionable places; an old-fashioned expression. EG *He's quite a man about town these days.* ● See also **ladies' man.** ● PHR = socialite

9 An Oxford **man**, Cambridge **man**, etc is a man who is or was a student at Oxford University, Cambridge University, etc. EG *He liked the idea of his daughter marrying an Oxford man... He's a Reading University man, isn't he?* N COUNT : AFTER N PROPER

10 A **man** is also **10.1** an ordinary soldier, as opposed to an officer. EG *They killed in all some 70,000 officers and men.* N COUNT = private **10.2** a male worker. EG *The farmer can't get a new man... I never employ extra men, no matter how big the job.* N COUNT **10.3** a servant; an old-fashioned use. ● See also **right-hand man.** N COUNT **10.4** a man who works for or represents a particular company or organization. EG *The man from the New York Times was here to interview us... They always had their trade union man telling them all their rights.* N COUNT+SUPP ⇑ representative

10.5 one of the pieces that you move in a game of chess or draughts. N COUNT = piece

11 People sometimes address a man as **'man'** when they are angry or impatient with him. EG *Don't sit there talking, man. Get going!... For heaven's sake, man, can't you see she's had enough?* N VOC

12 People used to address a man as **my man** or **my good man** when they considered him to be socially inferior to themselves. EG *All right, my man, that will be all for today... Thank you very much, my good man.* PHR : USED AS VOC

13 If you say that someone **is his own man**, you mean that he is able to make his own decisions and plans without having to obey other people. EG *Listen, I'm my own man and no one's going to tell me when to retire.* PHR : VB INFLECTS ⇑ be independent

14 If you describe a man as **a man's man**, you mean that he has qualities which make him popular with other men rather than with women. EG *Theodore Roosevelt was a man's man, through and through.* PHR : USU USED AS C

15 If something **makes a man out of** a young man, it causes him to behave like an adult man, rather than a boy; used showing approval. EG *The army made a man out of little Arnold Sims.* PHR : VB INFLECTS

16 If you **are man enough** for something, you have the necessary courage or ability to do it; used showing approval. EG *He's not man enough for the job.* PHR : VB INFLECTS, USU + *for/to*-INF

17 If a difficult or dangerous situation **separates the men from the boys** or **sorts the men from the boys**, it shows who can cope with difficulty or danger, and who cannot. EG *Necessity separates the men from the boys.* PHR : VB INFLECTS

18 If you **man** something such as a machine, you are in charge of it or available to operate it. EG *They manned the phones all through the night... The rebels refused to man the barricades during the uprising.* ● See also **manned.** V+O

-man, -men. **1 -man** is added to some adjectives and nouns in order to form nouns referring to a man who comes from a particular country or county. EG *...English→Englishman... ...Yorkshire→Yorkshireman.* SUFFIX : FORMS COUNTS

2 -man also combines with numbers to indicate that something involves or is designed for the number of people or men mentioned. EG *...a six-man expedition down the Amazon... ...a two-man canoe.* COMB : FORMS ADJ CLASSIFS

manacle /mænəkə⁰l/, **manacles, manacling, manacled.** **1 Manacles** are metal devices attached to a prisoner's wrists or legs in order to prevent the prisoner from moving easily or escaping. EG *Carleson locked the manacles around the man's wrists.* N COUNT : USU PL ⇑ device = fetters, shackles

2 To **manacle** someone means to attach manacles to their wrists or legs in order to prevent them moving easily or escaping. EG *Were any of them manacled to the floor?* V+O : USU PASS ⇑ restrain = fetter, shackle

manage /mænɪdʒ/, **manages, managing, managed.** **1** If you **manage** to do something, especially something difficult, you succeed in doing it. EG *How he managed to find us is beyond me... Did you manage to get anything to eat before you came?.. We'll manage it somehow, I'm sure.* V OR V+O/ *to*-INF : USU V+ *to*-INF

2 If you **manage** an organization, business, system, etc, you are responsible for controlling it. EG *Private banks are being nationalised, and are to be managed with workers' participation... It would appear to be better managed than the other auto companies... If government is going to manage the economy effectively, it needs their agreement.* V+O ⇑ administer = run

3 If you **manage** an object or device that is difficult to control, you succeed in controlling it. EG *I could not manage my boots, and tripped over my laces... ...the ironing board which I hadn't got the patience to manage.* V+O

4 If you can **manage** a period of time, you can spend that time on doing something. EG *I wish you could manage the time to come and talk to us... I could manage from about half-past seven till nine.* V OR V+O = make, spare

5 If you **manage** , you succeed in living when you do V not have much money. EG *I don't want charity. I can manage... I've always managed on a teacher's salary.*

manageable /mænɪdʒəbəᵒl/. You say that something is **manageable** when you can deal with it, because it is not too big or complicated. EG *Books and documents are manageable in small numbers... It is a perfectly manageable task to tackle systematically.* ADJ QUALIT ⇑ controllable

management /mænɪdʒməˀnt/, **managements**. 1 **Management** is the control and organizing of a business or other organization. EG *She began to take over the management of the estate... It's a question of good management.* ▸ **Management** also refers to the people who do this. EG *It's a question of management and unions coming together... I acted as official spokesperson in discussions with the management... They are part of my management team.* N UNCOUNT; ▸ N UNCOUNT/COUNT = bosses

2 **Management** is also the way you control someone or something. EG *The author's management of the plot is admirable... The baby can be greatly influenced by the parents' management... ...the management of money.* N UNCOUNT

manager /mænɪdʒə/, **managers**. A **manager** is 1 a person who is responsible for running a particular section or department of a business or other organization. EG *What you need is advice from your bank manager... ...the general manager of Philips Ltd in Singapore... ...an educated class of managers and bureaucrats.* N COUNT ⇑ organizer 2 a person who is responsible for the business interests of a singer, pop group, actor, etc. EG *John had now abandoned accountancy to become his manager.* N COUNT ⇑ organizer 3 a person who is responsible for organizing and training a sports team. EG *The Arsenal manager refused to comment after the match.* N COUNT ⇑ organizer = boss

manageress /mænɪdʒəres/, **manageresses**. A **manageress** is a woman who is responsible for running a shop, office, etc. EG *The manageress was tall and terrifying... ...the manageress of a bookshop.* N COUNT ⇑ organizer

managerial /mænɪdʒɪərɪəl/ means relating to the work of a manager or manageress. EG *...technical and managerial skills... She was promoted into some kind of managerial job... They reserved the right to make managerial decisions.* ADJ CLASSIF: ATTRIB ⇑ executive

managing director, managing directors. The **managing director** of a company is the most important working director, and is in charge of the way the company is managed. EG *He's now managing director of English National Opera... One day the managing director sent for him... As Managing Director she was an extremely good negotiator.* N COUNT ⇑ head

mandarin /mændərɪn/, **mandarins**. 1 A **mandarin** 1.1 is a person who has an important job in the Civil Service; an informal British English use. EG *...the mandarins in the Foreign Office... ...Whitehall's mandarins.* N COUNT: USU+SUPP ⇑ civil servant 1.2 was an important government official in China in former times. N COUNT

2 **Mandarin** is a Chinese language spoken mainly in Northern China and around Peking and by most educated Chinese people. It is the official language of China. EG *They speak Mandarin at work.* N PROPER

3 A **mandarin** is also a small orange which is easy to peel. N COUNT

4 A **mandarin** was, in former times, an important government official in China. N COUNT

mandate /mændeɪt/, **mandates**. 1 A government's **mandate** is the authority that it has to carry out particular policies as a result of winning an election. EG *The President, strengthened by a powerful conservative mandate, has called for increases in defence spending... The General Election gave Labour no such mandate.* N COUNT

2 A **mandate** is also 2.1 a particular task that you are instructed to carry out; a formal use. EG *Peter's mandate was to find the best available investment.* N COUNT = job 2.2 authority given to someone to govern a particular territory. EG *The British were ruling the area under a mandate from the League of Nations.* N COUNT/UNCOUNT

mandatory /mændətəᵒriˡ/. If something is **mandatory**, you are legally required to do it, without any possibility of not doing it. EG *Is the appointment of worker-directors to be mandatory?.* ADJ CLASSIF = compulsory, obligatory

mandible /mændɪbəᵒl/, **mandibles**. A **mandible** is a jawbone, especially the jawbone of an animal, bird, or fish; a technical term. N COUNT ⇑ bone = jaw bone

mandolin /mændəlɪn/, **mandolins**; also spelled **mandoline**. A **mandolin** is a musical instrument like a small guitar with four pairs of metal strings. EG *He had Nino playing the mandolin as accompaniment.* N COUNT

mandrake /mændreɪk/, **mandrakes**. A **mandrake** is a plant with purplish flowers and a forked root. People used to think that the root had magic powers. N COUNT

mandrill /mændrɪl/, **mandrills**. A **mandrill** is a large West African monkey with a blue and red face. N COUNT ⇑ baboon

mane /meɪn/, **manes**. 1 A horse's or lion's **mane** is the long thick hair that grows from its neck. EG *...the streaming manes.* N COUNT

2 If you refer to a person's hair as their **mane**, you mean that they have a lot of hair. EG *He had a mane of thick white hair.* N COUNT

man-eater, man-eaters. A **man-eater** is an animal which eats human beings. N COUNT ⇑ carnivore

man-eating. A **man-eating** animal is an animal which eats human beings, or which people believe might eat human beings. EG *...man-eating tigers.* ADJ CLASSIF: ATTRIB ⇑ carnivorous

maneuver /mənuːvə/. See **manoeuvre**.

maneuverable /mənuːvəᵒrəbəᵒl/. See **manoeuvrable**.

maneuvering /mənuːvəᵒrɪŋ/. See **manoeuvring**.

manfully /mænfʊliˡ/. If you do something **manfully**, you do it in a very determined way; often used humorously. EG *One teacher is manfully coping with a wide range of tasks... I could see Simon manfully wielding a shovel.* ADV WITH VB ⇑ bravely = valiantly

manganese /mæŋgəniːz/ is a greyish-white metal that is used in making steel. N UNCOUNT ⇑ metal

manger /meɪndʒə/, **mangers**. A **manger** is a feeding box in a stable or barn. EG *The horses were crunching their straw and oats at their manger.* N COUNT

mangle /mæŋgəᵒl/, **mangles, mangling, mangled**. 1 If something **is mangled**, it is crushed or twisted so forcefully that you cannot see what its original shape was. EG *...the mangled cabs of overturned lorries.* V+O: USU PASS = mutilate

2 A **mangle** is a device consisting of two rollers in a frame. You pass wet clothes between the rollers which squeeze the water out. EG *...a huge old wooden-rollered mangle.* N COUNT = wringer

mango /mæŋgəʊ/, **mangoes** or **mangos**. A **mango** is a tree with large sweet yellowish fruit which grows in hot countries. EG *...a mango grove.* ▸ used of the fruit. EG *He and his mates were out picking mangoes.* N COUNT

mangrove /mæŋgrəʊv/, **mangroves**. A **mangrove** is a tree that stands on roots which are above the ground. Mangroves grow very close to each other along coasts or on the banks of large rivers in hot countries. N COUNT

mangy /meɪndʒiˡ/, **mangier, mangiest**. A **mangy** animal is one that has lost a lot of its hair through disease, or that looks uncared-for. EG *Rose was sitting in her rocking chair with a mangy cat upon her knee.* ADJ QUALIT: USU ATTRIB ⇑ diseased = scruffy

manhandle /mænhændəᵒl/, **manhandles, manhandling, manhandled**. 1 If you **manhandle** someone, you treat them very roughly, for example when you are taking them somewhere. EG *There were complaints of racial slurs and manhandling.* V+O ⇑ handle

2 If you **manhandle** something such as cargo, packets, or baggage, you move it by hand from place to place as part of your job. V+O

manhole /mænhəʊl/, **manholes**. A **manhole** is a hole in a road or path covered by a metal plate that can be removed. Workers climb through manholes when they want to inspect or clean drains or sewers. EG *...an open manhole... ...manhole covers.* N COUNT ⇑ hole

manhood /mænhʊd/. 1 **Manhood** is 1.1 the state of being a man rather than a boy. EG *...the dubious rewards of manhood... ...the foremost of their manhood duties.* N UNCOUNT ≠ womanhood 1.2 the period of a man's life during which he is a man rather than a boy. EG *He had millions of dollars to play with in his early manhood.* N UNCOUNT ⇑ adulthood

2 American **manhood**, French **manhood**, etc is American men, French men, etc, regarded as a group. EG *...everything that was good and clean and manly in French young manhood.* N UNCOUNT: MOD+N

man-hour, man-hours. A **man-hour** is the amount of work that one person can do in an hour; used as a measurement when you are considering how long a job has taken or will take, or how many people you will need to do a job in a particular time. EG *One firm spent a total of 370,000 man-hours on the job.* N COUNT: USU PL

manhunt /mænhʌnt/, **manhunts**. A **manhunt** is a search for someone who has escaped or disappeared. EG *...the biggest manhunt the country had known... ...a manhunt for a fugitive American.* [N COUNT: IF + PREP THEN *for*]

mania /meɪnɪə/, **manias**. A **mania** is 1 a strong liking for something; used showing amusement or disapproval. EG *...her inordinate mania for romance... ...spending mania.* [N COUNT/UNCOUNT: IF + PREP THEN *for* = craving] 2 a mental illness. EG *...persecution mania.* [N UNCOUNT: AFTER N]

maniac /meɪnɪæk/, **maniacs**. 1 A **maniac** is a mad person who is violent and dangerous. EG *She was attacked by a maniac.* [N COUNT = madman] ● If you say that someone does something **like a maniac**, you mean that they do it in an extreme way, as if they were mad. EG *Everyone drives like a maniac in this town... I've been revising like a maniac these last three days.* [● PHR: USED AS AN A]

2 **Maniac** behaviour is behaviour that is so foolish and reckless that it is like that of a mad person; used showing disapproval. EG *What kind of a maniac plan was this?* ▸ used of people and groups. EG *Rick drove up to see who the maniac pilot was.* [ADJ CLASSIF: ATTRIB; ▸ = crazy, lunatic]

3 In informal English, you can also refer to someone with an extremely strong interest in a particular activity as a **maniac**; used showing amusement or disapproval. EG *He's a baseball maniac with little taste for politics.* [N COUNT = enthusiast, freak, fan]

maniacal /mənaɪəkəl/. **Maniacal** behaviour is violent or dangerous and uncontrolled. EG *His maniacal raving alarmed the butler... She was shrieking maniacal invective at the terrified girl.* [ADJ QUALIT ⇑ mad = insane] ◇ **maniacally**. EG *Flynn laughed maniacally.* [◇ ADV WITH VB]

manic /mænɪk/. **Manic** behaviour is behaviour in which you do something extremely quickly or energetically for a period of time, for example because you are very excited or anxious about something. EG *Weston finished his manic typing... ...outbursts of drunken violence, and manic activity and creativity.* [ADJ QUALIT = frenzied]

manic-depressive, manic-depressives. A **manic-depressive** is a person who is sometimes excited and confident and at other times very depressed, and who cannot control these feelings. EG *He's a bit of a manic-depressive.* [N COUNT ⇑ neurotic] ▸ used of people's behaviour and personalities. EG *...protection against manic-depressive behaviour... Mother may have had a manic-depressive personality.* [▸ ADJ CLASSIF]

manicure /mænɪkjʊə/, **manicures, manicuring, manicured**. If you **manicure** someone's hands or nails, you care for them by softening the skin and cutting and polishing the nails. EG *She was sitting manicuring her nails... He placed his manicured hands on the table.* [V+O] ▸ used as a noun. EG *His sister gave him a manicure once a month... ...a manicure set.* [▸ N COUNT/UNCOUNT ⇑ grooming]

manicurist /mænɪkjʊərɪst/, **manicurists**. A **manicurist** is a person whose job is manicuring people's hands and nails. EG *I decided to treat myself and go to the manicurist.* [N COUNT ⇑ beautician]

manifest /mænɪfɛst/, **manifests, manifesting, manifested**; a formal word. 1 If something is **manifest**, people can easily see that it exists or that it is true. EG *It was not just his manifest disapproval that stopped her short... It's not been made manifest to me that they are different.* [ADJ QUALIT ⇑ clear = plain, evident] ◇ **manifestly**. EG *Hopper was manifestly too important to be left off the guest list.* [◇ ADV]

2 If you **manifest** something or if it **manifests** itself, people are made aware of it. EG *It was a question of how we should manifest our resistance... His inventiveness most often manifested itself as a skill in lying.* [V+O (NG/REFL) ⇑ express = demonstrate]

manifestation /mænɪfɛsteɪʃən/, **manifestations**. A **manifestation** is a sign to people that something is happening or that something exists; a fairly formal word. EG *...the first manifestations of the Computer Revolution... These were manifestations of the darker side of his character.* [N COUNT + SUPP]

manifesto /mænɪfɛstəʊ/, **manifestos** or **manifestoes**. A **manifesto** is a written statement published by a group of people, especially a political party, in which they say what their aims and policies are. EG *I was involved in the preparation of Labour's manifesto... ...Shirley Williams' election manifesto.* [N COUNT: USU + SUPP = platform]

manifold /mænɪfəʊld/. Things that are **manifold** are of many different kinds; a literary word. EG *Her good works were manifold... His manifold absurdities might have been forgotten.* [ADJ CLASSIF = various]

manila /mənɪlə/; also spelled **manilla**. A **manila** envelope, folder, etc is made from a strong paper that is usually brown. EG *...a stack of manila envelopes... He held up the three manila folders.* [ADJ CLASSIF: ATTRIB]

manipulate /mənɪpjʊleɪt/, **manipulates, manipulating, manipulated**. 1 If you **manipulate** people, you skilfully cause them to behave in the way that you want them to. EG *Small children sometimes manipulate grown-ups... They were mere puppets manipulated by men in search of other ends.* [V+O ⇑ control] ◇ **manipulation** /mənɪpjʊleɪʃən/, **manipulations**. EG *...the reality of female manipulation.* [◇ N UNCOUNT/COUNT]

2 If you **manipulate** a situation, system, etc, you cause it to develop or operate in the way that you want it to. EG *It is a simple matter to manipulate such a situation... The job of a manager is to manipulate and control a complex system.* [V+O = manage] ◇ **manipulation**. EG *...the careful manipulation of circumstances... ...computers can do sums and manipulations very rapidly... ...the consequences of weather manipulation.* [◇ N UNCOUNT/COUNT]

3 If you **manipulate** a piece of equipment, you control it in a skilful way. EG *It is guided towards the target by a control wire manipulated by the engineer... Lawrence manipulated the knobs on his tape recorder.* [V+O ⇑ use = handle] ◇ **manipulation**. EG *I had bent to watch the mechanic's manipulations.* [◇ N COUNT/UNCOUNT]

4 If you **manipulate** someone's bones or muscles, you skilfully move and press them with your hands in order to remove tension or push the bones into their correct position; a technical term. EG *Is it true that you manipulate people's bones?* [V+O] ◇ **manipulation**. EG *What you need is a bit of manipulation.* [◇ N UNCOUNT]

manipulative /mənɪpjʊlətɪv/. **Manipulative** behaviour is behaviour in which you skilfully cause people to behave in the way that you want them to; a fairly formal word. EG *...the manipulative powers of the ruler... ...the early manipulative techniques of the three-year-old.* [ADJ QUALIT: USU ATTRIB ⇑ skilful]

manipulator /mənɪpjʊleɪtə/, **manipulators**. A **manipulator** is a person who skilfully controls events, systems, or people. EG *...the expert financial manipulator... He was a manipulator and behind-the-scenes man.* [N COUNT]

mankind /mænkaɪnd/. You can refer to all human beings as **mankind** when considering them as a group. EG *You have performed a valuable service to mankind... I want to work for the good of mankind... Mankind's ability to absorb change is limited.* [N UNCOUNT ⇑ humankind = humanity]

manly /mænli/, **manlier, manliest**. People describe a man's behaviour, character, or appearance as **manly** when they think that it is typical of, or suitable for, a man rather than a woman or boy; used showing approval. EG *He laughed a deep, manly laugh... It wasn't manly to wish for such indulgences... Clem stalked the woods pursuing manly activities.* [ADJ QUALIT = masculine, male] ◇ **manliness**. EG *...the need to prove his manliness.* [◇ N UNCOUNT]

man-made. Something that is **man-made** is made by people, rather than formed naturally. EG *We live in an entirely man-made environment... ...the man-made deserts of North Africa... ...man-made fibres.* [ADJ CLASSIF ⇑ artificial]

manna /mænə/ was, in the Old Testament of the Bible, a food which appeared miraculously in the desert and prevented Moses and his people from dying of hunger. EG *Our ancestors ate manna in the desert.* [N UNCOUNT] ● If something appears **like manna** or **like manna from heaven**, it appears suddenly as if by a miracle and helps you in a difficult situation. EG *The girl dropped in his path like manna... Maybe money will rain down on us like manna from heaven.* [● PHR: USED AS AN A ⇑ miraculousl]

manned /mænd/. A **manned** vehicle is a vehicle that is controlled by the people travelling in it. EG *They released special underwater manned vehicles.* [ADJ CLASSIF ⇑ driven]

mannequin /mænɪkɪn/, **mannequins**. A **mannequin** is a person who displays clothes, hats, or shoes by wearing them, especially in fashion shows or in fashion photographs; an old-fashioned word. [N COUNT = model]

manner /mænə/, **manners**. 1 The **manner** in which you do something is the way that you do it. EG *They filed the report in a routine manner... In this manner the undercover war went on... Their manner of rearing their young is extremely unusual.* [N SING WITH DET + = fashion] ● If you describe a book, painting, etc as being **in a particular manner**, you mean that it has been written, painted, etc in a style which is typical of a particular writer, artist, etc. EG *There had been a list of characters in the manner of La Bruyère... The production was* [● PHR: USED AS AN A] *entirely in black and white in the manner of Beardsley drawings.*

2 Your **manner** is **2.1** the way in which you behave and talk on a particular occasion. EG *The judge had been impressed by his manner... Her voice and manner changed suddenly.* **2.2** the way in which you usually behave and talk. EG *He was fat, with a lazy manner.* • **bedside manner**: see **bedside**. — N SING WITH DET = tone; N SING WITH DET = demeanour

3 **Manners** are ways of behaving or speaking, particularly when they are considered as good or polite. EG *She had beautiful manners... His manners were charming... It's about time he learnt some manners... Little was required of him except good manners... It is bad manners to point.* • See also **table manners**. — N PLURAL : USU ADJ+N ⇑ conduct

4 The **manner** of person you are is the kind of person that you are; an old-fashioned or literary use. EG *What manner of man is he?... It was difficult to tell what manner of woman was hidden beneath the woollen cloak.* — N SING WITH DET +of : USU what+N = sort, type

5 **All manner of** objects, people, etc means objects, people, etc of many different kinds. EG *There were four canvas bags filled with all manner of tools... He learnt tractor maintenance and all manner of things.* — PHR : USED AS O = all kinds

6 You say that something is not true **by any manner of means**, in order to emphasize that it is not true. EG *I'm not the only one by any manner of means... I certainly wouldn't call the evidence conclusive by any manner of means.* — PHR WITH BROAD NEG : USED AS AN A

7 You say **in a manner of speaking** when you realize that what you have just said is not absolutely or literally true, but is nevertheless true in a general way. EG *If he hadn't been her boss, in a manner of speaking, she would have reported him to the police... He was likely to get his knuckles rapped in a manner of speaking.* — PHR : USED AS ADV SEN

mannered /mænəd/. If someone's speech or behaviour is **mannered**, it seems very artificial, as if they were trying to impress people; used showing disapproval. EG *His conversation is a trifle mannered.* ▸ used of people and groups. EG *They thought me mannered and rather effeminate.* — ADJ QUALIT = affected

-mannered combines with words such as 'well' and 'bad' to indicate how well or badly someone behaves. EG *...charming, well-mannered young men... I couldn't believe that a child should be so ill mannered.* — COMB : FORMS ADJ QUALITS

mannerism /mænərɪzəᵒm/, **mannerisms**. A **mannerism** is a gesture or way of speaking which is very characteristic of a person or group, and which they often use. EG *As she grew older, her mannerisms became more pronounced... He had picked up some English mannerisms.* — N COUNT ⇑ idiosyncrasy, quirk

mannish /mænɪʃ/. People describe a woman's behaviour, voice, or appearance as **mannish** when they think that it is more like a man's behaviour, voice, or appearance than a woman's; often used showing disapproval. EG *Her voice was low and almost mannish... ...her mannish shirt and tie.* ▸ used of women; an offensive use. EG *She was mannish, a sergeant-major in skirts.* ◇ **mannishly**. EG *'Bill' turned out to be a woman dressed mannishly.* — ADJ QUALIT = masculine; ◇ ADV WITH VB

manoeuvrable /mənuːvəᵒrəbəᵒl/; also spelled **maneuverable** in American English. Something that is **manoeuvrable** can be easily moved into different positions. EG *...trucks with high, manoeuvrable platforms.* — ADJ QUALIT ⇑ moveable

manoeuvre /mənuːvə/, **manoeuvres, manoeuvring, manoeuvred**; also spelled **maneuver** in American English. 1 If you **manoeuvre** something into or out of a particular place or position, you succeed in moving it into or out of the place or position when this requires care or skill. EG *The Soyuz craft was manoeuvred to within 150 metres of Enterprise... Hooper started the car and manoeuvred out of the parking space... She held the door open while I manoeuvred the suitcases into the back.* ▸ used as a noun. EG *Most people seem to manage this manoeuvre without causing havoc.* — V OR V+O : USU+A ⇑ move; ▸ N COUNT = operation

2 A **manoeuvre** is also something clever and skilful which you do or say in order to change a situation and make things happen the way that you want them to. EG *These results have been achieved by a series of political manoeuvres... Suddenly, by a brilliant manoeuvre, he completely reversed the situation.* — N COUNT/UNCOUNT ⇑ move = ploy, dodge

3 If you have **room for manoeuvre**, you have the opportunity to change your plans or to behave in a different way if it becomes necessary or desirable. EG *That doesn't leave you much room for manoeuvre.* — PHR : USED AS O ⇑ scope

4 **Manoeuvres** are the moving around of soldiers and equipment in a large area of countryside in order to train the soldiers to fight battles. EG *The manoeuvres would increase in scope... ...a designated manoeuvre area.* — N COUNT/UNCOUNT : USU PL ⇑ movements = exercises

manoeuvring /mənuːvəᵒrɪŋ/, **manoeuvrings**; also spelled **maneuvering** in American English. **Manoeuvring** is the clever and skilful changing of a situation so that you can benefit from it. EG *He was well-known for his political manoeuvring... ...the manoeuvrings of the Byzantines... ...Harold's financial manoeuvrings.* — N UNCOUNT/COUNT ⇑ behaviour = manipulation

manor /mænə/, **manors**. 1 A **manor** is a large private house and land in the country, especially one which was built in the Middle Ages. EG *...the restoration of their ancient halls and manors... ...their Oxfordshire home, Kelmscott Manor... The Manor was put up for sale.* — N COUNT : ALSO IN NAMES AFTER N ⇑ property = estate

2 The **manor** of a division of a police force is the district that it is responsible for; used in very informal British English. EG *...a similar case within their own manor.* — N COUNT ⇑ area = patch

manor house, manor houses. A **manor house** is The main house that is or was on a medieval manor. EG *...the eldest son of a wealthy family, brought up in a manor house.* — N COUNT

manorial /məˈnɔːrɪəl/ means relating to a medieval manor or manors. EG *The manorial system was already well established... ...manorial records.* — ADJ CLASSIF : ATTRIB

manpower /mænpauə/. People refer to workers in general as **manpower** when they are considering them as a means of producing goods, etc, in contrast to machines and equipment. EG *What this country is in need of is manpower... We've not got the manpower to do a regular check... There was no manpower shortage at the time.* — N UNCOUNT ⇑ staffing

manqué /mɒŋkeɪ/. An actor **manqué**, writer **manqué**, etc is a person who never succeeded in becoming a professional actor, writer, etc although they tried to become one or, in your opinion, might have become one. EG *My father was a barber manqué... ...a master printer manqué.* — ADJ AFTER N ⇑ unfulfilled

manse /mæns/, **manses**. A **manse** is the house provided for a minister in certain Christian churches, for example in the Methodist Church. EG *The manse he lived in was old and damp.* — N COUNT

manservant /mænsɜːvənt/, **menservants**. A **manservant** is a man who works as a servant in a private house; an old-fashioned word. EG *The door was opened by a manservant.* — N COUNT ⇑ servant = man

mansion /mænʃəᵒn/, **mansions**. 1 A **mansion** is a large house. EG *I spent two nights in the mansion... ...a sober late eighteenth-century mansion.* — N COUNT

2 **Mansions** is a name given to some blocks of flats. EG *...Sloane Avenue Mansions.* — N PLURAL IN NAMES AFTER N

manslaughter /mænslɔːtə/ is the killing of a person by someone who may intend to hurt or injure them but who does not intend to kill them; a legal term: compare **murder**. EG *He was sentenced to two years for manslaughter... He pleaded not guilty to murder but guilty to manslaughter.* — N UNCOUNT

mantel /mæntəᵒl/, **mantels**; also spelled **mantle**. A **mantel** is a mantelpiece; an old-fashioned word. EG *He set the glass on the mantel... ...the ornate gilded mirror above the mantel.* — N COUNT ⇑ shelf

mantelpiece /mæntəᵒlpiːs/, **mantelpieces**; also spelled **mantlepiece**. A **mantelpiece** is a wood or stone shelf which is the top part of a border round a fireplace. EG *There was a Chinese clay horse on the mantelpiece... Miss Callender remained standing by the mantelpiece.* — N COUNT : USU SING = mantelshelf

mantelshelf /mæntəᵒlʃɛlf/, **mantelshelves**; also spelled **mantleshelf**. A **mantelshelf** is a mantelpiece; an old-fashioned word. EG *He took his keys off the mantelshelf.* — N COUNT

mantis /mæntɪs/, **mantises**. A **mantis** is the same as a praying mantis. — N COUNT ⇑ insect

mantle /mæntəᵒl/, **mantles**. 1 If you take on the **mantle** of something such as a profession or an important job, you take on the responsibilities and duties which must be fulfilled by anyone who has this profession or job; a literary use. EG *...those who would inherit the mantle of office... He had assumed the mantle of newspaper proprietorship.* — N SING : the+N+of

2 A **mantle** is **2.1** a layer of something covering a surface, for example a layer of snow on the ground; a literary use. EG *The earth bore a thick green* — N COUNT+SUPP

mantle of vegetation. **2.2** a piece of clothing without sleeves that people used to wear over their other clothes. N COUNT ↑ garment = cloak

3 See also **mantel**.

mantlepiece /mæntə⁰lpiːs/. See **mantelpiece**.

mantleshelf /mæ̲tə⁰lʃelf/. See **mantelshelf**.

man-to-man. A **man-to-man** conversation, discussion, etc involves two people talking honestly and openly, treating each other as equals. EG *I think we need to have a man-to-man discussion about this some time.* ADJ CLASSIF : ATTRIB ↑ open = frank

manual /mæ̲njʊ⁰əl/, **manuals**. **1 Manual** work is work in which you use your hands or your physical strength rather than your mind. EG *They regarded manual work as degrading... ...the productivity of manual workers.* ADJ CLASSIF : USU ATTRIB = blue-collar

2 A **manual** action, gesture, etc is one in which you use your hand or hands; a rather formal use. EG *The Victorian public speaker was noted for his manual gestures... I was unable to switch it on, let alone execute feats of manual dexterity.* ADJ CLASSIF : ATTRIB

3 Manual also means operated by hand, rather than by electricity or a motor. EG *...a five-speed manual transmission.* ◊ **manually**. EG *Such pumps can be operated manually.* ADJ CLASSIF : ATTRIB ◊ ADV WITH VB

4 A **manual** is a book which tells you how to do something or how a piece of machinery works. EG *Their instruction manuals are printed in German.* N COUNT = handbook

manufacture /mænjə⁴fæ̲ktʃə/, **manufactures, manufacturing, manufactured**. **1** If you **manufacture** something, you make it in a factory. EG *Many companies were manufacturing desk calculators... They are among the most sophisticated aircraft now being manufactured... Britain would buy less manufactured goods but more raw materials.* V+O = produce

▸ used as a noun. EG *We need better regulations governing the manufacture and maintenance of vehicles... IBM is in the forefront of computer manufacture.* ◊ **manufacturing**. EG *New England's economy is largely based on manufacturing, farming and tourism... India and China had built up important manufacturing industries.* ▸ N UNCOUNT ↑ making ◊ N UNCOUNT = production

2 A **manufacture** is something which has been made in a factory; a technical use. EG *They could afford to buy all the manufactures they needed.* N COUNT : USU PL ↑ item = product

3 If you **manufacture** something such as a piece of news, you invent it, intending that people will believe that it is true. EG *She had manufactured the terrorist story to put everyone off... He had manufactured and planted evidence.* V+O = concoct, fabricate

manufacturer /mænjə⁴fæ̲ktʃə⁰rə/, **manufacturers**. A **manufacturer** is a person or group of people who own a business that makes goods in large quantities. EG *I'm a manufacturer of farm machinery... He was a wealthy soap manufacturer... Have it serviced according to the manufacturer's instructions.* N COUNT = producer

manure /mənjʊ̲ə/ is animal faeces, sometimes mixed with chemicals, that is spread on the ground in order to make plants grow healthy and strong. EG *If farm-yard manure is used it must be well rotted... ...the powerful odour of stables and horse manure.* N UNCOUNT ↑ excrement = fertilizer, dung

manuscript /mæ̲njə⁴skrɪpt/, **manuscripts**. A **manuscript** is **1** a handwritten or typed document, especially the typed version of a book before it is printed. EG *I suggest that you offer your manuscript to a publisher at a later date... It was the first time I had seen the book, which I had read in manuscript.* **2** an old document that was written by hand on paper or parchment before printing was invented. EG *...treasured Arabic books and parchment manuscripts from ancient Timbuktu.* N COUNT, OR *in*+N ↑ writing = draft; N COUNT = script, scroll

Manx /mæ̲ŋks/ is used to describe people or things that belong to or concern the Isle of Man and the people who live there. ADJ CLASSIF

many /me̲ni¹/. The comparative for the quantifier explained in paragraph 1 is **more**, and the superlative is **most**: these words are dealt with separately in this dictionary. **1** You use **many** to refer to a large number of things or people when you are emphasizing how large the number is. EG *Many people have been killed... It was, in many ways, a nice room... He was very active everywhere, influencing as many people as he could... ...the many brilliant speeches that had been made... Many of the old people were blind... These families, like so many today, are child-centred... The invitations are rich, the temptations many.* QUANTIF+N IN PL ↑ several = lots of

● **Many a** time, **many a** woman, etc means many times, many women, etc. EG *That's happened many a time to me... I've spent many a moonlit night here... His bones were in a condition that many a young man might envy.* ● **many happy returns**: see **return**. ● **not in so many words**: see **word**. ● PHR+N IN SING

2 You use **as many as** before a number when you want to say how surprisingly large it is. EG *He has written as many as five books in eighteen months.* PHR+NUM+N IN PL

3 You use **a good many** or **a great many** to emphasize that you are referring to a large number of things or people. EG *I remember going to London a good many years ago... The information has proved useful to a great many people.* PHR+N IN PL ↑ many

4 You use **many's the time, many's the night**, etc when you want to say that something happens or happened very often. EG *Many's the time our sisters used to say that.* PHR : USED AS AN A

5 You also use **many** to ask questions about numbers or quantities, or sometimes to give information about them. EG *How many children has she got?... I used to get a lot of sweets. As many as I liked... There are about 35,000 species of crustacean, four times as many as there are of birds.* QUANTIF : *as/how*+QUANTIF+N IN PL

6 You use **the many** to refer to the majority of people considered separately from a small minority, especially because they share a particular quality or disadvantage that the minority do not have. EG *The many are left to house themselves.* N PLURAL : *the*+N

many-sided. Something that is **many-sided** is composed of many different parts or aspects. EG *...so many-sided a concept... The views which Plato formulates there are many-sided... Rabinsky became fascinated by the many-sided Arab character.* ADJ CLASSIF = complex

map /mæp/, **maps, mapping, mapped**. **1** A **map** is **1.1** a drawing of a particular area, for example a continent, a country, or a city, as it would appear to you if you saw it from above. A map shows the main features of the area and the way that they relate to each other. EG *On the map it is quite a brief strip of road... Maps can be obtained from the Tourist Office in the main square.* **1.2** a similar drawing that gives a special kind of information about an area. EG *Now look at the rainfall maps on page nineteen... He can even present you with local dialect maps for some parts of the world.* N COUNT ↑ diagram = chart, plan; N COUNT : MOD+N ↑ diagram = chart

2 If you **map** an area, you make a map of it. EG *...techniques that allow them to map the earth's crusts.* V+O = chart

3 Someone or something that **puts** a place **on the map** makes it become well-known and important. EG *This development at last put Hillingdon on the map.* PHR : VB INFLECTS

map out. If you **map out** something that you are intending to do, you work out in detail how you will do it. EG *We began to map out plans for our counter offensive... They met and mapped out their task.* PHRASAL VB : V+O+ADV ↑ plan = prepare

maple /meɪpə⁰l/, **maples**. A **maple** is a tree with five-pointed leaves that grows in countries which do not have hot climates, such as Canada. EG *The fields and walks were shaded by chestnut, maple, and cherry trees.* ▸ **Maple** is used to refer to the wood of this tree. EG *...the shining maple floorboards.* N COUNT ▸ N UNCOUNT

mar /mɑ̲ː/, **mars, marring, marred**. If you **mar** something, you spoil its appearance. EG *He didn't want to have his face marred by a broken nose... Graffiti marred the sides of buildings.* ● If you will **make or mar** something, you will cause it either to succeed or to fail. EG *...the power of Governments to make or mar inner city initiatives.* V+O = disfigure ● PHR : VBS INFLECT

Mar. is an abbreviation for March.

marathon /mæ̲rəθə⁰n/, **marathons**. **1** A **marathon** is a race in which people have to run about 26 miles (about 42 km) along roads. EG *Such a time would be the envy of many of today's marathon runners... I'm hoping to be in the London marathon next year.* N COUNT

2 A **marathon** job, task, etc is one that takes a long time to do and that is very tiring. EG *You need stamina to get through such a marathon production... He revealed this in his marathon press conference the day after.* ADJ CLASSIF : ATTRIB = lengthy, exhausting

marauder /mərɔ̲ːdə/, **marauders**. A **marauder** is a person or animal that roams around looking for something to steal or kill. EG *There are too many marauders along the land route... ...foxes, crows, and other marauders.* N COUNT ↑ robber = predator

marauding /mərɔ:dɪŋ/. A **marauding** person or animal is one that roams around looking for something to steal or kill. EG *He sensed behind them the marauding forces... Along them were sharp-pointed stakes to cripple any marauding animals or humans.* ADJ CLASSIF : ATTRIB ⇑ roaming = predatory

marble /mɑ:bəᵒl/, **marbles**. 1 **Marble** is a type of very hard rock which feels cold when you touch it and which shines when it is cut and polished. Statues and parts of buildings are sometimes made of marble. EG *...white Italian marble... ...a marble fireplace... ...a monument in black marble.* N UNCOUNT, OR N BEFORE N

2 **Marbles** is a children's game played with small balls, usually made of coloured glass. You roll a ball along the ground and try to hit an opponent's ball with it. EG *The little boys are playing marbles.* N UNCOUNT

3 A **marble** is 3.1 one of the small balls used by children in the game of marbles. N COUNT 3.2 a sculpture made of marble; a technical use. EG *The marbles are still on display.* N COUNT

4 If you say that someone **has lost** their **marbles**, you mean that they have gone mad; an informal humorous expression. EG *He must have lost his marbles.* PHR : VB INFLECTS = go mad

marbled /mɑ:bəᵒld/. Something that is **marbled** has a pattern or colouring like that of marble; a literary word. EG *...the marbled flush of her palms... There was a marbled moon coming up.* ADJ CLASSIF ⇑ mottled

march /mɑ:tʃ/, **marches, marching, marched**. The word **march** is spelled with a capital letter for paragraph 1. 1 **March** is the third month of the year in the western calendar. EG *He was assassinated in March 1978.* N UNCOUNT

2 If you **march**, you walk with very regular steps, like a soldier. EG *They marched through Norway... Play a band and they begin to march... Nobody can march thirty miles a day.* V : USU+A ▸ used as a noun. EG *We were woken in the middle of the night for a long march.* ▸ N COUNT ◊ **marching**. EG *They had mastered the techniques of marching... We heard the sounds of marching feet. ...an enormous procession of horses and marching troops.* ◊ N UNCOUNT, OR ADJ CLASSIF : ATTRIB ● **A day's march** is the distance that you can march in one day. EG *The base was within a day's march.* ● PHR : USED AS O/C/S ● If part of an army is **on the march**, they are going somewhere by marching there. EG *We were three days on the march.* ● PHR : USED AS AN A

3 A **march** is also 3.1 a piece of music with a regular rhythm that you can march to. EG *...the March from the Coronation of Poppea by Monteverdi... ...a funeral march.* N COUNT 3.2 the steady development or progress of something. EG *...the onward march of intellect... ...the slow march to socialism.* N SING WITH DET +SUPP

4 If people **march**, they walk together in a large group, usually through a town, in order to express their ideas or to protest about something. EG *The crowds of demonstrators marched down the main street.* V : USU+A ▸ used as a noun. EG *A million people took part in last year's march... She'd been on a few marches.* ▸ N COUNT = demonstration

5 If you **march** somewhere, you walk there quickly and in a determined way, for example because you are angry. EG *He marched out of the store... She turned and marched back into the kitchen.* V+A

6 If you **march** someone somewhere, you force them to walk there with you by grasping their arm tightly. EG *He took me by the arm and marched me out of the door... I marched her to the car.* V+O+A

7 If you **steal a march** on someone, you start doing something before they do it in order to gain an advantage over them. EG *We were afraid they might steal a march on us... They thought I was stealing a march by keeping fitter than the rest of them.* PHR : VB INFLECTS, IF+ PREP THEN *on*

8 If you give someone their **marching orders**, you tell them that you no longer want them or need them, for example as your employee or as your lover. EG *Pa gave her her marching orders... You'll get your marching orders pretty soon.* PHR : DETPOSS+ PHR, USED AS O

marcher /mɑ:tʃə/, **marchers**. A **marcher** is someone who is marching, either as a soldier or in a protest march. EG *The drums stopped and the marchers halted.* N COUNT ⇑ walker

marchioness /mɑ:ʃənɪˈs/, **marchionesses**. A **marchioness** is the wife or widow of a marquis, or a woman with the same rank as a marquis. N COUNT : ALSO IN TITLES

mare /meə/, **mares**. A **mare** is an adult female horse. N COUNT ≠ stallion

margarine /mɑ:dʒəri:n/ is a yellow substance that looks like butter and is made from vegetable oil, animal fat, and water. You can spread it on bread or use it for cooking. EG *Melt the margarine in a frying pan.* N UNCOUNT = marge

marge /mɑ:dʒ/ is margarine; an informal word. EG *Would you prefer butter or marge on your toast?* N UNCOUNT

margin /mɑ:dʒɪn/, **margins**. 1 A **margin** is the amount, for example the amount of votes in an election, which separates a winning candidate or party from a losing candidate or party. EG *Muskie should have won by a huge margin... They won by the small margin of five seats.* N COUNT : USU+ SUPP ⇑ difference

2 The **margin** on a written or printed page is the blank space at the side of the page. EG *They get a nice red tick in the margin to show that it's right.* N COUNT ⇑ edge

3 If there is a **margin** of something, there is a little bit more of it than is actually necessary to survive or succeed, and this extra amount allows you more freedom of choice or action. EG *What is the margin of safety?... Living at social security level leaves little margin for personal adornment... I hope they will allow a margin for error.* N COUNT/ UNCOUNT+SUPP

4 The **margin** of a place or area is the extreme edge of it. EG *We came to the margin of the wood... Another small frog builds its own ponds on the margins of forest pools.* N COUNT : USU+ *of* ⇑ periphery

5 The **margin** of a group, activity, situation, etc is the part that is furthest from what is typical of that group, activity, situation, etc. EG *There were multitudes of people living on the margin of society... We shall attract new things at the margin, new research institutes.* N COUNT : IF+ PREP THEN *of* ⇑ periphery = fringe

marginal /mɑ:dʒɪnəᵒl/, **marginals**. 1 Something that is **marginal** is small and not very important. EG *The effect will be marginal... The challenge to man's future cannot be met by making marginal adjustments here and there.* ADJ QUALIT = insignificant

2 A **marginal** politician, writer, artist, etc is one who is not very important and not involved in the main events or developments. EG *He has remained a rather marginal political figure.* ADJ QUALIT ⇑ unimportant

3 A **marginal** seat or constituency is a political constituency where elections are usually won by a very small majority, so that control often changes from one party to another; used especially in British English. EG *What happened in Croydon was that a marginal seat in a mid term election changed hands.* ADJ QUALIT : USU ATTRIB = uncertain ≠ safe ▸ used as a noun. EG *What will happen in the marginals?* ▸ N COUNT

4 **Marginal** land is on the edge of a fertile area and so is not able to grow very much grain, corn, wheat, etc. EG *The current land project is transforming 37,500 acres of marginal land into a thriving dairy centre.* ADJ CLASSIF : ATTRIB ⇑ unproductive

marginally /mɑ:dʒɪnəᵒliˡ/ means to only a small extent. EG *Miss Garlick was marginally kinder than the other teachers... Their faces were only marginally different.* ADV : USU+ADJ/ ADV = slightly

marigold /mæriˡgəʊld/, **marigolds**. A **marigold** is a type of yellow flower. N COUNT

marijuana /mærɪjuɑ:nə/ is a drug which is made from the dried leaves and flowers of the hemp plant, and which can be smoked in cigarettes; also used to refer to the hemp plant. EG *He is often high on marijuana... ...a marijuana cigarette.* N UNCOUNT = cannabis

marina /məri:nə/, **marinas**. A **marina** is a small harbour or area of water where people keep yachts and other small boats. N COUNT

marinade /mærɪneɪd/, **marinades, marinading, marinaded**. 1 A **marinade** is a sauce of oil, vinegar, spices, etc, which you pour over meat or fish before you cook it, in order to add flavour, or to make the meat or fish softer. EG *Brush the fillets with the marinade.* N COUNT ⇑ mixture

2 To **marinade** means the same as to marinate. EG *Allow the chicken to marinade for 1-2 hours.* V-ERG

marinate /mærɪneɪt/, **marinates, marinating, marinated**. If you **marinate** meat or fish, or if it **marinates**, you keep it in a mixture of oil, vinegar, spices, etc, before cooking it, so that it can develop a special flavour, or become softer. EG *It is best to marinate the meat for three days in wine and vinegar.* V-ERG ⇑ soak = steep ◊ **marinated**. EG *...marinated lamb.* ◊ ADJ CLASSIF

marine /məri:n/, **marines**. 1 A **marine** is 1.1 a soldier in the American Marine Corps. EG *...a brigade of US marines.* N COUNT 1.2 a British soldier who serves with the navy, and who is not a specialist sailor. N COUNT

2 **Marine** is used 2.1 to describe things relating to the sea, and to the animals and plants that live in the ADJ CLASSIF : ATTRIB

sea. EG ...*marine life... ...marine biology.* **2.2** to describe things concerned with ships and their movement at sea. EG *This is the accepted marine gesture for 'Help!'* ADJ CLASSIF : ATTRIB = maritime, nautical

Marine Corps. The **Marine Corps** is a particular section of soldiers who are part of the American Navy. N PROPER : *the*+N

mariner /mærɪnə/, **mariners**. A **mariner** is a sailor; an old-fashioned or literary word. EG *Many shipwrecked mariners died along this coast.* N COUNT = seaman

marionette /mærɪənet/, **marionettes**. A **marionette** is a puppet which you control by strings or wires. N COUNT ↑ doll

marital /mærɪtəl/ is used to describe things relating to marriage. EG ...*marital problems.* ADJ CLASSIF : ATTRIB

marital status. If someone asks what your **marital status** is, they want to know whether you are married, single, or divorced; a formal expression. EG *Please indicate your marital status.* N UNCOUNT

maritime /mærɪtaɪm/ is used to describe things relating to the sea and to ships. EG *We used to be a maritime nation... ...the National Maritime Museum.* ADJ CLASSIF : ATTRIB

marjoram /mɑːdʒərəm/ is a plant with small pale purple flowers and sweet-scented leaves, which is used as a herb. N UNCOUNT

mark /mɑːk/, **marks, marking, marked**. **1** A **mark** is a small part of a surface which is a different colour because something has been dropped on it, or because it has been damaged or changed in some way. EG *This is good for grease marks... I'm sorry, there seems to be a dirty mark on it.* N COUNT = stain, blemish

2 If you **mark** something, or if it **marks**, it gets a mark on it because of the effect of something on it. EG *Vinegar, lemon juice, egg and salt can mark cutlery... This type of cloth marks very easily.* V-ERG = stain

3 A **mark** is also **3.1** a written or printed symbol, for example a short line or a letter of the alphabet. EG *The page was covered with dozens of little marks... McNicoll made a few marks with his pen.* N COUNT **3.2** a written symbol such as a number or a letter which is used by a teacher to indicate how good or bad a student's work is. EG *When the final marks were posted for the term, Rudolph had an A in history... Give yourself the mark you think you deserve.* N COUNT = grade **3.3** a point that is given for a correct answer or for doing something well in an exam or competition. EG *You need 120 marks out of 200 to pass... I got really good marks in my exam... You get full marks for getting the right answer.* N COUNT ↑ score **3.4** a number or a point on a scale which is important or significant in some way. EG *Unemployment is now well over the three million mark... Once past the half-way mark he found that he was running more easily.* N COUNT : MOD+N ↑ level **3.5** a characteristic feature that enables you to recognize something. EG *Our words and our buildings still display the mark of early Greek influence... The scene bore all the marks of a country wedding.* N COUNT+SUPP ↑ sign

4 A **mark** of something is a type of behaviour or an event which shows that a certain situation or emotion exists. EG *They removed their hats as a mark of respect... ...a mark of friendship.* N COUNT+*of* ↑ symbol = sign

5 If you **mark** something, **5.1** you put a written symbol on it as an instruction or a warning. EG *He had the right to read reports marked Top Secret... The exit sign was marked with an arrow... I checked the map for mines but there was nothing marked.* V+O : USU PASS ↑ label **5.2** you put a written symbol on it, usually with a pen or pencil, in order to identify it in some way. EG *See that everything is marked with your initials... In her phrase book she had marked some pages for 'Asking Directions.'* V+O ↑ label

6 If a teacher **marks** an essay or some other piece of academic work, he or she decides how good it is and writes a number or letter on it to indicate this opinion. EG *I find poetry very difficult to mark... He was marking a student's essay.* V+O ↑ assess = grade

7 If something **marks** a place, position, spot, etc, it shows where something else is or where it used to be. EG *The area of burned clay marks the position of several Roman furnaces... Four brass rosettes in the floor mark the spot where the speaker's chair stood.* V+O ↑ indicate

8 If you **mark** your place, you show by some means where you are when you stop what you are doing, especially when reading a book, so that when you come back to it you can start again without any difficulty. EG *She had her finger pressed to the page as if marking her place.* V+O

9 Something that **marks** a particular stage or point is a sign that something different is about to happen. EG *The film marks a turning point in Allen's career... Her resignation marks the end of an era.* V+O ↑ indicate

10 If you do something to **mark** an event or occasion, you do it to indicate that you are aware of the importance of the event or occasion. EG *The concert is to mark the 75th Anniversary year of the composer's death... He made his promise at a rally to mark the opening of the congress.* V+O ↑ commemorate

11 If a particular quality **marks** an activity or a person's life or career, it is often demonstrated and is usually something that should be admired. EG *His cricket has always been marked by courage and determination... The missionary element has marked his glittering career.* V+O = characterize

12 Someone or something that **marks** someone as a particular type of person indicates that they are that type of person. EG *These signs marked him as a bachelor eager to wed... They put me in jail and marked me as an enemy of society.* V+O+A *(as)* = label

13 A **mark** is also **13.1** the unit of money that is used in West Germany and East Germany. It is also the name of the unit of money used in Finland. EG ...*the strength of the German Mark... I was paying eighty marks a month for my room.* N COUNT **13.2** a coin which is worth one mark. N COUNT

14 **Mark** is used before a number **14.1** to indicate the level of temperature in a gas oven. EG *Cook in oven at gas mark 5 for about an hour.* N UNCOUNT+NUM **14.2** to indicate a particular version or model of a machine, vehicle, or modern weapon. EG *The Mark II received enormous amounts of publicity.* N UNCOUNT+NUM = type

15 You say **'mark my words'**, often as a warning, when you want someone to pay attention to what you are saying. EG *And you mark my words, you haven't heard the last of him.* PHR : USED AS ADV SEN ● You say **'mark you'** to give emphasis to something you have just said and to make other people notice it because you think it is important. EG *He's very ambitious–like most men, mark you.* ● PHR : USED AS ADV SEN ↑ note = mind you

16 **On your marks** is a command given to runners at the beginning of a race in order to get them into the correct position to start. EG *On your marks! Get set! Go!* CONVENTION = ready

17 If you are **slow off the mark**, you are slow to understand something, for example a joke, or slow to start doing something. EG *You were a bit slow off the mark, there.* PHR : USED AS C ● If you are **quick off the mark**, you are eager and willing to do something without delay. EG *Neighbours were always pretty quick off the mark to ask him round whenever his wife was away.* ● PHR : USED AS C ↑ keen

18 If you **make** your **mark** or **make a mark**, you make people notice you because of something unusual or impressive that you have done. EG *It was here that Tony made his mark... ...a scholar who has made a mark in the history of ideas.* PHR : VB INFLECTS ↑ impress

19 If you **leave** your **mark** or **leave a mark**, you make important changes which will last and for which you will be remembered. EG *Another eminent Victorian left his mark on Gloucestershire... These policies have left indelible marks on British society.* PHR : VB AND N INFLECT ↑ affect

20 If something is **on the mark**, it is absolutely correct. If something is **off the mark**, it is incorrect. EG *The description seemed right on the mark... No, he's way off the mark.* PHR : USED AS AN A ● If something is **wide of the mark**, it is a long way from being correct. EG *His assessment of the situation might be rather wide of the mark.* ● PHR : USED AS = off

21 If something is **up to the mark**, it is good enough. EG *He told me my art wasn't up to the mark... These measures will generally keep him up to the mark.* PHR : USED AS AN A = up to standard

22 If you **mark time**, **22.1** you lift your feet up and down in a regular rhythm while staying in the same place, so that it looks as if you are marching. EG *The soldiers were marking time on the parade ground.* PHR : VB INFLECTS **22.2** you wait for something more interesting to happen, especially when you are doing something that you do not enjoy. EG *I've been marking time for a few days... School was a bore and a place where one marked time until the doors opened again.* PHR : VB INFLECTS

23 See also **birthmark, black mark, bookmark, exclamation mark, hallmark, landmark, postmark, punctuation mark, question mark, quotation mark, trademark.**

24 See also **marked, marking.**

mark down. **1** If you **mark** something **down**, **1.1** PHRASAL VB : V-you write it down. EG *If you witness an accident, mark down the licence of the car.* **1.2** you make its price lower than it has been. EG *Trousers are marked down from £39.95 to £20.00.* — O+ADV; PHRASAL VB : V+O+ADV = reduce

2 If a teacher **marks** a student **down**, he or she puts a lower grade on the student's work because of a mistake that has been made. EG *Wrong spellings get you marked down in exams.* — PHRASAL VB : V+O+ADV ⇑ reduce

3 If you **mark** someone **down** as a particular type of person, you consider that they have the qualities which make them that type of person. EG *I would have marked him down as a budding genius.* — PHRASAL VB : V+O+ADV+A *(as)*

4 See also **mark-down**.

mark off. **1** If you **mark off** a piece of ground, you separate it from everything around it, usually by making a fence or some other physical barrier. EG *He has marked off the area with lengths of string.* — PHRASAL VB : V+O+ADV

2 If something **marks** one thing **off** from another, it makes the two things very different from one another. EG *This characteristic marks her off from her brother.* — PHRASAL VB : V+O+ADV, IF+PREP THEN *from* ⇑ distinguish

3 If you **mark off** a date on a calendar or an item on a list, you put a line through it or next to it, in order to show that it has been completed or dealt with. EG *Each day was marked off with a neat X.* — PHRASAL VB : V+O+ADV = cross off

mark out. **1** If you **mark out** an area of land, you draw special lines on it so that it may be used for a particular sport or some other purpose. EG *Football pitches are usually marked out with white paint.* — PHRASAL VB : V+O+ADV

2 If a particular quality or feature **marks** a person **out**, it is unusual or special and makes them seem noticeably different from other people. EG *There was a stillness about Ralph that marked him out.* — PHRASAL VB : V+O+ADV ⇑ distinguish

mark up. If you **mark** something **up**, you increase its price. ● See also **mark-up**. — PHRASAL VB : V+O+ADV

mark-down, mark-downs. A **mark-down** is a reduction in the price of something. — N COUNT

marked /mɑːkt/. **1** If something is **marked**, it is very obvious and easily noticed. EG *He has shown marked improvements in spelling and writing... This kind of elitism is even more marked in schools.* — ADJ QUALIT = noticeable

◇ **markedly** /mɑːkɪdli¹/. EG *Business in Nigeria is markedly different from that in Europe.* — ◇ ADV = noticeably

2 If you describe someone as a **marked** man or woman, you mean that they are in danger from someone who wants to harm or kill them. EG *The bishop was a marked man.* — ADJ CLASSIF : USU ATTRIB ⇑ doomed

marker /mɑːkə/, **markers.** **1** A **marker** is an object which is used to show the position of something. EG *The post served as a boundary marker... There are no longer any markers to tell us when we are entering the danger zone.* — N COUNT ⇑ signpost

2 A **marker** or a **marker pen** is a pen with a thick tip made of felt, which is used for drawing and for colouring things. — N COUNT ⇑ felt pen

market /mɑːkɪt/, **markets, marketing, marketed.** **1** A **market** is a place, usually in the open air, where goods are bought and sold. Markets are sometimes held on particular days and some markets deal mainly in animals. EG *These women sell matches, fish, mirrors, or kerosene in the markets... ...a cattle market... ...a market stall... Cheltenham had been a small market town with a population of 1500.* — N COUNT

2 The **market** for a particular commodity is **2.1** the number of people who want to buy it. EG *...the declining commercial vehicle market... The West has artificially depressed the market for third world commodities.* **2.2** an area of the world in which the commodity is sold. EG *There is a vast overseas market... Access to new foreign markets was assured.* — N COUNT+SUPP : USU SING = demand; N COUNT+SUPP

3 The **market** is the total amount of a commodity sold in a particular period, in a particular country, etc, and is used to indicate how successful a company or country has been. EG *In 1980 Japan seized slightly over a fifth of the market... Importers have now lifted their share of the market so far this year from 24.5 to 30.3 per cent.* — N SING : *the*+N

4 If you **market** a product, you sell it, especially in an organized way and on a large scale. EG *The felt-tip pen was first marketed by a Japanese firm.* — V+O

5 **Market** is used to describe an economic situation in which the price of something is decided by how much there is of it to sell and how many people want to buy it. EG *We must respond to market forces... They have never had to operate in a market economy.* — N BEFORE N

6 **Market** is used in the expressions **a buyer's market** and **a seller's market** when you are describing a situation that is good financially for someone either buying or selling something such as a commodity or shares. EG *It's a seller's market at the moment.* — PHR : USED AS C

7 If something is **on the market**, it is available for people to buy. EG *A talking watch will shortly be on the market... Its one of the slowest cars on the market.* — PHR : USED AS AN A
● When something **comes onto the market**, it becomes available for people to buy. EG *Many labour-saving devices have come onto the market.* — ● PHR : VB INFLECTS
● When a company **brings** something **onto the market**, they make it available for people to buy. — ● PHR : VB INFLECTS

8 If something is **on the open market**, it is freely available for people to buy, for example in shops. EG *You'll never get a picture as good as this one on the open market.* — PHR : USED AS AN A

9 If a person or company **is in the market** for something, they are interested in taking part in a particular business deal. EG *Exxon might well be in the market to buy up a competitor too.* — PHR+*for/to*-INF : VB INFLECTS ⇑ want = be eager

10 The **market** in something is the activity of buying or selling it. EG *...this illegal market in live animals.* ● See also **black market**. — N SING WITH DET : USU+*in* ⇑ activity = trade

11 The stock market is sometimes referred to as the **market**. EG *In June the market collapsed to a five-and-a-half-year low.* — N SING : *the*+N

12 The **market** for jobs is the people who are looking for work and the jobs available for them to do. EG *I'm on the job market again... Among the less privileged groups in the labour market, women figured prominently.* — N SING : *the*+MOD+N

marketable /mɑːkɪtəbə⁰l/. Something that is **marketable** is able to be sold because people want to buy it. EG *...their only marketable commodity... Nothing is more marketable than the memoirs of an ex-President.* — ADJ QUALIT

market garden, market gardens. A **market garden** is a small farm where vegetables and fruit are grown for sale; used mainly in British English. — N COUNT

market gardener, market gardeners. A **market gardener** is a person who works on a market garden; used mainly in British English. — N COUNT

market gardening is the business of growing vegetables and fruit for sale; used mainly in British English. — N UNCOUNT

marketing /mɑːkɪtɪŋ/ is the part of business which is concerned with the way in which a product is sold, for example deciding on its price, the particular shops or areas in which it should be sold, the way it should be advertised, etc. EG *...the importance of effective marketing... ...marketing directors.* — N UNCOUNT ⇑ sale = distribution

marketplace/mɑkɪtpleɪs/, **marketplaces**; also spelled with a hyphen and as two words. **1** The **marketplace** is the activity of buying and selling and the places where this occurs. EG *Its products must compete in the international market place... In a capitalist world, the forces of the market-place prevail.* — N COUNT : *the*+N IN SING ⇑ trade

2 A **marketplace** is a small area in a town or city where there are no buildings and where goods are bought and sold. In small towns, the marketplace is usually a square area at the centre of the town. EG *There was a statue of Mozart in the market place... ...beggars crowded in every market-place.* — N COUNT

market research is the activity of collecting and studying information about what people want, need, and buy, especially because a company wants to find out whether a product or idea is likely to be successful before it spends more time, money, or effort on it. EG *I got a job in market research, interviewing housewives in the Leeds area.* — N UNCOUNT ⇑ research = consumer survey

marking /mɑːkɪŋ/, **markings.** **1** **Markings** are coloured shapes or designs on the surface of something, especially for decoration or identification. EG *Look at the markings on the petals... The plane had no markings.* — N COUNT : USU PL ⇑ mark

2 **Marking** is the work a teacher does when he or she reads a student's work and gives it a grade. EG *There is just no way of keeping up with all the marking.* — N UNCOUNT

marking ink is ink that is used for marking cloth, usually with your name, and which cannot be removed by washing. — N UNCOUNT

marksman /mɑːksmə³n/, **marksmen**. A **marksman** is a person who can shoot very accurately with a gun. EG *My father was an expert marksman.* N COUNT ⇑ shot

marksmanship /mɑːksmə³nʃɪp/ is the ability to shoot accurately. EG *It was an impressive display of marksmanship.* N UNCOUNT ⇑ shooting

mark-up, mark-ups. A **mark-up** is an increase in the price of something, for example the difference between its cost and the price that you sell it for. N COUNT

marmalade /mɑːməleɪd/. 1 **Marmalade** is a jam-like food made from oranges, lemons, or other fruit and usually eaten on bread or toast at breakfast. EG *...toast and marmalade.* N UNCOUNT ⇑ preserve

2 A **marmalade** cat has orangey-brown stripes. ADJ CLASSIF

marmoset /mɑːməzet/, **marmosets**. A **marmoset** is a very small South American monkey, which has claws on its fingers and toes. N COUNT

maroon /mərʊːn/, **maroons, marooning, marooned**. 1 Something that is **maroon** is dark reddish-purple in colour. EG *...a maroon jacket.* ▸ used as a noun. EG *The peaks were turning a plummy maroon.* ADJ COLOUR ▸ N UNCOUNT

2 If someone **is marooned**, they are left in a place, for example on an island, which it is difficult or impossible for them to escape from. EG *Five fishermen were marooned on a rock in a gale... It is a story about a group of young boys marooned on a desert island.* ◇ **marooned**. EG *The breakfast arrived and he went at it like a marooned mountaineer.* V+O : USU PASS, USU+A = strand ◇ ADJ CLASSIF = abandoned

3 If you **are marooned**, you are in a situation in which you feel alone and helpless, and which you cannot escape from. EG *I had been marooned on the outer fringes of the party, and was getting bored.* ◇ **marooned**. EG *Joy, marooned in her flat since her lover went back to his wife, became more and more depressed.* V+O : ONLY PASS, USU+A ⇑ be left = be abandoned ◇ ADJ CLASSIF ⇑ left = stuck

marquee /mɑːkiː/, **marquees**. A **marquee** is a large tent which is used at a fair, garden party, or other outdoor event, usually for eating and drinking in. EG *Strawberries and cream are in the marquee.* N COUNT = pavilion

marquis /mɑːkwɪs/, **marquises**; sometimes also spelled **marquess** in British English. A **marquis** is a male member of the nobility who has the rank between duke and earl. EG *...the Marquis of Stafford... ...the Marquess of Salisbury.* N COUNT : ALSO IN TITLES

marriage /mærɪdʒ/, **marriages**. 1 A **marriage** is 1.1 the relationship between a husband and wife. EG *It has been a happy marriage... Our marriage nearly broke up... Her fifth marriage lasted only a month.* N COUNT
1.2 the act of marrying someone, or the ceremony at which this is done. EG *I was one of her bridesmaids at the marriage... Victoria's marriage to her cousin was not welcomed by her family.* N COUNT/ UNCOUNT : IF+ PREP THEN *to* ⇑ union

2 **Marriage** is the state of being married. EG *I never wanted marriage... ...the institution of marriage.* N UNCOUNT

marriageable /mærɪdʒəbə⁰l/. Someone who is **marriageable** is suitable for marriage, especially with regard to age. EG *I have three marriageable daughters... My son's not of marriageable age.* ADJ CLASSIF = eligible

married /mærɪd/. 1 If you are **married**, you have a husband or wife. EG *...a married woman... She's married to an Englishman... He was thirty-five, married with two children.* ADJ CLASSIF : IF+ PREP THEN *to* = wedded

2 **Married** is used to describe things that involve marriage or take place during marriage. EG *The next chapter describes their early married life.* ADJ CLASSIF : ATTRIB = wedded

3 If you **are married to** something, you are so involved with it and dedicated to it that you have little time or interest for anything else. EG *They were married to the company they served... I am married to my music.* PHR : VB INFLECTS = be wedded to

marrow /mærəʊ/, **marrows**. 1 A **marrow** is a long, thick, green vegetable with soft white flesh, which you can cook and eat; used mainly in British English. N COUNT/ UNCOUNT

2 **Marrow** is the soft fatty substance which fills the space at the centre of the bones of humans and animals. EG *...a bone marrow transplant.* N UNCOUNT

3 If you are chilled, shocked, etc **to the marrow**, you are affected by cold weather or fear very intensely. EG *They looked chilled to the marrow... He was shocked to his marrow.* PHR : USED AS AN A = to the core

4 The **marrow** of something is the most important part of it. EG *This is the meaning and marrow of existence.* N SING : *the*+N+ *of* = essence

marrow bone, marrow bones. A **marrow bone** is a bone that contains a lot of marrow and that is used in cooking. N COUNT/ UNCOUNT

marry /mæri¹/, **marries, marrying, married**.
1 If you **marry** someone or if you **get married**, you form a legal relationship with a person of the opposite sex in a ceremony during which you make particular promises to that person and become their husband or wife. EG *I wanted to marry him... They are in love with each other and wish to marry... If I ever married, I wouldn't want to live my life here... When are you getting married?* V OR V+O : RECIP ⇑ unite = wed

2 When a clergyman or registrar **marries** two people, he or she unites them in a legal relationship as husband and wife. EG *You'll have to go and ask the vicar if he'll marry you in church.* V+O

3 If someone **marries** their child, they find a suitable partner for their child to marry. EG *He had married all his daughters and settled his sons.* V+O = settle

4 If you **marry** two things together, you join them together in some way. EG *Their racism at home has been married with their racism abroad... ...the marrying together of a number of different scientific disciplines.* V+O, OR V+O+A (to/with/ together) : RECIP

marry off. If you **marry** someone **off**, you find a suitable person for them to marry. EG *Oh, Mother stop it–you're always trying to marry me off!* PHRASAL VB : V+ O+ADV, IF+ PREP THEN *to*

marry up. If you **marry** something **up** with something else, you make them fit neatly together. EG *I'm trying to marry up the pattern on the wallpaper.* PHRASAL VB : V+ O+ADV, IF+ PREP THEN *with, to*

marsh /mɑːʃ/, **marshes**. A **marsh** is an area of land which is very wet and muddy because it is flat or low-lying and water cannot drain away properly. EG *I made my way slowly out of the marsh... To the east there is a dense date plantation bounded by marsh.* N COUNT/ UNCOUNT = bog

marshal /mɑːʃə⁰l/, **marshals, marshalling, marshalled**; also spelled **marshaling** and **marshaled** in American English. 1 If you **marshal** people or things, you gather them together and arrange them in order to achieve something. EG *He hesitated, marshalling his thoughts... He tried to marshal support for the scheme... Shipping was being marshalled into convoys.* V+O ⇑ collect

2 A **marshal** is 2.1 an official who helps to organize or run a public event. EG *It is unusual for a golfer to batter one of the marshals with his putter.* N COUNT 2.2 an official in a court of law. EG *I was led into the courtroom by a marshal.* N COUNT 2.3 a police officer in the United States who controls and organizes a particular area or district. N COUNT : ALSO IN TITLES 2.4 an officer who has the highest rank in an army or an air force. EG *...the air marshals... ...Marshal Montgomery.* N COUNT : ALSO IN TITLES, USU MOD+N

marsh gas is the gas methane, produced by vegetation decomposing under water. N UNCOUNT

marshland /mɑːʃlə³nd/, **marshlands**. **Marshland** is land that is covered in marshes. EG *Most of the area was marshland... Thunder rumbles through the marshlands.* N UNCOUNT/ COUNT = swamp

marshmallow /mɑːʃmæləʊ/, **marshmallows**. **Marshmallow** is a soft, sweet, spongy food that is used to make sweets or cakes. ▸ used of a sweet made from marshmallow. EG *We toasted marshmallows over the fire.* N UNCOUNT ▸ N COUNT

marshy /mɑːʃi¹/, **marshier, marshiest**. **Marshy** land is covered in marshes. EG *...a stretch of marshy coastline.* ADJ QUALIT ⇑ wet = boggy

marsupial /mɑːsj⁰uːpɪəl/, **marsupials**. A **marsupial** is an animal such as a kangaroo or an opossum. Female marsupials carry their babies in a pouch at the front of their body until the babies are fully mature and can live by themselves. EG *The opossum became the first marsupial to be known in Europe.* N COUNT

mart /mɑːt/, **marts**. A **mart** is a place, such as a market, where things are bought and sold, especially things that people collect. EG *...a stamp mart.* N COUNT+SUPP

marten /mɑːtɪn/, **martens**. A **marten** is a small animal rather like a weasel with thick fur and a bushy tail. EG *...the pine marten.* ▸ used of this animal's fur. EG *...a marten collar.* N COUNT ▸ N UNCOUNT

martial /mɑːʃəl/ is used to describe things relating to soldiers, war, or military matters. EG *They assumed that this martial behaviour would be accepted by the British Government... ...martial music.* ● See also **court martial**. ADJ CLASSIF : USU ATTRIB ⇑ aggressive = military

martial art, martial arts. A **martial art** is one of the philosophies and techniques of self-defence that N COUNT ⇑ fighting come from the Far East, for example Kung Fu, karate, or judo. EG *...a master of the martial arts.*

martial law is control of an area that is established and maintained by soldiers instead of civilians. EG *The country has now spent more than eight years under martial law.* N UNCOUNT

Martian /mɑ:ʃən/, **Martians.** 1 A **Martian** is an imaginary creature from the planet Mars. N COUNT

2 Something that is **Martian** exists on or relates to the planet Mars. EG *...Martian landings.* ADJ CLASSIF : USU ATTRIB

martin /mɑ:tɪn/, **martins.** A **martin** is a small bird with a forked tail. EG *...a sand martin.* N COUNT

martinet /mɑ:tɪnet/, **martinets.** A **martinet** is a person who believes in strict discipline and expects you to obey all orders; a formal word. EG *Denis was quite a martinet.* N COUNT ↑ disciplinarian = tyrant

martyr /mɑ:tə/, **martyrs, martyring, martyred.** 1 A **martyr** is 1.1 a person who suffers or is killed because of their religious or political beliefs, and therefore gives strength to people who share those beliefs. EG *St Sebastian was a Christian martyr... If he dies, he will become a martyr.* N COUNT ↑ sufferer 1.2 a person who suffers; often used showing disapproval to refer to someone who pretends to suffer or exaggerates their suffering in order to get sympathy or praise from other people. EG *Why do you have to be such a martyr all the time?* N COUNT = misery

2 If you **are a martyr to** something, you suffer greatly from it. EG *She was a martyr to migraine.* PHR : VB AND N INFLECT

3 If someone **is martyred** they are killed or made to suffer very greatly, because of their religious or political beliefs. EG *This is where St Peter was supposed to have been martyred... ...a martyred hero.* V+O : USU PASS = torture, pillory

4 See also **martyred.**

martyrdom /mɑ:tədəm/ is 1 the murder or enforced suffering of someone because of their religious or political beliefs. EG *...the martyrdom of St Thomas.* N UNCOUNT 2 a feeling of suffering; often used showing disapproval to refer to this feeling when it is exaggerated or deliberately experienced in order to gain sympathy or praise from other people. EG *She had smothered her children with her martyrdom.* N UNCOUNT

martyred /mɑ:təd/. A **martyred** expression or way of speaking is one that shows that you have suffered a lot, especially when you are exaggerating the suffering in order to get sympathy or praise from someone. EG *...a brave, martyred sigh... Mr Rogers wore a martyred expression.* ADJ CLASSIF : ATTRIB ↑ pathetic = long-suffering

marvel /mɑ:vəᵒl/, **marvels, marvelling, marvelled**; also spelled **marveling** and **marveled** in American English. 1 If you **marvel** at something, you are filled with surprise and admiration. EG *Early travellers marvelled at the riches of Mali... They listened to Jocasta and marvelled... 'My God,' Foster marveled, 'I've never seen so much money!'... I marvel that there are not more murderers in the world.* V, V+REPORT-CL/QUOTE, OR V+A (at)

2 A **marvel** is a thing or person that causes you to be filled with admiration and surprise. EG *Paestum is one of the marvels of Greek architecture... It's a marvel that I'm still alive... Oh, Albert, you're a marvel! How did you do it?* N COUNT = wonder, glory

3 **Marvels** are wonderful achievements that might have been thought impossible. EG *You've done marvels... Do not expect marvels.* N PLURAL = wonders

marvellous /mɑ:vəᵒləs/; also spelled **marvelous** in American English. Someone or something that is **marvellous** is excellent or wonderful and even better than you expected. EG *Two ounces! Oh, Robin, that's marvellous!... Flora, you're marvellous... Irving was marvellous as Cassius... I think Miss Birdbrain's a marvellous name for her.* ADJ QUALIT = splendid ◊ **marvellously.** EG *Children often cope marvellously when one parent dies... I slept marvellously well.* ◊ ADV = tremendously

Marxism /mɑ:ksɪzəᵒm/ is the political philosophy based on the writings of Karl Marx which states that the struggle between people of different social classes is the most important part of history. Marxism believes that people will develop through socialism towards a communist society. N UNCOUNT

Marxist /mɑ:ksɪst/, **Marxists.** 1 Something that is **Marxist** is based on or relates to Marxism. EG *...Marxist theory... ...Marxist-Leninists.* ADJ CLASSIF ↑ communist

2 A **Marxist** is a person who believes in Marxism. EG *Would you call yourself a Marxist?* N COUNT ↑ communist

marzipan /mɑ:zɪpæn/ is a paste made of almonds, sugar, and egg. It is sometimes put on top of cakes, or used to make small sweets. N UNCOUNT = almond paste

masc. is an abbreviation for 'masculine'.

mascara /mæskɑ:rə/ is a substance which people, usually women, put on their eyelashes in order to make them a different colour and seem thicker. EG *She was wearing lipstick and mascara.* N UNCOUNT ↑ make-up

mascaraed /mæskɑ:rəd/. **Mascaraed** eyes have mascara on the eyelashes. EG *There was fury in Miss Lenaut's dark, mascaraed eyes.* ADJ CLASSIF ↑ made-up

mascot /mæskəˀt/, **mascots.** A **mascot** is an animal, toy, doll, etc which is associated with a particular organization, and which is thought to bring good luck. EG *The regimental mascot is a goat called Winston.* N COUNT = emblem, talisman

masculine /mæskjəˀlɪn/. 1 Something that is **masculine** relates to or is considered typical of men, in contrast to women. EG *I think it must have something to do with masculine pride... ...the traditionally masculine language of the political intelligentsia... She said the atmosphere was too masculine.* ADJ QUALIT ↑ male ≠ feminine

2 If you describe a woman as **masculine,** you mean that she has a lot of qualities which make her seem more like a man; used showing disapproval. EG *The system makes boys effeminate and girls masculine... ...a rather masculine-looking lady.* ADJ QUALIT ↑ male

3 A room, piece of furniture, etc which is **masculine** is of the type that people expect men to have, for example because it is large, strong, and solid. EG *This boardroom is very masculine, with great heavy chairs.* ADJ QUALIT ↑ male

4 A **masculine** noun, pronoun, etc, in some languages, belongs to a particular class of nouns, pronouns, etc. Words that are masculine have sets of inflections which are different from those of feminine and neuter words. EG *In French, 'jardin' is a typical masculine noun.* ADJ CLASSIF

masculinity /mæskjəˀlɪnɪtiˡ/. 1 **Masculinity** is the fact of being a man. EG *In society we assume that masculinity has certain characteristics.* N UNCOUNT ≠ femininity

2 A man's **masculinity** consists of the qualities, especially sexual qualities, which are considered to be typical of men. EG *His masculinity was now in question... Some men measure their masculinity by anything from their jobs to their drinking habits.* N UNCOUNT : USU POSS+N ↑ virility = manhood

mash /mæʃ/, **mashes, mashing, mashed.** 1 If you **mash** potatoes or other vegetables, you crush them after they have been cooked. EG *Would you mash the potatoes for me, please.* V+O ◊ **mashed.** EG *...chicken, mashed potatoes and peas.* ◊ ADJ CLASSIF

2 In informal British English, **mash** is potatoes which have been boiled and mashed, often with butter and milk. EG *...bangers and mash.* N UNCOUNT

mask /mɑ:sk/, **masks, masking, masked.** 1 A **mask** is 1.1 something which you wear over your face in order to hide your face or make yourself look different, and which usually has holes for your eyes. EG *The thieves were wearing masks... Most of the actors were in beautifully modelled masks.* N COUNT ↑ disguise 1.2 something you wear over all or part of your face for protection. EG *...a welder's mask... ...a surgical mask.* N COUNT ↑ shield 1.3 behaviour which hides your real feelings or character. EG *He may learn to conceal his annoyance with a mask of measured politeness... ...a mask of indifference.* N COUNT : USU+SUPP 1.4 a substance which you spread over your face and leave for some time in order to improve your skin. EG *Her face was encased in a beauty mask.* N COUNT ↑ cosmetic = face pack ● See also **death mask, gas mask.**

2 If you **mask** something, you cover it so that it is difficult to see. EG *Her eyes were masked by huge, round sunglasses.* V+O = conceal, hide

3 If you **mask** your feelings, you make it difficult for people to tell what you really feel. EG *Our opponents mask their antagonism behind sweet words.* V+O = conceal, hide

masked /mɑ:skt/. Someone who is **masked** is wearing a mask. EG *Three armed and masked men suddenly burst in.* ADJ CLASSIF ↑ disguised

masked ball, masked balls. A **masked ball** was a dance held in former times at which all the guests wore masks. N COUNT

masking tape is plastic or paper tape which is sticky on one side and is used, for example, to protect part of a surface that you are painting. N UNCOUNT

masochism /mæsəᶿkɪzəᵒm/ is 1 behaviour in which someone seems to get pleasure and satisfaction from physical or mental suffering. EG *It was a combination* N UNCOUNT *of boredom and masochism that had attracted her to Christopher.* 2 sexual behaviour in which someone allows another person to cause them physical pain, for example by beating them, because they obtain sexual pleasure from such pain. — N UNCOUNT ⇑ perversion ≠ sadism

masochist /mæsə⁶kɪst/, **masochists**. A **masochist** is 1 a person who seems to get pleasure from physical or mental suffering. EG *Unless you are a complete masochist, you are unlikely to derive much pleasure from the show.* — N COUNT 2 a person who gets sexual pleasure from suffering physical pain. — N COUNT ≠ sadist

masochistic /mæsə⁶kɪstɪk/. **Masochistic** behaviour is behaviour in which a person suffers physical or mental pain in order to feel pleasure or satisfaction. EG *He took a masochistic delight in watching United get beaten every week... There are some actors with strong masochistic streaks who wish to hear only criticisms.* — ADJ QUALIT ⇑ perverse ◊ **masochistically**. — ◊ ADV

mason /meɪsə⁰n/, **masons**. 1 A **mason** is a person who is skilled at making or building things with stone. EG *He carved marble faster than any mason.* — N COUNT ⇑ craftsman = stonemason

2 A **Mason** is the same as a Freemason. — N COUNT

Masonic /məsɒnɪk/ is used to describe things relating to the beliefs, traditions, or organization of Freemasons. EG *...a Masonic dinner... ...a masonic lodge.* — ADJ CLASSIF : ATTRIB

masonry /meɪsənri¹/ is 1 bricks or pieces of stone which have been stuck together with cement as part of a wall or building. EG *Large chunks of masonry were beginning to fall... It had arched windows and ornate masonry... ...a masonry drill.* — N UNCOUNT ⇑ brickwork 2 the skill of making or building things with stone. EG *We offer a course in masonry.* — N UNCOUNT ⇑ craft

masquerade /mæskəreɪd/, **masquerades, masquerading, masqueraded**; a formal word.

1 If you **masquerade** as something, you pretend to be that thing. EG *He might try to masquerade as a policeman... He might even now be masquerading under an assumed name... There were many heated little speeches from the floor masquerading as questions.* — V+A *(as/under)* = pose

2 A **masquerade** is an attempt to deceive people about the true nature or identity of something. EG *I refuse to take part in such a masquerade.* — N COUNT ⇑ deception = pretence

mass /mæs/, **masses, massing, massed**. 1 A **mass** of things is a large number of them grouped together. EG *Bruce stuffed a mass of papers into his briefcase... A mass of hands went up.* — N PART : SING+N IN PL = load

2 A **mass** of something is a large amount of it. EG *There is a mass of detail to be worked out... His fine face was framed in a mass of long grey hair.* — N PART : SING+N UNCOUNT = lot

3 **Masses** of something means a great deal of it; an informal use. EG *They ate masses and masses of food... You can do that in masses of ways.* — N PART : PLURAL ⇑ lots = loads

4 A **mass** is 4.1 an amount of a solid substance, a liquid, or a gas, especially a large amount which has no definite shape. EG *The base of the rock cracked and the whole mass toppled into the sea... The contents have shrunk to a small dark mass... Rain occurs when a mass of warm air laden with water vapour rises.* — N COUNT : IF+ PREP THEN *of* 4.2 a large area of land. EG *The air over the great land mass of Asia heats up in summer and rises.* — N COUNT

5 **Mass** is used to describe something which involves or affects a very large number of people. EG *...the power of mass communication... ...mass unemployment... He was accused of mass murder.* — ADJ CLASSIF : ATTRIB ● If something exists or is done **on a mass scale**, it involves or affects a very large number of people. EG *Civil Disobedience on a mass scale was first used in 1920-1... We want to promote literacy on a mass scale.* — ● PHR : USED AS AN A = on a large scale ≠ in a modest way, on a small scale

6 The **masses** are the ordinary people in society considered as a group in contrast to the leaders or the highly educated people. EG *We want to produce opera for the masses... ...the power of the organized masses.* — N PLURAL : *the*+N = workers

7 The **mass** of people are most of the people in a country, society, or group. EG *They felt cut off from the mass of the population... The mass of pensioners are treated as children.* — N SING : *the*+N+*of* = bulk, majority

8 A **mass** of people, vehicles, etc is a large crowd of them. EG *...a chaotic mass of pedestrians and vehicles... He disappeared into a mass of bobbing heads.* — N PART

9 When people or things **mass**, or when you **mass** them, they gather together into a large crowd or group. EG *The students massed in Paris in May... The general was massing his troops... Thunderclouds were massing in the north-west.* — V-ERG

10 If something is a **mass** of things, it is covered with them or full of them. EG *His bare back was a mass of dark freckles... Poor Thelma was a mass of nerves.* — N PART : SING, a+N

11 The **mass** of an object is the amount of physical matter that it has; a technical term in physics. EG *The velocity depends on the mass of the object... Jupiter has 318 times the mass of Earth, yet only one-fourth its density.* — N UNCOUNT/COUNT

12 The religious ceremony called **Mass** is a ceremony in a Christian church, especially a Roman Catholic or Orthodox church, during which people eat bread and drink wine in order to remember the last meal of Jesus Christ. EG *He goes to Mass every Sunday.* — N UNCOUNT/COUNT = Communion

13 A **Mass** is a piece of music which uses the prayers from the Christian ceremony of Mass as words for singing. EG *...Bach's Mass in B Minor.* — N COUNT ⇑ composition

14 See also **massed**.

massacre /mæsəkə/, **massacres, massacring, massacred**. 1 A **massacre** is 1.1 the killing of a very large number of people at the same time in a violent and cruel way. EG *...the massacre of a village... The children were evacuated to save them from massacre.* — N COUNT/UNCOUNT = slaughter 1.2 a contest, match, election, etc in which one side suffers an extremely heavy defeat; an informal use. EG *The second round was an absolute massacre.* — N COUNT

2 If people **massacre** a large number of other people, they attack and kill them in a violent and cruel way. EG *The soldiers massacred almost all the survivors.* — V+O = slaughter

3 If you **massacre** someone, you make them suffer an extremely heavy defeat in a contest, game, election, etc; an informal use. EG *Benfica were massacred in the replay.* — V+O = thrash, slaughter

massage /mæsɑːd⁰ʒ/, **massages, massaging, massaged**. 1 If you **massage** a person or part of their body, you rub a part of their body, pressing their skin firmly, in order to make them relax or to stop their muscles from being painful. EG *Could you massage the back of my neck?... The nurse came to massage Miss Burton every afternoon.* — V+O

2 **Massage** is the action of rubbing a part of someone's body and pressing their skin firmly, in order to make them relax or to stop their muscles from being painful. EG *We can relax our tired muscles by massage... Let me give you a massage.* — N UNCOUNT/COUNT

3 If you **massage** statistics, figures, or evidence, you change or arrange them in order to deceive people. EG *He accused the government of massaging the evidence.* — V+O = doctor

masse. See **en masse**.

massed /mæst/ is used 1 to describe plants, trees, and their leaves and branches when they are growing thickly and in large quantities. EG *...the massed foliage of the shrub oak... ...banks of massed ferns.* — ADJ CLASSIF : ATTRIB ⇑ abundant = dense 2 to describe people who have been brought together in large numbers for a particular purpose. EG *...massed artillery... ...the massed groups of rival supporters.* — ADJ CLASSIF : ATTRIB ⇑ assembled 3 to describe something which exists in large quantities as a result of a long period of growth or being collected together. EG *...the massed weight of human opinion.* — ADJ CLASSIF : ATTRIB = collective

masseur /mæsɜː/, **masseurs**. A **masseur** is a person whose job is to give massage. — N COUNT

masseuse /mæsɜːz/, **masseuses**. A **masseuse** is a woman whose job is to give massage. — N COUNT

massif /mæsiːf/, **massifs**. A **massif** is a group of mountains that form part of a mountain range. — N COUNT

massive /mæsɪv/. Something that is **massive** 1 is extremely large in size or quantity. EG *He opened the massive oak front doors... ...a massive man in shirt sleeves... ...a massive increase in oil prices... These village boys are going to see massive changes.* — ADJ CLASSIF = colossal ◊ **massively**. EG *She got massively fat... We invested massively in West German machinery.* — ◊ ADV 2 happens on a very large scale and over a very wide area. EG *...massive air and missile attacks... She has been the subject of massive media coverage.* — ADJ CLASSIF ⇑ extensive = large-scale ≠ restricted

mass media. The **mass media** are the various ways by which information and news is given to large numbers of people, especially television, radio, newspapers, and magazines. EG *The mass media now play an increasing role in shaping our opinions.* — N SING : *the*+N VB CAN BE SING OR PL

mass noun, mass nouns, In grammar, a **mass noun** is a special kind of uncount noun which has a plural in certain circumstances, for example when you mean measures or brands of the thing that the word stands for. Nouns of this type are described as N MASS in this dictionary. See ☐ at N MASS. N COUNT

mass-produce, mass-produces, mass-producing, mass-produced. If you **mass-produce** something, you make it in large quantities, especially by using machines to do the work. EG *We lack the ability to mass-produce on large-scale assembly lines... Once the chip has been designed and etched out, they can be mass-produced.* ◇ **mass-produced**. EG *...cheap mass-produced exports.* V OR V+O ⇑ manufacture ◇ ADJ CLASSIF

mass-production; also spelled as two words. **Mass-production** is the production of something in large quantities, especially by using machines to do the work. EG *Soon the car will go into mass-production... It takes years for a new plane to move from drawing board to mass production.* N UNCOUNT

mast /mɑːst/, **masts**. 1 A **mast** is 1.1 a long vertical pole that is used to support the sails and flags on sailing ships and yachts. EG *She tied on the flag and ran it up the mast.* N COUNT 1.2 a long vertical pole that is used as an aerial to transmit radio sound or television pictures. EG *...a television mast.* N COUNT

2 If you **nail** your **colours to the mast**, you make it completely clear to people what your view is about something or who you support. EG *They've nailed their colours to the mast of independence.* PHR : VB INFLECTS

mastectomy /mæstektəmi¹/, **mastectomies**. A **mastectomy** is a surgical operation to remove a woman's breast. N COUNT

master /mɑːstə/, **masters, mastering, mastered**. 1 A **master** is a man who has authority over someone such as a servant or slave. EG *Sometimes there was no dispute between a master and his slave... George looked at his master rather doubtfully.* N COUNT ⇑ person ▸ A dog's **master** is its owner. EG *It might at times resemble the relationship of master and dog.* ▸ ⇑ owner

2 If a person is **master** of a situation or area of activity, they have complete power and control over it. EG *This was before man was total master of his environment... Agriculture was the only line where one could be master of all one did.* N UNCOUNT + *of* ⇑ controller

3 If you **master** a difficult situation, you succeed in controlling it. EG *Confrontations must be mastered as they arise... I breathed through my mouth and mastered the nausea.* V+O = overcome

4 If you **master** something, you learn how to do it properly or manage to understand it completely. EG *Slowly, one begins to master the complex skills involved... He worked resolutely to master peerage law... I mastered the local dialect.* V+O

5 **Master** is used to describe a skilled worker in a particular job, who is qualified to train others. EG *...master bakers... ...a master plumber.* ADJ CLASSIF : ATTRIB ▸ used as a noun. EG *He should apprentice himself to a master.* ▸ N COUNT

6 A **master** is also 6.1 a person who has reached the highest level of ability in a particular activity. EG *He is a master of both the written and spoken word.* N COUNT = expert ▸ used as an adjective. EG *...a master forger... ...the master spy, George Blake.* ▸ ADJ CLASSIF 6.2 in British English, a male teacher at a school: compare **mistress**. EG *...the science master... Grudges between masters and pupils never lasted.* N COUNT : USU MOD+N 6.3 an original copy of something, for example a film or a tape recording, that can be used to produce other copies. EG *From the clear master, make a second copy.* N COUNT ▸ used as an adjective. EG *Where's the master copy filed?* ▸ ADJ CLASSIF 6.4 a famous painter of the past. EG *A painting by the eighteenth-century French Master François Boucher has been bought for £80,000.* ● See also **old master**. N COUNT : ADJ+N = artist

7 A **master's** or a **master's degree** is the university degree of Master of Arts or Master of Science. EG *Mary-Lou took her business school master's degree at a college near Paris.* N COUNT = MA, M.Sc.

8 **Master** is used 8.1 by the followers of a male religious teacher or leader as a way of addressing him or referring to him. EG *I do not understand, Master.* N COUNT/VOC 8.2 before a boy's name as an old-fashioned way of addressing him. EG *Yes, Master Oliver.* N IN TITLES

master bedroom, master bedrooms. The **master bedroom** in a large house is the largest bedroom. N COUNT ⇑ room

masterful /mɑːstəful/. 1 Someone who is **masterful** behaves in a way which shows that they are in charge and can tell other people what to do. EG *She knows that he would be too masterful for her.* ADJ QUALIT ⇑ powerful ▸ used of a person's behaviour, voice, etc. EG *His voice had become more masterful.* ▸ = authoritative

2 **Masterful** behaviour or actions show great skill. EG *He resigned with masterful timing... Her answer was masterful.* ADJ QUALIT ⇑ able = skilful

master key, master keys. A **master key** is a key that can be used to open any of a particular set of locks, each of which is normally opened by its own individual key. N COUNT = pass key

masterly /mɑːstəli¹/. Something that is **masterly** has been done extremely well, and shows the highest level of ability. EG *This is a masterly, logical analysis... It was a masterly performance.* ADJ QUALIT ⇑ good = brilliant ▸ used to describe people. EG *He was masterly in dealing with people.* ▸ = excellent

mastermind /mɑːstəmaɪnd/, **masterminds, masterminding, masterminded**. 1 If you **mastermind** a difficult or complicated activity, you plan it in detail and then make sure that it happens successfully. EG *He masterminded a number of brutal terrorist attacks... A young accountant masterminded the take-over of the company... The series is masterminded by Jack Good.* V+O ⇑ instigate

2 The **mastermind** is the person who is responsible for planning and organizing a difficult or complicated activity; often used of criminals who plan big robberies. EG *The mastermind of the expedition was a Frenchman.* N COUNT

Master of Arts, Masters of Arts. A **Master of Arts** is an MA degree, or a person with that degree. N COUNT

master of ceremonies, masters of ceremonies. A **master of ceremonies** is 1 the person who announces the names of speakers at some state occasions, banquets, formal dinners, etc. N COUNT 2 the person who introduces the singers, comedians, actors, etc who appear in a variety show. N COUNT

Master of Science, Masters of Science. A **Master of Science** is an M.Sc. degree, or a person with that degree. N COUNT

masterpiece /mɑːstəpiːs/, **masterpieces**. 1 A **masterpiece** is 1.1 an extremely good painting, novel, film, etc. EG *One day I'll paint a masterpiece... It is one of the great masterpieces of European art.* N COUNT ⇑ work of art 1.2 a brilliant example of something. EG *It was a masterpiece of deceit.* N COUNT : IF+ PREP THEN *of* ⇑ epitome

2 An artist's, writer's, or composer's **masterpiece** is the best work of art that they produce in their career. EG *'Gulliver's Travels' is Swift's masterpiece.* N COUNT : WITH POSS

master plan, master plans. A **master plan** is a clever plan that is intended to help someone succeed in a very difficult or very important task. EG *My master plan worked.* N COUNT

masterstroke /mɑːstəstrəuk/, **masterstrokes**. A **masterstroke** is something you do which is unexpected but very clever and which helps you to achieve something. EG *Phoning your mother was a masterstroke.* N COUNT ⇑ deed = coup

master switch, master switches. A **master switch** is a switch that can be used to turn on or turn off all the lights, machines, etc of a particular set at the same time. EG *The lights in the corridor and cells were turned off by a master switch.* N COUNT

mastery /mɑːstəᵒri¹/ is 1 excellence in a particular skill or art. EG *...the mastery of Duke Ellington... They decided that his mastery of the language made him the ideal candidate.* N UNCOUNT : IF+ PREP THEN *of* 2 complete power or control over something. EG *His sons were struggling to obtain mastery of the country... Man gradually achieved a greater mastery over his environment.* N UNCOUNT : IF+ PREP THEN *of/over*

masthead /mɑːsthed/, **mastheads**. 1 A ship's **masthead** is the highest part of its mast. EG *A green flag flew from the masthead.* N COUNT ⇑ top

2 A newspaper's **masthead** is its name as it appears in big letters at the top of the front page. N COUNT ⇑ title

masticate /mæstɪkeɪt/, **masticates, masticating, masticated**. If you **masticate**, you chew; a formal word. EG *Rhoda went on masticating her toast.* V OR V+O

mastiff /mæstɪf/, **mastiffs**. A **mastiff** is a large, powerful, short-haired dog. N COUNT

masturbate /mæstəbeɪt/, **masturbates, masturbating, masturbated**. If someone **masturbates**, they stroke or rub their own genitals in order to get sexual pleasure. ◇ **masturbation** /mæstəbeɪʃəᵒn/. V ◇ N UNCOUNT

mat /mæt/, **mats**. 1 A **mat** is 1.1 a piece of cloth, card, plastic, etc which is put on top of a larger surface either for protection or for decoration. EG *She set his food on the mat before him... ...a beer mat.* — N COUNT
1.2 a small piece of carpet or other thick material which is put on the floor for protection, decoration, or comfort. EG *A tall girl was standing on the mat outside... ...a 'welcome' mat.* — N COUNT ⇑ rug

2 A **mat** of something such as grass or moss is a thick layer of it. EG *He lay hidden by a mat of creepers.* — N PART = tangle

3 See **matt**.

4 See also **matted**, **matting**.

matador /mætədɔː/, **matadors**. A **matador** is a person in a bullfight who is supposed to kill the bull. — N COUNT = bullfighter

match /mætʃ/, **matches, matching, matched**.

1 A **match** is an organized game of football, cricket, chess, or other sport. EG *...a football match... Are you going to the match?* — N COUNT ⇑ competition

2 A **match** is also a small thin stick of wood, or sometimes cardboard, which is covered at one end with a chemical substance. This end of the match produces a flame when you brush it hard against the side of a matchbox or some other rough surface. EG *Don't strike a match if you smell gas... ...a box of matches... He lit the paper with a match.* — N COUNT

3 If one thing **matches** something else or if the two things **match**, they are the same as one another, or have similar qualities. EG *Sometimes his inner thoughts and his outer actions do not match... The captain's feelings clearly matched my own... We have developed a throw-away mentality to match our throw-away products... The windmill blades will be adjustable to match wind speeds.* — V OR V+O : RECIP = correspond

4 If you **match** two things or if you **match** them **up**, you make them the same. EG *She tried to match up her gestures with those of her companions.* — V+O, OR PHRASAL VB : V+O+ADV = co-ordinate

5 If you **match** or **match up** one thing with another, you decide that one is suitable for the other, or that there is a connection between them. In some tests or puzzles you have to match pairs of things from a list. EG *All you have to do is correctly match the famous personalities with the towns they come from... The children are carefully matched to the couples who are adopting them... Can you match the tops up with the bottoms?* — V+O, OR PHRASAL VB : V+O+ADV = pair

6 If one thing **matches** something else, or if the two things **match**, they are the same colour or design as one another. EG *All her towels match... She was dressed in a yellow sari with yellow ribbons to match in her hair... The lampshades matched the curtains.* — V OR V+O : RECIP

7 A **match** is also a combination of colours or designs which are the same as one another. EG *This paint should be all right. It's not a perfect match, but it's not bad.* — N SING : USU MOD+N ⇑ equivalent

8 If you **match** something, you are as good as it, or equal to it in speed, size, or quality. EG *They are trying to upgrade their cars to match the foreign competition... She walked at a pace that Morris's short legs could hardly match... She writes with an audacity that has rarely been matched.* — V+O = emulate

9 If you **match** one thing against another, you make them compete against one another to see which one is better. EG *I've tried matching my brain against the computer's.* — V+O+A (against) = pit

10 If one thing **is no match for** something else, it is inferior to it and is unable to compete successfully with it. EG *A machine gun is no match for a tank... They were no match for us.* — PHR : VB INFLECTS ≠ measure up to

11 If you **meet** your **match**, you find that you are competing or fighting against someone or something that you cannot beat. EG *She's never yet met her match.* — PHR : VB INFLECTS

12 If you say that a man and a woman are or make a good **match**, you mean that they are likely to have a successful relationship or marriage. EG *Don't they make a good match?* ▸ used to say that someone would be a good person to marry, especially from a financial point of view. EG *Farmers' sons are considered good matches.* — N COUNT : MOD+N ⇑ partnership = couple ▸ ⇑ partner

13 See also **matched**, **matching**.

match up to. If something **matches up to** something else, it is of the quality, size, or standard that you expected. EG *The hotel didn't match up to our expectations... Did you think the book matched up to its brilliant review?* — PHRASAL VB : V+ADV+PREP = come up to

matchbox /mætʃbɒks/, **matchboxes**. A **matchbox** is a small box that you buy with matches in it. Usually two of the sides are rough, and covered with sandpaper or a special chemical so that you can strike matches on them. — N COUNT ⇑ container

matched /mætʃt/. 1 If two people are well **matched**, perfectly **matched**, etc, they are suited to one another and are likely to have a happy and successful relationship. EG *I thought we were perfectly matched... She said how wonderfully well matched her daughter and I were.* — ADJ CLASSIF : ADV+ADJ

2 If two people, teams, or groups are well **matched**, evenly **matched**, etc, they are of the same strength or ability so that it is not clear who is likely to win. EG *Government and rebel soldiers are evenly matched.* — ADJ CLASSIF : ADV+ADJ

matching /mætʃɪŋ/ is used to describe something which is the same colour or design as something else that you have just mentioned. EG *The room had plain, light-coloured walls with matching curtains... ...a blue suede jacket with matching shirt.* — ADJ CLASSIF : ATTRIB = coordinating

matchless /mætʃlɪ²s/. If you describe something as **matchless**, you mean that it is so exceptionally good or strong that you think no other could be as good or strong. EG *...men and women of matchless honesty... His vengeance was matchless.* — ADJ CLASSIF = unparalleled, unrivalled

matchmaker /mætʃmeɪkə/, **matchmakers**. A **matchmaker** is someone who tries to encourage other people they know to form relationships or to get married. EG *She is the village gossip and matchmaker.* — N COUNT ⇑ intermediary

matchmaking /mætʃmeɪkɪŋ/ is the activity of encouraging people you know to form relationships or get married. EG *He loved matchmaking.* — N UNCOUNT

match point, match points. A **match point** is a situation in a game of tennis when the player who is in the lead can win the match if they win the next point. EG *At match point, she served a double fault... Connors has two match points.* — N COUNT/UNCOUNT ⇑ score

matchstick /mætʃstɪk/, **matchsticks**. A **matchstick** is the stick of wood from a match. EG *He was removing the ashes from the bowl of his pipe with a matchstick.* — N COUNT = match

matchwood /mætʃwʊd/ is used in expressions like 'reduced to matchwood' or 'smashed to matchwood' when you want to say that something wooden has been completely destroyed and is in a lot of little bits. EG *The table had been smashed to matchwood.* — N UNCOUNT = smithereens

mate /meɪt/, **mates, mating, mated**. 1 Someone's **mate** is their friend; an informal use, used mainly by men. EG *He found himself separated from his mates... He had supposed his old mate Kowalski would be with them.* — N COUNT = pal

2 People, especially men, sometimes use **mate** as an informal way of addressing a man. EG *OK, mate, you win... She'll be all right, mate.* — N VOC = squire, pal

3 A **mate** is an animal's sexual partner. EG *Camels hate leaving their mates... Female orang-utans are about half the size of their mates.* ▸ used also of a person's sexual partner, especially a person's husband or wife. EG *...two young couples merrily swapping mates.* — N COUNT

4 When animals **mate**, a male and a female come together as a pair and have sex. EG *The great majority of amphibians still mate in water... The queen bee is likely to mate with two or three drones.* — V OR V+A (with) : RECIP ⇑ unite = couple
◊ **mating**. EG *Mosquitoes also use sound as a mating call.* — ◊ ADJ CLASSIF : ATTRIB

5 If you **mate** animals, you bring a pair of them together so that they will produce young. — V+O

6 A **mate** is also 6.1 a workman's assistant. EG *I think he got a job as a plumber's mate for a short time after that.* — N COUNT : USU MOD+N
6.2 an officer on a merchant ship. EG *The illness of mate and bosun made for exceptional circumstances.* — N COUNT ⇑ sailor

7 In chess, **mate** is the same as checkmate. EG *White to play and mate in two.* — N UNCOUNT

material /mətɪərɪəl/, **materials**. 1 A **material** is a solid substance, for example one which is found in the natural world, especially when you think of it as something that can be used. EG *We need a cheap abundant material to make the electrodes out of... Industry has increasingly found synthetic substitutes for natural materials.* ● See also **raw material**. — N COUNT/UNCOUNT

2 **Material** is 2.1 cloth, such as cotton or wool, that you can use to make clothes and other things. EG *The traditional materials, cotton and wool, have begun to become more popular again... The sleeping bags are made of quilted or acrylic material.* — N UNCOUNT/COUNT = fabric
2.2 ideas, information, or something you have written that you — N UNCOUNT = stuff

can use as the basis for a book, play, film, etc. EG *He wrote a good deal of the material himself... She hoped to find material for some articles... They researched a lot of background material.*

3 Material is used to describe something which is **3.1** concerned with possessions, money, and the conditions in which people live, rather than with emotional or spiritual life. EG *...the material comforts of life... In material terms, he is supremely privileged... People who travel have to keep their material possessions to a minimum.* ◇ **materially**. EG *Children can gain materially and psychologically when both parents work.* **3.2** concerned with the real world and physical objects, rather than with the abstract or the spiritual world. EG *...material existence... ...material objects.* — ADJ CLASSIF : USU ATTRIB ≠ moral, spiritual; ◇ ADV WITH VB; ADJ CLASSIF = concrete

4 Materials are the equipment or things that you need for a particular activity. EG *I packed all my books and writing materials... ...cleaning materials.* — N PLURAL : USU + SUPP = gear

5 Material is used to refer to someone from the point of view of whether or not they are capable of doing a particular job or of achieving something. EG *He is not university material at all... Keep an eye on your secretary as potential executive material.* — N UNCOUNT : MOD + N

6 Material evidence or information is relevant and important for a particular court case. EG *An individual has a legal duty not to withhold material evidence from a grand jury.* — ADJ CLASSIF = pertinent

materialise /mətɪərɪəlaɪz/. See **materialize**.

materialism /mətɪərɪəlɪzəᵒm/ is **1** the attitude that someone has when they think that money and possessions are more important than anything else in their life. EG *They were determined to renounce the materialism of the society they had been brought up in... This century has seen an increasing competitiveness and materialism.* **2** the belief that only physical matter exists, and that there is no spiritual world. — N UNCOUNT; N UNCOUNT = worldliness

materialist /mətɪərɪəlɪst/, **materialists**. A **materialist** is someone who wants a lot of money and possessions and believes that these are the only important things in life. EG *You're such a materialist!* ▸ used as an adjective. EG *A lot of people are prepared to turn their back on the materialist way of life.* — N COUNT ⇑ person; ▸ ADJ QUALIT = acquisitive

materialistic /mətɪərɪəlɪstɪk/. A **materialistic** person or society wants a lot of money and possessions and believes that these are the only important things in life. EG *This society has made people greedy and materialistic.* — ADJ QUALIT = acquisitive, mercenary

materialize /mətɪərɪəlaɪz/, **materializes, materializing, materialized**; also spelled **materialise**. **1** If a possible event **materializes**, it actually happens. EG *The irreversible surge of revolt that they had predicted did not materialize... The problems will really begin if the anticipated Gulf crisis materializes.* — V ⇑ appear = come about

2 If a person or thing **materializes**, they suddenly appear, after they have been invisible or in another place. EG *Derek had materialized through the steam... If Shakespeare were suddenly to materialize in London or New York today, he would get a huge shock.* — V = emerge

maternal /məˈtɜːnəᵒl/. **1** A woman who is **maternal** feels or behaves in the way a mother does towards her child. EG *She was unable to be maternal to any of her offspring.* ▸ used of people's behaviour or feelings. EG *...maternal feelings.* — ADJ QUALIT = motherly

2 Maternal is used to describe things relating to a mother, motherhood, or the mother's side of a family. EG *When the baby arrived, she slipped into the maternal role with ease and delight... He still bore the scars of maternal rejections... My father's maternal grandmother was a Turk.* — ADJ CLASSIF : ATTRIB

maternity /məˈtɜːnɪˈtiˡ/. **1 Maternity** is used to describe things relating to the assistance and medical care given to a woman when she is pregnant and when she actually gives birth. EG *...maternity hospitals... ...a maternity ward... Until now women have been granted a year's maternity leave after giving birth.* — N BEFORE N

2 Maternity is the state of being a mother. — N UNCOUNT

matey /meɪtiˡ/. Someone who is being **matey** is being very friendly, as if they were your close friend; an informal word; used mainly in British English. — ADJ QUALIT = pally

math /mæθ/ is the same as maths; used in American English. EG *His math teacher thought he was lazy... They all have strong math and science backgrounds.* — N UNCOUNT

mathematical /mæθəmætɪkəᵒl/. **1** Something that is **mathematical** involves numbers and calculations. EG *...mathematical calculations... ...a mathematical formula.* ◇ **mathematically**. EG *This theory was to be demonstrated mathematically over a century later.* — ADJ CLASSIF : ATTRIB ⇑ numerical; ◇ ADV ⇑ numerically

2 If you have a **mathematical** mind, you are clever at doing calculations or understanding problems that involve numbers. EG *Obviously Pamela's got a mathematical mind.* ◇ **mathematically**. EG *Here's a problem for those of you who are mathematically inclined.* — ADJ QUALIT : ATTRIB ⇑ scientific; ◇ ADV ⇑ scientifically

mathematician /mæθəmətɪʃəᵒn/, **mathematicians**. A **mathematician** is **1** a person who is trained in the study of numbers and calculations. EG *For decades mathematicians have wrestled with this elusive problem.* **2** a person who is good at doing calculations and using numbers. EG *They only took me on because I was a good mathematician.* — N COUNT ⇑ scientist; N COUNT

mathematics /mæθəmætɪks/. **1 Mathematics** is a subject which involves the study of numbers, quantities, shapes, etc; used especially of the academic subject which is studied at schools and universities. EG *He didn't want to study mathematics... ...professor of mathematics at Cambridge.* — N UNCOUNT

2 The **mathematics** of a problem is the calculations that are involved in it. EG *I'm not quite sure about the mathematics, but it seems to work out right.* — N UNCOUNT

maths /mæθs/ is the same as mathematics; used in British English. EG *I know nothing about modern maths... Women do better at maths in single-sex schools... ...a maths teacher.* — N UNCOUNT

matinee /mætɪneɪ/, **matinees**; also spelled **matinée**. A **matinee** is a play or film which is performed or shown in the afternoon. EG *I stood at the back of the packed theatre at a matinee... I went to a matinee... ...a matinee performance.* — N COUNT ⇑ performance

matins /mætɪnz/; also spelled **mattins**. **Matins** is a Christian religious service which is held in the morning. EG *I'll see you after Sunday matins.* — N UNCOUNT

matriarch /meɪtriˡɑːk/, **matriarchs**. A **matriarch** is **1** a woman who rules in a society in which power passes from mother to daughter. **2** an old and powerful female member of a family, for example a grandmother. — N COUNT; N COUNT

matriarchal /meɪtriˡɑːkəᵒl/. **1** A **matriarchal** society or system is one in which the ruler is female and the power is passed from mother to daughter. EG *There are traces of the old matriarchal society still present in their culture.* — ADJ CLASSIF

2 A **matriarchal** system of inheritance is one in which family property is traditionally inherited from women and not from men. — ADJ CLASSIF ⇑ female

matriarchy /meɪtriˡɑːkiˡ/, **matriarchies**. **Matriarchy** is **1** a system of government in which the ruler is female and the power is passed from mother to daughter. **2** a system of inheritance in which family property is traditionally inherited from women and not from men. — N UNCOUNT/COUNT; N UNCOUNT/COUNT

matrices /meɪtrɪsiːz, mæ-/ is the plural of **matrix**.

matriculate /məˈtrɪkjəˈleɪt/, **matriculates, matriculating, matriculated**. If you **matriculate**, you register formally as a student at a university, or you satisfy the academic requirements necessary for registration for a course. ◇ **matriculation** /məˈtrɪkjəˈleɪʃəᵒn/. EG *Work for a degree counts only from the date of matriculation.* — V = enrol; ◇ N UNCOUNT = enrolment

matrimonial /mætrɪməʊnɪəl/ means concerning marriage or married people; a formal word used, for example, in law. EG *...family and matrimonial law... ...sexual and matrimonial difficulties.* — ADJ CLASSIF : USU ATTRIB = marital

matrimony /mætrɪməniˡ/ means the same as marriage; a formal word used especially in legal and religious contexts. EG *They unite themselves in love and holy matrimony.* — N UNCOUNT

matrix /meɪtrɪks/, **matrices**. A **matrix** is **1** the environment or context in which something such as a society develops and grows; a formal use. EG *We need to look at the cultural matrix that makes a work of art sensible... Attitudes are formed in a matrix of psychological and social complications.* **2** a rectangular arrangement of numbers, symbols, or letters written in rows and columns and used in solving certain mathematical problems; a technical mathematical term. — N COUNT + SUPP = framework; N COUNT ⇑ array

matron /meɪtrən/, **matrons**. A **matron** is **1** a very senior nurse who is usually in charge of all the nursing staff in a hospital. **2** a middle-aged married — N COUNT : ALSO IN TITLES; N COUNT woman, especially one who is solemn and rather fat; often a humorous usage. **3** a woman who looks after the health and hygiene of children in boarding schools. N COUNT : ALSO IN TITLE

matronly /meɪtrənli¹/. A woman who is **matronly** is middle-aged and rather fat. EG *Mrs Frieda was solid and matronly.* ADJ QUALIT ⇑ mature

matt /mæt/; also spelled **mat**. A **matt** colour, paint, surface, etc is dull rather than shiny. EG *...matt black... Raspberries have a matt, spongy surface... ...a matt finish.* ADJ CLASSIF ≠ gloss

matted /mætɪ²d/. Something that is **matted** is twisted together, often because it is wet, so that a thick, untidy mass is formed. EG *Their hair was matted and dirt caked their faces... Her hair was now matted with snow... Steel plows sliced through the matted roots.* ADJ QUALIT ⇑ tangled

matter /mætə/, **matters, mattering, mattered.** **1** A **matter** is an event, situation, or subject which you have to deal with or think about, especially one that involves problems. EG *It was a purely personal matter... Will you report the matter to the authorities?... She's very honest in money matters... This is a matter for the police... The House of Commons is due to debate the matter.* • **a matter of life and death**: see **life**. • **a matter of record**: see **record**. N COUNT+SUPP = affair

2 Matters are the situation you are talking about, especially when something is affecting the situation in some way. EG *The murder of Jean-Marie will not help matters... There is only one applicant, which simplifies matters... They kept quiet about it until matters took a disturbing new turn.* N PLURAL = things • If something **makes matters worse**, it makes a difficult situation even more difficult. EG *The absence of electricity made matters worse... To make matters worse, they were almost always unreliable.* • PHR : VB INFLECTS ⇑ aggravate

3 Matter is **3.1** written material, especially books and newspapers. EG *Their reading matter included 'The Voyages of Captain Cook'... ...printed matter... He read everything, even the advertising matter in books of stamps.* N UNCOUNT+SUPP **3.2** part of a magazine, newspaper, book, film, etc, especially the most important part. EG *The journal's editorial matter is largely composed of enthusiastic articles on modern technology.* N UNCOUNT+SUPP = content **3.3** the physical part of the universe consisting of solids, liquids, and gases. EG *An atom is the smallest indivisible particle of matter... My research is concerned with the way matter behaves at the very lowest temperatures.* N UNCOUNT ⇑ substance **3.4** a particular type of substance. EG *The termites feed almost entirely on vegetable matter... His eyes were gummy with some yellowish matter.* • See also **subject-matter**. N UNCOUNT+SUPP = material

4 You say something like 'What's **the matter**?' or 'Is anything **the matter**?' to someone when you want to know what the problem is, for example because they seem upset or excited, or because something is not working properly. EG *What's the matter, Cynthia? You sound odd... What's the matter with your hand?... What's the matter with you?... I heard him shouting from the bathroom and went in to see what was the matter... We told them that there was nothing the matter.* PHR : USED AS C, WITH BROAD NEG = wrong

5 If something **matters**, it is important and is something that you care about or something that worries you. EG *The family, the Cottage and Twickenham were all that mattered to me... Your happiness, that's the only thing that matters.* V : NO CONT, NO IMPER ⇑ interest

6 If something does not **matter**, it does not make a difference to the situation. EG *It does not matter which method you choose... It never mattered what time of day or night it was... Is the idea clear? It doesn't matter about the actual numbers.* V WITH BROAD NEG : NO CONT, NO IMPER = make any difference

7 You say **'it doesn't matter'** **7.1** to tell someone who is apologizing to you that you are not angry or upset, and that they should not worry. EG *'I've only got dried milk.'–'It doesn't matter.'* CONVENTION = never mind **7.2** when someone offers you a choice between two or more things and you do not mind which is chosen. EG *'Do you want your coffee black?'–'It doesn't matter.'* CONVENTION = as it comes

8 no matter. 8.1 You say **'no matter'** after you have just asked a question or mentioned an idea or doubt and you have decided that it is not really important, interesting, or worth discussing. EG *Had Mary Jane slept there? No matter. She stretched out on the bed... That may have spared me a bloody nose. But no matter. I had my revenge in due time.* CONVENTION = never mind **8.2** You use **no matter** in expressions like 'no matter how' and 'no matter what' to say that something is true or happens in all circumstances and that it makes no difference what the particular circumstances are. EG *I told him to report to me after the job was completed, no matter how late it was... They smiled almost continuously, no matter what was said... Brown shirts are never smart, no matter who's wearing them.* PHR+WH ⇑ despite = irrespective of, never mind **8.3** You use **no matter what** to emphasize that you think that something is definitely going to happen. EG *They're going to win no matter what... The government will guarantee their salaries through mid-1988–no matter what.* PHR : USED AS AN A = regardless

9 The word **matter** is also used in the following expressions. **9.1** If you do something **as a matter of** principle, policy, etc, you do it for that reason or purpose. EG *I am prepared to go to prison as a matter of principle, rather than pay this tax... Merchant banks recruit women as a matter of policy.* PHR : USED AS AN A = because of **9.2** If you are going to do something **as a matter of** urgency, priority, etc, you are going to do it as soon as possible, because it is important. EG *The city needs, as a matter of urgency, £45m for the schools.* PHR : USED AS AN A **9.3** If something is done **as a matter of course**, it is done as part of a normal situation and is not regarded as unusual or exceptional. EG *The father does his share of the housework as a matter of course when at home.* PHR : USED AS AN A = automatically **9.4** You use **matter** in expressions such as 'a matter of weeks' when you are drawing attention to how small an amount is or how short a period of time is. EG *Within a matter of weeks she was crossing the Atlantic... I think it's only a matter of a day or two, isn't it?* N SING : a+N+*of* **9.5** If something is just **a matter of time**, it is certain to happen and will probably happen quite soon. EG *It appeared to be only a matter of time before they were caught.* PHR : USED AS C ⇑ inevitable **9.6** If something is just a **matter of** doing something, it is easy and can be done just by doing the thing that is mentioned. EG *Skating's just a matter of practice... I think you'll find that it's just a matter of putting these numbers in.* PHR : USED AS C = a question of **9.7** If you say that a statement is **a matter of opinion**, you mean that it is not a fact, and that other people, including yourself, do not agree with it. EG *'City are as good a team as United.'–'That's a matter of opinion.'* PHR : USED AS C = debatable **9.8** You say **as a matter of fact** to draw attention to what you are saying, especially when you are adding a comment which is relevant to what you have just been talking about, or when you are giving extra information which contradicts what someone has just said. EG *As a matter of fact I bought a copy of it this afternoon... I've got to go out again at once, as a matter of fact... It's my mother-in-law's birthday present, as a matter of fact.* PHR : USED AS ADV SEN = actually, as it happens **9.9** You say **for that matter** to emphasize that a statement you have made is also true in another situation, for another person, etc. EG *He's shaking with the cold. So am I, for that matter... We have no troops east of Dover, or west of it for that matter.* PHR : USED AS ADV SEN = come to that **9.10** If something is **no easy matter**, it is difficult to do it. EG *It was no easy matter to divert the little girl's attention.* PHR : USED AS C, USU+*to*-INF **9.11** If you say that something is **no laughing matter**, you mean that it is very serious and not something that you should laugh or joke about. EG *Look, it's no laughing matter you know! I might have been killed!* PHR : USED AS C = no joke **9.12** You say **the fact of the matter** or **the truth of the matter** when you state a fact which supports what you are saying or which is not widely known, perhaps because it is a secret. EG *The fact of the matter is, Cynthia said she'd meet me at the zoo today... I exhausted myself too early, that's the truth of the matter.* PHR : USED AS S/● = the truth is **9.13** If you say that something is **another matter** or **a different matter**, you mean that it is very different from the situation that you have just discussed or is an exception to a rule or general statement that you have just made. EG *The distribution of sex cells, however, was a different matter... But Asia was another matter altogether.* PHR : USED AS C **9.14** You add **but that is another matter** to a statement to indicate that it is outside the main subject and you do not want to discuss it any more. EG *I hated him; but that's another matter.* PHR **9.15** If a person in authority says **that's the end of the matter** or **that's an end to the matter**, they mean that a decision that has been taken must not be changed or discussed any more. EG *I won't agree to it as long as I'm here–and that's the end of the matter!* PHR = that's final

matter-of-fact. Someone who is **matter-of-fact** shows no emotion, for example no enthusiasm, anger, or surprise, in their speech or behaviour, especially in a situation where people expect them to be emotional. EG *'I see,' she said, trying to seem matter-of-fact.* ▸ used of people's behaviour or attitudes. EG *She said it calmly and firmly in a matter-of-fact voice... His matter-of-fact ideas were dull.* ◇ **matter-of-factly.** EG *'She died sir, six years ago, I think,' Scylla said matter-of-factly.* ◇ **matter-of-factness.** EG *...the matter-of-factness of his reply.* ADJ QUALIT ⇑ unemotional = down-to-earth ◇ ADV WITH VB

matting /mætɪŋ/ is strong thick material, usually made from a material like rope or straw, which is used as a floor covering. EG *There was rush matting on the floor.* ● See also **coconut matting.** N UNCOUNT

mattins /mætɪnz/. See **matins.**

mattock /mætək/, **mattocks.** A **mattock** is a tool with a blade at the end of a long handle which is used for breaking up hard soil. N COUNT

mattress /mætrɪ²s/, **mattresses.** A **mattress** is a large, flat cushion exactly the same size as a bed, which is put on a bed in order to make it soft to lie on. EG *...feather mattresses... He kept his life's savings under his mattress.* N COUNT

maturation /mætjə⁴reɪʃən, mætʃə⁴-/ is the process of becoming mature; a formal word. EG *Some species have a more rapid rate of early maturation.* N UNCOUNT ⇑ growth

mature /mətjʊə/, **matures, maturing, matured; maturer, maturest.** 1 When a child or young animal **matures,** it becomes an adult. EG *Girls mature about the end of their twelfth year... She had matured into a self-possessed and articulate young woman.* V ⇑ grow

2 When something **matures,** it reaches a state of complete development. EG *The new seeds matured in only 120 days... Her style had not yet matured.* V ⇑ develop

3 If you say that someone is of **mature** years, you mean that they are middle-aged and are close to being considered old; a polite use. EG *He was a neurotic widower of mature years... A marriage contracted in maturer years often turns out best.* ADJ CLASSIF : ATTRIB = advanced

4 If a person **matures,** they become more fully developed in their personality and emotional behaviour. EG *He had matured and quietened down considerably.* V = grow up

5 Someone who is **mature** is fully developed and balanced in their personality and emotional behaviour. EG *She's in some ways mature and in some ways rather a child.* ▸ used to describe something that a person has written or done. EG *This is the most mature of his books.* ADJ QUALIT = grown-up ≠ childish ▸ = adult

6 If you **mature** something such as wine or cheese, or if it **matures,** it is left for a time to allow its full flavour or strength to develop. EG *This whisky achieves its taste and colour by being matured in old wood... Hams improve with maturing.* V-ERG ⇑ age

7 Cheese, wine, etc that is **mature** has been left for a time to allow its full flavour or strength to develop. EG *This is a very palatable, mature wine.* ADJ QUALIT ⇑ ripe

8 When an investment, policy, etc **matures,** it becomes due for repayment. EG *The market value is bound to rise as the stock ages and matures... ...a maturing insurance policy.* V

mature student, mature students. A **mature student** is a student who is over 25 years old in a British college or university. N COUNT

maturity /mətjʊərɪ¹ti¹, -tʃʊə-/. 1 **Maturity** is the state of being fully developed or adult. EG *Only half of the young birds may live to reach maturity... ...physical maturity.* N UNCOUNT ⇑ development

2 Someone's **maturity** is their quality of being fully adult in their personality and emotional behaviour. EG *I have long felt that you lacked maturity... He conducted himself with a maturity beyond his experience.* N UNCOUNT = wisdom

3 The **maturity** of an investment, policy, etc is the time when it becomes due for repayment. EG *Interest is paid at the maturity of the investment.* N UNCOUNT : USU +SUPP

maudlin /mɔːdlɪn/. If you become **maudlin,** you become sad and sentimental about your life; often used of people who have been drinking alcohol. EG *Don't get so maudlin.* ▸ used of the way someone speaks or writes. EG *She continued in the same rather maudlin tone.* ADJ QUALIT = mawkish ▸ = weepy

maul /mɔːl/, **mauls, mauling, mauled.** 1 If someone **is mauled** by a person or an animal, they are savagely attacked by the person or animal and badly injured. EG *She had been severely mauled by a lion.* V+O : USU PASS

2 If critics or reviews **maul** a particular performance, show, film, etc, they criticize it very severely. EG *The following morning, the play was mauled by the critics.* V+O = tear to shreds

Maundy Thursday /mɔːndi¹ θɜːzdi¹/ is the Thursday before Easter Sunday. N UNCOUNT ⇑ day

Mauritian /mərɪʃə⁰n/, **Mauritians.** 1 Something that is **Mauritian** belongs or relates to Mauritius or to its people. ADJ CLASSIF

2 A **Mauritian** is a person who comes from Mauritius. N COUNT

mausoleum /mɔːsəlɪəm/, **mausoleums.** A **mausoleum** is 1 a building which contains the grave of a famous person or the graves of a rich family. EG *...an old mausoleum of blackened stone.* 2 a house that you feel is too large, empty, and old, and is therefore depressing to live in. EG *Do we have to live in this mausoleum?* N COUNT = tomb; N COUNT ⇑ building

mauve /məʊv/, **mauves.** Something that is **mauve** is of a pale purple colour. EG *...mauve writing paper.* ▸ used as a noun. EG *...the delicate mauve of a pigeon's breast.* ADJ COLOUR ▸ N MASS

maverick /mævə⁰rɪk/, **mavericks.** A **maverick** is someone who thinks and acts independently, and does not always do the same as the group that they belong to. EG *You're a maverick and you'll try anything.* ▸ used as an adjective. EG *He is a self-confessed maverick Marxist.* N COUNT = independent, loner ▸ ADJ CLASSIF : ATTRIB

maw /mɔː/, **maws.** If you describe something as a **maw,** you mean that it is like a huge mouth which eats or consumes everything around it; a literary word. EG *The furnace consumed fuel like a giant ravenous maw that had to be appeased by hurling tons of coal into its belly.* N COUNT : USU SING

mawkish /mɔːkɪʃ/. Something that is **mawkish** shows too much affection, admiration, or some other emotion and seems rather awkward or silly. EG *...mawkish verses... Claud's flat bovine face glimmered with a mawkish pride.* ◇ **mawkishness.** ADJ QUALIT ⇑ emotional = maudlin, gushing ◇ N UNCOUNT

max. is an abbreviation for 'maximum'; used especially after a number or amount, or to indicate the highest temperature in a period of time. EG *...max. 17°C... The total cost will be £90 max.*

maxim /mæksɪm/, **maxims.** A **maxim** is a rule for good or sensible behaviour, especially one which is in the form of a proverb or short saying. EG *Instant action: that's my maxim... 'Discipline is the soul of an army' was his favourite maxim.* N COUNT = motto

maximize /mæksɪmaɪz/, **maximizes, maximizing, maximized;** also spelled **maximise.** If you **maximize** something, you make it as great in amount or importance as you can. EG *The company's main objective is to maximize profits... We needed a strategy that would maximize the use of the country's existing airports.* ◇ **maximization** /mæksɪmaɪzeɪʃə⁰n/. EG *Our goal is the maximization of profits.* V+O ⇑ increase ◇ N UNCOUNT : USU+*of* ⇑ increase

maximum /mæksɪməm/. 1 The **maximum** amount or quantity of something is the largest that is possible, allowed, or safe. EG *It usually reaches its maximum height of 80,000 feet in about ten minutes... Never exceed the maximum daily dosage of 150 mg... They enlarged the window so that the maximum amount of light could shine into this room.* ADJ CLASSIF : ATTRIB ⇑ greatest

2 The **maximum** is the largest amount or quantity of something that is possible, used, or stated. EG *Conscription should be limited to a maximum of six months' service... Four wives is the maximum.* N SING WITH DET ⇑ limit

3 **Maximum** security, efficiency, etc is as great as it can be. EG *The plan must be carried out with maximum speed and discretion... They held the prisoner in isolation and under maximum security conditions.* ADJ CLASSIF : ATTRIB ⇑ greatest = full

4 If something has a particular value or rate **maximum** or **at the maximum,** this is the greatest value or rate it could possibly have or should have, and it might well be lower than that. EG *He has an IQ of 50 at the maximum... Cut your shopping down to twice a week maximum.* ADV AFTER NG, OR PHR : USED AS AN A = at the most

5 If you do something **to the maximum,** you do it to the greatest degree possible. EG *We must exploit tactical surprise to the maximum... The idea of integral organization has been carried to the maximum.* PHR : USED AS AN A = to the full

may /meɪ/. The word **may** is spelled with a capital letter for paragraph 8. 1 When you say that something **may** happen or be true, you mean that it will possibly happen or be true in the future, but you cannot be certain. EG *These tablets may cause sleepiness... We may be here a long time... We may never know the truth... If you don't listen to me, you may not have your job much longer... 'You're going to move out?'–'Yeah well, I may, I don't know.'* MODAL = might

2 When you say that something **may** be true, you mean that there is a possibility that it is true, but you cannot be certain. EG *This may or may not be true... I think we may have a problem... It may be that you want reassuring... Breathing our air may be hazardous to health.* • **be that as it may**: see **be**. MODAL : USU + *be* = might

3 When you say that something **may have** happened or **may have** been true, you mean that it is possible that it happened or was true, but you do not know for certain. You sometimes use **may have** when you are giving a possible explanation for something. EG *'Was he late?'–'He may have been.'... This allegation may have been true... A gigantic meteorite may have wiped out the dinosaurs 65 million years ago... He may have believed it because he wanted to.* MODAL + PAST PART = might have

4 If something **may** be done, it is possible to do it. EG *The fat in our diet may be reduced by buying low-fat milk... An example may be taken from a culture in which there is no notion of private property.* MODAL : USU + *be* = can

5 You use **may** 5.1 to say that someone is allowed to do something. EG *The child may bathe only when there is a life-saver present... The Roman law, according to which a girl may marry at twelve, was adopted by the Church... If the verdict is unacceptable, the defendant may appeal.* MODAL = can 5.2 in questions and after 'if' when you are asking for permission to do something or asking whether you can help. EG *May I have a word with you, please?... May I look round now?... I'll take a seat if I may... Hello. May I help you?* MODAL : USU WITH *I/we* 5.3 in speech as a polite way of interrupting someone, asking a question, or introducing what you are going to say next. EG *May I make a suggestion?... Did you, may I ask, get any results?... May I continue?... May I invite you gentlemen for a drink?* MODAL : USU WITH *I/we* = can, might

6 You also use **may** 6.1 when you mention the reaction or point of view that you think someone is likely to have, so that you can contradict it or explain something about it. EG *You may think it's silly, Edward, but it's honestly what I did... You may consider this sort of information trivial. But I can assure you it is extremely important... You may laugh, but just check it out for me, will you?* MODAL ↑ probably = might 6.2 to indicate that, although something is true, it is contradicted by another fact or argument which you are going to give. EG *They may be seven thousand miles away but they know what's going on over here... Ingenious though these techniques may be, they can hardly be regarded as practical.* MODAL : USU + *be* = might 6.3 when you add a comment which is not absolutely essential, but just interesting. EG *This, it may be added, greatly strengthened him in his resolve... It may be mentioned in passing that worms are very good for your garden.* MODAL : USU + *be* ↑ could 6.4 after expressions like 'so that' when you are stating the purpose for something. EG *They struggle to cure diseases so that people may live longer... I wish to clear the air so that we may breathe freely in future.* MODAL : USU *so that* + NG + MODAL ↑ will = can

7 You also use **may** in formal English to introduce a hope or wish that you have. EG *May he justify our hopes and rise to the top... Long may she live.* MODAL + NG + INF

8 **May** is the fifth month of the year in the Western calendar. EG *The meeting is on the 5th of May.* N UNCOUNT

maybe /meɪbi:/. **Maybe** makes what you say less definite. You use **maybe** 1 to indicate that something is possible or may be true, but you are not certain. EG *Maybe he'll be a prime minister one day... Well, maybe you're right... I heard you speak at Heidelberg. Maybe you remember me... Maybe she's not quite such a clot as we thought.* ADV SEN ↑ possibly = perhaps 2 to indicate that you are considering a course of action or to suggest a course of action to other people. EG *Maybe I ought to grow a moustache... He thought maybe he'd stay for a day or two... Maybe we should begin by introducing ourselves.* ADV SEN = perhaps 3 to offer an explanation for something, when you are not sure whether this explanation is true or not. EG *Maybe today seems so beautiful because yesterday was so dull... Why she'd chosen a Scots name I didn't know: maybe she just liked the sound of it.* ADV SEN = perhaps 4 when you are making a rough guess at a number, quantity, or value, rather than stating it exactly. EG *There were maybe half a dozen men drinking in there quietly... He's in his fifties, I'd say. Fifty-five, maybe... He was here for maybe 10 days.* ADV SEN ↑ approximately = perhaps, roughly 5 to indicate that, although a comment is partly true, there is also another point of view that should be considered. EG *Trivial? Well, maybe, but it's interesting all the same... 'I thought you said your dad was a drunk.'–'Maybe he was. But he was also a great singer.'* ADV SEN : USU WITH *but* = perhaps 6 as a reply when you do not want to say either 'yes' or 'no'. EG *'Are you going out with Sam?'–'Maybe'.* CONVENTION = perhaps

May Day, May Days. **May Day** is the first of May, which is celebrated as a holiday in several countries, especially as a workers' day in Socialist countries. N UNCOUNT/COUNT

mayday /meɪdeɪ/, **maydays**. A **mayday** or a **mayday signal** is a radio signal which someone in a plane or ship sends out as a call for help when the plane is going to crash or the ship is going to sink. N COUNT

mayfly /meɪflaɪ/, **mayflies**. A **mayfly** is an insect which lives near water and only lives for a very short time as an adult. N COUNT

mayhem /meɪhɛm/ is a situation in which there is no control or order, and a lot of people behave in an uncontrolled and often violent way. EG *The kids began to create mayhem in the washrooms... There was complete mayhem.* N UNCOUNT = chaos

mayn't /meɪnt/ is a spoken form of 'may not'.

mayonnaise /meɪəneɪz/ is a cold sauce which is thick and creamy and is made from egg yolks and oil. It is usually eaten with salads. N UNCOUNT

mayor /mɛə/, **mayors**. The **mayor** of a town or city is the person who has been elected to be the head of the town or city for one year, and to represent it at some official occasions. N COUNT : ALSO IN TITLES

mayoress /mɛərɪ²s/, **mayoresses**. A **mayoress** is the wife of a man who is the mayor of a town. When the mayor is a woman she chooses a woman friend or relative to be the mayoress. N COUNT : ALSO IN TITLES ↑ partner

may've /meɪəv/ is a spoken form of 'may have', especially when 'have' is an auxiliary verb.

maze /meɪz/, **mazes**. A **maze** is 1 a system of passages or pathways which it is difficult to find your way through because many of the passages do not lead anywhere. Some mazes are made of hedges. EG *The lawn was screened from prying eyes by woods and mazes and pavilions... Some worms were trained to find their way through a simple maze.* N COUNT ↑ network = labyrinth 2 a large number of ideas or subjects which are all connected with each other in a complicated way, and which you find difficult to distinguish clearly. EG *He lost himself in a maze of thoughts... It was all covered within the maze of publication law already in force.* N COUNT : IF + PREP THEN *of* ↑ tangle = web, morass

3 a puzzle in the form of a set of lines printed on paper. You have to draw a single line from the outside of the maze to the centre, without crossing any of the printed lines. N COUNT

MBE /ɛm bi: i:/, **MBEs**. An **MBE** is a British honour granted to a person by the King or Queen for a particular achievement; an abbreviation for 'Member of the Order of the British Empire'. The letters are used after the name of the person who has been awarded the honour. EG *...Miss May Walley MBE.* N COUNT : ALSO IN TITLES

MC, MCs. **MC** is an abbreviation for 'master of ceremonies'. EG *'Welcome back,' says the MC after the first act.* N COUNT : ALSO IN TITLES

McCoy /məkɔɪ/. If you describe someone or something as **the real McCoy**, you mean that they are the genuine person or thing and not an imitation or fake; a fairly informal expression. PHR : USED AS C

MCP, MCPs. **MCP** is an abbreviation for 'male chauvinist pig'; a man who behaves in a way that shows he thinks that men are superior to women and far more important than them. MCP is an informal, fairly offensive expression, used mainly by women. EG *He's a real MCP!* N COUNT

MD, MDs. **MD** is 1 an abbreviation for 'Doctor of Medicine'; a degree awarded to a person who has studied medicine and who has qualified as a doctor. The letters are usually used after a person's name. EG *...Richard Selzer, M.D.* N COUNT : ALSO IN TITLES AFTER NAME 2 an abbreviation for 'managing director'. EG *The MD wants to see you.* N COUNT : USU *the* + N IN SING

me /mi¹/ is used as the object of a verb or preposition. A speaker or writer uses **me** to refer to himself or herself. See **I**. EG *He told me about it... Give me* PRON : SING, USED AS O *your key... He looked at me reproachfully... It seems to me that this does no good... He was like you and me, but worse.*

mead /miːd/ is an alcoholic drink made of honey, spices, and water. N UNCOUNT

meadow /medəʊ/, **meadows**. A **meadow** is a field which has grass and flowers growing in it. N COUNT

meagre /miːgə/; also spelled **meager** in American English. Something that is **meagre** is very small in quantity or amount, and only just enough. EG *It was difficult to live on his meagre earnings... I hunched over my meagre fire.* ADJ QUALIT = measly, miserable

meal /miːl/, **meals**. 1 A **meal** is **1.1** an occasion such as breakfast, lunch, or dinner, when people eat. EG *They enjoyed their meals together... When the meal was over, Thomas went out.* N COUNT **1.2** the food that is eaten on one of these occasions. EG *We always had three good meals a day... ...a simple meal of bread and cheese.* N COUNT = repast

2 If you say that someone is **making a meal of** something, you mean that they are using more time and energy to do it than is necessary; an informal expression. PHR : VB INFLECTS

3 **Meal** is a rough powder made by crushing grain. It is used for flour or for animal food. N UNCOUNT

meals-on-wheels are hot meals that are taken to the homes of very old or sick people. They are provided as a service in Britain, usually by a local authority. EG *Mother is getting meals-on-wheels.* N PLURAL

meal ticket, meal tickets. A **meal ticket** is 1 a luncheon voucher; used in American English. N COUNT 2 somebody or something that gives you an income or enables you to earn one; used in informal English. EG *I can't leave Bob. He's my meal ticket.* N SING WITH DET

mealtime /miːltaɪm/, **mealtimes**. A **mealtime** is a period when you eat breakfast, lunch, or dinner. EG *I had a glass of juice three times a day at mealtimes.* N COUNT/ UNCOUNT, SING = PL = meal

mealy /miːli¹/, **mealier, mealiest**. Vegetables or fruit that are **mealy** are dry and powdery. EG *We ate flavourless mealy bananas.* ADJ QUALIT = chalky

mealy-mouthed. Someone who is **mealy-mouthed** is unwilling to speak in a simple or open way because they want to avoid talking directly about something unpleasant; used showing disapproval. EG *...mealy-mouthed politicians.* ▸ used to describe what people say. EG *...mealy-mouthed excuses.* ADJ QUALIT = evasive, pussyfooting ▸ = evasive

mean /miːn/, **means, meaning, meant; meaner, meanest**. Paragraphs 1 to 20 explain the verb **mean**, paragraphs 21 to 25 explain the noun **means**, paragraphs 26 to 30 explain the adjective **mean**, and paragraph 30 also explains the noun **mean**. 1 If you ask what a word, expression, gesture, etc **means**, you want it to be explained to you. EG *What does 'imperialism' mean?... What is meant by the term 'mental activity'?... The nod meaning yes is used in a great many societies.* V+O : NO CONT, NO IMPER ⇑ represent = signify ● If a word or phrase **means something to** you, you have heard it before and you know what it means. EG *Does 'Formula One' mean something to you? It doesn't mean anything to me.* ● PHR : VB INFLECTS

2 If you say that something **means** something, you are emphasizing how it should be understood, especially because it is not obvious or is very important. EG *An invitation for eight really means eight-thirty to nine... 'Stop! Stop!' she shrilled. 'And that means you too!'... Don't forget that 9 months' notice means just that.* V+O/REPORT-CL : NO CONT, NO IMPER ⇑ indicate

3 If you ask someone what they **mean**, you are asking them to explain exactly what they are thinking about or referring to, for example because they have not expressed it clearly enough for you to understand. EG *But what do we mean by 'education'?... I know the guy you mean... I thought you meant you wanted to take your own car... What's that supposed to mean?... 'I'm all right.'–'What do you mean–all right?'* V+O/REPORT-CL : IF O+PREP THEN *by* ⇑ refer to

4 You say **'I mean' 4.1** when you are explaining something more clearly or justifying a statement or comment that you have just made. EG *Does she drink? Heavily, I mean... If you haven't any climbing boots, you can borrow them. I mean dozens of people have got boots... This is a waste of time. I mean, what is the point?* PHR : USED AS ADV SEN = that's to say **4.2** when you are correcting something that you have just said. EG *This is Herbert, I mean Humbert... She's so authoritative, I mean authoritarian.* PHR : USED AS ADV SEN = sorry

5 You add **'you mean?'** at the end of a question when you are asking someone to explain in greater detail what they are really saying or what they are referring to. EG *'You could do with some help, couldn't you?'–'In the form of legal advice, you mean?'* PHR

6 If something **means** something to you, it is important to you in some way. EG *These were the friends who had meant most to her since childhood... Ten dollars would mean a lot to me.* V+O : IF+PREP THEN *to*, NO CONT, NO IMPER = matter

7 If something such as a name or title **means** something, it represents particular ideas or values to people. EG *'Made in Britain' does still mean something, if not very much.* V+O : NO CONT, NO IMPER = stand for

8 If one thing **means** another, **8.1** it shows that the second thing exists, is true, or will happen. EG *Water running down the outside of a wall may mean that the gutters are blocked... But don't you see what that phone call means?... She knew that it meant trouble.* V+O/REPORT-CL : NO CONT, NO IMPER ⇑ indicate = signify **8.2** it inevitably leads to the second thing happening. EG *A cut in taxes will mean a cut in government spending... I could always get a job on another paper, but it would mean moving to another city... The fact that you never see them doesn't mean that you shouldn't write to them occasionally.* V+O/REPORT-CL/-ING : NO CONT, NO IMPER

9 If you know **what it means** to do or be something, you know everything that is involved in that activity or experience, especially the effect that it has on your lifestyle or attitudes. EG *I now knew what it meant to be a star.* PHR+*to*-INF : VB INFLECTS

10 If you **mean** what you say, you are serious about it and not joking, exaggerating, or just being polite. EG *I'm going. I mean it... Did you really mean it about Christmas?... Anyone can programme a computer. And I do mean anyone.* V+O : NO CONT, NO IMPER

11 If you **mean** to do something, you do it quite deliberately and knowing what the effects or implications will be. EG *I'm sorry, I didn't mean to be rude... 'That hurts!'–'It's meant to!'... Did Einstein really mean to state that truth was a function of time?* ● To **mean business**: see **business**. V+*to*-INF : NO IMPER = intend

12 If someone **means well**, they are trying to be kind and helpful, even though they might have upset you or caused you problems. EG *Don't be too hard on him. He means well.* PHR : VB INFLECTS = be well-intentioned

13 If you say that someone **doesn't mean any harm** or **doesn't mean anything,** you are saying that they did not intend to upset people or to cause problems, even though they may in fact have done so. EG *I said something pleasant to her, meaning no harm, and she burst into tears... She's a big tease, but she doesn't mean anything.* PHR WITH BROAD NEG : VB INFLECTS

14 If you **mean** to do something, you plan to do it. EG *Roy couldn't remember a single thing he had meant to say... I meant to ring you but I'm afraid I forgot... I mean to be there tonight.* V+*to*-INF : NO IMPER = intend

15 If you **mean** something to be a particular thing or to do a particular thing, you intend that it should be or do that thing; used especially when you fail to do or achieve what you intended to. EG *Castle sat over what he meant to be his final report... Sorry, I'm not very good at drawing, but that's meant to be a cube... This was the way it was meant to work.* V+O+*to*-INF : USU PASS, NO IMPER ⇑ plan

16 If something **is meant** for something, it is designed or made for use in a particular situation. EG *These building techniques were meant for soft sand.* V+O+A *(for)* : ONLY PASS = be intended

17 If you **mean** something for a particular person or group, you intend that they should receive or use it. EG *His smile was meant for me.* V+O+A *(for)* : USU PASS

18 If something **is meant** to happen, it is very strongly expected to happen, almost as though there is a law or rule which orders it. EG *Are parents meant to love all their children equally?... I found a road that wasn't meant to be there.* V+O+*to*-INF : ONLY PASS = supposed to

19 If something **is meant** to have a particular quality or characteristic, it has a reputation for being like that. EG *They're meant to be good cars.* V+O+*to*-INF : ONLY PASS = thought

20 If you say that something **is meant**, or **is meant** to happen in a particular way, you believe it was intended and made to happen by God or fate, and not simply a coincidence or an accident. EG *They felt that their meeting must have been meant in some way... Perhaps, Mr Woods, you are meant to become a journalist rather than a lawyer.* V+O, OR V+O+*to*-INF : ONLY PASS = destined

21 The **means** of doing something is the method, instrument, or process which makes it possible. **Means** is both the singular and the plural form for this use. EG *Scientists are working to devise a means of storing this type of power... She could find no* N COUNT+SUPP = way

means of escape other than jumping out of the window... The essential means of transport for the islanders remained the donkey... We have the means to kill people on a massive scale... An attempt was made to sabotage the ceremony by violent means.

● If something is **a means to an end**, it is something that you do only because it will enable you to achieve what you want, and not because you are interested in doing it. EG *I never enjoyed the college, it was just a means to an end.* — ● PHR : USED AS C; ⇑ tool

22 If you do something **by means of** a particular method, instrument, or process, you do it using that method, instrument, or process. EG *The rig is anchored in place by means of steel cables.* — PREP

23 You say **'by all means'** as a way of telling someone that you are very willing to allow them to do what is being suggested. EG *If you feel you need to ask any questions, by all means do so... 'Would it be all right if I left a bit early?'–'Yes, yes, by all means.'* — CONVENTION; ⇑ of course; = feel free

24 **By no means, not by any means,** and **by no manner of means** are expressions used to emphasize that something is not true. EG *It is by no means certain that this is what he did... Not all of these people, by any means, opt for town life... I'm not the only one by any manner of means.* — PHR : USED AS AN A; = not at all

25 Your **means** are the money which you earn or have inherited and which you can use for your living expenses. EG *Sutcliffe has a house in Mayfair so he obviously has means... Bessie has good taste, and she has the means to gratify it.* ● If you **are living beyond** your **means**, you are spending more money than you actually have. ● If you **are living within** your **means**, you are spending less money than you actually have. — N PLURAL; = income; ● PHR : VB INFLECTS; ● PHR : VB INFLECTS, USU CONT

26 Someone who is **mean** is 26.1 unwilling to spend much money or to use very much of a particular thing. EG *Don't be mean with the tip, he's such a nice young man... I used to be very mean about hot water.* ◊ **meanness.** EG *These employers were famous for their meanness.* **26.2** unkind to someone, for example by hurting their feelings or by not allowing them to do something. EG *She had apologized for being so mean to Rudolph the day she left... I feel mean bothering him about a personal problem when I know he's so busy...* ◊ **meanly.** EG *He put down the receiver, meanly, before she could reply.* **26.3** capable of being very bad-tempered and deliberately cruel; used in American English. EG *After the seventh bourbon he begins to get mean.* — ADJ QUALIT : IF+ PREP THEN *about/with*; = stingy; ≠ generous; ◊ N UNCOUNT; ADJ QUALIT : IF+ PREP THEN *to*; ⇑ nasty; ≠ kind, nice; ◊ ADV; ADJ QUALIT; = vicious

27 A place that is **mean** looks poor and dirty; a fairly formal use. EG *We lived in the meanest hovel on the mountain road.* — ADJ QUALIT; = shabby

28 If you say that someone plays a **mean** trumpet, mixes a **mean** cocktail, etc, you are saying that they play the trumpet very well, mix cocktails very well, etc; an informal use. EG *Old Ronnie certainly mixes a mean cocktail.* — ADJ CLASSIF : ATTRIB; = great

29 If someone is **no mean** writer, golfer, etc, they are of a high standard or quality. EG *Sir George Gilbert Scott, himself no mean architect, approved the plans.* ▸ used of achievements. EG *Persuading John to come was no mean feat.* — PHR+N; ⇑ good; ▸ = some

30 The **mean** is a number that is either the average of a set of numbers or that represents the mid-point between the biggest and smallest numbers. EG *What you do first is to calculate the mean.* ▸ used as an adjective. EG *What is the mean height?* — N COUNT : IF SING *the*+N; = norm; ▸ ADJ CLASSIF : ATTRIB

31 See also **meaning**.

meander /mi¹ændə/, **meanders, meandering, meandered.** 1 If a river or road **meanders**, it has a lot of large bends in it and does not go directly from one place to another. EG *A stream meandered towards the sea... The road meanders a little.* — V : USU+A; = zigzag

2 A **meander** is a very large bend in a river. EG *The plain was crossed by the broad meanders of great rivers.* — N COUNT; = coil

3 If you **meander**, you travel or move slowly and not in any particular direction. EG *She liked to meander through familiar streets.* — V+A; = wander

meandering /mi¹ændəʳrɪŋ/. 1 A **meandering** river or road is one that meanders. EG *...a lazy, meandering river.* — ADJ CLASSIF : ATTRIB; = winding

2 A **meandering** speech, account, or piece of writing is one that does not have any order or structure at all but keeps moving from one subject to another. EG *...meandering editorials.* — ADJ QUALIT : USU ATTRIB; = rambling

meanie /mi:ni¹/, **meanies.** A **meanie** is a person who is unkind to someone, for example by hurting their feelings or by not allowing them to do something; an informal word used in British English. — N COUNT; = beast

meaning /mi:nɪŋ/, **meanings.** 1 The **meaning** of a word, expression, or gesture is the thing or idea that it refers to or represents and which can be explained using other words. EG *The word 'guide' is used with various meanings... Do you know the meaning of the phrase 'cock-and-bull story'?... Semantics is the study of meaning.* ● If you say that a person **doesn't know the meaning of the word**, you mean that they have never really experienced the thing you mention. EG *Hungry? You don't know the meaning of the word!... He doesn't know the meaning of the word 'fear'.* — N COUNT/ UNCOUNT; = sense; ● PHR : VB INFLECTS

2 The **meaning** of what someone says or of a book, film, etc is the thoughts or ideas that are intended to be expressed by it. EG *The meaning of the remark was clear... I don't understand the meaning of Pollock's paintings... There must be a deeper meaning than that.* ● If you **get** someone's **meaning**, you understand what they are really saying; an informal expression. EG *My aunt's gone a bit funny, if you get my meaning.* — N UNCOUNT/ COUNT; ⇑ sense; = significance; ● PHR : VB INFLECTS; = follow

3 You say **'What's the meaning of this?'** when you are asking what the reason is for an action or for behaviour that you disapprove of. — CONVENTION

4 If something that you do has **meaning**, it has a special importance with regard to its emotional effect on people or its practical value. EG *My prayers had real meaning for me at a very early age... If that's the case, his sacrifice no longer has any meaning.* — N UNCOUNT; = significance

5 **Meaning** is the quality which makes you feel that what you are doing has a purpose and is worthwhile. EG *We yearn for beauty, truth, and meaning in our lives... ...a world without meaning.* — N UNCOUNT; ⇑ rationale

meaningful /mi:nɪŋfʊl/. 1 A **meaningful** word, mark, gesture, etc has a definite meaning which can be explained using other words. EG *...a meaningful sign... Their children were all given meaningful names.* — ADJ QUALIT; ⇑ significant

2 A **meaningful** explanation, result, etc is one that you understand and that makes sense to you. EG *Nobody has ever explained electricity to me in a meaningful way... We failed to obtain any meaningful results from these experiments.* ◊ **meaningfully.** — ADJ QUALIT; = comprehensible; ◊ ADV WITH VB

3 A **meaningful** smile, look, etc is intended to express something, usually to a particular person, without anything being said. EG *...a meaningful look.* ◊ **meaningfully.** EG *'Goodnight, and call again. Anytime,' Boon added meaningfully.* — ADJ QUALIT; ⇑ expressive; = eloquent; ◊ ADV WITH VB; = pointedly

4 A **meaningful** relationship, experience, discussion, etc is serious and important in some way, especially emotionally or intellectually. EG *He felt the need to establish a more meaningful relationship with people... ...a deep and meaningful discussion.* — ADJ QUALIT; = profound; ≠ superficial

5 If your life is **meaningful**, it has a purpose and is worthwhile. EG *Could I acquire some wisdom? Could I make my life meaningful?* ◊ **meaningfully.** EG *At least you'd be filling your time meaningfully.* — ADJ QUALIT; ⇑ useful; ◊ ADV WITH VB; ⇑ usefully

meaningless /mi:nɪŋlɪ²s/. 1 Something that is **meaningless** 1.1 has no meaning. EG *They agreed on a special set of signals that would be meaningless to the others... These songs are largely meaningless.* **1.2** is of no importance or relevance. EG *Taxes made the bonus meaningless.* — ADJ QUALIT; ADJ QUALIT; = worthless

2 If something that you do is **meaningless**, it has no purpose and is not at all worthwhile. EG *People arrive at a factory and perform a totally meaningless task from eight to five.* — ADJ QUALIT; = futile

means test, means tests. A **means test** is a test in which your income is assessed in order to see if you are eligible for certain state grants or benefits. If your income is above a certain amount, you are not eligible. — N COUNT : USU SING; ⇑ evaluation

means-tested. A grant or benefit that is **means-tested** varies in amount depending on a means test. EG *...means-tested benefits.* — ADJ CLASSIF; ⇑ evaluated

meant /mɛnt/ is the past tense and past participle of **mean**.

meantime /mi:ntaɪm/. 1 **In the meantime** means in the period of time between two events. EG *His case won't come to court for several months, and in the meantime more than half the people think him guilty... At long last we were released. In the meantime of course, our friends had informed the news-* — PHR : USED AS ADV SEN; ⇑ during; = meanwhile papers. ▸ You can also say **meantime**. EG *But that's going to take quite a while. Meantime I wonder if we can turn our attention to a different problem.* ▸ ADV SEN = meanwhile

2 **For the meantime** means for a period of time from now until something else happens. EG *Nevertheless this action does patch up, for the meantime, the quarrel that was developing between them.* PHR : USED AS ADV SEN = for the moment

meanwhile /mi:nwaɪl/. **1** **Meanwhile** means while a particular thing is happening. EG *She ate an olive and tried to sit still. Nick, meanwhile, was talking about Rose.* ADV SEN ⇑ during

2 **Meanwhile** or **in the meanwhile** means in the period of time between two events. EG *But meanwhile a number of steps will have to be taken... Of course it will all end one day. In the meanwhile I enjoy the game we're all playing.* ADV SEN, OR PHR : USED AS ADV SEN = in the meantime

3 You can also use **meanwhile** to introduce a different aspect of a particular situation, especially one that is completely opposite to the one previously mentioned. EG *Big cuts in the tax on luxury goods benefited only a few. Meanwhile thousands of families were on the breadline.* ADV SEN

measles /mi:zəˀlz/ is an infectious illness that gives you a high temperature and red spots on your skin. EG *Sam's got measles... ...a mild case of measles.* ● See also **German measles**. N UNCOUNT ⇑ disease

measly /mi:zli¹/, **measlier, measliest**. Something that is **measly** is very small or inadequate; an informal word used showing disapproval. EG *One measly tomato, that's all we've had from this plant... ...all for a measly 40p!* ADJ QUALIT ⇑ insufficient = miserable

measurable /mɛʒəˀrəbəˀl/. If something is **measurable**, **1** it is large enough to be noticed or to be significant; a formal word. EG *Some measurable progress had been made.* ◇ **measurably**. EG *Their domestic performances have been measurably more effective.* **2** it can be measured. EG *...the statistically measurable rate of job turnover... ...measurable school tasks such as reading.* ADJ CLASSIF = perceptible ◇ ADV + ADJ/ADV ADJ CLASSIF

measure /mɛʒə/, **measures, measuring, measured**. **1** If you **measure** something, **1.1** you determine its exact size or extent. You can measure the length of something by using a ruler, for example. EG *He measured the diameter of the artery... The explosive force is measured in tons... Inflation, as measured by the consumer price index, fell.* ● See also **measuring**. **1.2** you decide what value or usefulness it has. EG *The performance of enterprises was measured by profits... We explain to people that we don't measure success by tests.* V+O = gauge V+O : IF+PREP THEN *by* ⇑ estimate = assess

2 If something **measures** a particular distance, its length, width, etc is equal to that distance. EG *The giant crab measures over three metres from claw to claw... ...small slivers of glass measuring a few millimetres across.* V+C ⇑ be

3 A **measure** of something is a certain amount of it. EG *Everyone is entitled to some measure of protection... We did reach a considerable measure of agreement... Survival in this world requires at least a measure of cooperation.* N PART : SING = degree

4 A **measure** is also **4.1** a unit in which you express size, speed, etc. EG *Inches aren't such a good measure–feet are more appropriate.* **4.2** a device such as a container or ruler that you use for measuring things. EG *...a glass measure marked in ounces... ...a yard measure.* ● See also **tape measure**. **4.3** an official standard amount of alcohol that is served in a bar, pub, hotel, etc. **4.4** an amount of alcoholic drink in a glass. EG *He poured himself another generous measure of cognac.* **4.5** a standard that you use when you are making a judgement about something. EG *Don't worry about the exam: it's just a measure of how you're getting on.* **4.6** an action carried out by a government or other authority in order to achieve a particular result. EG *Measures had been taken to limit the economic decline... Day nurseries were started as a war-time measure to allow mothers to work.* **4.7** a proposal that is being discussed in Parliament and that may become a law. EG *The party announced that it would not vote against the measure in Parliament.* N COUNT : USU SING; N COUNT : USU MOD+N; N COUNT; N PART = portion; N SING WITH DET +*of* = yardstick; N COUNT; N COUNT ⇑ legislation

5 If something exists or is true **in some measure**, **in large measure**, etc, it exists or is true to a small extent, to a great extent, etc; a fairly formal use. EG *We think of ourselves as in some measure emancipated from nature... Its internal unity was in large measure fictional.* PHR : USED AS AN A

6 If something affects your feelings **beyond measure**, it affects them more than you would normally think possible; a literary expression. EG *I was irritated beyond measure by the noise of the radio... ...subtle and exotic talents, fascinating beyond measure.* PHR : USED AS AN A = beyond belief

7 If you do something, give something, etc **for good measure**, you do it or give it in addition to something else that you have already done or given. EG *The waiter had taken away the plates and, for good measure, had removed his glass... They were charged with having instigated the riots, and, for good measure, with being responsible for the death of two policemen.* PHR : USED AS ADV SEN

8 If you **take** or **get** someone's **measure**, you estimate their abilities or intentions. EG *All the while they were taking the measure of the two shopkeepers... By now the enemy had got the measure of them.* PHR : VB INFLECTS ⇑ assess = size up

measure against. If you **measure** someone or something **against** another person or thing, you judge their value using the other person or thing as a standard. EG *It is sad to have to measure yourself against comparative strangers... Accountants can measure performance against them without difficulty.* PHRASAL VB : V+O+PREP

measure out. If you **measure out** a certain amount of a substance, you pour or empty the substance into a container until you have the amount that you need. EG *She carefully measured out a double whisky.* PHRASAL VB : V+O+ADV ⇑ apportion

measure up. If you **measure up** to a standard or to someone's expectations, you are good enough to achieve the standard or fulfil the person's expectations. EG *The state of repair failed to measure up to their exacting standards.* PHRASAL VB : V+ADV, WITH BROAD NEG, USU+*to* = come up

measured /mɛʒəd/. Something that is **measured** is careful and deliberate. EG *...walking at the same measured pace... ...a measured assessment of the trends.* ADJ CLASSIF

measurement /mɛʒəməˀnt/, **measurements**. **1** A **measurement** is a result that you obtain by measuring something. EG *Check the measurements first... Every measurement was mathematically exact.* N COUNT

2 **Measurement** is the activity or process of measuring something. EG *...the first actual measurement of the speed of sound.* N UNCOUNT : IF+PREP THEN *of*

3 Your **measurements** are the size of your waist, chest, hips, etc, used when you are buying clothes. N PLURAL : USU WITH POSS

MEASUREMENT □ This entry shows some ways of expressing measurements, for example sizes, distances, weights, temperatures, and speeds. In speech, the actual words that refer to the unit of measurement, for example 'metres', 'miles', 'kilos', 'litres', or 'degrees', are often left out when the context makes it clear what you are measuring and what units of measurement you are using. Some units of measurement, especially 'foot' and 'stone', do not always add 's' to form the plural. When measurements are used like adjectives in front of a noun, you never add 's' to the units of measurement. For example, you say 'a two-litre bottle' and 'a twenty-mile walk'. The following examples show ways of expressing measurements. EG *It was close on **ten feet in height**... ...building **ten-foot** concrete walls around the base... The visitor stood about **six feet tall**... ...people who are over **six foot**... ...heavy planks of wood about **three inches thick**... ...a tiny windowless cell **four feet wide** and **seven long**... The area they are working in is no more than **thirty metres square**... ...a block of ice **one cubic foot in size**.* The following examples show ways of expressing weights. EG *The largest brain possessed by any dinosaur weighed about a kilogram... ...14,000 metric tons of potatoes... ...a sixteen-ounce bar of soap.* The following examples show ways of expressing temperatures. EG *...a temperature of **four hundred degrees centigrade**... The temperature touched **100°F Fahrenheit** in Los Angeles that day... It had been **fourteen below zero** when they woke up... The temperature was well above **freezing point**.* The following examples show ways of expressing speed. EG *The cars are streaming by at **sixty miles an hour**... Cars were passing them at **seventy miles per hour**.* In the following examples, the speaker or writer is referring to clothing sizes or shoe sizes. EG *'What size do you take?'–'Ten.'... ...a size 9 shoe.* Numbers are also used in expressing other sorts of measurements, for example angles, the wind, and camera or gun sizes. EG *...a slope of perhaps ten degrees... A force nine gale had whipped up... We were able to use the 16mm camera... ...a .41 calibre revolver.*

measuring /mɛʒəˀrɪŋ/. A **measuring** jug, spoon, etc is a jug, spoon, etc specially designed for measur- ADJ CLASSIF : ATTRIB ing quantities, especially in cooking. EG *You can use any measuring jug marked in ounces... You need a set of measuring spoons.*

meat /miːt/, **meats**. **Meat** is flesh taken from an animal that has been killed so that people can cook it and eat it. EG *I prefer fresh meat and vegetables... Dogs need a balanced diet, not just meat... Meat prices may fall... ...cooked meats.* N MASS ↑ food

meaty /miːti¹/, **meatier, meatiest**. 1 A **meaty** person has a fat, heavy body, which reminds you of a piece of meat. EG *Along came the porters, immensely meaty, in bloodstained blue or white.* ▸ used of part of a person's body. EG *He extended his meaty, jeweled hands... ...his meaty lips.* ADJ QUALIT = beefy ▸ = fleshy

2 A meal that is **meaty** contains a lot of meat. EG *...a meaty meal... They liked an occasional meaty supplement to their diet.* ADJ QUALIT

mecca /mɛkə/, **meccas**. 1 **Mecca** is a city in Saudi Arabia, which is the holiest city in Islam because the Prophet Mohammed was born there. All Muslims face towards Mecca when they say their prayers. EG *...the pious Muslim on his way to Mecca... He would make a pilgrimage to Mecca.* N PROPER

2 A **mecca** is a place that many people go to, because it is famous or because it has something that they want. EG *The United States is still a Mecca for film-makers... ...tourist meccas... London in the fifties was a mecca for nationalist leaders.* N COUNT+SUPP : USU SING

mechanic /mɪ²kænɪk/, **mechanics**. 1 A **mechanic** is someone whose job is to repair and maintain machines and engines, especially car engines. EG *There's not a mechanic or technician who hasn't had this problem... A mechanic had told him the plate was hard to get on... ...car mechanics.* N COUNT ↑ worker

2 The **mechanics** of something is the way in which it works or the way in which it is done. EG *...the mechanics of the market... ...the mechanics and government of a workers' state... ...the mechanics of reading.* N PLURAL : *the*+N, USU+*of*

3 **Mechanics** is also the part of physics that deals with forces acting on moving or stationary objects. EG *...a practical science based on mathematics and mechanics.* N UNCOUNT

mechanical /mɪ²kænɪkə⁰l/. 1 A **mechanical** device has moving parts and uses power from an engine or from electricity in order to do a particular type of work. EG *They were using a mechanical shovel to clear up the streets... There were no mechanical devices available... ...a mechanical means of producing and reproducing images.* ◊ **mechanically**. EG *The glass doors slid open mechanically as she approached them... ...synthetic speech produced mechanically.* ADJ CLASSIF : USU ATTRIB = automatic ◊ ADV WITH VB = automatically

2 Someone who is **mechanical** understands how machines work and knows how to repair them. EG *I'm not a bit mechanical, I'm afraid.* ▸ used of a person's ability. EG *...a given level of mechanical ability... ...a boy with a mechanical bent.* ◊ **mechanically**. EG *I'm just not mechanically minded.* ADJ QUALIT ↑ skilled ▸ ADJ CLASSIF : ATTRIB ◊ ADV

3 Your behaviour is **mechanical** when you are doing something without thinking about it, because it is very uninteresting or because you have done it many times before. EG *When invention is left out, dancing becomes mechanical and dull... The checks became formal, the routines mechanical.* ◊ **mechanically**. EG *'Oh, fine, thanks,' said Philip mechanically... Sam shook hands mechanically with the newcomers.* ADJ QUALIT = routine, automatic ≠ creative ◊ ADV WITH VB = automatically

mechanise /mɛkənaɪz/. See **mechanize**.

mechanism /mɛkənɪzə⁰m/, **mechanisms**. A **mechanism** is 1 a part of a device or machine that does a particular task. EG *A steel disc had been welded on to the mechanism... ...the mechanism of the rifle... ...a locking mechanism.* 2 a special way of getting something done within a particular system. EG *There's no mechanism for changing the decision... ...the governing mechanism of the new EEC.* 3 a part of your behaviour that is automatic and that helps you to survive or to cope with a difficult situation. EG *During this regime, the defence mechanism of disbelief operated... Rabbits, too, have their survival mechanisms.* N COUNT : USU SING+SUPP; N COUNT+SUPP = procedure; N COUNT+SUPP ↑ process

mechanistic /mɛkənɪstɪk/. A **mechanistic** explanation is a way of explaining something such as a natural process as if it were a complicated machine; a technical term in science and philosophy. EG *...the mechanistic science of the nineteenth century... ...a purely mechanistic interpretation of the origins of man.* ADJ QUALIT

mechanize /mɛkənaɪz/, **mechanizes, mechanizing, mechanized**; also spelled **mechanise**. If you **mechanize** a process, you cause it to be done by a machine or machines, when it was previously done by people. EG *...the stimulus to mechanize production... Private firms may mechanize to avoid the troubles of a militant labour force.* ◊ **mechanized**. EG *...the mechanized and scientific agricultural industry... Housework has become highly mechanised.* ◊ **mechanization** /mɛkənaɪzeɪʃə⁰n/. EG *...the mechanisation of the postal service... Mechanization is eliminating jobs at every stage.* V OR V+O = automate ◊ ADJ QUALIT = automated ◊ N UNCOUNT

medal /mɛdə⁰l/, **medals**. A **medal** is a small piece of metal in the shape of a circle, cross, etc. It is given as an award for bravery or as a prize in a sporting event. EG *He was wearing full army uniform complete with badges and medals... ...the Distinguished Service Medal.* N COUNT

medallion /mɪ²dæljən/, **medallions**. A **medallion** is a piece of metal which looks like a coin and which you wear as an ornament, especially on a chain round your neck. EG *He wore a medallion of some sort round his neck.* N COUNT

medallist /mɛdə⁰lɪst/, **medallists**. A **medallist** is a person who has won a medal in sport. EG *She's an Olympic medallist.* N COUNT ↑ winner

meddle /mɛdə⁰l/, **meddles, meddling, meddled**. If you **meddle** in something, you involve yourself in it when it does not really concern you and you try to influence what happens; used showing disapproval. EG *What had induced the woman to meddle in his affairs?... I dared not meddle with my wife's plans.* V : IF+PREP THEN *in/with* ↑ participate = interfere

meddler /mɛdlə/, **meddlers**. A **meddler** is someone who becomes involved in things that do not really concern them and tries to influence what happens; used showing disapproval. EG *...this incorrigible meddler in the affairs of others.* N COUNT ↑ person

meddlesome /mɛdə⁰lsəm/ describes behaviour in which someone becomes involved in things that do not really concern them and tries to influence what happens; used showing disapproval. ▸ used of people. EG *Her detachment was a mask for a meddlesome nature... ...meddlesome parents.* ADJ QUALIT = interfering ▸ = interfering

media /miːdɪə/. 1 The **media** are television, radio, and newspapers regarded as a group. The media entertain or spread news and information to a large number of people. EG *The news media are interested only in bad news... The media is biased... Figures have been boosted by the pre-sales publicity in the media... The policy shift was an apparent response to heavy media coverage.* ● See also **mass media**. N SING : *the*+N, VB CAN BE SING OR PL ↑ communications

2 **Media** is a plural of **medium**.

mediaeval /mɛdiiːvə⁰l/. See **medieval**.

median /miːdɪən/. The **median** value of a set of values is the middle value when the values are arranged in order; a technical term in statistics. EG *2.7 billion people live in countries with a median income below £300 a head... The median age group in unfurnished renting was sixty to sixty-five.* ADJ CLASSIF : ATTRIB ↑ average

mediate /miːdi¹eɪt/, **mediates, mediating, mediated**. 1 If you **mediate**, you try to settle an argument between two groups of people, by talking to both groups and by trying to find things that they can both agree to. EG *They asked the courts and governments of Europe to mediate... Mediating between the two sides in this dispute will be a delicate business... The state must mediate the struggle for resources.* ◊ **mediation** /miːdɪeɪʃə⁰n/. EG *They paid small attention to the Vatican's offer of mediation.* V OR V+O : IF+PREP THEN *between* = arbitrate ◊ N UNCOUNT = arbitration

2 If something **is mediated** by an event, experience, or set of circumstances, it is changed slightly by it; a formal or literary use. EG *Biological processes may be mediated by specific social and historical conditions... Their contact was now mediated by consciousness.* V+O : USU PASS, USU+*by* = be modified

mediator /miːdi¹eɪtə/, **mediators**. A **mediator** is someone who tries to settle an argument between two groups of people by talking to both groups and by trying to find things that they can both agree to. EG *I was suggested as a possible candidate for the job of mediator... The University has proposed that a mediator be nominated to chair negotiations.* N COUNT = arbitrator

medic /mɛdɪk/, **medics**. A **medic** is a doctor or medical student; an informal word. EG *I waited in the* N COUNT *clearing for two hours with a wounded medic... ...a final year medic... The place is usually full of medics.*

medical /me̱dɪkəºl/, **medicals**. 1 **Medical** means relating to medicine or the to care of people's health. EG *She had to undergo medical treatment... The medical profession was baffled... ...a medical student... ...lack of adequate medical care.* ◊ **medically**. EG *Each child is medically examined at least three times a year.* — ADJ CLASSIF: ATTRIB; ◊ ADV ⇑ physically

2 A **medical** is a thorough examination of your body by a doctor, for example before you start a new job. EG *They were all set to give him a medical.* — N COUNT = check-up

medicament /məˀdɪ̱kəməˀnt/, **medicaments**. A **medicament** is a medicine; a formal word. EG *Morell gave him more and more powerful medicaments.* — N COUNT: USU PL

medication /me̱dɪke̱ɪʃəºn/, **medications**. **Medication** is 1 medical treatment. EG *Some of us were having medication.* 2 medicine. EG *...a cart loaded with medication... ...the use of antibiotic medication... The doctor can prescribe both medications.* — N UNCOUNT; N UNCOUNT/COUNT = medicament

medicinal /mɛdɪ̱sɪnəºl/. A **medicinal** substance acts as a medicine. EG *He was sent back to India to fetch a medicinal herb... ...the medicinal qualities of a plant.* ◊ **medicinally**. — ADJ CLASSIF ⇑ beneficial = healing; ◊ ADV

medicine /me̱dɪºsɪn/ medicines. 1 **Medicine** is the treatment of illness and injuries by doctors, nurses, and other trained people. EG *He was devoted to the practice of medicine... Geriatrics is the least popular branch of medicine... ...the importance of preventative medicine... ...the professions of medicine, dentistry and teaching.* — N UNCOUNT ⇑ healing

2 A **medicine** is a chemical substance, usually a liquid, tablets, or a powder, that you drink or swallow in order to cure an illness. EG *...a medicine for his cold... Medicine bottles fell off the shelves... Some illnesses are caused through people not using medicines properly.* — N COUNT/UNCOUNT = medication

medieval /me̱dɪi:vəºl/; also spelled **mediaeval**. Something that is **medieval** relates to or dates from the period between 1100 AD and 1500 AD, especially in European history. EG *He was giving us lectures on medieval German literature... ...a medieval church... ...feudalism in medieval Europe.* — ADJ CLASSIF: USU ATTRIB

mediocre /mi̱:dɪəʊkə/. Something that is **mediocre** is of a poor standard; used especially of something that does not show much skill or imagination. EG *There have been good, mediocre, and bad women artists... He spent much of his time reading mediocre paperbacks.* — ADJ QUALIT ⇑ bad = second-rate

mediocrity /mi:dɪɒkrɪ¹ti¹, me̱d-/, **mediocrities**. 1 The **mediocrity** of something is its poor standard. EG *He was dismayed by the mediocrity of the people working with him.* — N UNCOUNT = inferiority

2 A **mediocrity** is someone who is not very good at what they do. EG *You'll wind up a rich mediocrity.* — N COUNT = nonentity

meditate /me̱dɪteɪt/, **meditates, meditating, meditated**. 1 If you **meditate** or **meditate** on something, you think about it very carefully and deeply for a long time. EG *Spend some time meditating on the problem... The old man lay back and meditated.* — V: IF+PREP THEN *on/upon* = ponder, reflect

2 If you **meditate**, you remain in a silent and calm state for a period of time, as part of a religious training or so that you are more able to deal with the problems and difficulties of everyday life. EG *He used to meditate for ten minutes a day.* — V = contemplate

meditation /me̱dɪte̱ɪʃəºn/, **meditations**. 1 **Meditation** is 1.1 the act of thinking about something very carefully and deeply for a long time. EG *Miss Clare was deep in meditation... I hope we will not disturb your meditations.* 1.2 the act of remaining in a silent and calm state for a period of time, as part of a religious training or so that you are more able to deal with the problems and difficulties of everyday life. EG *He was deeply interested in meditation, the East, and yoga... She spent a night in prayer and meditation.* — N UNCOUNT/COUNT: IF COUNT THEN USU PL, SING=PL; N UNCOUNT = contemplation

2 A **meditation** is a detailed study in your mind of a particular subject. EG *I was prepared to plunge into a bitter meditation on the irony and malice of fate.* — N COUNT: IF+PREP THEN *on/upon* = deliberation

meditative /mɛdɪtətɪv/. If something that you do is **meditative**, it shows that you are thinking carefully about something. EG *His face went gently meditative... Daniel took a meditative sip of milky tea.* ▸ used of people. EG *Jim was quiet and meditative.* ◊ **meditatively**. EG *He was leaning meditatively on his elbow.* — ADJ CLASSIF ⇑ thoughtful = pensive; ◊ ADV WITH VB = pensively

Mediterranean /me̱dɪtəre̱ɪnɪən/. 1 The **Mediterranean** is a large sea which is between southern Europe and North Africa from north to south and the Straits of Gibraltar and western Asia from east to west. EG *Ships were moving into the Mediterranean... ...the Mediterranean resort town of Cannes.* ▸ used to refer to the countries around this sea. EG *...the migrant workers of the Mediterranean.* — N PROPER: *the*+N; ▸ ⇑ region

2 Something that is **Mediterranean** is characteristic of or belongs to the people or region around the Mediterranean Sea. EG *...a blazing display of Mediterranean ardour... The cool mountain air warms up and becomes mediterranean in temperature.* — ADJ QUALIT

medium /mi̱:dɪəm/, **mediums, media**. The plural of the noun can be either **mediums** or **media** in paragraph 2. The form **mediums** is the plural in paragraph 3.

1 **Medium** is used to describe 1.1 the size of something which is not large or small, but approximately half way between the two. EG *A large and a medium screwdriver should be sufficient... The man we are looking for is of medium height or smaller, with a long hooked nose.* 1.2 a colour which is not light or dark, but approximately half way between the two. EG *It came in two colours, medium brown or medium grey.* 1.3 something which is average in degree or amount, or approximately half way along a scale between two extremes. EG *Only 4 per cent of soils in the region have even medium fertility... This attitude was to be found at the higher and medium levels of command.* ● If you **strike a happy medium**, you find the right balance between doing too much and doing too little. — ADJ CLASSIF: USU ATTRIB; ADJ CLASSIF: USU ATTRIB = mid-; ADJ CLASSIF: USU ATTRIB; ● PHR: VB INFLECTS

2 A **medium** is 2.1 a way or means of expressing your ideas or of communicating with people. EG *I went to secondary school in a country where English is not the medium of instruction... He would prefer to be remembered for his talents in mediums other than photography.* 2.2 a substance or material which is used for a particular purpose or in order to produce a particular effect. EG *Air is a medium for sound... I think water colour is an extremely difficult medium to work with.* — N COUNT = form; N COUNT

3 A **medium** is also a person who claims to be able to contact and speak to people who are dead, and to pass messages between them and people who are still alive. — N COUNT ⇑ intermediary

4 See also **media**.

medium-dry wine or sherry is not very sweet. — ADJ CLASSIF

medium term. The **medium term** is the period of time which lasts a few months or years beyond the present time, in contrast with the short term or the long term. EG *We must now look at the medium term and see how costs can be reduced... ...medium-term programming.* — N SING: *the*+N, OR N BEFORE N

medium wave is a range of sound waves between 100 and 1000 metres long; used especially to refer to a range of sound waves used by radios. EG *There's cricket on medium wave until close of play... ...the medium-wave transmitter.* — N UNCOUNT

medley /me̱dli¹/, **medleys**. 1 A **medley** of different things is a mixture of them, especially one that produces an odd or interesting effect. EG *The skyline was a medley of great and small domes.* — N COUNT/PART = assortment

2 A **medley** is also 2.1 a collection of different tunes or songs that are played one after the other as a single piece of music. EG *And now, with a medley of forties favourites, here's Vera Lynn.* 2.2 a swimming race in which the four main swimming strokes must be used one after the other. — N COUNT ⇑ variety; N COUNT

meek /mi̱:k/, **meeker, meekest**. Someone who is **meek** is gentle and quiet, and likely to do what other people say. EG *She looked meek, but had the heart of a lion.* ◊ **meekly**. EG *'I'm sorry dear,' Gretchen said meekly.* ◊ **meekness**. EG *He agreed with surprising meekness.* — ADJ QUALIT ⇑ submissive = timid ≠ assertive; ◊ ADV; ◊ N UNCOUNT = docility

meet /mi̱:t/, **meets, meeting, met**. 1 If you **meet** someone or **meet up** with them, 1.1 you happen to be in the same place as them and start talking to them. You may know the other person, but be surprised to see them, or you may not know them at all. EG *I met a Swedish girl on the train from Copenhagen... I have never met anyone so attractive... I don't think we've met, have we?... We're all destined to meet up with someone who's better than we are.* 1.2 you both go to the same place, which you have earlier arranged to do, so that you can talk or do something together. — V OR V+O: RECIP, NO PASS, OR PHRASAL VB: V+ADV: IF+PREP THEN *with* ⇑ encounter; V OR V+O: RECIP, NO PASS, OR PHRASAL VB: V+ADV:

EG *After that they met every day... Meet me under the clock. We planned to meet up with them later in Florence.* IF+PREP THEN with

2 If you **meet** someone, you are introduced to them and begin talking to them and getting to know them. EG *Come and meet Tony and Rick... Now, who would you like to meet?* ▸ used when you greet or say goodbye to someone you have only just met. EG *Pleased to meet you... Nice to have met you.* V+O : NO PASS

3 If you **meet** someone or **meet** their train, plane, or bus, you go to the station, airport, or bus-stop at the time that they arrive there, so that you can greet them, talk to them, etc. EG *I was met by my daughter and son-in-law... Dan came to the airport to meet me.* V+O = collect

4 If one bus, train, boat, etc **meets** another, it arrives somewhere in time to take passengers or goods from the other bus, train, boat, etc. EG *They sent a steamer to meet the vessel carrying her to Africa.* V+O

5 When a group of people such as a committee **meet**, they gather together for a purpose. EG *Most regional committees meet four times a year... I hear that teachers in Tokyo meet to discuss our methods.* V = assemble, congregate

6 If something **meets** a need, requirement, or condition, it is of a sufficient quantity or quality to fulfil it. EG *His income is inadequate to meet his basic needs... Certain standards must be met.* V+O = satisfy

7 If you **meet** something such as a problem or difficulty, you deal satisfactorily with it. EG *These problems would simply have to be met as they came... This is the challenge. How are we to meet it?* V+O = cope with

8 If you **meet** the cost of something, you provide the money that is needed for it. EG *They offered to meet the entire cost of the chapel... Certain expenses are met for all committee members.* V+O = pay

9 If you **meet** a situation, attitude, problem, etc, you experience or become aware of it. EG *Sometimes he meets a situation for which his moral rules do not provide... Where had I met this kind of genial ignorance before?* V+O = come across

10 When a moving object **meets** another object, it comes into contact with it. EG *The heavy club met his head with a crack... Her mouth met his.* V OR V+O : RECIP, NO PASS ⇑ touch

11 If your **eyes meet** someone else's, you both look at each other at the same time, for example because you both realize that you have had a similar thought or because you are sexually attracted to one another. EG *Their eyes meet, and they smile... Her eyes rose to meet mine.* PHR : VB INFLECTS, RECIP ● When you **meet** someone's **eyes** or **gaze**, you notice that they are looking at you and you look at them at the same time. EG *She briefly met his eyes... The man met the girl's gaze.* ● PHR : VB INFLECTS ● If something, especially something surprising or impressive, **meets** your **eyes**, you see it. EG *The sight that met my eyes made it hard to keep a straight face.* ● PHR : VB INFLECTS ● You say **'there's more to this than meets the eye'** when you think the situation is not as simple as it seems to be. ● PHR

12 If two areas, especially areas of land or sea, **meet**, they are next to one another. EG *The foothills flattened out to meet the Bay shore... We had rounded Cape Point, where the Atlantic meets the Indian Ocean.* V OR V+O : RECIP, NO PASS = join

13 If two or more things **meet** or **meet up**, they join together at a particular place. EG *The road comes up from the north and meets the one from Lairg... Parallel lines never meet... This track should meet up with the main road.* V OR V+O : RECIP, NO PASS, OR PHRASAL VB : V+ADV : IF+PREP THEN with

14 If two sportsmen, teams, or armies **meet**, they compete or fight against one another. EG *Weaver must defend against James Tillis before meeting Cooney... Arsenal meet Spurs in the next round of the Cup.* V OR V+O : RECIP, NO PASS = take on

15 If someone **meets** their **death, meets a violent death**, etc, they die in a particular way, at a particular age, etc. EG *He met his death as the result of a conspiracy.* PHR : VB INFLECTS

16 A **meet** is an event in which athletes come to a particular place in order to take part in a race or races. EG *...a track meet.* N COUNT = meeting

17 ● See also **meeting.** ● to **make ends meet**: see **end.** ● to **meet** someone **halfway**: see **halfway.** ● to **meet** your **match**: see **match.**

meet with. 1 If something such as a suggestion, proposal, new book, etc **meets with** a particular reaction, it gets that reaction from people. EG *All appeals for aid meet with bureaucratic refusal... Almost everything else in the report meets with my approval.* PHRASAL VB : V+PREP, HAS PASS ⇑ receive

2 If you **meet** something **with** a particular reaction, you react to it in this way. EG *The men had met this refusal with indifference... His approaches had been met with ill-concealed disdain.* PHRASAL VB : V+O+PREP = treat with

3 If you **meet with an accident**, you have an accident; a fairly formal expression. EG *...an inquest on a child who met with an accident... I'm afraid that jug you bought me met with an accident.* PHR : VB AND N INFLECT

4 If you **meet with success, meet with failure**, etc, you are successful, unsuccessful, etc. EG *Strikes met with little success... My friend's plans met with some successes and some failures.* PHR : VB INFLECTS

5 In American English, to **meet with** someone means to go to the same place as them, which you have earlier arranged to do, so that you can talk to them or do something else together. EG *We can meet with the professor Monday night... The committee directed its legal staff to meet with CIA lawyers.* PHRASAL VB : V+PREP, HAS PASS

meeting /miːtɪŋ/, **meetings**. A **meeting** is **1** an event in which a group of people meet, usually inside a building, in order to discuss proposals, make decisions, etc. EG *There is a different chairman at each meeting... A meeting of physicists had been called in Paris.* ▸ used of the group of people. EG *The meeting agreed with him... The meeting votes that the sentence be quashed.* **2** an event in which you meet someone, intentionally or accidentally. EG *Christopher Milne remembers his first meeting with Alice... It's easy to imagine those romantic meetings in the gardens.* **3** an event in which a group of Quakers meet in order to worship together. EG *Have you been to a Quaker meeting?* N COUNT = assembly, gathering; ▸ N SING WITH DET; N COUNT = encounter; N COUNT ⇑ gathering

meeting house, meeting houses; also spelled with a hyphen. A **meeting house** is a building in which a group of nonconformist Christians, for example Quakers, meet in order to worship together. N COUNT

meeting place, meeting places; also spelled with a hyphen. A **meeting place** is a place where people meet; especially used of a place where two people, or a group of people, meet regularly. EG *Their house became a meeting place for all the radical students.* N COUNT = rendezvous

mega- is **1** added to nouns that refer to units of measurement in order to form other nouns referring to units that are a million times bigger. EG *...ton→megaton... ... watt→megawatt.* **2** used at the beginning of nouns and adjectives that refer to things that are very large or important; an informal use. EG *...mega-star... ...mega-visual.* PREFIX; PREFIX ⇑ super-

megahertz /mɛgəhɜːts/. **Megahertz** is both the singular and the plural form. A **megahertz** is a unit of frequency, used especially for radio frequencies. One megahertz equals one million cycles per second. EG *...a persistent beeping at 20.005 megahertz.* N COUNT : NUM+N = MHz

megalith /mɛgəlɪθ/, **megaliths**. A **megalith** is a very large stone that stands on the ground and that is thought to have been put there by people a long time ago; a technical term in archaeology. EG *...a ring of megaliths on some local hill.* N COUNT

megalomania /mɛgə⁰lə⁶meɪnɪə/ is the belief that you are more powerful and important than you really are. Megalomania is sometimes a mental illness. EG *Early success may lead to megalomania.* N UNCOUNT ⇑ vanity

megalomaniac /mɛgələ⁶meɪnɪæk/, **megalomaniacs**. A **megalomaniac** is someone who enjoys being powerful, or who believes that they are more powerful or important than they really are. EG *He was a megalomaniac who loved to wield power.* N COUNT ⇑ person

megaphone /mɛgəfəʊn/, **megaphones**. A **megaphone** is a device for making your voice sound louder in the open air. It is shaped like a hollow cone with open ends. You speak into the small end. EG *He grabbed a megaphone and stepped on to the bridge.* N COUNT = loudhailer

megaton /mɛgətʌn/, **megatons**. A **megaton** is one million tons. A one megaton nuclear weapon has the same power as one million tons of TNT; a technical term. EG *...a 15 megaton thermonuclear device.* N COUNT : NUM+N ⇑ measurement

melancholia /mɛlənkəʊlɪə/ is a feeling of great melancholy or depression; a formal or literary word. EG *She was given to lengthy bouts of melancholia.* N UNCOUNT ⇑ sadness

melancholic /mɛlənkɒlɪk/, **melancholics**. **1** If you feel **melancholic**, you feel very sad; a literary word. EG *...his melancholic smile.* ADJ QUALIT ⇑ unhappy

2 A **melancholic** is a person who suffers from melancholy. EG *I was becoming a melancholic.* — N COUNT

melancholy /mɛlənkɒli¹/. 1 **Melancholy** is an intense feeling of sadness which lasts for a long time and which strongly affects your behaviour and attitudes. EG *When he left, she sank into melancholy... I snapped out of this melancholy the moment a friend arrived.* — N UNCOUNT = despondency, gloom

2 If you feel **melancholy**, you feel very sad. EG *He was growing more melancholy every hour... ...a melancholy bachelor... ...a mood of melancholy introspection.* — ADJ QUALIT = sorrowful, gloomy

3 You describe something that you see or hear as **melancholy** when it gives you a feeling of sadness. EG *...the obscure, melancholy shapes of empty chairs... We acquainted him with the melancholy truth.* — ADJ QUALIT ⇑ sad = dismal

mélange /mɛlɑːnʒ/; also spelled **melange**. A **mélange** is a mixture of people or things. EG *A strange mélange of women emerged from the cells... ...a subtle melange of odours.* — N SING WITH DET : USU+*of* ⇑ collection = assortment

mêlée /mɛleɪ/, **mêlées**. A **mêlée** is a crowd of people rushing about in different directions and doing different things. EG *I was caught in the mêlée... His turban had fallen off in the mêlée.* — N COUNT : USU SING = scrimmage

mellifluous /mɪ²lɪfluəs/. A **mellifluous** voice, piece of music, etc is very pleasant to listen to; a formal word used showing approval. EG *They all had mellifluous voices... I particularly savoured the mellifluous second movement.* — ADJ QUALIT ⇑ smooth = melodious

mellow /mɛləʊ/, **mellower, mellowest; mellows, mellowing, mellowed**. 1 **Mellow** light makes things appear golden, soft, and rich in colour; used showing approval. EG *...the mellow Venetian light... ... the mellow sunlight.* — ADJ QUALIT

2 **Mellow** stone or brick has a smooth surface and a pleasant soft colour as a result of age and exposure to the weather; used showing approval. EG *...the lovely mellow stone of centuries... ...a strange Tudor building in mellow brick.* ▸ used of buildings. EG *...his mellow country house in Oxfordshire.* — ADJ QUALIT : USU ATTRIB

3 **Mellow** fruit is ripe fruit that has a soft golden brown colour; used showing approval. EG *They are at their best in the autumn, when they are at their fattest and most mellow.* — ADJ QUALIT = juicy

4 A **mellow** sound is smooth and pleasant to listen to; used showing approval. EG *Her voice sounded mellow and exciting... ...a warm, mellow sound.* — ADJ QUALIT = velvety

5 If someone **mellows** or if they **are mellowed** by something such as alcohol or good food, they become easier to talk to and more pleasant to be with. EG *Some bosses tend to mellow with lunch and are at their most approachable in the afternoon... The rum began to mellow her.* — V-ERG ⇑ relax = soften

6 If someone **mellows** or if age **mellows** them, they become kinder or less extreme in their behaviour as they grow older. EG *He mellowed considerably as he got older... I watched young politicians age and mellow... He says that age should have mellowed me.* — V-ERG ⇑ develop = soften

7 When someone becomes **mellow**, they mellow. EG *I got pretty mellow... Patrick, pleasantly mellow, was very willing to oblige him... I've seen him grow more mellow over the years.* — ADJ QUALIT : PRED ⇑ relaxed

melodic /mɪ²lɒdɪk/ means relating to melody; a technical term in music. EG *Handel's operas contain wonderful melodic inventions... The instruments produce one melodic line.* — ADJ CLASSIF : ATTRIB ⇑ musical

melodious /mɪ²ləʊdiəs/. A **melodious** sound is pleasant to listen to; a fairly formal word. EG *His voice was as melodious as a great actor's... He answered by a low melodious laugh.* — ADJ QUALIT ⇑ attractive = mellifluous

melodrama /mɛlə⁶drɑːmə/, **melodramas**. A **melodrama** is a story or play in which a lot of exciting, tragic, or serious things happen and in which people's emotions are very exaggerated. EG *...a wildly old-fashioned melodrama about a female spy... ...the traditional melodrama of the wicked squire and rustic tenant.* — N COUNT/ UNCOUNT

melodramatic /mɛlə⁶drəmætɪk/. **Melodramatic** behaviour is behaviour in which someone treats a situation as much more serious than it really is. EG *Must you be so insistently melodramatic?... I think we're getting a bit too melodramatic there.* — ADJ QUALIT = dramatic
◊ **melodramatically**. EG *He began melodramatically beating his head with his fist... His voice deepened melodramatically.* — ◊ ADV WITH VB = dramatically

melody /mɛlədi¹/, **melodies**. A **melody** is a tune; a fairly formal word. EG *...the grandest melody that Sibelius ever wrote.* — N COUNT

melon /mɛlən/, **melons**. A **melon** is a large fruit which is sweet and juicy inside and has a hard green or yellow skin. EG *...a large melon... They had melon and a small roast chicken for dinner.* — N COUNT/ UNCOUNT

melt /mɛlt/, **melts, melting, melted**. 1 When something **melts** or when you **melt** it, it changes from a solid to a liquid, usually because it has been heated. EG *The lakes become ice-free and the snow melts... Melt two ounces of butter in a saucepan... ...pans full of melted wax.* ◊ **melting**. EG *This might result in the melting of the polar ice caps.* ● **Butter wouldn't melt in** someone's **mouth**: see **butter**. — V-ERG ⇑ liquefy ≠ solidify; ◊ N UNCOUNT = thawing

2 When something **melts** or **melts away**, it gradually becomes smaller and then disappears. EG *Lynn's inhibitions melted... Their differences melted away... A great empire has melted away.* — V, OR PHRASAL VB : V+ADV ⇑ diminish = fade

3 If you **melt** into something such as a crowd of people, you hide among them without anyone noticing that you are doing it. EG *They often wanted to melt into the teeming millions... They rely for their defence on concealment, melting away into the undergrowth.* — V+A *(into)* ⇑ disappear = vanish

melt down. If you **melt down** an object, you heat it until it melts, so that you can use the material in order to make something else. EG *Railings were melted down for cannon... It is now economically viable to melt down old glass.* — PHRASAL VB : V+O+ADV ⇑ liquefy

melting point, melting points. The **melting point** of a substance is the temperature at which it melts when you heat it. EG *...the melting point of iron... Gold has quite a low melting point.* — N COUNT

melting pot, melting pots. A **melting pot** is a place or situation in which people, ideas, etc of different kinds gradually get mixed together. EG *...a melting pot of races.* — N COUNT : USU SING ⇑ mixture

member /mɛmbə/, **members**. 1 A **member** of a group is one of the people, animals, or things belonging to the group. EG *Babies on average have milder colds than older members of the family... ...a member of the opposite sex... The weaver bird is a member of the sparrow family.* — N COUNT+SUPP ⇑ individual

2 A **member** of an organization such as a club or a political party is a person who has joined the organization in order to take part in its activities. EG *He was a member of an exclusive New York city club... ...a Labour Party member.* — N COUNT : USU+SUPP

3 A **member** country, **member** state, etc is one of the countries that has joined an international organization or alliance. EG *All the member countries are under pressure to conform... The different priorities of various member states became apparent.* — ADJ CLASSIF : ATTRIB ⇑ associate

4 A **member** is also a Member of Parliament. EG *...John Parker, the Labour member for Dagenham.* — N COUNT : USU+*for*

Member of Parliament, Members of Parliament. A **Member of Parliament** is a person who has been elected by the people of a particular town or district in Britain to represent them in the House of Commons. EG *We can count upon the support of a few Labour Members of Parliament.* — N COUNT ⇑ politician = MP, member

membership /mɛmbəʃɪp/. 1 **Membership** of an organization is the state of being a member of it. EG *Deacon was questioned about his membership of the Nationalist Party... The criteria for membership are not so strict as in other clubs.* — N UNCOUNT ⇑ belonging

2 The **membership** of an organization is **2.1** the people who belong to it. EG *...20 people elected from the membership.* **2.2** the number of people who belong to it. EG *Membership declined to half a million.* — N SING : WITH *the/POSS*; N UNCOUNT

membrane /mɛmbreɪn/, **membranes**. A **membrane** is a thin piece of skin which connects or covers parts of a person or animal's body. EG *...the delicate membranes of the throat.* — N COUNT = tissue

memento /mɪ²mɛntəʊ/, **mementos, mementoes**. The plural can be either **mementos** or **mementoes**. A **memento** is an object which you keep because it reminds you of a person or a special occasion. EG *...the Presley napkin, a memento of the singer's farewell concert... ...one of the precious mementoes of his Presidency.* — N COUNT : IF+PREP THEN *of* = souvenir, keepsake

memo /mɛməʊ, miːməʊ/, **memos**. A **memo** is a short official note that is written to someone about something, especially at work. EG *...a memo to the* — N COUNT = memorandum

War Department asking for more soldiers... He wrote down a name and address on a memo pad.

memoir /mɛmwɑː/, **memoirs**. 1 A person's **memoirs** are a book which they write about people who they have known and events that they remember. EG *He was writing his memoirs of his career abroad... ...Memoirs of a Conservative.*
N PLURAL : USU WITH POSS = reminiscences

2 A **memoir** is a book or article that you write about someone who you have known well; a formal use. EG *I was writing a memoir of Colonel Burr.*
N COUNT ⇑ account

memorabilia /mɛməʳrəbɪlɪə/ are things that you collect because they are connected with a person, organization, etc in which you are interested. EG *He had a large collection of war memorabilia.*
N PLURAL ⇑ souvenirs

memorable /mɛməʳrəbəʳl/. Something that is **memorable** is worth remembering or likely to be remembered, because it is special or unusual. EG *The visit was memorable in many ways... I had a memorable train journey.* ◊ **memorably**. EG *He made a memorably conciliatory speech.*
ADJ QUALIT = unforgettable
◊ ADV = notably

memorandum /mɛmərændəm/, **memoranda**. A **memorandum** is 1 a written statement that you prepare specially for a person or committee in order to give them information about a particular matter. EG *He received a disturbing memorandum from the chief agent of the Party... They prepared a 45-page memorandum for the Select Committee.* 2 a short official note that you write to a person or to several people, especially people who you work with. EG *...an office memorandum.*
N COUNT = report
N COUNT = memo

memorial /mɪ²mɔːrɪəl/, **memorials**. 1 A **memorial** is an object built on the ground or placed on the wall of a building in order to remind people of a famous person or event. EG *The cars swirl round the memorial... ...a memorial to Queen Alexandra... ...the Albert Memorial.*
N COUNT : ALSO IN NAMES AFTER N ⇑ monument

2 A **memorial** event or prize is held or awarded as a way of remembering someone who has died. EG *He was often to be seen at funerals and memorial services... The book won the 1981 George Orwell Memorial Prize.*
ADJ CLASSIF : ATTRIB, ALSO IN NAMES ⇑ commemorative

memorize /mɛməraɪz/, **memorizes, memorizing, memorized**; also spelled **memorise**. If you **memorize** something, you learn it thoroughly so that you can repeat it exactly using only your memory. EG *I was able to read a whole page and memorise it in under three minutes.*
V+O = learn by heart

memory /mɛməʳrɪ¹/, **memories**. 1 Your **memory** is your ability to retain and recall information, ideas, images and thoughts. EG *The accuracy of their memory is astounding... I have a bad memory for such things... This gives an advantage to people whose mothers have good memories... A few things stand out in my memory.*
N COUNT : USU POSS+N IN SING

2 A **memory** is something that you remember from the past. EG *My memories of a London childhood are happy ones.*
N COUNT : IF+ PREP THEN *of* = recollection

3 Your **memory** of someone who has died is the things that you remember about them. EG *She worshipped his memory throughout her long widowhood.*
N SING : USU POSS +N

4 A computer's **memory** is the part of the computer where information is stored, especially for a short time before it is transferred to magnetic tapes or disks; a technical term.
N COUNT ⇑ store

5 The word **memory** is also used in the following expressions. **5.1** If you **lose** your **memory**, you can no longer remember things that you used to know. EG *He lost his memory for names.* **5.2** If you **commit** something **to memory**, you learn it thoroughly so that you can repeat it exactly using only your memory. **5.3** If you recite a poem, play a piece of music, etc **from memory**, you do it without looking at anything written or printed. EG *Sometimes she played from memory, sometimes from music... I quote from memory.* **5.4** If something has happened or existed **within** your **memory**, it has happened or existed during the period of time since you first started noticing and remembering things. EG *He had never actually owned anything within his memory.*
PHR : VB AND N INFLECT
PHR : VB INFLECTS = memorize
PHR : USED AS AN A
PHR : USED AS AN A

5.5 If something has happened or existed **within living memory**, it has happened or existed since the earliest time that can be remembered by anyone who is still alive. EG *The earthquake in San Francisco is well within living memory.* **5.6** If you do something **in memory of** someone who has died, you do it so that people will remember that person. EG *A fund was launched to set up a monument in memory of the dead men.*
PHR : USED AS AN A
PHR + NG, USED AS AN A ⇑ commemorating

memsahib /mɛmsɑːʰɪb/, **memsahibs**. A **memsahib** is used to refer to a white woman in India, especially during the period of British rule, or sometimes to an upper-class Indian woman; an old-fashioned word. EG *...a traditional memsahib out shopping in the bazaar.* ▸ used as a form of address. EG *I know of such a boy, Memsahib.*
N COUNT
▸ N IN TITLES ⇑ madam

men /mɛn/ is the plural of **man**.

menace /mɛnɪ¹s/, **menaces, menacing, menaced**. 1 A **menace** is **1.1.** something which is likely to cause serious harm to a person or thing. EG *...the menace of totalitarianism... ...a menace to democracy... There was anger and menace in his eyes.* **1.2** a nuisance; an informal use. EG *Rooks are a menace and there are far too many of them... You're a menace!*
N COUNT/ UNCOUNT ⇑ danger = threat
N COUNT

2 If something **menaces** you, it is likely to seriously harm you. EG *...the formidable threat that menaces Europe... One danger menaced his future.*
V+O = threaten

3 If a person **menaces** you, they intend or threaten to harm you. EG *We were menaced by drunks... The Marines would menace them away at rifle point.*
V+O = frighten

menacing /mɛnɪ¹sɪŋ/. If someone's behaviour is **menacing**, they seem to be intending to harm you. EG *The man's tone became slightly menacing... He advanced on me in a menacing fashion.* ◊ **menacingly**. EG *Joy scowled at him and waved her knife menacingly.*
ADJ QUALIT ⇑ dangerous = threatening
◊ ADV WITH VB

menage /mɛnɑːʒ/, **menages**; also spelled **ménage**. A **menage** is a group of people living together in one house; a formal word. EG *...a member of the O'Shea menage... ...a lurid account of the Marx menage.*
N COUNT : MOD+ N, USU SING = household

ménage à trois /meɪnɑːʒ ə⁹ trwɑː/, **ménages à trois**. You refer to three people as a **ménage à trois** when they live together, especially when one of them is having a sexual relationship with both of the others; a literary expression. EG *I'm not asking you to come out and join a ménage à trois.*
N COUNT : USU SING ⇑ household

menagerie /mə²nædʒəʳrɪ¹/, **menageries**. A **menagerie** is a collection of wild animals. EG *In this place the king kept his menagerie.*
N COUNT = zoo

mend /mɛnd/, **mends, mending, mended**. 1 If you **mend** something that is broken or not working, you repair it, so that it can be used again. EG *I mended some toys for her... I've just had to pay to have the television mended... He spent the evening sewing on buttons and mending socks.*
V+O

2 If you **mend**, you get better after you have been ill or have had an injury; a fairly formal or old-fashioned use. EG *It took over a year for her to mend.* ▸ used of a part of your body. EG *Her bones were too old to mend.* ● *If you are* **on the mend**, you are recovering from an illness or an injury; an informal expression. EG *He had some colour in his cheeks and was plainly on the mend.*
V ⇑ improve = recover
▸ = heal
● PHR : USED AS AN A = getting better

3 If someone **mends** their **ways**, they begin to behave well after they have been behaving badly. EG *You've got to mend your ways or you'll be out on your ear... She'll never mend her ways, if you ask me.*
PHR : VB INFLECTS ⇑ improve = reform

mendacious /mɛndeɪʃəs/. A **mendacious** statement, remark, etc is not truthful; a formal word.
ADJ QUALIT = lying

mendacity /mɛndæsɪtɪ¹/ is the quality of lying, rather than being truthful; a formal word. EG *The editorials were characterized by malevolence and mendacity.*
N UNCOUNT = falsehood

mending /mɛndɪŋ/ is 1 the sewing and repairing of clothes that have got holes in them. EG *I've got a lot of mending to do.* 2 clothes that you have collected together to be mended. EG *...his mother's basket of mending.*
N UNCOUNT
N UNCOUNT

menfolk /mɛnfəʊk/. When women talk about their **menfolk**, they mean the men in their family or society. EG *The women have a lot to do with their menfolk leaving the land.*
N PLURAL : DETPOSS+N

menial /miːnɪəl/, **menials**. 1 **Menial** work is very boring and tiring and has a low status. EG *I was made to do a good deal of menial work... ...menial tasks.*
ADJ QUALIT = lowly

2 A **menial** is a person who does the most boring and tiring jobs in an office or factory. EG *There is a positive attitude here, from the boss down to the lowliest menial.*
N COUNT ⇑ worker = minion

meningitis /mɛnɪndʒaɪtɪs/ is a serious illness in which the outer part of your brain and spinal cord
N UNCOUNT ⇑ disease

becomes very inflamed. Meningitis is caused by infection.

menopause /mɛnəᵒpɔːz/. The **menopause** is the time during which a woman gradually stops menstruating, usually when she is about fifty years old. N SING WITH DET, OR N UNCOUNT = change of life

men's room, men's rooms. The **men's room** is a toilet for men; used in American English. EG *We went out into the hallway to find the men's room.* N COUNT : USU the+N IN SING = gents

menstrual /mɛnstrʊᵒəl/ means relating to the time when a woman is menstruating. EG *...the menstrual cycle... ...menstrual periods.* ADJ CLASSIF : ATTRIB

menstruate /mɛnstrʊeɪt/, **menstruates, menstruating, menstruated**. When a woman **menstruates**, a flow of blood comes from her womb. Women who are fertile menstruate once a month unless they are pregnant, when they do not menstruate at all. ◊ **menstruation** /mɛnstrʊeɪʃəᵒn/. EG *...the onset of menstruation.* V ◊ N UNCOUNT

menswear /mɛnzwɛə/ is clothing for men. N UNCOUNT

-ment is 1 added to verbs in order to form nouns that refer to the doing or making of something or to things that are done or made. EG *...replace→replacement... ...enlarge→enlargement.* 2 added to verbs in order to form uncount nouns that refer to mental states. EG *...excite→excitement... ...disappoint→disappointment.* SUFFIX : FORMS NOUNS; SUFFIX : FORMS N UNCOUNTS

mental /mɛntəᵒl/. 1 **Mental** means 1.1 relating to the activity of your mind or brain, for example in thinking. EG *All humans do have some kind of innate mental ability... ...mental effort.* ◊ **mentally**. EG *Learning to wear contact lenses is tiring and mentally exhausting.* 1.2 relating to the health of your mind. EG *Children impose great strain on both the mental health of women and on their marriages... ...mental illness... ...mental patients.* ◊ **mentally**. EG *He was a sick man, mentally and physically... ...the rights of the mentally handicapped.* ADJ CLASSIF : ATTRIB ≠ physical; ◊ ADV ≠ physically; ADJ CLASSIF : ATTRIB = psychological; ◊ ADV ≠ physically

2 A **mental** act is one that is done in your thoughts, rather than by writing something down or talking about it. EG *...mental arithmetic.* ◊ **mentally**. EG *I have kicked myself mentally a hundred times for that stupidity.* ● If you **make a mental note** of something, you make an effort to store it in your memory so that you will not forget it. ADJ CLASSIF : ATTRIB; ◊ ADV WITH VB = inwardly; ● PHR : VB INFLECTS

3 **Mental** also means very stupid or foolish; used in very informal British English. EG *He must have been mental to do that!* ADJ QUALIT = mad

mental age, mental ages. A person's **mental age** is the age which they are considered to have reached in their thinking ability, by comparing their ability with the average ability for people of various ages; used especially of people who are mentally handicapped. EG *He is over 30, but he has a mental age of seven.* N COUNT : USU SING

mental hospital, mental hospitals. A **mental hospital** is a hospital for people who are suffering from mental illness. N COUNT

mentality /mɛntælɪtiˡ/, **mentalities**. Your **mentality** is the particular attitude or way of thinking that you have, especially when this is fixed or habitual; often used showing disapproval. EG *You have an accountant mentality... He is able to understand the mentality of the nation.* N COUNT+SUPP : USU SING = personality

menthol /mɛnθɒᵒl/ is a substance that smells a bit like peppermint, and that you can use to clear your nose when you have a cold. N UNCOUNT

mentholated /mɛnθəleɪtɪ²d/. Something that is **mentholated** contains menthol. EG *...mentholated throat lozenges.* ADJ CLASSIF

mention /mɛnʃəᵒn/, **mentions, mentioning, mentioned**. 1 If you **mention** something, you 1.1 say it, but do not spend very long talking about it. EG *I mentioned to Tom that I was thinking of going back to work... Jeremy mentioned having seen me on television the previous evening... As I've mentioned before, a president is sometimes deceived by his advisors.* 1.2 refer to it, usually briefly. EG *The priest mentioned the disappearance of his passport in church last Sunday... Penny decided not to mention her cold.* V+REPORT-CL/QUOTE : IF+PREP THEN *to* ⇑ communicate; V+O : IF+PREP THEN *to* = allude to

2 You say **'don't mention it'** to tell someone that they do not need to thank you for something you have done for them. EG *'Thanks for your help.'–'Oh, that's okay. Don't mention it.'* CONVENTION

3 You use **not to mention** when you want to add extra information which emphasizes even more strongly the point that you are making. EG *He felt that there was prestige in having a wife, not to mention a comfortable home... For the picnic I'd like some eggs and cheese and wine, not to mention sausage and bread and fruit.* PHR : NG+PHR+NG

4 A **mention** is a reference, usually brief, to a person or thing. EG *Once or twice there were mentions in the newspapers of the Queen having been ill... The first mention of the discovery appeared in an article last year... Mention was made earlier of the new university course in Japanese.* N COUNT/UNCOUNT : IF+PREP THEN *of* = announcement

5 If you **mention** someone or something, or you **mention** a name, you refer to someone or something by name. EG *Did I mention the name of the film I went to last night?... My grandfather mentioned me in his will.* V+O

6 The **mention** of someone or something is reference to them by name. EG *My brother used to go purple in the face at the very mention of my name... The mention of his sister made him angry.* N COUNT/UNCOUNT : USU N IN SING+*of*

7 If you **mention** someone, you put their name in an official list or report because of something brave or special that they have done. EG *His war record was outstanding. He was twice mentioned in despatches.* ▸ used as a noun. EG *At the age of sixty-seven, he had earned another mention in despatches... I must give my own honourable mention for the radio production of Harold Pinter's 'The Caretaker'.* V+O : USU PASS = cite; ▸ N COUNT/UNCOUNT = citation

mentor /mɛntɔː/, **mentors**. A person's **mentor** is someone who teaches them and gives them a lot of advice over a period of time; a formal word. EG *She had no literary mentor.* N COUNT ⇑ teacher = guru

menu /mɛnjuː/, **menus**. A **menu** is 1 a list of all the food that you eat during a formal meal, or that you can order in a restaurant. EG *What's on the menu?* 2 a list that you can ask for on a computer which tells you the possible things that you can do with the information stored in the computer. N COUNT; N COUNT

MEP /ɛm iː piː/, **MEPs**. **MEP** is an abbreviation for 'Member of the European Parliament'; a person who represents an area of the United Kingdom at the European Parliament, an organization which is part of the EEC. N COUNT : ALSO IN TITLE AFTER N

mercantile /mɜːkəntaɪl/ means relating to merchants or trading; a formal word. EG *...the overseas expansion of European mercantile and industrial civilization.* ADJ CLASSIF : ATTRIB = commercial

mercenary /mɜːsɪnəᵒriˡ/, **mercenaries**. 1 A **mercenary** is a soldier who is paid to fight by a country or group that he or she does not belong to. N COUNT ⇑ fighter

2 Someone who is **mercenary** is interested only in the money that they can get from a person or out of a situation; used showing disapproval. ADJ QUALIT

merchandise /mɜːtʃəndaɪz/ is goods that you sell, buy, or trade with; a formal or technical word. EG *I'd like to to examine the merchandise... ...a very long front window filled with signs and merchandise.* N UNCOUNT = wares

merchant /mɜːtʃənt/, **merchants**. 1 A **merchant** is a person who buys or sells goods in large quantities, especially one who imports and exports them. EG *...a textile merchant.* N COUNT = trader

2 **Merchant** describes sailors or ships that are not part of a country's armed forces but are involved in carrying goods for trade. EG *He served for many years in the British Merchant Navy... ...a merchant seaman... ...merchant shipping.* ADJ CLASSIF : ATTRIB

merchant bank, merchant banks. A **merchant bank** is a bank that deals mainly with business firms, investment, and foreign trade. N COUNT

merciful /mɜːsiˡfʊl/. 1 You describe an event or situation as **merciful** when you think it is fortunate or lucky, because it brings an end to pain or unhappiness. EG *Death came as a merciful release.* ◊ **mercifully**. EG *He thought he must be dreaming. And then, mercifully, he was... I could see it was going to be mercifully uncrowded.* ADJ QUALIT = blessed; ◊ ADV, OR ADV SEN = thankfully

2 Someone who is **merciful** behaves in a way that shows kindness and forgiveness to people who are in their power. EG *I begged him to be merciful.* ▸ used of actions and behaviour. EG *Sparing him was a merciful act.* ADJ QUALIT ⇑ kind; ▸ = humane

merciless /mɜːsiˡlɪ²s/. Someone who is **merciless** is very strict or cruel and does not show any forgiveness towards people. EG *He picked up a reputation as a merciless foe of gambling and pornography.* ◊ **mercilessly**. EG *Unarmed peasants were beaten mercilessly.* ADJ QUALIT ⇑ severe = implacable, relentless; ◊ ADV : USU WITH VB

mercurial /mɜːkjʊərɪəl/. Someone who is **mercurial** frequently changes their mind or mood without warning; a formal or literary word. EG *He was as mercurial as the weather.* ▸ used of a person's mind or character. EG *...a mercurial temperament.*
ADJ QUALIT ⇑ changeable = unpredictable ▸ = volatile

mercury /mɜːkjə⁴ri¹/ is a silver-coloured metal that is usually in a liquid form. It is used especially in thermometers and barometers.
N UNCOUNT

mercy /mɜːsi¹/, **mercies**. 1 **Mercy** is kind and considerate treatment that you show to someone, especially when you forgive them or do not punish them. EG *He pleaded for mercy... I'd have no mercy on them.*
N UNCOUNT = pity, compassion

2 If you describe an event or situation as a **mercy**, you mean that it is a piece of good luck for you. EG *What a mercy it was that Maisie had given up drinking... Be thankful for small mercies.*
N COUNT = blessing

3 The word **mercy** is also used in the following expressions. **3.1** If someone in power or authority does something **in** their **mercy**, they do it in a forgiving way. EG *In his mercy, Allah had seen fit to spare Juffure once again.* **3.2** If you **throw** yourself **upon** someone's **mercy**, you beg them to forgive you or to treat you with kindness. **3.3** If you are **at the mercy of** someone or something, you are in a situation where they have complete power over you. EG *This would leave a President at the mercy of any powerful faction in Congress... Now you are at my mercy.* **3.4** If you **are left to the mercies of** someone, or **to the tender mercies of** someone, you are put in a situation where you are helpless and will probably be treated badly or unfairly. EG *I hope you haven't been left to the tender mercies of our tourist industry, Mr Sudbury.*
PHR : USED AS ADV SEN = generously; PHR : VB INFLECTS; PHR : USED AS AN A; PHR : VB INFLECTS

mercy killing, mercy killings. A **mercy killing** is an act of killing someone who is very ill, in order to stop them suffering any more pain.
N COUNT/ UNCOUNT = euthanasia

mere /mɪə/, **merest**. **Mere** usually occurs immediately after any determiner that there is in a noun group. It does not have a comparative form, and the superlative form is used to give emphasis, rather than in comparisons. **Mere** is 1 used to emphasize how unimportant or useless a particular object, action, person, or quality is. EG *They were mere puppets manipulated by men in search of power... He often received an embrace, but more usually a mere handshake... Some experts say that was a mere coincidence... His behaviour was the merest childish exhibitionism.* 2 used when a quality or action that is usually unimportant has a very important or strong effect. EG *They feared the impact the mere presence of a political prisoner would have... A nervous boss can become hysterical at the mere mention of money... The merest suggestion of marital infidelity sends him into a flat spin.* 3 used to emphasize how small a particular amount or quantity is. EG *In Tanganyika, a mere 2 per cent of the population lived in towns... Our office lies a mere hundred yards from Leicester Square... She shook her head the merest fraction.*
ADJ CLASSIF : ATTRIB = simple, common; ADJ CLASSIF : ATTRIB; ADJ CLASSIF : ATTRIB, USU *a* + ADJ = bare

merely /mɪəli¹/. 1 You use **merely 1.1** to emphasize that something or someone is no more important, useful, or valuable than you say they are. EG *This is not genuine. It's merely a reproduction... We accept ideas like this merely because they have never been challenged... 'I killed him,' said Stevens, as casually as if they were merely discussing the weather.* **1.2** to emphasize that a particular amount, quantity, or period of time is very small. EG *January was merely a month away.*
ADV = simply, just; ADV = just

2 You use **not merely** to emphasize how important or surprising something is by comparing it with something else that is less important or surprising. EG *I am not merely anti-London, but anti-Londoners as well... The saints have known God–not merely believed in him... Much of this new industry was not merely in India; it was Indian-owned.*
ADV

meretricious /mɛrɪtrɪʃəs/. Something that is **meretricious** looks attractive but is in fact of little value; a formal word. EG *Advertisements convey an impression, however meretricious, of the importance of the goods being sold.*
ADJ QUALIT = spurious, false

merge /mɜːdʒ/, **merges, merging, merged**. 1 If one thing **merges** with another, or if you **merge** them, they are combined together to make one whole thing. EG *They advised their clients to take over or merge with another company... The former borough of Holborn was merged with St Pancras and Hampstead... The two roads merge here.*
V-ERG : ALSO V OR V+A *(with)* : RECIP ⇑ unite

2 If something **merges** into the darkness, the shadows, etc, it moves gradually to a place where you can no longer see it as a separate object. EG *His bulky form merged into the shadows.*
V+A *(into)* = melt

3 If two colours, sounds, substances, etc **merge**, they join together gradually and without any sudden change. EG *The lights flickering ahead of him merged together... The voices merged with one another... The designs merge and overlap.*
V OR V+A *(together/with)* : RECIP = blend

merger /mɜːdʒə/, **mergers**. A **merger** is the joining together of two separate companies, organizations, etc so that they become one. EG *Almost every day we hear of mergers and take-overs... They had both agreed to move toward a merger between the two organisations... The President called for a merger of the departments of Labour and Commerce.*
N COUNT ⇑ union

meridian /mə²rɪdɪən/, **meridians**. A **meridian** is an imaginary line from the North Pole to the South Pole. Meridians are drawn on maps to help you describe the position of a place.
N COUNT

meringue /mə²ræŋ/, **meringues**. A **meringue** is a very sweet cake that you make by whipping together sugar and the whites of eggs and then baking the mixture.
N COUNT

merit /mɛrɪt/, **merits, meriting, merited**. 1 If something has **merit**, it is good or worthwhile. EG *Have they got sufficient artistic merit?... It is difficult not to see some merit in the philosophy... His work is totally devoid of merit.* ● If something **has the merit of being** a particular quality, it has that quality, in contrast with alternatives which do not have that quality. EG *The first version certainly has the merit of being clear.*
N UNCOUNT ⇑ value = worth; ● PHR : VB INFLECTS ⇑ be

2 The **merits** of something are its advantages or other good points. EG *...the relative merits of cinema and drama as mediums of communication.* ● If you judge something **on** its **merits**, you come to a decision about it based on how good or worthwhile it is, rather than deciding beforehand or taking other factors into account. EG *We endeavour to assess any case on its merits.*
N PLURAL : USU WITH POSS; ● PHR : USED AS AN A

3 If something **merits** a particular action or treatment, it is good enough or important enough to be worth this action or treatment; a fairly formal use. EG *This experiment merits closer examination... It was not important enough to merit a special discussion.*
V+O/-ING : USU V +O = warrant, deserve

meritocracy /mɛrɪtɒkrəsi¹/, **meritocracies**. A **meritocracy** is a society or social system in which people have power or prestige because of their abilities and intelligence, rather than because of their wealth or social status; also used to refer to the people themselves.
N COUNT/ UNCOUNT

meritorious /mɛrɪtɔːrɪəs/. Something that is **meritorious** has qualities which make it good or worthwhile; a formal word. EG *...a lifetime of meritorious service.*
ADJ QUALIT ⇑ valuable = honourable

mermaid /mɜːmeɪd/, **mermaids**. In stories and legends, a **mermaid** is a woman who has a fish's tail instead of legs and who lives in the sea.
N COUNT

merrily /mɛrɪli¹/. If you do something **merrily**, you do it without realizing that there are a lot of problems that you have not thought about. EG *Before you skip merrily on to the next page, pause... ...two young couples merrily swapping mates.* ● See also **merry**.
ADV WITH VB ⇑ happily = blithely

merriment /mɛrɪmə²nt/ is 1 laughter which lasts a long time, because you find something very funny. EG *He roared out his merriment... His explanation produced an outbreak of merriment... She put a hand to her mouth to stifle her merriment.* 2 the behaviour of people who are enjoying themselves in a noisy way, for example by telling jokes or teasing each other. EG *Sounds of merriment came from behind the closed doors... The louder the merriment, the unhappier he became.*
N UNCOUNT ⇑ amusement = mirth; N UNCOUNT ⇑ enjoyment = revelry

merry /mɛri¹/, **merrier, merriest**; a rather old-fashioned word. 1 If you are **merry**, you are **1.1** happy and cheerful. EG *My in-laws, a merry band from Bath, had joined us... They were in a very merry mood.* ▸ used of someone's appearance. EG *He looked at Etta with a merry twinkle... ...a man with a merry pink face.* ◊ **merrily**. EG *Dr Mason laughed merrily.* **1.2** slightly drunk; an informal use. EG *I was beginning to feel a bit merry.*
ADJ QUALIT = jolly, jovial; ▸ = cheery; ◊ ADV WITH VB; ADJ QUALIT : PRED

2 A **merry** sound, sight, etc makes you feel cheerful.
ADJ QUALIT

EG ...*a merry tinkle of sounds.* ◊ **merrily**. EG *The fire was burning merrily.* ◊ ADV WITH VB = cheerfully

3 People say **Merry Christmas** at Christmas time. They mean that they hope that you will have a happy time during the Christmas holidays. The words 'Merry Christmas' are also printed in Christmas cards and you can see them in newspapers, shop windows, etc at Christmas. EG *Merry Christmas, Patrick!... A Merry Christmas to all our readers.* CONVENTION

4 See also **merrily**. ● to **play merry hell**: see **hell**.

merry-go-round, merry-go-rounds. A **merry-go-round** is a large circular platform which rotates and which you often see at funfairs. It has plastic or wooden animals, cars, etc on it which children can pretend to ride or drive when it turns round. EG *The little boy was trying to get off the merry-go-round.* N COUNT = carousel, roundabout

merry-making is the activities of people who are enjoying themselves together by singing, dancing, drinking alcohol, etc. EG *The merry-making continued late into the night.* N UNCOUNT = revelry

mesh /meʃ/, **meshes, meshing, meshed**. **1** **Mesh** is material like a net made from wire, thread, etc. EG ...*wire mesh... Flora fitted her toes into the light stretchable mesh of her tights.* N UNCOUNT = netting

2 If two things **mesh** or **mesh together**, they fit together closely. EG ...*the meshing of various cogs and gears... The orbits of ship and satellite meshed for a second time.* V OR V+A *(together)* = interlock

mesmerize /mezməraɪz/, **mesmerizes, mesmerizing, mesmerized**; also spelled **mesmerise**. If you **are mesmerized** by something, you are so interested in it or so attracted to it that you cannot think about anything else. EG *Blanche was mesmerized by his voice and his way of touching her... She was mesmerised by what was being said about her... The country ceased to be mesmerized by the success of its economic miracle.* ◊ **mesmerizing**. EG ...*the mesmerizing inanity of television.* V+O: USU PASS = fascinate, magnetize; ◊ ADJ QUALIT: ATTRIB

mess /mes/, **messes, messing, messed**. **1** If you say that something is a **mess**, you mean that it is in an untidy state. EG *I know the place is a mess, but make yourself at home... They went back to see how much mess they'd left behind.* N UNCOUNT

2 If you describe a situation, your life, etc as a **mess**, you mean that it is full of trouble, problems, etc. EG *My life is such a mess... It seemed a way out from the whole mess I'd got myself into... Students often make a mess of this type of question.* N COUNT: USU SING = muddle

3 If you say that something is **in a mess**, you mean that it is untidy or disorganized. EG *Her hair was in a terrible mess... The US economy is now in a mess.* PHR: USED AS AN A

4 A **mess** is also **4.1** something that has been spilt or burnt. EG *Keep an old tea towel to mop up any mess... ...a nasty burnt mess in your saucepan.* N COUNT/UNCOUNT **4.2** a room or building in which members of the armed forces eat. EG ...*a bomb attack on an officers' mess.* N COUNT: USU *the*/POSS+N ▸ used of the people who eat in the mess. EG *The whole mess burst out laughing.* ▸ ⇑ diners

5 People say **no messing** to emphasize that they are telling the truth; an informal expression in British English. EG *Honest, that's what he told me; no messing!* PHR = no kidding

mess about; an informal expression. **1** If you **mess about** or **mess around**, **1.1** you spend time doing things without any particular purpose or plan. EG ...*talking, playing, messing about together... Some of the lads had been messing around when they should have been working.* PHRASAL VB: V+ADV = muck about **1.2** you interfere with things in a harmful way; used showing disapproval. EG *She didn't want you coming and messing about with things.* PHRASAL VB: V+ADV, USU+*with* **1.3** you behave in a joking, teasing, or silly way. EG *Stop messing about! I'm trying to tell you something important.* PHRASAL VB: V+ADV = fool around

2 If you **mess** someone **about** or **mess** them **around**, you treat them badly, for example by not being honest with them, or by continually changing plans which affect them. EG *You've been messing me about all summer, and I'm fed up with it.* PHRASAL VB: ORDER V+O+ADV

mess up; an informal expression. **1** If you **mess up** something that has been carefully made or done, you spoil it. EG *That will mess up the whole analysis.* ● See also **mess-up**. PHRASAL VB: V+O+ADV = cock up

2 If you **mess up** a place, for example a room, you make it untidy or dirty. EG *I was used to him messing up the kitchen.* PHRASAL VB: V+O+ADV

mess with. If you **mess with** something dangerous or harmful, you become involved with it; an informal American expression. EG *We don't mess with grass or heroin or any of that stuff.* PHRASAL VB: V+PREP, HAS PASS

message /mesɪdʒ/, **messages**. **1** A **message** is **1.1** a request, piece of information, etc that you send to someone or leave somewhere for them when you cannot speak to them directly. EG *Oh, there was a message. Professor Marvin rang. He'd like to meet you on Tuesday... Tom squinted at the message. He recognized the handwriting... The pilot's radio caught a message that a ship was lost in the fog.* N COUNT ⇑ communication **1.2** an idea that someone tries to communicate to a lot of people in a series of speeches, articles, etc over a period of time. EG *There was nothing ambiguous in the message thumped out in his newspaper editorials... ...the message of black liberation... ...the Christian message of grace.* N SING WITH DET = tidings, concept

2 The **message** of a book, play, film, etc is a general statement that the author, director, etc is trying to express through it. EG *The play's reassuring message is that in the end good and right always triumph.* N COUNT ⇑ meaning = moral

3 If you say that someone **has got the message**, you mean that they have understood what you have been trying to tell them; an informal expression. EG *If we keep complaining, hospitals, doctors and nurses will eventually get the message.* PHR: VB INFLECTS ⇑ comprehend = catch on

messenger /mesɪndʒə/, **messengers**. A **messenger** takes a message to someone, or takes messages regularly as their job. EG *By the time the messenger reached him, the damage had been done... I sent it to him by messenger and within minutes I was called to his room.* N COUNT, OR *by*+N = courier

messenger boy, messenger boys. A **messenger boy** is **1** a boy who is employed to take messages to people. EG *We have plenty of messenger boys.* N COUNT **2** anyone whose work seems to consist of nothing more than taking messages between people; used showing disapproval. EG *We're nothing but messenger-boys... You're just acting as a messenger boy for David.* N COUNT = errand boy

messiah /mɪˈsaɪə/, **messiahs**. **1** The **Messiah** is, **1.1** for Jews, the King of the Jews, who will be sent to them by God. EG ...*the coming of the Messiah.* N PROPER **1.2** for Christians, Jesus Christ. EG ...*the birth of the Messiah.* N PROPER = Christ

2 A **messiah** is any person who promises to rescue or succeeds in rescuing people from a very difficult or dangerous situation. EG *In our history we have been plagued with false messiahs.* N COUNT = prophet

messianic /mesiænɪk/; a formal word. **Messianic** means **1** relating to the belief that a divine being has been born, or will be born, who will change the world. EG ...*messianic cults.* ADJ CLASSIF: ATTRIB **2** relating to the belief that there will be a complete change in the social order in a country or in the world. EG *Social democracy is not a messianic creed that promises to change the world... ...the messianic dream of world revolution.* ADJ CLASSIF: ATTRIB

messily /mesɪli[1]/. See **messy**.

Messrs /mesəz/. **1** is used before the names of two or more people as part of the name of a business. EG *Messrs Brant and Prout are dealers in hats.* N IN TITLES: USU N+N PROPER+*and*+N PROPER **2** is the plural of 'Mr'.

mess-up, mess-ups. A **mess-up** is a situation in which something has been done very badly or wrongly; an informal word. EG *There was some mess-up over the availability of dates... What did you think of the mess-up he made of his commentary?* N COUNT = cock-up

messy /mesi[1]/, **messier, messiest**. **1** **Messy** activities make people or a place dirty or untidy. EG *I hate picnics; they're messy... It is a messy and difficult business doing dairy work.* ADJ QUALIT = mucky, chaotic ▸ used of people and groups. EG *Sometimes I'm neat, sometimes I'm messy... You have the messiest friends in the whole world.* ▸ = sloppy ◊ **messily**. EG *Ten minutes into the film somebody is messily and bloodily blown up.* ◊ ADV WITH VB = untidily

2 Something that is **messy** is unpleasant to see or touch because it is dirty or sticky. EG ...*messy bits of food.* ADJ QUALIT = mucky

3 A **messy** place is dirty or untidy. EG *I disliked the messy farmyard.* ADJ QUALIT = mucky

4 A **messy** situation is confused or complicated, and therefore unsatisfactory. EG *I hate the whole messy business... It was developing into a very messy situation... ...a messy clandestine love affair.* ADJ QUALIT = awkward, sticky

met /met/ is **1** the past tense and past participle of 'meet'. **2** an abbreviation for 'meteorological'. EG ...*the Met Office... Met reports indicate severe frosts.*

metabolic /mɛtəbɒlɪk/ means relating to a person's or animal's metabolism; a technical term. EG *...the gradual slowing down of metabolic processes... ...basic metabolic needs.* ADJ CLASSIF: ATTRIB

metabolism /mɪ²tæbəlɪzə⁰m/, **metabolisms.** Your **metabolism** is the way that chemical processes in your body cause food to be used in an efficient way, for example to make new cells and to give you energy; a technical term. EG *Some people's metabolism is more efficient than others... Their rate of metabolism may slow down.* N UNCOUNT/COUNT

metal /mɛtə⁰l/, **metals.** A **metal** is a hard substance such as iron, steel, copper, or lead. Metals are used for making tools, coins, machinery, wire, etc. There are many kinds of metal. EG *I think brass is the best metal of all... This tool will cut metals like copper and silver.* ▸ used as an adjective. EG *Metal dustbins make a noise and get bent.* ● See also **heavy metal.** N MASS ▸ ADJ CLASSIF

metalled /mɛtə⁰ld/. A **metalled** road has a level surface made of many small pieces of stone; a technical term. EG *A metalled road runs about a third of the way... ...metalled highways.* ADJ CLASSIF ⇑ surfaced

metallic /mɪ²tælɪk/. **1** A **metallic** click, thud, tinkle, etc sounds like one piece of metal hitting another. EG *I heard the metallic click of a door handle... ...a distant metallic clunk from across the valley.* ADJ QUALIT: USU ATTRIB ⇑ hard

2 A **metallic** voice has a harsh unpleasant sound. EG *...singing in strange, metallic voices.* ADJ QUALIT: USU ATTRIB

3 Metallic eyes, hair, etc seem to shine like metal. EG *...your blue metallic eyes... Her hair was a metallic gold... ...the snow monkey with its metallic golden coat.* ADJ CLASSIF: USU ATTRIB ⇑ shining

4 Something that has a **metallic** finish has been coated with a substance in order to make it look like shiny metal. EG *Metallic finish is standard on this model.* ▸ used of objects that have been treated like this. EG *I put on the green metallic helmet.* ADJ CLASSIF: USU ATTRIB ⇑ shining

5 Something that tastes **metallic** has a bitter unpleasant taste. EG *...a metallic taste like blood in her mouth.* ADJ QUALIT = sour

6 Metallic also means consisting wholly or partly of metal. EG *Under these conditions hydrogen liquefies and becomes metallic... ...metallic ores.* ADJ CLASSIF

metallurgist /mɛtæləd͡ʒɪst/, **metallurgists.** A **metallurgist** is an expert in metallurgy. N COUNT ⇑ chemist

metallurgy /mɛtæləd͡ʒi¹/ is the scientific study of the properties and uses of metals. EG *...a young assistant professor in metallurgy.* N UNCOUNT ⇑ chemistry

metalwork /mɛtə⁰lwɜːk/. **1 Metalwork** is the activity of making objects out of metal in a skilful way. EG *She's good at woodwork, metalwork, and painting.* N UNCOUNT ⇑ craft

2 The **metalwork** is the metal part of something. EG *The police had discovered round holes in the metalwork.* N UNCOUNT: USU the+N

metamorphose /mɛtəmɔːfəuz/, **metamorphoses, metamorphosing, metamorphosed.** When someone or something **metamorphoses** or is **metamorphosed**, they change to something completely different; a formal word. EG *The headstrong girl metamorphoses into the loving wife and mother... Young girls are metamorphosed into stunning stars of the screen.* V-ERG: IF+PREP THEN *into* ⇑ transform = transfigure

metamorphosis /mɛtəmɔːfəsɪs/, **metamorphoses** /-iːz/. A **metamorphosis** is an event or process in which someone or something changes to something completely different. EG *When you get money you go through a metamorphosis... Science fiction may be undergoing a metamorphosis.* N COUNT/UNCOUNT ⇑ transformation

metaphor /mɛtəfə⁸/, **metaphors. 1** A **metaphor** is **1.1** an imaginative way of describing something by referring to something else which has the qualities that you are trying to express. For example, if you want to say that someone is very shy and timid, you might say that they are a mouse. EG *He is famous for his extensive use of golfing metaphors.* **1.2** something that you say, write, draw, etc that does not have its ordinary meaning but that is meant to be a symbol of something else that you are trying to express. EG *She sees the play as a metaphor for the prisons we create for ourselves... Central to Picasso's work was the metaphor of the bullfight.* N COUNT/UNCOUNT; N COUNT/UNCOUNT ⇑ image

2 If you **mix your metaphors**, you say something that consists of parts of two well-known phrases or sayings. People do this accidentally, or sometimes deliberately as a joke. EG *It's a case of shutting the stable door after the cat's out of the bag, if I may mix my metaphors... We have to make use of any gift horses that may come to hand-to use a slightly mixed metaphor.* PHR: VB INFLECTS

metaphorical /mɛtəfɒrɪkə⁰l/. You use the word **metaphorical** to indicate that you are not using words with their ordinary meaning, but are trying to describe a situation, feeling, etc by using images or symbols. EG *I had sprouted metaphorical wings... These meetings are ideal for the newcomer dipping a metaphorical toe in the water.* ◇ **metaphorically.** EG *I was literally as well as metaphorically wrapped in cotton wool... I was speaking metaphorically.* ADJ CLASSIF ⇑ symbolic ≠ literal, actual; ◇ ADV WITH VB ≠ literally

metaphysical /mɛtəfɪzɪkə⁰l/ means relating to theories about what exists and how we know that it exists. EG *...the metaphysical and religious ideas in his writings... ...the metaphysical truths which lay at the root of human suffering.* ADJ CLASSIF ⇑ philosophical

metaphysics /mɛtəfɪzɪks/ is the part of philosophy which is concerned with theories about what exists and how we know that it exists. EG *At the time I was not at all interested in metaphysics... ...the problem of demarcating science from metaphysics.* N UNCOUNT

mete /miːt/, **metes, meting, meted.** If you **mete out** a particular punishment, you officially order that someone shall be punished that way; a formal expression. EG *This punishment was meted out to me because of my political beliefs... Magistrates meted out fines of as much as £1,000.* PHRASAL VB: V+ADV, IF+PREP THEN *to* ⇑ give = dole out

meteor /miːtɪə⁸/, **meteors.** A **meteor** is a piece of rock or metal that burns very brightly when it enters the earth's atmosphere from space. EG *On a clear night scores of meteors streak the sky.* N COUNT

meteoric /miːtɪɒrɪk/. **1** A **meteoric** rise to power, fame, etc happens very quickly. EG *He enjoyed a meteoric rise to power in Callaghan's government... Until his meteoric rise to fame, he had never been outside the Congo.* ADJ CLASSIF ⇑ fast = lightening

2 If someone's career is **meteoric**, it is very successful very quickly. EG *His ecclesiastical career was meteoric.* ADJ CLASSIF = spectacular

3 Meteoric also means relating to meteors; a technical term. EG *...meteoric dust... ...meteoric impacts.* ADJ CLASSIF: ATTRIB

meteorite /miːtɪəraɪt/, **meteorites.** A **meteorite** is a large piece of rock or metal from space that has landed on the earth. EG *Scientists didn't realize, until 150 years ago, that meteorites come from space... ...an ancient meteorite crater.* N COUNT

meteorology /miːtɪərɒləd͡ʒi¹/ is the study of the processes in the earth's atmosphere that cause weather conditions. Meteorology is used especially for giving weather forecasts. EG *The areas most likely to benefit are medical science and meteorology.* ◇ **meteorological** /miːtɪərəlɒd͡ʒɪkə⁰l/. EG *...the Meteorological Office... Meteorological conditions were reasonably good.* ◇ **meteorologist.** EG *...the latest forecasts of the meteorologists.* N UNCOUNT ⇑ science; ◇ ADJ CLASSIF: ATTRIB; ◇ N COUNT = weather forecaster

meter /miːtə/, **meters, metering, metered. 1** A **meter** is **1.1** a device that measures and records something such as the amount of gas or electricity that you have used or the amount of money that you must pay for a taxi ride. EG *He went into the hall and examined the meter... Someone comes to read the gas and electricity meters... ...a fleet of taxis, each one with a broken meter.* **1.2** a parking meter. EG *I decided to park at a meter, and walk around for a while.* N COUNT; N COUNT

2 To **meter** something such as gas or electricity means to measure and record how much of it people use by means of meters in their houses. EG *Nuclear power would be 'too cheap to meter'... ...his metered domestic electricity supply.* V+O

3 See also **metre.**

methane /miːθeɪn/ is a colourless gas that has no smell. Natural gas consists mostly of methane. EG *Methane and carbon-dioxide are produced.* N UNCOUNT

method /mɛθəd/, **methods.** A **method** is a particular way of doing something. EG *...a change in the method of electing the party's leader... ...a special method for teaching languages... They made whisky by the old method... No one knows why they use this method.* N COUNT/UNCOUNT: USU COUNT = technique, system

methodical /mɪ²θɒdɪkə⁰l/. **Methodical** behaviour is behaviour in which you do something very carefully and in a particular order. EG *...the methodical manner in which I have always prided myself... ...the methodical exploitation of human beings.* ▸ used of people. EG *John was a methodical man.* ADJ QUALIT ⇑ careful = systematic; ▸ = orderly

◊ **methodically**. EG *Carefully and methodically Robin began his briefing... Methodically he listed in his mind the problems.* ◊ ADV = systematically

Methodism /mɛθədɪzəᵒm/ is the beliefs and practices of Methodists. EG *The programme is devoted to the history of Methodism.* N UNCOUNT

Methodist /mɛθədɪst/, **Methodists**. 1 **Methodists** are Christians who follow the teachings of John Wesley and who have their own branch of the Christian church and their own kind of worship. EG *His family were strict Methodists.* N COUNT 2 **Methodist** means relating to Methodists, their church, and their beliefs. EG *...the Methodist church... ...his local Methodist chapel... ...methodist preachers.* ADJ CLASSIF

methodology /mɛθədɒlədʒi¹/, **methodologies**. A **methodology** is a system of methods and principles for doing something, for example for teaching or for carrying out research; a formal or technical word. EG *...practical teaching methodology... ...a postgraduate course in research methodology... That's a difference of methodology rather than principle.* N COUNT/UNCOUNT

meths /mɛθs/ is methylated spirits; an informal word. EG *Use a spot of meths by itself on a piece of cotton wool... ...meths drinkers.* N UNCOUNT

methylated spirit /mɛθə¹leɪtɪ²d spɪrɪts/, **methylated spirits**. **Methylated spirits** or **methylated spirit** is a liquid made from alcohol and other chemicals. It is used for removing stains and as a fuel in small lamps and heaters. It is very dangerous to drink, but is sometimes drunk by people who are alcoholic. EG *We set off to clean up the house, with mops and methylated spirits... Try a little methylated spirit rubbed on with a soft cloth... ...a methylated spirit lamp for keeping toast hot.* N UNCOUNT = meths

meticulous /mɪ²tɪkjə⁴ləs/. A **meticulous** person does things very carefully and with great attention to detail. EG *...a meticulous young man... ...the neatest and most meticulous of girls.* ▸ used to describe the way that something is done. EG *He had prepared himself with meticulous care... ...meticulous observations of infants and small children.* ◊ **meticulously**. EG *The arrangements were planned meticulously... ...a pile of meticulously folded newspapers.* ◊ **meticulousness**. EG *...the meticulousness of their work.* ADJ QUALIT ⇑ careful = fastidious ▸ = painstaking ◊ ADV = precisely ◊ N UNCOUNT

metier /mɛtɪeɪ/, **metiers**; also spelled **métier**. Your **metier** is the type of work that you have a natural talent for and do well. EG *This was assuredly not my metier... He's found his metier at last.* N COUNT : USU POSS+N IN SING ⇑ vocation = calling

metre /miːtə/, **metres**; also spelled **meter** in American English. A **metre** is 1 a metric unit of length. It is equal to 100 centimetres in the metric system, or to 39.37 inches in the imperial system. EG *A squirrel was crouching motionless half a metre away... The blue whale grows to over 30 metres long... ...a thousand metre airstrip... It lives in depths of about two or three hundred metres... ...a speed of 3 metres a second.* N COUNT/PART ⇑ measurement 2 the regular and rhythmic arrangement of syllables in poetry; a technical term. N COUNT/UNCOUNT

metric /mɛtrɪk/ means relating to the metric system. EG *...the new metric sizes for clothes and shoes.* ADJ CLASSIF ⇑ decimal

metrication /mɛtrɪkeɪʃəᵒn/ is the process of changing from measuring things in imperial units to measuring them in metric units. N UNCOUNT

metric system. The **metric system** is the system of measurement that uses metres, centimetres, grammes, litres, etc. N SING : the+N

metric ton, metric tons. A **metric ton** is 1,000 kilograms. EG *...14,000 metric tons of potatoes.* N COUNT = tonne

metro /mɛtrəʊ/, **metros**. The **metro** or **Metro** is the underground railway system in some cities, for example in Paris. EG *I travelled south on the Metro... ...the Moscow metro system.* N COUNT : USU the+N = subway

metronome /mɛtrənəʊm/, **metronomes**. A **metronome** is a device which is used by people playing music to indicate the speed of a piece of music. It has an arm which swings from side to side making a clicking sound, and which can be adjusted to make the sound at different speeds. EG *The metronome ticked on slowly... ...the composer's metronome markings.* N COUNT ⇑ timer

metropolis /mɪ²trɒpəlɪs/, **metropolises**. A **metropolis** is a large city that is the main city in a country or region. EG *It took him sixteen days to reach the metropolis.* N COUNT

metropolitan /mɛtrəpɒlɪtəᵒn/, **metropolitans**. 1 **Metropolitan** means 1.1 belonging to or typical of a large busy city. EG *I could not hope to enjoy the metropolitan delights of cinemas and theatres... ...the Metropolitan Opera House.* ADJ CLASSIF : ATTRIB 1.2 relating to a country, rather than to its colonies; a technical term. EG *...the seventeen police districts of metropolitan France.* ADJ CLASSIF : ATTRIB

2 A **metropolitan** is an important priest in the Orthodox and Catholic Churches. He has authority over other priests and is in charge of a particular area. EG *...Metropolitan Nikodim.* N COUNT : ALSO IN TITLES

Metropolitan Police. The **Metropolitan Police** is the part of the British police force that works in London. EG *...the Commissioner of the Metropolitan Police.* N PLURAL : the+N

mettle /mɛtəᵒl/. 1 If you are **on** your **mettle**, you are ready to do something as well as you can, because you know that you are being tested or challenged. EG *I felt I was on my mettle. It was my first big chance in America... The new speed restrictions will put a keen driver on his mettle.* PHR : USED AS AN A ⇑ alert = on your toes

2 If you **show** your **mettle** or you **prove** your **mettle**, you show that you are capable of doing something well. EG *He had no chance to show his mettle.* PHR : VB INFLECTS = prove yourself

mew /mjuː/, **mews, mewing, mewed**. **Mews** is both the singular and plural of the noun in paragraph 2.

1 When a cat **mews**, it makes a soft high-pitched noise. EG *The cat was mewing for its supper.* ▸ used as a noun. EG *...a high-pitched mew.* V ▸ N COUNT

2 A **mews** is a yard or street surrounded by houses that were originally built as stables. EG *...a rear exit into a quiet mews.* ▸ used of the houses. EG *You can meander among mews and terraces... ...a tiny mews flat... ...14 Fishacre Mews.* N COUNT ▸ N COUNT : ALSO IN NAMES AFTER N ⇑ residences

Mexican /mɛksɪkən/, **Mexicans**. 1 Something that is **Mexican** belongs or relates to Mexico or to its people. EG *...a town on the Mexican border.* ADJ CLASSIF

2 A **Mexican** is a person who comes from Mexico. EG *We have always dealt honourably with Mexicans.* N COUNT

mezzanine /mɛzəniːn, mɛtsəniːn/, **mezzanines**. A **mezzanine** is a small floor which is built between two stories in a building, for example between the ground floor and the first floor. EG *...his office on the executive mezzanine.* N COUNT

mezzo /mɛtsəʊ/, **mezzos**. **Mezzo** means the same as mezzo-soprano; an informal word. EG *I limit myself to music that's for contralto or mezzo.* N COUNT/UNCOUNT

mezzo-soprano /mɛtsəʊ səprɑːnəʊ/, **mezzo-sopranos**. A **mezzo-soprano** is a female singer who sings with a higher range than a contralto but a lower range than a soprano. EG *She was a large mezzo-soprano who'd once had a good voice.* ▸ used of a woman's singing or speaking voice. EG *Sophia spoke in an unexpectedly passionate mezzo-soprano.* N COUNT ▸ N UNCOUNT

mg is a written abbreviation for 'milligrams'. EG *It contained 65mg of Vitamin C.*

Mgr (pronounced as 'Monsignor') is a written abbreviation for 'Monsignor'; used before the name of the priest.

MHz is a written abbreviation for 'megahertz'.

MI5 /ɛm aɪ faɪv/ is a British government organization which is concerned with the security of the United Kingdom; an abbreviation for 'Military Intelligence Section 5'. EG *Lady Hargreaves had been vetted by MI5.* N PROPER

MI6 /ɛm aɪ sɪks/ is a British government organization which tries to obtain secret information about the political and military affairs of other countries; an abbreviation for 'Military Intelligence Section 6'. EG *...the daily report from MI6.* N PROPER

miaow /mi¹aʊ/, **miaows, miaowing, miaowed**. A **miaow** is the short high-pitched sound that a cat makes. EG *...the miaow of a cat.* ▸ used as a verb. EG *I could hear Blackie miaowing outside.* N COUNT = mew ▸ V

miasma /mɪ⁵æzmə/, **miasmas**. A **miasma** is a very unpleasant smell in the air all around you; a literary word. EG *It covered the entire ranch in a foul miasma... ...a miasma of mothballs.* N COUNT/UNCOUNT = stench, odour

mica /maɪkə/ is a hard mineral which is found as small flat crystals in rocks. It has a great resistance to heat and electricity. EG *...the flash of mica in gray rock.* N UNCOUNT

mice /maɪs/ is the plural of **mouse**.

mickey /mɪki¹/. If you **take the mickey** out of someone, you make fun of them, either in a friendly or an unkind way; an informal expression. EG *Mustn't take the mickey out of George... You're always taking the mickey.* PHR : VB INFLECTS, IF+PREP THEN *out of* ⇑ tease

micro /maɪkrəʊ/, **micros**. A **micro** is a small computer, often used for word processing. EG *...the generation of computers before the micros.* N COUNT = micro-computer

micro- is used to form nouns referring to something that is a very small example of a particular type of thing. EG *...computer→microcomputer... ...processor→microprocessor... ...organism→micro-organism.* PREFIX

microbe /maɪkrəʊb/, **microbes**. A **microbe** is a very small living thing, which you can only see if you use a microscope. EG *...parasites, microbes and fungi... This orchid needs particular soil microbes.* N COUNT ⇑ organism

microbiology /maɪkrə⁶baɪɒlədʒi¹/ is the branch of biology which deals with the study of micro-organisms and their effects on people. EG *...courses in microbiology... ...the Centre for Applied Microbiology.* ◊ **microbiological** /maɪkrə⁶baɪə⁶lɒdʒɪkə⁶l/. EG *...microbiological research.* ◊ **microbiologist**. EG *...a leading microbiologist.* N UNCOUNT ⇑ science ◊ ADJ CLASSIF ◊ N COUNT ⇑ scientist

microchip /maɪkrə⁶tʃɪp/, **microchips**. A **microchip** is a very small piece of silicon inside a computer. It has electronic circuits on it and can hold large quantities of information or perform mathematical or logical operations; a technical term. EG *Large books, perhaps even sets of books, can be put on a single microchip.* N COUNT = chip

micro-computer, micro-computers. A **micro-computer** is the same as a micro. EG *...personal micro-computers.* N COUNT

microcosm /maɪkrə⁶kɒzə⁰m/, **microcosms**. A **microcosm** is a place, a society, or an activity that has all the main features of a much larger place, society, or activity, so that it seems like a miniature version of it. EG *Bristol was a microcosm of urban England in the 1970s... To me it seemed a microcosm of what the whole country could become.* N COUNT : IF+ PREP THEN *of* ⇑ representation

microelectronic /maɪkrə⁶ɛlektrɒnɪk/, **microelectronics**. 1 **Microelectronics** is the branch of electronics that deals with miniature electronic circuits, as used in computers. EG *...current developments in microelectronics.* N UNCOUNT

2 **Microelectronic** means relating to miniature electronic circuits. EG *...the manufacture of microelectronic components and equipment.* ADJ CLASSIF : ATTRIB

microfiche /maɪkrə⁶fiːʃ/, **microfiches**. A **microfiche** is a small sheet of film on which writing or other information is stored. The information is greatly reduced in size, and you read it by putting the microfiche into a machine which magnifies it. EG *The Periodicals Catalogue is now on microfiche.* N COUNT/ UNCOUNT

microfilm /maɪkrə⁶fɪlm/, **microfilms, microfilming, microfilmed**. 1 **Microfilm** is film that is used for photographing information so that it can be stored. The information is greatly reduced in size, and you read it by putting the film into a machine which magnifies it. EG *The library has a lot of Russian newspapers on microfilm... ...a microfilm reader.* N UNCOUNT/ COUNT

2 If you **microfilm** maps, documents, etc, you photograph them using a microfilm. EG *They waited while the plans were microfilmed... ...900,000 rolls of microfilmed documents.* V+O

micro-organism /maɪkrəʊ ɔːgənɪzə⁰m/, **micro-organisms**; also spelled as one word. A **micro-organism** is a microbe; a technical word. EG *...bacteria, viruses, and other microorganisms.* N COUNT

microphone /maɪkrə⁶fəʊn/, **microphones**. A **microphone** is the device that you speak into when you record or amplify your voice. A microphone converts sounds into electrical energy. EG *He was talking into a microphone... ...hidden microphones.* N COUNT

microprocessor /maɪkrə⁶prəʊsɛsə/, **microprocessors**. A **microprocessor** is the same as a micro. EG *...a typewriter with a microprocessor built into it.* N COUNT = micro

microscope /maɪkrə⁶skəʊp/, **microscopes**. A **microscope** is an instrument which magnifies very small objects so that you can look at them and study them. EG *A drop of water from a pond, viewed through a microscope, is full of tiny organisms... They are carefully prepared and examined under the microscope.* N COUNT

microscopic /maɪkrə⁶skɒpɪk/. 1 Something that is **microscopic** is 1.1 so small that you can only see it through a microscope. EG *...microscopic creatures.* ADJ CLASSIF

1.2 extremely small, when compared to other things of the same kind. EG *No-one could decipher my microscopic script... ...leaders of microscopic religious sects.* ◊ **microscopically**. EG *...a microscopically small Bolshevik party.* ADJ CLASSIF : USU ATTRIB ◊ ADV+ADJ/ ADV

2 A **microscopic** examination of something is very thorough and detailed. EG *...a microscopic study of medieval customs.* ◊ **microscopically**. EG *Was that examined microscopically?* ADJ CLASSIF : USU ATTRIB ◊ ADV = minutely

microsecond /maɪkrəʊsɛkənd/, **microseconds**. A **microsecond** is one-millionth of a second. EG *The earth was slowing down by ten to fifteen microseconds a day.* N COUNT ⇑ period

microwave /maɪkrə⁶weɪv/, **microwaves**. 1 A **microwave** cooker or oven is a cooker or oven which cooks food very quickly by electromagnetic radiation rather than by heat. EG *Mum has just won a microwave cooker... A bell rang on the microwave oven.* ADJ CLASSIF : ATTRIB

2 A **microwave** is a microwave cooker or oven. EG *I haven't got a microwave.* N COUNT

mid- is 1 used to form nouns or expressions that refer to the middle part of a particular period of time. EG *...afternoon→mid-afternoon... ...the nineteen fifties→the mid nineteen fifties.* 2 used to form nouns or adjectives that refer to the middle part of a particular place. EG *...Wales→mid-Wales... ...ocean→mid-ocean.* PREFIX PREFIX

mid-air. If something happens in **mid-air**, it happens in the air, rather than on the ground. EG *The bird turned in mid-air and darted away... ...a mid-air collision in which hundreds of people died.* N UNCOUNT : USU *in*+N, OR N BEFORE N

midday /mɪddeɪ/ is 1 twelve o'clock in the middle of the day. EG *Just before midday the telephone rang... The Prime Minister would speak to the nation on television and radio at midday.* 2 the middle part of the day, from late morning to early afternoon. EG *He was browned by the midday heat of Burma.* N UNCOUNT : USU PREP+N = noon N UNCOUNT : USU BEFORE N = noonday

middle /mɪdə⁶l/, **middles**. 1 The **middle** of a two-dimensional shape or area is the part of it that is furthest from all its sides, edges, or boundaries. EG *...a luminous green circle with a cross in the middle... In the middle of the lawn was a great cedar tree... Foster was standing in the middle of the room... ...a huge hall in the middle of the Staffordshire countryside.* • **the middle of nowhere**: see **nowhere**. N COUNT : USU N IN SING+SUPP = centre

2 The **middle** of a line or row is the part of it that is furthest from its two ends. EG *He sat down in the middle of the front row.* N COUNT : USU N IN SING+SUPP = centre

3 The **middle** object or person in a row of objects or people is the one that has an equal number of objects or people on each side. EG *She touched the middle button of her black leather coat... The statue stands in front of the middle tree.* ADJ CLASSIF : ATTRIB = central

4 The **middle** of a road, path, river, etc is the part of it that is furthest from its sides, edges, or banks. EG *...white lines painted along the middle of the highway.* N COUNT : USU N IN SING+SUPP = centre

5 The **middle** of a three-dimensional object, especially one shaped like a ball, is the inside part of it. EG *...conditions in the middle of neutron stars.* N COUNT : USU N IN SING+SUPP = core

6 Your **middle** is the part of your body around your stomach; an informal use. EG *He lay in his bunk, with both forearms wrapped round his middle... He dug both his fists into the soldier's middle.* N COUNT : USU POSS+N = midriff

7 The **middle** of an event or period of time is the part that comes after the first part and before the last part. EG *We landed at Canton in the middle of a torrential storm... ...the middle of the day... ...the middle of December... ... the middle of the 1960s.* ▸ used as an adjective. EG *...the middle fortnight of July... He was in his middle thirties.* N SING : *the*+N+*of* ▸ ADJ CLASSIF : ATTRIB

8 If you are **in the middle of** doing something, you are busy doing it and do not want to be interrupted. EG *I'm in the middle of washing... He's in the middle of planning his departmental budget.* PHR+-ING

9 The **middle** child in a family has equal numbers of younger and older brothers and sisters. EG *She was the middle child of the three... ...Martin, the middle son, aged twelve.* ADJ CLASSIF : ATTRIB

10 The **middle** course, way, etc is a moderate course of action that lies between two opposite and extreme courses; used showing approval. EG *Between Fascism or revolution there is a middle course... It was easy to mock his views for he knew no middle way.* ADJ CLASSIF : ATTRIB ≠ extreme

11 If you divide or split something **down the middle**, you divide or split it into two equal halves or groups. EG *I believe in dividing all tasks equally down the middle... The organisation split down the middle over the issue.* PHR : USED AS AN A ⇑ apart = in half

middle age, middle ages. 1 **Middle age** is the period in your life when you are no longer young but have not yet become old. Middle age is usually considered to take place between the ages of 40 and 60. EG *...a grave, courteous man in late middle age... He was growing stout with middle age.* N UNCOUNT

2 **Middle-age spread** is the fat that appears around many people's waists when they become middle-aged; an informal expression. EG *Virginia was showing signs of middle-age spread.* PHR : USED AS O/C/S = spare tyre

3 The **Middle Ages** were, in European history, the period between about 1000 AD and 1400 AD. EG *...the cities of Europe in the Middle Ages.* N PLURAL : *the*+N ⇑ era

middle-aged. 1 Someone who is **middle-aged** is neither young nor old. People between the ages of 40 and 60 are usually considered to be middle-aged. EG *She was fat and middle-aged... ... a middle-aged businessman.* ▸ used as a noun. EG *What about the middle aged?* ADJ CLASSIF = ageing ▸ N PLURAL : *the*+N

2 **Middle-aged** is used to describe attitudes and behaviour that are considered to be typical of a middle-aged person, for example by being conventional or old-fashioned; used showing disapproval. EG *...young people with comfortable jobs and a middle-aged outlook.* ADJ QUALIT = stuffy

middlebrow /mɪdəˀlbraʊ/, **middlebrows;** also spelled with a hyphen. 1 A **middlebrow** book, television programme, etc is interesting and enjoyable without requiring much thought. EG *They were conveniently known as middle-brow classics.* ADJ QUALIT ⇑ ordinary ≠ highbrow, lowbrow

2 A **middlebrow** is someone who reads middlebrow books, watches middlebrow television programmes, etc. EG *British television is regarded by middlebrows as the best in the world... They lost their licences if they displeased middlebrow committees.* N COUNT

middle class, middle classes. 1 The **middle class** or **middle classes** are the people in a society who are not working class or upper class. Business people, managers, doctors, lawyers, and teachers are usually regarded as middle class. EG *...the children of the middle class... ...the new Indian middle classes.* ▸ used as an adjective, usually spelled with a hyphen. EG *... a middle-class background... Watson's upbringing was comfortably middle-class... ...middle class families.* N COUNT : ALSO SING=PL = bourgeoisie ▸ ADJ CLASSIF = bourgeois

2 People sometimes describe attitudes and values as **middle class** when they think that they are typical of middle class people, for example in regarding possessions as very important; often used showing disapproval. EG *...middle-class consumer values... ...middle class attitudes.* ADJ QUALIT = bourgeois

middle distance. The **middle distance** is the area or space between the foreground and the distance in a view or a painting. EG *He stood at the helm, gazing into the middle distance... The Bay filled the middle distance, stretching out of sight on both sides.* N SING : *the*+N

Middle East. The **Middle East** is a part of Asia. It includes Iran and all the countries in Asia that are to the west and south-west of Iran. EG *...the wars in the Middle East... ...the 1974 Middle East conflict.* N PROPER : *the*+N

Middle Eastern means relating to the Middle East. EG *...Middle Eastern oil.* ADJ CLASSIF : ATTRIB

middleman /mɪdəˀlmæn/, **middlemen.** A **middleman** is someone who buys things from the people who produce them and sells them to the people who want to buy them. EG *...the profiteering of the middleman... Let's cut out the middleman.* N COUNT ⇑ intermediary = distributor

middle name, middle names. A person's **middle name** is a name that they have which comes between their first name and their surname. EG *I thought Penrose was his middle name.* N COUNT ⇑ forename

middle-of-the-road opinions, policies, etc are moderate, and usually between two political extremes. EG *...middle-of-the-road views... The party tries to stick to middle-of-the-road policies.* ▸ used of politicians, governments, etc. EG *I'd say we were middle-of-the-road... ...middle-of-the-road Labour MPs.* ADJ QUALIT ≠ extreme, controversial ▸ ≠ radical

middle school, middle schools. A **middle school** is, in Britain, a state school that children go to between the ages of 8 or 9 and 12 or 13. EG *They go from a first school to a middle school... ...Preston Middle School... ...exams taken at middle-school level.* N COUNT, OR *at/in/to*+N

Middle West. The **Middle West** is the central part of the United States of America. EG *...my home town in the Middle West.* N PROPER : *the*+N = Midwest

middling /mɪdlɪŋ/ is used to describe something which is not very good or very bad, but somewhere in the middle. EG *...a woman of middling intellectual attainments.* ADJ CLASSIF : USU ATTRIB = average, medium, mediocre

midge /mɪdʒ/, **midges.** **Midges** are very small insects which fly in groups, appearing to dance up and down in the air. Some kinds of midges bite human beings. N COUNT ⇑ insect = gnat

midget /mɪdʒɪt/, **midgets.** 1 A **midget** is a person who is very short, especially one who works in a circus as a clown. N COUNT = dwarf

2 **Midget** is used to describe something which is very small. EG *...a midget radio.* ADJ CLASSIF : ATTRIB

Midlands /mɪdləndz/. The **Midlands** is the region or area in the central part of a country, in particular the central part of England. EG *...industry in the Midlands... The play is set in a small Midlands village.* N PROPER : *the*+N, VB CAN BE SING OR PL

midnight /mɪdnaɪt/. 1 **Midnight** is twelve o'clock in the middle of the night. EG *It was nearly midnight... They are perfectly willing to wait until 11 or even midnight.* N UNCOUNT : USU PREP+N ≠ noon, midday

2 **Midnight** is used to describe something which happens or appears at midnight or in the middle of the night. EG *We were always having midnight parties on beaches.* N BEFORE N ⇑ night-time

3 If someone **is burning the midnight oil,** they are staying up very late in order to study or do some other work. PHR : VB INFLECTS

midpoint /mɪdpɔɪnt/, **midpoints.** 1 The **midpoint** of something long such as a line is the point on it that is the same distance from both ends. EG *At the midpoint of the bridge he stopped.* N COUNT/UNCOUNT ⇑ point = middle

2 The **midpoint** of an event is the time halfway between the beginning and the end of it. N COUNT, OR *at*+N

midriff /mɪdrɪf/, **midriffs.** Your **midriff** is the middle part of your body, between your waist and your chest. EG *He was up to his midriff in hot water.* N COUNT : USU POSS+N

midst /mɪdst/. 1 If you are **in the midst of** a group of people or things, you are surrounded by them or among them. EG *Sudhir found him in the midst of a group of his usual friends.* PREP = amidst

2 **In the midst of** is used to indicate what is taking place or being done when something else happens or at a particular point in time. EG *In the midst of this humiliating scandal, news arrived of Mr Hodge's resignation... Brody was in the midst of swallowing a bite of egg salad sandwich.* PREP = during

3 You say that someone is **in** your **midst** or **in** your **very midst** when you are drawing attention to the fact that they are in your group; a formal expression. EG *We have in our midst two Nobel prize-winners.* PHR : USED AS AN A ⇑ with

midstream /mɪdstriːm/. 1 Someone or something that is in **midstream** is in the middle of a river, where the current is strongest. EG *He unlocked the boat and they were soon in midstream.* N UNCOUNT : USU *in*+N = centre

2 If someone who has been speaking for a while stops or pauses **in midstream,** they stop speaking, often before continuing. EG *Cogg stopped in midstream to look round.* PHR : USED AS AN A

midsummer /mɪdsʌmə/ is the period in the middle of the summer. EG *The pruning should be done about midsummer... ...a hot midsummer day in July.* N UNCOUNT

Midsummer Day or **Midsummer's Day** is the 24th of June. N PROPER

midway /mɪdweɪ/ means 1 at or towards the middle of a place, area of land, or distance between two points. EG *St Germain is midway between Cherbourg and Granville... The taxi stopped midway down the street.* 2 at or towards the middle of a period of time or of an event or process. EG *Garfield visited the Yorkshire locations midway through filming.* ADV WITH VB : USU+PREP *(between/down)* ADV WITH VB : USU+PREP *(between/through)*

midweek /mɪdwiːk/. If you do something **midweek,** you do it in the middle of the week. EG *The Councils meet midweek... More than 1,100 people had been arrested by midweek.* ▸ used as an adjective. EG *...a midweek performance.* ADV WITH VB ▸ ADJ CLASSIF : ATTRIB

Midwest /mɪdwest/. The **Midwest** is the central part of the USA. EG *...retired farmers from the Midwest... ...midwest grassland.* N PROPER : *the*+N ⇑ region

Midwestern /mɪdwestən/. Something that is **Midwestern** belongs to or involves the Midwest. EG *...the Midwestern states of North America.* ADJ CLASSIF : USU ATTRIB = central

midwife /mɪdwaɪf/, **midwives.** A **midwife** is a nurse, usually a woman, who is trained to deliver babies and to advise pregnant women. N COUNT

midwifery /mɪdwɪfəºri¹/ is the work of a midwife and the skills it involves. N UNCOUNT ⇑ nursing

midwinter /mɪdwɪntə/ is the period in the middle of the winter, especially the end of December and the month of January. EG *It is a depressing place in midwinter... ...a lovely midwinter morning.* N UNCOUNT

mien /miːn/. Someone's **mien** is their general appearance and manner, especially the expression on their face, which shows what they are feeling or thinking; a literary word. EG *There was assurance in his mien... His gentle mien reminded me of his mother.* N SING WITH DET : USU POSS + N = manner

miffed /mɪft/. If you are **miffed**, you are slightly annoyed and hurt because of something which someone has said or done to you; an informal word. EG *She sounded miffed... Many union workers were miffed at his coolness.* ADJ QUALIT : PRED, IF + PREP THEN *at/by* = offended, peeved

might /maɪt/. **1** When you say that something **might** happen or be true, you mean that it will possibly happen or be true in the future, but you cannot be certain. EG *You might find that the trains are a bit cold... I might even lose my job... I might go to a concert tonight... 'Why don't you go back home and wait for him?'–'I might.'* MODAL = may

2 When you say that something **might** be true, you mean that there is a possibility that it is true, but you cannot be certain. EG *Don't eat it. It might be a toadstool... We might be wrong... If your zip sticks it might be because a thread has caught in it... Might not the reverse be true?... It might be wise to consult the wine waiter.* MODAL = could, may

3 Might is used, especially in subordinate clauses, as a past tense of 'may': see **may**. EG *I thought I might find you here... It hadn't occurred to him that we might feel excluded... She asked the young labourer's wife if she might borrow a pen and paper.* MODAL ⇑ would

4 If you say that something **might have** happened, you mean that **4.1** it was possible for it to have happened although it did not in fact happen. EG *A lot of men died who might have been saved... I daren't think about what might have happened... Things might have been so different.* MODAL + INF *(have)* + PAST PART = could have **4.2** it will possibly have happened by the time mentioned. EG *They might have got there by now... It might very well not have occurred yet.* MODAL + INF *(have)* + PAST PART = may have

5 When you say that something **might have** happened or been true, you mean that it is possible that it happened or was true but you do not know for certain. You sometimes use **might have** when you are giving a possible explanation for something. EG *He might well have said that. I just don't remember... She was in a summer dress her mother might have worn in the 1940s... People thought he might have shot his wife.* MODAL + INF *(have)* + PAST PART = could have, may have

6 Might is used in speech as a polite and rather formal way of interrupting someone, asking a question, or introducing what you are going to say next. Sometimes **might** is used because it sounds more aggressive than 'may'. EG *Might I inquire if you are the owner?... Might I suggest that you offer your manuscript to another publisher?... And how much did you give to our baby, might I ask?* MODAL : USU MODAL + I + INF

7 You also use **might 7.1** when you give advice to someone or suggest that they do something. EG *If the noise in your own home exhausts you, you might try double glazing and draught proofing... The other thing you might find out is who owns the land.* MODAL : USU *you* + MODAL = could **7.2** when you suggest to someone that they do something with you. EG *I thought we might have some lunch... There are a few things we might compare notes on.* MODAL **7.3** when you make a comment which justifies or supports a statement you are making. EG *That, one might argue, is not too terrible... The professions, as you might expect, guard their secrets closely.* MODAL **7.4** to indicate that someone ought to do something because it is right for them to do it. EG *You might do the washing up for a change!* MODAL ⇑ should ● If you say that someone **might have** done something, you are showing that you are angry or upset because they did not do something that you think they should have done. EG *You might have told me... They might have waited for us!* ● MODAL + INF *(have)* + PAST PART ⇑ could **7.5** to indicate that although something is true it is contradicted by another fact or argument which you are going to give. EG *They might preach liberty, equality, and fraternity, but their record on human rights is pretty awful.* MODAL = may

8 You use **might** in expressions such as 'I might have known' when you have learnt something that is disappointing or upsetting, to indicate that you are not surprised at it, because of the nature of the person or circumstances involved. EG *'I'm afraid we've run out of coffee.'–'I might have known'... You might have guessed then what he was up to.* MODAL

9 Might is power or strength; a formal use. EG *The government prepared to face the full might of union opposition to the plan... They would have little chance to survive against our might.* N UNCOUNT + SUPP ● If you do something **with all** your **might** or **with all** your **might and main**, you do it using all your strength and energy. EG *I tied the rope around the tree and heaved with all my might... She flew into a rage and screamed out with all her might and main.* ● PHR : USED AS AN A

mightily /maɪtɪli¹/ means **1** to a great extent or degree; an old-fashioned use. EG *Their economy flourished mightily... I rejoice mightily at the news.* ADV = heartily **2** with great strength and power; a literary use. EG *He hit the peg mightily on the top with a mallet.* ADV WITH VB

mightn't /maɪtəºnt/ is a spoken form of 'might not'.

might've /maɪtəv/ is an informal form of 'might have', especially when 'have' is an auxiliary verb.

mighty /maɪti¹/, **mightier, mightiest**. **1** Something that is **mighty** is **1.1** very powerful or strong; a literary use. EG *...this mighty nation... We know we're dealing with forces that are mightier than ourselves.* ADJ QUALIT **1.2** large and impressive, and gives an impression of great strength or power; a literary use. EG *...a mighty ship... ...two of Asia's mightiest rivers, the Ganges and the Brahmaputra.* ADJ QUALIT

2 In informal American English, **mighty** means very. EG *It's going to be mighty embarrassing to everybody.* ADV + ADJ/ADV

3 See also **high and mighty**.

migraine /miːgreɪn, maɪ-/, **migraines**. **Migraine** is an extremely painful headache that makes you feel very ill indeed. EG *Do you suffer from migraine?... The experience had brought on one of her migraines.* N UNCOUNT/COUNT

migrant /maɪgrənt/, **migrants**. A **migrant** is **1** a person who moves from one place to another, especially in order to find work. EG *Forest clearance brought more and more migrants flooding into the cities... Those factories are staffed to a very high degree by migrant workers.* N COUNT ⇑ itinerant **2** a bird, fish, or animal which migrates from one part of the world to another. EG *Summer migrants from Africa fly along the North African coast.* N COUNT

migrate /maɪgreɪt/, **migrates, migrating, migrated**. **1** If people **migrate**, they move from one place to another, especially in order to find work or to live there for a short time. EG *Millions have migrated to the cities because they could not survive in rural areas.* V : USU + A ◊ **migration** /maɪgreɪʃəºn/, **migrations**. EG *Migration for work is accelerating in the Third World... The tourist industry profits from mass migrations to the Mediterranean in the summer.* ◊ N UNCOUNT/COUNT

2 When birds, fish, or animals **migrate**, they move at a particular time or season from one part of the world or of a country to another, usually in order to breed or to find new feeding grounds. EG *Every spring they migrate towards the coast... ...migrating birds.* V ◊ **migration, migrations**. EG *Swallows begin their migration south in early autumn.* ◊ N UNCOUNT/COUNT

migratory /maɪgrətəºri¹/; a technical term. **1** A **migratory** bird, fish, or animal is one that migrates every year. ADJ CLASSIF : ATTRIB

2 Migratory means relating to migration. EG *...the migratory movements of salmon.* ADJ CLASSIF : ATTRIB

mike /maɪk/, **mikes**. A **mike** is a microphone; an informal word. EG *Is the mike turned on?* N COUNT

milch /mɪltʃ/. A **milch** cow or goat is one that is kept for milk; an old-fashioned word. ADJ CLASSIF : ATTRIB

mild /maɪld/, **milder, mildest**. **1** If someone or their behaviour is **mild**, they are gentle, kind, and warm-hearted. EG *His eyes were no longer mild but glittered with a suppressed fury... ...my loving wife's mild nature.* ADJ QUALIT ⇑ gentle ◊ **mildly**. EG *'No need to shout,' he said mildly.* ◊ ADV WITH VB ◊ **mildness**. EG *There was a mildness about his mouth and eyes that proclaimed gentleness and sensitivity.* ◊ N UNCOUNT

2 Mild weather is warmer than is usual for the time of year. EG *The weather was comparatively mild through December... It's very mild today.* ADJ QUALIT ⇑ temperate ◊ **mildness**. EG *The mildness of the air astonished him.* ◊ N UNCOUNT + SUPP

3 Food, cigarettes, etc that are **mild** are not strong, sharp, or bitter in taste or smell. EG *...a mild curry... ...a mild cheese.* ADJ QUALIT ≠ hot, strong

4 **Mild** soap, washing-up liquid, etc feels soft and pleasant to your skin and does not contain anything which might damage the things you want to wash. EG *Use a mild soap for sensitive skin... ...a mild detergent.* ◊ **mildness.** ADJ QUALIT ⇑ gentle ◊ N UNCOUNT

5 A **mild** illness is not very serious. EG *A slight fever often accompanies a mild infection.* ◊ **mildness.** EG *...the mildness of the attack.* ADJ QUALIT ◊ N UNCOUNT+SUPP

6 **Mild** is used to describe a quality, attitude, or emotion that is not very great in degree. EG *It was of mild academic interest only... We looked at each other in mild astonishment.* ◊ **mildly.** EG *He was mildly jealous... It was mildly amusing.* ADJ QUALIT ⇑ slight ◊ ADV+ADJ/ADV

7 A **mild** attempt, protest, etc is weak and not determined enough to have an effect. EG *There was a mild attempt to open the door of our room.* ◊ **mildly.** EG *Judy mildly protested.* ADJ QUALIT ◊ ADV WITH VB

8 In British English, **mild** is a clear, dark-coloured beer. EG *A pint of mild, please.* N UNCOUNT

mildew /mɪldjuː/ is a white, soft fungus that grows on plants, leather, food, etc when they are warm and damp. EG *The hall smelt of mildew.* N UNCOUNT ⇑ fungus = mould

mildewed /mɪldjuːd/. Something that is **mildewed** has mildew growing on it. ADJ CLASSIF

mildly /maɪldli[1]/. 1 See **mild.**

2 You use **to put it mildly** to indicate that you are describing something in language that is much less strong, direct, or critical than language you could have chosen. EG *The majority of college students have, to put it mildly, misgivings about military service... To call him a thief is putting it mildly.* PHR : VB INFLECTS, USED AS ADV SEN ⇑ understate

mild-mannered. Someone who is **mild-mannered** is always gentle, kind, and polite. ADJ QUALIT

mile /maɪl/, **miles**. 1 A **mile** is 1.1 a unit of distance that is 1760 yards. A mile is equal to 1.6 kilometres. EG *The island is only 29 miles long and 16 miles wide... The lecture halls were about a mile away from the halls of residence... ...a thirty mile drive.* N COUNT **1.2** a race that is one mile long. EG *Bannister was the first man to break the four minute mile... I think he held the record for the mile.* N SING WITH DET : USU *the*+N

2 **Miles** is used, especially in the expression 'miles away', to refer to a long distance. EG *'Frogstone Road? Where's that?'–'Miles away'... I had walked for miles and miles.* N PLURAL = far

3 In informal English, **miles** or **a mile** is used with the meaning 'a long way' or 'very much' in order to emphasize the difference between two things or qualities, or the difference between what you aimed to do and what you actually achieved. EG *'Is the answer 125?'–'No, you're miles out.'... I missed the target by a mile... This is better by miles.* N COUNT : USU PL

4 If you **are miles away**, you are unaware of what is happening or of what someone is saying, because you are thinking deeply about something else; an informal expression. EG *'Did you hear me?'–'No, sorry, I was miles away.'* PHR : VB INFLECTS = daydream

5 If you say that you can **see, recognize**, etc something **a mile off**, you mean that it is very obvious and easy to recognize; an informal expression. EG *You can tell he's a policeman a mile off... You could smell the booze on his breath a mile off.* PHR : VB INFLECTS, IF+PREP THEN *from* ⇑ easily

6 If you say that something **sticks** or **stands out a mile**, you mean that it is very obvious and easy to recognize; an informal expression. EG *Critics praised Bomberg's early work as 'standing out a mile from everything else done in England'.* PHR : VB INFLECTS

7 If you say that someone would **run a mile** when faced with doing a particular thing, you mean that they would be very frightened or unwilling to do it; an informal expression. PHR : VB INFLECTS

mileage /maɪlɪdʒ/, **mileages**. 1 Your **mileage** is the distance that you have travelled, measured in miles. EG *...the approximate mileage for the complete journey.* N COUNT/UNCOUNT : USU SING

2 The **mileage** of a vehicle is the number of miles that it can travel using one gallon of petrol. EG *...a smaller, lighter car with better mileage.* N COUNT/UNCOUNT : USU SING ⇑ total

3 The **mileage** in a particular course of action is its usefulness in getting you what you want. EG *There is more mileage in this policy... He was getting mileage out of this.* N UNCOUNT+*in/out of* ⇑ potential

milepost /maɪlpəʊst/, **mileposts**. A **milepost** is an important event in the history or development of something. EG *The time scale between mileposts of achievement differs from child to child.* N COUNT

milestone /maɪlstəʊn/, **milestones**. A **milestone** is 1 an important event in the history or development of something. EG *...a milestone in the history of broadcasting... ...one of the great milestones of human intellectual development.* N COUNT **2** a stone by the side of a road showing the distances to particular places. EG *Every milestone he passed showed the distance to Stonehenge.* N COUNT

milieu /miːljɜː/, **milieux, milieus**. The plural can be either **milieux** or **milieus**. The **milieu** in which you live or work is the group of people that you live among or work among; a formal word. EG *I was born in a social milieu where further education was a luxury... Frank Lloyd Wright tried to create a milieu that would be conducive to the study of architecture.* N COUNT : USU+SUPP = environment, surroundings

militancy /mɪlɪtənsi[1]/ is the behaviour of people who are militant. EG *The League is well known for its militancy.* N UNCOUNT

militant /mɪlɪtənt/, **militants**. 1 Someone who is **militant** is very active in trying to bring about political or social change, and often willing to use force. EG *They have become more militant in pressing for better pay and conditions... ...a militant feminist... ...militant trade unionists.* ◊ **militantly.** EG *They became consciously and militantly nationalistic... ...this failure to act militantly.* ADJ QUALIT ⇑ aggressive ◊ ADV ⇑ fiercely

2 A **militant** is a militant person. EG *...a number of well-known militants.* N COUNT = activist

militarism /mɪlɪtərɪzə[0]m/ is the desire to strengthen and use the armed forces of your country in order to make it more powerful; used showing disapproval. EG *...the militarism which led to the First World War.* ◊ **militarist, militarists.** EG *He was thrown out of his country by a clique of militarists... It made a militarist regime inevitable.* N UNCOUNT ⇑ policy ◊ N COUNT : USU BEFORE N ⇑ person

militaristic /mɪlɪtərɪstɪk/. Someone who is **militaristic** is eager to strengthen and use the armed forces of their country in order to make it more powerful; used showing disapproval. EG *...an immense militaristic state.* ADJ QUALIT ⇑ warlike

militarized /mɪlɪtəraɪzd/; also spelled **militarised.** A **militarized** area or region has members of the armed forces and military equipment in it. EG *...one of the most heavily militarized zones in the world.* ADJ QUALIT ⇑ armed

military /mɪlɪtə[0]ri[1]/. 1 **Military** means 1.1 relating to the armed forces of a country. EG *Since World War 2 there has been a trebling in military spending... ...military leaders... ...direct military action.* ◊ **militarily.** EG *They were deeply involved both politically and militarily in the Middle East.* ADJ CLASSIF : ATTRIB ⇑ martial ◊ ADV **1.2** relating to or belonging to the army, rather than to the navy or the air force. EG *...the naval, air, and military commands.* ADJ CLASSIF : ATTRIB

2 The **military** are the armed forces of a country, especially officers of high rank. EG *The politicians and the military will do nothing.* N PLURAL : *the*+N, VB CAN BE SING OR PL

3 If you do something in a **military** way, you do it in an exact and disciplined way, like a soldier. EG *He obeyed his orders with military precision.* ADJ QUALIT

military police. The **military police** are part of an army, navy, or air force, and act as its police force. EG *He was picked up by one of the military police... ...military-police jeeps.* N SING : *the*+N, VB CAN BE SING OR PL

military policeman, military policemen. A **military policeman** is a member of the military police. N COUNT

militate /mɪlɪteɪt/, **militates, militating, militated**. If something **militates** against something else, it makes it less likely to happen or succeed; a formal word. EG *Family tensions can militate against learning... Their very environment militated against competing on an equal footing.* V+A *(against)* ⇑ influence = hinder

militia /mɪlɪʃə/, **militias**. A **militia** is an organization that operates like an army but whose members are not professional soldiers. EG *...a building guarded by the local police and militia.* N COUNT/UNCOUNT : IF SING, VB CAN BE SING OR PL ⇑ force

militiaman /mɪlɪʃəmə[3]n/, **militiamen**. A **militiaman** is a member of a militia. N COUNT ⇑ person

milk /mɪlk/, **milks, milking, milked**. 1 **Milk** is the white liquid produced by cows, goats, etc which people drink and from which you can make cheese, butter, and yoghurt. EG *He only drinks milk in tea or coffee... ...a glass of milk... Put out the milk bottles.* N UNCOUNT
● See also **condensed milk, evaporated milk, skimmed milk.**

2 When someone **milks** a cow, goat, etc, they get milk from it by pulling its udders. EG *I've got a cow to milk, a calf to tend and an old sow to feed.* V OR V+O
◊ **milking**. EG *...the boy who was doing the milking... I had to install milking equipment.* ◊ N UNCOUNT ⇑ task
3 **Milk** is also **3.1** the white liquid from a woman's breasts which babies drink. EG *Although the mother has plenty of milk, the baby may not feed well.* N UNCOUNT **3.2** a white liquid produced inside coconuts. EG *He went to get some fresh coconut milk.* N UNCOUNT
4 If you **milk** a situation, place, etc, you get as much benefit or profit as you can from it, without caring about the effects on other people; used showing disapproval. EG *They'll milk it for all it's worth... The island was milked by the invaders for five centuries.* V+O = exploit
5 To **cry over spilt milk** means to spend time regretting something that has happened and that cannot be put right, instead of turning your attention to other things. EG *It's no use crying over spilt milk... Ferdinand is not one to cry over spilt milk.* PHR : VB INFLECTS

milk float, milk floats; used in British English. A **milk float** is a small van with a roof and no sides which is used to deliver milk to people's houses. Milk floats usually have an electric motor. N COUNT

milkmaid /mɪlkmeɪd/, **milkmaids**. A **milkmaid** was, in former times, a woman who worked in a dairy and who milked cows and made butter and cheese. N COUNT

milkman /mɪlkmə³n/, **milkmen**. A **milkman** is a person who delivers milk regularly to people's houses. EG *Empty bottles clinked as the milkman put them into his crate.* N COUNT

milk-shake, milk-shakes; also spelled without a hyphen or as one word. A **milk-shake** is a cold drink made by mixing milk with a flavouring, ice cream, or fruit, and stirring the mixture very fast until it becomes frothy. EG *We stopped and had a strawberry milkshake.* N MASS

milk tooth, milk teeth. Your **milk teeth** are the first teeth that grow in your mouth, which later fall out and are replaced by a second set. N COUNT : USU PL

milky /mɪlki¹/, **milkier, milkiest**. Something that is **milky** 1 is a pale white colour. EG *...clouds of milky smoke... ...her delicate milky-white face.* ADJ QUALIT 2 contains a lot of milk. EG *We always had milky coffee at lunchtime.* ADJ QUALIT

Milky Way. The **Milky Way** is the pale strip of light consisting of many stars that you can see stretching across the sky at night. N PROPER : *the*+N

mill /mɪl/, **mills, milling, milled**. 1 A **mill** is **1.1** a building in which grain is crushed and ground to make flour. EG *He sends his crop to a large mill instead of grinding it himself.* ● See also **windmill, water-mill**. N COUNT **1.2** a small device used for grinding coffee beans, pepper, etc into powder. EG *...a pepper mill.* N COUNT : MOD+N **1.3** a factory used for making a particular material, for example cotton, wool, or steel. EG *He had been in a cotton mill, then a motor firm... He had worked in a Solingen steel mill.* N COUNT : MOD+N
2 If you **mill** wheat, pepper, etc, you crush and grind it in a mill. EG *I went to get the grain milled... ...freshly milled pepper.* V+O ⇑ process
3 If you **put** someone **through the mill**, you make them answer a lot of difficult questions or do a lot of difficult things, usually because you are testing them. EG *I was put through the mill by my immediate superiors.* PHR : VB INFLECTS ⇑ test
4 ● **grist to the mill**: see **grist**. ● See also **milling, run-of-the-mill**.

mill around. When a crowd of people **mill around** or **mill about**, they move around within a particular place or area, so that the movement of the whole crowd looks very confused. EG *There were hundreds of boys and girls milling around on the lawn... Students and staff were milling about.* PHRASAL VB : V+ADV/PREP

millennium /mɪleniəm/, **millennia, millenniums**; a formal word. The plural can be either **millennia** or **millenniums**. 1 A **millennium** is **1.1** a thousand years. EG *They occupied Japan's northern region for at least a millennium... Over the millennia the wind and rain destroyed them.* N COUNT ⇑ era **1.2** one of the periods of a thousand years before or after the birth of Jesus Christ. 1987 is in the second millennium A.D. EG *...the fourth millennium B.C.... ...the remaining quarter century of the millennium.* N COUNT : USU *the*+N
2 The **millennium** is a period of a thousand years during which Christ will rule on earth, according to the belief of some Christians. EG *...sects that promise the millennium tomorrow.* N SING : *the*+N ⇑ era

miller /mɪlə/, **millers**. A **miller** is a person who owns or operates a mill in which grain is crushed and ground to make flour; a rather old-fashioned word. N COUNT

millet /mɪlɪt/ is a tall grass that is cultivated for its seeds or for hay. N UNCOUNT

milli- is added to some nouns that refer to units of measurement in order to form other nouns referring to units a thousand times smaller. EG *...metre→millimetre... ...gramme→milligramme... ...second→millisecond.* PREFIX

milligram /mɪlɪgræm/, **milligrams**; also spelled **milligramme**. A **milligram** is a metric unit of weight that is equal to one thousandth of a gramme. Its abbreviation is 'mg'. EG *...0.3 milligrams of mercury.* N COUNT/PART

millilitre /mɪlɪliːtə/, **millilitres**; also spelled **milliliter** in American English. A **millilitre** is a metric unit of volume for liquids and gases that is equal to a thousandth of a litre. Its abbreviation is 'ml'. EG *...45 millilitres of alcohol.* N COUNT/PART

millimetre /mɪlɪmiːtə/, **millimetres**; also spelled **millimeter** in American English. A **millimetre** is a metric unit of length that is equal to a tenth of a centimetre or a thousandth of a metre. Its abbreviation is 'mm'. EG *...small slivers of material measuring a few millimetres across... ...a silicon chip less than a millimetre thick.* N COUNT/PART

milliner /mɪlɪnə/, **milliners**. A **milliner** is a person whose job is making or selling women's hats. N COUNT

millinery /mɪlɪnə⁰ri¹/ is used to refer to hats made or sold by a milliner. EG *...a millinery display in a shop window.* N UNCOUNT

milling /mɪlɪŋ/. The people in a **milling** crowd move around within a particular place or area, so that the movement of the whole crowd looks very confused. EG *She escaped unnoticed into the milling crowds.* ADJ CLASSIF : ATTRIB ⇑ moving

million /mɪljən/, **millions**. A **million** or one **million** is the number 1,000,000: see □ at **number, age, measurement**, and **money**. EG *...Malaysia's 3.9 million Chinese... ...30 million dollars... ...£980 millions... 'How much?'-'Half a million.'* NUM : USU a/NUM+*million* ▸ A **million** or **millions** is often used to mean an extremely large number. EG *...millions of mosquitoes... Her books continue to give pleasure to millions.* ▸ NUM WITH PL : USED AS N PART

millionaire /mɪljənɛə/, **millionaires**. A **millionaire** is a very rich person who has money or property worth at least a million pounds, dollars, francs, etc. EG *She said her father was a millionaire... ...millionaire industrialists.* N COUNT

millionth /mɪljənθ/, **millionths**. 1 The **millionth** item in a series is the one you count as number one million: see □ at **number** and **age**. EG *Six years later the one-millionth Ford rolled off an assembly line.* ORDINAL
2 A **millionth** is one of a million equal parts of something. EG *...a millionth of a second... ...one ten millionth of an inch.* N COUNT : USU+*of* ⇑ fraction

millipede /mɪlɪpiːd/, **millipedes**. A **millipede** is a very small creature with a long, narrow body made of small segments, each with two pairs of legs. N COUNT

millstone /mɪlstəʊn/, **millstones**. 1 A **millstone** is a large flat round stone which is one of a pair of stones that, in former times, were used to grind grain into flour. N COUNT ⇑ stone
2 If something is **a millstone round your neck**, it is a very unpleasant problem or responsibility that you cannot escape from. EG *The debt becomes an even bigger millstone round the poor man's neck.* PHR

mime /maɪm/, **mimes, miming, mimed**. 1 **Mime** is the use of movements and gestures in order to express something or tell a story without using speech. EG *I had been conversing with him in mime... ...the re-enactment of the legends in mime and song... She was a member of a mime troupe.* N UNCOUNT ⇑ action
2 A **mime** is **2.1** an occasion or theatrical performance in which someone uses mime in order to describe or express something. EG *In a brilliant mime, he showed how he managed to support the tray.* N COUNT **2.2** a person who mimes things, especially as their job. N COUNT
3 If you **mime** something, you describe or express it using mime rather than speech. EG *'Dinner,' I said, and mimed cutting meat... They all vigorously mimed that I should speak as quietly as they did.* V OR V+O/-ING/REPORT-CL

Mimeograph /mɪmɪə⁶græf, -grɑːf/, **Mimeographs, Mimeographing, Mimeographed.** **Mimeograph** is a trademark. 1 A **Mimeograph** or **Mimeograph machine** is a machine that prints copies of letters or drawings on special paper. N COUNT
2 A **Mimeograph** is also a copy that has been produced by a Mimeograph. N COUNT
3 If you **Mimeograph** copies of something, you produce them using a Mimeograph. EG *...a Mimeographed list of names.* V+O ⇑ reproduce

mimetic /mɪmetɪk/. **Mimetic** movements or actions are ones in which you imitate something; a technical or formal word. EG *They perform their mimetic movements... She went through the mimetic actions of hearing a moan in the dark.* ADJ CLASSIF : USU ATTRIB ⇑ dramatic = representational

mimic /mɪmɪk/, **mimics, mimicking, mimicked.** 1 If you **mimic** the actions or voice of a person or animal, you imitate it in a way that is meant to be amusing or entertaining. EG *She'd had fun mimicking the aunt's smugness... I can mimic Cockney speech reasonably well... ...birds which he taught me to mimic.* V+O = copy
2 If someone or something **'mimics** another person or thing, they try to be like them or are in fact like them, although they are not really that person or thing. EG *The social climbers in the colonies started to mimic their conquerors.* V+O ⇑ copy = ape
3 A **mimic** is a person who is able to mimic people or animals. EG *One of my brothers is a wonderful mimic.* N COUNT ⇑ imitator

mimicry /mɪmɪkri¹/ is the action of mimicking someone or something. EG *...his fine talent for mimicry.* N UNCOUNT ⇑ imitation

min. is a written abbreviation for 'minimum, or for 'minutes' or 'minute'.

Min. is a written abbreviation for 'Ministry'.

minaret /mɪnəret/, **minarets.** A **minaret** is a tall, thin tower with several balconies around it which is part of a mosque or is built near a mosque. N COUNT

minatory /mɪnətə⁰ri¹/ means threatening; a formal word. EG *...minatory and ferocious women.* ADJ CLASSIF : ATTRIB

mince /mɪns/, **minces, mincing, minced.** 1 **Mince** is beef which has been cut into very small pieces; used mainly in British English. N UNCOUNT ⇑ meat
2 If you **mince** meat, you cut it into very small pieces. EG *Mince the lean meat finely.* ◊ **minced.** EG *...minced beef.* V+O ◊ ADJ CLASSIF : ATTRIB
3 If you **do not mince** your **words**, you tell someone something unpleasant without making any effort to be polite or to avoid upsetting them. EG *They certainly don't mince their words, do they?... I never mince words, you know that.* PHR : VB INFLECTS = be blunt
4 If you **mince** or if you **mince** your way somewhere, you walk with quick small steps in a very affected or effeminate way. EG *Off he goes, mincing his way across the department store.* ● See also **mincing.** V OR V+C ⇑ move

mincemeat /mɪnsmiːt/. 1 **Mincemeat** is 1.1 a sticky mixture of small pieces of dried fruit and other sweet things. Mincemeat is usually cooked in pastry to make mince pies. 1.2 in American English, meat that has been minced. N UNCOUNT; N UNCOUNT = mince
2 If you **make mincemeat of** someone, you defeat them easily and completely in an argument or fight; an informal expression. EG *He'll make mincemeat of you!* PHR : VB INFLECTS = demolish

mince pie, mince pies; also spelled with a hyphen. A **mince pie** is a small pie which contains sweet mincemeat. Mince pies are usually eaten at Christmas. N COUNT

mincer /mɪnsə/, **mincers.** A **mincer** is a machine which cuts meat and bone into very small pieces. N COUNT

mincing /mɪnsɪŋ/. A **mincing** walk consists of quick small steps and looks very affected or effeminate. EG *...mincing steps.* ▸ also used to describe a way of talking that seems very affected or effeminate. EG *...an effeminate mincing voice.* ◊ **mincingly.** EG *Rudolph had to walk delicately, almost mincingly, to keep from slipping.* ADJ QUALIT = dainty ▸ = affected ◊ ADV WITH VB

mind /maɪnd/, **minds, minding, minded.** 1 Your **mind** is 1.1 where your thoughts are. People often use the word 'mind' as if it is a box that thoughts come into or go out of. When something is 'in your mind', you are thinking about it; when something is 'at the front of your mind' or 'uppermost in your mind', you are thinking about it a lot. EG *All this confusion in the minds of young people was bound to lead to violence... She let her mind wander... There were two thoughts uppermost in my mind–who would do such a thing and why?... Agate couldn't get the woman's reply out of his mind... My mind's gone blank.* 1.2 your intellectual ability or knowledge. EG *You have a good mind... Jane knew she could improve her mind with good books... The study of logic trains the mind.* 1.3 your power to think, in contrast to your physical powers and your power to feel emotions. EG *You must be strong in mind and body... What is the human mind?* N COUNT : WITH POSS = head, brain; N COUNT = intellect; N COUNT/UNCOUNT ⇑ faculty
2 If you have a particular type of **mind**, you have a particular way of thinking which is part of your character or a result of your education or professional training. EG *You've got a very suspicious mind, Smithy... You have the mind of a child... Anne's got a scientific mind.* N COUNT + SUPP : USU SING = mentality
3 You can refer to someone as a particular kind of **mind** as a way of saying that they are clever, intelligent, or imaginative. EG *Billy was one of the most talented, abrasive minds I had ever worked with... ...a team of the brightest minds available... Great minds think alike.* N COUNT : USU + SUPP ⇑ person = thinker
4 The following expressions are used when referring to what someone is thinking about or what someone can remember. 4.1 If you **go over** something **in** your **mind** or **turn** it **over in** your **mind**, you think about it very carefully or repeatedly, because you want to understand it properly or find a solution to a problem. PHR : VB INFLECTS = chew over 4.2 If something **sticks in** your **mind**, it remains firmly in your memory. EG *For some reason, her name did stick in my mind.* PHR : VB INFLECTS 4.3 If something is **at the back of** your **mind**, you can only vaguely remember it. EG *Somewhere at the back of my mind, I had the feeling I'd seen him before.* PHR : USED AS AN A 4.4 If your **mind is on** something or you **have** your **mind on** something, you are thinking about that thing rather than something else. EG *Her mind was not on the announcements she was making... My mind was on other things.* PHR : VB INFLECTS 4.5 If something **brings** or **calls** another thing **to mind**, it reminds you of that other thing because it is similar in some way. EG *All those boats brought Bellini's Venetian landscape to mind.* PHR : VB INFLECTS = be reminiscent of 4.6 If you say **'out of sight, out of mind'**, you mean that people quickly forget someone if he or she goes away. PHR 4.7 If you **get** your **mind round** something that is complicated or difficult to understand, you manage to understand it. EG *It's a bit late to get one's mind round a puzzle like that.* PHR : VB INFLECTS ⇑ comprehend 4.8 If something **takes** your **mind off** a problem or unpleasant situation, it helps you to forget about it for a while. EG *Our little talk seemed to take our minds off the awful things that were happening.* PHR : VB INFLECTS 4.9 If something **slips** your **mind** or **goes out of** your **mind**, you forget to do it. EG *Maybe it had slipped my mind. I was, after all, incredibly busy that day.* PHR : VB INFLECTS 4.10 If something **comes to mind** or **springs to mind**, or if something **crosses** or **enters** your **mind**, you think of it suddenly and without making any effort. EG *I just pick up whatever groceries come to mind... Scotland springs to mind as an example... The thought never crossed my mind.* PHR : VB INFLECTS = enter your head 4.11 If something **puts** you **in mind of** something else, it reminds you of it because it is similar to it or is usually associated with it. EG *That joke puts me in mind of a funny thing that happened to me when I was on holiday.* PHR : VB INFLECTS = bring to mind 4.12 If you tell someone to **bear** something **in mind** or to **keep** something **in mind**, you are reminding or warning them about something important which they should remember. EG *It shouldn't be difficult for you. Bear in mind that these are sixty-five-year-old men... It is worth bearing in mind that, under such circumstances, we would have no alternative but to find another buyer.* PHR : VB INFLECTS, USU IMPER = note ≠ forget
5 The following expressions are used when referring to what is worrying someone. 5.1 If something is **on** your **mind**, you are worried or concerned about it and think about it a lot. EG *He won't admit this to me, but I know it's on his mind... The people at home had other things on their minds.* PHR : USED AS AN A 5.2 If something that happens is **a load** or **a weight off** your **mind**, it causes you to stop worrying, for example because it solves a problem that you had. PHR : USED AS C OR O = a relief 5.3 If you **set** or **put** someone's **mind at rest**, you tell them something that stops them worrying. EG *Let me set your mind at rest. There is nothing wrong with your heart.* PHR : VB INFLECTS = reassure
6 The following expressions are used when referring to what someone intends to do. 6.1 If you **have it in mind to** do something, you intend or want to do it. EG *I have it in mind to get a new coat for the winter.* PHR : VB INFLECTS 6.2 PHR : VB

If you ask someone what they **have in mind**, you want to know in more detail about an idea or wish they have. EG *What kind of rifle did you have in mind?... Who exactly did you have in mind?*
INFLECTS = be thinking of

6.3 If you do something **with** a particular thing **in mind**, you do it for that reason or with that purpose. EG *She wrote it with eventual publication in mind.*
PHR : USED AS AN A

6.4 If you **have a mind to** do something, you want or choose to do it. EG *They can stay on at school until they are sixteen if they have a mind to... If they had a mind to, they could easily get it published.*
PHR : VB INFLECTS

6.5 If you say that you **have a good mind to** do something or **have half a mind to** do something, you mean that you have a strong desire to do it, although you do not actually do it. EG *I've a good mind to punish you for behaving so badly... I had half a mind to walk out there and then.*
PHR : VB INFLECTS

6.6 If you **set** your **mind on** doing something, you are determined to do it. EG *They had their minds set on reform.*
PHR + -ING : VB INFLECTS

6.7 If you **put** your **mind to** something, you devote a lot of your energy, effort, and attention to it. EG *You could easily get a job in London, if you put your mind to it.*
PHR + NG/-ING : VB INFLECTS

7 The following expressions are used when referring to opinions and decisions. **7.1** If you **give** someone a **piece of** your **mind**, you tell them exactly what you think of them or their behaviour when you think they have behaved very badly; a fairly informal expression. EG *I'd like to give her a piece of my mind.*
PHR : VB INFLECTS ⇑ reprimand

7.2 If you **speak** your **mind**, you say firmly and honestly what you think about a situation, rather than keeping it a secret or being afraid.
PHR : VB INFLECTS

7.3 If a number of people are **of one mind, of like mind**, or **of the same mind**, they all agree about something.
PHR : NG + PHR ⇑ agreed

7.4 If you **know** your **own mind**, you are clear about your opinions or what you like, and are not easily influenced by other people.
PHR : VB INFLECTS

7.5 You use **to my mind** to indicate that the statement you are making is your own opinion. EG *The worst part of air travel to my mind is the hanging around in airport lounges... To my mind, Jackson never really exploited her potential.*
PHR : USED AS ADV SEN = in my opinion

7.6 If you have **an open mind**, you avoid forming an opinion or making a decision until you know all the facts. EG *The committee tried to keep an open mind... He approached the problem with a very open mind.*
PHR : USED AS O

7.7 If you have **a closed mind**, you are unwilling to consider new ideas on something, because you have firm opinions about it already.
PHR : USED AS O

7.8 If you **make up** your **mind** or **make** your **mind up**, you decide which of a number of possible things you will have or do. EG *We have to make up our minds quickly, or they'll go without us... She's incapable of making up her mind.*
PHR : VB INFLECTS = make a decision

7.9 If your **mind is made up**, you have decided something and will not alter your decision. EG *My mind's made up.*
PHR : AUX INFLECTS

7.10 If you **change** your **mind**, you change a decision you have made or an opinion that you had, especially so that you do or think the opposite. EG *All of a sudden I changed my mind and decided not to go anywhere... I'm not going to change my mind about the divorce.*
PHR : VB INFLECTS = have second thoughts

7.11 If you **change** someone's **mind**, you persuade them to change a decision they have made or an opinion that they had. EG *Even Lynn could not change Judy's mind.*
PHR : VB INFLECTS ⇑ influence

7.12 If you are **in two minds**, you are uncertain about what to do, especially when you have to choose between two courses of action. EG *I was very much in two minds whether or not to apply for the Cambridge job.*
PHR : USED AS AN A ⇑ unsure = undecided

8 The following expressions are used when talking about someone's mental state or amount of common sense. **8.1** If you say that someone is **out of** their **mind**, you mean that they are mad or very foolish. EG *Have you gone out of your mind?... I must be out of my mind.*
PHR : USED AS AN A = crazy

8.2 If someone is **losing** their **mind**, they are becoming mad or senile. EG *Perhaps I was losing my mind.*
PHR : USED AS C

8.3 If you say that someone is **bored out of** their **mind, stoned out of** their **mind**, etc, you mean that they are extremely bored, strongly affected by drugs, etc; an informal use.
PHR : USED AS C

8.4 If you say that nobody **in** their **right mind** would do something, you mean that it is an irrational thing to do and you would be surprised if anyone did it. EG *Nobody in their right mind would enjoy this show... What woman in her right mind would marry a man like that?*
PHR : USED AS AN A ⇑ sensible

9 The word **mind** is also used in the following expressions. **9.1** If you see something in your **mind's eye**, you imagine it and have a clear picture of it in your mind. EG *I tried to see him in my mind's eye... In her mind's eye, all that morning, she had pictured herself in the new house.*
PHR : USU DETPOSS + PHR = head

9.2 Mind over matter is used to describe situations in which a person seems to be able to control events and physical objects using their mind. EG *I don't know how she survived. Just a case of mind over matter, I suppose.*
PHR : USED AS C OR O

9.3 If you say that something such as an illness is **all in the mind**, you mean that the person concerned is probably imagining it.
PHR : USED AS C ≠ real

9.4 Your **state of mind** is your mental state at a particular time. EG *She was in a fairly disturbed state of mind.*
PHR : USED AS S OR O

9.5 If you **read** someone's **mind**, you guess what they are thinking, especially because you know them very well. EG *As though reading his mind, Boylan said, 'I do believe you ought to apply for the job.'*
PHR : VB INFLECTS

10 If you do not **mind** something or if you do not **mind**, you are not annoyed or bothered by something. EG *I don't mind personal questions at all... You probably do mind, but you're too polite to say so... I don't mind walking... I hope you don't mind, I came early... Nobody seemed to mind.*
V OR V + O/-ING/ REPORT-CL : USU WITH BROAD NEG = object

11 Mind is used in the expressions 'do you mind?' and 'would you mind?' as a polite way of asking permission or asking someone to do something. EG *Do you mind if I wait?... You don't mind if I'm rather informal, do you?... Would you mind waiting outside a moment?... 'Shall I spell that for you?'–'Well, if you wouldn't mind.'*
CONVENTION

12 If you are offered a choice and you say **'I don't mind'**, you mean that you will be happy with either of the things offered. EG *'Tea or coffee?'–'I don't mind.'*
CONVENTION

• You can also say **'I don't mind'** as a rather weak and casual way of saying 'yes'. EG *'Cup of tea?'–'Yeah, I don't mind.'*
• CONVENTION = fine

• You say **'I don't mind if I do'** as a way of accepting something that someone has offered you, especially food or drink.
• CONVENTION = I won't say no

13 If you say that you **wouldn't mind** something, you mean that you would quite like it. EG *I wouldn't mind a cup a tea... I wouldn't mind being a manager of a store, or something like that.*
PHR = fancy

14 You use the expression **if you don't mind** when rejecting someone's offer or suggestion. EG *I'll do it my own way if you don't mind... 'Come and have some more champagne.'–'If you don't mind, I'll stay here near the phone.'*
PHR : USED AS ADV SEN

• You use the expression **if you don't mind me saying so** or **if you don't mind my saying so** when you are expressing an opinion that you think might offend the person you are speaking to and you do not want to upset them. EG *That seemed to me rather unnecessary, if you don't mind me saying so.*
• PHR : USED AS ADV SEN

15 You say **'don't mind me'** to apologize for your presence when you think this might embarrass someone, and to tell them to carry on with what they were doing or about to do.
CONVENTION = go ahead

16 Mind is used in the expressions 'you mustn't mind them' and 'don't mind them' to apologize for someone else's behaviour which you think might have offended the person you are speaking to. EG *You mustn't mind Captain Van Donck.*
PHR : ONLY IMPER, IF + PREP THEN *about*

17 You use **never mind 17.1** to try and make someone feel better, when they have failed to do something or something unpleasant has happened to them; used mainly in spoken English. EG *Never mind, dear, you can't win them all.*
PHR : ONLY IMPER, IF + PREP THEN *about*

17.2 to indicate that something is not important, especially when someone is apologizing to you. EG *Some of their towels are soaking wet, but never mind.*
PHR : ONLY IMPER, IF + PREP THEN *about*

17.3 to tell someone that they need not do something, because it is not important or because you will do it yourself. EG *What's it like? Oh, never mind, I'll go and see for myself... Never mind about those, Sam!*
PHR : ONLY IMPER, IF + PREP THEN *about* = don't worry

17.4 when you are indicating in an emphatic way that someone cannot do a particular thing, after mentioning something easier that they cannot do. EG *He couldn't raise a guinea pig never mind a child... With this knee injury, I can't walk, never mind run.*
PHR = let alone

17.5 to tell someone to ignore something because it is not true or not important. EG *The pike was just a rumour, never mind what your father said.*
PHR

18 You use **never you mind** to tell someone not to ask about something because it is private and nothing to do with them; an informal expression. EG *'Who's that letter from?'–'Never you mind!'*
CONVENTION

19 If you tell someone to **mind** something, you are warning them to be careful so that they do not hurt themselves or other people, or damage something.
V + O : ONLY IMPER = watch

EG *Mind the step... Mind my specs!* ● You say **'mind out'** as an urgent warning to someone that they are about to hurt themselves, hurt someone else, or damage something; used in informal British English. ● EXCLAM = watch out

● Some people say **'mind how you go'** when they are saying goodbye to someone who is leaving; an informal expression. ● CONVENTION = take care

20 If you tell someone, especially a child, to **mind** their **language, tongue, manners,** etc, you are telling them to speak or behave properly and politely and not to be rude. EG *You should mind your tongue.* ● to **mind** your **P's and Q's**: see **P**. PHR

21 In informal American English, to **mind** someone means to pay attention to them and obey them. EG *Go on, kids. Mind your momma, don't be like me.* V+O = listen to

22 You use **mind** when you are reminding someone of something they must do. EG *Mind you pay the gas bill today!* V+REPORT-CL : ONLY IMPER = be sure

23 If you **mind** a child or something such as a shop or luggage, you look after it for someone else for a while. EG *She got a neighbour to come in and mind the child, while she did part-time jobs... Would you mind the bags?... My mother is minding the office.* V+O = keep an eye on

24 You use **mind you** or **mind 24.1** when you are adding a piece of information to something you have said, especially when the new information explains what you have said, or introduces a contrast. EG *I haven't seen her for a year. I don't know whether Donald has, mind you... I'll tell you one thing, mind, it's the most inexpensive holiday we've had.* PHR : USED AS ADV SEN, OR ADV SEN = however, though **24.2** when you are warning somebody that you mean what you say and they should consider it seriously. EG *You can read this. It's confidential, mind.* ADV SEN = mark you **24.3** to emphasize a particular part of what you are saying; usually used after repeating the part you wish to emphasize. EG *The first night we started–started, mind–with a platter of smoked salmon.* ADV SEN

25 See also **minded**.

mind-blowing. Something that is **mind-blowing** is really astonishing; an informal word. EG *The effect was truly mind-blowing.* ADJ QUALIT ⇑ surprising = staggering

mind-boggling. Something that is **mind-boggling** is so enormous or complicated that it is very hard to imagine; an informal word. EG *The concept is mind-boggling... ...mind-boggling wealth.* ADJ QUALIT ⇑ surprising = staggering

minded /maɪndɪd/. If someone is **minded** to do something, they want or intend to do it; a formal word. EG *He might hesitate to attack a country which seems minded to offer him total resistance... The reader can stop here if he is so minded.* ADJ CLASSIF : PRED, USU + *to*-INF

-minded 1 combines with adjectives and adverbs to indicate the nature of someone's character, attitude, or opinions. EG *...a narrow-minded Puritanical sect... He is very obedient, but so absent-minded and careless and untidy... ...the single-minded determination to use their power... As liberally-minded people, his parents taught him to think for himself.* COMB : FORMS ADJS **2** combines with adverbs to indicate that someone is interested in a particular subject or is able to think in a particular way. EG *There was a politically minded group at the CBC.* COMB : FORMS ADJS **3** combines with nouns to indicate that someone has a particular aim or goal. EG *...acquisition-minded companies... ...marriage-minded girls.* COMB : FORMS ADJS = oriented **4** combines with adjectives to indicate how good someone's ability to think is. EG *...simple minded flower people... ...a sharp-minded actress.* COMB : FORMS ADJS

minder /maɪndə/, **minders**. A **minder** is **1** a person whose job is to look after something, for example a child or an animal. EG *...a baby-minder... ...a child-minder... Industrialization would turn the masses into mere machine minders.* N COUNT+SUPP **2** a person whose job is to protect someone, especially a businessman, and do other tasks such as driving their car for them. N COUNT = bodyguard

mindful /maɪndful/. If you are **mindful** of something, you think about it and consider it when taking action. EG *Be mindful of the needs of others... Mindful of these criticisms, I shall attempt to justify my action.* ADJ QUALIT : PRED+*of*/REPORT-CL = conscious

mindless /maɪndlɪ^{2}s/. **1 Mindless** is used to describe actions which are regarded as stupid and usually as being destructive or anti-social. EG *...mindless violence... ...the mindless pollution of our cities.* ADJ CLASSIF : ATTRIB = senseless

2 A **mindless** job or activity is one that is so simple or is repeated so often that you do not need to think about it at all. EG *He spends the day performing mindless routine tasks.* ADJ CLASSIF = tedious

mind reader, mind readers. A **mind reader** is a person who claims or seems to be able to know what people are thinking. N COUNT

mine /maɪn/, **mines, mining, mined. 1** A speaker or writer uses **mine** to indicate that something belongs or relates to himself or herself. See **I**. EG *Margaret was a very old friend of mine... I sat beside her and took her hands in mine... He gave it to me, it's mine.* PRONPOSS

2 A **mine** is a place where people dig deep holes and tunnels into or under the ground in order to get out coal, diamonds, gold, etc. EG *...gold mines... ...a coal mine.* N COUNT

3 If you **mine** or if you **mine** coal, diamonds, gold, etc, you obtain that substance from the ground by digging deep holes and tunnels. EG *Uranium has not yet been mined in this country... They mine their own coal and ore... We are mining for coal.* V OR V+O : IF+PREP THEN *for* ⇑ dig

4 If you **mine** an area, you get coal, diamonds, gold, etc out of the ground there. V+O

5 A **mine** is also a device containing explosives which is hidden under the ground or in water in order to destroy ships, vehicles, or people as they pass over it or near it. EG *They laid mines in the vicinity of the pipelines... The ships all struck mines and sank.* ● See also **land mine**. N COUNT ⇑ bomb

6 If you **mine** an area of land or water, you place mines under the ground or in the water in order to destroy ships, vehicles, or people. EG *Eight miles of ground had been heavily mined.* V+O ⇑ booby-trap

7 If you say that a person or book is a **mine of information**, you mean that they have a great deal of information that you can make use of or enjoy. EG *He was an endless mine of information.* PHR : USU USED AS C ⇑ source = store

8 See also **mining**.

minefield /maɪnfi:ld/, **minefields. 1** A **minefield** is an area of land or water where explosive mines have been hidden. N COUNT

2 If you describe a situation as a **minefield**, you mean that it is a situation where there are a lot of hidden dangers or problems, and where you need to behave with care since things could easily all go wrong. EG *This could be a political minefield... We will need to tread warily through the minefield of departmental politics.* N COUNT

miner /maɪnə/, **miners**. A **miner** is a person who works underground in mines in order to obtain coal, diamonds, gold, etc. EG *My grandfather was a coal miner.* N COUNT

mineral /mɪnə^{0}rəl/, **minerals. 1** A **mineral** is a substance such as tin, salt, uranium, or sulphur that is formed naturally in rocks and the earth. EG *This is a continent exceptionally wealthy in minerals... ...the exploitation of mineral resources... They have discovered rich mineral deposits.* N COUNT

2 Sweet, flavoured fizzy drinks can be referred to as **minerals** in formal British English. N COUNT : USU PL ⇑ soft drinks

mineralogy /mɪnəræləd͡ʒi^{1}/ is the scientific study of minerals. ◊ **mineralogist, mineralogists.** N UNCOUNT ◊ N COUNT

mineral water is water that comes from a natural spring and often contains minerals that are thought to be good for your health. N UNCOUNT

minestrone /mɪnɪstrəuni^{1}/. **Minestrone** or **minestrone soup** is a type of soup which is made from meat stock and contains small pieces of vegetables and pasta. N UNCOUNT

minesweeper /maɪnswi:pə/, **minesweepers**. A **minesweeper** is a ship that is used to clear away explosive mines in the sea. N COUNT

mingle /mɪŋgə^{0}l/, **mingles, mingling, mingled. 1** If things such as sounds, feelings, or smells **mingle** or **are mingled**, they become mixed together but are usually each recognizable. EG *His cries mingled with theirs... It was a cry that mingled fright with surprise... He loved the mingled smell of jasmine and food in the air... John watched her with mingled dismay and pleasure.* V-ERG : ALSO V OR V+A (*with*) : RECIP ⇑ mix

2 If you **mingle**, you move around in a group of people, especially at a party when you chat to people you do not know. EG *Get out and mingle a bit... I used to train in a local park and mingle with the other runners.* V : IF+PREP THEN *with* = mix

mingy /mɪnd͡ʒi^{1}/, **mingier, mingiest**; an informal word. **1** Someone who is **mingy** is mean and unwilling to give or use very much of something. EG *She's rather mingy about food.* ADJ QUALIT = stingy

2 Something that is **mingy** is smaller in size or ADJ QUALIT amount than you expect or than you think is proper. EG *They gave us a mingy amount of cheese... ...a mingy profit.*

mini /mɪni¹/, **minis**. 1 A **Mini** is a trademark for a kind of small car. N COUNT

2 A **mini** is a mini-skirt. N COUNT

mini- is used to forms nouns referring to something which is a smaller or less important version of something else. EG *Does the Chancellor's mini budget represent a departure from stated Government policy?... The company now has 40% of the American mini-computer market.* PREFIX = small-scale

miniature /mɪnɪtʃə/, **miniatures**. 1 **Miniature** is used to describe something which is very small, especially a very small version of something which is normally much bigger. EG *...streets of decorated houses, tiny squares and miniature archways... They look like miniature sharks.* ADJ CLASSIF : ATTRIB = tiny

2 If you describe something as something else **in miniature**, you mean that it is smaller in size or scale than the other thing but otherwise exactly the same. EG *It was an Austrian chalet in miniature.* PHR AFTER N

3 A **miniature** is a very small painting, especially of a person. EG *I collect early English miniatures.* N COUNT

miniaturize /mɪnɪtʃəraɪz/, **miniaturizes, miniaturizing, miniaturized**; also spelled **miniaturise**. If you **miniaturize** something such as a machine, you produce a very small version of it. EG *We miniaturize spacecraft components.* V+O
◇ **miniaturized**. EG *...a miniaturized video recorder.* ◇ ADJ CLASSIF
◇ **miniaturization** /mɪnɪtʃəraɪzeɪʃə⁰n/. EG *...the miniaturization of electronic components.* ◇ N UNCOUNT

minibus /mɪni¹bʌs/, **minibuses**; also spelled with a hyphen. A **minibus** is a van which has seats in the back for passengers to sit on, and windows along its sides. EG *We went to school by minibus.* N COUNT, OR *by*+N

minicab /mɪnɪkæb/, **minicabs**; also spelled with a hyphen. A **minicab** is a small car used as a taxi. N COUNT, OR *by*+N

minim /mɪnɪm/, **minims**. A **minim** is a musical note that has a time value equal to half a semibreve. N COUNT = half-note

minimal /mɪnɪmə⁰l/. Something that is **minimal** is very small in quantity or degree, often of the smallest quantity or degree possible. EG *My knowledge of German was minimal... Playgroups are of minimal cost to local authorities.* ◇ **minimally**. EG *At first, Einstein's theories were only minimally more adequate than the ones they replaced.* ADJ CLASSIF = negligible; ◇ ADV = marginally

minimize /mɪnɪmaɪz/, **minimizes, minimizing, minimized**; also spelled **minimise**. If you **minimize** something, 1 you reduce it to the lowest amount or degree possible, or prevent it increasing beyond that amount or degree. EG *Our aim must be to minimize the risks... Crop rotations will help to minimise disease.* V+O ⇑ restrict
2 you make it seem smaller or less important than it really is. EG *She plays up her strong points and minimizes her weaknesses... I have no wish to minimize his role or his achievement.* V+O ⇑ reduce = play down

minimum /mɪnɪmə⁹m/. 1 The **minimum** amount or quantity of something is the smallest that is possible, allowed, or required. EG *They are going to raise the minimum level of taxation... I only had the minimum qualifications, but luck was with me... You'll need a minimum deposit of $20,000.* ADJ CLASSIF : ATTRIB = lowest, least

2 The **minimum** is the smallest amount or quantity of something that is possible, allowed, or required. EG *Two hundred's the bare minimum... He's someone who likes doing the minimum... He's gone out into the pouring rain with the minimum of clothing on... Practise each day for a minimum of twenty minutes.* N SING WITH DET : USU+SUPP

● If you **keep** something **to a minimum**, you keep it as small in amount or quantity as possible. EG *The priority for every flyer is to keep weight to a minimum.* ● PHR : VB INFLECTS

3 **Minimum** or **at the minimum** is used after a number or amount to indicate that this is the smallest number or amount that is possible, allowed, or required, and that it can be greater. EG *Allow 1-2 feet minimum.* PHR : USED AS AN A

mining /maɪnɪŋ/ is the industry and activities connected with getting coal, diamonds, gold, etc from the ground. EG *The country is still dependent on mining... ...a small mining town.* N UNCOUNT

minion /mɪnjən/, **minions**. A **minion** is a person who has a very unimportant job, especially one who carries out someone else's orders; a fairly formal word. EG *He was brutal in dealing with his minions.* N COUNT = underling

mini-skirt /mɪnɪskɜːt/, **mini-skirts**; also spelled as one word or two words. A **mini-skirt** is a very short skirt. Mini-skirts were very popular in the late 1960s. N COUNT ⇑ skirt = mini

minister /mɪnɪstə/, **ministers, ministering, ministered**. A **minister** is 1 a person who is in charge of a particular government department. EG *...Patrick Jenkin, the Minister of Health and Social Security... ...the minister for Scottish affairs.* ● See also **Prime Minister**. N COUNT : USU+SUPP ⇑ politician
2 a person who officially represents their government in a foreign country and has a lower rank than than an ambassador. EG *...the Spanish Minister in Washington... ...the US Minister in Madrid.* N COUNT : USU MOD+N ⇑ diplomat
3 a member of the clergy, especially in Protestant churches. EG *Women are allowed to be Nonconformist ministers but not Catholic priests.* N COUNT

minister to. If you **minister to** people or their needs, comforts, etc, you serve them or help them by making sure that they have everything they need or want; used in fairly formal English. EG *Anne had spent her life ministering to the needs of her husband.* PHRASAL VB : V+PREP, HAS PASS

ministerial /mɪnɪstɪərɪəl/ means belonging to or relating to a government minister or ministry. EG *Herr Ballin had rejected the offer of a ministerial post in Germany... We cannot afford the luxury of a ministerial crisis every six months.* ADJ CLASSIF : ATTRIB

ministrations /mɪnɪstreɪʃə⁰nz/. A person's **ministrations** are the things they do to help or care for someone in a particular situation; a literary word. EG *I sat in the kitchen waiting for O'Shea to finish his ministrations... I thanked him for his spiritual ministrations.* N PLURAL : USU WITH POSS

ministry /mɪnɪstri¹/, **ministries**. 1 A **ministry** is 1.1 a government department that deals with a particular area of administration within a country, for example employment, defence, or transport. EG *He worked in the Air Ministry... ...the Ministry of Energy... The ministry will have no alternative but to cut its expenditure.* N COUNT : USU+SUPP
1.2 the work that is done by a member of the clergy or by a religious person according to their religious beliefs. EG *A remarkable old Irish priest whose ministry was the hospital... The central message of Christ's ministry was the concept of grace.* N COUNT : USU SING

2 The **ministry** consists of members of the clergy, usually Protestant ones, and their beliefs and work. EG *Michael, deeply religious, had intended to join the ministry but was killed in the war.* N SING : *the*+N

mink /mɪŋk/, **minks**. 1 **Mink** is a very expensive fur that is used to make coats, hats, etc. EG *I'm very fond of mink... ...a mink coat.* N UNCOUNT

2 A **mink** is a small furry animal, from which mink is obtained. N COUNT

minnow /mɪnəʊ/, **minnows**. A **minnow** is a very small freshwater fish. N COUNT

minor /maɪnə/, **minors**. 1 Something that is **minor** has very little importance, significance, or seriousness, especially in relation to other things of the same sort. EG *I was rather more impressed by their similarities than by their minor differences... The police had been called to quell a minor disturbance... I'd always thought of him as a rather minor artist till then.* ADJ QUALIT : USU ATTRIB = small, lesser ≠ major

2 A **minor** illness, operation, etc is not likely to be dangerous to someone's life or health. EG *He's going in for a minor operation... ...minor injuries.* ADJ QUALIT : USU ATTRIB ≠ major

3 A **minor** key is one of the two types of key in which most European music is written. It is based on a scale of notes in which the third note is one and a half tones higher than the first note. EG *...Chopin's Scherzo in B flat minor.* ADJ CLASSIF : ATTRIB, OR AFTER N ≠ major

4 A **minor** is a person who is still legally a child. In Britain, people are minors until they reach the age of eighteen. N COUNT ≠ adult

5 **Minor** is used after a boy's name in some British schools in order to show that he is the younger of two boys with the same name. EG *He was called Jones Minor to distinguish him from the other Jones.* ADJ AFTER N ≠ major

minority /mɪ⁵nɒrɪti¹/, **minorities**. 1 The **minority** of people or things in a larger group is a number of them that form less than half of the larger group; used especially when the number is much less than half of the larger group. EG *Except for a fortunate minority, old age is intolerable... Only a small minority of children get a chance to benefit from this* N SING WITH DET : ALSO N + OF +N IN PL ≠ majority *system.* ▸ used as an adjective. EG *They are a minority group... ...a minority interest.* ● If a person or group is **in a minority** or **in the minority**, they belong to a number of people or things that form less than half of a larger group. EG *Artistic people are in a tiny minority in this country.* ▸ ADJ CLASSIF ● PHR : USED AS AN A

2 A **minority** is a group of people of the same race, religion, etc, who live in a place where most of the people around them are of a different race, religion, etc. EG *Our aim is to improve relations between police and the ethnic minorities.* ▸ used as an adjective. EG *In China I saw street signs in Korean and other minority languages.* N COUNT ▸ ADJ CLASSIF : ATTRIB

minstrel /mɪnstrəl/, **minstrels**. A **minstrel** was, in medieval times, a singer and musician who used to travel around and perform to noble families. N COUNT ⇑ entertainer

mint /mɪnt/, **mints, minting, minted**. **1** **Mint** is a small plant whose leaves have a strong smell and taste. It is used in cooking. EG *...a sprig of mint... ...mint tea.* N UNCOUNT

2 A **mint** is a sweet with a peppermint flavour. EG *...a packet of mints.* N COUNT

3 A **mint** is also **3.1** the place where the official coins of a country are made. EG *The Mint has decided to issue the coins next year... ...a medieval mint.* **3.2** a very large amount of money; an informal use. EG *They spent a mint of money putting it all back as it was.* N COUNT : USU SING; N SING : a+N+of +N UNCOUNT = pile

4 To **mint** coins, medals, etc means to make them in a mint. EG *One of the coins, dated 1693, was minted in Portuguese Africa.* V+O

5 If you **mint** a new word or phrase, you invent it and start using it. EG *...newly minted jargon.* V+O = coin

6 If something is **in mint condition**, it is in very good condition, as if it was new. EG *The book was still in mint condition.* PHR : USED AS AN A = immaculate

mint julep, mint juleps. A **mint julep** is an alcoholic drink made from rye whiskey, sugar, ice, and mint leaves. N COUNT

mint sauce is a sauce made from vinegar, mint leaves, and sugar. It is often eaten with lamb. N UNCOUNT

minus /maɪnəs/, **minusses, minuses**. The plural can be either **minusses** or **minuses**. **1** **Minus** is used to show that one number is being subtracted from another. 'Five minus three' means the same as 'three subtracted from five'. You represent this in figures as '5 - 3'. EG *Twenty-eight minus two is twenty-six.* = less

2 A **minus** is a minus sign. EG *There should be a minus there.* N COUNT

3 **Minus** four, **minus** seven, etc means four less than zero, seven less than zero, etc. EG *Temperatures there are colder than minus 120°C.* ADJ CLASSIF + NUM

4 **Minus** is also used in grading work in schools and colleges. An A minus is a better grade than a B plus, but it is not as good as an A. EG *I got an A minus.* ADJ AFTER N

5 If something is **minus** a leg, **minus** a handle, etc, it has a leg, handle, etc missing from it. EG *The statue survived though minus a leg.* PREP ⇑ without

minuscule /mɪnəskju:l/. Something that is **minuscule** is very small indeed. EG *He had to live in this minuscule room... ...street opera on a minuscule scale.* ADJ QUALIT = miniature

minus sign, minus signs. A **minus sign** is the sign (−) which is put between two numbers in order to show that the second number is being subtracted from the first one. It is also put before a number to show that the number is less than zero. N COUNT

minute, minutes, minuting, minuted; minutest. The word **minute** is pronounced /mɪnɪt/ when it is a noun or a verb, and /maɪnju:t/ when it is an adjective. **1** A **minute** is one of the sixty equal parts that an hour is divided into. EG *Davis was ten minutes late... This will take about twenty minutes to do... I'll be back in five minutes... An accident had taken place only a few minutes before... ...a fifteen minute introduction of the topic... It's twelve and a half minutes past six.* N COUNT : USU NUM/QUANTIF+N ⇑ period

2 **A minute** is also used in spoken English to mean a short time. EG *Will you excuse me if I sit down for a minute?... One minute, Ida. I'm just coming down... Can I just finish doing this? I won't be a minute... The maid will bring you your wine in a minute... Wait there a minute. I'll find something for you.* N SING : USU a/one+N ⇑ period = moment

3 The word **minute** is also used in the following expressions relating to time. **3.1** If something happens **within minutes** of something else, it happens very soon after it. EG *They were on the scene within minutes of the detonation... Death occurs within minutes.* **3.2** If you do something **the minute** that something else happens, you do it as soon as the other thing happens. EG *Ask for help the minute you're stuck... I knew it the minute I saw him.* **3.3** If you do something **at the last minute**, you do it at the last time that it can possibly be done. EG *They were only rescued at the last minute... I applied at the very last minute... Why do you always leave things to the last minute?* ● See also **last-minute**. **3.4** If you say that something is happening or being done **at this minute**, you are saying and emphasizing that it is happening or being done at the time that you are speaking. EG *She's feeding the baby at this minute.* PHR + NG, OR PHR : USED AS AN A; PHR ⇑ when; PHR : USED AS AN A = the last moment; PHR : USED AS AN A ⇑ now = right now

3.5 If you say that something must be done **this minute**, you mean that it must be done immediately. EG *Ma doesn't have to make a decision this minute... Do it now. This minute... I'm going right back to the shop this very minute.* **3.6** If you say that something will or may happen **at any minute**, you mean that it is likely to happen very soon. EG *Mrs Curry was going to cry any minute... It may snap at any minute.* **3.7** People often say **wait a minute** or **just a minute** when they want to stop you doing or saying something. EG *'Wait a minute,' says Howard, 'are you sure you've come to the right place?'... 'Now, just a minute, sir,' Mr Boggis said, raising a finger.* **3.8** See also **up-to-the-minute**. PHR : USED AS AN A = at once; PHR : USED AS AN A = at any moment; CONVENTION = hang on

4 **Minutes** are written records of the things that are said or decided at a meeting. EG *...the minutes of the Debating Society... You must learn how to take minutes.* N PLURAL

5 If you **minute** a meeting, you make a written record of the things that are said or decided at it; a formal use. EG *The discussion was duly minuted.* V+O : USU PASS

6 Something that is **minute** is extremely small. EG *They were adding minute amounts of fluoride to the water supply... ...not only gigantic bones but minute ones... I had remembered in minute detail everything that had happened.* ADJ QUALIT = tiny

minutely /maɪnju:tli[1]/; a fairly formal word. **1** If you examine something **minutely**, you examine it very carefully, paying attention to small details. EG *She began examining it minutely from all angles... ...a minutely detailed study.* ADV = meticulously

2 If something moves **minutely**, it moves very slightly. EG *His fingers trembled minutely.* ADV WITH VB

3 If something has been rolled, folded, etc **minutely**, it has been rolled, folded, etc until it is very small. EG *...the minutely folded piece of paper.* ADV WITH VB = finely

minutiae /maɪnju:ʃii:/ are small, unimportant details. EG *He has little time for the minutiae of the game.* N PLURAL

miracle /mɪrəkə[0]l/, **miracles**. **1** A **miracle** is **1.1** a wonderful and surprising event that people believe was caused by God. EG *People said that it was a miracle of God.* ▸ used as an adjective. EG *All that weekend I was like a man after a miracle cure.* **1.2** a very surprising and fortunate event. EG *My father got a job. It was a miracle... He survived, fetched up by some miracle on an island 40 miles to the North.* N COUNT ⇑ action; ▸ ADJ CLASSIF; N COUNT

2 People refer to a new invention as a **miracle** when it does things that they had previously thought were impossible. EG *The radio has developed from a fragile miracle to a cheap commonplace... We have accomplished technological miracles.* N COUNT = wonder

3 If you say that something or someone is a **miracle** of ingenuity, loveliness, etc, you mean that they are extremely ingenious, lovely, etc; used showing approval. EG *...speeches that would be miracles of eloquence... ...an even greater miracle of perception.* N COUNT+of = masterpiece

miraculous /mɪrækjə[4]ləs/. You describe something as **miraculous** **1** when it is very surprising and fortunate. EG *Success would have been miraculous in this case... I had been expecting some miraculous change to occur.* ◇ **miraculously**. EG *Two years later, the Captain, his sanity miraculously restored, was released... The two girls seemed, miraculously, to have survived this treatment.* **2** when you think that it is beautiful or interesting to an unusual degree. EG *The blazing red dress set off that miraculous complexion... ...fossils of a near miraculous perfection.* ◇ **miraculously**. EG *...a miraculously beautiful island.* ADJ QUALIT = amazing, phenomenal; ◇ ADV OR ADV SEN = incredibly; ADJ QUALIT ⇑ fine = unbelievable; ◇ ADV

mirage /mɪrɑ:ʒ/, **mirages**. A **mirage** is **1** something which you see in a hot region and which appears to be quite near, but is actually a long way N COUNT ⇑ illusion away, or is only an image and does not really exist. **2** something in the future that you look forward to, but that never actually happens. EG *They lead the nation towards the mirage of the technological paradise... The promised land that migrants hope for turns out to be a mirage.* N COUNT ⇑ dream = illusion

mire /maɪə/. You can refer to an unpleasant or difficult situation as a **mire** of some kind; a literary word. EG *They have dragged the planet deeper into the mire of militarism, tension, and war... We are still stuck in the nuclear mire.* N SING WITH DET = morass

mirror /mɪrə/, **mirrors, mirroring, mirrored. 1** A **mirror** is a flat piece of glass which reflects light, so that when you look at it you can see yourself reflected in it. EG *There was a full length mirror in the bedroom... She stared at herself in the mirror.* N COUNT

2 If water **mirrors** something, it reflects it, like a mirror; a literary use. EG *The clear water mirrored the blue sky.* V+O ⇑ reflect

3 If something **mirrors** something else, it has similar features to it, and therefore seems like a copy or representation of it. EG *Our discussion mirrors the dialogue or division between the groups... The inequalities between the sexes were mirrored in life in general.* V+O : IF PASS THEN+*in/by* ⇑ reflect

mirror image, mirror images; also spelled with a hyphen. If something is a **mirror image** of something else, it is like a reflection of it, either because it is exactly the same or because it is the same but reversed. EG *The room beyond proved to be a mirror-image of the first room... To him West Indian communities in London were mirror images of black communities in North America.* N COUNT ⇑ reflection = replica

mirth /mɜːθ/ is amusement which you express by laughing. EG *There came sounds of suppressed mirth... His anger gave place to mirth.* N UNCOUNT = hilarity

mirthless /mɜːθlɪ²s/. If you give a **mirthless** laugh or smile, people can see that you are not really amused. EG *He gave a short, mirthless laugh.* ◊ **mirthlessly**. EG *Card laughed mirthlessly.* ADJ CLASSIF : ATTRIB ≠ amused ◊ ADV WITH VB

mis- is added to some words in order to form other words, often ones which refer to things being done badly or wrongly. EG *...understand→misunderstand... ...use→misuse... ...calculation→miscalculation... ...conception→misconception.* PREFIX

misadventure /mɪsədventʃə/, **misadventures**. A **misadventure** is an unfortunate incident; a formal word. EG *He told a wonderfully funny story about a friend's misadventure... The coroner recorded a verdict of death by misadventure.* N COUNT/ UNCOUNT = mishap

misanthrope /mɪzənθrəup/, **misanthropes**. A **misanthrope** is a person who does not like other people; a formal word. EG *I have a dread of being thought a misanthrope.* N COUNT

misanthropic /mɪzənθrɒpik/. **Misanthropic** behaviour is behaviour which shows that someone does not like other people; a formal word. EG *He takes refuge in misanthropic fantasy.* ▸ used of people. EG *The horror of man led the misanthropic prophet to implacable hatred of the world.* ADJ QUALIT

misanthropy /mɪzænθrəpi¹/ is dislike of people; a formal word. EG *He felt himself plunging into misanthropy.* N UNCOUNT ⇑ hatred

misapplication /mɪsæplɪkeɪʃ⁰n/, **misapplications**. The **misapplication** of something is the use of it for a purpose for which it is not intended. EG *...the misapplication of techniques... ...the misapplication of resources.* N UNCOUNT/ COUNT = misuse

misapply /mɪsəplaɪ/, **misapplies, misapplying, misapplied**. If you **misapply** something, you use it for a purpose for which it is not intended. EG *The term seemed to me to be misapplied.* V+O : USU PASS = misuse

misapprehend /mɪsæprə¹hend/, **misapprehends, misapprehending, misapprehended**. If you **misapprehend** something, you understand it wrongly; a formal word. EG *It is all too easy to misapprehend its nature.* V+O = misunderstand

misapprehension /mɪsæpri¹henʃ⁰n/, **misapprehensions**. A **misapprehension** is a wrong idea or impression that you have about something. EG *I was still under a misapprehension as to the threat contained in the letter... What an unlucky misapprehension!* N COUNT/ UNCOUNT = misunderstanding

misappropriate /mɪsəprəupri¹eɪt/, **misappropriates, misappropriating, misappropriated**. If you **misappropriate** money, you take it and use it for your own purposes, when it does not belong to you. EG *Liddy had misappropriated some of the money, using it to finance his own business.* ◊ **misappropriation** /mɪsəprəupri¹eɪʃ⁰n/. EG *He had been held responsible for the misappropriation of certain funds.* V+O = embezzle ◊ N UNCOUNT = embezzlement

misbehave /mɪsbi¹heɪv/, **misbehaves, misbehaving, misbehaved**. If someone, especially a child, **misbehaves**, they behave in a way that is not acceptable to other people. EG *When children misbehave, their parents shouldn't become angry.* V : IF IMPER ONLY NEG ⇑ behave = play up

misbehaviour /mɪsbi¹heɪvjə/; also spelled **misbehavior** in American English. **Misbehaviour** is behaviour that is not acceptable to other people. EG *This leads to more misbehaviour on the child's part... He had heard reports about Shimanov's misbehaviour.* N UNCOUNT = misconduct

miscalculate /mɪskælkjə⁴leɪt/, **miscalculates, miscalculating, miscalculated**. If you **miscalculate**, you make a mistake in judging a situation or in making a calculation, with the result that you then do something badly or wrongly. EG *I must have miscalculated... He badly miscalculated the response to his proposal... He kept trying to jump over ditches and ponds, miscalculating, and then falling in.* ◊ **miscalculation** /mɪskælkjə⁴leɪʃ⁰n/, **miscalculations**. EG *These miscalculations had two serious consequences... The risks of miscalculation are greater than they were.* V OR V+O ⇑ misjudge ◊ N COUNT/ UNCOUNT ⇑ misjudgement

miscarriage /mɪskærɪdʒ/, **miscarriages**. A **miscarriage** is the act of giving birth to a foetus before it is properly formed, with the result that it cannot live: compare **abortion**. EG *She had had a miscarriage in early life.* N COUNT/ UNCOUNT

miscarriage of justice, miscarriages of justicc. A **miscarriage of justice** is a wrong decision made by a court, which has the result that an innocent person is punished. EG *He was 'reasonably convinced that there was a miscarriage of justice'.* N COUNT ⇑ error

miscarry /mɪskæri¹/, **miscarries, miscarrying, miscarried. 1** If a woman **miscarries**, she gives birth to a foetus before it is properly formed, with the result that it cannot live. EG *Emma miscarried and nearly died.* V

2 If a plan, scheme, etc **miscarries**, it goes wrong and fails. EG *Our scheme had miscarried... If a plan miscarries, he tries another.* V = misfire

miscast /mɪskaːst/. If someone who is acting in a play is **miscast**, the role that they have is not suitable for them, so they appear unconvincing or silly. ADJ QUALIT : USU PRED

miscellaneous /mɪsəleɪnɪəs/ is used to describe a group of things or people that are very different from each other. EG *...a miscellaneous collection of tools... ...miscellaneous enemies of authority.* ADJ QUALIT ⇑ various = assorted

miscellany /mɪseləni¹/, **miscellanies**. A **miscellany** is a collection or group of things that are very different from each other. EG *...a miscellany of little shops... The room was filled with a miscellany of objects.* N COUNT : IF+ PREP THEN *of* ⇑ variety = assortment

mischance /mɪstʃaːns/, **mischances**; a formal word. **1 Mischance** is bad luck. EG *This might have been the merest mischance.* N UNCOUNT = misfortune

2 A **mischance** is something that happens to you that is unlucky for you. EG *Deprivation is a common mischance... ...a series of mischances.* N COUNT = misfortune

mischief /mɪstʃɪf/. **1 Mischief** is **1.1** behaviour that is intended to cause trouble for people. EG *He's a shrewd organiser of mischief... ...the mischief that goes on in international politics.* **1.2** eagerness to have fun, especially by embarrassing people or by playing harmless tricks. EG *Her face was kind, her eyes full of mischief... There was about him an air of mischief.* **1.3** naughty behaviour by children. EG *She tried to stir up mischief among the other pupils... He was old enough to get into mischief and get beaten.* N UNCOUNT = monkey business; N UNCOUNT ⇑ liveliness; N UNCOUNT = trouble

2 Mischief is also the harm that someone or something does. EG *I always try to get the parent to undo the mischief.* N UNCOUNT = damage

3 If you **do** someone **a mischief** or **do** yourself **a mischief**, you injure someone or injure yourself; an informal expression. EG *He's intending to do us a mischief... Lally said that we'd do ourselves a mischief, if we weren't careful.* PHR : VB INFLECTS ⇑ harm = hurt

mischief-maker, mischief-makers; also spelled with a hyphen. A **mischief-maker** is a person who says or does things which are intended to cause N COUNT = troublemaker trouble between people. EG *She dismissed Sorel as a muddle-headed mischief-maker... The worst mischief makers had been transferred elsewhere.*

mischievous /mɪstʃɪvəs/. 1 A **mischievous** person 1.1 says or does things which are intended to cause trouble for people. EG *...an idle, mischievous woman.* ▸ used of behaviour. EG *His next manoeuvres were transparently mischievous... ...mischievous half-truths.* 1.2 is eager to have fun, especially by embarrassing people or by playing harmless tricks. EG *He was saucy and mischievous when he was working.* ▸ used of someone's voice or expression. EG *He heard her mischievous whispered voice in his ear... ...a mischievous smile.* ◊ **mischievously**. EG *Kitty winked mischievously.*

ADJ QUALIT ⇑ unkind; ▸ = malicious; ADJ QUALIT ⇑ playful = roguish ≠ serious; ▸ = impish; ◊ ADV WITH VB = roguishly

2 A **mischievous** child is often naughty but does not do any real harm. EG *She always was a mischievous child.* ▸ used of a child's behaviour. EG *He was continually being called in before the principal for his mischievous deeds.*

ADJ QUALIT

misconceived /mɪskə⁷nsi:vd/. A **misconceived** plan, method, etc is not the right one for dealing with a particular problem or situation and is therefore not likely to succeed. EG *His grand plans were misconceived... Their whole approach was misconceived.*

ADJ QUALIT : USU PRED ⇑ wrong = mistaken

misconception /mɪskənsɛpʃə⁰n/, **misconceptions**. A **misconception** is a wrong idea that you have about something. EG *It is a common misconception that gentlemen prefer blondes... People have the oddest misconceptions about doctors.*

N COUNT : USU + SUPP, IF + PREP THEN *about* = fallacy, delusion

misconduct /mɪskɒndʌkt/ is bad or unacceptable behaviour, especially by a professional person. EG *...a serious case of misconduct... They were victims of government misconduct.*

N UNCOUNT = malpractice

misconstruction /mɪskənstrʌkʃə⁰n/, **misconstructions**. A **misconstruction** is a wrong interpretation of something that happens or something that is said; a formal word. EG *There may be some error or misconstruction... The last scene is open to misconstruction.*

N COUNT/UNCOUNT = misinterpretation

misconstrue /mɪskənstru:/, **misconstrues, misconstruing, misconstrued**. If you **misconstrue** something that happens or something that is said, you interpret it wrongly; a formal word. EG *I said something that might have been misconstrued as an apology... You know how things get misconstrued in a small community.*

V+O ⇑ misunderstand = misinterpret

misdeed /mɪsdi:d/, **misdeeds**. A **misdeed** is a bad or evil act; a fairly formal word. EG *They had profited by his misdeeds... They tend to blame society for individual misdeeds.*

N COUNT ⇑ deed = misdemeanour

misdemeanour /mɪsdə¹mi:nə/, **misdemeanours**; also spelled **misdemeanor** in American English. A **misdemeanour** is 1 an act that is considered shocking or unacceptable by many people, although it does not really harm anyone; a fairly formal use. EG *They listened to accounts of his misdemeanours.* 2 a crime that is not as serious as a felony; a former legal term. EG *They were fined for their misdemeanours.*

N COUNT/UNCOUNT ⇑ crime = offence; N COUNT

misdirect /mɪsdɪrɛkt/, **misdirects, misdirecting, misdirected**. 1 If something **is misdirected**, it is used wrongly or inappropriately; a fairly formal use. EG *Those qualities of leadership could be misdirected.* ◊ **misdirected**. EG *...a misdirected and profit-oriented economic system.*

V+O : USU PASS ⇑ abuse; ◊ ADJ CLASSIF

2 If you **misdirect** someone, you send them to the wrong place. EG *Passengers for half a dozen flights had been misdirected to the same gate.*

V+O ⇑ direct

miser /maɪzə/, **misers**. A **miser** is a person who enjoys saving money and hates spending it; used showing disapproval. EG *Soon she discovered she had married a miser.*

N COUNT = skinflint

miserable /mɪzə⁰rəbə⁰l/. 1 If you are **miserable**, you are very unhappy. EG *Rudolph felt depressed and miserable... She wondered whether he knew how miserable he looked.* ▸ used of a person's voice or expression. EG *They all had miserable faces.* ◊ **miserably**. EG *He looked up miserably.*

ADJ QUALIT; ◊ ADV

2 If you describe a place or situation as **miserable**, you mean that it makes you feel unhappy or depressed. EG *...a miserable working-class district... Being without a grant is really miserable.*

ADJ QUALIT ⇑ unpleasant = depressing

3 If you describe the weather as **miserable**, you mean that it makes you feel depressed, because it is cold or raining. EG *...a miserable Monday morning... It was miserable and cold.*

ADJ QUALIT ⇑ unpleasant = depressing

4 You can describe a person as **miserable** when you do not like them, because they are bad-tempered or unfriendly. EG *You'll never see that miserable brat again.*

ADJ CLASSIF : ATTRIB ⇑ unpleasant = ill-tempered

5 You can describe something as **miserable** when you think that it is much smaller than it ought to be; used showing disapproval. EG *The company donates a miserable seven million a year... He was given a miserable little cubbyhole.* ◊ **miserably**. EG *There was one miserably small piece left.*

ADJ CLASSIF = paltry; ◊ ADV + ADJ/ADV

6 A **miserable** failure is very disappointing or humiliating. EG *The play was a miserable failure.* ◊ **miserably**. EG *I failed miserably.*

ADJ CLASSIF : ATTRIB; ◊ ADV WITH VB

miserly /maɪzəli¹/. 1 Someone who is **miserly** is very mean in the way that they spend money; used showing disapproval. EG *...a miserly old lady.* ▸ used of people's behaviour. EG *Don't spoil things by being miserly.*

ADJ QUALIT = parsimonious

2 A **miserly** amount of something is a very small amount; used showing disapproval. EG *She was left with a miserly amount of compensation.*

ADJ QUALIT = paltry

misery /mɪzə⁰ri¹/, **miseries**. 1 **Misery** is 1.1 great unhappiness. EG *He could have no excuse for increasing her misery... I am ill with misery... ...the miseries of unemployment.* 1.2 the way of life and unpleasant living conditions of people who are very poor. EG *He talked about the incredible misery of his people in India... They argued for a law to insure people against poverty and misery.*

N UNCOUNT/COUNT : ALSO SING = PL; N UNCOUNT = squalor, deprivation

2 If you say that someone is a **misery**, you mean that they are always complaining; used in informal English showing disapproval. EG *She's a real misery.*

N COUNT ⇑ person = pain

3 If someone **makes your life a misery**, they behave in an unpleasant way towards you over a period of time and make you very unhappy.

PHR : VB INFLECTS

4 If you **put** someone **out of their misery**, you tell them something that they are very anxious to know; a humorous expression. EG *Go on. Put him out of his misery... I decided that I must put her out of her misery.*

PHR : VB INFLECTS

5 If you **put** an animal **out of** its **misery**, you kill it because it is ill or injured and cannot be cured or healed.

PHR : VB INFLECTS

misfire /mɪsfaɪə/, **misfires, misfiring, misfired**. If a plan **misfires**, it goes wrong and does not have the results that you intend it to have. EG *Your plan has misfired... The use of force in support of their demands had misfired.*

V ⇑ failed = miscarry

misfit /mɪsfɪt/, **misfits**. A **misfit** is a person who has different attitudes or beliefs from other people in society or in a group, and so is not easily accepted by them. EG *In such societies there have always been misfits.*

N COUNT

misfortune /mɪsfɔ:tʃən/, **misfortunes**. A **misfortune** is something very undesirable that happens to you. EG *We all know of your daughter's misfortune... The violinist had the misfortune to turn over two pages at once... They had suffered their share of misfortune.*

N COUNT/UNCOUNT

misgiving /mɪsgɪvɪŋ/, **misgivings**. If you have **misgivings** about something that is being proposed or done, you feel that it is not quite right, and that it may have undesirable consequences. EG *The firm's collapse seemed to confirm their misgivings... She acts in this way with no misgivings... I was filled with misgiving.*

N PLURAL/UNCOUNT ⇑ doubt = uncertainty

misguided /mɪsgaɪdɪ²d/. **Misguided** opinions and attitudes are wrong, because they are based on mistakes or misunderstandings. EG *Official sources indicated that Sir Terence's view was misguided... ...misguided idealism.* ▸ used of people. EG *...my poor, misguided child... His contemporaries dismissed him as a misguided genius.*

ADJ QUALIT ⇑ mistaken; ▸ = misinformed

mishandle /mɪshændə⁰l/, **mishandles, mishandling, mishandled**. If you **mishandle** something, you deal with it badly or inefficiently. EG *My case was badly mishandled by my solicitors.*

V+O ⇑ treat

mishap /mɪshæp/, **mishaps**. A **mishap** is something that happens to you that is undesirable but not very serious. EG *She went home to inform her husband of the mishap... Through a combination of mishaps, the meeting was a failure... Tell your mother you have arrived here without mishap.*

N COUNT/UNCOUNT ⇑ accident

mishear /mɪshɪə/, **mishears, mishearing, misheard**. If you **mishear** what someone says, you hear it wrongly, so that you think that they said

V OR V+O ⇑ hear

something different from what they actually said. EG *I was sure I had misheard her question.*

misinform /mɪsɪnfɔːm/, **misinforms, misinforming, misinformed.** If you **are misinformed**, you are told something that is wrong or inaccurate. EG *I may have been misinformed about that.* ◊ **misinformed.** EG *The teachers I met were utterly misinformed about what was happening... The minister replied that the paper was misinformed.*

V+O : USU PASS, IF+PREP THEN *about* ⇑ inform = mislead
◊ ADJ CLASSIF : PRED, IF+PREP THEN *about*

misinformation /mɪsɪnfəmeɪʃən/ is information which is incorrect, often on purpose. EG *...a piece of blatant misinformation.*

N UNCOUNT

misinterpret /mɪsɪntɜːprɪt/, **misinterprets, misinterpreting, misinterpreted.** If you **misinterpret** something, you understand it wrongly, or you represent it wrongly to other people. EG *He saw the smile and misinterpreted it as friendliness... My work is misinterpreted a great deal.* ◊ **misinterpretation** /mɪsɪntɜːprɪteɪʃən/, **misinterpretations.** EG *The new version was less open to misinterpretation... They are quite unscrupulous in their misinterpretation of Scripture.*

V+O, OR V+O+A *(as)* ⇑ interpret = misread
◊ N UNCOUNT/COUNT ⇑ interpretation = misreading

misjudge /mɪsdʒʌdʒ/, **misjudges, misjudging, misjudged.** If you **misjudge** someone or something, you form an incorrect idea or opinion about them, and often you make a wrong decision as a result of this. EG *He knew that he had misjudged her... I had rather misjudged the timing of the operation.*

V+O ⇑ judge = miscalculate

misjudgement /mɪsdʒʌdʒmənt/, **misjudgements**; also spelled **misjudgment.** A **misjudgement** is the forming of an incorrect idea or opinion about someone or something, especially when you then make a wrong decision as a result of this. EG *There was a misjudgement as to what the public reaction to the film would be... They were guilty of a serious misjudgement.*

N COUNT/UNCOUNT ⇑ judgement = miscalculation

mislay /mɪsleɪ/, **mislays, mislaying, mislaid.** If you **mislay** something, you put it somewhere and then forget where you have put it. EG *She appears to have mislaid every box he sent her... They had failed to send it or it had been mislaid.*

V+O : IF IMPER ONLY NEG ⇑ lose

mislead /mɪsliːd/, **misleads, misleading, misled.** If you **mislead** someone, you make them believe something which is not true, either by telling them a lie or by giving them a wrong idea or impression. EG *He used his popular newspapers to mislead and frighten his readers... They were misled into buying a car... The public has been misled by the optimism surrounding the agreement.*

V+O : IF+PREP THEN *into*+-ING ⇑ misinform = deceive

misleading /mɪsliːdɪŋ/. Something that is **misleading** gives you a wrong idea or impression. EG *...misleading information... Statistics can be presented in ways that are misleading... Her appearance was misleading.* ◊ **misleadingly.** EG *The children looked misleadingly angelic.*

ADJ QUALIT = deceptive
◊ ADV = deceptively

misled /mɪsled/ is the past tense and past participle of **mislead.**

mismanage /mɪsmænɪdʒ/, **mismanages, mismanaging, mismanaged.** If you **mismanage** something, you organize it or deal with it badly. EG *The local people thought that education was being mismanaged.*

V+O = mishandle

mismanagement /mɪsmænɪdʒmənt/. If there is **mismanagement** of a system, organization, etc, it is being organized or dealt with badly. EG *Tree diseases are largely a result of mismanagement... ...problems of economic mismanagement.*

N UNCOUNT = mishandling

misnamed /mɪsneɪmd/. Something that is **misnamed** has a name that describes it badly or incorrectly. EG *...the grotesquely misnamed National Government.*

ADJ CLASSIF ⇑ named

misnomer /mɪsnəʊmə/, **misnomers.** A **misnomer** is a word or expression that is used to refer to something but which describes it wrongly or inaccurately; a formal word. EG *The very term 'positive discrimination' is a misnomer.*

N COUNT : USU *a*+N IN SING ⇑ name

misogynist /mɪsɒdʒɪnɪst/, **misogynists.** A **misogynist** is a man who hates women. EG *He quickly gained the reputation of being a misogynist.*

N COUNT

misplaced /mɪspleɪst/. 1 A **misplaced** feeling or action is inappropriate, or directed towards the wrong thing or person. EG *Her fears had been ludicrously misplaced... He had some sympathy, misplaced maybe, with the father... 'And very charming she looks too,' he commented, with misplaced gallantry.*

ADJ QUALIT

2 Something that is **misplaced** has been put in the wrong position or place. EG *Half a point would be taken off for a spelling mistake or a misplaced accent.*

ADJ CLASSIF

misprint /mɪsprɪnt/, **misprints.** A **misprint** is a mistake in the way something is printed, for example a spelling mistake. EG *There was a misprint in her name.*

N COUNT

mispronounce /mɪsprənaʊns/, **mispronounces, mispronouncing, mispronounced.** If you **mispronounce** a word, you pronounce it wrongly.

V+O ⇑ say

mispronunciation /mɪsprənʌnsɪeɪʃən/, **mispronunciations.** A **mispronunciation** is a wrong pronunciation of a word.

N COUNT/UNCOUNT

misquote /mɪskwəʊt/, **misquotes, misquoting, misquoted.** If you **misquote** someone or what someone has said or written, you repeat inaccurately what they have said or written. EG *He began to misquote Shakespeare... I think the conversation has been recorded, so I had better not misquote it.*

V+O ⇑ quote

misread, misreads, misreading. The form **misread** is used in the present tense, and is also the past tense and past participle. It is pronounced /mɪsriːd/ when it is used in the present tense and /mɪsred/ when it is the past tense or past participle.

1 If you **misread** a situation, someone's behaviour, etc, you misunderstand it. EG *Their behaviour was usually misread as indifference... He was unconsciously misreading their actions.*

V+O, OR V+O+A *(as)* ⇑ interpret = misinterpret

2 If you **misread** something that has been written or printed, you read it wrongly, so that you think that it says something that it does not say. EG *Nora would misread words, read on, then sense the mistake... She had misread a date in the Tour Book.*

V+O ⇑ read

misrepresent /mɪsreprɪzent/, **misrepresents, misrepresenting, misrepresented.** If you **misrepresent** someone or what they have said or written, you give a wrong or inaccurate account of what they have said or written. EG *Witnesses claim to have been seriously misrepresented... He says that I have misrepresented his views in my pamphlet.* ◊ **misrepresentation** /mɪsreprɪzenteɪʃən/, **misrepresentations.** EG *All political policies are open to misrepresentation.*

V+O, OR V+O+A *(as)* ⇑ represent = distort
◊ N UNCOUNT/COUNT = distortion

misrule /mɪsruːl/, **misrules, misruling, misruled.** To **misrule** a country means to govern it unfairly or inefficiently. EG *They misuse their powers and misrule our country.* ▸ used as a noun. EG *...petty tyrants whose subjects groan under their misrule.*

V+O ⇑ rule
▸ N UNCOUNT

miss /mɪs/, **misses, missing, missed.** 1 You use **Miss** 1.1 in front of the surname of a girl or woman who is not married or who is not using her husband's surname. You use 'Miss' in this way when you address her, write to her, or talk about her, especially if you do not know her well. EG *Good morning, Miss Haynes... Dear Miss Stephenson, I was very pleased to receive your letter... I do not know very much about Miss Ravenscroft.* ▸ The **Misses** is sometimes used in front of the plural form of a surname in order to address or refer to unmarried sisters, especially in old-fashioned English. EG *...the rich and settled spinsters, the Misses Bagnalls.* **1.2** in front of the name of a town, country, etc to refer to the woman who has been chosen in a competition as the most beautiful woman from that place. EG *...Miss Italy 1982... ...the Miss America competition.* **1.3** on its own to address a woman. In some schools, children address their women teachers as 'Miss'. 'Miss' is not a normal form of address in English. EG *My mam could help you, Miss.*

N IN TITLES
▸ N PL IN TITLES : *the*+N
N IN TITLES
N VOC

2 If you **miss** something, **2.1** you fail to notice it. EG *...a small detail which many might have missed... He doesn't miss much... You can't miss it, it's on the first floor.* **2.2** you fail to hit it, when you have thrown something at it, fired a gun at it, etc. EG *She had thrown her plate at his head and missed.* ▸ used as a noun. EG *We had a few near misses in the first raid.* **2.3** you regret that you no longer have it, are no longer doing it, etc. EG *I find I miss the telephone, since we've moved... I knew I should miss living in the Transkei.*

V+O = overlook
V OR V+O ≠ hit
▸ N COUNT ≠ hit
V+O/-ING

3 If you **miss** someone, **3.1** you regret that they are no longer with you, because you like them very much or feel lonely without them. EG *The two boys miss their father a great deal... She bent over and kissed him. 'Did you miss me?' she said.* **3.2** you

V+O
V+O

notice that they are not in a place where you had expected to see them. EG *We missed you at the meeting last night.*

4 If you **miss** the meaning or importance of something, you fail to understand or appreciate it. EG *The bishop concluded that she had missed his point entirely.* V+O

5 If you **miss** a chance or opportunity, you fail to take advantage of it. EG *It was a good opportunity which it would be a pity to miss.* V+O = let slip

6 If you **miss** a plane, train, etc, you arrive too late to catch it. EG *She was going to miss her plane if her husband didn't hurry... Daniel nearly missed his flight.* V+O ≠ catch

7 If you **miss** something such as a meeting or an activity, 7.1 you deliberately do not go to it, or do not take part in it. EG *I couldn't miss a departmental meeting... He would not have missed it for the world.* V+O = forego, skip

7.2 you are not able to go to it or take part in it, when you would have liked to. EG *The children are acutely aware of what they have missed... Ringo tried to cheer her up, telling her she wasn't missing much.* V+O = be deprived of

8 If you **give** something **a miss**, you decide not to do it or not to go to it; an informal expression. EG *D'you fancy going for a drink tonight?–I think I'll give it a miss, if you don't mind.* PHR : VB INFLECTS = skip

9 If an engine **misses**, it fails to operate, usually for a short time. EG *The engine started missing, popping and spluttering.* V ⇑ fail

10 • to **miss the boat**: see **boat**. • to **never miss a trick**: see **trick**. • See also **missing, hit and miss**.

miss out. 1 If you **miss out** something or someone, you fail to include them in something. EG *You can miss out a comma because you're writing too quickly.* PHRASAL VB : V+O+ADV ⇑ omit = leave out

2 If you **miss out on** something or **miss out**, you are not involved in something, or do not take part in it, when it would be of interest or benefit to you. EG *I miss out on all these kind of opportunities... You may miss out on some of the latest company gossip.* PHRASAL VB : V+ADV+PREP, OR V+ADV = lose out

misshapen /mɪsʃeɪpəᵒn/. Something that is **misshapen** does not have a normal or natural shape; often used showing disapproval. EG *...the misshapen handles on the old chest of drawers... Her misshapen old fingers twitched at her beads.* ADJ QUALIT ⇑ distorted

missile /mɪsaɪl/, **missiles**. A **missile** is 1 a weapon like a rocket that moves long distances through the air and explodes when it reaches its target. EG *Each is armed with sixteen powerful nuclear missiles... ...missile bases.* • See also **cruise missile, guided missile**. N COUNT 2 any object that you throw at someone. EG *Demonstrators attacked police cordons using sticks and assorted missiles.* N COUNT ⇑ weapon = projectile

missing /mɪsɪŋ/. 1 If something is **missing**, it is not in its usual place, and you cannot find it. EG *A blanket had gone missing... She thought some of her jewellery was missing.* ADJ CLASSIF ⇑ gone = absent

2 If a part of something is **missing**, it has been removed and has not been replaced. EG *The car was a wreck, with all its wheels missing... Half his front teeth are missing, knocked out in a brawl.* ADJ CLASSIF ⇑ gone

3 You say that something is **missing** from a statement, report, etc when it has not been included in it and you think that it should have been. EG *Two vital things are missing from the Scarman Report.* ADJ CLASSIF : USU PRED, IF+PREP THEN *from* ⇑ lacking

4 A **missing** person has disappeared completely, and their family do not know whether they are alive or dead. EG *I want to report a missing person... ...Larry Burrows, missing and presumed dead since 1971.* ADJ CLASSIF ⇑ lost • If a member of the armed forces is **missing in action**, they have not returned from a battle, their body has not been found, and they are not thought to have been captured. EG *...prisoners of war and those missing in action.* • PHR : USED AS C

missing link, missing links. The **missing link** is the piece of information or evidence that you need in order to make your knowledge or understanding of something complete. EG *Suddenly, this week, the missing link fell into place.* N COUNT : USU SING

mission /mɪʃəᵒn/, **missions**. 1 A **mission** is 1.1 an important task that you are given to do, especially one that involves travelling to another country. EG *He has repeatedly been on confidential missions to Berlin... They sent me on a mission there at the end of the war... Magee flew back to Rome, his mission a failure.* N COUNT 1.2 a group of people who have been sent to a foreign country to carry out an official task. EG *He became head of the Ugandan mission there... Mr Kaul was head of the economic mission at the International Conference of Civil Servants.* N COUNT : USU MOD+N = delegation ▸ used also to refer to the building that they use. EG *The German Mission had been blown up.* ▸ ⇑ building

2 A **mission** is also 2.1 the sending of military aircraft, especially bombers, to carry out a particular task. EG *...a bombing mission... In the next few years Foster flew four hundred missions.* N COUNT ⇑ operation = raid 2.2 the sending of a rocket into space. EG *A Soyuz 49 mission was launched with a two-man crew.* N COUNT ⇑ despatch

3 If you have a **mission**, there is something that you believe that you must try to achieve, as your duty. EG *...one of those girls who had a mission in life... The old world had an historic mission to fulfil in giving birth to new nations.* N SING WITH DET, OR N UNCOUNT ⇑ vocation = calling

4 A **mission** is also 4.1 the activities of a group of Christians who have been sent to a foreign country to teach people about Christianity. EG *They conducted five-day evangelistic missions around Britain.* N COUNT ⇑ campaign 4.2 a building or group of buildings in which missionary work is carried out. EG *...Ombachi Mission... ...St John's College, an Anglican mission school.* N COUNT : ALSO IN NAMES AFTER N ⇑ church

missionary /mɪʃənəᵒri¹/, **missionaries**. 1 A **missionary** is a Christian who has been sent to a foreign country to teach people about Christianity. EG *One of the college girls became a missionary and went out to Africa.* N COUNT ⇑ teacher = evangelist

2 **Missionary** zeal, **missionary** enthusiasm, etc is great enthusiasm for an idea, cause, etc that makes you want to get other people to support it. EG *We have to beware that missionary zeal doesn't blind us to the reality... Their belief in their cause is total and their missionary spirit is awesome.* ADJ CLASSIF : ATTRIB ⇑ enthusiastic

missive /mɪsɪv/, **missives**. A **missive** is a letter or other message that someone sends; a literary or old-fashioned word. EG *I accepted this gloomy missive as gravely as I could.* N COUNT

misspell /mɪsspe̱l/, **misspells, misspelling, misspelled, misspelt**. The forms **misspelled** and **misspelt** are both used as the past participle and past tense. If you **misspell** a word, you spell it wrongly. EG *The name, she noticed, was misspelled... Each misspelt word should be put right immediately.* V+O ⇑ spell

misspend /mɪsspe̱nd/, **misspends, misspending, misspent**. If you say that someone has **misspent** time or **misspent** money, you mean that they have wasted it, and could have spent it in better ways; used showing disapproval. EG *I'll tell him about my misspent life... They have misspent their scarce funds on facilities that nobody needs.* V+O : USU PAST OR PAST PART ⇑ waste = fritter away

missus /mɪsɪz, -ɪs/. 1 A man's **missus** is his wife; an informal word used humorously. EG *If my missus was like his missus, I'd leave home... I'll have to ask the missus.* N SING WITH DET : *the*+N

2 In some parts of Britain, people say **missus** to a woman as a very informal way of addressing her, when they do not know her name. EG *Did you hear him, missus?* N VOC = lady, madam

mist /mɪst/, **mists, misting, misted**. 1 A **mist** consists of a large number of tiny drops of water in the air, as a result of condensation near the ground. When there is a mist, you cannot see very far. EG *Everything was shrouded in mist... The sun started to show through the mist... ...the mists of early morning.* N UNCOUNT/COUNT ⇑ vapour

2 A **mist** is also a small cloud of tiny drops of liquid in the air. It is produced, for example, by an aerosol can or by your breath on a cold day. EG *The pressure sprayer releases a fine mist... Your breath turns to mist in front of you.* N UNCOUNT/COUNT ⇑ vapour

mist over. 1 When a piece of glass **mists over** or **mists up**, it becomes covered with tiny drops of moisture, so that you cannot see through it easily. EG *His spectacles misted over... Could you pass that cloth, the windscreen has misted up again.* PHRASAL VB : V+ADV = steam up

2 If your eyes **mist over** or **mist**, you cannot see easily, because there are tears in your eyes. EG *Grandpa Hindley's eyes still misted over when he told the tale... He shook her hand, his eyes misting a little.* PHRASAL VB : V+ADV, OR V = cloud over

mistake /mɪsteɪk/, **mistakes, mistaking, mistook, mistaken**. 1 A **mistake** is 1.1 an action or opinion that is incorrect or foolish, or that is not what you intended to do, or whose result is undesirable. EG *He had made a terrible mistake but he* N COUNT, OR *by*+N = error *wasn't going to admit it... Perhaps it is a mistake to seek a single universal explanation... We made the mistake of leaving our bedroom window open last night... The chances of being shot by mistake in Soho are a million to one against... I said there must be some mistake because it wasn't my birthday... The European countries have learned from their mistakes.* **1.2** something or part of something which is incorrect or not right. EG *There's a spelling mistake in the third line... Her new book is full of mistakes.* N COUNT = error

2 If you **mistake** something, you have a wrong belief about it. EG *At first he thought he had mistaken the address... I think you're mistaking how far the responsibility goes.* • If you say **there's no mistaking** someone or something, you mean that they could not possibly be wrongly thought to be someone or something else. EG *There was no mistaking her... There can be no mistaking his meaning... There was no mistaking the menace in his voice.* V+O, OR V+WH = misjudge • PHR : VB INFLECTS

3 If you **mistake** someone or something for another person or thing, you wrongly think that they are that person or thing. EG *With their brilliant green colour they are often mistaken for another deadly snake... You mustn't mistake lack of formal education for lack of wisdom.* V+O+A *(for)* ⇑ take

mistaken /mɪsteɪkən/. **1** If you are **mistaken** about something, you have a wrong belief about it. EG *I told her she must be mistaken... How could she have been mistaken about a thing like this?... 'That was it!' he exclaimed. 'I knew I wasn't mistaken!'* ADJ QULAIT : PRED, IF+PREP THEN *about/in*

2 If you have a **mistaken** belief, opinion, etc, you believe something which is not true. EG *It's a totally mistaken belief... The discovery of adrenalin came about through a mistaken impression.* ◇ **mistakenly**. EG *The parents may mistakenly believe that they are to blame for their child's illness.* ADJ QUALIT ⇑ wrong = erroneous ◇ ADV WITH VB ⇑ wrongly

mister /mɪstə/. **1** See **Mr.**

2 Men are sometimes addressed in a very informal way as **mister**, especially by children and especially when the person addressing them does not know their name. EG *Is that a walrus, mister?* N VOC

mistime /mɪstaɪm/, **mistimes, mistiming, mistimed**. If you **mistime** something, you do it at the wrong time, so that it is not successful. EG *He had mistimed his operations... There are disastrous results if the farmer mistimes the planting of his crops.* V+O ⇑ time

mistletoe /mɪsəˀltəʊ/ is a plant with white berries that grows on the branches of trees. Mistletoe is used in Britain as a Christmas decoration. N UNCOUNT

mistook /mɪstʊk/ is the past tense of **mistake**.

mistreat /mɪstriːt/, **mistreats, mistreating, mistreated**. If you **mistreat** a person or an animal, you treat them badly, especially by making them suffer physically. EG *If we mistreated our wives, they would all protest... No animal was killed or mistreated for the purpose of making this film.* V+O ⇑ harm = ill-treat

mistress /mɪstrɪˀs/, **mistresses**. **1** A man's **mistress** is a woman who he has a sexual relationship with but is not married to; usually used showing disapproval. EG *He keeps a mistress... He was accused of slaughtering his mistress and his child.* N COUNT

2 A **mistress** is also, in British English, a female schoolteacher. EG *...the hockey mistress at her school... ...Mademoiselle Girand, the French mistress.* N COUNT : USU MOD+N ⇑ teacher

3 A servant's **mistress** is the woman who employs him or her. EG *She was only carrying out her mistress's orders... The housekeeper said that her mistress had been rather odd in her manner.* N COUNT : USU WITH POSS

4 A dog's **mistress** is the woman who owns and looks after it. EG *The dog was said to be devoted to its mistress.* N COUNT : USU POSS+N ⇑ owner

5 If a woman is the **mistress** of a situation, she has control over the way that it will develop. EG *Etta was not the acknowledged mistress of the situation.* N COUNT+*of*

6 If a woman **is** her **own mistress**, she can choose what she wants to do, and does not have to depend on the wishes of other people. EG *I'm my own mistress, I say what's to be done... She was her own mistress now, and could please herself where she went.* PHR : VB INFLECTS

7 If a woman is a **mistress** of something such as a profession, she is extremely good at it. EG *She was the finest actress in England, a mistress of comedy and domestic drama.* N COUNT+*of* = queen

mistrust /mɪstrʌst/, **mistrusts, mistrusting, mistrusted**. **Mistrust** is the feeling that you have relating to someone who you do not trust. EG *She gazed on me with a sudden fear and mistrust... She had an ingrained mistrust of politicians.* ▸ used as a verb. EG *The child soon learns to mistrust offers of affection.* N UNCOUNT ▸ V+O

mistrustful /mɪstrʌstfʊl/. If you are **mistrustful** of someone or their actions, you do not trust them. EG *He was innately mistrustful of everyone and everything.* ADJ QUALIT ⇑ suspicious

misty /mɪstiˡ/, **mistier, mistiest**. **1** If it is **misty**, there is a lot of mist in the air. EG *It was still misty outside... ...a misty autumn morning... The night was cold and misty.* ▸ used of places. EG *We drove through the misty streets... ...the misty shores of Normandy.* ADJ QUALIT ⇑ foggy

2 **Misty** rain consists of tiny drops of rain that together look like a mist. EG *The roofs gleamed in the misty rain... ...misty drizzle.* ADJ CLASSIF : ATTRIB ⇑ fine

3 When a piece of glass is **misty**, it is covered with tiny drops of liquid, so that you cannot see through it. EG *His goggles were misty.* ADJ QUALIT = steamed up

4 If your eyes are **misty**, you cannot see easily, because there are tears in your eyes. EG *He looked at her through misty eyes.* ADJ QUALIT ⇑ clouded

5 A **misty** colour is a pale colour that looks as though you are seeing it through a mist. EG *It's coloured a misty blue.* ADJ CLASSIF : ATTRIB

misunderstand /mɪsʌndəstænd/, **misunderstands, misunderstanding, misunderstood**. If you **misunderstand** someone or what they say or write, you do not understand properly what they say or write. EG *I'm sure you've misunderstood him... She misunderstood my question... Like all satire, it can be misunderstood... Don't misunderstand me; we're not making any promises.* V OR V+O = misinterpret

misunderstanding /mɪsʌndəstændɪŋ/, **misunderstandings**. A **misunderstanding** is **1** a failure to understand something properly, for example a situation or a person's remarks. EG *This whole criticism seems to rest on a misunderstanding... This was a minor misunderstanding which could be instantly cleared up... ...a new source of suspicion and misunderstanding.* **2** a disagreement or slight quarrel. EG *He could not face the thought of any misunderstanding between himself and the old hunter... They usually sort out their misunderstandings.* N COUNT/UNCOUNT N COUNT : IF+PREP THEN *between/with* ⇑ argument

misuse, misuses, misusing, misused. The word **misuse** is pronounced /mɪsjuːs/ when it is a noun, and /mɪsjuːz/ when it is a verb. The **misuse** of something is its use in an incorrect, improper, or careless manner or for a wrong or dishonest purpose; used showing disapproval. EG *...the misuse of company assets... She cared deeply about words, and hated their misuse.* ▸ used as a verb. EG *He wanted to prevent science from being misused... In some cases, pesticides are deliberately misused.* N UNCOUNT/COUNT : IF+PREP THEN *of* ▸ V+O = abuse

mite /maɪt/, **mites**. **1** A **mite** is a very small amount; a rather old-fashioned or formal use. EG *Anybody with a mite of common sense could see how useless it was... The old lady won't be a mite of trouble.* • If someone or something is **a mite** old, a **mite** too big, etc, they are rather old, rather too big, etc; a rather old-fashioned or informal use. EG *I admit to feeling a mite sentimental as she crossed the threshold... I have a bed a mite softer than this one.* N PART : SING+N UNCOUNT ⇑ bit • PHR+ADJ/ADV = somewhat

2 A **mite** is also **2.1** a very tiny creature that lives on plants, in the fur of animals, etc. There are very many kinds of mite. EG *...red spider mites.* **2.2** a small child, especially one that you feel sorry for; an informal use. EG *It's cruel–the poor little mite.* N COUNT N COUNT = wretch

mitigate /mɪtɪgeɪt/, **mitigates, mitigating, mitigated**. To **mitigate** something means to make it less unpleasant, serious, or painful; a formal word. EG *Governments should endeavour to mitigate distress... It is often impossible to mitigate the results of deprivation.* V+O ⇑ reduce = alleviate

mitigating /mɪtɪgeɪtɪŋ/ circumstances make a bad action, especially a crime, easier to understand and excuse, and may result in the person responsible being punished less severely; a formal word and a legal term. EG *He could always plead the book as a mitigating circumstance at his trial... They may wish to deny the offence or plead mitigating circumstances.* ADJ CLASSIF : ATTRIB

mitigation /mɪtɪgeɪʃəˀn/. **1** If a court is told something **in mitigation**, it is told something that makes a crime easier to understand and excuse, usually in the hope that the court will decide to punish the PHR : USED AS AN A person responsible less severely; a formal expression and a legal term. EG *In mitigation, she could offer evidence of a deprived childhood... Mr Bertram tendered a plea in mitigation.*

2 Mitigation is also a reduction in the unpleasantness, seriousness, or painfulness of something; a formal use. EG *Some partial mitigation had occurred, but the situation was still regarded as critical.* — N UNCOUNT = alleviation

mitre /maɪtə/, **mitres**; also spelled **miter** in American English. A **mitre** is a tall pointed hat that is worn by bishops and archbishops on ceremonial occasions. EG *He was wearing an impressive new cope and mitre.* — N COUNT

mitt /mɪt/, **mitts**. **1 Mitts** are **1.1** the same as mittens. EG *Ingram was pulling on heavy mitts.* **1.2** in very informal English, a person's hands. EG *Keep your mitts off it!* — N COUNT : USU PL; N COUNT : USU PL = paw

2 In baseball, a **mitt** is also a glove worn by a catcher or first baseman. — N COUNT

mitten /mɪtə⁰n/, **mittens**. **Mittens** are gloves which have one section that covers your thumb and another section for your four fingers together. EG *She put on her mittens... For milder weather, caps and mittens are unnecessary.* — N COUNT : USU PL, ALSO *a pair of*+N

mix /mɪks/, **mixes, mixing, mixed**. **1** If you **mix** two substances, you stir or shake them together, or combine them in some other way, so that they become a single substance. EG *The mug had been used for mixing flour and water... The children were mixing dust and water into mud... Mix a tiny pinch of colouring into a big jar of face cream... This paint mixes easily with water... They drink whisky mixed with beer.* — V-ERG : ALSO V OR V+A *(with)* : RECIP

2 If you **mix** something, you prepare it by mixing other things together. EG *She went over to her cocktail cabinet and mixed Clarissa a drink... His wife carefully mixed the cement.* — V+O, V+O+O OR V+O+A *(for)* ⇑ make

3 A **mix** is a powder containing the correct amounts of all the substances that you need in order to make something such as a cake, cement, etc. You buy the mix in a packet and add water or another liquid to the powder. EG *...cake mixes... She bought a packet of patent cement mix.* — N MASS : MOD+N ⇑ mixture

4 A **mix** is also two or more things combined together. EG *We should try and keep a broad mix of subjects in our schools... His mind was a brilliant mix of sophisticated wit and savage humour... I find the mix of politics and literature very interesting.* — N COUNT : USU SING+SUPP ⇑ mixture = combination

5 If you **mix** two activities or **mix** one activity with another, you do them both at the same time. EG *I see no harm in mixing business with pleasure.* — V+O, OR V+A *(with)* : RECIP

6 If you **mix** with other people, you meet them and talk to them at a social event such as a party. EG *They no longer mix freely with foreigners... They were making no effort to mix... I cannot mix easily.* — V : IF+PREP THEN *with* = socialize

7 See also **mixed.**

mix up. **1** If you **mix up** two things or people, you confuse them, so that you think that one of them is the other one. EG *I have somehow mixed up two events... People even mix us up and greet us by each other's names.* — PHRASAL VB : V+O+ADV

2 If you **mix up** a number of things that are in a special order or arrangement, you change the order or arrangement, so that it becomes difficult to find particular things; used showing disapproval. EG *Don't mix those cards up, I've just sorted them out!... My papers have got all mixed up.* — PHRASAL VB : V+O+ADV ⇑ rearrange = muddle up

3 See also **mixed up, mix-up.**

mixed /mɪkst/. **1 Mixed** is used to describe something which **1.1** includes or consists of different things of the same general kind. EG *...mixed nuts... ...a mixed salad.* **1.2** involves people from two or more different races. EG *...a mixed marriage... He is of mixed parentage: half English, half Dutch.* — ADJ CLASSIF : ATTRIB; ADJ CLASSIF

2 Mixed education, accommodation, etc is intended for both males and females. EG *Do you prefer single-sex schools or mixed schools?* ● If you do something **in mixed company**, you do it in the presence of both men and women; used especially to talk about polite behaviour. EG *You shouldn't swear in mixed company.* — ADJ CLASSIF; ● PHR : USED AS AN A

3 Mixed is used to describe feelings, reactions, reviews, etc which consist of both some good and some bad things. EG *He has mixed feelings at times towards his wife... She had a rapturous audience on the first night, followed by very mixed reviews in the papers.* — ADJ QUALIT ⇑ different

mixed ability is used to describe a class or teaching system in which pupils are taught a subject together in the same class, even though some are very clever at the subject and others are not. EG *...mixed ability teaching.* — ADJ CLASSIF : ATTRIB ⇑ comprehensive

mixed bag. If you describe a situation or a group of things or people as a **mixed bag**, you mean that it contains some good items, features, or people and some bad ones. EG *The students are a bit of a mixed bag this year, I'm afraid... It's very much a mixed bag of activities.* — N SING : *a*+N ⇑ assortment = ragbag

mixed blessing, mixed blessings. If you describe someone or something as a **mixed blessing**, you mean that they may be helpful or enjoyable in some ways, but cause problems in other ways. EG *Children can be a mixed blessing!* — N COUNT

mixed doubles is a match in some sports, especially tennis and badminton, in which a man and a woman play as partners against another man and woman. EG *...a game of mixed doubles.* — N UNCOUNT ⇑ game

mixed economy, mixed economies. A **mixed economy** is an economic system in a country in which some companies are owned by the state and some are owned privately. — N COUNT

mixed farming is a system of farming that involves growing crops and keeping animals on the same farm. — N UNCOUNT

mixed grill, mixed grills. A **mixed grill** is a meal of grilled food, often including bacon, liver, chops, sausages, tomatoes and mushrooms. — N COUNT

mixed up; also spelled with a hyphen. **1** If you are **mixed up**, or if your mind is **mixed up**, you are confused, often because of emotional or social problems. EG *I got mixed up and forgot which one I'd gone to first... ...your mixed-up students... Tim was in a strange mixed-up frame of mind.* — ADJ QUALIT

2 If you are **mixed up** in something such as a crime or a scandal, you are involved in it. EG *I wasn't mixed up in it myself... He would rather not have to get mixed up in it.* — ADJ QUALIT : PRED, IF+PREP THEN *in*

3 If you are **mixed up** with a group of people, you are spending a lot of time with them; often used showing disapproval. EG *He felt that it had been a mistake to get mixed up with the French radicals.* — ADJ QUALIT : IF+PREP THEN *with* ⇑ involved

mixer /mɪksə/, **mixers**. **1** A **mixer** is a machine used for mixing things together. EG *...a food mixer... ...an electric mixer... ...a cement mixer.* — N COUNT : USU MOD+N

2 If you describe someone as a good or bad **mixer**, you mean that they are good or bad at talking to people they have not met before, especially at parties. — N COUNT ⇑ person

mixing bowl, mixing bowls. A **mixing bowl** is a large bowl used for mixing ingredients in when making cakes, bread, etc. — N COUNT

mixture /mɪkstʃə/, **mixtures**. **1** A **mixture** of things consists of several different sorts of the same thing, that are used, done, or found together in the same place. EG *I swallowed a mixture of pills... At the conference you could hear an amazing mixture of languages.* — N SING WITH DET +*of* ⇑ variety = assortment

2 A **mixture** is **2.1** something you get by putting together or experiencing at the same time two or more qualities, feelings, or other things which are quite different from one another. EG *She stared at the cold green soup in a mixture of disgust and hungry apprehension... He's got Spanish blood as well as Flemish–what a mixture!* **2.2** a substance, especially in a liquid or sticky form, consisting of two or more other substances which have been stirred or shaken together so that they can no longer be easily separated. EG *This is a mixture of water and household bleach... Take great care not to spill the mixture... We've experimented with different mixtures.* — N SING WITH DET : IF+PREP THEN *of* ⇑ combination; N COUNT

mix-up, mix-ups. A **mix-up** is a mistake or a failure in something that was planned, usually as a result of a misunderstanding or bad organization; an informal word. EG *Due to some administrative mix-up the letters had not been sent out... I think there's been a mix-up.* — N COUNT

Mk is an abbreviation for 'mark'; used to refer to a particular model or design of a car or machine. EG *...the Mk 4 Cortina.* — N UNCOUNT+NUM

ml is an abbreviation for **1** 'millilitre' or 'millilitres'. EG *...180ml of water.* **2** 'mile' or 'miles'.

mm is an abbreviation for 'millimetre' or 'millimetres'. EG *...35mm film... It measures 16 x 25 mm.*

Mm is used in writing to represent a sound that you make when someone is talking, to indicate that you are listening to them, that you agree with them, or that you are preparing to say something. EG *'It's quite hot in that part of Spain then is it?'-'Mm, it's very nice'... 'How long are you going for?'-'Mm, 2 weeks or 3 weeks.'*

mnemonic /nɪ'mɒnɪk/, **mnemonics**. A **mnemonic** is a word, short poem, sentence, etc that is intended to help you remember things such as scientific rules, spelling rules, etc. For example, 'i before e, except after c' is a mnemonic to help people remember how to spell words like 'believe' and 'receive'. ▸ used as an adjective. EG *These codes need to have some mnemonic value.* — N COUNT ⇑ formula; ▸ ADJ CLASSIF

mo /məʊ/. A **mo** is a very short length of time; a rather old-fashioned, informal word. EG *I'll be out in a mo.* — N SING: a+N = tick

MO /ɛm əʊ/, **MO's**. An **MO** is a doctor who works in the armed forces; an abbreviation for 'medical officer'. — N COUNT

moan /məʊn/, **moans, moaning, moaned**. 1 If you **moan**, 1.1 you make a low and miserable cry because you are in pain or suffering in some other way. EG *Otto moaned from the pain... He lay on his back, moaning, holding his broken arm.* — V = groan 1.2 you say something in a way that indicates you are really unhappy or anxious. EG *'What am I going to do?' she moaned... She wept and moaned that her husband had abandoned her.* — V+REPORT-CL/QUOTE = wail

2 If someone **is moaning** or **is moaning** about something, they are complaining about it; an informal use showing disapproval. EG *You're always moaning about money... Don't moan, it doesn't help solve your problems.* — V: IF+PREP THEN *about*, OR V +QUOTE/REPORT-CL = whinge

3 A **moan** is 3.1 a low and miserable cry expressing pain or other suffering. EG *Each time she moved her leg she let out a moan.* — N COUNT = groan 3.2 a complaint, often one that is expressed in a miserable voice; an informal use. EG *There are the usual moans if tea is late on the table... His constant moan is that no one understands him.* — N COUNT

4 If the wind **moans**, it blows with a low and rather sad sound. EG *The wind came moaning through the boughs of the trees.* ▸ used as a noun. EG *...the moan of the south wind.* — V = howl; ▸ N COUNT = wail

moaner /məʊnə/, **moaners**. A **moaner** is a person who is always complaining; an informal word used showing disapproval. EG *Don't worry about him; he's a real moaner.* — N COUNT

moat /məʊt/, **moats**. A **moat** is a deep and wide ditch which people used to dig round a hill or castle and then fill with water, in order to protect the place from people attacking it. EG *The castle had a tower at each corner and a moat all round.* — N COUNT

mob /mɒb/, **mobs, mobbing, mobbed**. 1 A **mob** is 1.1 a large and disorganized crowd of people, especially people who are angry about something and who behave in a violent way. EG *The police faced a mob throwing bricks and petrol bombs... It was then that there occurred the ugliest scenes of mob violence, rioting and looting.* — N COUNT = gang, mass 1.2 a group of people who spend a lot of time together, or who have a similar way of life and similar interests; an informal use. EG *I spent the afternoon with Weston and his mob... We've just been having a game of tennis, and all the mob were there.* — N SING WITH DET = crowd

2 If people **mob** someone, they gather round this person in a large crowd, in order to express feelings of anger or admiration. EG *Pop stars are always moaning about being mobbed by their fans.* — V+O ⇑ surround

mobile /məʊbaɪl/, **mobiles**. 1 Something that is **mobile** is able to move freely or be moved easily from place to place. EG *Most antelopes are so well developed that they are fully mobile as soon as they are born... The squadron was protected by a highly mobile anti-tank and air defence.* — ADJ QUALIT ⇑ movable

2 If you are **mobile**, 2.1 you can move or travel easily from place to place; used in informal English, especially to indicate that you are not physically injured or disabled or that you have a vehicle of your own. EG *The old man isn't mobile yet; he still has to stay in bed... Now I've bought a car, I'm mobile.* — ADJ CLASSIF: PRED ⇑ unrestricted 2.2 you are able to move to a different job, social class, or place to live, because you have the qualifications or personal qualities, or because the society you live in allows or encourages you to do so; a rather formal use. EG *Professional and technical populations are among the most mobile of all Americans... People who are geographically mobile are quite likely to be occupationally mobile as well.* — ADJ QUALIT: PRED ⇑ moving

3 If someone has a **mobile** face, the expression on their face changes quickly as their feelings change. EG *He had a mobile, expressive, animated face.* — ADJ QUALIT ⇑ changing

4 A **mobile** is a light structure which you hang from a ceiling as a decoration. It usually consists of several small objects which move as the air around them moves. — N COUNT

mobile home, mobile homes. A **mobile home** is a large caravan that people live in and that usually remains in the same place, but which can be pulled to another place using a car or van. — N COUNT = trailer

mobile library, mobile libraries. A **mobile library** is, in Britain, a van which takes books and library facilities from place to place, for example in rural areas or for people who are unable to get to the library because of their age or ill health. — N COUNT

mobility /məʊbɪlɪti[1]/ is 1 easy movement from place to place. EG *With the aeroplane, people achieved a physical mobility never before dreamed of... The increased battlefield mobility of the new tanks enabled us to achieve greater tactical surprise.* — N UNCOUNT

2 easy movement to a different job, social class or place to live, for example because of someone's qualifications or personal qualities, or because the society they live in allows or encourages such movement. EG *In times of economic recession, there is less social mobility.* — N UNCOUNT

mobility allowance, mobility allowances. A **mobility allowance** is, in Britain, a sum of money which the government pays to a person who is physically handicapped, in order to help them with the extra transport expenses that they have. — N COUNT/UNCOUNT ⇑ grant

mobilize /məʊbɪlaɪz/, **mobilizes, mobilizing, mobilized**; also spelled **mobilise**. 1 If you **mobilize** a group of people, you gather them together in one area or place so that they can take part in a particular activity. EG *If you can mobilize enough of your friends, your house will be decorated in no time.* — V+O ⇑ organize = assemble ◇ **mobilization** /məʊbɪlaɪzeɪʃəⁿn/. EG *The building of the canal required the mobilization and direction of large masses of labour.* — ◇ N UNCOUNT = organization

2 If you **mobilize** support, opinion, or a political movement, you succeed in encouraging people to take action, especially political action; a rather formal use. EG *The Trade Union Congress is prepared to mobilize the whole movement to defeat the bill... If he continues to make these public statements, he will never mobilise support.* — V+O ⇑ activate = marshal, muster ◇ **mobilization**. EG *Politically, of course, socialists were committed to mobilization of the workers and the peasantry.* — ◇ N UNCOUNT

3 If a country **mobilizes** or **mobilizes** its armed forces, its armed forces are given orders to prepare to fight a war; a formal or technical use. EG *The country was ordered to mobilize.* — V OR V+O ◇ **mobilization**. EG *Defence chiefs urged mobilization at once.* — ◇ N UNCOUNT

mobster /mɒbstə/, **mobsters**. A **mobster** is a member of an organized group of violent criminals; used mainly in American English. — N COUNT = gangster

moccasin /mɒkəsɪn/, **moccasins**. A **moccasin** is a soft, leather shoe which has a low heel, and a raised seam at the front above the toe. — N COUNT

mock /mɒk/, **mocks, mocking, mocked**. 1 If you **mock** a person or something that they do, you make them appear foolish, for example by saying something funny about them, or by imitating their behaviour. EG *He had mocked her modest ambitions... He always felt that Mrs Mount was mocking him a little... It is cruel to mock at the afflicted.* — V, V+O/QUOTE, OR V+A *(at)* ⇑ ridicule = poke fun at

2 You can use **mock** to describe something which is deliberately made to look older or more expensive than it really is, often using more modern methods or cheaper materials. EG *...mock-Georgian windows... ...mock cut-glass sherry glasses.* — ADJ CLASSIF: ATTRIB ⇑ false = imitation

3 You can also use **mock** to describe an emotion or feeling which a person pretends to have, usually as a joke. EG *Robert squealed in mock terror, then in real pain... 'I am doomed,' said Boylan, with mock melodrama.* — ADJ CLASSIF: ATTRIB ⇑ fake = feigned ≠ genuine

4 A **mock** examination, battle, etc is one that is intended to be like the real event so that people can practise and prepare themselves for the real event. EG *The marks in the mock A level exams were rather* — ADJ CLASSIF: ATTRIB ⇑ simulated

disappointing... The boys were told to re-enact the strategies in mock battles.
5 **Mocks** are practice exams that you take as part of your preparation for real exams; used mainly in informal British English. EG *You'll get the results of your mocks next Thursday.* — N PLURAL ↑ rehearsal

mockers /mɒkəz/. To **put the mockers on** an activity means to spoil it or prevent it from taking place; a very informal expression in British English. EG *The rain seems to have put the mockers on our little picnic.* — PHR : VB INFLECTS = wreck

mockery /mɒkəºriˡ/. 1 **Mockery** is the scornful attitude that you express in your speech or behaviour when you think someone is foolish, stupid, or inferior. EG *There was a tone of mockery in his voice... He had ignored Helen's mockery.* — N UNCOUNT ↑ scorn = derision
2 If something **makes a mockery of** something, it makes it appear foolish and worthless. EG *If he succeeds, it will make a mockery of parliamentary democracy.* — PHR : VB INFLECTS ↑ ridicule
3 If you describe an event or situation as a **mockery**, you mean that it is very unsuccessful, and insulting to other people taking part or watching, because the people who are in charge are not capable enough, or do not take the event seriously. EG *The interview was a mockery from start to finish.* — N SING : a+N ↑ failure = farce, travesty

mocking /mɒkɪŋ/ behaviour indicates that you have no respect for someone or something because you think they are stupid or inferior. EG *...a mocking smile... She stared at him in her mocking way.* — ADJ QUALIT ↑ disrespectful = scornful, superior
◊ **mockingly**. EG *'Do I shock you?' she said mockingly.* — ◊ ADV WITH VB

mock-up, mock-ups. A **mock-up** of something such as a machine or building is a model of it which is made, for example, to do tests on, to show people what it will look like, or to use in a film or television programme. EG *Here's a mock-up of the central section of the submarine.* — N COUNT : IF+ PREP THEN *of*

mod /mɒd/, **mods**. **Mods** are, in Britain, young men and women who wear a special kind of clothes, ride motor-scooters, and like a particular kind of pop music. Many young people were mods in the early 1960s. — N COUNT ↑ youth

MoD /ɛm əʊ diː/ is, in British English, an abbreviation for 'Ministry of Defence'; the government department that deals with matters affecting the defence of the United Kingdom. EG *...the MoD building in Whitehall.* — N PROPER : *the*+N

MOD □ In this dictionary MOD is used in the grammar entries beside words to describe words which come in modifying position, that is before a noun. 1 It is used to indicate that a noun must have a modifier before it, which can be either a noun or an adjective. An example is of a word which must have a modifier is **eater**. EG *Tim was a* ***slow*** *eater... She is a* ***non-meat*** *eater... I know I'm a* ***messy*** *eater.* 2 It is also used beside nouns which end in an 's' and which keep the 's' when they are used in modifying position. These nouns are described in the grammar notes as PL FORM WHEN MOD. An example is **fireworks** in **firework 2**. EG *...Britain's biggest fireworks display.*

modal /məʊdəºl/, **modals**. In grammar, a **modal** or a **modal auxiliary** is a word such as *can* or *would* which is used in a verbal group and which expresses possibility, intention, necessity, etc. For grammatical information about modals, see □ at MODAL. For explanations of the meanings of modals, see the individual entries. — N COUNT

MODAL □ In this dictionary MODAL is used in the grammar notes beside entries to refer to a small group of words in English, sometimes called 'modal auxiliaries' or 'modal verbs'. They are: *can, could, may, might, must, ought to, shall, should, will,* and *would.* (Another group of words *need, dare* and *used to* are called SEMI-MODAL. See □ at NEED, DARE and USED.) Modals behave in the following ways: 1 They can be followed only by a verb in the infinitive form. Examples are **must** and **ought to**. EG *We* ***must*** *get there before seven... You* ***must*** *give her all the help you can... Somebody* ***ought to*** *do something about it... They really* ***ought to*** *print the instructions on the side.* 2 They do not inflect. You do not say 'He musts' or 'She musted'. 3 In questions the modal comes before the subject. Examples are **can** and **will**, EG *Where* ***can*** *I get my book published?...* ***Can*** *I just finish doing this?...* ***Will*** *you meet me there?... Where* ***will*** *you be?* 4 In negative clauses the modal comes before the negative word *not*, and in *cannot* the two words are joined together. The word *not* has a short form *n't* which can be added to modals, as in *mustn't* and *shouldn't*. With **can**, **shall**, and **will** further changes are made to form the shortened negative. These are *can't, won't,* and *shan't*. Examples of modals used with negatives are **would** and **might**. EG *A picnic* ***wouldn't*** *be any fun without you... We're terribly sorry, it just* ***wouldn't*** *be convenient... I* ***might not*** *see him again... It* ***mightn't*** *be a bad idea to say that at the start.* 5 A modal can be used as a verbal group on its own when it is in contrast with another full verbal group. It is not necessary to repeat the main verb. The effect is to draw attention to the contrast. Examples are **might** and **can**. EG *I haven't strangled him yet but I* ***might****... 'Will you stay for lunch?'–'I* ***can't****,' the colonel said... I* ***can't*** *do it'.–'Yes, you* ***can****'.* 6 They are used in question tags, as in *You will be there,* ***won't*** *you?... You can tell,* ***can't*** *you.* 7 Only one modal can be used in a verbal group.

mod cons /mɒd kɒnz/ are the modern facilities in a house, for example hot water and heating, that make the house easy and pleasant to live in; used mainly in British English, in advertisements and humorously in informal use. EG *...complete with all mod cons.* — N PLURAL = amenities

mode /məʊd/, **modes**; a rather formal word. 1 A **mode** of life, behaviour, etc is a particular way of living, behaving, etc. EG *...conventionally acceptable modes of life... ...the mode of action which protesters adopt today... She always chose this mode of transport.* — N COUNT+SUPP, IF+PREP THEN *of* ↑ form
2 A **mode** is also a particular style in art, literature, dress, etc. EG *Each year brings a new mode and a new crop of artists... Their acting is kept very much in the comic mode.* • See also **à la mode**. — N COUNT+SUPP : USU SING = fashion

model /mɒdəºl/, **models, modelling, modelled**; also spelled **modeling, modeled** in American English. 1 A **model** is 1.1 a physical representation that shows what an object looks like or how it works. The model is often smaller than the object it represents. EG *...a special model of a section of the brain in action... ...scale models of well known Navy ships.* — N COUNT = mock-up, miniature
▸ used as an adjective. EG *I had a model theatre, for which I used to design scenery.* — ▸ N BEFORE N
1.2 a system that is being used and that people might want to copy in order to achieve similar results; a formal use. EG *This system seemed a relevant model for the new Africa... ...economic growth on the western model.* — N COUNT+SUPP ↑ example = pattern
2 A **model** of a system or process is a theoretical description that can help you understand how the system or process works, or how it might work; a technical term. EG *...the construction of mathematical models to understand the nature of evolution.* — N COUNT = framework
▸ used as a verb. EG *It is possible to model such a system mathematically.* — ▸ V+O = illustrate
3 Something that is a **model** of clarity, fairness, etc is exceptionally clear, exceptionally fair, etc. EG *This clause was a model of lucidity... ...a model of discretion.* — N COUNT+*of* ↑ example = pattern
4 A **model** wife, **model** teacher, etc is an excellent wife, excellent teacher, etc. EG *Jane has turned into a model mother... They are model students.* — ADJ CLASSIF : ATTRIB ↑ good = exemplary
5 A **model** hospital, **model** farm, etc has been specially built and organized to demonstrate how efficiently a hospital, farm, etc can function. EG *He built a model bakery... ...the model prison.* — ADJ CLASSIF : ATTRIB ↑ ideal
6 If you **model** yourself on someone or you **model** your behaviour on their behaviour, you copy the way that they do things, because you admire them and want to be like them. EG *The children have their parents on which to model themselves... Mary had modelled her handwriting on Sister Catherine's.* — V+O (NG/REFL) +A *(on)* = base
7 A **model** is also 7.1 a particular type of car, washing machine, etc. EG *The first production model should be ready in 1993... The Granada is the most popular model.* — N COUNT : USU MOD+N ↑ sort = version
7.2 a person whose job is to pose for a painter or photographer. EG *She was one of Rossetti's favourite models.* — N COUNT = sitter
▸ used as a verb. EG *You could see if the art college needs someone to model for them.* — ▸ V
7.3 a person who displays clothes, hats, etc by wearing them, especially in a fashion show or in fashion photographs. EG *She's a former fashion model... He got a job there as a male model.* — N COUNT = mannequin
8 If you **model** clothes, hats, etc, you display them by wearing them. EG *He models cardigans in knitting books... Gretchen was too fat to model.* — V OR V+O ↑ exhibit
◊ **modelling**. EG *Tom says she's not to do modelling while she's still at school.* — ◊ N UNCOUNT
9 If you **model** shapes or figures, you make them out of clay, plasticine, etc. EG *The children were asked to model an aeroplane out of balsa-wood... The original figure was modelled by Landseer.* — V OR V+O ↑ craft

moderate, moderates, moderating, moderated. The word **moderate** is pronounced /mɒdərət/ when it is an adjective or a noun, and /mɒdəreɪt/ when it is a verb. **1 Moderate** political opinions, policies, etc are not extreme. They are usually concerned with slow or small changes in a system, rather than with sudden or large ones. EG *...a woman with moderate views... The government continues to follow moderate policies.* ▸ used of people or groups. EG *The movement drew its support from moderate conservatives... They offer a chance to moderate people in both communities.*
ADJ QUALIT = middle-of-the-road

2 A **moderate** is a person whose political opinions and activities are not extreme. EG *The moderates have plenty to be anxious about... I began to regard myself as a moderate.*
N COUNT ≠ extremist, hardliner

3 A **moderate** amount, distance, speed, etc is neither large nor small. EG *The sun's rays, in moderate quantities, are important for health... There's a big dining room and a moderate sized kitchen... ...solving routine problems at a moderate pace.* ◊ **moderately.** EG *...moderately fast... ...a moderately long beard.*
ADJ QUALIT = reasonable, average ◊ ADV+ADJ/ADV

4 A **moderate** change in something is a change that is not great. EG *The chest X-ray showed moderate enlargement of the heart.* ◊ **moderately.** EG *Tobacco smoking has only declined moderately since the link with lung cancer was established.*
ADJ CLASSIF = slight ◊ ADV WITH VB = slightly

5 Moderate behaviour is behaviour that is not extreme. EG *Parents can get good results with either moderate strictness or moderate permissiveness.*
ADJ QUALIT: ATTRIB = reasonable

6 If you **moderate** something or if it **moderates**, it becomes less extreme or violent and more manageable or acceptable. EG *She had been given instructions to moderate her tone... The bad weather had moderated.* ◊ **moderating.** EG *They tried to exert a moderating influence on the crisis.*
V-ERG ⇑ reduce = calm ◊ ADJ CLASSIF: ATTRIB

moderately /mɒdəᵒrətli¹/. **1** Something that is **moderately** good, **moderately** likely, etc. is fairly good, fairly likely, etc. EG *Her handwriting was moderately good... When he died he left her moderately well off.* **2** Other meanings of **moderately** can be found in paragraphs **3** and **4** of the entry for **moderate.**
ADV+ADJ/ADV = quite

moderation /mɒdəreɪʃəᵒn/ is control of your behaviour that stops you acting in an extreme way. EG *It took a degree of moderation and responsibility on all sides to come to an agreement... He has not displayed the same moderation in his political behaviour as in his private life.* ● If you smoke, drink alcohol, etc **in moderation**, you do not smoke too much, drink too much, etc. EG *Even if you only smoke in moderation this is a good time to stop... It will not harm the baby if the mother drinks coffee or tea in moderation.*
N UNCOUNT = restraint ● PHR: USED AS AN A = a bit ≠ excessively

modern /mɒdə⁵n/. **1 Modern** means relating to the period of history that you live in, for example relating to the present decade or to the present century. EG *Marx still has much to say to the modern world... The social problems in modern society are mounting... ...the efficiency of their methods under modern conditions.*
ADJ CLASSIF: ATTRIB = contemporary, present-day ≠ past

2 Modern also means new and involving the latest ideas, latest equipment, etc; often used showing approval. EG *Japan successfully built up a modern capitalist economy... They share a common vested interest in a strong modern army... 'Did you like Stockholm itself?'–'Yes, it's very modern, isn't it?'* ◊ **modernity** /məⁱdɜːnɪti¹/. EG *...industries half way between tradition and modernity.*
ADJ QUALIT = up-to-date ≠ old-fashioned ◊ N UNCOUNT = innovation

3 People are sometimes described as **modern** when they have opinions or ways of behaviour that have not yet been accepted by most people in a society. EG *The Kirks are a modern couple, and believe in dividing all tasks equally... You're a modern man with advanced ideas.*
ADJ QUALIT = progressive ≠ orthodox

4 Modern is also used to describe styles of art, dance, architecture, etc that have developed in recent times; a technical term. EG *Modern art generally ignores traditional skills and crafts... ...the blend of modern and classical dance.*
ADJ CLASSIF: ATTRIB = avant-garde, contemporary

modern-day is used to describe something in the present that corresponds to something similar that existed or happened in an earlier period of history. EG *He was convinced that he was a modern-day Messiah... ...a modern-day feud over a proposed national park.*
ADJ CLASSIF: ATTRIB = latter-day

modernise /mɒdənaɪz/. See **modernize.**

modernism /mɒdənɪzəᵒm/ is the ideas and methods of modern art, especially when they are contrasted with earlier ideas and methods; a technical term. EG *...that moment when modernism first discovered itself... ...American Late Modernism.*
N UNCOUNT

modernist /mɒdənɪst/, **modernists. 1 Modernist** means relating to the ideas and methods of modern art; a technical term. EG *The market in modernist work failed to boom... ...Late Modernist formalism.*
ADJ CLASSIF: ATTRIB

2 A **modernist** is an artist who uses the ideas and methods of modern art; a technical term. EG *...the work of two of the greatest European modernists... ...the Late Modernists.*
N COUNT

modernistic /mɒdənɪstɪk/. A **modernistic** building, piece of furniture, etc has been designed and constructed in a noticeably modern way. EG *...the modernistic campus growing on the old estate... ...shiny tables in modernistic designs.*
ADJ QUALIT ≠ traditional

modernize /mɒdənaɪz/, **modernizes, modernizing, modernized**; also spelled **modernise.** If you **modernize** something such as a system or a factory, you change it by replacing old methods, equipment, etc with new ones; used showing approval. EG *...a twenty year programme to modernise Britain's transport system... The republican revolution of 1911 attempted to modernize China... ...12 million pounds spent by Courtaulds in modernizing its old Greenfield factory.* ◊ **modernization** /mɒdənaɪzeɪʃəᵒn/. EG *...plans for modernisation of the Post Office.*
V OR V+O ⇑ improve = update ◊ N UNCOUNT = updating

modern languages refer, especially in Britain, to the modern European languages, for example French, German, and Russian, especially when considered as a subject of study at school or university. EG *...a BA in Modern Languages... His wife is a modern languages teacher.*
N PLURAL

modest /mɒdɪ²st/. **1** A **modest** house, flat, etc is not large or expensive. EG *He moved from his hotel suite into a modest flat... ...modest two-family dwellings with tiny lawns.*
ADJ QUALIT = unassuming

2 A **modest** amount, **modest** rate, **modest** improvement, etc is relatively small. EG *Prices tended to rise year by year, but at a modest rate... ...a small theatre with a modest budget... ...modest inflation.* ◊ **modestly.** EG *He still gambled modestly.*
ADJ QUALIT = moderate, limited ◊ ADV WITH VB

3 A **modest** wage, **modest** success, etc is not large, but is considered to be sufficient or satisfactory. EG *He made a modest living by painting... She has enjoyed modest critical acclaim... They enjoyed material security and modest wealth.*
ADJ CLASSIF = reasonable, moderate

4 A **modest** person **4.1** avoids talking about their abilities, qualities, or possessions; used showing approval. EG *Brando was very self-conscious and modest... He's got a drawer full of medals but he's too modest to wear them.* ◊ **modestly.** EG *He talks quietly and modestly about his farm.* **4.2** is shy and easily embarrassed, especially by nudity or anything relating to sex. EG *That such a modest man should be unclothed seems highly improbable.* ◊ **modestly.** EG *They slipped out of their garments modestly.*
ADJ QUALIT = unassuming ≠ arrogant ◊ ADV WITH VB; ADJ QUALIT = bashful ◊ ADV WITH VB = discreetly

modesty /mɒdɪ²sti¹/ is **1** behaviour in which you avoid talking about your abilities, qualities, or possessions. EG *They are here to teach people modesty and humility... He was a warm soothing man, with surprising modesty.* **2** shyness or embarrassment, especially when relating to nudity or sex. EG *She covered herself with a sheet, respecting my modesty.*
N UNCOUNT; N UNCOUNT ⇑ shyness

modicum /mɒdɪkəm/. A **modicum** of something, especially something that is useful, necessary, or desirable, is a small amount of it; a rather literary word. EG *There was a modicum of comfort for the government in the latest set of banking figures... To build a big house required a modicum of taste.*
N PART: SING ⇑ bit = shred

modification /mɒdɪfɪkeɪʃəᵒn/, **modifications. 1** A **modification** to a vehicle, engine, etc is a small change which you make to it in order to improve it or to make it more suitable for a particular purpose; a rather technical use. EG *An urgent programme of modification to vehicles and weapons was put in hand... The engine was pulled apart for modifications and then reassembled.*
N COUNT/UNCOUNT ⇑ alteration

2 A **modification** to a plan, law, policy, etc is a small change which is made to it, usually in order to make it more acceptable; a formal use. EG *This led to powerful modifications of conservative theory and practice... The resolution includes key modifications*
N COUNT/UNCOUNT ⇑ alteration = adjustment, revision

calculated to win popular approval... I said I thought the idea might need modification.

modifier /mɒdɪfaɪə/, **modifiers**. In grammar, a **modifier** is a noun, adjective, etc that comes before a noun in the noun group and selects and restricts the meaning of the noun. See also □ at MOD. N COUNT

modify /mɒdɪfaɪ/, **modifies, modifying, modified**. **1** If you **modify** a plan, law, policy, etc, you change it slightly, often in order to make it more acceptable. EG *The present Government has modified this approach... English laws have had to be modified as a result of this.* V+O ⇑ alter = moderate

2 If you **modify** a vehicle, engine, etc, you make small changes to it in order to improve it or make it more suitable for a particular purpose. EG *Jaguar and Harrier aircraft were extensively modified and improved.* V+O ⇑ alter = adapt

3 In grammar, when a noun, adjective, etc **modifies** another noun, it comes before it in the noun group and selects and restricts the meaning of the noun. See also □ at MOD. V+O

modish /məʊdɪʃ/. Something that is **modish** is fashionable; a rather literary word. EG *Our modish outfits lay in a heap on the floor... ...modish magazines.* ADJ QUALIT

modular /mɒdjə^{4}lə/ is used in technical English and means, **1** in building, relating to the construction of buildings in parts called modules. EG *Even many supposedly 'permanent' buildings today are constructed on a modular plan.* ADJ CLASSIF **2** in education, relating to the teaching of courses at college or university in units called modules; used mainly in British English. EG *Does the modular system work in the 3rd year as well?* ADJ CLASSIF

modulate /mɒdjə^{4}leɪt/, **modulates, modulating, modulated**. **1** If you **modulate** your voice, you change or vary the way that it sounds, for example its loudness, pitch, or tone, according to the effect you are trying to create or the emotion you want to express. EG *Sam was so excited that he did not modulate his voice as he greeted her.* V+O ⇑ control = regulate ◇ **modulated**. EG *...her beautifully modulated voice... He continued in his carefully modulated actor's tones.* ◇ ADJ CLASSIF ⇑ controlled

2 If you **modulate** an activity or process, you alter or adjust it in order to make it more suitable for a particular set of circumstances; a formal use. EG *Attacks on industrial capital were modulated to attacks on monopoly and speculators.* V+O ⇑ control = moderate ◇ **modulation** /mɒdjə^{4}leɪʃə^{0}n/, **modulations**. EG *...all the modulations necessary to a decision-making process.* ◇ N COUNT/UNCOUNT

module /mɒdju:l/, **modules**; a technical term. A **module** is **1** in building, one of a set of parts from which some buildings are made. Each module is made separately, and the completed modules are then joined together to form the building. EG *Gantry cranes lift the modules into position... The apartment modules can be shifted around as needed.* N COUNT = component, unit **2** in engineering, a part of a machine, especially a computer, which performs a particular function. EG *...a computerized imaging module.* N COUNT = unit **3** in space technology, a part of a spacecraft which can carry out certain tasks independently of the other parts, often a part which can separate from and rejoin the spacecraft under its own power. EG *The lunar module is now in orbit around the moon... ...the command module.* N COUNT **4** in education, one of the units of a course taught in units at a college or university; used mainly in British English. EG *We have a syllabus which says that they do 10 modules... Most teachers approach each module with a concern for balance.* N COUNT

modus operandi /məʊdəs ɒpərændaɪ/. A **modus operandi** is a particular way of doing a task; used in formal English. EG *I came up with a modus operandi which served my own work.* N SING WITH DET ⇑ method

modus vivendi /məʊdəs vɪvendaɪ/. A **modus vivendi** is an arrangement which allows people who have different attitudes to live or work together; used in formal English. EG *A modus vivendi can be reached.* N SING WITH DET = compromise

moggy /mɒgi^1/, **moggies**; also spelled **moggie**. Some people refer to a cat as a **moggy**; used in informal British English. N COUNT

mogul /məʊgə^{0}l/, **moguls**. **1** A **Mogul** was a Muslim ruler in India in the sixteenth to eighteenth centuries. EG *The Moguls had been the military enemies of the British... ...the Mogul empire.* N COUNT

2 A **mogul** is an important, rich, and powerful businessman, especially one in the film or television industry. EG *He's a magnate, a movie mogul... ...a television mogul determined to win.* N COUNT : USU MOD+N

mohair /məʊheə/ is a very soft wool made from the outer hairs of Angora goats. EG *...a suit made from wool and mohair... ...a mohair coat.* N UNCOUNT

Mohammedan /mə^{6}hæmɪdə^{0}n/, **Mohammedans**. **Mohammedan** means the same as Muslim; an old-fashioned word. EG *A large number of them subscribe to the Mohammedan faith... Representation of the human body was forbidden to Mohammedans.* ADJ CLASSIF OR N COUNT

Mohammedanism /mə^{6}hæmɪdə^{0}nɪzə^{0}m/ is the religion of Islam; an old-fashioned word. N UNCOUNT

moist /mɔɪst/, **moister, moistest**. Something that is **moist** is slightly wet. EG *The seeds that land on a moist site develop into new plants... His eyes were huge and moist.* ADJ QUALIT = damp ≠ dry

moisten /mɔɪsə^{0}n/, **moistens, moistening, moistened**. If you **moisten** something, you make it slightly wet. EG *The girl moistened her lips with her tongue.* V+O

moisture /mɔɪstʃə/ is tiny drops of water in the air, on a surface, or in the ground. EG *A great deal of moisture is given off... The kitchen's stone floor was shiny with moisture... Trees have enormous roots that can reach out for moisture far below the surface.* N UNCOUNT ⇑ wetness

molar /məʊlə/, **molars**. A **molar** or **molar tooth** is a large tooth at the side of your mouth. Molars are used for crushing and chewing food. EG *...the baby's first set of molars.* N COUNT

molasses /mə^{6}læsɪz/ is a sweet, thick, dark brown syrup which is produced when sugar is refined. It is used in cooking. EG *He poured milk and molasses into a bowl.* N UNCOUNT

mold /məʊld/. See **mould**.

molder /məʊldə/. See **moulder**.

molding /məʊldɪŋ/. See **moulding**.

moldy /məʊldi^1/. See **mouldy**.

mole /məʊl/, **moles**. **1** A **mole** is a dark spot or small, dark lump on someone's skin which remains there from childhood onwards. EG *She had a tiny mole on her cheek.* N COUNT ⇑ growth

2 A **mole** is also a small animal with tiny eyes and dark fur, which is very good at digging. Moles eat insects and worms, and live mostly in tunnels in the ground. EG *...an ancient mole returning to its burrow.* N COUNT

3 In informal English, if you refer to someone as a **mole**, you mean that they are secretly working against the government, administration, or other organization of which they are a member. EG *There is some gossip in Westminster that there is a mole in the Thatcher cabinet.* N COUNT ⇑ spy

4 A **mole** is also a large stone wall built from the shore into the sea in order to reduce the force of the waves. EG *Old men sat along the mole and fished.* N COUNT = breakwater

molecular /mə^{6}lekjə^{4}lə/ means relating to molecules or a molecule; a technical term. EG *...molecular biology... ...the structure of a polymer at the molecular level.* ADJ CLASSIF : ATTRIB

molecule /mɒlɪkju:l/, **molecules**. A **molecule** is the smallest amount of a chemical substance which can exist by itself without changing or breaking apart; a technical term. EG *The haemoglobin molecule contains only four atoms of iron.* N COUNT

molehill /məʊlhɪl/, **molehills**. A **molehill** is a small pile of earth on the ground that has been left by a mole that has been digging there. EG *He stumbled over a molehill.* N COUNT ⇑ mound ● If you **make a mountain out of a molehill**, you make an unimportant fact or difficulty seem like a serious one. EG *Aren't we all making a mountain out of a molehill?* ● PHR : VB AND N INFLECT ⇑ exaggerate

molest /mə^{7}lest/, **molests, molesting, molested**. **1** Someone who **molests** a woman or a child interferes with them in a sexual way against their will and can be arrested by the police for this; a formal use. EG *You are fortunate you did not sexually molest that poor girl or I'd put you behind bars for life... She had killed a man who was molesting her.* V+O ⇑ assault = abuse ◇ **molestation** /mɒlesteɪʃə^{0}n/. EG *...child molestation.* ◇ N UNCOUNT

2 If you **molest** someone, you annoy them and prevent them from doing something or going somewhere, often by using physical violence; an old-fashioned use. EG *They feared they would be molested by the angry crowd... Kindly do not molest us.* V+O ⇑ annoy = bother

molester /mə^{7}lestə/, **molesters**. A **molester** is a person who interferes with women or children in a N COUNT sexual way against their will, and can be arrested by the police for this.

moll /mɒl/, **molls**. A gangster's **moll** is a woman who lives with him and has a sexual relationship with him; used mainly in old-fashioned American English. N COUNT : USU POSS+N

mollify /mɒlɪfaɪ/, **mollifies, mollifying, mollified**. If you **mollify** someone, you make them less upset or angry. EG *Francis immediately set about mollifying her... Mrs Pringle allowed herself to be mollified.* ◊ **mollified**. EG *Even Susy Williams looked mollified.* V+O ⇑ calm = appease, placate ◊ ADJ QUALIT : PRED

mollusc /mɒləsk/, **molluscs**. A **mollusc** is an animal such as a snail, slug, clam, or octopus, which has a soft body and no backbone. Many types of mollusc have hard shells which protect them, and many molluscs live in water. N COUNT

mollycoddle /mɒlɪkɒdə0l/, **mollycoddles, mollycoddling, mollycoddled**. If you **mollycoddle** someone, you do too many things for them and you protect them from unpleasant experiences; used showing disapproval. EG *A man must not allow himself to be mollycoddled.* V+O ⇑ spoil = pamper

Molotov cocktail /mɒlətɒv kɒkteɪl/, **Molotov cocktails**. A **Molotov cocktail** is a simple bomb made by putting petrol and cloth into a bottle. EG *The rioters were throwing Molotov cocktails.* N COUNT

molt /məʊlt/. See **moult**.

molten /məʊltə0n/ rock or metal has been heated to a very high temperature and has become a hot thick sticky liquid. EG *...a great mass of molten rock... Molten metal ran out on to the flagstones.* ADJ QUALIT : USU ATTRIB

mom /mɒm/, **moms**. Some people address or refer to their mother as **mom**; used mainly in informal American English. EG *When I was born, Mom was forty and Dad forty-six... 'Hey, mom,' said Billy, 'what's that around your neck?'* N PROPER/VOC : ALSO N COUNT

moment /məʊmə2nt/, **moments**. **1** A **moment** is a very short period of time, for example a few seconds. EG *She hesitated for only a moment... There was a moment of silence... A few moments later he heard footsteps... Wait a moment. Stay there... The fridge hasn't given a moment's trouble.* N COUNT

2 The word **moment** is used with this meaning in the following expressions. **2.1** If you do something at **the last moment**, you do it at the last possible time that it could be done. EG *We escaped from Saigon at the last moment... They waited until the very last moment.* PHR : USU PREP+PHR **2.2** If you say that you will do something **in a moment**, you mean that you will do it very soon. EG *I shall get angry in a moment... I'll come back to that in a moment.* PHR : USED AS AN A **2.3** If you say that something has **just this moment** happened, you are emphasizing that it has only just happened. EG *It's just this moment stopped raining... 'Would you like to go to the shops for me?'–'But I've only just this moment sat down.'* PHR : USED AS AN A **2.4** In a story, **'the next moment'** is used to emphasize that one event happens immediately after another. EG *The next moment he collapsed.* PHR : USED AS AN A **2.5** If you say that you do not believe something **for a moment** or **for one moment**, you are emphasizing that you do not believe it at all. EG *I don't believe it for one moment... I don't think for a moment he believed my reason.* PHR : USED AS AN A

3 A **moment** is also the actual point in time at which something happens. EG *At that precise moment, Miss Pulteney came into the office... ...the moment of death.* N SING WITH DET +SUPP = instant

4 The word **moment** is used with this meaning in the following expressions. **4.1** If you say that something is happening **at this moment**, you are emphasizing that it is happening at the time that you are speaking. EG *There's an exhibition at this moment at the Whitechapel Art Gallery.* PHR : USED AS AN A ⇑ now **4.2** You use the expressions **at the moment, at the present moment**, and **at this moment in time** when you want to emphasize that a particular situation exists at the time when you are speaking, although it may change in the future. EG *The biggest problem at the moment is unemployment... I'm sorry, but she's not in at the moment... The world uses very little energy at the present moment... At this moment in time, more and more women are losing their jobs.* PHR : USED AS AN A ⇑ now **4.3** If you say that you will not or cannot do something **for the moment**, you mean that you will not or cannot do it at the time when you are speaking, but you will probably be able to do it later. EG *I don't want to discuss this for the moment... I want to leave this for the moment and talk about something else... ...some Swedish workers whose names for the moment escape me.* PHR : USED AS AN A ▸ N COUNT **4.4** If you say that something happened **the moment** something else happened, you mean that the two things happened at almost the same time. EG *The moment I saw this, it appealed to me.* CONJ SUBORD ⇑ when = as soon as **4.5** The excitement **of the moment**, confusion **of the moment**, etc is the excitement, confusion, etc that exists at the time about which you are talking. EG *...the Islamic confusion of the moment.* PHR : NG+PHR **4.6** The hero **of the moment**, idol **of the moment**, etc is the person who is regarded as the most important hero, idol, etc at the time about which you are talking, especially when you are emphasizing that their status as hero or idol did not last or may not last for very long. EG *They're readily swayed by pop stars and the idol of the moment.* PHR : NG+PHR **4.7** ● **on the spur of the moment**: see **spur**. See also **spur-of-the-moment**.

5 A **moment** is also a particular occasion which is very important, memorable, or suitable for doing something. EG *...at such a critical moment in his career... There have been moments when everything seemed very bleak... It causes me moments of acute embarrassment... What's the best moment, do you think?* N COUNT : USU+SUPP = time ● If you say that someone **has** their **moments** or something **has** its **moments**, you mean that there are periods of time in that person's life or in a particular process or activity which involve great excitement, success, despair, etc, although the rest of the time they are ordinary and dull. EG *God, I have my moments.* ● PHR : VB INFLECTS

6 Something that is **of great moment** is very important; a formal or old-fashioned use. EG *...a matter of the greatest moment.* PHR : USED AS C, OR NG+PHR

momentary /məʊməntə0ri1/. Something that is **momentary** lasts for a very short period of time, for example for a few seconds. EG *There was a momentary pause.* ◊ **momentarily**. EG *She shivered momentarily... I had momentarily forgotten.* ADJ CLASSIF ⇑ temporary = brief, fleeting ◊ ADV WITH VB ⇑ temporarily

moment of truth, moments of truth. A **moment of truth** is an important time when you must make a decision quickly and whatever you decide will have important consequences in the future. EG *The moment of truth came when she got to the airport.* N COUNT

momentous /mə6mentəs/ decisions, events, etc are very important, often because of the effects that they will have in the future; a rather formal or literary word. EG *A great question had to be answered, a momentous decision made... There was no doubt it would be a momentous occasion.* ADJ CLASSIF = critical

momentum /mə6mentəm/ is **1** the ability that something has to keep developing in a particular way. EG *Such is the momentum of change in the second half of the twentieth century... It was necessary to crush the rebel movement before it had a chance to gather momentum.* N UNCOUNT ⇑ force = impetus **2** in physics, the mass of a moving object multiplied by its velocity; a technical term. EG *...the rate of change of momentum.* N UNCOUNT

momma /mɒmə/, **mommas**. The forms **mommy** /mɒmi1/ and **mommies** are also used. Some people address or refer to their mother as **momma** or **mommy**; used mainly in informal American English. EG *God bless Mommy and Daddy... My momma had six girls... Mommy, do you know what I want for Christmas?* N PROPER/VOC : ALSO N COUNT

Mon. is a written abbreviation for 'Monday'.

monarch /mɒnək/, **monarchs**. A **monarch** is a king, queen, or other royal person who reigns over a country or an empire. EG *The visitor was the monarch in person... ...the London home of the Monarch.* N COUNT ⇑ ruler

monarchical /mɒnɑːkɪkə0l/ means relating to a monarch or monarchs. EG *...the monarchical principle... ...monarchical and feudal institutions.* ADJ CLASSIF : ATTRIB ⇑ ruling

monarchist /mɒnəkɪst/, **monarchists**. A **monarchist** is a person who believes that their country should have a hereditary ruler such as a king or queen. EG *...a group of Hungarian monarchists.* N COUNT = royalist

monarchy /mɒnəki1/, **monarchies**. A **monarchy** is a system in which a monarch reigns over a country and in which the next monarch will be another member of the same family. EG *We want to abolish the monarchy... ...the stability and independence of the English monarchy.* ▸ used also to refer to a country that has this system. EG *France was an* N COUNT : USU the+N, OR UNCOUNT *absolute monarchy.* ▸ used also to refer to the monarch and his or her family. EG *...the aristocratic ways of the old Italian monarchy.* ▸ N COUNT : USU the+N = royalty

monastery /mɒnəstri¹/, **monasteries**. A **monastery** is a building or collection of buildings in which a group of monks live together and do their religious practices. Monasteries are usually situated away from towns and cities. N COUNT

monastic /mə⁷næstɪk/; a formal or literary word. 1 **Monastic** means relating to monks or to a monastery. EG *...monastic buildings.* ADJ CLASSIF ⇑ religious

2 If you live a **monastic** life, you live simply, without any luxuries. EG *...my austere, monastic life... ...monastic frugality.* ADJ QUALIT ⇑ simple

Monday /mʌndi¹/, **Mondays**. **Monday** is one of the seven days of the week. It is the day after Sunday and before Tuesday. Most people start their week's work on a Monday. EG *It was windy here last Monday... He had a plan for reducing ticket prices on Mondays.* N UNCOUNT/ COUNT

monetarism /mɒnɪ²tə⁰rɪzm/ is the control of a country's economy by regulating the total amount of money that is available and in use at any one time; a technical term. EG *She can't claim that monetarism has worked as it was meant to.* N UNCOUNT

monetarist /mɒnɪ²tə⁰rɪst/, **monetarists**; a technical term. 1 **Monetarist** means relating to monetarism. EG *...a result of monetarist policies... ...Mrs Thatcher's monetarist government.* ADJ CLASSIF

2 A **monetarist** is someone who believes that their country's economy should be controlled by regulating the total amount of money that is available and in use at any one time. EG *The monetarists are at least partly right.* N COUNT ⇑ person

monetary /mɒnɪ²tə⁰ri¹/ means relating to money, especially the total amount of money in a country; a formal word. EG *He is turning Washington's tight monetary policy to political advantage... ...techniques of monetary control.* ADJ CLASSIF : ATTRIB = financial

money /mʌni¹/. The plural forms **monies** and **moneys** are only used in paragraph 3. 1 **Money** is the coins or bank notes that you use when you buy something, or when you pay for a service. The money that a person has includes their savings in a bank, building society, etc, but does not include their other possessions. EG *Do you have any money on you?... I spent all my money on sweets... I had very little money left... He earns a lot of money... They might not accept English money... The money will be sent by cheque.* N UNCOUNT

2 The word **money** is used in the following expressions in informal English. 2.1 If you **make money**, you obtain money by earning it or by making a profit. EG *They made a lot of money last year... He made good money when he worked... How much money did you make?* PHR : VB INFLECTS 2.2 If you are **in the money**, you have a lot of money to spend. EG *She seems to be in the money these days.* PHR : USED AS AN A 2.3 If you **get your money's worth**, you get good value for the money that you spend. EG *I always insist on getting my money's worth.* PHR : VB INFLECTS 2.4 If you say that someone **has money to burn**, you mean that they have more money than they need or that they spend their money on things that you think are unnecessary; used showing disapproval. EG *Many oil-rich countries have money to burn.* PHR : VB INFLECTS

3 **Monies** refer to several separate sums of money that form part of a larger amount that is received or spent; a formal and old-fashioned use, also a legal term. EG *...public monies... The project received community monies.* N PLURAL ⇑ funds

4 • **money for old rope**: see **rope**. See also **blood money, danger money, hush money, pocket money**.

MONEY □ This entry shows some ways of referring to amounts of money. When you express amounts of money in writing, the main unit of currency that you are using is usually shown by a symbol or letter in front of the figures. For example, £100 means one hundred pounds, $100 means one hundred dollars, and DM100 means one hundred German marks. If an amount of money consists of both the main unit and a smaller unit, for example pounds and pence, or dollars and cents, then you usually show only the symbol or letter for the main unit, and you separate the two units by a full stop. For example, $2.50 means two dollars and fifty cents. If an amount of money consists of only a smaller unit, for example only pence or cents, then the symbol or letter usually follows the figures. For example, 50p means fifty pence. When you say aloud amounts of money that have been written in this way, the full word for the unit of currency is pronounced, and it is said after the numbers rather than before them. For example, £10 is said as 'ten pounds'. In speech, the actual words that refer to the unit of currency, for example 'pounds', 'pence', 'dollars', etc are often left out altogether. However, the context usually makes it clear exactly how much you are referring to, and also which currency you are referring to. The following examples show a few ways of expressing amounts of money. EG *He was making ninety dollars a week... It costs 35 pounds a kilo... ...a million and a half dollars... ...the ten-cent packet of balloons... The machine wouldn't take 10p pieces... Total British losses were close to a quarter of a million pounds.*

money-box, money-boxes; also spelled without a hyphen. A **money-box** is a small box with an opening at the top, into which a child puts coins as a way of saving money. EG *I took twenty cents out of my money-box.* N COUNT = piggy bank

moneyed /mʌni¹d/. See **monied**.

moneylender /mʌni¹lɛndə/, **moneylenders**; also spelled with a hyphen. A **moneylender** is a person who lends money which has to be paid back at a high rate of interest; a rather old-fashioned word. EG *He had the misfortune to owe a huge sum to a moneylender.* N COUNT = loan shark

money-maker, money-makers; also spelled without a hyphen. A **money-maker** is 1 a person whose chief concern is to make a lot of money; often used showing disapproval. EG *Montreal was the money-makers' Mecca... Have the manners and morals of the moneymakers improved?* N COUNT ⇑ capitalist 2 a business project or investment that yields a good profit; used in informal English showing approval. N COUNT

money market, money markets. A country's **money market** consists of all the institutions such as the government and commercial banks that deal with short-term loans, capital, and foreign exchange; a technical term. EG *They use that money to put into the money markets at a profit... The banks may well be in touch with the money markets... ...money-market funds.* N COUNT

Mongol /mɒŋgə⁰l/, **Mongols**. 1 The **Mongols** were a nomadic Asiatic people who conquered large areas of China and Central Asia under the leadership of Genghis Khan and Kublai Khan in the 12th and 13th centuries A.D. N COUNT

2 **Mongol** means belonging or relating to the Mongols. EG *They threw off Mongol rule in 1480.* ADJ CLASSIF

3 A **mongol** is an offensive term for someone who suffers from **Down's syndrome**. N COUNT

Mongolian /mɒŋgəulɪən/, **Mongolians**. 1 **Mongolian** is the language that is spoken by people who live in Mongolia. N UNCOUNT

2 **Mongolian** also means belonging or relating to Mongolia, or to its people or language. ADJ CLASSIF

3 A **Mongolian** is a person who comes from Mongolia. N COUNT

mongolism /mɒŋgəlɪzə⁰m/ is an offensive term for **Down's syndrome**. N UNCOUNT ⇑ disease

mongoose /mɒŋgu:s/, **mongooses**. A **mongoose** is a small furry animal with a long tail that lives in hot countries and kills snakes. N COUNT

mongrel /mʌŋgrəl/, **mongrels**. A **mongrel** is a dog with parents of different breeds. EG *If you want a dog, you can get a mongrel from a pet store.* N COUNT

monied /mʌni¹d/; also spelled **moneyed**. A **monied** person has a lot of money; a rather old-fashioned word. EG *...a few monied families in the neighbourhood.* ADJ QUALIT ⇑ wealthy = rich

monitor /mɒnɪtə/, **monitors, monitoring, monitored**. 1 If you **monitor** something, you regularly check how it is changing or progressing over a period of time. EG *The child's progress is being monitored... Microprocessors monitor tyre wear and brake power on the cars.* V+O

2 If you **monitor** sounds, especially radio broadcasts from other countries, you record them or listen carefully to them in order to obtain information. EG *They were getting news by monitoring BBC broadcasts... Patrol ships monitored the noise made by submarines in the vicinity.* V+O

3 A **monitor** is 3.1 a machine that is used to check or record things, for example processes or substances inside a person's body. EG *The patient was connected to the monitor.* N COUNT 3.2 a television set used in a television studio when a programme is being made, N COUNT

especially for watching and checking the picture and sound. EG *An image of the area seen by the television camera is displayed on a monitor screen.* **3.3** a school pupil who is chosen to do special duties to help the teacher; a rather old-fashioned use in British English. N COUNT

monk /mʌŋk/, **monks**. A **monk** is a man who has made a special set of solemn religious promises, especially not to marry or possess any wealth, and usually lives in a male religious community that is separated from the rest of society. EG *This magnificent Abbey was founded by a monk from Northumbria... ...medieval monks.* N COUNT

monkey /mʌŋki[1]/, **monkeys, monkeying, monkeyed**. **1** A **monkey** is an animal that lives in hot countries, and has a long tail and skilful hands which it uses for climbing trees and for moving from branch to branch. There are lots of different kinds of monkey. EG *Twenty or thirty monkeys were huddled along the thick branches.* N COUNT

2 In informal English, if you refer to a child as a **monkey**, you mean that it is very lively and naughty. EG *Stop it, you little monkey!* N COUNT/VOC = imp, scamp

monkey about; also **monkey around**. In informal English, if someone **is monkeying about**, **1** they are behaving in a silly and playful way. EG *The twins have been monkeying about in the attic again.* **2** they are interfering with what you are doing in a way that annoys you. EG *...coming and monkeying about in my affairs.* PHRASAL VB : V+ADV; PHRASAL VB : V+ADV ⇑ interfere = meddle

monkey about with; also **monkey around with**. In informal English, if someone **monkeys about with** something, they do something to it in a careless or ignorant way and may damage it or break it. EG *It would have been all right if you hadn't monkeyed about with the plug.* PHRASAL VB : V+ADV+PREP, OR V+PREP, HAS PASS = tinker with, tamper with

monkey business is slightly unacceptable, dishonest, or illegal behaviour; used in informal and rather old-fashioned English. EG *I knew there had been some monkey business going on.* N UNCOUNT ⇑ activity = hanky panky

monkey nut, monkey nuts; also spelled with a hyphen and as one word. A **monkey nut** is the same as a peanut; used in informal English. N COUNT

mono /mɒnəʊ/ is used to describe a record or a system of playing music in which all the sound is directed through one speaker only. EG *I've only got an old mono recording... We could only listen in mono.* ADJ CLASSIF, OR N UNCOUNT : in+N

mono- is used at the beginning of nouns and adjectives that have 'one' as part of their meaning. EG *...monologue... ...monochrome... ...monotone.* PREFIX

monochrome /mɒnəkrəʊm/; a technical term. **1** A **monochrome** painting is painted using only one colour in various shades. EG *I did a monochrome painting.* ADJ CLASSIF

2 Films, photographs, or televisions that are **monochrome** show black, white, and shades of grey, but no other colours. EG *...negatives, colour and monochrome transparencies.* ADJ CLASSIF

monocle /mɒnəkə[0]l/, **monocles**. A **monocle** is a glass lens which people in former times wore in front of one of their eyes to improve their ability to see with that eye. EG *He had wavy white hair and a monocle dangling from a ribbon.* N COUNT

monogamous /mə[7]nɒgəməs/ is used in formal English to describe **1** relationships in which people have only one husband or wife at a particular time, or to describe societies in which this is the custom. EG *Patriarchy based itself on monogamous marriage for women.* **2** animals who have only one mate for all their lives, or during one season. EG *Some females and some males are monogamous. Other males will mate with many females.* ADJ CLASSIF; ADJ CLASSIF

monogamy /mə[7]nɒgəmi[1]/ is the state or custom of being married to only one person at a particular time; a formal word. EG *Monogamy was the law of the land... Lifelong monogamy has other drawbacks.* N UNCOUNT ≠ polygamy

monogram /mɒnəgræm/, **monograms**. A **monogram** is a design based on someone's initials, and is usually marked on things they own such as a cigarette case, stationery, or clothing. EG *I picked up the lighter and examined it. There was a monogram on it.* N COUNT

monogrammed /mɒnəgræmd/ means marked with a design that includes a person's initials. EG *...his monogrammed hair brushes.* ADJ CLASSIF = initialled

monograph /mɒnəgræf, -grɑːf/, **monographs**. A **monograph** is a book which is a detailed study of only one subject. EG *Rainer Crone published a monograph on Warhol.* N COUNT

monolith /mɒnə[6]lɪθ/, **monoliths**. A **monolith** is a very large, upright piece of stone. Some monoliths were erected in ancient times. EG *He stumbled towards the huge, solitary monolith which had attracted his attention... There is magnetism emanating from these prehistoric monoliths.* N COUNT

monolithic /mɒnə[6]lɪθɪk/. **1** An organization or system that is **monolithic** is very large and gives the impression that it will never change or cease to exist, and that the people or parts in it are all very similar to each other. EG *...undermining the monolithic character of the main political parties... Don't think that Europe is monolithic and all countries in Europe must make the same decision.* ADJ QUALIT ⇑ impenetrable = intractable

2 Something that is **monolithic** is very large and impressive, so that everything else seems to be very small by comparison. EG *The great monolithic rock was surrounded by fertile flats... Monolithic buildings shaded out the sun.* ADJ QUALIT = colossal, monumental

monologue /mɒnəlɒg/, **monologues**. A **monologue** is **1** a long speech by one person during a conversation, which prevents other people from talking or expressing their opinions. EG *It wasn't so much a discussion as a monologue... He went into a long monologue, only part of which I understood.* **2** a long speech which is spoken by one person in a play; a technical term in the theatre. EG *I often returned to see her famous monologues.* N COUNT ≠ conversation; N COUNT/UNCOUNT ≠ dialogue

monopolistic /mə[7]nɒpə[6]lɪstɪk/. A firm or business company that is **monopolistic** controls or tries to control as much of an industry as it can; a formal or technical word. EG *We were intent on preventing monopolistic price increases by any of the big firms... He issued a statement denouncing the deal as monopolistic and dangerous.* ADJ QUALIT ⇑ controlling

monopolize /mə[7]nɒpəlaɪz/, **monopolizes, monopolizing, monopolized**; also spelled **monopolise**. **1** If you **monopolize** something, you have a very large share of it and you prevent other people from having a share. EG *The Dutch wanted to monopolize the profitable spice trade from the East... The landlords try to monopolize the extra profits.* V+O ⇑ control = dominate

◇ **monopolization** /mə[7]nɒpə[6]laɪzeɪʃə[0]n/. EG *Indonesians were barred from business by Dutch and Chinese monopolization.* ◇ N UNCOUNT = domination

2 If something **monopolizes** you, it demands a lot of your time and attention, so that there is very little time left for anything else. EG *My thoughts had been monopolized by the problem of finding a lawyer.* V+O = dominate

monopoly /mə[7]nɒpəli[1]/, **monopolies**. **1** A **monopoly** is **1.1** complete control of a particular subject or activity by one person or a group of people, so that other people find it difficult or impossible to compete with them. EG *The Americans lost the nuclear weapon monopoly when the Soviets exploded their first atomic bomb... I don't believe the medical profession has a monopoly on morality.* N COUNT : IF+PREP THEN of/on ⇑ domination

▸ also used to refer to a thing or place that the person or group has control over. EG *The South Shore used to be the exclusive monopoly of early Dutch and English landowners.* ▸ N COUNT ⇑ property

1.2 control of a large proportion or the whole of an industry by only one or a few large firms. EG *The partnership was small enough not to constitute a monopoly... They were trying to find economic alternatives outside monopoly capitalism.* N COUNT/UNCOUNT

2 Monopoly is a trademark for a board game using dice and in which the players try to buy land and buildings, charge rent for them, build new property on the land, etc, and win the game by making the other players lose all their money so that the winner owns everything. N PROPER

monorail /mɒnə[6]reɪl/, **monorails**. A **monorail** is a system of transport in which trains travel along a single rail which is usually high above the ground. EG *Monorail systems could help ease traffic congestion.* N COUNT, OR by+N

monosyllabic /mɒnə[6]sɪlæbɪk/ is used to describe a word that has only one syllable or a style of speaking in which a person says very little indeed. EG *She said she'd be along in an hour, to which I grunted something monosyllabic.* ▸ used also to describe a person who is speaking in this way. ADJ CLASSIF = terse

monosyllable /mɒnə⁶sɪləbə⁰l/, **monosyllables**. N COUNT : USU PL A **monosyllable** is a very short word, for example 'yes' or 'no'. You speak to someone in monosyllables when you do not want to have a conversation with them or give them any details. EG *He was answering only in monosyllables... He grunted at them in monosyllables, which was all that was necessary.*

monotone /mɒnətəun/, **monotones**. 1 A **monotone** is a sound or way of speaking in which the tone and loudness of the sound or voice does not vary at all and makes it very boring to listen to. EG *He droned on in the steady monotone that was later to become so familiar.* N COUNT : USU SING = drone

2 **Monotone** sounds and colours do not have any variations or shades; a rather formal use. EG *It was a monotone, steady beat which went on for ten minutes.* ADJ CLASSIF : ATTRIB ⇑ uniform

monotonous /mə⁷nɒtənəs/. Something that is **monotonous** has a dull and regular pattern which seems as if it will never change, and which makes you feel bored. EG *The juniors were caned once a fortnight with monotonous regularity... Barrack life is shown to be at once squalid and monotonous... Are you trying to suggest that a west country accent is monotonous and boring?* ◇ **monotonously**. EG *The day had been monotonously routine.* ADJ QUALIT = boring, tedious ◇ ADV

monotony /mə⁷nɒtəni¹/ is any pattern that is monotonous. EG *It is more and more difficult to get people to accept the monotony of work on the assembly line... They broke up the monotony of the days... The Victorians reacted with fervour against monotony.* N UNCOUNT : IF + PREP THEN *of* ⇑ regularity = repetition

Monsignor /mɒnsiːnjɔː/, **Monsignors**; the form **Monsignori** is also used for the plural. **Monsignor** is the title of a priest of high rank in the Catholic Church. EG *...Monsignor Glemp, Poland's new Primate.* N COUNT : ALSO IN TITLES

monsoon /mɒnsuːn/, **monsoons**. The monsoon is 1 the season in Southern Asia when there is a lot of very heavy rain. EG *Even during the monsoons the afternoons were warm and clear... ...thick monsoon mists.* 2 the wind that brings the monsoon rains in Southern Asia. In summer it blows from the South West, in winter from the North East. EG *And what if they attack before the monsoons blow south?... The air was heavy, damply hot; the monsoon was being promised and prayed for.* N COUNT : IF SING *the*+N, SING = PL = the rains; N COUNT : IF SING *the*+N

monster /mɒnstə/, **monsters**. 1 A **monster** is 1.1 a large imaginary creature that looks extremely frightening. EG *...hairy white monsters covered in metal... ...Dracula, Frankenstein, and every horrible monster you could think of... Is it possible to create new creatures, perhaps even monsters, by genetic engineering?* 1.2 something that is extremely large, such as a machine or a building. EG *...a great yellow monster of a bulldozer... The area has been obliterated by monsters in brick.* N COUNT; N COUNT ⇑ giant = monstrosity

2 **Monster** means extremely and surprisingly large. EG *...a contraption that is, essentially, a monster torch... ...the monster Piccadilly hotel.* ADJ CLASSIF : ATTRIB = gigantic

3 A **monster** is also a cruel, frightening, or evil person. EG *She recounted her tales of the monsters that once ruled Hollywood... You're a monster. A detestable, abominable monster.* N COUNT/VOC = fiend

monstrosity /mɒnstrɒsɪti¹/, **monstrosities**. A **monstrosity** is something that is extremely ugly, usually something large. EG *They lived in a five bedroom Edwardian monstrosity near the centre of town.* N COUNT = eyesore

monstrous /mɒnstrəs/. 1 If you describe a situation or event as **monstrous**, you mean that it is extremely shocking or unjust. EG *How could any scientist work on such a monstrous development?... The court's judgement was absolutely monstrous.* ◇ **monstrously**. EG *His decision was monstrously unjust.* ADJ QUALIT = abhorrent; ◇ ADV ⇑ terribly = awfully

2 If you describe something such as an object or place as **monstrous**, you mean that it is 2.1 unnatural or ugly in appearance which makes it extremely frightening. EG *...this dense and monstrous urban wilderness... Even the most harmless objects are twisted into monstrous shapes.* 2.2 extremely large in size or quantity. EG *They went from one state building to another in a fleet of monstrous vehicles.* ADJ QUALIT = grotesque; ADJ QUALIT = enormous

montage /mɒntɑːʒ/, **montages**. A **montage** is a picture, film, or piece of music, which consists of several different items that are put together, often in an unusual combination or sequence; a technical term. EG *...a montage of variegated scraps of paper... I merged all these colours together in a kind of montage.* N COUNT

month /mʌnθ/, **months**. 1 A **month** is 1.1 one of the twelve periods of time that a year is divided into, for example January or February. EG *It's happened three times this month... I'm going away later in the month... The pay will be five hundred pounds a month... The licence is valid for six months.* 1.2 a period of about four weeks. EG *He was kidnapped just over a month ago... Four months later she died of typhoid... ...for a month or two... We may not have that in a month's time.* N COUNT ⇑ period; N COUNT

2 You can use **months** when you mean a long time. EG *It could take months before a solution is found... The parcel lay on the shelf for months and months.* N PLURAL ⇑ ages

3 The word **month** is also used in the following expressions. 3.1 You can say **a month of Sundays** when you mean a very long time; used mainly in informal British English. EG *He had such a beating from his father that he couldn't sit down for a month of Sundays.* 3.2 If something happens **month after month**, it happens regularly every month or happens continuously for several months. EG *We can't sustain that kind of effort month after month.* 3.3 If something changes or develops **month by month**, it changes or develops during each period of one month, often at the same rate or in the same way. EG *Month by month, with almost boring predictability, the sales figures fell.* 3.4 If something happens **month in, month out**, it happens all the time, with the situation never seeming to change or improve. EG *Why did he hit me every week, month in, month out?* PHR : USU PREP + PHR WITH BROAD NEG ⇑ ages; PHR : USED AS AN A ⇑ continually; PHR : USED AS AN A ⇑ regularly; PHR : USED AS AN A ⇑ continuously

monthly /mʌnθli¹/, **monthlies**. 1 **Monthly** is used to describe 1.1 something that happens, is done, or appears once a month or every month. EG *...a monthly meeting.* ▸ used as an adverb. EG *Most of our staff are paid monthly.* 1.2 the amount of something that is measured during a period of one month or is valid or correct for a period of one month. EG *...the average monthly rainfall... My monthly income was over two hundred pounds.* ADJ CLASSIF : ATTRIB; ▸ ADV; ADJ CLASSIF : ATTRIB

2 A **monthly** is a magazine that is published once a month. N COUNT ⇑ periodical

monument /mɒnjə⁴mə²nt/, **monuments**. 1 A **monument** is 1.1 a large structure, usually made of stone, which is built to remind people of an event in history or of a famous person. Monuments often have a statue or picture of the person or event and some writing about them. EG *Across the north side of the grass is the monument to F D Roosevelt... The cloisters are rich in graves and monuments.* 1.2 a building, castle, bridge, etc which was built a long time ago and is regarded as an important part of a country's history. EG *...an ancient monument... The area was designated a national monument.* N COUNT = memorial; N COUNT

2 If you describe something as a **monument** to a particular quality that someone has, you mean that they were responsible for it and it is a very good example of the results or effects of that quality. EG *The picnic was a monument to Mrs Hochstadt's good management... I regard modern cities as monuments of man's folly.* N COUNT + *to/of* ⇑ symbol = testament

monumental /mɒnjə⁴mɛntə⁰l/. 1 A **monumental** building or sculpture is very large and historically or artistically important. EG *...the monumental facade of the Royal School... ...the creation of new and monumental sculptural forms.* ADJ CLASSIF : ATTRIB = immortal

2 **Monumental** means relating to the making of gravestones. EG *...a monumental mason... ...monumental alabaster.* ADJ CLASSIF : ATTRIB

3 A **monumental** book or musical work is very impressive, likely to be important for a long time, and large in scale. EG *...Wedderburn's monumental work, 'The Worker and the Law'... ...a monumental Symphony.* ADJ CLASSIF : USU ATTRIB = immortal

4 In informal English, you can use **monumental** to describe something that you think is extremely good, bad, severe, etc. EG *That night there was a monumental hailstorm... It was a case of monumental bad-manners.* ◇ **monumentally**. EG *It sounds monumentally dull.* ADJ CLASSIF : USU ATTRIB = terrific, stupendous; ◇ ADV = immensely

moo /muː/, **moos, mooing, mooed**. When a cow utters a long, loud sound, it **moos**. EG *We could hear* V = low the cows mooing in the cowshed. ▸ used as a noun. EG *Daisie replied with a low moo.* ▸ N COUNT

mooch /mu:tʃ/, **mooches, mooching, mooched.** 1 If you **mooch** about, you walk about slowly with no particular purpose. EG *He mooched about the house in his pyjamas... Jack and I, hands in pockets, mooched silently up the lane.* V+A = wander

2 In informal American English, if you **mooch** something, you ask someone to give it to you as a favour. EG *I'll come by next week and mooch a meal off you.* V+O : IF+PREP THEN *off/from* = cadge

mood /mu:d/, **moods.** 1 Your **mood** is the way you are feeling about things at a particular time, especially how cheerful or how angry you are. EG *He was always in a good mood... She was in one of her bad moods... At midday, my mood began to change.* ● If you are **in the mood** for something, you feel like doing it. EG *Mr Stokes wasn't in the mood for being helpful... He seemed to be annoyed and in the mood to question everything.* ● If you are **in no mood** for something, you do not feel like doing it. EG *She was in no mood for their brainless gossip this afternoon... He wasn't in any mood to do a deal with me.* N COUNT = humour; ● PHR : USED AS AN A, IF+PREP/VB THEN *for/to-INF* = inclined; ● PHR : USED AS AN A, IF+PREP/VB THEN *for/to-INF*

2 If you are in a **mood**, you are angry and impatient with everyone. EG *When Chris was in one of his moods, he was unpleasant to everyone... She was in a bit of a mood this morning.* N COUNT : USU *in*+N = temper

3 The **mood** of a group of people is the way that they think and feel about an idea, event, or question at a particular time. EG *The debate took place amid a mood of growing political despair... The mood of this week's meeting has been one of cautious optimism.* N SING WITH DET : USU+SUPP = atmosphere

4 In grammar, the **moods** of a verb or verb group are the set of forms which express a particular attitude towards what is being said or written or towards the person being addressed. For example, in English, you use the indicative mood when you are stating what you consider to be a fact, the imperative mood when you are telling or ordering someone to do something, and the subjunctive mood when you are expressing wishes, possibilities, or doubts. N COUNT

moody /mu:di[1]/, **moodier, moodiest.** Someone who is **moody** 1 is depressed or unhappy, and indicates this by not talking very much, or by being impatient with other people. EG *He's only moody because things aren't working out at home.* ◇ **moodily.** EG *She drank her coffee moodily.* ◇ **moodiness.** EG *Like the rest of his friends, he tolerated Alec's moodiness.* 2 often changes in their feelings, for example from being cheerful to being angry, within a short period of time. EG *He was generally moody and unpredictable.* ◇ **moodiness.** EG *Moodiness is a common feature of growing up.* ADJ QUALIT = morose, doleful; ◇ ADV WITH VB; ◇ N UNCOUNT; ADJ QUALIT = temperamental; ◇ N UNCOUNT

moon /mu:n/, **moons, mooning, mooned.** 1 The **moon** is 1.1 the round object in the sky that goes round the Earth once every four weeks and that you can often see at night. EG *We have landed men on the moon.* 1.2 the particular shape or appearance of the moon. EG *The sky was a brilliant silver from the full moon... A bright moon was coming up over the hills... ...a crescent moon.* N SING : *the*+N; N SING WITH DET

2 A **moon** is an object like a small planet that travels round a planet. EG *How many moons does Jupiter have?* N COUNT ⇑ satellite

3 If you **are mooning** or **mooning** around or about, you are spending time doing nothing in particular, for example because you feel unhappy or lazy, or are worried about something. EG *Most of that afternoon he mooned around.* V : USU+A = mope

4 If you are **over the moon**, you are very pleased about something; an informal expression. EG *I was over the moon to get your letter.* PHR : USED AS AN A = overjoyed

5 If you **want the moon** or **cry for the moon**, you want something which it is impossible for you to have; an informal expression. PHR : VB INFLECTS

6 If you say that something happens **once in a blue moon**, you mean that it happens very rarely. PHR : USED AS AN A

moon over. If you **moon over** someone, you pass your time just thinking about them because you are in love. EG *She was always mooning over that bloke.* PHRASAL VB : V+PREP, HAS PASS

moonbeam /mu:nbi:m/, **moonbeams.** A **moonbeam** is a ray of light from the moon. N COUNT

moon-faced. Someone who is **moon-faced** has a very round face. ADJ CLASSIF

moonless /mu:nlı[2]s/. A **moonless** sky or night is dark because there is no moon in the sky. ADJ CLASSIF

moonlight /mu:nlaıt/, **moonlights, moonlighting, moonlighted.** 1 **Moonlight** is the light that comes from the moon at night. EG *The field looked like water in the moonlight... Our meeting took place by moonlight.* N UNCOUNT

2 If you **moonlight**, you have a second job in addition to your main job, especially when this involves some dishonesty, for example because you do not inform your main employers or the tax office; an informal use. EG *She moonlighted as a waitress.* V ⇑ work

moonlit /mu:nlıt/. Something that is **moonlit** is made light or bright by moonlight. EG *I've spent many a moonlit night here... ...the beauty of the moonlit forest.* ADJ CLASSIF ⇑ illuminated

moonshine /mu:nʃaın/ is 1 foolish thoughts, ideas, or talk that are not based on reality. EG *I am tired and sick of war–its glory is all moonshine.* 2 whisky that is made illegally; used mainly in American English. N UNCOUNT ⇑ nonsense; N UNCOUNT ⇑ alcohol

moony /mu:ni[1]/. If you say a person has **moony** eyes, you mean their eyes are big and round and make the person seem vague or dreamy. ADJ CLASSIF

moor /mʊə, mɔ:/, **moors, mooring, moored.** 1 A **moor** is an area of open, uncultivated, and usually high land with poor soil that is covered mainly with grass and heather. EG *The mists had vanished from the moor... He used to go for long walks on the moors.* N COUNT : SING=PL = heath

2 If a boat **is moored** somewhere, it is at that place, attached to the land with a rope or cable so that it cannot drift away. EG *Boats were moored on both sides of the river.* V+O : USU PASS ⇑ secure = tie up

3 The **Moors** were a dark-skinned Muslim people who established a civilization in North Africa and Spain between the 8th and the 15th century A.D. N COUNT

4 See also **mooring.**

moorhen /mʊəhɛn, mɔ:-/, **moorhens.** A **moorhen** is a medium-sized black bird that lives near water. N COUNT ⇑ fowl

mooring /mʊərıŋ, mɔ:-/, **moorings.** 1 A **mooring** is the place on land or the particular object such as a metal ring to which a boat is tied. EG *During the storm boats were torn from their moorings... The mooring ropes were hauled in.* N COUNT

2 **Moorings** are the rope, anchors, or chains used to moor a boat or ship. EG *The bigger dinghy dragged her moorings.* N PLURAL ⇑ equipment

Moorish /mʊərıʃ, mɔ:-/. Something that is **Moorish** relates to or is characteristic of the Moors. EG *...the Moorish Empire... ...Moorish architecture.* ADJ CLASSIF

moorland /mʊələ[3]nd, mɔ:-/, **moorlands. Moorland** is land which consists of moors. EG *20 per cent of moorland on Exmoor has been lost since 1960... ...the beauty of Britain's moorlands... ...moorland sheep.* N UNCOUNT/PLURAL

moose /mu:s/. **Moose** is both the singular and the plural form. A **moose** is a large North American deer that has very flat antlers. N COUNT = elk

mooted /mu:tıd/. If something **is mooted**, it is suggested or introduced as a subject that you want people to discuss; a rather formal and old-fashioned word. EG *A holiday in France had been mooted earlier in the term.* V+O : ONLY PASS = proposed

moot point /mu:t pɔınt/, **moot points.** A **moot point** is a statement or idea that may or may not be true, or that people cannot agree about. EG *How serious he was about this issue is a moot point... It is a moot point which issue is most important.* N COUNT : IF SING, USU *a*+N ≠ certainty

mop /mɒp/, **mops, mopping, mopped.** 1 A **mop** is a tool for washing floors, dishes, etc which has a sponge, many pieces of string, or a cloth attached to a handle. Mops for cleaning the floor have a long handle. N COUNT

2 If you **mop** something such as a floor, you clean it with a mop. EG *I've spent all morning mopping the floors.* V+O, OR V

3 If you **mop** a liquid from a surface, you wipe the surface with a dry cloth so that the liquid is absorbed. EG *Remove the stain as fast as possible with cold water, mopping with a towel... He mopped the sweat from his face.* V+O, OR V = sponge

4 If you **mop** your face, you wipe it with a handkerchief or towel, for example in order to remove sweat or tears. EG *He mopped his sweating brow... She mopped her eyes.* V+O = dab

5 A **mop** is also a large amount of loose or untidy hair. EG *...a coarse mop of black hair... She had a mop of dusky curls.* N COUNT/PART = shock

mop up. 1 If you **mop up** or you **mop up** a liquid that has been spilt, you wipe it with a cloth, towel, etc so that the liquid is absorbed. EG *Mother started* PHRASAL VB : V+ADV, OR V+O+ADV *mopping up the oil... I love mopping up sauce with crusts of bread... I've mopped up with a bit of old cloth.*

2 To **mop up** the last parts of a job, the last members of a group, etc means to do something so that the job is completed, all the group have been dealt with, etc. EG *School leavers will be mopped up by youth opportunity schemes.* PHRASAL VB : V+O+ADV = absorb, account for

3 When an army **mops up** resistance, it deals with any people who are still fighting against it. EG *All resistance will be mopped up within two hours.* PHRASAL VB : V+O+ADV = eliminate

mope /məʊp/, **mopes, moping, moped.** If you **mope**, you feel miserable and are not interested in anything apart from yourself. EG *He just sits about, moping in an armchair.* V = languish

mope about. If you **mope about** or **mope around**, you wander around aimlessly, looking and feeling unhappy. EG *I moped around the house for a few days.* PHRASAL VB : V+ADV = moon

moped /məʊpɛd/, **mopeds.** A **moped** is a small motorcycle which you can also pedal like a bicycle. N COUNT

moral /mɒrəºl/, **morals. 1 Morals** are principles and values based on what a person or society believes are the right, proper, or acceptable ways of behaving. EG *It was difficult to doubt the excellence of his morals... Business morals nowadays are very low... Films like this are a danger to public morals.* N PLURAL ⇑ standards

2 Moral means concerned with the question of whether people's behaviour is right, proper, or acceptable. EG *I'm in a moral dilemma... I have witnessed a fall in moral standards... She feels responsible for the girl's moral welfare.* ADJ CLASSIF : ATTRIB = ethical

3 Moral courage, duty, responsibility, etc is based on what you know or believe is right, proper, or acceptable, rather than on what the law or a contract says should be done. EG *He had that moral courage which enables a man to stand alone... He roused the American people to an outburst of moral indignation... It is our moral duty to stay.* ADJ CLASSIF : ATTRIB ⇑ righteous

4 Someone who is **moral** behaves in a way that they know is right, proper, or acceptable. EG *Why do you have to be so moral?* ADJ QUALIT = virtuous

5 If you give **moral support** to someone, you do not give them any practical help but you encourage them by expressing approval and enthusiasm for what they are doing. EG *I looked across to give moral support to my colleagues.* PHR : USED AS O ⇑ encouragement ● If you say that the result of a contest is **a moral victory** for the person or side that lost, you mean that they have succeeded in demonstrating that, despite the result, they in fact have the better skills or qualities or that their cause is right and just. ● PHR : USU USED AS C, N INFLECTS

6 A **moral** story or lesson teaches good behaviour. EG *The story of my father is a sad moral tale.* ADJ QUALIT

7 The **moral** of a particular situation, story, or event is what it teaches you about how you should or should not behave. EG *The moral is clear: you must never marry for money... I don't know what moral to draw from all this.* N COUNT ⇑ lesson = message

morale /mɒrɑːl/ is the amount of confidence and optimism that a person or group of people feel in a difficult, dangerous, or important situation. EG *The morale of the men was good... The news was a boost to morale... The past 15 months have destroyed morale.* N UNCOUNT ⇑ feelings

moralise /mɒrəlaɪz/. See **moralize.**

moralist /mɒrəlɪst/, **moralists.** A **moralist** is someone who has strong ideas about what is right and what is wrong behaviour, and who teaches other people about it or tries to force them to behave according to these ideas. EG *My grandfather was a stern moralist.* N COUNT

moralistic /mɒrəlɪstɪk/. If you are **moralistic**, you make judgements about other people on the basis of your own beliefs and ideas about what is right; used showing disapproval. EG *...a moralistic society.* ▸ used of attitudes, approaches, etc. EG *She had rebuked David for his moralistic attitude to his clients.* ADJ QUALIT = didactic

morality /məʳrælɪti¹/, **moralities. 1 Morality** is **1.1** the idea that some forms of behaviour are right, proper, and acceptable and that other forms of behaviour are bad or wrong, either in your own opinion or in the opinion of society. EG *Sexual morality was enforced by the fear of illegitimacy... ...the decline in traditional morality.* N UNCOUNT = decency, principles **1.2** the quality or state of being right, proper, or acceptable, or of knowing what is right, proper, or acceptable in a particular situation. EG *We need their morality and wisdom.* N UNCOUNT ⇑ goodness = integrity

2 A **morality** is a system of principles and values concerning people's behaviour, which is generally accepted by a society or by a particular group of people. EG *Conflicts must arise between the two moralities.* N COUNT

3 The **morality** of something is the degree to which it is right, proper, or acceptable. EG *We talked about the morality of fox-hunting.* N UNCOUNT+*of* ⇑ rightness

moralize /mɒrəlaɪz/, **moralizes, moralizing, moralized.** If you **moralize**, you discuss or consider a situation only in the ways that it relates to your own beliefs or values of what is right and wrong, and often tell other people your opinions without being asked to. EG *Sam Dekker was not one for moralizing on the events of his life.* V : IF+PREP THEN *on/about/to*

morally /mɒrəli¹/. **1 Morally** means from the point of view of whether or not people's behaviour is right, proper, or acceptable. EG *I hold you morally responsible for her death... It is morally wrong not to do more to help the poor.* ADV+ADJ = ethically

2 If you behave or act **morally**, you behave or act in a way that you know is right, proper, or acceptable. EG *I try to live morally.* ADV WITH VB

morass /məræs/, **morasses. 1** If you describe a situation as a **morass**, you mean that it is extremely complicated and confused. EG *These gentlemen are usually bogged down in a morass of superfluous paperwork... Corporate tax is an ethical morass.* N COUNT : USU SING+SUPP = jungle, quagmire

2 A **morass** is an area of marshy or muddy ground. EG *There was still a morass of mud beneath the surface.* N COUNT : USU SING ⇑ marsh

moratorium /mɒrətɔːrɪəm/, **moratoriums.** The form **moratoria** is also used for the plural. A **moratorium** is the stopping of a particular activity or process for a fixed period of time as a result of an official agreement; a formal word. EG *The meeting did agree to extend the moratorium on the building of new warships.* N COUNT : IF+PREP THEN *on* ⇑ suspension

morbid /mɔːbɪd/. If someone or something is **morbid**, they express or involve too great an interest in unpleasant things or events, especially in death. EG *It's morbid to dwell on cemeteries and such like... ...morbid imaginations.* ADJ QUALIT = ghoulish ◊ **morbidly.** EG *She peered morbidly into the darkness.* ◊ ADV WITH VB

mordant /mɔːdənt/ humour or wit is very sarcastic and sharply critical; a formal or literary word. EG *The book sparkles with mordant humour.* ADJ QUALIT = biting ▸ used of people. EG *The mordant Ambrose Bierce was forty-five.* ▸ = waspish

more /mɔː/. **1** You can use **more** to indicate that there is a greater number of things or a greater amount of something than before or than is involved in something else. EG *Do you spend more time teaching, or doing research?... Better management may enable one man to milk more cows... There are usually many more applicants than posts in surgery... I'm changing my job for four times more money... Most men still earn much more than their wives.* QUANTIF+N IN PL OR N UNCOUNT : COMPAR ≠ less ● You can use **more than** with a number or amount to say that the actual number or amount is even greater, especially when you want to emphasize how large the actual number or amount is. EG *He saw more than 800 children, dying of starvation... The ringing went on and on for more than half-an-hour... The dog had attacked its mistress more than once.* ● PHR+NUM/NG = over ● You can use **no more than** or **not more than** with a number or amount to say that the actual number or amount is even smaller, especially when you want to emphasize how small the actual number or amount is. EG *The boats are not more than 45 feet long... The area they are working in is no more than thirty metres square.* ● PHR+NUM/NG = not above

2 More also means to a greater extent or degree. EG *The books that are true to life will attract them more... He had nothing waiting for him in Bombay any more than she had... I became more than ever convinced that the theatre was for me...* ADV COMPAR : WITH VB ≠ less ● **all the more**: see **all.**

3 You can use **more 3.1** to refer to an additional amount of something or an additional number of things. EG *In the next hour he found two more diamonds... Have you any more problems you'd like to discuss today?... Will you take some more coffee, Vicar?... Visit your doctor to find out more about free prescriptions.* QUANTIF+N IN PL OR N UNCOUNT ⇑ further **3.2** to indicate that there are other QUANTIF : ONLY things, people, events, etc as well as the ones mentioned, but you do not want to specify or identify them. EG *There's a lot more in his book besides music.* AS PRON

4 You can use **more** in front of adjectives or adverbs to form comparatives. EG *Your child's health is more important than the doctor's feelings... We are encouraging schools to become more aware of the aims of university education... Next time, I will choose more carefully.* ADV COMPAR + ADJ/ADV ≠ less

5 You can use **more** with adjectives or adverbs to say that a particular quality is present to a larger degree or extent than the average. EG *I want to talk about the problems that the more developed countries are facing... We hope to make programmes for the more discerning viewer.* ADV COMPAR + ADJ ≠ less

6 You can use **more** to indicate that something continues to happen for a further period of time. EG *They talked a bit more.* ● You can use **no more** or **not any more** to indicate that something has stopped happening or is no longer true. EG *I just wrote to apologize and thought no more about it... The employers don't want quality work any more.* ● If you do something **once more, twice more,** etc, you do it again once, twice, etc. EG *She wanted to perform it once more before she died.* ADV COMPAR AFTER VB ● PHR ≠ still ● PHR : USED AS AN A

7 You can use **more and more** to indicate that something or a group of things or people is becoming greater all the time in extent, degree, or amount. EG *More and more people grew ill... They began to dance, slowly at first, then more and more quickly... We became more and more friendly to Mr Dekker.* PHR ⇑ increasingly

8 You can use the structure **more...than** when you are expressing a contrast by saying that something is truer, greater, better, etc than something else which you mention later. EG *He always seemed old to me, more like a grandfather than a father... They were more amused than concerned.* ⇑ rather

9 You can use **more or less** to indicate that something is true in a general way, or that it is almost accurate but not completely. EG *'And that was how it all started?'–'Well, more or less.'... Brian more or less implied that we were lying... She had become more or less an invalid.* PHR : USED AS ADV SEN ⇑ roughly = broadly speaking

10 You can use **more** in expressions like 'no more, no less' and 'neither more nor less' to indicate that what you are saying is exactly true or correct and that you are not leaving anything out or adding anything extra. EG *Each mower took eleven rows of corn on his blade, no more and no less... They look to me just what they are, neither more nor less.* PHR : USED AS ADV SEN

11 You can use **no more than, nothing more than, not much more than,** etc to emphasize that something is not very important, valuable, or impressive, or that it is hardly worth considering. EG *He thought women were no more than commodities... At the moment our tree looks like nothing more than a branch... It wasn't much more than a formality.* PHR : V + PHR + C ⇑ merely

12 You can use **more than** to indicate and emphasize that you are deliberately expressing a statement in mild or cautious words which you are sure would still be true if expressed very strongly or forcefully. EG *You'll have more than enough money for any equipment you need... This was a more than generous arrangement... The ease of mind will more than compensate for any loss you may incur.* PHR + ADJ ⇑ extremely

13 You can use **what is more** or **what's more** to introduce an extra piece of information which emphasizes the point that you are making. EG *What's more, he adds, there are no signs of a change.* PHR : USED AS ADV SEN = furthermore

moreover /mɔːr<u>əʊ</u>və/ is used to introduce a piece of information, a statement, or an opinion that adds to or supports the previous one. EG *The Opposition have consistently accused the Government of corruption. Moreover, they have named names... Even though the packet of cigarettes lay open and was, moreover, of a very expensive brand, he took a crumpled packet out of his pocket and lit one of his own.* ADV SEN ⇑ and = furthermore

mores /m<u>ɔː</u>reɪz/. The **mores** of a particular place or group of people are the customs and habits that are typically found in that place or group; a formal word. EG *The last thirty years have seen great changes in social mores... What do we learn of the manners and mores of the New Zealand people from this film?* N PLURAL : USU + SUPP ⇑ conventions

morgue /m<u>ɔː</u>g/, **morgues**. A **morgue** is a building where dead bodies are kept before being cremated or buried. EG *...the city morgue.* N COUNT = mortuary

moribund /m<u>ɒ</u>rɪbʌnd/. Something that is **moribund** is about to come to an end because it no longer performs a worthwhile function; a formal word. EG *The moribund Post Office Advisory Board was replaced... ...moribund industries.* ADJ QUALIT ⇑ dead = ineffectual

Mormon /m<u>ɔː</u>mən/, **Mormons**. A **Mormon** is a person who belongs to the religious group called the Church of Jesus Christ of Latter-Day Saints. ▸ used as an adjective. EG *...the Mormon Church.* N COUNT ⇑ Christian ▸ ADJ CLASSIF : ATTRIB

morn /m<u>ɔː</u>n/, **morns**. **Morn** means the same as morning; a literary word. EG *He looked for her from morn till night.* N UNCOUNT/COUNT

morning /m<u>ɔː</u>nɪŋ/, **mornings**. 1 The **morning** is 1.1 the part of each day between the time that people usually wake up and noon or lunch-time. EG *The next morning I got up early and ate my breakfast... His plane left this morning... He had spent all morning preparing the meal... I read all the papers in the morning... The museums may open only in the mornings... She left after breakfast on Saturday morning.* ▸ used as an adjective. EG *I was reading the morning paper... ...the morning sun.* **1.2** the part of a day between midnight and noon. EG *She died in the very early hours of this morning.* N COUNT/UNCOUNT ▸ N BEFORE N N COUNT

2 The expression **in the morning** is used in the following ways. **2.1** If you say that something will happen **in the morning**, you mean that it will happen during the morning of the following day. EG *You'll feel awful in the morning, if you drink so much.* **2.2** If you say that something happened at one o'clock, two o'clock, etc **in the morning**, you mean that it happened at one o'clock, two o'clock, etc between midnight and noon, and not in the afternoon. EG *It was five o'clock in the morning.* PHR : USED AS AN A PHR : USED AS AN A = a.m.

morning coat, morning coats. A **morning coat** is a man's coat, usually black or grey, that is longer at the back than at the front and is worn as part of morning dress. N COUNT

morning dress is a suit of clothes that is worn by men on very formal occasions such as weddings. Morning dress normally consists of a morning coat worn with grey trousers, a white shirt, a grey tie, and often a top hat of the same colour as the coat. N UNCOUNT

morning room, morning rooms; also spelled with a hyphen. A **morning room** is a sitting-room in a large house, which is designed to get the sun in the mornings; an old-fashioned word. N COUNT

morning sickness is a feeling of sickness that some women have in the morning in the first few months of pregnancy. N UNCOUNT

Moroccan /mə[7]r<u>ɒ</u>kən/, **Moroccans**. 1 **Moroccan** means belonging or relating to Morocco or to its people. ADJ CLASSIF

2 A **Moroccan** is a person who comes from Morocco. N COUNT

morocco /mər<u>ɒ</u>kəʊ/ is a soft leather that is used for making things such as shoes and the covers of books. EG *...morocco slippers.* N UNCOUNT

moron /m<u>ɔː</u>rɒn/, **morons**. If you describe someone as a **moron**, you mean that they are very stupid; an offensive word used in informal English. EG *Louise is in love with that moron.* N COUNT/VOC ⇑ fool = idiot

moronic /mə[8]r<u>ɒ</u>nɪk/. If you say that someone is **moronic**, you mean that they are very stupid; an offensive word used in informal English. EG *He really is moronic.* ▸ used of a person's actions or behaviour. EG *I'm tired of your moronic attempts to impress me.* ADJ QUALIT

morose /mər<u>əʊ</u>s/. Someone who is **morose** is miserable, bad-tempered, and not willing to talk much to other people. EG *He was big, dark and morose.* ▸ used of a person's state of mind or behaviour. EG *The experience was accompanied by periods of doubt and morose depression.* ◇ **morosely**. EG *The man followed me morosely round the museum.* ADJ QUALIT = dour ▸ = moody ◇ ADV WITH VB = gloomily

morphia /m<u>ɔː</u>fɪə/ is the same as morphine; an old-fashioned word. N UNCOUNT ⇑ drug

morphine /m<u>ɔː</u>fiːn/ is a drug made from opium, which is used to relieve pain. N UNCOUNT = morphia

morris dancer /m<u>ɒ</u>rɪs d<u>ɑː</u>nsə/, **morris dancers**. A **morris dancer** is a person who takes part in morris dancing. N COUNT

morris dancing is a type of old English country dancing which is performed by people who wear a special costume, often with bells on it. N UNCOUNT

morrow /mɒrəʊ/. In old-fashioned English, the **morrow** means the day after today, or the day following the one you have just mentioned. EG *We must see what the morrow will bring... I'll see you on the morrow, then.* — N SING: the+N, USU AFTER on = next day

morse /mɔːs/. **Morse** or **morse code** is an international code which is used for sending messages. It uses a system of written dots and dashes, or short and long sounds, to represent each letter of the alphabet. EG *He tapped out his initials in morse.* — N UNCOUNT

morsel /mɔːsəˡl/, **morsels**. A **morsel** is a very small amount of something, especially a very small piece of food. EG *He had a morsel of food caught between one tooth and another... The dog often gets a nice morsel.* — N PART+N UNCOUNT = scrap

mortal /mɔːtəˡl/, **mortals**. 1 When you describe people as **mortal**, you are referring to the fact that they have to die and cannot live forever. EG *Remember that you are mortal... There was no mortal man who could hurt them now.* — ADJ CLASSIF ≠ immortal

2 You can refer to a **mortal** when you are want to emphasize that you are talking about an ordinary person, rather than someone who has power or has achieved something; sometimes used humorously. EG *They are now reduced to the status of ordinary mortals... He passed first time, something which we mortals couldn't manage.* — N COUNT = human

3 A **mortal** wound or blow results in the person's death; a literary use. ◇ **mortally**. EG *Blake was mortally wounded.* — ADJ CLASSIF ◇ ADV

4 If two people are in **mortal** combat, they are trying to kill each other. EG *They were locked in mortal combat.* — ADJ CLASSIF: ATTRIB = deadly

5 A **mortal** enemy, threat, etc is extremely serious and causes you to feel strong fear or hatred. EG *They regard the police as their mortal enemies... We are all in mortal danger.* ◇ **mortally**. EG *I was mortally afraid.* — ADJ CLASSIF: ATTRIB = deadly ◇ ADV+ADJ

6 In informal old-fashioned English, the word **mortal** is used to emphasize the word which follows, and to indicate that you are angry or annoyed. EG *I now had to do every mortal thing myself.* — ADJ CLASSIF: ATTRIB = blessed

mortality /mɔːtælɪtiˡ/ is 1 the fact that all people must die. EG *He grew up with an ever present sense of mortality.* 2 the number of people who die within a particular period of time or on a particular occasion. EG *Infant mortality has been reported by some at 200 per 1,000 births.* — N UNCOUNT ↑ death; N UNCOUNT = death

mortal sin, mortal sins. In the Roman Catholic Church, a **mortal sin** is an extremely serious one and will result in the person responsible being damned if he or she does not confess it, repent, and obtain forgiveness. EG *It is a mortal sin to take a human life.* — N COUNT/UNCOUNT

mortar /mɔːtə/, **mortars**. 1 A **mortar** is a short cannon which fires missiles high into the air for a short distance. EG *We returned fire with mortars and machine-guns.* — N COUNT

2 **Mortar** is a mixture of sand, water, and cement or lime, which is put between bricks to make them stay firmly together when you are building walls. EG *The new buildings were solid brick and mortar.* — N UNCOUNT

3 A **mortar** is also a bowl used for crushing dry grains or spices with a pestle until they are a fine powder that you can use in cooking. EG *He ground the spices himself with a mortar and pestle.* — N COUNT

mortarboard /mɔːtəbɔːd/, **mortarboards**; also spelled with a hyphen or as two words. A **mortarboard** is a stiff black cap with a flat, square top and a tassel hanging from it. Mortarboards are sometimes worn on formal occasions by university students and teachers. — N COUNT

mortgage /mɔːgɪdʒ/, **mortgages, mortgaging, mortgaged**. 1 A **mortgage** is a loan of money which you get from a bank, building society, or other financial institution in order to buy a house. EG *We can't get a mortgage... ...the mortgage rate.* — N COUNT

2 If you **mortgage** your house, land, etc, you use it as a guarantee to a company in order to borrow money from them. If you fail to repay the money you have borrowed, the company has the right to take possession of your property. EG *He will have to mortgage his land for a loan... The house was mortgaged.* — V+O ↑ pledge

mortice /mɔːtɪs/. See **mortise**.

mortician /mɔːtɪʃəˡn/, **morticians**. A **mortician** is a person whose job is to look after the bodies of people who have died, and to arrange their funerals; used in American English. — N COUNT ↑ undertaker

mortify /mɔːtɪfaɪ/, **mortifies, mortifying, mortified**. If you **are mortified**, you feel great shame and embarrassment. EG *I was mortified... Mortified, he knew his father had heard every word.* ◇ **mortifying**. EG *There were some mortifying setbacks.* ◇ **mortification** /mɔːtɪfɪkeɪʃəˡn/. EG *Davie was hiding his head in his hands with mortification.* — V+O: USU PASS = horrified; ◇ ADJ QUALIT; ◇ N UNCOUNT = chagrin

mortise /mɔːtɪs/, **mortises**; also spelled **mortice**. A **mortise** is a rectangular slot which is cut into a piece of wood, stone, etc. Another piece, called a tenon, goes into this slot. — N COUNT ↑ cavity

mortise lock, mortise locks. A **mortise lock** is a type of lock which fits into a hole cut into the edge of a door rather than being fixed to one side of it. The lock cannot be seen or unscrewed when the door is closed. — N COUNT

mortuary /mɔːtʃuˡəriˡ/, **mortuaries**. A **mortuary** is a special building or a room in a hospital where dead bodies are kept before they are buried or cremated. — N COUNT = morgue

mosaic /məʊzeɪɪk/, **mosaics**. A **mosaic** is a design which consists of small coloured pebbles or pieces of coloured glass set in concrete or plaster. EG *...a Roman mosaic.* — N COUNT

mosey /məʊziˡ/, **moseys, moseying, moseyed**. If you **mosey** somewhere, you go slowly along in a particular direction or round a particular place, often without any purpose except to see what is there; used mainly in informal American English. EG *I think I'll mosey down to the shops.* ▸ used as a noun. EG *I've just had a mosey round the garden.* — V+A = amble; ▸ N SING: a+N = saunter, stroll

Moslem /mɒzləˡm/. See **Muslim**.

mosque /mɒsk/, **mosques**. A **mosque** is a building where Muslims go to worship. Many mosques have high towers and domes. — N COUNT

mosquito /məskiːtəʊ/, **mosquitoes** or **mosquitos**. A **mosquito** is a small insect which lives in damp places and bites people or animals and sucks their blood. One type of mosquito can cause malaria. — N COUNT

mosquito net, mosquito nets. A **mosquito net** is a curtain made of very fine cloth, which is hung round a bed in order to keep mosquitoes and other insects away from a person who is sleeping. — N COUNT

moss /mɒs/, **mosses**. 1 **Moss** is a very small green plant which grows on damp soil, or on wood or stone. Many moss plants usually grow close together in a clump. EG *He flopped back down onto the soft moss... The bark was covered with moss.* — N MASS

2 If you say that **a rolling stone gathers no moss**, you mean that a person who keeps wandering casually from place to place will never enjoy the benefits of a settled life, such as a family, a home, a career, or close friends, but will also avoid the difficult things such as responsibilities, lack of freedom, boredom, etc. — PHR

mossy /mɒsiˡ/, **mossier, mossiest**. Something that is **mossy** is covered with moss. EG *...a flight of mossy stone steps.* — ADJ QUALIT

most /məʊst/. 1 You can use **most** to refer to the majority of a group of things or people or the largest part of something. EG *Most Arabic speakers understand Egyptian... He used to spend most of his time in the library... I saw most of the early Shirley Temple films... Most of us have strong views on politics.* — QUANTIF+N IN PL OR N UNCOUNT ≠ least

2 You can use 'the **most**' 2.1 to refer to an amount that is greater than the amount that anyone or anything else has, or that is more than has ever existed before. EG *Who has the most money?... This is the area that attracts most attention... The most my dad ever got in one night was fifteen pounds... Coolidge had most, Hoover least.* — QUANTIF+N IN PL OR N UNCOUNT: SUPERL ≠ least. 2.2 to refer to the largest amount of something that is possible. EG *They were making the most money that they could... That was the most that could be said against her.* — QUANTIF: SUPERL ↑ maximum. ● If you **make the most of** something, you get the maximum use, help, or advantage from it. EG *Governments should face up to the situation and make the most of it.* — ● PHR: VB INFLECTS

3 You can use **most** in front of adjectives or adverbs to form superlatives. EG *It was one of the most important discoveries ever made... He is one of the America's ten most wanted criminals... The head is the most sensitive part of the body... These are the works I respond to most strongly.* — ADV SUPERL+ADJ/ADV ≠ least

4 You can use **most** to indicate that something is true or happens to a larger degree or extent than — ADV SUPERL WITH VB

anything else. EG *What he most feared was being left alone... I liked him the most... Which do you value most-wealth or health?... This is the thing that worries me most of all... As everyone knew, most of all me, Kurt had always been a gentleman.* ⇑ much = above all ≠ least

5 You can also use **most** to emphasize an adjective or adverb; a rather formal use. EG *The trading results show a most encouraging trend... The film is most disturbing... I would most certainly love a drink... He always acted most graciously.* ADV + ADJ/ADV ⇑ very = highly, extremely

6 You can use **at most** or **at the most** **6.1** to indicate and emphasize that a number or amount that you have mentioned is the maximum possible or likely, and that the actual number or amount is probably smaller or should be smaller. EG *My job will only last two years at most... I only have fifteen minutes or twenty minutes at the most... There would be at most a couple of hundred people listening.* PHR WITH NG = at maximum **6.2** to emphasize that the statement you are making indicates the maximum which can be achieved or expected, or the strongest quality or feeling that someone could possibly have, and that the actual results, qualities or feelings are likely to be less in effect or intensity. EG *He offers, at most, stability... It is causing at most a minor nuisance... There is only at most room for one person.* PHR : USED AS ADV SEN

7 You can use **for the most part** to indicate that something is generally true, although not always or not completely. EG *The New Guinea forest is, for the most part, dark and wet... For the most part they sit in silence... Visibility, for the most part, was excellent.* PHR : USED AS ADV SEN = mostly, largely

-most is added to adjectives in order to form other adjectives that describe something as being further in a particular direction than other things of the same kind. EG *...southern→southernmost... ...inner→innermost... ...top→topmost.* SUFFIX : FORMS ADJS

mostly /məʊstli¹/ is used to indicate that a statement is generally true, for example true about the majority of a group of things or people, true most of the time, or true in most features. EG *The men at the party were mostly fairly young... She had had a very exciting career, mostly in Birmingham... She was busy writing, poetry mostly... A rattlesnake hunts mostly at night.* ADV OR ADV SEN ⇑ partly = mainly, chiefly

MOT /ɛm əʊ tiː/, **MOTs**. In Britain, an **MOT** is a test which, by law, must be made each year on all road vehicles that are more than 3 years old, in order to check that they are safe to drive. EG *Our ageing minibus failed its MOT.* N COUNT

motel /məʊtɛl/, **motels**. A **motel** is a hotel intended for people who are travelling by car, which has space to park cars near the rooms. N COUNT : ALSO IN NAMES AFTER N

moth /mɒθ/, **moths**. A **moth** is an insect with large wings, which usually flies about at night and is attracted to bright lights. N COUNT

mothball /mɒθbɔːl/, **mothballs**. A **mothball** is a small white ball made of a chemical such as naphthalene, which you can put amongst clothes or blankets in order to keep moths away and prevent them from making holes in them. N COUNT

moth-eaten. Clothes that are **moth-eaten** look very old and ragged with holes in. EG *She was wearing the same moth-eaten old coat.* ADJ QUALIT = tatty

mother /mʌðə/, **mothers, mothering, mothered**. **1** Your **mother** is the woman who gave birth to you. EG *I always did everything my mother told me... There is usually a strong relationship between mother and child.* N COUNT ⇑ parent ▸ **Mother** is also used to address or refer to your mother. EG *You are looking wonderful, Mother.* ▸ N PROPER/VOC = mum, ma, mummy

2 You can use **mother** to describe something that is the original thing of its kind or group, from which other things develop. EG *Our mother company is in New York... From this mother race, two distinct branches originated.* ADJ CLASSIF : ATTRIB

3 When you describe a condition or quality as the **mother** of an activity or situation, you mean that it is the original cause or source of the activity or situation. EG *Necessity is the mother of invention.* N SING WITH DET + *of* ⇑ creator

4 If you **mother** someone, **4.1** you look after them and bring them up, usually when you are their mother. EG *Female monkeys who were badly mothered became bad mothers themselves.* V+O : USU PASS = rear **4.2** you treat them with great care and affection, and often spoil them. EG *She mothers all her lodgers... He really enjoys being mothered.* V+O

mother country, mother countries. Someone's **mother country** is the country in which they were born and to which they still feel emotionally linked, wherever they might live. N COUNT : USU SING WITH *the*/POSS

mother figure, mother figures; also spelled with a hyphen. If you consider someone as a **mother figure**, you think of them as a person to whom you can turn for help, advice, or support. N COUNT

motherhood /mʌðəhʊd/ is the state of being a mother. N UNCOUNT

Mothering Sunday is the same as Mother's Day; used in rather formal British English. N UNCOUNT

mother-in-law, mothers-in-law. Someone's **mother-in-law** is the mother of their husband or wife. N COUNT ⇑ relative

motherland /mʌðələ³nd/ **motherlands**. Your **motherland** is the country in which you were born and to which you still feel emotionally linked. N COUNT : USU *the*/POSS + N

motherless /mʌðələ²s/. If someone is **motherless**, their mother has died, or has left them and gone away. EG *What a bad thing it is to leave a child motherless.* ADJ CLASSIF

motherly /mʌðəli¹/. A **motherly** action or attitude expresses warm, kind, and protective feelings like those of a mother. EG *Motherly hands touched him lightly, lovingly.* ADJ QUALIT ⇑ caring = maternal

Mother Nature is sometimes used to refer to nature, especially when it is being considered as a force that affects human beings; a literary expression. EG *We cannot control the caprices of Mother Nature.* N UNCOUNT

Mother of God is another name for the Virgin Mary, the mother of Jesus Christ; a term in Christianity. N PROPER

mother-of-pearl is the hard, smooth substance which forms a layer on the inside of the shells of some shellfish. It shines in various colours and is often used to make buttons or to decorate things. N UNCOUNT

Mother's Day is a special day in some countries on which mothers receive gifts and cards from their children. N UNCOUNT

mother ship, mother ships. A **mother ship** is a ship from which other smaller ships get supplies. N COUNT

mother superior, mother superiors. A **mother superior** is the head nun in a convent. N COUNT : ALSO IN TITLES

mother-to-be, mothers-to-be. A **mother-to-be** is a woman who is pregnant, especially for the first time. N COUNT

mother-tongue, mother-tongues. Your **mother-tongue** is the language that you learn from your parents when you are a child. N COUNT

motif /məʊtiːf/, **motifs**. A **motif** is **1** a design which is used as a decoration or as part of an artistic pattern. EG *...wallpaper that had a motif of motorbikes and crash-helmets... There were white curtains with black and red motifs on them.* N COUNT : USU + SUPP **2** a theme or idea that is frequently repeated throughout a piece of music or literature. EG *A motif that runs through the play is Hedda's thin hair... ...the musical motif.* N COUNT

motion /məʊʃəⁿn/, **motions, motioning, motioned**. **1** **Motion** is the process of continually changing position or moving from one place to another. EG *The bed swayed with the motion of the ship... ...a gibbon in motion in the tree tops.* • See also **slow motion**. N UNCOUNT ⇑ movement

2 A **motion** is an action, gesture, or movement. EG *He made stabbing motions with his spear... With a quick motion of her hands, she did her hair up in a knot... She was going up and down with the motions of the vehicle.* N COUNT : USU + SUPP

3 A **motion** in a meeting or debate is a formal proposal which the people present discuss and then vote on. EG *He proposed the motion that 'the Public Schools of England should be abolished.'... Councillors have tabled an amendment to the main motion for debate.* N COUNT

4 If you **motion** to someone, you make a movement with your hand in order to show them where you want them to go or to indicate to them what they should do. EG *Boylan motioned to Rudolph to sit down... Usually he would motion me to an easy chair or sofa.* V+A *(to)*, OR V+O+A *(to)* ⇑ indicate = wave

4 If you **go through the motions**, **4.1** you say or do something that is expected of you, without being very sincere or serious about it. EG *He caught my eye and went through the motions of sympathetically clapping... We all said goodnight and went through* PHR : VB INFLECTS ⇑ pretend

the motions. **4.2** you pretend to do something by making the movements associated with a particular action. EG *I can go through the motions of putting imaginary food into my mouth.*
PHR : VB INFLECTS, USU + *of*

5 A process or event that is **in motion** is happening already and continues to happen for a long period of time. EG *The changes are already in motion and have been for a decade or so.* ● If you **set** something **in motion** or you **put the wheels in motion**, you take the necessary action to make something start happening. EG *He set into motion a long negotiating process... We'll set the wheels in motion, Mrs Harris, and you'll be hearing from us in a few weeks.*
PHR : USED AS AN A = under way
● PHR : VB INFLECTS

6 Some people, especially doctors or nurses, say **motion** when they are referring in a polite way to a person's act of defecation or the faeces produced.
N COUNT

motionless /məʊʃəⁿnlɪ²s/. Someone or something that is **motionless** is not moving at all. EG *Rudolph sat motionless... ...wisps of white cloud hanging motionless in the sky.*
ADJ CLASSIF = still, frozen

motion picture, motion pictures; often used before another noun and spelled with a hyphen. A **motion picture** is the same as a film in the cinema; used in rather formal American English. EG *The series was used as the basis for a motion picture... ...the motion-picture industry.*
N COUNT = movie

motivate /məʊtɪveɪt/, **motivates, motivating, motivated. 1** If you or your actions **are motivated** by something, especially an emotion, it causes you to behave in a particular way or provides the reason for your behaviour. EG *...groups motivated by envy and the lust for power... My decision to make this trip was motivated by a simple desire to leave the country... He was studying the nature of revolution, the forces of history that motivate it.* ◊ **motivated**. EG *...a tightly knit group of politically motivated men.* ◊ **motivation** /məʊtɪveɪʃəⁿn/, **motivations**. EG *...the motivations behind our organization... There's a political motivation for these actions.* **2** If you **are motivated** to do something, you are caused to feel determined to achieve something and willing to work hard in order to succeed. EG *You have first got to motivate the children and then to teach them.* ◊ **motivated**. EG *Each individual was motivated to survive... ...highly motivated and enthusiastic people.* ◊ **motivation**. EG *She insists her success is due to motivation rather than brilliance... Some students feel a lack of motivation in their course.*
V+O : USU PASS ⇑ influence = inspire, prompt
◊ ADJ QUALIT = impelled
◊ N COUNT/UNCOUNT
V+O : USU PASS ⇑ inspire = stimulate
◊ ADJ QUALIT : USU ADV+ADJ
◊ N UNCOUNT = drive

motive /məʊtɪv/, **motives. 1** A person's **motive** is their aim or purpose which influences the way they behave. EG *Was there some more sinister motive for their action?... I urge you to question his motives.*
N COUNT = reason

2 Motive power provides energy that can be used to operate machinery. EG *Electricity is just one form of motive power.*
ADJ CLASSIF : ATTRIB = activating

motley /mɒtli¹/. A **motley** collection or group of people or things is one in which the people or things are all of different types or appearance so that the group seems rather odd; used showing disapproval. EG *...a motley crew of servants... ...a motley collection of hats and coats.*
ADJ QUALIT : ATTRIB ⇑ various = ill-assorted

motor /məʊtə/, **motors, motoring, motored. 1** A **motor** is **1.1** the part of a vehicle or machine that changes fuel such as petrol or diesel oil into energy, so that the vehicle moves or the machine works. EG *He got into the car and started the motor... The boat has a small outboard motor.* ▸ used as an adjective to describe vehicles with motors. EG *...motor vehicles of every description... The police use a motor launch to patrol the harbour.* **1.2** a device in which power, often electric power, is changed into movement in order to make something work. EG *The washing machine is powered by an electric motor.* **1.3** a car; used in informal British English. EG *That's a smashing new motor you've got.*
N COUNT = engine
▸ N BEFORE N
N COUNT
N COUNT

2 Motor also means concerning or relating to cars, trucks, buses, and other vehicles with a petrol or diesel engine. EG *High oil prices led to the decline of the motor industry... ...a motor mechanic... He was badly hurt in a motor accident... ...motor racing.*
ADJ CLASSIF : ATTRIB = car

3 If you **are motoring** somewhere, you are travelling there in a car, usually for pleasure; an old-fashioned use. EG *They spent a week motoring through Italy.*
V : USU CONT+A ⇑ travel = drive

motorbike /məʊtəbaɪk/, **motorbikes**; also spelled with a hyphen. A **motorbike** is the same as a motorcycle; a fairly informal word used in British English. EG *...a seaside town where youths on 500cc motorbikes roar up and down the promenade.*
N COUNT

motorboat /məʊtəbəʊt/, **motorboats**; also spelled with a hyphen. A **motorboat** is a boat that is driven by a small engine.
N COUNT ⇑ boat

motorcade /məʊtəkeɪd/, **motorcades**. A **motorcade** is a line of slowly-moving cars carrying important people, usually as part of a public ceremony. EG *The president was in an open car at the head of a long motorcade.*
N COUNT ⇑ procession

motor car, motor cars; also spelled with a hyphen and as one word. A **motor car** is the same as a car; a formal, rather old-fashioned term.
N COUNT

motorcycle /məʊtəsaɪkəⁿl/, **motorcycles**. A **motorcycle** is a two-wheeled vehicle that is similar to a bicycle but is much bigger and heavier and is driven by an engine.
N COUNT = motorbike

motorcyclist /məʊtəsaɪklɪst/, **motorcyclists**. A **motorcyclist** is a person who rides a motorcycle. EG *...an accident involving a lorry and a motorcyclist.*
N COUNT ⇑ rider

motoring /məʊtəⁿrɪŋ/ means concerning or relating to cars and the people who drive them. EG *The new law increases the fines for certain motoring offences... The main reason for joining a motoring organization is for its emergency services.* ● See also **motor**.
ADJ CLASSIF : ATTRIB

motorised /məʊtəⁿraɪzd/. See **motorized**.

motorist /məʊtəⁿrɪst/, **motorists**. A **motorist** is a person who drives a car.
N COUNT = driver

motorized /məʊtəⁿraɪzd/; also spelled **motorised**. **1** A vehicle that is **motorized** is fitted with an engine. EG *...motorized transport.*
ADJ CLASSIF

2 A **motorized** group of soldiers is equipped with motor vehicles. EG *A motorized infantry regiment followed up.*
ADJ CLASSIF

motorway /məʊtəweɪ/, **motorways**. A **motorway** is a road that has been specially built for fast travel over long distances. Motorways have two or three lanes in each direction and a restricted number of places at which drivers enter and leave them; used in British English. EG *You're not supposed to abandon your car on the motorway... ...motorway cafés.*
N COUNT = expressway

mottled /mɒtəⁿld/. Something that is **mottled** is covered with patches of different colours which do not form a regular pattern. EG *His face was mottled red and white... ...a mottled camouflage jacket.*
ADJ QUALIT : NOT WITH *very* ⇑ marked

motto /mɒtəʊ/, **mottoes, mottos**. The plural can be either **mottoes** or **mottos**. A **motto** is a short sentence or phrase that expresses a rule for good or sensible behaviour. It is often chosen by a person, school, or institution as their own special saying. EG *'Live and let live' was his motto... ...the school motto, 'To strive, to seek, to find.'*
N COUNT

mould /məʊld/, **moulds, moulding, moulded**; also spelled **mold** in American English. **1** If you **mould** a person, you influence them over a long period of time so that you cause their character or attitudes to develop in a particular way. EG *The deep motive is to mould the child into a disciplined creature... You cannot mould the character of a cat.*
V+O = shape

2 If you **mould** something, you create it or change it over a long period of time so that it develops in a way that is satisfactory or suitable for you. EG *We have spent the past year creating and moulding this industry... I think he can mould a coalition in the middle, between the extreme right and the left... The television pundits play a dominant role in moulding public opinion.*
V+O ⇑ develop = construct

3 If you **mould** a soft substance such as plastic or clay, you make it into a particular shape or into an object. EG *...clay moulded into battleships... ...the thick, smooth mud that the men used to mould walls for the new huts... ...black plastic chairs, their seats moulded to the shape of some average universal person.*
V+O ⇑ form = sculpt

4 When something **moulds** round an object or when you **mould** it there, it fits round the object tightly so that the shape of the object can still be seen. EG *Her clothes moulded perfectly to the lithe body.*
V-ERG+A ⇑ fit

5 A **mould** is a container that you use to make something into a particular shape. You pour a soft or liquid substance such as melted metal or jelly into the mould, and when the metal or jelly becomes solid you take it out and it has the same shape as the mould. EG *There was a leak in the mould; molten metal ran out on to the floor.*
N COUNT = cast

6 When a person fits or is cast in a **mould** of a particular kind, they have the characteristics, attitudes, behaviour, or lifestyle that are typical of a particular type of person. EG *He's a complex man who doesn't fit into the conventional mould of the typical retired army officer... They were all cast in the same contemporary mould, with flowing shoulder-length hair... She won't have the guts to break out of the mould and move to another company.*
N COUNT: USU+SUPP ⇑ pattern

7 Mould is **7.1** a soft grey, green, or blue substance that sometimes forms in spots on old food or on damp walls or clothes. Mould spreads quickly and can cover something completely. EG *The inside may be spotted with nasty green mould... Peanuts, when they go bad, produce a mould.* **7.2** a mixture of rotting leaves and twigs, which you dig into soil in order to make the soil more fertile. EG *...the fermenting autumn mould... ...leaf mould.*
N COUNT/UNCOUNT ⇑ fungus = mildew; N UNCOUNT

moulder /məʊldə/, **moulders, mouldering, mouldered**; also spelled **molder** in American English. Something that **is mouldering** is decaying slowly in the place where it has been left. EG *The leaves at the top rot and moulder... ...mouldering corpses.*
V: USU+A *(away)* ⇑ decay = decompose

moulding /məʊldɪŋ/, **mouldings**; also spelled **molding** in American English. A **moulding** is a strip of plaster or wood along the top of a wall or round a door, which has been made into an ornamental shape or decorated with a pattern. EG *...black and gold mouldings on the walls.*
N COUNT = cornice

mouldy /məʊldi[1]/, **mouldier, mouldiest**; also spelled **moldy** in American English. Something that is **mouldy** is covered with mould. EG *...food which has become partly mouldy... It has a nasty mouldy smell.*
ADJ QUALIT ⇑ bad

moult /məʊlt/, **moults, moulting, moulted**; also spelled **molt** in American English. When an animal or bird **moults**, it loses its fur, hair, or feathers by a natural process so that new fur, hair, or feathers can grow in the same place. EG *After they have begun to breed they may continue to moult... ...a moulting stork.*
V

mound /maʊnd/, **mounds**. A **mound** is **1** a pile of earth, stones, etc like a very small hill. EG *Each home was separated from the next by a circular mound of earth... The site consisted of a few grass mounds and some yards of flint wall.* **2** a large and rather untidy pile of objects. EG *He lay in his bunk under a mound of blankets... We had mounds of tasteless rice.*
N COUNT = hillock; N PART = heap

mount /maʊnt/, **mounts, mounting, mounted**.
1 If you **mount** a campaign or a particular course of action, you prepare it and carry it out. EG *Newspapers mounted a campaign of support for the rebels... We mounted a sustained attack on the government... No rescue or relief operations could be mounted.*
V+O ⇑ organize = launch

2 If you **mount** an exhibition, display, etc, you organize and present it. EG *We mounted an exhibition of recent books... Fifty such displays are being mounted over the next few days.*
V+O = put on

3 If something **mounts**, it becomes bigger or higher. EG *Social problems in modern society are mounting... The temperature mounted rapidly.* ◇ **mounting**. EG *He admitted that the mounting cost was 'a matter of serious concern'... Everywhere there is mounting unemployment.*
V ⇑ increase; ◇ ADJ CLASSIF = rising, escalating

4 If you **mount** steps or stairs, you go up them; a slightly formal use. EG *Walter mounted the steps and pressed the bell... She mounted the last flight to the sixth floor.*
V+O ⇑ ascend = climb

5 If you **mount** a stage or a platform, you climb up on to it from the floor or the ground; a slightly formal use. EG *I mounted the podium to stare into 10,000 faces.*
V+O ⇑ ascend

6 If you **mount** a horse, pony, etc or a bicycle, you climb on to its back or onto the saddle so that you can ride it. EG *The brothers watched as she mounted the mare.* ● See also **mounted**.
V OR V+O ⇑ get on

7 Your **mount** is the horse, pony, etc that you are riding. EG *Their mounts grew weaker and weaker.*
N COUNT ⇑ animal = steed

8 When a male animal **mounts** a female, it rests its front legs on the female's back or climbs on to it, in order to have sex; a technical term.
V+O ⇑ climb

9 If you **mount** an object in a particular place, you fix it there firmly on something that will support it. EG *The sword was mounted in a mahogany case... Mounting the engine in this way was an improvement... Machine guns had been mounted on top of the police stations.*
V+O: USU+A ⇑ attach

10 Mount is used as part of the name of a mountain. EG *...Mount Erebus.*
N UNCOUNT: USED IN NAMES

11 If you **mount a guard** over something, you get someone to guard it. EG *Strong police guards were mounted at all hospitals.* ● If you **mount guard** over something, you guard it yourself. EG *She had been asked to mount guard over a number of dogs.*
PHR: VB INFLECTS; ● PHR: VB INFLECTS

mount up. If something **mounts up**, it gets bigger or greater, because more and more is being added to it. EG *The soil becomes more and more acidic as pollution mounts up... You put a little by each week and you'll be surprised how it mounts up.*
PHRASAL VB: V+ADV ⇑ increase = build up

mountain /maʊntɪn/, **mountains**. **1** A **mountain** is a very large raised part of the earth's surface with steep sides which are usually difficult to climb. A mountain is bigger and higher than a hill. EG *She was silent while we climbed the mountain... We want a pleasant hotel in the mountains... ...a mountain road.* ▸ used as part of a name. EG *...the Rocky Mountains.* ● **Make a mountain out of a molehill**: see **molehill**.
N COUNT ⇑ projection; ▸ N COUNT

2 A **mountain** is also **2.1** a large heap of stones or other objects. EG *...a mountain of rubble... ...a mountain of dusty old-fashioned furniture.* **2.2** a very large amount of anything; an informal use. EG *A mountain of evidence has accumulated... I've got mountains of work to do.*
N PART+N UNCOUNT/N IN PLURAL; N PART+N UNCOUNT/N IN PLURAL = mass

mountaineer /maʊntɪnɪə/, **mountaineers**. A **mountaineer** is a person who is skilful at climbing the steep sides of mountains. EG *...a party of mountaineers going up the mountain.*
N COUNT ⇑ climber

mountaineering /maʊntɪnɪərɪŋ/ is the activity of climbing the steep sides of mountains as a hobby or sport. EG *Walking and mountaineering are now very popular.*
N UNCOUNT

mountainous /maʊntɪnəs/. **1** A **mountainous** place has a lot of mountains. EG *I was walking through mountainous country... The south and east regions are mountainous.*
ADJ QUALIT ⇑ hilly ≠ flat

2 A **mountainous** thing or person is unusually large or high. EG *...mountainous seas.*
ADJ CLASSIF: ATTRIB

mountain range, mountain ranges. A **mountain range** or **range of mountains** is a row of mountains that were formed at the same time in the earth's history. EG *We could just see beyond the next mountain range.*
N COUNT

mountainside /maʊntɪnsaɪd/, **mountainsides**. A **mountainside** is one of the steep sides of a mountain. EG *They walked a quarter of a mile down the mountainside.*
N COUNT ⇑ side

mountebank /maʊnti[1]bæŋk/, **mountebanks**. A **mountebank** is a person who tries to deceive people by claiming to be able to do wonderful things; a literary word, used showing disapproval. EG *The nation was led astray by a mountebank... You get fakes, cheats, mountebanks the world over.*
N COUNT = charlatan

mounted /maʊntɪ[2]d/. **Mounted** police, soldiers, etc ride horses when they are on duty. EG *The demonstrators were attacked by mounted police... ...the Transkei Mounted Rifles.*
ADJ CLASSIF: ATTRIB

mourn /mɔːn/, **mourns, mourning, mourned**.
1 If you **mourn** someone or you **mourn** for them or you **mourn** their death, you are very sad because they have died, and you show how sad you are in the way that you behave. EG *I remained to mourn him in Chicago... I shall always love Guy and mourn for him... The time to mourn my father's death is near.* ● See also **mourning**.
V+O, OR V+A *(for)* ⇑ lament = grieve for

2 If you **mourn** for something or you **mourn** over it, you are very sad because you no longer have it or because you can no longer hope to have it. EG *I mourned for the loss of my precious expectations... I mourn for what might have been... He mourned over what he was never going to see any more.*
V+A *(for/over)* ⇑ regret = grieve for

mourner /mɔːnə/, **mourners**. A **mourner** is a person who attends a funeral, especially as a relative or friend of the dead person. EG *I went out into the garden to join the mourners... Mourners thronged to the funeral.*
N COUNT

mournful /mɔːnfʊl/. **1** If you are **mournful**, you are very sad. EG *Jefferson looked mournful... The bells made her mournful.* ▸ used of a person's voice or appearance. EG *He addressed Thomas in an mournful voice... Their eyes were dark and mournful.* ◇ **mournfully**. EG *He shook his head mournfully.*
ADJ QUALIT = sorrowful, melancholy; ◇ ADV WITH VB

2 A **mournful** sound makes you think that it is made
ADJ QUALIT

by someone who is very sad. EG *The little train kept up its mournful howl... ...the mournful cry of a jackal pack.*

mourning /mɔːnɪŋ/. 1 **Mourning** is 1.1 public behaviour in which you show sadness and regret about a person's death. EG *Beards were shaved off as a sign of the deepest mourning... Today formal mourning is only observed for heads of state.* 1.2 a loud crying sound that people make in some societies when a person dies. EG *There was a steady mourning and a bitter grief... Gradually the terrible mourning subsided.* 1.3 special clothes that people wear in some societies when a member of their family dies. EG *Waldemar was wearing all the mourning he could find.* — N UNCOUNT ⇑ sorrow = grief; N UNCOUNT = wailing; N UNCOUNT = black

2 If you are **in mourning**, you are dressed or behaving in a particular way because a member of your family has died. EG *He was in mourning for his wife... Lammie arrived in deep mourning.* — PHR : USED AS AN A

mouse /maʊs/, **mice**. A **mouse** is a small furry animal with a long tail. There are many kinds of mouse; some live in people's houses and some live in the fields. EG *There's a mouse in my room... The cat was there to keep the mice and rats out of the kitchen.* • a **game of cat and mouse**: see **cat**. — N COUNT

mousetrap /maʊstræp/, **mousetraps**. A **mousetrap** is a small device that kills mice. It works by means of a powerful spring. — N COUNT ⇑ trap

mousey /maʊsi[1]/. See **mousy**.

moussaka /mʊsɑːkə/, **moussakas**. Moussaka is a food made with meat and aubergines and baked in an oven. — N MASS

mousse /muːs/ is a sweet food made from eggs and cream, with fruit or chocolate added to give it flavour. It is eaten cold. EG *...chocolate mousse.* — N MASS ⇑ dessert

moustache /məstɑːʃ/, **moustaches**; also spelled **mustache** in American English. A man's **moustache** is the hair that grows on his upper lip. If it is very long, it is sometimes referred to as his 'moustaches'. EG *...a tall man with a moustache... He licked his black moustache... He frowned and twirled his moustaches.* — N COUNT : SING=PL

mousy /maʊsi[1]/, **mousier, mousiest**; also spelled **mousey**. 1 A **mousy** person is very quiet and shy. EG *She had a mousy husband who appeared occasionally.* — ADJ QUALIT ≠ assertive

2 **Mousy** hair is a dull light brown colour; used showing disapproval. EG *Her mousy hair had been cheaply permed.* — ADJ QUALIT

mouth, mouths, mouthing, mouthed. The word **mouth** is pronounced /maʊθ/ when it is a singular noun and /maʊð/ when it is a verb. The plural noun is pronounced /maʊðz/. 1 Your **mouth** is the opening into which you put food when you eat. The word **mouth** sometimes refers only to your lips and the gap between them; it can also refer to the space inside your head where your tongue and teeth are. People, animals, fish, and insects have mouths, but birds have beaks. EG *She closed her eyes and opened her mouth... There was a cynical smile on his mouth... Mr Geard had his mouth full of sponge cake... Its long tongue flickers in and out of its tiny mouth.* — N COUNT ⇑ orifice

2 The word **mouth** is also used in the following expressions. 2.1 If you look **down in the mouth**, you look unhappy; an informal expression. EG *You look very down in the mouth today, Iris.* 2.2 If you hear something **from the horse's mouth**, you hear it from someone who is in a position to know that it is true. EG *I got it straight from the horse's mouth.* 2.3 If you **keep** your **mouth shut** about something, you do not talk about it. EG *I kept my mouth shut as much as possible... He found it hard to keep his mouth shut.* — PHR : USED AS AN A; PHR : USED AS AN A = first-hand; PHR : VB INFLECTS = keep quiet

2.4 If food **makes** your **mouth water**, the sight or smell of it makes you want to eat it very much. EG *The smell made his mouth water, but he turned his head away.* 2.5 If you have a number of **mouths to feed**, you have the responsibility of earning enough money to feed and look after that number of people, usually because they are your family. EG *They add to the number of mouths to feed.* 2.6 If you do not **open** your **mouth**, you do not say anything. EG *She didn't open her mouth all evening... He didn't dare open his mouth.* • **by word of mouth**: see **word**. • **to put words into someone's mouth**: see **word**. • **to take the words out of someone's mouth**: see **word**. • **to shoot your mouth off**: see **shoot**. • **shut your mouth**: see **shut**. • See also **big mouth**, **hand-to-mouth**, **loud-mouthed**, **open-mouthed**, **mouth-watering**. 3 If you **mouth** something, 3.1 you say it either without believing it or without understanding it. EG *Only yesterday she had been mouthing platitudes to the sixth form.* 3.2 you form the words with your lips without making any sound, so that people can understand what you mean by watching your lips. EG *She mouthed the word no... Jane caught her eye, mouthed 'Water?' and fetched her some.* — PHR : VB INFLECTS; PHR : USED AS O = dependants; PHR = utter a word; V+O ⇑ utter = spout; V+O/QUOTE ⇑ indicate

4 A **mouth** is also 4.1 the entrance to something such as a cave or hole. EG *There was a vicious snarling in the mouth of the shelter... From the observation platform you looked across the mouth of the excavation.* 4.2 the open end of a bottle or a glass. EG *'Enough,' said Ellen, tipping the mouth of the bottle up.* 4.3 the part of a river where it flows into the sea. EG *We lived near the mouth of the Bashee River.* — N COUNT : USU+of; N COUNT : USU+of; N COUNT : USU+of

mouthful /maʊθfʊl/, **mouthfuls**. 1 A **mouthful** of drink or food is the amount that you put into your mouth at any one time when you are drinking or eating. EG *He took another mouthful of whisky... She spoke through a mouthful of chicken... 'Don't you like me?' she asked between mouthfuls.* — N COUNT/PART

2 In informal English, a **mouthful** can also mean a long word or phrase that is difficult to say. EG *Now that's a bit of a mouthful... It's too much of a mouthful to say one million five hundred thousand.* — N COUNT ⇑ difficulty

mouth organ, mouth organs. A **mouth organ** is a small musical instrument. You play it by moving it across your lips and by blowing and sucking air through it. — N COUNT = harmonica

mouthpiece /maʊθpiːs/, **mouthpieces**. 1 The **mouthpiece** of a telephone is the part that you speak into. EG *He muttered 'Very good, thank you' into the mouthpiece... She had her hand over the mouthpiece.* — N COUNT

2 The **mouthpiece** of a musical instrument and of some other devices is the part that you put into your mouth. EG *He took the mouthpiece out of his mouth.* — N COUNT

3 The **mouthpiece** of a person or organization is the person who publicly states their opinions, policies, etc. EG *...a notable journalist who was his mouthpiece... He became the official mouthpiece of the moderate leadership.* ▸ used also to refer to a newspaper. EG *His mouthpiece was the Evening Post.* — N COUNT : USU WITH POSS, OR a/the+N+for = spokesperson; ▸ = organ

mouthwash /maʊθwɒʃ/, **mouthwashes**. A **mouthwash** is a liquid that you rinse your mouth with, in order to clean and freshen it. EG *She brushed her teeth, and gargled with mouthwash.* — N MASS

mouth-watering. **Mouth-watering** food looks or smells delicious, so that you want to eat it very much. EG *They showed us their mouth-watering wares.* ▸ used also of descriptions of food. EG *The menu is mouth-watering.* — ADJ QUALIT = appetizing; ▸ ⇑ enticing

movable /muːvəbə[0]l/; also spelled **moveable**. 1 Something that is **movable** is able to be moved from one place or position to another. EG *The room is divided by movable screens... A violent wind suddenly rose, blowing movable objects from the decks.* — ADJ CLASSIF ≠ fixed

2 A **movable** feast or festival does not happen on exactly the same date each year. Easter is a movable feast. — ADJ CLASSIF : ATTRIB ≠ fixed

move /muːv/, **moves, moving, moved**. 1 When you **move** something or when it **moves**, its position changes and it does not remain still. EG *He was laughing and moving his head from side to side... Workmen were moving a heavy wardrobe in a bedroom... The curtains behind began to move... I'll have to move the car... You work the whole system by moving a control rod up or down.* — V-ERG

2 If you **move**, 2.1 you change your position or go to a different place. EG *I was so scared I couldn't move... Can you move, you're squashing me?... He moved around, pulling books off shelves... Can you move down the bus, please?* ▸ used as a noun. EG *One move out of you and we'll start shooting... ...they followed his every move.* 2.2 you leave a place. EG *We ought to be moving. The sun's going down.* 2.3 you act or you begin to do something. EG *If we are going to go ahead, let us move fast.* — V : USU+A; ▸ N SING WITH DET = movement; V OR V+O (REFL); V

3 If you **move** or you **move** house, you leave the house where you have been living, and you go and live in a different house, taking your possessions with you. EG *Last year my parents moved from Hyde to Stepney... Send me an address if you move... He* — V OR V+O : IF V, USU+A ⇑ transfer

moved house in April. ▸ used as a noun. EG *I wrecked a good stereo on my last move.* ▸ N COUNT ⇑ relocation

4 If people in authority **move** someone, they make that person go from one place or job to another one. EG *Promising young executives are being moved around from one subsidiary company to another... They moved George to another prison.* V+O : IF+PREP THEN *from/to* = send, transfer

5 If you say that you cannot **move** in a place, you mean that it is very crowded and there is not much room. EG *You can't move in town this morning.* V : USU INF, USU WITH BROAD NEG = budge

6 If you are **on the move**, you are going from one place to another. EG *On the move again, we eventually came to a halt beside an old church... Billie Jean is constantly on the move.* PHR : USED AS AN A ⇑ move

7 If you say that something such as a vehicle can **move**, you mean that it can go very fast; an informal use. EG *This car can really move.* V = shift, go fast

8 If you **move** an event or the date of an event, you change the time at which it happens. EG *We'll have to move the date of the party... Is there any chance of moving forward the negotiations?* V+O : USU+A

9 If you **move** from one job or interest to another, you change from one job or interest to another. EG *He'd moved to the BBC from publishing... It's fun to move from project to project.* ▸ used as a noun. EG *The frequent moves at the upper levels ensure senior management is of the highest calibre.* V : USU+A ⇑ go = transfer ▸ N COUNT

10 If you **move** from one subject or activity to another, you change your attention from one subject or activity and concentrate on another. EG *The effort has moved from producing hardware to developing software... Let's move off this subject.* V+A

11 If you **move** in a particular direction, you change your situation or your attitude, opinions, policies, etc in that direction. EG *We are moving rapidly into the nuclear age... Economists had moved slowly to the right over the last year... Public opinion was moving strongly in favour of disarmament.* ▸ used as a noun. EG *This was the first step in his move away from the Labour party.* V+A = develop ▸ N COUNT

12 If you will not **move** or will not **be moved**, you have come to a decision and nothing will change your mind. EG *I shall not move in the matter.* V, OR V+O : USU PASS, WITH BRAOD NEG = budge

13 If a situation or process **is moving**, it is developing or progressing, rather than staying still. EG *Things are really moving now... Events now moved swiftly... A writer must keep the story moving.* V = develop, progress

14 If you **move** someone to do something, you influence them and cause them to do it. EG *What has moved the President to take this step?... My conscience was moved to action.* V+O+*to*-INF, OR V+O+A *(to)* ⇑ motivate = prompt

15 If something **moves** you, it has an effect on your emotions and causes you to feel sadness or sympathy for another person. EG *The whole incident had moved her profoundly... Amy had been moved almost to tears by the boy's story.* ◊ **moved**. EG *He was too moved to speak.* ● See also **moving**. V+O ⇑ affect ◊ ADJ QUALIT

16 If you **move** in a particular society, circle, world, etc, you know people in a particular social class or group and spend most of your time with them. EG *I expect you move in the highest social circles.* V+A = mix

17 If you **move** a motion or amendment, you formally propose it at a meeting so that everyone present can vote for or against it. EG *He rose to move a motion dealing with the training of social workers... She moved that the meeting be adjourned.* V+O/REPORT-CL = put

18 If you **move** a stain or mark, you remove it by cleaning. V+O = shift

19 If you **move** your **bowels**, or if your **bowels move**, you get rid of faeces from your body when you go to the toilet. PHR : VB INFLECTS = defecate

20 A **move** is **20.1** an act of going from one place to another; used especially when you are talking about a large group such as an army or company. EG *Last year the firm made a move to Glasgow... The men are ready for a move forward.* **20.2** an action that you take in order to achieve something. EG *Accepting this job was a very good move... The first real move towards disarmament... The County Council's move to appoint the 10 new teachers was condemned today by the unions.* **20.3** an act of putting a counter, chess piece, etc in a different position on a board when it is your turn to do so in a game. EG *That was a clever move... Whose move is it?* N COUNT ⇑ advance; N COUNT : USU SING ⇑ act; N COUNT

21 If you **make a move**, **21.1** you prepare or begin to leave one place and go somewhere else; an informal expression. EG *For a good half hour neither she nor any of the others made a move... Come on, it's time we were making a move... She made no move to rise from her chair.* **21.2** you take a course of action which you know someone else will respond to in some way; an informal expression. EG *For six days neither side made a move... I thought I had better make the first move.* PHR : VB INFLECTS; PHR : VB INFLECTS, ALSO+*to*-INF ⇑ act

22 The word **move** is also used in the following informal expressions. **22.1** If you tell someone to **get a move on**, you mean that they should hurry to do something. EG *Get a move on, you two.* **22.2** If you tell someone to **get moving**, you mean that they should leave as quickly as possible or do something as quickly as possible. EG *You had better get moving.* **22.3** If things **get moving**, they begin to develop and make progress. EG *I hope, when the thing gets moving, that you'll come again.* **22.4** If you **get** something **moving**, you cause it to begin and to make progress. EG *It was quite a struggle getting things moving and overcoming the difficulties.* PHR : VB INFLECTS; PHR : VB INFLECTS, USU IMPER; PHR : VB INFLECTS; PHR : VB INFLECTS

move about. If you **move about** or **move around**, **1** you keep going from one part of a place or room to another part. EG *She moved about the office, wafting scent... He thought he heard Sue moving around.* **2** you keep changing your job or keep changing the place where you live. EG *I've moved around a bit... She moved about from place to place.* PHRASAL VB : V+ADV/PREP = go about; PHRASAL VB : V+ADV

move along. If someone, especially a police officer, tells you to **move along**, they mean that you should leave and not stand around in a particular place. EG *Move along there, please.* PHRASAL VB : V+ADV ⇑ go = move on

move away. If you **move away**, you go and live in a different town or area of a country. EG *They had decided to retire from farming and move away.* PHRASAL VB : V+ADV

move down. If you **move down**, you go to a lower level, grade or class. EG *When they fail their mathematics exams they move down a year, and take them again... If I changed departments I'd probably have to move down a grade.* PHRASAL VB : V-ERG+ADV, USU +A = go down, drop down

move in. **1** When you **move in** or **move into** a different house or place, you begin to live in a different house or place. EG *We had moved in at the height of the summer... We were the first black family to move into that area.* PHRASAL VB : V+ADV/PREP ≠ move out

2 If someone **moves in** or **moves in** with you, they come to live with you. EG *He moved in with Mrs Camish... Are your parents going to move in?* PHRASAL VB : V+ADV, IF+PREP THEN *with* ≠ move out

3 If you **move in**, **3.1** you go towards a place or person in order to attack them. EG *They were under orders to move in from France... He began to move in on Tom.* **3.2** you become involved in a particular activity and take over from another person or group, perhaps in an unfair way; used showing disapproval. EG *Professional drug pushers moved in and organized the trade.* PHRASAL VB : V+ADV = close; PHRASAL VB : V+ADV, IF+PREP THEN *on* = muscle in

move off. If you **move off**, you start moving away from a place. EG *The gleaming fleet of cars prepared to move off... We move off on the cycles as fast as possible.* PHRASAL VB : V+ADV ⇑ go = set off, leave

move on. **1** When you **move on**, you leave the place where you have been staying or waiting and go somewhere else, or continue your journey. EG *After three weeks in Hong Kong, we moved on to Japan... 'Move on, boys', the policeman said.* PHRASAL VB : V+ADV

2 If someone such as a policeman **moves** you **on**, they order or cause you to leave a particular place and go somewhere else. EG *I used to play the violin in the street, but I was always being moved on by the police.* PHRASAL VB : V+O+ADV

3 If you **move on**, **3.1** you finish one thing and turn your attention to something else. EG *Can we move on to the second question?... Let's leave it there and move on... The men moved on to talk about something else.* **3.2** you leave your present job and start another one which will be better for you. EG *John wanted to move on from the Post to a bigger paper... It's time to move on.* PHRASAL VB : V+ADV, IF+PREP/VB THEN *to*/*to*-INF = go on; PHRASAL VB : V+ADV = graduate, progress

4 If time, the days, the months, etc **move on**, they pass or happen. EG *As the months moved on, I realized how inadequate these measures were.* PHRASAL VB : V+ADV = pass by, wear on

move out. If you **move out**, **1** you stop living in a particular house or place and you go to live somewhere else. EG *The fellow that lived there moved out without a trace... I want to move out of Birmingham.* **2** you stop living with a person and live somewhere else. EG *He threatened to move out.* PHRASAL VB : V+ADV, IF+PREP THEN *of* ⇑ move = leave; PHRASAL VB : V+ADV/PREP

move over. If you **move over**, **1** you change from PHRASAL VB : V+

one system or way of doing something to another. EG *There have been suggestions that we ought to move over towards a more liberal kind of economy.* 2 you leave your job in order to let someone else have it. EG *She decided to move over and make way for one of the younger women to take over.* 3 you change your position in order to make room for someone else. EG *Move over a bit, will you?*

ADV, USU+A = transfer
PHRASAL VB : V+ADV = step aside
PHRASAL VB : V+ADV ⇑ move = budge up

move up. 1 If you **move up**, 1.1 you change your position, especially in order to be nearer someone or to make room for someone else. EG *She moved up so close to my chair... Move up, John, let the lady sit down.* 1.2 you go to a higher level, grade, or class. EG *He's moved up the class... She blamed the system of children moving up year by year.*

PHRASAL VB : V+ADV ⇑ move
PHRASAL VB : V+ADV/PREP = go up

2 When soldiers, policemen, etc **move up** or when they **are moved up**, they are ordered to go to a particular position and be ready to act. EG *Two army groups had been moved up.*

PHRASAL VB : V-ERG+ADV ⇑ advance

moveable /mu̲ːvəbəˈl/. See **movable**.

movement /mu̲ːvməˈnt/, **movements**. 1 **Movement** is 1.1 the fact or activity of someone or something changing position or going from one place to another. EG *He heard movement in the hut... ...the soft movement of the flags.* 1.2 an act of going from one place to another or of travelling about in a particular area. EG *When services are in progress, movement of visitors is restricted... Men must have a certain freedom of movement... They tried to establish control over refugee movements* . 1.3 the process or act of transporting goods. EG *...the movement of oil cargoes.* 1.4 a change in number or amount. EG *...movements in commodity prices... ...upward movement of temperature.* 1.5 the fact or process of people changing their position in an organization or society. EG *There is less movement between the classes, less social mobility.*

N UNCOUNT
N UNCOUNT/COUNT ⇑ action
N UNCOUNT/COUNT
N UNCOUNT/COUNT+SUPP
N UNCOUNT/COUNT+SUPP = interchange

2 A **movement** is 2.1 an act of changing position; used especially when a person moves part of their body. EG *The proud movement of the head... Tom lit a cigarette with quick, jerky movements... In the shadows he saw a movement.* 2.2 a planned change in position that an army makes during a battle or military exercise. EG *...US naval force movements and exercises.* 2.3 a gradual development or change of an attitude, opinion, policy, etc. EG *...the party's general leftward movement... There was a movement towards a revival of conscription.*

N COUNT = motion
N COUNT = manoeuvre
N COUNT/UNCOUNT+SUPP = tendency, trend

3 Your **movements** are everything which you do or plan to do during a period of time. EG *I don't know why you have any interest in my movements it... What are your movements this week?*

N COUNT : USU POSS+N IN PLURAL ⇑ action

4 A **movement** is also 4.1 a group of people who share the same beliefs or ideas or who are trying to achieve a particular aim. EG *...the Trade Union Movement... They were unsuitable leaders for dynamic mass movements of this kind... ...the successful movement to abolish child labour.* 4.2 a major section of a symphony, concerto, or other piece of classical music. EG *There is an immensely long first movement.*

N COUNT : USU+SUPP, ALSO IN NAMES = organization
N COUNT

5 The **movement** of a clock or watch consists of the parts inside which cause the hands to move round. EG *It has the same precision as the wheels of a Swiss watch: a diamond movement.*

N COUNT ⇑ mechanism

mover /mu̲ːvə/, **movers**. 1 If you describe a person or animal as a particular kind of **mover**, you mean that they move at that speed or in that way. EG *All ant-eaters are fairly slow movers... She's a beautiful mover.*

N COUNT : ADJ+N

2 A **mover** is the person who puts forward a proposal or amendment at a meeting so that people can vote for or against it.

N COUNT = proposer

3 See also **prime mover**.

movie /mu̲ːviˈ/, **movies**. 1 A **movie** is, the same as a film; used mainly in American English. EG *...a new science-fiction movie... After dinner they went to a movie... ...movie stars... I bought a cine camera for seven quid to make some home movies.*

N COUNT = picture

2 In American English, the cinema is sometimes called the **movies**. EG *We decided to spend the afternoon at the movies.*

N PLURAL : *the*+N = flicks, pictures

moviegoer /mu̲ːviˈgəʊə/, **moviegoers**; also spelled with a hyphen. A **moviegoer** is a person who often goes to the cinema; used mainly in American English.

N COUNT

moving /mu̲ːvɪŋ/. 1 Something that is **moving** has a strong effect on your emotions, usually so that you feel pity or sympathy. EG *There is a graphic and moving account of his father's death... My visit was a moving experience.* ◇ **movingly**. EG *Her childhood is movingly described.*

ADJ QUALIT ⇑ emotional = touching
◇ ADV = touchingly

2 **Moving** means relating to the process of moving from the house where you have been living. EG *Moving costs have risen considerable.*

ADJ CLASSIF : ATTRIB = removal

3 A **moving** model or part of a machine moves or is able to move.

ADJ CLASSIF : ATTRIB

4 **The moving spirit** or **the moving force** is a person or thing that caused an activity to start and to keep going, and that influenced people to take part in it. EG *Janice was the moving spirit behind this venture.*

PHR USED AS S/O/C = driving force, inspiration

moving picture, moving pictures. A **moving picture** is a film; an old-fashioned expression.

N COUNT = motion picture

mow /mə̲ʊ/, **mows, mowing, mowed, mown**. The forms **mowed** and **mown** are both used as the past participle of the verb. 1 If you **mow** an area of grass, you cut it using a lawn mower. EG *Everyone was mowing their lawns.*

V OR V+O

2 If you **mow** corn, wheat, etc, you cut it with a machine or with a hand tool.

V OR V+O

mow down. To **mow down** a large number of people means you kill them all violently at one time, for example by shooting them. EG *Several children had strayed onto an airport runway and been mown down by a jet.*

PHRASAL VB : V+O+ADV = slaughter

mower /mə̲ʊə/, **mowers**. A **mower** is 1 the same as a lawn mower. 2 a machine that has sharp blades which go round in order to cut corn, wheat, etc. 3 a person who cuts grass, corn, wheat, etc.

N COUNT
N COUNT
N COUNT

MP, MPs. An **MP** is, in Britain, a person who has been elected by the people of a particular town or district to represent them in the House of Commons; an abbreviation for 'Member of Parliament'. EG *The Liberal MP Donald Wade demanded a debate... ...the MP for South East Bristol... ...Mr Tom King MP.*

N COUNT : ALSO IN TITLES AFTER NAME

mpg is an abbreviation for 'miles per gallon'; used especially after a number to indicate how many miles a vehicle can travel using one gallon of fuel. EG *It does 20 mpg.*

N PLURAL : USU NUM+N

mph is an abbreviation for 'miles per hour'; used especially after a number to indicate the speed of something such as a vehicle. EG *These cars are reasonably economical at a steady 56 mph.*

N PLURAL : USU NUM+N

Mr /mɪ̲stə/. 1 **Mr** is used before a man's name when you are speaking or referring to him; it is the written abbreviation for 'Mister'. EG *...Mr Jenkins... ...Mr John Watson.*

N IN TITLES

2 **Mr** is sometimes used before words like 'president' and 'chairman' when you are addressing the person who holds that position. EG *Yes, Mr President.*

N IN TITLES

3 See also **Messrs**.

Mrs /mɪ̲sɪz/ is used before the name of a married woman when you are speaking or referring to her. EG *...Mr and Mrs Clark... ...Mrs Carstairs... ...Mrs Julia Carstairs.*

N IN TITLES

Ms /mə̲z/ is used, especially in written English, before a woman's name when you are speaking to her or referring to her. If you use Ms, you are not specifying if the woman is married or not. EG *I wrote to Ms Walters and gave her my opinion.*

N IN TITLES

ms., mss. ms. is an abbreviation for 'manuscript'.

N COUNT

MS is an abbreviation for 'multiple sclerosis'.

N UNCOUNT

MSc., MScs. MSc. is an abbreviation for 'Master of Science'; a degree awarded by universities to people who have studied a scientific subject at a very advanced level. EG *The work was submitted as part of his MSc.*

N COUNT : ALSO IN TITLES AFTER NAME

Msgr is the written abbreviation for **monsignor**.

N IN TITLES

Mt, Mts. **Mt** is 1 a written abbreviation for 'mount'; used as part of the name of a particular mountain. EG *...Mt Etna.* 2 an abbreviation for mountain; used as part of the name of a particular mountain or range or mountains. EG *...Holyhead Mt... ...the Rocky Mts.*

N IN NAMES BEFORE N
N COUNT : ALSO IN NAMES AFTER N = Mountain

much /mʌ̲tʃ/. The comparative for the adverb and for the quantifier explained in paragraph 4 is **more**, and the superlative is **most**: these words are dealt with separately in this dictionary. 1 **Much** means to a large extent; used to emphasize strong qualities, feelings, actions, etc. EG *Myra and I are looking forward very much to the party... Thank you very much... He is very much at ease in life... He returned to Parliament a changed and much politicized man...*

ADV ⇑ greatly

He was as much a part of the community as the doctor.

2 You use **much** **2.1** to emphasize that something happens very often. EG *She doesn't talk about them much... Education is a much debated subject.* **2.2** to emphasize how large the difference is between things when you are comparing them. EG *Now I feel much more confident... It is much less likely... I'm treated so much better than Judy was... I thought that he was much the best speaker.*

ADV / ADV+COMPAR/SUPERL = considerably, far

3 **Much** is also used in the expressions 'much as' and 'much the same' to emphasize that something is very similar to something else. EG *The mountainous landscape was then much as it is today... The two poems convey much the same emotional tone.*

ADV+*as/the same* ⇑ almost = virtually

4 You also use **much** **4.1** to refer to a large amount or a large proportion of something. EG *We hadn't got much money... She spends so much time here... Much of the recent trouble has come from outside... It costs too much.* **4.2** to refer generally to a large amount of something when you are simply emphasizing the amount without stating specifically what it refers to. EG *There wasn't much to do... She had endured so much... Much has been gained from our discussions.*

QUANTIF+N UNCOUNT = a lot of / QUANTIF : ONLY AS PRON = a lot

5 You also use **much** to ask questions about amount or degree, or to give information about the amount or degree of something. EG *How much money have you got left?... How much did he tell you?... He's done as much as I have.*

QUANTIF : *as/how*+QUANTIF+N UNCOUNT

6 **So much for** is used, especially in spoken English, **6.1** to indicate that you have finished talking about a subject. EG *So much for music. Now for some of the other festivities.* **6.2** to refer in a rather bitter or sarcastic way to something that you had hoped would be useful but in fact has not been at all successful or helpful. EG *So much for that idea.*

PHR+NG / PHR+NG

7 The word **much** is also used in the following expressions. **7.1** **Not so much** is used to introduce the first part of a contrast when you are saying that something is not as true, great, appropriate, etc as something else which you mention later. EG *It was not so much an argument as a monologue.* **7.2** **Much as** is used to introduce and emphasize a fact which makes the other part of the sentence rather surprising because it seems partly to conflict with the fact mentioned. EG *Much as she likes him she would never consider marrying him.* **7.3** **Nothing much** means nothing that you think is worth mentioning or considering. EG *There's nothing much left.* **7.4** If a situation or action is **too much** for you, it makes you feel depressed and helpless because it is so difficult, tiring, worrying, etc. EG *It was too much for John to take.* **7.5** If you say that a person or thing is **too much**, you mean that they are so annoying that you can hardly bear it. **7.6** If you say that it was **as much as you could do** to do something, you mean that you found it very difficult to do and you could not manage anything more. EG *It was as much as I could do just to stop her crying.* **7.7** If you describe something as **not much of a** something, you mean that it is of weak or poor quality, for example when you think that someone is not very good at something or that something is hardly worth considering. EG *I'm afraid I'm not much of a cook... I haven't had much of a holiday this year.* **7.8** If you are **not much of a one for** something, you do not like it very much; a fairly informal expression. EG *I'm not much of a one for scotch.* **7.9** If you do not **so much as** do a particular thing, you do not even do the minimum that could be expected. EG *He just left without so much as saying goodbye... If you mention it by so much as a whisper, I'll be sent packing.* **7.10** If you **do not see much of** someone, you do not see them very often. EG *They didn't see much of each other.* **7.11** If you **do not hear much of** someone, you do not hear about them very often. EG *I haven't heard much of John lately.* **7.12** You say **'I thought as much'** after you have just been told something which you expected to happen or be true, to say in a disapproving or pessimistic way that you expected it to happen or to be true. EG *'I'm afraid he never arrived.'–'Yes, I thought as much.'* **7.13** • **not up to much**: see **up**. • **a bit much**: see **bit**.

PHR+NG+*as*+NG / CONJ SUBORD ⇑ although / PHR = not a lot / PHR : USED AS C / PHR : USED AS C / PHR : USED AS C / PHR+NG : USED AS O/C / PHR : USED AS C / PHR+INF/-ING/NG = even / PHR : VB INFLECTS / PHR : VB INFLECTS / CONVENTION

muchness /mʌtʃnɪ²s/. If two or more things are **much of a muchness**, they are very similar. EG *In general appearance they were all much of a muchness.*

PHR : USED AS C

muck /mʌk/, **mucks, mucking, mucked**; an informal word. **Muck** is **1** dirt or excrement. EG *They were digging holes and flinging muck at each other... There was muck everywhere.* **2** manure. EG *...a muck heap... ...two bags of muck.* **3** something such as food or writing that is of bad quality. EG *What are you reading that muck for?*

N UNCOUNT / N UNCOUNT / N UNCOUNT = rubbish

muck about. If you **muck about** or **muck around**, you behave in a stupid way so that you waste your time or do not achieve what you want to achieve. EG *She was mucking about with a jug of flowers on the table... You mustn't start mucking around.*

PHRASAL VB : V+ADV = mess about

muck in. If you **muck in**, you join in with an activity or you help other people with a job. EG *If we all muck in, we'll have the job done in no time.*

PHRASAL VB : V+ADV, IF+PREP THEN *with*

muck out. If you **muck out** stables, horses, etc, you clean the place where animals live. EG *She's mucking out the stables at the moment... Don't forget to muck out the horses.*

PHRASAL VB : V+ADV, OR V+O+ADV ⇑ clean out

muck up. If you **muck** something **up**, you do something very badly so that you do not achieve what you wanted to achieve. EG *I've taken my driving test twice, and both times I've mucked it up.*

PHRASAL VB : V+O+ADV = bungle, mess up

muckraker /mʌkreɪkə/, **muckrakers**; also spelled with a hyphen. A **muckraker** is someone who tries to find and spread scandal relating to well-known people.

N COUNT = stirrer

muckraking /mʌkreɪkɪŋ/; also spelled with a hyphen. **Muckraking** is the act of finding and spreading scandal relating to public figures. EG *The muckraking has begun.*

N UNCOUNT = stirring

mucky /mʌki¹/, **muckier, muckiest**; an informal word. **1** Something that is **mucky** is very dirty. EG *We were walking through a mucky wet forest.*

ADJ QUALIT

2 A **mucky** book or film is one that describes or shows a lot of sexual activity.

ADJ QUALIT ⇑ pornographic

mucous membrane /mjuːkəs membreɪn/, **mucous membranes**. A **mucous membrane** is a thin piece of skin that produces mucus to prevent itself from becoming dry. It covers delicate parts of the body such as the inside of your nose; a technical term in biology or medicine.

N COUNT

mucus /mjuːkəs/ is a liquid that is produced by some parts of your body, for example the inside of your nose. Mucus is also produced by some animals such as snails, in order to keep their skin moist and to help them to move.

N UNCOUNT

mud /mʌd/. **1** **Mud** is **1.1** a wet and sticky mixture of earth and water. EG *She was covered in mud... My cousin stamped around in the mud.* **1.2** earth that is used for buildings and becomes hard when it dries. EG *They make their houses out of mud and stones... They lived in round mud huts.*

N UNCOUNT ⇑ substance / N UNCOUNT

2 If at a particular time your **name is mud**, you are very unpopular and people do not have a very good opinion of you; an informal expression.

PHR : VB INFLECTS

muddle /mʌdə⁰l/, **muddles, muddling, muddled**. **1** A **muddle** is a state of untidiness or disorder. EG *With the right government, the country wouldn't be in such a muddle... No one came to sort out the worsening muddle of her finances.*

N COUNT : USU SING = mess

2 If you **muddle** something or you **muddle it up**, you cause one or more things to become confused or out of order. EG *I wish you wouldn't muddle my books and drawings... Later they may muddle up your names with those of your cousins.* ◇ **muddled**. EG *You've got the story muddled up.*

V+O, OR PHRASAL VB : V+O+ADV = mix up / ◇ ADJ QUALIT = mixed up

3 If you **muddle** someone, especially a very old person, you cause them to become confused. EG *Don't muddle her with too many suggestions.* ◇ **muddled**. EG *You wouldn't believe how tired and muddled she has become.*

V+O / ◇ ADJ QUALIT

4 A **muddle** is also a state of confusion in the mind. EG *I have got into a muddle... Her stare betrayed nothing but muddle and inattention.*

N COUNT/UNCOUNT = quandary

muddle along. If you **muddle along**, you live or exist without a proper plan or purpose in your life. EG *The church has lost its way, muddling along from Sunday to Sunday.*

PHRASAL VB : V+ADV ⇑ progress

muddle through. If you **muddle through**, you manage to do something even though you do not have proper equipment or a real policy. EG *The children are left to muddle through on their own.*

PHRASAL VB : V+ADV = get by

muddle-headed. If you are **muddle-headed**, you are confused or incapable of thinking clearly about

ADJ QUALIT = woolly

something. EG *...He was dismissed as a muddle-headed mischief-maker.*

muddy /mʌdi¹/, **muddier, muddiest; muddies, muddying, muddied.** 1 Something that is **muddy** contains mud or is covered in mud. EG *The brook was a bit muddy... The road became bumpier and bumpier, muddier and muddier.* ADJ QUALIT

2 If you **muddy** something, you make it muddy. V+O
◊ **muddied.** ◊ ADJ QUALIT

3 **Muddy** is used to describe a colour which is dull and brownish. EG *The landscape turns a mottled, muddy brown.* ADJ+ADJ COLOUR = murky

4 If you **muddy** a situation or issue, you make it seem less clear and less easy to understand. EG *The issue has been muddied by allegations of bribery.* V+O ⇑ confuse = cloud

mudflat /mʌdflæt/, **mudflats.** A **mudflat** is an area of flat empty land at the coast which is covered by the sea only when the tide is in. EG *...on the salt marsh and mudflats of Wigtown Bay.* N COUNT

mudguard /mʌdgɑːd/, **mudguards.** A **mudguard** is a curved piece of metal or plastic which is placed above the wheels of a bicycle or other vehicle, and which prevents too much water or mud from being thrown up behind. EG *...tearing around the country-side on a racing bike with no mudguards.* N COUNT

muesli /mjuːzli¹/ is a mixture of chopped nuts, dried fruit, and grains that you eat for breakfast with milk or yoghurt. N UNCOUNT ⇑ food

muezzin /muːɛzɪn/, **muezzins.** A **muezzin** is an official of a mosque who calls from its tower when it is the time of day for Muslims to say their prayers. N COUNT ⇑ official

muff /mʌf/, **muffs, muffing, muffed.** 1 If you **muff** something, you do something badly or you make a mistake while you are doing it, so that even if you finish it, it is not successful; an informal use. EG *I muffed a catch at cricket... She was determined that I should be born in London, but she muffed that through no fault of her own.* V+O = bungle, fluff

2 A **muff** is a piece of fur or thick cloth shaped like a short hollow cylinder. You might wear a muff on your hands to keep them warm in cold weather. EG *I used to clench my hands inside the muff.* N COUNT ⇑ garment

muffin /mʌfɪn/, **muffins.** A **muffin** is a kind of small round bread roll which you eat hot and with butter. EG *He was eating muffins with real solemnity.* N COUNT

muffle /mʌfə⁰l/, **muffles, muffling, muffled.** 1 If a sound **is muffled**, the volume is reduced so that it is less clear and difficult to hear. EG *The sound of a car passing on the street below was muffled.* V+O : USU PASS ⇑ diminish = deaden
◊ **muffled.** EG *Brody heard some muffled conversation... 'That's all very well' came the muffled reply.* ◊ ADJ QUALIT = faint

2 If you **are muffled** or **muffled up**, you are wearing a lot of heavy clothes so that very little of your body or face is visible. EG *Smithy was heavily clad and muffled almost to the eyebrows... A boy muffled up in a blue scarf was busy scribbling on a scrap of paper.* V+O, OR PHRASAL VB : V+O+ADV, USU PASS

3 If you **muffle** something such as an emotion or an effect, you reduce its strength or severity. V+O = soften

muffler /mʌflə/, **mufflers.** A **muffler** is 1 the same as a scarf; an old-fashioned word. EG *A long, dirty, knitted muffler was twined around her neck.* 2 in American English, the silencer on a car. N COUNT; N COUNT

mug /mʌg/, **mugs, mugging, mugged.** 1 A **mug** is a large, deep cup, usually one which has straight sides and a handle on one side. A mug usually does not have a saucer. EG *I was given the tin mug to drink out of... ...a chipped mug.* ▸ **Mug** also refers to the liquid inside a mug or the amount of liquid that it holds. EG *He drank a whole mug of coffee.* N COUNT = beaker; ▸ N PART+N UNCOUNT

2 If someone **mugs** you, they attack you in order to steal your money; an informal use. EG *They would lurk in the dark side streets and mug any passers-by.* V+O ⇑ assault
◊ **mugging, muggings.** EG *Mugging in the streets, even in broad daylight, was not uncommon... There has been a great increase in football hooliganism, vandalism and muggings.* ◊ N UNCOUNT/COUNT = robbery

3 Someone's **mug** is their face; a very informal use. EG *It was fixed to the wall between a crooner's mug and the lashes of a movie actress... Keep your ugly mug out of this.* N COUNT : USU POSS+N = mush

4 If you say that someone is a **mug**, you mean that they are stupid and easily deceived or misled by other people; a very informal use. EG *He was no mug though and took the proffered couple of pounds.* N COUNT ⇑ fool

5 If you say that something is **a mug's game**, you mean that it is an activity from which a person does not earn much money or get any satisfaction; a very informal expression. EG *'Not that I'd want to be a cameraman. A mug's game. No. I want to produce.'* PHR : USED AS C

mug up. If you **mug up** a subject, you study it quickly, for example before taking an examination, so that you can remember the main facts about it; an informal expression used mainly in British English. EG *She's upstairs mugging up history or geography or something.* PHRASAL VB : V+O+ADV = swot up

mugger /mʌgə/, **muggers.** A **mugger** is a person who attacks someone violently in a street in order to steal money from them. N COUNT ⇑ robber

muggins /mʌgɪnz/. If you refer to someone as **muggins**, you mean that you think they are stupid and so have been taken advantage of by other people; an informal expression. N SING : USED AS PRON

muggy /mʌgi¹/. If the weather is **muggy**, it is unpleasantly warm and damp, and makes you feel uncomfortable or tired. EG *I was stepping out of the plane and into the muggy, perfumed air of West Africa... It's very muggy today.* ADJ QUALIT = clammy, heavy

mug shot, mug shots. A **mug shot** is a photograph taken by the police of a person who has been charged with a crime or who is suspected of a crime; an informal expression. EG *Many hours passed before the mug shots and fingerprints were finally taken.* N COUNT

Muhammadan /mə⁶hæmədə⁰n/, **Muhammadans.** See **Mohammedan.**

Muhammadanism /mə⁶hæmədə⁰nɪzə⁰m/. See **Mohammedanism.**

mulberry /mʌlbə⁰ri¹/, **mulberries.** A **mulberry** is a tree which has small purple berries which you can eat. ▸ used also of the berries that grow on the tree. N COUNT

mulch /mʌltʃ/, **mulches, mulching, mulched.** A **mulch** is a mixture of rotting leaves and twigs which you put round the roots of plants in order to protect them and to help them to grow. EG *A good, nourishing annual mulch is a great help.* N COUNT = compost

mule /mjuːl/, **mules.** A **mule** is 1 an animal whose parents are a horse and a donkey. Mules are often used to carry people or goods in mountainous areas. EG *He spoke about his journeys into the Andes on a mule... All the equipment had been brought over the mountains on the backs of mules.* 2 a shoe or slipper which is open round the heel. N COUNT; N COUNT : USU PL

mulish /mjuːlɪʃ/. Someone who is **mulish** is unwilling to change their attitude or to do what other people tell them to do. EG *He's a very headstrong and mulish person most of the time, but underneath I think he's quite vulnerable.* ADJ QUALIT ⇑ difficult = pig-headed

mull /mʌl/, **mulls, mulling, mulled.** If you **mull** something **over**, you think for a long time about a problem or about something that has happened, often before deciding what to do. EG *Nell began to mull over the injustices of her new role... I sat there and tried to mull things over in my mind.* PHRASAL VB : V+O+ADV = review, turn over

mullah /mʊlə, mʌlə/, **mullahs.** A **mullah** is a Muslim who has studied Islamic religion and laws. N COUNT : ALSO IN TITLES

mulled /mʌld/. **Mulled** wine is wine to which sugar and spice have been added and which has then been heated. EG *They ordered mulled wine.* ADJ CLASSIF : ATTRIB

mullet /mʌlɪt/. **Mullet** is both the singular and the plural form. A **mullet** is a small sea fish that people cook and eat. N COUNT

multi- means 'many'. It is added to the beginning of nouns and adjectives. EG *... multilateral... ... multifarious... ... multi-storey.* PREFIX

multicoloured /mʌlti¹kʌləd/; also spelled with a hyphen. Something that is **multicoloured** has many different colours. EG *In the middle are multicoloured paving stones.* ADJ CLASSIF = kaleidoscopic

multifarious /mʌltɪfɛərɪəs/. Something that is **multifarious** is very many in number and of many different kinds; a formal word. EG *...the problem of inertia in all its multifarious forms... We have had to accommodate to the multifarious demands of a totally new city culture.* ADJ CLASSIF = diverse

multilateral /mʌltɪlætə⁰rəl/. Something that is **multilateral** involves at least three different groups of people or nations. EG *Such moves, he argued, could lead to multilateral nuclear disarmament... We are in favour of the holding of tripartite, bilateral, or even multilateral talks.* ADJ CLASSIF

multilingual /mʌltɪlɪŋgwəl/. 1 Something that is **multilingual** is written or said in several different languages. EG *...a multilingual pamphlet.* ADJ CLASSIF = polyglot

2 Someone who is **multilingual** is able to speak more than two languages very well.
ADJ CLASSIF

multi-millionaire, multi-millionaires; also spelled as one word. A **multi-millionaire** is a very rich person who has money or property worth several million pounds, dollars, francs, etc.
N COUNT

multinational /mʌltɪnæʃəᵒnəl/, **multinationals**; also spelled with a hyphen. 1 A **multinational** company has branches or subsidiary companies in many different countries. EG *Many of the West's large multinational companies have substantial operations in the poorer African countries... The multinational mining giant has quictly bought up all the land in this area.* ▸ also used as a noun to refer to this kind of company. EG *Local firms have to compete for skilled men with multinationals paying higher rates.*
ADJ CLASSIF = international
▸ N COUNT

2 **Multinational** also describes **2.1** something that involves people from several different countries. EG *...the multinational forces deployed under the treaty.*
ADJ CLASSIF = international

2.2 a country or region whose population is made up of people of several different nationalities, who were previously independent and had their own governments. EG *The USSR is also a multi-national state.*
ADJ CLASSIF

multiple /mʌltɪpəᵒl/, **multiples**. 1 Something that is **multiple** consists of many parts, involves many people, or has many uses. EG *There have been several multiple collisions in fog this winter... Old folk with multiple locks on the doors may feel a little safer.*
ADJ CLASSIF

2 A **multiple** is a number which can be divided by a smaller number an exact number of times. EG *24 is a multiple of 8.*
N COUNT+*of* = product

multiple-choice. A **multiple-choice** examination or question is one in which you have to choose the correct answer from several possible answers that are listed on the examination paper. EG *Psychologists designed a range of written and multiple-choice tests.*
ADJ CLASSIF

multiple sclerosis is a disease in which the substance that covers the nerves in a person's body is gradually destroyed. People who have multiple sclerosis gradually become weaker, and often suffer from double vision and slurred speech.
N UNCOUNT

multiplex /mʌltɪplɛks/. Something that is **multiplex** is complicated and involves many different people or things.
ADJ CLASSIF = complex

multiplication /mʌltɪplɪkeɪʃəᵒn/. **Multiplication** is 1 the process of calculating the total of one number which is multiplied by another number. EG *The process is still far simpler than routine multiplication and division.* 2 a large increase in the number or amount of something. EG *The result has been a huge multiplication nationally of men and women becoming involved in such schemes.*
N UNCOUNT ⇑ calculation
N UNCOUNT : USU +*of* = rise

multiplication table, multiplication tables. A **multiplication table** is a a list of the multiplications of numbers between one and twelve. Children often have to learn multiplication tables at school. EG *You needed a command of the multiplication tables, and the ability to spell.*
N COUNT = table

multiplicity /mʌltɪplɪsɪti¹/. A **multiplicity** of things is a large number or a large variety of them. EG *The structure of the Soviet State has been based upon a multiplicity of Union Republics... We sleep, troubled by a multiplicity of dreams.*
N SING WITH DET +*of* = host

multiply /mʌltɪplaɪ/, **multiplies, multiplying, multiplied**. 1 When something **multiplies** or when you **multiply** it, it increases greatly in number or amount. EG *The shops themselves began in consequence to multiply, eventually springing up in almost every town in the area... Problems of isolation in old age are greatly multiplied by physical isolation in a city.*
V-ERG

2 When animals and insects **multiply**, they increase in number by giving birth to large numbers of young. EG *In the filth, the lice as well as the fleas had multiplied by the thousand... The creatures began to multiply very rapidly.*
V = reproduce

3 If you **multiply** or you **multiply out**, you calculate the total which you get when you add a number to itself a particular number of times; for example 2 multiplied by 3 is equal to 2 plus 2 plus 2, which equals 6. EG *Add up the weekly costs of doing your job, then multiply it by fifty-two to get the rough annual outlay.*
V, V+O : USU+*by*, OR PHRASAL VB : V+O+ADV

multiracial /mʌltɪreɪʃəl/; also spelled with a hyphen. Something that is **multiracial** consists of or involves people of many different nationalities and cultures. EG *We live in a multiracial society... The handbook also became more multi-racial in content as well as in ideology.*
ADJ QUALIT

multi-storey; also spelled as one word. A **multi-storey** building or car park has several floors at different levels above the ground. EG *They are cut off from the rest of the world in a flat in a multi-storey block... ...a multi-storey carpark.*
ADJ CLASSIF

multitude /mʌltɪtju:d/, **multitudes**. 1 A **multitude** of things or people is a very large number of them. EG *It didn't work out quite like I intended it to, for a multitude of reasons... The job requires a multitude of people with special knowledge... These systems are capable of performing multitudes of different tasks.*
N COUNT/PART = host, mass

2 If something **covers** or **hides a multitude of sins**, it deliberately conceals things by appearing to be much better than it really is. EG *'Fitted carpets,' said the uncle, 'hide a multitude of sins...' These laws can cover a multitude of sins.*
PHR : VB INFLECTS

3 A **multitude** is a very large number of people. EG *'We are keeping our options open,' he had told the assembled multitude... This is a civilization that kills multitudes in mass warfare.*
N COUNT = population

4 The **multitude** is the great majority of people in a particular country or situation. EG *We are imposing this limit in the hope of satisfying the needs of the multitude... This factor must be set in the balance against the right of the multitudes to eat.*
N COUNT : *the*+N, SING=PL = masses

mum /mʌm/, **mums**. 1 Your **mum** is your mother; an informal use. EG *She said you'd gone to live with your mum and dad... My mum used to live here... I've been put in the special class, Mum.*
N PROPER/VOC : ALSO N COUNT ⇑ parent = ma

2 If you **keep mum** about something, you keep it a secret and don't tell anyone about it; an informal expression. EG *They launched a murderous attack on their enemy.*
PHR : VB INFLECTS = keep quiet

3 You might say **'Mum's the word'** when you are telling someone to keep secret something that you have told them, or when you are agreeing to keep secret something that they have told you; an informal expression.
CONVENTION = don't let on

mumble /mʌmbəᵒl/, **mumbles, mumbling, mumbled**. If you **mumble** or **mumble** something, you speak very quietly and indistinctly so that the words are difficult to understand. EG *Stop mumbling, for goodness sake... He took my hand and mumbled, 'Don't worry, you'll be all right'... He mumbled his apologies for disturbing her.* ▸ used as a noun. EG *His comment was heard only as a mumble.*
V, V+O/QUOTE/REPORT-CL, OR V+O+A (*to*) = mutter
▸ N COUNT ⇑ utterance

mumbo jumbo /mʌmbəʊ dʒʌmbəʊ/; also spelled with a hyphen. If you say that something is **mumbo jumbo**, you mean that it does not seem to make any sense at all to you; an informal expression. EG *The order of the alphabet is mumbo-jumbo to a child who cannot write his name... It was all mumbo jumbo and I didn't understand a word.*
N UNCOUNT = gibberish, nonsense

mummify /mʌmɪfaɪ/, **mummifies, mummifying, mummified**. If people **mummify** the body of someone who has died, they preserve it by rubbing it with oils and wrapping it in cloth. In ancient Egypt the bodies of important people used to be mummified. ◊ **mummified**. EG *St Denis's shrivelled, mummified body lies in an ornate coffin in the church.*
V+O = embalm
◊ ADJ CLASSIF ⇑ preserved

mummy /mʌmi¹/, **mummies**. 1 **Mummy** means mother; used informally, especially by children. EG *Mummy put me on the train at Victoria... ...love from Mummy and Daddy.*
N PROPER/VOC : ALSO N COUNT ⇑ parent = mum

2 A **mummy** is the body of a person which has been preserved after they have died by being rubbed with oils and wrapped in cloth. The bodies of important people in ancient Egypt were usually treated in this way. EG *...a gilded Egyptian mummy case.*
N COUNT ⇑ corpse

mumps /mʌmps/ is a disease usually caught by children. It causes a mild fever and painful swelling of the glands in the neck. EG *Jenny's just had mumps.*
N UNCOUNT

munch /mʌntʃ/, **munches, munching, munched**. If you **munch** or **munch** something, you eat it by chewing it steadily and thoroughly. EG *The father and son sat there, munching thin bread and butter... There was an old dog in the back yard munching on his food with great care.*
V OR V+O = chomp

mundane /mʌndeɪn/. Something that is **mundane** is very ordinary, and not especially interesting or unusual. EG *On a mundane level, we see all around us*
ADJ QUALIT = prosaic ≠ remarkable

people like this... ...a mundane description of the party.

municipal /mju:nɪsɪpəºl/ means associated with or belonging to a city or town which has its own local government. EG *This was the first big municipal housing scheme to get underway after the war... He was a genius with flowers, tending the municipal gardens with loving care.* ADJ CLASSIF: ATTRIB

municipality /mju:nɪsɪpælɪti¹/, **municipalities.** A **municipality** is a city or town which has authority to appoint a local council and local officials to administer its internal affairs; used also to refer to the local government of the city or town. EG *It was a big park, and the municipality did not have enough money to keep it tidy.* N COUNT

munificent /mju:nɪfɪsənt/ is used to describe something, for example a gift or an amount of money, which is large and very generous; a formal word. EG *He then conceived what I take to be the magnificent and munificent idea of the Marshall Plan.* ▸ used also of people who are generous. EG *...a munificent mother.* ADJ QUALIT; ▸ ADJ QUALIT

munitions /mju:nɪʃəºnz/ are military equipment and supplies, especially bombs, shells, and guns. EG *They were using both high explosive and chemical munitions... Women wanted to 'win the war' by working in munitions factories.* N PLURAL

mural /mjʊərəl/, **murals.** A **mural** is a picture which is painted directly onto the wall of a room or building. EG *...a mural of goddesses of ancient Crete.* N COUNT ⇑ painting = fresco

murder /mɜːdə/, **murders, murdering, murdered.** 1 **Murder** or a **murder** is the deliberate and unlawful killing of a person. EG *He pleaded guilty to seven counts of attempted murder... ...the rising number of murders in San Francisco... ...a murder charge.* N COUNT/ UNCOUNT

2 If you **murder** someone, you kill them deliberately and in an unlawful way. EG *They charged Williams with murdering Cater... The invaders captured, tortured, and murdered... His father, mother, and sister were all murdered by the terrorists.* V OR V+O

3 If someone **gets away with murder**, they can do whatever they like without anyone trying to control them or punish them if they do anything wrong; an informal expression. PHR: VB INFLECTS

4 If someone **screams blue murder** or **shouts bloody murder**, they make a lot of noise and fuss because something is happening or has happened that they do not like; an informal expression. PHR: VB INFLECTS ⇑ protest

5 You say that something **is murder** when you want to emphasize how bad, difficult, dangerous, or unpleasant it is; an informal use. EG *It was absolute murder in town on the first day of the sales.* PHR: VB INFLECTS = be hell

murderer /mɜːdəºrə/, **murderers.** A **murderer** is someone who deliberately and unlawfully kills another person. EG *They were all convicted murderers, thieves, or other criminals.* N COUNT ⇑ killer

murderess /mɜːdəºrɪ¹s/, **murderesses.** A **murderess** is a woman who deliberately and unlawfully kills another person. N COUNT ⇑ killer

murderous /mɜːdəºrəs/. 1 Someone who is **murderous** is likely to murder someone and is perhaps already guilty of murder. EG *They sent in the tanks and murdered the murderous dictator... The girl might have murderous tendencies.* ▸ used of people's behaviour. EG *They launched a murderous attack on the enemy shortly before dawn.* ADJ CLASSIF: USU ATTRIB = homicidal; ▸ ADJ CLASSIF: ATTRIB = deadly

2 If you have a **murderous** look about you, you look intensely angry or mad, as though you might kill someone. EG *The men sat with murderous hatred on their faces... His eyes have a murderous glint.* ADJ CLASSIF: ATTRIB = deadly

3 Something that is **murderous** is 3.1 extremely dangerous and could lead to people being killed. EG *...murderous slides and gorges.* 3.2 in informal English, extremely unpleasant and difficult. EG *It was absolutely murderous in town today.* ADJ QUALIT = lethal; ADJ QUALIT

murk /mɜːk/ is darkness or dense cloud, which is very difficult for light to shine through. EG *Through the murk the dull red sun slowly penetrated.* N SING: the+N = gloom

murky /mɜːki¹/, **murkier, murkiest.** 1 Places that are **murky** are dark and rather unpleasant because there is not sufficient light to see anything clearly. EG *The murky rooms were lit by naked, smoke-blackened lightbulbs... We looked out into the murky streets.* ADJ QUALIT = gloomy, dim

2 Water that is **murky** is dark in colour and has a lot of mud or leaves in it so that you cannot see through it. EG *All the fish had died in the murky water... ...murky ponds.* ADJ QUALIT ⇑ dirty

3 **Murky** is also used to describe something which is not easy to understand or which you do not know very much about, but which you suspect involves something dishonest or shameful. EG *There has been another murder in a shopping centre and murky goings-on in a local picture gallery... Tell us about your murky past.* ADJ QUALIT ⇑ obscure = shady

murmur /mɜːmə/, **murmurs, murmuring, murmured.** 1 If you **murmur** or you **murmur** something, you say it very quietly, so that not many people can hear what you are saying. EG *'Darling,' she murmured and they lay still... She sat there, tears in her eyes, murmuring his name... 'I suggest we climb Ben Nevis tomorrow.' They murmured agreement.* V, V+O/REPORT-CL/QUOTE, OR V+A (to)

2 A **murmur** is 2.1 a statement or utterance which can hardly be heard. EG *I knocked and went inside in response to a barely heard murmur... The audience were suddenly concentrating, with not a murmur in the auditorium.* 2.2 a continuous, low, indistinct sound, like the noise of a river or of voices far away. EG *There was a low murmur of conversation in the other room... It was too early for that murmur of insects which is the usual background noise in the evenings.* 2.3 a quiet complaint. EG *There are many murmurs from the sociologists at the Chairman's decision... The baby went back to sleep without a murmur.* 2.4 an abnormal sound which is made by the heart and which shows that there is probably something wrong with it. N COUNT; N SING WITH DET +SUPP = hum, drone; N COUNT; N SING: a+N

3 If you **murmur**, you complain gently about something. EG *He never murmured even faintly that he might prefer not to go out that evening.* V OR V+O/ REPORT-CL/ QUOTE, OR V+A (to)

muscle /mʌsəºl/, **muscles, muscling, muscled.** 1 A **muscle** is something inside your body which connects two different bones, and which you use when you make a movement. You can develop your muscles by playing sports or by lifting heavy weights. EG *The boys couldn't help admiring their bulging muscles... He flexed his jaw muscles and looked us square in the eye.* • If you say that someone didn't **move a muscle**, you mean that they stayed absolutely still. EG *He watched it all without moving a muscle.* N COUNT/ UNCOUNT ⇑ tissue = sinew; • PHR: VB INFLECTS ⇑ move

2 If someone has **muscle**, they have the strength and power which allow them to do something which they would otherwise find difficult. EG *It might also give muscle to ministers of health... The campaign, however inspired, was valueless without the muscle of an organisation behind it.* N UNCOUNT = clout

muscle in. If you **muscle in** on something or **muscle** your **way in**, you force your way into a situation where you have no right to be and where you are not welcome, in order to gain some advantage for yourself. EG *They are jealous of your success and resent the way you are muscling in on the territory over which they have jurisdiction... I don't like the way he's muscled his way in here.* PHRASAL VB: V+ADV+*on*, OR ORDER V+O+ADV ⇑ intrude = push in

muscular /mʌskjə⁴lə/. 1 **Muscular** means using your muscles or affecting your muscles. EG *Great muscular effort is needed... ...muscular pain.* ADJ CLASSIF: ATTRIB

2 Someone who is **muscular** is very fit and strong, and has firm muscles which are not covered with a lot of fat. EG *He was somewhat shorter, stockier, and more muscular than his father.* ADJ QUALIT = brawny

muscular dystrophy is a disease in which your muscles become gradually more and more weak so that you are eventually unable to move at all. N UNCOUNT

muse /mjuːz/, **muses, musing, mused.** 1 If you **muse** or **muse** about something, you think about it carefully, and for quite a long time, especially if it is something that has happened or is a decision you have to make; used mainly in written English. EG *'Europe, then,' mused Topson. 'Greece, Italy?'... The eminent science fiction author William Tenn once mused about the possibilities of genetic manipulation.* V+QUOTE, OR V: USU+A = ponder, speculate

2 A **muse** is an imaginary force which helps a person to do something, especially to paint or to write poetry or music, by giving them ideas and inspiration. A muse is often imagined to be a woman. EG *...the muse of music.* N COUNT

museum /mju:zɪəm/, **museums.** A **museum** is a place or building where large numbers of interesting and valuable objects are preserved and studied, and N COUNT: ALSO IN NAMES displayed to the public. Some museums contain works of art or historical objects; others contain specimens of plants and stuffed animals. EG *...the Museum of Modern Art... She is the curator of the small local museum.*

museum piece, museum pieces. A **museum piece** is an object or building which is very old and unusual. EG *The gun was a museum piece. It hadn't been fired for years... The house is now something of a museum piece.* — N COUNT ⇑ antique = showpiece

mush /mʌʃ/, **mushes.** **Mush** is a very thick soft paste; an informal word. You sometimes use the word **mush** to refer to food which has no particular taste or which has been cooked for too long. EG *He stirred the thick mush.* — N MASS = gunge

mushroom /mʌʃru⁴m/, **mushrooms, mushrooming, mushroomed.** 1 A **mushroom** is a fungus with a short stem and a round top which is wider than the stem. You can eat some kinds of mushroom, but others are poisonous. EG *I liked helping to pick mushrooms in the wet fields... ...a salmon and mushroom quiche.* — N COUNT

2 The word **mushroom** is also used to refer to a large cloud of dust which is shaped like a mushroom and which rises into the sky after a nuclear explosion. EG *There was an enormous mushroom cloud above the totally devastated centre of the city... ...the nuclear mushroom.* — N COUNT

3 If a place, event, or organization **mushrooms**, it develops very quickly from one which is small into one which is large and important. EG *The organization was founded in 1955 and quickly mushroomed into a mass movement of the middle classes... I did not know that this skirmish was going to mushroom into open warfare... ...a mushrooming suburb.* — V ⇑ grow = develop

4 If something **mushrooms**, it appears or comes into existence very quickly. EG *Factories mushroomed on the former mudflats of Jurong... Military slang mushrooms overnight.* — V = spring up

mushy /mʌʃi¹/. 1 Vegetables and fruit that are **mushy** are too soft and have lost most of their shape. EG *If mushrooms stew in their own liquid, they become limp and mushy.* — ADJ QUALIT

2 Stories that are **mushy** are very sentimental; used showing disapproval. EG *The film is a mushy, but strangely moving story of young love... ...mushy fiction.* — ADJ QUALIT ⇑ emotional = mawkish

music /mju:zɪk/. 1 **Music** consists of sounds that are put together in a pattern and performed by people either using instruments or singing, in order to give them or other people pleasure. EG *She'd had the radio on playing dance music... ...the music of Irving Berlin and Jerome Kern... To begin the programme, some music from the north of the continent... ...the broadcaster and rock music critic, Paul Gambaccini.* — N UNCOUNT ⇑ sound

2 **Music** is 2.1 the art of putting sounds together so that they produce a pleasant pattern. EG *I had a very underdeveloped appreciation of music and the theatre as a child... He plans to make his career in music... One of his granddaughters was having her music lesson.* — N UNCOUNT 2.2 the written representation of musical sounds. EG *Not one of them could read a note of music... She placed the music on the piano and sat down... Sometimes she played from memory, sometimes from music.* — N UNCOUNT ⇑ writing

3 If something that you hear is **music to** your **ears**, it makes you feel very pleased and happy. EG *He pretended not to hear, but it was music to his ears.* — PHR : USED AS C ⇑ good news

● to **face the music**: see **face**.

musical /mju:zɪkə⁰l/, **musicals.** 1 **Musical** is used to describe events, education, etc that are concerned with the playing or studying of music. EG *Herschel came back to England to try his luck at a musical career... ...one of London's most important musical events... Their musical education could hardly be regarded as comprehensive.* — ADJ CLASSIF : ATTRIB ⇑ artistic ◇ **musically.** EG *There is a lot going on musically every night in London.* — ◇ ADV WITH VB ⇑ artistically

2 Someone who is **musical** has a natural ability and interest in music. EG *He came from a musical family... 'Are you musical, too, Julie?' Boylan asked... One of Jenny's musical friends married a design student.* — ADJ QUALIT ⇑ talented ◇ **musically.** EG *Oh, you're obviously not musically inclined, then.* — ◇ ADV WITH VB ⇑ artistically

3 Sounds that are **musical** are tuneful and pleasant to hear. EG *A musical bell softly sounded somewhere in the passageway.* — ADJ QUALIT = melodious ◇ **musically.** EG *The coins rattled musically in the collecting box.* — ◇ ADV WITH VB

4 A **musical** or a **musical comedy** is a play or film that uses singing and dancing as part of the story. EG *The manager had seen a recent musical and liked the tunes... She appeared in the musical 'Oklahoma'.* — N COUNT ⇑ entertainment

musical box, musical boxes. A **musical box** is a box that contains a clockwork mechanism which plays a tune when you open the lid. — N COUNT

musical chairs. 1 **Musical chairs** is a game in which children run around a row of chairs while music is played. As soon as the music stops they all try and sit on a chair, but there is always one chair less than the number of children, so one child has to stop playing each time. In the end, only one child is left and he or she is the winner of the game. — N UNCOUNT

2 You can also use the term **musical chairs** to describe a situation in which people exchange jobs or positions very often. EG *It was time for political musical chairs again in the country... The premiership at this time was a prize in a game of musical chairs.* — N UNCOUNT ⇑ change

musical instrument, musical instruments. A **musical instrument** is an object such as a piano, guitar, or violin which you play in order to produce music. EG *They learned to play a variety of musical instruments.* — N COUNT ⇑ device

music hall, music halls; used in British English. 1 A **music hall** is a theatre that presents shows consisting of a series of performances by comedians, singers, and dancers. EG *It was the only time I have ever appeared in a music hall.* — N COUNT

2 **Music hall** is entertainment in the theatre consisting of a series of performances by comedians, singers, and dancers. Music hall was very popular in the early years of the twentieth century, but is now not very common. EG *...a popular music-hall ballad.* — N UNCOUNT = vaudeville

musician /mju:zɪʃə⁰n/, **musicians.** A **musician** is a person who plays a musical instrument well, especially when that is their job. EG *Henry was an accomplished musician... The musicians began packing their instruments away.* — N COUNT ⇑ artist

musicianship /mju:zɪʃə⁰nʃɪp/ is the skill that is involved when you play a musical instrument. EG *His scholarship and formal musicianship were not all they might have been.* — N UNCOUNT ⇑ artistry

music stand, music stands; also spelled with a hyphen. A **music stand** is a device that holds pages of music in position while you play a musical instrument. EG *If you're going to take up the violin, I suppose we'll have to get you a music stand.* — N COUNT ⇑ support

musk /mʌsk/ is a substance with a strong sweet smell that is used in making perfume. — N UNCOUNT

musket /mʌskɪt/, **muskets.** A **musket** is a gun with a long barrel. Muskets were used before rifles were invented. — N COUNT

musky /mʌski¹/ means smelling like musk. EG *...a sweet musky perfume.* — ADJ QUALIT ⇑ scented

Muslim /muzlɪm, mʌz-/, **Muslims.** 1 A **Muslim** is a person who believes in Islam and lives according to its rules. EG *...a pious Muslim on his way to Mecca.* — N COUNT = Mohammedan

2 **Muslim** is used to describe someone or something that belongs or relates to Muslims or to Islam. EG *Mohammed Ibn Arabi was perhaps the greatest of the medieval Muslim philosophers.* — ADJ CLASSIF = Mohammedan

muslin /mʌzlɪn/ is very thin cotton cloth. EG *...waitresses in crisp muslin aprons.* — N UNCOUNT

mussel /mʌsə⁰l/, **mussels.** A **mussel** is a shellfish that lives inside a dark-coloured shell which has two sides that fit tightly together. Mussels are often gathered for food. EG *Rocks are crammed with limpets, mussels, and clams.* — N COUNT ⇑ creature

must /mʌst/. 1 If you say that someone **must** do something, you mean that you think it is very important or necessary for them to do it. If you say that someone **must not** do something, you mean that you think it is very important or necessary for them not to do it. EG *Your family and children must always come first... You must learn to remain calm... People who qualify must apply within six months... You mustn't worry about me... You mustn't tease me like that, Mary... I feel I must write to thank you for all your help over the last few weeks... I mustn't stay gossiping with you any longer... It must be said that she is good at her job... It mustn't be forgotten that we do all make mistakes.* — MODAL ⇑ should

2 If you say that something **must** happen, you mean that you think that it is very important or necessary for it to happen. If you say that something **must not** — MODAL ⇑ have to

happen, you mean that you think it is very important or necessary for it not to happen. EG *The dreadful problems of Ethiopia must be solved... Schools must teach children the difference between right and wrong... If published, it must be published in its entirety... There must be no mistake... Things must change... All further plans must inevitably be re-thought.*

3 If you say that you **must** do something, you mean that you want to do it and intend to do it fairly soon. EG *I must come over and see you when he's away... I must go and make a phone call.* — MODAL ⇑ will

4 If you tell someone that they **must** do something, you are suggesting that they should do it or inviting them to do it. EG *I shall tell the Captain. You must play at the ship's concert... You must come and visit me... You must come round for a meal some time.* — MODAL : *you*+ MODAL ⇑ have to

5 If you ask why someone **must** do something, you are angry or upset about it and do not understand why they are doing it. EG *Why must she be so nasty to me? I don't know why you must always fuss so much.* — MODAL : AFTER *why* ⇑ need to

6 You say **'if I must'** when you do not want to do something but know that really you have got to do it. EG *Well, OK, I'll talk to him if I must.* — CONVENTION ⇑ have to

7 You say **'if you must'** when you know that you cannot stop someone doing something, but think that they are wrong or stupid to do it. EG *Write and ask them yourself if you must.* — CONVENTION ⇑ have to

8 You say **'if you must know'** when you tell someone something that you did not want them to know and you want to suggest that you think they were wrong to ask you about it. EG *If you must know, I'm going to help him look for an apartment.* — CONVENTION

9 **Must** is also used sometimes as a way of showing how eager or enthusiastic you are to do something. EG *Patrick's dancing the tango? This I must see!* — MODAL ⇑ want to

10 If you say that something **must** be true, you mean that you think that it is very likely to be true. EG *This must be the worst winter we've had for years... If he's sure, then it must be true... I must be even more tired that I thought... You must be Florrie Brown... You must be very fond of her... It must be pretty depressing.* — MODAL+*be* ⇑ have to

11 If you say that someone **must** have done something or that something **must** have happened, you mean that you are assuming or guessing that they did it or that it happened, although you are not actually certain. EG *We must have taken the wrong road... She had predicted that just such a creature must have existed... It must have been dreadfully difficult... It must've been terrifying for the people around you.* — MODAL+*have*

12 If you say that one thing **must have** happened in order for something else to happen, you mean that it is necessary for the first thing to have happened before the second thing can happen. EG *In order to qualify for Unemployment Benefit, you must have paid at least 26 Class 1 contributions.* — MODAL+*have* = should have

13 If you refer to something as a **must**, you mean that it is absolutely necessary; an informal use. EG *Rubber gloves are a must if your skin is sensitive to washing powders.* — N SING : a+N, USED AS A/C = necessity

mustache /məstɑ:ʃ/. See **moustache**.

mustard /mʌstəd/. **1** **Mustard** is **1.1** a yellow or brown paste which tastes hot and spicy. You often have a small amount of mustard with meat such as beef or ham. EG *...hot dogs dripping with mustard... ...a dash of French mustard.* — N UNCOUNT ⇑ condiment **1.2** a small plant with yellow flowers and long seed pods. The seeds can be used to make mustard. — N UNCOUNT

2 If clothes or paint are **mustard** in colour, they are brownish yellow. — ADJ COLOUR

muster /mʌstə/, **musters, mustering, mustered. 1** If you **muster** something such as strength, energy, or support, you gather together all that you can get in order to help you do something difficult or dangerous. EG *I hit him with all the force I could muster... The group cannot muster sufficient working class support.* — V+O = collect, summon

2 When people such as soldiers **muster** or when you **muster** them, they gather together in one place. EG *The group has mustered an average of 400 to 500 delegates per conference... ...the avenue of trees behind which the Twelfth Division mustered.* — V-ERG

3 If someone or something **passes muster**, they are good enough for the thing they are needed for. EG *With fashionable clothes and good make-up she might have passed muster.* — PHR : VB INFLECTS

muster up. If you **muster up** your courage, you find as much courage as you can to do something that you think is difficult or dangerous. EG *I mustered up enough courage to put in a request for a rise.* — PHRASAL VB : V+O+ADV = summon up

mustn't /mʌsənt/ is the usual spoken form of 'must not'.

must've /mʌstəv/ is a spoken form of 'must have', especially when 'have' is an auxiliary verb.

musty /mʌsti/, **mustier, mustiest**. Something that is **musty** smells stale and damp. EG *They pushed open the door and inhaled the familiar musty smell... The Women's prison was old, musty, dreary, and dim.* — ADJ QUALIT ⇑ unpleasant = fusty

mutant /mju:tənt/, **mutants**. A **mutant** is an animal or plant that is physically different from others of the same species as the result of a change in its genetic structure. — N COUNT = mutation

mutate /mju:teɪt/, **mutates, mutating, mutated.** If an animal or plant **mutates**, it develops unusual or new physical characteristics as the result of a change in its genetic structure. EG *That the planet could be populated by mutated humans is not as far-fetched as some people think.* — V : IF+PREP THEN *into*

mutation /mju:teɪʃən/, **mutations**. A **mutation** is **1** a change in the genetic structure of an animal or plant which causes a new sort of animal or plant to develop. EG *A series of mutations has resulted in larger grains of wheat... ...an increased frequency of gene mutations.* — N COUNT/UNCOUNT **2** a very important change in the structure or organization of something such as a society. EG *...profound mutations in culture and attitudes.* — N COUNT/UNCOUNT

mute /mju:t/, **mutes, muting, muted. 1** Someone who is **mute 1.1** is silent and does not speak. EG *Sally Jones was staring mute and awestruck before Mrs Geard's preparations for her party.* — ADJ CLASSIF ▸ used of people's behaviour. EG *Fanny clasped her hands in mute protest... With a mute bow he indicated to them his gratitude.* — ▸ ADJ CLASSIF : ATTRIB **1.2** is unable to speak; a rather old-fashioned word. ● See also **deaf-mute**. — ADJ CLASSIF = dumb

2 If you **mute** a noise or sound, you lower its volume. EG *She had closed all the windows to mute the sounds from the town.* — V+O = muffle ◊ **muted**. EG *...a strange, muted sound that seemed to vibrate through the ceiling... ...people spoke in muted voices.* — ◊ ADJ CLASSIF ⇑ quietened = muffled

3 If you **mute** your feelings, emotions, or activities, you reduce their strength. EG *The leadership encouraged them to mute their resistance.* — V+O = silence ◊ **muted**. EG *On the whole, criticism was muted... Ominously, enthusiasm was even more muted.* — ◊ ADJ QUALIT = subdued

4 If a colour **is muted**, it is soft and gentle as opposed to being bright and garish. EG *His shirt looked out of place against the muted greys and blues of the Chinese.* — V+O : USU PASS ⇑ subdue = soften

mutilate /mju:tɪleɪt/, **mutilates, mutilating, mutilated. 1** If someone **is mutilated**, they have been very severely injured, usually by having part of their body violently removed. EG *Both bodies had been mutilated... ...the mutilated victims of the rocket attack... He was temporarily insane when he attacked and mutilated the women.* — V+O : USU PASS ⇑ injure = maim

2 If you **mutilate** something, you damage it, either by destroying part of it or by changing its appearance or character. EG *They send out cards marked 'do not fold or mutilate'.* — V+O : USU PASS = disfigure

3 If a document or message **is mutilated**, its contents have been changed so that the original meaning is removed or lost. EG *The telegrams which Cynthia encoded were now more mutilated than ever.* — V+O : USU PASS ⇑ change = adulterate

mutilation /mju:tɪleɪʃən/, **mutilations. 1** A **mutilation** is a very serious injury which a person suffers, such as the loss of an arm or a leg. EG *...the variety of deaths and mutilations the war offered.* — N COUNT

2 **Mutilation** is the deliberate causing of a mutilation to someone. EG *These were men to whom the death or mutilation of wholly innocent men and women was of no consequence.* — N UNCOUNT = maiming

mutineer /mju:tɪnɪə/, **mutineers**. A **mutineer** is a person who takes part in a mutiny. — N COUNT ⇑ rebel

mutinous /mju:tɪnəs/. Someone who is **mutinous** shows that they are strongly dissatisfied with a person's authority and that they are likely to rebel against it. EG *The crew, who disliked the new Captain, were restive and mutinous.* — ADJ CLASSIF ⇑ rebellious

mutiny /mju:tɪni¹/, **mutinies, mutinying, mutinied**. A **mutiny** is a rebellion by a group of people who refuse to accept a person's authority any longer and try to take control of power from that person. EG *...a slave ship after a successful mutiny... Mutiny can lead to riot.* ▸ used as a verb. EG *Several units of the French Army mutinied against the government.* — N COUNT/UNCOUNT; ▸ V ⇑ rebel

mutt /mʌt/, **mutts**. If you call someone a **mutt**, you mean that they are stupid; an informal word. — N COUNT: USU MOD+N

mutter /mʌtə/, **mutters, muttering, muttered**. If you **mutter**, you speak very quietly so that you cannot easily be heard, often because you are complaining about something or because you are speaking to yourself. EG *Denis could be heard muttering to himself about my stupidity... A voice was heard to mutter that I was trying to ruin the meeting... He refused her invitation with a muttered excuse.* ▸ used as a noun. EG *He heard near his right ear a low mutter.* ◊ **muttering, mutterings**. EG *There was angry muttering from those who disagreed with the decision.* — V: USU+A, V+A (to), OR V+O/QUOTE/REPORT-CL = mumble; ▸ N COUNT; ◊ N COUNT/UNCOUNT ⇑ speech

mutton /mʌtə⁰n/ is the meat from an adult sheep which is eaten as food. EG *...a leg of mutton.* ● If you describe someone as **mutton dressed as lamb**, you mean that they are trying to look younger than they are, often in order to appear sexually attractive to other people; an informal expression. — N UNCOUNT; ● PHR: USED AS C

mutual /mju:tʃʊ⁰əl/ is used **1** to describe something that you do or that you give to someone when it is also something which they do or give to you. EG *Single parents can join self-help groups for social life and mutual help... They are in danger of mutual destruction.* **2** to describe an emotion when two or more people feel the same emotion towards each other at the same time. EG *I didn't like him and I was sure the feeling was mutual... What mattered was the mutual respect that existed on both sides.* **3** to describe something such as an interest which two or more people share. EG *They had discovered a mutual interest in rugby football... He sent an emissary who was a mutual friend to ask me to reconsider my decision.* — ADJ CLASSIF: ATTRIB ⇑ exchanged; ADJ CLASSIF = shared, reciprocal; ADJ CLASSIF: USU ATTRIB ⇑ common = joint

mutually /mju:tʃʊ⁰əl/. **1 Mutually** is used to refer to a situation in which two or more people feel the same emotion towards each other at the same time. EG *He enjoyed a mutually respectful relationship with them.* — ADV+ADJ

2 If two ideas or statements are **mutually exclusive**, **mutually contradictory**, etc, only one of them can be true or factual, because they cannot both be true at the same time. EG *There is no reason why these two functions should be mutually exclusive... The principles on which it is based are mutually contradictory.* — PHR: USED AS C ⇑ incompatible

Muzak /mju:zæk/ is a trademark. **Muzak** is recorded light music that is played as background music in shops, restaurants, etc; often used showing disapproval. — N UNCOUNT ⇑ music

muzzle /mʌzə⁰l/, **muzzles, muzzling, muzzled**. **1** The **muzzle** of an animal such as a dog is **1.1** its nose and mouth. **1.2** a wire cover or strap that is put over its nose and mouth, usually so that it cannot bite people. — N COUNT; N COUNT ⇑ guard

2 The **muzzle** of a gun is the open end where the bullets come out when it is fired. — N COUNT: USU+of

3 If you **muzzle** a dog or other animal, you put a muzzle on it. EG *All dogs are supposed to be muzzled and on leads in the streets.* — V+O ⇑ restrain

4 If you **muzzle** someone or a group of people, you prevent them from expressing their views freely. EG *...muzzling of the press.* — V+O ⇑ silence = gag

muzzy /mʌzi¹/. **1** Someone who feels **muzzy** is confused and unable to think clearly, often because they have drunk a lot of alcohol. EG *I'm feeling a bit muzzy in the head.* — ADJ QUALIT = groggy

2 Something that is **muzzy** is blurred and unclear. EG *...looking through the muzzy green of the holly bushes.* — ADJ QUALIT = fuzzy

MW is a written abbreviation for 'medium wave'; written on radios to help you find a particular radio station which is broadcast on medium wave. — N UNCOUNT: NUM+N

my /maɪ/. **1** A speaker or writer uses **my** **1.1** to indicate that something belongs or relates to himself or herself. See **I**. EG *My name is Alan Jones... I closed my eyes... He asked me about my work... ...in my own home.* **1.2** in front of a noun or name when he or she is speaking to someone and showing them affection. EG *Don't worry, my darling... My dear Mary.* **1.3** in some titles when he or she addresses or refers to someone with that title. EG *...my Lord.* — DETPOSS; DETPOSS+N VOC/PROPER; DETPOSS: USED IN TITLES

2 My is also used in some exclamations of surprise or shock. EG *Oh my God, he must have been killed... My goodness!* — DETPOSS+NG: USED AS EXCLAM

myopia /maɪəʊpɪə/ is the inability to see clearly things which are far away from you; a formal word. — N UNCOUNT

myopic /maɪəʊpɪk/. Someone who is **myopic** **1** is unable to see clearly things which are far away from them; a formal use. EG *She thinks Dolly is myopic and should see a good optician.* **2** is unable to realize what the consequences of an action will be, for example how other people will react to something they do. EG *Unfortunately, this is a somewhat myopic view.* — ADJ CLASSIF = shortsighted; ADJ QUALIT

myriad /mɪrɪəd/, **myriads**; a formal word. A **myriad** of people or things is a very large number of them. EG *...a myriad of political action groups... ...a feathery plant with myriads of tiny yellow flowers.* ▸ used as an adjective. EG *...today's myriad and multiplying instances of bad government.* — N PART+N IN PLURAL ⇑ lot = army, score; ▸ ADJ CLASSIF: ATTRIB

myself /maɪsɛlf/. **1** A speaker or writer uses **myself** as the object of a verb or preposition in a clause where 'I' is the subject or 'me' is a previous object. See **I**. EG *I want to enjoy myself... I was thoroughly ashamed of myself... I poured myself a small drink.* ▸ **Myself** is also used to emphasize the subject or object of a clause. It is usually used in addition to a subject or object, although it is sometimes used instead of 'me' as an object. EG *I myself feel that Muriel Spark is very underrated... I am not myself a particularly punctual person... I find it a bit odd myself... My first pupil today is a Pole like myself.* — PRON REFL: SING, USED AS O; ▸ PRON REFL: SING

2 Myself is also used by a speaker or writer in expressions such as 'I did it myself' in order to say that he or she did something without any help or interference from anyone else. EG *I dealt with it myself... I'll take it down to the police station myself.* — PRON REFL: SING ⇑ alone

mysterious /mɪstɪərɪəs/. **1** Something that is **mysterious** is strange and cannot be explained or understood. EG *Their grandson died of a mysterious illness... The islanders had no idea what the mysterious flakes could be.* ◊ **mysteriously**. EG *The American had mysteriously disappeared.* — ADJ QUALIT = curious, puzzling; ◊ ADV WITH VB = inexplicably

2 Someone or something that is **mysterious** has qualities or characteristics which give you a feeling of wonder and curiosity. EG *We were introduced to the mysterious and fascinating Baroness Blixen... ...the great black strip of land that lay mysterious and silent on the other side of the river... Then he got very mysterious and told me to think about it.* ◊ **mysteriously**. EG *They smiled mysteriously and said nothing.* — ADJ QUALIT ⇑ wonderful = enigmatic; ◊ ADV WITH VB = secretively

mystery /mɪstə⁰ri¹/, **mysteries**. **1** A **mystery** is **1.1** something strange that cannot be explained or understood. EG *These two deaths have remained a mystery... It's a mystery how he found it.* **1.2** a story in which strange things happen that are not explained until the end. EG *The majority of the books were mysteries and romances.* **1.3** a strange, rather secret and magical quality that a person or a place has. EG *The place continues to fascinate visitors, cloaked in its mystery... I was in love with the mystery of him.* **1.4** something that seems wonderful and impossible to explain because no people or only very few people have the knowledge to be able to understand it. EG *...the mystery of God... For most people physics probably remains one of those mysteries of life.* — N COUNT = puzzle; N COUNT; N UNCOUNT ⇑ strangeness; N COUNT: USU+of = wonder

2 A **mystery** person or thing is one whose identity is not known and which is often intended as a surprise, for example a parcel with unknown contents or a journey with an unknown destination. EG *...the mystery voice... ...a mystery tour... ...a mystery package.* — ADJ CLASSIF: ATTRIB

mystic /mɪstɪk/, **mystics**. **1** A **mystic** is a person who practises or believes in religious mysticism. — N COUNT ⇑ believer

2 Mystic means mystical. EG *...a performer in a mystic rite.* — ADJ QUALIT: ATTRIB

mystical /mɪstɪkə⁰l/. **1** Something that is **mystical** involves or relates to religious or spiritual powers and influences that most humans are unable to understand. EG *...a mystical or quasi-religious experience.* — ADJ QUALIT = mystic

2 A **mystical** group is one that practises religious mysticism. EG *...religious sects or mystical cults.* — ADJ CLASSIF: ATTRIB

mysticism /mɪstɪsɪzəᵒm/ is a religious practice in which people search for truth, knowledge, and unity with God through meditation and prayer. N UNCOUNT ⇑ religion

mystify /mɪstɪfaɪ/, **mystifies, mystifying, mystified.** Something that **mystifies** you amazes you because it is strange and impossible to explain or understand. EG *Some of these theorems we are beginning to understand. Others mystify us.* V+O = baffle
◇ **mystified.** EG *The audience was fascinated and mystified... He had a mystified look on his face.* ◇ ADJ QUALIT = baffled
◇ **mystifying.** EG *These rituals are totally mystifying to visitors from other lands.* ◇ ADJ QUALIT
◇ **mystification** /mɪstɪfɪkeɪʃəᵒn/. EG *Professor Marvin looks round in some mystification.* ◇ N UNCOUNT

mystique /mɪstiːk/ is a sense or atmosphere of mystery and secrecy which is associated with a particular person or thing; a formal word. EG *This book may help to dispel some of the mystique surrounding doctors.* N UNCOUNT

myth /mɪθ/, **myths.** A **myth** is 1 a story that people have made up in the past in order to explain how the world and mankind began or to justify religious beliefs and social customs. EG *Medusa was the unfortunate woman in the Greek myth who was loved by the god of the sea.* ▸ used as an uncount noun to refer to myths as a whole. EG *...matriarchies in history, legend, and myth.* N COUNT ▸ N UNCOUNT ⇑ stories
2 an untrue idea or explanation; often used showing disapproval. EG *The prevailing myth is that poverty is a punishment for irresponsible behaviour... ...the myth of love at first sight.* N COUNT ⇑ untruth = fallacy, delusion

mythic /mɪθɪk/ means the same as mythical. EG *...mythic power... ...mythic culture.* ADJ CLASSIF : USU ATTRIB

mythical /mɪθɪkəᵒl/. Something that is **mythical** 1 is imaginary and only exists in myths. EG *...mythical monsters.* ADJ CLASSIF : USU ATTRIB
2 is untrue or does not exist, even though some people say that it is true. EG *They trekked out to the west coast in search of the mythical opportunities open there.* ADJ CLASSIF : USU ATTRIB ⇑ unreal

mythology /mɪθɒləʤiʲ/ is a particular group of myths, or myths regarded as a subject to study. EG *Prometheus in Greek mythology brought fire to man.* N UNCOUNT
◇ **mythological.** EG *Jupiter was the Roman mythological king of the heavens.* ◇ ADJ CLASSIF : USU ATTRIB

Nn

N, n /ɛn/, **Ns, n's.** 1 **N** is the fourteenth letter of the English alphabet. N COUNT
2 **n** is used 2.1 in mathematics to represent a number whose value is not stated. EG *...two over one to the power n minus one.* 2.2 in informal spoken English to mean a large number. EG *There are n ways of doing it, you know.* = countless
3 **N** is also a written abbreviation for 'neutral'; used on electrical plugs.
4 **N** or **n** is also an abbreviation for other words beginning with N or n, such as 'north', 'northern', 'neuter', or 'noun'.

> **N** □ In this dictionary N is used in the grammar notes beside entries to mean 'noun'. It introduces information about the kind of word the noun is. For explanations of different kinds of nouns, see □ at NAME, N BEFORE N, N COUNT, N MASS, N PART, N PLURAL, N PROPER, N SING, N UNCOUNT, and TITLE.

'n' is used on informal written signs to represent the word 'and'. EG *Fish 'n' chips.* CONJ COORD

N.A.; also sometimes written **n/a. N.A.** is an abbreviation for 'not applicable'; used when you are filling in a form and a question or category on it is not relevant to you. CONVENTION

nab /næb/, **nabs, nabbing, nabbed.** If you **nab** someone, you catch them doing something wrong or arrest them; an informal word. EG *It was the CID who'd nabbed Peters.* V+O = collar

nacreous /neɪkrɪəs/. **Nacreous** things look like mother-of-pearl; a literary word. EG *...the nacreous glow that filled the heavens.* ADJ CLASSIF : ATTRIB = pearly

nadir /neɪdɪə, næ-/. 1 The **nadir** of something such as someone's career or the history of an organization is its worst time; a literary word. EG *...a government at the nadir of its unpopularity... ...when the fortunes of Trotskyism reached their nadir.* N SING : USU WITH POSS = depths
2 The **nadir** is the point in the sky that is directly opposite the zenith and directly below your feet when you are looking at it; compare **zenith.** N SING : *the*+N ≠ zenith

nag /næg/, **nags, nagging, nagged.** 1 If someone **nags** you, they complain to you continually in an irritating way. EG *He used to nag me endlessly about the family's money... ...a middle-aged clerk and his nagging wife.* V OR V+O/QUOTE
2 If something such as a doubt or worry is **nagging** at you, it is constantly worrying or annoying you. EG *Something else that she had said had been nagging at him ever since she had said it.* V+*at*
◇ **nagging.** EG *I have a nagging suspicion that one of the wheels has a puncture.* ◇ ADJ CLASSIF : ATTRIB = niggling
3 A **nag** is a horse, especially one that is too old to work; an old-fashioned use. N COUNT

nail /neɪl/, **nails, nailing, nailed.** 1 A **nail** is a small sharp piece of metal, usually with a flat end, which you hit with a hammer in order to push it into something, for example to join two pieces of wood together. EG *He handed her the bag of nails and the hammer... ...the oval mirror that hung from a nail on the wall.* N COUNT
● If you say that someone has **hit the nail on the head**, you mean that what they have just said was exactly right and exactly relevant. EG *He had hit the nail on the head mentioning the dump at breakfast.* ● PHR : VB INFLECTS ⇑ be accurate
2 If you **nail** something somewhere, you fix it or attach it there using a nail or nails. EG *They nail plastic sheets over their windows... There were signs nailed to the trees all along Bear Creek.* V+O+A ⇑ secure = tack, pin
3 Your **nails** are the thin hard areas that cover the end of each of your fingers and toes. EG *It was a female hand with neat nails and a wedding ring... He keeps biting his nails.* N COUNT : USU PL
4 If you **nail** someone, you catch them and prove that they have been breaking the law; an informal use. EG *He had been praised for his skill in nailing insurance frauds.* V+O = nab
5 If you **nail a lie**, you prove that it really is a lie; an old-fashioned, informal expression. PHR : VB INFLECTS
6 The word **nail** is also used in the following expressions, which are explained at other places in this dictionary. ● a **nail** in someone's **coffin**: see **coffin.** ● **hard as nails**: see **hard.** ● to **fight tooth and nail**: see **tooth.** ● to **nail** your **colours to the mast**: see **colour.**

nail down. 1 If you **nail** something **down**, you fix it firmly to the wall or to the floor so that it cannot move. EG *They'll take everything that isn't nailed down.* PHRASAL VB : V+O+ADV ⇑ secure
2 If you **nail** someone **down**, you force them to agree to something or confirm something definitely; an informal use. EG *He's very unwilling to cooperate but we're still trying to nail him down.* PHRASAL VB : V+O+ADV
3 If you **nail down** an agreement, you manage to reach a firm agreement with a definite result; a fairly informal use. EG *What the bishops hope to do now is to nail down a reasonably long-term policy.* PHRASAL VB : V+O+ADV ⇑ fix

nail up. If you **nail** something **up**, 1 you fix it to a wall or other vertical surface. EG *...the warning notice that he had nailed up on the pole.* PHRASAL VB : V+O+ADV
2 you close it completely and fix the lid or covering with nails. EG *It was nailed up in a barrel and cast into the sea.* PHRASAL VB : V+O+ADV ⇑ confine

nail brush, nail brushes; also spelled as one word. A **nail brush** is a small brush that you use for cleaning your nails. N COUNT

nail file, nail files; also spelled as one word. A **nail file** is a small strip of metal or sandpaper that you rub on the end of your fingernails and toenails to make them smooth and give them a rounded shape. N COUNT

nail polish; also spelled with a hyphen. **Nail polish** is the same as nail varnish. EG *Manicured hands complete with colourless nail polish.*
N UNCOUNT = nail varnish

nail scissors; also spelled with a hyphen. **nail scissors** are small scissors that you use for cutting your nails.
N PLURAL

nail varnish; also spelled with a hyphen. **Nail varnish** is a thick, usually pink or reddish-coloured liquid that you paint on your nails, especially as a cosmetic.
N UNCOUNT = nail polish

naive /naɪiːv/; also spelled **naïve**. Someone who is **naive** believes that things are much less complicated, difficult, or dangerous than they really are, for example because they have very little knowledge or experience of life; mainly used showing disapproval. EG *We're surely not so naive as to think that this will change anything... He was always careless about money and naive in the ways of the world.* ▸ used of people's ideas or behaviour. EG *...a naive hope of building heaven on earth.* ◊ **naively**. EG *They naively assume things can only get better.*
ADJ QUALIT = simple-minded, unrealistic
◊ ADV WITH VB

naivety /naɪiːvti¹/; also spelled **naïvety** or **naïveté**. **Naivety** is behaviour which shows simple and naive beliefs and a lack of knowledge or experience of life. EG *Basic assumptions are treated with a naivety which emphasizes how fanatical these people really are.*
N UNCOUNT = innocence

naked /neɪkɪ²d/. **1** Someone who is **naked** is **1.1** not wearing any clothes. EG *The sight of a naked girl might well have shocked him... He was naked except for a pair of bright red socks... The men's naked bodies shone with sweat.* ◊ **nakedness**. EG *...enough clothing to hide your nakedness.* **1.2** helpless and unprotected. EG *The children go out naked into the world.*
ADJ CLASSIF ⇑ uncovered = nude, unclothed
◊ N UNCOUNT
ADJ QUALIT : ATTRIB = defenceless

2 Animals, especially young animals, that are **naked** are not covered by hair, fur, or feathers. EG *In the nest they are still naked.*
ADJ CLASSIF ⇑ uncovered

3 Something that is **naked** does not have a cover over it, usually when you would normally expect it to have some sort of covering. EG *...naked electric light bulbs... Never look for a gas leak with a naked flame... ...a cliff of naked red earth and rock.*
ADJ CLASSIF : ATTRIB ⇑ uncovered = exposed

4 **Naked** emotions are clearly noticeable because they are too strongly felt to be hidden. EG *His face broke into an expression of naked anxiety.* ◊ **nakedly**. EG *The horror of this, so nakedly terrifying, held them all silent.*
ADJ CLASSIF : ATTRIB ⇑ obvious
◊ ADV = starkly

5 **Naked** actions or situations are quite open, with no attempt to hide what is happening, and are often unpleasant, violent, or dishonest. EG *The home employment offered to housewives is naked exploitation... ...naked dictatorship.*
ADJ CLASSIF : ATTRIB = blatant

6 If you can see something with the **naked** eye, you can see it without having to use any special equipment. EG *They are just large enough to see with the naked eye... ...microscopic hairs, invisible to the naked eye.*
ADJ CLASSIF : ATTRIB ⇑ unaided

namby-pamby /næmbi¹ pæmbi¹/. Someone who is **namby-pamby** is considered to be very sentimental or prim; used showing disapproval. EG *He was rather a namby-pamby sort of young man, I thought.*
ADJ QUALIT = wishy-washy, insipid

name /neɪm/, **names, naming, named**. **1** The **name** of a person, animal, place, etc, is the word that is used to identify and refer to them, and which distinguishes them from others of the same kind or sort. EG *His name is Richard Arnason... What was her name?... I cannot describe the officers or refer to them by name... She had first acted under the name of Phyllida Terson... ...tinnitus (the medical name for unceasing noises in the head).*
N COUNT : USU WITH POSS, OR *by* +N

2 When you **name** someone or something, **2.1** you give them a name, usually at the beginning of their life or existence. EG *She had wanted to name the baby Colleen... ...a supersonic aeroplane, eventually named the Concorde... I name this ship 'Ark Royal'.*
V+O+O/NAME = call, christen

2.2 you reveal their identity by stating their name, especially when it is someone who has done something in secret. EG *...rumours about a Minister whom he did not venture to name... I'm not going to sit here and name names for you.* **2.3** you identify them by saying their name, either in order to prove that you know it, or in order to provide some information about them. EG *On his death certificate she was again named as his wife... ...a profusion of flowers of all types; clematis, roses, snapdragons and tobacco plants, to name only a few... Name me the last five captains of Arsenal.*
V+O = identify
V+O, V+O+O : USU IMPER, OR V+O+A *(as)*

3 If you **name** someone or something **after** another person or thing, you give them the same name as the other person or thing, usually because there is a special relationship or link between them. EG *The College in Holborn is named after her... ...the International Omo Expedition named after the river in Kenya.*
V+O+A *(after)*

4 To **name** someone or something **for** another person or thing means the same as to name them after the other person or thing; used in American English. EG *Hayman Creek was named for Charles Hayman.*
V+O+A *(for)*

5 If you **name** something, you mention it or specify it, for example if you are making arrangements about something. EG *Name the place, we'll be there... He named a price he thought would scare me off.*
V+O = nominate, suggest

6 If you refer to someone's **name**, you are talking about their reputation. It is usually a good reputation unless it is modified by 'bad'. EG *Our shop had quite a name for making these belts... Grey spoke out in public to clear Haldane's name... We were accused of giving the country a bad name overseas.*
N COUNT : USU SING

7 A **name** is also someone who is famous, especially in the world of entertainment. EG *He had become a big name, a real pop hero.*
N COUNT : USU MOD+N = star

8 **in the name of**. **8.1** If something is registered or recorded **in the name of** someone, it officially belongs to them, is allocated to them, or is reserved for them. EG *The room was reserved in the name of Peters... The gun was registered in my name... He put the passport in the name of Duggan.* **8.2** If something is done or said **in the name of** an ideal or group of people, it is done or said by someone who represents that ideal or group. EG *The group claims to speak in the name of 'the simple people of the country'.* **8.3** If you say that something was done or said **in the name of** an ideal or group, you mean that it was done or said by someone who uses the ideal or group as a justification for their actions; used especially when suggesting that the person is mistaken in believing that their actions are right or good. EG *...creating three million unemployed in the name of controlling inflation... ...those who, in the name of religious conviction, devote their lives to terrorism.*
PHR WITH NAME/POSS : USED AS AN A
PHR+NG/NAME : USED AS AN A ⇑ for = on behalf of
PHR+NG/-ING : USED AS AN A

9 The word **name** is also used in the following expressions. **9.1** You use **by name** after a proper noun to indicate that you are stating precisely a person or an organization that you are talking about. EG *...the grocer, Jackson by name.* **9.2** You use **by the name of** to say what someone is called, especially when you do not know them very well and are talking about them in a formal way. EG *...a Swedish engineer by the name of George Scheutz... He goes by the name of El Cordobes.* **9.3** If you **call** someone **names** or **call** them **a name**, you insult or offend them by using unpleasant words to name them or describe them. EG *I lashed out at Kurt, calling him every name under the sun... ...having toes stepped on, being called a name, being the target of real goading.* **9.4** If you say that a situation or position exists **in all but name**, you mean that it is not officially recognized but that it is actually the case. EG *She had been for six years a wife in all but name.* **9.5** If you say that a situation or position exists **in name only**, you mean that the situation or position does not exist in the way that it has been described. EG *...the colonial territories which they ruled in name only... Many of these branches are inactive, existing in name only.* **9.6** You use the expression **the name of the game** to describe a particular activity or idea that is the most important in a particular situation; an informal expression. EG *We're beginning to understand what the name of the game is, it's getting people to express themselves without fear.* **9.7** If you **make a name for yourself**, you do something so successfully that you become well-known and admired for it. EG *George Eliot had already made a name for herself as a writer of considerable talent.*
PHR : NAME+PHR
PHR+NAME : USED AS AN A ⇑ named
PHR : VB AND N INFLECT ⇑ abuse
PHR : USED AS AN A ⇑ really
PHR : USED AS AN A = nominally
PHR : USED AS C/O/S
PHR : VB INFLECTS

10 The word **name** is also used in the following expressions, which are explained at other places in this dictionary. ● **a name to conjure with**: see **conjure**. ● **to give a dog a bad name**: see **dog**. ● to **lend** your **name to** something: see **lend**. ● **not have a penny to** your **name**: see **penny**. ● to **take** someone's **name in vain**: see **vain**. ● See also **brand name**,

Christian name, given name, maiden name, pet name.

NAME □ In this dictionary ALSO IN NAMES in the grammar notes beside an entry refers to the fact that an ordinary noun may be used to form part of a proper name. See **proper name** and □ at N PROPER. If the noun normally occurs in a particular place within the proper name, this information is given in the grammar notes. For example, **crescent** is given the notation N COUNT: ALSO IN NAMES AFTER N. This means that it is a count noun, and that it is often used after another noun to form a name. EG *We live in a small house in a* ***crescent...*** *We left Grosvenor Crescent at about five minutes to ten.* If the noun only occurs as part of a name, the grammar notes beside the entry read N IN NAMES. An example is **St**, as in *...High St.*

named /neɪmd/ is used to describe someone or something as having a particular name; used especially to refer to a person who you do not know or who you have never met. EG *I had to arrest Frau Doring and a man named Springer... They spoke highly of a lecturer named Harold Levy, and I joined his class... ...a building in Cardiff named the Temple of Peace.* — ADJ CLASSIF: PRED+NAMES = called

name-dropping is the habit of referring often to famous people as though they were friends, in order to impress people who are listening; used showing disapproval. EG *There was a good deal of academic name-dropping.* — N UNCOUNT ⇑ mentioning

nameless /neɪmlɪ²s/. 1 You use **nameless** 1.1 to describe someone or something whose name you do not know. EG *...the 'old tradesmen', as he calls them: the nameless ones who built and adorned the village... Fuller's brother had given his life to take some nameless town in Germany.* — ADJ CLASSIF: ATTRIB = anonymous, unknown **1.2** to describe someone or something that has not yet been given a name. EG *Were these all contributory factors to my new and nameless disease?* — ADJ CLASSIF = unknown

2 If you say that someone or something will be or remain **nameless**, you mean that you will not give the name of the person or thing that you are referring to, often in order not to embarrass them. EG *...cleaning up after others, who shall be nameless... I remember one movie which shall remain nameless that was described as 'two hours of sheer boredom'.* — ADJ CLASSIF: PRED = anonymous ≠ named

3 Nameless emotions are ones that you do not want to describe or specify. EG *He felt a nameless terror and sensed that death was near... ...pacing up and down, struggling with nameless thoughts.* — ADJ CLASSIF: ATTRIB ⇑ indescribable = shapeless

namely /neɪmli¹/. You can use **namely** to introduce detailed and specific information that adds to or explains what you have just said. EG *...three famous physicists, namely Simon, Kurte and Mendelsohn... ...to enforce the play's message, namely that mirage and reality merge in love... He could not do anything more than what he had promised–namely, to look after Charlotte's estate.* — ADV SEN = that is

name plate, name plates; also spelled with a hyphen or as one word. A **name plate** is a small, flat piece of metal or wood on or near the door of a room or building, showing the name and occupation of a firm or the person who works there. EG *...the shining new name plate on the wall of the building.* — N COUNT ⇑ sign

namesake /neɪmseɪk/, **namesakes**. The **namesake** of someone or something has the same name as they do. EG *Remember what happened to your namesake–stabbed in the back by a friend... ...Birmingham's namesake in Alabama.* — N COUNT: WITH POSS, USU SING

nanny /næni¹/, **nannies**. A **nanny** is a woman who is paid by parents to look after their children. EG *If they want a trained nanny, they will have to pay a high salary... It reminds me of Nanny Burton.* — N COUNT: ALSO IN TITLES ⇑ employee

nanny goat, nanny goats. A **nanny goat** is a female goat. — N COUNT

nap /næp/, **naps, napping, napped**. 1 A **nap** is a short sleep that you have during the day. EG *It was time for her to take a nap... He ate his meal and had a little nap.* — N COUNT = snooze

2 If you **nap**, you have a short sleep during the day. EG *That afternoon while Wendy was napping, I went to the cellar.* — V = doze

3 If someone is **caught napping**, something happens to them when they are not prepared for it; an informal expression. EG *The British were caught napping again.* — PHR

4 The **nap** of a carpet or cloth, especially velvet, is the top layer of short threads, which usually lie smoothly in only one direction. — N SING WITH DET ⇑ surface

napalm /neɪpɑ:m, næ-/, **napalms, napalming, napalmed**. 1 **Napalm** is a substance containing petrol, which is used to make bombs that burn and destroy people and plants. EG *Weapons such as fragmentation bombs and napalm should be banned.* — N UNCOUNT ⇑ weapon

2 If people **napalm** other people or places, they attack and burn them using napalm. EG *They can be napalmed and starved into retreat.* — V+O

nape /neɪp/, **napes**. The **nape** of your neck is the back of it. EG *...long brown hair, caught in a bow at the nape of her neck.* — N COUNT: USU SING+*of*

napkin /næpkɪn/, **napkins**. A **napkin** is a small piece of cloth or paper that you use when you are eating to protect your clothes, or to wipe your mouth or hands. EG *She set his dinner down and handed him a napkin... ...a paper table napkin.* — N COUNT = serviette

nappy /næpi¹/, **nappies**. A **nappy** is a piece of soft thick cloth or paper which is fastened round a baby's bottom in order to soak up its urine and faeces; used in British English. EG *After changing its nappy, she laid it gently down on its bed.* — N COUNT = diaper

narcissi /nɑ:sɪsɪ⁵/ is a plural form of **narcissus**.

narcissism /nɑ:sɪsɪzə⁰m/ is the habit of always thinking about yourself and admiring yourself instead of thinking about other people; a formal word. EG *His poetry shows evidence of narcissism.* — N UNCOUNT ⇑ egotism

narcissistic /nɑ:sɪsɪstɪk/. People who are **narcissistic** think about themselves a lot and admire themselves greatly; a formal word. ▸ used of people's behaviour and actions. EG *There is a strong narcissistic element in your work.* — ADJ QUALIT ⇑ self-centred

narcissus /nɑ:sɪsəs/, **narcissi**. The plural can be either **narcissus** or **narcissi**. A **narcissus** is a yellow, white, or orange flower which looks like a daffodil. Narcissi bloom in the spring. EG *There was a bowl of narcissus on the desk.* — N COUNT

narcotic /nɑ:kɒtɪk/, **narcotics**. 1 A **narcotic** is a drug which makes you sleepy and unable to feel pain, especially one which you can become addicted to. EG *...those who seek satisfaction in danger, narcotics, or sexual adventures.* — N COUNT: USU PL

2 Something that is **narcotic** has the effect of making you feel sleepy and slightly unreal. EG *In fact no parts of the common field poppy are narcotic.* — ADJ QUALIT

narrate /nəreɪt/, **narrates, narrating, narrated**. 1 If you **narrate** a story, you tell it from your own point of view, describing the things that happened in the correct order. EG *Some of the story was narrated in the film.* — V+O = relate, recount

2 If you **narrate** a film or documentary programme, you speak the words which accompany it and which tell what is happening. EG *We wanted Richard Burton to narrate it, but he was too busy in Switzerland.* — V OR V+O

narration /nəreɪʃə⁰n/, **narrations**. 1 **Narration** is **1.1** the telling of a story or of things that have happened. EG *The richness of his novel comes from his narration of it.* — N UNCOUNT = description **1.2** the speaking of words which have been written to accompany a film, documentary programme, etc. EG *...a taped narration to a slide show.* — N UNCOUNT = commentary

2 A **narration** is a story or narrative. — N COUNT

narrative /nærətɪv/, **narratives**. 1 A **narrative** is a story or an account of events and experiences. EG *The narrative of her battle against suicidal depression makes fascinating reading... Maybe all of that is true, but that's not what the narrative is about.* — N COUNT = tale

2 Narrative is the presentation in a novel of the events that happen in the story. EG *...an advanced course in the writing of extended narrative... ...the narrative structure of the book... She taught herself the techniques of narrative and dialogue.* — N UNCOUNT

narrator /nə³reɪtə/, **narrators**. A **narrator** is 1 a person in a book, film, television broadcast, etc, who tells the story or who explains what is happening. EG *He is the narrator of 'Your Life in Their Hands'.* — N COUNT **2** a person who is telling a story. EG *So he listens and waits for the narrator to explain more.* — N COUNT

narrow /nærəʊ/, **narrower, narrowest; narrows, narrowing, narrowed**. 1 Something that is **narrow** has a very small distance from one side to the other, especially in comparison to its length or height. EG *We turned left off the main road into a narrow lane... John reduced his eyes to two narrow slits... ...narrow cliff ledges.* ◇ **narrowness**. — ADJ QUALIT ≠ wide; ◇ N UNCOUNT

2 If something **narrows**, it becomes less wide. EG *The river narrowed and curved sharply to the left.* — V

3 If you **narrow** your eyes or if your eyes **narrow**, — V-ERG you almost close them, for example because you are angry or because you are trying to concentrate on something. EG *Kitty narrowed her eyes and glared at Karen... 'I want you back here in five minutes,' he growled, narrowing his eyes to ominous slits.*

4 Ideas, attitudes, beliefs, etc that are **narrow** do not reflect all the important features of a subject, and have a very limited range. EG *I think you are taking too narrow a view... In this section their education, in the narrower sense of the word, will be described.* ◊ **narrowness**. EG *He criticized the narrowness of the range of opinion represented.* — ADJ QUALIT = restricted; ◊ N UNCOUNT = limitation

5 If something **narrows** or if you **narrow** it, you reduce its extent, range, or scope. EG *The gap between the rich and the poor is probably narrowing... We have moved much closer, narrowed our differences.* ◊ **narrowing**. EG *...the progressive narrowing of the individual's field of choice.* — V ERG = diminish; ◊ N UNCOUNT+SUPP

6 A **narrow** result after a contest or difficult situation is one in which the difference between success and failure is very small. EG *It was a narrow victory, by only five votes... ...the narrow defeat of Baldwin.* ◊ **narrowness**. ● **on the straight and narrow**: see **straight**. — ADJ QUALIT : USU ATTRIB = marginal; ◊ N UNCOUNT : USU+*of*

narrow down. If you **narrow** something **down**, you are more precise about the fact or subject that you are discussing and eliminate any unnecessary or unwanted factors. EG *Can we narrow it down a bit, David?... They narrowed the choice down to about a dozen sites.* — PHRASAL VB : V-ERG+ADV

narrowly /nærə⁶li¹/. 1 You use **narrowly** to say that you are going to explain what you mean in a more exact and detailed way. EG *...between Montreal and New York, or more narrowly, between Toylestown and Blake.* — PHR : USED AS ADV SEN = specifically

2 If you do something **narrowly**, you do it with close and careful attention, so that you notice every important detail. EG *She watched him narrowly.* — ADV WITH VB = closely

3 If someone or something wins or loses **narrowly**, the difference between success or failure is very small. EG *Adams only narrowly escaped with his life... The Senate narrowly defeated the Bill.* — ADV WITH VB = barely, just

narrow-minded; also spelled as one word. Someone who is **narrow-minded** is unwilling to think seriously about opinions or aspects of a subject which they do not already believe in; used showing disapproval. EG *How stupid and bigoted and narrow-minded he had become.* ▸ used of people's attitudes and behaviour. EG *...a narrow-minded approach to broadcasting.* ◊ **narrow-mindedness**. — ADJ QUALIT = small-minded; ▸ = insular; ◊ N UNCOUNT

NASA /næsə/ is an American government organization which is concerned with developing the exploration of space; an abbreviation for 'National Aeronautics and Space Administration'. — N PROPER

nasal /neɪzə⁰l/. 1 When the air passes through your nose as well as through your mouth while you are speaking, the sounds you produce are **nasal**. EG *'It's worth bearing in mind,' he said in a nasal voice... In their moments of rage their nasal accents were similar.* ◊ **nasally**. EG *The man in the blazer was complaining nasally to the steward.* — ADJ QUALIT = adenoidal; ◊ ADV WITH VB

2 **Nasal** is used to describe things relating to the nose and the functions it performs; a formal use. EG *The internal nasal passages are very much reduced... ...a drop of nasal discharge.* — ADJ CLASSIF : ATTRIB

nascent /næsə⁰nt, neɪ-/. **Nascent** things or processes are just beginning, and are expected to become stronger or to grow bigger; a formal word. EG *...nascent industries and old traditional ones.* — ADJ CLASSIF : ATTRIB = budding

nasturtium /nə³stɜːʃə⁰m/, **nasturtiums**. **Nasturtiums** are low plants with long trailers along the ground and colourful, trumpet-shaped flowers. — N COUNT

nasty /nɑːsti¹/, **nastier, nastiest**; a fairly informal word. 1 Something that is **nasty** is 1.1 very unpleasant to see, experience, or feel. EG *This place has a very nasty smell... Once again, I got that nasty feeling that I was being followed.* ◊ **nastiness**. EG *In fact, natural poisons frequently can surpass in nastiness the chemist's creations.* 1.2 considered to be unattractive, undesirable, and in bad taste. EG *It's a tacky, nasty little movie, frankly.* ◊ **nastiness**. 1.3 very difficult and worrying to deal with. EG *This presented a nasty problem to Mayor Lindsay... ...a nasty question.* — ADJ QUALIT : USU ATTRIB = horrible; ◊ N UNCOUNT; ADJ QUALIT : USU ATTRIB; ADJ QUALIT = tricky

2 A **nasty** injury, cut, disease, etc is one which is considered to be especially unpleasant because it looks horrible or has a serious effect on your body. EG *A nasty bruise rose where the handbag had landed... Rats carry very nasty diseases.* — ADJ QUALIT

3 Someone who is **nasty** behaves in an unkind and unpleasant way towards other people. EG *I want us to be friends. Why must she be so nasty to me?... He's nasty about his family... I knew she could be very nasty, so I braced myself.* ◊ **nastily**. EG *Gareth interrupted, though not nastily.* ◊ **nastiness**. EG *I was quite surprised at the nastiness there was at that board meeting.* — ADJ QUALIT = mean, disagreeable; ◊ ADV WITH VB; ◊ N UNCOUNT = malice

nation /neɪʃə⁰n/, **nations**. A **nation** is an individual country considered together with its social and political structures. EG *...a supremely powerful imperial and commercial nation... What we as a nation want is not words but deeds... ...the great accomplishments of their nation.* ▸ The **nation** is also used to refer to all the people who live in a particular country. EG *He appealed to the nation for self-restraint... It was announced that the Prime Minister would speak to the nation on television at midday.* — N COUNT; ▸ N SING : *the*+N ⇑ population

national /næʃə⁰nəl, -ʃənə⁰l/, **nationals**. 1 **National** is used 1.1 to describe things involving or relating to the whole of a country or nation rather than to part of it or to other nations. EG *It made the headlines in the national newspapers... ...special stamps to mark national and international events... ...discussions at local and national level.* ◊ **nationally**. EG *Should housing policy be decided nationally or locally?* 1.2 to describe things that are typical of the people or customs of a particular country or nation. EG *Common sense is certainly a national characteristic... ...national dress.* — ADJ CLASSIF : USU ATTRIB; ◊ ADV; ADJ CLASSIF : ATTRIB

2 A **national** of a particular country is a person who has citizenship of that country, especially when they are staying in another country. EG *Much of the workforce was made up of foreign nationals... ...a German national.* — N COUNT : MOD+N = citizen

national anthem, national anthems. A **national anthem** is a nation's official song which is played on public occasions. — N COUNT

national government, national governments. A **national government** is a coalition government, especially one that is formed during a crisis. — N COUNT/UNCOUNT

National Health Service. In Britain, the **National Health Service** or the **National Health** is the system which provides free or cheap medical care to everybody. It is paid for by taxes. EG *...having a tooth out on the National Health... ...National Health doctors.* — N PROPER : USU *the*+N

national insurance is the system in which a government collects money regularly from employers and employees so that it can pay money to people who are ill, unemployed, or retired. EG *The social security scheme is paid for by national insurance contributions.* — N UNCOUNT : USU BEFORE N

nationalise /næʃə⁰nəlaɪz/. See **nationalize**.

nationalism /næʃə⁰nəlɪzə⁰m/ is 1 a desire for the political independence of your nation. EG *...nineteenth-century Czech nationalism.* 2 love of your nation, which is often associated with the belief that your nation is better than any other; sometimes used showing disapproval. EG *...chauvinistic nationalism and ethnic prejudice.* — N UNCOUNT; N UNCOUNT = patriotism

nationalist /næʃə⁰nəlɪst/, **nationalists**. **Nationalist** ideas, movements, groups, etc, are involved with trying to obtain or keep political independence for a particular country. EG *...the nationalist movements of French West Africa.* ▸ used as a noun to refer to people with nationalist ideas. EG *...a great Indonesian nationalist.* — ADJ CLASSIF : ATTRIB; ▸ N COUNT

nationalistic /næʃə⁰nɪstɪk/. Someone who is **nationalistic** is very proud of their nation and believes that it is better than any other nation; often used showing disapproval. EG *...an attempt to arouse nationalistic passions against the foreigner.* — ADJ QUALIT = jingoistic

nationality /næʃə⁰nælɪti¹/, **nationalities**. 1 Your **nationality** is your state of belonging to a particular country, because you were born there or because you have been legally accepted as belonging to it. EG *...British nationality... I want him to have dual nationality... Discussion has taken place among scientists of different nationalities.* — N UNCOUNT/COUNT : USU WITH SUPP

2 A **nationality** is a group of people who have the same racial origins, especially when they do not have their own independent country. EG *...the nationalities inhabiting Tsarist Russia... ...European* — N COUNT : USU = race

nationalities struggling for cultural and political autonomy.

nationalize /næʃəⁿnəlaɪz/, **nationalizes, nationalizing, nationalized**; also spelled **nationalise**. If people **nationalize** a company or industry, they change its ownership so that it is no longer private but owned by the state and controlled by the government. EG *There are people in the Party who want to nationalise 200 companies.* ◊ **nationalized**. EG *Gas and coal were nationalized industries.* ◊ **nationalization** /næʃəⁿnəlaɪzeɪʃəⁿn/. EG *He argued for nationalisation on grounds of efficiency.* V+O; ◊ ADJ CLASSIF: ATTRIB; ◊ N UNCOUNT

national park, national parks. A **national park** is a large area of land which is protected by the government because of its natural beauty, plants, or animals, and which the public can usually visit. EG *...the head ranger of this vast national park.* N COUNT

national service is compulsory service in the armed forces, which young people in certain countries have to do by law. EG *I did two years national service.* N UNCOUNT

nation-state, nation-states. A **nation-state** is an independent state which includes all of a nation rather than part of it. N COUNT

nationwide /neɪʃəⁿnwaɪd/. **Nationwide** activities or situations happen or exist all over a particular country. EG *...a nationwide campaign to recruit women into trade unions.* ▸ used as an adverb. EG *She had lectured nationwide to various organizations.* ADJ CLASSIF: ATTRIB = national; ▸ ADV WITH VB

native /neɪtɪv/, **natives**. **1** Your **native** country or area is the country or area where you were born and brought up. EG *She made her way home from Central Europe to her native Russia.* ADJ CLASSIF: ATTRIB ⇑ home

2 A **native** of a particular country or region is someone who is born in that country or region. EG *...John Magee, a native of Northern Ireland.* ▸ used as an adjective. EG *They took on the humble and low paid work that native Britons would not touch.* N COUNT+SUPP; ▸ ADJ CLASSIF: ATTRIB

3 A **native** is someone who was born and lives in a non-Western country and who belongs to the race or tribe that forms the majority among its inhabitants, especially when they are poor and uneducated; an old-fashioned use, now fairly offensive. EG *...bands of black natives wandering over the veldt.* ▸ used as an adjective. EG *...remote native tribes.* N COUNT = local; ▸ ADJ CLASSIF: ATTRIB

4 Your **native** language or tongue is the first language that you learned to speak when you were a child. EG *She had spoken in her native language... He read a poem, in his native Hungarian.* ADJ CLASSIF: ATTRIB = mother tongue

7 Plants or animals that are **native** to a particular region live or grow there naturally and have not been brought there by people. EG *These are the only lilies native to Great Britain.* ▸ used as a noun. EG *Sugar cane, a native of Bengal, became the chief produce of the West Indies.* ADJ CLASSIF: IF+PREP THEN *to* ⇑ local; ▸ N COUNT+*of*

8 A **native** ability or quality is one that you possess naturally without having to learn it. EG *They want to get some measure of each man's native mental powers... This is not due to any native physical superiority of baseball players.* ADJ CLASSIF: ATTRIB = innate

9 If someone who is abroad **goes native**, they try to live and dress like the local people. EG *On a visit to Uganda in 1952 he went native, and has been there ever since.* PHR: VB INFLECTS

native speaker, native speakers. A **native speaker** of a language is someone who speaks that language as their first language rather than having learnt it as a foreign language. EG *...the kind of language that's used by the native speaker of English.* N COUNT

Nativity /nətɪvɪti¹/. The **Nativity** is the birth of Jesus, which is celebrated by Christians at Christmas. EG *...like a child hearing the story of the Nativity.* N SING: *the*+N ⇑ event

nativity play, nativity plays. A **nativity play** is a play about the birth of Jesus, usually one performed by children at Christmas time. N COUNT

NATO /neɪtəʊ/ is an international organization which consists of the USA, Canada, the UK, and other European countries who have agreed to support one another if they are attacked; an abbreviation for 'North Atlantic Treaty Organization'. EG *These missiles are now deployed by NATO in very considerable numbers... ...NATO forces.* N PROPER

natter /nætə/, **natters, nattering, nattered**. When people **natter**, they talk casually for a long time about unimportant things; an informal word. EG *We just want to natter together about old times.* ▸ used as a noun. EG *They like to have a bit of a natter.* V = chat, jaw; ▸ N SING: *a*+N = chinwag

natty /næti¹/, **nattier, nattiest**; an informal word. **1** Someone who is **natty** is smart and neat in appearance. EG *...a small man, brisk and natty... He's a very natty dresser.* ▸ used of people's clothes. EG *...natty headgear.* ADJ QUALIT = dapper; ▸ = chic

2 Something that is **natty** is smart and cleverly designed. EG *...a natty metal tool box.* ADJ QUALIT = nifty

natural /nætʃəⁿrəⁿl/, **naturals**. **1** If you say that it is **natural** for someone to react or act in a particular way, you mean that you would expect them to react or act in this way in the particular circumstances mentioned. EG *She's upset. It's natural, isn't it? Today's the funeral... It is natural and rational that the older generation should be suspicious of the young... It is natural for trade unions to adopt an aggressive posture... She has a feeling that she is doing the most natural thing in the world.* ADJ QUALIT: USU PRED ⇑ normal ≠ unnatural, surprising

2 A **natural** way of behaving is one which is instinctive and has not been learned. EG *If you're an animal you follow your own natural inclinations.* ADJ CLASSIF: USU ATTRIB = inborn

3 A **natural** skill or gift is one that you were born with rather than one that you have learnt. EG *He had a natural gift for making things work... Only a few people have a natural aptitude for lateral thinking.* ADJ CLASSIF: ATTRIB = inborn, instinctive

4 If you say that someone is **a natural**, you mean that they can do something very well, not because they have been taught it, but because they were born with that skill. EG *He is a great craftsman, a natural.* N COUNT: IF SING *a*+N

5 If someone is **natural** or if they behave in a **natural** way, they behave in a way that shows that they are relaxed and are not trying to hide anything or pretend in any way. EG *...walking slowly, in a relaxed, natural manner, from one side of the stage to the other... There was something not quite natural about her speech.* ◊ **naturalness**. EG *I was impressed by their friendliness, ease and naturalness, and their total lack of shyness.* ADJ QUALIT = genuine, spontaneous ≠ contrived; ◊ N UNCOUNT = artlessness

6 Natural is used **6.1** to describe things that are not made or caused by people, but found in nature and the physical world around us. EG *The city has superb natural defences... Teeth are a natural weapon that man has... ...protection from many natural disasters... Scientists have found synthetic substitutes for natural materials.* **6.2** to describe things that do not use or involve chemicals or industrial processes. EG *They opened a shop selling natural foods... Deep freezing is the simplest natural way of preserving food.* **6.3** to describe people who are able to learn something mentioned very easily and to do it very well. EG *The children proved to be natural performers... She was a natural organizer and hostess.* ADJ CLASSIF: ATTRIB ≠ artificial, man-made; ADJ CLASSIF: ATTRIB ≠ processed, artificial; ADJ CLASSIF: ATTRIB = born, instinctive

7 If someone dies of **natural causes**, they die because they were ill and not because they were murdered or committed suicide. EG *The post mortem showed that death was due to natural causes.* PHR: PREP+PHR

8 Someone's **natural** mother or father is their actual mother or father, as opposed to one who has adopted or fostered them. EG *She claimed Prince Yousoupoff as her natural father... These children spend time in care before returning to their natural parents or being adopted.* ADJ CLASSIF: ATTRIB ⇑ real

9 Someone's **natural** child is their illegitimate child. EG *In her will there was a considerable sum of money left to her natural son, Desmond.* ADJ CLASSIF: ATTRIB = bastard

10 A musical note which is **natural** is the ordinary note, not its sharp or flat form. EG *She played B natural not B flat.* ▸ used as a noun. EG *Is that F a natural or a sharp?* ADJ AFTER N; ▸ N COUNT

natural childbirth is a method of childbirth in which the mother is given no anaesthetics but instead is prepared with and uses special breathing and relaxation exercises. EG *More and more women want to have their babies by natural childbirth.* N UNCOUNT

natural gas is methane gas which is found underground or under the sea. It is collected and stored, and piped into people's houses to be used for cooking and heating. EG *New reserves of oil, natural gas or even coal must be found if we are to survive the twenty-first century.* N UNCOUNT

natural history is the study of animals and plants. N UNCOUNT = nature study

naturalise /nætʃrəlaɪz/. See **naturalize**.

naturalism /nætʃrəlɪzəⁿm/ is a theory in art and literature which states that people and objects N UNCOUNT ⇑ realism should be shown as they actually are, rather than in an idealistic or unnatural way.

naturalist /nætʃrəlɪst/, **naturalists**. A **naturalist** is a person who is interested in and studies plants, animals, insects, and other living things. EG *Nearby is the bird sanctuary, memorial to the great naturalist W.H. Hudson.* N COUNT ⇑ biologist

naturalistic /nætʃrəlɪstɪk/ describes people or things that believe in, practise, or are characteristic of the theory of naturalism in art and literature. EG *You think of Hogarth as a naturalistic artist drawing the world as he thought it really was.* ADJ QUALIT : ATTRIB ⇑ realistic

naturalize /nætʃrəlaɪz/, **naturalizes, naturalizing, naturalized**; also spelled **naturalise**. If someone **is naturalized**, they become a citizen of a country which they were not born in. EG *All persons born or naturalized in the United States are entitled to vote.* ◇ **naturalized**. EG *Her German husband was a naturalised Englishman.* V+O : USU PASS ◇ ADJ CLASSIF : ATTRIB

naturally /nætʃrəli[1]/. **1** You use **naturally** to indicate that you think something is very obvious and not at all surprising. EG *Dena was crying, so naturally Hannah was upset... 'Do you propose to take account of that?'-'Naturally.'... Publishers naturally enough are hesitant about committing large sums of money to such a project.* ADV SEN = obviously

2 If one thing develops **naturally** from another, it develops as a normal consequence or result of the first thing. EG *Pocket calculators are an invention which sprang naturally out of the discovery of logarithms... This leads us fairly naturally into what career advisers call careers counselling.* ADV WITH VB = logically

3 If something happens or occurs **naturally**, it was not made or caused by people, but is found in nature or is a natural process. EG *He found there some rock that does not occur naturally within 30 kilometres... Scientists have long tried to reproduce artificially what they observed to happen naturally or accidentally... Some of the men will die naturally at sixty-five.* ADV WITH VB ≠ artificially

4 If someone behaves **naturally**, they behave in a way that shows that they are relaxed and are not trying to hide anything or pretend in any way. EG *The children are probably too much in awe of her to behave naturally... He stood there smiling, his hands resting naturally on his hips.* ADV WITH VB

5 If someone **naturally** has a particular characteristic, quality, or skill, it is something which they were born with rather than something that they have learned or developed. EG *...people who are naturally brilliant... She had a naturally cheerful and serene expression... She was naturally blonde.* ADV+ADJ ≠ artificially

6 If something **comes naturally** to someone, they find it an easy and obvious thing to do. EG *Politics came naturally to Tony.* PHR : VB INFLECTS, IF+PREP THEN *to*

natural resources are all the land, forests, and sources of energy and mineral wealth that occur naturally in a country and that can be used by human beings. EG *There is a plan to open up the vast region with its wealth of natural resources... ...a society that's not going to run out of natural resources.* N PLURAL

natural selection is a process which results in those animals and plants that are best suited to their environment surviving and producing young, while those that are less well suited die. In this way new characteristics become selected and retained and so species evolve. N UNCOUNT

nature /neɪtʃə/, **natures**. The word **nature** can also be spelled with a capital letter in paragraph 1. **1 Nature** is **1.1** everything in the world that is neither caused nor controlled by human beings, including all animals and plants and natural phenomena. EG *...the diversity of nature... It's Nature's way of being sure that life will continue as before.* **1.2** processes and events in the world which are neither caused nor controlled by human beings. EG *He wanted to challenge the premise that in nature genes interchange with each other.* **1.3** the aspects of our environment which appeal to us and which stimulate our senses. EG *A sunset is one of the most beautiful sights in nature... ...the beauty of nature... I'm a nature lover.* N UNCOUNT N UNCOUNT N UNCOUNT

● If you talk about going **back to nature**, you are referring to a desire that many people have to return to a simpler, less sophisticated way of life than the one which they are leading, for example when they are living in cities and working in commerce or industry. EG *...the 'Back to Nature' cult.* ● PHR : USED AS AN A, OR BEFORE N

2 The **nature** of something is its essential quality or fundamental character. EG *It is the nature of fire to burn... Such a situation is by nature painful... Their argument concerned the very nature of nuclear warfare.* N COUNT+SUPP USU SING, OR *by*+N

3 Someone's **nature** is their character, as shown by the way they behave or react to other people. EG *Rob had a very sweet nature... She is aristocratic in nature if not in name... ...a woman with a wildly passionate nature... He eventually revealed his real nature.* N COUNT+SUPP, OR *by*+N = disposition, temperament

4 The word **nature** is also used in the following expressions, where it has the general meaning of 'character'. **4.1** If a way of behaving is **in** your **nature**, it is a part of your character and so you behave in that way. EG *It was not in her nature to tell lies... It has never been in my nature to take life easy.* **4.2** If someone has a particular characteristic or quality **by nature**, it is a part of their character. EG *I am an optimist by nature... He was polite by nature.* PHR : USED AS A, IF+VB THEN *to*-INF PHR : USED AS A ⇑ naturally

4.3 If you talk about someone's **better nature**, you are referring to their feelings of kindness and desire to help other people. EG *...to manipulate people by appeals to their better nature.* **4.4** If a way of behaving is **second nature** to you, you do it almost without thinking because it is automatic or obvious to you. ● See also **human nature**. PHR : POSS+PHR = conscience PHR : USED AS C IF+PREP THEN *to*

5 If you say that something is of a particular **nature**, you mean that it has the characteristic or quality mentioned. EG *They suffered injuries of a very serious nature... The music he played was of a romantic rather than classical nature... These problems are political in nature.* N SING WITH DET +SUPP, OR *in*+N : AFTER ADJ = kind, sort

6 If you say that something is **in the nature of things**, you mean that it you would expect it to happen because it happens naturally. EG *It is in the nature of things that people will lie to save themselves.* PHR : USED AS A

7 If something is **in the nature of** a particular thing, it has some of the characteristics of that thing. EG *For me a detective story is in the nature of a race.* PHR+NG : USED AS AN A ⇑ like

8 If you say that you will do or have a particular thing **or something of that nature**, you mean that you will do or have that thing or something else which is similar to it. EG *I'll give them a meat dish, or something of that nature.* PHR : USED AFTER O

9 If you say that something has a particular characteristic **by** its **nature** or **by** its **very nature**, you mean that it has that characteristic because the kind of thing that it is always has that characteristic. EG *Cash is, by its very nature, universally transferable... Trade unions are by their nature conservative bodies... By their nature most businesses take risks.* PHR : USED AS A

10 A **call of nature** is a need to urinate or defecate; used when you want to be polite. EG *He went to answer a call of nature.* PHR : USED AS

nature study is the study of animals and plants at a very basic level by looking at them directly, for example as it is taught in schools to young children. N UNCOUNT = natural history

nature trail, nature trails. A **nature trail** is a route which is signposted through an area of countryside, pointing out animals, plants, rocks, etc which are particularly interesting. N COUNT ⇑ walk

naturism /neɪtʃər[o]ɪzə[o]m/ is the same as nudism. ◇ **naturist, naturists**. EG *There are two swimming pools, one for naturists.* N UNCOUNT ◇ N COUNT = nudist

naught /nɔːt/. See **nought**.

naughty /nɔːti[1]/, **naughtier, naughtiest**. **1** A child who is **naughty** behaves badly or is disobedient. EG *Don't be a naughty boy... He was sent to bed for being naughty.* ◇ **naughtiness**. EG *She knows when she is getting away with too much naughtiness.* ADJ QUALIT = bad ◇ N UNCOUNT

2 Something that is **naughty** is slightly rude or indecent. EG *...little boys who used naughty words... I can't see what harm he does with a naughty book or two.* ◇ **naughtiness**. EG *They enjoy stories about adult naughtiness.* ADJ QUALIT = dirty ◇ N UNCOUNT

nausea /nɔːzɪə, -sɪə/ is the condition of feeling sick and as if you are going to vomit. EG *Another wave of nausea hit him.* N UNCOUNT = sickness

nauseam /nɔːzi[1]æm/. see **ad nauseam**.

nauseate /nɔːzɪeɪt, -sɪ-/, **nauseates, nauseating, nauseated**. If something **nauseates** you, **1** it makes you feel sick and as if you are going to vomit. EG *The thought of food nauseated him.* **2** it is V+O = sicken V+O unpleasant and causes you to feel strong feelings of disgust or dislike. EG *The idea of Uncle Harold outside Nicola's door nauseated him.* ◊ **nauseating**. EG *...an ashtray full of old cigarette stubs, a nauseating sight... He droned on at nauseating length about his new job.* ◊ ADJ QUALIT = sickening

nauseous /nɔːzɪəs, -sɪəs/. **1** If you feel **nauseous**, you feel sick and as if you are likely to vomit. EG *I felt dizzy and nauseous.* ADJ QUALIT : PRED = queasy

2 Something that is **nauseous** is unpleasant and causes you to feel strong feelings of disgust or dislike. EG *...the nauseous ugliness of the nightmare.* ADJ QUALIT = revolting

nautical /nɔːtɪkəˀl/ is used to describe people or things relating to or involved with the sea and ships. EG *Captain Gulliver was a middle-class, nautical man... ...a placid elderly man in a nautical uniform.* ADJ CLASSIF : USU ATTRIB = seafaring

nautical mile, nautical miles. A **nautical mile** is a unit of measurement used at sea. It is equal to 1852 metres. N COUNT

naval /neɪvəˀl/ is used to describe people or things that belong to, relate to, or involve a country's navy. EG *It had been attacked by Norwegian naval and air forces... ...a French naval officer.* ADJ CLASSIF : ATTRIB

nave /neɪv/, **naves**. The **nave** of a church or cathedral is the long central part where the congregation worships. EG *...the long nave of the abbey.* N COUNT : USU *the*+N IN SING

navel /neɪvəˀl/, **navels**. Your **navel** is the small hollow in the middle of your tummy. N COUNT = belly button

navigable /nævɪgəbəˀl/. A river or other waterway that is **navigable** is wide enough or deep enough for a boat to travel safely. EG *Settlements were scattered along the banks of navigable rivers.* ADJ CLASSIF

navigate /nævɪgeɪt/, **navigates, navigating, navigated**. If you **navigate**, **1** you work out which direction to go while you are travelling by using maps and a compass or the sun and stars. EG *Some birds navigate by the stars... We didn't talk because Andy had to navigate.* V OR V+O = steer **2** you travel safely, especially through a difficult or dangerous place, because you know the route or work it out carefully. EG *...my ability to navigate through these hills.* V OR V+O

navigation /nævɪgeɪʃəˀn/ is **1** the process or skill with which people work out their position, direction, and speed when they are travelling, especially when they are travelling as a member of the crew of a ship or aeroplane. EG *...useful developments in navigation... Moving at such speeds, navigation becomes critically important.* N UNCOUNT **2** the act of navigating. EG *...the problems of sonar navigation.* N UNCOUNT = steering

navigational /nævɪgeɪʃəˀnəl, -ʃənəˀl/ is used to describe things relating to navigation. EG *...the jet plane's automatic navigational system.* ADJ CLASSIF : ATTRIB

navigator /nævɪgeɪtə/, **navigators**. A **navigator** is someone who works out the direction in which a ship or aeroplane is travelling. EG *He had many years experience as a sea captain and navigator... He is studying to be a navigator of planes.* N COUNT

navvy /nævi¹/, **navvies**. A **navvy** is a person who is employed to do hard physical work, for example building roads or canals; used especially of men in the nineteenth century. EG *...a colonel who had once been a navvy.* N COUNT ⇑ labourer

navy /neɪvi¹/, **navies**. **1** A **navy** is a country's military force that fights at sea; also used to refer to the ships and equipment it uses. EG *My father's in the Navy... The US, British and French navies have cooperated... ...a navy man.* N COUNT : USU *the*+N : IF SING, VB CAN BE SING OR PL : ALSO IN NAMES

2 Something that is **navy** or **navy-blue** is very dark blue in colour. EG *She tried on a navy suit... ...a navy-blue polo-necked jumper.* ADJ COLOUR

nay /neɪ/. **1 Nay** means no; an old-fashioned use. EG *They are trained to say nay.* CONVENTION

2 You use **nay** to emphasize your opinion by introducing a correction to what you have just said; a formal use. EG *It also enabled, nay, compelled me to pass through Portsmouth... Restriction of freedom begins with birth. Nay, it begins long before birth.* ADV SEN

NB is used, especially in writing, to draw someone's attention to what you are about to say or write. EG *N.B. The root of the plant is poisonous.*

> **N BEFORE N** □ In this dictionary N BEFORE N is used in the grammar notes beside entries to indicate that one noun modifies another. Examples are **capacity 2** and **capital 2**. EG *...a **capacity** audience... ...**capital** investment.* This feature is indicated only if it is the only or the most common way in which the word is used.

NCO /ɛn siː əʊ/, **NCO's**. **NCO** is an abbreviation for 'non-commissioned officer'; a soldier who has a rank such as sergeant or corporal, and who has authority over ordinary soldiers. EG *He had a minute staff of four officers, one NCO and eight men.* N COUNT

> **N COUNT** □ In this dictionary N COUNT is used in the grammar notes beside entries to mean that a noun is a count noun. N COUNTS behave in the following ways: **1** They have a plural form, usually made by adding -s. **2** When they are singular, they must have a determiner in front of them, such as *a*, *the*, or *her*. Examples are **shirt**, **table**, and **pen**. EG *He put on a clean white **shirt**... They've moved the **tables** for the party... She picked up her **pen**... Do you have a **pen**?* You do not say 'He put on clean white shirt' and you do not say 'Do you have pen?'

> □ N COUNT/UNCOUNT: see N UNCOUNT/COUNT.

-nd is added to a number that ends in 2 and is written in figures in order to form an ordinal number or a fraction. 2nd is pronounced 'second'. EG *...2→2nd... ...42→42nd.* SUFFIX : FORMS ORDINALS

NE; pronounced as 'north-east' or /ɛn iː/. **NE** is an abbreviation for 'north-east'; used on a compass or in descriptions of where a particular place is situated. ADJ CLASSIF : ATTRIB

Neanderthal /nɪændətɑːl/ is used to describe the people who lived in Europe before 12,000 BC, and their society. ADJ CLASSIF : ATTRIB

near /nɪə/, **nearer, nearest; nears, nearing, neared**. **1** If something is situated **near** or **near to** a place, thing, or person, it is only a short distance from them. EG *He stood near the door... ...on a country road near Belfast... I wish I lived nearer London... I stood very near to them... I looked at the books nearest to where I stood... No birds or animals came near... ...as they drew nearer... He pulled her nearer to him.* PREP, ADV AFTER VB, OR ADJ QUALIT = close to ≠ far from ◊ **nearness**. EG *All the while I was acutely aware of her nearness... ...factors like local costs and nearness to London.* ◊ N UNCOUNT+SUPP = proximity

2 If someone or something is **near** or **near to** a particular situation or state, they have almost reached it or are almost in it. EG *It cannot truthfully be said that Britain was ever near collapse as an ordered society... Her father was angry, her mother near tears... It came near to breaking point... She seemed very near to falling down.* PREP = close to

3 If something is similar to something else or closely related to it, it is **near** it or **near to** it. EG *Most views were fairly near the truth... That's near my own sort of work... The leaves of the plane trees can be nearer gold than green... He is the nearest we have to an English Leonardo da Vinci... Such systems can be seen to approach nearest to the ideal of the rational society.* PREP, OR ADV AFTER VB ⇑ like

4 If you are **near** or **near to** someone, you have a very close friendship with them and are very fond of them. EG *None of us could really get near her... She kept goldfish. Which brought her nearer to me than the fact she spent hours with my sister.* PREP, OR ADV AFTER VB = close to

5 If something happens **near** or **near to** a particular date or point in time, it happens a short time before or after it. EG *...near the beginning of the play... ...on or near October sixteenth... As the wedding day drew near, Vita felt no qualms... The dawn was near... ...as ten o'clock rolls nearer.* PREP, OR ADV AFTER VB = close to ≠ far from ● If you refer to things which will happen **in the near future**, you are referring to things that will happen quite soon. EG *Growth will be accelerating in the near future... These things will be available to us all in the very near future.* ● PHR : USED AS AN A

6 You use **near 6.1** to say that something is a little more or less than an amount or number stated. EG *...at something near the 10 per cent annual rate of growth... ...in fact it cost nearer three million dollars... He said it would take half a day, but I would have thought nearer half an hour.* PREP = close to **6.2** to say that someone is involved with a particular situation, activity, or person. EG *She left school at 11, and had not been near any kind of education or training since then... I wouldn't trust him near Nathan.* PREP : USU WITH BROAD NEG

7 If you refer to the **near** one of two things or people, you mean the one that is closer to you. EG *...the rider on the near horse... ...in the nearer houses... We walked to the nearest house.* ADJ QUALIT

8 Your **near** relatives are people who are closely related to you, for example your grandparents, cous- ADJ QUALIT : ATTRIB ins, aunts, and uncles, as well as your parents, your brothers, and your sisters. EG *...my near relations... ...his nearest relatives.* ● Your **nearest and dearest** are the people who you are closely related to or very fond of, especially your family or lover. EG *It comes as a shock only when the nearest and dearest are involved.* ● PHR : USED AS S/O/C

9 You also use **near 9.1** to say that something almost has the quality or identity mentioned. EG *...standing on a dock in near darkness... Very often tragedies or near tragedies occurred... ...a story about his near fall from the eleventh floor of a building.* ADJ CLASSIF : ATTRIB **9.2** to say that something almost happens in a particular way. EG *...Cambodia and its near catastrophic economic troubles.* ADV+ADJ = nearly

10 You use **near** in expressions such as **near enough**, **as near as makes no difference**, and **as near as no matter** in order to modify a statement and to say that although it is not completely and exactly true, it is nevertheless almost true and can be considered as true. EG *I'd near enough got it right... He paid a £100, or as near as makes no difference.* PHR : USED AS AN A = just about

11 If you say that something was **a near thing**, **11.1** you mean that a particular situation was almost a disaster or a failure. EG *The list of what could have gone badly wrong is a long one. It was certainly a very near thing.* PHR : USED AS C = a close shave **11.2** you mean that in a vote, election, or competition the winner only just managed to win. EG *'Oh, do you think he's going to get in?'–'It'll be a very near thing because the opposition will be so strong.'* PHR : USED AS C = touch and go

12 When something has a lot of the characteristics of a particular type of thing, and nothing else seems to be a better example of it, you can say that it is **the nearest thing to** that type of thing. EG *Soho is the nearest thing in Central London to a red light district... He is an astute politician and the nearest thing to a world-class statesman that Cambridge has ever produced.* PHR+NG/-ING : USED AS C

13 You use **nowhere near** and **not anywhere near** to make a clause negative and so emphasize that something is not the case; used mainly in spoken English. EG *It's nowhere near finished... Lions are nowhere near as fast as the cheetah... No list can be anywhere near complete.* PHR : USED AS AN A, NEG ⇑ not = not nearly

14 When you **near** a place, you get near it or nearer to it; a fairly formal use. EG *...as they neared the harbour... We were nearing the point where the lane curved.* V+O = approach

15 When you **near** a particular date or point in time, or when the date or time **nears**, it comes closer so that it will happen sooner; a fairly formal use. EG *...a great and original Australian writer, nearing 80, Christina Stead... ...when the time neared for the prayer.* V-ERG = approach

16 If a situation **nears** a particular state, it almost reaches it; a fairly formal use. EG *The crisis in Northern Ireland neared a flash point last week... It was confusion, nearing hysteria.* V+O = border on

nearby /nɪəbaɪ/; also spelled as two words or with a hyphen. If something is **nearby**, it is only a short distance from the place, thing, or person just mentioned, or from where you are. EG *We decided to walk to the cottage, as there was a river nearby... I got a place at a teachers' training college near by... ...Nottingham and nearby towns... He took the bag and tossed it into some nearby bushes.* ADJ CLASSIF

Near East. The **Near East** is the same as the Middle East. EG *...an archaeological excavation in the Near East.* N PROPER : *the*+N

nearly /nɪəli[1]/. **1 Nearly** means almost, but not completely, totally, or exactly. EG *Brody had been sitting there for nearly an hour... I think about it nearly all the time... She was nearly as tall as he was... It was nearly dark... I can nearly swim a width.* ADV = practically

2 You use **not nearly** as an emphatic way of making a clause negative and saying that something is not the case. EG *I haven't spent nearly long enough here... The deeper water was not nearly as good as the water close to the shore... Vegetarians like us don't have nearly so many foods to choose from as ordinary people.* PHR : USED AS AN A ⇑ not = nowhere near

near miss, near misses; also spelled with a hyphen. A **near miss** is **1** a bomb or shot which just misses the target, although it is very close. N COUNT **2** a situation where you nearly had an accident or disaster but just avoided it. EG *Most aircraft accidents or near misses are caused by pilot error.* N COUNT = narrow escape **3** an attempt to do something which nearly succeeds, but just fails to do so. N COUNT ⇑ failure

nearside /nɪəsaɪd/. The **nearside** of a vehicle is the side that is nearest the edge of the road where the vehicle is being driven normally. EG *The mini had just touched the offside of this truck with its nearside wing... ...a dent on the nearside.* N SING : WITH *the*/POSS, USU BEFORE N

near-sighted; also spelled as one word. **Near-sighted** means the same as short-sighted. EG *He was near-sighted and wore glasses.* ADJ QUALIT

neat /niːt/, **neater, neatest**. **1** Something that is **neat** is made or kept very tidy, clean, and smart. EG *His clothes were neat, his desk was neat, his office was neat... She had small, neat writing.* ADJ QUALIT ≠ disorderly, scruffy, shabby ◇ **neatly**. EG *It comes all neatly wrapped up in its own little cellophane bag.* ◇ ADV WITH VB = carefully ◇ **neatness**. EG *...a terrace of houses of the most fastidious neatness.* ◇ N UNCOUNT = orderliness

2 Someone who is **neat** is careful, tidy, and efficient in their appearance and behaviour. EG *Ethel was clean and neat and politely spoken... She used to be the neatest of girls.* ADJ QUALIT ≠ scruffy, slovenly ▸ used of people's behaviour. EG *...a neat businesslike manner.* ▸ = precise ◇ **neatly**. EG *...hanging his jacket neatly on the back of a chair.* ◇ ADV WITH VB

3 A **neat** way of organizing something or solving something is clever and convenient. EG *...neat patterns and chains of cause and effect... ...the neat division of the year into wet and dry seasons.* ADJ QUALIT = nice ◇ **neatly**. EG *The theories and measurements fitted together neatly.* ◇ ADV WITH VB = nicely

4 If you say that something is **neat**, you mean that you think it is very good; an informal use in American English. EG *That's a neat idea.* ADJ QUALIT = great

5 A **neat** alcoholic drink has nothing else added to it or mixed with it. EG *He never added water, always gulping the neat brandy down in one draught... ...if you take your whisky neat and don't have any soda water.* ADJ CLASSIF ⇑ pure ≠ diluted

nebulous /nebjə[4]ləs/. An idea that is **nebulous** is vague and difficult to talk about, either because you do not have enough information about it or because it is not properly organized. EG *I still had a nebulous notion of an afterlife... ...a nebulous concept.* ADJ QUALIT ⇑ imprecise = hazy

necessarily /nesɪ[2]sə[0]rɪli[1], nesɪ[2]serɪli[1]/. **1** If you say that something is not **necessarily** the case, you mean that it is not always the case. EG *Fleas and bedbugs are not necessarily associated with dirt... Documentaries don't necessarily need interviewers.* ADV WITH VB, WITH BROAD NEG = automatically

2 If you say that something **necessarily** happens or is the case, you mean that it has to happen in this way or has to be the case and cannot be any different. EG *Decisions were necessarily slow.* ADV = inevitably

necessary /nesə[2]sə[0]ri[1]/. **1** Something that is **necessary 1.1** is needed in order to obtain the result or effect you want. EG *Are we teaching undergraduates the necessary skills?... Make a soft dough, using a little more water if necessary... ...the colours and patterns necessary for perfect camouflage... I don't want to stay longer than necessary.* ADJ CLASSIF ⇑ important = required **1.2** is very important. EG *It is necessary to examine this claim before we proceed any further.* ADJ QUALIT = crucial **1.3** happens or exists only as the direct result of a particular event or situation, and cannot be any different. EG *There is no necessary connection between industrial democracy and productivity.* ADJ CLASSIF = inevitable

2 If you **do the necessary**, you do something that is necessary or important in a particular situation; an informal expression used in British English. EG *Leave it to me. I'll do the necessary.* PHR : VB INFLECTS

necessitate /nɪ[2]sesɪ[1]teɪt/, **necessitates, necessitating, necessitated**. If something **necessitates** an action, event, or situation, it makes it necessary; a fairly formal word. EG *The Government's action had necessitated a by-election... This would not necessitate taking an innocent life... It would indeed necessitate strong measures.* V+O/-ING = require

necessity /nɪ[2]sesɪ[1]ti[1]/, **necessities**. **1** If you say that there is a **necessity** for a particular thing to happen, you mean that it must happen. EG *With Allen on the scene the necessity for her to cope with her problems was removed... ...the necessity of protecting the free world... There was no necessity to devise anything at all... She went to work not out of choice but necessity.* N UNCOUNT : IF PREP THEN *of* TO-INF ⇑ need

2 A **necessity** is **2.1** something which you have to do, or which has to happen, and which you cannot avoid or prevent. EG *For many families relocation is a* N COUNT : USU SING = inevitabil

necessity, a consequence of unemployment. **2.2** something, such as food or clothing, that you need to have in order to live or in order to do something. EG *It was supplied with all the necessities of life... Television is considered a necessity by some... She was busy picking up some last-minute necessities and flinging them into her handbag.*
N COUNT = essential ≠ luxury

3 If you say that something happens **of necessity**, you mean that it must happen in this way because nothing else is possible or practical in the circumstances. EG *The account given here is of necessity extremely brief and over-simplified... Herdsmen must, of necessity, move with the herds.*
PHR : USED AS AN A = inevitably

neck /nɛk/, **necks, necking, necked. 1** Your **neck** is the part of your body which joins your head to the rest of your body. EG *She threw her arms around his neck and hugged him... The cat had a blue collar round its neck... He splashed his face and the back of his neck with water.*
N COUNT

2 The **neck** of a shirt, dress, jumper, or other garment is the part which goes over your shoulders and round or below your neck. EG *...a long dress with a lace neck... His shirt was open at the neck.*
N COUNT : USU *the*/MOD+N ⇑ edge

3 Neck is meat from an animal's neck. EG *...neck of lamb.*
N UNCOUNT : IF+ PREP THEN *of*

4 The **neck** of something such as a bottle or a violin is the long part at one end of it which is narrower than the main part of it. EG *He picked up the violin carefully by the neck.*
N COUNT : USU+ SUPP

5 A **neck** of land is a long, narrow strip of land which has the sea on both sides of it. EG *The cottage was on the neck of the little peninsula.*
N COUNT : IF+ PREP THEN *of* = causeway

6 The word **neck** is also used in the following expressions. **6.1** If something goes **down** your **neck**, it goes under your collar and down your back. EG *The rain was dripping down our necks.* **6.2** If something such as a problem is **around** your **neck** or if it is **hanging round** your **neck**, you are responsible for it, and you worry about it a great deal. EG *He had debts hanging round his neck... A screaming child is the last thing one wants around one's neck in the supermarket.* **6.3** If you talk about **breaking** or **wringing** someone's **neck**, you are angry with them and want to express this feeling, although you will not actually break their neck. EG *I ought to break his neck for doing that.* **6.4** If you say that you are **up to** your **neck** in a situation or activity, you mean that you are deeply involved in it and cannot get away from it or avoid it; an informal expression. EG *You were up to your neck in trouble with the press.* **6.5** If you say that someone is **breathing down** your **neck**, you mean that they are watching you very closely in order to check everything that you do. EG *They should not have the shareholders breathing down their necks all the time.* **6.6** If you say that someone is **risking** their **neck**, you mean that they are doing something that is very dangerous, usually in order to try and achieve a particular result. EG *I thanked him for risking his neck for me.* **6.7** If you **stick** your **neck out**, you do or say something in a way that draws attention to yourself and makes you open to the risk of criticism or danger; a fairly informal expression. EG *He was only too pleased to let someone else stick their neck out and take responsibility.*
6.8 If someone **gets it in the neck**, they are punished or criticized severely; an informal expression. EG *You'll get it in the neck if you aren't careful.* **6.9** If a racehorse or other competitor **wins by a neck**, it wins a race or other competition by a very small margin. **6.10** If two competitors are **neck and neck**, they are level with each other and appear to have an equal chance of succeeding or winning. EG *They were neck and neck right up to the finishing line.*
6.1 PHR : USED AS AN A; 6.2 PHR : USED AS AN A, OR PHR : VB INFLECTS; 6.3 PHR : VB INFLECTS = murder; 6.4 PHR : USED AS AN A, USU+*in* = knee deep; 6.5 PHR : VB INFLECTS ⇑ observe; 6.6 PHR : VB INFLECTS = take a risk; 6.7 PHR : VB INFLECTS = take a risk; 6.8 PHR : VB INFLECTS; 6.9 PHR : VB INFLECTS = scrape home; 6.10 PHR : USED AS C

• **dead from the neck up**: see **dead**. • the **scruff of** your **neck**: see **scruff**. • to **have a millstone round** your **neck**: see **millstone**.

7 If two people **neck**, especially teenagers, they kiss each other passionately; an informal use. ◊ **necking.** EG *Going to a dance with a boy usually led to necking.*
V : USU CONT; ◊ N UNCOUNT = snogging

neckerchief /nɛkətʃi[1]f/, **neckerchiefs.** A **neckerchief** is a piece of cloth folded diagonally to form a triangle, which people sometimes wear round their necks. EG *The brightly coloured silk neckerchief completed the effect.*
N COUNT ⇑ scarf

necklace /nɛklɪs/, **necklaces.** A **necklace** is a piece of jewellery, such as a chain or string of beads, which is worn round the neck, usually by women. EG *...a necklace of silver, glass, and amber.*
N COUNT

neckline /nɛklaɪn/, **necklines.** The **neckline** of a dress, jumper, or other piece of clothing is the shape or position of the top edge as it goes around your neck. EG *Her dress had an extremely low neckline.*
N COUNT : USU SING ⇑ line = neck

necktie /nɛktaɪ/, **neckties.** A **necktie** is a long narrow piece of material that is worn under a shirt collar, especially by men, and tied round the neck in a knot with the ends hanging down at the front; used in American English or old-fashioned British English. EG *Tom held Claude roughly by his necktie.*
N COUNT = tie

necromancy /nɛkrə[6]mænsi[1]/ is black magic or witchcraft; a formal word.
N UNCOUNT

nectar /nɛktə/ is a sweet liquid produced by flowers, which bees and other insects collect. EG *...bees spending the summer collecting nectar and turning it into honey.*
N UNCOUNT

nectarine /nɛktə[0]rɪn/, **nectarines.** A **nectarine** is a kind of peach which has a smooth skin.
N COUNT

née /neɪ/ is used before a woman's former name to indicate that it was her name before she changed it, for example when she got married. EG *...Jane Carmichael, née Byers.*
PREP : N PROPER +PREP+N PROPER = born

need /ni:d/, **needs, needing, needed. 1** If you **need** something, **1.1** you must have it because it is a basic necessity and because you depend on it in order to live and be healthy. EG *These animals don't hibernate; they need food throughout the winter... Infants usually know how much food they need... Children need to feel they matter to someone... Nearly half of Britain's single mothers need Family Income Supplement.* **1.2** you must have it if you are going to do a job, solve a problem, or achieve a particular result successfully. EG *You don't need a degree in mathematics to run a computer... The party has been unable to attract the funds needed for an election deposit... You'll need a minimum deposit of £20,000... There's no doubt that you need glasses.*
1.3 you want it very much because you think you would benefit from it. EG *Nature, the simple life, that's what I need desperately... If you need any help, just give me a ring... That is what we need so badly: a real professional theatre.* **1.4** you want it because you do not already own one or because the one you have is broken; used especially of things which are considered to be useful and not just luxuries. EG *Do you need a new telephone?*
1.1 V+O/*to*-INF ⇑ require; 1.2 V+O/*to*-INF = require; 1.3 V+O/*to*-INF = could do with; 1.4 V+O/*to*-INF

2 If you **need** to do something, you must do it, for example because it is an essential part of a process or development. EG *Before we answer this question, we need to look briefly at the world environment... A number of points need to be made about this.*
V+*to*-INF = have to

3 If you say that nothing **need** be done, or that nobody **need** do anything, you mean that there is no good reason why a particular thing should happen or a particular state of affairs come into existence. EG *No one need ever know that Dolly committed murder... Nothing need be said about it.*
SEMI-MODAL : WITH BROAD NEG

4 If you tell someone that they **need not** do something, you are telling them or advising them that there is no good reason why they should do it. EG *You needn't worry... You really needn't be scared.*
SEMI-MODAL : WITH BROAD NEG = don't have to

5 If you say that something **need not** happen, you mean that it might happen but that it is not necessary that it will happen. EG *Such tax cuts need not be inflationary... It needn't cost very much... There need be no real barrier between arts and science... It need not be so.*
SEMI-MODAL : WITH BROAD NEG

6 If you say that something that has happened **need not have** happened, you mean that it was not really necessary and could have been avoided. EG *I need not have worried... A lot of people died of physical diseases that need not have proved fatal... Nell needn't have worked... This had made things even more difficult than they need have been.*
SEMI-MODAL : WITH BROAD NEG +PAST PART

7 If you say that something **needs** a particular action or that an action **needs** doing, you mean that this action will benefit or improve a situation. EG *...the shed needs a good clean out... Keep a list of all the jobs that need doing... The top rim needs to be cut off.*
V+O/-ING/*to*-INF = want, could do with

8 If you say **'Who needs** a particular thing?', you are suggesting that this thing is unnecessary and not useful. EG *Who needs great pictures?*
PHR+NG : USED AS CONVENTION

9 If you say that we **need** something, or that something **is needed**, you mean that a particular action
V+O = require

would serve a useful purpose, although you may not intend to do that action yourself. EG *We need firmer rules about exact working hours... We need fewer prisoners in better prisons... We need more European co-operation... ...careful irrigation control is needed.*

10 If you tell someone that they **need** to do something or to have something, you mean that it is necessary or a good idea for them to do it or to have it; often used when you are giving advice. EG *You might need to visit a specialist... At this point you may need to get a lawyer and an accountant.* V+to-INF = have to

11 A **need** is 11.1 something that you must have in order to live and be healthy. EG *He had not even been able to satisfy her simple needs... The poor man is even less able to meet his needs and sinks further into debt... Never let your wants outstrip your needs.* N COUNT: USU POSS+N ⇑ essential = requirement

11.2 a strong feeling that you want something or want to do something, because you feel that you would benefit from it or that it would help you in some way. EG *I began to feel the need of somewhere to retreat... They do not touch each other, having no need... She felt no need to speak.* N SING WITH DET: IF+PREP THEN of/for, OR +to-INF ⇑ desire = necessity

11.3 something which is required in order to do a job, solve a problem, or achieve a particular result. EG *These groups are obviously answering a need... Their need for money is rising fast... Harris saw the need to organize his air forces... The programme starts with the needs of students at college level.* N COUNT: IF+PREP THEN of/for, OR+to-INF ⇑ requirement

12 **Need** is a situation in which people do not have enough to eat or enough money to live; an old-fashioned use. EG *She imagined a new world in which the problem of need had been solved... He sent her monthly cheques when she was seventy and in need.* N UNCOUNT: USU in+N = poverty ≠ plenty

13 You use the expression **if need be** or **if needs be** to say that an action mentioned will be carried out if it is considered to be necessary. EG *She said she would stay with me for months and years if need be... It is ready to guide the torpedo if need be.* PHR: USED AS AN A = if necessary

14 **in need of.** 14.1 If you are **in need of** something, you feel strongly that you want it, because you would benefit from it or because it would help you in some way. EG *She was in need of something stronger than ginger ale... I am badly in need of advice.* PREP = could use

14.2 If you say that someone or something is **in need of** attention, help, or change, you mean that it is necessary to give them something or do something to them. EG *The hospital was badly in need of decorating and refurnishing... The Shops Act is in need of revision... ...children in need of help.* PREP = in want of

15 **no need.** 15.1 If you **have no need of** something, you are able to continue your normal activities easily without it. EG *The country had no need of Western weapons.* PHR: VB INFLECTS = can do without

15.2 If you say that **there is no need** to do a particular thing, or behave in a particular way, you are telling someone that you disapprove of what they are doing or saying or the way in which they are behaving. EG *There's no need to get so worked up about it... All right, no need to rub it in.* PHR+to-INF/for ⇑ don't

15.3 If you say that there is **no need** for a particular action or that there is **no need** to do it, you mean that the action is not necessary because the situation you are in will still be satisfactory if it is not done. EG *'I'll wipe the dishes.'–'There's no need.'... He really had no need to work at all... 'I'll bring them up.'–'No need; one of my men will be waiting below.'* PHR: USED AS C, IF+PREP THEN for, OR to-INF

16 You use **without the need** to say that something can happen without a particular action being necessary. EG *His replacement takes over without the need for a by-election... An attack could be made without the need for reinforcement.* PHR+for/to-INF

17 You use expressions such as **I need hardly say** and **need I say** to suggest that what you are going to say is obvious and that the person or people listening to you will probably already know it. EG *Of course I need hardly say that this money would have been better spent on other things... I need hardly tell you what a delight it would be... Such a situation, need I say, could have been avoided.* PHR: USED AS ADV SEN ⇑ obviously

> **NEED** □ In this dictionary **need** is described as a SEMI-MODAL in the grammar notes beside paragraphs 3, 4, 5, and 6 of the entry for **need** because it can be used like the modals when it occurs with a negative. See □ at MODAL and at BROAD NEG. This box only concerns 'need' as a semi-modal. See the rest of the entry for other uses. **Need** as a semi-modal behaves in the following ways: 1 It is followed by an infinitive without *to.* EG *You needn't worry... We need not grudge them their mindless pleasures.* 2 It does not inflect. EG *He need not do anything.* 3 It is normally used with a negative such as *not* or *never* following it. EG *It need not cost very much... You need never worry about money.* It can be joined with the shortened form of the negative *-n't.* EG *I needn't say any more.* 4 *Need not* and *needn't* can be used without an infinitive after them, to refer back to a previous verbal group. EG *'I'll tell you as much as I know.'–'You needn't. I'm not asking you to.'* 5 In rather old-fashioned English, *need* can be used before the subject to form questions. EG *Need I say more?*

needful /niːdfʊl/ means necessary; an old-fashioned word. EG *...to provide the food, clothing, and shelter needful for the maintenance of health.* ADJ QUALIT

needle /niːdəˡl/, **needles, needling, needled.** 1 A **needle** is 1.1 a small, very thin piece of polished metal which is used for sewing. It has a sharp point at one end and a hole in the other end for a thread to go through. EG *I can't even thread a needle... Then we get a needle and cotton and sew up the hole.* N COUNT ⇑ tool

1.2 a thin stick that is used for knitting. It is usually made of plastic or metal and has a point at one end. EG *...a roomful of old ladies knitting away with steel needles.* N COUNT = knitting needle

1.3 a thin hollow metal rod with a sharp point, forming part of a syringe, which is used to inject a medicine or drug into someone's body. EG *It is injected like serum from a hypodermic needle.* N COUNT

1.4 a long thin metal rod with a point which a doctor who does acupuncture sticks into a patient's body. EG *She went to a man who stuck needles all over her and cured her instantly.* N COUNT

1.5 the small pointed instrument on a record player that touches the record and picks up the sound signals. EG *The needle jumped and scratched the record.* N COUNT = stylus

1.6 the long thin piece of metal or plastic on the dial of an instrument that can move backwards and forwards, giving information about measurements. EG *The speedometer needle swings back and forth.* N COUNT ⇑ indicator

1.7 one of the thin, hard, pointed leaves that grow on pine trees and other plants. EG *There was nothing on the ground except a thick layer of pine needles.* ● a **needle in a haystack**: see **haystack**. ● See also **pins and needles.** N COUNT

2 If someone **needles** you, they annoy you continually, especially by criticizing you; an informal use. EG *She was needling me about Doris... Alexander was needled by her manner.* V OR V+O: USU V +O = niggle

needless /niːdlɪ²s/. 1 Something that is **needless** is completely unnecessary. EG *The result was needless slaughter... It was a needless risk to run.* ◇ **needlessly.** EG *This may upset a mother needlessly.* ADJ CLASSIF = uncalled-for ◇ ADV

2 You say **needless to say** when you want to emphasize that what you are going to say is obvious and that the person or people listening to you will probably know it already. EG *Needless to say, there were reprisals for our actions... This new social awareness will, needless to say, bring big changes.* PHR: USED AS ADV SEN = of course

needlewoman /niːdəˡlwʊˡməˡn/, **needlewomen.** A **needlewoman** is a woman who does a lot of sewing, especially one who does it well; a rather old-fashioned word. EG *She was a clever needlewoman.* N COUNT = seamstress

needlework /niːdəˡlwɜːk/ is sewing or embroidery that is done by hand. EG *...the basket in which she kept her needlework.* ▸ used of the activity of sewing or embroidering. EG *Often such girls spend much time doing needlework.* N UNCOUNT

needn't /niːdəˡnt/ is the usual spoken form of 'need not'.

needy /niːdiˡ/, **needier, neediest.** Someone who is **needy** is very poor and does not have enough food or clothing or good enough housing to live healthily. EG *It is an organisation helping needy old people throughout the world... They are among the neediest children in Britain today.* ADJ QUALIT = poverty-stricken

nefarious /nɪ²fɛəriˡəs/. Something that is **nefarious** is wicked and immoral; a literary word. EG *...a nefarious system erected to exploit people.* ADJ QUALIT = despicable

> **NEG** □ In this dictionary NEG is used in the grammar notes beside entries to mean 'negative'. See □ at ADV BRD NEG and BROAD NEG. NEG is also used in the following ways. 1 It is used in the grammar notes for words such as *never, nobody,* and *nothing* to indicate that the word makes the clause in which it occurs negative. An example is **nobody**, which is described in the grammar notes as PRON INDEF: SING,NEG. EG *There was **nobody** in the room... **Nobody** cooks as well as she does.* No other negative word is used in the same clause. You do not say 'There wasn't nobody in

the room'. NEG is used in the grammar notes beside the word *not* to indicate its negative effect upon the verb that it is being used with.

neg. is a written abbreviation for 'negative'.

negate /nɪ²geɪt/, **negates, negating, negated**; a fairly formal word. If someone or something **negates** something, 1 they cause it to become wasted or valueless when it was previously useful or worthwhile. EG *The denial of the importance of someone negates all our efforts on their behalf... The decline of community life is negating the work of the State welfare services.* 2 they say that it does not exist. EG *Such reasoning seems to negate the distinctions inherent in logic.* — V+O; ⇑ counteract; = nullify, undo; V+O; ⇑ deny; = repudiate

negation /nɪ²geɪʃəⁿn/; a fairly formal word. 1 **Negation** is 1.1 a person's disagreement with someone or refusal of something. EG *The office shook with the impresario's negation of whatever was under discussion.* 1.2 the act of saying that something does not exist. EG *...the negation by the State authority of the rights of its citizens.* — N UNCOUNT; = contradiction; N UNCOUNT; = denial

2 The **negation** of a quality or ideal is its complete opposite or its complete absence. EG *The very possibility of divorce is the negation of Christian marriage... ...the very negation of the spirit of kindness.* — N SING WITH DET : USU+*of*

negative /nɛgətɪv/, **negatives**. 1 **Negative** is used to describe something that gives or suggests the answer 'no'. EG *We expected to receive a negative answer.* ◊ **negatively**. EG *The public responded negatively.* — ADJ CLASSIF; ≠ affirmative, positive; ◊ ADV WITH VB; ≠ positively

2 A **negative** is a word, expression, gesture, etc that means or suggests the meaning 'no,' 'not,' etc. See □ at BROAD NEG. — N COUNT; ≠ affirmative

3 **in the negative**. 3.1 If an answer is **in the negative**, it is 'no'. EG *This question had long since been answered in the negative.* 3.2 If a sentence is **in the negative**, it contains a word such as 'no', 'not', or 'never'. EG *'I went' in the negative is 'I did not go'.* — PHR : USED AS AN A; PHR : USED AS AN A

4 If someone is **negative** or if they have a **negative** attitude, they consider only the disadvantages and bad aspects of a situation, rather than the advantages and good aspects. EG *No one else I met ever had such a negative view of Alice Springs... He was especially negative about my written work... That's a slightly negative way of looking at the problem.* ◊ **negatively**. EG *Why do you always look at things so negatively?* — ADJ QUALIT; ≠ constructive, positive; ◊ ADV WITH VB

5 A feeling or experience that is **negative** is harmful or unpleasant in some way. EG *There are normal negative feelings connected with a pregnancy... Do you see prison as being a wholly negative experience?* ◊ **negatively**. EG *...affecting their behaviour negatively.* — ADJ QUALIT; ⇑ bad; ≠ positive; ◊ ADV WITH VB; = adversely

6 If a medical or other scientific test is **negative**, it shows no evidence of the medical condition or substance that you are looking for. EG *...a negative pregnancy test.* — ADJ CLASSIF

7 A **negative** is also the photographic image that is first produced when you use a camera, and which the final photograph is developed from. The negative of a black and white photograph is dark in the places where the photograph is light, and light where the photograph is dark. EG *...making prints from negatives.* — N COUNT

8 **Negative** also means having the same electrical charge as an electron; a technical term in physics. EG *Electrons are negative... ...a negative charge.* — ADJ CLASSIF; ADV WITH VB

9 A number, quantity, or measurement that is **negative** is less than zero. — ADJ CLASSIF; = minus

neglect /nɪ²glɛkt/, **neglects, neglecting, neglected**. 1 If you **neglect** someone or something, 1.1 you fail to look after them properly. EG *...the peasant farmer who mistreats the soil or neglects his crops.* ◊ **neglected**. EG *The child looked neglected, scruffy and unloved... ...dusty exhibits in a neglected provincial museum.* 1.2 you fail to give them the degree of attention, recognition, or consideration that they deserve. EG *...George Stubbs, so long neglected as being a mere horse-painter... I think we neglect the emotions in this area.* ◊ **neglected**. EG *...Bernard Shaw's neglected one-act comedy, 'A Village Wooing'.* — V+O; ◊ ADJ QUALIT; = uncared-for; V+O; ⇑ ignore; = overlook; ◊ ADJ QUALIT : ATTRIB

2 If you **neglect** to do something that you ought to do, you fail to do it. EG *I neglected to bring a gift... ...neglecting to exercise due care and control... I feel I'm neglecting my duty.* — V+O/*to*-INF

3 **Neglect** is 3.1 failure to look after someone or something properly. EG *It was the mother's neglect of her infant that caused its death... The government has been criticized because of its neglect of working class areas.* 3.2 the condition of not being looked after properly. EG *...estates suffering from vandalism and neglect... The area has still not recovered from more than a decade of neglect.* — N UNCOUNT; N UNCOUNT; ≠ attention

neglectful /nɪ²glɛktful/; a formal word. Someone who is **neglectful** 1 fails to look after someone or something properly. EG *...a neglectful father.* 2 fails to do something or give attention to something that they ought to do or consider. EG *...neglectful of his duties... The hospital had been neglectful.* — ADJ QUALIT; ADJ QUALIT : IF+ PREP THEN *of*; = careless

negligee /nɛglɪʒeɪ/, **negligees**; also spelled **négligée**. A **negligee** is a woman's dressing gown which is made of a very thin fabric, often with a lace pattern on it. EG *...a black silk negligee.* — N COUNT; ⇑ garment

negligence /nɛglɪdʒəns/ is failure to do something which you ought to do, or failure to show proper care and concern for something that you are responsible for. EG *The chairman of the Party had been dismissed for negligence... The authorities' negligence toward the prisoners' health was most disturbing... The accident was caused by the negligence of the other motorist.* — N UNCOUNT; = carelessness

negligent /nɛglɪdʒənt/. 1 Someone who is **negligent** fails to deal with something or someone with the right amount of care or concern, or fails to do something which they ought to do. EG *The committee heard that he had been negligent in his duty... They were not negligent of Alexandra.* ◊ **negligently**. EG *They may act foolishly or negligently.* — ADJ QUALIT : PRED; ⇑ careless; = neglectful; ◊ ADV WITH VB; ⇑ carelessly

2 If someone's way of behaving or way of dressing is **negligent**, it is informal and relaxed. EG *The hat was extremely becoming to him, as was the negligent air with which he wore it.* ◊ **negligently**. EG *...leaning negligently against the table.* — ADJ QUALIT; = nonchalant, casual; ◊ ADV WITH VB; = casually

negligible /nɛglɪdʒəbəⁿl/. Something that is **negligible** is so small or unimportant that it is not worth considering or worrying about. EG *The cost in human life had been negligible.... He predicted that this would have a negligible effect on the temperature.* — ADJ CLASSIF; = insignificant

negotiable /nɪ²gəʊʃəbəⁿl/. 1 Something that is **negotiable** can be changed or agreed by means of discussion. EG *The price is negotiable.* — ADJ CLASSIF; ≠ fixed

2 Contracts or assets that are **negotiable** can be transferred to another person in exchange for money. EG *The land was divided up into small private plots with negotiable freehold titles... There was a lot of money involved, not in hard cash but in negotiable securities.* — ADJ CLASSIF; ⇑ transferable

3 An area of land that is **negotiable** is easy to cross or travel through. EG *It was to provide a negotiable way through this landscape that the highway was built.* — ADJ QUALIT

negotiate /nɪ²gəʊʃieɪt/, **negotiates, negotiating, negotiated**. 1 If you **negotiate** something or **negotiate** for something, you have discussions with people who have different interests from you, especially in business, politics, or international affairs, in order to come to an agreement, solve problems, or make plans or arrangements. EG *He succeeded in negotiating British entry into the European Community... Paul will graduate as a chemical engineer and is already negotiating for a job worth £18,000... In 1967 he negotiated a technology and trade agreement with several African countries... The National Council negotiates directly with the British Gas Corporation.* — V OR V+O : IF+ PREP THEN USU *with/for*; ⇑ discuss

2 If you **negotiate** something such as a difficult area of land, you successfully travel over it or around it. EG *Taxi-drivers refused to negotiate the knee-deep potholes of the roads around the station.* — V+O

negotiating table. If you say that people are at the **negotiating table**, you mean that they are having serious discussions about something on which they disagree, and that they are trying to reach an agreement. EG *The Russians and the Americans have come to the negotiating table.* — N SING WITH DET

negotiation /nɪ²gəʊʃieɪʃəⁿn/, **negotiations**. **Negotiations** are discussions that take place between people who have different interests, especially in business, politics, or international affairs, in order for them to be able to come to an agreement about something, solve a problem, or make arrangements. EG *The early stages of their negotiations with the Government were unsuccessful... Negotiations are* — N COUNT : USU PL; ⇑ talk *not expected to resume until early next year... ...tax negotiations.* ▸ used as an uncount noun. EG *We need to allow more time for negotiation... The settlement was achieved by peaceful negotiation.* ▸ N UNCOUNT = bargaining

negotiator /nɪ²gəʊʃɪeɪtə/, **negotiators**. A **negotiator** is a person who takes part in negotiations in business, politics, or international affairs. EG *American negotiators adopted a low profile at last week's economics conference... I think our negotiators must expect a rather tough time in the next few weeks.* N COUNT ↑ representative

Negress /niːgrɪ²s/, **Negresses**. A **Negress** is a woman with black skin who comes from Africa or whose ancestors came from Africa; an old-fashioned word that some people find offensive. N COUNT

Negro /niːgrəʊ/, **Negroes**. A **Negro** is someone with black skin who comes from Africa or whose ancestors came from Africa; a fairly old-fashioned word that some people find offensive. EG *There were two Negro boys sitting behind me on the bus... ...American Negroes.* N COUNT

Negroid /niːgrɔɪd/. **Negroid** features are the physical features that black people from Africa have. ADJ CLASSIF

neigh /neɪ/, **neighs, neighing, neighed**. When a horse **neighs**, it utters a loud sound. EG *It galloped away, neighing.* ▸ used as a noun. EG *The horse gave a loud neigh.* V = whinny ▸ N COUNT = whinny

neighbour /neɪbə/, **neighbours**; also spelled **neighbor** in American English. 1 A **neighbour** is 1.1 someone who lives near you. EG *...your next-door neighbour... The children of many of their friends and neighbors have ended up in prison... Don't be afraid of what the neighbours will think.* N COUNT ↑ person 1.2 someone who is standing or sitting next to you or something which is next to something else of the same kind. EG *Rudolph turned his head slightly towards his neighbour... ...each shop striving to outdo its neighbour... The young plant risks being overshadowed by its neighbours.* N COUNT : WITH POSS

2 The **neighbour** of a country, county, state, etc is another country, county, state, etc that is next to it. EG *...bitter battles between Angola and her neighbours... ...the wishes and expectations of our French neighbours.* N COUNT : WITH POSS

3 Your **neighbour** is a person who you have dealings with; an old-fashioned use. EG *...the duty we owe to our neighbour... Love your neighbour as yourself.* N COUNT : WITH POSS

neighbourhood /neɪbəhʊd/, **neighbourhoods**; also spelled **neighborhood** in American English. 1 A **neighbourhood** is one of the parts of a town where people live. EG *...a very wealthy neighbourhood... She'd just moved into the neighbourhood from Connecticut... ...neighbourhood nursery schools.* N COUNT ↑ district ● A **friendly neighbourhood** institution or person is one that is situated or lives near you and is willing to help you; a humorous usage. EG *If you get lost, just ask your friendly neighbourhood policeman for directions.* ● PHR + NG ↑ local

2 The **neighbourhood** of a place or person is the area or the people around them. EG *We were heading for a destination in the neighbourhood of the Lofoten Islands... He tries to pin the fault on someone in his immediate neighbourhood.* N SING WITH DET : USU *the*+N = vicinity

3 **In the neighbourhood of** means approximately; used when you want to mention the price, size, etc of something but do not know exactly what it is. EG *He paid in the neighbourhood of £7000 for that car.* PREP = roughly

neighbouring /neɪbəᵒrɪŋ/; also spelled **neighboring** in American English. **Neighbouring** is used to describe something that is nearby or near something else. EG *Whole families came from neighbouring villages to look at her... The lock to the door of the neighbouring coach was shattered.* ADJ CLASSIF : ATTRIB

neighbourly /neɪbəli¹/; also spelled **neighborly** in American English. If someone who lives near you is **neighbourly**, they are kind, friendly, and helpful. EG *People were more neighbourly then.* ▸ used of people's actions. EG *That's a neighbourly thing to do... ...a sort of neighbourly friendliness.* ADJ QUALIT = hospitable, considerate

neither /naɪðə, niːðə/. 1 You use **neither** 1.1 in front of the first of two or more alternatives, when you are emphasizing that none of the alternatives mentioned is true, possible, or likely to happen. The other alternatives are introduced by 'nor'. EG *He spoke neither English nor French... Neither Margaret nor John was there... She neither drinks, smokes, nor eats meat.* CONJ COORD : NEG, *neither...nor* ↑ not 1.2 to refer to each of two things, people, situations, etc when you are making a negative statement that includes both of them. EG *Neither of us was having any luck... Neither was suffering pain... 'Does that mean yes or no?'–'Neither.'* PRON SING : NEG, ALSO+*of* ▸ used as a determiner. EG *They may end up being happy in neither situation.* ▸ DET+N COUNT IN SING : NEG 1.3 after a negative statement to introduce a clause and to say that the previous statement is also true of the person or thing that you are about to mention. EG *'I don't normally drink at lunch.'–'Neither do I.'... I was not happy and neither were they.* ADV : NEG = nor 1.4 after a negative statement to introduce another negative statement which contrasts with or adds information to the previous one; a fairly formal use. EG *I do not wish to be rude to you but neither do I wish to be rude to the others... She hadn't seen Guppy for weeks, neither had he telephoned.* ADV : NEG = nor

2 If you say that something is **neither here nor there**, you mean that it does not matter, because it is not relevant to what you are discussing. EG *This may be neither here nor there but I have to say it.* PHR : USED AS C ↑ irrelevant

nemesis /nemɪsɪs/. The **nemesis** of something such as a society is a disastrous period in its history that seems to you to be a just punishment for something that is wrong or immoral about it. EG *Every civilization seems to have its nemesis.* N SING WITH DET ↑ retribution

neo- is added to nouns and adjectives that refer to past ideologies, artistic styles, etc, in order to form other nouns and adjectives that refer to modern forms of these ideologies or styles. Words created in this way are usually spelled with a hyphen, but sometimes as one word. EG *...imperialism→neo-imperialism... ...expressionist→neo-expressionist... ...Freudian→neo-Freudian.* PREFIX

neoclassical /niːəʊklæsɪkəᵒl/. **Neoclassical** architecture or art dates from the late 18th century and uses designs, motifs, etc drawn from Roman and Greek architecture and art. ADJ CLASSIF

neo-colonialism is economic control or political influence that one country has over another country that is in theory independent, especially by having control of its businesses or financial institutions. N UNCOUNT

neolithic /niːəlɪθɪk/ is used to describe things relating to the period of prehistory when people had started farming but still used stone for their weapons and tools. The period lasted from 9000 to 6000 B.C. in south-west Asia and 4000 to 2400 B.C. in Europe. EG *...in neolithic times... ...neolithic weapons.* ADJ CLASSIF ↑ stone age

neologism /niːɒlədʒɪzəᵒm/, **neologisms**. A **neologism** is a new word or expression in a language, or a familiar word or expression that is now being used with a new meaning; a formal word. EG *I refuse to use the hideous neologism 'nicemanship'.* N COUNT

neon /niːɒn/. 1 **Neon** is a gas which occurs in very small amounts in the atmosphere. It is used in glass tubes for lights and illuminated signs. N UNCOUNT ↑ gas

2 **Neon** is used to refer to places, signs, etc that are lit by neon lights. EG *...neon signs... ...a tacky neon city.* N UNCOUNT : USU BEFORE N

neon light, neon lights. A **neon light** is a bright electric light that consists of a glass tube filled with the gas neon. Neon lights are sometimes bent into shapes or letters to form signs. EG *The front of the buildings glittered with bright neon lights.* N COUNT/ UNCOUNT

neophyte /niːəʊfaɪt/, **neophytes**. A **neophyte** is someone who is new to a particular activity; a formal or literary word. EG *America was a neophyte on the world stage... ...a political neophyte.* N COUNT ↑ newcomer = novice

nephew /nevjuː, nef-/, **nephews**. Someone's **nephew** is the son of their sister or brother. N COUNT ↑ relation

nepotism /nepətɪzəᵒm/ is the action of someone who has power or authority using their authority to get jobs for members of their family. EG *...the nepotism and corruption of their civil service.* N UNCOUNT ↑ favouritism

nerve /nɜːv/, **nerves, nerving, nerved**. 1 A **nerve** is a long, thin thread-like fibre in your body that transmits messages and feelings between your brain and other parts of your body. EG *This terrible disease causes physical atrophy of the optic nerves... ...a simple network of nerve fibres.* N COUNT

2 If you refer to someone's **nerves**, 2.1 you are referring to their ability or inability to cope successfully with emotional stress, tension, danger, etc. EG *Hoping to calm our nerves, we decided to spend the afternoon at the lake... Your nerves will not stand much more of this... Her authority was based on inner calm and strong nerves.* N PLURAL 2.2 you are referring to nervous, anxious, or tense feelings that they have, N PLURAL ↑ anxiety

especially because they are afraid or worried. EG *All during the lunch hour he had been in a state of nerves.*

3 Nerve is the courage and determination that you need in order to be able to do or complete a particular thing, especially in a difficult or dangerous situation. EG *Nobody in Rothermere's entourage had the nerve to remind him that he was several hours late already.... Finally she got up enough nerve to ask me to explain what communism was... His nerve, understandably, began to crack.* N UNCOUNT ↑ bravery

4 If you **nerve** yourself to do something difficult or frightening, you make yourself feel brave enough to do it. EG *At last the government nerved itself to work out a new policy.* V+O (REFL)+ *to*-INF, OR V+O (REFL) : IF+PREP THEN *for*

5 The word **nerve** is also used in the following expressions. **5.1** If you say that someone **strains every nerve** to do something, you mean that they use as much effort as they can in order to succeed in doing it. EG *They would strain every nerve to entertain him.* PHR : VB INFLECTS, IF+VB THEN *to*-INF ↑ try **5.2** If you say that you have **touched a raw nerve**, you mean that you have upset someone by being insensitive to something that they care about or feel strongly about. EG *I think I touched a raw nerve when I mentioned last night's meeting.* PHR : VB INFLECTS **5.3** If someone or something **gets on** your **nerves**, they annoy or irritate you very much; an informal expression. EG *He got on my nerves tonight with his damned fishing stories.* PHR : VB INFLECTS **5.4** If someone **is living on** their **nerves**, they are continually worried and anxious about the circumstances that they are in. EG *I was living on my nerves at the time, expecting at any moment to be arrested.* PHR : VB INFLECTS ↑ worry **5.5** If you **lose** your **nerve**, you suddenly panic and become afraid about something that you are doing. EG *The men inside the building lost their nerve and opened fire on the crowd.* PHR : VB INFLECTS = go to pieces **5.6** When you say that someone **had a nerve** or **had the nerve** to do something, you mean that they have angered or shocked you by doing something rude or disrespectful; an informal expression. EG *He had the nerve to say Fleet Street was corrupting me.* N SING WITH DET : USU+*to*-INF = cheek, effrontery

nerve centre, nerve centres. The **nerve centre** of an organization is the place from where the activities of the organization are controlled and where the leaders of the organization meet. EG *This office is the union's nerve centre.* N COUNT

nerve gas, nerve gases. Nerve gas is a poisonous gas that is used in war to paralyse people and even kill them. N MASS

nerveless /nɜːvlɪ²s/. **1 Nerveless** fingers and hands are numb and do not have any strength because of cold, fear, tiredness, etc. EG *Plate after plate dropped from his nerveless fingers and smashed on the tiles.* ADJ QUALIT : ATTRIB ↑ weak

2 Someone who is **nerveless** is extremely brave and shows no fear at all. EG *A few men, nerveless and cool, slept soundly.* ADJ QUALIT ↑ courageous

nerve-racking; also spelled **nerve-wracking**. Something that is **nerve-racking** makes you feel very tense and worried. EG *It was a nerve-racking and soul-searching period for us all.* ADJ QUALIT = harrowing

nervous /nɜːvəs/. **1** Someone who is **nervous** is worried and frightened, and shows this in their behaviour. EG *Both actors were exceedingly nervous on the day of the performance.* ADJ QUALIT ↑ anxious = jittery, tense ◇ **nervously.** EG *He laughed nervously and asked me what I meant.* ◇ ADV = uneasily ◇ **nervousness.** EG *'Pa,' Rudolph began, trying to conquer his nervousness.* ◇ N UNCOUNT = agitation

2 A **nervous** person is very tense, sensitive, and easily upset. EG *These pills will help you to control your nervous disposition... Sam's a nervous child.* ADJ QUALIT : ATTRIB

3 If you are **nervous** about something, you feel slightly afraid of it and worried about it. EG *People are so nervous about believing anything to be right... He's nervous of thieves in that little shop of his.* ADJ QUALIT : PRED+*about/of* ↑ apprehensive ◇ **nervousness.** EG *There was nervousness even in the White House at what might happen.* ◇ N UNCOUNT ↑ anxiety

4 A **nervous** illness or condition is one that affects your emotions and your mental state. EG *But she had suffered a lot of nervous strain and shock and general worry... He retired to his sick-bed in a state of nervous exhaustion.* ADJ CLASSIF : ATTRIB

nervous breakdown, nervous breakdowns. A **nervous breakdown** is an illness in which someone suffers from deep depression, worry, and tiredness, and so has psychiatric treatment; a term used by ordinary people and not a technical term. EG *I thought of a young boy I knew who had had a nervous breakdown... You'll give yourself a nervous breakdown going on working like this.* N COUNT

nervous system, nervous systems. Your **nervous system** is all the nerves in your body together with your brain and spinal cord, which control your movement and reflexes as well as your thoughts and feelings. N COUNT

nervous wreck, nervous wrecks. If you say that someone is a **nervous wreck**, you mean that they are extremely nervous or worried about something; an informal expression. EG *I waited so long that by the time my turn came I was a nervous wreck.* N COUNT : USU AS C

nervy /nɜːvi¹/. Someone who is **nervy** tends to be very tense, anxious, and easily upset. EG *She never recovered from it, and she was very nervy afterwards.* ADJ QUALIT ↑ nervous

-ness is added to adjectives to form nouns which often refer to a state or quality. For example 'sadness' is the state of being sad and 'kindness' is the quality of being kind. Uncountable nouns such as these are not always defined in this dictionary but are often included in the entry for the adjective. EG *...frank→frankness... ...happy→happiness... ...watchful→watchfulness... ...weak→weakness.* SUFFIX : FORMS N UNCOUNTS

nest /nest/, **nests, nesting, nested. 1** A **nest** is **1.1** a place made by a bird to lay its eggs in, using twigs, leaves, moss, mud, etc. EG *Did you see how many eggs there were in that nest?* ● to **feather** your **nest**: see **feather**. N COUNT **1.2** the place that groups of insects or other animals make in which to live and to give birth to their young. EG *We had a wasp's nest in the roof... There was a nest of field mice in the back of the car.* N COUNT **1.3** a comfortable home or place to stay in. EG *...a really cosy nest... He converted the room into a love nest.* N COUNT **1.4** a set of objects that fit into or inside each other. EG *...a nest of tables.* N COUNT/PART+ N IN PL

2 When a bird **nests** somewhere, it builds a nest and settles there to lay its eggs. EG *Hornbills nest in holes in trees... Some terns nest well north of the Arctic Circle.* V : USU+A ◇ **nesting.** EG *They each have their favoured nesting sites... ...a nesting box.* ◇ ADJ CLASSIF : ATTRIB

nest egg, nest eggs; also spelled with a hyphen. A **nest egg** is a sum of money that you are saving for some purpose; an informal expression. EG *They squandered their little nest-egg.* N COUNT = savings

nestle /nesəºl/, **nestles, nestling, nestled. 1** If you **nestle** somewhere, you move into a comfortable position, especially by pressing against someone or something soft. EG *They nestled together on the sofa.* V+A : ALSO V+O +A = snuggle

2 If something **nestles** somewhere, it is in that place or position and seems safe or sheltered. EG *The house was detached but had other houses nestling against it on both sides.* V+A

nestling /nestºlɪŋ/, **nestlings.** A **nestling** is a young bird that has not yet learnt to fly. EG *...the male passes food to his mate and nestlings.* N COUNT = fledgling

net /net/, **nets, netting, netted**; also spelled **nett** in British English for paragraphs 8, 9, and 10. **1 Net** is a kind of cloth made of very fine cotton or nylon threads that are woven together so that there are small equal spaces between them and you can see through the cloth. EG *The bride wore a veil of white net... All the windows have net curtains.* ● See also **netting**. N UNCOUNT ↑ fabric

2 A **net** is **2.1** a piece of netting which is used, for example, to protect vegetables or fruit from birds or insects. EG *You'd better put a net over your strawberries to keep the birds off.* N COUNT ↑ cover **2.2** a container or bag made from netting and used, for example, to hold shopping or to keep something in place. N COUNT **2.3** a bag made from a piece of netting, sometimes one on the end of a pole, which is used for catching animals, especially fish or butterflies. EG *It was only when he had the trout in the net that he looked up... ...a butterfly net.* N COUNT ↑ trap **2.4** the piece of netting across the centre of a tennis court, badminton court, etc which the ball should go over. EG *Often she would hit an easy one into the net... The net was up and the daily volleyball game was in progress.* N COUNT ↑ barrier **2.5** a framework with netting over it, attached to the back of the goal on a football pitch or a hockey pitch. EG *He slammed the ball into the back of the net.* N COUNT ↑ structure **2.6** something such as a system that is considered to be controlling or affecting a lot of people or things in some way. EG *The redistribution of national wealth requires that* N COUNT = web *no one should escape the net... All sorts of strange characters are caught within the net.* • See also **hairnet, safety net.**

3 If someone **slips through the net**, they escape from something, such as a system or a trap, that was meant to catch them or deal with them. EG *The police are determined not to let him slip through the net a second time.* PHR : VB INFLECTS = get away

4 If you **cast** your **net wider**, you consider or try a greater variety of things. EG *We must cast our net wider and observe this incident in a broader social context.* PHR : VB AND N INFLECT

5 If you **net** a fish or other animal, you catch it in a net. EG *At last he managed to net the fish.* V+O = land

6 If you **net** something, you manage to get it, especially by using skill. EG *They like revealing how clever they have been in netting what others could not get... He was netting his third and largest fortune.* V+O = acquire

7 If you **net** a particular amount of money, you gain it as profit when all expenses have been paid. EG *The plastics began netting £1 billion a year for the company.* V+O, V+O+O, OR V+O+A *(for)* = bring in

8 A **net** profit or loss is one which remains when everything that should be subtracted from it has been subtracted. EG *That gave him a net profit of just over 23%... Last year he made a profit of £20,000 net.* ADJ CLASSIF : ATTRIB, OR AFTER N ⇑ actual = clear

9 The **net** weight of something is its weight without its container or wrapping. EG *The net weight is 250g... It weighs 250 g net.* ADJ CLASSIF : ATTRIB, OR AFTER N ⇑ actual

10 A **net** result is one that is final, when everything that is necessary has been considered or included. EG *The net effect of these changes is that the diesel car is becoming more attractive... The net result is a massive and growing labour surplus.* ADJ CLASSIF : ATTRIB

netball /nɛtbɔ:l/ is a game played by two teams of seven players, usually women. Each team tries to score goals by throwing a ball through a net which is on a hoop at the top of a pole at each end of the court. N UNCOUNT ⇑ sport

nether /nɛðə/ is used to describe the lower part of a thing or place; an old-fashioned word. EG *Her parents retreated gracefully into the nether regions of the house.* ADJ CLASSIF : ATTRIB ⇑ bottom

nett /nɛt/. See **net**.

netting /nɛtɪŋ/ is a fabric or material made of pieces of thread or string, or metal wires, that are woven or knotted together so that there are equal spaces between them. EG *The dog scratched impatiently at the netting... With a curse he disentangled his head from the netting.* N UNCOUNT = net

nettle /nɛtə⁰l/, **nettles**. **1** A **nettle** is a wild plant with spiky leaves covered with little hairs, usually ones that sting. EG *I pushed her in the nettles... ...fields covered with stinging nettles.* N COUNT ⇑ weed

2 If you **grasp the nettle**, you deal with a problem or do something that is unpleasant quickly and in a determined way. EG *I think we've got to grasp this nettle and find a solution.* PHR : VB INFLECTS ⇑ act

nettled /nɛtlə⁰d/. If you are **nettled**, you are annoyed or offended. EG *Judy was a bit nettled.* ADJ QUALIT = piqued

nettle rash; also spelled with a hyphen. **Nettle rash** is a rash of small itchy red or white lumps on a person's skin which are usually caused by a stinging nettle. N UNCOUNT

network /nɛtwɜ:k/, **networks, networking, networked**. **1** A **network** is **1.1** a large number of lines or things that look like lines, for example roads or veins, which cross each other or meet at many points. EG *There was a network of tiny red veins running over her white skin... ...the network of back streets in the Latin Quarter.* N COUNT ⇑ group **1.2** a large number of people, groups, institutions, etc that have a connection with each other and work together as a system. EG *...a network of clinics... We have well developed marketing networks... ...the public telephone network... ...the supportive network of the extended family.* N COUNT+SUPP ⇑ group **1.3** a radio or television company or group of companies that usually broadcast the same programmes at the same time in different parts of the country. EG *She gave an informal interview on a national television network.* N COUNT : USU MOD+N ⇑ organization = station

2 When a television or radio programme **is networked**, it is broadcast at the same time by several different television stations. EG *...decisions about which programmes were to be networked.* V+O : USU PASS

neural /njʊərəl/ is used to describe things relating to a nerve or to the nervous system; a technical term in biology or medicine. EG *There is evidence of the existence of a specific neural mechanism that carries out this function... ...the neural system.* ADJ CLASSIF : ATTRIB

neuralgia /njʊəræld͡ʒə/ is very severe pain along the whole length of a nerve; a technical term in medicine. EG *I suffer from very painful facial neuralgia.* N UNCOUNT

neurological /njʊərə⁶lɒd͡ʒɪkə⁰l/ is used to describe things relating to the nervous system; a technical term in medicine. EG *...a progressive neurological disease.* ADJ CLASSIF : USU ATTRIB

neurology /njʊrɒləd͡ʒi¹/ is the study of the structure, function, and diseases of the nervous system; a technical term in medicine. ◇ **neurologist, neurologists.** EG *Finally my doctor advised me to see a neurologist and I agreed.* N UNCOUNT ⇑ science ◇ N COUNT ⇑ scientist

neuron /njʊərɒn/, **neurons**. A **neuron** is a cell that is part of the nervous system and that conducts messages to and from the brain; a technical term in biology. N COUNT

neurone /njʊərəʊn/, **neurones**. A **neurone** is the same as a neuron. EG *The human brain consists of neurones, blood cells and chemical elements.* N COUNT

neurosis /njʊərəʊsɪs/, **neuroses** /njʊərəʊsi:z/. **1** **Neurosis** is a mental illness which causes people to have continual and unreasonable fears and worries. EG *Such problems can distort personality and lead to neurosis... ...curing a neurosis in a child.* N UNCOUNT/COUNT ⇑ disorder

2 A **neurosis** is something that someone worries about a lot or fears a lot. EG *...my parents' neurosis about murderers.* N COUNT = phobia

neurotic /njʊərɒtɪk/, **neurotics**. **1** Someone who is **neurotic** **1.1** continually shows great and unreasonable anxiety, especially about something in particular. EG *Nothing is more distracting than a neurotic boss... They are becoming neurotic about their careers.* ADJ QUALIT = paranoid, manic **1.2** is affected by neurosis. ADJ CLASSIF

2 A **neurotic** is someone who suffers from neurosis. N COUNT

neuter /nju:tə/, **neuters, neutering, neutered**.
1 A **neuter** noun, pronoun, etc, in some languages, belongs to a particular class of nouns, pronouns, etc. Words that are neuter have sets of inflections which are different from those of masculine and feminine words. ADJ CLASSIF

2 When an animal **is neutered**, its organs of reproduction are removed. EG *My two kittens were being neutered down at the vet hospital.* V+O : USU PASS

neutral /nju:trə⁰l/, **neutrals**. **1** A country or person that is **neutral** does not officially support anyone in a disagreement or war. EG *Throughout the hostilities they remained neutral... ...neutral and friendly governments... Because I was neutral in the conflict I was a welcome visitor.* ADJ CLASSIF = non-aligned ▸ used as a noun. EG *It is essential that we transform them from active enemies into passive neutrals.* ▸ N COUNT ◇ **neutrality** /nju:trælɪti¹/. EG *He was not a pacifist but an advocate of armed neutrality.* ◇ N UNCOUNT = non-alignment

2 A **neutral** position or point of view is one that does not help or support either side in a disagreement, dispute, or war. EG *I undertake to preserve a strictly neutral position during this debate... You're not getting a neutral, unbiased view on this.* ADJ QUALIT = impartial, unbiased ◇ **neutrality**. EG *We have a tradition of political neutrality for our civil servants.* ◇ N UNCOUNT = impartiality

3 If someone is **neutral** or if something that they do is **neutral**, they do not show any emotions or any preference or bias. EG *Their decision was neutral on the question of the closed shop... I waited, but her eyes were neutral.* ADJ CLASSIF = uncommitted ◇ **neutrality**. EG *This represents an attitude of neutrality towards religion.* ◇ N UNCOUNT = detachment

4 A voice that is **neutral** does not reveal any obvious emotions and does not show any obvious characteristics. EG *'Look,' she said in a neutral voice... ...a neutral accent like Brian's.* ADJ QUALIT = indeterminate ≠ distinctive

5 Something that is **neutral** does not cause any overall change because it involves two equal and opposite qualities, ideas, or amounts. EG *Hence, an equal cut in taxes and in spending is neutral in the short run.* ADJ QUALIT

6 **Neutral** is the position between the gears of a car or other vehicle, in which the gears are not connected to the engine and the vehicle will not move. EG *Hendricks pushed the handle into neutral.* N UNCOUNT

7 The **neutral** wire in an electric flex or plug is the wire that is not earth or live and that is needed to complete the circuit so that the electric current can ADJ CLASSIF flow. EG *Cut back the covers of the neutral and live wires about 1 inch.*

8 Neutral is used **8.1** to describe things that are pale greyish or brownish in colour. EG *The water was of a pale, neutral colour, a sort of ashen grey... Nothing surrounded it except a vague, neutral greyness.* **8.2** to describe things that contain no colour at all or that are suitable to be used for any colour. EG *...a neutral shoe cream.* **8.3** in physics, to describe things such as atomic particles that have neither a positive nor a negative charge. **8.4** in chemistry, to describe things that are neither acidic nor alkaline. ADJ COLOUR = toneless, dull; ADJ COLOUR; ADJ CLASSIF ↑ charged; ADJ CLASSIF

neutralism /njuːtrəlɪzəm/ is the policy or practice of remaining neutral and not aligning with any of the large power blocs. EG *...growing neutralism in Western Europe.* N UNCOUNT = neutrality

neutralize /njuːtrəlaɪz/, **neutralizes, neutralizing, neutralized**; also spelled **neutralise**. If someone or something **neutralizes** something, **1** they prevent it from having any effect. EG *Their aim is to neutralize the Council's propaganda campaign... The incident seems likely to neutralise whatever goodwill has been generated.* **2** they prevent it from working properly. EG *All aircraft on the ground were neutralized until repairs could be effected.* V+O = counteract; V+O = incapacitate

◇ **neutralization** /njuːtrəlaɪzeɪʃən/. EG *...the neutralization of some 120 artillery batteries.* ◇ N UNCOUNT: USU+of

neutron /njuːtrɒn/, **neutrons**. A **neutron** is an atomic particle that has no electrical charge. EG *When an atom is split it releases neutrons.* N COUNT

neutron bomb, neutron bombs. A **neutron bomb** is a nuclear weapon that is designed to kill people and animals without a large explosion and without destroying buildings or causing serious radioactive pollution. EG *...missiles and neutron bombs.* N COUNT

never /nevə/. **1 Never** means **1.1** at no time in the past or at no time in the future. EG *I've never been to Europe... I shall never forget this day... I'd never seen a dead man before... I never eat breakfast on Sundays... Never in my life have I seen anyone drink as much as you.* **1.2** not in any circumstances at all. EG *What is morally wrong can never be politically right... Bringing up children in an inner city is never easy.* ADV: NEG ↑ not; ADV: NEG

2 Never ever is an emphatic expression for 'never'; used mainly in spoken English. EG *Things will never ever be the same again... She never ever wears a hat.* PHR: USED AS AN A

3 You use **never** with the simple past tense to mean 'did not'; used mainly in spoken English. EG *My bus never arrived... The summit never took place... Good gracious! I never knew that.* ADV+VB: NEG

4 If you say that something **will never do** or **would never do**, you mean that you think it is not good enough or not suitable. EG *I'm sorry, but these curtains will never do.* CONVENTION

5 You also use **never** in exclamations to indicate how surprised or shocked you are by something. EG *'I've started taking yoga classes.'–'Never! Really?'... You've never sold the house? I don't believe it!* ADV WITH VB, OR EXCLAM = surely not

6 If you say **'Well, I never'**, you are indicating that you are very surprised about something that you have just seen or found out; an informal expression. EG *Well, I never. It's Mrs Oliver.* • **never mind**: see **mind.** • **never fear**: see **fear**. EXCLAM = blow me

never-ending. Something that is **never-ending** seems to last a very long time, especially because it is depressing or boring. EG *It was a drab, never-ending afternoon... ...the never-ending flow of refugees.* ADJ CLASSIF = interminable

never-never. If you buy something **on the never-never**, you buy it by hire purchase or on credit; an informal expression used in old-fashioned British English. EG *He bought the car on the never-never.* PHR: USED AS AN A

never-never land is an imaginary land where everything is nice and pleasant; an informal expression. N UNCOUNT

nevertheless /nevəðəles/ means in spite of what has just been said. EG *He had not slept that night. Nevertheless, he led the rally with his usual vigour... She saw Clarissa immediately, but nevertheless hovered there a moment longer and pretended to look around for her.* ADV SEN = nonetheless

new /njuː/ **newer, newest; news**. The forms **new, newer, newest** are used for the adjective explained in paragraphs 1 to 10. The form **news** is used for the noun in paragraphs 11 to 16. **1** Something that is **new 1.1** has been recently created, made, or built, or is in the process of being created, made, or built. EG *...smart new houses... I haven't really had a new idea in years... ...major new discoveries... There is nothing new in the fact that he feels betrayed... That failure takes on a new significance in the light of what you have just said.* **1.2** has not been used or owned by anyone else. EG *It took me a year to save up for a new hat... He has a new car every year... Slip the old washer out, put a new one in... They cost over twenty dollars new.* **1.3** is different, either because it has changed recently, or because you have not experienced it or been involved in it before. EG *Not long after that, he got a new job... Try and get me her new address... Whenever will I find a new place to live?... Keep looking for new ways to save your time and energy.* ADJ QUALIT; ADJ CLASSIF; ADJ CLASSIF: ATTRIB

◇ **newness**. EG *...the intrusion of novelty, newness into our existence.* **1.4** has been designed, developed, or invented recently, and is considered to be better or more advanced than the thing that it replaces. EG *...100 models promoting two new Fiat cars... ...a new type of bandage that stops minor bleeding almost immediately... The new system has been running for a number of months... ...a newer and better tank, the T-80.* **1.5** has only recently been discovered or noticed. EG *...a new star. ...the discovery of new oilfields in the North Sea.* ◇ N UNCOUNT; ADJ CLASSIF: ATTRIB ↑ modern; ADJ CLASSIF: ATTRIB

2 A **new** country is one that has recently achieved independence. EG *...the new nations... ...the newer Asian countries.* ADJ CLASSIF: ATTRIB

3 A **new** day, year, etc, is the beginning of the next day or year. EG *Claim before the new benefit year which starts on 4th January... ...on the eve of a new era... He greets each new day in the knowledge that he may not see its end.* ADJ CLASSIF: ATTRIB

4 New is used to describe a person or country that has recently achieved or acquired a particular status. EG *...from the new mother's point of view.* ◇ **newness**. EG *He's still excited because of the newness of the position.* ADJ CLASSIF: ATTRIB ≠ long-standing; ◇ N UNCOUNT

5 Someone who is **new** has recently arrived in a particular place or job, or has recently joined a group or organization. EG *This year the Festival has a new director... The society welcomes new members... Only Florrie, the new girl, saw Ida slip a note into Madeleine's hand.* ADJ CLASSIF

6 If you are **new** to a situation or place, or if the situation or place is **new** to you, you have not previously seen it or had any experience of it. EG *...a part of England completely new to him... ICAM is a new set of initials to me... I am new to this game.* ADJ QUALIT: PRED+to ↑ strange = unfamiliar

7 New potatoes or carrots are produced early in the season for such vegetables and are usually small with a rather sweet flavour. EG *There were no more new potatoes.* ADJ CLASSIF: ATTRIB

8 If you say that something is **as good as new**, you mean that it is now working very well or is in very good condition, after it has been damaged and then repaired. EG *I'm really pleased–it's as good as new now.* PHR: USED AS C

9 The adjective **new** is also used in the following expressions, which are explained at other places in this dictionary. • **new blood**: see **blood.** • **a new lease of life**: see **lease.** • **pastures new**: see **pasture.** • **to turn over a new leaf**: see **leaf.** • See also **brand-new**.

10 See also **newly**.

11 News is **11.1** information about a recent event or a recently changed situation. EG *I've got some good news for you... ...a fascinating piece of news... News travels pretty fast... ...after receiving the news of my acceptance... ...'friends' who delight in breaking bad news.* **11.2** information that is published in newspapers and broadcast on radio and television about recent events in the country or the world. EG *...a half hour of world and domestic news... He's recently been in the news again... The news media should have provided more coverage... Their talks had been held under a news blackout.* N UNCOUNT, OR N SING WITH the/POSS; N UNCOUNT, OR N SING: USU+the+N

12 The **news** is a programme on television or radio which consists of information about recent events in the country or the world. EG *Have you listened to the news today?... It was on the news at 9.30... We all watch the telly news.* N SING: the+N ↑ broadcast

13 If you say that someone or something is **news**, you mean that they are considered to be interesting and N UNCOUNT: USED AS C important at the moment, and that people want to hear about them on the radio and television and in newspapers; an informal use. EG *By now Trevino was news wherever he went... There is no question that someone killed by a shark is news.*

14 In informal English, if you say that someone or something is **bad news**, you mean that they will cause you trouble or problems. If you say that someone or something is **good news**, you mean that they will be helpful or useful to you, and that you approve of them. EG *I had no choice but to look the young man over, and hope he was good news.* PHR : USED AS C

15 If you say **'That's news to me'**, you mean that you did not previously know what you have just been told and that you are rather surprised by it. CONVENTION

16 People say **'No news is good news'** in order to encourage themselves when they are worried about a situation but have not heard any news about it for some time. CONVENTION

new- combines with the past participle of some verbs to make words or expressions which indicate that an action has been done or completed very recently. EG *...a lovely smell, like new-cut grass... ...thousands of new-made graves.* PREFIX

newborn /nju:bɔ:n/; also spelled with a hyphen. A **newborn** baby or child is one that has been born recently. EG *Newborn babies sleep in short bursts.* ADJ CLASSIF ⇑ young

new broom, new brooms. A person who has just started a new job and who intends to make a lot of changes may be referred to as a **new broom**; an informal expression. EG *'Daintry,' the Brigadier explained, 'is our new broom.'* N COUNT : USU SING ⇑ newcomer

newcomer /nju:kʌmə/, **newcomers**. A **newcomer** is a person who has recently arrived to live in a place, joined an organization, or started a job. EG *For the thousands of newcomers, however, city life is strange... ...the head of Section 6, Watson, is a relative newcomer... ...newcomers to the neighbourhood.* N COUNT

newel /nju:ə⁰l/, **newels**. A **newel** or a **newel post** is the thick post at the top or bottom of a staircase, supporting the hand rail. N COUNT

new-fangled. A **new-fangled** idea or piece of machinery has been recently devised, created, or invented; a fairly informal word, used showing disapproval. EG *No doubt they'll produce some new-fangled gadget to dispose of it.* ADJ CLASSIF : ATTRIB ⇑ modern

new-found. A **new-found** quality, ability, or person is one that you have discovered recently. EG *...this new-found confidence... Your new-found enthusiasm for running will soon fade away... We don't need to be tied by the rules of any new-found friends.* ADJ CLASSIF : ATTRIB ⇑ recent

new-laid. **New-laid** eggs are very fresh because they have been laid very recently. ADJ CLASSIF : ATTRIB

newly /nju:li¹/ is used before past participles to indicate that a particular action is or was very recent. EG *...the newly-married couple... ...a newly formed consortium of businessmen... ...newly discovered pieces of evidence.* ADV+PAST PART

newlyweds /nju:li¹wɛdz/; also spelled with a hyphen. **Newlyweds** are a man and woman who have recently got married. EG *...Britain's royal newlyweds on their honeymoon cruise.* N PLURAL ⇑ couple

new moon, new moons. 1 A **new moon** is the moon when it appears as a thin crescent shape at the start of its four-week cycle of appearing to become larger and then smaller. EG *Clouds shrouded the new moon.* N COUNT

2 The **new moon** is the time, occurring about once a month, during which the new moon appears in the sky. EG *It happened a few days before the new moon.* N COUNT : IF SING, *the*+N

news agency, news agencies. A **news agency** is an organization which collects news stories from all over the world and sells them to newspapers, magazines, and television and radio stations. EG *...a deal that would make Reuters the largest news agency in the world.* N COUNT

newsagent /nju:zeɪdʒənt/, **newsagents**. A **newsagent's** or **newsagent** is a shop which sells newspapers and magazines, and often cigarettes, sweets, and stationery. EG *I bought a midday edition of the Evening Standard at the newsagent's in Shepherds Market.* ▸ A **newsagent** is also the person who runs a newsagent's. N COUNT = paper shop ▸ ⇑ shopkeeper

newscaster /nju:zkɑ:stə/, **newscasters**. A **newscaster** is a person who reads the news on a television or radio broadcast. N COUNT ⇑ announcer

news conference, news conferences. A **news conference** is the same as a press conference; used in American English. EG *The Senator called a news conference to deny the CBS report.* N COUNT

newsflash /nju:zflæʃ/, **newsflashes**. A **newsflash** is an interruption that is made to a radio or television programme to announce an important piece of news. N COUNT ⇑ announcement

newsletter /nju:zlɛtə/, **newsletters**. A **newsletter** is a printed sheet or several sheets of paper containing information about a group or organization that is sent regularly to its members. EG *They keep in touch with their members by issuing a quarterly news letter.* N COUNT = bulletin

newsman /nju:zmə³n/, **newsmen**. A **newsman** is a reporter for a newspaper or a television or radio news programme. EG *Sharp-eyed newsmen had spotted it.* N COUNT

newspaper /nju:zpeɪpə/, **newspapers**. 1 A **newspaper** is 1.1 a publication consisting of a number of large sheets of folded paper, on which news, advertisements, and other information is printed. Some newspapers are produced every day from Monday to Saturday, and others once a week. EG *People were rushing to buy copies of the newspaper... ...a weekly newspaper... ...a newspaper article... ...a famous writer on a Sunday newspaper... ...copies of France's leading daily newspaper Le Figaro.* **1.2** an organization that produces a newspaper. EG *I work for a newspaper... These laws empowered them to close down any newspaper arbitrarily... He took a firm grip on the management side of the newspaper.* N COUNT; N COUNT ⇑ business

2 **Newspaper** consists of pieces of old newspapers, especially when they are being used for another purpose such as wrapping things up. EG *Wedge it with a wad of newspaper.* N UNCOUNT ⇑ paper

newspaperman /nju:zpeɪpəmə³n/, **newspapermen**. A **newspaperman** is a reporter who works for a newspaper. EG *Hearst mingled with newspapermen day and night... What wouldn't a newspaperman give to get a picture of that!* N COUNT = newsman, journalist

newsprint /nju:zprɪnt/ is 1 the cheap, fairly rough paper on which newspapers are printed. EG *...bales of newsprint.* 2 the text that is printed in newspapers. EG *...to enable literacy students to deal with a page of newsprint.* N UNCOUNT; N UNCOUNT ⇑ print

newsreel /nju:zri:l/, **newsreels**. A **newsreel** is a short film which gives an account of recent events in the country or the world, made especially for showing in cinemas. EG *She had spent hours viewing newsreel footage of Princess Anne.* N COUNT

newsroom /nju:zru⁴m/, **newsrooms**. A **newsroom** is an office at a newspaper or in a broadcasting organization where news reports are written and edited before they are printed or broadcast. EG *Leaving his office I peeped into the newsroom, where the reporters were clattering on typewriters.* N COUNT

news-stand, news-stands. A **news-stand** is a movable stand or stall in the street or at a railway station from which newspapers are sold. EG *She went to the news-stand at the end of the platform and bought a paper.* N COUNT

newsworthy /nju:zwɜ:ði¹/. Something that is **newsworthy** is sufficiently interesting to be reported as news on the radio or television or in the newspapers. EG *...their selection of newsworthy events and interpretations.* ADJ QUALIT = notable

newsy /nu:si¹/. A **newsy** letter is full of interesting news about yourself, your family, and your friends; an informal word. ADJ QUALIT

newt /nju:t/, **newts**. A **newt** is a small creature which has a moist skin, short legs, and a long tail. Newts live partly on land and partly in water. N COUNT ⇑ amphibian

New Testament. The **New Testament** is the part of the Bible that deals with the life of Jesus Christ and with Christianity in the early Church. N PROPER : *the* N

new town, new towns. A **new town** is a town that has been planned and built as a whole, including shops, houses, factories etc, rather than one that has developed gradually. N COUNT

new wave, new waves. A **new wave** is a movement in art, music, film, politics, etc which intentionally introduces new ideas instead of following traditional or conventional ideas. EG *...one of the young producers from the new wave of British music... This 'new wave' can boast an array of gifted directors.* N COUNT

New World. The **New World** is used to refer to the western hemisphere of the world, especially the land mass of North and South America. EG *...the great voyages of discovery to the New World.* N PROPER : the+N

New Year. 1 **New Year** or the **New Year** is the time when people celebrate the start of a year. EG *We had a marvellous time over New Year... That's the only New Year's resolution I have kept.* ● People say **'Happy New Year'** to each other as a greeting at New Year. N UNCOUNT, OR N SING : the+N; ● CONVENTION

2 The **New Year** is also used to refer to the first few weeks of a year. EG *Sarah had to go there in the New Year... In the new year they moved into a cottage at Wytham.* N SING : the+N

New Year's Day is the first day of a year. In Western countries this is January 1st. EG *New Year's Day is a national holiday... ...on a bitterly cold New Year's day.* N UNCOUNT

New Year's Eve is the last day of the year, the day that comes before New Year's Day. N UNCOUNT

New Zealander /nju: zi:lə³ndə/, **New Zealanders**. A **New Zealander** is a person who comes from New Zealand. N COUNT

next /nekst/. 1 The **next** minute, day, or other period is the one which happens immediately after the present one. EG *The next five years are of vital importance... Over the next few months their work pattern changed... The next day, I left better prepared... Next day, it was still raining... I'm getting married next month... He may no longer be Chancellor next April... My pulse was 40 one minute and 100 the next.* ▸ used after the name of a day of the week or a month. EG *The boots will be ready by Wednesday next.* ORDINAL ⇑ following; ▸ ORDINAL : AFTER N UNCOUNT

2 The **next** concert, election, or other event is the first one that will occur after the time at which you are speaking. EG *I may vote for her at the next election.* ORDINAL

3 The **next** thing or person is 3.1 the thing or person that you are going to deal with when you finish dealing with something else. EG *My next question is, 'What is art?'... Next patient, please... What's next on the agenda?... The next thing is, does Mr McPherson feel he can work with us?... Before they had finished one show, they were already putting together material for the next... ...trudging from one 'No Vacancies' sign to the next.* 3.2 the thing or person that comes after the one you are considering, in a group of things or people that occur in a particular order. EG *Her next sister was the great actress Ellen Terry.* ORDINAL; ORDINAL

4 If you say that you are as good, bad, etc **as the next** person, you mean that you are no different from anyone else in the respect mentioned. EG *He enjoyed praise as much as the next man.* PHR+NG

5 The **next** place or person is the one that is nearest to you or the first one that you come to. EG *The telephone was ringing in the next room... ...in the valley beyond the next mountain range... Pull into the next lay-by... He whispered the words to the next man... Take the next on the right, then the second on the left... We missed Junction 12 and came off at the next.* ORDINAL : the+ORDINAL = neighbouring

6 You also use **next** 6.1 to say what happens or comes immediately after something else. EG *Next, we did the Merchant of Venice... The audience does not know what is going to happen next... It's your turn next.* 6.2 to mention what you intend to discuss or do now that you have finished discussing or doing something else. EG *We turn next to Dorothy Sayers... Next, I'd like to show you some pictures.* 6.3 to refer to the first occasion on which something that has already happened happens again. EG *When they next went on deck, he had to be helped up... It was some years later when I next saw her... What shall I say when we next meet?* 6.4 to refer to something or someone that has the greatest amount of a particular quality except for one other thing or person. EG *The best kind of story is the one with a happy ending; the next best is the one with an unhappy ending... Maurice was next in size among the boys to Jack.* ADV WITH VB; ADV SEN; ADV WITH VB; ADV+SUPERL/PREP

7 In informal spoken English, you can say **next thing** or **the next thing I knew** to suggest that a new situation which you are describing was surprising because it happened very suddenly. EG *The next thing I knew, I was in hospital... The next thing, he was gone... Next thing I was aboard a great big container ship.* PHR ⇑ then

8 **The week after next, the month after next**, etc, is the month, week, etc that follows the next one. For example, when it is May, the month after next is July. EG *This was where he had to go the week after next... The term after next I'm going to do some philosophy.* PHR : USED AS AN A

9 **next to. 9.1** Someone or something that is **next to** a place, thing, or person is at the side of it. EG *She went and sat next to him... There was a bowl of goldfish next to the bed... The two graveyards were next to each other... ...the building next to the old Chapel.* **9.2** You use **next to** before a negative or a word that suggests a negative to mean almost, but not completely. EG *I knew next to nothing about him... The photographs were next to useless but they were all we had.* **9.3** You can use **next to** in order to give your second choice when you are stating your likes and dislikes. EG *Next to Rome, I like Paris.* PREP ⇑ near = beside; ADV+ADJ/PRON INDEF : WITH BROAD NEG = virtually; PREP

next door. 1 You use **next door** to refer to one of the houses or flats that are nearest to yours or to someone else's on each side. EG *She lived next door to the Wilsons... I'm going next door to tell that woman to stop playing that music so loud.* ▸ used as an adjective, usually spelled with a hyphen. EG *...our next-door neighbour, Joan Pearce.* ▸ used to refer to the person or people who live next door to you. EG *...next door's cat.* ADV WITH VB : IF +PREP THEN to ⇑ beside; ▸ ADJ CLASSIF : ATTRIB; ▸ N UNCOUNT

2 If you talk about the place, building, object, etc **next door**, you are referring to the one that is nearest to you; an informal use. EG *At the table next door was a pretty girl.* ADJ CLASSIF : ATTRIB, OR ADV WITH VB : IF+ PREP THEN to

next of kin. Your **next of kin** is the person who is your closest relative; used especially in official or legal documents. EG *The only next of kin seems to be a cousin in Droitwich... You require the consent of the next of kin.* N SING WITH DET, OR N UNCOUNT

nexus /neksəs/. **Nexus** is both the singular and the plural form. A **nexus** is a connection or a series of connections and links within a particular situation or system; a formal word. EG *The cash nexus cast its net to cover the world... They have gradually been sucked into this nexus of non-opposition.* N COUNT+SUPP ⇑ network

> **NG** □ In this dictionary **NG** is used in the grammar notes beside entries to mean noun group. Noun groups always have a noun or a pronoun as their headword, i.e. a noun or pronoun is the main word in the group. The headword of a noun group may either occur on its own, or it may have a determiner, adjectives, or other modifiers in front of it. Examples of noun groups with **house** as headword, and with different types of modifiers are *...the house... ...his smelly old house... ...my beautiful Georgian country house.* The headword may be followed by a relative clause or a prepositional group, as part of the noun group. Words which follow the headword and which are part of the noun group are often called qualifiers. Examples of noun groups with **house** as headword and with modifiers and qualifiers are *...the town house of Sir Winston Churchill... ...the new house that they have built.*

NHS is an abbreviation for 'National Health Service'. EG *...treatment on the NHS... ...free NHS dental treatment.* N PROPER : the+N

NI /ɛn aɪ/ is an abbreviation for 'national insurance'. EG *You don't have to pay NI contributions while you are out of work.* N UNCOUNT : USU BEFORE N

nib /nɪb/, **nibs**. A **nib** is a small pointed piece of metal at the end of a fountain pen, which controls the flow of ink as you write. N COUNT

nibble /nɪbə⁰l/, **nibbles, nibbling, nibbled**. 1 If you **nibble** something, or **nibble** at it, 1.1 you eat it slowly by taking small bites out of it, for example when you are not very hungry. EG *Just nibble a piece of bread... She nibbled at her food.* 1.2 you bite it very gently. EG *She nibbled my ear lobe playfully.* V+O, OR V : USU +A (at/on) = pick at; V+O, OR V+A (at)

2 When a mouse or other small animal **nibbles** something, it takes small bites out of it quickly and repeatedly. EG *They like to nibble at their food throughout the day... It was nibbling a carefully chosen leaf.* V+O, OR V : USU +A (at/on)

3 A **nibble** is 3.1 an act of biting something gently or quickly. EG *A few licks and nibbles quickly put him off.* 3.2 in informal English, a light meal which you eat when you are in a hurry or when you are not very hungry. EG *Do you fancy a nibble?* N COUNT; N SING : a+N = snack

nice /naɪs/, **nicer, nicest**. **Nice** is a very common word, especially in informal spoken English, which is used to express pleasure, approval, or admiration of a very general kind. 1 You can use **nice** when you want to say or ask whether something is enjoyable or pleasant. EG *It would be nice to keep bees... This is the nicest thing that has ever happened to me... 'Did you have a nice time at the party?'* ADJ QUALIT = good

2 You can use **nice** in expressions such as 'Nice to meet you' when you meet someone for the first time, 'Nice to see you' when you meet someone you have met before, or 'Nice to have met you' when you are saying goodbye to someone you have met for the first time. EG *It's so nice to see you... 'The name's Weaver.'–'Mr Weaver. How nice.'... It's been nice meeting you.* ADJ QUALIT: USED IN CONVENTIONS

3 If you say that something is **nice**, **3.1** you mean that you find it attractive or pleasant. EG *How nice you look... It doesn't taste very nice.* ◊ **nicely**. EG *I always think Bessie dresses very nicely.* **3.2** you mean that you admire it or like it. EG *'What do you think of my new pictures?'–'Very nice.'... There's some nice carving on this chair... She has a really nice way of putting things.* ◊ **nicely**. EG *I think Edward nicely pointed out the absurdity of the situation.* ADJ QUALIT ◊ ADV WITH VB ADJ QUALIT = good, attractive ◊ ADV WITH VB = cleverly

4 If you say that someone does or says something **nice**, you mean that you think they are being kind and thoughtful; sometimes used as a way of thanking them. EG *It's nice of you to say that... How nice of you to come... He said some very nice things about my poetry.* ADJ QUALIT = good

5 If you say that someone is **nice**, you mean that they are friendly and pleasant and that you like them. EG *He's very nice... He was a terribly nice man... They were nice enough people, but the conversation was a bit dull.* ◊ **niceness**. EG *She smiled with an extraordinary niceness.* ADJ QUALIT = likeable ≠ unpleasant ◊ N UNCOUNT

6 If you **are nice** to people, you behave in a friendly and pleasant way towards them. EG *Promise me you'll be nice to her when she comes back... She could be quite nice sometimes when she was feeling in the mood... I wish I'd been nicer to him.* PHR : VB INFLECTS, IF + PREP THEN *to*

7 Behaviour or manners that are **nice** are polite and acceptable. EG *Mind you, he had very nice manners, didn't he?* ◊ **nicely**. EG *You may have a biscuit if you ask nicely... They said please and thank you and ate nicely.* ADJ QUALIT = charming ◊ ADV WITH VB = politely

8 If the weather is **nice**, it is warm and pleasant. EG *It's not a very nice day, is it?* ADJ QUALIT = fine

9 You can also use **nice** in an ironic way to indicate that you do not like something, such as an unfriendly remark made by another person. EG *'You're so stupid!'–'Oh that's nice. That's very nice.'... Nice friends you've got. They've just walked off with my radio.* ADJ QUALIT = charming

10 **nice one**; an informal expression. **10.1** If someone says **'nice one'**, they are praising something that they have just seen or heard, especially something clever or funny. EG *'Checkmate in four moves.'–'Nice one, Robert.'* **10.2** You can use **nice one** as an ironic response when someone has just told you about something stupid or embarrassing that they have done. EG *'How did it go?'–'Not too well. I ran into the back of the driving instructor's car.'–'Oh, nice one.'* CONVENTION ↑ very good CONVENTION

11 You can also use **nice** to give extra emphasis to an adjective or adverb which is describing something that you think is pleasant, attractive, or necessary. EG *We had a nice long chat... Give her a nice big smile now.* ADV + ADJ/ADV = good

12 If you say that something is **nice and** peaceful, **nice and** gentle, etc, you are emphasizing a quality that you like, admire, or think is desirable in a particular situation. EG *That's nice and convenient for you... It's so nice and peaceful here... You'll have to get up nice and early.* ADV WITH VB, OR ADJ QUALIT : PRED ↑ extremely

13 A **nice** idea, point, or distinction is very precise and exact and needs very careful thought before you can understand it; a formal use. EG *There's a nice distinction between 'continuous' and 'continual'... We happen to be making quite nice judgements on people.* ◊ **nicely**. EG *The twelve characters are all nicely differentiated.* ADJ QUALIT = fine, subtle ◊ ADV WITH VB = subtly

nice-looking. Someone who is **nice-looking** is physically attractive. EG *He was a nice-looking fellow.* ADJ QUALIT = good-looking

nicely /naɪsli¹/. 1 Something that is happening or operating **nicely** is working in a satisfactory way or in the way that you want it to happen. EG *The generator is ticking over nicely... You need some form of identification. Your driver's licence will do nicely... He thought he could manage quite nicely without them.* ADV AFTER VB = well enough

2 If someone says that you are **doing very nicely** or that you are **doing very nicely for yourself**, they mean that you are successful and in a good financial position. EG *She's doing very nicely for herself these days... The managing director is alive and well and doing very nicely, thank you.* PHR : VB INFLECTS, USU CONT = prosper

3 Other meanings of **nicely** can be found in the entry for **nice** in paragraphs 3, 7, and 13. ADV

nicety /naɪsɪti¹/, **niceties**. 1 A **nicety** is a small detail, especially with regard to polite behaviour and good manners. EG *Can we cut the niceties and get quickly to the point?... In diplomacy the niceties of etiquette must be observed.* N COUNT : USU PL, IF + PREP THEN *of* = subtlety

2 If something is done **to a nicety**, it is done with complete accuracy regarding details. EG *It is exquisite! It suits the words to a nicety.* PHR : USED AS AN A

niche /niːʃ/, **niches**. A **niche** is 1 a hollow area in a wall which can be used to hold a statue, or a natural hollow part in a hillside or cliff. EG *...the little statue of the saint in his niche near the pulpit... Madeleine placed it carefully in the rocky niche.* **2** a job or position which is exactly suitable for someone and which they want to keep. EG *You can then find your own niche in public life.* N COUNT ↑ recess N COUNT = slot

nick /nɪk/, **nicks, nicking, nicked**. 1 If you **nick** something or **nick** yourself, you make a small cut into the surface of the object or into your skin, usually by accident. EG *He shaved badly, nicking himself in a couple of places.* V+O (NG/REFL)

2 A **nick** is a very slight cut made in the surface of something. EG *I felt with my bare fingers for nicks in their metal.* N COUNT = notch

3 If someone **nicks** something, they steal it; an informal use. EG *My typewriter had been nicked.* V+O

4 If someone **is nicked**, they are arrested by the police. EG *You haven't got a record have you? Haven't been nicked for anything?* V+O : USU PASS = pick up

5 The **nick** is prison; an informal use. EG *He's in the nick again.* N SING : *the*+N

6 If something happens **in the nick of time**, it happens successfully, but at the last possible moment; an informal expression. PHR : USED AS A A

7 If you say that something is **in good nick**, **in bad nick**, etc, you mean that it is in good or bad condition; used in informal English. EG *It's in terrible nick, your typewriter.* PHR : USED AS A A

nickel /nɪkəºl/, **nickels**. 1 **Nickel** is a silver-coloured metal that can be mixed with other metals to form an alloy. EG *Copper pans should be lined with silver, nickel, or tin.* N UNCOUNT

2 A **nickel** is an American or Canadian coin that is worth five cents. N COUNT

nickname /nɪkneɪm/, **nicknames, nicknaming, nicknamed**. 1 A **nickname** is an informal name for someone, especially one that is used by their friends or relations. EG *He aptly referred to Gordon as 'Bullhead', a nickname that quickly stuck.* N COUNT = label

2 If you **nickname** someone or something, you give them an informal name. EG *For a brief while, Mrs Thatcher was nicknamed 'Tina'.* V+O+C

nicotine /nɪkətiːn/ is 1 an addictive substance that is contained in tobacco. EG *Many smokers who are chemically addicted to nicotine cannot cut down easily.* **2** the substances in cigarettes and tobacco such as tar and nicotine itself, which leave a yellowish-brown stain on things. EG *...teeth browned by nicotine.* N UNCOUNT N UNCOUNT

niece /niːs/, **nieces**. Someone's **niece** is the daughter of their sister or brother. EG *She was Lady Astor's niece.* N COUNT ↑ relation

nifty /nɪfti¹/, **niftier, niftiest**. Something that is **nifty** is neat and pleasing or cleverly done; an informal word. EG *That was a nifty piece of work... ...a nifty station wagon.* ADJ QUALIT

Nigerian /naɪdʒɪəriən/, **Nigerians**. 1 Something that is **Nigerian** belongs or relates to Nigeria or to its people. ADJ CLASSIF

2 A **Nigerian** is a person who comes from Nigeria. N COUNT

niggardly /nɪgədli¹/. Someone who is **niggardly** is not very generous, either with money or with praise. EG *I don't want to seem niggardly.* ▸ used of amounts. EG *...a niggardly salary.* ADJ QUALIT ↑ mean ▸ = beggarly

nigger /nɪgə/, **niggers**. **Nigger** is an extremely offensive word for a black person, especially a Negro. N COUNT

niggle /nɪgəºl/, **niggles, niggling, niggled**; an informal word. 1 If something **niggles** you, it causes you to worry slightly over a long time. EG *It's been niggling me all week; I can't remember where I put it.* ◊ **niggling**. EG *...little niggling doubts.* V OR V+O ⇑ trouble = bother ◊ ADJ CLASSIF

2 If you **niggle** or if you **niggle** a person, you criticize the person or fuss continually about small things. EG *Critics niggled that the rapid production of planes was dangerous... Matthews niggled Luce on the China issue.* V OR V+O/ REPORT-CL = nag, carp

3 A **niggle** is 3.1 a small worry or doubt that you keep thinking about. EG *There is not the slightest niggle at the back of your mind that you should be spending your time more usefully?* N COUNT = misgiving 3.2 a small criticism about something. EG *I just have one small niggle about this book.* N COUNT = quibble

nigh /naɪ/. 1 If someone says that an event is **nigh**, they mean that it will happen very soon; an old-fashioned use. EG *He declared that the end of the world was nigh.* ADV AFTER VB = close, near

2 You use **well nigh** in front of an adjective, especially a negative one such as 'impossible' or 'intolerable', to mean nearly or almost. EG *I think it's well nigh impossible to draw the line between carelessness and negligence.* ADV+ADJ/ADV: WITH BROAD NEG = virtually

3 **Nigh on** an amount, number, age, etc, means almost that amount, number, or age; an old-fashioned use. EG *My youngest son looks after me: he is nigh on forty but he doesn't think about getting married at all.* PREP+NUM = nearly

night /naɪt/, **nights**. 1 The **night** is 1.1 the part of each period of twenty-four hours when it is dark outside. EG *He went out late at night when the streets were empty... The night was very still... We walked for six days and six nights... The rainstorms lasted all night long.* N COUNT/ UNCOUNT ≠ day 1.2 the period of time between the end of the afternoon and midnight, or between the end of the afternoon and the time when you go to bed. EG *I was out that night... I didn't get a dance all night... I went on Saturday night... ...on the night of 13th of August.* N COUNT/ UNCOUNT = evening 1.3 the period of time when it is dark and when most people are sleeping. EG *He woke in the night with a dreadful pain... I cannot sleep at nights... Try these pills if you can't sleep at night.* N COUNT, OR *at*+N

2 **Night** things, services, events, etc happen, are done, or are active at night. EG *I took the night train from Copenhagen... I'm on night duty tonight.* N BEFORE N ≠ day

3 **Night** is the darkness that there is when it is not daytime. EG *Night is falling.* N UNCOUNT ≠ light

4 A particular **night** is a particular evening performance of, for example, a play or a concert. EG *...the last night of the proms... There were no tickets left for the press night... The first night was a great success.* N COUNT+SUPP: USU MOD+N

5 The word **night** is also used in the following expressions relating to time. 5.1 If it is a particular time **at night**, it is between the time when it gets dark and midnight. EG *...eleven o'clock at night... ...nine at night.* PHR: USED AS AN A = p.m. 5.2 If something happens **day and night** or **night and day**, it happens all the time without stopping. EG *They were being guarded night and day.* PHR: USED AS AN A = constantly 5.3 If you **have a bad night**, you sleep badly during the night. EG *She had another bad night last night.* PHR: VB INFLECTS 5.4 If you **have an early night**, you go to bed early. If you **have a late night**, you go to bed late. EG *I haven't had an early night for weeks... I can't afford to have another late night this week.* PHR: VB INFLECTS 5.5 If you **make a night of it**, you spend a whole evening doing something enjoyable. EG *Let's make a night of it!* PHR: VB INFLECTS

nightcap /naɪtkæp/, **nightcaps**. A **nightcap** is 1 a drink that you have just before you go to bed, often an alcoholic drink. N COUNT = toddy 2 an old-fashioned kind of soft hat that people used to wear in bed. N COUNT

nightclothes /naɪtkləʊðºz/ are clothes that you wear in bed, such as pyjamas or nightdresses. N PLURAL = nightwear

nightclub /naɪtklʌb/, **nightclubs**. A **nightclub** is a social establishment which is open in the evenings or late at night, and where people go to drink, and to dance or see a show. EG *She had become a nightclub hostess.* N COUNT

nightdress /naɪtdrɛs/, **nightdresses**. A **nightdress** is a sort of dress that women or girls wear in bed. N COUNT = nightie

nightfall /naɪtfɔːl/ is the time of day when it starts to get dark. EG *By nightfall I was feeling hungry and sleepy... We both wanted to get out of there before nightfall.* N UNCOUNT = dusk

nightgown /naɪtgaʊn/, **nightgowns**. A **nightgown** is 1 the same as a nightdress; used especially in formal or American English. N COUNT 2 the same as a nightshirt; an old-fashioned use. N COUNT

nightie /naɪtiˡ/, **nighties**. A **nightie** is a nightdress; an informal word. N COUNT

nightingale /naɪtɪŋgeɪl/, **nightingales**. A **nightingale** is a small brown European bird. The male nightingale is considered to sing very beautifully. N COUNT

nightlife /naɪtlaɪf/; also spelled with a hyphen or as one word. **Nightlife** is the entertainment and social activities, such as nightclubs, theatres, and bars, that are available at night in towns or cities. EG *...the exotic nightlife of Montmartre and Pigalle.* N UNCOUNT

nightlight /naɪtlaɪt/, **nightlights**; also spelled with a hyphen. A **nightlight** is a very dim light that can be left on at night in a bedroom. N COUNT

nightly /naɪtliˡ/. A **nightly** action or event happens or is done regularly every night. EG *I was watching the nightly television news... ...his nightly reading of the Bible.* ADJ CLASSIF: ATTRIB ⇑ regular ▸ used as an adverb. EG *My mother prayed nightly that I would not choose a theatrical career.* ▸ ADV WITH VB

nightmare /naɪtmɛə/, **nightmares**. A **nightmare** is 1 a very frightening and upsetting dream. EG *He rushed to her room when she had nightmares and comforted her... In his nightmares they burned his house.* N COUNT 2 a very frightening, unpleasant, or worrying situation. EG *The first day was a nightmare, but it was far from a total disaster... ...or they would all die in this nightmare place.* N COUNT ⇑ horror

nightmarish /naɪtmɛərɪʃ/. If you describe a situation or event as **nightmarish**, you mean that it is extremely frightening. EG *I had these endless nightmarish visions of what could go wrong.* ADJ QUALIT: USU ATTRIB = terrifying

night owl, night owls. A **night owl** is someone who regularly stays up late at night, or who prefers to work at night; an informal expression. N COUNT

night porter, night porters. A **night porter** is a person whose job is to be on duty at the main reception desk of a hotel throughout the night. N COUNT ⇑ receptionist

night school, night schools; also spelled with a hyphen. **Night school** is a school where adults can go to educational courses in the evenings. N UNCOUNT/ COUNT = evening classes

nightshade /naɪtʃeɪd/. See **deadly nightshade**.

night shift, night shifts; also spelled with a hyphen. A **night shift** is a period of work that is done at night on a regular basis as part of a job, for example in a hospital or factory. EG *It is illegal in many countries for women to work on night shift.* N COUNT/ UNCOUNT ▸ The **nightshift** is also used to refer to the people who work on a night shift. EG *They waited until the night shift arrived.* ▸ N SING: *the*+N, VB CAN BE SING OR PL ⇑ workers

nightshirt /naɪtʃɜːt/, **nightshirts**. A **nightshirt** is a long, loose shirt that men and boys can wear in bed. N COUNT

nightstick /naɪtstɪk/, **nightsticks**. A **nightstick** is a truncheon; used in American English. N COUNT

night-time is the part of the day between the time when it gets dark and the time when it gets light again. EG *Who would see smoke at night-time anyway?... The night-time cold kept you awake.* N UNCOUNT, OR N BEFORE N = night

night-watchman /naɪt wɒtʃməºn/, **night-watchmen**; also spelled without a hyphen. A **night-watchman** is a person whose job is to guard buildings at night. N COUNT

nightwear /naɪtwɛə/ is clothing that you wear in bed, such as pyjamas or nightdresses; a fairly formal word. N UNCOUNT = nightclothes

nihilism /naɪhºɪlɪzm/ is a belief which rejects all political or religious authority and current ideas in favour of the individual. EG *In early youth we wear our nihilism with a certain bravado.* N UNCOUNT ◊ **nihilist, nihilists**. EG *It was enough to turn you into a nihilist.* ◊ N COUNT

nil /nɪl/. 1 If you say that something is **nil**, you mean that it does not exist at all. EG *Our international sales would probably have been nil... You can reduce the danger to almost nil.* N UNCOUNT = nothing, nought

2 You use **nil** when you are saying what the score is in a sport such as football, rugby, or hockey, to indicate that a team has not scored any goals or points. EG *Wales beat England three nil.* N UNCOUNT = nothing, zero

nimble /nɪmbəºl/, **nimbler, nimblest**. 1 Someone who is **nimble** is able to move their fingers, ADJ QUALIT = agile hands, or legs quickly, lightly, and easily. EG *By now, he was quite nimble on his wooden leg... People get to be very nimble at operating the keyboard.* ▸ used of people's movements. EG *He had very round cheeks, twinkling eyes, nimble movements, and a shrill voice.* ◇ **nimbly**. EG *Nimbly, he swung himself out of the car.* ◇ ADV WITH VB = smartly

2 Someone who has a **nimble** mind is very quick and clever in the way that they think and understand things. ADJ QUALIT = lively, alert

nimbus /nɪmbəˢs/, **nimbuses**. A nimbus is a large dark grey cloud that brings rain or snow; a technical term in meteorology. N COUNT

nincompoop /nɪnkəʳmpu:p, nɪŋ-/, **nincompoops**. If you refer to someone as a **nincompoop**, you mean that they are rather silly and do not think about what they are doing properly; an informal word. EG *I felt such a nincompoop!* N COUNT = fool

nine /naɪn/, **nines**. 1 **Nine** is the number 9: see □ at NUMBER, AGE, DATE, MEASUREMENT, MONEY, and TIME. EG *It had been nine years since she had seen her brother.* NUM
● **nine times out of ten**: see **time**.

2 If you **dress yourself up to the nines**, you put on very smart and fashionable clothes, especially in order to create an impression; an informal expression. EG *She had dressed herself up to the nines and put on her tallest shoes.* PHR : VB INFLECTS = doll yourself up

nineteen /naɪnti:n/. 1 **Nineteen** is the number 19: see □ at NUMBER, AGE, DATE, MEASUREMENT, MONEY, and TIME. EG *The ceremony was performed at the same time in nineteen other countries.* NUM

2 If you say that someone **talks nineteen to the dozen**, you mean that they talk very fast; an informal expression. PHR : VB INFLECTS

nineteenth /naɪnti:nθ/. The **nineteenth** item in a series is the one that you count as number nineteen: see □ at NUMBER, AGE, and DATE. EG *...the industrialism of the nineteenth century.* ORDINAL

ninetieth /naɪntɪɪʳθ/. The **ninetieth** item in a series is the one that you count as number ninety: see □ at NUMBER and AGE. EG *In his ninetieth year he had lost the ability to speak.* ORDINAL

ninety /naɪnti¹/, **nineties**. **Ninety** is the number 90: see □ at NUMBER, AGE, DATE, MEASUREMENT, and MONEY. EG *He was making ninety dollars a week... 'Eighty nine and I'll never live to be ninety,' he wheezed.* NUM

ninny /nɪni¹/, **ninnies**. If you refer to someone as a **ninny**, you mean that they are rather silly; an informal word. EG *That was the one good result of our son marrying a rich ninny.* N COUNT = fool

ninth /naɪnθ/, **ninths**. 1 The **ninth** item in a series is the one that you count as number nine: see □ at NUMBER, AGE, and DATE. EG *...the ninth floor of the Hotel.* ORDINAL

2 A **ninth** is one of nine equal parts of something. EG *In exchange for this work they get one ninth of the crop.* N COUNT : USU + *of* ⇑ fraction

nip /nɪp/, **nips, nipping, nipped**. 1 If you **nip** somewhere, usually somewhere nearby, you go there quickly or for a short time; an informal use. EG *I'll just nip out and post these letters... I was nipping up and down the stairs most of the time.* V+A = pop

2 If you **nip** someone or something, you pinch them or bite them lightly. EG *The horse nipped me on the back of the head... ...its beak nipping at my chin... ...to nip a feather off an ostrich.* ▸ used as a noun. EG *He gave her a nip, and then something of a bite, on the lips.* V+O : USU + A, V + A *(at)*, OR V ▸ N COUNT : USU SING = nibble

3 A **nip** is a small sip or amount of strong alcoholic drink. N PART = dram

4 If you say there is **a nip in the air**, you mean that it is rather cold; an informal expression. PHR : USED AS C

5 **Nip** is also an extremely offensive word for a Japanese or oriental person. N COUNT

nipper /nɪpə/, **nippers**. A **nipper** is a child; an informal word. EG *He's known the place since he was a nipper.* N COUNT = kid

nipple /nɪpəᵒl/, **nipples**. 1 The **nipples** on someone's body are the two small pieces of slightly hard flesh on their chest. Babies suck milk from their mothers' breasts through their mothers' nipples. EG *Infection can enter the breast through the nipple.* N COUNT

2 A **nipple** is also a piece of rubber or plastic in the shape of a nipple which is fitted to the top of a baby's bottle. N COUNT = teat

nippy /nɪpi¹/; an informal word. 1 If you say that the weather is **nippy**, you mean that it is rather cold. EG *The air was nippy outside.* ADJ QUALIT = chilly

2 Someone or something that is **nippy** moves very quickly. EG *You'll catch him if you're nippy.* ADJ QUALIT = quick

nirvana /nɪəvɑ:nə, nɜ:-/, **nirvanas**. **Nirvana** is 1 the ultimate state of spiritual enlightenment which can be achieved in the Hindu and Buddhist religions. EG *...spiritual progress towards nirvana.* 2 a state of complete happiness and peace. EG *They would live in a Nirvana of perpetual happiness.* N UNCOUNT ⇑ release; N UNCOUNT/COUNT = paradise

nit /nɪt/, **nits**. 1 A **nit** is 1.1 a stupid or silly person; an informal British English use. EG *You nit... You thought he was an Old Etonian nit.* 1.2 the egg of a kind of louse that often lives in people's hair. EG *They looked to see if you have nits in your hair.* N COUNT; N COUNT : USU PL ⇑ parasite

2 If you say that someone is **picking nits**, you mean that they are finding fault with someone or something by concentrating on small and unimportant details. EG *He spent his time picking nits in their work.* PHR : VB INFLECTS ⇑ criticize = pick holes

nitpicking /nɪtpɪkɪŋ/; also spelled with a hyphen. When you refer to someone's **nitpicking**, you mean that they concentrate on small and unimportant details, especially so that they can find fault with something; used showing disapproval. EG *I'm sick of all this nitpicking.* ▸ used as an adjective. EG *...a legal process which is long, laborious, and nitpicking.* N UNCOUNT = quibbling ▸ ADJ QUALIT

nitrate /naɪtreɪt/, **nitrates**. A **nitrate** is a chemical compound that includes nitrogen and oxygen. Nitrates are used as fertilizers in agriculture. N COUNT/UNCOUNT

nitrogen /naɪtrədʒəˡn/ is a colourless element that has no smell and is usually found as a gas. It forms about 78% of the earth's atmosphere, and is found in all living things. N UNCOUNT

nitty-gritty /nɪti¹ grɪti¹/. The **nitty-gritty** of a matter, situation, activity, etc is the basic and most important parts of it or facts about it; an informal word. EG *We had to set out the nitty-gritty of our aims.* N SING : *the*+N = core

nitwit /nɪtwɪt/, **nitwits**. A **nitwit** is a stupid or silly person; an informal word used in British English. EG *They're a bunch of nitwits.* N COUNT = nit, twit

> **N MASS** □ In this dictionary N MASS is used in the grammar notes beside entries to mean that a noun is a mass noun. An N MASS normally behaves like an uncount noun. See □ at N UNCOUNT. However, unlike an uncount noun, it can also treat the things that it refers to as countable, and in this case it shows the usual distinction between the form with an 's' and the form without an 's'. Therefore, when the noun refers to a particular type, brand, or measure of something, it can be used in the plural. For example, *three* **teas** *means three cups of tea* or *three types of tea*; *three* **sugars** *means three spoonfuls of sugar* or *three types of sugar*; *they're different* **reds** *means they are different shades of red.* Some uncount nouns, especially those which refer to goods that you can buy, can be used as mass nouns by people who know a lot about them and who work with them. For example, in some technical situations you could talk about *steels* as in *High-grade steels are not suitable.* In this dictionary only nouns of this type which are commonly used with a plural have been called N MASS. Examples of mass nouns are **cheese** 1, **ink** 1.1, and **jam** 1. EG *...a piece of Swiss* **cheese**... *Five kinds of* **cheese** *on a wooden platter... ...imported Italian salami, hams and* **cheeses**... *This new* **ink** *dries very quickly... ...large angular writing in purple* **ink**... *...drawings we did when we were children, in green and purple* **inks**... *We were making* **jam**... *...fruit and vegetables with which to make* **jams**.

no /nəʊ/, **noes, no's**. The plural can be either **noes** or **no's**. 1 You use **no** in speech to express different sorts of responses and reactions, normally to indicate a negative response. You say **'No'** 1.1 as an answer to a question, when the answer could be 'yes' or 'no'. EG *'Did you see that programme last night?'–'No, I didn't.'... 'Do they speak any other language?'–'No'.* 1.2 to tell someone that they have made a false statement or answered a question wrongly. EG *'They go round kissing one another when they meet.'–'No they don't.'–'Yes they do. I've seen them doing it.'... No, I don't agree with you.* 1.3 to order someone not to do something. EG *No! Stop that at once.* 1.4 to refuse an offer; usually used with 'thanks' or 'thank you' in polite English. EG *'Do you want a biscuit?'–'No thanks.'* 1.5 to say that you are unwilling to agree to something that someone has asked you. EG *'Can you lend me ten quid?'–'No, I* CONVENTION : NEG; CONVENTION : NEG ⇑ wrong; EXCLAM; CONVENTION : NEG; CONVENTION : NEG *can't.'... After all, the worst the boss can do is say no if you ask him.* ● If you say that someone **will not take no for an answer**, you mean that they will not accept that you have refused to agree to something, so that they go on asking you to agree. ● PHR : VB INFLECTS, USU INF

2 You use **no** in conversation **2.1** to indicate your involvement in the conversation and to say that you agree with, accept, or understand a negative statement that the previous speaker has made. EG *'It's not difficult, you see.'-'No, it must be quite easy when you know how.'... 'They don't want to open longer than necessary.'-'No, of course.'* CONVENTION **2.2** as a polite way of introducing an objection to a negative statement that the previous speaker has made. EG *'The cars aren't meant to be fast.'-'No, but they can cruise quite comfortably.'... 'It's not that long really, is it?'-'No, but the thing is, sometimes it seems like it.'* CONVENTION **2.3** as a way of introducing a correction to what you have just said. EG *What are you going to be doing next year, Rajeev? No, not next year, the year after?... ...500 grams, no, a little less than that.* CONVENTION **2.4** to introduce a new topic or an explanation into a conversation. EG *No, to go back to what I was saying earlier, we really need to think again about this policy... 'Oh, I didn't expect you,' I said.-'No, well, I've just found out that I won't have to leave after all.'* CONVENTION ⇑ well **2.5** to express shock, disappointment, annoyance, or sadness at something that has happened or that you have just realized. EG *'Michael's fallen off his bike.'-'Oh no, not again.'* EXCLAM

3 You use **no** at the beginning of a noun group **3.1** to mean not any or not one, even though people might expect there to be one or some. EG *He has given no reason for his decision... I do it all on my own. I have no help at all... They had no immediate plans to change... She had no intention of spending the rest of her life working for them... There's no sense in making people unhappy... No country can insulate itself from the affairs of others.* DET : NEG **3.2** to emphasize that someone or something definitely does not have the characteristic or identity mentioned. EG *She is no friend of mine... No true believer is so bigoted as a convert... Beatty's no fool, I'm telling you.* DET + N COUNT IN SING : NEG **3.3** to mean that the thing mentioned is very small or unimportant; often used as an understatement of something that is in fact quite large or serious. EG *It's no distance at all... He had no wounds worth mentioning.* DET : NEG = hardly any

4 You also use **no** **4.1** in front of an adjective to make the adjective mean its opposite. EG *The seats have been replaced, which is no bad thing... This is no great handicap in the short run.* DET + ADJ + N : NEG **4.2** in front of a comparative adjective to say that something has either exactly the quality or amount mentioned, or less of it, but certainly not more. EG *The whole gun was no longer than eighteen inches... Winners will be notified by post no later than 31st August.* ADV + ADJ/ADV IN COMPAR : NEG **4.3** in front of a comparative adjective to emphasize the level, standard, or size of something, and to express surprise, scorn, or admiration at it. EG *He committed no fewer than 91 errors... ...a job that was no better than a common labourer's.* ADV + ADJ/ADV IN COMPAR : NEG ⇑ not

5 **No** is also used in statements without a main verb **5.1** in notices or instructions which say that a particular thing or activity is forbidden. EG *No smoking... No talking.* DET : NEG **5.2** in protests. EG *No Cruise missiles... No wage cuts!* DET : NEG = down with

6 If you say **there is no** doing a particular thing, you mean that it is very difficult or impossible to do that thing. EG *There was no denying it, he was an intelligent man... There's no arguing with my father.* PHR + -ING : VB INFLECTS

7 A **no** is a person who has answered 'no' to a question or who has voted against something; also used to refer to their answer or vote. EG *There were fifteen noes and one don't know.* N COUNT = nay

8 The word **no** is also used in the following expressions, which are explained at other places in this dictionary. ● **no doubt**: see **doubt**. ● **no way**: see **way**. ● **no less than**: see **less**. ● **no longer**: see **long**. ● **no more**: see **more**.

No., Nos.; also written with a small initial letter. **No.** is a written abbreviation for 'number', and is pronounced as 'number'. EG *He lives at No. 14 Sumatra Road... ...Chanel No. 5... ...Ray Keene, the no. 2 seed.* N UNCOUNT/ COUNT + NUM

nob /nɒb/, **nobs**. A **nob** is a person who is rich or who comes from a much higher social class than you; a rather old-fashioned word. EG *...the nobs attending the royal wedding.* N COUNT = toff

no ball, no balls. A **no ball** is a ball that is bowled in cricket in a way that is not allowed by the rules, for which an extra run is given to the batting side. N COUNT

nobble /nɒbəºl/, **nobbles, nobbling, nobbled**; an informal word. If you **nobble** someone, **1** you get their attention so that you can talk to them. V+O **2** you bribe or threaten them so that they will do something that you want them to do. V+O

nobility /nəʊbɪlɪti¹/. **1** **Nobility** is **1.1** the quality of being noble and admirable in behaviour and character. EG *He had nobility in defeat... He followed his principles with nobility.* N UNCOUNT = dignity **1.2** the condition of belonging to the nobility of a society. EG *The silken rope which was the privilege of nobility.* N UNCOUNT = rank

2 The **nobility** of a society are all the people who hold titles and high social rank. EG *The new rich of early commerce and industry aped the nobility... ...the entrenched power of the landed nobility.* N SING : the + N, VB CAN BE SING OR PL = aristocracy

noble /nəʊbəºl/, **nobler, noblest; nobles**. **1** Someone who is **noble** **1.1** is honest, brave, and unselfish, and deserves admiration and respect. EG *Among them were some of the greatest and noblest men in our history.* ▸ used of people's character and behaviour. EG *...a man of noble character... ...the noble impulse to save people from themselves.* ADJ QUALIT ⇑ admirable = worthy ▸ = lofty ◊ **nobly**. EG *She had nobly served the cause of Christianity.* ◊ ADV WITH VB **1.2** belongs to a high social class and has a title. EG *...young men of noble birth... ...the sons of noble families.* ADJ CLASSIF = aristocratic

2 Something that is **noble** is of superior and impressive quality or appearance. EG *...an old man with a noble head and a bristling moustache... ...noble brandies... ...one of the noblest collections of art in England.* ADJ QUALIT = fine, distinguished ◊ **nobly**. EG *The tower is made of brick, and nobly striped.* ◊ ADV = splendidly

3 A **noble** is someone who belongs to a high social class and has a title such as 'Baron' or 'Duke'; used mainly in former times. EG *Every great noble in the land wanted to marry the king's daughter.* N COUNT = lord, peer

nobleman /nəʊbəºlmə³n/, **noblemen**. A **nobleman** is a man who is a member of the nobility. EG *...the daughter of a Spanish nobleman.* N COUNT = aristocrat

noblewoman /nəʊbəºlwʊ¹məºn/, **noblewomen**. A **noblewoman** is a woman who is a member of the nobility. N COUNT

nobody /nəʊbə⁷di¹/, **nobodies**. The form **no-one** is also used. You use **nobody** and **no-one** when you are talking about people rather than things. Compare **nothing**. **1** **Nobody** or **no-one** means not a single person, or not a single member of a particular group or set. EG *Nobody seems to notice... There was nobody on the bridge at all... They had seen no-one else all afternoon... Well, I'm sorry but there's no-one here called Nikki.* PRON INDEF : NEG

2 A **nobody** is someone who does not matter to anyone, and has no authority or important position. EG *Miss Watkins was a nobody. She was a drifter. No family, no close friends.* N COUNT : IF SING, a + N = nonentity

nocturnal /nɒktɜːnəºl/. **1** Something that is **nocturnal** happens during the night. EG *You are now free to resume your nocturnal sightseeing tour of our city.* ADJ CLASSIF ⇑ night-time

2 An animal that is **nocturnal** is active mostly at night. EG *Leopards are essentially nocturnal.* ▸ used of animals' behaviour. EG *Their nocturnal habits make long-eared owls hard to see.* ADJ CLASSIF

nocturne /nɒktɜːn/, **nocturnes**. A **nocturne** is a short gentle piece of music, often one written to be played on the piano. EG *...Chopin's Nocturne in D flat.* N COUNT

nod /nɒd/, **nods, nodding, nodded**. **1** If you **nod**, **1.1** you move your head quickly down and up to show that you are answering 'yes' to a question, or to show agreement, understanding, or approval. EG *'Is it true?' She nodded... He nodded his head... I nod in agreement.* V OR V+O **1.2** you bend your head once in a particular direction in order to indicate something or to give someone a signal to do something. EG *'Ask him,' said Ringbaum, nodding towards Philip... She nodded to him to follow her.* V+A = gesture **1.3** you bend your head once when you meet or leave someone or when they leave you, as a way of saying hello or goodbye. EG *The ladies greeted me with a smile. I nodded to them and sat down... They all nodded a final good-night.* V OR V+O : IF + PREP THEN at/to **1.4** you keep letting your head fall forward because you are falling asleep while sitting down. EG *They sat in a triangle, nodding like old men in the sun.* V

2 If something **nods**, it bends or moves gently up and down. EG *There was not even a little breeze to make the poppies nod.* [V]

3 A **nod** is a quick movement of your head down and up. EG *From time to time, he gave him an encouraging nod... 'There it is,' she said indicating the car with a nod of her head.* [N COUNT: IF SING, USU a+N ⇑ movement]

4 The word **nod** is also used in the following expressions. **4.1** If you **give the nod** or if you **give** someone **the nod**, you give permission for something to be done; an informal expression. [PHR: VB INFLECTS] **4.2** If a proposal is accepted **on the nod**, it is accepted without being questioned or argued about; an informal expression. EG *It had gone through 'on the nod'.* [PHR: USED AS AN A ⇑ easily] **4.3** If you are **on nodding terms** with someone, you recognize them because you see them quite often and you perhaps say hello to them, but you do not know them well. EG *He knew nearly all of them by sight. He was even on nodding terms with a few of them.* [PHR: USED AS AN A, IF+PREP THEN+*with* ⇑ acquainted] • **a nodding acquaintance**: see **acquaintance**. • **a nod is as good as a wink**: see **wink**.

nod off. If you **nod off**, you fall asleep while you are sitting down, especially when you had not intended to fall asleep; an informal expression. EG *They just sit and chat to each other, or nod off... His remarks left delegates nodding off.* [PHRASAL VB: V+ADV = doze off]

noddle /nɒdə⁰l/, **noddles**. Your **noddle** is your head; an informal word. [N COUNT]

node /nəʊd/, **nodes**. A **node** is **1** the place on the stem of a plant from which a branch or leaf grows; a technical term in biology. [N COUNT] **2** a place on a diagram where two lines or branches meet. [N COUNT]

nodule /nɒdju⁴l/, **nodules**. A **nodule** is **1** a small round lump on something, especially the root of a plant. EG *...the bacteria in the root nodules of beans.* [N COUNT ⇑ protuberance]
2 a small rounded lump of rock, especially one surrounded by another type of rock; a technical term in geology. EG *Embedded in the limestone are nodules of flint.* [N COUNT ⇑ protuberance]

Noel /nəʊel/ means Christmas; used especially in greetings and on cards that you send to people at Christmas. [N PROPER]

noggin /nɒgɪn/, **noggins**. A **noggin** is a small amount of an alcoholic drink; an old-fashioned word. EG *Meantime we might as well have a noggin.* [N COUNT = dram]

no-go area, no-go areas. A **no-go area** is a district or place which is controlled by a group of people who use force to prevent the army, police, or other people from entering it or being there. EG *The Catholics set up no-go areas on their side... 90 per cent of the country had become no-go areas.* [N COUNT]

noise /nɔɪz/, **noises, noised**. **1** A **noise** is a sound that someone or something makes. EG *A sudden noise made Brody jump... The branches snapped with a dry cracking noise... The old lady made some noises to the horse, and pulled at the reins... Dolphins produce a great variety of noises.* [N COUNT]

2 Noise is **2.1** a loud or unpleasant sound. EG *Try not to make so much noise... ...the noise of music from the jukebox... They didn't seem to notice the pollution and the noise.* [N UNCOUNT/COUNT = racket, row] **2.2** enthusiastic discussion about a particular subject or interest in that subject. EG *The political noise comes mainly from the businessmen.* [N UNCOUNT/COUNT ⇑ reaction]
2.3 interference that occurs in a signal and prevents you from hearing sounds properly. [N UNCOUNT]

3 If something **is noised** about or abroad, people talk about it so that it becomes generally known. EG *It had been noised abroad that the departments would shortly be amalgamated.* [V+O/REPORT-CL +A (*about/abroad/around*): USU PASS]

4 The word **noise** is also used in the following expressions. **4.1** If you **make a noise about** something, you complain or argue a lot about it in order to draw attention to it. EG *The women were making a lot of noise about having a room of their own.* [PHR: VB INFLECTS = fuss] **4.2** If you **make noises**, you indicate particular feelings or ideas by the way you talk rather than by mentioning or discussing them directly. EG *They were denying involvement and making placatory noises... Why are you making noises about supporting them?* [PHR: VB INFLECTS] **4.3** If you **make the right noises** or **make all the right noises**, you show concern or enthusiasm about something because you know you ought to rather than because you really want to. EG *She said I would have to come and visit her. I made the right noises, then changed the subject... Mr Howell made all the right noises about this, but what we need is action.* [PHR: VB INFLECTS] **4.4** See also **big noise**.

noiseless /nɔɪzlɪ²s/. Something that is **noiseless** does not make any sound. EG *...a totally noiseless fan.* [ADJ QUALIT = silent]
◊ **noiselessly**. EG *I sat down beside my wife noiselessly.* [◊ ADV WITH VB]

noisome /nɔɪsəm/. Someone or something that is **noisome** is offensive and extremely unpleasant; a formal word. EG *...the most noisome politicians of this or any other century... ...noisome vapours.* [ADJ QUALIT = noxious]

noisy /nɔɪzi¹/, **noisier, noisiest**. **1** Someone or something that is **noisy** makes a lot of noise, especially loud or unpleasant noise. EG *The audience was large and noisy... ...noisy children... Her noisy efforts with the sink plunger proved unsuccessful.* [ADJ QUALIT ≠ quiet] ◊ **noisily**. EG *He sipped noisily at his coffee... My sister was crying noisily.* [◊ ADV WITH VB = loudly]

2 Noisy behaviour and actions attract people's attention to a subject by repeatedly mentioning and discussing it. EG *...the noisy opportunism of their political line.* [ADJ QUALIT = strident, vociferous]

3 A place that is **noisy** is full of a lot of noise, especially loud or unpleasant noise. EG *They complained that Canton was hot and noisy and they wanted to leave... The living-room was as crowded as ever and just as noisy.* [ADJ QUALIT ≠ quiet, peaceful]

nomad /nəʊmæd/, **nomads**. A **nomad** is a person who belongs to a tribe which travels from place to place rather than living in one place all the time. EG *...the nomads of Central Asia.* [N COUNT ⇑ traveller]

nomadic /nəʊmædɪk/. **1** A **nomadic** society or group of people travel from place to place rather than living in one place all the time. EG *...the nomadic hunting societies of Siberia.* [ADJ CLASSIF ⇑ travelling]

2 A **nomadic** way of life is one in which you travel from place to place and do not have a settled home. EG *...a nomadic way of life... ...a carefree nomadic existence.* [ADJ QUALIT ⇑ travelling]

no-man's land. **1 No-man's land** is land that is not owned or controlled by anyone, for example the land between two boundaries. EG *...carrying the white flag into no-man's land.* [N UNCOUNT ⇑ place]

2 A **no-man's land** is a situation in which nothing seems clear or definite; a literary use. EG *...a no-man's land between sleeping and waking.* [N SING WITH DET = grey area]

nom de plume /nɒm də plu:m/, **noms de plume**. The singular and the plural are pronounced in the same way. A **nom de plume** is the name that an author uses instead of his or her real name; a formal expression. EG *Why would a lady choose a nom de plume such as George Eliot?... He intended using a nom de plume in case our English friends disliked his views.* [N COUNT]

nomenclature /nə⁶menklətʃə/. The **nomenclature** of a particular set of things is the system of naming those things; a formal word. EG *...scientific nomenclature.* [N UNCOUNT ⇑ classification]

nominal /nɒmɪnə⁰l/. **1** Something that is **nominal** is supposed to have a particular identity or status, but in reality does not have it. EG *We were charged with directing the operation, though under the nominal leadership of a guerrilla general.* [ADJ CLASSIF ⇑ apparent = ostensible, theoretical] ◊ **nominally**. EG *Dad, nominally a Methodist, entered churches only for weddings and funerals.* [◊ ADV = theoretically ≠ in practice]

2 A **nominal** price or sum of money is very small in comparison with the real cost or value of the thing you are buying or selling. EG *At a nominal price, the settlers got the rest of the land.* [ADJ CLASSIF: ATTRIB ⇑ minimal = token]

nominate /nɒmɪneɪt/, **nominates, nominating, nominated**. **1** If you **nominate** someone, you formally suggest them as a candidate in an election or competition or for a job. EG *I've been nominated for a Senior Lectureship... He was nominated by the Democrats to stand against Theodore Roosevelt.* ▸ You can also **nominate** things, for example for awards. EG *...one of the songs that were nominated for the Oscar.* [V+O: IF+PREP THEN *for* = propose, put forward]

2 If you **nominate** someone for a job or to a position, you formally choose them to hold that job or position. EG *A third of the committee members are nominated by the local authority... Trade unions nominate representatives to public bodies.* [V+O, V+O+A (*as/for/to*), OR V+O+*to*-INF = appoint, assign]

nomination /nɒmɪneɪʃə⁰n/, **nominations**. **1** A **nomination** is an official suggestion of someone as a candidate in an election or competition or for a job. EG *...a list of nominations for senior lectureships... Humphrey had no real chance of winning the nomination.* [N COUNT] ▸ used as an uncount noun. EG *Membership of* [▸ N UNCOUNT] *the committee is by nomination from within the party.*

2 The **nomination** of someone to a particular job or position is their appointment to that job or position. EG *...Judge Sandra Day O'Connor's nomination to the Supreme Court.* N UNCOUNT/COUNT : USU+SUPP ⇑ choice = election

nominative /nɒmɪnətɪv/, **nominatives**. In the grammar of some languages, for example Latin, the **nominative** case is the case that shows that a noun or pronoun is the subject of a verb. ▸ used as a noun. EG *It's in the nominative.* ADJ CLASSIF ▸ N SING : *the*+N

nominee /nɒmɪniː/, **nominees**. A **nominee** is someone who is nominated for or to something. EG *Dave is this year's nominee for the Exchange scheme.* N COUNT = candidate

non- is 1 added to adjectives and nouns that describe something or someone as having a particular property or quality, to form other adjectives and nouns describing something or someone as not having that property or quality. EG *...violent→non-violent... ...existent→non-existent... ...socialist→non-socialist.* PREFIX 2 added to nouns that refer to a particular kind of action, to form other nouns referring to a failure or refusal to take this kind of action. EG *...cooperation→non-cooperation... ...acceptance→non-acceptance... ...aggression→non-aggression... ...appearance→non-appearance.* PREFIX 3 added to nouns to form other nouns that describe something as not being the thing that it is supposed or intended to be. EG *...event→non-event... ...answer→non-answer... ...art→non-art.* PREFIX

non-aggression is the idea or plan that countries should not attack, fight, or try to harm each other in any way. EG *He met top Soviet leaders, which led to a non-aggression pact between the two countries.* N UNCOUNT

non-alcoholic. A **non-alcoholic** drink does not contain alcohol. EG *...non-alcoholic lager.* ADJ CLASSIF

non-aligned. A country that is **non-aligned** does not support or is not part of any politically linked group of countries, especially one headed by the United States or USSR. EG *...a policy of friendship toward the developing and non-aligned countries.* ADJ CLASSIF ⇑ neutral

non-alignment is the state or policy of being non-aligned. EG *No change in our position of nonalignment is contemplated.* N UNCOUNT ⇑ neutrality

nonchalance /nɒnʃələns/ is the quality of being very calm and of seeming not to worry or care very much about things. EG *The answers are given with so much confidence and such nonchalance.* N UNCOUNT = equanimity, unconcern

nonchalant /nɒnʃələnt/. Someone who is **nonchalant** behaves calmly and in a way which suggests that they do not worry or care very much about things. EG *He tried to sound cheerful and nonchalant.* ▸ used of people's behaviour. EG *Be polite in a teasing, nonchalant manner.* ◊ **nonchalantly**. EG *The officer waved a hand nonchalantly.* ADJ QUALIT = carefree, unconcerned ▸ = casual ◊ ADV WITH VB = carelessly

non-combatant, **non-combatants**. A **non-combatant** is someone who does not actually fight in a war, although they may be in the armed forces or involved in the war in some way. N COUNT ≠ participant

non-commissioned officer, **non-commissioned officers**. A **non-commissioned officer** is a person who holds a military rank such as sergeant or corporal and who has been appointed to this rank from the lower ranks, rather than by receiving a commission. N COUNT

noncommittal /nɒnkəmɪtəl/. If someone is **noncommittal**, they do not express their opinion or decision clearly and firmly. EG *On planning the government is studiously noncommittal... 'She's a pleasant girl', I said, trying to be non-committal.* ▸ used of things that people say or do. EG *I received a noncommittal letter in return.* ◊ **noncommittally**. EG *'I see', I said noncommittally.* ADJ QUALIT ⇑ vague = evasive, politic ◊ ADV WITH VB = cautiously

non compos mentis /nɒn kɒmpəs mentɪs/. If someone is **non compos mentis**, they are unable to understand what they are doing, for example because they are mentally ill, and therefore they are not legally responsible for their actions; a legal term. ADJ CLASSIF : PRED ⇑ insane

nonconformist /nɒnkənfɔːmɪst/, **nonconformists**; also spelled with a hyphen, and with a capital letter for paragraph 3. 1 A **nonconformist** is someone who behaves in an unusual or rebellious way. EG *The present system severely pressures all nonconformists, intellectuals, artists, and so on.* N COUNT = rebel, individualist

2 Ideas or ways of behaving that are **nonconformist** are unusual, original, or eccentric. EG *I've got rather nonconformist ideas on this.* ADJ QUALIT = unconventional

3 A **Nonconformist** is a Protestant in Great Britain who does not belong to the Church of England. EG *...a committee which includes Catholics, Anglicans, and Nonconformists... ...a Nonconformist chaplain.* N COUNT ⇑ Christian

nonconformity /nɒnkənfɔːmɪti/ is unusual or rebellious behaviour. EG *...the product of middle-class nonconformity and dissent.* N UNCOUNT

non-contributory. If a pension scheme is **non-contributory**, regular contributions to it are made by the employer rather than by the employee. ADJ CLASSIF : USU ATTRIB

non-cooperation /nɒn kəʊɒpəreɪʃən/ is a way of protesting in which you do not do any work apart from the work that you are officially required to do. EG *They adopted a policy of non-cooperation with management.* N UNCOUNT

nondescript /nɒndɪskrɪpt/. Something that is **nondescript** is fairly dull, uninteresting, and unexciting in appearance or design. EG *...a complex of nondescript buildings... The women were dressed in nondescript clothes.* ADJ QUALIT ⇑ ordinary = characterless

none /nʌn/. 1 **None** means 1.1 not any or not one; often used instead of a structure with 'not' and 'any' in order to emphasize something or to suggest that the situation is unexpected or unusual. EG *'You had no difficulty in finding it?'–'None at all.'... This created a class of large landowners where none had existed before... She showed none of the belligerence and arrogance I had learned to expect... I have answered every single question. My opponent has answered none.* PRON : NEG, ALSO +*of* 1.2 no people at all or no members of a particular group or set. EG *None of us understood the play... He wasn't much use, and none of the other staff were either... Most people are kind. Lots of them very kind. But none so kind as Otto... None could afford the books or food.* PRON : NEG, ALSO +*of* ⇑ nobody

2 If you say that you will **have none of** something, you mean that you refuse to tolerate it; an informal expression. EG *Alfred would have none of it... I'm having none of that language here.* PHR : VB INFLECTS ≠ tolerate

3 **None but** means only; a fairly formal expression. EG *He said that he had none but the most friendly feelings towards her.* PHR+NG = purely

4 You use **none too** in front of an adjective or adverb as a way of making it negative; a fairly formal expression. EG *We don't really understand it. We argue, but we're none too sure what we're arguing about... He turned back to her and hauled her none too gently to her feet.* PHR+ADJ/ADV : NEG ⇑ not

5 You use **none the** to say that someone or something does not have any more of a particular quality than they did before. EG *She looks none the better for her holiday... He returned none the wiser.* PHR+ADJ/ADV IN COMPAR : NEG = no

6 The word **none** is also used in the following expressions, which are explained at other places in this dictionary. • **none of** someone's **business**: see **business**. • **none of your concern**: see **concern**. • **none other than**: see **other**. • **none the worse**: see **worse**. • **second to none**: see **second**. • See also **nonetheless**.

nonentity /nɒnentɪti/, **nonentities**. 1 A **nonentity** is a person who is unimportant and insignificant. EG *Gant came from a family of nonentities.* N COUNT ≠ VIP, bigwig

2 **Nonentity** is the state of being unimportant or insignificant. EG *They had rescued him from nonentity.* N UNCOUNT ⇑ insignificance

non-essential. Things that are **non-essential** are not absolutely necessary. EG *Leave behind all non-essential items... We must cut back non-essential private motoring.* ADJ CLASSIF = unnecessary ≠ essential

nonetheless /nʌnðəles/ means the same as **nevertheless**; a fairly formal word. EG *Admittedly legal training may be a bit wider and may include elements of economics and political science. But it is nonetheless a law-dominated training... She couldn't act at all. Nonetheless she was a very hot box office attraction.* ADV SEN = however

non-event, non-events. If you say that something was a **non-event** you mean that it was uninteresting or disappointing, although you had expected it to be interesting or exciting. N COUNT ⇑ disappointment = anticlimax

non-existence is the fact of not existing. EG *He spoke at length about the nonexistence of philosophical problems.* N UNCOUNT ⇑ absence ≠ existence

non-existent. Something that is **non-existent** does not exist or is not in a particular place although you expect it to exist or to be in that place. EG *The animals are small, the trees virtually non-existent...* ADJ CLASSIF

...*a certain Englishman masquerading as a non-existent Frenchman called André Martin.*

non-fiction is writing that is based on fact and truth rather than a story or an account that has been invented. EG *In non-fiction books with illustrations, the text is often poor.* — N UNCOUNT ≠ fiction

non-flammable. If a fabric or substance is **non-flammable**, it will not catch fire. — ADJ CLASSIF ⇑ fireproof

non-human means not human; used especially of animals and other living creatures. EG ...*the non-human primates–chimpanzees and the like.* — ADJ CLASSIF : USU ATTRIB ≠ human

non-intervention is the practice or policy of not becoming involved in a dispute or disagreement between other people and of not helping either side. EG ...*an overall commitment to the principle of non-intervention.* — N UNCOUNT ≠ intervention

non-iron. **Non-iron** clothes do not need to be ironed because they are made of fabrics that do not crease. — ADJ CLASSIF = drip dry

non-member, non-members. A **non-member** of a particular club or organization is someone who is not a member of it; used for example of someone who visits the club with a member and has to pay a different entrance fee. — N COUNT ⇑ outsider ≠ member

no-no. If something is a **no-no**, it is considered undesirable or unacceptable; an informal word. EG *He didn't quite grasp why photos were a no-no.* — N SING : a+N = forbidden

non-nuclear means not using or involving nuclear weapons or nuclear power. EG ...*the deployment of non-nuclear weapons...* ...*non-nuclear countries.* — ADJ CLASSIF : ATTRIB

no-nonsense means firm, efficient, and concerned only with things that are important and relevant. EG *I liked his no-nonsense approach to the whole matter.* — ADJ CLASSIF : ATTRIB = straightforward

non-payment is a failure to pay a sum of money that is owed. EG *Joy's stepfather was in prison for non-payment of fines.* — N UNCOUNT ≠ payment

nonplussed /nɒnplʌst/. If you are **nonplussed**, you feel confused and unsure how to react. EG ▸ *Swallow looked nonplussed. She opened her mouth a number of times... Mr Hatchett was completely nonplussed by the inexplicable Mrs Taswell.* — ADJ QUALIT ⇑ uncertain = at a loss

non-profit-making. An organization or charity that is **non-profit-making** is not run with the intention of making a profit. — ADJ CLASSIF

non-proliferation is the limiting of the production and spread of something such as nuclear or chemical weapons. EG ...*a non-proliferation treaty.* — N UNCOUNT ⇑ restriction

non-resident, non-residents. A **non-resident** is someone who is not living in a particular place such as a country or not staying in a particular building such as a hotel. EG *Is the hotel bar open to non-residents?* — N COUNT ⇑ person ≠ resident

nonsense /nɒnsəns/. **1 Nonsense** is **1.1** words, speech, or texts that do not mean anything and do not make sense. EG *You can throw the computer program out of joint by typing in nonsense...* ...*a nonsense answer.* — N UNCOUNT = rubbish **1.2** something spoken or written that you disagree with because you consider it untrue, stupid, or meaningless. EG *A lot of nonsense is talked about the temperature of wine... 'You see, I am her father.'–'Nonsense,' he said. 'You are not'... Their policy on defence is military nonsense.* ● **stuff and nonsense**: see **stuff**. — N UNCOUNT, OR EXCLAM = rubbish **1.3** foolish behaviour that makes a particular situation very difficult. EG *Stop this nonsense, Louisa, for God's sake... We should put a stop to all this nonsense and make it clear who is in charge... It would patently be a nonsense to put him in complete control.* — N UNCOUNT, OR N SING WITH DET = foolishness **1.4** poetry or writing that is specially written to be amusing without meaning anything or making sense. EG *I recalled the charming nonsense verse I used to write her...* ...*Edward Lear's Nonsense Poems.* — N UNCOUNT : USU BEFORE N

2 Nonsense is sometimes used after a noun or adjective in order to show that you dislike or disapprove of the activity, situation, or thing described by the noun or adjective. EG *We were warned not to get caught up in any sort of publicity nonsense, interviews or photographs... I look forward to the day when all this atomic nonsense is abandoned.* — N UNCOUNT : MOD +N = rubbish, stuff

3 To **make a nonsense of** something or to **make nonsense of** it means to cause it to lose its good, important, or useful qualities, and to become ridiculous, pointless, or a waste of time. EG *The rest of his policies made nonsense of his call for moderation... The video tape collection makes nonsense of sitting in a cinema.* — PHR : VB INFLECTS

nonsensical /nɒnsɛnsɪkəl/. Something that is **nonsensical** is stupid, ridiculous, or untrue. EG *All this talk about a shortage of energy looks rather nonsensical... This attitude seemed nonsensical to the general public.* — ADJ QUALIT = absurd

non sequitur /nɒn sɛkwɪtə/, **non sequiturs**. A **non sequitur** is a statement, remark, or conclusion that does not follow naturally or logically from what has just been said; a formal word. EG *This is a complete non sequitur from what's been going on.* — N COUNT

non-shrink. Fabric that is **non-shrink** has been specially treated so that it does not shrink when it is washed. — ADJ CLASSIF

non-smoker, non-smokers. A **non-smoker** is someone who does not smoke. EG *I am a confirmed non-smoker.* — N COUNT ⇑ person ≠ smoker

non-smoking. A **non-smoking** area in a public place such as a train or cinema is an area in which people are not allowed to smoke. EG *Do you prefer the smoking or non-smoking section?* — ADJ CLASSIF ≠ smoking

non-standard. Words, expressions, or pronunciations that are **non-standard** are different in some way from the standard language used by most educated speakers, and are often regarded as incorrect. — ADJ CLASSIF ⇑ atypical

non-starter, non-starters. A **non-starter** is someone or something, such as a plan or idea, that has no chance of success. EG *They accepted that United Nations sponsorship was a non-starter and that the only alternative was private funding... I was perfectly content to remain a non-starter as a cricketer.* — N COUNT : USU USED AS C

non-stick. A saucepan, frying-pan, or baking tin that is **non-stick** has a thin layer of a special coating on its inside, which prevents food from sticking to it. EG ...*non-stick saucepans.* — ADJ CLASSIF

non-stop. Something that is **non-stop** continues without any pauses or interruptions. EG *They keep up a more or less non-stop conversation...* ...*taking the non-stop flight to London.* — ADJ CLASSIF ⇑ continuous

non-U. Behaviour or language that is **non-U** is characteristic of the lower classes and is therefore considered unacceptable among the upper classes; used in British English. — ADJ QUALIT ⇑ inferior ≠ U

non-union. An organization or company that is **non-union** does not employ workers who belong to a trade union. EG ...*workers from non-union businesses.* ▸ also used of people who do not belong to a trade union. EG ...*non-union labour.* — ADJ CLASSIF = non-unionized

non-unionized; also spelled **non-unionised**. People who are **non-unionized** do not belong to a trade union. EG *Can non-unionised employees participate?* ▸ also used of jobs that employ people who do not belong to a trade union. EG ...*those who have spent their lives in non-unionised, low paid employment.* — ADJ CLASSIF = non-union ≠ unionized

non-verbal. A form of communication that is **non-verbal** does not involve the use of language. EG *Art, like gesture, is a form of non-verbal expression... Children's ability was measured by verbal and non-verbal reasoning tests.* — ADJ CLASSIF ⇑ wordless ≠ verbal

non-violence is the use of peaceful methods that do not harm or injure people in order to try to make changes happen, especially political changes. EG *He was interested in Gandhian ideas of non-violence.* — N UNCOUNT ⇑ pacifism ≠ violence

non-violent. Actions, policies, attitudes, etc that are **non-violent** involve or support the use of peaceful methods that do not hurt or injure people in order to try and make changes happen, especially political changes. EG *It is to be a peaceful, non-violent protest...* ...*Martin Luther King's non-violent policies.* — ADJ CLASSIF ⇑ pacifist ≠ violent

non-white, non-whites. Someone who is **non-white** is a member of a race of people who are not of European origin. EG *Of all the members of the Metropolitan Police Force, only 119 are non-white.* — ADJ CLASSIF = black, coloured ≠ white ▸ used as a noun. EG *Such economic policies are hurting non-whites badly.* — ▸ N COUNT

noodle /nuːdəl/, **noodles**. **Noodles** are long thin strips of pasta which usually contain egg. Noodles are often used in Chinese, Italian, and other cookery and are sometimes put into soup. — N COUNT : USU ⇑ food

nook /nʊk/, **nooks**. A **nook** is a small and sheltered place; a rather literary word. EG ...*a secluded nook... I longed for a safe nook out of the wind.* — N COUNT = corner ● If you talk about **every nook and cranny** of a place, you are emphasizing that you mean all the parts of it. EG *Every nook and cranny of this place brought back memories... They poke into every nook and cranny, finger the carving in the furniture.* — ● PHR : USED A S/O

noon /nuːn/. 1 **Noon** is twelve o'clock in the middle of the day. EG *The visitor turned up at noon.* N UNCOUNT = midday

2 **Noon** means happening or appearing in the middle part of the day. EG *We do our shopping before the noon heat.* N BEFORE N = midday, noonday

noonday /nuːndeɪ/. 1 **Noonday** means happening or appearing in the middle part of the day. EG *It was lit by a flash brighter than the noonday sun.* N BEFORE N = midday, noon

2 **Noonday** also means twelve o'clock in the middle of the day; an old-fashioned or literary use. EG *At around noonday two people entered the grove.* N UNCOUNT = noon, midday

no-one /nəʊ wʌn/; also spelled as two words. **No-one** means the same as nobody: see **nobody 1**.

noose /nuːs/, **nooses**. A **noose** is a piece of rope that is tied into a circle, being used for example to hang people. EG *...the hangman's noose.* N COUNT

nope /nəʊp/ is sometimes used instead of 'no' as a response in informal English. EG *'Can you start tomorrow?'-'Nope. Monday's the earliest.'* CONVENTION ≠ yes

nor /nɔː/ is used 1 after 'neither' in order to introduce the second alternative or the last of a number of alternatives in a negative statement. EG *Neither Margaret nor John was there... My father could neither read nor write... He neither drinks, smokes nor eats meat... Her eyes showed neither amusement nor embarrassment nor nervousness.* CONJ COORD: NEG, *neither...nor* 2 after a negative statement in order to add something else that the negative statement applies to. EG *This is not the whole story, nor anything like the whole story... Melanie was not to be found-not that day, nor the next day, nor the day after that.* CONJ COORD: NEG = and not 3 after a negative statement in order to introduce another negative statement which adds information to the previous one. EG *I could not afford to eat in restaurants and nor could anyone I knew... I couldn't understand a word they said, nor could they understand me.* ADV SEN+AUX/MODAL+S: NEG = neither

Nordic /nɔːdɪk/. 1 **Nordic** means relating to the countries of northern Europe, especially Scandinavia. EG *He considers that the British political landscape resembles that of the Nordic countries.* ADJ CLASSIF

2 Someone who looks **Nordic** has blond hair, blue eyes, and a fair skin, and is fairly tall. EG *The colonel was a handsome man, with his strong Nordic face and white-blond hair.* ADJ CLASSIF ⇑ Germanic

norm /nɔːm/, **norms**. 1 A **norm** is 1.1 a way of behaving that is considered normal and usual and that people expect from you, for example in society or in a particular situation. EG *...the conventional norms of polite European society.* N COUNT: USU PL ⇑ convention 1.2 an official standard or level of achievement that you are expected to reach. EG *The factory has been built strictly to central government norms.* N COUNT ⇑ requirement

2 If you say that a situation is **the norm**, you mean that it is usual and expected. EG *In Russia, working wives have been the norm throughout the Soviet era.* N SING: *the*+N = typical

normal /nɔːməᵒl/. 1 Something that is **normal** is usual and ordinary, in accordance with what people expect. EG *Can she lead a fairly normal life?... Traffic was normal for an August weekend... In normal circumstances I would have resigned immediately... The new plaster has shrunk slightly, as is normal.* ADJ QUALIT = typical ≠ abnormal

2 Someone who is **normal** 2.1 behaves in a way that is considered acceptable and usual. EG *Barter's the most normal person I've ever met.* ADJ QUALIT ≠ odd 2.2 is generally healthy in body and mind, without any major defects or problems. EG *This is a perfectly normal baby... ...a completely normal child.* ADJ CLASSIF

normalcy /nɔːməᵒlsi¹/ is the same as normality; an old-fashioned and formal word. N UNCOUNT

normality /nɔːmælɪti¹/ is a situation in which everything is normal, usual, and as people would expect. EG *He nursed her back to normality... People have a longing for normality.* N UNCOUNT

normalize /nɔːməlaɪz/, **normalizes, normalizing, normalized**; also spelled **normalise**. When you **normalize** a situation or when it **normalizes**, it becomes normal. EG *If you can talk to her you stand a better chance of normalising the situation.* V-ERG

normally /nɔːməli¹/. If you say that something **normally** happens or that you **normally** do a particular thing, you mean that 1 it is what usually happens or what you usually do. EG *I don't normally drink at lunch... Meetings are normally held three or four times a year... How many patients does a practitioner normally have on his list?* ADV: USU WITH VB, OR ADV SEN 2 it happens in a way that is usual and in accordance with what people expect. EG *The important thing is that she's eating normally.* ADV WITH VB

Norman /nɔːmən/. 1 A **Norman** is someone who comes from northern France, especially one of the people who invaded and conquered England in 1066, or their descendants. N COUNT

2 **Norman** is also used to refer to the period of history in Britain from the late 11th century until the end of the 12th century, and in particular to the style of architecture of that period. ADJ CLASSIF

normative /nɔːmətɪv/ means creating or stating particular norms or rules of behaviour. EG *We must provide some normative guidelines... ...a normative judgment about equality.* ADJ CLASSIF

north /nɔːθ/; often spelled with a capital letter, especially when used to refer to a region. 1 The **north** is 1.1 the direction which is on your left when you are looking towards the direction where the sun rises. EG *The land to the north and east was low-lying... ...operating from Norwegian airfields in the far north... Set the compass to north and then work out the direction we have to walk.* • See also **magnetic north, true north**. N SING: *the*+N, OR N UNCOUNT 1.2 the part of a place, country, or region which is towards the north. EG *He became quite a figure in the north of England.* N SING: *the*+N, IF+PREP THEN +*of*

2 **North** means towards the north or to the north of a place or thing. EG *They were heading north... It's 150 miles or so north of Salisbury... Due north lay the highest cliffs of the island... I remember we were on a vacation up north.* ADV WITH VB: USU AFTER VB

3 The **north** part of a place, country, or region is the part which is towards the north. EG *The organization is run from a basement flat in north London... We flew over the deserted mountains of North Arizona... ...the north face of the Eiger... ...the Labour MP for Aberdeen North.* ADJ CLASSIF: ATTRIB, OR IN NAMES

4 A **north** wind blows from the north. ADJ CLASSIF

northbound /nɔːθbaund/. **Northbound** roads, cars, trains, etc lead or are travelling towards the north. EG *An accident has closed the northbound section of the Dartford Tunnel... ...platform 1 northbound, platform 2 southbound.* ADJ CLASSIF

north-east; also spelled without a hyphen, and often spelled with a capital letter or capital letters when used to refer to a region. 1 The **north-east** is 1.1 the direction which is halfway between north and east. EG *Our route lay somewhere to the north-east... We attack from the north-east in two waves.* N SING: *the*+N 1.2 the part of a place, country, or region which is towards the north-east. EG *...the north-east of England... All the kids in the North-East in those days had street teams.* N SING: *the*+N, IF+PREP THEN +*of*

2 **North-east** means towards the north-east or to the north-east of a place or thing. EG *It had turned away north-east and passed out of view... It's a small town about fifteen kilometers northeast of Uppsala.* ADV WITH VB: USU AFTER VB

3 The **north-east** part of a place, country, or region is the part which is towards the north-east. EG *The oldest part is close to the north-east entrance... A donkey cart trots down a road in north-east Brazil, headed for Recife.* ADJ CLASSIF: ATTRIB = north-eastern

4 A **north-east** wind blows from the north-east. ADJ CLASSIF

north-easterly; also spelled without a hyphen. 1 A **north-easterly** point, area, or direction is to the north-east or towards the north-east. EG *All the streams were flowing in a north-easterly direction to the coast.* ADJ QUALIT

2 A **north-easterly** wind blows from the north-east. ADJ CLASSIF

north-eastern; also spelled without a hyphen. **North-eastern** means in or from the north-east of a region or country. EG *In September 1975, floods in north-eastern India made 233,000 people homeless.* ADJ CLASSIF: USU ATTRIB

northerly /nɔːðəli¹/. 1 A **northerly** point, area, or direction is to the north or towards the north. EG *...the wet, northerly slopes... One convoy was proceeding along a more northerly route and another along a more southerly track.* ADJ QUALIT = northern

2 A **northerly** wind blows from the north. ADJ CLASSIF

northern /nɔːðəˢn/ means in or from the north of a region or country. EG *It lies in the Magdalena valley between two arms of the northern Andes... These cliffs are the finest bird breeding grounds in the Northern Hemisphere.* ADJ CLASSIF: USU ATTRIB

northerner /nɔːðənə/, **northerners**. A **northerner** is a person who was born in or who lives in the north of a place or country. EG *More civil service* N COUNT *posts and contracts would be likely to go to Northerners.*

northernmost /nɔːðəˢnməʊst/. The **northernmost** part of an area or the **northernmost** thing in a line is the one that is farther towards the north than any other. EG *That was only possible in his country on its northernmost island, Hokkaido.* ADJ CLASSIF : ATTRIB ≠ southernmost

North Pole. The **North Pole** is the place on the surface of the earth which is farthest towards the north. EG *We were flying high, high above the North Pole.* N PROPER : *the*+N ≠ South Pole

northward /nɔːθwəd/or **northwards** means towards the north. EG *The engine droned on and on as we flew northward... She battered her way northwards through the wild seas.* ▸ **Northward** is also used as an adjective. EG *...the northward offensive of the Eighth Army.* ADV WITH VB ▸ ADJ CLASSIF

north-west; also spelled without a hyphen, and often spelled with a capital letter or capital letters when used to refer to a region. **1** The **north-west** is **1.1** the direction which is halfway between north and west. EG *At the bridge the lake curves to the north-west.* N SING : *the*+N **1.2** the part of a place, country, or region which is towards the north-west. EG *I love the soft speech of the people away up in the north-west... There's a large hilly area in the north-west... I returned to the Pacific Northwest, where I had a fellowship.* N SING : *the*+N, IF+PREP THEN *of*

2 North-west means towards the north-west or to the north-west of a place or thing. EG *Some 300 miles north-west of Kampala, there is an abandoned customs post.* ADV WITH VB : USU AFTER VB

3 The **north-west** part of a place, country, or region is the part which is towards the north-west. EG *It's an extensive Roman settlement in north-west England... ...the north-west frontier of India remained a battleground.* ADJ CLASSIF : ATTRIB = northwestern

4 A **north-west** wind blows from the north-west. ADJ CLASSIF

north-westerly; also spelled without a hyphen. **1** A **north-westerly** point, area, or direction is to the north-west or towards the north-west. EG *We took the more picturesque north-westerly route.* ADJ QUALIT

2 A **north-westerly** wind blows from the north-west. ADJ CLASSIF

north-western; also spelled without a hyphen. **North-western** means in or from the north-west of a region or country. EG *He was with Kurdish tribes in northwestern Iran... Gary found work on a cattle station in Northwestern Australia.* ADJ CLASSIF

Norwegian /nɔːwiːdʒəⁿn/, **Norwegians**. **1 Norwegian** means belonging or relating to Norway, or to its people or their language. EG *...a Norwegian scientific expedition spent nine months there.* ADJ CLASSIF ⇑ Scandinavian

2 A **Norwegian** is someone who comes from Norway. EG *...the Norwegians and Danes flatly rejected the evidence.* N COUNT

3 Norwegian is the language spoken by people who live in Norway. EG *I haven't spoken Norwegian since the war.* N UNCOUNT

nose /nəʊz/, **noses, nosing, nosed**. **1** Your **nose** is **1.1** the part of your face which sticks out above your mouth. It is used for smelling and breathing. EG *My nose is itching... Johnny punched me in the nose.* N COUNT **1.2** your sense of smell. EG *His nose told him that he was getting near the cow shed.* N COUNT : IF SING POSS+N

2 The **nose** of a car or aeroplane is the front part of it. EG *...pictures from a camera in the nose of the plane... I saw the car's nose appear round the corner.* N COUNT+SUPP

● If cars and other vehicles are **nose to tail**, they are standing with the nose of one vehicle close behind the back part or tail of another. EG *Traffic stood nose to tail right the way down the Strand.* ● PHR : USED AS AN A

3 If a person, animal, or vehicle **noses** in a certain direction, it moves slowly and carefully in that direction. EG *A police car came nosing silently along the street... Rhoda nosed past them.* V+A = nuzzle

4 The word **nose** is also used in the following informal expressions. **4.1** If you say that something **gets up** your **nose**, you mean that it annoys you. EG *His selfishness really gets up my nose.* PHR : VB/N INFLECT **4.2** If you say that someone **is keeping** their **nose clean**, you mean that they are behaving well and keeping out of trouble. EG *I'm just trying to keep my nose clean and get on with my job.* PHR : VB/N INFLECT **4.3** If you **keep** your **nose to the grindstone**, you are working very hard. EG *I've got exams in two weeks, so I'm keeping my nose to the grindstone just at the moment.* PHR : VB/*nose* INFLECT = slog **4.4** If you **pay through the nose** for something, you pay a very high price for it. EG *Country people have to pay through the nose for their goods... It's a terrible car, and what annoys me is that I paid through the nose for it.* PHR : VB/N INFLECT **4.5** If you **rub** someone's **nose in** something that they do not want to think about, for example a failing or a mistake that they have made, you remind them repeatedly about it. EG *There's no need to rub my nose in the fact that she's so much more attractive than I am.* PHR : VB/N INFLECT ⇑ gloat **4.6** If you **thumb** your **nose at** someone, you behave in a way that shows that you do not care what they think. EG *In his own way, he was thumbing his nose at all those grown-up phoneys down there.* PHR : VB/N INFLECT

4.7 If someone **has** their **nose in a book**, they are reading it, so that they do not notice what is going on around them. EG *You've always got your nose in a book.* PHR : VB/NOUNS INFLECT **4.8** If you do something **under** someone's **nose**, you do it right in front of them, without trying to hide it from them. EG *Cheating was going on under the teacher's nose... It happened under our very noses.* PHR : USED AS AN A, N INFLECTS ⇑ blatantly

4.9 If you say that someone can **see no further than** their **nose**, you mean that they only consider things that are very obvious, and have no imagination for other possibilities. PHR : VB/N INFLECT **4.10** If you **look down** your **nose at** someone or something, you treat them with disrespect, because you think that they are inferior; used showing disapproval. EG *I think he looks down his nose at my work.* PHR : VB/N INFLECT ⇑ disdain = sneer at **4.11** If you **turn up** your **nose at** something, you reject it because you think that it is not good enough for you; used showing disapproval. EG *She turned up her nose at the meal I had cooked.* PHR : VB/N INFLECT

4.12 If you say or do something **with** your **nose in the air**, you do it in a way that shows that you believe that you are better than other people. EG *She always used to walk around with her nose in the air.* PHR : USED AS AN A, *nose* INFLECTS = haughtily **4.13** If you say that someone **has a nose for** something, you mean that they have an instinctive ability to find it or recognize it. EG *She had a good nose for rare jazz records.* PHR : VB INFLECTS **4.14** If you **follow** your **nose**, you make decisions and behave in a particular way because you feel instinctively that this is what you should do, rather than because you are following any guidelines or rules. EG *Be ready to follow your nose when you start a new job.* PHR : VB/N INFLECT **4.15** If you **keep** your **nose out** of something, you do not interfere with it if it does not concern you. EG *Keep your nose out of my business affairs!* PHR : VB/N INFLECT ≠ poke your nose in **4.16** If you **poke** or **stick** your **nose into** something, you try to interfere with it even though it does not concern you. EG *He shouldn't poke his nose into their business.* PHR : VB/N INFLECT = meddle **4.17** If you **cut off** your **nose to spite** your **face**, you do something intended to hurt someone else because you are angry or upset, although in fact what you do will hurt you more than it hurts the person that you are angry with. PHR : VB INFLECTS **4.18** If a woman says that she is going to **powder** her **nose**, she means that she is going to the toilet; a very old-fashioned expression. EG *I want to powder my nose before we go.* PHR : VB/N INFLECT **4.19** to **put** someone's **nose out of joint**: see **joint**.

nose about or **nose around**. If you **nose about** or **nose around**, you look around a place that belongs to someone else, to see if you can find something interesting; an informal expression. EG *Stay outside the door and see that no one comes nosing around.* PHRASAL VB : V+ADV/PREP

nose out. If you **nose out** information, you discover it by searching thoroughly; an informal expression. EG *I am not interested in nosing out the details of someone else's agony.* PHRASAL VB : V+O+ADV = discover

nosebag /nəʊzbæg/, **nosebags**. A **nosebag** is a bag containing food for a horse, which is hung over the horse's head. N COUNT

nosebleed /nəʊzbliːd/, **nosebleeds**. If someone has a **nosebleed**, blood comes out from inside their nose. N COUNT

nosedive /nəʊzdaɪv/, **nosedives, nosediving, nosedived**; also spelled with a hyphen. **1** A **nosedive** is **1.1** a quick steep drop which an aeroplane makes with its nose pointing towards the ground. EG *...like an airplane in the movies, pulling out of a nosedive... The machine went into a deliberate nose-dive.* N COUNT **1.2** a sudden fast drop in prices or exchange rates. EG *Share prices took a nosedive on the stock market.* N COUNT

2 If an aeroplane **nosedives**, it flies very fast and at a very steep angle towards the ground. V ⇑ drop

3 If prices or exchange rates **nosedive**, they fall very suddenly. EG *They fell below $2 in value on 5 March and then nosedived to $1.71.* V = plummet

nosegay /nəʊzgeɪ/, **nosegays**. A **nosegay** is a small bunch of flowers, for example one that is pinned to a woman's dress or that is carried by a woman at her wedding. N COUNT = posy

nosey /nəʊzi[1]/. See **nosy**.

nosey-parker, nosey-parkers. A **nosey-parker** is someone who is interested in things which do not concern them; an informal expression. EG *'Do you think I'm a terrible nosey-parker?'* N COUNT = snooper, busybody

nosh /nɒʃ/is food that has been prepared and is ready to eat; a very informal word. EG *Here's Ruth with the nosh.* N UNCOUNT, OR N SING WITH DET = grub

nosiness /nəʊzɪnɪ[2]s/. See **nosy**.

nostalgia /nɒstældʒɪ[0]ə/ is a slightly sad and very affectionate feeling you have for the past, especially for a particularly happy time. EG *...nostalgia for the good old days... Many people look back with nostalgia to feudal times.* N UNCOUNT : IF + PREP THEN *for* = yearning

nostalgic /nɒstældʒɪk/. **1** Something that is **nostalgic** causes you to feel nostalgia. EG *Pollock's earliest works are nostalgic evocations of rural America.* ADJ QUALIT ↑ evocative

2 Someone who is or who feels **nostalgic** is thinking affectionately and longingly about a happier time in the past. EG *...talking about Christmases in her childhood, she made me feel nostalgic.* ◊ **nostalgically**. EG *...talking nostalgically of the good old days.* ADJ QUALIT = sentimental ◊ ADV

nostril /nɒstrɪl/, **nostrils**. A person's or animal's **nostrils** are the two openings at the end of their nose, through which they breathe. EG *...the smell of smoke in my nostrils... All South American monkeys have flat noses with widely spaced nostrils.* N COUNT

nostrum /nɒstrəm/, **nostrums**; an old-fashioned word, used showing disapproval. A **nostrum** is **1** a kind of medicine which is prepared and sold by someone who is not properly qualified. **2** someone's favourite idea or theory, which is intended to solve a particular problem. EG *...the old nostrum of public ownership.* N COUNT; N COUNT = cure-all

nosy /nəʊzi[1]/, **nosier, nosiest**; also spelled **nosey**. Someone who is **nosy** is interested in things which do not concern them, and interferes with other people's affairs; an informal word. EG *'I don't think she meant to be nosy,' said Mother.* ◊ **nosiness**. ADJ QUALIT ↑ curious = inquisitive, prying ◊ N UNCOUNT

not /nɒt/. You use **not** to make a negative statement, question, or phrase. It is generally used after an auxiliary or modal verb; if there is no auxiliary or modal verb in the corresponding positive clause, the auxiliary 'do' is used. In spoken and informal written English, it often occurs in the form **n't** added to the auxiliary or modal verb. The full form **not** is used in formal and written English and for emphasis. **1** Typically, **not** makes a whole clause negative. EG *It's not a good idea... He did not laugh... I don't agree with everything he says... There wasn't enough room for everybody... I couldn't do it... It isn't unusual... It's not unusual.* NEG

2 When **not** is used with verbs such as 'want', 'think', and 'seem', which express intentions, opinions, or appearances, the negative effect of **not** belongs to the following clause or infinitive. For example, 'I don't think we need to worry' means 'I think we do not need to worry'; 'He did not want to go' means 'He wanted not to go'. NEG + VB + REPORT-CL/ *to*-INF

3 You use **not**, usually in the form **n't**, in question tags after a positive statement: see **tag**. EG *That's a new one, isn't it?... You've seen this, haven't you?... They can do this, can't they... She made a remarkable recovery, didn't she.* NEG AFTER MODAL/AUX

4 You can use **not** to make questions **4.1** expressing surprise about something. EG *Don't they like strawberries?... Have you not read it?* **4.2** as a polite way of making a suggestion. EG *Don't you think we should try the other spanner?... Shouldn't they have their coats on?* NEG; NEG

5 You can use **not** to represent the negative of a word, group, or clause that has just been used without repeating it. EG *'Can you come?'–'I'm afraid not.'... They'd be bound to know if it was all right or not... More often than not I could tell what they were thinking.* NEG ≠ so

6 You can use **not** in front of 'all' or 'every' when you want to say something that applies only to some members of the group that you are talking about. EG *Not all scientists are as honest as Pasteur was... Not everyone agrees with me.* ● If you say that something is **not always** the case, you mean that sometimes it is the case and sometimes it isn't; for example 'We didn't always succeed' means that sometimes we succeeded and sometimes we did not. NEG + *all/every*; ● PHR : USED AS AN A, NEG

7 You can use **not** or **not even** in front of 'a' or 'one' as emphatic ways of saying that there is none at all of what is being mentioned. EG *They had no Western products at all, not even a gun... Not an original house remains, not one.* NEG + *a/one*

8 You can use **not** in front of a word referring to a distance, length of time, or other amount to say that the actual distance, time, or amount is less than the one mentioned. EG *The taxi was not five yards away... Not ten seconds later he was violently sick.* NEG + NUM

9 You can use **not** to introduce a negative part of a structure, in order to contrast something that is untrue with something that is true. EG *We wept, not because we were frightened but because we were ashamed.... Each finger ends with a sharp claw, not a flat blunt nail... It was a reaction not so much of strength as of weakness and desperation.* NEG

10 You use **not only** when you are mentioning two things or situations. 'Not only' introduces the one that you consider to be less informative, less surprising, or less important. It is usually contrasted with a second clause or phrase introduced by 'but' or 'but also'. The expressions **not just, not simply,** and **not merely** are used in the same way. EG *He now determined to be not only commander-in-chief but also his own principal adviser... It became a widespread craze, not just one confined to a few people... ...not merely in Afro-Asia, but in the rest of the world too.* PHR

11 Not that is used to introduce a negative clause that increases the force of a previous statement. EG *They had vanished before I ever got to the customs shed. Not that it mattered much.* CONJ SUBORD : NEG

12 Not at all is **12.1** an emphatic way of saying 'No' or of agreeing that the answer to a question is 'No'. EG *'Does that seem nonsense to you?'–'Not at all.'... 'Would you mind?'–'Not at all, of course I wouldn't mind.'* **12.2** a polite, rather formal way of acknowledging a person's thanks. EG *'Thanks.'–'Not at all.'... 'May I?'–'It would be very kind of you.'–'Not at all.'* CONVENTION : NEG ↑ no; CONVENTION : NEG = forget it

13 ● **if not**: see **if.** ● **not half**: see **half.** ● **not least**: see **least.** ● **not to mention**: see **mention.** ● **nothing if not**: see **nothing.** ● **not for nothing**: see **nothing**.

notability /nəʊtəbɪlɪti[1]/, **notabilities**. A **notability** is an important or famous person. N COUNT = VIP

notable /nəʊtəbə[0]l/, **notables**. **1** Something that is **notable** is important, interesting, or remarkable. EG *With a few notable exceptions this trend has continued... ...a nation which produced some of the most notable political thinkers in Europe... 'Divide-and-rule' policies have been more notable for their ultimate failure than for their short-term success.* ADJ QUALIT = noteworthy, famous

2 A **notable** is an important person. EG *...a dinner for sixty notables.* N COUNT : USU PL = VIP

notably /nəʊtəbli[1]/. You use **notably 1** to specify an important or typical example of something that you are talking about. EG *Some people, notably his business associates, had learned to ignore his moods... The organization had many enemies, most notably among feminists.* **2** to emphasize a particular quality that someone or something has. EG *Thus far, Wall Street, at least, has been notably unimpressed.* ADV + NG/PREP ↑ particularly; ADV + ADJ, OR ADV SEN = markedly

notary /nəʊtə[0]ri[1]/, **notaries**. A **notary** is a person, usually a lawyer, who is legally empowered to witness the signing of documents in order to make them legally valid. N COUNT

notation /nəʊteɪʃə[0]n/, **notations**. A **notation** is **1** a set of written symbols that are used to represent a system of thought such as music, logic, or mathematics. EG *It was impossible to write down in the usual musical notation... ...long numbers which build up using binary notation.* **2** one or more symbols that have been written down. EG *...wishing he could decode the notations on the slips.* N UNCOUNT/ COUNT + SUPP; N COUNT

notch /nɒtʃ/, **notches, notching, notched**. **1** A **notch** is **1.1** a small cut, usually V-shaped, in the surface or edge of something. EG *He put his cigarette into the notch of a white ashtray... These beetles have notches at the sides of the wing covers.* **1.2** a particular level on a scale of achievement or ability; an informal use. EG *My regard for Smithy went up another notch... Lyle seems unable to lift his game that extra notch that is required when the prize is great.* N COUNT ↑ indentation; N COUNT = degree

2 If you **notch** something, you make one or more V + O small V-shaped cuts in its surface or edge. EG *...the notched edge.*

notch up. If you **notch up** something such as a score or total, you achieve it. EG *The Tory candidate had notched up eleven hundred more votes than Mr Jones.*
PHRASAL VB : V+O+ADV

note /nəʊt/, **notes, noting, noted**. 1 A **note** is 1.1 a short, usually informal letter. EG *She left a note saying she would see us again... She wrote a note to the chief of police... Enclose a note of explanation.*
N COUNT ⇑ message

1.2 something that you write down so that you can refer to it again and remember something, for example what someone said or what you intended to say. EG *I'll make a note of that... ...people speaking from notes... Our people took notes or operated tape recorders.*
N COUNT ⇑ record

1.3 a short piece of additional information in a book, article, document, etc, often one that gives extra information about the main text. EG *...pretentious programme notes... Yugoslavia is a different matter (see note on the Yugoslav situation, below).*
N COUNT = annotation

1.4 a short document that has to be signed by someone and that gives official information about something. EG *Ask your doctor for a sick note... ...delivery notes.* • See also **promissory note**.
N COUNT : USU MOD+N

1.5 a piece of printed paper that is used as money. EG *He handed me a pound note... ...twenty five-pound notes... ...several paid on the spot in notes.* • See also **banknote**.
N COUNT

2 If you **make**, **have**, or **keep a mental note** of something, you make a special effort to remember it. EG *He made a mental note to tell Lamin later who these men were.*
PHR : VB/N INFLECT, USU+ *to*-INF/*of*

3 If you **compare notes** with someone, you talk to them about something and find out whether they have the same opinion, information, or experiences of it as you. EG *I think there are a few things we might compare notes on.*
PHR : VB INFLECTS, IF+ PREP THEN *on* ⇑ discuss

4 If you **note** something such as a fact, 4.1 you become aware of it. EG *Note that the report does not carry any form of official recommendation... His audience, I noted with regret, were beginning to look bored... It is important for us to note three basic facts.*
V+O/REPORT-CL : NO CONT = observe, notice

4.2 you write it down as a record of what has happened. EG *The sale is noted in the gunsmith's logbook... Often, he noted the exact time and place on the sketch.*
V+O = log, register

4.3 you mention it in order to draw people's attention to it. EG *Wages have, as already noted, a dual function in the economy... A government report released last week noted an alarming rise in racial harassment.*
V+O/REPORT-CL/QUOTE = observe, remark

5 If you **take note** of something, you pay attention to it because you think that it is important or significant. EG *I found that he had taken note of everything I had said... I had to start taking some note of political developments.*
PHR : VB INFLECTS, IF+ PREP THEN *of*

6 Someone or something that is **of note** is important, worth mentioning, or well-known. EG *...an artist of some note... ...an ancient Welsh chieftain who had done little of note other than to sell his army to the English.*
PHR : USED AS AN A, OR AFTER N = consequence

7 A **note** is also 7.1 a sound of a particular pitch, especially one made by a musical instrument or a human voice when singing. EG *...the slow music rang out, note by solemn note.*
N COUNT

7.2 a written symbol that represents a sound of a particular pitch and length. EG *Not one of them could read a note of music.*
N COUNT

7.3 one of the keys of a musical instrument that has a keyboard, such as a piano.
N COUNT

7.4 a continuous sound that something is making. EG *...the variation in the depth of the engine note... The boar's note changed to a squeal.*
N SING WITH DET

7.5 a particular quality in someone's voice that shows how they are feeling. EG *There was a note of triumph in her voice... His voice took on a new note of uncertainty.*
N SING WITH DET +SUPP = tone

7.6 a particular feeling, impression, or atmosphere. EG *I would, on a slightly more serious note, caution the Party against overconfidence... Sensing this would be a good note on which to end the interview, I got up.. This will strike the correct note.*
N SING WITH DET +SUPP

note down. If you **note** something **down**, you write down the important points quickly, so that you will be able to refer to them later. EG *I'll give you time to note down where to send off for them.*
PHRASAL VB : V+O+ADV ⇑ record

notebook /nəʊtbʊk/, **notebooks**. A **notebook** is a small book for writing notes in. EG *Beynon put his notebook and pen inside his jacket.*
N COUNT

noted /nəʊtɪ²d/. Someone or something that is **noted** is well-known and admired for a particular characteristic that they have. EG *...a noted American writer... ...a Scottish family noted for its intellect... ...a town not noted for its picturesque scenery.*
ADJ CLASSIF : USU PRED+*for* = renowned, famous

notepad /nəʊtpæd/, **notepads**. A **notepad** is a pad of paper that you use for writing notes or letters on.
N COUNT = jotter

notepaper /nəʊtpeɪpə/ is paper that you use for writing letters on. EG *...the letter, dated 15 September, was on notepaper headed 'Executive Committee'.*
N UNCOUNT

noteworthy /nəʊtwɜːði¹/. A fact or event that is **noteworthy** is interesting, remarkable, or significant. EG *It was noteworthy that the Count was the only person who did not seem to care.... One noteworthy fact is that members of the staff seldom complain.*
ADJ QUALIT = notable, striking

nothing /nʌθɪŋ/, **nothings**. You use **nothing** to make negative statements when you are talking about things, events, or ideas, rather than people. Compare **something**, **nobody**. 1 You use **nothing** to say that no objects, events, or ideas are present, even though people might expect that some would be present. EG *She shook the bottle over the glass; nothing came out... The man nodded but said nothing... There's nothing to worry about... I had nothing else to do... Nothing much was happening there at the time.*
PRON INDEF : NEG

2 If you say that an action or event was about **nothing**, you mean that it was about something very unimportant and trivial. EG *A fight started over nothing... ...a long transatlantic phone call about nothing.*
PRON INDEF : *about/over*+ PRON

3 If you say that something cost **nothing** or is worth **nothing**, you mean that it cost or is worth a surprisingly small amount of money. EG *They sold their land for nothing.*
PRON INDEF : USED AS O

4 You can also use **nothing** before an adjective, to refer to a situation, event, or activity and to say that it does not have the particular quality mentioned. EG *There is nothing new about this technique... He usually drank nothing stronger than beer... I didn't know that Davis was ill. It's nothing serious, I hope.*
PRON INDEF+ ADJ QUALIT : NEG

5 You can use **nothing** before 'so' and an adjective, or before a comparative adjective, to refer to a particular quality and to emphasize how strong or great it is. EG *There's nothing more satisfying than a good laugh... Personally, I can think of nothing more unpleasant... There's nothing so embarrassing as when things go wrong.*
PRON INDEF+ ADJ IN COMPAR/ +*so (...as)* : NEG

6 In informal English, if you say that someone or something is **nothing**, you mean that they have no worthwhile or interesting characteristics. EG *All that was nothing, absolutely nothing, to the joy that I felt when I saw her... I hate you. You're disgusting. You're nothing... This man is a petty criminal. He's nothing compared to most people we go after.* ▸ used as a count noun. EG *...these loafers, these worthless nothings, who sit here chattering like old fishwives.*
ADJ CLASSIF : PRED = nobody ▸ N COUNT

7 If you say that someone or something is or means **nothing** to you, you mean that you do not care about them at all. EG *He meant nothing to her now... Suspension means nothing to us... Of course, in those days time was nothing. Now it is everything.*
PRON INDEF : NEG

8 If you say **'It's nothing'**, you are saying that something is not as important, serious, or significant as other people might think. EG *'What's the matter with you?' Claud asked.–'It's nothing,' he gasped. 'I'll be all right in a minute.'*
CONVENTION

9 The word **nothing** is also used in the following expressions. 9.1 If you say that an action was done **for nothing**, you mean that it was done either without a good reason or without achieving any worthwhile results. EG *It is hard to believe that they died for nothing... Why should I waste my time and bother people for nothing?*
PHR : USED AS AN A ⇑ unnecessarily

9.2 If you say that it was **not for nothing** that something happened, you mean that there was a very good reason for it to happen. EG *It was not for nothing that the Algerians had followed their example... Not for nothing is there a public outcry.*
PHR : USED AS AN A

9.3 If you say that someone is getting **something for nothing, money for nothing,** etc, you mean that they are getting money or something that they want without having to give anything or do anything for it. EG *You're always expecting something for nothing. Go out and earn it for a change.*
PHR : USED AS C/

9.4 If you say about a story, report, etc, that there is **nothing in it** or **nothing to it**, you mean that it is
PHR : USED AS C

untrue. EG *I'm checking a rumour. Probably there's nothing in it... It was all nonsense. Nothing to it at all.*

9.5 If you say about something that you have done that there was **nothing to it**, you mean that it was easy. PHR : USED AS C

9.6 Nothing of the sort is used as an emphatic way of refusing permission or of denying something. EG *You will do nothing of the sort... People have said that history should show us proof. It shows us nothing of the sort.* PHR = no such thing

9.7 You can use **all or nothing** to say that either something must be done fully and completely or else it cannot be done at all. EG *It's got to be all or nothing... It is a mistake to believe that the language system acts in an on/off, all-or-nothing way.* PHR : USED AS C, OR BEFORE N

9.8 You can use **nothing less than** to emphasize your next words, often indicating that something seems very surprising or important. EG *What was needed was nothing less than a new industrial revolution... His life has been ruined, utterly destroyed by nothing less than education... This was nothing less than tragic.* PHR+NG/ADJ = nothing short of

9.9 You can use **nothing more than** in order to say that something is very simple and not at all complicated. EG *The fence consisted of nothing more than three single strands of naked wire... Poor Clarissa wanted nothing more than to have someone to talk to... The Captain is suffering from nothing more serious than a cold.* PHR+NG/ADJ/*to*-INF = just, merely

9.10 If you say that someone or something is **nothing if not** good, bad, clever, comfortable, etc, you mean that they clearly have a lot of the particular quality mentioned. EG *The Texans are nothing if not considerate.* PHR+ADJ : USED AS C ⇑ very

9.11 Nothing but a particular thing means only that thing. EG *She could see nothing but his head and his knees... ...thirty years of nothing but war.* PHR+NG = just

9.12 In British English, if you say that **there is nothing for it** but to take a particular action, you mean that it is the only possible course of action that you can take, even though it might be unpleasant. EG *There was nothing for it but to try the heavy stuff... There was nothing for it now except to go straight ahead with the plan.* PHR+*but*/*except*+*to*-INF/INF : VB INFLECTS

9.13 In very informal English, you can say **'Nothing doing'** when you want to say that something is not happening or cannot be done. EG *I wanted to get this one mended but nothing doing I'm afraid... I tried to find her a place to stay. But there was nothing doing in Rummidge that night.* PHR : USED AS C, OR CONVENTION

10 The word **nothing** is also used in the following expressions which are explained at other places in this dictionary. • **to say nothing of**: see **say**. • **nothing short of**: see **short**. • **to stop at nothing**: see **stop**. • **to think nothing of**: see **think**. • See also **sweet nothings**.

nothingness /nʌθɪŋnɪ(ə)s/ is **1** the fact of not existing. EG *Time reduces all such works to nothingness.* N UNCOUNT **2** complete emptiness or a complete absence of things, feelings, etc. EG *When I woke up it was into nothingness. Grey nothingness. I was ill.* N UNCOUNT

notice /nəʊtɪs/, **notices, noticing, noticed.** **1** If you **notice** something or someone, you become aware of them through your senses or through your experience. EG *I suddenly noticed a fat man sitting in the front row... Ralph noticed a rapid tapping noise... She noticed with a kind of horror that he was staring at her... She noticed him scratching his head... I've noticed that computers never go wrong in my favour... I couldn't help noticing the change in him.* V, V+O/REPORT-CL, OR V+O+-ING/INF : NO CONT ⇑ perceive

2 The word **notice** is used in the following expressions relating to awareness. **2.1** If you **take notice** of a particular fact or situation, you behave in a way that shows that you are aware of it. EG *I hope the heads of schools will take notice of my comments.* PHR : VB INFLECTS, IF+PREP THEN *of* = pay attention to

2.2 If you **take no notice** of someone or something, you do not allow them to affect what you think or what you do. EG *Take no notice of him. He's always rude to people... No-one took any notice after that.* PHR : VB INFLECTS, IF+PREP THEN *of* = pay no attention to

2.3 If you **bring** something **to** someone's **notice**, you make them aware of it, for example by mentioning it to them. EG *...the things that were brought to my notice by Mrs Oliver... We bring to the notice of the committee things that ought to be done.* PHR : VB INFLECTS

2.4 If something **comes to** your **notice**, you become aware of it because it is mentioned to you or because you notice it yourself. EG *Many cases have come to my notice since I started looking.* PHR : VB INFLECTS

2.5 If something **escapes** your **notice**, you fail to recognize it or realize it. EG *It did not escape her notice that he kept glancing at her... This has not escaped the notice of the police force.* PHR : VB INFLECTS, USU WITH BROAD NEG

3 If someone gets **notice** from other people, they receive attention and admiration or respect from them. EG *He achieved some public notice in later life... Nevertheless, they deserve notice and respect.* N UNCOUNT = recognition

4 Notice is also an announcement or warning in advance that you are going to do something or that something is going to happen. EG *The union was to give 28 days' notice of indefinite strikes... She could have done it if she'd had a bit more notice... We reserve the right to eject without notice any objectionable person.* N UNCOUNT : USU +SUPP = warning

5 The word **notice** is also used in the following expressions relating to advance warnings. **5.1** If something can or must be done **at short notice**, it can or must be done very soon, and without very much warning. EG *He had to leave his previous quarters at short notice... It was going to be difficult to fix things at such short notice.* PHR : USED AS AN A ⇑ suddenly

5.2 If something can or must happen **at a moment's notice, at five minutes' notice**, etc, it can or must happen within the amount of time that is mentioned. EG *The leading group is to move back at five minutes' notice... ...ready to be switched on at a moment's notice.* PHR : USED AS AN A

5.3 To **serve notice** means to give a warning that something is going to happen or is likely to happen. EG *The Council served notice of its intention to close the swimming pool... This serves notice that many of Britain's voters are looking for an alternative.* PHR : VB INFLECTS, IF+PREP THEN *of*/*to* ⇑ tell

5.4 If a situation is said to exist **until further notice**, it will continue for an uncertain length of time until someone changes it. EG *The beaches are closed until further notice.* PHR : USED AS AN A ⇑ indefinitely

5.5 If an employer **gives** an employee **notice,** the employer tells the employee that he or she must leave his or her job, usually within a short and fixed period of time. EG *He had received orders that morning to give her notice... On Friday she had been given two weeks' notice at the Works.* PHR : VB INFLECTS ⇑ dismiss

5.6 If you **hand in** your **notice,** you tell your employer that you intend to leave your job soon, within a set period of time. EG *I handed in my notice last week... He was going to give in his notice.* PHR : VB INFLECTS ⇑ resign

6 A **notice** is **6.1** a general announcement giving information, which is written or printed and put in a place where it can be read by everyone who goes past it. EG *At the main entrance gates, there was a large notice which said 'Visitors welcome at any time'... Someone put up a notice about it the other day.* N COUNT **6.2** a formal announcement in a newspaper or magazine about something that has happened or is going to happen. EG *Shortly after, they ceased to publish notices in the Evening Post... One can still see notices to 'beloved Nanny' in the 'Deaths' column.* N COUNT **6.3** one of a number of similar or identical letters that an organization sends to a number of people giving them some information or asking them to do something. EG *The computer can issue invoices and reminder notices.* N COUNT **6.4** a review of a play, film, concert, etc, in a newspaper or magazine. EG *It had had encouraging notices.* N COUNT : USU PL = write-up

noticeable /nəʊtɪsəb(ə)l/. Something that is **noticeable** is very obvious, so that it is easy to see, hear, or recognize. EG *It did not have any noticeable effect upon the rate of economic growth... It was noticeable that the knuckles of his right hand were bruised.* ADJ QUALIT = conspicuous, perceptible

◊ **noticeably.** EG *Their house was noticeably warmer than the Foxes' great draughty mansion.* ◊ ADV = perceptibly

noticeboard /nəʊtɪsbɔːd/, **noticeboards.** A **noticeboard** is a board, usually on a wall, on which notices are displayed; a British English term. EG *The corridor seemed to be decorated entirely with posters and noticeboards.* N COUNT = bulletin board

notifiable /nəʊtɪfaɪəb(ə)l/. A **notifiable** disease, crime, etc is one that must be reported to the authorities whenever it occurs, because it is considered to be extremely dangerous to the community. ADJ CLASSIF

notification /nəʊtɪfɪkeɪʃ(ə)n/, **notifications.** **1 Notification** is the act of informing someone officially about something. EG *There had been the usual notification through the head of Military Intelligence... Mutual notification of naval movements was agreed.* N UNCOUNT ⇑ communication

2 A **notification** is a formal or official announcement about something. EG *You will normally be sent an official notification of the results of your interview by post.* N UNCOUNT/COUNT+SUPP ⇑ notice

notify /nəʊtɪfaɪ/, **notifies, notifying, notified.** If you **notify** someone of something, you inform V+O : IF+PREP THEN *of*+, OR V+

them officially about it. EG *The Housing Department is notified of all planning applications... The worker nearest the breakdown would notify his foreman.* O+REPORT-CL ⇑ tell = apprise

notion /nəʊʃəⁿn/, **notions**. A **notion** is 1 an opinion or belief about a particular subject. EG *The notion that the earth is flat was rejected long ago... ...the notion of equal pay for equal work... He had only the vaguest notion of what it was all about.* N COUNT : USU+ of+/REPORT-CL ⇑ idea = concept 2 a slight desire or intention. EG *I've a notion to go and find him.* N COUNT : IF+VB THEN+to+-INF = mind

notional /nəʊʃənəⁿl/. Something that is **notional** exists only in theory or as a suggestion or idea, but not in reality. EG *...a notional rent element was included in the calculation.* ADJ CLASSIF = hypothetical

notoriety /nəʊtəraɪɪ¹ti¹/ is the fact of being well known for something that is bad or undesirable. EG *...terrorists who acquired international notoriety for the kidnapping of government figures.* N UNCOUNT : IF+ PREP THEN for ⇑ fame

notorious /nəⁿtɔːrɪəs/. Someone or something that is **notorious** is well known for something that is bad or undesirable. EG *The area was notorious for murders... The most notorious example is America's Love Canal... Despite his notorious arrogance, I felt I could do business with him.* ADJ QUALIT : IF+ PREP THEN for = infamous ≠ famous ◊ **notoriously**. EG *Elsewhere, rainfall is notoriously variable and unreliable.* ◊ ADV+ADJ/ ADV

notwithstanding /nɒtwɪθstændɪŋ, -wɪð-/. **Notwithstanding** means that the particular thing mentioned has no effect on the situation that you are describing, although people might expect it to; a formal word. EG *Computing remains a growth area and one in which, notwithstanding economic recessions, the outlook looks bright... Concern over human rights, international agreements notwithstanding, probably did as much as anything to foster the new note of realism.* PREP : ALSO AFTER NG, OR CONJ SUBORD ⇑ despite

nougat /nuːgɑː/ is a kind of hard chewy pink or white sweet, containing nuts and sometimes fruit. N UNCOUNT

nought /nɔːt/, **noughts**. **Nought** is the number 0: see ☐ at NUMBER. EG *...nought point two... Using binary notation is in fact just manipulating ones and noughts.* NUM = zero

noughts and crosses is a pencil-and-paper game for two players, played on a piece of paper divided into a square in which there are nine spaces. The players take turns and compete to be the first to fill in a row of three crosses or of three noughts in the spaces; used in British English. N UNCOUNT

noun /naʊn/, **nouns**. In grammar, a **noun** is a word which is used to refer to a person, a thing, or an abstract idea such as a feeling or quality. In this dictionary, the abbreviation N is used in the grammar notes beside entries to mean 'noun'. See ☐ at N COUNT, NG N MASS, N PART, N PLURAL, N PROPER, N SING, and N UNCOUNT. N COUNT

nourish /nʌrɪʃ/, **nourishes, nourishing, nourished**. 1 To **nourish** a person, animal, or plant means to provide them with the food that is required for life, growth, and good health. EG *It is better to nourish schoolchildren by feeding them good food... A great variety of animals nourish themselves on vegetable foods.* V+O (NG/REFL) ⇑ sustain = feed ◊ **nourishing**. EG *They still look thin, even when they have the most nourishing food to eat... Blackcurrants are extremely nourishing.* ◊ ADJ QUALIT = nutritious ◊ **nourished**. EG *...badly nourished babies.* ◊ ADJ QUALIT

2 To **nourish** a feeling or belief means to allow it to grow or to encourage it to grow. EG *They nourish their passion for a while in secret... The illusion of unlimited powers was nourished by astonishing scientific and technological progress.* V+O = foster

nourishment /nʌrɪʃm²ənt/ is 1 the food that is required by the human body or by any other living thing to grow and remain healthy. EG *He should have been taking nourishment and even walking around a little... The seeds are full of nourishment.* N UNCOUNT 2 the action of nourishing somebody or something or the experience of being nourished. EG *Illness can be caused by poor nourishment, especially in winter.* N UNCOUNT = nutrition

nous /naʊs/ is intelligence or common sense; an old-fashioned informal word. EG *He has a certain amount of social nous.* N UNCOUNT

nouveau-riche /nuːvəʊ riːʃ/, **nouveaux-riches**. The plural is pronounced the same as the singular. A **nouveau-riche** is someone who has recently become rich, but who comes from a lower social class than other rich people and has tastes, manners, or a lifestyle that others consider vulgar. EG *...the number of nouveaux-riches who appeared on the scene.* N COUNT = parvenu ▸ used as an adjective. EG *He was supposed to be above such things now that he was nouveau riche.* ▸ ADJ CLASSIF

Nov. is an abbreviation for November.

novel /nɒvəⁿl/, **novels**. 1 A **novel** is a long written story about people and events that have been invented by the author. EG *She had written a book about her childhood, and a novel about the strikes in Jarrow... ...like a scene from a novel by Henry James.* N COUNT ⇑ book

2 Something that is **novel** is unlike anything that has been done, experienced, or created before, especially in a way that is interesting, unusual, or clever. EG *The computer produced a completely novel proof of a well known theorem... The group suggested new ideas and novel approaches to the problems faced by the community.* ADJ QUALIT ⇑ new = innovative, fresh

novelette /nɒvəlet/, **novelettes**. A **novelette** is a short novel, usually one that is not about a very serious subject. EG *...television soap operas and cheap novelettes.* N COUNT ⇑ story

novelist /nɒvəⁿlɪst/, **novelists**. A **novelist** is a person who writes novels. N COUNT ⇑ writer

novelty /nɒvəⁿlti¹/, **novelties**. 1 **Novelty** is the quality of being different, new, and unusual. EG *Will you still be happy after the novelty of the first few weeks is over?... The novelty soon wears off... The demand is for increasing quality, variety and novelty.* N UNCOUNT ≠ boredom

2 A **novelty** is 2.1 something that is unusual, different, new, or unlike anything that you have done or experienced before. EG *When I first arrived in the United States one of the novelties that fascinated me was the drive-in movies.* N COUNT 2.2 a cheap, unusual object, especially one without a useful purpose that is sold as a gift or put into a Christmas cracker. EG *...a shop selling novelties and souvenirs... ...novelty ashtrays.* N COUNT

November /nəʊvembə/ is the eleventh month of the year in the Western calendar. EG *The current agreement ends on November 24.* N UNCOUNT

novice /nɒvɪs/, **novices**. A **novice** is 1 someone who has been doing a job or other activity for only a short time and who is not experienced at it. EG *He's still a novice as far as film acting is concerned... Look at a novice workman and compare his results with those of an expert.* N COUNT ⇑ learner 2 a person who has recently entered a monastery or a convent, and who is not yet a full monk or nun. N COUNT ⇑ probationer

now /naʊ/. 1 **Now** is used 1.1 to refer to the present time, often in contrast to a time in the past or the future. You may be talking about what is actually happening at the moment or about the present stage of your life or about the present stage of history. EG *It is now just after one o'clock... What if a shark came along right now?... I'm going home now... Calculators are now owned by a high percentage of school children... She has three children now... ...a now historic production of Under Milk Wood.* ADV = at present ▸ used as the subject of a verb, or after a preposition. EG *Now is the time to find out... Goodbye for now... From now on, you are free to do what you like.* 1.2 to specify the length of time that something has lasted, from the time it started until the present time. EG *'How long have you been keeping bees?'-'For five years now'... It's two weeks now since I wrote to you... How long have you lived here now?* ADV WITH VB : AFTER NG/A

2 **Now** is also used with the past tense, especially in novels and stories, to refer to the particular time in the past that you are speaking or writing about, as opposed to any later or earlier time. EG *It was ten o'clock now... They were walking more slowly now... By now the country had changed dramatically.* ADV WITH VB : ALSO AFTER PREP

3 **Just now** means a very short time ago. EG *I apologize for my outburst just now... I was talking to him just now.* PHR : USED AS A ⇑ recently

4 If you say **'It's now or never'**, you mean that something must be done immediately, because if it is not done immediately there will not be another chance to do it. CONVENTION

5 You can say **'Now for...'** when you are going to change the subject and talk about something different. EG *...and now for some more of your letters... Now for the question of your expenses.* PHR+NG

6 If you say that something will happen **any day now**, **any moment now**, or **any time now**, you mean that it will happen very soon. EG *Any day now, the local authority is going to announce a major housing scheme... They should arrive any time now.* PHR : USED AS A

7 If you say that something happens **now and then** or PHR : USED AS

every now and then, you mean that it happens sometimes but not very often or regularly. EG *Now and again my method appears to work... Every now and then there is a confrontation.* A = occasionally

8 Now also means as a result of what has recently happened. EG *I was hoping to see you tomorrow. That won't be possible now... It's the most beautiful city I have ever seen. Now I understand why you come back so often.* ADV WITH VB

9 Now that or **now** is used when you want to say that the effect of something that has happened is that something else takes place. EG *Now that she's found him, she'll never let him go... Now that I am old, I can read all the books I've always meant to read... I like him a lot now he's older.* CONJ SUBORD ↑ because

10 Now is also used **10.1** at the beginning of a sentence, to introduce information which is relevant to the part of the story or account that you have reached and which needs to be known before you can continue. EG *Daisy's only dangerous fault was her willingness to kick. Now, a camel can kick you in any direction, within a radius of six feet... Now this king had three daughters.* ADV SEN = well **10.2** in spoken English, to introduce a contrast. EG *I don't know anything about car engines. Now, if Richard was here, he'd be able to help you.* ADV SEN = however **10.3** in informal spoken English, as something to say while you think of what to say next. EG *Well now, I've got the following suggestions... Now, let's stop for a moment there... I've got her address somewhere. Now let me see.* **10.4** to give a slight friendly emphasis to a request or command. EG *I must get back to work. Run along, now... Be very careful now... Give me the gun. Quick now!* **10.5** in spoken English, as a friendly way of trying to calm or comfort someone. EG *There now, don't cry... Now, come on. Be sensible.*

11 Now, now is used in spoken English **11.1** as a friendly way of trying to comfort someone. EG *'Now, now,' the doctor said, taking her gently by the hand. 'You mustn't get so upset.'* CONVENTION = there there **11.2** as a friendly way of introducing a warning to someone not to behave in a particular way. EG *Now, now, there's no need to be nasty.* CONVENTION

12 Now then is used in spoken English to attract people's attention when you want to say something to them. EG *Now then, sleepyhead! It's time to go to bed... Now then, who's for a cup of tea?* = right

nowadays /naʊədeɪz/ means at the present time in general, in contrast with the past. EG *At one time only birds and stars were sighted in the skies. Nowadays they are joined by aeroplanes, rockets, and satellites... Kids nowadays are lazy... Why don't we ever see Jim nowadays?* ADV WITH VB ↑ now = these days

nowhere /nəʊweə/. **1** You use **nowhere** to make negative statements about places, for example to say that a suitable or appropriate place does not exist. EG *There was nowhere to hide... She had absolutely nowhere else to go... 'Where are we going?'-'Nowhere in particular.'... Nowhere have I seen any serious mention of this.* ADV WITH VB : NEG = no place

2 If you say that something or someone appears **from nowhere** or **out of nowhere**, you mean that they have appeared suddenly and that you do not know where they have come from. EG *Two men suddenly appeared from nowhere... There were sudden rivers formed out of nowhere.* PHR : USED AS AN A = out of the blue

3 If you say that a place is **in the middle of nowhere**, you mean that it is isolated and a long way from anywhere civilized or interesting; an informal expression. EG *We were sitting in the middle of nowhere... ...a little village in the middle of nowhere.* PHR : USED AS AN A = in the sticks

4 If you say that you **are nowhere**, that you **are getting nowhere**, or that something **is getting** you **nowhere,** you mean that all your efforts are unsuccessful and are not producing any worthwhile results. EG *I keep going off on tangents that get me nowhere... Calling me yellow will get you nowhere... Without them I would be nowhere.* PHR : VB INFLECTS

5 If you say that something is **nowhere near** the case, you mean that it is not true at all, and that the truth is quite different. EG *Lions are nowhere near as fast as the cheetah.* PHR : NEG, PHR + as...as

noxious /nɒkʃəs/. **1** A **noxious** gas or substance is harmful or poisonous. ADJ CLASSIF : USU ATTRIB

2 Something that is **noxious** is extremely unpleasant. EG *They gave off a most noxious smell... She would never harm an insect, however noxious.* ADJ QUALIT = nasty, foul

nozzle /nɒzəˀl/, **nozzles**. A **nozzle** is a small, narrow end piece fitted to a tube or pipe, used to control the flow of a liquid coming out of it. EG *She turned the nozzle and the spray concentrated down to a stream.* N COUNT

N PART □ In this dictionary N PART is used in the grammar notes beside entries to mean that a noun is a partitive noun. A partitive noun is one that is typically followed by *of* in a partitive construction, for example *two pints of beer, a piece of furniture, a herd of cows.* Partitive constructions provide a way of referring to parts of items which are difficult to divide or to items which are grouped together in particular ways. There are three main kinds of partitive nouns. **1** Some N PARTS are used as a way of measuring things that are typically expressed by uncount nouns or mass nouns. Examples are **pint**, **ton**, and **cup**. EG *...two **pints** of beer... ...five **tons** of coal... ...a **cup** of sugar.* **2** Some N PARTS are used as a way of referring to individual items of something that is expressed by an uncount noun. Examples are **bit** and **piece**. EG *...a **bit** of paper... ...a little **bit** of work... It's attached to a **piece** of string... I've a fascinating **piece** of news.* **3** Some N PARTS are collective nouns, where the noun following *of* is a plural count noun. Examples are **herd** and **flock**. EG *...a **herd** of cows... ...a huge **flock** of sheep.*

N PLURAL □ In this dictionary N PLURAL is used in the grammar notes beside entries to mean that a noun is used with a plural verb when it is the subject of the verb. If a pronoun is used to stand for the noun, then it is a plural pronoun such as 'they' or 'them'. Examples are **clothes, police**, and **contents**. EG *Her **clothes were** elegant but simple. She bought **them** at Harrods... Where will you go if the **police** find out?... She tested the **contents** by squirting **them** onto her hand.* Plural nouns which have the plural ending *-s* generally lose the *-s* when they are used as modifiers. An example is **trousers**. EG *He slipped it into one **trouser** pocket.* However, a few nouns keep the *-s* when they are used as modifiers. The grammar note beside these nouns says PL FORM WHEN MOD. An example is **fireworks**. EG *...a **fireworks** display.* Some plural nouns which end in *-s*, such as *jeans, binoculars,* and *glasses*, refer to a single object which has two main parts. With these, you sometimes refer to the item as *a pair of jeans, a pair of binoculars*, etc. These are described in the grammar notes as N PLURAL: ALSO *a pair of* N. An example is **scissors**. EG *The **scissors** are over there on the desk... I was sent out to buy **a pair of scissors**... I wish I'd brought some **scissors**.*

N PROPER □ In this dictionary N PROPER is used in the grammar notes beside entries to mean that a noun is a proper noun. An N PROPER refers to one particular person, place, or institution. Proper nouns behave in the following ways: **1** Most proper nouns are used without a determiner before them. Examples are **Asia, Hell**, and **Father Christmas**. EG *...the largest country in **Asia**... ...a descent into **Hell**... the pains of **Hell**... Colin wants to meet **Father Christmas**.* **2** There are some proper nouns which always have *the* before them. These are described in the grammar notes as N PROPER: *the*+N. Examples are **BBC** and **Church of England**. EG *How should **the BBC** be financed?... She'd moved to **the BBC** from publishing... I'm not a member of **the Church of England** myself... It would have to be accepted in **the Church of England**.* **3** Sometimes the same word can be used as a count noun and a proper noun. Nouns like this are described as N COUNT/PROPER and N COUNT/PROPER: *the*+N. An example of a word which is described as N COUNT/PROPER: *the*+N is **prime minister**. EG *...the conference of Commonwealth **Prime Ministers**...* (N COUNT) *There was room for everyone, whether a messenger boy or **a prime minister**...* (N COUNT) ***The Prime Minister** has now agreed to our proposal.*(N PROPER: *the*+N).

nr is a written abbreviation for 'near'; used especially as part of an address. EG *Offchurch, nr Leamington Spa, Warwicks.* PREP

N SING □ In this dictionary N SING is used in the grammar notes beside entries to mean that the noun is a singular noun. N SINGS behave in the following ways. **1** They are always singular. **2** They are always used with a determiner. If it does not matter which determiner is used, the grammar note reads N SING WITH DET. Examples are **business 8, jumble 1.1**, and **vicinity**. EG *We must get to the bottom of **this business**... There was something unreal about **the whole business**... It was a difficult **business** altogether... ...**a jumble** of signs and lettering... He thrust it away. It simply added to **the** ghastly **jumble**... ...somewhere in **the vicinity** of the Orinoco River... All the birds in **their vicinity** went silent.* **3** Some N SINGS are always used with a particular determiner, and this is shown in the grammar note beside the entry. Examples are **brink**

(N SING: *the*+N), **standstill** (N SING: *a*+N), and **colouring 2** (N SING: POSS+N). EG *They were on* ***the brink*** *of war... Europe had really reached* ***the brink****... The machine came to* ***a standstill*** *at last... Everything had ground to* ***a standstill****... Her son had inherited* ***her colouring****...* ***My colouring*** *was the same as Mark's, olive skin, dark hair.*

-n't. See **not**.

nth /ɛnθ/. The **nth** item in a series is the highest or most recent item, even though you do not know how many other items there are. **Nth** is often used to suggest that someone has done something or that something has happened a lot of times. EG *...smoking his nth cigarette... She had to repeat for the nth time the details of her conversation.* — ORDINAL = umpteenth

nuance /nju:ɑ:ns, nju:ɑ:ns/, **nuances**. A **nuance** is a slight and subtle difference in sound, colour, feeling, appearance, or meaning. EG *He practised until he could imitate every gesture and nuance of her speech... It is a strange smile. It lacks the subtle nuances of an ordinary smile.* — N COUNT = nicety, refinement
▸ used as an uncount noun. EG *...the range of nuances in the painter's touch.* — ▸ N UNCOUNT = subtlety

nub /nʌb/, **nubs**. The **nub** of a situation, problem, or argument is the central and most basic part of it. EG *We ought to get down to the nub of the matter... It reduces her case to its legal nub.* — N SING WITH DET : USU+SUPP = core, crux

nubile /nju:baɪl/. A woman who is **nubile** is young, physically mature, and sexually attractive. EG *...a nubile Hollywood actress.* — ADJ QUALIT = lissom

nuclear /nju:klɪə/ means **1** relating to the structure or behaviour of atoms and the nuclei of atoms.. EG *...nuclear physics... ...nuclear fission.* — ADJ CLASSIF : ATTRIB
2 relating to, involving, or using power that is produced from the energy released by atoms when they are split. EG *...the risks associated with nuclear power... ...nuclear energy... ...the nuclear industry.* — ADJ CLASSIF : USU ATTRIB = atomic
3 relating to, involving, or using weapons that explode by using the energy released by atoms. EG *...an agreement on the use of nuclear weapons... There are no winners in nuclear war... ...his father's interest in nuclear disarmament.* — ADJ CLASSIF : USU ATTRIB = atomic

nuclear family, nuclear families. A **nuclear family** is a family consisting only of parents and their children and not including aunts, uncles, cousins, etc. EG *...her reaction against the nuclear family.* — N COUNT

nuclear-free. A **nuclear-free** place is a place where nuclear weapons and nuclear energy are forbidden. EG *I should like to see Europe as a nuclear-free zone.* — ADJ CLASSIF : ATTRIB

nuclear reactor, nuclear reactors. A **nuclear reactor** is a device which is used to produce nuclear energy. EG *...the extremely high temperatures of a nuclear reactor... ...a byproduct of nuclear reactors is plutonium.* — N COUNT ⇑ generator = atomic pile

nucleus /nju:klɪəs/, **nuclei**/nju:klɪaɪ/. **1 A nucleus** is the central part of an atom. The nucleus is positively charged and is made up of protons and neutrons. EG *The fundamental particles make nuclei, the nuclei join in atoms.* — N COUNT ⇑ centre
2 The **nucleus** of a cell is the part that contains the chromosomes and controls the growth and reproduction of the cell. EG *It is possible to transplant chromosomes in cell nuclei.* — N COUNT
3 The **nucleus** of something such as a system of ideas or a group of people is a small group that is important because it is the centre or foundation of a much larger system or group. EG *These councils would form the nucleus of a future regime.* — N COUNT : IF+ PREP THEN *of* ⇑ basis = kernel, core

nude /nju:d/. **1** Someone who is **nude** or **in the nude** is not wearing any clothes. EG *...portraits of nude women.* — ADJ CLASSIF, OR PHR : USED AS AN A = naked
2 A nude is a picture or statue of a person who is not wearing any clothes. EG *...the tradition of the male nude in art.* — N COUNT

nudge /nʌdʒ/, **nudges, nudging, nudged. 1** When you **nudge** someone, you push or poke them gently, usually with your elbow, in order to draw their attention to something or to make them move. EG *He was tone deaf and had to be nudged whenever the band went into the national anthem... The twelve girls grinned and nudged each other.* — V+O = prod
▸ used as a noun. EG *Neil, give your companion a nudge.* — ▸ N COUNT = prod, dig
2 If you **nudge** something or someone into a place or position, you gently push them there. EG *She nudged the door shut with her knee... Helen nudged me back onto my side.* — V+O+A
3 If you **nudge** someone into doing something, you gently persuade them to do it. EG *People began to nudge the couple into going away.* — V+O+A = push
▸ used as a noun. EG *...a middle-man trying to give us a nudge in the required direction.* — ▸ N COUNT = push
4 If something **nudges** a particular amount, level, or state, it almost reaches it. EG *The speedometer moved up to nudge sixty... His fortunes were also at a low ebb, nudging bankruptcy.* — V+O = approach

nudism /nju:dɪzəᵒm/ is the practice of not wearing clothes, especially because you believe that it is a good thing not to wear clothes. EG *In some countries nudism is against the law.* — N UNCOUNT = naturalism
◊ **nudist**. EG *The beach was reserved for nudists... ...a nudist club.* — ◊ N COUNT = naturalist

nudity /nju:dɪti¹/ is the state of wearing no clothes. EG *...full frontal nudity on stage and screen... The boys treated nudity as a natural thing.* — N UNCOUNT = nakedness

nugget /nʌgɪ²t/, **nuggets**. A **nugget** is **1** a small rough lump of something, especially gold. EG *His father occasionally sent him solid gold nuggets.* — N COUNT
2 a piece of interesting or valuable information. EG *...curious and enlightening nuggets of information... They came up with the nugget that in 1918 he had been involved in dubious business speculations.* — N COUNT = titbit

nuisance /nju:səns/, **nuisances**. If you say that someone or something is a **nuisance**, you mean that they annoy you or cause you problems. EG *It was a nuisance for them to have all these visitors sitting around.... It's such a nuisance that you live so far away... He was nothing but a nuisance and a rascal... I'm sorry to have been such a nuisance.* — N COUNT : USU SING = bore, drag
● If you **make a nuisance of** yourself, you behave in a way that annoys or irritates other people. EG *...teenagers who make nuisances of themselves.* — ● PHR : VB/N INFLECT

nuke /nju:k/, **nukes, nuking, nuked**; an informal word used mainly in American English. **1 A nuke** is a nuclear weapon. EG *No more nukes!* — N COUNT
2 If one country **nukes** another, it bombs it using nuclear weapons. — V+O

null /nʌl/. If a contract or agreement is **null and void**, it is not legally valid. EG *The contract was declared null and void.* — PHR : USED AS C ⇑ invalid

nullify /nʌlɪfaɪ/, **nullifies, nullifying, nullified. 1** To **nullify** something means to make it ineffective. EG *This had the effect of nullifying our original advantage... The whole team's effectiveness can be nullified.* — V+O = cancel out
◊ **nullification** /nʌlɪfɪkeɪʃəᵒn/. — ◊ N UNCOUNT
2 To **nullify** a legal decision or procedure means to declare it not legally valid. EG *Each state had the right to nullify the federal government's laws.* — V+O = invalidate
◊ **nullification**. — ◊ N UNCOUNT

NUM □ In this dictionary NUM is used in the grammar notes to mean that a word is a number. NUMS behave in the following ways. **1** A NUM can occur in a noun group. It comes before the head noun and before any adjectives in the group. If there is a determiner, eg *the, these,* or *those,* the NUM comes after it. Except for *hundred, thousand, million,* and *billion,* NUMS do not occur with the determiner a or an. An example is **two.** EG *...two chairs... ...the* ***two*** *major decisions of his life.* **2** A NUM can be used as the head of a noun group, without a noun, when the text or situation makes it clear what it refers to, as in *There were* ***twenty*** *or more waiting for him.* **3** It is possible to use a prepositional group starting with *of* after a NUM, as in *They are* ***two of*** *the nicest people I've ever met... The* ***twelve of*** *us became very close during those four weeks.* Information about combining numbers and other uses of numbers is given in □ at NUMBER. See also □ at ORDINAL.

numb /nʌm/, **numbs, numbing, numbed. 1** If a part of your body is **numb**, it is unable to feel pain or any other physical sensation. EG *When I woke my left arm was asleep, wholly numb and almost useless.* — ADJ CLASSIF : IF+ PREP THEN *with* = dead
◊ **numbness**. EG *She was fighting off the numbness of frostbite.* — ◊ N UNCOUNT
2 If you are **numb** with grief, shock, fear, etc, you are unable to react normally or express emotion because you are so shocked, frightened, unhappy, etc. EG *Numb with shock, Kunta stood watching blankly.* — ADJ QUALIT : IF+ PREP THEN *with* = stunned
◊ **numbness**. EG *I felt the numbness I last felt when I heard that President Kennedy had been assassinated.* — ◊ N UNCOUNT
◊ **numbly**. EG *Numbly, he watched through one of the windows.* — ◊ ADV WITH VB = dully
2 If something **numbs** you or **numbs** a part of your body, it prevents you from feeling pain or any other physical sensation. EG *A stone numbed his shoulder... The bleeding stopped, and the constant walking* — V+O = deaden

numbed the pain. ◊ **numbed.** EG *...his cold numbed hands.* ◊ ADJ QUALIT = numb

3 If an event or experience **numbs** you or **numbs** your mind, you can no longer think clearly or feel emotions very strongly. EG *We are numbed by repeated disappointments... His mind, once sharp, has been numbed by half a lifetime of hardship.* V+O = deaden ◊ **numbed.** EG *He stood there in a numbed daze.* ◊ ADJ QUALIT

number /nʌmbə/, **numbers, numbering, numbered. 1** A **number** is **1.1** any of the words such as 'two', 'nine', or 'eleven', or the symbols such as 1, 3, or 47. You use numbers when counting or calculating, or to say how many things you are referring to. EG *Multiply that number by five, and write down the answer... 861 is a three-figure number.* N COUNT **1.2** a figure or series of figures that is used to identify or distinguish something or someone. Number in this sense is often abbreviated to 'No.' EG *Do you know what your bank account number is?... We lost our way; it was too dark to see the house numbers... I got on a number 61 bus.* N COUNT, OR N+NUM **1.3** the special series of digits that you dial when you are making a telephone call to someone. EG *I couldn't ring her as I hadn't got her number.* N COUNT ● **wrong number**: see **wrong**.

2 You refer to a particular **number** of things or people when you are saying how many there are; often used when you do not know exactly how many. EG *A surprising number of men never marry... ...cities with large numbers of children in care... Suitable computer programs were few in number... They were produced in vast numbers.* N COUNT OR *in*+N: USU+SUPP, ALSO SING=PL ⇑ amount ● **A number** of things or people means several. EG *There are a number of reasons why this happened... A number of people disagreed.* ● PHR: USU PHR +*of*+N IN PL ● **Any number** of things or people means a large quantity of them. EG *I'd warned her about it any number of times... Missing information about any number of things could lead to a sale falling through.* ● PHR: USU PHR +*of*+N IN PL = a lot ● If you refer to things or people **beyond number** or **without number**, you mean that there are so many of them that it would be impossible to count them all; a literary expression. EG *She saw people beyond number... There were daffodils without number in that field.* ● PHR: N IN PL+PHR

3 A **number** is also **3.1** a copy of a magazine or periodical that has been published at a particular time, usually one in a series. EG *Is that this week's number of 'Nature'?* N COUNT+SUPP = issue **3.2** a short piece of music, a song, or a dance that is performed. N COUNT **3.3** a smart piece of clothing or set of clothes that you wear together; an informal use. EG *They looked so elegant in their smart black numbers and their hats... ...Janice's little blue number.* N COUNT: ADJ+N ⇑ dress

4 One of a group of people's **number** is a member of that group. EG *We were all saddened when one of our number was killed.* PHR: USED AS S/O/C

5 The word **number** is also used in the following informal expressions. **5.1** If you **have** someone's **number**, you know all about them and so have an advantage over them. PHR: VB INFLECTS **5.2** If someone's **number comes up**, it is their turn to experience something unpleasant. EG *Their number was coming up.* PHR: VB INFLECTS **5.3** If you say that someone's **number is up**, you mean that they are going to die. EG *I thought my number was up.* PHR: VB INFLECTS **5.4** If you say that there is **safety in numbers**, you mean that you are safer doing something if there are a lot of people doing it rather than doing it alone. PHR: USED AS C

6 In grammar, **number** indicates whether a noun or verb is singular or plural. N UNCOUNT

7 If a group of people or things **numbers** a particular total or amount, there is that number or amount of them. EG *The force numbered almost a quarter of a million men.* V+O (NUM) = add up to

8 If you **number** something, you give it a number in a series and mark it with that number. EG *All the boxes were labelled and numbered... The essay is in a horrible muddle because I haven't numbered the pages.* V+O

9 If someone or something **is numbered** among a particular group, they are believed to belong in that group. EG *She can be numbered among the great musicians of our time.* V+O+A (*among*): USU PASS ⇑ include

10 If you say that someone's or something's **days are numbered**, you mean that there only remains a short time before something unpleasant will happen to them, for example that they will die. EG *Her days were numbered... The days of the project are numbered.* PHR: VB INFLECTS

NUMBER □ See page 986.

numberless /nʌmbəlɪ²s/ means too many to be counted. EG *He had had bad digestion, fevers and numberless other illnesses.* ADJ CLASSIF = countless

number one; an informal expression. **1 Number one** means better, more important, or more popular than anything else of its kind. EG *...the Stones, the number one rock group.* ADJ CLASSIF ⇑ best
2 If you **look out for number one**, you think of yourself and no one else. EG *He only ever looks out for number one.* PHR: VB INFLECTS

number plate, number plates. A **number plate** is a sign on the front or back of a vehicle that shows its registration number; used mainly in British English. N COUNT = license plate

Number Ten is often used to refer to 10 Downing Street, London, the official home of the British Prime Minister; often used with reference to the discussions that are held there or the decisions that are made there. EG *There has been no response from Number Ten.* N PROPER

numbskull /nʌmskʌl/. See **numskull**.

numeracy /nju:mə⁰rəsi¹/ is the ability to do arithmetic. N UNCOUNT

numeral /nju:mə⁰rəl/, **numerals.** A **numeral** is a symbol or group of symbols used to represent a number. EG *In Arabic numerals, the year is written 1983, but in Roman numerals it is written MCMLXXXIII.* N COUNT

numerate /nju:mə⁰rət/. Someone who is **numerate** is able to do arithmetic. ADJ CLASSIF

numerical /nju:merɪkə⁰l/ means written or expressed in numbers. EG *...the actual numerical value of pi... ...numerical data.* ADJ CLASSIF ◊ **numerically.** EG *A numerically correct answer is vitally important.* ◊ ADV

numerous /nju:mə⁰rəs/. **1** If you refer to **numerous** things or people, you mean that there are a lot of them. EG *We had numerous discussions on the meaning of communism... The Government has made its position clear on numerous occasions... We want especially to thank the numerous friends who gave us encouragement... George was the only survivor into boyhood of her numerous children.* QUANTIF+N IN PL ⇑ many = countless
2 Things or people that are **numerous** exist or are present in large numbers. EG *Small enterprises have become more numerous... They are by far the most numerous amphibians alive today... A large picture on the wall showed a numerous family eating in a garden... The cast is large, though nothing like as numerous as one might suppose.* ADJ QUALIT ≠ rare, scarce

numinous /nju:mɪnəs/ means holy, awe-inspiring, and mysterious; a formal word. EG *The numinous power of the rock shook him.* ADJ QUALIT ⇑ divine

numskull /nʌmskʌl/, **numskulls**; also spelled **numbskull.** A **numskull** is a silly or stupid person; an old-fashioned informal word. N COUNT: ALSO VOC = fool

nun /nʌn/, **nuns.** A **nun** is a member of a female religious community. N COUNT

N UNCOUNT □ In this dictionary N UNCOUNT is used in the grammar notes beside entries to mean that a noun is an uncount noun. N UNCOUNTS behave in the following ways: **1** They do not treat the things that they refer to as countable, and therefore there is no choice between a form with an *-s* and a form without an *-s*. In order to treat the things that they refer to as countable, they are involved in a partitive construction such as *two pieces of* and *five chunks of* before the N UNCOUNT. See □ at N PART. See also N MASS. Examples of N UNCOUNT are **furniture** and **happiness**. EG *The room was small, low and overcrowded with* ***furniture****... I believe that the aim of life is to find* ***happiness****.* **2** They do not usually have a determiner in front of them. When they do have a determiner, further information about the noun is usually given to explain it more fully. This further information may be in the form of a modifier before the noun or a relative clause or prepositional group after the noun. See □ at SUPP. EG *He started smashing up all the* ***furniture****... ...the ultimate goal of all revolutions: the* ***happiness*** *of the individual... ...a* ***happiness*** *that he had never expected.*

NUMBER □ In this dictionary, information about the ways in which numbers are used in English is given both in the entries for individual words and also in □ at AGE, DATE, MEASUREMENT, MONEY, and TIME. The way that numbers behave grammatically is explained in □ at NUM and ORDINAL.

This entry shows some ways of saying numbers and of expressing ideas such as quantities, fractions, percentages, ratios, and approximate amounts. The chart that accompanies this entry shows ways of counting and expressing numbers.

The numbers 'hundred', 'thousand', 'million', and 'billion' are usually preceded by another number, or by the determiner 'a' if you are referring to only one hundred, one thousand, etc. EG *...a thousand dollars... ...over thirty thousand inhabitants.*

For numbers greater than a hundred, it is usual to say 'and' before the part of the number which is less than a hundred. For example, 351 is said as 'three hundred and fifty-one' and 49,280 is said as 'forty-nine thousand two hundred and eighty'.

There are different ways of saying numbers greater than a hundred. For example, 250 can be said as 'two hundred and fifty', 'two fifty', or 'two five oh'. 2,500 can be said as 'two thousand five hundred' or 'twenty-five hundred'. For longer numbers such as telephone numbers or account numbers, it is usual to say the figures individually. For example, you would say the number 131274 as 'one three one two seven four'. The number 0 is usually said as 'oh', although 'zero' and 'nought' are sometimes used instead.

The following examples show some ways of referring to quantities. EG *The number of congress members declined from 371 to 361.. I went back there half a dozen times after that first meeting... She was elected by more than 5,000 votes... An enormous number of photographs were taken, of which the Imperial War Museum has about eight thousand.*

The following examples show some ways of expressing fractions, decimals, percentages, proportions, and ratios. EG *...two fifths of the forest... ...a quarter of all children in this area... A third is almost the same as point three three... 80% of the workforce voted for a strike in a secret ballot... Only one in ten of the residents objected... Inflation is now running 70 per cent higher than it was in 1960... It's worth a hundred times more than that... ...in the ratio of approximately 2:1... The female/male ratio was 19 to 1.*

NUMBERS	
0	zero, nought, nothing
1	one
2	two
3	three
4	four
5	five
6	six
7	seven
8	eight
9	nine
10	ten
11	eleven
12	twelve
13	thirteen
14	fourteen
15	fifteen
16	sixteen
17	seventeen
18	eighteen
19	nineteen
20	twenty
21	twenty-one
22	twenty-two
23	twenty-three
24	twenty-four
30	thirty
31	thirty-one
40	forty
41	forty-one
50	fifty
51	fifty-one
60	sixty
61	sixty-one
70	seventy
71	seventy-one
80	eighty
81	eighty-one
90	ninety
91	ninety-one
100	a hundred
101	a hundred and one
102	a hundred and two
110	a hundred and ten
111	a hundred and eleven
120	a hundred and twenty
200	two hundred
1,000	a thousand
1,001	a thousand and one
1,010	a thousand and two
2,000	two thousand
10,000	ten thousand
20,000	twenty thousand
100,000	a hundred thousand
1,000,000	a million
2,000,000	two million
1,000,000,000	a billion

ORDINALS	
1st	first
2nd	second
3rd	third
4th	fourth
5th	fifth
6th	sixth
7th	seventh
8th	eighth
9th	ninth
10th	tenth
11th	eleventh
12th	twelfth
13th	thirteenth
14th	fourteenth
15th	fifteenth
16th	sixteenth
17th	seventeenth
18th	eighteenth
19th	nineteenth
20th	twentieth
21st	twenty-first
22nd	twenty-second
23rd	twenty-third
24th	twenty-fourth
30th	thirtieth
31st	thirty-first
40th	fortieth
41st	forty-first
50th	fiftieth
51st	fifty-first
60th	sixtieth
61st	sixty-first
70th	seventieth
71st	seventy-first
80th	eightieth
81st	eighty-first
90th	ninetieth
91st	ninety-first
100th	hundredth
101st	hundred and first
102nd	hundred and second
110th	hundred and tenth
111th	hundred and eleventh
120th	hundred and twentieth
200th	two hundredth
1,000th	thousandth
etc	etc

FRACTIONS	
$\frac{1}{2}$	a half
$\frac{1}{3}$	a third
$\frac{1}{4}$	a quarter
$\frac{1}{5}$	a fifth
$\frac{1}{6}$	a sixth
$\frac{1}{7}$	a seventh
$\frac{1}{8}$	an eighth
$\frac{1}{9}$	a ninth
$\frac{1}{10}$	a tenth
etc	etc

N UNCOUNT/COUNT □ In this dictionary N UNCOUNT/COUNT in the grammar notes beside entries means that the noun can be used both as an uncount noun and as a count noun. See □ at N UNCOUNT and N COUNT. An example is **velocity**. EG *He experiences a feeling of increasing **velocity**... ...the **velocity** of light... ...aircraft flying away from one another at **velocities** that amaze us.* If count uses are more common than uncount uses, the notation N COUNT/UNCOUNT is used.

nunnery /nʌnəri¹/, **nunneries**. A **nunnery** is a house or institution in which nuns live; an old-fashioned word. EG *She refused marriage and entered a nunnery.* — N COUNT = convent

nuptial /nʌptᵒʃəᵒl/, **nuptials**; a formal, old-fashioned word. **1 Nuptial** means relating to a wedding or to marriage. EG *...nuptial bliss.* — ADJ CLASSIF : ATTRIB

2 Someone's **nuptials** are their wedding celebrations. EG *Naturally I watched the nuptials of the Prince and Princess of Wales.* — N PLURAL

nurse /nɜːs/, **nurses, nursing, nursed. 1** A **nurse** is **1.1** a person whose job it is to care for ill people, especially in hospital. EG *She spent long hours talking with the nurses and doctors. She's a trained nurse... Nurse Lore was on the telephone.* — N COUNT : ALSO IN TITLE **1.2** a person who is trained to look after young children. EG *...a children's nurse from the Norland Institute.* ● See also **wet-nurse**. — N COUNT

2 If you **nurse** someone, you care for them when they are ill. EG *She discovered that he was ill and stayed to nurse him... Back home, and without medical help, he nursed her back to normality.* — V+O ⥣ look after

3 If you **nurse** an illness or injury, you allow it to get better by resting. EG *Do you want to go to bed and nurse that tooth?* — V+O ⥣ rest

4 When a baby **nurses** or when its mother **nurses** it, it feeds by sucking milk from its mother's breast. EG *A small, premature baby may be too weak to nurse... Mothers now have six weeks off from work to nurse their new-born babies.* — V-ERG = suckle

5 If you **nurse** an emotion, for example a hope or wish, you feel it very strongly for a long time. EG *Mr Wilson had long nursed a desire to build his own yacht... For years he had nursed a grudge against her.* — V+O = harbour

6 If you **are nursing** your **pride**, you feel sorry for yourself after an experience in which you have failed or been made to look foolish. EG *In Rome at the weekend Ernie James was nursing his pride after a 'disappointing' performance.* — V+O

7 If you **nurse** something that you are holding, you hold it carefully for a long time. EG *Philip was now nursing his fourth gin and tonic.* — V+O

8 See also **nursing**.

nursemaid /nɜːsmeɪd/, **nursemaids**. A **nursemaid** is a woman or girl who is paid to look after young children. EG *He decided to hire the girl as a nursemaid for his two small children.* — N COUNT = nurse

nursery /nɜːsəᵒri¹/, **nurseries. 1** A **nursery** is **1.1** a room in a family home in which the young children of the family sleep or play. — N COUNT **1.2** a place where very young children can be looked after while their parents are at work, shopping, etc. EG *She wished she had been able to send her children to such a nursery when they were small... Standards of care are low in some factory nurseries.* — N COUNT **1.3** a place where plants, young trees, etc are grown in order to be sold or to be planted in other places. EG *Gardening in a market garden or nursery can be a fulfilling job.* — N COUNT

2 Nursery means relating to the education of young children who are between three and five years old. EG *Nursery education is provided in many areas... Local mothers have been invited to bring their children along to playgroups or nursery classes.* — N BEFORE N

3 See also **day nursery**.

nursery nurse, nursery nurses. A **nursery nurse** is a person who has been trained to look after very young children. EG *She is assisted by nursery nurses who have trained for two years.* — N COUNT

nursery rhyme, nursery rhymes. A **nursery rhyme** is a short poem or song for young children. Most nursery rhymes are old, traditional, and very well known. EG *...a book of nursery rhymes.* — N COUNT

nursery school, nursery schools. A **nursery school** is a school for young children who are between three and five years old. EG *We need to open more playgroups and nursery schools in country areas... ...after dropping the kids off at nursery school.* — N COUNT/UNCOUNT = kindergarten

nursery slopes are the gentle slopes on a mountain that are used by people who are learning to ski. EG *There was hardly any snow at all on the nursery slopes this year.* — N PLURAL

nursing /nɜːsɪŋ/ is **1** the job or skill in which you look after people who are ill. EG *She ran courses in domestic skills and home nursing... ...the medical and nursing professions.* — N UNCOUNT **2** the period of time during which a mother feeds her baby with milk from her breasts. EG *The other precaution during pregnancy and nursing is to avoid putting on excess weight.* — N UNCOUNT = breast-feeding

nursing home, nursing homes. A **nursing home** is **1** a private hospital or residential home, especially for old people. EG *She was in a nursing home somewhere and she was not in good health at all.* — N COUNT ⥣ institution **2** a private maternity hospital; used mainly in British English. — N COUNT

nurture /nɜːtʃə/, **nurtures, nurturing, nurtured**; a formal word. **1** If you **nurture** a young child or a young plant, you care for and protect it while it is growing and developing. EG *A mother's duty to nurture her children... He walked round the garden looking fondly at the plants he had nurtured... The National Trust does its best to nurture the land it holds.* — V+O

2 To **nurture** plans, ideas, or people such as employees means to take action to encourage their development and success. EG *After spending two years nurturing this project, Bains came to England... The company structure continues to nurture high-grade personnel.* — V+O = cultivate

3 If you **nurture** an emotion, you feel it for a long time and encourage it. EG *I had nurtured such extraordinary passion for this girl.* — V+O = harbour

4 Nurture is care, protection, and encouragement that is given to someone or something while they are growing and developing. EG *...the early nurture of the infant.* — N UNCOUNT

nut /nʌt/, **nuts. 1** A **nut** is the hard fruit of certain trees, which grows inside a very hard shell. The nuts of many kinds of trees can be eaten. EG *I want to buy some cashew nuts... The cakes have chopped nuts in them.* — N COUNT : USU PL

2 A **nut** is also a small piece of metal with a hole in it through which a bolt goes. Nuts and bolts are used to hold together things such as pieces of machinery. EG *Take your spanner and tighten the nut... Replace the nuts and bolts on the wheel, then tighten.* — N COUNT ● If you talk about the **nuts and bolts** of a subject or activity, you are referring to detailed practical aspects of it rather than abstract ideas about it; an informal expression. EG *Our administrator does the day-to-day nuts and bolts and nitty-gritty.* — ● PHR : USED AS O

3 If you refer to someone as a **nut**, **3.1** you mean that they are mad or crazy; an informal use. EG *We think it was a nut who did this murder.* — N COUNT ⥣ lunatic **3.2** a person who is extremely enthusiastic about a particular subject or activity; an informal use. EG *She is one of those vegetarian nuts.* — N COUNT : MOD+N = freak

4 If you say that someone is **nuts**, you mean that they are mad; an informal use. EG *These kids must be nuts... You must have been really nuts to leave this place.* — ADJ CLASSIF : PRED = crazy

5 Your **nut** is your head; a very informal use. EG *Mind your nut on that door.* — N COUNT = noddle

6 If you say that someone **is doing** their **nut**, you mean that they are extremely angry; a very informal use. EG *Mum will do her nut if you take her car.* — PHR : VB/N INFLECT = be furious

7 If you say that something is **a hard nut to crack** or **a tough nut to crack**, you mean that it is difficult to do or understand; an informal expression. EG *This one is a hard nut to crack.* — PHR : USED AS C ● If you refer to someone, especially a man, as a **tough nut**, you mean that they are obstinate or difficult to deal with; an informal expression. — ● PHR : USED AS C = hard man

nut-brown. Something that is **nut-brown** is dark reddish brown in colour. — ADJ COLOUR

nutcase /nʌtkeɪs/, **nutcases**. A **nutcase** is someone who is crazy or insane; a very informal word. — N COUNT = nut

nutcracker /nʌtkrækə/, **nutcrackers**. A **nutcracker** or a pair of **nutcrackers** is a tool for cracking the shell of a nut to get to the edible part inside. — N COUNT, OR N PLURAL : ALSO *a pair of*+N IN PL

nuthouse /nʌthaʊs/, **nuthouses**. A **nuthouse** is a psychiatric hospital; a very informal word. N COUNT

nutmeg /nʌtmɛg/ is a spice made from the large dried fruit of a tree that grows in the tropics, especially in the Far East. It is used to flavour food. EG *Season the pudding with grated fresh nutmeg.* N UNCOUNT
▸ used to refer to the tree. EG *The fleshy fruit of the nutmeg tree is like an apricot... There was a nutmeg growing in the garden.* ▸ N COUNT

nutrient /njuːtrɪənt/, **nutrients**. A **nutrient** is a substance that is absorbed into a plant or into the body of an animal and that helps it to grow. EG *Excessive rainfall washes out valuable minerals and nutrients from the soil... ...oxygen from her lungs and nutrients derived from her food.* N COUNT

nutriment /njuːtrɪməᵊnt/, **nutriments**. **Nutriment** is the food or nourishment that is required by all living things in order for them to grow and remain healthy. EG *There were other sources of nutriment.* N UNCOUNT ⇑ food ▸ used as a count noun. EG *...drying out the soil, extracting nutriments.* ▸ N COUNT = nutrient

nutrition /njuːtrɪʃəᵊn/ is 1 the process of taking food or nutrients into the body and absorbing them. All living things need nutrition in order to grow and stay healthy. EG *Because of his poor nutrition, he has grown weaker and weaker... The scheme involves changing dietary habits and improving nutrition generally.* N UNCOUNT = diet **2** all the proteins, vitamins, minerals, etc which are contained in food and which help your body to grow and be healthy. EG *...foods that have a high nutrition content.* N UNCOUNT

nutritional /njuːtrɪʃəᵊnəl, -ʃənəᵊl/ means involving or relating to the food that you eat and the proteins, vitamins, minerals, etc in your food which help you to remain healthy. EG *From a nutritional point of view, quality of food matters more than quantity... ...the nutritional value of steak.* ADJ CLASSIF : ATTRIB

nutritious /njuːtrɪʃəs/. Food that is **nutritious** contains proteins, vitamins, minerals, etc which help your body to grow or be healthy. EG *Hummingbirds have discovered that nectar and pollen are very nutritious.* ADJ QUALIT = nourishing

nutritive /njuːtrɪtɪv/ means the same as nutritional. EG *Since their vegetable food was so poor in nutritive value, the herbivores had to eat a great deal of it.* ADJ CLASSIF : ATTRIB

nutshell /nʌtʃɛl/. **In a nutshell** means stated in an extremely concise way that summarizes the main point. EG *You've really put in a nutshell the reasons why we failed... That, in a nutshell, is what we're doing.* PHR : USED AS ADV SEN ⇑ concisely = briefly, in a word

nutter /nʌtə/, **nutters**. A **nutter** is someone who is mad; a very informal word. N COUNT = nutcase

nutty /nʌti¹/, **nuttier, nuttiest**. 1 Something that is **nutty** tastes of nuts, has the texture of nuts, or is made with nuts. EG *They all have a fresh, nutty flavour.* ADJ QUALIT

2 Someone or something that is **nutty** is insane or very foolish; used in informal English. EG *She was a bit nutty... ...this utterly nutty idea.* ADJ QUALIT = loony

nuzzle /nʌzəᵊl/, **nuzzles, nuzzling, nuzzled**. If you **nuzzle** someone or something, you gently rub your nose and mouth against them, especially to show affection. EG *'Ellen,' he said, nuzzling her neck... I could see the horse nuzzling at Ned's coat.. She nuzzled closer and her hair tickled his chin.* V+O, OR V+A

NW is an abbreviation for 'north-west' or 'north-western'. ADJ CLASSIF : ATTRIB

nylon /naɪlɒn/, **nylons**. 1 **Nylon** is a strong, flexible artificial material which is used for making cloth, clothes, and other things. EG *...use picture wire or nylon cord to hang pictures... ...sheets made of nylon.* N UNCOUNT ⇑ synthetic

2 **Nylons** are stockings or tights made of nylon; an old-fashioned term. N PLURAL : ALSO *a pair of*+N

nymph /nɪmf/, **nymphs**. A **nymph** is 1 in Greek and Roman mythology, one of the spirits of nature, who were believed to take the form of young women and live in trees, rivers, and mountains. N COUNT ⇑ goddess **2** a young woman; used in old-fashioned poetic English. N COUNT **3** the larva of an insect such as a dragonfly or mayfly, which develops into an adult without going through the stage of being a pupa. N COUNT

nympho /nɪmfəʊ/, **nymphos**. A **nympho** is a nymphomaniac; an informal word. N COUNT

nymphomaniac /nɪmfəᵊmeɪnɪæk/, **nymphomaniacs**. A **nymphomaniac** is a woman who makes it very obvious that she likes to have sex, especially with a lot of different men; used showing disapproval. N COUNT

Oo

O, o /əʊ/, **O's, o's**. 1 **O** is the fifteenth letter of the English alphabet. N COUNT

2 **O** is used, in spoken English, to mean nought or zero, for example when you are telling someone a telephone number, or the number of a year such as '1908'. EG *That is equal to point o eight nine... ...one seven nine double o.* NUM

3 **O** is used in exclamations, especially when you are expressing strong feelings. EG *O God, I want to go home... O the joy of those Saturday afternoons... O yes, he's very good.* EXCLAM = Oh

4 **O** is an abbreviation for various words beginning with O or o, such as 'old', 'organization', 'officer', and 'of'.

> **O** ☐ In this dictionary o is used in the grammar notes beside entries to mean object. See ☐ at V+O, V+O+A, V+O+C, V+O+O, V-ERG, and RECIP.

o' /ə/ is used, in written English, to represent the word **of** pronounced in a particular way. EG *...a cup o' tea... ...a lot o' money... ...one o' them.* PREP

oaf /əʊf/, **oafs**. An **oaf** is a clumsy or stupid person; used showing disapproval. EG *Paul, you are a big oaf!* N COUNT ⇑ idiot
◊ **oafish**. EG *...women who are weary of their oafish husbands.* ◊ ADJ QUALIT = loutish

oak /əʊk/, **oaks**. An **oak** or **oak tree** is a large tree that often grows in woods and forests. EG *...a forest of oaks... ...an immense oak tree.* N COUNT ▸ used of the wood from the tree, which is strong and hard. EG *...a square oak table... ...the oak-panelled corridor.* ▸ ADJ CLASSIF

oaken /əʊkəᵊn/ means made of wood from an oak tree; a rather literary word. EG *...the heavy oaken door.* ADJ CLASSIF ⇑ wooden

OAP /əʊ eɪ piː/, **OAP's**. An **OAP** is, in Britain, a man over the age of 65 or a woman over the age of 60; an abbreviation for 'old-age pensioner'. EG *Fares generally must be reduced for OAP's.* N COUNT

oar /ɔː/, **oars**. An **oar** is a long pole that is used for rowing a boat. The oar is fixed across the side of the boat, you pull the handle, and the wide, flat part at the other end moves through the water and causes the boat to move. EG *The oar got entangled in the weeds... ...balancing the blades of the oars above the water.* N COUNT ● If you **get, put,** or **stick** your **oar in**, you interfere with what someone else is doing, interrupt them, or express your opinion about something without being asked to; an informal expression, used showing disapproval. ● PHR : VB INFLECTS = meddle

oasis /əʊeɪsɪs/, **oases** /əʊeɪsiːz/. 1 An **oasis** is a small area in a desert where water and plants are found. N COUNT ⇑ place

2 An **oasis** is also any pleasant place or situation which is surrounded by unpleasant ones. EG *The town was an oasis of prosperity in a desert of poverty... The holidays had been oases in a dry wilderness of lessons.* N COUNT : USU USED AS C = island, haven

oat /əʊt/, **oats**. 1 **Oats** are the grains of a cereal that is used especially for making porridge or for feeding animals. EG *...fields of wheat and barley and oats... ...oat flour.* N PLURAL

2 ● If you say that someone **is getting** their **oats**, you mean that they are having sex regularly; a very ● PHR : VB INFLECTS

informal expression in British English. EG *David hadn't got his oats for some time.* • to **sow** one's **wild oats**: see **wild**.

oath /əʊθ/, **oaths**. 1 An **oath** is a promise, especially the promise that you make to tell the truth in a court of law. EG *...an oath of allegiance to Spain... ...a man taking the oath in court.* • See also **Hippocratic oath**. • If someone is **on** or **under oath**, they have made a promise, especially a promise to tell the truth in a court of law. EG *Witnesses sometimes lie on oath... I was a doctor and under oath to save life.* — N COUNT; • PHR : USED AS AN A

2 An **oath** is also an offensive expression or a swearword; an old-fashioned use. EG *He was answered with a torrent of French oaths.* — N COUNT

oatmeal /əʊtmiːl/. 1 **Oatmeal** is a coarse flour made by crushing oats. EG *...oatmeal biscuits... ...oatmeal and milk... ...herring in oatmeal.* — N UNCOUNT

2 Something that is **oatmeal** is a very pale creamy colour with a brownish tone. EG *...an oatmeal coat and brown trousers... ...oatmeal wallpaper.* — ADJ COLOUR

obduracy /ɒbdjəʳrəsi[1]/. Someone's **obduracy** is their behaviour when they are stubborn and determined not to change their mind about something; a formal word, used showing disapproval. EG *...the obduracy of his silence... ...his obduracy over China.* — N UNCOUNT ⇑ determination = stubbornness

obdurate /ɒbdjəʳrə[1]t/. If someone is **obdurate**, they are stubborn and determined not to change their mind about something; a formal word, used showing disapproval. EG *...her obdurate leadership... The headman remained obdurate.* ◇ **obdurately**. EG *She waited obdurately for a taxi.* — ADJ QUALIT ⇑ determined = obstinate, unbending; ◇ ADV WITH VB

obedience /ə[6]biːdɪəns/ is your behaviour when you do what someone asks or tells you to do, especially someone in authority. EG *She failed to show proper obedience and respect to the elders... He did it in obedience to her wishes... ...obedience to authority.* — N UNCOUNT : IF + PREP THEN *to* ⇑ submission = deference

obedient /ə[6]biːdɪənt/. Someone who is **obedient** behaves as they are asked or told to do, especially willingly. EG *She was an obedient little girl... We sat down, obedient to the wishes of Oliver.* ◇ **obediently**. EG *'Try it,' Clem ordered. Obediently I picked up the cup.* • **Your obedient servant** is an old-fashioned or informal way of ending a letter before signing your name. — ADJ QUALIT ⇑ submissive ≠ rebellious; ◇ ADV WITH VB = dutifully; • CONVENTION

obeisance /əʊbeɪsəns, əʊbiː-/, **obeisances**; a formal word. 1 **Obeisance** is respect or obedience for someone or something. EG *...the obeisance of subordinates... While paying obeisance to general principles, it left the decision to its individual members.* — N UNCOUNT : IF + PREP THEN *to* = homage

2 An **obeisance** is a physical gesture, especially a bow, that you make in order to show your respect for someone or something. EG *Making a very low obeisance, she received a kiss from him.* ▸ used as an uncount noun. EG *The emperor made obeisance to this image.* — N COUNT = curtsy; ▸ N UNCOUNT

obelisk /ɒbə[2]lɪsk/, **obelisks**. An **obelisk** is a tall stone pillar that has been built in honour of a person or an important event. EG *...a granite obelisk commemorating the battle... ...an Egyptian obelisk.* — N COUNT ⇑ monument

obese /əʊbiːs/. Someone who is **obese** is very fat; a formal word. EG *In the window was an obese man reading the paper... He has become obese and lazy.* ◇ **obesity** /ə[6]biːsɪti[1]/. EG *Obesity is a real health hazard.* — ADJ QUALIT ⇑ overweight = stout; ◇ N UNCOUNT = corpulence

obey /ə[6]beɪ/, **obeys, obeying, obeyed**. If you **obey** a person, a command, or an instruction, you do what you are told or advised to do. EG *The troops were reluctant to obey orders... They obeyed me without question... Be careful to obey the manufacturer's washing instructions.* — V OR V+O : USU V +O = follow

obfuscate /ɒbfʌskeɪt/, **obfuscates, obfuscating, obfuscated**. To **obfuscate** or **obfuscate** something means to deliberately make it seem confusing and difficult to understand; a formal word. EG *I do not know why you obfuscate... The ruling classes obfuscate the minds of the exploited.* ◇ **obfuscation** /ɒbfʌskeɪʃə[0]n/. EG *...an obfuscation of the real issues.* — V OR V+O ⇑ confuse; ◇ N UNCOUNT = clouding

obituary /ə[6]bɪtjʊ[0]əri[1]/, **obituaries**. An **obituary** is a piece of writing about the character and achievements of someone who has just died. EG *I read Sewell's obituary in the Daily News... Evans wrote an obituary of Stalin... ...the obituary page of the Times.* — N COUNT ⇑ article

obj. is an abbreviation for 'object'.

object, objects, objecting, objected. Object is pronounced /ɒbdʒɪ[2]kt/ when it is a noun, and /ə[7]bdʒekt/ when it is a verb. 1 An **object** is something that has a fixed shape or form, that you can touch or see, and that is not alive. EG *...the shabby, black object he was carrying... ...a solid object... ...mats, bowls, and other objects.* — N COUNT

2 A person's **object** or the **object** of what they are doing is the person's aim or purpose. EG *The minder's object is to keep the child asleep... To journey for months with the sole object of finding and filming a rare creature... ...the object of Haldane's visit.* — N COUNT : USU WITH POSS ⇑ intention = objective

3 The **object** of a particular feeling or reaction is **3.1** the thing or person that it is directed towards. EG *This difficulty was the object of ridicule in some quarters... ...young Eileen, the object of his desires.* — N COUNT : USU + *of* ⇑ recipient

3.2 the thing or person that causes it. EG *I was an object of embarrassment to the college authorities... The fertile land became the object of violent struggles for possession.* • See also **sex-object**. — N COUNT : USU + *of* = subject

4 In grammar, the object of a verb or a preposition is the word or phrase which completes the structure begun by the verb or preposition. All prepositions require an object; for example, if you use the word 'of', you have to add an object. Many verbs, like 'make', also need an object. The object is usually a noun, pronoun, or noun group. See ☐ at V+O, V+O+A, V+O+C, V+O+O, V-ERG, RECIP. — N COUNT

5 If you say that something such as money is **no object**, you mean that it is not important or a problem, either because you have a lot of it, or because other things are more important. EG *Money, it seemed, was no object... He had the appearance of a man to whom time was no object.* — PHR : USED AS C ⇑ unimportant = irrelevant

6 If you **object** to something, you express your opposition, dislike, or disapproval of it. EG *We object to the selection of Haldane... You may object that the system makes boys effeminate... The men objected and the women supported their protest... I don't object to the early start. I've always been an early riser.* — V : IF + PREP THEN *to*, OR V + REPORT-CL ⇑ disagree = protest ≠ accept, approve

objection /ə[7]bdʒekʃə[0]n/, **objections**. An **objection** is something that you say in which you express your opposition to something or your disapproval of it, giving reasons for your opinion. EG *They raised objections to Seagram's bid... Simpson met every objection with sound arguments... The objection that he had no experience was ignored... I've no objection to anybody coming into my lesson... 'Why not?' he said gently. 'Do you have any objection?'.* — N COUNT : IF + PREP THEN *to* ≠ approval

objectionable /ə[7]bdʒekʃə[0]nəbə[0]l/. If you describe someone or something as **objectionable**, you mean that you strongly disapprove of them, because you consider them offensive and unacceptable. EG *...politicians whose views he found objectionable... ...arms sales to objectionable regimes... ...a vulgar, irritating and objectionable person.* — ADJ QUALIT ⇑ unpleasant = obnoxious

objective /ə[7]bdʒektɪv/, **objectives**. 1 Your **objective** is what you are trying to achieve by a particular course of action. EG *Mobil's primary objective is to win... ...political objectives... If this policy is reversed we shall never achieve our objectives.* — N COUNT = aim, goal

2 Information that is **objective** relates to or is based on facts and things that can be seen or measured. EG *There is no objective evidence of anything of the kind... ...a search for objective data.* ◇ **objectively**. EG *Realities which exist independently and objectively.* ◇ **objectivity** /ɒbdʒektɪvɪti[1]/. — ADJ CLASSIF ⇑ real = factual; ◇ ADV ⇑ actually; ◇ N UNCOUNT

3 If you describe a person or their opinion as **objective**, you mean that they are trying to be fair and base their opinions on facts, rather than on personal feelings. EG *...a book on communism written by an astonishingly objective author... Help them to come to a more objective view of their situation.* ◇ **objectively**. EG *It was desirable to view these things objectively.* ◇ **objectivity**. EG *Although historians may strive after objectivity, they are necessarily men of their time.* — ADJ QUALIT = detached, impartial ≠ subjective; ◇ ADV WITH VB; ◇ N UNCOUNT

object lesson, object lessons. An **object lesson** is an action, event, or situation that demonstrates the correct or best way to do something or demonstrates the truth or wisdom of a particular principle; often used showing approval. EG *Thank you, that was an object lesson in how to handle a difficult customer!* — N COUNT ⇑ demonstration

objector /ə[7]bdʒektə/, **objectors**. An **objector** is someone who states or shows that they oppose or disapprove of something. EG *The objectors did not challenge the museum's need... ...the inquiry for which the objectors had asked.* • See also **conscientious objector**. — N COUNT = dissenter, protester

objet d'art /ɒbʒeɪ dɑː/, **objets d'art**. An **objet d'art** is a small ornament or object that is considered to have artistic merit. N COUNT

obligated /ɒblɪgeɪtɪ²d/. If you feel **obligated** to do something, you feel that it is your duty to do it; a rather formal word. EG *I felt obligated to turn up on time.* ADJ CLASSIF: PRED, USU+to/to-INF = bound

obligation /ɒblɪgeɪʃə⁰n/, **obligations**. An **obligation** is something that you must do because you have promised to do it or because it is your duty to do it. EG *We had to go home because of family obligations... The city does indeed have an obligation to keep the schools open... We are under no obligation to give him what he wants.* N COUNT/UNCOUNT: IF+PREP/VB THEN to/to-INF = commitment

obligatory /ə⁷blɪgətə⁰ri¹/. If something is **obligatory**, you must do it, especially because of a custom, a rule, or a law. EG *I fixed a perimeter fence round it–this was obligatory in those days... It is not obligatory to answer.* ADJ CLASSIF = compulsory

oblige /ə⁶blaɪdʒ/, **obliges, obliging, obliged**. 1 If something **obliges** you to do something, it makes you feel that you must do it. EG *Old-world politeness, however, obliged me to go on with the ordeal... I felt obliged to invite him into the parlour.* V+O+to-INF = compel

2 To **oblige** someone means to be helpful to them by doing what they have asked you to do. EG *'Who did you ask to drive?'–'Charlie Kirch. He's only too glad to oblige.'... A girl reporter obliged Hearst by 'fainting' in the main street.* V OR V+O ↑ help

● People sometimes say **much obliged, I am obliged to you**, etc, in order to indicate that they are very grateful to you. These are rather old-fashioned expressions. EG *'Alright?'–'Yes, yes, much obliged.'... I am immensely obliged to you.* ● CONVENTION, OR PHR: VB INFLECTS

● If you say that you **would be obliged** if someone would do something, you are telling them in a very formal and polite way that you want them to do it. EG *I'd be obliged if you'd mind your own business.* ● PHR = kindly

obliging /ə⁶blaɪdʒɪŋ/. Someone who is **obliging** is willing and eager to be helpful; used showing approval. EG *Mr Carston is a very obliging, amiable gentleman.* ◊ **obligingly**. EG *Her full name and title had obligingly been printed on a board outside.* ADJ QUALIT = accommodating ◊ ADV WITH VB

oblique /ə⁷bliːk/, **obliques**. 1 If you describe a statement, reference, comment, etc, as **oblique**, you mean that it is indirect and therefore difficult to understand. EG *...an oblique compliment... Alexander took this as an oblique reference to his own affairs.* ▸ used to describe people and their behaviour. EG *He has a curiously oblique manner.* ◊ **obliquely**. EG *Was suicide mentioned, however obliquely?* ADJ QUALIT ↑ obscure ▸ = evasive ◊ ADV WITH VB = indirectly

2 An **oblique** line is one that slopes at an angle, rather than being vertical, horizontal, or perpendicular to another line. EG *...a script which had oblique strokes after every phrase... He walked away at an oblique angle.* ◊ **obliquely**. EG *Rays from the sun strike more obliquely towards the poles.* ADJ CLASSIF ≠ slanting ◊ ADV WITH VB = diagonally

3 An **oblique** is a line that is sloping, rather than vertical or horizontal. N COUNT

obliterate /ə⁷blɪtəreɪt/, **obliterates, obliterating, obliterated**. 1 If something **obliterates** an object or place, it destroys it completely. EG *I watched bombs obliterate the villages... The path had been obliterated by cattle.* ◊ **obliteration** /ə⁷blɪtəreɪʃə⁰n/. EG *Each side is committed to the obliteration of the other.* V+O = annihilate ◊ N UNCOUNT+of = annihilation

2 If you **obliterate** something such as a memory, emotion, or thought, you remove it completely from your mind; a rather literary use. EG *In a few years she had managed to obliterate all memories of the incident... Anne was eager to obliterate her error.* ◊ **obliteration**. V+O = cancel ◊ N UNCOUNT

oblivion /ə⁷blɪviən/ is 1 the state of not being aware or conscious of what is happening around you. EG *I sank back into oblivion.* 2 the state of having been forgotten or of no longer being considered important. EG *No one said anything about the episode and it began to sink into oblivion.* N UNCOUNT; N UNCOUNT = obscurity

oblivious /ə⁷blɪviəs/. If you are **oblivious** to something or **oblivious** of it, you are not aware of it. EG *She seemed oblivious of the attention she was drawing to herself... He was totally oblivious to the fact that he had almost been killed.* ADJ QUALIT: USU PRED+to/of = ignorant ≠ conscious

oblong /ɒblɒŋ/, **oblongs**. An **oblong** is a shape which has two long sides and two short sides and in which all the angles are right angles. EG *The only bathroom was a tiny oblong between the landing and my room.* ▸ used as an adjective. EG *...an oblong table.* N COUNT = rectangle ▸ ADJ CLASSIF

obnoxious /ə⁷bnɒkʃəs/. If you describe someone as **obnoxious**, you mean that they are very unpleasant. EG *He has some obnoxious qualities, but he is reliable... ...his obnoxious daughter.* ◊ **obnoxiously**. EG *...an obnoxiously trendy teacher.* ADJ QUALIT = loathsome, odious ◊ ADV

oboe /əʊbəʊ/, **oboes**. An **oboe** is a wooden orchestral instrument that is shaped like a tube and played by blowing through a reed inserted at its top. EG *'You play the oboe, I see,' said Simon.* N COUNT

oboist /əʊbəʊɪst/, **oboists**. An **oboist** is someone who plays the oboe. N COUNT ↑ musician

obscene /ə⁷bsiːn/. 1 Something that is **obscene** shocks and offends people, especially because it is related in an unpleasant way to naked people, sex, or bodily functions. EG *The Herald had been prosecuted for printing obscene and indecent advertising... Try to deal with obscene telephone calls by putting the phone down immediately.* ADJ QUALIT ↑ offensive = filthy

2 You can also refer to someone or something as **obscene** when you disapprove of them very strongly. EG *'I think you're obscene,' says Carmody, turning and opening the door... It's obscene. Reducing such things to politics... ...the obscene gap between city and rural incomes.* ADJ QUALIT = disgusting

obscenity /ə⁷bsenɪti¹/, **obscenities**. 1 **Obscenity** is behaviour that shocks and offends people because it involves nudity, sex, violence, bodily functions, etc, in an unpleasant or indecent way. EG *Existing laws on obscenity are to be tightened.* N UNCOUNT

2 An **obscenity** is 2.1 a word or expression that is rude and offensive because it relates to sex or bodily functions. EG *They started yelling abuse and obscenities at the cops.* 2.2 an event or action that shocks or angers you very much because it is so unjust and immoral. EG *This massacre is one of the towering obscenities of our time.* N COUNT: USU PL; N COUNT = atrocity

obscurantism /ɒbskjə⁴ræntɪzə⁰m/ is the practice or activity of deliberately making something vague and difficult to understand, especially in order to prevent people from finding out the truth. EG *Indeed, obscurantism had become the official policy.* N UNCOUNT

obscurantist /ɒbskjə⁴ræntɪst/. Something that is **obscurantist** is deliberately vague and difficult to understand, especially in order to prevent people from finding out the truth. EG *...an obscurantist attitude.* ▸ used of people. EG *...a number of obscurantist theologians.* ADJ CLASSIF

obscure /ə⁷bskjʊə/, **obscures, obscuring, obscured; obscurer, obscurest**. 1 Something that is **obscure** is 1.1 known by only a few people. EG *...obscure operas... ...an obscure Austrian mountain village... ...an eighteenth-century book so obscure I can't even remember the name of it.* 1.2 complex and not easily understood. EG *...obscure points of theology or semantics... France's relationship to new organization is extremely obscure.* 1.3 difficult to see or hear. EG *He saw the hideous, obscure shape rise slowly to the surface.* ADJ QUALIT; ADJ QUALIT ≠ straightforward; ADJ QUALIT = indistinct

2 To **obscure** something means 2.1 to make it difficult to know or difficult to understand. EG *Words that obscure the truth must be discarded... The central issue in your campaign must not be allowed to obscure the wider political issues.* 2.2 to prevent it from being seen or heard properly. EG *An enormous piece of sticking plaster obscured one half of his face... Some areas were obscured by patches of fog... A loud brassy chord rang down the corridor, obscuring the sound of her voice.* V+O ↑ hide = cloud; V+O ↑ hide

obscurity /ə⁷bskjʊərɪti¹/ is 1 the state of being known by only a few people. EG *He has risen from obscurity to international fame... My proposals disappeared for the most part into obscurity.* 2 darkness or very dim light. EG *He peered into the obscurity beneath the trees.* 3 the quality of being difficult to understand. EG *Dixon didn't mind the obscurity of the reference.* N UNCOUNT = insignificance; N UNCOUNT = gloom; N UNCOUNT

obsequious /ə⁷bsiːkwiəs/. People who are **obsequious** are too eager to help you, listen to what you say, agree with you, etc; used showing disapproval. EG *...obsequious shop assistants.* ◊ **obsequiously**. EG *They smiled obsequiously when she said such things.* ◊ **obsequiousness**. EG *...cunning obsequiousness.* ADJ QUALIT = servile, fawning ◊ ADV WITH VB ◊ N UNCOUNT

observable /ə⁷bzɜːvəbə⁰l/. Something that is **observable** can be seen or noticed. EG *It is an action that is observable in almost all countries in the world... ...observable events.* ◊ **observably**. EG *He was observably growing thinner about the waist.* ADJ CLASSIF = visible ◊ ADV = visibly

observance /ə⁷bzɜːvəns/, **observances**. The **observance** of something such as a law or custom is the practice of obeying or following it completely. EG *...observance of speed limits and traffic lights... ...the observance of agreed procedures.* ▸ used as a count noun. EG *...religious observances.*
N UNCOUNT + SUPP = obeying ▸ N COUNT

observant /ə⁷bzɜːvənt/. Someone who is **observant** has the ability to notice things that are not usually noticed; used showing approval. EG *You're very observant, Cathy... He was not an especially observant man.*
ADJ QUALIT = perceptive

observation /ɒbzəveɪʃə⁰n/, **observations**. 1 **Observation** is the action or process of carefully watching someone or something, especially in order to learn or understand something about them. EG *...new information gathered by observation or experiment... ...our observation of others... He has been taken into hospital for observation.* ● If you are **under observation**, you are being watched carefully, especially by some authority such as the police, the government, or a hospital. EG *It would be as well if she was put under observation in some nursing home.*
N UNCOUNT = study, examination ● PHR : USED AS AN A

2 An **observation** is 2.1 something that you have learned or understood by seeing or watching something and thinking about it. EG *...clinical observations.* 2.2 a comment or remark that you make about something, especially as a result of having watched or thought about it a lot. EG *I wish to make a few general observations about your work so far... ...one or two dry observations which might have passed for humour.*
N COUNT ⇑ discovery; N COUNT : USU + A OR REPORT-CL

3 **Observation** is also the ability to notice things that are not usually noticed. EG *...keen powers of observation.*
N UNCOUNT = perception

observational /ɒbzəveɪʃə⁰nəl, -ʃənə⁰l/; a formal word. **Observational** means 1 relating to people's ability to notice things. EG *...your observational faculties.* 2 relating to the watching of something in order to learn new things. EG *As an observational device, it is primitive.*
ADJ CLASSIF : USU ATTRIB; ADJ CLASSIF : USU ATTRIB

observatory /ə⁷bzɜːvətə⁰ri¹/, **observatories**. An **observatory** is a special building from which scientists can study and watch things like the stars, the sky, and weather patterns.
N COUNT : ALSO IN NAMES

observe /ə⁷bzɜːv/, **observes, observing, observed**. 1 If you **observe** someone or something, you 1.1 watch them carefully, especially in order to learn or understand something about them. EG *The team spent months observing the way mothers take care of their babies.* 1.2 see or notice them; a rather formal use. EG *He looked out through the window and observed me walking along the boat deck... It was difficult to observe any change in his expression.*
V OR V+O = study; V+O = remark

2 If you **observe** that something is the case, you make a remark or comment about it, especially when it is something you have noticed or thought about a lot; a rather formal use. EG *'People aren't interested in spiritual things,' observed the actress... I would only observe that he is well qualified for the post.*
V+REPORT-CL/QUOTE ⇑ say

3 If you **observe** something such as a law or custom, you obey or follow it completely. EG *I didn't enjoy the party, but the conventions had been observed.*
V+O = honour

observer /ə⁷bzɜːvə/, **observers**. An **observer** is 1 someone who spends time watching an activity or event in order to see what happens, but without actually taking part. EG *...political observers and media commentators.* 2 someone who sees or notices something. EG *A casual observer may get the wrong impression.*
N COUNT ⇑ watcher; N COUNT

obsess /ə⁷bsɛs/, **obsesses, obsessing, obsessed**. If something **obsesses** you or if you **are obsessed** with it or by it, you keep thinking about it over a long period of time, and find it difficult to think about anything else. EG *He became absolutely obsessed with a girl reporter on television... Ellen was obsessed by marriage... The image of Madeleine obsessed him.*
V+O : USU PASS = preoccupy

obsession /ə⁷bsɛʃə⁰n/, **obsessions**. An **obsession** is something that you cannot stop thinking about because it is very important to you. EG *Taylor's fascination with bees developed into an obsession.*
N COUNT = fixation

obsessional /ə⁷bsɛʃə⁰nəl, -ʃənə⁰l/ means the same as obsessive. EG *...an obsessional need to win.* ◊ **obsessionally**. EG *He was obsessionally attached to her throughout his life.*
ADJ QUALIT ◊ ADV WITH VB

obsessive /ə⁷bsɛsɪv/. You say that an attitude or kind of behaviour is **obsessive** when someone keeps thinking or behaving in this way, and seems unable to stop it. EG *Obsessive tidiness in the office is a bad sign.* ◊ **obsessively**. EG *He was obsessively interested in every single detail about my early life.*
ADJ QUALIT = obsessional ◊ ADV WITH VB

obsolescence /ɒbsəlɛsəns/ is the state of being no longer needed or no longer desirable because something newer or more efficient has been invented. EG *...an educational system whose obsolescence becomes more evident every day.*
N UNCOUNT = redundancy

obsolescent /ɒbsəlɛsənt/. Something that is **obsolescent** is nearly obsolete or becoming obsolete.
ADJ CLASSIF = waning

obsolete /ɒbsəliːt/. Something that is **obsolete** is no longer needed or no longer desirable because something newer or more efficient has been invented. EG *'Reading and writing,' he suggested, 'will become obsolete skills.'*
ADJ CLASSIF = outmoded

obstacle /ɒbstəkə⁰l/, **obstacles**. An **obstacle** is 1 an object that makes it difficult for you to go where you want to go, because it is in your way. EG *Bats can not only sense obstacles in their path, but also identify them.* 2 a situation or event that stops you from doing something or that makes it difficult for you to do something. EG *The bureaucratic obstacles to getting her son over from Jamaica seemed insurmountable.*
N COUNT; N COUNT = hindrance

obstetric /ə⁷bstɛtrɪk/, **obstetrics**. **Obstetric** is an adjective and **obstetrics** is an uncount noun. 1 **Obstetrics** is the branch of medicine that is concerned with pregnancy and childbirth; a technical term in medicine. EG *By this time I had decided that my future lay in obstetrics and gynaecology.*
N UNCOUNT

2 **Obstetric** means concerned with obstetrics. EG *...obstetric nurses.*
ADJ CLASSIF : ATTRIB

obstetrician /ɒbstətrɪʃə⁰n/, **obstetricians**. An **obstetrician** is a doctor who is specially trained to deal with childbirth and the care of pregnant women; a technical term in medicine.
N COUNT ⇑ specialist

obstinacy /ɒbstɪnəsi¹/ is the strong determination that someone has to do exactly what they want and not to change their mind or be persuaded to do anything else. EG *He denounced the obstinacy of the Transport Minister... I detected a certain obstinacy in his attitude.*
N UNCOUNT = stubbornness

obstinate /ɒbstɪnət/. 1 Someone who is **obstinate** is very determined to do what they want, and will not change their mind or be persuaded to do something else. EG *...an obstinate, rebellious child with a violent temper.* ▸ used of people's behaviour. EG *He retained an obstinate regard for appearances.* ◊ **obstinately**. EG *'But it's impossible,' William kept obstinately repeating.*
ADJ QUALIT = stubborn, headstrong ▸ = dogged ◊ ADV WITH VB = stubbornly

2 You describe things as **obstinate** when they are difficult to move, change, or destroy. EG *These weeds are really obstinate.* ◊ **obstinately**. EG *Unemployment figures are remaining obstinately high.*
ADJ QUALIT = persistent ◊ ADV

obstreperous /ə⁷bstrɛpərəs/. Someone who is **obstreperous** is noisy and difficult to control. EG *Drunks were rarely charged unless they became obstreperous.*
ADJ QUALIT = stroppy

obstruct /ə⁷bstrʌkt/, **obstructs, obstructing, obstructed**. 1 If something **obstructs** a road, path, entrance, etc, it blocks it, so that people or vehicles cannot get past. EG *The crash obstructed the road for several hours.*
V+O

2 If you **obstructs** someone or something, you stop them from moving forward by blocking their path. EG *We had been told that the charge was 'obstructing pedestrian traffic'.*
V+O = block

3 To **obstruct** something such as justice or progress means to prevent it from happening properly or from developing. EG *It is a crime for the President to obstruct justice.*
V+O ⇑ impede

obstruction /ə⁷bstrʌkʃə⁰n/, **obstructions**. 1 An **obstruction** is something that blocks a road, path, entrance, etc. EG *These obstructions could take some vital weeks to clear from the canals.*
N COUNT ⇑ blockage

2 **Obstruction** is the act of deliberately delaying something or preventing something from happening, especially in business, law, parliament, etc. EG *...the serious charge of 'obstruction of justice'.*
N UNCOUNT

obstructionism /ə⁷bstrʌkʃə⁰nɪzə⁰m/ is the practice or policy of deliberately delaying or preventing legal, business, or parliamentary operations.
N UNCOUNT

obstructive /ə⁷bstrʌktɪv/. Someone who is **obstructive** deliberately causes difficulties for other
ADJ QUALIT ⇑ difficult

people; used showing disapproval. EG *She's just being obstructive... He behaved in a very obstructive fashion.* ◇ **obstructiveness**. EG *...the bureaucratic obstructiveness of the customs officials.* ◇ N UNCOUNT

obtain /ə⁷bteɪn/, **obtains, obtaining, obtained**.
1 To **obtain** something means to get it or achieve it; a rather formal use. EG *She obtained her degree in 1951... Scientists realized that it was possible to obtain energy by splitting the atom... Both of these books can be obtained from the Public Library.* V+O

2 If a situation, custom, etc **obtains**, it exists; a formal use. EG *That unfortunately is the situation that obtains today.* V = prevail

obtainable /ə⁷bteɪnəbə⁰l/. Something that is **obtainable** can be obtained easily. EG *Savings up to 65% are obtainable under this scheme.* ADJ CLASSIF : USU PRED ⇑ available

obtrude /ə⁷btruːd/, **obtrudes, obtruding, obtruded**. 1 When something **obtrudes** or when you **obtrude** it, it becomes noticeable in an undesirable way; a formal or literary use. EG *Gertrude now clearly felt that she had obtruded her sorrow... Those measures obtruded on his privacy.* V-ERG

2 If an object **obtrudes**, it sticks out. V

obtrusive /ə⁷btruːsɪv/. Something that is **obtrusive** is noticeable in an unpleasant way. EG *Equally obtrusive was the graffiti that had started to appear .. The dog was huddled under the bench as if to be less obtrusive.* ◇ **obtrusively**. EG *Hawke got up and walked obtrusively out of the building.* ADJ QUALIT ⇑ obvious ◇ ADV WITH VB ⇑ obviously

obtuse /ə⁷btjuːs/. 1 Someone who is **obtuse** has difficulty understanding things, or makes no effort to understand them; used in rather formal English, showing disapproval. EG *Are you normally stupid or just being deliberately obtuse?* ▸ used of what they say. EG *...obtuse and ignorant remarks.* ◇ **obtuseness**. EG *...the cowardly obtuseness of white liberals.* ADJ QUALIT = thick, slow ◇ N UNCOUNT : USU+SUPP

2 An **obtuse** angle is between 90 and 180; a technical term in mathematics. ADJ CLASSIF

obverse /ɒbvɜːs/. The **obverse** of an opinion, situation, or argument is its opposite; a rather formal word. EG *How we live depends on where we live. And the obverse is true... The obverse of expansion at the top was contraction at the bottom.* N SING : the+N, IF+PREP THEN of = reverse

obviate /ɒbvieɪt/, **obviates, obviating, obviated**. To **obviate** something such as a problem or a need means to remove it or make it unnecessary; a formal word. EG *Energy conservation obviates the need for further generating capacity... He destroyed the letter to obviate any suspicion that might fall on him.* V+O = avert

obvious /ɒbviəs/. 1 Something that is **obvious** is easily seen or understood, and cannot be doubted. EG *It was painfully obvious that I knew very little about it... For obvious reasons, I preferred my house to his... Curzon was the obvious choice... There's no obvious answer.* ADJ QUALIT ⇑ clear

2 If you describe something that someone says as **obvious**, you mean that it is unnecessary or shows lack of imagination; used showing disapproval. EG *Tove made such an obvious remark... You shouldn't tell such obvious lies.* ● If you say that someone is **stating the obvious**, you mean that they are saying something that everyone already knows and understands. EG *There didn't seem much point in stating the obvious.* ADJ QUALIT ⇑ predictable ● PHR : VB INFLECTS

obviously /ɒbviəsli¹/. You use **obviously** 1 to indicate or introduce something that you expect everyone to understand or know about. EG *There are obviously decisions that have to be made... Obviously I don't need to say how important this project is.* 2 to indicate that something is easily seen, noticed, or recognized. EG *The soldier was obviously badly hurt... One of the beds had obviously been slept in.* ADV SEN = clearly; ADV = plainly

occasion /əkeɪʒə⁰n/, **occasions, occasioning, occasioned**. 1 An **occasion** is 1.1 a case of something happening or the time when it happens. EG *I met him only on one occasion... There are occasions when you must not refuse... When the occasion demands it, you will have to go.* 1.2 an important event, ceremony, or celebration, usually one of a formal or public kind. EG *They have the date fixed for the big occasion... The Oval Office will be used for ceremonial occasions... ...an important social occasion.* 1.3 an event or situation that provides a reason or opportunity for something to happen or be done; a rather formal use. EG *For the girls, nature study was an occasion for lazy walks and idle picnics... The gun will stay where it is until I have occasion to use it.* N COUNT; N COUNT = function; N UNCOUNT OR N SING WITH DET : USU+SUPP/ to-INF/for

2 If something happens **on occasion**, or **on occasions**, it happens sometimes, but not very often. EG *It has, on occasion, created trouble for the bank... You have on occasions surprised people.* PHR : USED AS AN A = occasionally

3 If someone **rises to the occasion**, they successfully do what is necessary to overcome a difficult situation or unexpected problem. EG *Dekker had risen to the occasion with an insight that surprised us all.* PHR : VB INFLECTS

4 To **occasion** something means to cause it; a formal use. EG *...deaths occasioned by police activity... The discovery occasioned me no surprise... This occasioned great suffering among the Indians.* V+O, V+O+O, OR V+O+A (for)

occasional /əkeɪʒə⁰nəl, -ʒənə⁰l/ means happening or being present sometimes, but not regularly or often. EG *...an occasional trip as far as Aberdeen... ...architects, planners, and the occasional sociologist... Apart from the occasional article, he hadn't published anything... ...occasional flashes of light.* ◇ **occasionally**. EG *Friends visit them occasionally... He was arrogant and occasionally callous.* ADJ CLASSIF : USU ATTRIB ⇑ infrequent = odd ◇ ADV WITH VB

occidental /ɒksɪdentə⁰l/ means relating to the countries of Europe and America; a formal word. EG *...all religions, oriental and occidental.* ADJ CLASSIF = western ≠ oriental

occult /ɒkʌlt/. The **occult** is the knowledge and study of supernatural or magical forces, powers, and skills. EG *...the enthusiasm for astrology and the occult.* ▸ used as an adjective. EG *...books on occult subjects... ...fantastic occult powers that he was said to possess.* N SING : the+N ▸ ADJ CLASSIF : ATTRIB

occupancy /ɒkjə⁴pənsi¹/ is the fact of living or working in a room, building, etc, especially for a particular period of time; a rather formal word. EG *Another publishing firm had taken over the occupancy... ...on the first evening of his occupancy.* N UNCOUNT

occupant /ɒkjə⁴pənt/, **occupants**. 1 The **occupant** of a building or room is the person who lives or works there. EG *At the next house Mr King told the occupant: 'You can't vote for Reynolds.'... A tidy office means that the occupant doesn't want things disturbed.* N COUNT = occupier

2 An **occupant** is also someone who is in a room, vehicle, seat, bed, etc at a particular time. EG *...a bus in which all the occupants have seats facing the front... The room's sole occupants were the boy and a big hound.* N COUNT

occupation /ɒkjə⁴peɪʃə⁰n/, **occupations**. 1 An **occupation** is 1.1 a job or profession. EG *...a poorly paid occupation... ...everyone, irrespective of age, sex or occupation.* 1.2 an activity that you do for pleasure or as part of your daily life. EG *Riding was her favourite occupation... Washing up is considered the basest of all occupations.* N COUNT/ UNCOUNT; N COUNT = pursuit

2 The **occupation** of a place or country by a group of people or an army is the act of moving into and staying in it in order to gain control of it. EG *...the French occupation of North Africa... ...an attempted occupation of the Iranian embassy... Holland came under German occupation.* N UNCOUNT+ SUPP = invasion

3 Someone's **occupation** of a building is their living or working in it. EG *...Nixon's occupation of the White House... The local authority should help owner occupation.* N UNCOUNT+ SUPP = occupancy

occupational /ɒkjə⁴peɪʃə⁰nəl, -ʃənə⁰l/ means relating to a person's job or profession. EG *...new educational, occupational and recreational options... Lawyers were the most numerous occupational group.* ◇ **occupationally**. EG *...equality for women politically, occupationally and economically.* ADJ CLASSIF : ATTRIB ◇ ADV

occupational hazard, occupational hazards. An **occupational hazard** is something unpleasant that you may suffer or experience in the course of doing your job, hobby, etc. EG *...occupational hazards like dusts which harm the lungs... ...the occupational hazards of motorcycle riding.* N COUNT ⇑ danger

occupational therapy is a way of helping people who have been ill or injured to develop or regain skills by giving them work to do. EG *In hospital he read, wrote poetry, participated in occupational therapy.* N UNCOUNT

occupier /ɒkjə⁴paɪə/, **occupiers**. The **occupier** of a house, flat, piece of land, etc is the person who lives or works there; used when you do not know their name or when their name is unimportant. EG *The occupier of the premises has applied for planning permission..* N COUNT = occupant

occupy /ɒkjə⁴paɪ/, **occupies, occupying, occupied.** 1 To **occupy** a building or place means to live, stay, or work in it. EG *Houses occupied by the aged must be centrally heated... They occupy neighbouring offices.*
V+O = inhabit

2 If something **occupies** a particular area or place, it fills or covers it, or exists there. EG *Dry lands occupy a third of the world's surface... The fourth wall is occupied by a blackboard.*
V+O = take up

3 If something such as a toilet or chair **is occupied**, someone is using it, so that it is not available for anyone else to use. EG *The third chair was occupied by an actress... At the pub, his usual corner was occupied.* ◇ **occupied.** EG *She found the toilet occupied.*
V+O: ONLY PASS ≠ vacant
◇ ADJ CLASSIF = engaged

4 If a group of people or an army **occupies** a place or country, they move into it and stay there in order to gain control of it. EG *The plan was to occupy Zagreb... The students occupied the Administration Block.* ◇ **occupied.** EG *...the occupied Eastern Quarter.*
V+O = take over, seize
◇ ADJ CLASSIF

5 If someone or something **occupies** a particular place in a system, process, or plan, they belong to the system, process, or plan and do what their position requires. EG *...workers occupying key positions... The demonstration occupies a central place in their political campaign.*
V+O = hold

6 If something **occupies** you or if you **occupy** yourself or **occupy** your time or your mind with it, you are busy doing it or thinking about it. EG *It was just a matter of keeping her occupied... He needed something to occupy his mind or his hands... They were occupying themselves in growing their own food... How do you occupy your time?*
V+O (NG/REFL): IF REFL+PREP THEN *in/with* ⇑ involve

7 If something **occupies** you, it requires your efforts, attention, or time. EG *That work was to occupy him for the rest of his life... His attention was occupied with other matters... ...squadrons occupied in routine surveillance.*
V+O: IF PASS THEN+A (*in/with*) = involve, engage

8 If something **occupies** a particular period of time, it happens while that amount of time passes. EG *The episode occupied many millions of years.*
V+O = last

occur /ə⁷kɜː/, **occurs, occurring, occurred.** When something **occurs**, 1.1 it happens. EG *The attack occurred about six days ago... ...the chances of an accident occurring... Mistakes are bound to occur... The changes which have occurred in the past fifty years... Gosse was informed of what occurred by a friend.* 1.2 it exists or is present in a particular place. EG *The phrase occurs often in the Quran... ...two other commonly occurring weeds... Racism and sexism occur in all institutions.*
V = take place
V+A

2 If a thought or idea **occurs** to you, you suddenly think of it or realize it. EG *As soon as that thought occurred to him, he felt worse... It never occurred to me to ask... It had never occurred to her that he might insist on paying.*
V+A (*to*): NO CONT

occurrence /ə⁷kʌrəns/, **occurrences.** 1 An **occurrence** is something that happens; a rather formal word. EG *...weeks before the tragic occurrence... Just such an occurrence took place in 1963.*
N COUNT ⇑ event = incident

2 The **occurrence** of something is the fact that it happens or is present in a particular situation. EG *...the occurrence of physical violence... We may reduce the occurrence of cancer by fifty per cent.*
N UNCOUNT+SUPP

ocean /əʊʃə⁰n/, **oceans.** 1 The **ocean** is 1.1 the sea; a rather literary use. EG *I went down to the ocean and took a swim... This creature lives in the depths of the ocean... ...the ocean breeze.* 1.2 one of the five very large areas of sea on the Earth's surface. EG *...the seas and oceans of the world... ...the Atlantic Ocean.*
N SING: *the*+N
N COUNT: IF SING *the*+N, ALSO IN NAMES AFTER ADJ

2 An **ocean** of something is a very large area of it; a literary use. EG *...that terrible ocean of sand... The ocean of flat empty land stretched before us.*
N PART = expanse

3 If you say there are **oceans** of something, you mean that there is a very large amount of it; an informal use. EG *...oceans of beef, turkey, and chicken.*
N PART = lashings

ocean-going ships are designed for travelling on the sea rather than on rivers, canals, or lakes.
ADJ CLASSIF: ATTRIB

oceanic /əʊʃi¹ænɪk/ means belonging or relating to an ocean or to the sea. EG *...oceanic currents... ...oceanic life forms.*
ADJ CLASSIF: ATTRIB ⇑ marine

oceanography /əʊʃi⁰ənɒgrəfi¹/ is the scientific study of the sea, sea currents, the rocks on the sea bed, and the fish and animals that live in the sea. EG *...oceanography and oil prospecting.*
N UNCOUNT ⇑ science

◇ **oceanographer, oceanographers.** EG *...an oceanographer on a diving expedition.* ◇ **oceanographic** /əʊʃi⁰ənəgræfɪk/. EG *A naval oceanographic research ship located the wreckage.*
◇ N COUNT
◇ ADJ CLASSIF: ATTRIB

och /ɒx/ is used, in Scottish or Irish English, when someone begins speaking, expresses surprise at something, or wants to emphasize their agreement or disagreement with what has just been said. EG *'Och,' says the girl, 'you're Dr Kirk.'... You're better out of it. Och aye.*
EXCLAM = O, Oh

ochre /əʊkə/; also spelled **ocher** in American English. **Ochre** is coloured earth, usually red or yellow, that is used to make dyes and paints. EG *They used red ochre to stain their blankets...* ▸ used of the colour. EG *...a plateau of red and ochre... ...green tiles, ochre paint, red wood.*
N UNCOUNT
▸ ADJ COLOUR, OR N UNCOUNT

o'clock /əklɒk/. You use **o'clock** 1 after numbers from one to twelve to state a time which is that particular number of complete hours past midday or midnight; see also ☐ at TIME. EG *At two o'clock in the morning Castle was still awake... It was 11 o'clock at night... ...the Nine O'Clock News... ...the 12 o'clock train.* ● See also **five o'clock shadow.** 2 to indicate a train, bus, aircraft, or boat that is due to arrive or depart at a particular time; an informal use. EG *She'll be on the six o'clock, and she'll want her supper.*
ADV AFTER NUM
N SING: *the*+NUM+N ⇑ vehicle

Oct. is an abbreviation for 'October'.

octagon /ɒktəgən/, **octagons.** An **octagon** is a geometrical shape that has eight straight sides.
N COUNT

octagonal /ɒktægənə⁰l/. Something that is **octagonal** has eight straight sides. EG *...the octagonal tower.*
ADJ CLASSIF

octane /ɒkteɪn/ is a chemical substance that exists in petrol and that is used to measure and describe the quality of petrol. EG *This petrol has a lower octane value, which means a drop in engine efficiency.... ...high octane petrol.*
N UNCOUNT: USU BEFORE N

octave /ɒktɪv/, **octaves.** An **octave** is the musical interval between the first note and the eighth note of a scale; used also of the eighth note. EG *The piano has a range of seven octaves.*
N COUNT

October /ɒktəʊbə/ is the tenth month of the year in the Western calendar. EG *They will be on show at the Museum until October next year.*
N UNCOUNT

octogenarian /ɒktə⁶dʒɪneərɪən/, **octogenarians.** An **octogenarian** is a person who is between eighty and eighty-nine years old.
N COUNT

octopus /ɒktəpəs/, **octopuses. Octopus** can also also be used as the plural form. An **octopus** is a sea creature with eight tentacles that it uses to catch food. Some people cook and eat octopus.
N COUNT

oculist /ɒkjə⁴lɪst/, **oculists.** An **oculist** is an optician; used mainly in American English.
N COUNT

odd /ɒd/, **odder, oddest; odds.** 1 If you say that something is **odd**, you mean that it is strange or unusual. EG *The odd thing was that the others began to be ill six months later... Isn't that a bit odd?... There's something rather odd about its shape... It was considered odd that she still lived at home.* ◇ **oddly.** EG *Marsha found the play oddly disappointing.* ◇ **oddness.** EG *...the slight oddness in her voice.* ● You say **'oddly enough'** when you think that your next statement is going to surprise the person you are talking to. EG *Oddly enough, it was through him that I met Carson.*
ADJ QUALIT = peculiar, queer
◇ ADV = peculiarly
● PHR: USED AS ADV SEN = strangely

2 Someone who is **odd** behaves in an unusual way or has an unusual appearance. EG *We thought she was rather odd.* ◇ **oddly.** EG *The drug made him behave quite oddly.*
ADJ QUALIT = peculiar
◇ ADV

3 If you talk about **the odd** something or **an odd** something, you mean that the amount, number, or quality of it is not large or important; an informal use. EG *You can add bones, the odd vegetable, herbs and chopped onions... Have you got an odd bit of paper?*
ADJ CLASSIF: ATTRIB

4 If you talk about **odd** things, you mean that they are of various different types. EG *I usually write odd notes in the back of my diary... He could do odd jobs about the place to earn a bit of money.* ● See also **odds and ends.**
ADJ CLASSIF: ATTRIB = miscellaneous

5 You use **odd** after a number to indicate that you are only stating an approximate number; an informal use. EG *We first met twenty odd years ago.*
ADV: NUM+ADV +N IN PL ⇑ approximately

6 **Odd** numbers are those which cannot be divided exactly by the number two. EG *3, 15, and 179 are all odd numbers... Put even numbers on one side, odd numbers on the other.*
ADJ CLASSIF: ATTRIB ≠ even

7 **Odd** items are those which do not belong in a set or
ADJ CLASSIF:

pair of similar items. EG *You can't go out wearing odd socks.*
ATTRIB

8 The **odd man out**, **odd woman out**, or **odd one out** in a particular situation is a person who is different from the other people in it. EG *I was the odd one out; all my friends were in couples.*
PHR : USU *the*+ PHR
= misfit

9 The **odds** in a particular situation represent the degree of probability that something will or will not happen or that someone will or will not succeed. Odds are often stated in numbers, especially in gambling. If you bet one pound on a horse whose odds are '10 to 1', you will receive ten pounds if the horse wins. EG *...a cool assessment of the military odds... Nobody would put any money on the horse at those odds.* ● If you say that the **odds are in favour of** someone or something, you mean that the person is likely to succeed or the thing is likely to happen. EG *The odds were 10-1 in favour of him going... The odds in favour of our winning are two to one.* ● If you say that the **odds are against** someone or something, you mean that the person is likely to fail or the thing is unlikely to happen. EG *The odds against another attack were very high.* ● See also **odds-on**.
N PLURAL : *the*+ N
↑ chances
● PHR : VB INFLECTS
● PHR : VB INFLECTS

10 If you say that **the odds are** that something will happen or that something is true, you mean that it is likely to happen or likely to be true; an informal expression. EG *The odds are that it will rain tomorrow.*
PHR+REPORT-CL
= chances are

11 If something happens **against all the odds**, **in the face of** overwhelming **odds**, etc, it happens although it seemed impossible or very difficult. EG *She manages to sustain her optimism against all the odds... She will succeed against all odds... ...a strategic withdrawal against overwhelming odds... ...in the face of unbelievable odds.*
PHR : USED AS AN A

12 **at odds**. 12.1 If someone is **at odds** with someone else or if two people are **at odds**, they are disagreeing or quarrelling with each other. EG *She is at odds with her boss... The allies are at odds over how to respond to the threat.* 12.2 If one part of something is **at odds** with another part of it, the two parts do not match or suit each other. EG *The glossy, colourful cover was totally at odds with its dull academic content.*
PHR OR PHR + *with* : RECIP, USED AS AN A
= at loggerheads
PHR OR PHR + *with* : RECIP, USED AS AN A
= out of tune

13 If you say **'It makes no odds'** in a particular situation, you mean that whatever you do or whatever choice you make is unimportant; an informal expression. EG *Tea or coffee? Give me either, it makes no odds... Whatever he did, it made no odds to her.*
PHR : VB INFLECTS

oddball /ɒdbɔːl/, **oddballs**. An **oddball** is a person who behaves in a way which most people find unusual or peculiar; an informal word. EG *...an oddball who painted rocks on the sea shore.*
N COUNT
= eccentric

oddity /ɒdɪti¹/, **oddities**. 1 An **oddity** is 1.1 a very unusual person or thing. EG *...a shop devoted to oddities: rubber fruit, explosive cigars... A career woman is still regarded as something of an oddity.*
N COUNT : USU PL
= curiosity

1.2 a very unusual characteristic that someone or something has. EG *...those personal oddities in his drawing... ...the oddities and absurdities of the language.*
N COUNT
= peculiarity

2 **Oddity** is the quality of being or appearing unusual or strange. EG *...the oddity of her behaviour.*
N UNCOUNT

odd-job man, odd-job men. An **odd-job man** is a man who is paid to do various manual jobs, usually in somebody's home, for example clearing drains or cleaning windows.
N COUNT
↑ workman

odd-looking; also spelled as one word. Someone or something that is **odd-looking** is unusual or peculiar in appearance. EG *...the oddlooking stranger they had seen... ...an odd-looking package.*
ADJ QUALIT

oddment /ɒdmə²nt/, **oddments**. **Oddments** are objects of any kind, especially ones that are old or left over from a larger group that has been used up. EG *...old postcards and scraps, all sorts of oddments... ...oddments of furniture.*
N COUNT : USU PL
= bit, scrap

odds and ends are small unimportant objects, jobs, etc; an informal expression. EG *I had a trunk filled with various odds and ends that I would need for camping... I'll finish the last few odds and ends tomorrow.*
N PLURAL
= bits and pieces

odds-on; also spelled as two words. An **odds-on** chance is very likely to win or to be the case; an informal word. EG *Calderwood is the odds-on favourite... It was odds-on that there was no killer.*
ADJ CLASSIF
↑ probable

ode /əʊd/, **odes**. An **ode** is a poem that is usually written in praise of a particular person, thing, or event, and that contains lines of different lengths and metres.
N COUNT

odious /əʊdɪəs/. You describe people or things as **odious** when you find them extremely unpleasant. EG *I shouldn't dream of telling the odious woman anything of the sort... His love-making was odious to her.*
ADJ QUALIT
= hateful

odium /əʊdɪəm/ is the dislike, disapproval, or hatred that people feel for a particular person, usually because of something that the person has done; a formal word.
N UNCOUNT
= abhorrence

odor /əʊdə/. See **odour**.

odorous /əʊdə⁰rəs/. Something that is **odorous** has a particular smell, especially a pleasant one; a literary word. EG *...the sweetly odorous premises of big stores.*
ADJ QUALIT
= fragrant

odour /əʊdə/, **odours**; also spelled **odor** in American English. An **odour** is a particular and distinctive smell. EG *...the warm odour of freshly-baked scones... A faint, sweet, woody odour hung in the air.* ● See also **body odour**.
N COUNT : USU+ SUPP
= aroma, scent

odyssey /ɒdɪsi¹/, **odysseys**. An **odyssey** is a long exciting journey in which a lot of things happen. EG *...dream holidays and youthful odysseys.*
N COUNT

o'er /ɔː/ means the same as 'over'; an old-fashioned word used mainly in poetry. EG *Fierce raged the tempest o'er the deep.*
PREP

oesophagus /iːsɒfəgəs/, **oesophaguses**; also spelled **esophagus**. A person or animal's **oesophagus** is the part of their body that carries the food from their throat to their stomach.
N COUNT
= gullet

oestrogen /ɛstrədʒən, iːstrə-/; also spelled **estrogen**. **Oestrogen** is a hormone produced in the ovaries of female animals. Oestrogen controls the reproductive cycle and prepares the body for pregnancy.
N UNCOUNT

of /ə⁷v/. 1 You use **of** 1.1 after nouns expressing quantities, groups, measurements, or amounts. EG *...a collection of essays... ...an old pair of trousers... The number of dogs is increasing... ...jewellery worth millions of pounds... ...25 gallons of hot water... ...a sheet of paper... ...a jar of paint... ...a big piece of apple pie... ...a nice cup of tea... ...a paper bag of sandwiches... Half of the boats sank... Natural gas accounts for about 10% of our total energy consumption.* 1.2 to specify an amount or value. EG *...a price increase of 2%... She was paid the going rate of seventeen dollars a day... ...a town of 13,000 people.* 1.3 to say how old someone is. EG *He was a boy of nineteen... He came to school at the age of five... a baby of 6 months* 1.4 when you are talking about one or more things among a number of similar ones. EG *This is the first of a short series of programmes... One of the problems is that we have very little time... Two of the three managed to escape... Many of the students come from English-speaking countries.* 1.5 to indicate that a meeting, organization, or group is attended by particular people. EG *...a meeting of the Social Democratic parliamentary group... ...the House of Representatives.* 1.6 to say that something shows, represents, or describes something. EG *...a map of Sweden... ...a picture of the newcomers... ...an account of the event.*
PREP AFTER N
PREP AFTER N
PREP+NUM : AFTER N
PREP AFTER NUM/QUANTIF
PREP AFTER N
PREP AFTER N
= portraying

2 You use **of** 2.1 to say that someone has a particular attitude, reaction, characteristic, etc. EG *We need the permission of the judge... We must do it with the approval of the trade unions... ...the religious and moral beliefs of the peasant communities... He had to face the disapproving stares of Rummidge students... The average age of commercial farmers in Vermont is now over 50... ...essays written in the style of F.R. Leavis.* 2.2 to indicate that something or someone is associated with a particular person or owned by them. EG *Have you still got that book of mine?... Imagine a child of yours being run over by a car... She's a friend of Stephen's... I'd love to have a house of my own... ...the Conservative government of Mr Edward Heath... ...the traditional role of women.* 2.3 to indicate the person you are talking about when you are saying that an action was kind, generous, unpleasant, etc. For example, 'It was kind of her' means 'She was kind'. EG *It was kind of her to take me in... That was nasty of him!*
PREP AFTER N
PREP AFTER N
PREP AFTER ADJ

3 You use **of** 3.1 to say that something is attached to something or forms part of something. EG *She clutched the sleeve of his robe... ...the corners of a triangle... ...the lace-curtained window of the bedroom... ...any day of the week... ...Act V of Macbeth.*
PREP AFTER N

3.2 to say that someone is involved in or works for an organization or group in the particular way mentioned. EG *He is General Secretary of the Tobacco Workers' Union... He was a member of a famous golf club... ...representatives of the workers.* **3.3** in titles of government departments or ministers to say what a particular department or minister is concerned with. EG *...the Department of Employment... ...the Ministry of Defence... ...the Minister of Health and Social Security.* PREP AFTER N / PREP AFTER N

4 You use **of** with the names of places. It is used **4.1** to indicate that someone is living in or associated with a particular place. EG *...the Mayor of Moscow... ...the people of France.* **4.2** in descriptions of places in towns or cities. EG *...the streets of London... ...industrial areas of Belfast.* **4.3** in the names of companies, organizations, etc, to indicate that they are situated or based in a particular town, city, or country. EG *...the University of California... ...The Times of London.* **4.4** after words like town, city, village, etc to introduce the name of that town, city, village, etc. EG *...the village of Fairwater Green... ...the City of London.* PREP : N+PREP +N PROPER / PREP : N+PREP +N PROPER / PREP : N+PREP +N PROPER / PREP : N+PREP +N PROPER

5 You use **of** **5.1** after nouns that have been formed from verbs. The noun group following 'of' is either the object or the subject of the verb. EG *It's a thriller based on the kidnapping of a royal child... There has been a reorganisation of the health service... Protection of the environment is an important consideration... ...the failure of emergency talks... ...the arrival of the next train.* **5.2** after nouns meaning 'someone who does a particular action' to introduce the direct object of the action they do. For example, 'a signer of the Declaration of Independence' is someone who signs the Declaration of Independence. EG *He was a fervent spectator of baseball and football... ...the planners of the traffic system... ...a pioneer of scientific photography.* PREP AFTER N / PREP AFTER N

6 You use **of** **6.1** to specify or give more information about a particular attitude, reaction, process, action, etc. EG *She had no intention of spending her whole life working in a bank... You wouldn't dream of wasting your money on things like that... This is a further blow to their hopes of a reconciliation... This is something I'm very proud of... ...the fear of losing their jobs... ...an act of faith.* **6.2** to indicate a particular subject. EG *They want every detail of what happened... ...the whole concept of economic growth... ...his new theory of vision... They were not told of this new privilege.* **6.3** to say that something consists of a particular thing. EG *I had strong feelings of jealousy... There was an atmosphere of friendly co-operation... ...gifts of olive oil... Enterprises are moving from a position of profit to one of relying on government subsidy... Her vocabulary of abuse dated from earlier in the century... This is a town where there's a large population of old people.* **6.4** to say that someone or something has a particular characteristic or quality. EG *She's a woman of iron character... ...men and women of matchless honesty... She helped him to a gin and tonic of giant proportions... There is very little laughter of any kind in that house.* **6.5** in expressions that indicate that you are thinking about a particular person or thing. EG *It all reminds me of a boy from North Dakota... The social landscape is more reminiscent of the Latins... ...in memory of John Roberts.* PREP / PREP ⇑ about / PREP AFTER N / PREP AFTER N/be / PREP

7 You use **of** **7.1** to say that something is made or formed from a particular substance. EG *...a dress made of cotton... ...a rod of steel... ...a necklace of solid gold.* **7.2** to say that something is created or formed as a result of something; a formal use. EG *Of such trivia are lifelong complexes formed.* PREP / PREP ⇑ from

8 You use **of** **8.1** after nouns that refer to size, structure, etc. EG *The width of each road varies a great deal... It was impossible to estimate the size of the crowd... ...a discussion on the ideal structure of a reorganized university.* **8.2** after words like 'kind', 'sort', 'version', etc. EG *It was some sort of epidemic thing... That sort of complexity keeps you looking... ...shades of green... ...a concert version of Telemann's opera 'Pimpinone'.* **8.3** after words like 'beginning', 'end', 'outbreak', 'increase', etc. EG *It's a plot with a victory at the end of it... ...the outbreak of the Civil War... ...the beginning of the Industrial Revolution.* **8.4** after words like 'result', 'consequence', 'cause', etc, to express causal relationships between things. EG *This was partly the consequence of his own success... ...the effects of crime... Unemployment has not been a major cause of the recent events... Police are seeking an explanation of the deaths of two children.* PREP AFTER N / PREP AFTER N / PREP AFTER N / PREP AFTER N

9 You use **of** in comparisons **9.1** to say that something resembles the thing that is mentioned after 'of'. For example 'the colour of blood' means 'the same colour as blood'. EG *...a boil the size of a golf ball.* **9.2** to say that something is like the thing that is mentioned before 'of'. For example, 'a giant of a man' means 'a man like a giant.' EG *...a crumbling shipwreck of a Victorian castle.* PREP AFTER N ⇑ like / PREP : N+PREP +a/an+N

10 You use **of** in expressions relating to time. It is used **10.1** to say that something happened at a particular time or relates to a particular time. EG *...the recession of 1974-75... ...the great conflicts of the past ten years.* **10.2** to indicate that something is the best or worst thing to happen during a particular period of time. EG *That was the real highlight of the morning... ...the disaster of the week.* **10.3** after a word like day, time, week, etc, to indicate what happens or happened during that period of time. EG *...the day of his inauguration... This was at the time of the earthquake.* **10.4** to say that something often happens at a particular time; an old-fashioned use. EG *I like to stroll down to the allotment of an afternoon.* **10.5** to say what time it is by indicating how many minutes there are before the hour mentioned; used in American English. EG *...a quarter of eight.* **10.6** to say what date it is. EG *...the 17th of June... ...the 1st of October.* PREP AFTER N / PREP : N+PREP +the+N / PREP AFTER N / PREP ⇑ every / PREP / PREP : ORDINAL +PREP+N

11 You use **of** **11.1** to say that a disease or medical condition is affecting a particular part of your body. EG *...cancer of the stomach... ...inflammation of the lungs.* **11.2** to say that someone died from a particular illness. EG *She died of pneumonia.* **11.3** to indicate that something is removed or taken away from someone or something. EG *It is quite difficult to rid clothes of cooking smells or tobacco fumes... She was cured of cancer.* PREP AFTER N / PREP / PREP

12 'Of' is used in this dictionary in the expression 'used of...' to indicate what kinds of things a particular word can describe or refer to. PREP

of course. See **course**.

off /ɒf/. In paragraphs 1 and 2, **off** is used to refer to movement and position. **1** You use **off** **1.1** to indicate that something is removed from somewhere, especially a surface. EG *He took his hand off her arm... I dropped the teapot and the handle broke off... He was wiping sweat off his face... Miss Archer fell off her chair in a swoon... The paint was peeling off... You can leave the top off.* **1.2** to indicate that one part of something is separated from another. EG *They decided that the railway would be fenced off... He had marked off the area with lengths of string.* **1.3** to indicate that something which has moved towards a surface and touched it moves away from it again. EG *Something hit the windscreen and bounced off... Light is shone on to them and then reflected off them.* **1.4** to indicate that you leave a place or move away from it, for example to go somewhere else or to do a particular activity. EG *He started the motor of the car and drove off abruptly... He limped off, down the shabby street... Morris hurried off eagerly to get a cab... When are you off to America?... I'm off. See you in the morning... I'm off home now... He had gone off to work... I just had to send Matthew off to bed.* ● **'They're off'** is used by radio and television reporters to say that a race has begun. **1.5** to say where someone or something is, especially when they are a long way away from where you are. EG *She's off in Florida at some labour conference... The university is off to the right... He was off in a corner having a nervous breakdown... A lot of men were off fighting.* **1.6** to indicate that you leave a bus, train, or other form of transport. EG *The train slowed to a halt and a few people got off... He got off his bicycle... They got off the bus at Grafton.* **1.7** to indicate that someone or something moves away from a place or is no longer in or on that place. EG *The last dancers drifted off the floor... Get the car off the road as fast as possible... He walked in off the street... When they reached Fifty-fifth Street, they turned off Fifth Avenue... We swerved off the freeway.* **1.8** to say that you remove a piece of clothing or that you are not wearing it. EG *Rudolph would have liked to sit down* PREP, OR ADV WITH VB / ADV AFTER VB ⇑ apart / PREP, OR ADV WITH VB / ADV AFTER VB / ● CONVENTION / ADV+PREP/-ING : AFTER be / ADV AFTER VB, OR PREP / PREP, OR ADV AFTER VB / ADV WITH VB

and take his boots off... She kicked off her shoes... He took off his jacket... He was sitting there with his shoes and socks off... Let me help you off with your coat.

2 You use **off** to say that someone or something is **2.1** away from a place or outside it. EG *A lot of students are in private accommodation off campus... There is ice cream for sale off the premises... I kept off the main roads... In Scotland you have no right to keep people off your land unless they are doing damage... Please keep off the grass.* **2.2** fairly near a road. EG *We stayed in a motel off the main highway.* **2.3** in or on the sea and quite close to the coast. EG *...two islands off the mainland of China... ...two miles off shore... We had caught several sharks off the end of Long Island.* **2.4** at the side of and leading from a particular room. EG *The kitchen's off the dining room... ...two high carved wooden doors leading off the hallway.*
PREP ≠ on · PREP · PREP ⇑ near · PREP

3 You also use **off** **3.1** to say that you are not doing a particular activity or participating in something. EG *He's been off the committee for months... I'll be off duty at four.* **3.2** to refer to a period of time when you do not have to go to work, for example because you are ill or on holiday. EG *Tonight is his night off... She's off work with a bad cold... I would love to have a year off... Never think twice about asking for time off.* **3.3** to indicate that you are not thinking or talking about a particular subject. EG *It's the only thing that takes your mind off your problem.* **3.4** to indicate that someone is not taking drugs or receiving medical treatment. EG *We need to take you off antibiotics for a while.* **3.5** to say that a machine, electrical appliance, etc is not functioning. EG *He stood up and turned off the machine... Boylan switched off the headlights... All the lights were off... Do you think we could turn that thing off?* **3.6** to say that something such as a sports event or an agreement has been cancelled. EG *It's raining and golf is therefore off... They have called off next year's baseball season... The deal's off.* **3.7** to refer to a time in the future. EG *The day may not be far off when there are colonies on the Moon... Control over the mind is not as far off as we think... We're still a long way off achieving this.* **3.8** to indicate where you obtained something from; a fairly informal use. EG *It's a book he bought second-hand, years ago, off a sixpenny stall... I bought it off my father... I borrowed a few pounds off him.* **3.9** to indicate the direction that the wind is coming from. EG *A warm breeze was coming off the sea.* **3.10** to indicate that something succeeds or works by means of a particular thing. EG *There is a special wire cutter which works off a battery... We lived off beans and bacon... There were a lot of merchants who had made fortunes off the black market.* **3.11** to indicate a reduction in the price of something. EG *You can get ten per cent off with a student card... I managed to knock 100 pounds off the price.*
PREP ≠ on · ADV AFTER VB, OR ADV/PREP AFTER N ⇑ away · PREP · PREP · ADV AFTER VB, OR ADJ CLASSIF : PRED · ADV AFTER VB, OR ADJ CLASSIF : PRED · ADV/PREP AFTER N/ADJ = away · PREP · PREP · PREP = on · PREP, OR ADV AFTER VB

4 If food is **off**, **4.1** it tastes and smells unpleasant because it is going bad. EG *This cream is off... The milk's gone off.* **4.2** it is not available for you to eat in a restaurant. EG *I'm sorry, sir, but the duck's off.*
ADJ CLASSIF : PRED · ADJ CLASSIF : PRED

5 If you are **off** something, you no longer like it; an informal use. EG *I'm off beer at the moment... I used to like opera but I've gone off it recently.*
PREP

6 If you are badly **off**, well **off**, etc, you are as poor or as rich as the adverb suggests. EG *In the cities the poor are as badly off as they were in the villages... You were better off before... He reckoned he'd be something like two pounds a week worse off.* • If you ask someone **how** they are **off for** something, you are asking them how much of it they have; an informal expression. EG *How are you off for money at the moment?... How are we off for milk?*
ADJ CLASSIF : PRED AFTER ADV · • CONVENTION

7 If you are feeling **off**, you are feeling slightly unwell. EG *I'm feeling a bit off today.*
ADJ QUALIT

8 If you say that someone's behaviour is **a bit off**, you mean that you find it unacceptable and rude; an informal expression. EG *I really thought it was a bit off the way she behaved.*
PHR : USED AS C ⇑ bad

9 You also use **off** to indicate that you relieve pain or discomfort in the way mentioned. EG *I often get a stitch and find the best thing is to walk it off... I spent the day sleeping off a hangover.*
ADV AFTER VB

10 **Off and on** means the same as 'on and off': see **on**. EG *I've been coming here off and on for years.*
PHR : USED AS AN A

offal /ɒfəˡl/ is the internal organs of animals, for example their hearts and livers, when people cook them and eat them. EG *...offal mixed with onions and oatmeal.*
N UNCOUNT ⇑ meat

off-balance. If someone is **off-balance**, **1** they are not standing firmly and can easily fall or be knocked over. EG *She was running, off-balance, with her feet wrongly positioned... He was thrown off-balance.* **2** they are not expecting a particular event or piece of news and are extremely surprised or upset by it. EG *Her casual announcement caught me completely off-balance.*
ADJ CLASSIF : PRED, OR ADV WITH VB ⇑ unsteady · ADJ QUALIT : PRED, OR ADV WITH VB = off-guard

offbeat /ɒfbiːt/; also spelled with a hyphen. Something that is **offbeat** is unusual and often humorous; a fairly informal word. EG *We'll have no more offbeat dialogue.*
ADJ QUALIT = unorthodox

off-centre. If something is **off-centre**, it is not exactly in the middle of a space or surface. EG *The assembly can be mounted slightly off-centre so that it swings aside.*
ADJ QUALIT, OR ADV WITH VB

off-chance; also spelled as one word. If you do something **on the off-chance**, you do it because you hope that it will succeed or be useful, although you think that this is unlikely. EG *She walked up to Rose Cottage on the off-chance of finding Mrs Meek in... He collected an enormous amount of information on the off-chance that he might later have a use for it.*
PHR : USED AS A A, USU + *of*/REL CL ⇑ in case

off-colour. If you are **off-colour**, you are slightly ill. EG *He's been a bit off-colour for the past two days.*
ADJ QUALIT : PRED

off-day, off-days. If you have an **off-day**, in informal English, you do not work or perform as well as usual. EG *We all have our off-days, of course.*
N COUNT

off duty; often used before another noun and spelled with a hyphen. When someone is **off duty**, they are not working for a period of time; used of people like nurses who work unusual hours. EG *What do you do when you're off duty?... ...an off-duty policeman.*
ADJ CLASSIF ≠ on duty

offence /əˈfens/, **offences**; also spelled **offense** in American English. **1** An **offence** is a crime, especially one that breaks a particular law and requires a particular punishment. EG *...a criminal offence... They were arrested for drug offences... ...an offence against the state... Thirteen people were charged with offences including obstruction and resisting arrest.* • **a capital offence**: see **capital**.
N COUNT ⇑ wrong

2 **Offence** or an **offence** is behaviour which causes people to be upset or embarrassed. EG *His calmly rational voice somehow robbed his words of all offence... The chapel was called, to avoid offence, the Contemplation Centre... He committed the equally serious offence of interrupting the conversation.*
N UNCOUNT

3 The word **offence** is also used in the following expressions. **3.1** If you **cause offence** or **give offence** to someone, you upset or embarrass them, for example by being rude or tactless. EG *The play is liable to give offence to many people.* **3.2** If you **take offence** at something someone says or does, you feel upset, often unnecessarily, because you think they are being rude to you; often used showing disapproval. EG *He was always so quick to take offence.* **3.3** Some people say **'no offence'** to reassure you that they do not want to upset you, although what they are saying may seem rude. EG *No offence, but there's a terrible smell in here.*
PHR : VB INFLECTS, IF + PREP THEN *to* ⇑ offend · PHR : VB INFLECTS, IF + PREP THEN *at* = take umbrage · CONVENTION

offend /əˈfend/, **offends, offending, offended.**
1 If you **offend** someone, you upset or embarrass them by doing something rude or tactless. EG *She was terribly afraid of offending anyone... They took care never to offend their visitors.* ◊ **offended.** EG *Clarissa looked offended.*
V+O = insult, hurt · ◊ ADJ QUALIT PRED

2 If something **offends** a law, rule, or principle or **offends** against it, it breaks it; a formal use. EG *This new process offends every known natural law... This would offend against the principle of fairness.*
V+O, OR V+A *(against)* ⇑ go against

3 To **offend** also means to commit a crime or crimes; a formal use. EG *Certain criminals are more likely to offend again when they're released.*
V : IF + PREP THEN *against* = break the law

offender /əˈfendə/, **offenders.** An **offender** is **1** a person who has committed a crime; a formal use. EG *In 1965, 42% of convicted offenders ended up in prison... ...thieves, vandals, sex offenders and muggers... ...the harsh treatment of young offenders.* **2** one of a number of people or things that cause a particular kind of harm. EG *Television is the worst offender of the lot.*
N COUNT ⇑ criminal · N COUNT = culprit

offending /əˈfendɪŋ/. You use **offending** to describe something that is causing a problem and that needs
ADJ CLASSIF : ATTRIB

to be dealt with, for example by getting rid of it or by repairing it. EG *Smear the juice on the offending areas... He tapped the offending bulge with a pencil... The offending washer and nut should be clearly visible.*

offense /əˈfɛns/. See **offence**.

offensive /əˈfɛnsɪv/, **offensives**. 1 Something that is **offensive** upsets or embarrasses people because it is rude or insulting; used showing disapproval. EG *The advertisements were highly offensive to women... That was an extremely offensive remark.* ADJ QUALIT = objectionable
◊ **offensively**. EG *The examiners were often offensively rude to candidates.* ◊ ADV = insultingly
2 An **offensive** is 2.1 a strong military attack. EG *...a two-week military offensive... ...the enemy's air offensive.* ▸ used as an adjective. EG *We took immediate offensive action... ...a strategic and offensive role, rather than a purely defensive one.* N COUNT = onslaught ▸ ADJ CLASSIF : USU ATTRIB
2.2 a strong action or actions that express your anger or disapproval. EG *...a propaganda offensive against the government.* N COUNT = attack
3 If you **go on the offensive, go over to the offensive,** or **take the offensive**, you begin to take strong action in order to express your disapproval of something. EG *If all else fails, I'll go over to the offensive.* PHR : VB INFLECTS

offer /ɒfə/, **offers, offering, offered**. 1 If you **offer** something to someone, you 1.1 ask them if they would like to have it or use it. EG *Meadows stood up and offered her his chair... I was offered a place at Harvard University.* V+O, V+O+O, OR V+O+A *(to)* ⇑ give
1.2 hold it out to them so that they can look at it or take it. EG *He turned, and offered his identity card... ...an apple which he offered to his friend.* V+O, V+O+O, OR V+O+A *(to)* = proffer
2 If you **offer** to do something, you say that you are willing to do it. EG *Gopal offered to take a group of us to Mysore... 'We could take it for you,' offered Dolly... We've offered to see their leaders.* V+*to*-INF, OR V+QUOTE = volunteer
3 An **offer** is something that someone says they will give you or do for you if you want them to. EG *Their offer of mediation was rejected... She accepted the offer of a cigarette... ...Kirk's offer to take me to the clinic... After 'Julius Caesar', I had no film offers for a while.* N COUNT
4 If you **offer** someone information, advice, or praise, you give it to them because they have asked for it or expect it or because you feel that they need or deserve it. EG *They didn't ask Liebermann's name and Liebermann didn't offer it... Do you have any advice to offer parents?... May I offer my congratulations... Kunta offered her no explanation for his behaviour.* V+O, V+O+O, OR V+O+A *(to)*
5 If you **offer** someone love, friendship, etc, you show them that you love them, feel friendly towards them, etc in your behaviour or speech. EG *Children who are offered little affection develop slowly... Her blue eyes seemed to offer friendship.* V+O, V+O+O, OR V+O+A *(to)* ⇑ give
6 To **offer** prayers, praise, or a sacrifice to God means to worship Him in one of those ways. EG *Offer thanks to God for blessing our efforts.* V+O, V+O+O, OR V+O+A *(to)* ⇑ give
7 If something such as an organization **offers** something, it has an important or useful quality or provides a particular opportunity, service, or product. EG *The new car plant offers the prospect of 5,000 jobs... ...the facilities and equipment offered by the playgroup... Racal offers a portable telephone unit at a reasonable price.* V+O, V+O+O, OR V+O+A *(to)* ⇑ supply = provide
8 If someone or something **has** something **to offer,** they have a particular quality or ability that makes them important, attractive, or useful. EG *...the delights that the natural world has to offer... ...the latest that technology has to offer.* PHR : *have* INFLECTS ⇑ possess
9 An **offer** in a shop or by a company that sells things is a specially low price for a particular product or something extra that you get by buying this product, usually for a short period of time. EG *...cut price offers... ...special offers.* N COUNT = reduction
10 If something is **on offer**, 10.1 it is available to be used or bought. EG *The high rates of interest on offer do involve penalties... ...the weird and wonderful range of gear on offer.* PHR : USED AS AN A
10.2 its price is specially reduced for a particular period of time. EG *This item is on offer for a limited period.* PHR : USED AS AN A ⇑ cheap
11 If you **offer** a particular amount of money for something, you say that you will pay that much to buy it. EG *I'll offer you nine pounds for it... They offered Rayos 2,000 pesos an acre.* V+O, V+O+O, OR V+O+A *(to)*
12 An **offer** is also the amount of money that someone says they will pay to buy something. EG *Murgatroyd's offer was the most attractive... I'll make you one final offer. Twenty pounds.* N COUNT
● If you are **open to offers**, you are willing to sell something if someone will pay a price that you think is reasonable. EG *The original price was ten thousand but I'm open to offers.* ● PHR : USED AS C

offer up. To **offer up** prayers, praise, or a sacrifice to God means to worship Him in one of those ways. EG *...the five daily prayers that are offered up to Allah.* PHRASAL VB : V+O+ADV

offering /ɒfəʳrɪŋ/, **offerings**. An **offering** is 1 something that is specially produced to be sold. EG *...last week's offerings of caviar and smoked salmon... 'Motorway' is the latest solo offering from Wilko Johnson.* N COUNT
2 something that is offered to God as a sacrifice. EG *...small offerings of food to appease the rain gods.* ● **burnt offering**: see **burnt**. N COUNT ⇑ gift

off-guard. If someone is **off-guard**, they are not expecting a surprise or danger that suddenly occurs. EG *It is easy to be taken off-guard.* ADJ CLASSIF = unawares

off-hand; also spelled without a hyphen. 1 If someone behaves in an **off-hand** manner, 1.1 they are not friendly or polite, and show little interest in what other people are doing or saying; used showing disapproval. EG *He became increasingly off-hand with Victoria... ...the off-hand contempt with which she treated most men.* ADJ QUALIT ⇑ casual = perfunctory
1.2 they are not formal or stiff; used showing approval. EG *...a more relaxed off-hand manner.* ADJ QUALIT = easy-going
2 If you say something **off-hand**, you say it without needing to think hard or prepare your statement. EG *Off-hand, I can think of three examples.* ADV WITH VB = off the cuff

office /ɒfɪs/, **offices**. 1 An **office** is 1.1 a room, usually not in your home, where you do your job, especially when it involves work of a clerical, administrative, or professional kind. EG *He called me into his office... On the wall of his office was a large map.* N COUNT
1.2 a building or set of rooms where people do clerical, administrative, or professional work. EG *You didn't go to the office today?... ...a modern office block... ...outside office hours.* ▸ **Office** is also used to refer to the people who work there. EG *The whole office knows that... ...a letter from the head office in Wimbledon.* N COUNT N COUNT : USU SING ▸ ⇑ employees
1.3 a department of an organization, especially the government, where people deal with a particular kind of administrative work. EG *...your local education office... ...the tax office dealing with his firm.* ● See also **post office, registry office.** N COUNT : USU+SUPP
▸ **Office** is also used in the names of some government departments. EG *...the Scottish Office in London... ...the Central Office of Information.* ● See also **Foreign Office, Home Office.** ▸ N COUNT : USED IN NAMES AFTER N
1.4 a small building or room where people can go for information, tickets, or a service of some kind. EG *...the ticket office... ...the enquiry office... ...a left luggage office at Cardiff station.* ● See also **booking office, box office, lost property office.** N COUNT : USU MOD+N
2 **Office** is an important job or position of authority in government or in an organization. EG *The President of the BMA holds office for one year... ...Baldwin's second term of office as Premier... The office of JP is an honorary one... ...two men in high office.* N UNCOUNT
● When someone is **in office**, they are in a position of authority to which they were elected or appointed, especially in the government of a country. EG *Labour was in office... ...during his first year in office.* ● PHR : USED AS AN A ⇑ ruling = in power
● If someone is **out of office**, they are no longer in the position of authority that they were previously elected or appointed to. EG *Churchill was out of office.* ● PHR : USED AS AN A
● When someone **takes office**, they are elected or appointed to a position of authority, especially in the government of a country, and begin to do their duties. EG *...as soon as President Kennedy took office... The new Conservative Government took office.* ● PHR : VB INFLECTS ⇑ start
3 Someone's **good offices** are the help that they give to other people who are trying to achieve something; a formal use. EG *Through the good offices of an American journalist, Northcliffe sent money to them... May I count on your good offices to raise these matters at the next meeting?.* PHR : WITH POSS = support

office boy, office boys; also spelled with a hyphen. An **office boy** is a young man, especially one who has just left school, who is employed in an office to do simple tasks; a rather old-fashioned word. EG *Dickens worked for a bit as office-boy.* N COUNT ⇑ employee

office-holder, office-holders. An **office-holder** is a person who has an important official position in an organization; a formal word. EG *...a former office-holder in the Oxford Union... The two principal office-holders wield enormous power.* N COUNT

officer /ɒfɪsə/, **officers**. An **officer** is 1 a person who has a position of authority in the armed forces. EG *...a retired army officer... He takes his responsibilities as an officer very seriously... ...a crew of three hundred and fifty officers and men.* ● See also **commanding officer**, **non-commissioned officer**, **petty officer**, **warrant officer**. 2 a person who has an important position in an organization, especially in public or government service. EG *...a Careers Officer... ...a regional officer of the Transport Union... ...prison officers.* ● See also **probation officer**, **returning officer**. 3 a member of the police force. EG *Inspector Darroway was the officer in charge of the investigation... ...senior CID officer Barbara Kelly.* ▸ used to address a policeman or policewoman. EG *Listen, Officer, why do you need all this information?* N COUNT ⇑ soldier; N COUNT : USU MOD+N ⇑ employee; N COUNT : ALSO IN TITLES ⇑ policeman; ▸ N AS VOC

official /əfɪʃəˀl/, **officials**. 1 Something that is **official** is 1.1 published, approved, or done by the government or by someone else in authority. EG *The official figures for the year were published in January... ...official recognition by the Ministry... ...official policy... ...the increasing number of strikes, official and unofficial.* 1.2 given a special position of importance by an organization or person. EG *...his official biography... Arabic is the official language of Morocco... ...the official wedding photographer.* 1.3 used by, done by, or involves a person in a position of authority, as part of their job or position rather than as a private individual. EG *...the Prime Minister's official residence... ...an official visit... I had not done this in any official capacity.* 1.4 part of a formal event or ceremony that is done so that it becomes publicly known or recognized. EG *...the official opening of the new bridge.* ◊ **officially**. EG *They were not officially engaged... The war officially ended the following year.* ADJ CLASSIF ⇑ authorized; ADJ CLASSIF : ATTRIB ⇑ approved; ADJ CLASSIF : ATTRIB; ADJ CLASSIF : ATTRIB; ◊ ADV WITH VB ⇑ formally

2 The **official** reason or explanation for something is something incorrect that people are told in the hope that they will believe it, because the truth is embarrassing; often used humorously. EG *Visiting his aunt was only the official motive.* ◊ **officially**. EG *Officially she shares a flat with some girlfriend... Officially I don't smoke.* ADJ CLASSIF : ATTRIB = alleged ≠ actual; ◊ ADV SEN = theoretically

3 An **official** is a person who holds a position of authority in an organization. EG *'Today,' says an official of the university, 'We're pulling back on research.'... ...government officials... ...trade union officials.* N COUNT ⇑ employee

officialdom /əfɪʃəldəˀm/ is used to refer to government officials or the officials of some other organization and to the way in which they work. People use this word especially when they disapprove of the officials' rules and regulations, their slowness, or their unhelpfulness. EG *...his persecution at the hands of officialdom... This leaves the individual at the mercy of officialdom.* N UNCOUNT

official receiver. The **official receiver** is the person appointed by the government to deal with the affairs of a person or company after they have gone bankrupt. N SING : the+N

officiate /əfɪʃieɪt/, **officiates, officiating, officiated**. When someone **officiates** at a ceremony or formal occasion, he or she is in charge and performs the official part of the ceremony. EG *Who officiated at your wedding?* V : IF+PREP THEN at ⇑ preside

officious /əfɪʃəs/. Someone who is **officious** is too eager to tell people what to do; used showing disapproval. EG *She liked them because they were not officious.* ADJ QUALIT = interfering

offing /ɒfɪŋ/. If you say that something is **in the offing**, you mean that it is likely to happen soon. EG *A wedding is in the offing... War was already in the offing.* PHR : USED AS AN A = imminent

off-key. If you say that music is **off-key**, you mean that it is not in tune. EG *Sheila was singing loudly in an off-key soprano.* ADJ CLASSIF = out of tune

off-licence, off-licences; also spelled without a hyphen. In Britain, an **off-licence** is a shop which sells beer, wine, and other alcoholic drinks. EG *Russell's shop was now the off-licence.* N COUNT

off limits; also spelled with a hyphen and as one word, especially when used before another noun. If somewhere is **off limits** to you, you are not allowed to go there; used especially in American English. EG *The Eastern Zone was now off-limits to me.* ADJ CLASSIF : PRED

offload /ɒfləʊd/, **offloads, offloading, offloaded**. If you **offload** something that you do not want, you get rid of it, especially by giving it to someone else; a rather informal word. EG *I'm trying to offload some of my work onto him.* V+O : IF+PREP THEN onto = dump

off-peak is used to describe something that happens or that is used at a time when there is little demand for it, so that it is cheaper than usual. EG *The price of off-peak electricity has gone up... I always get an off-peak train into town.* ADJ CLASSIF : ATTRIB

off-putting. You describe someone or something as **off-putting** when you find them rather unpleasant and do not want to know them better. EG *She has a rather off-putting manner... His behaviour is deliberately intended to be off-putting.* ADJ QUALIT = antipathetic

off season. The **off season** is the part of the year when not many people go on holiday and when hotels, plane tickets, etc are often cheaper. EG *We like to go there in the off season... Off-season tickets are a lot cheaper.* N SING : the+N, OR ADJ CLASSIF ≠ high season

offset /ɒfsɛt/, **offsets, offsetting, offset**. If one quantity or amount **is offset** by another quantity or amount, the two quantities or amounts are made to balance, so that an advantage or disadvantage is cancelled out. EG *They argued that their wage increases would be offset by higher prices... His welfare entitlements would be offset against his tax payments.* V+O : IF+PREP THEN against

offshoot /ɒfʃuːt/, **offshoots**. An **offshoot** is something which has developed from something else. EG *The Committee was an off-shoot from the Nationwide Liaison Committee... Afrikaans is an offshoot of Dutch.* N COUNT+SUPP = spin-off

offshore /ɒfʃɔː/. Something that is **offshore** is situated in the sea at a distance from the coast, or moving away from the coast towards the open sea. EG *...offshore oil terminals... A gentle current carried him slowly offshore.* ADJ CLASSIF, OR ADV WITH VB

offside /ɒfsaɪd/. The **offside** of a vehicle is the side of it that is furthest from the pavement when you are driving; used mainly in British English. EG *The mini had touched the offside of the truck with its nearside wing... ...the offside wheel.* N SING WITH DET ≠ nearside

offspring /ɒfsprɪŋ/. **Offspring** is both the singular and the plural form. Your **offspring** are your children; a rather formal word, often used humorously. EG *How do parents pass genes on to their offspring?... ...his large and lumpy offspring.* ▸ used of animals. EG *If you take mice or any other animal, their offspring are basically the same animal.* N COUNT : USU WITH POSS = progeny; ▸ N COUNT/UNCOUNT = young

off-stage; also spelled without a hyphen. **Off-stage** is used to refer to 1 sounds in a play that happen in the part of a theatre that is just behind the stage or to the side of the stage. EG *There were tremendous roars off stage... ...off-stage thunder.* 2 the behaviour of actors and actresses in real life, when they are not acting in a play or film. EG *Offstage she is direct, honest, and forceful... ...Ernest's off-stage voice.* ADJ CLASSIF : ATTRIB, OR ADV WITH VB; ADV WITH VB, OR ADJ CLASSIF : ATTRIB

off-the-cuff. An **off-the-cuff** remark is spoken without being planned or practised in advance. EG *His off-the-cuff replies convulsed the audience.* ADJ CLASSIF OR ADV = spontaneous

off-the-peg. **Off-the-peg** clothes are bought in a shop and not made especially for a particular person. EG *This street is notable for off-the-peg gents' clothing.* ▸ used as an adverb. EG *Hilary bought a wedding dress off the peg at C & A, and flew out to join him... ...a dress which could have come off the peg at any department store.* ADJ CLASSIF ≠ made-to-measure; ▸ ADV WITH VB

off-the-record. **Off-the-record** remarks, statements, etc are made unofficially and are not intended to be made public. EG *...an off-the-record chat... ...an off-the-record briefing to the American press.* ADJ CLASSIF : ATTRIB, OR ADV WITH VB

off-white. Something that is **off-white** is not pure white, but slightly grey or yellow. EG *...a tatty off-white dress.* ADJ COLOUR

oft /ɒft/ means the same as 'often' and is usually used in compounds like 'oft-repeated,' 'oft-heard,' etc; a rather literary word. EG *...the oft-quoted statement that 'numbers always lie.'* ADV WITH VB

often /ɒfəˀn/. In informal English, people sometimes say **oftener** and **oftenest** rather than 'more often' and 'most often'. 1 If something happens **often**, it happens many times or much of the time. EG *We often get very wet cold winters here... I've often* ADV WITH VB : NO COMPAR = frequently *thought about this... It's not often you meet someone who's really interested... Women are often very successful in advertising.*

2 You use **often** when you are asking or talking about how frequently something happens. EG *How often do you need to weigh the baby?... The sun shone less often... We had to stop more and more often... She didn't write very often... John came as often as he could.* ADV WITH VB

3 **Often** is used in the following phrases. 3.1 If you say that something happens **more often than not**, you mean that it usually happens. EG *More often than not the patient recovers.* PHR : USED AS AN A = generally 3.2 If you say that something happens **as often as not**, you mean that it happens fairly often. EG *These paintings as often as not end up in America.* PHR : USED AS AN A 3.3 If you say that something happens **every so often**, you mean that it happens occasionally over a period of time. EG *Every so often, she takes a weekend in London.* PHR : USED AS AN A = now and then

ogle /əʊgəᵒl/, **ogles, ogling, ogled**. If someone **ogles** someone else, they stare at them, especially in a way that indicates a sexual interest; used showing disapproval, or sometimes humorously. EG *The men ogled her lasciviously.* V+O = eye up

ogre /əʊgə/, **ogres**. An **ogre** is 1 a character in fairy stories who is large, cruel, frightening, and often eats people. N COUNT 2 a person or situation that you consider to be cruel, evil, or to cause harm. EG *Grim stark poverty was the ogre of my past.* N COUNT ↑ monster

oh /əʊ/ has very little meaning. You use it 1 to introduce a response or a comment on something that has just been said. EG *'I'll give it to you now.'–'Oh thanks.'... Oh well, never mind... 'He's got bald patches where he fell on his head.'–'Oh, poor man.'... 'I have a flat in London.'–'Oh yes, whereabouts?'... 'How's your brother then?'–'Oh he's fine.'... 'I didn't realise he was 25.'–'Oh I think he must be.'* EXCLAM 2 when you are hesitating while speaking, for example because you are not sure of the facts, or because you are searching for the right word. EG *It was about, oh, half past five when I got home... We didn't stay long in Romania, we only went to, oh, what was the place, Mamaia, on the Black Sea.* EXCLAM = er 3 to express a feeling such as surprise, pain, grief, annoyance, or joy. EG *She covered her face with her hands and cried, 'Oh! Oh!'... 'He wants to see you immediately,' I said. 'Oh!' she said. Her smile vanished.* EXCLAM

ohm /əʊm/, **ohms**. An **ohm** is a unit which is used to measure electrical resistance; a technical term in physics. EG *...a resistance of forty ohms.* N COUNT

O.H.M.S. is the abbreviation for 'On Her Majesty's Service' or 'On His Majesty's Service'. It is used on official letters from British or Commonwealth government offices.

oil /ɔɪl/, **oils, oiling, oiled**. 1 **Oil** is 1.1 a smooth thick sticky liquid that is used as a fuel and for lubricating machines. Oil is found underground, and it can also be manufactured. EG *...fuels such as coal or oil... ...the oil and gas industries.* ● to **pour oil on troubled waters**: see **water**. ● to **burn the midnight oil**: see **midnight**. N UNCOUNT ↑ substance 1.2 a smooth thick sticky liquid that is made from plants or animals. Some oils are used for cooking and some for rubbing into things. EG *...cooking oil... ...olive oil.* N UNCOUNT : USU MOD+N 1.3 a smooth thick liquid that is often scented and that you rub into your skin, add to your bath, or use as a cosmetic in another way. EG *...some sort of delicious bath oil... ...sun tan oil.* N UNCOUNT : USU MOD+N

2 If you **oil** a machine, you put oil into it in order to make it work smoothly. EG *He has to oil and wind the clock... The gun was kept well oiled.* V+O = lubricate ● If you **oil the wheels** of something, you act in a way that will help it to run smoothly and successfully. EG *Business lunches can be very useful in oiling the wheels of commerce.* ● PHR : VB INFLECTS

3 If you **oil** your skin, your hair, etc, you rub oil onto it. EG *He had wavy, oiled hair.* V+O

4 **Oils** are 4.1 oil paintings. EG *...an exhibition of watercolours and oils by Turner... He had some very nice oils.* N COUNT : USU PLURAL 4.2 oil paints. EG *...a portrait in oils.* N PLURAL

oilcan /ɔɪlkæn/, **oilcans**; also spelled with a hyphen. An **oilcan** is a container for oil that has a long spout and that is used when oiling machinery. N COUNT

oilcloth /ɔɪlklɒθ/ is a cotton fabric with a shiny waterproof surface, formerly used for tablecloths or other covers. N UNCOUNT ↑ cloth

oilfield /ɔɪlfi:ld/, **oilfields**; also spelled as two words. An **oilfield** is an area of land or seabed under which oil is found and from which oil is removed. EG *...the oilfields of Indonesia and Burma.* N COUNT

oil-fired. Things that are **oil-fired**, for example radiators or central heating systems, use oil as a fuel. ADJ CLASSIF ↑ powered

oilman /ɔɪlməˀn/, **oilmen**. An **oilman** is a man who owns an oil company or who works in the oil business, for example on an oilrig. EG *...a Denver oilman.* N COUNT ↑ worker

oil paint, oil paints. **Oil paint** is a thick paint, used especially by artists, that is made from a coloured powder and linseed oil. EG *...tubes of oil paint.* N UNCOUNT/COUNT

oil painting, oil paintings. An **oil painting** is a painting for which oil paint has been used. EG *...really valuable oil paintings.* N COUNT

oilrig /ɔɪlrɪg/, **oilrigs**; also spelled as two words. An **oilrig** is a structure on land or in the sea that people use as a base when drilling for oil. N COUNT

oilskin /ɔɪlskɪn/, **oilskins**. An **oilskin** is a coat, pair of trousers, or other piece of clothing that is made from thick waterproof cotton. EG *...sea boots and oilskins.* N COUNT ↑ garment

oil slick, oil slicks; also spelled with a hyphen. An **oil slick** is a layer of oil that is floating on top of the sea, a lake, etc as the result of an accident. N COUNT ↑ patch

oil tanker, oil tankers; also spelled with a hyphen. An **oil tanker** is a ship, lorry, or other vehicle that is used for transporting oil. N COUNT

oil well, oil wells; also spelled with a hyphen. An **oil well** is a hole which is drilled into the ground or the seabed in order to remove the oil which lies underground. N COUNT

oily /ɔɪliˡ/, **oilier, oiliest**. 1 Something that is **oily** 1.1 is covered with oil. EG *...oily rags... ...oily fried potatoes.* ADJ QUALIT 1.2 looks or feels like oil. EG *...an oily substance.* ADJ CLASSIF = slimy

2 You describe someone as **oily** when you find them unpleasant because of the way that they flatter people or behave in an excessively polite way. EG *...gross oily stupid fellows.* ADJ QUALIT = smarmy

oink /ɔɪŋk/ is used to represent the sound that a pig utters. = grunt

ointment /ɔɪntməˀnt/, **ointments**. An **ointment** is a smooth thick substance that is put on sore skin or a wound to help it heal. EG *...zinc ointment.* N MASS = salve ● You describe something as a **fly in the ointment** when it spoils a situation or activity and prevents it from being as successful as you had hoped or expected. EG *The only fly in the ointment was that his own son refused to co-operate.* ● PHR = obstacle

OK /əʊ keɪ/. See **okay**.

okay /əʊkeɪ/, **okays, okaying, okayed**; also spelled **OK**. **Okay** is an informal word that is used in many different ways and for many different purposes. Here are some of the main uses. 1 You can use **okay** 1.1 to say that you quite like someone, or that you find a situation, event, someone's behaviour, etc, acceptable. The actual tone of voice you use shows the degree of enthusiasm you feel. EG *I asked Jenny how she thought it all went. 'Okay,' she said... I'll have another coffee and then I'll be going, if that's okay... Sub-titles or dubbing are okay for Europe but not for America... She wanted to know if the trip was OK with the government.* ADJ CLASSIF : PRED = all right 1.2 to say that someone is safe or well, or that an object or machine is in good working order and able to be used. EG *'Where's Jane?'–'Just back there. She's okay. Just shocked.'... Stick with me and you'll be okay, don't you worry... 'That's gazpacho. Soup.'–'Are you sure it's okay?'* ADJ CLASSIF : PRED = all right

2 You can use **okay** 2.1 when you are agreeing to something, for example to an arrangement that is being made. EG *'I'll be back at a quarter past one.'–'OK. I'll see you then.'... I asked if he could see me in the early afternoon. He said okay... 'I must go and make a phone call.'–'Yeah OK.'* CONVENTION = fine 2.2 to check whether the person you are talking to understands what you have just said and accepts it. EG *I'll be back in fifteen minutes. OK?* CONVENTION = right 2.3 as a way of stopping people from arguing with you or criticizing you any more by showing that you accept the points that they want to make, although you don't really agree with them. EG *And did I notice tears in his eyes? I mean, okay, the title was at stake, but tears!... 'What* CONVENTION = fair enough

do you know about life in England?'–'Okay, so I wasn't born here. But I've spent a lot of time here.'

3 Okay is sometimes used in conversations or discussions to mark the end of a particular topic, and to show someone that you want to start talking about or doing something else. EG *Okay, do you mind if we speak a bit of German now?... Okay, now – underneath the photographs you'll see printed captions.* CONVENTION = right

4 If someone in authority **okays** something, they officially agree to it or allow it to happen. EG *I'm blowed if I know why, but I'll okay this overdraft.* V+O ⇑ approve

5 If you **are doing okay**, you are being successful, especially with money, and feel that life is enjoyable and satisfactory. EG *When we were working in the post office during Christmas rush, we were doing okay.* PHR : VB INFLECTS, USU CONT = do all right

6 If someone in authority **gives the okay** to something, they give someone permission to do it. EG *I don't want to go on really before he's given the OK.* PHR : VB INFLECTS

okra /əʊkrə/ is a vegetable in the form of long green pods. N UNCOUNT

old /əʊld/, **older, oldest**. **1** Someone who is **old** has lived for many years and is no longer young. EG *...his old mother... ...a little old lady... I wondered how a man as old as he could be in such good physical shape.* ▸ The **old** is used to refer to people who are old. EG *...the particular needs of the old and infirm.* ADJ QUALIT = aged ≠ young ▸ N PLURAL : the+N

2 Something that is **old 2.1** has existed for a long time and is no longer new. EG *...a massive old building of crumbling red brick... ...old paintings... ...old, valuable carpets.* ADJ QUALIT = ancient **2.2** is no longer in a good or new condition because of its age or because it has been used a lot. EG *The cellar was stacked with old boxes... ...wardrobes full of old clothes.* ADJ QUALIT = tatty **2.3** is now no longer used or has been replaced by a newer version. EG *She was speeding out of Brussels along the old E40 highway towards Namur... I was directed into the old dining room... The re-establishment of the old order was clearly impossible.* ADJ QUALIT : ATTRIB = former

3 If you say that someone or something is a particular number of years, months, etc **old**, you mean that they have lived or existed for that length of time. EG *She's about 50 years old... 'How old are you?'–'I'll be eight next year'... He wasn't old enough to understand what we said... She was a couple of years older than me.* ADJ QUALIT

4 Old is used in combination with numbers to specify a person of a particular age. EG *Is there any point in teaching 18- and 19-year-olds about the French Revolution?... ...twelve-year-olds... ...a 40-year-old man.* N COUNT : NUM+year+N

5 A situation or behaviour that is described as **old** has been in existence or happening for a long time. EG *...an old dispute with a neighbour... It's just an old habit of mine.* ADJ QUALIT : USU ATTRIB = long-standing

6 Old traditions and ways of doing things were started many centuries ago and have hardly changed at all; usually used showing approval. EG *The old traditions died hard... He was brought up in the old ways... All the old skills are gone.* ADJ QUALIT : USU ATTRIB = time-honoured

7 You use **old** to describe **7.1** friends, enemies, etc that you have known for many years and that you still know. EG *Pete's an old friend of mine... ...old enemies.* ADJ QUALIT : ATTRIB **7.2** things that are well known because they have often been repeated. EG *There's an old saying that opposites attract each other... ...an old joke.* ADJ QUALIT : ATTRIB, NO COMPAR/SUPERL **7.3** things that you had or people that you knew in the past, but no longer have or know. EG *...his old job at the publishing company... ...an old tutor... One of her old admirers wrote to her.* ADJ QUALIT : ATTRIB, NO COMPAR/SUPERL = former

8 If you use **old** to describe a place, you are referring to that place as it was at an earlier time or period in history. EG *...the American fondness for Old England.* ADJ CLASSIF : ATTRIB ⇑ early

● If you talk about something that happened **in the old days** or **in the olden days**, you are talking about something that happened many years ago. EG *Hong Kong was a shopper's paradise in the old days.* ● **the good old days**: see **day**. ● PHR : USED AS AN A = once

9 Of old. 9.1 If you talk about ships **of old**, knights **of old**, etc, you are referring to ships or knights that existed in the past, and that no longer exist; a literary expression. PHR AFTER N **9.2** If you say that you **know** someone or something **of old**, you mean that you have known them for a long time. PHR : VB INFLECTS

10 You can use **old** to express affection or familiarity when you are talking to or about someone that you know; an informal use. EG *Take care, old boy... I got a letter from good old Lewis... Remember old Waxy at school?* ADJ CLASSIF : ATTRIB

11 any old; an informal expression. **11.1** You use **any old** to emphasize that the quality of something is not important, as long as it can be used for a particular purpose. EG *...wine glasses in any old shape or size... Any old bit of cloth will do.* PHR BEFORE N **11.2** If you say that that something is not **any old** thing, you are emphasizing how special or famous it is. EG *This is not just any old painting, it's a Rembrandt.* PHR BEFORE N

old-age pensioner, old-age pensioners. An **old-age pensioner** is the same as an OAP. N COUNT

old boy, old boys; used in British English. **1** An **old boy** of a particular school or college is a man who used to be a pupil there. ● When people talk about the **old-boy network**, they are referring to the situation in which people who knew each other at public school or university use their positions of influence to help each other; usually used showing disapproval. EG *He arrived on the board through the old-boy network.* N COUNT ● PHR ⇑ patronage **2** An **old boy** is also any old or middle-aged man; a rather old-fashioned informal use. EG *She can twist the old boy round her little finger.* N COUNT

olde /əʊld/ is used in names of places and in advertising to make people think that something is very old and interesting. EG *...a smart cottage called The Olde Forge.* ADJ CLASSIF : ATTRIB

olden /əʊldə[°]n/. **in the olden days**: see **old**.

old-fashioned. **1** Something that is **old-fashioned** is no longer considered appropriate in style or design, especially because it has been replaced by something that is more modern. EG *...the old-fashioned internal combustion engine... He was wearing old-fashioned plastic-rimmed glasses.* ADJ QUALIT = outmoded

2 If you are **old-fashioned**, you believe in and behave according to the values and standards of the past. EG *I am very old-fashioned.* ▸ used of people's attitudes and behaviour. EG *...a charming old-fashioned custom... ...old-fashioned ideas.* ADJ QUALIT ⇑ traditional ≠ progressive

old flame, old flames. An **old flame** is someone who you once had a romantic relationship with. EG *...an old flame of Charlotte's.* N COUNT

old girl, old girls; used in British English. **1** An **old girl** of a particular school or college is a woman who used to be a pupil there. N COUNT

2 An **old girl** is also any old or middle-aged woman; a rather old-fashioned informal use. EG *The old girl is slightly dotty.* N COUNT

old guard. When people talk about the **old guard**, they are referring to a group of people who have worked together for a long time and who are regarded as rather old-fashioned. EG *Tensions began to arise between the old guard and some of their newer members.* N SING : the+N, VB CAN BE SING OR PL

old hand, old hands. An **old hand** is a person who is very skilled at something because they have a lot of experience; often used showing approval. EG *...a few old hands in the press corps.* N COUNT = veteran

old hat. See **hat**.

old maid, old maids. **1** People sometimes refer to an old or middle-aged woman as an **old maid** when she has never married and they think that it is unlikely that she ever will marry; an offensive expression. N COUNT = spinster

2 An **old maid** is also a man or woman who is very cautious and timid; used showing disapproval. EG *He's nothing more than a ridiculous old maid.* N COUNT = old woman

old man; an informal expression. Your **old man** is **1** your father. EG *The first letter I got from my old man told me how proud he was of me.* N SING WITH DET **2** your husband. EG *Her old man's run off with someone else.* N SING WITH DET

old master, old masters. An **old master** is a famous painter of the past. ▸ used of a painting by an old master. EG *...beautiful posters or reproductions of old masters.* N COUNT ▸ ⇑ picture

old school. the **old school**: see **school**.

old school tie. In British English, when people talk about the **old school tie**, they are referring to the situation in which people who knew each other at public school or university use their positions of influence to help each other; usually used showing disapproval. N UNCOUNT

Old Testament. The **Old Testament** is the first part of the Bible. It contains Jewish writings and is especially concerned with the history of the Jewish people. N PROPER : the+N

old-timer, old-timers; an informal word, used mainly in American English. An **old-timer** is 1 someone who has been in a particular place or job for a long time. 2 an old man. N COUNT = veteran; N COUNT

old wives' tale, old wives' tales. An **old wives' tale** is a common belief that is based on traditional ideas and that is often considered to be foolish or superstitious. N COUNT

old woman, old women. An **old woman** is a man or woman who is fussy or timid; an informal word, used showing disapproval. EG *He's a bit of an old woman.* N COUNT

ole /əʊl/ is used in written English to represent the word 'old' pronounced in a particular way. EG *Don't mess around with ole Clem... Where's your ole lady?* ADJ QUALIT : ATTRIB

oleander /əʊli¹ændə/, **oleanders**. An **oleander** is an evergreen tree or shrub that has white, pink, or purple flowers. Oleanders grow in Mediterranean countries and in some parts of Asia and Australia. N COUNT

O level, O levels. An **O level** is an educational qualification in a particular subject. O levels are awarded in England, Wales, and Northern Ireland. Schoolchildren usually take O level examinations at the age of 15 or 16, after they have studied for them for 2 or 3 years. O level examinations are being replaced by GCSE examinations. EG *I think you can do it for GCE O Level... He got O-level Maths... I wish they would keep their minds on their O-levels.* N COUNT

olfactory /ɒlfæktə⁰ri¹/ means concerned with the sense of smell; a formal or technical word. EG *...delicate olfactory nerves... It arouses their olfactory sense.* ADJ CLASSIF : ATTRIB ⇑ sensory

oligarchy /ɒlɪgɑ:ki¹/, **oligarchies**. 1 An **oligarchy** is a small group of people who control and run a particular country or organization. EG *...the ageing oligarchy that constitutes its leadership.* N COUNT

2 **Oligarchy** is a situation in which a country or organization is run by an oligarchy. N UNCOUNT

olive /ɒlɪv/, **olives**. 1 An **olive** is a small green or black oily fruit that has a bitter taste. Olives can be eaten as a snack or with a meal, or used in cooking. Olives are also pressed to make olive oil. EG *...a plate of salami, olives and bread.* ▸ also used to refer to the tree on which olives grow. EG *Magpies strutted between the olives... ...olive groves.* N COUNT; ▸ N COUNT

2 Something that is **olive** or **olive green** is yellowish-green in colour. EG *...his olive National Guard uniform... ...olive green towels.* ADJ COLOUR

olive branch; also spelled with a hyphen. If you offer an **olive branch** to someone, you say or do something in order to show that you want to end a disagreement or quarrel. EG *They conceded the point, accepting his olive branch, and we all shook hands... I shall extend the olive branch to that poor misguided child.* N SING WITH DET ⇑ peace offering

olive oil; also spelled with a hyphen. **Olive oil** is oil that is obtained by pressing olives. It is used for putting on salads or for cooking. N UNCOUNT

-ological is used to replace '-ology' at the end of some nouns in order to form adjectives. These adjectives describe something as relating to a particular science or subject. For example, 'biological' means relating to biology. Adjectives formed in this way are not usually defined in this dictionary, but may be found at the entry for the noun. EG *...theology→theological.* SUFFIX : FORMS ADJS

-ologist is used to replace '-ology' at the end of some nouns in order to form other nouns that refer to people who are concerned with a particular science or subject. For example, a biologist is concerned with biology. Nouns formed in this way are not usually defined in this dictionary, but may be found at the entry for the noun ending in '-ology'. EG *...psychology→psychologist.* SUFFIX : FORMS N COUNTS

-ology is used at the end of some nouns that refer to a particular science or subject. EG *...geology... ...sociology... ...ecology.* SUFFIX : FORMS NOUNS

Olympian /əlɪmpɪən/ means very powerful, large, or impressive; a rather literary word. EG *...disasters on an Olympian scale... ...this vast Olympian landscape... ...his Olympian calm.* ADJ CLASSIF : USU ATTRIB = phenomenal

Olympic /əlɪmpɪk/, **Olympics**. 1 **Olympic** means relating to the Olympic Games. EG *...judo, golf and fencing to Olympic standard... ...an Olympic finalist.* ADJ CLASSIF : ATTRIB ⇑ international

2 The **Olympics** are the Olympic Games; an informal word. EG *Didn't she win a gold medal at the Olympics?* N PLURAL : PL FORM WHEN MOD

Olympic Games. The **Olympic Games** are a set of international sports competitions which take place every four years, each time in a different country. EG *...the showjumping at the 1948 Olympic Games.* N PLURAL : the+N = Olympics

ombudsman /ɒmbudzmə³n/, **ombudsmen**. The **ombudsman** is an official who is appointed by the government to investigate complaints that people make against the government or public organizations. N COUNT ⇑ investigator

omega /əʊmɪgə/ is the last letter of the Greek alphabet. N UNCOUNT

omelette /ɒmlɪ²t/, **omelettes**; also spelled **omelet** in American English. 1 An **omelette** is a food made by beating eggs and cooking them in a flat pan. N COUNT

2 If you say **'You can't make an omelette without breaking eggs'**, you mean that you often can't achieve something in a particular situation without damaging or destroying things that already exist. PHR

omen /əʊmə²n/, **omens**. An **omen** is something that you think indicates what is going to happen in the future and whether it will be good or bad. EG *An eclipse of the sun is the worst of bad omens... It was a good omen for the trip.* N COUNT ⇑ sign = portent

ominous /ɒmɪnəs/. Something that is **ominous** is worrying or frightening because it makes you think that something unpleasant is going to happen. EG *There was an ominous silence... The present crisis is far more ominous.* ◇ **ominously**. EG *Black clouds were piling up ominously.* ADJ QUALIT = menacing, sinister; ◇ ADV

omission /ə⁶mɪʃə⁰n/, **omissions**. 1 An **omission** is something that has not been included or not been done, either deliberately or accidentally. EG *My failure to register had been an innocent omission... The reports were full of errors, ambiguities and omissions.* N COUNT ⇑ mistake ≠ inclusion

2 **Omission** is the act of not including someone or something or of not doing something. EG *...the omission of women from these studies... The occasion called for a special prayer, and its omission was inexcusable.* N UNCOUNT ⇑ exclusion ≠ inclusion

omit /ə⁶mɪt/, **omits, omitting, omitted**. 1 If you **omit** something, you do not include it in an activity or piece or work, deliberately or accidentally. EG *...again omitting any mention of his own work... Two groups were omitted from the survey–the old and women.* V+O = leave out

2 If you **omit** to do something, you do not do it; a formal use. EG *Hotels often omit to check guests' cars... He omitted to say whether these men would be armed.* V+*to*-INF = fail, neglect

omnibus /ɒmnɪbə⁹s/, **omnibuses**. An **omnibus** is 1 a book which contains a large collection of stories or articles, often by a particular person or about a particular subject. EG *...the Sherlock Holmes omnibus.* 2 a radio or television broadcast which contains two or more similar programmes that were originally broadcast separately. EG *...the omnibus edition of The Archers.* N COUNT : USU SING = anthology; N COUNT : USU SING ⇑ programme

omnipotence /ɒmnɪpətəns/ is the state of having total authority or power; a formal word. EG *...God's omnipotence.* N UNCOUNT

omnipotent /ɒmnɪpətənt/. Someone or something that is **omnipotent** has complete power over things or people; a formal word. EG *...an omnipotent central committee.* ADJ CLASSIF = all-powerful

omnipresent /ɒmni¹prezə⁰nt/. Something that is **omnipresent** is present everywhere or affects everyone at the same time; a formal word. EG *The fear of failure was omnipresent... ...the omnipresent coal dust.* ADJ CLASSIF = pervasive

omniscient /ɒmnɪsɪənt/. Someone who is **omniscient** knows or seems to know everything; a formal word. EG *God is eternal, omniscient... The woman goes as a patient to an omniscient professional.* ADJ CLASSIF ⇑ knowledgeable

omnivorous /ɒmnɪvərəs/. 1 An **omnivorous** person or animal eats all kinds of food, including both meat and plants; a technical or formal use. EG *...the change from a vegetarian to an omnivorous diet.* ADJ CLASSIF

2 **Omnivorous** also means liking a wide variety of things of a particular kind; a rather formal use. EG *...an omnivorous newspaper reader.* ADJ CLASSIF

on /ɒn/. 1 You use **on** in phrasal verbs, for example in 'cotton on', 'keep on', and 'sign on', and after some other verbs such as 'rely', 'depend', and 'insist'. See individual verb and phrasal verb entries for such items, which are not treated here.

2 You use **on 2.1** to describe the position of a person PREP

or thing when they are touching the upper surface of an object and their weight is supported by that object. EG *Two cushions lay on the floor... ...a cow grazing on a hill... He put his letter on top of his desk... Flora sits on the sofa.* **2.2** to specify a surface or place which something moves towards and where it lands, falls, or stops. EG *He dropped it on the floor... She threw cold water on her face.* PREP = onto **2.3** to say that something is touching or attached to the side of a surface or object, or is seen there. EG *...the posters on the walls... ...a sticker on her car... They show their pictures on a screen.* PREP = upon **2.4** to say that something is touching or attached to the underneath of something. EG *On the ceiling hung dustpans and brushes... On the roof of the cave were several bats.* PREP = upon **2.5** to say that you are touching a part of someone's body. EG *She kissed him on the mouth... He laid a hand on my shoulder.* PREP = upon **2.6** to say what part of your body supports your weight or what part of an object supports its weight. EG *Howard lay on his back... Turn it over on its side.* PREP = upon **2.7** to say that something is attached to the end of something, or hanging from it. EG *Her coat was hanging on the hook... ...a bunch of balloons on a string.* PREP ⇑ upon **2.8** to say that something is attached to something and is considered to be a part of it. EG *...the handle on the window... ...the buttons on his shirt.* PREP **2.9** to refer to the position of the lid of a box, top of a bottle, etc when it is securely in place. EG *Put the top back on the bottle when you've finished... Be careful, the lid's not on properly.* ADV AFTER VB, OR PREP

3 You use **on 3.1** to specify the material or object on which something is written, painted, or printed. EG *She wrote it down on a piece of paper... ...the table on the back page of the book... ...a card with his name on... On the map it seems much smaller.* PREP **3.2** to specify a colour or pattern over which another colour or pattern has been painted or printed. EG *...a red cross on a white background.* PREP = upon **3.3** to say that something is included as part of a list, timetable, etc. EG *The item was not on the agenda... A dozen Building Societies on my list pay 10 per cent or more.* PREP

4 You use **on 4.1** to suggest a general area where something is or where something happens, rather than a precise position. EG *My father worked on a farm... The house is on Pacific Avenue... ...on the horizon... ...on the banks of the river... ...on the fourth floor... There was one on each side.* PREP **4.2** to say that something is situated very close to a river or lake. EG *...a house on the river... ...Stratford on Avon.* PREP = upon **4.3** to say that you are travelling along a road or river. EG *We were driving on a California freeway... They stood and watched the boats on the river.* PREP

5 You use **on 5.1** to say that someone is wearing something. EG *She had her coat on... She put her good shoes on... Hogan was clipping on his seat belt.* ADV AFTER VB **5.2** to say that someone is carrying something, especially something small which they could carry in a pocket. EG *He had an air pistol hidden on him... I didn't have any money on me.* PREP **5.3** to say that someone's face shows a particular expression, such as a smile. EG *She had a puzzled expression on her face.* PREP = upon

6 You use **on 6.1** to specify the particular form of transport that someone is using or the way in which they are walking. EG *She was the only passenger on the plane... He was very careful and walked on tiptoe... I preferred to enter on foot... ...on the midnight train from London... ...on horseback... ...on a bicycle.* PREP • **on all fours**: see **four**. **6.2** to say that someone is boarding a particular form of transport in order to begin a journey. EG *Afterwards they got on a bus and went to a cinema.* PREP = onto

7 You use **on** to specify a day, date, or occasion. EG *...on a Sunday afternoon in November 1973... Your presence is essential on an occasion like this... Caro was born on April 10th... ...on the first day of term... ...on Thursday night.* PREP

8 You use **on 8.1** to specify the subject of a book, discussion, etc. EG *...books on philosophy, art, and religion... She was questioning him closely on the subject of rents... Get legal advice on this... ...ideas on how films should be made... Ellmann commented on it at length... ...a talk on agriculture.* PREP ⇑ about **8.2** to refer to an agreement or decision. EG *We shook hands on it... They agreed on three points.* PREP ⇑ about • to **sleep on** something: see **sleep**.

9 You use **on 9.1** to say what tool or instrument you are using in a particular activity. EG *...waltzes played on the violin... He puffs on his pipe.* PREP **9.2** to specify the cause of injury or damage, especially to a person's body. EG *He cut himself on the gatepost... I almost choked on my food... He gashed his arm on a window.* PREP **9.3** to say what fuel or form of power is used to make something work. EG *Most cars run on petrol... My radio works on batteries.* PREP ⇑ using **9.4** to specify the system used to store information. EG *Everybody's records are on file... The information is recorded on a computer.* PREP **9.5** to specify the medium, such as radio, television, film, or theatre, through which something is produced or performed. EG *I heard it on the radio... Reagan will appear on television later this week... That would look marvellous on stage.* PREP • **on the telephone**: see **telephone.** • **on the phone**: see **phone.** **9.6** to specify the financial or legal arrangement under which something is bought or sold. EG *I bought it on credit... The house is on a 99-year lease... I'll give you a little on account.* PREP **9.7** to specify a qualification, such as passing an examination or winning a vote, as a result of which a decision is made. EG *He was offered a place at college on his A level results... You will be judged on your performance.* PREP • **on account of**: see **account.** **9.8** to specify the reason or feeling that causes you to do something. EG *I had to vote for him, of course, on principle... He frequently acted on a hunch... She bought it on impulse.* PREP **9.9** to specify the particular method, system, or set of principles that is being used. EG *They work on a rota system... Burglar alarms operate on a variety of principles... ...organized on a short-term basis.* PREP ⇑ using **9.10** to specify the intensity or scale of an activity. EG *To talk on any deep level was impossible... We're going to build on a large scale.* PREP

10 You use **on 10.1** to say that something has begun and is happening at the time mentioned. EG *The war was on then... Our summer sale is now on... There was a scare on about lead pollution.* ADJ CLASSIF : PRED ⇑ in progress **10.2** to say that a film, play, etc is being shown currently, or that a social event is taking place. EG *Look at the paper and see what's on... Is there anything on at the Odeon?... The play went on in Sweden... The exhibition is on at the Tate.* ADV WITH VB, OR ADJ CLASSIF : PRED

11 If you say that someone **has a lot on, does not have much on**, etc you are talking about the amount of work or the number of activities they are doing at the time, and whether they are busy or not; an informal expression. EG *I asked her to do it but she's got such a lot on that she won't have time.* PHR : VB INFLECTS

12 You use **on 12.1** to say that you are continuing to do something. EG *I read on... They walked on... Babbage pressed on alone.* ADV AFTER VB **12.2** to say that someone or something moves forward, or continues to move in the same direction. EG *'Move on, boys,' he used to say... She went on upstairs... He walks on down the corridor.* ADV WITH VB **12.3** to say that something happens immediately after you have done something or at the same time that you do something; a formal use. EG *...his shock on accidentally looking into a mirror... 'It's so unfair,' Clarissa said on her return... On arrival, they were silent for a while... On being called 'young lady', she laughed... ...on evidence of death.* PREP+NG/-ING = upon

13 On is also used in the following expressions referring to processes. **13.1** If you say that something happens **on and on**, you mean that it continues to happen for a very long time. EG *It was easy to talk on and on... The list goes on and on.* PHR : USED AS AN A **13.2** If you say that something happens **on and off**, you mean that it happens occasionally and not in a regular or continuous way. EG *I've been writing my thesis on and off for years.* PHR : USED AS AN A = intermittently **13.3** If you are **on at** someone, or go, keep, or get **on at** them, you repeatedly criticize them, complain about something that they do, or ask them to do something. EG *He's always on at me about the way I dress... I went on at my father to have seat belts fitted in the car.* PHR : USED AS AN A **13.4** If you are **on about** something, or go or keep **on about** it, you talk a lot about the same subject, especially in a way which is boring or confusing; an informal expression. EG *He's always on about yoga... Bill was on about you the other day... What are you on about?* PHR : USED AS AN A = rabbiting on **13.5** You say **from now on, from this time on, from this moment on**, etc to indicate that something starts to happen at the time mentioned and continues to happen afterwards. EG PHR : USED AS AN A

From this time on, I felt less guilty... From now on, do exactly what I tell you.

14 You use **on** to emphasize how late or early something is in time, or how far something is away from you. EG *Later on, he was up in his bedroom... I found a tree a little further on.* ● **just on**: see **just**. ● **nigh on**: see **nigh**. [ADV AFTER ADJ/ADV]

15 You use **on** to say that a machine, electrical appliance, etc is functioning. EG *The television set remained on... Turn the heater on... A tap had been left on.* [ADV AFTER VB, OR ADJ CLASSIF : PRED]

16 If you say that something **is not on** or **is just not on**, you mean that it is unacceptable or impossible; an informal expression. EG *That sort of writing just isn't on... It just wasn't on.* [PHR : USED AS AN A; ⇑ unsatisfactory]

17 You use **on 17.1** to specify the activity that you are doing, especially to say whether you are working or not. EG *I was on holiday in Italy... I came home on leave... A policeman was on duty outside the palace... They went on strike... The girls often came on our expeditions.* [PREP] **17.2** to specify the kind of job that you are doing, or the kind of life that you are living. EG *I applied for a job on the railway... They were on the dole.* ● **on the scrounge**: see **scrounge**. ● **on the beat**: see **beat**. ● **on the door**: see **door**. ● **on call**: see **call**. [PREP] **17.3** to say that you are working as a member of a committee, council, or other group of people in authority. EG *She has been on a number of committees... Mr Grantham served on the Council... ...the four women on its executive.* [PREP = in] **17.4** to specify who is paying for something. EG *The drinks are on me... ...treatment on the National Health Service.* ● **on the house**: see **house**. [PREP] **17.5** to specify what you are eating or drinking or what you are giving as food to someone else or to an animal. EG *Soon they were feasting on steak and chips... What do you feed your dog on?* [PREP] **17.6** to say that you are taking medicine or drugs regularly. EG *I'm not on the pill at the moment... He was on drugs.* [PREP] **17.7** to specify the amount of money that you are living on or the source of the money. EG *...people on a low income... She's on a student grant... 200 rupees! How can I manage on that?* [PREP]

18 You use **on 18.1** to say who an action affects. EG *The pressure on him was enormous... The news did not seem to have much effect on her... You blame it on each other.* [PREP = upon] **18.2** to say who an action is intended to harm. EG *...an assassination attempt on the Governor... Police opened fire on a mob... ...attacks on EEC ministers.* [PREP = against, upon] **18.3** to say who or what you are looking at or thinking about. EG *Their eyes were all on him... My mind's on other things at the moment.* [PREP = upon] **18.4** to say what your thoughts or energies are directed towards achieving. EG *She was concentrating on her personal life... Howard insisted on being present... ...more emphasis on community projects.* [PREP = upon] **18.5** to say what you are trying to produce. EG *Scientists are working on chips which will hold a million words... He had been at work on a book.* [PREP] **18.6** to say whether something wastes or saves money, fuel, or material. EG *This car is more economical on fuel... How much could be saved on wages?* [PREP] **18.7** to say for what purpose you are spending or giving your money, time, or effort. EG *...the amount of money he spent on clothes... I've wasted too much time on him.* [PREP = upon] **18.8** to say what you are comparing something or someone to, when you say they are better or worse. EG *Trade in August was 12.5 per cent down on a year ago... He is a marked improvement on his predecessor.* [PREP] **18.9** to say what items are involved in taxes, fines, profits, etc. EG *...a new sales tax on luxury goods... You pay interest on your mortgage... They have to pay fines on their books... Profits on books will be down.* [PREP ⇑ for]

19 ● **and so on**: see **so**. ● **on behalf of**: see **behalf**.

once /wʌns/. **1** If you do something **once**, **1.1** you do it on one occasion only. EG *I've been out with him once, that's all... I met her just the once... Even if you only do it once, it will never be forgotten.* [ADV WITH VB, OR N SING : *the/this* +N] **1.2** you do it one time only. EG *He walked away without looking back once... The phone rang more than once.* [ADV WITH VB]

2 If something happens **once** a day, week, month, etc, it happens regularly one time in each day, week, month, etc. EG *Once a week, on Tuesdays, she wrote a letter to her mother.* [ADV]

3 If something happens **once every** day, **once every** two weeks, etc, it happens regularly one time every day, every two weeks, etc. EG *Some trees only bear fruit once every twenty-five years.* [PHR+NG]

4 Once means **4.1** in the past, but no longer. EG *Texas was once ruled by Mexico... It once belonged to my father.* [ADV WITH VB] **4.2** at one time or on one occasion only in the past. EG *You said once that Man would never reach the moon... We once had a hilarious day making recordings of our own songs... I had worked with him once before.* [ADV WITH VB]

5 Once also means as soon as something happens. EG *Once the sun had set, the air turned cold... What would happen to the infant once it was born?... Once inside her flat, she opened the letter.* [CONJ SUBORD ⇑ when]

6 At once. 6.1 If you do something **at once**, you do it immediately, without any delay or hesitation. EG *I knew at once that something was wrong... She stopped playing at once.* [PHR : USED AS AN A = instantly] **6.2** If a number of different things happen **at once**, they all happen at the same time. EG *Everybody is talking at once... ...if you are cooking several different meals at once.* [PHR : USED AS AN A = simultaneously]

7 All at once. 7.1 If several different things happen **all at once**, they all happen at the same time. EG *A number of things happened all at once... He looked at me as if I'd smoked eighty cigarettes all at once.* [PHR : USED AS AN A = simultaneously] **7.2** If something happens **all at once**, it happens suddenly, often when you are not expecting it to happen. EG *All at once she felt afraid... All at once, Ralph was dancing around the lamp.* [PHR : USED AS AN A]

8 The word **once** is also used in the following expressions. **8.1** If you have done something **once or twice**, you have done it a few times, but not very often. EG *She had been to London once or twice before.* [PHR : USED AS AN A ⇑ occasionally] **8.2** If something happens **once in a while**, it happens sometimes, but not very often. EG *Once in a while we go to the cinema.* ● **Once in a blue moon**: see **moon**. [PHR : USED AS AN A = now and then] **8.3 For once** is used to emphasize that something happens on this particular occasion, even if it has never happened before, and may never happen again. EG *She was able, for once, to relax... Just for once I am completely lost.* [PHR : USED AS AN A = for a change] **8.4 Once and for all** means completely or finally, in such a way as to end any doubt or uncertainty. EG *They had to be defeated once and for all... The trip proved once and for all that I hated travelling.* [PHR : USED AS AN A = conclusively] **8.5 Once upon a time** means a long time ago in the past. It is used especially at the beginning of children's stories. EG *Once upon a time there were three princes.* [PHR : USED AS AN A] **8.6** If something happens **once again** or **once more**, it happens one more time. EG *If you do that once again, I'll scream!... She wanted to see him once more before she died.* [PHR : USED AS AN A]

once-over. If you **give** someone or something **the once-over**, you quickly look at or inspect them; an informal expression. EG *I'll give it the once-over when you've finished.* [PHR : VB INFLECTS ⇑ examine]

oncoming /ɒnkʌmɪŋ/ means moving towards you. EG *Nothing could stop the oncoming waves... ...oncoming traffic.* [ADJ CLASSIF : ATTRIB ⇑ approaching]

one /wʌn/, **ones**. **1 One** is the number 1: see ☐ at NUMBER, AGE, DATE, MEASUREMENT, MONEY, and TIME. EG *Of these four suggestions, only one is correct... Ten minus one is nine... ...precisely one hundred miles... It is nearly one o'clock.* [NUM]

2 You use **one 2.1** to say that you are referring to a single thing or person, rather than to different things or people, or to several things or people. EG *The two friends share one job... He couldn't stay in one place... They would be working on as many as 20 rescues at any one time.* [NUM] **2.2** to emphasize that something or someone is the only thing or person of their kind in a particular situation. EG *Their one aim in life is to go to University... She is the one person with enough medical knowledge to make it possible.* [NUM+N COUNT IN SING = sole]

3 One can be used **3.1** instead of 'a' to emphasize the following noun. EG *If there was one thing Julie couldn't do without, it was tea... One person I would like to meet is Marilyn Monroe.* [DET+N COUNT IN SING] **3.2** instead of 'a' to emphasize the following adjective or expression; an informal use. EG *He's one worried man... There was one hell of a row when they came on.* [DET+MOD+N COUNT IN SING] **3.3** in front of someone's name to indicate that you do not know them personally or very well; a fairly formal use. EG *The big man is one Bert Lance, an old, dear friend of the President.* [DET+N PROPER]

4 You can also use **one** to refer to the first of two or more things that you are comparing. EG *I have found one firm ten times more expensive than another...* [DET+N COUNT IN SING, OR PRON : SING]

There were four bunks in the cell, two on one side and two on the other.

5 One is also used **5.1** to refer to a thing or person of a particular kind, especially when you want to describe them or to give new information about them. EG *I'll have this one, thank you... These trousers aren't as tight as the other ones... The airport is one of the best equipped in the region... ...buying old houses and building new ones.* **5.2** to refer to a thing or person that has not been mentioned before, for example when you are going to give information about them. EG *We had one case which dragged on for a couple of years... 'They criticise me all the time,' wrote one divorced woman.*

PRON : HAS PL
DET+N COUNT IN SING, OR PRON : SING+*of*

6 One can refer to **6.1** a particular time in the past when you are not stating the time precisely. EG *One day, she went for a swim in the ocean... I took Andrea out to dinner one evening.* **6.2** a time in the future when you are not stating the time precisely. EG *...one day when you are feeling strong... He would take it round to Mrs Swallow one evening.*

DET+N COUNT IN SING
DET+N COUNT IN SING
= some

7 One can also refer to **7.1** something that is spoken, such as a joke, story, remark, or a problem or issue that is being discussed. EG *I leave you to think about this one yourselves... Oh, that's a difficult one to answer, isn't it... Have you heard the one about the actress and the bishop?* **7.2** an alcoholic drink, in expressions such as 'a quick one' or 'one for the road'. EG *Do you fancy a quick one?... I think he's had one too many.*

PRON : SING WITH DET
⇑ subject
PRON : SING

8 You can also use **one** as a way of addressing or referring to someone you are fond of or admire; an old-fashioned or formal use. EG *Come along now, little ones, off to bed... Goodbye, dear one.*

PRON+SUPP : HAS PL

9 In informal English, **one** is used after a verb that means 'hit', in order to give emphasis to the verb. EG *I belted him one... Go on, thump him one.*

PRON : SING

10 One is also a personal pronoun and can be used as a subject or an object. A speaker or writer uses **one** in formal English **10.1** to refer to people in general, for example in statements about what usually happens in a particular situation. EG *One can eat well here... The law should guard one against this sort of thing.* **10.2** to refer to himself or herself when giving an opinion, in order to make it less personal, and to suggest that it is an opinion which is widely held. EG *One tends to think of their characteristics as being more or less identical... ...a time in the future which one hopes will never come to pass.*

PRON : SING
= you
PRON : SING

11 The word **one** is also used in the following expressions. **11.1** If you **are one for** something, you like or approve of it or you are good at doing it. EG *He's a great one for football.* **11.2** If you say that someone is **not one** to do something, you mean that they are not likely to do it, because of their character or habits. EG *Uncle Harold was not one to underestimate the problem.* **11.3** If you say that someone **is a one**, you are pretending to be slightly shocked by their attitude or behaviour, even though you are not really shocked and perhaps even admire them; an informal expression. EG *You are a one!* **11.4** You use the expression **one by one** to say that only one person does something at a particular time, or that only one thing is dealt with or happens at that time. EG *One by one they stood up... She swallows the aspirin, sipping them down with water one by one.* **11.5 One or two** means a very few. EG *'Are those pictures genuine?'-'One or two are reproductions.'... One or two of the girls help in the kitchen.* **11.6** If people or things are **in ones and twos**, there are only a very few of them at a particular time or in a particular place. EG *...standing around in ones and twos.* **11.7** If someone says to you, **'you've got it in one'**, they mean that you have immediately understood their point or what they are suggesting; an informal expression. EG *Got it in one! That's right.* **11.8** If you are or have **one up on** someone, you have an advantage over them; an informal expression. EG *She'd got one up on me.* **11.9** If you describe someone or something as **one in a million** or **one in a thousand**, you mean that they are very remarkable or special in some way. **11.10 A hundred and one, a thousand and one**, etc, mean a great many. EG *There must be a thousand and one books of this sort on the market... I've got a million and one things to do, so don't bother me now.* **11.11** If something is described as **two in one, three in one**, or **all in one**, it is a single unit, but is made up of several different parts or has several different functions. EG *...a film that is tragedy, comedy, political comment, all in one... ...a three-in-one gardening implement.* **11.12** If a group of people does something **as one**, all the people do the same thing at the same time or in the same way; a formal or literary expression. EG *They rose as one.* **11.13** If something is **all one** to you, you do not mind or care which of the several possibilities in the situation happens or is chosen. EG *It's all one to her... But that's all one as far as she's concerned.* **11.14** When people are **at one**,they are in agreement with each other, and living or working peacefully together; an old-fashioned expression. EG *They were at one with each other.* **11.15** You can use **for one** to emphasize that a particular person is definitely behaving or reacting in a particular way, whatever other people do or say. EG *But I for one feel very grateful and very satisfied... Patrick for one is worried.*

PHR : VB INFLECTS
PHR+*to*-INF : USED AS C
PHR : VB INFLECTS
PHR : USED AS AN A
⇑ individually
PHR : USED AS NUM
PHR : USED AS AN A
CONVENTION
⇑ correct
PHR : USED AS C/O
PHR : USED AS C
⇑ rare
PHR : USED AS NUM
⇑ lots
PHR
PHR : USED AS AN A
⇑ together
PHR : USED AS C, IF+PREP THEN *to*
⇑ unimportant
PHR : USED AS C, IF+PREP THEN *with*
= in harmony
PHR AFTER N
⇑ certainly

12 The word **one** is also used in other expressions, which are explained at other places in this dictionary. ● **one and all**: see **all.** ● **ten to one**: see **ten.** ● **one and only**: see **only.** ● **one after another**: see **another.** ● **one after the other**: see **other.** ● **six of one and half a dozen of the other**: see **six.** ● See also **number one.**

one-armed bandit, one-armed bandits. A **one-armed bandit** is the same as a fruit machine. EG *They play roulette and take on the one-armed bandits.*

N COUNT

one-horse. 1 A **one-horse** town is a very small, dull, and old-fashioned town. EG *...a little one-horse town miles from anywhere.*

ADJ CLASSIF : ATTRIB

2 A **one-horse** vehicle is a vehicle that is drawn by one horse. EG *...the one-horse bus that travelled between the villages.*

ADJ CLASSIF : ATTRIB

one-liner, one-liners. A **one-liner** is a funny remark or a joke told in one sentence, for example in a play or comedy programme; an informal word. EG *There were some good one-liners.*

N COUNT
⇑ witticism

one-man. 1 A **one-man** performance or business is done by only one man rather than by several people. EG *...a one-man show... ...a one-man taxi business.*

ADJ CLASSIF : ATTRIB

2 A **one-man** vehicle or tool is designed for one man or person to use. EG *...a one-man canoe.*

ADJ CLASSIF : ATTRIB

3 A **one-man** woman is a woman who likes to have only one man as her partner; an old-fashioned use. EG *I'm a one-man woman.*

ADJ CLASSIF : ATTRIB

one-man band, one-man bands. A **one-man band** is a street entertainer who wears and plays a lot of different instruments at the same time, for example drums, cymbals, and the mouth organ, using different parts of their body.

N COUNT
⇑ musician

one-night stand, one-night stands. A **one-night stand** is **1** a very brief sexual relationship, usually involving having sex with a particular person on only one occasion. EG *I'm tired of one-night stands.*

N COUNT
⇑ affair

2 a performance that is given in a particular place on only one evening, rather than on several evenings in a row. EG *I played a few one-night stands around the country.*

N COUNT

one-off, one-offs. A **one-off** is something that is made or happens only once. EG *'A one-off,' he said delightedly. 'A tailor-made gun.'* ▸ used as an adjective. EG *...one-off, hand-made items from skilled craftsmen.*

N COUNT
= original
▸ = unique
ADJ CLASSIF : ATTRIB

one-parent family, one-parent families. A **one-parent family** is a family that consists of one parent and his or her children living together, for example when the other parent has died or the parents are divorced. EG *...children from one-parent families.*

N COUNT

one-piece is used to describe clothing, for example a swimming costume, which consists of one piece only, rather than two or more separate parts. EG *Both wore one-piece swimsuits.*

ADJ CLASSIF : ATTRIB

onerous /ɒnərəs, əʊ-/. Work or tasks that are **onerous** are difficult or unpleasant; a formal word. EG *The studies involved were less onerous than those for being a lawyer.*

ADJ QUALIT
= burdensome

one's /wʌnz/. **1** A speaker or writer uses **one's** to indicate that something belongs or relates to people in general, or to himself or herself. See paragraph **10** of the entry for **one.** EG *Naturally, one wanted only the best for one's children... ...the yearning for a home of one's own.*

DET POSS

2 One's is also a spoken form of 'one is' or 'one has',

especially when 'has' is an auxiliary verb. EG *One's never quite sure exactly how things are going to turn out... 'I'll have another one,' said Ellen. 'This one's almost finished.'... One only gets the quality that one's paid for.*

oneself /wə'nself/. 1 A speaker or writer uses **oneself** 1.1 as the object of a verb or preposition in a clause where 'one' is the subject or a previous object. See paragraph **10** of the entry for **one**. EG *One must keep such interests to oneself... But how could she tell? One cannot trust oneself too far.* ▸ **Oneself** is also used to emphasize the subject or object of a clause. It is usually used in addition to a subject or object, although it is sometimes used instead of 'one' as an object. EG *Others might find odd what one finds perfectly normal oneself.* 1.2 as the object of a verb or preposition, even though 'one' has not previously been used in the clause. EG *...how to handle oneself in social situations... ...the treatment of other people and even oneself as helpless 'animals'.* — PRON REFL : SING, USED AS O; ▸ PRON REFL : SING; PRON REFL : SING, USED AS O

2 To do something **oneself**, in formal English, means to do it without any help or interference from anyone else. EG *One will have to do it oneself, then.* — PRON REFL : SING ⇑ alone

one-sided. 1 If an activity or relationship is **one-sided**, one of the people or groups involved does much more than the other or is much stronger than the other. EG *...one-sided conversations... ...a one-sided relationship.* — ADJ QUALIT ≠ balanced

2 People who are **one-sided** consider only one side of an argument, issue, or event; used showing disapproval. EG *They accused us of being one-sided.* ▸ used of things that people say or write. EG *...a one-sided account of the affair.* — ADJ QUALIT = biased

one-time; also spelled as one word. **One-time** is used to describe a job, position, or role which someone used to have, or something which happened or existed in the past. EG *...Fred Dunn, a onetime stockyard worker... A blue plaque announces the one-time presence of Canaletto.* — ADJ CLASSIF : ATTRIB = former

one-to-one. 1 A **one-to-one** relationship is one in which someone deals with only one other person. EG *Children benefit from one-to-one adult attention... ...one-to-one tuition.* — ADJ CLASSIF : ATTRIB = individual

2 A **one-to-one** comparison is one in which something is compared with something else that is broadly equivalent or similar to it. EG *These terms are not one-to-one translatable.* — ADJ CLASSIF : ATTRIB

one-track mind, one-track minds. Someone who has a **one-track mind** thinks about and is interested in only one thing. — N COUNT ⇑ obsession

one-upmanship /wʌn ʌpmənʃɪp/ is the practice of trying to appear better than someone else and make them feel inferior. — N UNCOUNT

one-way. 1 **One-way** streets or traffic systems are ones in which vehicles can only travel along in one direction. EG *...a one-way street.* — ADJ CLASSIF : USU ATTRIB

2 **One-way** describes journeys or tickets which go just to one place, rather than to that place and then back again. EG *...a one-way ticket to Jersey... ...a one-way trip.* — ADJ CLASSIF : USU ATTRIB

3 A **one-way** mirror is a mirror which acts as a window when looked through from the other side and which is often used for secretly watching people, for example prisoners. EG *He studied the prisoner by means of a one-way mirror.* — ADJ CLASSIF : ATTRIB

4 A **one-way** relationship is one in which one of the people or groups involved does everything for the other one and receives nothing in return. EG *Latin American feudalism is a one-way business... ...a relationship built up of one-way acts of service.* — ADJ CLASSIF : USU ATTRIB = one-sided

one-woman. 1 A **one-woman** performance or business is done by only one woman, rather than by several people. EG *...a thought-provoking one-woman show.* — ADJ CLASSIF : ATTRIB ⇑ solo

2 A **one-woman** man likes to have only one woman as his partner; an old-fashioned use. — ADJ CLASSIF : ATTRIB

ongoing /ɒngəʊɪŋ/. An **ongoing** situation has been happening for quite a long time and which is continuing to happen. EG *...an ongoing economic crisis... There is an ongoing discussion within the party about this.* — ADJ CLASSIF : ATTRIB ⇑ continuous

onion /ʌnjən/, **onions**. An **onion** is a small round white vegetable that grows underground and has a strong, sharp smell and taste. EG *...tomatoes and onions from the garden... ...onion soup.* ▸ used to refer to the whole plant. ● If you **know your onions**, you know or have learnt a lot about a particular subject; an informal expression. — N COUNT/UNCOUNT; ● PHR : VB INFLECTS

onlooker /ɒnlʊkə/, **onlookers**. An **onlooker** is someone who watches an event take place, without taking part in it. EG *She blew a kiss to the shivering onlookers.* — N COUNT = spectator

only /əʊnli[1]/. 1 **Only** can be placed almost anywhere in a sentence. In written English it is usually considered correct to place 'only' immediately before the thing it refers to. In spoken English, however, stress often indicates what 'only' refers to, and so there is not as much need to be careful about the position of 'only.'

2 **Only** is used to indicate that something is the one thing that is done, that happens, or that is relevant in a particular situation, in contrast to all the other possible things that are not done, do not happen, or are not relevant. EG *I'm only interested in finding out what the facts are... He could see only Kowalski, no one else... He read only paperbacks... The video is to be used for teaching purposes only... You're only here tonight because I asked for you.* ● You use **only if** to say that one thing will not happen unless another thing happens. EG *I will come only if nothing is said to the press... These snakes only attack if they feel cornered or threatened.* — ADV ⇑ exclusively; ● CONJ SUBORD ⇑ providing

3 When **only** is used with the following meanings, it usually occurs immediately after any determiner that there is in a noun group. You use **only** to describe 3.1 the single example or occurrence of something, when there are no others at all. EG *...the only survivor... I was the only one smoking... The only English city he enjoyed working in was Manchester... It was the only way out.* 3.2 the person or thing which you think is the best of a particular group and which you therefore prefer. EG *Flying is the only way to travel... Champagne really is the only drink.* ● In informal English, **the one and only** is often used in front of the name of a singer, actor, or other celebrity when they are being introduced on a show. EG *Ladies and gentlemen, please welcome the one and only Diana Ross!* — ADJ CLASSIF : ATTRIB ⇑ sole; ADJ CLASSIF : ATTRIB; ● PHR BEFORE N

4 An **only** child is a child who has no brothers or sisters. EG *I was an only child.* — ADJ CLASSIF : ATTRIB

5 You can also use **only** when you want to indicate that something is no better, worse, more important, more interesting, etc than you say it is. EG *I was only kidding... He's only a boy... It was only a squirrel... They ruled in name only.* — ADV = just, merely

6 **Only just**. You use **only just** 6.1 to say that something is true, but by such a small degree that it is almost not true at all. EG *He could only just hear them... The heat was only just bearable.* 6.2 to say that something happened a very short time ago. EG *I've only just arrived... The real work has only just begun.* — PHR : USED AS AN A = barely; PHR : USED AS AN A ⇑ just

7 You can also use **only** to indicate that you are talking not about the whole of an amount, but about a part or sample. EG *These are only some of the ways you can help... Only a tiny minority of postgraduate students were married.* — ADV + NG = just

8 **Only** can also be used 8.1 to emphasize how small an amount or number is or how short a length of time is. EG *We only paid £26... It only took half an hour... She is still only in her early forties... A chairman is elected for one meeting only... I saw them only briefly.* 8.2 to emphasize that something happened surprisingly recently. EG *This beetle has only recently been discovered... It seems like only yesterday... Peel's Police Act was only passed in 1829.* — ADV = just; ADV = just

9 You use **not only** when you are linking two statements which are remarkable or surprising in some way. The second statement is even more remarkable or surprising than the first. EG *Chimps not only use tools but make them... Not only are you funny, but you're actually witty as well... That would not only be regrettable, it would be quite disastrous.* — PHR : USED AS CONJ COORD

10 You can use **only** in front of a verb to indicate that the result of something is unfortunate or undesirable and is likely to make the situation worse rather than better. EG *This only widened the gulf between the Town Hall and the tenants... Don't expect too much. You'll only be disappointed.* — ADV WITH VB = just, merely

11 If you say you **have only to** do something, you are mentioning the simple thing that someone must do in order to understand that something is true, or to — PHR : VB INFLECTS = just, simply

prove it. EG *The gardening industry is booming. You have only to go round the nurseries at the weekend... You've only got to read the newspapers to see what can happen to hitch-hikers.*

12 Only is often used after 'can' or 'could' to emphasize that it is impossible to do anything other than the thing that is mentioned. EG *She could only obey... One can only wonder at his cheek... At first I said I would not go. I could only think it was a trick to get me there.*
ADV : MODAL + ADV + INF

13 You can also use **only** to emphasize a wish or hope. EG *I only hope the fans will have compassion... I only wish I had the money.* • **if only**: see **if**.
ADV WITH VB = just

14 In informal English, **only** can be used to add a comment which qualifies or limits what you have just said. EG *Rattlesnake is just like chicken, only tougher... But for her it's just life as usual, only lonelier... We'll wait for you. Only hurry up!*
CONJ SUBORD = but, except

15 In informal English, **only** can also be used after a conditional clause to indicate the reason why you are not going to do something. EG *I would come, only I've nothing to wear.*
CONJ SUBORD = but

16 Only can also be used before an infinitive to introduce something which happens immediately, and which you find rather surprising or unfortunate. EG *He broke off, only to resume almost at once... I finally found my watch, only to discover that it had stopped.*
ADV + *to*-INF

17 Only is also used to emphasize how appropriate a certain course of action or type of behaviour is. EG *It is only natural that she will have mixed feelings about your promotion... You really should ask before using the phone. It's only polite... It's only fair to point this out.* • **Only too** is used to emphasize that something happens or exists to a much greater extent than you would expect or like. EG *He is normally only too pleased to be advised by a woman... She remembered that night only too clearly.*
ADV + ADJ; • PHR + ADJ/ADV ⇑ very = all too

o.n.o. is an abbreviation for 'or near offer'. It is used after a price in an advertisement to indicate that the person who is selling something is willing to accept slightly less money than the sum they have mentioned. EG *...£600 o.n.o.*

onomatopoeia /ɒnəmætəpiːə/ is the formation and use of words which sound like the noise or the thing that they are describing or representing. 'Hiss,' 'buzz,' and 'rat-a-tat-tat' are examples of onomatopoeia.
N UNCOUNT ⇑ language

onomatopoeic /ɒnəmætəpiːɪk/. Language that is **onomatopoeic** uses onomatopoeia.
ADJ CLASSIF

onrush /ɒnrʌʃ/. The **onrush** of something such as a feeling or emotion is the sudden quick development of it, which happens so fast and so forcefully that you cannot control it; a fairly formal word. EG *She shut her eyes in alarm against the onrush of her tears... ...an overpowering onrush of pain.*
N SING WITH DET + *of* ⇑ onset = surge

onset /ɒnsɛt/. The **onset** of something is the beginning of it, especially when it is something unpleasant. EG *...the onset of war... ...his brave response to the onset of blindness.*
N SING : *the* + N + *of* ⇑ start

onshore /ɒnʃɔː/. **Onshore** means **1** happening or moving towards the land. EG *...a light onshore breeze.*
ADJ CLASSIF, OR ADV WITH VB

2 happening on or near land, rather than at sea. EG *The ship will be built onshore in dry dock.*
ADJ CLASSIF, OR ADV WITH VB

onslaught /ɒnslɔːt/, **onslaughts**. An **onslaught** is a very violent attack against someone or something. EG *...a co-ordinated onslaught on enemy airfields... Conservatives criticized the bill for its onslaught on family values.*
N COUNT + SUPP = assault

on-the-job. **On-the-job** training or experience is training or experience which you are given or gain while you are working.
ADJ CLASSIF : ATTRIB

on-the-spot is used to describe something that happens in a place where other things have already happened or are happening, especially when there is not time for a great deal of preparation. EG *...on-the-spot field work... ...on-the-spot investigations.*
ADJ CLASSIF : ATTRIB

onto /ɒntu/; also spelled **on to**. **1 Onto** is used to refer to movement or position in the following ways: **1.1** to indicate the place where something is put or falls, especially where it is touching or attached to something else. EG *She slammed the bottle down onto the tray... He screwed the lid tightly onto the top of the jar... The bird hopped up on to a higher branch.*
PREP ⇑ on

1.2 to indicate the place towards which someone moves or something is directed. EG *They came out of the bar onto the street... The door opened on to a dark staircase... We let our gazes drift onto other objects in the room.*
PREP

1.3 to indicate that you move into a particular position. EG *He got down onto his knees... He was pulled onto his feet.*
PREP

1.4 to indicate that you move into a bus, train, or other form of transport. EG *She watched the people get onto the train... Our equipment was being loaded onto a bus.*
PREP = on

2 Onto is also used **2.1** to introduce a new subject which is going to be discussed or a new activity which you are going to start. EG *The conversation shifts onto art and music and theatre... Let's leave it there and move onto another question... I want to come onto that in a minute.*
PREP

2.2 to indicate the person towards whom an action or emotion is directed. EG *The education of the village boys has been forced onto us... The feeling began rubbing off onto me.*
PREP = on

2.3 to say that something or someone becomes included as a part of a list or group of people. EG *She flatly refused to go onto the electoral register... ...extra workers who will come onto the labour market.*
PREP = on

3 If you are **onto** something, you are in the process of discovering it, especially when it is more important, more exciting, or better than you had previously thought. EG *They saw a royal seal so they knew that they were onto something... I think we're onto something big... As soon as the authorities get onto it, it's not allowed any more.*
PREP

onus /əʊnəs/. If you say that the **onus** is on someone to do something, you mean it is their duty or responsibility to do it; a formal word. EG *The onus was on me to earn enough to support the family... The onus of proof must lie with them.*
N SING : USU *the* + N ⇑ obligation

onward /ɒnwəd/, **onwards**. When it is an adverb, the form **onwards** is normally used in British English, and **onward** in American English or old-fashioned or formal British English. **1 Onward** means **1.1** moving forward or continuing a journey. EG *...the onward motion of the boat... ...a flight to Mykonos, with an onward boat journey to Paros.* ▸ used as an adverb. EG *Miss Ryan hurried onward... ...from China to India, and onwards to East Africa.*
ADJ CLASSIF : ATTRIB; ▸ ADV AFTER VB = forwards, on

1.2 developing, progressing, or becoming more important over a period of time. EG *...this onward march of the Labour movement.* ▸ used as an adverb. EG *The world was moving onward... In the Civil Service, he might have gone onwards and upwards.*
ADJ CLASSIF : ATTRIB; ▸ ADV AFTER VB = on

2 From then onward, from 1960 onwards, etc is used to say that something begins to happen at the time or date mentioned, and continues to happen after that: see also **on**. EG *From that time onward he had never spoken to her again... ...from the seventies onwards... ...from January of next year onwards.*
PHR : USED AS AN A

onyx /ɒnɪks/ is a semi-precious stone which can be various colours. It is used for making ornaments, jewellery, etc.
N UNCOUNT

oo /uː/. See **ooh**.

oodles /uːdəᵊlz/. **Oodles** of something means a very large quantity of it; an informal word. EG *...corn on the cob with oodles of butter.*
N PART : PLURAL

ooh /uː/; also spelled **oo**. People say **ooh** when they are surprised, looking forward to something, or find something pleasant or unpleasant; an informal word. EG *Oo, I like going swimming... Ooh, you are awful... Ooh, that feels nice.*
EXCLAM

oomph /ʊmf/ means the forceful energy or liveliness that someone or something has; an informal word. EG *They want to show that Jamaica's got oomph... He gave it all the extra oomph he could.*
N UNCOUNT = verve, vitality

oops /ʊps, uːps/. You say **oops** to indicate that there has been a slight accident or mistake, or to apologise to someone for it; an informal word. EG *'Oops, sorry.'... 'Oops! He's fallen down.'*
EXCLAM = whoops

ooze /uːz/, **oozes, oozing, oozed**. **1** When a thick or sticky liquid **oozes**, or something **oozes** it, it flows slowly and in small quantities. EG *...blood oozing from his wounds... The yolk oozes out... His sandals oozed black slime.*
V : USU + A = trickle, seep

2 Ooze is any thick, sticky, liquid substance, especially the mud at the bottom of a river, lake, or the sea. EG *...ooze and sand.*
N UNCOUNT = sludge

3 If someone **oozes** a quality or feeling, or **oozes** with it, they show or express it too strongly, often when they do not really have or feel it; used showing disapproval. EG *His letter, oozing remorse, appeared*
V + O, OR V + A *(with)* = drip

in all the newspapers... Her voice oozed with politeness.

op /ɒp/, **ops**; an informal word. An **op** is 1 a medical operation. EG *She was in hospital to have an op.* 2 a military operation. EG *...the Ops room... ...whenever he went on ops.* N COUNT; N COUNT : USU PL

op. is an abbreviation for 'opus'. EG *...Three Pieces for Orchestra, op.6.* N UNCOUNT + NUM

opacity /əʊpæsɪti[1]/; a formal word. **Opacity** is 1 the quality of being difficult to see through. EG *...the opacity of the paper.* 2 the quality of being difficult to understand. EG *...Coleridge's opacity.* N UNCOUNT; N UNCOUNT = obscurity

opal /əʊpə[0]l/, **opals**. An **opal** is a precious stone which is usually colourless or of a milky white colour, but which seems to change in colour according to its surroundings. N COUNT/ UNCOUNT

opalescent /əʊpəlesənt/ means colourless or milky white like an opal, or changing colour like an opal. EG *...an opalescent veil... The sky was covered with an opalescent vapour.* ADJ CLASSIF : USU ATTRIB = iridescent

opaque /əʊpeɪk/; a formal or literary word. 1 An object or substance that is **opaque** has enough thickness or colour to prevent you from seeing through it, or light from passing through it. EG *...the opaque windows of the jail.* ADJ QUALIT ≠ transparent

2 Someone or something that is **opaque** is difficult to understand. EG *Their intentions remained opaque.* ADJ CLASSIF : USU PRED

op. cit. is used after an author's name to refer to a book of theirs which has already been mentioned; a formal expression used in written English. EG *...Simone de Beauvoir, op. cit.*

OPEC /əʊpɛk/ is an organization of countries who produce and sell oil, which tries to develop a common policy and system of prices; an abbreviation for 'Organization of Petroleum-Exporting Countries'. EG *...fuel bought from OPEC... ...the OPEC countries.* N PROPER

open /əʊpə[0]n/, **opens, opening, opened.** 1 If you **open** something such as a door, or if it **opens**, you change its position or unlock it so that air, light, things or people can pass through. EG *She opened the door with her key... The door opened.* ▸ used as an adjective. EG *...the open window... The drawer slid open... He pushed open the front door.* ● If an action **opens the door** or **opens doors** to something, it makes a situation possible or allows people to do something which was not possible before. EG *The country opened the door to imports... Use your contacts to open doors and meet the people who matter.* V-ERG ⇑ move ≠ close; ▸ ADJ CLASSIF ≠ closed; ● PHR : VB AND N INFLECT

2 If you **open** a bottle, box, or other container, you remove or unfasten the lid, cork, or other device that keeps it closed. EG *Open the toolbox... I opened a can of beans.* ▸ used as an adjective. EG *...an open packet of cigarettes... Boylan couldn't get the bottle open.* V+O; ▸ ADJ CLASSIF

3 If you **open** a letter or parcel, you cut or tear the envelope, or remove its wrapping. EG *I'll open the mail after breakfast.* ▸ used as an adjective. EG *...the open telegram on her desk... He tore open the envelope.* ● See also **open letter**. V+O; ▸ ADJ CLASSIF

4 If you **open** a book, you move its covers apart in order to read or write on the pages inside. EG *Open the book at page 23.* ▸ used as an adjective. EG *...the open Bible... She kept her diary open.* ● If you describe someone as an **open book**, you mean that it is easy to know what they are thinking or why they are doing something. V+O ≠ close, shut; ▸ ADJ CLASSIF; ● PHR : USED AS C

5 If you **open** your mouth, you move your lips and teeth apart, for example in order to eat, speak or express surprise or shock. EG *'Open wide and point to the tooth that hurts.'* ▸ used as an adjective. EG *Angelica looked at me with her mouth open.* ● See also **open-mouthed**. V+O, OR V+A *(wide)* ≠ close, shut; ▸ ADJ CLASSIF ≠ closed

6 If you do not **open** your mouth on a particular occasion, you do not say anything; an informal use. EG *No man dared open his mouth, or out he went!... 'For goodness sake don't open your mouth.'* V+O = say a word

7 If you **have** or **keep** your **ears open**, 7.1 you are listening very hard to hear a noise. EG *Can you keep your ears open for the phone?* 7.2 you are paying great attention to what people say around you because you want to know some particular information. PHR : VB INFLECTS; PHR : VB INFLECTS

8 If you **open** your eyes, you move your eyelids upwards, for example when you wake up, so that you can see. ● If you **open** your **eyes wide**, you are expressing surprise or shock. EG *She opened her eyes wide and stared at me.* ● If you **open** your **eyes** or someone's **eyes** to something, you make yourself or them realize the truth about a situation, especially when the truth is unpleasant. EG *Now my eyes have been opened, I shall never trust him again.* V+O; ● PHR : VB INFLECTS; ● PHR : VB INFLECTS

9 If you **have** or **keep your eye** or **eyes open, 9.1** you are looking for something that you want to find, for example when it has been lost. **9.2** you are being very careful because there is a possibility of danger. EG *Keep your eyes open for trouble.* PHR : VB INFLECTS; PHR : VB INFLECTS = watch out

10 If you **open** your hand, you unfold your fingers so that the palm of your hand can be seen, usually in order to reveal what you have been hiding in it. V+O = unclasp

11 If you **open** your arms, you stretch them wide apart in front of you, for example when you are going to hug someone. ● If you accept or welcome a person, situation, or idea **with open arms**, you accept or welcome them with a lot of pleasure and enthusiasm. EG *Our teaching degree is welcomed with open arms in many countries.* V+O = throw wide; ● PHR : USED AS AN A = enthusiastically

12 If you **open** your mind to new ideas, you become ready and willing to accept and to try and understand their good qualities and possible benefits. EG *Open your mind to some new thoughts.* ◊ **openness.** EG *...his openness of mind on historical evidence.* ▸ used as an adjective. EG *She tried to keep an open mind on such subjects.* to **open** your **heart**: see **heart**. ● See also **open-minded**. V+O; ◊ N UNCOUNT; ▸ ⇑ receptive; ADJ CLASSIF ⇑ receptive

13 If you describe someone or their character as **open**, you mean they are honest and do not want or try to hide anything or to deceive anyone. EG *Judy had an open and trusting nature... ...an open friendly smile.* ◊ **openness.** EG *...their relaxed openness.* ADJ QUALIT = candid, frank; ◊ N UNCOUNT

14 If you are **open** to ideas, suggestions, etc, you are ready and willing to accept them and to try and understand their good qualities and possible benefits. EG *He was always open to ideas... We are open to suggestions.* ADJ QUALIT : PRED + *to* = receptive

15 If you say that a person, idea, system, etc is **open** to criticism, blame, praise, etc you mean they are likely to receive it because of the qualities they possess or the effects they have had. EG *The critic is open to attack... Such a description is open to misunderstanding.* ADJ CLASSIF : PRED + *to* = susceptible

16 When a shop, office, or public building **opens** or you **open** it, **16.1** its doors are unlocked, the people in it start working, and customers or clients can use it. EG *He sat outside, waiting for the bar to open... When does the library open?* ▸ used as an adjective. EG *The firm kept its office open in Delhi.* ◊ **opening.** EG *The Gallery is experimenting with evening opening.* ● See also **opening hours, opening time**. **16.2** it starts operating for the first time. EG *They're opening an office in Birmingham... Philips opened up four new factories last year.* V-ERG ≠ close, shut; ▸ ADJ CLASSIF; ◊ N UNCOUNT; V-ERG = set up

17 If you **open** a building, public area, or institution you declare officially, usually at a public ceremony, that it is now ready to be used or to start operating. EG *When Parliament is opened, the Queen enters under Victoria Tower.* ◊ **opening.** EG *...the opening of the new theatre.* ▸ used as an adjective. EG *Lord Shawcross declared the hotel open.* V+O; ◊ N UNCOUNT; ▸ ADJ CLASSIF : PRED

18 If you **open** a private place such as a house or garden, you specially allow people to visit it at certain times, usually because it is very old or connected with a famous person. EG *The Colonel opens his garden for the National Gardens scheme.* ▸ used as an adjective. EG *Hagley Hall is often open to the public at weekends.* ● See also **open day, open house**. V+O; ▸ ADJ CLASSIF : PRED

19 If a country **opens** its **borders** or **frontiers**, it starts to allow people and goods to pass freely between it and other countries. EG *The Japanese opened their borders to Western goods in 1853.* PHR : VB INFLECTS

20 When a public event such as a conference, or an artistic event like a play or film **opens**, it begins to take place, be shown, or be performed for a limited period of time. EG *The trade union conference opened last week... We went on tour before opening in London in 'The Three Sisters.'* ◊ **opening, openings.** EG *...the opening of 'Nicholas Nickleby' on Broadway.* ● See also **opening night**. V ⇑ start; ◊ N UNCOUNT + SUPP/N COUNT = first night

21 If a person or activity **opens** or **opens** a particular event, they start the event by being the first person to perform or the first activity to occur, when other people or activities will follow. EG *Driberg opened with a question on finance... Senator Denton opened* V OR V+O = commence

the hearing by reminding us of our duty... Gooch opened the batting for England.

22 If a military action **opens** or you **open** it, it begins. EG *The Allies opened a general offensive against them.* V-ERG ⇑ start

23 If you **open fire**, you start shooting. EG *Police opened fire on a mob of rioters.* PHR : VB INFLECTS

24 If you **open** an account with a bank or a commercial organization, you begin to use their services, by giving them some money to look after or invest, or by buying goods from them on credit. EG *I'm opening an account to save up for a new car.* V+O ⇑ start

25 If someone or something **opens** the way to a new state or situation, **opens** opportunities for it, etc, they allow it to develop by changing the circumstances, people's attitudes, etc. EG *Wealth opened new opportunities for education.* V+O = create

26 If you **open** something that is blocked or it **opens**, the obstruction is removed and you can pass through. EG *It took three days to clear the snow and open the road to traffic... The crowd opened and let us pass.* ▸ used as an adjective. EG *They try to keep the Pass open all winter.* V-ERG ▸ = passable ≠ blocked ADJ CLASSIF

27 If a place **opens** to, into, or onto another place, **27.1** you can go straight from one to the other, for example through a door. EG *These rooms have doors opening directly to the garden.* V+A = lead **27.2** it gradually becomes larger or wider until you reach the second place. EG *The passage opened out into a cavern.* V+*out* ⇑ widen

28 When flowers **open**, they change from being buds and their petals spread out. EG *Roses opened and fell within the day.* ▸ used as an adjective. EG *The small white flowers are open in May.* V = unfold ▸ ADJ CLASSIF : USU PRED

29 If you say **the clouds, the heavens,** or **the skies open**, you mean that it starts to pour with rain; a literary expression. EG *The clouds opened and there was a terrific thunderstorm.* PHR : VB INFLECTS

30 An **open** area of land, sea, etc is a large area that is not blocked or obstructed, for example the land has few buildings or trees, or the sea is not close to land and has few islands. EG *The road stretched across open country... ...the wide open spaces... ...cut off from the open sea.* ◇ **openness**. EG *...the openness of Vincent Square.* ADJ CLASSIF : ATTRIB ◇ N UNCOUNT

31 An **open** structure or object is not covered or completely enclosed. EG *The wind roared across the open car... ...an open fire in the lounge.* ● See also **open-plan**. ADJ CLASSIF : ATTRIB ⇑ uncovered

32 If you do something **in the open**, you do it outdoors rather than in a house or other building. EG *The children enjoyed sleeping out in the open.* ● See also **open air**. PHR : USED AS AN A = outside

33 An **open** wound, sore, etc is one in which the skin is damaged and blood or pus is oozing out. ADJ CLASSIF

34 If something that you are wearing, for example a jacket, is **open**, it is not fastened by buttons, a zip, etc. EG *...an open black raincoat.* ● See also **open-necked**. ADJ CLASSIF = undone

35 An **open** situation, attitude, or way of behaving is one that is not kept hidden or secret. EG *Their dispute finally broke out into open war... ...open government... ...open criticism.* ● See also **open secret**. ◇ **openness**. EG *...the openness of the reporting of the war.* ADJ CLASSIF : ATTRIB ◇ N UNCOUNT = frankness

36 If an attitude or situation is **in the open**, or is brought out **into the open**, etc, people are told about it or made aware of it, and it is no longer kept secret. EG *The hostility was out in the open now... Problems may be brought out into the open.* PHR : USED AS AN A

37 If a meeting, invitation, or competition is **open**, anyone is allowed to join in, accept, or compete in it. EG *Most Council meetings are open to the public at all times... The discussion was thrown open to all present.* ● See also **open market**. ADJ CLASSIF ≠ closed

38 If you describe a situation or topic as **open**, you mean that it is being discussed or considered, or has been deliberately left undecided, for example because all the facts are not yet known. EG *I let joining the Party remain an open question... They had left their options open... Whether they actually are friends is open to debate.* ● See also **open-ended**. ADJ CLASSIF : IF+ PREP THEN *to* ≠ settled, resolved

39 If you describe opportunities as **open** to someone, you mean that they are freely available to them. EG *We should use the opportunities now open to us.* ADJ CLASSIF : PRED+*to*

40 If a job is **open**, it is available for someone to have or to apply for. EG *I'm afraid the vacancy is no longer open.* ADJ CLASSIF : PRED = vacant

41 **Open** is used to describe sports events in which anyone can compete, especially an annual golf tournament in which both amateurs and professionals can play. EG *...the Women's Open Golf Championship.* ▸ used as a noun. EG *Nicklaus won the Open at St Andrews in 1978.* ADJ CLASSIF : ALSO IN NAMES ▸ N SING : *the*+N, ALSO IN NAMES

open out. If someone **opens out**, they start to say exactly what they think or feel about something or someone. EG *She found it difficult to open out to people.* PHRASAL VB : V+ ADV

open up. **1** If someone **opens up**, they start to say exactly what they think or feel about something or someone. EG *She was disappointed that he hadn't opened up about Gretchen.* PHRASAL VB : V+ ADV, USU+*about* ⇑ speak

2 When an opportunity **opens up**, or when a situation **opens up** an opportunity, the situation gives you that opportunity. EG *All sorts of possibilities began to open up... Politics opens up incomparable opportunities.* PHRASAL VB : V-ERG+ADV ⇑ form

3 If a place or area **opens up**, or you **open** it **up**, it becomes easier to get to, or provides opportunities for development. EG *Brunel opened up the West... The land is beginning to open up.* PHRASAL VB : V-ERG+ADV

4 If someone with a gun **opens up**, they start shooting. EG *They opened up as the convoy came abreast of them.* PHRASAL VB : V+ ADV ⇑ shoot

5 When you **open up** a building or when you **open up**, you unlock and open the door so that people can get in. EG *'Open up! It's snowing out here.'* PHRASAL VB : V+ ADV, OR V+O+ ADV

open air; often used before another noun and spelled with a hyphen. The **open air** means outside rather than in a building. EG *Dry clothes in the open air, if possible... ...heated open-air swimming pools.* N SING : *the*+N = outdoor

open-and-shut. A problem, legal matter, or dispute that is **open-and-shut** is easily decided or solved because the facts are very clear. EG *An open-and-shut murder case.* ADJ CLASSIF = straightforward

open-cast; also spelled as one word. An **open-cast** mine is a mine in which the coal or other minerals are near the surface and underground passages are not needed. ADJ CLASSIF

open day, open days. An **open day** is a special occasion on which a school, university, or other institution is open for the public to visit. EG *You can see his work and meet the teacher on open days.* N COUNT

open-ended. A discussion or activity that is **open-ended** is started or done without the intention of achieving a particular decision or result. EG *They had an open-ended discussion on the problem... The experiments may be genuinely open-ended... ...open-ended questions.* ADJ CLASSIF ⇑ indefinite

opener /əʊpə^{o}nə/, **openers**. **1** An **opener** is a tool which is used to open containers such as tins or bottles. EG *Where did you hide the can opener?... ...a tin opener... ...a bottle opener... ...a letter opener.* ● See also **eye-opener**. N COUNT : MOD+ N

2 **For openers** is used **2.1** to emphasize that something is only the first action or stage in a process or situation; an informal expression. EG *'Is that good enough?'–'For openers,' Rudolph said... For openers, he'd take the job at the Met.* PHR : USED AS AN A = for starters **2.2** to emphasize that an amount is only an approximate guess and that it is likely to be more; an informal expression. EG *'I'd say about a million dollars, for openers.'* PHR : USED AS AN A = for starters

open house is used to refer to a situation in which people allow friends or visitors to come to their house whenever they want to. EG *It was open house to a fairly closed circle of friends... They keep open house.* N UNCOUNT

opening /əʊpə^{o}nɪŋ/, **openings**. **1** **Opening** is the act of opening something: see **open**. N UNCOUNT

2 The **opening** item or part of something is the item or part that comes first. EG *...his opening remarks... ...the opening stages of fighting... ...the opening scene of the play.* ADJ CLASSIF : ATTRIB ⇑ beginning

3 An **opening** is **3.1** the first part of something, for example a book or a concert. EG *The main characters are established in the opening of the book.* N COUNT ⇑ beginning **3.2** the first moves in a game of chess, especially a series of moves that is often used. N COUNT

4 An **opening** is also **4.1** a hole or empty space through which air, light, things, or people can pass. EG *A small opening is left at the top... We slid through the opening into the field.* N COUNT **4.2** a good opportunity to do something, for example to talk about a particular subject. EG *Charlotte herself provided me with an opening.* N COUNT : IF+ PREP THEN *for* **4.3** a job that is available. EG *There were* N COUNT *openings in the police force... A degree can lead to many openings in public service.*

opening hours are the times during which a shop, bank, library, or pub are open for business. EG *Banks often have very short opening hours.* N PLURAL

opening night, opening nights. The **opening night** of a play, opera, etc is the first night on which a particular production of it is performed. EG *I was at the opening night with my parents.* N COUNT = premier

opening time is the time that a shop, bank, library, or pub opens for business. EG *Men would be hanging around the pub doors at opening time.* N UNCOUNT

open letter, open letters. An **open letter** is a letter that is published in a newspaper or magazine and is written by one famous person to another, usually in order to protest or complain about something. EG *...an article headed 'Open Letter to Dr. Verwoerd'... They organised an open letter to the Labour movement.* N COUNT

openly /əʊpəᵒnliˡ/. If you do something **openly**, you do it without trying to hide any facts or your feelings. EG *His mother wept openly... Margaret was openly angry at the other women... It's better to admit it openly.* ADV ≠ secretly

open market. The **open market** is used to refer to the normal process of buying and selling goods, in which the goods are advertised and sold publicly and not privately: compare **black market**. EG *He was able to sell his work in the open market... You won't get a picture as good as this on the open market.* N SING : the+N

open-minded. Someone who is **open-minded** is willing to listen to and consider other people's ideas and suggestions. EG *...an intelligent, open-minded man... ...an open-minded approach to new techniques.* ◊ **open-mindedness**. ADJ QUALIT ⇑ receptive ◊ N UNCOUNT

open-mouthed. Someone who is **open-mouthed** is very surprised about something and has their mouth open. EG *She was staring open-mouthed at a picture of her father... Bowman leaned forwards in open-mouthed astonishment.* ADJ CLASSIF ⇑ amazed

open-necked. If you are wearing an **open-necked** shirt or blouse, you are wearing a shirt or blouse with the top button unfastened and no tie. EG *...dressed in open-necked shirt and shorts.* ADJ CLASSIF : ATTRIB

open-plan. A building or room that is **open-plan** has no walls that divide it into smaller areas. EG *Her first job was in an open-plan office.* ADJ CLASSIF

open secret, open secrets. An **open secret** is something which is supposed to be a secret, but that many people know about. EG *It is an open secret that he has just become engaged.* N COUNT

Open University. The **Open University** is a university in Britain that runs degree courses on the radio and television for students who do not have the proper qualifications and want to study part-time or mainly at home. Students send their work by post to their tutors. EG *After two years she had four of the six credits needed for her B.A. at the Open University.* N PROPER : the+N

opera /ɒpəᵒrə/, **operas**. 1 An **opera** is 1.1 a play with music in which most of the words are sung. EG *...tickets for the opera... ...a Wagner opera.* ● **Soap opera**: see **soap**. 1.2 an organization or group of people who perform operas. EG *...the English National Opera.* N COUNT ⇑ entertainment; N IN NAMES

2 **Opera** is the branch of music and drama that relates to operas. EG *Are you interested in opera?... A book on Italian opera... ...an opera singer.* N UNCOUNT ⇑ genre

opera house, opera houses. An **opera house** is a theatre that is specially designed for the performance of operas. EG *...the Royal Opera House.* N COUNT : ALSO IN NAMES

operate /ɒpəreɪt/, **operates, operating, operated**. 1 When a business or organization **operates** or you **operate** it, the people in it work in a planned way over a period of time or in a particular place. EG *The multinational companies which operate in their country... He operates an Afghan news service here... ...package tours operating from the States.* ◊ **operation**. EG *...in the bus service's first year of operation.* V-ERG; ◊ N UNCOUNT

2 When military forces **operate** in a particular region, they are there in order to carry out their orders, usually as part of a larger plan or campaign. EG *Police patrols operated throughout the area... ...Canadian aircraft operating from Newfoundland.* V+A ⇑ act

3 When a rule, system, or force **operates**, it works in a particular way or has a particular effect. EG *Laws of the same kind operate in nature... We discussed how language operates... Two sorts of forces operate on it.* ◊ **operation**. EG *...to try to limit the operation of the contract.* V = function; ◊ N UNCOUNT

4 To **operate** a particular method of doing something means to choose to use it when organizing or running a larger system. EG *These countries operate variants of the capitalist system... Will you operate a voluntary policy of wage restraint?* V+O

5 When you **operate** a machine or device, or it **operates** , you make it work. EG *...how to operate the safety equipment... ...the way calculators operated.* ◊ **operation**. EG *...instructions for the operation of machinery.* V-ERG; ◊ N UNCOUNT

6 When doctors **operate**, they cut open a person's body in order to remove, replace or repair a diseased or damaged part of it. EG *They operated but it was too late... His knees have been operated on three times.* ◊ **operating**. EG *...an old man on the operating table.* V; ◊ ADJ CLASSIF : ATTRIB

operatic /ɒpəræ̱tɪk/ means relating to opera. EG *...symphonic, choral and operatic elements... ...operatic roles.* ADJ CLASSIF : USU ATTRIB ⇑ musical

operating theatre, operating theatres. An **operating theatre** is a special room in a hospital where surgeons carry out medical operations. N COUNT

operation /ɒpəreɪ̱ʃəᵒn/, **operations**. 1 An **operation** is 1.1 a planned activity that involves many actions or many people doing different things. EG *...the biggest police operation in French history... Learn about the company's operations... ...taxes at each stage of the operation.* 1.2 a complicated action or a series of actions that is done to produce a particular result. EG *...certain machine tool operations... The operations are repeated for each circuit.* N COUNT : USU+SUPP; N COUNT

2 A military **operation** is an action that is usually part of a larger plan. EG *...the most successful operation of the war... ...military operations in Europe.* N COUNT

3 An **operation** is also a business or company; used especially when you indicate the type of commercial activity they are involved in. EG *Multiponics, a large-scale farming operation, went bankrupt in 1971.* N COUNT : USU MOD+N = enterprise

4 A medical **operation** is a form of treatment in which a doctor cuts open a patient's body in order to remove, replace, or repair a diseased or damaged part of it. EG *Her mother was about to undergo a major operation... ...heart operations... I had an operation on my spine.* N COUNT

6 **In operation**. 6.1 If a machine or device is **in operation**, it is working. EG *...gas drilling rigs in operation in the USA.* 6.2 If a plan or system is **in operation**, it is being used. EG *Similar schemes were in operation in other countries.* PHR : USED AS AN A; PHR : USED AS AN A = in use

7 If a rule, system, or plan **comes into operation** or you **put** it **into operation**, you begin to use it. EG *When's that syllabus coming into operation? The plans were put into operation immediately.* PHR : VB INFLECTS = be implemented

8 See also **operate**.

operational /ɒpəreɪ̱ʃəᵒnəl, -ʃənəᵒl/. 1 A machine or piece of equipment that is **operational** is working or able to be used. EG *...fifty operational warships... ...a fully operational rifle.* ADJ CLASSIF ⇑ usable

2 **Operational** is used to describe actions, situations, or problems that occur when a plan or system is being carried out in practice. EG *...operational difficulties... They move to their operational positions.* ADJ CLASSIF : ATTRIB

operative /ɒpəᵒrətɪv/, **operatives**. 1 Something that is **operative** is working or having an effect. EG *The scheme was fully operative by 1975... ...the operative side of the business.* ADJ CLASSIF

2 If you describe a word that has been used as **the operative word**, you want to draw attention to it because you think it is important or exactly true in a particular situation, and often when you are making a joke by using it with a slightly different meaning. EG *'He's a hard nut to crack,' said Sergeant Yates. 'Nut being the operative word,' said Flint. '...a couple of thousand other music lovers.'–'The operative word is lovers,' said Jean.* PHR : USED AS C

3 An **operative** is 3.1 a worker, especially one with a manual skill; a formal use. EG *...each operative on a production line... ...the Federation of Building Trades Operatives.* 3.2 a spy or secret service agent; used especially in American English. EG *...a secret overseas operative... ...FBI operatives.* N COUNT; N COUNT

operator /ɒpəreɪtə/, **operators**. 1 An **operator** is 1.1 a person who works at a telephone exchange or at the switchboard of an office or hotel. EG *He dialled* N COUNT OR VOC ⇑ worker

the operator... 'Hello?'-'Operator?'-'Yes'.-'Can you help me?' **1.2** a person who is employed to operate or control a machine. EG *...computer operators... ...farm-machine operators.* **1.3** a person who runs a business; often used showing disapproval. EG *...tour operators... ...unscrupulous operators... ...small-time operators.*
N COUNT+SUPP ⇑ worker
N COUNT+SUPP

2 If you call someone a good **operator**, you mean that they are skilful at achieving what they want, often in a slightly dishonest way; an informal use. EG *You're a great operator, why don't you talk to them?... He was a really smooth operator.*
N COUNT : MOD+N ⇑ person

operetta /ɒpərɛtə/, **operettas**. An **operetta** is a type of opera which is light-hearted and often comic and has some of the words spoken rather than sung. EG *...Viennese operetta... ...the operettas of Gilbert and Sullivan.*
N COUNT/UNCOUNT ⇑ entertainment

ophthalmic /ɒfθælmɪk/ means relating to or concerned with the medical care of your eyes and your eyesight; a formal word. EG *...dental, ophthalmic and nursing staff... ...an ophthalmic optician.*
ADJ CLASSIF : ATTRIB

opiate /əʊpɪət/, **opiates**; a formal word. **1** An **opiate** is a drug that contains opium. Opiates can reduce pain or cause you to sleep. EG *...repeated doses of opiates.*
N COUNT

2 If you call something an **opiate**, you mean it makes people think less or spend less time on important activities. EG *They rejected the cinema as a mindless opiate that would destroy good conversation... ...the Marxist view of religion as the opiate of the poor.*
N COUNT : USU+SUPP ⇑ pacifier

opine /ə⁶paɪn/, **opines, opined**. To **opine** means to express your opinion; a very formal and old-fashioned word. EG *I opine that at this end of the table we have an obvious candidate... 'It's quite long enough,' she opined.*
V+QUOTE/REPORT-CL, NO CONT ⇑ say

opinion /əpɪnjən/, **opinions**. **1** An **opinion** is **1.1** a statement of what someone thinks or believes about something. EG *The students were eager to express their opinions... If you want my honest opinion, I don't think it will work... ...a personal opinion.* ● You add **in my opinion, in their opinion**, etc to a statement to emphasize that it is what you or someone else thinks, and not necessarily a fact. EG *'Very sensible, in my opinion.'... Information of this nature was valuable, in his opinion.* **1.2** someone's judgement of another person's character or ability. EG *My opinion of Mr Smith rose sharply... After their bad results, they are not likely to have a very good opinion of themselves.*
N COUNT : USU POSS+N IN SING ⇑ belief
● PHR : USED AS ADV SEN
N SING : USU WITH POSS/MOD, N+*of* = estimation

2 If someone **is of the opinion** that something is the case, it is their firm belief. EG *He is of the opinion that money is not important... They were of the opinion that Jack had done the right thing... Many of his friends were of the same opinion.*
PHR : VB INFLECTS = feel

3 Opinion is **3.1** the way in which someone thinks, especially about what is right and what is wrong. EG *We want a broad range of interest and opinion... Difficulties arise where there's a difference of opinion.* ● **Matter of opinion**: see **matter**. **3.2** beliefs or views which are held by a large group of people. EG *...changes in public opinion... ...international opinion... ...the impact on world opinion.*
N UNCOUNT ⇑ belief
N UNCOUNT : USU MOD+N ⇑ feeling

4 An **opinion** from an expert is the advice or judgement that they give you in the subject that they know a lot about. EG *Get an independent opinion before you buy the house... My doctor asked a specialist for a second opinion on my X-rays.*
N COUNT : USU SING

opinionated /əpɪnjəneɪtɪ²d/. Someone who is **opinionated** is very sure that what they believe is right; used showing disapproval. EG *...this inexperienced but opinionated newcomer... ...when they are older and more opinionated.*
ADJ QUALIT

opinion poll, opinion polls. An **opinion poll** is an organized process of asking people for their opinion on a particular subject, especially concerning politics. EG *...a public opinion poll conducted by the German government... Opinion polls suggest that the Social Democrats will gain few seats.*
N COUNT

opium /əʊpɪəm/ is a drug made from the seeds of a type of poppy. It is used in medicines that reduce people's pain and cause them to sleep, but is also used by some people who want to experience its effects. Opium is illegal in many countries. EG *I shall give her a dose of opium... He smoked opium and hashish.*
N UNCOUNT

opossum /əpɒsəm/, **opossums**. An **opossum** is a small animal that lives in America. It carries its young in a pouch on its body, and has thick fur and a long tail.
N COUNT ⇑ marsupial

opp. is an abbreviation for 'opposite'.

opponent /əpəʊnənt/, **opponents**. An **opponent** is **1** a person who is against you in a disagreement, fight, contest, or game. EG *...their political opponents... He beat his opponent three sets to love... ...a massive punch to the jaw of his opponent.* **2** a person who disagrees with something and criticizes it or tries to change it. EG *...opponents of apartheid... ...a leading opponent of the budget cuts.*
N COUNT : USU POSS+N = adversary
N COUNT : IF+PREP THEN *of* = enemy

opportune /ɒpətju:n/ means happening at the time that is most convenient for someone or most likely to lead to success; a formal word. EG *It was most opportune that Mrs Davenport should arrive... The call came at an opportune moment for me.*
ADJ QUALIT = providential

opportunism /ɒpətju:nɪzə⁰m/ is a way of behaving in which you are quick to use any opportunity that occurs in order to gain money or power, and do not worry about whether your actions are right or wrong; a formal word, used showing disapproval. EG *He was accused of commercial opportunism... ...the sort of cynical opportunism the British media expected.*
N UNCOUNT

opportunist /ɒpətju:nɪst/, **opportunists**. An **opportunist** is someone who takes advantage of any situation that will help them personally, without considering whether their actions are right or wrong; a formal word, used showing disapproval. EG *...no heroes, only opportunists committed to survival.* ▸ used as an adjective. EG *The party grew more reformist and opportunist... ...a purely opportunist view.*
N COUNT = adventurer
▸ ADJ QUALIT = self-seeking

opportunistic /ɒpətju:nɪstɪk/ means behaving in an opportunist way, or having opportunist ideas; a formal word. EG *...an opportunistic foreign policy... His unprincipled and opportunistic changes of position.*
ADJ QUALIT = unscrupulous

opportunity /ɒpətju:nɪti¹/, **opportunities**. An **opportunity** is a situation that makes it possible for you to do something that you want to do. EG *...equal pay and opportunities for women... It will give you an opportunity to meet all kinds of people. ...their lack of opportunity.* ● If you do something **at the earliest** or **first opportunity**, you do it as soon as you are able to. EG *Contact us at the earliest opportunity... They would return to power at the first opportunity.* ● If you do something **at every opportunity**, you do it whenever it is possible. EG *...their willingness to help at every opportunity.*
N COUNT/UNCOUNT ⇑ possibility = prospect
● PHR : USED AS AN A
● PHR : USED AS AN A

oppose /əpəʊz/, **opposes, opposing, opposed**. **1** If you **oppose** someone or something, you express your strong disagreement with them or disapproval of them, often in a formal way by making speeches or writing letters. EG *Your father opposed your wish to become a sculptor... He opposed the founding of the Gallery... The measure is opposed by the Treasury Department.*
V+O = contest

2 If you **are opposed to** something, you strongly disapprove of it because you think it is wrong, evil, or stupid. EG *He was opposed to the development of nuclear weapons... The civil service was strongly opposed to the new Ministry.*
PHR : AUX INFLECTS = be against

3 If you **oppose yourself to** someone or something, you express your firm disagreement with a particular view, belief, or person; a formal use. EG *Golub opposed himself to this view.*
PHR : VB INFLECTS = contest

4 You use **as opposed to** when you are contrasting two things and you want to emphasize the first one. EG *He was wearing a grey lightweight suit as opposed to his usual check sports jacket... There's a need for technical colleges as opposed to universities.*
PREP

5 If you **oppose** one thing to another thing, you deliberately contrast them in order to emphasize a particular point of view. EG *'Art', when it is opposed to 'Science', is often romantic.*
V+O+A *(to)* ⇑ compare

opposed /əpəʊzd/ is used to describe two ideas, systems, etc that are very different from each other, especially when the people involved have very strong feelings against each other. EG *...two bitterly opposed schools of socialist thought... ...a strategy which is diametrically opposed to that of the previous government.*
ADJ CLASSIF : IF PRED, +*to* = opposite, conflicting

opposing /əpəʊzɪŋ/ is used to describe two ideas that are too different to fit into the same system or plan. EG *There are two opposing tendencies in your recent work... Parents and children are on opposing*
ADJ CLASSIF = opposite

sides of most arguments... We held almost diametrically opposing points of view.

opposite /ɒpəzɪt, -sɪt/, **opposites**. 1 If one thing is **opposite** another, it is on the other side of a space from it. EG *The hotel is opposite a railway station... Lynn was sitting opposite him... The man opposite lifts down her case... Opposite is St. Paul's Church.* PREP OR ADV

2 **Opposite** is used to describe something or the part of something that is furthest away from you or from something else. EG *...on the opposite side of the street... Ellen and Hooper were sitting at opposite ends of the couch... She burst in through the opposite door.* ADJ CLASSIF : USU ATTRIB = far

3 Something that is **opposite** something else on a list, an official form, or other piece of writing is next to it or on the same line. EG *Opposite his own name was a small tick... The man wrote 'fifty dollars' opposite the word VALUE.* PREP OR ADV = by

4 The **opposite** of someone or something is the person or thing that is most different from them. EG *My brother is just the opposite... In many ways, passion is the opposite of love.* N COUNT : USU *the*+N IN SING = reverse

5 **Opposite** is used to describe something that is completely different from another thing that you have mentioned, or to describe two things that are completely different from each other. EG *I wanted to impress them but probably had the opposite effect... ...two opposite ways of improving it... Paul turned and walked in the opposite direction... ...two drums rotating in opposite directions... Sherlock Holmes took the opposite point of view.* ADJ CLASSIF : USU ATTRIB ● **The opposite sex** refers to men if you are a woman or talking about women, and refers to women if you are a man or talking about men. EG *We all begin to miss contact with the opposite sex... The teenage period is crucial in learning about the opposite sex.* ● PHR : USU USED AS O

opposite number, opposite numbers. Your **opposite number** is a person who has the same job or rank as you, but works in a different department, firm, or organization. EG *I only had contact with my opposite number, not with the Foreign Secretary... French Trotskyists met their British opposite numbers at a conference.* N COUNT : POSS+N = counterpart

opposition /ɒpəzɪʃəⁿn/. 1 **Opposition** is strong, angry, or violent disagreement and disapproval. EG *It was only built after much opposition from the planners... He faced formidable opposition in carrying through this policy... Industrialists inevitably found themselves in opposition to the Government.* N UNCOUNT

2 When **opposition** is used with the following meanings, it can be used with a singular or a plural verb. The **opposition** is used to refer to 2.1 the politicians, political party, or group of parties that form part of a country's parliament but are not in the government. EG *...leader of the Opposition... ...two new opposition parties... The Opposition motion was defeated.* N SING : USU *the* +N 2.2 all the people who disagree strongly with a person, a group, or an idea. EG *The opposition consisted of chiefs and elders.* N SING : *the*+N 2.3 the person or team you are competing against in a sports event. EG *One player makes the break through the opposition's defence.* N SING : *the*+N

oppress /əˢpres/, **oppresses, oppressing, oppressed**. 1 To **oppress** someone means to treat them unfairly or cruelly, and to prevent them from having the same opportunities, freedom, benefits, etc as others. EG *...institutions that oppress women.* V+O ⇑ suppress ◇ **oppressed**. EG *...the sufferings of oppressed people everywhere.* ◇ ADJ CLASSIF ▸ The **oppressed** is used to refer to people who are oppressed. EG *...the poor, the exploited, and the oppressed.* ▸ N PLURAL : *the* +N = downtrodden

2 If something **oppresses** you, it causes you to feel depressed, anxious, and uncomfortable. EG *Somehow, though, the room oppressed him.* V+O

oppression /əˢpreʃəⁿn/, **oppressions**. **Oppression** is 1 the act of oppressing a person or group, or the state of being oppressed. EG *...the oppression of the weak and defenceless.* N UNCOUNT/COUNT = persecution ▸ used as a count noun. EG *...the social, economic and religious oppressions in fourteenth century England.* ▸ N COUNT 2 a feeling of depression and anxiety, especially when it is caused by a place or situation. EG *Passing the place, my sense of oppression increased.* N UNCOUNT = despondency

oppressive /əˢpresɪv/. 1 An atmosphere or weather that is **oppressive** is hot and humid, so that you feel very uncomfortable and sometimes ill. EG *The atmosphere became close, oppressive... ...the oppressive heat of the plains.* ADJ QUALIT = stifling ◇ **oppressively**. EG *The room was oppressively hot.* ◇ ADV+ADJ/ADV

2 A situation that is **oppressive** is one that you find difficult to deal with, and that causes you to feel depressed and anxious. EG *It's unbearable at home. Oppressive... ...an oppressive mortgage.* ADJ QUALIT

3 Laws, societies, and customs that are **oppressive** prevent a particular person or group from having the same opportunities, freedoms, or benefits as others; used showing disapproval. EG *...an oppressive bureaucracy... ...the present oppressive system.* ADJ QUALIT ⇑ unjust

oppressor /əˢpresə/, **oppressors**. An **oppressor** is someone who oppresses other people. EG *They didn't have the will to stand up against their foreign oppressors.* N COUNT = persecutor, tyrant

opprobrious /əprəʊbrɪəs/. Language that is **opprobrious** expresses scorn or contempt for someone or something; a formal word. ADJ QUALIT ⇑ scornful

opprobrium /əprəʊbrɪəm/ is the state of being disliked and criticized very much because of something that you have done; a formal word. EG *The opprobrium and enmity he incurred were caused by his outspoken brashness.* N UNCOUNT = censure

opt /ɒpt/, **opts, opting, opted**. If you **opt** for something, or **opt** to do something, you choose it or decide to do it in preference to anything else. EG *My father left the choice of career to me, and I opted for law... In Latin America, the Church has opted to be on the side of the poor and under-privileged.* V+A *(for)*, OR V+*to*-INF = plump

opt out. If you **opt out**, you choose to be no longer involved in something. EG *Today there is a growing tendency for people to opt out... He tried to opt out of political and economic decision-making.* PHRASAL VB : V+ADV, IF+PREP THEN *of*

optic /ɒptɪk/, **optics**. **Optic** is an adjective and **optics** is an uncount noun. 1 **Optic** means relating to eyes or to sight. EG *...the optic nerves.* ADJ CLASSIF : ATTRIB

2 **Optics** is the branch of science concerned with vision, sight, and light. EG *Newton published his first work on optics.* N UNCOUNT ⇑ physics

optical /ɒptɪkəⁿl/. 1 **Optical** instruments, devices, or processes are concerned with vision, light, or images. EG *...an optical microscope.* ADJ CLASSIF : ATTRIB

2 **Optical** means relating to the appearance of things or the way that people see them. EG *...pleasurable optical effects.* ADJ CLASSIF : ATTRIB = visual

optical illusion, optical illusions. An **optical illusion** is something such as an object or design that deceives your eyes and causes you to see something different from what is really there. EG *It was merely a clever optical illusion.* N COUNT ⇑ trick

optician /ɒptɪʃəⁿn/, **opticians**. An **optician** is someone whose job involves testing people's eyesight, and making and selling glasses and contact lenses. N COUNT ⇑ specialist

optimism /ɒptɪmɪzəⁿm/ is the feeling of being hopeful about the future and the belief that a particular situation or course of action will be successful. EG *...a man of great optimism... There was a definite air of optimism at the headquarters.* N UNCOUNT ⇑ hope = confidence ◇ **optimist, optimists**. EG *I'm an optimist by nature.* ◇ N COUNT

optimistic /ɒptɪmɪstɪk/. 1 Someone that is **optimistic** is hopeful about the future, and believes that things will happen in the best possible way. EG *But then people were optimistic and hopeful... ...an optimistic mood... ...the optimistic and expanding 1960's.* ADJ QUALIT = confident ◇ **optimistically**. EG *John says optimistically, 'I'm going to enjoy this.'* ◇ ADV WITH VB ⇑ hopefully

optimum /ɒptɪməm/ is used to describe the best amount, rate, etc, or the one that gives the greatest advantages; a fairly formal word. EG *...trying to achieve the optimum rate of economic growth... The optimum feeding time is around dawn.* ADJ CLASSIF : ATTRIB = ideal ▸ used as a noun. EG *They are not functioning at their optimum.* ▸ N SING WITH DET

option /ɒpʃəⁿn/, **options**. 1 An **option** is something that you can choose to do in preference to one or more alternatives. EG *They urged the Chancellor to go for the first option... He had, I would say, two options... ...the option of another referendum.* N COUNT ⇑ possibility = choice ● If you **keep** or **leave** your **options open**, you avoid making a decision about something. EG *She was determined not to be foolish. That meant keeping options open... They had left their options open.* ● PHR : VB INFLECTS ≠ commit yourself

2 **Option** is also used to refer to the right, need, or ability to choose between two or more alternative courses of action. EG *He was given the option: give them up or lose your job. ...the children of mothers* N SING WITH DET

who have no option but to work... That is their only option.

3 An **option** is also **3.1** an agreement or contract that gives someone the right to buy or sell something such as a house or shares at a future date, if they decide they want to do so. EG *...an option to buy up to 2.5 million Shearson shares... In 1973 both Pan Am and TWA cancelled all their options.* **3.2** a subject which a student can choose to study as a part of their main course. EG *I did a special option in phonetics.* N COUNT; N COUNT

optional /ɒpʃəᵊnəl, -ʃənəᵊl/. If something is **optional**, you can choose whether you do it or not. EG *Games are optional at this school... ...optional courses on linguistics and French cinema.* ADJ CLASSIF = voluntary ≠ compulsory

opulence /ɒpjə⁴ləns/ is great wealth; a formal word. EG *His eyes had never beheld such opulence.* N UNCOUNT = affluence

opulent /ɒpjə⁴lənt/; a formal word. **1** Someone who is **opulent** is very wealthy. EG *...the privileges of an opulent society.* ADJ QUALIT = affluent

2 Something that is **opulent** looks as if it cost a lot of money, especially because it is very richly decorated. EG *...the magnificently opulent marble altar... ...opulent furnishings.* ADJ QUALIT = sumptuous

opus /əʊpəs/, **opuses, opera**. The plural can be either **opuses** or **opera**. An **opus** is **1** a musical composition, for example a symphony or concerto. 'Opus' is often used with a number indicating when the composition was written; a formal use. EG *...Brahms Variations on a Hungarian Song, Opus 21 No 2.* **2** a great artistic work, such as a piece of writing or a painting; an informal use. EG *I had after all a learned opus to write.* N COUNT: USU N +NUM; N COUNT: USU SING = creation

or /ɔː, ə/. **1 Or** is used **1.1** to link a number of alternatives. EG *Do you want your drink up there or do you want to come down for it?... ...scotch or Bourbon?... Are you going with your parents or by yourself?... ...teaching English as a foreign or second language... Don't tell Ma or Pa... Have you any brothers or sisters?* **1.2** to give another alternative, when the first alternative is introduced by 'either' or 'whether'. EG *Most aircraft accidents occur at either take-off or landing... He didn't know whether he wanted to laugh or cry... Don't you think we'd better wait and see whether or not the operation was successful?* **1.3** between two numbers to indicate that you are giving an approximate amount. EG *You are supposed to polish your car three or four times a year... She had only seen him once or twice in her life... Forty or more people were already assembled.* CONJ COORD; CONJ COORD: *either/whether...or*; CONJ COORD

2 Or is also used **2.1** after a statement to introduce a comment which qualifies, explains, corrects, etc what you have just said. EG *So the popular preconception remains intact. Or did until last week... The company is paying the rent or at least contributing to it... I am waiting until Labour is returned to office in a couple of years. Or not, as the case may be.* **2.2** when you are giving another word for something you have just mentioned, because the second word is more accurate or easier to understand than the first word. EG *He is the owner of the largest network of 'frontons', or arenas, in the country... ...Margaret. Or Molly as she was called.* CONJ COORD; CONJ COORD

3 You can also use **or 3.1** to link two clauses, when the first clause gives an instruction or advice, and the second clause gives the result of not following this instruction or advice. EG *Don't put anything plastic in the oven or it will probably start melting... You've got to be very careful or else you'll miss the turnoff into our place.* **3.2** to introduce something which is an explanation or justification for a statement you have just made. EG *He can't be that bad, can he, or they wouldn't have allowed him home?* CONJ SUBORD ⇑ because = otherwise; CONJ SUBORD ⇑ because = otherwise

4 If you say something like 'family **or no** family', 'work **or no** work', etc, you are emphasizing that a particular thing makes no difference to what is going to happen. EG *Family or no family, he should have said no... You'll have to go to the door, dog or no dog.* PHR: USED AS CONJ COORD

5 The word **or** is also used in the following expressions, which are explained at other places in this dictionary. • **or else**: see **else**. • **or so**: see **so**. • **or other**: see **other**. • **or something**: see **something**.

-or is used at the end of nouns that refer to people who do a particular type of work or take a particular type of action. EG *...author... ...sailor... ...supervisor... ...sponsor... ...donor... ...instigator.* SUFFIX: FORMS N COUNTS

oracle /ɒrəkəᵊl/, **oracles**. An **oracle** is **1** a priest or priestess in ancient Greece, who made predictions about the future or told people the truth about a particular situation. EG *Socrates had been told by the Delphic oracle that he was the wisest of men.* **2** a prophecy or other statement made by an oracle. N COUNT ⇑ prophet; N COUNT

oracular /ɒrækjə⁴lə/. Something that is **oracular** comes from or is related to an oracle; a formal word. EG *...oracular guidance for the future.* ADJ CLASSIF ⇑ prophetic

oral /ɔːrəl/, **orals**. **1** Something that is **oral 1.1** is spoken rather than written. EG *...an oral test in German.* ◇ **orally**. EG *The candidate shall be examined orally and in writing by the Examiners.* **1.2** is used by or done with your mouth. EG *...an oral vaccine... ...the oral contraceptive pill.* ◇ **orally**. EG *...a pill taken orally.* ADJ CLASSIF; ◇ ADV WITH VB; ADJ CLASSIF; ◇ ADV WITH VB

2 An **oral** is an exam that is spoken rather than written, especially in a foreign language. EG *In some examinations the oral follows a written paper.* N COUNT

orange /ɒrɪndʒ/, **oranges**. **1** Something that is **orange** is of a colour between red and yellow. EG *...an orange silk scarf.* ▸ used as a noun. EG *His shirt was a bright orange.* ADJ COLOUR; ▸ N MASS

2 An **orange** is a round fruit that is juicy and sweet. It has a thick skin that is orange in colour, and is divided into sections inside. EG *...a crate of oranges... ...banana plantations and orange groves.* N COUNT

3 Orange is also a drink that is made from or tastes of oranges. EG *...fizzy orange... She was drinking gin and orange... ...orange juice.* N UNCOUNT

orangeade /ɒrɪndʒeɪd/ is a sweet orange-coloured drink that tastes of oranges. Orangeade is sometimes fizzy, and sometimes mixed with water; used mainly in British English. EG *She asked us if we'd like some orangeade.* N UNCOUNT

orange blossom consists of the white flowers of an orange tree. Orange blossom is sweetly scented and traditionally carried by European and American brides at their wedding. N UNCOUNT

orangery /ɒrɪndʒəᵊri¹/, **orangeries**. An **orangery** is a conservatory or greenhouse in which orange trees are grown. N COUNT ⇑ greenhouse

orangey /ɒrɪndʒi¹/. Something that is **orangey** is slightly orange in colour. EG *She was wearing a sort of orangey blouse.* ADJ COLOUR

orang-outang /ɔːræŋ uːtæŋ/, **orang-outangs**; also spelled **orang-utan**. An **orang-outang** is a large ape with long arms that comes from the rain forests of Borneo and Sumatra. N COUNT

oration /ɔːreɪʃən/, **orations**. An **oration** is a formal speech made in public. EG *He asked for no funeral oration... ...a short oration in Boxer's honour.* N COUNT = address

orator /ɒrətə/, **orators**. An **orator** is someone who makes formal speeches in public, or who is skilled at making speeches. EG *He is a marvellous orator.* N COUNT ⇑ speaker

oratorical /ɒrətɒrɪkəᵊl/ means relating to or using oratory; a formal word. EG *...oratorical skills... ...a long oratorical speech.* ADJ CLASSIF: ATTRIB = declamatory

oratorio /ɒrətɔːrɪəʊ/, **oratorios**. An **oratorio** is a piece of music that has a religious subject and is written for singers and an orchestra. EG *...a dramatic oratorio such as Bach's 'St Matthew Passion'.* N COUNT

oratory /ɒrətəᵊri¹/, **oratories**. **1 Oratory** is the art of making formal speeches in public and showing skill in expressing yourself or in stirring people's feelings; a formal use. EG *He roused the troops with his oratory... ...people skilled in the use of oratory.* N UNCOUNT ⇑ speaking = rhetoric

2 An **oratory** is a room or building where people go to pray. N COUNT ⇑ place

orb /ɔːb/, **orbs**. An **orb** is **1** something that is shaped like a ball, for example the sun or moon; a formal or literary use. EG *...that great red orb, now sinking down towards the Bristol Channel... ...the dusty yellow orbs of street lamps.* **2** a small, ornamental ball with a cross on top that is carried by a king or queen in important ceremonies, for example when they are being crowned. N COUNT = sphere; N COUNT ⇑ sphere

orbit /ɔːbɪt/, **orbits, orbiting, orbited**. **1** An **orbit** is the curved path in space that is followed by an object going round and round another, larger object, for example a planet going round the sun. EG *...the orbit of the planet Mercury... How much does it cost to put a satellite into orbit?* N COUNT, OR *into/in*+N ⇑ circuit

2 If something such as a satellite or moon **orbits** a planet or sun, it moves in a continuous, curving path around that planet or sun. EG *...the first American astronaut to orbit in space... This asteroid takes 238 years to orbit the sun.* V OR V+O ⇑ circle

3 Orbit is also used to refer to the area over which a N SING WITH DET particular person, group or institution has influence. EG *...my re-entry into the family orbit... ...out of the Labour Party's orbit.*

orbital /ɔ:bɪtəºl/ is used to describe **1** a road that goes all the way round a large city. EG *...the orbital motorway.* **2** the orbit of an object in space. EG *...orbital space stations.* ADJ CLASSIF : ATTRIB / ADJ CLASSIF : ATTRIB

orchard /ɔ:tʃəd/, **orchards**. An **orchard** is an area of land on which fruit trees are grown. EG *...an apple orchard.* N COUNT

orchestra /ɔ:kɪ²strə/, **orchestras**. An **orchestra** is a large group of musicians who play a variety of different instruments together. An orchestra usually plays classical music: compare **band**. EG *The orchestra played the Russian national anthem... ...the London Philharmonic Orchestra.* ● See also **chamber orchestra**. N COUNT : ALSO IN NAMES

orchestral /ɔ:kɛstrəºl/ means consisting of or relating to music that is played by an orchestra. EG *...Mozart's orchestral pieces... ...orchestral musicians.* ADJ CLASSIF : ATTRIB ⇑ musical

orchestra pit, orchestra pits. The **orchestra pit** in a theatre is the space reserved for the musicians, immediately in front of or under the stage. N COUNT ⇑ area

orchestrate /ɔ:kɪ²streɪt/, **orchestrates, orchestrating, orchestrated**. **1** To **orchestrate** something means to carefully organize it in order to produce a particular result or situation, sometimes in an unfair or deceitful way. EG *He personally orchestrated that entire evening.* ◊ **orchestrated**. EG *...a brilliantly orchestrated campaign of persuasion and protest.* ◊ **orchestration**. EG *They suspected heavy Russian infiltration and orchestration.* V+O ⇑ arrange = stage-manage / ◊ ADJ QUALIT : ATTRIB / ◊ N UNCOUNT

2 To **orchestrate** a piece of music means to rewrite it so that it can be played by an orchestra. EG *I orchestrated the 'Song of the Volga Boatmen'.* V+O = arrange

orchestration /ɔ:kɪ²streɪʃəⁿn/, **orchestrations**. An **orchestration** is a piece of music that has been rewritten so that it can be played by an orchestra. EG *...his orchestrations of Bach, Handel, and Brahms.* N COUNT = arrangement

orchid /ɔ:kɪd/, **orchids**. An **orchid** is a plant that has very unusual and beautiful flowers and is found in many different places in the world; also used to refer to the flower. Some people collect orchids. EG *...hot mornings spent wandering in search of orchids.* N COUNT

ordain /ɔ:deɪn/, **ordains, ordaining, ordained**. **1** When someone **is ordained**, they are made a member of the clergy in a religious ceremony. EG *When I was first ordained, I served as a hospital chaplain.* ◊ **ordained**. EG *...the Reverend Young, an ordained minister.* V+O : USU PASS ⇑ invest / ◊ ADJ CLASSIF : ATTRIB

2 If someone in authority **ordains** something, they order that it should happen or be in existence; a formal use. EG *She believed that love had been ordained by God... Lady Sackville ordained complete discretion.* V+O/REPORT-CL = decree

ordeal /ɔ:di:l/, **ordeals**. An **ordeal** is a difficult and extremely unpleasant experience or situation. EG *The Rosses' dreadful ordeal finally ended at 9 a.m. on the Monday morning... ...an ordeal such as imprisonment, illness, or disaster.* N COUNT : USU SING

order /ɔ:də/, **orders, ordering, ordered**. **1 In order to** and **in order that** are used to introduce an explanation of why someone does or did something. EG *He had to hurry in order to reach the next place on his schedule... Rose trod with care, in order not to spread the dirt... They are learning English in order that they can study a particular subject.* CONJ SUBORD

2 An **order** is something that you are told to do by someone in authority. EG *Quickly he gave his orders... He had received orders that morning to continue with the work... George went away to carry out this order... An official inquiry was set up on the orders of the Minister of Health.* ● **A tall order**: see **tall**. ● If you are **under orders** to do something, you have been told to do it by someone in authority. EG *This group was under orders to carry out an armed reconnaissance.* N COUNT : ALSO SING=PL = instruction / ● PHR : USED AS AN A, IF+VB THEN *to*-INF

3 If you **order** someone to do something, you tell someone of a lower position or rank to do something. EG *He ordered me to fetch the books... The President said he would order his aides not to appear... Harriet was ordered to keep away from my cell... 'Sit down!' he ordered.* V+O+*to*-INF, OR V+QUOTE = command

4 If you **order** someone into or to a particular place, you tell someone of a lower position or rank to go there. EG *I ordered him outside... He ordered me out of the building.* V+O+A

5 If someone in authority **orders** something, they give instructions that it should be done. EG *Sherman ordered an investigation into her husband's death... A district court ordered the hospital closed... The Captain ordered the ship's masts to be cut down.* V+O/REPORT-CL, OR V+O+*to*-INF/ PAST PART

6 If you **order** something that you are going to pay for, such as food, drink, furniture, etc, you ask for it to be brought to you, sent to you, made for you, etc. EG *Davis had ordered a second whisky... She ordered an extra delivery of coal... What do you want? I'll order now.* V, V+O, V+O (NG/REFL)+O, OR V+O+A *(for)* ⇑ request

7 An **order** is also **7.1** something that you ask to be brought to you, sent to you, made for you, etc, and that you are going to pay for. EG *A waiter came to take their order... The wholesale suppliers arrived to take an order for goods... We will continue to deal with overseas orders...* ● See also **mail order**. **7.2** a legal document that states that something must be done. EG *You will need an order signed by the Home Secretary... They had obtained a High Court order forbidding the sale... ...a custody order.* **7.3** a small printed paper that can be exchanged for money at a bank or a post office and that is sent to someone, for example as payment of their pension. EG *You will get a book of orders to cash each week at the post office... Each order is for one week's pension in advance.* ● See also **banker's order, postal order, standing order**. **7.4** a group of monks or nuns who have special religious beliefs and aims and who spend their lives trying to achieve these aims. EG *We felt we needed to found an order like that... ...the Order of St Benedict.* **7.5** a group of people whose members are appointed by someone such as a king or queen as a reward for their services or achievements. EG *...the Order of the Garter.* **7.6** a group within a species of animals or plants that are very similar to each other, and that are regarded as a single group for the purposes of classification; a technical term in zoology, botany, biology, etc. EG *These plants are classified in an order of their own.* N COUNT / N COUNT / N COUNT / N COUNT : ALSO IN NAMES ⇑ community / N COUNT : ALSO IN NAMES ⇑ society / N COUNT ⇑ category

8 Order is **8.1** the way a set of things is arranged or done when one thing is placed or done first, another thing second, another thing third, and so on. EG *The names are not in alphabetical order... Decide in what order the rooms will be cleaned... Grown-ups have a different order of priorities.* ● See also **pecking order**. **8.2** the state that something is in when its different parts are related in a way that can be recognized and understood, especially when someone or something has made it this way. EG *I felt it would create some order in our lives... ...a need for intellectual order in the minds of individuals.* **8.3** the state that exists in a place or among a group of people when normal activities are taking place and laws or rules of behaviour are being obeyed. EG *Some semblance of order had been established... Without order, stability is impossible... One look from him was enough to enforce order and obedience.* ● See also **law and order**. ● To **keep order** or **keep** someone **in order** means to prevent a person or a group of people from disobeying laws or rules of behaviour. EG *To keep order among forty-five vigorous children is no easy matter... It was seen as a weapon to keep the working classes in order.* N COUNT/ UNCOUNT ⇑ arrangement / N UNCOUNT ⇑ organization ≠ confusion / N UNCOUNT = discipline / ● PHR : VB INFLECTS ⇑ control

9 When people talk about a particular **order**, they mean the way society is organized in a particular place. EG *They don't accept the existing order... No man could have hated the old order more bitterly... After 1945 a new world order was constructed.* N SING WITH DET +SUPP = system

10 In order. 10.1 If something is done **in order**, it is done in a sequence that was decided earlier to be correct, in which one thing is placed or done first, another thing second, and so on. EG *In correct order I recited the twelve things I was supposed to do.* **10.2** If something is **in order** or put **into order**, it is arranged tidily or according to a system. EG *Chairs were arranged and printed material put in order... Gretchen combed her hair into some sort of order.* **10.3** If something is **in good order, in perfect order**, etc, it is in good condition. EG *The cement is slightly cracked but otherwise in good order... The house was deserted but in good order.* **10.4** A machine, device, or vehicle that is **in order** or **in working order** is in a good enough condition to be used. EG *We soon put Jim's bike in order... He was always finding* PHR : USED AS AN A = in sequence / PHR : USED AS AN A / PHR : USED AS AN A / PHR : USED AS AN A *cars in good working order.* **10.5** If you describe someone or their behaviour at a meeting or in a committee, etc, as being **in order**, you mean that they are correct, according to the rules of the meeting, committee, parliament, etc. EG *I think this is in order, since the agenda permits us to make suggestions... Whether I am in order or not, I call him a liar.* PHR : USED AS AN A ⇑ right

11 Out of order. 11.1 If something is **out of order**, it is in a different sequence from one that was decided earlier to be correct, in which one thing is placed or done first, another thing second, and so on. EG *The books are all out of order.* PHR : USED AS AN A = out of line **11.2** A machine, device, or vehicle that is **out of order** is broken or damaged, and therefore not able to be used. EG *The tractors are out of order and there are no spare parts... Your secretary's typewriter is out of order.* PHR : USED AS AN A ≠ working **11.3** If you describe someone or their behaviour at a meeting or in a committee, etc, as being **out of order**, you mean that they are incorrect, according to the rules of the meeting, committee, parliament, etc. EG *The resolution was ruled out of order... Sir Kelvin was out of order.* ● See also **point of order**. PHR : USED AS AN A ≠ in order

12 To **order** something means **12.1** to cause the different parts of something to be related in a way that can be recognized and understood. EG *One can't order one's feelings... Things could be ordered differently... ...changes in the way society is ordered and run.* V+O ⇑ arrange **12.2** to group similar species of animals or plants together for the purposes of classification; a technical term in zoology, botany, biology, etc. V+O ⇑ classify

13 If you refer to something of a particular **order**, you mean something of a particular kind; a fairly formal use. EG *Quality of this order is still to be found... ...an anti-nuclear campaigner of the highest order... Its prices are much of the order I have been describing.* N SING WITH DET = kind ● **In the order of** and **of the order of** mean approximately. EG *Britain's contribution is something in the order of 5 per cent... Wind speeds at the airport were of the order of 160 kilometres per hour.* ● PREP

14 The word **order** is also used in the following expressions. **14.1** If something such as a belief or attitude is **the order of the day**, it is very common among a particular group of people. EG *Permissiveness became the order of the day.* PHR : USED AS C = prevalent **14.2** If you do something **to order**, you do it whenever you are asked to do it. EG *A great actress can usually weep to order.* PHR : USED AS AN A = on demand **14.3** Something that is **on order** at a shop, factory, etc, has been asked for by someone, and sometimes paid for, but not yet received by them, for example because they are waiting for it to be made. EG *I've got a sewing machine on order at Woolworth's.* PHR : USED AS AN A **14.4 'Order!'** is used by the chairman or chairwoman of a meeting to tell someone that they must stop breaking the rules of the meeting or causing a disturbance. CONVENTION

order about. If you **order** someone **about**, or **order** them **around**, you always tell them what to do in a bossy and unsympathetic way; used showing disapproval. EG *Don't try to order them about... It was intolerable that those two fat slobs could order her around.* PHRASAL VB : V+O+ADV

ordered /ɔːdəd/. Something such as a system or society that is **ordered** is properly arranged, planned, or controlled. EG *...a tendency to make the system more and more ordered... ...an ordered society... In Mrs Kaul's house everything was so well ordered and expensive.* ADJ QUALIT ≠ chaotic, formless

orderliness /ɔːdəlɪnɪ[1]s/ is **1** the state of being well organized or well arranged. EG *We pride ourselves on the orderliness of our way of life.* N UNCOUNT ≠ chaos **2** the habit of doing things in a neat and well organized way. EG *Flora maintains a certain orderliness in all these things.* N UNCOUNT = neatness

orderly /ɔːdəli[1]/, **orderlies**. **1** Something that is **orderly** is well organized or arranged. EG *...a system of orderly government... He tried to exercise power in a humane, civilised and orderly way.* ADJ QUALIT = ordered

2 An **orderly** is an untrained male hospital attendant who does heavy work, such as moving trolleys. EG *I sat at the end of the ward with the orderly.* N COUNT ⇑ worker

> **ORDINAL** □ In this dictionary ORDINAL is used in the grammar notes beside entries to mean that the word is an ordinal number, like *second, third, tenth* and *forty-fifth*. Ordinal numbers usually follow a determiner like *the* or *my*. They are often used to modify nouns, except where the text or situation makes it clear what you are referring to. An example is **third**. EG *...my* ***third*** *husband... ...Japan's* ***third*** *largest city.*

ordinal number, ordinal numbers. An **ordinal number**, or an **ordinal**, is a number that tells you what position something has in an ordered group of things: compare **cardinal number**. N COUNT

ordinance /ɔːdɪnəns/, **ordinances**. An **ordinance** is an official rule or order; a formal word. EG *In 1972 the city passed an ordinance compelling all outdoor lighting to be switched off at 9.00 p.m.* N COUNT = regulation

ordinand /ɔːdɪnænd/, **ordinands**. An **ordinand** is a man who is being trained to be a priest. N COUNT ⇑ trainee

ordinary /ɔːdɪ[1]nri[1]/. **1** Something that is **ordinary** **1.1** is not special or different in any way, especially because it is very common. EG *...ordinary everyday objects... What do ordinary people really think about universities?... Ordinary grass seed won't grow there.* ADJ QUALIT ≠ unusual, rare **1.2** is rather dull because it is not special in any way; used showing disapproval. EG *She is likeable enough, but very ordinary.* ADJ QUALIT = pedestrian

2 **Ordinary** means normal and usual. EG *'Of course,' she added in her ordinary voice... It was an ordinary working day for them.* ADJ CLASSIF : ATTRIB ◇ **ordinarily**. EG *I learned later that this room was ordinarily used by the doctor.* ◇ ADV = normally ● **In the ordinary way** means normally and is used to suggest that the present situation is different from normal. EG *I wouldn't go there in the ordinary way, but this time I have to.* ● PHR : USED AS AN A

3 Something that is **out of the ordinary** is unusual or different. EG *I'd like to bring her something a little out of the ordinary.* PHR : USED AS AN A = special

4 An **ordinary** degree is an undergraduate degree that is lower than an honours degree. EG *...an ordinary degree in chemistry.* ADJ CLASSIF : ATTRIB

ordination /ɔːdɪneɪʃə[0]n/, **ordinations**. An **ordination** is a religious ceremony in which someone is made a member of the clergy in the Christian Church. EG *I'm going to an ordination in France next Sunday.* N COUNT ▸ used as an uncount noun. EG *...the ordination of women.* ▸ N UNCOUNT

ordnance /ɔːdnəns/ consists of military supplies, especially weapons. EG *...Royal Ordnance Factories.* N UNCOUNT

Ordnance Survey. The **Ordnance Survey** is the British government organization that produces detailed maps of Britain and Ireland. N PROPER : *the*+N

ordure /ɔːdjʊə/ is excrement; a formal word. EG *...a bucketful of ordure.* N UNCOUNT

ore /ɔː/, **ores**. **Ore** is rock or earth from which metal can be obtained. EG *...iron ore.* N MASS

oregano /ɒrɪgɑːnəʊ/ is a herb that is used in cooking; used also to refer to the whole plant. EG *Season with a little salt, oregano, and soy sauce.* N UNCOUNT

organ /ɔːgən/, **organs**. **1** An **organ** is a part of your body that has a particular purpose or function, for example your heart or lungs. Most of your organs are inside your body. EG *Children's bones and organs are very sensitive to radiation... ...reproductive organs.* N COUNT

2 **Organ** is used to refer to an organization such as a company or newspaper that is controlled or influenced by a larger, more powerful organization, and that is used by them as a means of getting things done or giving information to the public. EG *They decided to close the independent newspaper and launch it again as a government organ.* N COUNT : USU+SUPP = mouthpiece

3 An **organ** is also a large musical instrument that has many pipes of different lengths through which air is forced, and which is played rather like a piano with keys and pedals. EG *Schubert sang in the choir and played the organ... ...organ music... ...a cinema organ.* ● See also **barrel organ, mouth organ**. N COUNT

organdie /ɔːgəndi[1]/; also spelled **organdy** in American English. **Organdie** is a fine, slightly stiff cotton fabric that is used for making dresses. EG *...a white organdie blouse.* N UNCOUNT

organ-grinder, organ-grinders. An **organ-grinder** is an entertainer who plays a barrel organ in the streets. N COUNT

organic /ɔːgænɪk/. **1** Something that is **organic** is produced by or found in plants or animals. EG *The rocks were carefully searched for organic remains.* ADJ CLASSIF : USU ATTRIB ⇑ living

2 **Organic** is used to describe methods of farming and gardening that use only natural animal and plant products as fertilizers, pesticides, fungicides, etc, rather than chemicals. EG *...organic farming... ...or-* ADJ CLASSIF : USU ATTRIB ≠ chemical *ganic crops.* ◇ **organically.** EG *...organically grown vegetables.* ◇ ADV WITH VB ≠ chemically

3 Organic describes change, development, or progress that happens gradually and naturally rather than in a sudden or forced way; a formal use. EG *That's the problem with large-scale modern industry. Instead of organic growth, there have been abrupt, discontinuous changes.* ◇ **organically.** EG *The growth of payed employment did not emerge organically out of these societies.* ADJ CLASSIF ⇑ natural ◇ ADV WITH VB

4 If a structure or society is described as **organic**, it is considered to be made up of many different parts which all contribute to the way the whole structure or society works; a formal use. EG *The society is undifferentiated, organic, undivided.* ADJ CLASSIF ⇑ united

organisation /ɔːgənaɪzeɪʃəⁿn/. See **organization.**

organisational /ɔːgənaɪzeɪʃəⁿnəl, -ʃənəⁿl/. See **organizational.**

organise /ɔːgənaɪz/. See **organize.**

organiser /ɔːgənaɪzə/. See **organizer.**

organism /ɔːgənɪzəⁿm/, **organisms.** An **organism** is 1 an animal or plant, especially one that is very simple or so small that it cannot be seen without a microscope. EG *These creatures are descended from simpler organisms like corals and jellyfish.* 2 something that seems to be like a living creature, especially because it seems to grow and develop and because it has a complex structure. EG *Factories and cities are more complex organisms than self-sufficient villages.* N COUNT ⇑ creature; N COUNT ⇑ thing

organist /ɔːgənɪst/, **organists.** An **organist** is someone who plays the organ. EG *He is a very fine organist.* N COUNT ⇑ musician

organization /ɔːgənaɪzeɪʃəⁿn/, **organizations;** also spelled **organisation.** 1 An **organization** is a group, society, club, or business, especially a large one that has particular aims. EG *...student organizations... ...problems of turning the Post Office into a profitable organisation... ...the World Health Organisation.* N COUNT

2 **Organization** is 2.1 the structure of something, especially the way in which its different parts are related and how they work together. EG *There has been a total technological change in the organization of society... ...a report on party organisation in 1965.* N UNCOUNT ⇑ arrangement

2.2 the act of making the arrangements for a particular activity in order to make sure that everything happens as planned. EG *There are more than fifty full-time party workers for the organisation of conferences and rallies... I don't want to get involved in the actual organisation of things.* 2.3 efficiency and the ability to do things in a well-planned and ordered way; used showing approval. EG *There's a complete lack of organization–it's disgraceful!* 2.4 the act of forming a group or society such as a trade union in order to have more power to achieve something, or the state of being formed into such a group or society. EG *In industries where there is strong union organisation, basic wages and conditions are normally better... I'm in favour of widespread organisation of labour.* N UNCOUNT = running; N UNCOUNT ⇑ planning; N UNCOUNT

organizational /ɔːgənaɪzeɪʃəⁿnəl, -ʃənəⁿl/; also spelled **organisational. Organizational** means 1 relating to the way that something is planned and arranged and the ability to do this efficiently. EG *It was created by an organizational genius named Alfred P. Sloan... ...new organizational methods were introduced.* 2 relating to the structure of a society, business, or system and the relationship between the various parts. EG *At the very top of the Church of England's organisational structure are the Church Commissioners.* 3 relating to groups, clubs, societies, or businesses. EG *The group has no political or organisational links with the terrorists* ADJ CLASSIF : ATTRIB; ADJ CLASSIF : ATTRIB ⇑ structural; ADJ CLASSIF : ATTRIB ⇑ group

organize /ɔːgənaɪz/, **organizes, organizing, organized;** also spelled **organise.** 1 If you **organize** something, 1.1 you make all the arrangements for it and are in charge in order to make sure that everything happens as planned. EG *We organized a concert in the village hall... He was organizing the search for survivors... I thought that meeting was badly organized.* 1.2 you give a particular structure to something or put things into order. EG *He needed a little time to organize his response to the criticism... Papers are organized in enormous filing cabinets.* V+O ⇑ arrange; V+O = marshal

1.3 you make someone or something efficient so that they work in the best, most effective way. EG *Older students were having difficulty in studying and organizing themselves.* V+O (NG/REFL) ⇑ control

2 When workers or employees **organize,** they form into a group or society such as a trade union in order to have more power to achieve something. EG *Their poverty prevents them from organizing effectively to improve their wages... ...the forces of outside capital and of organized labour.* V ⇑ unite

organized /ɔːgənaɪzd/; also spelled **organised.** 1 Something that is **organized** is planned and controlled on a large scale and involves a lot of people all taking part in the same type of activity. EG *Do you mean to say you're going on an organized holiday?... ...organised religion... ...companies linked to organized crime.* ADJ CLASSIF : ATTRIB

2 Someone or something that is **organized** is very efficient and works in a very effective way. EG *How well organised you are!... ...a highly organized industry... All you need to get organized is a writing surface, a chair, and a pen and paper.* ADJ QUALIT ⇑ orderly

organizer /ɔːgənaɪzə/, **organizers;** also spelled **organiser.** An **organizer** is the person who makes all the arrangements for something and makes sure that it happens as planned. EG *She brought a prosecution against the organizers for an indecent exhibition.* N COUNT

orgasm /ɔːgæzəⁿm/, **orgasms.** An **orgasm** is 1 the moment of greatest pleasure and excitement in sexual activity. EG *I never have an orgasm with him.* N COUNT ⇑ climax

2 any experience that involves a lot of pleasure or excitement; a formal word. EG *...this aesthetic orgasm.* N COUNT+SUPP = frenzy

orgasmic /ɔːgæzmɪk/ means 1 relating to a sexual orgasm; a technical term in medicine. 2 very enjoyable or exciting; an informal use. EG *The war was the orgasmic experience of his newspaper career.* ADJ CLASSIF; ADJ CLASSIF ⇑ best = climactic

orgiastic /ɔːdʒiˈæstɪk/ means involving extreme pleasure. EG *...moods of orgiastic intoxication.* ADJ CLASSIF = riotous

orgy /ɔːdʒiˈ/, **orgies.** An **orgy** is 1 a party in which people behave in a very uncontrolled way, especially involving sexual activity. EG *Judges had been engaging in sexual orgies... ...a drunken orgy.* 2 any activity that is done to an extent that is considered excessive; used showing disapproval. EG *I indulged in an orgy of housework... ...an orgy of destruction.* N COUNT; N COUNT+SUPP = surfeit, frenzy

orient /ɔːriənt/, **orients, orienting, oriented.** 1 The **Orient** refers to the part of the world that includes India, China, and Japan; a literary or old-fashioned use. EG *In the markets, I breathed the smells of the Orient... ...political theory in the West and in the Orient.* N PROPER : *the*+N = East, Far East

2 If you **orient** yourself to a new situation, you learn about it and prepare yourself to deal with it; a formal use. EG *The discussions helped me orient myself to the language... The newcomer has to orient himself.* V+O (REFL) = acclimatize

3 If someone or something **is oriented** to or towards a particular aim, idea, or person, they work or act with that aim, idea, or person in mind; a formal use. EG *The union is oriented towards welfare capitalism... Education was oriented to theory and distant facts... We have been too much oriented towards the Americans.* ● See also **oriented.** V+O : ONLY PASS, USU+*to/towards*

oriental /ɔːriɛntəⁿl/, **orientals.** 1 Something that is **oriental** comes from or is associated with the part of the world that includes India, China, and Japan. EG *...Oriental philosophy... ...her oriental features... ...oriental carpets.* ADJ CLASSIF = eastern

2 An **Oriental** is a person who comes from the part of the world that includes India, China, and Japan; often considered an offensive word. EG *...olive-skinned Orientals.* N COUNT

orientate /ɔːriɛnteɪt/, **orientates, orientating, orientated.** 1 If someone or something **is orientated** to or towards a particular subject, place, or person, they are very interested in them and concentrate their efforts on them. EG *We're orientated towards the social sciences... ...new firms orientated towards China... It was orientated towards Anthony.* V+O : ONLY PASS, USU+*to/towards* ⇑ be directed

2 When you **orientate** yourself, 2.1 you make sure of where you are by looking at a map, or by searching for places or objects that you are familiar with. EG *...trying to orientate myself on the map... ...the traveller who is well orientated within London.* 2.2 you learn about the new situation you are in and prepare to deal with it. EG *Her son was still trying to orientate himself.* V+O (REFL) = orient; V+O (REFL) = acclimatize

orientated /ɔːrɪenteɪtɪ[2]d/ If someone is politically **orientated**, family **orientated**, business-**orientated**, etc, they are particularly interested in politics, family, business, etc. EG *The whole group became more child orientated... ...a commercially orientated theory... ...career-orientated women.*
COMB : FORMS ADJS ⇑ directed = oriented

orientation /ɔːrɪenteɪʃə[0]n/, **orientations**. 1 The **orientation** of an organization, system, etc means the activities it is interested in and the aims that it has. EG *...the party's revolutionary orientation... ...suggestions for a different orientation to the campaign... The school has an orientation towards practical skills.*
N COUNT+SUPP ⇑ direction = inclination

2 The **orientation** of a physical object is the direction it faces or the direction of the line along which it exists. EG *...the orientation of magnetic crystals in rocks... ...the orientation of the wall... Its orientation is north and south.*
N COUNT : USU WITH POSS

3 **Orientation** is information or training that you need in order to understand a new subject, job, activity, or situation. EG *...a three-day orientation course... I needed some orientation at this stage.*
N UNCOUNT = briefing

oriented /ɔːrɪentɪ[2]d/. If someone is politically **oriented**, family **oriented**, business-**oriented**, etc, they are particularly interested in politics, family, business, etc. EG *...politically oriented men... ...export-oriented industries.*
COMB : FORMS ADJS = orientated

orienteering /ɔːrɪentɪərɪŋ/ is a sport in which people run from one place to another, using a compass and a map to guide them between points that are marked along the route.
N UNCOUNT

orifice /ɒrɪfɪs/, **orifices**. An **orifice** is an opening or hole, especially one in your body such as your mouth; a formal word often used in a humorous way. EG *An endless flow of words streamed from the same orifice... ...the building's orifices.*
N COUNT

origin /ɒrɪdʒɪn/, **origins**. 1 The **origin** or **origins** of something means the beginning of it, often referring to the reasons for it beginning, the time when it began, etc. EG *The unrest has its origins in economic problems... ...the origin of the universe... ...the origins of the word 'jazz'... It may be of more recent origin... It is agricultural in origin.*
N COUNT : USU WITH POSS, SING=PL, OR N UNCOUNT = source

2 A person's **origin** or **origins** means the country, race, or social class of their parents or ancestors. EG *...a woman of Pakistani origin... ...your working-class origins... Trevino's origins were humble.*
N COUNT : USU POSS+N, SING=PL, OR N UNCOUNT = birth

original /ərɪdʒɪnə[0]l/, **originals**. 1 **Original** is used to describe the appearance, character, or parts of something when it began to exist, or when it was first made, thought of, etc. EG *They will restore the house to its original state... Of the original twenty, only twelve remained... ...the original steam engine... The original idea came from Dr Ball... ...in answer to your original question.* ◊ **originally**. EG *I stayed longer than I originally intended... It was originally a toy factory.*
ADJ CLASSIF : ATTRIB ⇑ earliest = initial
◊ ADV WITH VB = initially

2 If you refer to the **original**, when talking about an important document or famous work of art, you mean the one that the author or artist wrote or made themselves, and not any copies or translations of them. EG *The original is in the British Museum... The translation was faithful to the intention of the original... The lions were cast from a single original modelled by Landseer.* ▸ used as an adjective. EG *...an original Gordon Craig sketch... ...working on original documents.* • You say **in the original, in the original French**, etc, to refer to the language that a book, play, etc was first written in. EG *I read Simone de Beauvoir in the original... It was performed in the original Sanskrit.*
N COUNT ≠ copy, reproduction
▸ ADJ CLASSIF = genuine
• PHR : USED AS AN A

3 A piece of writing or music that is **original** is recently written and has never been published or performed before. EG *...her first collection of short stories, some original, some reprinted... ...the award for Best Original Play.*
ADJ CLASSIF ⇑ new

4 If you describe someone, their ideas, or their work as **original**, you mean that they are very imaginative and clever and use new ideas or methods; used showing approval. EG *...a daring and original idea... ...a most original guitar player.* ◊ **originality** /ərɪgɪ[1]nælɪti[1]/. EG *...a sculptor of genius and great originality... Its ideology is lacking in originality.*
ADJ QUALIT = creative, unusual
◊ N UNCOUNT = inventiveness

original sin is, according to some Christians, the wickedness of character that all human beings are born with because the first human beings, Adam and Eve, disobeyed God.
N UNCOUNT

originate /ərɪdʒɪneɪt/, **originates, originating, originated**. When something **originates** or you **originate** it, it begins to happen or exist; a formal word. EG *The bullfight originated in Spain... These beliefs originated in the 19th century... The idea originates with the woman who wrote the music.*
V-ERG : USU+A ⇑ start

originator /ərɪdʒɪneɪtə/, **originators**. The **originator** of an action or idea is the person who first thinks of it, begins it, or causes it; a formal word. EG *The originator of the idea was a young professor... ...the originator of the crime.*
N COUNT : IF+ PREP THEN *of* ⇑ creator = author

ornament /ɔːnəmə[2]nt/, **ornaments, ornamenting, ornamented**. 1 An **ornament** is 1.1 a small object that you display in your home because it is attractive. EG *...the ornaments on the mantlepiece... ...painted china ornaments.* 1.2 an object that is worn by a person, for example jewellery, to make them look more attractive. EG *...an ear ornament... ...gold ornaments, bracelets, rings.*
N COUNT
N COUNT

2 **Ornament** consists of the parts of an artistic work such as a book, sculpture, or piece of music, that are added to make it more elaborate and attractive. EG *He sang without ornament or embellishment... ...decorated with gold ornament.*
N UNCOUNT ⇑ decoration

3 If you **ornament** something, you add decorative objects or patterns to it in order to make it look more attractive. EG *...highly ornamented rooms... The sand was ornamented with shells and seaweed.* ◊ **ornamentation** /ɔːnəmə[2]nteɪʃə[0]n/. EG *The bookcase is four feet long with ornamentation carved near the ends.*
V+O : USU PASS ⇑ improve = decorate
◊ N UNCOUNT = decoration

4 If you describe someone as an **ornament**, you mean that they are admired by people and help to increase the good reputation of the group or organization that they belong to; an old-fashioned use. EG *...the head waitress, Lily, a much-loved ornament of the club... His son could have become an ornament to the firm.*
N COUNT : USU+ SUPP ⇑ asset

ornamental /ɔːnəmentə[0]l/. Something that is **ornamental** is intended to be attractive rather than practical or useful. EG *...an ornamental pond... ...ornamental bushes.*
ADJ CLASSIF = decorative

ornate /ɔːneɪt/. Something that is **ornate** has a lot of decoration, especially curving patterns. EG *...ornate necklaces... ...ornate lettering.* ◊ **ornately**. EG *...an ornately carved chair.*
ADJ QUALIT = elaborate
◊ ADV WITH VB = elaborately

ornery /ɔːnəri[1]/. Someone who is **ornery** is stubborn, bad-tempered, and uncooperative; a very informal word used in American English. EG *Quint got ornery when he was bored.*
ADJ QUALIT = awkward

ornithology /ɔːnɪθɒlədʒi[1]/ is the study of birds; a formal word. EG *I've taken up ornithology.* ◊ **ornithological**. EG *I spent three years doing ornithological research.* ◊ **ornithologist, ornithologists**. EG *...a famous ornithologist.*
N UNCOUNT
◊ ADJ CLASSIF
◊ N COUNT

orphan /ɔːfən/, **orphans, orphaning, orphaned**. 1 An **orphan** is a child whose parents are dead. EG *She became an orphan at twelve... ...an orphan boy from London.*
N COUNT

2 If someone **is orphaned**, their parents have died. EG *We adopted the twins when they were orphaned.* ◊ **orphaned**. EG *...a home for orphaned girls.*
V+O : ONLY PASS
◊ ADJ CLASSIF

orphanage /ɔːfə[0]nɪdʒ/, **orphanages**. An **orphanage** is a place where children who are orphans are looked after. Orphanages are usually run by charities or religious groups.
N COUNT ⇑ institution

orthodox /ɔːθədɒks/. 1 **Orthodox** beliefs, methods, or systems are those that are accepted or believed by most people. EG *...the traditional beliefs of orthodox Christianity... ...orthodox medicine.*
ADJ CLASSIF : ATTRIB = conventional

2 People who are **orthodox** 2.1 believe in the older and more traditional ideas of their religion, or the political party or system that they support. EG *...a fairly orthodox socialist... ...Orthodox Jews.* 2.2 are regarded as normal and ordinary in their actions, behaviour, and thinking. EG *The child has less orthodox ambitions for herself... That project had advanced no further than his more orthodox ones.*
ADJ CLASSIF
ADJ QUALIT = conventional

orthodoxy /ɔːθədɒksi[1]/, **orthodoxies**; a formal word. 1 The **orthodoxy** in a particular area of human thought or activity means the ideas or methods that are popular or most widely used at a particular time. EG *...the prevailing orthodoxy on this delicate problem... Conceptual art became the seventies orthodoxy.*
N COUNT ⇑ philosophy

2 **Orthodoxy** is 2.1 the traditional and accepted beliefs of a particular religion or philosophy. EG
N UNCOUNT : USU MOD+N

...*Islamic orthodoxy... ...Marxist orthodoxy.* **2.2** the degree to which a person believes in and supports the ideas of their religion or political party. EG ...*an argument over the questioned orthodoxy of Rabbi Jacobs... ...the rigid conservative orthodoxy of Mr Mzali.* N UNCOUNT : USU WITH POSS = traditionalism

orthography /ɔːθɒgrəfi[1]/ means the way words are spelled or should be spelled; a formal word. N UNCOUNT = spelling

orthopaedic /ɔːθəpiːdɪk/; also spelled **orthopedic**, especially in American English. **Orthopaedic** means concerning the medical care of the bones in the bodies of humans and animals, especially the treatment or prevention of injuries or defects; a technical term in medicine. EG ...*the Orthopaedic Hospital... ...orthopaedic patients... ...orthopedic boots.* ADJ CLASSIF : ATTRIB

-ory is **1** added in place of the '-e' at the end of some verbs and nouns in order to form adjectives. EG ...*advise→advisory... ...sense→sensory.* SUFFIX : FORMS ADJS **2** added in place of the '-ion' at the end of some uncountable nouns in order to form adjectives. EG ...*illusion→illusory... ...exploration→exploratory.* SUFFIX : FORMS ADJS

OS /əʊ ɛs/ is **1** an abbreviation for 'outsize'; used especially on labels on clothes, or in advertising clothes for sale. ADJ CLASSIF **2** an abbreviation for 'Ordnance Survey'. EG ...*OS maps.* N BEFORE N

oscillate /ɒsɪleɪt/, **oscillates, oscillating, oscillated**; a formal or technical word. **1** If something **oscillates**, it moves repeatedly from one position to another and back again. EG *Its wings oscillate up and down a hundred times a second... ...the oscillating motion of the waves.* V : USU+A ⇑ swing ◇ **oscillation, oscillations.** EG ...*the oscillation of the pointer on weighing machines.* ◇ N UNCOUNT/COUNT ⇑ swinging

2 If you **oscillate** between two moods, attitudes, or types of behaviour, you keep changing from one to another and back again. EG *He oscillates between conservatism and radicalism... His mood oscillated between co-operation and aggression.* V+A *(between)* = waver, hover ◇ **oscillation.** EG *Her continual oscillation from mobility to immobility.* ◇ N UNCOUNT/COUNT = change

3 An electric current that **oscillates** changes in amount or in the direction of its flow at regular intervals of time. EG ...*a high frequency oscillating electrical current.* V = fluctuate

oscillation /ɒsɪleɪʃəⁿn/, **oscillations**. An **oscillation** is an increase or decrease in an amount that happens frequently or regularly. EG ...*the short-term oscillation of the share index.* N COUNT = fluctuation

osier /əʊzɪə/, **osiers**. An **osier** is a willow tree whose twigs are used for making baskets; also used of the twigs. N COUNT

osmosis /ɒzməʊsɪs, ɒs-/ is **1** the process by which a liquid passes through a thin piece of solid substance such as the roots of a plant; a technical term in physics and biology. N UNCOUNT ⇑ movement **2** the way in which people or ideas influence each other gradually and without any obvious signs. EG ...*a kind of sisterly osmosis... ...by some obscure process of imperial osmosis.* N UNCOUNT ⇑ process

ossify /ɒsɪfaɪ/, **ossifies, ossifying, ossified**. If you say that an idea, system, or organization **ossifies**, or something **ossifies** it, you mean that it becomes fixed and difficult to change; a formal word, used showing disapproval. EG *The State ossifies class relationships.* V-ERG = fossilize ◇ **ossified.** EG ...*a large, bureaucratic and ossified system... Things became ossified in the late 17th century.* ◇ ADJ CLASSIF = stagnant ◇ **ossification** /ɒsɪfɪkeɪʃəⁿn/. EG ...*social ossification and the denial of individual rights.* ◇ N UNCOUNT = fossilization

ostensible /ɒstɛnsɪbəⁿl/ is used to describe something that seems to be true or is officially stated to be true, but about which you or other people have doubts; a formal word. EG ...*the ostensible purpose of his excursion... The ostensible cause was the currency reform in West Germany.* ADJ CLASSIF : ATTRIB ⇑ pretended = alleged ≠ actual ◇ **ostensibly.** EG *Rose left the room, ostensibly to explain about dinner to the cook... ...photocopies made ostensibly for the legal department... ...ostensibly fair and reasonable prices.* ◇ ADV SEN, OR ADV = seemingly

ostentation /ɒstɛnteɪʃəⁿn/ means doing things or buying things in order to impress people with your wealth or importance; a formal word, used showing disapproval. EG *More than two telephones is pure ostentation... ...my distaste for any ostentation.* N UNCOUNT

ostentatious /ɒstɛnteɪʃəs/; a formal word. **1** Something that is **ostentatious** costs a lot of money and is intended to impress people; used showing disapproval. EG ...*a magnificent and ostentatious palace... ...hotels that catered in ostentatious luxury for a hundred guests at a time.* ADJ QUALIT = extravagant

2 Someone who is **ostentatious** wants to impress people with their wealth, importance, or a quality that they think they have; often used showing disapproval. EG *We Americans are lavish, generous, and ostentatious... They were neither aggressive, inept nor ostentatious.* ADJ QUALIT = flashy, flamboyant ◇ **ostentatiously.** EG *They were never ostentatiously dressed.* ◇ ADV WITH VB = flashily

3 Ostentatious actions or behaviour are done deliberately and in an exaggerated way in order to draw people's attention to you, and often in order to make them react in a particular way. EG *She sets the door, with an ostentatious precision, half ajar.* ADJ QUALIT ⇑ obvious = conspicuous ◇ **ostentatiously.** EG *I started ostentatiously clearing the table... ...preparations ostentatiously made for blocking the Straits.* ◇ ADV WITH VB = conspicuously

osteopath /ɒstiˈəⁿpæθ/, **osteopaths**. An **osteopath** is a person who treats illnesses by massaging people's bodies and bending them in different ways, especially in order to reduce pain or stiffness. EG *He went to an osteopath; one crack and never a twinge of pain since.* N COUNT

ostracism /ɒstrəsɪzəⁿm/ is the state of being ostracized or the act of ostracizing someone; a formal word. EG *The mothers of these children feared social ostracism... They faced hostility, contempt, ostracism.* N UNCOUNT ⇑ exclusion

ostracize /ɒstrəsaɪz/, **ostracizes, ostracizing, ostracized**; also spelled **ostracise**. If someone **is ostracized**, people deliberately behave in an unfriendly way towards them and do not allow them to take part in any of their social activities; a formal word. EG *He was ostracized from Cape Town society... Their children were ostracized by teachers and pupils alike.* V+O : USU PASS ⇑ exclude = cold-shoulder

ostrich /ɒstrɪtʃ/, **ostriches**. An **ostrich** is a large African bird that cannot fly. It has long legs, a long neck, a small head, and large soft feathers. N COUNT

other /ʌðə/, **others**. When 'other' follows the determiner 'an', it is written as one word: see **another**. When 'other' is used as an adjective, it usually occurs immediately after any determiner that there is in a noun group. **1** You use **other 1.1** to refer to an additional thing or person like one that has been mentioned or is known about. EG *There were some other people in the compartment... May I make one other point?... He and two others were sentenced to death... ...in our family, as in many others.* ADJ CLASSIF : ATTRIB, OR PRON : HAS PL **1.2** to refer to someone or something that is not the person or thing already mentioned or known about, or that is different from them. EG *That's true for Italy, but not for most other European countries... I've got other things to think about... There was no other way to do it... ...neither tomorrow, nor Friday, nor any other day... Many sites are near rivers. Others are close to main roads... Some projects are shorter than others.* ADJ CLASSIF : ATTRIB, OR PRON : HAS PL **1.3** at the end of a list or a group of examples, to refer generally to people or things like the ones just mentioned. EG ...*Malaysia, Indonesia and other places... ...toys, paints, books and other equipment... ...schools or other institutions.* ADJ CLASSIF : ATTRIB ⇑ etc ▸ used as a noun to refer to people or organizations. EG ...*architects and planners and others.* ▸ N PLURAL **1.4** after 'among' in expressions such as **among other things, among others**, etc to say that there are several more facts, things, people, etc like the one or ones mentioned but that you do not intend to discuss them in detail. EG *Your father is–among other things–a very private person... Professor Barry, among others, has drawn attention to this problem... ...fish found in, among other places, the coastal waters of Japan.* PHR : USED AS AN A **1.5** to refer to places or times which are not the place or time you are in. EG ...*people of other times... Results in other countries are impressive.* ADJ CLASSIF : ATTRIB ⇑ different

2 You also use **other 2.1** to refer to the second of two things or people when the first has been mentioned or when their identity is known. EG ...*the other side of the street... ...the other end of the room... ...a man coming the other way... He had his papers in one hand, his hat in the other... ...two daughters, one a baby, the other a girl of twelve.* ADJ CLASSIF : ATTRIB, OR PRON, USU *the+other* **2.2** to refer to the rest of the people or things in a group. EG ...*the other members of the class.* ADJ CLASSIF : ATTRIB ▸ used as a noun. EG *He sat far away from the others... I shall wait until the others come back.* ▸ N PLURAL **2.3** to refer to people in general. EG *One ought not to inflict one's problems on other people.* ADJ CLASSIF : ATTRIB

▸ used as a noun. EG *Working for others can be most fulfilling.* **2.4** to refer to one of two or more people, things, or groups that have a connection or relationship, or that affect one another in some way. You usually use 'each' or 'one' to refer to the one you mention first, and 'other' to the one you mention next. EG *One shot the other and then shot herself... Each recognized the other as the key to success.*

▸ N PLURAL; PRON : SING, *the* + PRON

3 You also use **other** in expressions of time such as **the other day, the other evening, the other week,** etc to refer to a day, evening, or week in the recent past. EG *I saw Davis the other day... Have you forgotten what happened the other night?... My sister came down the other week.*

PHR : USED AS AN A; ⇑ recently

4 other than. 4.1 You use **other than** after a negative or broad negative to say that the person, item, or thing that follows is the only exception to the statement you have just made. EG *She never discussed it with anyone other than Derek... I don't have a thing with me other than this coat... There was no noise other than a muted organ.* **4.2** You use **no other than** and **nothing other than** to introduce a decision, reason, or result and emphasize that it is the only one possible in the situation. EG *They did it for no other reason than sheer frustration... He reread every page with no other purpose than to pass the time... There's no choice other than to reopen his case... The signal could mean nothing other than a halt to the advance.* **4.3** You use **none other than** and **no other than** to emphasize the name of a person or thing when it is surprising in a particular situation. EG *It was none other than the famous Mr Victor Hazel himself... He was talking to no other person than Millington Harwood.* **4.4** If you **are other than** you appear or people expect, you are different or surprising in your character, behaviour, or occupation. EG *He may be quite other than he seems... We cannot pretend to be other than we are.*

PREP OR CONJ SUBORD : WITH BROAD NEG; = apart from, except; PHR + NG/*to*-INF/INF; PREP; = no less; PHR : VB INFLECTS; ⇑ differ

5 every other. 5.1 You use expressions such as **every other** day, **every other** person, etc to refer to the first or second of each pair of days, people, etc in a longer period of time, a larger group of people, etc. EG *We wrote every other day... Their local committees are usually held every other month.* **5.2** You also use **every other** to emphasize that you are referring to all the rest of the people or things in a group. EG *...along with every other female in the village.*

PHR + N IN SING; ⇑ regularly; = every second; PHR + N IN SING

6 The word **other** is also used in the following expressions. **6.1** You use the expression **on the other,** meaning 'on the other hand', to introduce the second part of an argument or discussion when the first part was introduced by 'on the one hand'. EG *On the one hand, we would have done as they did; on the other, we suspect that this is not the whole story.* **6.2** You use **one after the other** to emphasize that actions or events happen with very little time between them, or in a very similar way, and not separately, differently, or at exactly the same time. EG *Stone, Prattley and Unwin came forward one after the other... ...a series of days, one after the other... We saw the three plays one after the other.* **6.3** You say **or other** after words such as 'some', 'something', or 'somehow' to emphasize that you cannot or do not want to be more precise about the information that you are giving; used mainly in spoken English. EG *For some reason or other your name was omitted... I went back into the house for something or other... Somehow or other, he reached the Alps... He was called Nat something or other.* **6.4** You use **one or other** to refer to one or more things or people in a group, when it does not matter which particular one or ones are thought of or chosen. EG *One or other current must be altered... ...the position of the beads in relation to one or other end of the frame... ...the MPs who supported one or other of the journals... ...a simple sentence in one or other language.* **6.5** You also use **other** in several expressions which are explained at other entries in this dictionary: ● **each other**: see **each.** ● **your other half**: see **half.** ● **this, that, and the other**: see **this.** ● **in other words**: see **word.**

PHR : USED AS AN A; PHR : USED AS AN A; = in succession; PHR; PHR; ⇑ any

otherness /ʌðənɪ²s/ is the quality that someone or something has which is strange or different from yourself or from the things that you have experienced. EG *...the otherness of Australia.*

N UNCOUNT; ⇑ strangeness

otherwise /ʌðəwaɪz/. You use **otherwise 1** to say what the result or consequence would be if the previously mentioned situation, fact, idea, etc was untrue or was not the case. EG *It's perfectly harmless, Mabel, otherwise I wouldn't have done it... Wash five times a day. You're not properly clean otherwise... This makes the show more exciting than it would otherwise be.* **2** to emphasize that a particular event or feature mentioned is an exception to the general situation. EG *The cement is slightly cracked but otherwise in good order... That was a sudden outbreak in an otherwise blameless career.* **3** to refer to the opposite of something, or something very different from what was previously stated, believed, or known; a rather formal use. EG *Life was splendid. I had no reason to think otherwise... Stiff and formal, the man was incapable of acting otherwise... ...these places, otherwise known as New Towns.* **4** in the expression **or otherwise,** to refer to the opposite of the preceding word, especially in situations where either of them may be correct. EG *He said nothing of her attractiveness or otherwise... Both sides understand, consciously or otherwise, the limitations of the treaty.... It had no effect on its users, beneficial or otherwise.* **5** in the expressions **or otherwise** or **and otherwise,** to indicate that other things are possible in addition to what was mentioned previously. EG *You should wear gloves, rubber or otherwise... ...no evidence of treachery, British or otherwise... ...a slow trend to freedom, political and otherwise.* **6** to indicate that other ways of doing something are possible in addition to the way already mentioned. EG *His mother will spank him or otherwise show disapproval... The child is fed and otherwise attended to.*

ADV SEN; ADV + ADJ/ADV/PREP; ADV WITH VB; ⇑ differently; PHR : USED AS AN A; ⇑ or not; PHR : USED AS AN A; ADV WITH VB

other-worldly means more concerned with spiritual matters than with daily life. EG *...other-worldly, unrealistic people... ...traditional, other-worldly religions, such as Hinduism.*

ADJ QUALIT : USU ATTRIB; ≠ worldly

otter /ɒtə/, **otters.** An **otter** is a small animal with brown fur, short legs, and a long tail. Otters swim well and catch and eat fish.

N COUNT

ouch /aʊtʃ/ is used **1** to express sudden pain. EG *Ouch! That hurt!* **2** to express surprise or shock at something unpleasant; used in a rather humorous way. EG *'They cost about forty pounds each.'–'Ouch,' Farnbach said.*

EXCLAM; EXCLAM

ought /ɔːt/. You use **ought 1** to say that you think that an action or someone's behaviour is morally right. If you say 'ought not', you think it is morally wrong. EG *They ought to be free, oughtn't they?... People in a university oughtn't to get away with it... Ought he to be forced out of the Presidency?... Somebody ought to do something about it.* **2** to say that you think it is a good idea and important for you or someone else to do a particular thing, and that it would be slightly wrong of you or them not to do it. EG *Oughtn't we to phone for the police?... We ought to order, oughtn't we?... Rudolph didn't know whether he ought to sit down or not... Someone ought to turn that tap off... She ought to see the doctor.* **3** to criticize someone's attitude or behaviour, when you expect them to behave in a particular way and think that they should feel guilty if they have not done so. EG *'I don't care,' he said. 'Well, you ought to,' she said... He ought to know better.* **4** to say that a statement that you make or a feeling that you have is reasonable in a particular situation. EG *I really oughtn't to be surprised.* **5** to indicate the correct way to do something or the correct position for something. EG *It's gone too far–it ought to go over to there.* **6** to say that something is probably true or will probably happen in the way mentioned. EG *That ought to interest you... It ought to be quite easy... It ought to be possible to mend it... He ought to be out of jail by now.* **7** to say that you think it is the right point in a piece of writing or speech to explain something or add new information, because it is important and relevant. EG *That's interesting. I think we ought to talk about that one... Perhaps we ought to pause for a moment to find out what other people think.* **8** in the expressions **ought to have** and **ought not to have,** when you realize that you or someone else has made a mistake and you are suggesting how it could have been avoided. EG *I ought to have said yes... I ought not to have come here... The strike ought not to have been allowed to succeed... Sam ought to have realised how dangerous it was.* **9** to

MODAL; = should; MODAL; = should; MODAL; MODAL; = should; MODAL; = should; MODAL; = should; MODAL : WITH *I/we*; = should; MODAL; MODAL

tell someone that you must do something, for example that you must leave; a polite use. EG *It's getting late; I think I ought to go if you don't mind.*

oughtn't /ɔːtəⁿnt/ is a spoken form of 'ought not'.

ounce /aʊns/, **ounces**. 1 An **ounce** is 1.1 a unit of weight used in Britain and the USA that is a sixteenth of a pound, and is equal to 28.35 grams; see also □ at MEASUREMENT. EG *...an ounce of tobacco... The baby gains 6 to 8 ounces a week... ...an ounce above her regular weight.* 1.2 a unit of liquid capacity equal to 0.028 litres. EG *...a measuring jug marked in ounces.* 2 You also talk about an **ounce** of effort, an **ounce** of sense, etc meaning a small amount of effort, sense, etc; an informal use. EG *...using every ounce of strength he possessed... ...anyone with an ounce of intelligence.*
N COUNT/PART = oz; N COUNT/PART; N PART: USU SING+N UNCOUNT ⇑ bit = scrap

our /aʊə/. A speaker or writer uses **our** to indicate that something belongs or relates both to himself or herself and to one or more other people as a group. See **we**. EG *...our children... ...the future of our society... This could change our lives... We were on our own.*
DET POSS

ours /aʊəz/. A speaker or writer uses **ours** to indicate that something belongs or relates both to himself or herself and to one or more other people as a group. See **we**. EG *It is a very different country from ours... ...a school such as ours... This is a friend of ours.*
PRON POSS

ourselves /aʊəsɛlvz/. 1 A speaker or writer uses **ourselves** 1.1 as the object of a verb or preposition in a clause where 'we' is the subject or 'us' is a previous object. See **we**. EG *I think we may find ourselves without any real choice... We almost made ourselves ill... In 1968 we built ourselves a new surgery.* ▸ **Ourselves** is also used to emphasize the subject or object of a clause. It is usually used in addition to a subject or object, although it is sometimes used instead of 'us' as an object. EG *In teaching, we ourselves have to do a lot of learning.* 1.2 instead of 'us', especially after a preposition, when the subject of the clause is not 'we'; used to express politeness or emphasis. EG *With the exception of a few Algerians and ourselves, everyone spoke Spanish.*
PRON REFL: PL, USED AS O; ▸ PRON REFL: PL; PRON REFL: PL, USED AS O

2 **Ourselves** is also used by a speaker or writer in expressions such as 'we did it ourselves' in order to say that he or she, together with one or more other people, did something without any help or interference from anyone else. EG *We were allowed to go down ourselves.*
PRON REFL: PL ⇑ alone

-ous is added to some nouns in order to form adjectives. These adjectives describe something or someone as having a particular quality. When the noun ends in '-y', the '-y' always changes to '-i' in the adjective. When the noun ends in '-e', the '-e' also sometimes changes to '-i' in the adjective. EG *...outrage→outrageous... ...hazard→hazardous... ...mystery→mysterious... ...grace→gracious.*
SUFFIX: FORMS ADJS

oust /aʊst/, **ousts, ousting, ousted**. If you **oust** someone from a job, position of power, or place, you cause them to leave it, often by force or illegal means; a formal word. EG *...the coup which ousted the President... He was ousted from his job... ...ousting landowners and peasants from their lands.*
V+O ⇑ remove = throw out

out /aʊt/. In paragraphs 1 and 2 **out** is used to refer to movement and position. 1 You use **out** 1.1 to indicate movement away from a place, for example from a room, a building, or a vehicle. EG *She rushed out of the house... The lift doors opened and they stepped out into the empty foyer... He was already on his way out... I got up to see him out... She's just got out of bed... It dropped out of the sky.* 1.2 to indicate that someone is away from their usual place in order to do a particular job. EG *A search party is out looking for survivors... They sent three fire engines out.* 1.3 to indicate that someone is absent from their home or work for a short time. EG *He came when I was out... All my friends are out of town... I just slipped out for a packet of fags.* ● If you are **out and about**, you are going out, meeting people, and leading a normal life again after you have recovered from an illness. EG *I should be out and about again by next week.* 1.4 to indicate that someone is absent from home for a social activity, such as going to the cinema or to a restaurant. EG *Do you eat out a lot?... We don't go out much... They were invited out by Howard's head of department... ...an evening out.* 1.5 to indicate that someone is away from or leaving a town or city or that a place is outside a town or city. EG *...a week-end resort about twenty-five miles out of town... I don't want to live any further out... I can't wait to get out of Birmingham.* 1.6 to indicate that someone is travelling towards a distant place or is in it. EG *They went out as pioneers in 1890... Her husband was out in Africa somewhere.* 1.7 to indicate movement or a position that is towards the centre of an area and away from the edge. EG *She tosses the bottle out into the river... They stood right out in the middle of the road... We put out to sea.* 1.8 to indicate that something is in a position that is further away than usual from a particular place or from its normal position. EG *I slipped and put out my arm to save myself... She opened her fingers and held out a painted egg... His stomach stuck out.* 1.9 to indicate that someone is looking through a window or door towards the things that are outside a particular building or place, or that something is facing in that direction. EG *She stared out at the rain... It looks out over a golf course... She was standing looking out of the window.*
ADV AFTER VB/N: IF+PREP THEN USU *of*; ADV AFTER VB/N; ADV AFTER VB ≠ in; ● PHR: USED AS AN A ⇑ better; ADV AFTER VB/N ≠ in; ADV AFTER VB, OR ADV+*of*; ADV AFTER VB; ADV AFTER VB; ADV AFTER VB; ADV AFTER VB

1.10 to indicate that something is situated or happens in the open air, rather than in a room or building. EG *There are so many people sleeping out... It's hot out... He's out in the garden.* 1.11 to indicate that a number of things are distributed to several places or in several directions. EG *Howard gives out drinks to all the guests... We sent out a leaflet to every household.* 1.12 to indicate that someone or something occupies a large area, or a larger area than before. EG *She stretched herself out on the sofa... ... a display of paperbacks spread out on the pavement.* 1.13 to indicate that light, smell, heat, etc comes from a particular place or thing. EG *It throws out an intense smell of tea leaves.* 1.14 to indicate that someone or something makes a particular sound, especially a loud sound. EG *She let out a shriek... The sirens blared out... Loud rock music wells out of a boutique.*
ADV AFTER VB = outside; ADV AFTER VB; ADV AFTER VB; ADV AFTER VB; ADV AFTER VB

2 You use **out** 2.1 to indicate that something is removed from a container or place where it is enclosed. EG *She opened a lacquered box and took out a cigarette... She had the key out and was fumbling at the door... He got out a book and read... She tore several sheets of paper out of the back of the book... Could you take it out of the fridge for me?... The fossils are carefully chipped out of the rock.* 2.2 to indicate that someone is removing something from a place where it has been stored or kept safe. EG *I must get some money out of the bank... Get a book out of the library... She drew out all her savings.* 2.3 to indicate that someone is leaving an institution or has left it.. EG *Someone else I know has just come out of hospital... I had been out of university a year... Once out of high school, she started singing in night clubs.* 2.4 to indicate that someone or something is prevented from entering a place or from participating in a situation. EG *It's designed to keep out intruders... They are pricing the country out of international markets.* 2.5 to indicate that someone is removing or getting rid of someone or something that they do not want. EG *I hope you kicked him out... They're too good to throw out... I want him out!... Get these kids out of here!... She brushed out the wrinkles in her dress... They're determined to stamp out political extremism.* 2.6 to indicate that someone is no longer involved or no longer taking part in something, especially because they find it difficult or unpleasant. EG *Face up to it and get out before it's too late... Count me out... I want out... ...the only way out of a hopeless situation.*
ADV AFTER VB, OR PREP; ADV AFTER VB, OR PREP; ADV AFTER VB; ADV AFTER VB ≠ in; ADV AFTER VB; ADV AFTER VB/N ≠ in

2.7 to indicate that information or facts that were secret have been revealed. EG *The word got out that he would, after all, go ahead... He thought he had blurted out quite enough... She coaxed out of me what I really felt... The secret's out.* ● If you say **'Out with it'**, you are asking someone to tell you something that they do not want to tell you or that they have tried to hide from you. EG *Come on. Out with it!*
ADV AFTER VB; ● CONVENTION = spit it out

2.8 to indicate that something is or becomes available to the public. EG *His book had come out... She has now brought out a second album... ...the most up-to-date geography book out.*
ADV AFTER VB/N

3 You use **out** 3.1 to indicate that something is no longer burning, shining, functioning, etc. EG *He turned the light out... She stubbed out her cigarette.*
ADV AFTER VB

3.2 to indicate that someone is asleep or unconscious. EG *I was knocked out... She went out like a light.* 3.3 to indicate that something is considered to be impossible or unacceptable; an informal use. EG *That's right out, I'm afraid... Romance is making a come back. Reality is out.* 3.4 to indicate that fashions, styles, clothes, etc are unfashionable. EG *Long skirts are definitely out this year... It's terribly out of fashion.*
ADV AFTER VB
ADV AFTER VB ≠ in
ADV AFTER VB ≠ in

4 You use **out of** 4.1 to indicate why someone does something. EG *He wrote that review out of pure spite... Gretchen felt that he was silent out of embarrassment.* 4.2 to indicate that someone derives pleasure, profit, etc from something. EG *They all got something out of it... We don't get great pleasure out of it... You did well out of Saving Certificates.* 4.3 to indicate that something happens as a result or consequence of something else. EG *The new law came out of Government's concern over rising house prices... Arising out of that, they've extended their work into other fields.* 4.4 to indicate that someone no longer does a particular thing. EG *I've got out of the habit of writing letters... He's managed to stay out of trouble for two years now.* 4.5 to indicate that someone no longer has a particular thing. EG *We're out of paper.* 4.6 to indicate that a particular substance or material is used in order to make something. EG *You can make petroleum out of coal and you can make it out of gas... ...a small basket formed out of wire.* 4.7 to indicate that someone is using a particular sum of money in order to pay for something. EG *Is he paying for your trip out of parish funds?* 4.8 to indicate that something happens to one person, group, set, etc selected from a larger group or set. EG *One out of every 10 people is likely to suffer from a mental illness at some time in their life... ...nine times out of ten... He chooses out of a set of options.* 4.9 to indicate that someone manages to obtain something from someone else, for example information or a particular reaction. EG *I prised the information out of him... You won't get any sympathy out of her.* 4.10 to indicate that something is similar to something from a particular book, film, etc. EG *It was like something out of an old Charlie Chaplin film... He looked like a character out of a Dickens novel.* 4.11 to indicate that someone is sheltered from a particular kind of weather. EG *You ought to stay out of the sun... We'll have to get in out of the rain.*
PREP = from
PREP
PREP = from
PREP
PREP
PREP = from
PREP = from
PREP
PREP
PREP = in
PREP ≠ in

5 When plants or flowers are **out**, they have flowers that are fully open. EG *The daffodils are out.*
ADJ CLASSIF: PRED

6 If someone is **out** for something, they want or intend to achieve that thing. EG *He's out for power... You might feel that they're out to use your house as a free hotel.*
ADJ CLASSIF: PRED+for/to-INF ⇑ aiming

7 If workers are **out**, they are on strike; used in informal English. EG *We've been out for two and a half months and we're not going back until we get what we're asking for.*
ADJ CLASSIF: PRED

8 You also use **out** to indicate that a particular period of time is finished. EG *They had sold over a million copies before the year was out.*
ADJ CLASSIF: PRED = over

9 If you say that something such as a calculation or measurement is **out**, you mean that it is incorrect. EG *All the calculations were out... It's only a couple of degrees out.*
ADJ CLASSIF: PRED ⇑ wrong ≠ correct

10 • **inside out**: see **inside**.

out- is added to some verbs to form other verbs that describe someone or something as doing a particular action much better than another person or thing. EG *...run→outrun... ...climb→outclimb... ...fight→outfight.*
PREFIX

out-and-out. You use **out-and-out** when you are describing a person or thing of a particular type and you want to emphasize how completely they have all the characteristics of that type of person or thing. EG *He's an out-and-out villain... ...an out-and-out professional... ...out-and-out mayhem.*
ADJ CLASSIF: ATTRIB = absolute

outback /autbæk/. The **outback** refers to the isolated and remote areas of Australia where very few people live. EG *We've always lived in the outback.*
N SING: the+N ⇑ countryside

outbid /autbɪd/, **outbids, outbidding, outbidded, outbid**. The forms **outbidded** and **outbid** are both used as the past tense and the past participle. If you **outbid** someone, you offer more money than they do for something that you both want to buy. EG *We'll be outbid at every auction... They are outbidding other potential buyers.*
V+O = top

outboard motor, outboard motors. An **outboard motor** is a motor with a propeller that can be fixed to the back of a small boat.
N COUNT

outbreak /autbreɪk/, **outbreaks**. An **outbreak** of something unpleasant such as a war or disease is a sudden occurrence of it. EG *...the outbreak of the Second World War... ...a severe outbreak of food poisoning.*
N COUNT+SUPP

outbuilding /autbɪldɪŋ/, **outbuildings**. An **outbuilding** is a building such as a barn or stable which is near to a large house and which is owned by the people who own the house. EG *...a big farmhouse with a cluster of outbuildings around it.*
N COUNT: USU PL

outburst /autbɜːst/, **outbursts**. An **outburst** is 1 a sudden and strong expression of emotion, especially anger. EG *I apologize for my outburst just now... He roused the American people to an outburst of moral indignation.* 2 a sudden period of violent activity. EG *...degrading outbursts of drunken violence.*
N COUNT = explosion
N COUNT+SUPP

outcast /autkɑːst/, **outcasts**. An **outcast** is someone who is not accepted by a group of people or by society. EG *They are treated as outcasts.*
N COUNT = pariah

outclass /autklɑːs/, **outclasses, outclassing, outclassed**. If you **outclass** someone, you are a lot better than they are at a particular activity. EG *He was totally outclassed.*
V+O = outshine

outcome /autkʌm/, **outcomes**. The **outcome** of something such as an action or process is the result of it. EG *There were not many people who dared predict the outcome of the general election... It was a complicated sequence of events that led to this most extraordinary outcome.*
N COUNT: USU SING, OR N SING: the+N+of

outcrop /autkrɒp/, **outcrops**. An **outcrop** is a large rock or group of rocks sticking out of the ground. EG *...a massive outcrop of granite.*
N COUNT: USU+SUPP

outcry /autkraɪ/, **outcries**. An **outcry** is a reaction of strong disapproval and anger shown by the public or media about an event, a government policy, etc. EG *There was a public outcry about selling arms to the rebels.*
N COUNT: USU+PREP = protest

outdated /autdeɪtɪ²d/ is used to describe ideas or ways of behaving which are old-fashioned and no longer useful. EG *He accused parents of spoiling their children's lives by forcing on them outdated beliefs, outdated manners, outdated morals.*
ADJ QUALIT = outmoded

outdid /autdɪd/ is the past tense of **outdo**.

outdistance /autdɪstəns/, **outdistances, outdistancing, outdistanced**. If you **outdistance** someone, 1 you are a lot better and more successful than they are at a particular activity. EG *He easily outdistanced men like Castle, who was of an older generation.* 2 you beat all your opponents easily in a race. EG *She outdistanced all the opposition.*
V+O = outstrip
V+O = outstrip

outdo /autduː/, **outdoes, outdoing, outdid, outdone**. If you **outdo** someone, you are a lot more successful than they are at a particular activity. EG *Robertson found that a heavy person can outdo a lighter one in certain jobs.*
V+O ⇑ beat

outdoor /autdɔː/, **outdoors**. 1 **Outdoor** activities, clothes, etc happen or are used outside and not in a building. EG *It was outdoor work, and fairly healthy... He was fully dressed in his outdoor clothes.*
ADJ CLASSIF: ATTRIB ≠ indoor

2 **Outdoor** people enjoy doing things outside in the fresh air. EG *'I like it here,' he said. 'I'm an outdoor man.'... She's definitely the outdoor type.*
ADJ CLASSIF: ATTRIB ≠ indoor

3 **Outdoors** means outside in the fresh air rather than in a building. EG *He spent little time outdoors... Children of all ages should be outdoors several hours a day.*
ADV AFTER VB = out of doors

4 The **outdoors** refers to a way of life or activities in which you spend a lot of time outside in the fresh air, especially in the countryside. EG *...the great outdoors.*
N SING: the+N

outer /autə/ is used to describe 1 things which contain or enclose something else. EG *Using a knife, peel off the outer plastic cover of the flex... The building's outer walls and doors are all of brown glass.* 2 things that are situated towards the edge of a place. EG *The family lived in the outer suburb of Le Vesinet... He sits in the outer office.*
ADJ CLASSIF: ATTRIB ⇑ exterior
ADJ CLASSIF: ATTRIB

outermost /autəməust/ is used to describe the one thing of a group of things which is situated furthest from the centre. EG *We had arrived in the outermost group of islands... Saturn was the outermost of the planets known in ancient times.*
ADJ CLASSIF: ATTRIB

outer space is the planets and space which are very far away from the earth. EG *...a creature from outer space.* — N UNCOUNT

outfit /aʊtfɪt/, **outfits**. An **outfit** is 1 a set of clothes, especially one that you wear for a special occasion. EG *He was dressed in an immaculate white outfit... ...sports outfits.* — N COUNT : USU+SUPP = ensemble
2 a group of people who work together; a fairly informal use. EG *I joined this outfit hoping to get abroad... They should have employed a public relations outfit.* — N COUNT : USU+SUPP = crew
3 all the equipment that you need in order to do a particular job. EG *...a complete anti-snake bite outfit.* — N COUNT : MOD+N = kit

outfitter /aʊtfɪtə/, **outfitters**. **Outfitters** can also be used as the singular form. An **outfitter** or **outfitters** is a shop that sells men's clothes; an old-fashioned word. EG *...a gentlemen's outfitter.* — N COUNT

outflank /aʊtflæŋk/, **outflanks, outflanking, outflanked**. 1 If one army **outflanks** another, it succeeds in getting round the side of it in order to attack it. EG *...an attempt to outflank the main force.* — V+O
2 If you **outflank** someone, you succeed in getting into a position where you can defeat them, for example in an argument. EG *He found himself outflanked over incomes policy.* — V+O = outdo

outflow /aʊtfləʊ/, **outflows**. An **outflow** is a place where water or some other liquid flows out of a lake, reservoir, etc. EG *The fungus was found in a sewage outflow in Sardinia.* — N COUNT

outfox /aʊtfɒks/, **outfoxes, outfoxing, outfoxed**. If you **outfox** someone, you are a lot more clever or cunning than they are and so defeat them in some way. EG *We managed to outfox him.* — V+O = outsmart

outgoing /aʊtgəʊɪŋ/. 1 **Outgoing** is used to describe someone or something that is leaving a place or a job. EG *...the outgoing president... This box is for outgoing mail.* — ADJ CLASSIF : ATTRIB
2 Someone who is **outgoing** is very friendly and open in their behaviour; used showing approval. EG *Adler was an outgoing, sociable kind of man.* — ADJ QUALIT = extrovert
3 You use **outgoings** to refer to the money which you have to spend regularly, for example in order to pay your rent or bills. EG *Try to reduce as many outgoings as possible.* — N PLURAL = expenses

outgrow /aʊtgrəʊ/, **outgrows, outgrowing, outgrew, outgrown**. 1 If one thing **outgrows** another thing, it grows until it is bigger than the other thing. EG *Left alone, the young weeds would outgrow and choke the rice crop.* — V+O
2 If you **outgrow** a particular piece of clothing, you grow bigger so that you can no longer wear it. EG *You're going to outgrow these shoes very soon.* — V+O
3 If you **outgrow** a particular way of behaving or thinking, you change and become more mature, so that you no longer behave or think in the way that you did before. EG *She had now outgrown her juvenile sense of humour.* — V+O = grow out of

outgrowth /aʊtgrəʊθ/, **outgrowths**. An **outgrowth** of something is a natural development from it or result of it. EG *This theory was an outgrowth of Einstein's 'unified field theory'.* — N SING WITH DET +SUPP = consequence

outhouse /aʊthaʊs/, **outhouses**. An **outhouse** is a small building which is near to or adjoining a house and which is owned by the people who own the house. EG *Behind the cottage was an old outhouse.* — N COUNT

outing /aʊtɪŋ/, **outings**. An **outing** is a trip to a place of interest, for example a museum or the seaside, or to the theatre, cinema, etc. EG *I think perhaps we should postpone the outing.* — N COUNT = excursion

outlandish /aʊtlændɪʃ/. Something that is **outlandish** is very strange and unusual; used showing disapproval. EG *They've read the most outlandish things.* — ADJ QUALIT = bizarre

outlast /aʊtlɑːst/, **outlasts, outlasting, outlasted**. If one thing **outlasts** another thing, it lives or exists longer than the other thing. EG *Even those leafless beech trees would outlast him.* — V+O = outlive

outlaw /aʊtlɔː/, **outlaws, outlawing, outlawed**. 1 When something **is outlawed**, it is made illegal. EG *The use of poison gas was outlawed.* — V+O = ban
2 An **outlaw** is someone who has done something illegal and who is hiding from the authorities; a rather old-fashioned use. EG *...a band of outlaws.* — N COUNT ⇑ criminal = fugitive

outlay /aʊtleɪ/, **outlays**. An **outlay** is an amount of money that you spend as an investment. EG *The scheme required an initial outlay of 3,000,000 pounds.* — N COUNT : USU+SUPP ⇑ expenditure

outlet /aʊtlɪ²t/, **outlets**. An **outlet** is 1 a means of expressing and releasing emotions, feelings, or ideas which you have inside you. EG *...outlets for political expression.* — N COUNT = channel
2 a market for a product. EG *There is a huge sales outlet for pocket calculators.* — N COUNT
3 a shop or organization which sells the goods made by a particular manufacturer. EG *Several commercial outlets had already expressed an interest.* — N COUNT
4 a hole or pipe through which water or air can flow out. EG *Clean the sink outlet... ...the outlet of the water supply.* — N COUNT ⇑ exit

outline /aʊtlaɪn/, **outlines, outlining, outlined**. 1 To **outline** something such as an idea or plan means to explain it in a general way, without giving all the details. EG *He listened as I outlined my reasons... We distributed leaflets outlining the legal rights of wives.* — V+O = sketch out
2 An **outline** is 2.1 a general explanation or description of something which does not give all the details. EG *The course gave us a brief outline of European art... ...the outline of an idea.* — N SING WITH DET, OR *in*+N = delineation
2.2 the shape of something, especially when you cannot see it clearly and can only see its profile and not the details. EG *He saw the outline of a house against the sky... ...an outline drawing.* — N SING WITH DET, OR *in*+N
3 When light **outlines** something, it shows the profile of the object without all the details, especially because it is shining from behind the object. EG *He was clearly outlined in the light of a lamp... The light was just sufficient to outline a few ruins that stood apart on a little hill.* — V+O = silhouette

outlive /aʊtlɪv/, **outlives, outliving, outlived**. 1 To **outlive** someone means to continue to live after they have died. EG *Olivia had outlived Pepita by eighteen years.* — V+O = survive
2 To **outlive** something means to continue to exist after something else has disappeared or been replaced. EG *This system has managed to outlive changes in telephone design.* — V+O = survive
● If something **outlives** its **usefulness**, it has existed for too long and so is no longer useful or necessary. EG *People even wondered whether the organization had outlived its usefulness.* — ● PHR : VB INFLECTS

outlook /aʊtlʊk/, **outlooks**. 1 Your **outlook** is your general attitude towards life. EG *My whole outlook on life had changed... They are European in outlook... Their outlooks are so similar.* — N COUNT : POSS+N, OR *in*+N = perspective
2 The **outlook** is 2.1 the general impression that a situation gives about how it is going to develop, especially whether it is going to improve or get worse. EG *The economic outlook is bright... The outlook for food and energy prices is good.* — N SING : *the*+N, USU+SUPP = prospect
2.2 the weather forecast for the next day or the next few days. EG *...the outlook for the weekend.* — N SING : *the*+N

outlying /aʊtlaɪɪŋ/ is used to describe places that are very far away from the major towns and cities of a country or far from the centre of a town or city. EG *...Hong Kong's outlying territories... ...outlying areas.* — ADJ CLASSIF : ATTRIB ⇑ distant = remote

outmanoeuvre /aʊtmənuːvə/, **outmanoeuvres, outmanoeuvring, outmanoeuvred**; also spelled **outmaneuver** in American English. To **outmanoeuvre** someone means to gain an advantage over them in a particular situation by behaving in a clever and skilful way. EG *We were outmanoeuvred.* — V+O = outsmart

outmoded /aʊtməʊdɪ²d/. Something that is **outmoded** is old-fashioned and no longer useful. EG *...outmoded techniques... ...a rather outmoded view.* — ADJ QUALIT = outdated

outnumber /aʊtnʌmbə/, **outnumbers, outnumbering, outnumbered**. If one group of people or things **outnumbers** another group, it is greater in number than the other group. EG *Nationally men outnumber women... They are certainly outnumbered by the Social Democrats... They were outnumbered twelve to one.* — V+O

out of date; spelled with hyphens when used before a noun. Something that is **out of date** is old-fashioned and no longer useful. EG *You will find that the dictionaries are out of date and mislead you on this point... This is rather an out-of-date concept.* — ADJ QUALIT = outmoded

out of doors; also spelled with hyphens. **Out of doors** means outside in the fresh air and not in a building. EG *Sam and I will stay out of doors... We sat out-of-doors beneath tall elms.* — ADV WITH VB = outdoors
▸ used as a noun. EG *She had to be introduced gently to the out-of-doors.* — ▸ N SING : *the*+N

out-of-the-way places are 1 very far from towns and cities and so rather isolated. EG *Our expeditions have been to some out-of-the way places.* — ADJ QUALIT ⇑ remote
2 not well-known. EG *Tim took her to funny out-of-the-way pubs.* — ADJ QUALIT

out of work; spelled with hyphens when used before a noun. Someone who is **out of work** is unemployed. EG *...an out-of-work actress.* — ADJ CLASSIF

out-patient, out-patients; also spelled as one word. An **out-patient** is someone who receives treatment at a hospital during the day but does not stay there overnight. EG *They are being treated in hospital as out-patients... ...an out-patient clinic.* N COUNT

outpost /aʊtpəʊst/, **outposts**. An **outpost** is a small settlement in a foreign country or distant part of a country which is used for trading or military purposes. EG *Government officers established the first outposts and settlements.* N COUNT

outpouring /aʊtpɔːrɪŋ/, **outpourings**. 1 An **outpouring** of something is a great amount of it that is produced very rapidly. EG *...a prolific outpouring of ideas and energy.* N COUNT : USU+ of = flood

2 **Outpourings** are things that you say or write which seem uncontrolled and irrational and indicate that you are very angry or upset about something. EG *...the hysterical outpourings of fanatics.* N PLURAL+SUPP = rantings

output /aʊtpʊt/, **outputs, outputting, output**. 1 Someone's **output** is the amount of something that they make or produce. EG *The party maintains a constant output of pamphlets... ...the literary output of the post-war period... EEC countries are steadily increasing agricultural output.* N UNCOUNT : USU +SUPP = yield

2 When a computer **outputs** something, it sorts and produces information as the result of a particular program or operation; a technical use. EG *The program will output it into a file.* V+O

3 **Output** is also **3.1** the information which a computer sorts out and produces as the result of a particular program or operation. EG *...output data... There's something wrong with this output.* N UNCOUNT/ COUNT **3.2** the amount of electric current that is produced by a power station. EG *...a new hydro-electric scheme with an output of 405 megawatts.* N UNCOUNT/ COUNT

outrage /aʊtreɪdʒ/, **outrages, outraging, outraged**. 1 If something **outrages** you, it makes you feel extremely shocked, angry, or upset. EG *Members of Parliament were outraged by the news of the assassination... I once outraged them by arguing that English food is the best in Europe.* ◊ **outraged**. EG *Ginny shot him a look of outraged disbelief.* V+O = scandalize, shock ◊ ADJ QUALIT = furious

2 **Outrage** is a very strong feeling of anger and shock. EG *Her brow wrinkled with outrage... ...a sense of outrage.* N UNCOUNT = indignation

3 An **outrage** is an act or event which people find very shocking, especially one that involves violence. EG *There have been more reports of bomb outrages in the north of the country... ...outrages against society.* N COUNT = atrocity

outrageous /aʊtreɪdʒəs/. You describe something as **outrageous** when it is 1 very unusual and slightly shocking. EG *She used to say some outrageous things.* ◊ **outrageously**. EG *She was outrageously greedy.* ADJ QUALIT **2** very shocking and socially or morally unacceptable. EG *He's cutting spending on education while he's increasing the military budget. Outrageous!... Nearly every day from then on, some new outrageous incident would take place.* ◊ **outrageously**. EG *He was behaving outrageously.* ADJ QUALIT = scandalous ◊ ADV WITH VB

outran /aʊtræn/ is the past tense of **outrun**.

outré /uːtreɪ/. Something that is **outré** is very unusual and strange, and rather shocking; a formal word. EG *...Thelma's outré garb.* ADJ QUALIT = freakish

outrider /aʊtraɪdə/, **outriders**. An **outrider** is a policeman, policewoman, or other official who rides on a motorcycle or horse beside or in front of an official vehicle, in order to escort and protect the people in the vehicle. EG *Eight police outriders escorted the minister's car.* N COUNT ⇑ guard

outright /aʊtraɪt/. 1 **Outright** is used to describe behaviour and actions that are open and direct, rather than hidden or indirect. EG *It was an outright refusal... ...outright attacks on religion... ...a coldness that was just short of outright hostility.* ▸ used as an adverb. EG *If I ask outright I get nowhere.* ADJ CLASSIF : ATTRIB ⇑ obvious ▸ ADV WITH VB = openly

2 **Outright** also means complete and total. EG *Her characters are never outright villains... They can now establish outright dictatorship.* ADJ CLASSIF : ATTRIB = absolute

3 If you have something or do something **outright**, you have it or do it completely, so that there can be no doubt about it. EG *The government has banned it outright... They own outright all their machinery.* ADV AFTER VB = completely

● If a person or animal **is killed outright**, they are killed at once, for example in an accident, rather than being injured and dying slowly. EG *All three were killed outright.* ● PHR : VB INFLECTS

outrun /aʊtrʌn/, **outruns, outrunning, outran, outrun**. 1 If you **outrun** someone, you run faster than they do, and therefore are able to escape from them or to arrive somewhere before they do. EG *She managed to outrun them.* V+O = outstrip

2 If one thing **outruns** another thing, it develops faster than the other thing. EG *City growth far outran the general population boom.* V+O = exceed

outsell /aʊtsel/, **outsells, outselling, outsold**. If a product **outsells** another product, it is sold faster or in larger quantities than the other product. EG *In some places American skis are outselling Scandinavian, Swiss, and Austrian ones.* V+O

outset /aʊtset/. **At the outset** means at the beginning of an event, a process, or a period of time. If something is done **from the outset**, it is done from the beginning. EG *You should explain this to him at the outset... The police had participated from the outset... They were discouraged from marrying at the outset of their careers.* PHR : USED AS AN A

outshine /aʊtʃaɪn/, **outshines, outshining, outshone**. If you **outshine** someone at a particular activity, you are better than they are at it. EG *He felt sure he could outshine them all.* V+O ⇑ surpass

outside /aʊtsaɪd/, **outsides**. 1 The **outside** of something, such as a container or building, is the part which surrounds or encloses the rest of it. EG *...the outside of the bottle... ...a row of houses whose outsides were falling to pieces... Examine the property closely from the outside.* ▸ used as an adjective. EG *...a long wooden shed that stood against the outside wall.* N COUNT+USU SUPP ⇑ exterior ≠ inside ▸ ADJ CLASSIF : ATTRIB

2 You use **outside** to refer to something that is **2.1** situated or happening outside a building. EG *It was dark outside... Let's go outside... There was a demonstration outside the Social Security office.* ▸ used as an adjective. EG *We only had an outside lavatory.* ADV WITH VB, OR PREP ≠ indoor, inside ▸ ADJ CLASSIF **2.2** on the other side of the door of a room or on the other side of a gate, etc. EG *I put them on the chair outside my room... He's on the landing outside... He directed me to sit on a bench outside a closed door.* ADV WITH VB, OR PREP ≠ inside

3 You also use **outside** to refer to **3.1** the community or life in general when it is considered to be frightening and hostile compared to your own family, friends, and way of life. EG *They don't want to go out into the outside world... ...the cold, uncaring world outside... They have few links with the outside community.* ADJ CLASSIF **3.2** the way of life of someone who is not in prison or another institution. EG *Is life outside as dangerous as all that?... ...life on the outside.* ADJ CLASSIF, OR N SING : the+N

4 An **outside** line or an **outside** call is a telephone line or call that is connected to people or places away from the building that you are in. EG *You always had to pay if you made an outside call... I can't get an outside line.* ADJ CLASSIF : ATTRIB

5 You use **outside** to describe people or places that are **5.1** away from or not in a particular town, city, or country. EG *Nobody outside California knew much about him... This is the largest Chinese settlement outside Asia... Meanwhile, there is still war outside Europe.* PREP OR ADV+ of : USU PREP ≠ in **5.2** near to a particular town or city but not actually inside it. EG *...a small, pleasant village, just outside Birmingham... We live outside of London.* PREP OR ADV+of ⇑ beside

6 The **outside** lanes of a wide road are the lanes nearest to its centre, along which the fastest vehicles drive. EG *We were going along at 90 in the outside lane.* ADJ CLASSIF : ATTRIB, OR N SING : the+N

7 You also use **outside** to refer to the part of something which is furthest from its centre and nearest to its edge. EG *Start at the outside edge of the stain and work inwards.* ADJ CLASSIF : ATTRIB, OR N SING : the+N = outer

8 If your shirt or blouse is **outside** your trousers or skirt, it is hanging over them rather than being tucked in. EG *You're wearing your shirt-tails outside your jeans.* PREP

9 **Outside** is used to refer to **9.1** people who are not included in or not members of a particular group or organization. EG *The bill was supported by a mass movement outside Parliament.* ▸ used as an adjective or noun. EG *Since 1974, no outside body has questioned the advice... We smuggled a number of copies in from the outside.* PREP ▸ ADJ CLASSIF : ATTRIB, OR N SING : the+N **9.2** something that is not included in a particular range of things. EG *The surviving pipeline was outside his range of responsibility... How people kill for pleasure is totally outside my understanding.* PREP = beyond ≠ within **9.3** something that does not happen during a particular period of time, espe- PREP ≠ in

cially when this is a period of time when you should be working. EG *You'll have to do it outside office hours.*

10 You use **at the outside** to say that you think that a particular amount is the largest possible in a particular situation, or that a particular time is the latest possible time for something to happen. EG *I'd have said twenty-three miles at the outside... We should be there by four at the outside.* PHR : USED AS AN A

outside broadcast, outside broadcasts. An **outside broadcast** is a radio or television programme that is not recorded or filmed in a studio, but in another building or in the open air. EG *...the problems of doing an outside broadcast.* N COUNT ⇑ transmission

outsider /aʊtsaɪdə/, **outsiders.** An **outsider** is **1** someone who is not involved with a particular group of people or with a particular organization or way of life. EG *We will have to engage the services of an outsider... To an outsider this looks like an idyllic life.* N COUNT

2 someone who is not accepted by a particular group of people, or who feels that they do not fit into the group, for example because they are different in some way. EG *He was something of an outsider... They feel like outsiders.* N COUNT = odd man out **3** a horse or dog which is taking part in a race and which is considered unlikely to win. EG *The race was won by an outsider.* N COUNT ≠ favourite

outsize /aʊtsaɪz/. **1 Outsize** means the same as **outsized.** EG *...a blonde with outsize spectacles.* ADJ CLASSIF : USU ATTRIB

2 Outsize clothes are clothes for very large people. Usually you have to buy outsize clothes in special shops. EG *Available in large, extra large, and outsize.* ADJ CLASSIF : USU ATTRIB

outsized /aʊtsaɪzd/ is used to describe something which is much larger than other things of its kind, or much larger than you would expect. EG *...an outsized book on poverty in America.* ADJ CLASSIF = outsize

outskirts /aʊtskɜːts/. The **outskirts** of a city or town are the parts of it that are furthest away from its centre. EG *The garage was on the outskirts of town... The march should reach the outskirts of London on May 27th.* N PLURAL : *the*+N, USU+*of* ⇑ edge

outsmart /aʊtsmɑːt/, **outsmarts, outsmarting, outsmarted.** If you **outsmart** someone, you use your intelligence or a clever trick to defeat them or to gain an advantage. EG *She had to outsmart the enemy... The council outsmarted us by releasing their own press statement.* V+O = outwit

outspoken /aʊtspəʊkən/. If you are **outspoken**, you give your opinions about things openly and honestly, even if they are likely to shock or offend people. EG *You are younger and more outspoken than they are... ...an outspoken critic of extremists... ...clear, outspoken statements.* ◊ **outspokenness.** EG *They were penalized for their outspokenness.* ADJ QUALIT = forthright ◊ N UNCOUNT

outspread /aʊtspred/. If something is **outspread,** it is stretched or spread out as far as possible. EG *...supporting himself on his outspread fingers... ...perched on a crag, its wings outspread... ...the outspread newspaper.* ADJ CLASSIF

outstanding /aʊtstændɪŋ/. **1** If you describe a person, their abilities, or their work as **outstanding,** you are saying that their abilities or achievements are very remarkable and impressive; used showing approval. EG *She would never be an outstanding actress... These companies have done outstanding work in human relations... His war record was outstanding.* ADJ QUALIT ⇑ good

2 Something that is **outstanding** is very obvious or important. EG *There are significant exceptions, of which oil is the outstanding example.* ADJ CLASSIF : ATTRIB = notable

3 Money that is **outstanding** has not yet been paid and is still owed to someone. EG *There is fifty pounds outstanding, I believe... ...£28 million in outstanding fines.* ADJ CLASSIF ⇑ owing

4 Work or problems that are **outstanding** have not yet been done or solved. EG *...an outstanding problem that needs working on.* ADJ CLASSIF ⇑ remaining

outstandingly /aʊtstændɪŋli[1]/ is used to indicate an extreme degree of a quality. EG *She must be outstandingly good... ...an outstandingly successful director... I realized how outstandingly dull he was.* ADV+ADJ/ADV = exceptionally

outstay /aʊtsteɪ/, **outstays, outstaying, outstayed.** If you **outstay** your **welcome,** you stay somewhere, for example at someone's house or party, longer than they want you to or expect you to. EG *He decided to leave before he outstayed his welcome.* PHR : VB INFLECTS

outstretched /aʊtstretʃt/. If a part of the body of a person or animal is **outstretched,** it is stretched out as far as possible. EG *...balancing himself with outstretched arms... The little cage wobbled in her outstretched hand... They stand on the rocks, wings outstretched.* ADJ CLASSIF

outstrip /aʊtstrɪp/, **outstrips, outstripping, outstripped.** To **outstrip** someone or something means to become greater in amount, degree, wealth, or importance than they are. EG *His personal wealth far outstripped Northcliffe's... Demand appeared to outstrip the capital available for investment... They found themselves outstripped in education, in commerce... His newspaper outstripped its rivals in circulation.* V+O ⇑ overtake = surpass

out tray, out trays. An **out tray** is a tray or shallow basket used in offices to put letters and documents in before they are sent out of the office. N COUNT

outvote /aʊtvəʊt/, **outvotes, outvoting, outvoted.** If you **are outvoted,** more people vote against what you are proposing than vote for it, so that your proposal is defeated. EG *Shop stewards recommending strike action have been outvoted... I have a lot of confidence in him–but I was outvoted.* V+O = vote down

outward /aʊtwəd/, **outwards.** When it is an adverb, the form **outwards** is normally used in British English and the form **outward** is used in American English and in formal or old-fashioned British English. **1** You use **outward** or **outwards** to indicate **1.1** that something moves, faces, or extends in a direction away from the place that you are in or from the place that you are talking about. EG *He swam outwards into the bay... The door opened outwards... He stared outwards at the sea... The fields sweep outward to the base of the mountain.* ADV AFTER VB ⇑ out **1.2** that someone points or stretches a part of their body away from them. EG *Turn your knees outwards... ...lips pushed outward like a spout.* ADV AFTER VB ⇑ out

2 An **outward** journey is a journey that you make away from a place that you are intending to return to later. EG *We met on the outward journey.* ▸ Used as an adverb. EG *Our journey outwards was delayed at the airport... ...the outward bound troop ship.* ADJ CLASSIF : ATTRIB ▸ ADV AFTER VB/N ≠ back

3 You use **outward** to describe **3.1** a person's feelings or attitudes as they seem to other people, rather than as they actually are. EG *...the importance you put on outward appearances... I said it with what I hoped was outward calm... MPs kept up their outward allegiance to the parties they belonged to.* ADJ CLASSIF : ATTRIB ⇑ external **3.2** the part of something which you see when you look at it from the outside. EG *They retain the outward shape they had in life... The symptoms are the outward and visible signs of the disease.* ADJ CLASSIF : ATTRIB ⇑ external

4 Outwards is used to indicate that a person's actions concern or affect people other than themselves or the group or country that they belong to. EG *He advised his countrymen to turn their attention outwards, to foreign affairs... Such action is directed outwards against society.* ADV AFTER VB = outward

outwardly /aʊtwədli[1]/. You use **outwardly 1** to indicate that a situation or opinion may seem to be true to someone who does not know much about it or does not think about it very carefully, but that the real situation is different. EG *Outwardly they have much in common... I suppose outwardly the evening must have seemed pleasant enough.* ADV SEN = on the surface **2** to describe a person's behaviour or actions, when you are saying that what they are feeling or thinking is different. EG *His brain is seething, but outwardly he remains composed... It is what she really thinks that matters, not just what she does outwardly.* ADV WITH VB

outweigh /aʊtweɪ/, **outweighs, outweighing, outweighed.** If one thing **outweighs** another, it is of greater importance, benefit, or significance than the other thing; a formal word. EG *The benefits far outweighed the risk to any individual... National interest outweighed local objections... Their superiority in speed would be outweighed by their unreliability.* V+O

outwit /aʊtwɪt/, **outwits, outwitting, outwitted.** If you **outwit** someone, you use your intelligence or a clever trick to defeat them or to gain an advantage over them. EG *I already knew how to outwit him.* V+O = outsmart

outworn /aʊtwɔːn/. A belief or custom that is **outworn** is old-fashioned and no longer has any ADJ CLASSIF ⇑ outdated meaning or usefulness. EG *There is no point in pandering to outworn superstition.*

ouzo /u:zəʊ/ is a strong, aniseed-flavoured alcoholic drink that is made in Greece. N MASS ↑ alcohol

ova /əʊvə/ is the plural of **ovum**. N COUNT

oval /əʊvə⁰l/, **ovals**. An **oval** is a shape that is like a flattened circle. EG *...her lovely oval face... ...oval-shaped eyes... ...a wardrobe with an oval mirror.* N COUNT, OR ADJ CLASSIF

ovary /əʊvə⁰ri¹/, **ovaries**. An **ovary** is the organ that produces reproductive cells in the body of a woman, or of any female animal, bird, or fish; a technical term in biology. N COUNT

ovation /ə⁶veɪʃə⁰n/, **ovations**. An **ovation** is a long burst of applause from an audience for a particular performer, speaker, etc; a formal word. EG *She received a tremendous ovation... The crowd broke into a long, thunderous ovation.* ● If you receive a **standing ovation**, the audience all stand up in order to applaud you, as a sign of extreme approval or pleasure. EG *The speech was accorded a standing ovation.* N COUNT : USU SING ● PHR : USED AS O ↑ tribute

oven /ʌvə⁰n/, **ovens**. An **oven** is a part of a cooker that is like a box with a door, inside which food is placed to be cooked. EG *She took the pie out of the oven and turned the gas off.* N COUNT

ovenproof /ʌvə⁰npru:f/. An **ovenproof** dish is one that has been specially made to be used in an oven without being damaged by the heat. ADJ CLASSIF : USU ATTRIB

over /əʊvə/. **1** You use **over** in phrasal verbs, for example in 'boil over', 'give over', and 'tick over', and after some other verbs such as 'fly', 'pour' and 'worry'. See individual verb and phrasal verb entries for such items, which are not treated separately here.

2 You use **over** **2.1** to say that something is in the sky above a particular place or area. EG *The sun is over the mountain by ten every morning... ...a warning satellite over the Indian Ocean... There's an aircraft coming over.* PREP, OR ADV AFTER VB **2.2** to say that one thing is higher than another and above it, with a space between them. EG *The lamp hung over the table.* PREP **2.3** to say that someone or something is in a higher part of a building, directly above a lower part. EG *He lived over a bakery... The bathroom is over the kitchen.* PREP **2.4** to say that one thing is on top of another and touching it so as to cover it or close it. EG *Fit the plunger over the sink hole and pump several times.* PREP

3 You use **over** **3.1** to say that light or a liquid or gas is covering someone or something. EG *Brilliant light poured over me... Students were spraying paint over each other.* PREP ↑ onto **3.2** to say that one piece of clothing is being worn on top of another and partly or completely covers it. EG *She was wearing a short robe over her bathing suit.* PREP **3.3** to say that a piece of clothing covers a particular part of your body. EG *He climbed down the fire escape with a jacket over his head... Her tight dress was wrinkled over her hips.* PREP ↑ on **3.4** to say that one thing is supported by another and its ends are hanging down on each side of it. EG *Willie's suit was carefully folded over her arm.* PREP **3.5** to say that a layer of something is covering or spread on a surface. EG *Spray splashed over the deck... Get all the rust off, then paint over it.* PREP **3.6** to say that one part of someone's body is covering or partly covering another. EG *He put a hand over his mouth... Her hair hung down over her eyes.* PREP **3.7** to say that a particular expression appears on someone's face. EG *A look of bliss came over his face.* PREP ↑ across

4 all over. **4.1** You use **all over** or **over** to refer to everywhere in the world or everywhere in a particular country. EG *They come from all over the world... I've been all over Austria... The figures are compared over the whole country... Adults the world over have faced this problem.* PREP, OR ADV AFTER N **4.2** If you say that a piece of news or information is **all over** a particular place, you mean that it has become known to everyone in that place; an informal use. EG *Dolly told the Captain, and it was all over the ship in no time.* PREP **4.3** If you say that someone is **all over** another person, you mean that they are too affectionate or considerate towards them; an informal use. EG *Ooh, she was all over him!* PREP **4.4** If you say **'That's him all over'**, **'That's** her **all over'**, etc, you mean that what someone has just done is typical of them; an informal use. PHR : VB INFLECTS **4.5** If you say that a situation or activity is **all over** or **over**, you mean that it is completely finished. EG *On December 13th our troubles will be all over... ...the uncertainty was over... Rodin's search was over.* PHR : USED AS C ↑ ended

5 You use **over** **5.1** to say that a person is looking across and above the top of an object, often while doing something else. EG *She was watching him over the rim of her cup... The ponies would come and look over the wall... We talked over his yard gate.* PREP **5.2** to say what can be seen from a particular place, such as a room or a window. EG *The windows look out over a park.* PREP = onto **5.3** to say that someone is looking at the whole of something, usually quickly. EG *He ran his eye over one particular paragraph... His eyes glanced over the contents of the motor car.* PREP **5.4** to say that someone is looking in a particular direction or at a particular object. EG *She glanced over at William's empty chair... He looked over at his son with genuine surprise.* ADV AFTER VB : USU+A **5.5** to say that someone is looking downwards, especially from the edge of a higher place down to a lower place. EG *I looked over the precipice.* PREP

6 You use **over** **6.1** to indicate movement from one place to another. EG *The doctor walked over to the door... I rushed over to Paris... He met her on the plane coming over... I've got some friends coming over tonight... Elizabeth, come over here.* ADV AFTER VB **6.2** to indicate a position on the other side of a road, river, area of land, etc. EG *Eastwards over the Severn lie the hills... Trinity Square is just over the road.* PREP = across **6.3** to indicate movement across a boundary, river, etc. EG *...on the way back over the Channel... We moved through fields and over ditches... We crossed over into Tennessee very late that night.* PREP, OR ADV AFTER VB **6.4** to say that you are giving or passing something to someone. EG *He picked up the phone and passed it over... Chuck that book over, will you?* ADV AFTER VB = across **6.5** to say that something is moving across a surface. EG *He watched the towel run over her skin... ...running their tongues over their lips... His pen flowed rapidly over the paper.* PREP **6.6** to say that someone or something moves across an area of land or that a road leads across it. EG *She ran back, skipping over the grass... ...travelling with him over Salisbury Plain... The track winds over hills and ridges.* PREP **6.7** to say that someone or something moves above and across something and comes down on the other side of it. EG *Castle stepped over the dog and went into the hall... I saw the car disappearing over the hill.* PREP, OR ADV AFTER VB

7 Over is used **7.1** to say that someone or something falls towards or onto the ground or the floor, often suddenly or violently. EG *She fell over in the mud... He slumped over in his seat... He was knocked over by a bus.* ADV AFTER VB ↑ down **7.2** to say that something moves downwards from the edge of a high place towards the ground, the sea, etc. EG *They just chucked it over the side.* PREP, OR ADV AFTER VB **7.3** to say that someone is not in an upright position, and that a part of their body is above something. EG *He crouched over a typewriter... She bent over the desk... Grimes was leaning forward over the steering wheel.* PREP **7.4** to say that someone leans or stretches in a particular direction, especially sideways. EG *Pat leaned over and picked it up... The Prince leaned over to me and said, 'That's him.'* ADV AFTER VB = across **7.5** to say that someone or something is bent or folded, especially so that two parts touch each other. EG *She was doubled over, her face in anguish.* ADV AFTER VB = up **7.6** to say that someone turns their body so that it faces another direction, while they are lying on the ground or in bed. EG *He rolled over and peered into Jack's face... I turned over and fell out of bed.* ADV AFTER VB **7.7** to say that you move an object with the result that it faces a different direction, that another part of it can be seen, or that it is upside down. EG *He turned the page over... She tipped the pan over and a fish flopped out.* ADV AFTER VB

8 If you are **over** an illness or an experience, it has finished and you have recovered from its effects. EG *She was still getting over her bereavement... He was supposed to be over all that by now... It took a long while to get over it.* PREP

9 If something is **over** a particular measurement, amount, or age, it is more than that measurement, amount, or age. EG *...just over a thousand yards in width... She was well over fifty... ...people aged 80 or over... She did it for over a week... They paid out over 3 million pounds.* PREP, OR ADV AFTER NUM

10 If something occurs or is required **over and above** what is normal or known about, it occurs or is required in addition to the normal or known thing, PREP = besides, p and is often surprising or unreasonable. EG *...confusions in our dealings with foreigners, over and above language difficulties... ...and over and above that, she didn't want him to go to college.*

11 If you hear one sound **over** another sound or other sounds, it is louder than the other sound or sounds. PREP = above

12 If you say that you have some food or money **over**, you mean that it remains after you have used all that you need. EG *Was there any money left over?... If there's any meat over, put it in the fridge.* ADV AFTER VB/N ⇑ remaining

13 You use **over 13.1** to say that someone controls, rules, or has power over other people, an organization, a country, etc. EG *The leadership had absolute control over the organization... ...his authority over them... ...a means of breaking his hold over me.* PREP **13.2** to say that someone or something is stronger, more powerful, or more important than someone or something else, especially after defeating them. EG *...the triumph of the strong over the weak... ...victory over capitalism... National independence takes priority over class struggle.* PREP **13.3** to say that a different person or group takes control of a person, organization, or country. EG *The homelands pass over to black rule... We handed her over to the police.* ADV AFTER VB **13.4** to say that you are guarding someone or something, or watching them very carefully. EG *She had been asked to mount guard over a number of dogs.* PREP **13.5** to say that someone changes the group or party they belong to, or changes their opinions. EG *The students tried to win over the working class to their campaign... Had he been able to buy him over, we would have had a majority.* ADV AFTER VB

14 You use **over 14.1** to say who is affected by a particular problem, worry, or fear. EG *He held the will over her like a threat... There's a question mark over her future with us.* PREP **14.2** to say what is being dealt with, discussed, argued about, etc. EG *They take enormous trouble over any complaints they receive... ...disagreements over administrative policies... They were always quarrelling over women.* PREP **14.3** to indicate the cause or source of someone's feelings or problems. EG *I've been getting into trouble over that... ...the anxiety which the Commander suffered over it... I found him still chuckling over a telephone call he had received.* PREP = because of **14.4** to say that you are discussing something or thinking about it very carefully and for a long time. EG *Talk it over with Daddy... He loves to talk over old times... He cast his mind back over the day.* PREP, OR ADV AFTER VB

15 You use **over 15.1** to indicate a particular period of time during which something happens. EG *Read their work over the vacation... He'd had flu over Christmas... ...a process developed over many decades.* PREP **15.2** to say that someone does something while they are doing something else. EG *The leaders met over informal lunches... ...sitting down with friends over coffee... They discussed it over a game of golf.* PREP ⇑ during

16 If you say that something happened **twice over, three times over**, etc, you are stating the number of times that it happened and emphasizing that it happened more than once. EG *He became a father many times over.* PHR : USED AS AN A

17 If you say that something happened **over again** or **all over again**, you are unhappy that it is happening for a second time, usually because it took a long time, a lot of effort, or was unpleasant when it first happened. EG *It was like the War all over again... It was almost as bad as getting divorced all over again... We couldn't stand to see the same films over again, so we went out.* PHR : USED AS AN A

18 If you say that something happens **over and over** or **over and over again**, you mean that it happens many times. EG *Men did the same job over and over again... I read it over and over again... Over and over, the same stories kept cropping up.* PHR : USED AS AN A = again and again

19 Over is used in the following ways when a radio, television, or telephone is involved. **19.1** You use **over** to say that you give or receive information by means of the radio or telephone. EG *They talked about it over the telephone... I heard it over the radio.* PREP = on **19.2** The presenter of a radio or television programme says **'Over to'** someone to indicate the person who will speak next. EG *Over to you, Peter... And now over to our correspondent in Belfast.* PREP **19.3** People say **'Over'** to indicate that they have finished speaking and are waiting for a reply, when they are communicating by radio, for example in the army, police, an airport control tower, etc. EG *Repeat, please, Colonel. I didn't get all that. Over.* CONVENTION **19.4** People say **'Over and out'** to officially end a radio conversation in the army, police, an airport control tower, etc. CONVENTION

20 You use **over** to say that a particular figure or amount is divided by another figure or amount; a technical term in mathematics and physics. EG *...four hundred and four over eighty-two.* PREP : NUM + PREP + NUM

over- is placed before an adjective or verb to indicate **1** that a quality exists or an action is done to too great an extent; used showing disapproval. EG *...an over-confident young man... The plan was over-ambitious... ...over-ripe fruit... ...the over-centralized system... I was an only child and my mother had always over-protected me.* PREFIX **2** a very high or extreme degree of a quality. EG *I was overtired at work the next day... ...over-expensive housing.* PREFIX

overact /əʊvərækt/, **overacts, overacting, overacted.** If you **overact**, you exaggerate your emotions and gestures, especially when acting in a play; used showing disapproval. EG *I knew I had been overacting.* V

overall /əʊvərᵊɔːl/, **overalls. 1 Overall** is used to describe a situation in general, including everything but not considering the details. EG *...the overall pattern of his life... The overall impression was of a smoky industrial scene.* ▸ used as an adverb. EG *Overall, imports account for half of our stock.* ADJ CLASSIF : ATTRIB ≠ specific ▸ ADV SEN = broadly

2 Overalls are a single piece of clothing that combines trousers and a jacket. You wear overalls over your clothes in order to protect them from dirt, paint, etc while you are working. EG *The breast pocket of his overalls was filled with tools.* N PLURAL : ALSO *a pair of*+N ⇑ garment

3 An **overall** is a piece of clothing shaped like a coat. You wear an overall over your clothes in order to protect them from dirt while you are working. EG *Wear an overall, not an apron.* N COUNT ⇑ garment

overarm /əʊvərɑːm/ is used to describe actions that you do, such as throwing a ball, in which you stretch your arm over your shoulder. EG *She would throw overarm... ...his strong overarm strokes.* ADV AFTER VB, OR ADJ CLASSIF

overawe /əʊvərɔː/, **overawes, overawing, overawed.** If you **are overawed** by someone or something, you are very impressed by them and a little afraid. EG *Don't be overawed by what the experts say.* V+O : USU PASS = intimidate

overbalance /əʊvəbæləns/, **overbalances, overbalancing, overbalanced.** If you **overbalance**, you fall over or nearly fall over, because you are not in a firm position. EG *He overbalanced and fell backwards on to a coffee table.* V

overbearing /əʊvəbeərɪŋ/. Someone who is **overbearing** tries to make other people do what he or she wants in an unpleasant and forceful way; used showing disapproval. EG *...her jealous, overbearing mother-in-law.* ADJ QUALIT = domineering

overboard /əʊvəbɔːd/. **1** If you fall **overboard**, you fall over the side of a ship into the water. EG *Gardner might have fallen overboard... He had to hang on to avoid being washed overboard.* ADV AFTER VB

2 You can use the word **overboard** in the following informal expressions. **2.1** If you say that someone **is going overboard**, you mean that they are doing something to a greater extent than is necessary or reasonable; used showing disapproval. EG *Now listen, Liebermann, you're going a little bit overboard.* PHR : VB INFLECTS ⇑ exaggerate **2.2** If you **go overboard for** someone, you find them extremely attractive or fall in love with them. PHR : VB INFLECTS **2.3** If you **throw** a plan or idea **overboard**, you decide it is no longer useful and abandon it. PHR : VB INFLECTS ⇑ discard

overburdened /əʊvəbɜːdᵊnd/. If you are **overburdened** with work, problems, etc, you have more work, problems, etc than you can cope with. EG *You're not overburdened with work just now?... She did not want to trouble relatives already overburdened with stress.* ADJ QUALIT

overcame /əʊvəkeɪm/ is the past tense of **overcome**.

overcast /əʊvəkɑːst/. You describe the sky or the weather as **overcast** when there are a lot of clouds and the light is poor. EG *The rain had lessened, but it stayed overcast... ...the grey, overcast sky.* ADJ QUALIT ⇑ cloudy

overcharge /əʊvətʃɑːdʒ/, **overcharges, overcharging, overcharged.** If someone **overcharges** you, they charge you too much money for V OR V+O ⇑ cheat their goods or services. EG *The taxi-driver tried to overcharge her.*

overcoat /əʊvəkəʊt/, **overcoats**. An **overcoat** is a thick, warm coat that you wear in winter. N COUNT = topcoat

overcome /əʊvəkʌm/, **overcomes, overcoming, overcame, overcome**. The form **overcome** is used in the present tense and is also the past participle. **1** If you **overcome** a problem or a feeling, you successfully deal with it or control it. EG *I was still trying to overcome my fear of the dark... We tried to overcome their objections to the original plan.* V+O = overthrow

2 If you **are overcome** by a feeling, you feel it very strongly. EG *I was overcome by a sense of failure... He was overcome with astonishment.* V+O : USU PASS = be overwhelmed

overcrowded /əʊvəkraʊdɪ²d/. You describe a place as **overcrowded** when there are too many things or people in it. EG *...overcrowded cities... ...the overcrowded sitting-room.* ADJ QUALIT ↑ crowded

overcrowding /əʊvəkraʊdɪŋ/. You say that there is **overcrowding** when there are more people living in a place than the place was designed for. EG *There is serious overcrowding in our prisons.* N UNCOUNT ↑ crowding

overdo /əʊvəduː/, **overdoes, overdoing, overdid, overdone**. If you **overdo** something, **1** you behave in an exaggerated way in a particular situation; used showing disapproval. EG *Wish them good luck, but don't overdo it or they may become suspicious.* V+O : USU V+*it* ↑ exaggerate **2** you try to do more than you are physically capable of, for example when you are ill or tired. EG *Don't overdo it. It's very hot in the sun... Don't overdo these exercises, especially at first.* V+O : USU V+*it*

overdone /əʊvədʌn/. You say that food such as meat is **overdone** when it has been cooked for too long or at too high a temperature; used showing disapproval. ADJ QUALIT : USU PRED = overcooked

overdose /əʊvədəʊs/, **overdoses**. If someone takes an **overdose** of a drug, they take more of it than is safe, either accidentally or deliberately. EG *Alice took an overdose after a row with her mother... ...a massive overdose of sleeping pills.* N COUNT : USU SING ↑ dose

overdraft /əʊvədrɑːft/, **overdrafts**. An **overdraft** is an agreement that you make with your bank that allows you to spend more money than you actually have in your account; also used of the extra amount allowed. EG *She asked him for a fifty-pound overdraft... We're not supposed to authorize overdrafts... ...overdraft facilities.* N COUNT

overdrawn /əʊvədrɔːn/. If a person is **overdrawn** or if their bank account is **overdrawn**, the person has spent more money than they have in their account. EG *I'm overdrawn this month, but it should balance out next month... ...interest charged on overdrawn accounts.* ADJ QUALIT = in the red

overdressed /əʊvədrɛst/. You say that someone is **overdressed** when you think that they are wearing too many clothes or clothes which are too formal for a particular occasion; used showing disapproval. ADJ QUALIT

overdue /əʊvədjuː/. **1** If someone is **overdue**, they have not arrived and it is after the time when they were expected to arrive. they arrive or occur later than you expected or wanted them to. EG *They're half an hour overdue. I wish they'd come.* ADJ QUALIT ↑ late

2 You say that something such as a change is **overdue** when you think that it should already have been carried out. EG *Reform in all these areas is long overdue.* ADJ QUALIT

3 If money or a book borrowed from a library is **overdue**, you still have the money or the book, although it is now later than the date when it should have been paid or returned. EG *I've got three books that are overdue... The rent on his apartment was three weeks overdue.* ADJ QUALIT ↑ late

3 You say that a baby is **overdue** or that a pregnant woman is **overdue** when the baby has not been born, although it is later than the time that it was expected to be born; an informal use. ADJ QUALIT : PRED ↑ late

overeat /əʊvər⁰iːt/, **overeats, overeating, overeaten**. If you **overeat**, you eat more than you really need to or more than is healthy; used showing disapproval. EG *She has a tendency to overeat.* V
◊ **overeating**. EG *Obesity is only partly caused by overeating.* ◊ N UNCOUNT

overemphasize /əʊvər⁰ɛmfəsaɪz/, **overemphasizes, overemphasizing, overemphasized**; also spelled **overemphasise**. If you **overemphasize** something, you give it more importance than it deserves or than is considered appropriate. EG *I hope nobody will overemphasize the importance of these little essays... I cannot overemphasize how delicate this business is.* V+O/REPORT-CL

overestimate /əʊvər⁰ɛstɪmeɪt/, **overestimates, overestimating, overestimated**. **1** If you **overestimate** something, you think that it is greater in amount or importance than it really is. EG *Do not overestimate the importance of the economic problems... We greatly overestimated the time this would take.* V+O ↑ misjudge

2 If you **overestimate** a person or **overestimate** their qualities, you think that they are better or have more of the quality than is the case. EG *Obviously I overestimated your sense of humour.* V+O = overrate

overflow /əʊvəfləʊ/, **overflows, overflowing, overflowed**. **1** If a liquid **overflows** or if a river, lake, etc **overflows**, it becomes too great in quantity for the container or place it is in and flows over its edges or boundaries. EG *He was careful to see that the jar did not overflow... Rivers often overflow their banks.* V OR V-ERG ↑ flood

2 You say that people **overflow** a room or building when there are too many of them in it and some of them have to move out. EG *The crowd overflowed the auditorium... They overflowed onto the steps and pavement.* V OR V-ERG = flood

3 If something **is overflowing** with things, it is very full of them. EG *The table was overflowing with clothes... ...overflowing dustbins.* V+A *(with)* = burst ● If you describe something as full **to overflowing**, you mean that it is extremely full. EG *The ashtrays were full to overflowing... The theatre filled to overflowing.* ● PHR : USED AS AN A ↑ extremely

4 If someone **is overflowing** with a feeling or if the feeling **overflows**, the person experiences it very strongly and expresses it in their behaviour or actions. EG *...a nurse overflowing with love... The resentment would overflow... ...overflowing passion.* V OR V+A *(with)* = brim over

● If you describe someone as full **to overflowing** with a feeling, you mean that they are feeling it extremely strongly. EG *Full to overflowing with emotion, he gave them the farewell speech.* ● PHR : USED AS AN A ↑ extremely

5 An **overflow** is **5.1** a hole or pipe that allows liquid to flow out of a container when it gets too full. EG *...the sink overflow... ...overflow pipes.* N COUNT ↑ outlet **5.2** the extra things or people that something cannot contain or deal with because it is not large enough. EG *The camp took in the overflow from other prisons.* N COUNT : USU *the*+N IN SING ↑ excess

overgrown /əʊvəgrəʊn/. If a place is **overgrown**, it is thickly covered with plants and weeds, usually because it has not been looked after for a long time. EG *...a large house, overgrown with brambles... ...the overgrown path.* ADJ QUALIT

overhang /əʊvəhæŋ/, **overhangs, overhanging, overhung**. **1** If one thing **overhangs** another thing, **1.1** it is higher than the other thing and sticks out sideways above it. EG *His balcony overhung a large cage... ...the shadow of an overhanging rock... ...ponds with overhanging birch trees.* V OR V+O **1.2** it is supported by the other thing and hangs down its sides. EG *...wet clothes overhanging the tub... ...the walls of the garden, overhung with roses.* V OR V+O

2 An **overhang** is the part of something that sticks out sideways above something else. EG *...the strip of beach beneath the cliff overhang... The window is shaded by an overhang or an extended roof.* N COUNT : USU SING = ledge

overhaul /əʊvəhɔːl/, **overhauls, overhauling, overhauled**. **1** If you **overhaul** a machine or other equipment, you repair it, clean it, and check it thoroughly. EG *The engines were overhauled completely before our departure... The aircraft is not new, but it has been recently overhauled.* V+O = service ▸ used as a noun. EG *The pistons no longer fitted and an overhaul was needed.* ▸ N COUNT = service

2 If you **overhaul** an idea, system, etc, you examine it again very carefully and make changes to it in order to improve it. EG *The company needs to overhaul its techniques and methods... The churches are overhauling the old doctrines.* V+O ▸ used as a noun. EG *...a major overhaul of the country's educational system.* ▸ N COUNT : USU SING

3 If one person or vehicle **overhauls** another, they overtake the other person or vehicle because they are able to move faster. EG *The fastest boat on the run had suddenly been overhauled by this new liner... I had no chance of overhauling him.* V+O ↑ pass = overtake

overhead /əʊvəhed/, **overheads**. **Overhead** is an adjective and **overheads** is a noun. 1 You say that something is **overhead** when it is above you or above the place that you are talking about. EG *Seagulls were circling overhead... Feet were pounding on the deck overhead... The guard switched on an overhead light.* ADV AFTER VB/N, OR ADJ CLASSIF

2 The **overheads** of a business are its regular and essential expenses such as rent and the cost of telephones, stationery, etc. EG *...reducing expenditure on overheads... He's got heavy overheads.* N PLURAL

overhear /əʊvəhɪə/, **overhears, overhearing, overheard**. If you **overhear** someone or **overhear** what they are saying, you hear what they are saying when they are not talking to you and do not know that you are listening. EG *Judy overheard him telling the children about it... I was too far away to overhear their conversation... I wouldn't like to be overheard.* V OR V+O

overheat /əʊvəhiːt/, **overheats, overheating, overheated**. If something **overheats** or if you **overheat** it, it becomes hotter than is necessary or desirable. EG *The engine stalled; it was overheating... ...the overheated bedroom.* ◊ **overheating**. EG *...overheating of the detector boxes.* V-ERG ⇑ heat ◊ N UNCOUNT ⇑ heating

overheated /əʊvəhiːtɪ²d/. You say that someone is **overheated** when they are angry or annoyed and arguing forcefully about something. EG *Sir John becomes overheated if he sees the word 'chairperson' in a newspaper... Their conversation seemed disagreeably overheated.* ADJ QUALIT = agitated

overhung /əʊvəhʌŋ/ is the past tense and past participle of **overhang**.

overjoyed /əʊvədʒɔɪd/. If you are **overjoyed**, you are extremely pleased about something. EG *Francis was overjoyed to see him... They were overjoyed at this treatment.* ADJ CLASSIF: PRED = delighted

overkill /əʊvəkɪl/. You say that there is **overkill** when something is spoiled by being done to a much greater extent than is necessary; used showing disapproval. EG *We must beware of overkill... ...the media's overkill coverage.* N UNCOUNT ⇑ excess

overland /əʊvəlænd/. An **overland** journey is a long journey made across land by vehicle or on foot, on horseback, etc when this is a difficult or unusual way to travel. EG *I find the overland journey more exciting... ...an overland march across the desert... You travelled overland to India?* ADJ CLASSIF, OR ADV AFTER VB

overlap /əʊvəlæp/, **overlaps, overlapping, overlapped**. 1 If one thing **overlaps** another or if the two things **overlap**, a part of one thing covers a part of the other. EG *The circles overlap... It's not directly underneath, but overlaps slightly... A quilt must overlap the sides of the bed.* V OR V+O : RECIP

2 If two ideas, systems, activities, etc **overlap** or if one **overlaps** the other, they involve some of the same subjects, people, or periods of time. EG *The two theories obviously overlap... We worked overlapping shifts so there were always two of us on duty.* ▸ used as a noun. EG *...the overlap of responsibilities... There is considerable overlap between the two systems.* V, V+O, OR V+A (with) : RECIP ▸ N UNCOUNT/ COUNT

overlay /əʊvəleɪ/, **overlays, overlaying, overlaid**. 1 If something **is overlaid** with something else, it is covered by it. EG *Silt from rivers will overlay the ground... ...broken slabs overlaid with rubble.* V+O : USU PASS + with

2 If you **overlay** one type of behaviour, attitude, or idea with another, you add one to the other, often in a superficial way. EG *These feelings were overlaid by the child's need for a father.* ▸ used as a noun. EG *It was said with an overlay of good humour.* V+O : USU PASS ▸ N SING WITH DET

overleaf /əʊvəliːf/ is used in books and magazines to say that something is on the next page. EG *Some of the animals are illustrated overleaf.* ADV AFTER VB

overload /əʊvələʊd/, **overloads, overloading, overloaded**. 1 If you **overload** something such as a vehicle, you put more things or people into it or onto it than it was designed to carry. EG *The aircraft was dangerously overloaded... ...boats overloaded with desperate people... ...overloaded open trucks.* V+O : USU PASS

2 If a part of a transport system **is overloaded**, more people or vehicles use it than it was designed for. EG *Heathrow Airport was already overloaded by 1972... ...overloaded roads.* V+O : ONLY PASS

3 If you **overload** an electrical system, you try to use more electricity than it was designed for, and damage it. EG *Your fuse has blown because you have overloaded the circuit.* V+O

4 If you **overload** someone, you give them more work, problems, or information than they can cope with. EG *Medical services were overloaded with casualties... Students were overloaded with facts.* ▸ used as a noun. EG *...the sheer mental overload.* V+O : USU PASS + with ▸ N COUNT

overlook /əʊvəlʊk/, **overlooks, overlooking, overlooked**. 1 If a building, window, etc **overlooks** a place, you can see the place clearly from the building, window, etc. EG *Elegant buildings overlooked the square... ...a room which overlooked the garden... ...windows overlooking the playground.* V+O = look over

2 If you **overlook** a feature of something or a fact, you ignore it, do not notice it, or do not realize its importance. EG *They overlook the enormous risks involved... The Army overlooked the fact that the caves were on the other side.* V+O = disregard

3 If you **overlook** someone's faults or bad behaviour, you forgive them and do not criticize or punish them. EG *I decided to overlook his unkindness.* V+O = excuse

overlord /əʊvəlɔːd/, **overlords**. An **overlord** was a person in former times who had power over many people. EG *...an excellent overlord, who protected his people from bandits.* N COUNT ⇑ master

overly /əʊvəli¹/ means more than is normal, necessary, or reasonable; a formal or slightly old-fashioned word. EG *My friends and I were not overly eager to enter... Don't start being overly generous... I'm not overly keen on him.* ADV+ADJ ⇑ too = over

overmanned /əʊvəmænd/. If a place or particular type of work is **overmanned**, there are too many people working there or doing the work. EG *The industry is not only heavily overmanned but also in financial difficulties.* ADJ QUALIT = overstaffed

overmanning /əʊvəmænɪŋ/. If there is **overmanning** in a place or type of work, there are too many people working there or doing the work. N UNCOUNT

overmuch /əʊvəmʌtʃ/. If something happens **overmuch**, it happens too much or very much; a formal word. EG *The rumours she heard did not bother her overmuch.* ▸ used as an adjective. EG *He had done her a disservice by showing overmuch affection.* ADV WITH VB AND BROAD NEG = unduly ▸ ADJ CLASSIF : ATTRIB

overnight /əʊvənaɪt/. 1 **Overnight** means 1.1 during the whole night. EG *If you leave your bike around here overnight, it's likely to disappear... For an overnight stay the Hotel Claravallis is perfect.* 1.2 at some point during the night. EG *I woke to find that he had disappeared overnight.* ADV, OR ADJ CLASSIF : ATTRIB; ADV WITH VB

2 **Overnight** cases, clothes, etc, are ones that you take with you when you go somewhere to stay for one or two nights. EG *He was carrying a little overnight bag.* ADJ CLASSIF : ATTRIB

3 You also say that something happens **overnight** when it happens suddenly or extremely quickly, especially when this is rather unexpected. EG *Things can sometimes go out of fashion overnight.* ADV WITH VB

overpaid /əʊvəpeɪd/. If you say that someone is **overpaid** or that their job is **overpaid**, you mean that they are paid too much for the work that they do. EG *He was grossly overpaid... In most countries such jobs are overpaid in relation to the average income.* ADJ QUALIT

overpass /əʊvəpɑːs/, **overpasses**. An **overpass** is a road which goes over the top of another road; used mainly in American English. N COUNT = flyover

overplay /əʊvəpleɪ/, **overplays, overplaying, overplayed**. 1 If you **overplay** something, you make it seem more important than it really is. EG *He's been overplaying his promotion a bit.* V+O ⇑ exaggerate

2 If you **overplay** your **hand**, you behave as if you are in a stronger position than you actually are. PHR : VB AND N INFLECT

overpopulated /əʊvəpɒpjə⁴leɪtɪ²d/. A city, town, or country that is **overpopulated** has too many people living in it. EG *The city had always been noisy, overpopulated, and polluted.* ADJ CLASSIF = overcrowded

overpopulation /əʊvəpɒpjə⁴leɪʃə⁰n/. If there is **overpopulation** in a place there are too many people living there. EG *Many problems are caused by poverty and overpopulation.* N UNCOUNT = overcrowding

overpower /əʊvəpaʊə/, **overpowers, overpowering, overpowered**. 1 If you **overpower** someone, you completely defeat them because you are stronger than they are. EG *The bank robber was overpowered by two cashiers.* V+O

2 If something such as a smell, emotion, or sensation **overpowers** you, it makes you feel weak and helpless. EG *The smell of decaying meat overpowered Crompton.* V+O = overwhelm

overpowering /əʊvəpaʊərɪŋ/. 1 A feeling or emotion that is **overpowering** is so strong or powerful ADJ QUALIT

that you cannot resist it. EG ...*an overpowering feeling of failure.*
2 An **overpowering** smell is so strong that you cannot smell anything else. EG ...*the overpowering scent of English garden flowers.* ADJ QUALIT = powerful

overpriced /əʊvəpraɪst/. You say that goods are **overpriced** when you think that they are too expensive; used showing disapproval. EG *He spent his money on overpriced and tasteless clothes.* ADJ QUALIT

overran /əʊvəræn/ is the past tense of **overrun**.

overrate /əʊvəreɪt/, **overrates, overrating, overrated**. If you **overrate** someone or something, you think that they are more important or valuable than they really are. EG *We feel that maths is somewhat overrated as a school subject.* V+O : USU PASS = overvalue

overreach /əʊvəriːtʃ/, **overreaches, overreaching, overreached**. If you **overreach** yourself, you fail by trying to be too clever or by trying to do more than you can. EG *'It isn't wise to be too clever,' I said. 'Sometimes you overreach yourself.'* V+O (REFL) ⇑ defeat

overreact /əʊvərɪækt/, **overreacts, overreacting, overreacted**. If someone **overreacts** to something that happens, they react to it by being more angry, upset, afraid, etc, than they need to be. EG *People tend to overreact when they hear about a shark attack.* V ⇑ react

override /əʊvəraɪd/, **overrides, overriding, overrode, overridden**. **1** If one thing **overrides** another thing, it replaces the other thing or reduces its importance, because it is more powerful. EG *The day-to-day struggle for survival overrode all other things.* V+O
2 If you **override** someone or **override** their decisions, you cancel their decisions because you have more power or authority than they have. EG *As managing director, he will be able to override their decisions.* V+O = overrule

overriding /əʊvəraɪdɪŋ/. Something that is **overriding** is more important than anything else. EG *The overriding need in the world is to promote peace.* ADJ CLASSIF : ATTRIB = major

overrule /əʊvəruːl/, **overrules, overruling, overruled**. **1** If judges or law courts **overrule** a decision, they decide that it is not valid. EG *The judgement was overruled by the State Supreme Court.* V+O = overturn
2 If you **overrule** someone or **overrule** their objections or arguments, you decide that what they are saying is not allowed or is not valid. EG *The objection was overruled.* V+O = quash

overrun /əʊvərʌn/, **overruns, overrunning, overran, overrun**. **1** If an army **overruns** a country, it succeeds in occupying it very quickly. V+O
2 If animals or plants **overrun** a place, they spread quickly all over it. EG *A million years ago, the species began to overrun the earth... The city is overrun by rodents.* V+O = cover
3 If something such as an event or meeting **overruns**, it lasts longer than it is intended to. EG *The meeting overran by an hour.* V OR V+O = overshoot

overseas /əʊvəsiːz/ means relating to or belonging to foreign countries that are on the other side of a sea or ocean. EG *There is a vast overseas market for our goods... ...overseas students.* ▸ used as an adverb. EG *These companies are investing large sums overseas... Roughly 4 million Americans travel overseas each year.* ADJ CLASSIF : ATTRIB ▸ ADV WITH VB = abroad

oversee /əʊvəsiː/, **oversees, overseeing, oversaw, overseen**. **1** If you **oversee** something such as a job, you make sure that it is done properly by watching someone while they do it. EG *He had started, overseen, and finished the job.* V+O = supervise
2 If you **oversee** someone, you watch or spy on them, especially in order to control their actions; a formal use. EG *He was like a single-minded big brother overseeing every act and thought of the people.* V+O

overseer /əʊvəsiːə/, **overseers**. An **overseer** is someone who watches work being done to make sure that it is done properly. N COUNT ⇑ supervisor

oversell /əʊvəsel/, **oversells, overselling, oversold**. If you **oversell** something or someone, you exaggerate their merits or abilities. EG *It would be foolish to oversell the powers of science.* V+O

oversexed /əʊvəsekst/. If you describe someone as **oversexed**, you mean that they are more interested in sex or more involved in sexual activities than you think they should be; used showing disapproval. EG *...a tough, oversexed, working-class kid.* ADJ CLASSIF

overshadow /əʊvəʃædəʊ/, **overshadows, overshadowing, overshadowed**. **1** If something such as a mountain or a tall building **overshadows** a place, it is close to the place and much higher than the place is. EG *...Irun, overshadowed by the Pyrenees.* V+O : USU PASS = dwarf
2 If someone **overshadows** someone else, they cause the other person to seem less important or interesting. EG *She was sometimes overshadowed by the more talkative members of the family.* V+O : USU PASS = eclipse
3 If a feeling, attitude, or someone's behaviour **overshadows** an event or situation, it makes it seem less happy and enjoyable. EG *A great sense of responsibility seemed to overshadow the gathering.* V+O : USU PASS = cloud

overshoe /əʊvəʃuː/, **overshoes**. An **overshoe** is a large shoe, often made of rubber or plastic, that you wear over an ordinary shoe in order to protect it, for example in the snow or rain. N COUNT : USU a pair of+N

overshoot /əʊvəʃuːt/, **overshoots, overshooting, overshot**. **1** If you **overshoot** a place when you are driving, you pass the place by mistake, when you had intended to stop or turn there. EG *We had overshot that turning again.* V OR V+O
2 You say that someone **has overshot the mark** when make a mistake as a result of misjudging a situation. EG *You've overshot the mark there.* PHR : VB INFLECTS

oversight /əʊvəsaɪt/, **oversights**. An **oversight** is a careless mistake that you make because you have failed to notice something important. EG *I consider this a gross oversight on your part.* N COUNT/ UNCOUNT = omission

oversimplify /əʊvəsɪmplɪfaɪ/, **oversimplifies, oversimplifying, oversimplified**. If you **oversimplify** something, you describe or explain it too simply so that what you say is inaccurate. EG *We must be careful not to oversimplify the issue... You oversimplify things as always.* V OR V+O ⇑ simplify

oversize /əʊvəsaɪz/. **Oversize** clothes are much bigger than usual or much too big for the person who is wearing them. EG *...a three-year-old girl in an oversize pair of slacks.* ADJ CLASSIF = outsize

oversized /əʊvəsaɪzd/ means the same as 'oversize'. ADJ CLASSIF

oversleep /əʊvəsliːp/, **oversleeps, oversleeping, overslept**. If you **oversleep**, you sleep longer than you intended to and wake up late. EG *Sorry I'm late–I overslept.* V

overspill /əʊvəspɪl/ is an arrangement by which people are moved from an overcrowded city and are accommodated in new houses or flats in smaller towns where they can live in better conditions; a technical term. EG *...London overspill plans... These flats are an overspill development.* N UNCOUNT OR ADJ CLASSIF : ATTRIB

overstaffed /əʊvəstɑːft/. You say that a place is **overstaffed** when there are too many people working there. EG *...the overstaffed kitchen.* ADJ QUALIT

overstate /əʊvəsteɪt/, **overstates, overstating, overstated**. If you **overstate** something, you describe or explain it in a way that suggests that it is more important or serious than it really is. EG *It is impossible to overstate the importance of religion in explaining these customs... I don't want to overstate the case but this is probably the most important event in my life.* V+O ⇑ exaggerate = overemphasize

overstatement /əʊvəsteɪtməⁱnt/, **overstatements**. An **overstatement** is a way of describing something that makes it seem more important or serious than it really is. EG *'Vast' proved to be something of an overstatement.* N COUNT/ UNCOUNT = exaggeration

overstay /əʊvəsteɪ/, **overstays, overstaying, overstayed**. If you **overstay** your time or your welcome, you stay somewhere longer than people want you to. EG *I'd already overstayed my time by a week.* V+O = outstay

overstep /əʊvəstep/, **oversteps, overstepping, overstepped**. If you **overstep** something such as the rules of a system or the rules of polite behaviour, you go beyond what is considered acceptable; used showing disapproval. ● If you **overstep the mark**, you behave in a way that is not acceptable by breaking particular social rules, for example by being rude or impolite. EG *This last week he's overstepped the mark... ...those who publicly overstep the mark by their ostentation.* V+O ● PHR : VB INFLECTS = go too far

overt /əʊvɜːt/. Something that is **overt**, for example behaviour or an action, is done or shown in an open and obvious way. EG *...overt hostility.* ◇ **overtly**. EG *His jokes got more and more overtly malicious.* ADJ QUALIT ◇ ADV

overtake /əʊvəteɪk/, **overtakes, overtaking, overtook, overtaken**. 1 If you **overtake** a vehicle, person, or animal on a road or path, you pass them because you are moving faster than they are. EG *I found myself behind the gigantic truck that had overtaken us.* V OR V+O

2 If something such as an event, change, etc **overtakes** you, it happens to you unexpectedly or suddenly when you are not prepared for it. EG *...all the changes that have overtaken Shetland recently.* V+O = befall

3 If something such as an emotion **overtakes** you, it has an overpowering effect on you; a rather literary use. EG *Utter weariness overtook me an hour later.* V+O = engulf

4 If one thing **is overtaken** by another thing, it is replaced by it, because the other thing is more powerful. EG *His fear was slowly overtaken by embarrassment.* V+O : USU PASS = succeed

overtax /əʊvətæks/, **overtaxes, overtaxing, overtaxed**. 1 If you **overtax** yourself or **are overtaxed**, you are physically or mentally exhausted. EG *I was afraid that he would overtax himself... They were dangerously overtaxed... My overtaxed brain rebelled and everything went blank.* V+O : USU PASS = overwork

2 If a government **overtaxes** a country or its people, it makes them pay too much tax. EG *They believed that Britain was overtaxed.* V+O : USU PASS

overthrow /əʊvəθrəʊ/, **overthrows, overthrowing, overthrew, overthrown**. 1 If a group of people **overthrow** a leader, government, or regime, they remove them by force. EG *He has been under arrest since March for attempting to overthrow the present regime.* V+O = topple ▸ used as a noun. EG *...the overthrow of the right-wing dictatorship.* ▸ N COUNT

2 If values or standards **are overthrown**, they are replaced by other values or standards. EG *Laws are openly violated, standards of behaviour are overthrown.* V+O : USU PASS = bring down

overtime /əʊvətaɪm/. 1 **Overtime** is extra time that you spend working at your job, in addition to your normal working hours. EG *He had worked hard all his life, putting in overtime at the factory whenever he could.* N UNCOUNT

2 You also say that someone **works overtime** when they use a lot of energy, effort, and enthusiasm in doing something; an informal expression. EG *This weekend he has been working overtime to persuade the members to support him.* PHR : VB INFLECTS, USU + *to*-INF

overtone /əʊvətəʊn/, **overtones**. If something has **overtones** of a particular kind, it has traces of an idea, emotion, or attitude which is not openly expressed. EG *There were even overtones of blackmail... The play has heavy political overtones.* N COUNT + SUPP : USU PL ⇑ hint = undercurrent

overtook /əʊvətʊk/ is the past tense of **overtake**.

overture /əʊvətjʊə/, **overtures**. 1 An **overture** is 1.1 a fairly short piece of music played by an orchestra, often one that was written as an introduction to an opera or play. EG *...Elgar's 'Cockaigne' Overture.* N COUNT 1.2 something that is deliberately said or done as a preparation for something else. EG *I sensed that this was the overture to an argument.* N COUNT : USU + SUPP = prelude

2 If you make **overtures** to someone, you try to begin a friendly or romantic relationship with them. EG *...overtures of friendship... ...romantic overtures.* N PLURAL : USU + SUPP ⇑ gesture

overturn /əʊvətɜːn/, **overturns, overturning, overturned**. 1 If something **overturns** or if you **overturn** it, it turns upside down or on its side. EG *She overturned the chairs and hurled the cushions about... Pollock's car crashed into a clump of trees and overturned... ...overturned army lorries.* V-ERG = upturn

2 If someone **overturns** a legal decision, they change it by using their higher authority and power. V+O = overrule

3 If someone **overturns** a government or regime, they remove it or destroy it, especially by using violence. EG *They expressed their desire to overturn the existing regime.* V+O = overthrow

overvalue /əʊvəvæljuː/, **overvalues, overvaluing, overvalued**. If you **overvalue** someone or something, you think that they are much more important or valuable than they really are. EG *We generally tend to overvalue money and undervalue art.* V+O = overrate

overview /əʊvəvjuː/, **overviews**. An **overview** of a complicated situation is a a clear understanding or description of it as a whole, without bothering about all the details. EG *Posy felt she had an overview of the situation.* N COUNT : USU + *of* = grasp

overweening /əʊvəwiːnɪŋ/. **Overweening** pride, arrogance, etc is very great power, arrogance, etc; a formal word, used to emphasize your disapproval. EG *This was merely the outcome of her overweening pride... ...his overweening impatience.* ADJ CLASSIF : ATTRIB = immoderate

overweight /əʊvəweɪt/. If someone is **overweight**, they are too fat, and therefore unhealthy. EG *Nearly half the people in this country are overweight.* ADJ QUALIT : USU PRED = obese

overwhelm /əʊvəwelm/, **overwhelms, overwhelming, overwhelmed**. 1 If something **overwhelms** you, it makes you feel completely helpless, astonished, or embarrassed. EG *He was overwhelmed by the intensity of her love... The horror of it all had overwhelmed me.* V+O : USU PASS

2 If an army or group of people **overwhelms** another, they gain complete victory or control over them because they are stronger or more skilful. EG *Their mission was to seize the bridges and overwhelm the garrison.* V+O ⇑ defeat

overwhelming /əʊvəwelmɪŋ/. 1 Something that is **overwhelming** makes you feel so helpless, surprised, embarrassed, etc that you cannot think clearly. EG *...an overwhelming sense of powerlessness.* ADJ QUALIT = overpowering ◇ **overwhelmingly**. EG *The reception on the first night had been overwhelmingly appreciative.* ◇ ADV

2 **Overwhelming** is used to emphasize that an amount or quantity is much greater than other amounts or quantities. EG *An overwhelming majority of people are opposed to this plan.* ADJ CLASSIF = vast ◇ **overwhelmingly**. EG *It is still an overwhelmingly rural country.* ◇ ADV = predominantly

overwork /əʊvəwɜːk/, **overworks, overworking, overworked**. 1 If you **are overworking** or if someone **is overworking** you, you are working too hard, and are likely to become very tired or ill. EG *He wanted to make sure they didn't overwork and have heart attacks... I hope you're not overworking that poor boy.* V-ERG ▸ used as a noun. EG *Signs of overwork are nervous tension, irritability, and depression.* ▸ N UNCOUNT ⇑ strain

2 If you **overwork** something, you use it too much; an informal use. EG *'Crisis' has become one of the most overworked words of modern British politics.* V+O

overwrought /əʊvərɔːt/. Someone who is **overwrought** is very nervous, worried, and upset. EG *She was tired and overwrought.* ADJ QUALIT = on edge

ovulate /ɒvjə⁴leɪt/, **ovulates, ovulating, ovulated**. When a woman or female animal **ovulates**, she produces ova from her ovary; a technical term in physiology and biology. V ◇ **ovulation** /ɒvjə⁴leɪʃə⁰n/. EG *These hormones appear in highest concentration around the time of ovulation.* ◇ N UNCOUNT

ovum /əʊvəm/, **ova**. An **ovum** is one of the reproductive cells of a woman, female animal, or bird. It is fertilized by a male sperm to produce young; a technical term in biology and medicine. N COUNT = egg

ow /aʊ/. People say **'Ow!'** when they suddenly feel pain. EG *'Ow!' he screamed... Ow! Stop it! You're hurting!* EXCLAM = ouch

owe /əʊ/, **owes, owing, owed**. 1 If you **owe** money to someone you need to pay it back to them because they have lent it to you. EG *You owe me a fiver... He owed a hundred and eighty nine pounds.* V+O, V+O+O, OR V+O+A *(to)*

2 If someone or something **owes** a particular quality or ability to someone or something else, they only have it because of the other person or thing. EG *She owed her technique entirely to his teaching... The plains of the Ganges owe their fertility to the minerals deposited there by the river... Alfred owed everything to him.* V+O+A *(to)*

3 If you **owe** someone something such as thanks, gratitude, etc, you feel that you must behave in that way towards them, for example because of something that they have done for you. EG *We owe you our thanks, Dr Marlowe... Neither he nor Melanie owe me any explanation.* V+O+O, OR V+O +A *(to)* ● To **owe** someone **a living** means to have a duty to look after them or support them. EG *She seems to think that the world owes her a living.* ● PHR : VB INFLECTS

4 You use **owing to** when you are introducing a reason for something. EG *I missed my flight owing to a traffic hold-up.* PREP = due to

owl /aʊl/, **owls**. An **owl** is a bird with a flat face, large eyes, and a small sharp beak. There are many kinds of owl. Usually owls obtain their food by hunting small animals at night. EG *...the hoot of an owl coming from the direction of the cottage.* N COUNT

owlish /aʊlɪʃ/. Someone who is **owlish** looks rather like an owl and seems to be very serious and clever. EG *Jimmie was almost owlish in his earnest solemnity.* ◊ **owlishly.** EG *Patrick peered owlishly at us through his horn-rimmed glasses.* ADJ QUALIT ◊ ADV WITH VB

own /əʊn/, **owns, owning, owned.** When **own** is used as an adjective, it usually occurs immediately after the determiner or possessive in the noun group.

1 You use **own** 1.1 to emphasize that something belongs to a particular person. EG *I gathered she'd killed her own children... My own view is that there are no serious problems... His background was rather similar to my own.* ADJ CLASSIF: ATTRIB, OR PRON: POSS+own 1.2 to indicate that something is used by, or is characteristic of, only one person, thing, or group. EG *Each city has its own peculiarities... They usually do a good job in their own way... His style is very distinctive, very much his own.* ADJ CLASSIF: ATTRIB, OR PRON: DETPOSS +own ↑ individual 1.3 to indicate that someone does or makes something without any assistance or interference from other people. EG *They will be expected to make their own beds... Make your own decisions... I said what about lunch, and he said, oh, get your own.* ADJ CLASSIF: ATTRIB, OR PRON: DETPOSS +own

2 **On** your **own.** 2.1 If you are **on** your **own**, you are alone. EG *She lived on her own... He would sit in a corner on his own... We were in the park on our own.* PHR: USED AS AN A = alone 2.2 If you do something **on** your **own**, you do it without any help or assistance from anyone else. EG *We can't solve this problem all on our own... From now on, you're on your own.* PHR: USED AS AN A = by yourself

3 You refer to people as your **own** when you feel loyal to them and want to protect or support them, especially because you are related to them. EG *We look after our own.* PRON: DETPOSS +PRON

4 The word **own** is used in the following expressions. 4.1 You can say **each to his own, each to their own,** etc, to mean that although you do not share someone's taste or liking for a particular thing, everyone has a right to like and do different things. EG *He's really keen on opera–it's not my sort of thing, but each to his own.* PHR 4.2 You use **of** his **own, of** her **own,** etc to emphasize that something belongs or relates to a particular person. EG *She has troubles of her own... I had a proposal of my own to make... He then set up a small travel business of his own.* PHR AFTER N 4.3 If you say that a person or thing has something **of** their **own** or **all of** their **own**, you are emphasizing that a particular quality or characteristic belongs to only that person or thing. EG *This type of glass has a colour and character all of its own... It developed a unique personality of its own.* PHR AFTER N ↑ individual 4.4 If you **make** something your **own**, you become involved with it in such a way that it is thought of by other people as being related only to you or belonging only to you, rather than to anyone else. EG *Edith Evans made the part her own.* PHR: VB INFLECTS 4.5 If you **get** your **own back** on someone, you have your revenge on them because of something that they have done to you; an informal expression. EG *At last he was getting his own back.* PHR: VB INFLECTS ↑ be revenged ● to **call** your **own**: see **call.** ● To **hold** your **own**: see **hold.**

5 If you **own** something, you have it as your property because you bought it or because it was given to you. EG *Julie's father owned a business that dealt in bulk orders... ...a huge old house owned by an Irish doctor... Who owns this bit of land?* V+O ↑ possess ● If you say that someone does something **like** or **as if** they **own the place**, you mean that they do it in a very arrogant and confident way; an informal expression, used showing disapproval. EG *...three or four men who acted like they owned the place... I watched the cat cross the lawn to the house, walking as though it owned the whole place.* ● PHR: USED AS AN A ↑ arrogantly

6 To **own** something or **own** that something is true means to admit that it is true; an old-fashioned use. EG *She owned to having had doubts at first. ...people who would rather die than own themselves cowards.* V+REPORT-CL, V +A (to+-ING), OR V+O+C = confess

own up. If you **own up** to something wrong that you have done, you tell someone that you did it, especially when you find this difficult. EG *Come on, own up! Who did it?... No-one owned up to taking the money.* PHRASAL VB: V+ ADV, IF+PREP THEN to ↑ admit = confess

owner /əʊnə/, **owners.** The **owner** of something is the person to whom it belongs. EG *The owner of the bookstore was sitting at his desk... The average American car owner drives 10,000 miles per year... The wardrobe had been left behind by previous owners.* ● See also **homeowner, landowner.** N COUNT ↑ possessor

owner-occupier, owner-occupiers. An **owner-occupier** is a person who owns the house or flat that they live in. EG *Most of the grants had been taken up by owner-occupiers.* N COUNT = homeowner

ownership /əʊnəʃɪp/ is the state of owning something, especially something large such as a business or an area of land. EG *...public ownership of land, finance, and the building industry... In the United States today the desire for home ownership is still strong... ...proof of ownership.* N UNCOUNT ↑ possession = proprietorship

ox /ɒks/, **oxen.** An **ox** is a castrated bull that is usually used for pulling vehicles or carrying things. EG *...a plough pulled by two oxen.* N COUNT

Oxbridge /ɒksbrɪdʒ/ is used to refer to the universities of Oxford and Cambridge, considered together and separately from all other British universities. EG *...Oxbridge graduates.* N PROPER

oxcart /ɒkskɑːt/, **oxcarts.** An **oxcart** is a cart pulled by an ox or oxen. EG *This road was built for oxcarts, not for cars.* N COUNT

oxidation /ɒksɪdeɪʃəⁿn/ is a process in which a chemical substance changes because of the addition of oxygen, for example when something rusts; a technical word. N UNCOUNT ↑ reaction

oxide /ɒksaɪd/, **oxides.** An **oxide** is a compound of oxygen and another chemical element. EG *...iron oxide... ...oxides of nitrogen.* N COUNT/ UNCOUNT: USU MOD+N

oxidize /ɒksɪdaɪz/, **oxidizes, oxidizing, oxidized**; also spelled **oxidise.** When a substance **oxidizes** or **is oxidized**, it changes chemically because of the effect of oxygen on it. For example, when a metal becomes rusty, it oxidizes. EG *Aluminium doesn't oxidise in wet weather.* V-ERG

oxtail /ɒksteɪl/ is the tail of an ox which is used as meat and for making soup. EG *...oxtail soup.* N UNCOUNT

oxyacetylene /ɒksiˈəsetəliˑn/ is a mixture of two gases, oxygen and acetylene. It burns with a very hot, bright flame and is used for cutting and welding metal. EG *You can cut anything open with an oxyacetylene flame.* N UNCOUNT: USU BEFORE N

oxygen /ɒksɪdʒəⁿn/ is a colourless gas that forms a major part of the air and that is necessary for most plants, animals, insects, etc to be able to live, and for things to burn. EG *Fish have gills through which oxygen is absorbed from the water.* N UNCOUNT

oxygenate /ɒksɪdʒəneɪt/, **oxygenates, oxygenating, oxygenated.** To **oxygenate** something means to mix or dissolve oxygen into it. ◊ **oxygenated.** EG *...oxygenated water.* V+O ◊ ADJ CLASSIF

oxygen mask, oxygen masks. An **oxygen mask** is a bowl-like object which is attached to a cylinder of oxygen by means of a tube. It is placed over a patient's nose and mouth so that they can be given more oxygen and can therefore breathe more easily. EG *She was breathing using an oxygen mask.* N COUNT ↑ equipment

oxygen tent, oxygen tents. An **oxygen tent** is a clear tent that is put over a patient who is very ill in hospital and filled with pure oxygen to help them breathe. N COUNT ↑ equipment

oyster /ɔɪstə/, **oysters.** 1 An **oyster** is a fairly large, flat shellfish. There is one type of oyster that can be eaten and another that produces pearls. EG *...smoked salmon and oysters... ...mushroom and oyster pie.* ● If you say that **the world is** someone's **oyster**, you mean that they can do anything or go anywhere that they want to. EG *You have passed the first hurdle and the world is your oyster.* N COUNT ● PHR: VB INFLECTS

oyster bed, oyster beds. An **oyster bed** is a place where oysters live or are kept, so that they can be used as food or for producing pearls. EG *We started off down the long dyke, through the oyster beds.* N COUNT

oystercatcher /ɔɪstəkætʃə/, **oystercatchers.** An **oystercatcher** is a black and white wading bird with a long red beak. It lives near the sea and eats small shellfish. N COUNT

oz. Oz is both the singular and the plural form. **oz** is a written abbreviation for 'ounce' or 'ounces'. It is used after a number to indicate a measurement of weight. EG *...3 oz of butter.* N COUNT: NUM N

ozone /əʊzəʊn/. 1 **Ozone** is a form of oxygen. There is a layer of ozone high above the earth's surface. EG *...the ozone layer, which cuts off most of the ultraviolet radiation from the sun.* N UNCOUNT ↑ gas

2 People sometimes use **ozone** to refer to the air at the seaside, which is regarded as clean and healthy. N UNCOUNT

Pp

P, p /piː/, **Ps, p's.** The plural of the abbreviation in paragraph 4 is **pp. 1 P** is the sixteenth letter of the English alphabet. N COUNT

2 If you have to **mind** your **p's and q's**, you have to be very careful not to say anything impolite; an informal expression. EG *You two mind your p's and q's or I'll take the back of my hand to you!* PHR : VB INFLECTS

3 p is an abbreviation for 'pence' or 'penny'. EG *It's only 10p.* N UNCOUNT : NUM+N

4 p. is used before a number as a written abbreviation for 'page'. EG *See p. 72.* N COUNT+NUM

5 p is written on a piece of music to show that the part indicated should be played quietly.

6 P or **p** is also an abbreviation for other words beginning with p or P, such as 'parking' and 'per'.

pa /pɑː/, **pas.** Someone's **pa** is their father; an informal, old-fashioned word used especially in American English. EG *Hi, Pa... Don't tell Ma or Pa.* N PROPER/VOC : ALSO N COUNT

p.a. is a written abbreviation for 'per annum'. EG *I shall be paid £12,000 p.a.* ADV : USU VB+ NUM+ADV

PA /piː eɪ/, **PA's. PA** is **1** an abbreviation for 'personal assistant'. EG *Suggest that he needs a PA rather than a secretary.* N COUNT : USU SING **2** an abbreviation for 'public address': see **public address system.** EG *I heard the bark of the PA system.* N SING WITH DET

pace, paces, pacing, paced. The word **pace** is pronounced /peɪs/ for every paragraph except paragraph 10, and /peɪsi¹/ for paragraph 10. **1** The **pace** of something is the speed at which it happens or is done. EG *The sale resumed at a brisk pace, as if nothing had happened... Despite the breakneck pace of change, people eagerly called for more... Harassment of dissidents gathered pace again.* N UNCOUNT : USU +SUPP

2 Someone's **pace** is **2.1** the speed at which they do something. EG *He criticized the Government's snail-like pace in implementing a road safety programme.* N SING : USU POSS +N

2.2 the speed at which they walk. EG *He proceeds at a leisurely pace... He quickened his pace... The pace he set was too fast for the others.* N SING WITH DET : USU+SUPP = tempo

3 keep pace. 3.1 If someone or something **keeps pace**, they change, progress, or increase as quickly as someone or something else. EG *Any country which fails to keep pace with these developments will soon be in trouble... Earnings have not kept pace with inflation.* PHR : VB INFLECTS, IF+ PREP THEN *with* = keep up **3.2** If you **keep pace** with someone, you succeed in walking as fast as them when you are going somewhere with them or trying to follow them. EG *Rodney knew I was trying very hard to keep pace with him.* PHR : VB INFLECTS, IF+ PREP THEN *with* = keep up

4 If you do something or walk **at your own pace**, you do it or walk at the speed that is comfortable for you. EG *...the ability to tackle it at his own pace... I will also allow the prefects to walk to church at their own pace.* PHR : USED AS AN A

5 If you can **stand the pace**, you are able to live or work somewhere where you have to do a lot of things quickly, without becoming ill or unhappy as a result. EG *They can't stand the pace in the city.* PHR : VB INFLECTS

6 If you **force the pace** of something, you make it happen more quickly than it would naturally happen. PHR : VB INFLECTS

7 A **pace** is **7.1** a step of normal length that you take when you walk. EG *The keeper took two quick paces forward.* N COUNT = stride **7.2** the distance you move when you take a step. EG *He stopped when he was a few paces away... ...guns that will kill at a thousand paces.* N COUNT : USU PL = yard

8 If you **go through** your **paces** or **show** your **paces**, you show someone how well you can do something. If someone **puts** you **through** your **paces**, they make you show how well you can do something. EG *The crowd of simple country people showed their paces in Portuguese.* PHR : VB INFLECTS

9 If you **pace** a particular place, you keep walking within a small area, often because you are anxious or impatient. EG *She paced the room angrily... She began to pace round the office... Harold paced nervously up and down the platform.* V+O, OR V+A ⇑ walk

10 You say **pace** a particular person when stating an opinion to indicate politely that you realize you are disagreeing with them; a formal use. EG *They are more successful in an atmosphere of economic expansion than they are (pace Sir Geoffrey Howe) if the economy is squeezed.* PREP

pace out. If you **pace out** or **pace off** a distance, you walk a particular number of paces from a particular point in order to work out where something should be put, or you walk from one point to another in order to count the number of paces between them. EG *Placing the gun beside a tree he paced out a hundred and fifty paces.* PHRASAL VB : ORDER V+ADV+ O ⇑ measure

pacemaker /peɪsmeɪkə/, **pacemakers.** A **pacemaker** is **1** a device that is put next to someone's heart, usually under their skin, in order to make their heart beat in the right way. N COUNT **2** a competitor who is in front of other competitors during part of a race and who therefore causes that part of the race to be run at a particular speed. N COUNT

pachyderm /pækɪdɜːm/, **pachyderms.** A **pachyderm** is a large thick-skinned animal such as an elephant or rhinoceros; a technical zoological term. N COUNT

Pacific /pəsɪfɪk/. **1** The **Pacific** or the **Pacific Ocean** is a very large area of sea to the west of North and South America, and to the east of Asia and Australia. N PROPER : *the*+ N

2 Pacific is used to describe things in or relating to the Pacific Ocean. EG *...Pacific islands.* ADJ CLASSIF : ATTRIB

3 Something that is **pacific** is peaceful or intended to result in peace; a formal use. EG *...their pacific intentions.* ADJ CLASSIF = peaceable

pacifier /pæsɪfaɪə/, **pacifiers.** A **pacifier** is a child's dummy; used in American English. EG *His grandson was toddling around with a pacifier in his mouth.* N COUNT

pacifism /pæsɪfɪzə⁰m/ is the belief that war and violence are always wrong. N UNCOUNT

pacifist /pæsɪfɪst/, **pacifists.** A **pacifist** is a person who believes in pacifism and does not take part in wars. EG *In matters of defence he was not a pacifist but an advocate of armed neutrality... ...the pacifist movement.* N COUNT

pacify /pæsɪfaɪ/, **pacifies, pacifying, pacified.** If you **pacify** someone, you cause them to become calm, quiet, or satisfied when they have been angry or upset. EG *He tried to pacify the mob... He pacified his conscience by promising himself he would start work tomorrow.* V+O = placate, appease ◊ **pacification** /pæsɪfɪkeɪʃə⁰n/. EG *...the pacification of the island.* ◊ N UNCOUNT

pack /pæk/, **packs, packing, packed. 1** If you **pack** a bag or if you **pack**, you put your belongings in a case, bag, or trunk, usually because you are leaving one place and going to another. EG *He packed his bags and left... I packed my gear and walked outside... He walked back to the hotel to pack and pay his bill... I packed the tools away.* V OR V+O ◊ **packing.** EG *Have you started your packing?* ◊ N UNCOUNT

2 If you **pack** things, especially in a factory, you put them into containers or parcels so that they can be transported and sold, or sent to people. EG *She spent all summer packing apricots.* V+O ◊ **packing.** EG *Send 25p extra for postage and packing.* ◊ N UNCOUNT

3 If you **pack** people or things into a place or if they **pack** a place, so many of them are in that place that they are very close together and the place is full. EG *About 300 of us were packed into a half-built mansion... Thirty thousand people packed into the stadium to hear him... ...clusters of houses tightly packed together... Americans of all ages stream over the highways and pack the airports.* V-ERG+A, OR V+ O = cram ● If a play, film, etc **packs them in**, lots of people go to see it; an informal expression. EG *'Star Wars' was really packing them in.* ● PHR : VB INFLECTS = pull in

4 If you **pack** a jury, committee, or audience, you make sure that lots of people who support you are in it. V+O

5 A **pack** is a bag containing your belongings that you carry on your back or that is carried on the back of an animal when you are travelling. EG *I took a bottle of scotch from my pack... ...climbing up the hill with a pack on your back.* N COUNT = backpack

6 A **pack** is also **6.1** a packet; used especially in American English. EG *...a pack of cigarettes... ...a* N COUNT

cornflakes pack... *Vegetables are available in five-pound packs.* **6.2** a complete set of playing cards; used especially in British English. EG *...a pack of cards.* **6.3** a group of animals that hunt together, especially wolves or dogs. EG *...packs of hounds... ...the leading hounds in the pack.* **6.4** a group of people who go around together and do things together. EG *The boys always went about as a pack... ...the leader of the pack... They're like a pack of kids!* **6.5** an organized group of brownies or cubs. **6.6** the forwards in a rugby team when they are in a scrum.
N COUNT = deck; N COUNT OR N PART; N COUNT: ALSO N +of+N IN PL = gang; N COUNT; N COUNT

7 If you say that an account is **a pack of lies**, you mean that it is completely untrue. EG *He told me a pack of lies.* PHR: USED AS C/O

8 If someone or something **packs** a lot of force or power, they have this force or power which can have a strong effect. EG *Each submarine packs enough nuclear missiles to destroy vast areas of territory... He packs a fair punch.* V+O ⇑ possess

9 If you **send** someone **packing**, you tell them in an angry way to leave; an informal expression. PHR: VB INFLECTS ⇑ dismiss

10 See also **packed, packing, face pack.**

pack in. If you **pack** something **in**, you stop doing it, usually because you are tired of doing it; an informal expression used in British English. EG *It's a good job. I don't think he'd pack it in.* PHRASAL VB: V+O+ADV = jack in ● When someone is saying or doing something annoying, you tell them to **pack it in** as an informal and fairly rude way of telling them to stop saying or doing it. EG *I can't stand any more of this, Nell. For God's sake pack it in.* ● CONVENTION

pack off. If you **pack** someone **off** somewhere, you send them there to stay for a period of time, usually because you do not want them with you; an informal expression. EG *They pack their sons off to boarding school... I packed her off to bed with a hot water bottle.* PHRASAL VB: V+O+ADV ⇑ dispatch

pack up. 1 If you **pack up** your belongings or if you **pack up**, you put all your belongings in a case, bag, etc, usually because you are leaving one place and going to another. EG *We suggested Verity should pack up her few belongings immediately... Once term finishes we all pack up and go home.* PHRASAL VB: V+ADV, OR V+O+ADV

2 If you **pack up**, you stop doing a piece of work and sometimes also tidy things away; a fairly informal use. EG *I think I'll pack up and go home now.* PHRASAL VB: V+ADV

3 If a machine **packs up**, it stops working because it has broken or gone wrong; an informal use. EG *The engine packed up just before we reached Paris.* PHRASAL VB: V+ADV = break down

package /pækɪdʒ/, **packages, packaging, packaged. 1** A **package** is **1.1** a small parcel. EG *She pulled out a small package wrapped in tissue paper.* N COUNT **1.2** in American English, a packet. EG *He took a package of cigarettes out of his pocket.* N COUNT

2 When an amount of something **is packaged**, it is put into packets to be sold. EG *The cereal is packaged in plain boxes.* V+O: USU PASS

3 A **package** is also a set of suggestions or proposals that are presented as one thing so that all of them have to be accepted or none of them. EG *There was an announcement by the government of a fresh package of spending cuts... They offered a package worth sixty million dollars.* N COUNT

package deal, package deals. A **package deal** is an offer which includes a number of items, all of which must be accepted if the offer as a whole is accepted. EG *They rejected the package deal put forward by the management.* N COUNT: USU SING

package holiday, package holidays. A **package holiday** or a **package tour** is a holiday where a travel company books your travel and accommodation for you. N COUNT

packaging /pækɪdʒɪŋ/ is the container that something is sold or sent in, or the material used to make the container. EG *...the foolish extravagance of much modern packaging.* N UNCOUNT

pack animal, pack animals. A **pack animal** is an animal such as a horse or donkey that is used to carry things on journeys. N COUNT

packed /pækt/. **1** A place that is **packed** is very crowded. EG *The theatre was packed... ...a vast room packed with excited people... The coffee house was packed tight.* ADJ QUALIT: IF+PREP THEN *with* = crammed

2 Something that is **packed** with things or **packed** full of something contains a very large number of things or a very large amount of something. EG *...jets packed with electronic devices... The book is packed full of information.* ADJ CLASSIF: PRED: IF+PREP THEN *with* ⇑ filled

3 Someone who is **packed** has put their belongings in a bag because they are about to leave. EG *She was all packed and ready to leave.* ADJ CLASSIF: PRED

packed lunch, packed lunches. A **packed lunch** is food, wrapped in paper or in a container, that you take to school or on an outing and eat for lunch. N COUNT

packed out. If a place is **packed out**, it is completely full of people; an informal expression used in British English. EG *The cinema was packed out.* ADJ CLASSIF: PRED = jam-packed

packer /pækə/, **packers.** A **packer** is a person whose job is to pack things into containers. N COUNT ⇑ worker

packet /pækɪt/, **packets. 1** A **packet** is **1.1** a box made of thin cardboard or a bag, envelope, or wrapper made of paper or plastic, in which a quantity of items are sold. EG *...a packet of cigarettes... ...a packet of carrot seed... ...cereal packets... ...packet soup.* **1.2** a small flat parcel. N PART ⇑ container = package; N COUNT

2 In informal British English, people refer to a lot of money as a **packet**. EG *He made a packet out of selling holidays to students.* N SING: *a*+N = fortune

3 A **packet** or a **packet boat** is a boat that carries passengers, cargo, and post from one place to another. Packet boats were used more in former times. N COUNT

pack ice is an area of ice that is floating on the sea and is made up of pieces of ice that have been pushed together. N UNCOUNT

packing /pækɪŋ/ is paper, plastic, etc which is used to put round things that are being sent or moved somewhere in containers, in order to stop them getting damaged. ● See also **pack 1, 2.** N UNCOUNT

packing case, packing cases; also spelled with a hyphen. A **packing case** or a **packing crate** is a large wooden box in which things are put in order to be stored or transported somewhere. N COUNT = tea chest

pact /pækt/, **pacts.** A **pact** is a formal agreement between two or more people or governments to do a particular thing or to help each other. EG *A similar pact was signed in 1967, banning all military activity... This led to a non-aggression pact between the two countries.* ● See also **suicide pact.** N COUNT

pad /pæd/, **pads, padding, padded. 1** A **pad** is a fairly thick, flat piece of a soft or firm substance, especially cloth or foam rubber, which is used for example to clean something, to protect something from pressure, or to give more shape to something. EG *Dab the wound with a cotton wool pad soaked in antiseptic liquid... Polish it with a soft cloth folded into a pad... ...scouring pads... ...dresses with shoulder pads... Elbow pads and knee pads are essential on a skateboard.* N COUNT

2 A **pad** of fat or flesh is a thick piece of fat or flesh under someone's skin. EG *...the pad of fat on her rear.* N COUNT = cushion

3 If you **pad** something, you put something soft in it or over it in order to make it less hard, to protect it, or to give it a different shape. EG *I padded my costume in order to make myself look fat.* ◊ **padded.** EG *The steering wheel is padded with real leather... ...a padded bra... ...a padded sofa... Jackets were shorter and shoulders were less padded.* V+O ⇑ stuff; ◊ ADJ CLASSIF: IF+PREP THEN *with* ⇑ stuffed

4 If someone's body or a part of it **is padded**, it is covered with a thick layer of fat under the skin. ◊ **padded.** EG *She was now padded with spare fat... ...her heavily padded hips.* V+O: USU PASS; ◊ ADJ CLASSIF

5 The **pads** of an animal such as a cat or dog are the soft, fleshy parts on the bottom of its paws. N COUNT: USU ⇑ sole

6 A person or animal that **pads** somewhere walks there with steps that are fairly quick and heavy but not very loud. EG *Hooper came loping up the lane with the dog padding quick and soft-footed at his heels... Uncle Harold padded out of the room, barefoot.* V+A

7 A **pad** is also **7.1** a number of pieces of paper which are fixed together along the top or the side, in such a way that each piece can be torn off when it has been used. EG *He took a pad and pencil from his pocket... Mrs Oliver made a brief note on the telephone pad... ...a pad of paper.* **7.2** a platform or an area of flat, hard ground from which helicopters can take off or rockets can be launched. EG *The helicopter was already in the air, hovering about a metre above the pad.* N COUNT: ALSO +of+N UNCOUNT; N COUNT

8 Someone's **pad** is the place, especially a flat, where they are living; an informal use. EG *...his bachelor pad in Davies Street.* N COUNT ⇑ residence

9 See also **Brillo pad.**

pad out. If you **pad out** a piece of writing or a PHRASAL VB:

speech with unnecessary words or pieces of information, you include them in it to make it longer and hide the fact that you have not got very much to say. EG *She has a habit of padding out her essays with a lot of long quotes.* O+ADV, IF+PREP THEN *with* ⇑ lengthen

padded cell, padded cells. A **padded cell** is a small room with padded walls in a psychiatric hospital, where mentally ill people can be put if it is thought that they might hurt themselves in an ordinary room. N COUNT

padding /pædɪŋ/ is 1 something soft that is put in or over something else in order to make it less hard, to protect it, or to give it a different shape. EG *...a big wad of padding.* N UNCOUNT = wadding 2 unnecessary words or information used to make a piece of writing or a speech longer. N UNCOUNT = waffle

paddle /pædə⁰l/, **paddles, paddling, paddled**. 1 A **paddle** is 1.1 a short pole with a wide, flat part at one end or both ends, which is held in both hands and used to move a canoe or other small boat through the water. N COUNT 1.2 a flat part of a machine, for example a water wheel, which is pushed by a liquid or which pushes against a liquid. EG *The wheel's paddles are pushed round by water flowing beneath it.* N COUNT

2 If you **paddle** a boat or **paddle** somewhere, you move the boat through the water using a paddle. EG *...a boat paddled by chanting Africans... The people here paddle from place to place in canoes.* V+O, OR V : USU +A = row

3 If you **paddle** along, you move fairly slowly through water by moving your hands or feet up and down. EG *She lay flat on the raft and paddled with both arms... ...the geese paddling along a few yards astern.* V : USU+A

4 If you **paddle**, you walk or stand in shallow water, especially at the edge of the sea, for fun. EG *We were paddling, like elderly trippers at Southend... It was too cold for paddling.* ▸ used as a noun. EG *After lunch we had a bit of a paddle in the sea.* V = wade ▸ N COUNT : USU SING

paddle boat, paddle boats; also spelled as one word. A **paddle boat** or a **paddle steamer** is a large boat that is pushed through the water by the movement of large wheels that have flat boards fitted to them and are turned by a steam engine. N COUNT, OR *by*+N

paddling pool, paddling pools. A **paddling pool** is a shallow artificial pool for children to paddle in. N COUNT

paddock /pædək/, **paddocks**. 1 A **paddock** is a small field where horses are kept. N COUNT

2 At a race course, the **paddock** is the place where the horses are put and shown to the public before each race. N COUNT = enclosure

paddy /pædi¹/, **paddies**. 1 A **paddy** or a **paddy field** is a flooded field in which rice is grown. EG *...rice paddies in Bangkok.* N COUNT

2 Someone who is **in a paddy** is angry, usually about something unimportant; an informal expression. PHR : USED AS AN A

3 A **Paddy** is an Irishman; an informal and usually offensive use. N COUNT/VOC

padlock /pædlɒk/, **padlocks, padlocking, padlocked**. 1 A **padlock** is a lock which is used for fastening two things or two parts of something together. It consists of a block of metal with a U-shaped bar attached to it, one end of which is released when the padlock is unlocked with a key. EG *We put a chain and a padlock on the back gate.* N COUNT

2 If you **padlock** something, you lock it or fasten it to something else using a padlock. EG *The cupboards were padlocked... She padlocked her bike to the railings.* V+O

padre /pɑːdri¹/, **padres**. A **padre** is a Christian priest, especially a chaplain to the armed forces; a fairly informal word. EG *The padre never used that prayer again... Good evening, Padre.* N COUNT/VOC ⇑ clergyman

paean /piːən/, **paeans**. A **paean** is a piece of music, writing, or film that expresses praise, admiration, or joy; a literary word. EG *The film is a paean to nature.* N COUNT = eulogy

paediatrician /piːdɪətrɪʃə⁰n/, **paediatricians**; also spelled **pediatrician**. A **paediatrician** is a doctor who specializes in treating children's illnesses. N COUNT

paediatrics /piːdɪætrɪks/; also spelled **pediatrics**. **Paediatrics** is the area of medicine that is concerned with children's illnesses and their treatment. N UNCOUNT

paella /paɪelə/ is a dish cooked especially in Spain which consists of rice mixed with small pieces of vegetables, fish, and chicken. N UNCOUNT ⇑ food

paeony /piːəni¹/. See **peony**.

pagan /peɪgə⁰n/, **pagans**. 1 Some people use **pagan** to describe people, beliefs, and practices that do not belong to any of the main religions of the world, especially when they existed or are thought to have existed long before these religions. EG *...the pagan emperor Diocletian.* ▸ used of things and beliefs. EG *...an ancient pagan festival... ...pagan gods.* ADJ CLASSIF = heathen

2 A **pagan** is a person who has pagan beliefs or practices. EG *They burnt thousands of pagans and heretics.* N COUNT = heathen

paganism /peɪgənɪzə⁰m/ is the state of having pagan beliefs or practices. N UNCOUNT

page /peɪdʒ/, **pages, paging, paged**. 1 A **page** is 1.1 one side of one of the pieces of paper in a book, magazine, or newspaper, usually with a number printed at the top or bottom. EG *For details of how pensions will be increased, see page 16... The next day's journal allotted its front page to the case.* N COUNT, OR N+NUM 1.2 one of the pieces of paper in a book, magazine, or newspaper. EG *Ellen aimlessly turned the pages of her magazine.* N COUNT

2 You can refer to an important event or period of time as a **page** of history; a literary use. EG *...a glorious page in our history.* N COUNT+SUPP = chapter

3 When someone employed in a hotel, a large shop, an airport, etc **pages** a particular person, they call out that person's name, sometimes using a loud speaker system, in order to attract his or her attention and give him or her a message. EG *Paging Peter Smith. Would you go to reception please.* V+O ⇑ summon

4 In former times, a **page** was a young boy who was a knight's servant and was learning to be a knight. N COUNT

5 A **page** is also the same as a page-boy: see **page-boy 1**. N COUNT

pageant /pædʒənt/, **pageants**. A **pageant** is 1 a show, often performed out of doors, which is made up of several historical or literary scenes. N COUNT ⇑ play 2 a very grand and colourful ceremony or public display. EG *...the pageant of the Duke's immense, sumptuous funeral.* N COUNT = spectacle

pageantry /pædʒəntri¹/ is the grand, colourful appearance and actions of people and things involved in a special formal event, especially a royal one. EG *The week of the royal wedding is crammed with festivities and pageantry.* N UNCOUNT ⇑ ceremony

pageboy /peɪdʒbɔɪ/, **pageboys**; also spelled with a hyphen. 1 A **pageboy** is a small boy who is one of the bride's attendants at a wedding. N COUNT

2 A **pageboy** or a **pageboy** hairstyle is a hairstyle in which all the hair is smooth and the same medium length and the ends are curled under. N COUNT : USU SING OR BEFORE N

pagination /pædʒɪneɪʃə⁰n/. The **pagination** of a book, magazine, etc is the way that the pages have been numbered; used especially when there is a mistake in the sequence of numbers; a formal word. EG *The pagination is wrong–there's no page 56.* N UNCOUNT : USU *the*+N = numbering

pagoda /pəgəʊdə/, **pagodas**. A **pagoda** is a tall building which is used for religious purposes, especially by Buddhists, in China, Japan, and South-East Asia. Pagodas are usually very ornately decorated and consist of many storeys. N COUNT ⇑ temple

pah /pæ/ is an old-fashioned exclamation used to express scorn or disgust. EXCLAM

paid /peɪd/. 1 **Paid** is the past tense and past participle of **pay**.

2 **Paid** work is work that you are given money for doing. EG *...if you will be doing some paid work after retirement.* ▸ used with an adverb to indicate how much money you are given. EG *...women in low paid jobs.* ADJ CLASSIF : USU ATTRIB ▸ ADJ CLASSIF : ADV+ADJ

3 **Paid** workers are given money for the work they do. EG *Most of the work is done by paid staff.* ▸ used with an adverb to indicate how much money they are given. EG *The people who will suffer most will be the low paid.* ADJ CLASSIF ▸ ADJ CLASSIF : ADV+ADJ

4 If you have **paid** holiday or **paid** leave, you are given your wages or salary while you are on holiday. ADJ CLASSIF : ATTRIB

5 Something that **puts paid to** something else, for example someone's hope or chance of doing something, ends or destroys it. EG *In the end, bad weather put paid to their chances of winning the match.* PHR : VB INFLECTS = ruin

paid-up. Someone who is a **paid-up** member of a particular group 1 has paid the money required to join the group. EG *Over three million people in Britain are paid-up members of conservation groups.* ADJ CLASSIF : ATTRIB

2 is recognized definitely as a member of the group, or is an enthusiastic member of it. EG *All, however, are paid-up members of the Media Mob, faces that appear on every chat show.* ADJ CLASSIF : ATTRIB = committed

pail /peɪl/, **pails**. A **pail** is a bucket, especially one made of metal or wood; a slightly old-fashioned word. EG *...large metal pails filled to the brim with milk.* ▸ **Pail** is also used to refer to the contents of a pail or the amount it contains. EG *They boiled five or six pails of water.*
N COUNT ⇑ container
▸ N PART+N UNCOUNT = bucketful

pain /peɪn/, **pains, paining, pained**. 1 **Pain** or a **pain** is an unpleasant feeling which you have in a part of your body because you have been hurt or are ill. EG *He was in pain... Where is the pain?... A searing pain shot up his arm... She complained of severe pains in her chest... Adults said they suffered abdominal pains.*
N UNCOUNT/COUNT ⇑ discomfort

2 **Pain** is also the feeling of deep unhappiness that you have when unpleasant or upsetting things happen. EG *How well I understood the confusion and pain of her parents... I remember, with pain, his tears.*
N UNCOUNT = anguish

3 Something that **pains** you makes you feel upset or unhappy. EG *It pained him that his father talked like that... It pains me to hear that you are leaving... Such remarks always pained him.*
V+O : NO CONT = distress

4 If a part of your body **pains** you, it hurts; an old-fashioned or literary use. EG *On nights like this, his wounded foot pained him.*
V+O = trouble

5 The word **pains** is used in the following expressions relating to effort or care. 5.1 If, when you have done something which involved quite a lot of work or effort, you get a particular thing **for your pains**, you get that thing as a reward for what you have done or as the result of it; used especially when it is disappointing. EG *A cup of tea was all I got for my pains.*
PHR : USED AS AN A = for your trouble

5.2 If you **take pains** to do something or with something, or **go to great pains** to do something, you make a great effort to do it or to do it properly. EG *She took great pains to conceal this from her parents... He always took great pains with his stage make-up.* 5.3 Someone who **is at pains** to do something is very eager to do it carefully and thoroughly. EG *Mr Thompson was at pains to emphasize that he was threatening nobody.*
PHR : VB INFLECTS, USU+*to*-INF ⇑ try
PHR+*to*-INF : VB INFLECTS = be anxious

6 If you say that someone or something is **a pain** or a **pain in the neck**, you mean that you find them very annoying or irritating; an informal expression. **A pain in the arse**, **backside**, etc is a rude, very informal variation of this expression. EG *He's a right pain, that man... She's such a pain in the neck... The car isn't mended yet, which is a pain.*
PHR : USED AS C = nuisance

7 If you have to do something **on** or **under pain of** a particular punishment, you have to do it or else you will suffer that punishment; a formal expression. EG *They were ordered not to cross the border, on pain of death.*
PREP

pained /peɪnd/. Someone who looks or sounds **pained** seems hurt or offended. EG *She only raised her eyebrows and looked pained.* ▸ used of people's expressions and behaviour. EG *Mrs Kaul departed in pained silence... Albert's great bearded face took on a pained and puzzled look.*
ADJ QUALIT = aggrieved, reproachful

painful /peɪnful/. 1 If a part of your body is **painful**, it hurts because it is injured or because there is something wrong with it. EG *My back is so painful that I cannot stand upright any more.*
ADJ QUALIT = sore

2 Something that is **painful** 2.1 causes someone physical pain. EG *My boots are still painful... ...a long and painful illness.* ◊ **painfully**. EG *She struck him, quite painfully, with the ruler.* 2.2 is upsetting and unpleasant. EG *...the painful process of growing up... It's a very painful subject... It was painful to admit that I was wrong.* ◊ **painfully**. EG *His blush reminded him painfully how young he was.* 2.3 is done slowly and with a lot of effort. EG *Progress is rather painful... His writing was slow and painful.* ◊ **painfully**. EG *...a convict who could scarcely write but had painfully scrawled out a statement.*
ADJ QUALIT = agonizing
◊ ADV WITH VB
ADJ QUALIT = distressing, traumatic
◊ ADV
ADJ QUALIT = laborious
◊ ADV WITH VB = laboriously

3 A performance or entertainment that is **painful** is so bad that it is distressing to watch or listen to; an informal use. EG *...a painful romantic comedy.*
ADJ CLASSIF = excruciating

painfully /peɪnfuli[1]/. You use **painfully** to emphasize a quality or situation that is upsetting or undesirable. EG *I was always painfully aware of my shortcomings... ...a painfully dull speech... It was painfully obvious from my silence that I knew nothing about horses.* ● See also **painful**.
ADV ⇑ very = acutely

painkiller /peɪnkɪlə/, **painkillers**. A **painkiller** is a pill or other form of drug which reduces or stops physical pain.
N COUNT = analgesic

painless /peɪnlɪ[2]s/. Something that is **painless** 1 causes or involves no physical pain. EG *Quite painless, wasn't it?... Death from drowning was a relatively easy and painless way to go.* ◊ **painlessly**. EG *My tooth came out quite painlessly.* 2 does not involve much effort or unhappiness. EG *...the painless way to learn German... There is no painless transition to socialism.* ◊ **painlessly**. EG *Industrialization in western countries was achieved painlessly.*
ADJ QUALIT ≠ painful
◊ ADV WITH VB
ADJ QUALIT = easy
◊ ADV WITH VB = effortlessly

painstaking /peɪnsteɪkɪŋ/. Someone who is **painstaking** carries out tasks extremely carefully and thoroughly. EG *He had been an efficient and painstaking worker.* ▸ used of work and qualities. EG *...painstaking research... The picture had been cleaned with painstaking care.* ◊ **painstakingly**. EG *He painstakingly records details of every race.*
ADJ QUALIT ⇑ careful = scrupulous
◊ ADV = scrupulously

paint /peɪnt/, **paints, painting, painted**. 1 **Paint** is 1.1 a coloured liquid that you put onto an object using a brush, roller, etc, usually in order to protect its surface or make it look nice. EG *...a tin of pink paint... ...modern non-drip paints... Slogans were splashed in red paint against the cliffs.* 1.2 a coloured liquid or thick paste, or a coloured substance that can be mixed with a liquid, that people put on surfaces to make pictures or designs. EG *...tubes of oil paint... In the art room, the brushes and paints had been set out.* 1.3 the covering of dried paint that an object has. EG *The metal is all still perfect under the paint... The paint was flaking off the walls.*
N MASS ⇑ substance
N MASS
N SING WITH DET : *the*+N

2 When you **paint** a picture or **paint** a person, scene, or object, you do a picture of something on a piece of paper, canvas, etc using paint. EG *Whistler painted his mother in a rocking chair... He had received a commission to paint a picture for the Canadian Ambassador... Hopper painted in a 'realist' style.* ● See also **painting**.
V OR V+O ⇑ portray

3 When you **paint** something, for example a wall or a piece of furniture, you cover it with paint. EG *The rooms were painted green.* ◊ **painted**. EG *...painted furniture.*
V, V+O, OR V+O+C (ADJ COLOUR)
◊ ADJ CLASSIF : ATTRIB

4 If you **paint** something on an object or **paint** an object, you put a design on it or write on it using paint. EG *Teenagers use aerosol cans to paint messages on lavatory walls... ...the white lines painted along the middle of the road.* ◊ **painted**. EG *...a painted egg... ...a screen painted with mythological figures... ...the wastebasket with the painted roses.*
V+O+A, OR V+O : RECIP ⇑ mark
◊ ADJ CLASSIF : IF+PREP THEN +*with* ⇑ marked

5 If someone **paints** a part of their body, they put a coloured substance on it, usually in order to make it look attractive. EG *Taking out her lipstick, she began to paint her lips... I had nothing to do all day but paint my nails and look pretty.* ◊ **painted**. EG *'Thank you, George,' said the painted girl at the table... The Chief turned a bleak, painted face towards him.*
V+O ⇑ adorn
◊ ADJ CLASSIF : ATTRIB = made-up

6 If you **paint** a liquid on something, you put the liquid onto its surface using a brush. EG *Paint the varnish on and leave it to dry for at least four hours.*
V+O+A ⇑ apply

7 If you **paint a gloomy picture**, **a vivid picture**, etc of a situation or thing, you give a description of it that is gloomy, vivid, etc. EG *She paints a dismal picture of the future.*
PHR : VB INFLECTS

8 When someone **paints the town red** or **paints the town**, they go out and have a good time in a lively way, especially by drinking a lot, often to celebrate something.
PHR : VB INFLECTS = make whoopee

paint over. If you **paint over** a mark, word, etc, you cover it with paint so that it is hidden.
PHRASAL VB : ORDER V+ADV+O

paintbox /peɪntbɒks/, **paintboxes**. A **paintbox** is a small flat tin containing a number of little blocks of paint which can be made wet and used to paint a picture.
N COUNT

paintbrush /peɪntbrʌʃ/, **paintbrushes**; also spelled with a hyphen. A **paintbrush** is a brush which you use for putting paint onto something.
N COUNT

painter /peɪntə/, **painters**. A **painter** is 1 an artist who paints pictures. EG *...famous British water-colour painters... ...painters and sculptors... ...a landscape painter.* 2 someone whose job is painting the walls, doors, window frames, etc of buildings. EG *My cousin's a painter and decorator.*
N COUNT
N COUNT ⇑ workman

painting /peɪntɪŋ/, **paintings**. 1 A **painting** is a picture which someone has produced using paint. EG *...a large painting by Rossetti... ...a fourteenth-century painting of Richard II... ...surrealistic paintings... ...oil paintings.*
N COUNT

2 **Painting** is 2.1 the activity of painting pictures. EG *...the skills of painting, sculpture, and drawing.* 2.2
N UNCOUNT
N UNCOUNT

the activity of painting walls, doors, furniture, etc.
2.3 the pictures painted by a particular artist or group of artists, and the style in which they are painted. EG *The gallery houses a collection of British painting from 1500 to the present day... ...the tradition of Western painting.* N UNCOUNT+SUPP ⇑ art

paint stripper is a substance, usually a thick liquid, which you use in order to remove the old paint from things such as doors or pieces of furniture. N UNCOUNT

paintwork /peɪntwɜːk/. The **paintwork** of a building or vehicle is the covering of paint on it or the parts that are painted. EG *Use warm water and detergent to wash paintwork... The paintwork was chipped.* N UNCOUNT

pair /pɛə/, **pairs, pairing, paired.** 1 A **pair** of things are two things of the same size and shape that are intended to be used together, for example shoes. EG *He bought a pair of hiking boots... Dragonflies have two pairs of wings.* N PART+N IN PLURAL, IF SING VB CAN BE SING OR PL ⇑ set

2 Something consisting of two main parts which are of the same size and shape, for example trousers, glasses, or scissors, is referred to as a **pair** of trousers, glasses, scissors etc. EG *I put on a pair of golfing slacks... Does anyone have a pair of tweezers?* N COUNT : USU N +*of*+N IN PL

3 Two people who are together in a particular place, who are doing something together, or who are involved in a relationship together can be referred to as a **pair**. EG *They were a somewhat sinister pair... They'd always been a devoted pair... They would be seen walking in pairs.* N COUNT : IF SING VB CAN BE SING OR PL

4 Two animals, birds, or fish that mate with each other and produce young are referred to as a **pair**. EG *Breeding pairs lay from three to eight eggs annually.* N COUNT : ALSO N +*of*+N IN PL, IF SING VB CAN BE SING OR PL

5 You can refer to one thing as the **pair** of another thing if the two things are of the same size and shape and are intended to be used together. EG *I perched beside a statue which had lost its arms and head. Its pair had once stood at the other side of the courtyard.* N COUNT : POSS+N = mate

6 See also **au pair**.

pair off. When people **pair off** or when someone **pairs** them **off**, they become grouped in pairs. EG *They'll probably pair off for company... People are paired off according to their level of competence.* PHRASAL VB : V-ERG+ADV

pair up. If you **pair up** with someone, you agree to do something together. EG *He paired up with Timothy but they lost eventually.* PHRASAL VB : V+ADV, OR V+ADV +A *(with)*

paisley /peɪzli¹/ is a special pattern of curving shapes and colours, used especially on cloth fabric. N UNCOUNT

pajama /pədʒɑːməz/. See **pyjama**.

Pakistani /pɑːkɪstɑːni¹/, **Pakistanis**. 1 Something or someone that is **Pakistani** comes from, relates to, or belongs to Pakistan. ADJ CLASSIF

2 A **Pakistani** is a person who comes from Pakistan. N COUNT

pal /pæl/, **pals, palling, palled**. 1 A **pal** is a friend; an informal use. N COUNT

2 People sometimes use **pal** to address someone when they do not feel very friendly towards them; an informal use. EG *Listen pal, you'd better be careful what you say!* N VOC = mate

pal up. If you **pal up** with someone, you become friends with them; an informal expression. EG *We first palled up when we met in Majorca on holiday.* PHRASAL VB : V+ADV, OR V+ADV +A *(with)*

palace /pælɪs/, **palaces**. 1 A **palace** is a very large, richly decorated house, especially one which is the home of a king, queen, or president. EG *The palace ceased to be a main royal residence in 1960... The Queen appeared with her family on the balcony of Buckingham Palace.* ▸ The **Palace** is used to refer to the people who live in a royal palace, especially when referring to an official opinion expressed by a king or queen. EG *'You'll have to question the Palace,' said the official... It was rumoured that the Palace was enchanted by what it had heard.* N COUNT : ALSO IN NAMES ⇑ building ▸ N SING : *the*+N

2 A **palace** is also any large grand building which looks as though it might be the home of an important person. EG *Later came limousines, luxury hotels, palaces in Florida.* N COUNT

3 **Palace** is used as part of the name of some theatres, cinemas, hotels, or similar public places. EG *We went to see a film at the Palace... He was asleep in his suite in the Palace Hotel.* N IN NAMES

palatable /pælətəbə⁰l/. 1 Food or drink that is **palatable** is pleasant to taste. ADJ QUALIT = tasty

2 An experience, suggestion, idea, etc that is **palatable** is acceptable and perhaps pleasant. EG *Under such circumstances, death might have seemed more palatable.* ADJ QUALIT

palate /pælə¹t/, **palates**. 1 Your **palate** is the top part of the inside of your mouth. • See also **cleft palate**. N COUNT

2 The **palate** is the sense of taste and the ability to judge good food and drink. EG *No one had a finer palate than Watteau; he could taste every delicate flavour... Gradually the palate becomes educated to sweeter wines.* N COUNT

palatial /pəleɪʃə⁰l/. A house that is **palatial** is large and splendid like a palace. ADJ QUALIT ⇑ grand

palaver /pəlɑːvə/ is unnecessary fuss and bother about the way something is done; an informal word. EG *What a palaver it was!* N UNCOUNT = to-do

pale /peɪl/, **paler, palest; pales, paling, paled**. 1 Something that is **pale** is whitish and not strong or bright in colour. EG *He had on a pale blue sports shirt... The house is built of red brick, with pale stone edgings.* ADJ QUALIT ⇑ light

2 If someone looks **pale**, the skin of their face looks whiter than usual, usually because they are ill, frightened, or shocked. EG *You look awfully pale: are you all right?... Joan collapsed, pale and trembling.* ▸ used as a verb. EG *His cheeks paled. He mopped his sweating brow.* ◊ **paleness**. EG *Symptoms are unusual paleness and tiredness.* ADJ QUALIT = wan ▸ V ◊ N UNCOUNT = pallor

3 A light that is **pale** is very weak and dim. EG *They drove through stripes of long shadows and pale sunshine down the treelined highway... I watched a pale dawn streak the cliffs.* ADJ CLASSIF = faint

4 If something **pales** in comparison with something else, it becomes less serious or important, or appears inferior to the thing that it is being compared with. EG *Such things paled in comparison with what was at stake... Her beauty seemed to pale beside her mother's.* V+A = fade

5 If you say that something is **beyond the pale**, you mean that it is not considered to be acceptable. EG *John's behaviour is beyond the pale!* PHR : USED AS AN A ⇑ unacceptable

Palestinian /pælɪ²stɪnɪən/, **Palestinians**. 1 Something that is **Palestinian** comes from, belongs to, or relates to the region between the River Jordan and the Mediterranean Sea which used to be called Palestine, or to the Arabs who come from this region. ADJ CLASSIF

2 A **Palestinian** is an Arab who comes from the region that used to be called Palestine. N COUNT

palette /pælɪ²t/, **palettes**. A **palette** is 1 a flat piece of wood or plastic on which an artist mixes colours for painting. N COUNT 2 the range of colours that are characteristic of a particular artist or school of painting. EG *The lighter palette of the impressionists suited her femininity.* N COUNT

palette knife, palette knives. A **palette knife** is a knife with a broad, flat, flexible blade, used in cookery. N COUNT

palindrome /pælɪndrəʊm/, **palindromes**. A **palindrome** is a word or a phrase that is the same whether you read it backwards or forwards, for example the word 'refer'. N COUNT

palings /peɪlɪŋz/ are a fence that is made of a series of long, thin, pointed, upright pieces of wood or metal. EG *Mrs Burt stuck her head over the palings wearing her husband's hat.* N PLURAL = railing

palisade /pælɪseɪd/, **palisades**. A **palisade** is a fence of wooden posts which are driven into the ground in order to protect people from attack. N COUNT = stockade

pall /pɔːl/, **palls, palling, palled**. 1 A **pall** is 1.1 a cloth used to cover a coffin at a funeral. N COUNT 1.2 a coffin at a funeral. N COUNT

2 A **pall** of smoke is a flat cloud of smoke that hangs over something. N COUNT : USU+*of*

3 If a **pall** of silence, gloom, fear, etc falls on or hangs over a person or a situation, the person or situation is affected by a heavy and long-lasting atmosphere of silence, gloom, fear, etc. EG *The pall of silence fell upon us again... A pall of mystery seems to hang over it all.* N SING WITH DET +SUPP : USU+*of* +N UNCOUNT = cloud

4 If something **palls**, it begins to seem uninteresting or boring, often because it has lasted or continued for too long. EG *It's one of the few delights that never palls.* V

pallbearer /pɔːlbɛərə/, **pallbearers**. A **pallbearer** is a person who helps to carry the coffin or walks beside it at a funeral. N COUNT ⇑ mourner

pallet /pælɪ²t/, **pallets**. A **pallet** is 1 a narrow mattress filled with straw which is put on the floor for someone to sleep on. 2 a hard, narrow bed. 3 a flat wooden platform on which goods are stacked so that they can be lifted and moved using a fork-lift truck. N COUNT N COUNT

palliative /pælɪətɪv/, **palliatives**. 1 A drug or medical treatment that is a **palliative** is one which relieves suffering without treating the cause of the suffering. EG *...its effectiveness as a cure or palliative for so many ailments.* N COUNT ⇑ relief

2 An action that is a **palliative** is intended to make someone feel less angry or concerned about a problem, but does not actually solve the problem. EG *He was not readmitted, but this palliative proved quite inadequate... This can be seen as an official palliative to the evident inequity of the system.* ▸ used as an adjective. EG *...the application of palliative methods... ...palliative words.* N COUNT ▸ ADJ CLASSIF = soothing

pallid /pælɪd/. Someone or something that is **pallid** is 1 unattractively or unnaturally pale in appearance. EG *His dry pallid face often looked gaunt... A pallid moon shone fitfully between the ragged clouds.* 2 weak and unexciting, with no positive qualities. EG *...a world in which their pallid acceptance was becoming absurd... ...all perfectly innocuous in their pallid fashion.* ADJ QUALIT = colourless ADJ QUALIT = insipid

pallor /pælə/ is an unusual or unhealthy pale appearance, especially of someone's skin. N UNCOUNT = paleness

pally /pæli¹/. If you are **pally** with someone, you are friendly with them; an informal word. ADJ QUALIT: IF + PREP THEN *with*

palm /pɑːm/, **palms, palming, palmed**. 1 A **palm** or a **palm tree** is a tree which grows in hot countries and has long pointed leaves that grow out of the top of a tall trunk with no branches. There are several kinds of palm trees. EG *He sat in the shade beneath the palms... Among the familiar trees were large growths of palm and cactus.* N COUNT

2 The **palm** of your hand is the inside surface which your fingers can bend towards, but not including the fingers themselves. EG *She placed the money in his palm... Claud spat on the palms of his hands and rubbed them together.* N COUNT: WITH POSS

3 If a fortune teller reads your **palm**, she or he looks at the position and shape of the lines on the palm of your hand and tells you what these lines are believed to indicate about your life and future. N COUNT: POSS+N

4 The word **palm** is also used in the following expressions. 4.1 If you **grease** someone's **palm**, you bribe them; an informal expression. EG *You won't get any help unless you suitably grease their palms.* 4.2 If you ask someone to **cross** your **palm** or **cross** your **palm with silver**, you are asking them to pay you a small amount of money, for example when you are giving them information or predicting their future. PHR: VB INFLECTS PHR: VB INFLECTS

4.3 If you say that you have someone **in the palm of** your **hand**, you mean that they always do whatever you want them to do. PHR: USED AS AN A

5 If someone **palms** something, usually as part of a trick, they make it seem to disappear by hiding it skilfully in their hand. V+O ⇑ conceal

palm off. 1 If someone **palms** something **off** on you, they give or sell you something that they don't really want as an easy way of getting rid of it. EG *'What happened to that old car he had?'–'He palmed it off onto some young couple.'* PHRASAL VB: V+O+ADV, IF+PREP THEN *on/onto* = unload onto

2 If you **palm** someone **off** with an excuse or a lie, you tell them something in order to get rid of them and stop them from bothering you or someone else. EG *I palmed him off with the excuse that I had no money.* PHRASAL VB: V+O+ADV, IF+PREP THEN *with* = fob off

palmistry /pɑːmɪstri¹/ is the practice and art of telling what people are like and what will happen in their future life by examining the lines on the palms of their hands. N UNCOUNT

palm oil is a yellow oil which comes from the fruit of certain palms and is used in making soap and sometimes as a fat in cooking. N UNCOUNT

Palm Sunday is the Sunday before Easter. N UNCOUNT

palomino /pæləmiːnəʊ/, **palominos**. A **palomino** is a horse which is golden or cream in colour and has a white mane and tail. N COUNT

palpable /pælpəbə⁰l/. 1 Something that is **palpable** is so obvious that it can easily be seen or felt. EG *The president's scepticism was palpable... ...a palpable lie.* ◊ **palpably**. EG *It was palpably unjust... The excuse was so palpably untrue that he felt sorry for Daintry.* ADJ QUALIT = evident ◊ ADV

2 An atmosphere, emotion, etc that is described as **palpable** is so intense that it seems as if it can be touched or felt physically. EG *The air was warm, close, palpable as cotton wool... The peace of the Temple was palpable.* ◊ **palpably**. EG *A sudden awkwardness entered, palpably, almost like an unwelcome intruder.* ADJ QUALIT = tangible ◊ ADV

palpitate /pælpɪteɪt/, **palpitates, palpitating, palpitated**. 1 If someone's heart **palpitates**, it beats very fast and irregularly because they are frightened or anxious. EG *My palpitating heart only calmed down near the end.* V = flutter

2 If something **palpitates**, it trembles or moves quickly backwards and forwards, or seems to move in this way. EG *Inside the crowded courtroom, the silence palpitated with the frustration of people powerless to do anything.* V = throb

palpitation /pælpɪteɪʃə⁰n/, **palpitations**. **Palpitations** or **palpitation** is a condition in which the heart beats very fast and with an irregular beat. EG *...blood circulation or palpitation of the heart... I got palpitations when I read the name.* N UNCOUNT OR N COUNT: USU PL

palsied /pɔːlzɪd/. Someone who is **palsied** is unable to control their muscles because of illness, and often as a result, their limbs shake uncontrollably. EG *...problems of paraplegic, spastic and palsied children... ...brass padlocks that a blind and palsied picklock could have opened.* ADJ CLASSIF

palsy /pɔːlzi¹/ is an illness which results in paralysis. There are several kinds of palsy. • See **cerebral palsy**. N UNCOUNT

paltry /pɔːltri¹/. 1 A **paltry** sum of money or amount of something is very small and not of much use or value. EG *...a paltry wage... The deal cost him a paltry £100... Computer memories have grown much larger since the paltry hundred or so bits of store of the earliest machines.* ADJ QUALIT: ATTRIB = meagre

2 A person, action, or attitude that is described as **paltry** is not considered to be of any worth or value. EG *I dare say he's a puny, posturing, paltry fellow... Your ambitions are only paltry.* ADJ QUALIT = trifling

pampas /pæmpəz/. The **pampas** is the large areas of flat, grassy land in South America where no trees grow. N SING: *the*+N ⇑ plains

pampas grass is a tall plant which has large, feathery, cream-coloured flower heads on the end of long stalks. N UNCOUNT

pamper /pæmpə/, **pampers, pampering, pampered**. If you **pamper** someone, you treat them too kindly and do too much for them in order to make them comfortable. EG *...children pampered by nannies.* V+O = cosset

pamphlet /pæmflɪ²t/, **pamphlets**. A **pamphlet** is a thin book with only a few pages and a paper cover, which is produced to tell people about a particular subject. N COUNT = booklet

pamphleteer /pæmflɪ²tɪə/, **pamphleteers**. A **pamphleteer** is a person who writes pamphlets, especially about political subjects. N COUNT ⇑ writer

pan /pæn/, **pans, panning, panned**. 1 A **pan** is 1.1 a container with a long handle that is used for cooking things in, usually on top of a cooker. Pans are usually round in shape and made of metal. EG *He started tipping beans into a pan... ...pots and pans.* N COUNT = saucepan

1.2 in American English, a shallow metal container used for baking things in. EG *...metal cake pans.* N COUNT = tin

2 The **pan** on a set of scales is the container into which you put the substance to be weighed. N COUNT ⇑ dish

3 When a film camera **pans**, it moves in a wide sweep, for example to follow a moving object. EG *Occasionally the camera pans back to reveal a nervous foot tapping.* V, OR V-ERG: U+A

4 If someone **pans** for gold, they use a shallow dish to sift gold from a river. EG *Hundreds of men came to pan the rivers and get rich quick.* V OR V+O: IF+PREP THEN *fo*

5 If someone **pans** something, they criticize it severely; an informal use. EG *His work was panned by his boss.* V+O = slate

6 A lavatory **pan** is the bowl-shaped part of a toilet. N COUNT

7 See also **frying pan**. • **a flash in the pan**: see **flash**.

pan out. When you talk about the way that things **pan out**, you are saying that this is the way that things develop from a particular situation; an informal expression. EG *...if things pan out as we think they will.* PHRASAL VB: ADV = work out

pan- is added to the beginning of adjectives and nouns in order to form other adjectives and nouns that describe something as connected with all places or people of a particular kind. EG *...the Pan-African Congress... ...Pan-American Airways... ...Pan-Islamism.*
PREFIX

panacea /pænəsɪə/, **panaceas**. A **panacea** is something that is supposed to be a cure for any problem or illness; often used showing disapproval. EG *...an obsession with technology as a panacea for life's ills... ...abortion and divorce–those two contemporary panaceas for all matrimonial ills.*
N COUNT: USU USED AS C ⇑ remedy

panache /pənæʃ, -nɑːʃ/. If someone has **panache** or if they do something with **panache**, they behave or do something in a very confident, stylish, and elegant way. EG *He offered it to me with all the panache of a ballet dancer presenting a rose.*
N UNCOUNT ⇑ style = dash

panama hat /pænəmɑː hæt/, **panama hats**. A **panama hat** or a **panama** is a hat, worn especially by men, that is made of straw and has a rounded crown with quite a wide brim.
N COUNT

panatella /pænətelə/, **panatellas**; also spelled **panatela**. A **panatella** is a long thin cigar.
N COUNT

pancake /pænkeɪk/, **pancakes**. A **pancake** is a thin, flat circle of cooked batter made of milk, flour, and eggs. Pancakes are usually rolled up or folded and eaten hot with a sweet or savoury filling inside. • **as flat as a pancake**: see **flat**.
N COUNT

Pancake Day is the Tuesday before Ash Wednesday; an informal expression. People traditionally eat pancakes on Pancake Day.
N UNCOUNT

pancake landing, pancake landings. If an aircraft makes a **pancake landing**, it makes an emergency landing in which it comes down to a height of a few feet and then drops flat onto the ground.
N COUNT

pancake roll, pancake rolls. A **pancake roll** is a small pancake that is filled with Chinese style vegetables and perhaps meat, and then rolled up.
N COUNT

pancreas /pæŋkrɪəs/, **pancreases**. Your **pancreas** is an organ in your body that is situated behind your stomach. It produces insulin and enzymes that help in the digestion of food.
N COUNT

panda /pændə/, **pandas**. A **panda** is a large black and white animal, rather like a bear, which lives in the bamboo forests of China.
N COUNT

panda car, panda cars. A **panda car** is a small police patrol car; used in British English.
N COUNT

pandemic /pændemɪk/, **pandemics**. A **pandemic** is something that affects everybody over a very wide area; a formal word. EG *...a universal pandemic of despair... Children are now suffering an epidemic, even a pandemic, of low-grade intoxication.* ▸ used as an adjective. EG *It was discovered to be pandemic.*
N COUNT = plague; ▸ ADJ CLASSIF ⇑ widespread

pandemonium /pændɪməʊnɪəm/ is a state or situation of noisy confusion and disorder. EG *When the lawyers and spectators heard about this ploy, pandemonium broke loose.*
N UNCOUNT = chaos

pander /pændə/, **panders, pandering, pandered**. If you **pander to** someone or to their wishes, you do everything that they want, even though it is not good for them, often in order to get some advantage for yourself. EG *Big business firms pander to the teenagers of today... The older children are encouraged to pander to their slightest whim.*
PHRASAL VB: V+PREP, HAS PASS = indulge

pandit /pændɪt/, **pandits**. A **pandit** is a wise man, especially in India. ▸ used as a title. EG *Pandit Dayanand formed this association.*
N COUNT, OR N IN TITLES

p & p is an abbreviation for 'postage and packing'; used when stating the cost of packing something in a parcel and sending it through the post. EG *...cost £4.50 + p & p... ...£20 p.&p. incl.*
N UNCOUNT

pane /peɪn/, **panes**. A **pane** of glass is a flat sheet of glass used in a window or door. EG *We'll have to smash a pane in the kitchen window... A pane of glass in the study was cracked.*
N COUNT: ALSO N + of + N UNCOUNT

panegyric /pænɪdʒɪrɪk/, **panegyrics**. A **panegyric** is a formal speech or piece of writing that praises someone or something; a formal word. EG *He breaks into a lengthy panegyric on English culture.*
N COUNT = eulogy

panel /pænəl/, **panels, panelling, panelled**; also spelled **paneling** and **paneled** in American English. **1** A **panel** of people is a small group of people who are chosen, for example, to discuss or give their opinions on a particular subject in public, or to hear evidence and make a decision. EG *Does the panel think that the proposed sale of these nationalized industries is beneficial to the country? ...an interviewing panel for a new dance teacher.*
N COUNT: VB CAN BE SING OR PL = team

2 A **panel** is a flat, rectangular or square piece of wood, metal, china, etc that forms part of a larger object, for example a section of a door. EG *It is completed by slipping white wall panels between the uprights of the frame... ...a screen composed of little pivoting panels of Victorian engraved glass... There was glass in the upper panels of the door... ...a silk kimono with a few choice panels of embroidery.* • See also **solar panel**.
N COUNT

3 A control **panel** or instrument **panel** is a board or surface which contains switches and controls to operate one or more pieces of equipment. EG *...a panel of instruments.*
N COUNT

4 If you **panel** a wall or other surface, you cover it with decorative panels of wood.
V+O ⇑ decorate

panelled /pænəld/. A **panelled** room has decorative wooden panels covering its walls. EG *She led the way across a small panelled hall... His parliamentary office was enormous, panelled in dark wood.* ▸ used also of walls. EG *On the panelled wall were paintings of horses.*
ADJ CLASSIF: USU ATTRIB ⇑ decorated

2 A **panelled** door does not have a flat surface but has square or rectangular areas set into its surface. EG *He leaned against the heavy panelled door.*
ADJ CLASSIF: USU ATTRIB

panelling /pænəlɪŋ/ is decorative boards or strips of wood that cover a wall inside a building.
N UNCOUNT ⇑ covering

panellist /pænəlɪst/, **panellists**. A **panellist** is a person who sits on a panel and speaks in public, especially on a radio or television programme.
N COUNT ⇑ speaker

panel pin, panel pins. A **panel pin** is a thin nail with a small head.
N COUNT

pang /pæŋ/, **pangs**. A **pang** is a sudden, sharp feeling, usually of sadness or pain. EG *She felt a sudden pang of regret... Their hunger pangs were sharper than my pangs of conscience.*
N COUNT: USU + of = twinge

panic /pænɪk/, **panics, panicking, panicked**. **1** **Panic** or a **panic** is a feeling of anxiety which is so great that you either cannot do anything at all, or you act without thinking about what would be the best thing to do. EG *Sandy was close to panic... These rumours spread panic... Some of them got into their cars and took off in a panic... Jenny succumbed to a last minute panic.* ▸ A **panic** is also a situation in which people are affected by this strong feeling of anxiety. EG *...dreams, nightmares and childhood panics... We didn't want to start a panic on the Stock Exchange.*
N COUNT/UNCOUNT ⇑ fear; ▸ N COUNT = scare

2 If you **panic**, you are affected by a sudden feeling of strong anxiety which makes you unable to act sensibly and calmly. EG *I hadn't rehearsed it properly and I panicked... Don't panic. Sit still and keep calm.*
V: IF IMPER ONLY NEG = flap

3 In informal English, a **panic** is a very great hurry, when you have a great deal to do and very little time to do it in. EG *I was in the usual mad panic–dashing here and there!... What's the panic?... Any time will do. There's no panic.*
N SING WITH DET = rush

panicky /pænɪki[1]/. A **panicky** feeling or **panicky** behaviour is characterized by panic. EG *...a panicky feeling that lasts for a moment before each exam... ...a panicky reaction.*
ADJ QUALIT ⇑ scared

panic-stricken. Someone who is **panic-stricken** is panicking a great deal. EG *...a panic-stricken crowd... She heard a rustle behind her and turned, panic-stricken.* ▸ used of actions and behaviour. EG *...a panic-stricken outburst of crying.*
ADJ CLASSIF = terrified

pannier /pænɪə/, **panniers**. A **pannier** is **1** one of two bags or boxes for carrying things in which are fixed on each side of the wheel of a bicycle or motorbike, usually at the back. **2** a large basket, especially one of two that are put over an animal used for carrying loads.
N COUNT ⇑ container; N COUNT ⇑ container

panoply /pænəpli[1]/. A **panoply** of things or people is a magnificent collection or array of them, especially associated with a particular ceremonial event; a formal word. EG *Their wedding had been formal and formidable, with a full panoply of relatives... ...the entire panoply of courtly love.*
N UNCOUNT: USU + of

panorama /pænərɑːmə/, **panoramas**. **1** A **panorama** is a view where you can see a very long way over a wide area of land, usually because you are on high ground. EG *All the world lay below me in a vast panorama of windswept mountain tops.*
N COUNT: IF + PREP THEN of = vista

2 People refer to the whole range and variety of a subject, or a wide range of different things or people seen in one place as a **panorama**. EG *...the infinitely*
N COUNT: IF + PREP THEN of = kaleidoscope

crowded panorama of written history... Karen watched the panorama of passing people with wide eyes.

panoramic /pænəræmɪk/. A **panoramic** view is one where you can see a very long way over a wide area. EG *...a panoramic view of the valley floor.* ADJ CLASSIF = sweeping

panpipes /pænpaɪps/ are a musical instrument made of a number of short wooden pipes of different lengths. They are played by blowing across the open ends of the pipes. N PLURAL

pansy /pænzi[1]/, **pansies**. 1 A **pansy** is a small garden plant which has flowers with very large, rounded petals that are usually purple, yellow, or cream in colour. N COUNT

2 If you refer to someone as a **pansy**, you are saying in a rather rude way that they behave in a very weak, ineffective, and rather effeminate way; an informal use. N COUNT/VOC = sissy

3 A **pansy** is also a homosexual man; an offensive use. N COUNT/VOC

pant /pænt/, **pants, panting, panted**. 1 **Pants** are 1.1 in British English, a piece of clothing worn under your other clothes, which has two holes to put your legs through and elastic around the hips or waist to keep them up. EG *He took off his shorts and pants and stood there naked... Waterproof pants over the nappies are a special help.* N PLURAL : ALSO a pair of+N ⇑ underwear 1.2 in American English, trousers. EG *He started to unbutton his pants... He fumbled in his pants pocket for his whistle.* N PLURAL : ALSO a pair of+N

2 If you **pant**, you breath quickly and loudly with your mouth open because you have been doing something energetic. EG *Don't hurry, don't pant, breathe in slowly... We lugged the branch underneath, panting and puffing... 'Let me go,' she panted.* V OR V+QUOTE/REPORT-CL = gasp

3 The word **pants** is also used in the following informal expressions. 3.1 If you **catch** someone **with** their **pants down**, they are unprepared to do what you have asked, or you have caught them in an embarrassing situation. PHR : VB INFLECTS 3.2 If someone or something **scares the pants off** you, you are very scared indeed. If someone or something **bores the pants off** you, you are very bored indeed. PHR : VB INFLECTS 3.3 If you do something **by the seat of** your **pants**, you rely on your instinct and experience instead of using elaborate equipment or following a carefully prepared plan. PHR : USED AS AN A ⇑ instinctively

pantaloons /pæntəlu:nz/ are long trousers with very wide legs, gathered at the ankle. N PLURAL : ALSO a pair of+N

pantechnicon /pæntɛknɪkən/, **pantechnicons**. A **pantechnicon** is a large covered lorry, especially one used for moving equipment or furniture about from one place to another. N COUNT ⇑ vehicle

pantheism /pænθi[1]ɪzə[0]m/ is 1 the religious belief that God is in everything in nature and the universe. N UNCOUNT ◊ **pantheist, pantheists**. 2 a willingness to worship and believe in all gods. N UNCOUNT

pantheistic /pænθi[1]ɪstɪk/. Religion or belief that is **pantheistic** involves the acceptance of the idea that God is in everything in nature and the universe. EG *His religion was pantheistic and humanist... ...a certain mystical, pantheistic idealism.* ADJ CLASSIF

pantheon /pænθi:ən, pænθɪən/, **pantheons**. 1 A **pantheon** is a building which is erected to honour all the gods or dead heroes of a nation. N COUNT : USU SING ⇑ shrine

2 You can refer to a group of important people as a **pantheon** of stars, artists, etc. EG *It took Blake some time to find his place in the pantheon of national artists.* N COUNT+SUPP : USU SING = galaxy

panther /pænθə/, **panthers**. A **panther** is a large wild animal that belongs to the cat family and is usually black in colour. N COUNT

panties /pæntɪz/ are underpants that are worn by women or children. N PLURAL : ALSO a pair of+N

panto /pæntəʊ/, **pantos**. A **panto** is a pantomime; an informal word. N COUNT

pantomime /pæntə[6]maɪm/, **pantomimes**. 1 A **pantomime** is 1.1 a funny musical play for children, that is based on a fairy story and usually performed at Christmas time. N COUNT = panto 1.2 a mime. EG *She enacted a pantomime of strangling herself.* N COUNT = dumb show

2 If you refer to a situation or event as a **pantomime**, you mean that it is a silly situation in which silly or confused things happen. N COUNT : USU SING = farce

pantry /pæntri[1]/, **pantries**. A **pantry** is a small room or large cupboard in a house, usually near the kitchen, where food is kept. N COUNT = larder

panty hose; also spelled as one word. **panty hose** is nylon tights worn by women. N UNCOUNT ⇑ hosiery

pap /pæp/. 1 Information, entertainment, etc that is described as **pap** is considered to be of no worth, value, or serious interest. EG *Students today are unwilling to go on being fed the pap that the schools dispense so readily.* N UNCOUNT = drivel

2 **Pap** is also any soft or liquid food, especially for babies or people who are ill. N UNCOUNT = mush

papa, papas. The word **papa** is pronounced /pəpɑ:/ in formal or old-fashioned English, and /pæpə/ in American English or when used in an informal or childish way. Someone's **papa** is their father. EG *Papa, over here Papa!... How are your papa and mama?* N PROPER/VOC : ALSO N COUNT

papacy /peɪpəsi[1]/. The **papacy** is the position, power, and authority of the Pope, including the length of time that a particular person holds this position; a formal word. EG *One of the first acts of Pope Paul's papacy was the appointment of this commission... There was strong pressure for the papacy to be returned to Rome.* N SING WITH DET

papadom /pɒpədəm/. See **poppadum**. N COUNT

papal /peɪpə[0]l/ is used to describe things relating to the Pope or to the papacy. EG *...a papal election.* ADJ CLASSIF : ATTRIB

papaya /pəpaɪə/, **papayas**. A **papaya** is a fruit with a green skin, sweet yellow flesh, and small black seeds. Papayas grow on trees in hot countries such as the West Indies. N COUNT/UNCOUNT = pawpaw

paper /peɪpə/, **papers, papering, papered**. 1 **Paper** is 1.1 the material that you write on or wrap things with, for example a page of this book. EG *Rudolph picked up the piece of paper and gave it to her... ...a paper bag.* N UNCOUNT ⇑ substance 1.2 wallpaper. EG *The paper in the living-room is ghastly.* N UNCOUNT

2 A **paper** is a newspaper. EG *I read about the riots in the papers... When you get your daily paper, which page do you read first?... The society papers naturally spoke of 'an alliance'.* N COUNT

3 **Papers** are 3.1 sheets of paper with information on them. EG *Always file important papers as soon as they have been dealt with... He pretended to consult the papers on his knee.* N COUNT : USU PL = documents 3.2 official documents that prove who you are or that give you official permission to do something, for example a passport, visa, and identity card. EG *Each person travelled under false name and papers.* N PLURAL ⇑ identification 3.3 a collection of documents relating to a person's private and public life, for example letters, diaries, etc. EG *The general sold his private papers to the Thomson Organisation.* N PLURAL

4 A **paper** is also 4.1 an exam paper. EG *He failed the history paper... You have two hours for each paper.* N COUNT ⇑ test 4.2 a long essay written on an academic subject, especially one that is published in journals or read to an audience of colleagues. EG *I've been asked to give a paper on nuclear fission at Toronto University.* N COUNT = treatise

5 A **paper** agreement, qualification, etc is one that is written down and officially recognized or agreed, but perhaps not useful or valuable. EG *...paper evidence... I didn't have to be a doctor, which my paper qualifications declared me to be.* N BEFORE N

6 If you **paper** a room or a wall, you put wallpaper onto a wall in a room in order to decorate it. V+O ⇑ cover

7 **on paper**. 7.1 If you put your thoughts down **on paper**, you write them down rather than just thinking or talking about them. EG *He had been stupid to put his suggestions down on paper... It is much easier to work things out on paper.* PHR : USED AS AN A = in writing 7.2 If something has a particular quality **on paper**, it seems to have this quality in theory but does not necessarily have it in reality. EG *The project looks impressive enough on paper.* ADV SEN = theoretically

8 When you **put pen to paper**, you start writing something. EG *Even though I had a lot of ideas, it took me a long time to actually put pen to paper.* PHR : VB INFLECTS ⇑ write

9 If you say that something is **not worth the paper it's written on**, you mean that although it is written down and should therefore be official, it is worthless, for example because whatever is promised or agreed will not be carried out. PHR : USED AS C = valueless

10 See also **Green Paper, White Paper**.

paper over. If someone **papers over** a difficulty or problem, they deliberately give the impression that things are going well and try to hide the difficulty or problem. EG *This is a device to paper over the cracks in government policy... There is no papering over* PHRASAL VB : ORDER V+ADV O = cover up *the fact that basic disputes exist... In the General Election of 1964 the differences were papered over.*

paperback /peɪpəbæk/, **paperbacks**. A **paperback** is a printed book which has a thin cardboard cover. EG *He read only paperbacks... ...both a hardback and a cheap paperback edition.* N COUNT

paperboy /peɪpəbɔɪ/, **paperboys**. A **paperboy** is a boy who delivers newspapers to people's homes. N COUNT

paperclip/peɪpəklɪp/, **paperclips**; also spelled with a hyphen and as two words. A **paperclip** is a small piece of bent wire, used to fasten papers together. N COUNT ⇑ fastener

paper-knife, paper-knives; also spelled as two words. A **paper-knife** is a blunt knife-shaped object which is used for opening envelopes. N COUNT

paper money is money which is made of paper. N UNCOUNT

paper round, paper rounds. A **paper round** is a job of delivering newspapers to houses along a certain route. EG *Andrew does a paper round on Saturday mornings.* N COUNT

paper shop, paper shops. A **paper shop** is a shop that sells newspapers. N COUNT = newsagent

paper tiger, paper tigers. A **paper tiger** is a country, institution, or person that seems powerful but is not so in reality. N COUNT

paperweight /peɪpəweɪt/, **paperweights**. A **paperweight** is a small, heavy object which is placed on papers to prevent them from being scattered. N COUNT ⇑ weight

paperwork /peɪpəwɜːk/ is the part of a job which is routine and which involves dealing with letters, reports, and records. N UNCOUNT

papery /peɪpəri[1]/. Something that is **papery** is thin and dry like paper. EG *...papery leaves.* ADJ CLASSIF

papier-mâché /pæpjeɪmæʃeɪ/ is a substance made of pieces of paper that are mixed with paste or glue. It is then made, while still damp, into boxes, bowls, ornaments, etc. EG *She brought home a little doll made of papier-mâché... ...a papier-mâché box.* N UNCOUNT

paprika /pæprɪkə/ is a mild-tasting red powder used for flavouring food, especially meat. N UNCOUNT ⇑ spice

papyrus /pəpaɪrəs/, **papyruses, papyri**. The plural can be either **papyruses** or **papyri**. 1 **Papyrus** is 1.1 a tall water plant that grows in Africa. N UNCOUNT 1.2 a type of paper made from papyrus stems that was used in ancient Egypt, Rome, and Greece. N UNCOUNT

2 A **papyrus** is an ancient document written on papyrus. N COUNT

par /pɑː/. 1 If someone or something is **on a par** with someone or something else, the two people or things are equally good or bad, or similar in some way. EG *He put Warhol on a par with Titian... Forcing a child to learn is on a par with forcing a man to adopt a religion.* PHR : USU + *with*, USED AS AN A ⇑ equal

2 **below par, under par, not up to par**. 2.1 Someone who is **below par** or **under par** or **not up to par** feels rather ill or tired and cannot work as effectively as normal. EG *If for whatever reason the teacher is under par, the children are likely to suffer.* PHR : USED AS C = off colour 2.2 Something that is **below par** or **under par** or **not up to par** is below the standard that it ought to be. EG *Your work isn't up to par these days.* PHR : USED AS C ⇑ unsatisfactory

3 **Par** is the number of strokes which it is thought that a good golfer should take for a hole or for all the holes on a particular golf course. EG *The eleventh hole is a par three... ...the competitors who are playing the course under par.* N UNCOUNT, OR N + NUM

4 Something that is **par for the course** is what you would expect to happen, because it has often happened in the past. EG *I would often dismiss her behaviour as par for the course.* PHR : USED AS C = typical

para /pærə/, **paras**. A **para** is a paratrooper; an informal word. EG *The First Colonial Paras were in the mutiny almost to a man.* N COUNT : USU PL

para., paras. Para. is an abbreviation for 'paragraph'. EG *See paras. 2 and 3 on p. 10.* N COUNT, USU + NUM

parable /pærəbə[0]l/, **parables**. A **parable** is a short story about everyday things which is told in order to make a moral or religious point, especially the ones told by Jesus. EG *...the parable of the talents.* N COUNT

parabola /pəræbələ/, **parabolas**. A **parabola** is a type of curve such as the path of something that is thrown up into the air and comes down in a different place. N COUNT = arc

parabolic /pærəbɒlɪk/. A **parabolic** object or curve is shaped like a parabola. EG *...a 42m diameter parabolic reflector.* ADJ CLASSIF : USU ATTRIB

parachute /pærəʃuːt/, **parachutes, parachuting, parachuted**. 1 A **parachute** is a very large circle of thin cloth which is folded up and attached by strings to a person or thing that is about to jump or be thrown from an aircraft. When they are in the air, the parachute opens out so that they land safely. EG *...the corpse of a young paratrooper whose parachute had failed to open.* N COUNT = chute

2 If someone **parachutes** somewhere, they jump from an aircraft using a parachute. EG *...a young captain who had parachuted into enemy territory... He now spends weekends skydiving and parachuting.* V : USU + A

3 If someone **parachutes** a person or thing somewhere, they drop that person or thing there from an aircraft with a parachute attached. EG *He had got a medal in the war for being parachuted behind the lines and blowing up enemy installations.* V + O : USU + A

parachutist /pærəʃuːtɪst/, **parachutists**. A **parachutist** is a person who jumps from an aircraft using a parachute. N COUNT

parade /pəreɪd/, **parades, parading, paraded**.

1 A **parade** is 1.1 a procession of people to celebrate a special day or event. EG *When the war was over there was a parade in London.* N COUNT ⇑ celebration 1.2 an occasion on which soldiers march and do drill together in front of important soldiers or other spectators. EG *She attended the passing-out parade of her son as a second lieutenant.* N COUNT ⇑ ceremony ● Soldiers who are **on parade** are standing or marching at a formal occasion. ● PHR : USED AS C

2 When a group of people **parades** or when you **parade** them, they walk together, especially in a formal group, so that people can see them. EG *The army paraded round drill squares... The captured criminals were paraded in chains through the streets.* V-ERG = march

3 If you **parade** somewhere, you walk about so that people can see you and admire you. EG *Young men paraded up and down the street in striped blazers... He paraded in front of the mirror in his new uniform.* V + A = strut

4 If you **parade** a thing that you have or a real or pretended feeling, you show it to people or make it obvious, usually in order to make them admire or envy you. EG *He paraded his girlfriends and his car in front of me... She seldom or never paraded this knowledge... Rhoda was parading such an air of tender dedication that he felt uneasy.* V + O = flaunt

5 A **parade** of something that you have or of a real or pretended feeling is a display of it. EG *But this parade of force was only for show... ...the dockers' parade of support for the leader of their union.* N SING WITH DET + *of* = show

6 If you **parade** something as a particular good or important thing, you say in an enthusiastic or pompous way that it is that thing, usually when it is not. EG *These changes were paraded as progress.* V + O + A *(as)* = claim

7 A **parade** is also a short row of shops, usually set back from the main street. N COUNT : ALSO N + *of* + N IN PL

8 **Parade** is also used as part of the name of a street. EG *...the fashionable road known as Church Parade.* N IN NAMES AFTER N

9 See also **hit parade**.

parade ground, parade grounds. A **parade ground** is an area of ground at a place where soldiers live, which is used for practising marching on and holding parades. N COUNT

paradigm /pærədaɪm/, **paradigms**. A **paradigm** is 1 an example or model for something which explains it or shows how it can be produced; a technical term. EG *...particular models or paradigms of society and how it functions.* N COUNT = pattern 2 a clear and typical example of something. EG *This episode may serve as a paradigm of industry's problems.* N COUNT

paradise /pærədaɪs/. 1 **Paradise** is 1.1 Heaven, where good people are believed to go after they die. EG *My beloved wife went to Paradise after a nine-month illness... They were told they were going to a paradise where all their earthly infirmities would be taken from them.* N PROPER, OR N SING WITH DET + SUPP 1.2 another name for the garden of Eden where Adam and Eve lived in the Bible. EG *...the sin which caused Adam and Eve to be expelled from Paradise.* N PROPER

2 You can refer to a place that is very beautiful as a **paradise**; a literary use. EG *The King retired to this mountain paradise to escape the oppressive heat of the Plains.* N SING WITH DET

3 You can refer to a place or situation that seems perfect and has everything that you want as **paradise** or a **paradise**. EG *...a choice between a world* N UNCOUNT/SING WITH DET = heaven

transformed either into a paradise or into a disaster area... This stage of the project was very trying indeed; but it was paradise compared with the third and final phase... It was a technological paradise.

● You can refer to a place that has everything that someone who likes a particular thing or activity could want as **a shopper's paradise, a nature-lover's paradise,** etc. EG *Hong Kong was a shopper's paradise in the old days... All the pillars and concealed entrances make this court an eavesdropper's paradise.* ● See also **fool's paradise**.
● PHR

paradox /pæ̱rədɒks/, **paradoxes**. A **paradox** is 1 a situation or thing which is strange because it has or involves two opposite facts or qualities which you would think could not both be true at the same time. EG *It was busy and crowded and yet at the same time peaceful. This was a paradox she discovered over and over again... This is perhaps the central paradox of British politics.* 2 a statement in which it seems that if one part of it is true, another part of it cannot be. EG *The audience took this for a joke or a paradox... The answer to the question is full of paradox.*
N COUNT ⇑ puzzle
N COUNT/UNCOUNT ⇑ contradiction

paradoxical /pæ̱rədɒ̱ksɪkəᵒl/. A **paradoxical** situation or thing has or involves two opposite facts or qualities which you would think could not both exist at the same time. EG *It was paradoxical that, in a country where free speech was enshrined in the constitution, people were persecuted for their views... The need to conquer was only one part of Napoleon's paradoxical character.*
ADJ QUALIT ⇑ illogical

paradoxically /pæ̱rədɒ̱ksɪkəᵒli¹/. You use **paradoxically** to introduce or indicate a statement about a situation that you think is surprising or paradoxical. EG *Paradoxically, the parent who allows secrets is the one to whom the child is more likely to come with a problem.*
ADV SEN ⇑ surprisingly

paraffin /pæ̱rəfɪn/ is a clear, strong-smelling liquid which is used as a fuel, for example in heaters and lamps. EG *I lit the paraffin lamp.*
N UNCOUNT = kerosene

paraffin wax is a white wax obtained from petrol or coal which is used for making candles and sealing containers.
N UNCOUNT

paragon /pæ̱rəgəᵒn/, **paragons**. Someone who is a **paragon** is perfect or has a lot of a particular good quality. EG *We adults are no paragons of virtue... Compared with our cousin, he was a paragon of honesty and uprightness... We expect top athletes to be moral paragons.*
N COUNT : USU+SUPP ⇑ ideal

paragraph /pæ̱rəgrɑːf/, **paragraphs**. A **paragraph** is a section of a piece of writing. It consists of a sentence or a series of sentences. The first sentence of a paragraph always begins on a new line, and the first word is often slightly to the right of the first words of other lines. EG *Brody read the paragraph Vaughan had indicated... ...the rules outlined in paragraph 90 of the agreement... While on holiday, he saw a paragraph in an English newspaper that interested him.*
N COUNT, OR N+NUM

parakeet /pæ̱rəkiːt/, **parakeets**. A **parakeet** is a small parrot with a long tail. There are many different kinds of parakeet.
N COUNT ⇑ bird

parallel /pæ̱rəlɛl/, **parallels, paralleling, paralleled**; also spelled **parallelling** and **parallelled** in British English. 1 A **parallel** is 1.1 something that is very similar to something else, but that exists or happens in a different place or at a different time. EG *...a book which has no parallel that I know of in the English language... You do not have to go far to find a living parallel for these prehistoric organisms.* 1.2 a similarity between two different things. EG *There are curious parallels between medicine and law... Their work has parallels with that of the women's group... There are such great differences that close parallels cannot be drawn.*
N COUNT = equivalent
N COUNT : USU PL, IF+PREP THEN *between/to/with*

2 Something that **parallels** something else 2.1 is the same as it in some way, especially as good as it. EG *...the idea of computers with intellects paralleling or exceeding Man's... ...with a devotion and dedication not often paralleled in the history of letters... His career has almost exactly paralleled that of Hopper.* 2.2 takes place at the same time as it and often seems to be connected with it. EG *The major increases in street lighting in the Fifties and Sixties were paralleled by similar rises in the crime rate.*
V+O = match, equal
V+O ⇑ accompany

3 A **parallel** change, event, situation, or thing takes place at the same time as another one that is mentioned, or is similar to it. EG *...an endless process of destruction whose effects have to some extent been mitigated by a parallel process of re-creation... ...the divergence of originally parallel political movements... Running parallel with this there was an increase in her blood pressure.*
ADJ CLASSIF : IF+PREP THEN *to/with*

4 Something that occurs **in parallel** with something else occurs at the same time as it. EG *Increasing world affluence advances in parallel with a decreasing requirement to work.*
PHR : USU+*with*, USED AS AN A ⇑ together

5 Two lines, two long things, or two lines of movement that are **parallel** are the same distance apart all along their length. EG *The telescopic sight and the barrel were exactly parallel... The boys were marching in two parallel lines... Vanderhoff Street ran parallel to Broadway... The fish had been moving parallel to the shoreline.*
ADJ CLASSIF : IF+PREP THEN *to/with*

6 A **parallel** is also an imaginary line round the earth that is parallel to the equator. EG *...situated within about 25 miles of the 38th parallel.*
N COUNT

7 Two electrical components that are **in parallel** in a circuit are arranged so that the same voltage is applied to both of them; a technical term.
PHR : USED AS AN A, IF+PREP THEN *with*

parallelogram /pæ̱rəlɛ̱ləgræm/, **parallelograms**. A **parallelogram** is a four-sided geometrical figure in which every side is parallel to the side opposite it.
N COUNT ⇑ quadrilateral

paralyse /pæ̱rəlaɪz/, **paralyses, paralysing, paralysed**; also spelled **paralyze** in American English. 1 Something that **paralyses** a person or animal causes them to have no feeling in all or part of their body and to be unable to move. EG *A stroke paralysed half his face... Wasps catch spiders and paralyse them with a sting.* ◊ **paralysed**. EG *...a person paralysed from the neck down.*
V+O ⇑ immobilize
◊ ADJ CLASSIF = immobilized

2 Something that **paralyses** a person, organization, or place causes them or it to become unable to take any action or function properly. EG *Great cities are paralysed by strikes, power failures, and riots... He was paralysed by uncertainty.* ◊ **paralysed**. EG *What he saw left him paralysed with fright.* ◊ **paralysing**. EG *...the paralysing northern winters... ...paralysing loneliness.*
V+O = cripple
◊ ADJ QUALIT
◊ ADJ QUALIT = numbing

paralysis /pəræ̱lɪsɪs/ is 1 the loss of feeling in all or part of the body, and the inability to move. EG *One drop would be enough to induce paralysis and blindness.* 2 the condition of being unable to take action or function properly. EG *The administration had been centralized to the point of near paralysis.*
N UNCOUNT ⇑ immobility
N UNCOUNT

paralytic /pæ̱rəlɪ̱tɪk/, **paralytics**. 1 A **paralytic** is a person whose body, or part of it, is paralysed.
N CLASSIF ⇑ invalid

2 Someone who is **paralytic** is extremely drunk, often so drunk that they can hardly walk; an informal use.
ADJ QUALIT = legless

paramedic /pæ̱rəmɛ̱dɪk/, **paramedics**. A **paramedic** is a person who helps do medical work.
N COUNT

parameter /pəræ̱mə¹tə/, **parameters**. A **parameter** is a factor or limit which affects the way that something can or should be done or made. EG *It is necessary to be aware of all the parameters that have a bearing on the design process... ...a solution that falls within certain critical parameters (including cost and location).*
N COUNT : USU PL ⇑ consideratio

paramilitary /pæ̱rəmɪ̱lɪtəᵒri¹/. 1 A **paramilitary** organization is similar to an army but is not the official army of a country. EG *...a paramilitary terrorist group.* ▸ The **paramilitary** is used to refer to such an organization. EG *The paramilitary look after their own.*
ADJ CLASSIF : USU ATTRIB ⇑ military
▸ N PLURAL : *the*+N

2 **Paramilitary** is used 2.1 to describe something relating to or done by a paramilitary organization. EG *...increasing sabotage and paramilitary operations.* 2.2 to describe something that helps the official army of a country. EG *We have a paramilitary capability in case of general war.*
ADJ CLASSIF : ATTRIB
ADJ CLASSIF : ATTRIB

paramount /pæ̱rəmaʊnt/. Something that is **paramount** or of **paramount** importance is more important than anything else. EG *The interests of the child are paramount... Conservation is of paramount importance... ...our paramount national asset.*
ADJ CLASSIF = foremost

paranoia /pæ̱rənɔ̱ɪə/ is 1 a mental illness in which someone believes that other people are trying to harm them or that they are much more important than they really are; a technical psychiatric term. 2 intense suspicion, fear, and distrust of other people. EG *...my growing paranoia.*
N UNCOUNT ⇑ insanity
N UNCOUNT

paranoiac /pærənɔɪk/, **paranoiacs**. **Paranoiac** means the same as paranoid. ADJ QUALIT, OR N COUNT

paranoid /pærənɔɪd/, **paranoids**. Someone who is **paranoid 1** is much more suspicious, distrustful, or afraid of other people than is normal. EG *You're getting paranoid... I may be paranoid but I've noticed that computers never go wrong to my advantage.* ADJ QUALIT = neurotic
▸ used of ideas, feelings, and behaviour. EG *...a paranoid terror of young people.* ▸ = obsessive
2 has the mental illness of paranoia; a technical psychiatric term. EG *...a paranoid schizophrenic.* ADJ CLASSIF = paranoiac
▸ used as a noun. EG *...an angry paranoid who will rush in one day in a rage.* ▸ N COUNT

paranormal /pærənɔːməºl/. A **paranormal** event or power, for example the appearance of a ghost, is one that does not seem to be in accordance with scientific laws and is thought to involve strange, unknown forces. EG *...paranormal phenomena.* ADJ CLASSIF = supernatural
▸ The **paranormal** is used to refer to paranormal events or matters. EG *Far from being terrified by the paranormal, I find myself mildly amused.* ▸ N SING : *the*+N = supernatural

parapet /pærəpɪ²t/, **parapets**. A **parapet** is a low wall along the edge of a bridge, roof, balcony, etc. EG *They leaned over the low stone parapet and stared into the pool.* N COUNT

paraphernalia /pærəfəneɪlɪə/. **1** You refer to a large number of objects that someone has with them or that are involved in a particular activity as **paraphernalia**. EG *The girls began to gather their hockey sticks, satchels, and other paraphernalia... He was glad to be free of the paraphernalia of smoking.* N UNCOUNT : USU +SUPP ⇑ articles
2 You can also refer to the things and events that are involved in a particular activity or system as **paraphernalia**. EG *...elections, opinion polls, public meetings, and all the paraphernalia of a lively democracy.* N UNCOUNT : USU +SUPP = trappings

paraphrase /pærəfreɪz/, **paraphrases, paraphrasing, paraphrased**. **1** A **paraphrase** is an account, sentence, or expression that gives the meaning of another account, sentence, or expression in a different way. EG *The article was clearly either a close paraphrase or a direct translation of Dixon's own original article.* N COUNT : IF+ PREP THEN *of* = version
2 If you **paraphrase** something written or spoken, or the person who said it, you give its meaning using different words. EG *We must, to paraphrase Socrates, bring out the knowledge that people have inside them... 'This house is a sanctuary,' she said. (I paraphrase for there is no copy of the speech anywhere.)* V OR V+O

paraplegia /pærəpliːdʒɪə/ is paralysis of the lower half of the body. N UNCOUNT

paraplegic /pærəpliːdʒɪk/, **paraplegics**. A **paraplegic** is someone whose lower half of their body, including their legs, is paralysed, for example as the result of an injury to their spine. N COUNT ⇑ invalid
▸ used as an adjective. ▸ ADJ CLASSIF

parapsychology /pærəsaɪkɒlədʒi¹/ is the study of strange mental abilities that seem to exist but are impossible according to accepted scientific theories. N UNCOUNT

parasite /pærəsaɪt/, **parasites**. **1** A **parasite** is a small animal or plant that lives on or in a larger animal or plant of a different type and gets its food from it. EG *...sheep parasites.* N COUNT
2 A person who is a **parasite** expects other people to provide him or her with money, food, and accommodation and does not do any work or give anything in return; used showing disapproval. EG *You're a parasite, a scrounger.* N COUNT = leech

parasitic /pærəsɪtɪk/. **1 Parasitic** animals or plants live and feed on larger animals or plants. EG *...tiny parasitic insects.* ADJ CLASSIF
▸ used to describe things caused by or relating to parasitic animals or plants. EG *...parasitic diseases.* ▸ ADJ CLASSIF : ATTRIB
2 A **parasitic** person or organization does no real work but gets money or food because of the work done by other people. EG *These measures could eliminate the profiteering of parasitic middlemen.* ADJ QUALIT
◊ **parasitical**. EG *...the worthless, parasitical human beings.* ◊ ADJ QUALIT

parasol /pærəsɒl/, **parasols**. A **parasol** is an object like an umbrella that you carry or that is over a table so that you are protected from the sun. EG *She twirled her parasol in a bored way.* N COUNT = sunshade

paratrooper /pærətruːpə/, **paratroopers**. A **paratrooper** is a soldier who is a member of a group of paratroops. N COUNT = para

paratroops /pærətruːps/ are soldiers who are trained to be dropped by parachute into battle or into enemy territory. EG *...light weapons, of the kind that might be used by paratroops... ...paratroop attacks.* N PLURAL ⇑ troops

parboil /pɑːbɔɪl/, **parboils, parboiling, parboiled**. If you **parboil** food, often vegetables, you boil it until it is partly cooked. V+O

parcel /pɑːsəºl/, **parcels, parcelling, parcelled**; also spelled **parceling** and **parceled** in American English. **1** A **parcel** is an object or group of objects wrapped in paper, especially so that it can be sent by post. EG *He started undoing a little newspaper parcel tied with string... International charities sent parcels of food and clothes to the refugees.* N COUNT : IF+ PREP THEN *of* = package
2 When you **parcel** something **up**, or **parcel** it, you wrap it up into a parcel. V+O+A *(up)*, OR V+O
3 A **parcel** of something, or of things or people, is an amount of it, or a quantity of them. EG *Ari did not wish to marry until he could get a parcel of land and build a home... ...children who are left to the ineffectual care of a parcel of servants.* N COUNT+*of*+N UNCOUNT/N IN PL
• **part and parcel**: see **part**.

parcel out. When you **parcel** something **out**, you divide it into several parts or amounts and give them to different people. EG *...the parcelling out of the land.* PHRASAL VB : V+O+ADV ⇑ distribute

parch /pɑːtʃ/, **parches, parching, parched**. If the sun **parches** something, especially the ground or plants, it makes it completely dry. EG *The hot sun parched the bare earth below.* V+O = bake

parched /pɑːtʃt/. **1** Something that is **parched** has become very dry; used especially of earth, plants, or someone's mouth. EG *She touched her wet fingertips to her parched lips... The parched soil soaked up the rain.* ADJ QUALIT = dehydrated
2 If you say that you are **parched**, you mean that you are very thirsty; an informal use. ADJ CLASSIF : PRED

parchment /pɑːtʃmə²nt/, **parchments**. **1 Parchment** is **1.1** the yellowish-cream skin of a sheep or goat that was used in former times for writing on. EG *...an ancient piece of parchment... His face was yellow like parchment.* N UNCOUNT
1.2 thick yellowish-cream paper. N UNCOUNT
2 A **parchment** is a document written on parchment. N COUNT

pardon /pɑːdəºn/, **pardons, pardoning, pardoned**. **1** When you **pardon** someone, you forgive them for doing something bad or wrong; a rather old-fashioned use. EG *...a banner saying 'Jesus pardons, Jesus saves'... She asked him to pardon her rudeness.* V OR V+O
2 Pardon is forgiveness; a rather old-fashioned use. EG *He is pitiless and has never been heard to speak of pardon.* N UNCOUNT
• If you **beg** someone's **pardon**, you say you are sorry for doing something. EG *He begged her pardon for arriving too early.* ● PHR : VB INFLECTS ⇑ apologize
3 If you say that someone may **be pardoned** for doing a particular thing, you mean that it is a reasonable and understandable thing to do, in the circumstances. EG *Someone faced with a choice between French and Baxter may be pardoned for making no choice at all... Admiral Foster may be pardoned a certain understandable exaggeration.* V+O+A *(for+ -ING)*, OR V+O+O : USU PASS = be excused
4 If someone who has been found guilty of a crime is given a **pardon**, they are officially allowed to go free and are not punished. EG *She wrote to the Queen asking for a pardon for her son.* N COUNT/ UNCOUNT
▸ used as a verb. EG *I hope that poor fellow may be pardoned for whatever crime he has committed.* ▸ V+O
• See also **free pardon**.
5 The word **pardon** is also used in the following expressions. **5.1** You say **pardon?** or **I beg your pardon?** when you have not heard or understood what someone has just said and want them to repeat it, or when you find it surprising or offensive. EG *'How old is she?'–'Pardon?'–'I said how old is she?'... 'Where the devil did you get her?'–'I beg your pardon?'* CONVENTION
5.2 You say **I do beg your pardon** or **I beg your pardon** as a way of apologizing for accidentally doing something, for example stepping on someone's foot, disturbing them, or burping. CONVENTION = sorry
5.3 You say **I beg your pardon** or **pardon me** or **I beg his or her pardon** as a way of apologizing for making a mistake in what you are saying, or for using the wrong word. EG *It is treated in the sentence as a noun–I beg your pardon–as an adjective... I'd also like to thank Brock–uh–Rock, I beg his pardon–for doing the lighting.* CONVENTION = sorry
5.4 You say **pardon me** or **pardon me for interrupting, asking, etc** or **pardon my interrupt-** CONVENTION = excuse me

ing, asking, etc to get someone's attention, for example before asking a question, and to apologize for bothering them. EG *Pardon me, Sergeant, I wonder if you'd do me a favour?... Pardon my asking, but I'm curious. Are you an actor?* **5.5** You say **pardon me** or **I beg your pardon**, politely, before disagreeing with someone. EG *Pardon me, but I think in fact it starts tomorrow, not today.* **5.6** You say **pardon me** for doing or being a particular thing, or **pardon my bluntness, interference**, etc as a way of indicating that you realize you are saying something that might be thought rude or wrong. EG *Pardon me if I sound cynical, but what did you expect?* **5.7** You say **pardon me for existing, living, breathing**, etc in a hurt, sarcastic way when someone says something angrily to you, to indicate that you think they are being unfair; an informal expression. **5.8** You say **if you'll pardon the expression** just before or after using a rude word when you think it might offend people; an informal expression. EG *I think they're full of–pardon the expression–bull.*

CONVENTION = excuse me; CONVENTION = forgive me; CONVENTION; CONVENTION

pardonable /pɑːdəºnəbəºl/. You describe a bad action or attitude as **pardonable** when you understand why someone did it or has it and think that they can be forgiven for it in the circumstances. EG *It was an exaggeration, but a pardonable one... 'I won,' I said with pardonable smugness.* — ADJ QUALIT = excusable

pare /pɛə/, **pares, paring, pared**. **1** When you **pare** something or **pare** part of it off, you cut off the skin or top layer of it. EG *Mother was paring apples... She pared the two corns on her little toes... The remains of the brown outer layer should be pared off with a knife.* ● See also **paring**. — V+O, OR V+O+A (off) ↑ trim

2 When you **pare** something such as the amount of money you spend, you reduce it because you have to. EG *This would mean slicing into food budgets already pared to the bone.* — V+O, OR V+A ↑ cut

pare down. When you **pare** something **down**, **1** you make it smaller by cutting thin pieces off it. EG *...pared-down fingernails.* **2** you reduce it or make it less extensive. EG *I did want to pare down my political involvements to a minimum... I had pared my possessions down to almost nothing.* — PHRASAL VB: V+O+ADV; PHRASAL VB: V+O+ADV, IF+PREP THEN *to*

parent /pɛərənt/, **parents**. **1** Your **parents** are your father and mother. EG *Her parents are well-off... ...the bond between parents and children.* ● **foster parents**: see **foster 1**. — N COUNT ↑ relation

2 The **parents** of an animal are the adult animals that have produced it. EG *The first larvae to hatch have to be fed by their parents... ...one of the parent crows.* — N COUNT, OR N BEFORE N

3 The **parent** plant of a particular plant is the plant that it comes from or is produced by. EG *This then germinates while still attached to the parent plant.* — N BEFORE N = mother

4 The **parent** organization of a particular organization is the organization that created it and usually still owns it or has some control over it. EG *...subsidiaries that are represented on the board of directors of the parent company.* — N BEFORE N

parentage /pɛərəntɪdʒ/. Your **parentage** is the fact of who your parents are, what nationality they are, what class they are, etc. EG *...children of racially mixed parentage... They still did not know her place of birth or her parentage.* — N UNCOUNT = origin

parental /pərɛntəºl/ is used to describe something that comes from or relates to parents in general, or that comes from or relates to one or both of the parents of a particular child. EG *...problems caused by a lack of parental control... She dares not stay out late for fear of a parental rebuke... ...parental love.* — ADJ CLASSIF: USU ATTRIB

parenthesis /pərɛnθɪsɪs/, **parentheses** /pərɛnθɪsiːz/. **1** A **parenthesis** is a remark or extra part that is put into a sentence. In writing, a parenthesis is separated from the main part of the sentence by commas, dashes, or brackets. ● If you say something **in parenthesis** while you are talking, you interrupt yourself to say it and then go on with what you were saying before. — N COUNT ↑ comment = aside; ● PHR: USED AS AN A

2 Parentheses are a pair of brackets that are put round a word or sentence; a technical term. — N COUNT: USU PL = bracket

parenthetical /pærənθɛtɪkəºl/. A **parenthetical** remark or section is put into something written or spoken but is not an essential part of it; a formal word. EG *There is a parenthetical section in the middle of the poem.* ◇ **parenthetically**. EG *She mentioned parenthetically that her mother had been ill.* — ADJ CLASSIF ↑ additional; ◇ ADV WITH VB = in passing

parenthood /pɛərənthud/ is the state of being a parent. EG *...young people facing the new responsibility of parenthood.* — N UNCOUNT

parenting /pɛərəntɪŋ/ is the activity of bringing up and looking after your child. EG *...the effects of bad parenting.* — N UNCOUNT

parent-teacher association, parent-teacher associations. A **parent-teacher association** is an organization formed so that the parents and teachers of children at a particular school can discuss school matters that affect the children. — N COUNT = PTA

par excellence /pɑːrº ɛksəlɑːns/. You say **par excellence** when you want to emphasize that something is the best possible example of a particular thing; a formal or literary expression. EG *She was strongly committed to her job, a policewoman par excellence... This is the chicken-and-egg situation par excellence.* — ADV SEN

pariah /pəraɪə/, **pariahs**. A person who is a **pariah** is disliked so much by other people that they refuse to associate with him or her; a formal word. — N COUNT = outcast

paring /pɛərɪŋ/, **parings**. A **paring** is a thin piece that has been cut off something, especially a nail or fruit or vegetable. EG *...a fingernail paring... ...potato parings.* — N COUNT = clipping

parish /pærɪʃ/, **parishes**. **1** A **parish** is an area, for example a village or part of a town, which has its own church and clergyman. EG *...the parish of St Mark's, Sambourne Fishley... ...the medieval parish church... ...my parish priest.* ▸ **Parish** is also used to refer to the people who live in a parish. EG *The parish has welcomed the new vicar with open arms.* — N COUNT

2 A **parish** is also a small area, especially a country area, which has its own local government. EG *The community has its own parish council... Stroud parish has a census population of only 20,000.* — N COUNT

parishioner /pərɪʃənə/, **parishioners**. Someone who is a **parishioner** of a particular clergyman lives in his parish; used especially of someone who goes to church regularly. EG *She had been one of his parishioners in Shropshire.* — N COUNT

Parisian /pərɪziən/, **Parisians**. **1** A **Parisian** person or thing belongs to or relates to Paris or to its people. EG *...the latest Parisian fashions.* — ADJ CLASSIF

2 A **Parisian** is a person who comes from Paris. — N COUNT

parity /pærɪtɪ¹/; a fairly formal word. **1 Parity** is the state of being equal. EG *...the theoretical parity in powers between the two Houses of Parliament... Their policy on pensions is parity of retirement age... Women workers at the factory went on strike for parity with men in 1968.* — N UNCOUNT ↑ equality

2 If there is **parity** between the units of currency of two countries, the exchange rate is such that the units are equal to each other; a technical term in economics. — N UNCOUNT

park /pɑːk/, **parks, parking, parked**. **1** A **park** is **1.1** an area of land with grass and trees, usually in a town, where people go in order to relax or enjoy themselves. EG *She took her children for a walk in the park... ...Hyde Park... ...old men sitting on park benches.* **1.2** in British English, an area of grass and trees around a large country house. EG *The stream divides Lord Upminster's park from the agricultural land.* **1.3** an area of land which is used for a particular purpose. EG *...the new industrial park... We drove past the amusement park.* — N COUNT: ALSO IN NAMES AFTER N; N COUNT ↑ grounds; N COUNT: MOD N

2 When you **park** a vehicle, or **park** somewhere, you move the vehicle into a position where it can stay for a period of time, and usually leave it. EG *She parked in front of the library... I paid a £15 fine for parking on a double yellow line... We could just see the lights of a parked car.* — V: USU+A OR V+O

3 If you **park** yourself somewhere, or **park** an object somewhere, you put yourself there and stay there, or put the object there and leave it there, sometimes without asking the necessary permission; an informal use. EG *She parked herself on the sofa and stayed there all evening... The girl parked her chewing gum on the back of the telephone.* — V+O (NG/REFL)+A = deposit

4 See also **car park, national park**.

parka /pɑːkə/, **parkas**. A **parka** is a jacket or coat which has a quilted lining and a hood with fur round the edge. — N COUNT

parking /pɑːkɪŋ/ is **1** the action of moving a vehicle into a position where it can be left for a period of time. EG *Parking is something I'm very bad at... ...a 'No parking' sign... I drove slowly along, looking for a* — N UNCOUNT: U BEFORE N *parking space... ...a parking offence.* **2** space for parking a vehicle in. EG *There's plenty of parking.* N UNCOUNT

parking lot, parking lots. A **parking lot** is an area of ground where people can leave their cars, usually if they pay a small amount of money; used in American English. N COUNT = car park

parking meter, parking meters. A **parking meter** is a device beside a parking space in the road which you put money into in order to pay for the right to park there for a particular period of time. N COUNT

parking ticket, parking tickets. A **parking ticket** is a piece of paper with instructions to pay a fine, which a traffic warden puts on your car when you have parked illegally. EG *I've had three parking tickets in the last week.* N COUNT

Parkinson's disease /pɑːkɪnsənz dɪsiːz/ is a disease which causes a person's limbs to shake and become uncontrollable. N UNCOUNT ⇑ illness

Parkinson's Law /pɑːkɪnsənz lɔː/ is the belief or fact that work expands to fill the amount of time you have to do it in. N UNCOUNT

parkland /pɑːklænd/, **parklands.** is land with grass and trees on it, especially around a large country house. N UNCOUNT/COUNT: SING=PL ⇑ grounds

parkway /pɑːkweɪ/, **parkways.** A **parkway** is a wide road with grass and trees on either side; used in American English. N COUNT

parky /pɑːki[1]/. If you say it is **parky**, you mean it is rather cold; an informal word used in British English. ADJ QUALIT = nippy

parlance /pɑːləns/. You say **in common parlance, in medical parlance**, etc just before or after using a particular word or expression to indicate what style of speech it is or what group of people usually use it. EG *It had been proved–'beyond a reasonable doubt,' in judicial parlance–that there had been a cover-up... ...the stage when, in Civil Service parlance, it is taken on board.* PHR: USED AS AN A

parley /pɑːli[1]/, **parleys, parleying, parleyed.** **Parley** or a **parley** is a discussion, especially between two people or groups who are opposed to each other but who want to come to an agreement; a rather old-fashioned word. EG *One of the warring families wanted to make peace and arrange a parley... The man started the car without further parley.* N UNCOUNT/COUNT ▸ used as a verb. EG *Whatever the reason, Mathews refused to parley.* ▸ V: IF+PREP THEN *with*

parliament /pɑːlə[1]mə[2]nt/, **parliaments.** **1** The **parliament** of a country is a group of people who meet in a particular place to make or change the country's laws. The members of the parliament are either elected by the people or are in it because they hold high office or rank. EG *...proposals for the creation of Welsh and Scottish parliaments.* N COUNT ⇑ government ▸ You can refer to the parliament of your country or of the country that you are talking about as **Parliament.** EG *The amount of this increase is approved each year by Parliament... He was the second farm-worker to get into Parliament... There was no debate whatsoever, not even in Parliament.* ● See also **Member of Parliament, Houses of Parliament.** ▸ N PROPER

2 A particular **parliament** is a particular period of time in which a parliament is doing its work, between two elections or between two periods of holiday. EG *The new system should only come into force at the dissolution of the present parliament... They discussed the policies that they would like to see implemented in the next parliament.* N COUNT+SUPP ⇑ session

parliamentarian /pɑːlə[1]mɛnteəriən/, **parliamentarians.** **1** A **parliamentarian** is a Member of Parliament who is an expert on the rules and procedures of Parliament and takes an active part in debates. EG *It was during this time that he made his reputation as a parliamentarian.* N COUNT ⇑ politician

2 In the English Civil War, the **Parliamentarians** were the people who supported Parliament and opposed the King. N COUNT

parliamentary /pɑːlə[1]mɛntə[0]ri[1]/ is used to describe things that are connected with a parliament or with Members of Parliament. EG *...at the start of each parliamentary session... ...parliamentary democracy... He was adopted as a Liberal parliamentary candidate.* ADJ CLASSIF: ATTRIB

parlour /pɑːlə/, **parlours**; also spelled **parlor** in American English. A **parlour** is **1** a sitting-room; an old-fashioned use. EG *She was lying on a small settee in the parlour.* N COUNT **2** a place of business which is comfortably furnished for the customers; used mainly in American English. EG *He took her into ice cream parlours and ordered huge whipped cream sundaes.* ● See also **beauty parlour.** N COUNT

parlour game, parlour games. A **parlour game** is a game that is played indoors by families or at parties, for example a guessing game or word game. N COUNT

parlourmaid /pɑːləmeɪd/, **parlourmaids**; also spelled with a hyphen. A **parlourmaid** was, in former times, a female servant whose job involved waiting at table. N COUNT

parlous /pɑːləs/. Something that is in a **parlous** state is in a bad situation or in bad condition; an old-fashioned or literary word. EG *...the parlous state of the roof.* ADJ QUALIT: USU ATTRIB = dire

Parmesan /pɑːmɪzæn/ or **Parmesan cheese** is a hard Italian cheese with a strong flavour which is usually grated and used in cooking or sprinkled over food. N UNCOUNT

parochial /pə[3]rəʊkɪəl/. **1** People who are **parochial** think only about their own local affairs and interests; used showing disapproval. EG *Even now we are still far too parochial, far too insular.* ▸ used of ideas and attitudes. EG *This is a narrow and parochial view.* ADJ QUALIT ⇑ limited = narrow-minded

2 Parochial is used to describe things that belong or relate to the parish connected with a particular church. EG *...the parochial church council.* ADJ CLASSIF: ATTRIB

parochialism /pə[3]rəʊkɪəlɪzə[0]m/ is the quality of being parochial and self-centred; used showing disapproval. N UNCOUNT

parodist /pærədɪst/, **parodists.** A **parodist** is a person who writes or creates parodies. N COUNT ⇑ humorist

parody /pærədi[1]/, **parodies, parodying, parodied.** **1** A **parody** is a piece of writing, drama, or music which copies the style of someone well-known, or perhaps represents a familiar situation or person, in a humorous and exaggerated way. EG *...a careful and loving Raymond Chandler parody by two authors... The film was a brilliant parody of American life... ...real modern verse, not parody.* N COUNT/UNCOUNT = spoof

2 When someone **parodies** a particular work, thing, or person, they make or perform a parody of it. EG *He parodied Daniel, making his eyes wide with false disapproval... I am beginning to parody his style.* V+O = mimic

3 If something is a **parody** of a particular thing, it is meant to be that thing but is not genuinely that thing or is of very low quality. EG *...a scruffy red parody of a wig... ...with my face twisted into the parody of a smile.* N COUNT: USU+*of* = travesty

parole /pərəʊl/, **paroled.** **1** If a prisoner is given **parole**, he or she is freed before their prison sentence is due to end, on condition that he or she behaves well. EG *Prisoners are entitled to apply for parole... ...the parole board.* N UNCOUNT ⇑ release ● A prisoner who is **on parole** has been allowed to leave prison but has to visit a parole officer at a police station regularly. EG *He was released on parole.* ● PHR: USED AS AN A

2 Someone's **parole** is the period of time during which they are freed from prison on condition that they behave well. EG *Her parole was comparatively brief.* N SING WITH DET, OR N UNCOUNT

3 A prisoner who **is paroled** is given parole. EG *A month before he was due to be released, Gus was paroled.* V+O: USU PASS

paroxysm /pærəksɪzə[0]m/, **paroxysms**; a fairly formal word. **1** A **paroxysm** of rage, jealousy, etc is a sudden very strong feeling of rage, jealousy, etc. EG *In a sudden paroxysm of rage, Wilt picked it up and hurled it across the room... ...paroxysms of jealousy and possessiveness.* N COUNT+*of* = fit

2 A **paroxysm** is a sudden series of violent, uncontrollable movements that your body makes because you are coughing, laughing, or in great pain. EG *...a painful paroxysm of coughing... I was doubled over in paroxysms of laughter... This only intensified the paroxysms, and the old lady expired within the hour.* N COUNT: IF+PREP THEN *of* ⇑ spasm = fit

parquet /pɑːkeɪ/ is a floor covering made of small rectangular blocks of wood fitted together in a pattern. EG *...the highly polished parquet floor... The dog dribbled onto the parquet.* N UNCOUNT: USU MOD ⇑ flooring

parricide /pærɪsaɪd/, **parricides**; a formal word. **1** A **parricide** is someone who has killed one of their parents. N COUNT ⇑ murderer

2 Parricide is the crime of killing one of your parents. N UNCOUNT ⇑ murder

parrot /pærət/, **parrots, parroting, parroted.** **1** A **parrot** is a tropical bird with a curved beak and N COUNT grey or brightly-coloured feathers. There are many kinds of parrot. Parrots are sometimes kept as pets and sometimes copy what people say.

2 If you **parrot** something that someone else has said, you repeat it, often without understanding what it means, rather than thinking what to say yourself. EG *...people who find that parroting a theory is easier than testing it.*
V+O = echo

3 If you say something **parrot fashion**, you repeat it after someone else, without having to understand it or think about it. EG *The children learn things parrot fashion.*
PHR : USED AS AN A = by rote

4 A **parrot** cry or phrase is an expression that is taken up and used by a lot of people. EG *...the charges and counter-charges that have become parrot cries during the campaign.*
N BEFORE N

parry /pæri[1]/, **parries, parrying, parried**. 1 If you **parry** a question or argument, you cleverly avoid answering it or dealing with it. EG *Instead of answering he parries with another question... He parried arguments with devastating repartee.*
V+O, OR V+A (with) = counter

2 If you **parry** a blow from someone who is attacking you, you push aside their arm or weapon so that you are not hurt. EG *She aimed a blow at him, which he parried, simply covering his face with his arm.* ▸ used as a noun. EG *...a skilful parry.*
V OR V+O ↑ deflect ▸ N COUNT

parse /pɑːz/, **parses, parsing, parsed**. If you **parse** a sentence, you work out what grammatical type each word and clause in it is.
V+O ↑ analyse

parsimonious /pɑːsɪməʊnɪəs/. Someone who is **parsimonious** is very unwilling to spend money; a formal word used showing disapproval.
ADJ QUALIT = stingy

parsimony /pɑːsɪməni[1]/ is extreme unwillingness to spend money; a formal word used showing disapproval. EG *His parsimony was legendary throughout the film world.*
N UNCOUNT = stinginess

parsley /pɑːsli[1]/ is a small plant with curly leaves that are used for flavouring or decorating savoury food.
N UNCOUNT ↑ herb

parsnip /pɑːsnɪp/, **parsnips**. A **parsnip** is a long, thick, pale cream vegetable that grows under the ground; also used of the plant that produces this vegetable.
N COUNT/UNCOUNT ↑ root

parson /pɑːsə[n]n/, **parsons**. A **parson** is a vicar or other member of the clergy without special rank; a rather old-fashioned word.
N COUNT ↑ clergyman

parsonage /pɑːsə[n]nɪdʒ/, **parsonages**. A **parsonage** is the house where a parson lives; a rather old-fashioned word.
N COUNT

parson's nose. The **parson's nose** of a cooked bird is the fatty piece of flesh at the tail end.
N COUNT : USU SING

part /pɑːt/, **parts, parting, parted**. The nouns and adverb are dealt with in paragraphs 1-11, the expressions in paragraphs 12-28, and the verbs in paragraphs 29-32. **1 A part** of something is **1.1** one of the pieces that make up an object, for example a machine. EG *Unscrew the plug. It is now in two parts, a top and a bottom... We'll describe the various parts of the flower... These devices have no moving parts... Remove the handle part... ...a group of workers who make parts for generators.*
N COUNT : IF+ PREP THEN USU (of/for) = bit

1.2 a particular area or section of something, for example a country or someone's body. EG *I don't know this part of London very well... This is still a major problem in some parts of the world... The lower part has been damaged... Test the stain remover on an unimportant part of the fabric... The head is the most sensitive part of the body.* ● See also **private parts**.
N COUNT : IF+ PREP THEN of = bit

1.3 a period of time within a larger period of time, or a section of an event. EG *...in the latter part of the twentieth century... She spent the first part of her honeymoon in hospital... Youth is the best part of your life.*
N COUNT : USU MOD+N IN SING+ of

1.4 a section of something written or spoken, or of a film, play, programme, or piece of music. EG *...the freshness and charm of the early part of the novel... The first part of that statement is a lie... You missed the good part. You should have been here five minutes ago.* ▸ used in the title of a section of a piece of writing, programme, etc or of one of a series of related pieces of writing or programmes. EG *Part Two. Chapter One. 'Shedding Burdens'... After the break, in Part Three, we'll be looking at some answers to these questions... ...Question 2, Part A.*
N COUNT : IF+ PREP THEN of = bit

1.5 a division or feature of something, for example a system or someone's character. EG *...the different parts of the social services system... I look over the various parts of my character with perplexity... Some parts of housekeeping are pleasant... The exam is divided into two parts, the written part and the practical.* ▸ used in the title of a section of a degree course. EG *Hans is still doing Part One Maths isn't he?*
N COUNT : IF+ PREP THEN of ↑ section

1.6 a particular aspect of a situation, activity, or thing. EG *The most awful part about the whole thing was it was not even my fault... Finding the money would be the hard part.*
N SING : the+N+ SUPP = bit

2 Something or someone that is **part** of a particular thing or is a **part** of it is one of the pieces, sections, areas, or things of which it is made up, or is one aspect of it; often used when emphasizing that something is included in something else rather than being outside it or separate from it. EG *The bridge is part of the main north-south road... Economic measures must form part of any solution to this crisis... One suspects this was only part of the story... Dependency is an intrinsic part of love... They are very much part of the day-to-day life of all human beings... It was all part of the job.*
N UNCOUNT/N SING : a+N, IF+ PREP THEN of

3 When you refer to **part** of something or a **part** of it, you are referring to some of it or to a section of it. EG *Part of the ceiling collapsed... Part of the Missouri was frozen over... My brothers went to school for part of the day and to work for the rest of it... The scales reflect back only a part of the light that falls on them.*
N PART

4 If **part** of you or a **part** of you wants or feels a particular thing, you have that desire or feeling but also have the opposite one or other ones. EG *Part of him wanted to die... A part of us yearns, hopes, for something better.*
N UNCOUNT/N SING : a+N, IF+ PREP THEN of ≠ all

5 If you say that something is **part** one thing, **part** another, you mean that it is partly the first thing and partly the second. EG *This extraordinary document is part fiction and part fact... The 'revolution of women' is part cause, part consequence, of the challenge to family structure that has occurred in recent years.*
ADV = partially

6 A **part** is a variable quantity used when measuring substances that are mixed together. For example, if you have to mix two parts of disinfectant with three parts of water, you mix two pints, buckets, spoonfuls, etc of the disinfectant with three pints, buckets, or spoonfuls of water, depending on the quantity you need. EG *Wipe the skin with one part spirits to five parts water... Mix together equal parts of coarse salt and soda crystals... ...a concentration of only five parts per million.*
N COUNT : ALSO N +of+N UNCOUN[T] ↑ amount

7 If something is a particular number of **parts** one thing and another number of **parts** another thing, it is both those things in the proportion indicated by the numbers. For example, if a feeling is eight **parts** fear and two **parts** excitement, it is roughly eight tenths fear and two tenths excitement.
N COUNT : NUM+N+N UNCOUNT

8 **Parts** is used in rather old-fashioned expressions such as 'three parts' and 'nine parts' to mean 'three-quarters', 'nine-tenths', etc. EG *On the table was a scotch bottle, three parts empty.*
N COUNT : NUM+N+ADJ

9 A particular **part** in a play or film is a particular role and the words and actions involved; also used to refer to a particular copy of these words. EG *Brutus is certainly the most difficult part in the play... She plays the part of Jennet, the witch... I knew the part by heart.*
N COUNT = character

10 A particular **part** in a piece of music that a group of people sing or play together is the tune sung or played by a particular section of that group, for example people with voices of a particular pitch or who play a particular instrument; also used to refer to a written copy of this tune. EG *The soprano part is very difficult.*
N COUNT

11 Your **part** in a particular activity, event, or situation is the way in which you are involved in it and the extent to which you are involved. EG *He was being arrested for his part in the demonstrations... What are you doing in this? What is your part in it?... Leave her alone–she has no part in this.*
N SING : USU PO[SS] +N ↑ involveme[nt]

12 If you **do** your **part**, you do what is required of you when you and others are attempting to achieve something. EG *I have thought of a way to save Dolly, if only Dolly can do her part.*
PHR : VB INFLECTS

13 When you are referring to what a particular person thinks, does, or experiences, you say **for** their **part** they think, do, or experience that thing, especially when contrasting them with someone else. EG *Christopher's family despised my family, and they,*
PHR : USED AS A[N] A

for their part, hated Christopher's... For my part, personally, I do not agree.

14 For the most part means mostly, in most places, or usually; a slightly formal expression. EG *The New Guinea forest is, for the most part, dark and wet... The majority do attend for the most part regularly.* PHR : USED AS AN A = by and large

15 In large part means mostly or to a very large extent; a formal expression. EG *It was in large part a clay-like swamp... We live in a society which is in large part determined by the underlying structure of our ethical beliefs.* PHR : USED AS AN A = mainly

16 In part means to some extent but not completely; often used when you are discussing the causes of something or reasons for something. EG *The company's eventual collapse in part stemmed from these events... The improvement was brought about in part by the Trade Union Movement.* PHR : USED AS AN A = partly

17 In or **round these parts** or **in those parts** means in the place you are referring to; an informal expression, often used when referring to a small village or an area far from home or civilization. EG *He has been called simply 'Master' in these parts since he was a boy... What's a girl like you doing in these parts?* PHR : USED AS AN A = round here

18 On the part of a particular person means expressed, done, or felt by that person; a rather formal expression. EG *A frank question on his part led to a frank answer on mine... It will arouse deep suspicions on the part of our allies... I consider this a gross oversight on your part.* PHR + NG : USED AS AN A

19 Something that is **part and parcel of** something else is necessarily involved or included in it. EG *These things happen to be part and parcel of my everyday reality... It also has mild drawbacks, which are part and parcel of its virtues.* PHR + NG : USED AS C ⇑ part of

20 You use expressions such as **a good part of** something and **a large part of** something to refer to quite a large proportion or section of a particular thing. EG *Children's needs account for a good part of the family budget... A large part of Linda's day is spent on the telephone... A sizeable part of the labour force now live in the cities... It is the older ones who do by far the greatest part of the damage.* PHR + NG : USED AS C = a lot of

21 You use the expressions **the best part of** something, **the better part of** something, or **the greater part of** something when you are referring to most of a particular thing. EG *The men stayed out for the best part of a year... I struggled against it throughout the better part of two years.* PHR + NG : USED AS C = nearly

22 If you say, when discussing the reasons for something or causes of something, that **part of it is** a particular fact, you are saying that this fact is one of the reasons or causes. EG *Why exactly she hated him I don't know. Part of it was of course, that he had insulted her... I think that's part of it.* PHR OR PHR + REPORT-CL

23 If someone or something **plays a part** in a particular situation, event, or thing, they are involved in it and have an effect on it. EG *Accountants now play a much more active part in the shaping of international business... Examinations seem to play a large part in education and in schools... He is denying that racism played any part in the riots... Psychiatry already plays its part in encouraging conformity... Air power had a crucial part to play.* PHR : VB INFLECTS, USU + in ⇑ influence

24 If you **play a part**, or **play** or **act the part of** a particular person, you deliberately behave in a way that hides your real character or feelings, or in a way that is typical of a particular person. EG *He was playing a part and she knew it... It fell to Philip Crow to act the part of host to everybody.* PHR : VB INFLECTS

25 If you **take** a criticism or joke made against you **in good part**, you are not annoyed or upset by it. PHR : VB INFLECTS

26 When you **take part** in a particular activity, you do something together with other people. EG *I asked her if she'd take part in a discussion about the uprising... I'm sure she would like to come and take part... They want to take an active part in their country's affairs... He denied that he took any part in the cover-up.* PHR : VB INFLECTS, IF + PREP THEN in = participate

27 If you **take** someone's **part** when other people are criticizing them or disagreeing with them, you defend them or support them. EG *She had through loyalty taken Rose's part.* PHR : VB INFLECTS = side with

28 If you **want no part of** something or **want no part in** it, you do not want to be involved in it, for example because you consider it to be wrong. PHR : VB INFLECTS ⇑ reject

● **greater/more than the sum of its parts**: see **sum**.

29 If you **part** something or if it **parts**, two parts of it move or are moved in opposite directions, so that there is a space between them. EG *'Look,' she said, and very gently parted the grasses before her... Ralph's lips parted in a delighted smile... His lips were parted in a half smile.* V-ERG

30 When you **part** your hair, you comb it in two different directions so that it lies flat on either side of a straight line running from the front of your head to the back. EG *She has thin black hair parted in the middle.* V + O : USU PASS ⇑ arrange

31 When two people **part**, or **part** from each other, they leave each other, often for ever at the end of a relationship; a formal use. EG *We parted with many expressions of mutual goodwill... A year ago they had parted for ever.* ● to **part company**: see **company**. V + A (from) : RECIP = separate

32 If two people **are parted**, they are prevented from being together. EG *It would kill her to be parted from him for any length of time... We still theoretically marry 'until death do us part'.* V + O : USU PASS ⇑ be separated

33 See also **parting, partly**.

part with. If you **part with** something that is valuable or that you would prefer to keep, you give it or sell it to someone else. EG *I took the book, thanked her, and told her I would never part with it... She didn't want to part with the money.* PHRASAL VB : V + PREP = surrender

part- combines with adjectives, nouns, and verbs to mean partly but not completely the thing mentioned. EG *Glenys was part-Aboriginal... He is part-owner of two Colorado radio stations.* PREFIX

partake /pɑːteɪk/, **partakes, partaking, partook, partaken**; an old-fashioned, formal word. **1** If you **partake** of food or drink, you eat or drink some of it. EG *He refused to partake of the modest meal Serafina had prepared.* V : USU + A (of)

2 If you **partake** in an activity, you take part in it. EG *...people deprived of the right to partake in social decision-making.* V + A (in) = participate

3 If something **partakes** of a particular quality, it has it to some extent. EG *Here the process of education partakes of the nature of discovery.* V + A (of)

partial /pɑːʃəl/. **1** A **partial** state or quality is not complete or whole. EG *I could give it only partial support... ...partial victory... ...partial truths.* ADJ CLASSIF : USU ATTRIB ≠ total

2 If you are **partial** to a particular thing or type of thing, you like it very much; a slightly formal word. EG *The vicar is very partial to roasted pheasant.* ADJ QUALIT : PRED + to

◊ **partiality** /pɑːʃiælɪti¹/. EG *He had a partiality for fast cars.* ◊ N UNCOUNT

3 Someone who is **partial** supports or favours a particular person or thing, for example in a competition or dispute, when they should be completely fair and unbiased. ◊ **partiality**. EG *Show no partiality in your decisions.* ADJ QUALIT = biased; ◊ N UNCOUNT = bias

partially /pɑːʃəli¹/ means to some extent, but not completely. EG *A horse, partially hidden by the trees, grazes peacefully... Dolly might have been partially responsible for it.* ADV = partly

participant /pɑːtɪsɪpənt/, **participants**. Someone who is a **participant** in a particular activity, action, or system takes part in it. EG *She was a willing participant in these campaigns... The weather tended to favour the British participants.* N COUNT : IF + PREP THEN in ⇑ person

participate /pɑːtɪsɪpeɪt/, **participates, participating, participated**. If you **participate** in a particular activity, action, or system, you take part in it. EG *We asked high school students to participate in an anti-drugs campaign... In a modern democracy people want to be invited to participate more fully.* V : IF + PREP THEN in = be involved, join in

◊ **participation** /pɑːtɪsɪpeɪʃən/. EG *The success of the festival depended upon the participation of the whole community... The theatre, unlike television, still offers true audience participation.* ◊ N UNCOUNT : IF + PREP THEN in = involvement

participatory /pɑːtɪsɪpeɪtəri¹/; a fairly formal word. A **participatory** system, activity, or role involves a particular person or group of people taking part in it. EG *...participatory democracy.* ADJ CLASSIF : USU ATTRIB

participial /pɑːtɪsɪpɪəl/ means relating to a participle; a technical term in grammar. ADJ CLASSIF : ATTRIB

participle /pɑːtɪsɪpəl/, **participles**. In grammar, a **participle** is a form of a verb that can be used in compound tenses of the verb, or as an adjective. There are two types of participle in English: the past participle, which usually ends in '-ed', and the present participle, which usually ends in '-ing'. See ☐ at PAST PART and -ING. N COUNT ⇑ word

particle /pɑːtɪkəl/, **particles**. **1** A **particle** of something such as a substance, quality, or emotion is N COUNT/PART : USU + SUPP a very small piece or amount of it. EG *...particles of metal... ...food particles... They will not give up the smallest particle of their liberty.*

2 In physics, a **particle** is a very small piece of matter which is smaller than an atom, for example an electron or a proton. EG *...the properties of basic particles.* N COUNT

3 In grammar, a **particle** is a word that has a function rather than a meaning, for example a preposition or an adverb. N COUNT

particular /pətɪkjə⁴lə/, **particulars**. 1 When you refer to a **particular** thing, person, or group, you are emphasizing that you are talking about that thing, person, or group, and not about other things or people of the same kind. EG *That is the end of the growth of that particular part of the plant... ...a man who wishes to make a particular woman fall in love with him... Let me ask you about one particular artist... She was not permanently attached to any particular city... Suddenly and for no particular reason she remembered the dog she had had as a child.* ADJ CLASSIF: ATTRIB = specific

2 A **particular** quality, state, or possession is separate and different from other things of the same kind, and belongs to one thing, person, or group. EG *They are a minority group with a particular point of view... Each species has its own particular place on the reef.* ADJ CLASSIF: ATTRIB = distinct

3 You use **in particular** 3.1 to indicate that what you are saying applies especially to the thing or person mentioned, or that it applies especially in the situation or place mentioned. EG *Joan Greenwood in particular I thought was wonderful... This gesture is found in particular in Brazil... ...stories of Bombay in general and the film world in particular.* PHR = particularly **3.2** to introduce a statement giving the most important example of the kind of thing that you have just mentioned, after you have just made a general statement about something. EG *In particular, he was criticized for pursuing a policy of conciliation and reform.* PHR: USED AS ADV SEN = specifically

4 Expressions such as **anything in particular** and **anyone in particular** mean a particular, specific thing, person, etc, rather than just anything or anyone. EG *Are you looking for anything in particular?* PHR

5 Expressions such as **nothing in particular** and **nobody in particular** mean nothing or nobody important or special, or no one thing, person, etc more than any other. EG *They chat about nothing in particular.* PHR

6 If you talk about the **particular**, you are referring to individual things, cases, or events as opposed to a general situation or theory. EG *The particular may have to be sacrificed to the general.* N SING: *the*+N

7 You can use **particular** to emphasize that something, especially a feeling or quality, is greater or more intense than usual, or greater than that relating to other things. EG *The battle was waged with particular ferocity... The shortage of airfields gave particular concern... ...a lecture on health with particular reference to personal hygiene.* ADJ QUALIT: ATTRIB+N UNCOUNT ⇑ much = especial

8 **Particulars** are facts or details relating to something or someone; a formal use. EG *Renshaw jotted down a few particulars in his notebook... She refused to go into particulars.* N PLURAL

9 A **particular** is a part or detail of something such as a statement or belief; a formal use. EG *He knew that her account was false in one material particular.* N COUNT ⇑ matter

10 Someone who is **particular** is not easily satisfied, for example when they are choosing or buying something. EG *They're quite particular about their personnel.* ADJ QUALIT: PRED, IF+PREP THEN *about* = fussy

particularize /pətɪkjə⁴ləraɪz/, **particularizes, particularizing, particularized**; also spelled **particularise**. If you **particularize** something you have been talking about in a general way, you give details or specific examples of it. V OR V+O = spell out

particularly /pətɪkjə⁴ləli¹/. 1 You use **particularly** to indicate that what you are saying applies especially to the thing or person mentioned or especially in the situation or place mentioned. EG *This was hard for young children, particularly when they were ill... This has been challenged by a number of workers, particularly Gibson... He particularly dislikes quiz shows.* ADV

2 **Particularly** also means more than usually or normally. EG *She was looking particularly attractive today, he thought... This is not particularly difficult to do... 'It's really gruesome, is it?'-'No, not particularly.'* ADV

parting /pɑːtɪŋ/, **partings**. 1 **Parting** or a **parting** is an occasion on which one person leaves another. EG *George said no more until their final parting... She felt unable to bear the strain of parting... I recalled Mr Starke's kind parting words.* N COUNT/ UNCOUNT

2 The **parting** of something is the action of moving two parts of it apart. EG *...the parting of the Red Sea.* N UNCOUNT/ COUNT

3 The **parting** in someone's hair is the line running from the front to the back of their head where their hair has been combed in opposite directions. N COUNT

4 When you refer to a **parting of the ways**, you are referring to a time or place at which two people who have been working together stop working together, or two people who have been travelling together go in different directions. PHR ⇑ divergence

parting shot, parting shots. A **parting shot** is a remark, usually an unpleasant one, that you make at the end of a conversation, just before leaving. EG *Lionel paused to deliver a parting shot at the door.* N COUNT: USU SING ⇑ comment

partisan /pɑːtɪzæn/, **partisans**. 1 Someone who is **partisan** strongly supports a particular person, cause, etc; used especially when they do this without thinking carefully about the matter. EG *There are, he agrees, real dangers in a partisan Civil Service.* ▸ used of opinions, attitudes, etc. EG *...partisan political passions.* ADJ QUALIT = prejudiced

2 Someone who is a **partisan** of a particular person or thing is a strong supporter of them or it. EG *I was not aware, Mr Leggett, that you were such a partisan of General Jackson.* N COUNT = champion

3 A **partisan** is also a member of an armed force that is formed in a country occupied by enemy soldiers in order to fight them unofficially. EG *...those who fought in the hills and forests as partisans.* N COUNT ⇑ fighter

partition /pɑːtɪʃəⁿn/, **partitions, partitioning, partitioned**. 1 A **partition** is a screen or thin wall that separates one part of a room or vehicle from another. EG *In one corner behind a partition was a lavatory... The room had been divided into little cubicles with wooden partitions.* N COUNT ⇑ barrier

2 If you **partition** a room, you separate one part of it from another by placing a partition between the two parts. EG *They had partitioned the inside into offices.* V+O ⇑ divide

3 **Partition** is the dividing of a country into parts so that each part becomes an independent country. EG *...the partition of India in 1947.* ▸ used as a verb. EG *One plan involved partitioning the country.* N UNCOUNT ⇑ division ▸ V+O ⇑ divide

partition off. If you **partition off** part of a room or vehicle you separate that part from the rest of the room or vehicle by placing a partition between the two parts. PHRASAL VB: V+O+ADV ⇑ wall off

partitive /pɑːtɪtɪv/, **partitives**. In grammar, a **partitive** is a word or expression that comes before a noun and indicates that part of a particular thing is being referred to rather than the whole of it. See □ at N PART. ▸ used as an adjective. N COUNT ▸ ADJ CLASSIF

partly /pɑːtli¹/ means to some extent, but not completely. EG *The brass handles are partly obscured by white paint... Nations had been overrun or partly overrun in wars for centuries past... The actors were not very happy with my production, partly because of the scenery... I think this is partly a political and partly a legal question.* ADV = partially

partner /pɑːtnə/, **partners, partnering, partnered**. 1 Your **partner** is **1.1** the person you are married to or are having a romantic or sexual relationship with. EG *A marriage is likely to last if you and your partner are similar in personality.* N COUNT: USU POSS+N ⇑ companion **1.2** the person you are doing something with, for example if you are dancing or playing a game against another pair of people. EG *If she is a bad dancer, she will not have many dance partners... He had operated as partner of another gunman who was still at large.* N COUNT

2 The **partners** in a firm or business are the people who share the ownership of it. EG *She was a partner in a firm of solicitors.* N COUNT

3 If you **partner** someone, you are their partner in a game or at a social occasion. EG *He found himself partnering Mrs Keppel at bridge.* V+O

4 The **partner** of a country or organization is the country or organization, or one of the countries or organizations, with which they have an alliance or N COUNT = associate

agreement. EG *This move will not please Britain's EEC partners... ...the Moderate Party, the largest and most conservative partner in the coalition.*
5 A man can address another man as **partner** when he is being friendly; used in informal American English. N VOC

partnership /pɑ:tnəʃɪp/, **partnerships.** 1 **Partnership** or a **partnership** is 1.1 a relationship in which two or more people, organizations, or countries work together as partners. EG *Remember that your aim is to establish a working partnership with your child's teachers... ...new forms of partnership between management and workers.* 1.2 the state of being a partner in a business. EG *Gerran had taken him into full partnership in his company... They've offered me a partnership.* N UNCOUNT/COUNT: IF+PREP THEN between/of/with = alliance; N UNCOUNT/COUNT
2 A **partnership** is also a business owned by two or more people. EG *...Johnson Marshall and Partner, one of Britain's biggest partnerships.* N COUNT

part of speech, parts of speech. A **part of speech** is a particular grammatical class of word, for example noun, adjective, or verb. N COUNT

partook /pɑ:tʊk/ is the past tense of **partake.**

partridge /pɑ:trɪdʒ/, **partridges;** **partridge** can also be used as the plural form. A **partridge** is a wild bird with brown feathers, a round body, and a short tail. In Britain some people shoot partridges for sport or for food. N COUNT

part-singing is the singing of songs in which three or more tunes are sung at the same time. N UNCOUNT

part-time. A **part-time** worker or student, or someone who has a **part-time** job, works or studies for only part of each working week or day. EG *We employ a staff of five part-time receptionists... The single mother's answer may be part-time work... She is paid on a part-time basis.* ▸ used as an adverb. EG *40 per cent of women work part-time.* ADJ CLASSIF: USU ATTRIB ≠ full time; ▸ ADV WITH VB ≠ full time

part-timer, part-timers. A **part-timer** is a person who works part-time. N COUNT ⇑ worker

part way; also spelled with a hyphen and as one word. **Part way** means part of the way or partly; an informal expression. EG *Part way through the meal she became suspicious... The window was partway open.* ADV: USU+PREP = halfway

party /pɑ:ti[1]/, **parties.** 1 A **party** is a political organization whose members all have the same basic aims and beliefs, usually an organization that tries to get its members elected to the government of a country or state. EG *He's a member of the Labour Party... At the age of thirteen he joined the Communist Party... ...the party leader.* N COUNT: ALSO IN NAMES ⇑ group
2 A **party** is also a social event, often in someone's home, at which a number of adults or children enjoy themselves by eating, drinking, dancing, talking, playing games, etc. Parties are often held to celebrate a special occasion. EG *I asked her to the party... ...a birthday party... They gave a farewell party for her... ...her new party dress.* ● See also **garden party, hen party, stag party.** N COUNT
3 A **party** of people is a group of people who are doing something together, for example travelling together. EG *He took a party of fellow Americans on a tour... We had to get into our seats 15 minutes before the Royal party... The survivors worked together in rescue parties.* ● See also **search party, working party.** N COUNT/PART
4 A particular **party** is also a person who is one of the people involved in something such as a legal dispute or the signing of a contract or agreement; a formal use. EG *He is obviously within his rights in expecting the guilty party to pay up... Difficulties arise only when one or another party oversteps the limits... Residents and other interested parties were free to come.* ● See also **third party.** N COUNT+SUPP = individual
5 Someone who **is a party to** a particular action, agreement, etc, or who **is party to** it, is involved in it, and therefore partly responsible for it. EG *They simply wouldn't be a party to such a ridiculous enterprise... They fined or imprisoned all those party to illegal agreements.* PHR: VB INFLECTS = be mixed up in
6 You can also use **party** in informal and rather old-fashioned English to refer to a person. EG *This party came up to me and asked for a light.* N COUNT

partying /pɑ:ti[1]j[0]ɪŋ/ is the activity of going to parties; an informal word. N UNCOUNT

party line, party lines. 1 The **party line** on a particular issue is the official view taken by a political party, which its members are expected to support. EG *They could be guaranteed to trot out the party line on all issues.* ● to **toe the party line:** see **toe.** N COUNT ⇑ stance
2 A **party line** is a telephone line shared by two or more houses, offices, etc. N COUNT

party piece, party pieces. Someone's **party piece** is something that they often do to entertain people, especially at parties, for example singing a particular song or saying a particular poem; used in informal English. N COUNT

party political broadcast, party political broadcasts. A **party political broadcast** is a short broadcast on radio or television made by a political party, especially before an election, in which its policies are explained and other parties are often criticized. N COUNT

party politics. When politicians engage in **party politics,** they do things to try and improve people's opinions about their party instead of doing things for the good of the country; often used showing disapproval. N UNCOUNT

party wall, party walls. A **party wall** is a wall that is shared by two houses or other buildings that are joined together. N COUNT

parvenu /pɑ:vənju:/, **parvenus.** You refer to someone as a **parvenu** when they have suddenly acquired wealth or high status, but you think they are not very cultured or well-educated; a formal word used showing disapproval. N COUNT = upstart

pas de deux. **Pas de deux** is both the singular and the plural form. Both forms are pronounced /pɑ: də dɜ:/; the plural form can also be pronounced /pɒ: də dɜ:z/. In ballet, a **pas de deux** is a dance in which two dancers dance alone together. N COUNT

pass /pɑ:s/, **passes, passing, passed.** 1 To **pass** someone or something means to go past them without stopping. EG *We passed the New Hotel... The crowd opened and let us pass... Each passing car threw up a cloud of white dust.* V OR V+O
2 If you **pass** a moving vehicle when you are driving along a road, you drive faster than it and go past it. EG *Nigel drove fast and well, passing cars only when it was safe.* V OR V+O = overtake
3 When someone or something **passes** somewhere, for example in a particular direction or through a particular thing, they move in that direction or through that thing. EG *I had to pass this way to reach my car... They passed through an arched gateway... Pre-cut slabs of toffee pass along a conveyor belt... The gas is then passed along a pipe... A meal taken by a human being normally passes through the body in about twenty-four hours.* V+A ⇑ go
4 If something such as a road, river, or pipe **passes** in a particular direction or along a particular route, it continues or extends in that direction or along that route. EG *The stream and the road pass through green and stony fields... The two gates controlled the roadway where it passed through the palace grounds... The pipe passed under the city sewer.* V+A = go, run
5 If you **pass** something to someone, you take it in your hand and give it to them. EG *She passed me her glass... Pass me Philip's card, would you?... Photos were passed from hand to hand.* V+O, V+O+O, OR V+O+A *(to)*
6 If you **pass** something through, over, or under a particular thing, you arrange it in that position, for example by threading it through, over, or under the thing. EG *Tie the string to the switch and pass it under the hook.* V+O+A = run, thread
7 If something **passes** from one person or group to another, the second person or group becomes the new owner or controller of it instead of the first. EG *Her property passes to her next of kin... Responsibility for security there would now pass to Westminster.* V+A *(to)* ⇑ go
8 If you **pass** the ball to someone else in your team during a game of football, hockey, basketball, etc, you kick, hit, or throw it to them. EG *Robson passes to Lineker on the right wing.* V+A OR V+O: USU+A ⇑ send
9 When a period of time **passes,** it begins, continues, and finishes. EG *The first few days passed... The time seems to have passed so quickly.* V = elapse, go by
10 If you **pass** your life or a period of time in a particular way, you spend your life or the time in that way, for example doing a particular kind of work or living in particular conditions. EG *Men pass their lives farming their small plots of land... Am I to* V+O+-ING/A

pass all my life abroad?... We passed a pleasant afternoon together.

11 To **pass** through a particular period of time or series of stages means to exist before, during, and after that period or those stages and to be affected by this. EG *Mrs Yule had to pass through a few years of much bitterness... Humanity was believed to pass through four great ages... The revolutionary movement has passed through a succession of distinctive phases.*
V+A *(through)*

12 If something **comes to pass**, it happens; a very old-fashioned or literary expression. EG *Yet this all came to pass with barely a demurring voice.*
PHR : VB INFLECTS = come about

13 If something **passes**, it comes to an end, especially in a slow way. EG *The crisis passed... The old aristocratic order is passing.*
V = disappear

14 If you **pass** a test or an examination or if the examiner **passes** you, you are successful in it. EG *I passed my driving test in Holland... She told me that I had passed... If you don't pass in your subsidiary subject you can't get a degree.*
V, OR V+O

15 If something **passes** a test, trial, or requirement, it is considered to be satisfactory, when judged in a particular way. EG *Whatever is alive has passed the test. Whatever is extinct has failed... A suit in the English style might pass.*
V OR V+O

16 If a growing total **passes** a particular amount or level, it becomes greater than that amount or level as it increases. EG *Contributions for 1986 have already passed the £600,000 mark.*
V+O = surpass, exceed

17 If an official group of people **passes** something such as a new law or a proposal, they formally approve it or agree to it. EG *Many of the laws passed by Parliament are never enforced... ...the passing of the 1870 Education Act... Congress passed a resolution accepting his services... We'll get local union branches to pass motions.*
V+O

18 If someone in authority **passes** something, they officially allow it to be used, seen, read, or heard by the people who live in a particular place. EG *This drug has been passed by the US Food and Drug Administration... ...her terrifying remark (which the censor must have passed).*
V+O = approve

19 To **pass** a sentence or verdict on someone or something means to officially give an opinion on them, for example to say what punishment will be given to a person who has committed a crime. EG *Sentence had not been passed... We have decided to pass a sentence of imprisonment of 6 months.*
V+O

20 If something **passes** for a particular thing or if someone **passes** as a particular type of person, they are generally accepted to be that thing or type of person, even though they do not necessarily have the right qualities. EG *...that brief period that passes for summer in those high latitudes... A strip of space 4 feet wide passed as a kitchen... You may pass as a remarkably witty man... His invitation might have passed as casual.*
V+A *(for/as)*

21 If you **pass** a remark or comment, you say something. EG *It was a policy with her never to speak or pass any comment when she was in their company... They did pass one compliment, however, in spite of their misgivings.*
V+O ⇑ make

22 If something such as remarks, greetings, or jokes **pass** between two or more people, they are spoken by them to each other. EG *...the usual greetings that passed between them... ...the indecent jokes that passed between her and old Walters.*
V+A *(between/among)* = be exchanged

23 If something **passes** without comment or reaction, nobody comments on it or reacts to it. • If you **let** something **pass**, you do not say or do anything in response to it. EG *'Training,' she said; and I let it pass... For the moment, we'll let that pass.*
V+A/C • PHR : FIRST VB INFLECTS ⇑ ignore

24 If something or someone **passes** unnoticed or unseen, they are not noticed or seen. EG *Social change was so slow that it would pass unnoticed in one person's lifetime.*
V+C ⇑ go unnoticed

25 If someone **passes** a dud cheque, a bad cheque, etc, they pay for something with a cheque that will not be accepted by a bank, for example because it is stolen or because the account does not have enough money in it. EG *I swear I've never passed a dud cheque in my life.*
V+O ⇑ cash

26 If someone **passes** something such as blood, there is blood in their faeces or urine; a formal use. EG *He passed blood in his urine again last night.* • If someone **passes water**, they urinate; a formal expression.
V+O • PHR : VB INFLECTS

27 If you say **'pass'** or **'I pass'** in answer to a question or during a game, you mean that you cannot answer the question or that you are unwilling to take part in the next stage of the game. EG *'What is the largest British bird?'–'Pass'... He refused to play the next round. 'I pass,' he said.*
CONVENTION

28 A **pass** is **28.1** the act of kicking, hitting, or throwing the ball to another member of your team during a game of football, hockey, basketball, etc. EG *Hughes intercepted a pass by Jones.* **28.2** the result that you get when you have succeeded in an examination or test. EG *She got seven passes in her 'O' levels... I suppose you could set a pass mark at 60 per cent.* **28.3** a document that allows you to do something, for example to visit a particular place or to travel on trains or buses without paying. EG *I have a pass to go from New York to East Hampton... ...journalists were issued with separate passes... On Saturday the train would be full of soldiers on weekend passes.* **28.4** a route between two mountains that are very close to each other. EG *We rode down out of the pass onto a small green plain... ...the Khyber Pass.* **28.5** an unpleasant or difficult situation; a literary use. EG *The problems that have brought us to this pass.*
N COUNT ⇑ play; N COUNT; N COUNT ⇑ authorizatio = permit; N COUNT, ALSO IN NAMES = defile; N SING WITH DET = crisis, dilemma

29 If someone **makes a pass** at you, they try to begin a romantic or sexual relationship with you; an informal expression.
PHR : VB INFLECTS, USU+ *at*

30 The word **pass** is also used in the following expressions, which are explained at other places in this dictionary. • **to pass the buck:** see **buck.** • **to pass judgement**: see **judgement.** • **to pass muster:** see **muster.** • **to pass the time**: see **time.** • **to pass the time of day with** someone: see **time.** • **to pass the word: see word.**

31 see also **passing.**

pass around. To **pass** something **around** means the same as to pass it round. EG *I've got a couple of pictures you might like to pass around.*
PHRASAL VB : V+O+ADV/PREP

pass away. 1 If you say that someone **passed away**, you mean that they died; used especially when you want to avoid saying the word 'die'. EG *Your husband sent the letter to us shortly before he passed away.*
PHRASAL VB : V+ADV

2 When something **passes away**, it slowly disappears. EG *...the fashions and tendencies that have emerged and passed away... A hurt look appeared in Jack's eyes and passed away.*
PHRASAL VB : V+ADV ⇑ go

pass by. If you **pass by** something, you go past it. EG *We pass by another marker... I was just passing by and I saw your car.*
PHRASAL VB : V+ADV, OR V+O+ADV

pass down. If you **pass down** something such as stories, traditions, or characteristics, you tell, teach, or give it to someone who belongs to a younger generation than you. EG *...stories his own father had passed down to him.*
PHRASAL VB : V+O+ADV = hand down

pass off. 1 If you **pass** something **off** as a particular thing, especially a more valuable or important thing than it really is, you convince people that it is that thing. EG *The painting had been passed off as early Flemish, or Dutch... The man who made the cabinet passed it off as an antique.*
PHRASAL VB : V+O+ADV, USU *as*

2 If an event **passes off** in a particular way, especially in a satisfactory way, it happens and ends in that way. EG *That passed off rather well, don't you think?... Most of these situations pass off without mishap.*
PHRASAL VB : V+ADV+A = go off

3 If something such as a feeling or condition **passes off**, it gradually disappears. EG *Fortunately the effects of the gas passed off relatively quickly.*
PHRASAL VB : V+ADV = wear off

pass on. 1 If you **pass** something **on** to someone, you give it to them, for example after you have used it or after someone else has given it to you. EG *He handed a typewritten sheet to King to pass on to Smith... They take it, look at it, and then pass it on... He only had shoes which other folk passed on to him.*
PHRASAL VB : V+O+ADV, USU+*t* = hand

2 If you **pass on** something such as a message, story, or information to someone, you tell them something that has been told to you. EG *When the information was given to me I was to pass it on to her... Philip assured her that he had passed on the invitation.*
PHRASAL VB : V+O+ADV, USU+*t* ⇑ repeat

3 If you **pass on** costs to someone else, you cause them to pay for something that you should pay for. EG *Governments have tried to prevent firms from passing on cost increases.*
PHRASAL VB : V+O+ADV, IF+PREP THEN *to* ⇑ transfer

4 If you **pass on** to a different subject while you are writing or speaking, you begin to talk about it. EG *They passed on to other matters.*
PHRASAL VB : V+ADV, IF+PREP THEN *to*

5 If you **pass on** to a different place, you go there, especially as part of a journey or tour; a fairly formal use. EG *We passed on to a small pantry and entered the dining room.*
PHRASAL VB : V+ADV, USU+A = move on, proceed

6 If you say that someone **passed on**, you mean that they died; used especially when you want to avoid using the word 'die'. EG *I'm sorry to have to tell you that she passed on in the night.*
PHRASAL VB : V+ADV

pass out. 1 If someone **passes out**, they faint or collapse; an informal use. EG *I thought I was going to pass out.*
PHRASAL VB : V+ADV = black out

2 When a police, army, navy, or air force cadet **passes out**, he or she satisfactorily finishes his or her course of training.
PHRASAL VB : V+ADV

pass over. 1 If you **pass** someone **over for a job or position,** you do not choose them for that job or position, but choose instead a person who is younger or who has less experience. EG *He got it into his head he was being passed over for promotion... Neither of us got the job. We were both passed over.*
PHRASAL VB : V+O+ADV = reject

2 If you **pass over** a particular topic in a conversation, you do not discuss it. EG *He didn't give a reason and Robertson passed it over in silence... He passed over the events of that week.*
PHRASAL VB : V+O+ADV = ignore

3 See also **Passover.**

pass round. If you **pass** something **round** a group of people, you give it to each person in turn, or you give it to one person who then gives it to someone else. EG *Just take a light and pass the matches round.*
PHRASAL VB : V+O+ADV/PREP

pass up. If you **pass up** something such as an opportunity, you do not take advantage of it. EG *I wouldn't have passed up the chance for a million dollars...*
PHRASAL VB : V+ADV+O ⇑ miss = let go

> **PASS** □ In this dictionary PASS is used in the grammar notes beside entries to refer to the passive form of a verb. This is formed by the verb *be* followed by a past participle, so the passive of *to reject* is *to be rejected.* The passive allows you to mention an action without saying who did it. For example, *Your application **was rejected*** avoids saying who rejected the application. In the corresponding active clause you have to say who did the rejecting, as in *The committee rejected your application.* If you want to mention who did it in a passive clause, you use a prepositional group with the preposition *by.* EG *Your application **was rejected** by the committee.* The subject of the passive clause is the same as the object of the active clause. Only transitive verbs can have a passive.

passable /pɑːsəbəl/. 1 If you say that something is **passable**, you mean that its quality or standard is satisfactory. EG *They make passable sandals out of old car tyres... ...some very passable small restaurants.* ◊ **passably.** EG *...a very passably forged document... It reminded me that Jane had once played passably.*
ADJ QUALIT = adequate, acceptable
◊ ADV WITH VB = adequately

2 If a road or path is **passable**, it is not completely blocked, and so people are able to travel along it. EG *Many of these roads are not passable in bad weather.*
ADJ CLASSIF = clear

passage /pæsɪdʒ/, **passages.** 1 A **passage** is 1.1 a long, narrow space with walls or high fences on both sides, which connects one place or room with another. EG *At the end of the narrow passage was a bathroom... We went up the side of the house and along a little passage to the garden.*
N COUNT ⇑ corridor = passageway

1.2 an empty space that allows you to move through a crowd of people or large number of obstructions. EG *Her aides had to go on ahead of her to clear a passage.*
N SING WITH DET = path

1.3 a tube or long, narrow hole which connects one part of the body with another and along which air or liquid can pass. EG *...the nasal passages.*
N COUNT : USU MOD+N ⇑ duct

2 A **passage** in a book, speech, or piece of music is a short section of it that you are considering separately from the rest. EG *There's one brilliant passage in the book, where the Italian gets trapped in the lift... Read the following passage and answer the questions below... The piano and the clarinet both have long solo passages.*
N COUNT

3 The **passage** of someone or something is 3.1 their movement as they go past a place or from one place to another. EG *The wind of the train's passage ruffled his hair.*
N UNCOUNT : USU WITH POSS ⇑ passing

3.2 the way in which they progress from one stage in their development or situation to another. EG *...his rapid passage into senior philosophical circles.*
N SING WITH DET +SUPP

4 A **passage** is also a journey by ship from one country to another. EG *The passage across to Belfast was one of the roughest I've known.* ● If you **work** your **passage** to a particular place, you get a temporary job on a boat which is going there, so that you do not have to pay the fare.
N COUNT = crossing
● PHR : VB INFLECTS

5 If you are granted **passage** through a country or area of land, you are given permission or the right to go through it; a formal use.
N UNCOUNT ⇑ access

6 The **passage** of a particular period of time is the process or fact of its passing; a fairly formal use. EG *...despite the passage of two thousand years... Their friendship has survived the passage of time.*
N SING : *the*+N+*of*

7 The **passage** of a bill or act through a parliament is the official acceptance of it by the parliament. EG *The situation changed considerably with the passage of the Companies Act in 1975.*
N UNCOUNT : USU WITH POSS = enactment, passing

passageway /pæsɪdʒweɪ/, **passageways.** A **passageway** is a long, narrow space with walls or high fences on both sides, which connects one place or room with another.
N COUNT ⇑ way = passage

passant /pæsɑːŋ/. See **en passant.**

passé /pæseɪ/. Something that is **passé** is no longer regarded as fashionable. EG *It was fashionable in the sixties, okay in the seventies but definitely passé in the eighties.*
ADJ QUALIT ⇑ unfashionable = old hat

passenger /pæsɪndʒə/, **passengers.** A **passenger** is 1 a person who travels in a vehicle, boat, aeroplane, etc, but who is not the driver or a member of the crew. EG *The ferry service handles 400 passengers a week... He lifted the briefcase into the passenger seat.*
N COUNT ⇑ traveller

2 a person in a team or group who does not do his or her share of the work; used in British English showing disapproval. EG *There's no room for passengers on this project.*
N COUNT

passer-by /pɑːsə baɪ/, **passers-by**; also spelled without a hyphen. A **passer-by** is a person who is walking past something or someone. EG *One of the boys had stopped a passer-by and asked him to phone an ambulance... Passers-by could hear our rising voices.*
N COUNT ⇑ pedestrian

passim /pæsɪm/. In indexes and notes, **passim** indicates that a particular name or subject occurs frequently throughout a particular piece of writing or section of a book. EG *...Johnson, S: pp. 102-114 passim.*

passing /pɑːsɪŋ/. 1 **Passing** events, activities, fashions, etc last for only a short period of time. EG *...passing glimpses of pale flowers... ...the fleeting, passing contacts of city life.*
ADJ CLASSIF : ATTRIB ⇑ brief = fleeting, transitory

2 The **passing** of a period of time is the fact or process of its beginning and continuing. EG *The passing of time brought news of them.*
N UNCOUNT : USU *the*+N+*of*

3 If something changes **with each passing day, with every passing week,** or **with each passing year,** etc it changes continuously. EG *The situation gets more difficult with each passing day.*
PHR : USED AS AN A

4 The **passing** of a tradition or habit is the fact or process of its coming to an end and not being used any more. EG *People have become sentimental about the passing of ways and customs.*
N UNCOUNT : USU *the*+N+*of* ⇑ disappearance

5 If you mention something **in passing**, you mention it briefly while you are talking or writing about something else. EG *Sociologists like Wirth have referred in passing to the transitory nature of human ties... We can note, in passing, the rapid expansion of private security organisations.*
PHR : USED AS AN A = incidentally

passion /pæʃən/, **passions.** 1 **Passion** is 1.1 a feeling of very strong sexual attraction for someone. EG *I had felt such extraordinary passion for this girl... Flirtations often develop into passions.*
N UNCOUNT/COUNT ⇑ obsession

1.2 a very strong feeling about something or belief in it. EG *Anna hated them with passion... He admired the intensity and passion of Bevan... ...their attempt to arouse nationalistic passions against the foreigner.*
N UNCOUNT/COUNT = fervour

2 If you have a **passion** for something, you have a very strong interest in it and like it very much. EG *Biology is their great passion at the moment... She had developed a passion for the natural world, for gardens, for birds.*
N COUNT ⇑ liking

3 Christians refer to the sufferings and death of Jesus Christ as the **Passion.**
N SING : *the*+N

passionate /pæʃənət/. Someone who is **passionate** 1 expresses very strong feelings about something or has very strong beliefs in it. EG *...a passionate social*
ADJ QUALIT = fervent

reformer. ▸ used of their behaviour. EG *...a passionate speech... She burst into passionate sobbing.* ◊ **passionately.** EG *People care deeply and passionately about this issue... I argued with him passionately.* [◊ ADV WITH VB ⇑ strongly] **2** has strong romantic or sexual feelings and often expresses them in their behaviour. EG *...a passionate and lonely woman.* ▸ used of their behaviour. EG *...passionate love.* ◊ **passionately.** EG *They were kissing passionately.* [ADJ QUALIT ⇑ warm] [◊ ADV WITH VB = ardently]

passion fruit; **passion fruit** is both the singular and plural form. A **passion fruit** is a small egg-shaped fruit that is produced by certain kinds of flower which grow in hot countries. [N COUNT/UNCOUNT]

passion play, passion plays. A **passion play** is a play which tells the story of the suffering and death of Jesus Christ. [N COUNT]

passive /pæsɪv/. **1** Someone who is **passive** does not respond actively to things that are said or done to them. For example they do not show their feelings, or they do not resist things that they do not like. EG *The ideals of womanhood have been produced by men who desire women to be passive... She was so enraged that she could remain passive no longer.* ▸ used of their behaviour. EG *His response was passive... There had been a widespread rejection, active or passive, of many of the traditional moral values.* ◊ **passively.** EG *They accept passively every law that is passed.* ◊ **passivity** /pəˈsɪvɪti/. EG *The long passivity of the National Council had come to an end.* [ADJ QUALIT = unresponsive, idle] [◊ ADV WITH VB] [◊ N UNCOUNT = inertia]

2 Passive resistance, **passive** action, etc is the activity of showing resistance to governments, authority, or the law by non-violent methods, such as fasting, peaceful demonstrations, or refusal to co-operate. EG *...responding to police action with passive resistance methods–lying down or standing in the middle of the road.* [ADJ CLASSIF]

3 In grammar, the **passive** is the form of the verb which is made up of the auxiliary verb 'be' and the past participle of a main verb. See ☐ at PASS. [N UNCOUNT]

passivize/pæsɪvaɪz/, **passivizes, passivizing, passivized**; also spelled **passivise.** If you **passivize** a verb or a structure that contains a verb, you make the verb passive. [V-ERG]

Passover /pɑːsəʊvə/ is a Jewish festival that begins in late March or early April and that lasts for eight days. [N UNCOUNT]

passport /pɑːspɔːt/, **passports. 1** A **passport** is an official document containing your name, photograph, and personal details, which you need to show at the border when you go into a foreign country. EG *The pastor had left his passport on the bedside table... My husband has not got a British passport.* [N COUNT ⇑ permit]

2 A **passport** to success, achievement, a career, etc is something that makes it possible. EG *A good education is the passport to success.* [N COUNT : IF + PREP THEN *to* = key]

password /pɑːswɜːd/, **passwords.** A **password** is a secret word or expression that you must say in order to be allowed into a particular place. [N COUNT]

past /pɑːst/, **pasts. 1** The **past** is the time that existed before the present time, together with the things that happened during that time. EG *He was highly praised in the past as head of the National Security Agency... ...the great Sanskrit dramas of the past... If we forget the past, we are doomed to repeat it.* [N SING : *the*+N]

2 Someone's or something's **past** is all the things which have happened to them in the time before the present. EG *...Britain's imperial past... He never discussed his past... ...a man without a past.* [N SING : USU POSS +N ⇑ history]

3 In grammar, the **past** of a verb is its past tense. [N COUNT]

4 You can use **past** to describe things that happened in the past, or things that used to exist, or people who used to have a particular job, position, status, etc. EG *...sound judgement based on past experience... He refused to respond to questions about his past business dealings... He lamented his past leniency... ...past members of the department... They criticised past Governments for spending £3,500m on military aid.* [ADJ CLASSIF : ATTRIB = former]

5 You can also use **past** to describe a period of time **5.1** which happened a very long time ago. EG *We must search many past centuries for a parallel... His family had settled in the village in years past... ...the junk of decades past.* [ADJ CLASSIF : ATTRIB, OR ADJ AFTER N] **5.2** which has lasted from an earlier point in time up until the present. EG *I've spent most of the past eight years at sea... No summit meeting in the past quarter century has ever achieved so little.... He couldn't believe what he'd been through in the past hour.* [ADJ CLASSIF : ATTRIB = last]

6 When you are telling the time, you use **past** in order to say how many minutes it is after the hour mentioned: see ☐ at TIME. EG *It's ten past eleven... We have consulting sessions every day from half past eight in the morning till eleven... 'What's the time now?'–'It's quarter past.'* [PREP, OR ADV AFTER N]

7 You can also use **past** in order to indicate that the time now is later than a particular time that is mentioned. EG *It's long past bedtime.* ▸ used as an adverb. EG *He felt tired–the hour had struck long past for his bed.* [PREP] [▸ ADV AFTER N = ago]

8 If something such as a situation or feeling is **past**, it has completely disappeared or has finished and gone. EG *They were preparing themselves to descend, as all danger was now past... She refused to let her mind linger on alternatives long past.* [ADJ CLASSIF : PRED = over]

9 If someone or something goes **past** a particular thing, person, or place, they go from one side of it to the other while they are moving somewhere. EG *He walked past Lock's hat shop... He turned his head aside and drove straight past me.* ▸ used as an adverb. EG *People ran past laughing.* [PREP = by] [▸ ADV AFTER VB]

10 If you look, point, shout, etc **past** someone or something, you do not look, point, shout, etc directly at them but at someone or something behind them. EG *He stared past me out of the window.* [PREP = beyond]

11 If something is situated **past** a particular place, it is situated farther on or farther away than that place. EG *Past Doctor Ford's surgery was the grocer's... The body was carried to the burying place, not far past the village.* [PREP = beyond]

12 Past a particular point or level means to a greater extent than that point or level. EG *I can't count past four... She never managed to get past the second chapter... The temperature soared up past 100.* [PREP = beyond]

13 If someone or something is **past** a particular condition or stage of development, they are no longer in that condition or at that stage. EG *The machines were long past their prime... She is past her peak.* [PREP = beyond]

14 If you are **past** a particular kind of activity or thing, you are no longer interested in it or able to do it. EG *When the kids were younger, they nearly drove me silly, but they're past all that now.* [PREP = beyond] ● If you say that someone is **past it**, you mean that they are too old to do something which they could have done when they were younger; an informal expression. [● PHR : USED AS C]

15 If you say that something is **past** description, hoping, doubting, etc, you mean that you cannot properly describe it or sensibly hope for it or doubt it, etc. EG *It was exhilaration past description... They offered salaries past dreaming.* [PREP = beyond]

16 If you say that you **would not put it past** someone to do a particular thing, you mean that they are quite likely to do it and that you would not be surprised if they did. EG *I wouldn't put it past him to pinch the whole lot while we're away.* [PHR : *put* INFLECTS]

pasta /pæstə/, **pastas. Pasta** is a type of food that is made from a mixture of flour, eggs, and water and that is then formed into different shapes. Spaghetti, macaroni, and noodles are types of pasta. [N MASS]

paste /peɪst/, **pastes, pasting, pasted. 1 Paste** is **1.1** a soft, wet, often sticky, mixture of a substance and a liquid, which can be spread easily. EG *Mix the butter and flour into a paste.* [N COUNT/UNCOUNT] **1.2** a mixture of water and flour or starch that is used for sticking paper to things. EG *...wallpaper paste.* [N MASS ⇑ adhesive] **1.3** a soft, smooth, sticky mixture of food that you spread onto bread or toast. EG *...sandwiches filled with potted duck paste... ...anchovy paste.* [N MASS : USU AFTER N] **1.4** a hard shiny glass that is used for making imitation jewellery. EG *...a necklace of paste emeralds.* [N UNCOUNT]

2 When you **paste** paper or something made from paper, you put paste on it so that you can stick it to a surface or stick it together. EG *They were cutting and pasting long paper chains.* [V+O]

3 When you **paste** something on a surface or when you **paste** a surface with it, you stick it on that surface using paste. EG *Labels with dates and the names of newspapers were pasted to some of the clippings... The children were kept busy pasting gold stars on a chart... The walls were pasted with pictures of aircraft.* [V+O+A]

4 See also **pasting.**

pastel /pæstəl, pæstel/, **pastels.** 1 **Pastel** colours are pale, light, and soft. EG *...pastel green... ...pastel shades of pink, blue, and brown.*
ADJ CLASSIF: ATTRIB

2 **Pastels** are **2.1** colours that are pale, light, and soft. EG *Our new range of paints includes some new subtle pastels.*
N COUNT: USU PL ⇑ shades

2.2 small sticks of waxy chalk of different colours that are used in drawing and making pictures.
N COUNT: USU PL ⇑ crayons

▸ A **pastel** is also a picture that has been made using pastels. EG *...a pastel portrait of his father.*
▸ N COUNT: USU MOD

pasteurize /pɑːstjəraɪz/, **pasteurizes, pasteurizing, pasteurized**; also spelled **pasteurise.** When milk or cream **is pasteurized**, bacteria are removed from it by means of a special heating process.
V+O: USU PASS ⇑ sterilize

◊ **pasteurized.** EG *...pasteurized milk.*
◊ ADJ CLASSIF

◊ **pasteurization** /pɑːstjəraɪzeɪʃən/. EG *Pasteurisation kills off any harmful bacteria that may be present.*
◊ N UNCOUNT ⇑ sterilization

pastiche /pæstiːʃ/, **pastiches.** A **pastiche** is a piece of writing, music, or a picture, in which the style is copied from someone or something else, or which contains a mixture of different styles; a formal word.
N COUNT = imitation, parody

pastille /pæstɪl/, **pastilles.** A **pastille** is a small, round sweet that has a fruit flavour. Some pastilles contain medicine and you can suck them if you have a sore throat or a cough. EG *...a strawberry fruit pastille.*
N COUNT: USU MOD+N

pastime /pɑːstaɪm/, **pastimes.** A **pastime** is something that you do because you enjoy it or are interested in it, rather than as work. EG *...leisurely pastimes, like gardening, woodwork, music and toy-making.*
N COUNT ⇑ recreation = hobby, interest

pasting /peɪstɪŋ/; an informal word. If someone gives you a **pasting,** 1 they criticize you severely. EG *Robin took rather a pasting from Morris Zapp at the last Staff Seminar... The reviewers gave me quite a pasting.*
N SING WITH DET ⇑ attack = knock

2 they defeat you heavily in a game or competition. EG *United received a 5-0 pasting this afternoon.*
N SING WITH DET = thrashing

past master, past masters. If you are a **past master** at something, you are very skilful at it because you have had a lot of experience of doing it. EG *...a speciality at which they are past masters.*
N COUNT = adept

pastor /pɑːstə/, **pastors.** A **pastor** is a member of the Christian clergy, especially one who is not a member of the Catholic or Anglican churches. EG *We have no pastor at present: the church is run by five deacons.*
N COUNT

pastoral /pɑːstərəl/. 1 A **pastoral** way of life is one in which people live in the country and farm the land, especially by keeping animals that feed on the grass. EG *...the ordinary pastoral life of people... They began to be dependent on an entirely pastoral economy.* ▸ used of people who live in this way. EG *...the pastoral nomads and their animals.*
ADJ CLASSIF: ATTRIB = rural

2 A **pastoral** place, atmosphere, idea, etc is characteristic of or relates to peaceful country life and scenery; a literary word. EG *...a sheltered pastoral scene with little lambs and yellow flowers... This stretch of land was a peaceful, pastoral Eden... ...pastoral fantasies.*
ADJ CLASSIF: ATTRIB = bucolic, rustic

3 The **pastoral** duties and activities of clergy in the Christian churches relate to the general needs of people, rather than just their spiritual or religious needs. EG *...a pastoral visit.*
ADJ CLASSIF: ATTRIB

4 The **pastoral** duties and activities of teachers in schools relate to the the general needs of the pupils, rather than just their educational needs.
ADJ CLASSIF: ATTRIB ⇑ help

> **PAST PART** □ In this dictionary PAST PART is used in the grammar notes beside entries to refer to the past participle of a verb. The past participle of most verbs in English is formed with an *-ed* ending, for example *helped* and *walked.* These have the same spelling as the past tense of the verb. A few verbs have irregular past participle forms, for example *broken* and *given.* The past participle is used in forming two main kinds of verbal group in English: perfect tenses and passives. When it is used to form a perfect tense, the past participle comes after a form of the auxiliary *have.* EG *You **have helped** me a lot... He **had walked** along this road before.* When it is used to form a passive, it comes after a form of the auxiliary *be.* EG *She **was** greatly **helped** by psychotherapy.* See □ at PASS. The past participle of some verbs is used as an adjective. You can say *She has **broken** his heart,* and you can also say *...a **broken** heart* and *His heart is **broken**.*

past participle, past participles. In grammar, the **past participle** of a verb is a form which usually ends in -ed or -en. It is used to form some tenses and the passive voice, and is also used to modify nouns. See also □ at PAST PART.
N COUNT

past perfect. You use the **past perfect** tense of a verb when you are describing an action that took place before another action which is also mentioned.
N SING: *the*+N = pluperfect

pastrami /pəstrɑːmi[1]/ is strongly seasoned smoked beef.
N UNCOUNT

pastry /peɪstri[1]/, **pastries.** 1 **Pastry** is a food made of flour, fat, and water that is mixed into a dough and then rolled flat. It is used for making pies and flans.
N MASS

2 A **pastry** is a type of small cake made with sweet pastry. EG *...pastries filled with custard or whipped cream.*
N COUNT

past tense. In grammar, the **past tense** or the **past** is used in contrast with the present tense to refer mainly to things that happened or existed before the time when you are speaking or writing.
N SING: *the*+N

pasture /pɑːstʃə/, **pastures, pasturing, pastured.** 1 **Pasture** is land that has grass growing on it and that is used for farm animals to graze on. EG *...five acres of pasture... ...the lush green pastures of Ireland.*
N UNCOUNT/COUNT = pastureland

▸ used to refer to the grass itself. EG *The famine is so severe that there is no pasture for our flocks.*
▸ N UNCOUNT

2 **out to pasture. 2.1** If you send or put animals **out to pasture,** you move them out to the fields so that they can eat the grass there. EG *The stallions are put out to pasture every Spring.*
PHR: USED AS AN A

2.2 If you **put** someone **out to pasture,** you force them to stop work because you think they are getting too old; an informal expression. EG *It's time old Jones was put out to pasture.*
PHR: VB INFLECTS = retire

3 You use expressions like **pastures new, greener pastures,** and **lusher pastures** to refer to places or situations that seem much more attractive than the one which you were in previously or are in now. EG *She departed for newer and lusher, not to say greener, pastures in the United States.*
PHR: USED AS O/C

pastureland /pɑːstʃəlænd/ is land that has grass growing on it and that is used for farm animals to graze on.
N UNCOUNT = pasture

pasty, pastier, pastiest; pasties. The word **pasty** is pronounced /peɪsti[1]/ when it is an adjective and /pæsti[1]/ when it is a noun. 1 If you are **pasty** or if you have a **pasty** face, you look pale and unhealthy. EG *They looked pasty and red-eyed.*
ADJ QUALIT = anaemic, wan

2 A **pasty** is a small pie which consists of pastry folded around meat, vegetables, cheese, etc. EG *...a Cornish pasty.*
N COUNT

pat /pæt/, **pats, patting, patted.** 1 If you **pat** something, you tap it or hit it lightly, for example with your fingers. EG *He patted the tree trunk softly... Dr Hochstadt leaned forward and patted Etta's hand.*
V+O

▸ used as a noun. EG *...a friendly pat on the shoulder.*
▸ N COUNT

2 If you give someone **a pat on the back** or if you **pat** them **on the back,** you tell them that you approve of what they have done or are trying to do. EG *I think she deserves a pat on the back.*
PHR: USED AS O, OR PHR: VB INFLECTS

3 A **pat** is also a small lump of something soft; used especially of butter. ● See also **cowpat.**
N PART+N UNCOUNT

4 A **pat** answer or remark is something you say that sounds prepared, for example an answer to a question that you are expecting to be asked. EG *I unfailingly gave my pat reply... They come up with a nice, pat generalisation.*
ADJ CLASSIF: ATTRIB = rehearsed, glib

● If you **have** something **off pat,** you have learned it thoroughly so that you can say it at any time. EG *She had all the answers off pat.*
● PHR: VB INFLECTS ⇑ memorize

patch /pætʃ/, **patches, patching, patched.** 1 A **patch** is **1.1** a piece of material which you use to cover a hole in something that you are mending. EG *All of them had patches on their clothes... I mended holes in the sheets by sewing on square patches.*
N COUNT ⇑ covering

1.2 a small piece of material which you wear to cover an injured eye. EG *...an eye patch.*
N COUNT ⇑ protection

2 If you **patch** something, you fasten a patch over a hole or tear in it in order to mend it. EG *She earned money by patching and selling old clothes... They patched the leaking roofs... ...patched jeans.*
V+O ⇑ repair

3 A **patch** is also **3.1** a part of a surface or area which is different in appearance from the surface or area around it. EG *...the damp patch at the corner of the ceiling... ...patches of snow... He had fat hairy arms, and a bald patch on his head.*
N COUNT+SUPP = spot, bit

3.2 a part or small section of something which you are considering
N COUNT+SUPP

separately from the rest of it. EG *There are some wonderful patches in this poem... ...the difficult patches in their relationship.* **3.3** a small area of ground which is used for growing vegetables or fruit. EG *...a cabbage patch.* [N COUNT+SUPP = plot] **3.4** a district where a policeman or other official person works, and which they know very well; used in British English. EG *There's been no trouble on my patch for weeks.* [N SING WITH DET = beat]

4 If you have or go through **a bad patch** or **a sticky patch**, you experience a time when your life is full of difficulties and problems; used in British English. EG *I went through a bad patch a few years ago.* [PHR : USED AS O/C ⇑ period]

5 If you say that someone or something **is not a patch on** someone or something else, you mean that they are not nearly as good as the other person or thing; an informal expression. EG *Joe's not a patch on her at swimming.* [PHR : VB INFLECTS ≠ measure up to]

patch together. If you **patch** something **together**, you form it from a number of parts in a hurried or careless way. EG *A new government was patched together with the help of the military... She couldn't, as some writers do, just patch together old material.* [PHRASAL VB : V+O+ADV = cobble together]

patch up. 1 If you **patch up** something which is damaged, you mend or patch it so that it can be used. EG *They have to patch up the mud walls that the rains have battered.* [PHRASAL VB : V+O+ADV ⇑ repair]

2 If you **patch up** a quarrel or relationship with someone, you try to be friends again and not to quarrel any more. EG *It's time you started patching up this quarrel... She tried to patch things up.* [PHRASAL VB : V+O+ADV ⇑ settle = make up]

patchwork /pætʃwɜːk/, **patchworks. 1 Patchwork** is needlework that is done by sewing together pieces of material which are of different colours and shapes. EG *She does beautiful patchwork... ...embroidery and patchwork quilts made by women.* [N UNCOUNT]

2 If you describe something as a **patchwork**, you mean that it is made up of different parts or pieces. EG *...this marvellous patchwork of meadows and marsh.* [N COUNT+SUPP = mosaic]

patchy /pætʃiˡ/, **patchier, patchiest.** If something is **patchy**, **1** it is not spread evenly, but scattered around in small quantities. EG *If you dye the clothes in too small a pan, the colour will be patchy... ...patchy fog.* [ADJ QUALIT ⇑ irregular ≠ uniform] **2** it is correct in some parts, but not in all parts, and is therefore considered incomplete and unsatisfactory. EG *The evidence is a bit patchy, isn't it?... He has a rather patchy grasp of history.* [ADJ QUALIT ⇑ incomplete = sketchy]

pate /peɪt/, **pates.** Your **pate** is the top of your head; an old-fashioned word. EG *He mopped the sweat from his bald pate.* [N COUNT : USU POSS+ADJ+N]

pâté /pæteɪ/, **pâtés. Pâté** is a mixture of meat, fish, or vegetables with various flavourings. The ingredients are blended together into a paste and eaten. [N MASS]

patella /pətelə/, **patellae.** Your **patella** is your kneecap; a medical term. [N COUNT]

patent /peɪtəᵒnt/, **patents, patenting, patented.** The word **patent** can also be pronounced /pætəᵒnt/ for the meanings in paragraphs 1 and 2. **1** A **patent** is an official right to be the only person or company allowed to make or sell a new product for a certain period of time; used also to refer to the document you are given when you obtain this right. EG *The first English patent for a typewriter was issued in 1714... To protect his precious device he even took out a patent on it.* [N COUNT] ▸ used as an adjective. EG *...a packet of a patent cement mix.* [▸ N BEFORE N]

2 If you **patent** something, you obtain a patent for it. EG *In the early 1870s he patented a new kind of sugar.* [V+O ⇑ register] ◊ **patented.** EG *This century there have been over a hundred patented devices to extract energy from the waves.* [◊ ADJ CLASSIF : ATTRIB ⇑ registered]

3 Something that is **patent** is obvious, and easy to notice or recognize; a fairly formal use EG *It was a patent impossibility.* [ADJ CLASSIF = manifest] ◊ **patently.** EG *It would patently be a nonsense to pretend nothing was wrong.* [◊ ADV = clearly]

4 Patent or **patent leather** is leather or plastic which looks like leather, has a very hard shiny surface, and is used especially to make shoes and handbags. EG *...black trousers, black patent shoes and white gloves... ...a pair of black patent leather shoes.* [N UNCOUNT : USU BEFORE N]

patent medicine, patent medicines. A **patent medicine** is **1** a medicine that is supposed to have secret ingredients which will suddenly cure you and make you healthy. Patent medicines are usually sold by people who have no medical knowledge and simply want to get your money. [N COUNT = cure-all] **2** a medicine or [N COUNT] drug that is produced and patented by one particular firm.

paterfamilias /peɪtəfəmɪlɪæs/, **paterfamiliases.** When you refer to a man as a **paterfamilias**, you are referring to him in his role as a father and head of a household; a formal word. EG *He was a natural paterfamilias.* [N COUNT : USU SING = patriarch]

paternal /pətɜːnəᵒl/ means **1** characteristic of the feelings or behaviour that a father shows towards his child. EG *...lack of proper paternal love... ...a paternal duty.* [ADJ CLASSIF : ATTRIB ⇑ parental = fatherly] ◊ **paternally.** EG *He smiled paternally at me as I passed.* [◊ ADV WITH VB] **2** related through or descended from a person's father rather than his or her mother. EG *...our paternal grandmother.* [ADJ CLASSIF : ATTRIB]

paternalism /pətɜːnəlɪzəᵒm/ is an attitude which is shown by a government or other authority that makes all the decisions for the people for whom it is responsible, thus taking away personal responsibility. EG *...a philosophy flavoured with paternalism.* [N UNCOUNT ⇑ policy] ◊ **paternalist.** EG *...a paternalist state.* [◊ ADJ QUALIT]

paternalistic /pətɜːnəlɪstɪk/. **Paternalistic** systems or beliefs reflect or are characteristic of paternalism. EG *...a paternalistic society... ...paternalistic attitudes.* [ADJ QUALIT]

paternity /pətɜːnɪtiˡ/ is the state or fact of being the father of a particular child. EG *He acknowledged his paternity of Pepita's three daughters.* [N UNCOUNT ⇑ parenthood]

paternity leave. If a man has **paternity leave,** his employer allows him some time off work because his child has just been born. [N UNCOUNT]

paternity suit, paternity suits. If a woman starts or takes out a **paternity suit**, she asks the help of a law court to establish that a particular man is the father of her child, often in order to claim financial support from him. [N COUNT = affiliation proceedings]

paternoster /pætənɒstə/, **paternosters. 1** A **paternoster** is a type of lift which consists of a chain of open compartments that move slowly in a loop up and down inside a building without stopping. [N COUNT]

2 The Lord's Prayer is sometimes called the **Paternoster**, especially by Catholics and especially when the prayer is said in Latin. [N SING : *the*+N, OR N COUNT]

path /pɑːθ/, **paths. 1** A **path** is **1.1** a long, thin line of ground that has been marked by people walking, for example through a forest or up a mountain. EG *The path was easy to follow, then it just stopped... He took her off up one of the long grassy paths far away from us.* [N COUNT ⇑ way = footpath, track] **1.2** a strip of ground, often covered with concrete or gravel, intended for people to walk on. Paths are often made in gardens, parks, or along the sides of roads. EG *His steps were slow as he went up the path to his front door.* [N COUNT ⇑ walkway = pathway]

2 Your **path** is the space ahead of you towards which you are moving or through which you intend to move. EG *On arrival he found his path barred... It moves forward killing anything in its path.* [N COUNT : USU POSS+N = way] ● If you **cross** someone's **path** or if your **paths cross**, you meet them by chance. EG *Our paths had crossed many years before.* [● PHR : VB INFLECTS]

3 The **path** of a particular person or thing is the line along which he, she, or it moves when going in a particular direction. EG *The bullet had scored its path across the skin of the fruit... ...the flight path of the 747 carried it directly overhead... ...far beyond the path of Saturn.* [N COUNT : WITH POSS = course]

4 A **path** is also a particular course of action or way of doing something. EG *I criticized the path the government was taking... ...the broad path of success... He saw public ownership as only one of many paths to achieving a socialist society.* [N COUNT = pathway]

pathetic /pəθetɪk/. If you describe someone or something as **pathetic**, **1** you mean that they are sad and weak, or helpless and ineffectual, and that they cause you to have feelings of pity and sadness. EG *It was pathetic to see a man to whom reading meant so much become almost totally blind... The kitten was so tiny and sweet and pathetic.* [ADJ QUALIT = pitiable] ◊ **pathetically.** EG *He looked pathetically defenceless.* [◊ ADV] **2** you mean that they are so bad or weak that they make you feel impatient or angry; used showing disapproval. EG *Our efforts so far have been really rather pathetic... It was all just a stupid pathetic joke.* [ADJ QUALIT = feeble]

pathfinder /pɑːθfaɪndə/, **pathfinders.** A **pathfinder** is someone whose job is to find routes across areas. [N COUNT ⇑ scout]

pathological /pæθəlɒdʒɪkəᵒl/. **1** If you describe a person or his or her behaviour as **pathological**, you [ADJ QUALIT = compulsive] mean that he or she behaves in an extreme way and cannot control himself or herself easily; used showing disapproval. EG *...a pathological liar... He has a pathological urge to succeed.*

2 Pathological also means relating to or concerned with pathology. EG *...pathological work.*
ADJ CLASSIF

pathologist /pəˈθɒlədʒɪst/, **pathologists**. A **pathologist** is someone who studies or investigates diseases and illnesses.
N COUNT ⇑ scientist

pathology /pəˈθɒlədʒiˈ/ is the branch of medicine that is concerned with the study of the way diseases and illnesses begin and develop.
N UNCOUNT

pathos /peɪθɒs/ is a quality in something such as a situation, film, or play that causes feelings of sadness and pity in people watching, hearing, or reading about it; a fairly formal word. EG *...the pathos of his situation... They have eyes full of sadness, loneliness and pathos.*
N UNCOUNT = poignancy

pathway /pɑːθweɪ/, **pathways**. A **pathway** is **1** a path along which you can walk or a route which you can take. EG *Marsha could make out a possible pathway through the wire... They walked along the pathway toward the house.* **2** a particular course of action or way of doing something. EG *We have to decide which alternative pathways to choose, which cultural styles to pursue... Complete passivity of mind and body were the pathway to pleasure.*
N COUNT; N COUNT = path

patience /peɪʃəns/. **1** If you have or show **patience**, **1.1** you are able to control your feelings so that you do not get annoyed, even in situations which other people would find annoying or frustrating. EG *It took a vast amount of patience not to shout at him... I've lost all patience with you and your excuses.* **1.2** you are able to wait calmly for something or to do something very difficult or uninteresting without complaining or giving up. EG *Paul was waiting his turn with patience... It's a great book if you only have the patience... We may not have the time or the patience to give much thought to this problem.*
N UNCOUNT ⇑ self-control = tolerance; N UNCOUNT ⇑ calmness

2 If you **try** someone's **patience**, you annoy them so much that it is very difficult for them to keep their temper. EG *I tried her patience to the limits.*
PHR : VB INFLECTS

3 Patience is also a card game for only one player. There are many different games of patience.
N UNCOUNT = solitaire

patient /peɪʃənt/, **patients**. **1** If you are **patient**, **1.1** you are able to control your feelings so that you do not get annoyed, even in situations which other people would find annoying or frustrating. EG *He was very patient with me... I'm a patient woman, you know that.* ▸ used of your behaviour. EG *The young cashier gave a patient sigh.* ◊ **patiently**. EG *He answered my questions patiently.* **1.2** you are able to wait calmly for something or to do something very difficult or uninteresting without complaining or giving up. EG *Just be patient... One moment sir. If you would be a little patient... ...an exact and patient scientist.* ◊ **patiently**. EG *James waited patiently for her to finish.*
ADJ QUALIT = forbearing, tolerance; ◊ ADV WITH VB; ADJ QUALIT ⇑ calm; ◊ ADV WITH VB

2 A **patient** is a person who is receiving medical treatment from a doctor or hospital, or who is registered with a particular doctor. EG *Next patient, please... How many patients does a practitioner normally have on his or her list?*
N COUNT

patina /pætɪnə/; a formal word. **1** The **patina** of an object is a fine layer of something that forms or appears on its surface. EG *The directories were piled high, with a patina of grey-brown grease.*
N SING+SUPP = coating

2 The **patina** of an antique or other old object is a soft shine that develops on its surface as it grows older. EG *...the patina of age.*
N SING+SUPP = sheen

patio /pætiəʊ/, **patios**. A **patio** is a paved area or area of concrete in a garden, close to a house, where people can sit in chairs. EG *She was sitting in a deck chair on the patio... ...elegant patio furniture.*
N COUNT ⇑ terrace

patio doors are glass doors that lead onto a patio.
N PLURAL

patisserie /pətiːsəriˈ/, **patisseries**. A **patisserie** is a shop where you can buy cakes and pastries.
N COUNT ⇑ bakery

patois. **Patois** is both the singular and the plural form. The singular form is pronounced /pætwɑː/ and the plural form is pronounced /pætwɑːz/. A **patois** is a form of a language that is spoken by the ordinary people in a particular area of a country. It has different pronunciations, words, and grammar from the other forms of the language. EG *Mouriere works methodically, chatting freely in patois.*
N COUNT/ UNCOUNT = dialect

patriarch /peɪtriˈɑːk/, **patriarchs**. A **patriarch** is **1** the male head of a family or tribe. EG *Each family of gorillas is led by a great silver-backed patriarch.* **2** the head of one of a number of Eastern Christian Churches. EG *...Pope Shenauda III, patriarch of the Coptic Church.*
N COUNT; N COUNT ⇑ bishop

patriarchal /peɪtriˈɑːkəˈl/. **1** A **patriarchal** society, family, or system is one in which men have all or most of the power and importance. EG *We live in a patriarchal society... Some men still try and recreate their traditional, patriarchal role.*
ADJ CLASSIF = male-dominated

2 A **patriarchal** man is quite old and looks impressive and powerful. EG *He was a large and splendidly patriarchal figure with piercing blue eyes and a white beard.*
ADJ QUALIT

patriarchy /peɪtriˈɑːkiˈ/, **patriarchies**. **1 Patriarchy** is a system in which men have all or most of the power and importance in a society or group. EG *...the dawn of 'civilisation' and patriarchy.*
N UNCOUNT

2 A **patriarchy** is a patriarchal society.
N COUNT

patrician /pətrɪʃəˈn/, **patricians**. **1** Someone who is **patrician** comes from a family of high social rank, or looks or behaves as if he or she does; a formal word. EG *...a patrician face... ...local magnates and patrician families.*
ADJ QUALIT = aristocratic

2 A **patrician** is a person who comes from a family of high social rank.
N COUNT = aristocrat

patricide /pætrɪsaɪd/, **patricides**. **1 Patricide** is the crime of killing your own father.
N UNCOUNT ⇑ murder

2 A **patricide** is someone who has killed their own father.
N COUNT ⇑ murderer

patrimony /pætrɪməniˈ/, **patrimonies**. Someone's **patrimony** is the possessions that they have inherited from their father or ancestors; a formal word.
N COUNT ⇑ inheritance

patriot /pætriət, peɪt-/, **patriots**. Someone who is a **patriot** loves their country and feels very loyal towards it. EG *I am a fervent patriot... ...Swiss patriots.*
N COUNT = nationalist

patriotic /pætriɒtɪk, peɪt-/. Someone who is **patriotic** loves their country and feels very loyal towards it. EG *...patriotic young men.* ▸ used of things and behaviour. EG *...a patriotic song... ...a tide of patriotic fervour.* ◊ **patriotically**. EG *Crowds cheered, patriotically waving flags and banners.*
ADJ QUALIT = nationalistic; ◊ ADV

patriotism /pætriətɪzəˈm, peɪt-/ is love for and loyalty towards your country. EG *Her patriotism would not permit her to buy a foreign car.*
N UNCOUNT

patrol /pətrəʊl/, **patrols, patrolling, patrolled**. **1** When soldiers, police, etc **patrol** a particular area or building, they move around the area or building, usually as part of a regular process, in order to make sure that there is no trouble or danger there. EG *The Marines went back to patrolling the hills... I saw women patrolling the streets with rifles on their backs... They still patrolled beyond the perimeter.*
V OR V+O ⇑ guard

2 When soldiers, police, etc are on **patrol**, they are patrolling a particular area. EG *Two policemen on patrol saw the thief running away... An entire platoon was ambushed during a patrol and wiped out... ...a patrol boat.*
N COUNT, OR *on*+N

3 A **patrol** is a group of soldiers, vehicles, ships, etc that are patrolling a particular area. EG *A battalion of Marines was sent to reinforce the patrols.*
N COUNT

patrol car, patrol cars. A **patrol car** is a police car with a radio telephone used for patrolling streets and motorways. EG *The police came in a black unmarked patrol car.*
N COUNT = squad car

patrolman /pətrəʊlməˈn/, **patrolmen**. A **patrolman** is, **1** in American English, a uniformed policeman who patrols a particular area. EG *One of the patrolmen shone his flashlight into Joe's face... ...Patrolman Len Hendricks.* **2** in British English, a person employed by a motorists' association who is based in a particular area and goes to help motorists when, for example, their cars break down.
N COUNT : ALSO IN TITLES; N COUNT

patron, patrons. The word **patron** is pronounced /peɪtrən/ for the meanings in paragraphs 1, 2, and 3 and /pætrɒn/ for the meaning in paragraph 4. A **patron** is **1** a person who supports and gives money to artists, writers, musicians, etc. EG *His portraits did not always please his patrons... ...a natural entrepreneur and patron of the arts.* **2** an important person who is interested in a particular charity, group, or campaign and who allows his or her name to be used for publicity purposes. EG *Our Chamber Music Society has the Lord Mayor as its patron.* **3** a person who uses a particular shop, hotel, etc, especially one who
N COUNT ⇑ supporter; N COUNT = sponsor; N COUNT = client

uses it frequently; a fairly formal use. EG *We had arguments which would have mystified the patrons in English pubs... Patrons are requested to wear neat attire.* 4 a person who runs a restaurant, bar, or hotel, especially in France. EG *We were effusively welcomed by the patron and his wife.* N COUNT ⇑ restaurateur

patronage /pætrənɪdʒ/. 1 **Patronage** is 1.1 the help and financial support given by someone to a person or a group such as a charity. EG *...public patronage of the arts... Dalton the physicist received lavish patronage in his formative years.* N UNCOUNT = backing 1.2 the power that a person has to make appointments to important jobs, give contracts for work, etc. EG *The power of the court aristocracy now lay in its power of patronage... Mr White has been able to protect his own patronage appointments.* N UNCOUNT 1.3 patronizing remarks or behaviour towards someone. EG *...the insolent and offensive patronage of her husband by the Prime Minister.* N UNCOUNT

2 If you give your **patronage** to a particular shop, hotel, etc, you become a customer and spend money there; a fairly formal use. EG *Her patronage of Felicity Fashions had consisted of the purchase of one dress.* N UNCOUNT

patronize /pætrənaɪz/, **patronizes, patronizing, patronized**; also spelled **patronise**. 1 If you **patronize** someone, you speak or behave towards them in a way which seems friendly, but which shows that you think that you are superior to them in some way; used showing disapproval. EG *She seemed to think that experience gave her the right to patronise... Don't patronize me!* V OR V+O

2 If you **patronize** a particular shop, hotel, etc, you use it frequently; a fairly formal use. EG *She tried to persuade people not to patronize the store until it agreed to hire black assistants.* V+O = frequent

3 Someone who **patronizes** artists, writers, musicians, etc supports them and gives them money. EG *Henry VII patronized a Flemish artist, Mabuse.* V+O = sponsor

patronizing /pætrənaɪzɪŋ/; also spelled **patronising**. Someone who is **patronizing** speaks or behaves towards you in a way which seems friendly, but which shows that they think that they are superior to you in some way; used showing disapproval. EG *He was rather patronizing when we lunched together.* ▸ used of behaviour, remarks, etc. EG *'It's quite a nice little story,' added Amy in a patronising tone... ...his patronizing arrogance.* ◊ **patronizingly**. EG *He was now smiling patronizingly.* ADJ QUALIT = condescending ▸ = condescending ◊ ADV WITH VB

patron saint, patron saints. The **patron saint** of a particular group of people, place, or thing is someone, usually a saint, who is believed to give them special protection. EG *...St Hubert, the patron saint of hunters... ...Peter Pan, the park's unofficial patron saint.* N COUNT : IF+ PREP THEN *of* ⇑ protector

patsy /pætsi¹/, **patsies**. If you refer to someone as a **patsy**, you mean that they are rather stupid and are easily cheated or badly treated by other people; used in informal American English. N COUNT

patter /pætə/, **patters, pattering, pattered**. 1 If something **patters** on a surface, it hits it quickly several times, making a series of quiet, tapping sounds. EG *Spots of rain pattered on the window... Dead leaves, blown on the wind, pattered against the walls.* V : USU+A = beat

2 When you **patter** somewhere, you walk quickly, making a series of tapping sounds with your feet. EG *I could hear him pattering along the corridor in his bare feet.* V+A = scurry

3 A **patter** is a quick series of quiet, tapping sounds. EG *They heard a quick patter of paws on matting as the dog came to meet them... They fell with a soft little patter, like raindrops on dry leaves.* N SING WITH DET

4 When you talk about **the patter of tiny feet**, you are referring to a baby that someone is going to have, or might be going to have; a humorous expression. EG *We might hear the patter of tiny feet all over again.* PHR : USED AS O

5 Someone's **patter** is a speech or talk that they have learned in advance and that they recite quickly in order to entertain or influence people. Comedians, conjurers, and salespeople often use patter. EG *I would mimic a sudden toothache to explain the breaks in my patter... He gave the usual patter about watertight boxes.* N UNCOUNT = spiel

pattern /pætə⁰n/, **patterns, patterning, patterned**. 1 A **pattern** is 1.1 a particular, recognizable way in which something is done or organized; used when this is the way in which it is usually done. EG *Over the next few months their work pattern changed... ...behaviour patterns... It fits in with the pattern of her family life... Their studies revealed a consistent pattern in the history of the country's economy... ...closed empires on the traditional Chinese pattern.* N COUNT 1.2 a particular physical form or arrangement. EG *What will be the shape and size and pattern of engines in the future?... ...a computer card with a particular pattern of holes in it.* N COUNT 1.3 a design made up of an arrangement of lines or shapes, especially one in which the same shape is repeated at regular intervals over a surface. EG *Jack was drawing a pattern in the sand with his forefinger... ...a frock with a pattern of little red apples... ...an artist with a very good sense of pattern... Old trees had fallen, forming a criss-cross pattern of trunks.* N COUNT/UNCOUNT

1.4 a diagram or shape that you can use as a guide when you are making something such as a model or a piece of clothing. EG *...sewing patterns.* N COUNT ⇑ guide

2 If something new **is patterned** on something else that already exists, it is deliberately made or created so that it has similar features to it. EG *The 'Daily Dispatch' was patterned on the British press.* V+O+A *(on)* : USU PASS = model

patterned /pætə⁰nd/. Something that is **patterned** is covered with a pattern or design. EG *...patterned carpets... ...ties patterned with flowers.* ADJ CLASSIF : IF+ PREP THEN *with* ⇑ decorated ≠ plain

patterning /pætə⁰nɪŋ/. 1 **Patterning** is the forming of fixed ways of behaving or doing things, by repetition or copying; a formal use. EG *...social patterning.* N UNCOUNT

2 Lines, spots, and other patterns, for example on the body of an animal, are referred to as **patterning**. N UNCOUNT = markings

patty /pæti¹/, **patties**. A **patty** is a small, round, meat pie; mainly used in American English. N COUNT

paucity /pɔːsɪti¹/. If you say that there is a **paucity** of something, you mean that there is an insufficient amount of it; a formal word. EG *There is a paucity of academic work on 'fringe' political groups... The very paucity of evidence tells a tale.* N SING WITH DET +*of* = dearth

paunch /pɔːntʃ/, **paunches**. If a man has a **paunch**, he has a fat stomach. EG *His tunic bulged over a premature paunch.* N COUNT = pot belly

paunchy /pɔːntʃi¹/, **paunchier, paunchiest**. Someone who is **paunchy** has a fat stomach. ADJ QUALIT

pauper /pɔːpə/, **paupers**. A **pauper** is a very poor person; a rather old-fashioned word. EG *Jefferson died a pauper... Let's face it, none of the boys are paupers.* N COUNT

pauperism /pɔːpərɪzə⁰m/ is the state of being very poor; an old-fashioned word. N UNCOUNT = poverty

pauperize /pɔːpəraɪz/, **pauperizes, pauperizing, pauperize**; also spelled **pauperise**. If something **pauperizes** a group of people, it causes them to become very poor. EG *Smallholders are being pauperized and turned into landless labourers... This imperialism pauperized an entire nation.* V+O = beggar

pause /pɔːz/, **pauses, pausing, paused**. 1 If you **pause** while you are speaking, you stop speaking for a short time, for example in order to think before you continue. EG *'Damn it, Martin!' he shouted, then paused for a moment, struggling to calm himself... He paused and then went on in a low voice.* V = break off

2 If you **pause** while you are moving or doing something, you stop for a moment. EG *He paused with a hand on the doorknob... He does not pause for breath until he reaches the top floor... He can do this without looking up and without pausing in his work.* V

3 If you **pause** before doing something, you wait for a moment before doing it, for example in order to think about what you are intending to do. EG *I cabled it without pausing to consider what the consequences might be... 'What is it?' asked Mrs Bixby. 'Try to guess.' Mrs Bixby paused. Be careful, she told herself.* V

4 A **pause** is 4.1 a moment of silence that occurs when a sound, for example speech or music, stops before beginning again. EG *'I'm leaving you,' she said. There was a long pause. Then he said, 'I suppose I can't stop you.'... She continued after a pause... My signal will be three knocks, a pause, then two more.* N COUNT = gap 4.2 a short period when you stop doing what you are doing, for example to have a rest, before continuing again. EG *He went on for 35 minutes without a pause... The insect moves slowly and laboriously, with frequent pauses to gather strength.* N COUNT = break 4.3 in music, a moment when a note or a short silence is made to N COUNT

last slightly longer than such a note or silence usually does, in order to give a special effect.

5 If something **gives** you **pause**, it makes you hesitate and think carefully about the situation before doing what you had been intending to do; a formal use. EG *The gale raging outside was sufficient to give pause to even the most courageous climber.* PHR : VB INFLECTS

pave /peɪv/, **paves, paving, paved.** 1 When a road or an area of ground **is paved** or **is paved over**, it is covered with blocks of stone, bricks, concrete, etc so that it is suitable for walking or travelling on. EG *The Strand end of the road was not paved until 1532.* ◊ **paved.** EG *...a steep causeway paved with slabs of granite... A dirt road led from the paved main road to a small village.* V+O, OR PHRASAL VB : V+O+ADV : USU PASS ◊ ADJ CLASSIF : IF+PREP THEN *with/in*

2 If one thing **paves the way** for another, it creates a situation in which the other thing is more likely to happen or can happen more easily. EG *His work paved the way for Denis Burkitt's theories.* PHR : VB INFLECTS, USU+*for*

3 If you say that the streets of a particular city are **paved with gold**, you mean that it is easy to become rich there. PHR : USED AS C

4 See also **paving**.

pavement /peɪvmə²nt/, **pavements.** A **pavement** is 1 in British English a path with a hard surface by the side of a street. EG *He was standing on the pavement outside the bank... Shoppers hurry along the pavements.* 2 a paved area or surface. EG *...a fountain surrounded by a stone pavement.* 3 in American English, the surface of a roadway. N COUNT = sidewalk; N COUNT/UNCOUNT

pavement artist, pavement artists. A **pavement artist** is a person who draws pictures on the pavement with coloured chalks and who is given small amounts of money by people who walk past. N COUNT

pavilion /pəvɪljən/, **pavilions.** A **pavilion** is 1 a building on the edge of a sports ground, especially a cricket field, where players can change their clothes and wash; used in British English. EG *...a cricket pavilion.* 2 a temporary structure, especially a large tent, which is used at an outdoor public event, for example an exhibition. EG *They're looking round the Russian pavilion.* 3 an ornamental building in a park or country estate. N COUNT; N COUNT; N COUNT

paving /peɪvɪŋ/ is a paved area or surface. EG *...a little rectangle of brick paving... His suede shoes slap lightly on the paving.* ● See also **crazy paving**. N UNCOUNT

paving stone, paving stones; also spelled with a hyphen. A **paving stone** is a flat piece of stone, usually rectangular or square in shape, that is used for making pavements. EG *Blades of grass poked up between the paving stones.* N COUNT : USU PL = flagstone

paw /pɔ:/, **paws, pawing, pawed.** 1 The **paw** of an animal such as a cat, dog, or bear is its foot, which has claws for gripping things and soft pads for walking and running. EG *...a black cat with white paws.* N COUNT

2 When an animal **paws** something or **paws** at it, it draws its paw, hoof, etc over that thing or hits at it. Some animals, for example horses and bulls, paw the ground when they are angry. EG *The horse snorts and paws the ground... The dog pawed at the doorknob again and again.* V+O, OR V+A *(at)*

3 Someone's **paw** is their hand; used in informal English. EG *She placed her little hand on my clumsy paw.* N COUNT = mitt

4 If you **paw** someone, you touch or stroke them in a manner that offends them, especially in a sexual manner. EG *I didn't like being pawed.* V+O = grope

pawn /pɔ:n/, **pawns, pawning, pawned.** 1 If you **pawn** something that you own, you leave it with a pawnbroker, who gives you money for it and who has the right to sell it if you do not pay back the money within a particular period of time. EG *Brian didn't have a watch–he had pawned it some years ago.* V+O = hock

2 A **pawn** is the smallest and least valuable playing piece in chess. Each player has eight pawns at the start of the game. N COUNT

3 If you refer to someone as a **pawn**, you mean that they are being used by someone else and do not realize it or cannot prevent it. EG *They are simply pawns in the hands of larger powers.* N COUNT : USU USED AS C = puppet

pawnbroker /pɔ:nbrəʊkə/, **pawnbrokers.** A **pawnbroker** is a person who will lend you money if you give them a possession of yours. When you repay the money, the pawnbroker gives you back your possession, but if you do not repay the money within a particular period of time, the pawnbroker can sell it. ▸ The **pawnbroker** or the **pawnbroker's** is used to refer to a pawnbroker's shop. N COUNT

pawn shop, pawn shops. A **pawn shop** is a pawnbroker's shop. N COUNT

pawpaw /pɔ: pɔ:/, **pawpaws.** A **pawpaw** is a fruit with green skin, sweet yellow flesh, and black seeds that grows in the West Indies. N COUNT = papaya

pax /pæks/. Children say **pax** to indicate that they want to end a fight or argument that they are involved in. They sometimes cross their fingers at the same time. CONVENTION

pay /peɪ/, **pays, paying, paid.** 1 When you **pay** an amount of money to someone, you give them the money because you are buying something from them or because you owe it to them. When you **pay** a bill, debt, fare, etc, you pay the amount that is owed or required. EG *He had paid £5,000 for the boat... Willie paid for the drinks... I'll pay by cheque... I've left you some money to pay the window cleaner... After all, we pay our taxes... ...the interest you pay on your mortgage... He paid his bill and left.* ● to **pay through the nose**: see **nose**. V, V+O, V+A, V+O+O, OR V+O+A

2 When your employers **pay** you, they give you your wages or salary. EG *She was being paid sixty dollars a week... You're not paid to ask questions... We refused to pay them their wages... The company pays well.* V+O, V+A, V+O+O, OR V+O+A

3 The **pay** that someone receives is the money that they receive as their wages or salary. EG *The pay is dreadful... She lost three weeks' pay... ...a pay rise of £20 a week.* ● See also **back pay**. N UNCOUNT ⇑ earnings

4 If a job, deal, investment etc **pays** a particular amount, it brings you that amount of money. EG *She complained about her husband's job and how poorly it paid... It's not a hard job when a day's work pays £2,500.* V+O, OR V+A

5 If a business, deal, etc **pays**, it brings you a profit. EG *You've got to be able to make your business pay.* V

6 If something that you buy eventually **pays** for itself, it is so efficient that over a period of time you save as much money as you bought it for, because it results in you having to spend less than you would have done otherwise. EG *Loft insulation should pay for itself within two years.* V+A *(for)*

7 If a particular course of action **pays**, it results in some advantage or benefit for you. EG *It pays to keep on the right side of your boss... Crime doesn't pay.* V OR V+*to*-INF/*for* = be worthwhile

8 If you **pay** for something, you suffer as a consequence of doing or having it, or have to give up something in order to have it. EG *He paid dearly for his mistake... You failed, and you must pay the penalty... The women paid with their lives... This is a small price to pay for independence.* V : USU+A, OR V+O

9 You also use **pay** with some nouns, for example in the expressions 'to pay a visit' and 'to pay attention', to indicate that something is given or done. EG *It would be nice if you paid me a visit sometime... I paid very little attention to what I heard... His tearful family came to pay their last respects... It was probably the greatest compliment I could have paid her.* V+, OR V+O+O

10 If you say that someone **is in the pay of** a person or group that you regard as your enemy, you mean that they are being paid by that person or group to work on their behalf, often secretly. PHR : VB INFLECTS

11 If you **pay** your **way**, you pay for things that you use or get rather than making or letting other people pay for them. PHR : VB INFLECTS

12 See also **paid**.

pay back. 1 If you **pay back** an amount of money that you have borrowed from someone, you return the money to them. EG *If I take out a loan, it could take me years to pay it back... I'll pay you back next week.* PHRASAL VB : V+O+ADV = repay

2 If you **pay** someone **back** for doing something unpleasant to you, you make them suffer for what they did. PHRASAL VB : V+O+ADV ⇑ punish

pay into. When you **pay** money **into** a bank account or **pay** it **in**, you put it into the account or transfer it there. PHRASAL VB : V+O+PREP/ADV

pay off. 1 If you **pay off** a debt, bill, etc, you give someone the amount of money that you owe them. PHRASAL VB : V+O+ADV

2 If you **pay** someone **off**, 2.1 you give them money so that they do not cause you trouble. EG *They'll just keep coming back until you pay them off.* 2.2 you give them the wages that you owe them and dismiss them from their job. PHRASAL VB : V+O+ADV; PHRASAL VB : V+O+ADV

3 If an action **pays off**, it is successful; used when it was quite likely that it would fail. EG *It was a risk and it paid off.* PHRASAL VB : V+ADV = succeed

4 See also **payoff**.

pay out. **1** If you **pay out** money, especially a large amount of money, you spend it on a particular thing or activity. EG *He had paid out good money to educate Julie at a boarding school.* PHRASAL VB : V+O+ADV

2 When you **pay out** a rope or cable, you unwind it in a controlled way. PHRASAL VB : V+O+ADV

pay up. If you **pay up**, you give someone the money that you owe them, even though you would prefer not to. EG *Come on, pay up.* PHRASAL VB : V+ADV

payable /peɪəbəl/. **1** If an amount of money is **payable**, it has to be paid or can be paid. EG *The annual interest payable on these loans was vast... A tax refund may be payable if the dead person was paying tax.* ADJ CLASSIF : PRED = due

2 If a cheque is made **payable** to a particular person or company, it has their name written on it to indicate that they are the person to whom the money should be paid. EG *Cheques should be made payable to Trans Euro Travel Ltd.* ADJ CLASSIF : PRED+*to*

pay-bed, pay-beds. A **pay-bed** is a bed in a free hospital that is used by a patient who is paying for treatment. N COUNT

pay-day; also spelled without a hyphen. **Pay-day** is the day on which a worker is paid his or her salary or wages. EG *Can you lend me £5 till pay-day?* N UNCOUNT

PAYE /piː eɪ waɪ iː/ is a system of paying income tax in which your employer pays your tax directly to the government, and then subtracts this amount from your salary or wages; an abbreviation for 'pay as you earn'. N UNCOUNT

payee /peɪiː/, **payees**. The **payee** of a cheque, banker's order, etc is the person who is to be given the money; a technical word. N COUNT ⇑ recipient

payer /peɪə/, **payers**. Someone who is a good **payer** always pays bills or debts quickly. Someone who is a bad **payer** pays bills or debts late, or not at all. • See also **taxpayer, ratepayer**. N COUNT : ADJ+N

paying guest, paying guests. A **paying guest** is a person who pays to stay with someone in their home, usually for a short period of time. N COUNT

paying-in book, paying-in books. A **paying-in book** is a book of paying-in slips. N COUNT

paying-in slip, paying-in slips. A **paying-in slip** is a form that you fill in when you pay cash or cheques into a bank account. N COUNT

payload /peɪləʊd/, **payloads**. **1** The **payload** of an aircraft or other form of transport is the amount of things or people that it can carry. EG *It was to be the first supersonic airliner that would fly with a commercial payload.* N COUNT/UNCOUNT ⇑ load

2 The **payload** of a missile is the quantity of explosives it contains. N COUNT ⇑ charge

paymaster /peɪmɑːstə/, **paymasters**. A **paymaster** is a person or organization that pays for an activity or project to be carried out, and that therefore has some control over it. N COUNT

payment /peɪməᵊnt/, **payments**. **1 Payment** is the act of paying money or of being paid. EG *Was the payment of rent to be optional?... When can I expect payment?* N UNCOUNT

2 A **payment** is an amount of money that is paid to someone, especially as one of a series, or an act of paying money to them. EG *...the government's commitment to making a weekly cash payment to mothers... Some said that social security payments were too high... He was unable to keep up the payments on his car.* • See also **balance of payments**. N COUNT

payoff /peɪɒf/, **payoffs**; also spelled with a hyphen. A **payoff** is **1** a result of a particular action, usually a good or desirable one. EG *Some carry out research without daring to hope that there could be a practical pay-off... One of the immediate payoffs was an increase in productivity.* N COUNT = reward **2** a payment made to someone so that they do not cause trouble for you, or when you have dismissed them. EG *It was usually possible to make a payoff to a high police official to keep quiet.* N COUNT ⇑ bribe

pay packet, pay packets; also spelled with a hyphen. Your **pay packet** is the envelope containing your wages, which you are given at the end of every week; used in British English. EG *...pieces of torn pay packets outside the factory gates.* ▸ used to refer to someone's wages or salary. EG *They assume that people work simply for money, for the pay-packet at the end of the week.* N COUNT ▸ ⇑ earnings

pay phone, pay phones; also spelled with a hyphen. A **pay phone** is a coin-operated telephone, usually in a public place such as a restaurant, theatre, etc. N COUNT

payroll /peɪrəʊl/, **payrolls**. If you are on an organization's **payroll**, you are employed by and paid by that organization. EG *She was no longer on their payroll... That year British Aluminium added about 1,000 workers to its UK payroll.* N COUNT ⇑ staff

payslip /peɪslɪp/, **payslips**. A **payslip** is a piece of paper given to an employee at the end of each week or month, which states how much money he or she has earned and how much tax, national insurance, etc, has been deducted. N COUNT ⇑ record

PC, PCs. A **PC** is a police constable; used especially as the title of a male police constable. EG *...PC Cooper.* N IN TITLES

pcm is a written abbreviation for 'per calendar month'; used especially in advertisements for flats when indicating how much the rent will be. EG *...£130 pcm.*

pd is a written abbreviation for 'paid'. It is written on a bill to indicate that it has been paid.

Pde is a written abbreviation for 'Parade'; used on maps and when writing addresses. EG *...North Pde, Summerton.*

PE /piː iː/ is a lesson in which schoolchildren do physical exercises or take part in physical games or sports; an abbreviation for 'physical education'. EG *We had two lessons of PE a week.* N UNCOUNT = PT

pea /piː/, **peas**. **1 Peas** are round green seeds which grow in pods and are eaten as a vegetable. EG *...chicken, mashed potatoes, and peas... ...a packet of frozen peas... ...pea soup.* N COUNT : USU PL

2 A **pea** is a climbing plant with small white flowers and green pods that contain peas. N COUNT

3 If you say that two people or things are **like two peas in a pod**, you mean that they are exactly alike. PHR : USED AS AN A

peace /piːs/. **1** If you have **peace**, you are not being disturbed, and you are in calm, quiet surroundings. EG *I shall need some peace and quiet in which to practise... Go away and leave us in peace... He chose to return to the relative peace of his childhood village... He gave her no peace until she agreed.* N UNCOUNT ⇑ calmness

2 If you have a feeling of **peace** or are at **peace**, you feel contented and calm and not at all worried. EG *...the search for this elusive inner peace... If only for your own peace of mind you should find out what really happened... ...a child of grace and happiness, at peace with her surroundings.* N UNCOUNT

3 When a country has **peace** or is at **peace**, it is not involved in a war. EG *Their activities threaten world peace... ...peace negotiations... ...in times of peace... ...a lasting peace... ...one day when the world is at peace.* N UNCOUNT

4 A **peace** is an agreement that ends a war between two or more countries. EG *...an honourable peace... ...a negotiated peace in Europe.* N SING WITH DET

5 Peace also means relating to campaigns for disarmament, especially nuclear disarmament. EG *...the European Peace Movement.* N BEFORE N

6 If there is **peace** among a group of people or if they live at **peace** with each other, they live or work together in a friendly way and do not quarrel or fight. EG *She had done it for the sake of peace in the family... The government place the peace and good order of society at the head of their list of priorities.* N UNCOUNT ⇑ unity = harmony

7 If someone disturbs or breaks the **peace**, they behave in a noisy or violent way that causes trouble and disorder; a technical term in law. EG *The youths were littering the beaches and disturbing the peace.* • See also **breach of the peace**. • **Justice of the Peace**: see **JP**. N SING : *the*+N ⇑ order

8 If you say that someone **is at peace**, you mean that they are dead, and that perhaps they are no longer unhappy. PHR : VB INFLECTS

9 If you **hold your peace** or **keep your peace**, you do not speak, even though there might be something you want to say. EG *He told her to concentrate upon what she was doing and hold her peace.* PHR : VB INFLECTS = keep quiet

10 If a person or group of people comes **in peace**, they come as friends and have no intention of fighting with the people they are approaching. PHR : USED AS A

11 If you **keep the peace**, **11.1** you prevent people from arguing violently or fighting with each other. EG PHR : VB INFLECTS

I looked on as an arbiter and kept the peace. **11.2** you make sure that people are behaving in a peaceful and lawful way; a technical use. EG *The police are there to enforce the law and to keep the peace.* PHR : VB INFLECTS **11.3** you behave in a lawful way and do not cause any trouble; a technical use. EG *He was found guilty of assault and bound over to keep the peace.* PHR : VB INFLECTS

12 If you **make peace** with someone or **make** your **peace** with them, you put an end to your quarrel with them, especially by apologizing. EG *She went to her mother's room to make peace... He was obliged to make his peace with the salesman.* PHR : VB INFLECTS, IF + PREP THEN *with* ⇑ apologize

13 When they are referring to someone who is dead, some people say **may** they **rest in peace** in order to show respect for the dead person and to express the hope that their spirit is untroubled. EG *His mother, may she rest in peace, brought up sixteen children.* ▸ **Rest in Peace** is also sometimes written on gravestones. PHR

peaceable /pi:səbə⁰l/. **1** Someone who is **peaceable** tries to avoid quarrelling or fighting with other people. EG *...peaceable citizens.* ADJ QUALIT = peace-loving

2 Something that is **peaceable** is free from violence or disorder. EG *It advocates peaceable, non-violent methods.* ADJ CLASSIF = peaceful ◊ **peaceably**. EG *The constitution gives people the right 'peaceably to assemble'.* ◊ ADV WITH VB = peacefully

Peace Corps. The **Peace Corps** is an American organization that sends young people as volunteers to help with projects in developing countries. N SING : *the*+N

peaceful /pi:sfʊl/. **1** A **peaceful** place or time is quiet and calm and free from disturbance. EG *It's so nice and peaceful here... ...peaceful parks and gardens... It was going to be a far from peaceful Christmas.* ADJ QUALIT = tranquil ◊ **peacefully**. EG *They lived there peacefully, happily.* ◊ ADV WITH VB

2 Someone who feels or looks **peaceful** is free from worry or anxiety. EG *He looked curiously peaceful as he lay there.* ▸ used of things. EG *...peaceful memories.* ADJ QUALIT = serene, untroubled ◊ **peacefully**. EG *That night he slept peacefully.* ◊ ADV WITH VB

3 Something that is **peaceful** **3.1** is free from trouble or violence. EG *...peaceful demonstrations in Bonn.* ADJ QUALIT ≠ violent ◊ **peacefully**. EG *They decided that they would protest peacefully.* ◊ ADV WITH VB **3.2** does not involve war. EG *The country has achieved a peaceful parliamentary transition to independence... ...the first international conference on The Peaceful Uses of Atomic Energy.* ADJ QUALIT ◊ **peacefully**. ◊ ADV WITH VB

4 Peaceful people try to avoid quarrelling or fighting with other people. EG *...the most peaceful nation on earth.* ADJ QUALIT ◊ **peacefully**. ◊ ADV WITH VB

peace-keeping; also spelled as one word. A **peace-keeping** force is an armed force that is sent to a country where there is war or fighting, in order to try to prevent more violence. Peace-keeping forces are usually made up of troops from several different countries. ADJ CLASSIF : USU ATTRIB

peace-loving people try to avoid quarrelling or fighting with other people. ADJ QUALIT = peaceable

peacemaker /pi:smeɪkə/, **peacemakers**; also spelled with a hyphen. A **peacemaker** is a person who tries to stop people or countries from quarrelling or fighting by talking with the people concerned. N COUNT ⇑ mediator

peace offering, peace offerings; also spelled with a hyphen. A **peace offering** is something that is given or said to someone as a kind of apology to end a quarrel. EG *I bought Mum some flowers as a peace offering.* N COUNT

peacetime /pi:staɪm/; also spelled with a hyphen. **Peacetime** is a period of time during which a country is not at war. EG *...the party which had freed the nation from military conscription in peacetime... ...peacetime exercises and training.* N UNCOUNT

peach /pi:tʃ/, **peaches**. **1** A **peach** is a round, juicy fruit with sweet yellow flesh and slightly furry, yellow and red skin. Peaches grow in warm countries. EG *...tinned peaches... She was twenty-eight and had skin like a peach.* N COUNT

2 Something that is **peach** is pale pinky-orange in colour. EG *...soft peach chiffon.* ▸ used as a noun. ADJ COLOUR ▸ N UNCOUNT

3 If you describe someone or something as a **peach**, you mean that you think they are very pleasing or good; used in informal English. EG *That was a peach of a shot!* N SING : *a*+N = beauty

peach melba /pi:tʃ mɛlbə/, **peach melbas**. **peach melba** is a dessert made from peaches, ice cream, and raspberry sauce. N UNCOUNT/COUNT

peacock /pi:kɒk/, **peacocks**. **1** A **peacock** is a large bird of the pheasant family. The male has a very large tail which it can spread out like a fan and which is marked with beautiful blue and green spots. EG *Peacocks strutted on the lawn... ...peacock feathers.* N COUNT

2 If you describe someone, especially a man, as a **peacock**, you mean that they are rather proud of themselves and like wearing attractive clothes and looking good; used showing disapproval. N COUNT = dandy

3 Something that is **peacock** or **peacock blue** is deep greenish-blue in colour. EG *...a peacock corduroy jacket.* ▸ used as a noun. ADJ COLOUR ▸ N UNCOUNT

pea-green. Something that is **pea-green** is bright green in colour, like the colour of peas. ADJ COLOUR

peahen /pi:hɛn/, **peahens**. A **peahen** is a female peacock. N COUNT ⇑ bird

peak /pi:k/, **peaks, peaking, peaked**. **1** The **peak** of a process of development or of an activity is the point or stage at which it is at its strongest, most fully developed, most successful, etc. EG *They were trained to a peak of physical fitness... Computer technology has not yet reached its peak... He's going to be at his peak in a couple of years... Membership was already near its peak.* N COUNT : USU SING

2 When something or someone **peaks**, they reach the highest value or the highest level of success. EG *The annual workload no longer peaks at harvest time.* V

3 The **peak** level or value of something is its highest level or value. EG *...the peak voltage... The average span between introduction and peak production was thirty-four years.* ADJ CLASSIF : ATTRIB = maximum

4 Peak times are the times when there is most demand to buy a product or use a service. EG *...hotels are obviously more expensive in peak season... ...the peak demand for electricity.* ADJ CLASSIF : ATTRIB ⇑ busy

5 The **peak** of a mountain is the pointed top of it. ▸ also used of the mountain itself. EG *It is one of the highest peaks in the Alps.* N COUNT ⇑ summit

6 The **peak** of a cap is the part at the front that sticks out above your eyes. EG *He wore a brown cloth cap with the peak pulled down low over his eyes.* N COUNT

peaked /pi:kt/. **1** A **peaked** cap is one that has a pointed or rounded part that sticks out over your eyes. ADJ CLASSIF

2 If someone looks **peaked**, they look pale and rather ill. EG *Ever since then he had been peaked, red-eyed, and miserable.* ADJ QUALIT ⇑ unwell

peaky /pi:ki¹/, **peakier, peakiest**. If someone looks **peaky**, they look pale and rather ill; an informal word. ADJ QUALIT

peal /pi:l/, **peals, pealing, pealed**. **1** When bells **peal**, they ring one after the other, making a musical sound. ▸ used as a noun. EG *...a peal of bells.* V+O = chime ▸ N COUNT

2 A **peal** of sound, especially of laughter or thunder, consists of a long, loud series of notes. EG *...bursting into peals of laughter... The first clear peals from the trumpets sounded... ...a peal of thunder.* N COUNT+SUPP

peanut /pi:nʌt/, **peanuts**. **1 Peanuts** are small hard oval seeds that grow under the ground. Peanuts are often eaten as a snack, especially roasted and salted. EG *Two bags of salted peanuts... ...peanut oil.* N COUNT = groundnut

2 If you refer to an amount of money as **peanuts**, you mean that it is a very small amount indeed; an informal expression. EG *But this was peanuts compared to the wealth that my father amassed.* N PLURAL : USED AS C = nothing

peanut butter is a brown paste made out of crushed peanuts, which you can spread on bread and eat. EG *...peanut butter sandwiches.* N UNCOUNT

pear /pɛə/, **pears**. A **pear** is a sweet, juicy fruit which is narrow near its stalk, and wider and rounded at the bottom. Pears have white flesh and thin green or yellow skin, and grow on trees. ▸ used of the tree on which a pear grows. EG *...a long garden full of pear and apple trees.* N COUNT/UNCOUNT ▸ N BEFORE N

pearl /pɜ:l/, **pearls**. **1** A **pearl** is a hard, round, object which is creamy white in colour with a pale, silvery shine. Pearls grow inside the shell of an oyster and are used for making valuable jewellery. EG *She was wearing a single string of pearls... ...small pearl buttons.* ● See also **cultured pearl**, **mother-of-pearl**. N COUNT/UNCOUNT ⇑ jewel

2 If you refer to something or someone as a **pearl**, you mean that they are especially good or beautiful. N COUNT = jewel

3 If you say that someone **is casting pearls before swine**, you mean that they are wasting their time by offering something that is very helpful or valuable to PHR : VB INFLECTS someone who does not appreciate or understand it. EG *I don't know why I bother to talk to you, I'm just casting pearls before swine!*

pearl barley is small grains of barley which have been ground smooth. Pearl barley is used especially in making soups. N UNCOUNT

pearl-grey. Something that is **pearl-grey** is a pale bluish grey colour. ADJ COLOUR

pearly /pɜːli¹/. Something that is **pearly** has the appearance of pearls; used showing approval. EG *...pearly teeth... ...pearly pink light.* ADJ CLASSIF

peasant /pezə⁰nt/, **peasants**. 1 A **peasant** is an agricultural worker, especially one who works on a small piece of land in a poor country and who is considered to be of low social status. EG *The party's appeal is strongest among workers and peasants... Thibon was himself of peasant origin.* N COUNT

2 **Peasant** clothes or customs are considered to be typical of the way of life or behaviour of a peasant. EG *...velvet and lace and fashionable peasant embroidery... ...a peasant skirt... ...peasant life.* ADJ CLASSIF : ATTRIB = rustic

3 If you refer to someone as a **peasant**, you are saying that they are rude or ignorant; an informal and offensive use. EG *He's a real peasant... Richard Strauss, not Johann Strauss, you peasant!* N COUNT : ALSO VOC

peasantry /pezə⁰ntri¹/. The **peasantry** is all the peasants in a particular country. EG *The new middle classes were no friends of the peasantry... ...backward countries where the peasantry are the revolutionary class... The peasantry has shrunk from 74.6 millions to 65.5.* N SING WITH DET : VB CAN BE SING OR PL

pease pudding /piːz pʊdɪŋ/ is a dish of dried peas that have been soaked and boiled until they are soft; used in old-fashioned British English. N UNCOUNT = mushy peas

peashooter /piːʃuːtə/, **peashooters**; also spelled with a hyphen. A **peashooter** is a tube used by children as a weapon for blowing small objects such as dried peas at people. N COUNT ⇑ toy

pea-souper /piː suːpə/, **pea-soupers**; also spelled as one word. A **pea-souper** or a **pea-soup** fog is a very thick, dirty fog; used in informal British English. N COUNT

peat /piːt/. **Peat** is black or brown decaying plant material which is found under the ground in cool, wet, moorland regions. Peat can be added to soil or compost, or burnt on fires instead of coal. EG *...the smoke of burning peat, rising from cottage hearths... ...a peat bog.* N UNCOUNT

peaty /piːti¹/, **peatier, peatiest**. **Peaty** soil or land contains a large quantity of peat. ADJ QUALIT

pebble /pebə⁰l/, **pebbles**. A **pebble** is a smooth, rounded stone which is found on seashores and river beds. EG *He picked up a large shiny pebble on the beach... ...river pebbles.* N COUNT

pebbledash /pebə⁰ldæʃ/ is a covering for the outside walls of a house which is made of small stones set in plaster; used in British English. N UNCOUNT : USU BEFORE N

pebbly /pebli¹/, **pebblier, pebbliest**. A **pebbly** beach or river bed is covered in pebbles. EG *I prefer sandy beaches to pebbly ones.* ADJ QUALIT ⇑ stony

pecan /pɪkæn, piːkən/, **pecans**. A **pecan** is a nut with a thin, smooth shell that grows on trees in the southern United States and that can be eaten. N COUNT

peccadillo /pekədɪləʊ/, **peccadillos** or **peccadilloes**. A **peccadillo** is a small, unimportant sin or fault; a rather old-fashioned word. N COUNT = misdemeanour

peck /pek/, **pecks, pecking, pecked**. 1 When a bird **pecks** or **pecks** something, it bites at something with a sudden forward movement of its beak. EG *...a plump brown hen, pecking around for stray grains of corn... A pigeon pecked at the chipping putty... She chided the birds for pecking her fingers... Larger birds may come and peck holes in their eggs.* ▸ used as a noun. EG *When she tried to touch the eggs, it gave her a peck.* V : USU+A, OR V+O = nibble, poke ▸ N COUNT ⇑ bite

2 If you **peck** someone on the cheek, you give them a quick, light kiss. EG *She pecked his cheek... Howard laughs and pecks Flora on the cheek.* ▸ used as a noun. EG *She gave him a quick peck on the cheek.* V+O : USU+A ▸ N COUNT

3 If you **peck** at your food, you eat only small amounts of it, especially because you are ill or not hungry, or because you don't like the food; an informal use. V+A *(at)* = pick

pecker /pekə/, **peckers**. If you tell someone to **keep** their **pecker up**, you are encouraging them to be cheerful in a difficult situation; an informal expression. PHR : VB INFLECTS

pecking order, pecking orders. The **pecking order** in a group is the order of seniority or power within the group. EG *He didn't like being at the bottom of the pecking order.* N COUNT : USU the+N IN SING ⇑ hierarchy

peckish /pekɪʃ/. If you are **peckish**, you are slightly hungry; used in informal British English. EG *'I expect you're feeling rather peckish.'* ADJ QUALIT : USU PRED

pectin /pektɪn/ is a substance that is found in ripe fruit. It is used in the manufacture of jam to help it set. N UNCOUNT

pectoral /pektə⁰rəl/, **pectorals**. 1 The **pectorals** are the large chest muscles that help you to move your shoulders and your arms. EG *...strong women with bulging pectorals.* N COUNT : USU PL

2 A **pectoral** is also a pectoral fin. N COUNT : USU PL

pectoral fin, pectoral fins. The **pectoral fin** of a fish is a fin that is just behind its head and that helps it to control the direction in which it moves. N COUNT : USU PL

peculiar /pɪ²kjuːlɪə/. 1 If you describe someone or something as **peculiar**, you mean that they are strange, often in an unpleasant way. EG *That lemon is a very peculiar shape indeed... The girl was wearing a very peculiar trouser suit... Once or twice she acted in a very peculiar manner... She gave him a peculiar look.* • **funny peculiar**: see **funny**. ADJ QUALIT = bizarre, odd

2 If you say that you feel **peculiar**, you mean that you feel slightly ill, dizzy, or sick. EG *Seeing blood makes me feel a bit peculiar inside.* ADJ QUALIT : PRED = queasy

3 If something is **peculiar** or if it is **peculiar** to a particular thing or person, it is unique or only found in particular circumstances. EG *There is a peculiar bond of sympathy and understanding between them... She really was a bit sorry for me in her own peculiar way... ...the style of decoration peculiar to the late 1920s and early 1930s... Some of this change is not peculiar to London but is national.* ADJ CLASSIF : USU +to ⇑ special

peculiarity /pɪ²kjuːlɪærɪti¹/, **peculiarities**. 1 A **peculiarity** is 1.1 a strange or unusual habit or characteristic. EG *It was one of Boylan's peculiarities that he wanted to humiliate her.* 1.2 a thing or quality which is unique, and only relates or belongs to one particular place or person. EG *Is this prudery a British peculiarity?... Each city has its own peculiarities, its own history and character.* N COUNT : USU WITH POSS N COUNT : USU WITH POSS = characteristic

2 **Peculiarity** is the quality of being strange, often in an unpleasant way. EG *...his feeling of solitude, of peculiarity... ...the peculiarity of the Colonial situation.* N UNCOUNT/COUNT

peculiarly /pɪ²kjuːlɪəli¹/. 1 If someone behaves or does something **peculiarly**, they act in a very strange way. EG *Molly is behaving rather peculiarly... Sylvia looked at me peculiarly.* ADV = oddly

2 You also use **peculiarly** to emphasize that someone or something has a special or unique quality. EG *It's an idiom that people can recognise as peculiarly English... He was prone to outbursts of a peculiarly stupid and vicious kind.* ADV = particularly

pecuniary /pɪ²kjuːnɪəri¹/ means concerning or involving money; a formal word. EG *There can be few places in the world where pecuniary self-interest is pursued more diligently.* ADJ CLASSIF = financial

pedagogic /pedəgɒdʒɪk, -gɒg-/. **Pedagogic** or **pedagogical** means concerning the methods and theory of teaching; a formal word. EG *...pedagogic and pediatric authorities.* ◇ **pedagogically**. ADJ QUALIT ⇑ educational ◇ ADV WITH VB

pedagogue /pedəgɒg/, **pedagogues**. A **pedagogue** is a teacher; a very old-fashioned formal word. N COUNT

pedagogy /pedəgɒgi¹, -gɒdʒi¹, -gəʊdʒi¹/ is the study and theory of the methods and principles of teaching; a formal word. N UNCOUNT

pedal /pedə⁰l/, **pedals, pedalling, pedalled**; also spelled **pedaling, pedaled** in American English.

1 The **pedals** on a bicycle are the two parts that you push with your feet in order to make the bicycle move. N COUNT

2 When you **pedal** a bicycle, you push the pedals around with your feet to make it move. EG *His legs were aching from pedalling too fast.* V OR V+O

3 When you **pedal** somewhere, you go there on a bicycle. EG *I pedalled in to work that night... It was time to pedal the three miles to the restaurant.* V+A = cycle

4 A **pedal** in a car or on a machine is a lever that you press with your foot in order to control the car or machine. N COUNT

5 See also **soft-pedal**.

pedal bin, pedal bins. A **pedal bin** is a waste bin that has a lid controlled by a pedal and that you keep in the kitchen. N COUNT ⇑ container

pedant /pedənt/, **pedants.** A **pedant** is someone who pays too much attention to minor details; used showing disapproval. N COUNT

pedantic /pɪ²dæntɪk/. Someone who is **pedantic** is excessively careful and too concerned with minor, unimportant details; used showing disapproval. EG *...some fussy and pedantic middle-aged clerk... They would sound terribly pedantic if they spoke classical Greek.* ▸ used of what someone says or does. EG *If I understood his pedantic German correctly, he was expressing an admiration for her.* ADJ QUALIT

pedantry /pedəⁿntri¹/ is unnecessarily great attention to details or rules; used showing disapproval. N UNCOUNT

peddle /pedəⁿl/, **peddles, peddling, peddled.** 1 Someone who **peddles** goods goes from place to place selling small objects; a rather old-fashioned use. EG *...a jolly old man who peddled ice-cream.* V OR V+O

2 Someone who **peddles** drugs sells illegal drugs. EG *The police want to keep the streets free of crime and dope peddling.* V+O = push

3 If someone **peddles** an idea or information, they try, in a very persistent way, to get people to accept it. EG *...the unreliable gossip that had been peddled for so long... His newspapers were peddling the twin policies of appeasement and optimism.* V+O ⇑ promote

peddler /pedlə/, **peddlers.** 1 A **peddler** is someone who sells small objects, usually by taking them round from house to house. EG *...the cries of London peddlers loudly hawking their wares.* N COUNT = pedlar

2 A drug **peddler** is a person who sells illegal drugs. EG *...hustlers and dope peddlers and receivers of stolen goods.* N COUNT = pusher

3 Someone who is a **peddler** of particular ideas, often expresses these ideas to other people. EG *...peddlers of dreams.* N COUNT : USU+*of* = pedlar

pedestal /pedɪ²stəⁿl/, **pedestals.** 1 A **pedestal** is the base on which something such as a statue or a column stands. EG *At the very top of the steps was a bust of Shakespeare on a pedestal.* N COUNT = stand

2 A **pedestal** basin is one that is supported by a single column. EG *There is a rear bathroom with panelled bath and pedestal lavatory basin.* ADJ CLASSIF : ATTRIB

3 If you **put** someone **on a pedestal**, you admire that person very much and show this in the way you behave towards them, the way you talk about them, etc. EG *I put you on a pedestal: I would have died for you.* PHR : VB AND N INFLECT = idolize

4 If you **knock** someone **off their pedestal**, you cause people to stop admiring them by showing that his or her good reputation is not deserved. PHR : VB AND N INFLECT = show up

pedestrian /pɪ²destrɪən/, **pedestrians.** 1 A **pedestrian** is a person who is walking, especially in a town or a city, rather than travelling in a vehicle. EG *Pedestrians jostled them on the pavement... This man is very keen on the rights of pedestrians... You may be considered to be obstructing pedestrian traffic.* N COUNT ⇑ walker

2 Something that is **pedestrian** is ordinary, dull, and not at all interesting; used showing disapproval. EG *Baker brings a touch of style to a government whose members are pretty pedestrian.* ADJ QUALIT ⇑ mediocre

pedestrian crossing, pedestrian crossings. A **pedestrian crossing** is a place where pedestrians can cross a street and where motorists must stop to let them cross. N COUNT

pedestrianize /pɪ²destrɪənaɪz/, **pedestrianizes, pedestrianizing, pedestrianized**; also spelled **pedestrianise.** To **pedestrianize** a street or shopping area means to make it into an area that is intended mainly for pedestrians, and where vehicles are not usually allowed. EG *They have decided to pedestrianise the centre of Plymouth.* ◊ **pedestrianized.** EG *There are cafés, boutiques, and a post office, all set in a now prettily pedestrianised enclave.* V+O; ◊ ADJ CLASSIF : ATTRIB

pedestrian precinct, pedestrian precincts. A **pedestrian precinct** is a street or part of a town that is used only by pedestrians and where vehicles are not usually allowed to go. EG *Parliament Square might even become a pedestrian precinct.* N COUNT

pediatrician /piːdɪətrɪʃəⁿn/. See **paediatrician.**

pediatrics /piːdɪætrɪk/. See **paediatrics.**

pedicure /pedɪkjʊə/, **pedicures. Pedicure** is treatment and care of the feet, either by a medical expert or by a beautician. N UNCOUNT/COUNT

pedigree /pedɪgriː/, **pedigrees.** 1 The **pedigree** of a cat, dog, cow, etc is its recorded ancestry. An animal is considered to have a good pedigree when all its known ancestors are of the same type. EG *He had cost a lot of money and perhaps his pedigree was a little too perfect... ...the fine dogs with pedigrees... ...a pedigree registration certificate.* N COUNT ⇑ ancestry

2 A **pedigree** animal is descended from animals which have all been of a particular type. The owner of a pedigree animal should have a document to prove this. EG *Don't buy a pedigree dog without a registration certificate.* ADJ CLASSIF : ATTRIB = thoroughbred

3 Someone's **pedigree** is **3.1** their ancestry; used especially where their ancestors are royal or are members of an aristocracy. EG *Sir Francis Galton, in his studies of pedigree in Victorian society, came to believe that all human qualities were inherited.* **3.2** their background, especially when this is considered to have affected and formed their attitudes and beliefs. EG *He had a criminal pedigree... Party activists with lower middle class pedigrees are numerous.* N COUNT : USU WITH POSS, OR UNCOUNT = ancestry; N COUNT : USU+SUPP ⇑ history

pediment /pedɪmə²nt/, **pediments.** A **pediment** is a piece of stone, wood, etc, usually three-sided, that is built over a doorway or window as a decoration. N COUNT

pedlar /pedlə/, **pedlars.** 1 A **pedlar** is someone who sells small objects, especially by taking them round from house to house. EG *The family had given shelter to an old pedlar.* N COUNT = peddler

2 Someone who is a **pedlar** of particular ideas often expresses these ideas to other people. EG *...a pedlar of gloom and despondency... ...a pedlar of dreams.* N COUNT : USU+*of* = peddler

pee /piː/, **pees, peeing, peed**; an informal word. 1 When someone **pees**, they urinate. Some speakers consider this usage to be rude and unacceptable. ▸ used as a noun. EG *I must go for a pee.* V = wee; ▸ N SING : *a*+N

2 **Pee** is urine. Some speakers consider this usage to be rude and unacceptable. N UNCOUNT

peek /piːk/, **peeks, peeking, peeked.** If you **peek** at something or someone, you have a quick look at them, especially secretly or quietly. EG *She peeked over the top of her menu... ...peeking at yourself in the mirror.* ▸ used as a noun. EG *I took a peek at the list... He had climbed the balcony to have a peek at it.* V : USU+A = peep; ▸ N COUNT : USU *a*+N

peekaboo /piːkəbuː/ is a game for young children where you cover your face with your hands or hide behind something and then suddenly take your hands away or peep out, saying 'peekaboo!'. N UNCOUNT OR EXCLAM = peepbo

peel /piːl/, **peels, peeling, peeled.** 1 The **peel** of a fruit is its skin, especially when it has been removed from the fruit. **Peel** is only used to refer to the skin of certain fruits that have thicker skins, for example oranges, grapefruit, or apples. EG *...grated lemon peel.* N UNCOUNT

2 When you **peel** fruit or vegetables, you remove their skins. EG *I hate peeling potatoes... Would you peel me an apple please?.* V+O, V+O+O, OR V+O+A *(for)*

3 If a surface, especially a painted surface, **is peeling**, it is gradually losing its outer surface, especially as a result of age or neglect. EG *The walls are peeling through neglect... ...an old peeling noticeboard.* ▸ used of the paint or other substance that is coming off the surface. EG *The paint was peeling from the woodwork... Too much heat will make the bark wrinkle and peel... All the paint's peeling off.* V : USU CONT; ▸ V : IF+PREP THEN *off*, USU CONT

4 If you **peel**, you lose small pieces of the top layer of your skin because of sunburn. EG *My back's peeling very badly.* ▸ used of the skin that comes off. EG *...the skin peeling off his nose.* V : USU CONT; ▸ V : IF+PREP THEN *off*, USU CONT

5 ● to **keep** your **eyes peeled**: see **eye.**

peel off. 1 If you **peel** something **off** a surface, you remove it by pulling it off gently in one piece. EG *I peeled some moss off the wood.* PHRASAL VB : V+O+ADV/PREP, HAS PASS

2 If you **peel off** a tight piece of clothing, you take it off by pulling it slowly. EG *She peeled off her sweater.* PHRASAL VB : V+O+ADV

3 If part of a group of moving vehicles, people, etc **peel off**, they leave the group following a course that curves away to one side. EG *The police motorcycle escort had to peel off and go down the next road.* PHRASAL VB : V+ADV

peeler /piːlə/, **peelers.** A **peeler** is a special knife used for removing the skin from fruit and vegetables. EG *He's still got my potato peeler.* N COUNT ⇑ device

peelings /piːlɪŋz/ are pieces of skin from a vegetable or fruit when it has been peeled. EG *...potato peelings... We always put tea leaves and vegetable peelings on the compost heap.* N UNCOUNT : USU MOD+N

peep /piːp/, **peeps, peeping, peeped.** 1 If you **peep** at something, you look at it very quickly, especially secretly and quietly. EG *They crept up to the glass doors and peeped inside.* ▸ used as a noun. EG *We went upstairs to have a peep at the new baby... Tom did take a peep.* V: USU+A = peek ▸ N COUNT: USU a+N = peek

2 If something **peeps** out from behind or under something, it appears for a short time, or a small part of it begins to appear. EG *The sun peeped through the clouds.* V+A = emerge

3 A **peep** is also a short, high-pitched noise such as that made by young birds or the horns of some cars. EG *Peep! peep! went the little car.* N COUNT ⇑ sound

4 If you say that you haven't heard a **peep** out of someone, you mean that they have not said anything or made any noise; an informal use. EG *I don't want to hear another peep out of you children until you've finished your homework!* N SING: a+N, USU WITH BROAD NEG = sound

peepbo /piːpbᵊəʊ/. is a game for young children where you cover your face with your hands or hide behind something and then suddenly take your hands away or peep out, saying 'peepbo!'. N UNCOUNT OR EXCLAM = peekaboo

peephole /piːphᵊəʊl/, **peepholes.** A **peephole** is a small hole in a door or wall through which you can look secretly at what is happening on the other side. N COUNT

Peeping Tom, Peeping Toms. Someone who is referred to as a **Peeping Tom** secretly looks at other people when they believe they are not being watched, especially when they are undressing. N COUNT = voyeur

peepshow /piːpʃəʊ/, **peepshows**; also spelled as two words. A **peepshow** is a box containing moving pictures which you can look at through a small hole. Peepshows were formerly found at fairs as a form of entertainment. N COUNT

peer /pɪə/, **peers, peering, peered.** 1 If you **peer** at something, you look carefully at it, bending your head in the direction you are looking; used especially when you have difficulty in seeing something. EG *Walter peered anxiously at his father's face... Howard sat next to Henry, peering through the windscreen.* V+A = gaze

2 A **peer** is a person who is a member of the nobility. EG *Some Conservative peers feared that reform might lead to the end of the House of Lords.* ● See also **life peer.** N COUNT ⇑ nobleman

3 Your **peers** are the people who are the same age, social status, ability, etc as you. EG *Comparing students with their peers outside university, they are more likely to have emotional problems.* N COUNT: USU PL ⇑ equals

peerage /pɪərɪdʒ/, **peerages.** 1 The **peerage** consists of all the peers of a country. EG *Succession to the peerage means disqualification from the House of Commons.* N SING: the+N ⇑ nobility

2 A **peerage** is the title and position in society which a person has when they are a peer. EG *A new principle by which an heir to a peerage may renounce his peerage.* N COUNT ⇑ rank

peeress /pɪərɪ²s/, **peeresses.** A **peeress** is a woman who is a member of the nobility. N COUNT

peer group, peer groups. A **peer group** is a group of people of about the same age or social status who are considered to share values and interests. EG *Some children attach more importance to the peer group than to their parents.* N COUNT ⇑ contemporaries

peerless /pɪəlɪ²s/. Something that is **peerless** is so magnificent, beautiful, or perfect that you feel that nothing can equal it; a formal word. EG *It was another peerless day.* ADJ CLASSIF = matchless

peer of the realm, peers of the realm. A **peer of the realm** is a member of the nobility in Britain who has the right to sit in the House of Lords. N COUNT

peeve /piːv/, **peeves, peeving, peeved.** If something **peeves** you, you feel irritated and annoyed by it; an informal use. EG *It really peeves me that he chose to behave in that way.* ◊ **peeved.** EG *He sounded very peeved in his letter.* V+O = rile, bug ◊ ADJ QUALIT

peevish /piːvɪʃ/. Someone who is **peevish** is irritated and complains a lot. EG *...a peevish child... He sounded peevish and his hands made pointless, nervous movements.* ▸ used of behaviour, emotion, and actions. EG *...a peevish expression... a general feeling of peevish regret.* ◊ **peevishly.** EG *'Where have you been?' she asked peevishly.* ADJ QUALIT ⇑ irritable = petulant ▸ = petulant ◊ ADV WITH VB

peewit /piːwɪt/, **peewits.** A **peewit** is a bird found in the countryside, especially on moorland. Peewits are black and white in colour. N COUNT = lapwing

peg /peg/, **pegs, pegging, pegged.** 1 A **peg** on a wall or door is a thin piece of wood, metal, or plastic that is attached to the wall or door and used for hanging things on. EG *He takes his leather coat from the peg.* N COUNT

2 A **peg** is also 2.1 a device used for attaching washing to a line while the washing is being dried. Pegs consist either of two small pieces of wood joined by a spring, or a shaped piece of wood with a slot up the middle. N COUNT 2.2 a small piece of metal or wood that is used for fastening something to something else. EG *The wooden pegs that held it together could be removed.* N COUNT

3 If you **peg** something somewhere, you fasten it there with a peg. EG *Mamma came out and pegged wet clothes on the line... Peg this down with string.* V+O+A ⇑ attach

4 If you say that something is a **peg** higher, lower, more important, etc when you are considering it as being on a scale, you mean that it is at the next point up or down; an informal use. EG *This soon brought down by several pegs the emotional excitement.* N COUNT: USU+ ADV (COMPAR) ⇑ degree

5 If you say that someone should **be brought down a peg or two**, you mean that they should be made to realize that they are not as important or wonderful as they think they are. EG *It's time he was brought down a peg or two.* PHR: VB INFLECTS ⇑ humble

6 Something that is described as a **peg on which to hang** something else is something which can be used to explain something else, or which can be used as a way of trying to achieve something else. EG *Some issues may be merely pegs on which to hang individual hostilities.* PHR: USED AS O/C

7 Someone who is described as a **square peg in a round hole** is doing something or in a situation that does not suit them at all. PHR: USED AS C = misfit

8 If the price, value, level, etc of something **is pegged** at a particular level or to the level of something else, it is fixed at the level indicated or adjusted according to the level of something else; an informal use. EG *The federal deficit for 1982 could be pegged at 42.5 billion dollars... ...however high the hotel pegged its prices.* V+O: IF+PREP THEN *at/to* ⇑ set

peg away. If you **peg away** at something, you keep doing it in a very determined way; often used when you are not succeeding or achieving very much; an informal use. EG *He would rather keep on pegging away at a beginner's book.* PHRASAL VB: V+ ADV, IF+PREP THEN *at* ⇑ persist

peg out. 1 If someone **pegs out,** 1.1 they die; an informal use. EG *He looked as if he was going to peg out at any minute.* PHRASAL VB: V+ ADV 1.2 they are too exhausted to carry on with what they have been doing; an informal use. EG *I did try a marathon once, but I pegged out half way through.* PHRASAL VB: V+ ADV

2 If you **peg out** clothes, sheets, etc, you fasten them to a washing line with pegs. EG *She trudged up the garden and began to peg out the clothes on the line.* PHRASAL VB: V+ O+ADV = hang out

3 If you **peg** something **out,** you spread it out, for example on the ground, and fasten it there with pegs. EG *...a sheepskin pegged out on the grass.* PHRASAL VB: V+ O+ADV

peg-leg, peg-legs. A **peg-leg** is an artificial leg, especially a wooden one; an old-fashioned and informal word. N COUNT

pejorative /pədʒɒrətɪv/. A **pejorative** word or expression is one which is critical. EG *I didn't think he was using inequality in a pejorative sense... ...justification of the pejorative term 'junk' food.* ADJ QUALIT = disparaging

pekinese /piːkɪniːz/, **pekineses**; also spelled **pekingese.** A **pekinese** is a small dog with long hair, short legs, and a short, flat nose. N COUNT

pelican /pelɪkən/, **pelicans.** A **pelican** is a large water bird which catches fish and keeps them in the bottom part of its beak which is shaped like a big bag. N COUNT

pelican crossing, pelican crossings. A **pelican crossing** is a place where pedestrians can cross a road by pressing a button which operates traffic lights to stop the traffic. N COUNT

pellagra /pəleɪgrə, -læ-/ is a disease caused by poor diet and which is characterized by skin and central nervous system disorders and tiredness. N UNCOUNT ⇑ illness

pellet /pelɪ²t/, **pellets.** A **pellet** is 1 a small round object, sometimes made by rolling a bit of soft material between your fingers. EG *Sudhir took the opportunity to throw a paper pellet at Judy... Beetles bury pellets of dung and lay their eggs within them.* N COUNT: USU+ SUPP ⇑ ball

2 a small metal ball fired from a gun. EG *I fired some shotgun pellets into the air.* N COUNT ⇑ bullet

pell-mell /pe̲l me̲l/. If you dash, run, fall, etc **pell-mell** somewhere, you move in a hurried, and disorderly way. EG *I dashed pell-mell into the drawing room.* — ADV WITH VB

pellucid /pelu̲:sɪd/. Something that is **pellucid** is extremely clear; a literary word. — ADJ CLASSIF = limpid

pelmet /pe̲lmɪ²t/, **pelmets**. A **pelmet** is a long, narrow piece of wood or fabric which is fixed at the top of a window for decoration and to hide the curtain rail. — N COUNT ⇑ cover

pelt /pe̲lt/, **pelts, pelting, pelted**. 1 A **pelt** is the skin and fur of an animal which can be used to make clothing or rugs. EG *Its thick pelt makes the brown bear a favourite target.* — N COUNT

2 If you **pelt** someone with something, you throw lots of things at them as a way of attacking them. EG *He was pelted with eggs when he arrived.* — V+O+A *(with)* = bombard

3 If someone **is pelted** with questions, they are asked a great number of questions one after the other. — V+O+A *(with)*: NO IMPER

4 If it **is pelting** with rain or if it **is pelting down**, it is raining very hard; an informal use. EG *It's pelting with rain out there!... The rain was pelting down outside.* — V, V+A *(with)*, OR PHRASAL VB: V+ADV, USU CONT = pour

5 If someone **pelts** somewhere, they run there very fast; an informal use. EG *She went pelting down the street.* — V+A = belt

6 Something or someone that is moving **at full pelt** is moving very fast indeed; an informal expression. EG *He was caught driving his car at full pelt down the road.* — PHR: USED AS AN A

pelvic /pe̲lvɪk/ means near or relating to your pelvis. — ADJ CLASSIF: ATTRIB

pelvis /pe̲lvɪs/, **pelvises**. Your **pelvis** is the large, wide, curved group of bones at the base of your spine at the level of your hips. EG *It extends right down the front of the animal's chest and is actually connected with its pelvis.* — N COUNT

pen /pe̲n/, **pens, penning, penned**. 1 A **pen** is a long thin object with which you write in ink. **Pen** can refer to a ballpoint or a fountain pen. EG *He took out his pen and wrote down his name and address... You can borrow that pen if you want to.* — N COUNT ⇑ implement

2 If someone **pens** a letter, note, etc, they write it; a formal or literary use. EG *Infuriated, he penned a blistering reply... ...a novel of 65,000 words penned in a clear childish hand.* — V+O = draft

3 A piece of writing, idea, etc that is described as being from the **pen** of a particular writer has been written by that person. EG *There has been much discussion of these serious issues from his pen this year.* — N SING: WITH POSS

4 A **pen** for farm animals is a small enclosure with a fence round it in which they are put for a short time, for example at market. EG *The pigs were huddled together at the far end of the pen.* — N COUNT

5 If animals **are penned** somewhere or **are penned up**, they are kept together in a pen. — V+O: USU+A

6 **A slip of the pen** is a small mistake in something that you have written. EG *It was just a slip of the pen... I noticed the slip of my pen in the preceding paragraph.* — PHR: USED AS C/O ⇑ error

7 If you **put pen to paper**, you write something; a formal or literary use. EG *At last I managed to put pen to paper.* — PHR: VB INFLECTS

7 • **ballpoint pen**: see **ballpoint**. • **felt-tip pen**: see **felt-tip**. • See also **play pen**.

penal /pi̲:nə⁰l/. 1 **Penal** means relating to the punishment of criminals. EG *...the British penal system... I'm chairman of the Howard League for Penal Reform.* — ADJ CLASSIF: ATTRIB

2 A **penal** institution, establishment, colony, etc is one that is used or designed as a place for punishment, especially imprisonment. EG *He was moved to the penal settlement on the Isle of Pines... ...a penal colony.* — ADJ CLASSIF: ATTRIB

3 A **penal** fine, tax, etc is very severe. EG *...penal taxation.* — ADJ CLASSIF: ATTRIB

penal code, penal codes. The **penal code** consists of all the laws in a country that are concerned with crime and punishment. — N COUNT

penalize /pi̲:nəlaɪz/, **penalizes, penalizing, penalized**; also spelled **penalise**. 1 If someone **is penalized** for doing something which is against the rules or instructions, they are punished for it by being made to suffer some disadvantage. EG *The council will be penalised for spending too much last year... You will be penalized if you don't answer all the questions... The referee penalized Smith for handling the ball.* — V+O: USU PASS

2 If someone **is penalized** by their situation, they are treated in a way that is unfair and to their disadvantage as a result of their position. EG *Why should I be penalized just because I'm a woman?... It would be unfair to penalise those without a job.* — V+O: USU PASS

penal servitude is the punishment of being sent to prison and forced to do hard physical work. EG *In 1922 he was sentenced to seven years' penal servitude.* — N UNCOUNT

penalty /pe̲nə⁰lti¹/, **penalties**. A **penalty** is 1 a legal punishment, such as imprisonment or a fine. EG *There are now stiffer penalties for drunken drivers... The court considers a financial penalty to be appropriate punishment.* — N COUNT 2 a punishment in the form of a disadvantage for breaking the rules or for not fulfilling the terms of an agreement or contract. EG *The borough of Hackney is facing grant penalties worth 2 million pounds.* — N COUNT 3 an unpleasant result of something that you do or of your state or position. EG *I had to pay the penalty for the wrong decisions I made.* — N COUNT = price 4 a disadvantage which a player or team is given for doing something against the rules. EG *...a time penalty of twelve seconds.* — N COUNT 5 a chance to kick the ball towards the goal from a position in front of the goal without players from the other team being allowed to tackle you. Penalties are given in football and other sports against a team that commits a foul. EG *The referee gave a penalty... United scored from a first-half penalty.* — N COUNT

penalty area, penalty areas. The **penalty area** on a football pitch is an area in the shape of a rectangle which is in front of the goal. Within this area the goalkeeper is allowed to handle the ball and a penalty is given if a foul is committed by the attacking team. — N COUNT = penalty box

penalty box, penalty boxes. 1 The **penalty box** in football is the penalty area. — N COUNT

2 The **penalty box** in ice hockey is an area in which players who have been penalized have to sit for the period of time of their penalty. — N COUNT

penalty clause, penalty clauses. A **penalty clause** in a contract is a clause which states what the penalty is for breaking the agreement, for example how much money must be paid. EG *Surprisingly he did not insert a penalty clause.* — N COUNT

penance /pe̲nəns/, **penances**. 1 **Penance** is 1.1 something that you willingly do as a punishment to show that you are sorry for something serious that you have done wrong. EG *We must do penance for our sins.* — N UNCOUNT/COUNT 1.2 in the Roman Catholic Church, an attempt to gain forgiveness for sins by confessing to a priest and doing something such as saying prayers. EG *...the sacrament of penance.* — N UNCOUNT = atonement

2 A **penance** is also something that you must do, for example because it is your duty, but which you dislike very much. EG *It was a real penance for me to go round the shops with the kids.* — N COUNT: USU SING = trial

pen-and-ink. A **pen-and-ink** drawing is drawn using a pen rather than a pencil. EG *...a pen-and-ink drawing of Zinoviev.* — ADJ CLASSIF: ATTRIB

pence /pe̲ns/ is a plural form of **penny** or **p.** EG *...a ten pence coin... It costs fifteen pence.* — N PLURAL: USU NUM+N

-pence is the form that was used to combine with a number in order to indicate an amount of money in old pence before decimalization in Britain. EG *...sixpence... ...ninepence.* — COMB: FORMS NOUNS

penchant /pe̲nt⁰ʃənt, pɒnʃɒn/. If someone has a **penchant** for something, they have a special liking or tendency for it; a formal word. EG *The Americans, he considered, had a penchant for being disconcertingly frank.* — N SING WITH DET: USU a+N+*for* = fondness

pencil /pe̲nsə⁰l/, **pencils, pencilling, pencilled**. 1 A **pencil** is an object that you use for writing or drawing. It consists of a long thin piece of wood with a piece of graphite in the middle. — N COUNT ⇑ implement • If you write or draw something **in pencil**, you do it with a pencil. EG *The last three items on the list were added in pencil.* See also **blue pencil, propelling pencil**. — • PHR: USED AS AN A

2 If someone **pencils** a note, letter, symbol, etc, they write or draw it with a pencil. EG *He pencilled his initials at the end.* — V+O ◊ **pencilled**. EG *...a pencilled note.* — ◊ ADJ CLASSIF

pencil in. If you **pencil in** a word, note, letter, or part of a drawing, you add the thing mentioned to a piece of writing or a drawing using a pencil. EG *Their names had been pencilled in.* — PHRASAL VB: V+O+ADV

pendant /pendənt/, **pendants**; also spelled **pendent** in paragraph 2. 1 A **pendant** is a piece of jewellery which is attached to a chain or thong and which you wear round your neck. EG *...a long amber pendant.* N COUNT ↑ ornament

2 If you describe something as **pendant**, you mean that it is hanging, either over the edge of something or suspended from something; a literary use. EG *...pendent creepers.* ADJ CLASSIF = dangling

pending /pendɪŋ/; a fairly formal word. 1 Something that is **pending** 1.1 is going to happen soon. EG *He knew my examination was pending.* ADJ CLASSIF 1.2 is waiting to be finally settled or decided. EG *The offer is left pending until their examination results are known... ...a pending lawsuit in Boston.* ADJ CLASSIF = undecided ≠ definite

2 If something is done **pending** a particular event, it is done while someone is waiting for the event to happen, or until it happens. EG *Pending our move to the new house we moved to temporary accommodation in London... An interior administration is to be set up, pending elections.* PREP ↑ awaiting

pendulous /pendjə⁴ləs/. Something that is **pendulous** hangs downwards and swings freely, especially in an unattractive way; a formal word. EG *His stomach was distended and pendulous.* ADJ QUALIT = sagging

pendulum /pendjə⁴ləm/, **pendulums**. 1 A **pendulum** on a clock is a large weight which hangs at the bottom of a piece of metal or rope, and which swings from side to side in order to regulate the mechanism of the clock. N COUNT

2 When you refer to the **pendulum** of something and to the way it swings, you are referring to a change from one state of affairs, opinion, belief, etc to the opposite one. EG *...the pendulum of upper class fashion... The pendulum has swung too far away from local initiatives.* N SING : *the*+N+SUPP

penetrate /penɪtreɪt/, **penetrates, penetrating, penetrated**. 1 If you **penetrate** a particular area that is difficult to get into, you succeed in getting into it. EG *This was the territory of enemies, penetrated only for the purposes of trade and war... They penetrated into territory where no man had ever gone before.* ◊ **penetration** /penɪtreɪʃə⁰n/, **penetrations**. EG *...the penetration of hostile defences.* V+O, OR V+A ↑ enter ◊ N UNCOUNT/COUNT

2 If someone **penetrates** an enemy group or organization, they succeed in joining it in order to gather information, cause trouble, etc. EG *You're much better placed than we are to penetrate the Party.* ◊ **penetration**. EG *...agent penetrations of the L.A.F. and other groups.* V+O = infiltrate ◊ N UNCOUNT/COUNT

3 If something **penetrates** something that it is difficult to get through, it succeeds in getting through. EG *The sun was not high enough or hot enough yet to penetrate the thick foliage overhead... Even if the shell did not penetrate, it could still cause damage.* ◊ **penetration**. EG *Penetration at one or more points was inevitable.* V OR V+O = break through ◊ N UNCOUNT/COUNT

4 If you **penetrate** something that is difficult to understand, you succeed in understanding it; a fairly formal use. EG *I attended his lectures, which helped me to penetrate the mysteries in the Manifesto... She could always be depended upon to penetrate what I was thinking.* ◊ **penetration**. EG *They approach their own faith with the same vigour and the same penetration.* V+O = fathom, grasp ◊ N UNCOUNT

5 If someone **penetrates** a disguise, they are not deceived by it. EG *Not many people managed to penetrate my disguise.* V+O = see through

6 When a man **penetrates** a woman during sex, he inserts his penis into her vagina. V+O = enter

penetrating /penɪtreɪtɪŋ/. 1 A **penetrating** sound is loud and very unpleasant to listen to. EG *...short, penetrating blasts of a whistle... ...the Cockney's penetrating voice...* ADJ QUALIT

2 A **penetrating** look is one that makes you feel uncomfortable because it seems to reach inside your thoughts. EG *He had an extraordinarily penetrating gaze.* ▸ used of someone's eyes. EG *Her hair was flaming red, and her eyes penetrating and resentful.* ADJ QUALIT ↑ deep = piercing

3 Someone who has a **penetrating** mind is able to understand a subject or problem quickly and in great depth. ▸ used of what someone says or writes when it shows this ability. EG *I was trying to think up another penetrating question.* ADJ QUALIT = sharp, keen

pen-friend, pen-friends; also spelled as one word. If you have a **pen-friend**, especially one in a foreign country, you write to this person regularly, and build up your friendship through your letters. Pen-friends often never meet each other. N COUNT = pen pal

penguin /peŋgwɪn/, **penguins**. A **penguin** is a large black and white bird found especially in the Antarctic. Penguins cannot fly but use their wings for swimming in water. N COUNT

penicillin /penɪsɪlɪn/ is an antibiotic medicine that is used to treat pneumonia and other diseases caused by bacteria. N UNCOUNT

penile /piːnaɪl/ means relating to a penis; a formal word. EG *...penile cancer.* ADJ CLASSIF : ATTRIB

peninsula /pɪ²nɪnsjə⁴lə/, **peninsulas**. A **peninsula** is a long narrow piece of land that is almost surrounded by water but that is joined to the mainland. N COUNT : ALSO IN NAMES AFTER N

penis /piːnɪs/, **penises**. A man's **penis** is the part of his body that he uses when urinating and when having sex. N COUNT

penitence /penɪtəns/ is sincere regret for wrong or evil things that you have done. EG *The spirit of penitence was in the air.* N UNCOUNT = repentance

penitent /penɪtənt/. Someone who is **penitent** is very sorry for something wrong or evil that they have done, and sincerely regrets their actions. ADJ QUALIT = repentant

penitential /penɪtenʃə⁰l/ means expressing deep sorrow and regret at having done something wrong; a formal word. EG *...a penitential pilgrimage.* ADJ CLASSIF

penitentiary /penɪtenʃə⁰ri¹/, **penitentiaries**. A **penitentiary** is a prison; used in American English. N COUNT

penknife /pennaɪf/, **penknives**. A **penknife** is a small knife with blades that fold back into the handle. N COUNT

penmanship /penmə³nʃɪp/ is the art and skill of writing by hand; a formal word. N UNCOUNT

pen name, pen names; also spelled with a hyphen. A writer's **pen name** is the name that he or she uses on books and articles instead of his or her real name. N COUNT = nom de plume

pennant /penənt/, **pennants**. A **pennant** is a long narrow flag, usually triangular in shape, especially one used by ships as a signal. N COUNT

pennies /peni¹z/ is the plural of **penny**.

penniless /penɪlɪ²s/. Someone who is **penniless** has hardly any money at all. EG *If Miss Drew gave me notice I'd be penniless.* ADJ QUALIT ↑ poor

penny /peni¹/, **pennies, pence**. The form **pence** is only used for the plural in sense 1.2, and otherwise the form **pennies** is used. The abbreviation **p** is more commonly used for senses 1.1 and 1.2, as the word 'penny' suggests the old large penny that was in use in Britain before currency was decimalized in 1971. 1 A **penny** is 1.1 a small bronze-coloured British coin which is worth one hundredth of a pound. N COUNT 1.2 the amount of money which a penny is worth. EG *You haven't got 50 pence I could borrow?... Ten pence isn't a lot of money.* N COUNT : IF PL, VB IS SING 1.3 a large bronze-coloured British coin used before 1971 that used to be worth one twelfth of a shilling. N COUNT 1.4 in American English, a coin that is worth one cent. N COUNT

2 **Penny** is also used in negative expressions and with words like 'every' to emphasize that absolutely nothing is spent or that you are referring to absolutely all of a sum of money. EG *It won't cost me a penny... Nobody will bet one penny that they will succeed... To Mr Hazel it was worth every penny.* N SING WITH DET

3 The word **penny** is also used in the following expressions. 3.1 If someone **doesn't have a penny to their name**, they are very poor indeed. EG *He didn't have a penny to his name when she married him.* PHR : AUX INFLECTS 3.2 If you **don't have two pennies to rub together**, you have so little money that you can hardly afford to buy anything; used mainly in British English. PHR : AUX INFLECTS 3.3 If something costs **a pretty penny**, it costs a large amount of money. PHR : USED AS O = a fortune 3.4 If you say **'take care of the pennies and the pounds will take care of themselves'**, you are advising someone to be careful not to waste small amounts of money because it is easy to waste a large amount of money over a long period of time in this way. PHR ↑ economize 3.5 If you say to someone who has been very quiet and thoughtful **'a penny for your thoughts'**, you are asking them to tell you what they are thinking about. PHR 3.6 If you say **the penny dropped**, you mean that someone has understood something that they have been unaware of or not understood for a long time. EG *I stared at him for a long time and then the penny dropped. 'So this is it,' I said.* PHR : VB INFLECTS = it clicked 3.7 If you go to **spend a penny**, you go to the toilet; an old-fashioned, polite expression used in PHR : VB INFLECTS

British English. **3.8** If you say **'in for a penny in for a pound'**, you are saying that you have committed youself to doing something and so you might as well do it to the fullest extent possible and get involved completely; used mainly in British English. EG *'Oh well, in for a penny, in for a pound,' he said. 'Why don't you ask your family to come too?'* — PHR

3.9 Things that are said to be **two a penny** or **ten a penny**, are so common that there is nothing special about them and they are easily available. EG *We have fifty men like that–drivers are two a penny.* — PHR : USED AS C; = a dime a dozen

3.10 If someone unwanted or unacceptable keeps **turning up like a bad penny**, they are continually appearing when and where they are not wanted; used especially to indicate that people would rather forget about them but cannot do so. — PHR : VB INFLECTS

-penny combines with a number to indicate the amount in pence that something costs. This use now tends to suggest an amount in old currency before decimalization in Britain, and it is more common to use **p** instead. EG *I'd like four eightpenny stamps, please.* — COMB : FORMS ADJ CLASSIFS

penny-farthing, penny-farthings. A **penny farthing** is an old style of bicycle that had a very large front wheel and a small back wheel. — N COUNT

penny-pinching is the practice of being too careful about money and being unwilling to spend even small amounts. EG *Good preventative health care means we cannot allow penny-pinching.* — N UNCOUNT ▸ used as an adjective. EG *She muttered something to herself about penny-pinching miserly old men.* — ▸ ADJ QUALIT = parsimonious

penny whistle, penny whistles. A **penny whistle** is a cheap musical instrument, consisting of a metal tube with holes in it and a mouthpiece that you blow into. — N COUNT = tin whistle

pennyworth /pɛnəθ, pɛnɪwəθ/. A **pennyworth** of something is the amount of it that can be bought for a penny; a rather old-fashioned word. EG *...a pennyworth of mustard pickle... ...the common things that people buy by the pennyworth.* — N SING WITH DET : IF+PREP THEN *of*

pen pal, pen pals. A **pen pal** is the same as a penfriend; an informal word. — N COUNT

penpusher /pɛnpʊʃə/, **penpushers**; also spelled with a hyphen. A **penpusher** is a person whose work consists of a lot of boring, repetitive jobs that involve writing. — N COUNT = clerk

pension /pɛnʃən/, **pensions, pensioning, pensioned.** The word **pension** can also be pronounced /pɒnsjɒn/ in paragraph 2. **1** Someone who has a **pension** receives a sum of money that is paid regularly by the State or a former employer because they have retired, or because they are widowed or disabled. EG *My parents lived long enough to draw their old age pension... ...a retired judge living on a state pension.* — N COUNT ⇑ allowance

2 A **pension**, especially in Europe, is a small hotel. EG *He had stayed at the Pension Kleist for a fortnight.* — N COUNT : ALSO IN NAMES

pension off. 1 If someone **is pensioned off**, they are made to retire from work and given a pension. EG *We were pensioned off at the age of forty-five.* — PHRASAL VB : V+O+ADV, USU PASS

pensionable /pɛnʃənəbəl/ means relating to someone's entitlement to receive a pension. EG *...anybody over pensionable age... The poor have no savings and no cushy, pensionable positions.* — ADJ CLASSIF

pension book, pension books. A **pension book** or a **pension order book** is a small booklet issued to pensioners by the Department of Health and Social Security in Britain. It contains payment slips that can be exchanged for the pension money at a Post Office each week. — N COUNT

pensioned /pɛnʃənd/ means receiving a pension. EG *...the pensioned professionals.* — ADJ CLASSIF : ATTRIB

pensioner /pɛnʃənə/, **pensioners.** A **pensioner** is someone who receives a pension, especially the pension paid by the State to elderly people. EG *...old age pensioners.* — N COUNT

pension scheme, pension scheme. A **pension scheme** is a financial scheme which enables you to receive a pension after you have contributed to it for a certain period. — N COUNT

pensive /pɛnsɪv/. Someone who is **pensive** is very thoughtful and quiet, and perhaps sad. EG *He became so pensive that she did not like to break into his thoughts.* — ADJ QUALIT = meditative ▸ used of expressions and behaviour. EG *...his pensive silence.* — ▸ = dreamy ◊ **pensively.** EG *He is playing the flute quietly, pensively, badly.* — ◊ ADV WITH VB

pentagon /pɛntəgɒn/, **pentagons. 1** The **Pentagon** is the building in Washington that is the headquarters of the US department of Defence. — N PROPER : *the*+N ▸ used of the military leaders who work there and the decisions that are taken by them. EG *The Pentagon is already planning new developments in the field.* — ▸ N PROPER : *the*+N, IF SING, VB CAN BE SING OR PL

2 A **pentagon** is a shape which has five sides and five angles. — N COUNT ⇑ polygon

pentameter /pɛntæmɪtə/, **pentameters.** A **pentameter** is a line of poetry that has five strong beats in it. — N COUNT/UNCOUNT

pentathlon /pɛntæθlən/, **pentathlons.** A **pentathlon** is a sporting competition in which contestants compete in five sports, usually swimming, fencing, shooting, running, and riding. — N COUNT, OR N SING : *the*+N

Pentecost /pɛntiˈkɒst/ is **1** a Jewish religious festival that takes place 50 days after Passover, and that celebrates the harvest. — N UNCOUNT **2** a Christian religious festival that celebrates the sending of the Holy Spirit to the first apostles. — N UNCOUNT

penthouse /pɛnthaʊs/, **penthouses.** A **penthouse** or a **penthouse** suite or apartment is a very luxurious flat or set of rooms in a hotel, especially one near the top of a tall building. — N COUNT ⇑ residence

pent-up. Pent-up emotions, energies, or forces are held back and not allowed to be expressed or released. EG *The reactions were partly the product of pent-up frustration... ...sports in which they can get rid of some of their pent-up energy.* — ADJ CLASSIF : USU ATTRIB

penultimate /pɪnʌltəˈmət/. The **penultimate** thing in a set or series of things is the last but one. EG *This is the penultimate volume in Marchand's marvellous series.* — ADJ CLASSIF

penurious /pɪnjʊərɪəs/. Someone who is **penurious** is very poor indeed; a formal word. — ADJ QUALIT

penury /pɛnjəˈri/ is great poverty; a formal word. EG *They would face penury unless they could secure employment very soon.* — N UNCOUNT = destitution

peony /piːəni/, **peonies**; also spelled **paeony.** A **peony** is a medium-sized garden plant that has large round flowers, usually pink, crimson, or white in colour. — N COUNT

people /piːpəl/, **peoples, peopling, peopled. 1 People** are men, women, and children. EG *There were 120 people at the lecture... We'll talk to the people concerned and see how they feel... The amount of potatoes and bread people buy has dropped... There has been a complete change in people's ideas on the subject recently.* — N PLURAL

2 When you refer to the **people**, you are referring to ordinary men and women in contrast to a group such as the government or the aristocracy with power or high social status. EG *I don't think MPs really represent the people as such... ...power to the people.* — N PLURAL : *the*+N = masses

3 Your **people** are your relatives or family; a rather old-fashioned use. EG *My people came from the North.* — N PLURAL : POSS +N = folk

4 You sometimes use **people** in spoken English when you are talking to or about a particular group of people in order to refer to the members of that group. EG *He spent a long time on that explanation and I think people got rather bored... How did you get on? Did people find it difficult to speak for as long as ten minutes?* — N PLURAL

5 If you refer, for example, to the electricity **people** or television **people,** you are referring to the men and women who are involved in or deal with electricity or television, perhaps as their job; a fairly informal use. EG *I'll have to get the electricity people in... This is being investigated by the urban studies people.* — N PLURAL : *the*+N

6 A **people** is all the men, women, and children of one particular country, nation, or race. EG *...the beliefs of various peoples across the world... ...the Ethiopian people.* — N COUNT

7 If an area or country **is peopled** by a particular group or number of people, that group or number of people live there. EG *...Istanbul, now peopled by 4 million Turks... ...the humid regions, many of which are sparsely peopled.* — V+O : USU PASS+ *by/with* = be inhabited

8 If something **is peopled** with particular things or people, or if they **people** it, they are present in it; a fairly literary use. EG *The earth is peopled only with echoes... ...the racists that peopled my childhood...* — V+O : USU PASS+ *by/with*

pep /pɛp/, **peps, pepping, pepped**; an informal word. **Pep** is liveliness and energy. EG *It puts colour* — N UNCOUNT = vitality *in the cheeks and gives more pep to humans of all ages.*

pep up. 1 If you try to **pep** something **up**, you try to make it more lively or interesting. EG *He realized that the conference needed pepping up a bit... ...the company is trying to pep up its product line.*
PHRASAL VB : V+O+ADV = liven up ≠ tone down

2 If you give someone something to **pep** them **up**, you give them something that will give them more energy. EG *I gave him an extra dose of glucose to pep him up.*
PHRASAL VB : V+O (NG/REFL)+ADV = liven up ≠ tone down

pepper /pɛpə/, **peppers, peppering, peppered.** 1 **Pepper** is a spicy-tasting black or cream-coloured powder which is used to flavour food. EG *...freshly ground black pepper... Do you need pepper and salt?*
N UNCOUNT ↑ seasoning

2 A **pepper** is a vegetable which is hollow and roughly round in shape. Peppers are usually red, green, or yellow, and can be cooked or eaten raw in salads. EG *Add the sweetcorn and the diced green or red pepper.*
N COUNT/UNCOUNT : USU ADJ COLOUR+N = capsicum

3 If someone or something **peppers** a surface with pieces of something, these pieces are thrown at or scattered on the surface. EG *...pepper the surface with slug pellets... 'There,' he insisted, his abrupt English peppering the air with faint showers of spittle.*
V+O+A *(with)* ↑ cover = dot, scatter, sprinkle

4 If someone **peppers** something, they shoot at it repeatedly. EG *They like to pepper you in the legs at about fifty yards... Two more ships came along and peppered the hills until we'd passed.*
V+O = pelt, riddle

5 If you **pepper** food, you add pepper to it.
V+O

pepper-and-salt. A **pepper-and-salt** pattern on fabric consists of tiny dark and white specks of colour.
ADJ CLASSIF : ATTRIB ↑ grey

peppercorn /pɛpəkɔːn/, **peppercorns.** A **peppercorn** is a small, dried berry which comes from a pepper plant, and which is crushed in order to produce pepper.
N COUNT ↑ spice

peppered /pɛpəd/. 1 Food that **is peppered** has had pepper added to it to give it a spicy flavour. EG *That night's pot of soup was heavily peppered and spiced.*
V+O : USU PASS ↑ season

2 Something that is **peppered** with things has many of the things mentioned all over its surface, or contains a lot of them. EG *...assuming that the universe is peppered with these planets... His French is heavily peppered with Americanisms.*
ADJ QUALIT : PRED, IF+PREP THEN *with*

peppermint /pɛpəmɪnt/, **peppermints.** 1 **Peppermint** is a strong sharp flavour that is used especially to flavour sweets; also used to refer to the plant from which this flavouring is obtained. EG *...a large peppermint humbug.*
N UNCOUNT : USU BEFORE N = mint

2 A **peppermint** is a hard white sweet which has a flavour of peppermint.
N COUNT = mint

pepperpot /pɛpəpɒt/, **pepperpots.** A **pepperpot** is a container for pepper that is used during meals. A pepperpot is usually small, with a lot of holes in the top for shaking out the pepper.
N COUNT ↑ cruet

peppery /pɛpəri[1]/. 1 Food that is **peppery** has a strong taste of pepper.
ADJ QUALIT ↑ spicy

2 Someone who is described as **peppery** is irritable and bad-tempered. EG *...the familiar type of the peppery old colonel.*
ADJ QUALIT = gruff

pep pill, pep pills. A **pep pill** is a pill which someone takes to make themselves feel happier or more active; an informal word.
N COUNT : USU PL = upper ≠ downer

pep talk, pep talks. A **pep talk** is a speech which is intended to encourage people to work harder, try to win, feel more confident, etc; an informal expression. EG *Mr Reagan gave a pep talk to House Republican members.*
N COUNT

peptic ulcer /pɛptɪk ʌlsə/, **peptic ulcers.** A **peptic ulcer** is an ulcer that occurs in the digestive system of people or animals.
N COUNT

per /pɜː/. 1 When you express rates, ratios, prices, or measurements, you can use **per** to say how many units apply to each of the items being measured, charged, etc. EG *The dwellings have more than six people per room... We spend something like 20 million pounds per year... ...sixty miles per hour... Output per worker has been growing at a tremendous rate.*
PREP : USU NUM +PREP

2 If something happens or is done **as per** a particular system, plan, or set of instructions, it happens or is done in the way that the plan, system, or set of instructions says it should be done; a fairly formal expression. EG *We shall proceed as per the instructions specified in the letter.*
PREP = according to, in accordance with

3 If you say that something happens **as per usual** or **as per normal**, you mean that it happens in the usual or normal way; a fairly informal expression.
PHR : USED AS AN A = as usual

perambulate /pəræmbjə[4]leɪt/, **perambulates, perambulating, perambulated**; a very old-fashioned word. When someone **perambulates**, they walk about for pleasure, without going in a particular direction. ◊ **perambulation** /pəræmbjə[4]leɪʃə[0]n/. EG *Hyde Park has always been a place for a promenade, for perambulation.*
V OR V+O = ramble, stroll, wander ◊ N UNCOUNT

perambulator /pəræmbjə[4]leɪtə/, **perambulators**; a very old-fashioned or formal word. A **perambulator** is a pram. EG *Children are pushed in a perambulator.*
N COUNT

per annum. If you state an amount **per annum**, you are stating that the amount applies to each period of one year. EG *It costs 125 pounds per annum.*
ADV : NUM+ADV = p.a., per year, yearly

per capita. When you are talking about the distribution of money, land, etc, if you state an amount **per capita** you are stating the amount that applies to each person in the country or area. EG *Per capita incomes have grown and grown... What is the average wage per capita?*
ADJ CLASSIF : ATTRIB, OR ADV

perceive /pəsiːv/, **perceives, perceiving, perceived.** If you **perceive** something, 1 you realize, notice, see, or hear it, especially when it is not obvious to other people. EG *He perceived what was not seen by many others... Many insects can perceive colours of the spectrum that are invisible to us.*
V+O/REPORT-CL = spot

2 you understand it or come to a particular opinion about it by studying, observing, reading, etc. EG *It is important that the president be perceived as moving the country forward... ...this theory expresses the truth as I perceive it.*
V+O = view

per cent /pəsɛnt/. If you express an amount as being, for example, 28 **per cent** (28%) of a total, you are saying that if the total were divided into 100 parts, the amount that you are stating would represent 28 of these 100 parts. EG *He won 28.3 per cent of the vote... Poland is 90 per cent Roman Catholic... A good tumbler drier can also reduce ironing by 80 per cent... The interest is three per cent a month.* ● **a hundred per cent**; see **hundred**.
PHR : NUM+PHR

percentage /pəsɛntɪdʒ/, **percentages.** A **percentage** is a fraction or amount of something which, if the whole thing were divided into 100 parts, is equal to a particular number of these parts. EG *What is the percentage of nitrogen in air?... ...areas with a very high percentage of immigrants... It's a tiny percentage of the total income.*
N COUNT : IF+PREP THEN USU *of*

perceptible /pəsɛptɪbə[0]l/. Something that is **perceptible** can just be seen or noticed. EG *...the first, barely perceptible touches of autumn... These changes were already perceptible before the war.* ◊ **perceptibly.** EG *The skin under the brown eyes was perceptibly darker than it had been earlier.*
ADJ QUALIT ↑ noticeable ≠ imperceptible ◊ ADV

perception /pəsɛpʃə[0]n/, **perceptions.** 1 Someone who has **perception** has the ability to realize or notice things that are not obvious to other people. EG *...a person of extraordinary perception... He was scared by the quickness of her perception.*
N UNCOUNT ↑ awareness = insight

2 A **perception** is a belief or opinion that you have as a result of realizing or noticing something, especially something which is perhaps not obvious to other people. EG *He has found a way of meaningfully representing his perceptions and experiences through his painting... It didn't mean anything to me, except a vague perception that it didn't sound good.*
N COUNT = insight

3 **Perception** is the awareness of things that you have by means of your senses, especially the sense of sight. EG *...visual perception... ...man's perception of time.*
N UNCOUNT

perceptive /pəsɛptɪv/. Someone who is **perceptive** is good at noticing or realizing things quickly, especially things that other people might not notice or realize. EG *I'm not really perceptive as far as literature goes... ...a perceptive critic.* ▸ used of someone's remarks or thoughts. EG *...a very perceptive comment.* ◊ **perceptively.** EG *Jenkins has written perceptively on the politics of the eighteenth century.* ◊ **perceptiveness.** EG *...moments of great hilarity, satire, perceptiveness, extreme wit.*
ADJ QUALIT ↑ observant ≠ show ◊ ADV WITH VB ◊ N UNCOUNT

perch /pɜːtʃ/, **perches, perching, perched.** **Perch** can also be used as the plural form for the noun in paragraph 5. 1 If you **perch** somewhere, you sit on the edge of a chair or object that is not intended to be a seat, usually for a short period of
V+A

time. EG *Dr Quilty perched on the corner of his desk.* ◇ **perched**. EG *Flora, perched on the side of the bath, laughs.* ◇ ADJ CLASSIF : PRED+A

2 If something **perches** somewhere or if you **perch** it there, it is in a position on top of something or on the edge of it, where it looks as if it might fall off. EG *The stone buildings perch on a hill crest between vertical cliffs.* ◇ **perched**. EG *...a little village perched above the lake.* V-ERG+A ≠ nestle; ◇ ADJ CLASSIF : PRED+A

3 When a bird **perches** on something, for example a branch or a wall, it stands there, usually for a short period of time. EG *It fluttered to the branch and perched there for a moment or two... ...a sparrow perched on the saddle.* V : USU+A

4 A **perch** is 4.1 a short rod which has been designed for a bird to stand or rest on. EG *She unhooked one bird from his perch.* N COUNT 4.2 a place where you sit, especially one that is not intended as a seat. EG *We found a perch on the ruins of a low stone wall... He climbed all the way to his favourite perch near the top.* N COUNT

5 A **perch** is also an edible fish that lives in lakes, ponds, and rivers. EG *...fishing for perch.* N COUNT

perchance /pətʃɑːns/ means perhaps; an old-fashioned or literary word. ADV SEN = maybe

percipient /pəsɪpɪənt/. Someone who is **percipient** is good at noticing or realizing things quickly, especially things that other people might not notice or realize; a formal word. EG *...a very percipient author... ...as the more percipient local residents may have realized.* ADJ QUALIT = acute, observant, perceptive

percolate /pɜːkəleɪt/, **percolates, percolating, percolated**. 1 If something **percolates** somewhere, it passes slowly through something that has very small holes or gaps in it. EG *...filled with mysterious light percolating through stained-glass windows... The heated sea water percolating downwards becomes very corrosive.* V+A = filter, trickle

2 When coffee **percolates** or when you **percolate** it, you make it using a percolator. V-ERG

3 If an idea, information, feeling, etc **percolates** through a group of people, it spreads slowly through the group. EG *Structuralist ideas percolated through the academic community.* V+A ⇑ spread

percolator /pɜːkəleɪtə/, **percolators**. A **percolator** is a pot in which coffee is made and served. Boiling water circulates up a central tube and down through ground coffee beans. N COUNT

percussion /pəkʌʃəⁿn/. In music, **percussion** consists of the instruments such as drums, cymbals, and tambourines that are played by striking them with another object. EG *We had Dailey on the percussion, and Flannery on the clarinet... ...a complex percussion solo... ...the percussion section of an orchestra.* N UNCOUNT, OR N SING : the+N ⇑ musical instruments

percussion cap, percussion caps. A **percussion cap** is a small device containing explosive powder that is used as a detonator or in toy guns. EG *He carefully fitted a bullet, until only the brass percussion caps showed to view.* N COUNT

percussionist /pəkʌʃənɪst/, **percussionists**. A **percussionist** is a person who plays percussion instruments. N COUNT ⇑ musician

perdition /pɜːdɪʃəⁿn/ is the state of never-ending punishment after death; a literary word. EG *...one more step down the road to perdition.* N UNCOUNT = hell, damnation ≠ salvation

peregrination /perɪgrɪneɪʃəⁿn/, **peregrinations**. A **peregrination** is a long journey which involves wandering about from place to place; a formal word. N COUNT

peregrine falcon /perɪgrɪn fɔːlkən/, **peregrine falcons**. A **peregrine falcon** or a **peregrine** is a large bird of prey, which has a dark-coloured back and is lighter coloured underneath. N COUNT

peremptory /pəremptəⁿri¹/. Someone who says or does something in a **peremptory** way behaves in a way that shows that they expect to be obeyed immediately and with no argument; used showing disapproval. EG *With a peremptory note in his voice he told the officer in charge to fetch the papers. Our conversation was interrupted by a peremptory thudding at the door.* ▸ used of people. EG *'Have you finished?' asked a peremptory woman.* ◇ **peremptorily**. EG *'Come!' he said peremptorily, taking hold of John by the elbow.* ADJ QUALIT = imperious ≠ hesitant; ◇ ADV WITH VB = imperiously

perennial /pɪ²renɪəl/, **perennials**. 1 A situation that is described as **perennial** lasts for a long time or for ever. EG *...the perennial problems of isolation in old age... ...the perennial conflict between government and opposition.* ◇ **perennially**. EG *...the intense blue of a perennially cloudless sky.* ADJ CLASSIF = constant, everlasting, perpetual; ◇ ADV = constantly

2 A **perennial** is a plant that lives for several years. EG *Daffodils, tulips, and snowdrops are what we call perennials... ...perennial plants.* N COUNT

perfect, perfects, perfecting, perfected. The adjective and the noun are pronounced /pɜːfɪ²kt/ and the verb in paragraph 6 is pronounced /pəfekt/. 1 Something that is **perfect** 1.1 is completely correct or accurate, or is done so well that it could not be done any better. EG *The figure was a perfect circle... She speaks perfect English... Ian has a perfect photographic memory... The seam was so perfect that it was not even noticeable.* ADJ CLASSIF = faultless ≠ imperfect, inaccurate 1.2 is in a completely whole, new, pure, or undamaged condition. EG *The metal is all perfect still under the paint... He smiled at her, his teeth white and perfect... You're in perfect health.* ADJ CLASSIF = immaculate ≠ imperfect

2 If you say that something is **perfect**, you mean that 2.1 it is wonderful and you are very pleased with it. EG *We had a perfect day... He could see for miles. It was perfect... Everything now seemed as perfect as could be.* ADJ CLASSIF ⇑ lovely = excellent ≠ awful 2.2 it is the best possible and ideal for the particular purpose or situation. EG *We're calling her Frieda. It's the perfect name for a baby... They make a perfect couple... This was the perfect moment for the enemy to move in... I've got the perfect solution... The actor was perfect for the part.* ADJ CLASSIF = exact, right ≠ wrong

3 Someone who is **perfect** is considered to behave in an ideal way and have no faults in their character. EG *Lionel was perfect to me in those days... OK, so I made a mistake. Well, nobody's perfect, are they?* ADJ CLASSIF : PRED ⇑ good

4 If you describe someone as the **perfect** gentleman, woman, landlady, etc you mean that their behaviour or character is typical of what is expected of such a person; used showing approval. EG *Rudolph was the perfect gentleman... We know all the traditional images of the 'perfect woman' at home.* ADJ CLASSIF : ATTRIB ⇑ ideal = complete, essential, ultimate

5 **Perfect** can be used to give emphasis to the noun following it. EG *You're behaving like a perfect idiot... They are perfect strangers... I have a perfect right to be here... It makes perfect sense to me... 'I will never talk to him. Ever,' I said with perfect calm.* ADJ CLASSIF : ATTRIB ⇑ utter = absolute, complete

6 If you **perfect** something, you improve or work on it so that it becomes perfect. EG *They perfected their plans during the day... She hoped to perfect her technique... They are bent on improving and perfecting existing weaponry.* V+O = polish ≠ spoil

7 In grammar, the **perfect** tense of a verb in English is the tense that is formed with the present tense of the auxiliary 'have' and the past participle of the main verb. ADJ CLASSIF : ATTRIB

8 If you say **practice makes perfect**, you mean that if someone keeps trying to do something and practising it, they will eventually become skilled at it. EG *'I'll never be any good at this!'–'Come on, practice makes perfect.'* PHR = if at first you don't succeed

perfection /pəfekʃəⁿn/. 1 **Perfection** is the quality of being perfect. EG *They were looking for peace and for perfection... There's no such thing as perfection in poetry... Those small, well-secluded gardens of incredible perfection.* N UNCOUNT ⇑ goodness ≠ imperfection

2 If something is done **to perfection**, it is done so well that it could not be done any better. EG *The dress fitted her to perfection... People are so often able to fake a smile to perfection.* PHR : USED AS AN A = perfectly ≠ imperfectly

3 The **perfection** of something is the act or process of improving it so that it becomes perfect. EG *We are interested in the perfection of production methods.* N UNCOUNT : USU +of ⇑ improvement

perfectionism /pəfekʃənɪzəⁿm/ is the state or quality of being a perfectionist. EG *It was a blow to Phoebe's pride and perfectionism.* N UNCOUNT

perfectionist /pəfekʃənɪst/, **perfectionists**. A **perfectionist** is a person who refuses to accept anything that is not perfect; often used to suggest that someone is being too fussy. EG *Morris was always a perfectionist... In this shabby office we cannot afford to be perfectionists... Precision isn't maintained for any romantic or perfectionist reasons.* N COUNT ⇑ idealist

perfectly /pɜːfɪ²ktli¹/. 1 **Perfectly** can be used to emphasize something, often because you think that people do not believe it or because it might seem unlikely. EG *There's nothing to worry about. This is a perfectly normal baby... 'You're not ill, are you, Louisa?'–'I'm perfectly all right, thank you very* ADV+ADJ/ADV = completely, absolutely, totally, utterly *much.'... I think this is a perfectly reasonable thing to do... He knows his duty perfectly well but he won't do it. It's perfectly disgusting!... I'll be perfectly frank with you... I don't think much of this, to be perfectly honest.*

2 **Perfectly** means in a completely perfect or accurate way; used showing approval. EG *Nobody speaks English perfectly... The climate suited Len perfectly... The crystal is perfectly symmetrical... Her straight, black hair was always perfectly brushed... Teddy did everything perfectly.* ADV ⇑ well = accurately, correctly ≠ badly

perfect pitch. Someone who has **perfect pitch** is able to identify or sing a musical note perfectly. N UNCOUNT

perfidious /pəfɪdɪəs/. Someone who is **perfidious** is treacherous or untrustworthy; a literary word. ADJ CLASSIF = false

perfidy /pɜːfɪdi¹/ is treacherous actions or behaviour; a literary word. N UNCOUNT = betrayal

perforate /pɜːfəreɪt/, **perforates, perforating, perforated.** 1 If something **is perforated**, it has a number of small holes made in it for a particular purpose. EG *...a perforated steel plate.* V+O : USU PASS

2 If something **perforates** something else, it pierces it or causes it to have a hole or holes in it. EG *...perforated ear drums.* V+O ⇑ puncture

perforation /pɜːfəreɪʃə⁰n/, **perforations. Perforations** are small holes or slits that are made in something; used especially of holes made in a piece of paper so that part of it can be torn off easily. N COUNT : USU PL

perforce /pəfɔːs/ is used to indicate that something happens or is the case because it is unavoidable or inevitable rather than because it is intended or desired; a formal, old-fashioned word. EG *This freedom at last gave back a voice to those who had perforce been silent for so long... Much of what is said about the behaviour of ancient man is, perforce, guesswork.* ADV SEN ⇑ necessarily

perform /pəfɔːm/, **performs, performing, performed.** 1 When you **perform** a task or action, especially one that is complicated, you do it or carry it out. EG *About 200 heart operations a year are performed at the Brook Hospital... Most young birds seem to be able to perform the complex movements of flying... The ceremony was performed at the same time in nineteen other countries... How he performed these miracles nobody ever quite knew.* V+O

2 If something **performs** a particular service or function, it does the thing mentioned or has the effect indicated. EG *This organization performs a vital contemporary service.* V+O = fulfil

3 When you **perform** or when you **perform** a play, a piece of music, a dance, etc, you do something in order to entertain an audience. EG *He performed for them a dance of his native Samoa... We had to perform on a temporary stage... ...performing monkeys.* V OR V+O

4 If something or someone **performs** well, badly, or in a particular way, they work, function, or do a particular thing well, badly, or in the way indicated. EG *...the difficulty of finding a rifle which will perform satisfactorily under those conditions... Although she had never been interviewed on TV before, she performed well.* V : USU+A

performance /pəfɔːməns/, **performances.** 1 A **performance** is the acting of a play or role, the playing of a piece of music, the doing of a dance, etc in front of an audience. EG *I think Roger Rees gives a remarkable performance... After the performance I went round to see her in her dressing room... ...an amateur performance of Macbeth.* N COUNT ⇑ rendition

2 Someone's or something's **performance** is how well they do or how successful they are. EG *How is a company to measure its performance?... ...despite Great Britain's poor economic performance in the 1970's... Many people are extremely disappointed with the performance of this government.* N UNCOUNT : USU WITH POSS = achievement ▸ used of a particular occasion on which something or someone does well or does badly. EG *...after a disappointing performance in the 220-yards handicap.* ▸ N COUNT : MOD/POSS+N = showing

3 The **performance** of a car or other vehicle is its ability to go fast and accelerate quickly. EG *Unnecessarily high speeds are bad for fuel economy and do little for performance... ...high performance cars.* N UNCOUNT ⇑ functioning

4 You describe what someone says or does as a **performance** 4.1 when they are saying or doing it in order to produce a particular effect on other people. EG *'See you tomorrow.'–'Bye.' It was not a bad performance.* N SING WITH DET = act 4.2 when you think that they are behaving badly. EG *I wonder what brought on that little performance!* N SING WITH DET 4.3 when it takes a long time and you think it is boring or unnecessary. EG *It's a bit of a performance, I know, but it's worth it in the end.* N SING WITH DET = rigmarole

5 The **performance** of a task or action is the doing of it. EG *...the performance of his Presidential duties... ...as if it were the performance of some elaborate court ritual.* N SING WITH DET : USU+*of* = execution

performer /pəfɔːmə/, **performers.** 1 A **performer** is a person who acts, sings, plays an instrument, etc to entertain an audience. EG *...a gifted performer.* N COUNT ⇑ entertainer

2 Someone or something that is a particular kind of **performer** does a particular thing in the way indicated or to the standard indicated. EG *His supporters are all wondering why he is such a rotten performer on television when he is such a brilliant speaker in Parliament... He earned a useful living as a night club performer.* N COUNT : ADJ+N ⇑ doer

performing arts. Dance, drama, music, and other forms of entertainment that are usually performed live in front of an audience are referred to as the **performing arts.** EG *...the John F Kennedy Center for the Performing Arts.* N PLURAL : *the*+N

perfume /pɜːfju⁴m/, **perfumes.** A **perfume** is 1 a liquid that smells pleasant and that you put on your skin or clothing to make it smell nice. EG *...a faint smell of perfume... ...a small bottle of perfume... ...an expensive perfume.* N MASS = scent 2 a fragrant, pleasant smell. EG *The familiar perfumes of wild flowers filled her nostrils.* N COUNT = fragrance

perfumed /pɜːfju⁴md/. Something that is **perfumed** has a sweet, pleasant smell, either naturally or because perfume has been put on it. EG *...perfumed flowers... The air was cool and sweet, perfumed with the scent of sub-tropical vegetation... He handed her a perfumed towel.* ADJ QUALIT = scented

perfunctory /pəfʌŋktə⁰ri¹/. A **perfunctory** action is done quickly, casually, and carelessly; a formal word. EG *There was a perfunctory search of his bags at London Airport... Max gave his wife a perfunctory kiss.* ADJ QUALIT = cursory, negligent ◇ **perfunctorily** . EG *'Where's Albert Morris?' Brody said to Vaughan after perfunctorily greeting the others.* ◇ ADV WITH VB

pergola /pɜːgələ/, **pergolas.** A **pergola** is an arch or roofed structure in a garden, which consists of a framework over which climbing plants can be grown. N COUNT

perhaps /pəhæps/. 1 If you say that **perhaps** a particular thing will happen or has happened, or **perhaps** a particular thing is the case, you mean that you think it is possible or likely, although you are not sure about it. EG *Perhaps God does not exist... Perhaps I'll come. Perhaps not... Perhaps Andrew is right after all... Nobody would believe it, except, perhaps, Jill.* ADV SEN = maybe ≠ certainly

2 You use **perhaps** when you are offering an explanation for something and you are not sure whether this explanation is true or not. EG *Not many people used to go there, perhaps because it was on the edge of town... He said nothing of his stay with her. Perhaps he had forgotten... Has it been thrown away, perhaps?* ADV SEN = maybe ≠ certainly

3 You also use **perhaps** when you are mentioning a member of a particular group, as an example, and it is not important which member you mention. EG *You could act a scene from one of Shakespeare's plays–'Hamlet' or 'Macbeth' perhaps.* ADV SEN = maybe

4 You can also use **perhaps** when you are making a rough guess at a number, quantity, or value rather than stating it exactly. EG *There are perhaps fifty women here... He sat there silently for perhaps half a minute.* ADV SEN = maybe

5 If you say that something should **perhaps** be done, you are suggesting that it should be done, because you think it is probably the right thing to do, although you are not absolutely sure. EG *Should he arrange it? Perhaps he should... Perhaps it would be best if he didn't let them know about his money problems.* ADV SEN = maybe

6 You can also use **perhaps** when making a polite request or offer. EG *Perhaps I might keep these, for a day or two?... Can I offer you anything–a drink, perhaps?* ADV SEN = maybe

7 You say **perhaps** when expressing an opinion to indicate that you are prepared to accept that other people might disagree with you or in order to be polite when criticizing something. EG *I think that's* ADV SEN = possibly

perhaps her finest picture... The roast beef was perhaps a little overdone... Perhaps I am wrong, but I feel that he has made a serious mistake.

8 When you are speaking on a formal or public occasion, you say **perhaps** to indicate in a polite, informal way that you intend to say or do something. EG *Perhaps first I had better explain what we try to do here at the Centre.* ADV SEN = maybe

9 You can also use **perhaps** to indicate that even though a particular thing is or may be true, there are other related aspects or points that should be considered. EG *He is a little small, perhaps. But small dogs are often a lot tougher than large ones... Perhaps she liked him, but I didn't.* ADV SEN = maybe

10 You say **perhaps** in reply to a question when you disagree or would like to say 'no' but wish to be polite. EG *A phenomenal price? Well, perhaps.* CONVENTION = maybe

11 You can also use **perhaps** when you are talking about something and you decide to correct yourself and explain things more clearly. EG *I took a magnificent photo of him–or perhaps I should say a photo of him looking magnificent... Colonel Dainty had an angry or perhaps a sullen expression on his face.* ADV SEN : USU *or* +ADV = maybe

per head. If a group of people have, give, or are given a particular amount of something **per head**, the average for each person is that amount. EG *Meals were being subsidized by up to £16 per head... So the average amount of land per head is declining.* ADV : USU NUM+ADV

peril /pɛrɪl/, **perils**; a fairly formal word. **1** A **peril** is something that is very dangerous. EG *...the perils of being a fugitive... The arms race is the greatest single peril now facing the world.* N COUNT = danger, hazard

2 Peril is very great danger. EG *Tell him that he stands in great peril... ...mythical heroes who were aided in their moments of greatest peril by birds and beasts.* N UNCOUNT

3 If you say that someone does a particular thing **at** their **peril**, you mean that it is dangerous and likely to result in harm for them. This expression is used especially when warning someone not to do something. EG *You become neglectful at your peril.* PHR : USED AS AN A

perilous /pɛrɪləs/. Something that is **perilous** is dangerous or risky; a fairly formal word. EG *The first leg of the perilous journey was over... ...but to neglect the town was equally perilous.* ADJ QUALIT = hazardous ≠ safe ◊ **perilously**. EG *...an incident in which it came perilously close to destruction... She bumped into the lectern, which swayed perilously forward.* ◊ ADV WITH VB = precariously

perimeter /pərɪmɪtə/, **perimeters**. The **perimeter** of an area of land or a flat geometrical shape is its whole outer edge or boundary. EG *...the square stone posts that marked the camp's perimeter... Dog patrols had been intensified around the perimeter fence... ...round the perimeter of the clearing.* N COUNT : IF+PREP THEN *of* = border ▸ used of the whole length of this edge. EG *...the perimeter divided by the number of sides.* ▸ ⇑ measurement

period /pɪərɪəd/, **periods**. **1** A particular **period** is **1.1** a particular length of time. EG *...over a period of several months... ...in a 24-hour period... Long periods of rain will be interrupted by short periods of showers... He was in therapy for a long period of time... The magazine was forced to close down for a period.* N COUNT : USU+SUPP = spell **1.2** a length of time when the activity mentioned is taking place or is planned to take place. EG *...long and expensive training periods... The main business of the meeting comes first, and then the question period afterwards.* N COUNT : USU MOD+N = session **1.3** a time in the life of a person, organization, society, etc, that is characterized by a particular kind of activity or event. EG *It was an extremely important period for us... ...a period of intense radical activity... ...during his period of office in 1962 as Minister of Justice... ...Picasso's Blue Period.* N COUNT+SUPP ⇑ stage **1.4** a particular time in history. EG *...in the Edwardian period... ...the Middle Ages and other remote periods of time... ...in later geological periods... ...Italian opera of that period.* N COUNT : USU+SUPP = age, era

2 A **period** is one of the divisions of time in a day at school, college, or university when a particular subject is taught. EG *There were five periods of French a week... Teachers these days don't get many free periods.* N COUNT = lesson

3 Period is used of things whose style is typical of an earlier time in history and which either date from that time or are deliberately made in that style. EG *...period costumes... ...period furniture.* N BEFORE N ⇑ historical

4 A woman's **period** is the bleeding from her womb that happens for a few days each month when she is not pregnant. EG *...menstrual periods.* N COUNT

5 A **period** is also the same as a full stop; used mainly in American English. N COUNT

6 You say **period** after stating a fact or opinion to emphasize that you are definite about it and to say that you are not going to discuss it further; used mainly in fairly informal American English. EG *I could have prevented them, and I didn't. Period.* ADV SEN : ALWAYS AT END OF SENTENCE = full stop

periodic /pɪəriˈɒdɪk/. A **periodic** event or situation happens occasionally and at fairly regular intervals. EG *...special clinics where the elderly may have periodic health check-ups... ...problems such as diseases or periodic droughts.* ADJ CLASSIF : ATTRIB = periodical

periodical /pɪəriˈɒdɪkəl/, **periodicals**. **1** A **periodical** is a journal or newspaper on a particular subject, especially an academic one, that is published at regular intervals, for example every month. EG *...periodicals like the New York Review of Books.* N COUNT ⇑ publication

2 Periodical means the same as periodic. EG *These mood shifts are periodical and recurring.* ADJ CLASSIF : ATTRIB

periodically /pɪəriˈɒdɪkəli/. Something that happens **periodically** happens occasionally and at fairly regular intervals. EG *We met them periodically during the summer break.* ADV WITH VB = regularly

periodic table. The **periodic table** is a table showing the chemical elements arranged according to their atomic numbers. N SING : *the*+N

peripatetic /pɛrɪpətɛtɪk/. A **peripatetic** person travels around and stays for short periods of time in different places, often in order to work in those places; a formal word. EG *...the son of a peripatetic engineer.* ADJ CLASSIF : ATTRIB = itinerant ▸ used of a way of life. EG *I began my peripatetic existence, working more and more away from home.* ▸ = nomadic

peripheral /pərɪfərəl/, **peripherals**. **1** Something that is **peripheral** is of little importance in comparison with other parts or aspects of something or with other similar things. EG *Therefore energy is now not a peripheral but a central issue in the economy... ...the peripheral features of religion... The men are somewhat peripheral to this society.* ADJ QUALIT ⇑ minor ≠ crucial

2 Peripheral also means on or relating to the edge of an area or a group of things or people. EG *...Russia's peripheral provinces... This gives greater peripheral vision.* ADJ CLASSIF

3 Peripherals or **peripheral** devices are extra devices that can be attached to or put in a computer; a technical term. N COUNT : USU PL, OR BEFORE N

periphery /pərɪfəri/, **peripheries**; a fairly formal word. **1** The **periphery** of an area or a group of things is the edge of it. EG *The cost of land on the expanding periphery of Calcutta went up by 1300 per cent... Other animals were depicted on the periphery of the group... ...on the periphery of my field of vision.* N COUNT : IF+PREP THEN *of*

2 The **periphery** of something, for example a field of activity, is the part of it that is not as important or basic as other parts or that does not get as much attention. EG *There had always been those on the periphery of the movement who had advocated violence... ...projects working on the periphery of education.* N COUNT : IF+PREP THEN *of* = fringes ≠ centre

periscope /pɛrɪskəʊp/, **periscopes**. A **periscope** is a vertical tube with mirrors in it that are arranged so that when you look in the lower end of the tube, you can see things which are otherwise out of sight. Periscopes are used especially in submarines in order to see above the surface of the water. EG *'Up periscope,' he ordered.* N COUNT ⇑ device

perish /pɛrɪʃ/, **perishes, perishing, perished**.

1 If people, animals, or plants **perish**, they die as a result of very hard conditions or are killed; a formal or literary use. EG *She left her little ones to perish from starvation and disease.* V

2 If something **perishes**, it comes to an end or is destroyed for ever; a literary use. EG *Your state is corrupt and deserves to perish... The old religion is perishing.* V = collapse

3 If rubber, leather, or a fabric **perishes**, it starts to fall to pieces. V ⇑ disintegrate

4 If food **perishes**, it goes bad or rots. V

5 If you say **perish the thought**, you mean that you find a suggestion or possibility that has just been mentioned very unpleasant or ridiculous; a fairly informal expression. EG *Not that I'd ever stand for Parliament myself–perish the thought.* CONVENTION = God forbid

6 See also **perishing**.

perishable /pe̱rɪʃəbəᵒl/, **perishables**. Something, especially food, that is **perishable** goes bad quite quickly. EG *...a perishable cargo.* ▸ used as a plural noun. EG *Freight supervisors were nervously watching perishables.*
ADJ QUALIT
▸ N PLURAL
⇑ goods

perisher /pe̱rɪʃə/, **perishers**. You can refer to a child as a **perisher** when you are annoyed with it or feel sorry for it; an informal word, used in old-fashioned English. EG *The poor little perisher died in my arms.*
N COUNT
= blighter

perishing /pe̱rɪʃɪŋ/. 1 If the weather is **perishing** or **perishing cold**, it is extremely cold. EG *I was up in Minnesota during its perishing winter... It's perishing cold this morning.*
ADJ CLASSIF
= freezing

2 You can use **perishing** to emphasize something when you dislike it or are annoyed; an informal and old-fashioned use, used in British English. EG *'Why don't you throw that thing out?'–'What thing, dear?'–'That perishing clock.'*
ADJ CLASSIF : ATTRIB
= blasted

peritonitis /pe̱rɪtənaɪtɪs/. If you have **peritonitis**, the inside wall of your abdomen is inflamed and very painful; a technical term in medicine.
N UNCOUNT

periwinkle /pe̱ri¹wɪŋkəᵒl/, **periwinkles**. A **periwinkle** is 1 an evergreen plant that grows along the ground and has blue flowers. 2 an edible creature like a snail that lives in or near the sea.
N COUNT
N COUNT
⇑ mollusc

perjure /pɜ̱:dʒə/, **perjures, perjuring, perjured**; a formal or legal word. 1 If you **perjure** yourself in a court of law, you lie although you have promised to tell the truth. EG *You can't expect me to perjure myself in the witness-box.*
V+O (REFL)
= forswear

2 If you **perjure** someone or something in a court of law, you lie about them. ◊ **perjured**. EG *Keeler's evidence in the Gordon case was perjured.*
V+O
◊ ADJ CLASSIF
= false

perjury /pɜ̱:dʒəri¹/, **perjuries**. **Perjury** is the crime of lying in a court of law although you have promised to tell the truth; a formal or legal word. EG *She was subsequently charged with perjury and sentenced to nine months' imprisonment... He committed a number of perjuries.*
N UNCOUNT/ COUNT
= falsehood

perk /pɜ̱:k/, **perks, perking, perked**. A **perk** is something extra, such as a car or free accommodation, which you may receive in addition to your salary if you work for a particular company or if you have a particular job; an informal use. EG *There are nice perks with the job such as help with your mortgage.*
N COUNT
= fringe benefit

perk up. When someone or something **perks up**, they become more cheerful, interested, or exciting; an informal expression. EG *John was being a bore. A proper misery. He perked up when we got there, though... I tried to think of some ways to perk up her appetite.*
PHRASAL VB : V-ERG+ADV
= enliven

perky /pɜ̱:ki¹/, **perkier, perkiest**. If someone is **perky** or if they behave in a **perky** way, 1 they are cheerful, lively, and full of enthusiasm; used showing approval. EG *We were accompanied by a perky little widow in her 70s.* 2 they have a bold and confident manner that may seem impolite; used showing disapproval. EG *He is all perky awareness, a bustling busybody.*
ADJ QUALIT
= bright, jaunty
ADJ QUALIT
= brash, spirited

perm /pɜ̱:m/, **perms, perming, permed**. 1 If you have a **perm**, your hair is treated with chemicals in order to make it curly or wavy. The curls last for several months.
N COUNT
⇑ hairstyle

2 If your hair **is permed**, it is treated with chemicals in order to make it curly or wavy.
V+O : USU PASS
⇑ curl

permafrost /pɜ̱:məfrɒst/ is land that is permanently frozen to a great depth, even though the surface may thaw slightly in the summer. EG *...the permafrost of the North.*
N UNCOUNT

permanence /pɜ̱:mənəns/. If something has **permanence**, it remains the same for a long time or for ever. EG *The fight had to be led by a party with more permanence in its membership and structure... How could peace be built without some assurance of permanence with regard to our economic life?*
N UNCOUNT
= constancy, continuity
≠ impermanence, transience

permanency /pɜ̱:mənənsi¹/, **permanencies**. 1 A **permanency** is someone or something that is always present or that stays the same for a long time or for ever. EG *He seems to have become a permanency in her life.*
N COUNT
= fixture

2 **Permanency** also means the same as permanence. EG *...an air of permanency.*
N UNCOUNT
= constancy

permanent /pɜ̱:mənənt/. Something that is **permanent** 1 lasts for ever or for a very long time. EG *Some drugs taken in large quantities cause permanent brain damage... Hiroshima in Japan gained itself a permanent place in history.* ◊ **permanently**. EG *My imprisonment was likely to scar me permanently.* 2 is present all the time or happens all the time. EG *In many parts of the world the only permanent water supply lies below the ground... I began to live in an almost permanent state of fear.* ◊ **permanently**. EG *My wife and children are staying there permanently... The doors were kept permanently locked.*
ADJ QUALIT
◊ ADV WITH VB
ADJ CLASSIF
= constant
◊ ADV WITH VB
= constantly

permeable /pɜ̱:mɪəbəᵒl/. If something is **permeable**, liquids are able to pass through its surface; a formal word. EG *The insect's skin is permeable.*
ADJ QUALIT
= absorbent
≠ impervious

permeate /pɜ̱:mɪeɪt/, **permeates, permeating, permeated**; a formal word. 1 When something such as an idea or feeling **permeates** a particular thing, it influences that thing or affects every part of it. EG *The fear of bureaucracy permeates their thought... This reflected the sense of optimism which permeated the times... They encourage their basic principles to permeate slowly through the consciousness.*
V+O, OR V+A *(through)*
= pervade, dominate

2 When something **permeates** a particular thing, it passes through its surface and spreads into it. EG *Damp and mould can easily permeate the wood... If the tip leaks, dangerous chemicals may permeate through rocks and soil into rivers.*
V+O, OR V+A *(through)*
⇑ spread
= penetrate

permissible /pəmɪ̱səbəᵒl/. If something is **permissible**, it will be allowed, because it does not break any rules, laws, or conventions; a fairly formal word. EG *Her request is perfectly permissible... ...the maximum permissible levels of radiation... I understood that it was permissible to ask a question.*
ADJ CLASSIF
= admissible

permission /pəmɪ̱ʃəᵒn/. If you have or are given **permission** to do something, someone has said that they will allow you to do it. EG *He gave me permission to go... The Minister refused permission for it... You can't do it without permission.*
N UNCOUNT
= authorization

permissive /pəmɪ̱sɪv/. A **permissive** society, person, way of behaving, etc allows or tolerates things which other people disapprove of, especially freedom in sexual behaviour. EG *We live in a permissive age... ...the frequency of divorce in the 'permissive society'.* ◊ **permissiveness**. EG *The child began to take advantage of our permissiveness... ...sexual permissiveness.*
ADJ QUALIT
⇑ tolerant
◊ N UNCOUNT

permit, permits, permitting, permitted. The word **permit** is pronounced /pəmɪ̱t/ when it is a verb, and /pɜ̱:mɪt/ when it is a noun. 1 If you **permit** someone to do something, you allow them to do it, and if you **permit** something, you allow it to exist, happen, or be done; a fairly formal use. EG *Her father would not permit her to eat sweets... No admissions are permitted in the hour before closing time... The doctor has permitted him only two meals a day... We were permitted into the hall five minutes before the exam.*
V+O+*to*-INF, V+O, OR V+O+O, OR V+A
⇑ let

2 If you **permit** yourself to do something, you let yourself do it, especially when it is something that you do not usually do or that you do not feel completely free to do; a fairly formal use. EG *He permitted himself a slight smile... I permitted myself potatoes only once a week.*
V+O (REFL)+O/ *to*-INF
= allow

3 If something **permits** a particular thing, it makes it possible or provides the opportunity for it; a fairly formal use. EG *Had time permitted, we would have stayed longer... Why shouldn't we use the garden, weather permitting?... His health had improved enough to permit him a beer or two before dinner.*
V, V+O+O, OR V+O+*to*-INF
= allow

4 If something **permits** of a particular thing, it makes it possible; a very formal use. EG *The crime permits of no defence.*
V+A *(of)*
= admit

5 A **permit** is a written statement by an official body which says that you may do something, such as work in a foreign country. EG *She could not get in without a permit... ...work permits.*
N COUNT
= pass

permutation /pɜ̱:mju:teɪʃəᵒn/, **permutations**. A **permutation** is a variation in the way in which a number of things are ordered or arranged; a formal word. EG *You can form any and every number out of permutations of these symbols.*
N COUNT : USU PL +*of*

pernicious /pənɪ̱ʃəs/. If you describe something as **pernicious**, you consider that it is very harmful; a formal word. EG *The government's policy is indistinguishable from that of its Labour rival, and equally pernicious... ...shameful and pernicious nonsense.*
ADJ QUALIT
= injurious

pernickety /pənɪkɪti¹/. Someone who is **pernickety** worries too much about small, unimportant details; an informal word. EG *She was a trifle pernickety.* ADJ QUALIT ⇑ fussy

peroration /perəreɪʃə⁰n/, **perorations**. A **peroration** is the last part of a speech, particularly the part where the speaker summarizes his or her main points; a formal word. N COUNT ⇑ oration

peroxide /pərɒksaɪd/. **Peroxide** or hydrogen **peroxide** is a chemical that is often used for bleaching hair or as an antiseptic. N UNCOUNT

perpendicular /pɜːpə²ndɪkjə⁴lə/. 1 Something that is **perpendicular** stands or rises straight up from the ground. EG *...the great perpendicular red face of the cliffs.* ADJ CLASSIF ⇑ upright = vertical

2 If something is **perpendicular** to something else, it is at an angle of 90 degrees to it; a technical or formal use. EG *The two lines of bones are set perpendicular to one another.* ADJ CLASSIF: PRED, IF+PREP THEN *to* = at right angles

3 If you describe the position or angle of something in relation to the **perpendicular**, you are describing it in relation to an imaginary line that is completely vertical and at an angle of 90 degrees to the ground. EG *The pillar had been restored to the perpendicular.* N SING: *the*+N ≠ horizontal

perpetrate /pɜːpɪ²treɪt/, **perpetrates, perpetrating, perpetrated**. If someone **perpetrates** a crime or other harmful or immoral act, they successfully commit it. EG *There was a great deal of fraud perpetrated by various members.... ...the horrors perpetrated on the South American continent.* V+O: USU PASS

perpetrator /pɜːpɪ²treɪtə/, **perpetrators**. A **perpetrator** is a person who has committed a harmful or immoral act; a formal word. EG *...the perpetrator of the crime.* N COUNT

perpetual /pəpetju⁰əl/. Something that is **perpetual** 1 never ends or changes. EG *They hoped to live in a world of perpetual happiness... These bats live in deep caves in perpetual darkness.* ◊ **perpetually**. EG *...Freetown, the perpetually rainy capital of Sierra Leone.* 2 happens repeatedly and therefore seems never to end or change; used showing disapproval. EG *I got tired of his perpetual questions... They always break the bedtime rules and make themselves a perpetual nuisance.* ◊ **perpetually**. EG *She was perpetually answering the doorbell.* ADJ CLASSIF: USU ATTRIB ◊ ADV = continually ADJ CLASSIF: ATTRIB = continual, constant ◊ ADV WITH VB

perpetuate /pəpetjuːeɪt/, **perpetuates, perpetuating, perpetuated**. To **perpetuate** a system, belief, situation, etc means to do something that allows it to continue. EG *...an education system that perpetuates poverty and inequality... ...their determination to perpetuate the conspiracy.* ◊ **perpetuation** /pəpetjuːeɪʃə⁰n/. EG *...the perpetuation of inequality.* V+O ⇑ preserve ◊ N UNCOUNT+*of*

perpetuity /pɜːpɪ²tjuːɪti¹/. If something is done **in perpetuity** or **for perpetuity**, it is intended to last for ever; a formal expression. EG *The plots where they were buried were dedicated in perpetuity to the United States.* PHR: USED AS AN A

perplex /pəpleks/, **perplexes, perplexing, perplexed**. To **perplex** someone means to cause them to feel confused and slightly worried because they do not completely understand. EG *He perplexed people; they didn't quite know what to make of him.* ◊ **perplexed**. EG *Mrs Jane looked perplexed.* ◊ **perplexing**. EG *This might seem very perplexing to somebody who knows nothing about it.* V+O = bewilder, puzzle ◊ ADJ QUALIT ◊ ADJ QUALIT

perplexity /pəpleksɪti¹/, **perplexities**. 1 **Perplexity** is a feeling of confusion and slight worry which you have because there is something that you do not completely understand. EG *She looked at us in some perplexity.* N UNCOUNT = puzzlement

2 A **perplexity** is something that is complicated and difficult to understand; a formal use. EG *Perhaps we shall find answers to the great perplexity.* N COUNT ⇑ problem = riddle

perquisite /pɜːkwɪzɪt/, **perquisites**. A **perquisite** is the same as a perk; a formal word. EG *They are rewarded in pay, power and perquisites.* N COUNT: USU PL ⇑ extra

per se /pɜː seɪ/. **Per se** is a formal expression which is used to say 1 that you are considering a particular subject only from a general or theoretical point of view, rather than taking into account the practical aspects or your own experiences. EG *Most people know very little about the educational process per se.* 2 that something has a particular quality simply because it is what it is. EG *Anything socially practical is good per se.* ADV: NG+ADV = as such ADV: ADJ+ADV = in itself

persecute /pɜːsɪkjuːt/, **persecutes, persecuting, persecuted**. If someone **persecutes** you, 1 they treat you cruelly and unfairly and make you suffer, especially because of your political or religious beliefs. EG *Members of these sects are ruthlessly persecuted and suppressed.* 2 they keep bothering or annoying you and making your life difficult. EG *He said she was persecuting him and following him.* V+O = maltreat, oppress V+O = harass, hound

persecution /pɜːsɪkjuːʃə⁰n/, **persecutions**. 1 A **persecution** is a time when a group of people are treated cruelly and unfairly, especially because of their political or religious beliefs. EG *He had fled from France at the time of the persecution.* N COUNT = oppression

2 **Persecution** is cruel and unfair treatment of a person or group, especially because of their political or religious beliefs. EG *...the persecution of nonconformists and minorities.* N UNCOUNT

persecutor /pɜːsɪkjuːtə/, **persecutors**. A **persecutor** is someone who treats a person or group unfairly and cruelly, especially because of their political or religious beliefs. N COUNT = tormentor

perseverance /pɜːsɪvɪərəns/. If you do something with **perseverance** or if you have **perseverance**, you keep trying to do it and you do not give up, even though it is very difficult. EG *It allowed him to finally benefit from his perseverance and hard work.* N UNCOUNT ⇑ effort = persistence

persevere /pɜːsɪvɪə/, **perseveres, persevering, persevered**. If you **persevere** with something, you keep trying to do it and you do not give up, even though it is very difficult. EG *Everyone had to persevere and face up to innumerable setbacks... This is one reason why we persevered with the diary.* ◊ **persevering**. EG *The child is so persevering, when she knows she is unwanted.* V: IF+PREP THEN *with* ⇑ continue = persist ◊ ADJ QUALIT = persistent

Persian /pɜːʃə⁰n/, **Persians**. 1 Something that is **Persian** belongs or relates to the ancient kingdom of Persia or to the modern state of Iran, or to its people or language; a rather old-fashioned use. ADJ CLASSIF

2 **Persian** carpets and rugs come from Persia. They have geometric patterns in rich colours and are made by hand from silk or wool. ADJ CLASSIF

3 **Persian** is the language that is spoken by people who live in Iran or who used to live in the ancient kingdom of Persia. N UNCOUNT

persimmon /pɜːsɪmən/, **persimmons**. A **persimmon** is a sweet red fruit which grows on trees in hot countries. N COUNT

persist /pəsɪst/, **persists, persisting, persisted**. 1 If something **persists**, it continues to exist, even after you have tried to make it disappear. EG *Political differences still persist... The pain persisted into the morning.* V = last

2 If you **persist** in or with something, you continue to do it with determination, even though it is difficult or other people are against it. EG *There was no doubt what consequences would ensue if I persisted... People still persist in thinking that standards are going down... He persisted with his policy of conciliation... 'And what,' persisted Casson, 'is to prevent us waiting?'* V, V+A, OR V+QUOTE = keep on

persistence /pəsɪstəns/. 1 The **persistence** of something is the fact of its continuing to exist for a long time. EG *Because of the suddenness and persistence of the depression I saw my doctor... This persistence of ties with the countryside is not uncommon.* N UNCOUNT ⇑ existence

2 If you have **persistence**, you continue to do something with determination, even though it is difficult or other people are against it. EG *She managed it by persistence and ambition.* N UNCOUNT ⇑ strength = perseverance

persistent /pəsɪstənt/. 1 Something that is **persistent** continues to exist, even after you have tried to make it disappear. EG *...a time of high and persistent unemployment... How do you get rid of a persistent nasty smell?* ADJ QUALIT = constant

2 If your behaviour is **persistent**, you continue to do something with determination, even though it is difficult or other people are against it. EG *...a just reward for hard work and persistent effort... ...persistent requests for action.* ▸ used of people. EG *I think you have to be persistent, if people say no to you.* ADJ QUALIT ⇑ firm = relentless

persistently /pəsɪstəntli¹/ means 1 happening again and again. EG *They persistently drew the wrong conclusions... We simply can't allow a free rein for those who persistently break laws.* 2 done with determination, even though it is difficult or other people are against it. EG *It was his enemies who so persistently predicted his early fall.* ADV WITH VB = continually, repeatedly ADV WITH VB ⇑ firmly = determinedly

person /pɜːsən/, **persons**. The form **persons** is mainly used in very formal or legal language, and the word 'people' is usually used instead to refer to more than one person: see the entry at **people**. **1** A **person** is an individual man or woman. EG *There was far too much meat for one person... I want to see the person responsible for dealing with accounts... Are you the type of person who thrives on activity?... She was an absolutely charming person... The bomb exploded, killing 111 persons and injuring 188.* ▸ used to refer to a man or woman when you are considering him or her from the point of view of his or her real nature. EG *Is Jane Fonda, the actress, at odds with Jane Fonda, the political person?... ...the marvellous way he writes about Britten as a person.*

N COUNT ⇑ human being
▸ = character

2 You use **person** in expressions such as 'I'm a great outdoors person' or 'I'm not a coffee person' when you are saying whether or not you like a particular kind of activity or thing; an informal use. EG *I'm not much of a city person myself.*

N COUNT : MOD + N = type

3 Your **person** is your body; a rather old-fashioned or formal use. EG *The accused was found to have an offensive weapon concealed about his person.*

N COUNT : POSS + N

4 In grammar, a **person** is a person in a conversation. The first **person** is the speaker, the second **person** is the person addressed, and the third **person** is anyone else listening but not taking part in the conversation.

5 If you do something **in person**, you do it yourself rather than letting a substitute do it for you. If you talk to someone or meet, see, or hear them **in person**, they are actually present in the same place as you, for example rather than being on television, on the telephone, etc. EG *He wished he had gone to the house in person... He chose to address Congress in person... Now I had the chance to hear her speak in person... They talk a lot to one another, over the telephone and in person.*

PHR : USED AS AN A ⇑ directly

6 In the person of is used in front of the name of someone when you want to say that they have particular characteristics or are in a particular position. EG *We had, in the person of Susan Smith, an outstanding leader... He found one new problem in the person of Max Jones.*

PREP

-person, -persons. -person is used instead of '-man' or '-woman' in words such as 'spokesman' or 'chairwoman' when you want to refer to a person who holds a particular job or who carries out a particular activity, and when you do not want to make assumptions or show prejudices about the sex of the person. EG *He spoke to CND chairperson Joan Ruddock.*

SUFFIX : FORMS N COUNTS

persona /pəsəʊnə/, **personas** or **personae**; a formal word. Your **persona** is the aspect of your character or nature that you present to other people, perhaps in contrast to your real character or nature. EG *He decided to adopt an entirely new persona.* ● See also **persona non grata**.

N COUNT = image

personable /pɜːsənəbəl/. Someone who is **personable** has a pleasant appearance and character; a slightly old-fashioned word. EG *...a personable young man.*

ADJ QUALIT = presentable

personage /pɜːsənɪdʒ/, **personages**. A **personage** is a famous or important person; a fairly formal word. EG *...an important personage... ...funerals of great personages.*

N COUNT

personal /pɜːsənəl/ means **1** expressing the ideas or wishes of an individual person rather than of an organization or official group. EG *This is a personal opinion: I feel that the union should have a ballot... She applied for legal aid to bring a personal action against Sutcliffe.* **2** done directly by a particular person rather than by a substitute or representative; often used to suggest that the result is therefore much better. EG *The book was translated from the German under the personal supervision of the author.* **3** relating to an individual person. EG *...a personal challenge... ...a matter of personal preference... ...personal liberty.* **4** relating to your deepest feelings and most private activities that you do not usually talk to other people about. EG *...the most intimate details of their personal lives... It was difficult to speak about anything very personal... ...personal problems.* **5** referring to the appearance or character of a particular person in a way that is rude or offensive. EG *...finely veiled personal insults... I'd like to change the subject because I think we're getting too personal.* **6** belonging to a particular person or only for that person's attention or use. EG *...personal belongings... ...a letter marked 'personal'... ...a cheque drawn on his personal bank account.* **7** relating to your body. EG *...personal hygiene.*

ADJ CLASSIF : ATTRIB (1)
ADJ CLASSIF : ATTRIB (2)
ADJ CLASSIF : ATTRIB (3)
ADJ QUALIT (4)
ADJ QUALIT (5)
ADJ CLASSIF : ATTRIB (6)
ADJ CLASSIF : ATTRIB (7)

personal assistant, personal assistants. A **personal assistant** is someone who is employed to help a particular person with his or her work, especially with the secretarial and administrative part of the work.

N COUNT

personal column, personal columns. The **personal column** in a newspaper is a column which contains messages for individual people or advertisements of a private nature.

N COUNT

personal computer, personal computers. A **personal computer** is a fairly small computer that is used mainly by people at home rather than by a business.

N COUNT ≠ mainframe

personalise /pɜːsənəlaɪz/. see **personalize**.

personality /pɜːsənælɪti/, **personalities**. **1** Your **personality** is your whole character and nature. EG *The fact that they reacted so differently was a reflection of their very different personalities... He has a wonderful personality... ...the belief that the environment shapes personality... He was a very amusing and original personality.*

N COUNT + SUPP, OR N UNCOUNT

2 A **personality** is a famous person, especially in entertainment, broadcasting, or sport. EG *...TV personalities... Brian Johnston was named Radio Sports Personality of the year... ...four US Senators and other prominent American personalities.*

N COUNT = celebrity ≠ nobody

3 Personalities are rather rude remarks referring to a person's character or appearance; a rather old-fashioned use. EG *But the fight never degenerates into personalities; there is no feeling of bitterness.*

N PLURAL ⇑ insults

personalize /pɜːsənəlaɪz/, **personalizes, personalizing, personalized**; also spelled **personalise**. **1** If you **personalize** an argument, discussion, idea, or issue, you consider it from the point of view of individual people and their characters or relationships, rather than considering the facts in a general or abstract way. EG *We don't want to let the argument become personalized.* ◊ **personalization** /pɜːsənəlaɪzeɪʃən/. EG *...the absurd personalization of the issue.*

V+O
◊ N UNCOUNT

2 If you **personalize** something, **2.1** you mark it with the name, address, or initials of the owner, for example by printing, engraving, or embroidering it. ◊ **personalized**. EG *...personalized writing paper and pens... ...personalized cheques.* **2.2** you do or design it specially according to the needs of an individual rather than doing it in the same way for everyone. ◊ **personalized**. EG *... a personalized service.*

V+O ⇑ label
◊ ADJ CLASSIF
V+O ⇑ adapt
◊ ADJ CLASSIF

personally /pɜːsənəli/. **1** You use **personally** in order to emphasize that you are giving your own opinion. EG *Personally, I do not agree... I like German wines personally... Well, personally, I feel that this is very difficult.*

ADV SEN

2 You also use **personally** **2.1** to say that you are talking about someone from the point of view of their character and nature. EG *...our relationships with each of the people we know personally.* **2.2** to say that something is done directly by a particular person rather than by a substitute or representative. EG *Since then I have undertaken all the enquiries personally... It's a question you would have to raise with Mr Gerran personally.* **2.3** to say that something relates to an individual person. EG *I wasn't referring to you personally but to the department as a whole... It would be unjust for him to bear personally the great expenses involved.* **2.4** to say that something refers to the appearance or character of a particular person in a way that is rude or offensive. EG *Don't take it personally.*

ADV WITH VB
ADV WITH VB, OR ADV AFTER N
ADV WITH VB
ADV WITH VB

personal pronoun, personal pronouns. **personal pronouns** refer to the people who are involved in conversations. There are special forms for the subject position and for the object position. Personal pronouns are called PRON in the grammar notes beside the words. See ☐ at PRON.

N COUNT

persona non grata /pɜːsəʊnə nɒn grɑːtə/, **personae non gratae**. A **persona non grata** is someone who is unacceptable or unwelcome; a formal expression. EG *I felt I was persona non grata.*

N COUNT

personify /pəsɒnɪfaɪ/, **personifies, personifying, personified**. **1** If something abstract such as a quality **is personified** in a piece of literature, it is

V+O : USU PAST PART

represented in the form of a person; a technical term. EG *...angelic powers personified as gods.* ◊ **personification** /pəˢsɒnɪfɪkeɪʃəⁿn/. EG *...the personification of natural forces.* ◊ N UNCOUNT

2 If you say that someone **personifies** a particular thing or quality, you mean that they are a perfect example of that thing or possess that quality to a great degree or extent. EG *She felt that he seemed to personify the evil that was in the world... She is beauty personified.* ◊ **personification.** EG *He is the personification of the political power of industrial unions.* V+O : USU PAST PART ⇑ represent ◊ N UNCOUNT ⇑ representation

personnel /pɜːsənel/. 1 The **personnel** of a particular organization, business, or other establishment are the people who work there. EG *We were unable to offer this service because I hadn't got the personnel to cope with it... We've advertised for extra security personnel... ...personnel managers.* N PLURAL = staff

2 **Personnel** is a department in a large company or organization that deals with the employees, keeps their records, and helps with any problems they might have. EG *I work in personnel... She is the head of personnel for a big company.* N UNCOUNT

3 When you refer to **personnel** in the armed forces, you are referring to the people employed there, as opposed to machines or equipment. EG *...space launches which would convey cargo and personnel into orbit... ...personnel carriers.* N PLURAL

perspective /pəspektɪv/, **perspectives.** 1 A particular **perspective** is a particular way of thinking about or viewing something, especially one that is influenced by your beliefs or experiences. EG *He wanted to leave the country in order to get a better perspective on things... It was impossible for me to identify with his religious perspective... This report may have given me a distorted perspective... He always argued from a strange perspective that made it impossible to answer him.* N COUNT : USU + SUPP = view, outlook

2 **Perspective** is 2.1 the ability to think clearly and sensibly about a situation and consider it in relation to everything else. EG *She had a tough time keeping her perspective.* N UNCOUNT = objectivity 2.2 a method used by artists to represent objects in a picture so that they appear to be near or far away, and large or small in relation to each other. EG *We had a lesson in drawing class on perspective.* N UNCOUNT ⇑ technique 2.3 the visual effect that makes things that are further away seem smaller than things which are closer and makes parallel lines seem to meet at a point in the distance. N UNCOUNT

3 If you consider something **in perspective** or get it **into perspective,** you think about it sensibly and consider it in relation to everything else. EG *The president's role, judged in perspective, was even more reprehensible... It will help to put in perspective the vast gulf that separates existing groups... First of all we ought to get it into some kind of perspective.* PHR : USED AS AN A

4 If an object in a picture is **in perspective**, it has the correct size and position in relation to other things in the picture, and so looks realistic. If it is **out of perspective**, it has the wrong size and position. PHR : USED AS AN A

Perspex /pɜːspeks/ is a trademark for a strong, clear plastic which is sometimes used instead of glass. N UNCOUNT

perspicacious /pɜːspɪkeɪʃəs/. Someone who is **perspicacious** notices, realizes, and understands things quickly; a formal word. EG *Even the most perspicacious of students of human nature may fail to notice this trait in his character.* ADJ QUALIT = astute ≠ slow

perspicacity /pɜːspɪkæsɪti¹/ is the quality of being perspicacious; a formal word. N UNCOUNT

perspiration /pɜːspəreɪʃəⁿn/ is the salty colourless liquid which comes out onto the surface of your skin to cool your body, for example when you are hot, ill, or very frightened; a fairly formal word. EG *There were beads of perspiration on his upper lip.* N UNCOUNT = sweat

perspire /pəspaɪə/, **perspires, perspiring, perspired.** When you **perspire**, a salty colourless liquid comes out onto the surface of your skin to cool your body; a fairly formal word. EG *Hot and perspiring, John toiled up the dusty ascent.* V = sweat

persuade /pəsweɪd/, **persuades, persuading, persuaded.** 1 If someone or something **persuades** you to do something that you were at first unwilling to do, they cause you to do it by giving you a good reason for doing it. EG *Marsha was still trying to persuade Posy to change her mind... They had no difficulty in persuading him to launch a new paper... He is the sort of man that could be persuaded into anything... ...as the threat of unemployment persuades workers to moderate their pay demands.* V+O, V+O+ *to*-INF, OR V+O+A ⇑ influence

2 If someone **persuades** you that something is the case or is true, they cause you to believe that it is the case, especially by talking to you. EG *We worked hard to persuade them that we were genuinely interested in the project... I had persuaded myself that I could continue indefinitely like this.* ◊ **persuaded.** EG *She gradually became persuaded that market research was a community service... Few of them are persuaded of the benefits of the village shop.* V+O (NG/REFL), V+O (NG/REFL)+ REPORT-CL/A *(of)* = convince ◊ ADJ CLASSIF : PRED = convinced ≠ sceptical

persuasion /pəsweɪʒəⁿn/, **persuasions.** 1 **Persuasion** is the act of persuading someone to do something or persuading them to believe that something is the case. EG *I had to adopt other methods of persuasion... You could, with a little persuasion, get some of these people to help.* N UNCOUNT

2 If you are of a particular **persuasion**, you hold a particular belief or set of beliefs, especially religious or political beliefs; a fairly formal use. EG *...those who are not of the Roman Catholic persuasion... Many people in your organization may be of this persuasion.* ▸ used of someone who holds a particular set of beliefs. EG *This policy seemed to suit most political persuasions.* N COUNT : USU MOD+N IN SING

3 You can describe someone as being **of** a particular **persuasion** as a formal, humorous way of saying that they are of the type mentioned. EG *...singers of the Peggy Lee persuasion.* PHR : USED AS AN A = school

persuasive /pəsweɪsɪv/. Something or someone that is **persuasive** is likely to persuade someone to believe or do a particular thing. EG *...a very persuasive argument... He was eloquent and persuasive.* ◊ **persuasively.** EG *Her arguments are very lucidly and persuasively set out in this book.* ADJ QUALIT = convincing ≠ unconvincing ◊ ADV WITH VB

pert /pɜːt/. Someone, usually a young woman, who is **pert** is prim, neat, and cheeky. EG *...a pert, spiteful-looking woman.* ▸ used of things. EG *Her voice was pert, almost coquettish... ...her pert little nose.* ADJ QUALIT = saucy

pertain /pəteɪn/, **pertains, pertaining, pertained.** Something that **pertains** to something else belongs, relates, or applies to it; a formal word. EG *The 201 file contains all the documents that pertain to a given agent... The rules pertaining to one set of circumstances do not necessarily pertain to another.* V+A *(to)* = be relevant

pertinacious /pɜːtɪneɪʃəs/. Someone who is **pertinacious** continues doing something or trying to achieve something rather then giving up quickly; a formal word. EG *She was a skilful and experienced advocate, quiet but pertinacious.* ADJ QUALIT = persistent, tenacious

pertinent /pɜːtɪnənt/. Something that is **pertinent** is relevant to or connected with something else, especially a subject that is being discussed, and should be given attention because of this. EG *I asked him a lot of pertinent questions about the original production... ...medical documents which were highly pertinent to the question of Gregory's sanity.* ADJ QUALIT

perturb /pətɜːb/, **perturbs, perturbing, perturbed.** If something **perturbs** you, it makes you feel worried; a fairly formal word. EG *His behaviour had been perturbing me more than I had cared to admit.* ◊ **perturbed.** EG *They are not the slightest bit perturbed by it... She was perturbed about a rash which had come out on her face... The vicar looked perturbed.* V+O = alarm, disturb, trouble ◊ ADJ QUALIT : PRED = alarmed, troubled

perturbation /pɜːtəbeɪʃəⁿn/ is anxiety and worry; a formal word. EG *They had been pressing for a tight incomes policy, to the growing perturbation of the unions.* N UNCOUNT = concern

perusal /pəruːzəⁿl/. The **perusal** of a piece of writing is the action of reading it fairly quickly and without concentrating very hard on it; a fairly formal word. EG *Clare handed it over for my perusal... A perusal of the White Paper suggests otherwise.* N UNCOUNT : USU +SUPP = examination

peruse /pəruːz/, **peruses, perusing, perused.** When you **peruse** a piece of writing, you read it fairly quickly and without concentrating very hard on it; a fairly formal word. EG *He took the letter and perused it.* V+O = study

Peruvian /pəruːvɪən/, **Peruvians.** 1 A **Peruvian** person or thing belongs or relates to Peru, or to its people. EG *Other affected areas are the Peruvian coast and north-east Brazil.* ADJ CLASSIF

2 A **Peruvian** is a person who comes from Peru. N COUNT

pervade /pə⁵veɪd/, **pervades, pervading, pervaded.** Something, especially a quality or smell, that **pervades** a particular place or thing is present throughout it and is a noticeable feature of it. EG *An atmosphere of contentment and tolerance pervades the school... There was a smell of coffee pervading the atmosphere... This error pervades all present-day systems.* — V+O = permeate

pervasive /pə⁵veɪsɪv/. Something, especially a quality, effect, or smell, that is **pervasive** is present or felt throughout a place or thing. EG *...a pervasive atmosphere of fear... ...the Church's all pervasive influence... Certainly TV is the most powerful and pervasive of the media.* — ADJ QUALIT ⇑ widespread

perverse /pəvɜːs/. 1 Someone who is **perverse** deliberately does things that are unreasonable or that will result in harm, especially because someone else wants them to do the opposite. EG *He was extremely perverse and unpredictable... It would be perverse to refuse to support this plea.* ▸ used of actions, feelings, etc. EG *He takes a perverse delight in irritating people... I felt a perverse desire to accept his challenge... ...her perverse, wicked refusal to give them a chance in life.* ◇ **perversely.** EG *They persisted, perversely, in trying to grow grain.* — ADJ QUALIT = contrary; ▸ = wayward; ◇ ADV = wilfully

2 **Perverse** is sometimes used to describe sexual behaviour that is considered unacceptable and disgusting. Some people consider this use incorrect. — ADJ QUALIT = kinky, deviant

perversion /pəvɜːʃəⁿn/, **perversions.** 1 **Perversion** or a **perversion** is sexual behaviour or a sexual desire that is considered abnormal and unacceptable. EG *...bizarre sexual perversions.* — N COUNT/UNCOUNT ⇑ abnormality

2 The **perversion** of something is the changing of it so that it is no longer what it used to be or should be. EG *...the systematic perversion of the truth.* — N COUNT/UNCOUNT+*of* = corruption

3 A **perversion** is also something wrong, unnatural, or harmful that is the result of something being changed so that it is no longer what it used to be or should be. EG *The worker himself is turned into a perversion of a free being.* — N COUNT = travesty

perversity /pəvɜːsɪti¹/. 1 Someone who shows **perversity** deliberately does things that are unreasonable or does things that they know people do not want them to do. EG *...her perversity as a child... ...the perversity of fate.* — N UNCOUNT = contrariness

2 **Perversity** is also sometimes used to mean sexual perversion. Some people consider this use incorrect. — N UNCOUNT

pervert, perverts, perverting, perverted. The word **pervert** is pronounced /pəvɜːt/ when it is a verb, and /pɜːvɜːt/ when it is a noun. 1 If you **pervert** something, for example a process or society, you change it or interfere with it so that it is not as good as it used to be or should be. EG *Their traditional ceremonies were perverted into meaningless rituals... The country's obsession with the western way of life has perverted its development... He was accused of conspiring to pervert the course of justice.* — V+O ⇑ distort

2 A **pervert** is a person whose behaviour, especially sexual behaviour, is unacceptable and harmful or disgusting. EG *...perverts who rape and strangle small girls in parks.* — N COUNT = deviant

3 If someone **perverts** someone else, they cause them to develop unacceptable behaviour or ideas, especially unacceptable sexual behaviour. — V+O ⇑ corrupt

perverted /pəvɜːtɪ²d/. 1 Someone who is **perverted** has unacceptable or disgusting behaviour or ideas, especially sexual behaviour or ideas. EG *He had called the Headmaster arrogant and perverted.* ▸ used of actions and behaviour. EG *She regarded their relationship as more naughty than perverted.* — ADJ QUALIT = kinky, twisted; ▸ = unhealthy

2 Something that is **perverted** is wrong, unnatural, or harmful. EG *She realized that it was futile to try to understand the perverted logic of her jailers... ...the inventions of a perverted imagination... ...perverted values.* — ADJ QUALIT = warped

peseta /pəseɪtə/, **pesetas.** The **peseta** is the unit of money that is used in Spain. — N COUNT : USU NUM+N

pesky /peski¹/, **peskier, peskiest.** Something that is **pesky** is irritating; an informal word, used mainly in American English. EG *Pesky flies!* — ADJ QUALIT = tiresome

peso /peɪsəʊ/, **pesos.** The **peso** is the unit of money that is used in Portugal and in many of the countries in South America. — N COUNT : USU NUM+N ⇑ currency

pessary /pesəri¹/, **pessaries.** A **pessary** is 1 a solid medicine for curing infections. A woman puts it into her vagina and it dissolves there. — N COUNT
2 a contraceptive device which looks rather like a pill and contains a chemical which kills sperm. A woman puts it into her vagina and it dissolves there. — N COUNT

pessimism /pesɪmɪzəⁿm/ is the habitual belief that bad things will happen or are happening, or the belief that a particular thing will be unsuccessful or bad. EG *He had three weeks in which to prove to himself that his pessimism was unjustified.* — N UNCOUNT ⇑ attitude = despondency

pessimist /pesɪmɪst/, **pessimists.** A **pessimist** is someone who is always pessimistic or who is pessimistic about a particular thing. EG *Pessimists tell us that the family as we know it is doomed.* — N COUNT = cynic

pessimistic /pesɪmɪstɪk/. Someone who is **pessimistic** always thinks that bad things will happen or are happening, or thinks that a particular thing will be unsuccessful or bad. EG *Success now seemed very remote and Bernard felt pessimistic.* ▸ used of opinions and attitudes. EG *This is too pessimistic a view.* ◇ **pessimistically.** EG *Plan pessimistically.* — ADJ QUALIT = despondent ≠ hopeful; ▸ = bleak; ◇ ADV WITH VB

pest /pest/, **pests.** 1 A **pest** is an insect, rat, or other small animal which damages food supplies or crops. EG *Cold kills off lots of diseases and pests in the soil... If you see a rat call the town hall and ask for the pest controller.* — N COUNT

2 You describe someone, especially a child, as a **pest** when they keep bothering you or doing annoying things; an informal use. EG *He would give him a slap if he was too much of a pest.* — N COUNT : ALSO VOC = nuisance

pester /pestə/, **pesters, pestering, pestered.** If you **pester** someone, you keep asking or telling them to do something, or keep bothering them. EG *Everyone pestered me so much that I gave it up... For years Desiree had been pestering him to take her to Europe... We always pestered her for more.* — V+O = badger, nag

pesticide /pestɪsaɪd/, **pesticides.** **Pesticide** or a **pesticide** is a chemical which farmers put on their crops to kill harmful animals, especially insects. EG *...using all the latest seeds, fertilizers, and pesticides.* — N MASS

pestilence /pestɪləns/, **pestilences.** **Pestilence** or a **pestilence** is a disease that spreads quickly and kills large numbers of people; a literary word. — N COUNT/UNCOUNT = plague

pestle /pesəⁿl/, **pestles.** A **pestle** is a stick, usually made of marble or pottery, with a thick, round end. A pestle is used for crushing herbs, grain, etc in a bowl called a mortar. — N COUNT ⇑ implement

pet /pet/, **pets, petting, petted.** 1 A **pet** is a tame animal that you keep and look after in your home to give you company and pleasure. Dogs, cats, and rabbits are common pets. EG *It is against the rules to keep pets... The little boy saw his pet dog hurt by a car... ...a pet shop.* — N COUNT

2 Someone's **pet** theory, project, subject, etc is one that they have particularly strong feelings about or particularly like or support. EG *We were listening to yet another careful gardener with his pet theories... Smoking is one of my pet hates.* — ADJ CLASSIF : ATTRIB = personal

3 Someone who is the **pet** of someone in a position of authority is treated with special kindness and favour by them, often in a way that is unfair to others. EG *She's the teacher's pet.* — N COUNT : USU POSS+N = favourite

4 You can call someone **pet** as a sign of affection or friendliness; an informal use. EG *'Here, pet,' Boylan said kindly... I'll go into that tomorrow, my pet.* — VOC = darling

5 You describe someone as a **pet** when you think that they are sweet and nice; used in informal English. EG *He's quite an old pet, but useless as a source of information.* — N COUNT = poppet

6 If you **pet** someone, especially a child, you treat them with special kindness and favour. EG *Everybody liked me, everybody petted me.* — V+O = spoil

7 If you **pet** a person or animal, you pat or stroke them affectionately. EG *Give the infant as much hugging and petting as you can... She was holding the cat in her arms and petting it tenderly.* — V+O ⇑ touch

8 When two people, especially a teenage couple, **pet,** they kiss and stroke each other; an informal use. — V ⇑ embrace

petal /petəⁿl/, **petals.** The **petals** of a flower on a plant or tree are the coloured or white parts which are joined at the base and form the main part of the flower. EG *...rose petals... The wind shakes a little shower of white petals from a thorn tree on the bank.* — N COUNT

petard /pɪ²tɑːd/. If someone who has planned to harm someone else is **hoist with** their **own petard,** their plan in fact results in harm for themselves. — PHR : VB INFLECTS

peter /piːtə/, **peters, petering, petered.** If something **peters out,** it gradually comes to an end. — PHRASAL VB : V+ADV

EG *The tracks petered out a mile or two later... The meeting petered out after two hours.*

Peter. If you say that someone **is robbing Peter to pay Paul**, you mean that they are taking money or something else from one group of people in order to give it to another one, instead of finding extra money for the second group. PHR : VB INFLECTS

petite /pəti:t/. A woman who is **petite** is small and slim; used showing approval. EG *I vaguely remember her as being dark and petite.* ADJ QUALIT = dainty

petit-four /peti fɔ/, **petit-fours, petits-fours**; also spelled without a hyphen. The plural can be either **petit-fours** or **petits-fours**. A **petit-four** is a very small sweet cake or biscuit, often made of marzipan. N COUNT

petition /pɪ²tɪʃə⁰n/, **petitions, petitioning, petitioned**. 1 A **petition** is 1.1 a document which is signed by a lot of people and which asks the government or another official group to do a particular thing. EG *He presented a petition signed by 10,357 electors.* N COUNT 1.2 a formal request which is made to someone in authority; a formal use. N COUNT 1.3 an application to a court of law for some legal action to be taken. EG *She has filed a petition for divorce.* N COUNT

2 If a person or group of people **petitions** someone in authority or **petitions** for something, 2.1 they present a document which asks that a particular thing be done. EG *They petitioned the government to abolish hanging.* V OR V+O ⇑ request 2.2 they make a formal request; a formal use. EG *It is my clear duty to petition the court to declare this action illegal.* V OR V+O = call upon

petitioner /pɪ²tɪʃənə/, **petitioners**. A **petitioner** is 1 a person who presents or signs a petition. N COUNT 2 a person who asks the court for a divorce. N COUNT

pet name, pet names. A **pet name** is a special name that you use to address a close friend or a member of your family. EG *Teddy was her pet name for him.* N COUNT = nickname

petrify /petrɪfaɪ/, **petrifies, petrifying, petrified**. 1 If something **petrifies** you, it makes you feel very frightened indeed, perhaps so frightened that you cannot move. EG *The warning whistle started to blow. The sound petrified him.* V+O ⇑ scare = terrify ◊ **petrified**. EG *If I hadn't been alone I wouldn't have been nearly so petrified.* ◊ ADJ QUALIT = terrified

2 When something dead **petrifies**, it gradually changes into stone. V-ERG ◊ **petrified**. EG *The mountain range loomed menacingly like some petrified prehistoric monster.* ◊ ADJ CLASSIF : ATTRIB ◊ **petrification** /petrɪfɪkeɪʃə⁰n/. ◊ N UNCOUNT

3 If something such as a society or institution **petrifies** or if something else **petrifies** it, it ceases to change and develop; a formal use. EG *Militarism and xenophobia petrified the social order... ...if civilization was not to wither or petrify.* V-ERG = stagnate ◊ **petrification**. EG *These statements, taken too literally, lead to the petrification of meaning.* ◊ N UNCOUNT = stagnation

petrochemical /petrəukemɪkə⁰l/, **petrochemicals**. A **petrochemical** is a chemical that is obtained from petroleum or natural gas. EG *...the petrochemical industry.* N COUNT

petrol /petrəl/ is a liquid which is obtained from petroleum and which is used as a fuel to drive motor vehicles; used in British English. EG *Petrol only costs around 30p per gallon there... ...a petrol pump.* N UNCOUNT = gasoline

petrol bomb, petrol bombs. A **petrol bomb** is a simple bomb consisting of a bottle filled with petrol. The bottle also contains a cloth that is lit just before the bottle is thrown. EG *They were found guilty of possessing petrol bombs and assaulting police.* N COUNT

petroleum /pə²trəulɪəm/ is oil which is found under the surface of the earth or sea bed and from which petrol, paraffin, and other substances can be obtained. EG *Oil and petroleum refining is going to be a major industry here.* N UNCOUNT = crude oil

petroleum jelly is a soft, clear jelly which is obtained from petroleum and which is used as an ointment for putting on your skin, or to grease surfaces. N UNCOUNT

petrol station, petrol stations. A **petrol station** is a garage by the side of the road where petrol is sold and put into vehicles; used in British English. EG *...a self-service petrol station.* N COUNT = filling station

petticoat /petɪ¹kəut/, **petticoats**. A **petticoat** is a piece of clothing like a skirt that is worn under a skirt or dress. N COUNT = slip

pettifogging /petɪ¹fɒgɪŋ/. Someone who is **pettifogging** pays unnecessary attention to unimportant, boring details; a rather old-fashioned word. EG *They were small men with the low suspiciousness of pettifogging attorneys.* ADJ CLASSIF

pettish /petɪʃ/. Someone who is **pettish** shows childish irritation and anger over something that is not really important. EG *He was getting more and more pettish and hysterical.* ADJ QUALIT = petulant

petty /petɪ¹/, **pettier, pettiest**. 1 **Petty** things are small and unimportant. EG *But these were petty details... She was familiar with their petty social problems, and they bored her.* ADJ QUALIT : USU ATTRIB = trifling, trivial

2 If you describe an action or someone's behaviour as **petty**, you mean that it shows that they care too much about small, unimportant matters and perhaps that they are unnecessarily mean and unkind. EG *...petty jealousies... How foolish and petty it would have been to deny oneself this small luxury.* ADJ QUALIT : USU PRED = small-minded ◊ **pettiness**. EG *Even from you I hadn't expected such pettiness.* ◊ N UNCOUNT

3 **Petty** is also used of people or actions that are comparatively low in importance, rank, seriousness, or scale. EG *Authority was distributed among hundreds of petty leaders... This move was accompanied by a sharp rise in petty crime.* ADJ CLASSIF : ATTRIB = minor ≠ important, major

petty cash is money that is kept in the office of a company, ready to be used for making small payments if necessary. EG *Give Lexington fifteen dollars out of the petty cash.* N UNCOUNT

petty larceny is the theft of property that is not very valuable; a legal term. N UNCOUNT ⇑ crime

petty officer, petty officers. A **petty officer** is a non-commissioned officer in the navy. N COUNT : ALSO IN TITLES

petulance /petjə⁴ləns/ is unreasonable, childish bad temper over something unimportant. EG *...an exhibition of petulance and arrogance.* N UNCOUNT = sulkiness

petulant /petjə⁴lənt/. Someone who is **petulant** is unreasonably angry and upset in a childish way about something unimportant. EG *He was petulant, selfish, arrogant, and occasionally callous... The expression around her mouth was petulant.* ADJ QUALIT = sulky, peevish ◊ **petulantly**. EG *'You're always giving me advice,' Calderwood said petulantly.* ◊ ADV WITH VB = sulkily

petunia /pɪ²tju:nɪə/, **petunias**. A **petunia** is a garden plant with pink, white, or purple trumpet-shaped flowers. N COUNT

pew /pju:/, **pews**. 1 A **pew** is a long wooden seat with a back, which people sit on in church. N COUNT ⇑ pew

2 You can say **'take a pew'** as an informal, humorous way of inviting someone to sit down. EG *Come in. Come in. Take a pew. Cigarette?* PHR : VB INFLECTS

pewter /pju:tə/ is a grey metal made by mixing tin and lead. Pewter was often used in former times to make containers and ornaments. EG *...an eighteenth-century room, all dark oak and pewter mugs and plates.* N UNCOUNT ⇑ alloy

pfennig /fenɪg/, **pfennigs**. A **pfennig** is a small German coin, worth one hundredth of a mark. N COUNT

pH. The **pH** of a solution indicates how acid or alkaline the solution is. Acidic solutions have a pH of less than 7 and alkaline solutions have a pH of more than 7. N SING WITH DET

phalanx /fælæŋks/, **phalanxes, phalanges**. The plural can be either **phalanxes** or **phalanges**. A **phalanx** is a closely-packed group of people who are united for a particular purpose, for example to fight; a formal or technical word. EG *...a phalanx of infantrymen.* N COUNT/PART

phallic /fælɪk/. Something that is **phallic** is shaped like a phallus or symbolic of male sexual powers. EG *...the great stone pillar that rose like a phallic symbol from the earth.* ADJ QUALIT

phallus /fæləs/, **phalli** or **phalluses**. A **phallus** is 1 a model of a penis, especially one used as a symbol in old religions. N COUNT 2 a penis; a formal use or a technical term in psychology. N COUNT

phantasmagoria /fæntæzməgɔ:rɪə/, **phantasmagorias**. A **phantasmagoria** is a confused, dream-like sight made up of lots of different things; a literary word. EG *There hovered round the body in the coffin a phantasmagoria of dream-like thoughts.* N COUNT ⇑ vision

phantom /fæntə⁰m/, **phantoms**. 1 A **phantom** is something, especially a human form, which you think you see or hear but which is not real; a rather literary use. EG *I found myself staring at her as if she were a phantom.* N COUNT = ghost

2 **Phantom** is also 2.1 used of something which you think you see or hear but which is not real; a fairly ADJ CLASSIF : ATTRIB

literary use. EG ...*a phantom presence... I heard nothing but phantom bells ringing inside my own skull.* 2.2 used of something which you wrongly think you have or are experiencing. EG ...*a phantom pregnancy.* ADJ CLASSIF : ATTRIB ≠ real

3 **Phantom** is used in humorous expressions such as 'the **phantom** wine drinker' and 'the **phantom** bell ringer' that refer to an unknown person who does something or keeps doing something, especially something criminal. EG *The phantom wine drinker strikes again!* ADJ CLASSIF : ATTRIB = mysterious

pharaoh /fɛərəʊ/, **pharaohs**. A **pharaoh** was a king of ancient Egypt. EG ...*Thutmose III, an Egyptian pharaoh of the XVIII dynasty.* ▸ The pharaoh at a particular time is sometimes referred to as **Pharaoh**. EG ...*the closing of the Red Sea on Pharaoh's army.* N COUNT : ALSO IN TITLES ▸ TITLE

Pharisee /færɪsi:/, **Pharisees**. 1 The **Pharisees** were a group of Jews, mentioned in the Bible, that believed in strictly obeying the laws of Judaism. N COUNT : USU PL

2 A **Pharisee** is also a person who pretends to be very moral or religious but who is not moral or religious in a true, deep way; a formal use. N COUNT ⇑ hypocrite

pharmaceutical /fɑ:məsju:tɪkə⁰l/, **pharmaceuticals**. **Pharmaceutical** is an adjective and **pharmaceuticals** is a plural noun. 1 **Pharmaceutical** means connected with the professional preparation of drugs and medicines. EG ...*the world's largest pharmaceutical company... ...modern pharmaceutical products.* ADJ CLASSIF : ATTRIB ⇑ medical

2 **Pharmaceuticals** are drugs and medicines. EG ...*ten big consignments of pharmaceuticals.* N PLURAL

pharmacist /fɑ:məsɪst/, **pharmacists**. A **pharmacist** is a person who is qualified to prepare and sell drugs and medicines. ▸ A **pharmacist** or a **pharmacist's** is a shop in which drugs and medicines are sold by a pharmacist. N COUNT = chemist

pharmacology /fɑ:məkɒlədʒi¹/ is the branch of science relating to drugs and medicines. ◊ **pharmacologist, pharmacologists**. N UNCOUNT ◊ N COUNT

pharmacy /fɑ:məsi¹/, **pharmacies**. 1 **Pharmacy** is the job or art of preparing drugs and medicines. EG *She's at university doing pharmacy... Modern pharmacy has solved the problem of sleeplessness.* N UNCOUNT

2 A **pharmacy** is a shop, or part of a shop, where drugs and medicines are sold or given out. EG *Try the pharmacy on the corner.* N COUNT

phase /feɪz/, **phases, phasing, phased**. 1 A particular **phase** is a particular stage in a process, or in the gradual development of something such as a society or person's life or career. EG *When this happens, society enters a dangerous phase... It covers all phases of Picasso's work... World War II opened up the final phase in the disintegration of imperialism... Don't worry–it's just a phase he's going through.* N COUNT : USU+SUPP = period

2 If you **phase** a change or the introduction of something over a period of time, you cause it to happen gradually and in stages. EG *It involved a phased programme going over a twenty-five-year period.* V+O = stagger

3 The **phases** of the moon are the different shapes which the moon appears to have at different times during a month. N COUNT+SUPP

4 If two or more things are **out of phase**, they are not happening or working together as they should be, or are not in harmony with each other. If they are **in phase**, they are happening or working together as they should be, or are in harmony with each other. EG *Their national moods and public philosophies are out of phase... The lights come on in phase.* PHR : USED AS AN A, IF+PREP THEN *with*

phase in. If you **phase in** something, for example a new way of operating, or **phase it into** a system, you introduce it gradually. EG *Technology offers many alternatives that could be phased in.* PHRASAL VB : V+O+ADV/PREP, HAS PASS = bring in

phase out. If you **phase** something **out**, you gradually withdraw it from use. EG *This type of weapon was now being finally phased out.* PHRASAL VB : V+O+ADV ⇑ remove

PhD, PhDs. A **PhD** is a degree awarded to people who have done advanced research into a particular subject and have written an account of it; an abbreviation for 'Doctor of Philosophy'. EG *He's got a PhD in psychology... ...Jenny Remfrey PhD... ...a PhD thesis.* N COUNT : ALSO IN TITLES AFTER NAME ⇑ qualification

pheasant /fɛzə⁰nt/, **pheasants**. **Pheasant** can also be used as the plural form. A **pheasant** is a long-tailed bird often shot as a sport or for eating. Male pheasants are usually brightly coloured. EG ...*a cock pheasant.* ▸ used of the meat of a pheasant. EG *I like pheasant if it isn't tough.* N COUNT ▸ N UNCOUNT

phenomena /fɪ²nɒmɪnə/ is the plural of **phenomenon**.

phenomenal /fɪ²nɒmɪnə⁰l/. Something that is **phenomenal** is so great or good that it is very unusual indeed. EG *I think he's a pianist of absolutely phenomenal talent... ...the phenomenal growth of opera in Italy a century or so ago.* ◊ **phenomenally**. EG *There were a number of phenomenally expensive shops... Factory industry grew phenomenally from the 1880's onwards.* ADJ QUALIT ⇑ remarkable = incredible ◊ ADV ⇑ extremely = incredibly

phenomenon /fɪ²nɒmɪnən/, **phenomena**. 1 A **phenomenon** is something that happens or exists and can be seen or experienced; used especially when the event or thing is being considered in a scientific or academic way. EG *Constable looked at natural phenomena in a way that few painters before him had... ...the dreaded phenomenon of physical death... The employment problem tends to be a city phenomenon.* N COUNT : USU+SUPP

2 Someone who is a **phenomenon** is remarkable for a particular quality or achievement. EG *He was a phenomenon, a titanic force in the history of modern art.* N COUNT : USU USED AS C = prodigy

phew /fju:/ is used to represent the soft whistling sound that you make when you breathe out quickly, for example when you are very hot or have been running, or when you are relieved about something. EG *'Phew,' she said, 'it's hot out.'* EXCLAM

phial /faɪəl/, **phials**. A **phial** is a tube-shaped glass bottle used, for example, to hold medicine. N COUNT/PART

philanderer /fɪlændə⁰rə/, **philanderers**. A **philanderer** is a man who flirts a lot or has a lot of casual love affairs with women; a formal word used showing disapproval. N COUNT

philanthropic /fɪlənθrɒpɪk/. A **philanthropic** person or organization freely gives money and other help to people who need it. EG ...*a private philanthropic trust.* ADJ CLASSIF ⇑ charitable

philanthropist /fɪlænθrəpɪst/, **philanthropists**. A **philanthropist** is a person who freely gives money and other help to people who need it. EG ...*the most truly noble of Victorian philanthropists, the 7th Earl of Shaftesbury.* N COUNT ⇑ benefactor ≠ miser

philanthropy /fɪlænθrəpi¹/ is the giving of money and other help to people who need it, without wanting anything in return. EG ...*an organization not noted for its philanthropy.* N UNCOUNT ⇑ charity

philatelist /fɪlætəlɪst/, **philatelist**. A **philatelist** is a person who collects and studies postage stamps; a technical term. N COUNT ⇑ collector

philately /fɪlætəli¹/ is the hobby of collecting and learning about postage stamps; a technical term. N UNCOUNT

Philippine /fɪlɪpi:n/. A **Philippine** person or thing belongs or relates to the Philippines or to the people of the Philippines. ADJ CLASSIF = Filipino

philistine /fɪlɪstaɪn/, **philistines**. The word **philistine** is spelled with a capital letter for paragraph 3 and sometimes for paragraph 1. 1 A **philistine** is a person who does not understand or like good art, music, literature, etc and does not think they are important; used showing disapproval. EG ...*Philip Ridgeway, a big, coarse philistine from somewhere in the north of England.* N COUNT = boor

2 Someone who is **philistine** does not understand or like good art, music, literature, etc; used showing disapproval. EG *From Chelsea he raged at a philistine public.* ▸ used of things and actions. EG ...*a stunningly philistine article in New York magazine.* ADJ QUALIT = lowbrow ≠ cultured

3 The **Philistines** were a tribe of people in ancient Palestine. N COUNT : USU PL

philistinism /fɪlɪstɪnɪzə⁰m/ is the attitude or quality of not caring about, understanding, or liking good art, music, literature, etc; used showing disapproval. EG *She wrote an article lamenting the philistinism of an egalitarian culture.* N UNCOUNT

philology /fɪlɒlədʒi¹/ is the study of words, especially the words in a particular language, and how they have developed or changed. EG ...*those wishing to specialize in Slavonic philology.* ◊ **philologist, philologists**. N UNCOUNT ⇑ linguistics ◊ N COUNT ⇑ linguist

philosopher /fɪlɒsəfə/, **philosophers**. 1 A **philosopher** is a person who creates or studies theories about the nature of existence, knowledge, thought, etc or about how people should live and behave. EG *Haldane was a lawyer, philosopher, and politician...* N COUNT ⇑ theorist

...the Greek philosopher Thales... ...a question that has puzzled philosophers since the beginning of time.
2 If you describe someone as a **philosopher**, you mean that they think deeply and seriously about life and other basic, important matters. EG *You're obviously a bit of a philosopher.* N COUNT: USU USED AS C ⇑ thinker

philosophic /fɪləsɒfɪk/ means the same as philosophical. ADJ CLASSIF

philosophical /fɪləsɒfɪkəºl/. **1 Philosophical** means concerned with or relating to philosophy. EG *I read some of his philosophical and political essays... They used to have long philosophical conversations.* ADJ CLASSIF: USU ATTRIB ⇑ theoretical
◇ **philosophically**. EG *...a great and philosophically most profound view of the world.* ◇ ADV
2 Someone who is **philosophical 2.1** does not get upset when disappointing or disturbing things happen; used showing approval. EG *He was a plump, placid boy with a philosophical approach to life... Eddie spoke in a tone of philosophical resignation.* ADJ QUALIT = stoical
◇ **philosophically**. EG *He accepted their conclusion philosophically.* ◇ ADV WITH VB **2.2** thinks deeply and seriously about life and other basic, important matters. ADJ CLASSIF ⇑ thoughtful

philosophize /fɪlɒsəfaɪz/, **philosophizes, philosophizing, philosophized**; also spelled **philosophise**. Someone who **philosophizes** talks about basic, important subjects such as life, often in a boring, pretentious way. EG *This is not just empty philosophizing.* V: USU CONT ⇑ theorize

philosophy /fɪlɒsəfi¹/, **philosophies**. **1 Philosophy** is the study or creation of theories about the nature of existence, knowledge, thought, etc or about how people should live and behave. EG *She read philosophy at Oxford... ...moral philosophy.* ▸ also used of these theories themselves. EG *...an expert on Eastern philosophy.* N UNCOUNT ⇑ subject
2 A particular **philosophy** is **2.1** a particular theory or set of ideas that a philosopher has. EG *...the political philosophies of the West.* **2.2** a particular belief or theory that someone has about how to live or how to deal with a particular situation. EG *The move was consistent with the President's non-interventionist philosophy... ...new philosophies of child rearing... He was an angry, embittered, rich man, with no philosophy of life beyond self-indulgence.* N COUNT+SUPP = ideology; N COUNT+SUPP = principle

phlegm /flem/. **1 Phlegm** is the thick yellowish substance that develops in your throat and at the back of your nose when you have a cold. EG *Pa was coughing up some phlegm.* N UNCOUNT ⇑ mucus
2 If someone shows **phlegm**, they are very calm when they are experiencing something exciting or distressing; a fairly formal use. EG *What struck me was the remarkable bravery–or phlegm–of the cameramen in continuing to film.* N UNCOUNT

phlegmatic /flegmætɪk/. Someone who is **phlegmatic** stays calm even when exciting or distressing things happen, perhaps when they should be showing more emotion. EG *He was a phlegmatic, rather unemotional, certainly undemonstrative man.* ADJ QUALIT = stolid

phobia /fəʊbɪə/, **phobias**. A **phobia** is **1** an irrational fear or hatred of something, which is so strong that it is like an illness. EG *Another pupil had a phobia of poison... ...school phobia.* **2** a very strong dislike of something. EG *I've got a phobia about dust.* N COUNT; N COUNT

phobic /fəʊbɪk/, **phobics**. **1** A **phobic** feeling, reaction, etc results from or is related to a strong, irrational fear or hatred of something. EG *...phobic anxieties about going out.* ADJ CLASSIF: ATTRIB
2 Someone who is **phobic** has a strong, irrational fear or hatred of something. EG *There is a general feeling that to be phobic is to be an incomplete person.* ADJ CLASSIF
▸ used as a noun. EG *...school phobics.* ▸ N COUNT

phoenix /fiːnɪks/, **phoenixes**. A **phoenix** is an imaginary bird which, according to ancient myths, burns itself to ashes every five hundred years and is then born again. EG *Religion, like a phoenix, has been resurrected from the ashes of the revolution.* N COUNT

phoenix-like . Something that is **phoenix-like** returns or is created again after seeming to disappear or be destroyed. EG *Out of the ashes of the Suffragette Movement, phoenix-like, a new feminist militancy was being born.* ADJ CLASSIF ⇑ reborn

phone /fəʊn/, **phones, phoning, phoned**. **1** The **phone** is an electrical system of communication that makes it possible for you to talk directly to someone else in a different place who has a phone, usually by dialling a number on a piece of equipment and speaking into it. EG *We have heard from her by phone a couple of times... Most of the advisory work is carried out over the phone... I must go and make a phone call... Could you give me Frau Doring's address and phone number?* N SING: *the*+N, OR *by*+N UNCOUNT = telephone
2 A **phone** is the piece of equipment that you speak into when you talk to someone by phone. EG *I'm scared to answer the phone... The phone rang. It was Jimmy Breslin.* ▸ used to refer to the part of this piece of equipment that you pick up when you are using it. EG *She picked up the phone and dialled a number.* N COUNT = telephone
3 When you **phone** someone or **phone** their number, you dial their phone number and speak to them by phone. EG *I went back to the motel to phone Jenny... Harland phoned to tell me what time the bus was due.* V OR V+O = ring, call
4 If someone is **on the phone**, **4.1** they are speaking to someone else by phone. EG *I spent an hour on the phone trying to sort things out... She told me on the phone about the accident.* **4.2** they have a phone in their home or place of work, so that they can be contacted by phone. EG *I'm not on the phone.* PHR: USED AS AN A; PHR: USED AS AN A

phone up. When you **phone** someone **up**, you dial their phone number and speak to them by phone, especially about something not very important. EG *I must phone her up tonight.* PHRASAL VB: V+ADV, OR V+O+ADV = ring up, call up

phone book, phone books. A **phone book** is a book that contains the telephone numbers of the people in a particular town or area, next to their names and addresses. EG *I took the liberty of looking you up in the phone book.* N COUNT = telephone directory

phone booth, phone booths; also spelled with a hyphen. A **phone booth** is **1** a place in a station, hotel, or other public building where there is a public telephone. **2** in American English, a small shelter in the street in which there is a public telephone. N COUNT; N COUNT = call box

phone box, phone boxes; also spelled with a hyphen. A **phone box** is a small shelter in the street in which there is a public telephone, EG *Every phone box in Selly Oak had been vandalized.* N COUNT = call box

phone-in, phone-ins. A **phone-in** is a programme on radio or television in which people telephone with questions, ideas, or opinions and their calls are broadcast. EG *...a late-night phone-in programme.* N COUNT

phonetic /fə⁶netɪk/, **phonetics**. **Phonetic** is an adjective and **phonetics** is an uncount noun. They are technical terms in linguistics. **1 Phonetics** is the study of speech sounds. N UNCOUNT
2 Phonetic means relating to the sound of a word or to the sounds used in languages. ADJ CLASSIF: ATTRIB
3 A **phonetic** system of spelling is one in which each sound is represented by only one written symbol and each written symbol represents only one sound. ADJ CLASSIF
◇ **phonetically**. EG *We were taught to spell phonetically.* ◇ ADV WITH VB

phoney /fəʊni¹/, **phoneys**; **phonier, phoniest**; also spelled **phony**. **Phoney** is an informal word. **1** Something that is **phoney** is false rather than genuine; often used showing disapproval. EG *He gave a phony name and a phony address... She spoke with a phoney British accent.* ADJ CLASSIF = fake, sham
2 Someone or something that is **phoney** is insincere or pretentious. EG *He thought all grown-ups were phony... The company had a phoney Latin name which inspired no confidence.* ADJ QUALIT ⇑ false
3 Someone who is a **phoney 3.1** is insincere and pretentious. EG *I suddenly realized what a phoney he is.* **3.2** is not who or what they pretended they were. EG *They'll be furious when they find out he's a phony.* N COUNT = fraud; N COUNT

phonograph /fəʊnəgrɑːf, -græf/, **phonographs**. A **phonograph** is a record player; used in American English or in old-fashioned British English. EG *We played cards and listened to the phonograph.* N COUNT = gramophone

phonology /fə⁶nɒlədʒi¹/ is the study of the speech sounds in a particular language; a technical term in linguistics. ◇ **phonological** /fɒnəlɒdʒɪkəºl/. EG *...important phonological distinctions.* N UNCOUNT; ◇ ADJ CLASSIF: ATTRIB

phony /fəʊni¹/. See **phoney**.

phooey /fuːi¹/; an informal word. You say **phooey 1** to express, in a rather rude way, your belief that someone is talking nonsense. **2** when you are disappointed or annoyed about something. EXCLAM = rubbish; EXCLAM

phosphate /fɒsfeɪt/, **phosphates**. A **phosphate** is a chemical compound that contains phosphorus. Phosphates are often used in fertilizers. EG *...uranium, tin, phosphates, and other minerals.* N COUNT/UNCOUNT

phosphorescence /fɒsfərɛsəns/ is a glow or brightness which is produced without using heat. EG ...*letters that shine with a fearful phosphorescence.* N UNCOUNT = luminescence

phosphorescent /fɒsfərɛsənt/. Something that is **phosphorescent** glows with a soft light but gives out little or no heat. EG ...*cultures of phosphorescent bacteria... ...cloudy phosphorescent gas.* ADJ CLASSIF

phosphorus /fɒsfərəs/ is a poisonous whitish element that glows faintly and that burns when it is in contact with air. N UNCOUNT

photo /fəʊtəʊ/, **photos.** A **photo** is a photograph; an informal use. EG *I took a magnificent photo of him.* N COUNT

photo- is added to nouns and adjectives in order to form other nouns and adjectives which refer or relate to photographs or photographic processes, or to light. EG ...*journalism→photo-journalism... ...montage→photomontage... ...engraving→photoengraving.* PREFIX

photocopier /fəʊtə⁶kɒpɪə/, **photocopiers.** A **photocopier** is a machine which quickly copies documents or drawings onto pieces of paper by photographing them. N COUNT

photocopy /fəʊtə⁶kɒpi¹/, **photocopies, photocopying, photocopied.** 1 A **photocopy** is a copy of a document made using a photocopier. EG *We need to make a photocopy to send to staff members.* N COUNT

2 If you **photocopy** a document, you make a copy of it using a photocopier. V+O

photo finish. If the finish of a race is a **photo finish,** two of the competitors cross the finishing line so close together that a photograph has to be examined to find out who has won. N SING : a+N

Photofit /fəʊtəʊfɪt/; a trademark. A **Photofit** picture is a picture of someone wanted by the police that is made up of several photographs of different facial features. N BEFORE N ⇑ composite

photogenic /fəʊtədʒɛnɪk/. Someone or something that is **photogenic** looks nice in photographs. EG *Photogenic girls were sought for a series of adverts.* ADJ QUALIT

photograph /fəʊtəgrɑːf, -græf/, **photographs, photographing, photographed.** 1 A **photograph** is a picture that is made using a camera containing film which changes when light falls on it and which is then printed on special paper. EG *I take photographs of things that interest me... It's a very good photograph of her... They contacted the police after seeing his photograph in a newspaper.* N COUNT ⇑ image = photo

2 When you **photograph** someone or something, you use a camera to obtain a photograph of them. EG *She photographed the pigeons in Trafalgar Square... He doesn't like being photographed.* V+O

photographer /fətɒgrəfə/, **photographers.** A **photographer** is 1 a person whose job consists of taking photographs. EG ...*Robert L. Beck, photographer for Life magazine.* N COUNT 2 someone who takes photographs. EG *Florrie had never been a good photographer.* N COUNT+SUPP

photographic /fəʊtəgræfɪk/. 1 **Photographic** means connected with photographs or photography. EG ...*expensive photographic equipment... ...a photographic record of the chick's development.* ADJ CLASSIF : ATTRIB

2 Someone who has a **photographic** memory is able to remember things very accurately and in great detail after they have seen them. ADJ CLASSIF : ATTRIB ⇑ accurate

photography /fətɒgrəfi¹/ is the craft, job, or process of taking or producing photographs. EG *Fox-Talbot was a pioneer of photography.* N UNCOUNT ⇑ representation

photostat /fəʊtə⁶stæt/, **photostats, photostating, photostated;** also spelled **photostatting, photostatted. Photostat** is a trademark. 1 A **Photostat** is a particular type of photocopy. EG ...*a photostat of the actual report.* N COUNT ⇑ copy

2 If you **photostat** a document, you photocopy it. V+O

PHR □ In this dictionary PHR is used in the grammar notes beside entries to mean 'phrase' or 'expression'. Examples are **for life,** at **life 12.2, a blessing in disguise,** at **blessing,** and **keep tabs on,** at **tab.** Where a phrase normally has a particular clause function, such as adjunct, complement, or object, this function is mentioned in the grammar note. Thus, **for life** is described as PHR: USED AS AN A because it normally functions as an adjunct. EG *She agreed to be my friend **for life**... Their faces were scarred **for life**.* **A blessing in disguise** is described as PHR: USED AS C because it normally functions as a complement. EG *A crisis can be **a blessing in disguise**... This attack proved **a blessing in disguise** for France.* In many phrases, one or more of the words in the phrase can be inflected to fit into different clause structures. Where this is so, it is mentioned in the grammar note. An example is **to keep tabs on,** described as PHR: VB INFLECTS. The verb inflects but the noun *tabs* is always used, as shown, in the plural. EG ***I kept tabs on him.*** You cannot say 'I kept a tab on him'. In other cases, the wording of the phrase cannot normally be inflected. Examples are **a fly in the ointment** at **ointment,** and **wouldn't hurt a fly** at **fly 18.** You say ***The fly in the ointment** is that they don't want to go.* You cannot say 'These problems are flies in the ointment'. You say *Peter **wouldn't hurt a fly**.* You cannot say 'Peter did not hurt a fly' or 'Peter wouldn't hurt flies'. In this dictionary, additional information is given where necessary to show restrictions on the phrase or to indicate what follows it. An example is **turn a deaf ear** at **deaf 5,** described as PHR: VB INFLECTS, IF+PREP THEN *to.* This means that the verb *turn* inflects, although the noun *ear* does not, and that if the whole phrase is followed by a prepositional phrase, the preposition *to* starts the prepositional phrase. EG *Young people sometimes seem to **turn a deaf ear** to the words of their anxious parents.* Another example is **take a delight,** at **delight 2,** described as PHR: VB INFLECTS, USU+*in*+-ING. This means that the verb *take* inflects, although the noun *delight* does not, and that the whole phrase is usually followed by *in* + a verb in its -ING form. EG *He **takes a positive delight** in being hurt.*

PHRASAL VB □ In this dictionary PHRASAL VB is used in the grammar notes beside entries to mean 'phrasal verb'. Phrasal verbs are explained at the end of the relevant verb entry. A phrasal verb is a combination of two words with a single meaning. One word is a common verb and the other word is a preposition or one of the common adverbs such as *up, down,* and *across.* In a few cases, both an adverb and a preposition can be used. Examples of phrasal verbs are **come across,** meaning 'discover', as in *I **came across** a problem,* and **take off,** meaning 'mimic', as in *She used to **take off** Mrs Thatcher.* If the verb is used with a preposition (PREP), it must be followed by a noun group, which functions as a prepositional object. If it is used with an adverb (ADV), it does not need to be followed by anything. In addition to the ADV or PREP, the verb itself may be transitive or intransitive. The main patterns of phrasal verbs are as follows: 1 V+ADV describes a phrasal verb in which the verb is intransitive and is followed by an adverb. Examples are **burn down** and **butt in.** EG *The mansion **burned down** four years ago... You can't just **butt in** when other people are talking.* 2 V+PREP describes a phrasal verb in which the verb is intransitive and is followed by a preposition. Examples are **come across 1** and **stand by 3.** EG *I **came across** an old French saying about priests... In that case I **stand by** what I said.* Sometimes the prepositional object can become the subject of a passive clause. When this is possible, the grammar note says V+PREP, HAS PASS. Examples are **look after 1** and **see to.** You can say *The children **were looked after** by a succession of young girls* as well as *A succession of young girls **looked after** the children.* You can say *It's all right, it **is being seen to*** as well as *It's all right, someone **is seeing to** it.* Extra information is sometimes given about what follows the prepositional object. An example is **take to,** as in *He **took to** wearing leather jackets,* which is described as PHRASAL VB: V+PREP+-*ing,* because the preposition is followed by an *-ing* form. 3 V+O+ADV describes a phrasal verb in which the verb is transitive and is followed by an adverb. Examples are **bring up 1** and **iron out.** EG *I had a struggle to **bring** the family **up**... Some women choose to stay at home and **bring up** their children... Technology enables us to **iron out** the natural problems.* These transitive phrasal verbs can be used in the passive, unless the grammar note tells you that they cannot. EG *The children **were brought up** by their mother... There are anomalies which **will be ironed out**.* In this type of phrasal verb, the object of the verb can normally come either before or after the adverb. If the object is a pronoun, it comes before the adverb, as in *They **took** him **on**.* If the object is a longer noun group, it usually comes after the adverb, as in *They **took on** nearly a hundred school leavers and young trainees.* If the object is a fairly short noun group, it may come before or after the adverb. There are some phrasal verbs of this type where the object of the verb comes before the adverb. There are others where the object comes after the adverb, unless the object is a pronoun. These are described in the grammar notes as PHRASAL VB: ORDER V+O+ADV and PHRASAL VB: ORDER V+ADV+O. Examples are **keep down** and **give up.** EG *The main aim is to **keep** development costs **down**... I am trying to **give up** smoking.* You do not normally say 'I am trying to give smoking up.' 4 V+O+PREP describes a phrasal verb that is transitive and is followed by a prepositional group. Examples are **talk into, drag into,** and **hold against.** EG *We **talked** Donald **into** leaving his job... I pointed out that it was the politicians who **were dragging** politics **into** sport... They **will hold** that **against** you when you apply next time.* 5 V+ADV+PREP describes a phrasal verb in which the verb is intransitive and is followed by an adverb and a preposition. The preposition always comes after the adverb. Examples are **look forward to, get away with,** and **go through with.** EG *I began to **look forward to** their visits... We **got away with** it... She vowed she would **go through with** it.* 6

V+O+ADV+PREP describes a phrasal verb in which the verb is transitive and is followed by an adverb and a preposition. The preposition always comes after the adverb. The object of the verb can come between the verb and the adverb, or after the adverb and before the preposition. An example is **take out on**. EG *She **took out** her unhappiness **on** her husband... She **took** her unhappiness **out on** her husband.* 7 V+ADV/PREP describes a phrasal verb in which the verb is intransitive and is followed by a word which can be used as either an adverb or a preposition. Examples are **break through** and **branch off**. EG *I struggled up the side of the gully and **broke through** the nettles* (V+PREP)... *After a while I **broke through** and saw him* (V+ADV)... *The road to Lutterworth **branches off** here* (V+ADV)... *It **branches off** the main road* (V+PREP). 8 V+O+ADV/PREP describes a phrasal verb in which the verb is transitive and is followed by a word which can be used as either an adverb or a preposition. Examples are **cross off** and **pass around**. EG *I **crossed** my name **off** the list* (V+O+PREP)... *She **crossed** her name **off*** (V+O+ADV)... *I've got a couple of pictures you might like to **pass around*** (V+O+ADV)... *We **passed** it **around** the room* (V+O+PREP). 9 V-ERG+ADV describes a phrasal verb that consists of an ergative verb followed by an adverb. See □ at V-ERG.

phrasal verb /frəɪzəˀlvɜːb/, **phrasal verbs**. A **phrasal verb** is a combination of a verb and an adverb or preposition, used together to have a particular meaning. In this dictionary, phrasal verbs have PHRASAL VB in the grammar notes beside the entries. See □ at PHRASAL VB. — N COUNT

phrase /freɪz/, **phrases, phrasing, phrased**. 1 A **phrase** is 1.1 a short group of words that people often use as a way of referring to something or saying something, especially a group of words that is memorable or whose meaning is not obvious from the words contained in it. Phrases that are given an explanation in this dictionary are referred to as 'expressions'. They are given the label PHR in the grammar notes beside the entries. See □ at PHR. EG *People still use the phrase 'doctor's orders'... The French-speaking Africans even have a phrase for this state of affairs... It was Asa Briggs who originally coined the phrase 'redrawing the map of learning'.* — N COUNT = expression

1.2 a small group of words which forms a unit, either on its own or within a sentence. EG *He punctuated every phrase by slapping the counter... My German was practically nil–a few phrases here and there... FORTRAN and BASIC use English words and phrases.* — N COUNT

2 If you **phrase** something in a particular way, you express it in words in that way. EG *The moment I'd said it, I could see that I'd phrased it wrong... A more bluntly phrased view came from the Leader of the Opposition.* — V+O+A ⇑ say = word

3 The word **phrase** is also used in the following expressions relating to speech. 3.1 You say **in a** particular person's **phrase** or **to use a** particular person's **phrase** when you are repeating a phrase that someone else has used. EG *In Mao's graphic phrase, China 'stood up'... ...a 'trained incapacity', to use Merton's phrase.* — PHR : USED AS ADV SEN 3.2 A particular **turn of phrase** is a particular way of expressing something in words. EG *You have a nice turn of phrase.* — PHR+SUPP : USED AS O/S 3.3 If you can **turn a phrase**, you can express things in a clever and original way. EG *He knew how to turn a phrase.* — PHR ● **to coin a phrase**: see **coin**.

4 A **phrase** is also a small group of musical notes which form a unit that is part of a longer piece of music; a musical term. EG *It was a single short phrase being sung over and over again.* — N COUNT

phrase book, phrase books. A **phrase book** is a book used by people travelling abroad that has lists of useful words and expressions in a foreign language together with the translation of each word or expression. EG *...a French phrase book.* — N COUNT

phraseology /freɪziɒlədʒiˡ/. If something is expressed using a particular type of **phraseology**, it is expressed in words and expressions of the style and type indicated; a rather formal word. EG *...the Latin phraseology of legal documents... ...the sort of phraseology used by some journalists about illiterates.* — N UNCOUNT+SUPP = parlance

phrasing /freɪzɪŋ/. 1 The **phrasing** of something that is said is the exact words that are used to say it. EG *...the careful phrasing of the Minister's statement.* — N UNCOUNT : USU +SUPP = wording

2 The **phrasing** of someone who is singing, playing a piece of music, acting, or reading poetry is the way in which they divide up the work that they are performing by pausing slightly in appropriate places. EG *Her phrasing was faultless.* — N UNCOUNT : USU WITH POSS ⇑ performance

phrenology /frɪˀnɒlədʒiˡ/ is the science of finding out what people's characters and abilities are by measuring the natural bumps on their skulls. — N UNCOUNT ◊ **phrenologist**. — ◊ N COUNT

phut /fʌt/. If something, especially a machine, **goes phut**, it goes wrong and stops working; an informal word. EG *The computer's gone phut.* — PHR : VB INFLECTS ⇑ fail

physical /fɪzɪkəˀl/, **physicals**. 1 **Physical** qualities, actions, or things are connected with a person's body, rather than with their mind, emotions, or soul. EG *All his physical and emotional needs would be attended to... Their physical strength was their pride... He never once used physical punishment on me.* — ADJ CLASSIF : USU ATTRIB ⇑ bodily ◊ **physically**. EG *He looked physically fit... She didn't attract me physically.* — ◊ ADV

2 **Physical** also means 2.1 relating to the structure, size, or shape of something that can be touched and seen, or involving things that can be touched and seen. EG *...the physical properties of substances... ...the physical characteristics of the earth... ...the overall physical size of a computer.* — ADJ CLASSIF : ATTRIB 2.2 connected with physics or the laws of physics. EG *...basic physical laws.* — ADJ CLASSIF : ATTRIB ⇑ scientific

3 **Physical** is also used of objects that can be touched and seen. EG *...the apparent ability of the mind to affect and move physical objects... ...a further step towards the replacement of physical money by electronic money.* — ADJ CLASSIF : ATTRIB

4 Someone's **physical** surroundings are the objects, structures, or natural features around them, rather than the society or group that they are in. EG *...an opportunity for children to look at the nature of the physical world around them... No irretrievable damage to the physical environment has yet been done... ...the appalling physical conditions in prisons.* — ADJ CLASSIF : ATTRIB

5 A **physical** fact, state, or quality is a real and actual one. EG *...the physical presence of the telephone... They would face poverty unless they could secure physical possession of oil-producing areas.* — ADJ CLASSIF : ATTRIB ◊ **physically**. EG *Some religions suppose that there is a Heaven physically above the earth.* — ◊ ADV ⇑ actually

6 Someone who is **physical** often touches people that they are with; a fairly informal use. — ADJ QUALIT

7 A **physical** is an examination of someone's body by a doctor to see how fit they are. — N COUNT

physical education consists of children at school doing physical exercises and playing physical games and sports. — N UNCOUNT = PE, PT

physical jerks are physical exercises that people do to keep fit; a rather old-fashioned expression. — N COUNT

physical science, physical sciences. The **physical sciences** are branches of science such as physics, chemistry, and geology that are concerned with things that do not have life and with natural forces. EG *...the uneven race between the life sciences and the physical sciences... ...the division of physical science into chemistry and physics.* — N PLURAL/N UNCOUNT

physical training is the same as physical education; a rather old-fashioned expression. — N UNCOUNT

physician /fɪzɪʃəˀn/, **physicians**. A **physician** is a doctor; an American or rather old-fashioned word. EG *It is unlikely that the number of consultant physicians in geriatric medicine will increase.* — N COUNT

physicist /fɪzɪsɪst/, **physicists**. A **physicist** is a person who studies physics or who does research connected with physics. EG *Physicists are still interested in magnetism... ...a well-known nuclear physicist.* — N COUNT ⇑ scientist

physics /fɪzɪks/ is the scientific study of forces and qualities such as heat, light, sound, pressure, gravity, and electricity, and the way that they affect objects. EG *According to our present ideas of physics, nothing can travel faster than light... ...nuclear physics... There's a desperate shortage of physics teachers.* — N UNCOUNT ⇑ science

physio /fɪziəʊ/, **physios**; an informal word. 1 **Physio** is physiotherapy. — N UNCOUNT

2 A **physio** is a physiotherapist. — N COUNT

physiognomy /fɪziɒnəmiˡ/, **physiognomies**; a formal word. 1 Your **physiognomy** is your face; used especially when your face is considered to show your character. EG *He kept his eyes fixed upon the old-world physiognomy of Mr Didlington.* — N COUNT : USU WITH POSS = features

2 The **physiognomy** of an area of countryside is its shape and the geographical features in it, such as hills and rivers. — N SING : *the*+N+*of* ⇑ appearance

physiological /fɪziəlɒdʒɪkəˀl/. 1 Something that is **physiological** relates to the way that a person's or — ADJ CLASSIF ⇑ biological animal's body functions, or to the way that a plant functions. EG *...the physiological processes of an animal's body... ...physiological changes that are beyond our control.*

2 Physiological is also used of things relating to the science of physiology. EG *...Pavlov's physiological theories.* — ADJ CLASSIF : ATTRIB ⇑ biological

physiology /fɪzɪɒlədʒi^1/. **1 Physiology** is the scientific study of how people's and animals' bodies function, and of how plants function. EG *She was awarded the Nobel Prize for physiology and medicine.* ◊ **physiologist**. — N UNCOUNT ⇑ biology; ◊ N COUNT

2 The **physiology** of a particular animal or plant, or of a particular biological part or process, is the way that it functions. EG *He was interested in the physiology of bulls... ...the anatomy, physiology, and psychology of pregnancy.* — N SING : the+N+of ⇑ biology

physiotherapist /fɪzɪəʊθerəpɪst/, **physiotherapists**. A **physiotherapist** is a person whose job is doing physiotherapy. — N COUNT = physio

physiotherapy /fɪzɪəʊθerəpi^1/ is treatment that someone is given, especially to help them regain their ability to move, which involves doing exercises or having part of their body massaged or warmed. — N UNCOUNT ⇑ therapy = physio

physique /fɪziːk/, **physiques**. Someone's **physique** is the shape and size of their body and muscles; used especially when referring to a man's body. EG *...a good-looking lad with a fine physique, powerful and attractive.* — N COUNT : USU SING, OR N UNCOUNT = build

pi /paɪ/ is a number, approximately 3.142, which is equal to the circumference of a circle divided by its diameter. It is usually represented by the Greek letter π. — NUM

pianissimo /pɪənɪsɪməʊ/. A piece of music that is played **pianissimo** is played very quietly; a musical term. ▸ used as an adjective. EG *Sh! It's the pianissimo section next.* — ADV WITH VB ≠ fortissimo; ▸ ADJ CLASSIF : ATTRIB

pianist /pɪənɪst/, **pianists**. A **pianist** is a person who plays the piano, especially one who earns money by playing the piano. EG *...the great Brazilian pianist Guiomar Novaes.* — N COUNT ⇑ musician

piano /pi^{1}ænəʊ/, **pianos**. **1** A **piano** is **1.1** a large musical instrument with a row of black and white keys. When these keys are pressed down by the player's fingers, little hammers hit wire strings and different notes are played. EG *Her house had a piano in every room... I hear you play the piano... ...my weekly piano lessons.* ▸ used as an uncount noun. EG *I don't know of any duets for piano and trumpet... ...Hines, the father of jazz piano.* ● See also **grand piano**. — N COUNT; ▸ N UNCOUNT

2 A piece of music that is played **piano** is played quietly; a musical term. — ADV WITH VB ≠ forte

pianoforte /pi^{1}ænəʊfɔːteɪ/, **pianofortes**. A **pianoforte** is a piano; a formal or old-fashioned word. — N COUNT/ UNCOUNT

piazza /pɪætsə, -ædzə/, **piazzas**. A **piazza** is a large open square, especially in an Italian town. EG *They walked out of the cafeteria, and across the piazza.* — N COUNT : ALSO IN NAMES BEFORE N

picaresque /pɪkəresk/. A **picaresque** story is one in which a dishonest but likeable hero travels around and has lots of exciting adventures; a literary term. ▸ used of the hero or events in such a story. EG *...after adventures as picaresque and unlikely as those of any hero of romance.* — ADJ QUALIT

piccalilli /pɪkəlɪli^1/ is a sharp-tasting yellow sauce made from chopped and pickled vegetables. — N UNCOUNT ⇑ relish

piccolo /pɪkələʊ/, **piccolos**. A **piccolo** is a very small musical instrument that is shaped like a flute but that produces higher notes. — N COUNT ⇑ wind instrument

pick /pɪk/, **picks, picking, picked**. **1** If you **pick** a particular person, thing, or way of doing something, you choose that one. EG *Next time let's pick somebody who can fight... Just pick what suits you and leave the rest... I could not have picked a better way to travel.* ◊ **picked**. EG *Most nations now give military training to a picked quota of their young men.* ● If you **pick and choose**, you make the choice that you want to make and reject things that you do not want; a fairly informal expression. EG *You always did like to pick and choose... A good secretary can pick and choose her job.* — V+O = select, opt for; ◊ ADJ CLASSIF = selected; ● PHR : VBS INFLECT ⇑ be particular

2 If you **have** your **pick** of a group of things, you are able to choose any of them that you want. — PHR : VB INFLECTS

3 If you **take** your **pick**, you choose or take whichever one of a group of things that you want. EG *Take your pick. Choose whichever one of the three methods you fancy.* — PHR : VB INFLECTS

4 The best things or people in a particular group can be referred to as the **pick** of that group. EG *After a day's fishing, the pick of the catch was served up at the inn that evening.* — N SING : the+N, IF+PREP THEN of = cream

5 When you **pick** flowers, fruit, etc from plants or trees, you break them off and take or collect them. EG *I liked helping to pick mushrooms in the wet fields... How nice of the children to remember her and pick her some flowers.* — V+O, V+O+O, OR V+O+A (for) = gather, pluck

6 If you **pick** something from a particular place, you take it in your hand and move it. EG *He picked his blazer off a chair... ...picking the volume off the shelf... They had to stop to pick out thorns from their feet.* — V+O+A = pluck, remove

7 If you **pick** your nose, teeth, or another part of your body, you try to remove something from it with your fingernail or a small tool. EG *My sister was wrinkling her eyes and picking her nose... He had just had a meal and was picking his teeth after it... She started picking a spot on her chin.* — V+O

8 If a person or animal **picks** meat from a bone or **picks** the bone clean, they eat the small pieces of meat that remain on it. EG *Their bones had been picked clean by the birds.* — V+O+A, OR V+O +C

9 If you **pick** a fight or quarrel with someone, you deliberately cause a fight or quarrel; a fairly informal use. EG *Hell's Angels picked fights with delegates in the streets... He had ceased, of his own free will, to pick quarrels with her.* — V+O : IF+PREP THEN with ⇑ start

10 If someone, for example a thief, **picks** a lock, they open it without a proper key by moving the mechanism inside it with a piece of wire, hairpin, or other small tool. — V+O

11 If you **pick** your **way** across an area where there are lots of things on the ground, you walk very carefully, looking at the ground to see where to put your feet. EG *He began to pick his way over the tumbled rocks.* — PHR : VB INFLECTS+A

12 A **pick** is a tool consisting of a thin, curved piece of metal with a point at one or both ends and a long handle joined to the middle of the metal. Picks are used for breaking up the ground or rocks. EG *I got torn and bleeding hands working with a pick and shovel.* — N COUNT

13 The word **pick** is also used in the following expressions, which are explained at other places in this dictionary. ● to **have a bone to pick with someone**: see **bone**. ● to **pick someone's brains**: see **brain**. ● to **pick holes in** something: see **hole**. ● to **pick someone's pocket**: see **pocket**. ● See also **handpicked, pickings**.

pick at. **1** If you **pick at** the food that you are eating, you eat only very small amounts of it. EG *The Prime Minister glanced at Laing, picking morosely at his salad.* — PHRASAL VB : V+PREP, HAS PASS

2 If you **pick at** something, you keep pulling it or scratching it with your fingers. EG *Monkeys pick at one another's fur as a social ritual.* — PHRASAL VB : V+PREP, HAS PASS

pick off. **1** If someone **picks off** people, aircraft, etc, they shoot them down one by one, aiming at them from a distance. — PHRASAL VB : V+O+ADV

2 When you **pick** yourself **off** the ground or floor after you have fallen or been knocked down, you stand up rather slowly. EG *As I picked myself off the ground I saw him disappear round the corner.* — PHRASAL VB : V+O (REFL)+PREP = get up

pick on. **1** If you **pick on** someone, you unfairly speak to them in an unpleasant way or treat them unkindly; an informal use. EG *Why are you always picking on me?... The older men pick on the boys and are always looking for faults.* — PHRASAL VB : V+PREP, HAS PASS = get at

2 If you **pick on** a particular person or thing, you choose that one. EG *Of all the girls in town, he had to pick on Mr Zapp's daughter.* — PHRASAL VB : V+PREP, HAS PASS

pick out. **1** If you **pick out** someone or something, **1.1** you recognize them when they are among a large group of similar people or things, or when it is difficult to see them. EG *He could pick out a good cook in a crowd... One could just pick out the letters AGR.* — PHRASAL VB : V+O+ADV = spot **1.2** you choose them from among others. EG *My job is the job they picked out for me.* — PHRASAL VB : V+O+ADV

2 If part of something that is painted **is picked out** in white or in a bright colour, it is painted in that colour so that it can be seen clearly beside the other parts. EG *...mouldings picked out in white.* — PHRASAL VB : V+O+ADV, USU PASS = highlight

3 If you **pick out** a tune on a musical instrument, you play it slowly and awkwardly because you do not — PHRASAL VB : V+O+ADV know exactly which notes to play. EG *I can just about pick out 'Greensleeves' with one finger.*

pick over. If you **pick over** a quantity of things, especially fruit, you examine them so that you can throw away or reject the bad ones. PHRASAL VB : ORDER V+ADV+O

pick up. 1 When you **pick** something **up**, you lift it up from a particular place. EG *He stooped down to pick up the two pebbles... The telephone rang and Judy picked it up... The air was full of flying objects, picked up by the tearing winds.* PHRASAL VB : V+O+ADV ⇑ take up

2 When you **pick** yourself **up** after you have fallen or been knocked down, you stand up rather slowly. EG *He picked himself up and walked away.* PHRASAL VB : V+O (REFL) +ADV ⇑ get up

3 When you **pick up** something or someone that is waiting to be collected, you go to the place where they are and take them away. EG *I'll pick it up on my way to work... I might get my brother to come and pick me up.* PHRASAL VB : V+O+ADV = collect

4 If someone who is driving a vehicle **picks** someone **up**, they stop for them and then take them where they want to go. EG *People usually stop and pick up a fisherman.* PHRASAL VB : V+O+ADV

5 If someone **is picked up** by the police or another group, they are arrested or taken somewhere to be asked questions; an informal use. EG *I don't want you to be picked up for vagrancy... He was picked up by government agents for questioning.* PHRASAL VB : V+O+ADV, USU PASS

6 If you **pick up** a skill, habit, or attitude, you acquire it over a period of time as a result of being in a particular place, doing a particular thing, or being with a particular group of people, rather than because you have tried hard to acquire it; a rather informal use. EG *Lo had had ample time to pick up the rudiments of driving... Did you pick up any Swedish?... It's an affectation picked up from some friends of mine.* PHRASAL VB : ORDER V+ADV+O

7 If you **pick up** an idea or a piece of information, you get it into your mind from something that you hear, read, or see; an informal use. EG *Only seconds later I was wondering where I'd picked up this piece of blatant misinformation... I may pick up a couple of useful ideas for my book.* PHRASAL VB : ORDER V+ADV+O = glean

8 If you **pick up** something that you buy, you pay only a small amount of money for it; an informal use. EG *Her mother had liked to pick up bargains in basement sales... ...an old car he picked up for £250.* PHRASAL VB : ORDER V+ADV+O

9 If you **pick up** an illness, you get it from somewhere or something. EG *...some kind of food poisoning that they picked up at dinner... Babies can easily pick up thrush, a mild fungus infection.* PHRASAL VB : ORDER V+ADV+O = catch, contract

10 If you **pick up** something, for example a particular reputation or a prize, you gain it or win it; a fairly informal use. EG *He picked up a reputation as a merciless foe of gambling... It picked up the Best Musical Award... He returned to his home town, picked up a degree in journalism, and married his childhood sweetheart.* PHRASAL VB : ORDER V+ADV+O ⇑ get = acquire

11 If someone **picks up** a particular amount of money for the work they do, they earn that amount of money; an informal use. EG *A welding overseer picks up £400 a week.* PHRASAL VB : ORDER V+ADV+O ⇑ get

12 If you **pick up** someone you do not know, you start talking to them and behaving in a friendly way towards them, often because you want to have a casual sexual relationship with them; an informal use. EG *I doubt whether Tony ever picked up a woman in his life.* PHRASAL VB : V+O+ADV

13 If a person or animal **picks up** a faint smell or a quiet sound, they become aware of it. EG *He sniffed the air, trying to pick up their scent... Kunta's ears picked up a strange, muted sound.* PHRASAL VB : ORDER V+ADV+O = detect

14 If you **pick up** a radio or television signal that is being broadcast, especially a faint one, you receive it and are able to hear or see what is being broadcast. EG *It was easier to pick up Radio Luxembourg than the Light Programme.* PHRASAL VB : ORDER V+ADV+O

15 If you **pick up** something by radar, a sign of it appears on the radar screen and you know that it is there. PHRASAL VB : ORDER V+ADV+O ⇑ detect

16 If you **pick up** a particular feature, especially a mistake, in something that is written or said, you notice it as you read or listen; a rather informal use. EG *Read your work through so that if there is a mistake you'll pick it up.* PHRASAL VB : V+O+ADV

17 If you **pick up** a particular point or topic that someone has mentioned, you go back to it and say something relating to it. EG *I'd like to pick up the point David made... The President picked up the theme.* PHRASAL VB : ORDER V+ADV+O ⇑ discuss

18 If you **pick up** something that you had stopped doing or being involved in, you continue it, especially from the point where you had stopped. EG *So you came back expecting to pick up where we left off, did you?... We picked up the conversation from where we had left it.* PHRASAL VB : V+ADV, OR V+O+ADV

19 If you **pick** someone **up** on something that they have said or done, you mention it and tell them that you think that it is wrong. EG *May I just pick him up on what he said about women.* PHRASAL VB : V+O+ADV ⇑ correct

20 If trade or the economy of a country **picks up**, it improves. EG *The economy is picking up.* PHRASAL VB : V+ADV

21 If you **pick up** the bill or **pick up the tab**, you pay the bill; an informal use. EG *They went, leaving us to pick up the bill for the materials.* PHRASAL VB : ORDER V+ADV+O

22 When you **pick up the pieces** after a disaster, you do what you can to get the situation back to normal again or to make it better. EG *When the confusion dies down, we can try to pick up the pieces.* PHR : VB INFLECTS

23 When a vehicle **picks up speed**, it begins to move more quickly. EG *The car pulled slowly away, then gradually picked up speed until it was out of sight.* PHR : VB INFLECTS = accelerate, gather speed

24 See also **pick-up**.

pickaxe /pɪkæks/, **pickaxes**; also spelled **pickax** in American English. A **pickaxe** is a large tool consisting of a thin, curved piece of metal with a point at one or both ends and a long handle joined to the middle of the metal. Pickaxes are used for breaking up the ground or rocks. N COUNT ⇑ pick

picker /pɪkə/, **pickers**. A fruit **picker**, cotton **picker**, etc is a person who is picking fruit, cotton, etc, usually for money. EG *...strawberry pickers... They do not employ any professional pickers.* N COUNT : USU MOD+N ⇑ worker

picket /pɪkɪt/, **pickets, picketing, picketed**. 1 A **picket** is one of a group of people, especially trade union members, who are standing outside a factory or other place in order to protest about something, prevent people from going in, or persuade the workers to join a strike. EG *We could hear the chanting of the pickets... Members of the Court of Governors had to push their way through student pickets to attend their meeting yesterday afternoon.* ▸ also used to refer to the group of people. EG *They marched to the factory and formed a picket.* ● See also **flying picket**. N COUNT

2 When a group of people, especially trade union members, **picket** a factory or other place, they stand outside it in order to protest about something, prevent people from going in, or persuade the workers to join a strike. EG *The plan was to picket docks and power stations... Fifty women and children picketed the local office of the Department of Health.* V OR V+O

◊ **picketing**. EG *...before the mass picketing and its consequent mass arrests began.* ◊ N UNCOUNT

3 A **picket** is also the picketing of a factory or other place, especially during a strike. EG *...the historic picket at Saltley coke depot.* N COUNT

picket line, picket lines; also spelled with a hyphen. A **picket line** is a line or group of pickets outside a factory or other place. EG *He told me never to cross a picket line... ...the presence of students on picket lines.* N COUNT

pickings /pɪkɪŋz/. You can refer to the money that can be made easily in a particular place, enterprise, or area of activity as the **pickings**. EG *Others found rich pickings in the field of insurance... You think you can find easier pickings here.* N PLURAL : USU MOD+N = spoils

pickle /pɪkᵊl/, **pickles, pickling, pickled**. 1 **Pickles** are vegetables or fruit, sometimes cut into pieces, which have been kept in vinegar or salt water for a long time so that they have a strong sharp taste. EG *...a jar of pickles... She can make jams, chutneys, and pickles.* N COUNT/N MASS ⇑ food

2 When you **pickle** food, you keep it in vinegar or salt water so that it does not go bad and it develops a strong sharp taste. V+O ⇑ preserve

3 **Pickle** is also the liquid in which food is pickled. EG *Meat can be preserved in pickle.* N UNCOUNT

4 If you are in a **pickle**, you are in a difficult and awkward situation; an informal use. EG *So how did you get yourself in this pickle?* N SING WITH DET = mess, jam

5 You can call a rather naughty child a **pickle** when you are not really cross with him or her; used in informal British English. N COUNT/VOC

pickled /pɪkᵊld/. 1 **Pickled** vegetables, meat, etc have been kept in vinegar or salt water to preserve ADJ CLASSIF : ATTRIB them. EG *His breath smelled of beer and pickled onions... ...pickled herring.*

2 Someone who is **pickled** is drunk; a very informal use. ADJ QUALIT : PRED

pick-me-up, pick-me-ups. A **pick-me-up** is a drink that you have in order to make you feel healthier and more energetic; a fairly informal word. N COUNT = restorative, tonic

pickpocket /pɪkpɒkɪt/, **pickpockets.** A **pickpocket** is a person who steals things from people's pockets, handbags, etc in public places. N COUNT ⇑ thief

pick-up, pick-ups; also spelled as one word. 1 A **pick-up** or a **pick-up truck** is a small truck with low sides that can be easily loaded and unloaded. EG *He drove in to Fort Dodge in his pick-up two or three times a week.* N COUNT

2 When a **pick-up** takes place, **2.1** someone starts talking to a person they do not know and behaving in a friendly way towards them, often because they want to have a casual sexual relationship with that person; an informal use. EG *But the girl clearly knows a pick-up when she sees one.* **2.2** someone picks up a person or thing that is waiting to be collected. EG *Groups of agents see the shipments through from the pick-up point to their destinations in Britain.* N COUNT; N COUNT

3 The **pick-up** of a record-player is the arm with the needle at the end of it. N COUNT

picky /pɪki¹/, **pickier, pickiest.** Someone who is **picky** is difficult to please and only likes a small range of things; an informal word. ADJ QUALIT = choosy, fussy

picnic /pɪknɪk/, **picnics, picnicking, picnicked.** 1 A **picnic** is an occasion on which you eat a meal that you have brought with you out of doors, usually in a field or wood or at the beach. EG *They went on picnics and small trips in the Alfa Romeo... He often talks of that picnic we had last summer... We used to take a picnic lunch and eat it on the beach.* N COUNT OR N BEFORE N ⇑ outing

2 When people **picnic**, they eat a picnic somewhere. EG *The woods might be full of people picnicking... He swam down the river while families picnicking on the banks looked on in amazement.* V : USU+A

3 If you say that a task or activity **is no picnic**, you mean that it is not easy to do and involves a lot of problems; an informal expression. EG *Travel abroad is no picnic.* PHR : VB INFLECTS

picnicker /pɪknɪkə/, **picnickers.** A **picnicker** is someone who is having a picnic. N COUNT ⇑ person

pictorial /pɪktɔ:rɪəl/ means relating to or using pictures. EG *They acquired the skilful use of certain pictorial conventions... They had insisted on a full pictorial coverage of the event.* ADJ CLASSIF : ATTRIB ⇑ artistic

picture /pɪktʃə/, **pictures, picturing, pictured.** 1 A **picture** consists of lines and shapes that are drawn, painted, or printed on a surface and that show a person, thing, or scene. EG *It is the single most important picture Picasso ever painted... Most of my pictures are etchings, engravings, or screen prints... He finally picks up a book to look at the pictures.* N COUNT

2 A **picture** is also **2.1** a photograph, especially one that is taken quickly. EG *We all had our pictures taken... There was a picture of them both in the paper.* **2.2** an image or a series of images which is seen on a television screen and which shows a real event, person, or thing. EG *We have all seen television news pictures of their forces in action.* **2.3** a film, especially one that is seen at a cinema; used especially in American English. EG *We worked together in the last picture I made... The soldier left before the end of the picture... She had been a star in the silent pictures.* ● See also **motion picture**. N COUNT = photo, snap; N COUNT : USU PL; N COUNT = movie

3 If you go to the **pictures**, you go to a showing of a film at a cinema; used mainly in informal British English. EG *She met him at the pictures.* N PLURAL : *the*+N = the cinema

4 When you refer to the **picture** that a television has, you are referring to the images which are seen on the screen, with regard to how clear and sharp they are. EG *The picture needs adjusting.* N SING WITH DET

5 If someone or something **is pictured** in a newspaper, magazine, poster, etc, or on television in an information programme, they appear in a photograph or picture, or on television. EG *Mr Lionel Murray was pictured in The Times the other day sharing a platform with Mostyn.* V+O : USU PASS+A/-ING

6 A **picture** is also **6.1** an idea or memory of someone or something that you can see in your mind as if you were actually seeing it with your eyes. EG *...a mental picture of clouds scudding across the sky... A picture flashed through Kunta's mind of the panther springing at him.* **6.2** an idea or belief about something. EG *They can get quite a distorted picture of what's going on... I imagine we all have a picture in our minds of how and where our friends will retire.* **6.3** a description in words or a representation in a film of what something, especially a situation, is like. EG *Mr Hamilton gives a most interesting picture of Monty's family background... You paint a rather bleak picture... The winner in this category is a wry picture of life in a Northern town.* N COUNT = image; N COUNT : USU SING; N COUNT : USU SING+SUPP

7 When you **picture** something in your mind, you think of it so that you have a clear idea of what it is like or what it would be like. EG *He could picture all too easily the consequences of being caught... In her mind's eye she had pictured herself spreading out a splendid repast.* V+O (NG/REFL) ⇑ imagine

8 If you **picture** something in a particular way, you describe it in that way. EG *Lloyd George pictured vividly in the Commons the magnitude and gravity of the problem... Day after day Mr Hearst is picturing the President of the United States as a buffoon.* V+O : USU+A

9 When you refer to the **picture** in a particular place or with regard to a particular thing or group, you are referring to the situation there or to the situation with regard to that thing or group. EG *In Nigeria, paradoxically, the picture at first appears to be different... The economic picture is far from good.* N SING : USU *the*+N

10 The word **picture** is also used in the following informal expressions. **10.1** If you say that someone is **in the picture**, you mean that they are involved in the situation that you are talking about. If you say that they are out of the **picture**, you mean that they are not involved in the situation. EG *She must have hated being out of the picture... If there were no children in the picture, he couldn't understand why she didn't just leave the man... This is how Rita enters the picture.* **10.2** If you **get the picture**, you understand a particular situation, especially one which someone is describing to you; an informal expression. EG *I get the picture. You want to keep the whole thing quiet.* **10.3** If you **put** someone **in the picture**, you tell them about a situation which they need to know about; an informal expression. EG *Let me put you in the picture about the situation there.* **10.4** If you say that someone is **a picture of health, the picture of misery**, etc, you are emphasizing that they appear to have as much of the quality mentioned as it is possible to have. EG *Vidal was a picture of sophisticated detachment.* N SING : *the*+N = scene; PHR : VB INFLECTS; PHR : VB INFLECTS ⇑ inform; PHR : USED AS C ⇑ example = model, epitome

picture book, picture books; also spelled with a hyphen. A **picture book** is a book with a lot of pictures in it and not much writing, often a children's book. N COUNT

picture rail, picture rails; also spelled with a hyphen. A **picture rail** is a narrow piece of wood which is sometimes fixed to the walls of a room just below the ceiling. Pictures can be hung from it using string and hooks. N COUNT

picturesque /pɪktʃəresk/. 1 A **picturesque** place, building, costume, etc is attractive and interesting to look at, usually because it is old and unspoiled. EG *...a small hotel overlooking the picturesque fishing harbour of Zeebrugge... ...the picturesque and antique uniform of the Beefeaters.* ◇ **picturesquely**. EG *...a small town situated picturesquely in a deep, narrow, wooded valley.* ADJ QUALIT = charming; ◇ ADV WITH VB

2 **Picturesque** words and expressions make a strong impression on you because they are unusual, interesting, or rude. EG *That was, in Frank's picturesque phrase, like pouring water into a bucket... He told me, in picturesque language, to go away.* ◇ **picturesquely**. EG *...a place picturesquely known as Valley of Troublesome Creek.* ADJ QUALIT = colourful, striking; ◇ ADV WITH VB = colourfully

piddle /pɪdə⁰l/, **piddles, piddling, piddled.** When someone **piddles**, they urinate; an informal word used mainly by children. ▸ used as a noun. V; ▸ N SING : *a*+N

piddling /pɪdlɪŋ/. Something that is **piddling** is small or unimportant; an informal use showing disapproval. EG *They gave me piddling little jobs to do.* ADJ CLASSIF ⇑ trivial = piffling

pidgin /pɪdʒɪn/, **pidgins.** A **pidgin** is a language which is a mixture of two other languages. A pidgin is not usually anyone's native language but is used when people from two different countries do business with each other. ▸ used as an adjective. EG *They spoke pidgin English.* N COUNT/UNCOUNT; ▸ ADJ CLASSIF : ATTRIB

pie /paɪ/, **pies**. 1 A **pie** consists of food, usually meat, vegetables, or fruit, which is baked in pastry and which has pastry on the top. In American English, the word **pie** is also used to refer to food which is baked in pastry but which does not have pastry on the top. EG *...slices of cold chicken pie... ...a big piece of apple pie... We sat on the grass, each with our bottle of Cola and a hot pie.* N COUNT/UNCOUNT

2 If you describe or refer to something that is promised or planned as **pie in the sky**, you mean that you think that it is very unlikely to happen; an informal expression. EG *They were promised dignity, self-rule, pie in the sky... Can society really believe in the pie-in-the-sky promises of Professor Arthur Grant?* PHR : USU USED AS O/C = daydream, mirage

3 The word **pie** is also used in the following expressions, which are explained at other places in this dictionary. • **a finger in every pie**: see **finger**. • to **eat humble pie**: see **humble**. • See also **cottage pie**, **shepherd's pie**.

piebald /paɪbɔːld/. Something, especially an animal, that is **piebald** has patches of two different colours on it, usually black and white. EG *...a thin piebald pony.* ADJ CLASSIF ⇑ marked

piece /piːs/, **pieces, piecing, pieced**. 1 A **piece** is 1.1 a bit or part of something that has been broken off, torn off, or cut off. EG *He came back dragging a great big piece of a tree... ...loosely folded pieces of cloth... He tore both letters into small pieces.* N COUNT/PART = fragment 1.2 one of the individual parts or sections which make up an object, especially a part or section that can be removed. EG *Piece by piece he assembled the rifle... His bicycle was at present lying in pieces at home in the garage... ...like pieces fitting into a jigsaw puzzle.* N COUNT : IF + PREP THEN *of*

1.3 a part or section of something, considered separately. EG *The satellite will be looking down on a particular piece of the earth... I'm the editor of this paper, and I own a piece of it.* N COUNT/PART

2 A **piece** of something that you can eat, for example a cake, a loaf of bread, or a joint of meat, is a slice or portion that has been cut from it. EG *Lally was spreading marmalade on a piece of toast... She cut the cake and gave me a piece.* N COUNT OR N PART + N UNCOUNT

3 You can refer to an individual item or object of a particular type as a **piece** of clothing, furniture, equipment, etc. EG *The only piece of clothing she had bought in months was a red jumper... He moved around the room examining the furniture one piece at a time... Have you got a piece of paper I could write on?... ...a cumbersome piece of machinery.* N PART + N UNCOUNT = article, bit

4 You can refer to an individual group of facts or opinions, an individual action, or an individual product or creation as a **piece** of information, work, writing, etc. EG *...a thoughtful piece of research... ...this piece of advice... ...a piece of music... ...a simple piece of arithmetic.* N PART + N UNCOUNT ⇑ item = bit

5 You can describe an event or action as a **piece** of luck, impudence, etc, when you think that it is an example of the quality, behaviour, or activity mentioned. EG *Meeting Mrs Hooke was a piece of good fortune... ...a piece of blatant egotism.* N PART + N UNCOUNT ⇑ instance = bit

6 A **piece** is also 6.1 something that is written or created, for example an article, play, or short musical composition. EG *...a thoughtful piece about President Roosevelt... It was a classic piece called Forever Is For Us... Rigid with nervousness, I played the piece I had been practising for months.* N COUNT ⇑ work 6.2 an object, for example a vase or a table, that is considered valuable or interesting. EG *He refused to buy a single piece from Chippendale's Chinese period.* N COUNT = item 6.3 a gun, especially one that is large and powerful; a military use. EG *Helicopters brought in the heavier artillery pieces.* N COUNT

7 A 10p **piece**, a fifty cent **piece**, etc is a coin that is worth the amount mentioned. EG *The machine wouldn't take 10p pieces... ...a silver lighter that was no bigger than a 50p piece.* N COUNT : MOD + N = bit

8 The **pieces** which you use when you play a board game such as chess or backgammon are the specially shaped objects which you move around or onto the board when you play the game. EG *They cleared the chessboard and put the pieces in their box.* N COUNT = man

9 You can refer to someone as a particular kind of **piece** as a way of describing their character or behaviour; used in rather old-fashioned, informal English. EG *She was a flighty piece.* N COUNT + SUPP ⇑ person

10 **to pieces**. 10.1 If something is smashed or taken to **pieces** or falls **to pieces**, it is broken or taken apart or comes apart so that it is in separate pieces. EG *The poster had been ripped to pieces... He took to pieces and reassembled an entire engine... Halfway home the body of the car literally fell to pieces.* PHR : USED AS AN A = to bits 10.2 If you say that someone or something was torn **to pieces**, shot **to pieces**, etc, you are emphasizing that they were very badly injured or damaged. EG *...the little town that had been torn to pieces by the enemy's guns.* PHR : USED AS AN A = apart, to bits 10.3 If someone **goes to pieces**, they are so upset, frightened, or nervous that they can no longer cope or do what they should do; an informal expression. EG *He did not go to pieces as I feared he might.* PHR : VB INFLECTS = crack up

10.4 If someone **tears** you **to pieces** or **pulls** your work or ideas **to pieces**, they criticize you, your work, or your ideas very severely; an informal expression. EG *He never praised you and he never tore you to pieces... I explained my theory and he just pulled it to pieces.* PHR : VB INFLECTS

11 If something, for example a plan or system, is **in pieces**, it has been destroyed or is no longer useful or effective. EG *The strategy it thought it had lies in pieces, demolished by changes in the balance of power.* PHR : USED AS AN A = in ruin, in shreds

12 If something or someone is still **in one piece**, for example after a dangerous journey or experience, it is safe and not damaged, injured, or harmed. EG *Surprisingly, most of the crockery was still in one piece.* PHR : USED AS AN A ⇑ whole

13 If something with several different parts is **all of a piece**, it is the same throughout or consistent in some way. If one thing is **of a piece** with another, it is consistent with it; a fairly formal expression. EG *'It's all of a piece when you think of it,' said Nancy... Pimlico is still remarkably of a piece, architecturally.* PHR : USED AS C, IF + PREP THEN *with* ⇑ alike = of a kind

14 When you **say** your **piece**, you say what you want to say about a particular matter. EG *Right, now I've said my piece, I'll sit down.* PHR : VB INFLECTS

15 The word **piece** is used in the following expressions, which are explained at other places in this dictionary. • **bits and pieces**: see **bit**. • **a piece of cake**: see **cake**. • to **give someone a piece of your mind**: see **mind**. • to **pick up the pieces**: see **pick up**. • See also **museum piece**.

piece together. 1 If you **piece together** the truth about something or the nature or meaning of something, you gradually discover it or understand it by becoming aware of different facts or by considering how they fit together. EG *I found out the truth by piecing together hints and rumours that I heard at school... She had not yet been able to piece together exactly what had happened.* PHRASAL VB : V + ADV + O/REPORT-CL = deduce, work out

2 If you **piece** something **together**, you gradually make or form it by joining several things or elements together. She pieced together the torn-up drawing... EG *...a nation struggling to piece together a new identity.* PHRASAL VB : V + O + ADV ⇑ assemble

-piece combines with numbers to indicate that a set of things contains a particular number of items or members. EG *...a 36-piece dinner service... ...men in dark, three-piece suits.* COMB : FORMS ADJ CLASSIFS

pièce de résistance /pjes də rezɪstɑːns/. The **pièce de résistance** of a group or series of things is the most important or impressive item in it. N SING WITH DET ⇑ climax

piecemeal /piːsmiːl/. A **piecemeal** change, action, or process happens or is done gradually or at irregular intervals, rather than being done as a single action or in a continuous controlled way. EG *...gradual and piecemeal change.* ▸ used as an adverb. EG *Films are financed piecemeal; the distributor doles out money little by little.* ADJ CLASSIF : USU ATTRIB ⇑ random ▸ ADV AFTER VB = by degree

piecework /piːswɔːk/; also spelled with a hyphen. If you do **piecework**, you are paid according to the amount of work you do rather than being paid for working a particular length of time. EG *The drivers of these trucks were all on piece-work, which meant that the more trips they did, the more they got paid.* N UNCOUNT ⇑ work

pied-à-terre /pjeɪdəteə/, **pieds-à-terre**. The plural is pronounced the same as the singular. A **pied-à-terre** is a small house or flat, especially in a town, which you own but only use occasionally. N COUNT ⇑ home

pie-eyed. Someone who is **pie-eyed** is drunk; an informal word. ADJ QUALIT

pier /pɪə/, **piers**. A **pier** is 1 a large structure like a bridge which sticks out into the sea at a seaside town and which people can walk along. Piers usually have N COUNT : ALSO IN NAMES AFTER N places of entertainment on them. EG *...a postcard showing a view of the pier at Worthing... ...on Blackpool Pier.* **2** a structure made of wood or stone which has a flat top and sticks out into the sea, a lake, or a river so that boats can stop there and people can get on and off. EG *He walked along the wooden pier and climbed down the short ladder into the boat... ...a fishing pier on the shore of the lake.* N COUNT ⇑ jetty

pierce /pɪəs/, **pierces, piercing, pierced. 1** If an object, especially a sharp object, **pierces** something or if you **pierce** something with a sharp object, the object goes into it and makes a hole in it or through it. EG *When the snake's fangs pierce its victim's flesh, the venom is injected... The pointed end of the stick pierced through its throat into its mouth... The woman screamed as if he had pierced her with a knife.* V+O, OR V+A (*USU through/into*) ⇑ penetrate = puncture

2 If you have your ears **pierced**, you have holes made through them so that you can wear pieces of jewellery in them. V+O : USU PASS

3 If someone or something **pierces** something that acts as a barrier, they manage to get through it. EG *One of these gunmen pierced the protective cordon around the President's house... The bitter wind pierced even the folds of her warm fur coat.* V+O, OR V+A (*through*) ⇑ penetrate

4 If a light **pierces** the darkness, it shines through it. EG *No gleam pierces the dark.* V+O ⇑ penetrate

5 If a sound **pierces** the silence, it is suddenly and unexpectedly heard. EG *A cry of 'God Almighty' pierced the silence.* V+O ⇑ penetrate

6 If you **are pierced** by a painful feeling or emotion, you suddenly experience it; a literary use. EG *Her heart was pierced by a curious pang.* V+O : USU PASS, OR V+A (*through/into*)

7 If you **pierce** a person's unfriendly or unemotional attitude, or their lack of understanding, you manage to make them feel or understand something or respond to you. EG *For the moment there was no point at which he could pierce her composure.* V+O, OR V+A (*through*) = break through

8 If something **pierces** something else, it is in it or is seen against it and makes a contrast with it; a literary use. EG *The spire of St Patrick's pierced the grey sky like a pointed finger.* V+O, OR V+A (*through*)

pierced /pɪəst/. A **pierced** object has had holes made in it, for example as a form of decoration. EG *...pierced wooden screens.* ADJ CLASSIF

piercing /pɪəsɪŋ/. **1** A **piercing** sound or voice is high-pitched and very sharp and clear in an unpleasant way. EG *I was jolted out of my exhaustion by piercing screams... ...a very young voice, shrill and piercing.* ◊ **piercingly.** EG *Piercingly, the conductor blew his whistle.* ADJ QUALIT ⇑ penetrating = shrill ◊ ADV WITH VB = shrilly

2 If someone's eyes are **piercing**, they are bright and seem to look at you very hard and see things very clearly. EG *He was over six feet tall, with piercing blue eyes.* ▸ used of a look or glance. EG *Liz gave her a very piercing glance.* ◊ **piercingly.** EG *She looked at me piercingly.* ADJ QUALIT ⇑ penetrating = probing ◊ ADV WITH VB

3 Something that is **piercing** causes you to feel a very strong, intense emotion, especially sadness. EG *...a piercing appeal... ...a smile of piercing sweetness.* ◊ **piercingly.** EG *He was piercingly reminded of his homeland.* ADJ QUALIT ◊ ADV WITH VB

4 A **piercing** wind makes you feel very cold. EG *I was trembling in a piercing draught.* ADJ QUALIT = biting

pierrot /pɪərəʊ/, **pierrots.** A **pierrot** is a clown or entertainer who wears a white costume and a white pointed hat and whose face is covered with white make-up. N COUNT

piety /paɪɪti[1]/ is belief in God or in a particular religion, and behaviour or actions that show that you have this belief and are trying to behave in a good, religious way. EG *They were drawn to the church not by piety but by curiosity... ...men of true piety.* N UNCOUNT = devotion, holiness

piffle /pɪfəl/. If you describe what someone says as **piffle**, you mean that you think that it is nonsense; an informal word. N UNCOUNT = rubbish, twaddle

piffling /pɪflɪŋ/. Something that is **piffling** is small or unimportant, and ridiculous; an informal word. EG *...the steps taken are so minuscule, so piffling in the face of the enormity of the problem.* ADJ QUALIT ⇑ trivial = trifling

pig /pɪg/, **pigs, pigging, pigged. 1** A **pig** is a pink, or sometimes black, animal with short legs, floppy ears, and not much hair on its skin. Pigs are often kept on farms for their meat. EG *The pig squealed... They sat gobbling their food like pigs at a trough.* N COUNT ⇑ mammal = hog

2 If you call someone a **pig**, you mean that you think that they are unpleasant in some way, especially that they are greedy, dirty, unkind, or oppressive; an informal, offensive use. N COUNT : USU MOD+N, ALSO VOC

3 Some people use the word **pig** to refer to a policeman; a very informal offensive use. N COUNT

4 You can refer to a difficult or awkward task as a **pig** of a job; used in informal British English. N SING : a+N ⇑ problem

5 If you **pig** yourself, you eat a great deal on a particular occasion; an informal use showing disapproval. V+O (REFL) = scoff

6 To **make a pig of** yourself means the same as to pig yourself; used in informal English. PHR : VB INFLECTS

7 If you **make a pig's ear of** something that you do, you do it very badly so that the result is of very low quality; used in informal British English. PHR : VB INFLECTS = bungle

8 You can describe something that is offered for sale as a **pig in a poke** when you cannot examine it or find out all about it before you buy it, so that it may in fact not be a good thing to buy; an informal expression. EG *'You know I'm not going to buy that kind of pig in a poke.'* PHR : USED AS O/C ⇑ risk = gamble

9 If you say **pigs might fly** after someone has said that a particular thing might happen, you mean that you think that it is very unlikely indeed to happen; an informal humorous expression. EG *'He might pay it back.'–'Yeah, and pigs might fly!'* CONVENTION

10 pig in the middle: see **piggy in the middle.** ● See also **guinea pig.**

pigeon /pɪdʒɪn/, **pigeons. 1** A **pigeon** is a bird, usually grey in colour, which has a fat body and makes long soft sounds. Pigeons often live in towns. EG *A pigeon was cooing up in one of the elms... Tourists photographed the pigeons in Trafalgar Square.* N COUNT

2 If you say that something **is** a particular person's **pigeon**, you mean that it is their responsibility and they should deal with it; an informal, rather old-fashioned expression. EG *That's your pigeon, Cynthia.* PHR : VB INFLECTS

3 If someone **sets** or **puts the cat among the pigeons**, they do or say something that causes a lot of argument or that makes people angry. EG *The President set the cat among the pigeons by halting commercial processing of nuclear waste.* PHR : VB INFLECTS

pigeon-hole, pigeon-holes, pigeon-holing, pigeon-holed. 1 A **pigeon-hole** is one of the sections in a wooden frame on a wall, or in a writing desk, where mail and messages can be left for a particular person or where documents can be kept. EG *Howard strolled over to the long rows of pigeon-holes to collect his mail... She went over to the desk, and took an old crumpled press cutting out of a pigeon-hole.* N COUNT ⇑ compartment

2 You can also use the word **pigeon-hole** to refer to a class, category, or role into which someone or something is put or to which they are considered to belong; a fairly informal use. EG *In traditional communities, the individual had his pigeon-hole ordained from birth.* N COUNT = niche, slot

3 If you **pigeon-hole** someone or something, you decide that they belong to a particular class or category; used in fairly informal English, often showing disapproval. EG *They called us 'women's libbers', since their desire to categorize us, pigeon-hole us, was so strong.* V+O = label, stereotype

piggery /pɪgəri[1]/, **piggeries.** A **piggery** is a farm or a part of a farm where pigs are kept. N COUNT

piggy /pɪgi[1]/, **piggies**; an informal word. **1** Young children often refer to a pig as a **piggy**. N COUNT

2 Someone who is **piggy** is greedy or selfish; a rather childish use. ADJ QUALIT

3 If someone has **piggy** eyes, their eyes are small and unattractive. ADJ CLASSIF : ATTRIB

piggyback /pɪgi[1]bæk/, **piggybacks.** If you give someone, usually a child, a **piggyback** or a **piggyback** ride, you carry them high on your back, supporting them under their knees; a fairly informal word. EG *Children need hugging and piggyback rides.* ▸ used as an adverb. EG *He carried them all piggyback across the stream.* N COUNT, OR BEFORE N ▸ ADV WITH VB

piggybank /pɪgi[1]bæŋk/, **piggybanks**; also spelled with a hyphen. A **piggybank** is a small container, usually shaped like a pig, with a slot in it to put coins in. Piggybanks are used by children to save money in. N COUNT

piggy in the middle. 1 Piggy in the middle or **pig in the middle** is a game in which two children throw N UNCOUNT a ball to each other while a third child stands between them and tries to catch it.

2 If someone **is piggy in the middle** or **is pig in the middle**, they are unwillingly involved in or affected by a quarrel between two other people or groups. EG *I'm sick of being piggy in the middle all the time!* PHR : VB INFLECTS

pig-headed; also spelled as one word. Someone who is **pig-headed** refuses to change their mind about things; a fairly informal word used showing disapproval. EG *They can be stupid, intransigent, and pigheaded, just as anyone else can be.* ADJ QUALIT ⇑ stubborn = obstinate

piglet /pɪglɪ²t/, **piglets**. A **piglet** is a very young pig. N COUNT

pigment /pɪgmə²nt/, **pigments**. A **pigment** is a substance that gives something a particular colour; a formal word. EG *The larvae are coloured blood red by hemoglobin, a pigment that speeds the diffusion of oxygen... The ink used contained traces of an artificial pigment not developed until about 1920.* N COUNT/ UNCOUNT

pigmentation /pɪgmə²nteɪʃə⁰n/. The **pigmentation** of a person, animal, or plant is the natural colouring it has; a formal word. EG *...the dark skin pigmentation of people living near the equator.* N UNCOUNT

pigmy /pɪgmi¹/. See **pygmy**.

pigpen /pɪgpɛn/, **pigpens**. A **pigpen** is the same as a pigsty; used in American English. N COUNT

pigskin /pɪgskɪn/ is a fine leather made from the skin of pigs. EG *She had a new pig-skin case.* N UNCOUNT OR N BEFORE N

pigsty /pɪgstaɪ/, **pigsties**. 1 A **pigsty** is a hut with a yard where pigs are kept on a farm. N COUNT = pen, sty

2 If you describe a room or a house as a **pigsty**, you mean that it is very dirty and untidy; an informal use. N COUNT : USU SING = tip, dump

pigtail /pɪgteɪl/, **pigtails**. A **pigtail** is a length of hair that has been divided into three and then plaited; used especially of hair worn in this way by young girls or men, rather than by women. EG *They wore their hair braided in long pigtails... A girl with a blonde pigtail down her back came out of the house.* N COUNT ⇑ plait = braid

pike /paɪk/, **pikes**. **Pike** can also be used as the plural form for sense 1. A **pike** is 1 a large fish that lives in rivers and lakes, and that eats other fish. EG *He said that there was a pike in the River Ouse almost a yard long... The rivers were rich in salmon and pike.* N COUNT 2 a weapon used in former times that consisted of a pointed metal blade on the end of a long pole. N COUNT

pikestaff /paɪkstɑːf/. If something is **as plain as a pikestaff**, it is very obvious or easy to see; a rather old-fashioned expression. EG *There it was in black and white, as plain as a pikestaff: 'No pets allowed.'* PHR : USED AS AN A

pilaf /pɪlæf/; also spelled **pilaff**. **Pilaf** is the same as pilau. N UNCOUNT

pilau /pɪlaʊ/. **Pilau** or **pilau** rice is a dish consisting of rice flavoured with spices, often mixed with pieces of meat or fish. N UNCOUNT

pilchard /pɪltʃəd/, **pilchards**. A **pilchard** is a small fish that lives in the sea. In Britain pilchards are often sold in tins. EG *We had pilchards on toast.* N COUNT : USU PL

pile /paɪl/, **piles, piling, piled**. 1 A **pile** is 1.1 a quantity of things which have been put somewhere so that they form a mass which is high in the middle and has sloping sides, or a quantity of a substance which forms a mass like this. EG *There in front of me was a great pile of old tin cans... He tipped a pile of raisins into his hand... ...a pile of sand... Sort your dirty washing into piles.* N PART+N UNCOUNT = heap, mound **1.2** a quantity of things which have been put neatly somewhere so that each thing is on top of the one below. EG *The dirty plates have been stacked in a pile on the kitchen bench... The man lifted a pile of books from the bedside table.* N PART+N IN PL/ N UNCOUNT ⇑ group = stack

2 If you **pile** a quantity of things somewhere, you put them there, forming a pile. EG *Brody picked up the heap of papers and piled them on top of a radiator... My sister started piling the hymn books on top of each other... Sam piled on more branches... Her hair was piled high on her head.* • to **pile on the agony**: see **agony**. V+O+A, OR V+A = stack

3 If something, for example a surface, **is piled** with a quantity of things, it is covered with or filled with a pile of them or with piles of them. EG *His desk was piled with papers... They brought me a plate piled high with Italian salami.* V+O : USU PASS+ *with* = heap, stack

4 If you refer to a **pile** of something or to **piles** of something, you are emphasizing that there is a large amount of it; an informal use. EG *He's got an enormous pile of hush money stashed away... There's a whole pile of features that they share... I've got piles of work to do.* N PART+N UNCOUNT/N IN PL : SING=PL ⇑ a lot = loads, tons

5 If you **make a pile**, you make a large amount of money; an informal use. EG *My brother made a pile selling videos.* PHR : VB INFLECTS = bomb

6 Someone who is at **the bottom of the pile** is low down in society or in an organization and has little power or money. Someone who is at **the top of the pile** is high up in society or in an organization and has a lot of power or money. These expressions are used in informal English. EG *If you are at the bottom of the pile, your first efforts must be directed to changing your status... ...people who have fought their way to the top of the human pile.* PHR : PREP+ PHR, USED AS A ⇑ system = heap

7 If a group of people **pile** into or out of a vehicle, they all get into or out of it in a rather disorganized way. EG *His guests piled out of cars behind him... The troops piled into the coaches.* V+A ⇑ pour = bundle, swarm

8 A **pile** is also **8.1** a large impressive building. EG *...Badminton, the Duke of Beaufort's Palladian pile.* N COUNT **8.2** a column of wood, concrete, or metal which is pushed into the ground as part of the foundations for large buildings and bridges; a technical term. EG *The house has to be built on piles which are sunk down through the top layer of the soil.* N COUNT : USU PL = post, support

9 **Piles** are swellings that appear in the blood vessels inside a person's anus and then develop into painful growths. N PLURAL = haemorrhoids

10 The **pile** of a carpet or of a fabric such as velvet is its soft surface, which consists of lots of little threads standing on end. EG *The pile's wearing a bit thin... She stepped onto the luxurious deep pile carpet.* N UNCOUNT = nap, flock

pile up. 1 If you **pile up** a quantity of things or if they **pile up**, you put them somewhere or they accumulate somewhere, forming a pile. EG *All her possessions were piled up there... Her hair had been piled up on top of her head... The papers she was meant to be reading piled up untouched on her desk.* PHRASAL VB : V-ERG+ADV = heap up

2 If a quantity of things **piles up** or if someone **piles** them **up**, more and more of them are acquired or occur, so that the quantity of them increases. EG *I've got a huge backlog of work that's been piling up while I was on holiday... All these disasters piled up on the unfortunate Bangladeshis... Last year alone, the company piled up losses totalling £4 billion.* PHRASAL VB : V-ERG+ADV = mount up

pile-up, pile-ups; also spelled as one word. A **pile-up** is a road accident in which several vehicles crash into each other. EG *There had been a twenty-car pile-up on the M1.* N COUNT

pilfer /pɪlfə/, **pilfers, pilfering, pilfered**. Someone who **pilfers** things, usually inexpensive things, steals them. EG *...Major Eatherly, who pilfered from supermarkets... There is remarkably little pilfering.* V OR V+O

pilgrim /pɪlgrɪm/, **pilgrims**. A **pilgrim** is a person who makes a journey to a holy place for a religious reason. EG *The Pope received a group of Polish pilgrims.* N COUNT ⇑ believer

pilgrimage /pɪlgrɪmɪdʒ/, **pilgrimages**. A **pilgrimage** is a journey that someone makes to a holy place for a religious reason. EG *She made the pilgrimage to Lourdes... ...a place of pilgrimage.* N COUNT/ UNCOUNT

pill /pɪl/, **pills**. 1 A **pill** is a small, round mass of medicine that you swallow whole. EG *At 3 a.m. I took a sleeping pill.* N COUNT = tablet

2 The **pill** is a type of pill that is taken regularly by a woman so that she does not become pregnant. EG *Three million women take the pill... I'm not on the pill.* N SING : *the*+N ⇑ contraceptive

3 If you describe something that happens as **a bitter pill** or say that it is **a bitter pill to swallow**, you mean that you find it very disappointing or unpleasant. PHR : USU USED AS C = a blow

4 If someone **sugars the pill** or **sweetens the pill** when they do something that the people affected by it will dislike, they try to make it less unpleasant or they do something pleasant at the same time. EG *The government's tried to sweeten the pill.* PHR : VB INFLECTS

pillage /pɪlɪdʒ/, **pillages, pillaging, pillaged**. **Pillage** is the stealing of property in a rough, violent way, usually by a group of people; a formal word. EG *Their business was war, murder, pillage and rape.* N UNCOUNT ⇑ theft = looting, plunder ▸ used as a verb. EG *Their villages were pillaged and their crops destroyed.* ▸ V OR V+O = despoil

pillar /pɪlə/, **pillars**. 1 A **pillar** is a tall, narrow, solid structure, which is usually used to support part of a building together with other pillars. EG *I was so tired I fell asleep leaning against a pillar on some-one's porch.* N COUNT ⇑ post = column

2 A **pillar** of something is a tall, narrow mass or amount of it. EG *A characteristic feature of this area is the detached pillars of rock that stand in the sea.* N COUNT+SUPP

3 Someone who is a **pillar** of a particular group that they belong to is an active and important member of it. EG *I thought you had to be a pillar of the community to foster children... ...pillars of society.* N COUNT : USU+ of = rock, mainstay, upholder

4 If you go **from pillar to post**, you go from one place to another, especially when you are trying to do a lot of things quickly. EG *I was the apprentice, rushing from pillar to post merely to be freshly inundated with work.* PHR : USED AS AN A

pillar box, pillar boxes; also spelled with a hyphen. In British English, a **pillar box** is a tall, red, iron cylinder with a narrow hole in it where you can put letters to be collected by a postman. Pillar boxes stand on pavements. N COUNT = mailbox

pillared /pɪləd/. A **pillared** building or part of a building has pillars supporting it. EG *...under the pillared arcade.* ADJ CLASSIF

pillbox /pɪlbɒks/, **pillboxes**; also spelled with a hyphen. A **pillbox** is a tiny tin or box which you can use to carry pills in. N COUNT

pillion /pɪljən/. When you ride **pillion** on a motor-cycle or a horse, you sit behind the person who is controlling the motorcycle or horse. ADV AFTER VB

pillory /pɪləri[1]/, **pillories, pillorying, pillo-ried**. 1 If someone **is pilloried**, they are criticized severely or said to be silly by a large number of people, especially in newspapers or on radio and television. EG *He was pilloried in the newspapers and his resignation demanded.* V+O : USU PASS ⇑ shame

2 A **pillory** is a wooden frame with holes for the head and hands. In Europe in the Middle Ages criminals were locked in a pillory for a period of time as a punishment. N COUNT

pillow /pɪləʊ/, **pillows, pillowing, pillowed**. 1 A **pillow** is a rectangular cushion which you rest your head on when you are in bed. EG *She lay with her face in the pillow, muffling her sobs... I slept with a gun under my pillow.* N COUNT

2 If your head **is pillowed** on something, usually something soft, it is resting comfortably on it. EG *He lay with his head pillowed on a clump of moss.* V+O : USU PASS, IF+PREP THEN on

pillowcase /pɪlə[6]keɪs/, **pillowcases**. A **pillow-case** is a cover for a pillow, made of cotton or other fabric, that can be removed and washed. N COUNT = pillowslip

pillowslip /pɪlə[6]slɪp/, **pillowslips**. A **pillowslip** is the same as a pillowcase. N COUNT ⇑ cover

pillow talk. Conversations that people have when they are in bed together can be referred to as **pillow talk**. N UNCOUNT

pilot /paɪlət/, **pilots, piloting, piloted**. 1 A **pilot** is 1.1 a person who is trained to fly an aircraft. EG *...an experienced fighter pilot... The airline blamed pilot error for the crash.* 1.2 a person who steers a ship through a difficult stretch of water, for example through the entrance to a harbour. The pilot usually gets onto the ship specially to do this. N COUNT; N COUNT ⇑ navigator

2 When someone **pilots** an aircraft or ship, they act as its pilot. EG *...a burly, jolly man who piloted his own airplane.* V+O

3 If you **pilot** a new law or scheme, you try to introduce it and look after it as it goes through the process of being introduced. EG *He was keen to see through the Bill which John Silkin was piloting on sub-contracting.* V+O

4 A **pilot** scheme, study, etc is used to test whether a particular scheme or product will be successful before introducing it or manufacturing it on a large scale. EG *This year we are trying a pilot scheme.* ADJ CLASSIF : ATTRIB ⇑ trial

5 A **pilot** is also the pilot light on a gas cooker, boiler, or fire. N COUNT ⇑ flame

pilot light, pilot lights. A **pilot light** is 1 a small gas flame in a cooker, boiler, or fire, which burns all the time and which lights the main large flame when the gas is turned fully on. EG *Don't leave your oven with the pilot light on.* 2 a small electric light, usually red, on an electrical appliance which shows that the appliance is switched on. N COUNT; N COUNT

pimento /pɪmentəʊ/, **pimentos**. A **pimento** is a mild-tasting red pepper. N COUNT ⇑ vegetable

pimp /pɪmp/, **pimps**. A **pimp** is a man who con-trols prostitutes, gets clients for them, and takes a large part of their earnings. EG *Willie is a convicted pimp.* N COUNT = ponce, procurer

pimple /pɪmpə[0]l/, **pimples**. A **pimple** is a small red spot, especially on your face. EG *He knew that eating sweets causes pimples.* N COUNT

pimply /pɪmpli[1]/. Someone who is **pimply** has a lot of pimples, especially on their face. EG *He was an ugly, pimply little boy.* ADJ QUALIT = spotty

pin /pɪn/, **pins, pinning, pinned**. 1 A **pin** is a very small, thin, round piece of metal with a point at one end. Pins can be stuck through things, for example through two pieces of cloth, in order to fasten them together. • See also **drawing pin**. N COUNT

2 You can also refer to a safety pin, a hairpin, a hatpin, or a panel pin as a **pin** when you have already mentioned it using its full name or when it is obvious what you are referring to. N COUNT

3 If you **pin** something somewhere, you fasten it to something else by sticking a pin, a drawing pin, or a safety pin through it and then into or through the second thing. EG *If you haven't any curtains to draw, pin a sheet over the window... Pin it on the back of the kitchen door... She wore a white leather rose pinned to her blouse.* V+O+A

4 A **pin** is also 4.1 a small brooch or badge with a pin attached to the bottom of it for fastening it to a person's clothing. EG *...a big coral pin her father had brought her from Naples.* 4.2 the clip on a hand grenade that prevents it from exploding and that is pulled out when you want the grenade to explode. N COUNT; N COUNT

5 If someone or something **pins** someone or some-thing else in a particular position or place, they hold them or press down on them firmly so that they cannot move. EG *Victor's left arm encircled him, pinning both the accountant's arms to his side... His strong arms were around me, pinning me down.* V+O+A ⇑ trap

6 If you **pin** the blame for something on someone, you say, often unfairly, that they did it or caused it. EG *You can't pin that on me.* V+O+A *(on/ upon)* = accuse

7 If you **pin** your hopes or your faith on something or someone, you hope that it will solve a particular problem or help you to get a particular thing, because it is the only thing that possibly can. EG *He increasingly pinned his hopes on the prospect of a split in the opposition party... I pin my faith on public opinion.* V+O+A *(on/ upon)* ⇑ rely

8 Your **pins** are your legs; an informal old-fashioned use. EG *I'm not too steady on my pins these days.* N PLURAL : DETPOSS+N

9 If you say that **for two pins** you would do a particular thing, you mean that you would very much like to do it and have not done it only because it would not be very polite, sensible, etc. EG *For two pins I'd tell him what I think of his silly idea.* PHR : USED AS ADV SEN

10 You say **pin back your ears, pin back your lugholes**, etc as an informal, humorous way of telling someone to listen to what you are going to say. PHR : VB INFLECTS

pin down. 1 If you try to **pin down** something which is hard to define or describe, you try to say exactly what it is or what it is like. EG *The courts have found obscenity impossible to pin down as a punishable offence.* PHRASAL VB : V+O+ADV

2 If you **pin** someone **down**, you cause them to make an exact and clear statement about something, usu-ally when they have been trying to avoid doing so. EG *He was anxious to pin the Minister down to some definite commitment.* PHRASAL VB : V+O+ADV ⇑ commit

pin up. 1 If you **pin up** something such as a poster or a notice, you pin it to a wall or another vertical surface so that it can be seen easily. EG *The map was pinned up and became the centre of attention.* PHRASAL VB : V+O+ADV ⇑ put up

2 If you **pin up** part of a piece of clothing, a curtain, etc, you pin the bottom of it to a part of it that is higher up. EG *At last the hem was pinned up.* PHRASAL VB : V+O+ADV

3 If a woman **pins** her hair **up**, she makes it into a bun or a similar hairstyle and fixes it in place with hairpins. EG *Her hair was pinned up, but wisps escaped here and there.* PHRASAL VB : V+O+ADV

4 See also **pin-up**.

pinafore /pɪnəfɔː/, **pinafores**. A **pinafore** or a **pinafore dress** is a dress with no sleeves, which is worn over a blouse or sweater. N COUNT

pinball /pɪnbɔːl/ is a game in which a player tries to keep a small ball from rolling to the bottom of a pin-table, by getting it to bounce off obstructions on the surface of the pin-table. N UNCOUNT

pinball machine, pinball machines. A **pinball machine** is the same as a pin-table. N COUNT

pince-nez /pænsneɪ, pɪns-/ are an old-fashioned kind of spectacles and consist of two lenses in a frame that fits tightly onto the top of the nose. EG *He was the only man I'd ever seen wearing pince-nez.* N PLURAL: ALSO *a pair of*+N ⇑ glasses

pincer /pɪnsə/, **pincers.** 1 **Pincers** are a tool consisting of two pieces of metal that are hinged in the middle. Pincers are used for gripping things or for pulling things out. EG *Pull them out with a pair of pincers.* N PLURAL: ALSO *a pair of*+N

2 The **pincers** of an animal such as a crab or lobster are their front claws, which consist of two curved parts. N COUNT: USU PL

pincer movement, pincer movements. A **pincer movement** is an attack by an army or other group in which they attack their enemies in two places at once with the aim of surrounding them. N COUNT ⇑ manoeuvre

pinch /pɪntʃ/, **pinches, pinching, pinched.** 1 If you **pinch** something, especially part of a person, you squeeze it quickly between your thumb and first finger. EG *Dr. Hochstadt pinched Judy's cheek as she passed... I pinched myself to make sure I wasn't dreaming.* V+O = tweak

2 A **pinch** is a quick squeeze which you give to something using your thumb and first finger. N COUNT = tweak

3 A **pinch** of a powder or a substance made up of small pieces is the amount of it that you can hold between your thumb and your first finger. EG *Season with a little salt and a pinch of cinnamon... He took a vigorous pinch of snuff.* • to **take** something **with a pinch of salt**: see **salt**. N PART+N UNCOUNT ⇑ quantity

4 If something **pinches** something else, it squeezes it or holds it tightly. EG *The hinge pinched Billy's skin and he gave a grunt of pain.* V+O

5 If your shoes **pinch**, they hurt your feet because they are too tight. V

6 If you **pinch** something, you steal it; an informal use. EG *I pinched fourpence from the box... Quite a few people have tried to pinch this idea.* V+O = nick, lift

7 **At a pinch** means if absolutely necessary and if there is no alternative. EG *At a pinch the new doctor would do.* PHR: USED AS AN A

8 If you **feel the pinch**, you are able to afford fewer things than before, usually as the result of a change, for example in the economy. EG *The big couture establishments have been feeling the pinch lately.* PHR: VB INFLECTS

9 If you **pinch and scrape, pinch and save**, etc, you spend as little money as possible and use everything that you have very carefully and for as long as you can. EG *For years my parents pinched and scraped to provide us with the things they wanted us to have.* PHR: VBS INFLECT ⇑ economize

pinched /pɪntʃt/. If someone's face is **pinched**, it looks thin and pale, usually because they are ill, starving, frightened, or cold. EG *Her face was white and pinched.... He lay on his bed, looking pinched and worn.* ADJ QUALIT = drawn

pincushion /pɪnkuʃəⁿn/, **pincushions.** A **pincushion** is a very small cushion that you stick pins and needles into so that you can get them easily when you need them. N COUNT

pine /paɪn/, **pines, pining, pined.** 1 A **pine** or a **pine tree** is a tall evergreen tree which has long, thin, sharp leaves and a fresh smell. Pine trees grow in cool parts of the world. EG *...the lower slopes of a pine forest... Mountain lakes and pines lay below them.* N COUNT ⇑ conifer

2 **Pine** is the pale coloured wood of pine trees, which is often used for making furniture. EG *...the stripped pine dresser.* N UNCOUNT = pinewood

3 If you **are pining** for something, you very much want to have it or very much want it to happen, and feel rather sad because you think that it is not likely to happen soon. EG *He had been pining for a moment like this... Most of them were already pining to be recognized and admitted as citizens.* V: USU CONT, IF+ PREP/VB THEN *for/to-INF* = long

4 If you **pine** for someone who has died or gone away, you feel very unhappy all the time because they have gone and you do not want to eat or do anything. EG *She sat in the house day after day, pining for her lover.* V: USU CONT, IF+ PREP/VB THEN *for/to-INF* = grieve

pine away. If someone **pines away**, they gradually become weaker and die because they are so unhappy that a particular person has died or left them. EG *I believe she actually pined away–lost her will to live.* PHRASAL VB: V+ ADV ⇑ grieve

pineapple /paɪnæpəⁿl/, **pineapples.** A **pineapple** is a large oval fruit that is sweet, juicy, and yellow inside and is covered with a thick, hard, woody skin. EG *...a slice of pineapple... You need two fresh pineapples... ...pineapple juice.* N COUNT/ UNCOUNT

pinecone /paɪnkəʊn/, **pinecones**; also spelled with a hyphen. A **pinecone** is a small oval seed case that is produced by a pine. N COUNT = cone

pine-needle, pine-needles. Pine-needles are long, thin, sharp leaves that grow on pine trees. They look rather like needles. N COUNT: USU PL

pinewood /paɪnwʊd/, **pinewoods.** 1 A **pinewood** is a wood which consists of pine trees. N COUNT

2 **Pinewood** is wood that has come from a pine tree. N UNCOUNT

ping /pɪŋ/, **pings, pinging, pinged.** 1 If something such as a bell or a piece of metal **pings**, it makes a high-pitched noise that stops very quickly. EG *The bell pings; the lift doors open.* ▸ used as a noun. EG *There was a loud ping.* V ⇑ sound

ping-pong /pɪŋ pɒŋ/ is the game of table tennis. EG *...the ping-pong champion of China... ...a ping-pong ball... ...a novel electronic ping-pong game.* N UNCOUNT: USU BEFORE N

pinhead /pɪnhɛd/, **pinheads.** A **pinhead** is a small metal or plastic ball on the end of a pin. ▸ often used to indicate how small something is. EG *You could place half a dozen of them on a pinhead.* N COUNT

2 If you refer to someone as a **pinhead**, you are suggesting in a rather insulting way that they are stupid. EG *...the questions some pinhead from the BBC had asked him.* N COUNT/VOC = idiot, fool

pinion /pɪnjən/, **pinions, pinioning, pinioned.** If you **pinion** someone, you prevent them from moving or escaping, especially by holding or tying their arms. EG *...pinioned by the press of men around them, they were unable to move.* V+O: USU PASS ⇑ restrain

pink /pɪŋk/, **pinker, pinkest; pinks, pinking, pinked.** 1 Something that is **pink** is of a colour that is between red and white. EG *The tree was covered with beautiful pink blossom... Her cheeks were pinker and her eyelids darker than they had been earlier in the day.* ▸ used as a noun. EG *The bathroom was decorated in pink.* ADJ COLOUR ▸ N MASS

2 If someone goes **pink**, their face turns a slightly redder colour than usual because they are embarrassed, angry, or have been doing something energetic. EG *He went very pink, and looked away.* ADJ COLOUR = flushed

3 A **pink** is a small garden plant that has very narrow blue-green leaves and pink, white, or red sweetly-scented flowers; used also of the flowers themselves. N COUNT

4 If the engine of a vehicle **pinks**, it makes a metallic squeaking or knocking sound because it is not working properly; used in British English. V = knock

5 Someone who is described as **being pink** with reference to their political beliefs supports Socialist policies only to a very slight or weak degree and so is considered to be very moderate in their beliefs. ADJ QUALIT

6 If you **pink** the edge of a piece of material, you cut it with pinking shears to prevent it fraying. V+O

7 Someone who is **in the pink** is in very good health. EG *You certainly look in the pink!* • to **be tickled pink**: see **tickle**. PHR: USED AS AN A ⇑ well

pinkie /pɪŋkiˡ/, **pinkies**; also spelled **pinky**. Someone's **pinkie** is the smallest finger on their hand; an informal use. N COUNT = little finger

pinking shears are special scissors that have blades with V-shaped teeth and that give zigzag edges to anything that they cut. They are used especially to cut cloth, so as to prevent its edges from fraying. N PLURAL: ALSO *a pair of*+N

pinkish /pɪŋkɪʃ/ means slightly pink in colour. EG *...a faint pinkish glow.* ADJ COLOUR

pin money is small amounts of extra money that someone earns in order to buy things that they want but that they do not really need. N UNCOUNT

pinnacle /pɪnəkəⁿl/, **pinnacles.** 1 A **pinnacle** is a pointed cone-shaped piece of stone or rock. EG *...a pinnacle of rock.* N COUNT

2 The **pinnacle** of a system, or of someone's ambitions or hopes, is the highest or most successful point or degree. EG *It represents the pinnacle of intellectual capability.* N COUNT: USU SING+*of* ⇑ height = peak

pinny /pɪniˡ/, **pinnies.** A **pinny** is an apron; an informal word. N COUNT

pinpoint /pɪnpɔɪnt/, **pinpoints, pinpointing, pinpointed.** 1 If you **pinpoint** the cause of something, you discover or explain exactly what is causing or preventing it. EG *You can pinpoint any danger and we can deal with it.* V+O ⇑ show = identify

2 If you **pinpoint** the position of something, you discover or show someone its exact position. EG *'Just here,' he said, pinpointing it on the map.* — V+O = locate

3 A **pinpoint** of light is a very small spot of light. — N COUNT

pinprick /pɪnprɪk/, **pinpricks**. 1 A **pinprick** is something that annoys you for a short time. EG *...the hundred daily pinpricks of family life.* — N COUNT ↑ annoyance = irritation

2 A **pinprick** of light is a very small spot of light. — N COUNT+SUPP

pins and needles. If you get **pins and needles** in part of your body, it is affected by sharp tingling pains for a period of time because it has been in an awkward or uncomfortable position. — N UNCOUNT

pinstripe /pɪnstraɪp/. **Pinstripe** cloth has very narrow vertical stripes. EG *He wore a carnation and a new pin-stripe suit.* — ADJ CLASSIF: ATTRIB ↑ striped

pint /paɪnt/, **pints**. 1 A **pint** is 1.1 in Britain, a unit of measurement for liquids that is equal to one-eighth of an imperial gallon or 568 cubic centimetres. EG *...one pint of milk... 'Two pints of bitter,' says Henry, standing at the bar... He drank his tea from his own pint mug.* — N COUNT/PART+N UNCOUNT **1.2** in America, a unit of measurement for liquids that is equal to one-eighth of an American gallon or 473 cubic centimetres. — N COUNT/PART+N UNCOUNT

2 If you have a **pint** in a pub, you have a pint of beer. EG *He likes having a couple of pints with his lunch... Do you fancy going out for a pint?* — N COUNT: ALSO N +*of*+N UNCOUNT

pin-table, pin-tables. A **pin-table** is a sloping surface with pins and other obstructions on it, on which the game of pinball is played. The obstructions are often electrically wired to light up and ring a bell when the ball touches them. — N COUNT = pinball machine

pint-size. Someone or something that is described as **pint-size** or **pint-sized** is very small. — ADJ CLASSIF = petite

pin-up, pin-ups; also spelled as one word. A **pin-up** is a picture of an attractive woman or man, often a famous person or a model wearing very few clothes. People sometimes fix pin-ups to a wall, so that they can look at them and cheer themselves up. EG *The bathroom wall was plastered with pin-ups of film stars... ...pin-ups of prize fighters.* — N COUNT ▸ used as an adjective. EG *...pin-up artists... ...pin-up girls.* — ▸ ADJ CLASSIF: ATTRIB

pioneer /paɪənɪə/, **pioneers, pioneering, pioneered**. 1 Someone who is referred to as a **pioneer** in a particular area of activity is one of the first people to be involved in it and develop it. EG *He was a pioneer of photography... ...her pioneer work in organizing militant groups of pensioners... ...the great pioneer Socialist Jimmy Maxton.* — N COUNT OR N BEFORE N

2 Someone who **pioneers** a new activity, invention, or process is one of the first people to do it. EG *...a general hospital which pioneered open heart surgery in this country... ...the two-way wrist radio that Dick Tracy pioneered.* — V+O

3 A **pioneer** is also a person who is one of the first people to live, farm, etc in a new or unknown country or area of a country. EG *They all went out as pioneers, with little or nothing.* — N COUNT = settler

pioneering /paɪənɪərᵒɪŋ/ means doing something that has not been done before, for example developing or using new inventions or processes or belonging to a new political movement. EG *...a pioneering and innovative banker... ...the pioneering Asian socialists... Maggie Thompson personifies the pioneering spirit... This meeting also heard about pioneering work in the London borough of Hounslow.* — ADJ CLASSIF: USU ATTRIB

pious /paɪəs/. 1 Someone who is **pious** 1.1 believes in God or in a particular religion very deeply and shows this belief in the way they behave and live. EG *Mrs Smith was a very pious woman who attended Church services regularly...* — ADJ QUALIT ↑ respectful = devout, religious ▸ used of what someone says or does. EG *...pious utterances.* **1.2** pretends to be very religious but is not really sincere; used showing disapproval. — ADJ QUALIT ↑ hypocritical = sanctimonious

2 **Pious** hopes are unlikely to be achieved. EG *Congress had done no more than set out some pious hopes.* — ADJ QUALIT: ATTRIB = improbable

pip /pɪp/, **pips, pipping, pipped**. 1 A **pip** is one of the small hard seeds in a fruit such as an apple, orange, or pear. — N COUNT

2 The **pips** on the radio are a series of six short, high-pitched sounds that are used as a time signal. — N COUNT = bleep

3 If you **pip** someone **at the post**, you just beat them in a competition or something that you are both trying to achieve. — PHR: VB INFLECTS ↑ defeat

4 If you say that someone **gives** you **the pip**, you mean that you do not like them because they annoy you or because you feel that they are strange in some way; an informal use. — PHR: VB INFLECTS = irritate

pipe /paɪp/, **pipes, piping, piped**. 1 A **pipe** is **1.1** a long round hollow object usually made of metal or plastic which is used for carrying liquids or gas. EG *...hot water pipes... No home can be warm or comfortable if the pipes are frozen or burst...* — N COUNT **1.2** an object which is used for smoking tobacco or other substances. You put the tobacco into a small container at one end of the pipe, light it, and inhale the smoke through a narrow tube. EG *He was sitting quietly in his armchair, smoking a pipe and reading the morning paper... ...pipe-smoking teachers in tweeds.* — N COUNT

2 To **pipe** a liquid or gas somewhere means to transfer it from one place to another through a pipe. EG *Hot water is piped to all the rooms.* — V+O: USU+A ↑ carry

3 To **pipe** is used to indicate that someone is speaking in a high-pitched voice. EG *'It's for you,' he piped, waving a purple envelope.* — V+QUOTE/O

4 An organ **pipe** is one of the long hollow tubes in which air vibrates and produces a musical note. EG *...the widest pipe of the largest cathedral organ.* — N COUNT

5 **Pipes** are a musical instrument consisting of a bag and a series of wooden tubes. The bag is filled with air and the air is forced through the tubes, one of which has holes in it which you play with your fingers to produce the tune. EG *Amid the sound of pipes and a flurry of sand the troops left.* — N PLURAL

6 See also **piping, piping hot**.

pipe down. If you tell someone who is talking a lot or talking loudly to **pipe down**, you are telling them to stop talking; an informal use. — PHRASAL VB: V+ADV, NO CONT = be quiet

pipe up. If someone who has been silent for a while **pipes up**, they start speaking. EG *'It's all very well for you, Elizabeth,' he piped up.* — PHRASAL VB: V+ADV, NO CONT, USU+QUOTE

pipe cleaner, pipe cleaners. A **pipe cleaner** is a piece of wire covered with a soft woolly substance which is used for cleaning a tobacco pipe. — N COUNT

piped music is music which is played through loud speakers in large supermarkets, stations, and other public places. — N UNCOUNT = Muzak, canned music

pipe dream, pipe dreams; also spelled with a hyphen. A **pipe dream** is an idea that you have about something which you would like to happen in the future but which is impossible in reality. EG *It's only a pipe dream, but I wish I could meet him.* — N COUNT

pipeline /paɪplaɪn/, **pipelines**. 1 A **pipeline** is a large, very long pipe which is used for carrying oil or gas over a long distance, often underground. EG *They feed the gas into the existing pipeline from the Brent field to shore.* — N COUNT: ALSO *by*+N

2 If something is **in the pipeline**, it is already planned or begun and about to happen or be completed soon. EG *...more improvements were in the pipeline.* — PHR: USED AS AN A ↑ imminent

piper /paɪpə/, **pipers**. A **piper** is a musician who plays the bagpipes. EG *...the piper who played sweetly on his pipes.* — N COUNT

pipette /pɪpet/, **pipettes**. A **pipette** is a thin glass tube which is used in scientific experiments for carrying or measuring small amounts of liquid. — N COUNT

piping /paɪpɪŋ/. 1 **Piping** is **1.1** metal, plastic, or other substances made in the shape of a pipe or tube. EG *...glass piping.* — N UNCOUNT **1.2** a narrow tube of fabric that looks rather like a piece of thick string. Piping is used to decorate clothing and things such as cushions. — N UNCOUNT

2 If someone says something in a **piping** voice, they say it in a high-pitched voice. EG *In a piping but determined voice she ordered me to sit down. ...from the piping choirboys to the sonorous bass.* — ADJ CLASSIF: ATTRIB = shrill

piping hot. Food or water that is **piping hot** is very hot; usually used showing approval. EG *...piping hot pudding... The water's piping hot.* — ADJ CLASSIF

pipsqueak /pɪpskwi:k/, **pipsqueaks**. If you refer to someone as a **pipsqueak**, you are saying that they are unimportant and showing your contempt for them. — N COUNT/VOC = squirt

piquancy /pi:kənsi[1]/. If something adds **piquancy** to a situation, it adds interest and excitement, perhaps with a slight mystery. EG *Heckling is something they would not wish to change for it adds piquancy to the contest.* — N UNCOUNT

2 **Piquancy** is also a pleasantly spicy taste. EG *...using herbs or spices to give variety and piquancy.* — N UNCOUNT

piquant /piːkənt, -kɑːnt/. 1 Food that is **piquant** has a pleasantly spicy taste. EG *...a piquant sauce.* ADJ QUALIT

2 Something that is **piquant** is interesting and intriguing but also shows signs of being puzzling and slightly mysterious. EG *...a piquant incident, you must admit... ...a most piquant face with large appealing dark-blue eyes.* ADJ QUALIT

pique /piːk/ is a feeling of anger and resentment caused by someone's pride being hurt. EG *Although she was ashamed of it, she sulked. Simon found such pique amusing... She flounced off the stage with an air of pique.* ● If someone does something **in a fit of pique**, they do it because they are angry and resentful that their pride has been hurt. EG *He withdrew in a fit of pique.* N UNCOUNT ● PHR: USED AS AN A

piqued /piːkt/. If someone is **piqued**, they are angry and resentful because their pride has been hurt. EG *I was piqued and prepared not to like him one bit... 'You were pretty certain, weren't you?' asked Casson, piqued at being predicted in this manner.* ADJ QUALIT

piracy /paɪrəˈsɪ/ is robbery carried out by pirates, originally by pirates on the sea but now more usually by people who illegally take other people's work or property. EG *...illegal migration and labour piracy started up.* N UNCOUNT

piranha /pɪrɑːnə/, **piranhas**. **Piranha** can also be used as the plural form. A **piranha** is a small fierce fish with sharp teeth which lives in South American rivers and eats meat. N COUNT

pirate /paɪrəˈt/, **pirates, pirating, pirated**. 1 A **pirate** is a person, especially in former times, who sailed on the sea and stole from other people's ships. EG *Pirates boarded the vessels and robbed the passengers... ...a wave of pirate raids on merchant ships.* N COUNT ⇑ robber = buccaneer

2 You can refer to someone as a **pirate** when they take and use someone else's work or property without having the right to do so. EG *I met one of these pirates recruiting labour on a rubber estate.* N COUNT

3 A **pirate** is also a person or a company that broadcasts illegally; an informal use. EG *There are at least a dozen pirates transmitting in London alone.* N COUNT

4 Someone who is **pirating** video tapes, cassettes, or books is copying, publishing, and selling them when they have no right to do so because the contents legally belong to someone else. ◊ **pirated**. EG *There were a lot of pirated editions.* V+O ⇑ illicit ◊ ADJ CLASSIF

pirate radio, pirate radios. **Pirate radio** is the broadcasting of radio programmes illegally, for example by transmitting from a ship in the sea. EG *There was evidence of pirate radios interfering with shipping... ...a pirate radio station.* N UNCOUNT/COUNT ⇑ illegal

pirouette /pɪruɛt/, **pirouettes, pirouetting, pirouetted**. 1 A **pirouette** in ballet is a fast turn of the dancer's body which is done on the toes or the ball of the foot. ▸ used as a verb. EG *She pirouetted on to the stage.* N COUNT ▸ V

piss /pɪs/, **pisses, pissing, pissed**; an informal word. Many speakers consider this to be a rude word and avoid using it. 1 To **piss** means 1.1 to urinate. V

2 If someone has a **piss**, they urinate. N SING: *a*+N

3 **Piss** is urine. N UNCOUNT

4 If it **is pissing** with rain, it is raining very heavily. V: USU CONT+ *with*

piss about. If someone **pisses about** or **pisses around**, 1 they waste a lot of time doing a lot of little things that do not really need doing, especially when there are more important things waiting to be done. PHRASAL VB: V+ADV

2 they behave in a silly, childish way that annoys other people. PHRASAL VB: V+ADV

piss down. If it **is pissing down**, it is raining very hard indeed. PHRASAL VB: V+ADV

piss off. 1 If a person tells someone else to **piss off**, that person is telling them in a rude way to go away, usually because they have done something very annoying. PHRASAL VB: V+ADV, USU IMPER

2 If someone is **pissed off** with something or if something **pisses** them **off**, they feel bored and irritated by it. PHRASAL VB: V+ADV, OR V+O+ADV

pissed /pɪst/. Someone who is **pissed** is drunk; a very informal word. ADJ QUALIT: USU PRED

pistol /pɪstəˀl/, **pistols**. A **pistol** is a small gun that is held in the hand. EG *It sounded like a small pistol going off.* N COUNT ⇑ handgun

piston /pɪstəˀn/, **pistons**. A **piston** is a cylinder or metal disc that is part of an engine. Pistons slide up and down inside tubes under the force of pressure or an explosion causing various parts of the engine to move. N COUNT

pit /pɪt/, **pits, pitting, pitted**. 1 A **pit** is 1.1 a large hole that is dug in the ground, usually for a particular purpose. EG *The inside of the pit was stacked completely around with ammunition... ...an inspection pit dug in the ground under a bamboo shelter.* ● See also **sandpit**. 1.2 a small, shallow hole, usually one of several holes, in the surface of something. EG *I'm trying to avoid all these pits in the road.* 1.3 a coal mine. EG *How did the men manage for baths coming home from the pit?... ...losses incurred through the postponement of pit closures.* N COUNT; N COUNT: USU PL; N COUNT = colliery, mine

2 A gravel **pit**, clay **pit**, etc is a very large hole that is left where gravel or clay has been dug from the ground. N COUNT+SUPP = working

3 The **pit** in a theatre is the area at the back on the ground floor; a rather old-fashioned word. EG *They went and sat in the pit.* ● See also **orchestra pit**. N COUNT: IF SING *the*+N = rear stalls

4 You can refer to very deep feelings that you seem to feel in the area of your body around your stomach as being felt in **the pit of your stomach**. EG *No-one should underrate the worry in the pit of their stomach as a new volunteer... The ache in the pit of her stomach was no worse than the one in her heart.* PHR: USU USED AS O

5 In motor racing, the **pits** are the areas at the side of the track where drivers stop for refuelling and repairs during the race. N COUNT: USU PL

6 If you refer to someone or something as **the pits** you mean that they are the worst of their kind. EG *This town really is the pits.* PHR: USED AS C

7 If you **pit** your **wits against** someone, you compete with them in a test of knowledge, intelligence, etc. EG *Here is your chance to pit your wits against the experts.* PHR: VB INFLECTS

8 See also **pitted**.

pit-a-pat /pɪt ə pæt/ is a way of referring to a sound that consists of a series of short, light taps, like the sound of raindrops falling on a surface. = pitter-patter

pitch /pɪtʃ/, **pitches, pitching, pitched**. 1 A football **pitch**, hockey **pitch**, cricket **pitch**, etc is an area of ground that is marked out and used for playing that particular game. EG *On the hockey pitch Miss Cadogan was umpiring a game... On bad pitches we need very good batsmen.* N COUNT: USU MOD+N = field

2 If you **pitch** something somewhere, you throw it with quite a lot of force, usually aiming it carefully. EG *She pitched the ball as far as she could... He was busy pitching a penny at a crack in the sidewalk.* V+O: USU+A

3 In the game of baseball or rounders, when you **pitch** the ball, you throw it to the batsman. V+O

4 If someone or something **pitches** somewhere, they fall forwards suddenly and with a lot of force. EG *He would have been unable to prevent himself from pitching over the low guard rails... He suddenly pitched headlong to the ground.* V+A

5 If a boat **pitches**, it moves violently up and down with the movement of the waves when the sea is rough. EG *The ferry pitched and rolled more than usual.* V = toss

6 If someone **is pitched** into a new situation, they are suddenly forced into it. EG *This pitched him into the political arena.* V+O: USU+A = throw, thrust

7 The **pitch** of a sound is its degree of highness or lowness. EG *The scream died away, changing pitch as it faded... Her voice dropped to a lower, more confidential pitch.* ● See also **perfect pitch**. N UNCOUNT

8 If you **pitch** your voice or other sound at a particular level, you produce the sound at the level indicated. EG *The voice was calm, but pitched slightly higher than Brody remembered... His wife gave out a little high-pitched yell.* V+O

9 If you **pitch** something at a particular level, rate, degree of complexity, etc, you set it at that level or rate. EG *Her lectures are pitched directly at the level of the students... The prices of these cars are pitched extremely competitively.* V+O+A

10 If something rises to a **pitch**, it rises to a very high level or degree. EG *Her dilemma was mounting up to a pitch of blind anger.* N SING WITH DET: USU+SUPP

11 **Pitch** is also a black substance that is sticky when it is hot and very hard when it is dry. It is used on the bottoms of ships and boats and on the roofs of houses to prevent water from getting in. N UNCOUNT

12 When you **pitch** a tent, you put it into an upright position using the poles and fix it securely to the ground. EG *We pitched the tent and took our goods out of the car.* V+O = erect

13 If someone **queers the pitch for** someone else, PHR: VB

they spoil their plans and opportunities; an informal expression. INFLECTS

pitch in. If you **pitch in**, you join in with an activity or you help other people with a job that they are doing. EG *They will be expected to pitch in and make their own beds.* PHRASAL VB : V+ADV = muck in

pitch into. If a person **pitches into** someone else, he or she attacks them, either by hitting them, or by insulting and criticizing them. EG *The boss really pitched into me and told me I wasn't working hard enough.* PHRASAL VB : V+PREP, HAS PASS = lay into

pitch-black. If a place or the night is **pitch-black** or **pitch-dark**, it is completely dark. EG *We started off through the pitch-black woods.* ◇ **pitch blackness**, **pitch darkness**. EG *...a place of pitch blackness.* ADJ CLASSIF : USU ATTRIB ◇ N UNCOUNT

pitched /pɪtʃt/. A **pitched** roof is one that slopes quite steeply as opposed to one that is flat. ADJ QUALIT ⇑ sloping

pitched battle, pitched battles. A **pitched battle** is a very fierce and violent fight. EG *Police fought a pitched battle with about 40 youths.* N COUNT

pitcher /pɪtʃə/, **pitchers**. 1 A **pitcher** is 1.1 a jug; used in American English. EG *He poured the milk out of the pitcher.* N COUNT ⇑ container 1.2 a large container made of clay, usually rounded and having a narrow neck and two ear-shaped handles. Pitchers are usually used for holding and pouring water. N COUNT

2 In baseball, the **pitcher** is the person who throws the ball to the batsman. EG *Most baseball teams carry nine or ten pitchers and might expect to use three or four in any one game.* N COUNT ⇑ bowler

pitchfork /pɪtʃfɔːk/, **pitchforks**. A **pitchfork** is a large fork with two prongs and a long handle that is used for lifting hay, grass, straw, etc. N COUNT ⇑ tool

piteous /pɪtɪəs/. Something that is **piteous** is so sad or in such a sorrowful or weak state that you feel great pity. EG *There were piteous sounds of suffering and pain... She gave so piteous a description of her plight.* ◇ **piteously**. EG *Fanny cried out piteously at the same moment... She looked piteously up at Liz.* ADJ QUALIT = pitiful ◇ ADV WITH VB = pitifully

pitfall /pɪtfɔːl/, **pitfalls**. A **pitfall** is something harmful that might happen if a particular course of action is taken. EG *Some concern has been expressed about the pitfalls of pursuing such a drastic policy... What are the pitfalls?* N COUNT : USU PL ⇑ consequence = danger, hazard

pith /pɪθ/. 1 The **pith** of an orange, lemon, or other citrus fruit is the white substance that is between the peel and the fruit itself. N UNCOUNT

2 The **pith** of something is the most essential or important part of it. EG *The pith of the matter was in those two phrases... This principle is the whole pith of right-to-work legislation in America.* N SING : *the*+N+*of* ⇑ point = crux

pithead /pɪthɛd/, **pitheads**. The **pithead** at a coalmine is all the buildings and machinery, etc which are above the ground. EG *He was accosted by his men at the pithead... It was agreed that there would be a pithead ballot.* N COUNT : IF SING USU *the*+N

pithy /pɪθi[1]/, **pithier, pithiest**. A **pithy** comment or piece of writing is concise, yet sensible and full of meaning. EG *...pithy sayings... An excellent pithy little guidebook is 'Deep Freezing' by Mary Norwak.* ADJ QUALIT ⇑ terse

pitiable /pɪtɪəbə[0]l/. Something or someone that is **pitiable** is in such a sad, weak, or unfortunate situation that you feel pity for them. EG *They are as pitiable a sight as you could imagine... ...so miserable, so pitiable was the broken man before me.* ◇ **pitiably**. EG *The daughter's dowry or wedding feast is so pitiably small.* ADJ QUALIT = pitiful ◇ ADV = pitifully

pitiful /pɪtɪfʊl/. Something or someone that is **pitiful** is so sad, weak, or unfortunate that you feel great pity for them. EG *It is pitiful to see old people degraded like that... ...his thin, bony legs and his pitiful arms... ...a pitiful sound of a human being in unbearable pain.* ◇ **pitifully**. EG *He looked at me pitifully and scrambled to his feet.* ADJ QUALIT = pitiable ◇ ADV = pathetically

pitiless /pɪtɪlɪ[2]s/. 1 Someone or something that is **pitiless** shows absolutely no feelings of pity or mercy. EG *...his office face, cool and pitiless, replacing his former cordiality. The creature looked at me with pitiless eyes.* ◇ **pitilessly**. EG *They watched and judged us and were pitilessly spiteful.* ADJ CLASSIF ◇ ADV = mercilessly

2 Something, especially the weather, that is **pitiless** is very harsh or severe and shows no signs of improving. EG *The sky was cold, pale blue and pitiless.* ADJ QUALIT ⇑ unremitting = relentless

pittance /pɪtə[0]ns/. If someone receives a **pittance**, they receive only a very small amount of money; used showing disapproval. EG *Women often prefer to look after their children well, rather than working for a pittance... She has several sidelines, none of which pay more than a pittance.* N SING : *a*+N

pitted /pɪtɪ[2]d/. If the surface of something is **pitted**, it is covered with a lot of small, shallow holes. ADJ QUALIT = scarred

pitter-patter /pɪtə pætə/ is a way of referring to a sound that consists of a series of short, light taps like the sound of raindrops falling on a surface. EG *...the pitter-patter of tiny feet.* N SING OR ADV = pit-a-pat

pituitary /pɪtjuːɪtə[0]ri[1]/, **pituitaries**. The **pituitary** or **pituitary gland** is a gland that is attached to the base of the brain. It produces hormones which affect growth, sexual development, and other functions of the body. N COUNT : USU SING

pity /pɪti[1]/, **pities, pitying, pitied**. 1 If you feel **pity** for someone, you feel very sorry for them because they are experiencing great misfortune, unhappiness, or sorrow. EG *She felt pity, of course, for the child... She walked away in an agony of hopeless grief and pity.* N UNCOUNT ⇑ compassion

2 If you **pity** someone, you feel pity for them. EG *In that society, of course, cripples were to be pitied and shunned... He shook his head sorrowfully, pitying himself for what had been done to him.* V+O

3 If you say that it is a **pity** that something is the case, you mean that it is a circumstance or state of affairs that causes disappointment or regret. EG *It seemed a pity to eat it after all the trouble they'd taken in making it... It will be a terrible pity if this should happen.... Pity you missed that film last night.* N SING : *a*+N ⇑ misfortune = shame

● You can say **a thousand pities** when you want to say that it is a very great pity that something is the case. EG *It's a thousand pities to see the way things are being wasted.* ● PHR : USED AS C

4 If you add **more's the pity** to a comment you have just made or in response to something that you have been told, you are expressing your disappointment or regret about something. EG *We've got to tell the tax office, more's the pity.* PHR : USED AS ADV SEN ⇑ unfortunately

5 If you **take pity on** someone who has a problem or is upset about something, you feel sorry for them and help them. EG *A man who spoke English took pity on us and translated for us.* PHR : VB INFLECTS

6 **For pity's sake** is used when you are annoyed, displeased, or exasperated. EG *For pity's sake leave me alone!... For pity's sake, Linda! Where do you pick up such ways.* PHR : USED AS ADV SEN

7 **Pity** is also an attitude which shows forgiveness and mercy towards someone. EG *No pity will be shown to thieves.* N UNCOUNT ⇑ clemency

pitying /pɪti[1]ɪŋ/. A **pitying** look shows that someone feels pity and perhaps slight contempt. EG *Angelica gave me a pitying smile.* ◇ **pityingly**. EG *He shook his head pityingly from side to side.* ADJ CLASSIF : ATTRIB ◇ ADV WITH VB

pivot /pɪvət/, **pivots, pivoting, pivoted**. 1 A **pivot** is the pin or the central point on which something balances or turns. EG *We watched the compass needle as it swung resolutely round on its pivot... There are some moments in life that are like pivots around which your existence turns.* N COUNT ⇑ fulcrum

2 If something **pivots**, it turns on a central point, or as if it were on a pivot. EG *The helicopter lifted to the top of the monument, banked, pivoted, and swooped back into the darkness... Now bring your body forward with a straight back, pivoting from the hips... Michael stopped, pivoted and walked back in.* V

3 A **pivot** is also the central or most important thing around which everything else is based or arranged. EG *The great chamber was the ceremonial pivot of the house... Their daughter was the pivot of their lives... My days revolved around two pivots, my home and my studio.* N COUNT = crux

pivot on. If something **pivots on** something else, it depends on this thing which is very important to its success or progress. EG *Success or failure pivoted on a single exam.* PHRASAL VB : V+PREP

pivotal /pɪvətə[0]l/. A **pivotal** point, factor, role, etc is one that is very important and affects the success or development of the larger thing that it is involved in. EG *This scene is probably the pivotal point of the whole book... 1941 was the pivotal year of the war.* ADJ CLASSIF

pixie /pɪksi[1]/, **pixies**. A **pixie** is an imaginary little creature like a fairy and which has pointed ears and a pointed hat. Pixies are found in many children's stories. N COUNT

pixie hat, pixie hats. A **pixie hat** is a pointed woollen hat. N COUNT

pizza /piːtsə/, **pizzas**. A **pizza** is a flat, round piece of dough or pastry spread with tomatoes, cheese, herbs, etc and then baked in an oven. Pizzas originally came from Italy. EG *...a plate of pizza... He heated up a frozen pizza.*
N COUNT/UNCOUNT

pizzazz /pɪtsæz/. Someone or something that has **pizzazz** is exceptionally exciting or attractive; an informal use. EG *The polls showed that the candidate was thought to have no charisma, no pizzazz, no passion.*
N UNCOUNT ↑ flamboyance

pizzicato /pɪtsɪkɑːtəʊ/. If a string instrument such as a violin is played **pizzicato**, it is played by plucking the strings with the fingers rather than by using the bow; a technical term in music.
ADV WITH VB

pl is a written abbreviation for 'plural' or 'place'.

placard /plækɑːd/, **placards**. A **placard** is a large cardboard or wooden notice that is carried in a march or demonstration or displayed in a public place. EG *Students paraded round the campus carrying placards... He held a placard saying 'Disarm Now!'*
N COUNT ↑ poster

placate /plə³keɪt/, **placates, placating, placated**. If **placate** someone, you try to stop them feeling angry or resentful by doing or saying things that will please them. EG *Nobody would tell her the truth: they were all too anxious to placate and to soothe... ...the desire of politicians to placate the public.* ◊ **placating**. EG *Her hand hovered near his sleeve, placating and gentle.*
V OR V+O ↑ soothe = appease, mollify
◊ ADJ QUALIT = pacifying

placatory /pləkeɪtəºri¹/. A **placatory** remark or action is intended to stop someone feeling angry or resentful by doing or saying things that will please them. EG *The President's speech seemed astonishingly placatory... They were making placatory gestures.*
ADJ QUALIT ↑ soothing = appeasing

place /pleɪs/, **places, placing, placed**. **1** A **place** is **1.1** somewhere, for example an area, a point, or a building. EG *We were looking for a good place to camp... The place where they landed was relatively green... The cellar was a very dark place... He had 150 photographs of people and places taken during his travels abroad... They seem to have scheduled the president to be in two places at once.* **1.2** a town, country, island, or other specific area that usually has a name. EG *...Steelhead, the place where I was staying... ...a place called Doulting.* **1.3** an area, town, building, institution, etc that has been mentioned or whose identity is understood; an informal use. EG *He was going to blow the place up... Mr Evans seemed to know the place well... Come on, you know you're going to miss this place.* **1.4** somewhere that provides a service or entertainment, for example a hotel, pub, hospital, or institution. EG *Do you know a place called The Farmer's Inn?... We'd got into a nice place in Ullapool so we thought we'd spend 4 nights there... I was writing off to various places in Britain asking about courses.*
1.1 N COUNT — 1.2 N COUNT = location — 1.3 N SING: *the/this* +N — 1.4 N COUNT = establishment

2 In informal English, if you refer to someone's **place**, you mean the house, flat, room, etc where they are living or staying. EG *Could I stay at your place for a bit, Rob?... We had gone on to Aunt Clare's place... 'What sort of place do they have?'-'Two furnished rooms.'*
N COUNT: USU POSS+N IN SING

3 The word **place** is used after another word in order to refer to somewhere that is used for the particular activity, purpose, or event indicated. EG *...in a Tipperary market-place... ...a meeting place... ...the bracken around their hiding-place... ...Shakespeare's birthplace.* ● See also **fireplace**.
N COUNT: MOD+N

4 Someone's **place** of work, **place** of birth, etc is the address or town where they work, were born, etc. EG *Please give your name, address, age, place of birth, and religion.*
N COUNT+*of* ↑ location

5 If you say that somewhere is the **place** for someone or for a particular purpose, you mean that it is very suitable for that person or purpose. EG *Of course it was no place to raise a child with damaged lungs... The saloon, I decided, was the place for me.*
N SING WITH DET +*for/to-INF*

6 Something's **place** is the position or actual point where it is or was, where it belongs, or where it should be. EG *She put the book back in its place on the shelf... Mrs Kaul had to leave her place and go to the back of the room to reprimand the boys... Don't park your car in the wrong place... I keep these cards in a very safe place.*
N COUNT: USU SUPP/POSS+N

7 The word **place** is also used in the following expressions referring to position. **7.1** If something is **in place** or put **into place**, it is in its correct or usual position, or put into the correct position. EG *He held the handle in place while the glue set... Jane then, screwed the grille back into place... A chair still stands in place at the top of the stairs.* **7.2** If something is **out of place**, it is not in its correct or usual position. EG *She was slightly out of breath but not one hair was out of place.* **7.3** If you **take** your **place**, you go and sit or stand in your correct position. EG *I took my place in class.*
7.1 PHR: USED AS AN A — 7.2 PHR: USED AS AN A — 7.3 PHR: VB INFLECTS

8 If you **place** something somewhere, you put it in a particular place or position, especially in a careful, firm, or deliberate way. EG *She placed the music on the piano and sat down... Chairs had been placed in rows all down the room... Each stone is firmly and correctly placed.*
V+O+A = set

9 When something **takes place**, it happens, especially in a controlled or organized way or as a result of something. EG *The next attack took place four hours later... The talks will take place in Vienna... Profound political changes have been taking place in the country... The pressure becomes so great that an explosion takes place.*
PHR: VB INFLECTS, USU+A = occur

10 all over the place. 10.1 If something is happening **all over the place**, it is happening in a lot of different places or over a very large area. EG *Our fashions sell in London and Paris and New York and all over the place... If he wasn't careful, there would be fuses blowing all over the place.* **10.2** If things are **all over the place**, they are very untidy or disorderly. EG *There were clothes and old shoes all over the place... My brother's hair is all over the place.*
10.1 PHR: USED AS AN A = everywhere — 10.2 PHR: USED AS AN A

11 If someone **screams the place down, howls the place down**, etc, they scream or cry very loudly and for a long time.
PHR: VB INFLECTS

12 If you go **places**, you go to different places or to places that are not described in detail; used in American English. EG *She was always wanting to tag along when we went places with our friends... They had a yacht and went places.*
ADV AFTER VB ↑ somewhere

13 If you say that someone **is going places**, you mean that they are showing a lot of talent or ability in their work and are likely to become very successful.
PHR: VB INFLECTS

14 The word **place** can be used after the determiners 'any', 'no', 'some', or 'every' instead of the adverbs 'anywhere', 'nowhere', 'somewhere', or 'everywhere'; used especially in informal American English. EG *You are not going any place... He had no place else to go.*
N SING WITH DET

15 A **place** within a larger area is a specific point or area within that larger area. EG *I've just been bruised in two places getting off the bus... She twisted around to show the place on her back... Fires were still burning in many places.*
N COUNT = spot

16 If something has particular characteristics or features **in places**, it has them at several points within an area. EG *As I remember, the path was steep in places... The country was flat, covered in tall scrub in places, and dotted with lakes.*
PHR: USED AS AN A = in patches

17 A **place** on a seat, at a table, in a hotel, etc is a seat, bed, or room in a hotel or hostel, or a space that is available for someone to use or fill. EG *There was only one possible place left for him to sit... I had a place reserved at the Youth Hostel in Stockholm... She couldn't find a place in the car park.*
N COUNT: USU+A/*to*-INF

18 A **place** at a table is also a space for one person to sit at a table during a meal, as shown by the knives, forks, spoons, glasses, etc that have been arranged on the table ready for one person to use. EG *Every day 12 places are laid for dinner... There were three glasses in front of each place, and a lot of cutlery.*
N COUNT ↑ setting

19 If you have a **place** on a committee, at a particular college, etc, you are a member or have the opportunity of being a member of the committee, are able to go to that college, etc. EG *I got a place at a teachers' training college nearby.... ...university places... Harper failed to win a place on the committee.*
N COUNT: USU+SUPP

20 If you refer to someone's **place** or something's **place** in a society, system, situation, etc, you are referring to their position or role in relation to other people or things, sometimes when you want to say how significant or right this is. EG *...Britain's place in the world... I had to learn my place among other individuals... Superstition had no place in their teaching... The demonstration occupies a central place in their political campaign... I want to see women going*
N COUNT: USU WITH POSS, USU+A

out into the world and taking their place side by side with men.

21 You can use **place** when you refer to the relative importance of something or someone, especially when you describe them as less important than something or someone else. EG *They decided to relegate the massed frontal attack to second place and to concentrate on a small-scale offensive... Adults in the commune took second place to the children.* N COUNT : USU ORDINAL/*first/last*+N IN SING ⇑ priority

22 People in **high places** or in a **high place** are the most powerful people in a government, society, or organization; used especially in relation to their influence, dishonesty, or remoteness from other people. EG *...rumours of corruption in high places... ...some evil influence in a high place.* PHR : USED AS O, USU *in*+PHR ⇑ the top

23 If you talk about how well someone **is placed**, you are talking about their position in relation to other people or to a situation, especially with regard to how successful they are or how many advantages they have. EG *He talked about how well we're placed with regard to America and Japan... As for finance, we're better placed than people think... Such an organization could help and encourage those similarly placed today.* V+O : USU PAST PART

24 If you **place** someone or something in relation to other people or things, you consider or judge them with regard to these other people or things. EG *This salary should be placed against an average of £9,000 in the rest of the profession... She is placed amongst the leading poets of her generation.* V+O+A = put, set

25 Someone's **place** in a race or competition or when they are being considered on a scale, is their position at the end of the race or on the scale. First place is the winning, leading, or top position. EG *She took first place in the Highlands and Islands Crafts Fair... Thus the US leapt from sixth place to second in the league of world war fleets.* N COUNT : USU ORDINAL/*first/last*+N IN SING

26 If someone **is placed** first, second, last, etc, they come in that position in a race, competition, or scale. EG *I was quite satisfied to be placed third.* V+O : ONLY PASS +ORDINAL/*first/last*

27 In a race or competition, a person, horse, car, etc that **is placed** finishes in first, second, or third position. Sometimes, the person or thing that comes fourth is also referred to as being placed. EG *His horse Glenavon wasn't even placed.* V+O : ONLY PASS

28 A good, appropriate, sensible, etc **place** in a particular situation, event, speech, activity, etc is a suitable point at which to do something. EG *This could be a very good place to start... This is not the place for a detailed description of all his problems... We'll deal with that in its proper place.* N COUNT : USU SING+SUPP = time

29 Your **place** in a book, speech, description, etc is the point that you have reached. EG *Her finger was pressed to the page as if marking her place... He pretended to have lost his place in his notes.* N COUNT : USU POSS+N IN SING

30 If you refer to a particular **place** in a situation, piece of work, book, film, etc, you are referring to a specific part of it. EG *There are scores of places in this film where I was moved to tears.* N COUNT

31 If you have been trying to understand something puzzling and then everything **falls into place, clicks into place, fits into place**, etc, you suddenly begin to understand how different bits of information are connected and everything becomes clearer. EG *So this was where all the money had gone. It all fell into place... Then all sorts of things started tumbling into place and I knew that was it.* PHR : VB INFLECTS

32 You use **in the first place** when you are referring to what happened or what something was like at the beginning of a situation or before a series of other events or changes. EG *Nobody can remember what was agreed in the first place... How did she become interested in the French Revolution in the first place?... I didn't want to come here in the first place.* PHR : USED AS AN A

33 You use the expressions **in the first place, in the second place**, etc to introduce or draw attention to one of a series of points or reasons. **In the first place** can also be used to emphasize a very important point or reason. EG *...information that, in the first place, would have been very difficult for me to obtain and, in the second place, would have been useless anyhow.* PHR : USED AS ADV SEN

34 If someone **places** a person or thing in a particular state or situation, they cause that person or thing to be in that state or situation. EG *The agreement was thus not placed at risk... Chamberlain placed the Cabinet in a difficult situation... They are coping with a major life-change, one which places them outside the traditional social order.* V+O+A = put

35 If someone **places** a thing or person on a list or record or in a particular situation, condition, category, etc, they put that thing or person there; a slightly formal use. EG *There were no specific, concrete proposals placed before the people in attendance... Many of the teachers had been placed on the blacklist... These assets must be placed into a special fund.* V+O+A

36 If you have authority over someone and you **place** them somewhere, you arrange for them to work or stay there; a fairly formal use. EG *She was placed once more in medical care... His employer placed him at the head of his factory.* V+O : USU+A = set

37 To **place** someone means to find a home or job for them; used especially when a home is being found for a child who is being fostered or adopted; a formal use. EG *Two of the children still haven't been placed.* V+O : USU+A

38 If you **place** something such as responsibility, pressure, a restriction, etc on someone, you give it to them or force it on them. EG *The responsibility placed upon us is too heavy to be borne... Renewed pressure will be placed on the Government this week... Nature has placed considerable limitations on agriculture.* V+O+A *(on/upon)* = impose, lay

39 If you **place** emphasis on something or **place** the blame, hope, etc for something on a person or thing, you are showing clearly the attitude indicated towards that person or thing. EG *The New Left placed much emphasis on the role of culture... The government had placed reliance on their powers... Vita seemed to be placing most of the blame on her mother.* V+O : USU+A = lay, put

40 If you **place** an order, an advert in a paper, or a telephone call to a particular place, you go through the procedure that is necessary to get the thing done. EG *Dad placed the order... We placed an advert in the evening paper... She walked to the back of the cafe where the telephone was situated and placed a local call.* V+O

41 If you say that you cannot **place** someone, a voice, etc, you mean that you are unable to identify a person, remember where you first met them, or recognize who the voice belongs to. EG *She was looking at me as if she could not quite place me... I know the name well enough but can't place him for some silly reason.* V+O : USU WITH MODAL AND BROAD NEG

42 When you are stating a number which includes a decimal point, you indicate how many numbers are to the right of the decimal point by stating the number of decimal **places**. EG *The value of pi is 3.142, correct to three decimal places.* N COUNT : USU NUM+N ⇑ figure

43 **Place** is used as part of the name of a square or short street in a town, especially one where the houses are all of a similar type. EG *...Waterloo Place.* N IN NAMES ⇑ road

44 In the House of Commons, MPs refer to the House of Lords as **the other place** or **another place**. These expressions are also used in the House of Lords to refer to the House of Commons. PHR : USED AS S/O

45 The word **place** is also used in the following expressions. **45.1** If something or someone appears or is substituted **in place of** something or someone else, they replace the other thing or person, or are put there instead of the other thing or person. EG *The factory has been pulled down, and in its place a new hospital has been put up... Assembly is carried out by computer-programmed robots in place of human workers... He was wondering whom to promote in Davis's place.* PHR : USED AS AN A **45.2** If you **take** or **fill** someone's **place**, you begin to do what they were previously doing. If something **takes the place of** something else, it begins to exist instead of that thing. EG *Armed soldiers were soon to take the place of diplomats... The old system has died and a new one has sprung up to take its place... But who will fill Daniel's place?... They certainly would not like to take the mother's place.* PHR : VB INFLECTS = replace **45.3** If you **change places** with another person, you change situations or roles in life with them. EG *One day we shall change places, and you will stay at home and I shall go to work... But we like having children, and we wouldn't change places with a childless couple for anything.* PHR OR PHR+*with* : RECIP, VB INFLECTS **45.4** When you are giving someone advice, if you say **in their place**, you would act in a particular way, you mean that if you were in their situation and having the same experiences as they are, you would act in this way. PHR : USED AS AN A

EG *Then it occurred to me that anyone in John's place would have done the same thing... Put yourself in my place.* 45.5 If you tell someone that **it is not** their **place** to do a particular thing, you mean that it is wrong or inappropriate for them to do it. EG *Frank felt it was not his place to raise any objection... It was hardly my place to say so.*

PHR : VB INFLECTS, USU + *to*-INF

45.6 If you say that someone should be shown their **place**, should be kept in their **place**, etc, you mean that they should be made aware of their unimportance and low social position in society, made to show respect to their superiors, and should be prevented from gaining any power. EG *Children need to be shown their place... A repressive police system was formed to keep them in their place.*

N COUNT : USU POSS + N, SING MAY = PL = station

45.7 If you **put** someone in their **place**, you show them that they are much less important, intelligent, wonderful, etc than they think they are. EG *I decided to put this upstart politely in his place... She rightly put me in my place.*

PHR : VB INFLECTS ⇑ chastise = humble

45.8 If a person or action is **out of place** in a particular situation, that person or action is inappropriate, wrong, or does not fit easily into the situation. EG *I never quite overcame the sense of being out of place, of being an outsider... It is described with a degree of detail which might seem out of place in a book so limited on scope.*

PHR : USED AS AN A = awkward, uncomfortable

46 ● **pride of place**: see **pride**.

placebo /pləsiːbəʊ/, **placebos**. A **placebo** is **1** a harmless, inactive substance that a doctor gives to a patient instead of a drug, for example when testing the effects of a drug, or when the patient has imagined their illness. EG *Some will get the new drug while others receive an inert placebo... ...a placebo vaccine.*

N COUNT

2 something that is done, said, or given to a person who feels discontented or depressed in order to please or comfort them. EG *...a box of placebos for the children: soft drinks, toys, games, books.*

N COUNT

placement /pleɪsməˀnt/, **placements**. **1** The **placement** of something is the act or process of putting something or someone in a particular place or position. EG *I spent a week directing the placement of the boulders.*

N UNCOUNT/COUNT : USU WITH *the*/POSS, N + *of*

2 If someone, especially someone on a training course, gets a **placement**, they get a job for a period of time which will give them experience in the work they are training for. EG *For Clive there was a possibility of a placement at the zoo... Amongst other placements, he spent some months at the Children's Hospital.*

N COUNT

3 The **placement** of someone in a job or home is the act or process of finding them a job or a home. EG *...the rehabilitation of offenders through placement in community work situations.*

N UNCOUNT : USU WITH POSS

placenta /pləsentə/, **placentas**. The **placenta** is the mass of veins and tissue inside the womb of a pregnant woman or animal, which the foetus is attached to.

N COUNT

place setting, place settings. A **place setting** is a complete set of equipment including knives, forks, spoons, and glasses, that is arranged on a table for the use of one person at a meal.

N COUNT

placid /plæsɪd/. **1** A **placid** person or animal is calm and does not easily become excited, angry, or upset. EG *He was a plump, placid boy with a philosophical approach to life.*

ADJ QUALIT = even-tempered

◊ **placidly**. EG *'They will learn. One day,' she said placidly... Beyond we could see Samson, Mr Robert's cow, placidly grazing.*

◊ ADV WITH VB

◊ **placidity** /pləsɪdɪti¹/. EG *They try to keep them in a state of drugged placidity.*

◊ N UNCOUNT

2 A **placid** place or area of water is calm and peaceful. EG *...the placid harbour waters... Switzerland is much too placid for my taste.*

ADJ QUALIT

plagiarism /pleɪdʒərɪzəᵒm/, **plagiarisms**. **1** **Plagiarism** is the action of using or copying someone else's idea or work and pretending that you thought of it or created it; used showing disapproval. EG *It was a shameless piece of plagiarism.*

N UNCOUNT = piracy

2 A **plagiarism** is an idea or a piece of writing or music that has been secretly copied from someone else's work; used showing disapproval. EG *His book was full of plagiarisms.*

N COUNT

plagiarist /pleɪdʒərɪst/, **plagiarists**. A **plagiarist** is someone who plagiarizes other people's ideas and work.

N COUNT

plagiarize /pleɪdʒəraɪz/, **plagiarizes, plagiarizing, plagiarized**; also spelled **plagiarise**. If you **plagiarize** someone else's idea, or part of a piece of writing or music by someone else, you use it in your own work and pretend that you thought of it or created it; used showing disapproval. EG *She said she plagiarized the phrase from 'Lady Chatterley's Lover'... He's constantly plagiarizing other people's research.*

V OR V+O ⇑ copy

plague /pleɪg/, **plagues, plaguing, plagued**. **1** A **plague** is a disease, such as cholera or typhoid, that spreads quickly and kills large numbers of people. EG *...disasters such as wars, plagues, earthquakes, and famine.*

N COUNT = epidemic

2 **Plague** or the **plague** is a very infectious and usually fatal disease, in which the patient has a severe fever and swellings on his or her body. EG *...an epidemic of plague was feared.*

N UNCOUNT, OR N SING : *the*+N

3 A **plague** of unpleasant things is a large number of them that arrive or happen at the same time and are difficult to deal with. EG *...a plague of locusts... Their time will be taken up in coping with a new plague of anti-social forces.*

N COUNT + *of* + N IN PL = epidemic

4 If you describe something as a **plague**, you mean that it is annoying or troublesome. EG *London's fogs used to be a plague to residents but an adventure to visitors.*

N COUNT : USU SING = curse

5 If bad or unpleasant things **plague** you, they keep happening and cause you a great deal of trouble, difficulty, or suffering. EG *The system is still plagued by technical faults... He suffered severe back injuries, which plague him to this day... Even experienced soldiers were sceptical and plagued by doubts... I don't know why we have been plagued with such ill luck.*

V+O ⇑ afflict

6 If you **plague** someone, you keep bothering them or asking them for something. EG *The readers were urged to plague their MP with letters of protest.*

V+O : IF + PREP THEN *with* = pester

7 If you say that you **avoid** someone or something **like the plague**, you are emphasizing that you deliberately avoid them completely. EG *Avoid like the plague any sort of piecework.*

PHR : VB INFLECTS = shun

8 You say **a plague on** a particular person or thing when you are very irritated by them and do not want to bother with them any more; a rather old-fashioned expression. EG *A plague on you and your damned percentages!*

PHR + NG : USED AS CONVENTION

plaice /pleɪs/. **Plaice** is both the singular and the plural form. **Plaice** or a **plaice** is an edible sea fish with a flat body. EG *We're having plaice for dinner.*

N UNCOUNT/COUNT

plaid /plæd/, **plaids**. **1** **Plaid** is material with a tartan or other check design on it; also used of the tartan design itself. EG *She wore a plaid shirt and blue jeans... ...their fondness for plaids and checks.*

N MASS ⇑ fabric

2 A **plaid** is a long piece of tartan material which is worn over the shoulder as part of Scottish Highland national dress.

N COUNT ⇑ shawl

plain /pleɪn/, **plains; plainer, plainest**. **1** A **plain** is a large, flat area of land with very few trees on it. EG *On the plain were more buffalo than they had ever seen... ...vast plains covered in yellow grasses.*

N COUNT = prairie

2 A **plain** object or surface is entirely in one colour and has no pattern, design, or writing on it. EG *They are set against a plain background with carefully controlled lighting... I'll tell them to put it in a plain envelope.*

ADJ CLASSIF : ATTRIB ≠ patterned, fancy

3 **Plain** clothing, food, architecture, etc is very simple in form or style. EG *She felt ashamed of her plain dress... I enjoy good plain food; nothing fancy.*

ADJ QUALIT : USU ATTRIB ≠ elaborate

4 If a fact or situation is **plain**, it is easy to recognize or see. EG *Whatever the terms used, the facts are plain enough... It was plain that Eddie wanted to get back to sleep... I've made it plain to the Chairman that we need you here... Their difficulty is plain.* ● **plain as a pikestaff**: see **pikestaff**.

ADJ QUALIT : USU PRED = clear

5 **Plain** statements are direct and easy to understand, and perhaps not very polite. EG *The eve of battle is the time for plain words... ...a plain statement of fact.* ▸ used of someone who is speaking. EG *He was plain about this.*

ADJ QUALIT = blunt

6 You can use **plain** before a noun, a noun group, or an adjective in order to emphasize it. EG *All of these facts, surmises and plain guesses rest on a central supposition... Logical judgment can also be just plain wrong.*

ADJ CLASSIF : ATTRIB, OR ADV + ADJ/ADV = downright

7 You can use **plain** before a name to emphasize how simple or ordinary it is, especially when you are comparing it with another, more unusual or impressive, name. EG *In those days she was plain Norma Jean Mortenson.*

ADJ CLASSIF : ATTRIB + N PROPER ⇑ ordinary

8 Someone who is **plain** is not at all beautiful. EG *...a plain plump girl with pigtails.* ADJ QUALIT = homely

9 In knitting, **plain** is the most basic type of stitch. N UNCOUNT

10 An official, usually a police officer, who is **in plain clothes** is wearing ordinary clothes instead of a uniform. EG *The officer, travelling in plain clothes and using civil airlines, arrived eventually in Beira.* PHR : USED AS AN A

11 **plain sailing**: see **sailing**.

plain chocolate is dark brown chocolate that has a stronger and less sweet taste than milk chocolate. N UNCOUNT

plain-clothes; also spelled as one word. A **plain-clothes** official, especially a police officer, is wearing ordinary clothes instead of a uniform. EG *Lebel ordered a plain-clothes detective to check into the hotel.* ADJ CLASSIF : ATTRIB ≠ uniformed

plain flour is flour that does not have chemicals added to it that make cakes increase in size when they are cooked. N UNCOUNT

plainly /pleɪnli^1/. 1 If you say that something is **plainly** the case or is **plainly** a particular thing, you mean that it is clearly or obviously the case; often used when you are trying to convince someone else. EG *The man was plainly demented... The woman's appearance had plainly disturbed him... Plainly, these new techniques have a long way to go.* ADV SEN = manifestly

2 If you can see, hear, or smell something **plainly** or if it is **plainly** visible or audible, you can see, hear, or smell it easily. EG *You could see the oysters quite plainly, lying all over the sea-bed... The holes in my tights were plainly visible.* ADV = clearly

3 If you say something **plainly**, you say it in a way that is easy to understand and cannot be mistaken. EG *The judge said that quite plainly.* ADV WITH VB

plainsong /pleɪnsɒŋ/ is a type of church music in which a group of people sing one tune together, without having musical instruments played at the same time. N UNCOUNT ↑ singing

plainspoken /pleɪnspəʊkə^{0}n/; also spelled with a hyphen. Someone who is **plainspoken** says exactly what they think; usually used showing approval. ADJ QUALIT = blunt

plaint /pleɪnt/, **plaints**. A **plaint** is a complaint or a sad cry; a literary word. EG *...the moans and plaints of their children.* N COUNT

plaintiff /pleɪntɪf/, **plaintiffs**. A **plaintiff** is a person who brings a legal case against someone in a court of law. EG *The court established that the plaintiff had not received medical treatment for the injury.* N COUNT ↑ accuser

plaintive /pleɪntɪv/. A **plaintive** sound, voice, question, etc is sad and high-pitched. EG *...a plaintive wail... ...a plaintive flute.* ◊ **plaintively**. EG *'Why are you like this?' her husband was asking plaintively.* ADJ QUALIT ◊ ADV WITH VB

plait /plæt/, **plaits, plaiting, plaited**. 1 If you **plait** three or more lengths of hair, grass, rope, etc together, you twist them over and under each other to make one thick length. EG *Her thick brown hair was plaited in a single braid down her back... My sister was plaiting a bracelet out of water grasses... ...long ropes of plaited rushes.* V+O

2 A **plait** is 2.1 a length of hair that has been divided into three and then plaited. EG *...her long gold plaits, each tied with a red ribbon.* N COUNT 2.2 a length of plaited grass, rope, etc. N COUNT

plan /plæn/, **plans, planning, planned**. 1 A **plan** is a method of achieving something that you have worked out in detail beforehand. EG *I told them of my plan... The conference drew up a five-point plan to revive the socialist cause... ...her plan for union reform... The committee is now attempting to put its plans into operation.* N COUNT = strategy

2 If you **plan** what you are going to do, you decide in detail what you are going to do and how you are going to do it. EG *At breakfast I planned my day... Everything must be exactly planned and organized in advance... We must plan for the future... The concert is going ahead as planned.* ◊ **planned**. EG *There was something meaningful and planned in the boy's revelations.* V, V+O/to-INF, OR V+A (for) ↑ prepare ◊ ADJ QUALIT = premeditated

3 If you **plan** to do a particular thing, you intend to do it. EG *What do you plan to do after college?... I was planning a career in law... There are two windmills planned.* ◊ **planned**. EG *News of the planned sale of 50,000 acres of state forests has been released.* V+O/to-INF = propose ◊ ADJ CLASSIF = proposed

4 If you have **plans**, you are intending to do a particular thing. EG *Do you have any plans for the weekend?... Weekend gales forced him to change his plans... He was always making grandiose plans to sell or mortgage his house.* N PLURAL : USU + for/to-INF = projects

5 When you **plan** something that you are going to make, build, or create, you decide what the main parts of it will be and how they will be arranged. EG *How do you plan a book?... ...the art of planning a garden.* V+O = design, think out

6 A **plan** is also 6.1 a list or diagram of the main parts that are going to be included in something, for example a piece of writing. EG *...a plan of a story.* N COUNT = outline 6.2 the shape and design of a garden, building, or group of buildings. EG *...the plan and overall design of the building.* N COUNT = layout 6.3 a detailed drawing that shows what each floor of a building looks like from above, what the inside of a machine looks like, etc. It often gives the measurements of each part of the building or machine. EG *Make a neat plan of your new home.* N COUNT = diagram 6.4 a drawing that shows where people are to sit around a table. EG *Numbers would be drawn to determine the seating plan.* N COUNT = arrangement

7 The word **plan** is also used in the following expressions. 7.1 A **plan of action** or a **plan of campaign** is a series of actions that you have decided to take in order to achieve something. EG *What's your plan of action?* PHR : USED AS O/C/S = strategy 7.2 If something happens **according to plan**, it happens at the time that it was arranged or intended to happen and in the way that it was intended to happen. EG *The whole thing was going according to plan.* PHR : USED AS AN A

8 See also **planning**.

plan for. If you have not **planned for** a particular thing, you have not realized that it might happen and so have not considered it when making your arrangements. EG *I hadn't planned for so many people.* PHRASAL VB : V+PREP, HAS PASS = planned on

plan on. 1 If you **plan on** doing a particular thing, you intend to do it; used in fairly informal English. EG *I plan on staying in London for the foreseeable future.* PHRASAL VB : V+PREP, HAS PASS = propose

2 If you have not **planned on** a particular thing, you have not realized that it might happen and so have not considered it when making your arrangements. EG *I hadn't planned on the bad weather.* PHRASAL VB : V+PREP, HAS PASS ↑ expected

plan out. If you **plan out** what you are going to do, you decide in detail what you are going to do and how you are going to do it. EG *I hadn't even planned out the route coherently yet.* PHRASAL VB : V+O+ADV ↑ prepare

plane /pleɪn/, **planes, planing, planed**. 1 A **plane** is a vehicle with wings and one or more engines that enable it to fly through the air. EG *We bought the cigarettes on the plane... We went by plane... He got killed in a plane crash... My plane leaves at eleven.* N COUNT, OR by+N ↑ vehicle = aeroplane

2 If a number of points, positions, or lines are in the same **plane**, one flat surface could pass through them all. EG *Such joints can only move in one plane.* N COUNT ↑ level

3 In technical language, a **plane** is a flat surface or a thin, flat object, especially one sloping at a particular angle. EG *...an elaborate structure of coloured planes.* N COUNT

4 You can refer to a particular type or level of living, awareness, conversation, etc as a particular **plane**, especially when talking about a change from one type or level to another. EG *I entered a plane of existence where nothing mattered... She tried to lift the conversation onto a more elevated plane.* N COUNT+SUPP

5 A **plane** is also a tool that has a flat bottom with a sharp blade in it. You move the plane over a flat piece of wood in order to remove thin pieces of its surface. N COUNT

6 If you **plane** a piece of wood, you make it smaller or make it level or smooth by using a plane. EG *Get a carpenter to plane jammed windows.* V+O = shave

7 If something, especially a boat, **planes** across water, it moves quickly across it, just touching the surface. V+A = skim

8 A **plane** is also the same as a plane tree. N COUNT

planet /plænɪ^{1}t/, **planets**. A **planet** is a large, round object in space that goes round a star; used especially of the nine large objects, including Earth, that go round the sun. EG *They have the capacity to kill every human being on the planet... ...the orbit of the planet Mars.* N COUNT

planetarium /plænɪ^{1}tɛərɪəm/, **planetariums**. A **planetarium** is a building where lights are shone on the ceiling to represent the planets and the stars and to show how they appear to move. N COUNT

planetary /plænɪ'təⁿri'/ means relating to or belonging to planets. EG *...the planetary exploration programme... ...the computation of planetary orbits.* ADJ CLASSIF: ATTRIB

plane tree, plane tree. A **plane tree** is a large tree with broad leaves that often grows in towns. N COUNT

plangent /plændʒəⁿnt/. A **plangent** sound is deep, loud, and perhaps sad; a literary word. EG *Once more he played those plangent chords.* ADJ QUALIT

plank /plæŋk/, **planks.** 1 A **plank** of wood is a long rectangular piece of wood which is fairly thin and which has been roughly cut. See also **gangplank.** N COUNT: ALSO N +*of*+N UNCOUNT = board

2 In former times, if a sailor was made to **walk the plank** as a punishment, he was forced to walk on a plank over the edge of the ship into the sea so that he drowned. PHR: VB INFLECTS

3 The main **plank** of the campaign of a group or political party is the main principle on which it bases its campaign, or its main aim. EG *Unilateral nuclear disarmament was one of the two main planks of union policy... ...this belief, often a key plank in the proposals for nationalization... She could never stand on a platform which had violence as its main plank.* N COUNT: USU MOD+N = policy

planking /plæŋkɪŋ/ is wood which has been cut into planks. EG *He felt an odd vibration from the hard rough planking he lay on.* N UNCOUNT = boarding

plankton /plæŋktən/ is a layer of tiny animals and plants that live in the surface layer of the sea. N UNCOUNT

planner /plænə/, **planners.** 1 The **planners** in local government are the people who are responsible for deciding how land should be used and what new buildings should be built. EG *The city has changed drastically in recent years. The planners saw to that... ...David Lewis, an architect and city planner.* N COUNT: USU PL ⇑ designer

2 A **planner** is a person who works out in detail what is going to be done in the future and how it is going to be done. EG *By nature a long-range planner, he spent his first few months studying his surroundings... ...TV programme planners.* N COUNT: USU MOD+N

planning /plænɪŋ/ is 1 the process of deciding in detail how to do something before you actually start to do it. EG *Anything is possible with enough time and planning... The project is still in the planning stage.* ● See also **family planning.** 2 control by the local government of the way that land is used in an area and what new buildings are built. EG *...the concrete deserts created by modern planning at its worst... I was in the planning department.* N UNCOUNT ⇑ preparation; N UNCOUNT

planning permission is official permission that you must get from the local authority before a new building can be built or an extension made to an existing building. EG *The occupier of the above premises has applied for planning permission.* N UNCOUNT

plant /plɑ:nt/, **plants, planting, planted.** 1 A **plant** is a living thing that grows in the earth and that has a stem, leaves, and roots; not usually used to refer to trees. EG *I had to root up all the plants and burn them... ...aquatic plants... ...the great plant collector E H Wilson.* ● See also **bedding plant, eggplant, pot plant, rubber plant.** N COUNT ⇑ organism

2 When you **plant** something such as a seed, plant, or young tree, you to put it into the ground so that it will grow there. EG *The people of Juffure needed all their strength to plant crops for the new harvest... I'd better go and see if the gardener has planted those cabbages.* ◇ **planting.** EG *Autumn planting does away with this cumbersome procedure.* V+O; ◇ N UNCOUNT

3 When someone **plants** a piece of land or a pot or hanging basket with a particular type of plant or crop, they put plants or seeds into the piece of land to grow them there. EG *Alongside the road was a field planted with what he recognized as maize... He looks at the garden he has planted... ...small front gardens planted with rose trees.* V+O: USU+A *(with)*

4 A **plant** is also a factory or place where power is generated. EG *The Brick and Tile Works and the cement plant were going full blast... ...an active group at British Leyland's Cowley plant... ...the reopening of a nuclear plant after an accident.* N COUNT ⇑ establishment

5 **Plant** is large machinery that is used in connection with an industrial process. EG *The company plans to spend nearly £1 billion on new plant and equipment... ...a factory where heavy plant is being shunted about.* N UNCOUNT ⇑ equipment

6 If you **plant** something somewhere, you put it down firmly in that place. EG *I planted my deckchair beside hers... He stood in front of her, his legs planted apart.* V+O+A = plonk

7 If you **plant** a kiss, a blow, a kick, etc somewhere, you give someone a kiss, a blow, or a kick on a particular part of their body. EG *'Hello,' she said, turning her head so David could plant a kiss on her cheek.* V+O: USU+A ⇑ place

8 If someone **plants** something somewhere, for example a bomb or a tape recorder, they hide it in the place where they want it to function. EG *They had planted the bomb beneath the house... I haven't planted a microphone in your desk.* V+O: USU+A ⇑ secrete

9 If someone **plants** something such as a weapon or drugs on someone, they put it somewhere that is associated with that person in order that they will be wrongly accused of something. EG *I'm convinced the evidence was planted in John's flat.* V+O: USU+A ⇑ incriminate

10 If an organization **plants** an informer or a spy somewhere, they send that person there so that they can do something secretly or illegally, for example obtain important information. EG *The CIA had planted its agents and informers in all the strategic areas... Perhaps she's been planted to catch me.* V+O: USU+A ⇑ infiltrate

11 A **plant** is also a person who is sent to a particular place so that they can do something secretly or illegally there, for example obtain important information. EG *One of them must be a plant, but which one?* N COUNT = infiltrator

12 If you **plant** an idea or a story in someone's mind, you cause them to begin to accept or believe it without them knowing that it is you who are the cause. EG *Someone else would have to plant the idea in his mind... He might want to plant a false rumour.* V+O: USU+A ⇑ cultivate

plant out. When you **plant out** seedlings or young plants, you plant them in the ground in the place where they are to be left to grow. EG *We had to rear it in a nursery and plant it out.* PHRASAL VB: V+O+ADV

plantain /plæntɪn/, **plantains.** A **plantain** is 1 a large green banana; also used of the tree on which it grows. 2 a wild plant with broad leaves and a head of tiny green flowers on a long stem. N COUNT; N COUNT

plantation /plɑ:nteɪʃəⁿn/, **plantations.** A **plantation** is 1 a large piece of land especially in a tropical country, where crops such as cotton, tea, sugar, or rubber are grown. EG *They bought land or just seized it to set up plantations... ...a date plantation.* 2 a large number of trees that have been planted together in a particular place. N COUNT; N COUNT ⇑ wood

planter /plɑ:ntə/, **planters.** A **planter** is a person who owns or manages a plantation. EG *...the wages and living conditions of tea planters and their families... He was the son of a wealthy planter.* N COUNT ⇑ farmer

plant pot, plant pots. A **plant pot** is a round pot, usually made of clay or plastic, that you fill with earth in order to grow plants in it. N COUNT ⇑ container = flowerpot

plaque /plæk, plɑ:k/, **plaques.** 1 A **plaque** is a flat plate or tablet, usually made of metal, wood, or stone, which is fixed to a wall or monument in memory of a famous person or event. EG *...a memorial plaque at the crematorium... ...a little bronze plaque in the pavement... At No. 58, a blue plaque marks where Sir Arthur Sullivan once lived.* N COUNT ⇑ memorial

2 **Plaque** is a deposit that forms on the surface of a tooth consisting of saliva, bacteria, and food. Plaque causes gum disease. N UNCOUNT

plasma /plæzmə/ is the clear, yellow fluid part of blood which contains the corpuscles and cells. N UNCOUNT

plaster /plɑ:stə/, **plasters, plastering, plastered.** 1 **Plaster** is a smooth paste made of sand, lime, and water which dries and forms a hard layer. Plaster is used to cover walls and ceilings especially inside buildings. EG *The walls were in a dreadful condition–their yellow plaster was peeling off... Cracks appear at the joints between new plaster and old... ...a plaster replica of the Venus de Milo.* N UNCOUNT ⇑ cement

2 If you **plaster** a wall or ceiling, you cover it with a smooth layer of plaster. EG *...a wall that was poorly plastered.* ◇ **plastering.** EG *Has the man come to do the plastering yet?* V OR V+O; ◇ N UNCOUNT

3 If you **plaster** a surface with things, especially pieces of paper, you stick a lot of them all over it. EG *The outer windows had been plastered with posters. Photographs plastered every surface.* ◇ **plastered.** EG *The walls of his tiny shop were plastered with pictures of actors and actresses.* V+O: IF+PREP THEN *with* ⇑ cover; ◇ ADJ CLASSIF: PRED+*with* ⇑ covered

4 A **plaster** is a strip of sticky material used for covering small cuts on your body. EG *I dabbed the cut* N COUNT ⇑ bandage

and applied a plaster... Sticking plaster leaves sticky patches on your finger.
5 If you have a leg or arm **in plaster**, you have a cast made of plaster of Paris around your leg or arm to protect a broken bone and allow it to mend. PHR : USED AS AN A
6 See also **plastered.**

plasterboard /plɑːstəbɔːd/ is thin rectangular boards in the form of sheets of cardboard held together with plaster. Plasterboard can be used to cover walls and ceilings inside a building. N UNCOUNT

plaster cast, plaster casts; also spelled with a hyphen. A **plaster cast** is a case made of plaster of Paris, which is used for protecting broken bones by keeping part of the body stiff and rigid, and can also be used as a mould for sculptures. N COUNT

plastered /plɑːstəd/. 1 If something is **plastered** to a surface, it is sticking to the surface. EG *His wet hair was plastered to his forehead... His fair hair was plastered over his eyebrows.* ADJ CLASSIF : PRED+A
2 If something is **plastered** with a sticky substance, it is covered with it. EG *Her back was thickly plastered with sun-tan oil.* ADJ QUALIT : PRED+with
3 If a story, article, set of pictures, etc is **plastered** somewhere, for example over the front page in a newspaper, it is printed or displayed in a very prominent or obvious position. EG *Some atrocity–a rape or murder–was plastered all over the front page.* ADJ CLASSIF : PRED
4 If someone is **plastered**, they are very drunk; an informal use. EG *Your idea of drinking is to get as plastered as you can.* ADJ QUALIT : PRED = sloshed

plasterer /plɑːstərə/, **plasterers**. A **plasterer** is a person whose job it is to cover walls and ceilings with plaster. EG *You need a plasterer to do that job properly.* N COUNT ⇑ decorator

plaster of Paris /plɑːstər əv pærɪs/ is a type of plaster made from white powder and water, which dries quickly and is used to make plaster casts. N UNCOUNT

plastic /plæstɪk/, **plastics**. 1 **Plastic** is a material which is produced by a chemical process and which is used to make many objects and coverings. It is light in weight, can be formed easily into shape when heated, and does not break easily. EG *The roofs are covered in winter by sheets of plastic... Don't use abrasive cleaners on any plastics as they may scratch... ...plastic-wrapped fruit from a supermarket... Today the plastics industry produces a vast range of materials.* N UNCOUNT/N PLURAL
2 Something that is **plastic** is 2.1 made of plastic. EG *Village potters become redundant as cheap plastic bowls and buckets flood the market... ...a plastic shopping bag... The plastic seating was uncomfortable... ...a plastic bullet.* ADJ CLASSIF 2.2 soft and able to be pressed into different shapes. EG *Tidal heating may be keeping the crust of Europe plastic.* ADJ QUALIT = flexible, pliable ◊ **plasticity** /plæstɪsɪti[1]/. EG *...the plasticity of flesh.* ◊ N UNCOUNT 2.3 easily changed or influenced. EG *Their rhetoric is two-dimensional and plastic.* ADJ QUALIT = adaptable ◊ **plasticity**. EG *Visual images have a fluidity and plasticity that words can never achieve.* ◊ N UNCOUNT
3 If you describe something as **plastic**, you mean that it looks or tastes unnatural or false because it is artificial and man-made; used showing disapproval. EG *...the plastic rat-race world... ...glamorous models with plastic smiles... He settled for plastic hamburgers again.* ADJ QUALIT ⇑ unreal = phoney

plastic bomb, plastic bombs. A **plastic bomb** is a small bomb which contains plastic explosive. EG *...the wave of plastic bombs exploding in cinemas and cafés.* N COUNT

plastic explosive is soft material which explodes and is used to make bombs, and which can be pressed into different shapes. N UNCOUNT ⇑ explosive

Plasticine /plæstɪsiːn/ is a trademark for a soft coloured substance like clay which is used by children for making little models. N UNCOUNT

plastic surgery is the practice and skill of performing operations to repair or replace skin which has been damaged, or to improve people's appearance by changing features of the body. EG *One of the survivors needed plastic surgery.* N UNCOUNT

plat du jour /plæ də ʒʊə/, **plats du jour**. The **plat du jour** in a restaurant is the dish which has been specially prepared in a restaurant on a particular day. N COUNT

plate /pleɪt/, **plates, plating, plated**. 1 A **plate** is 1.1 a round or oval flat dish that is used to hold food. Plates are sometimes used to hold other things such as money that is being collected. EG *The dirty plates have been stacked in a pile on the kitchen table... He looked at the food on his plate... Behind him was a little plate for tips.* N COUNT ▸ also used to refer to the food on a plate or the amount of food it contains. EG *I could have eaten the whole plate!... She finally threw her plate of fish and chips at his head... Judy passed from group to group with plates of sandwiches and cakes.* ▸ N COUNT : ALSO N+*of*+N IN PL/N UNCOUNT = plateful 1.2 a flat sheet of metal, especially one that is a cover for part of a piece of machinery or a building. EG *Suddenly a plate on the side of the boiler cracked and steam roared out... We got into the cellar through a round hole covered by a metal plate.* N COUNT 1.3 a small flat piece of metal with someone's name written on it, which you usually find beside the front door of an office or house, near the doorbell. EG *I read her name on the polished brass plate... There were two name plates on the door.* N COUNT : USU MOD+N ⇑ sign
2 The **plates** on a car are the pieces of metal or plastic attached to the front and back of the car, showing a set of numbers and letters which identify the car or the country where it comes from. EG *It was a car bearing Irish licence plates... Philip tried to read their number plates at the traffic lights... There was a smattering of foreign plates: GB, B, D, I, NL, and others.* N COUNT : USU MOD+N ⇑ sign
3 A **plate** on a cooker is one of the electric rings or discs on the top which provide heat for cooking. N COUNT = ring
4 **Plate** is 4.1 dishes, bowls, mugs, and cups that are made of precious metal, especially silver, gold, or pewter. EG *We would prefer church plate and other treasures to be concealed in bank storerooms.* N UNCOUNT 4.2 things made of cheap metal that have been covered thinly with precious metal, such as gold or silver. EG *Just look at these goblets–I reckon they're silver plate.* N UNCOUNT : USU MOD+N
5 Metal that **is plated** has been covered with a thin layer of precious metal such as gold or silver. EG *...a copper salver, plated with silver.* V+O : USU PAST PART ▸ used as an adjective. EG *...gold-plated brooches... ...a nickel-plated cigarette box.* ▸ COMB : FORMS ADJ CLASSIFS
6 To **plate** something means to cover it with metal plates. V+O
7 A **plate** used in printing and engraving is a sheet of metal which is carved or treated with chemicals so that it can then be used to print text or pictures. EG *He engraved the plate carefully... ...Hogarth's second plate for the 'Industry and Idleness' series.* N COUNT
8 A **plate** in a book is a picture or photograph which takes up a whole page in a book and which is usually printed on higher quality paper than the rest of the book. See also **book plate**. N COUNT ⇑ illustration
9 The **plates** that form part of the bodies of some animals are wide, flat, thin pieces of horn or bone that grow on their bodies to protect their skin. EG *The plate covering the gills fits closely to the fish's body... They have heavy scales attached to bony plates in the skin.* N COUNT : USU PL ⇑ covering
10 A **plate** that is used with a microscope is a small rectangular piece of glass onto which you put a small amount of the substance that you want to look at. You then slide the plate under the microscope to look at the substance. N COUNT = slide
11 A **plate** that is used in photography is a thin sheet of glass that is covered with a layer of chemicals which react to the light and on which an image can be formed. EG *I have the developed plates and all the negatives of the photographs.* N COUNT = slide
12 A dental **plate** is a piece of metal or plastic which is shaped to fit the roof of a person's mouth and to which a set of false teeth are attached. ▸ also used to refer to the set of false teeth that are fixed onto a plate. EG *He would first provide me with provisional plates until the gums settled.* N COUNT
13 In geology, a **plate** is a large piece of the earth's surface, perhaps as large as a continent, which moves around very slowly; a technical term. EG *...the zones where the drifting continental plates that form the earth's crust meet.* N COUNT ⇑ crust
14 The word **plate** is also used in the following expressions. 14.1 If you **clean** or **empty** your **plate**, you finish eating all the food on your plate so that it is completely empty. EG *Children should not be pressurized to eat or to empty their plates.* PHR : VB INFLECTS 14.2 If you **have a lot on** your **plate**, you have a lot of work to do or a lot of things to deal with; an informal PHR : VB INFLECTS

expression. EG *I know you've got a lot on your plate–take it easy... She worries about how much Barbara has on her plate.* **14.3** If you **hand** something to someone **on a plate**, you allow them to get or achieve something easily; an informal expression. EG *She got the job handed to her on a plate... You can't expect people to give you all the answers on a plate, you know.* PHR : VB INFLECTS, USU PASS

plateau /plætəʊ/, **plateaus, plateaux**. The plural can be either **plateaus** or **plateaux**. **1** A **plateau** is a large area of fairly flat land which is much higher than the land around it. N COUNT

2 If an activity or process reaches a **plateau** in its development, it reaches a stage during which there is no change or development. EG *In the seventies the US space programme seemed to have reached a plateau of development... ...a learning plateau.* N COUNT

plateful /pleɪtfʊl/, **platefuls**. A **plateful** of food is an amount of food that is on a plate and fills it. EG *...a plateful of sandwiches.* N COUNT : USU+ *of*+N UNCOUNT/ N IN PL

plate glass; often used before another noun and spelled with a hyphen. **plate glass** is glass made in large, flat pieces, which is used especially to make large windows and doors. EG *The building was constructed of white brick, slates and plate glass... ...a new plate-glass window.* N UNCOUNT OR N BEFORE N

platform /plætfɔːm/, **platforms**. **1** A **platform** is **1.1** a flat structure, usually made of wood, on which people stand when they make speeches or give a performance, in order that they can be seen by the audience. EG *The speaker mounted the platform... Chopin's performances on the platform were always brilliant.* N COUNT ⇑ surface = stage ● If someone **appears on the same platform** as someone else or **shares a platform** with them, they both make speeches at a particular public meeting. EG *Last week she appeared on the same platform as her main political opponent.* ● PHR : VB INFLECTS, RECIP *(with/as)* **1.2** the area in a railway station beside the rails and higher than them, where you wait for or get off a train. EG *Jordache paced nervously up and down the platform... She was waiting on Platform 14 for the train to London.* N COUNT **1.3** a flat raised structure or area, usually one on which something can stand or land, or from which it can leave. EG *A chain of helicopter landing platforms could be anchored in the Thames... ...loading platforms... The nests are roughly built platforms of twigs.* N COUNT

2 If a particular person or group has a **platform**, they have an opportunity to tell people what they think or want, or what they can offer. EG *It provides a platform for the consumer's viewpoint... He used this personal battle as a platform from which to campaign for reform.* N COUNT : USU+ SUPP

3 The **platform** of a political party or candidate is what they say they will do if they are elected. EG *He campaigned on a socialist platform... ...the people who put together political platforms.* N COUNT : USU+ SUPP = manifesto

4 In a bus, the **platform** is the area of floor at the front or back where you get on and off. EG *She jumped off the platform while the bus was still moving.* N SING : *the*+N

5 Platform shoes or **platforms** are shoes with a very thick layer of wood or plastic underneath both the front part and the heel. N BEFORE N, OR N PLURAL

plating /pleɪtɪŋ/ is a thin layer of metal on something, or a covering of metal plates. N UNCOUNT

platinum /plætɪnəm/. **1 Platinum** is a very valuable, silvery-grey metal. It is often used for making jewellery. N UNCOUNT

2 Platinum hair is very fair, almost white. EG *...a platinum blonde.* ADJ COLOUR ⇑ blonde

platitude /plætɪtjuːd/, **platitudes**. A **platitude** is a statement which is considered boring and unsatisfactory because it has been made many times before in similar situations; a rather formal word. EG *Given his liking for platitudes, he might well have added that, if a job was worth doing, it was worth doing well... ...empty platitudes about democracy.* N COUNT = cliché, banality

platitudinous /plætɪtjuːdɪnəs/. A **platitudinous** remark or speech is boring and unoriginal; a rather formal word. EG *...a platitudinous statement affirming 'the right of the individual to live freely.'* ADJ CLASSIF = clichéd, banal

Platonic /plətɒnɪk/. **1** A **Platonic** relationship or feeling of affection does not involve sex. EG *As Platonic love went out of fashion, sex entered the picture... Her interest in him was entirely platonic.* ADJ CLASSIF ⇑ spiritual ≠ sexual

2 Platonic also means relating to the ideas of the Greek philosopher Plato. EG *He had some extraordinary Platonic notion of the perfect human soul.* ADJ CLASSIF : USU ATTRIB

platoon /plətuːn/, **platoons**. A **platoon** is a small group of soldiers which is one section of a company and which is commanded by a lieutenant. EG *...a platoon of infantry... In his platoon he had thirty-two men.* N COUNT : IF SING, VB CAN BE SING OR PL ⇑ team

platter /plætə/, **platters**. A **platter** is a large, flat plate used for serving food; used in American English or in rather old-fashioned British English. EG *There were five kinds of cheese on a wooden platter... I was presented with a silver platter.* ▸ also used to refer to an amount of food on a platter. EG *We had a platter of smoked fish.* N COUNT = dish ▸ N+*of*+N UNCOUNT/N IN PL ⇑ plateful

plaudits /plɔːdɪtz/. If a particular person or thing receives **plaudits** from a particular group of people, those people express their admiration for or approval of that person or thing; a formal word. EG *The building won immediate plaudits from architects and laymen alike.* N PLURAL = commendation

plausible /plɔːzəˈbəºl/. **1** A **plausible** explanation, argument, or statement is one that seems likely to be true or valid. EG *Such a theory seems very plausible... ...a plausible answer.* ◊ **plausibly**. EG *It could plausibly be argued that this diversity is accidental.* ◊ **plausibility** /plɔːzəbɪlɪti[1]/. EG *Let us consider the charges she faces, and the legal plausibility of those charges.* ADJ QUALIT = reasonable ◊ ADV WITH VB ◊ N UNCOUNT = credibility

2 Someone who is **plausible** seems to be telling the truth and is likely to be believed; used especially of someone who is in fact lying. EG *...an extraordinarily plausible liar.* ADJ QUALIT = believable

play /pleɪ/, **plays, playing, played**. **1** When children, animals, or perhaps adults **play**, they spend time doing enjoyable things, such as using toys, taking part in games, chasing each other, etc. EG *The kids went off to play on the swings... I played with the children all day... Her grandchildren enjoy playing with her old toys... I like to work hard and play hard.* V : USU+A, OR V+O = amuse yourself

2 The enjoyable activities that children spend time doing are referred to as **play**. EG *The very uselessness of play is its greatest asset.* ● Children who are **at play** are playing. N UNCOUNT = recreation ● PHR : USED AS AN A

3 When you **play** a particular sport, game, or match, you take part in it. EG *Ray and I played squash at least three times a week... Do you play chess?... I used to play for the village cricket team... He played in 44 Test matches... Peterborough haven't played their third round match yet.* V+O, OR V : USU +A

4 When one person or team **plays** another one, they compete against them in a sport or game. EG *Did you see McEnroe playing Connors the other day?... I saw Australia play against England at Lords.* V+O, OR V+A *(against)*

5 If the people in charge of a sports team **play** a particular person, they include that person as a member of the team. EG *They had decided not to play their best player because she had a bad cold.* V+O = use

6 If you **play** a particular position in a sports team, for example a football team or a hockey team, you have that position. EG *Stan O'Brien played full-back... I played in defence for a change.* V+C, OR V+A

7 When you **play** the ball or **play** a shot or a stroke in a game of football, cricket, golf, etc, you hit or kick the ball. EG *As a golfer you know that in playing a shot the worst mistake is to take your eye off the ball.* V+O ⇑ strike

8 When someone who is taking part in a game of cards **plays** a card, they put it down on the table as part of the game when it is their turn to do so. EG *Colin played a king, so I played my ace.* V+O

9 A person who is in charge of a game or competition or who is commenting on it can give the score by saying '15 **plays** 12', '25 **plays** 40', etc. NUM+V+NUM

10 Play is also the playing of a game, especially cricket, for a period of time. EG *Rain stopped play... Play should be over by six o'clock.* N UNCOUNT

11 You can refer to a particular standard or type of **play** as a way of saying how well or in what way the people taking part in a game play. EG *There was some nice play from United in the second half.* N UNCOUNT+ SUPP

12 If the ball being used in a game is **in play**, it is in a position where, according to the rules, it can be kicked or hit. If the ball is **out of play**, it is not in a position where it can be kicked or hit. EG *Robson managed to keep the ball in play.* PHR : USED AS AN A

13 If someone **plays** something such as casinos or V+O the stock market, they gamble or speculate. EG *He made most of his money by playing the stock market.*

14 If you **play** a joke or a trick on someone, you deceive them or do something else that affects them which you think is amusing or which helps you to gain an unfair advantage. EG *I presumed someone was playing a rather sick joke... They played a dirty trick on us.*
V+O : IF+PREP THEN *on* = perpetrate

15 If you **play** it cool, **play** it safe, **play** it for real, etc, you deliberately behave in a particular situation in the way indicated or deal with a situation in the way indicated; used in fairly informal English. EG *They agreed that they would play it cool if they saw the boys again... They certainly seemed to be playing it for real... I think this is probably the best way of playing it.*
V+O+C/A ⇑ treat

16 A **play** is a piece of writing which is intended to be performed in a theatre, on the radio, or on television, and which consists of the words that a set of characters say. EG *Wesker has written four major plays since then.* ▸ also used to refer to a performance of a play. EG *I saw the play a couple of years ago... My daughter is in the school play.*
N COUNT = drama

17 If an actor **plays** a particular role or character in a play or film, he or she says the words and performs the actions of a particular character. EG *Brutus was played by James Mason... Gwen Taylor played the part of Christine.*
V+O = portray, act

18 When actors **play** in a particular play or **play** it, they perform in it. EG *I was asked to play in a revival of 'Ghosts'... I learnt a great deal about playing Shakespeare... We played to ninety per cent audiences.*
V+A, OR V+O = act

19 If a play **is playing** at a particular place or **is playing** a particular place, it is being performed there. EG *Don't miss 'The Way of the World,' now playing at the Haymarket... I asked him how he felt about 'Bent', which played the Criterion this year.*
V+A, OR V+O : USU CONT = be on

20 If you **play** the innocent, the dutiful daughter, etc or if you **play** dumb, nervous, etc, you behave as if you are the kind of person mentioned or as if you have the quality or feeling indicated, usually in order to create a particular effect. EG *Don't you play the wise old professor with me, Franz... So you want to play nervous today?* ● If you **play hard to get**, you pretend not to be interested in another person or in something that another person is trying to persuade you to do. EG *'Maybe she doesn't like me.'-'No, I think she's just playing hard to get'.*
V+C = act ● PHR : VB INFLECTS

21 If you **play** host, **play** God, **play** soldier, etc, you perform the duties or functions of the type of person mentioned. EG *This year we're playing host to the New Sussex Opera... Scientists should never play God.*
V+C/O : NO PASS = act as

22 If you **play** a musical instrument or **play** a tune or a note on a musical instrument, you produce music from it. EG *Out on the balcony, a man stood playing a trombone... Doesn't he play beautifully?... The child played him a tune.* ◊ **playing**. EG *He revolutionized jazz saxophone playing.*
V+A, V+O, OR V+O+O ◊ N UNCOUNT

23 If you **play** a record or tape or **play** a record player, tape machine, or radio, you put a record or tape on a piece of equipment, or switch on the radio, so that you can listen to it. EG *I'll play you the tape in a minute... Passengers must not play radios or cassettes.*
V+O OR V+O+O

24 If a musical instrument, a radio, etc **is playing** music, or if music **is playing**, music is being produced. EG *I heard a cornet playing in Leicester Square... He could hear music playing faintly.*
V-ERG : USU CONT

25 If you say that something such as light **plays** on a particular thing or **plays** about a particular place, you mean that it keeps touching that thing lightly or moving quickly about; a literary use. EG *The glossy patches of sunshine played over their bodies... I could feel the soft peach chiffon playing around my legs... Lightning played across the sky.* ▸ used as a noun. EG *...the play of light on the water.* ● If you say that **a smile plays on** someone's **lips** or **over** someone's **lips**, you mean that they smile only a little or look as if they are going to smile; a literary expression.
V+A ▸ N SING ● PHR : VB INFLECTS

26 If a fountain or sprinkler **is playing**, it is sending out water.
V : USU CONT

27 If someone **plays** a hose on a particular thing or part of something, they point the hose at it so that water goes onto it.
V-ERG

28 If someone who is fishing with a rod and line **plays** a fish that is caught on the hook, they allow it to become tired by forcing it to pull repeatedly on the line.
V+O

29 The **play** of forces, feelings, etc is the way in which they influence each other's strength and effect. EG *All human actions are determined by a complex play of motives and forces.*
N SING WITH DET +*of* ⇑ interaction

30 If there is some **play** in a rope or in part of a structure or object, the rope or part is able to move, rather than being firmly fixed.
N UNCOUNT = give

31 When a particular thing **comes into play** or **is brought** or **called into play**, it begins to be used or to have an effect on a situation; used in fairly formal English. EG *All kinds of forces will come into play when the decision is made public... Computer systems were brought into play to draw up attack strategies.*
PHR : VB INFLECTS

32 If something **gives** or **allows full play to** someone's imagination or ability, it allows them to use it freely. If it **gives no play to** it, it prevents them from using it freely. EG *Radio allows full play to one's imagination.*
PHR : VB INFLECTS

33 If a person or animal does something **in play**, they do it as a joke or a game rather than seriously. EG *I used to throw cushions at her, in play.*
PHR : USED AS AN A = in fun

34 If you **make great play of** or **about** a particular fact or feature, **make a lot of play of** it, etc, you give it great emphasis when you mention it. EG *I made great play about the fact that computers could do the job in a fraction of the time... The novel does make a lot of play of the setting, the Villa itself.*
PHR : VB INFLECTS

35 When you **make** your **play** or **make a play for** something, you make a deliberate and obvious attempt to achieve or gain something. EG *Now we have made our play, we will have to wait and see what happens.*
PHR : VB INFLECTS

36 If something or someone **plays a part** or **plays a role** in a particular situation, event, or thing, it is involved in it and has an effect on it. EG *Examinations seem to play a large part in education... Television pundits play a dominant role in moulding public opinion... ...a struggle in which both force and persuasion played their part.*
PHR : VB INFLECTS

37 If you **play for time**, you try to get something to happen at a later time, in order that you can achieve something or think what to do before it happens. EG *She was playing for time.*
PHR : VB INFLECTS ⇑ delay

38 When you refer to the **state of play**, you are referring to the state of a situation, relationship, activity, etc at a particular time. EG *What's the state of play?*
PHR : USED AS S/O/C

play along. If you **play along** with someone or their plans, you agree to do what they want you to do as part of their plans, although you intend to stop doing this after a period of time. EG *I'll play along with them for the moment.*
PHRASAL VB : V+ADV, USU+*with* = go along

play around. **1** If you **play around** with a problem or a group of things, you think about the different parts of it or move the things around in order to find the best solution or arrangement; an informal expression. EG *I'll play around with it later and see if I can come up with an answer... I put the shells on a screen and played around with them until I got something attractive.*
PHRASAL VB : V+ADV, USU+*with* = juggle

2 If you **play around**, you have sex with people other than the person you are married to or have a close sexual relationship with; an informal expression used showing disapproval. EG *You don't think he's playing around, do you?*
PHRASAL VB : V+ADV = sleep around

play around with. **1** If you **play around with** something, you deal with it or treat it in a careless or irresponsible way. EG *I think it's slightly frightening that people are going to play around with the hormone content of plants.*
PHRASAL VB : V+ADV+PREP, HAS PASS

2 If you **play around with** the idea of doing something, you consider doing it, although you will probably not do it.
PHRASAL VB : V+ADV+PREP = toy with

3 If you **play around with** something, you keep moving it with your hands without thinking about what you are doing, for example because you are bored or nervous. EG *We spent the whole afternoon playing around with bits of string.*
PHRASAL VB : V+ADV+PREP, HA PASS = fiddle with

play at. **1** If you **play at** a particular activity, you do
PHRASAL VB : V

it casually and without any real effort. EG *I realized that I had been only playing at politics at university.* PREP = flirt with

2 If someone, especially a child, **plays at** being a particular kind of person or being in a particular kind of situation, they pretend to be that person or be in that situation, usually as a type of game. EG *They played at being huntsmen.* PHRASAL VB : V+PREP

3 If you ask **what** someone **is playing at**, in an angry way, you are showing that you think that they are doing something stupid or wrong; used in informal English. EG *What do you think you're playing at?... I don't know what these postmen are playing at.* PHR

play back. **1** When you **play back** a tape or film on which you have recorded sound or pictures, you operate the machine it is in so that you can listen to the sound or watch the pictures. • See also **playback**. PHRASAL VB : V+O+ADV

play down. If you **play down** a fact or feature, you try to make people think that it is unimportant, or less important than it really is. EG *He played down his recent promotion... He will play down the financial difficulties of the company.* PHRASAL VB : V+O+ADV

play off against. If you **play** two or more people or groups **off against** each other, you cause them to compete against each other or to oppose each other so that you will gain an advantage. EG *The multinational companies can play individual markets off against each other... Annie played one parent off against the other.* PHRASAL VB : V+O+ADV+PREP, HAS PASS

play on. **1** If you **play on** the feelings or attitudes of the people listening to you, you say things which make use of those feelings or attitudes in order to persuade them about something. EG *He used to play on their prejudices and their fears.* PHRASAL VB : V+PREP, HAS PASS = exploit

2 If a writer or speaker **plays on** a particular idea or word, he or she cleverly makes use of different aspects of it, often for a humorous effect. EG *Arbuthnot's satire plays on the idea of society as a human body.* PHRASAL VB : V+PREP, HAS PASS ↑ exploit

play out. If people **play out** a scene, drama, fantasy, etc, they take part in events which seem fated to happen or which seem to be part of a story or dream. EG *One day this scene would have to be played out between them... We're just playing out fantasies.* PHRASAL VB : V+ADV = enact

play up. **1** If you **play up** a fact or feature, you emphasize it and try to make people think that it is more important than it really is. EG *The temptation is to play up the sensational aspects of the story.* PHRASAL VB : V+O+ADV = exaggerate

2 If a machine or a part of your body is **playing up** or is **playing** you **up**, it is not working properly or is hurting and is therefore causing problems; used in informal English. EG *Our phone is playing up again... My arm is playing me up this morning.* PHRASAL VB : V+ADV, OR V+O+ADV, USU CONT

3 If a group of children are **playing up**, they are being naughty and are difficult to control; used in informal English. EG *The kids are playing up again.* PHRASAL VB : V+ADV = misbehave

play upon. To **play upon** something means the same as to play on it. PHRASAL VB : V+PREP, HAS PASS

play with. **1** If you **play with** the idea of doing something, you consider doing it, although you will probably not do it. EG *Thomas played with the idea of letting Coyne make all the arrangements.* PHRASAL VB : V+PREP, HAS PASS = toy with

2 If you **play with** something, you keep moving it with your hands without thinking about what you are doing, for example because you are bored or nervous. EG *I sat there playing with a bottle of suntan lotion.* PHRASAL VB : V+PREP = fiddle with

3 If you **play with** your food, you push it around your plate instead of eating it, because you are not hungry. PHRASAL VB : V+PREP, HAS PASS

4 If a writer or speaker **plays with** words or ideas, he or she uses them in a clever and unusual way for a special effect. PHRASAL VB : V+PREP = manipulate

5 If you say that someone **is playing with** someone else, you mean that they are behaving towards them in an insincere way. EG *'Albert,' she said, 'Stop playing with me like this.'* PHRASAL VB : V+PREP, USU CONT

6 If someone **plays with** themselves, they masturbate; an informal expression. PHR : VB INFLECTS

7 If you **have** a particular amount of **time** or **money to play with**, you have that amount of time or money available to do something; used in fairly informal English. EG *How much money have we got to play with?* PHR : VB INFLECTS

play-act, play-acts, play-acting, play-acted. Someone who **is play-acting** is pretending to have feelings or attitudes that they do not really have. EG *I wasn't really hurt–I was just play-acting.* V : USU CONT = sham, fake

playback /pleɪbæk/. The **playback** of a tape is the operation of the machine it is in so that you can listen to the sound recorded on it or watch the pictures recorded on it. EG *The noise caused by the continual playback of films and video programmes was deafening... Then all you have to do is press the playback button.* N UNCOUNT = replay

playbill /pleɪbɪl/, **playbills**. A **playbill** is a piece of paper which tells the public when and where a play will be performed. N COUNT ↑ advertisement

playboy /pleɪbɔɪ/, **playboys**. A **playboy** is a rich man who spends most of his time enjoying himself in expensive ways. EG *Her fourth husband was a wealthy Irish playboy.* N COUNT

player /pleɪə/, **players**. **1** A **player** is **1.1** a person who takes part in a sport or game. EG *...Gerald Davies, the former Welsh rugby player... There is a shortage of talented young players today.* N COUNT **1.2** a person who performs music on a musical instrument. EG *He's one of the most original guitar players in jazz.* N COUNT ↑ musician **1.3** an actor; used in formal or rather old-fashioned English. EG *The players came on stage with their backs to the audience.* N COUNT

2 See also **cassette player, record player**.

playful /pleɪful/. **1** A **playful** action or remark is light-hearted and friendly rather than serious or hostile. EG *She gave Philip's hand a little playful squeeze... Davis made a playful pretence at seizing Castle's briefcase.* ▸ used of people. EG *He was just being playful.* ◊ **playfully**. EG *He grasped her wrist playfully.* ADJ QUALIT = good-natured, teasing ◊ ADV WITH VB

2 A **playful** animal or person is lively and happy. EG *...a playful kitten.* ADJ QUALIT = frisky

playground /pleɪgraʊnd/, **playgrounds**. **1** A **playground** is a piece of land where children can play. A playground is either part of a school or is a public area with equipment to play on such as swings and slides. EG *He could hear the children in the playground nearby... ...a school playground.* • See also **adventure playground**. N COUNT

2 If you describe a particular place or area of activity as the **playground** of a particular person or group, you mean that they are able to have a very enjoyable and active time in that place or taking part in that activity. EG *...the millionaires' playgrounds of the Mediterranean coast... He considered journalism his playground.* N COUNT+SUPP = domain

playgroup /pleɪgruːp/, **playgroups**. A **playgroup** is an informal kind of school for very young children where they learn things by playing. EG *Children living in remote places cannot get to the playgroup... ...while the children are at playgroup.* N COUNT/UNCOUNT = nursery

playhouse /pleɪhaʊs/, **playhouses**. A **playhouse** is **1** a theatre. EG *We saw a show at the local playhouse... Dan was stage-managing at the Playhouse.* **2** a small structure that looks like a house and is big enough for children to play in. N COUNT : ALSO IN NAMES AFTER N ; N COUNT ↑ toy

playing card, playing cards. A **playing card** is a rectangular piece of thin cardboard with a number or picture printed on it, which is part of a set of 52 that you use to play games. EG *I had a pack of playing cards.* N COUNT

playing field, playing fields; also spelled with a hyphen. A **playing field** is a large area of grass where people play sports, especially one owned by a school or a university. EG *The voices from the playing field had died down... Our teachers were as friendly on the playing-fields as they were strict in the classroom.* N COUNT

playlet /pleɪlɪᵊt/, **playlets**. A **playlet** is a short play. N COUNT

playmate /pleɪmeɪt/, **playmates**. A child's **playmate** is another child, or perhaps an animal or an adult, with whom he or she often plays. EG *Over the summer my playmates were my cousins.* N COUNT = companion

playoff /pleɪɒf/, **playoffs**; also spelled with a hyphen. A **playoff** is an extra game or match which is played to decide the winner of a competition when two or more people have got the same score. EG *Nicklaus won in an 18-hole playoff against Billy Casper and Bob Stone.* N COUNT

play on words, plays on words. A **play on words** is an amusing use of a word that has more than one meaning, or that sounds like another word N COUNT : USU SING = pun with a different meaning, so that what you say has two different meanings.

playpen /pleɪpen/, **playpens**; also spelled with a hyphen. A **playpen** is a small structure which is designed for a baby or young child to play safely in. It has bars or a net round the sides and is open at the top. N COUNT ⇑ enclosure

playroom /pleɪruᵘm/, **playrooms**; also spelled with a hyphen. A **playroom** is a room in a house for children to play in. N COUNT

plaything /pleɪθɪŋ/, **playthings**; a fairly formal word. 1 A **plaything** is a toy or other object that a child plays with. EG *I used to get them new playthings to keep them quiet.* N COUNT

2 If you say that someone is the **plaything** of a particular person or force, you mean that the person or force does things with them for their own amusement and does not care about them. EG *He wanted to have me as a plaything for some time longer... We are the playthings of fate.* N COUNT

playtime /pleɪtaɪm/ is a period of time between lessons at school when children can play outside. N UNCOUNT = break

playwright /pleɪraɪt/, **playwrights**. A **playwright** is a person who writes plays. EG *...Gwyn Thomas, a novelist and playwright from South Wales.* N COUNT = dramatist

plaza /plɑːzə/, **plazas**. A **plaza** is an open square, especially in a town in Spain or a Spanish-speaking country. N COUNT: ALSO IN NAMES AFTER N

PLC is an abbreviation for 'public limited company'. It is used after the name of a company whose shares can be bought by the public. EG *...National Westminster Bank PLC.* N IN NAMES

plea /pliː/, **pleas**. A **plea** is 1 an intense, emotional request or the emotional giving of a reason why something should be done; a fairly formal use. EG *She at last responded to his pleas for help... His speech included an 'urgent plea to this nation not to neglect its sick and elderly'... She insisted that they should live in London, despite his plea that he could work better in the country.* N COUNT ⇑ appeal, entreaty 2 the answer which someone charged with a crime makes to the charge in a court of law, in which they say whether they are guilty or not; a legal term. EG *I agreed to enter a plea of guilty if the Crown would drop the charge against my friend.* N COUNT 3 an excuse which is given for doing something or for not doing something; a formal use. EG *Our plea of national poverty rings a little hollow.* N COUNT ⇑ justification

pleached /pliːtʃt/. **Pleached** trees have had their young branches bent under and over each other in order to form a particular shape. ADJ CLASSIF

plead, pleads, pleading, pleaded, pled. The forms **pleaded**, **plead**, and **pled** are all used as the past tense and past participle. The word **plead** is pronounced /pliːd/ when it is used in the present tense and /pled/ when it is used as the past tense and past participle. 1 If you **plead** with someone to do something, you ask them in an intense, emotional way to do it, because you very much want them to do it and you are afraid that they will not. EG *He was pleading with her to control herself... 'Take me with you,' he pleaded... She wrote to the Prime Minister pleading for restraint... His parents pleaded that he should be given one more chance.* V+QUOTE/REPORT-CL, OR V+A = beg, entreat

2 If someone, especially a lawyer, **pleads** someone else's case or cause or **pleads** for them, they speak in support or defence of them; a formal use. EG *Of course his mother does her best to plead his case... ...posters which plead the special cause of working-class women... I heard him plead in court only once... Who will plead for us?* V+O, OR V+A ⇑ argue

3 If you **plead** a particular thing as an excuse for doing something or for not doing something, you give it as your excuse; a formal use. EG *The Government might find it convenient to plead ignorance... Whenever she invites him to dinner, he pleads a prior engagement... I pleaded that I felt ill.* V+O/REPORT-CL ⇑ allege = protest

4 When someone charged with a crime **pleads** guilty or **pleads** not guilty, they say in a court of law that they are guilty or not guilty of the charge against them; a legal term. EG *'How do you plead?'-'Not guilty'... I have to plead guilty... ...making decisions about the defendant's fitness to plead.* V OR V+C

pleading /pliːdɪŋ/, **pleadings**. 1 A **pleading** expression, gesture, or tone of voice is one that shows that you very much want the person you are with to do something. EG *Then he saw his brother's pleading expression and his heart softened.* ◇ **pleadingly**. EG *He looked up pleadingly at his father's startled face.* ADJ CLASSIF: ATTRIB = beseeching ◇ ADV WITH VB

2 **Pleading** is asking someone in an intense, emotional way to do something. EG *After days of tearful pleading and sulking, she stayed... It was hard to resist his daughter's pleadings.* N UNCOUNT/N PLURAL entreaty

pleasant /plezəᵊnt/, **pleasanter, pleasantest**. 1 Something that is **pleasant** is rather nice and enjoyable or attractive. EG *...a pleasant chat... The chapel is a pleasant square building of red brick... It was pleasant to slip outside and sit under the apple tree... It is one of the pleasantest places I know.* ADJ QUALIT ⇑ good = agreeable, charming ◇ **pleasantly**. EG *I was pleasantly surprised.* ◇ ADV

2 Someone who is **pleasant** is friendly and likeable. EG *They were pleasant lads... Try and be a bit more pleasant to your sister.* ▸ used of someone's voice, behaviour, etc. EG *A salesman came up to me and said in a pleasant voice, 'Can I help you?'... Dr Lake wrote a very pleasant letter to my father.* ADJ QUALIT = nice ◇ **pleasantly**. EG *'Please come in,' she said pleasantly.* ◇ ADV WITH VB

pleasantry /plezəᵊntriˡ/, **pleasantries**. A **pleasantry** is a casual, friendly remark which is said in order to be polite. EG *We stood about exchanging a few pleasantries.* N COUNT = courtesy

please /pliːz/, **pleases, pleasing, pleased**. 1 You say **please** 1.1 when you are politely asking someone to do something. EG *'Follow me, please,' the guide said... Please don't interfere, Boris... I can't tell you, Father. Just lend me the money. Please... Will you please bring your slide rule to every class.* ADV SEN 1.2 when you are politely asking for something or ordering something, or asking if you can do something. EG *I'd like to make an appointment to see one of the doctors this morning please... Hello. Could I speak to Sue, please?* ADV SEN 1.3 when you are accepting something politely. EG *'Do you want some milk?'-'Yes please.'... 'Shall I read to you?'-'Yes, please.'... 'Coffee?'-'Please.'* CONVENTION = thank you 1.4 to indicate that you want someone to stop doing something or to stop speaking, especially because you find it unpleasant or upsetting. EG *Graham, please, they're not used to your kind of language... 'I wish you'd all go to hell!'-'Oh please, Clarissa. That's enough.'* ADV SEN 1.5 to indicate politely that someone should not bother to do something because you do not consider that it is necessary. EG *'I'll pay you back, of course.'-'Mr Liebermann, please! You're a guest in our home; it's your telephone too.'* ADV SEN 1.6 to attract someone's attention; used especially by children to attract the attention of a teacher or other adult. EG *Please miss, why is that wrong? You've marked it wrong.* CONVENTION = excuse me

2 If someone or something **pleases** you, they make you feel happy and satisfied, or give you enjoyment and pleasure. EG *You're an impossible man to please, Emmanuel... Neither idea pleased me... Rose was plain and anxious to please... It pleases me that he should want to talk about his work.* V OR V+O ⇑ satisfy

3 **Please** is used in expressions such as 'as she pleases', 'anyone he pleases', and 'whatever you please' to indicate that someone can do or have whatever they wish. EG *Judy had a right to come and go as she pleased... Then make it up into whatever form you please... He can get almost anyone he pleases to work with him.* V OR V+O = choose, like

4 You say **if you please** 4.1 to indicate that you find a fact or situation that you have just mentioned or that you are just about to mention difficult to believe, or that you are surprised or rather angry about it. EG *...a passenger called Jago-Rodney Jago, if you please.* PHR: USED AS A 4.2 as a very polite and formal way of attracting someone's attention. EG *Captain Imrie stopped me at the door. 'If you please, Dr Marlowe, a word with you.'* CONVENTION

5 You say **please God** to emphasize a very strong hope, wish, or desire that you have. EG *He's an honest man. Always was, and always will be, please God.* PHR: USED AS A

6 You say **'please yourself'** to show in an informal, rather rude way that you do not mind or care whether the person you are talking to does a particular thing or not. EG *'Do you mind if I wait?' I asked. Melanie shrugged: 'Please yourself.'* CONVENTION

pleased /pliːzd/. 1 If you are **pleased**, you are happy about something or satisfied with something. EG *He dared not show that he was pleased... She seemed very pleased that he had come... I am so pleased to have seen you again... He was pleased with my* ADJ QUALIT: PRED = delighted *progress... Amy seemed pleased at the idea.* ▸ used of an expression. EG *The pleased smile went from her face.* ▸ ADJ QUALIT : ATTRIB = contented

2 If you say that someone is not **pleased**, you mean that they are very annoyed about something or very dissatisfied with something. EG *She did not look at all pleased... The captain wasn't too pleased about my having seen that.* ADJ QUALIT : PRED = happy

3 If you are **pleased** with yourself, you are happy about something that you have done and feel proud of yourself, perhaps in a way that other people find rather annoying or unpleasant. EG *She looked pleased with herself.* ADJ QUALIT : PRED + *with* + REFL = satisfied

4 If someone is or will be **pleased** to do something, they are very willing to do it. EG *They will be only too pleased to let someone else take the risk... The local hospital will always be pleased to accept them.* ADJ QUALIT : PRED + *to*-INF = happy

5 You can say **'pleased to meet you'**, **'pleased to make your acquaintance'**, etc as a polite way of greeting someone who you are meeting for the first time. CONVENTION

pleasing /pliːzɪŋ/. Something that is **pleasing** gives pleasure and satisfaction to someone; a fairly formal word. EG *She is most pleasing in manner and appearance... ...a pleasing piece of news... ...a building which is pleasing to the eye.* ADJ QUALIT = agreeable

pleasurable /plɛʒəᵒrəbəᵒl/. Something that is **pleasurable** is pleasant and enjoyable; a fairly formal word. EG *...a pleasurable sensation... Dixon felt none of the pleasurable excitement he'd expected... Not every child expects reading to be pleasurable.* ADJ QUALIT = agreeable
◇ **pleasurably**. EG *He had often pleasurably anticipated the moment when he would be free of school for ever.* ◇ ADV WITH VB

pleasure /plɛʒə/, **pleasures**. **1 Pleasure** is **1.1** a feeling of happiness, satisfaction, or enjoyment. EG *McPherson could scarcely conceal his pleasure at my resignation... They take pleasure in their children's accomplishments... I'd travel a thousand miles just for the pleasure of meeting you... I can't understand how people can kill for pleasure.* N UNCOUNT **1.2** the activity of enjoying yourself, especially rather than working or doing what you have a duty to do. EG *He was a man who lived for pleasure... She is a disciplined creature who will put duty before pleasure... Whether you're in San Francisco for business or pleasure, it is a crime not to cross the Golden Gate Bridge... He set off on another of his European pleasure tours.* N UNCOUNT ⇑ recreation

2 A **pleasure** is an activity, experience, or aspect of something that you find very enjoyable and satisfying. EG *They were talking about what a pleasure it would be to hunt in the nearby forests... They look on it as more of a duty than a pleasure... ...the pleasures of choral singing.* N COUNT = delight

3 You can describe or refer to the experience of meeting someone, having them as a guest or a partner, etc as a **pleasure** when you are being polite and friendly, often in a formal way. EG *She greeted him vivaciously. 'What a great pleasure.'... Mr and Mrs Oliver Barrett request the pleasure of your company at the wedding of their daughter... May I have the pleasure of this dance?... Perhaps you'll do me the pleasure of joining me in a drink.* N SING WITH DET = honour

4 You can say **'It was a pleasure'**, **'My pleasure'**, **'A pleasure'**, etc as a polite way of replying to someone who has just thanked you for doing something. EG *'Thank you very much for coming and talking to us about your research.'–'It's a pleasure.'* CONVENTION = you're welcome

5 You can say **'With pleasure'** as a polite way of saying that you are very willing to do something that someone has asked you to do. EG *'Quick! Come over here!'–'With pleasure.'* CONVENTION = certainly

6 If you do something **at** someone's **pleasure**, you do it because they wish you to and for as long as they wish you to; a formal expression. EG *If this were so, the President would remain in office at the pleasure of the Senate.* PHR : USED AS AN A

pleat /pliːt/, **pleats, pleating, pleated. 1** A **pleat** in a piece of clothing is a permanent fold that is made in the cloth by folding one part over another and stitching the top of the fold. ● See also **box pleat**. N COUNT : USU PL

2 If you **pleat** the cloth when you are making a piece of clothing, you make pleats in it by folding and stitching it. ◇ **pleated**. EG *...a brown pleated skirt.* V+O ◇ ADJ CLASSIF

pleb /plɛb/, **plebs**. A **pleb** is the same as a plebeian; an informal word. N COUNT

plebeian /pləʼbiːən/, **plebeians**. **1** A **plebeian** is a member of the lower social classes; used showing disapproval. EG *...his dislike of what he called the plebeians.* N COUNT

2 Something that is **plebeian** is connected with, or typical of, the lower social classes; used showing disapproval. EG *He had gone back to his rather plebeian job... He had a rather thick, short, plebeian neck.* ADJ QUALIT = lower-class

plectrum /plɛktrəm/, **plectrums**. A **plectrum** is a small thin piece of plastic, wood, metal, etc that is held between the finger and thumb and used for plucking the strings of a guitar, banjo, mandolin, etc. N COUNT

pled /plɛd/ is a past tense and past participle form of **plead**.

pledge /plɛdʒ/, **pledges, pledging, pledged. 1** A **pledge** is a solemn promise or guarantee to do or provide something, especially one that is made by a government, politician, etc. EG *The Government should fulfil its 1979 Manifesto pledge... The pledge of independence for Cuba was honoured... He gave a pledge to handle the affair in a friendly manner... This appeal brought at least five more pledges of £10.* N COUNT

2 If someone **pledges** something, they promise solemnly that they will do or provide a particular thing. EG *He once pledged his vote to me, without my asking... He is prepared to pledge his wholehearted allegiance to the party... A lot of people have pledged a lot of money this evening.* V+O/REPORT-CL/*to*-INF = guarantee, offer

3 If you **pledge** yourself or someone else to something or to do something, you commit yourself or that person solemnly to follow a particular course of action or to support a particular person, group, or idea. EG *The new organization pledged itself to the revolutionary overthrow of the dictator... He pledged himself to support the legislation reforms... The letter to the IMF pledged Britain to £200 million surplus in 1968.* V+O (NG/REFL) + A (*to*)/*to*-INF = dedicate

4 If you **pledge** your **word**, you make a solemn promise, implying that if you do not fulfil it you will not expect people to believe you ever again. PHR : VB INFLECTS

5 A **pledge** is also something valuable that you leave with someone else as a guarantee that you will pay a much larger amount or fulfil an agreement later. EG *She left her watch as a pledge with the taxi-driver.* ▸ used as a verb. EG *The property was pledged as security for loans.* N COUNT ⇑ token ▸ V+O

plenary /pliːnəri¹, plɛn-/, **plenaries**. A **plenary** session or meeting is attended by everyone who has the right to attend. EG *A plenary meeting was called for.* ▸ used as a noun. EG *The plenary petered out after half an hour.* ADJ CLASSIF : USU ATTRIB ▸ N COUNT

plenipotentiary /plɛnɪpətɛnʃəri¹/, **plenipotentiaries**. A **plenipotentiary** is someone who has full power and authority to act as a representative of a country, organization, etc. EG *One of the plenipotentiaries actually refused to sign the treaty.* ▸ used as an adjective. EG *...plenipotentiary powers.* N COUNT ▸ ADJ CLASSIF

plentiful /plɛntɪful/. Something that is **plentiful** exists in large amounts or numbers, so that there is enough for people's wants or needs. EG *Food became more plentiful each day... Rhinoceroses were plentiful in this section of the country... The Governor has laid in a plentiful supply of champagne and Havana cigars.* ◇ **plentifully**. EG *This little plant grows plentifully on heaths and other dry, grassy places.* ADJ QUALIT ⇑ sufficient = abundant, copious ◇ ADV WITH VB

plenty /plɛnti¹/. **1** If there is **plenty** of something or if there are **plenty** of things, there is a large amount of something or a large number of things; often used to indicate that there is enough of something or more than you need. EG *We've got plenty of time... There are always plenty of jobs to be done... They would have plenty to eat... There had been plenty going on... 'Have you anything to say?'–'Plenty'... 'A fiver should be plenty.'* QUANTIF = lots

2 If there are things **in plenty**, the thing mentioned exists or happens in large amounts or numbers. EG *Food and drink had been consumed in plenty... All the signs were there in plenty.* PHR : USED AS AN A = in abundance

3 If you **see plenty of** someone you see them often; an informal use. EG *I'm sure we shall see plenty of you.* PHR : VB INFLECTS

4 Plenty is a situation in which people have a lot to eat or a lot of money to live on; a formal use, sometimes used in connection with the economic state of a country. EG *Starvation spreads in the midst* N UNCOUNT = prosperity *of plenty... We are using new technology to help us along the road to peace and plenty.*

5 Plenty is also used to emphasize a quality that is very strong; an informal use. EG *They are both plenty bright enough.* — ADV+ADJ/ADV

plethora /plεθərə/. A **plethora** of something is an amount of it that is much greater than you want, need, or can cope with; a fairly formal use. EG *He stood there, surrounded by that plethora of microphones, amplifiers, speakers, and reporters.* — N SING WITH DET +*of*+N IN PL = excess, superfluity

pleurisy /plʊərɪsi[1]/ is a serious illness in which the lungs are inflamed, breathing is difficult, and coughing causes great pain. — N UNCOUNT

plexus /plεksəs/. See **solar plexus**.

pliable /plaɪəbə[0]l/. **1** Something that is **pliable** is easily bent without cracking or breaking. EG *The gelatine must be soaked in cold water until pliable... ...a soft and pliable material.* — ADJ QUALIT = supple

2 Someone who is **pliable** is easily influenced and controlled by other people. EG *She had from birth been trained to be sweet, pliable, forgiving, and compassionate.* — ADJ QUALIT = compliant

pliant /plaɪənt/. **1** Someone who is **pliant**, is easily influenced and controlled by other people. EG *The Democrats may not be as pliant as they appear.* — ADJ QUALIT = compliant

2 Something that is **pliant** is easily bent without cracking or breaking. — ADJ QUALIT = supple

pliers /plaɪəz/ are a tool used for holding or pulling out small things such as nails or for bending or cutting wire. You use a pair of pliers by squeezing together the two handles in your hand, which pushes together the two specially shaped pieces at the other end. — N PLURAL : ALSO *a pair of*+N

plight /plaɪt/, **plights, plighting, plighted. 1** If someone is in a **plight**, they are affected by a situation that is distressing and full of problems. EG *Seeing the people's plight, he kneeled down and prayed... We want to raise funds and to spotlight the plight of the mentally handicapped... In fifteen years' time we will be in a sad plight.* — N SING WITH DET : USU WITH POSS ⇑ condition

2 In literary English, when two people **plight** their **troth**, they say they love each other and want to marry. — PHR : VB INFLECTS

plimsoll /plɪmsəl/, **plimsolls**. A **plimsoll** is a shoe made of canvas with a flat rubber sole, which people wear for sports and leisure. — N COUNT : USU PL = pump, gym shoe

Plimsoll line, Plimsoll lines. The **Plimsoll line** on a ship is a line painted on the outside and which marks how deep the ship should lie in the water when it is fully loaded. — N COUNT = load line

plinth /plɪnθ/, **plinths**. A **plinth** is a square block made of stone on which a statue or a pillar stands. — N COUNT ⇑ base

plod /plɒd/, **plods, plodding, plodded. 1** If someone **plods** along, they walk slowly as if their feet are too heavy to lift up properly. EG *He plodded along the white road over Salisbury Plain... I turned and plodded back the way I had come.* — V : USU+A = trudge

2 If someone **plods** on or **plods** along with a job, they work slowly and steadily and without enthusiasm at something that they find difficult or uninteresting. EG *I found that playing different parts was a strain. However, we plodded on and many people liked that last Hamlet best of all... He would have plodded on in the Board of Trade for years.* — V+A

plodder /plɒdə/, **plodders**. Someone who is a **plodder** works slowly and steadily to finish a job, but who shows no signs of enthusiasm or inspiration; used showing disapproval. — N COUNT

plonk /plɒŋk/, **plonks, plonking, plonked. 1** If you **plonk** something somewhere, you put it down or drop it heavily and carelessly. EG *Bottles of beer were plonked on the wooden table... Neil Armstrong achieved the goal of plonking an American boot on the moon... He plonked himself down on the sofa and sat there all evening!* — V+O+A ⇑ set down

2 A **plonk** is a heavy, hollow sound. EG *The mug came down with a plonk.* — N COUNT : USU SING

3 If someone is **plonking** away on a piano, they are playing it rather heavily or badly. — V+A, OR V+O

4 Plonk is cheap or poor quality wine; an informal use. EG *Shall we get a bottle of plonk?* — N MASS

plop /plɒp/, **plops, plopping, plopped. 1** A **plop** is a soft gentle sound, like the sound made by something light dropping into water without a splash. EG *I saw my hat go floating through the air and land with a plop in the bucket.* ▸ also used to represent a sound of this kind. EG *I threw another pebble-plop!* — N COUNT ⇑ noise

2 If something **plops** somewhere, especially into liquid, it drops with a soft gentle sound. EG *The float plopped into the water and bobbed gently on the surface... Great big tears plopped into her soup... ...plopping sounds.* — V+A

3 If you **plop** something somewhere, you put it there rather heavily and carelessly, so that it makes a slight noise. EG *Walking over to the chair, she plopped down into it.* — V+A, OR V+O+A ⇑ put down

plot /plɒt/, **plots, plotting, plotted. 1** A **plot** is a secret plan by a number of people to do something that is illegal or wrong, usually against a person or a government. EG *On 14th February another plot to assassinate the General was uncovered... Ward was the victim of a plot by the Establishment.* — N COUNT = conspiracy

2 If people **plot** something or **plot** to do something, they plan secretly to do it. Usually it is something that is illegal or wrong, usually against a person or a government. EG *Anyone convicted for plotting against the king will be executed... They were accused of plotting to overthrow the government... He was always plotting trouble and strikes.* — V, V+O, V+ *to*-INF, OR V+A *(against)* = conspire

3 The **plot** of a film, novel, or play is the story and the way in which it develops. EG *They were having some difficulty in following the plot... Tell me the plot.* — N COUNT = story line

4 A **plot** of land is a small piece of land, especially one that has been measured or marked out for a special purpose, such as for building houses or for farming or growing vegetables. EG *His land is split up into several widely scattered plots... She had five acres of pasture, a plot for growing vegetables, and a flower garden.* — N COUNT

5 When someone **plots** the position or course of a plane or ship, they mark it on a map or chart in order to see what course or direction it is taking. EG *They now plotted the new positions of each vessel.* — V+O

6 When you are drawing a graph, you **plot** the points on it by marking them at the appropriate places to form the graph. EG *These figures can be plotted on a graph.* — V+O

7 To **plot** the progress or development of something means to make a plan or diagram of it in order to show how it has developed in the past or will develop in the future. EG *They are trying to plot the way forward for adult literacy education.* — V+O = chart

plotter /plɒtə/, **plotters**. A **plotter** is **1** a person who secretly plans with others to do something that is illegal or wrong, usually against a person or a government. EG *The arrest of the plotters soon followed.* — N COUNT : USU ⇑ planner = conspirato **2** a person or instrument that marks the position of something, for example a ship or plane, on a map or chart. — N COUNT

plough /plaʊ/, **ploughs, ploughing, ploughed**; also spelled **plow** in American English. **1** A **plough** is a large farming tool with sharp blades which is attached to a tractor or an animal such as a horse. A plough is pulled across the soil to turn it over, usually before seeds are planted. EG *Some landlords would let their land only to peasants owning a bullock and plough.* ● See also **snowplough**. — N COUNT

2 When someone **ploughs** an area of land, they turn over the soil using a plough. EG *In Sri Lanka a small tractor can plough an acre in six to nine hours... It's difficult to use machines to plough down hills.* — V OR V+O ⇑ till

◇ **ploughed**. EG *The old people can remember this area as ploughed fields.* — ◇ ADJ CLASSIF

3 If someone or something **ploughs** on, **ploughs** their way through something, etc, they continue moving through something or trying to complete something, although it needs a lot of effort because it is so difficult or awkward. EG *The fighters ploughed on to their destination airfields... Jimmie hesitated for a moment and then ploughed on with his speech... Bob sat in a corner, gloomily ploughing his way through an enormous plate of food.* — V+A

4 If something **ploughs** into something else, it continues moving, especially in a clumsy or careless way, with the result that a crash or collision is caused. EG *The car ploughed into his garden wall... Four tank regiments ploughed into the two brigades on the left.* — V+A *(into)* ⇑ collide

5 If someone **ploughs** money into a business or company, they put large sums of money into it in order to make it into a bigger or better one. EG *The* — V+O+A (USU *into*) = invest *huge sums of money which were ploughed into computing soon began to pay off... They ploughed their profits back into further investment.*

6 The **Plough** is a group of seven bright stars in the Northern Hemisphere which are thought to look like a plough. N PROPER : the+ N

7 If an area of land **goes under the plough**, it is ploughed for the first time and its use is changed to that of growing crops. EG *The park had gone under the plough.* PHR : VB INFLECTS

plough in. If someone **ploughs in** a crop or what remains of a crop after it has been harvested, they plough the land causing the plants to be turned into the soil to fertilize the land. EG *The stalks are left to be ploughed in for the next planting.* PHRASAL VB : V+O+ADV

plough up. If an area of land **is ploughed up**, the soil is turned over using a plough, especially on land which is being changed from grassland to land which will be used for growing crops; often used showing disapproval. EG *Nearly half of Wiltshire's chalk grassland was ploughed up to grow corn.* PHRASAL VB : V+ADV, USU PASS

ploughman /plaumə³n/, **ploughmen**. A **ploughman** is a person whose job is to plough the land, especially using a plough pulled by animals. N COUNT

ploughman's lunch, ploughman's lunches; used in British English. A **ploughman's lunch** or a **ploughman's** is a snack consisting of bread, cheese and pickles. It is usually bought and eaten in a pub. N COUNT

ploughshare /plauʃɛə/, **ploughshares**. If you talk about people **turning swords into ploughshares**, you are talking about people who have been fighting or quarrelling making peace with each other. EG *It is time to turn swords into ploughshares.* PHR : VB INFLECTS

plover /plʌvə/, **plovers**. A **plover** is a bird with long wings and a short straight beak that lives mainly on the seashore. N COUNT

plow /plau/. See **plough**.

ploy /plɔɪ/, **ploys**. A **ploy** is a way of behaving that you have planned carefully in order to achieve a secret purpose or advantage for yourself. EG *Men have a number of ploys which they use to make their inferiors feel awkward... The announcement was a clever ploy to deflect criticism of the government... This headache was clearly a delaying ploy.* N COUNT = stratagem, tactic

pluck /plʌk/, **plucks, plucking, plucked**. **1** If you **pluck** something, especially a fruit, flower, or leaf, you take it in your hand and pull it in order to remove it from its stalk or from where it is attached to. EG *These primates used their hands for plucking fruit and leaves... He plucked another tomato and offered it to Hilda... Ben plucked off for himself some of the ripened fruits.* V+O = pick

2 If you **pluck** something from somewhere, **pluck** at something, etc, you take hold of it and pull it with a sharp movement. EG *He laughed briefly and plucked the paper from my hand... She plucked off his mask... He plucked me by the sleeve to lead me out... Rough hands plucked at my jacket.* V+O : USU+A, OR V+A = grasp, tug

3 If you **pluck** a chicken or other dead bird, you pull its feathers out to prepare it for cooking. EG *They'd been busy cleaning and plucking the birds for the Christmas feast.* V+O

4 If someone **plucks** their eyebrows, they pull out the hairs that they do not want to be there using tweezers. V+O

5 If you **pluck** someone from an unpleasant or dangerous situation, you rescue them. EG *Boats that fisherman usually dodge have sometimes plucked them off foundering vessels... ...plucking these fellows out of their prison.* V+O+A

6 When someone **plucks** a musical instrument such as a violin or guitar, they pull the strings with their fingers and let them go, so that they make a sound. EG *...plucking the mandolin for a few harsh chords... He idly plucked the strings of the lute... She was plucking at a lyre with only one string.* V+O, OR V+A ⇑ strum

7 Someone who has **pluck** has courage and strength which they show when they are in difficulty or afraid. N UNCOUNT = nerve

8 If someone **plucks** an idea, an answer, etc **out of the air**, the idea or answer comes to them unexpectedly and without having been carefully thought about. PHR : VB INFLECTS

9 If you **pluck up the courage** to do something, you make yourself put aside your fears and worries and give yourself courage to do it. EG *I eventually plucked up enough courage to go in... Sheila plucked up her courage to ask for a pay rise.* PHR : VB INFLECTS, USU+to-INF

plucky /plʌki¹/, **pluckier, pluckiest**. Someone who is **plucky** has courage and strength which they show when they are in difficulty or afraid. EG *This schoolgirl story featured a plucky heroine.* ADJ QUALIT = brave, daring

plug /plʌg/, **plugs, plugging, plugged**. **1** A **plug** in an electrical system is **1.1** a small plastic device that connects the wire from an appliance to the electricity supply, by means of small metal pieces which fit into the holes in a socket. EG *...a three-pin plug... Do you know how to wire a plug?... ...13-amp plugs.* N COUNT **1.2** a device which connects the wire from one piece of equipment to a socket in another, for example from an amplifier to a loudspeaker or from a computer terminal to a keyboard. N COUNT **1.3** a socket that is a source of electricity, usually in the wall of a room; an informal use. EG *You could run it off a mains plug... Use the plug in the spare bedroom.* N COUNT

2 A **plug** is also **2.1** a thick, circular piece of rubber or plastic that you use to block the hole in a bath, sink, etc when you want to fill it with water. EG *Where's the sink plug?... Every time we took the plug out, the kitchen flooded.* N COUNT **2.2** a small tube of plastic or wood that you put into a hole, especially in a wall, in order to make a screw fit tightly into it. EG *Never screw directly into a wall, always use wall plugs... Always insert plugs at right angles to a wall.* N COUNT : USU+SUPP **2.3** a small piece of cotton wool or wax that you put in your nose when it is bleeding or in your ears to protect them from noise. EG *...two cotton-wool plugs for his nose... Finally, I tried ear plugs.* N COUNT+SUPP

3 A **plug** in the engine of a motor vehicle is a device which produces the electrical spark that ignites the fuel. EG *Keeping plugs in good condition will cut your fuel consumption.* N COUNT = spark plug

4 If you **plug** a hole, you block it with something. EG *He plugged the cracks with paper... Have you plugged all the leaks?... Mark plugged his ears with cotton wool.* V+O

5 If you **plug** a book, film, etc, especially on the radio or television, you mention or praise it in order to encourage people to buy it, see it, etc; an informal use. EG *The radio stations are plugging the record like mad... People are always plugging their books on TV chat shows.* ▸ used as a noun. EG *Can I quickly give our new show a plug?* V+O ▸ N COUNT : USU SING

6 If you **plug** someone, you shoot them with a gun; used in informal American English. EG *I wanted to plug that bully full of lead.* V+O

plug away. If you **plug away** at something, you keep trying very hard to do something which you consider difficult or uninteresting. EG *He told them that they must keep plugging away... She plugged away at her maths.* PHRASAL VB : V+ADV, IF+PREP THEN at ⇑ persevere

plug in. **1** If you **plug in** a piece of electrical equipment or **plug** it **into** a source of electricity, you push its plug into an electric socket so that it can work. EG *I plugged in the kettle... Plug it into the mains... She plugged the lamp into a wall-socket... A television set is a fire risk if left plugged in overnight.* PHRASAL VB : V+O+ADV/PREP, USU+A ⇑ connect

2 If you **plug** one piece of electrical equipment **into** another, or **plug** it **in**, you connect the two together so that one operates the other. EG *He put on a record and plugged in the earphones... Portable computers can be plugged into TV sets... He has a flash gun plugged into his camera.* PHRASAL VB : V+O+ADV/PREP

3 If a piece of electrical equipment **plugs in** or **plugs into** a source of electricity or another piece of equipment, it is designed to be powered by electricity or to be connected to the other piece of equipment. EG *The one we have at home plugs into the mains... That plugs in here.* PHRASAL VB : V+ADV/PREP

4 If you **plug** something **into** a hole or slot or **plug** it **in**, you fit it into the hole or slot. EG *...balls of wax which you plug into your ear... He has a hearing device plugged into his ear.* PHRASAL VB : V+O+ADV/PREP

5 If you **plug into** a group of people or their ideas, or **plug in**, you find out about them and try to understand them; used mainly in informal American English. EG *What I'm really trying to do is to plug into people's fantasies... Politicians have been kept plugged in to the public relations operation.* PHRASAL VB : V+ADV/PREP = tune in

plugged /plʌgd/. If a part of your body such as your nose is **plugged**, it is blocked by mucus or other ADJ CLASSIF substance, usually because you are ill. EG *...a plugged tear duct... My nostrils were plugged with mucus.*

plughole /plʌghəul/, **plugholes.** 1 A **plughole** is a small hole in a bath, sink, etc which allows the water to flow away, and into which you can put a plug. N COUNT

2 If you say that something has gone **down the plughole**, you mean it has failed completely or been wasted. EG *Eighteen months' work had disappeared down the plughole.* PHR : USED AS AN A

plum /plʌm/, **plums.** 1 A **plum** is a small fruit with a thin, dark-red or yellow skin, which is juicy and yellow inside and has a large stone in the middle; used also of the tree on which it grows. EG *...a bag of plums... ...plum jam.* N COUNT

2 Something that is **plum** is dark-red or purple in colour; a rather literary use. EG *...a plum velvet suit... ...her plum-coloured skirt... Harris's face went a deep plum red.* ADJ COLOUR

3 If you say that something, especially a job, is a **plum**, you mean that it is very desirable and that the person who gets it is very lucky; an informal use. EG *...the plum the President gave him–chairman of the new corporation... They held most of the plum jobs before independence... She was given another plum part: the lead in a £3m film.* N COUNT : USU BEFORE N = choice

plumage /plu:mɪdʒ/. 1 A bird's **plumage** is all the feathers on its body; used especially when you are talking about the colour of the feathers. EG *...a bird of brilliant plumage... Its plumage had turned grey.* N UNCOUNT ↑ coat

2 Someone's **plumage** is the colourful and unusual clothes that they wear; a humorous use. EG *...the magnificence of her plumage and her smile.* N UNCOUNT ↑ clothing

plumb /plʌm/, **plumbs, plumbing, plumbed.** 1 If you **plumb** something that is difficult to understand, you succeed in understanding it fully; a literary use. EG *The soul of man cannot be plumbed... Man's capacity to plumb the truth.* V+O = fathom

2 If someone or something **plumbs the depths** of an unpleasant emotion or quality, they experience or express it to an extreme degree. EG *The story shows how she plumbs the depths of humiliation... This song plumbs the depths of bad taste.* PHR : VB INFLECTS

3 If you say that something is **plumb** in a particular place, you mean that it is exactly in that place; an informal use. EG *...the ship's approach, plumb through the middle of the gap... The match landed plumb in the middle of the ashtray.* ADV+PREP = bang, slap

4 **Plumb** is used to emphasize that something is true in an extreme degree; an informal American use. EG *I think you're plumb crazy... You plumb embarrass me... I was plumb tired.* ADV = completely

plumb in. If you **plumb** something **in**, for example a bath, toilet, or washing machine, you connect it to the water and drainage pipes in a building. EG *The shower can be plumbed into the existing central heating system... The bath needs to be plumbed in.* PHRASAL VB : V+O+ADV, OR V+O+PREP ↑ install

plumber /plʌmə/, **plumbers.** A **plumber** is a person whose job is to connect and repair water and drainage pipes, baths, toilets, etc. EG *The plumbers came to mend the pipes... If it still leaks, call a plumber.* N COUNT ↑ worker

plumbing /plʌmɪŋ/. 1 The **plumbing** in a building consists of the water and drainage pipes, baths, toilets, etc in the building. EG *Will it need new wiring and plumbing?... ...a house with superb plumbing and full central heating... ...the removal of dangerous lead plumbing in buildings.* N UNCOUNT

2 **Plumbing** is the work of connecting and repairing water and drainage pipes, baths, toilets, etc in a building. EG *...a course in plumbing... ...minor plumbing repairs.* N UNCOUNT

plumb line, plumb lines; also spelled with a hyphen. A **plumb line** is a piece of string with a weight attached to the end, which is used to check that something such as a wall is vertical or slopes at the correct angle. N COUNT

plume /plu:m/, **plumes, pluming, plumed.** 1 A **plume** is 1.1 a large, usually bright-coloured, bird's feather or a group of such feathers, sometimes used as a decoration on people's hats. EG *The male birds of paradise carry their plumes for several months... ...an ostrich plume... ...a short woman with a long, grey plume on her hat.* 1.2 a bunch of long, thin strands of hair or soft material, tied tightly at one end and flowing loosely at the other. Plumes are usually attached to soldiers' helmets, horses' heads, etc, as decoration. EG *...plain helmets with no plume... ...four horses with black plumes... ...the red plumes of the Royal Horse Guards.* N COUNT; N COUNT

2 A **plume** of smoke or water is a rather large quantity of it that rises into the air in a small column before thinning out or scattering; a rather literary use. EG *A thunderous plume of spray leapt halfway up the cliff... The last plume of blue smoke curled away.* N COUNT+of

3 See also **nom de plume**.

plume on. If you **plume** yourself **on** something, you are proud of it. EG *Men plume themselves on the improvement of society... She was pluming herself on her figure.* PHRASAL VB : V+O (REFL)+PREP

plumed /plu:md/ means decorated with a plume or plumes, or shaped like a plume; a rather literary word. EG *...his plumed helmet... ...brightly plumed pheasants... ...a slow sway of his plumed tail.* ADJ CLASSIF

plummet /plʌmɪt/, **plummets, plummeting, plummeted.** 1 If someone or something **plummets** downwards, it falls very quickly. EG *She would plummet to the ground... ...jumping in and plummeting straight to the bottom... The explosion sent the aircraft plummeting towards the sea.* V+A = plunge

2 If an amount, rate, or price **plummets**, it decreases quickly and suddenly. EG *The price of waste paper plummeted... ...governments with plummeting revenues... The number of farms has continued to plummet.* V = plunge, drop

3 If the level or degree of something **plummets**, it quickly and suddenly becomes lower or worse. EG *His popularity has plummeted... The standard of English has plummeted during the last few years... Staff morale plummeted.* V = deteriorate

plummy /plʌmi[1]/, **plummier, plummiest.** 1 If you say that someone has a **plummy** voice or accent, you mean that they speak in a rather old-fashioned, upper-class English way. ADJ QUALIT

2 Something that is **plummy** is dark red in colour; a literary use. EG *The peaks were turning a plummy maroon.* ADJ COLOUR

plump /plʌmp/, **plumper, plumpest; plumps, plumping, plumped.** 1 Someone or something that is **plump** is rather fat or large; often used to show affection or approval. EG *...a plump, red-faced man... The hens were plump and creamy-brown... ...plump mangoes.* ◇ **plumply.** EG *A child perched plumply on his knee... The cat fell plumply and noisily to the ground.* ◇ **plumpness.** EG *She was a little inclined to plumpness... His body had the soft plumpness of a bird.* ADJ QUALIT = chubby, rounded; ◇ ADV WITH VB; ◇ N UNCOUNT

2 If you **plump** something soft or **plump it up**, you squeeze and shake it back into its proper shape. EG *She plumped the cushions and emptied the ashtrays... ...plumping up her pillow.* V+O, OR PHRASAL VB : V+O+ADV = fluff

plump down. 1 If you **plump down**, you sit down suddenly or clumsily. EG *He plumped down in one of the chairs... Clara plumped herself down on the bed.* PHRASAL VB : V+ADV, OR V+O (REFL)+ADV

2 If you **plump down** something, you put it down suddenly and carelessly. EG *I plumped down my shopping bag.* PHRASAL VB : V+O+ADV

plump for. If you **plump for** someone or something, you choose them, often suddenly after a lot of hesitation or careful thought. EG *The judges had eventually plumped for Rushdie's novel... In the event, they plumped for a three-stage conference... She plumped for the eclair, to my surprise.* PHRASAL VB : V+PREP = opt for

plum pudding, plum puddings. A **plum pudding** is a special pudding that is eaten at Christmas, made with dried fruit, spices, and suet; a rather old-fashioned expression. EG *...their standard feast – roast goose and plum pudding.* N COUNT/UNCOUNT = Christmas pudding

plunder /plʌndə/, **plunders, plundering, plundered**; a formal word. 1 If someone **plunders** someone or something, they steal property from them, using force and often causing damage. EG *The conquerors plundered their wealth and burnt their cities... Imperialist governments plunder the weaker nations... Instead, he chooses to plunder and kill.* V OR V+O = despoil, lo

2 **Plunder** is 2.1 the activity of stealing property from people or places, using force and often causing damage. EG *...engaged in colonial plunder... Plunder was their principal occupation.* 2.2 property that is stolen, using force and often causing damage. EG *He escaped with his plunder.* N UNCOUNT = pillage; N SING WITH D = booty

plunge /plʌndʒ/, **plunges, plunging, plunged.** 1 If someone or something **plunges** in a particular direction, they fall, rush, or throw themselves in that direction. EG *They plunged into the pool together...* V+A = dive

She slipped and plunged forward... I found a door open and plunged inside... The car plunged into the river.

2 If you **plunge** an object into something, you push or place it quickly or violently into it. EG *She plunged her hands into her coat pockets... He plunged the knife into her breast... I never plunge vegetables into boiling water.* V+O+A ⇑ stick = thrust

3 To **plunge** into a state or condition or to **plunge** someone or something into it means to suddenly experience it or cause them to experience it. EG *I plunged into the blackest despair... The hall was plunged into darkness... ...the danger of plunging society into chaos and anarchy.* V-ERG+A ⇑ descend = sink

4 If you **plunge** into an activity, you get involved in it suddenly, without thinking carefully or preparing for it. EG *She plunged bravely into the debate... ...socialists who plunge into trade union activities... Father plunged into a financial gamble.* V+A *(into)* = charge, leap

5 If you **plunge** into a subject, you get deeply involved in it. EG *Academic research plunges into the past and emerges with few facts... The men did not plunge deeply into any subject.* V+A *(into)* = delve

6 If an amount or rate **plunges**, it decreases quickly and suddenly. EG *Sales have plunged by 24%... The franc plunged to its lowest rate against the dollar... The war could send prices plunging... ...the plunging cost of water turbines.* V ⇑ fall = plummet, drop

7 A **plunge** is 7.1 a sudden downward or forward movement by a person or thing. EG *The sun started its plunge behind the hills... They were relying on the plunge into icy waters to kill me... It was a thirty-five-foot plunge.* N COUNT = fall 7.2 the sudden beginning of an activity, often without careful thought or preparation. EG *...her plunge into further education.* N COUNT 7.3 a sudden decrease in an amount, especially a price. EG *Prices started a downward plunge.* N COUNT = fall

8 If you **take the plunge**, you decide on a course of action which you consider is difficult or risky and which you will not be able to reverse later. EG *Take the plunge and start your own firm, or join a large company... Washington has taken the plunge: its Metro system is scheduled to open next year... We took the plunge and got married.* PHR : VB INFLECTS

plunger /plʌndʒə/, **plungers**. A **plunger** is a device for unblocking pipes, sinks, etc, consisting of a piece of rubber on the end of a stick. You press the plunger up and down over the pipe or the hole in the sink, and the suction you create moves the blockage. EG *...a sink plunger... ...a toilet plunger.* N COUNT

plunging /plʌndʒɪŋ/. A **plunging** neckline on a woman's dress is one that is cut very low down with a steep V-shape. ADJ CLASSIF : ATTRIB ⇑ low

plunk /plʌŋk/, **plunks, plunking, plunked**; an informal word. 1 A **plunk** is a dull, metallic sound. EG *It rolled onto the ice with a dull plunk... ...the plunk of a guitar.* N COUNT : USU SING

2 If you **plunk** something down, you put it down without great care. EG *I plunked the cardboard crown on the head of the winner.* V+O = plonk

plunk down. If you **plunk down** or **plunk** yourself **down**, you sit down heavily and clumsily. EG *She plunked down in an armchair and lit a cigarette.* PHRASAL VB : V+ADV, OR V+O (REFL)+ADV

pluperfect /pluːpɜːfɪ²kt/ is the term used in grammar for the tense of a verb describing actions that were completed in the past before another event in the past. The pluperfect in English is formed using 'had' followed by the past participle of the verb, as in the sentences 'I had gone by then' and 'She'd eaten them before I arrived'. N SING : the+N, OR ADJ CLASSIF : ATTRIB = past perfect

plural /pluərəl/, **plurals**. 1 In grammar, **plural** is the term used for the state or form of a noun, pronoun, determiner, adjective, or verb when it refers to two or more people, things, or groups. See also ☐ at N PLURAL. EG *Use the first person plural... The singular is 'louse' and the plural is 'lice'.* N COUNT, ADJ CLASSIF, OR ADJ AFTER N ≠ singular

2 Something that is **plural** consists of 2.1 more than one person or thing. EG *...plural occupancy of the throne.* ADJ CLASSIF = multiple 2.2 different kinds of people or things. EG *A democratic society is a plural society... We need a plural system of education, with different kinds of institutions.* ADJ CLASSIF = diverse

pluralism /pluərəlɪzə⁰m/; a formal word. **Pluralism** is 1 the existence of a variety of different people, opinions, or principles within the same society, system, or philosophy. EG *...the contemporary condition of pluralism and relativity... ...the pluralism and complexity of the real issues.* N UNCOUNT ◊ **pluralist**. EG *...a pluralist political system... ...a society that was increasingly multi-racial and pluralist.* ◊ ADJ QUALIT = mixed 2 the belief that it is good for a society, system, or philosophy to have a variety of different people, opinions, or principles. EG *...a one-system world whose opposite is pluralism, a chaos of opinions... The same push towards pluralism is evident in painting, too.* N UNCOUNT = diversification ◊ **pluralist, pluralists**. EG *'Are you a pluralist, then?'–'I'm a kind of anarchist, I suppose'... ...the promotion of humane, pluralist values.* ◊ N COUNT

pluralistic /pluərəlɪstɪk/. 1 A society, system, or philosophy that is **pluralistic** consists of a variety of different people, opinions, or principles. EG *...a pluralistic power structure... ...a complex, pluralistic society.* ADJ CLASSIF = pluralist

2 Someone who is **pluralistic** believes that it is good for a society, system, or philosophy to have a variety of people, opinions, or principles. EG *...a pluralistic approach to leisure.* ADJ CLASSIF = pluralist

plurality /pluəræləti¹/, **pluralities**. 1 A **plurality** of things is the existence of more than one of them. EG *It is necessary to acknowledge a plurality of aims... ...the plurality of belief systems in modern society.* N SING WITH DET +of = multiplicity

2 If a person or party has a **plurality** in an election, they have more votes than any other individual person or party, but not more than the total votes received by all the other people or parties. EG *They have a plurality in Congress but are just short of a majority.* N COUNT

plus /plʌs/, **pluses**. The form **plusses** is also used for the plural of the noun. 1 **Plus** is used 1.1 to show that one number or quantity is being added to another. 'Five plus three' is represented in figures as '5 + 3'. EG *What's seventeen plus nine?... Work out the full weekly rent, plus your rates... It costs £29 a bottle plus VAT.* PREP ≠ minus 1.2 after a number to show that the real number is more than the number mentioned. EG *...in my 25 years plus as a police officer... They take the exams at 13 plus.* ADJ AFTER N

2 A **plus** is a plus sign. EG *You need a plus there.* N COUNT

3 **Plus** five, **plus** eight, etc means five greater than zero, eight greater than zero, etc. EG *If the input voltage is plus three, it comes out as minus six.* PREP ≠ minus

4 **Plus** is also used in grading work in schools and colleges. A B plus is a better grade than a B, but it is not as good as an A minus. EG *Your marks seem to go up and down a bit, don't they?: C plus, D minus, B, D plus.* ADJ AFTER N ≠ minus

5 **Plus** is also used to introduce an additional item to one or more that you have already mentioned; an informal use. EG *Now five people, plus Val, are missing... You'll need a sense of humour, plus tolerance and patience... ...plus the fact that the woman is still regarded as the man's dependant... He wore strange scarves and beads, plus he was English.* CONJ COORD, OR PREP = as well as

6 A **plus** is also an advantage or good feature about a particular situation, course of action, etc; an informal use. EG *The offer had a number of plusses for us... On the plus side, you will have a private bath and telephone... This is certainly a plus point.* N COUNT = bonus

plush /plʌʃ/, **plusher, plushest**. 1 Something that is **plush** is very smart, comfortable, and expensive. EG *...his plush car with its reclining seats... ...a plush suburban house.* ADJ QUALIT = luxurious

2 **Plush** is a thick, soft material like velvet, used especially to cover furniture. EG *...deep red plush on the chairs... ...curtains of crimson plush.* N UNCOUNT

plushy /plʌʃi¹/, **plushier, plushiest**. Something that is **plushy** is very smart, comfortable, and expensive; an informal word. EG *...plushy interiors.* ADJ QUALIT = luxurious

plus sign, plus signs. A **plus sign** is the sign (+) which is put between two numbers in order to show that the second number is being added to the first one. It can also be put before a number to show that the number is more than zero (+3), and after a number to show that the real number is more than the one mentioned (18+). N COUNT ⇑ symbol

plutocracy /pluːtɒkrəsi¹/, **plutocracies**; a formal word. **Plutocracy** is the political system in which a country is ruled by its wealthiest people; also used to refer to the country or the people who rule it. EG *Newspapers are the organs of plutocracy.* N UNCOUNT/COUNT

plutocrat /pluːtə⁶kræt/, **plutocrats**. A **plutocrat** is someone who is powerful only because they are rich; a formal word used showing disapproval. EG *You're* N COUNT *nothing but a plutocrat... Bureaucrats and plutocrats thrive in every European capital.*

plutonium /plu:təʊnɪəm/ is a radioactive element used especially in nuclear weapons and as a fuel in nuclear power stations. EG *...nuclear explosive materials such as uranium or plutonium... ...plutonium radiation.* N UNCOUNT

ply /plaɪ/, **plies, plying, plied**; a rather literary word except in paragraph 6. 1 If you **ply** someone with food or drink, you keep on giving them more of it. EG *Dolly plied me with sweets... They had plied him with too much drink.* V+O+A(with) ⇑ supply

2 If you **ply** someone with questions, you keep asking them questions. EG *I plied him with questions about his novel.* V+O+A(with)

3 If a ship or boat **plies** somewhere, it makes regular journeys there, carrying people or goods. EG *...a new passenger liner to ply the North Atlantic route... Boats plied along the lake... ...the ferry that plies between Dover and Boulogne.* V+O, OR V+A ⇑ travel

4 If you **ply** a trade, you do a particular kind of work regularly as a profession. EG *Its difficult for window cleaners to ply their trade round here... Jim marvelled at the way his idol plies his craft... Hawkers plied up and down the platform.* V OR V+O : USU V+O

5 If you **ply** a tool, you use it. EG *They plied their paste brushes madly... The expert uses these three tools and plies them with patience.* V+O

6 **Ply** is 6.1 the thickness of wool, rope, etc, which is measured by the number of strands it is made from. EG *What ply wool will I need?... Two-ply would be best.* 6.2 the same as plywood. EG *...made of bonded ply, asbestos, and aluminium.* N UNCOUNT; N UNCOUNT ⇑ wood

plywood /plaɪwʊd/ is wood that consists of thin layers of wood stuck together. EG *...sheets of plywood... ...the flimsy plywood door.* N UNCOUNT

p.m. is used after a number to refer to a particular time between noon and midnight. EG *Can you come on Tuesday about 4 p.m.?... Some of the shops stay open until 7 p.m.* ADV : NUM+ADV

PM is an abbreviation for 'Prime Minister'; an informal use. EG *...the PM's speech to the conference... ...something that every previous PM has failed to do.* N PROPER : the+N

pneumatic /nju:mætɪk/. **Pneumatic** is used to describe something which is 1 operated by compressed air and is usually very powerful. EG *...a pneumatic drill... ...pneumatic hammers.* 2 pumped full of air. EG *...a pneumatic chair... ...pneumatic bags to lift the wings.* ADJ CLASSIF : ATTRIB; ADJ CLASSIF : ATTRIB

pneumonia /nju:məʊnɪə/ is a serious disease which affects your lungs and makes it difficult for you to breathe. EG *She nearly died of pneumonia.* N UNCOUNT

PO /pi: əʊ/is an abbreviation for 'Post Office' or 'postal order'.

poach /pəʊtʃ/, **poaches, poaching, poached**. 1 If someone **poaches** fish, animals, or birds, they illegally catch them on someone else's property. EG *He had been poaching deer... They can't poach herring from our waters.* ◇ **poaching**. EG *...the methods he used to discourage poaching.* V OR V+O; ◇ N UNCOUNT

2 If you **poach** a member of another organization or a player from another team, you secretly or dishonestly persuade them to join your one. EG *...charges of poaching members.* V+O

3 If someone **poaches** an idea, a book, etc, they dishonestly or illegally use the idea, publish the book, etc. EG *The paper regularly poaches other papers' scoops.* V+O = steal

4 If someone **poaches** on someone else's territory, they start doing a job or activity that is the other person's responsibility or privilege. EG *We shall see the computer beginning to poach on the preserves of human beings.* V+A = encroach

5 If you **poach** an egg, you remove its shell and cook the egg gently in boiling water. EG *...poached eggs and beans.* V+O

6 If you **poach** food such as fish, you cook it gently in boiling water or milk. EG *...poached salmon.* V+O = simmer

poacher /pəʊtʃə/, **poachers**. A **poacher** is someone who illegally catches fish, birds, or animals on someone else's property. N COUNT ⇑ person

PO Box is used before a number to refer to an address to which you can send letters, money, etc, which the Post Office keeps until they are collected by the person who has paid for the service. EG *...PO Box 48.* N COUNT : USU+NUM ⇑ box

pock /pɒk/, **pocks**. **Pocks** are small hollows on the surface of someone's skin, which are caused by disease. N COUNT

pocked /pɒkt/. Something that is **pocked** has pock-marks all over its surface. ADJ QUALIT

pocket /pɒkɪt/, **pockets, pocketing, pocketed**.
1 A **pocket** in a piece of clothing is a small bag that is sewn into the garment or onto the outside of it, and that is used for carrying small things such as money or a handkerchief. EG *She put her hand in her coat pocket.* N COUNT ⇑ pouch

2 If someone **pockets** something, 2.1 they put it in their pocket; a formal use. EG *I locked the door and pocketed the key.* 2.2 they take money or something valuable, especially when they have not got the right to do so. EG *She must have pocketed the rest of the money.* V+O; V+O ⇑ steal

3 **Pocket** is also used before a noun to indicate that something is small enough to fit into a pocket. EG *Wrapped in a white woollen scarf lay a pocket automatic.* N BEFORE N

4 A **pocket** in, for example, a suitcase or a car door is a pouch or bag which is attached to the object and which is used for putting things in. EG *Have you left the map in the driver's door pocket?* N COUNT

5 If you say that something will affect someone's **pocket**, you mean it will affect the amount of money that they have; an informal use. EG *Going to the opera isn't very good for my pocket.* N COUNT : USU POSS+N ⇑ income

6 A **pocket** of something is a small area where something is happening or which has a particular quality, and which is separated from other areas like it. EG *There were only pockets of fighting after the cease-fire... We sat in the pocket of warmth by the fire.* ● See also **air pocket**. N COUNT/PART

7 The **pockets** on a billiard, snooker, or pool table are the holes around the edge of the table and the pouches underneath which catch the balls. N COUNT ⇑ cavity

8 When a player **pockets** a ball in billiards, snooker, or pool, the ball goes into one of the pockets around the edge of the table. V+O : NO CONT

9 The word **pocket** is also used in the following fairly informal expressions. 9.1 If you **have** someone in your pocket or if they are **in your pocket**, they are willing to do whatever you tell them; used especially to indicate that that person is weak. EG *The mayor has the local police in his pocket.* 9.2 If people **live in each other's pockets**, they are always together and are very dependent on each other; used showing disapproval. 9.3 If someone **picks** your **pocket**, they steal something from your pocket, and you do not usually realize it until it has gone. 9.4 If someone is accused of **lining** their **pockets**, they are making a lot of money, especially dishonestly or by doing something unacceptable. EG *The nuclear arms race is lining the pockets of the arms manufacturers.* 9.5 If you have to **put** your **hand in** or **into your pocket**, you have to pay or give money to someone. EG *Will you put your hand in your pocket for the Spastics Society?* 9.6 If you are **out of pocket** after a financial exchange or deal with someone, you have less money than you should have or less than you had originally. EG *I don't want you to end up out of pocket.* PHR : VB INFLECTS; PHR : VB INFLECTS; PHR : VB AND N INFLECTS; PHR : VB INFLECTS ⇑ accumulate; PHR : VB AND N INFLECTS ⇑ spend; PHR : USED AS A ⇑ poorer

pocketbook /pɒkɪtbʊk/, **pocketbooks**. A **pocketbook** is 1 a small book or notebook which is small enough to carry in your pocket. 2 a woman's handbag which does not have straps for carrying it; used in American English. 3 a wallet or small case which is used for carrying money and papers; used in American English. N COUNT; N COUNT ⇑ bag; N COUNT

pocket calculator, pocket calculators. A **pocket calculator** is an electronic machine which does arithmetic calculations and is small and cheap enough to be used by many people. EG *Many children these days use pocket calculators in school.* N COUNT

pocketful /pɒkɪtfʊl/, **pocketfuls**. A **pocketful** of something is 1 the amount that a pocket will hold. EG *I collected two pocketfuls of shells from the beach.* 2 a lot of something, especially money; an informal use. EG *He must make pocketfuls of money in that job.* N COUNT/PART; N COUNT/PART

pocket handkerchief, pocket handkerchiefs. A **pocket handkerchief** is a small handkerchief; a rather old-fashioned word. N COUNT ⇑ cloth = hanky

pocket knife, pocket knives; also spelled as one word. A **pocket knife** is a small knife having several N COUNT = penknife blades which fold into the handle so that you can carry it around with you safely.

pocket money; also spelled with a hyphen. **Pocket money** is 1 money which is given to a child by his or her parents every week; used in British English. EG *When he was ten, his pocket money was 50p. a week... I only get a pound a week pocket money.* 2 a small amount of money that you use for small personal expenses. N UNCOUNT = allowance; N UNCOUNT = spending money

pocket-sized. Something that is **pocket-sized** is smaller than the usual size; an informal use. EG *This explains why two pocket-sized nations are at war.* ADJ CLASSIF

pockmark /pɒkmɑːk/, **pockmarks**. Pockmarks are small hollows on the surface of someone's skin which are caused by disease. N COUNT : USU PL ⇑ mark

pockmarked /pɒkmɑːkt/. If the surface of something is **pockmarked**, it has small hollow marks covering it. EG *The plane was making its approach to the pockmarked landing strip.* ADJ QUALIT = pitted

pod /pɒd/, **pods**. A **pod** is a seed container that grows on some plants such as peas or beans. N COUNT

podgy /pɒdʒi¹/. Someone who is **podgy** is fairly fat. EG *...a small, podgy girl.* ADJ QUALIT = chubby

podium /pəʊdɪəm/, **podiums**. A **podium** is a small platform on which someone stands in order to give a lecture, conduct an orchestra, etc. EG *He mounted the podium, to stare into 10,000 faces.* N COUNT = dais

poem /pəʊɪm/, **poems**. A **poem** is a piece of writing in which the words are chosen for their beauty, sound, or imagery and carefully arranged, often in short lines which rhyme. EG *...a selection of Robert Browning's poems... Get somebody to write a little poem which Edith could recite.* N COUNT

poet /pəʊɪt/, **poets**. A **poet** is a person who writes poems. EG *He was a journalist, poet, and writer of short stories.* N COUNT ⇑ writer

poetic /pəʊetɪk/. 1 Something that is **poetic** or **poetical** is very beautiful and expressive, or shows great depth of feeling, understanding, or sensitivity. EG *...a poetic and beautiful picture of the landscape... ...her father's resonant voice repeating the great poetical chapters in Isaiah.* ◊ **poetically**. EG *...as one Nigerian chief poetically remarked.* ADJ QUALIT; ◊ ADV WITH VB

2 **Poetic** or **poetical** also means relating to, or in the form of, poetry. EG *...poetic prose... ...a poetic tradition older than writing.* ADJ CLASSIF : ATTRIB

poetic justice. If you describe something that happens to someone as **poetic justice**, you mean that you consider it to be perfectly suitable or right, because of the very good or very bad things that that person has done in the past. EG *It was maybe poetic justice that I should now be on the receiving end.* N UNCOUNT ⇑ deserved

poetic licence is freedom from the normal rules of language and truth, such as is found in poetry. EG *We have to allow him a bit of poetic licence.* N UNCOUNT

poet laureate, poet laureates, poets laureate. The plural form can be either **poet laureates** or, in more formal English, **poets laureate**. The **poet laureate** is the poet who is chosen and paid by the British queen or king for the rest of the poet's lifetime and who writes poems for special occasions. N COUNT : ALSO IN TITLES

poetry /pəʊɪtri¹/ is 1 poems in general, considered as a form of writing or literature. EG *...a book of poetry... They print poetry and drama... ...a fine drawing room where poetry recitals were held.* 2 the art or skill of writing poems and the effect that is produced by the type of language used in poems. EG *Roger McGough revitalized poetry in England in the 1960s... The glory of the play and its magnificent poetry took you out of yourself.* 3 a quality of beauty, sadness, or greatness that people see or experience in something, and the powerful emotional effect that it has on them. EG *...the poetry of human existence... ...the magnificent poetry of his sculpture.* N UNCOUNT; N UNCOUNT ⇑ literature; N UNCOUNT + SUPP

pogo stick /pəʊgəʊ stɪk/, **pogo sticks**. A **pogo stick** is a toy consisting of a long metal pole with a spring in the lower end and a bar on which you can stand. You jump up and down on the bar, holding onto the top of the pole, and bounce along the ground. N COUNT

pogrom /pɒgrəm/, **pogroms**. A **pogrom** is an organized, official persecution which usually leads to mass killing of a group of people, usually for racial or religious reasons. EG *The Jews were periodically reminded of their status by pogroms encouraged by the State.* N COUNT = massacre

poignancy /pɔɪnj⁰ənsi¹/ is deeply felt distress or sorrow; a formal word. EG *It was a moment of extraordinary poignancy... There was a poignancy in the air.* N UNCOUNT ⇑ pathos

poignant /pɔɪnj⁰ənt/. Something that is **poignant** makes you feel great sorrow, because the distress is obviously very deeply felt. EG *One of the most poignant sights of childhood is the toddler howling for his mother... His cry of protest is still poignant today... ...narratives describing poignant tales of missed opportunities.* ◊ **poignantly**. EG *He poignantly describes poverty as it existed in his own childhood... I felt poignantly my daughter's grief, as well as my own.* ADJ QUALIT ⇑ moving = distressful; ◊ ADV WITH VB ⇑ movingly

poinsettia /pɔɪnsetɪə/, **poinsettias**. A **poinsettia** is a plant with groups of bright red or pink leaves that grows naturally in Central America and is popular as a houseplant. N COUNT ⇑ shrub

point /pɔɪnt/, **points**. 1 The word **point** is used in a number of different ways to refer to something that is said in a discussion, argument, or debate. 1.1 A **point** is something that you say and that expresses a particular fact or idea. EG *That's a very good point... We had quite a long argument on this point... There are a few points you might like to bear in mind... I want to make several quick points... This was a point I put to her in the interview.* 1.2 Someone's **point** is what they are saying and trying to persuade other people to accept. EG *Let me tell you a little story to illustrate my point... The bishop concluded that she had missed his point entirely.* 1.3 The **point** is the most important part of what you are saying, or the most important part of a discussion or conversation. EG *That's just the point... The point was that Dookie could not walk... You've all missed the point... Sorry, we're getting away from the point... The major point about this book is its scope.* N COUNT ⇑ statement; N SING : POSS+N ⇑ argument; N SING : *the*+N ⇑ essence

2 If you say that someone has **a point**, you are accepting what they have said and are going to think more carefully about it, even changing your own plans and opinions because of it. EG *'But it may be raining.'–'Well, that's a point. Shall we take an umbrella?'... You've got a point there.* N COUNT : USU a +SING

3 The word **point** is also used in the following expressions which refer to what people are saying in a discussion, argument, or debate. 3.1 If you can **see** someone's **point**, you understand what they mean or why they have been saying or doing particular things. EG *I see your point... He was irritated by their constant racism, and I could see his point.* 3.2 If you say to someone **'I take your point'**, you mean that you accept that what they are saying is true. EG *I take your point about needing new recordings.* 3.3 If you say to someone **'point taken'**, you are admitting to them that they are right and you are wrong in the argument or discussion. EG *OK, OK, point taken. Forget I said that.* 3.4 When someone **comes** or **gets to the point**, they start talking about the thing that is most important to them, rather than having an ordinary, unimportant conversation. EG *Philip, I may as well come straight to the point. I'm pregnant... 'Sit down, McFee,' I said, 'and get to the point.'* 3.5 If you **make** your **point** or **prove** your **point**, you prove that something is true, either by arguing about it in a discussion or writing, or by your actions or behaviour. EG *OK, OK, you can turn down the music now–you've made your point... To prove his point, Mr Higgerson gave me the letter.* 3.6 If you **get the point**, you understand something that people have been trying to show, prove, or explain to you. EG *Do you get the point?... I didn't even have to speak and she got the point.* 3.7 Something that is **beside the point** is not relevant to the subject that you are considering or discussing. EG *That's beside the point... In art as a whole the notion of taste is beside the point.* 3.8 Something that is **to the point** is relevant to the subject that you are considering or discussing, or expressed neatly without wasting words or time. EG *Her words were precise and to the point... His memos and letters are intelligible and to the point.* PHR : VB INFLECTS; CONVENTION; CONVENTION ⇑ understood; PHR : VB INFLECTS; PHR : VB INFLECTS; PHR : VB INFLECTS = get it; PHR : USED AS AN A = irrelevant; PHR : USED AS AN A ≠ wordy, inconsequential

4 You use the expression **'not to put too fine a point on it'** to say that you are about to speak plainly and directly, in a way that some people might find rude; used mainly in spoken English. EG *She was–not to put too fine a point on it–stupid and inept.* PHR : USED AS ADV SEN ⇑ frankly

5 A **point** is 5.1 a detail or particular aspect of something. EG *These two projects have some inter-* N COUNT, OR N UNCOUNT + *by*+N

esting points in common... On a point of information, Mr Chairman, may I correct the speaker?... This is just a minor point of criticism... The court dismissed the charges on a technical point... Taking it point by point, what do you think are the advantages and disadvantages of the scheme?. UNCOUNT **5.2** one of the items on a list or in an arrangement or process. EG *...the new five-point action programme... The main point on the agenda was left till the end of the meeting.* N COUNT : USU+SUPP **5.3** a particular characteristic, quality, or ability that someone has. EG *That's his best point, I think... Your strong points are your creativity and inventiveness... Thorpe's got his bad points but I like him on the whole.* N COUNT : MOD+N ⇑ feature

6 The word **point** is also used in the following expressions which refer to details or aspects of something. **6.1** The **finer points** of something are the details or aspects of it which are the most complicated and therefore the hardest to understand. EG *...the finer points of socialist-feminist theory... He alone truly appreciates its finer points.* PHR : USED AS S/O, WITH POSS = subtleties **6.2** If you say that something **has its points**, you mean that although you are criticizing it, you think that it does have some good qualities as well. EG *I suppose it's quite pretty in its way. It has its points.* PHR : VB INFLECTS **6.3** If someone in authority **stretches a point**, they allow another person to break the rules, because there are special reasons for doing so. EG *One might even stretch a point and let her off this time.* PHR : VB INFLECTS = bend the rules **6.4** ● **case in point**: see **case.** ● **in point of fact**: see **fact.** ● **sore point**: see **sore.** ● See also **selling point, talking point.**

7 If you **make a point of** doing something or **make it a point to** do something, you do something in a very deliberate way, especially so that other people will notice your behaviour. EG *You make a point of forgetting everything I have said... I made a special point of being sociable... I make it a point to look as healthy and attractive as I can.* PHR : VB INFLECTS

8 If you talk about the **point** of something, or say that there is no **point in** something, you are referring to its purpose or to how useful it is. EG *There's no point in talking to you... There was not much point in thinking about it... I didn't see the point of boring you with all this... What was the point in attempting to live together?* N SING WITH DET : USU+SUPP = sense

9 A **point** is also **9.1** a particular place or position, especially a precise one where a particular thing happens or is done. EG *We were nearing the point where the lane curved round to the right... Her gaze shifted to a point over my left shoulder... He walked up a driveway to reach a point from which he could survey the beach... An earthquake can strike at almost any point on the globe... The tanks turned off before reaching the ambush point.* N COUNT+SUPP = spot **9.2** a particular position on a line, shape, or object, or in a diagram or map. In drawings, this position is usually represented by a dot. EG *The circle passes through those two points... We'll label the points A and B.* N COUNT : USU+SUPP **9.3** one of the 32 marks on a compass that show direction, especially North, South, East, or West. N COUNT+SUPP **9.4** a dot that you can see in the distance, especially a dot of light. EG *...a light rotating around a moving point... The sky around those points of light was neither grey nor black.* N COUNT : USU+SUPP = speck **9.5** See also **focal point, jumping-off point, vantage point.**

10 The **point** of something such as a pin, needle, or knife is the thin, sharp end of it. EG *His moustache had been rolled into two tight points... It just has a short point.* N COUNT ⇑ tip

11 If you are at gun **point**, rifle **point**, etc, someone is pointing a gun or rifle at you and forcing you to do something. EG *Their opponents were excluded at gun point... He held me up at the point of a gun... The guardsmen herded them back at bayonet point.* N UNCOUNT+SUPP

12 A ballet dancer's **points** are the toes of his or her shoes. EG *Can you stand on your points?* N PLURAL

13 On a coastline, a **point** is a long thin piece of land which stretches away from the mainland into the sea. EG *Go east as far as the point... We rounded Cape Point, where the Atlantic meets the Indian Ocean.* N COUNT : USU SING, ALSO IN NAMES ⇑ peninsula

14 On a railway track, **points** are the levers and rails at the place where a single line divides into two or more lines. EG *The train rattled noisily over some points.* N COUNT : USU PL ⇑ junction

15 In spoken English, you use **point** to refer to the dot or mark that in decimal numbers separates the whole numbers from the fractions. EG *We take point nine six and multiply it by forty... ...four point eight kilohertz.* N UNCOUNT+NUM ⇑ symbol

16 You also use **point** to refer to **16.1** a particular time or moment. EG *At one point, I was dreadfully rude to a young woman... At this point the girl slowly sat up on the sofa... At the point of death, the old woman suddenly clutched his hand... There will come a point in the future when computers will be able to detect smells.* N COUNT+SUPP : USU SING = instant **16.2** a particular stage in the development of something, often when changes take place or something new begins to happen. EG *Do you ever reach a point where you just can't agree with her?... There comes a point in your school career when you find you have no respect for your teachers... The Trade Unions brought the economy to crisis point.* N COUNT+SUPP : USU SING

17 The word **point** is also used in the following expressions which refer to time or to a stage in a process or in the development of something. **17.1** You can use **at this point in time** to refer to the present time; an informal expression. EG *At this point in time we don't know.* PHR : USED AS AN A ⇑ now **17.2** The **high point** of a process or period of time is its best stage or moment. EG *His dinner had been the high point of his evening... This was the high point of their civilization.* PHR : USED AS C/O/S = zenith **17.3** The **low point** of a process or period of time is its worst stage or moment. EG *To the Kirks the summer represents the low point of the year.* PHR : USED AS C/O/S = nadir **17.4** If you say that someone is weak **to the point of** exhaustion, you mean that they are so weak that they are almost exhausted. EG *Claudia was sensitive to the point of self-consciousness... He was puzzled to the point of embarrassment... She hated him to the point of frenzy... I could not fall asleep unless I exercised to the point of exhaustion.* PHR+NG : USED AS AN A **17.5** If you are **on the point of** something, you are just about to do it. EG *As they were on the point of setting out, a light rain began to fall.... Capitalism was on the point of collapse and revolution was imminent.* PREP **17.6** If something happens **up to a point**, it happens only a little or to a certain extent. EG *He is indeed right, but only up to a point... Up to a point I totally agree with Catherine... 'You did not enjoy it?'–'Up to a point I did.'* PHR : USED AS ADV SEN ≠ totally **17.7** ● See also **boiling point, freezing point, starting point, turning point, vanishing point.** ● **point of no return**: see **return.** ● **saturation point**: see **saturation.**

18 In sport, competitions, games, etc, a **point** is one of the individual marks or scores that together make up a total mark or score. EG *She had a scorecard on which she kept track of the points they gained against each other... The panel of judges gave him the highest points.* ● to **score points** off someone: see **score.** N COUNT

19 A **point** is also **19.1** one of a set of equal marks on a scale that measures things, such as a weighing machine or a thermometer. N COUNT **19.2** an electric socket; used in British English. EG *The room contained a wash-basin, an electric-shaver point, a bed, a table, and a chair.* N COUNT

20 If you **point** at something, you show it to people by holding out your finger or an object such as a stick, so that if people look in the direction of your finger or the stick, they will see what you are showing. EG *My friend didn't say anything, he just pointed... He pointed at her as if he meant her to stand up... 'Over there,' she said and pointed to the bathroom door... He pointed a shaking finger at my friend and hissed with rage.* ● to **point the finger at** someone: see **finger.** V OR V+O : IF+PREP THEN *at/to* ⇑ gesture

21 If something **points** in a particular direction, it shows that direction, as for example when words are written on road signs or when footprints are left on a soft surface. EG *There was a street sign that pointed back down towards the cemetery.* V+A = indicate

22 To **point the way** means to show the direction in which something will progress or develop well, usually by providing a good example. EG *Our plan tries to point the way forward to a better life... She pointed the way in which care of the aged must proceed.* PHR : VB INFLECTS, USU+

23 If you **point** someone **in the direction** of something, you give them instructions on how to get there or how to do something; an informal expression. EG *Just point them in the right direction and send them to our department.* PHR : VB INFLECTS ⇑ direct

24 If something **points** in a particular direction, it is facing in that direction. EG *One of its four toes* V+A *pointed backwards... The snake lies with its body quite straight and pointing directly at its prey.*

25 If you **point** something at someone, you hold it so that the tip or end of it is nearest to that person. EG *They were horrified when I told them I had actually pointed a gun at someone... But is it acceptable to make such a film, to point the camera so relentlessly at a dying man?* — V+O+A ⇑ direct = level

26 If you **point** your toes, you stretch them outwards and downwards, especially when you are dancing. — V+O

27 If something **points** to a situation, it indicates that that situation exists or is likely to exist in the future. EG *Her questions point to a desire to know some vital truth... All of the forces that point to weak economic activity are evident... If one considers the direction in which this points, the outcome must be obvious.* — V+A

28 If you **point** to something that has happened or that is happening, you are using it as proof or evidence that a particular situation exists. EG *They pointed proudly to the administration's success in recent years... Critics point to the continuing instability of the company.* — V+A *(to)* = call attention

29 If you **point** a wall or a building, you put mortar or cement into the gaps between the bricks or stones so that the surface becomes sealed again. — V+O

30 See also **pointed, pointing.**

point out. If you **point** something **out**, **1** you cause people to notice it or to look at it, especially when you want them to recognize a particular person or thing amongst a group of similar people or things. EG *On car journeys we all used to shout and point out lovely places along the way... I can always remember and recognize plants after they have been pointed out to me... I'll point him out to you.* — PHRASAL VB: V+O+ADV ⇑ show **2** you make a comment that gives people an important new piece of information or corrects their mistaken ideas. EG *She pointed out that he was wrong... 'It's a golden opportunity, really,' Johnson pointed out... Mr Merritt pointed this problem out to you the other day.* — PHRASAL VB: V+O+ADV, OR V+ADV+QUOTE/REPORT-CL ⇑ indicate

point up. If you **point up** something, you emphasize it; a formal expression. EG *US officials pointed up the similarities in these policies.* — PHRASAL VB: V+O+ADV = highlight

point-blank. 1 If you say something **point-blank**, you say it very directly, or even rudely, without any apologies or explanations. EG *She refused the offer point-blank... The Chancellor denied it point-blank... ...a point-blank refusal to discuss any matters concerning her sister.* — ADV, OR ADJ CLASSIF: ATTRIB = outright

2 If you shoot someone or something **point-blank**, you shoot them when the gun is touching or almost touching them. EG *I shot him in the brain, point-blank... ...shooting at point-blank range.* — ADV, OR ADJ CLASSIF: ATTRIB

pointed /pɔɪntɪ[2]d/. **1** Something that is **pointed** has a point at one end. EG *His daughter has a pointed nose... Its jaws are pointed.* — ADJ CLASSIF ⇑ sharp

2 Comments or behaviour that are described as **pointed** express unpleasant reactions such as criticism or warning in a very obvious way. EG *Etta gave another pointed look in their direction... She made two pointed comments.* — ADJ QUALIT = barbed ◊ **pointedly.** EG *She kept sighing and looking pointedly out of the window... 'How old is he?' Freya asked pointedly.* — ◊ ADV WITH VB

pointer /pɔɪntə/, **pointers.** A **pointer** is **1** something such as a piece of advice which helps you to understand a situation or to find a way of working or making progress. EG *She gave him a few more pointers... ...a list of things that seemed to be pointers to the truth of what happened.* — N COUNT ⇑ indication **2** a long, thin stick that teachers use to point to maps, screens, and large charts or diagrams. — N COUNT: USU SING **3** the long thin piece of metal that moves along a dial or the face of a measuring instrument, pointing at numbers so that you can read measurements. EG *The pointer on a good weighing machine should be very accurate.* — N COUNT: USU SING = needle **4** a hunting dog that shows where wild animals or birds are hiding, by standing very still and pointing towards them with its nose. — N COUNT

pointing /pɔɪntɪŋ/ is a way of repairing the outside of a building by filling in the holes between the bricks or stones. EG *...the way people do pointing on stonework.* ▸ also used to refer to the cement between bricks or stones in a wall. EG *We've got leaking drainpipes and worn pointing.* — N UNCOUNT

pointless /pɔɪntlɪ[2]s/. Something that is **pointless** has no use, sense, or purpose. EG *...pointless violence... It all seemed pointless to me... It is pointless to try to apportion blame.* — ADJ QUALIT = senseless ◊ **pointlessly.** EG *He had pointlessly hurt her.* — ◊ ADV WITH VB = senselessly

point of order, points of order. A **point of order** is an objection that someone makes in a formal debate because the proper rules of behaviour or organization have been broken; a formal expression. EG *On a point of order from the chairman, the constitution was amended.* — N COUNT: USU SING

point of reference, points of reference. A **point of reference** is something which you use to help you understand a situation or to communicate with someone. EG *We have nothing in common to talk about, no points of reference.* — N COUNT

point of view, points of view. 1 A **point of view** is **1.1** the opinions or attitudes that a particular person or group has about something. EG *I take a different point of view... We understand your point of view.* — N COUNT = viewpoint **1.2** a way of looking at or considering something. EG *An outsider who can offer a fresh point of view may stimulate new ideas.* — N COUNT: USU SING = angle

2 If you discuss or consider something **from a** particular **point of view** or **from the point of view of** a particular thing, you are using one particular aspect of a situation in order to judge or assess that situation. EG *From a practical point of view it is quite irrelevant... From the commercial point of view, they have little to lose... We'll consider the problem from the point of view of the way it was handled.* — PHR: USED AS AN A

poise /pɔɪz/ is **1** a calm, dignified, self-controlled manner. EG *She received me with incredible poise for one so young.* — N UNCOUNT = aplomb **2** a graceful, very controlled way of standing and moving. EG *...a beautiful girl of about fourteen with the grace and poise of a natural model.* — N UNCOUNT = elegance

poised /pɔɪzd/. **1** If a part of your body is **poised**, you are holding it in the air so that it is completely still but ready to move at any moment. EG *He waited with fingers poised over the keys... His hand was poised halfway to his mouth with an empty pipe.* — ADJ CLASSIF: PRED, USU+A = suspended

2 If someone is **poised** to do something, they are completely ready to take action at any moment. EG *...powerful military forces, poised for invasion... He was poised to become champion.* — ADJ CLASSIF: PRED, USU+*to*-INF/*for* = all set

3 If you are **poised**, you are calm, dignified, and self-controlled. EG *She was poised and diplomatic on the telephone.* — ADJ QUALIT: PRED = self-possessed

poison /pɔɪzə[n]n/, **poisons, poisoning, poisoned. 1 Poison** is a substance that harms or kills people or animals if it is swallowed or absorbed by them. EG *It was deadly poison and if he drank it he'd probably die... The use of poisons in Britain is controlled by legislation.* — N UNCOUNT/COUNT • If you hate something **like poison**, you hate it very much indeed; an informal expression. EG *They all hate them like poison.* — • PHR: VB INFLECTS ⇑ greatly • If you say that someone **is poison**, you mean that they are extremely unpleasant and nasty; a rather old-fashioned expression. EG *She's absolute poison.* — • PHR: VB INFLECTS

2 If you **poison** a person or animal, you deliberately kill them or make them very ill by means of poison. EG *He had been poisoned with strychnine... It was quite common for dogs to be poisoned this way.* — V+O ⇑ harm ◊ **poisoning.** EG *The poisoning had not been accidental.* — ◊ N UNCOUNT

3 If you **are poisoned** by a substance, it makes you very ill. EG *You can also be poisoned by agricultural and industrial wastes... ...the total number of people poisoned by pesticides in the developing world.* — V+O: USU PASS ⇑ be harmed ◊ **poisoning.** EG *Thousands of swans die of lead poisoning each year.* — ◊ N UNCOUNT: USU MOD+N • See also **blood poisoning, food poisoning.**

4 If something such as food, drink, or a weapon **is poisoned**, it has had poison added to it so that it can be used to harm or kill a person or animal. EG *They killed huge elephants with tiny, poisoned darts... ...a poisoned whisky bottle.* — V+O: USU PASS

5 If water, air, land, etc, **is poisoned**, it has been damaged by harmful substances, for example chemicals. EG *The countryside is poisoned and devastated... ...our poisoned air and polluted streams and lakes.* — V+O: USU PASS = be contaminated

6 To **poison** a situation, relationship, etc, means to spoil it in an unpleasant and nasty way so that you no longer feel happy and optimistic about it. EG *...the despair that poisoned the Romantic movement... He had poisoned the political life of the nation... ...an atmosphere poisoned by fascism.* — V+O = taint

7 If someone **poisons** your **mind** against another person, they make you dislike that person, especially — PHR: VB INFLECTS, USU+

by telling you things that are not true; used showing disapproval. EG *She had poisoned their minds against him.* — against

poisoner /pɔɪzə⁰nə/, **poisoners**. A **poisoner** is someone who has killed or harmed another person or other people by using poison. — N COUNT ↑ killer

poison gas is a gas that is poisonous and usually used to kill people, for example in war or to execute criminals. EG *The use of poison gas was outlawed by international convention.* — N UNCOUNT ↑ weapon

poisonous /pɔɪzə⁰nəs/. 1 Something that is **poisonous** will kill people or animals or make them ill if it is swallowed or absorbed by them. EG *...a poisonous plant... Never eat rhubarb leaves–they're poisonous.* — ADJ QUALIT ↑ dangerous = toxic

2 An animal that is **poisonous** produces a poison that will kill you or make you ill if you are bitten by the animal or if you eat it. EG *...one of the most poisonous snakes in the world.* — ADJ QUALIT ↑ dangerous

3 If you describe something as **poisonous**, you mean that it is extremely unpleasant and likely to spoil or destroy a good relationship, situation, etc; a formal use. EG *The article contained some fairly poisonous allegations about his social behaviour... ...the poisonous egotism of Hamilton.* — ADJ QUALIT = vicious

4 If you describe someone as **poisonous**, you mean that they are very unpleasant and you feel that you cannot trust them. EG *You are the most poisonous man I know.* — ADJ QUALIT = venomous

poison-pen letter, poison-pen letters. A **poison-pen letter** is a very unpleasant letter that tells you nasty things about yourself or someone close to you in order to upset you or to cause trouble. EG *Imagine receiving a poison-pen letter or an obscene telephone call.* — N COUNT

poke /pə͟ʊk/, **pokes, poking, poked**. 1 If you **poke** someone or something, you quickly push them with something sharp, for example your finger. EG *People poked and prodded the students with their umbrellas... He's always poking me in the eye with his elbow... You almost poked my eye out... Ralph sat down and began to poke little holes in the sand.* — V+O = dig, jab
▸ used as a noun. EG *Len gave him an affectionate poke.* — ▸ N COUNT = prod

2 If you **poke** one thing into another, you make a pushing movement with the first thing so that it goes into the second thing. EG *Never poke a finger or scissors into an electric socket.* — V+O+A = insert

3 If you **poke** a fire, you push it with a poker so that it burns better. EG *She was on her knees, poking the fire.* — V+O, OR V+A (at)

4 If something **pokes** out of or through something else, it appears from behind or underneath something else, while still remaining partly hidden. EG *A bottle of wine poked out of a silver ice bucket... Blades of grass poked up between the paving stones... ...an old armchair with a rusty spring poking through the fabric.* — V+A = stick, jut

5 If you **poke** your head out of or through an opening or it **pokes** out of or through an opening, you push it through the opening, especially so that you can see someone or something more easily. EG *The driver slowed down and poked his head out of the window to stare... His secretary poked her head through the door.* — V-ERG+A = stick

6 • to **poke fun at** someone: see **fun**. • a **pig in a poke**: see **pig**.

poke about. If you **poke about** or **poke around** for something, you search for it in a particular place, usually by moving lots of objects around in a rather vague manner; an informal expression. EG *He poked about in the undergrowth... He was lying flat on his stomach, poking around under the bed with his arm.* — PHRASAL VB: V+ADV, USU+A = grope around

poke at. If you **poke at** something, you make lots of little pushing movements at it with something sharp. EG *The chef poked at his little pile of ashes.* — PHRASAL VB: V+PREP, HAS PASS = prod

poker /pə͟ʊkə/, **pokers**. 1 **Poker** is a card game that people usually play in order to win money. EG *His main hobby was poker... Ray was playing poker with two friends.* — N UNCOUNT

2 A **poker** is a metal bar which you use to move coal or wood in a fire so that it burns better. EG *She stirred the fire with the poker.* — N COUNT ↑ rod

poker face, poker faces. A **poker face** is an expression on your face that shows none of your thoughts or feelings; an informal expression. EG *Keep calm, keep a poker face and proceed methodically.* — N COUNT = straight face

poker-faced. If you are **poker-faced**, you have a calm expression on your face which shows none of your thoughts and feelings; an informal word. — ADJ CLASSIF = impassive

poky /pə͟ʊki¹/, **pokier, pokiest**; also spelled **pokey**. A room or house that is **poky** is uncomfortably small and ugly; an informal word. EG *Her flat has three poky little rooms and a kitchen.* — ADJ QUALIT = cramped

polar /pə͟ʊlə/. 1 **Polar** means concerned with or related to the area around the North and South Poles. EG *...the melting of the polar ice caps... Most insects do not live in polar regions.* — ADJ CLASSIF: ATTRIB

2 **Polar** also describes things which are completely opposite in character, quality, type, etc; a formal use. EG *...the polar extremes of 'totalitarianism' and 'democracy.'* — ADJ CLASSIF: ATTRIB

polar bear, polar bears. A **polar bear** is a large white bear which lives near the North Pole. — N COUNT

polarise /pə͟ʊləraɪz/. See **polarize**.

polarity /pə⁵lærɪti¹/, **polarities**. If you talk about the **polarity** between two people or things, you mean that they are completely different from each other because they have opposite qualities, principles, opinions, etc. EG *We must not view politics exclusively in terms of the left/right polarity. ...the polarities of good and evil.* — N UNCOUNT/COUNT = polarization

polarize /pə͟ʊləraɪz/, **polarizes, polarizing, polarized**; also spelled **polarise**. If people **polarize** or something **polarizes** them, they form into two separate groups which hold opposite or conflicting positions or opinions. EG *In countries like Britain the political debate is polarized between two major parties... The hunger strike has further polarized Ulster's population... The socialist movement had become polarised by 1880.* ◊ **polarization** /pə͟ʊləraɪzeɪʃə⁰n/. EG *...a growing world polarisation between rich and poor countries.* — V-ERG: USU PASS ↑ divide = split; ◊ N UNCOUNT ↑ division

Polaroid /pə͟ʊlərɔɪd/, **Polaroids**. 1 A **Polaroid** is a photograph taken with a Polaroid camera. — N COUNT

2 **Polaroid** is a trademark for a special substance that is used to treat glass, so that the amount of glare shining through the glass from bright light is reduced. EG *...Polaroid glasses.* — N UNCOUNT

3 **Polaroids** are sunglasses which have been treated with Polaroid in order to reduce the glare of the sun. EG *I must get myself a new pair of Polaroids.* — N PLURAL: ALSO a pair of+N

Polaroid camera, Polaroid cameras. A **Polaroid camera** is a trademark for a small camera that can take, develop, and print a photograph in a few seconds. EG *A Polaroid camera can be extremely useful at times.* — N COUNT

pole /pə͟ʊl/, **poles**. 1 A **pole** is 1.1 a long, thin piece of wood or metal, used especially for supporting things or for pushing a small boat along. EG *...tent poles... ...telegraph poles... He climbed down the pole to the ground.* 1.2 one of the two ends of the earth's axis, or of the axis of any other planet. • See also **North Pole, South Pole**. 1.3 one of two completely opposite qualities, opinions, beliefs, etc. EG *Political theories have tended to crystallize around two opposite poles, with many variations in between.* • If you say that two people are **poles apart**, you mean that they hold completely different beliefs and opinions. EG *Politically they were poles apart.* — N COUNT ↑ stick; N COUNT: USU MOD+N; N COUNT = extreme; • PHR: USED AS AN A = worlds apart

2 A **Pole** is someone who comes from Poland. EG *...a Pole of genius, Joseph Conrad.* — N COUNT

poleaxe /pə͟ʊlæks/, **poleaxes, poleaxing, poleaxed**. 1 A **poleaxe** is a very large axe, usually used for killing cattle. — N COUNT

2 To **poleaxe** a person or animal means to hit them so hard that they become unconscious. EG *He collapsed as if poleaxed.* — V+O ↑ stun

poleaxed; an informal word. If you are **poleaxed**, 1 you are so surprised or shocked that you do not know what to say or do. EG *I was completely poleaxed by the news.* 2 you are extremely drunk. EG *He was really poleaxed the other night.* — ADJ QUALIT: PRED; ADJ QUALIT: PRED

polecat /pə͟ʊlkæt/, **polecats**. A **polecat** is a small, fierce, wild animal rather like a weasel, which lives in Europe, Asia and North Africa. Polecats have a very unpleasant smell. — N COUNT

polemic /pəlemɪk/, **polemics**. 1 A **polemic** is a fierce written or spoken attack on a particular doctrine, belief, or opinion, or a defence of a doctrine, belief, or opinion. EG *Williams wrote a splendid polemic in my favour... ...Sartre's great polemics against his friends... ...an endless swirl of discussion, debate, and polemic.* — N COUNT/UNCOUNT ↑ argument

2 Polemics is the skill or practice of arguing passionately for or against a doctrine, belief, or opinion. EG *This could lead to less polemics and a more practical attitude towards talks.*
N UNCOUNT

polemical /pəlemɪkə⁰l/ means arguing fiercely and passionately for or against a doctrine, belief, or opinion. EG *...a polemical book arguing the case for better adult education in Britain... When I made that statement I was being polemical.*
ADJ CLASSIF ↑ argumentative

polemicist /pəlemɪsɪst/, **polemicists**. A **polemicist** is someone who is skilled at arguing passionately for or against a doctrine, opinion, or belief; a formal word.
N COUNT ↑ debater

Pole Star. The **Pole Star** is the star that is nearest to the North Pole in the Northern hemisphere.
N SING : *the*+N

pole vault, pole vaults. A **pole vault** is a very high jump which athletes make over a high bar, using a long, flexible pole to help lift themselves up.
N COUNT

police /pə⁰liːs/, **polices, policing, policed**. 1 The **police** are **1.1** the official organization in a country responsible for making sure that people obey the law, for protecting people and property, and for arresting criminals. EG *The police were called... Contact the police as soon as possible after a burglary... Three police cars arrived.* ● See also **military police, secret police**. **1.2** men and women who are members of this organization. EG *280 people were arrested and 117 police and demonstrators injured... The protesters surrendered to police after about an hour.*
N PLURAL : *the*+N; N PLURAL ↑ people

2 To **police** a place means to preserve law and order in it by means of the police or another organization such as the army. EG *It is impossible to police such a vast area.* ● See also **community policing**.
V+O ↑ control

police constable, police constables. A **police constable** is a policeman or policewoman of the lowest rank. EG *...Police Constable Jones... ...a uniformed police constable.*
N COUNT : ALSO IN TITLES = PC

police force, police forces. A **police force** is the police organization in a particular country or area. EG *We have the finest police force in the world... ...the Greater Manchester Police Force.*
N COUNT : ALSO IN NAMES

policeman, policemen. The word **policeman** is pronounced /pə⁰liːsmə⁰n/ in both the singular and the plural. A **policeman** is a man who is a member of the police force. EG *He had been a policeman for six years... ...the death of two policemen.*
N COUNT = police officer

police officer, police officers. A **police officer** is a policeman or policewoman.
N COUNT

police state, police states. A **police state** is a state or country in which the government controls people's freedom by means of the police, especially secret police; used showing disapproval.
N COUNT

police station, police stations. A **police station** is the local office of a police force in a particular area. EG *A youth was being questioned at Cannon Row police station... I once spent a night in a police station.*
N COUNT : ALSO IN NAMES

policewoman, policewomen. The word **policewoman** is pronounced /pə⁰liːswʊ¹mə⁰n/ in the singular and /pə⁰liːswɪmɪn/ in the plural. A **policewoman** is a woman who is a member of the police force.
N COUNT

policy /pɒlɪsi¹/, **policies**. A **policy** is **1** a general set of ideas or plans that has been officially agreed on by people in authority and which is used as a basis for making decisions, especially in politics, economics, or business. EG *I give you my word there is no change in our policy... He was criticized for pursuing a policy of reconciliation... ...two television debates on economic and foreign policy.* **2** a document which shows the agreement that you have made with an insurance company. EG *It is advisable to read the small print on your policy... This service is free to policy holders.*
N COUNT/UNCOUNT : USU+SUPP ↑ plan; N COUNT

polio /pəʊlɪəʊ/ is a serious infectious disease caused by a virus. It often causes paralysis in the person who has the disease. EG *She had been crippled by polio.*
N UNCOUNT = poliomyelitis

poliomyelitis /pəʊlɪəʊmaɪəlaɪtɪs/ is the same as polio; a technical word. EG *...vaccinations for poliomyelitis and tetanus.*
N UNCOUNT

polish, polishes, polishing, polished. The word **polish** is pronounced /pɒlɪʃ/ for paragraphs 1 to 3 and the phrasal verbs. It is spelled with a capital letter and pronounced /pəʊlɪʃ/ for paragraphs 4 and 5. **1 Polish** is a substance that you put on the surface of an object in order to clean it, protect it, and make it shine. EG *You should use wax polish on wooden furniture... ...silver polish... ...liquid polish.*
N UNCOUNT : USU MOD+N

2 If you **polish** something, **2.1** you put polish on it. EG *Leather needs polishing with good quality cream.* ▸ used as a noun. EG *He wanted to give it a real polish.* ◊ **polished**. EG *She slipped and fell on the polished wooden floor.* **2.2** you rub it with a cloth to make it shine. EG *He polishes his spectacles with a handkerchief before answering.* ▸ used as a noun. EG *She gave her glasses a quick polish.* ◊ **polished**.
V OR V+O; ▸ N SING : *a*+N; ◊ ADJ QUALIT; V OR V+O; ▸ N SING : *a*+N; ◊ ADJ QUALIT

3 Polish is also the pleasing and elegant style of something which makes it of better quality than other similar things; used showing approval. EG *It's an honest book but it hasn't got polish.*
N UNCOUNT = poise, elegance

4 Polish means belonging or relating to Poland, its people, or their language. EG *Her mother was Polish... It was a dramatic moment in Polish history.*
ADJ CLASSIF

5 Polish is also the language spoken by people who live in Poland.
N UNCOUNT

polish off. **1** If you **polish off** food, you eat all of it. EG *We can polish off this plate of bacon and eggs easily.*
PHRASAL VB : V+O+ADV ↑ finish

2 If you **polish off** a job, you finish it completely and quickly. EG *Last year's papers were polished off in half an hour.*
PHRASAL VB : V+O+ADV ↑ complete

polish up. **1** If you **polish up** a particular ability or skill, you improve it by working at it. EG *I want to go to evening classes to polish up my French.*
PHRASAL VB : V+O+ADV = perfect

2 If you **polish up** an object, you rub it with a cloth to make it shine. EG *My sister had the spoons and was polishing them up with a yellow duster.*
PHRASAL VB : V+O+ADV

polished /pɒlɪʃt/. **1** Someone who is **polished** shows confidence and sophistication in social situations. EG *She is a polished woman... He had the most polished, sophisticated manner.*
ADJ QUALIT = refined, suave

2 If you describe an ability or skill as **polished**, you mean that it is of a very high standard. EG *My German was not very polished.*
ADJ QUALIT = accomplished

polisher /pɒlɪʃə/, **polishers**. A **polisher** is a machine that is used for polishing something. EG *...a floor polisher.*
N COUNT

Politburo /pɒlɪtbjʊərəʊ/, **Politburos**. The **Politburo** in a communist country is the chief committee that makes policies and decisions. EG *The Politburo decided that he should be stripped of his power.*
N COUNT : USU *the*+SING

polite /pəlaɪt/, **politer, politest**. **1** Someone who is **polite** has good manners and behaves in a way that is socially correct and considerate of other people's feelings. EG *One could always rely on him to be polite and do the right thing... It's polite to ask before you help yourself... He was very polite to his superiors... If you write for a leaflet it is polite and sensible to enclose a stamped addressed envelope... ...a polite refusal... That was the politest way he could think of saying it.* ◊ **politely**. EG *He thanked me politely... An embarrassed Derek was trying to explain politely that he needed his meal now... After knocking politely at the door, he went in.* ◊ **politeness**. EG *I do expect reasonable politeness and consideration.*
ADJ QUALIT = courteous; ◊ ADV WITH VB = courteously; ◊ N UNCOUNT = courtesy

2 Polite describes things that you say or do simply because it is socially correct to do or say them, rather than because you mean them sincerely. EG *Emma was talking about the weather and trying to make polite conversation... ...a polite smile.* ◊ **politeness**. EG *Such feelings tend to remain submerged beneath a mask of social politeness.*
ADJ CLASSIF ↑ civil; ◊ N UNCOUNT ↑ civility

3 Polite society and **polite** company refer to the people in society who consider themselves to be socially superior to others and who feel that they are setting a standard of behaviour for other people to follow. EG *...the conventional norms of polite European society.*
ADJ CLASSIF : ATTRIB = refined

politic /pɒlɪtɪk/, **politics**. **Politic** is an adjective and **politics** is an uncount noun. **1 Politics** refers to the actions or activities which people use to achieve power in a country, society, or organization or which ensure that power is used in a particular way. EG *He has remained active in British politics and in the politics of the wider world... Emily has never had the slightest interest in politics... He was active in Liberal politics... ...an awareness of the realities of politics and diplomacy... ...local politics... ...office politics.*
N PLURAL/UNCOUNT

2 Someone's **politics** are their beliefs about how a country ought to be governed. EG *...the early influence of socialist ideas on his politics... I have no*
N PLURAL : USU WITH POSS

politics... Her politics at this time could be described as radical.

3 Politics also refers to the study of the ways in which a country is governed and power is acquired and used in that country. EG *She went up to Cambridge at the age of seventeen to read Politics, Philosophy and Economics.* N UNCOUNT

4 If you say that something is **politic**, you mean that it seems to you to be the most sensible or prudent thing to do in the circumstances, particularly with regard to your own interests so that you gain an advantage or achieve a goal; a formal use. EG *It might be more politic to tell him yourself than let him find out from someone else... ...the politic thing to do.* ADJ QUALIT ↑ tactful = expedient

political /pəlɪtɪkəºl/. **1 Political** means relating to politics. EG *...the British political scene... ...the major political parties... ...political developments... ...serious political discussion... He was sent to jail for his political views... These years proved to be the climax of his political career... ...demands for political and religious freedom.* ◊ **politically**. EG *We must change our attitudes if we want to continue to participate politically in Europe... The public services ought to be politically impartial... It's a country which is peaceful, politically stable and prosperous.* ADJ CLASSIF: USU ATTRIB ◊ ADV

2 Someone who is **political** is interested in politics and holds strong beliefs about it. EG *He was always very political... I had never been a political animal.* ADJ QUALIT

political asylum is the protection given by a government to foreigners who leave their own country for political reasons. EG *She asked for political asylum in this country and was refused.* N UNCOUNT ↑ asylum

political economy is the study of the way in which a government influences or organizes a nation's wealth. N UNCOUNT ↑ economy

political prisoner, political prisoners. A **political prisoner** is someone who has been imprisoned because they have expressed views that are hostile to or critical of their own government. N COUNT

political science is the study of the ways in which power is acquired and used in a country, especially by those who govern the country. EG *He has agreed to give guest lectures in political science at ten different colleges this year.* N UNCOUNT

political scientist, political scientists. A **political scientist** is someone who studies and lectures about political science. N COUNT

politician /pɒlɪtɪʃəºn/, **politicians**. A **politician** is someone whose job is politics, especially one who is a member of parliament or who is involved in some way in governing a country. EG *Haldane was a Scottish lawyer, philosopher and politician... ...professional diplomats and politicians.* N COUNT

politicize /pəlɪtɪsaɪz/, **politicizes, politicizing, politicized**; also spelled **politicise**. If you **politicize** someone or something, you make them more political or make them more involved in or aware of politics. EG *I believe that it is absurd to politicize the content and subject matter of text books... The environmental movement became increasingly politicized.* ◊ **politicization** /pəlɪtɪsaɪzeɪʃəºn/. EG *...the increasing politicization of the country.* V+O ◊ N UNCOUNT

politicking /pɒlɪtɪkɪŋ/ is political activity that people take part in, usually to gain votes or for their own personal advantage; often used showing disapproval. EG *There was little in his frenetic politicking which gave any hint of future statesmanship.* N UNCOUNT

politico /pəlɪtɪkəʊ/, **politicoes**. A **politico** is a politician; an offensive word, used showing disapproval. EG *I was accused by a visiting politico of being a bourgeois individualist.* N COUNT

politico- is added to adjectives to form other adjectives that describe something as being both political and the other thing that is mentioned. EG *...a politico-economic strategy.* PREFIX

polity /pɒlɪti¹/, **polities**. A **polity** is an organized society, such as a nation, city, or church, together with its government and administration; a formal word. EG *...the classic conservative yearning for an ordered polity... ...geographical India, consolidated into a polity by Britain.* N COUNT

polka /pɒlkə/, **polkas**. A **polka** is a fast, lively dance that was popular in the nineteenth century and at the beginning of the twentieth century; also used of a piece of music composed in the rhythm of this dance. N COUNT

polka dot, polka dots. **Polka dots** are lots of spots printed on a piece of cloth; used especially when the cloth is part of a woman's dress. N COUNT: USU PL ↑ dot

poll /pəʊl/, **polls, polling, polled**. **1** A **poll** is a survey in which people are asked their opinions about something such as a famous person or a political party, usually in order to find out how popular something is or to predict what will happen in the future. EG *On all the reputable public opinion polls the Tories have lost a lot of ground... Late last year the polls gave the President a 10 to 15 point lead.* N COUNT

2 To **poll** someone means to ask them what they think about something such as a famous person or political party. EG *A majority of those polled wanted 'stricter law enforcement'.* V+O ↑ canvass

3 The **polls** means a political election. EG *A massive attempt to convince people to boycott the polls... The party won a convincing victory at the polls with an overall majority of ninety-seven seats... We'll still be squabbling about it when we go to the polls.* N PLURAL: the+N

4 If a political party or a candidate **polls** a particular number of votes, they get that number of votes as a result of an election. EG *In 1959 they only polled 43.7% of the votes... He polled 1,781 votes... We had polled heavily in provincial elections.* V+O, OR V+A ↑ amass = net

5 ● See also **deed poll, polling**.

pollarded /pɒlɑːdɪ²d/. A **pollarded** tree has had its top branches cut off so that it grows more bushy; a technical term. EG *A hawk was hovering in the air above some pollarded willows.* ADJ CLASSIF: ATTRIB ↑ pruned

pollen /pɒlən/ is a fine powder produced by flowers that fertilizes other flowers of the same species so that they produce seeds. N UNCOUNT

pollen count, pollen counts. A **pollen count** is a measurement of the amount of pollen in the air at a particular place and time. EG *We can expect a high pollen count over the next week or so.* N COUNT

pollinate /pɒlɪneɪt/, **pollinates, pollinating, pollinated**. To **pollinate** a plant or tree means to fertilize it with pollen. EG *The plant may pollinate itself.* ◊ **pollination** /pɒlɪneɪʃəºn/. EG *Planting trees in groups rather than long thin lines helps pollination.* V+O ◊ N UNCOUNT

polling /pəʊlɪŋ/ is the act of voting in an election. EG *The result of the polling will be known tomorrow morning.* N UNCOUNT

polling day, polling days. **Polling day** is the day on which people vote in an election. EG *Will you need transport on polling day?* N UNCOUNT/COUNT ↑ date

polling station, polling stations. A **polling station** is a place where people go to vote at an election. It is often a school or other public building. N COUNT

pollutant /pəluːtənt/, **pollutants**. A **pollutant** is a substance that pollutes the environment, especially a poisonous chemical that is produced as a waste product of an industrial process. EG *The main pollutants in this country are sulphur dioxide and smoke.* N COUNT ↑ contaminant

pollute /pəluːt/, **pollutes, polluting, polluted**. To **pollute** the water, air, atmosphere, etc means to make it dirty, impure, and dangerous for people and animals to live in or to use, especially by means of poisonous chemicals. EG *Our water supply is becoming polluted with nitrates... ...the polluted atmosphere of towns and cities.* V+O = contaminate

pollution /pəluːʃəºn/ is **1** the process of polluting the water, air, atmosphere, etc, especially by means of poisonous chemicals. EG *...changes in the climate due to pollution of the atmosphere by industrial waste... ...environmental pollution.* **2** the unpleasant substances that pollute the water, air, atmosphere, etc. EG *She was horrified by all the pollution on the beach.* N UNCOUNT ↑ impurity = contamination; N UNCOUNT ↑ contamination

polo /pəʊləʊ/ is a game played between two teams of players. The players ride horses and use long-handled wooden hammers to hit a ball in an attempt to score goals. EG *...a polo match.* N UNCOUNT

polo-necked. A **polo-necked** or **polo-neck** sweater has a thick fold of material at the top which covers most of a person's neck. EG *...a navy-blue polo-necked jumper.* ADJ CLASSIF: ATTRIB

poltergeist /pɒltəgaɪst/, **poltergeists**. A **poltergeist** is an invisible force that some people believe can move furniture, throw objects, etc, in a house, and which they often think of as a type of ghost. EG *...the reality of flying saucers and poltergeists.* N COUNT

poly /pɒli¹/, **polys**. A **poly** is the same as a polytechnic; an informal word, used mainly in British English. EG ...*a poly student.* N COUNT ⇑ college

polyandry /pɒli¹ændri¹/ is the custom in some societies in which a woman can be married to more than one man at the same time; a technical term. N UNCOUNT ⇑ polygamy

polyester /pɒli¹ɛstə/ is a substance that is produced by a chemical process and used especially to make clothes. EG ...*polyester skirts.* N UNCOUNT ⇑ fabric

polyethylene /pɒli¹ɛθı¹li:n/ is the same as polythene; used mainly in American English. EG ...*a waterproof material such as polyethylene.* N UNCOUNT ⇑ plastic

polygamy /pəlɪgəmi¹/ is the custom in some societies in which someone can be married to more than one person at the same time; a technical term. N UNCOUNT ⇑ marriage

polyglot /pɒli¹glɒt/, **polyglots**. **Polyglot** is used to describe a book, society, etc, in which several different languages are used; a formal word. EG ...*a polyglot culture.* ▸ used to refer to a person who speaks or understands many languages. ADJ CLASSIF = multilingual ▸ N COUNT ⇑ linguist

polygon /pɒli¹gɒn/, **polygons**. A **polygon** is a shape made by three or more straight lines or sides; a technical term in geometry. N COUNT ⇑ figure

polymath /pɒli¹mæθ/, **polymaths**. A **polymath** is a person who is very knowledgeable in many different subjects; a formal word. N COUNT ⇑ expert

polymer /pɒli¹mə/, **polymers**. A **polymer** is a chemical compound with large molecules made of many smaller molecules of the same kind. Some polymers exist naturally and others are produced in laboratories and factories. EG *Most modern paints are based on polymers... ...a degree in polymer science.* N COUNT

Polynesian /pɒlıni:ʒı⁰ən/, **Polynesians**. **1** A **Polynesian** person or thing comes from or relates to Polynesia. EG ...*Polynesian carvings... ...Polynesian girls.* ADJ CLASSIF **2** A **Polynesian** is a person who comes from Polynesia. EG ...*the needs of the Polynesians.* N COUNT

polyp /pɒlıp/, **polyps**. A **polyp** is **1** a small animal that lives in the sea. It has a hollow body like a tube and tentacles around its mouth. EG ...*coral polyps... ...strange growths of coral, polyp, and weed.* N COUNT/UNCOUNT **2** a small, unhealthy growth on a surface inside your body, especially inside your nose. N COUNT

polyphony /pə⁷lıfəni¹/ is the playing of several different melodies, the singing of different lines of a song, etc, at the same time in a piece of music; a technical term. EG ...*rhythmic polyphony... ...twelve-part polyphony.* N UNCOUNT

polystyrene /pɒli¹staıri:n/ is a very light, plastic substance used especially to make containers or as an insulating material. EG ...*shapes cut from cardboard or polystyrene... ...polystyrene ceiling tiles.* N UNCOUNT

polysyllable /pɒli¹sıləbə⁰l/, **polysyllables**. A **polysyllable** is a word that has more than two syllables; a technical term. N COUNT ≠ monosyllable

polytechnic /pɒli¹tɛknık/, **polytechnics**. A **polytechnic** is a college, especially in Britain, where you can go after leaving school in order to study academic subjects at various levels up to degree level or to train for particular jobs. EG ...*a course in drama at Manchester Polytechnic... ...universities, polytechnics, teacher training colleges.* N COUNT : ALSO IN NAMES

polythene /pɒli¹θi:n/ is a type of plastic usually made into thin sheets or bags and used especially to keep food fresh or to keep objects dry. EG *Cover it tightly with polythene... ...a polythene bag.* N UNCOUNT

polyunsaturated /pɒli¹ʌnsætjə⁴reıtı²d/ is used to describe substances such as oil and margarine that are made mainly from vegetable fats and are thought to be better for your health than those made from animal fats. EG *Ground nut oil has a high percentage of polyunsaturated fatty acids... ...butter on her toast instead of polyunsaturated margarine.* ADJ CLASSIF

polyurethane /pɒli¹jʊərəθeın/ is a plastic material used especially to make paint or types of foam and rubber which prevent water or heat from passing through them. EG ...*polyurethane paints.* N UNCOUNT

pom /pɒm/, **poms**. A **pom** is the same as a pommy.

pomegranate /pɒmi¹grænıt/, **pomegranates**. A **pomegranate** is a round fruit with a thick, reddish skin. It contains lots of small seeds with juicy flesh around them; used also of the tree on which it grows. EG ...*figs, pomegranates, and olives.* N COUNT

pommel /pʌmə⁰l, pɒm-/, **pommels, pommelling, pommeled**. **1** A **pommel** is **1.1** the knob on the end of the handle of a sword. N COUNT **1.2** the part of a saddle that rises up at the front, or a knob that is fixed there. N COUNT

2 To **pommel** means to **pummel**; used in American English. V OR V+O

pommy /pɒmi¹/, **pommies**. The singular is sometimes spelled **pommie**. A **pommy** is an English person; a slightly offensive word used mainly in Australian English. N COUNT : ALSO VOC

pomp /pɒmp/ is the use of a lot of people, fine clothes, decorations, etc, usually at a public ceremony. EG ...*coming ashore with pomp and ceremony... ...the mystery, awe, and pomp surrounding royalty.* N UNCOUNT ⇑ display

pom-pom /pɒm pɒm/, **pom-poms**. A **pom-pom** is a small ball of wool or other material used to decorate caps, furniture, etc. EG ...*a black knitted cap with a red pom-pom.* N COUNT

pomposity /pɒmpɒsıti¹/ is very serious behaviour or speech which shows that you think you are more important than you really are; a formal word, used showing disapproval. EG *'At the Foreign Office? You'd find out what pomposity really means there!'... They were annoyed by my pomposity, my insistence on taking the blame for the whole affair.* N UNCOUNT ⇑ self-importance

pompous /pɒmpəs/. **1** Someone who is **pompous** tries to behave or speak in a very serious way, because they think they are more important than they really are; used showing disapproval. EG *Anything I say now is bound to sound pompous... 'You pompous idiot! Can't you see what you've done?'... ...a pompous document of over 500 pages.* ADJ QUALIT ⇑ self-important = grandiose ◇ **pompously**. EG *Universities ought to stand for, putting it rather pompously, improving the human condition.* ◇ ADV WITH VB

2 A **pompous** building or ceremony is built or arranged in a grand and very elaborate style. EG ...*a pompous monument... ...a pompous celebration.* ADJ QUALIT ⇑ magnificent

ponce /pɒns/, **ponces, poncing, ponced**; a very informal word. **1** A **ponce** is the same as a pimp. N COUNT ▸ used as a verb. EG *If you walk down the road with a boyfriend, he's accused of poncing.* ▸ V

2 If you call a man a **ponce**, you are insulting him because you think that he is too fussy in the way he dresses and in his manners. EG *That little ponce!* N COUNT : ALSO VOC

3 If you say that someone **is poncing** about or **poncing** around, you mean that they are not doing something properly, quickly, or seriously; used showing disapproval. V+A *(about/around)*

poncho /pɒntʃəʊ/, **ponchos**. A **poncho** is a piece of clothing that consists of a long piece of material, usually wool, with a hole cut in the middle through which you put your head. Some ponchos are made of waterproof material and have a hood. EG ...*a Peruvian wool poncho.* N COUNT ⇑ cloak

pond /pɒnd/, **ponds**. A **pond** is a small area of water, smaller than a lake, often one that has been artificially created. EG ...*an ornamental pond they had in the garden... Another frog builds its own ponds on the margins of forest pools... ...pond weeds.* N COUNT = pool

ponder /pɒndə/, **ponders, pondering, pondered**. If you **ponder**, you think about something carefully; a rather literary word. EG *Hooper seemed to ponder for a moment, then he nodded... Mary pondered bitterly upon the meaning of life... ...pondering what to do... I wanted to ponder the next move quietly.* V OR V+O : USU+REPORT-CL/*on/upon* ⇑ consider = cogitate

ponderous /pɒndə⁰rəs/; a rather literary word. Someone or something that is **ponderous** is **1** very dull and serious, with no excitement or humour. EG *He spoke in a slow, ponderous way... ...the ponderous nature of their play... ...the ponderous guards with their rifles.* ADJ QUALIT ⇑ solemn = pedestrian ◇ **ponderously**. EG *She nodded ponderously... His manner was ponderously formal.* ◇ ADV **2** large and heavy. EG ...*a table with ponderous legs... ...ponderous royal tombs.* ADJ QUALIT = massive **3** very slow or clumsy in their movements. EG ...*taking a ponderous swing at the ball.* ADJ QUALIT = laboured ◇ **ponderously**. EG *Slowly, ponderously, the vehicle shifted a few inches... Pringle was moving ponderously about.* ◇ ADV WITH VB = laboriously

pong /pɒŋ/, **pongs, ponging, ponged**. **1** A **pong** is an unpleasant smell; a very informal word, used in British English. EG *There was a pong in the room.* N COUNT = stink ▸ used as a verb. EG *The bazaars ponged of spices... 'Pooh! It pongs!'* ▸ V : IF+PREP THEN *of*

2 See also **ping-pong**.

pontiff /pɒntıf/, **pontiffs**. The **pontiff** is the pope; a formal word. N PROPER : *the*+N

pontifical /pɒntıfıkə⁰l/. If someone behaves in a **pontifical** way, they behave as if they have total ADJ QUALIT ⇑ authoritative knowledge or complete authority in a situation; a formal word, often used showing disapproval. EG *'Mrs Waites,' said Mr Willet, in his pontifical manner, 'is well-meaning, but ignorant.'... The lawyer, with pontifical gravity, sat on a high chair.*

pontificate /pɒntɪfɪkeɪt/, **pontificates, pontificating, pontificated**; a formal word. 1 If someone **pontificates**, they state their opinions as if they are the only correct ones and nobody could possibly argue against them. EG *A man pontificated that all good ideas are simple... He was always pontificating.* — V OR V+REPORT-CL; ⇑ expound = hold forth

2 The **pontificate** of a pope is the period of time during which he is pope. EG *...the sadly brief pontificate of Pope John Paul I.* — N COUNT: WITH POSS

pontoon /pɒntu:n/, **pontoons**. 1 A **pontoon** is a floating platform, often one used to form or support a bridge. EG *...pontoon bridges... They float on pontoons.* — N COUNT

2 **Pontoon** is a card game in which players try to collect a set of cards which do not add up to more than twenty-one. — N UNCOUNT

pony /pəʊni^1/, **ponies**. A **pony** is a type of horse which is smaller in size than an ordinary horse. EG *...riding our ponies all over the farm... ...wild ponies... ...pony carts.* — N COUNT

ponytail /pəʊni^{1}teɪl/, **ponytails**; also spelled with a hyphen and as two words. A **pony tail** is a hairstyle used especially by young girls in which their hair is tied up at the back of the head and hangs down like a tail. EG *...her hair tied back in a pony tail... ...her pony tail swinging down over her face.* — N COUNT

poodle /pu:dəl/, **poodles**. A **poodle** is a type of dog with thick, curly hair. EG *...a breeder of pedigree poodles.* — N COUNT

poof /pʊf, pu:f/, **poofs**; also spelled **pouf**; an informal word, used in British English. 1 A **poof** is a homosexual man; an offensive use. — N COUNT/VOC

2 Some people say **poof 2.1** to indicate that something happened very suddenly. EG *...just like that, poof!* — EXCLAM **2.2** to express scorn, disbelief, or impatience. EG *Poof! There's nothing to talk about. If you can't, you can't.* — EXCLAM = pooh, bah

pooh /pu:/; an informal word. 1 **Pooh** is used **1.1** to express disapproval or scorn. EG *Pooh! That's an old idea and it's never worked.* — EXCLAM **1.2** to express disgust at an unpleasant smell; used mainly in British English. EG *Pooh! It stinks in here!* — EXCLAM

2 **Pooh** is excrement; used in British English and mainly by children. — N UNCOUNT

pooh-pooh /pu: pu:/, **pooh-poohs, pooh-poohing, pooh-poohed**. If someone **pooh-poohs** an idea or suggestion, they consider it foolish, impractical, or unnecessary; an informal word. EG *He pooh-poohed Thomas's anxieties about it... Sally pooh-poohed the idea that you need three meals a day.* — V+O; ⇑ dismiss = deride

pool /pu:l/, **pools, pooling, pooled**. 1 A **pool** is **1.1** a small area of still or slow-moving water. EG *...stretches of sand with rocks and pools... ...the pool where the waterfall is... The river dries up into a string of stagnant pools.* — N COUNT; ⇑ pond **1.2** a swimming pool. EG *She went swimming in the hotel pool... ...pools, tennis courts, and stables.* — N COUNT

2 A **pool** of liquid, light, etc is a small area of it on a surface. EG *He was lying dead in a pool of blood... A spotlight threw a pool of violet light onto the stage... ...a pool of paint.* — N COUNT+*of*; = puddle

3 A **pool** of people, money, things, etc is a quantity or number of them that are deliberately collected together to be used or shared by several people or organizations. EG *...27 players and a pool arrangement in which all clubs would participate... ...car pools... ...the pool of trained men... ...the remaining pools of cash.* — N COUNT+SUPP; ⇑ supply = fund

4 If people or organizations **pool** their money, knowledge, workers, or equipment, they allow them to be collected and used for a particular purpose or to be shared by all of them. EG *We pooled our money, bought a van, and travelled... They pooled their food resources... ...pooling their information.* — V+O; = combine

5 **Pool** is a game played on a table with six holes around the edges. Players use long, thin cues to hit hard, coloured balls with numbers on them into the holes. EG *...the pool room... ...a pool table.* — N UNCOUNT

6 If you do the **pools**, you take part in a type of gambling competition in which people try to win money by guessing correctly the results of football matches; used in British English. EG *...pools coupons... They won 300,000 pounds in the Pools.* — N PLURAL: *the*+N

poop /pu:p/, **poops**. The **poop** of an old-fashioned sailing ship is the raised structure at the back end of it. — N COUNT

pooped /pu:pt/. If you are **pooped**, you are very tired; used mainly in informal American English. EG *Morris was pooped, but curiosity kept him moving along.* — ADJ QUALIT: PRED; = exhausted

poor /pʊə, pɔ:/, **poorer, poorest**. 1 Someone who is **poor** has very little money and few possessions. EG *I was a student then, and very poor... ...a poor family... He was also one thousand pounds poorer.* — ADJ QUALIT; = impoverished, indigent
▸ The **poor** is used to refer to people who are poor. EG *In the cities the poor are as badly off as they were in the villages... ...the rural poor.* — ▸ N PLURAL: *the*+N; = needy

2 A **poor** country, part of a country, part of a city, etc is inhabited mainly by people with very little money and few possessions. EG *...a poor part of Stratford... ...aid to the poorer countries... The gap between rich and poor regions widened.* — ADJ QUALIT; ≠ rich

3 If you say **'Poor girl'**, **'Poor Bill'**, etc, you are expressing sympathy for someone who is ill, unhappy, or unfortunate, or regret for someone who has died. EG *Poor little thing!... Poor old Dennis, he can't do a thing right... I heard over the radio that poor Barry had been murdered.* — CONVENTION

4 An object that is **poor** in quality or condition has not been made very well or looked after very carefully. EG *...books in a very poor condition... ...poor housing conditions... The quality of the photograph was poor.* — ADJ QUALIT; = bad, unsatisfactory ◇ **poorly**. EG *...a very narrow road, poorly maintained... ...poorly designed equipment.* — ◇ ADV WITH VB; = badly

5 An action, activity, or event that is **poor** is not done skilfully or organized efficiently, and is therefore unsuccessful or unsatisfactory. EG *Maurice did a rather poor dive... He had made a poor job of it... I had a poor education... ...Britain's poor economic performance.* — ADJ QUALIT; = feeble ◇ **poorly**. EG *...the excursions were poorly planned.* — ◇ ADV WITH VB

6 If you say that someone is a **poor** worker, athlete, etc, you mean that they are not very skilful in an activity. EG *He was a poor performer at sports... I am a poor businessman... She was a very poor swimmer.* — ADJ QUALIT: ATTRIB; ⇑ bad = rotten ◇ **poorly**. EG *I spoke Spanish so poorly.* — ◇ ADV WITH VB

7 If someone has **poor** eyesight, a **poor** memory, etc, they are not able to see very well, remember things, etc, for example because they are not well or are getting old. EG *...poor lungs... I've got a very poor memory.* — ADJ QUALIT; ⇑ bad = deficient ◇ **poorly**. EG *The child is eating poorly... She had been sleeping poorly.* — ◇ ADV WITH VB

8 If someone is in **poor** health, they are ill. EG *My father was a cripple, my mother in poor health... In spite of poor health, I was able to continue working.* — ADJ QUALIT; ⇑ bad

9 If you describe an amount, number, or rate as **poor**, you mean that it is less than expected or than is considered reasonable. EG *The pay was poor... ...educational results for boys are poorer... ...the poor attendance at dinner that night.* — ADJ QUALIT; ⇑ small = low ◇ **poorly** . EG *...a poorly paid occupation... ...poorly funded and under-equipped.* — ◇ ADV WITH VB

10 When the weather is **poor**, it is cold, cloudy, foggy, or rainy. EG *...poor weather conditions.* — ADJ QUALIT; ⇑ bad

11 If you describe something as **poor** in a desirable quality or valuable substance, you mean that it contains very little of it. EG *The water was tepid and poor in oxygen... Their food was poor in nutritive value.* — ADJ QUALIT: PRED+*in*; ⇑ inadequate

-poor is used after nouns to form adjectives indicating that something has very little of the thing mentioned, usually a thing that is considered desirable or valuable, EG *...energy-poor countries.* — COMB: FORMS ADJ CLASSIFS; ≠ -rich

poorhouse /pʊəhaus, pɔ:-/, **poorhouses**; also spelled with a hyphen. In former times in Britain, a **poorhouse** was an institution in which poor people could live. It was paid for by the public. EG *...the Dickensian image of a nineteenth-century poorhouse.* — N COUNT

poorly /pʊəli^1, pɔ:-/. If someone is **poorly**, they are ill; an informal word, used in British English. EG *They were all feeling very poorly... Your brother's had an operation and he's quite poorly.* • See also **poor**. — ADJ QUALIT: PRED; = sick

poor relation, poor relations. If you describe one thing as a **poor relation** of another, you mean that it is similar to or part of the other thing but inferior to it. — N COUNT; ⇑ version

pop /pɒp/, **pops, popping, popped.** 1 **Pop** is 1.1 modern music that is popular among young people and usually has a strong rhythm and uses electric or electronic equipment. EG *...pop music... ...pop concerts... ...a pop group... ...the rapidly changing pop culture.* 1.2 a flavoured fizzy drink such as lemonade; an informal use. EG *...soda pop... ...a bottle of pop.* N UNCOUNT / N MASS

2 **Pop** is used to refer to or to address your father; used mainly in informal American English. EG *Pop and I went for walks... This goose is great, Pop.* N PROPER/VOC = dad, pa

3 **Pop** is used to represent a short sharp sound, for example the sound made by bursting a balloon or by pulling a cork out of a bottle. EG *The cork came out with a loud pop... The light bulb went pop.* N COUNT OR ADV

4 If something **pops**, it makes a short sharp sound. EG *The engine began coughing and popping ... The cork popped and flew out of her hand.* V

5 You say that your ears **pop** to describe the feeling in your ears when you move very quickly upwards or downwards, for example in a lift. V

6 If you say that someone's eyes **pop**, you mean that they are very surprised or excited; an informal use. EG *Frankie's eyes were popping with amazement.* ● See also **pop-eyed**. V : USU+A *(out)* = protrude = bulge

7 When something **pops** or you **pop** it, it bursts open, usually with a short sharp sound. EG *Colin popped the balloon with a pin... His pot belly was popping the buttons on his shirt.* V-ERG

8 If you **pop** something somewhere, you put it there; an informal use. EG *He popped a piece of gum into his mouth.* V+O+A

9 If you **pop** your head, face, or nose into a room, office, etc, you briefly look inside or do something quickly and leave. EG *A man popped his head into the room and said, 'Next, please.'* V+O+A

10 If someone or something **pops** from a position where they were hiding or could not be seen, they suddenly move into a position where you can see them. EG *Suddenly she popped out from behind a bush... Just then a letter popped through the letterbox.* V+A ⇑ emerge

11 If you **pop** somewhere, you go there for a short time and often unexpectedly. EG *Why don't you pop in for a coffee and a chat... I'm just popping out for a haircut... The cook kept popping up from the kitchen.* V+A = nip

12 ● to **pop the question**: see **question**.

pop off. If someone **pops off**, they die; an informal expression, used mainly in British English. EG *He could pop off any day now.* PHRASAL VB : V+ADV

pop on. 1 If you **pop on** a piece of clothing, you put it on; an informal expression. EG *Pop your coat on.* PHRASAL VB : V+O+ADV

2 If you **pop on** a piece of equipment, you switch it on so that it works; an informal expression. EG *I'll just pop the kettle on.* PHRASAL VB : V+O+ADV

pop up. If someone or something **pops up**, they appear in a place or situation unexpectedly. EG *Your name has popped up from time to time... If a person tries to bury such feelings they only pop up somewhere else-as tenseness, for example.* ● See also **pop-up**. PHRASAL VB : V+ADV = crop up

pop. is an abbreviation for 'population'; used especially before a number to indicate the total population of a city or country. EG *...pop. 120 million.*

popadam /pɒpədəm/. See **poppadum**. N COUNT

pop art is a style of modern art which began in the 1960's. It uses bright colours, styles of drawing from popular sources such as advertising and comics, and objects from modern everyday life as its subjects. N UNCOUNT

popcorn /pɒpkɔːn/ consists of grains of maize that are heated until they burst and become large and light in texture. You can add salt or sugar to the popcorn before eating it. EG *...a bag of popcorn.* N UNCOUNT ⇑ corn

Pope /pəʊp/, **Popes.** The **Pope** is the head of the Roman Catholic Church. EG *The Emperor was crowned by the Pope... ...Pope John Paul II.* N PROPER/N COUNT : ALSO IN TITLES

popery /pəʊpəri[1]/ is used to refer to the beliefs, practices, and teachings of Roman Catholics by people who are opposed to them. N UNCOUNT

pop-eyed. If you say that someone is **pop-eyed**, you mean that their eyes are wide open because they are surprised or excited; an informal word. EG *...sauntering, pop-eyed tourists.* ADJ QUALIT : ATTRIB = goggle-eyed

popish /pəʊpɪʃ/ is used to describe the beliefs, practices, and teachings of Roman Catholics by people who are opposed to them. ADJ CLASSIF : ATTRIB

poplar /pɒplə/, **poplars.** A **poplar** is a type of tall, thin tree; used also of the wood from this tree. EG *...a country road lined with poplars... ...a bench under a poplar tree.* N COUNT/UNCOUNT

poplin /pɒplɪn/ is a type of cotton material used to make clothes. EG *...a dress of striped poplin... ...a poplin blouse.* N UNCOUNT ⇑ fabric

poppa /pɒpə/. Your **poppa** is your father; an informal word, used mainly in American English. N PROPER/VOC

poppadum /pɒpədəm/, **poppadums**; also spelled **papadom, popadam**, etc. A **poppadum** is a very thin, circular crisp made from a mixture of flour and water which is fried in oil. Poppadums are usually eaten with Indian food. N COUNT

popper /pɒpə/, **poppers.** A **popper** is a device for fastening clothes, bags, etc. It consists of two pieces of plastic or metal, one with a small lump on it and the other with a small hole in it. You press the two bits together in order to fasten the popper; used in British English. N COUNT

poppet /pɒpɪt/, **poppets. Poppet** is used in informal British English to refer to or address a child or someone you are very fond of. EG *'Whatever you say, poppet.'* N COUNT : ALSO VOC = pet, sweetie

poppy /pɒpi[1]/, **poppies.** A **poppy** is 1 a plant with a large, delicate, red flower. Opium is obtained from one type of poppy. EG *...a big bunch of poppies.* 2 an artificial poppy which is worn in Britain on a particular day in November in memory of those who died in the two world wars. EG *Would you like to buy a poppy?* N COUNT / N COUNT

poppycock /pɒpi[1]kɒk/ is used to refer to something which you think is nonsense; an old-fashioned and informal word. EG *You're talking utter poppycock.* N UNCOUNT = drivel, rubbish

Poppy Day is the day in Britain on which people remember those who died in the two world wars; an informal expression. EG *...the Queen laying her Poppy Day wreath.* N PROPER/N COUNT

Popsicle /pɒpsɪkə[0]l/, **Popsicles.** A **Popsicle** is a trademark in the USA for a piece of ice flavoured with fruit that is frozen onto a stick and eaten as a sweet. EG *...sucking on a coconut Popsicle.* N COUNT

populace /pɒpjə[4]ləs/. The **populace** of a country refers to all its people, especially the ordinary people in contrast to the leaders; a formal word. EG *They represented only a fraction of the general populace... The populace went wild... ...uniting the broad masses of the populace.* N SING : *the*+N ⇑ inhabitants = masses

popular /pɒpjə[4]lə/. 1 Something that is **popular** is enjoyed or liked by a lot of people. EG *The Tower of London is the most popular tourist attraction in Britain... Swimming is very popular with all ages... ...popular music.* ◇ **popularity** /pɒpjə[4]lærɪti[1]/. EG *...the popularity of science fiction films... In Britain, lager is gaining in popularity.* ADJ QUALIT ≠ unpopular / ◇ N UNCOUNT = appeal

2 **Popular** ideas or attitudes are those which are approved of or held by most people. EG *There is genuine popular support for these proposals... Contrary to popular belief, science does not offer us certainties... ...the popular image of feminism.* ADJ CLASSIF : USU ATTRIB = widespread, general

3 **Popular** newspapers, television programmes, etc are aimed at the needs or tastes of ordinary people and not the specialists in a particular subject. EG *The popular press is obsessed with the Royal Family... Television can be both informative and popular... ...a series of popular talks on medicine.* ADJ CLASSIF : USU ATTRIB

4 Someone who is **popular** is liked by most people, or by most people in a particular group. EG *He has always been popular among Conservatives... She is very popular with the general public... He became a popular Governor.* ◇ **popularity** /pɒpje[4]lærɪti[1]/. EG *...his immense popularity with radio audiences... ...the popularity of the new President.* ADJ QUALIT / ◇ N UNCOUNT = appeal

5 **Popular** is used to describe political activities which are open to or involve all people, and not just members of parliament, members of a particular party, etc; a formal use. EG *...not a mere party issue, but deserves wider popular debate... ...her advocacy of popular democracy... Arguments among its supporters destroyed the campaign as a popular movement.* ADJ CLASSIF : ATTRIB = democratic, public

popularize /pɒpjə[4]ləraɪz/, **popularizes, popularizing, popularized**; also spelled **popularise.** 1 To **popularize** something means to make a lot of people interested in it and able to enjoy it. EG *Television has done a lot to popularize snooker.* V+O

2 To **popularize** an academic subject, a scientific V+O

idea, etc, means to make it more easily understandable to ordinary people; a formal use. EG *Scientific notions soon become slipshod and inaccurate when they are popularized.*

popularly /pɒpjə⁴ləli¹/ is used to indicate 1 that a name or term you mention is used by most ordinary people but is not the official name or term. EG *The statue is popularly known as the 'Golden Man and Horse'... This theory was popularly called the Big Bang.* 2 that an idea you mention is believed by most people, although it may not be true. EG *It is popularly believed that eating carrots makes you see better in the dark.*
ADV WITH VB ↑ widely = commonly
ADV WITH VB ↑ widely = commonly

populate /pɒpjə⁴leɪt/, **populates, populating, populated.** 1 If an area **is populated** by people or animals, those people or animals live there, often in large numbers. EG *The town is heavily populated by immigrants... The water was populated by slimy, savage things... The rabbits who so thickly populated the area.* ◊ **populated.** EG *...the less populated islands... ...the densely populated countryside.*
V+O : USU PASS ↑ inhabit
◊ ADJ QUALIT ↑ inhabited

2 To **populate** an area means to cause plants, animals, or people to live there. EG *Convicts from France were sent to populate the islands... ...a socialist miracle that would populate the desert.*
V+O : IF+PREP THEN with

population /pɒpjə⁴leɪʃə⁰n/, **populations.** The **population** of a country or area refers to 1 all the people who live in it. EG *The country is unable to feed its population... ...13% of the population.* 2 the number of people who live in it. EG *What is the population of Calcutta?... Kandahar has a population of 230,000... ...a population explosion... ...the increase in population.* 3 all the people or animals of a particular type in it. EG *...civilian populations... ...a prison population of 44,000... In these areas, populations of mosquitoes are greatly reduced.*
N COUNT
N COUNT/ UNCOUNT
N COUNT : USU+ SUPP

populism /pɒpjə⁴lɪzə⁰m/ refers to political activities or ideas that are based on the interests and opinions of ordinary people, sometimes involving the use of people's fears or prejudices in order to achieve political success; a formal word. EG *...the party's abandonment of populism and its surrender to the middle-class socialists... It was a short step from populism to racism.* ◊ **populist, populists.** EG *Its ideology was more populist than bourgeois... ...a populist senator.*
N UNCOUNT ↑ democracy
◊ ADJ CLASSIF/N COUNT

populous /pɒpjə⁴ləs/. A **populous** country or area has a lot of people living in it; a formal word. EG *...the less populous areas of London... ...the world's fifth most populous country.*
ADJ QUALIT = populated

pop-up. 1 A **pop-up** book, usually a children's book, has pictures that stand up when you open the pages.
ADJ CLASSIF : ATTRIB

2 A **pop-up** toaster has a mechanism that pushes slices of bread up when they are toasted.
ADJ CLASSIF : ATTRIB

porcelain /pɔːsə⁰lɪ³n/ is a hard, shiny substance made by heating clay. It is used to make delicate and expensive cups, plates, and ornaments. EG *...antique pottery and porcelain... ...a porcelain statue.*
N UNCOUNT ↑ china = bone china

porch /pɔːtʃ/, **porches.** A **porch** is 1 a sheltered area at the entrance to a building. It has a roof and sometimes has walls. EG *...the church porch... ...a big house with a glass porch.* 2 a raised platform built along the outside wall of a house and often covered with a roof; used mainly in American English. EG *...sitting beside me on the back porch... She was wheeled out on to her porch, as if it were a stage.*
N COUNT ↑ shelter
N COUNT ↑ terrace = veranda

porcine /pɔːsaɪn/. If you describe someone as **porcine**, you mean that they look like a pig; a literary word. EG *...a bald porcine old man... She had faintly porcine features.*
ADJ QUALIT

porcupine /pɔːkjə⁴paɪn/, **porcupines.** A **porcupine** is an animal that has many long, thin, sharp quills on its back. The quills stick out as protection when it is attacked.
N COUNT ↑ rodent

pore /pɔː/, **pores, poring, pored. Pores** are 1 the small holes in the skin of people and animals. EG *...the pores round his nose.* 2 the small holes on the surface of plants. EG *...mushrooms with minute yellow pores.* 3 the tiny gaps or cracks in rocks and soil. EG *...water trapped in pores in rocks... They clog the pores of the soil.*
N COUNT ↑ cavity
N COUNT ↑ orifice
N COUNT ↑ cavity

pore over. If you **pore over** information, especially in the form of writing, maps, or charts, you look at it and study it very carefully. EG *Monks pored over ancient texts... ...poring over the statistics.*
PHRASAL VB : V+ PREP, HAS PASS

pork /pɔːk/ is meat from a pig, usually fresh and not smoked or salted. EG *...pork chops... ...bacon, ham, and pork.*
N UNCOUNT

pork pie, pork pies. A **pork pie** is a round pie with cooked pork inside the pastry. EG *...pork pies and sausage rolls.*
N COUNT/ UNCOUNT

porn /pɔːn/; an informal word. The form **porno** /pɔːnəʊ/ is also occasionally used. 1 **Porn** means the same as pornography. EG *...the porn shops of Soho.* ● See also **hard porn, soft porn.**
N UNCOUNT

2 **Porn** also means the same as pornographic. EG *...porn movies... ...glossy porno magazines.*
ADJ CLASSIF : ATTRIB

pornographic /pɔːnəgræfɪk/. Something that is **pornographic** is designed to cause sexual excitement by showing naked people, referring to sexual acts, etc; used showing disapproval. EG *...pornographic films and magazines... Adverts become more and more pornographic.*
ADJ QUALIT

pornography /pɔːnɒgrəfi¹/ refers to books, magazines, films, etc that are designed to cause sexual excitement by showing naked people, referring to sexual acts, etc; used showing disapproval. EG *...a merciless foe of gambling and pornography... ...pornography in the cinema.*
N UNCOUNT

porous /pɔːrəs/. Something that is **porous** has many small holes in it, through which water, air, etc can pass. EG *...compacting the soil, making it less porous... ...the partly porous walls of our digestive system.*
ADJ QUALIT

porphyry /pɔːfɪri¹/ is a hard rock with large crystals in it. It is polished and used to make large ornaments, to decorate parts of buildings, etc. EG *...a portable altar in silver and porphyry... ...an Egyptian porphyry jar.*
N UNCOUNT

porpoise /pɔːpəs/, **porpoises.** A **porpoise** is a sea animal that looks like a dolphin or a small whale. Porpoises usually swim about in groups.
N COUNT ↑ mammal

porridge /pɒrɪdʒ/. 1 **Porridge** is a thick, sticky food made from oats cooked in water or milk and eaten hot, especially for breakfast; used also to describe similar food made from other cereals. EG *...a plate of porridge.*
N UNCOUNT ↑ cereal

2 **Porridge** also refers to a period of time spent in prison; an informal use, used in British English. EG *He's done porridge.*
N UNCOUNT

port /pɔːt/, **ports.** 1 A **port** is 1.1 a town by the sea or on a river which has a harbour. EG *...a fishing port... ...coastal ports... ...Port Elizabeth.* 1.2 the harbour area with docks, warehouses, etc, where ships load or unload goods or passengers. EG *...a massive port development... ...the port authorities.*
N COUNT : ALSO IN NAMES
N COUNT

2 The **port** side of a ship or aircraft is the left side when you are facing towards the front end of it; a technical term. EG *...the port side of the cockpit... A wave caught the trawler on her port bow.* ▸ used as a noun. EG *...a few hundred yards to port.*
ADJ CLASSIF ≠ starboard
▸ N UNCOUNT

3 **Port** is a strong, sweet wine, usually dark red, which you drink after a meal. EG *...a glass of port... I'm fond of vintage port.*
N MASS

4 If you say **'any port in a storm'**, you mean that when someone is in trouble, they accept help from anyone, even from people they would normally avoid.
PHR

portable /pɔːtəbə⁰l/, **portables.** A machine or device that is **portable** is designed to be easily carried or moved. EG *...a little portable TV... They're very cheap and extremely portable.* ▸ used as a noun. EG *We wound up the black portable... ...dancing to a little portable.* ◊ **portability** /pɔːtəbɪlɪti¹/. EG *...ease of maintenance and portability.*
ADJ QUALIT ↑ movable
▸ N COUNT
◊ N UNCOUNT

portal /pɔːtə⁰l/, **portals.** A **portal** is a large and impressive doorway at the entrance to a building; a literary word. EG *...the main portal of the cathedral... ...villas with huge marble portals.*
N COUNT

portcullis /pɔːtkʌlɪs/, **portcullises.** A **portcullis** is a strong gate above an entrance to a castle, fort, etc, which used to be lowered to the ground in order to keep out enemies.
N COUNT

portend /pɔːtend/, **portends, portending, portended.** If something **portends** something, it indicates what is likely to happen in the future, whether it will be good or bad, etc; a formal word. EG *The berries on your hedge portend an early and severe winter... ...an omen portending our future victory... What do these changes portend for food production?*
V+O ↑ foretell = foreshado[w]

portent /pɔːtent/, **portents**; a formal word. 1 A **portent** is something that indicates what is likely to happen in the future, whether it will be good or bad,
N COUNT ↑ sign = omen

etc. EG *Are dreams a portent of things to come?... ...amazed that he ignored the portents for so long... ...a hopeful portent.*

2 **Portent** is the quality of being important, especially in indicating or affecting future events. EG *It's a day of portent... ...extravagant manifestations but without portent.* N UNCOUNT ⇑ significance

portentous /pɔːtentəs/; a formal word. 1 Something that is **portentous** is very important, especially in indicating or affecting future events. EG *Its consequences were historically portentous... Nothing portentous was happening to me.* ADJ QUALIT = ominous, momentous

2 If someone's behaviour is **portentous**, 2.1 they behave very seriously because they are about to do or say something unpleasant to someone. EG *Mary's face became portentous. She said seriously, 'Just listen to this.'* ◊ **portentously**. EG *He portentously rolled up his sleeve... Calderwood cleared his throat portentously.* 2.2 they behave, speak, or write more seriously than necessary because they want to impress other people. EG *His essay is perhaps a little portentous... ...the portentous way in which he wrote his name.* ◊ **portentously**. EG *She came back to announce portentously: 'A curate has come to call.'* ADJ QUALIT = ominous; ◊ ADV WITH VB = ominously; ADJ QUALIT = pompous, pretentious; ◊ ADV WITH VB = pompously

porter /pɔːtə/, **porters**. A **porter** is 1 a person whose job is to look after a building such as a hotel, especially to be in charge of its entrance. EG *...throwing open doors like a hotel porter... ...the hall porter... ...the porter of the block of flats where you live.* ● See also **night porter**. 2 a person whose job is to carry things, for example to carry people's luggage at a railway station. EG *He applied for a job as a porter... ...a railway porter... ...market porters.* N COUNT = doorman, janitor; N COUNT

portfolio /pɔːtfəʊliəʊ/, **portfolios**. A **portfolio** is 1 a thin, flat case for carrying papers, drawings, etc in. EG *...zipping up his portfolio.* 2 a set of items that represent someone's work, especially an artist's drawings or paintings, and which they use when entering competitions or applying for work. EG *I collected a portfolio of my drawings and showed them to the publisher... ...a portfolio of photographs.* N COUNT; N COUNT : IF+ PREP THEN *of* ⇑ collection = sample

3 a minister's responsibility for a particular area of a government's activities; a formal use. EG *None of them holds key portfolios... ...the transport portfolio.* N COUNT : USU+ SUPP

● A minister **without portfolio** is one who is given the rank of minister without being given responsibility for any particular area of a government's activities; a formal expression. 4 a combination of shares and other investments that a particular investor has; a technical use. EG *...a portfolio of stocks and bonds... Never invest more than 10% of the portfolio in any one security.* ● PHR : USED AS AN A; N COUNT : IF+ PREP THEN *of*

porthole /pɔːthəʊl/, **portholes**. A **porthole** is a small round window, especially on the side of a ship or aircraft. EG *...the portholes of the cabin... ...a modern residence with porthole windows.* N COUNT

portico /pɔːtɪkəʊ/, **porticos**. The form **porticoes** is also used for the plural. A **portico** is a large, covered area at the entrance to a building, with pillars supporting the roof; a technical term in architecture. EG *...the hotel portico... ...a palace with a huge marble portico.* N COUNT ⇑ porch

portion /pɔːʃəⁿn/, **portions, portioning, portioned**. 1 A **portion** of a physical object is a part of it that has a particular quality or feature. EG *...in the centre of the flattened portion... The sloping portion is difficult to reach... ...the lower portion of the counter.* N PART = section, area

2 A **portion** of an area or country is a smaller area within it. EG *...outlying portions of the estate... ...this portion of England.* N PART = region

3 A **portion** of a group of things or people consists of some of them but not all of them. EG *The police were aware of a portion of his activities... ...less favoured portions of the community.* N PART = section

4 A **portion** of a document or book is a part of it. EG *...a portion of the autobiography... I gave him portions of manuscript to read.* N PART = extract

5 A **portion** is also one of several equal parts into which something is divided or of which it consists. EG *Divide it into eight portions... ...equal portions of vodka and orange juice.* N PART = segment

6 A **portion** of a sum of money is a part of it. EG *...an appreciable portion of the university budget... A large portion of this money would come to her.* N PART ⇑ amount = share

7 A **portion** of food is the amount that is given to one person at a meal. EG *He held out his plate for a second portion... He asked for a small portion... 'Two portions of chips, please.'* N PART ⇑ quantity

8 Someone's **portion** is their fate or destiny; a literary use. EG *Utter disaster was my portion... What would be my portion on the day the enemy invaded?* N SING : POSS+N = lot

portion out. If you **portion out** something, you share it out among a group of people. EG *...the food that Tim was carefully portioning out... The presents were then portioned out.* PHRASAL VB : V+ O+ADV

portly /pɔːtliˡ/, **portlier, portliest**. Someone who is **portly** is rather fat; a rather old-fashioned word used in polite English to avoid causing offence. EG *...portly middle-aged gentlemen... ...portly ladies.* ADJ QUALIT = stout

portmanteau /pɔːtmæntəʊ/, **portmanteaus**. The form **portmanteaux** /pɔːtmæntəʊz/ is sometimes used for the plural. 1 A **portmanteau** is a large travelling case which opens out into two equal compartments; an old-fashioned use. EG *...stuffing shirts into his portmanteau.* N COUNT ⇑ suitcase

2 **Portmanteau** is used to describe 2.1 a word that combines parts of the forms and meanings of two other words. For example, 'brunch' is formed from 'breakfast' and 'lunch' and means a meal that is eaten in the middle of the morning; a technical use. ADJ CLASSIF : ATTRIB = blend

2.2 someone or something that combines many different features or uses. EG *...one of those portmanteau expressions... ...a portmanteau title.* ADJ CLASSIF : ATTRIB

port of call, ports of call. A **port of call** is 1 a place where a ship stops during a journey. EG *Our next port of call was Cyprus.* 2 any place where you stop for a short time, especially during a day when you visit several places, shops, people, etc; an informal use. EG *His last port of call was the chemist's.* N COUNT ⇑ port; N COUNT

portrait /pɔːtrɪ³t/, **portraits**. A **portrait** is 1 a painting, drawing, or photograph of a person, often showing only their face. EG *...a famous portrait of the musician... She painted landscapes and portraits... ...a good portrait photograph.* ● See also **self-portrait**. 2 a piece of writing, a film, etc, that gives a particular impression or opinion of someone or something by summarizing their character or by emphasizing some of their features. EG *...her portrait of the novelist as a kind of crook... The film is a love story, with routine portraits of a conductor and an ambitious violinist.* N COUNT ⇑ picture; N COUNT : USU+ *of* = portrayal, depiction

portraiture /pɔːtrɪ³tʃə/ is the art of painting or drawing portraits; a technical term. EG *...a master of portraiture.* N UNCOUNT

portray /pɔːtreɪ/, **portrays, portraying, portrayed**. To **portray** someone or something means 1 to show them by artistic means, for example in a book, film, or play. EG *Writers who tried to portray London in words... The animals were portrayed by actors in masks.* 2 to give a particular impression or opinion of them by emphasizing some of their features. EG *Advertising tends to portray women in a very traditional role... Minor mishaps were portrayed as major tragedies.* V+O = depict; V+O+A = depict

portrayal /pɔːtreɪəl/, **portrayals**. A **portrayal** is 1 the representation of someone or something by artistic means, especially an actor's performance in a play or film. EG *He got the award for his portrayal of Willy Loman in 'Death of a Salesman'... ...an eye-catching portrayal of the beautiful Madame Chiang.* N COUNT : USU+ *of* = depiction

2 the particular impression or opinion of someone or something which is given in a speech or piece of writing. EG *It was very fair in its portrayal of the Army... ...the portrayal of labour as the source of wealth... ...his portrayal by the media as an enemy of democracy.* 3 an act of showing or describing something. EG *...deeply offended by portrayals of sexual behaviour... He specialised in the portrayal of heroism.* N COUNT : USU+ *of* = representation; N COUNT : USU+ *of* = description

Portuguese /pɔːtjə⁴giːz/. The plural form of the noun in paragraph 2 is also **Portuguese**.

1 Something that is **Portuguese** comes from or relates to Portugal, its people, or its culture. EG *...the great Portuguese navigators.* ADJ CLASSIF

2 A **Portuguese** is a person who comes from Portugal. EG *A Portuguese was elected to the board.* N COUNT

3 **Portuguese** is the language spoken in Portugal, Brazil, Angola, and Mozambique. EG *'That's all right,' he said in Portuguese.* N UNCOUNT

pos. is a written abbreviation for 'positive'.

pose /pəʊz/, **poses, posing, posed**. 1 If someone **poses**, 1.1 they stand in a particular place or in a particular manner, for example so that someone can V : USU+A take a photograph of them or paint their portrait. EG *The bride and groom pose for the photograph... They wanted her to pose naked... She loved to pose in front of the mirrors.* **1.2** they behave in an exaggerated way because they want people to look at them; used showing disapproval. EG *She dances, smiles, poses, and shouts... I loved trailing my cloak, posing and being emotional.* V = posture

2 If someone **poses** as another person, they pretend to be that person in order to deceive people. EG *...a friend posing as my lawyer... ...an agent posing as a telephone engineer.* V+A *(as)* = masquerade

3 If someone or something **poses** problems, threats, dangers, etc, they cause those problems, threats, dangers, etc. EG *Its length must pose considerable steering problems... He posed a serious threat to their authority.* V+O : USU+A = present

4 If someone **poses** a question or idea, they ask or state that question or idea; a fairly formal use. EG *This brings me back to the question you posed earlier... He was the first to pose an alternative concept of the world.* V+O = raise

5 A **pose** is **5.1** a particular position or manner in which someone is standing, sitting, etc. EG *...hundreds of photographs in various poses... He tried to keep an alert pose.* N COUNT+SUPP = posture **5.2** a way of behaving that is intended to give a particular impression, often in order to deceive or impress people. EG *His pose as the champion of the proletariat... ...younger rock bands striking fashionable poses.* N COUNT : USU+SUPP ⇑ behaviour = image

poser /pəʊzə/, **posers**. A **poser** is **1** a poseur. EG *How I hate posers.* N COUNT **2** a difficult problem or puzzle; an informal use. EG *I remember putting the familiar poser to my father.* N COUNT = riddle

poseur /pəʊzɜː/, **poseurs**. If you call someone a **poseur**, you mean that they are behaving in a particular way merely in order to impress people or deceive them; used showing disapproval. EG *It says you're a radical poseur... ...a hypocritical poseur.* N COUNT : ALSO VOC = poser, show-off

posh /pɒʃ/, **posher, poshest**; an informal word. **1** Something that is **posh** is smart in appearance, fashionable, and expensive. EG *She had stayed in posh hotels... ...a posh London restaurant.* ADJ QUALIT = swish, grand

2 If you describe someone as **posh**, you mean that they belong to or behave like the upper classes. EG *...your posh friends... ...putting on her posh voice.* ADJ QUALIT = la-di-da, refined

3 If you say that someone **talks posh**, you mean that they are speaking in an upper class accent; sometimes used showing disapproval. EG *Make him promise not to talk posh!* PHR : VB INFLECTS

posit /pɒzɪt/, **posits, positing, posited**. If you **posit** something, you suggest or assume it as the basis for an argument or calculation; a formal word. EG *...the features that we posit as characteristics of democracy... The Metro's financial performance is posited on one million passengers a day.* V+O : USU+A = postulate

position /pəzɪʃə°n/, **positions, positioning, positioned**. **1** The physical **position** of someone or something is **1.1** the exact place where they are, often at a particular moment in time. EG *They tell the time by the position of the sun... The house is in a very exposed position... He had shifted position from the front to the back of the room.* N COUNT/UNCOUNT = location **1.2** the particular way in which they are occupying a space, for example the direction they are facing, whether they are upright or horizontal, etc. EG *I helped her to a sitting position... She remained in that position, head up, hand on hip... Hold it in an upright position.* N COUNT+SUPP, OR N UNCOUNT ⇑ posture **1.3** the way in which several of them are arranged in relation to one another. EG *...the position of the beads in relation to one another... ...the position of the pieces on the board.* N UNCOUNT/COUNT ⇑ arrangement **1.4** the particular position which a switch, lever, or other movable device is in, especially whether it is on or off. EG *He pushed the safety catch down into the ready position... Switch it to the on position.* N COUNT : USU *the*+MOD+N IN SING ⇑ place = setting **1.5** a particular place where an army has put soldiers or equipment; a technical use. EG *The Marines fired on his position with mortars... ...troops in forward positions... ...a machine gun position.* N COUNT+SUPP = emplacement

2 If someone or something is **in position** or is put **into position**, **2.1** they are in the correct place, usually according to a plan or rule. EG *By 8.05 the groups were in position... ...pulling into position in the line of cars waiting to turn.* PHR : USED AS AN A **2.2** they are in the correct position for a particular purpose, for example facing the correct direction, upright, etc. EG *...the reeds are driven into position... Keep it in position with a rubber band.* PHR : USED AS AN A = in place

3 If someone or something is **out of position**, they are no longer in the correct place, facing the correct direction, etc. PHR : USED AS AN A ≠ in place

4 If you **position** someone or something, you put them in a particular place or in their correct position, usually in a careful, firm, or deliberate way. EG *...positioning her legs a certain way... The boy positioned himself near the door... ...the guns positioned around the airfields.* V+O (NG/REFL) : USU+A

5 Your **position** within society is the importance that you have compared to other people. EG *Women hold a very strong position in Aboriginal society... ...people in positions of power and influence... The army might maintain its position indefinitely by force.* N COUNT : WITH POSS/SUPP ⇑ place

6 Position is the state of great importance that someone has. EG *...respect for the qualities of position, education, and wealth... The farm-worker has no position, no status.* N UNCOUNT = consequence

7 A **position** in a company or organization is a job or post in it, usually involving professional, managerial, or clerical work, not manual work. EG *...top management positions... ...a more senior position... Thorn lost his position as steward.* N COUNT ⇑ place

8 The **position** of a person or team in a race or competition is their place in the order at its finish or at a particular point during it. EG *She sprinted hard to hold third position... ...the top five positions in the League... ...lying in fourth position after two rounds.* N COUNT : USU NUM/ORDINAL+N

9 Someone's **position** at a particular point in time is the situation they are in, often because of something that has just happened. EG *It puts me in a rather difficult position... You are in the fortunate position of having no responsibilities... Ask her how she would cope in your position... This helped everyone's tax position.* N COUNT : WITH POSS/SUPP ⇑ state

10 If someone is **in a position** to do something, they are able to do it, for example because they have sufficient money, authority, or knowledge. If someone is **in no position** to do something, they are unable to do it. EG *I would then be in a position to do that for her... They were in no position to help... I'm in no position to say... She was in a better position to appreciate its significance.* PHR : USED AS AN A+*to*-INF

11 If you say that you are **in no position** to criticize or make fun of someone, you mean that you do not want to, because you know that you are just as guilty or foolish as they are. EG *...nor are we in any position to reproach them.* PHR : USED AS AN A+*to*-INF ≠ justified

12 A **position** that you have on a particular subject or situation is your attitude towards it or your opinion of it; a formal use. EG *If you take a multilateralist position... What is their position on the proposed sale of aircraft?... ...this change in position by the President.* N COUNT, OR *in*+N = viewpoint, stance

13 The **position** of a player in a team game is the particular role that they play, for example whether they attack or defend. EG *He played in six different positions in his first season.* N COUNT

positive /pɒzɪtɪv/. **1** If someone is **positive** about a fact or decision, they are very sure that it is true or correct and have no doubts. EG *'Are you sure you don't want her address?'–'Positive.'... He was positive that he had seen it in the newspaper.* ADJ CLASSIF : PRED, USU+REPORT-CL/*about* = certain

2 If someone is **positive**, they feel hopeful or confident. EG *Our conversation did make me feel better, more positive... Etta was now taking a more positive attitude.* ADJ QUALIT = optimistic

3 An action or decision that is **positive** is done or made in a very deliberate and forceful way that is likely to have good results. EG *Now's the time for positive thinking... ...a very positive decision... That was a very positive shot from Davis.* ADJ QUALIT = decisive ◊ **positively**. EG *They should participate more positively in the process.* ◊ ADV WITH VB = actively

4 A feeling, achievement, etc that is **positive** is considered to be morally good or practically useful in some way. EG *Positive feelings like tenderness and joy... What would you regard as your positive achievements?* ADJ QUALIT = constructive

5 A reaction, reply, etc that is **positive** expresses agreement, approval, or encouragement. EG *Public response was positive... Another positive sign was a statement by Mr Dirk.* ADJ QUALIT = constructive ≠ negative ◊ **positively**. EG *Thomson replied positively: 'There will be no change in policy.'* ◊ ADV WITH VB = affirmatively

6 A **positive** instruction, order, etc is very clear and definite, so that there can be no confusion about what is meant. EG *But I gave you positive instructions.* — ADJ CLASSIF : USU ATTRIB = explicit

7 **Positive** evidence gives definite proof of the truth or identity of something, so that there can be no doubt about it. EG *Positive identification of the blood type was impossible... I was looking for some positive evidence that Barney came to the flat.* — ADJ CLASSIF : USU ATTRIB = conclusive
◊ **positively.** EG *The body has been positively identified.* — ◊ ADV WITH VB = definitely

8 If a test or its result is **positive**, it shows evidence of the particular medical condition, substance, etc that you are looking for. EG *I'm happy to tell you the results are positive... ...a positive pregnancy test.* — ADJ CLASSIF ≠ negative

9 A **positive** number, quantity, measurement, etc is greater than zero; a technical term in mathematics. EG *If x is positive, y must be negative... ...positive and negative numbers.* — ADJ CLASSIF ≠ negative

10 If something has a **positive** electrical charge, it has the same charge as a proton and the opposite charge to an electron; a technical term. EG *The current flows from positive to negative.* ◊ **positively.** EG *...the positively charged terminal.* — ADJ CLASSIF ≠ negative; ◊ ADV WITH VB

11 You also use **positive** to emphasize **11.1** that something is true to an extreme degree. EG *I usually find cooking a positive pleasure... Your room is a positive disgrace.* — ADJ CLASSIF : ATTRIB = absolute **11.2** that something is true, even though it may be surprising. EG *It seems no harm and may be some positive good... Life in a town brings positive advantages to children.* — ADJ CLASSIF : ATTRIB = actual

positive discrimination is the policy of deliberately treating one group of people better than others because they have previously been treated unfairly. — N UNCOUNT ⇑ favouritism

positively /pɒzɪtɪvli^{1}/. **1** You use **positively** to emphasize that you really mean what you are saying, even though it may sound surprising or extreme. EG *It's quite positively the last time that you'll see me.* — ADV SEN = definitely **2** the particular word that follows, even though it may sound surprising or extreme. EG *Her friends had been positively abusive... She positively flowed into my arms... The task looks positively frightening.* — ADV **3** the presence of a particular effect or attitude, when its absence or its opposite might be expected. EG *I didn't object. I positively approved her initiative... I finished the journey feeling positively refreshed... Mary never refused his advances, but she never positively invited them either.* ● See also **positive**. — ADV = actively, actually

positive vetting is the thorough checking of a person by a government before they are trusted with official secrets; a formal word used mainly in British English. EG *I'm not so happy about Davis, in spite of the positive vetting.* — N UNCOUNT

positivism /pɒzɪtɪvɪzm/ is a philosophical system which accepts only things that can be seen or proved. EG *...religious mysticism and scientific positivism.* ◊ **positivist, positivists.** EG *a logical positivist... ...the positivist approach.* — N UNCOUNT = empiricism; ◊ N COUNT

> **POSS** □ In this dictionary POSS is used in the grammar notes beside entries to indicate that a noun is usually used with a possessive form. The possessive form may be one of three types, as follows: (a) a possessive pronoun as determiner (see □ at DETPOSS); one of *my, your, his, her, its, our, their.* (b) a noun or name with an added *'s* (apostrophe *'s*), such as *John's, Professor Smith's, the writer's*; also *someone's* etc. If the noun is plural already, or if the singular form already ends in *-s*, the possessive is formed by adding only the apostrophe, as in *the teachers'*, compared with *the teacher's.* (c) a prepositional group following the noun, as in *...the diary of the deceased.* The noun following *of* may also be in the possessive, as in *...a book of my father's.* When the grammar notes say N WITH POSS, they refer to any of these three types. When they say POSS+N, they refer to (a) and (b) only.

poss. /pɒs/ is an abbreviation for 'possible'; used especially in informal British English. EG *I'll do it as soon as poss.*

posse /pɒsi^{1}/, **posses.** A **posse**, in the United States, was a group of men on horses, who were brought together by the local sheriff to help him chase and capture a criminal. EG *...the outlaw Jesse James, pursued by a posse.* — N COUNT

possess /pəzɛs/, **possesses, possessing, possessed**; a fairly formal word. **1** If you **possess** something, you own or have it. EG *How I longed to possess a suit like that... They were found guilty of possessing petrol bombs.* — V+O : NO CONT, NO IMPER

2 If something **possesses** a particular feature or part, it has it. EG *For hundreds of years London possessed only one bridge... Television possesses a unique if superficial magic.* — V+O : NO CONT, NO IMPER

3 If you **possess** a quality, ability, etc, you have it. EG *He possessed the qualities of a war leader... ...skills they do not possess.* — V+O : NO CONT, NO IMPER

4 If someone **is possessed of** a thing, a quality, an ability, etc, they own or have it; a formal or literary expression. EG *He was possessed of the dubious distinction of being my son-in-law... The Allies were possessed of superior resources.* — PHR : VB INFLECTS = enjoy

5 If someone or something **possesses** a person, they strongly influence or control that person's behaviour or thinking. EG *A violent rage possessed him... I was possessed with the notion that I was not alone... Why am I so possessed by her?* — V+O : IF PASS THEN *with/by*, NO CONT, NO IMPER = obsess

6 If you ask **'What possessed** someone **to** do something?', you are expressing great surprise that they have done something which you consider foolish or dangerous. EG *What on earth possessed you to come here?* — PHR

7 If someone **is possessed**, their mind and body are controlled by an evil spirit or by the devil. — V+O : USU PASS

possession /pəzɛʃə$^{\circ}$n/, **possessions. 1 Possession** is the state of having something which belongs to you or which you have obtained or achieved. EG *The possession of a degree does not guarantee you a job... Freedom depended on the possession of land... I had in my possession a portion of the money... The document came into the possession of the Daily Mail.* — N UNCOUNT : USU WITH POSS, OR N +*of* ⇑ ownership

2 If someone **is in possession of** something, especially something valuable or important or something which they were not expected to have, they have it; a formal expression. EG *MacDonald has been in possession of the letter for some weeks... ...a person who is in possession of their faculties and a clear mind.* — PHR : VB INFLECTS

3 **Possession** is also **3.1** the crime of having or owning something illegally; a technical use. EG *...arrested for possession of drugs... ...illegal possession of firearms.* — N UNCOUNT : IF+ PREP THEN *of* ⇑ ownership **3.2** the state of physically occupying or controlling a house, area of land, or country, whether you own it or not. EG *The tenant has already got possession of the house... They took possession of the island.* — N UNCOUNT : IF+ PREP THEN *of* = hold **3.3** control of the ball by one team in a game such as football or hockey, which usually indicates that they are the better team. EG *Everton have had most of the possession.* — N UNCOUNT **3.4** control of a person's mind and body by an evil spirit or by the devil. EG *This charm would protect a man from possession by evil spirits while he slept.* — N UNCOUNT

4 Your **possessions** are **4.1** the things that you own or have with you at a particular time. EG *He had few possessions... Check your possessions on arrival... ...money, property, possessions.* — N COUNT : USU PL = belongings **4.2** countries or territories which are controlled by another country. EG *...the British possessions... ...colonial possessions.* — N COUNT : USU PL = colony

possessive /pəzɛsɪv/, **possessives. 1** Someone who is **possessive 1.1** wants all the attention and love of another person; used showing disapproval. EG *She was very possessive about Rod... I had always been aware of the possessive streak in her.* — ADJ QUALIT ⇑ jealous ◊ **possessiveness.** EG *...a child's possessiveness towards its mother.* — ◊ N UNCOUNT **1.2** does not like their things to be used by other people. EG *I am possessive about my car... People become very possessive about little things.* — ADJ QUALIT ⇑ selfish ◊ **possessiveness.** EG *The village men have the same possessiveness about their gardens.* — ◊ N UNCOUNT ⇑ selfishness

2 **Possessive** is a grammatical term used to describe or refer to words that indicate the person or thing that an object, feature, quality, etc belongs to. For example, 'my' is a possessive adjective and 'yours' is a possessive pronoun. See also □ at POSS and DETPOSS. — ADJ CLASSIF, OR N COUNT

possessor /pəzɛsə/, **possessors.** A **possessor** is the person that something belongs to; a formal or literary word, often used in a humorous way. EG *I was the proud possessor of two tickets to the opera... Beauty puts a tremendous strain on its possessor.* — N COUNT : USU WITH POSS = owner

possibility /pɒsɪbɪlɪti^{1}/, **possibilities.** A **possibility** is **1** something that might be true or might happen. EG *We must accept the possibility that we might be wrong... There was now no possibility of success... Yes, that is a possibility.* — N UNCOUNT/ COUNT : USU+ SUPP OR REPORT-CL **2** something that you are able to do and that you might do. EG *I considered the possibility of joining the Communist* — N COUNT, OR N UNCOUNT+SUPP = opening, prospect

Party... All sorts of possibilities had begun to open up... That was one of the possibilities that was suggested.

possible /pɒsɪbəºl/, **possibles**. 1 Something that is **possible** 1.1 is able to be done or achieved. EG *It is possible for us to measure his progress... They are doing everything possible to take care of you.* 1.2 may happen or be done by someone in the future, but is not certain to happen or to be done by them. EG *His staff warned him of the possible consequences... A breakthrough may be possible next year... America and Russia were both possible financiers of the dam.* ADJ CLASSIF = feasible; ADJ CLASSIF = likely

2 You can say that a fact, theory, or solution is **possible** in order to indicate that you do not know whether it is true, correct, or the best, but you accept that it might be. EG *That's one possible answer... It is possible that he said these things.* ADJ CLASSIF = conceivable ≠ impossible

3 If you do something **as soon as possible, as much as possible**, etc, you do it to the greatest degree or extent that you are able to in a particular situation. EG *Go as soon as possible... I like to know as much as possible about my patients... He sat as far away from the others as possible.* PHR : USED AS AN A

4 If you say that something is **the best possible, the biggest possible**, etc, you mean that it is the best, biggest, etc that is available, can exist, or can be achieved. EG *We provide the best possible accommodation for our students... ...the harshest possible conditions... ...specialisation to the highest degree possible.* PHR+N

5 If you do something **where possible, wherever possible, whenever possible**, etc, you do it on every occasion that you have the opportunity to do it. EG *We traded with the British wherever possible... They wished, where possible, to avoid new conflicts... Whenever possible, loads were parachuted in.* PHR : USED AS AN A

6 You add **if possible, if at all possible**, etc to a wish, intention, or ambition, to indicate that although it is what you really want, you realize that in a particular situation you may have to accept something less or something different. EG *He wanted to bring hundreds of people, thousands if possible, to City Hall... 'When do you want to go?'-'This weekend, if possible.'* PHR : USED AS ADV SEN

7 A **possible** is one of several people or things that have the right qualities or qualifications for a particular purpose, and may eventually be chosen for it. EG *He sounds like a possible... The first three houses were all possibles... There were ten possibles in all.* N COUNT = candidate ≠ reject

possibly /pɒsɪbliˡ/. You use **possibly** 1 to indicate that you are not sure whether something is true or might happen. EG *Television is possibly to blame for this... The threat was possibly not very great... This must have been a little reading-room, possibly Leo's study.* 2 in questions, to emphasize that you are surprised, puzzled, or shocked by something you have seen, heard, or been asked to do. EG *I wondered how on earth they could possibly understand... 'The police? What could they possibly want with me?'... How could you possibly expect me to eat that?* 3 to emphasize that someone has tried their hardest to do something, or has done it as well as they can in a particular situation. EG *He will do everything he possibly can to aid you... He planned to come back again as soon as he possibly could... I have made myself as comfortable as I possibly can.* 4 with a negative, to emphasize that someone is unwilling or unable to do something, or that it cannot happen or be done by anyone. EG *I can't possibly stay in all the weekend... They couldn't possibly afford another... Nobody could possibly tell the difference.* ADV SEN = perhaps; ADV : ADV+VB = conceivably; ADV : ADV+VB = conceivably; ADV : ADV+VB

possum /pɒsəm/, **possums**. 1 A **possum** is an opossum; used in informal American English. N COUNT ↑ marsupial

2 If you **play possum**, you pretend that you are asleep or that you do not know something in order to deceive someone; an informal expression. EG *She's just playing possum.* PHR : VB INFLECTS ↑ mislead

post /pəʊst/, **posts, posting, posted**. 1 **The post** is the public service by which letters and parcels are collected and delivered; used mainly in British English. EG *Winners will be notified by post... You'll get these through the post.* N SING : the+N, OR by+N = mail

2 If something is **in the post**, it has been sent by post and is in the process of being delivered. EG *There is a cheque for you in the post.* PHR : USED AS AN A

3 If you are trying to **catch the post**, you are trying to put a letter or parcel in a post-box or take it to a post office before the next official time for collection. PHR : VB INFLECTS

4 **Post** consists of the letters and parcels that are delivered to you, especially on one particular occasion. EG *There is some post for you... Rose was reluctant to answer her post... Your letter arrived second post.* N UNCOUNT = mail

5 If you **post** a letter, parcel, etc, you send it to someone by putting it in a post-box or by taking it to a post office. EG *I'm going to post a letter... I'll be glad to post you details... Post it to the social security office.* V+O, V+O+O, OR V+O+A (to) = mail

6 If you **post** a notice, sign, or other piece of written information somewhere, or you **post** it **up** somewhere, you fix it to a wall, noticeboard, etc so that everyone can see it. EG *I shall post it up for all to see... When the final marks were posted, Rudolph had an A in French... I was obeying all posted speed limits.* V+O, OR PHRASAL VB : V+O+ADV, USU+A = display

7 If you **keep** someone **posted**, you inform them about developments in a situation as they occur, or tell them when something happens that they are waiting for. EG *David promised to keep them posted.* PHR : VB INFLECTS

8 **Post** is often used in the names of newspapers. EG *...The Evening Post... ...The Birmingham Post and Mail.* N IN TITLES

9 **A post** is 9.1 a strong, upright pole made of wood or metal which is fixed in a particular place, for example to support something or to tie things to. EG *A dog sat chained to a post outside... ...a row of fence posts.* 9.2 a goalpost; an informal use. EG *And he's hit the post!* 9.3 a post which marks the finishing point on a horse-racing track. EG *And first past the post is Golden Fleece.* N COUNT; N COUNT; N SING : the+N

10 The **first past the post** system in political elections is the system in which the winner is the person with more votes than any other candidate, even though the winner may receive only a small proportion of the total number votes; used mainly in British English. PHR+N

11 A **post** in a company or organization is a job or official position in it, usually involving some degree of responsibility; a formal use. EG *...a post at the High School... She is well qualified for the post... He offered to resign his post.* N COUNT

12 A **post** in an office, a ship, a battle, etc is a particular place in it where someone is commanded or expected to be in order to do their job or when a particular situation happens. EG *Everyone was at his post... He had to leave his post and flee... ...lookout posts where sentries kept watch... ...an observation post 500 metres further west.* N COUNT : POSS/MOD+N = station, position

13 If a company, organization, or person in authority **posts** someone somewhere, 13.1 they send that person to another town or country to work for them there. EG *I have been posted to Paris.* 13.2 they make that person stand in a particular place, for example to supervise an activity or guard the place. EG *Brody had posted two officers on the beach... We posted a guard to keep watch.* V+O+A = assign; V+O : USU+A ↑ put = position

14 ● See also **lamp-post, posting.** ● to **pip** someone at the post: see **pip.** ● **by return of post**: see **return.**

post- is used to form words that describe something as taking place after a particular date, event, or stage of development. EG *...1945→post-1945. ...school→post-school... ...colonial→post-colonial.* PREFIX

postage /pəʊstɪdʒ/ is the money that you have to pay for sending letters, parcels, etc by post. EG *Send 25p extra for postage and packing.* N UNCOUNT

postage stamp, postage stamps. A **postage stamp** is a small piece of gummed paper which you have to buy and stick on an envelope or parcel before you post it; a formal expression. EG *It was only the size of a postage stamp... ...the Museum's collection of postage stamps.* N COUNT = stamp

postal /pəʊstəºl/ is used to describe 1 people or things that are connected with the service of carrying letters, parcels, etc. EG *...increases in postal charges... The postal services threatened to go on strike.* 2 activities that involve sending things by post. EG *...postal ballots... The war stopped postal communication between the two countries.* ADJ CLASSIF : ATTRIB; ADJ CLASSIF : ATTRIB

postal order, postal orders; used mainly in British English. A **postal order** is a piece of paper representing a sum of money, which you buy at a post office when you want to send money to someone by post. They must sign it or pay it into an N COUNT = money order account when they receive it, so it is safer to use than cash. EG *...a one-pound postal order... The application form and the postal order were sent off to the Passport Office.*

postbag /pəustbæg/, **postbags**. A **postbag** is **1** a bag in which a postman carries letters and parcels. N COUNT
2 the letters that are received by an important person, a newspaper, a television company, etc, especially when they represent public opinion on a particular subject; an informal use. EG *The statement brought Rodgers his biggest postbag to date... The power of the postbag must never be underestimated.* N SING : USU WITH POSS ⇑ post

post-box, post-boxes. A **post-box** is **1** a metal box with a hole in it, which you can put letters into to be collected by a postman. Post-boxes are fixed in public places, often on street corners. EG *Marion, run down to the post-box with this letter.* N COUNT = letter-box, mail-box **2** a metal box which a postman puts letters into when he delivers them, especially at the entrance to a block of flats or offices. EG *...a dozen grey post-boxes in the hallway.* N COUNT = mailbox, letterbox

postcard /pəustkɑːd/, **postcards**. A **postcard** is a piece of thin card, often with a picture on one side, which you can write on and send to people by post without using an envelope. EG *I sent her a postcard from Eastbourne.* N COUNT

postcode /pəustkəud/, **postcodes**. A **postcode** is a short sequence of numbers or letters at the end of an address. Postcodes make it easier and quicker for post to be delivered to the correct address; used in British English. N COUNT ⇑ code = zip code

postdate /pəustdeɪt/, **postdates, postdating, postdated**. If you **postdate** a document such as a cheque or letter, you write a date on it that is later than the date when you actually write it, in order to allow yourself a period of time before it becomes officially or legally valid. V+O

poster /pəustə/, **posters**. A **poster** is a large notice or picture that you stick on a wall or noticeboard, especially to advertise something. EG *...cinema posters... ...posters for political parties... ...colourful posters of Paris and Venice.* N COUNT = advertisement

poste restante /pəust restɑːnt/ is a service operated by post offices by which letters and parcels that are sent to you are kept at a particular post office until you collect them; used mainly in British English. EG *The clerk at the poste restante counter... ...a poste restante address.* N UNCOUNT, OR N BEFORE N ▸ used as an adverb. EG *You'd better send it poste restante.* ▸ ADV WITH VB

posterior /pɒstɪərɪə/, **posteriors**. **1** Someone's buttocks can be referred to as their **posterior**; a formal or humorous use. EG *He paused a moment to raise his posterior from the chair.* N COUNT
2 Posterior describes something that is situated at the back of something else; a technical use in medicine, architecture, etc. EG *...the posterior muscles.* ADJ CLASSIF : ATTRIB = rear

posterity /pɒsterɪti[1]/; a formal word. When you talk about **posterity**, you are referring to all the future generations of people, especially when you are considering how they will be affected by things happening or existing now, or what opinion they will have of them. EG *What will posterity decide about these people?... This fine building should be preserved for posterity.* N UNCOUNT

poster paint is a type of paint similar to watercolour paint. EG *...tins of poster paints.* N COUNT/ UNCOUNT

postgraduate /pəustgrædjuːət/, **postgraduates**. A **postgraduate** is a student who has a first degree from a university and is studying or doing research at a more advanced level; used mainly in British English. EG *...2,200 undergraduates and 400 postgraduates... Many students go on and do postgraduate work... ...postgraduate students.* N COUNT = graduate

posthumous /pɒstjə[4]məs/ is used to describe something that happens after someone's death but relates to their activities or achievements before they died. EG *He received a posthumous award for bravery... ...a posthumous publication.* ◇ **posthumously**. EG *Posthumously, the Webbs have won their battle.* ADJ CLASSIF ◇ ADV WITH VB

post-industrial is used to describe the present state of many Western societies, referring especially to the changes in types of industry, methods of manufacture, and people's lifestyles. EG *...the post-industrial computer age... ...the merits of a post-industrial leisure society.* ADJ CLASSIF : ATTRIB

posting /pəustɪŋ/, **postings**. A **posting** is a job that you are given by your employers, which involves going to a different town or country. EG *I've been given an overseas posting to Japan... He had a posting to a weapons training course for six months.* N COUNT ⇑ assignment

postman /pəustmə[3]n/, **postmen**. A **postman** is a man whose job is to collect and deliver letters and parcels that are sent by post. N COUNT ⇑ employee

postmark /pəustmɑːk/, **postmarks**. A **postmark** is a mark which is printed on letters and parcels at a post office and shows the time and place of posting. EG *...an envelope with a London postmark.* N COUNT

postmaster /pəustmɑːstə/, **postmasters**. A **postmaster** is a man who is in charge of a post office. EG *...the village postmaster.* N COUNT

postmistress /pəustmɪstrɪ[2]s/, **postmistresses**. A **postmistress** is a woman who is in charge of a post office. EG *The postmistress was a widow.* N COUNT

post-mortem /pəust mɔːtəm/, **post-mortems**. A **post-mortem** is **1** a medical examination of a dead person's body in order to find out the cause of his or her death. EG *The post-mortem indicated cirrhosis... You'll have to carry out a post-mortem... ...a post-mortem examination.* N COUNT ⇑ dissection = autopsy **2** an examination of something that has recently happened, especially something that has failed or gone wrong. EG *There will be a post-mortem when the boss gets back... ...the post-mortem on the election results.* N COUNT ⇑ analysis

post-natal means happening after the birth of a baby. EG *...post-natal care... Mothers may suffer from post-natal depression.* ADJ CLASSIF : ATTRIB

post office, post offices. **1** The **Post Office** is, in Britain and many other countries, the national organization that is responsible for postal services. EG *The government encouraged the Post Office to establish its own banking service.* N SING : the+N
2 A **post office** is a building where you can go to use any of the services provided by the national postal service, for example to buy stamps or post letters and parcels. EG *From the city's main post office he sent off two telegrams... ...a giro cheque which you can cash at the post office.* N COUNT

postpone /pə[6]stpəun/, **postpones, postponing, postponed**. If you **postpone** an event, you delay it happening or arrange for it to take place at a later time than was originally planned or agreed. EG *Could you postpone your departure for five minutes?... The flight had been postponed until eleven o'clock... The decision cannot be postponed indefinitely.* V+O : USU PASS = defer, put off

postponement /pə[6]stpəunmə[2]nt/, **postponements**. A **postponement** is the act of delaying something or arranging for it to take place at a later time than originally planned or agreed. EG *...the postponement of the new parliamentary session... I'd like to apply for a postponement... ...the costs of cancellation or postponement.* N COUNT/ UNCOUNT ⇑ delay = deferral

postscript /pəustskrɪpt/, **postscripts**. A **postscript** is **1** a message written at the end of a letter after you have signed your name. EG *Cott had added a postscript to his letter.* N COUNT ⇑ addition = PS **2** an addition to a finished story, account, or statement, which gives new information; an informal use. EG *There's a postscript to this story... Postscript: Gladys died in 1976.* N COUNT

postulate, postulates, postulating, postulated; a formal word. The word is pronounced /pɒstjə[4]leɪt/ when it is a verb and /pɒstjə[4]lət/ when it is a noun.
1 If you **postulate** something, you suggest it as the basis for a theory, argument, or calculation, or assume that it is the basis. EG *Professor Wilson is postulating a genetic change... Functionalism postulates an inborn need to solve problems... They postulate excessive increases in population.* V+O/REPORT-CL ⇑ suppose
2 A **postulate** is an idea that is suggested as or assumed to be the basis for a theory, argument, or calculation. EG *Is this a reasonable postulate?... ...the postulates of Marxism.* N COUNT = assumption, hypothesis

posture /pɒstʃə/, **postures, posturing, postured**. **1** A **posture** is **1.1** a particular position or manner in which you stand, sit, etc, which often expresses your feelings or character. EG *...his stiff, upright posture... ...hands held out in the imploring posture of a beggar... These exercises help to develop good posture.* N COUNT/ UNCOUNT : USU+ SUPP = pose **1.2** an attitude that you have towards a particular subject, situation, or problem. EG *They are trying to adopt a more co-operative posture.* N COUNT+SUPP : USU SING = outlook, stance
2 If someone **is posturing**, **2.1** they are behaving in an exaggerated way because they want other people V : USU CONT = pose

to look at them. EG *...posturing impudently on the table... He'll love posturing and posing in that T-shirt.* **2.2** they are trying to give a particular impression to other people, often in order to deceive them. EG *...posturing to project an air of knowledge.* V: USU CONT

post-war; also spelled as one word. **Post-war** is used to describe something that happens or exists in the period of time after a war, especially soon after it. EG *...a serious challenge to any post-war government... ...a relic of the postwar era... ...a postwar apartment building.* ADJ CLASSIF: ATTRIB

posy /pəʊzi[1]/, **posies**. A **posy** is a small bunch of flowers. N COUNT/PART ⇑ bouquet

pot /pɒt/, **pots, potting, potted**. **1** A **pot** is **1.1** a deep round container used for cooking, especially one used for cooking stews and soups. EG *...glazed clay pots.* N COUNT ⇑ receptacle ▸ also used to refer to the food inside a pot or the amount of food that it contains. EG *...a big steaming pot of stew.* ▸ N PART **1.2** a container with a handle and a spout, from which coffee or tea is served. EG *...a coffee pot.* N COUNT ⇑ receptacle ▸ also used to refer to the tea or coffee inside the pot. EG *I'll just go and make a fresh pot of tea.* ▸ N PART **1.3** a deep bowl or cylindrical container for paint, jam, or any other thick liquid. EG *There were old paint pots stacked on the shelves.* N COUNT ⇑ receptacle ▸ also used to refer to the liquid contained in such a container. EG *We'll have that pot of cream with the gooseberries.* ▸ N PART ⇑ receptacle **1.4** a container, usually made of earthenware or plastic, which is used for growing plants in. EG *Pots of geraniums stood on the window-sill.* N COUNT = flowerpot **1.5** a deep bowl used instead of a toilet, especially by small children and adults who cannot walk to the bathroom. N COUNT = chamber pot, potty ● See also **chimney pot, lobster pot, melting pot, potted.**

2 If you say that something is a case of **the pot calling the kettle black**, you mean that one person is criticizing another person for faults which in fact they both have. PHR: USED AS C

3 If you invite someone to take **pot luck**, you invite them to be your guest and to eat with you in your home, although you have not planned to invite them and do not know what is going to be available. EG *Come this evening. I'm afraid it will be rather pot luck.* PHR: VB INFLECTS

4 If someone has **pots** of something such as money, they have a lot of it; an informal use. N PART: PLURAL

5 The **pot** is **5.1** a sum of money to which each player in a card game has contributed, which is won as a prize by the player who wins the game. N SING: *the*+N = kitty, pool **5.2** a sum of money to which two or more people contribute, which is used for a joint purpose, for example to buy food for all the contributors; used in American English. N SING: *the*+N ⇑ fund = kitty

6 A cup that is given as the prize in a sports competition is sometimes referred to as a **pot**; an informal use. N COUNT

7 If you **pot** a plant, you put it into a pot filled with earth, so that it can grow there. EG *I was helping him pot the cuttings.* ● See also **potting compost, potting shed.** V+O

8 If you **pot** a billiard ball, you succeed in hitting it into one of the pockets in a game of snooker or billiards. EG *Davies only needs to pot one more red to be sure of winning this frame.* V+O ⇑ score = pocket ▸ used as a noun. EG *...another brilliant pot by Davies.* ▸ N COUNT ⇑ stroke

9 If you **pot** a small animal such as a rabbit or hare, you shoot it and kill it, usually because you want to cook it and eat it. EG *Old men with even older shotguns roam the hills at weekends potting rabbits, partridge, pigeons, etc.* V+O

10 If you **take a pot at** something or someone, you shoot at it without taking the time to aim carefully; an informal expression. PHR: VB INFLECTS

11 A **pot** is also the same as a pot belly; an informal use. EG *He had hairy arms and an enormous pot.* N COUNT

12 If you say that something has **gone to pot**, you mean that it has lost all its good qualities because nobody has looked after it or worked at it; an informal expression. PHR: VB INFLECTS ⇑ deteriorate

13 Pot is cannabis; an informal use. EG *He was said to have smoked pot occasionally.* N UNCOUNT ⇑ marijuana

potash /pɒtæʃ/ is a white powdery substance, obtained from the ashes of burnt wood. It is used especially as a fertilizer. N UNCOUNT

potassium /pətæsɪəm/ is a soft silvery-white chemical element, which occurs mainly in compounds. These compounds are used especially in making glass, soap, detergents, and fertilizers. N UNCOUNT

potato /pəteɪtəʊ/, **potatoes**. **1** A **potato** is a round white vegetable with a brown or red skin. Potatoes grow underground. EG *He's digging up potatoes in the vegetable garden... ...something starchy such as potato or cereal.* N COUNT/UNCOUNT ⇑ tuber

2 You can refer to a difficult subject, for example one about which different people have very strong and conflicting views, as **a hot potato.** EG *The subject of abortion became a hot potato.* PHR: USED AS C

pot-bellied. Someone who is **pot-bellied** has got a pot belly. ADJ QUALIT

pot belly, pot bellies. Someone who has a **pot belly** has a round, fat stomach which sticks out, caused either by eating or drinking too much or else by bad-quality food and starvation. N COUNT

pot-boiler, pot-boilers; also spelled without a hyphen. A **pot-boiler** is a piece of writing, music, or other work which a writer, musician, or other artist has created in order to earn money quickly rather than as a work of artistic merit. EG *These short stories were written as pot boilers to get him out of debt.* N COUNT

pot-bound. A plant that is **pot-bound** is growing in a pot which is too small for it, so that the roots cannot continue to grow. ADJ CLASSIF

potency /pəʊtənsi[1]/ is **1** the power and influence that a person, action, or idea has to affect or change people's lives or beliefs. EG *Princess Ida's spell lost its potency... The play conjures up the potency of evil in all its frightening seductiveness.* N UNCOUNT: USU WITH POSS ⇑ force **2** the ability of a man to have sex. EG *This can be seen as insulting to a man's sexual potency.* N UNCOUNT

potent /pəʊtənt/. **1** Something that is **potent** is very effective and powerful. EG *Potent new weapons will shortly be available... ...potent antibiotics and other drugs... The schools have been potent instruments of westernization... ...a potent argument.* ADJ QUALIT ⇑ strong

2 A man who is **potent** is capable of having sex or of having a lot of sex. EG *In early adulthood you are at your most potent.* ADJ QUALIT

potentate /pəʊtənteɪt/, **potentates**. A **potentate** is a ruler who has direct power over his people. EG *...Princes, Maharajahs and other potentates.* N COUNT = autocrat

potential /pətenʃəl/. **1** You use **potential** to say that something or someone may develop into the particular kind of thing or person mentioned, but has not done so yet. EG *All 92 countries are customers or potential customers of the United States... ...a massive potential market, big enough for everyone... The dispute has scared away potential investors... ...advertisements appealing for potential foster parents.* ADJ CLASSIF: ATTRIB ⇑ possible ◇ **potentially**. EG *Electricity is potentially dangerous, so treat it with respect.* ◇ ADV+ADJ/ADV

2 A person's **potential** is the range of abilities and talents that he or she was born with, although these abilities and talents may not be in full use yet. EG *We inherit a certain disposition–a potential for intelligence, perhaps... Many children do not achieve their potential.* N UNCOUNT+SUPP ⇑ capability

3 If someone has **potential,** they have an ability to succeed or to do something well, although this may not be happening yet. EG *Has this woman got executive potential?* N UNCOUNT ⇑ capability

4 If something has a particular **potential,** it has the necessary qualities to enable it to develop in the way mentioned, although it may not actually be doing so yet. EG *...the very considerable potential of fast computers for code-cracking... Water the seedlings well to allow them to grow to their full potential.* N UNCOUNT+SUPP ⇑ possibility

potentiality /pətenʃiælɪti[1]/, **potentialities**. A **potentiality** for something is the possibility that a thing or a person has for growth, development, or coming into existence; a formal word. EG *...the potentiality for disorder in the social realm... He was swift to publicise the potentialities of motoring and flight.* N COUNT/UNCOUNT+SUPP = potential

pot herb, pot herbs; also spelled with a hyphen. A **pot herb** is a plant whose dried leaves or stems are used in cooking as a flavouring. N COUNT

pothole /pɒthəʊl/, **potholes**; also spelled with a hyphen. A **pothole** is **1** a large hole in the surface of a road, caused by traffic and bad weather. EG *The jeep lurched dangerously as it hit a large pothole in the road.* N COUNT **2** a deep hole in the ground in a limestone area, often leading to a network of underground caves and tunnels. N COUNT ⇑ cave

potholer /pɒthəʊlə/, **potholers**; also spelled with a hyphen. A **potholer** is someone who explores underground caves as a sport. N COUNT

potholing /pɒthəʊlɪŋ/; also spelled with a hyphen. **Potholing** is the sport of exploring underground caves. N UNCOUNT ↑ caving

potion /pəʊʃəⁿn/, **potions**. A **potion** is a drink that contains medicine, poison, or something that is supposed to have magic powers. EG *...a medicine chest stuffed with drugs, potions, ointments and bandages... He made up and sold love potions.* N COUNT : USU MOD+N

pot plant, pot plants. A **pot plant** is a plant which is grown indoors in a flowerpot. N COUNT

potpourri /pəʊpʊri¹/, **potpourris**. A **potpourri** is 1 a mixture of dried petals and leaves from different flowers in a bowl. Potpourris are used to make rooms smell pleasant. N COUNT/ UNCOUNT **2** a collection of various different items which were not originally intended to form a group. EG *...a whole potpourri of useless gadgets.* N COUNT ↑ medley = miscellany

pot roast, pot roasts; also spelled with a hyphen. A **pot roast** is a piece of meat that is cooked very slowly with a small amount of liquid in a covered pot. N COUNT/ UNCOUNT ↑ joint

pot-shot, pot-shots; also spelled without a hyphen. If you take a **pot-shot** at something or someone, you shoot at them without taking the time to aim carefully; an informal expression. N COUNT

potted /pɒtɪ²d/. **1** A **potted** plant is growing in a container indoors. EG *Their offices are filled with potted palms and other greenery.* ADJ CLASSIF : ATTRIB ↑ cultivated

2 **Potted** meat or fish has been cooked and then put into a small sealed container to be kept until needed. EG *...potted shrimps.* ADJ CLASSIF : ATTRIB ↑ preserved

3 A **potted** biography, history, etc contains the main facts about someone or something in a short and often over-simplified form. EG *One page of the programme is devoted to a potted history of the theatre.* ADJ CLASSIF : ATTRIB ↑ abridged = condensed

potter /pɒtə/, **potters, pottering, pottered**. A **potter** is someone who makes pottery, usually by hand and not in a factory. N COUNT ↑ craftsman

potter about. If you **potter about** or **potter around**, you pass the time in a gentle, unhurried way, doing pleasant but unimportant things; used in British English. EG *He loved to potter around in the garden.* PHRASAL VB : V+ ADV/PREP = putter

potter's wheel. A **potter's wheel** is a piece of equipment with a flat disc which spins round, on which a potter puts soft clay in order to shape it into a pot. N COUNT

pottery /pɒtəⁿri¹/, **potteries**. **1** **Pottery** is **1.1** pots, dishes, and other articles which are shaped from clay and then baked in an oven in order to make them hard. EG *...a sale of antique pottery and porcelain.* N UNCOUNT ↑ earthenware **1.2** the craft or activity of making pottery, usually by hand or using a potter's wheel. EG *My hobbies are pottery and basket-weaving.* N UNCOUNT

2 A **pottery** is a factory or workshop where pottery is made. N COUNT

potting compost is soil that is specially prepared to help young plants to grow. N UNCOUNT

potting shed. A **potting shed** is a shed in a garden, in which you can keep seeds, garden tools, etc. N COUNT

potty /pɒti¹/, **potties; pottier, pottiest**. **1** A **potty** is a deep bowl which a small child uses instead of a toilet. N COUNT ↑ receptacle = pot

2 If you say that someone or something is **potty**, you mean that they are crazy or foolish; an informal word. EG *They thought she was potty, going camping in Scotland in December... It drives you potty.* ADJ QUALIT ↑ mad = daft

3 If you are **potty about** someone or something, you like them very much; an informal expression. PHR : VB INFLECTS

potty-trained. When a small child is **potty-trained**, it is able to use a potty and therefore does not need to wear nappies any more; an expression used in British English. ADJ CLASSIF ↑ continent

potty-training is the process of teaching a small child to use a potty, so that it will not need to wear nappies any more; an expression used in British English. N UNCOUNT

pouch /paʊtʃ/, **pouches**. A **pouch** is **1** a flexible container like a small bag, used to keep things in, for example papers or tobacco. EG *He took the cards and put them in the leather pouch on his belt... He was going to make a tobacco pouch out of them.* N COUNT **2** a loose fold of skin hanging down under each eye of a person who is old or tired. EG *Under my eyes the pouches were heavy.* N COUNT : USU PL = bag **3** a baglike pocket of skin on an animal. Female kangaroos and other marsupials have pouches on their stomachs in which their babies grow. Rodents such as hamsters have pouches in their cheeks in which they keep food. EG *The eggs eventually hatch inside the mother's pouch... They stuff what they don't need into their cheek pouches.* N COUNT

pouf /pu:f/. See **poof**.

pouffe /pu:f/, **pouffes**. A **pouffe** is a low, soft piece of furniture which is used for sitting on or for resting your feet on. N COUNT ↑ stool

poultice /pəʊltɪs/, **poultices**. A **poultice** is a bandage with a mixture of soft ointments on it. The ointments are heated and the bandage is put over a painful or swollen part of someone's body. EG *...a poultice for inflamed eyes... She treated the swelling with poultices of herbs.* N COUNT ↑ dressing

poultry /pəʊltri¹/. **Poultry** is both the singular and the plural form.

1 **Poultry** is meat from farm birds such as chickens, turkeys, and ducks. EG *They sell a wide range of cooked, frozen and fresh poultry... Red wine is drunk with meat, game and poultry.* N UNCOUNT

2 **Poultry** are birds which are kept on farms to produce eggs and to be killed for food. EG *Nowadays, most poultry live in battery houses.* N PLURAL ↑ fowl

pounce /paʊns/, **pounces, pouncing, pounced**. **1** When an animal or bird **pounces** on something, it leaps on it and grabs it, in order to eat it. EG *Twice he had seen leopards pouncing on unsuspecting young baboons... ...the characteristic snorting of a lion just as it pounces.* V : IF+PREP THEN *on/upon* ↑ seize

2 If someone **pounces** on you, they come up to you suddenly and take hold of you. EG *The police were about to pounce upon us... With a harsh cry of recognition, the man pounced upon me.* V : IF+PREP THEN *on/upon* ↑ seize

3 If someone **pounces** on something such as a mistake, they draw attention to it in order to get it corrected. EG *Local politicians are quick to pounce on any trouble... His teacher is pouncing on every error... The press always seems ready to pounce.* V : IF+PREP THEN *on/upon* = leap

pound /paʊnd/, **pounds, pounding, pounded**. **1** A **pound** is **1.1** a unit of money which is used in Britain. One pound is divided into one hundred pence. EG *I was being paid about fifty pounds a week... He owns some 20 million pounds worth of property in Mayfair... ...his assets, including his thirty-five thousand pound house.* N COUNT : USU a/ NUM+N **1.2** the British currency system. EG *...a 13% fall in the pound against the dollar.* N SING : *the*+N **1.3** a unit of money or the currency system in some other countries, for example Ireland, Egypt, Syria, Lebanon, Israel, and Cyprus. N COUNT, OR N SING : *the*+N **1.4** a coin or banknote which is worth one pound. EG *Can you change a pound, Debbie?* N COUNT

2 A **pound** is also a unit of weight used mainly in Britain, America, and other countries where English is spoken. One pound is equivalent to 0.454 kilograms. EG *He eats barely one pound of rice a day... The meat was sold for over $7 a pound... He's about six feet tall and weighs about 140 pounds.* N COUNT/PART : USU a/NUM+N ● If you say that someone is demanding their **pound of flesh**, you mean that they are insisting on getting something that they are legally entitled to have, even though it may bring them little or no benefit and may cause great distress to the person from whom it is demanded. ● PHR : USED AS O, USU POSS+PHR ↑ dues

3 A **pound** is also **3.1** a place where stray domestic animals are taken and kept until they are claimed by their owners. If they are not claimed, they are destroyed. EG *Her constant companion was a dog whom she had saved from a pound.* N COUNT ↑ enclosure **3.2** a place where cars that have been parked illegally are taken by the police and kept until they are claimed by their owners. EG *Redeeming your car from the pound can be expensive.* N COUNT ↑ enclosure

4 If you **pound** something or **pound** on it, you hit it loudly and repeatedly. EG *They began pounding on the walls... In frustration she would pound the dining-room table for immediate service.* V+O, OR V+A ↑ strike = hammer ◊ **pounding**. EG *The pounding of the drums grew louder and louder... The constant pounding of the surf had worn the rocks smooth.* ◊ N UNCOUNT ↑ hammering

5 If you **pound** something such as a typewriter or a musical instrument, you use it energetically and noisily, but not necessarily very skilfully. EG *She was crouched over a typewriter which she pounded furiously.* V+O, OR V+A ↑ hit

6 To **pound** something also means to crush it into a paste or a powder or into very small pieces. EG *The women of the village pounded grain in their mortars... ◊* **pounded**. EG *...sweet cakes made of pounded rice and honey.* V+O = pulverize ◊ ADJ CLASSIF : ATTRIB

7 If your heart or a part of your body **is pounding,** it is beating or throbbing with an unusually strong and fast rhythm. EG *My heart pounded with joy... His head was pounding.* ◊ **pounding**. EG *I felt only the pounding of my heart... With a madly pounding heart he took the steps three at a time.* V ◊ N UNCOUNT OR ADJ CLASSIF

8 If someone **pounds** into or towards a place, they run there with heavy, noisy steps. EG *Without a word he pounded up to the house... A dozen men came pounding down the stairs into the dark room.* V+A = hammering

-pounder, -pounders. A six- or eight-**pounder** is 1 an animal or fish that weighs six or eight pounds. EG *...a smoked salmon, one of a dozen thirteen-pounders her husband had caught.* 2 a gun that fires a shell weighing six or eight pounds. COMB : FORMS N COUNTS

pounding /paʊndɪŋ/; an informal word used mainly in British English. If someone or something gets a **pounding**, 1 they are severely injured or damaged. EG *The city was taking a pounding as the battle approached its suburbs.* 2 they are severely defeated in a sports match or competition. EG *United gave Spurs a real pounding last night.* ● See also **pound**. N SING : a+N = battering; N SING : a+N = thrashing

pour /pɔː/, **pours, pouring, poured**. 1 If you **pour** a liquid or other substance, you cause it to flow out of a container by holding the container at a particular angle. EG *The waiter poured the wine into her glass... I poured the rest down the sink... She poured the salt carefully into the pot.* V+O : USU+A ⇑ transfer = decant

2 If you **pour** someone a drink, you fill a cup or glass with the drink so that they can drink it. EG *He poured Ellen a glass of wine... Lally poured herself another cup of tea... She poured a drink for herself... Shall I pour?* V, V+O, V+O+O, OR V+O+A *(for)* ⇑ serve

3 If a container **pours** well, the substance inside it flows out quickly, easily and without spilling, because it has been well designed or well made. If a container **pours** badly, the substance inside it flows out slowly or messily. EG *This teapot doesn't pour very well.* V+ADV

4 When a liquid or other substance **pours** somewhere, it flows there quickly and in large quantities. EG *The rain poured through a hole in the roof... The sweat began to pour down his face... ...fumes pouring from the backs of buses.* V+A = stream

5 When it **pours** or when it **pours** with rain, it rains very heavily. EG *It was absolutely pouring with rain... In London it poured all the time... The rain had been pouring down all night.* ◊ **pouring**. EG *Don't go out into the pouring rain.* V : *it*+V, OR V+A = bucket ◊ ADJ CLASSIF : ATTRIB = teeming

6 If people or animals **pour** into a particular place, they go there quickly and in large numbers. EG *Refugees are now pouring into this country... It was wonderful to see the fans pouring through the entrance.* V+A ⇑ rush = stream

7 If something such as information **pours** in to an organization, **pours** from a person, etc, a lot of it is obtained, received, or given. EG *Messages of encouragement poured in from people of all kinds... Reports of the devastation poured in... ...the lies that poured from headquarters... The words poured out of her.* V+A = flood, stream

8 If you **pour** money or energy into an activity or organization, you use a lot of it in order to do that activity or help the organization. EG *The state is pouring money into further education... They poured their energies into religious reform.* V+O+A *(into)* ⇑ put = pump

9 If you **pour scorn on** something or someone, you say that they are foolish or worthless. EG *He merely poured scorn on my arguments.* PHR : VB INFLECTS = sneer at

10 If you **pour cold water on** an idea or plan, you criticize it a lot so that people lose their enthusiasm for it. ● to **pour oil on troubled waters**: see **water**. PHR : VB INFLECTS = discourage

pour out. 1 If you **pour out** a drink, you fill a cup or glass with the drink. EG *Castle poured out two glasses of whisky.* PHRASAL VB : V+O+ADV ⇑ serve

2 If you **pour out** your thoughts, feelings, or experiences, you tell someone all about them, especially quickly. EG *I was on the verge of pouring out all my feelings... He poured out a horrifying story.* PHRASAL VB : V+O+ADV = reveal

pout /paʊt/, **pouts, pouting, pouted**. If you **pout**, you stick out your lips as a way of showing or pretending that you are annoyed or dislike someone or something. EG *She tossed back her hair and pouted... ...girls with pouting mouths.* ▸ used as a noun. EG *...smiles and sneers, shrugs and pouts... ...with a pout of her lips.* V ⇑ sulk ▸ N COUNT ⇑ expression

poverty /pɒvəti¹/. 1 **Poverty** is the state of being extremely poor. EG *There are thousands living in poverty... ...a community suffering poverty and injustice.* N UNCOUNT = penury, hardship

2 You can use **poverty** to refer to any situation in which there is not enough of something or its quality is poor; a formal use. EG *...the poverty of most people's ideas about computers... ...the poverty of the soil.* N UNCOUNT+*of* = paucity

poverty-stricken. If a person, area, or organization is **poverty-stricken**, they are suffering extremely badly because of lack of money. EG *...poverty-stricken peasants... ...the poverty-stricken National Health Service.* ADJ CLASSIF ⇑ poor = impoverished

pow /paʊ/ is used in very informal English to indicate the suddenness of an event or the sound of an explosion. EG *I stopped for some gas and pow!, he drove off... I landed, pow! Right in a jam!... Pow, pow–you're dead.* EXCLAM ⇑ noise

POW /piː əʊ dʌbəᵒljuː/ is an abbreviation for 'prisoner of war'. EG *They tried to warn the POWs... ...a POW camp.*

powder /paʊdə/, **powders, powdering, powdered**. 1 **Powder** consists of very tiny particles of a solid substance. EG *Their bones turn to powder... ...washing powders... She put on some lipstick and dusted her face with powder.* N MASS ⇑ granules

2 If you **powder** yourself, you cover your body or parts of it with scented powder. EG *After her bath, she powdered herself and brushed her teeth... She lightly powdered her face.* ◊ **powdered**. EG *You could see each wrinkle on her powdered face.* V+O (NG/REFL) = dust ◊ ADJ CLASSIF ⇑ covered

3 Some women say they want to **powder** their **nose** as a polite way of saying that they want to use the toilet. PHR : VB INFLECTS

powdered /paʊdəd/ is used to describe products which are sold in the form of a powder. EG *...powdered milk... ...powdered coffee.* ● See also **powder**. ADJ CLASSIF : ATTRIB

powder puff, powder puffs; also spelled with a hyphen. A **powder puff** is a round piece of soft, thick material which women use to put powder on their faces. N COUNT

powder room, powder rooms; also spelled with a hyphen. A **powder room** is a room for women in public buildings such as hotels, where they can use the toilet, have a wash, etc. N COUNT = ladies

powdery /paʊdəᵒri¹/. Something that is **powdery** looks or feels like powder. EG *...powdery snow... ...powdery chalk.* ADJ QUALIT ⇑ crumbly

power /pɑʊə/, **powers, powering, powered**. 1 If someone has **power**, they have control over other people or over events or activities. EG *...his yearning for power... They didn't have that power before... It gave the President too much power.* N UNCOUNT = authority, domination

2 If someone has a particular **power**, 2.1 they have a particular physical ability, skill, or opportunity to do something. EG *They did not have the power of speech... They lose the power to walk... They were equals except in earning power.* 2.2 they have official authority or permission to do something, for example to make decisions, arrest people, etc. EG *The chairman has power to fine noisy citizens... The Government curbed the Lords' powers... ...the power of veto.* 2.3 they have the ability to strongly affect people's thoughts or feelings by their artistic skills or intelligence. EG *...the power of his ideas... ...a fine actor of great power.* N SING WITH DET OR N UNCOUNT+SUPP ⇑ capability; N COUNT/UNCOUNT+SUPP ⇑ right; N COUNT/UNCOUNT+SUPP = force, intensity

3 If a person or group of people take **power** or come to **power**, they take charge of a country's affairs, for example by winning an election or by using military force. EG *...when Hitler came to power... The Tories were restored to power for more than four years... The military regime took power in 1964.* ● If a person or group of people is **in power**, they are in charge of a country's affairs. EG *The Tories were in power at the time.* N UNCOUNT ⇑ rule ● PHR : USED AS AN A = governing

4 If you refer to a person or group of people as **the power** in a particular situation, you mean that they have control over it, especially when people generally do not realize this. EG *...the power behind the throne... The press saw these two men as the real power in the land.* N COUNT : USU SING

5 A **power** is a country that is very rich, important, N COUNT+SUPP

or has strong military forces. EG *...a major naval power... ...a country wedged between two opposing power blocs.*

6 If you refer to sea **power**, air **power**, etc you mean warships or military aircraft and their ability to defend or attack an area or fight an enemy in a war. EG *They were potent instruments of sea power... Ships themselves required the protection of air power.* N UNCOUNT : MOD +N ⇑ strength

7 The physical **power** of a person or animal or of a natural force or device is the strength that they have to move, damage, or destroy things. EG *...the power of the wind... I underestimated the power of the explosion.* N UNCOUNT

8 Power is the energy that is obtained by burning a fuel or by using the wind or sun, especially when it is used to make a machine work or to produce electricity. EG *He had planned to use steam power for his later version... ...water or wind power... ...a cheap source of power.* N UNCOUNT

9 Power is also used to mean electricity. EG *A hydro-electric scheme would generate 300 megawatts of power... Just turn the power on, would you?* N UNCOUNT

10 A **power** tool, device, or system is mechanically or electrically operated. EG *...a power mower... ...the new model with a 2.2 litre engine and power steering.* ADJ CLASSIF : ATTRIB

11 In mathematics, a **power** is a number which is written in small size at the top and to the right of another number or a letter. It indicates how many times the number must be multiplied by itself in order to get a particular result. For example, 2 to the power of 3 (or 2^3) is 2 x 2 x 2, or 8. N COUNT+*of* = exponent

12 To **power** a machine or activity means to provide the energy that it needs in order to work or be possible. EG *The gas cylinders that powered the cookers ran out... Its radar equipment was powered by a nuclear reactor.* V+O = fuel

13 The word **power** is also used in the following expressions. **13.1** If someone is **at the height of** their **powers**, they are doing something, especially something that requires skill or imagination, better than at any other time during their life; a literary expression. PHR : USED AS AN A **13.2** If you say that something will **do** you **a power of good**, you mean that it will benefit you greatly. EG *His holiday will do him a power of good.* PHR : VB INFLECTS
13.3 If you are **in** someone's **power**, they have complete control over you. EG *The Count had them in his power... We were completely in her power.* PHR : USED AS AN A **13.4** If it is **in** or **within** someone's **power** to do something, they are able to do it, for example because they have the strength, money, or authority. EG *It was in her power to deny me many things... It may not be within their power to help in practical matters.* PHR : USED AS AN A, USU+*to*-INF **13.5** If you do **everything in** your **power** to achieve something, you try as hard as you can to achieve it. EG *I did everything in my power to give her a really good time... We should be doing everything in our power to develop viable alternatives to petrol.* PHR : USED AS O = all you can **13.6** If you refer to **the powers that be**, you mean the people in authority in a particular situation, especially when you disapprove of them or the way that they control things. EG *Because you are old, the powers that be presume that you no longer have needs... The powers-that-be are worried that it won't look nice.* PHR : USED AS S/O = the authorities, high-ups

powerboat /pauəbəut/, **powerboats**. A **powerboat** is a very fast, powerful motorboat. N COUNT

power cut, power cuts; also spelled with a hyphen. A **power cut** is a period of time when the electricity supply to a particular building or area is interrupted, sometimes deliberately. N COUNT

-powered is used to form adjectives that describe machines or vehicles which work or move by means of a particular type of power. EG *...nuclear-powered submarines... ...electrically-powered cars.* • See also **high-powered.** COMB : FORMS ADJ CLASSIFS

power failure, power failures. A **power failure** is a period of time when the electricity supply to a particular building or area is interrupted, for example because of damage to the cables. N COUNT/UNCOUNT

powerful /pauəful/. **1** A person, government, or organization that is **powerful** is able to control or influence events or other people's behaviour. EG *They organize themselves in powerful and effective trade unions... ...the most powerful government in western Europe.* • See also **all-powerful.** ADJ QUALIT ⇑ strong = influential

2 A person, animal, or part of a body that is **powerful** is physically strong. EG *He had broad shoulders and powerful arms... ...a powerful man.* ◊ **powerfully.** EG *He was powerfully built.* ADJ QUALIT = hefty ◊ ADV WITH VB

3 You use **powerful** to say that someone can do something vigorously and well because they are physically strong. EG *She was a powerful swimmer.* ADJ QUALIT : ATTRIB ⇑ good

4 A **powerful** blow, kick, etc is done with great force. EG *The stallion will attack with powerful kicks and bites... It kills with a powerful crunch of its teeth.* ADJ QUALIT ⇑ strong ≠ gentle

5 A **powerful** machine, device, substance, etc is one that is very effective, for example because it is strong and efficient or because it can be used with great force. EG *...a powerful engine... ...the world's most powerful computer. They had just exploded a powerful hydrogen bomb. ...a powerful and quick-acting medicine.* ADJ QUALIT

6 A **powerful** smell is strong and unpleasant. EG *There was always a powerful smell of kippers in the living-room.* ◊ **powerfully.** EG *...a room smelling powerfully of cats.* ADJ QUALIT = pungent ◊ ADV WITH VB = strongly

7 A **powerful** voice is loud and can be heard from a long way away. ADJ QUALIT = strong

8 A **powerful** light, especially an artificial light, is very bright. EG *...the car's powerful headlights.* ADJ QUALIT = dazzling

9 You also use **powerful** to say that something has a very strong effect on the person or people involved. EG *I find his argument very powerful... We have powerful evidence for this... Religion has a very powerful part to play... He produced a series of extraordinarily powerful paintings... ...the powerful emotions which that music evokes.* ◊ **powerfully.** EG *Picasso's 'Guernica' powerfully influenced him.* ADJ QUALIT ≠ weak, insignificant ◊ ADV WITH VB ⇑ strongly

power game, power games. When you refer to the **power game**, you are referring to a situation in which different people or groups are competing for power. EG *...his next move in the power game.* N COUNT : USU SING

powerhouse /pauəhaus/, **powerhouses**. A **powerhouse** is someone who is very energetic; an informal word. EG *Mel was a powerhouse of disciplined energy.* N COUNT : USU+*of*

powerless /pauələs/. **1** If you are **powerless**, you are unable to control or influence things. EG *Without the full support of the party, the Cabinet is powerless... Prisoners are powerless and helpless creatures.* ◊ **powerlessness.** EG *She experienced an overwhelming sense of powerlessness.* ADJ CLASSIF = impotent, helpless ◊ N UNCOUNT = impotence

2 If you are **powerless** to do a particular thing, you are completely unable to do it. EG *You're powerless to stop it... I stood there watching, feeling powerless to help.* ADJ CLASSIF : PRED+*to*-INF ≠ able

power line, power lines. A **power line** is a cable, especially above ground, along which electricity is conveyed to an area or building. N COUNT

power plant, power plants. A **power plant** is a place where electricity is generated. N COUNT

power point, power points. A **power point** is a device that is connected to an electricity supply and fitted into a wall. If a plug is pushed into it, electricity can pass through the plug and into another device such as a television or an electric fire. N COUNT = mains socket

power-sharing; also spelled without a hyphen. **Power-sharing** is a system in which people who would not normally take part in the government of their country, the management of their factory, etc, are allowed to do so. EG *...the demand for power-sharing from the unions.* N UNCOUNT

power station, power stations. A **power station** is a place where electricity is generated on a large scale. EG *To keep the power stations going they need either coal or oil.* N COUNT

power worker, power workers. A **power worker** is someone who works at a power station. N COUNT

pox /pɒks/. The **pox** is syphilis; an informal word. See also **chicken pox, smallpox.** N SING : *the*+N

pp is written before a person's name at the bottom of some formal or business letters. It means 'for and on behalf of', and indicates that someone else has signed the letter for them. EG *...J.R. Adams, pp D. Philips.* PREP

pp. is the plural of 'p', and means 'pages'.

PR is **1** an abbreviation for 'public relations'. EG *Arrangements had been made by his PR man and aide.* **2** an abbreviation for 'proportional representation'.

practicable /præktɪkəbəl/; a formal word. **1** If a task, plan, or idea is **practicable**, it is capable of ADJ CLASSIF ⇑ possible

being carried out successfully. EG *The noise will be reduced as far as is practicable... State intervention to aid private industry was both practicable and beneficial.* ◇ **practicability** /præktɪbəbɪlɪti¹/. EG *I am not qualified to suggest improvements or comment on the practicability or desirability of legislation.*
◇ N UNCOUNT = feasibility

2 Something that is **practicable** is suitable to be used for a particular purpose. EG *A dark fabric is easily the most practicable for upholstery.*
ADJ QUALIT = practical

practical /præktɪkəºl/, **practicals**. 1 **Practical** problems, ideas, or activities are concerned with aspects of a real situation and with events that actually happen, rather than just with ideas and theories about the situation. EG *The SDP faces practical difficulties of organization and finance... Much of the information he gleaned was of no practical use... Practical experience of broadcasting and journalism would be valuable.*
ADJ CLASSIF : ATTRIB ≠ theoretical

2 If you are **practical**, 2.1 you are able to make sensible decisions and deal efficiently with problems in real life without letting your emotions or imagination affect you. EG *Start being as methodical and practical about it as you can... What a very practical mind you have.*
ADJ QUALIT = businesslike
2.2 you are good at doing jobs with your hands. EG *I am more practical than you.*
ADJ QUALIT = handy

3 **Practical** ideas and methods are likely to be effective or successful in a real situation. EG *Their ideas are too opposed to our way of thinking to be considered practical... How long will it be before nuclear fusion becomes practical?*
ADJ QUALIT = feasible, viable

4 Clothes, household equipment, etc that are **practical** are sensible, useful, and effective for a particular purpose rather than fashionable or attractive. EG *Ceramic tiles are very hard on the feet, though practical.*
ADJ QUALIT = functional

5 You use **practical** to emphasize that something very nearly achieves the state that you mention. EG *It was a practical certainty... The first night was a practical sell-out.*
ADJ CLASSIF : ATTRIB = virtual

6 A **practical** is an examination or a lesson in which you make things or do experiments rather than simply write; an informal use. EG *I use that book for writing up physics practicals.*
N COUNT

practicality /præktɪkælɪti¹/, **practicalities**. 1 The **practicalities** of a situation are the aspects of it which are concerned with real events rather than with ideas and theories about it. EG *He turned out to know very little about the practicalities of living... ...the practicality of planned parenthood.*
N COUNT : USU PL, OR N UNCOUNT ⇑ reality

2 **Practicality** is the ability to react to a situation in a positive and successful way without worrying about ideas or theories. EG *He has the English mixture of extreme practicality and dreaminess.*
N UNCOUNT

practical joke, practical jokes. A **practical joke** is a trick that is intended to embarrass someone or make them look ridiculous. EG *They loved practical jokes.*
N COUNT = prank

practically /præktɪkəºli¹/. **Practically** means 1 almost, but not completely or exactly. EG *The town was practically deserted... He knew practically no English... I had visitors practically every night... She practically forced him into joining the army.*
ADV = virtually
2 involving real actions or events, rather than just ideas or theories. EG *The work this term is more practically based.*
ADV WITH VB ≠ theoretically

practice /præktɪs/, **practices, practicing, practiced**. 1 The **practice** of an activity involves carrying it out in accordance with your beliefs or theories. EG *We must combine theory with practice... The practice of reason can be our only hope.*
N UNCOUNT ⇑ application

2 A **practice** is an activity or habit that you do regularly because it has become a custom or tradition. EG *We must respect the practices of cultures different from our own... Benn began the practice of holding regular meetings... ...the ancient Japanese practice of binding the feet from birth.*
N COUNT

3 Normal or standard **practice** is a normal or accepted way of doing things, for example as accepted within one particular organization or institution. EG *This was standard practice... The authorities agreed to review his residence permit, against normal practice.*
N UNCOUNT : ADJ +N = procedure

4 **Practice** is regular training or exercise that you do in order to improve your skill at a sport or an activity such as music. EG *Skating's just a matter of practice... It takes practice... In time and with practice it becomes less of an effort... I sometimes help them with their homework or music practice.*
N UNCOUNT
▸ used to refer to a period of time that you spend doing this. EG *Mr Donnelly, the track coach, ended the day's practice early... How was the target practice?*
▸ N SING WITH DET = work-out

5 If you have had **practice** at an activity, you have had experience that has helped you develop your skill at it. EG *When it comes to washing up I've had as much practice as anybody... It's all good practice... I felt I hadn't had enough practice.*
N UNCOUNT = training

6 A doctor's or lawyer's **practice** is the place where they work, often with a group of other doctors or lawyers, and where their patients or clients go to see them. EG *...a medical practice... Some prefer to consult a doctor with a private practice who takes paying patients... He had a solid career in a country law practice.*
N COUNT ⇑ business
▸ used as an uncount noun to refer to the work of a doctor or lawyer who has a practice. EG *These doctors lived on their earnings from private practice... He's going into general practice.*
▸ N UNCOUNT : USU MOD+N

7 The word **practice** is also used in the following expressions. 7.1 If you **put** something **into practice**, you carry it out in accordance with your beliefs or theories. EG *I'm not sure how effective these methods will be when put into practice... He had yet to attempt to put principles into practice.*
PHR : VB INFLECTS ⇑ apply
7.2 If you describe the way something happens **in practice**, you are talking about what actually happens in a real situation, especially in contrast to ideas or theories about the situation. EG *In practice, he exerted little influence over the others... What it means in practice is that he does twice the work for half the money.*
PHR : USED AS ADV SEN = in actual fact ≠ in theory, in principle
7.3 If you are **in practice**, you have had a lot of regular experience recently at an activity. If you are **out of practice**, you have not had much experience recently.
PHR : USED AS AN A
7.4 If you say **practice makes perfect**, you mean that it is possible to learn something or develop a skill if you practise enough. People often say 'practice makes perfect' to someone to encourage them to continue practising.
CONVENTION

8 To **practice** means the same as to **practise**; used in American English.

practise /præktɪs/, **practises, practising, practised**; also spelled **practice** in American English. 1 If you **practise**, you do exercises in an activity such as a sport or playing music in order to improve your skill at it. EG *No matter how hard one practises, there is no substitute for match conditions... I played the piece I had been practising for months... They just want to use you for practising their English.* ● See also **practised**.
V OR V+O

2 If people **practise** particular activities, 2.1 they do them as a custom or traditional way of behaving. EG *The pleasures of watching these two tribes practising their own habits and customs are immense... Infanticide was practised by many early cultures... ...a charming old-fashioned custom still practised in the suburbs.*
V+O ⇑ carry out = observe
2.2 they carry them out in accordance with a particular belief or theory. EG *How are we expected to be democratic if we have never been allowed to practise democracy?*
V+O = pursue

3 If you **practise** something unpleasant on someone, you treat them in an unpleasant or cruel way. EG *I am horrified when I think of the cruelty practised on these helpless victims... Torture was certainly practised by Europeans upon Europeans.*
V+O+A = perpetrate

4 If you **practise** a profession such as law, you work as a lawyer. EG *He went on to study law and practise it... He's in Hull practising medicine just now... Many doctors in country districts still practise from their own houses.* ◇ **practising**. EG *He is now a practising doctor in Essex.*
V OR V+O
◇ ADJ CLASSIF : ATTRIB

practised /præktɪst/. Someone who is **practised** at doing something is good at it because they have had experience and have developed their skill at it. EG *A practised searcher rarely leaves any trace of his presence.*
ADJ CLASSIF = experienced
▸ used of people's qualities and achievements. EG *He allowed his practised eye to travel slowly over the landscape... His was a practised performance.*
▸ = expert

practitioner /præktɪʃəºnə/, **practitioners**; a formal word. A **practitioner** is 1 a person who regularly does a particular activity. EG *...the new practitioners of art history.*
N COUNT + *of*
2 a person who works as a doctor or lawyer. EG *He's a medical practitioner.*
N COUNT : USU MOD+N

praesidium /prɪsɪdɪəm/. See **presidium**.
N COUNT

praetorian guard, /prɪtɔːrɪən gɑːd/, **praetorian guards**. A **praetorian guard** is a group of people
N COUNT

who are supposed to be loyal to a particular person, but who are often more interested in their own aims and ambitions. EG *...that Praetorian Guard of foreigners around the President.*

pragmatic /prægmætɪk/, **pragmatics**. 1 **Pragmatic** ideas, reasons, attitudes, etc deal with a situation or problem in a practical way rather than in a theoretical way; a formal use. EG *He argued the case for increased state intervention on wholly pragmatic grounds... This is not just ideology, but pragmatic politics.* ◊ **pragmatically**. EG *My father pragmatically and empirically built up his knowledge of boat-building.*
ADJ QUALIT ⇑ practical = realistic
◊ ADV WITH VB ⇑ practically

2 **Pragmatics** is the study of the way language is used in particular situations, and is therefore concerned with the functions of words as opposed to their forms. It deals with the intentions of the speaker, and the way in which the hearer interprets what is said; a technical term in linguistics.
N UNCOUNT

pragmatism /prægmətɪzəᵒm/ is a way of thinking or of dealing with problems in a practical way rather than by using theory or abstract principles; a formal word. EG *There had been too much pragmatism of late and not enough principle... ...the voice of American pragmatism.* ◊ **pragmatist, pragmatists**. EG *Pragmatists though we may sometimes be, it's just not possible to expect us to agree under those terms.*
N UNCOUNT ⇑ attitude = practicality
◊ N COUNT ⇑ realist

prairie /prɛəri¹/, **prairies**. In North America, a **prairie** is a large flat area of grassy land with very few trees. EG *I used to dream of a million dollars for buying prairie... ...the prairie farmer's wheat... The depression hit the prairies.*
N UNCOUNT/ COUNT, OR N SING : the+N ⇑ grassland

praise /preɪz/, **praises, praising, praised**. 1 If you **praise** someone or something, you express strong approval for their qualities or achievements. EG *Sylvia had a stern father who never praised her... Gaitskell praised his 'passionate intensity'... They praised his speech for its clarity and humour... I remember praising the picture she had over the mantelpiece.*
V+O ⇑ approve = compliment

2 **Praise** is what you say or write about someone when you are praising them. EG *Three other entrants were singled out for special praise... She finds it hard to give praise... 'The Times' newspaper was more specific in its praise.*
N UNCOUNT = commendation

3 If you **sing** someone's **praises**, you praise them in an enthusiastic or exaggerated way. EG *Liz is forever singing your praises... He's now singing the praises of Iain Macleod.*
PHR : VB INFLECTS = laud

4 If you **sing your own praises**, you boast about how good or clever you are; used showing disapproval. EG *He's always singing his own praises.*
PHR : VB INFLECTS = brag

5 If you **praise** God or **praise** the Lord, you express your respect, honour, and thanks to God, for example during a church service or in your prayers. EG *They experience an ability to praise God in unknown languages.*
V+O ⇑ worship

6 **Praise** is also the expression of respect, honour and thanks to God. EG *...a hymn of praise... Give praise to the Lord.*
N UNCOUNT ⇑ worship

7 You can also use **praise** in expressions like 'praise be', 'praise be to God', or 'praise God', when you want to say that you are very relieved about something.
CONVENTION

praiseworthy /preɪzwɜːði¹/. Something that is **praiseworthy** is considered to be admirable or worthy of praise. EG *...a significant and praiseworthy increase in computer intelligence.*
ADJ QUALIT = commendable

pram /præm/, **prams**. A **pram** is a baby's cot on wheels. EG *...a young mother pushing a pram.*
N COUNT

prance /prɑːns/, **prances, prancing, pranced**.
1 If someone **prances**, they walk or move around with exaggerated movements because they want people to look at them and admire them; often used showing disapproval. EG *When it was Vic's turn, he pranced about, lifting his knees high.* ◊ **prancing**. EG *The father turned and walked with a curious little prancing stride over to the bed.*
V+A = strut, parade
◊ ADJ CLASSIF : ATTRIB = mincing

2 If an animal such as a horse **prances**, it moves with quick, high steps. EG *A couple of yards away the buck is prancing up and down.*
V : USU+A ⇑ = cavort

prank /præŋk/, **pranks**. A **prank** is a trick that is intended to embarrass someone or to make them seem foolish; a rather old-fashioned word.
N COUNT

prankster /præŋkstə/, **pranksters**. A **prankster** is someone who plays tricks and practical jokes on people; a rather old-fashioned word.
N COUNT ⇑ joker

prat /præt/, **prats**. If you call someone a **prat**, you mean that they are very stupid or foolish; an offensive word, used in informal British English.
N COUNT : ALSO VOC = twit

prattle /prætəᵒl/, **prattles, prattling, prattled**; an informal word, often used showing disapproval. If someone **prattles** on about something, they talk a great deal without saying anything important, especially just for the sake of talking. EG *Brigadier Tomlinson prattled on.* ▸ used as a noun. EG *He was impervious to her laughter and prattle.*
V : USU+A (on) = babble
▸ N UNCOUNT = babble

prawn /prɔːn/, **prawns**. A **prawn** is a small shellfish, similar to a shrimp, which can be eaten. EG *...a buffet with big prawns and fillet steak.*
N COUNT ⇑ crustacean

prawn cocktail, prawn cocktails. A **prawn cocktail** is a dish that consists of prawns, salad, and a sauce. It is usually eaten at the beginning of a meal.
N COUNT/ UNCOUNT

pray /preɪ/, **prays, praying, prayed**. 1 If you **pray**, you speak to the God that you believe in, in order to give thanks or to ask for his help. EG *He kneeled down and prayed to Allah... The men entered the mosque to pray for forgiveness... Now all I had to do was pray... I have prayed so hard that he will live.*
V : USU+A, OR V +REPORT-CL

2 If you **pray** for something or **pray** that something might happen, you hope for it or want it very strongly. EG *Praying she would not see me, I hurried down the street... He got what he had prayed for, a beautiful little puppy... I would never have believed that Londoners would pray for rain.*
V+A (for), OR V+ REPORT-CL

3 You can use **pray** to add politeness or sarcasm to a question or a command; an old-fashioned use. EG *Pray sit down and tell me what I can do for you... 'Who, pray, invited you?' said James.*
ADV SEN

prayer /prɛə/, **prayers**. 1 **Prayer** is the activity of praying to God. EG *It was time for prayer and the Muslims kneeled... Her eyes were shut and her lips were moving in prayer.*
N UNCOUNT ⇑ devotion

2 A **prayer** is all the words which you say when you are praying. EG *I got into bed after I had said my prayers... I made a brief prayer for her swift and complete recovery... Our prayer for his return has been answered.* **2.2** a set form of words which is said during a religious service. EG *We will now say the Lord's Prayer.* **2.3** a hope which you have for the future, and which you sometimes ask God to help you achieve. EG *My one prayer is that I don't live to be really old.*
N COUNT
N COUNT
N COUNT

3 **Prayers** can refer to a short religious service, often informal, at which people gather especially to pray. EG *The next morning I was returning from prayers at the mosque... There were family prayers every evening in the chapel.*
N PLURAL

4 If you say that someone **hasn't got a prayer**, you mean that it is impossible for them to succeed in what they are trying to do; an informal expression.
PHR : VB INFLECTS

prayer book, prayer books; also spelled with a hyphen. A **prayer book** is a book which contains the prayers which are used in church or at home.
N COUNT

pre- is used to form words that describe something as taking place before a particular date or event. EG *...marital→pre-marital... ...war→pre-war... ...1914→pre-1914... ...trial→pre-trial.*
PREFIX

preach /priːtʃ/, **preaches, preaching, preached**. 1 If a member of the clergy **preaches** or **preaches** a sermon, he or she gives a talk on a religious or moral subject during a church service. EG *The chaplain came and preached to a packed church.*
V OR V+O ⇑ speak

2 If someone **preaches** a particular belief or way of life, they try and convince people to accept those beliefs or to take a particular course of action. EG *They preach peace while preparing for war... His father used to go round the villages preaching Socialism.*
V+O/REPORT-CL = advocate

3 If you **preach** at someone, you give them advice about what they should do in a very boring, moralizing way; used showing disapproval. EG *I've had enough of you preaching at me all the time–just leave me alone!*
V : IF+PREP THEN at ⇑ advise = lecture

4 If you say that someone **practises** what they **preach**, you mean that they do themselves what they encourage other people to do. EG *He practises what he preaches, which is more than you do.*
PHR : VBS INFLECT

preacher /priːtʃə/, **preachers**. A **preacher** is a person who preaches sermons as part of a church service. Preachers are often members of the clergy. EG *Tony inherited his eloquence from his father, a*
N COUNT ⇑ teacher

Christian preacher... His father had been a lay preacher.

preamble /priːæmbəˡl/, **preambles**. A **preamble** is an introduction that comes before something you say or write; a formal word. EG *...an intensely long preamble... Without preamble, he told Stuart the whole story again.* N COUNT/ UNCOUNT

prearranged /priːəreɪndˡʒd/; also spelled with a hyphen. Something that is **prearranged** has been planned or arranged before the time when it actually happens. EG *They were certain the riot couldn't have been prearranged... ...a prearranged signal.* ADJ CLASSIF ↑ predetermine

precarious /priˡkeəriəs/; a fairly formal word. 1 Something that is **precarious** is in a dangerous state or position because it is not securely held in place and seems likely to fall down or collapse at any moment. EG *Even in the dry season the streams have to be crossed by precarious rows of half bricks... Baby monkeys cling to their mother's fur in what seems to be a most precarious fashion.* ADJ QUALIT ↑ unstable = hazardous
◇ **precariously**. EG *For the rest of the journey I sat precariously on the roof of the cabin.* ◇ ADV WITH VB

2 If your situation or position is **precarious**, you are not secure because you are not in complete control of events and might fail in what you are doing. EG *The management of the unit was then in a precarious position... Life for most people will be more precarious in the year 2000 than it is now.* ADJ QUALIT ↑ risky = insecure
◇ **precariously**. EG *I found myself living, somewhat precariously, from one assignment to another.* ◇ ADV WITH VB

precaution /priˡkɔːʃəˡn/, **precautions**. A **precaution** is an action that is intended to prevent something dangerous or unpleasant from happening. EG *I had taken the precaution of swallowing two sea sickness tablets... ...fire precautions... As a precaution, I had brought an extra sweater with me.* N COUNT ↑ care

precautionary /priˡkɔːʃənəˡriˡ/. **Precautionary** actions are taken in order to prevent something dangerous or unpleasant from happening; a formal word. EG *I would have to take precautionary steps to keep him out.* ADJ CLASSIF ↑ safety

precede /priˡsiːd/, **precedes, preceding, preceded**; a fairly formal word. 1 If one event or period of time **precedes** another, it happens before the second event or period of time. EG *...the sudden drop in temperature that precedes a heavy thunder storm... The children's dinner was preceded by party games.* V+O ↑ happen = come before ≠ come after, follow, succeed
◇ **preceding**. EG *I knew that he had been in Cuba the preceding summer... Enrolments had risen by 50 per cent in the preceding decade.* ◇ ADJ CLASSIF : ATTRIB ↑ previous

2 If someone or something **precedes** you somewhere, they go there in front of you. EG *She slung the bag over her shoulder and preceded him across the vast hallway... We were preceded by a huge man called Teddy Brown.* V+O = lead

3 Words, sentences, etc, that **precede** something are spoken written, or printed just before it. EG *...it was preceded by a set of random words.* V+O ≠ follow
◇ **preceding**. EG *I noticed the slip of my pen in the preceding paragraph... In the four preceding chapters, I have diagnosed the sickness of contemporary society.* ◇ ADJ CLASSIF : ATTRIB ↑ above = previous, last

4 If someone **precedes** you in a particular job or position, they had your job or position before you did. EG *He preceded me as chairman of the Society.* V+O

precedence /presɪdəns/; a formal word. 1 If something **takes precedence over** another thing, it is treated as being more important and is dealt with before the other thing. EG *The peaceful ordering of human society takes precedence over every other consideration... In my case, practicality takes precedence over superstition.* PHR : VB INFLECTS

2 **Precedence** is the formal order of priority that is given to people at ceremonial occasions. EG *Officers and wives entered in strict order of precedence.* N UNCOUNT

precedent /presɪdənt/, **precedents**; a formal word. 1 A **precedent** is 1.1 an action or official decision that can be referred to in order to justify taking a similar action or decision. EG *His Lordship went on to look at other precedents... Newton's case had already established the precedent... The Supreme Court, he went on, had already set a precedent.* N COUNT = example, model
1.2 something of the same type that has happened or existed before. EG *There was no precedent for the riots.* N COUNT = forerunner

2 **Precedent** is the way that something has always been done and therefore the way that is considered to be correct. EG *He broke with precedent by making his maiden speech on a controversial subject... It would be contrary to legal precedent to hear him.* N UNCOUNT = custom

precept /priːsept/, **precepts**. A **precept** is a general rule that helps you to decide how you should behave in particular circumstances; a formal word. EG *...the simple precept 'Do as you would be done by'.* N COUNT = maxim, principle

precinct /priːsɪŋkt/, **precincts**. 1 A **precinct** is 1.1 a specially built shopping area in the centre of a town or city, in which cars are not allowed; used in British English. EG *...a shopping precinct... ...a pedestrian precinct... Howard goes on down the precinct to the supermarket.* N COUNT
1.2 an enclosed area around a large building, which is surrounded by a boundary or wall; a fairly formal use. EG *...the rambling courts and precincts of the Palace... ... the precincts of Westminster Cathedral.* N COUNT : SING=PL
1.3 an area or district which is part of a city and has its own police force, fire service, etc; used in American English. EG *Stevens put his life in danger by entering a precinct where police officers had been shot.* N COUNT

2 The **precincts** of an institution or organization are its buildings and land, especially when they are considered to represent the institution or organization; a formal use. EG *Gambling is prohibited within the precincts of the University.* N PLURAL = area, environs

precious /preʃəs/. 1 Something that is **precious** is 1.1 considered to be important, valuable, and useful, and therefore should not be wasted or used badly. EG *The one resource more precious than any other was land... They have lost precious working time... My life is more precious to me than my property... His knowledge of foreign affairs is too precious to be dispensed with.* ADJ QUALIT = prized
1.2 worth a lot of money because it is rare. EG *...salt is nearly as precious as gold in many places.* ADJ QUALIT ↑ expensive = valuable

2 **Precious** possessions or memories are very important to you because they are concerned with people or events in your life which you remember with pleasure. EG *To me our friendship is a very precious thing... I imagine he treasures that evening as one of the precious mementoes of his Presidency.* ADJ QUALIT = cherished, treasured

3 **Precious** is used in informal English to express your dislike for something that someone else thinks is very important, but which makes you angry or bored. EG *I'm sick and tired of your precious brother-in-law... How sentimental you are about your precious ideas.* ADJ CLASSIF : ATTRIB ↑ damned = beloved

4 If you say that someone is **precious**, you mean that they behave in a formal and unnatural way because they are concerned with unimportant details and try too hard to be perfect; used showing disapproval. EG *He's a wee bit precious... Was I being too precious about this thing?* ▸ used of people's behaviour and actions. EG *He has a slightly precious prose style.* ADJ QUALIT = affected, mannered

5 If you say that there is **precious little** of something, you mean that there is only a small amount of it. EG *There's precious little they can learn from us... He was a man with no charm at all and precious few virtues.* PHR : USED AS QUANTIF

precious metal, precious metals. A **precious metal** is a valuable metal such as gold or silver, which is often used for making jewellery. N COUNT/ UNCOUNT

precious stone, precious stones. A **precious stone** is a valuable stone that is used for making jewellery. Diamonds, rubies, and sapphires are precious stones. N COUNT = gem, jewel

precipice /presɪpɪs/, **precipices**. A **precipice** is 1 a very steep side on a mountain or rock. EG *...I looked over the precipice... At the edge of the precipice he sat down.* N COUNT ↑ edge = cliff
2 a dangerous situation in which you are extremely close to disaster or failure. EG *Britain was speeding towards an economic precipice... It took a serious illness to push him over the precipice into debt.* N COUNT ↑ danger = brink

precipitate, precipitates, precipitating, precipitated; a formal word. The word **precipitate** is pronounced /priˡsɪpɪteɪt/ when it is a verb, and /priˡsɪpəˡtəˡt/ when it is an adjective. When it is a noun, it can be pronounced either /priˡsɪpəˡtəˡt/ or /priˡsɪpɪteɪt/.

1 If something **precipitates** a new event or situation, it causes it to happen, usually suddenly and unexpectedly. EG *Its effect would be to precipitate a change in the law... All this would reduce profits and precipitate an economic crisis.* V+O = hasten, bring about

2 A **precipitate** action happens suddenly, and usually faster than people consider to be sensible or reason- ADJ QUALIT ↑ rash

able. EG *All this meant a precipitate advance to socialism.* ◊ **precipitately**. EG *The visit ended precipitately when four shots were fired.* ◊ ADV WITH VB

3 A **precipitate** is a solid substance that becomes separated from a liquid during a chemical reaction; a technical term in chemistry. EG *A white precipitate had gathered at the top of the glass.* N COUNT

precipitation /pri'sɪpɪteɪʃə⁰n/ is **1** a process in a chemical reaction which causes solid particles to become separated from a liquid; a technical term in chemistry. N UNCOUNT **2** rain, snow, hail, etc that falls as water or ice after it condenses in the atmosphere; a technical term in meteorology. N UNCOUNT **3** extreme haste in the way you carry out an action; a formal use. EG *Europe looked like sliding down a slope, and with precipitation, into an abyss of war.* N UNCOUNT

precipitous /pri'sɪpɪtəs/; a formal word. **1** A **precipitous** area is very high and has very steep sides. EG *We bumped over the precipitous road to the ferry.* ADJ QUALIT

2 Precipitous actions happen quickly and often without being planned. EG *This, however, was far too precipitous and reckless for Frank to accept.* ADJ QUALIT ⇑ quick = hasty

précis /preɪsi'/. **Précis** is both the singular and the plural form. It is pronounced /preɪsi'z/ when it is the plural.

A **précis** is a short piece of writing which contains the main points of a book or report, but not the details. EG *...a comprehensive and convincing précis of the main points of the case.* N COUNT = summary ▸ used as an uncount noun. EG *...exercises in précis and comprehension.* ▸ N UNCOUNT

precise /pri'saɪs/. **1** You use **precise** to emphasize that you are describing something accurately, correctly, and exactly. EG *At that precise moment we were interrupted by the telephone... The precise nature of the disease has not yet been established... These transmitters send out warning signals identifying their precise location.* ADJ CLASSIF: ATTRIB = exact, very

2 Something that is **precise** is accurate and complete in all its details. EG *Mr Jones gave him clipped and precise instructions... The timing had to be very precise.* ADJ QUALIT ⇑ fine

3 Someone who is **precise** is extremely careful and particular about details and in the way they act. EG *He was very precise in his manner.* ADJ QUALIT ⇑ meticulous

4 You say **'to be precise'** to indicate that you are now giving more detailed information or a slight correction that relates to what you have been saying. EG *I have to be up early–4 a.m. to be precise.* PHR : USED AS AN A

precisely /pri'saɪsli'/. **1 Precisely** means accurately and exactly. EG *He made the knots precisely, losing no time... Let me explain to you precisely what I am going to do.* ADV WITH VB

2 You can use **precisely** to emphasize the exact truth or accuracy of what you are saying. EG *It is precisely the richest societies which pursue the most aggressive politics... He was furious, precisely because he had not been consulted... It seems to me that he is precisely the kind of writer to whom the Nobel Prize should be awarded... I'll tell you precisely how your father makes his money.* ADV+N/CONJ/REPORT-CL

3 If you say **'precisely'**, you are agreeing with someone or emphasizing that you believe what they said was exact. EG *'Precisely,' was the Bishop's opinion.* CONVENTION = exactly, quite

precision /pri'sɪʒə⁰n/ is the quality of being exact and accurate. EG *The attack was carried out with clockwork precision... He had established a reputation for unfailing precision in his job.* N UNCOUNT = accuracy, exactness

preclude /pri'klu:d/, **precludes, precluding, precluded**; a formal word. **1** If something **precludes** an event or action, it prevents that event or action from happening. EG *This should not preclude a search for a better hypothesis... Popular revolt was virtually precluded... This would preclude many types of commercial development.* V+O = prohibit, inhibit

2 If a set of circumstances **precludes** you from doing something or going somewhere, they make it impossible for you to do it or go there. EG *Its methodology would preclude critics from explaining why one book is better than another... It sets limits on the powers of the Government, and precludes it from acting unconstitutionally.* V+O+A *(from)* ⇑ prevent = debar

precocious /pri'kəʊʃəs/. **1 Precocious** children behave in a way that makes them appear to be older than they really are, usually because they are cleverer than other children of the same age; often used showing disapproval. EG *He was rather a precocious child with a mind of his own... I have a really brilliant, precocious pupil in my class.* ADJ QUALIT ⇑ mature = forward ◊ **precociously**. EG *...his own precociously articulate and tirelessly inquisitive child.* ◊ ADV ◊ **precociousness**. EG *They encouraged this precociousness.* ◊ N UNCOUNT

2 Someone or something that is **precocious** has developed to an advanced stage earlier or more quickly than is usual. EG *The precocious development of literature in an otherwise undeveloped culture.* ADJ CLASSIF ⇑ early

3 If someone achieves something at a **precocious** age, they are considered to be surprisingly young to be so successful. EG *She achieved the rank of full professor at a precocious age.* ADJ QUALIT: ATTRIB ⇑ early

precocity /pri'kɒsɪti'/ is the quality or state of being very advanced in your behaviour; a formal word. EG *Impressed by my precocity, the General offered me a place on his staff.* N UNCOUNT ⇑ development = forwardness

preconceived /pri:kənsi:vd/. If you have **preconceived** ideas about something, you have already made up your mind about it before you have had enough information or experience to form a fair opinion; often used showing disapproval. EG *We have preconceived ideas about the capabilities of our minds... The development of the idea depended on getting away from preconceived notions.* ADJ CLASSIF: ATTRIB ⇑ biased

preconception /pri:kə⁷nsepʃə⁰n/, **preconceptions**. A **preconception** is a belief that you already have about something before you know enough information or have enough experience to form a fair opinion about it. EG *The popular preconception remains intact... He tries to deny information that challenges his preconceptions.* N COUNT ⇑ idea = prejudice

precondition /pri:kə⁷ndɪʃə⁰n/, **preconditions**. A **precondition** is something which must happen, be true, or be done first, before it is possible for something else to happen; a formal word. EG *Redistribution is a precondition for any transition to a stable society... ...countries where economic growth is a precondition of any kind of human advance.* N COUNT : USU *for/of* = requirement, prerequisite

pre-cooked food has been prepared and cooked in advance so that it can be heated quickly before you eat it. EG *Pre-cooked and dry cereals absorb a lot of milk.* ADJ CLASSIF

precursor /pri'kɜ:sə/, **precursors**. A **precursor** is something that happened or existed before something else, especially when it is considered to have had an influence on future events. EG *The railways were the precursors of what was to come... Learning the Highway Code was a precursor to any driving.* N COUNT : IF+PREP THEN *of/to* = forerunner, predecessor

> **PRED** □ In this dictionary PRED is used in the grammar notes beside an adjective to mean that the adjective is used in predicative position after the verb 'be' or after some other verbs such as 'become', 'feel', and 'seem'. If an adjective always occurs after a verb it is described as PRED. If it usually occurs after a verb it is described as USU PRED. An example is **asleep**. EG *The baby is **asleep** at last.* You do not say '...an asleep baby'.

predate /pri:deɪt/, **predates, predating, predated**. If you say that one thing **predated** another, you mean that the first thing happened or existed some time before the second thing; a formal word. EG *The building of the Nansera airfield predated the building of the Shiraz by several years.* V+O : IF+PREP THEN *by*

predator /predətə/, **predators**. A **predator** is **1** an animal that kills and eats other animals. EG *The whiting is a major predator on smaller fish... In New Zealand, there were no predators before the arrival of man.* N COUNT ⇑ hunter ≠ prey **2** a person who is eager to gain something out of someone else's weakness or suffering, and who shows no sympathy or mercy; used showing disapproval. EG *They distort the facts to present the police as dictatorial predators.* N COUNT = opportunist, vulture

predatory /predətə⁰ri'/. **1 Predatory** animals live by killing other animals for food. EG *She was safe from predatory birds on the verandah.* ▸ used of their behaviour. EG *They lie in shallow water to escape the predatory attentions of bigger fish.* ADJ CLASSIF: ATTRIB ⇑ aggressive

2 Predatory people or organizations are eager to gain something out of someone else's weakness or suffering and show no sympathy or mercy. EG *...the drawing-rooms of predatory new-rich women.* ADJ CLASSIF: ATTRIB ⇑ greedy = voracious

predecessor /pri:dɪsesə/, **predecessors**. **1** Your **predecessor** is the person who had your job before you started doing it. EG *She wasn't being paid the same wage as her male predecessor.* N COUNT : USU POSS+N

2 The **predecessor** of an object, machine, etc is the N COUNT : USU thing which came before it in a sequence or process of development. EG *Only the name links the new Cavalier with its predecessor.* WITH POSS = forerunner

predestination /pri:dɛstɪneɪʃən/ is the belief that human beings have no control over events because they have already been decided by God or by fate. EG *...as irreconcilable as the notions of predestination and free will.* N UNCOUNT = destiny

predestined /pri:dɛstɪnd/. If you say that a situation was **predestined**, you mean that nobody had any control over it because it had already been decided by God or by fate. EG *I was therefore predestined to be a slave... Do you think it was predestined since the beginning of the world?* ADJ CLASSIF = destined

PREDET □ In this dictionary PREDET is used in the grammar notes beside entries to mean that the word is a predeterminer. The predeterminers are *such, what, all, both, half, double, twice, treble, thrice* and *quadruple*. They come right at the start of a noun group, even before a DET (determiner) if there is one. If there are restrictions on which determiner and/or noun follows a predeterminer, this is indicated in the grammar notes. An example is **all 1.2**, for which the grammar note says PREDET+N UNCOUNT OR N IN PLURAL.

predetermined /pri:dɪtɜ:mɪnd/. If something is **predetermined**, its form, position, or result has already been decided by previous events or by a person, and has not developed by chance; a formal word. EG *He believes that we're all genetically predetermined... The energy industries expanded at their own predetermined rate.* ADJ CLASSIF: ATTRIB = prearranged

predeterminer /pri:dɪtɜ:mɪnə/, **predeterminers**. In grammar, a predeterminer is a word that is used before a determiner, and that gives you more information about the noun in the noun group, for example, 'all' in 'all the time', 'both' in 'both our children', and 'half' in 'half an hour'. Words which are predeterminers have PREDET in the grammar note beside the entry. See also □ at PREDET. N COUNT

predicament /pri¹dɪkəmə²nt/, **predicaments**. A **predicament** is an unpleasant situation that you are in and that is difficult to get out of; a fairly formal word. EG *He hasn't realized his predicament yet... Smith had misled them into a worse predicament than ever before.* N COUNT+SUPP ⇑ state = dilemma, fix

predicate, predicates, predicating, predicated. The word **predicate is pronounced** /prɛdɪkət/ when it is a noun, and /prɛdɪkeɪt/ when it is a verb.

1 In some systems of grammar, the **predicate** of a sentence or clause is the part of it that is not the subject. For example, in the sentence: 'I decided what to do', 'decided what to do' is the predicate; a technical use. N COUNT

2 If you **predicate** something, you state that you believe it is true; a formal use. EG *It has been predicated that a seismic shock was the cause of these phenomena.* V+O/REPORT-CL ⇑ imply

3 If you say that one idea or situation **is predicated** on another, you mean that the first idea or situation can be true or real only if the second one is true or real; a formal use. EG *Everything was predicated on getting to the airport with time to spare.* V+O: USU PASS+on/upon = rely

predicative /pri¹dɪkətɪv/. If an adjective is in **predicative** position, it comes after a verb. See □ at PRED. ADJ CLASSIF: ATTRIB

predict /pri¹dɪkt/, **predicts, predicting, predicted**. If you **predict** an event or action, you say that you believe that it will happen, or that it will happen in a particular way. EG *I predict that we will survive his temporary absence... He predicted a brilliant future for the child... You can't predict what these things are going to do.* V+O/REPORT-CL/QUOTE = foresee

predictable /pri¹dɪktəbə⁰l/. Something that is **predictable** happens in a way that you are able to know about in advance, for example because it always or very often happens like that. EG *The outcome is not always predictable... Certain conditions have led to fairly predictable kinds of behaviour.* ◊ **predictably**. EG *Predictably, the affair went hopelessly wrong... ...conventional situations where everyone behaves predictably.* ◊ **predictability** /prə¹dɪktəbɪlɪti¹/. EG *They do not expect predictability from other adults.* ADJ QUALIT = foreseeable; ◊ ADV SEN, OR ADV WITH VB; ◊ N UNCOUNT

prediction /pri¹dɪkʃə⁰n/, **predictions**. If you make a **prediction** about something, you say that you believe it will happen, or that it will happen in a particular way. EG *...a number of alternative predictions about the future of Higher Education... ...a prediction of the likely outcome of the next election.* ▸ used as an uncount noun. EG *...the study of probability and simple methods of prediction that can be used in one's personal life.* N COUNT = forecast, prognostication; ▸ N UNCOUNT = forecasting

predictive /pri¹dɪktɪv/. Speech or writing that is **predictive** is concerned with information about future events; a formal word. ADJ CLASSIF = prophetic

pre-digested. If you describe information as **pre-digested**, you mean that it has been made simpler or easier to understand; used showing disapproval. EG *The local press is particularly vulnerable to pre-digested news.* ADJ CLASSIF: ATTRIB ⇑ simplified

predilection /pri:dɪlɛkʃə⁰n/, **predilections**. If you have a **predilection** for something, you have a strong liking for it; a formal word. EG *This explained her predilection for chiffon scarves.* N COUNT: USU+for = fondness

predispose /pri:dɪspəʊz/, **predisposes, predisposing, predisposed**. If something **predisposes** you to a particular belief or way of life, it has influenced you, and is one of the reasons why you have that belief or follow that way of life; a formal word. EG *The stranger's role predisposes him to a distinctly 'objective' attitude.* ◊ **predisposed**. EG *She was perhaps predisposed to be critical.* V+O+A (to/towards) = incline, prompt; ◊ ADJ CLASSIF: PRED

predisposition /pri:dɪspəzɪʃə⁰n/, **predispositions**. If someone has a **predisposition** towards a particular attitude, action, or state, they have a tendency towards it because of the sort of person they are; a formal word. EG *She may have inherited the predisposition to murder the man she marries... There is an ideological predisposition in favour of public enterprise.* N COUNT = inclination

predominance /pri¹dɒmɪnəns/; a fairly formal word. 1 If there is a **predominance** of one particular type of person or thing in a group, there are many more of that type than of the other types represented there. EG *...the predominance of traders and businessmen in the party's ranks.* N UNCOUNT: USU+of = preponderance

2 Someone or something that has **predominance** has the greatest amount of power or importance in a particular set of people or things. EG *We now have total predominance in the European market.* N UNCOUNT = dominance

predominant /pri¹dɒmɪnənt/. Something that is **predominant** is more important or noticeable than anything else in a particular set of people or things; a fairly formal word. EG *Italian opera became absolutely predominant at the end of the 17th century... The predominant mood among policy-makers working in the field is one of despair.* ADJ CLASSIF = dominant

predominantly /pri¹dɒmɪnəntli¹/. You can use **predominantly** to indicate that you are describing the feature or quality that is most apparent in a situation. EG *The debates were predominantly about international affairs... Their first reaction to pregnancy was predominantly one of dismay.* ADV = largely, mainly

predominate /pri¹dɒmɪneɪt/, **predominates, predominating, predominated**; a formal word. 1 If you say that a particular type of person or thing **predominates**, you mean that they exist in greater numbers than any other type in the group that they belong to. EG *Westernized intellectuals were bound to predominate in such a party.* V ⇑ abound

2 If a particular feature or quality **predominates**, it is the most important or noticeable one in a situation. EG *Feelings rather than facts predominate... Unemployment still predominates.* V = prevail

pre-eminence /pri: ɛmɪnəns/ is the quality of being more important, powerful, or capable than other people or things in a group; a formal word. EG *No one doubted the pre-eminence of my father in financial matters.* N UNCOUNT = superiority

pre-eminent /pri: ɛmɪnə²nt/. Someone or something that is **pre-eminent** has more outstanding qualities or abilities than the other people or things in a group; a formal word. EG *For the next thirty years Bryce was the pre-eminent figure in Canadian economic policy.* ADJ CLASSIF = foremost

pre-eminently /pri: ɛmɪnəntli¹/ means to a very great extent. EG *This attitude is at the same time pre-eminently political.* ADV = predominantly

pre-empt /pri: ɛmpt/, **pre-empts, pre-empting, pre-empted**; a formal word. 1 If you **pre-empt** an action, you prevent it from happening by doing something which makes it pointless or V+O = frustrate

impossible. EG *...the desire to pre-empt possible moves by one superpower.*
2 If you **pre-empt** something, you take possession of it in a way that prevents anyone else from having it. V+O = appropriate

pre-emptive /pri: emptɪv/. A **pre-emptive** attack or strike is intended to damage or destroy your enemy's weapons before they can be used against you; a technical term. EG *Neither side has the ability to launch a pre-emptive strike.* ADJ CLASSIF: ATTRIB

preen /pri:n/, **preens, preening, preened.** **1** If you **preen** yourself, you spend a lot of time making yourself look neat and tidy; often used showing disapproval. EG *He preened himself in front of the mirror.* V+O (NG/REFL)
2 If you **preen**, you are self-satisfied and proud of yourself because of something that you know or have done; often used showing disapproval. EG *He began to preen himself on his superior intelligence... Doreen preened with pleasure.* V OR V+O (REFL)
3 When birds **preen**, they clean their feathers and arrange them neatly using their beak. EG *A wild peacock pecked and preened on the lawn.* V OR V+O (NG/REFL)

prefab /pri:fæb/, **prefabs.** A **prefab** is a house built with parts which have been made in a factory and then quickly put together; used in British English. EG *...a wartime prefab of great character.* N COUNT

prefabricated /pri¹fæbrɪkeɪtɪ²d/. **Prefabricated** buildings are built with parts which have been made in a factory so that they can be easily carried and put together in any place. EG *...a prefabricated steel building.* ADJ CLASSIF: ATTRIB

preface /prefɪs/, **prefaces, prefacing, prefaced.** **1** A **preface** is an introduction at the beginning of a book, which explains why the book was written or what it is about. EG *Granville-Barker had written a fine preface to the play.* N COUNT: IF+PREP THEN *to* = foreword
2 If you **preface** an action or speech, you say or do something first before you go on to the main part of what you intend to say or do. EG *Baynton prefaced his entrance with tremendous roars offstage... Each girl who spoke prefaced her remarks with 'sorry'.* V+O+A (*with/by*) = precede

prefect /pri:fekt/, **prefects.** A **prefect** is an older pupil at a British school who carries out special duties and who helps the teachers to control the younger pupils. N COUNT

prefer /pri¹fɜ:/, **prefers, preferring, preferred.** **1** If you **prefer** someone or something, you like that person or thing better than another, and so are more likely to choose them if there is a choice. EG *A glass of sherry? Or would you prefer a cocktail of some kind?... I infinitely prefer Barber to his deputy... There are those who prefer to suffer deprivation rather than claim legal aid... I prefer not to think about it... I'd prefer that he remain forgotten... The Head Master prefers them to act plays they have written themselves.* V+O/REPORT-CL/*to*-INF, OR V+O+A(*to*)/*to*-INF: NO CONT, NO IMPER ◇ **preferred.** EG *...'Danny,' whose preferred name is 'Dan'.* ◇ ADJ CLASSIF: ATTRIB
2 If the police **prefer charges** against someone, they make a formal accusation against that person, which has to be decided in a court of law; a technical expression. EG *Police yesterday detained a man for questioning, but no charges have yet been preferred.* PHR: VB INFLECTS

preferable /prefəᵒrəbəᵒl/. Something that is **preferable** is more desirable or suitable than something else, and is therefore more likely to be done or chosen if there is a choice. EG *Gradual change is preferable to sudden, large-scale change... Many people find this method immensely preferable... Would it be preferable to transfer all my accounts?* ADJ CLASSIF: USU +*to* = better
◇ **preferably.** EG *Clean the car from the top, preferably with a hose and warm water.* ◇ ADV SEN

preference /prefəᵒrəns/, **preferences.** **1 Preference** is **1.1** the desire to have, do, or choose one thing rather than another, because you like it better, or because it is more convenient for you. EG *'Do you have a preference for tragedy or comedy?'–'No, I have no preference.'... I still continue to live in this country by preference... I took the non-stop flight to London, in preference to the two-stage journey via New York... Each of us is likely to develop personal preferences for certain types of entertainment.* N UNCOUNT/COUNT ⇑ liking **1.2** an advantage that you give someone by treating them more favourably than other people. EG *Preference was given to those who had overseas experience.* N UNCOUNT = precedence
2 A **preference** is the thing in a group that you like better than other things in the group. EG *My own preference is traditional jazz.* N COUNT: USU POSS+N

preferential /prefərenʃəl/. **Preferential** is used to describe treatment which is deliberately better for some people than for others, and which therefore gives them an advantage. EG *What entitles you to this preferential treatment?* ADJ CLASSIF: ATTRIB = privileged ◇ **preferentially.** EG *No one should be treated preferentially.* ◇ ADV WITH VB ⇑ specially

preferment /pri¹fɜ:mə²nt/ is promotion to a better and more influential job; a very formal word. EG *...a man whose sole claim to preferment was his wealth.* N UNCOUNT = advancement

prefigure /pri:fɪgə/, **prefigures, prefiguring, prefigured.** If something **prefigures** something else, it is a first indication which suggests or determines that the second thing will happen. EG *He had significantly prefigured the whole subsequent history of 'pure' painting.* V+O ⇑ predict

prefix /pri:fɪks/, **prefixes.** A **prefix** is **1** a letter or group of letters which is added to the beginning of a word in order to make a new word. See □ below. N COUNT **2** a word or title that is used before someone's name, for example 'Mr', 'Ms', or 'Dr'; a rather old-fashioned use. N COUNT

> **PREFIX** □ In this dictionary PREFIX is used in the grammar notes beside an entry which cannot normally be used as a word by itself. It is placed before another word to form a new word in the same word class. Sometimes the two parts are written as one word, sometimes they are joined by a hyphen (-). An example is **semi-**. You can say ***semicircular*** and ***semi-permanent.*** The adjectives **circular** and **permanent** and the added prefixes form new adjectives.

pregnancy /pregnənsi¹/, **pregnancies.** **Pregnancy** is the condition of being pregnant or the period of time during which a female is pregnant. EG *The breasts enlarge during pregnancy... The pregnancy was complicated... Numbers of unwanted pregnancies resulted.* N UNCOUNT/COUNT

pregnancy test, pregnancy tests. A **pregnancy test** is a medical test which women have in order to find out whether they have become pregnant. EG *Wait until six weeks after your last period and get a pregnancy test.* N COUNT

pregnant /pregnənt/. **1** If a woman or female animal is **pregnant**, she has a developing baby or babies in her body. A woman normally gives birth to a baby after she has been pregnant for nine months. EG *She had married and immediately got pregnant... She was three months pregnant... My mother was pregnant with me at the time... Sarah was pregnant by another man.* ADJ CLASSIF: IF+PREP THEN *with/by*
2 A **pregnant** moment has a special meaning or significance which is not obvious, but which people are aware of; a literary use. EG *There followed a pregnant pause... She kept a silence which was pregnant with indications of how much more she could say.* ADJ CLASSIF: IF+PREP THEN *with* ⇑ significant = loaded

preheat /pri:hi:t/, **preheats, preheating, preheated.** If you **preheat** an oven, you switch it on and allow it to reach a certain temperature before you put food inside it. EG *Preheat the oven to gas mark 4... Bake in a preheated oven at 375°F.* V+O ⇑ heat

prehensile /pri¹hensaɪl/. Something that is **prehensile** is able to curl round objects and grip them; a technical term, used of parts of an animal's body. EG *...the African monkey's prehensile tail.* ADJ CLASSIF

prehistoric /pri:hɪstɒrɪk/ means relating to the time in history before information was written down. EG *...prehistoric and primitive peoples.* ADJ CLASSIF: USU ATTRIB

prehistory /pri:hɪstəᵒri¹/ is the time in history before any information was written down. N UNCOUNT

pre-industrial refers to the time before machines were introduced to produce goods on a large scale. EG *The pre-industrial family was a self-sufficient unit... ...the transformation of pre-industrial into advanced industrial societies.* ADJ CLASSIF: ATTRIB

prejudge /pri:dʒʌdʒ/, **prejudges, prejudging, prejudged.** If you **prejudge** a situation, you form an opinion about it before you know all the facts; a formal word. EG *We should try not to prejudge the issue.* V OR V+O ⇑ judge

prejudice /predʒʊdɪs/, **prejudices, prejudicing, prejudiced.** **1 Prejudice** is an unreasonable dislike of or preference for something, for example a particular group of people in society. EG *Prejudice against women is becoming less se-* N UNCOUNT/COUNT = discrimination, bias *vere... ...racial prejudice... Barber was a man of strong views and strong prejudices.*

2 If you **prejudice** someone, you influence them in an unfair way so that they form an unreasonable opinion about something. EG *Circumstances have prejudiced his mother against his early marriage... We were not allowed to mention Griffiths' record for fear of prejudicing the jury.* V+O = bias

3 If someone **prejudices** your situation, they do something that makes your opportunities worse than they should be; a formal use. EG *I don't want to prejudice your chances in any way.* V+O ⇑ harm = spoil

4 If you take an action **without prejudice to** an existing situation, your action does not change or harm that situation; a formal expression. EG *They continued hostile attacks without prejudice to their negotiations.* PREP

prejudiced /prɛdʒʊdɪst/. Someone who is **prejudiced** has an unreasonable dislike of or preference for something, for example a particular group of people in society; used showing disapproval. EG *People were prejudiced against her... Public opinion is based on incorrect or very prejudiced information.* ADJ QUALIT = biased

prejudicial /prɛdʒʊdɪʃəl/. **Prejudicial** actions or situations are harmful, especially to people's health, their safety, or their way of life; a formal word. EG *Such actions were clearly prejudicial to the health and safety of the public.* ADJ CLASSIF: PRED, USU+*to* = deleterious

prelate /prɛlɪt/, **prelates**. A **prelate** is a clergyman of high rank, for example a bishop or an archbishop; a technical term. N COUNT

preliminary /prɪˈlɪmɪnə⁰riˈ/, **preliminaries**. **1** **Preliminary** activities happen at the beginning of a sequence of events, often as a form of preparation. EG *...preliminary arrangements... They are taking some of the preliminary steps in preparation for a possible war.* ADJ QUALIT: ATTRIB = initial

2 A **preliminary** is **2.1** something that you do at the beginning of an activity, often as a form of preparation. EG *He spent a long time on polite preliminaries... This action is regarded as a necessary preliminary to the formation of a mass party.* N COUNT: USU PL **2.2** the first part of a competition, which decides who will go on to the main competition. EG *He did well to get through the preliminaries.* N COUNT ⇑ contest

prelude /prɛljuːd/, **preludes**. A **prelude** is **1** an event which comes before another more important event, and which prepares people for it or which acts as an introduction to it. EG *This speech has been hailed by his friends as the prelude to his return to office.* N COUNT: USU+*to* = preface **2** a short piece of music for the piano or organ; a technical term. EG *...a Chopin prelude.* N COUNT: ALSO IN NAMES

premarital /priːmærɪtə⁰l/ means relating to the time before people get married, especially when they are intending to get married soon. EG *...premarital sex... ...gossip about the latest premarital pregnancies.* ADJ CLASSIF: ATTRIB

premature /prɛmətjʊə/. **1** Something that is **premature** **1.1** happens earlier than usual or earlier than people expect. EG *This disease produces premature aging of the brain... ...the premature departure of the visitors... His tunic bulged over a premature paunch.* ADJ CLASSIF ⇑ early ◇ **prematurely**. EG *The warden retired prematurely with a nervous disorder.* ◇ ADV **1.2** is not appropriate, because it happens or is done too early or before everything is ready. EG *The final word 'goodbye' had been premature... It's a bit premature to be thinking about having one's biography written.* ADJ QUALIT ⇑ inappropriate

2 A **premature** baby is born before the date when it is due to be born. EG *A small, premature baby may be too weak to nurse... Twins are often premature and small.* ADJ CLASSIF ⇑ early ◇ **prematurely**. ◇ ADV WITH VB

premeditated /priˈmɛdɪteɪtɪ²d/. Something such as a crime that is **premeditated** is done after it has been carefully planned or thought about. EG *There's nothing premeditated about it, you know–it just happened... ...a premeditated act of murder.* ADJ CLASSIF = deliberate ≠ spontaneous

premeditation /priˈmɛdɪteɪʃə⁰n/ is thinking about something or planning it before you actually do it; a formal word. EG *The door of his study was open, and without premeditation he turned into it.* N UNCOUNT

premier /prɛmjə/, **premiers**. **1** A **premier** is a president or prime minister who is the head of the government of his or her country; used mainly in newspapers and broadcasting. EG *...the French premier... ...Premier Francisco Pinto Balsemao.* N COUNT/N PROPER: ALSO IN TITLES ⇑ leader

2 **Premier** is used to describe something that is considered to be the most important or the best in quality when compared with other things of the same type. EG *The article referred to Hull as Europe's premier port.* ADJ CLASSIF: ATTRIB = foremost

premiere /prɛmɪɛə, prɛmɪə/, **premieres**. A **premiere** is the first public performance of a new play or film. EG *The film had its world premiere at San Sebastian... I had three tickets to the premiere of 'The Nightingale'.* N COUNT ⇑ showing = opening

premiership /prɛmjəʃɪp/ is the position of being the leader of a government, or the time during which someone holds this position. EG *He should never have been considered for the premiership... ...one of the most important political crises of his premiership.* N UNCOUNT ⇑ leadership

premise /priˈmaɪz, prɛmɪs/, **premises, premised**; also spelled **premiss** for the meaning in paragraph 2. **1** The **premises** of a business or an institution are all the property, including the buildings and land, that are on one site and are occupied by the business or institution. EG *Some of the food was grown on the premises... In 1971 the firm moved to new premises in Bethnal Green.* N PLURAL

2 A **premise** is something that you suppose is true and that you use as a basis for developing an idea or statement; a formal use. EG *He avoided criticizing the hospital on the premise that submissiveness would lead to release... I'm rather questioning whether the whole premise is correct... I wouldn't concede his premiss, so naturally, I don't draw his conclusion.* N COUNT, OR N COUNT+REPORT-CL = assumption

3 If a theory or system **is premised** on an idea or belief, you have assumed that the idea or belief is correct and have used it as the basis for your theory; a formal use. EG *Technocratic planning was premised on hierarchy.* V+O: ONLY PASS ⇑ be based

premium /priːmɪəm/, **premiums**. **1** A **premium** is **1.1** a sum of money that is added to something, for example to someone's earnings or to the price of goods, in order to encourage people to work hard or to produce the goods. EG *Investors were even more willing to pay a premium for companies that offered such a potential for growth... ...the Regional Employment Premium.* N COUNT ⇑ bonus **1.2** a sum of money that you pay regularly to an insurance company for an insurance policy. EG *...tax relief on life insurance premiums.* N COUNT ⇑ payment

2 **Premium** prices are higher than usual, for example because goods are in short supply. EG *They usually pay a premium price for their small orders.* ADJ CLASSIF: ATTRIB = inflated

3 **at a premium**. **3.1** If something is sold **at a premium**, it is sold at a higher price than usual, for example because it is in short supply. EG *Fertilizer is sold at a premium by government officials.* PHR: USED AS AN A = over the odds **3.2** If something is **at a premium**, it is wanted or needed, but is difficult to get or achieve. EG *Real sleep was at a premium... Student flats are also at a premium.* PHR: USED AS AN A = in demand

4 If you **put** or **place a high premium** on a quality or characteristic, you regard that quality or characteristic as especially important. EG *A high premium comes to be placed on discipline and unity... We do put a very high premium on common sense.* PHR: VB INFLECTS ⇑ value

premium bond, premium bonds. **Premium bonds** are numbered tickets that the government sells through post offices in Britain. Each month, a computer randomly selects several numbers, and the people whose tickets have those numbers win a sum of money. N COUNT

premonition /prɛmənɪʃə⁰n/, **premonitions**. If you have a **premonition**, you have a feeling that something is about to happen, often something unpleasant, even though you do not have a rational reason for believing it. EG *He had had a sudden premonition that she had run away with another man... His hand shook violently and he had a premonition of failure.* N COUNT: USU+*of*/REPORT-CL = presentiment, foreboding ▸ used as an uncount noun. EG *'Certainly,' she said, knowing with dismal premonition what she would see.* ▸ N UNCOUNT = foreboding

premonitory /priˈmɒnɪtə⁰riˈ/. **Premonitory** feelings or events make you think that something unpleasant is about to happen; a formal word. EG *Daniel felt a premonitory malaise just watching the crowd gather.* ADJ CLASSIF: USU ATTRIB = ominous

prenatal /priːneɪtə⁰l/ is used to describe things relating to the medical care of women during pregnancy. EG *...prenatal classes for expectant mothers.* ADJ CLASSIF: ATTRIB

preoccupation /priːɒkjəˈpeɪʃə⁰n/, **preoccupations**. **1** **Preoccupation** is a state of mind in which you think about something so much that you do not N UNCOUNT = obsession consider other things to be important. EG *Let me explain my preoccupation with beautiful architectural sites... He was capable of total preoccupation.*

2 A **preoccupation** is something that you think about a lot because it is important to you. EG *Keeping warm was Morris's main preoccupation in his first few days there.*
N COUNT = concern

preoccupied /priːɒkjəˈpaɪd/. Someone who is **preoccupied** thinks a lot about a particular idea or problem, and is therefore hardly aware of other things. EG *His wife becomes more and more preoccupied with the children... She seemed rather preoccupied and distant... He strode along with a preoccupied frown.*
ADJ QUALIT : IF+PREP THEN *with* = absorbed

preoccupy /priːɒkjəˈpaɪ/, **preoccupies, preoccupying, preoccupied.** If something **preoccupies** you, you think about it a great deal, so that it takes up a lot of your time; a fairly formal word. EG *This is a question which increasingly preoccupies me.*
V+O ⇑ concern = absorb

preordained /priːɔːdeɪnd/. Something that is **preordained** is believed to be happening in the way that has been decided by God or by fate; a formal word. EG *Certain people are preordained to a higher status by an omniscient God.*
ADJ CLASSIF = predestined

PREP □ In this dictionary PREP is used in the grammar notes beside an entry to indicate that it is a preposition. All prepositions take an object. The preposition and its object form a prepositional group. The prepositional object is usually a noun group. In the prepositional group *on the table*, the preposition 'on' takes the prepositional object 'the table'. Some prepositions are typically followed by the -ING form of a verb. These are called PREP OR PREP+-ING in the grammar notes in this dictionary. An example is **by**. EG *By these actions he achieved his aim... **By doing** this, he achieved his aim.*

pre-packed. **Pre-packed** goods are packed or wrapped before they are sent to the shop where they are sold.
ADJ CLASSIF

prepaid /priːpeɪd/; also spelled with a hyphen. **Prepaid** items are paid for in advance, before the time when you would normally pay for them. EG *Prepaid postcards had been provided.*
ADJ CLASSIF : ATTRIB

preparation /prepəreɪʃəⁿn/, **preparations.** 1 **Preparation** is 1.1 the activity of getting something ready for use or for a particular purpose. EG *Benn was involved in the preparation of Labour's manifesto... Education should be a preparation for life... ...food preparation... ...the end of the planning and preparation stage... The area will be cleared soon in preparation for work on the recreational field.*
N UNCOUNT : USU +SUPP

1.2 schoolwork, usually done at home, for a particular lesson or examination; a formal use. EG *You have your corrections to do and your preparation.*
N UNCOUNT = homework

2 **Preparations** are all the things that are done and the arrangements that are made before an event that will happen in the future. EG *Preparations for a summit meeting continued... He'll have to make preparations for the funeral... Elaborate preparations were being made to get me out of prison.*
N PLURAL

3 A **preparation** is a mixture that has been prepared for use as food, medicine, cosmetics, etc. EG *...beauty preparations.*
N COUNT ⇑ substance

preparatory /prəˈpærətəⁿriˈ/; a formal word. 1 **Preparatory** actions are done at the beginning of an activity as a form of introduction or preparation. EG *...a preparatory report... This was where we were to have our preparatory language courses.*
ADJ CLASSIF : ATTRIB = introductory

2 If one action happens **preparatory to** another, the first thing happens or exists before the second. EG *He dusted the shirts down preparatory to draping them over a hanger.*
PREP = prior to

preparatory school, preparatory schools. A **preparatory school** is the same as a prep school; a formal expression.
N COUNT/UNCOUNT

prepare /priˈpeə/, **prepares, preparing, prepared.** 1 If you **prepare** someone or something, you make them ready for an event or action that will happen in the future. EG *By making us do lesson-plans, they're making sure we prepare our classes... She was expecting me, a room was prepared.*
V+O : IF+PREP THEN *for*

2 If you **prepare** for an event or action that will happen soon, 2.1 you get yourself ready for it. EG *The guests prepared for their departure... I must prepare for church... He ordered his crew to prepare for action... I jumped up and prepared to defend myself.*
V, V+*to*-INF, OR V+O (REFL) : USU +*for* = make ready

2.2 you make plans for it so that it will be organized when it happens. EG *They preach peace while waging or preparing for war... He knew that he would now have to prepare actively to fight an open democratic battle.*
V : USU+*to*-INF/*for*

3 If you **prepare** food, you clean it, cook it, etc so that it is ready to be eaten. EG *He had spent all morning preparing the meal... She had prepared a thermos of hot onion soup.*
V+O, V+O+O, OR V+O+A (*for*) = make

4 If you **prepare** someone for a new situation, you get them used to the idea that things are going to change, often in ways that they will not like. EG *Prepare yourself for a shock... Problems sometimes arise for mothers who have suddenly taken on full-time work without preparing their children... The children have been well prepared for their father's death.*
V OR V+O (NG/REFL) : USU+*for* ⇑ accustom

prepared /priˈpeəd/. 1 If you are **prepared** to do something, you are willing and able to do it. EG *What sort of risks are you prepared to take?... I'm prepared to say I was wrong... Many countries seem prepared to consider nuclear energy.*
ADJ CLASSIF : PRED+*to*-INF ⇑ ready

2 If you are **prepared** for something, you are ready for it, and are therefore not surprised when it happens. EG *I was not really prepared for her fits of boredom... Be prepared for power cuts by buying lots of candles.*
ADJ QUALIT : PRED, IF+PREP THEN *for*

3 Something that is **prepared** has been organized, made, or written beforehand, so that it is ready when it is needed. EG *He read out a prepared statement... ...a specially prepared fluorescent screen.*
ADJ CLASSIF

preparedness /priˈpeədnɪˈs/ is the state of being ready for something to happen, especially for war to be declared; a formal word. EG *...the need for military preparedness.*
N UNCOUNT ⇑ readiness

preponderance /priˈpɒndəⁿrəns/. If there is a **preponderance** of one particular type of person or thing in a group, there are more of that type than of any others; a formal word. EG *There is a definite preponderance of women among those who study English Literature.*
N UNCOUNT : USU +*of* = predominance

preponderant /priˈpɒndəⁿrənt/. If a particular type of person or thing is **preponderant**, that type is in the majority, or is more important than the others in its group; a formal word. EG *...a group among whom Germans would be preponderant.*
ADJ CLASSIF = predominant

◊ **preponderantly.** EG *Its supporters remain preponderantly students rather than workers.*
◊ ADV = chiefly

preposition /prepəzɪʃəⁿn/, **prepositions.** In grammar, a **preposition** is a word such as 'by', 'for', 'into', or 'with', which usually has a noun group as its object. Words which are prepositions have PREP in the grammar notes beside the entry. See □ at PREP.
N COUNT

prepossessing /priːpəzesɪŋ/. Someone or something that is **prepossessing** is attractive or pleasant in appearance.
ADJ QUALIT = appealing, fetching

preposterous /priˈpɒstəⁿrəs/. If you describe something as **preposterous**, you mean that it seems so strange that it is unreasonable or unlikely; a fairly formal word. EG *The situation was preposterous and became even more so... ...a preposterous idea.*
ADJ QUALIT = absurd, outrageous

◊ **preposterously.** EG *The rooms inside the town hall were as preposterously grandiose as the exterior.*
◊ ADV = ludicrously

prep school, prep schools. A **prep school** is a private school in Britain where children are educated until the the age of 11 or 13, after which they go to a public or other secondary school.
N COUNT/UNCOUNT

prepubescent /priːpjuːbesənt/ means relating to the time just before someone reaches puberty; a formal or technical word.
ADJ CLASSIF

Pre-Raphaelite /priː ræfəlaɪt/, **Pre-Raphaelites.** 1 The **Pre-Raphaelites** were a group of British painters in the nineteenth century who concentrated on themes from history, romantic myth, and folklore. ▸ used as an adjective to refer to the style of the Pre-Raphaelites. EG *...a whole section on Pre-Raphaelite landscape.*
N COUNT
▸ ADJ CLASSIF : USU ATTRIB

2 If you describe a woman as **Pre-Raphaelite**, you mean that she looks like a character in a Pre-Raphaelite picture, for example because she has long wavy hair and a young delicate face.
ADJ QUALIT ⇑ romantic

pre-recorded. Something that is **pre-recorded** has been recorded in advance so that it can be broadcast or played later. EG *These programmes are pre-recorded and then relayed to Brighton.*
ADJ CLASSIF

prerequisite /priːrekwɪzɪt/, **prerequisites.** A **prerequisite** is something that must happen or exist
N COUNT : USU+*for/of/to*

before another thing is possible; a formal word. EG *This is a great bonus, but it is not a prerequisite for high intelligence... The profitability of a mixed economy is an essential prerequisite of economic growth.* ▸ used as an adjective. EG *He made this a prerequisite condition of the deal going through.* ↑ requirement = precondition ▸ ADJ CLASSIF = essential

prerogative /pri¹rɒgətɪv/, **prerogatives**. Someone's **prerogative** is a special privilege or power that they have or are allowed to have; a formal word. EG *Unfortunately new ideas are not the prerogative of those who spend a long time doing research... He was never in work, but still held the male prerogative of receiving every penny of the family income.* N COUNT : USU the+N+of = right

presage /prɛsɪdʒ/, **presages, presaging, presaged**. If something **presages** a situation or event, it is considered to be a warning or sign of what is about to happen; a formal word. EG *The drive for equality often presages chaos, disruption, and unhappiness.* V+O = portend

presbytery /prɛzbɪtə⁰ri¹/, **presbyteries**. A **presbytery** is the house in which a Roman Catholic priest lives; a technical term. N COUNT

pre-school is used to describe things relating to the care and education of children before they reach the age when they have to go to school. EG *...a pre-school playgroup... ...private nursery schools for pre-school children.* ADJ CLASSIF : ATTRIB = nursery

prescience /prɛsɪəns/ is the ability to see what is likely to happen in the future and to take appropriate action; a formal word. EG *It was an act of prescience, much criticized at the time.* N UNCOUNT = foreknowledge

prescient /prɛsɪənt/. If you say that someone or something was **prescient**, you mean that they were able to know or predict what was going to happen in the future; a formal word. EG *It was a prescient film about what later happened in Three Mile Island.* ADJ QUALIT = prophetic

prescribe /pri¹skraɪb/, **prescribes, prescribing, prescribed**. 1 If a doctor **prescribes** treatment or medicine for you when you are ill, he or she orders it for you. EG *There are various medications that the doctor may prescribe... The doctor will analyse the symptoms and prescribe a course of treatment.* V+O

2 If someone **prescribes** an activity or duty, they state that it must be done or carried out as if it were a rule. EG *The factory laws prescribed a heavy fine for every day of contravention.* ◊ **prescribed**. EG *The list of prescribed duties has been drawn up by the federation... They were assigned to the countryside for a prescribed period of time.* V+O ↑ order = dictate ◊ ADJ CLASSIF : ATTRIB = set

prescription /pri¹skrɪpʃə⁰n/, **prescriptions**. A **prescription** is 1 a piece of paper on which a doctor writes an order for medicine and which you give to a chemist in exchange for the medicine. EG *These pills can be obtained by prescription only... Just sign the declaration on the back of the prescription form.* N COUNT ↑ form 2 medicine which a doctor orders for you. EG *I'm not sleeping even with the prescription Ackerman gave me... You can get free prescriptions if you are over pension age.* N COUNT 3 an instruction which states what must happen or be done in particular circumstances; a formal use. EG *There is growing political support for his economic prescriptions.* N COUNT = direction

4 If you can only get a particular medicine **on prescription**, you cannot buy it at the chemist without first getting a prescription for it from a doctor. PHR : USED AS AN A

prescriptive /pri¹skrɪptɪv/. Something that is **prescriptive** sets down rules and states what should and should not happen in certain circumstances; a formal word. EG *He is a man free of prescriptive social norms... His account was descriptive rather than prescriptive.* ADJ QUALIT = strict

presence /prɛzəns/, **presences**. 1 Someone's **presence** in a particular place is the state of them being there. EG *He tried to justify his presence in Belfast... He was aware of her presence... He had to cope with the presence of her family.* N UNCOUNT : WITH POSS ≠ absence

2 If you say that someone has **presence**, you mean that they impress people by their appearance and manner; used showing approval. EG *He had a tremendous physical presence... She certainly had presence.* N UNCOUNT = personality

3 A **presence** is a person, or a being with human characteristics, which you cannot see, but which you are aware of in a particular place; a literary use. EG *There was another presence in the saloon with me... ...a mysterious winged presence, felt rather than seen.* N COUNT = entity

4 A country that has a military **presence** somewhere, especially somewhere abroad, has soldiers stationed there. EG *The Navy had a strong presence along the east coast... Soon there would be no military presence east of Suez... ...keeping a naval presence in the Mediterranean.* N UNCOUNT : USU +A

5 If you are **in** someone's **presence**, you are in the same place as they are, and can be seen or heard by them. EG *I had felt comfortable in her presence... The guest is then ushered into his presence... Haldane repeated his statement in the presence of the chairman.* PHR : USED AS AN A

6 If you **make** your **presence felt**, you do something which forces people to pay attention to you. PHR : VB INFLECTS

presence of mind is the ability to act quickly and sensibly in a difficult or dangerous situation. EG *Richard had the presence of mind to step forward and pick it up.* N UNCOUNT = wits

present, presents, presenting, presented. The word **present** is pronounced /prɛzənt/ when it is an adjective or noun, and /pri¹zɛnt/ when it is a verb. 1 You use **present** to describe people, situations, things, etc that exist now, especially when you want to distinguish them from others that they have replaced or that will replace them in the future. EG *The present system has many failings... The present chairperson is a woman... The present General Council will oppose the move... Economic planning cannot succeed in present conditions.* ADJ CLASSIF : ATTRIB = existing, current ● **The present day** is the period of history that is taking place now. EG *This tradition has continued till the present day.* ● PHR : USED AS O = today ● See also **present-day**.

2 The **present** is the period of time or the part of your life that is taking place now. EG *We have to come to terms with the present... I felt too remote from the present... If you can't live for the present, there's no point in living at all.* N SING : the+N ≠ future, past

3 If you say that something exists or is happening **at present**, or **at the present time**, you mean that it exists or is happening at the time when you are writing or speaking, rather than in the future. EG *I don't want to get married at present... He is at present serving a life sentence... It is only a remote possibility at the present time.* PHR : USED AS AN A ↑ now = at the moment

4 If a situation exists **for the present**, it exists now and will continue until something happens which will cause it to change. EG *For the present she continues with the antibiotics... That's all for the present, Miss Livingstone.* PHR : USED AS AN A = provisionally

5 If someone is **present** somewhere, they are there, for example when something happens. EG *He had been present at the dance... Howard insisted on being present... There was a photographer present.* ADJ CLASSIF : PRED = in attendance

6 A **present** is something that you give to someone and that you hope they will like, for example on their birthday or when you visit them at their home. EG *She bought us all a present... I gave him an atlas as a birthday present... He had brought home a present for her.* N COUNT = gift

7 In grammar, the **present** of a verb is its present tense. N COUNT

8 If you **present** someone with something such as a prize or a document, or if you **present** it to them, you give it to them in a formal or official way. EG *Monica Sims, Controller of Radio 4, presented Mr Morgan with his prize... The Awards were presented by Sir Robin Day... One of his constituents presented a petition to the Commons.* V+O : IF+PREP THEN to, OR V+O +A (with/)

9 If something **presents** a difficulty, challenge, etc, it causes or provides this difficulty, challenge, etc so that you have to work hard in order to succeed in what you are trying to do. EG *The Tornado presented the Island with severe problems... Everest presented a challenge to Hilary... This may present certain hazards... It was not a problem which had ever really presented itself to her.* +O : IF+PREP THEN to, OR V+O +A (with/) = pose

10 If you **present** people with information, you give it to them in a formal or precise way. EG *Figures can be presented in many ways... Today I want to present the student view... Teachers were presenting us with an accurate picture of history.* V+O : IF+PREP THEN to/in, OR V +O+A (with)

11 If someone or something **presents** a particular view, they cause you to see them in that way. EG *She continued to present me with a view of the crown of her head... The far side of our steep little street presented a peculiar sight... Only part of the diagram is presented to each retina.* V+O : IF+PREP THEN to, OR V+O +A (with) = affords

12 If you **present** someone or something in a particular way, you describe them in that way, especially when this involves making them appear better or worse than they really are. EG *Her lawyer wanted to present her in the most favourable light... It is customary to present the British as the colonialist oppressor... They endeavoured to present the mixed economy as an ideal.* V+O+A *(as/in)* = portray

13 If you **present** yourself somewhere, you officially arrive there, for example in order to attend an interview or to keep an appointment. EG *The next morning I presented myself at their offices... The visitor presented himself at the vicarage.* V+O (REFL)+A

14 If something such as an opportunity **presents** itself, it becomes apparent to you, often at a time when you do not expect it. EG *Was he going to do it again if the opportunity presented itself?* V+O (REFL) = offer

15 If you **present** something such as a performance or an exhibition, you organize it so that the public can come and see it or watch it. EG *She came to see every one of the new plays he was presenting... The Museum of Modern Art is presenting a complete retrospective of Ray's work.* V+O = put on

16 If you **present** a programme on radio or television, you introduce the separate parts of it, especially when it is a programme that gives news or information. EG *...'University Link', compiled and presented by Dr Brian Smith.* V+O

17 If you **present** someone to an important person, you officially introduce them; a formal use. EG *Margaret had been presented at Court... May I present Mr Rudolph Wallace.* V+O : USU+A

presentable /pri'zentəbə⁰l/. Someone or something that is **presentable** is considered to be attractive or pleasant, and suitable to give or show to other people. EG *She still looked quite presentable... We tried to arrange the material in a presentable manner.* ◊ **presentably.** ADJ QUALIT ⇑ acceptable ◊ ADV

presentation /prezənteɪʃə⁰n/, **presentations.** 1 The **presentation** of information, news, etc involves making it available to people, for example by broadcasting it or by printing it, and the way in which this is done. EG *...the presentation of new data... ...the presentation of the case by the Attorney-General... His presentation was clear and incisive.* N UNCOUNT : IF+ PREP THEN *of* = exposition

2 **Presentation** is the appearance of something and the impression that it gives to people. EG *Competition by price is giving way to an accent on presentation.* N UNCOUNT = display

3 A **presentation** is **3.1** a formal event or ceremony in which someone is given something such as a prize or a reward. EG *We all had to troop across the ground for some presentations underneath the stand.* N COUNT **3.2** something that is performed before an audience, for example a play or a ballet. EG *The cultural presentation given by the Cuban delegation was most impressive... ...a theatrical presentation of 'Danton's Death'.* N COUNT+SUPP = performance

present-day. You use **present-day** to describe people or situations that exist now, especially when you want to distinguish them from similar people or things that existed at an earlier time, or to distinguish a thing or a place from the same thing or place as it used to be in the past. EG *...present-day Japanese children... ...social conditions in present-day India.* ADJ CLASSIF : ATTRIB = modern, latter-day

presenter /pri'zentə/, **presenters**. A **presenter** is a person who introduces the separate parts of a television or radio programme, especially a programme that gives news or information. N COUNT ⇑ broadcaster

presentiment /pri:sentɪmə²nt/, **presentiments**. A **presentiment** is a feeling that a particular event, for example someone's death, will soon take place; a formal word. EG *Mel had not forgotten the vague unease, the presentiment of danger he had felt while on the plane.* N COUNT : IF+ PREP THEN *of*, OR +REPORT-CL = premonition

presently /prezəntli¹/. 1 You use **presently** when you are giving an account to indicate that one thing happened soon after another that you have just mentioned. EG *Presently I got the whole story... 'It's young Mr Dekker,' said Cordelia presently, 'I know his voice.'* ADV SEN, OR ADV WITH VB = before long

2 If you say that something will happen **presently**, you mean that it will happen soon. EG *The Prince of Wales will be here presently.* ADV WITH VB = shortly

3 If you say that something is **presently** happening, you mean that it is happening at the time when you are writing or speaking. EG *The oil and gas rigs are presently in operation... America and Japan are presently working on chips which will hold a million words.* ADV WITH VB ⇑ now = currently

present participle, present participles. In grammar, the **present participle** of an English verb is the form that ends in 'ing'. It is used to form some tenses, and to form adjectives and nouns from a verb. See □ at -ING. N COUNT

present perfect. In grammar, the **present perfect** tense of an English verb is the tense that is formed with the present tense of the auxiliary 'have' and the past participle of the main verb. N SING : *the*+N

present tense. In grammar, the **present tense** or the **present** is used in contrast with the past tense to refer mainly to things that happen or exist at the time of speaking or writing. N SING : *the*+N

preservative /pri'zɜ:vətɪv/, **preservatives**. A **preservative** is a chemical substance that prevents things from decaying. Some preservatives are added to food, and others are used to treat wood or metal. EG *The timber should also be treated with a preservative.* N MASS

preserve /pri'zɜ:v/, **preserves, preserving, preserved.** 1 If you **preserve** something, you make it remain the way it is, and protect it from changing or stopping. EG *The main thing as far as education is concerned is to preserve standards... We are interested in preserving world peace... I stood there, determined to preserve my dignity... Your old employer must preserve your right to a guaranteed minimum position.* ◊ **preservation** /prezəveɪʃə⁰n/. EG *...the preservation of democracy.* V+O ⇑ keep = maintain ◊ N UNCOUNT

2 If you **preserve** something, you take action to save it or protect it from damage, loss, destruction, or decay. EG *As a doctor, it was my duty to preserve life... ...a paint spray which would preserve it from corrosion... ...one of those big houses, which had been preserved as a sort of museum... ...his efforts to preserve a language that only a few people still spoke.* ◊ **preservation.** EG *...the Society for the Preservation of Fine Furniture.* V+O ⇑ keep ◊ N UNCOUNT

3 If you **preserve** food, you prevent it from decaying so that you can store it for a long time. There are several ways of preserving food, such as freezing, drying, or pickling. EG *Deep freezing is the simplest natural way of preserving food. ...the sale of preserved food.* V+O ⇑ treat

4 **Preserves** are foods such as jam, marmalade, or pickle, that are made by cooking fruit or vegetables with a large amount of sugar, salt, or vinegar so that they can be stored for a long time. N MASS

6 A particular **preserve** is an area of life or an activity that seems to allow only one sort of person to be involved in it or to take part in it; a formal use. EG *Banking has remained a male preserve... ...working-class preserves, such as pigeon-racing... Whole city districts become preserves of people of one particular ethnic origin.* N COUNT+SUPP = domain

7 A **preserve** is an area of land or water where animals are protected. EG *Except for such preserves, the mountains have offered the elk their safest habitat.* N COUNT = reservation

preserved /pri'zɜ:vd/. Something that is well **preserved**, perfectly **preserved**, etc is in a good state or a perfect state even though it is very old. EG *There are some excellently preserved fossilized tree stumps... ...Islamic Cairo, the best preserved mediaeval township in the world.* ADJ QUALIT = conserved

preserver /pri'zɜ:və/, **preservers**. A **preserver** of a particular tradition or of a region is someone who tries to prevent the end or decline of the tradition or region. EG *...a celebrated restorer and preserver of the old Cornish language.* N COUNT : IF+ PREP THEN *of*

pre-set, pre-sets, presetting. The form **pre-set** is used in the present tense and is also the past tense and past participle of the verb. If you **pre-set** a piece of equipment, you set the controls in advance of the time when you want it to work. EG *She preset the video recorder before she went out.* ▸ used as an adjective to refer to equipment that has been pre-set. EG *Bake in a pre-set oven for 45 minutes.* V+O ▸ ADJ CLASSIF : ATTRIB

preside /pri'zaɪd/, **presides, presiding, presided.** 1 If you **preside** over a formal gathering such as a meeting, you act as the chairperson. EG *He had presided over a seminar for theoretical physicists... He could not have been more gracious in the way he presided at table.* V : USU+A *(over/at)*

2 If you **preside** over an event, you are considered by V : USU+A *(over)*

other people to be responsible for it and in a position to control it. EG ...*the men presiding over this quiet revolution.*
3 If an object **presides** over a place, it is larger or taller than anything around it and therefore dominates the area; a formal use. EG *A large figure in stone presides massively over the approach to the museum... ...Hanover Square and its presiding statue of Pitt.* V+A *(over)* = dominate

presidency /prezɪdənsi¹/, **presidencies**. **1** The **presidency** is the position or function of a president. EG *He is to be nominated for the presidency... It took several years before he achieved the presidency.* N COUNT: USU *the*+N IN SING, OR N UNCOUNT
2 Someone's **presidency** is the period of time during which they are president. EG *From the beginning of your presidency I beg that we should work together... ...the coming presidency of Governor Dewey of New York.* N COUNT: WITH POSS, USU SING

president /prezɪdənt/, **presidents**; often spelled with a capital letter. **1** The **president** of a republic is the person who has the highest political position, and who is also the head of state. EG *The French president arrived in the United States this week... ...a letter from the President of the United States... ...the assassination of President Kennedy... He was running for president in 1960.* N COUNT/UNCOUNT: ALSO IN TITLES ⇑ leader
2 The **president** of an organization or society is the person who has the highest position in it. EG *...the former President of the Royal Academy... She was given a warm welcome by the president of Harvard University.* N COUNT ⇑ head
3 In the United States, the **president** of a company is the head of it. N COUNT ⇑ executive

president-elect, **president-elects**. The **president-elect** is the person who has been elected as the next president but who has not yet started work as president. N COUNT: ALSO IN TITLES ⇑ politician

presidential /prezɪdenʃə⁰l/. **Presidential** activities or things relate or belong to a president or presidency. EG *...John Kennedy's presidential airplane... ...the next presidential election... An American presidential campaign lasts for eighteen months.* ADJ CLASSIF: ATTRIB ⇑ official

presidium /prɪsɪdɪəm/, **presidiums**; also spelled **praesidium**. A **presidium** is a permanent administrative committee, especially in communist countries; a technical term in politics. N COUNT ⇑ council

press /pres/, **presses, pressing, pressed**. **1** If you **press** something somewhere, you hold it firmly against something else by pushing it gently onto the other thing. EG *Stroganov pressed his hand to his heart... He stayed a moment with the receiver pressed against his ear... She pressed her palms together.* V+O+A ⇑ push
2 If you **press** a part of a device, you push it with your finger in order to make the device work, for example to call a lift or to ring a doorbell. EG *The young man pressed a button... He could press the buzzer and wake her... Mrs Carstairs pressed an electric bell... He just hadn't pressed the right knob.* V+O
▸ used as a noun. EG *All this can be called up at the press of the right button.* ▸N COUNT
3 If you **press** on something, you push hard against it with your hand or your foot. EG *He pressed heavily on his companion's wrist... The driver may press harder on the accelerator... She pressed down upon the velvet cloth... Ralph used one hand as a fulcrum and pressed down with the other.* V: USU+A
4 If you **press** yourself somewhere, you push your body against a surface such as a wall or the ground, often in order to avoid being seen. EG *He pressed himself to the ground... The animal presses itself against a tree trunk... They pressed back against the wall.* V+O (REFL)+A, OR V+A ⇑ flatten
5 If you **press** someone's hand, you briefly squeeze it as a way of showing affection or encouragement. EG *I pressed her hand and told her I must go... He pressed the lad's arm with his free hand.* V+O = clasp
6 If you **press** clothes, you iron them in order to get rid of the creases. EG *I learnt how to press my uniform... He always pressed his trousers before wearing them.* V+O
7 If you **press** plants, you keep them squeezed between two flat surfaces until they become dry so that you can preserve them or use them for making a picture. V+O ⇑ flatten
8 If you **press** grapes, olives, etc, you crush them with a lot of force in order to squeeze out all the juice from inside them. V+O
9 If you **press** for something, you try hard to achieve it or obtain it by working to persuade a government or other authority that it is important. EG *He pressed for full public ownership... He continued to press for a peaceful solution... The landless labourers formed a union to press for higher wages.* V+A *(for)* = campaign
10 If you **press** someone, you try hard to persuade them to do something, to accept something, or to talk about something. EG *French immediately pressed him to visit the British Forces... He pressed me to have a cup of coffee with him... Don't press me on this point... Brooke, when pressed, replied: 'I am not prepared to look at this.'* V+O: USU+ *to*-INF/*on* = urge
11 If you **press** someone into an activity, you force them to become involved in it or to take it up. EG *I was pressed into rugby under compulsion... She found herself pressed into the role of assistant astronomer... He pressed her into service as his servant and companion.* V+O+A *(into)* = rope
12 If you **press** a subject or opinion, you work hard to get it discussed or recognized, because it is important to you that other people should understand it and accept it. EG *It enabled Benn to press his own ideas more openly... Bergson relentlessly pressed the issue of determinism... ...a large group working hard to press the consumer viewpoint.* V+O = push
13 If you **press** something on someone, you give it to them in a very forceful way so that they cannot avoid taking it, even if they do not really want it. EG *His aunts were pressing upon him cups of tea and chocolate cookies... They were flattered enough by the gifts that were pressed upon them.* V+O+A *(upon/on)* = thrust, force
14 If you **press** charges against someone, you make an official accusation against them which has to be decided in a court of law. EG *They decided against pressing charges... Mr Haggerty doesn't wish to press a charge.* V+O: IF+PREP THEN *against* = prefer
15 If something such as a danger or difficulty **presses** on you, it affects you unpleasantly and in a way that you cannot avoid. EG *The same needs press upon the socialist bloc... The realities of the present pressed down on them... ...the dangers which press upon us.* V: IF+PREP THEN *on/upon* = weigh
16 When people in a crowd **press**, they move with difficulty because there is not enough space for everyone to move easily. EG *Shoppers and pedestrians press along the pavements... A group of people pressed through a door at the other end of the room.* V+A = mill
17 If you **press** your **advantage** or **press an advantage**, you make sure that you use whatever opportunity you have to do or say what you want; a literary expression. EG *He rejoiced and pressed his advantage... I resolved to press my advantage and spend a good deal of time there... He would press any advantage with the utmost vigour.* PHR: VB INFLECTS
18 The **Press** is **18.1** all the newspapers that are published in a particular place, especially the main newspapers of a country. EG *The Daily Dispatch was patterned on the British press... I saw you advertising in the press... ...an amusing story in the press... Press comments could be merciless.* N SING: *the*+N, VB CAN BE SING OR PL ⇑ media = papers **18.2** a particular group of journalists, for example the journalists who write for the main newspapers of a country, or the journalists who go to an event or place in order to describe what is happening there. EG *I got to know a lot of the American press... Granville-Barker would never meet the press... A friend of mine was rung up by the press.* ● See also **gutter press**. N SING: *the*+N = newspapermen, reporters
19 If someone or something **gets a good press** or **gets a bad press**, they are praised or criticized in the newspapers, or on television or radio. EG *The Lords tend to get rather a poor press... I hope he'll get a fairer press in his own country.* PHR: VB INFLECTS
20 A **press** is a machine that is used for printing. EG *I resolved to acquire my own press... Since then the presses have scarcely stopped turning.* N COUNT
21 When a newspaper or magazine **goes to press**, the next edition of it starts being printed. EG *This happened just as the Economist was going to press... This edition is, at the time of going to press, I hope up to date.* PHR: VB INFLECTS
22 See also **pressed, pressing**.

press ahead. If you **press ahead**, you begin or continue doing something in a determined way, PHRASAL VB: V+ADV, USU+*with* knowing that it may take a long time or may be very difficult. EG *He has pressed ahead with talks.*

press on. If you **press on,** 1 you continue doing something in spite of difficulties or disappointments. EG *They courageously pressed on with their vital repair work... Babbage pressed on alone, achieving little... We are just pressing on regardless.* 2 you continue with a journey, even though it is becoming more difficult or more dangerous. EG *Otto would press on with all speed for Bear Island... The rest of us said a prayer and pressed on.*

PHRASAL VB : V+ADV, USU+*with* = carry on ≠ give up
PHRASAL VB : V+ADV+A = keep going

press box, press boxes. A **press box** is a room at a sports ground which is reserved for journalists to watch sporting events.

N COUNT

press conference, press conferences. When a famous person such as a politician or film star gives a **press conference,** he or she holds a meeting in order to answer questions put by a number of newspaper and television reporters. EG *The day that we returned, an important press conference was held... At his next press conference he was asked how he felt about the result.*

N COUNT ⇑ interview

press corps. The **press corps** is a group of reporters who are all working in the same place; used in American English. EG *I had friends in the press corps... I attached myself to the White House press corps.*

N SING : *the*+N, VB CAN BE SING OR PL ⇑ journalists

press cutting, press cuttings. A **press cutting** is a report that you cut out of a newspaper and keep, usually because it refers to you or to someone you know or admire. EG *She took an old crumpled press cutting out of her bag.*

N COUNT ⇑ extract

pressed /prɛst/. If you are **pressed** for something such as money or time, you do not have enough at the moment, and are not sure how you will manage. EG *He was always pressed for money... I'm a bit pressed for time, I'm afraid.* ● See also **hard-pressed.**

ADJ QUALIT : PRED, IF+PREP THEN *for* = pushed

pressgang /prɛsgæŋ/, **pressgangs, pressganging, pressganged;** also spelled with a hyphen. 1 In former times, a **pressgang** was a group of men who used to capture men and boys and force them to join the navy.

N COUNT : IF SING, VB CAN BE SING OR PL

2 If you **are pressganged** into doing something, you are made to do it, even though you do not really want to. EG *A couple of months later, I found myself press-ganged into standing at the election.*

V+O+A *(into)* : USU PASS = press

pressing /prɛsɪŋ/. Something that is **pressing** needs to be dealt with immediately. EG *Management of the economy ceased to be a pressing issue... Allen had more pressing claims on my attention... I remembered a pressing appointment with the ship's doctor... It's something I know she wants, but it's not pressing.*

ADJ QUALIT ⇑ important = urgent

pressman /prɛsmə[3]n/, **pressmen.** A **pressman** is a reporter, especially a man, who works for a newspaper or magazine; used in British English. EG *He passed on Mr Thompson's reply to waiting pressmen.*

N COUNT = newspaperman

press officer, press officers. A **press officer** is a person who is employed by an organization to give information about the organization to the press.

N COUNT ⇑ employee

press release, press releases. A **press release** is a written statement about a matter of public interest given to the press by an organization that is concerned with the matter. EG *We considered issuing some sort of press release afterwards.*

N COUNT ⇑ bulletin

press-up, press-ups; also spelled as one word. If you do **press-ups,** you lie with your face towards the floor and push down with your hands to raise your body off the floor. When your arms are straight, the weight of your body is on your hands and toes. People do press-ups as an exercise for strengthening their muscles. EG *In that three hours he must have done 600 press-ups.*

N COUNT : USU PL

pressure /prɛʃə/, **pressures, pressuring, pressured.** 1 **Pressure** is 1.1 the force that you produce when you press hard on something. EG *It took a bit of pressure to make the lid close... Gas could be released by pressure on a trigger... He disliked the pressure of her hand... It bent when the slightest pressure was put upon it.* 1.2 the force that a quantity of gas or liquid has on any surface that it touches. Pressure is measured by the amount of force that is exerted over a particular area such as a square metre or a square foot. EG *I'll just check the tyre pressure... The water pressure may need adjusting... ...a pressure of five tons per square metre.* 1.3 an attempt to persuade or force someone to do something by carrying out a series of actions or by strongly expressing your opinion. EG *For a long time he's been trying to put pressure on us... The strong pressure of public opinion drove him from office... In Europe the main pressure for change is coming from the unions.* 1.4 the strong need to perform a lot of tasks, make a lot of decisions, etc, especially when you have very little time to do each thing. EG *Parents can suffer from too much pressure... We do our best work under pressure... ...the pressures of public life.*

N UNCOUNT
N UNCOUNT+SUPP
N UNCOUNT : USU +SUPP
N UNCOUNT/N PLURAL : UNCOUNT=PL = stress, strain

2 If you **bring pressure to bear** on someone, you use your influence to try and make them do something which they do not really want to do, but which you think they should do; a formal expression. EG *Reform only came about through the public bringing unceasing pressure to bear on Parliament... The committee can however still bring pressure to bear.*

PHR : VB INFLECTS

3 If you are **under pressure** from someone **to do** something, you are being persuaded very strongly that you must do it. EG *I'm under a lot of pressure from my partners... We came under increasing pressure from Government officials.*

PHR : USED AS AN A

4 If you **pressure** someone to do something, you persuade them forcefully that they must do it. EG *The present system severely pressures all nonconformists... The children are not pressured to eat or to empty their plates... Some young people are pressured into staying on at school.*

V+O, OR V+O+*to*-INF/*into* = pressurize

5 See also **blood pressure.**

pressure cooker, pressure cookers; also spelled with a hyphen. A **pressure cooker** is a large saucepan with a lid that fits tightly, in which you can cook food quickly using steam at a high pressure.

N COUNT

pressure group, pressure groups. A **pressure group** is an organized group of people whose aim is to persuade a government or other authority to take a particular course of action, for example to change a law. EG *They have no pressure group working on their behalf... They tried to organize themselves into a really effective pressure group.*

N COUNT : IF SING, VB CAN BE SING OR PL = lobby

pressurize /prɛʃəraɪz/, **pressurizes, pressurizing, pressurized;** also spelled **pressurise.** 1 If you **pressurize** someone to do something, you persuade them or force them to do it, even though they do not really want to. EG *It was a move designed to pressurise workers to return earlier... He saved me from myself by pressurizing me to plead not guilty.*

V+O, OR V+O+*to*-INF/*into* = oblige

pressurized /prɛʃəraɪzd/; also spelled **pressurised.** 1 A **pressurized** container or area is in a state where the pressure outside is different from the pressure inside. For example, when an aeroplane is flying at a high altitude, the cabin is pressurized so that it has a similar air pressure to that on the ground. EG *...the pressurized cabin of a Boeing 707.*

ADJ CLASSIF

2 **Pressurized** liquids or gases have been compressed so that they are very compact, either in order to store them or to use them in industrial processes. EG *...pressurised water reactors.*

ADJ CLASSIF

prestige /prɛstiːʒ/. If you have **prestige,** other people admire you because of the high quality of your work or your position in society. EG *They had other means of acquiring wealth, prestige, and power... He is looking for a job with some prestige attached to it... The days when air travel abroad on business was a prestige activity are over.*

N UNCOUNT = status

prestigious /prɛstɪdʒɪ[o]əs/. Something that is **prestigious** is important, influential, and admired by people. EG *...one of the most prestigious universities in the country.*

ADJ QUALIT = reputable

prestressed concrete /priːstrɛst kɒnkriːt/ is concrete that has steel wires inside it to strengthen it.

N UNCOUNT

presumably /pri[1]zjuːməbli[1]/. You use **presumably** to say that, although you are not certain that what you are saying is true, you think that it is very likely to be true. EG *He writes the words to suit the tune, presumably... The statue is presumably not intended as a likeness of the Duke.*

ADV SEN ⇑ probably

presume /pri[1]zjuːm/, **presumes, presuming, presumed.** 1 If you **presume** that something is the case, you decide that it is very likely to be the case, although you cannot be certain. EG *I presume that they just send out a folder... If you do not come, I shall presume the deal is off... 'When? Saturday?'–'I presume so.'*

V+REPORT-CL/*so/not* = assume

2 If something **is presumed** to be the case, people

V+O+*to*-INF/C :

believe that it is the case, although they cannot be certain. EG *...a village presumed to be under Vietcong control... Larry Burrows, missing and presumed dead since 1971... He got away and is presumed to be living in Spain.*
USU PASS

3 You can say **'I presume'** to mean 'presumably', especially if you are expecting that the person you are talking to will say whether you are right or wrong. EG *You are married, I presume?*
PHR : USED AS ADV SEN = I take it

4 If you say that someone **presumes** to do something, you mean that they do it even though they have no right to do it; a formal or literary use. EG *I did not presume to interpret them.*
V+*to*-INF = venture

5 If one idea, theory, or branch of knowledge **presumes** another, it regards it as true without analysing it, so that it can be used as the basis for further ideas and theories; a formal use. EG *Logic presumes a separation of subject from object... Technology presumes there's just one right way to do things.*
V+O/REPORT-CL = presuppose

presumption /prɪ¹zʌmpʃəⁿn/, **presumptions**. 1 A **presumption** is something that is presumed to be true. EG *...based on the presumption that heaven has four walls... I don't think that's a false presumption.*
N COUNT : USU+REPORT-CL/*of*/SUPP = assumption

2 **Presumption** is behaviour in which someone does something that they have no right to do; a fairly formal use. EG *He lacked the energy even to be angry with her for her presumption... We have the presumption to believe that we can foresee the ultimate effects of our actions.*
N UNCOUNT = nerve, audacity

presumptive /prɪ¹zʌmptɪv/ is used to describe things that are based on presumptions about what is probably true, rather than on certainty. EG *...a presumptive diagnosis of thrombosis... ...heir presumptive.*
ADJ CLASSIF : ATTRIB, OR ADJ AFTER N

presumptuous /prɪ¹zʌmptjʊəs/. Someone who is **presumptuous** does things that they have no right or authority to do. EG *I hope you'll not think me presumptuous... It is dangerous and presumptuous to interfere between parents and children.* ◊ **presumptuously**. EG *...far-out playhouses that presumptuously described themselves as non-profit-making.* ◊ **presumptuousness**. EG *I hated them for their lies and presumptuousness.*
ADJ QUALIT ⇑ interfering
◊ ADV WITH VB
◊ N UNCOUNT

presuppose /priːsəpəʊz/, **presupposes, presupposing, presupposed**. If one state of affairs **presupposes** another, the first state of affairs cannot be true unless the second is also true. EG *The whole myth of the Ascension presupposes there is a Heaven physically above the Earth.*
V+O/REPORT-CL = assume

presupposition /priːsʌpəzɪʃəⁿn/, **presuppositions**. A **presupposition** is something that you assume to be true, especially something which you must assume is true in order to continue with what you are saying or thinking; a formal word. EG *People can be persuaded to believe things which contradict their former presuppositions.*
N COUNT : USU+SUPP/REPORT-CL = preconception

pretence /prɪ¹tens/, **pretences**; also spelled **pretense** in American English. 1 A **pretence** is an action or way of behaving that could deceive people into believing something that is not true. EG *There's an enormous pretence of intellectual torment, but in fact it's facile despair... Work is not available to them even though we make a pretence that it still is... The industry has abandoned any pretence of restraint.*
N COUNT : USU SING+*of/at*/REPORT-CL, OR N UNCOUNT ⇑ deception

2 If someone makes no **pretence** to have a particular quality, they do not claim to have that quality. EG *She has never made any pretence to ladylike behaviour.*
N UNCOUNT+*to/at* : WITH BROAD NEG

3 If you do something under **false pretences**, you do it while allowing people to believe that your intentions are different from what they really are. EG *...obtaining public money under false pretences for a lost cause.*
PHR : USED AS O

pretend /prɪ¹tend/, **pretends, pretending, pretended**. If you **pretend** that something is the case, you act in a way that could make people believe that it is the case, even though in fact it is not. EG *He pretended to fall over... Philip politely pretended not to have heard this remark... Her father tried to pretend that nothing unusual had happened.*
V+*to*-INF/REPORT-CL

pretender /prɪ¹tendə/, **pretenders**. A **pretender** is someone who claims the right to a particular position which they do not have, when their claim is disputed by other people.
N COUNT ⇑ claimant

pretension /prɪ¹tenʃəⁿn/, **pretensions**. If you attempt to make people believe that you are better or more important than you really are, your behaviour may be referred to as **pretension** or **pretensions**. EG *The countries she'd visited had unanimously rejected her pretensions... He is evidently a person of some social pretension.*
N UNCOUNT/COUNT : IF+PREP THEN *to/of*, UNCOUNT=PL

pretentious /prɪ¹tenʃəs/. If you say that someone or something is **pretentious**, you mean that they claim to be important, but you do not think that they are important. EG *It sounds a bit pretentious... ...one of the most pretentious films of all time.* ◊ **pretentiousness**. EG *He hated the pictures, their pretentiousness, their pompous sentimentality.*
ADJ QUALIT = pompous ≠ modest
◊ N UNCOUNT

preternatural /priːtənætʃrəl/ is used to describe something that is unusual or exceptional in a way that might make you believe that superhuman forces are involved; a formal word. EG *...his drive towards a preternatural clarity.* ◊ **preternaturally**. EG *She was preternaturally calm.*
ADJ CLASSIF = abnormal
◊ ADV+ADJ/ADV

pretext /priːtekst/, **pretexts**. A **pretext** is a reason that you pretend has caused you to do something; usually used as an excuse for doing something that is considered wrong or bad. EG *The Government invented a 'plot' as a pretext for arresting opposition leaders... He refused to see them, put them off on one pretext or another... ...under the pretext of defence needs... The organization withdrew its support on an ideological pretext.*
N COUNT

prettify /prɪtɪfaɪ/, **prettifies, prettifying, prettified**. If you **prettify** something, especially something that is basically ugly, you make it look pretty, for example by adding ornaments and decorations to it; a formal word. EG *She tried to prettify her office with a few plants and picture postcards.*
V+O ⇑ improve = smarten up

pretty /prɪti¹/, **prettier, prettiest**. 1 Someone, especially a woman or girl, who is **pretty** is nice to look at and attractive in a delicate way. EG *She was very young, very pretty and great fun... Who's that pretty little girl?... She looked as pretty as a picture in her long white dress... She had such a pretty face.* ◊ **prettily**. EG *'John's so jealous,' she says, blushing prettily.* ◊ **prettiness**. EG *...her dark prettiness.*
ADJ QUALIT = good-looking, bonny
◊ ADV WITH VB
◊ N UNCOUNT

2 A place or a thing that is **pretty** is nice to look at in a rather conventional or superficial way. EG *It's one of the prettiest views in London... ...a very pretty garden... The wallpaper was very pretty, covered in roses and lilac.* ◊ **prettily**. EG *It was prettily engraved with flowers on the back.* ◊ **prettiness**. EG *...the fairy-tale prettiness of the towns.*
ADJ QUALIT = charming, attractive
◊ ADV
◊ N UNCOUNT = charm

3 You can also use **pretty** to describe music, ideas, and other things that you cannot see that are charming and pleasing but not deeply serious. EG *We heard some very pretty music.* ◊ **prettily**. EG *'Oh, I should be ashamed,' she said prettily.*
ADJ QUALIT = nice
◊ ADV WITH VB

4 If you say that something is **not a pretty sight**, you mean that it is unpleasant or distressing to look at; an informal expression often used ironically. EG *Her face, disfigured by emotion, was not a pretty sight... 'He was beside himself with rage.'–'I see. Not a pretty sight, I imagine.'*
PHR : USED AS C

5 You can also use **pretty** in informal English to give mild emphasis to an adjective or adverb, meaning 'quite', 'rather', or 'very'; often used as an understatement. EG *I thought it was pretty good really, for a first attempt... I'm pretty certain she enjoys it... I must say, this is pretty ridiculous... If you don't mind my saying so, that's pretty strange.* ● If you describe something as **pretty fair**, you mean that it is quite good or very good. EG *I had a pretty fair idea of the answer to this question.*
ADV+ADJ/ADV = kind of
● PHR : USED AS C, OR BEFORE N = shrewd

6 **Pretty much** means almost exactly or to a great extent; an informal expression. EG *I told him pretty much what you just told me.*
PHR : USED AS AN A

7 **Pretty nearly** means almost; an informal expression. EG *...pretty nearly true desert.*
PHR : USED AS AN A

8 **Pretty well** is an informal expression meaning 8.1 almost. EG *...a superb illustrated book which contains pretty well everything that is known about lilies... ...she hated pretty well all of them.* 8.2 as well as can be expected in the circumstances. EG *She can care for herself pretty well for a person who can't say a word.*
PHR : USED AS AN A = nearly
PHR : USED AS AN A

9 If you say that someone **is sitting pretty**, you mean that they are in a good, safe, or comfortable position, while other people are still suffering or having to work hard; an informal expression.
PHR : AUX INFLECTS

10 The word **pretty** is also used ironically in some informal expressions, when you mean that something is really not at all pleasing or pretty. EG *Well,*
ADJ CLASSIF : ATTRIB ⇑ bad = fine

this is a pretty state of affairs. **10.1** If you say that things have come to **a pretty pass**, you mean that the situation has become really bad; a rather old-fashioned expression. EG *Things have come to a pretty pass, I must say, if the British police have to carry guns.* **10.2** If you say that something **cost a pretty penny**, you mean that it was expensive. EG *That stereo must have cost you a pretty penny.* ● to **lead** someone **a pretty dance**: see **dance**.

PHR : USED AS O

PHR : VB INFLECTS

pretzel /pretsəl/, **pretzels**. A **pretzel** is a small, crisp biscuit made in various fancy shapes, glazed and salted on the outside.

N COUNT

prevail /priˈveɪl/, **prevails, prevailing, prevailed**. **1** If something such as a custom or a way of thinking **prevails** in a particular place at a particular time, it is normal or generally accepted in that place at the time you are talking about. EG *...the traditions of liberal empiricism and scepticism that have prevailed in Britain since the 17th century... Different doctrines prevail at different periods.*

V+A ⇑ exist = be present

2 If something such as a proposal or a principle **prevails**, it gains a position of controlling influence, often after a long struggle against something else. EG *In the end, common sense prevailed... A cornerstone of democracy is its notion that majority opinion prevails... Political arguments had prevailed over economic sense.*

V : IF+PREP THEN *over* ⇑ win = triumph

prevail upon. If you **prevail upon** or **prevail on** someone to do something, you succeed in persuading them to do it; a fairly formal expression. EG *Brother Ted had been prevailed upon to bring his flute.*

PHRASAL VB : V+PREP, HAS PASS = talk into

prevailing /priˈveɪlɪŋ/. **1 Prevailing** is used to describe whatever is normal, usual, or most common at a particular time. EG *The prevailing view shifted still further... ...in the light of prevailing cultural standards... ...excluded from the prevailing political system.*

ADJ CLASSIF : ATTRIB = current

2 The **prevailing** wind in a particular region is the one that usually blows, coming from a particular direction. EG *It has a long coastline and strong prevailing winds.*

ADJ CLASSIF : ATTRIB

prevalence /prevələns/. The **prevalence** of something is the fact that it is widespread and occurs commonly. EG *...the prevalence of snobbery in Britain.*

N SING : *the*+N+*of*

prevalent /prevələnt/. Something that is **prevalent** exists or occurs to a great extent or as a common practice or belief. EG *...the liberal atmosphere prevalent in the late 1960s... ...one current theory prevalent among waste-disposal scientists.*

ADJ QUALIT = prevailing

prevaricate /priˈværɪkeɪt/, **prevaricates, prevaricating, prevaricated**. If you **prevaricate**, you deliberately avoid doing something that you ought to do or avoid telling people something that they want you to tell them. EG *The doctors prevaricated, arguing the need for additional clinical tests.*

V = equivocate, hedge

◊ **prevarication** /priˈværɪkeɪʃəⁿn/, **prevarications**. EG *This law is still not properly in force, prevarication by industry and bureaucrats having caused the delay.*

◊ N UNCOUNT/COUNT = equivocation

prevent /priˈvent/, **prevents, preventing, prevented**. **1** If you **prevent** someone from doing something, you stop them doing it. EG *My only idea was to prevent him from speaking... Are you instructed to prevent me entering?... Cotton mittens will prevent the baby from scratching his own face... It was as much as he could do to prevent himself from turning aside.*

V+O (NG/REFL) +*from*/-ING

2 If people or things **prevent** something from happening, they ensure that it cannot happen. EG *...silicones, which prevent the fibres from adhering to each other.*

V+O+*from*/-ING = stop

3 If you **prevent** something such as an event, you make sure that it cannot happen. EG *Some of these rods are necessary to prevent a destructive explosion... It was not enough to prevent war... They even threatened to prevent my going on my trip.*

V+O ⇑ stop

preventable /prɪventəbəⁿl/. Something that is **preventable** can be prevented from occurring. EG *Rheumatic fever is now a preventable disease.*

ADJ CLASSIF ⇑ avoidable

preventative/priˈventətɪv/ means the same as **preventive**.

ADJ CLASSIF : ATTRIB

prevention /priˈvenʃəⁿn/ is action that prevents something from happening. EG *...the prevention of cruelty to animals... ...crime prevention.*

N UNCOUNT : IF+PREP THEN *of*

preventive /priˈventɪv/. **Preventive** actions are intended to help stop things such as disease or crimes from occurring. EG *Preventive measures are essential... ...preventive medicine... ...the emergency preventive detention of dangerous persons.*

ADJ CLASSIF : ATTRIB

preverbal /priːvɜːbəⁿl/. The **preverbal** stage in a child's life is the one before he or she can speak; a formal or technical word. EG *She sank at times into a preverbal baby stammer.*

ADJ CLASSIF : ATTRIB

preview /priːvjuː/, **previews**. A **preview** is an opportunity to see something such as a film or an art exhibition before it is officially shown to the public. EG *Welcome to the press preview of the Seyer Street exhibition... He had just shown them his latest masterpiece in a sneak preview.*

N COUNT ⇑ viewing

previous /priːvɪəs/. **1** A **previous** event is one that happened at some time earlier than something else of the same kind. EG *He had children from a previous marriage... We were always told how valuable our previous career experience would be... This problem has been mentioned in a previous chapter.*

ADJ CLASSIF : ATTRIB

2 The **previous** day, week, year, etc is the one that occurred immediately before the events or period that you are talking about. EG *They had spirited him across the frontier the previous night... The Colonel spent the previous winter riding over ploughed fields... The previous Government had decided to build it... I think we can now answer the question posed at the end of the previous chapter.*

ADJ CLASSIF : ATTRIB = preceding

previously /priːvjəsliˡ/. **1 Previously** means at some time before the period or events that you are talking about. EG *I had previously lived the life of a miserly savage... He was previously British consul in Atlanta, Georgia.*

ADV WITH VB = formerly

2 You also use **previously** to say exactly how much earlier one event was than another event. EG *This load had actually been dispatched three months previously... They had officially retired ten years previously.*

ADV WITH VB = before

pre-war /priː wɔː/; also spelled without a hyphen. **Pre-war** refers to the period before a war, especially the Second World War. EG *...the prewar telephone network.*

ADJ CLASSIF : ATTRIB

prey /preɪ/, **preys, preying, preyed**. **1** The **prey** of an animal or bird is the creatures that it hunts and eats in order to live; also used of wild animals that a man tries to catch and kill. EG *Hawks circled overhead looking for prey... A mole must have some way of finding its prey.* ● See also **bird of prey**.

N UNCOUNT : USU WITH POSS = quarry

2 If something **falls prey to** something else, it is seized or taken over by it. EG *...to help prevent the company falling prey to a Stock Exchange raid.*

PHR : VB INFLECTS

3 If someone **is prey to** something unpleasant, they are severely affected by it; a literary expression. EG *She was prone to isolation, prey to doubt... ...if you are prey to fear, stress or anxiety.*

PHR : VB INFLECTS

prey on. **1** An animal or bird that **preys on** another kind of animal, bird, fish, or insect lives by catching and eating creatures of the other kind. EG *The amphibians were hunters, preying on worms, insects and other invertebrates.*

PHRASAL VB : V+PREP, HAS PASS = live off

2 If something **preys on** your **mind**, you worry a lot about it and cannot stop thinking about it. EG *The decision preyed on his mind.*

PHRASAL VB : V+PREP = trouble

price /praɪs/, **prices, pricing, priced**. **1** The **price** of something is the amount of money that you must pay in order to buy it. EG *The price of firewood has risen steeply... The price is still only £1.05... Petrol will continue to drop in price... Oil prices are stable for the first time in years.* ● See also **cut-price, list price, retail price index**.

N COUNT : USU+SUPP, OR *in*+N = cost

2 The **price** that you **pay** for something is an unpleasant thing that you have to do or an unpleasant situation that you have to endure in order to get something desirable. EG *This was the price that had to be paid for progress... The question is whether the price is worth paying... This is a small price to pay for independence.*

PHR : VB INFLECTS = penalty

3 at any price. 3.1 If you want something **at any price**, you are determined to get it or obtain it, even if unpleasant or undesirable things happen as a result. EG *...the desire to win at any price... His slogan is peace at any price.* **3.2** If you say that something will not be agreed to or accepted **at any price**, you are emphasizing that someone will not agree to it or accept it at all. EG *Most men can't stand it at any price.*

PHR : USED AS AN A = at any cost

PHR : USED AS AN A

4 If you get something **at a price**, you get it with something unpleasant or undesirable happening as a

PHR : USED AS AN A

result. EG *Such is Ford's grip on the market, though it is one obtained at a price.*

5 If you say **'What price** something?', you are saying that you think that there is very little chance of something happening, usually because something else has recently happened which makes it seem unlikely or impossible. EG *What price the two-party system in the future?... What price England winning the Test Match now?* PHR

6 If you **price** something that you intend to sell, you decide how much you will charge for it. EG *The least expensive will be priced at £7,000... ...reasonably priced accommodation.* V+O : USU PASS

7 If you **price** something that does not belong to you, you estimate how much it costs, or how much it would cost if it were for sale. EG *She glanced around, mentally pricing the other woman's possessions.* V+O ⇑ value

8 If you **price** yourself **out of the market**, you offer goods for sale at such a high price that no one will buy them, especially when similar goods can be bought more cheaply from someone else. EG *If they're not careful, they're going to price themselves out of the market... Nuclear energy has priced itself out of the market.* PHR : VB INFLECTS

priceless /praɪslɪ²s/. 1 A piece of jewellery, furniture, etc that is **priceless** is very valuable. EG *...a beautiful priceless sapphire... ...the wanton destruction of a priceless harpsichord.* ADJ CLASSIF ⇑ precious

2 Something such as information or an unusual skill that is described as **priceless** is extremely useful. EG *This priceless asset has enabled him to win innumerable tournaments... The findings could be priceless.* ADJ CLASSIF = invaluable

3 If you describe someone or their behaviour as **priceless**, you mean that you find them very amusing or amazing. ADJ QUALIT

pricey /praɪsi¹/, **pricier, priciest**. Something that is **pricey** is expensive; an informal word. EG *It's quite pricey, isn't it?* ADJ QUALIT = costly

prick /prɪk/, **pricks, pricking, pricked**. 1 If you **prick** something or **prick** holes in it, you make small holes in it with a sharp object such as a pin. EG *Prick the sausages before you fry them... I pricked little holes in the plastic wrapping.* V+O : USU+A ⇑ pierce = jab

2 If something sharp **pricks** you, it scratches or pierces your skin. EG *I remember getting pricked terribly when I went picking berries.* V+O = lacerate

3 If something **pricks** a part of your body, it causes a slight tickling or burning feeling. EG *I could feel the hairs pricking on the back of my neck... Tears pricked the backs of her eyes.* ◊ **pricking**. EG *...that sharp pricking pain all the way down his spine.* V+O, OR V : USU +A ⇑ prickle = sting ◊ ADJ CLASSIF : ATTRIB

4 A **prick** is a feeling of slight sharp pain that you get when something pricks you. EG *She felt anxiety like the prick of an insect.* N COUNT = sting

5 A **prick** is also 5.1 a man's penis; a very informal and offensive use. 5.2 a man that you dislike very much, usually because he thinks that he is clever and important and you think that he is not; a very informal and offensive use. N COUNT N COUNT/VOC = bastard

prick up. If an animal **pricks up** its **ears** or if its **ears prick up**, its ears suddenly stand up straight or point sharply towards a sound. EG *The dog's ears were pricked up straight.* PHR : VB INFLECTS

2 If you **prick up** your **ears** or if your **ears prick up**, you listen eagerly when you suddenly hear an interesting sound or an important piece of information. EG *He pricked up his ears at the sound of his father's voice... My ears pricked up when I heard them mention her name.* PHR : VB INFLECTS

prickle /prɪkə⁰l/, **prickles, prickling, prickled**. 1 A **prickle** is a small, sharp point that sticks out from a leaf or from the stalk of a plant. EG *The leaf was darkish and had prickles on it.* N COUNT : USU PL = thorn

2 If a part of your body, especially your skin, **prickles**, 2.1 it feels as if a lot of small sharp points are being stuck into it. EG *The shirt I was wearing made my skin prickle.* 2.2 it tingles, usually because you feel a strong emotion such as fear or excitement. EG *My skin prickled with fear... For an instant his flesh had prickled with alarm.* ▸ used as a noun. EG *...a prickle of pleasure.* V = smart V : IF+PREP THEN *with* = crawl ▸ N COUNT : IF+ PREP THEN *of*

prickly /prɪkli¹/. 1 Something that is **prickly** has a lot of prickles. EG *The leaves were long and prickly... ...prickly thorn bushes.* ADJ QUALIT = thorny

2 Someone who is **prickly** loses their temper very easily. EG *...a prickly and tiresome man.* ADJ QUALIT = touchy

prickly heat is a condition caused by very hot weather, in which your skin becomes hot and itchy and is covered with lots of tiny bumps. EG *Prickly heat usually starts round the neck.* N UNCOUNT

prickly pear, prickly pears. **Prickly pear** can also be used as the plural form. A **prickly pear** is a kind of cactus that has round fruit with prickles on; also used of the fruit itself, which you can eat. N COUNT

pride /praɪd/, **prides, priding, prided**. 1 **Pride** is a good feeling of happiness and eagerness for praise, which you have when you or people that you like have done something good, or when you own something that you think is good. EG *Pride shone in John's eyes... Claud was triumphant, bursting with pride and excitement... His mother looked at him with affection and pride... She pointed with pride to the fine horses she had trained.* N UNCOUNT ⇑ satisfaction

2 If you **have** or **take pride** in something that you have or do, you feel pleased and happy because of it. EG *...the childish pride he has in his latest gadgets... I take very great pride in the success of my children... We take no pride in what goes on in our country.* PHR : VB INFLECTS+*in* = revel

3 If you **pride** yourself on something that you have or do, you are very proud of it and usually make sure that other people are aware of it too. EG *Mrs Hochstadt prided herself on her intelligence... The restaurant prided itself on its continental cuisine.* V+O (REFL)+A *(on)*

4 If someone or something is your **pride and joy**, they make you feel very happy and glad, for example because they are your most important possession, your best piece of work, or your favourite friend or child; used showing approval. EG *Their baby daughter was their pride and joy.* PHR : POSS+PHR, USED AS C = treasure

5 **Pride** is also 5.1 a sense of dignity and self-respect that a person has. EG *My pride did not allow me to complain too often... Pride alone prevented her from giving up... The setback was a blow to his political pride.* 5.2 a feeling of being superior to others which makes a person boast and ignore other people's feelings and advice; used showing disapproval. EG *There is a lot of pride in the phrase 'no one can fool me'.* N UNCOUNT = self-esteem N UNCOUNT = arrogance, vanity

6 If you **swallow** your **pride**, you decide to behave in a way that you do not admire or respect, because you want or need something that is very important to you. EG *He swallowed his pride and accepted the money.* PHR : VB INFLECTS

7 If you are **nursing** your **pride**, you are trying to recover your sense of dignity after you have been made to appear foolish or stupid. EG *He was nursing his pride after losing the competition.* PHR : VB INFLECTS

8 If something has **pride of place**, it is the most important thing in a group of things. EG *The table was loaded down with all kinds of delicious dishes, but the roast turkey took pride of place... Musical composition will take pride of place in the festivities.* PHR : USED AS O

9 A **pride** of lions is a group of lions that live together. EG *A pride of lions killed his entire herd of goats... On occasion, members of a pride will hunt as a team.* N PART : USU SING+N IN PLURAL

priest /priːst/, **priests**. A **priest** is 1 a man who is a member of the Christian clergy, especially in the Catholic, Anglican, or Orthodox church. EG *...an Anglican priest... ...a remarkable old Irish priest... In the Roman Catholic church women cannot become priests.* 2 a man in many non-Christian religions who has particular duties and responsibilities in the place where people worship. EG *...a Buddhist priest.* N COUNT ⇑ clergyman N COUNT

priestess /priːstɛs/, **priestesses**. A **priestess** is a woman in many non-Christian religions who has particular duties and responsibilities in the place where people worship. N COUNT

priesthood /priːsthʊd/. The **priesthood** is 1 the position and office of being a priest; a technical term in theology. EG *...the responsibilities of the priesthood.* 2 all the members of the Christian clergy, especially in a particular Church or region. EG *...the Catholic priesthood.* N SING : *the*+N N SING : *the*+N

priestly /priːstli¹/ is used to describe things that belong or relate to a priest. EG *...priestly duties... ...a priestly blessing.* ADJ CLASSIF : ATTRIB = pastoral

prig /prɪg/, **prigs**. A **prig** is an irritating person who carefully obeys rules of good behaviour and who behaves as if he or she is better than other people; used showing disapproval. EG *Jason was a self-righteous prig.* N COUNT/VOC = snob

priggish /prɪgɪʃ/. Someone who is **priggish** is irritating because they carefully obey rules of good behaviour and behave as if they are better than other people; used showing disapproval. EG *...a rather priggish young man... I'm sick of your priggish little ways!* ◊ **priggishness**.
ADJ QUALIT = snobbish, self-righteous
◊ N UNCOUNT

prim /prɪm/, **primmer, primmest**. Someone who is **prim** behaves very correctly and is easily shocked by anything rude or improper; often used showing disapproval. EG *She had a very prim voice.* ▸ used of people's behaviour and actions. EG *There was a prim avoidance of the issue.* ◊ **primly**. EG *His sister sat primly with her legs together... 'Excuse me,' Mr Boggis answered primly.*
ADJ QUALIT ↑ correct = prissy
◊ ADV WITH VB = demurely

prima ballerina /priːmə bælərиːnə/, **prima ballerinas**. A **prima ballerina** is the most important female dancer in a ballet or a ballet company. EG *...the Bolshoi's prima ballerina.*
N COUNT : USU SING

primacy /praɪməsi[1]/. Something that has **primacy** in a particular situation is the most important or most powerful thing in that situation; a formal word. EG *America should give greater recognition to Indian primacy in South Asia... ...the primacy of the Third World in liberation theology.*
N UNCOUNT : IF + PREP THEN *of* = supremacy

prima donna /priːmə dɒnə/, **prima donnas**. A **prima donna** is 1 the main female singer in an opera. EG *...the world-famous prima donna.*
N COUNT : USU SING

2 someone whose moods change very quickly and suddenly and who is therefore very difficult to deal with; used showing disapproval. EG *...a prima donna who is also an intensely serious artist.*
N COUNT : USU SING

primaeval /praɪmiːvəl/. See **primeval**.

prima facie /praɪmə feɪʃi[1]/ is used to describe something which seems to be true when you consider it for the first time; a formal expression. EG *There is indeed some prima facie evidence to support such a thesis... ...a prima facie case of murder.*
ADJ CLASSIF : ATTRIB, ADV SEN, OR ADV + ADJ

primal /praɪməl/ is used to describe something that relates to the causes or origins of things; a formal word. EG *...the primal cause of all life.*
ADJ CLASSIF : ATTRIB ↑ original

primarily /praɪmərəli[1]/. You use **primarily** to say what is mainly true in a particular situation. EG *Most linguists would say they were concerned primarily with the structure of languages... Although research is important, the university exists primarily for the students... The issue was not primarily a political one but essentially moral.*
ADV WITH VB = chiefly, essentially

primary /praɪməri[1]/, **primaries**. 1 **Primary** is used to describe 1.1 something that is extremely important, so that it happens or is dealt with before anything else. EG *This was a primary concern of Gandhi... One of Europe's primary requirements was minerals... Policemen were the primary targets and suffered most of the casualties... She gets her primary satisfaction from her career.* 1.2 the education of children between 5 and 11 years old in Britain. EG *...primary education... I enjoy working with the primary age group.*
ADJ CLASSIF : USU ATTRIB = chief, main
ADJ CLASSIF : ATTRIB = elementary

2 A **primary** is an election in an American state in which people vote for someone to become a candidate for a political office. EG *We lost the New Hampshire primary.*
N COUNT

primary colour, primary colours. A **primary colour** is one of the three colours red, yellow, or blue, which can be mixed together in different ways to make all other colours.
N COUNT

primary school, primary schools. A **primary school** is a school in Britain for children between 5 and 11 years old. EG *I started primary school when I was 5 years old.*
N COUNT/UNCOUNT

primate /praɪmət/, **primates**. 1 A **primate** is one of the group of mammals which is the most intelligent and highly developed and which includes humans, monkeys, and apes. EG *All primates are facially expressive... ...an ancestral form from which all the higher primates are descended... ...the ancient primate habit of vegetarianism.*
N COUNT

2 The **Primate** of a particular country or region is the archbishop of that country or region; a formal use. EG *...the Primate of Ireland, Cardinal O'Fiaich.*
N COUNT : ALSO IN TITLES

prime /praɪm/, **primes, priming, primed**. 1 **Prime** is used to describe 1.1 something that is most important or fundamental to a particular situation. EG *What was said was of prime importance... Maths is no longer a prime requirement for a career in accountancy... High sugar intake is the prime villain in arterial and heart disease.* 1.2 something that is of the best possible quality. EG *...a piece of prime beef... He wants his herd delivered to the cattle market in prime condition... Artists vied for the prime sites to paint.* 1.3 something that is absolutely typical of a particular situation or type of thing. EG *We had, a few years ago, a prime example of the power of the press to embarrass.*
ADJ CLASSIF : ATTRIB ↑ main = primary
ADJ CLASSIF : ATTRIB = choice
ADJ CLASSIF : ATTRIB = classic

2 Someone or something's **prime** is the stage in their development when they are at their strongest, most fully developed, most successful, etc. EG *I had been a good player in my prime... ...machines long past their prime.*
N SING : WITH POSS ↑ best = heyday

3 Someone who is **in the prime of life** is at the time of their life when they feel strongest, healthiest, and most active. EG *He's only just over forty–in the prime of life.*
PHR : USED AS AN A

4 If you **prime** someone about something, you give them information about it before it happens or before they are involved in it, so that they are prepared for it. EG *I had primed Eddie enough for him to expect the odd photo and autograph request... He is well primed to enter the profession.*
V+O : USU+A = brief, prepare

5 If you **prime** wood, you cover it with special paint in order to prepare it for the main layer of paint. EG *Prime bare wood and paint it as soon as possible.*
V+O

6 If you **prime** a gun, bomb, etc, you prepare it so that it is ready to fire or explode. EG *The gun was primed and ready.*
V+O

Prime Minister, Prime Ministers. A **Prime Minister** is the leader of the government of a country. EG *...Prime Minister Margaret Thatcher... It was announced that the Prime Minister would speak to the nation on television.*
N PROPER/N COUNT : ALSO IN TITLES = premier, PM

prime mover, prime movers. Someone or something that is a **prime mover** of a plan, idea, situation, etc has an important influence in starting it. EG *They were prime movers in the enterprise... For the Europeans, profit was usually the prime mover.*
N COUNT = driving force

prime number, prime numbers. A **prime number** is a whole number greater than 1 that cannot be divided exactly by any whole number except itself and the number 1; a technical term in mathematics. EG *2, 3, 7, and 11 are prime numbers.*
N COUNT

primer /praɪmə/, **primers**. 1 **Primer** is a type of paint that is put onto wood in order to prepare it for the main layer of paint. EG *Use primer before applying the main coat.*
N MASS

2 A **primer** is a book containing basic facts about a subject, which is used by someone who is beginning to study that subject. EG *...Longman Green's basic English Primer.*
N COUNT : ALSO IN NAMES

primeval /praɪmiːvəl/; also spelled **primaeval**. **Primeval** is used to describe 1 things that belong to a very early period in the history of the world. EG *...primeval forests... ...the primeval tribe... His howling sounded like some primeval beast's.* 2 feelings and emotions that are very ancient and instinctive. EG *...primeval terror... ...primeval stirrings of foreboding.*
ADJ CLASSIF : ATTRIB ↑ old = primordial
ADJ CLASSIF : ATTRIB = primordial

primitive /prɪmɪtɪv/. Something that is **primitive** 1 belongs to a society of people who live in a very simple way, usually without industries or a writing system. EG *...anthropologists who have lived with and studied primitive tribes... ...the history of primitive religion... The most commonly cited example of a primitive device is the abacus.* 2 belongs to a very early period in the development of something, for example an early type of animal. EG *The okapi is a short-necked primitive cousin of the giraffe... ...primitive cereals... He was driven by the most primitive of instincts.* 3 is very simple in style or very old-fashioned; often used showing disapproval. EG *Conditions were often primitive... The sleeping accommodation is somewhat primitive when judged by normal standards.*
ADJ QUALIT : USU ATTRIB ≠ civilized, sophisticated
ADJ QUALIT ↑ original = elementary
ADJ QUALIT = crude ≠ sophisticated

primordial /praɪmɔːdɪəl/ is used to describe things that have existed from a very early time or since the beginning of the world; a formal word. EG *...the primordial moment when everything began... ...a wild, haunting, primordial sound.*
ADJ CLASSIF : ATTRIB = primeval

primrose /prɪmrəʊz/, **primroses**. 1 A **primrose** is a wild plant which has pale yellow flowers in spring; also used of the flower itself.
N COUNT

2 Something that is **primrose** or **primrose yellow** is pale yellow in colour. EG *Mrs Kaul's bathroom was all in primrose yellow.*
ADJ COLOUR

primula /prɪmjəˈlə/, **primulae, primulas**. The plural can be either **primulae** or **primulas**. A **primula** is a type of primrose with very brightly coloured flowers; also used of the flower itself. N COUNT

Primus /praɪməs/, **Primuses**; a trademark. A **Primus** or a **Primus stove** is a small cooker that burns paraffin and is often used in camping. EG *The kettle was steaming away on the Primus stove.* N COUNT : USU SING

prince /prɪns/, **princes**. **1** A **prince** is **1.1** a male member of a royal family, especially the son of the king or queen of a country. EG *...a little school play about princes and princesses... ...a statue of Prince Charles' grandfather.* N COUNT : ALSO IN TITLES **1.2** the male, royal ruler of a small country or state. EG *...Prince Louis Alexander of Battenburg.* N COUNT : ALSO IN TITLES

2 If you call a man the **prince** of a particular area or type of work, you mean that you consider him to be the best man in that area or type of work; an informal use. EG *...General Weyler, whom the Journal had denounced as the prince of all cruel generals.* N COUNT : USU SING+SUPP = epitome

princely /prɪnsliˈ/. **1** Something that is **princely** belongs to a prince or is suitable for a prince. EG *...the princely courts of Asia.* ADJ CLASSIF

2 A **princely** amount, especially an amount of money, is a large amount. EG *We're managing to sell them at a princely 25 pounds a time.* ADJ QUALIT : ATTRIB = handsome

Prince of Wales. The **Prince of Wales** is the eldest son of the king or queen of Britain. He is the person who will next rule the country. EG *Edward VII lived here for years as Prince of Wales.* N PROPER : *the*+N

princess /prɪnsɛs/, **princesses**. A **princess** is a female member of a royal family, usually the daughter of a king or queen or the wife of a prince. EG *...three young princesses from Nepal... In 1922 he married Princess Mary, only daughter of King George V.* N COUNT : ALSO IN TITLES

principal /prɪnsɪpəˈl/, **principals**. **1 Principal** means first in order of importance. EG *His principal interest in life was to be the richest man in Britain... ...the principal character in James Bernard Fagan's play.* ADJ CLASSIF : ATTRIB = main

2 A **principal** is the person in charge of a school or a college. EG *Complaints began arriving at the principal's office... ...Mr Patrick Miller, principal of Esher College.* N COUNT = head

principality /prɪnsɪpælɪtiˈ/, **principalities**. A **principality** is the country that is ruled by a prince or that a prince takes his title from. EG *...the Principality of Monaco.* N COUNT

principally /prɪnsɪpəˈliˈ/ means more than anything else. EG *He dealt principally with Ethiopia... There has been a massive build-up of nuclear weapons, principally by the two super-powers.* ADV = chiefly

principle /prɪnsɪpəˈl/, **principles**. **1** A **principle** is **1.1** a general rule that you try to obey in the way that you behave or in the way that you try to achieve something; used showing approval. EG *...a man of high principles... She abandoned her principles... She was a woman of principle... The government is torn between principle and expediency.* N COUNT/UNCOUNT ⇑ honour **1.2** a law or rule that shows how a particular theory or philosophy is put into practice. EG *...the principles of formal logic... ...a party organized on Leninist principles.* N COUNT+SUPP/REPORT-CL = tenet **1.3** a general scientific law which explains something such as a natural phenomenon or the way that a device or a machine works. EG *This will demonstrate the general principle... ...the principle of acceleration.* N COUNT+SUPP/REPORT-CL ⇑ rule

2 If you do something **on principle**, you do it because of a particular belief that you have. EG *I had to vote for him, of course, on principle.* PHR : USED AS AN A

3 in principle. **3.1** If something is possible **in principle**, it has never happened or has never been done, but there is no known scientific reason why it should not happen or should not be done. EG *The kind of thing I was doing was, in principle, applicable to great numbers of tests.* PHR : USED AS AN A = in theory **3.2** If someone agrees with or approves of something **in principle**, they generally agree to the idea of it but may be unable or unwilling to support it in practice. EG *I wish to know if you agree in principle to the idea... We are willing, in principle, to look afresh at the 1921 constitution.* PHR : USED AS AN A

principled /prɪnsɪpəˈld/. **1 Principled** behaviour is based on principles that people use to guide the way they act. EG *He had assumed a principled, unchanging position from the outset.* ADJ CLASSIF : ATTRIB

2 Someone who is **principled** acts in accordance with the principles that they hold. EG *I forgot you were so high principled.* ADJ QUALIT

print /prɪnt/, **prints, printing, printed**. **1** If you **print** a book, a newspaper, or a leaflet, you produce it in large quantities by means of a mechanical process. EG *I don't know who you think is going to print this book of yours... I asked him for an estimate to print a weekly paper for me... They had thousands of red stickers printed.* • See also **printing**. V+O

2 If you **print** a piece of speech or writing, you include it in a newspaper, magazine, or book. EG *The paper printed a big exclusive story about Margaret Thatcher... This interview was not printed in the local or national press... It won't appear in printed form for a number of months.* V+O : USU+A = publish

3 You use the expression **the printed word** to refer to any information that is printed in a book, newspaper, etc. EG *The impulse toward acceleration in communications is by no means limited to the printed word... He declared in a succession of books that the printed word was finished.* PHR : USED AS O/S

4 Print is the letters and numbers on a page of a book, newspaper, etc. EG *...paragraphs like the one in bold print below... The print is rather poor.* N UNCOUNT = type

5 The **small print** or the **fine print** of a legal document is the part which contains details of something such as an agreement or a guarantee, and which is often printed in smaller letters than the rest of the document. EG *She looked at the small print at the bottom of the section.* N UNCOUNT

6 If a book is **in print**, it is available from a publisher. If a book is **out of print**, it is no longer available from a publisher. EG *I think you'll find it's still in print... Most of the books were out of print... The Macmillan edition is out of print.* PHR : USED AS C

7 If a person or something that a person says is **in print** or gets **into print**, what he or she says is printed in a book, magazine, newspaper, etc. EG *This was not mentioned in print... He launched straight into print, with disastrous consequences... He had not been seen in print much over the last few years.* PHR : USED AS AN A

8 A **print** is **8.1** a picture that is copied from a painting by photography or made mechanically from specially prepared surfaces and dyes. Usually several copies of one print are made at the same time. EG *Frith issued a popular print which sold in tens of thousands... Lady Hargreaves wanted sporting prints.* N COUNT ⇑ copy **8.2** one of the photographs from a film that has been developed. EG *...simple black and white prints... The prints were underdeveloped.* N COUNT

9 If you **print** cloth or **print** a pattern on cloth, you reproduce the pattern many times on the cloth, usually by using dye and special machinery. EG *...a pattern which is printed onto the fabric by hand... She always dressed in cotton printed saris.* V+O

10 Print cloth has a pattern printed on it. EG *Janet wore a faded print apron.* ADJ CLASSIF : ATTRIB

11 A **print** is also **11.1** a footprint. EG *We had to choose which set of prints to follow... His feet left prints in the soft soil.* N COUNT : USU PL = track **11.2** a fingerprint. EG *The prints were compared.* N COUNT : USU PL

12 If you **print** or **print** words, you write in letters that are not joined together and that look like the letters in a book or newspaper. EG *There was a long, white, plain envelope on her desk, with her name printed on it... As long as you print fairly clearly, you don't have to learn any new typing skills.* ▸ used as a noun to refer to this type of writing. EG *The numbers are written in this rather stylized thick square print.* V OR V+O : USU+A ▸ N UNCOUNT

print out. When a computer, or a special machine attached to a computer, **prints out** information, it reproduces it on paper. EG *The projects are printed out, ready to use.* • See also **print-out**. PHRASAL VB : V+O+ADV

printable /prɪntəbəˈl/. If something that someone says is not **printable**, it is likely to offend people, and is therefore not suitable for printing in a newspaper or a magazine. EG *I doubt if my views on the Loch Ness monster were printable.* ADJ QUALIT : USU WITH BROAD NEG ⇑ acceptable

printer /prɪntə/, **printers**. A **printer** is **1** someone who prints books, newspapers, leaflets, etc, usually as an employee of a printing firm. EG *The printers tried to dictate how he should run his business.* N COUNT ⇑ worker **2** a machine that is connected to a computer and that prints out on paper information or calculations from the computer. EG *...a new line of computer printers.* N COUNT

printing /prɪntɪŋ/ is the process or activity of printing newspapers, books, leaflets, etc. EG *I taught* N UNCOUNT *myself the rudiments of printing... ...a Gloucester printing apprentice.*

printing press, printing presses. A **printing press** is a machine used for printing. EG *This six-colour printing press comes from Japan.*
N COUNT

printout /prɪntaut/, **printouts**; also spelled with a hyphen. A **print-out** is a piece of paper on which information from a computer has been printed, either by the computer itself or by a machine attached to the computer. EG *...people carrying computer printouts... ...a printout of the result.*
N COUNT/UNCOUNT

prior /praɪə/, **priors.** 1 If something happens **prior** to a particular time or event, it happens before that time or event; a fairly formal use. EG *It occurred in Dallas, Texas, just prior to President Kennedy's assassination... Most people in Britain prior to 1760 were country people.*
PREP = previous to

2 **Prior** is used to describe something that happens, exists, or is done or experienced before a particular time. EG *No prior knowledge should be required... Prior arrangements had to be made... I have a prior engagement.*
ADJ CLASSIF : ATTRIB = previous

3 A **prior** claim, obligation, duty, etc is more important than other claims, obligations, duties, etc and therefore needs to be dealt with first. EG *There are many others who have a prior claim on one's devotion... He feels a prior obligation to his job as a journalist.*
ADJ CLASSIF : ATTRIB = stronger

4 A **prior** is a monk who is in charge of a priory, or who is an abbot's deputy in a monastery.
N COUNT : ALSO IN TITLES

priority /praɪɒrɪti[1]/, **priorities.** 1 Something that is a **priority** must be done, dealt with, or provided as soon as possible. EG *Getting food was the main priority... Factories seemed to be China's highest priority.* ▸ used as an adjective. EG *The waiting list now contains a thousand priority cases.*
N COUNT+SUPP ⇑ objective = concern
▸ ADJ CLASSIF : ATTRIB

2 Someone's **priorities** are a set of problems, considerations, or courses of action which they need to deal with in a particular order because some are more important than others. EG *There is little attempt to find out the priorities of the public... Grown-ups have a different order of priorities... The policeman had his priorities right.*
N PLURAL ⇑ concerns

3 **Priority** is the importance that something has in relation to others, so that it is considered or dealt with before some things and after others. EG *Strict priority was agreed... ...the priority of the various tasks of government.*
N UNCOUNT

4 If you **give priority** to someone or something, you treat them as more important than anyone or anything else. EG *These children are given priority when day nursery places are allocated... The trade unions must give priority to protecting the interests of their members.*
PHR : VB INFLECTS

5 Someone or something that **takes** or **has priority** over someone or something else is regarded or treated as more important than them. EG *National independence takes priority over class struggle... The question of laser beams will take priority.*
PHR : VB INFLECTS = take precedence

priory /praɪəri[1]/, **priories.** A **priory** is a place where a small group of monks live and work together. EG *...the ruins of the Cluniac Priory of Stansgate.*
N COUNT : ALSO IN NAMES

prise /praɪz/, **prises, prising, prised**; also spelled **prize.** If you **prise** something open or **prise** it away from a surface, you force it to open or force it to come away from the surface. EG *He prised the lids off both tins of paint... I prised her arms free.*
V+O+A = lever

prise out. If you **prise** information **out** of someone, you succeed in getting them to tell you the information, especially when they are very unwilling to tell you it. EG *Morris had not been able to prise out any information about his own teaching programme... Christopher prized it out of her in an unguarded moment.*
PHRASAL VB : V+O+ADV = wheedle out

prism /prɪzə[0]m/, **prisms.** A **prism** is a solid, transparent object made of glass or plastic, which has many straight sides and angles. It separates the light which passes through it into the colours of the rainbow.
N COUNT

prismatic /prɪzmætɪk/; a formal word. **Prismatic** is used to describe 1 something that is very bright and clear. EG *...prismatic colours... ...that prismatic first light of morning.* 2 something that is related to or concerned with a prism.
ADJ CLASSIF : USU ATTRIB
ADJ CLASSIF : ATTRIB

prison /prɪzə[0]n/, **prisons.** 1 A **prison** is a building where criminals are kept in order to punish them and to protect other people from them. EG *He died in prison... He was eventually sent to prison for a very long time... We should try to keep young people out of prison... The prison officers threatened to strike.* ▸ used as an uncount noun to refer to the act of sending people to prison as punishment. EG *Are there alternatives to prison?*
N COUNT : ALSO IN NAMES, OR *in/out of*+N ⇑ institution
▸ N UNCOUNT ⇑ imprisonment

2 You can refer to something that you are involved in as a **prison** when it causes you to feel trapped against your will and unable to escape; a literary use. EG *The Kirks' marriage had become a prison... I had created my own prison by telling so many lies.*
N COUNT : USU SING ⇑ trap

prison camp, prison camps. A **prison camp** is a guarded camp where prisoners of war or political prisoners are kept. EG *...soldiers who have recently been released from prison camps.*
N COUNT

prisoner /prɪzə[0]nə/, **prisoners.** 1 A **prisoner** is 1.1 someone who is kept in a prison as a punishment. EG *He was the only prisoner permitted to enter my cell.*
N COUNT = convict, inmate

1.2 someone who has been captured by an enemy, for example in war. EG *...Russian prisoners being escorted to the train.* ● If you **hold** someone **prisoner**, you guard them so that they cannot escape. EG *The young private was held a prisoner by the guerrillas.* ● If you **take** someone **prisoner**, you capture them. EG *They took several soldiers prisoner and killed the rest... We might get taken prisoner by the enemy.*
N COUNT = captive
● PHR : VB INFLECTS ⇑ imprison
● PHR : VB INFLECTS

2 If you are a **prisoner** of a particular situation, you feel trapped by it; a literary use. EG *I felt trapped, a prisoner of my own dramatic visions... You're a prisoner of your own snobbery.*
N COUNT : USU SING+SUPP = captive

prisoner of war, prisoners of war. A **prisoner of war** is a soldier who is captured by the enemy during a war and kept as a prisoner until the end of the war. EG *...Italian prisoners of war.*
N COUNT = POW

prissy /prɪsi[1]/. Someone who is **prissy** always behaves very correctly and in a fussy way and is easily shocked by anything rude or improper; an informal word used showing disapproval. EG *She had a prissy way of talking.*
ADJ QUALIT = prim

pristine /prɪstaɪn, -tiːn/. Something that is **pristine** is or seems completely new, clean, and unused; a formal word. EG *He wiped his fingers on his pristine handkerchief.*
ADJ CLASSIF = immaculate

privacy /praɪvəsi[1], prɪvəsi[1]/. If you have **privacy**, you are alone or can be alone, so that you can do things without other people seeing you or disturbing you. EG *I hated the lack of privacy in the dormitory... I felt I needed privacy... ...the privacy of your own home... Perhaps you'd like to take it home with you and read it in privacy.*
N UNCOUNT ⇑ solitude ≠ publicity

private /praɪvɪ[1]t/, **privates.** 1 Something that is **private** is for the use of one person or group of people only, rather than for the general public. EG *All rooms have got private bath, shower and WC... The fields were private property... The garden is private... ...a private showing of a film.*
ADJ CLASSIF : USU ATTRIB ⇑ personal ≠ public

2 **Private** discussions, interviews, etc take place between a small group of people and are kept secret from other people. EG *I have asked the editors to apply to the Prime Minister for a private interview.* ◇ **privately.** EG *The notion was discussed privately between the two men at lunch.*
ADJ CLASSIF : ATTRIB = confidential ≠ public
◇ ADV WITH VB

3 If you do something **in private**, you do it without other people being present, usually because it is something that you want to keep secret. EG *Could we talk to you in private?... I don't mind what people do in private.*
PHR : USED AS AN A = privately ≠ publicly

4 You use **private** to describe activities and belongings that are connected with your personal life rather than with your work or business. EG *She never spoke about her past or her private life... I have an official diary and a private diary... Top directors will probably have all their private telephone bills paid by the company.*
ADJ CLASSIF : ATTRIB ≠ business, public

5 Your **private** thoughts, plans, etc are thoughts and plans which are personal to you and which you do not talk about to other people. EG *He was deep in his own private thoughts... He was engaged in a private quest of his own.* ◇ **privately.** EG *Privately Ben felt close to despair.*
ADJ CLASSIF : ATTRIB = secret
◇ ADV WITH VB

6 If you describe a place as **private**, you mean that it is quiet and you can be alone there without being interrupted or disturbed. EG *This place is quiet and private... ...a private place of meditation.* ● If you can **be private** in a particular place, you can be
ADJ QUALIT = secluded
● PHR : USU MODAL+PHR

alone there without being interrupted or disturbed by anyone. EG *There's no place to be private.*

7 A **private** person is very quiet by nature and does not share his or her thoughts and feelings with other people. EG *Away from the glare of publicity he becomes an intensely private man... They were very private people, with almost no friends.* ADJ QUALIT = reserved, withdrawn

8 Private is also used to describe services that you pay for or industries that are owned by an individual person or group, rather than services and industries that are controlled by the state. EG *...private education... ...private health insurance... All private banks are being nationalized.* ◊ **privately**. EG *These are privately owned firms.* ADJ CLASSIF: ATTRIB = independent ≠ state ◊ ADV WITH VB ≠ state

9 A **private** is a soldier who has the lowest rank in an army. EG *The young private had been held a prisoner by the guerrillas.* N COUNT: ALSO IN TITLES

10 Your **privates** are your genitals; an informal use. N PLURAL

private detective, private detectives. A **private detective** is a detective who works alone rather than in the police force and who you can hire to find missing people or do other kinds of investigation for you. EG *He hired a private detective to go out and make enquiries.* N COUNT = private eye

private enterprise is industry and business which is owned by an individual person or group and not supported financially by the government. EG *...rich societies organized along private enterprise lines.* N UNCOUNT

private eye, private eyes. A **private eye** is the same as a private detective; used in informal American English. N COUNT

private member's bill. The plural can be either **private member's bills** or **private members' bills**. A **private member's bill** is a law that is proposed by a member of parliament acting as an individual rather than as a member of his or her political party. EG *...her successful private member's Bill.* N COUNT

private parts. If you talk about someone's **private parts**, you are referring to the outer sex organs on their body in a polite way. EG *Even the women's private parts were inspected.* N PLURAL = genitals

private school, private schools. A **private school** is a school which is not supported financially by the government and which parents have to pay for their children to go to. EG *I went to an expensive private school.* N COUNT

private sector. The **private sector** is the part of a country's economy which is not controlled or supported financially by the government. EG *In the private sector, urban salaried workers have been able to obtain higher incomes.* N SING: the+N

privation /praɪveɪʃ(ə)n/, **privations**. If you suffer from **privation** or **privations**, you are deprived of things that are necessary to your life or that you feel are necessary; a formal word. EG *Life was riddled with petty privation... I had suffered such shameful privations.* N UNCOUNT/COUNT ⇑ hardship

privatize /praɪvətaɪz/, **privatizes, privatizing, privatized**; also spelled **privatise**. If a government **privatizes** a company, industry, or service that is owned and controlled by the state, it changes its ownership so that it becomes private and owned by an individual or group. EG *...plans to privatize coal.* ◊ **privatized**. EG *...the difference between privatized and collectivized home-ownership systems.* ◊ **privatization** /praɪvətaɪzeɪʃ(ə)n/. EG *...the privatisation of the telephone sevice... The Conservative government has extended its drive for privatization to the forestry business.* V+O ≠ nationalize ◊ ADJ CLASSIF: ATTRIB ◊ N UNCOUNT

privet /prɪvɪt/ is a type of bush with small leaves that stay green all year round. It is often grown in gardens to form hedges. EG *Most houses were separated by garages or privet hedges.* N UNCOUNT

privilege /prɪvɪ(ə)lɪdʒ/, **privileges**. **1** A **privilege** is a special right or advantage that is given to only one person or group and that puts them in a better position than other people. EG *One of the privileges of belonging to the club is that you can use its tennis courts... The children would resent any special privileges given to the staff.* N COUNT = perk, prerogative

2 Privilege is the power and advantages that belong to a small group of people, usually because of their wealth or their high social class. EG *...the accumulation of private wealth, property, and privilege.* N UNCOUNT

3 A **privilege** that you have is an opportunity to do something that gives you great pleasure or satisfaction, and that most people never have the opportunity to do. EG *It was a privilege to work with such a great actress... I had the privilege of meeting the Queen when she visited our school.* N COUNT: USU SING = honour

privileged /prɪvɪ(ə)lɪdʒd/. Someone who is **privileged** has special rights, advantages, or opportunities that most other people do not have. EG *I am privileged to have worked with her so often... They are a privileged group of people... ...a privileged guest.* ▸ The **privileged** is used to refer to people who are privileged. EG *...an impressive modern city reserved for the privileged.* ADJ QUALIT ⇑ lucky = honoured ▸ N PLURAL: the+N = elite

privy /prɪvi[1]/, **privies**. **1** A **privy** is a toilet, especially one that is in a small shed outside and at some distance from a house; an old-fashioned use. EG *...the ivy-covered privy at the end of his garden.* N COUNT

2 If you are **privy** to something secret, you are allowed to know about it; a formal use. EG *Very few of them were privy to the details of the conspiracy.* ADJ CLASSIF: PRED, USU+to ⇑ informed

Privy Council. In Britain, the **Privy Council** is a group of people who are appointed to advise the king or queen on political affairs. N PROPER: the+N

prize /praɪz/, **prizes, prizing, prized**. **1** A **prize** is **1.1** something of value, for example money or a trophy, that is given to someone who has the best results in a competition or game, or as a reward for doing good work. EG *I entered one or two competitions and won prizes... My pig won first prize at Skipton Fair... ...a Nobel prize-winner... What will you do with the prize money?* N COUNT ⇑ award **1.2** something that you consider to be very important and that you try very hard to obtain or achieve. EG *...a great strategic prize retained firmly in the grasp of the United States.* N COUNT ⇑ goal ● See also **consolation prize**.

2 If you say **no prizes for guessing** something, you mean that something is extremely obvious and therefore not at all difficult to guess; an informal expression. EG *No prizes for guessing the title.* PHR+NG/REPORT-CL

3 You use **prize** to describe **3.1** things that are of such good quality that they win prizes or deserve to win prizes. EG *...prize carnations.* ADJ CLASSIF: ATTRIB **3.2** something that is typical of a particular group or type of things and therefore a perfect example of that group or type. EG *...a prize example of the group's underhand behaviour.* ADJ CLASSIF: ATTRIB = classic **3.3** something that you own which you value very greatly. EG *...his prize possession... They stole my prize Ming vase.* ADJ CLASSIF: ATTRIB ⇑ cherished

4 If you **prize** something, you feel that it is valuable and important, so that you are very proud of it or try hard to obtain it. EG *The deer were prized for their tasty venison... ...a kind of glass which is now very rare and much prized.* ● See also **prise**. V+O: USU PASS ⇑ value = treasure

prize-fighter, prize-fighters. A **prize-fighter** is a boxer who fights to win money. N COUNT

prize-giving, prize-givings. A **prize-giving** is a ceremony where schoolchildren are given prizes for doing good work during the year. EG *...a school prize giving... It's prize-giving next week.* N COUNT/UNCOUNT

pro /prəʊ/, **pros**. **1** A **pro** is **1.1** a professional; an informal use. EG *He went to the golf course to play a round with the local pro... He is now turning pro.* N COUNT ≠ amateur **1.2** a prostitute; an informal use. EG *She's only an old pro.* N COUNT

2 The pros and cons of a situation are its advantages and disadvantages, which you think about and judge at the same time so that you can make a sensible decision. EG *...a rational weighing-up of the pros and cons... The pros and cons of strike action were discussed.* PHR: USED AS O/S

3 If you are **pro** a particular plan or belief, you agree with it or support it. EG *Are you pro or anti nuclear disarmament?* PREP = for

pro- is added to adjectives and nouns in order to form adjectives that describe someone as supporting or admiring a country, person, idea, etc. EG *...the Government's pro-American policy... ...the pro-nuclear lobby.* PREFIX

probability /prɒbəbɪlɪti[1]/, **probabilities**. **1** The **probability** of something happening is the fact that it is very likely to happen. EG *The probability of accident was overwhelming... The probability is that they will find themselves heavily in debt.* N UNCOUNT+SUPP, OR N COUNT = likelihood ● **In all probability** means very probably. EG *They could, in all probability, perform any kind of calculation.* ● PHR: USED AS ADV SEN = doubtless

2 A **probability** is a mathematical measurement of how likely it is that something will happen, expressed as a fraction or percentage. EG *Each event has a particular probability of occurring... He was working out the relative probabilities of each plan* N COUNT/UNCOUNT ⇑ chance

succeeding... ...a long series of measurements and probability estimates.

probable /prɒbəbə°l/. 1 Something that is **probable** is likely to be true or correct, or likely to happen. EG *It seems very probable that they are descended from a single ancestor... This is the most probable interpretation of the situation... The Belgians face a probable general election this autumn.* ADJ QUALIT ↑ possible

2 You use **probable** to describe a role or function that a person, thing, place, etc is likely to have. EG *...Mrs Thatcher's probable successor... ...the probable venue for the 1992 Olympics.* ADJ QUALIT : ATTRIB ↑ possible

probably /prɒbəbli¹/. You use **probably** to say that you think that something is likely to be the case, although you do not actually know whether it is the case or not. EG *He probably kept your examination papers... Next year I shall probably be looking for a job... The owner is probably a salesman... You're probably right.* ADV SEN = doubtless

probation /prə⁶beɪʃə°n/ is 1 a period of time during which someone who has committed a crime is not sent to prison, but has to keep the law and be under the supervision of a probation officer. EG *He's out on probation... She had been put on probation after six months in prison.* N UNCOUNT ↑ suspension 2 a period of time during which your character and personality are being assessed and tested, for example to see if you are suitable for a particular type of work. EG *He was a mechanic who was on probation.* N UNCOUNT = trial

probationary /prə⁶beɪʃənə°ri¹/ is used to describe 1 someone who has finished their training in a particular job or profession, but who is still being assessed to see if they will be allowed to continue. EG *...the probationary teachers in our school.* ADJ CLASSIF : ATTRIB 2 the time during which someone is assessed at the beginning of their career before they are allowed to continue. EG *You can become a qualified teacher and then do a probationary year... ...a six-month probationary period.* ADJ CLASSIF : ATTRIB = trial

probationer /prə⁶beɪʃə°nə/, **probationers**. A **probationer** is 1 a nurse who is still being trained. N COUNT 2 someone who has committed a crime and who is on probation rather than in prison. N COUNT ↑ offender

probation officer, probation officers. A **probation officer** is an officer working for a magistrate court who supervises and guides offenders put on probation by the court. EG *Mr Hutchings is senior probation officer at a special centre in Camberwell.* N COUNT

probe /prəʊb/, **probes, probing, probed**. 1 If you **probe**, you ask questions or make enquiries in an indirect way, in order to discover things that other people do not want you to know. EG *I began to probe and try to find out why they had employed her... We were probing for information relevant to our needs... 'Isn't there track practice today?' she probed... She asked me one or two questions, probing the nature of my interest.* V, V+A, OR V+O/QUOTE = investigate ▸ used as a noun. EG *Morris evaded his sister's probe.* ▸ N COUNT ◇ **probing**. EG *My probing was turning out to be quite successful.* ◇ N UNCOUNT ↑ questioning

2 If you **probe** a situation or **probe** into it, you examine it thoroughly in order to search for new information about it, especially when people are trying to keep the information secret. EG *The company's tax situation was rigorously probed by revenue officials.* V+O, OR V+A (into) = look into

3 A **probe** into a situation is a public enquiry which exposes new facts, especially when these facts are shameful or embarrassing and people have been trying to keep them secret. EG *...an ongoing probe into suspected drug dealing in Florida... Do you remember the probe into the British security services?* N COUNT : USU SING = investigation

4 A **probe** is also 4.1 a long thin metal instrument that is used by doctors and dentists to examine very delicate parts of the body. EG *The brain surgeon asked the nurse to pass her a probe.* N COUNT 4.2 a long, thin part of the body of an animal or insect, which is used to search for tiny hidden pieces of food. EG *This beetle has a bony probe on its head.* N COUNT = feeler

5 If you **probe** someone or something, you poke them with a probe or something similar in order to examine them or to find something that is hidden. EG *The bird was probing the mound with its bill.* V+O, OR V+A (for) = prod, explore ▸ used as a noun. EG *'Let's try and do a probe,' said the dentist.* ▸ N COUNT

probity /prəʊbɪti¹/ is a high standard of correct moral behaviour; a formal word. N UNCOUNT ↑ morality

problem /prɒbləm/, **problems**. 1 A **problem** is 1.1 a situation or a state of affairs that causes difficulties for people, so that they try to think of a way to deal with it. EG *...how families can try to solve these problems... ...the social problems in modern society... I think we may have a problem here... She has a weight problem... The problem is that she can't cook.* N COUNT ↑ trouble 1.2 a puzzle that requires logical thought or mathematical procedures to solve it. Problems are often invented as a test of people's ability to think logically or to use mathematical skills. EG *...the development of problem-solving programs.* N COUNT

2 **Problem** children or **problem** families continually cause difficulties for themselves and for other people, often because they have been affected by unhappy experiences. ADJ CLASSIF : ATTRIB = difficult

3 **'No problem'** is an informal expression used in spoken English to tell someone that you can and will do something that they want you to do. CONVENTION = sure

problematic /prɒbləmætɪk/. Something that is **problematic** is full of problems and difficulties, and therefore complicated to think about. EG *...the problematic nature of government-industry relations.* ADJ QUALIT = tricky ≠ straightforward

problematical /prɒbləmætɪkə°l/ means the same as problematic. EG *The relationship between private business and government remains problematical.* ADJ QUALIT

proboscis /prəubɒsɪs/, **proboscises**; a formal or technical term. A **proboscis** is 1 a long flexible tube that some kinds of insects have as a mouth. EG *...a small moth with a specially curved proboscis that enables it to gather pollen.* N COUNT : USU SING 2 an elephant's trunk. N COUNT

procedural /prə⁶siːdʒərəl/ means involving a formal procedure; a fairly formal word. EG *...a procedural agreement for dealing with disputes... ...procedural obstacles.* ADJ CLASSIF

procedure /prə⁶siːdʒə/, **procedures**. A **procedure** is a way of doing something, especially one that is formally or conventionally accepted as being correct. EG *There was no constitutional procedure for replacing the Vice-President... ...the proper procedure to be followed in decision-making.* N COUNT/UNCOUNT = formula, practice

proceed, proceeds, proceeding, proceeded. The verb is pronounced /prə⁶siːd/; the plural noun in paragraph 7 is pronounced /prəʊsiːdz/. 1 If you **proceed** to do something, you go on to do it after you have finished doing something else. EG *With this ambiguous remark, she proceeded to hand over the key to my room... He proceeded to explain... Kurt proceeded to outline my duties.* V+to-INF

2 If someone **proceeds** with something or **proceeds**, they continue to follow a course of action that they have already started; a fairly formal use. EG *Consult your local borough surveyor and proceed from there... It is necessary to examine this claim before we proceed any further.* V : IF+PREP THEN USU with = carry on

3 If something such as an activity or process **proceeds**, it goes on and does not stop. EG *Preparations had proceeded night and day... The flow of ideas proceeds more easily.* V ↑ continue

4 If someone **proceeds** in a particular direction, they go in that direction; a formal use. EG *He proceeded downstairs... ...as we were proceeding along Chiswick High Street.* V : USU+A

5 If something such as a road or path **proceeds** in a particular direction, it leads in that direction; a formal use. EG *The North Walk proceeds through grass and trees to the children's playground.* V : USU+A

6 If something such as a sound or smell **is proceeding** from a particular place, it is coming out of it; a formal use. EG *There was a smell proceeding from his person.* V+A (from) = issue

7 The **proceeds** of some event or activity are the amount of money that has been obtained from it. EG *The proceeds will be given away to a deserving charity... The land was bought out of the proceeds of the 1851 Exhibition.* N PLURAL : the+N, IF+PREP THEN of = takings

8 See also **proceeding**.

proceed against. To **proceed against** a person or organization means to begin a legal action against that person or organization. PHRASAL VB : V+PREP, HAS PASS

proceeding /prə⁶siːdɪŋ/, **proceedings**. 1 **Proceedings** are 1.1 a series of events that happen in a particular place, especially in a planned or controlled way. EG *Millions of people watched the proceedings on television... He closed the proceedings in three short sentences... He directed proceedings from his suburban mansion... This would be the only* N COUNT : USU the+PL

time during the whole proceeding when the blood flow would be cut off. **1.2** a written record of the discussions and decisions at a meeting. EG *The proceedings were published in the newspapers.*
N PLURAL : USU the+N ⇑ minutes

2 Legal **proceedings** are a legal action taken against someone. EG *I shall institute proceedings against you for unfair dismissal... No extradition proceedings had taken place.*
N PLURAL

process /prəʊses/, **processes, processing, processed.** **1** A **process** is **1.1** a series of actions which are carried out in order to achieve a particular result. EG *It has been a long process getting this information... ...a slow and laborious process.* **1.2** a series of developments which happen naturally and which result in a biological or chemical change. EG *...personality changes that accompany the aging process... ...the digestive processes... ...the process of fertilization.* **1.3** a series of actions or thoughts by which you come to a decision or find an answer. EG *The best solution can only be found by a process of trial and error.* **1.4** any method of treating raw materials in a factory in order to manufacture a finished product. EG *...an effort to bring advanced technology and new processes into British industry.*
N COUNT : USU+SUPP; N COUNT : USU+SUPP; N COUNT+SUPP = means; N COUNT : USU+SUPP = technique

2 If someone or something **is in the process of** doing something, they have started to do it and are still doing it. EG *She is still in the painful process of growing up... The whole world is now in a process of Westernization.*
PHR : VB INFLECTS

3 If someone who is doing something does something else **in the process**, they do the second thing while doing the first thing. EG *I got him out all right, but overbalanced in the process and fell sprawling.*
PHR : USED AS AN A ⇑ simultaneously

4 To **process** raw materials means to make changes to them industrially in order to make products that can be used or sold. EG *The first industries to develop are usually those processing locally produced materials.* ◇ **processing.** EG *...the processing and storing of radioactive materials... Calcutta became the centre of the jute-processing industry.*
V+O ⇑ treat; ◇ N UNCOUNT ⇑ treating

5 To **process** natural food means to treat it chemically, for example by adding colouring and preservative, before it is sold to the public. EG *Vegetables and fruit nowadays are all further processed before consumers buy them.* ◇ **processed.** EG *...promoting the use of whole, organic foods, rather than processed foods... ...a packet of processed cheese.* ◇ **processing.** EG *...the food processing industry.*
V+O; ◇ ADJ CLASSIF; ◇ N UNCOUNT

6 To **process** something such as information means **6.1** to put it through a system in order to deal with it. EG *The DHSS reckons your application will take a few weeks to process... I was processed carefully through the security network before being allowed in.* **6.2** to run programs on it in a computer. EG *Eight or ten computers are processing data in the group.* ● See also **data processing, word processing.**
V+O ⇑ examine; V+O ⇑ arrange

procession /prəˢseʃəⁿn/, **processions.** A **procession** is a line of people who are walking together, or riding in coaches or cars, as part of a public ceremony to celebrate an important event. EG *The actual wedding procession starts at 10.05 a.m. from Buckingham Palace... They had organized a Christmas procession through the centre of town.*
N COUNT, OR *in*+N = parade

processional /prəˢseʃəⁿnəl, -ʃənəⁿl/ means used for or taking part in a ceremonial procession. EG *Thousands of people lined the processional route.*
ADJ CLASSIF : ATTRIB

proclaim /prəˢkleɪm/, **proclaims, proclaiming, proclaimed.** **1** To **proclaim** something, often something of national importance, means to make a public announcement about it. EG *The Government proclaimed a state of emergency... The Daily Express proclaimed, 'End of the Crisis'... ...when the American colonies proclaimed their independence in 1776.*
V+O/QUOTE/REPORT-CL = declare

2 If something **proclaims** that something is the case, it shows clearly that it is the case, usually by means of something that can be seen. EG *There was a feather on the rock, proclaiming that a bird had been there.*
V+O/REPORT-CL = indicate

proclamation /prɒkləmeɪʃəⁿn/, **proclamations.** A **proclamation** is a public announcement about something, often something of national importance. EG *She was born only a few years after the Emancipation Proclamation of 1862, and her parents had been slaves... ...proclamations of independence.*
N COUNT, OR *by*+N = declaration

proclivity /prəˢklɪvɪti¹/, **proclivities.** A **proclivity** is a tendency to behave in a particular way or to like a particular thing, often a bad way or thing; a formal word. EG *I know they don't approve of my sexual proclivities... ...a proclivity for violence and authoritarianism.*
N COUNT+SUPP

procrastinate /prəˢkræstɪneɪt/, **procrastinates, procrastinating, procrastinated.** If you **procrastinate**, you are very slow to do something, because you keep leaving it until later; a formal word. EG *...if you can honestly admit that you are procrastinating about doing something unpleasant.* ◇ **procrastination** /prəˢkræstɪneɪʃəⁿn/. EG *There was now little cause for procrastination.*
V ⇑ delay = stall; ◇ N UNCOUNT = delay

procreate /prəʊkrieɪt/, **procreates, procreating, procreated.** When animals or people **procreate**, they produce offspring; a formal word, often used showing disapproval when used of people. EG *They are concerned only with eating, sleeping, and procreating.* ◇ **procreation** /prəʊkrieɪʃəⁿn/. EG *...the idea that sex is for procreation only.*
V OR V+O = breed, reproduce; ◇ N UNCOUNT = reproduction

procurator /prɒkjəˢreɪtə/, **procurators.** A **procurator** is an administrative official with legal powers, especially in the Soviet Union, the Roman Catholic Church, or the ancient Roman Empire.
N COUNT

procurator fiscal, procurators fiscals. The **procurator fiscal** is a legal officer in Scotland who performs the functions of a public prosecutor.
N COUNT

procure /prəkjʊə/, **procures, procuring, procured**; a formal word. **1** If you **procure** something, especially something that is difficult to obtain, you obtain it. EG *There is no hope of procuring military supplies in any quantity... He had meant to go out and procure a bottle of wine.*
V+O : IF+PREP THEN *for*, OR V+O+O ⇑ get

2 Someone who **procures** introduces prostitutes to clients.
V

procurement /prəkjʊəməˀnt/ is the act of obtaining something such as supplies for an army or other organization; a formal word.
N UNCOUNT = acquisition

procurer /prəkjʊərə/, **procurers**; a formal word. A **procurer** is **1** someone who obtains goods or supplies for an organization. **2** a man who introduces prostitutes to clients.
N COUNT; N COUNT

procuress /prɒkjəˢreˈs/, **procuresses**; a formal word. A **procuress** is a woman who introduces prostitutes to clients.
N COUNT

prod /prɒd/, **prods, prodding, prodded.** **1** If you **prod** something or someone, you poke them or push them with a short, quick movement of your finger or something such as a stick. EG *The young man prodded his donkey with special urgency... She prodded a bean with her fork... He prodded Kunta roughly towards the raised platform.*
V+O : USU+A ⇑ propel

2 If you **prod** someone to do something that needs to be done, you remind them to do it, often because you think that they are being slow or unwilling to do it. EG *...armaments companies who prod the defence ministry into action every now and again... You may have to prod him from time to time and generally keep him up to the mark.* ◇ **prodding.** EG *This was on their own initiative, without the least prodding from me.*
V+O+*to*-INF, OR V+O+A ⇑ urge = spur; ◇ N UNCOUNT = prompting

3 A **prod** is **3.1** an act of poking something or someone with your finger or with a stick. EG *Mrs Travers gave her a prod.* **3.2** an act of reminding someone to do something. EG *The Home Office took their time replying, despite numerous prods from Mr Harper.* **3.3** an object like a stick, which you push against an animal's body in order to make it move in a particular direction. EG *...electric cattle prods.*
N COUNT ⇑ push; N COUNT = reminder; N COUNT = goad

prod at. If you **prod at** something, you poke it several times or make poking movements towards it. EG *She prodded at the contents of the pan.*
PHRASAL VB : V+PREP = poke at

prodigal /prɒdɪgəⁿl/, **prodigals**; a literary word. Someone who behaves in a **prodigal** way spends a lot of money carelessly, without thinking about what they will do when they have no money left. EG *...this prodigal generosity... ...prodigal expenses on clothes... ...the parables of the lost sheep and the prodigal son.* ▸ used as a noun. EG *Alice had dreamed sentimentally that the prodigal would return.*
ADJ CLASSIF = extravagant, profligate; ▸ N COUNT

prodigious /prədɪdʒəs/. Something that is **prodigious** is so large in size or in amount that it causes amazement; a fairly literary word. EG *The cost has been prodigious... He has a prodigious capacity for beer.* ◇ **prodigiously.** EG *He ate prodigiously.*
ADJ QUALIT = colossal; ◇ ADV

prodigy /prɒdɪdʒi¹/, **prodigies.** A **prodigy** is **1** a person with an unusually great natural ability for
N COUNT : USU MOD+N

something such as music or mathematics, which shows itself at an early age. EG *He was a mathematical prodigy... Leibniz was another child prodigy.* 2 something amazing and wonderful. EG *His vacation was a reward for the prodigies he had already achieved.* N COUNT = marvel

produce, produces, producing, produced. The word **produce** is pronounced /prədju:s/ when it is a verb, and /prɒdju:s/ when it is a noun. 1 To **produce** something means to cause it to happen. EG *All our efforts have not produced an agreement... This drug has produced terrible effects on children... His comments produced an angry response.* V+O = bring about

2 To **produce** things such as foodstuffs or manufactured goods means to create them, usually in large quantities by an industrial or other process. EG *It produces a third of the nation's oil... Farmers must produce a good deal more than they themselves need... ...factories producing domestic electrical goods.* V+O

3 When animals, plants, or people **produce** things such as offspring, leaves and flowers, or natural substances such as sweat, these things form as the result of a biological process. EG *Flowers produce pollen or nectar throughout the day... Parents are responsible for the offspring they produce... Amphibians have glands in their skin which produce a slime that helps to keep it moist.* V+O ⇑ create

4 When a thing or process **produces** heat, sound, a gas, etc, heat, sound, a gas, etc comes from it or is created as a result of it. EG *The sun produces light and heat... Burning oil produces carbon dioxide... His band produce a beautifully deep and soothing backing sound.* V+O

5 If you **produce** a new idea or a work of art, you design it and make it. EG *Inventors and famous scientists usually produce a string of new ideas, not just one... These artists produce works of great beauty.* V+O

6 If you **produce** evidence or an argument for or against a particular point of view, you show it or explain it to people in order to get them to understand it or agree with you. EG *He produces no evidence for his belief... They had produced all kinds of arguments against her.* V+O: IF+PREP THEN *for/against* = present, advance

7 If you **produce** an object from somewhere such as your pocket or handbag, you bring it out into the open so that it can be seen. EG *He produced his passport... Poirot produced the letter from his pocket.* V+O: USU+A ⇑ show

8 If you **produce** something such as a meal, you prepare it and provide it for someone, often in a surprisingly short period of time. EG *I am always ready to produce a meal in emergencies.* V+O = supply

9 Someone who **produces** a play, film, television programme, or record organizes its preparation and gets it ready to present to the public. EG *The film was directed, written and produced by Mel Brookes... The girls and boys write and produce their own plays.* V OR V+O ⇑ manage

10 **Produce** is food or other agricultural material that is grown in large quantities to be sold. EG *Sugar became the chief produce of the Caribbean... British produce came under pressure from foreign competition.* N UNCOUNT ⇑ goods

producer /prədju:sə/, **producers.** A **producer** is 1 a person whose job is to organize the preparation of a play, film, television programme, or record. The producer of a film controls the money that is spent on it. EG *He is the producer of several TV shows.* 2 a company, country, or person that provides a large supply of something, especially something that is manufactured or grown to be sold to the public. EG *The Soviet Union is the world's leading crude oil producer... ...the mass producers of consumer goods.* N COUNT ⇑ organizer; N COUNT: USU+SUPP ⇑ provider

product /prɒdʌkt/, **products.** 1 A **product** is 1.1 something that is produced and sold in large quantities, often as the result of an industrial process. EG *...packaged foods and other consumer products... There are masses of car-cleaning products available... Manufacturers spend huge sums of money on advertising their products.* 1.2 something that is the result of a creative, scientific, or other process. EG *I stood back and admired the finished product.* N COUNT: USU PL ⇑ goods; N COUNT ⇑ creation

2 Someone who is a **product** of a particular type of society, education, or range of experiences has particular characteristics as a result of living in it or experiencing it. EG *She is a product of the 1970s... The elites who took over power were products of the colonial education system.* N COUNT+*of*

3 A situation that is a **product** of someone's efforts or a particular set of circumstances is the result of it. EG *The uniformity of the dancers was the product of hours of training... His reaction to events was the product of prejudice and fear.* N COUNT+*of*

4 The **product** of two numbers is the number that you get when you multiply them together; a technical term in mathematics. EG *The product of 4 and 3 is 12.* N COUNT: IF+PREP THEN *of*

production /prədʌkʃᵊn/, **productions.** 1 **Production** is 1.1 the process of manufacturing or growing something in large quantities in order to provide a supply to be sold to the public. EG *...more efficient methods of production... You need an efficient production manager... Plutonium is usable for the production of nuclear weapons.* 1.2 the amount of goods manufactured or grown by a company or country. EG *The firm exports 90% of its production... Industrial production has fallen by 20% over two years.* 1.3 the creation of something as a result of a process or activity, for example a natural or scientific process. EG *The mammalian sexual cycle involves the regular production of a new egg... Because of the slowing down of white blood cell production, infection sets in... ...the production of electricity.* 1.4 the act of showing something to someone, for example a card or ticket which will allow you to do something. EG *OAPs are issued with cheap tickets on production of a pension book... The production of fresh information changed people's views.* 1.5 the organization and preparation of plays, films, television programmes, or records, in order to present them to the public. EG *He was writing plays for production at the Blackfriars Theatre... I am hoping to go into television production.* N UNCOUNT; N UNCOUNT = output; N UNCOUNT+SUPP ⇑ formation; N UNCOUNT: USU+*of* = presentation; N UNCOUNT: USU+SUPP

2 A **production** is a play, opera, ballet, etc that has been prepared for presentation and is being performed at a theatre. EG *...Peter Hall's production of The Tempest at the Old Vic... What did the New York critics have to say about the production?* N COUNT ⇑ show

3 If you **make a production out of** something, you make a fuss about it and make it seem more important than it really is; an informal expression. EG *We can't afford to make a big production out of it.* PHR: VB INFLECTS

production line, production lines. A **production line** is an arrangement of machines in a factory in which each machine makes only one part of a product. The product passes from machine to machine until it is finished. EG *...cars coming off the production line at British Leyland.* N COUNT = assembly line

productive /prədʌktɪv/. 1 Something or someone that is **productive** manufactures or grows a large and profitable supply of goods. EG *Agriculture and industry both grew more productive... ...productive enterprises... ...productive workers.* ◊ **productively.** EG *...unless the land is used more productively.* ADJ QUALIT ⇑ efficient; ◊ ADV WITH VB

2 If something such as a meeting or experience is **productive**, good or useful things happen as a result of it. EG *The 1950s proved a productive decade for them... Something made that first meeting of two strangers into a productive friendship.* ◊ **productively.** EG *I had spent my afternoon productively.* ADJ QUALIT = fruitful, rewarding; ◊ ADV WITH VB

3 Something that is **productive** of a particular situation or feeling creates it; a fairly formal use. EG *Fights between the parents are confusing to the child and productive of anxiety.* ADJ CLASSIF: PRED+*of*

productivity /prɒdəktɪvɪti¹/ is a measure of the efficiency of a company or country, which is calculated by comparing the amount or value of goods produced with the time and money spent on producing them and the number of workers who produce them. EG *There have been enormous increases in agricultural productivity.* N UNCOUNT ⇑ efficiency

prof /prɒf/, **profs.** People sometimes refer to a professor as a **prof**; an informal, rather humorous word. N COUNT/VOC

Prof., Profs. Prof. is an abbreviation that is used in front of a person's name to indicate that he or she is a professor. EG *...Prof. Douglas Brewer.* N IN TITLES

profane /prəfeɪn/, **profanes, profaning, profaned**; a formal word. 1 Something that is **profane** 1.1 shows disrespect for a religion or religious things, so that it is considered sinful. EG *...profane utterances* ADJ CLASSIF ⇑ disrespectful

against the Church. ◇ **profanity** /prəfænɪti/. EG ...*shocking acts of profanity.* **1.2** is concerned with everyday life rather than religion and spiritual things. EG *Children are being brought up in an entirely profane environment.*
◇ N UNCOUNT
ADJ CLASSIF: ATTRIB ≠ spiritual

2 If someone **profanes** something holy or religious, they treat it with disrespect. EG *They have profaned the long upheld traditions of the Church.*
V+O = desecrate

profess /prəfes/, **professes, professing, professed**; a formal word. **1** If you **profess** to do or have something, you claim that you do or have it, sometimes when this is not the truth. EG *Nell didn't like her, or professed not to... His real interest was sports cars, about which he professed extensive knowledge.*
V+*to*-INF, OR V+O = allege

2 If you **profess** a particular feeling or opinion about something, you openly express that feeling or opinion. EG *Many have professed disgust at the use of weapons... She professed great relief at getting some rest.*
V+O = declare

3 If you **profess** a particular religion, you have that religion. EG *He saw no reason why slaves professing Christianity should be freed.*
V+O

professed /prəfest/ is used to indicate that someone claims to have the status, purpose, feeling, etc which is mentioned; a formal word. EG ...*the assassination of McKinley by a professed anarchist... ...a professed love of everything about that country.*
ADJ CLASSIF: ATTRIB ⇑ declared

profession /prəfeʃən/, **professions**. **1** A **profession** is **1.1** a type of job that requires special training and that brings a fairly high status, for example work connected with medicine, law, or education. EG *She decided on law or journalism as her ultimate profession... I am by profession a teacher.* **1.2** the group of people who have the same profession. EG *The medical profession are doing a very difficult job.*
N COUNT, OR *by*+N = career
N COUNT: IF SING, VB CAN BE SING OR PL

2 A **profession** of a particular belief or feeling is something that you say which expresses that belief or feeling. EG *There is something ludicrous in his professions of concern about the problem.*
N COUNT: USU+*of* = assertion

professional /prəfeʃənəl, -ʃənəl/, **professionals**. **1 Professional** means **1.1** relating to the work that a person does for an occupation, especially work that requires special training. EG *He started his professional life as a comedian... I have sought professional advice.* ◇ **professionally**. EG *They are professionally qualified.* **1.2** having a job that requires special training and that brings a fairly high status. EG *The flat is ideal for the professional single person.* **1.3** having a job in which you receive money for doing something that many people do as a hobby or do for themselves, for example sport, music, or cooking. EG *She left the shop in which she had been working and became a professional actress... ...professional cooks.* ◇ **professionally**. EG *He played the oboe professionally.*
ADJ CLASSIF: USU ATTRIB
◇ ADV WITH VB
ADJ CLASSIF: ATTRIB ⇑ working
ADJ CLASSIF: USU ATTRIB ≠ amateur
◇ ADV WITH VB

2 If something that someone does or produces is **professional**, it is very skilful and of a very high standard. EG *It is a very assured, professional performance... He had typed the whole scheme out in a very professional manner.* ▸ used of people. EG *They are very professional and competent.*
ADJ QUALIT = expert ≠ amateurish

3 If you say that someone is a **professional** busybody, a **professional** trouble-maker, etc, you mean that they often behave in the annoying or unpleasant way indicated.
ADJ CLASSIF: ATTRIB = full time

4 A **professional** is **4.1** a person who has a job that requires special training and brings a fairly high status. EG ...*nurses, doctors, social workers, and other professionals.* **4.2** a person with a job in which they receive money for doing something that many people do as a hobby or do for themselves. EG *He has 17 major championship victories as a professional plus two amateur titles.* **4.3** a person who shows great skill and high standards in the job or activity that they do; used showing approval. EG *We are all professionals at our jobs.*
N COUNT ⇑ worker
N COUNT = pro ≠ amateur
N COUNT: IF SING, *a*+N = expert

professionalism /prəfeʃənəlɪzəm/. If you show **professionalism** in what you do, **1** you show great skill and high standards. EG *The campus paper was produced with incredible speed and professionalism by the students.* **2** you show qualities that are typical or expected of a person in your profession. EG *He has learned to trust her professionalism more.*
N UNCOUNT = polish
N UNCOUNT

professor /prəfesə/, **professors**. **1** A **professor** in a British university has the highest rank of the teachers in a department. ▸ used as a title. EG ...*Professor Cole... He was Professor of English at Strathclyde University.*
N COUNT ⇑ academic
▸ N IN TITLES

2 A **professor** in an American or Canadian university or college is a teacher there. ▸ used as a title. EG ...*Professor Read of McGill University.*
N COUNT
▸ N IN TITLES

professorial /prɒfɪsɔːrɪəl/; a formal word. **Professorial** means **1** looking or behaving like a person who has great authority. EG ...*Murray McPherson, a professorial figure.* **2** relating to the work of a professor. EG *She will be there in her professorial capacity.*
ADJ QUALIT = imposing
ADJ CLASSIF

professorship /prəfesəʃɪp/, **professorships**. A **professorship** is the post of professor in a university.
N COUNT = chair

proffer /prɒfə/, **proffers, proffering, proffered**; a formal word. **1** If you **proffer** something to someone, you hold it towards them so that they can take it or touch it. EG *He helped himself from the sauce boat proffered to him... The Doctor shook the proffered hand.*
V+O: IF+PREP THEN *to*, OR V+O+O ⇑ offer

2 If you **proffer** something such as advice, friendship, or help to someone, you offer it to them so that they can accept it or make use of it. EG ...*her proffered opinions... She had already proffered her resignation.*
V+O, V+O+O, OR V+O+A *(to)* = volunteer

proficiency /prəfɪʃənsi/. If you show **proficiency** in something, you show ability or skill at it. EG *You need some proficiency in book-keeping for this job.*
N UNCOUNT: IF+PREP THEN *in*

proficient /prəfɪʃənt/. If you are **proficient** in something, you show ability or skill at it. EG *She is proficient in English... Do you think that calculators stop children becoming proficient at arithmetic?... ...a proficient swimmer.*
ADJ QUALIT: IF+PREP THEN *in/at* ⇑ skilled = competent

profile /prəʊfaɪl/, **profiles**. **1** Your **profile** is the outline of your face as it is seen when someone is looking at you from the side. EG *I had a glimpse of her calm pale profile... He had a beautiful profile.*
N COUNT

2 A **profile** of someone is a short description of them, their life, and their character in a newspaper or magazine or on television or radio. EG *She wanted to write profiles of the founders of the Party... ...a television profile of Clint Eastwood.*
N COUNT: IF+PREP THEN *of* ⇑ biography

3 If someone or something is seen **in profile**, they are seen from the side. EG *He turned his head to see himself in profile.*
PHR: USED AS AN A

4 If you **keep a low profile**, you avoid doing things that make people notice you. EG *Keep a low profile until you have had time to settle in.*
PHR: VB INFLECTS = lie low

profit /prɒfɪt/, **profits, profiting, profited**. **1** A **profit** is an amount of money that is gained in business or trade, for example when the cost of making something is less than the amount that it is sold for. EG *The company made a profit of 113 per cent... The biggest profits should come from computer chips... ...the pursuit of profit.*
N COUNT/UNCOUNT ⇑ gain = revenue

2 Profit is the advantage or benefit that you gain from a course of action; a formal use. EG *The company exploits natural resources to its own profit.*
N UNCOUNT = good

3 If you **profit** from or by something, you gain an advantage or benefit from it; a formal use. EG *I was grateful to him, and profited from his advice... They had profited by their experience with me.*
V+A *(from/by)*

profitable /prɒfɪtəbəl/. Something that is **profitable 1** makes a profit or is likely to result in a profit. EG *The farm is a highly profitable business... It was more profitable to export the crops.* ◇ **profitability** /prɒfɪtəbɪlɪti/. EG ...*a decline in the profitability of public transport.* ◇ **profitably**. EG *Can the motor vehicle industry operate profitably?* **2** is useful and results in some advantage or benefit for you. EG *He certainly made profitable use of the lessons he had learnt.* ◇ **profitably**. EG *There was little I could profitably do sitting at my desk.*
ADJ QUALIT ⇑ successful
◇ N UNCOUNT
◇ ADV WITH VB
ADJ QUALIT = valuable
◇ ADV WITH VB = usefully

profiteer /prɒfɪtɪə/, **profiteers**. A **profiteer** is a person who makes large profits by charging high prices for goods that are hard to get; used showing disapproval.
N COUNT

profiteering /prɒfɪtɪərɪŋ/ is the activity of making large profits by charging high prices for goods that are hard to get; used showing disapproval.
N UNCOUNT ⇑ exploitation

profit-making is the activity or fact of making a profit. EG *Businesses were scientific about profit-making.* ▸ used as an adjective. EG ...*a profit-making industry.*
N UNCOUNT
▸ ADJ CLASSIF = profitable

profit-sharing is a system by which all the people who work in a company have a share in its profits. EG ...*profit-sharing schemes.*
N UNCOUNT

profligacy /prɒflɪgəsi1/ is extravagance and being wasteful; a formal word. EG *...a profound dislike of waste, of profligacy and of misuse.* N UNCOUNT = squandering

profligate /prɒflɪgɪ1t/ means extravagant and wasteful; a formal word. EG *...our profligate use of resources.* ADJ QUALIT = reckless

profound /prə6faʊnd/; a fairly formal word. **1** A **profound** feeling or experience affects you very deeply and strongly. EG *...blissful love and profound hatred... He was in a state of profound shock.* ADJ QUALIT = extreme, great
◊ **profoundly**. EG *His mother profoundly disliked dogs... I am profoundly grateful for this opportunity to meet you.* ◊ ADV = intensely
2 A **profound** effect or change is one that affects or changes something very greatly. EG *The development was to have a profound effect on all our lives.* ADJ QUALIT = marked, great
◊ **profoundly**. EG *...a profoundly changing Britain.* ◊ ADV
3 **Profound** is also used to emphasize the seriousness or depth of something. EG *...profound differences... Her ignorance of foreign policy was profound.* ADJ QUALIT ⇑ deep
◊ **profoundly**. EG *It is profoundly undemocratic.* ◊ ADV
4 A **profound** person, idea, work, or way of thinking shows great intellectual depth and understanding. EG *It's a profound book... ...thinking in a profound and imaginative way.* ADJ QUALIT ⇑ thoughtful

profundity /prə6fʌndɪti1/, **profundities**; a formal word. **1** **Profundity** is great intellectual depth and understanding. EG *...their profundity in arguing socialist theory.* N UNCOUNT = erudition
2 If you refer to the **profundity** of a feeling, experience, change, etc, you mean that it is deep, powerful, or serious. EG *...the speed and profundity of the changes around us.* N UNCOUNT = greatness
3 A **profundity** is a remark that shows great intellectual depth and understanding; often used ironically. EG *...exchanging such profundities as 'Looks like rain today'.* N COUNT : USU PL ≠ banality

profuse /prə6fju:s/ is used to indicate that a quantity of something is very large. EG *There were profuse apologies for its absence... It brought him out into a profuse sweat.* ◊ **profusely**. EG *He was dragged off to the police station bleeding profusely... They thanked her profusely.* ADJ QUALIT; ◊ ADV WITH VB

profusion /prə6fju:zə0n/. If there is a **profusion** of something or if it occurs in **profusion**, there is a very large quantity of it. EG *...a profusion of new words... Everything was there in such profusion that we did not know what to take.* N UNCOUNT, OR N PART : SING+N IN PLURAL = abundance

progenitor /prəʊdʒɛnɪtə/, **progenitors**; a formal word. **1** A **progenitor** of someone is a direct ancestor of theirs. N COUNT = forefather
2 The **progenitor** of an idea which has developed is the person who first thought of it. N COUNT ⇑ originator

progeny /prɒdʒɪni1/; a formal word. **1** Your **progeny** are your children. N PLURAL
2 The **progeny** of a particular thing are the things that develop from it. EG *...these computers and their even faster, even smaller progeny.* N PLURAL = offspring

prognosis /prɒgnəʊsi:s/, **prognoses** /prɒgnəʊsɛs/; a formal word. A **prognosis** is **1** a prediction of how something that has already begun will develop or end. EG *The prognosis on unemployment in western Europe is poor.* N COUNT+SUPP : USU SING = forecast **2** a prediction by a doctor of how a particular illness will develop and how likely it is that the patient will be cured. N COUNT : USU SING

prognostication /prɒgnɒstɪkeɪʃə0n/, **prognostications**. A **prognostication** is a prediction about something; a formal word. EG *They took this prognostication seriously.* N COUNT/UNCOUNT = prognosis

program /prəʊgræm/, **programs, programming, programmed**. **1** A **program** is a set of instructions that a computer uses in order to perform a particular operation. EG *...computer programs... I decided to write a program for a microprocessor.* N COUNT
2 When you **program** a computer or when you **program**, you write a set of instructions that a computer can use in order to perform a particular operation. EG *Can computers be programmed to hold intelligent conversations?* ◊ **programming**. EG *...computer programming.* V OR V+O; ◊ N UNCOUNT
3 See also **programme**.

programme /prəʊgræm/, **programmes, programming, programmed**; also spelled **program** in American English. **1** A **programme** is **1.1** a detailed, large-scale plan which has been developed for a particular purpose, for example to provide a particular service or to deal with a particular problem. EG *...the development of a nuclear power programme... ...major programmes of research and development.* N COUNT : USU+SUPP = scheme **1.2** a plan of events, jobs, or activities that are to take place, including the times at which each thing should happen or be done. EG *...their programme of meetings, talks and exhibitions.* N COUNT : USU+SUPP = schedule **1.3** a play, show, talk, etc that you watch on television or listen to on the radio. EG *What is your favourite television programme?... ...the last programme in our series on education.* N COUNT ⇑ broadcast **1.4** a booklet or sheet of paper that you can buy when you go to a play, concert, or other event and that contains information about it. EG *...a theatre programme.* N COUNT **1.5** the series of pieces of music, acts, etc that are to be performed in a concert or a show. EG *The second work in the programme is the Piano Concerto.* N COUNT
2 If someone **is programmed** to behave in a particular way, they are likely to behave in that way, without thinking about it, because of the strong effect that their society or situation has on them. EG *The mother is programmed by Nature to risk her life for her young... They have been conditioned and programmed by their societies.* V+O : USU PASS, USU+*to*-INF
3 When you **programme** a machine or system, you set its controls so that it will work in a particular way or at particular times. EG *The radiators are programmed to come on at six every morning.* V+O : USU+*to*-INF

programmer /prəʊgræmə/, **programmers**. A **programmer** is a person whose job is to write programs for computers. EG *...a computer programmer.* N COUNT

progress, progresses, progressing, progressed. The word **progress** is pronounced /prəʊgres/ when it is a noun, and /prə6grɛs/ when it is a verb. **1** **Progress** is **1.1** the process of gradually getting nearer to achieving something or completing something. EG *She is making good progress with her German... They came in from time to time to check on my progress.* N UNCOUNT = headway **1.2** new developments and changes that are made in society in order to improve conditions or to create a more sophisticated way of life. EG *...technological progress.* N UNCOUNT ⇑ advancement
2 The **progress** of something such as a situation or action is the way in which it develops and changes over a period of time. EG *We discussed the progress of the jail suit... He followed the progress of hostilities with impatience.* N SING : *the*+N+*of* ⇑ development ● If something is **in progress** at a particular time, it is happening at that time. EG *There was a game in progress... A lot of work is in progress at the moment to try and improve the situation.* ● PHR : USED AS AN A = under way
3 The **progress** of a person, vehicle, etc is his, her, or its movement while travelling in a particular direction. EG *The two of them continued their progress down the road... He followed its progress as it gradually disappeared from view.* N UNCOUNT : WITH POSS
4 To **progress** means **4.1** to develop over a period of time to a stronger, more mature, or more desirable state. EG *You're not progressing quickly enough... Technology did not progress any further... She managed to progress to a senior position.* V : USU+A = advance **4.2** to happen gradually over a period of time. EG *My impressions changed radically as the trip progressed.* V **4.3** to move forwards from one place to another. EG *The storm progressed across country.* V+A = travel
5 If you **progress** to something new, you start doing something which follows on from what you were doing before, for example you change to a new topic of conversation. EG *From there we progressed to a discussion on politics.* V+A *(to)* = move on

progression /prə6grɛʃə0n/, **progressions**; a fairly formal word. **1** A **progression** is a gradual development from one state or situation to another over a period of time. EG *The progression from one extreme to the other is gradual.* N COUNT+SUPP ⇑ change
2 A **progression** of things is a number of things which come one after the other. EG *I leaned out and looked at the endless progression of lakes.* N COUNT+*of* = string
3 **Progression** is movement forwards from one place to another. EG *Progression is at a snail's pace.* N UNCOUNT = progress

progressive /prə6grɛsɪv/, **progressives**. **1** Someone who is **progressive** or has **progressive** ideas has modern opinions and ideas and is eager to change the existing way of doing things. EG *Some young parents are eager to be progressive... ...a progressive school... ...a more progressive policy.* ADJ QUALIT = enlightened, radical

2 A **progressive** is a progressive person. EG *She had a world-wide reputation as a progressive.* N COUNT = radical

3 A **progressive** change happens gradually over a period of time. EG *...the progressive industrialization of our society.* ◊ **progressively**. EG *It became progressively easier to see.* ADJ CLASSIF = gradual ◊ ADV = increasingly

prohibit /prə⁶hɪbɪt/, **prohibits, prohibiting, prohibited**. **1** If someone **prohibits** something, they forbid it by means of a law, rule, or official agreement. EG *She believes that nuclear weapons should be totally prohibited... The country has a law prohibiting employees from striking.* V+O : IF+PREP THEN *from* ≠ permit

2 If one thing **prohibits** another another thing from happening, it makes it impossible for that thing to happen. EG *The main problem prohibiting widespread use is the cost of these machines.* V+O = prevent ≠ permit

prohibition /prəuɪbɪʃə⁰n/, **prohibitions**. A **prohibition** is a law or rule which states that a particular thing is not allowed. EG *They are demanding the imposition of a prohibition on rent increases... ...the prohibition of strikes... I had broken the stern prohibitions of Uncle Nick.* N COUNT/ UNCOUNT ⇑ restriction

prohibitionist /prəuɪbɪʃənɪst/, **prohibitionists**. A **prohibitionist** is a person who believes that it should be illegal to sell or drink alcoholic drinks. N COUNT

prohibitive /prə⁶hɪbɪtɪv/. If the cost of something is **prohibitive**, it is so high that you cannot afford it. EG *The cost of making them by hand is prohibitive.* ◊ **prohibitively**. EG *The transport of heavy goods over long distances will soon become prohibitively expensive.* ADJ QUALIT ◊ ADV+ADJ/ ADV ⇑ extremely

project, projects, projecting, projected. The word **project** is pronounced /prɒdʒɛkt/ when it is a noun, and /prədʒɛkt/ when it is a verb. **1** A **project** is **1.1** an idea or plan that you intend to carry out in the future or that is being carried out at present. EG *We must have a good sensible discussion about our theatre project... We talked about very large scale projects for putting satellites into space.* N COUNT **1.2** a detailed study of a particular subject. EG *He's doing a project on Scottish oil.* N COUNT

2 If something **is projected**, it is planned to happen in the future. EG *There were demonstrations against the projected visit by the Foreign Minister... The buildings were standing in the path of a projected motorway and would have to be pulled down.* V+O : USU PASS ⇑ intend

3 If a future amount or statistic **is projected**, it is estimated. EG *The population of Britain is projected to rise slowly over the next ten years... They can expect to be consulted on the projected rate of economic growth.* V+O : USU PASS

4 To **project** something through the air means to cause it to move through the air with a lot of force; a fairly formal use. EG *Pieces of masonry and any loose objects were projected through the air by the explosion.* V+O+A ⇑ throw = hurl

5 To **project** a light, a film, or a picture onto a wall or screen means to make it appear there. EG *They were delighted to see their holiday slides projected on a screen.* V+O ⇑ show

6 If something **projects**, it sticks out above or beyond a surface or edge; a fairly formal use. EG *At the base of the cliffs, projecting from the seas, are sharp needles of rock... ...a projecting black lintel.* V : USU+A = protrude

7 If you **project** your voice, you speak loudly and clearly so that your voice can be heard at a distance. EG *You must learn to project your voice more.* V+O

8 If you **project** someone or something as a particular thing, you try to make people believe that they are that thing. EG *His electoral strategy was to project Labour as the party of progress... He had projected himself as a reformer.* V+O (NG/REFL) : USU+*as*

9 If you **project** your feelings upon other people, you imagine that other people have the same feelings as you. EG *She easily projects her own anxieties and insecurity upon other people.* V+O+A *(on/ upon)* = transfer

10 If you **project** yourself into a different time, place, or situation, you imagine that you are there. V+O (REFL)

projectile /prədʒɛktaɪl/, **projectiles**. A **projectile** is an object that is fired from a gun or other weapon; a formal word. N COUNT

projection /prədʒɛkʃə⁰n/, **projections**. **1** A **projection** is **1.1** a part of something that sticks out above or beyond a surface or edge; a fairly formal use. EG *...an odd-shaped structure with three leg-like projections on the bottom.* N COUNT **1.2** an estimation of the size of a future amount. EG *The company had made projections of sales of 3000 aircraft.* N COUNT ⇑ estimate **1.3** a representation on a flat surface of a three dimensional object or curved line; a technical term. N COUNT

2 Projection is the act of projecting a light or a film onto a wall or screen, usually using a projector. EG *...a projection room.* N UNCOUNT

projectionist /prədʒɛkʃənɪst/, **projectionists**. A **projectionist** is someone whose job is to work a projector, for example at a cinema. EG *...movie projectionists.* N COUNT ⇑ operator

projector /prədʒɛktə/, **projectors**. A **projector** is a machine that projects films or slides onto a screen or wall. EG *...a slide projector.* N COUNT

proletarian /prəulɪtɛərɪən/, **proletarians**; a rather old-fashioned word. **1 Proletarian** means relating to or involving the proletariat. EG *...the cause of establishing a new proletarian party.* ADJ CLASSIF : ATTRIB = working class

2 A **proletarian** is a member of the proletariat. N COUNT

proletariat /prəulɪtɛərɪət/. The **proletariat** is the class of people in a country who are paid wages for work that they do with their hands, especially in industry, and who do not own much of the country's property; a rather old-fashioned word. EG *He is not one of the proletariat... He identified himself with the proletariat and their struggles.* N SING WITH DET : VB CAN BE SING OR PL = working class

proliferate /prə⁶lɪfəreɪt/, **proliferates, proliferating, proliferated**. If things **proliferate**, they increase in number very quickly; a fairly formal word. EG *Other groups are now proliferating... Tropical vegetation proliferates.* ◊ **proliferating**. EG *...all these proliferating hotels.* V = spread ◊ ADJ CLASSIF : ATTRIB

proliferation /prə⁶lɪfəreɪʃə⁰n/; a fairly formal word. **1** The **proliferation** of something is its rapid increase in number. EG *We can prevent the proliferation of nuclear weaponry.* N UNCOUNT : IF+ PREP THEN *of*

2 If there is a **proliferation** of a particular kind of thing, that thing exists in very large numbers. EG *They were puzzled by the proliferation of pubs they found.* N PART = abundance ≠ paucity

prolific /prə⁵lɪfɪk/. **1** A writer, artist, or composer who is **prolific** produces a large number of novels, paintings, etc. EG *...a prolific novelist... Picasso had remained prolific.* ADJ QUALIT = productive

2 An animal or person that is **prolific** produces a large number of offspring or children. ADJ QUALIT

3 Something that is **prolific** exists or is being produced in large numbers. ADJ QUALIT = numerous

prolix /prəulɪks, prəulɪks/. A piece of writing that is **prolix** uses more words than is necessary; a formal word used showing disapproval. ADJ QUALIT = long-winded, verbose

prologue /prəulɒg/, **prologues**. **1** A **prologue** is a piece of text that is spoken or written at the beginning of a play or book in order to introduce it. EG *Noel Coward wrote a prologue to the play.* N COUNT : IF+ PREP THEN *to* ⇑ introduction = preface ≠ epilogue

2 If one event is a **prologue** to another one, it leads to it; a formal use. EG *The death of the President could only be the prologue to civil war.* N SING WITH DET +*to*

prolong /prə⁶lɒŋ/, **prolongs, prolonging, prolonged**. To **prolong** something means to make it last longer. EG *All the time people are seeking to prolong life... He wanted to prolong the experience.* V+O ⇑ lengthen = extend ≠ shorten

prolonged /prə⁶lɒŋd/. A **prolonged** event or an event that happens over a **prolonged** period of time continues for a long time, or for longer than was expected. EG *...a prolonged and bitter struggle... ...prolonged applause... Inflation may prove uncontrollable over a prolonged period of time.* ADJ QUALIT : USU ATTRIB ⇑ long ≠ short

prom /prɒm/, **proms**; used in informal British English. A **prom** is **1** a concert at which some of the audience stand rather than sit. EG *...the Last Night of the Proms.* N COUNT **2** a road or path that is built next to the sea or the beach at a seaside resort. N COUNT = promenade

promenade /prɒmənɑːd/, **promenades, promenading, promenaded**. **1** A **promenade** is **1.1** a road or path that is built next to the sea or the beach at a seaside resort. EG *She sat on a railed seat on the promenade.* N COUNT : USU *the*+N **1.2** a slow walk that you take for pleasure, especially in a public place; a rather old-fashioned, formal use. EG *The Park has always been a place for a promenade.* N COUNT = stroll **1.3** a path built for people to walk along for pleasure, especially in a public park. EG *The park's grandest promenade is the Broad Walk.* N COUNT

2 When you **promenade**, you go for a slow walk for pleasure, especially in a public place; a rather old-fashioned, formal use. V : USU+A = stroll

promenade concert, promenade concerts. A **promenade concert** is a concert at which some of the audience stand rather than sit; used in British English. EG *The Promenade Concerts were founded originally by Sir Henry Wood.*
N COUNT = prom

prominence /prɒmɪnəns/. 1 If someone or something is in a position of **prominence**, they are well-known and important. EG *Alan Travers had risen to prominence in his wife's organisation... Robertson was the man who brought Hoyland into prominence... ...issues such as ecology and the environment which have suddenly come into prominence.*
N UNCOUNT ⇑ importance ≠ insignificance

2 If something is in a position of **prominence**, it sticks out or is in a high, noticeable position. EG *The mansion was in a position of spectacular prominence.*
N UNCOUNT

prominent /prɒmɪnənt/. 1 Someone who is **prominent** is well-known and important. EG *...US Senators and other prominent American personalities... She had access to some very prominent people.*
ADJ QUALIT ≠ insignificant, unknown

2 Something that is **prominent 2.1** is very noticeable or important. EG *There was one prominent advertisement, among three pages of other ads... Occupying a prominent place in the room is a blackboard.*
ADJ QUALIT = significant ≠ insignificant

◊ **prominently.** EG *I was looking at a large photograph prominently displayed in her front room... In the labour market before 1974, women figured prominently.*
◊ ADV WITH VB

2.2 sticks out or sticks up. EG *He has a prominent Adam's apple... I think my nose is too prominent.*
ADJ QUALIT ⇑ projecting = protuberant

promiscuity /prɒmɪskjuːɪti[1]/ is the behaviour of a person who has many short sexual relationships with a lot of different people; used showing disapproval. EG *Relatives do sometimes worry about sexual promiscuity when a child reaches adolescence.*
N UNCOUNT = sleeping around

promiscuous /prəmɪskjuəs/. Someone who is **promiscuous** has many short sexual relationships with a lot of different people; used showing disapproval. EG *I'm not sexually promiscuous.* ▸ used of behaviour and attitudes. EG *...when a girl engages in promiscuous sexual behaviour.*
ADJ QUALIT ≠ chaste

promise /prɒmɪs/, **promises, promising, promised.** 1 If you **promise** that you will do something, you say to someone that you will definitely do it. EG *I'll be back at one o'clock, I promise... I promised to take my children to the fun-fair on Saturday... I promised your father that you should never know he had been in prison... The visitor turned up at noon, as promised.*
V, V+O/REPORT-CL/QUOTE/to-INF, OR V+O+REPORT-CL/QUOTE/to-INF = vow

2 If you **promise** a particular thing to someone, you tell them that you will definitely give it to them or that you will make sure that they have it. EG *He promised me a new car for my birthday... Dick was promised a job in Alaska... The government promise better homes for all who need them.*
V+O+O, OR V+O+A (to/for)

3 If a situation or event **promises** to develop in a particular way, it shows signs that it will develop in that way. EG *We woke up to a fine May morning that promised heat later... The debate during the election campaign promises to be lively.*
V+O, OR V+to-INF

4 A **promise** is a statement which you make to someone in which you say that you will definitely do something. EG *He's always making promises and then breaking them... They failed to fulfil their promises to revive the economy.*
N COUNT = vow

5 **Promise** is a sign or indication of something, for example success, that will or may happen in the future. EG *When she was young, she showed considerable promise as a tennis player... Their marriage held little promise of happiness... It was a good year for all of them, full of promise... The promise of the revolution was slow in being realized.*
N UNCOUNT

promising /prɒmɪsɪŋ/. Something that is **promising** shows signs that it is likely to be very good or successful. EG *The scandal threatened an abrupt end to a promising political career... Julie Walters was voted 'most promising new actress, 1980' for her performance in 'Educating Rita'... I consulted the menu. It looked promising.*
ADJ QUALIT

promissory note /prɒmɪʃəri[1] nəʊt/, **promissory notes.** A **promissory note** is a written promise that you make to pay a specified sum of money to a particular person either on a particular date or when you are asked for it; used in formal English.
N COUNT = IOU

promontory /prɒməntə[0]ri[1]/, **promontories.** A **promontory** is a cliff that stretches out into the sea. EG *The mansion was on a promontory, high over the Pacific.*
N COUNT ⇑ point

promote /prəməʊt/, **promotes, promoting, promoted.** 1 If people **promote** something, they help or encourage it to develop or succeed, for example by creating favourable conditions. EG *She accused the government of not doing enough to promote economic growth... The meeting was held in order to promote better understanding between the two countries.*
V+O = foster

2 If a firm **promotes** a product, it tries to increase the sales or popularity of that product, for example by special advertising. EG *The band are going on a nationwide tour to promote their new record.*
V+O = push

3 If someone **is promoted**, they are given a more important job in the organization they work for, and are paid more money. EG *She has been promoted twice since joining the company five years ago... He was promoted from corporal to sergeant.*
V+O : IF+PREP THEN from/to ≠ demote

promoter /prəməʊtə/, **promoters.** A **promoter** is 1 a person who helps to organize and finance something, especially a sports event. EG *...a boxing promoter.*
N COUNT

2 a person or thing that helps or encourages something to develop or succeed. EG *She was a tireless promoter of new causes.*
N COUNT+of = supporter

promotion /prəməʊʃə[0]n/, **promotions.** 1 If you are given **promotion**, you are given a more important job in the organization you work for, and are paid more money. EG *She took a computing course to improve her chances of promotion... You can expect promotion to management level after three or four years... What are your promotion prospects in this job?* ▸ used as a count noun. EG *I'm hoping for another promotion this year.*
N UNCOUNT ⇑ advancement; ▸ N COUNT

2 The **promotion** of a product is the way in which a firm tries to increase its sales or popularity, for example by means of special advertising. EG *There are government controls on the promotion of cigarettes... ...a promotion campaign... The new product was backed by mass media promotion and sophisticated marketing.*
N UNCOUNT

3 A **promotion** is a publicity campaign that is intended to increase the sales of something. EG *They're planning a big promotion for their new washing powder.*
N COUNT

4 The **promotion** of something such as an idea is the attempt to encourage it or help it to develop. EG *The promotion of good health is the department's most important job.*
N UNCOUNT+of = encouragement

promotional /prəməʊʃə[0]nəl, -ʃnə[0]l/. **Promotional** events or ideas are designed to increase the sales of a product or service. EG *...promotional advertising... ...promotional literature.*
ADJ CLASSIF : USU ATTRIB

prompt /prɒmp[0]t/, **prompts, prompting, prompted.** 1 If something **prompts** an event or action, it causes it to happen. EG *A strike had prompted the setting up of the committee... He was wondering what Lamin had overheard to prompt that question... My choice was prompted by a number of considerations.*
V+O = occasion

2 If something **prompts** you to do something, it causes you to decide to do it and then act on your decision. EG *The Times article prompted him to call a meeting of the staff... We listened so attentively that the Doctor felt prompted to expand on his theme... It was Anne's nagging which prompted me into this visit to the doctor.*
V+O+to-INF/A = motivate

3 When someone **prompts** an actor or actress during a rehearsal or performance, they remind him or her of the next words that he or she is supposed to say. EG *She needed to be prompted three times.* ▸ used as a noun. EG *I had to be given a prompt.*
V OR V+O; ▸ N COUNT

4 If you **prompt** someone, you say something which is intended to encourage them to continue talking about a subject when they have just stopped talking. EG *'Yes?' Morris prompted, after a pause.*
V+O/QUOTE ⇑ suggest = coax

5 **Prompt** means done immediately and without any delay. EG *Professor Hamburg got a prompt expression of regret in reply... Fortunately prompt medical attention was available... The newspaper demanded a prompt, searching and complete enquiry.*
ADJ QUALIT : USU ATTRIB = immediate, swift

6 If you are **prompt** to do something, you do it with very little delay. EG *The company was prompt in its response to these accusations... Mary was prompt to dismiss any suspicions I might have had.*
ADJ QUALIT : PRED+to-INF/A = quick ≠ slow

◊ **promptness.** EG *The manager replied with promptness and courtesy.*
◊ N UNCOUNT

7 If you say that something happens at a particular time **prompt**, you mean that it happens at that time exactly; a fairly informal use. EG *The meeting will begin at 8 o'clock prompt.* — ADV AFTER NG = on the dot, sharp

prompter /prɒmp⁰tə/, **prompters**. A **prompter** is the person in a theatre whose job is to remind an actor or actress of words that he or she has forgotten during a performance. — N COUNT

prompting /prɒmp⁰tɪŋ/, **promptings**. **Prompting** is the action of saying something in order to cause someone to do a particular thing. EG *I think he'll agree with a bit of prompting... She did it without any prompting... ...Mummy's constant promptings to be 'a nice, clever boy like your brother.'* — N UNCOUNT/COUNT ⇑ persuasion

promptly /prɒmp⁰tli¹/. If you do something **promptly**, **1** you do it immediately and without any delay at all. EG *When you receive orders you must obey them promptly without question... One continues to learn things in life, then promptly forgets them.* — ADV WITH VB = straightaway **2** you do it at exactly the time that has been arranged. EG *I arrived at the gates promptly at six o'clock.* — ADV : VB+ADV+A = punctually

promulgate /prɒməlgeɪt/, **promulgates, promulgating, promulgated**. If people **promulgate** a new law or a new idea, they announce it publicly and make it widely known; a formal word. EG *A Prices and Incomes policy was boldly conceived and promulgated.* — V+O

PRON □ In this dictionary PRON is used in the grammar notes beside entries to mean 'pronoun'. Pronouns are used like noun groups, and there are several different kinds of them. **1** Personal pronouns refer to the people involved in conversations. There are special forms for the subject position *(I, he, she, we, they)* and for the object position *(me, him, her, us, them)*. The pronouns *you* and *it* do not change in form. For further details, see the entries for each word. **2** The words *this, that, these,* and *those* are called demonstrative pronouns, and are used in referring to things that have been mentioned or that are present in the situation. EG ***That** is a nice dress... I do like **these**.* For further details, see the entries for each word. **3** Most pronouns act as noun groups and are not used with modifiers such as adjectives. The word *one* is often called a pronoun, but it has a different function, because it must have some sort of modifier or qualifier. EG *That's just **one** of the things I like about him... ...an easy **one** to handle.* **4** For other pronouns, see □ at PRON INDEF, PRONPOSS, and PRON REFL. **5** A number of other words in the noun group are called pronouns if there is no noun that they modify. Examples are determiners such as *some, enough,* and *all*; and a few adjectives such as *same*. EG *I think five dollars should be **enough**... ...the **same** as any other job... I bought a ticket and he did the **same**.* Pronouns of this type are often followed by *of*, and the grammar note says PRON: ALSO+*of*. EG *I've had **enough** of her temper for one day.*

prone /prəʊn/. **1** If you are **prone** to something, you have a tendency to be affected by that thing. EG *He was prone to indigestion after rich restaurant meals... The car industry is notoriously prone to strikes.* — ADJ QUALIT : PRED+*to*-INF/*to* ⇑ inclined = susceptible
2 If you are **prone**, you are lying flat with the front of your body on the ground; a formal use. EG *She was lying prone on the floor.* — ADJ CLASSIF

prong /prɒŋ/, **prongs**. The **prongs** of a fork are the long pointed parts. A fork usually has three or four prongs. — N COUNT

PRON INDEF □ In this dictionary PRON INDEF is used in the grammar notes beside entries to mean 'indefinite pronoun'. The indefinite pronouns are *anybody, anyone, anything, everybody, everyone, everything, nobody, no-one, nothing, somebody, someone,* and *something*. You use an indefinite pronoun when you cannot or do not want to refer to particular people or things. An indefinite pronoun is used with a singular verb. It cannot have a determiner. EG *She knew that **something** was wrong...* There was ***nobody** there.* An indefinite pronoun can be used with an adjective, in which case the adjective follows the pronoun. EG *He had **something** important to tell us... **Nobody** special went to the party.*

pronominal /prəʊnɒmɪnə⁰l/ means relating to a pronoun. — ADJ CLASSIF

pronoun /prəʊnaʊn/, **pronouns**. In grammar, a **pronoun** is a word that is used to replace a noun or a noun group that has already been mentioned or that will be mentioned later. 'He', 'she', and 'them' are all pronouns. Words that are pronouns have PRON in the grammar notes beside the entries. See □ at PRON. — N COUNT

pronounce /prənaʊns/, **pronounces, pronouncing, pronounced**. **1** To **pronounce** a word or sound means to say it in a particular way, usually in the accepted way for a particular language. EG *We can never be certain in English how an unfamiliar word should be pronounced... I can't pronounce his name... ...the town of Ixtlan, pronounced East-lon.* — V+O, OR V+O+O
2 If you **pronounce** something to be true, you state that it is true definitely or officially. EG *The victim was pronounced dead on arrival at Southampton Hospital... I now pronounce you man and wife.* — V+O+C/*to be* ⇑ declare
3 To **pronounce** also means to say something in a way which shows that you feel sure about what you are saying; a formal use. EG *'The letter is a forgery,' she pronounced.* — V+REPORT-CL/QUOTE = declare
4 If someone **pronounces** a verdict or decision, they give that verdict or decision formally and officially. EG *'Are the people ready to pronounce their verdict?'-'Guilty'.* — V+O ⇑ declare
5 If you **pronounce** on something, you give your opinion on it, usually because you are an expert on it; a formal use. EG *She was asked to pronounce on the merits of an eighteenth century table.* — V+A *(on)*

pronounced /prənaʊnst/. **1** Something that is **pronounced** is very obvious or noticeable. EG *His smile grew more pronounced... She has fine pronounced eyebrows... He spoke with a pronounced English accent.* — ADJ QUALIT ≠ faint
2 If you have **pronounced** views on something, you have very strong, definite views on it. EG *He has very pronounced views on education.* — ADJ QUALIT = decided ≠ uncertain

pronouncement /prənaʊnsmə²nt/, **pronouncements**. A **pronouncement** is a statement, usually a public and official one, on an important topic; a formal word. EG *Despite official pronouncements to the contrary, the Prime Minister was known to be considering resignation.* — N COUNT = declaration

PRONPOSS □ In this dictionary PRONPOSS is used in the grammar notes beside entries to mean 'possessive pronoun'. The possessive pronouns are *mine, yours, his, hers, ours,* and *theirs*. A possessive pronoun is used to say who something belongs to or relates to. It can never be used with determiners or adjectives. See also □ at DETPOSS. Examples are **ours, mine**, and **yours**. *At least your machines are modern. **Ours** are liable to break down any moment... They have different ideas to **ours**... Is this book **mine** or **yours**?* Possessive pronouns can also be used in a construction with *of*, following a noun group that starts with a determiner. EG *I want to introduce you to a friend of **mine**... What are we going to do about this idea of **yours**?*

PRON REFL □ In this dictionary PRON REFL is used in the grammar notes beside entries to mean 'reflexive pronoun'. The reflexive pronouns are *myself, yourself, herself, himself, itself, ourselves, yourselves, themselves,* and *oneself*. There are two main uses of reflexive pronouns. **1** A reflexive pronoun can be used as the object of a verb or preposition when the object refers to the same person or thing as the subject of the clause. EG *Ralph pulled **himself** out of the water... Dogs cannot cool **themselves** by sweating... Did you enjoy **yourself**?* The reflexive pronoun **yourself** can also be used as an object or prepositional object when the verb is imperative. EG *Enjoy **yourselves**!... Take care of **yourself**.* **2** A reflexive pronoun can also be used to emphasize that someone did something without any help from anyone else. EG *We did it **ourselves**... She made the cake **herself**.* If the pronoun comes immediately after the noun group, it emphasizes that noun group. EG *We **ourselves** did it... The girls **themselves** made all the presents.*

PRON REL □ In this dictionary PRON REL is used in the grammar notes beside entries to mean 'relative pronoun'. Relative pronouns are words such as *who, which, whose* and *that*. They introduce relative clauses.

pronto /prɒntəʊ/. If you say that something must be done **pronto**, you mean that it must be done quickly and immediately; an informal word. EG *You'd better get it done pronto.* — ADV AFTER VB = at once

pronunciation /prənʌnsieɪʃə⁰n/, **pronunciations**. **1** The **pronunciation** of a word or language is the way in which it is usually spoken. EG *English people often find the pronunciation of French difficult... Both pronunciations are acceptable.* — N UNCOUNT/COUNT
2 Someone's **pronunciation** of a word is the way in — N COUNT : USU

which they pronounce it. EG *My Italian friends are always correcting my pronunciation.*
SING WITH POSS

proof /pruːf/, **proofs.** 1 **Proof** or a **proof** of something is evidence or facts that show that it is true or that it exists. EG *If you have any proof of that allegation, may I suggest that you make it known... What proof have you that this was ordered?*
N UNCOUNT/COUNT: IF + PREP THEN *of*, OR + REPORT-CL = evidence

2 A **proof** is also a first printed copy of something, for example of a page of a book, that is made so that mistakes can be corrected before more copies are printed. EG *He worked away from home, correcting proofs... He took the proof of the editorial into Thomas Marlowe's room.*
N COUNT

3 If someone is **proof** against something, they cannot be harmed or affected by that thing; a formal use. EG *There is no man in the world who is proof against an assassin's bullet... Few are proof against all temptations.*
ADJ CLASSIF: PRED + *against* = secure ≠ vulnerable

4 **Proof** is also used after a number to give the alcoholic strength of a drink such as whisky or brandy, measured on a scale from 0 to 100 per cent. EG *It is 65% proof instead of the usual 70%.*
ADJ AFTER NUM

5 If you say that **the proof of the pudding is in the eating**, you mean that something new can only be judged to be good or bad after it has been tried or used.
CONVENTION

-proof combines with nouns to form adjectives which indicate that something cannot be damaged by the thing mentioned. EG *A thatch is wind-proof, frost-proof and good to look at... This building's supposed to be earthquake proof... High technology has made New England recession-proof.* ● See also **fireproof, waterproof.**
COMB: FORMS ADJS

proof-read, proof-reads, proof-reading. The form **proof-read** is used in the present tense and is also the past tense and past participle. In the present tense it is pronounced /pruːfriːd/; the past tense and past participle are pronounced /pruːfrɛd/. When you **proof-read** a text, you read it to find and mark mistakes that need to be corrected.
V OR V+O

proof-reader, proof-readers; also spelled without a hyphen. A **proof-reader** is a person who is employed to look at printed texts and to find and mark any mistakes that need to be corrected before the text is published.
N COUNT

prop /prɒp/, **props, propping, propped.** 1 If you **prop** an object on or against something, you support it in a particular position by putting something underneath it or resting it against something. EG *She propped her chin on her hand and surveyed him... His gun lay propped against the wall.*
V+O+A

2 A **prop** is 2.1 an object, for example a stick, that you use to support something in a particular position. EG *He used two sticks as props for the rope.*
N COUNT
2.2 the main person, group, or thing that gives strength to a system, institution, or person. EG *They ceased to be the prop of the imperial administration... Discussing everything was the prop of their marriage.*
N COUNT: USU SING = mainstay
2.3 an object or a piece of furniture that is used on a theatre stage when a play is being acted, or when a film is being made. EG *The sets, props and costumes were all ready.*
N COUNT: USU PL
2.4 a propeller; an informal use.
N COUNT

prop up. 1 If you **prop** an object up, you support it in a particular position by putting something underneath it or resting it against something. EG *His feet were propped up on the coffee table... The little mirror was propped up on the dressing table.*
PHRASAL VB: V+O+ADV, USU+A

2 If a government or group of people **props up** another government or an institution, it gives it support and helps it to survive. EG *The Government does not intend to prop up declining industries... We should prop up countries run on more or less liberal lines.*
PHRASAL VB: V+O+ADV = maintain, sustain

propaganda /prɒpəgændə/ is information, frequently exaggerated or false information, which is spread by political groups in order to influence the public; usually used showing disapproval. EG *It is essential to sort the truth from the propaganda... He launched an attack on the use of propaganda to intimidate the population.*
N UNCOUNT

propagandist /prɒpəgændɪst/, **propagandists.** 1 A **propagandist** is a person who works to spread propaganda, for example for a political group; often used showing disapproval. EG *...dedicated revolutionary activists and propagandists.*
N COUNT ⇑ promoter

2 **Propagandist** activities or publications are intended to help spread propaganda. EG *...a small propagandist group.*
ADJ CLASSIF: ATTRIB

propagandize /prɒpəgændaɪz/, **propagandizes, propagandizing, propagandized**; also spelled **propagandise.** If someone **propagandizes**, they try to influence other people by spreading propaganda; a rather formal word usually used showing disapproval.
V OR V+O

propagate /prɒpəgeɪt/, **propagates, propagating, propagated.** 1 If people **propagate** information or an idea, they spread it so that it will influence a lot of people; a formal use. EG *The group is doing what it can to propagate the rumour... She toured the principal cities to propagate her cause.* ◊ **propagation** /prɒpəgeɪʃəⁿn/. EG *...the propagation of knowledge.*
V+O = disseminate, promulgate
◊ N UNCOUNT

2 When animals **propagate**, they reproduce and therefore increase in numbers; a formal use. ◊ **propagation.** EG *These conditions have been tried, tested and found valuable for the better propagation of the species.*
V
◊ N UNCOUNT = procreation

3 If you **propagate** plants or if they **propagate**, they grow and increase in number; a technical term. EG *The new seeds will propagate themselves... The plants propagate quickly in warm temperatures.*
V-ERG

propane /prəʊpeɪn/ is a gas that comes from petroleum and is used for cooking and heating.
N UNCOUNT

propel /prəⁱpɛl/, **propels, propelling, propelled.** 1 To **propel** something in a particular direction means to cause it to move in that direction. EG *The boat continued to move, assisted by wind and tide as well as propelled by his own efforts... The fish moved silently through the water, propelled by short sweeps of its tail.*
V+O: USU+A ⇑ drive

2 If something or someone **propels** you in a particular direction, they encourage you very strongly to act in a particular way. EG *Often people's own daily problems can propel them in the direction of the revolutionary parties.*
V+O+A = drive

propellant /prəⁱpɛlənt/, **propellants.** A **propellant** is 1 something, for example a motor, chemical, or fuel, that causes something to move forwards. 2 a gas that is used in aerosol cans to force the contents out of the can when you press the button.
N COUNT
N MASS

propeller /prəⁱpɛlə/, **propellers.** A **propeller** is a device attached to an aircraft or boat consisting of two or more blades fixed to a central bar. The engine makes the propeller spin round, and this causes the boat or aircraft to move forward. EG *The water was thrashing and churning about under the propellers.*
N COUNT

propelling pencil, propelling pencils. A **propelling pencil** is a pencil with a metal or plastic case. The lead that you write with can be moved down as it is needed by turning the outside of the pencil.
N COUNT

propensity /prəpɛnsɪtiⁱ/, **propensities.** A **propensity** is a natural tendency that you have to behave in a particular way; a formal word. EG *The conference gave a foretaste of the party's propensity for mass gatherings... All of us recognize our own propensity to evil.*
N COUNT: USU SING + *for/to/to-INF* = disposition, inclination

proper /prɒpə/. 1 **Proper** is used 1.1 to describe things that are considered to be real and genuine, as opposed to things that are similar to them but less satisfactory in some way. EG *Have you been to a proper doctor?... He's never had a proper job... Lack of proper funding is making our job more difficult.*
ADJ CLASSIF: ATTRIB = true
1.2 to emphasize that something is definitely a part of a particular place, object, etc in order to distinguish it from other things which are sometimes regarded as part of it and sometimes not. EG *By the time I got to the village proper everyone was out to meet me.*
ADJ AFTER N
1.3 to emphasize that someone or something is exactly as you are describing them; an informal use. EG *She was a proper miser.*
ADJ CLASSIF: ATTRIB = real

2 If you say that a way of behaving is **proper**, you mean that it is acceptable according to the accepted standards of a particular society or group. EG *It wasn't proper for a man to show his emotions... It was right and proper that I should be present in the house.* ▸ used of people who behave in this way. EG *Gretchen was a neat, proper, beautiful girl... She was very proper.*
ADJ CLASSIF = decent, fitting ≠ improper
▸ ADJ QUALIT ⇑ correct

3 **Proper** also means correct. EG *What's the proper word for those things?... Everything was in its proper place.*
ADJ CLASSIF: ATTRIB = right

properly /prɒpəli¹/. 1 If something is done **properly**, it is done correctly and satisfactorily, according to an accepted standard. EG *The children are properly clothed and fed... I had not eaten properly for the past few days... The reviewers don't seem to be doing their job properly.* ADV WITH VB = adequately ≠ badly

2 If you say that someone behaves **properly**, you mean that they are behaving in a way that is considered to be acceptable and not rude or shocking. ADV WITH VB = decently

3 **Properly** also means to a very great degree; an informal use. EG *You looked properly fed up.* ADV+ADJ/ADV = really

proper noun, proper nouns. In grammar, a **proper noun** is a noun which is the name of a person, place, or institution. Proper nouns are often spelled with a capital letter at the beginning. Words that are proper nouns have N PROP in the grammar notes beside the entries. See □ at N PROP. N COUNT

propertied /prɒpətɪd/. **Propertied** people own land or property; a formal word. ADJ CLASSIF : ATTRIB

property /prɒpəti¹/, **properties**. 1 Someone's **property** is all the things that belong to them or something that belongs to them. EG *Their job is to protect private property... Her property passes to her next of kin... Most men no longer treat their women as property... ...the misuse of prison property.* N UNCOUNT = belongings, possessions

2 A **property** is a piece of land that is owned by a person or an institution, and the building or buildings that are on it; often used to refer to a house and its garden. EG *He's got his own property... There was a dam at one edge of the property.* N COUNT

3 The **properties** of a substance or object are the ways in which it behaves in particular conditions. EG *...the physical properties of substances... ...fundamental work on the properties of basic particles.* N COUNT : USU PL ⇑ characteristics

prophecy /prɒfɪsi¹/, **prophecies**. A **prophecy** is a statement that something will happen or will become true in the future. EG *The prophecy was fulfilled... Rudolph found Boylan's prophecies distasteful... It is a plausible bit of prophecy.* N COUNT/ UNCOUNT = prediction

prophesy /prɒfɪsaɪ/, **prophesies, prophesying, prophesied**. If you **prophesy** that something will happen, you say that it will happen in the future. EG *I prophesy that in ten years' time real income per head will be four times greater than now... I'm not going to prophesy about this.* V+O/REPORT-CL/ QUOTE/A = predict, foretell

prophet /prɒfɪt/, **prophets**. 1 A **prophet** is 1.1 a person who is believed to be chosen by God to say things that God himself wants to say to people, for example to tell them what they should do and what they should not do. EG *They listened to the word of the prophet.* N COUNT 1.2 a person who predicts that particular things will happen or will become true in the future. EG *The prophets of doom have been proved wrong before.* N COUNT+*of* = seer 1.3 someone who is strongly in favour of a particular idea and actively supports it. EG *...a prophet of peace... ...the first and perhaps most original prophet of socialism.* N COUNT+*of*

2 The **Prophet** is another name for Mohammed, the founder of Islam. EG *...the five centuries following the death of the Prophet.* N PROPER : *the*+N

prophetess /prɒfɪtɛs/, **prophetesss**. A **prophetess** is a woman who is a prophet. N COUNT

prophetic /prə⁶fɛtɪk/. Something that is **prophetic** describes or predicts things that eventually happen or become true. EG *His concluding remark was prophetic... These were prophetic words.* ADJ QUALIT

◇ **prophetically**. EG *He prophetically warned of the dangers of progress.* ◇ ADV WITH VB

prophylactic /prɒfɪlæktɪk/, **prophylactics**. 1 **Prophylactic** means concerned with preventing disease; a medical term. ADJ CLASSIF ⇑ preventive

2 A **prophylactic** is a substance or device used for preventing disease; a medical term. EG *It can be used as a prophylactic.* N COUNT

propinquity /prəpɪŋkwɪti¹/ is nearness to someone, either because you live near to them or because you are closely related to them; a formal word. EG *They value their friends because of their residential propinquity.* N UNCOUNT = closeness

propitiate /prə⁶pɪʃieɪt/, **propitiates, propitiating, propitiated**. If you **propitiate** a person or a god, you stop them being angry or impatient by doing something to please them; a formal word. EG *His face was blackened to propitiate the goddess of chance.* V+O ⇑ calm = appease, placate

◇ **propitiation** /prə⁶pɪʃieɪʃə⁰n/. ◇ N UNCOUNT

propitiatory /prə⁶pɪʃɪətri¹/. An action that is **propitiatory** is intended to stop someone from being angry with you by pleasing them; a formal word. ADJ CLASSIF = appeasing

propitious /prə⁶pɪʃəs/. If something is **propitious**, it is likely to give successful results; a formal word. EG *It was hardly a propitious time to join one of those newspapers... Conditions were propitious for development.* ADJ QUALIT ⇑ helpful = favourable ≠ unfavourable

proponent /prə⁶pəʊnənt/, **proponents**. If you are a **proponent** of a particular theory, point of view, or course of action, you actively support it. EG *...the proponents of conservation.* N COUNT : IF+ PREP THEN *of* ⇑ supporter

proportion /prəpɔːʃə⁰n/, **proportions**. 1 A **proportion** of a whole thing or group is a part of it; used when you are thinking about the relative sizes of the part and the whole. EG *A vast proportion of our revenue comes from advertisements... Courts are now sending a smaller proportion of offenders to prison... There is always a proportion of the crowd which wants to make trouble... What proportion of schools are funded by the state?* N COUNT : USU SING+*of* = percentage

2 The **proportion** of one kind of thing in a group is the amount or number of that kind of thing that is included in the group. EG *Sunday magazines always include a high proportion of advertisements for cars... The proportion of women in the total work-force has risen.* N COUNT : USU SING+*of* ⇑ quantity

3 The **proportion** of one thing to another is the relationship between the two in terms of how much there is of each thing. EG *The proportion of workers to employers was large... Mix the flour and fat in the proportion two to one... I hope the cake is okay. I may have got the proportions slightly wrong.* N COUNT : USU *the*+SING+*of* = ratio

4 If you refer to the **proportions** of something, you are referring to its size. EG *...the majestic proportions of the great Pyramid... ...a gin and tonic of giant proportions... Steps must be taken to reduce the problem to manageable proportions.* N PLURAL : USU MOD+N = dimensions

5 If you refer to the **proportions** in a work of art or a design, you are referring to the relative sizes of its different parts or dimensions. EG *He was satisfied with the proportions... A mirror can add space to a room, improve proportions or lighting.* N PLURAL ▸ used as an uncountable noun. EG *It's a colourful painting, but it lacks proportion.* ▸ N UNCOUNT = balance

6 If one thing increases or decreases **in proportion to** or **in proportion with** another thing, it increases or decreases at the same rate so that the two things are always in the same relationship with each other. EG *Western cities expanded in proportion with the growth of industry... Efficiency increases in direct proportion to the incentives offered... Time spent on a proposal varies in inverse proportion to its importance.* PREP

7 If you say that something is big or small **in proportion** to something else, you mean that it is big or small when you compare it with the other thing or measure it against the other thing. EG *Babies have big heads in proportion to their bodies.* PHR : USED AS AN A, IF+PREP THEN *to* = in relation to

8 If you say that something is **out of all proportion** to something else, you mean that it is far greater or more serious than is necessary or appropriate. EG *The fine was out of all proportion to the seriousness of the offence.* PHR : USED AS AN A, IF+PREP THEN *to* ≠ commensurate with

9 If you say that someone has **got** something **out of proportion**, you mean that they think it is more important or more worrying than it really is. EG *Haven't you got things just a little bit out of proportion?* PHR : VB INFLECTS

10 If someone has a **sense of proportion**, they know the difference between what is really important and what is not. EG *A sense of proportion is essential if you want to enjoy sport.* PHR : USED AS S/O

proportional /prəpɔːʃə⁰nəl, -ʃənə⁰l/. If one thing is **proportional** to another, it increases or decreases at the same rate as the other thing increases or decreases, so that there is always the same relationship between the two things. EG *The output should be proportional to the input... As a rule the suicide rates are proportional to the size of the city... The major powers should make proportional cuts.* ADJ CLASSIF : IF+ PREP THEN *to* = proportionate

◇ **proportionally**. EG *Males have proportionally longer legs and larger feet than females.* ◇ ADV

proportional representation is a system of voting in elections in which each political party is N UNCOUNT represented in parliament in proportion to the number of people who vote for it in an election.

proportionate /prəpɔːʃənət/ means the same as proportional. EG *After a run, your recovery time is proportionate to your fitness.* ◊ **proportionately.** EG *It is the middle classes which have proportionately lost more through the tax changes... Britain spent proportionately more on research and development than its competitors.* — ADJ CLASSIF: IF+ PREP THEN *to*; ◊ ADV WITH VB

-proportioned combines with adverbs to indicate that something is arranged so that the proportions of the different parts produce a certain effect. EG *The picture is carefully proportioned... He has well-proportioned features.* — COMB: FORMS ADJ QUALITS = balanced

proposal /prəpəʊzəºl/, **proposals.** 1 A **proposal** is 1.1 a suggested plan, often a formal written one, which is put forward for people to think about and decide upon. EG *There is controversy about a proposal to build a new nuclear power station... The two governments discussed a proposal for ending hostilities... I heard about some proposals for cheaper flights to the United States.* 1.2 a request to someone to marry you. EG *She told me that the second proposal of marriage which she received came from an Italian prince.* — N COUNT ⇑ suggestion; N COUNT: IF+ PREP THEN *of*

2 **Proposal** is the act of proposing something. — N UNCOUNT

propose /prəpəʊz/, **proposes, proposing, proposed.** 1 If you **propose** a plan or idea, you suggest it for people to think about and decide upon. EG *Even before they moved in, he had started to propose alterations to their new house... When he was very ill the priest had proposed to him that he might like to make a will.* — V+O/REPORT-CL, OR V+A *(to)*+ REPORT-CL ⇑ put forward

2 If someone **proposes** a motion in a debate, they introduce it and speak about why they agree with it. EG *Benn proposed the motion 'That this House has no confidence in the Prime Minister'.* — V+O ≠ oppose

3 If you **propose** a toast to someone or something, you ask people to drink a toast to that person or thing. EG *His brother-in-law proposed a toast to the happy couple.* — V+O: IF+PREP THEN *to*

4 If you **propose** to do something, you intend to do it; a formal use. EG *I do not propose to discuss this matter at all... I asked her what method of assessment she proposed to use in teaching.* ◊ **proposed.** EG *...my proposed trip to America.* — V+*to*-INF; ◊ ADJ CLASSIF: ATTRIB

5 If you **propose** to someone, you ask them to marry you. EG *Michael proposed to me in the corridor at work and I accepted.* — V OR V+O: IF+ PREP THEN *to*

proposer /prəpəʊzə/, **proposers.** A **proposer** is the person who introduces a subject in a debate or meeting or who suggests someone's name for a job or for membership of a club. — N COUNT

proposition /prɒpəzɪʃəºn/, **propositions, propositioning, propositioned.** 1 A **proposition** is 1.1 a carefully-worded statement which is put forward for discussion, especially in a formal situation such as parliament. EG *She defended the proposition that we could not afford to make any more cuts in spending on education... The students discussed the proposition that man is basically good.* 1.2 a person or a thing that is being considered from the point of view of success or failure. EG *The proceeds which could be made were not sufficient to make it a profitable proposition.* 1.3 an offer or arrangement which it is suggested that someone might be interested in. EG *He came to me one day with an extraordinary proposition... William, would you care to consider a proposition?* 1.4 a mathematical theorem or statement, which usually contains its proof. — N COUNT ⇑ idea; N COUNT: USU MOD+N; N COUNT ⇑ suggestion; N COUNT

2 If you **proposition** someone who you are not married to or having a romantic or sexual relationship with, you ask them to have sex with you. — V+O

propound /prəpaʊnd/, **propounds, propounding, propounded.** If you **propound** an argument, idea, or point of view, you suggest it for people to consider; a formal word. EG *This line of argument is propounded largely by the more influential US commentators.* — V+O ⇑ express = put forward

proprietary /prəºpraɪətəºriˡ/; a formal word. 1 **Proprietary** medicines, toiletries, cleaning materials, etc are ones that are sold under a trade name. EG *For grease marks try a proprietary dry cleaner... ...a proprietary medicine.* — ADJ CLASSIF: ATTRIB

2 If your behaviour is **proprietary**, you are behaving in a way that shows that you are, or that you think you are, the owner of something. EG *He spoke the name proudly and with a slight proprietary air.* — ADJ QUALIT

proprietor /prəºpraɪətə/, **proprietors.** A **proprietor** is the owner of a business, for example of a newspaper, a hotel, or a shop. EG *...the proprietor of the Financial News... ...the hotel proprietor.* — N COUNT: USU+ SUPP

proprietorial /prəºpraɪətɔːrɪəl/; a formal word. 1 **Proprietorial** means belonging to or relating to a proprietor. EG *...the abuse of proprietorial power.* — ADJ CLASSIF: ATTRIB

2 If your behaviour is **proprietorial**, you are behaving in a way that shows that you are, or that you think you are, the owner of something. EG *She had a proprietorial attitude towards the children.* — ADJ QUALIT: USU ATTRIB = proprietary

proprietorship /prəºpraɪətəʃɪp/ is ownership of a business, for example of a newspaper, a hotel, or a shop; a formal word. — N UNCOUNT

proprietress /prəºpraɪətrɪˀs/, **proprietresses.** A **proprietress** is a woman who is the owner of a business, for example a newspaper, hotel, or shop. EG *...the hotel proprietress.* — N COUNT: USU+ SUPP

propriety /prəºpraɪətiˡ/, **proprieties**; a formal word. 1 **Propriety** is correctness of behaviour in terms of what is considered socially or morally acceptable. EG *What is questionable is the propriety of diluting truth for the sake of a good story... I always try to write with propriety.* — N UNCOUNT

2 The **proprieties** are the standards of social behaviour which most people consider to be the correct ones to follow. EG *He was a stickler for the proprieties... She had so abandoned all sense of the proprieties as to be holding young Allen by the arm.* — N PLURAL: USU *the*+N

propulsion /prəpʌlʃəºn/ is the power that moves something, especially a vehicle, in a forward direction. EG *...jet propulsion... ...rocket propulsion.* — N UNCOUNT

pro rata. If something is paid for **pro rata**, it is paid for according to how much is used or received; a formal word. EG *Computer time is paid for pro rata... The orchestra is paid on a pro rata basis for concertos.* — ADV AFTER VB, OR ADJ CLASSIF: ATTRIB

prosaic /prəʊzeɪɪk/. Something that is **prosaic** is dull and unimaginative; a fairly formal word. EG *It's a shame that they make lovely music in such a prosaic building... Mine is an independent but perhaps a more prosaic existence.* ◊ **prosaically.** EG *It is officially and prosaically known as Boritaka 200 – more romantically as the Lost City.* — ADJ QUALIT ⇑ ordinary = mundane ≠ interesting; ◊ ADV WITH VB ≠ imaginatively

proscenium /prºəsiːnɪəm/, **prosceniums.** A **proscenium** or a **proscenium arch** is an arch in a theatre which separates the stage from the audience; a technical term. — N COUNT

proscribe /prəºskraɪb/, **proscribes, proscribing, proscribed.** If people in authority **proscribe** something, they publicly state that the existence or the use of that thing is forbidden; a formal word. EG *The State might proscribe private education altogether.* — V+O ⇑ condemn = ban ≠ endorse

proscription /prəºskrɪpʃəºn/. The **proscription** of something is the the act of stating that its existence or use is forbidden; a formal word. — N UNCOUNT: USU +*of* = prohibition

prose /prəʊz/, **proses.** 1 **Prose** is ordinary written language, in contrast to poetry. EG *...a piece of continuous prose... His descriptive prose is sound and clear... He works in both poetry and prose.* — N UNCOUNT

2 A **prose** is a piece of writing in a foreign language, done by a student in a language class; used mainly in British English. EG *Have you all done the French prose I set you?* — N COUNT

prosecute /prɒsɪkjuːt/, **prosecutes, prosecuting, prosecuted.** 1 If you **prosecute** someone, you accuse them of a crime and bring criminal charges against them. EG *In many cases shopkeepers will not prosecute... Trespassers will be prosecuted... He was prosecuted for drunken driving.* — V OR V+O

2 The person who **prosecutes** in a trial tries to prove that the person who is on trial is guilty. EG *...the district attorney prosecuting the case... ...the prosecuting lawyer.* — V OR V+O ≠ defend

prosecution /prɒsɪkjuːʃəºn/, **prosecutions.** 1 **Prosecution** is the bringing of criminal charges against someone. EG *He could still face criminal prosecution... Most cases have not resulted in prosecution... ...the prosecution of a bookseller.* ▸ used as a count noun. EG *The Smiths eventually brought a prosecution against the organizers... The prosecutions took place under the Public Order Act.* — N UNCOUNT; ▸ N COUNT

2 The **prosecution** in a trial is all the lawyers who are responsible for bringing criminal charges — N SING: *the*+N ≠ defence

against someone and trying to prove that they are guilty. EG *Mr Mervyn Griffith-Jones will lead for the prosecution... Today he will be questioned by the prosecution... ...a prosecution witness.*

3 The **prosecution** of a course of action is the carrying out of that course of action; a formal use. EG *...the prosecution of the war... I meet a wide range of people in the prosecution of my duties.* — N SING : *the*+N+*of* = pursuance

prosecutor /prɒsɪkju:tə/, **prosecutors**. A **prosecutor** is a lawyer who tries to prove in a trial that the person who is on trial is guilty. EG *...Archibald Cox, the special prosecutor for the government.* — N COUNT

proselytize /prɒsɪlɪtaɪz/, **proselytizes, proselytizing, proselytized**; also spelled **proselytise**. If you **proselytize**, you try very hard to persuade someone to leave their religious faith, political party, etc, and to join yours; a formal word. — V = convert

prospect, prospects, prospecting, prospected. The word **prospect** is pronounced /prɒspɛkt/ when it is a noun, and /prə^{7}spɛkt/ when it is a verb. 1 If there is some **prospect** of something happening, there is a possibility that it will happen. EG *There was little prospect of significant military aid... The prospects for revolution are remote.* — N UNCOUNT : USU +*of/for/* REPORT-CL = chance, likelihood

2 A **prospect** is something that you expect or know is going to happen. EG *She rejoiced at the prospect of the China trip... She did not relish the prospect of climbing another flight of stairs... You may well be daunted by this bleak prospect.* — N COUNT/ UNCOUNT : IF+ PREP THEN *of* ⇑ thought

3 Someone's **prospects** are their chances of being successful in their career, especially by being promoted quickly to a high position in an organization. EG *I tried to give a rosy picture of his prospects... Success or failure here would be crucial to his future prospects.* — N PLURAL : USU WITH POSS

4 A **prospect** is also a view from a particular place, especially of a large area of land, a large part of a city, etc; an formal, old-fashioned use. EG *...a prospect of spires, domes and towers.* — N COUNT = vista

5 If people **prospect** for oil, gold, etc, they look for it in a particular place with the intention of extracting it or mining it. — V : IF+PREP THEN *for* ⇑ search

prospective /prə^{7}spɛktɪv/ is 1 used of someone who intends to do a particular thing, for example to have a particular profession. EG *She is married to a prospective Member of Parliament... Godalming College has been forced to turn away 300 prospective students.* — ADJ CLASSIF : ATTRIB = aspiring, would-be 2 used of something that is likely to happen soon. EG *The organizers are unhappy about the prospective loss of playing fields.* — ADJ CLASSIF : ATTRIB = imminent

prospector /prə^{7}spɛktə/, **prospectors**. A **prospector** is a person who looks for oil or for valuable minerals such as gold. — N COUNT

prospectus /prə^{7}spɛktəs/, **prospectuses**. A **prospectus** is a document produced by a college, school, or company that gives details about it and its activities. EG *It's interesting to compare the two university prospectuses.* — N COUNT

prosper /prɒspə/, **prospers, prospering, prospered**. If people or businesses **prosper**, they are successful and make good progress, especially financially. EG *A lot of companies prospered... The farmers prospered.* — V = flourish, thrive

prosperity /prɒspɛrɪti^1/ is a condition in which a person or community is doing well economically and has a good standard of living. EG *...a period of unprecedented wealth and prosperity.* — N UNCOUNT = affluence ≠ poverty

prosperous /prɒspə^{0}rəs/. Someone who is **prosperous** is wealthy and successful. EG *His father was a prosperous farmer and coal merchant... ...the more prosperous sections of society.* ▸ used of places. EG *...a reasonably prosperous English city.* — ADJ QUALIT = affluent, well-off ≠ poor

prostate /prɒsteɪt/, **prostates**. The **prostate** or the **prostate gland** is an organ in the body of male mammals which is situated at the neck of the bladder and produces a liquid which forms part of the semen. — N COUNT

prostitute /prɒstɪtju:t/, **prostitutes, prostituting, prostituted**. 1 A **prostitute** is a person, especially a woman, who has sex with men in exchange for money. EG *He thought she was a prostitute... ...a male prostitute.* — N COUNT = hooker, streetwalker

2 If a woman **prostitutes** herself, she has sex with men in exchange for money; used showing disapproval. — V+O (REFL)

3 If you **prostitute** yourself or your talents, beliefs, etc, you behave in a way which is unworthy of you or use your talents for unworthy purposes, usually for money; used showing disapproval. — V+O (REFL/NG)

prostitution /prɒstɪtju:ʃə^{0}n/ is 1 the work of people who have sex with men in exchange for money. EG *A thriving trade in prostitution has grown up among women factory workers.* — N UNCOUNT 2 the misuse or exploitation of something important in exchange for money or other gains; used showing disapproval. EG *...the flagrant prostitution of true human values.* — N UNCOUNT+ SUPP = abuse

prostrate, prostrates, prostrating, prostrated. The word **prostrate** is pronounced /prɒstreɪt/ when it is a verb, and /prɒstreɪt/ when it is an adjective. 1 If you **prostrate** yourself, you lie stretched out flat on the ground with your face downwards, especially as an act of worship or submission. EG *I wanted to throw my arms about him, prostrate myself before him.* — V+O (REFL) ◊ **prostration** /prɒstreɪʃə^{0}n/. EG *I was willing to adopt this attitude of abject prostration.* — ◊ N UNCOUNT

2 If you are **prostrate**, 2.1 you are lying stretched out flat on the ground with your face downwards. EG *...the prostrate figure of Mr Green... They were chained prostrate along the rails.* — ADJ CLASSIF 2.2 you are so distressed by some awful experience that you are unable to do anything at all. EG *The shock took some time to hit me. But when it did I was prostrate... I was prostrate with grief.* — ADJ CLASSIF : IF+ PREP THEN *with* = devastated

3 If you **are prostrated** by something, especially an illness, you are completely exhausted by it. EG *The poor girl was prostrated and a doctor confined her to bed.* — V+O : USU PASS ⇑ incapacitated ◊ **prostration**. EG *...nervous prostration.* — ◊ N UNCOUNT

prosy /prəʊzi^1/, **prosier, prosiest**. Writing that is **prosy** is dull and uses too many words. — ADJ QUALIT = stodgy

protagonist /prə^{6}tægənɪst/, **protagonists**. 1 Someone who is a **protagonist** of an idea or political movement is a supporter of that idea or movement, especially a well-known one. EG *...a leading protagonist of the movement... She was herself a vehement protagonist of sexual equality.* — N COUNT : USU+ SUPP = champion

2 A **protagonist** is also an important character in a play or story; a formal use. — N COUNT

protean /prəʊti:ən, prəʊtɪən/. Someone or something that is **protean** has the ability to continually change their nature, appearance, or behaviour; a very formal word. EG *He has a protean nature.* — ADJ CLASSIF = changeable

protect /prə^{6}tɛkt/, **protects, protecting, protected**. 1 To **protect** someone or something means to keep them safe from injury, damage, loss, or other unpleasant effects or events. EG *She had his umbrella to protect her from the rain... Babies are protected against diseases like measles by their mothers' milk... The Common Law has always protected individual rights.* — V+O : USU+A *(from/against)* ⇑ keep safe

2 If a government **protects** an industry, it helps it by putting a tax on imported goods. EG *Is is sensible to protect a little inefficient remnant of a textile industry?* — V+O ⇑ aid

3 If an insurance policy **protects** you against a particular event, for example death, injury, or theft, it promises to give money to you or your family if that thing happens. — V+A *(against)*, OR V+O : USU+ *against* = insure

protection /prə^{6}tɛkʃə^{0}n/. 1 If something gives **protection** against unpleasant effects or events, it keeps someone or something safe from those effects or events. EG *The mud walls and straw roofs of these huts offer little protection against rats... ...protection from the sun's rays... Ships themselves required the protection of naval and air power... He packed a pistol for his own protection.* — N UNCOUNT ⇑ defence

2 If someone or something is **protection** against something unpleasant, they keep you safe from that thing. EG *She put on dark glasses as a protection against the strong light... God is our protection.* — N UNCOUNT ⇑ defence

3 If an insurance policy gives you **protection** against a particular event, for example death, injury, or theft, it promises to give money to you or your family if that thing happens. EG *This policy gives you protection against loss of earnings due to sickness or unemployment.* — N UNCOUNT

4 If a government has a policy of **protection**, it helps its own industries by putting a tax on imported goods. EG *His remedy for decline is trade protection.* — N UNCOUNT

5 If gangsters offer people **protection**, they demand money from them and in return promise not to hurt them or damage their property. EG *She has to pay protection money to thugs to stop them beating her* — N UNCOUNT : USU BEFORE N

up... *The brothers run a protection racket in London's East End.*

protectionism /prə⁶tekʃənɪzə⁰m/ is the policy a country has of helping its own industries by putting a tax on imported goods. EG *He is opposed totally to protectionism.* ◊ **protectionist.** EG *They want to introduce further protectionist legislation.* N UNCOUNT = free trade ◊ ADJ CLASSIF : ATTRIB

protective /prə⁶tektɪv/. 1 **Protective** means designed or intended to protect something or someone from danger or physical harm. EG *...protective clothing and equipment.* ADJ CLASSIF : USU ATTRIB

2 If someone is **protective** towards another person, they show a strong wish to keep that person safe from things that could hurt or frighten them. EG *She felt very protective towards her sister and loved her dearly.* ◊ **protectively.** EG *Rudolph sat up, an arm tightening protectively around Julie's shoulder.* ◊ **protectiveness.** EG *...parents' natural anxiety and protectiveness.* ADJ QUALIT : IF+ PREP THEN towards ◊ ADV WITH VB ◊ N UNCOUNT

protector /prə⁶tektə/, **protectors.** A **protector** is 1 someone who protects a person or thing. EG *He put himself forward as Gertrude's natural protector... ...ecologists and protectors of wildlife.* 2 a device that protects something from physical injury. EG *We had to wear cheek protectors–broad metal bands that go across the face.* N COUNT : USU WITH POSS/SUPP; N COUNT : USU MOD+N IN PL

protectorate /prə⁶tektərɪ³t/, **protectorates.** A **protectorate** is a country that is controlled and protected by a more powerful country. EG *He flew towards the British protectorate of Aden.* N COUNT ⇑ territory

protégé /prəʊtɪʒeɪ/, **protégés**; sometimes spelled **protégée** when you are referring to a woman. Someone who is the **protégé** of an older and more experienced person is helped and guided by him or her over a period of time. EG *Some of the film star's protégés and admirers were also there... ...a protégé of Lord Burlington.* N COUNT : WITH POSS ⇑ acolyte

protein /prəʊtiːn/, **proteins.** A **protein** is a substance found in meat, eggs, milk, etc. You need protein in order to grow and to have a healthy body. EG *Cassava flour is pure calories with no protein... ...protein deficiency.* N COUNT/ UNCOUNT

pro tem /prəʊ tem/. If something is happening **pro tem**, it is happening at the moment but is only temporary. ADV AFTER VB = for the time being

protest, protests, protesting, protested. The word **protest** is pronounced /prəʊtest/ when it is a noun, and /prətest/ when it is a verb. 1 If you **protest** about something or against something, you say or show publicly that you object to something that someone, especially someone in authority, is doing or is intending to do; used in British English. EG *Labour MPs took to the streets to protest against government economic policy... He was criticized for not protesting about Gerald Brook's imprisonment... I was shoved, protesting, into a side room... I protest.* V : USU+A (about/against/at) ⇑ criticize

2 If you **protest** something, you protest about it; used in American English. EG *He protested the action in a telephone call to the President.* V+O ⇑ criticize

3 If you **protest** that something is the case, you insist that it is the case, when other people think that it may not be. EG *They protested that they had never heard of him... 'You're wrong,' I protested... The mother protested her innocence.* V+REPORT-CL/ QUOTE/O

4 A **protest** is 4.1 the act of saying or showing publicly that you object to something that someone is doing or intending to do. EG *They joined in the protests against the government's proposals... There was a wave of student riots, in protest at university conditions... Fifty-five priests had signed the letter of protest.* 4.2 something that someone insists is true. EG *The police took him away, ignoring his protests that he had been with his girl-friend all evening.* N COUNT/ UNCOUNT ⇑ complaint; N COUNT ⇑ declaration = protestation

Protestant /prɒtɪ²stənt/, **Protestants.** 1 Someone or something that is **Protestant** belongs to the branches of the Christian church which separated from the Catholic church in the sixteenth century. EG *The students of Umtata High School were mostly Protestant.* ADJ CLASSIF

2 A **Protestant** is a person who belongs to a Protestant church. EG *The vast majority of the workers here are Protestants.* N COUNT ⇑ Christian

Protestantism /prɒtɪ²stəntɪzə⁰m/ is the set of Christian beliefs that are held by Protestants. N UNCOUNT ⇑ Christianity

protestation /prəʊtesteɪʃə⁰n/, **protestations.** A **protestation** is a strong declaration that something is true or not true; a formal word. EG *Despite her protestations she had been quite looking forward to the journey... ...protestations of friendship.* N COUNT = protest

protester /prətestə/, **protesters.** A **protester** is a person who protests publicly about something, for example by taking part in a demonstration. EG *The protesters surrendered to the police after about an hour.* N COUNT = demonstrator

protocol /prəʊtəkɒl/ is a system of rules about the correct way to act on important formal occasions, for example at meetings between the governments of different countries. EG *There is no protocol for enemy officers meeting like that... Beaton had to face a tricky problem of protocol.* N UNCOUNT

proton /prəʊtɒn/, **protons.** A **proton** is a particle which forms part of the nucleus of an atom and has a positive electrical charge; a technical term in physics. EG *They are bombarded by high-energy electrons, protons, and other ions.* N COUNT

protoplasm /prəʊtə⁶plæzəm/ is a colourless liquid from which plants and animals are formed; a technical term in biology. N UNCOUNT

prototype /prəʊtə⁶taɪp/, **prototypes.** A **prototype** is the first model that is made of something. The prototype is used as a basis for later improved models. EG *Funds for continued testing of the prototypes ran out last week... ...a prototype plane.* N COUNT ⇑ original

protracted /prə⁶træktɪ²d/. Something that is **protracted** lasts a long time, especially longer than usual or longer than expected. EG *She was late returning to the office after a protracted lunch... My recovery was uneventful though protracted.* ADJ QUALIT = extended, prolonged ≠ brief

protractor /prə⁶træktə/, **protractors.** A **protractor** is a flat, semicircular piece of plastic or metal which is used for measuring angles. N COUNT

protrude /prə⁶truːd/, **protrudes, protruding, protruded.** If something **protrudes** from somewhere, it sticks out; a formal word. EG *His teeth protrude like fangs... He tripped over a pair of boots protruding from under the table.* ◊ **protruding.** EG *He felt his own protruding ribs.* V : USU+A ◊ ADJ CLASSIF

protrusion /prə⁶truːʒə⁰n/, **protrusions.** A **protrusion** is something that sticks out from somewhere; a formal word. EG *...a jumble of spikes and jagged protrusions.* N COUNT ⇑ bump

protuberance /prə⁶tjuːbərəns/, **protuberances.** A **protuberance** is a rounded part that sticks out from the surface of something; a formal word. N COUNT = bulge, bump

protuberant /prə⁶tuːbərənt/. Something that is **protuberant** sticks out from a surface; a formal word. EG *...his rather protuberant ears.* ADJ QUALIT = protruding

proud /praʊd/, **prouder, proudest.** 1 If you feel **proud**, you feel glad about something that you or someone close to you has done or possesses, and think it is a good thing to have done or to possess. EG *They seemed proud of what they had accomplished... I felt proud of myself... Their country should be proud of them... I'm working-class and proud of it... We might soon be proud parents.* ◊ **proudly.** EG *She proudly displayed her collection of ornaments... He was grinning proudly, delighted with his achievement.* ADJ QUALIT ≠ ashamed ◊ ADV WITH VB

2 Someone who is **proud** 2.1 has or shows a sense of dignity and self respect which results from the fact that they refuse to behave like a servant towards other people; used showing approval. EG *He was a poor but very proud old man... They are a proud people.* ◊ **proudly.** EG *She is proudly independent of her husband.* 2.2 feels that they are superior to other people and more important than them; used showing disapproval. EG *She was too proud to apologize... She was proud and defiant... He had a proud, almost arrogant face.* ADJ QUALIT : USU +of/to-INF = dignified ≠ servile ◊ ADV; ADJ QUALIT = arrogant, vain ≠ humble

3 If you describe an object as **proud**, you mean that it stands very straight and tall and so seems more important than anything else around it; a literary use. EG *...tall poplars, their proud tops bowing gently in the wind... ...proud banners.* ADJ CLASSIF : ATTRIB ⇑ high = lofty, noble

4 Someone's **proudest possession** is a possession which they like and value more than all their other possessions. EG *The locket was my proudest possession.* PHR : POSS+PHR

5 If someone **does** you **proud**, they welcome you or treat you very well, giving you good food and lots of entertainment; an informal expression. EG *Mum did us all proud last Christmas.* PHR : VB INFLECTS

provable /pruːvəbəᵊl/. Statements and theories that are **provable** can be proved. EG *...a mathematically provable law.* — ADJ CLASSIF = verifiable

prove /pruːv/, **proves, proving, proved, proven**. **Proved** and **proven** are both used as the past participle. 1 To **prove** that something is true or correct means to show definitely that it is true or correct. EG *The autopsy proved that she had drowned... Statistics never prove anything... He has proved that his hypothesis is correct... It's been scientifically proven.* — V+O/REPORT-CL = confirm, verify ≠ disprove

2 If you **prove** someone or something to have a particular quality, you show that they have that quality. EG *I have proved it to be sound... He has proved himself untrustworthy... Our strategy was proven correct.* — V+O (NG/REFL) +C/to-INF ⇑ demonstrate

3 If someone or something **proves** to have a particular quality, they are shown to have that quality. EG *Our internal security has so far proved excellent... This information has proved useful to a great many people.* — V+C/to-INF = turn out

proven /pruːvəᵊn/. 1 **Proven** means having been definitely shown to be true or correct. EG *...our proven high standards... He is a proven liar.* — ADJ CLASSIF : USU ATTRIB = attested

2 **Proven** is also the past participle of **prove**.

provenance /prɒvɪᵊnəns/. The **provenance** of something is the place that it originally came from; a formal word. EG *There was doubt about its real provenance.* — N UNCOUNT : USU WITH POSS = origin, source

provender /prɒvɪndə/ is food for animals, especially corn and hay that is eaten by horses; an old-fashioned word. — N UNCOUNT = fodder

proverb /prɒvɜːb/, **proverbs**. A **proverb** is a short sentence that people often quote and that gives advice or tells you something about human life and problems in general. EG *There is a proverb my grandmother used to repeat: 'Half a loaf is better than no bread'... The old Jewish proverb runs 'a man is not a man until he has a son'.* — N COUNT ⇑ saying = maxim, saw

proverbial /prəvɜːbɪəl/. 1 **Proverbial** is used when you want to emphasize that what you are saying is a well-known proverb or expression, or part of one. EG *It is rather like looking for the needle in the proverbial haystack.* — ADJ CLASSIF : ATTRIB

2 Something that is **proverbial** is very well-known by a lot of people. EG *Their generosity is proverbial.* — ADJ CLASSIF ⇑ famous
◊ **proverbially**. EG *The weather there is proverbially unreliable.* — ◊ ADV+ADJ/ADV

provide /prəvaɪd/, **provides, providing, provided**. 1 If you **provide** something for someone, you give it to them or lend it to them so that they have it when they need it. EG *Most animals provide food for their young... The government cannot provide all young people with a job... Please place your litter in the receptacle provided.* — V+O, OR V+O+A (for/with) = supply

2 If something **provides** a desirable or useful feature or quality, it has or gives that feature or quality and you can benefit from it. EG *Her work provides intellectual satisfaction... There are jobs on the farm to which the machine provides no real answer... A victory next Sunday could provide the opportunity he needs... Kenya provides an example of the trend towards democratic government in Africa.* — V+O ⇑ give

3 If a law or decision **provides** that something will happen, it states that it will happen. EG *Their plans provided that control of all ships would be given to the senior admiral... The law provides that a child can be taken into care in those circumstances.* — V+REPORT-CL

4 See also **provided, providing**.

provide for. 1 If you **provide for** someone, you support them by giving them money and the things that they need. EG *Parents are expected to provide for their children... Is he provided for financially?... Our nursery provides for all the needs of very young children.* — PHRASAL VB : V+PREP, HAS PASS

2 If you **provide for** a possible future event, you take it into account when you plan or do something; a formal use. EG *We provide for the possibility of illness in the examination regulations.* — PHRASAL VB : V+PREP, HAS PASS

3 If a law or decision **provides for** something, it makes it possible; a formal use. EG *The Act provided for financial penalties to be imposed on all offenders.* — PHRASAL VB : V+PREP, HAS PASS ⇑ allow

provided /prəvaɪdɪᵈd/. If you say that something will happen **provided** or **provided that** something else happens, you mean that the first thing will happen only if the second thing also happens. EG *She was prepared to come, provided that she might bring her daughter... Children were permitted into the hall for these films, provided they sat at the back... He said he was prepared to give jobs to both of us provided I could assure him I intended to stay.* — CONJ SUBORD = on condition, as long as, providing

providence /prɒvɪdəns/ is an external force, for example a god, which is believed by some people to arrange our lives and the things that happen to us. EG *The money lender proposed that they let providence decide the matter.* — N UNCOUNT = fate

providential /prɒvɪdenʃəᵊl/. Something that is **providential** is lucky because it happens at exactly the right time but without the person it benefits having caused it in any way. EG *It had been a providential death.* ◊ **providentially**. EG *She was providentially elsewhere.* — ADJ CLASSIF = fortunate; ◊ ADV

provider /prəvaɪdə/, **providers**. A **provider** is someone or something that gives a person the things that they need or want. EG *Diana, her duties as a provider of food over, sat down in a corner... Government has become a substantial provider of manufacturing finance.* — N COUNT

providing /prəvaɪdɪŋ/. If you say that something will happen **providing** or **providing that** something else happens, you mean that the first thing will happen only if the second thing also happens. EG *It would be pleasant living in Glasgow providing you were living in a nice flat... Providing they remained at a safe distance, we would be all right.* — CONJ SUBORD = on condition, as long as, provided

province /prɒvɪns/, **provinces**. 1 A **province** is a section of country that has definite boundaries and its own administration. EG *He had a big house in the Cape Province... They want independence for Namibia, a province long administered by South Africa.* — N COUNT : ALSO IN NAMES ⇑ district

2 The **provinces** are all the parts of a country except the part where the capital is situated. EG *I recently led a tour of the provinces... ...teenage life in the provinces.* — N PLURAL : *the*+N = the regions ≠ the capital

3 If you say that a subject or activity is the **province** of a particular person, you mean that the person mentioned has a special interest in it, special knowledge about it, or special responsibility for it. EG *This will always remain the province of the specialist... Twentieth-century painting is the province of the Tate Gallery.* — N SING : WITH POSS = concern

provincial /prəvɪnʃəᵊl/, **provincials**. 1 **Provincial** means belonging to or connected with the parts of a country outside the capital. EG *...provincial newspapers... ...an English provincial theatre... ...provincial towns.* — ADJ CLASSIF : ATTRIB ⇑ regional

2 Someone or something that is **provincial** is narrow-minded and unsophisticated; used showing disapproval. EG *...a deeply provincial and conformist woman... His art is primitive and provincial.* — ADJ QUALIT = parochial

3 A **provincial** is a person who comes from the provinces of a country rather than from the capital. — N COUNT

provincialism /prəvɪnʃəlɪzəᵊm/ is a narrow outlook and lack of cultural sophistication which is supposed to exist in the provinces; used showing disapproval. EG *The provincialism of Birmingham bothered me.* — N UNCOUNT = insularity ≠ sophistication

provision /prəvɪʒəᵊn/, **provisions, provisioning, provisioned**. 1 The **provision** of something is the act of giving or lending it to someone so that they have it when they need it. EG *There are gaps in the provision of all kinds of government services... Plans have been made for nuclear war, including some provision of shelters and emergency stores of food.* — N UNCOUNT : USU +*of*

2 **Provision** for a future need is preparation for it. EG *Provision for old age was an important item in the government's plans.* — N UNCOUNT+*for*

3 If you **make provision for** something, you prepare for it by making arrangements. EG *They made provision for the defence of Britain... She did not make any provision for her children.* — PHR : VB INFLECTS = provide for

4 **Provision** is also money and facilities which have been provided, for example by the government, for people's needs. EG *Nursery provision is usually poor in country areas... Provisions for handicapped students are very good at some universities.* — N UNCOUNT/COUNT

5 **Provisions** are supplies of food and other things that are needed. EG *She had a basket of provisions on her lap... We set out with enough provisions for the day.* — N PLURAL

6 A **provision** in an agreement or law is a condition which is formally included in it. EG *The government had still to agree on the provisions of the Bill... The* — N COUNT = proviso

Act excluded from its provisions cases of death by murder.

7 If someone **is provisioned** with food or something else that is necessary, they are provided with it; a fairly formal use. EG *We were fully provisioned with fuel and water.* — V+O : USU PASS+ *with*; ⇑ supply

provisional /prəvɪʒəⁿnəl, -ʒənəⁿl/. Something that is **provisional** has been arranged or appointed for the present time, but may be changed in the future. EG *...a provisional government... There was a provisional diagnosis of schizophrenia... All these conclusions are provisional.* ◇ **provisionally**. EG *They have provisionally agreed.* — ADJ CLASSIF; ⇑ temporary; ◇ ADV WITH VB

proviso /prəvaɪzəʊ/, **provisos**. A **proviso** is a condition in an agreement. You agree to do something if this condition is fulfilled. EG *At last she consented, with the proviso that he should repay her as soon as he could... I agree, with one proviso.* — N COUNT : USU+ REPORT-CL; = provision

Provo /prɒvəʊ/, **Provos**. A **Provo** is a member of the Provisional I.R.A.; an informal word. — N COUNT

provocation /prɒvəkeɪʃəⁿn/, **provocations**. If you describe something that someone does as **provocation** or a **provocation**, you mean that you think that they did it deliberately in order to make you or someone else react in an angry or violent way. EG *They must not react to this provocation... He denounced the ceremony as a provocation designed to cause a clash between Catholics and Protestants... She will have a tantrum at the least provocation... Given sufficient provocation, I could have shot him without hesitation... ...things that any man might do under provocation.* — N UNCOUNT/ COUNT

provocative /prəvɒkətɪv/. 1 Something that is **provocative** 1.1 is intended to annoy people and make them react angrily. EG *He stuck provocative posters on boards when nobody was looking... They are being controversial and provocative just to spite us.* ◇ **provocatively**. EG *He glared at me provocatively.* — ADJ QUALIT; ≠ conciliatory, reassuring

1.2 includes a lot of controversial ideas and so makes you think or talk about interesting or exciting things. EG *We recommend Andrew Wader's provocative film 'Rough Treatment'... The question period was very challenging and provocative.* — ADJ QUALIT

3 Behaviour that is **provocative** is intended to make someone feel sexual desire. EG *...shaking her hips in a consciously provocative manner.* ◇ **provocatively**. EG *She smiled provocatively.* — ADJ QUALIT; = erotic; ◇ ADV WITH VB

provoke /prəvəʊk/, **provokes, provoking, provoked**. 1 If you **provoke** a person or animal, you deliberately annoy them and try to cause them to behave aggressively. EG *Rayos was trying to provoke them into fighting... Waving a red cape, Delgado provoked the animal to charge... They are armed and ready to shoot if provoked in the slightest way.* — V+O; ⇑ anger; ≠ placate

2 If something **provokes** a violent or unpleasant reaction to a situation, it causes it. EG *The petition provoked a storm of criticism... ...the violence provoked by the marches... ...the insult that had provoked the duel.* — V+O; = prompt

provost /prɒvəst/, **provosts**. A **provost** is 1 the head of a university college in Britain; used especially of colleges at Oxford and Cambridge. EG *...Lord Briggs, the provost of Worcester College.* 2 the chief magistrate of a Scottish borough. EG *...the Provost of Clydebank, Robert Fleming.* — N COUNT : ALSO IN TITLES; N COUNT : ALSO IN TITLES

prow /praʊ/, **prows**. The **prow** of a ship or boat is the front part of it. — N COUNT; = bow

prowess /praʊɪˢs/ is outstanding ability at doing a particular thing; a fairly formal word. EG *There are legends about his prowess as a jockey... ...her conversational prowess... ...a display of military prowess.* — N UNCOUNT; = aptitude

prowl /praʊl/, **prowls, prowling, prowled**. 1 When an animal or person **prowls**, they move around quietly and carefully, trying not to be noticed, for example when they are hunting another animal or person. EG *Tigers prowl through the forest in search of their prey.* ▸ used as a noun. EG *They set out on their nightly prowl.* — V : USU+A, OR V +O; = steal, stalk; ▸ N COUNT+ SUPP

2 If a person or animal is **on the prowl**, they are moving around quietly and carefully, and trying not to be noticed. EG *...the bark of a jackal setting out on the prowl for food.* — PHR : USED AS AN A

3 If you **prowl** around, you wander around with no specific aim or intention; an informal use. EG *We prowled around the second-hand music shops for hours... He prowled about between his office and the theatre.* — V+A; ⇑ stroll

prowl car, prowl cars. A **prowl car** is a police car that the police use for travelling around an area to see if there are any problems there; used in American English. — N COUNT; = panda car, patrol car

prowler /praʊlə/, **prowlers**. A **prowler** is an unknown man who follows women and children or hides near their houses, especially at night, in order to scare them or perhaps harm them; an informal word. — N COUNT

proximity /prɒksɪmɪti¹/. **Proximity** to a place is nearness to that place; a formal word. EG *Much of the town's attractiveness lies in its proximity to the northern cape of Japan... I had grown accustomed to the continual proximity of an animal... Keep your companion within close proximity.* — N UNCOUNT+ SUPP; = closeness

proxy /prɒksi¹/, **proxies**. 1 **Proxy** is the authority that is given to a person to act or make decisions for someone else who is not present, for example at a meeting or an election; a legal term. EG *...power of proxy.* ▸ used as an adjective. EG *There will be no proxy votes for delegations.* — N UNCOUNT; ▸ ADJ CLASSIF : ATTRIB

2 A **proxy** is a person who is given the authority to act or make decisions for someone else who is not present, for example at a meeting or an election. EG *...the role he played as a proxy for her.* — N COUNT; ⇑ delegate; = representative

3 If you do something **by proxy**, you arrange for someone else to do it for you. EG *You can create an international incident by proxy.* — PHR : USED AS AN A

prude /pru:d/, **prudes**. A **prude** is a person who is easily shocked by things that they think are rude, especially things relating to nudity or sex; used showing disapproval. EG *Come on Frank, don't be such a prude.* — N COUNT; = prig, puritan

prudence /pru:dəns/ is care and wisdom that someone shows when they are making judgements or decisions; a formal word. EG *I consider that I have acted with proper diligence and prudence.* — N UNCOUNT; = good sense; ≠ rashness

prudent /pru:dənt/. Someone who is **prudent** is sensible and careful; a formal word. EG *His wife was a prudent manager of money.* ▸ used of actions or decisions. EG *He now considered it prudent to carry a revolver... He seemed a more prudent choice.* ◇ **prudently**. EG *The offer was not rejected; acceptance was prudently postponed.* — ADJ QUALIT; ⇑ careful; ≠ daft, stupid; ◇ ADV WITH VB

prudential /pru:denʃəⁿl/ means the same as prudent; an old-fashioned and formal word. EG *He abstained, partly from prudential reasons.* — ADJ CLASSIF; = sensible; ≠ stupid

prudery /pru:dəri¹/ is prudish behaviour or attitudes; used showing disapproval. EG *This is no time for prudery.* — N UNCOUNT; = prudishness

prudish /pru:dɪʃ/. Someone who is **prudish** is easily shocked by things that they think are rude, especially things relating to nudity or sex; used showing disapproval. EG *Although he's a doctor, he is strangely prudish about sex.* ▸ used of behaviour and attitudes. EG *Her compressed lips registered a trace of prudish disapproval.* ◇ **prudishness**. EG *I was exasperated by her incredible prudishness.* — ADJ QUALIT; = priggish, prim; ◇ N UNCOUNT; = prudery

prune /pru:n/, **prunes, pruning, pruned**. 1 A **prune** is a type of dark purple plum that has been dried and can be eaten. — N COUNT; ⇑ fruit

2 When you **prune** a tree or other plant, you cut off some of the branches so that it will grow better the year after. EG *I am pruning my roses... He prunes every branch that does not bear fruit.* ◇ **pruning**. EG *The pruning should be done about midsummer.* — V+O; ⇑ trim; ◇ N UNCOUNT

3 If you **prune** something, for example a piece of writing or a play, you make it smaller, shorter, or cheaper by cutting out parts of it that are not needed. EG *If you could prune this essay it would improve it... The budgets of several departments will require pruning.* — V+O; ⇑ reduce; = cut

pruning hook, pruning hooks. A **pruning hook** is a tool like a curved knife with a hook on the end which is used for pruning trees and shrubs. — N COUNT

prurience /prʊərɪəns/ is a strong interest that someone shows in sexual matters; a formal word, used showing disapproval. — N UNCOUNT; = salaciousness; ≠ prudery

prurient /prʊərɪənt/. Someone who is **prurient** shows a strong interest in sexual matters; a formal word, used showing disapproval. EG *The girls were ogled by prurient officials.* — ADJ CLASSIF; = salacious; ≠ prudish

prussic acid /prʌsɪk æsɪd/ is an extremely poisonous acid. — N UNCOUNT

pry /praɪ/, **pries, prying, pried**. 1 When someone **pries**, they try to find out about someone else's private affairs, or look at their personal possessions, — V : IF+PREP THEN *into*; = snoop

often secretly; used showing disapproval. EG *Look, I'm not trying to pry. You don't have to tell me anything... So don't go prying into my affairs or you'll get hurt.*

2 If you **pry** something open or **pry** it away from something else, you force it open or force it to come away from the other thing; used in American English. EG *He took a screwdriver and pried open the cabinet door... He was trying to pry something out of the tractor engine... They got in through a grating that they had pried loose.* V+O+A, OR V+A = prise

3 If you **pry** information out of someone, you succeed in getting them to tell you the information, even though they are very unwilling to do this; used in American English. EG *I managed to pry out of the adults the reason for her disappearance.* V+O+A OR V+A = prise

PS, PSs. You use **PS** to introduce a further message at the end of a letter after you have signed it. EG *With love from us both, Dad. PS Mum asks me to remind you to bring back her duvet.* ▸ used to refer to such a message. EG *He added a PS.* ▸ N COUNT = postscript

psalm /sɑːm/, **psalms**. The **psalms** or **Psalms** are the 150 songs, poems, and prayers which together form the Book of Psalms in the Bible. EG *The psalm was the 137th Psalm, about the waters of Babylon.* N COUNT

psephology /sɪ²fɒləʤɪ¹/ is the study of how people vote in elections. ◊ **psephologist, psephologists**. N UNCOUNT ◊ N COUNT

pseud /sjuːd/, **pseuds**. If you say that someone is a **pseud**, you mean that they are trying to appear very knowledgeable, artistic, well-educated, etc, in a pretentious way; an informal word, used showing disapproval. EG *They're all such pseuds!* N COUNT = poser

pseudo- is added to some adjectives and nouns in order to form other adjectives and nouns. Adjectives and nouns formed in this way describe something as not being the thing that it is claimed to be. EG *...scientific→pseudo-scientific... ...Georgian→pseudo-Georgian... ...religion→pseudo-religion.* PREFIX

pseudonym /sjuːdənɪm/, **pseudonyms**. A **pseudonym** is a name which someone, especially a writer, sometimes uses as their name instead of their real name. EG *Henry Handel Richardson was the pseudonym of Ethel Florence Lindesay Richardson... Many of his best journalists wrote under pseudonyms.* N COUNT: IF+ PREP THEN *of/for* = assumed name, pen name

psych /saɪk/, **psychs, psyching, psyched**. The spellings **psyche, psyches** are also used. **psych out**. If you **psych out** your opponent in a contest, you try to make them feel less confident by behaving in a very confident or aggressive way; an informal expression. PHRASAL VB: V+O+ADV

psych up. If you **psych** yourself **up** before a contest or a difficult task, you prepare yourself for it mentally, especially by telling yourself that you can win or succeed; an informal expression. EG *I'm trying to psych myself up for the big race.* ◊ **psyched up**. EG *I'm all psyched up now.* PHRASAL VB: V+O (REFL)+ADV ◊ ADJ QUALIT: PRED

psyche /saɪki¹/, **psyches**. **1** Your **psyche** is your mind and your deepest feelings and attitudes, which form part of your nature; a formal or technical word. EG *These feelings probably lie deep in the male psyche... It is easy to understand how a person's psyche can be damaged by such experiences.* N COUNT: USU WITH MOD/POSS = being

2 See also **psych**.

psychedelic /saɪkədelɪk/. **1 Psychedelic** means relating to drugs, such as LSD, which affect your mind and cause you to think that you are seeing strange things. EG *...a psychedelic drug... ...the use of drugs in the pursuit of psychedelic experience.* ADJ CLASSIF: ATTRIB = hallucinogenic

2 Psychedelic clothing, art, etc is brightly coloured and strangely patterned in a way that is associated with the effects of psychedelic drugs. EG *He wore blue jeans and a psychedelic shirt... The walls were covered with psychedelic posters.* ADJ CLASSIF

psychiatric /saɪkɪætrɪk/ means **1** relating to the practice of psychiatry. EG *...a psychiatric hospital... ...the psychiatric profession.* **2** involving mental illness. EG *...psychiatric disorders... ...a mother with psychiatric problems.* ADJ CLASSIF: ATTRIB; ADJ CLASSIF: ATTRIB

psychiatrist /saɪkaɪətrɪst/, **psychiatrists**. A **psychiatrist** is a doctor who treats people suffering from mental illness rather than physical diseases. EG *I see a psychiatrist once a month... ...a child psychiatrist.* N COUNT = shrink

psychiatry /saɪkaɪətri¹/ is the branch of medicine concerned with the study and treatment of mental illness. N UNCOUNT

psychic /saɪkɪk/, **psychics**. **1** Someone who is **psychic** or who has **psychic** powers has strange mental powers which cannot be explained by scientists, such as being able to read the minds of other people or to see into the future. EG *'How did you know I was coming?'-'I must be psychic.'* ADJ CLASSIF

2 A **psychic** is a person who has psychic powers. N COUNT

3 Psychic also means relating to the mind rather than the body. EG *Psychologists have contended that most of the psychic damage to a child is done in the first five years.* ADJ CLASSIF = psychical ≠ physical

psychical /saɪkɪkə⁰l/ means the same as psychic. ADJ CLASSIF

psycho /saɪkəʊ/, **psychos**. **1** A **psycho** is someone whose mind and character is not normal, with the result that they do very bad things, often violent things, and do not feel sorry about the things that they do; an informal word. EG *...a raving psycho who kills just for kicks.* ▸ used as an adjective. EG *He was practically psycho.* N COUNT = psychopath ▸ ADJ CLASSIF: PRED

psycho- is added to words in order to form other words which describe or refer to things connected with the mind or with mental processes. EG *...social→psycho-social... ...linguistics→psycholinguistics... ...analyse→psychoanalyse.* PREFIX

psychoanalyse /saɪkəʊænəlaɪz/, **psychoanalyses, psychoanalysing, psychoanalysed**; also spelled **psychoanalyze** in American English. When a psychotherapist or psychiatrist **psychoanalyses** someone who is mentally ill or depressed, he or she examines or treats them using the method of psychoanalysis. V+O = analyse

psychoanalysis /saɪkəʊənælɪsɪs/ is the examination or treatment of someone who is mentally ill or depressed by asking them about their feelings and their past in order to discover hidden feelings or past experiences which may be causing their condition. N UNCOUNT = analysis

psychoanalyst /saɪkəʊænəlɪst/, **psychoanalysts**. A **psychoanalyst** is someone who treats people who are mentally ill or depressed using the method of psychoanalysis. N COUNT = analyst

psychoanalytic /saɪkəʊænəlɪtɪk/ means relating to psychoanalysis. EG *This is consistent with psychoanalytic theory.* ADJ CLASSIF

psychoanalyze /saɪkəʊænəlaɪz/. See **psychoanalyse**.

psychological /saɪkə⁰lɒʤɪkəl/. **1 Psychological** qualities, effects, etc are concerned with a person's mind and thoughts rather than, for example, with their body or with the social or economic aspects of their life. EG *Are there important psychological differences between the two sexes?... Such an experience may have long-term psychological effects... His dislike of the course may prove to be a psychological barrier he cannot overcome.* ◊ **psychologically**. EG *She was tough, both physically and psychologically.* ADJ CLASSIF = mental ≠ physical ◊ ADV

2 Psychological also means relating to psychology. EG *...psychological tests.* ADJ CLASSIF: ATTRIB

3 When you refer to **the psychological moment**, you are referring to the time at which you think someone is most likely to react favourably to a suggestion, request, or course of action. EG *I waited for the psychological moment to tell Colin about the car.* PHR: USED AS O

psychological warfare consists of attempts to make your enemy lose confidence, give up hope, or feel afraid, so that you can win. N UNCOUNT ↑ strategy

psychologist /saɪkɒləʤɪst/, **psychologists**. A **psychologist** is a person who studies the human mind and tries to explain why people behave in the way that they do. EG *...Dr Piaget, the Swiss child psychologist... This behaviour should not be confused with what psychologists call 'role-playing.'* N COUNT ↑ scientist

psychology /saɪkɒləʤɪ¹/. **1 Psychology** is **1.1** the scientific study of the human mind and the reasons for people's behaviour. EG *...a degree in psychology... ...the psychology of perception.* **1.2** the ability to understand the way that people think and feel so that you know the right thing to say to someone, or the right time to say it, in order to get them to react or behave in the way that you want them to. EG *'I told him just before he went on his holidays.'-'That was good psychology.'* N UNCOUNT; N UNCOUNT

2 The **psychology** of a particular person, type of person, or group is the kind of mind that they have, which causes them to think or behave in the way that they do. EG *...the psychology of the travelling salesman... ...research on mob psychology.* N UNCOUNT+SUPP ↑ character

psychopath /sa͟ɪkə⁶pæθ/, **psychopaths**. A **psychopath** is someone whose mind and character is not normal, with the result that they do very bad things, often violent things, and do not feel sorry about the things that they do. N COUNT = psycho

psychopathic /sa͟ɪkə⁶pæ͟θɪk/. Someone who is **psychopathic** is a psychopath. EG *...a psychopathic murderer.* ▸ used of someone's behaviour or mind. EG *...psychopathic acts.* ADJ CLASSIF : ATTRIB

psychosis /saɪkə͟ʊsɪs/, **psychoses**. **Psychosis** or a **psychosis** is madness of a severe kind; a medical term. EG *It is not uncommon for the psychosis to recur with every pregnancy.* N UNCOUNT/COUNT

psychosomatic /sa͟ɪkə⁶sə⁶mæ͟tɪk/. A **psychosomatic** illness is a physical illness which occurs because the patient is very worried, frightened, or unhappy. ADJ CLASSIF

psychotherapist /sa͟ɪkəʊθe͟rəpɪst/, **psychotherapists**. A **psychotherapist** is a person who treats people who are mentally ill or depressed using psychotherapy. N COUNT

psychotherapy /sa͟ɪkəʊθe͟rəpi¹/ is the use of psychological methods to treat people who are mentally ill or depressed, rather than using physical methods such as drugs or surgery. EG *...psychotherapy sessions.* N UNCOUNT ⇑ treatment

psychotic /saɪkɒ͟tɪk/, **psychotics**. **1** Someone who is **psychotic** is mad; a medical term. EG *His eldest son had become psychotic.* ▸ used of behaviour and feelings. EG *...his almost psychotic hatred of women.* ADJ CLASSIF
2 A **psychotic** is someone who is mad; a medical term. N COUNT

pt, pts. **pt** can also be used as the plural form. **pt** is a written abbreviation for 'pint' or 'pints' when you use it after a number. EG *...1 pt warm water.* N PART : USU NUM+N

PT /pi: ti͟:/ is the same as physical training. EG *...a PT instructor.* N UNCOUNT = PE

PTA /pi: ti: e͟ɪ/, **PTA's**. A **PTA** is a parent-teacher association. EG *We've even joined the PTA.* N COUNT : ALSO IN NAMES

Pte is a written abbreviation for 'Private' when it is used before a person's name as a military title. EG *...Pte John Ward.* N IN TITLES

pterodactyl /te͟rədæktɪl/, **pterodactyls**. A **pterodactyl** was a flying reptile that existed in prehistoric times. N COUNT ⇑ dinosaur

PTO /pi: ti: ə͟ʊ/ is a written abbreviation for 'please turn over'. It is written at the bottom of a page to indicate that there is more writing on the other side. CONVENTION

pub /pʌb/, **pubs**. A **pub** is a building, especially in Britain, Ireland, and Australia, where people can have drinks, especially alcoholic drinks, and talk to their friends. EG *We used to go drinking in a pub called the Soldier's Arms... He was in the pub most evenings and always offered us drinks.* ▸ also used to refer to the people in a pub. EG *Keep your voice down! The whole pub can hear you!* N COUNT = public house; ▸ N SING

pub crawl, pub crawls. A **pub crawl** is an activity in which someone goes from one pub to another having drinks in each one; an informal expression, used mainly in British English. EG *I used to go on pub crawls with him every weekend.* N COUNT ⇑ tour

puberty /pju͟:bəti¹/ is the stage in a person's life when he or she becomes physically able to have children and starts to become physically like an adult. EG *...a schoolboy who has just reached the age of puberty.* N UNCOUNT = adolescence

pubescent /pju:be͟sənt/. A **pubescent** girl or boy has reached the stage in their life when they are becoming physically like an adult. ADJ CLASSIF : ATTRIB

pubic /pju͟:bɪk/ means relating to the area just above a person's genitals. EG *...pubic hair.* ADJ CLASSIF : ATTRIB

public /pʌ͟blɪk/. **1** You can refer to people in general, or to all the people in a particular country or community, as the **public**. EG *All members of the public are welcome... The gardens are open to the public... The general public was not interested in his kind of music... They're not giving the public what they want.* N SING : the+N, VB CAN BE SING OR PL
2 You can refer to a particular set of people in a country who share a common interest, activity, or characteristic as a particular kind of **public**. EG *His books are read by a reasonably large public in France and Italy... ...literature available to the general reading public... I have my public to consider.* N SING WITH DET +SUPP : VB CAN BE SING OR PL ⇑ group
3 Public is **3.1** used of things that belong or relate to the people in a country or community as a whole. EG *The campaigners claim to have attracted significant public support... The problem was how to create and sustain public interest... This pollution is a hazard to public health.* ADJ CLASSIF : ATTRIB **3.2** used of things that belong or relate to the government or the state, or that are done by it for the people. EG *The government is reducing public spending... ...public officials.* ◊ **publicly**. EG *...a publicly owned company.* ADJ CLASSIF : ATTRIB ≠ private; ◊ ADV WITH VB **3.3** used of buildings, services, facilities, etc which are provided for everyone to use, and which are usually owned by the government or local authority and run or looked after by it. EG *Both of these books can be obtained from the Public Library... ...public transport... ...public telephones... The public footpath is on the other bank.* ADJ CLASSIF : ATTRIB ≠ private **3.4** used of people or their activities that are known about by many other people because they are often mentioned on television, in newspapers, etc. EG *...famous and highly respected public figures... Well-known people from all sections of public life give the scheme their support... ...the contrast between Hearst's public image and his private demeanour.* ADJ CLASSIF : ATTRIB ≠ private
4 A **public** statement, action, or event is made or done with members of the public present or able to know about it. EG *No public announcement had yet been made... Her very last public appearance was at the Old Vic... He resisted demands for a public enquiry... We hold weekly public meetings.* ▸ used of a speaker or performer. EG *...public speakers addressing large groups of people.* ◊ **publicly**. EG *I am going to say what I think of him openly and publicly.* ADJ CLASSIF : ATTRIB; ◊ ADV WITH VB ≠ privately
● If you say or do something **in public**, you say or do it when a group of other people are present, especially people you do not know. EG *He repeated in public what he had said in private.* ● PHR : USED AS AN A = publicly ≠ privately
5 If a fact is made **public** or becomes **public**, it becomes known to everyone rather than being kept secret. EG *The cause of death was not made public... Only rarely does he let his own views become public.* ADJ CLASSIF : PRED ≠ secret
6 A **public** place is one where people can come and go freely and where you can easily be seen and heard. EG *Please understand, sir, this is a very public place... Can we talk somewhere less public?* ADJ QUALIT ≠ private
7 If someone is **in the public eye**, they are known about by everyone and are often mentioned on television, in newspapers, etc. If they disappear **from the public eye**, they are no longer known about by everyone and are no longer mentioned. EG *Anders vanished from the public eye.* PHR : USED AS AN A
8 If a company **goes public**, it starts selling its shares to the public. EG *The company is going public next month.* PHR : VB INFLECTS

public address system, public address systems. A **public address system** is an electrical system including a microphone, amplifier, and loudspeakers which is used so that someone's voice, or music, can be heard by everyone in a large building, ship, etc. EG *The captain spoke to the passengers over the public address system.* N COUNT

publican /pʌ͟blɪkən/, **publicans**. A **publican** is a person who owns or manages a pub; a rather old-fashioned word in British English. N COUNT

publication /pʌ͟blɪke͟ɪʃə⁰n/, **publications**. **1** The **publication** of a book, magazine, article, etc is the act of printing it and sending it to shops to be sold. EG *...some years after the publication of his book... Several of her articles have already been accepted for publication... The book was sold out on the day of publication.* N UNCOUNT ⇑ issue
2 A **publication** is a book, magazine, etc that has been published. EG *...a respected scholar with a long and impressive list of publications to his name.* N COUNT
3 The **publication** of information or an opinion is the act of making it known to the public; a fairly formal use. EG *...the Government's annual publication of social trends.* N UNCOUNT ⇑ announcement

public bar, public bars. A **public bar** is a room in a British pub where the furniture is plain and where the prices of drinks are lower than in other bars. N COUNT ≠ lounge bar, saloon bar

public company, public companies. A **public company** is a company whose shares can be bought by the general public. N COUNT

public convenience, public conveniences. A **public convenience** is a toilet that is provided in a public place for everyone to use; used in British English. N COUNT

public enterprise is the ownership and management of industries and companies by the state rather than by individual people. N UNCOUNT

public house, public houses. A **public house** is a pub; used in British English. EG *...the customers of the public house called the Robin Hood.* N COUNT

publicise /pʌblɪsaɪz/. See **publicize**.

publicist /pʌblɪsɪst/, **publicists**. A **publicist** is a person who publicizes things, especially as a job in advertising or journalism. EG *...the Labour Party's publicists.* N COUNT ⇑ advertiser

publicity /pʌblɪsɪti[1]/ is **1** information or actions intended to attract the public's attention to someone or something. EG *There was some advance publicity for the book... We shall have a great publicity campaign.* N UNCOUNT ⇑ exposure **2** the public's attention and interest. EG *She sought out publicity... I refuse to have you stirring up a lot of publicity about a foolish thing like this.* N UNCOUNT

publicity agent, publicity agents. A **publicity agent** is a person whose job is to make sure that a large number of people know about an actor, show, etc so that the actor, show, etc is successful. N COUNT

publicize /pʌblɪsaɪz/, **publicizes, publicizing, publicized**; also spelled **publicise**. If you **publicize** a fact, event, campaign, etc, you make it widely known to the public. EG *This action drove him to make a much publicised attack on the Home Secretary... His programme for reform was well publicised in his newspapers.* V+O/REPORT-CL ⇑ advertise ≠ suppress

public nuisance, public nuisances. **1** If someone causes a **public nuisance**, they do something that harms members of the public and is illegal; a legal term. EG *...citizens who are behaving abnormally or causing a public nuisance.* N SING : a+N

2 You say that a person is a **public nuisance** when they annoy and bother other people. N COUNT ⇑ nuisance

public opinion is the opinion or attitude of the public regarding a particular matter. EG *The politicians have to respond to public opinion... Public-opinion polls showed Grant trailing Murray.* N UNCOUNT

public relations is **1** the part of an organization's work that is concerned with obtaining the public's approval for what it does. EG *Mrs Patel had shown a flair for public relations from the beginning... Sotheby's public relations people embarked on an ambitious programme.* N UNCOUNT ⇑ advertising = PR **2** the state of the relationship between an organization and the public. EG *It's good for public relations.* N PLURAL

public relations officer, public relations officers. A **public relations officer** is a person who is employed by an organization to try to make the public approve of what the organization does. EG *He's a public relations officer for the firm.* N COUNT

public school, public schools. **1** In Britain, a **public school** is a private, independent school that provides general secondary education which parents have to pay for. The pupils often live there in term-time. EG *He wanted to send his children to exclusive public schools.* N COUNT/UNCOUNT ≠ state school

2 In the USA, Australia, and some other parts of the world, a **public school** is a local school that is supported financially by the government and provides free education. N COUNT/UNCOUNT

public sector. The **public sector** is the part of a country's economy which is controlled or supported financially by the government. EG *...the giant institutions of the private and public sector.* N SING : the+N ≠ private sector

public-spirited. Someone who is **public-spirited** tries to help the community that they belong to; used showing approval. EG *She's a public-spirited woman who takes part in politics.* ADJ QUALIT ≠ selfish

public works are buildings, roads, etc that are built by the government for the public. EG *...by providing employment in public works projects.* N PLURAL

publish /pʌblɪʃ/, **publishes, publishing, published**. **1** When a company **publishes** a book, magazine, etc, it has copies of it printed, which are then sent to shops and sold. EG *Dr Johnson's dictionary was published in 1755... ...the Save and Prosper Book of Money, published by Collins... The group began publishing its own magazine called Worker's Power.* V OR V+O ⇑ print = issue

2 When the people in charge of a newspaper or magazine **publish** a piece of writing, they print it in their newspaper or magazine. EG *The Times would never publish any letter I sent in... I was thrilled to have an article published in the magazine.* V+O

3 If someone **publishes** a book or an article that they have written, they arrange to have it published. EG *Professor John Maynard Smith has just published a book on evolution... He has published quite a lot of articles.* V+O

4 If you **publish** information or an opinion, you make it known to the public by having it printed in a newspaper, magazine, etc. EG *He has just been sentenced to a long prison term for publishing his views... The latest figures for bank lending are to be published tomorrow.* V+O ⇑ publicize = broadcast

publisher /pʌblɪʃə/, **publishers**. A **publisher** is a person or a company that publishes books. EG *Poindexter, my publisher, had commissioned me to write a third novel... The publishers of the book are Collins.* N COUNT

publishing /pʌblɪʃɪŋ/ is the profession of publishing books. EG *I'd like a career in publishing... He had been a proof reader for a small publishing firm.* N UNCOUNT

publishing house, publishing houses. A **publishing house** is a company which publishes books. N COUNT = publishers

puce /pjuːs/. Something that is **puce** is a dark purple colour. EG *His complexion was puce in colour.* ▸ used as a noun. EG *The colours of the university are indigo and puce.* ADJ COLOUR ▸ N UNCOUNT

puck /pʌk/, **pucks**. The **puck** in the game of ice hockey is the small rubber disc that is used instead of a ball. N COUNT

pucker /pʌkə/, **puckers, puckering, puckered**. **1** When a part of your face **puckers** or when you **pucker** it, it becomes folded and creased because you are frowning, trying not to cry, etc. EG *His face puckered, the tears leapt from his eyes... He sucked air through thick puckered lips.* V-ERG ⇑ screw up

2 If something such as fabric **puckers**, it becomes wrinkled or creased, instead of lying smooth and flat. V-ERG
◇ **puckered**. EG *Some of the seams were puckered.* ◇ ADJ QUALIT

puckish /pʌkɪʃ/. Someone who is **puckish** is mischievous and enjoys playing tricks on people; a rather old-fashioned word. ▸ also used of behaviour or expressions. EG *...a puckish grin... ...a puckish sense of fun.* ADJ QUALIT = impish

pud /pʊd/, **puds**. **Pud** is the same as pudding; an informal word. EG *What's for pud today?* N COUNT/UNCOUNT

pudding /pʊdɪŋ/, **puddings**. **1** A **pudding** is **1.1** a cooked sweet food made with suet, rice, or flour, fat, and eggs. It is usually served hot and has the shape of the bowl that it was cooked in. EG *...steamed pudding... ...a treacle pudding.* ● See also **Christmas Pudding, plum pudding**. N COUNT/UNCOUNT ⇑ dish **1.2** the sweet course of a meal which is usually served after the main course; a rather informal use in British English. EG *What are we having for pudding?* N UNCOUNT/COUNT ⇑ dessert = afters

2 See also **black pudding, Yorkshire pudding**.

pudding basin, pudding basins. A **pudding basin** is a deep round bowl that is used in the kitchen, especially for mixing or for cooking puddings; used in British English. N COUNT

puddle /pʌdə[0]l/, **puddles**. A **puddle** is a small shallow pool of liquid that has spread on the ground or the floor. You can see puddles of water on roads and paths after it has been raining. EG *The road was filled with puddles from the rain... It was dark and damp and there were little puddles on the muddy floor.* N COUNT

puerile /pjʊəraɪl/. You describe behaviour as **puerile** when it is silly and childish. EG *She had me doing things I thought were puerile and degrading... His newspapers mounted a puerile campaign against him.* ADJ QUALIT = juvenile

puff /pʌf/, **puffs, puffing, puffed**. For paragraph 10, the noun is pronounced /pʊf/ and can be spelled **poof** or **pouf**. **1** If someone **puffs** a cigarette or pipe or if they **puff** away at it, they suck smoke into their mouth and blow it out again. EG *She looked calm and relaxed, puffing her cigarette... He puffed at his cigar... He puffed on his pipe with a little smile... George would light up and puff away for a while.* V+O, OR V+A

2 If someone takes a **puff** of a cigarette, they suck smoke into their mouth and blow it out again. EG *She raised the cigarette to her lips, intending to take a puff.* N COUNT : IF SING USU a+N = drag

3 If you **are puffing**, you are breathing loudly and quickly with your mouth open because you are tired or out of breath after a lot of physical effort. EG *We lugged the branch underneath, panting and puffing.* ● to **huff and puff**: see **huff**. ▸ used as a noun. EG *Her breath came in puffs and gasps.* V : USU CONT = pant ▸ N COUNT

4 If you haven't got any **puff** or if you are **out of puff**, N UNCOUNT, OR you are finding it difficult to breathe, usually because you have been doing something energetic; an informal use. EG *He spoke with difficulty at first because he hadn't got his puff back.* PHR: USED AS AN A = breath

5 A **puff** of air, smoke, dust, etc is a small, quick rush of it blown out from somewhere and often making small clouds. N COUNT: USU+ *of* ⇑ gust

6 If something such as smoke or steam **puffs** or **is puffed** out into the air, it is blown out in small clouds. EG *Can you see the steam puffing out at the top?... ...puffing clouds of smoke into the air.* V-ERG: USU+A *(out)*

7 If a vehicle **is puffing** along, it is moving while blowing out smoke or steam. EG *The train puffed slowly through the tunnel.* V+A

8 If a person **is puffing** along, he or she is walking or running while breathing loudly and quickly. EG *We saw him puffing up the hill behind us.* V+A

9 A **puff** is also a cake which is made from hollow puff pastry and is filled with cream, fruit, or jam. EG *...cream puffs.* N COUNT: AFTER N

10 If someone refers to a man as a **puff**, they are saying in an offensive way that he is a homosexual. N COUNT: ALSO VOC

11 See also **puffed**.

puff out. When something **puffs out**, it becomes larger and rounder, especially by being filled with air. EG *Their chests were puffed out like angry swans... They puffed out their cheeks.* PHRASAL VB: V-ERG+ADV ⇑ expand

puff up. If part of your body **puffs up** as a result of an injury, it becomes swollen. EG *Small areas on their arms or legs would puff up.* See also **puffed up**. PHRASAL VB: V+ADV ⇑ expand = swell

puffball /pʌfbɔ:l/, **puffballs**. A **puffball** is a fungus which bursts to release a cloud of spores when it is ripe. N COUNT

puffed /pʌft/. 1 If a part of your body is **puffed** or **puffed up**, it is swollen because of injury. EG *He was sore all over and his hands were puffed... ...her left eye is all puffed up.* ADJ QUALIT: PRED ⇑ enlarged

2 If you are **puffed** or **puffed out**, you are breathing with difficulty because you have been using a lot of energy; an informal use. EG *I was a bit puffed because it was quite a long way from the pub... By the time I got to the top I was pretty well puffed out.* ADJ QUALIT: PRED ⇑ tired

puffed sleeve, puffed sleeves. A blouse or dress with **puffed sleeves** has sleeves which form a raised round shape at the shoulder where the edge of the material is gathered. N COUNT

puffed up. Someone who is **puffed up** is very proud of themselves because they think that they are very important; used showing disapproval. EG *I was expecting that he would return all puffed up with himself... We had to listen to puffed-up males telling their stories of bravery.* ADJ QUALIT = boastful, conceited

puffin /pʌfɪn/, **puffins**. A **puffin** is a black and white bird with a large, brightly-coloured beak, which lives by the sea in northern areas of the world. N COUNT

puff pastry is a type of pastry which is very light and flaky. N UNCOUNT

puffy /pʌfi[1]/, **puffier, puffiest**. Something that is **puffy** has a round, swollen appearance. EG *One eye was a slit in his puffy cheek... Around midday, the fog lifted and puffy clouds floated across the sky.* ADJ QUALIT

pug /pʌg/, **pugs**. A **pug** is a small, fat dog with short hair and a flat nose. N COUNT

pugnacious /pʌgneɪʃəs/. Someone who is **pugnacious** is always ready to quarrel or start a fight; a fairly formal word. EG *Sonny was a strong, stocky boy, pugnacious and quick to take offence... Fassler searched him, looking pugnacious and determined.* ADJ QUALIT ⇑ aggressive = argumentative

◊ **pugnacity** /pʌgnæsɪti[1]/. EG *'So what?' he said, with his usual pugnacity.* ◊ N UNCOUNT

pug nose, pug noses. A **pug nose** is a short, flat nose. N COUNT

puke /pju:k/, **pukes, puking, puked**; a very informal word. 1 If someone **pukes**, they vomit. EG *The baby puked a couple more times.* V

2 **Puke** is the same as vomit. EG *I wiped the puke off my clothes.* N UNCOUNT

pull /pʊl/, **pulls, pulling, pulled**. 1 When you **pull** something, 1.1 you hold it firmly and use force in order to move it towards you or to remove it from somewhere. EG *The women's job was to pull the grass and weeds out of the corn... She pulled Paul's hair so hard that he yelled... He hoisted the rope over the branch, pulled with all his strength and down it came... She pulled him down on the couch next to her... The dog sniffed at Marsha's bags. The guard pulled her away... The wire was too strong and pulled a hook out of the floor.* ▸ used as a noun. EG *Give a pull now as I tell you.* V OR V+O: USU+A = yank ≠ push ▸ N COUNT

1.2 you hold it and move it towards you or out of its previous position. EG *I pulled down a dull-looking book from an upper shelf... He pulled forward a chair.* V+O+A = draw

2 When a vehicle, animal, or person **pulls** something such as a cart or piece of machinery, they are attached to it or hold it, so that it moves along behind them when they move forward. EG *Farmers were driving open carts pulled by donkeys... The trailer had come in the night before, pulled by a brand-new Landrover.* V+O = draw ≠ push

3 If you **pull** a part of your body or **pull** in a particular direction, you move that part of your body or move with force, especially when someone is holding you and you do not want them to. EG *'Let go of me,' she said, and pulled her arm savagely out of his grasp... He tried to tilt up her chin so he could kiss her, but she pulled away fiercely... The baby began to cry angrily and pulled her head back.* V+A, OR V+O+A = draw

4 If you **pull** yourself out of a place or **pull** yourself away from it, you hold onto something and use force to move the rest of your body out of the place or away from it. EG *Ralph pulled himself out of the water... They managed to pull themselves clear.* V+O (REFL)+A = drag

5 If you **pull** clothing or coverings round you, you wrap them round yourself quickly. If you **pull** clothes on or off, you take them on or off quickly. EG *The bitter east wind made the girl pull her black woollen scarf tightly round her neck... He got back into the warm bed, pulled the blankets up around him... He started to pull on his tattered shorts... He pulled off his shirt.* V+O+A

6 If you **pull** at something, you hold it and move it towards you before you let it go again. EG *They walked along the path to the bridge in silence, pulling at the tall summer grasses... 'Come home now, Jim,' she said, pulling at his sleeve.* V+A *(at)* = tug at

7 When you **pull** a curtain or blind, you move it across a window or other opening in order to cover or uncover the opening. EG *She slammed the window down and pulled the blind... She goes across to the window and pulls back the curtain.* V+O: USU+A = draw

8 When you **pull** a switch, handle, trigger, or other device, you move it towards you or downwards in order to operate a piece of equipment or machine. EG *He pulls the string of the switch... I shut my eyes involuntarily when I pulled the trigger.* V+O ≠ push

9 If you **pull** something apart or if you **pull** it to pieces, 9.1 you break it or take it apart without much care. EG *The chances are that if you pull apart one of the calculators you won't get it back together again... Try and stop the cat pulling the Christmas tree to bits.* V+O+A

9.2 you criticize it severely. EG *He pulled my essay to pieces.* V+O+A = tear

10 When a person **pulls** a gun or other weapon on someone or something, he or she takes out the gun or weapon and prepares to use it against them; an informal use. EG *The cop pulled his pistol and threatened to shoot the dog.* V+O: IF+PREP THEN *on* = draw

11 When you **pull** at an oar, you hold it and force it to move through the water so that the boat you are travelling in moves forward. EG *He let his oars sink into the water and commenced pulling with long furious strokes... In this position, each pulling at a separate oar, they rounded the point.* ▸ used as a noun. EG *Two more pulls and he was clear of the wreck.* V: USU+A *(at)* ▸ N COUNT = stroke

12 When someone **pulls** a pint, they move a handle which causes beer to flow from a large container, through a pipe, and into a glass, in order to serve a customer. If you say that someone **pulls** pints as a job, you mean that they work in a pub. V+O = draw

13 If you **pull** something to left or right or if it **pulls** to left or right, it moves to one side rather than going straight. If you **pull** to left or right when you are driving a car, you turn the car to the left or right. to move or to move it towards one side, rather than going straight. EG *The wheel pulled toward the right... The ball pulled away and was wide... Geraint pulled sharply to the left... She pulled her car around to the side of the station.* V+A, OR V+O+A = veer

14 If you **pull** ahead of or **pull** away from other people, you gradually become more skilful or successful than they are. EG *He's pulling way ahead of the others in all the science subjects.* V+A

15 When an engine or vehicle **pulls**, it works hard and uses a lot of effort in order to operate. EG *They all have a 2.5 litre, four-cylinder engine which pulls like a steam engine at low speeds... The vehicles pulled and wheezed up the hill.*
V; ⇑ strain

16 If something **pulls** you or your attitudes, thoughts, or actions, it strongly influences you in a particular way. EG *Rage had pulled my instincts in the very same direction... It pulls me back to reality at regular intervals.*
V+O : USU+A; = draw

17 To **pull** people means to attract them and their support or interest; an informal use. EG *It's something that should really pull the punters... He was much interested in the number of votes she would pull.*
V+O; ⇑ get; = draw, win; ≠ lose

18 If you **pull** for someone or on behalf of them, you use your influence to try to help them, especially in order to get them a job or promotion; an informal use. EG *A lot of officers here have been pulling for you.*
V+A *(for/on)*; = put in a word for

19 If someone or something **is pulled** off or **pulled** out of somewhere, they are removed from use or work and are no longer available; a fairly informal use. EG *The buses were pulled off the street after a van was booby-trapped... Telephone operators were pulled out on strike.*
V+O+A : USU PASS; = withdraw

20 If you **pull** a muscle or tendon, you injure it by straining it. EG *Despite their pulled muscles they managed to finish the race.*
V+O

21 If you **pull** at or on a cigarette or pipe, you take a long, deep breath when it is in your mouth. EG *'Oh, I'm not complaining,' Arnold said, pulling at his cigarette.* ▸ used as a noun. EG *Her husband took a long slow pull at his cigarette.*
V+A *(at/on)*; = draw; ▸ N COUNT; = draw

22 If you **pull** a trick on someone, you deceive or trick them in some way; an informal use. EG *'That's a lousy trick to pull,' he called... I think somebody's pulled a fast one here... Don't try to pull anything.*
V+O; = play

23 When someone **pulls** someone else, they succeed in attracting them sexually and having sex with them; an informal use.
V+O

24 A **pull** is also **24.1** a climb up a hill which involves a lot of effort and takes a long time. EG *It's a long pull up to the summit.* **24.2** a strong physical force which is difficult to resist and which causes things to move in a particular direction. EG *He swam towards the centre of the river, feeling the pull of the current.* **24.3** an emotional force which influences your behaviour in a particular way and which is difficult to resist. EG *The pull of your career remains strong... He felt a strange pull to visit his old house again.*
N COUNT : USU SING; N COUNT+SUPP : USU SING; = tug; N COUNT+SUPP : USU SING; ⇑ influence

25 If you have **pull**, you have power and are able to influence people. EG *Their economic power gives them political and social pull with local government and bank officials.*
N UNCOUNT; ⇑ strength; = weight

26 If you say to someone **'Pull the other one, it's got bells on'** or **'Pull the other one'**, you mean that you do not believe what they have just said and that they must be joking; an informal expression. EG *'Have you heard, we might get new contracts.'–'Go on, pull the other one.'–'No, seriously, I heard them discussing it this morning.'*
CONVENTION; = come off it, get away

27 The word **pull** also occurs in a large number of expressions, which are explained under other words in this dictionary. ● to **pull a face**: see **face**. ● to **pull** someone's **leg**: see **leg**. ● to **pull out all the stops**: see **stop**. ● to **pull punches**: see **punch**. ● to **pull rank**: see **rank**. ● to **pull** your **socks up**: see **sock**. ● to **pull strings**: see **string**. ● to **pull** your **weight**: see **weight**.

pull apart. **1** If you **pull apart** two or more people or animals that are fighting, you separate them, using force. EG *I rushed in and tried to pull the dogs apart.* **2** To **pull** someone **apart** means to cause them great mental suffering. EG *Their rows are enough to pull that kid apart.*
PHRASAL VB : ORDER V+O+ADV; PHRASAL VB : ORDER V+O+ADV; = tear apart

pull away. **1** When a vehicle **pulls away** or when its driver **pulls away**, the vehicle starts moving forward after being stationary. EG *The bus pulled away... The lights changed and I pulled away.*
PHRASAL VB : V+ADV; = draw away, pull off

2 If something **pulls away** from something else, it becomes separated from it. EG *The upper of the shoe had pulled away from the sole.*
PHRASAL VB : V+ADV+A *(from)*

pull back. **1** When an army **pulls back** or **is pulled back**, it leaves its position and retreats to a place which it can defend more easily, or it goes back to its own territory. EG *But the enemy is not willing to pull back from any of its present positions.*
PHRASAL VB : V-ERG+ADV; = withdraw

2 If you **pull back** from something, you decide not to proceed with it, because you are afraid of what might happen if you do. EG *At the last moment Gwyneth pulled back.*
PHRASAL VB : V+ADV; ⇑ withdraw

pull down. **1** If you **pull down** a building or other structure, you destroy it completely by removing or breaking the bricks, stones, etc which it is made of. EG *Why did they pull all those houses down?... It was a mistake not to pull down the barriers.*
PHRASAL VB : V+O+ADV; ⇑ demolish; = tear down; ≠ put up

2 If something **pulls** you **down**, **2.1** it makes you physically weaker than usual and depressed; an informal expression. EG *That bout of flu pulled him down quite a lot.* **2.2** it causes you to fail at something, or to do badly; an informal expression. EG *It was his mother that really pulled him down.*
PHRASAL VB : V+O+ADV; ⇑ weaken; = drag down; PHRASAL VB : V+O+ADV; = drag down

pull in. **1** When a vehicle or its driver **pulls in** somewhere, for example at a car park or garage, the driver drives the vehicle into the place and stops it there. EG *I pulled in for gas...*
PHRASAL VB : V+ADV, USU+A; ≠ pull out

2 When a train **pulls in** at a station, it arrives at the station and stops. EG *The London train pulled in to the branch line station.*
PHRASAL VB : V+ADV, USU+A; ≠ pull out

3 When the police **pull** someone **in**, they go to find them and arrest them; an informal expression in British English.
PHRASAL VB : V+O+ADV

4 If you **pull in** a particular amount of money, especially a large amount, you earn it; an informal expression. EG *He's pulling in about twenty thousand a year.*
PHRASAL VB : V+O+ADV; = rake in

5 To **pull** people **in** means to attract them in large numbers. EG *Higher wages in the cities pull in the rural poor.*
PHRASAL VB : V+O+ADV; = draw

6 See also **pull-in**.

pull off. **1** When a vehicle or its driver **pulls off** the road, the vehicle turns out of the road and into a parking space, side road, etc. EG *We pulled off into a filling station... I pulled off the road and stopped to see what was wrong.*
PHRASAL VB : V+ADV/PREP

2 When a vehicle or its driver **pulls off**, the vehicle starts moving forward after being stationary. EG *The car pulled off. 'Where are we going?' I asked brightly.*
PHRASAL VB : V+ADV; = draw away, pull away

3 If you **pull** something **off**, you succeed in doing something which is very difficult. EG *She had succeeded, triumphantly: she had pulled it off.*
PHRASAL VB : V+O+ADV; ⇑ accomplish; = carry off

pull out. **1** When a vehicle or its driver **pulls out** from a place, the driver drives the vehicle out of the place and into the road and then drives away. You also say that the vehicle or the driver **pulls out** when the driver drives the vehicle into another traffic lane, especially in order to overtake another vehicle. EG *He climbed in, they pulled out, and Sylvia waved... He pulled out to overtake the lorry and narrowly missed a car coming the other way.*
PHRASAL VB : V+ADV; = move out

2 When a train **pulls out** of a station, it leaves the station. EG *We watched from the bridge as the train pulled out of the station.*
PHRASAL VB : V+ADV; = draw out

3 If you **pull out** of a difficult situation or if someone **pulls** you **out** of it, you get out of it, or they help you to get out of it. EG *It's going to take us even longer to pull out of this particular recession... He said that we must pull the country out of this 'economic calamity'.*
PHRASAL VB : V-ERG+ADV

4 If you **pull out** of an activity, situation, or business deal, you withdraw from it. EG *You have to pay over a 10% deposit which you lose if you pull out before completion... He pulled his party out of the coalition.*
PHRASAL VB : V-ERG+ADV

5 If an army **pulls out** of a place or region or if it **is pulled out**, it leaves the place or region and no longer operates there. EG *Troops had begun to pull out of the area... The Prime Minister has reaffirmed his intention of pulling all 10,000 of them out by the end of June.*
PHRASAL VB : V-ERG+ADV; = withdraw

6 If you **pull out** something such as information or ideas from a lot of other things, you separate them from those things so that you can use them on their own. EG *The computer does a search through its file and pulls out all information relevant to that word.*
PHRASAL VB : V+O+ADV; = extract, take out

7 See also **pull-out**.

pull over. **1** When a vehicle or its driver **pulls over**, the driver drives the vehicle closer to the side of the road, either in order to stop the vehicle or to allow another vehicle to overtake. EG *Pull over, Oliver. Stop the car.*
PHRASAL VB : V+ADV

2 See also **pullover**.

pull round. When you **pull round**, **1** you become conscious again after you have been made unconscious. EG *She's beginning to pull round.* **2** you
PHRASAL VERB : V+ADV; PHRASAL VB : V+

recover from an illness. EG *He'll pull round, don't worry.* ADV

pull through. 1 When you **pull through** a serious illness, you recover from it. EG *The worst seems to be over, I think she'll pull through... The doctors managed to pull her through a long and difficult illness.* PHRASAL VB : V-ERG+ADV/PREP = come through

2 If you **pull through** something which causes you difficulty or if someone **pulls** you **through** it, you manage to succeed at it or survive it. EG *They managed to pull her through her exams somehow.* PHRASAL VB : V-ERG+ADV/PREP

pull together. 1 If people **pull together,** they co-operate with each other and ignore the things which they disagree about so that they can get through a difficult situation. EG *We all pulled together during the war... This is one thing we must all pull together on.* PHRASAL VB : V+ADV = join forces

2 If you **pull** something **together,** you organize it, for example by arranging many different things or parts in an orderly, controlled, or attractive way. EG *We had a final draft which I pulled together in a sort of editorial way... In the meantime, a campus-wide rally was being pulled together.* PHRASAL VB : V+O+ADV = draw together

3 When you **pull** yourself **together,** you bring your emotions under control so that you behave calmly and reasonably and think clearly. EG *That's quite enough of that. Pull yourself together now and stop this at once... Pulling herself together, Mrs Oliver managed to fight back her annoyance.* PHR : V+O (REFL)+ADV = get a grip on yourself

pull up. 1 When a vehicle or its driver **pulls up,** the driver makes the vehicle slow down and stop. EG *The rain stopped as we pulled up to the hotel.* PHRASAL VB : V+ADV = draw up

2 If you **pull up** something such as a chair, you move it closer to something or someone. EG *I now pulled up a chair and sat back to watch the news.* PHRASAL VB : V+O+ADV = bring up, draw up

3 If you **pull up** something which is fixed to the ground or the floor, you remove it with force by pulling it towards you, usually in order to destroy it completely. EG *They started pulling up the floorboards... ...pulling up weeds.* PHRASAL VB : V+O+ADV = rip up, tear up

4 If something **pulls** you **up** short or **pulls** you **up** with a jerk, you suddenly stop what you are doing and begin to question whether what you are doing is right. EG *The man's ingrained morality pulled him up short... He senses what is happening and pulls himself up with a jerk.* PHRASAL VB : V+O (NG/REFL)+ADV

5 If someone **pulls** you **up** on something, they scold or criticize you severely for something that you have done; an informal expression. EG *If they don't like what you're doing they'll soon pull you up on it.* PHRASAL VB : V+O+ADV = reprimand, tell off ≠ praise

6 If you **pull up** in something that you are learning, or if something or someone **pulls** you **up** in it, you improve at it and become nearly as good as other people or reach the standard required; an informal expression. EG *These marks seem to be satisfactory so that means you've pulled up quite a bit.* PHRASAL VB : V-ERG+ADV

7 You also say that someone **pulls up** when they become involved in fewer activities and rest more; an informal expression. EG *He said if I didn't pull up a bit I was in danger of a complete breakdown.* PHRASAL VB : V+ADV = ease up, slow down

pullet /pʊlɪt/, **pullets.** A **pullet** is a hen that is less than one year old. N COUNT

pulley /pʊli[1]/, **pulleys.** A **pulley** is a device which consists of a chain, belt, or piece of rope stretched over the rim of a wheel and attached to it at one end. You lift or lower heavy loads by attaching the free end of the rope to the load and winding or unwinding the rope on the wheel. N COUNT

pull-in, pull-ins. A **pull-in** is a cafe on a main road where you can get cheap meals; an informal word in British English. N COUNT

Pullman /pʊlmən/, **Pullmans.** A **Pullman** is a kind of railway carriage which is extremely comfortable and luxurious. A **Pullman** train is a train which consists of these carriages. N COUNT, OR *by*+N

pull-out, pull-outs. A **pull-out** is a section of a magazine, usually in the middle, which you can remove easily and keep. N COUNT

pullover /pʊləʊvə/, **pullovers.** A **pullover** is a knitted woollen garment that covers the upper part of your body, and usually your arms, and which you put on by pulling it over your head. N COUNT = sweater, jumper

pulmonary /pʌlmən[ə]ri[1], pʊl-/ means relating to your lungs; a formal word. EG *...pulmonary tuberculosis.* ADJ CLASSIF : ATTRIB

pulp /pʌlp/, **pulps, pulping, pulped.** 1 **Pulp** is 1.1 a substance which has become soft, smooth, and wet, often because it has been crushed or beaten. EG *We squashed the berries into a pulp.* N UNCOUNT 1.2 the soft inner part of a fruit or vegetable. EG *Scoop out the pulp and mash it with the cream.* N UNCOUNT = flesh 1.3 material which is made from crushed wood, rags, or other fibres and which is used to make paper. EG *...a paper and pulp manufacturer... The company guaranteed supplies of the wood pulp needed for the newsprint.* N UNCOUNT 1.4 If someone **beats** you **to a pulp,** they hit you hard again and again until you are helpless and badly injured. PHR : VB INFLECTS

2 People sometimes use **pulp** to refer to books or magazines which they consider to be of poor quality, for example because they were written quickly without much thought and try to shock people in a sensational way; used showing disapproval. EG *They seem satisfied with cheap tabloids, trite films, and the pulp library of crime.* N UNCOUNT : USU BEFORE N = trash

3 To **pulp** something means to crush it so that it becomes a pulp. EG *Once gnawed, ground, and pulped, the food has to be digested.* V+O

pulpit /pʊlpɪt/, **pulpits.** A **pulpit** is a small raised platform in church with a rail or barrier around it, where a member of the clergy stands to preach or to lead the prayers. N COUNT

pulpy /pʌlpi[1]/. 1 Something that is **pulpy** is soft, smooth, and wet; often used of the soft inner part of a fruit or vegetable or of a substance that has been crushed or beaten. ADJ QUALIT

2 **Pulpy** books and magazines are considered poor in quality, for example because they were written quickly without much thought and try to shock the reader in a sensational way; used informally showing disapproval. EG *...a pulpy novel.* ADJ QUALIT : ATTRIB ⇑ bad = trashy

pulsate /pʌlseɪt/, **pulsates, pulsating, pulsated.** If something **pulsates,** it 1 moves with strong, regular movements like the blood beating through your body. EG *The creature has no heart, only a number of pulsating arteries.* V : USU+A = throb ◇ **pulsation** /pʌlseɪʃ[ə]n/. EG *...the pulsation in every human organ necessary to life.* ◇ N UNCOUNT 2 shakes with strong, regular beating movements or beating sounds. EG *Her final top note pulsated with triumph... The young beast's flanks pulsated violently.* V : USU+A = quiver ◇ **pulsation.** ◇ N UNCOUNT

pulse /pʌls/, **pulses, pulsing, pulsed.** 1 Your **pulse** is the regular beating of blood through your body, which you can feel when you touch particular parts of your body, especially your wrist. EG *The artery at the wrist is used for feeling the pulse... Before the singer came on, her pulse started to race.* N COUNT : USU SING

● When someone **takes** your **pulse,** they find out the speed of your heartbeat by feeling the pulse in your wrist with their fingers and counting the number of beats in one minute. ● PHR : VB INFLECTS

2 A **pulse** is also 2.1 a regular beat in music, which is often produced by a drum. EG *The music's throbbing pulse was giving me a headache.* N COUNT : USU SING 2.2 a series of beats or vibrations which are produced in a regular rhythm, for example as a sound wave or electromagnetic signal; a technical use. EG *It signals information to the computer by emitting a pulse of electrons.* N COUNT ▸ A **pulse** is also a single beat or vibration in such a series. EG *Active sonar sends out a series of sound pulses.*

3 If you refer to the **pulse** of a group or society, you mean the ideas or opinions that it has at a particular time. EG *I'm hoping to see what the artistic pulse of the country is.* N SING : *the*+N+SUPP ● If you **have** or **keep** your **finger on the pulse,** you know all the latest news and developments. EG *When it comes to fashion he always has his finger on the pulse.* ● PHR : VB INFLECTS

4 **Pulses** are seeds from particular plants which can be cooked and eaten, for example peas, beans, and lentils. EG *...protein foods such as peanuts, fish, pulses, and wholemeal bread.* N COUNT : USU PL

5 If something **pulses,** it 5.1 moves with strong, regular movements like the blood beating through your body. EG *The blister throbbed and burned, pulsed and ached.* V : USU+A = throb 5.2 shakes with strong, regular beating movements or beating sounds. EG *... a soft rhythmic pulsing sound.* V : USU+A = quiver

pulverize /pʌlvəraɪz/, **pulverizes, pulverizing, pulverized;** also spelled **pulverise.** To **pulverize** something means 1 to make it into a powder by crushing it. EG *The processes involved pulverising the nuts.* V+O = grind 2 to do great damage to it or to destroy it completely. EG *Vast areas were pulverized by Nazi shot... Their proposal looks certain to be pulverised.* V+O = annihilate, demolish

puma /pjuːmə/, **pumas**. A **puma** is a wild animal that is a member of the cat family. Pumas are a similar size to lions. They have brownish-grey fur, eat other animals, and live in mountain regions of North and South America. N COUNT = cougar

pumice /pʌmɪs/. **Pumice** or **pumice stone** is a grey stone that is very light in weight and that you use to clean surfaces or to rub on your skin in order to soften it or to remove stains. N UNCOUNT

pummel /pʌməᵒl/, **pummels, pummelling, pummelled**; also spelled **pummeling, pummeled** in American English. If you **pummel** someone or something, you beat them again and again using your fists. EG *She tipped some water into the bowl of flour and fat, and pummelled it fiercely... ...little stubble-headed boys pummelling and shouting.* V OR V+O = pommel

pump /pʌmp/, **pumps, pumping, pumped**. 1 A **pump** is 1.1 a machine which is used to force a liquid or gas to flow in strong, regular movements in a particular direction. EG *We have several methods of getting energy using windmills, heat pumps and other devices.* N COUNT 1.2 a device for bringing water to the surface from below the ground. Pumps usually have an upright metal tube going into the ground and a handle that you push against in order to force the water upwards under pressure. EG *...water pumps... It was my morning job to fill four buckets from the pump.* N COUNT 1.3 a device that consists of a tube and a handle which you push in and out in order to force air into something under pressure, especially into the tyre of a vehicle. EG *...a bicycle pump.* N COUNT

2 A **pump** or a **petrol pump** is a machine with a hose attached to it from which you can fill your car with petrol. EG *She drove up in her 1940 Ford and stopped at a pump.* N COUNT

3 **Pumps** are canvas shoes with flat rubber soles which people wear for sports and leisure. EG *He looked very summery in his white flannels and pumps.* N COUNT : USU PL = plimsoll, gym shoe

4 To **pump** a liquid or gas in a particular direction means to force it to flow in strong, regular movements in that direction, using a pump or in the way that a pump does. EG *A new textile factory was pumping its waste upstream into the river... We can use the electricity to pump water back into a dam or a reservoir... The heart pumps blood into the veins.* V+O+A ⇑ push

5 To **pump** water, oil, or gas means to get a supply of it from below the surface of the ground, using a pump. EG *John went across the grass to a cast-iron pump and started pumping water to drink.* V+O ⇑ obtain

6 If you **pump** or **pump up** something such as a tyre on a vehicle or bicycle, you fill it with air by using a pump. EG *Do your tyres need pumping up?* V+O, OR PHRASAL VB : V+O+ADV ⇑ blow up

7 To **pump** someone's stomach or to **pump** it **out** means to remove the contents of someone's stomach using a pump, because they have swallowed poison or taken an overdose of drugs. EG *We rushed her to the casualty department to have her stomach pumped.* V+O, OR PHRASAL VB : V+O+ADV ⇑ empty

8 To **pump** or to **pump away** means 8.1 to move vigorously in and out or up and down. EG *The lungs are depressed and expanded as the abdomen pumps up and down... His heart was pumping away.* V, OR PHRASAL VB : V+ADV 8.2 to push down vigorously again and again on something. EG *Hold the edge of the plunger, fit it over the sink hole and pump several times... I looked at the carburettor and pumped the kick starter until I was exhausted.* V+O, OR PHRASAL VB : V+O+ADV

9 If you **pump** something such as money or energy into a particular thing, you put a lot of money, energy, etc into it; a fairly informal use. EG *Most governments have pumped all available funds into large-scale modern technological projects... This is an area into which increased effort is likely to be pumped in the near future.* V+O+A *(into)* = pour

10 If you **pump** someone about something, you keep asking them questions in order to obtain information about it; an informal use. EG *I pumped him discreetly about his past.* V+O : IF+PREP THEN *about* ⇑ question = grill

11 To **pump** or to **pump out** rounds from a machine gun or revolver means to fire a lot of shots from it very quickly. To **pump** someone or something full of bullets means to fire a lot of bullets into them. EG *They fired continuously, each gun pumping three or four rounds a minute.* V+O, OR PHRASAL VB : V+O+ADV

pump out. To **pump out** something means to produce or supply it continually in large amounts; a fairly informal use. EG *...a radio station pumping out pop music... He automatically pumps out articles each week, regardless of quality.* PHRASAL VB : V+O+ADV

pumpernickel /pʌmpənɪkəᵒl/ is a dark brown, heavy bread made from rye, which is eaten especially in Germany. N UNCOUNT

pumpkin /pʌmpᵒkɪn/, **pumpkins**. A **pumpkin** is a very large orange-coloured fruit that has thick skin and is soft inside with a lot of seeds. EG *...pumpkin pies.* ▸ also used to refer to the plant on which the fruit grows. N COUNT/UNCOUNT ▸ N COUNT

pun /pʌn/, **puns, punning, punned**. 1 A **pun** is a use of words that have more than one meaning, or words that have the same sound but different meanings, so that what you say has two different meanings and makes people laugh. An example of a pun is 'My dog's a champion boxer'. N COUNT ⇑ joke = play on words

2 If you **pun**, you try to amuse people by making a pun. V ⇑ joke

punch /pʌntʃ/, **punches, punching, punched**.

1 If you **punch** someone or something, you hit them hard with your fist. EG *I wanted to strike him on the face, to punch him for what he had done to me... Boylan punched him hard on the nose... He punched the pillow with all his strength.* V+O, OR V+A

2 A **punch** is a hard blow with your fist. EG *Ringbaum, swaying with the punch, kept his balance.* N COUNT

3 If you **punch** something such as the buttons on a keyboard, you touch them in order to operate a typewriter, computer, etc. If you **punch** letters, numbers, codes, etc into a computer or if you **punch** them out on it, you touch the appropriate buttons in order to give instructions to the computer. EG *When you punch the fourth button, a new network will flash on the screen... ...electronic locks which open when you punch in the appropriate combination... She rapidly punched out the numbers on the telephone.* V+O : USU+A = key

4 A **punch** is also a tool or device that you use for making holes in something. EG *He made a small hole in the belt with a leather punch.* N COUNT

5 If you **punch** holes in something, you make holes in it with a punch or with any kind of sharp instrument. EG *...old oil drums that have some holes punched in them for ventilation.* V+O

6 **Punch** is a drink usually made from wine or spirits mixed with hot water, sugar, lemons, and various spices. EG *We made gallons of rum punch for the party.* N MASS

7 If you say that something has **punch**, you mean that it has a special force or power which makes it particularly effective; an informal use. EG *His articles lack punch... Each missile carries enough of a nuclear punch to obliterate many cities.* N UNCOUNT, OR N SING : a+N

8 To **pull punches**. 8.1 If you **pull punches** when you are fighting with someone, you do not hit them as hard as you are capable of doing. PHR : VB INFLECTS 8.2 If you do not **pull punches** when you are criticizing someone or something, you say exactly what you think and do not soften your criticism in any way. EG *I was in no mood to pull punches or choose words carefully... My lunchtime lecture pulled no punches.* PHR : VB INFLECTS, USU WITH BROAD NEG

Punch and Judy show, Punch and Judy shows. A **Punch and Judy show** is a comic puppet show for children, in which Punch, a small, hook-nosed puppet, fights with his wife Judy. These shows are usually performed in a small booth at fairs or at the seaside. N COUNT

punchbag /pʌntʃbæg/, **punchbags**. A **punchbag** is a heavy leather bag, stuffed with horsehair or other material and hanging on a rope, which is punched hard by boxers and other sportsmen for training and exercise. N COUNT = punching bag

punchball /pʌntʃbɔl/, **punchballs**; also spelled with a hyphen. A **punchball** is a large leather ball fixed on a spring, which is punched rapidly by boxers and other sportsmen for training and exercise. N COUNT

punchbowl /pʌntʃbəʊl/, **punchbowls**. A **punchbowl** is a large bowl in which drinks, especially punch, are mixed and served. N COUNT

punch-drunk. Someone who is **punch-drunk** 1 shows signs of brain damage, such as unsteadiness and the inability to think clearly, usually because of having been a boxer and having suffered many blows on their head. ADJ CLASSIF ⇑ injured 2 is dazed and confused, for example because they have been working too hard or doing something very intensely, so that they feel ADJ CLASSIF ≠ fresh their brain can no longer absorb anything. EG *They're delighting in having got me punch-drunk with talk.*

punching bag, punching bags. A **punching bag** is the same as a punchbag; used especially in American English. N COUNT

punch-line, punch-lines; also spelled without a hyphen. The **punch-line** of a joke or funny story is its last sentence or phrase, which gives it its humour. N COUNT

punch-up, punch-ups; also spelled as one word. A **punch-up** is a fight or argument, often one which involves people hitting each other; an informal word used in British English. EG *'Looks as though you've been in a real punch-up,' says the barmaid.* N COUNT = brawl

punchy /pʌntʃi¹/, **punchier, punchiest.** 1 If you describe something such as a piece of writing as **punchy**, you mean that it is effective and forceful, because points are made clearly, briefly, and decisively; an informal word, used showing approval. EG *...a punchy little leaflet.* ADJ QUALIT = incisive ≠ rambling

2 **Punchy** also means the same as punch-drunk; an informal use. EG *I was punchy from the sheer volume of facts that had been thrown at me.* ADJ QUALIT

punctilious /pʌŋktɪlɪəs/. You say that someone is **punctilious** when they are very careful to behave correctly; a fairly formal word. EG *You are the most punctilious person I ever met... In public he was punctilious about such things.* ▸ used of their behaviour. EG *She displayed a punctilious lack of curiosity about such things.* ◇ **punctiliously.** EG *He thanked her punctiliously.* ADJ QUALIT = meticulous ≠ lax ◇ ADV

punctual /pʌŋktjuᵒəl/. Someone who is punctual 1 arrives somewhere or does something at exactly the right time. EG *I expect my guests to be punctual at the table for breakfast.* ◇ **punctually.** EG *Mary arrived at the New Inn punctually at ten o'clock.* 2 typically does things at the right time and is rarely late. EG *I am not myself a particularly punctual person.* ◇ **punctuality** /pʌŋktjuælɪti¹/. EG *Miss Talmadge had a reputation for punctuality.* ADJ CLASSIF: PRED = on time, prompt ◇ ADV WITH VB ADJ QUALIT ◇ N UNCOUNT

punctuate /pʌŋktjueɪt/, **punctuates, punctuating, punctuated.** 1 If something **is punctuated** by or with particular things, it is interrupted by them at intervals; a fairly formal use. EG *The old lady's words were punctuated by noise from outside... Bursts of growth were punctuated with periodic setbacks.* V+O: USU PASS+ by/with = intersperse

2 When you **punctuate** a piece of writing, you put punctuation in it. V+O

punctuation /pʌŋktjueɪʃəⁿn/ is 1 the marks such as full stops, commas, or question marks that you use in writing to divide words into sentences, clauses, etc. EG *The punctuation needs putting right.* 2 the way in which punctuation has been used in a piece of writing. EG *She is always meticulously accurate in punctuation and spelling.* N UNCOUNT N UNCOUNT

punctuation mark, punctuation marks. A **punctuation mark** is a sign such as a full stop, comma, or question mark that you use in writing to divide words into sentences, clauses, etc. N COUNT

puncture /pʌŋktʃə/, **punctures, puncturing, punctured.** 1 A **puncture** is a small hole in a car tyre or bicycle tyre that has been made by a sharp object and that damages the tyre because the air inside the tyre escapes. EG *One of the wheels has a puncture.* N COUNT

2 To **puncture** a tyre or something else that contains air or liquid means to make a small hole in it. EG *The shrapnel may puncture tyres, fuel tanks and radiators.* ◇ **punctured.** EG *...a punctured balloon.* V-ERG ⇑ pierce ◇ ADJ CLASSIF

3 If someone **is punctured** or if their feelings **are punctured**, something happens which stops them feeling confident or happy and makes them feel depressed or miserable. EG *Bernard was all alone. Punctured, utterly deflated, he dropped into a chair... The incident punctured his pride.* V+O: USU PASS = deflate

pundit /pʌndɪt/, **pundits.** A **pundit** is a person who knows a lot about a particular subject and is often asked to give information or opinions about it to the public; an informal word. EG *John Lowerson is one of our pundits on local history... The television pundits play a dominant role in moulding public opinion.* N COUNT: USU+ SUPP = expert

pungency /pʌndʒənsi¹/. 1 If something has **pungency**, it has a strong, sharp smell or taste. EG *...the pungency of burning peat.* N UNCOUNT

2 If speech or writing has **pungency**, it uses words and ideas that have a direct, powerful effect and often cleverly criticize something; a formal use. EG *She writes with relentless pungency.* N UNCOUNT ⇑ directness

pungent /pʌndʒənt/. 1 Something that is **pungent** has a strong, sharp smell or taste which is often so strong that it is unpleasant. EG *The pungent, choking smell of sulphur filled the air.* ADJ QUALIT = powerful ≠ delicate

2 Speech or writing that is **pungent** has a direct, powerful effect and often cleverly criticizes something; a formal use. EG *This short pungent novel displays Muriel Spark's wildness of imagination... This is the pungent and original argument.* ADJ QUALIT = biting, pointed

punish /pʌnɪʃ/, **punishes, punishing, punished.** 1 If you **punish** someone, you make them suffer in some way because they have done something wrong, for example committed a crime. EG *They discovered his crime and punished him for it... ...a recent government campaign to punish poachers... The drinking of alcohol was punished by death.* V+O, OR V+O+A (for) = penalize

2 To **punish** a crime means to punish anyone who commits that crime. EG *The early Hebrew fathers punished adultery with death... Crimes should be punished.* V+O, OR V+O+A (for) ≠ reward

punishable /pʌnɪʃəbəᵒl/. If a crime or particular way of behaving is **punishable**, people are punished if they commit that crime or behave in that way. EG *Possession of drugs is punishable by prison in some cases... Legislation was under way to make it a punishable offence.* ADJ CLASSIF

punishing /pʌnɪʃɪŋ/. Something that is **punishing** makes you very weak or helpless. EG *The purpose was to inflict a punishing defeat on the enemy armies.* ADJ QUALIT: ATTRIB ⇑ serious = crippling, debilitating

punishment /pʌnɪʃməˀnt/, **punishments.** 1 **Punishment** is the act of punishing someone. EG *Punishment and prison sentences cannot reform the hardened criminal... ...physical punishment.* N UNCOUNT ≠ reward

2 A **punishment** is a particular way of punishing someone. EG *What punishment do you think might be appropriate?... He maintained that the only true punishment for murder was death... ...one of the most horrible punishments imaginable.* N COUNT ≠ reward

3 **Punishment** is also severe physical treatment of any kind. EG *The car absorbed the punishment, and only the worst bumps disturbed the suspension... The crew were in no condition to withstand any further punishment from the sea.* N UNCOUNT ⇑ treatment

4 See also **capital punishment, corporal punishment.**

punitive /pjuːnɪtɪv/. Something that is **punitive** is intended to punish people and so is often harsh. EG *We will take no punitive action against those who have broken the rules... They dragged her away to the punitive isolation unit of the prison... The government's response to the recent riots was punitive.* ADJ CLASSIF = punishing

Punjabi /pʌndʒɑːbi¹/, **Punjabis.** 1 **Punjabi** is the language that is spoken by people who live in the Punjab. N UNCOUNT

2 A **Punjabi** is someone who comes from the Punjab. ▸ used as an adjective. EG *...a Punjabi woman.* N COUNT ▸ ADJ CLASSIF

punk /pʌŋk/, **punks.** 1 **Punk** or **punk rock** is rock music that has been popular among young people since the late 1970's. It is played in a fast, loud, and aggressive way and is often a protest against conventional attitudes and ways of behaving. EG *I'm not really a fan of punk... ...a punk rock concert.* N UNCOUNT ⇑ pop music

2 **Punk** is used to describe a style of clothes, art, design, etc which is associated with punk music and is typically bold and unconventional. EG *My mother wouldn't let me have a punk hairstyle.* ADJ CLASSIF: ATTRIB

3 A **punk** or a **punk rocker** is a young person who likes punk music and dresses in an unconventional and shocking way, for example by having brightly coloured hair and wearing metal chains. EG *They were mostly teenage punks at the club... ...punk rockers with safety pins in their ears.* N COUNT

punnet /pʌnɪt/, **punnets.** A **punnet** is a small, light, square box in which soft fruits, for example strawberries or raspberries, are often sold. ▸ also used to refer to the fruit inside a punnet or the amount of fruit that it contains. EG *I bought a punnet of strawberries.* N COUNT ▸ N PART+N IN PLURAL

punt /pʌnt/, **punts, punting, punted.** 1 A **punt** is a long boat with a flat bottom. You move the boat along by standing at one end and pushing a long pole down against the bottom of the river. EG *Two punts passed on their way downstream.* N COUNT

2 When you **punt**, you travel along a river in a punt. V

EG *I punted a bit farther out... We went punting on the river.*

punter /pʌntə/, **punters**; an informal word in British English. 1 A **punter** is a person who bets money on horse races. EG *Favourites, as any punter will tell you, do not always win.* N COUNT ⇑ gambler

2 When you talk about the **punters**, you are referring to all the people for whom you regularly do something or make something, especially when they are people who you are trying to please and who you never meet. For example a newspaper editor may refer to the readers of his newspaper as 'the punters'. EG EG *What was the punters' reaction to it?* N COUNT : USU PL, the+N

puny /pjuːni¹/, **punier, puniest**. Someone or something that is **puny** is very small or weak compared to other people or things of the same kind; often used showing disapproval. EG *What a puny old man... ...her puny efforts.* ADJ QUALIT = feeble, pathetic ≠ sturdy

pup /pʌp/, **pups**. A **pup** is 1 a young dog. EG *...a cocker spaniel pup.* N COUNT 2 a young animal such as a seal. EG *...a seal pup.* N COUNT

pupa /pjuːpə/, **pupae**. A **pupa** is an insect that is in the stage of development between a larva and a fully grown adult. It has a protective covering and does not move; a technical word in biology. EG *...a butterfly pupa.* N COUNT = chrysalis

pupil /pjuːpɪ⁰l/, **pupils**. 1 The **pupils** of a school are the children who go to that school. EG *...a school with more than 1300 pupils... ...the relationship between teacher and pupil... He is an unresponsive pupil who behaves badly.* N COUNT = schoolchild

2 A **pupil** of a painter, musician, or other expert is someone who studies under that expert and learns his or her skills. EG *Auerbach and Kossoff were pupils of David Bomberg... You can see his influence in the painting of his pupils.* N COUNT : WITH POSS ⇑ student

3 The **pupil** in your eye is the small round black hole in the centre of the iris. N COUNT

puppet /pʌpɪt/, **puppets**. 1 A **puppet** is a doll that you can move, either by pulling strings which are attached to it or by putting your hand inside its body and moving your fingers. EG *The story was wonderfully performed by stick puppets operated from behind a screen.* N COUNT = marionette

2 You also refer to people or countries as **puppets** when their actions are controlled by more powerful people or countries, although they may appear to be independent; used showing disapproval. EG *They made the rules but, in reality, they were mere puppets manipulated by other men... ...a puppet government.* N COUNT

puppeteer /pʌpɪtɪə/, **puppeteers**. A **puppeteer** is a person who gives shows using puppets. N COUNT ⇑ entertainer

puppy /pʌpi¹/, **puppies**. A **puppy** is a young dog. EG *Don't buy a puppy less than seven weeks old... Our dog has had three litters of puppies.* N COUNT = pup

puppy fat is fat that some children have on their bodies when they are young but that disappears when they grow older and taller. EG *She had a lot of puppy fat then.* N UNCOUNT

puppy love is romantic love that an adolescent feels for someone. Puppy love does not usually last long because adolescents' feelings change as they grow older. EG *It's only puppy love.* N UNCOUNT

purchase /pɜːtʃə¹s/, **purchases, purchasing, purchased**; a formal word. 1 When you **purchase** something, you buy it. EG *He sold the house he had purchased only two years before... I purchased a jumper from your Guildford store... The oil company announced that it was purchasing 5.1 per cent of its own shares.* V+O ⇑ obtain ≠ sell

2 **Purchase** is the act of buying something. EG *We need to know the exact day of purchase... He advised them on the purchase of their new car.* N UNCOUNT

3 A **purchase** is something that you buy. EG *Among his purchases were several tins of beans... He did not make more than one purchase at any one shop.* N COUNT

4 If you get or gain **purchase** somewhere, you find something that you can hold on to and that prevents you from falling. EG *...trying to get some purchase on the cliff.* N UNCOUNT

purchaser /pɜːtʃə¹sə/, **purchasers**. A **purchaser** is a person who buys something; a formal word. N COUNT = buyer

purchase tax is a tax that you pay when you buy something. It is included in the price that you pay for something. N UNCOUNT

purchasing power; a technical expression. 1 The **purchasing power** of an individual or a community is the amount of money that they have available in order to buy goods. EG *The value of the country's currency declined along with the purchasing power of its inhabitants... A rise in incomes will create increased purchasing power.* N UNCOUNT

2 The **purchasing power** of a currency is its value in terms of how much can be bought with it at any one time. EG *...the purchasing power of the pound.* N UNCOUNT : WITH POSS

purdah /pɜːdə/ is the custom practised in some Muslim and Hindu societies, in which women avoid the company of male strangers, for example by remaining in a special part of a house or covering their faces to avoid being seen by them. EG *I said that I did not agree with purdah.* ● If a woman lives **in purdah**, she lives in this way. EG *He kept her in purdah.* N UNCOUNT ● PHR : USED AS AN A

pure /pjʊə/, **purer, purest**. 1 A **pure** substance is 1.1 not mixed with anything else. EG *...a dress of pure silk.* ◊ **purity** /pjʊərɪti¹/. EG *A geological survey showed that the purity and thickness of the coal seams were not sufficient to justify opening a new mine.* ADJ CLASSIF ◊ N UNCOUNT 1.2 clean, healthy, and free from anything that might be harmful. EG *An advantage of breast feeding is that the milk is always pure... ...the pure, dry desert air that preserved the treasures.* ◊ **purity**. EG *...the importance of purity in the water supply.* ADJ CLASSIF ≠ contaminated ◊ N UNCOUNT

2 A **pure** person does not do or think anything sinful or bad; a rather literary use. EG *Teddy Boylan's not fit for your pure, beautiful little sister to marry... ...pure in mind and body.* ◊ **purity**. EG *...secret thoughts which defiled her purity.* ADJ CLASSIF = unsullied ◊ N UNCOUNT

3 A **pure** colour is so clear that you feel it is a perfect example of that particular colour. EG *The sky was pure azure as the clouds parted... ... pure white.* ADJ+ADJ COLOUR

4 A **pure** sound is very clear, is beautiful to hear, and stays on a particular note without wavering. EG *...a pure ringing sound... The singer's voice remained pure and clear throughout the evening.* ◊ **purity**. EG *...purity of tone.* ADJ CLASSIF ◊ N UNCOUNT

5 A form of art that is **pure** is produced or done exactly according to a standard, form, or pattern that is expected of such things; a formal use. EG *...the finest and purest Norman ecclesiastical architecture.* ◊ **purity** EG *We admired its purity of form.* ADJ QUALIT = unadulterated ◊ N UNCOUNT

6 **Pure** research or **pure** science is concerned only with theory and not with how this theory can be used in practical ways, for example, in industry or engineering. EG *...chemistry, both pure and applied... ... pure maths... It's entirely pure research.* ADJ CLASSIF : ATTRIB = theoretical ≠ applied

7 **Pure** also means complete and total. EG *He shut his eyes in pure bliss... He had got into Leeds University by pure academic effort... I came on the idea by pure chance.* ADJ CLASSIF : ATTRIB = sheer

8 **Pure and simple** is used to emphasize that a particular thing is the only thing involved and no others are considered. EG *It is a matter of investment, pure and simple.* PHR AFTER N

pure-bred. A **pure-bred** animal has parents, grandparents, etc that all belong to the same single breed. EG *By the first world war there were less than 100 pure-bred specimens of the English goat left.* ADJ CLASSIF : ATTRIB

puree /pjʊəreɪ/, **purees, pureeing, pureed**. 1 A **puree** is food which has been mashed or blended so that it forms a thick, smooth sauce. EG *...tomato puree... ...chestnut puree... An electric blender makes soups, purees, and puddings in a trice.* N MASS

2 If you **puree** food, you make it into a puree. EG *I use a blender to puree cooked meats, vegetables, and fruits.* V+O ⇑ mash

purely /pjʊəli¹/. 1 **Purely** means involving only one feature and not including anything else. EG *...something purely practical like mending a washing machine... Is it to be a purely educational organisation?... The reaction is purely involuntary... ...a purely casual acquaintance... There's nothing personal in all this, you know. Purely a routine check.* ADV ⇑ completely

2 **Purely and simply** is used to emphasize that a particular thing is the only thing involved and no others are considered. EG *Students are admitted purely and simply on merit.* PHR : USED AS ADV SEN = simply

purgative /pɜːgətɪv/, **purgatives**. A **purgative** is a medicine that causes you to defecate and so to get rid of unwanted substances from your body; a formal word. ▸ used as an adjective. N COUNT = laxative ▸ ADJ CLASSIF

purgatory /pɜːgətəºri¹/. The word **purgatory** is sometimes spelled with a capital letter in sense 1. 1 **Purgatory** is the place where Roman Catholics believe the spirits of dead people are sent to suffer for their sins on earth before they go to heaven. EG *...eternal Damnation and Purgatory.* N PROPER

2 You can also refer to a very unpleasant experience as **purgatory**. EG *I feel that I am in purgatory... It was a sort of purgatory that had to be endured.* N UNCOUNT = hell

purge /pɜːdʒ/, **purges, purging, purged**. 1 When people **purge** an organization or political party, they remove from it all the people who are no longer thought to be acceptable members, for example because their ideas are not the same as the ideas of the leaders. EG *They had done their best to purge extremists from the party... The organisation has been purged of many of its active members.* ▸ used as a noun. EG *They discovered that there were infiltrators inside the party. A purge began.* V+O : USU+A *(of/from)* ▸ N COUNT

2 If you **purge** your thoughts or your mind of something undesirable such as hatred or envy, you stop yourself from having such thoughts or being affected by them. EG *...an attempt to purge her mind and heart of a love which had possessed her for too many years... I tried desperately to purge myself of these dangerous desires.* V+O (NG/REFL) : USU+A *(of)* ⇑ free, rid

purify /pjʊərɪfaɪ/, **purifies, purifying, purified**. 1 If you **purify** a substance, you make it pure by removing any harmful, dirty, or inferior substances from it. EG *...specially purified water.* V+O ⇑ clean ≠ contaminate
◊ **purification** /pjʊərɪkeɪʃəºn/. EG *...the purification of the water supply.* ◊ N UNCOUNT

2 If a person **is purified**, their sins are removed from them by a religious ceremony. ◊ **purification**. V+O (NG/REFL) ◊ N UNCOUNT

purist /pjʊərɪst/, **purists**. A **purist** is a person who believes strictly in absolute correctness, especially in relation to a particular subject about which they have a lot of knowledge. EG *He has not endeared himself to purists in recent years... Musical purists were outraged at this innovation.* N COUNT ⇑ pedant

puritan /pjʊərɪtəºn/, **puritans**. The word **puritan** is sometimes spelled with a capital letter in sense 1.
1 The **puritans** or **Puritans** were a group of English Protestants who tried to get rid of all Roman Catholic influences in English churches in the sixteenth and seventeenth centuries. EG *...from the time of the Puritans onwards... ...a woman from a Puritan background... ...the puritan belief that Satan dwelt in nature.* N COUNT

2 You also describe someone as a **puritan** when they live according to strict moral or religious principles, especially by avoiding physical pleasures. EG *...an austere old New England puritan... They are the puritans of the revolutionary movement.* ▸ used as an adjective. EG *...puritan morality.* N COUNT ▸ ADJ QUALIT

puritanical /pjʊərɪtænɪkəºl/. Someone who is **puritanical** behaves according to strict moral or religious principles, especially by avoiding physical pleasures. EG *I was fastidious, even puritanical... Penny was anything but puritanical.* ▸ used of ideas and behaviour. EG *...a puritanical distaste for alcohol.* ADJ QUALIT

puritanism /pjʊərɪtənɪzm/ is behaviour or beliefs that are based on strict moral or religious principles, especially the principle that people should avoid physical pleasures. EG *I had felt that puritanism and sexual repression were essentially political... They have cultivated an image of working class puritanism.* N UNCOUNT

purl /pɜːl/, **purls, purling, purled**. 1 **Purl** is a stitch in knitting in which you put the needle into the back rather than the front of the stitch on the other needle. EG *...a row of purl.* N UNCOUNT, OR N BEFORE N

2 When you **purl** a stitch in knitting, you make it using a purl stitch. EG *...knit one, purl one.* V+O

purlieus /pɜːljuːz/. The **purlieus** of a place are the areas immediately surrounding it; a literary word. EG *...exploring the overgrown purlieus of the temple.* N PLURAL : USU WITH POSS = neighbourhood

purloin /pɜːlɔɪn/, **purloins, purloining, purloined**. If you **purloin** something, you steal it or borrow it without asking permission; a formal word. EG *I purloined his discarded newspaper after he left the room.* V+O ⇑ take = pinch

purple /pɜːpəºl/, **purples**. 1 Something that is **purple** is of a reddish-blue colour. EG *Jim changed, putting on clean jeans and a purple shirt.* ▸ used as a noun. EG *The birds are brilliantly coloured in reds, yellows, blacks and purples.* ADJ COLOUR ▸ N MASS

2 If someone turns **purple** in the face, their face becomes dark red in colour because they are extremely angry. EG *He referred to me as 'the enemy' and used to go purple in the face at the very mention of my name.* ADJ COLOUR

purple heart, purple hearts. The expression **purple heart** is spelled with capital letters in paragraph 1. 1 The **Purple Heart** is a medal that is given to members of the US Armed Forces who have been wounded during battle. N COUNT

2 **Purple hearts** are small, purple-coloured, heart-shaped pills containing amphetamine; used in British English. N COUNT ⇑ drug

purplish /pɜːplɪʃ/ means slightly purple in colour. EG *What's that purplish spot on your neck?* ADJ COLOUR

purport, purports, purporting, purported. The word **purport is pronounced** /pə⁵pɔːt/ when it is a verb, and /pɜːpɔːt/ when it is a noun; a formal word. 1 If you say that someone or something **purports** to do or be a particular thing, you mean that they claim to do or be that thing. Sometimes you also mean that in your opinion this claim is false. EG *There were advertisements for cosmetics purporting to delay the development of wrinkles... The Party purports to be the alternative government in Britain.* V+*to*-INF

2 The **purport** of a piece of speech or writing is its general meaning. EG *You need to grasp the general purport of each passage that you read.* N SING WITH POSS = content

purpose /pɜːpəs/, **purposes, purposing, purposed**. 1 The **purpose** of something is the reason for which it is made or done, for example the result that a course of action is intended to produce, or the function that an object is intended to perform. EG *The purpose of the meeting was to discuss the committee's report... The buildings are now used as a prison, but they weren't built for that purpose... It was agreed that the money could only be used for peaceful purposes.... We were given the loan for the purpose of buying a car.* N COUNT

2 Your **purpose** is the thing that you want to achieve, especially something that you are determined to do or get. EG *Her only purpose in life was to get rich... Complete secrecy was essential to our purposes.* N COUNT = intention, objective

3 **Purpose** is the feeling of having a definite aim and of being determined to achieve it. EG *She has given them a sense of purpose.* N UNCOUNT = resolve

4 If you **purpose** something, you intend to do it; an old-fashioned use. EG *I had not purposed to leave before nightfall... She was already purposing to be a nun.* V+O/*to*-INF = plan

5 The word **purpose** is also used in the following expressions. 5.1 You use the expression **for all practical purposes** to suggest that a situation is not exactly as you describe it but the effect is the same as if it were. EG *...in the third, and for all practical purposes, final phase... The rest are now, for all practical purposes, useless.* PHR : USED AS AN A = to all intents and purposes 5.2 If you do something **on purpose**, you do it deliberately and not by accident or chance. EG *He had gone there on purpose, to see what happened. Do you think I did it on purpose?... I'm sure nobody shot Jack on purpose. It was an accident.* PHR : USED AS AN A = intentionally ≠ accidentally 5.3 If something **serves a purpose**, it is useful and can help you to achieve a particular result. EG *I knew it would serve no purpose to argue with her... The place wasn't perfect but it would serve its purpose.* PHR : VB INFLECTS 5.4 If you say that something was **to no purpose**, you mean that no result, or no good result, came from it. If you say that it was **to good purpose**, you mean that it was useful. EG *It was all to no purpose... He used his past experience to good purpose.* PHR : USED AS AN A 5.5 If you say that something is **to the purpose**, you mean that it is very useful or relevant; a formal expression. EG *Everything she said was pointed and to the purpose.* PHR : USED AS AN A = to the point 5.6 **to all intents and purposes**: see **intent**.

purpose-built. A building that is **purpose-built** has been specially designed and built for the use it is being put to; used in British English. EG *...a purpose-built nursery school.* ADJ CLASSIF : USU ATTRIB

purposeful /pɜːpəsful/. If someone is **purposeful** or if they behave in a **purposeful** way, they show that they have a definite plan or purpose and a strong desire to achieve it. EG *They were striving to bring about change in a purposeful way... ...his busy, purposeful life.* ◊ **purposefully**. EG *She began walking slowly but purposefully towards the bridge.* ADJ QUALIT = determined, resolute ≠ aimless ◊ ADV WITH VB

purposeless /pɜːpəslɪ²s/. If an action is **purposeless**, it does not seem to have a sensible purpose or reason; used showing disapproval. EG *...casual, unprovoked and purposeless violence.* ▸ used of people. EG *His discovery left him feeling purposeless, stunned.* — ADJ QUALIT = pointless; ▸ = aimless

purposely /pɜːpəsli¹/. If you do something **purposely**, you do it deliberately and not by accident or chance. EG *She purposely sat in the outside seat... Her voice was purposely low.* — ADV = intentionally

purposive /pɜːpəsɪv/. A **purposive** action or activity is one that has a clear and definite purpose or aim; a formal word. EG *...the conscious, planned, purposive use of scientific progress.* — ADJ CLASSIF

purr /pɜː/, **purrs, purring, purred.** 1 When an engine or machine **purrs**, it makes a quiet, low-pitched, continuous vibrating sound. EG *I heard cars purr in the distance.* ▸ used as a noun. EG *She listened to the purr of the car... I could hear the gentle purr of a movie projector.* ◇ **purring.** EG *...the far-distant purring of a tractor.* — V ⇑ hum; ▸ N SING WITH DET; ◇ N UNCOUNT

2 When someone **purrs**, they speak in a soft, gentle voice because they are pleased about something. EG *'It's wonderful,' she purred delightedly.* — V+QUOTE = murmur

3 When a cat **purrs**, it makes a low vibrating sound with its throat because it is contented. EG *The cat began to purr loudly.* ▸ used as a noun. EG *The cat gave a short purr and Hallam stroked its head.* — V; ▸ N SING WITH DET

purse /pɜːs/, **purses, pursing, pursed.** 1 A **purse** is a very small bag that people, especially women, use to keep their money in. You usually keep your purse in your pocket or inside a larger bag; mainly used in British English. EG *She began hunting in her purse for some coins.* — N COUNT

2 A **purse** is also the same as a handbag; used in American English. EG *She took her large glossy black purse from the knob of the door.* — N COUNT ⇑ bag

3 The **purse** in a competition or contest, especially a boxing match, is the amount of money that is offered as a prize. — N COUNT

4 The word **purse** is sometimes used to refer to the total amount of money that a country, family, or group has; a formal use. EG *Inflation puts extra demands on the state purse.* — N COUNT ⇑ resources

5 If you **purse** or **purse up** your lips or mouth, you draw your lips into a small rounded shape. EG *He pursed his lips in distaste... Her little mouth was pursed up tight.* — V+O, OR PHRASAL VB : ORDER V+ADV+O

purser /pɜːsə/, **pursers.** The **purser** on a ship is an officer who deals with the accounts and official papers. On a passenger ship, the purser is also responsible for the welfare of the passengers. — N COUNT

purse strings; also spelled with a hyphen. If you say that someone holds or controls the **purse strings**, you mean that they control the way money is spent in a particular family, group, country, etc. — N PLURAL : *the*+N

pursuance /pəsjᵘuːəns/. If you do something **in pursuance of** a particular activity, you do it as part of carrying out that activity; a very formal word. EG *It was all done in pursuance of his duties.* — PREP ⇑ in the course of

pursue /pəsjᵘuː/, **pursues, pursuing, pursued**; a fairly formal word. 1 If you **pursue** something such as an activity, interest, or plan, you continue to do it or to carry it out. EG *Lyttleton pursued a policy of peace and order... His wealth enabled him to pursue his passionate interest in art... Mr Wigg had been pursuing his own inquiries... Immediate action should be pursued in these areas.* — V+O = carry out

2 If you **pursue** something such as a particular aim or result, you make efforts, often over a long period of time, to achieve it. EG *These are the objectives which businesses should seek to pursue... Growth must not be pursued at the expense of environmental pollution.* — V+O = strive for

3 If you **pursue** a particular subject, you try to find out more about it by asking questions. EG *I don't want to pursue that question now... I pursued that matter at dinner.* — V+O ⇑ go into

4 If you **pursue** people, vehicles, or animals, you chase or search for them in order to catch them. EG *Weasels pursue rats and mice as well as birds... The police pursued the wrong car.* — V+O

pursuer /pəsjᵘuːə/, **pursuers.** Your **pursuers** are people who are chasing or searching for you; a fairly formal word. EG *He managed to give his pursuers the slip.* — N COUNT : USU POSS+PL

pursuit /pəsjᵘuːt/, **pursuits**; a formal word. 1 Your **pursuit** of something is your attempts at achieving it. If you do something in **pursuit** of a particular result, you do it in order to achieve that result. EG *...the pursuit of happiness... How far should any of us go in pursuit of what we want?... People are having to retrain for new jobs and leave their homes in pursuit of them.* — N UNCOUNT+*of* ⇑ search

2 The **pursuit** of a particular plan, activity, or interest is the act of carrying it out. EG *He spent the summer in the vigorous pursuit of sport.* — N UNCOUNT+*of*

3 The **pursuit** of a person, vehicle, or animal is the act of chasing or searching for them. EG *...a gamekeeper in pursuit of a poacher... After counting sixty the rest set off in pursuit.* ● If you are **in hot pursuit** of someone, you are chasing after them with great determination. EG *He started running-with all the others in hot pursuit.* — N UNCOUNT; ● PHR : USED AS AN A

4 A **pursuit** is something that you spend time doing, especially an activity that you enjoy doing when you are not working. EG *...leisure pursuits... Games like chess are rather intellectual pursuits.* — N COUNT : USU PL +SUPP

purvey /pəveɪ/, **purveys, purveying, purveyed**; a formal word. 1 If you **purvey** something such as information, you tell it to people. EG *...the editor's comment that he was in business to purvey news.* — V+O = convey, transmit

2 If someone **purveys** goods or services, they provide them. — V+O

purveyor /pəveɪə/, **purveyors**; a formal word. 1 A **purveyor** of information is someone who provides it. — N COUNT+*of* ⇑ supplier

2 A **purveyor** of goods or services is a person or company that provides them. — N COUNT+SUPP ⇑ supplier

pus /pʌs/ is a thick yellowish liquid that forms in wounds when they are infected. — N UNCOUNT

push /pʊʃ/, **pushes, pushing, pushed.** 1 When you **push** something, 1.1 you press it using force, for example with your hand. EG *She pushed the button that locked the door... Turn the handle, lift, and push... He pushed on the punt pole.* ▸ used as a noun. EG *The gate slid open at the push of a button.* ● See also **bell push.** 1.2 you cause it to move or fall by pressing against it with some force. EG *She pushed the drawing across the desk towards Rudolph... Bulldozers pushed snow aside... Kids were pushing each other into the water... I pushed open the door.* 1.3 you cause it to move along in front of you by walking behind it and pressing against it continuously. EG *The child was pushing a pram... Castle pushed his bicycle up King's Road... If the car breaks down, we'll just have to get out and push.* ▸ used as a noun. EG *My car's broken down-would you give me a push down the road?* — V OR V+O ⇑ touch = shove; ▸ N COUNT : USU SING; V+O : USU+A = shove; V OR V+O; ▸ N COUNT : USU SING

2 If you **push** through or past things that are blocking you or if you **push** your **way** through them, you use force to move them slightly so that you can move past them. EG *Ralph pushed between them to get a better view... The men pushed past them towards the bar... I pushed my way through the people.* — V+A, OR PHR : V INFLECTS : USU+A = shove

3 If you **push** at something, you touch it repeatedly with a pushing movement. EG *He pushed petulantly at a lump of chicken skin... She pushed at her hair and laughed.* — V+A *(at)* = poke at

4 If you **push** yourself or a part of your body into a particular position, you use your muscles in order to move into that position. EG *He pushed himself abruptly to his feet... She suddenly pushed herself upright... He frowned and pushed out his lips.* — V+O (NG/REFL) +A

5 If an army **pushes** into a country that it is invading, it moves farther into it. EG *The troops pushed into the Republic.* ▸ used as a noun. EG *We made a substantial push into the New Territories.* — V+A = advance; ▸ N COUNT : USU SING

6 If you say that something such as a road or group of buildings **pushes** in a particular direction, you mean that it extends or lies in that direction; a rather literary use. EG *The chapel is dwarfed by the surrounding buildings, pushing ever upwards... The path pushed on farther into the valley.* — V+A ⇑ go

7 If something **pushes** or **is pushed** in a particular way, it changes or develops in that way. EG *This movement must push in the direction of socialism... In early pieces, he seemed to be pushing towards a new artistic style.* ▸ used as a noun. EG *Even if the push toward large cities is stopped, the problems will not disappear.* — V-ERG+A ⇑ move; ▸ N COUNT : USU SING = drive, shift

8 To **push** something such as a value or amount in a particular direction means to cause it to change in that way. For example, to **push** something up means — V+O+A

to make it increase, and to **push** it down means to make it decrease. EG *This oil boom can only push the basic inflation rate up to higher levels... International confidence in the mark has eroded, pushing it down more than 25 per cent against the dollar.* ▸ used as a noun. EG *Raw material costs gave a push to prices.* ▸ N COUNT : USU SING

9 If you **push** someone, **9.1** you try to help them to make progress in their work by constantly persuading and encouraging them; an informal use. EG *They pushed their son because they were ambitious for him... Girls were not pushed hard academically... You have to push yourself to get on in the academic world.* V+O (NG/REFL) ⇑ encourage **9.2** you try to persuade them to talk about something when they do not really want to; an informal use. EG *When we pushed her, she explained what she had meant earlier.* V+O = press **9.3** you force them to behave in a particular way or to do a particular thing; a slightly informal use. EG *No one's pushed me into this; I've decided to do it of my own accord... The government was pushed to desperate extremes... Pressure groups are trying to push governments in the direction of reform.* V+O : USU+A = pressurize ▸ used as a noun. EG *With a firm push from his wife, he became one of the most passionate opponents of the regime.* ▸ N COUNT : USU SING = shove

10 If you **push** for something, you make great efforts in order to achieve it; an informal use. EG *He is pushing for secret balloting in Party elections... The extreme Left were pushing for power.* V : IF+PREP THEN *for* = press for ▸ used as a noun. EG *France led the non-aligned nations into a push for sanctions.* ▸ N COUNT : USU SING+*for*

11 If you **push** something or someone **forward** or if you **push** them, you try to get people to pay attention to them. EG *There are so many new projects being pushed forward at the moment... We didn't like to push ourselves forward... He's always pushing himself and going on about what he's doing.* PHRASAL VB : V+O+ADV, OR V+O (NG/REFL)

12 To **push** something also means to try to increase its popularity or to attract people to it; an informal use. EG *...huge adverts pushing slimming drugs.* V+O = promote

13 If you **push** a particular subject, idea, or point, you try to make people listen to you, agree with you, or believe you. EG *I'd like to move away from that subject a little, unless you want to push it... I'm sure you all understand exactly what I mean without my having to push the point.* V+O

14 If you **push** something such as an advantage or opportunity, you take full advantage of it. EG *I pushed this advantage ruthlessly.* ● to **push** your **luck**: see **luck**. V+O = exploit

15 When someone **pushes** drugs, they sell them illegally; an informal use. EG *She was jailed for pushing heroin.* V OR V+O = hawk

16 A **push** is also a special effort that you make in order to get something done or finished. EG *You'll need all your strength for the final push.* N COUNT : USU SING

17 If you have **push**, you have the energy and determination to succeed in what you are doing. EG *...men like Northcliffe, men of push and go.* N UNCOUNT = drive

18 If you say that you could do something **at a push**, you mean that you could manage to do it, if you were really forced to, but that it would be difficult; an informal expression. EG *I could get five people in the car at a push.* PHR : USED AS AN A = just about ≠ easily

19 If someone **gives** you **the push** or if you **get the push**, **19.1** they end their relationship with you; an informal expression in British English. EG *He gave me the push last week.* PHR : VB INFLECTS **19.2** they dismiss you from your job; an informal expression in British English. PHR : VB INFLECTS

20 See also **pushed, pushing**.

push about. To **push** someone **about** means the same as to push them around; an informal expression. PHRASAL VB : V+O+ADV

push ahead. If you **push ahead**, you make progress with something. EG *They have pushed ahead with an optimistic development strategy.* PHRASAL VB : V+ADV, USU+*with* = advance

push along. To **push along** means the same as to push off; an informal expression. EG *I must be pushing along now, it's getting late.* PHRASAL VB : V+ADV ⇑ go = leave

push around. If someone **pushes** you **around**, they give you orders in a rude and insulting way or try to make you feel worthless compared with them; an informal expression. EG *We're not going to let them push us around any more... He began to push people around intellectually.* PHRASAL VB : V+O+ADV ⇑ order around = push about

push aside. If you **push** something **aside**, you treat it as unimportant and pay attention to something else instead. EG *These crucial issues tend to get pushed aside and forgotten.* PHRASAL VB : V+O+ADV

push in. When someone **pushes in**, they push in front of other people in a queue and move ahead of them unfairly. EG *Felicity pushed in next to Howard... Stop pushing in, and wait your turn.* PHRASAL VB : V+ADV = barge in

push off. **1** When you **push off**, you leave the person or place that you are visiting; an informal expression. EG *I'll be pushing off, then.* PHRASAL VB : V+ADV ⇑ go

2 If someone tells you to **push off**, they are telling you in a rude way to go away. EG *Push off. You're not wanted... The policeman told us to push off.* PHRASAL VB : V+ADV, USU IMPER

push on. **1** When you **push on**, you continue travelling somewhere, or start travelling again after you have stopped. EG *I felt restless and wanted to push on... He pushed on, staggering sometimes with his weariness.* PHRASAL VB : V+ADV ⇑ set off

2 When you **push on** with something that you are doing, you start doing it again after a short break. EG *I've got to push on with this file.* PHRASAL VB : V+ADV, USU+*with*

push out. To **push** something **out** means to produce a lot of it or send it out somewhere; an informal expression. EG *She sits for hours pushing out endless letters and articles... Computers can push out information to the external world at a very fast rate.* PHRASAL VB : V+O+ADV = churn out

push over. **1** If you **push** someone or something **over**, you push them so that they fall onto the ground. EG *The children were pushing each other over on the sand.* PHRASAL VB : V+O+ADV = knock over

2 See also **pushover**.

push through. If you **push** something **through**, you succeed in getting it accepted, often with difficulty. EG *The Opposition was against the new proposal, but the Government managed to push it through all the same.* PHRASAL VB : V+O+ADV

push bike, push bikes. A **push bike** is a bicycle which you move by turning the pedals with your feet, as opposed to a motorcycle; an informal word used in British English. N COUNT = cycle

push-button. A **push-button** machine or process is controlled by means of buttons or switches which you press in order to make it function. EG *...those push-button calculators.* ADJ CLASSIF : ATTRIB

pushcart /pʊʃkɑːt/, **pushcarts**. A **pushcart** is a small cart with a long handle for carrying small things; used mainly in American English. N COUNT = handcart

pushchair /pʊʃtʃɛə/, **pushchairs**. A **pushchair** is a small folding chair on wheels, in which a baby or small child can sit and be wheeled around; used in British English. N COUNT ⇑ pram

pushed /pʊʃt/. **1** If you are **pushed** for something such as time or money, you do not have enough of it; an informal use. EG *Sorry–can't stop–I'm a bit pushed for time... She's pushed for money at the moment... I can't take on that work now–I'm pushed as it is.* ADJ QUALIT : PRED, USU *for* ⇑ lacking

2 If you **are hard pushed** to do something or **are pushed** to do it, you find it very difficult to do it. EG *Most of us are hard pushed to understand how people can torture each other.* PHR : VB INFLECTS, USU+*to*-INF

pusher /pʊʃə/, **pushers**. A **pusher** is a person who sells illegal drugs; a fairly informal word. EG *Professional dope pushers moved in and organized the trade.* N COUNT ⇑ seller = peddler

pushing /pʊʃɪŋ/. If you say that someone is **pushing** a particular age, you mean that they are nearly that age; an informal expression. EG *Until a man is pushing sixty-five, he doesn't usually think about retirement... My older children are pushing university student age.* PREP = almost, going on

pushover /pʊʃəʊvə/, **pushovers**; an informal word. **1** You say that something is a **pushover** when it is easy to do or easy to get. EG *The English exam was a real pushover this year.* N COUNT : USU SING = cinch

2 You say that someone is a **pushover** when they are easy to persuade or influence. EG *You won't have much trouble with her–she'll be a pushover.* N COUNT : USU SING

push-up, push-ups. A **push-up** is the same as a press-up; used especially in American English. N COUNT

pushy /pʊʃi¹/, **pushier, pushiest**. Someone who is **pushy** wants to do better or get more than any one else, and constantly demands people's attention; an informal word showing disapproval. EG *He was cheeky, pushy, self-centred, and demanding.* ADJ QUALIT = forward ≠ retiring

pusillanimity /pjuːsɪlənɪmɪti¹/ is timidity and the fear of taking risks; a formal word, used showing disapproval. N UNCOUNT ⇑ cowardice ≠ bravery

pusillanimous /pju:sɪlænɪməs/. If someone is **pusillanimous** or if they behave in a **pusillanimous** way, they are timid and scared to take risks; a formal word, used showing disapproval. ADJ QUALIT ⇑ cowardly = wet ≠ brave

puss /pus/, **pusses**. People sometimes refer to a cat as a **puss** or address it as **puss**. EG *You're a pretty puss, aren't you?... Puss! Come here!* N COUNT : ALSO VOC = pussy

pussy /pusi[1]/, **pussies**. 1 A **pussy** or a **pussycat** is the same as a cat; used in informal English, often by children or when you are talking to children. EG *She sat down on a chair and said, 'Here, pussy, pussy,' to the cat.* N COUNT, ALSO VOC

2 A woman's **pussy** is her genitals; used in very informal English. For many people this is a rude use. N COUNT

pussyfoot /pusi[1]fut/, **pussyfoots, pussyfooting, pussyfooted**. If you say that someone **is pussyfooting**, you mean that they are behaving in a cautious way because they are not sure what to do and are afraid to commit themselves; an informal word, used showing disapproval. EG *Stop pussyfooting and get on with it.* V = prevaricate

pussy-willow, pussy-willows. A **pussy-willow** is a willow tree which has long, thin, furry white flowers in the spring. N COUNT

pustule /pʌstju:l/, **pustules**. A **pustule** is a pimple on the skin which contains pus; a medical term. N COUNT = boil

put /put/, **puts, putting, put**. The form **put** is used in the present tense and is the past tense and past participle of the verb. 1 When you **put** something in a particular place or position, you move it into that place or position. EG *She put her hand on his arm... I put her suitcase on the table... The women put a garland round her neck.* V+O+A ≠ remove

2 If you **put** someone somewhere, for example in an institution or room, you cause them to go there or be taken there, and to stay there for a period of time. EG *They had to put him into an asylum... I have to put the kids to bed.* V+O+A

3 When you **put** something such as an idea or remark in a particular way, you express it in that way. EG *They cannot put their feelings into words... He didn't put it quite as crudely as that... Let me put it this way: I find him very difficult indeed.* V+O+A ● When you want to quote something that someone has said or written and that expresses something which you yourself agree with, you can say **'as they put it'**. EG *As one couple put it: 'We are all victims of our culture.'... He was, as Sarah had once put it, 'going too far'.* ● PHR : USED AS ADV SEN ● You use expressions like **to put it briefly** and **to put it simply** just before you say something in order to comment on your way of saying it, for example to say that you are going to express yourself briefly or simply. EG *To put it briefly, we must attend to this problem immediately or accept the consequences... To put it in more general terms: man is moral, woman amoral.* ● PHR : USED AS ADV SEN ● to **put it mildly**: see **mildly**.

4 When you **put** your case or point of view, you state in detail your reasons for doing or thinking something. EG *He would have known how to put his case... She put her own point of view.* V+O = present

5 When you **put** a question to someone, you ask them a question or ask them to explain something. EG *I put this question to Dr Leslie Cook... Let me put to you a practical problem.* V+O : IF+PREP THEN *to*

6 If you **put it to** someone that something is the case, you suggest to them that it is true, especially when you think that they will be unwilling to accept or admit this. EG *I put it to him that, in fact, he was losing a good foreman... They put it to me that I knew all the time where the money was hidden.* PHR+REPORT-CL : VB INFLECTS

7 If you **put** someone or something in a particular state or situation, you cause them to be in that state or situation. EG *It puts me in a rather difficult position... The company closed several months ago putting 120 people out of a job... This would put the party into power... She put the matter beyond all doubt.* V+O+A = place

8 If you **put** something or someone in a particular class or group, you classify them in that way. If you **put** them, for example, above or below something or someone else, you judge them to be greater or less great than the other thing or person. EG *I'd put it among his earlier works... I wouldn't put him in the same class as Verdi... They put Warhol on a par with Titian.* V+O+A ⇑ consider ● If you **put** something **before, over**, or **above** something else, you consider that the first thing is more important than the second and you show this in your behaviour. EG *He always put duty before pleasure... ...the failure to put public before private interest.* ● PHR : VB INFLECTS

9 If you **put** your time, strength, energy, etc into a particular activity, you use it in doing that activity. EG *She put all her energy into tidying the place up... Rudolph took a solo on the trumpet, putting everything he had into it.* V+O+A *(into)* = apply

10 If you **put** money into something, you invest money in it. EG *Capitalists are encouraged to put their wealth into productive enterprises... I put a lot of money into it.* V+O+A *(into)* = sink

11 If you **put**, for example, additional work, responsibilities, pressure, or demands on someone, you give them additional work or responsibilities or try to make them do something. EG *It puts a tremendous responsibility on us... People felt free to put more demands on the system... Pursuit of these objectives puts a strain on the economic system.* V+O+A *(on/upon)* = place ≠ remove

12 If you **put**, for example, emphasis or reliance on something, you emphasize it or rely on it. If you **put** the blame for something on someone, you blame them for it. EG *She put all the stress on Bal and his ideas... Don't put too much reliance on this.* V+O+A *(on/upon)* = place

13 If you **put** a particular word, sentence, etc somewhere, you write or type it there. EG *He couldn't read what Ken had put for his address... Put all the details on the card.* V+O : USU+A

14 If you **put** pen to paper, spade to the ground, etc, you start writing, digging, etc; a literary use. EG *A week elapsed before I could put pen to paper... ...putting plough or spade to the earth.* V+O+A *(to)* = apply

15 When a ship **puts to sea**, it sails away from the sea shore or from a harbour; a rather old-fashioned expression. PHR : VB INFLECTS = set sail

16 If you say that you **don't know where to put** yourself, you mean that you are very embarrassed; an informal expression. PHR : AUX INFLECTS

17 The word **put** also occurs in a large number of expressions, which are explained under another word in this dictionary. For example: ● to **put** your **back into** something: see **back**. ● to **be hard put to do** something: see **hard**. ● to **put** someone**'s mind at rest**: see **mind**. ● to **put** someone **out of their misery**: see **misery**. ● to **stay put**: see **stay**. ● to **put** someone **to death**: see **death**.

put about. If you **put** something **about**, you tell it to people that you meet and cause it to become well-known. EG *Gossips have put it about that I am leaving next week... A rumour was put about to the effect that he had been drunk.* PHRASAL VB : V+O+ADV ⇑ say = put around spread

put across. When you **put** something **across**, you succeed in describing or explaining it to someone. EG *You need the skill to put your ideas across... It's very hard to put across the facts.* PHRASAL VB : V+O+ADV = convey, get across

put around. To **put** something **around** means the same as to put it about. PHRASAL VB : V+O+ADV/PREP

put aside. 1 If you **put aside** some work that you are doing, you stop doing it and put it somewhere in order to do something else. EG *My aunt put aside her sewing and picked up her book.* PHRASAL VB : V+O+ADV

2 If you **put aside** something that you might think about, you deliberately do not think about it. EG *It's a problem which they usually put aside.* PHRASAL VB : V+O+ADV = disregard

3 If you **put aside** a sum of money or supply of something, you place it in a bank, store, etc so that you can use it at a later time. EG *Your best plan is to put aside funds to cover these sudden calls for money.* PHRASAL VB : V+O+ADV ⇑ save = put by ≠ spend

put at. If a cost, value, age, etc **is put at** a particular amount, it is estimated to be that amount. EG *The pipeline's cost is now put at 2.7 billion pounds... The consensus of opinion put the date at 1900.* PHRASAL VB : V+O+PREP : HAS PASS = calculate

put away. 1 If you **put** something **away**, you put it tidily into a cupboard, drawer, pocket, etc. EG *I put away the shopping... Right–put your books away.* PHRASAL VB : V+O+ADV

2 If you **put** someone **away**, you cause them to stay in a prison, mental hospital, etc for a long time or for the rest of their life; an informal use. EG *They put him away for ten years... The doctor wanted me to have him put away.* PHRASAL VB : V+O+ADV ⇑ confine = lock up

3 To **put away** food or drink means to eat or drink a large amount of it; an informal use. EG *I had put away half a bottle of whisky.* PHRASAL VB : V+O+ADV ⇑ consume = down

4 If you **put** money **away** in a bank or savings PHRASAL VB :

account, you save it. EG *I've got a thousand pounds put away for a rainy day.*
O+ADV = stash away

put back. 1 If you **put** something **back** to a later time, you postpone it. EG *We've had to put back the seminar again.* • to **put the clock back**: see **clock**.
PHRASAL VB : V+O+ADV = defer, delay

2 To **put** something **back** also means to delay it or slow it down. EG *This will put production back at least a month.*
PHRASAL VB : V+O+ADV, USU+A ≠ speed up

3 If you **put back** alcoholic drink, you drink a large amount of it in a short time; an informal use. EG *I'd put back a fair amount of gin.*
PHRASAL VB : V+O+ADV = knock back

put by. If you **put by** a sum of money or supply of something, you place it in a bank, store, etc so that you can use it at a later time. EG *It's always a good idea to have something put by.*
PHRASAL VB : V+O+ADV ⇑ save = put aside ≠ spend

put down. 1 If you **put down** something that you are holding or carrying, you put it onto a surface, for example onto the floor or a table. EG *Marsha put her cup down... I put down my glass... Her chair was put down in the middle of the stage.*
PHRASAL VB : V+O+ADV ⇑ place = set down ≠ pick up

2 When you **put down** words, sentences, etc, you write or type them somewhere. EG *Put down what we've just said... For profession he put down simply 'business man'.*
PHRASAL VB : V+O+ADV

3 When soldiers, police, or other people in authority **put down** a riot or rebellion, they stop it by using force against the people who are taking part in it. EG *It was his duty to put down any internal trouble... Some of these riots are put down by the local police.*
PHRASAL VB : V+O+ADV = crush, suppress

4 If you **put** someone **down**, you behave in a way that makes them appear foolish, especially by ridiculing things that they say; an informal use. EG *A lot of people will be delighted to see him put down... ...her infuriating habit of putting people down in small ways.*
PHRASAL VB : V+O+ADV = humiliate, squash

5 When the driver of a vehicle **puts down** passengers, he or she stops in order to let them get out. EG *The bus put people down at every village along the way.*
PHRASAL VB : V+O+ADV = drop ≠ pick up

6 If someone **puts down** an animal that is old, ill, or dangerous, they kill it. EG *We had to have the cat put down.*
PHRASAL VB : V+O+ADV, USU PASS = destroy, put to sleep

7 See also **put-down**.

put down as. If you **put** someone or something **down as** a particular type of person or thing, you decide, often wrongly, that they are of that type. EG *He put me down as a moral crusader... Their labours were put down by historians as a calculated effort to police the world.*
PHRASAL VB : V+O+ADV+PREP = classify as, mark down as

put down for. If someone **puts** you **down for** a particular thing, they record your name, for example on a list, as intending to do it or being willing to do it. EG *I've put you down for a contribution of five pounds.*
PHRASAL VB : V+O+ADV+PREP

put down to. If you **put** something **down to** a particular thing, you believe that it is caused by that thing. EG *All this can be put down to advances in motor engineering... I put it down to arthritis.*
PHRASAL VB : V+O+ADV+PREP = attribute

put forth. If you **put forth** something such as an idea or theory, you make it known, for example by stating or publishing it; an old-fashioned formal word. EG *They discussed the matter, and put forth their conclusions.*
PHRASAL VB : V+O+ADV = state, set forth

put forward. 1 If you **put forward** something such as an argument or proposal, you produce it in order for people to consider and discuss it. EG *These were the arguments which Carson put forward... They rejected every proposal put forward.*
PHRASAL VB : V+O+ADV = advance, submit ≠ withdraw

2 If you **put** someone **forward** or if you **put** their name **forward**, you nominate them for a particular job or position. EG *The organization put forward eight candidates for the NUS executive... Too few women's names are put forward.*
PHRASAL VB : V+O+ADV = propose

put in. 1 If you **put in** a particular period of time or amount of effort doing something, you spend that period of time or that amount of effort doing it. EG *I put in fifteen hours of work daily... You've put in a lot of work... He put in an hour or so campaigning.*
PHRASAL VB : V+O+ADV ⇑ do

2 If you **put in** for something such as a job or if you **put in** a request, you apply for the job or make the request. EG *I put in a request for an interview... They put in a £20 a week pay claim... He put in for leave... Father put in for his job.*
PHRASAL VB : V+ADV, OR V+O+ADV, IF+PREP THEN *for* = submit ≠ withdraw

3 If you **put in** a remark or comment, you interrupt someone when they are saying something, usually to give some extra information about the subject. EG *'He was selling confectionery and bakery goods,' the bishop put in... 'But didn't you hear what I said?' put in Sally Jones.* • to **put in a good word for** someone: see **word**.
PHRASAL VB : V+ADV+QUOTE ⇑ say = interject

4 When voters **put in** a particular person, government, etc, that person or government is elected. EG *They put in a new regime... The voters turned that party out and put in its rival.*
PHRASAL VB : V+O+ADV = elect, vote in

5 When a ship **puts in** or **puts into** a harbour, it goes into harbour for a short time. EG *Sooner or later a ship will put in here... We might have to put into Hammerfest for shelter... We were refused permission to put in at Corfu.*
PHRASAL VB : V+ADV/PREP = dock ≠ set sail

6 If you **put** something **in**, you fix it, fit it, or plant it somewhere. EG *Sewerage facilities would be put in... We're having a new sink unit put in... ...the strawberry plants I'd seen her putting in earlier in the year.*
PHRASAL VB : V+O+ADV/PREP ⇑ install ≠ remove

put off. 1 If you **put** something **off**, you delay doing it. EG *They kept putting off signing the paper... Don't put it off till tomorrow.*
PHRASAL VB : V+O+ADV = postpone

2 If you **put** someone **off**, **2.1** you tell them that you are not yet able to do something that they have asked you to do. EG *I'm sorry, but I can't put him off any longer.*
PHRASAL VB : V+O+ADV

2.2 you cause them to change their mind and not do or have something that they were intending to do or have. EG *Nothing would put her off once she had made up her mind... Senator Ervin was not to be put off by the President's claim.* • to **put** someone **off their stroke**: see **stroke**.
PHRASAL VB : V+O+ADV/PREP = deter

3 To **put** someone **off** something means to disgust or offend them slightly so that they do not want to do, have, or experience it. EG *I had seen enough to put me off farmwork.*
PHRASAL VB : V+O+ADV/PREP

4 When a ship or vehicle **puts** someone **off**, it stops somewhere in order to let them get off. EG *They put him off at Calais.*
PHRASAL VB : V+O+ADV+A = drop ≠ take on

put on. 1 When you **put on** something such as a piece of clothing, you place it on or over a part of your body in order to wear it. EG *I put on my jacket... Morris put on his hat and gloves... He put on his glasses.*
PHRASAL VB : V+O+ADV/PREP = don ≠ take off

2 When you **put on** something such as make-up or ointment, you paint or spread it over a part of your skin. EG *She put lipstick on before every class... ...the cream that she put on to soothe her sunburn.*
PHRASAL VB : V+O+ADV/PREP = apply ≠ remove

3 When a person or company **puts on** a play, opera, show, etc, it is performed, produced, or organized by them. EG *He puts on working class plays... A French company has put on 'Peter Grimes'.*
PHRASAL VB : V+O+ADV = present, stage

4 When a person or organization **puts on** a particular kind of service, they provide that service. EG *The farmhouse puts on quite a decent spread... They're putting on a special train service.*
PHRASAL VB : V+O+ADV = lay on

5 If someone **puts on** weight, they become heavier. EG *Hasn't he put on weight?... She had put on over a stone.*
PHRASAL VB : V+O+ADV/PREP = gain ≠ lose

6 If you **put on** something such as an electrical or gas device, you cause it to work by pressing a switch, turning a knob, etc. EG *He put on the light... Shall I put the fire on?... She put the radio on.*
PHRASAL VB : V+O+ADV = turn on ≠ put off, turn off

7 If you **put on** the brake of a vehicle, you operate the brake. EG *She had to put on her brake rather suddenly... Put the brake on and leave the car in gear.*
PHRASAL VB : V+O+ADV = apply ≠ release

8 If you **put on** a record, tape, video, etc, you cause it to begin to play by putting it onto or into a record player, cassette player, video, etc. EG *We put on a record called 'Laughing Gas'... She put on the Brahms Second Piano Concerto... The teacher was asked to put on a tape.*
PHRASAL VB : V+O+ADV ≠ take off

9 If you **put on** a kettle, saucepan, etc, you place it onto a gas or electric cooker in order to boil water, cook a meal, etc. If you **put on** a meal, you begin to cook it. EG *They put the kettle on to make a cup of tea... She forgets to put the dinner on.*
PHRASAL VB : V+O+ADV/PREP ≠ take off

10 If you **put on** a bet, you make a bet. If you **put** a sum of money **on** something, for example a particular racehorse, you make a bet about it, for example that the horse will win. EG *Put a fiver on 'Stainless Stephen' for me.* • to **put** your **shirt on** something: see **shirt**.
PHRASAL VB : V+O+ADV/PREP

11 To **put** a particular amount **on** something means to add that amount to its cost or value. EG *That decision will put another 5p a gallon on petrol.*
PHRASAL VB : V+O+PREP = slap on ≠ knock off

12 To **put** a particular tax or restriction **on** something means to cause it to be taxed or restricted in that way. EG *A seventy per cent tax has been put on*
PHRASAL VB : V+O+PREP = impose

whisky... The government has put an embargo on all imports.

13 If you **put on** a look or way of speaking or behaving, you look, speak, or behave in a way that is not natural to you. EG *She put on that look of not caring... I don't see why you have to put on a phoney English accent.* ● to **put on a brave** or **good face**: see **face**. ● If you say that someone **is putting it on**, you mean that they are pretending to have strong or deep feelings about something in order to get attention or sympathy; an informal expression. EG *Putting it on a bit, aren't you?*

PHRASAL VB : V+O+ADV = assume, adopt
● PHR : VB INFLECTS

14 If someone is putting you **on**, they are teasing you by trying to make you believe something that is not true; an informal use. EG *'You're putting me on,' said Deirdre.*

PHRASAL VB : V+O+ADV = have on, kid

put onto. If you **put** someone **onto** something, you tell them about something that could benefit them; a fairly informal use. EG *One of his married friends put him on to Volunteer Service.*

PHRASAL VB : V+O+PREP

put out. **1** If something such as an announcement or story **is put out**, **1.1** it is told to or read by a lot of people. EG *He put out a statement denouncing the commission's conclusions... Various scare stories have been put out during the last few years.* **1.2** it is broadcast on radio or television. EG *The pilot put out a radio message... It was put out by the non-commercial network OXYZ.*

PHRASAL VB : V+O+ADV
PHRASAL VB : V+O+ADV

2 If you **put out** something such as a fire, a candle, or a cigarette, you cause it to stop burning. EG *He put the fire out... Sheldon put out his cigar.*

PHRASAL VB : V+O+ADV = extinguish ≠ light

3 If you **put out** an electric light, you cause it to stop shining by pressing or turning a switch. EG *He put out the light.*

PHRASAL VB : V+O+ADV = turn off ≠ put on

4 To **put out** something also means **4.1** to take it out of your house and leave it, for example, on the doorstep or ready for someone to collect. EG *Did you put the rubbish out?... She still can't remember to put out the milk bottles... It's as easy as putting out the cat at night.* **4.2** to put it somewhere, especially in a room, so that it will be noticed and used. EG *I put clean clothes out for you on the bed... Put out some ashtrays.*

PHRASAL VB : V+O+ADV ≠ bring in
PHRASAL VB : V+O+ADV ⇑ provide ≠ remove

5 If you **put out** your hand or both your hands, you move your hand or hands forward from your body, for example in order to protect yourself, to receive something, or to shake someone else's hand. EG *Judy put out her hands... I walked over to one young woman and put out my hand.*

PHRASAL VB : V+O+ADV = extend, hold out ≠ withdraw

6 If you **put** your tongue **out**, you poke it through your lips, especially as a rude gesture. EG *She put her tongue out at him.*

PHRASAL VB : V+O+ADV, IF+PREP THEN *at* = stick out

7 If you **put** your back, hip, shoulder, etc **out**, you accidentally cause a bone to be moved from its normal position; an informal use. EG *More backs may have been put out cleaning baths than in any other activity.*

PHRASAL VB : V+O+ADV = dislocate

8 If you are put out, someone or something has upset or annoyed you; an informal use. EG *Clarissa was too full of her own indignation to be put out by any lack of response.* ◊ **put out**. EG *Lally looked a bit put out... I was somewhat put out when the audience laughed loudly.*

PHRASAL VB : V+O+ADV, USU PASS
◊ ADJ QUALIT : PRED = piqued

9 If you **put** yourself **out** to do something, you do it even if it is inconvenient for you, especially in order to help someone; a fairly informal use. EG *John was always prepared to put himself out... He was putting himself out to please her.*

PHRASAL VB : V+O (REFL) + ADV = go to some trouble

10 If you **put** someone **out**, you cause them trouble or inconvenience; a rather old-fashioned use. EG *I hope I'm not putting you out.*

PHRASAL VB : V+O+ADV

put over. **1** When you **put** something **over**, you succeed in describing or explaining it to someone. EG *It is difficult for her to put over her own thoughts... How to put it over to the class, that's the trouble.*

PHRASAL VB : V+O+ADV = convey, get across

2 If someone **puts one over** on you, they deceive you and make you believe something such as a false claim or excuse; an informal expression. EG *I thought he was trying to put one over on me.*

PHR : VB INFLECTS, IF+PREP THEN *on* = pull a fast one

put round. To **put** something **round** means the same as to put it about. EG *It's just a rumour put round by students.*

PHRASAL VB : V+O+ADV = spread

put through. **1** If you **put through** a telephone call or **put through** the person making the call, you enable the person to speak to someone else by telephone. EG *She wanted to chat with the caller before putting the call through... 'It's Martha.'–'Okay. Put her through.'... 'Data Room, please.'–'I'll put you through.'*

PHRASAL VB : V+O+ADV = connect ≠ cut off

2 To **put through** something such as an agreement or plan means to succeed in getting it formally approved or agreed. EG *They put through the first nuclear arms agreements... They had at last succeeded in putting a meaningful reform through.*

PHRASAL VB : V+O+ADV

3 If you **put** someone **through** something such as a course of study or series of tests, you make them do it. EG *He put himself through several diploma courses... It's not right to put him through a lot of tests.* ● to **put** someone **through their paces**: see **pace**.

PHRASAL VB : V+O+PREP

4 If someone **puts** you **through** it, they do something to you or make you do something that is unpleasant for you; an informal use. EG *Did they put you through it, Janet?... I'm sorry to put you through this again.*

PHRASAL VB : V+O+PREP ≠ spare

put together. **1** If you **put** something **together**, **1.1** you join its different parts to each other so that it can be used. EG *He started to put his rod together.* **1.2** you organize or arrange it; a fairly informal use. EG *The whole production was somewhat hastily put together... The agency has put together the biggest ever campaign for a new car.*

PHRASAL VB : V+O+ADV
PHRASAL VB : V+O+ADV

2 You say **put together** after an expression that refers to a set of people or things when you want to indicate that another person or thing has, does, or uses more of something than the whole of the rest of the set. EG *He is smarter than all your colonels put together... The schools spend as much as the rest of the city put together.*

PHR AFTER N

put up. **1** To **put up** something such as a wall, a fence, or a building means to build it; a fairly informal use. EG *We shall have to put up a fence... ...a building that the authorities had put up.*

PHRASAL VB : V+O+ADV ⇑ construct = erect

2 If you **put up** something such as an umbrella, tent, or hood, you open, assemble, or arrange it so that it can be used. EG *I should put your umbrella up... I put up my tent on the outskirts of Camp Q... Why doesn't she put the hood up?*

PHRASAL VB : V+O+ADV = raise ≠ lower, take down

3 If you **put up** something such as a poster or sign, you stick or fasten it to a building, wall, fence, etc. EG *These posters were put up all over the place... She put up a large sign outside her house.*

PHRASAL VB : V+O+ADV ≠ take down

4 If you **put up** opposition or resistance to something, you oppose or resist it. EG *America has put up so much resistance to Concord... We had put up a fierce struggle.* ● to **put up a fight**: see **fight**. ● to **put up a good show**: see **show**.

PHRASAL VB : ORDER V+ADV+O = offer

5 If you **put up** something such as an argument or proposal, you produce it in order for people to consider and discuss it. EG *...the argument that the Vatican is putting up all the time... He wouldn't have put up half such a good case for himself.*

PHRASAL VB : ORDER V+ADV+O = advance, put forward ≠ withdraw

6 If you **put up** money for something, you provide the money that is needed to pay for it. EG *The banks will not put up money without government backing... They put up their own cash.*

PHRASAL VB : ORDER V+ADV+O

7 To **put up** the price or cost of something means to cause it to increase. EG *If we have couchettes, it'll put the price up even more.*

PHRASAL VB : V+O+ADV = raise ≠ bring down

8 If someone **puts** you **up** or if you **put up** somewhere, you stay with them or stay there for one or more nights. EG *I offered to put him up... She was put up at the Grand Hotel... We put up at Chestnut Court.*

PHRASAL VB : V-ERG+ADV, +A

9 If you **put up** or **are put up** in an election, you are chosen to be a candidate in the election. EG *They put up several candidates in Cornwall... He put up as an independent candidate.*

PHRASAL VB : V-ERG+ADV

10 See also **put-up**.

put upon. If you **are put upon**, someone treats you badly and takes advantage of your willingness to help them; an informal expression. EG *We are not prepared to be put upon.* ● See also **put-upon**.

PHRASAL VB : PREP, USU PASS = impose on

put up to. If you **put** someone **up to** something, you cause them to do something wrong or foolish, for example by suggesting that it would be a clever or amusing thing to do. EG *Julie herself had probably put them up to it.*

PHRASAL VB : V+O+ADV+PREP = incite ≠ deter

put up with. If you **put up with** something, you tolerate or accept it, even though you find it unpleasant or unsatisfactory. EG *I'm prepared to put up with it for the time being... The visitors could put up with any amount of boredom... The natives have to put up with gaping tourists.*

PHRASAL VB : V+ADV+PREP = endure

putative /pju:tətɪv/. If you describe someone or something as **putative**, you mean that they are

ADJ CLASSIF : ATTRIB

generally thought to be the particular thing mentioned; a formal or legal word. EG *...the putative father of her child.*

put-down, put-downs. A **put-down** is something that you say or do to someone which makes them appear foolish; an informal word. EG *The ultimate put-down is to be given a pat on the head.* N COUNT = snub

putrefaction /pju:trɪfækʃə⁰n/ is the process of rotting or decaying; a formal word. EG *...the smell of putrefaction.* N UNCOUNT = decomposition

putrefy /pju:trɪfaɪ/, **putrefies, putrefying, putrefied.** When something **putrefies**, it rots and produces a disgusting smell; a formal word. EG *Thousands of bodies were decomposing and putrefying.* V = decay, decompose

putrescent /pju:trɛsənt/. Something that is **putrescent** is beginning to rot and produce a disgusting smell; a formal word. EG *...a putrescent corpse.* ADJ CLASSIF = decaying

putrid /pju:trɪd/. 1 Something that is **putrid** is rotten and beginning to smell disgusting; a formal use. EG *... rotted and putrid mess.* ADJ CLASSIF = decaying

2 If you describe something as **putrid**, you mean that it is worthless or useless; an informal use. EG *It was absolutely putrid!* ADJ QUALIT = awful, terrible ≠ fine, great

putsch /pʊtʃ/, **putsches.** A **putsch** is a sudden attempt to get rid of a government by force. EG *...the military putsch of April 1961.* N COUNT ⇑ uprising = coup

putt /pʌt/, **putts, putting, putted.** A **putt** is a stroke in golf that you make with a special club when the ball has reached the green; a technical term. EG *I managed to miss a three-foot putt.* ▸ used as a verb. EG *He usually putted well with that club.* N COUNT ▸ V OR V+O : USU V

putter /pʌtə/, **putters, puttering, puttered.** 1 A **putter** is a club used for hitting a golf ball when it has reached the green; a technical term. N COUNT

2 When a boat or vehicle **putters**, its engine makes a slow throbbing sound as it moves. EG *A few fishing boats puttered past.* V : USU+A = chug

3 To **putter** also means the same as to potter about; used in American English. EG *He spent his days puttering in his rose garden.* V : USU+A = tinker

putting green, putting greens; also spelled with a hyphen. A **putting green** is a very small golf course on which the grass is kept short and on which there are no obstacles. N COUNT

putty /pʌti¹/ is a stiff paste used to fix glass panes into frames and to fill cracks or holes in woodwork. N UNCOUNT

put-up. **A put-up job** is something that has been arranged beforehand in order to cheat or deceive someone; an informal expression. EG *It was a put-up job, if ever there was one.* PHR : USED AS C = fix

put-upon. If you are **put-upon**, you have been treated badly by someone who has taken advantage of your willingness to help them; an informal word. EG *...the depressed and depressing Halliwell, his put-upon friend... I felt cheated and put-upon.* ADJ QUALIT ⇑ maltreated = used

puzzle /pʌzə⁰l/, **puzzles, puzzling, puzzled.** 1 To **puzzle** someone means to cause them to feel confused and often slightly worried because they cannot understand something. EG *There was one sentence which puzzled me deeply... O'Shea puzzled Morris.* ◊ **puzzling.** EG *This is a puzzling statement... I find this rather puzzling.* V+O = baffle, mystify ◊ ADJ QUALIT = baffling

2 If you **puzzle** your head or **puzzle** about something, you try hard to think of the answer or explanation for something. EG *He was still puzzling his head about the two names... They're puzzling in their minds what that word means.* V+O, OR V+A ⇑ ponder

3 A **puzzle** is 3.1 a person or thing that is hard to understand or does not seem to have an explanation. EG *The motives of the film-makers remain a puzzle.* N COUNT : USU SING = mystery

3.2 a question, game, or toy that you need skill or careful thought to answer correctly or to put together properly. EG *...mental puzzles.* ● See also **Chinese puzzle.** N COUNT ⇑ problem

puzzle out. If you **puzzle out** a problem, you find the answer to it by thinking hard about it. EG *I've been trying to puzzle out the answer all day.* PHRASAL VB : V+O+ADV ⇑ solve

puzzle over. If you **puzzle over** something, you think hard about it in order to try to understand it. EG *She puzzled over the letter all morning.* PHRASAL VB : V+PREP, HAS PASS ⇑ ponder

puzzled /pʌzə⁰ld/. Someone who is **puzzled** is confused and often slightly worried because they cannot understand something. EG *Madeleine looked puzzled... I am puzzled that she left without saying goodbye... He was puzzled why a man who used so much tobacco bought it in such small quantities.* ▸ used of expressions. EG *...a puzzled expression.* ADJ QUALIT = mystified, perplexed

puzzlement /pʌzə⁰lmə²nt/ is the confusion and slight worry that you feel when you do not understand something. EG *I looked at him in puzzlement.* N UNCOUNT = bafflement, perplexity

PVC /pi: vi: si:/ is a plastic material which is used for making clothing, pipes, tiles, etc. 'PVC' is an abbreviation for 'polyvinyl chloride'. N UNCOUNT

pw is a written abbreviation for 'per week'. It is used especially when stating the weekly cost of something. EG *...rent-£25 pw.* N UNCOUNT : USU NUM+N

pygmy /pɪgmi¹/, **pygmies**; also spelled **pigmy.** 1 **Pygmy** is used in order to refer to a species of animal which is the smallest of a group of related species; a technical use. EG *The pygmy marmoset has a body length of only ten centimetres.* N BEFORE N ⇑ small ≠ giant

2 A **pygmy** is a very small person, especially a person who comes from a racial group in which the people are all small. EG *...the pygmies of the Amazon jungle.* N COUNT

pyjama /pədʒa:mə/, **pyjamas**; also spelled **pajama** in American English. A pair of **pyjamas** consists of loose trousers and a loose jacket or top that people, especially men and children, wear in bed. EG *He was sitting there in striped pyjamas... ...his pyjama trousers.* N PLURAL : ALSO *a pair of*+N

pylon /paɪlə⁷n/, **pylons. Pylons** are very tall metal structures which hold electric cables high above the ground so that electricity can be transmitted over long distances. EG *...electricity pylons.* N COUNT

pyramid /pɪrəmɪd/, **pyramids.** 1 A **pyramid** is 1.1 an ancient stone building which was built over the tombs of dead kings and queens, especially in Egypt. Pyramids have triangular walls that slope upwards and inwards to a single point. EG *The Pyramids were among the Seven Wonders of the World.* N COUNT 1.2 an object or shape with a flat base and flat triangular sides that slope upwards and inwards to a point. N COUNT 1.3 something that is shaped like a pyramid. EG *They built a pyramid of leaves and twigs.* N COUNT

2 You can describe something as a **pyramid** when it is organized in levels so that the top level contains fewer people or things than the lower levels. EG *The universities are at the top of the pyramid of education.* N COUNT : USU SING+SUPP ⇑ hierarchy

pyramidal /pɪrəmɪdə⁰l/. Something that is **pyramidal** is shaped like a pyramid; a formal word. EG *...a pyramidal building.* ADJ CLASSIF

pyre /paɪə/, **pyres.** A **pyre** is a high pile of wood which is built outside in order to ceremonially burn dead bodies or religious offerings; a formal word. EG *...a funeral pyre... They built pyres and made burnt offerings to their god.* N COUNT ⇑ fire

Pyrex /paɪrɛks/ is a trademark for a type of strong glass which is used for making bowls, dishes, etc that do not break when you cook things in them. N UNCOUNT, OR N BEFORE N

pyrotechnics /paɪrə⁶tɛknɪks/. 1 **Pyrotechnics** is the making or displaying of fireworks. N UNCOUNT

2 People also sometimes refer to amazing displays of skill as **pyrotechnics.** N PLURAL : USU+SUPP

Pyrrhic victory /pɪrɪk vɪktə⁰ri¹/, **Pyrrhic victories.** If you describe a result as a **Pyrrhic victory**, you mean that although you have won or gained something, it was not worth the losses or sacrifices that you had to make. N COUNT

python /paɪθə⁷n/, **pythons.** A **python** is a large, very long snake that kills animals by squeezing them with its body. N COUNT

Qq

Q, q /kjuː/, **Qs, q's.** 1 **Q** is the seventeenth letter of the English alphabet. ● to **mind one's p's and q's**: see p. N COUNT
2 **Q** or **q** is an abbreviation for various words beginning with Q or q, such as 'question' and 'Queen'.

QC, QCs. In British English, a **QC** is a senior barrister; an abbreviation for 'Queen's Counsel'. QC is often used after a person's name. N COUNT: ALSO IN TITLES AFTER NAMES

Q.E.D. is used 1 to say that you have proved what you originally set out to prove; a technical term in mathematics. CONVENTION 2 in informal English, to indicate that something which has just been said or done is the answer to a question. CONVENTION

qua /kwɑː/ is used to indicate that you are talking about something as an ideal or as an abstract idea; a formal word. EG *It's the bourgeoisie he's after, not the English qua English.* PREP = as

quack /kwæk/, **quacks, quacking, quacked.** 1 When a duck makes a sound, it **quacks.** EG *...wild duck quacking on the river.* ▸ used as a noun. EG *Suddenly, he heard a quack.* V ⇑ call ▸ N COUNT
2 A **quack** is a doctor or an unqualified person who claims to be skilled in medicine; used showing disapproval. EG *...paying exorbitant fees to a quack who promises a magical cure.* N COUNT

quad /kwɒd/, **quads.** A **quad** is 1 one of four children who are born at the same time to the same mother. N COUNT ⇑ child 2 a quadrangle in a college at Oxford University or in a school; used in British English. N COUNT

quadrangle /kwɒdræŋgəºl/, **quadrangles.** A **quadrangle** is an open square area that has buildings round it, which is designed as part of the whole group of buildings. N COUNT ⇑ courtyard = quad

quadrilateral /kwɒdrɪˈlætəºrəl/, **quadrilaterals.** A **quadrilateral** is a geometrical shape that has four straight sides joined together. N COUNT

quadrille /kwəʼdriːl/, **quadrilles.** A **quadrille** is an old-fashioned dance for four or more couples. N COUNT

quadruped /kwɒdrupɛd/, **quadrupeds.** A **quadruped** is any animal with four legs; a formal word. N COUNT

quadruple /kwɒdrʊpəºl/, **quadruples, quadrupling, quadrupled.** 1 When an amount or number **quadruples** or when you **quadruple** it, it becomes four times as large. EG *In the last twenty years wheat production has almost quadrupled... We could quadruple output to around 10 million tons.* V-ERG ⇑ increase
2 An amount that is **quadruple** is four times as large as it had been previously or four times as large as average. EG *She poured him a quadruple measure of whisky.* ADJ CLASSIF

quadruplet /kwɒdrʊplɪˀt, kwɒdruːplɪˀt/, **quadruplets.** A **quadruplet** is one of four children who are born at the same time to the same mother. N COUNT = quad

quaff /kwɒf, kwɑːf/, **quaffs, quaffing, quaffed.** If you **quaff** a drink, you drink it quickly; an old-fashioned word. EG *He quaffed half the contents of his glass in one gulp.* V+O = swig

quagmire /kwægmaɪə, kwɒg-/, **quagmires.** A **quagmire** is 1 a soft, wet area of land, especially one which you sink into if you try to walk on it. EG *...heavy soils which turn into a quagmire when trodden.* N COUNT/UNCOUNT 2 an awkward, complicated, or embarrassing situation. N COUNT = dilemma

quail /kweɪl/, **quails, quailing, quailed.** The form **quail** can be used as the plural of the noun as well as **quails.** 1 A **quail** is a small bird of the partridge family; also used of the meat of this bird. EG *...a dog trainer who shot quail for the market... ...a large flock of quails.* N COUNT/UNCOUNT
2 If you **quail,** you feel very afraid. EG *She quailed before his angry bitterness.* V = cringe

quaint /kweɪnt/, **quainter, quaintest.** Something that is **quaint** is attractive because it is strange and rather old-fashioned. EG *...quaint little houses.* ADJ QUALIT = curious
◇ **quaintly.** EG *The building was quaintly old-fashioned.* ◇ **quaintness.** ◇ ADV ◇ N UNCOUNT

quake /kweɪk/, **quakes, quaking, quaked.** 1 If you **quake,** you tremble or shake because you are very afraid. EG *I just stood there quaking with fear.* V = quiver
2 A **quake** is an earthquake. EG *On average, there are four major quakes in a century.* N COUNT

Quaker /kweɪkə/, **Quakers.** A **Quaker** is a person who belongs to a Christian group called the Society of Friends. N COUNT

qualification /kwɒlɪfɪkeɪʃəºn/, **qualifications.** 1 A **qualification** is 1.1 an official record of achievement that you get when you have successfully completed a course of training or passed an exam. EG *No training or special qualifications are needed for the job... I have a secretarial qualification... I haven't got any qualifications at all in English Literature.* N COUNT 1.2 a quality or skill that you need for a particular activity or job. EG *One of the qualifications you need in advertising is a fertile mind... He had every qualification for the job except impartiality.* N COUNT ⇑ requirement = attribute 1.3 a detail or explanation that you add to a statement or description to make it less strong or less generalized. EG *Two qualifications need to be made... Throughout this book I have, with suitable qualifications and apologies, used the word 'intelligence' in connection with computers.* N COUNT/UNCOUNT ⇑ restriction
2 **Qualification** is the act of successfully completing a course of training or passing the exams that you need to pass in order to work in a particular profession. EG *Even after qualification jobs were hard to find.* N UNCOUNT

qualified /kwɒlɪfaɪd/. 1 Someone who is **qualified** 1.1 has successfully completed a course of training or passed the exams that they need to pass in order to work in a particular profession. EG *These tests have to be carried out by a qualified doctor... The ophthalmic optician is qualified to examine your eyes... They have exams and are fully qualified at the end of four years.* ADJ CLASSIF ⇑ trained 1.2 has the qualities or skills that are suitable for a particular activity or job. EG *He was well qualified to fulfil the role of dictator... She did not feel qualified to discuss it.* ADJ QUALIT: PRED, USU+*to*-INF ⇑ suited
2 **Qualified** agreement or praise is not total and suggests that you have doubts. EG *The reaction was one of qualified praise... Their allegiance to the party had remained somewhat qualified.* ADJ QUALIT ⇑ limited ≠ wholehearted

qualifier /kwɒlɪfaɪə/, **qualifiers.** A **qualifier** is a person or thing that qualifies for something, especially a person who is successful in the first part of a competition and qualifies for the main competition or the next round. N COUNT

qualify /kwɒlɪfaɪ/, **qualifies, qualifying, qualified.** 1 When someone **qualifies,** they successfully complete a course of training or pass the exams necessary in order to be entitled to work in a particular profession. EG *I was thirty-three before I qualified as a doctor... Did you take a degree at University before you qualified?* V
2 If you **qualify** a statement or description, you add a detail or explanation to it to make it less strong or less generalized. EG *I'll qualify what I said... If I said that Warsaw was grim and grey, that statement has to be qualified.* V+O = modify
3 If someone **qualifies** for something, they have the right to have it or do it. EG *By working all their lives, people ought to qualify automatically for their pensions... Boon had failed to qualify for a postgraduate grant.* V+A *(for)* = be eligible
4 When something **qualifies** as something or when you **qualify** it as something, you describe it as having a particular quality. EG *I qualify it as pathetic... ...the rare unfortunate occurrences that qualified as news.* V-ERG+A *(as)*
5 To **qualify** in a competition means to be successful in one part of it so that you go on to another competition or another round. EG *England failed to qualify for the next round.* V ⇑ succeed

qualitative /kwɒlɪtətɪv, -teɪt-/ means affecting or relating to the standard of something and also to what it is like. EG *They have done nothing to stop qualitative improvements... ...a qualitative change.* ADJ CLASSIF: USU ATTRIB
◇ **qualitatively.** EG *The job of cutting cane has become qualitatively different since the revolution.* ◇ ADV

quality /kwɒlɪtiˡ/, **qualities.** 1 **Quality** is 1.1 the standard of something, and how good or bad it is in relation to other things of the same kind. EG *...improvements in quality... ...standards of quality and* N UNCOUNT ⇑ level taste... The quality of the photograph was poor... ...the high quality of their transmissions... I've got some good quality paper... ...things that are of lower quality. There is growing concern with the quality of life... ...the quality of this relationship is vital. **1.2** a high standard, for example in the way something has been made or done. EG ...four American-made programs of quality, taste, and family interest... ...a reputation for scrupulous scholarship and for quality... ...quality Australian fiction... The employers don't want quality work any more. N UNCOUNT, OR N BEFORE N

2 A **quality** is **2.1** a characteristic like kindness, honesty, or magnificence that is part of the nature of a person or thing. EG *Asquith paid tribute to his personal qualities... I've actually got a list here of the qualities they look for in a teacher... These two great players shared many of the same fine qualities–generosity, diligence, modesty, simplicity.* N COUNT ⇑ feature = attribute **2.2** a physical characteristic of a substance or object. EG *The vehicles are well respected for their performance, handling qualities, and robustness... ...medical sermons preaching the lethal qualities of fats.* N COUNT+SUPP ⇑ feature = property **2.3** an impression that something gives about what it is like. EG *The skin on the baby's face had a pearly translucent quality... The parish church itself retains the mysterious quality of an ancient sacred place.* N COUNT+SUPP = character

3 The **quality** newspapers are newspapers which are generally thought to give serious accounts of the news and reports on business matters, industry, culture, and society. They are usually large-sized. ADJ CLASSIF : ATTRIB ▸ used as a noun to refer to these newspapers in general. EG *...a story in one of the qualities.* ▸ N PLURAL : the+N

quality control is the activity of checking that products are all of a satisfactory standard and quality, usually by testing samples of them. EG *They were trained in better management, quality control and marketing.* N UNCOUNT ⇑ check

qualm /kwɑːm/, **qualms**. A **qualm** is a feeling of doubt or nervousness that you have because you are not sure that what you are doing is right. EG *He felt no qualms as he waited... I sometimes have qualms about our teaching.* N COUNT : USU PL = misgiving, scruple

quandary /kwɒndəºri¹/, **quandaries**. A **quandary** is the state of not being able to decide or think what to do about a situation that you are involved in. EG *He found himself in a quandary.* N COUNT = dilemma

quanta /kwɒntə/ is the plural of **quantum**.

> **QUANTIF** ☐ In this dictionary QUANTIF is used in the grammar notes beside entries to describe a word such as *more, least,* or *several.* These words are used to indicate the general quantity or amount of something. QUANTIFS behave in the following ways: **1** They come before a noun and usually before any adjectives in the noun group. An example is **many 5**. EG *She was living **many** miles away... There aren't **many** gardeners of my ability left... It presents too **many** delivery problems.* **2** They are used in front of a particular type of noun. For example, *many* and *several* are used in front of N COUNTS in the plural; *little* and *much* are used in front of N UNCOUNTS. The grammar note beside each entry explains which type of noun the QUANTIF is used with, when there are restrictions on this. **3** They can be used before a prepositional group starting with *of.* Examples are **most 2** and **several**. EG *We spent **most** of Saturday on it... **Most** of my work is political in intent... I had acted in **several** of his plays... **Several** of the women told me that they had been to the film.* **4** They can be used in the position in the clause which would typically be taken by a noun group, where they often stand for or refer back to another noun group. An example is **little 6.4**. EG *She ate **little**... He should say as **little** as possible... We really know very **little** about them... They had **little** in common.*

quantify /kwɒntɪfaɪ/, **quantifies, quantifying, quantified**. If you **quantify** something, you represent it as an amount or number so that it can be counted, measured, or compared to other things. EG *If one could quantify joy, it is likely that for me it would be a new car.* V+O

quantitative /kwɒntɪtətɪv, -teɪt-/ means **1** involving or relating to the size or amount of something. EG *There has been a unique quantitative jump in industrial production.* ADJ CLASSIF : USU ATTRIB **2** represented as an amount or number. EG *It is not yet possible to make a quantitative assessment of the effectiveness of our investment.* ADJ CLASSIF : USU ATTRIB

quantity /kwɒntɪti¹/, **quantities**. **1** A **quantity** is an amount that you can measure or count. EG *You only need a very small quantity... ...a pound of anchovies and the same quantity of salt... Natural gas was discovered in large quantities beneath the North Sea... He threw into the flames a quantity of leaves from a certain bush.* N COUNT/PART : ALSO SING=PL

2 Quantity is **2.1** a large amount of something. EG *The meat is produced in quantity and sold in Eastern Europe... They are proud of the sheer quantity of the work they can shift in a day.* N UNCOUNT = bulk **2.2** the amount of something that there is; often used in contrast to its quality and how good it is. EG *Materials are being seen in terms simply of quantity rather than quality... The food supply has grown less, in quantity and quality, as economic rot sets in.* N UNCOUNT

3 If you say that someone or something is an **unknown quantity**, you mean that you do not know anything about them. EG *To Shanti the outside world was a totally unknown quantity.* PHR : USED AS C = mystery

quantity surveyor, quantity surveyors. A **quantity surveyor** is a person who works with builders and architects and whose job is to calculate how long particular pieces of work will take and how much they will cost. EG *I started off wanting to be a quantity surveyor.* N COUNT

quantum /kwɒntəºm/, **quanta**. **1** A **quantum** is a quantity of something, especially a very small quantity; used in formal English. EG *He supplies a quantum of effort or of energy which could as well be supplied by almost anyone else.* N PART ⇑ amount

2 Quantum is used to describe various theories in physics and mathematics which are concerned with the properties and behaviour of particles. N BEFORE N

quantum leap, quantum leaps. A **quantum leap** or a **quantum jump** is a very great change, increase, or advance. N COUNT

quarantine /kwɒrəntiːn/, **quarantines, quarantining, quarantined**. **1 Quarantine** is the period of time during which a person or animal that may have a disease is kept separate from other people or animals so that the disease does not have a chance to spread. A period of quarantine is usually necessary for animals arriving from abroad. EG *Sam was growing impatient after the long quarantine... Her dog was in quarantine.* N SING : the+N, OR N UNCOUNT ⇑ isolation

2 To **quarantine** a person or animal means to keep them separate from others for a period of quarantine. EG *We will have to quarantine you for a few days.* V+O ⇑ isolate

quarrel /kwɒrəºl/, **quarrels, quarrelling, quarrelled**. American English uses the spellings **quarreling, quarreled**. **1** A **quarrel** is **1.1** an angry argument between two or more people, especially one which continues for quite a long time. EG *I don't think this office should enter into a family quarrel... There wasn't any evidence of quarrels between them.* N COUNT ⇑ disagreement = row **1.2** a cause of disagreement or complaint, especially something that someone has said that you particularly disagree with. EG *My quarrel with Greenberg is that he conceded far too much... I wouldn't have any quarrel with this proposal myself.* N COUNT+*with* : USU SING

2 If one person **quarrels** with another person, or if two people **quarrel**, they have an angry argument. EG *They quarrelled quite often... I don't want to quarrel with you.* V OR V+A (*with*) : RECIP = argue, row ◇ **quarrelling**. EG *I hate all the quarrelling in the house.* ◇ N UNCOUNT = arguing

3 If you say that you would **quarrel** with something that someone has said, you mean that you disagree or find fault with it. EG *One thing I would quarrel with in your introduction is the suggestion that television causes violence... I think Canetti might quarrel with the use of the word 'madness'.* V+A (*with*) = take issue

quarrelsome /kwɒrəlsəm/. Someone who is **quarrelsome** is always arguing with people. EG *His brothers were greedy and quarrelsome.* ADJ QUALIT = argumentative

quarry /kwɒri¹/, **quarries, quarrying, quarried**. **Quarry** is used as both the singular and the plural form for sense 1.1. **1** A **quarry** is **1.1** an animal that is being hunted. EG *Move slowly, or you will startle your quarry into instant retreat... Their quarry were rhinoceros, elephant, and leopard.* N COUNT : USU POSS+N = prey **1.2** an open surface that has been dug out of a mountain or a piece of land for the purpose of extracting stone, slate, or some other mineral. EG *This mountain was the site for a quarry... In 1553 just one of the quarries, Cymerau, produced 762 tons of finished slate.* N COUNT ⇑ mine

2 To **quarry** a stone or mineral means to remove it V OR V+O from a quarry by digging, drilling, or blasting. EG *These limestones have been quarried for centuries.*

quart /kwɔ:t/, **quarts**. A **quart** is a unit of volume that is equal to two pints. EG *...a quart of mayonnaise... You'll need a saucepan or jug that holds a quart.* N PART ⇑ measurement

quarter /kwɔ:tə/, **quarters, quartering, quartered**. 1 A **quarter** is one of four equal or approximately equal parts of something. EG *...a quarter of a century... It took me something like an hour and a quarter to make a phone call.* ▸ used as an adjective. EG *The sudden strength of American art in the quarter century following the Second World War was astonishing.* ● See also **three-quarters**. N COUNT ⇑ fraction ▸ ADJ CLASSIF : ATTRIB

2 If you **quarter** something, **2.1** you divide it into four equal or approximately equal parts. EG *The apples should be peeled, quartered, and coarsely grated.* **2.2** you reduce it so that it is only one fourth of its previous size, amount, quantity, etc. EG *The price of wheat was quartered in a year.* V+O V+O

3 **Quarter** to or, in American English, **quarter** of a particular hour is fifteen minutes before that time: see □ at TIME. EG *It's quarter to five... They allowed you to go at a quarter to eight... At a quarter of eight, in the library, he resumed his letter.* N UNCOUNT+*of/to*, OR N SING : *a*+N+*of/to*

4 **Quarter** past a particular hour is fifteen minutes past that time: see □ at TIME. EG *We're due at Janet's at quarter past eleven... I went up at quarter past... ...a quarter past four exactly.* N UNCOUNT+*past*, OR N SING : *a*+N+*of/to*

5 A **quarter** is also **5.1** a period of three months. EG *In the last quarter of 1980 inflation rose by 1%... Your salary will be paid each quarter, in arrears, by a bank-giro cheque.* **5.2** an American or Canadian coin that is worth 25 cents. EG *I deposited a quarter and two dimes in the slot.* **5.3** a unit of weight that is equal to four ounces; used in informal British English when you are buying things that are normally sold in small quantities. EG *A quarter of toffees, please.* **5.4** a direction or point of the compass, especially in relation to the direction that the wind is blowing from; a fairly formal use. **5.5** an area in a town or city where a particular group of people live or work or that is considered to have particular characteristics. EG *...the Black quarters of New York, Detroit or Washington... ...the network of back streets in the Latin Quarter... They lived eight to a room in some unsanitary quarter.* N COUNT : USU SING · N COUNT · N PART : USU SING · N COUNT · N COUNT : USU MOD+N, USU SING = district

6 If you refer to a feeling or reaction being in certain **quarters** or coming from a particular **quarter**, you are referring rather vaguely to a person or group of people who are reacting in a particular way to something. EG *Male prejudice still exists in certain quarters... The product was withdrawn after warning from the most eminent scientific quarters... Then came help from another quarter.* N COUNT+SUPP : USU PL

7 **Quarters** are rooms or houses that are provided for people to live in, especially soldiers and their families. EG *He had to leave his previous quarters at short notice due to a fire... ...servants' quarters... ...sleeping quarters.* N PLURAL ⇑ accommodation

8 To **quarter** people or animals means to provide them with somewhere to stay and sleep for a period of time, usually because they have to do a job away from where they usually live. EG *...a more remote area where the camels were quartered... ...Smith's hotel, where we were quartered throughout the war.* V+O : USU+A, USU PASS ⇑ accommodate = house

9 **At close quarters** means from a place that is very near or close to someone or something. EG *It was a privilege to observe her at such close quarters... It will be marvellous to see the country at such close quarters.* PHR : USED AS AN A

10 **Quarter** is mercy or pity that you show towards someone who is in your power; an old-fashioned use. EG *But Bloom has got no quarter from the competitors whom he had forced out of business... ...and in such circumstances men give no quarter.* N UNCOUNT : USU USED AS O WITH BROAD NEG = clemency

quarterdeck /kwɔ:tədɛk/, **quarterdecks**; also spelled with a hyphen. The **quarterdeck** on a ship is the highest part of the deck, which is near the back of the ship. EG *Drenching spray now and then splashed over the quarterdeck.* N COUNT : USU SING

quarterfinal /kwɔ:təfaɪnə[0]l/, **quarterfinals**; also spelled with a hyphen. A **quarterfinal** is one of the four matches in a competition which decides which four players or teams will compete in the semi-final. EG *As expected, Liverpool won their quarterfinal convincingly.* ▸ The **quarterfinals** is the round of a competition in which these four matches are played. EG *We lost in the quarterfinals.* N COUNT ▸ N PLURAL : USU the+N

quarterly /kwɔ:təli[1]/, **quarterlies**. 1 If something happens **quarterly**, it happens regularly four times a year, at intervals of three months. EG *The committee meets quarterly... ...an annual salary paid monthly or quarterly.* ▸ used as an adjective. EG *This is what the quarterly conference is for.* ADV AFTER VB ⇑ periodically ▸ ADJ CLASSIF : ATTRIB

2 A **quarterly** is a magazine or journal that is published regularly four times a year, at intervals of three months. EG *...a new quarterly journal called Fourth International.* N COUNT, OR ADJ CLASSIF : ATTRIB ⇑ periodical

quartermaster /kwɔ:təmɑ:stə/, **quartermasters**; also spelled with a hyphen. A **quartermaster** is an army officer who is responsible for accommodation, food, and equipment. N COUNT

quartet /kwɔ:tet/, **quartets**. A **quartet** is 1 a group of four people who play musical instruments or sing together. EG *...a concert given by the Amadeus Quartet.* 2 a piece of music for four instruments or four singers. EG *The concert began with a Mozart quartet.* 3 a group of four people or things. EG *Behind the happy couple was a quartet of bridesmaids.* N COUNT : ALSO IN NAMES AFTER N, USU SING · N COUNT · N COUNT/PART

quarto /kwɔ:təʊ/, **quartos**. 1 **Quarto** is a size of paper which is about 20 centimetres by 26 centimetres in size. N UNCOUNT

2 A **quarto** is a book which has pages which are quarto size. N COUNT

quartz /kwɔ:ts/ is a kind of hard, shiny crystal. It is used in making electronic equipment and very accurate watches and clocks. EG *...a quartz watch.* N UNCOUNT ⇑ mineral

quasar /kweɪzɑ:, -sɑ:/, **quasars**. A **quasar** is an object in outer space which is like a star and which produces powerful radio waves and other forms of energy; a technical term. N COUNT

quash /kwɒʃ/, **quashes, quashing, quashed**. 1 If you **quash** a decision or judgement, you officially reject it and make it no longer legally valid. EG *Their prison sentences were quashed on appeal... He made use of the Official Secrets Act to quash a critical parliamentary question.* V+O = overrule, revoke

2 If you **quash** someone or their emotions, you cause them to become weaker or less active. EG *His guilt swelled, but he quashed it... In his childhood he was utterly quashed by serious, stern, duty-bound parents.* V+O = repress

quasi- /kweɪzaɪ/. 1 **Quasi-** combines with adjectives to indicate that someone or something has some but not all of the qualities referred to by the adjective. EG *I am talking about a mystical or quasi-religious experience. ...the quasi-academic world of research institutes.* PREFIX

2 **Quasi-** also combines with nouns to indicate that someone or something is almost but not quite the thing mentioned. EG *They have turned their countries into quasi-republics.* PREFIX ⇑ so-called

quatrain /kwɒtreɪn/, **quatrains**. A **quatrain** is a verse of poetry that has four lines; a technical word. N COUNT

quaver /kweɪvə/, **quavers, quavering, quavered**. 1 If someone 's voice **quavers**, it sounds unsteady, for example because they are nervous or uncertain. EG *Her voice quavered grotesquely.* V OR V+QUOTE = quake

◊ **quavering**. EG *The quavering voice grew louder.* ◊ ADJ CLASSIF

2 A **quaver** is **2.1** the uncertain and unsteady sound in someone's voice when they are feeling nervous. EG *I tried to imitate his accent and the quaver which could sometimes be heard in his voice.* **2.2** a musical note that has half the time value of a crotchet; a technical term in music. N SING WITH DET = quiver · N COUNT

quay /ki:/, **quays**. A **quay** is a long platform beside the sea or a river where boats can be tied up and loaded or unloaded. N COUNT = wharf

quayside /ki:saɪd/. The **quayside** is the area at the edge of a quay. EG *The crowds on the quayside began to move off.* N SING WITH DET

queasy /kwi:zi[1]/, **queasier, queasiest**. If you feel **queasy**, 1 you feel rather ill, as if you are going to be sick. 2 you feel uneasy and worried about something. EG *I had a queasy feeling about the whole thing.* ADJ QUALIT · ADJ QUALIT = uncomfortable

queen /kwi:n/, **queens**. 1 A **queen** is **1.1** a woman who rules a country as its monarch. Queens are not elected, but are born into a royal family. EG *Kings and queens wear crowns... Admiralty Arch was part of the national memorial to Queen Victoria.* **1.2** a woman who is married to a king. EG *Henry VIII* N COUNT : ALSO IN TITLES ⇑ sovereign · N COUNT : ALSO IN TITLES *married his first Queen in the Tower of London.* **1.3** a woman who is famous, and who is considered to be outstanding in some particular field or achievement. EG *She was one of the great movie queens of her time... ...the queen of the newscasters, Angela Rippon.* • See also **beauty queen**. **1.4** a large female bee, ant, or wasp which can lay eggs. There is usually only one queen in each group of insects. EG *Queens lay up to 2,000 eggs a day during the summer... In a hive you've got one queen bee.* **1.5** the most powerful piece in chess, which can move backwards, forwards, sideways, and diagonally. EG *A good chess-player avoids exposing his queen.* **1.6** a playing card with a picture of a queen on it. A queen is usually worth more than a jack and less than a king. EG *...the queen of spades.* **1.7** a homosexual man, especially one who behaves in a feminine way; an offensive word used in informal English.

N COUNT : USU SING+SUPP = star; N COUNT ⇑ insect; N COUNT ⇑ chessman; N COUNT : IF+ PREP THEN *of* ⇑ playing card; N COUNT = queer

2 If you say that a particular woman **is queen bee**, you mean that she behaves as if she was the most important woman in a group of people. EG *She likes to be queen bee at all their parties.*

PHR : VB INFLECTS

queenly /kwi:nli¹/. Someone or something that is **queenly** is like a queen, or is considered to be suitable for a queen. EG *Rose's status was not exactly queenly... ...Dante Gabriel Rossetti's queenly portraits of women.*

ADJ QUALIT ⇑ regal

Queen Mother, Queen Mothers. The **Queen Mother** is the mother of a ruling king or queen. EG *...the Queen Mother's favourite artist... They gave a tea party for Queen Elizabeth the Queen Mother.*

N COUNT : ALSO IN TITLES, *the*+N

queer /kwɪə/, **queers**; **queerer, queerest**. **1** Something that is **queer** is, unexpected, unnatural, or strange. EG *He's a queer character, my friend Evans... Something was definitely queer about this town... It gave her a queer sensation to shake hands with a murderer... It was the queerest feeling!* ◊ **queerly**. EG *She looked at me queerly and didn't seem to know how to answer.*

ADJ QUALIT = odd, weird; ◊ ADV = oddly

2 If you say that you feel **queer**, you mean that you feel slightly ill. EG *I came over all queer after half an hour.*

ADJ QUALIT : PRED = dizzy

3 If you say that someone is **queer**, you mean that they behave in a mad or unreasonable way; used in informal English. EG *He got knocked on the head last year and he was very queer afterwards... She thinks I'm queer in the head.*

ADJ QUALIT : PRED ⇑ unbalanced = funny

4 In very informal, old-fashioned English, a **queer** is a homosexual man; an offensive use. ▸ also used as an adjective.

N COUNT; ▸ ADJ CLASSIF

5 If you say that someone is **in queer street**, you mean that they are having difficulties, especially because they owe a lot of money; used in informal British English.

PHR : USED AS AN A = in debt

6 • to **queer** someone's **pitch**: see **pitch**.

quell /kwel/, **quells, quelling, quelled**. **1** To **quell** opposition, violent behaviour, etc, means to use force or persuasion to put an end to it. EG *The police had been called in to quell a minor disturbance... This statement won't quell disagreement over the Voting Rights Act.*

V+O ⇑ stop = subdue

2 If you **quell** unpleasant feelings such as fear or grief, you try and stop yourself having these feelings or stop them becoming stronger. EG *I was trying to quell a growing unease.*

V+O = stifle, suppress

quench /kwentʃ/, **quenches, quenching, quenched**. **1** If you **quench** your thirst, you have a drink so that you stop being thirsty.

V+O = slake

2 If someone **quenches** a fire, they stop it burning; a slightly old-fashioned use. EG *Marion struggled to quench the flames.*

V+O = extinguish

querulous /kwerjᵘʊləs/. Someone who is **querulous** is often complaining, especially in a sad, whining voice. EG *...querulous children.* ▸ used of people's voices and statements. EG *Otto spoke in a weakly querulous voice... ...Marsha's querulous enquiry.* ◊ **querulously**. EG *'Where have you been?' she asked querulously.*

ADJ QUALIT = fretful; ▸ = petulant; ◊ ADV WITH VB = peevishly

query /kwɪəri¹/, **queries. querying, queried**. **1** A **query** is **1.1** a question, especially one which expresses doubt about something. EG *The assistant accepted my cheque for £210 without query... He works for an insurance company and deals with all the queries that come in.* **1.2** a question mark.

N COUNT, OR *without*+N; N COUNT

2 If you **query** something, you check it by asking about it because you are not sure if it is correct or accurate. EG *The company accountant queried my travel expenses... Our legal advisers did query whether it was absolutely correct.*

V+O, OR V+WH = question

3 To **query** means to ask a question; used especially in American English. EG *'How much do I owe you?' I queried, fishing in the pocket of my jeans.*

V+QUOTE = enquire

quest /kwest/, **quests, questing, quested**; an old-fashioned or literary word. **1** A **quest** is a long and difficult search for something, especially something that you value. EG *Little did I know when I embarked on this quest how futile it would be... ...the quest for truth.* • If you are **in quest of** something, you are looking for it. EG *I went down the stairs in quest of Teresa.*

N COUNT : IF+ PREP THEN *for*; • PREP = in search of

2 To **quest** means to search or seek for something, especially something which you value. EG *His hand, questing for something else, touched the handle of the revolver.* ◊ **questing**. EG *Enderby's questing finger roamed round the class like a searchlight.*

V : IF+PREP THEN *for* = hunt; ◊ ADJ CLASSIF : ATTRIB = searching

question /kwestʃəⁿn/, **questions, questioning, questioned**. **1** A **question** is a form of words which you say or write in order to ask someone about something, for example if you need information, or if you want to know their opinion. EG *Jill began to ask Fred a lot of questions about his childhood... A panel of experts attempted to answer the questions on education which were put to them* • In informal English, if you **pop the question**, you ask someone to marry you. EG *He finally popped the question after the waiter had brought the bill.*

N COUNT = query; • PHR : VB INFLECTS = propose

2 If you **question** someone, you ask them a lot of questions about a particular subject. EG *I started questioning her about Jane and Anthony... Parents and teachers were questioned closely to find out what was wrong with the school... Many of the men questioned in a survey thought that married women should not work.* ◊ **questioning**. EG *The three men were taken to the police station for questioning... He had to sit four written papers followed by verbal questioning by a panel of three judges.*

V+O : IF+PREP THEN *about* = sound out; ◊ N UNCOUNT = interrogation

3 If you **question** something, you express your doubts about whether it is true or worthwhile. EG *In many countries now women are questioning their traditional role in society... You are challenging my competence as a teacher, and I question your right to do it... He questioned whether anybody could run a marathon in less than 2 hours.* ◊ **questioning**. EG *Her children all have questioning minds.*

V+O, OR V+WH; ◊ ADJ QUALIT : ATTRIB

4 If there is some **question** about something, there is a doubt or uncertainty about it. EG *There has been some question as to whether or not the President will resign... There was absolutely no question about the diagnosis: She had lung cancer.*

N UNCOUNT+ SUPP

5 The word **question** is also used in the following expressions relating to doubt and uncertainty. **5.1** If something is **beyond question**, there is no doubt at all about it. EG *She knew beyond question that I was a person who could be trusted.* **5.2** If something **brings** something else **into question**, it makes people think more seriously about this other thing. EG *Unemployment has brought into question the right of married women to work.* **5.3** If you **call** something **into question**, you express serious doubts about it, usually because you think it might be dishonest or immoral. EG *His honesty was called into question... The morality of government has frequently been called into question.* **5.4** If a statement or subject is **open to question**, it is not yet certain and is considered to be worth discussing. EG *Whether women are happier now they enjoy such freedom as they do now is open to question.* **5.5** If you say that something is **out of the question**, you mean that it is impossible and is not worth considering. EG *She knew that a holiday this year was out of the question... It has been so cold here that gardening has been out of the question most of the time.* **5.6** If you say **there is no question of** doing something or succeeding in something, you mean that it is impossible to do it. EG *The hotel was so noisy that there was no question of getting a full night's sleep... There was never any question of his being fit enough to play against Spain.* **5.7** If you do something **without question**, you do it obediently and without arguing or asking why it is necessary. EG *They obeyed me without question.*

PHR : USED AS AN A = for certain; PHR : VB INFLECTS; PHR : VB INFLECTS; PHR : USED AS C = debatable; PHR : USED AS AN A = unthinkable; PHR : VB INFLECTS; PHR : USED AS AN A

6 In question. **6.1** The time **in question**, the place **in question**, etc, is the time or place which you have already referred to and which is important in what you are talking about. EG *Did James have dinner with*

PHR AFTER NG

you on the night in question?... He was pleased to see the woman in question come out of the shop. **6.2** If something is **in question**, there is a doubt about it. EG *The survival of some tribes has always been in question.* [PHR : USED AS AN A; ⇑ doubtful]

7 A **question** is also **7.1** a problem or a point which needs to be discussed. EG *His resignation raised the question of his successor... It is difficult for unilateralists to admit there is another side to the missile question... This raises the question as to whether or not parents should teach their children to read before they start school.* [N COUNT+SUPP; = issue] ● If someone **begs the question**, they assume something which supports their point of view, even though they have not proved this assumption. [● PHR : VB INFLECTS] **7.2** a problem which is set in an examination in order to test a person's knowledge or ability. EG *In the English exam you have to answer four questions in two hours.* [N COUNT]

questionable /kwɛstʃənəbəˈl/. Something that is **questionable** is not absolutely certain because you think that there is something wrong or unsatisfactory about it. EG *It is questionable whether the rat is a suitable test model... ...questionable projects like convention centres.* [ADJ QUALIT; = doubtful, dubious]

questioner /kwɛstʃənə/, **questioners**. A **questioner** is a person who is asking a question. EG *There doesn't seem to be an immediate answer to this questioner's problem.* [N COUNT]

questioning /kwɛstʃənɪŋ/. **1** If someone has a **questioning** expression on their face, they look as if they are expecting to hear an answer to a question. EG *He looked at her with a questioning expression.* [ADJ QUALIT] ◊ **questioningly**. EG *We pointed to the bag and raised our eyebrows questioningly.* [◊ ADV WITH VB]

2 Other meanings of **questioning** can be found in the entry for **question** in paragraphs 2 and 3.

question mark, question marks. A **question mark** is **1** the punctuation mark (?) which is used in writing at the end of a question. [N COUNT] **2** a doubt which remains over someone or something. EG *A question mark hangs over the future of the Social Democratic Party in Britain.* [N COUNT; ⇑ uncertainty]

question-master, question-masters. A **question-master** is the person who asks the questions in a game or a quiz on the television or radio. [N COUNT; = quizmaster]

questionnaire /kwᵒɛstʃənɛə/, **questionnaires**. A **questionnaire** is a written list of questions which are answered by a lot of people in order to provide information for a report or a survey. [N COUNT]

question tag, question tags. A **question tag** is a very short clause at the end of a statement which changes the statement into a question. In *'She said half price, didn't she?'*, the words *'didn't she'* are a question tag. [N COUNT]

queue /kjuː/, **queues, queueing, queued**. The present participle is also spelled **queuing**. The word **queue** is used mainly in British English. **1** A **queue** is a line of people, cars, etc that are waiting for something, such as the opportunity to buy something. EG *Sheila was in the queue for coffee... ...a queue of people... We'd better join the queue.* [N COUNT]

2 If you **queue**, you stand in a line while waiting for something, such as the opportunity to buy something. EG *Queuing is our national passion... Queue here for 'Star Wars'... People queued at the standpipes for water.* [V]

queue up. To **queue up** means the same as to queue. EG *People were queueing up for his autograph.* [PHRASAL VB : V+ADV]

quibble /kwɪbəˈl/, **quibbles, quibbling, quibbled**. **1** If people **quibble**, they argue about a small matter which is not at all important. EG *One may quibble about the exact unemployment figures but the general trend is undeniable.* [V : IF+PREP THEN *about/over/with*]

2 A **quibble** is a minor objection that you have to something. EG *These are merely quibbles.* [N COUNT; = niggle]

quiche /kiːʃ/, **quiches**. A **quiche** is a tart filled with a savoury mixture of eggs, cheese, and other things and eaten either hot or cold. [N COUNT; ⇑ flan]

quick /kwɪk/, **quicker, quickest**. **1** Something or someone that is **quick** moves or performs actions with great speed. EG *She was precise and quick in her movements.* [ADJ QUALIT; = rapid, swift] ◊ **quickly**. EG *...trees which grow quickly... I walked quickly up the passage... ...if events move as quickly as some people think they will.* [◊ ADV WITH VB; = rapidly] ◊ **quickness**. EG *He moved with the quickness and lightness of the man of action.* [◊ N UNCOUNT] ● **Quick march** is used as a command to tell someone, especially a group of soldiers, to walk quickly. [● PHR : USED AS IMPER]

2 Something that is **quick 2.1** takes or lasts only a short time. EG *Let's just have a quick look at that... ...a quick visit... It's quicker if you use a large sponge.* [ADJ QUALIT] ◊ **quickly**. EG *He died quickly... They embraced quickly.* [◊ ADV WITH VB] **2.2** happens without any delay or with very little delay. EG *They are pressing for a quick resumption of arms negotiations... You're likely to get a quicker reply if you telephone... John was quick to help him.* [ADJ QUALIT; = swift] ◊ **quickly**. EG *She wants to get the whole thing over with as quickly as possible... 'Let's talk to Philip.'–'Not now,' she said quickly.* [◊ ADV WITH VB] ● **Quick as a flash**: see **flash**.

3 A **quick one** is, a drink, especially an alcoholic one, that you drink quickly before leaving somewhere; an informal expression. EG *Have you got time for a quick one before we take off?* [PHR : USED AS O; = quickie]

4 If someone has a **quick** temper, they are easily made angry. EG *...a man who was quick-tempered and brave.* [ADJ QUALIT : ATTRIB; = hot]

5 Someone who is **quick** is intelligent and able to understand, think, or notice things with great speed. EG *I find the average village person, well, not very quick, shall we say... ...his quick wit and chirpy humour... He was quick-witted, an enthusiast and an optimist.* [ADJ QUALIT; ⇑ clever = sharp] ◊ **quickness**. EG *...great quickness of mind.*

● **quick off the mark**: see **mark**. ● **quick on the uptake**: see **uptake**.

6 The **quick** on your fingernails or toenails is the area around the edge where the nail joins the finger or toe. EG *Her nails were bitten down to the quick.* [N SING : *the*+N]

● To **cut** someone **to the quick** means to make them feel very upset and hurt. EG *Her cruel remarks cut me to the quick.* [● PHR : VB INFLECTS; ⇑ distress]

quick- is added to words, especially present or past participles, in order to form adjectives which describe something as happening without any delay. EG *...quick-growing plants... ...a quick-acting poison... ...two cans of the quick-dry paint.* [PREFIX]

quicken /kwɪkəᵒn/, **quickens, quickening, quickened**. **1** When something **quickens** or when you **quicken** it, it moves or happens at a greater speed than before. EG *This thought made him quicken his pace... When he heard her name his heart would quicken.* [V-ERG; = accelerate]

2 If something **quickens** your interest or if your interest **quickens**, your interest becomes stronger and more active. EG *'Where?' asked Lebel with quickened interest.* [V-ERG; = increase]

quickie /kwɪkiˡ/, **quickies**. A **quickie** is, in informal English, something that only takes a short time to do or deal with, for example a drink or a question. EG *We've just got time for one more question, so let's have a quickie.* [N COUNT : USU a +N IN SING; = quick one]

quicklime /kwɪklaɪm/ is a white substance made by heating limestone that is used, for example for making cement. [N UNCOUNT; ⇑ chemical]

quicksand /kwɪksænd/, **quicksands**. **Quicksand** or **quicksands** is used to refer to deep wet sand that you sink into and get stuck in when you try to walk on it. EG *We might have to cross a swamp or quicksand.* [N UNCOUNT/COUNT, SING=PI]

quicksilver /kwɪksɪlvə/ is mercury; a rather old-fashioned word. [N UNCOUNT]

quickstep /kwɪkstɛp/. The **quickstep** is a ballroom dance with a lot of quick steps; also used of the music it is danced to. [N SING : *the*+N]

quid /kwɪd/. **Quid** is both the singular and the plural form. In informal British English, a **quid** is the same amount of money as a pound. EG *It's a quid a day... It cost 45 quid.* [N COUNT]

quid pro quo /kwɪd prəʊ kwəʊ/, **quid pro quos**. A **quid pro quo** is a gift or advantage that is given to someone in return for something they have done; a fairly formal term. EG *His promotion may be regarded as the quid pro quo for his support.* [N COUNT; ⇑ reward]

quiescent /kwɪɛsəᵒnt/. Something that is **quiescent** is, quiet and inactive; used in formal written English. EG *...careful portraits of quiescent animals... Once quiescent minorities are asserting their rights again.* [ADJ QUALIT; = dormant]

quiet /kwaɪət/, **quieter, quietest; quiets, quieting, quieted**. **1** Something or someone that is **quiet** makes only a small amount of noise or is making much less noise than usual. EG *Bal said in a quiet voice, full of dignity, 'I have resigned'... It is one* [ADJ QUALIT; ≠ loud] *of the quieter aircraft using Kennedy Airport.* ◇ **quietly**. EG *'I'm going to do it,' I said quietly.* ◇ ADV WITH VB

2 If a place is **quiet**, there is very little noise there. EG *It was very quiet in there; you could just hear the wind moving the trees.* ◇ **quietness**. EG *They venture through the door into the quietness of early-morning Watermouth.* ADJ QUALIT ≠ noisy ◇ N UNCOUNT = stillness

3 Quiet is the state of almost complete silence. EG *Ralph was on his feet too, shouting for quiet, but no one heard him... In the quiet of the studio it sounded like a small pistol shot.* N UNCOUNT = hush

4 If you are **quiet**, you do not say anything at all. EG *There was nothing to say to this so she kept quiet... Maisie had gone unnaturally quiet... 'Be quiet and listen.'* ◇ **quietly**. EG *We lay quietly for almost an hour.* ADJ QUALIT : PRED = silent ◇ ADV WITH VB

5 Someone who is **quiet** always behaves in a calm and gentle way and is not easily made angry, upset, or excited. EG *She is thoughtful, quiet and controlled... I had never seen the quiet Ryan so angry.* ◇ **quietly**. EG *He was quietly courteous to the staff.* ◇ **quietness**. EG *...a tall, imposing woman, with the quietness of authority about her.* ADJ QUALIT = placid, even-tempered ◇ ADV+ADJ ◇ N UNCOUNT

6 Something that is **quiet** happens in secret or in such a way that people do not notice. EG *He conducted some quiet diplomacy for the President during his world tour... He may have domestic problems; I'll have a quiet word with him.* ◇ **quietly**. EG *The multinational mining giant has quietly bought up nearly £100 million worth of stocks.* ● If something is done **on the quiet**, it is done secretly or in such a way that other people do not notice. EG *They've been building up quite a large shareholding on the quiet.* ● If you **keep quiet** about something or **keep** something **quiet**, you keep it secret. EG *And you must keep quiet about what you saw tonight.* ADJ QUALIT = unobtrusive, confidential ◇ ADV WITH VB = secretly ● PHR : USED AS AN A ● PHR : VB INFLECTS

7 If a place or institution is **quiet**, nothing very exciting or important happens there. EG *The village is so quiet now... 'How's your business?'–'Quiet, sir, very quiet.'* ▸ used as a noun. EG *In the country the quiet made them feel depressed.* ADJ QUALIT ⇑ calm ≠ active, busy ▸ N UNCOUNT

8 Quiet means peaceful and not disturbed by excitement, trouble, or worry. EG *...a married couple who lived quiet and happy lives together... Everything is quiet. There is no trouble here... What about going to the Golf and having a quiet drink there?* ◇ **quietly**. EG *I was standing in a corner quietly drinking a cup of tea.* ◇ **quietness**. EG *After the quietness of home and school, university had been almost frightening.* ADJ QUALIT = tranquil ≠ troubled ◇ ADV WITH VB = peacefully ◇ N UNCOUNT

9 An event that is **quiet** happens without a lot of ceremony, publicity, or fuss. EG *The funeral was as quiet as the marriage had been.* ◇ **quietly**. EG *They were married quietly in a little country church.* ADJ QUALIT = restrained ◇ ADV WITH VB = simply

10 A **quiet** feeling is not expressed aloud or shown to other people. EG *They lead lives of quiet despair... There are grounds for quiet optimism.* ◇ **quietly**. EG *...quietly admiring Claudia's honesty.* ADJ QUALIT : ATTRIB ◇ ADV WITH VB

11 Colours, clothes, or decorations that are **quiet** are not bright or very fashionable, but pleasant or of good quality. ADJ QUALIT = restrained

12 If something **quiets** or if you **quiet** it, it becomes less noisy or less active; used in American English. EG *Boon got in and quieted the engine... His sobs quieted.* V-ERG = quieten

quiet down. If something **quiets down** or if you **quiet** it **down**, it becomes less noisy or less active; used in American English. EG *The room quieted down.* PHRASAL VB : V-ERG+ADV

quieten /kwaɪətə^{0}n/, **quietens, quietening, quietened**. If you **quieten** something or someone, you make them become less noisy or less active. EG *Can't you do anything to quieten those children a bit?... ...in order to quieten European doubts about the credibility of the nuclear deterrent.* V+O ⇑ calm = subdue

quieten down. If something or someone **quietens down** or if you **quieten** them **down**, they become less noisy, less active, and more calm; used only in British English. EG *...a cunning stratagem to quieten down the rebellious peasants. He had matured and quietened down considerably.* PHRASAL VB : V-ERG+ADV = calm down

quietism /kwaɪətɪzə^{0}m/ is the belief that you must calmly accept what happens and that you should not try to change things; a formal word. N UNCOUNT

quill /kwɪl/, **quills**. A **quill** is **1** a pen made from a bird's feather. EG *...when people wrote with quills.* **2** a large, stiff feather on a bird's wing or tail. **3** one of the stiff, sharp points that porcupines and some other animals have on their bodies. N COUNT N COUNT N COUNT

quilt /kwɪlt/, **quilts**. A **quilt** is a cover filled with feathers or some other thick, warm, soft material, which you put over yourself when you are in bed. EG *Is your sleeping bag the sort which can be unzipped to use as a quilt?... ...terylene quilts... ...patchwork quilts.* N COUNT ⇑ bedding

quilted /kwɪltɪ^{2}d/. Something that is **quilted** consists of two layers of fabric with a layer of soft thick material between them, often decorated with lines of stitching which form a diamond pattern. EG *She was wearing a pink quilted bed-jacket... ...quilted nylon anoraks.* ADJ CLASSIF ⇑ padded

quin /kwɪn/, **quins**. A **quin** is one of five children who are born to the same mother at the same time. N COUNT = quintuplet

quince /kwɪns/, **quinces**. A **quince** is a hard fruit with an acid taste that is used for making jelly, marmalade, etc. EG *...quince marmalade.* N COUNT

quinine /kwɪniːn/ is a drug that is used to treat fevers such as malaria. N UNCOUNT

quintessence /kwɪntɛsəns/; a formal word. The **quintessence** of something is **1** the aspect of it which seems to represent its central nature. EG *That surely is the quintessence of possession.* **2** the most perfect or typical example of it. EG *She is the quintessence of sweetness.* N SING : *the*+N+*of* N SING : *the*+N+*of* = embodiment

quintessential /kwɪntɪ^{2}sɛnʃə^{0}l/ means seeming to represent the central nature of something in a pure, concentrated form; a formal word. EG *...the quintessential early Renaissance man.* ADJ CLASSIF : USU ATTRIB ⇑ fundamental

quintet /kwɪntɛt/, **quintets**. A **quintet** is a group of five singers or musicians singing or playing together; also used of a piece of music written for such a group. EG *...Schubert's 'Trout' quintet.* N COUNT

quintuplet /kwɪntjʊplɪ^{2}t, kwɪntjuːplɪ^{2}t/, **quintuplets**. A **quintuplet** is one of five children who are born to the same mother at the same time. N COUNT = quin

quip /kwɪp/, **quips, quipping, quipped**; a rather old-fashioned word. **1** A **quip** is an amusing or clever remark. EG *He appears once again with a ready quip.* N COUNT = witticism

2 If you **quip**, you say something funny or clever, in order to amuse people. EG *'I've read so much about him', Philip quipped.* V+QUOTE = jest

quirk /kwɜːk/, **quirks**. A **quirk** is **1** a habit or aspect of a person's character which is odd or unusual. EG *Everyone has his little quirks and oddities, and I am no exception.* **2** a strange occurrence that is unexpected and difficult to explain. EG *By a quirk of fate my father and I both applied for the same job... The belief that meteors were atmospheric quirks led to the term meteorology.* N COUNT = idiosyncrasy N COUNT : USU+SUPP = accident

quirky /kwɜːki^{1}/, **quirkier, quirkiest**. Something or someone that is **quirky** is rather odd in their behaviour, character, or appearance. EG *...the quirky brilliance of Miller... Copenhagen is full of churches with quirky spires.* ADJ QUALIT

quisling /kwɪzlɪŋ/, **quislings**. A **quisling** is a traitor who helps the enemy army that has invaded his or her own country; an old-fashioned word used showing disapproval. N COUNT = collaborator

quit /kwɪt/, **quits, quitting**. The form **quit** is used in the present tense and past tense, and it is also the past participle. **1** If you **quit** doing something, you stop doing it. EG *Jack wants to quit smoking... 'Quit punching me!'* V OR V+O/-ING ⇑ cease = pack in

2 If you **quit** or **quit** a job, you resign from it. EG *She quit her job... I'm going to quit psychiatry... I've had enough. I quit.* V OR V+O ⇑ leave = give up

3 If you **quit** a place, you leave it. EG *When all the other students had quit the room, he walked up to Miss Lenaut's desk... He quit Barcelona for Paris... He was given two months' notice to quit his house.* V+O = forsake

4 If two people **are quits**, neither of them owes the other anything. EG *If I buy you lunch, we're quits, aren't we?* PHR : VB INFLECTS = be even

5 To **call it quits** means to agree that an argument or fight should be ended since neither person any longer owes anything to the other one. EG *Take a million bucks and call it quits.* PHR : VB INFLECTS

quite /kwaɪt/. **1 Quite** means to a fairly great extent or to a greater extent than average. EG *He was quite young... Actually, that's quite nice, I like that... He calls quite often... I quite enjoy looking round museums... You can find books on that subject quite easily... It is quite likely that we will fail.* ADV = rather, relatively

2 Quite is used **2.1** to emphasize the complete degree or extent to which something is true or is the case. EG *I stood quite still... You're quite sure you don't mind?... You're quite right... I saw its driver quite clearly... I quite understand... Oh I quite agree... That's quite enough of that-pull yourself together... I quite frankly am too miserable to care.* **2.2** with a negative to say that something is almost the case or is very close to the state or situation stated; it is also used to reduce the force of the negative, for example for reasons of politeness or lack of certainty. EG *It doesn't look quite big enough... It somehow didn't quite fit together... I'm not quite sure... I didn't quite understand what it was all about.* **2.3** with a negative to express doubt and hesitancy about information, the nature of something, or how to act. EG *I don't know quite how to deal with that one... Dr Benson went out to Canada, I don't know quite where... No one knew quite where to start.* — ADV; ADV : WITH BROAD NEG = entirely; ADV : VB+ADV+ WH, WITH BROAD NEG = exactly, just

3 Quite a or **quite some** is used to say that a thing or person is of a very unusual, exceptional, or exciting nature. EG *It was quite a sight... My heavens, you have quite a memory. I'd forgotten that song.* ● If you say that someone or something is **quite something**, you mean that they are really special or remarkable; an informal expression used showing approval. EG *Her victory really was quite something. It has upset the whole political balance.* — PHR+N IN SING ⇑ amazing = phenomenal; ● PHR : USED AS C ⇑ good

4 You say **quite** or **quite so** to express your agreement with what someone has just said. EG *'It does a lot for police-public relations.'–'Quite.'* — CONVENTION ⇑ yes

quitter /kwɪtə/, **quitters**. A **quitter** is a person who gives up easily instead of finishing something that they have started. EG *I don't believe you're a quitter.* — N COUNT = defeatist

quiver /kwɪvə/, **quivers, quivering, quivered**. **1** If something **quivers**, it shakes or trembles with a fast and very light movement. EG *He tried to steady his fingers, but they quivered uncontrollably... The leaves quivered in the breeze.* ▸ used as a noun. EG *Her whole body gave a slight quiver.* — V = quake, shiver; ▸ N SING : a+N = shudder

2 A **quiver** is a container for carrying arrows in. — N COUNT

quixotic /kwɪksɒtɪk/ means having romantic and unrealistic ideas of things that are impossible or impractical; a formal word. EG *It's a play which often defies adequate production by its very poetic and quixotic nature... It seemed to John as if merely by making this blind quixotic effort he was on the way to insure a happy issue for their love.* — ADJ QUALIT = idealistic

quiz /kwɪz/, **quizzes, quizzing, quizzed**. **1** A **quiz** is a game or competition in which someone tests your knowledge by asking you questions. EG *...a television quiz show.* — N COUNT, OR N BEFORE N

2 If you **quiz** someone, you ask them questions, often because you want to discover some particular information; a rather old-fashioned use. EG *She couldn't be sure why he was quizzing her.* — V+O ⇑ question = grill

quizmaster /kwɪzmɑːstə/, **quizmasters**; also spelled with a hyphen. A **quizmaster** is the same as a question-master. — N COUNT

quizzical /kwɪzɪkəˀl/. A **quizzical** look or expression is one which suggests that you know something secret or confidential about the person you are looking at or talking to. EG *I could see from Miss Clare's quizzical glance that she knew exactly what was going on... She turned to me with what might have been an expression of quizzical amusement.* ◊ **quizzically**. EG *He removed his dark glasses and stared quizzically at the gunsmith.* — ADJ QUALIT ⇑ knowing = shrewd; ◊ ADV WITH VB ⇑ knowingly

quoit /kɔɪt/, **quoits**. **1 Quoits** is a game in which rings are thrown over a small post. — N UNCOUNT ⇑ game

2 A **quoit** is a ring that is used in the game of quoits. — N COUNT

quorum /kwɔːrəm/. A **quorum** is the smallest number of members of a group, committee, etc, that is officially necessary before a meeting is allowed to begin. EG *The quorum is eight... We now have a quorum, so we can begin.* — N SING WITH DET ⇑ minimum

quota /kwəʊtə/, **quotas**. A **quota** is **1** a limited number or quantity of something, such as goods imported into a country, which is officially allowed. EG *The Minister wants to impose a quota of 1.6m cars... ...a quota system.* **2** the share of something which you are normally expected to have, give, or receive. EG *I gave him his quota of 'Yes sirs' and shut up... Men have their full quota of emotions, of course.* — N COUNT ⇑ limitation = allowance; N COUNT : USU SING WITH POSS = ration

quotation /kwəʊteɪʃəˀn/, **quotations**. A **quotation** is **1** a phrase or passage from a book, poem, play, etc. EG *They are discussing a quotation from a novel by Somerset Maugham... She couldn't remember the source of the quotation.* **2** the price that someone says they would charge you to do a particular piece of work. EG *You should get a quotation for fitting double glazing... They submitted quotations and agreed prices.* — N COUNT : IF+ PREP THEN *from* ⇑ extract; N COUNT

quotation mark, quotation marks. **Quotation marks** are punctuation marks that are used in writing to show where speech or a quotation begins and ends. Quotation marks are also used round a word or phrase that you are talking about. They are usually written or printed as ' and '. — N COUNT : USU PL ⇑ symbol = quote

quote /kwəʊt/, **quotes, quoting, quoted**. **1** If you **quote** someone or something, you repeat the exact words that they have written or said. EG *He was quoted in his local evening paper as saying: 'A lot of people will suffer as a result of this decision.'... They believed that the working class were somehow 'different from us', to quote Lord Curzon... He wanted to show off his ability to quote from the Fourth Psalm... She quoted the Chinese proverb about lighting candles.* — V+O/QUOTE, OR V+A ⇑ state

2 If you **quote** something such as a law or fact, you refer to it as an example because it gives authority to what you are saying or arguing. EG *Can people in this country quote EEC law in our own courts?... They quote figures to compare the costs of adult education in different countries... I will quote only one or two examples.* — V+O = cite

3 If you **quote** a price, you suggest a price for which you are willing to do a particular piece of work or to sell a particular thing. EG *Ask the refuse department to come and quote for removing the stuff... They quoted us £350.* — V+A *(for)*, V+O, OR V+O+O ⇑ estimate

4 A **quote** is **4.1** a phrase or passage from a book, poem, play, etc. EG *A short quote from the Oration... They have a lot of good quotes about organization in that book.* **4.2** the price that someone says they would charge you to do a particular piece of work. EG *They accepted his high quote without argument... Try getting a quote from a caterer for a really big party.* — N COUNT : IF+ PREP THEN *from* = quotation; N COUNT

5 Quotes are, in informal English, quotation marks. — N PLURAL

6 In informal English, you can say **'quote'** in front of a word or phrase when you want to indicate that you are repeating what someone else wrote or said, and that you do not think it is the appropriate or right word to use. The word or phrase is often followed by 'unquote'. EG *It will not show up against quote 'similar' unquote backgrounds and this sort of thing.*

> **QUOTE** □ In this dictionary QUOTE is used in the grammar notes beside a verb to mean that it is used with quoted speech, also called direct speech. Examples are **say, shout**, and **suggest**. EG *'What are you doing, Henry?' **says** Myra... 'If anything comes up, Willie,' Nichols **was saying**, 'I'll let you know.'... A man came running out of the ward **shouting**: 'It's a girl!'... 'Albert!' she **shouted**... 'Perhaps,' he **suggested**, 'it was just an impulse.'* Verbs that take QUOTE usually also occur with reported speech. See □ at REPORT-CL.

quoth /kwəʊθ/ is a very old-fashioned word that means the same as 'said'. It is only used in the past tense, usually as a third person singular, and it always follows the subject of the verb. It is now used mainly humorously. EG *'Would it bore you very much,' quoth Hazel, 'to come with us tomorrow for a swim?'* — V+QUOTE

quotidian /kwəʊtɪdɪən/. **Quotidian** activities are normal, everyday activities; a formal word. — ADJ CLASSIF = daily

quotient /kwəʊʃəˀnt/, **quotients**. **1** A particular **quotient** is the degree or extent of the stated thing. EG *This job has a high stress quotient... Your vulnerability quotient was extremely high.* ● **intelligence quotient**: see **IQ**. — N SING WITH DET : MOD+N ⇑ rate = factor

2 A **quotient** is the number you get when you divide one number into another; a technical term in mathematics. — N COUNT ≠ product

Quran /kɔːrɑːn/; also spelled **Koran**. The **Quran** is the sacred book on which the religion of Islam is based. — N PROPER : *the* N

Quranic /kəˀrænɪk/; also spelled **Koranic**. **Quranic** is used to describe something which belongs or relates to the Quran. — ADJ CLASSIF : ATTRIB

Rr

R, r /ɑ:/, **Rs, r's.** 1 **R** is the eighteenth letter of the English alphabet. ● **the three R's**: see **three**. N COUNT

2 **R** is an abbreviation for 'registered'; used to show that a trademark has been registered legally and officially. It is written as an R inside a circle.

3 **R** is also an abbreviation meaning 'king' or 'queen'; an abbreviation for Latin 'rex' or 'regina'. EG *Elizabeth R.* N IN TITLES : AFTER N

4 **R** or **r** is also an abbreviation for other words beginning with R or r, such as 'road', 'right', 'river', and 'radius'.

-r . See **-er**.

rabbi /ræbaɪ/, **rabbis**. A **rabbi** is a Jewish religious leader, especially one who is in charge of a synagogue, is qualified to teach Judaism, or is an expert on Jewish law. N COUNT : ALSO IN TITLES

rabbit /ræbɪt/, **rabbits, rabbiting, rabbited.** 1 A **rabbit** is a small furry animal with long ears. Rabbits live in holes in the ground. N COUNT

2 **Rabbit** is meat or fur obtained from rabbits. N UNCOUNT

3 If you **go rabbiting**, you go hunting or shooting rabbits. PHR : VB INFLECTS

rabbit on. If you say that someone **is rabbiting on**, you mean that they are talking continuously in an unnecessarily long and boring way; an informal expression. PHRASAL VB : V+ADV, IF+PREP THEN *about* ⇑ talk = go on

rabble /ræbəᵊl/. 1 A **rabble** is a crowd of noisy, disorderly people. EG *...a rabble of boys and girls of all ages.* N SING WITH DET : USU+SUPP = mob

2 If you refer to a group of people as the **rabble**, you mean that you think they are coarse and unpleasant and you are superior to them. EG *He doesn't mix with the rabble in here.* N SING : *the*+N

rabble-rouser, rabble-rousers. A **rabble-rouser** is a clever speaker who can persuade a group of people to do violent or unruly things, often for his or her own political advantage. N COUNT ⇑ orator = demagogue

rabble-rousing is encouragement that a person gives to a group of people to do violent or unruly things, often for his or her own political advantage. EG *He deplored anti-Semitic rabble-rousing.* ▸ used as an adjective. EG *...a rabble-rousing newspaper.* N UNCOUNT ⇑ incitement ▸ ADJ CLASSIF : ATTRIB

rabid /ræbɪd, reɪ-/. 1 You use **rabid** to describe someone who you think has very strong and unreasonable opinions on a subject, especially in politics. EG *...a rabid feminist.* ADJ QUALIT : USU ATTRIB = fanatical

2 An animal that is **rabid** is infected with the disease of rabies. EG *...a rabid dog.* ADJ CLASSIF ⇑ diseased

rabies /reɪbiˡz/ is a serious disease which causes people and animals, especially dogs, to go mad and die. N UNCOUNT

R.A.C. The **R.A.C.** is a British motoring organization that helps members when their cars break down; an abbreviation for 'Royal Automobile Club'. N PROPER : *the*+N

raccoon /rəku:n/, **raccoons**; also spelled **racoon**. A **raccoon** is a small animal that has dark-coloured fur, black stripes on its face, and a long striped tail. Raccoons live in forests in North and Central America. N COUNT

race /reɪs/, **races, racing, raced.** 1 A **race** is 1.1 a competition to see who is the fastest, for example in running, swimming, or driving. EG *She came second in the race... The race is run through a forest... ...a horse race.* N COUNT 1.2 a situation in which people, countries, or organizations compete with each other for power or control. EG *The race for the White House is now on.... ...the arms race... ...the space race.* ● See also **rat race**. N SING WITH DET +SUPP

2 If you **race** someone or **race** against them, you compete with them in a race. EG *They would often race one another to the bus stop... She has raced against some of the best runners in the country.* V+A OR V+O

3 If you **race** an animal or vehicle, you prepare it for races and make it take part in races, especially as a hobby or profession. EG *He races pigeons... They race vintage cars.* V+O : NO PASS

4 The **races** are a series of horse races that are held at a racecourse, and where people go to watch and to bet on which horse will win. EG *He was celebrating a huge win at the races.* N PLURAL : *the*+N ⇑ event = race meeting

5 If you **race** somewhere, you go there as quickly as possible. EG *We had to race across London to get the train... He turned and raced after the others.* V+A = speed

6 If you say that something **races** towards a particular state or position, you mean that it moves or advances very quickly towards this state or position. EG *We're faced with the problem of population growth racing ahead of employment growth.* V+A

7 If your heart **races**, it beats much more quickly than usual, often because you are excited or afraid. EG *His heart raced as he saw the plane coming in to land.* V

8 **A race against time** is a situation in which you have to work very hard and fast in order to do something before a certain time. PHR : USED AS C ⇑ rush

9 A **race** is also one of the major groups into which human beings can be divided according to certain important physical features, such as the colour of their skin or the kind of hair they have. EG *...a political system that involved complete segregation of the races... ...the white race.* ▸ used as an uncount noun. EG *The law prohibits discrimination on the grounds of colour or race... The rules have to be applied without any class or race bias.* ● See also **human race**. N COUNT ⇑ division ▸ N UNCOUNT ⇑ condition

10 See also **racing**.

racecourse /reɪskɔ:s/, **racecourses**; also spelled with a hyphen and as two words. A **racecourse** is a course or track on which horses race; used in British English. N COUNT

racehorse /reɪshɔ:s/, **racehorses.** A **racehorse** is a horse that is kept and trained for running in races. N COUNT

race meeting, race meetings; also spelled with a hyphen. A **race meeting** is an occasion when a series of horse races are held at the same racecourse, often during a period of several days. N COUNT ⇑ event

racer /reɪsə/, **racers.** A **racer** is a vehicle, especially a car or bicycle, that is designed to be used in races and therefore travels fast. N COUNT

race relations are the ways in which people of different races in the same community live together and behave towards each other. EG *...efforts to improve race relations... ...race relations policy.* N PLURAL : PL FORM WHEN MOD

racetrack /reɪstræk/, **racetracks.** A **racetrack** is 1 a track for races between runners, cars, or bicycles. N COUNT 2 in American English, a racecourse. N COUNT

racial /reɪʃəᵊl/. 1 An unpleasant act that is **racial** is done to people because they belong to a particular race. EG *...the fight against racial discrimination... ...the crudest kind of racial prejudice... ...an alarming rise in racial harassment.* ◊ **racially.** EG *The attack was racially motivated.* ADJ CLASSIF : USU ATTRIB ◊ ADV

2 **Racial** is also used to describe 2.1 things that happen between people who belong to different races. EG *...our message of racial reconciliation... ...a struggle which transcended racial barriers... ...the racial inequality in our society.* ◊ **racially.** EG *...children of racially mixed parentage.* ADJ CLASSIF : USU ATTRIB ◊ ADV 2.2 things that affect or relate to people who are members of a particular race. EG *An old racial memory is stirred in us.* ADJ CLASSIF : USU ATTRIB

racialism /reɪʃəlɪzəᵊm/ is the same as racism; a rather old-fashioned word used in British English. N UNCOUNT

racialist /reɪʃəlɪst/, **racialists.** **Racialist** means the same as racist; a rather old-fashioned word used in British English. ADJ QUALIT, OR N COUNT

racing /reɪsɪŋ/. 1 **Racing** is 1.1 the sport of racing horses. EG *There is usually at least one page devoted to racing in the newspaper... ...racing stables.* N UNCOUNT 1.2 a sport in which races are held between a particular type of vehicle or animal. EG *...Formula One motor racing... ...pigeon racing.* N UNCOUNT : MOD +N

2 **Racing** is used to describe vehicles and other things that are designed for using in races. EG *...a racing car... ...a racing bike.* ADJ CLASSIF : ATTRIB

racism /reɪsɪzəᵊm/ is 1 the treatment of some people as inferior because they belong to a particular race; used showing disapproval. EG *...subtle forms of racism... ...the opportunity to live unhampered by racism.* N UNCOUNT ⇑ discrimination = racialism 2 the belief that some races are inferior to N UNCOUNT others; used showing disapproval. EG *...John's vehement racism.*

racist /rеɪsɪst/, **racists**. 1 **Racist** people, things, actions, etc treat some people as inferior, or believe that they are inferior, because they belong to a particular race; used showing disapproval. EG *...a clear demonstration of the racist nature of their justice... He went round sticking racist posters on walls.* [ADJ QUALIT ⇑ discriminatory = racialist]

2 A **racist** is a person who treats some people as inferior, or believes that they are inferior, because they belong to a particular race; used showing disapproval. EG *He's a racist and a sexist.* [N COUNT = racialist]

rack /ræk/, **racks, racking, racked**. The verb is also spelled **wrack** in American English. 1 A **rack** is 1.1 a piece of equipment, usually with hooks, pegs, bars, etc, that is used for holding things or for hanging things on. EG *The racks were crowded with new dresses... He rinsed the plates carefully and put them on the rack to drain... The girl searched in a rack of pigeon-holes behind her.* [N COUNT ⇑ framework] 1.2 a shelf over the seats in a bus, plane, or train on which you put bags, cases, and other pieces of luggage. EG *The little girl started to count all the bits of luggage on the racks.* [N COUNT]

2 Someone or something that **racks** you causes you great suffering or pain; a literary use. EG *He entered a realm where nightmares racked him... Although the world is still racked with wars, the danger of another world war seems to have receded... She stood there, racked by indecision, and began to cry.* [V+O: USU PASS+A *(by/with)* = torment, torture]

3 The **rack** was a piece of equipment on which people were tortured in former times by being tied to it and then stretched, with their legs being pulled in one direction and their arms in the other. EG *He lay there groaning like some prisoner stretched out on the rack.* [N COUNT: USU *the*+N IN SING] • If you say that someone is **on the rack**, you mean that they are suffering physical or mental pain. EG *That is why we are on the rack, forced into one of the longest strikes in living memory.* [• PHR: USED AS AN A]

4 If you **rack** your **brains**, you try very hard to think of something; an informal expression. EG *Racking his brains he couldn't think of a single example... 'What are the advantages?' Philip racked his brains, but couldn't think of any.* [PHR: VB INFLECTS]

5 If something **goes to rack and ruin**, it slowly decays and falls to pieces because it is neglected and nobody is looking after it. EG *Their farm was slowly going to rack and ruin... He felt great anger that so much had been allowed to go to rack and ruin.* [PHR: VB INFLECTS]

6 See also **racking**.

racket /rækɪt/, **rackets, racketing, racketed**; also spelled **racquet** in paragraphs 4 and 5. 1 If someone is making a **racket**, they are making a loud unpleasant noise. EG *...the ghastly non-stop racket that a healthy baby makes... The older boys set up a terrific racket, yelling out warnings and instructions.* [N SING WITH DET = din, row]

2 A **racket** is 2.1 an illegal activity that is used to make money. EG *They had in fact set up the Marshall Plan as an insurance racket... ...a small-time racket which he pulled from time to time.* [N COUNT: USU MOD+N = game, number] 2.2 a particular activity, business, or occupation; a humorous use. EG *I found myself in the psychoanalysis racket.* [N COUNT: MOD+N = game]

3 If people **racket**, they make a lot of noise or move about very noisily; a literary use. EG *...raucous female laughter that rackets about the kitchens... The world is racketing around at an ever madder pace.* [V: USU+A ⇑ rage]

4 A **racket** is also a bat with an oval frame and strings across and down it, which you hold in your hand when you are playing tennis, squash, or badminton. You hit the ball or shuttlecock with your racket. EG *I bought her a new tennis racket.* [N COUNT]

5 **Rackets** is a game which is similar to squash but which is played with a hard ball by two or four people. EG *At school, he played rackets and fives.* [N UNCOUNT]

racketeer /rækɪtɪə/, **racketeers**. A **racketeer** is a person who makes money in a dishonest way by threatening people or by selling them worthless, illegal, or immoral goods or services. EG *...the pimps and racketeers on the Avenue.* [N COUNT = villain]

racketeering /rækɪtɪərɪŋ/ is making money in a dishonest way by threatening people or by selling them worthless, illegal, or immoral goods or services. EG *...the racketeering bosses who ran the city.* [N UNCOUNT]

racking /rækɪŋ/. A **racking** pain or emotion is one which you feel very strongly. EG *She burst into terrible racking sobs.* [ADJ CLASSIF: ATTRIB]

raconteur /rækɒntɜː/, **raconteurs**. A **raconteur** is a person who can remember a lot of stories and who tells them in an interesting or amusing way. [N COUNT]

racoon /rəkuːn/. See **raccoon**.

racquet /rækɪt/. See **racket**.

racy /reɪsi[1]/, **racier, raciest**. A style of writing or way of behaving that is **racy** is intended to interest and amuse people by shocking or surprising them. EG *...a racy, romantic historical novel.* ◊ **racily**. EG *It's very racily written.* [ADJ QUALIT ⇑ popular = spicy; ◊ ADV WITH VB]

radar /reɪdɑː/ is a way of discovering the position and speed of machines such as ships and aircraft when they cannot be seen, by using radio signals shown on a screen. [N UNCOUNT]

radar trap, radar traps; also spelled with a hyphen. A **radar trap** is a device which uses radar to enable the police to catch motorists who are driving faster than they should. [N COUNT ⇑ speed trap]

radial /reɪdɪəl/, **radials**. 1 **Radial** is used to describe things that form the kind of pattern that you get when straight lines are drawn from the centre of a circle to a number of points round the outside. EG *...one of the radial streets leading out from the market square... ...radial roads.* [ADJ CLASSIF: USU ATTRIB]

2 A **radial** is a tyre whose sides are strengthened inside by cords that point towards the centre of the wheel instead of being arranged diagonally. Because of this, radials look softer and are less likely to skid than other tyres. [N COUNT]

radiance /reɪdɪəns/ is 1 glowing light shining from something or reflected on or around something. EG *The candle's light threw a faint radiance on the sleeping girl... Standing close in the headlight's radiance, the man turned.* [N UNCOUNT] 2 great happiness that shows in someone's face, often making them look very attractive. EG *...the dreamy sweet radiance of her features.* [N UNCOUNT]

radiant /reɪdɪənt/. 1 Someone who is **radiant** is so happy that their joy shows in their face, often making them look very attractive. EG *The bride looked radiant... The pictures show him radiant in the knowledge of his victory... The Cabinet was misled by Haig's radiant optimism.* ◊ **radiantly**. EG *...radiantly beautiful... 'They're going to make me a director,' he said radiantly.* [ADJ QUALIT ⇑ beautiful = glowing; ◊ ADV]

2 Something that is **radiant** glows brightly; a literary use. EG *Everything looked radiant in the morning sun.* ◊ **radiantly**. EG *The wall was shining radiantly like a gate of heaven.* [ADJ QUALIT = shining; ◊ ADV]

radiate /reɪdi[1]eɪt/, **radiates, radiating, radiated**. 1 If things **radiate**, they form a pattern that is like lines drawn from the centre of a circle to various points on the edge. EG *...roads that radiated before us... ...glossy green leaves, with radiating veins of pale yellow.* [V: USU+A]

2 If you **radiate** an emotion or quality or if it **radiates** from you, it is obvious from your expressions and behaviour that you have that quality or are experiencing that emotion. EG *They seemed to radiate inner contentment... In the evening Valentina was back, radiating confidence... There was a tenderness that radiated from her.* [V+O, OR V+A *(from)* = give off, emit]

3 If something **radiates** heat or light, heat or light comes from it. EG *The stones under our feet seemed to radiate heat... We could feel the heat radiating from the sandstone walls.* [V-ERG: IF V, THEN+A ⇑ emit]

radiation /reɪdi[1]eɪʃ[ə]n/ is 1 very small particles of a radioactive substance, produced for example by nuclear weapons, that can cause illness and death if your body is exposed to them. EG *Long term radiation effects are more frightening... Those exposed to a very large amount of radiation experience internal bleeding.* [N UNCOUNT] 2 energy, especially heat, that comes from a particular source, for example the sun. EG *...a building designed to trap and store radiation from the sun.* [N UNCOUNT]

radiation sickness is an illness that is caused by a person's body being exposed to too much radiation. EG *You would probably start to show the first signs of radiation sickness within two hours.* [N UNCOUNT]

radiator /reɪdieɪtə/, **radiators**. A **radiator** is 1 a hollow metal device, usually connected by pipes to a central heating system, that can be filled with hot water, oil, or steam and used to heat a room. EG *Sit by the radiator and get warm.* [N COUNT ⇑ heater] 2 a piece of apparatus connected to the engine of a motor vehicle, which contains the water that is used to cool the engine. EG [N COUNT ⇑ container]

If there is no water in your radiator your engine will overheat immediately.

radical /rædɪkəºl/, **radicals.** 1 Someone who is **radical** believes that there should be very great or extreme changes in society. EG *...a radical barrister and founder member of CND.* ▸ used also of organizations, newspapers, books, etc. EG *The League had become too radical... ...the radical left... ...radical bookshops.* ADJ QUALIT ⇑ fundamental

2 A **radical** is someone who believes in trying to produce very great or extreme changes in society. EG *He immediately established his reputation as a radical... ...socialists and radicals.* N COUNT ⇑ fundamentalist

3 **Radical** is also used to describe something that affects or relates to the most important or basic qualities of a situation or thing. EG *...a radical disagreement over fundamentals... Two radical advances in computer design have taken place.* ADJ QUALIT : USU ATTRIB ⇑ fundamental

◇ **radically.** EG *...a radically different approach... Attitudes towards education will have to change radically.* ◇ ADV

radicalism /rædɪkəlɪzəºm/ is radical beliefs, ideas, or behaviour. EG *...the radicalism of the Government... ...the traditions of radicalism and dissent.* N UNCOUNT

radicalize /rædɪkəlaɪz/, **radicalizes, radicalizing, radicalized**; also spelled **radicalise.** If someone **radicalizes** a situation, place, or group of people, they make it more radical; a formal word. EG *He was very active everywhere, radicalizing as many people as he could.* V+O

radii /reɪdɪaɪ/ is the plural of **radius.**

radio /reɪdɪəʊ/, **radios, radioing, radioed.** 1 **Radio** is 1.1 a system of sending sounds over a distance by transmitting electrical signals. EG *The phone lines are down but he may be able to reach it by radio... ...radio waves.* N UNCOUNT ⇑ process 1.2 the activity or industry of sending out programmes for the public to listen to, by using electrical signals broadcast in all directions from a transmitter. EG *He directed a Sherlock Holmes series for the radio... It was a song that had been on the radio a lot that winter... ...a radio play... ...a local radio station... ...a new adaptation for radio of Jane Austen's well-known novel.* N SING : *the*+N, OR N UNCOUNT ⇑ medium

2 A **radio** is 2.1 a piece of equipment that receives radio signals, which you can use to listen to programmes which are broadcast for the public. EG *She switched on the radio... ...regular advertisements on radio and television... A radio was blaring out pop music.* N COUNT, OR *on*+N ⇑ apparatus = wireless, receiver 2.2 a piece of equipment, for example on a ship or plane, that is used for sending and receiving messages by radio. EG *They were able to send urgent messages to their allies on their clandestine radio... We managed to establish radio communication with them.* N COUNT

3 If you **radio** someone, you send a message to them by radio. EG *I had radioed Rick and arranged to have a car waiting for me... The commander radioed to the Admiralty in London for instructions.* V+O, OR V : USU +A ⇑ communicate

radioactive /reɪdɪəʊæktɪv/. Something that is **radioactive** contains or consists of a substance that produces energy in the form of powerful and harmful rays, as a result of unstable atoms breaking up. EG *There are serious problems connected with nuclear radioactive waste disposal... It caused extensive and dangerous radioactive fallout.* ADJ QUALIT

radioactivity /reɪdɪəʊæktɪvɪti¹/ is 1 the quality that some substances have of producing powerful and harmful rays as a result of unstable atoms breaking up. EG *Jupiter's heat may be caused by radioactivity.* N UNCOUNT ⇑ property 2 radioactive energy. EG *...a serious leak of radioactivity.* N UNCOUNT = radiation

radiocarbon /reɪdɪəʊkɑːbən/ is a type of carbon which is radioactive, and which therefore breaks up slowly at a steady rate. Its presence in an object can be measured in order to find out how old the object is. EG *...radiocarbon dating.* N UNCOUNT = carbon 14

radio-controlled. A device that is **radio-controlled** works by receiving radio signals which operate it. EG *I once made a radio-controlled plane from a kit.* ADJ CLASSIF

radiogram /reɪdɪəʊgræm/, **radiograms.** A **radiogram** is a piece of equipment consisting of a cabinet that contains a record-player and a radio. Radiograms used to be very common but are now rare; used in British English. N COUNT ⇑ apparatus

radiograph /reɪdɪəʊgrɑːf, -græf/, **radiographs.** A **radiograph** is the same as an X-ray; an old-fashioned or technical word. N COUNT ⇑ photograph

radiographer /reɪdɪɒgrəfə/, **radiographers.** A **radiographer** is a person who is trained to take X-rays. N COUNT

radiography /reɪdɪɒgrəfi¹/ is the process of taking X-rays, especially for medical examinations. N UNCOUNT

radiologist /reɪdɪɒləd͡ʒɪst/, **radiologists.** A **radiologist** is a doctor who is trained in radiology. N COUNT

radiology /reɪdɪɒləd͡ʒi¹/ is the branch of medical science that deals with the use of radioactivity in making medical examinations and in treating diseases. N UNCOUNT ⇑ subject

radio-telephone, radio-telephones. A **radio-telephone** is a telephone which carries sound by sending radio signals rather than by using wires, and which is often used in cars. N COUNT

radio telescope, radio telescopes; also spelled with a hyphen. A **radio telescope** is an instrument that receives radio waves from space and finds the position of stars and other objects in space. N COUNT

radiotherapist /reɪdɪəʊθerəpɪst/, **radiotherapists.** A **radiotherapist** is a person who is trained in the treatment of diseases by radiation. N COUNT ⇑ doctor

radiotherapy /reɪdɪəʊθerəpi¹/ is the treatment of diseases such as cancer by using radiation. N UNCOUNT

radish /rædɪʃ/, **radishes.** A **radish** is a small, fat, red or white root vegetable with a fairly strong taste, which you can eat raw in salads. N COUNT

radium /reɪdɪəm/ is a radioactive element which is used in the treatment of cancer and other serious diseases. EG *...radium therapy.* N UNCOUNT

radius /reɪdɪəs/, **radii.** 1 The **radius** of a circle is the length of a straight line drawn between the centre and the outside edge. EG *...a circle with a radius of fifteen kilometres... I've indicated the value of these radii.* N COUNT

2 A **radius** of a particular distance is a circular area that stretches around a point or place for that distance in all directions. EG *The meeting attracted about 160 people from a 25-mile radius... A camel can kick you in any direction, within a radius of six feet.* N SING WITH DET +SUPP ⇑ range

RAF /ɑːr aɪ ef, ræf/. The **RAF** is the British air force; an abbreviation for 'Royal Air Force'. N PROPER : *the*+N

raffia /ræfɪə/ is a fibre made from the leaves of a type of palm tree, which can be used to make mats and baskets. EG *...coarse raffia string.* N UNCOUNT

raffish /ræfɪʃ/. Someone who is **raffish** is rather unrespectable, but in a way that seems quite attractive, daring, or stylish; a literary word. EG *They were a mixed and rather raffish lot.* ▸ used of places. EG *What raffish districts of London his friends inhabited!* ADJ QUALIT ◇ **raffishness.** EG *He had a raffishness that women found rather charming.* ◇ N UNCOUNT

raffle /ræfəºl/, **raffles, raffling, raffled.** 1 A **raffle** is a competition in which you buy tickets that have numbers on them. Some numbers are chosen later, and if you have bought a ticket that has one of these numbers you win a prize. EG *Mr Willet has kindly offered to sell raffle tickets.* N COUNT ⇑ lottery

2 If someone **raffles** something, they organize a raffle which has that thing as one of the prizes. EG *We're going to raffle a bottle of champagne.* V+O ⇑ dispose of

raft /rɑːft/, **rafts.** 1 A **raft** is 1.1 a floating platform made from large pieces of wood, oil-drums, etc, that are tied together. N COUNT ⇑ craft 1.2 an inflatable rubber or plastic mattress that floats on the water and that people sometimes use when they go swimming in the sea. EG *He stood up, grabbed his raft, and dragged it down to the water.* N COUNT

2 If you refer to **a raft of** things, you mean that there are a lot of them; an informal use in American English. EG *He went through a raft of mail inviting him to speak to conferences and meetings.* PHR+N UNCOUNT OR N IN PL

rafter /rɑːftə/, **rafters. Rafters** are the sloping pieces of wood that support a roof. EG *Most of these houses still have their original rafters.* N COUNT ⇑ beam

rag /ræg/, **rags, ragging, ragged.** 1 A **rag** is a piece of old cloth which you can use, for example, to clean or wipe things. EG *Wiping his hands on a rag, he went out to where the car was... She applied the dye with a cotton rag.* N COUNT ▸ used as an uncount noun. EG *...a crumpled piece of rag... The farmer's wife tied some rag round my hand.* ▸ N UNCOUNT

2 **Rags** are old, torn clothes which do not look respectable. EG *...beggars in dirty white rags which scarcely covered them.* ● See also **glad rags.** N PLURAL = tatters

3 A **rag** is also a piece of ragtime music: see N COUNT

ragtime. EG *He put the trumpet to his lips and began playing 'Tiger Rag'.*

4 In informal English, a **rag** is 4.1 a newspaper, especially one that you do not have a high opinion of. EG *Her photograph was in the local rag.* 4.2 a series of amusing and lively events that students arrange once a year in order to raise money for charity. N COUNT / N COUNT ⇑ stunt

5 If you **rag** someone, you tease them unkindly; a rather old-fashioned use. EG *They ragged him unmercifully about his new girlfriend.* V+O

6 **Rags to riches** is used to describe the way in which someone rapidly becomes very successful or rich after they have been quite poor; an informal expression. EG *...a kind of overnight rags-to-riches story.* PHR

7 If you describe something as **a red rag to a bull**, you mean that it is certain to make a particular person extremely angry; an informal expression used in British English. EG *...a retired colonel to whom anything modern was a red rag to a bull.* PHR : USED AS C ⇑ provocative

8 See also **ragged**.

raga /rɑːgə/, **ragas**. A **raga** is a piece of music that follows a traditional Indian form. N COUNT

ragamuffin /rægəmʌfɪn/, **ragamuffins**. A **ragamuffin** is a child who is dirty and wears torn clothes; an old-fashioned word. EG *He didn't want his boys to come in looking like ragamuffins.* N COUNT = urchin

rag-and-bone man, rag-and-bone men. A **rag-and-bone man** is a person who goes from street to street with a horse and cart trying to buy and sell things such as old clothes and furniture; used in British English. N COUNT

ragbag /rægbæg/, **ragbags**; also spelled with a hyphen. A **ragbag** of things is a group of things which do not have very much in common with each other, but which are being considered together at the same time; an informal word. EG *...that complicated cultural rag-bag of people's values.* N COUNT+SUPP = jumble

rag doll, rag dolls. A **rag doll** is a soft doll made from pieces of cloth. N COUNT

rage /reɪdʒ/, **rages, raging, raged**. 1 **Rage** is a feeling of extremely strong anger that is very difficult to control. EG *He smashed the picture in a fit of rage... She was trembling with rage and frustration.* ▸ used as a count noun. EG *I stormed out of the room in a passionate rage... She flew into a rage.* N UNCOUNT = fury, wrath / ▸ N COUNT = fury

2 If you **rage** about something, you feel intense anger about it and perhaps indicate it in the way you speak or behave. EG *The thought of the way she had been treated made her rage... He would rage about the unfairness of it all... ...raging at his own weakness.* V : USU+A ⇑ be cross

3 If something powerful or unpleasant **rages**, it continues with great force or violence. EG *There was a monsoon raging outside... The debate raged throughout the whole day... Fires still raged throughout the area.* V : USU+A

4 A particular **rage** is an activity, style of clothes, etc that is in fashion for a short time; an informal use. EG *We tended to go along with whatever was the current rage... At that time there was a great rage for 1920s clothes.* ● If something is **all the rage**, it is very popular and fashionable. EG *Jogging and aerobics were all the rage that year.* N SING WITH DET : IF+PREP THEN *for* ⇑ interest = craze, fad / ● PHR : USED AS C = the thing

5 See also **raging**.

ragged. When **ragged** is the past tense and past participle of **rag** it is pronounced /rægd/, but in the senses given here it is pronounced /rægɪd/. 1 Someone who is **ragged** is rather dirty and is wearing clothes that are old and torn. EG *...a ragged, skinny man of about fifty.* ◊ **raggedly**. EG *...raggedly dressed women.* ADJ QUALIT = tattered / ◊ ADV WITH VB

2 Clothes that are **ragged** are old and torn and rather dirty. EG *Little boys in ragged clothes would rush to the train begging... The collar of his ragged coat was turned up.* ADJ QUALIT = tattered, scruffy

3 Something that is **ragged** is untidy and uneven, usually because it has not been properly organized or made. EG *They were herded into a ragged line... He saw a man in a tattered tunic and a ragged beard.* ◊ **raggedly**. EG *The little engine runs raggedly and seems to lack power.* ADJ QUALIT / ◊ ADV WITH VB

4 An edge that is **ragged** is uneven and rough. EG *There were four ragged screw holes where a handle had been.* ADJ QUALIT : USU ATTRIB = jagged

5 If someone or something **runs** you **ragged**, they make you do so much that you become exhausted; an informal expression. PHR : VB INFLECTS = debilitate, exhaust

raggedy /rægɪdi¹/. Something that is **raggedy** has edges that are slightly rough and uneven; an informal word. EG *...long raggedy strands of material.* ADJ QUALIT = tatty

raging /reɪdʒɪŋ/. 1 **Raging** feelings or desires are very intense and severe. EG *...the raging anti-communism of the forties and fifties... ...a raging thirst.* ADJ CLASSIF : ATTRIB

2 **Raging** water flows and moves very forcefully and violently. EG *The river became a raging torrent when the rains came... ...a tower above the raging sea.* ADJ CLASSIF : ATTRIB = foaming

3 **Raging** weather is very bad and stormy. EG *...the season of bitter cold and raging blizzards.* ADJ CLASSIF

raglan /ræglən/. A **raglan** sleeve is one that joins the neckline and includes the shoulder of a piece of clothing. ▸ used of clothing that has raglan sleeves. EG *...a brown raglan coat with a matching hat.* ADJ CLASSIF : ATTRIB

ragtag /rægtæg/; also spelled with a hyphen. **Ragtag** people or organizations are badly organized and not considered to be respectable; an informal word. EG *...a ragtag army roadblock on the outskirts of the city.* ● **Ragtag and bobtail** means all sorts of people, including many who are not respectable. EG *...spies, actors, poets, loose women, and all the rag-tag and bobtail that followed a victorious army in those days.* ADJ QUALIT : ATTRIB = disorderly / ● PHR : ⇑ crowd = mob

ragtime /rægtaɪm/ is a kind of jazz music that became popular in America in the 1900s. EG *...whistling a ragtime tune.* N UNCOUNT

rag trade. The **rag trade** is the business and industry of making and selling clothes, especially women's clothes; an informal expression used in British English. EG *Forty years she spent in the rag trade.* N SING : *the*+N

rag week. In British English, **rag week** is a week once a year when students collect money for charity by arranging a series of amusing and lively events. N UNCOUNT

raid /reɪd/, **raids, raiding, raided**. 1 A **raid** is 1.1 a sudden military attack against an enemy, in which the purpose is to cause damage rather than to occupy the enemy's land. EG *Both the bridges were destroyed in enemy bombing raids... Commandos made another raid on the French coast.* 1.2 a sudden entering of a building by the police, for example when they are searching for illegal drugs or dangerous criminals. EG *They wrote to protest about police raids on members' homes... ...a drug squad raid.* 1.3 an act of entering a place in order to steal something secretly or by force. EG *The scandal was caused by a raid on the Party's headquarters... The gang had carried out a series of bank raids.* ● See also **air raid**. N COUNT : IF+PREP THEN *on* ⇑ invasion = incursion / N COUNT : IF+PREP THEN *on* ⇑ invasion / N COUNT : IF+PREP THEN *on* ⇑ foray

2 If people **raid** a place, they make a sudden armed attack against it. EG *Renegade supporters of the old chief are still raiding villages along the border.* ◊ **raiding**. EG *...a raiding party.* V+O ⇑ invade / ◊ ADJ CLASSIF

3 If the police **raid** a building, they enter it by force, for example in order to look for dangerous criminals or illegal drugs. EG *The police raided the house and uncovered a cache of weapons.* V+O ⇑ invade

4 If someone such as a burglar **raids** a place, they enter it secretly or by force in order to steal something from it. EG *Terrorists or criminals might raid a nuclear power station and seize a supply of plutonium... She made them promise they would never raid the larder again.* V+O ⇑ invade

raider /reɪdə/, **raiders**. A **raider** is 1 a soldier who is involved in a military raid. EG *The military command said the raiders attacked two power stations near the border.* 2 a police officer who is involved in a raid. EG *One police raider tore the top off a pool table.* 3 a person who steals something during a raid. EG *The three armed raiders escaped after a two mile car chase.* N COUNT ⇑ aggressor / N COUNT / N COUNT ⇑ criminal = robber

rail /reɪl/, **rails, railing, railed**. 1 A **rail** is 1.1 a horizontal bar that is firmly connected to posts or fixed round the edge of something. Rails act as fences or as supports for people to lean against. EG *Holding on to the rail with one hand, he pulled himself up... She leaned on the ship's rail... The crowds were so great that they had to put a special rail round the podium.* 1.2 a horizontal bar that is used to hang things on. EG *Remember to dust the tops of bookshelves and picture rails... ...a heated towel rail.* 1.3 one of the two metal bars fixed to the ground on which railway trains run. EG *The engine left the rails and ploughed into the bank.* N COUNT / N COUNT / N COUNT ⇑ girder

2 **Rail** is the method of travelling and transporting things in trains that run along rails fixed to the N UNCOUNT = railway

ground. EG *They travelled by road and rail through France... ...the disruption of rail communications.*

3 If someone **goes off the rails**, they start to behave in a way that does not seem acceptable to other people; an informal expression. PHR : VB INFLECTS ⇑ rebel

4 If you **rail** against someone or something, you complain loudly and bitterly about them; a rather old-fashioned use. EG *...the economic order they so often rail against... He had been railed at by them as a prig and a poser.* V : IF+PREP THEN *against/at* ⇑ curse = berate

rail in. If you **rail in** animals or people, you keep them inside a particular piece of land by putting a railing round it. EG *Pedestrians are railed in as if they were sheep.* PHRASAL VB : V+O+ADV ⇑ confine

rail off. If you **rail off** an area of land, you put a railing round it in order to keep people out. EG *So many people had fallen into the pond that it had to be railed off.* PHRASAL VB : V+O+ADV ⇑ fence off

railcard /reɪlkɑːd/, **railcards.** A **railcard** is an identity card that young people or pensioners in Britain can buy, which allows them to buy train tickets more cheaply. N COUNT

railing /reɪlɪŋ/, **railings.** A **railing** is a kind of fence made from metal bars. EG *He grasped the iron railing with both hands... I peered through the railings into the courtyard.* N COUNT : ALSO SING=PL ⇑ barrier

raillery /reɪləri¹/ is behaviour that involves friendly jokes and teasing remarks referring to what someone is or what they have done; a literary word. EG *There was a certain amount of raillery at Basil's expense.* N UNCOUNT = banter

railroad /reɪlrəʊd/, **railroads.** A **railroad** is the same as a railway; used in American English. EG *...railroad tracks.* N COUNT ⇑ transport

railway /reɪlweɪ/, **railways**; used in British English. A **railway** is **1** a method of travelling and of carrying things from one place to another by using trains of carriages or trucks which are pulled by a locomotive and which run on rails that are fixed to the ground. EG *All this changed with the invention of the railway... ...in the early days of railways... ...the railway station.* N COUNT : SING=PL ⇑ transport **2** a route between two places on a specially prepared track with rails fixed along it for trains to travel on. EG *...the railway to Addis Ababa... Railways and roads were sabotaged.* N COUNT **3** a company or organization that operates railway routes. EG *...a timetable of the Western Australian Government Railways.* N IN NAMES AFTER N : SING=PL

railway line, railway lines; used in British English. A **railway line** is **1** a railway route between two places. EG *...the railway line from London to Brighton.* N COUNT **2** the track or the rails on which trains run. N COUNT

railwayman /reɪlweɪmə³n/, **railwaymen.** A **railwayman** is a man who works for the railway; used in British English. N COUNT ⇑ worker

railway track, railway tracks. A **railway track** is a specially prepared strip of ground with metal rails on it that trains travel on; used in British English. EG *...just outside Ramsdale, between the railway tracks and Lakeview Hill.* N COUNT = permanent way

raiment /reɪmə³nt/ is clothing; a very old-fashioned word. EG *He put on the sober black raiment which was his usual wear.* N UNCOUNT

rain /reɪn/, **rains, raining, rained. 1 Rain** is water that falls from the clouds in small drops. EG *You can't go home in all this rain... The rain had been pouring all night... A light rain had begun to fall.* N UNCOUNT

2 When it **rains**, water falls from the clouds in drops as rain. EG *It had started to rain... Is it raining?... It was raining hard every day now.* V : *it*+V ● If you say that it **is raining cats and dogs**, you mean that it is raining very heavily; an informal expression. EG *It could be raining cats and dogs on a Monday but she'd still do the washing.* ● PHR : VB INFLECTS = pour

3 The **rains** are the seasons in tropical countries during which there is very heavy rain. EG *Up here the rains last only three or four months... When the rains come, however, these plants emerge in great numbers.* N PLURAL : *the*+N = monsoon

4 If something **rains** from above on to you, it falls rapidly and in large quantities. EG *Many times over the next 15 months ash rained from the sky.* V+A

5 A **rain** of things is a large number of things that fall from above at the same time and with great force. EG *Like a rain of bullets, blobs of sulphur would pour down on us.* N PART : *a*+N = hail, shower

6 If you say **come rain or shine**, you mean that something happens or used to happen regularly without being affected by influences such as the weather; an informal expression. EG *I got up at five o'clock in the morning, rain or shine.* PHR : USED AS AN A

7 If you say that someone is **as right as rain**, you mean that they are completely well or healthy again, for example when they have just recovered from an illness or a shock; an informal expression. EG *You'll be as right as rain in ten minutes.* PHR : USED AS C

8 If you say **'It never rains but it pours'**, you mean that an unfortunate or unhappy event has been or will probably be followed by another unfortunate or unhappy event. PHR

rain down. If things **rain down** or if people **rain** them **down** on to a person or place, they fall rapidly or are directed forcefully and in great numbers on to the person or place. EG *Their sticks rained down on him even harder... They closed in on Soumaoro's forces, raining down arrows from both sides.* PHRASAL VB : V+ADV, OR V-ERG+ADV

rain off. If a sports match **is rained off**, it has to stop, or it is not able to start, because it is raining. EG *Today's match between Yorkshire and Kent has been rained off.* PHRASAL VB : V+O+ADV, ONLY PASS

rainbow /reɪnbəʊ/, **rainbows. 1** A **rainbow** is **1.1** an appearance of an arch of different colours that can sometimes be seen in the sky opposite the sun when it is raining or after it has been raining. EG *...thousands of birds, in every colour of the rainbow.* N COUNT **1.2** a wide range of bright colours. EG *The big doors were fastened wide open, framing a rainbow of colours on the snowy street.* N PART = kaleidoscope

2 If you say that something is **at the end of the rainbow**, you mean that it is something that you have always wanted but never expect to get. EG *The World Championship was for me at the end of the rainbow.* PHR : USED AS AN A

rain check. If you say that you will **take a rain check** on an offer or a suggestion, you mean that you do not want to accept it straight away, but you might accept it later; an informal expression used mainly in American English. PHR : VB INFLECTS, IF+PREP THEN *on*

raincoat /reɪnkəʊt/, **raincoats.** A **raincoat** is a waterproof coat that you wear when it is raining to prevent your other clothes getting wet. N COUNT = mackintosh

raindrop /reɪndrɒp/, **raindrops.** A **raindrop** is a single drop of rain. N COUNT

rainfall /reɪnfɔːl/ is the amount of rain that falls in a particular area during a certain period. EG *This is half the average monthly rainfall of London's Kew Gardens.* N UNCOUNT

rainforest /reɪnfɒrɪst/, **rainforests**; also spelled as two words. A **rainforest** is a thick forest of tall trees which is found in tropical areas where there is a lot of rain. N COUNT

rainstorm /reɪnstɔːm/, **rainstorms.** A **rainstorm** is a fall of very heavy rain. N COUNT = downpour

rainwater /reɪnwɔːtə/ is water that has fallen as rain, especially when it has been stored. EG *Rainwater was collected in a lead tank on the roof.* N UNCOUNT

rainy /reɪni¹/, **rainier, rainiest. 1** If the weather, a place, or a time is **rainy**, it is raining a lot in that place or during that time. EG *Most tropical areas have rainy and dry seasons... ...a rainy Sunday afternoon... ...Freetown, the perpetually rainy capital of Sierra Leone.* ADJ QUALIT = wet

2 If you say that you are saving or keeping something **for a rainy day**, you mean that you are saving it until a time in the future when you might need it or want it. EG *They put part of the money in the savings bank for a rainy day.* PHR : USED AS AN A

raise /reɪz/, **raises, raising, raised. 1** If you **raise** something, you move it so that it is in a higher position or pointing towards a higher position. EG *He tried to raise the window, but the sash cord was broken... ...a chest of drawers set upon four carved legs that raised it about a foot from the ground... Ralph raised a hand for silence.* V+O = lift ● If you **raise** your **eyebrows**, you show surprise by moving the top of your face upwards so that your eyebrows move higher above your eyes. EG *He raised his eyebrows in extravagant surprise.* ● PHR : VB INFLECTS ● to **raise a finger**: see **finger**. ● to **raise hell**: see **hell**. ● to **raise the roof**: see **roof**.

2 If you **raise** yourself, you stretch your body so that you are standing up straight, or so that you are no V+O (REFL) = hoist, heave longer lying flat; a literary use. EG *She attempted to raise herself, saying frantically that she must go... Slowly she raised herself to her full height... Brody rolled over towards Ellen, raising himself up on one elbow.*

3 If you **raise** the rate or level of something, you increase it so that it becomes greater or larger. EG *The maximum speed was raised to roughly seventy miles per hour... A country in deficit abroad should raise its interest rates to attract foreign money.* V+O

4 Someone or something that **raises** the standard of an activity or task improves it so that it becomes better. EG *Putting teachers in day nurseries would raise standards.* V+O

5 If you **raise** your voice, you begin to speak more loudly, usually because you are becoming angry. EG *Gregory began to raise his voice in protest.* V+O

6 A **raise** is an increase in your wages or salary; used mainly in American English. EG *He thought about asking his boss for a raise.* N COUNT = rise

7 If you **raise** support for something such as a charity or an institution, you collect money for it or collect people's signatures to show their support. EG *They held a jumble sale to raise money for the church roof... A variety of events to raise funds were planned... They were aiming to raise fifteen million signatures in support of Attwell.* V+O ⇑ get

8 If you **raise** money, you manage to get the amount you need for a particular purpose, for example by cashing your savings, by selling your property, or by borrowing. EG *I could probably raise the extra two thousand pounds but I'd prefer not to.* V+O

9 If you **raise** a smile or other sign of emotion, you show that emotion, even though you may not feel it. EG *She raised a wan smile... 'He could carry me off tomorrow and I wouldn't raise a whimper!' she said.* V+O ⇑ make

10 If someone or something **raises** a particular emotion or type of behaviour in someone else, they cause it to occur. EG *For me it always raises fond memories of broad main streets... His jokes barely raised a smile.* V+O

11 Someone who **raises** a child is responsible for it until it is grown up. EG *His children were raised in the Catholic faith... I had been far too well raised to comment.* V+O = bring up

12 If you **raise** a particular type of plant, crop, or animal, you grow that type of plant or crop, or breed that type of animal. EG *...the plump, tender capons raised by a local farmer... Today the family raises beans, wheat, and sugar beet.* V+O ⇑ cultivate

13 If you **raise** a subject that you want to discuss, you mention it or state it to someone. EG *You would have to raise that with Mr Gerran personally... Mike still gets quite embarrassed whenever the subject is raised... The Foreign Office raised no objection.* V+O: IF+PREP THEN *with* = bring up

14 If someone **raises** a restriction or ban, they stop enforcing it. EG *There is mounting pressure to raise the oil embargo currently in force.* V+O ⇑ remove = lift

15 If you **raise** someone on the radio or telephone, you succeed in contacting them. EG *Hendricks tried to raise Kimble on the radio.* V+O

16 If you **raise** your opponent in a game of cards, you make a higher bid than he or she did. EG *I'll raise you £10.* V+O, OR V+O+O

raised /reɪzd/. A flat object or area that is **raised** is higher than its surrounding surface. EG *...a raised jetty four feet high... On her shoulder was a raised purple-pink swelling.* ADJ CLASSIF ⇑ elevated

raisin /reɪzən/, **raisins**. **Raisins** are dried grapes that you can eat raw or use in cooking cakes and puddings. N COUNT

raison d'être /reɪzɒn detrə/, **raisons d'être**. The **raison d'être** of someone or something is the most important reason for them existing in the way that they do; a formal expression. EG *Selling, after all, is their raison d'être.* N COUNT: USU SING

rake /reɪk/, **rakes, raking, raked**. **1** A **rake** is a garden tool consisting of a row of metal teeth attached to a long handle. You can use a rake to loosen the earth and make it level before putting in plants, or to gather together dead leaves. N COUNT

2 If you **rake** a surface, you move a rake across it in order to make it smooth and level. EG *Always rake the sand in the bunkers smooth after your shot.* V OR V+O: USU V+O

3 If you **rake** things such as leaves or weeds together, you move them together using a rake. EG *Rake the dead leaves into a pile... They set fire to the tall piles of weeds they had raked up.* V+O+A

4 If you **rake** around or through something such as a place or a pile of papers, you make a thorough search of it. EG *I'll have to rake around in my desk and see if it's there... We've been raking through all her papers.* V+A

5 If something such as a light or a gun **rakes** an area, it operates by moving slowly from side to side in order to cover as large an area as possible. EG *Enemy searchlights raked the sea... They raked us from stem to stern with automatic fire.* V+O ⇑ search = scan

6 A **rake** is also a man who is regarded as behaving in a rather immoral way, for example by gambling, drinking, or having sexual relationships with many women; a rather old-fashioned use. EG *He is a rake, a gambler, and a shallow-minded fellow.* N COUNT

7 The **rake** of a surface or object is the amount by which it slopes; used for example of the floor of a theatre that slopes so that all the audience can see the stage clearly. EG *At the Old Vic the rake was so steep that I could hardly keep my balance.* N SING WITH DET

rake in. If someone **is raking in** money, they are earning a lot of money fairly easily; an informal expression. EG *She must be raking in a fortune... They're raking it in!* PHRASAL VB: V+O+ADV, USU CONT = coin

rake over. If you **rake over** a subject, you keep returning to it and talking about it even though it is not particularly interesting or pleasant. EG *Why travel back into the past to rake over old worries?* PHRASAL VB: ORDER V+ADV+O

rake up. **1** If you **rake up** people or things, you bring them together for a particular purpose, especially when this is difficult to do. EG *I'll see if I can rake up a few people to help you.* PHRASAL VB: V+O+ADV ⇑ gather

2 If you **rake up** an embarrassing incident that happened in the past, you talk about it or remind someone about it, especially when they would rather forget it. EG *What was the point in raking up all that muck about his criminal record?* PHRASAL VB: V+O+ADV ⇑ revive = dredge up

raked /reɪkt/. If a surface such as the floor in a theatre is **raked**, it slopes quite steeply, for example so that all the audience can see the stage clearly. ADJ QUALIT

rake-off. A **rake-off** is an illegal share in profits that is taken by someone who has helped to arrange a business deal; an informal word. N SING WITH DET = cut, percentage

rakish /reɪkɪʃ/. **1** If a man is described as **rakish**, he is considered to have a rather immoral way of living; an old-fashioned word. EG *There was little she had not heard about his rakish, wandering existence.* ADJ QUALIT ⇑ dissolute
◇ **rakishly**. EG *He grinned rakishly.* ◇ ADV WITH VB

2 If you wear a hat at a **rakish** angle, it looks rather smart in a way that is intended to seem casual and confident. EG *...the cloak, the gloves, and a beret worn at a rakish angle.* ◇ **rakishly**. EG *...a round white cap rakishly tilted over her left ear.* ADJ QUALIT ⇑ fashionable = jaunty ◇ ADV WITH VB

rally /ræli[1]/, **rallies, rallying, rallied**. **1** A **rally** is **1.1** a large public meeting, often outdoors, that is held in order to show support or encourage support for something such as a political party. EG *She was invited to address a big anti-government rally in Hyde Park... About 3000 people attended the rally to mark the centenary of Karl Marx's death.* N COUNT = gathering **1.2** a recovery of health or strength, for example after a period of weakness or an illness. EG *The New York stock exchange staged a late rally this afternoon.* N COUNT **1.3** a competition in which cars or motorcycles are driven in timed stages over public roads. EG *...the Monte Carlo Rally.* N COUNT: ALSO IN NAMES

2 A **rally** in tennis, badminton, squash, etc is a continuous series of shots that the players exchange in the course of one point. EG *Rallies on grass courts tend to be shorter than on clay.* N COUNT

3 When people **rally** to something such as a political group or idea or when they **are rallied** by it, they become united in support of it. EG *She believed that the voters would rally to the Conservatives if an election were held... They made a final effort to rally their supporters on the day before the vote... ...an attempt to rally public opinion in favour of import controls.* V-ERG: IF V, THEN +A = assemble, gather

4 When people **rally** or when they **are rallied** by someone, they gather their strength to be able to continue a struggle, for example after a defeat or setback. EG *The enemy's forces rallied, and made a fresh attack on the town... ...the solemn tones of Winston Churchill, rallying Allied morale.* V-ERG ⇑ recover
◇ **rallying**. EG *...a rallying cry.* ◇ ADJ CLASSIF

5 If someone or something **rallies**, they begin to become stronger again after a setback such as an illness or a drop in prices. EG *The president rallied, but then died from his wounds nine days later... The stock market rallied today after yesterday's dramatic falls.*
V ⇑ recover

rally round. If people **rally round**, they come together and work as a group in order to support someone or something at a difficult time. EG *We all rallied round when the school was threatened with closure... The party rallied round him after his election defeat.*
PHRASAL VB : V+ADV/PREP

rallying point, rallying points. A **rallying point** is a place or idea which people consider to be symbolic and which they are attracted to in support of something such as a political group or idea. EG *Our theatre project will be a rallying point for those hundreds of amateur groups all over the country.*
N COUNT

ram /ræm/, **rams, ramming, rammed**. **1** If one vehicle such as a ship or car **rams** another, it crashes into it with great force, usually causing a lot of damage. EG *The ship had been rammed by a British destroyer.*
V+O

2 If you **ram** something somewhere, you push it there with great force. EG *He rammed the bolt back across the door.*
V+O+A

3 A **ram** is **3.1** an adult male sheep. **3.2** a device that is used for forcing things into place. • See also **battering ram**.
N COUNT

4 Someone or something that **rams** something **home** makes you fully understand or accept a fact or idea, for example by providing clear examples or proof. EG *The First World War rammed home the same lesson.*
PHR : VB INFLECTS ⇑ reinforce

5 If someone **rams** something **down** your **throat**, they try to make you learn it or believe it, especially when you are unwilling to do so, by continually repeating it. EG *I think they've got the point. There's no need to ram it down their throats.*
PHR : VB AND N INFLECT ⇑ impress upon

Ramadan /ræmədæn/ is the ninth month of the Muslim year, during which Muslims eat and drink nothing from sunrise to sunset.
N UNCOUNT

ramble /ræmb^{ə}l/, **rambles, rambling, rambled**. **1** A **ramble** is a long walk, usually to explore the countryside. EG *We were out on a country ramble.*
N COUNT ⇑ wander

2 If you **ramble**, **2.1** you go for a long walk in the countryside. EG *I was rambling over the hills of Yorkshire.* **2.2** you walk slowly and without purpose. EG *She rambled out of the room without saying a word.* **2.3** you talk or write in a confused way and without any order. EG *When he did talk he often rambled and said strange things.*
V+A ⇑ wander; V+A; V : NO IMPER

3 When a climbing plant **rambles**, it grows spreading out in many directions. EG *The honeysuckle rambled all over the fence.*
V : NO IMPER = straggle

ramble on. If someone **rambles on**, they talk or write for a long time in a confused way and without any order. EG *...listening to Miriam as she rambled on.*
PHRASAL VB : V+ADV, IF+PREP, THEN *about* = go on

rambler /ræmblə/, **ramblers**. A **rambler** is a person who goes on rambles in the countryside, usually as part of an organized group.
N COUNT ⇑ walker

rambling /ræmblɪŋ/. **1** A **rambling** building or town has no regular shape and spreads out in many directions. EG *We bought a rambling old house near the village.*
ADJ QUALIT ⇑ irregular = straggling

2 Rambling speech or writing continues for a long time in a confused way, without any order. EG *She wrote me a long rambling letter.*
ADJ QUALIT : USU ATTRIB = meandering

3 Rambling is the activity of going for long walks in the countryside.
N UNCOUNT ⇑ walking

ramification /ræmɪfɪkeɪʃ^{ə}n/, **ramifications**. A **ramification** is one of the many consequences or developments that complicate a decision, idea, or plan, especially the indirect ones that are not at first obvious to you; a fairly formal word. EG *Not many people actually understand the ramifications of these guidelines... We considered the proposal and all its ramifications.*
N COUNT+SUPP : USU PL ⇑ implication

ramp /ræmp/, **ramps**. A **ramp** is **1** a sloping surface that connects two places that are at different levels, for example one that has been built so that it can be used by cars or wheelchairs. EG *It's driven up a ramp and straight on to the train.* **2** a change in the level between two sections of a road, which is due to road works. **3** a small hump that is deliberately built on a road to make cars slow down when they drive over it. EG *Watch out for the ramps.*
N COUNT; N COUNT; N COUNT

rampage /ræmpeɪdʒ/, **rampages, rampaging, rampaged**. **1** If people or animals **rampage**, they rush about in a wild or violent way, often causing damage or destruction. EG *...elephants rampaging through the bush.*
V : USU+A

2 If you **are on the rampage** or **go on the rampage**, you rush about in a wild or violent way. EG *A section of the crowd broke loose and went on the rampage.*
PHR : VB INFLECTS

rampant /ræmpənt/. Something that is **rampant** is growing, spreading, or continuing to exist in an uncontrolled way; used especially of undesirable conditions, such as crime or disease. EG *Political apathy is rampant... They wanted to put an end to the rumours, which were rampant.*
ADJ QUALIT = unchecked, unrestrained

rampart /ræmpɑːt/, **ramparts**. A **rampart** is an earth bank, often with a wall on it, that is built to protect a fort, castle, or city. EG *Perhaps the tower was part of the ramparts of the city.*
N COUNT : USU PL

ramrod /ræmrɒd/, **ramrods**. **1** A **ramrod** is a long thin rod used for cleaning the barrel of a gun or for forcing gunpowder down the barrel of an old-fashioned gun.
N COUNT

2 If someone sits or stands **as stiff as a ramrod** or **as straight as a ramrod**, they sit or stand in a very stiff and upright way. EG *She sat there stiff as a ramrod.*
PHR : USED AS AN A

3 Ramrod is used to describe someone who is holding their body very straight and upright. EG *The small cortege swept past the ramrod guards... They stand ramrod straight.*
ADJ CLASSIF : ATTRIB, OR ADV

ramshackle /ræmʃæk^{ə}l/. A **ramshackle** building is badly made or badly looked after, and likely to fall down or fall apart. EG *...a ramshackle cottage.*
ADJ QUALIT : USU ATTRIB = dilapidated, rickety

ran /ræn/ is the past tense of **run**.

ranch /rɑːntʃ/, **ranches**. A **ranch** is **1** a large farm for raising cattle, sheep, or horses, especially in the United States. EG *In California ranch owners fly as much as 120 miles every day.* **2** in American English, any large farm on which a particular type of animal or crop is produced. EG *...a chicken ranch.*
N COUNT; N COUNT : MOD+N

rancher /rɑːntʃə/, **ranchers**. A **rancher** is a person who owns a ranch or works on a ranch; used mainly in American English. EG *The plan has been fiercely resisted by ranchers.*
N COUNT ⇑ farmer

ranching /rɑːntʃɪŋ/ is the activity of running a ranch; used mainly in American English. EG *...beef and sheep ranching.*
N UNCOUNT ⇑ farming

rancid /rænsɪd/. Butter, bacon, or other fatty foods that are **rancid** have gone bad and taste or smell stale and unpleasant. EG *The fridge smelled strongly of rancid butter.*
ADJ QUALIT = off, rank

rancorous /ræŋk^{ə}rəs/. Someone who is **rancorous** feels deep and bitter hatred; a formal word. EG *He had been incredibly rancorous toward McKinley.*
ADJ QUALIT ⇑ hostile

rancour /ræŋkə/; also spelled **rancor** in American English. **Rancour** is a feeling of deep and bitter hatred towards a person; a formal word. EG *He was shaken by rage and rancour... Ruth looked at Hugh, and he smiled without rancour.*
N UNCOUNT ⇑ hostility

random /rændə^{o}m/. **1** Something that is **random** happens or is chosen without a definite plan, pattern, or purpose. EG *The killings were random, gruesome, and baffling... The way the books were arranged seemed completely random... This is just a random selection of the complaints we have received.*
ADJ QUALIT : USU ATTRIB = ad hoc

◇ **randomly**. EG *Ink had been randomly squirted on the floor and the walls.*
◇ ADV = haphazardly

2 If something is done **at random**, it is done without a definite plan, pattern, or purpose. EG *Bullets were being fired into the crowd at random... He opened the book at random.*
PHR : USED AS AN A = randomly

randy /rændi^{1}/, **randier, randiest**. Someone who is **randy** is eager to have sexual intercourse; an informal word. EG *The heat made them both randy.*
ADJ QUALIT ⇑ lecherous

rang /ræŋ/ is the past tense of **ring**.

range /reɪnʒ/, **ranges, ranging, ranged**. **1** The **range** of something is the total area or extent within which it can operate effectively, and beyond which it is no longer effective. EG *Sonar also has a limited range and is affected by water temperatures... What is the range of their transmitters?... The sound has a frequency that is far above the range of our ears.*
N COUNT+SUPP : USU SING+*of* ⇑ capacity

2 The **range** of a gun or other weapon is the maximum distance to which it can fire bullets, shells, rockets, etc. EG *It's a powerful gun but its range is very limited... Their tanks stayed just beyond the*
N COUNT+SUPP : USU SING

range of our big guns... ...medium range ballistic missiles.

3 The **range** at which someone or something is shot is the distance that they are away from the gun that shoots them. EG *He shot the President twice at close range... She had been shot at point-blank range... It can kill at a range of 200 yards.* N UNCOUNT : *at*+N, WITH SUPP

4 The **range** of a ship, plane, car, or other vehicle is the distance that it can travel before it needs more fuel. N SING WITH DET

5 The **range** of a singer or musical instrument is the total extent between the highest and lowest musical notes that they can reach. EG *She had a marvellous voice with an extraordinary range... ...a voice in the low tenor range.* N SING WITH DET +SUPP

6 The **range** of an activity or influence is the total number of things that it includes or involves. EG *Her talk conveyed something of the range and diversity of research activities in the university... He said it was outside his range of responsibility.* N COUNT+SUPP : USU SING+*of* ⇑ extent = compass, scope

7 A **range** of things is a number of different things of the same general kind. EG *They were questioned about their attitudes on a range of subjects from politics to astrology... The new technology has opened up a very wide range of possibilities... ...a narrow range of options.* N SING WITH DET +*of*+N IN PL ⇑ set = variety

8 A **range** of products is a number of products of the same general kind that are produced by a company or sold by a shop. EG *They stock a wide range of electrical goods... ...a new car in the VW range.* N COUNT+SUPP ⇑ set

9 A **range** is the complete group that is included between two fixed points on a scale of measurement, quality, or evaluation. EG *There are three basic price ranges... ...children in the top 15 per cent of the ability range... ...a ship in the 8-10,000 ton range... The age range is from six months to forty-seven years.* N COUNT : MOD+N = bracket

10 Things that **range** between two points, or from one point to another, vary within these points on a scale of measurement, quality, or evaluation. EG *Prices range from £3 to £19... Their politics ranged from liberal to radical... The cost of the improvements would range between 2.5 million and 4 million pounds. They were offered increases ranging from £6.71 to £16.31 a week... It deals with Britain's industrial problems, ranging from technology gaps to lack of investment.* V+A *(from...to/ between...and)* : NO CONT

11 If a piece of writing or speech **ranges** over a particular topic or group of topics, it extends so as to include or deal with all of the topic or topics. EG *The book ranges historically as far back as the Florence of the Renaissance... The conversation ranged widely... Her lecture ranged over the Raj, Kipling, and a whole variety of subjects.* V+A

12 If people or animals **range** an area, they travel around in it, without any definite plan or destination; a fairly literary use. EG *They range the unsettled countryside unchecked... ...ranging over the hills and plains.* V+O : NO PASS, OR V+A *(over)* = roam, wander

13 If you **range** people or things, **13.1** you arrange them in a line or in lines. EG *Books were ranged on shelves on the walls... The boys ranged themselves in rows on the grass.* V+O *(NG/REFL)* +A **13.2** you cause them to join together against someone else in a conflict or argument. EG *The best protection would be to range all the most powerful nations on the same side... Their failure should be seen in the light of all the forces ranged against them.* V+O+A ⇑ align

14 A **range** is also **14.1** a large area of open grassy land, especially in the United States, where cattle can wander and graze. EG *They are driven north each spring across the open range.* N COUNT ⇑ tract = pampas, prairie **14.2** a number of hills or mountains that form a continuous line. EG *The plain lies beyond this range of hills... The high, dark Absaroka Range looms directly ahead.* N COUNT+SUPP : ALSO IN NAMES = chain **14.3** a place where people can practise shooting at targets or where missiles and other weapons can be tested. EG *...a missile range in the Nevada desert... ...a rifle range.* N COUNT : USU MOD+N ⇑ area **14.4** a large old-fashioned type of iron cooking stove with one or more ovens, usually heated by a fire. EG *She pokes away at the fire in the range.* N COUNT

rangefinder /reɪnʒfaɪndə/, **rangefinders**; also spelled with a hyphen. A **rangefinder** is an instrument used for measuring the distance of something that you are shooting at or photographing. EG *The tank has a high velocity 125 mm gun and laser rangefinder.* N COUNT

ranger /reɪndʒə/, **rangers**. A **ranger** is a person whose job is to look after a forest or park that belongs to the state or, in Britain, to the royal family. EG *...the head ranger of a vast national park.* N COUNT ⇑ keeper

rank /ræŋk/, **ranks, ranking, ranked**. **1** A **rank** is the position or grade that a person holds within an organization, for example in the armed forces or the police, which decides how much importance or authority they have. EG *A prisoner of war must only reveal his name, rank, and serial number... He wasn't getting the salary to which he was entitled by rank and seniority... She achieved the rank of full professor at the precocious age of 31... At the head of each committee was a minister of Cabinet rank.* N COUNT/ UNCOUNT ● If someone **pulls rank**, they make unfair use of the authority that their high position in an organization gives them. EG *She usually gets her way without needing to pull rank.* ● PHR : VB INFLECTS

2 When you say that something **ranks** in a particular position on a scale, you mean that it has that position on the scale. EG *The island ranks as one of the poorest and least developed of the whole region... The magazine ranked a lowly 52nd among British publications.* V-ERG+A : NO CONT = rate

3 The **ranks** are the ordinary members of an organization, especially of the armed forces, as opposed to those who hold important positions. EG *...a senior officer who had risen from the ranks... The announcement spread panic in the ranks.* N PLURAL : *the*+N = rank and file N PLURAL : *the*+N

4 The **ranks** of an organization or group of people are the people who belong to it. EG *...the growing ranks of the unemployed... The party was becoming increasingly intolerant of dissent within its own ranks... There are about 1,000 members, but their ranks are growing.* N PLURAL+SUPP

5 If you **break ranks**, you are disloyal or fail to support a group of which you are a member. EG *There was no tolerance for anyone who broke ranks.* PHR : VB INFLECTS ⇑ desert

6 If the members of a group **close ranks**, they support each other in a united way and oppose any attack on them or criticism of them. EG *If they're criticized they tend to close ranks.* PHR : VB INFLECTS = stick together

7 A **rank** is also **7.1** a row of people or things that extends from side to side. EG *Massed ranks of police guarded the entrance to the base... There they stood in dense ranks, 30 metres tall.* N COUNT : USU P ⇑ line **7.2** the social class that a person belongs to; a rather old-fashioned use. EG *...people from the upper and middle ranks of society... We cater for everyone, regardless of age or social rank.* N COUNT/ UNCOUNT ⇑ order **7.3** a taxi rank. EG *Only a single taxi remained on a rank a little way down Davies Street.* N COUNT = taxi stand

8 **Rank** is used to describe a quality, especially a bad or undesirable one, that is of an extreme and unmistakable kind. EG *I recognized this at once as an attitude of rank favouritism... ...rank stupidity.* ADJ CLASSIF : ATTRIB ⇑ absolute = utter

9 Something that is **rank** has a strong and unpleasant taste or smell; a fairly formal use. EG *He trudged heavily up the steps, rank with the sweat of his night's work.* ADJ QUALIT ⇑ pungent

10 Vegetation that is **rank** is growing thickly and uncontrollably; a formal use. EG *The house still stood among its rank acres of rhododendrons.* ADJ QUALIT = luxuriant

rank and file. The **rank and file** are the ordinary members of an organization such as a trade union, a political party, or an army, as opposed to the leaders or officers. EG *There are now considerable political differences between the leadership and the rank and file... There was a great deal of rank and file support for the strike.* N SING : *the*+N VB CAN BE SING OR PL

ranking /ræŋkɪŋ/, **rankings**. **1** A **ranking** is a position on a scale, especially one that shows how good a person is at a sport in relation to other people. EG *She currently holds the number two ranking.* N COUNT+SUPP = rating

2 In American English, the **ranking** officer is the one who has the highest rank of anyone who is present. EG *Were these orders given to you by a ranking officer?* ADJ CLASSIF : ATTRIB ⇑ senior

rankle /ræŋkəl/, **rankles, rankling, rankled**. Something that **rankles** you makes you feel angry or bitter. EG *The argument with Sam earlier on still rankled... His behaviour rankles with me still.* V ⇑ irritate

ransack /rænsæk/, **ransacks, ransacking, ransacked**. If someone **ransacks** a place, **1** they search every part of it very thoroughly. EG *I ransacked the kitchen for something better.* V+O = rummage **2** they steal V+O things from it and leave it in a mess. EG *...the man whose house he had burgled and ransacked.*

ransom /rænsəᵒm/, **ransoms, ransoming, ransomed.** 1 A **ransom** is an amount of money that has to be paid in order to set free someone who has been kidnapped. EG *The family paid a ransom of £50,000 for the child's release... They said he would be held until the ransom money was produced.* — N COUNT ↑ payment

2 If someone **holds** you **to ransom**, 2.1 they keep you as a prisoner until money is paid for you to be set free. EG *The minister's daughter was held to ransom.* — PHR : VB INFLECTS

2.2 they put you in a position in which you are forced to agree to unreasonable demands. EG *She accused them of holding the nation to ransom.* — PHR : VB INFLECTS

3 If you **ransom** someone, you get them set free by paying a ransom. — V+O ↑ rescue

rant /rænt/, **rants, ranting, ranted.** If someone **rants**, they say a lot of foolish things in a loud, excited, and often angry way; used showing disapproval. EG *He would rant like this till she could not bear it any more... I was ranting on about history and our English heritage.* — V : USU+A, OR V +QUOTE ↑ utter
◊ **ranting, rantings.** EG *...the rantings and ravings of the lunatic fringe... They were not listening to David's ranting.* — ◊ N COUNT : SING=PL
● To **rant and rave** means the same as to rant; used especially when you want to exaggerate. EG *He ranted and raved about it.* — ● PHR : VBS INFLECT

rap /ræp/, **raps, rapping, rapped.** 1 If you **rap** on something, or if you **rap** it, you hit it with a series of quick blows. EG *He rapped on the table and called for silence... ...rapping their knuckles with a ruler.* — V+A *(on/ADV)*, V +O, OR V+O+A = thump

2 A **rap** is 2.1 a quick hit or knock against something. EG *A light rap sounded at the door.* — N COUNT
2.2 a severe warning or criticism from someone in a position of authority. EG *After this sharp rap from the inspectors they will have to improve their safety measures.* — N SING WITH DET = rebuke, reprimand
● If you receive **a rap on the knuckles** or **a rap over the knuckles**, you receive a warning or criticism about something that you have done. EG *He could not spend a pound without a rap over the knuckles from the bank.* — ● PHR : USED AS O ↑ rebuke
● If you **take the rap**, you are blamed or punished for something, even if it is not your fault; an informal use. EG *When these things go wrong, the government tends to take the rap.* — ● PHR : VB INFLECTS, IF+ PREP THEN *for*

3 When people **rap**, they have a relaxed, friendly conversation; used in informal American English. EG *We could hear them in the room below, laughing and rapping.* — V ↑ talk = chat

rap out. If you **rap out** an order or a question, you say it quickly and sharply. EG *She rapped out the words urgently... 'Is that the truth?' he suddenly rapped out.* — PHRASAL VB : V+ ADV+O/QUOTE ↑ utter = snap

rapacious /rəpeɪʃəs/. Someone who is **rapacious** is extremely greedy, especially for money; a formal word. EG *...rapacious businessmen.* ▸ used of people's actions and feelings. EG *...selfish rapacious ventures.* — ADJ QUALIT = avaricious, grasping

rapacity /rəpæsɪtiˡ/ is extreme greed, especially for money; a formal word. EG *...the rapacity of humans.* — N UNCOUNT = avarice

rape /reɪp/, **rapes, raping, raped.** 1 When a man **rapes** a woman, he violently forces her to have sex with him when she does not want to. EG *...an organization to help women who have been raped.* — V+O
▸ used as a noun to refer to this crime, or to an instance of the crime. EG *...a rape victim... She had to testify to his attempts at rape... ...the violence witnessed in riots, rapes, and muggings.* — ▸ N UNCOUNT/ COUNT

2 The **rape** of the countryside or the earth is the destruction or spoiling of it; a formal use. EG *...the rape of the earth's riches.* — N SING WITH DET *+of*

3 **Rape** is also a plant which is grown on farms and has bright yellow flowers. The seeds are crushed to provide oil, and the leaves are given as food to sheep and pigs. — N UNCOUNT

rapid /ræpɪd/, **rapids.** 1 Something that is **rapid** 1.1 happens at a very fast rate or within a very short period of time. EG *Jobs tend to be plentiful at a time of rapid economic growth... People are worried about the rapid and massive increase in military spending.* — ADJ QUALIT ↑ quick = swift
◊ **rapidly.** EG *The situation had rapidly deteriorated... ...rapidly increasing divorce rates.* — ◊ ADV WITH VB
1.2 moves or operates with great speed. EG *She awoke in a state of extreme panic, with rapid heartbeats and heavy breathing... He took a few rapid steps towards the beach.* — ADJ QUALIT ↑ quick = swift
◊ **rapidly.** EG *They walked rapidly past the churchyard.* — ◊ ADV WITH VB ↑ swiftly

2 **Rapids** are parts of a river where the water moves very fast, often over rocks. EG *Further down the river there is another stretch of rapids.* — N PLURAL

rapidity /rəpɪdɪtiˡ/ is a very fast rate of movement, change, or development. EG *The film shows the rapidity of the changes in this area of medicine.* — N UNCOUNT ↑ speed

rapier /reɪpɪə/, **rapiers.** A **rapier** is a long, thin sword with a sharp point; a formal, rather old-fashioned word. — N COUNT

rapist /reɪpɪst/, **rapists.** A **rapist** is a man who has raped a woman. — N COUNT ↑ criminal

rapport /ræpɔː/. If people have a **rapport** with each other, they have a relationship in which they have a special ability to understand each other's feelings or points of view. EG *He had established a pleasant form of rapport with my mother... There is insufficient rapport between hospitals and family doctors.* — N UNCOUNT OR N SING WITH DET : IF+PREP THEN *between/with* ↑ exchange

rapprochement /rəˢprɒʃmɒŋ/. A **rapprochement** is an increase in friendliness in the relationship between two countries, groups, or individuals, after a period of time when they have not been friendly with each other; a formal word. EG *This prompted many Americans to call for a rapprochement with Latin America... He thought he could effect a rapprochement between Burke and Holmes.* — N SING WITH DET : IF+PREP THEN *between/ of/with* ↑ reconciliation

rapt /ræpt/. Someone who is **rapt** is so interested in something or so fascinated by it that they cannot stop looking at it or think about anything else. EG *Claud was staring at me, rapt.* ▸ used of people's appearance or behaviour. EG *For an hour my audience listened in rapt silence... I gazed bewildered at his rapt face.* — ADJ QUALIT ↑ attentive = absorbed

rapture /ræptʃə/, **raptures.** 1 **Rapture** is is an overpowering feeling of delight; a literary use. EG *...his face shining with rapture.* — N UNCOUNT = ecstasy
▸ used as a plural noun. EG *...during the first raptures of their honeymoon.* — ▸ N PLURAL

2 If you **go into raptures** about something, you express your strong liking for it or great enthusiasm about it. EG *I had gone into raptures over the country I had been travelling through.* — PHR : VB INFLECTS

rapturous /ræptʃərəs/. A **rapturous** feeling is one which in which you feel very great happiness or enthusiasm; a literary word. EG *...the rush of rapturous delight which this news brought to her.* ▸ used of events or action in which great happiness is expressed. EG *He was given a rapturous welcome in his home town.* — ADJ QUALIT = ecstatic

rare /rɛə/, **rarer, rarest.** 1 Something that is **rare** 1.1 is not common and is therefore interesting or valuable. EG *These wild flowers are so rare I want to do whatever I can to save them... Diane's hobby is collecting rare books... ...laws that ban trade in rare reptiles.* — ADJ QUALIT = scarce
1.2 is not done or does not happen very often. EG *Cases of smallpox are extremely rare... It's rare to come across any book which makes you laugh out loud... On the rare occasions when he spoke, his voice sounded very nervous.* — ADJ QUALIT ↑ unusual = infrequent

2 **Rare** is used to describe a quality that someone or something has which is extremely good or remarkable. EG *She was a rare beauty... ...her rare gift for comedy.* — ADJ QUALIT : ATTRIB = exceptional

3 Meat that is **rare** is cooked very lightly so that the inside is still red. EG *...a rare beef steak.* — ADJ QUALIT = underdone

4 Air that is **rare** does not contain much oxygen, with the result that it is difficult for people to breathe. The air in high places is rare. — ADJ QUALIT = rarefied

5 See also **rarely, raring, rarity.**

rarebit /rɛəbɪt/ is the same as Welsh rarebit. — N UNCOUNT

rarefied /rɛərɪfaɪd/; also spelled **rarified.** 1 A **rarefied** situation or place is one in which there is a very high academic or social standard, but which is separated from ordinary people and real life; used showing disapproval. EG *...the rather rarefied atmosphere of university and student life... ...the rarefied world of the very, very rich.* — ADJ QUALIT : USU ATTRIB ↑ exclusive = esoteric

2 Air that is **rarefied** does not contain much oxygen, with the result that it is difficult for people to breathe. The air in high places is rarified. — ADJ QUALIT = rare

rarely /rɛəliˡ/ means not very often. EG *I'd rarely seen a man look so unhappy... Rarely has so much time been wasted by so many people... Only rarely does he let his own views become public.* — ADV BRD NEG = seldom

raring /rɛərɪŋ/. If you are **raring** to do something, you are very eager to do it. EG *They were raring to fight for more victories.* — ADJ CLASSIF : PRED+*to*-INF
● If you are **raring to go,** you are very eager to start something; an informal expression. EG *We're all raring to go.* — ● PHR : USED AS C

rarity /rɛərɪti¹/, **rarities**. 1 A **rarity** is a person or thing that is interesting or valuable because it is so unusual. EG *It is not surprising to find that bat twins are a rarity... ...six bags of gold coins, many of which were rarities.* — N COUNT ⇑ exception

2 The **rarity** of something is its quality of not being very common and therefore being interesting or valuable. EG *Many animals are endangered by their rarity and beauty... The record does at least have a rarity value.* — N UNCOUNT = scarcity

rascal /rɑːskə⁰l/, **rascals**. 1 If you refer to a child as a **rascal**, you mean that they have behaved badly or played a trick, but you are not really angry with them. EG *You little rascal!* — N COUNT OR *you* +N VOC = rogue, scallywag

2 If you refer to someone, especially a man, as a **rascal**, you mean that they have a bad character and behave in a dishonest way; an old-fashioned use. — N COUNT OR *you* +N VOC = reprobate, rogue

rascally /rɑːskəli¹/. Someone who is **rascally** behaves badly or plays tricks, but in a way which does not really make you angry. — ADJ QUALIT ⇑ mischievous = roguish

rash /ræʃ/, **rashes**. 1 Someone who is **rash** does or says things that are foolish, because they act without thinking carefully first. EG *Don't be rash, Castle, we don't want to give away more than we have to.* — ADJ QUALIT ⇑ impulsive = hasty
▸ used of people's actions. EG *For God's sake, Emmanuel, don't do anything rash... It would be rash to suppose that this particular freedom will continue... I've got so many of those things that you buy in a rash moment and then never use.* — ▸ = reckless
◇ **rashly**. EG *Some people jumped rashly to the conclusion that something must be wrong.* — ◇ ADV WITH VB = hastily
◇ **rashness**. EG *He could not disguise his pleasure at the rashness of what he was doing.* — ◇ N UNCOUNT = recklessness

2 A **rash** is a lot of spots or rough areas that appear on your skin when you have certain illnesses or are allergic to something. EG *...a man with a rash on one side of his neck.* — N COUNT ⇑ inflammation

3 A **rash** of events or occurrences is quite a large number of them that all happen or appear within a short period of time. EG *From the mid-1950s to the early 1960s, there was a rash of books and articles elaborating this theory... A rash of robberies had suddenly struck the country.* — N PART+N IN PLURAL ⇑ series = spate

rasher /ræʃə/, **rashers**. A **rasher** of bacon is a thin slice of bacon. — N COUNT

rasp /rɑːsp/, **rasps, rasping, rasped**. 1 A **rasp** is 1.1 a rough harsh sound which is unpleasant to hear, like the sound of two things scraping together. EG *...the rasp of sandpaper on wood... There was an ugly rasp in his voice.* — N SING WITH DET = grate
1.2 a tool with a long blade covered with sharp teeth, which you use to make wood or metal smoother. — N COUNT

2 If someone or something **rasps**, they make a rough, harsh sound which is unpleasant to hear. EG *Crickets rasped loudly... 'It's frightful,' she rasped.* — V OR V+QUOTE = grate
◇ **rasping**. EG *...a dry rasping voice... With a rasping sound the gate was opened.* — ◇ ADJ QUALIT = grating

raspberry /rɑːzbə⁰ri¹/, **raspberries**. A **raspberry** is 1 a small red fruit which is soft and sweet and which you can eat; also used of the bush on which this fruit grows. EG *...home-made raspberry jam.* — N COUNT ⇑ berry
2 in informal English, a sound which you make by putting your tongue out and blowing. It is intended to insult someone or to make fun of them. EG *He then blew a loud and lengthy raspberry... His victory was announced to a chorus of raspberries.* — N COUNT

Rasta /ræstə/, **Rastas**. **Rasta** means the same as Rastafarian; an informal word. — N COUNT, OR ADJ CLASSIF

Rastafarian /ræstəfɛərɪən/, **Rastafarians**. A **Rastafarian** is a believer in a religion that originated in Jamaica. Rastafarians worship a former emperor of Ethiopia, Haile Selassie, as God. ▸ used as an adjective. — N COUNT; ▸ ADJ CLASSIF

rat /ræt/, **rats, ratting, ratted**. 1 A **rat** is a small animal which has a long tail and looks rather like a large mouse. EG *Rats carry very nasty diseases... How do I get rid of these rats and mice?* — N COUNT ⇑ rodent
● If you say that someone looks **like a drowned rat**, you mean that they look very wet and uncomfortable. — ● PHR : USED AS AN A
● to **smell a rat**: see **smell**.

2 If you call someone a **rat**, you mean that you dislike them because they are disloyal to you or have deceived you; an informal use. EG *Oh, you rat... They're all rats in our business.* — N COUNT OR *you* +N VOC

3 If you **rat** on someone, you are disloyal to someone by revealing secret information about them; an informal use. EG *So you ratted on Gertrude?* — V : IF+PREP THEN *on* ⇑ betray = grass

4 If you **rat** on an agreement or promise, you break it; an informal use. EG *I hope you're not thinking of ratting on the deal.* — V : IF+PREP THEN *on* = default

5 You say **rats** when you are annoyed or frustrated about something; an informal use. EG *A piece of crockery smashed in the kitchen. 'Oh rats!'* — EXCLAM = bother, damn

rat-a-tat /ræt ə tæt/. **Rat-a-tat** or **rat-a-tat-tat** is used to describe a repeated knocking or tapping sound, for example the sound of someone knocking on a door. EG *There was a knock at the door. Rat-a-tat-tat... ...the continual rat-a-tat of machine-gun fire.* — N SING WITH DET

ratchet /rætʃɪt/, **ratchets**. A **ratchet** is a wheel or bar with sloping teeth that is only able to turn in one direction because a piece of metal prevents the teeth from moving backwards. EG *...a mechanical toy with a broken ratchet... ...ratchet wrenches.* — N COUNT ⇑ mechanism

rate /reɪt/, **rates, rating, rated**. 1 The **rate** at which something happens is the speed at which it happens over a period of time. EG *...the rapid rate of change which the industrial world is facing... He was ordered to pay me at the rate of ten pounds a month... Toffler himself underestimated the rate at which things were going to move... ...an 8% inflation rate.* ● **at a rate of knots**: see **knot**. — N COUNT+SUPP

2 The **rate** of a particular phenomenon is the number of instances of it which occur during a period of time. EG *The divorce rate is fantastically high... What is your success rate?... There is a close link between a rising rate of unemployment and a rising suicide rate.* — N COUNT+SUPP ⇑ ratio

3 The **rate** of taxation or interest is the level of it. EG *Any money earned over that level is taxed at the rate of 59 per cent... It's a very good rate of interest compared with the other banks... ...the rise in the mortgage rate.* — N COUNT : USU+SUPP

4 If you say that **at this rate** something will happen, you mean that it will happen if things continue to develop or happen as they have been developing or happening. EG *At this rate we'll be millionaires by Christmas!... We shan't find what we're looking for at this rate.* — PHR : USED AS AN A

5 You use **at any rate** 5.1 to indicate that what you have just said might be too general or an exaggeration, and you want to be more precise. EG *Come early evening. After tea-time, at any rate... They felt, or at any rate Dan felt, both relieved and still frightened.* — PHR : USED AS ADV SEN = at least
5.2 to indicate that the important thing is what you are going to say now and not what has just been said, which is not necessarily even relevant or true. EG *I don't know exactly what he did–something in industry, I think. But at any rate he got a knighthood for it... I don't think there's been an edition since 1977; at any rate that's the one I'll be referring to.* — PHR : USED AS ADV SEN = anyway

6 **Rates** are a local tax in Britain which has to be paid by people who own buildings or rent unfurnished buildings. The money from the rates in an area is used to pay for local services and public facilities. EG *What do you pay for your rates and water rates?... For a while fares in London were subsidised by the rates... ...those who have won rate and rent rebates.* — N PLURAL

7 If you **rate** someone or something as having a particular quality, you consider that they have that quality. EG *Their goalkeeper was rated as being of county standard... He was a self-taught geologist, rated by his colleagues as one of the best.* — V+O (NG/REFL) +A/C : USU A *(as)*, NO CONT ⇑ evaluate = reckon

8 If you **rate** something highly, you consider that it is important. EG *Looks are never rated very highly when people are asked what basis they choose their friends on... The virtues of kindness and generosity tend to be rated above all others.* — V+O+C, OR V+O +A : NO CONT ⇑ value = rank

9 If someone or something **rates** as having a particular level of importance, quality, or ability, they are generally regarded as having that level of importance, quality, or ability. EG *On a scale of one to ten, it probably rated about number seven... Miss Swanson does not rate high as a picker of husbands.* — V+A, OR V+C (ADJ) : NO CONT = rank

10 If you **rate** something, 10.1 you have a good general opinion of it; an informal use. EG *I don't rate any of his family.* — V+O : NO CONT
10.2 you deserve it. EG *He rated twenty-five shillings a week at twenty-one... I became what they call a double agent, Sarah. I rate a lifetime in jail.* — V+O : NO CONT = merit

11 See also **rating**.

rateable value /reɪtəbə⁰l væljuː/, **rateable values**. In Britain, the **rateable value** of a building — N COUNT ⇑ valuation is a theoretical value based on its size and the facilities it has, which is used for calculating how much the owner must pay in rates: see **rate 6**.

ratepayer /reɪtpeɪə/, **ratepayers**; also spelled with a hyphen. In Britain, a **ratepayer** is a person who owns or rents a building and therefore pays rates. EG *It should be the factory that pays for its waste disposal, not the local ratepayers.* N COUNT ⇑ taxpayer

rather /rɑːðə/. **1 Rather** means **1.1** to a certain, limited, or slight extent; often used to reduce the force of a criticism or to avoid making a statement that is too direct. EG *I'm rather puzzled by this question... He looked rather pathetic standing in the slush outside... It stood rather like an old farm dog... I rather think it was three hundred and fifty pounds.* ADV = somewhat

1.2 to quite a large degree or extent; often used to emphasize or add force to a statement. EG *The company thought I did rather well... I'm in rather a hurry. I've got to go... She's got mumps rather badly.* ADV ⇑ very

2 You use **rather** to express a preference or to say what you want to happen. When you use it to say what you want someone else to do, it is always followed by a past tense even though the action refers to the future. EG *He's not terribly interested in the project, he'd rather be out playing golf... 'What was all that about?'-'I'm sorry, I'd rather not say'... 'May I go on?'-'I'd rather you didn't.'... Would you rather she came to see me?* ● If you say **'Rather you than me', 'Rather her than me'**, etc, you mean that you would certainly not want to do the thing that the other person is going to do. EG *'I'm going rock climbing this weekend.'-'Rather you than me!'* ADV SEN : *would/had*+*rather* = prefer to; ● PHR

3 You use **rather than** to say what someone does not do, when you are stating this in contrast to what they do actually do. EG *I have used familiar English names rather than scientific Latin ones... Rather than disappoint them he did two quick tricks.* PREP, OR CONJ SUBORD = instead of

4 You also use **rather 4.1** to introduce a correction or qualification to one of the words in a statement that you have just made, often in order to achieve a significant or humorous effect. EG *Suddenly there stood before him, or rather above him, a gigantic woman... That one picture speaks volumes. Or rather lies volumes.* ADV SEN : USU *or*+*rather* **4.2** to introduce a statement that expresses a different and often opposite opinion from the one that has just been expressed and to suggest that this second statement is a truer or better one. EG *This was no matter for congratulation, but rather a matter for vengeance.* ADV SEN

5 Rather is also an emphatic way of saying yes or of agreeing with someone; an old-fashioned use. EG *'I do think she was jolly good, don't you?'-'Rather!'* CONVENTION

ratify /rætɪfaɪ/, **ratifies, ratifying, ratified**. If you **ratify** a written agreement or document, you give your formal approval to it, usually by signing it, and in this way make it official; a formal word. EG *Over 90 countries ratified an agreement to ban the use of these chemicals.* ◊ **ratification** /rætɪfɪkeɪʃəⁿn/. EG *His objections prevented ratification of the proposals.* V+O ⇑ agree = confirm; ◊ N UNCOUNT = confirmation

rating /reɪtɪŋ/, **ratings**. **1** A **rating** is a score or assessment based on how much of a particular quality someone or something has. EG *...jobs which are currently assigned a low rating on the economic and social scale... ...an IQ rating roughly equivalent to eight-year-old children... Opinion polls showed Schmidt's popularity rating at an all-time low of 41.5 per cent.* N COUNT : USU MOD+N

2 Ratings are lists giving the number of people who watched each television programme during the week, so that the most popular and least popular programmes are known. EG *The ratings are a disaster and the reviews are worse... ...determined to win the ratings battle.* N PLURAL : PL FORM WHEN MOD ⇑ statistics

3 Your **rating** of something is your opinion about its quality. EG *Harold's rating of some of his brother's creations wasn't very flattering.* N SING WITH DET = assessment

4 A **rating** is also a sailor in a national navy who is not an officer. N COUNT

5 Rating is the assessment of the value of a property and the amount of rates that the owner or tenant must pay. N UNCOUNT

ratio /reɪʃɪəʊ/, **ratios**. A **ratio** is a relationship between two amounts or measurements, which shows how much greater one is than the other when they are compared. EG *...a high teacher/pupil ratio... ...a ratio of one tutor to five students... The ratio between attackers and defenders was roughly eight to one.* ● If you say that one thing is **in direct ratio to** another, you mean that there is a definite relationship between the change in one thing and the change in another, and that this can be expressed as a ratio. EG *Efficiency increases in direct ratio to incentive.* N COUNT : USU+SUPP = proportion; ● PHR : USED AS AN A

ration /ræʃəⁿn/, **rations, rationing, rationed**. **1** A **ration** is **1.1** a particular quantity of something scarce, for example food or petrol during a war, which each person is allowed to have. EG *...a 20 percent reduction in monthly meat rations.* **1.2** the amount of something, for example a quality or emotion, that you think is sufficient or normal for a person to have. EG *They have more than their ration of selfishness.* N COUNT ⇑ allowance; N COUNT+SUPP : USU SING ⇑ share = allowance

2 When a person or government **rations** something scarce, they limit the quantity of it which each person is allowed to have. EG *Meat was still rationed at the beginning of the fifties.* V+O ⇑ allocate

3 If you **ration** someone to a particular amount of something, you allow them to have only that amount of it. EG *I'm going to ration you to a cigarette a day.* V+O : IF+PREP THEN *to* ⇑ limit

4 Rations are all the food which is supplied to a soldier or a member of an expedition each day. EG *We have sufficient rations for three weeks... We'll be back on full rations tomorrow.* N PLURAL

5 See also **rationing**.

ration out. If you **ration out** something scarce, you distribute it to a group of people, giving each person only a small amount. EG *I rationed out the last of the food.* PHRASAL VB : V+O+ADV ⇑ apportion

rational /ræʃəⁿnəl, -ʃənəⁿl/. Someone who is **rational** is able to think clearly and to make decisions and judgements that are based on reason rather than emotions. EG *Let's talk about this like two rational people.* ▸ used of people's ideas and actions. EG *There is no rational explanation... Panic destroys rational thought.* ◊ **rationally**. EG *Let's discuss this rationally... You are hardly behaving rationally.* ◊ **rationality** /ræʃənælɪtiⁱ/. EG *The debate soon lost all semblance of rationality.* ADJ QUALIT ⇑ sensible = reasoning; ◊ ADV WITH VB = sensibly; ◊ N UNCOUNT

rationale /ræʃənɑːl/ is the set of reasons on which a particular course of action, practice, or belief is based; a fairly formal word. EG *What is the rationale for corporal punishment?* N SING WITH DET : IF+PREP THEN *for/of* = basis

rationalism /ræʃəⁿnəlɪzəⁿm/ is the belief that your opinions and the way you live your life should be based on reason and not emotions or religious beliefs. EG *...the great divide which separates rationalism from superstition.* N UNCOUNT ⇑ doctrine

rationalist /ræʃəⁿnəlɪst/, **rationalists**. **1** A **rationalist** is a person who bases their opinions and the way they live their life on reason and not on emotions or religious beliefs. N COUNT

2 Opinions and behaviour that are **rationalist** are based on reason and not on emotions or religious beliefs. EG *...the rationalist philosophy of the middle classes in Victorian England.* ADJ QUALIT = rationalistic

rationalistic /ræʃəⁿnəlɪstɪk/ means the same as rationalist: see **rationalist 2**. EG *...rationalistic theories.* ADJ QUALIT

rationalize /ræʃəⁿnəlaɪz/, **rationalizes, rationalizing, rationalized**; also spelled **rationalise**. **1** When you **rationalize** something, you think of reasons so that you can explain and understand a course of action, belief, or state of mind that you are unhappy about. EG *I rationalise it by saying that I need the money.* ◊ **rationalization** /ræʃəⁿnəlaɪzeɪʃəⁿn/, **rationalizations**. EG *The health argument is usually a rationalization.* V OR V+O/REPORT-CL = justify; ◊ N COUNT/UNCOUNT = justification

2 When people **rationalize** a company, system, or industry, they make it more efficient by removing staff and equipment that are not necessary. EG *Society and industry had been rationalized and modernized.* ◊ **rationalization**. EG *...the continuing rationalization of the British armed forces.* V+O = streamline; ◊ N UNCOUNT

rationing /ræʃəⁿnɪŋ/ is a system of limiting the quantity of food, petrol, water, etc, which each person is allowed to have, because there is a shortage. EG *I can remember petrol rationing... Despite rationing, they always had plenty of meat.* N UNCOUNT ⇑ allocation

rat race; also spelled with a hyphen. If you refer to a job or way of life as a **rat race**, you mean that the people in it all compete fiercely with each other to be successful; used showing disapproval. EG *He was* N SING WITH DET : USU *the*+N ⇑ competition *one of the few people I ever knew who got out of the rat race... We are all living in the rat-race.*

rat-tat /ræt tæt/. **Rat-tat** or **rat-tat-tat** is the same as rat-a-tat. EG *There was a rat-tat at the door.* N SING WITH DET

ratter /rætə/, **ratters**. A **ratter** is a dog or cat that catches and kills rats. N COUNT ⇑ animal

rattle /rætəºl/, **rattles, rattling, rattled**. 1 When something **rattles** or when you **rattle** it, it makes a lot of short, rapid knocking sounds because it is being shaken or hitting continually against something hard. EG *A cold November wind rattled the windows... The chains of playground swings rattled in the dark.* ▸ used as a noun. EG *The rattle of the engine became louder... ...the sound of squeaks and rattles.* V-ERG = clatter; ▸ N COUNT ⇑ noise = clatter

2 A **rattle** is also 2.1 a baby's toy that has bits inside that rattle when the baby plays with the toy. N COUNT 2.2 a wooden instrument that you shake to make a loud rattling sound, for example at a football match. N COUNT

3 If something **rattles** somewhere, it moves there and makes a lot of short sharp knocking sounds at the same time. EG *I had taken a taxi which rattled down the road... The small beans rattle to the bottom.* V+A = clatter

4 If something **rattles** you, it makes you worried, annoyed, or less calm. EG *His questions obviously rattled her... He seems rattled about our presence.* V+O = disconcert, unsettle

5 See also **rattling**.

rattle away. See **rattle on**.

rattle off. If you **rattle** something **off**, you say or write it very quickly and without much effort. EG *...a machine capable of rattling off thousands of calculations in a few minutes.* PHRASAL VB : V+O+ADV = reel off

rattle on. If you **rattle on** or **rattle away**, you talk quickly and for a long time, usually about something which is not very interesting or important. EG *Some of the women in our delegation would rattle on about sex.* PHRASAL VB : V+ADV, IF+PREP THEN *about* = chatter

rattle through. If you **rattle through** something, you deal with it quickly in order to finish it. EG *They rattled through the rest of the meeting.* PHRASAL VB : V+PREP, HAS PASS = whip through

rattler /rætlə/, **rattlers**. A **rattler** is the same as a rattlesnake; used in informal American English. N COUNT

rattlesnake /rætəºlsneɪk/, **rattlesnakes**. A **rattlesnake** is a poisonous American snake with bony rings at the end of its tail which make a rattling sound when the tail is shaken. N COUNT

rattling /rætlɪŋ/ is used to emphasize how good or pleasant something is; a rather old-fashioned informal word. EG *...a rattling good story.* ADV+ADJ/ADV ⇑ very = cracking

ratty /rætiˡ/, **rattier, rattiest**. If you are **ratty**, you show that you are easily annoyed; an informal use in British English. EG *What a ratty old couple we are.* ◇ **rattiness**. EG *I apologise for my rattiness yesterday.* ADJ QUALIT = crotchety; ◇ N UNCOUNT

raucous /rɔːkəs/. Something such as a sound that is **raucous** is loud and rough. EG *I could hear the sound of raucous laughter... We had had one or two memorable raucous evenings together.* ◇ **raucously**. ADJ QUALIT ⇑ noisy; ◇ ADV WITH VB

raunchy /rɔːntʃiˡ/, **raunchier, raunchiest**. Someone who is **raunchy** looks or sounds as though they have a strong and aggressive desire for sex; an informal word. EG *...some of the most brazen, raunchy people in the world.* ▸ used of someone's appearance or voice. EG *She has one of the raunchiest voices in rock music.* ADJ QUALIT ⇑ sexy

ravage /rævɪdʒ/, **ravages, ravaging, ravaged**; a formal word. 1 Someone or something that **ravages** something causes so much damage to it over a period of time that it is almost completely destroyed. EG *...the diseases which ravage Aboriginal populations... He came from a country ravaged by war.* V+O = devastate, lay waste

2 The **ravages** of the weather, time, war, etc are the damaging effects of it. EG *...the ravages of rain and sun... The State could not protect its citizens from the ravages of inflation.* N PLURAL+SUPP : USU+*of*

rave /reɪv/, **raves, raving, raved**. 1 If you **rave**, you talk in an excited and uncontrolled way, for example because you are very angry. EG *I must have raved at Richard for nearly five minutes.* ● to **rant and rave**: see **rant**. V : IF+PREP THEN *about/against/at* = rant

2 If you **rave** about something that you admire very much, you write or speak with great enthusiasm about it; an informal use. EG *The car magazines have been raving about the new model... Another newspaper raved: 'the most exciting play I have ever seen.'* V+A *(about)*, OR V+QUOTE ⇑ praise

3 A **rave** is 3.1 a piece of writing that praises something a lot, especially a work of art; an informal use. EG *...Tynan's famous rave for Look Back in Anger... Stoppard's new play has received rave reviews.* N COUNT ⇑ review 3.2 something which is very popular and fashionable for a short time, especially with young people; an informal use. EG *...the latest rave in party gear.* N COUNT = craze

4 **Rave** is used to describe something that is extremely popular and fashionable, especially with young people; an informal use. EG *...a list of all night rave places in Paris.* ADJ CLASSIF : ATTRIB = trendy

5 If you **rave it up**, you enjoy yourself by drinking, dancing, etc for a long time and behaving in a noisy and disorderly way; a rather old-fashioned, informal expression. EG *...a huge crowd raving it up in Trafalgar Square.* PHR : VB INFLECTS = revel

6 See also **raving**.

raven /reɪvəºn/, **ravens**. 1 A **raven** is a large bird which has shiny black feathers and a deep harsh call. N COUNT ⇑ crow

2 Something, especially hair, that is **raven** is a shiny black colour; a literary use. EG *...raven black hair... ...a raven-haired girl.* ADJ COLOUR : ATTRIB

ravenous /rævənəs/. If you are **ravenous**, you are very hungry indeed; an informal word. EG *By that time I was ravenous... Most infants have a ravenous appetite.* ◇ **ravenously**. EG *He looked ravenously at the table to see what they were having for dinner.* ADJ QUALIT : USU PRED = famished, starving; ◇ ADV

raver /reɪvə/, **ravers**. A **raver** is a person who is very lively and has an exciting social life; an informal word used in British English. EG *He's a bit of a raver.* N COUNT = swinger

rave-up, rave-ups. A **rave-up** is a very lively party where people dance and drink a lot; an informal word used in British English. EG *We're having a rave-up on Saturday night.* N COUNT

ravine /rəviːn/, **ravines**. A **ravine** is a very deep narrow valley which has steep sides and which has been made by a stream flowing through it. EG *...on the opposite side of the ravine... The city is built on layers of rock rising out of ravines.* N COUNT = gorge

raving /reɪvɪŋ/, **ravings**. 1 You use **raving** to describe someone who you think is completely mad; an informal use. EG *You're all raving lunatics... All of them are stark raving mad.* ADJ CLASSIF : ATTRIB, OR ADV-ADJ

2 **Ravings** are things that someone says which are disordered and do not make sense, like the talk of a person who is mad or seriously ill. EG *The statements made in The Times were just the ravings of a madman.* N PLURAL : USU WITH POSS = rantings

ravioli /rævɪəʊliˡ/ is an Italian food made from small squares of pasta which are filled with meat and served with a sauce. N UNCOUNT

ravish /rævɪʃ/, **ravishes, ravishing, ravished**; a formal or literary word. 1 If you **are ravished** by someone, it gives you great pleasure and delight, especially because it is very beautiful to look at. EG *He was ravished by the beauty of the language... ...paintings which ravish the eye.* V+O : USU PASS

2 If a man **ravishes** a woman, he rapes her; an old-fashioned use. V+O

3 If an army **ravishes** a town, it damages and robs it. V+O

ravishing /rævɪʃɪŋ/. Someone or something that is **ravishing** is very beautiful to look at. EG *I'd almost forgotten how ravishing you looked... ...a ravishing blonde... ...one of Van Dyck's last masterpieces, the ravishing Cupid and Psyche.* ◇ **ravishingly**. EG *She was ravishingly beautiful.* ADJ QUALIT = stunning; ◇ ADV = stunningly

raw /rɔː/. 1 Meat or other food that is **raw** is not cooked. EG *...a piece of raw meat... You can eat carrots cooked or raw.* ADJ CLASSIF = uncooked

2 **Raw** materials or substances are in a natural state before being used in a manufacturing process. EG *...Indian exports of raw cotton to Lancashire... ...raw rubber from Malaysia.* ADJ CLASSIF : ATTRIB = crude, untreated

3 **Raw** facts or data are not yet arranged or selected and so are not yet ready to be used. EG *We've gathered a mass of raw data.* ADJ CLASSIF : ATTRIB

4 **Raw** emotions and qualities are natural and basic and not weakened by being controlled too much. EG *You're going to kill someone one day with your raw power.* ADJ CLASSIF : ATTRIB = naked, pur

5 If a part of your body is **raw**, you have lost or burnt some of the skin covering it, so that it is very sore. EG ADJ QUALIT ⇑ painful

Every boy's feet had big, raw blisters on them... My back felt raw from the heat of the sun.

6 If you say that someone is **raw**, you mean that they are too young or too new in a job to know how to behave or how to do things properly; used in American English. EG *He's just a raw kid.* ADJ QUALIT ⇑ inexperienced = green

7 If the weather is **raw**, it is unpleasantly cold and wet. EG *He went out into the raw London night... ...a raw day in Sunderland.* ADJ QUALIT

8 A piece of writing or an account of something that is **raw** is very frank and truthful about a subject which is unpleasant or controversial. EG *His last piece, on Chief Justice Warren, was too raw to print.* ADJ QUALIT

9 **In the raw** means 9.1 in informal English, completely naked. EG *Afterwards we went for a swim in the raw.* PHR : USED AS AN A 9.2 in a brutal and uncivilized state. EG *Golding's books describe life in the raw.* PHR AFTER N

10 If you think that you have got **a raw deal**, you think that you have been treated unfairly or harshly, for example by not being paid or rewarded enough; an informal expression. EG *He thinks he's got a raw deal from life.* PHR : USED AS O

11 If you **touch a raw nerve** or **touch** someone **on the raw**, you hurt their feelings by talking about something which is painful to them. EG *His wife's words touched a raw nerve.* PHR : VB INFLECTS

raw-boned. Someone who is **raw-boned** is very thin. EG *...the tall raw-boned youth.* ADJ QUALIT = lean

rawhide /rɔ:haɪd/, **rawhides**; used in American English. 1 **Rawhide** is cow's leather that has not been treated. EG *...a rawhide belt.* N UNCOUNT

2 A **rawhide** is a whip that is made of rawhide. N COUNT

raw material, raw materials. 1 **A raw material** is a natural substance which is used to make something, for example in an industrial process. EG *...coal, oil, gas, and other raw materials... ...a source of raw materials for western industry.* N COUNT/ UNCOUNT : USU PL = staple

2 If you describe someone or something as **raw material** for a particular purpose, you mean that they can be used for that purpose if they are changed or developed in some way. EG *She makes use of people she meets as raw material for her fiction... ...the raw material of the army.* N UNCOUNT : USU +SUPP = basis

ray /reɪ/, **rays**. 1 A **ray** is a beam of heat or light. EG *The rays of the sun can be very harmful... ...exposure to ultraviolet rays... Long, orange-coloured rays of light fell horizontally across the field.* N COUNT : USU PL +SUPP

2 A **ray** of hope, comfort, or some other good feeling or quality is a small amount of it that you welcome because it makes a bad situation seem less bad. EG *There was now a ray of hope... She let a ray of originality into his humdrum life.* N PART = glimmer, trace

3 A **ray** is also a large sea fish which has a flat body, eyes on the top of its body, and a long tail. N COUNT

rayon /reɪɒn/ is a smooth fabric made from cotton, wool, or synthetic fibres. It looks and feels similar to silk. N UNCOUNT ⇑ material

raze /reɪz/, **razes, razing, razed**. If people **raze** a building, town, or forest, they completely destroy it so that nothing is left above the ground. EG *Cortes razed Tenochtitlan and founded Mexico City... Many villages were razed to the ground.* V+O : IF+PREP THEN *to* ⇑ demolish = flatten

razor /reɪzə/, **razors**. A **razor** is a tool that you use for removing hair from your skin. It cuts the hair close to the skin with a sharp blade. EG *...the fatal consequence of cutting herself with a razor... ...an electric razor.* N COUNT

razor blade, razor blades. A **razor blade** is a small, thin, flat piece of metal with a very sharp edge, that can be fastened to a razor and used for removing hair from your skin. EG *I'll just pop into the chemist for some razor blades... Sheet polythene can be cut with a razor blade and stuck to the window frame.* N COUNT

razor-sharp. Something that is **razor-sharp** is very sharp, like a razor-blade. EG *...a small knife made of a razor-sharp straight blade set into a short bamboo stick.* ADJ CLASSIF

razzle /ræzə⁰l/. If you **go on the razzle**, you go out and enjoy yourself in a lively and noisy way, for example by going to pubs or night clubs; an informal expression. EG *We're off on the razzle again tonight.* PHR : VB INFLECTS

RC, RC's. **RC** is an abbreviation for 'Roman Catholic'. N COUNT, OR ADJ CLASSIF

Rd is a written abbreviation for 'road'; used especially in addresses and on maps or signs. N IN NAMES AFTER N

-rd is added to a number that ends in 3 and is written in figures in order to form an ordinal number or fraction. 3rd is pronounced 'third'. EG *3rd... ...23rd... ...173rd.* SUFFIX : FORMS ORDINALS

re /ri:/. You use **re** in writing to introduce a subject or item which you are going to discuss or refer to in detail; used in formal written English. EG *Re your letter of 16 July 1985, I am pleased to inform you that you will shortly receive a cheque for £16-50 in settlement of your claim.* PREP

R.E. is a school subject in which children learn about religion; an abbreviation for 'religious education'. N UNCOUNT

re-. 1 **Re-** is added to verbs and nouns 1.1 in order to form other verbs and nouns that refer to the repeating of an action or process. For example, to 're-read' something means to read it again, and to 're-marry' means to marry again. EG *...tell→retell... ...use→reuse... ...election→re-election.* PREFIX 1.2 in order to form other verbs and nouns that refer to a process opposite to one that has already taken place. For example, to 'reappear' means to appear after disappearing, and to 'regain' something means to gain it after you have lost it. PREFIX

2 **Re-** is added to verbs to form other verbs describing the changing of the position or state of something. For example, to 'relocate' something means to locate it in a different place and to 'rearrange' something means to arrange it in a different way. EG *...distribute→redistribute... ...deploy→redeploy.* PREFIX

-'re is a shortened form of 'are'. In spoken English it is added to the end of the pronoun or noun which is the subject of the verb. For example, 'we are' can be shortened to 'we're'. EG *You're quite right... They're lovely... What're you waiting for?*

reach /ri:tʃ/, **reaches, reaching, reached**. 1 When you **reach** somewhere, you arrive there. EG *It was dark by the time I reached their house... Turn left when you reach the main road... It took three days for the letter to reach me.* V+O = get to, come to

2 If you **reach** somewhere, you stretch out your hand or arm in order to do something or in order to get something. EG *He reached into his inside pocket and produced a pen... She reached across the desk and shook my hand... He reached up and put the book back on the shelf... She reached for her bag and pulled out a gun... I reached out a hand and caught the ball.* V+A, OR V+O+A : USU V+A

3 When you **reach** something, you get it by stretching out your hand or arm, often to give it to someone else. EG *Could you reach a pot of jam out of the top cupboard, please?... She asked me to reach her the book from the shelf.* V+O, OR V+O+O = pass

4 If you say that you can **reach** something, you mean that you can touch it or take hold of it by stretching out your arm. EG *I can't reach that shelf unless I stand on a chair.* V+O = grasp

5 When you **reach** someone who is in another place, you speak to them or send a message to them, for example by telephoning them. EG *I tried to reach you at home several times, but no-one answered the phone.* V+O = contact

6 If something **reaches** a place, point or level, it extends as far as that place, point, or level. EG *When the water reached his waist, he had to start swimming... The ladder doesn't quite reach the top of the wall... She wore a long blue skirt reaching down to the ground... Rumours of an enemy invasion began to reach the capital... The only sound that reached his ears was the crashing of the waves.* V+O, OR V+A

7 If someone or something **reaches** a particular stage, condition, or level, they get to it, for example through natural development or gradual progression. EG *We have reached the point at which we are beginning to make a profit... Unemployment among young people has reached a very high level... Kangaroos can reach speeds of 60 kph... Most children stay at home until they reach school age.* V+O = attain

8 If you **reach** an agreement, decision, or result, you achieve it through time, effort, or thought. EG *After long negotiations, they managed to reach an agreement on rates of pay... We feel that we have now reached a clearer understanding of the problems.* V+O = arrive at

9 The **reach** of something or someone is the distance or limit to which they can stretch, extend, or travel. EG *Her powerful service and long reach give her a big advantage over her opponent... Keep all medi-* N UNCOUNT : USU AFTER PREP = compass, range

cines out of reach of children... The flat is within easy reach of the shops and the station... By escaping the country, she put herself beyond the reach of the authorities... Can these plants grow at depths beyond the reach of sunlight?

10 The **reaches** of a section of a river or a region of land are the large areas of land that it covers. EG *...a small community living on the upper reaches of the Amazon... Further to the north, there are great reaches of forest.*
N PLURAL + SUPP : USU + *of* = stretch, expanse

react /ri'ækt/, **reacts, reacting, reacted. 1** When you **react** to something that has happened to you, you behave in a particular way because of what has happened. EG *Sam didn't look up or react in any way... They tend to react to affection in a selfish way... She tends to react strongly if he lights a cigarette... I wondered how he'd react to such a blunt question.*
V : USU + A, IF + PREP THEN *to* = respond

2 If you **react** against something, you deliberately do something in a way that is different from the way that it has been done before. EG *They reacted against the formality of their predecessors... He was clearly reacting against Victorian traditions.*
V + A *(against)* ⇑ behave = rebel

3 If you **react** to a substance, usually a drug, that has got into your body, you are affected unpleasantly or made ill by it. EG *We were alarmed at the way in which Katie reacted to the drug.*
V : USU + A, IF + PREP THEN *to* ⇑ suffer

4 If one chemical substance **reacts** with another, it has an effect on it, for example by combining with it to form a new substance. EG *The water was reacting with the ferrous iron in the tank.*
V OR V + A *(with)* : RECIP ⇑ combine

reaction /ri'ækʃə⁰n/, **reactions. 1** A **reaction** is **1.1** something that you feel or do because of something that has happened or because you are in a particular place or with a particular person. EG *My immediate reaction was one of revulsion... She laughs about people's reaction to hearing that she is a Lloyd's broker... Vita's reaction to Italy was exactly what mine had been... We were not prepared for the violence of his reaction towards Sandy.* **1.2** a way of doing something that is intended to be different from another way of doing it, because you do not like the other way. EG *My work has never been a reaction against Abstract Expressionism.* **1.3** a change of public opinion in which something that has been popular becomes unpopular. EG *The decade ended in a huge reaction against the pill... The burden the Act placed on ratepayers led to a reaction against public expenditure.*
N COUNT/UNCOUNT + SUPP = response; N COUNT + *against*; N SING WITH DET : IF + PREP THEN *against*

2 Your **reactions** are your abilities to move quickly as a result of something that happens to you, especially something that might be harmful or dangerous. EG *Inevitably, our reactions get slower as we get older... They tried out a computer game meant to time their reactions.*
N PLURAL ⇑ reflexes

3 **Reaction** is the belief that things should not change and the attempt to prevent any changes, especially the political or social system of a country; used showing disapproval. EG *Once again the forces of reaction prevailed... Reaction and restrictive practices were putting a brake on enterprise.*
N UNCOUNT

4 A **reaction** is also **4.1** a process in which two substances combine together chemically and make another substance. EG *A chemical reaction occurs in the fuel cell... ...the reaction of ground water with the molten rock.* **4.2** an illness or other unpleasant effect that is caused by a substance, usually a drug, that gets into your body. EG *I'm afraid I usually have a bad reaction to penicillin.*
N COUNT : IF + PREP THEN *between...and/of...and/with*; N COUNT : IF + PREP THEN *to*

reactionary /ri'ækʃənə⁰ri¹/, **reactionaries.** Someone or something that is **reactionary** does not want any changes in a system, especially the political or social system of a country, and tries to prevent any changes from taking place; used showing disapproval. EG *This was a victory for reactionary forces... ...the public image of the House of Lords as reactionary.* ▸ used as a noun to refer to a person with such views. EG *...the need to appease powerful reactionaries in the Church.*
ADJ QUALIT ⇑ conservative; ▸ N COUNT ⇑ conservative

reactivate /ri'æktɪveɪt/, **reactivates, reactivating, reactivated.** If people **reactivate** a system or organization, they make it work again after it has not been working for a while. EG *The western allies were continuing their efforts to reactivate the Office of Strategic Services.* ◇ **reactivation** /ri'æktiveɪʃə⁰n/.
V + O ⇑ revive; ◇ N UNCOUNT

reactive /ri'æktɪv/. Something that is **reactive** is able to react chemically with a lot of different substances. EG *...these sensitive and highly reactive compounds.* ◇ **reactiveness.**
ADJ QUALIT ⇑ unstable; ◇ N UNCOUNT

reactor /ri'æktə/, **reactors.** A **reactor** is **1** the same as a nuclear reactor. EG *They are making the reactors as safe as they possibly can.* **2** a container, especially one that is used in industry, in which a chemical reaction takes place. EG *We have to know about rates of heat transfer in chemical reactors of one sort or another.*
N COUNT; N COUNT

read, reads, reading. The form **read** is used in the present tense and is also the past tense, and the past participle of the verb. In the present tense it is pronounced /ri:d/, and the past tense and past participle are pronounced /red/. **1** When you **read** written or printed words or symbols, **1.1** you look at them and understand them. EG *Have you read that article I gave you?... I remember reading about it in the paper... I have never been able to read music... I read through the whole paper and couldn't find it.* ▸ used as a noun. EG *There's nothing like a good read.* **1.2** you say them aloud. EG *Children everywhere love to have stories read to them... She loved to hear her own voice and she read, 'The day I wrote a name upon the Strand.'*
V OR V + O; ▸ N SING : *a* + N; V + O ⇑ speak

2 If you can **read**, you have the ability to look at and understand written words. EG *She taught all her children to read and write at an early age... My mother taught me how to read when I was four.*
V

3 If you **read** someone's **lips**, you understand what they are saying by looking at the movements of their lips. EG *Can he read your lips?*
PHR : VB INFLECTS

4 If you **read between the lines**, you are aware of something, for example another person's feelings, although it is not expressed openly. EG *Reading between the lines he knew there was something wrong.*
PHR : VB INFLECTS ⇑ interpret

5 If you **have a reading knowledge of** a language, you know it quite well but are not fluent in it.
PHR : VB INFLECTS

6 If a book or magazine is **a good read, an excellent read**, etc, it is very enjoyable to read. EG *That seems to me to be a very good read.*
PHR

7 If you refer to how well or badly a text **reads**, you are referring to how well it is written and how easy or pleasant it is to read.
V + A

8 If you **read** something in a particular way, you understand or interpret it in that way. EG *I think it could be read as the simple story of the narrator... This drawing could be read as an exemplar of classical expression... Conflicting parts of the ambivalent signal are both read as genuine and acted upon accordingly.*
V + O + A : USU PASS + A *(as)*

9 If you refer to what something **reads**, you are referring to what is written there. EG *The notice on the gate read 'Evacuee reception centre'... 'Durand', read the name plate screwed into the door frame.*
V + QUOTE ⇑ state

10 If you **read** someone or if you **read** their mood, you understand how they feel or why they behave in a particular way. EG *I've never been able to read him... He read other people's moods fast.*
V + O = work out

11 If you **read** someone, **11.1** you understand what they are saying. EG *Do you read me, Mrs Jordache?... 'I read you,' she said softly.* **11.2** you can hear them; used when you are talking to someone on a radio transmitter to say that the channel is clear. EG *This is mission control. We read you loud and clear.*
V + O; V + O

12 When you **read** a meter, gauge, or other measuring device, you look at it and record the figure on it. EG *We'd better read the gas meter.*
V + O

13 If a measuring device **reads** a particular amount, it shows that amount. EG *The thermometers are reading 108 degrees in the shade... Modern electricity meters read like the mileage recorder on the car dashboard.*
V + O, OR V + A

14 If you **read** a subject, you study it at university. EG *He went up to Oxford to read history... Tony is reading French at Warwick University.*
V + O

15 See also **reading**.

read into. If you **read** a meaning or quality **into** something, you find it there although it may not actually be there. EG *Some people read sex into the most innocent story.*
PHRASAL VB : O + PREP

read out. If you **read** a piece of writing **out**, you say it aloud as you read it. EG *Could you just read out this next paragraph?*
PHRASAL VB : O + ADV

read up. If you **read up** a subject or if you **read up**
PHRASAL VB :

on a subject, you read a lot about it so that you become informed on it. EG *I'll have to read up on this particular case... I left the entire topic till the last week and read up three centuries of art in one weekend.* ORDER V+ADV+O, OR V+ADV+PREP = bone up

readable /ri̲ːdəbəᵊl/. A book, article, etc that is **readable** is 1 interesting and worth reading. EG *It's a very readable book.* ADJ QUALIT 2 written or printed in a way that is clear or tidy enough to be read easily. ADJ CLASSIF = legible

reader /ri̲ːdə/, **readers**. A **reader** is 1 a person who reads. EG *I'm not much of a reader... All of them were keen readers of detective stories.* N COUNT 2 a person who reads a particular publication. EG *The paper is gathering one thousand new readers a week... The magazine was designed to shock the reader... As the reader may well imagine, by now I was exhausted.* N COUNT 3 a person who reads a written or printed text aloud, for example for a radio programme. EG *The programme was written and produced by John Powell, and the reader was Tom Jaffrey.* N COUNT 4 a person who reads books for a publisher in order to give an opinion on whether they should be published or not. N COUNT 5 a book of simplified literature, selected passages, and exercises used for teaching at school. EG *We've just published a new reader in French.* N COUNT 6 a machine that makes it possible to read what is on a microfilm by showing an enlarged image of it on a screen. EG *Then that's set up on a microfilm reader for them.* N COUNT ⇑ projector = microfiche 7 a machine that has a special lens that is capable of reading a text, for example in order to store it on a computer. EG *...a photo-electric reader capable of scanning characters.* N COUNT 8 a senior lecturer at a British university just below the rank of a professor. EG *He's a reader in mathematics.* N COUNT

readership /ri̲ːdəʃɪp/, **readerships**. 1 The **readership** of a book, newspaper, or magazine is all the people who read it. EG *...a readership of about ten million people.* N SING WITH DET +SUPP ⇑ audience

2 A **readership** is the post of a reader at a British university. EG *They offered me a readership at the University of London.* N COUNT : USU SING

readily /re̲dɪliˈ/. 1 If you do something **readily**, you do it in a way that shows that you are very willing to do it. EG *He readily accepted an invitation to dinner... Adorno had readily agreed to do the job.* ADV WITH VB ⇑ willingly

2 If something is **readily** noticeable or possible, it is very easy to notice or to do. EG *Personal computers are readily available these days... Pollock's muddle and confusion are readily apparent... He couldn't readily put his finger on any reason.* ADV ⇑ easily

readiness /re̲dɪnɪˈs/ is 1 the state of being prepared for something. EG *Long lines of vehicles stood loaded in readiness for the move... He faces it with calm readiness and resolute determination.* N UNCOUNT = preparation 2 willingness or eagerness to do something. EG *I restated our readiness to resume negotiations.* N UNCOUNT ⇑ desire

reading /ri̲ːdɪŋ/, **readings**. 1 **Reading** is the activity of looking at written or printed symbols and understanding them. EG *I don't do a lot of reading... Tell me what impressions you've got from the reading I asked you to do.* N UNCOUNT

2 A **reading** is 2.1 a text that is read aloud to an audience. EG *We all said 'Amen!' when the readings were done.* N COUNT ⇑ recital 2.2 a reading aloud of a play by actors when they are beginning to rehearse a new play. EG *The first reading of the play went pretty badly.* N COUNT ⇑ rehearsal 2.3 a social event where something, especially poetry, is read aloud, often by the author. EG *...activities such as plays, poetry readings, and specialist lectures.* N COUNT ⇑ recital 2.4 the figure or measurement shown by a meter, gauge, or other measuring device. EG *The failure was caused by a gauge which stuck, giving a wrong reading.* N COUNT 2.5 one of the three stages of presentation and discussion of a new bill in parliament before it can be passed as law. EG *The second reading of the new bill will be on Dec. 15.* N COUNT : USU ORDINAL+N

3 Your **reading** of a word, text, or situation is the way in which you understand or interpret it. EG *It seemed clear enough to him, from his reading of the matter.* N COUNT+SUPP ⇑ interpretation

4 If you say that something is good **reading**, difficult **reading**, boring **reading**, etc, you mean that it is good, difficult, boring, etc to read. EG *Everyone should have these books. They make excellent reading.* N UNCOUNT : ADJ +N

reading lamp, reading lamps; also spelled with a hyphen. A **reading lamp** is a small lamp that you keep on a desk or table. You can move its lampshade in order to direct the light to where you need it for reading. N COUNT

reading room, reading rooms; also spelled with a hyphen. A **reading room** is a quiet room in a library or museum where you can read and study. EG *He went down to the reading room of the British Museum.* N COUNT

readjust /riːədʒʌ̲st/, **readjusts, readjusting, readjusted**. 1 If you **readjust** or **readjust** yourself, you adapt to a new situation that you are in. EG *It is difficult to readjust to changing reality.* V OR V+O (REFL) : IF+PREP THEN to

2 If you **readjust** something, you move or alter the controls on it again so that it functions in a different way. EG *...peering through a microscope, continually readjusting the focus.* V+O

readjustment /riːədʒʌ̲stməˀnt/, **readjustments**. 1 **Readjustment** is adapting to a new situation. EG *...a period of readjustment.* N UNCOUNT OR COUNT

2 A **readjustment** to something is another movement or alteration to its controls so that it functions in a different way. N COUNT/UNCOUNT

ready /re̲diˈ/, **readies, readying, readied**. 1 If someone or something is **ready**, they are properly prepared for doing something. EG *Go and get the boat ready... The waitress strolled over to the table. 'Are you ready to order?'... Are you ready now? I'll drive you back to your flat... We were getting ready for bed.* ADJ CLASSIF : PRED, IF+PREP/VB THEN for/to-INF ● If someone or something is **ready and waiting**, they are specially prepared for a particular job or purpose. EG *...an impressive array of food, ready and waiting for the party in the evening... The Allied air forces were ready and waiting.* ● PHR : USED AS C ● If you say **ready when you are**, you are telling someone who is doing something for you that you are waiting for them to start; an informal expression. EG *Right Miss Jordache we're ready when you are.* ● PHR : USED AS C

2 If you are **ready** for something or **ready** to do something, you are able to do it or deal with it because you have the suitable experience for it or you are old enough and sensible enough for it. EG *...countries that are getting independence and are obviously not ready for it... You're nowhere near ready for such a job... She's certainly not ready to take on that kind of responsibility.* ADJ CLASSIF : PRED, USU+for/to-INF = prepared

3 If you are **ready** to do something, you are willing to do it. EG *...couples who are ready to move house in order to get work... That is something which we should not be ready to tolerate in a civilised society... ...a discontented group, only too ready to look elsewhere for support.* ADJ CLASSIF : PRED+to-INF

4 If you are **ready** for something, you need it or want it. EG *We were all ready for sleep.* ADJ CLASSIF : PRED+for

5 If something is **ready**, it is able to be used, taken, or bought after a period of preparation. EG *Your glasses will be ready in a fortnight... Lunch is ready... Their crops would soon be ready for harvesting.* ADJ CLASSIF : PRED, IF+PREP THEN for

6 If something is **ready** to do something, it is about to do it or likely to do it. EG *...an over-ripe plum, ready to fall... It was the dry season and everything was ready to catch fire.* ADJ CLASSIF : PRED+to-INF

7 If you have an answer or piece of information **ready**, you have prepared it in your mind so that you know what you are going to say. EG *She wanted to have her excuses ready if her father asked any questions.* ADJ CLASSIF : PRED

8 **Ready** is used to refer to things that are able to appear or be used very quickly and easily. EG *The tourists provided a ready market for Kashmir's specialities... ...the ready availability of equipment... I have no ready explanation for this fact... He had a ready, engaging smile.* ADJ CLASSIF : ATTRIB

9 **Ready** money is in the form of notes and coins rather than cheques, and so can be used immediately. EG *...£3,000 in ready cash.* ADJ CLASSIF : ATTRIB ▸ used as a plural noun to refer to such money; used in informal, mainly spoken English. EG *I need the readies by tomorrow.* ▸ N PLURAL

10 When you **ready** something, you prepare it for a particular purpose. EG *The satellite would be readied with all possible haste and sent up to relay messages.* V+O : IF+PREP THEN for

11 When you **ready** yourself, you prepare yourself for something; a formal use. EG *Standard Oil and Union Carbide are readying themselves for a monumental struggle.* V+O (REFL) : USU+to-INF/for

12 See also **readily, readiness**.

ready-made. 1 **Ready-made** things that you buy have already been made and so are able to be used ADJ CLASSIF : ATTRIB, OR ADV immediately. EG *...the black ready-made bow holding her hair... ...ready-made food... You can buy your greenhouse ready-made.* WITH VB ⇑ convenient

2 Something that is **ready-made** is extremely convenient or useful for a particular purpose. EG *...a ready-made experiment in sociology... ...a ready-made basis for negotiations.* ADJ CLASSIF

reaffirm /riːəfɜːm/, **reaffirms, reaffirming, reaffirmed.** If you **reaffirm** something, you state it again. EG *The ministers reaffirmed their intention not to surrender... She reaffirmed that she would give evidence against him.* V+O/REPORT-CL

real /rɪəl/. 1 Something that is **real** 1.1 actually exists and is not imagined, invented, or theoretical. EG *You must know the difference between what's real and make-believe... ...real or imagined feelings of inferiority... Robert squealed in mock terror, then in real pain.* ADJ CLASSIF: USU ATTRIB ⇑ true = genuine 1.2 is of the natural, proper, or traditional kind, and not artificial or imitation. EG *The steering wheel is padded with real leather... Rudolph couldn't tell whether the jewellery was real or not... ...fancy chocolates, with real liqueurs inside.* ADJ CLASSIF ⇑ true = genuine

2 **Real** is used to describe something that 2.1 has all the characteristics or qualities that such a thing typically has. EG *...the only real accident that I've ever had in fog and ice... I guess it's the first real letter I've ever received from you... I used to tell him he wasn't a real Christian.* ADJ CLASSIF: ATTRIB = proper 2.2 is the truest, most central, and most typical part of the thing. EG *South Africa never seems quite like the real Africa to me... I knew he had seen something of my real self before he took me on.* ADJ CLASSIF: ATTRIB = essential, genuine, true

3 You also use **real** to emphasize the existence of something, usually a physical object, that seems unusual, unexpected, or surprising in some way. EG *There was a great park all about it, and real hills which you could run up... Maria's lace-ups had got holes in the toes, real holes.* ADJ CLASSIF: ATTRIB = proper

4 If you say that something is **the real thing**, you mean that it is the proper or actual thing or event, and not an imitation or practice. EG *It is a poor copy of the real thing... 'You're being recorded now.'–'Is this the real thing?'* PHR ⇑ genuine

5 If you describe a problem, situation, or feeling as **real**, you mean that it definitely exists and is serious, important, or considerable. EG *I think it's a real problem... ...a mother who is suffering from real hardship... The growth and scale of Morgan's empire is a real achievement... The threat of attack was a very real one.* ADJ QUALIT ⇑ actual

6 If something happens **for real**, it happens or is done seriously, and is not pretended or imagined. EG *It was done. I was on my own. For real.* PHR: USED AS AN A ⇑ really = in earnest

7 The **real** value or cost of something is the final and genuine one, which you arrive at after you have subtracted or included all other amounts and taken into consideration all other factors such as inflation. EG *Multiply it by fifty-two to get the rough, real annual cost... The value of the dollar in real terms has fallen... ...real disposable income per head.* ADJ CLASSIF: ATTRIB ⇑ actual = net, overall

8 You also use **real** 8.1 with negatives to say that something cannot be correctly described as existing or being fully present, although it may be there to a limited extent. EG *There's no real cause for concern... Everyone knew that Humphrey had no real chance of winning the nomination... I doubt whether Lilian had any real understanding of Shakespeare.* ADJ CLASSIF: ATTRIB, WITH BROAD NEG = proper, true 8.2 in front of a noun to indicate that you are referring to the true or original thing of its kind, in contrast to one that people may wrongly believe to be true. EG *That is the real reason for the muddle... If only people would realise where their real interests lie... My real home is in Tshabo.* ADJ CLASSIF: ATTRIB 8.3 to emphasize your description of someone or something. EG *It's a real shame... Then we had a real stroke of good luck.* ADJ CLASSIF: ATTRIB

9 **Real** is used in American English meaning 'very'. EG *I was getting some real good stories here... You and I must have lunch together real soon.* ADV+ADJ/ADV = really

10 See also **really**.

real estate; spelled with a hyphen when used before another noun. 1 **Real estate** is property in the form of lands and buildings, rather than personal possessions. EG *Eventually he founded a firm and acquired a bit of real estate... They can go and invest in urban real estate, and become landlords again.* N UNCOUNT

2 **Real-estate** businesses or agents sell houses, buildings, and land; used in American English. EG *We called at several real estate offices until we agreed on a place... He was in the real-estate business.* N UNCOUNT: USU BEFORE N

realignment /riˈəlaɪnməˀnt/. A **realignment** of the way something is organized is a new order or arrangement of it; a formal word. EG *We believe that the need for a realignment of British politics must now be faced.* N UNCOUNT: USU DET+N+*of* = restructuring

realise /rɪəlaɪz/. See **realize.**

realism /rɪəlɪzəˀm/ is 1 awareness of the truth and facts about a situation, and readiness to accept it or deal with it in a practical way. EG *...the refreshing and welcome spirit of realism and common sense... She did as much as anything to foster the new note of realism.* N UNCOUNT = pragmatism, common sense 2 the quality of being very like the person, thing, or situation that is represented in a painting, film, play, book, etc. EG *...the vast and awesome realism of the Aztec sculptures... Extraordinary degrees of realism are reached in the film.* N UNCOUNT ⇑ likeness = verisimilitude 3 a style of art and literature that tries to represent what is familiar or typical in real life, rather than an idealized or romantic view of it. N UNCOUNT = naturalism

realist /rɪəlɪst/, **realists.** 1 A **realist** is someone who is aware of the truth and facts about a situation, and who is prepared to accept it or to deal with it in a practical way. EG *They are doing valuable work which idealists as well as realists would want to see done.* N COUNT = pragmatist 2 a painter, writer, etc who believes in and practises the theory of realism in art and literature. N COUNT

realistic /rɪəlɪstɪk/. 1 A person or attitude that is **realistic** shows awareness of the truth and facts about a situation, and is prepared to accept it or to deal with it in a practical way. EG *They were much more realistic about its long term commercial prospects... ...a realistic attempt to solve problems... ...taking a realistic view of human nature.* ADJ QUALIT ⇑ sensible ◇ **realistically.** EG *This can stop you viewing your situation realistically.* ◇ ADV WITH VB

2 A **realistic** painting, story, film, etc, is a very accurate and lifelike representation of the person, object, or situation that is being represented. EG *He and his actors tried to create a realistic portrayal of the Africans.* ADJ QUALIT ◇ **realistically.** EG *...a film that doesn't attempt to be realistically convincing.* ◇ ADV

reality /riˈælɪtiˈ/, **realities.** 1 **Reality** is the real existence and real nature of things, rather than what is imagined or invented. EG *...a sense of reality... He is out of touch with reality... She had never seemed able to face reality.* N UNCOUNT = actuality

2 The **reality** of a situation is the truth about it, especially when this is unpleasant or unwelcome. EG *...the harsh reality of daily life... ...an awareness of the realities of politics and diplomacy... ...the wider cultural and social realities.* N COUNT+SUPP ⇑ facts

3 If you talk about a **reality**, you are referring to the fact that something is true, exists, or is really happening. EG *The reality was that air transport had now become one of the major strategic manifestations of air power... The Popular Front was a reality in South Wales long before it was official in Europe... How many of her fine intentions have become reality?... Day-dreams had become realities.* N COUNT/UNCOUNT ⇑ truth

4 **In reality.** 4.1 You can use **in reality** to introduce a statement that contradicts, corrects, or contrasts with what has just been said. EG *They imagined that they made the rules but, in reality, they were mere puppets... People who seem at first 'stand-offish' in reality are often simply nervous.* PHR: USED AS ADV SEN = actually, in fact 4.2 **In reality** is also used to say that something actually exists, happens, or is done in real life, rather than in stories, plans, ideas, etc. EG *The sound was far more menacing in reality than in the movies.* PHR: USED AS A = in actuality

realizable /rɪəlaɪzəbəˀl/. 1 Ideas, aims, projects, etc that are **realizable** can be achieved or carried out, for example because the necessary knowledge, equipment, or money that is available. EG *Most of it is technically realizable at this moment.* ADJ CLASSIF ⇑ possible = feasible, attainable

2 Goods, property, investments, etc that are **realizable** can be sold easily, for example without any legal problems or official waiting period; a technical term in finance. EG *...realizable assets.* ADJ CLASSIF ⇑ saleable = convertible

realize /rɪəlaɪz/, **realizes, realizing, realized**; also spelled **realise.** 1 If you **realize** a particular fact, you understand or become aware of it, either by thinking about it and connecting together the information you have, or as a result of discovering new information. EG *It was a shock to realize afterwards that I had danced almost the whole evening with her* V+O/REPORT *husband... I didn't realise that you two lived so close... Do you realize you're the first girl I've been out with?... He is a much more remarkable man than many people realized... I came to realise in the end why this must be done... She realized the significance of what he was trying to do.* ◊ **realization** /rɪəlaɪzeɪʃ°n/. EG *This realization was shattering for all of us... ...a growing realization on the part of governments that national defence budgets were excessive.* ◊ N SING WITH DET+REPORT-CL = discovery, recognition

2 If you **realize** a design or idea, you put it into a physical form, for example by painting a picture, building a machine, etc; a formal use. EG *No design is too sophisticated for him to realize in iron, brass, or copper... ...the attempt to realize a world view through their painting... ...little houses which prevent a developer from realising his grand design for a site.* V+O ⇑ convert = reproduce, translate

3 If you **realize** a hope, desire, ambition, etc, you succeed in making it happen in reality; a formal use. EG *I don't suppose either of us will realise his dream... Our national aspirations could be realised.* ◊ **realized**. EG *The delight of a realised ambition overcame him.* ◊ **realization**. EG *...the realization of a lifelong dream... ...one practical step towards the realisation of this goal.* ● If you say that your **worst fears were realized**, you mean that something has happened which was the worst possible thing that you could imagine happening in that situation. EG *The teams went back onto the ice, where my worst fears were quickly realized; Cornell scored.* V+O ⇑ achieve = fulfil ◊ ADJ CLASSIF ◊ N SING WITH DET : USU+of ● PHR : VB INFLECTS

4 If you **realize** yourself or your potential, you achieve satisfaction by doing the best you can, according to your ability; a formal use. EG *The task is to realize our selves by changing the environment... He isn't really realising his potential... ...a loose framework in which men and women can realise their possibilities.* V+O (NG/REFL) ⇑ succeed = fulfil

5 To **realize** an amount of money or a profit means to obtain it by selling something; a technical term in finance. EG *Liquidation would have realized more than £60 a share for stockholders... ...Young Socialist summer fairs that have realized four figure sums for the organisation.* ◊ **realization**. EG *...the money obtained from the realisation of these assets.* V+O = fetch ◊ N UNCOUNT+SUPP

really /rɪəli¹/. 1 You can use **really** 1.1 to emphasize a statement that you are making or an opinion that you are giving; used mainly in spoken English. EG *It is really very difficult indeed... It really is beautiful, isn't it?... I really ought to go back inside... I don't mind in the least, I really don't... That was very good, I really enjoyed that... I really think I've had enough for the day.* 1.2 to give emphasis to an adjective or adverb; used especially in spoken English. EG *It was really good, wasn't it Andy?... These fires produce really obnoxious fumes... We're doing really well actually.* 1.3 to emphasize the exact truth or facts about a situation. EG *This year the grant was £380 with fees so that was really £440... He's not really going for a bath; he's going to sit in the garden... I want to know what really happened... What I'm really saying is, I'm delighted.* 1.4 in questions or negative statements when you want to make someone agree with you by answering 'no'; used mainly in spoken English. EG *Do you really think they bother to listen in to us?... But is there really anything new to say about him?... You don't really expect me to believe that.* 1.5 to emphasize that something happens to a much greater extent and more seriously than before. EG *It is at the postgraduate level that the pressure really begins.* 1.6 in opinions or statements in order to make them less definite and more hesitant. EG *Some of these programmes are very interesting, really... There was only me and her for lunch, so I ate quite a lot really.* 1.7 to slightly reduce the force of a negative in a statement or opinion. EG *He didn't really want to go to America by this time... It doesn't really matter... No, I'm not really in favour of that... 'Any more problems?'-'Not really, no.'... I don't know which is the better policy, really... I don't really know.* ADV SEN = honestly, truly; ADV+ADJ/ADV ⇑ very; ADV WITH VB = actually, truly; ADV WITH VB : USU WITH BROAD NEG = actually, honestly; ADV WITH VB = in earnest; ADV SEN = I suppose; ADV AFTER BROAD NEG

2 You can say **really** 2.1 when you are involved in a conversation and are listening with interest. EG *'It was quite close to the airport.'-'Really?'-'Across country about 20 minutes.'... 'We got out of the train and we went to the lounge and had breakfast...'-'Oh really?'-'...which was very nice.'* 2.2 to express surprise or disbelief at what someone has said, or to check that you have understood them properly. EG *'Nobody was allowed inside the Plaza unless he'd been injected by Doc Murray.'-'Really?'... 'Inflation's dropped faster under a Tory Government than it did under a Labour Government.'-'Has it really?'* CONVENTION = ah, oh; CONVENTION

3 You say **'really!'**, **'well really!'**, etc, when you are annoyed with someone. EG *'Really,' said Mrs Oliver to herself with some annoyance... Oh really! It's too bad of him.* EXCLAM = honestly

realm /rɛlm/, **realms**; a fairly formal word. A **realm** is 1 a particular area of interest, activity, or thought. EG *Public opinion plays a vital and healthy role in the political realm... What we seek in any realm of human thought is not absolute certainty... Clearly, we are in the realm of fertile imagination rather than historical fact.* 2 a country that has a king or queen as its head of state. EG *...the established church of the realm, the Church of England... He wrote to the Queen suggesting that she appoint him a peer of the realm.* 3 the area over which someone has control or authority. EG *Very soon a computer will not remain exclusively in the realm of scientists.* N COUNT+SUPP : SING=PL ⇑ field; N COUNT = kingdom, monarchy; N COUNT+SUPP : USU SING = kingdom

real time; spelled with a hyphen when used before another noun. **Real time** is a type of computer programming or data processing in which the amount of time that passes between each operation or stage is important and relevant; a technical term. EG *...real-time processing.* N UNCOUNT

realtor /rɪəltə⁸/, **realtors**. A **realtor** is an estate agent; used in American English. N COUNT

real world; spelled with a hyphen when used before another noun. **Real world**. If you talk about the **real world**, you are referring to the world and life in general, usually in contrast to a particular person's own life, experience, or ideas when this seems untypical or unrealistic in some way. EG *How do you manage to keep your students in touch with the real world?... We get worried about what is going on in the real world... ...real-world knowledge.* N SING : the+N ⇑ reality

ream /riːm/, **reams**. If you say that there are **reams** of something, you mean that there is a large amount of it; an informal use. EG *She's written reams of poetry.* N PART : USU PLURAL

reap /riːp/, **reaps, reaping, reaped**. 1 If someone **reaps** a crop such as corn, they cut it down and gather it. EG *There were crops to be sown and reaped... We reaped by hand.* V OR V+O : USU V+O ⇑ harvest

2 If you **reap** something that you want, you obtain it, often after you have worked hard or made careful plans to get it. EG *The time will come when we are reaping the full benefits of North Sea oil.* V+O ⇑ gain

reaper /riːpə/, **reapers**. A **reaper** is 1 a machine that is used to cut and gather crops. EG *A rabbit got caught in the blades of the reaper.* 2 a person who cuts and gathers crops by hand. N COUNT; N COUNT

reappear /riːəpɪə/, **reappears, reappearing, reappeared**. If someone or something **reappears**, they return again after they have been away or out of sight for some time. EG *The waiter reappeared at Dixon's side with a loaded tray... From time to time 'Gypsy' clothes reappear as a fashion.* V : USU+A ⇑ appear

reappearance /riːəpɪərəns/, **reappearances**. A **reappearance** is the appearance again of someone or something that has previously disappeared or been away. EG *I think we can expect his reappearance in public life before long.* N COUNT

reappraisal /riːəpreɪzə°l/, **reappraisals**; a formal word. The **reappraisal** of something such as an idea is the careful consideration of it, which helps you to decide whether to change what you think about it. EG *The Minister wants a reappraisal of the 1921 Anglo-Irish Treaty... All your ideas need a thorough reappraisal.* N COUNT/UNCOUNT = re-examination, review

reappraise /riːəpreɪz/, **reappraises, reappraising, reappraised**; a formal word. If you **reappraise** something such as an idea, you carefully consider it in order to decide whether to change what you think about it. EG *They have obliged politicians of all parties to reappraise the role of small businesses.* V+O = re-examine, review

rear /rɪə/, **rears, rearing, reared**. 1 The **rear** of something such as a building or vehicle is the part that is at the back of it. EG *He walked toward the rear of the house... ...seats facing the rear.* ▸ used as an adjective. EG *There was a rear entrance into the post office... I got out and examined the right rear wheel.* N SING : the+N, IF+PREP THEN of; ▸ ADJ CLASSIF : ATTRIB

2 The **rear** of a line of things or people is the position that is at the back of the line. EG *The motorcycles dropped back to a position at the rear of the convoy... Ralph walked in the rear.* • If someone **brings up the rear** or **takes up the rear**, they occupy a place at the back of a line of people or things. EG *Jack brought up the rear.* — N SING : the+N, IF+PREP THEN of; • PHR : VB INFLECTS

3 Someone's **rear** is the part of their body that they sit on; an informal use. EG *She slapped him on the rear.* — N COUNT ⇑ buttocks = behind

4 If you **rear** children, you bring them up until they are old enough to look after themselves. EG *Geraldo has adopted and reared four children. ...a child reared on self-indulgence.* — V+O = raise

5 If a person or animal **rears** young animals, they keep and look after them until they are old enough to be used for food or work, or until they can look after themselves. EG *I used to rear chickens... ...an ideal place for hatching and rearing young turtles.* — V+O ⇑ raise

6 If an animal **rears** or **rears** its legs, it moves the front part of its body upwards, so that its front legs are high in the air and it is standing on its back legs. EG *It's difficult to control a rearing horse.* — V OR V+O ⇑ stand

7 If you say that something such as a building or mountain **rears** over you, you mean that it is very tall and close to you. EG *A tree out in the street reared over the top of the wall.* — V+A (over) ⇑ rise = tower

8 If something unpleasant **rears its ugly head**, it starts to become apparent. EG *Dissension might so easily have reared its ugly head and wrecked our future plans.* — PHR : VB AND N INFLECT

rear up. If a person or animal **rears up**, they suddenly move the front part of their body upwards. EG *He reared up on his back legs in total fear.* — PHRASAL VB : V+ADV

rearguard /rɪəgɑːd/. 1 The **rearguard** is the group of soldiers who protect the back part of an army in a battle, especially when the army is retreating. — N SING WITH DET ≠ vanguard

2 If someone is **fighting a rearguard action**, they are making a determined effort to prevent something happening which they disapprove of, although it is probably too late for them to succeed. EG *Calderwood fought a stubborn rearguard action against the transformation of his section.* — PHR : VB INFLECTS ⇑ resist

rearm /riːɑːm/, **rearms, rearming, rearmed**. When a country **rearms**, it starts to build up a stock of military weapons again. EG *There was every reason to rearm.* — V-ERG, OR V+A (against) ⇑ arm

rearmament /riːɑːməməˀnt/ is the process of building up a new stock of military weapons. — N UNCOUNT ⇑ armament

rearmost /rɪəməʊst/. The **rearmost** thing in a line is the one that is nearest to the back of the line. EG *They jumped on to the rearmost carriages.* — ADJ CLASSIF : ATTRIB = last

rearrange /riːəreɪndʒ/, **rearranges, rearranging, rearranged**. 1 If you **rearrange** something, you organize it in a different way so that it now has a new order or arrangement. EG *She rearranged the furniture.* — V+O ⇑ change

2 If you **rearrange** an appointment that you have already made, you decide on a new time or date for it. EG *Can we rearrange the dinner for next week?* — V+O ⇑ change

rearrangement /riːəreɪndʒməˀnt/, **rearrangements**. A **rearrangement** is 1 a change in the way that things are ordered or arranged. EG *...the rearrangement of the examination system.* 2 a change of the time or date when something is due to happen. EG *...loudspeaker announcements advising passengers of delays and rearrangements.* — N COUNT/UNCOUNT; N COUNT/UNCOUNT

rear-view mirror, rear-view mirrors. A **rear-view mirror** is a mirror inside a car which enables you to see the traffic behind you while you are driving. — N COUNT

reason /riːzəˀn/, **reasons, reasoning, reasoned**. 1 The **reason** for something is a particular fact or situation which explains why it happens, or which causes it to happen. The fact or situation is usually described or specified either before or after the word 'reason'. EG *I asked the reason for the decision... One of the reasons for coming to England is to make money... Public pressure is towards more street lighting rather than less: the reason is, of course, that people feel safer in well-lit streets... There are several reasons why we can't do that... For reasons of space I have missed out some of the details.... There is reason to disbelieve him.* — N COUNT : USU+for/REPORT-CL/to-INF, OR N UNCOUNT+to-INF = ground

2 **Reason** is 2.1 the good and sensible reasons that make it understandable why a person has a particular belief or feeling. EG *If I have been a negative critic, I have had good reason for being so... I'm getting annoyed, and with reason.* • If you say **all the more reason** to do something, you are emphasizing that a statement that has just been made is a strong recommendation for a course of action which you believe is right. EG *'But I'm exhausted!'–'All the more reason to get back home as soon as possible.'* — N UNCOUNT = justification, cause; • PHR+for/to-INF

2.2 the ability that people have to think carefully about facts in order to make a judgement or to form an argument. EG *He had to rely less on reason than on the rousing of emotion... ...his lack of faith in reason.* — N UNCOUNT = rationality

2.3 a sensible and fair attitude towards making decisions or coming to conclusions. EG *I've tried appealing to reason but she won't agree.* — N UNCOUNT = common sense

3 **Reason** is also used in the following expressions relating to causes and judgements. 3.1 If you say that something happened or was done **for some reason**, you mean that you know that it happened, but you do not know why it happened. EG *For some reason we talked about death.* — PHR : USED AS AN A

3.2 When you do not know why someone has done something which you do not agree with, or which you think is not a good thing to do, you can say that he or she did it **for reasons best known to himself** or **herself**. EG *For reasons best known to herself she's decided to sell the car.* — PHR : USED AS AN A

3.3 If something happens **by reason of** something else, it happens because of that other thing; a fairly formal expression. EG *I enjoyed a measure of protection by reason of my age.* — PREP

3.4 If you **listen to reason**, you allow yourself to be influenced by sensible arguments from other people. — PHR : VB INFLECTS

3.5 If you **see reason**, you eventually act sensibly after considering advice from other people or thinking about what to do. EG *At last he saw reason and agreed to give me my money back.* — PHR : VB INFLECTS = see sense

3.6 If you think that something is **within reason**, you think it is fair and not too extreme. EG *There is the advantage that each person could, within reason, choose which one should be built.* — PHR : USED AS AN A

4 If you **reason**, 4.1 you think carefully about facts in order to make a judgement or to form an argument. EG *Human beings are able to reason.* ◊ **reasoned**. EG *She presented her case with reasoned argument.* — V; ◊ ADJ CLASSIF

4.2 you come to a particular conclusion by thinking carefully about all the facts. EG *Copernicus reasoned that the earth revolved around the sun... They would probably not report the matter to the police, he reasoned.* • See also **reasoning**. — V+REPORT-CL/QUOTE ⇑ argue

reason out. If you **reason** something **out**, you solve a problem or answer a question by considering all the relevant aspects of it. EG *Let's try and reason this out.* — PHRASAL VB : V+O+ADV ⇑ work out

reason with. If you **reason with** someone, you try to persuade them to do something or agree to something by using sensible arguments. EG *We all know how difficult it is to reason with a prejudiced person.* — PHRASAL VB : V+PREP, HAS PASS

reasonable /riːzəˀnəbəˀl/. 1 People who are **reasonable** behave in a fair and sensible way. EG *Our mother was always very reasonable... 'I can't do that, Morris. Be reasonable.'* ◊ **reasonableness**. EG *I thought I argued with great reasonableness.* — ADJ QUALIT ⇑ moderate; ◊ N UNCOUNT

2 Something such as a decision or judgement that is **reasonable** is fair and understandable because there are good reasons to suppose it is right. EG *There was no reasonable explanation for her decision... It was quite reasonable to suppose that he wanted the money too.* — ADJ QUALIT

3 Something that is **reasonable** is quite good, but not very good. EG *...a reasonable amount of luck... In Africa 36 per cent of the urban population has reasonable access to a safe water supply.* — ADJ QUALIT = fair, moderate

4 **Reasonable** prices are considered to be very fair and not too high. EG *A good range of drinkable wines at reasonable prices... The tickets will cost a very reasonable £30.* — ADJ QUALIT ⇑ acceptable

reasonably /riːzəˀnəbliˡ/. 1 **Reasonably** means to quite a good or great degree. EG *I'm reasonably broad across the shoulders... ...very good at reading and reasonably good at writing.* — ADV+ADJ/ADV = fairly

2 If someone behaves **reasonably**, they behave sensibly and fairly. EG *'Well, you can't do that now,' I said reasonably.* — ADV WITH VB

reasoning /riːzəˀnɪŋ/is 1 the process of coming to a particular conclusion by thinking carefully about all the facts. EG *The facts don't matter, nor does the quality of his reasoning... What is the reasoning behind that decision?... ...the reasoning powers of the* — N UNCOUNT

mind. 2 the actual arguments, statements, and conclusions that you produce by this process. EG *I won't bother you with pages of tedious chemical reasoning.*
N UNCOUNT

reassemble /riːəsembəˀl/, **reassembles, reassembling, reassembled.** 1 To **reassemble** something such as a machine means to put it back together after it has been taken apart. EG *It was reassembled in the physics labs at Harvard.*
V+O ⇑ assemble = reconstruct

2 When people or animals **reassemble** or when you **reassemble** them, they gather together again in a group. EG *Parliament reassembled to debate the issue of sanctions... The farmer used dogs to reassemble his goats, which had begun to wander.*
V-ERG ⇑ assemble = regroup

reassembly /riːəsembliˡ/is 1 the gathering together again of a group of people. EG *...the reassembly of Parliament in the New Year.* 2 the putting together of something such as a machine after it has been taken apart. EG *...instructions for reassembly of the rifle.*
N UNCOUNT ⇑ assembly; N UNCOUNT ⇑ assembly = reconstruction

reassert /riːəsɜːt/, **reasserts, reasserting, reasserted.** 1 If you **reassert** something such as authority or if you **reassert** yourself, you make it clear that you are once again in a position of power or in control of something. EG *He had made efforts to reassert his authority over them... We have a tough and dominant boss who will reassert himself as soon as he gets back.*
V+O (NG/REFL)

2 If something such as an idea, principle, or habit **reasserts** itself, it once again becomes significant in a particular situation. EG *The urge to survive reasserted itself.*
V+O (REFL)

reassess /riːəses/, **reassesses, reassessing, reassessed.** If you **reassess** a situation, you think about it again and decide whether you want to change your ideas or opinion about it. EG *Events speed past us, compelling us to reassess our assumptions... Edward Greenfield eagerly seized the chance to reassess Karajan's view of Sibelius.*
V+O ⇑ rethink = review

reassessment /riːəsesməˀnt/, **reassessments.** **Reassessment** is the process of reassessing something. EG *The time has come for a dramatic reassessment... My description of it needed reassessment.*
N UNCOUNT/COUNT ⇑ rethinking = reviewing

reassurance /riːəʃʊərəns/, **reassurances.** 1 **Reassurance** involves helping someone to stop worrying, often by saying something kind or friendly to them. EG *They turned nervously towards each other in search of reassurance... I found comfort in his words, and reassurance that I had made the right decision.*
N UNCOUNT ⇑ comfort

2 A **reassurance** is something that you say or do in order to reassure a person. EG *...they will be anxious to receive reassurances from established members.*
N COUNT ⇑ comfort

reassure /riːəʃʊə/, **reassures, reassuring, reassured.** If you **reassure** someone, you help them to stop worrying, often by saying something kind or friendly to them. EG *I was trying to reassure her that things weren't as bad as she thought... They need to be reassured by parents and teachers that they are still wanted.* ◊ **reassuring.** EG *The woman smiled at him in an extremely reassuring manner.* ◊ **reassuringly.** EG *She looked at me reassuringly.*
V+O (NG/REFL), OR V+O (NG/REFL)+REPORT-CL/QUOTE ⇑ comfort = calm; ◊ ADJ QUALIT ⇑ comforting; ◊ ADV

rebate /riːbeɪt/, **rebates, rebating, rebated.** A **rebate** is an amount of money which is paid back to you because you have paid more tax, rent, etc than you needed to. EG *You should get a tax rebate... ...a rebate on the rates.*
N COUNT ⇑ repayment = refund

rebel, rebels, rebelling, rebelled. The word **rebel** is pronounced /rebəˀl/ when it is a noun, and /rɪˡbel/ when it is a verb.

1 A **rebel** is 1.1 someone who is actively involved in fighting against the army of the government of their own country because they want to bring about a new political system. EG *Sources said that rebels had made regular attacks on the railways... The travellers said that rebel groups controlled the centre of the city.* 1.2 someone who behaves in a way that is different from the way they are expected to behave, because they have rejected the values of their parents or their society. EG *Neill is only a rebel against society.*
N COUNT : USU PL OR BEFORE N ⇑ fighter = insurgent; N COUNT = nonconformist

2 If you **rebel,** 2.1 you act with other people against the rulers of your country, often using violent methods, in order to force a change in the system of government. EG *...the Duke of Monmouth, who rebelled against his uncle James II in 1685.* 2.2 you behave in a way that is not usual or expected because you have rejected the values of your parents, society, or culture. EG *...adolescents who rebel and demand freedom and independence... Tony never rebelled against his upbringing.*
V : IF+PREP THEN *against* ⇑ fight = revolt; V : IF+PREP THEN *against*

3 If your body or part of your body **rebels,** it is no longer able to tolerate the level of pain or discomfort that it is experiencing. EG *I hammered the door until my knuckles rebelled... Lynn's healthy, non-smoking lungs were rebelling before she reached the door.*
V = give out

rebellion /rɪˡbeljən/, **rebellions.** 1 A **rebellion** is a violent, organized action taken by a large group of people against the rulers of their country, usually in order to force a change in the system of government. EG *The rebellion spread until it enveloped the land... There had been rebellion against the British before.*
N COUNT/UNCOUNT = revolt

2 **Rebellion** is 2.1 behaviour or statements by a group within a particular organization who have begun to oppose the leaders of the organization. EG *He faces a growing rebellion from the left wing of his party.* 2.2 the rejection of the values of your parents, society, or culture, which causes you to behave in a way that is different from the way you are expected to behave. EG *Youth has always been the time for rebellion... They embodied the spirit of the times, of progress and rebellion against authority.*
N UNCOUNT/COUNT ⇑ opposition = revolt; N UNCOUNT/COUNT ⇑ behaviour = revolt

rebellious /rɪˡbeljəs/. Someone who is **rebellious** 1 behaves in a way that is considered to be unacceptable, and refuses to do what people want them to do. EG *...an obstinate, rebellious child with a violent temper.* ◊ **rebelliously.** EG *'Nonsense,' said my assistant rebelliously.* ◊ **rebelliousness.** EG *Those with easy-going parents may show no open rebelliousness at all.* 2 is involved in taking violent action against the rulers of their country, usually in order to force a change in the system of government. EG *The tribesmen were as rebellious as ever... ...a rebellious province.*
ADJ QUALIT = defiant; ◊ ADV WITH VB; ◊ N UNCOUNT = defiance; ADJ QUALIT = mutinous

rebirth /riːbɜːθ/is a change that leads to a new period of growth and improvement. EG *...a more suitable climate for a rebirth of English football... We look forward to our rebirth as a nation.*
N UNCOUNT = renaissance, revival

reborn /riːbɔːn/. If you say that someone or something is or has been **reborn,** you mean that they have now become active again after a period of inactivity. EG *Hatred of the system had been reborn in him.*
ADJ CLASSIF : USU PRED ⇑ born

rebound, rebounds, rebounding, rebounded. The word **rebound** is pronounced /rɪˡbaʊnd/ when it is a verb, and /riːbaʊnd/ when it is a noun.

1 If something **rebounds,** it bounces or springs back after hitting a solid surface such as the floor or a wall. EG *It rebounded from the edge of her plate and fell to the floor.*
V : IF+PREP THEN *from* ⇑ move = bounce

2 If you say that someone is **on the rebound,** you mean that they have just ended a close personal relationship with a person who has rejected them, and are already beginning a new relationship with someone else. EG *She married him on the rebound.*
PHR : USED AS AN A

3 If an action or situation **rebounds** on you, it has an unpleasant effect some time after it originally happened. EG *I suspected, rightly, that her intervention only rebounded upon Fanny*
V+A *(on/upon)* ⇑ harm

rebuff /rɪˡbʌf/, **rebuffs, rebuffing, rebuffed.** 1 If you **rebuff** someone or **rebuff** a suggestion that they make to you, you refuse to listen to them or take any notice of what they are trying to say to you, even though they are trying to be helpful. EG *His suggestion was very sharply rebuffed... Sam was rebuffed again and again.*
V+O : USU PASS ⇑ reject = spurn

2 A **rebuff** is a rejection of something such as a suggestion or advice that someone has offered to you in a friendly or helpful way. EG *She didn't understand that her rebuff had hurt him.*
N COUNT

rebuild /riːbɪld/, **rebuilds, rebuilding, rebuilt.** 1 To **rebuild** a town or a building means to build it again, or to make a great many repairs and changes to it, usually because it has been badly damaged. EG *The way they rebuilt the pier spoiled people's view.*
V OR V+O : USU V+O ⇑ reconstruct

2 To **rebuild** something such as an organization or business means to develop it again so that it becomes as good as it was before it was destroyed or damaged. EG *The Party had been destroyed and would need rebuilding... ...the company's effort to rebuild its business.*
V OR V+O : USU V+O ⇑ repair = reconstruct

rebuke /rɪˈbjuːk/, **rebukes, rebuking, rebuked.** 1 If you **rebuke** someone, you speak severely to them because they have said or done something that you do not approve of. EG *She often rebuked David for his authoritarian attitude to his clients.* ▸ used as a noun. EG *He had received a stern rebuke from his superiors... He dared not do it for fear of parental rebuke.*
V+O : IF+PREP THEN *for* = censure; ▸ N COUNT/UNCOUNT = reprimand

rebut /rɪˈbʌt/, **rebuts, rebutting, rebutted.** If you **rebut** a charge or criticism that is made against you, you say or write something which proves that it is not true; a formal word. EG *I am writing this letter to rebut the suggestion that I have failed in my duty.*
V+O = disprove, refute

rebuttal /rɪˈbʌtəˈl/, **rebuttals.** A **rebuttal** is a statement which proves that a charge or a criticism that has been made against you is not true; a formal word. EG *It was a complete rebuttal of the charges against him... The trade minister offered a lukewarm rebuttal.*
N COUNT = refutation

recalcitrance /rɪˈkælsɪtrəns/ is a stubborn unwillingness to obey orders or to co-operate; a formal word. EG *In the end their recalcitrance was too much for him.*
N UNCOUNT ⇑ disobedience = rebelliousness

recalcitrant /rɪˈkælsɪtrənt/. Someone or something that is **recalcitrant** is stubbornly unwilling to obey orders or to co-operate; a formal word. EG *...dealing with a recalcitrant boy in his classroom.*
ADJ QUALIT = disobedient

recall /rɪˈkɔːl/, **recalls, recalling, recalled.** 1 If you **recall** something, you remember it by making a deliberate attempt, often because you want to tell someone about it. EG *'I ran outside to look for my children,' recalled Miriam... Deirdre recalled seeing a poster on his wall... As far as I could recall, everything was as I had left it.*
V+O/-ING, V+REPORT-CL/QUOTE = recollect

2 You can say 'as I **recall**' or 'you might **recall**', in order to remind someone about something which you both already know and which is relevant to what you are talking about. EG *Now as I recall, last lesson we were looking at the way plants scatter their seeds... They greeted their commander-in-chief who, as you may recall, is the President of the United States.*
V : *as*+S+V, OR S+*might/may*+V : USED AS ADV SEN = remember

3 **Recall** is the ability or act of remembering something that has happened in the past. EG *Why are some memories more available for recall than others?* ● If something is **beyond recall** or **past recall**, it is no longer possible to remember it.
N UNCOUNT = recollection; ● PHR : USED AS AN A

4 To **recall** a person or a group means 4.1 to order them to return, for example if they have been working abroad. EG *Eighteen months ago they recalled him to Mozambique... Parliament was hastily recalled from recess.* ▸ used as a noun. EG *He was angered by his recall.* 4.2 to bring them back into military service. EG *The government passed a bill to recall reservists.* ▸ used as a noun. EG *...arrangements were made for recall of reservists.*
V+O : USU+A = call back; ▸ N UNCOUNT; V+O ⇑ call up; ▸ N UNCOUNT ⇑ call-up

5 If a company **recalls** products, it asks shops and people who have bought the products to return them because there is something wrong with them. EG *The car was recalled for possible safety defects.*
V+O

recant /rɪˈkænt/, **recants, recanting, recanted.** If you **recant**, you say in public that you no longer have a particular set of beliefs; a formal word. EG *He was brought before the Inquisition on charges of heresy, and forced to recant... Under threat of death, men recanted their religion before the altar.*
V OR V+O ⇑ state = renounce, repudiate

recap /riːkæp/, **recaps, recapping, recapped.** When you **recap**, you repeat the main points of an explanation, description, or argument as a summary of it. EG *It was necessary to recap briefly the events of the period.* ▸ used as a noun. EG *Here is a recap of these suggestions.*
V OR V+O = recapitulate; ▸ N COUNT = résumé

recapitulate /riːkəpɪtjəˈleɪt/, **recapitulates, recapitulating, recapitulated.** When you **recapitulate**, you repeat the main points of an explanation, description, or argument, as a summary of it. EG *These points will recapitulate what has been established so far.* ◇ **recapitulation** /riːkəpɪtjəˈleɪʃəˈn/, **recapitulations.** EG *The next lesson will be a quick recapitulation of what we've done so far.*
V OR V+O = recap; ◇ N COUNT/UNCOUNT = résumé

recapture /riːkæptʃə/, **recaptures, recapturing, recaptured.** 1 If you **recapture** a pleasant emotion or sensation, you succeed in feeling it in the same way as you felt it on an earlier occasion. EG *She tried, but failed, to recapture her earlier mood... I wanted to recapture that feeling of freedom that I had somehow lost.*
V+O ⇑ regain = recover

2 If people **recapture** a place or a piece of land, they get it under their control again by attacking the people who had taken it from them. EG *The Turks had returned and recaptured their trench.* ▸ used as a noun. EG *They pressed ahead with the recapture of the fort.*
V+O ⇑ recover = regain; ▸ N SING : USU *the*+N+*of*

3 To **recapture** a person or an animal that has escaped from somewhere means to catch them again. EG *Most of the escaped prisoners were quickly recaptured.*
V+O ⇑ capture

recast /riːkɑːst/, **recasts, recasting.** The form **recast** is used in the present tense and is the past tense and the past participle form.

1 If you **recast** something, you change it by organizing it in a different way. EG *...recasting the subsidy system... The text had been recast into language comprehensible only to legal experts.*
V+O = remodel

2 If a part in a play **is recast**, it is given to a different actor or actress. EG *To everyone's surprise the part of Claudius had been recast.*
V+O ⇑ cast

recd. is a written abbreviation for 'received'.

recede /rɪˈsiːd/, **recedes, receding, receded.** 1 If something **recedes**, 1.1 it moves further away into the distance, usually before disappearing completely. EG *Now and then cars passed me, red tail-lights receding.* 1.2 it gradually becomes less clear or less bright, usually before disappearing completely. EG *The deep purple had begun to recede from his cheeks... Already the memory was receding.*
V; V = fade

2 If a man **is receding**, he is starting to go bald by losing hair at the front of his head. EG *He's receding a bit.* ▸ used also of his hair. EG *His hair is receding a bit at the temples.* ◇ **receding.** EG *...a receding hairline.*
V; ▸ = thin; ◇ ADJ CLASSIF : ATTRIB

receipt /rɪˈsiːt/, **receipts.** 1 A **receipt** is a piece of paper that you give or send to someone to confirm that you have received money or goods from them. EG *We've got receipts for each thing we bought... Ask for a receipt and make sure that you get it.*
N COUNT ⇑ record

2 **Receipts** are the amounts of money received during a particular period, for example in a shop or in a theatre. EG *The receipts from admission fees to Stonehenge fell sharply... ...tax receipts.*
N PLURAL = income, takings

3 **Receipt** is the act of receiving something; a formal use. EG *You have to sign here and acknowledge receipt... We are awaiting the receipt of further information... He was in receipt of an annual income.*
N UNCOUNT : IF+PREP THEN *of*

receive /rɪˈsiːv/, **receives, receiving, received.** 1 When you **receive** something, you get it after it has been given to you or sent to you. EG *Northcliffe received a letter from his brother... She always received the same reply... Did they receive money for their work?*
V+O

2 If you **receive** a reaction, attitude, or action that is directed towards you, you experience it. EG *The criticism he received in England hurt badly... Three policemen received minor injuries... She received a tremendous ovation.* ● If you **are on the receiving end** of something unpleasant, you are the person that the unpleasant thing is directed towards. EG *You may find yourself on the receiving end of my father's temper.*
V+O = meet with, suffer; ● PHR : VB INFLECTS, IF+PREP THEN *of*

3 When you **receive** a visitor or a guest, you welcome them, often in a formal way. EG *Tell her I shall be delighted to receive her... Fassler received Liebermann in his office.*
V OR V+O : USU+O

4 If you **receive** a person or thing in a particular way, you react in a way that indicates how you feel about that person or thing. EG *He had been warmly received wherever he went... Your latest novel has been very well received.*
V+O+A = greet

5 If people **receive** someone into a club, organization, or group of people, they accept them as a member. EG *Jane had been officially received into the Church a month previously.*
V+O+A *(into)* = admit

6 When a radio or television set **receives** signals, it changes them into sound or pictures. EG *...improvements in both receiving and transmitting sound.*
V OR V+O

7 If you **are receiving** someone, you are able to hear a message that they are sending you on a radio set. EG *Are you receiving me, Morris?*
V OR V+O : USU CONT = read

8 If an opening or container **receives** an object, the object is put inside it; a formal use. EG *...preparing the long rows to receive the seeds.*
V+O : NO CONT = accept

received /rɪˈsiːvd/ means based on authority rather than experience and generally accepted by people as being right and normal. EG ...*contrary to the received wisdom of the day.* ADJ CLASSIF : ATTRIB ⇑ given

Received Pronunciation is the standard accent used by speakers of southern British English; a technical term in language teaching or linguistics. N UNCOUNT

receiver /rɪˈsiːvə/, **receivers**. 1 A **receiver** is 1.1 the part of a telephone that you hold near to your ear and speak into. EG *She picked up the receiver and dialled the number... He replaced the receiver.* N COUNT 1.2 the equipment that changes radio or television signals into sound and pictures. A television or radio set is a receiver. EG *Do you have an FM receiver?* N COUNT ⇑ apparatus 1.3 a person who buys and sells stolen property that they know has been stolen. EG ...*receivers of stolen goods.* N COUNT ⇑ criminal = fence

2 A **receiver** is also someone who is officially appointed to look after the affairs of a company that has gone bankrupt and to distribute its funds; used in British English. EG ...*the appointment of Robert Courtney Smith as the official receiver... The receivers reported at the end of February 1970.* N COUNT : USU the+N ⇑ official

receivership /rɪˈsiːvəʃɪp/ is the state of being bankrupt and in the charge of the official receivers. EG *The company will go into receivership.* N UNCOUNT

recent /riːsənt/. Something that is **recent** 1 happened or appeared only a short time ago. EG *They talked about their recent trip to Africa.* ADJ QUALIT : USU ATTRIB 2 happened or appeared during a short period of time before the present. EG *Tonight we're going to have a look at recent developments in Biology... Few sights have become more familiar in recent times than the street demonstration.* ADJ QUALIT : USU ATTRIB ⇑ past

recently /riːsəntli¹/. 1 If something happened **recently**, it happened only a short time ago. EG *Recently, I lectured to seven hundred Swedes... It is only quite recently that I started painting... The problem has been ignored until very recently... This flower was discovered as recently as 1903.* ADV WITH VB

2 If you have done something **recently** or if it has happened **recently**, it has happened during a short period of time before the present. EG *I haven't heard from her recently... I wonder whether he's been writing recently.* ADV WITH VB = lately

receptacle /rɪˈseptəkəºl/, **receptacles**. A **receptacle** is an object such as a dish, tin, jar, or waste-paper bin, which is used to put or keep things in; a formal word. EG *Please put your cigarette ends into the receptacle provided.* N COUNT = container

reception /rɪˈsepʃəºn/, **receptions**. 1 The **reception** in a hotel, office, hospital, etc is the area which you go to when you first arrive and which deals with reservations, appointments, and enquiries. EG *I signed in at reception... Bob telephoned down to the reception desk... Would you make an appointment at reception?* N UNCOUNT ⇑ department

2 A **reception** is a formal party which is given in order to welcome a group of people or to celebrate a special event, for example a wedding. EG *We're going to the Dean's reception... The reception was held in the Albany.* N COUNT

3 The **reception** of someone or something is the public reaction to them or it. EG *I wrote to George about the enthusiastic reception of his book... Butler received a hostile reception in Bristol.* N COUNT+SUPP : USU SING

4 The **reception** of people is the act of formally welcoming them, especially when they are important guests; a formal use. EG ...*a room which was kept for the reception of visitors.* N SING WITH DET = greeting

5 **Reception** is the degree of clarity of the sound or picture which you get from a radio or television, and which usually depends on the strength of the electronic signal. EG *Radio reception kept fading... I'm getting perfect reception now, thanks.* N UNCOUNT ⇑ quality

reception centre, reception centres. A **reception centre** is a place which provides temporary accommodation for people who have nowhere else to live. EG *The Department for Family Welfare set up reception centres.* N COUNT ⇑ hostel

reception class, reception classes. A **reception class** in an infant school is the first class that children go into when they start school; a formal word. N COUNT

receptionist /rɪˈsepʃənɪst/, **receptionists**. A **receptionist** is a person who works in a hotel, office, doctor's surgery, etc, whose job is to deal with guests or clients when they first arrive, answer the telephone, and arrange reservations or appointments. EG *He handed back his room key to the receptionist... Make another appointment with the receptionist.* N COUNT ⇑ worker

reception room, reception rooms. A **reception room** is a room in a house where people can sit together, for example a living room or a dining room; used especially in advertisements of houses for sale. N COUNT

receptive /rɪˈseptɪv/. Someone who is **receptive** is willing to consider and accept new ideas or suggestions. EG *We need people who are receptive to new ideas... The public began to develop a more receptive attitude.* ◇ **receptiveness**. EG ...*this receptiveness to new notions.* ◇ **receptivity** /riːseptɪvɪti¹/. EG ...*their receptivity to his ideas.* ADJ QUALIT : IF+ PREP THEN *to/of* = open ◇ N UNCOUNT ◇ N UNCOUNT : USU+*to*

recess /riːses/, **recesses**. A **recess** is 1 a period of holiday between the sessions of work of a committee or parliament. EG *The Senate investigating committee is going into recess for a couple of weeks... Parliament was hastily recalled from recess.* N UNCOUNT/ COUNT = vacation 2 a small area in a room which is formed by one part of a wall being built further back than the rest of it and which gives extra space in the room. N COUNT = alcove 3 a deep or hidden part of something. EG *I pushed the problem down into the dim recesses of my mind.* N COUNT+SUPP : USU PL = corner

recessed /riːsest/ means hidden or placed in a recess in a wall. EG ...*the recessed doorway.* ADJ CLASSIF : ATTRIB

recession /rɪˈseʃəºn/, **recessions**. A **recession** is a period when the economy of a country becomes much less successful, with industry producing and selling less, and more people becoming unemployed. EG ...*a period of recession and under-employment... In spite of the recession, private car sales are 5 per cent up... Economic sanctions can be effective, particularly in a recession.* N COUNT/ UNCOUNT = depression, slump

recharge /riːtʃɑːdʒ/, **recharges, recharging, recharged**. To **recharge** a battery means to fill it with electricity again after it has been used, by connecting it to a special piece of electrical equipment. EG *Does your battery need recharging?* V+O ⇑ charge

rechargeable /riːtʃɑːdʒəbəºl/. A battery that is **rechargeable** can be recharged so that it can be used again. ADJ CLASSIF

recherché /reʃɜːʃeɪ/. Something that is **recherché** is very sophisticated and makes people think that it has been planned, made, or said by a knowledgeable and intellectual person. EG ...*a very recherché sort of film.* ADJ QUALIT

recidivist /rɪsɪdɪvɪst/, **recidivists**. A **recidivist** is someone who repeatedly commits crimes although they have already been punished or sent to prison. EG *Dawn was a hopeless recidivist.* N COUNT ⇑ criminal

> **RECIP** In this dictionary RECIP is used in the grammar notes beside some verb entries to indicate a special pattern that the verb makes with two noun groups. An example is **meet**. If we know that 'John met Mary', we also know that 'Mary met John' and that 'John and Mary met'. EG *In the third year of university he* **met** *Barbara... Barbara* **met** *him in London... Barbara and Howard* **met** *in a sociology lecture... The young couple* **met** *a week before the wedding... They* **met** *each other at a party.* RECIP verbs behave in the following ways. 1 The two noun groups can be either the subject or the object of the RECIP verb. Either noun group can be the subject or the object without altering the meaning of the verb. 2 The two noun groups can be linked by *and* as the subject of the RECIP verb, or the verb can have a plural noun or plural pronoun as its subject. The verb in this pattern does not have an object, except for the phrase *each other*, which emphasizes the reciprocal meaning. 3 In a few cases the RECIP verb makes its pattern with a preposition. An example is **argue**, which is described in the grammar notes as V OR V+A(*with*): RECIP. EG *We were* **arguing** *about money... I don't want to* **argue** *with you about it.*

recipe /resɪpi¹/, **recipes**. 1 A **recipe** is a list of ingredients and a set of instructions telling you how to mix and cook the ingredients in order to make a particular dish. EG *'Your paté is delicious,' said Dorothy. 'Will you give me the recipe?'... ...an old Polish recipe for beetroot soup.* N COUNT

2 If something **is a recipe for** a particular thing, it is very likely to make that thing happen. EG *In 1961 this policy appeared to be a recipe for disaster.* PHR : VB INFLECTS

recipient /rɪ²sɪpɪənt/, **recipients**. A **recipient** is someone who receives something; a formal word. EG ...*letters kept by the recipients... They would in time become the recipients of much criticism.* N COUNT : IF+ PREP THEN *of*

reciprocal /rɪ²sɪprəkə⁰l/ means done or given by someone because another person did or gave something similar to them. EG *In the case of countries belonging to the EEC, their social security system is linked to Britain's by a reciprocal agreement... We felt compelled to organize some kind of reciprocal display of strength.* ADJ CLASSIF : USU ATTRIB ⇑ mutual

reciprocate /rɪ²sɪprəkeɪt/, **reciprocates, reciprocating, reciprocated.** If you **reciprocate**, you do, give, or feel a particular thing because something similar has been done or given to you or felt about you. EG *Invitations to the home of a subordinate may often be accepted, but not reciprocated... By then she'd paid me so many compliments, I was beginning to feel the urge to reciprocate.* V OR V+O ⇑ return

reciprocity /rɛsɪprɒsɪti¹/ is behaviour between two people or groups of people in which each gives or concedes a lot to the other. EG *Many writers have sought to establish a relationship of real reciprocity and equality with their readers.* N UNCOUNT

recital /rɪ¹saɪtə⁰l/, **recitals.** A **recital** is a performance or music or poetry, usually given by one performer. EG *She had been asked to give a piano recital... ...a drawing-room where chamber concerts and poetry recitals were held.* N COUNT : USU + SUPP

recitation /rɛsɪteɪʃə⁰n/, **recitations.** 1 A **recitation** is a piece of writing or poetry that someone learns and speaks aloud. EG *The children did two beautiful recitations from 'Wind in the Willows.'* N COUNT : USU + SUPP

2 **Recitation** is 2.1 the saying aloud of a piece of poetry or writing that you have learnt. EG *She had arrived to interrupt his recitation.* N UNCOUNT/ COUNT 2.2 the saying aloud of a list of things. EG *...the recitation of our names and numbers.* N UNCOUNT/ COUNT

recite /rɪ¹saɪt/, **recites, reciting, recited.** 1 When you **recite** something such as a poem, you repeat it aloud after you have learned it. EG *Jenny recited the poem she had selected... She recited a speech from 'As You Like It.'* V OR V+O/ QUOTE : USU V+O ⇑ say

2 When you **recite** a list of things, you say it aloud. EG *...if I recited the whole inventory... She took pleasure in reciting the list of major events in the town's history.* V+O ⇑ state

reckless /rɛklɪ²s/. Someone who is **reckless** shows a complete lack of care about danger or about the results of their actions. EG *I don't like the way he drives. He's reckless.* ▸ used of people's actions. EG *They denounced the government for its reckless squandering of public funds.* ◊ **recklessly.** EG *She had recklessly agreed to lend them what they needed.* ◊ **recklessness.** EG *...his aggressiveness and recklessness.* ADJ QUALIT ⇑ irresponsible = foolhardy; ◊ ADV; ◊ N UNCOUNT = rashness

reckon /rɛkə⁰n/, **reckons, reckoning, reckoned.** 1 If you say that you **reckon** that something is true, you mean that you think that it is true; used in informal English. EG *She reckoned that there was a risk... Well, I reckon I may vote for her at the next election... I reckon he's barmy.* V+REPORT-CL

2 If something **is reckoned** to be true or if you **reckon** it to be true, you consider or believe that it is true. EG *About 40 per cent of the country is reckoned to be illiterate... The rules would be reckoned awkward by anyone else... It was reckoned a fine job but the money wasn't great.* V+O+C, OR V+O + *to*-INF : USU PASS = is regarded

3 If you **reckon** an amount, you calculate it; a formal or old-fashioned use. EG *The number of days lost through unemployment in 1968 can be reckoned at 146 million... She no longer anxiously reckoned the weeks and the months of her widowhood... Scylla reckoned on her fingers.* V OR V+O = work out

4 If you **reckon** to do something, you expect to do it. EG *They reckon to sell most of them abroad... They reckoned to overpower by sheer force of numbers.* V+*to*-INF

reckon in. If you **reckon in** something, you include it as part of a total. EG *When everything is reckoned in, they are not so badly paid.* PHRASAL VB : V+ O+ADV

reckon on. If you **reckon on** or **reckon upon** something, you feel certain that it will happen and so assume that it will happen. EG *He reckoned on a large reward if he succeeded... They had not reckoned on such a fight.* PHRASAL VB : V+ PREP, HAS PASS = bank on

reckon up. If you **reckon up** a set of figures, you add them together to find the total; an old-fashioned expression. EG *It won't take him a minute to reckon up the bill.* PHRASAL VB : V+ O+ADV = tot up

reckon with. 1 If you had not **reckoned with** something, you had not expected it and so were not prepared for it. EG *She had not reckoned with a surprise of this sort.* PHRASAL VB : V+ PREP, HAS PASS

2 If you say that there is someone or something **to be reckoned with**, you mean that you have to deal with them and it is difficult. EG *There was also Gertrude to be reckoned with... The Union has always been a major force to be reckoned with.* PHR : USU AFTER N

reckon without. If you say that you had **reckoned without** something, you mean that you had not expected it and so were unprepared for it; an informal expression. EG *They reckoned without Margaret's determination.* PHRASAL VB : V+ PREP, HAS PASS

reckoning /rɛkə⁰nɪŋ/, **reckonings.** A **reckoning** is 1 a calculation that you make about something. EG *It's only a rough reckoning... By his own reckoning, he had taken five hours to get there.* N COUNT/ UNCOUNT 2 the action of admitting things that you have done, especially when you are punished for them. EG *At some time there would have to be a reckoning with her.* N COUNT : USU SING ● **The day of reckoning** is the time when you pay or are punished for things that you have done wrong. EG *We merely put off the day of reckoning... The day of reckoning had not come for Harold Harmsworth.* ● PHR : USED AS S/O/C

reclaim /rɪ¹kleɪm/, **reclaims, reclaiming, reclaimed.** 1 If you **reclaim** something that you have lost or something that has been taken away from you, you ask for it back, because you think that you have a right to it. EG *You must present this ticket when you reclaim your luggage... Three customers have tried to reclaim their money.* V+O ⇑ demand = claim back

2 When people **reclaim** land, they make it suitable for farming or building, by draining it, irrigating it, protecting it from the sea, etc. EG *...efforts to reclaim large areas of marshland... ...lowland bogs have been reclaimed.* ◊ **reclaimed.** EG *...reclaimed land.* V+O ⇑ convert; ◊ ADJ CLASSIF

3 If people **reclaim** waste materials, they collect them so that they can be processed and used again. EG *Other metals are also reclaimed by Waste Disposal authorities.* V+O ⇑ recover

4 If you **reclaim** a person, you cause them to end their bad or criminal behaviour; an old-fashioned use. EG *...a reclaimed drunkard.* V+O : IF+PREP THEN *from* ⇑ save = reform

reclamation /rɛkləmeɪʃə⁰n/ is 1 the successful attempt to make desert, marshland, or other unusable land suitable for farming or building. EG *...the reclamation of marginal lands.* N UNCOUNT ⇑ conversion 2 the recovery of a substance found in rubbish, used products, waste materials, etc, so that it can be used again. EG *We should encourage reclamation and recycling.* N UNCOUNT

recline /rɪ¹klaɪn/, **reclines, reclining, reclined.** 1 If you **recline**, you sit or lie with the upper part of your body supported at an angle. EG *Humans sit, stand, squat, and recline in a whole range of different positions... He sat there, reclined against a foam rubber cushion.* V : USU + A

2 When a seat **reclines** or when you **recline** it, you lower the back of it so that you can lie down or rest your body in a leaning position. EG *He reclined his seat and soon began to doze... He drove away in his big plush car with its reclining seats.* V-ERG ⇑ adjust

recluse /rɪ¹klu:s/, **recluses.** A **recluse** is a person who lives alone and deliberately avoids other people. EG *...a scruffy elderly recluse.* N COUNT = hermit

reclusive /rɪ¹klu:sɪv/. Someone who is **reclusive** lives alone and deliberately avoids other people; a formal word. EG *His estranged wife, Becky, had become increasingly reclusive.* ADJ QUALIT ⇑ solitary

recognise /rɛkəg⁰naɪz/. See **recognize.**

recognition /rɛkəg⁰nɪʃə⁰n/. 1 **Recognition** is the act of recognizing someone when you see them or identifying something when you see it. EG *She just walked past me without so much as a glance of recognition... ...an exercise to test children's word recognition.* N UNCOUNT ⇑ identification

2 If something has changed **beyond recognition** or **out of all recognition**, it has changed to such an extent that it is no longer possible to recognize it. EG *The social structure has changed beyond recognition... The factory's productivity has been improved out of all recognition.* PHR : USED AS AN A ⇑ greatly

3 **Recognition** is also 3.1 understanding and acceptance of a fact or situation. EG *There has been insufficient recognition of the magnitude of the problem... This might lead to a recognition by both the superpowers that arms talks must be continued.* N UNCOUNT + SUPP = appreciation, realization 3.2 official acceptance that something is valid or proper. EG *Several countries withheld recognition of* N UNCOUNT

the new Administration. **3.3** favourable public attention that is given to someone because of their achievements or abilities. EG *He yearned for academic recognition.*
N UNCOUNT ⇑ approval = acknowledgement

4 If something is done **in recognition of** someone's achievements, it is done as a way of showing official appreciation of their achievements. EG *He was awarded a knighthood in recognition of his truly great contribution to the British cinema.*
PHR+NG/-ING : USED AS AN A

recognizable /rɛkəg⁰naɪzəbə⁰l/; also spelled **recognisable**. Something that is **recognizable** is easy to recognize or identify. EG *This situation produces recognisable stress symptoms... There was an old weathered statue barely recognisable as Charles II.*
ADJ QUALIT

◊ **recognizably**. EG *It has several recognizably distinct meanings.*
◊ ADV = perceptibly

recognize /rɛkəg⁰naɪz/, **recognizes, recognizing, recognized**; also spelled **recognise**. **1** If you **recognize** someone or something, you know who someone is or what something is when you see them or hear them, because you have seen them or heard them before. EG *She didn't recognise me at first... He didn't recognise the voice on the other end of the line... The postmistress recognised her at once as Mrs Pennington's daughter.*
V+O, OR V+O+A (as) : NO CONT

2 If you **recognize** something **2.1** you are able to identify it when you see it, for example because you have learned about it or had some previous experience of it. EG *They are specially trained to recognize the symptoms of radiation-sickness... There was a field planted with what he recognized as maize.*
V+O, OR V+O+A (as) : NO CONT

2.2 you have a clear awareness and understanding of it. EG *He was one of the few people to recognise the problem and foresee the dangers... They recognised that the success of the scheme was by no means certain.*
V+O/REPORT-CL, OR V+O+A (as) ⇑ perceive = appreciate

2.3 you accept the fact that it exists or is true. EG *They refused to recognise that a wrong decision had been made... We recognise this as a genuine need... His talent has been recognized and his pictures fetch very high prices.*
V+O/REPORT-CL, OR V+O+A (as) ⇑ acknowledge

3 If people **recognize** a government, an official document, etc, they officially accept that it is valid, proper, or lawful. EG *The new regime was at once recognized by China... Are qualifications gained in Britain recognized in other European countries?.*
V+O

4 If people **recognize** something that someone has done, they show official appreciation of it. EG *In 1975 the nation recognized her efforts by making her home a historical monument.*
V+O ⇑ acknowledge

recognized /rɛkəg⁰naɪzd/; also spelled **recognised**. **Recognized** means generally approved or accepted as having a particular quality or position. EG *There are several recognized techniques for treating this condition... She's a recognized authority on artificial intelligence.*
ADJ CLASSIF ⇑ known

recoil, recoils, recoiling, recoiled. The word **recoil** is pronounced /rɪ¹kɔɪl/ when it is a verb and /riːkɔɪl/ when it is a noun.

1 If you **recoil, 1.1** you move your body, or part of your body, quickly away from something because it gives you a painful or unpleasant feeling. EG *When he touched the man's arm, he recoiled in horror, for it was cold and rigid... He tried to put his arm round her, but she recoiled from him.*
V : USU+A = draw back

1.2 you have a strong and immediate feeling of fear, dislike, or horror about something that you see or hear about, so that you want to withdraw completely from the situation. EG *He recoiled in horror from the savagery which he witnessed... Parents may recoil at this kind of behaviour.*
V : IF+PREP THEN at/from ⇑ react = shrink

2 Recoil is **2.1** a quick backward movement that something or someone makes as a result of being hit by something or as a result of fear. EG *She must have felt his recoil.*
N UNCOUNT = wince

2.2 a quick backward movement that a gun makes, or that part of a gun makes, when the gun is fired. EG *His shoulder was bruised from rifle recoil.*
N UNCOUNT = kick

3 If an action **recoils** on the person doing it, it harms them or their family or friends in a way that is not intended; a formal word. EG *His attempts to impress his neighbours recoiled on his wife and family.*
V+A (on) = rebound

recollect /rɛkəlɛkt/, **recollects, recollecting, recollected**. If you **recollect** something, you are able to remember it; a slightly formal word. EG *He was unable to recollect the names too... He does not recollect how long they were in the house... In the old days, if you recollect, we used to play in this field.*
V+O/REPORT-CL = recall

recollection /rɛkəlɛkʃə⁰n/, **recollections**. **1** A **recollection** is something such as an event or episode from the past which you succeed in remembering. EG *I have a vivid recollection of the house where I lived as a child... ...my recollections of Australia.*
N COUNT ⇑ memory

2 Recollection is the remembering of something from the past. EG *She had a flash of recollection... With the shock of recollection he understood why.*
N UNCOUNT

3 If you say that something is true **to the best of** your **recollection**, you mean that you think that it is true but you do not remember it very well and so cannot be sure. EG *To the best of my recollection, I was seven when I last visited Edinburgh.*
PHR : USED AS AN A

recommend /rɛkəmɛnd/, **recommends, recommending, recommended**. **1** If you **recommend** someone or something, you praise them or suggest that they are suitable for a particular job or purpose. EG *I asked my friends to recommend a doctor who is good with children... Nell was successfully recommended for a job as a nursery governess... Margaret Drabble has just published a fine novel which I'd strongly recommend... He is a very highly recommended window cleaner.*
V+O : IF+PREP THEN as/to/for = commend

2 If you **recommend** a particular action, you suggest that it should be done. EG *The Committee must decide whether or not to recommend that the President should resign... Although my sister and her husband have eight children, they do not recommend other couples to have families of this size... The doctor may recommend limiting the amount of fat in your diet... They recommended a merger of the two biggest supermarket groups.*
V+O/-ING, V+REPORT-CL/QUOTE, OR V+O+to-INF ⇑ advise

3 If a particular quality **recommends** a person or thing, it makes that person or thing attractive or desirable. EG *It's an old hotel with very little to recommend it.*
V+O

recommendation /rɛkəmɛndeɪʃə⁰n/, **recommendations**. A **recommendation** is **1** the suggestion that something or someone is very good or is suitable for a particular job or purpose. EG *The best way to find a gardener is through personal recommendation... The prize is awarded annually on the recommendation of the teaching staff.*
N COUNT/UNCOUNT ⇑ advice

2 advice which is given to someone as to what is the best thing to do. EG *The decision that is taken will depend largely on what recommendation they make to the Prime Minister.*
N COUNT

recompense /rɛkəmpɛns/, **recompenses, recompensing, recompensed**. **1 Recompense** is something, usually money, that you give to someone to thank them for helping you or to say that you are sorry for harming them. EG *The boatman asked for recompense for the damage done... Would you accept this as a little recompense for all the trouble you have taken?*
N UNCOUNT : IF+PREP THEN for ⇑ compensation

2 If you **recompense** someone, you give them something, usually money, to thank them for helping you or to say that you are sorry for harming them. EG *We had to recompense the peasants for the loss of their goats.*
V+O : IF+PREP THEN for ⇑ compensate = reimburse

reconcile /rɛkə⁷nsaɪl/, **reconciles, reconciling, reconciled**. **1** If you **reconcile** two things that seem to be opposed to each other, you find a way in which they are in agreement. EG *I cannot reconcile the two points of view.... I asked how he would reconcile apartheid with Christianity.*
V+O : IF+PREP THEN to/with

2 If you **are reconciled** with someone, you have become friendly with them again after a quarrel or disagreement. EG *They had gone back to their home towns and had been reconciled with their families.*
V+O : IF+PREP THEN to/with, USU PASS

3 If you **reconcile** yourself to an unpleasant situation, you accept it and do not to try to change it or escape from it. EG *He told them to reconcile themselves to their misery on earth.*
V+O (REFL)+A (to)

reconciled /rɛkə⁷nsaɪld/. If you are **reconciled** to something, you agree to accept it although it is unpleasant. EG *After a while he grew reconciled to the situation... She became reconciled even to diplomatic parties.*
ADJ CLASSIF : PRED+to ⇑ accepted

reconciliation /rɛkə⁷nsɪli¹eɪʃə⁰n/, **reconciliations**. **Reconciliation** is **1** a process in which two people, or two groups of people, become friendly again after they have quarrelled or have not been in contact with each other. EG *...the dawning hopes of reconciliation in Western Europe... I told her that there could never be a reconciliation between us.*
N UNCOUNT/COUNT : IF+PREP THEN between/of/with ⇑ forgiveness

2 an act or process in which two things which seem to
N UNCOUNT : IF+PREP THEN

be opposed to each other are successfully brought together so that they are in agreement. EG *...the reconciliation of full employment with relatively low economic growth... ...two attitudes between which there can be no reconciliation.*
between/of/with
⇑ accommodation

recondite /rɪ¹kɒndaɪt, rɛkəndaɪt/. Something that is **recondite** is not known about by many people and is therefore difficult to understand; a formal word. EG *...this recondite area of learning... He felt his enigmas were becoming too recondite.*
ADJ QUALIT
= abstruse, esoteric

recondition /riːkəndɪʃəⁿn/, **reconditions, reconditioning, reconditioned**. To **recondition** a machine or piece of equipment means to repair or replace all the parts that are worn or broken. EG *This one's new, but the others have only been reconditioned.* ◇ **reconditioned**. EG *...a reconditioned cooker.*
V+O
⇑ overhaul
◇ ADJ CLASSIF

reconnaissance /rɪ²kɒnɪ¹səns/ is the process of obtaining military information about an army or an area by sending small groups of soldiers to explore or by using planes or satellites; a military term. EG *The decision was taken to step up reconnaissance of enemy naval movements... ...reconnaissance planes...*
N UNCOUNT
⇑ investigation

reconnoitre /rɛkənɔɪtə/, **reconnoitres, reconnoitring, reconnoitred**; also spelled **reconnoiter** in American English. To **reconnoitre** means to obtain information about the size and position of an army or about the geographical features of an area, by sending a small group of soldiers to explore or by using planes or satellites; a military term. EG *Small armoured task forces had reconnoitred the area.*
V OR V+O
⇑ investigate

reconsider /riːkə⁷nsɪdə/, **reconsiders, reconsidering, reconsidered**. If you **reconsider** something, you think about it again so that you can decide whether you ought to do something different. EG *He asked me to reconsider my decision... They urged the Government to reconsider their position... The military have had to reconsider how modern warfare should be waged.* ◇ **reconsideration** /riːkə⁷nsɪdəreɪʃəⁿn/. EG *This would allow time for debate and reconsideration... ...a reconsideration of the strategy of the war.*
V, V+O, OR V+REPORT-CL (WH)
= review
◇ N UNCOUNT
= review

reconstitute /riːkɒnstɪtjuːt/, **reconstitutes, reconstituting, reconstituted**. **1** To **reconstitute** an organization means to form it again in a different way. EG *The group was reconstituted after 26 March.* ◇ **reconstituted**. EG *...the reconstituted provisional government.*
V+O
⇑ regroup
◇ ADJ CLASSIF : ATTRIB

2 If you **reconstitute** a food that is dried, you change it back to its original form by adding water to it. EG *Use warm water to reconstitute dried yeast.*
V+O
⇑ restore

reconstruct /riːkə⁷nstrʌkt/, **reconstructs, reconstructing, reconstructed**. **1** To **reconstruct** a building that has been destroyed or badly damaged means to build it again. EG *When they started to reconstruct the building, they found a false wall.* ◇ **reconstructed**. EG *...the reconstructed royal palace.*
V+O
= restore
◇ ADJ CLASSIF
= restored

2 To **reconstruct** a system or policy means to replace it with one that works in a different way. EG *The present system should be reconstructed or abandoned... ...a systematic attempt to reconstruct race relations policy.*
V+O
= reorganize

3 If you **reconstruct** an event that happened in the past, you create a complete description of what it was like by combining a lot of small pieces of information. EG *He reconstructs in his books the details of unimportant lives... The historian tries to reconstruct societies in terms of what is familiar to him... The police were able to reconstruct the events leading to the girl's disappearance.*
V+O
⇑ conjecture

reconstruction /riːkə⁷nstrʌkʃəⁿn/, **reconstructions**. **1 Reconstruction** is the process of making a country normal again after a war, for example by replacing buildings that have been damaged or destroyed. EG *They played an active role in the reconstruction of post-war Britain.*
N UNCOUNT
= rebuilding

2 A **reconstruction** is a copy of something that no longer exists. EG *...a giant reconstruction of the skeleton of a dinosaur.*
N COUNT
= reproduction

3 The **reconstruction** of a building is the act of building it again. EG *The reconstruction of the Town Hall is scheduled to start next month.*
N UNCOUNT
= restoration

4 The **reconstruction** of a system is the act of forming it again in a different way. EG *Asquith announced the belated reconstruction of his government.*
N UNCOUNT
= reorganization

5 The **reconstruction** of an event that happened in the past is an attempt to recreate it by combining a lot of small pieces of information. EG *...a detailed reconstruction of some of the events.*
N UNCOUNT

record, records, recording, recorded. The word **record** is pronounced /rɪ¹kɔːd/ when it is a verb and /rɛkɔːd/ when it is a noun and adjective.

1 A **record** is an account of an event or piece of information which is kept in writing or some other form so that it is available for people to refer to. EG *Keep a record of any repair bills... Could I have your name and address for my records?... Record sheets must be filled in... ...medical records.*
N COUNT
⇑ evidence

2 If you **record** a piece of information, you keep it in writing or some other permanent form so that it is available for people to refer to. EG *All personnel details could be recorded on a computer... ...his lifelong habit of recording events and keeping a diary... ...throughout recorded history... Their every action and expression was recorded by concealed cameras.*
V+O
⇑ preserve
= document

3 To **record** something that has happened means to make it known in writing or some other form. EG *The minutes recorded that there had been a heated argument... The school magazine records an interesting debate... My father's reply is worth recording.*
V+O/REPORT-CL
⇑ relate

4 If you **record** your opinion, you express it publicly so that it can be written down or kept in some other permanent form and people will know what your opinion was. EG *I'd just like to record my reservations about the decision the committee has made.*
V+O
⇑ make known

5 If something **records** a measurement or value, it shows that measurement or value. EG *The clock records the time as seven forty-five... Every milestone he passed recorded the distance to Stonehenge.*
V+O
= give, indicate

6 If you **record** a piece of music, you perform it so that the sound can be copied onto a round flat piece of plastic and played later on a record-player. EG *I'd love Sinatra to record some of my songs... Did you ever record with Louis Armstrong?.*
V OR V+O

7 If you **record** something such as speech, a performance, or an event, you put it onto tape or film so that it can be heard or seen again later. EG *The film was recorded on video-tape... I'd like to record your voice... We had better be careful what we're saying since it's being recorded.* ◇ **recorded**. EG *...a recorded interview.*
V+O
◇ ADJ CLASSIF : ATTRIB

8 A **record** is also **8.1** a round flat piece of plastic on which sound, especially music, is recorded. The sound can be heard again by playing the record on a record-player. EG *I've got every record by Elvis Presley... We were playing jazz records... She made her debut album in 1973 for a minor record company.*
N COUNT
= disc

8.2 the music which is on a particular record or cassette, and which is available for people to buy. EG *That's a very good record.*
N COUNT

8.3 the time, distance, number of victories, etc which is the best that has ever been achieved in a particular sport or other activity. EG *The record is just over 10 seconds... He held the record for running the mile... Lewis could break world records in the 100 and 200 metres.*
N COUNT
⇑ standard

9 Record means higher, lower, better, etc than has ever been achieved before. EG *Unemployment was at a record high... The bank rate was increased to a record 8%.*
ADJ CLASSIF : ATTRIB

10 Someone's **record** is **10.1** all the facts that are known about their past achievements or character. EG *Mr Gerran has a very distinguished record... Such committees have had a poor record in the past... ...a man with a record of instability.*
N COUNT+SUPP

10.2 a list of the crimes that a person has been found guilty of and which is kept by the police. EG *He's got a record as long as my arm.*
N COUNT
= form

11 The word **record** is also used in the following expressions. **11.1** If something that you say is **off the record**, it is not official and not intended to be published or made known. EG *Now that remark was off the record, understand?... I don't mind frank talks off the record.*
PHR : USED AS AN A

11.2 If you **go on record** or if you **are on record** as saying something, you have said it publicly and officially and it has been written down, for example in a newspaper. EG *You're on record as saying that you will retire from football at the end of the year.*
PHR+as+-ING : VB INFLECTS

11.3 If you keep information **on record**, you keep an account of it in writing or in some other form so that it is available for people to refer to. EG
PHR : USED AS AN A
= on file

The police had kept his name on record. **11.4** If something is the best, highest, lowest, etc **on record**, it is the best, highest, lowest, etc that has ever been noticed and written down. EG *The highest monthly figures on record.* **11.5** If you **set** or **put the record straight**, you say or write something to explain that something which has been regarded as true is in fact not true. EG *Harold Begbie wrote a book to put the record straight.* **11.6** If you say that what you are going to say next is **for the record**, you mean that you are saying it publicly and officially and want it to be written down and remembered. EG *For the record I'd just like to say that I totally disagree with this decision.* **11.7** If something is **a matter of record**, it is well known and accepted as a fact because there is a lot of evidence to prove it. EG *Borg's brilliance on the tennis court is a matter of record.* PHR AFTER SUPERL / PHR : VB INFLECTS ⇑ correct / PHR : USED AS ADV SEN / PHR : USED AS C

12 See also **recording, track record.**

record-breaker, record-breakers. A **record-breaker** is someone who beats the previous record for a particular performance or achievement, especially in sport. EG *I don't think we'll see any record-breakers today.* N COUNT ⇑ competitor

record-breaking. Something that is **record-breaking** is better than the previous record for a particular performance or achievement. EG *The play enjoyed a record-breaking Christmas season.* ADJ CLASSIF : USU ATTRIB

recorded delivery. If you send a letter or parcel **recorded delivery**, you send it using a Post Office service which gives you an official record of the fact that the letter or parcel has been posted and delivered; used in British English. EG *Send all letters recorded delivery if you want to be certain they will arrive.* N UNCOUNT

recorder /rɪ'kɔːdə/, **recorders.** A **recorder** is **1** a musical instrument that you play by blowing down one end and putting your fingers in different positions over a series of holes. N COUNT ⇑ flute **2** a machine or instrument that keeps a record of something, for example in an experiment or on a vehicle. EG *...the mileage recorder on the car dashboard.* N COUNT : USU MOD+N **3** in England and Wales, a barrister or solicitor who is appointed as a part-time judge in the Crown Court. EG *The case was heard by the Recorder.* N COUNT **4** a tape-recorder. EG *He switched off the recorder... The recorder will be on all the time.* N COUNT ⇑ machine

recording /rɪ'kɔːdɪŋ/, **recordings. 1** A **recording** is a record, tape, or video of something, for example a piece of music, a television programme, or a conversation. EG *...a new recording of the Second Symphony... Very few recordings of Picasso's voice exist.* N COUNT

2 Recording means involved in making records, tapes, or videos. EG *...a recording engineer... ...recording equipment... I went up to the big recording studio in Maida Vale.* N UNCOUNT : USU BEFORE N

record library, record libraries. A **record library** is a library from which you can borrow records and cassettes with music on them. N COUNT

record player, record players; also spelled with a hyphen. A **record player** is a machine on which you can play the music or other sound on a record. EG *Nearly all teenagers have record players.* N COUNT = gramophone

recount, recounts, recounting, recounted. The word **recount** is pronounced /rɪ'kaʊnt/ in paragraph 1 and /riːkaʊnt/ in paragraph 2.

1 If you **recount** a story or event, you tell or describe it to people; a fairly formal use. EG *Nick recounted the story with real wit... The decisions taken have been recounted elsewhere.* V+O/REPORT-CL (WH) = relate

2 A **recount** is a second or further count, especially of votes in an election when the result is very close between two or more candidates. EG *The vote was close and a recount gave McClellan a lead of only 472... Williams called for a recount.* N COUNT

recoup /rɪ'kuːp/, **recoups, recouping, recouped.** If you **recoup** a sum of money that you have spent or lost, you get it back. EG *I recouped the initial cost within two years.* V+O = recover, regain

recourse /rɪ'kɔːs/. If you have **recourse** to something, you use it in order to help you in a difficult situation; a formal word. EG *He has no option other than to have recourse to violence... I couldn't tell which direction without recourse to a map... Industrial action is the only recourse we have.* N UNCOUNT : USU +*to* ⇑ resort

recover, recovers, recovering, recovered. The word **recover** is pronounced /rɪ'kʌvə/ in paragraphs 1 to 6, and /riːkʌvə/ in paragraph 7. **1** When you **recover** from something such as an illness, you become well again. EG *It was weeks before he fully recovered... He called to see if an elderly patient had recovered from an illness... He sustained a wound from which he did not recover.* V : IF+PREP THEN *from* = recuperate

2 If you **recover** from something such as an unhappy or unpleasant experience, you stop being emotionally affected by it. EG *They took a long time to recover from this shock... Her death was a great grief to him and I doubt if he ever recovered afterwards.* V : IF+PREP THEN *from* = get over

3 If something **recovers** from a period of weakness, difficulty, low value, etc, it improves, strengthens, or becomes more valuable again. EG *The economy began to recover about this time.* V : IF+PREP THEN *from* = rally

4 If you **recover** something, you get it back after it has been lost or stolen or after it has been in a place which is difficult or dangerous to reach. EG *'It would mean a lot to me to recover those documents,' he said... They recovered her body from the old mine-shaft.* V+O : IF+PREP THEN *from* ⇑ regain = retrieve

5 If you **recover** an ability or a state of mind that you have lost, you get it back. EG *He was beginning to recover the use of his voice... She had quickly recovered her composure... He died in hospital without recovering consciousness.* V+O (NG/REFL) = regain

6 If you **recover** an amount of money that you have spent or invested, you get the same amount back. EG *We recovered our purchase price in the first year... Some investors sought to recover losses sustained earlier in the week.* V+O = recoup

7 If you **recover** a chair, settee, etc, you replace the fabric on it. EG *This settee needs recovering.* V+O ⇑ refurbish

recoverable /rɪ'kʌvəᵒrəbəᵒl/. If something is **recoverable**, it is possible for you to get it back or have it returned to you. EG *...forgotten but still recoverable knowledge... Gambling debts, unlike all others, were not recoverable at civil law.* ADJ CLASSIF

recovered /rɪ'kʌvəd/. If you are **recovered**, you are in your normal state of health again after you have been ill. EG *The doctor advised him to stay at home until he was fully recovered.* ADJ CLASSIF : PRED ⇑ well

recovery /rɪ'kʌvəᵒriⁱ/, **recoveries. Recovery** is **1** the process of becoming well again after an illness. EG *The shock of the operation delayed his recovery... He made a good recovery from his stroke.* N UNCOUNT/COUNT : IF+PREP THEN *from* **2** an improvement in something such as the value of shares or the economy of a country after a period during which it has been in a bad state. EG *His advisers insisted that no economic recovery was in sight.* N UNCOUNT/COUNT = upturn **3** the process or fact of getting back something that has been lost or stolen or that is difficult or dangerous to reach. EG *An anonymous phone-call led to the recovery of most of the stolen property.* N UNCOUNT : USU +SUPP = retrieval **4** the process or fact of getting back something such as an ability or a state of mind that you had lost. EG *The news from home was sufficient to bring about the recovery of his equanimity.* N UNCOUNT : USU +SUPP **5** the process of getting back the same amount of money that you have spent or invested in a particular activity. EG *Recovery of travelling expenses can take up to a month.* N UNCOUNT : USU +SUPP

recreate /riːkri'eɪt/, **recreates, recreating, recreated.** To **recreate** something such as a former institution, situation, or way of life means to bring it back into existence. EG *This country can no longer hope to recreate its past... The opportunity could not be recreated.* V+O = restore

recreation, recreations. The word **recreation** is pronounced /rekri'eɪʃəᵒn/ in paragraph 1 and /riːkri'eɪʃəᵒn/ in paragraph 2. **1 Recreation** is enjoyable activity in which you exercise your body or use your mind when you are not working. EG *Sport and recreation have always been part of university life... The library was reserved for quieter recreations... We made our way directly to the recreation room.* N UNCOUNT/COUNT ⇑ activities = leisure

2 A **recreation** of something is an act of bringing it into existence again or doing something that makes people believe that it has come back into existence again. EG *One branch of the Party called for the recreation of the International. ...Radio Four's recreation of life in an Edwardian country house.* N UNCOUNT : IF+PREP THEN *of* = restoration

recreational /rekri'eɪʃənəᵒl/. **Recreational** means relating to activity in which you exercise your body or use your mind when you are not working. EG *We are being deprived of the recreational use of forests... The prisons were without showers or recreational facilities.* ADJ CLASSIF : USU ATTRIB = leisure

recreation ground, recreation grounds. A **recreation ground** is a piece of public land, usually in a town, where people can go to play sport and games. N COUNT ⇑ area

recrimination /rı2krımıneıʃə0n/, **recriminations.** **Recriminations** are accusations made by two people or two groups of people about each other's behaviour on a particular occasion. EG *...bitter recriminations.* ▸ used as an uncount noun. EG *...prolonged bouts of recrimination.* N PLURAL ⇑ reproach ▸ N UNCOUNT

recriminatory /rı2krımınətri1/. If something that you say or do is **recriminatory**, it involves you accusing someone of something. EG *...recriminatory arguments.* ADJ CLASSIF

recruit /rı1kru:t/, **recruits, recruiting, recruited.** 1 To **recruit** people for an organization or company means to find new members or workers to join it. EG *They set out to recruit a team of the brightest minds available... What disturbs me is that coloured people are not being recruited for the police force.* ◇ **recruiting.** EG *Other voluntary organizations reported sharp rises in recruiting... ...a recruiting centre for the army.* V : USU+A, V+O, OR V+O+A ⇑ get = enrol ◇ N UNCOUNT = recruitment

2 A **recruit** is a person who has recently joined an organization, company, or institution. EG *...the army, with its ranks swollen by these new recruits... They spent much of the trip interviewing possible recruits.* N COUNT ⇑ member

3 If you **recruit** someone for a particular purpose, you persuade them to do something for you. EG *Sisters and brothers were recruited to go out on sponsored walks in an effort to raise enough money... Mothers and fathers could be recruited to help.* V+O, OR V+O+*to*-INF = enlist

recruitment /rı1kru:tmə2nt/ is the act or activity of finding new members for an organization or new workers for a company or institution. EG *Her time was largely taken up with recruitment and training... ...the mass recruitment of volunteer teachers... We have a graduate recruitment scheme in the company.* N UNCOUNT = enrolment

rectangle /rektæŋgə0l/, **rectangles.** A **rectangle** is a shape which has four sides and four angles, each of which is a right angle. Each side has the same length as the side opposite to it. EG *He folded his newspaper into a neat rectangle... ...a little rectangle of bricked paving with chairs.* N COUNT = oblong

rectangular /rektæŋgjə4lə/. Something that is **rectangular** is shaped like a rectangle. EG *We came across a sort of trench, rectangular in shape.* ADJ CLASSIF = oblong

rectify /rektıfaı/, **rectifies, rectifying, rectified.** If you **rectify** something which is wrong, undesirable, or unsatisfactory, you change it so that it is correct or as you wish it to be; a fairly formal word. EG *Armed forces are expected to be sent in to rectify the situation... The tenant will be held responsible for rectifying any damage.* ◇ **rectification** /rektıfıkeıʃə0n/. V+O ◇ N UNCOUNT

rectilinear /rektılınıə/. Something that is **rectilinear** consists of straight lines or forms a pattern of straight lines; a formal word. EG *...rectilinear streets.* ADJ CLASSIF

rectitude /rektıtju:d/ is a quality or attitude that makes people behave honestly and virtuously according to accepted standards; a formal or literary word. EG *...striving for rectitude and righteousness.* N UNCOUNT

rector /rektə/, **rectors.** 1 A **rector** is a priest of the Church of England who is in charge of a parish. EG *Sometimes the Rector came up and preached a sermon.* N COUNT = vicar

2 In Scotland, a high-ranking university official elected by the students is called the **rector.** EG *He was elected by the students of Edinburgh University as their rector.* N COUNT ⇑ officer

rectory /rektə0ri1/, **rectories.** A **rectory**, in England or Wales, is the house in which a rector and his family live. EG *Many people visit the old rectory at West Putford.* N COUNT

rectum /rektəm/, **rectums.** Your **rectum** is the bottom end of the tube down which waste food passes out of your body. N COUNT ⇑ bowel

recumbent /rı1kʌmbənt/. If you are **recumbent**, you are lying down; a literary word. EG *I nodded towards the recumbent occupant of the other bed.* ADJ CLASSIF

recuperate /rı1kj0u:pəreıt/, **recuperates, recuperating, recuperated.** When you **recuperate**, you recover your health or strength, especially after you have been ill; a formal word. EG *I was just beginning to recuperate... I need time to recuperate from the shock.* ◇ **recuperation** /rı1kj0u:pəreıʃə0n/. EG *My mother has gone to Bath for a period of rest and recuperation.* V : IF+PREP THEN *from* ⇑ recover ◇ N UNCOUNT

recuperative /rı1kj0u:pə0rətıv/. Something that is **recuperative** helps you to recover after you have been ill; a formal word. EG *His recuperative powers were quite remarkable.* ADJ CLASSIF : USU ATTRIB ⇑ healing

recur /rı1kɜ:/, **recurs, recurring, recurred.** If something **recurs**, it happens again, either once or many times. EG *It was probable that the same circumstances would now recur... It was a phrase that was to recur again and again... A patient reported a dream that had recurred throughout her life.* V : USU+A ⇑ occur = be repeated

recurrence /rı1kʌrəns/, **recurrences.** A **recurrence** is a repetition of something that has happened before; a formal word. EG *He was aware of the possibility of a recurrence of his illness.* N COUNT/ UNCOUNT

recurrent /rı1kʌrənt/ means the same as recurring. EG *...a recurrent feeling of illness.* ADJ CLASSIF : USU ATTRIB

recurring /rı1kɜ:rıŋ/. **Recurring** events or feelings happen or occur many times. EG *Food scarcity will be a recurring problem in the future... ...a recurring nightmare.* ADJ CLASSIF : ATTRIB = recurrent

recycle /ri:saıkə0l/, **recycles, recycling, recycled.** If you **recycle** things that have already been used, such as bottles or sheets of paper, you process them so that they can be used again. EG *Fossil fuels cannot be recycled. Once they are gone they are gone for ever.* ◇ **recycled.** EG *...recycled paper.* V+O ◇ ADJ CLASSIF

red /red/, **redder, reddest; reds.** 1 Something that is **red** is the colour of blood or of a ripe tomato. EG *He had very red lips... There's nothing there but miles of broken red rock and dust.* ▸ used as a noun. EG *She was dressed all in red... ...brilliant paintings in reds and greens and blues.* ADJ COLOUR ▸ N MASS

2 If your face is **red**, it is much redder in colour than it normally is, usually because you are embarrassed or very angry. EG *She bends over, her face red, and begins to wipe up the mess... Ralph clenched his fist and went very red.* ● If you are as **red as a beetroot**, your face is very red, often because you are extremely embarrassed. ADJ COLOUR = flushed ● PHR : USED AS C ⇑ flushed

3 **Red** hair is between red and brown in colour. ADJ COLOUR

4 If the sky is **red**, it is pink in colour, usually when the sun is setting or rising. ADJ COLOUR

5 **Red** blood cells are the cells in your blood which carry oxygen and haemoglobin round the body. ADJ CLASSIF : ATTRIB

6 A **red** light is a signal to traffic to stop. EG *The bus had failed to stop at the red light.* ADJ COLOUR

7 If you are **in the red** or if your bank account is **in the red**, you have spent more money than you have in your account and so you are in debt to the bank. EG *I'm £100 in the red this month.* PHR : USED AS AN A = overdrawn

8 If you **see red**, you suddenly become very angry. EG *Suddenly I saw red.* PHR : VB INFLECTS

9 **Red** is red wine. EG *Would you prefer red or white?* N MASS

10 If you call someone a **red**, you mean that they support communism, socialism, or left-wing ideas in general; an informal expression used showing disapproval. EG *Our home is full of Reds and anti-government people.* N COUNT ⇑ leftist

11 People or ideas that are **red** support communism, socialism, or left-wing ideas in general; an informal word used showing disapproval. ADJ CLASSIF ⇑ leftist

12 ● to **paint the town red**: see **paint.** ● **like a red rag to a bull**: see **rag.**

red alert, red alerts. A **red alert** is a warning about an emergency that is given to hospitals and other organizations so that they can be ready to deal with it. N COUNT/ UNCOUNT

red-blooded. Someone who is **red-blooded** has lots of energy and strength; an informal word used showing approval. EG *'I'm a red-blooded, normal American boy,' Thomas said.* ADJ QUALIT

red-brick; also spelled as one word, especially for paragraph 2. 1 A **red-brick** building is built with bricks that are reddish-brown in colour. ADJ CLASSIF : ATTRIB

2 A **redbrick** university is one of the British universities that were established in large cities outside London in the late 19th and early 20th centuries, as opposed to much older universities, for example Oxford and Cambridge. ADJ CLASSIF : ATTRIB ⇑ provincial

red carpet. The **red carpet** is special treatment that is given to important or honoured visitors, for example the laying of a strip of red carpet for them to walk on. EG *We shall have to roll out the red carpet when he comes.* N SING : *the*+N ⇑ welcome

Red Crescent. The **Red Crescent** is an organization in Muslim countries that helps people who are suffering because of war, famine, or natural disaster. N PROPER : the+N

Red Cross. The **Red Cross** is an international organization that helps people who are suffering because of war, famine, or natural disaster. N PROPER : the+N

redcurrant /rɛdkʌrənt/, **redcurrants**. A **redcurrant** is an extremely small, bright red European fruit that grows in bunches on a bush; used also of the bush itself. N COUNT ⇑ currant

redden /rɛdə⁰n/, **reddens, reddening, reddened**. 1 If you **redden** or if your face **reddens**, your face becomes redder in colour, usually because of a strong emotion that you are feeling. EG *The soldier's face reddened in anger... I saw him redden with pleasure.* V-ERG

2 To **redden** something means to cause it to become red or more red in colour. EG *Was the liquid really blood or merely water reddened with betel juice?* V+O

reddish /rɛdɪʃ/ means slightly red in colour. EG *The women busily collected the ripened reddish berries.* ADJ COLOUR

redecorate /ri:dɛkəreɪt/, **redecorates, redecorating, redecorated**. To **redecorate** a building or a room means to paint it or put wallpaper on it again. EG *The lounge had been redecorated since his last visit.* ◇ **redecoration** /ri:dɛkəreɪʃə⁰n/. V+O ⇑ decorate ◇ N UNCOUNT

redeem /rɪ¹di:m/, **redeems, redeeming, redeemed**; a fairly formal word. 1 If someone or something **redeems** an unpleasant situation, they prevent it from being completely bad or unacceptable because of a quality that they have or because of something that they do. EG *...doing his best to redeem a boring dinner.* ◇ **redeeming**. EG *...an obscene book with no redeeming qualities.* V+O ⇑ relieve = rescue, save ◇ ADJ CLASSIF : ATTRIB

2 If you **redeem** yourself, you do something that will give people a better opinion of you again after you have behaved badly or made yourself unpopular. EG *He was trying to redeem himself for his earlier failure.* V+O (REFL) ⇑ reinstate

3 If you **redeem** something, you get it back from someone by repaying them money that you have borrowed from them. The item that you redeem has been kept by them as a guarantee that you will repay the money. EG *Pawnbrokers reckon they make most money when people redeem their jewellery.* V+O ⇑ regain = reclaim

4 If you **redeem** a debt or obligation, you pay someone money that you owe them or that you have promised to pay them. EG *If he does not redeem the debt, he will be landless... General Foods will redeem this voucher at face value.* V+O = discharge

5 In Christianity, to **redeem** someone means to free them from sin and evil by giving them faith in Jesus Christ. EG *She felt called to heal and redeem drunkards and junkies, to convert people to Christ.* V+O ⇑ save

redeemable /rɪ¹di:məbə⁰l/. If something is **redeemable**, it can be exchanged for a particular sum of money or for goods worth a particular sum. EG *...inexpensive gift certificates redeemable at local stores.* ADJ CLASSIF

redeemer /rɪ¹di:mə/, **redeemers**. 1 In Christianity, the **Redeemer** is Jesus Christ, who is believed to have freed people from the consequences of sin and evil. N PROPER : WITH the/POSS = saviour

2 A **redeemer** is any person who saves someone from a difficult or dangerous situation; a rather old-fashioned use. EG *Was it possible that Italy had found her redeemer?* N COUNT = saviour

redemption /rɪ¹dɛmp⁰ʃə⁰n/; a formal word. 1 **Redemption** is 1.1 the act of redeeming something or of being redeemed by something. 1.2 freedom from the consequences of sin and evil which Christians believe was made possible by Jesus Christ's death on the cross. EG *They visited the Shrine of Our Lady to pray for redemption.* N UNCOUNT; N UNCOUNT ⇑ grace = salvation

2 If you say that something or someone is **past** or **beyond redemption**, you mean that they are so bad that it is unlikely that anything can be done to improve or repair them. EG *'My complexion is past redemption,' she said dismally... The cause for which they had worked and fought was effectively beyond redemption.* PHR : USED AS AN A ⇑ hopeless = irredeemable

redemptive /rɪ¹dɛmp⁰tɪv/. In Christianity, something that is **redemptive** leads to freedom from the consequences of sin and evil; a formal word. EG *Christ's redemptive sacrifice.* ADJ CLASSIF : USU ATTRIB ⇑ saving

red ensign, red ensigns. A **red ensign** is a flag that is flown by ships of the British Merchant Navy. It is a red flag with a Union Jack in the top corner. N COUNT

redeploy /ri:dɪplɔɪ/, **redeploys, redeploying, redeployed**. To **redeploy** troops or forces means to distribute them in a different way so that they are ready for use or action. EG *The reconnaissance Tornados were redeployed to the south.* V+O ⇑ reorganize

redeployment /ri:di¹plɔɪmə²nt/ is the redistribution of troops, weapons, or resources so that they are ready for use or action. EG *There was a southward redeployment of Allied forces.* N UNCOUNT : USU +SUPP ⇑ reorganization

redevelop /ri:di¹vɛləp/, **redevelops, redeveloping, redeveloped**. To **redevelop** an area means to change it by removing existing buildings and roads, and by building new ones. EG *The whole of the city centre has now been redeveloped.* V+O ⇑ develop

redevelopment /ri:di¹vɛləpmə²nt/, **redevelopments**. **Redevelopment** is the changing of a part of a town or other area by removing existing buildings and roads, and building new ones. EG *The area is undergoing redevelopment... ...a proposed redevelopment of Soho.* N UNCOUNT/COUNT ⇑ development

red-faced. Someone who is **red-faced** has a face that appears red, for example because because they are embarrassed or because they drink a lot. EG *Everyone knew Tinker, a burly, red-faced man.* ADJ CLASSIF ⇑ ruddy

red-handed. If you **catch** someone **red-handed**, you catch them while they are in the act of doing something wrong. PHR : VB INFLECTS

redhead /rɛdhɛd/, **redheads**. A **redhead** is a person whose hair is a colour that is between red and brown. N COUNT

redheaded /rɛdhɛdɪ²d/. Someone who is **redheaded** is a redhead. ADJ CLASSIF

red herring, red herrings. A **red herring** is something irrelevant, which takes your attention away from the main subject or problem that you are considering. EG *They were using the issue as a red herring.* N COUNT = diversion

red-hot. 1 Metal that is **red-hot** is at such a high temperature that it has turned red. ADJ CLASSIF

2 Something that is **red-hot** is too hot for you to be able to touch safely or comfortably. EG *She burnt herself on a red-hot pan handle.* ADJ CLASSIF

3 **Red-hot** people, activities, or attitudes show great enthusiasm or excitement; an informal use. EG *...the red-hot patriotism of the defenders of the Republic... ...red-hot Socialists.* ADJ CLASSIF = ardent, burning

Red Indian, Red Indians. A **Red Indian** is a native North American Indian; a rather old-fashioned and offensive expression. N COUNT

redirect /ri:də¹rɛkt/, **redirects, redirecting, redirected**. 1 If you **redirect** your energy, resources, or ability, you begin to work in a different way because your aims have changed. EG *I needed to redirect my energies... Most industries were redirected to the needs of a wartime economy.* V+O ⇑ alter

2 To **redirect** something such as traffic means to change the course or direction that it has to follow. EG *All traffic is being redirected to avoid this stretch of the motorway.* V+O = divert

3 If you **redirect** someone's mail, you send it to their new address after it has been delivered to an address where they no longer live. EG *Please redirect all letters to the following address.* V+O = forward

redistribute /ri:dɪstrɪbju:t/, **redistributes, redistributing, redistributed**. To **redistribute** something such as money means to share it among people or organizations in a different way from the way that it had been previously shared. EG *Money would be redistributed from the traditional arts institutions.* ◇ **redistribution** /ri:dɪstrɪbju:ʃə⁰n/. EG *We do not envisage any redistribution of wealth and power.* V+O ⇑ distribute ◇ N UNCOUNT ⇑ distribution

red light, red lights; spelled with a hyphen in paragraph 3. 1 A **red light** is a traffic signal which shines red to indicate that drivers must stop. EG *...driving madly through red lights and down one-way streets.* N COUNT

2 If you **see a red light**, you know that you ought to stop what you are doing because you realize that it is dangerous or foolish. PHR : VB INFLECTS

3 The **red-light** district of a city is the area where prostitutes work. ADJ CLASSIF : ATTRIB

red meat is meat such as beef or lamb, which is dark brown in colour after it has been cooked. N UNCOUNT

redness /rɛdnɪ²s/ is the quality of being red in colour. EG *Her cheek was still slightly mottled where the redness was fading.* N UNCOUNT

redo /riːduː/, **redoes, redoing, redid, redone.** If you **redo** a piece of work, you do it again in order to improve it or change it. EG *I had to redo the stitching twice before I was satisfied.* V+O ⇑ do

redolent /rɛdə⁶lənt/; a literary word. If something is **redolent** of something else, 1 it has features that make you think of that other thing. EG *It was written in language redolent of the Lakeland Poets.* ADJ CLASSIF : PRED+of 2 it has a strong smell of that other thing. EG *Her colour was high and her breath redolent of gin and peppermint.* ADJ CLASSIF : PRED+of ⇑ smelling

redouble /riːdʌbə⁰l/, **redoubles, redoubling, redoubled.** If you **redouble** your efforts, you greatly increase the amount of energy you put into your activities when you are trying to achieve something. EG *Undaunted, he redoubled his efforts in the Labour Party... Was it fear that led John to redouble his furious strokes as he rowed their boat away?* V+O ⇑ augment

redoubt /rɪdaut/, **redoubts**; a formal word. A **redoubt** is 1 a place or situation in which someone feels safe because they know that no-one can spoil their peace or attack them. EG *The club was an all-female redoubt.* N COUNT ⇑ haven 2 an isolated and protected place which soldiers can hide in or retreat to in a battle. EG *...concrete bunkers and redoubts.* N COUNT ⇑ stronghold

redoubtable /rɪ¹dautəbə⁰l/. Someone who is **redoubtable** has a very strong character, which makes people respect and slightly fear them; a formal word. EG *She realised that the redoubtable Marie Tempest was coming her way.* ADJ QUALIT ⇑ impressive = formidable

red pepper, red peppers. 1 A **red pepper** is a ripe pepper that is used in cooking and can be eaten raw in salads. N COUNT ⇑ capsicum

2 **Red pepper** is a hot-tasting red powder that is made from red peppers and used to flavour food. N UNCOUNT = cayenne

redress /rɪ¹drɛs/, **redresses, redressing, redressed**; a formal word. 1 If you **redress** something such as a wrong or a grievance, you do something to correct it or to improve things for the person who has been badly treated. EG *He did all that he possibly could to redress the wrongs.* V+O = rectify, remedy ● If you **redress the balance** or the **imbalance**, you make two things more equal again because the fact that they were not equal was considered to be unfair or undesirable. EG *...the struggle to redress the balance between local authorities... We were refused the pay increase needed to redress the balance.* ● PHR : VB INFLECTS, IF+PREP THEN *between*

2 **Redress** is compensation for something wrong or unfortunate that has been done to you. EG *We are entitled to expect full and speedy redress for product or service failures.* N UNCOUNT = reparation

redskin /rɛdskɪn/, **redskins.** A **redskin** is a native North American Indian; an old-fashioned and offensive word. N COUNT

red tape is official rules and regulations that take a lot of time and usually seem unnecessary. EG *Applying for the grant involves a great deal of red tape.* N UNCOUNT ⇑ bureaucracy

reduce /rɪ¹djuːs/, **reduces, reducing, reduced.** 1 To **reduce** something means 1.1 to make it smaller in size or amount or less in degree. EG *They have promised to reduce public expenditure... The work-force would have to be reduced from 13,000 to 7,500... They used a stolen car to reduce the risk of detection.* ◊ **reduced.** EG *...a reduced rate of production.* V+O : IF+PREP THEN *from/to* ⇑ lessen = lower

1.2 to change it into a different and less complicated form, for example by separating it into its parts. EG *Every building in the area was reduced to rubble... This kind of analysis reduces the problem to its simplest form.* V+O+A *(to)*

2 To **reduce** someone to a particular state means to cause them to be in an undesirable state as a result of an unpleasant action or process. EG *Any survivors would be quickly reduced to the life of a hunter-gatherer.* V+O+A *(to)* ⇑ bring

3 If you **are reduced** to a particular way of working or behaving, the conditions that you are in force you to work or behave in this way, even though it is unpleasant or humiliating. EG *They were reduced to desperate measures to get an interview with her... We were reduced to selling the car to pay the phone bill.* V+O+A *(to+NG/-ING)* : USU PASS

4 When you **reduce** a liquid such as a sauce or when it **reduces**, you boil it in order to make it less in quantity and to make it thicker. EG *Boil all the ingredients together till they are reduced to half the quantity.* V-ERG : IF+PREP THEN *to*

reduction /rɪ¹dʌkʃə⁰n/, **reductions.** 1 **Reduction** is the act of making something smaller in size or amount or less in degree. EG *These problems stem from the reduction of the railway network in the 1960s.* N UNCOUNT : IF+PREP THEN *in/of* ⇑ contraction

2 A **reduction** is an amount by which something is made smaller or less. EG *They have made substantial reductions in labour costs... We do not expect to see any significant reduction in the number of civil servants... ...a 6 per cent reduction in industrial investment.* N COUNT : IF+PREP THEN *in* = cut

3 The **reduction** of something to a different form is the changing of it to a simpler form. EG *I objected to this reduction of the whole issue to a single question.* N SING WITH DET +*of*+NG+*to* = simplification

redundancy /rɪ¹dʌndənsi¹/, **redundancies.** 1 A **redundancy** is the dismissal of an employee because the company or institution that they work for has decided that their job is no longer necessary or is too expensive. EG *The trade unions accepted 3500 redundancies... They fear compulsory redundancies next month.* N COUNT : USU PL = job loss

2 **Redundancy** is 2.1 the state of no longer having a job because the company or institution which you worked for has decided that they no longer need or can no longer afford to have someone doing your job. EG *The possibility of redundancy was obviously present in their minds.* N UNCOUNT ⇑ unemployment 2.2 the state of no longer being needed because the original demand no longer exists or because the same function is being fulfilled by something else. EG *It's clear redundancy, wastefulness and inefficiency.* N UNCOUNT

3 **Redundancy** payments are sums of money that employers give to people that they make redundant as a form of compensation. EG *If you've worked there for 2 years, you should get a redundancy payment... Redundancy money does not last for ever.* ADJ CLASSIF : ATTRIB

redundant /rɪ¹dʌndənt/. 1 If you are **redundant**, you have been made unemployed because the company or institution which you worked for decided that they no longer need or can no longer afford to have someone doing your job. EG *Alumetal Ltd will be making 250 workers redundant at its processing plant next year... ...dozens of redundant film directors looking for work.* ADJ CLASSIF

2 Something that is **redundant** is no longer needed because its job is being done by something else, or because its job is no longer necessary or useful. EG *...skills which have been made redundant by technological advance... ...a large warehouse which faces onto three redundant docks.* ADJ QUALIT ⇑ unnecessary = superfluous

redwood /rɛdwud/, **redwoods.** A **redwood** is an extremely tall tree that grows in California; used also of the wood that comes from this tree. N COUNT/UNCOUNT ⇑ conifer

reed /riːd/, **reeds.** A **reed** is 1 a plant with a tall strong hollow stem. It grows in large groups in shallow water or on marshy ground. EG *We tried to avoid the beds of reeds at the river curves.* N COUNT/UNCOUNT : USU PL ⇑ grass 2 the strong hollow stem of a reed that is used for making materials such as the roofs of houses. EG *...a bed of woven reeds.* N COUNT/UNCOUNT : USU PL 3 a thin piece of cane or metal inside a musical woodwind instrument. When air is blown over it, it vibrates and makes a sound. N COUNT

reedy /riːdi¹/, **reedier, reediest.** 1 A place that is **reedy** has reeds growing all over it. EG *...a house by the reedy banks of Whitelake River.* ADJ QUALIT

2 If you describe a voice as **reedy**, you mean that it has a high and unpleasant sound. EG *Richard, in his thin, reedy voice, made a painfully dull ninety-minute speech.* ADJ QUALIT ⇑ high-pitched

reef /riːf/, **reefs.** A **reef** is a long line of rocks or sand that is just above or just below the surface of the sea. EG *Beyond the coral reef the open sea was dark blue.* N COUNT ⇑ ridge

reefer /riːfə/, **reefers.** 1 A **reefer** or **reefer jacket** is a short thick coat which is often worn by sailors. N COUNT

2 A **reefer** is also a cigarette which is made with marijuana and tobacco; an old-fashioned, informal use. N COUNT = joint

reef knot, reef knots. A **reef knot** is a type of double knot that will not come undone easily. N COUNT

reek /riːk/, **reeks, reeking, reeked.** 1 If someone or something **reeks** of a particular thing, they smell very strongly of it. EG *Thomas appeared within a minute, reeking powerfully of brandy... ...a small* V : IF+PREP THEN *of/with* = stink airless theatre crammed with children and reeking with popcorn.

2 If something **reeks**, it has a very strong, unpleasant smell. EG *...the urine, vomit, and faeces that reeked everywhere around him.* V = stink

3 The **reek** of something is its very strong and unpleasant smell. EG *...the sickening reek of blood... ...the familiar reek of cigarettes.* N SING WITH DET +SUPP : USU+*of* = stench

4 If a place **reeks** with something, it seems to contain an enormous amount of it. EG *The water was absolutely reeking with all kinds of fish with queer names... Glastonbury must have reeked with what you call 'superstition.'* V+A *(with)* = brim, teem

5 If something **reeks** of unpleasant ideas or principles, it gives a strong impression that it is firmly based on those ideas or principles. EG *The whole film reeks of racism.* V+A *(of)* ⇑ suggest = smack

reel /riːl/, **reels, reeling, reeled.** 1 A **reel** is 1.1 a cylindrical object which is used to hold long things such as thread or cinema film. The thread or film is wrapped round the reel so that it can be kept neatly together. EG *She took up some scissors and a reel of white string... Reels of magnetic tape were piled high on his desk.* N COUNT/PART 1.2 all the scenes and events that you see on a cinema screen when the cinema film on one reel is shown. EG *Saigon looked like the final reel of 'On the Beach'.* N COUNT+SUPP 1.3 a round device with a handle, attached to a fishing-rod. One end of the fishing line is wrapped round the reel, and when you catch a fish, you can pull it towards you by turning the handle. N COUNT

2 If you **reel** 2.1 you move about unsteadily and jerkily as if you are going to fall. EG *I reeled back into the room... She gave him a smack in the face that sent him reeling off the pavement.* V : USU+A = stagger, sway 2.2 you are very upset by an unpleasant experience. EG *We reeled from the shock of discovering that our own father was a liar.* V : IF+PREP THEN *from* = be stunned

3 If you say that your brain or mind **is reeling**, you mean that you are feeling very confused because you have too many things which you need to think about. EG *My brain reeled with all my plans for my new house... His mind was dazed and reeling with all that he had seen and heard.* V = swim

4 A **reel** is also a type of fast Scottish dance. N COUNT

reel in. If you **reel in** a fish, you pull it towards you by winding the line onto the reel of the your fishing rod. EG *You could throw a bare hook in the water and reel it in, and more often than not you'd catch a fish.* PHRASAL VB : V+O+ADV, OR V+ADV ⇑ pull in

reel off. If you **reel off** information, you repeat it from memory quickly and easily. EG *He could reel off the names of all the capitals of Europe.* PHRASAL VB : V+O+ADV = rattle off

re-elect, re-elects, re-electing, re-elected. If someone such as an MP or a trade union official **is re-elected**, they win a new election and are therefore able to continue in their position as MP or union official. EG *I was re-elected with a majority of over 4,300... The Council re-elected him President.* V+O : USU PASS, OR V+O+C ◇ **re-election.** EG *He stood again for re-election... Her re-election seemed assured.* ◇ N UNCOUNT

re-enact, re-enacts, re-enacting, re-enacted. If you **re-enact** a scene or incident, you repeat the movements that were made originally. EG *They used to re-enact this play, endlessly, in the playground.* V+O = act out

re-entry is the act of returning to a place that you have left, especially a country. EG *You should apply for a re-entry visa before you leave the country.* N UNCOUNT

re-examine, re-examines, re-examining, re-examined. When you **re-examine** ideas or beliefs that you hold, you think about them very carefully because you realize that you might have to change your opinion about them. EG *This forced researchers to re-examine their assumptions about man's early evolution.* V+O ⇑ reconsider ◇ **re-examination.** EG *This has prompted a re-examination of the purposes of education in modern Britain.* ◇ N COUNT/UNCOUNT : USU SING, IF+PREP THEN *of*

ref /ref/, **refs.** A **ref** is a referee in a football match, boxing match, etc; used in informal English. N COUNT

ref. is an abbreviation for 'reference'; often written at the top of business letters in front of a code which refers to a file where all the correspondence about the same matter is kept. EG *Our ref. 66/ADC/1986.*

refectory /rɪfektəʳri¹/, **refectories.** A **refectory** is a large dining hall, for example in a university or in a monastery; a formal word. N COUNT = canteen

refer /rɪ¹fɜː/, **refers, referring, referred.** 1 If you **refer to** a particular subject or person, you talk about them or mention them. EG *In his letters to Vita he rarely referred to political events... I am not allowed to describe the officers or refer to them by name... Her story has appeared in some newspapers: I refer to Miss Russell.* PHRASAL VB : V+PREP, HAS PASS = allude, discuss

2 If you **refer to** something or someone as a particular thing, you give them that name or say that that is what they are. EG *This kind of art is often referred to as 'minimal art'... ...the decline of what I refer to as the industrial working class.* PHRASAL VB : V+PREP+A *(as)*, HAS PASS

3 If something such as a name **refers to** a particular thing, situation, or idea, it relates to it or describes it in some way. EG *The serial number refers to the country in which the car was manufactured... The term 'elitism' seems to me to refer to those possessing some degree of power.* PHRASAL VB : V+PREP, HAS PASS

4 If you **refer to** a source of information such as a reference book, you look at it in order to find something out. EG *She could make a new dish without referring to any cookery books... ...a well trained clerk who could find his way around by referring to a filing system... ...information which can be referred to on future occasions.* PHRASAL VB : V+PREP, HAS PASS ⇑ check = consult

5 If you **refer** someone to a source of information, you tell them where they are likely to discover the information which they need, or which you think will interest them. EG *I refer you to a paper by Sutherland published recently... On two occasions at least Gray refers us to Chekhov.* V+O+A *(to)* ⇑ send = direct

6 To **refer** someone who is ill to a doctor or hospital means to officially send them there so that they can be treated. EG *He would have to refer Jenny to a specialist... She was referred by her doctor to a consultant.* V+O : USU+A *(to)*

7 If you **refer** a task or problem to a particular person or organization, you formally let them know about it so that they can deal with it. EG *She referred the matter to the European Court of Justice... Several established carpenters began to refer work to him... The death has been referred to the coroner.* V+O+A *(to)* ⇑ send = pass on

referee /refəriː/, **referees, refereeing, refereed.** 1 A **referee** is a person whose job is to control a sports match or contest. The person in charge of any kind of football game, or of a boxing or wrestling match, is called a referee. EG *The referee stopped the fight in the tenth round.* N COUNT ⇑ judge

2 When someone **referees** a sports match or contest, they act as the referee. V OR V+O ⇑ officiate

3 A **referee** is also a person who gives you a reference, for example when you are applying for a job. EG *Applicants are asked to give the names of three referees.* N COUNT

reference /refəʳrəns/, **references.** 1 **Reference** to someone or something is 1.1 the act of talking about them or mentioning them. EG *...the person to whom Philip had made such contemptuous reference... There is no further reference to him in her diary.* N UNCOUNT : IF+PREP THEN *to* = allusion 1.2 the act of referring to them for information or advice. EG *Decisions are taken by boards of directors without any reference to the CBI... They acted without reference to the local authority police committee... ...a wrist-size computer for quick reference and portability.* N UNCOUNT : IF+PREP THEN *to* = consultation

2 Information that you keep **for future reference** is information which you do not need immediately but which you think might be useful in the future. EG *A piece of advice fixed firmly in my brain for future reference... For future reference, I am living in Stockport and not Birmingham.* PHR : USED AS AN A

3 If you say or write something **with reference to** a particular thing, person, or quality, you mean that this thing, person, or quality is the subject of what you are saying or writing. EG *With reference to what we did last week I would like to read you this letter I received... ...a talk on contraception and health with particular reference to personal responsibility... The term was used with reference to students at universities as well as polytechnics.* PREP ⇑ about

3 A **reference** to a person or thing is something you say or write which mentions them. EG *A reference to 'the Party' always meant the Socialist party... The pamphlets contained hardly any references to nationalisation.* N COUNT : IF+PREP THEN *to* = allusion

4 A **reference** is 4.1 a word, phrase, or idea that comes from a book, poem, play, etc, which you use N COUNT : USU ADJ+N

as a way of talking about something or someone else. EG *He was always ready with a biblical reference–the patience of Job or something like that... ...literary allusions and references.* 4.2 something such as a number or name that tells you where you can obtain the information that you want, for example from a book, list, or map. EG *...the two page references that I gave you... ...map Reference 41° N 93° W.* 4.3 a letter that is written by someone who knows you, which describes your character and abilities. When you are applying for a job, an employer might ask for references, for example in order to make sure that you are reliable and honest. EG *I've got to get a reference from the University... I've given you a marvellous reference.* N COUNT; N COUNT ⇑ assessment

5 You look at **reference** materials, papers, documents, etc, in order to find information or advice about a particular subject. EG *...a valuable reference document... ...reference material... Works of reference that I had not yet been able to study.* ▸ also used to describe the part of a library or bookshop where reference works are kept. EG *He returned to the Reference Room and put the volume back... She couldn't take the Rayden volume home with her, as it was in the reference section.* N UNCOUNT : USU BEFORE N; ▸ N BEFORE N

6 See also **frame of reference**, **point of reference**, **terms of reference**.

reference book, reference books. A **reference book** is a book such as a dictionary or encyclopedia which contains detailed information, often about a particular subject. EG *...a list of reference books on his subject.* N COUNT

referendum /rɛ̲fərɛ̲ndəm/, **referenda, referendums.** The plural can be either **referenda** or **referendums**.

A **referendum** is a vote in which the people in a particular country or area are all asked to say whether they agree or disagree with a particular policy. EG *The citizens of Massachusetts voted yes in a referendum to cut property tax.* N COUNT ⇑ pole

refill /ri̲:fɪl/, **refills, refilling, refilled.** 1 If you **refill** something, you fill it again after it has been emptied. EG *Sue refilled Jennifer's glass... He went off to refill the aquarium.* V+O

2 A **refill** is 2.1 a drink that is poured into your glass when you have finished your previous drink; an informal word. EG *I handed her my cup for a refill.* N COUNT
2.2 a container that holds a substance and that replaces an empty container, for example the container in a ballpoint pen. N COUNT

refine /rɪ¹fa̲ɪn/, **refines, refining, refined.** 1 To **refine** a substance means to make it pure by using an industrial process to remove all other substances from it. EG *These companies also refine and market oil products... They were in competition with other sugar-refining companies.* V+O ⇑ purify

2 If you **refine** a theory, idea, etc, you improve it by making small alterations to it. EG *Their theories are continually being refined... I used these meetings to refine my ideas... The original model has to be refined.* V+O = hone

refined /rɪ¹fa̲ɪnd/. 1 Someone who is **refined** is very polite and well-mannered. EG *She was delicate, refined, sensitive, unused to hardship... ...a thin, blond, refined man in a bow-tie.* ADJ QUALIT ⇑ civilized = cultivated, genteel

2 Something that is **refined** 2.1 has been cleverly made or highly developed, and is therefore especially useful or effective. EG *They had a gigantic and very refined apparatus... The new model was larger, faster, and more refined than its predecessor.* 2.2 has been purified in an industrial process so that all other substances have been removed from it. EG *...refined foods such as sugar and white flour.* ADJ QUALIT = sophisticated; ADJ CLASSIF

refinement /rɪ¹fa̲ɪnmə²nt/, **refinements.** 1 A **refinement** is 1.1 a small alteration that you make to something such as a theory or an explanation in order to improve it. EG *The details and refinements of the explanation remained totally obscure... ...Godel's theorem and its later refinements by Church and Russell.* 1.2 an alteration or addition that you make to something such as a machine in order to make it more efficient or easier to use. EG *They need schools far more than they need new weapons or refinements to Concorde.* N COUNT/UNCOUNT ⇑ amendment; N COUNT ⇑ improvement = modification

2 **Refinement** is politeness and good manners, combined with a way of behaving which shows that you dislike anything vulgar. EG *Mr Willet's tone changed to one of genteel refinement.* N UNCOUNT ⇑ quality = cultivation

refinery /rɪ¹fa̲ɪnə⁰ri¹/, **refineries.** A **refinery** is a factory where substances such as oil or sugar are refined. EG *The next step was to expand the company's oil refinery... To his right were the oil refineries of St. Gabriel.* N COUNT

refit /ri̲:fɪ̲t/, **refits, refitting, refitted.** To **refit** a ship means to repair it or fit new parts to it. EG *The older ships had been retained, refitted and rearmed.* V+O

> **REFL** ☐ In this dictionary REFL is used in the grammar notes beside entries as an abbreviation for PRON REFL (reflexive pronoun) when it is given as part of a verb pattern. An example is **shoot 2**, which is described as V+O(NG/REFL). EG *He shot **himself**.* For information about reflexive pronouns see ☐ at PRON REFL.

reflate /ri̲:fle̲ɪt/, **reflates, reflating, reflated.** To **reflate** a country's economy means to increase the amount of money that is available for use in order to encourage more economic activity; a technical term in economics. EG *...government measures to reflate the economy.* ◇ **reflation** /ri̲:fle̲ɪʃə⁰n/. EG *The experiment of reflation could hardly come at a worse time.* V-ERG : USU V+O ⇑ inflate; ◇ N UNCOUNT ⇑ inflation

reflationary /ri̲:fle̲ɪʃənə⁰ri¹/. **Reflationary** economic activities cause an increase in the amount of money that is in circulation in a country; a technical term. EG *...a major reflationary programme... We must avoid any risky reflationary exercise.* ADJ CLASSIF ⇑ inflationary

reflect /rɪ¹flɛ̲kt/, **reflects, reflecting, reflected.** 1 If something **reflects** a particular attitude or situation, it has characteristics which indicate that it is caused by or is very similar to this attitude or situation. EG *The choice of school reflected Dad's hopes for us... Their stock prices fell to levels that did not reflect the true value of their assets... This impermanence is reflected in society in many subtle ways.* V+O = mirror

2 To **reflect** something means to give an impression of what it is like. EG *There are whole areas of human life that you can't reflect in a television documentary.* V+O ⇑ show = depict, portray

3 When light, heat, or other rays **reflect** or when a surface **reflects** them, they bounce back from the surface rather than pass through it. EG *Although it feels like a normal fabric it reflects heat back into the room... A lot of these materials absorb more energy than they reflect... It was a sunny day and the light reflected off the waiting cars.* • to **bathe in reflected glory**: see **glory**. V-ERG ⇑ rebound

3 When an object such as a mirror **reflects** a thing or person that is facing it, it shows the image of that thing or person. EG *...an oval mirror which reflected the entire room... I saw street lamps mistily reflected in black water... ...the mirrors where you see yourself reflected.* V+O ⇑ reproduce

4 When you **reflect**, 4.1 you think in a slow, deliberate way about something that involves ideas or opinions rather than definite facts. EG *I have of course had a chance to reflect and to think about whether or not this is a good thing... Rodin reflected long over Casson's argument.* 4.2 you make a comment that expresses your thoughts on something. EG *Well, I reflected, I couldn't say I hadn't been warned.* V : IF+PREP THEN *on/over/upon* ⇑ consider = ponder, meditate; V+REPORT-CL/QUOTE ⇑ think

5 If an action or situation **reflects** on another thing, it gives people a particular impression of that other thing. EG *Obviously your behaviour is going to reflect on the whole group... The story reflected badly on Amity and worse on Brody.* V+A *(on/upon)* ⇑ discredit

reflection /rɪ¹flɛ̲kʃə⁰n/, **reflections.** 1 A **reflection** is 1.1 something which informs you about a particular thing because it has similar characteristics or because it is based on that other thing. EG *Their behaviour in this respect was a reflection of their very different personalities... ...the novels of Charles Dickens as a reflection of life in nineteenth century Britain... Is it an accurate reflection of reality?* 1.2 a situation or event which has the effect of making people aware of a particular aspect of someone or something. EG *Obviously this issue is a very sad reflection on the state of the Labour Party... I thought this a very fair reflection upon the way in which she lived her life.* 1.3 light or an image of someone or something that can be seen in a mirror or on a shiny surface. EG *She was standing there* N COUNT+*of* ⇑ indication; N SING WITH DET +*on/upon* ⇑ discredit; N COUNT ⇑ duplicate *looking at her reflection in the mirror... The reflections from the fireworks twinkled in the river.*

2 Reflection is **2.1** the process which causes light, heat, and other rays to bounce back from some surfaces rather than pass through them. EG *He went on to explain the laws of reflection of light... ...sources of sound reflection.* N UNCOUNT ⇑ return **2.2** slow and deliberate thought about something that involves ideas or opinions rather than definite facts. EG *The intention was to distract prisoners from any prolonged reflection upon their wretched condition... Furious flashes of light jolted me out of my reflections... 'You ought to take it,' she said, after a moment's reflection.* N UNCOUNT/COUNT, SING=PL = meditation ● You say **on reflection** to indicate that you have thought very carefully about the various factors involved in a situation. EG *I suppose, on reflection, there is something immoral about it... I was astounded, but on reflection it seems to me that he didn't really have much alternative.* ● PHR : USED AS ADV SEN

3 A **reflection** is also a comment or thought that expresses your ideas about something. EG *It has aroused all kinds of philosophical reflections on work-sharing... Console yourself with the reflection that you are not the only one.* N COUNT : USU+SUPP

reflective /rɪˈflektɪv/. **1** If you are **reflective**, you are thinking in a slow, quiet way about something which involves ideas or opinions rather than definite facts. EG *It was a thoughtful and reflective Air Marshal who flew the remaining few miles.* ADJ QUALIT = pensive ▸ used also to describe people's behaviour. EG *She took a reflective draught from her glass.* ▸ = pensive ◇ **reflectively**. EG *Barney scratched his chin reflectively.* ◇ ADV WITH VB

2 If something is **reflective** of a particular situation or idea, it has qualities that make it typical of that situation or idea; a formal use. EG *These comments by Joy and Lester were reflective of the general attitude.* ADJ QUALIT : PRED+*of* = indicative

3 Something that is **reflective** causes light, heat, or other rays to bounce back as soon as they reach its surface. EG *...a special reflective jacket.* ADJ CLASSIF ⇑ shiny

reflector /rɪˈflektə/, **reflectors**. A **reflector** is **1** a small piece of specially patterned glass or plastic which is fitted to the back of a bicycle or car or to a post beside the road, and which glows when light shines on it. N COUNT ⇑ safety device **2** a type of telescope which has a spherical mirror; a technical term. N COUNT

reflex /riːfleks/, **reflexes**. **1** A **reflex** is a sudden and uncontrollable movement made by a part of your body, which is caused by pressure or a blow that affects a particular nerve. EG *The doctor checked my reflexes and could find nothing wrong... This is the normal reflex action which occurs during breast-feeding.* N COUNT ⇑ response **2** your ability to act quickly when something unexpected happens, for example when you are driving a car. EG *She had incredible reflexes, like some quick little grasshopper... All the old men had slow reflexes and diminished sight.* N PLURAL ⇑ response **3** something that you do or say immediately and without thinking about it whenever you have a particular kind of experience. EG *'No!' I interrupted as an instant reflex. 'Please don't.'... ...a bitter smile that was a reflex to almost all news of disaster.* N COUNT ⇑ response

reflexive /rɪˈfleksɪv/. **1** An action or movement that is **reflexive** is done immediately as a result of something happening. EG *It was a purely reflexive move on his part.* ADJ CLASSIF ⇑ reactive ◇ **reflexively**. EG *Reflexively, he stepped backwards.* ◇ ADV WITH VB

reflexive pronoun, reflexive pronouns. In grammar, a **reflexive pronoun** is one which refers back to the subject of a sentence or clause. For example, in the sentence 'you'll just have to do it yourself', the reflexive pronoun 'yourself' refers back to 'you'. N COUNT

reflexive verb, reflexive verbs. In grammar, a **reflexive verb** is a transitive verb in which the subject and object are the same person or thing. The object is always a reflexive pronoun. For example in the sentence 'He introduced himself', the object of the verb, 'himself', refers to the subject of the verb, 'he'. N COUNT

reforest /riːfɒrɪˀst/, **reforests, reforesting, reforested**. To **reforest** an area that no longer has any trees on it means to plant trees there in order to make a forest. EG *The government is making strenuous efforts to reforest the hills.* V+O ⇑ cultivate ◇ **reforestation** /riːfɒrɪˀsteɪʃəⁿn/. EG *Independent landowners took decisive steps towards reforestation.* ◇ N UNCOUNT

reform /rɪˈfɔːm/, **reforms, reforming, reformed**. **1 Reform** is a set of changes and improvements to something such as a law, a social system, or an institution. EG *He called for the reform of the divorce laws... I was in favour of social reform... ...the task of carrying through the necessary reforms.* N UNCOUNT/COUNT ⇑ change ● See also **land reform**.

2 To **reform** something such as a law, a social system, or an institution means to improve it by making changes. EG *...a serious attempt at reforming our assessment methods... ...proposals to reform the Labour Party... It is high time that the legal profession reformed itself.* V+O (NG/REFL) ◇ **reformation** /refəmeɪʃəⁿn/. EG *Lord Fulton proposed the reformation of the whole of the Civil Service.* ◇ N UNCOUNT

3 When someone **reforms** or when something **reforms** them, they stop doing something that society does not approve of, such as stealing or drinking too much alcohol, and they start to live differently. EG *You have had every chance to reform... Punishment and prison sentences cannot reform the criminal.* V-ERG ⇑ convert ◇ **reformed**. EG *...a reformed alcoholic.* ◇ ADJ CLASSIF

4 Reform is also the change that occurs in someone's way of life when they stop doing something that society does not approve of, such as stealing or drinking too much alcohol. EG *We should substitute ideas of reform and readjustment for the idea of punishment.* N UNCOUNT ⇑ correction = improvement

re-form /riːfɔːm/, **re-forms, re-forming, re-formed**. When something such as a pattern or organization **re-forms** or when someone **re-forms** it, they create it again after it has spent some time in a different form. EG *The group re-formed after the war.* V-ERG

reformer /rɪˈfɔːmə/, **reformers**. A **reformer** is a person who tries to improve something such as a law or a social system. EG *His early experiences turned him into a passionate social reformer.* N COUNT ⇑ philanthropist

reformist /rɪˈfɔːmɪst/, **reformists**. **Reformist** ideas, activities, or people are involved in trying to bring about reforms. EG *...the Government's adoption of reformist policies.* ADJ QUALIT : USU ATTRIB ▸ used of people. EG *...reformists like Benn.* ▸ N COUNT

refract /rɪˈfrækt/, **refracts, refracting, refracted**. When a ray of light or a sound wave **refracts** or when something **refracts** it, the path it follows bends at a particular point, for example where it enters water or glass. EG *...a soft flow of reflected and refracted light.* V-ERG : USU PASS ◇ **refraction** /rɪˈfrækʃəⁿn/. EG *The colours are separated by refraction.* ◇ N UNCOUNT

refractory /rɪˈfræktəⁿriˈ/. Someone who is **refractory** is stubborn and very difficult to work with or control; a formal word. EG *The whole enterprise revolves round a refractory individual genius like Frank.* ADJ QUALIT

refrain /rɪˈfreɪn/, **refrains, refraining, refrained**. **1** If you **refrain** from doing something, you deliberately do not do it, even though you would like to do it or had intended to do it; a slightly formal use. EG *I carefully refrained from looking at him... They both refrained from direct association with the president... Mr Greenfield almost sighed, but refrained.* V : IF+PREP THEN *from* = abstain, forbear

2 A **refrain** is **2.1** a short, simple part of a song, which you repeat many times when you sing the song. N COUNT = chorus **2.2** a comment or saying that someone often repeats to you. EG *'Make yourself useful, Mary,' had been a refrain from her childhood.* N COUNT

refresh /rɪˈfreʃ/, **refreshes, refreshing, refreshed**. **1** If something **refreshes** you when you have become hot or tired, it makes you feel cool or energetic again. EG *I do not think I have ever been so refreshed by a fortnight away.* V+O ◇ **refreshed**. EG *These trains are so luxurious that you can end a long journey feeling positively refreshed.* ◇ ADJ QUALIT : USU PRED

2 If you **refresh** yourself, you do something which will make you feel better after you have been uncomfortably hot or tired. EG *We were only too grateful when playtime came and we could refresh ourselves with a cup of tea.* V+O (REFL) = revive

3 If you **refresh** something, you make it seem as good and fresh as when it was new; a literary use. EG *We struggle to refresh our imagery, to keep it up-to-date... They try to widen and refresh their experience.* V+O = renew

4 If someone **refreshes your memory** about something, they tell you something that you have forgotten. PHR : VB AND N INFLECTS ⇑ remind

refresher course, refresher courses. A **refresher course** is a training course in which people improve their knowledge or skills and learn about new developments relating to the job that they do. N COUNT

refreshing /rɪ¹frɛʃɪŋ/. Something that is **refreshing** 1 is pleasantly different from what you are used to. EG *It was a refreshing change for her to meet a woman executive... I found a refreshing absence of industrial sprawl.* ◊ **refreshingly.** EG *The plot is refreshingly intelligent and original.* 2 has the effect of making you feel energetic or cool again after you have been uncomfortably tired or hot. EG *He enjoyed the refreshing swims in the nearby creek.* ADJ QUALIT = welcome; ◊ ADV; ADJ QUALIT = reviving

refreshment /rɪ¹frɛʃmə²nt/, **refreshments.** 1 **Refreshments** are drinks and often small amounts of food that are provided, for example during a meeting or a journey. EG *There was a stop for refreshments between Coalmont and Ramsdale... Will there be a refreshment bar?* N PLURAL ⇑ sustenance

2 **Refreshment** is 2.1 food and drink; a literary use. EG *Should you not come into the house for some refreshment?* 2.2 the process of refreshing yourself, especially by eating or drinking something. EG *He needs to stop fairly often for refreshment... He wanted a little refreshment.* N UNCOUNT = sustenance; N UNCOUNT

refrigerate /rɪ¹frɪdʒəreɪt/, **refrigerates, refrigerating, refrigerated.** If you **refrigerate** food, you make it very cold in order to preserve it. EG *Milk can be kept 3 days if it is well refrigerated.* ◊ **refrigeration** /rɪ¹frɪdʒərɛɪʃə⁰n/. EG *They had no air-conditioning and no refrigeration.* V+O : USU PASS ⇑ cool; ◊ N UNCOUNT

refrigerator /rɪ¹frɪdʒəreɪtə/, **refrigerators.** A **refrigerator** is a large container which is kept cool inside, usually by electricity, so that food and drink which you keep in it stays fresh. EG *Brody reached into the refrigerator and pulled out a beer.* N COUNT = fridge

refuel /riːfjuəl/, **refuels, refuelling, refuelled**; also spelled **refueling** and **refueled** in American English. 1 When an aircraft **refuels** or **is refuelled**, it is filled with more fuel so that it can continue its journey. EG *Concorde needs to refuel on flights of above 3,500 miles.* V-ERG ⇑ fuel

2 If something **refuels** your feelings or emotions, it makes them stronger. EG *Their shares inexplicably jumped 10p to 114p, refuelling speculation of a possible takeover.* V+O ⇑ renew

refuge /rɛfjuːdʒ/, **refuges.** 1 **Refuge** is 1.1 protection from unhappiness or unpleasantness which you hope to get from being in a particular situation or taking part in a particular activity. EG *He seeks refuge in silence... One must be careful not to take refuge in delusion.* 1.2 protection against something that is unpleasant or threatening, such as bad weather or danger. EG *I ran into the refuge of the crowd... Marie was entirely alone, without friends or refuge.* N UNCOUNT = sanctuary; N UNCOUNT = safety, shelter

2 A **refuge** is 2.1 a place where you can go for safety and protection. EG *A small cave was the only refuge from the cold.* 2.2 a place which gives accommodation and help to women who have suffered violence from their husbands. EG *More women who have been in refuges are now involved in local groups.* N COUNT : USU SING; N COUNT ⇑ hostel

3 If you **take refuge** somewhere, you go there because it is safe and you will feel protected there. EG *Whole families had taken refuge down the tunnels.* PHR : VB INFLECTS, USU+A ⇑ shelter

refugee /rɛfju⁴dʒiː/, **refugees.** A **refugee** is someone who has been forced to leave their country because there is a war or because of their political or religious beliefs. EG *...50,000 refugees from the war zone... ...a massive influx of refugees from neighbouring countries... ...a refugee camp.* N COUNT

refund /riːfʌnd/, **refunds, refunding, refunded.** 1 A **refund** is a sum of money which is returned to you, for example because you have paid someone too much money or because you have returned goods to a shop. EG *...a tax refund.* N COUNT = repayment

2 If you **refund** money to someone, you return it to them, for example because they have paid you too much for something. EG *At first I used to refund people their money, I felt so sorry for them... The shop should refund the twelve dollars.* V+O, V+O+O, OR V+O+A *(to)* = pay back

refurbish /riːfɜːbɪʃ/, **refurbishes, refurbishing, refurbished.** To **refurbish** a building or room means to clean it and decorate it and make it more attractive; a formal word. EG *The city's museum was being refurbished.* V+O = renovate

refusal /rɪ¹fjuːzə⁰l/, **refusals.** 1 Someone's **refusal** to do something is their behaviour and attitude when they deliberately choose not to do it. EG *In all his films we see his refusal to create outright villains... The curious national hypocrisy that involved a refusal to admit that people bet at all.* N UNCOUNT + to-INF

2 A **refusal** is 2.1 an act of saying or showing that you will not do what someone has asked you to do or ordered you to do. EG *...the refusal of the factory workers to use forklift trucks... I shook my head in adamant refusal.* 2.2 an act of refusing to give or grant something, such as your permission. EG *All appeals for aid met with bureaucratic refusal... My search for a job involved me in many applications and many refusals.* 2.3 an act of not accepting something that has been offered to you. EG *His refusal of a peerage caused the Prime Minister some embarrassment.* N COUNT/UNCOUNT ⇑ rejection; N COUNT/UNCOUNT ⇑ rejection; N UNCOUNT : IF+ PREP THEN *of* = spurning

3 If you give someone **first refusal** on something you are selling, you allow them to decide whether they want to buy it before you offer it to anyone else. PHR : USED AS O

refuse, refuses, refusing, refused. The word **refuse** is pronounced /rɪfjuːz/ when it is a verb, and /rɛfjuːs, -uːz/ when it is a noun. 1 If you **refuse** to do something 1.1 you deliberately choose not to do it. EG *The French refused to consider the proposal... He refused to accept the political advice which was offered... Their bosses refuse to allow them any responsibility.* 1.2 you say firmly that you will not do it. EG *I refuse to believe that it can't be done... Three employees were dismissed for refusing to join a union.* V OR V+to-INF = decline, resist; V OR V+to-INF ⇑ decline

2 If someone **refuses** you something, they use their authority over you to prevent you from having it. EG *The Council refused permission for them to live together... He was refused burial in consecrated ground... Only the president could refuse him a loan.* V+O+O, OR V+O : USU+A = deny

3 If you **refuse** something that is offered to you, you choose not to accept it. EG *I offered him wine but he refused it... It was an offer Lever felt he couldn't refuse.* V+O = decline, reject

4 **Refuse** is all the things that are not wanted in a house, shop, or factory, and that are regularly thrown away. EG *It has evolved from a dump for ordinary refuse into the largest toxic waste dump in Britain... This department is also responsible for refuse collection.* N UNCOUNT = rubbish, garbage, trash

refute /rɪ¹fjuːt/, **refutes, refuting, refuted.** If you **refute** something such as a theory or argument, you prove that it is wrong; a formal word. EG *The argument cannot be refuted at the moment... This piece of evidence would have refuted the charge of his main accuser.* ◊ **refutation** /rɛfjuːtɛɪʃə⁰n/, **refutations.** EG *For a long time there was neither confirmation nor refutation of these speculations... He produced an emphatic and written refutation by Horder.* V+O = disprove, rebut; ◊ N UNCOUNT/COUNT : IF+ PREP THEN *of* ⇑ negation

regain /rɪ¹geɪn/, **regains, regaining, regained.** 1 If you **regain** a desirable condition or state, you succeed in returning to it after a period during which you have been in a less desirable condition or state. EG *He never fully regained his health... I did my best to regain my composure... He never regained political power.* V+O = recover

2 If you **regain** a safe or familiar place, you succeed in arriving there after you have been lost or in danger; a formal use. EG *She turned and went back down the lane to regain the main road... We were thankful to regain the shore.* V+O

regal /riːgə⁰l/. Something that is **regal** belongs to a king or queen, or is considered suitable for a king or queen, usually because it is very splendid or magnificent. EG *...his regal suite in the Palace Hotel... ...a regal staircase leading into a vast reception hall.* ADJ QUALIT = royal

regale /rɪ¹geɪl/, **regales, regaling, regaled.** If you **regale** someone with stories, jokes, etc, you tell them a lot of stories or jokes, even if they do not want you to. EG *I used to have a dentist who regaled me with extraordinary stories.* V+O+A *(with)*

regalia /rɪ¹geɪlɪə/ refers to all the traditional clothes and items which someone such as a king or a judge wears or carries on official occasions; a formal word. EG *...a Judge of the Supreme Court in full regalia.* N UNCOUNT ⇑ costume

regard /rɪ¹gɑːd/, **regards, regarding, regarded.** 1 If you **regard** someone or something as being a particular thing or as having a particular quality, you believe that they are that thing or that they have that quality. EG *I regard it as one of my master-* V+O (NG/REFL) +A *(as)* ⇑ see = consider *pieces... Parents were still regarded as being responsible for the control of their children... She now regarded herself as a woman.*

2 If you **regard** something or someone with a particular feeling such as dislike or respect, you have that particular feeling for them. EG *He is regarded with some suspicion by the country's leaders... His visitors regarded him with a mixture of contempt, envy, and hope... They found that they were not regarded so highly or so positively by their teachers.* ◊ **regarded.** EG *The more highly regarded cameramen were kept very busy.*

V+O+A (USU *with*) = view
◊ ADJ QUALIT : ONLY ADV+ADJ

3 Regard for someone or something is a feeling of respect that you have for them. EG *My regard for him grew day by day... I have a high regard for Mike.*

N UNCOUNT : USU +*for* = esteem

4 If you say that something **regards** a particular subject, you mean that it is about that subject; a formal use. EG *The next item regards the state of the company's finances.*

V+O = concern

5 Regards is used in expressions like 'best regards' and 'with warm regards' as an informal way of expressing friendly sentiments towards someone, at the end of a letter, or when you are saying goodbye to someone. EG *Give my regards to your daughter... Hope to see you soon. With warm regards, Patricia.*

N PLURAL : USU POSS/MOD+N = good wishes

6 If you **hold** someone or something **in high regard**, you have a great deal of respect for them.

PHR : VB INFLECTS

7 If you **hold** someone or something **in low regard**, you do not have any respect for them.

PHR : VB INFLECTS

8 You say **with regard to** or **in regard to** a particular subject to state that what you are saying or writing is concerned with that subject; a fairly formal expression. EG *With regard to the gasfire, we hardly use it... My upbringing was fairly strict in regard to obedience and truthfulness.*

PREP = regarding

9 You can use **in this regard** or **in that regard** when what you are about to say is closely connected with the previous thing you have said; used in fairly formal English. EG *In this regard, the child may be thought of as having two homes.*

ADV SEN

10 You use **as regards** to say what you are talking or writing about. EG *In my opinion, she was no artist at all as regards dancing... As regards the car, I didn't forget to put an advertisement in the paper... His position as regards the report had been misunderstood.*

PREP = regarding

regarding /rɪˈgɑːdɪŋ/. You use **regarding** to say what you are talking or writing about. EG *There was always some question regarding education.*

PREP

regardless /rɪˈgɑːdlɪˀs/. **1** If you do something or if something happens **regardless of** a particular factor, you do it or it happens despite this factor, which is often a difficulty of some sort. EG *If they are determined to strike, they will do so regardless of what the law says.*

PREP ⇑ in spite of

2 If you say that someone did something **regardless,** you mean that they did it even though there were problems or factors which could have stopped them. EG *The injury was giving him great pain, but he carried on regardless.*

ADV AFTER VB

regatta /rɪgætə/, **regattas.** A **regatta** is a sports event consisting of races between yachts or rowing boats.

N COUNT : ALSO IN NAMES

regency /riːdʒənsiˈ/, **regencies. 1 Regency** is used to refer to the period in Britain at the beginning of the nineteenth century and to the style of architecture, literature, etc, that was popular at the time. EG *The house itself was full of family portraits and Regency furniture.*

ADJ CLASSIF : USU ATTRIB ⇑ Georgian

2 A **regency** is a period of time during which a country is governed by a regent.

N COUNT

regenerate /riˈdʒenəreɪt/, **regenerates, regenerating, regenerated.** To **regenerate** a place or a system means to develop and improve it and make it more active, successful, or important, especially after a period when it has been declining; a formal word. EG *We are looking for ways in which community participation could help regenerate the inner cities.* ◊ **regeneration** /riˈdʒenəreɪʃəⁿn/. EG *...the goal of economic regeneration... ...a regeneration of local democracy.*

V+O = revitalize, revive
◊ N UNCOUNT = revival

regenerative /riˈdʒenəˀrətɪv/. **Regenerative** actions, processes, etc, cause something to become more active, successful, or important again; a formal word.

ADJ CLASSIF = revitalizing

regent /riːdʒənt/, **regents**; also spelled with a capital letter. A **regent** is a person who rules a country when the king or queen is unable to rule, for example because they are too young or too ill. EG *She visited the Regent of Hungary... ...an estate designed for the Prince Regent.*

N COUNT : ALSO IN TITLES

reggae /regeɪ/ is a kind of West Indian popular music which has a very strong beat. EG *The record shows strong reggae influence.*

N UNCOUNT

regicide /redʒɪsaɪd/, **regicides**; a formal word. **1** A **regicide** is a person who kills a king.

N COUNT

2 Regicide is the act of killing a king.

N UNCOUNT

regime /reɪʒiːm/, **regimes**; also spelled **régime**. If you refer to a **regime**, you are talking about **1** a system or method of government; often used showing disapproval. EG *...a socialist 'Welfare State' regime... A regime where decision making is shared by all.* **2** a group of people who rule a country; often used showing disapproval. EG *...the corrupt and ignorant regime that had ruled since 1921... ...an attempt to overthrow the regime.*

N COUNT : USU+SUPP ⇑ management
N COUNT : USU+SUPP ⇑ government

3 A **regime** is also the same as a regimen; a formal use. EG *From now on you must keep to a really strict regime.*

N COUNT : USU+SUPP = regimen

regimen /redʒɪmen/, **regimens.** A **regimen** is a set of rules about food and exercise that some people follow in order to stay healthy; a formal word. EG *He kept to his prescribed regimen.*

N COUNT = regime

regiment /redʒɪməˀnt/, **regiments. 1** A **regiment** is a large group of soldiers usually under the command of a colonel. EG *...an infantry regiment... ...the Third Essex Regiment.*

N COUNT : ALSO IN NAMES AFTER N ⇑ army

2 A **regiment** of people or things is a large number of them. EG *They recruited a whole new regiment of messengers... Our bodies are equipped with whole regiments of different types of special cells.*

N PART+N IN PL ⇑ group

regimental /redʒɪmentəⁿl/ means belonging to a particular regiment. EG *They took their orders from the regimental commander.*

ADJ CLASSIF : ATTRIB

regimentation /redʒɪmenteɪʃəⁿn/ is very strict control over a group of people; used showing disapproval. EG *...the obstacles presented by social chaos or social regimentation.*

N UNCOUNT

regimented /redʒɪmentɪˀd/. Something that is **regimented** is very strictly controlled; used showing disapproval. EG *...the regimented life-style of the industrial world.*

ADJ QUALIT

region /riːdʒən/, **regions. 1** A **region** is **1.1** a large area of land with definite boundaries, which is one of the parts of a country that has been divided up for administrative purposes. EG *The country has nine autonomous regions... Fighting in the Central Region had developed during the last few days.* **1.2** a large area of land which has no definite boundaries but which has some feature or quality that makes it different from other areas. EG *...a humble priest in a small country region.*

N COUNT ⇑ division
N COUNT

2 The **regions** are all the parts of a country except the part where the capital is situated. EG *Now for our latest reports on unemployment in the regions.*

N PLURAL : USU *the*+N = the provinces

3 You can use **region** to refer to an area of knowledge, a part of a discussion, or a field of activity that you are talking about. EG *...and here we enter a region of moral ambiguity... To have access to the truth and so to pass beyond the region of mere opinion is to take great risks.*

N COUNT+SUPP = realm

4 You can use **region** to refer to a part of your body, for example when you want to indicate where you have a pain. EG *He was complaining of pains in the shoulder region.*

N COUNT+SUPP

5 You can use **in the region of** to indicate that a measurement or price that you are stating is only an approximate one. EG *...temperatures would be in the region of 500 degrees centigrade... It was going to be in the region of fifteen to thirty years before the debt would be paid off.*

PREP = about, roughly

regional /riːdʒəⁿnəl, -dʒənəⁿl/. **1 Regional** organizations and activities are involved in the administration of a particular region. EG *Most regional committees meet four times a year... Apply to your local Regional Hospital Board for details.*

ADJ CLASSIF : ALSO IN NAMES BEFORE N ⇑ area

2 Something that is **regional** belongs to, is typical of, or occurs only in a particular part of a country which is away from the capital. EG *She had a strong regional accent.*

ADJ CLASSIF = provincial

regionalism /riːdʒəⁿnəlɪzəⁿm, -dʒənəⁿlɪzəⁿm/ is a strong feeling of pride or loyalty that people in a region have for that region, often including a desire to have more power to govern themselves, or some-

N UNCOUNT = federalism

times the desire to be a separate country; a formal word.

register /rɛdʒɪstə/, **registers, registering, registered**. 1 A **register** is 1.1 an official list or record of names, objects, events, etc. EG *The teacher marks the register at the beginning of the lesson... ...the electoral register... ...the parish register of births, marriages, and deaths.* N COUNT ⇑ inventory 1.2 in American English, a machine in a shop, bar, or restaurant that is used to add up and record how much money people pay, and in which the money is kept. EG *He rang up the sale on the register.* N COUNT ⇑ till = cash register 1.3 a style of speaking or writing that is used in particular circumstances or social situations. N COUNT/UNCOUNT+SUPP 1.4 the range of a person's voice or of a musical instrument, from the lowest to the highest notes that it can reach. N SING WITH DET/POSS

2 When you **register**, you put your name on an official list, for example to enable you to receive a particular service. EG *We must register for work at the employment agency first... Have you registered at the hotel yet?... They're coming to register as students on the English course... He had failed to register with the local health centre.* V: USU+A ⇑ enrol ◊ **registered**. EG *...a registered childminder... ...a registered drug addict.* ◊ ADJ CLASSIF: ATTRIB = certified

3 If you **register** something, such as the name of someone who has just died, or the details of ownership of your car, you have these facts recorded on an official list. EG *One of the cars was registered in my name.* V+O: USU+A

4 When an amount or measurement **registers** or when something **registers** it, the amount or measurement is shown on a scale or recording instrument. EG *The inflation index registered a modest 7.8% annual rate... It was such a small amount that it didn't register on our machine.* V-ERG

5 If someone **registers** something such as a victory or a success, they achieve it, for example in an election or other contest; a rather formal or literary use. EG *The Party would probably register a significant advance in the forthcoming elections... England registered their first win of the competition last night.* V+O ⇑ gain = record

6 If you **register** your feelings or opinions about something, 6.1 you do something which is intended to let other people know exactly what you feel or think. EG *Thousands joined the march to register their opposition to the cuts in education.* V+O ⇑ express 6.2 they are clearly visible to other people because of the expression on your face. EG *He stared at me for a moment, his face registering disbelief... Smithy registered surprise, then shook his head.* V+O ⇑ show

7 If you say that a piece of information did not **register**, you mean that when you told it to someone, they did not really pay attention to what you were saying and may not remember it; an informal use. EG *I told them I would be leaving, but I don't think it registered.* V: USU WITH BROAD NEG = sink in

8 If you **register** a letter or parcel, you send it by a special form of postal service, for which you pay an extra amount to insure it in case it is not delivered. EG *If you're sending it through the post, it would be a good idea to register it.* V+O ◊ **registered**. EG *...a registered letter... ...registered mail.* ◊ ADJ CLASSIF: ATTRIB

register office, register offices. In Britain, a **register office** is the same as a registry office; an official term. N COUNT

registrar /rɛdʒɪstrɑː/, **registrars**. A **registrar** is 1 a person whose job is to keep official records, especially of births, marriages, and deaths. N COUNT 2 a senior administrative official in a college or university. N COUNT 3 a senior hospital doctor. N COUNT

registration /rɛdʒɪstreɪʃəⁿn/ is the recording of something such as a person's name or the details of an event in an official list or record. EG *...a certificate of registration of death... If the company's total income is over a certain amount, registration for VAT is compulsory.* N UNCOUNT ⇑ notification

registration number, registration numbers. A **registration number** is the series of letters and numbers that are shown at the front and back of a car or other road vehicle; used mainly in British English. N COUNT

registry /rɛdʒɪstri¹/, **registries**. A **registry** is a place where official records are kept. N COUNT ⇑ office

registry office, registry offices. A **registry office** is an office where births, marriages, and deaths are officially recorded, and where people can get married without a religious ceremony. N COUNT

regress /ri¹grɛs/, **regresses, regressing, regressed**; a formal word. If someone or something **regresses**, they return to a worse condition or way of life; a formal word. EG *She had to get out of this place before she regressed to infancy.* V: IF+PREP THEN *to* ⇑ degenerate ▸ used as a noun. EG *What was progress in modern society was regress for the individual.* ▸ N UNCOUNT

regression /ri¹grɛʃəⁿn/ is the process of changing back to a worse condition or way of life; a formal word. EG *We must beware of regression to authoritarianism.* N UNCOUNT: IF+PREP THEN *to* = reversion

regressive /ri¹grɛsɪv/. Behaviour, activities, or processes that are **regressive** are likely to cause a return to a worse condition or way of life; a formal word. EG *This kind of behaviour has been frowned upon as regressive and immature.* ADJ QUALIT ⇑ backward

regret /rɪ¹grɛt/, **regrets, regretting, regretted**. 1 If you **regret** something that has happened or something that you have done, you feel sorry and wish that you had not done it or that it had not happened. EG *I immediately regretted my decision... It made me regret that my student days are over... He regretted what he had said... Afterwards he regretted having spoken to them about it.* V+O/REPORT-CL/-ING = rue

2 **Regret** is a feeling of sadness, disappointment, or anger with yourself, which is caused by something that has happened or something that you have done. EG *Joe felt a sudden pang of regret... We informed them with regret of our decision... Linda has no regrets at having become a City banker.* N UNCOUNT, OR N COUNT: SING=PL ⇑ sorrow

3 If you say that you **regret** a particular situation, you are politely saying that you are sorry about it because you know that the people you are speaking to or writing to will not be pleased by it. EG *London Transport regrets any inconvenience caused by these repairs... Later, I regret to say, rents went up... The notice said 'Dr Beamish has a cold and regrets he cannot meet his classes today.'* V+O/REPORT-CL/*to*-INF: NO CONT

regretful /rɪ¹grɛtful/. If a person or their behaviour is **regretful**, they show that they feel regret about something. EG *He is neither proud nor regretful about what happened... He cast a last regretful glance toward the entrance.* ADJ QUALIT ⇑ sad = rueful ◊ **regretfully**. EG *He shook his head regretfully.* ◊ ADV WITH VB ⇑ sadly

regrettable /rɪ¹grɛtəbəⁿl/. Something that is **regrettable** is considered to be unfortunate and causes feelings of sadness or disapproval. EG *...the regrettable manifestations of cruelty to children... His tiredness caused him to make a regrettable error.* ADJ QUALIT

regrettably /rɪ¹grɛtəbli¹/. **Regrettably** is used 1 when you want to emphasize that something is true or exists to an extent that is unfortunate or unwelcome. EG *Regrettably few of them, if indeed any, have gone to university.* ADV+ADJ/ADV ⇑ very 2 when you want to say that a particular fact or situation is considered to be unfortunate or regrettable. EG *Regrettably, it is not an easy plant to grow in this country.* ADV SEN = sadly, unfortunately

regroup /riːgruːp/, **regroups, regrouping, regrouped**. When people **regroup** or when someone **regroups** them, they arrange themselves into a group again. EG *They regrouped and were ordered to open fire.* V-ERG ⇑ reorganize

regular /rɛgjə¹lə/, **regulars**. 1 Something that is **regular** 1.1 exists or occurs in a simple pattern or arrangement in which events happen or objects are placed with equal amounts of time or space between them. EG *He could hear her deep, regular breathing... The doctor examined the baby at regular intervals... There were regular lines of holes between the side windows.* ADJ QUALIT ⇑ even ◊ **regularly**. EG *A row of regularly spaced cabbages.* ◊ ADV WITH VB 1.2 has an even shape, with lines or parts that are equal in size or well-balanced in appearance. EG *The face was sun-tanned, with regular features... It's easy to draw because it's such a regular shape.* ADJ QUALIT = symmetrical

2 **Regular** events or activities happen 2.1 according to a definite arrangement or plan, for example so that they happen at the same time each day or week. EG *The orchestra was tuning up for its regular Sunday afternoon concert... You need to take regular exercise... Safety checks are made on a regular basis.* ADJ QUALIT ◊ **regularly**. EG *The members meet regularly in one another's homes.* ◊ ADV WITH VB 2.2 often, and over a long period of time. EG *Police made snap searches of passers-by after one of the regular bombings.* ADJ QUALIT

◇ **regularly**. EG *Local poverty is so acute that children are regularly abandoned.*
◇ ADV WITH VB = repeatedly

3 **Regular** customers, visitors, etc, go to the same shop or visit the same place frequently . EG *About ten per cent of the population are regular churchgoers... ...one of our regular customers.*
ADJ QUALIT : ATTRIB ⇑ habitual

4 **Regular** times, places, conditions, etc, are ones which are considered to be usual or normal. EG *It's past his regular bedtime... You can get in touch with a psychiatrist through your regular doctor.*
ADJ CLASSIF : ATTRIB

5 A **regular** verb, noun, or adjective inflects in the same way as most other verbs, nouns, or adjectives in the language.
ADJ CLASSIF ⇑ standard

6 **Regular** soldiers or troops work permanently in the armed forces, in contrast with people who are doing a short period of compulsory military service or have volunteered to fight during a war. EG *He had been a captain commanding a regular Marine company... ...a regular officer.*
ADJ CLASSIF : ATTRIB ⇑ permanent

7 You can use **regular** to emphasize that something is happening to a greater degree than was expected or than is usual; an informal use. EG *This is turning into a regular epidemic.*
ADJ CLASSIF : ATTRIB = veritable

8 Someone who is **regular** defecates every day and does not suffer from constipation; also used of women who menstruate at evenly-spaced intervals; used in informal English, for example by nurses, doctors, or parents of small children.
ADJ CLASSIF : PRED

9 A **regular** is **9.1** a person who goes somewhere or does something often, for example someone who is often a customer at the same shop or pub. EG *He was one of my regulars at the pub where I worked last year.* **9.2** a full-time professional member of one of the armed forces. EG *There were several reserve units manned by former regulars.*
N COUNT; N COUNT ⇑ serviceman

regularity /rɛgjəˈlærɪti¹/, **regularities. Regularity** is a state or situation in which things happen repeatedly, often according to a definite plan. EG *The same exam questions cropped up with unfailing regularity... They felt that all the regularities in nature have a purpose.*
N UNCOUNT/ COUNT

regularize /rɛgjəˈləraɪz/, **regularizes, regularizing, regularized**; also spelled **regularise**. To **regularize** something means to cause it to have a regular pattern or arrangement, often so that it can be given official approval or recognition. EG *Their status and area of work is thereby regularized.*
V+O : USU PASS

regulate /rɛgjəˈleɪt/, **regulates, regulating, regulated**. 1 To **regulate** an activity or process means to control it, usually by means of rules or laws. EG *The volume of economic activity was regulated by the supply of money... ...a body of rigid rules regulating all aspects of life.* ◇ **regulated**. EG *His life was too well regulated to be affected by affairs of the heart.*
V+O = govern; ◇ ADJ QUALIT = ordered

2 If you **regulate** a machine or device, you adjust it slightly in order to control the way it operates. EG *Do you know how to regulate the boiler?*
V+O

regulation /rɛgjəˈleɪʃəⁿn/, **regulations**. 1 A **regulation** is a written rule made by a government or another authority which is intended to control the way something is made or done, or the way people are allowed to behave. EG *There are specific regulations governing these types of machines... You can't do that. It's against the regulations.*
N COUNT : USU PL

2 **Regulation** is the controlling of an activity or process, usually by means of rules or laws. EG *We don't believe in more regulation. We believe in less... ...stricter regulation over toxic waste disposal.*
N UNCOUNT

3 A **regulation** condition or state is one that is required by a particular law or rule. EG *He had the short regulation haircut of a policeman.*
ADJ CLASSIF : ATTRIB = statutory

4 **Regulation** items, clothing, etc, are the usual or expected ones in a particular situation, even though they are not required by any rules or laws. EG *A stocky man in the regulation pin-striped suit... She stubbed out her cigarette in the regulation ashtray.*
ADJ CLASSIF : ATTRIB = orthodox, statutory

regulator /rɛgjəˈleɪtə/, **regulators**. A **regulator** is a device that automatically controls something such as the temperature or humidity in a room. EG *He used this knowledge to design new plant growth regulators.*
N COUNT

regurgitate /rɪˈgɜːdʒɪteɪt/, **regurgitates, regurgitating, regurgitated**. 1 If you **regurgitate** food, you bring it back up from your stomach before it is digested. EG *The young feed on regurgitated food from the parent birds.*
V+O = disgorge

2 If you **regurgitate** ideas or facts, you express them in a way that indicates that you are merely quoting them from a book or repeating what a teacher has said, but have not really understood them yourself. EG *The student is expected to regurgitate an answer to the teacher.*
V+O ⇑ repeat

rehabilitate /riːhᵊəbɪlɪteɪt/, **rehabilitates, rehabilitating, rehabilitated**. 1 If you **rehabilitate** someone who has been in prison or someone who has been very ill, you help them to live a normal life again. EG *...women who had been imprisoned or rehabilitated... He used exercise programmes to rehabilitate heart-attack victims.* ◇ **rehabilitation** /riːhᵊəbɪlɪteɪʃəⁿn/. EG *...the rehabilitation of drug addicts... ...a rehabilitation centre.*
V+O; ◇ N UNCOUNT

2 If a government **rehabilitates** someone, it considers them to be acceptable again after a period during which it had rejected them or severely criticized them. EG *...rehabilitated dissidents.*
V+O = reinstate

3 If you **rehabilitate** a building or an area, you improve its condition so that it can be used again. EG *There was no money to rehabilitate Collindeane Tower.* ◇ **rehabilitation** /riːhᵊəbɪlɪteɪʃəⁿn/. EG *...the rehabilitation of old streets.*
V+O = restore; ◇ N UNCOUNT = restoration

rehash /riːhæʃ/, **rehashes, rehashing, rehashed**. 1 A **rehash** is something that you write or say in which you use ideas and facts which are not original, often merely rearranging them so that they appear to be new; used showing disapproval. EG *His new book seems to be just a rehash of one of his earlier ones.*
N COUNT : USU SING+*of* = reworking

2 If you **rehash** ideas or facts, you use them again but in a slightly different way so that your work appears to be original although it is not. EG *Later writers have rehashed Fort's material.*
V+O = rework

rehearsal /rɪˈhɜːsəⁿl/, **rehearsals**. A **rehearsal** is a practice performance of a play, a dance, or a piece of music which is intended as a preparation for a public performance. EG *She was always word-perfect at the first rehearsal... He used to sketch the actors during rehearsals.* ● See also **dress rehearsal**.
N COUNT/ UNCOUNT = run-through

rehearse /rɪˈhɜːs/, **rehearses, rehearsing, rehearsed**. 1 If you **rehearse** a play, dance, or piece of music, you practise it in preparation for a public performance. EG *The actors began to rehearse a few scenes... I was tempted to stay and hear this superb orchestra rehearse.*
V OR V+O = try out

2 If you **rehearse** something that you are going to say, you silently practise it by imagining that you are saying it. EG *She was secretly rehearsing various amusing ways of telling what had happened.*
V+O = try out

3 If you **rehearse** something, you repeat it in detail; a formal word. EG *These arguments have been rehearsed on many occasions.*
V+O = go over

rehouse /riːhaʊz/, **rehouses, rehousing, rehoused**. If someone **is rehoused**, they are provided with a different house to live in, especially one that is better than their previous one. EG *Young families are being rehoused in New Towns... He was responsible for rehousing them.*
V+O : USU PASS ⇑ accommodate

reign /reɪn/, **reigns, reigning, reigned**. 1 If something **reigns**, it is the most powerful or noticeable feature of a situation or period of time. EG *...peace has reigned in Europe... Violence reigned supreme... ...the smug sense of comfort which reigned over the town.*
V : USU+A ⇑ exist = prevail

2 The **reign** of something is the period of time during which it is extremely powerful or noticeable; a formal use. EG *...the reign of the dinosaurs.*
N SING WITH DET +*of* = rule

3 A **reign of terror** is a period during which there is a lot of violence and killing by people who are in a position of power.
PHR : USED AS S/C, *reign* INFLECTS

4 The **reign** of a king or queen is the period during which he or she rules. EG *...George III's long reign... ...the reign of Elizabeth I.*
N COUNT : WITH POSS

5 When kings or queens **reign**, they rule a country. EG *The emperor Chia Ching reigned from 1522 to 1566. ...the reigning monarch.*
V : USU+A

reigning /reɪnɪŋ/. The **reigning** champion of a contest or competition is the person who won it most recently at the time when you are talking or about which you are talking. EG *John McEnroe, the reigning champion, was beaten in the first round.*
ADJ CLASSIF : ATTRIB ⇑ current

reimburse /riːɪmbɜːs/, **reimburses, reimbursing, reimbursed**. If you **reimburse** someone for something, you pay back to them money they have spent or lost while doing some-
V+O, V+O+O, OR V+O+A = refund

thing for you or as a result of your wrong actions. EG *I have promised to reimburse her for the damage to her car.* ▸ used also of the money that they have spent or lost. EG *The cash would be reimbursed from central funds.*

reimbursement /riːɪmbɜːsmə²nt/ is the repayment to someone of money they have spent or lost while doing something for someone else or as a result of someone else's wrong actions. EG *Who do I see about reimbursement of travelling expenses?* N UNCOUNT = refund

rein /reɪn/, **reins, reining, reined.** 1 **Reins** are 1.1 two thin leather straps that you use for controlling a horse when you are riding it or when it is pulling a vehicle. The reins are fastened to the bridle on the horse's head and you hold the loose ends. EG *He made some noises to the horse, and pulled at the reins.* N PLURAL 1.2 thin straps that you use for controlling a young child who has just learned to walk. The reins are fastened to a harness round the child's body and you hold a loop or the loose ends. N PLURAL

2 If you **give a free rein to** someone, you give them a lot of freedom, especially freedom to decide how they are going to do a particular task. EG *He has given a free rein to the Security Service in their current investigations... He gave his army free rein to crush rebels.* PHR : VB INFLECTS

3 If you **keep a tight rein on** someone or something, you control that person or thing firmly. EG *We will have to keep a tight rein on expenditure in the next few months... Lynn kept a tight rein on herself while she related the tragic events.* PHR : VB INFLECTS

4 If someone has the **reins** of government or of power, they are in control of a country or an organization. EG *He had finally taken over the reins of government... He had assumed the reins of power, following a civil war.* N PLURAL : USU *the*+N+*of*+N UNCOUNT

rein in. If you **rein in** a horse, you stop it or cause it to go more slowly by pulling its reins. PHRASAL VB : V+O+ADV

reincarnate /riːɪŋ¹kɑːneɪt/, **reincarnates, reincarnating, reincarnated.** If you say that someone **is reincarnated**, you mean that they are born again after death and live in the body of another living creature. EG *People ask me what I want to be reincarnated as.* V+O : USU PASS ⇑ reborn = come back ◊ **reincarnated.** EG *At one time I thought I was Michelangelo reincarnated.* ◊ ADJ CLASSIF ⇑ reborn

reincarnation /riːɪŋ¹kɑːneɪʃə⁰n/, **reincarnations.** 1 **Reincarnation** is the belief that after death the soul of a person passes into the body of another living creature. EG *I believe in reincarnation.* N UNCOUNT ⇑ rebirth

2 A **reincarnation** is a person or animal in whose body a person who has died is born again. EG *They all regarded us as reincarnations of their ancestors.* N COUNT

reindeer /reɪndɪə/. **Reindeer** is both the singular and the plural form. A **reindeer** is a deer that has large antlers. Reindeer live in northern areas of Europe, Asia, and America. EG *...herds of reindeer.* N COUNT

reinforce /riːɪnfɔːs/, **reinforces, reinforcing, reinforced.** 1 If something **reinforces** a feeling, situation, or process, it strengthens it. EG *This sort of experience reinforces their feelings of worthlessness... Such conclusions may reinforce existing prejudices... They hope to reinforce their domination in these countries... This reinforces the trend towards equality.* V+O ⇑ increase = confirm

2 If something **reinforces** an idea or point of view, it provides more evidence or support for it and makes it more likely to be true or valid. EG *This report reinforces practically everything that has been said so far... This reinforces what you're saying.* V+O = back up

3 To **reinforce** a physical object means to make it stronger or harder. EG *They were manufacturers of reinforced helmets... I had not thought of reinforcing the handles with leather.* V+O : IF+PREP THEN *with* ⇑ strengthen

4 To **reinforce** an army means to make it stronger by providing it with more soldiers or more weapons. EG *They managed to hold on until the armies were reinforced.* V+O ⇑ strengthen

reinforced concrete is concrete that is made with pieces of metal inside it to make it stronger. EG *The old bridge was replaced by a new structure of reinforced concrete.* N UNCOUNT

reinforcement /riːɪnfɔːsmə²nt/, **reinforcements.** 1 **Reinforcements** are soldiers who are sent to join an army or part of an army in order to make it stronger. EG *News reached them of the safe arrival of reinforcements and supplies... More reinforcements were on the way.* N PLURAL ⇑ troops

2 **Reinforcement** is 2.1 the process of reinforcing an army or part of an army in order to make it stronger. EG *An attack could be made without the need for reinforcement.* N UNCOUNT ⇑ strengthening 2.2 the strengthening of a feeling or attitude that someone already has. EG *More legislation will only lead to a reinforcement of existing prejudices.* N UNCOUNT/COUNT = confirmation 2.3 something that is added to a material or an object in order to make it harder or stronger. N UNCOUNT/COUNT

reinstate /riːɪnsteɪt/, **reinstates, reinstating, reinstated**; a rather formal word. 1 If you **reinstate** someone, you give them back a job or position of power which had been taken from them. EG *He was four times sacked and four times reinstated.* V+O ⇑ restore

2 To **reinstate** something means to cause it to exist or be important again. EG *...threats to reinstate this tax... The trip reinstated my faith in myself.* V+O = restore

reinstatement /riːɪnsteɪtmə²nt/ is the act of giving someone back a job or position of power which had been taken from them; a rather formal word. N UNCOUNT

reissue /riːɪʃuː, -ɪsjuː/, **reissues, reissuing, reissued.** 1 A **reissue** is something such as a book or a record that is published or produced again after it has not been available to be bought or obtained for some time. N COUNT : USU SING ⇑ issue

2 To **reissue** something such as a book or record means to publish or produce it again after it has not been available to be bought or obtained for some time. EG *The writings of Jean Rhys have recently been reissued.* V+O ⇑ issue

reiterate /riːɪtəreɪt/, **reiterates, reiterating, reiterated.** If you **reiterate** something, you say it again, either once or several times; a formal word. EG *In the face of their attack Butler simply reiterated the government's position... The president was reiterating that if it became necessary he would dissolve Parliament and hold a general election.* V+O/REPORT-CL/QUOTE = restate

reiteration /riːɪtəreɪʃə⁰n/, **reiterations.** A **reiteration** is a repetition of something that you have already said; a formal word. EG *...the weary reiteration of the same old arguments.* N COUNT/UNCOUNT = restatement

reject, rejects, rejecting, rejected. The verb is pronounced /rɪ¹dʒɛkt/ and the noun is pronounced /riːdʒɛkt/. 1 If you **reject** a proposal or request, you say that you have definitely or officially decided not to agree to it. EG *The Labour Party rejected offers to discuss the reform of the House of Lords... The amendment was rejected by 207 votes to 143.* V+O = turn down ◊ **rejection** /riːdʒɛkʃə⁰n/, **rejections.** EG *...his rejection of persistent requests for military action.* ◊ N UNCOUNT/COUNT

2 If you **reject** something such as a belief or a political system, you decide that you do not believe in it and do not want to live by its rules. EG *It was hard for me to reject my family's religious beliefs... Some people reject the idea of a mixed economy.* V+O = spurn, dismiss ◊ **rejection.** EG *There had been a widespread rejection of many of the traditional processes of political participation.* ◊ N UNCOUNT : IF+PREP THEN *of/by* = dismissal

3 If an employer **rejects** a person who has applied for a job, that person is not offered the job. EG *Many candidates were rejected.* V+O = turn down ◊ **rejection, rejections.** EG *After a week he received his rejection letter.* ◊ N UNCOUNT/COUNT

4 If you **reject** someone who wants to marry you, you say that you will not marry them. EG *He was afraid she would reject him because he was a foreigner.* V+O = turn down ◊ **rejection.** EG *He decided not to approach her for fear of rejection.* ◊ N UNCOUNT ≠ acceptance

5 If you **reject** someone who expects love, affection, or kindness from you, such as a member of your family, your lover, or a friend, you behave towards them in a very cruel or hostile way, sometimes even refusing to accept them any longer as a part of your family or as your lover or friend. EG *...children rejected by their natural parents.* V+O = disown ◊ **rejection.** ◊ N UNCOUNT

6 If you **reject** an object that has just been made, you throw it away or do not accept it because it is imperfect. EG *We'll have to reject these. They've got little cracks in them.* V+O = scrap

7 If a person's body **rejects** something such as a new heart that has been put into it by surgery, it tries to attack it and destroy it with antibodies; a technical term in medicine. EG *In replacement surgery we may find the body rejecting foreign material.* V+O ≠ accept ◊ **rejection, rejections.** EG *There is always the risk of rejection with a heart transplant.* ◊ N UNCOUNT/COUNT ≠ acceptance

8 If something such as a machine **rejects** a coin, the V+O

coin does not make the machine work. EG *The phonebox often jammed, or rejected perfectly good coins.*

9 A **reject** is a product that has not been accepted for use, because something is wrong with it. EG *The rejects were stacked in a corner until they could be removed.* — N COUNT

rejoice /rɪˈdʒɔɪs/, **rejoices, rejoicing, rejoiced**; a rather formal or literary word. 1 If you **rejoice**, you are very pleased about something. EG *The bankers heard the news, and rejoiced... She rejoiced in her new-found independence... They rejoiced to see peace return to their country at last.* — V, V+A *(in)*, OR V +REPORT-CL/ *to*-INF ⇑ be delighted

2 If you say that someone or something **rejoices in the name of** or **title of** something, you mean that they are called that and you find it an unusual or amusing name or title, or an inaccurate or misleading name or title considering their actual function or activities. EG *...a fat individual rejoicing in the name of Frederick Crispin Harbottle.* — PHR : VB INFLECTS = be named

rejoicing /rɪˈdʒɔɪsɪŋ/, **rejoicings**. **Rejoicing** is behaviour in which a lot of people show great delight about something, usually in a noisy way; a rather literary word. EG *It is a time for great rejoicing.* — N UNCOUNT = jubilation
▸ used as a plural noun. EG *There were terrific rejoicings on the day war ended.* — ▸ N PLURAL = festivities

rejoin, rejoins, rejoining, rejoined. The word **rejoin** is pronounced /riːˈdʒɔɪn/ in paragraphs 1 and 2, and /rɪˈdʒɔɪn/ in paragraph 3. 1 If you **rejoin** someone, you go back to them after having left them for a short time. EG *Instead of rejoining his friends, he went off to sit by himself... I rejoined him upstairs.* — V+O ⇑ join

2 If you **rejoin** a group or club, you become a member of it again after not being a member for a period of time. EG *He was determined to rejoin the RAF.* — V+O, OR V ⇑ join

3 If you **rejoin**, you make a quick reply to something that someone has said, usually in a witty or critical manner; a formal use. EG *'That is a matter that will be dealt with in due time,' I rejoined.* — V+QUOTE, OR V = retort

rejoinder /rɪˈdʒɔɪndə/, **rejoinders**. A **rejoinder** is a reply to a question or remark, especially a quick, witty, or critical one; a formal or literary word. EG *This brought a somewhat sharp rejoinder from Mr Harper.* — N COUNT = retort

rejuvenate /rɪˈdʒuːvɪneɪt/, **rejuvenates, rejuvenating, rejuvenated**; a rather formal word. 1 If something **rejuvenates** you, it makes you feel or look young again. EG *I think we were rejuvenated by the experience.* — V+O = regenerate
◇ **rejuvenating**. EG *...rejuvenating cosmetics.* — ◇ ADJ QUALIT

2 If you **rejuvenate** an organization or system, you make it more lively and more efficient, for example by introducing new ideas and new methods. EG *He resolved to rejuvenate the party with dynamic policies... She thought she could rejuvenate the British economy.* — V+O = revitalize
◇ **rejuvenating**. EG *The new manager had a rejuvenating effect on the organization.* — ◇ ADJ QUALIT = revitalizing
◇ **rejuvenation** /rɪˈdʒuːvɪneɪʃə^{0}n/. EG *He was responsible for the rejuvenation of several aspects of the company's operations.* — ◇ N UNCOUNT

rekindle /riːkɪndə^{0}l/, **rekindles, rekindling, rekindled**. If something **rekindles** an interest, feeling, or thought that you used to have, it makes you think about it or feel it again; a rather literary word. EG *We hoped we could rekindle his enthusiasm for cricket... My maternal longings were rekindled.* — V+O

relaid /riːleɪd/ is the past tense and past participle of **relay**.

relapse /rɪˈlæps/, **relapses, relapsing, relapsed**; a rather formal or literary word. When it is a noun, the word can also be pronounced /riːlæps/. 1 If you **relapse** into a way of behaving that is undesirable or that requires no effort, you start to behave in that way again. EG *She relapsed into depression... Cameron had relapsed into silence again.* — V : USU+*into* ⇑ lapse

2 A **relapse** is 2.1 a gradual change back to an undesirable way of behaving. EG *...her relapses into alcoholism.* — N COUNT : USU+ *into*
2.2 a change in a sick person's condition when his or her health suddenly gets worse after it has been improving; a slightly technical use. EG *...after several operations and relapses.* — N COUNT ⇑ deterioration

relate /rɪˈleɪt/, **relates, relating, related**. 1 If you say that one thing **relates** to another or if you **relate** one thing to another, you are stating or claiming that there is a connection or link between the two things. EG *There are rules for relating English spelling and pronunciation... ...the way that words in a sentence relate to each other.* — V-ERG OR V-ERG +A *(to)* : RECIP ⇑ connect
◇ **related**. EG *...the price of petrol and oil related products... Two important and closely related questions arise.* — ◇ ADJ CLASSIF ⇑ connected

2 If you say that something **relates** to a particular subject, you mean that it concerns that subject or is connected with it. EG *I wanted to ask you a question that relates to electricity.* — V+A *(to)* = appertain

3 If you can **relate** to other people, you are able to understand how they feel or behave and so are able to communicate with them or deal with them easily. EG *Children need to learn to relate to other children.* — V OR V+A *(to)* : RECIP ⇑ interact

4 If you can **relate** to something such as an idea, you feel that it has relevance or meaning for you. EG *Women relate more to this revolution in human thought.* — V : IF+PREP THEN *to*

5 If you **relate** a story or a series of events, you tell or describe it to people. EG *Davis related the experience of three Cuban girls... I related the whole story of the time Chris and I were stranded in the North of Scotland.* — V+O = recount

related /rɪˈleɪtɪ^{2}d/. 1 People who are **related** belong to the same family. EG *...four people closely related to each other.* — ADJ CLASSIF : IF+ PREP THEN *to* ⇑ connected

2 If different types of animal are **related** or if different languages are **related**, they have evolved from the same type of animal or language. EG *Termites are closely related to cockroaches... French and Spanish are related languages.* — ADJ CLASSIF : IF+ PREP THEN *to* ⇑ connected

3 Another meaning of **related** can be found in paragraph 1 of the entry for **relate**.

relating /rɪˈleɪtɪŋ/. **Relating to** a particular subject means concerning that subject or with reference to it. EG *They passed a law relating to noise... They meet weekly for discussion on matters relating to homemaking in all its aspects.* — PREP ⇑ about

relation /rɪˈleɪʃə^{0}n/, **relations**. 1 **In relation to** or **with relation to** something means with reference to it or in comparison with it. EG *Using this portable communications system, everybody knows exactly where they are in relation to everybody else... Wages are very low in relation to the cost of living.* — PREP = compared with

2 If you refer to the **relation** of one thing to another, you are referring to the connection or similarity between the two things. EG *She argued that literature has no relation to reality... The interpretation bore no relation to the actual words spoken.* ● See also **poor relation**. — N UNCOUNT : USU +*of/to*

3 A **relation** between two people or groups of people consists of all the feelings, connections, dealings, and communications that exist between them. EG *This disagreement did not spoil the relation between Britain and the United States.* — N COUNT : USU+ *between/with*, ALSO SING = PL = relationship

4 If someone is your **relation**, they belong to the same family as you. EG *I said that I was a distant relation of her first husband.* — N COUNT : USU WITH POSS = relative

5 **Relations** are 5.1 contacts between different people or groups of people and the way in which they behave towards each other, for example how they communicate or cooperate. EG *This fear is causing East-West relations to deteriorate... Management needs to maintain close relations with the unions... Relations between them were strained.* — N PLURAL : USU+ SUPP ⇑ interaction = communication
5.2 sexual activities, especially sexual intercourse; used in very polite English. EG *Sexual relations are less awkward in the dark for people who feel embarrassed or shy.* — N PLURAL

relationship /rileɪʃə^{0}nʃɪp/, **relationships**. 1 A **relationship** is 1.1 the way in which two people or groups of people behave towards each other and feel towards each other. EG *The old relationship between the friends was quickly re-established... Pakistan's relationship with India has changed dramatically.* ● a **love-hate relationship**: see **love**. — N COUNT : IF+ PREP THEN *between/with* ⇑ interaction
1.2 a close friendship between two people, especially involving romantic or sexual feelings. EG *When the relationship ended two months ago he said he wanted to die.* — N COUNT : IF+ PREP THEN *between/with* = affair

2 The **relationship** between two things is the way in which they are connected or linked. EG *What is the relationship between language and thought?* — N COUNT : IF+ PREP THEN *between/to/of*

3 Your **relationship** with someone is the particular way in which you are related to them by being a member of the same family. EG *'What is your relationship to the patient?'–'I'm his daughter'.* — N SING : USU WITH POSS ⇑ connection

relative /rɛlətɪv/, **relatives**. 1 You can use **relative** when you mean that something is 1.1 true to a certain degree or extent. EG *The head of the department is a relative newcomer... He chose to return to the relative peace of his childhood village.* — ADJ CLASSIF : ATTRIB = comparative
1.2 being — ADJ CLASSIF :

measured or judged by being compared to something else. EG *There was a discussion on the relative naval strengths of the two countries.* ATTRIB = respective

2 **Relative to** something means with reference to it or in comparison with it; a formal use. EG *There is a shortage of labour relative to the demand for it.* PREP = compared to

3 If someone is your **relative**, they belong to the same family as you. EG *His wife had to visit some of her relatives for a few days.* N COUNT : USU WITH POSS = relation

4 If you say that something is **relative**, you mean that it cannot be judged to be good or bad in itself, but needs to be considered and judged in the context of other things or with reference to its results or effects; a formal use. EG *All human values are relative.* ADJ CLASSIF ≠ absolute

relative clause, relative clauses. In grammar, a **relative clause** is a subordinate clause that is introduced by a relative conjunction or a relative pronoun and that modifies a noun or pronoun in the main clause. N COUNT

relative conjunction, relative conjunctions. In grammar, a **relative conjunction** is a conjunction such as 'when' or 'where' that is being used to introduce a relative clause. N COUNT

relatively /rɛlətɪvli¹/ means to quite a large extent or degree, but not to a very large extent or degree. EG *It was relatively easy to find her house... A relatively small number of people disagreed.* ADV + ADJ/ADV = comparatively

relative pronoun, relative pronouns. In grammar, a **relative pronoun** is a pronoun such as 'who' that is being used to introduce a relative clause. N COUNT

relativity /rɛlətɪvɪti¹/. 1 The theory of **relativity** is Einstein's theory concerning space, time, and motion; a technical term. N UNCOUNT

2 If you talk about the **relativity** of something, you mean the fact that it cannot be judged to be good or bad in itself, but needs to be considered and judged in the context of other things or with reference to its results or effects; a formal use. EG *They teach the relativity of all ethical ideas.* N UNCOUNT

relax /rɪ¹læks/, **relaxes, relaxing, relaxed.** 1 When you **relax** or when something **relaxes** you, you feel less worried and more calm. EG *He saw that nothing was wrong, and relaxed... Some people can't even relax when they are at home... Just lie back and relax.* V-ERG

2 When a part of your body **relaxes**, it becomes less stiff or firm. EG *The baby's whole body relaxed... She watched the muscles of his arms hardening and relaxing.* V-ERG

3 If you **relax** your grip or your hold on something, you hold it less tightly than before. EG *He relaxed his grip on her arm.* V-ERG = loose

4 If you **relax** a rule or your control over something, you make it less strict. EG *At the beginning of the century the rules were relaxed... He had no intention of relaxing his policies.* V+O = moderate

5 If you **relax** something such as your attention, you reduce or weaken it; a formal use. EG *I was determined not to relax my own vigilance... Somehow he had to relax the man's guard.* V+O

relaxation /riːlækseɪʃəⁿn/, **relaxations. Relaxation** is 1 a way of spending time that is pleasant and restful. EG *It was the only place for off-duty relaxation... It is so necessary for the mother to have some rest and relaxation... This had been his most pleasant relaxation of the week.* N UNCOUNT/COUNT = recreation 2 the act or process of making the control of something become less strict. EG *He was in favour of the relaxation of external controls... There must be no relaxation in our high standards... The authorities encouraged a general relaxation in child discipline.* N UNCOUNT : IF + PREP THEN *of/in* ⇑ lessening = slackening

relaxed /rɪ¹lækst/. Someone who is **relaxed** is not worried or anxious. EG *She gave the impression of being quite relaxed.* ▸ used also of actions and situations. EG *It was a relaxed and quite informal discussion... The children benefit from the relaxed atmosphere.* ADJ QUALIT = calm ≠ strained

relaxing /rɪ¹læksɪŋ/. Something that is **relaxing** helps you to become less anxious and worried. EG *It is a delightful, relaxing place for a short holiday break... The time spent was so pleasant, so relaxing.* ADJ QUALIT = restful

relay, relays, relaying, relayed, relaid. The word is pronounced /riːleɪ/ in paragraphs 1 and 2, /rɪ¹leɪ/ in paragraphs 3 and 4, and /riːleɪ/ in paragraph 5. The form **relayed** is the past tense and past participle of the verb in paragraphs 3 and 4, and the form **relaid** is the past tense and the past participle of the verb in paragraph 5. 1 A **relay** or a **relay race** is a race between two or more teams of runners, swimmers, etc. Each member of the team runs or swims one section of the race. EG *They were taking part in a relay race round London. ...a school relay team.* N COUNT ● If people do something **in relays**, they do it in small groups at different times. EG *The children at our school have to be fed in two relays.* ● PHR : USED AS AN A = in shifts

2 A **relay** is 2.1 an automatic device that controls something such as the turning on and off of a switch. EG *...a general purpose computer using magnetic relays... I've come to check the relay system.* N COUNT 2.2 a piece of equipment that receives television or radio signals from one place and sends them on to another place. EG *...communications satellites acting as relay stations in space.* N COUNT

3 If you **relay** something that has been said to you, you repeat it to another person. EG *McKenzie relayed the question to me... ...some news relayed to him the night before by his wife.* V+O : IF + PREP THEN *to* = pass on

4 To **relay** television or radio signals means to send them on or broadcast them. EG *The Sunday Concert will be relayed live on Radio Three.* V+O = transmit

5 If you **relay** something such as a carpet or a road surface, you lay it again. EG *She wanted to relay the carpet in her new home... The railway company were proposing to spend 1.5 million pounds on relaying a single track.* V+O

release /rɪ¹liːs/, **releases, releasing, released.** 1 If you **release** a person or animal that has been in captivity, you set the person or animal free. EG *They had just been released from prison... The terrorists released a kidnapped politician.* V+O : IF + PREP THEN *from* ⇑ liberate ▸ used as a noun. EG *Nearly a year after his release he was still unable to sleep properly.* ▸ N UNCOUNT/COUNT ⇑ liberation

2 **Release** is a feeling that you have of no longer suffering or no longer having to worry about something. EG *That first day brought her a feeling of release... He was looking for some form of release from an unbearable situation.* N UNCOUNT : IF + PREP THEN *from* ⇑ relief

3 If something **releases** you from something unpleasant, it frees you from it; a formal word. EG *I was released, for the first time, from all my guilty thoughts... This releases them from personal responsibility.* V+O : IF + PREP THEN *from* ⇑ relieve

4 If you **release** someone from their work, you allow them to spend a period of time away from their work. EG *He was released to complete the funeral arrangements for his sons.* V+O = excuse ▸ used as a noun. EG *The release of staff for training purposes is actively encouraged.* ● See also **day release**. ▸ N UNCOUNT : USU + SUPP

5 If someone in authority **releases** something, they make it available for people to use; a formal use. EG *We felt it was time the President released the Watergate tapes... I was waiting for the office to tell me to release the keys... Their aim was to release money for the schools... The statement had to be delivered to someone who could release it to the press.* V+O ⇑ give = hand over ▸ used as a noun. EG *His relatives finally agreed to the release of his private papers... The Government announced a month later the release of one million pounds.* ▸ N UNCOUNT : USU + SUPP

6 A **release** is an official statement or information that is given to the press or the media in written form, so that it can be published or broadcast. EG *We considered issuing some sort of statement or press release.* N COUNT = announcement

7 If you **release** something, you stop holding it and allow it to move or to be moved. EG *He quickly released her hand.* V+O = let go

8 If you **release** a missile or bomb, you fire it. EG *The bomb load was automatically released by the computer.* V+O = launch ▸ used as a noun. EG *The reported release of a missile over the Indian Ocean... He pressed the release button.* ▸ N UNCOUNT : USU + SUPP = launch

9 If you **release** a device, you make it able to move freely again, for example by moving something that is blocking it. EG *He made sure the brake had been fully released... I ran to the door and released the catch.* V+O

10 When a company **releases** a film or the video of a film, it lets the film be shown in public cinemas or makes the video available for people to buy. EG *Paramount Pictures planned to release the film* V+O ⇑ present = launch

before Christmas. ▸ used as a noun. EG *The London release of 'The Janitor' begins on Saturday.* ▸ N UNCOUNT = opening

11 If a film is **on release** or **on general release**, it is available for showing in public cinemas. EG *Her latest film is currently on release.* PHR : USED AS AN A = showing

12 When a company, a pop singer, or a pop group **releases** a new record or video, they make it available for people to buy. EG *Their new single has just been released.* V+O = issue

13 A **release** is also a new record or video that has just been made available for people to buy. EG *Their new release is called 'Tattoo You'.* N COUNT

14 When something **releases** heat, energy, radioactivity, etc, it causes them to leave a substance, container, or area and enter the surrounding area or surrounding objects. EG *High-pressure gas could be released by pressure on a trigger... It came quite close to releasing radioactivity into the environment.* V+O = emit ▸ used as a noun. EG *...a great release of explosive energy... ...the controlled release of water from reservoirs.* ▸ N UNCOUNT : USU+SUPP = emission

15 When you **release** a feeling that you have been hiding and trying not to show, you express it; used in formal English. EG *This can help us to release our latent anger.* V+O = give vent to ▸ used as a noun. EG *...a great release of joy... ...the harmless release of rebellious spirits.* ▸ N UNCOUNT : USU+SUPP ≠ suppression

relegate /rɛlɪ²geɪt/, **relegates, relegating, relegated.** 1 If you **relegate** something, you cause it to have a less important position or status. EG *Much of the existing text can safely be relegated to the footnotes... This kind of approach may relegate these problems somewhere down on the priority list.* V+O : USU+A (to) ⇑ downgrade

2 If a team that competes in a league competition is **relegated**, it starts competing in a lower division in the next competition, because it was one of the least successful teams in the higher division. EG *They've lost three matches in a row, but at least they are not likely to be relegated.* V+O : USU PASS, IF+PREP THEN to = demote ◊ **relegation** /rɛlɪ²geɪʃə⁰n/. EG *We're nearing relegation this year.* ◊ N UNCOUNT

relent /rɪ¹lɛnt/, **relents, relenting, relented.** If you **relent**, you agree to allow someone to do something that you originally refused to let them do; a formal word. EG *In certain circumstances, our parents would relent and permit us to meet.* V = soften

relentless /rɪ¹lɛntlɪ²s/; a rather literary word. 1 Something that is **relentless** never stops or never becomes less intense. EG *...the relentless beating of the sun on the roofs... The traffic noise is relentless... ...the relentless population increase.* ADJ CLASSIF = unrelenting, merciless ◊ **relentlessly.** EG *The chase relentlessly continues.* ◊ ADV WITH VB = mercilessly

2 Someone who is **relentless** is determined to do or achieve something and refuses to give in. EG *He could be a relentless enemy.* ADJ QUALIT = implacable ◊ **relentlessly.** EG *...a relentlessly ambitious politician.* ◊ ADV

relevance /rɛləvəns/ is 1 the connection that something has with what is being talked or written about. EG *She did not quite understand the relevance of his remarks.* N UNCOUNT : IF+PREP THEN to 2 the importance of something to something else, for example the importance of something you have read to your way of life. EG *He tried to explain to the children the relevance of what he was doing... He spoke about the religion of Islam and its relevance to Black people in the United States.* N UNCOUNT : IF+PREP THEN to = significance

relevant /rɛləvənt/. 1 If something is **relevant**, 1.1 it is connected with what is being talked or written about. EG *This point is not really relevant and we had better move on... ...highly relevant information... He could use all the material that was relevant.* ADJ QUALIT : IF+PREP THEN to = pertinent 1.2 it has an important connection with something else. EG *They accept that what you are doing is relevant to their problems... The North American experience may be highly relevant for the emergent countries... China's experience seemed more relevant in their situation than that of the USSR.* ADJ QUALIT : IF+PREP THEN to

2 **Relevant** also means appropriate or correct for a particular purpose or according to a set of rules. EG *They are made to conform with the relevant British Standards... Members are drawn from people living in the relevant area.* ADJ CLASSIF : ATTRIB

reliable /rɪ¹laɪəbə⁰l/. 1 If something or someone is **reliable**, you can trust them to work hard or well, or always to act, behave, or happen in the way that you want them to. EG *She is a charming and reliable person... ...the diesel engine is long-lasting and extremely reliable.* ADJ QUALIT = dependable ◊ **reliability** /rɪ¹laɪəbɪlɪti¹/. EG *These machines have always been noted for reliability.* ◊ N UNCOUNT ◊ **reliably.** EG *They worked reliably under battle conditions.* ◊ ADV WITH VB

2 Information that is **reliable** is likely to be true or correct, and can therefore be trusted and believed. EG *We have no reliable information about that.* ADJ QUALIT ⇑ certain ▸ used also of people who give you information. EG *The telegram was based on information from a reliable source.* ▸ = trustworthy ◊ **reliably.** EG *We are reliably informed that her new record will be released in the autumn.* ◊ ADV WITH VB

reliance /rɪ¹laɪəns/ is the quality or condition of being reliant on something or someone. EG *...complete reliance on drugs... ...the student's reliance on the teacher.* N UNCOUNT : USU +on/upon = dependence

reliant /rɪ¹laɪənt/. Someone who is **reliant** on something, needs that thing and often cannot live or continue to do their work without it. EG *They are often reliant on government funds.* ADJ QUALIT : PRED+on/upon = dependent

relic /rɛlɪk/, **relics.** A **relic** is 1 an object, custom or tradition which has survived from the past into the present and is still used or practised. EG *...relics of her distant past... These ideas are relics of Victorian discipline.* N COUNT : USU+SUPP ⇑ survival 2 something which is kept because it is associated with a famous person or important event from the past. EG *We visited a museum with relics of great explorers.* N COUNT : USU+SUPP 3 a remaining piece of something which was made or built in the past. EG *You can still see the last surviving relic of the old Palace of Westminster... We often dug up relics of the Civil War in our playground* N COUNT : USU+SUPP ⇑ remnant 4 the body of a saint or something closely associated with a saint, which is thought of as being holy. N COUNT

relief /rɪ¹li:f/, **reliefs.** 1 **Relief** is 1.1 a feeling of gladness that something unpleasant has not happened or is no longer happening. EG *The news brought a sense of relief... To my relief, he found the suggestion acceptable... I saw with relief that the visitor was Mr Beden... I breathed a sigh of relief.* N UNCOUNT, OR N SING WITH DET 1.2 a temporary pause in or the ending of an unpleasant feeling or experience for a particular person. EG *For me, their visits were a relief from loneliness.* N UNCOUNT : IF+PREP THEN from 1.3 money, food, or clothing that is provided, often from public funds, for people who are very poor or hungry. EG *She outlined what was being done to provide relief... ...a cricket match in aid of Flood Relief... ...Christmas relief funds.* N UNCOUNT ⇑ aid

2 **Light relief** or **comic relief** is a light-hearted or funny moment or part of a play, story, etc that is otherwise very serious or depressing. EG *I found the play utterly depressing. The only light relief was provided when the actors forgot their lines.* PHR : USED AS S/O = diversion

3 The **relief** of a town, fort, etc is the freeing of it after it has been surrounded by an enemy army; a military term. EG *The relief of Khe Sanh began on April 1.* N SING : the+N+of ⇑ rescue

4 A **relief** is a sculpture that is carved out of a flat vertical surface; a technical term in art. EG *...magnificent reliefs by Donatello.* N COUNT

5 **Relief** is also the quality that a surface has when different parts of it stick out, or appear to stick out, in contrast to when a surface looks completely flat. EG *I used to have a globe of the world in relief... ...a relief map of Europe.* N UNCOUNT, OR N BEFORE N ● If something **stands out in bold relief** or **sharp relief** or **clear relief**, it is very noticeable because it contrasts strongly with everything else around it. EG *A particular tree stood out in clear relief.* ● PHR : VB INFLECTS ⇑ be prominent

6 A **relief** is also a person who takes your place and continues to do the job or duty that you have been doing, when it is time for you to go home. Sometimes, this is a person who has been specially asked to come and do the work instead of a regular employee who is ill. EG *When does your relief come on duty?... They had to phone for a relief driver.* N COUNT

relieve /rɪ¹li:v/, **relieves, relieving, relieved.** 1 If something **relieves** an unpleasant feeling that you have, it makes it less unpleasant. EG *Anxiety may be relieved by talking to a friend... The passengers swallow to relieve the pressure on their eardrums.* V+O = ease, lessen

2 If someone or something **relieves** you, they remove an unpleasant feeling, difficulty, or problem that you have. EG *The news relieved him of some of his embarrassment... By writing down all your family's birthdays you relieve yourself of the burden of remembering them.* V+O (NG/REFL) +A (of) = rid

3 If you **relieve** someone of something that is heavy or that they want to get rid of, you take it away from them; a rather formal use. EG *He relieved her of the* V+O+A (of)

plates she was holding... Let me relieve you of your coat.

4 If you **relieve** someone **of** their **duties** or **of** their **post**, you dismiss them from their job; a formal expression. EG *I was relieved of my hospital duties... I was relieved of my position as director.* PHR : VB AND N INFLECT = sack

5 If you **relieve** someone, you take their place and continue to do the job or duty that they have been doing. EG *They sent an army unit to relieve the Marines... He returned to his room before relieving the porter in the afternoon.* V+O ⇑ replace

6 If an army **relieves** a town, fort, etc, it frees it after it has been surrounded by an enemy army; a military term. EG *Bremen was relieved by 20 August.* V+O ⇑ rescue

7 If you **relieve** yourself, you urinate; an old-fashioned expression used in polite English. EG *He went into the house to relieve himself.* V+O (REFL)

relieved /rɪˈliːvd/. If you are **relieved**, you feel pleased because something unpleasant is not true, is not as bad as you had feared, has not happened, or is no longer happening. EG *The Belgian looked relieved, and promptly sat down again... I am relieved to hear that this isn't true... He felt enormously relieved that they had taken the matter so calmly.* ADJ QUALIT : USU PRED, ALSO + REPORT-CL/ *to*-INF ⇑ glad

religion /rɪˈlɪdʒən/, **religions**. 1 **Religion** consists of the belief in a god or gods and the activities that are connected with this belief, such as prayer or worship in a church or temple. EG *Politics and religion were daily topics of conversation... The school placed strong emphasis on religion.* N UNCOUNT

2 A **religion** is a particular system of belief in a god or gods and the activities that are connected with this system. EG *...the Christian religion... Her religion is severe and uncompromising.* N COUNT = faith

religious /rɪˈlɪdʒəs/. 1 Something that is **religious** is about or connected with religion in general or one particular religion. EG *Virtually all religious activities were suppressed... ...people who have no religious faith... She could not accept the religious beliefs of her parents.* ADJ CLASSIF : USU ATTRIB

2 Someone who is **religious** has a strong belief in a god or gods. EG *The young woman was gentle and religious... Our parents were very religious and very patriotic.* ▸ used also of people's characters or things that they say or do which indicate that they have a strong belief in a god or gods. EG *I have always had a strongly religious temperament... ...Mozart's profoundly religious music.* ADJ QUALIT = devout

religiously /rɪˈlɪdʒəsli¹/. If you do something **religiously**, you do it very regularly by your own choice because of a feeling of duty. EG *The ornaments were all religiously dusted by Gertrude.* ADV WITH VB = dutifully

relinquish /rɪˈlɪŋkwɪʃ/, **relinquishes, relinquishing, relinquished**; a formal word. If you **relinquish** something such as authority, responsibility, or a job, you give it up. EG *England has been forced to relinquish her Empire... She relinquished the editorship of the newspaper... Step by step she has relinquished all responsibility* V+O = abandon

reliquary /rɛlɪkwəri¹/, **reliquaries**. A **reliquary** is a box in which a relic of a saint is kept; a technical term. N COUNT

relish /rɛlɪʃ/, **relishes, relishing, relished**. 1 If you **relish** something, you get a great deal of pleasure or enjoyment from it; a rather formal or literary use. EG *The truth is that he relishes the challenge of competition... Hendricks smiled, relishing his moment of command.* ▸ used as a noun. EG *In his book he exposed with relish all the evils of our present day... The sight of the dead bird ended my relish for shooting at anything live.* ● If you **relish the idea, thought**, or **prospect** of something, you are looking forward to it very much; a rather formal or literary expression. EG *...rebels who relish the prospect of conflict and violence... She didn't relish the idea of going on her own.* V+O ⇑ like = enjoy ▸ N UNCOUNT = enthusiasm ● PHR : VB INFLECTS

2 **Relish** is something such as a sauce or a pickle that you add to food in order to give it more flavour. EG *Try some of this relish with your pie.* N MASS

relive /riːlɪv/, **relives, reliving, relived**. When you **relive** something, you remember something that has happened in the past and imagine that you are experiencing it again. EG *I had a curious urge to relive my visit there with her... It's depressing if you spend too much time reliving old joys.* V+O

reload /riːləʊd/, **reloads, reloading, reloaded**. When you **reload** a gun, you load it again by putting in more bullets or explosive. EG *The captain stopped to reload.* V OR V+O

relocate /riːləʊkeɪt/, **relocates, relocating, relocated**; a formal word. When people or businesses **relocate** or when someone **relocates** them, they move to a different place. EG *Our headquarters has been relocated in Milton Keynes... The population had all been relocated... Semi-skilled workers find themselves compelled to relocate.* ◇ **relocation** /riːləʊkeɪʃᵊn/. EG *Priority must be given to the relocation of industry... For many families, relocation is an upsetting experience.* V-ERG ⇑ transfer ◇ N UNCOUNT ⇑ moving

reluctance /rɪˈlʌktəns/ is unwillingness to do something, especially something that you cannot avoid doing, and which you therefore do slowly and without enthusiasm. EG *We had considerable difficulty in overcoming their reluctance... They showed some reluctance to support the military measures required... They released her with reluctance.* N UNCOUNT : ALSO + *to*-INF ≠ willingness

reluctant /rɪˈlʌktənt/. If you are **reluctant** to do something, you are unwilling to do it and hesitate before doing it, or do it slowly and without enthusiasm. EG *He is reluctant to be photographed... Actresses used to be very reluctant to wear tight corsets... The reluctant bridegroom smiled for the first time.* ◇ **reluctantly**. EG *She reluctantly handed him his stick... A wage increase of 21% was reluctantly conceded.* ADJ QUALIT : ALSO + *to*-INF ≠ eager, keen ◇ ADV WITH VB = grudgingly

rely /rɪˈlaɪ/, **relies, relying, relied**. 1 To **rely** on something or someone means to need them and depend on them in order to survive or work properly. EG *She is forced to rely on social security money... Hong Kong's prosperity relies heavily on foreign businesses... They made little use of missiles, but relied upon tanks.* V+A (*on/upon*)

2 If you **rely** on someone or something, you trust them to work hard or well, or always to act, behave, or happen in the way that you want them to. EG *One could always rely on him to be polite and do the right thing... They cannot be relied upon to offer much support or advice.* V+A (*on/upon*) = count

remain /rɪˈmeɪn/, **remains, remaining, remained**. 1 To **remain** in a particular state or condition means to stay in that state or condition and not change. EG *Mrs Oliver remained silent... Her husband remained standing... The results of these experiments remain a secret.* V+C ⇑ continue

2 If you **remain** in a place, you stay there and do not move away. EG *I was allowed to remain at home... Otto was having the greatest difficulty in remaining in his seat.* V : USU + A

3 If something **remains**, 3.1 it still exists, especially when other parts or other similar things no longer exist. EG *Even today remnants of this practice remain... He was cut off from what remained of his family.* 3.2 it has not yet been done and still needs to be done. EG *Much still remains to be done... One hazard remained to be overcome.* V = survive; V+O+*to*-INF = be left

4 If a problem **remains**, it still exists and is still unsolved. EG *These problems remain... Many questions remain about the mechanics of Jupiter's atmosphere... The fact remains that they mean to destroy us.* V

5 If you say that something **remains to be seen**, you mean that it is not at all certain what will happen. EG *'Can he do it?' I asked. 'That remains to be seen,' she replied... It remains to be seen what the long term effects will be.* PHR : *remain* INFLECTS

6 The **remains** of something are the parts of it that are left after most of it has been taken away or destroyed. EG *She tore off the remains of the paper label... They drove past the remains of two bombed-out tanks... The remains of the meat sat on the kitchen table.* N PLURAL : USU + *of* = remnants

7 The **remains** of a person or animal are the parts of their body that are left after they have died, especially when they died in a violent way or have been dead for a long time. EG *She pleaded for his remains to be returned, so that he could be given a proper burial... ...the remains of a huge dinosaur.* N PLURAL : WITH POSS

8 **Remains** are things such as parts of buildings, pottery, etc from a much earlier period of history, especially from an earlier civilization, that have been found, usually buried in the ground. EG *They had a tremendous number of Roman remains there... ...the ancient remains of Ediacara.* N PLURAL

remainder /rɪˈmeɪndə/, **remaindered**. 1 The **remainder** of something is the part of it that remains after the other parts have gone or been dealt with. EG *Afterwards she went to Brighton where she lived for the remainder of her life... I will pay you a hundred pounds deposit and the remainder on delivery.* — N SING : *the*+N, IF+PREP THEN *of* = rest

2 The **remainder** in arithmetic is the amount left over when one number cannot be exactly divided by another. — N SING : *the*+N

3 If a book **is remaindered**, it is sold at a reduced price because it has not been selling very well and the publishers have decided not to produce any more copies of it. — V+O : ONLY PASS

remaining /rɪˈmeɪnɪŋ/ is used to describe the part of something or the people or things of a group which continue to exist after the rest of the thing or group has ceased to exist, or been used up, taken away, dealt with, or destroyed. EG *He began to pack the remaining sandwiches back into the hamper... ...the process of removing their remaining civil rights... ...the demise of her last remaining relatives.* — ADJ CLASSIF : ATTRIB

remake, remakes, remaking, remade. The word **remake** is pronounced /riːˈmeɪk/ when it is a verb, and /ˈriːmeɪk/ when it is a noun. 1 If someone **remakes** something, they make it again, especially in a way that is better than it was before. EG *They give prices for remaking old mattresses.* — V+O ⇑ make

2 A **remake** is a film that has the same story, and often the same title, as a film that was made earlier. EG *...the 1934 remake of 'Young Men in Spats'.* — N COUNT : USU + SUPP

remand /rɪˈmɑːnd/, **remands, remanding, remanded**. 1 If a judge or magistrate **remands** someone who is accused of a crime, the trial does not take place immediately, and the person is ordered to come back to court at a later date. EG *He was remanded for trial at the central criminal court.* — V+O : USU PASS ⇑ recall

2 **Remand** is the practice of delaying the start of a trial until all the evidence is ready. EG *He's due in court on Monday, but only for remand.* — N UNCOUNT

3 If someone accused of a crime **is remanded in custody**, they are kept in prison until their trial begins. — PHR : VB INFLECTS ⇑ imprison

4 If someone accused of a crime **is remanded on bail**, they are allowed to go home until their trial begins, but have to leave a sum of money with the court which will not be given back to them if they fail to return for the trial. — PHR : VB INFLECTS

5 If someone accused of a crime is **on remand**, they have appeared in court and are waiting for their trial to begin. — PHR : USED AS AN A

remand centre, remand centres. A **remand centre** is an institution where young people who have been accused of a crime are sent until their trial begins or while a decision about their punishment is being made. — N COUNT ⇑ prison

remark /rɪˈmɑːk/, **remarks, remarking, remarked**. 1 If you **remark** that something is the case, you say what you think about a particular subject or what you have noticed about it. EG *'Your grandfather was a good friend to me,' he remarked... As R.L.Stevenson remarked, 'To travel hopefully is a better thing than to arrive.'... Mary's friends remarked that she could hate as passionately as she could love... If any of his friends remarked on his sudden failure to appear I explained that he had gone to visit his father.* — V+QUOTE/ REPORT-CL, OR V +A *(on/upon)* = comment

2 A **remark** is something that you say, often in a casual or informal way. EG *At school some of the children used to make unkind remarks about my clothes... His opening remarks were serious and philosophical... He closed the discussion with the remark that 'the economy is showing signs of improving'.* — N COUNT ⇑ comment

remarkable /rɪˈmɑːkəbəˀl/. Someone or something that is **remarkable** is unusual or exceptional in some way that causes people to notice them and be surprised. EG *He prepared the dinner with remarkable speed and efficiency... His statement was remarkable for its clarity... She was altogether a rather remarkable woman... Her achievement was the more remarkable in that she had come from such a poor family.* ◇ **remarkably**. EG *He has recovered from the accident remarkably well... ...a great President but a remarkably boring man.* — ADJ QUALIT = outstanding, striking; ◇ ADV+ADJ/ ADV, OR ADV SEN = exceedingly

remarriage /riːˈmærɪdʒ/ is the act of remarrying. — N UNCOUNT

remarry /riːˈmæriˈ/, **remarries, remarrying, remarried**. If you **remarry**, you marry again after you and your previous husband or wife have obtained a divorce, or after your previous husband or wife has died. — V OR V+O

remedial /rɪˈmiːdɪəl/; a formal word. **Remedial** activities are 1 intended to improve someone's health when they are ill. EG *...remedial exercises for handicapped children.* 2 intended to improve someone's ability to read, write, etc when they have had difficulty learning to do these things. EG *What materials and aids would you recommend for a remedial English course?* 3 intended to correct something that has been done wrong or to change something that is considered to be harmful. EG *I've taken other modest remedial steps.* — ADJ CLASSIF : USU ATTRIB (1, 2, 3)

remedy /ˈrɛmɪˈdiˈ/, **remedies, remedying, remedied**; a fairly formal word. 1 A **remedy** is 1.1 a successful way of dealing with a problem or difficulty. EG *...a drastic remedy for lawlessness and disorder... ...a new political movement that saw remedies to the whole predicament.* — N COUNT : IF + PREP THEN *for* = answer, cure, solution. 1.2 something that is intended to cure you when you are ill or in pain. EG *He preferred home-made remedies to even the most modern pharmaceutical products.* — N COUNT

2 If someone **remedies** something that is wrong or harmful, they do something that corrects it or improves it. EG *Technicians laboriously tried to find and remedy faults... Such measures can do little to remedy the fundamental wrong.* — V+O = rectify

remember /rɪˈmɛmbə/, **remembers, remembering, remembered**. 1 If you **remember** people or events from the past, your mind still has an impression of them and you are able to think about them. EG *He said he remembered the man well... I remember cabling home for more money... I also remembered that the shop was on the way to Muswell Hill... I fell silent, remembering what I had heard... I remember him falling down the steps.* — V+O/REPORT-CL/ -ING, OR V+O+ -ING = recall, recollect

2 If you can **remember** something, you are able to bring it back into your mind by making an effort to do so. EG *I wake up early trying to remember the things I have to do... Something else was worrying her, but she could not remember what it was... 'And did she?'-'I don't know, I can't remember.'* — V, V+O/REPORT-CL/-ING, OR V+O +-ING ⇑ be aware of = recall

3 If you **remember** something that you have made an effort to learn, you are able to repeat it from memory. EG *She found it almost impossible to remember her lines... I remember long pieces of Shakespeare.* — V+O

4 If you **remember** to do something, you do it when you intended to. EG *She gave me a list of things to remember... Remember to go to the post office.* — V, V+O, OR V+ *to*-INF

5 If you tell someone to **remember**, you are emphasizing a particular fact which you think they already know and which is relevant to what you are saying. EG *That, you must remember, was before I was born... Remember that women did not gain the vote until 1918... It must be remembered that many of them would be over retirement age.* — V, OR V+O/ REPORT-CL

6 If you say **'you remember'** when you are talking to someone, you mean that you are telling them something that they already know. EG *Kennedy, you remember, was elected before that happened... Sometimes, as you remember, the drawing room was full of people.* — PHR : USED AS ADV SEN = recall

7 If someone **is remembered** for what they did, other people have noticed it and think it was important or interesting. EG *The thing for which he will be remembered by history is his honesty... He will be remembered as the losing candidate.* — V+O : USU PASS+ A ⇑ record

8 When people **remember** a person or event, they hold a ceremony in honour of that person or event. EG *On November 11th we remember the dead of two world wars.* — V+O

9 If you **remember** someone such as a waiter or a child, you give them a tip or a present. EG *My aunt always remembers me on my birthday.* — V+O

10 If someone **remembers** you **in** their **will**, they leave you money or property when they die. — PHR : VB AND N INFLECTS

11 If you ask someone to **remember** you to another person, you are asking them to pass your greetings to the other person. EG *Don't forget to remember me to your father.* — V+O+A *(to)* : NO CONT ⇑ greet

remembrance /rɪˈmɛmbrəns/, **remembrances**. 1 A **remembrance** is 1.1 a memory you have of someone, or of something that happened in — N COUNT

the past; a formal use. EG *We have many pleasant remembrances of my aunt.* 1.2 something which you keep because it reminds you of a person or event from the past; a formal use. EG *I took the photos as a pictorial remembrance of the trip.*
N COUNT : IF + PREP THEN *of* = memento, souvenir

2 **Remembrance** is the honouring of the memory of someone or something. EG *Ashes can be scattered in a garden of remembrance.*
N UNCOUNT = commemoration

Remembrance Day is the Sunday nearest to November 11 when people in Britain honour the memory of the people who died in the two World Wars.
N UNCOUNT

remind /rɪˈmaɪnd/, **reminds, reminding, reminded.** 1 If someone or something **reminds** you of a fact or event that you are already aware of, they do or say something which makes you think about that fact or event. EG *You do not need to remind people of their mistakes all the time... She had to remind him that he had a wife... 'Oh, that reminds me,' said John. 'Where's the football?'*
V+O : USU + *of/about*/REPORT-CL

2 When someone **reminds** you, they say something to you to make you remember a particular task or activity that you know you ought to deal with. EG *Remind me to speak to you about Davis... Don't forget to remind her about the party... He reminded himself to thank Mary for the present... Miss Lemon reminded him of two appointments.*
V+O (NG/REFL) + *to*-INF/REPORT-CL/A (*about/of*) ⇑ tell

3 If someone or something **reminds** you of someone or something else, they have certain characteristics which are very similar and which make you think of the other person or thing. EG *Your son reminds me of you at his age... He wasn't quite sure what it reminded him of.*
V+O+A (*of*)

reminder /rɪˈmaɪndə/, **reminders.** A **reminder** is 1 someone or something that makes you think of a particular person, event, or action. EG *Seeing her again was a painful reminder of how different things had been five years ago... Just a reminder that you can get those papers from my secretary... She sent him to bed with a reminder to hang up his clothes.*
N COUNT : USU + SUPP

2 a letter or note sent to tell you that you have not done something such as pay a bill or return library books. EG *I've had another reminder from the library.*
N COUNT

reminisce /rɛmɪnɪs/, **reminisces, reminiscing, reminisced**; a rather formal or literary word. If you **reminisce** about someone or something from your past, you remember them and write or talk about them, often with pleasure and affection. EG *Wartime experiences were something to reminisce about.*
V : IF + PREP THEN USU *about*

reminiscence /rɛmɪnɪsəns/, **reminiscences**; a rather formal or literary word. 1 A **reminiscence** is 1 something you remember from the past, which you talk or write about. EG *She continued with fascinating reminiscences of their marriage... I spoke with the hall porter and exchanged reminiscences about Robertson.* ▸ used as an uncount noun. EG *He lapsed into the silence of reminiscence.*
N COUNT : USU PL ⇑ memory = recollection
▸ N UNCOUNT = recollection

2 Someone's **reminiscences** are the stories and facts that they remember from their life and which they present in a book or other account. EG *He tells many stories in his reminiscences 'Time Was'.*
N PLURAL : USU WITH POSS ⇑ autobiography = memoirs

reminiscent /rɛmɪnɪsənt/; a rather formal or literary word. 1 If someone or something is **reminiscent** of another person or thing, they remind you of that other person or thing. EG *The atmosphere was reminiscent of spy movies... There was a sweetish smell, vaguely reminiscent of coffee.*
ADJ QUALIT : PRED + *of* ⇑ similar

2 If someone is **reminiscent**, they are talking or thinking about people or events from their past. EG *We listened to Captain Imrie speaking, quietly reminiscent... In her reminiscent moods she used to tell us about her childhood.*
ADJ CLASSIF ⇑ remembering

remiss /rɪˈmɪs/. If someone is **remiss**, they are careless about doing things which ought to be done; a formal word. EG *Unfortunately, sociologists have been remiss in countering such misconceptions.*
ADJ QUALIT : PRED = forgetful, negligent

remission /rɪˈmɪʃəⁿn/ is 1 the reduction of someone's prison sentence, usually because they have behaved well while they are in prison; a technical term. EG *...three months remission for good conduct.*
N UNCOUNT

2 forgiveness for breaking one of the laws or rules of your religion; a formal use. EG *...the remission of sins.*
N UNCOUNT = pardon

remit, remits, remitting, remitted; a formal word, pronounced /rɪˈmɪt/ when it is a verb and /riːmɪt/ when it is a noun. 1 If you **remit** money to someone, you send it to them as payment either for a service or for something that you are buying from them. EG *I promised to remit the balance, plus interest, in monthly instalments... The travel bureau was asking me to remit promptly.*
V OR V+O

2 The **remit** of a person, an official committee, a piece of research, etc is the area of activities or information that they are expected to or have authority to deal with. EG *Lord Scarman's remit for the second phase of his inquiry is still confined to Brixton.*
N SING WITH DET ⇑ brief

remittance /rɪˈmɪtəns/, **remittances.** A **remittance** is a sum of money that you send, usually through the post, as payment for something; a formal word. EG *Post the form with the remittance to the appropriate passport office.*
N COUNT

remnant /rɛmnənt/, **remnants.** 1 A **remnant** of something is a small part of it that is left over when the main part has been removed, destroyed, or no longer exists. EG *They still clutched at the remnants of their self-esteem... Even today remnants of this practice remain.*
N COUNT : USU + *of* ⇑ remains

2 A **remnant** is a small piece of material that is left over when the rest of a large piece has been used or sold.
N COUNT

remodel /riːmɒdəⁿl/, **remodels, remodelling, remodelled**; also spelled **remodeling, remodeled** in American English. If someone **remodels** a building or room, they give it a different form or shape. EG *The Kirks had remodelled their house... The building has been much altered and remodelled.*
V+O ⇑ alter = recast

remonstrance /rɪˈmɒnstrəns/ is protest about a situation or a person's behaviour, which you are trying to change or stop; a formal word. EG *She had abandoned all attempts at remonstrance with Thomas.*
N UNCOUNT = objection

remonstrate /rɛmənstreɪt/, **remonstrates, remonstrating, remonstrated.** If you **remonstrate** with someone, you protest to them about a situation or a person's behaviour and try to get it changed or stopped; a formal word. EG *He had gone to the manager to remonstrate... She remonstrated with the porter.*
V : IF + PREP THEN USU *with* = expostulate, object

remorse /rɪˈmɔːs/ is a strong feeling of guilt about something that you have done; a formal word. EG *I had been filled with remorse over hurting her... He shot his wife and then in a fit of remorse shot himself.*
N UNCOUNT ⇑ regret

remorseful /rɪˈmɔːsful/. Someone who is **remorseful** has strong feelings of guilt about something that they have done; a formal word. EG *There he stood, looking sad and remorseful, agreeing with every word.* ◇ **remorsefully.**
ADJ QUALIT ⇑ regretful
◇ ADV WITH VB

remorseless /rɪˈmɔːslɪ²s/; a formal word. 1 Someone who is **remorseless** continually behaves in a very unkind way towards other people, and has no pity for them or regret about this behaviour. EG *...the remorseless teacher at school, insisting that all the work must be done again.* ◇ **remorselessly.** EG *The Press still pursued their victim remorselessly.*
ADJ QUALIT = merciless, pitiless
◇ ADV WITH VB = ruthlessly

2 Something that is **remorseless** continues in an unpleasant and persistent way. EG *...the frightful, remorseless noise of the engines.* ◇ **remorselessly.** EG *I was woken before six by the rain hammering remorselessly against the bedroom window.*
ADJ CLASSIF = relentless
◇ ADV WITH VB

remote /rɪˈməʊt/, **remoter, remotest.** 1 Something that is **remote** is far away in distance or time. EG *...a village remote from the world... The Beatles carried Liverpool's fame to the remotest corners of the earth... ...research into the remote past.* ◇ **remoteness.** EG *They found the remoteness of the country a great problem.*
ADJ QUALIT = distant
◇ N UNCOUNT

2 A place or area that is **remote** is a long way from places where people live, and is therefore difficult to get to. EG *Television has begun to penetrate even the remote areas of Java... Many children living in remote places cannot get to the playgroup.* ◇ **remoteness.**
ADJ QUALIT = isolated, inaccessible, secluded
◇ N UNCOUNT

3 If something is **remote** from a particular subject or area of experience, it is not very relevant to it because it is very different. EG *Much new knowledge is remote from the immediate interests of the ordinary person... His stories are too remote from everyday life.*
ADJ QUALIT : IF + PREP THEN *from* = distant, removed

4 If you describe someone as **remote**, you mean that they behave in a way which indicates that they do not want to be friendly or closely involved with other people. EG *She was a silent girl, cool and remote...*
ADJ QUALIT = aloof, distant, reserved

The union leaders have to beware of getting too remote from their members. ◇ **remoteness.** EG *Chris seems to understand my remoteness... He criticised the remoteness of public authorities.* ◇ N UNCOUNT ⇑ aloofness

5 If the possibility of something happening is **remote,** it is very unlikely that it will happen at all. EG *Winning is only a remote possibility at the moment... ...in the remote event of any of them dying.* ADJ QUALIT = faint, slight, vague

6 If you **do not have the remotest idea** or **notion** about something, you know absolutely nothing about it at all. EG *None of these scientists had the remotest notion where his peculiar obsession was leading.* PHR : VB INFLECTS

remote control is a system of controlling a machine or a vehicle from a distance by using radio or electronic signals. EG *The missile is guided by remote control.* N UNCOUNT

remote-controlled. Something that is **remote-controlled** is controlled from a distance by the use of radio or electronic signals. EG *...remote-controlled unmanned aircraft.* ADJ CLASSIF

remotely /rɪˈməʊtliˈ/. 1 You can use **remotely** to add emphasis in negative clauses and in clauses with words like 'anything' and 'anyone'. EG *I've never seen anything remotely like it... He'll eat anything that looks remotely edible... She knew I wasn't even remotely serious... Agreement did not seem remotely possible at the time.* ADV+ADJ/ADV/PREP : USU WITH BROAD NEG = faintly, vaguely

2 If someone or something is **remotely** placed or situated, they are a long way from other people or places. EG *Living as remotely situated as she did, it was really very difficult to get to see her very often.* ADV WITH VB = distantly

remould, remoulds, remoulding, remoulded. The word **remould** is pronounced /riːməʊld/ in paragraph 1 and /riːməʊld/ in paragraph 2. 1 A **remould** is an old tyre which has been given a new surface and can be used again. N COUNT

2 To **remould** something such as a way of thinking means to change it so that it has a new structure or is based on different principles; a formal use. V+O

remount /riːmaʊnt/, **remounts, remounting, remounted.** When you **remount** a bicycle or horse, you get back on it after you have got off it or fallen off it. EG *The children remounted their ponies and trotted off... Why didn't you remount and ride back instead of just sitting there?* V OR V+O ⇑ mount

removable /rɪˈmuːvəbəˈl/. If something is **removable,** you can move it easily from the place where it is, for example because it is not heavy or not firmly fixed. EG *These bookshelves must be removable for storage and carrying.* ADJ CLASSIF ⇑ movable

removal /rɪˈmuːvəˈl/, **removals.** 1 The **removal** of something is the act of removing it from somewhere or of getting rid of it. EG *He consented to the removal of the flags... You should equip yourself with a stain removal kit... ...the removal of the threat of intervention.* N UNCOUNT : USU +SUPP

2 A **removal** company transports furniture from one building to another, for example when you leave one house and go to live in a different one. EG *A good removal firm packs everything... Removal men have special techniques for getting beds down stairs.* ▸ A **removal** is the process of transporting furniture from one building to another. N BEFORE N ⇑ transfer ▸ N COUNT : USU PL ⇑ transfer

remove /rɪˈmuːv/, **removes, removing, removed.** 1 If you **remove** something, you take it away from the place where it was. EG *The tea-ladies came in to remove the cups... The rubble and other debris from the lobby were removed from the hotel before dawn... He removed his hand from the man's collar.* V+O : IF+PREP THEN *from/to* ⇑ move

2 When you **remove** your clothing, you take it off. EG *Will you remove your shoes before you go in, please?* V+O

3 If you **remove** a stain from something, you treat it with a chemical or wash it and cause the stain to disappear. EG *This mixture can remove stains from metal and china.* V+O : IF+PREP THEN *from* = get rid of

4 To **remove** someone from a group such as a committee means to stop them being a member of that group, usually against their wishes. EG *They made an attempt to remove her from the General Council.* V+O : IF+PREP THEN *from* = oust

5 When people in authority **remove** someone from somewhere, they take them away, often to an institution where they will be supervised. EG *The local authority cannot suddenly remove the child before an adoption hearing.* V+O = spirit away

6 To **remove** an undesirable feeling, attitude, situation, etc, means to take action in order to get rid of it. EG *The situation can be helped by removing those inequalities... The regime tried to remove food subsidies in 1970... Instant publication would have removed suspicion.* V+O

7 In formal English, if you say that something is **at one remove from** another thing, you mean that it is quite closely related to it, and if you say it is **at many removes from** it, you mean it has very little connection with it. PREP

removed /rɪˈmuːvd/. 1 If you say that an idea or situation is far **removed** or distantly **removed** from something, you mean that it is very different from it. EG *His ideas on foreign policy were far removed from those of the Government.* ADJ QUALIT : PRED+*from*, USU ADV+ADJ

2 Your cousin once **removed** is the cousin of one of your parents, the cousin of one of your children, or the child of one of your cousins. ADJ : NG+*once*+ADJ

remover /rɪˈmuːvə/, **removers.** A **remover** is a substance that you use for removing unwanted stains, marks, etc. EG *Have we any stain remover?* N MASS : USU MOD +N ⇑ solvent

remuneration /rɪˈmjuːnəreɪʃəⁿn/, **remunerations. Remuneration** is the payment that is made to someone for work they have done; a formal word. EG *...the introduction of remuneration for councillors... A small remuneration and expenses are paid.* N COUNT/UNCOUNT ⇑ pay

remunerative /rɪˈmjuːnərətɪv/. A **remunerative** job or task is one which you are paid for; a formal word. EG *He is prepared to accept any remunerative chore, however demeaning.* ADJ QUALIT ⇑ paying

renaissance /rəˀneɪsəns/. 1 The **Renaissance** was the period in Europe in the 14th, 15th, and 16th centuries A.D., especially in Italy, during which there was a great revival of interest in art, literature, and learning. ▸ used as an adjective. EG *...Renaissance art.* N PROPER : *the*+N ▸ ADJ CLASSIF : ATTRIB

2 A **renaissance** is a revival of interest in a particular topic, especially a form of art, literature, or music. EG *...the explosive renaissance of the British theatre in the late fifties... ...two decades of cultural renaissance.* N SING+DET = rebirth

renal /riːnəˀl/ means concerning or relating to the kidneys in the body of a person or animal; a technical term in medicine. EG *...an experiment on the renal circulation.* ADJ CLASSIF : USU ATTRIB

rename /riːneɪm/, **renames, renaming, renamed.** If you **rename** something, you give it a new name in place of the name it had before. EG *Mr Haq has taken over the Carousel Cafe and renamed it The Pearl of India.* V+O : USU+C ⇑ name

rend /rend/, **rends, rending, rent**; a literary or old-fashioned word. 1 When a loud noise **rends** the air, it occurs very suddenly and violently. EG *The air was rent with their grunts and whistles... ...people who rent the night with the sound of drums and trumpets.* V+O = pierce

2 If you **rend** something, you tear or rip it apart violently. V+O

render /rendə/, **renders, rendering, rendered**; a formal word. 1 To **render** someone or something harmless, invisible, possible, etc means to cause them to become harmless, invisible, possible, etc. EG *I have often ordered equipment which has been rendered obsolete before it was ever used... It must have rendered him unconscious for a considerable period.* V+O+C

2 If you **render** someone help or assistance, you do something that helps them. EG *We would never have secured our independence without the aid you rendered.* V+O, V+O+O, OR V+O+A *(to)* = provide

3 If you **render** a bill or an account, you present it to the person who has to pay you for work that you have done for them. EG *He has an account to render for £3,000.* V+O, V+O+O, OR V+O+A *(to)* = submit

4 If you **render** a poem, play, etc, into another language, you translate it. V+O+A *(into/from)*

5 If you **render** a wall, you cover it with a layer of cement or plaster in order to protect it. V+O

rendering /rendəⁿrɪŋ/, **renderings.** A **rendering** of a play, poem, or piece of music is a particular performance of it. EG *They began with a loud rendering of the hymn 'Onward Christian Soldiers'.* N COUNT : USU+*of* = rendition

rendezvous /rɒndeɪvuː/, rendezvousing, rendezvoused; a rather formal word. The form **rendezvous** is pronounced /rɒndeɪvuːz/ when it is the plural of the noun or the third person singular of the verb. 1 A **rendezvous** is 1.1 a meeting, often a secret one, that N COUNT you have arranged with someone for a particular time and place. EG *I'd lie awake, wondering whether you'd come to our next rendezvous... We made a dawn rendezvous.* **1.2** the place where you have arranged to meet someone, often secretly. EG *I met him at a secret rendezvous outside the city.* N COUNT **1.3** a place which is frequently used by a particular group of people. EG *This is one of the great rendezvous of London for artists.* N COUNT = haunt

2 If you **rendezvous** with someone, you meet them at a time or place that you have agreed in advance. EG *The paratroops were expected to rendezvous with the First Support Group.* V OR V+A *(with)* : RECIP

rendition /rɛndɪʃəⁿn/, **renditions**. A **rendition** of a play, poem, or piece of music is a particular performance of it. EG *...a wonderful rendition of 'These Foolish Things'.* N COUNT : USU+ *of* = rendering

renegade /rɛnɪgeɪd/, **renegades**. A **renegade** is a person who abandons the religious, political, or philosophical beliefs that they used to have, and accepts opposing or different beliefs; usually used showing disapproval. EG *Renegade supporters of the deposed King are still raiding villages... ...structuralist renegade Rene Girard, professor of French literature.* N COUNT

renege /rɪ¹niːg, -neɪg/, **reneges, reneging, reneged**. If someone **reneges** on an agreement or promise that they have made, they do not keep to it; a formal word. EG *They had to return £400,000 because they had reneged on the deal... ...those who renege on their responsibilities.* V : IF+PREP THEN *on* = go back on

renew /rɪ¹njuː/, **renews, renewing, renewed**.

1 To **renew** an activity means to begin it again with greater force or power than before. EG *She renewed her efforts to open the window... He renewed his threat to resign... She at once renewed her attack on Judy.* ◊ **renewed**. EG *We must prepare for renewed efforts to recruit more members... The pressure for change seemed to gather renewed force.* V+O ◊ ADJ CLASSIF : ATTRIB ⇑ new

2 If you **renew** a relationship with someone, you start it again after you have not seen the other person for some time. EG *I hoped that we might renew our friendship.* V+O : IF+PREP THEN *with*

3 When you **renew** something such as a passport, a contract, a season ticket, etc, you extend the period of time for which it remains valid. V+O ⇑ prolong

4 When something **is renewed**, it grows again or is immediately replaced after it has been destroyed or lost, usually as part of a natural process. EG *Volcanic soils are very fertile, as they are renewed from new rock material.* V+O : USU PASS

5 When you **renew** part of a machine or device, you replace it with a new part in order to make it work properly. EG *A lot of the cost of maintenance goes into renewing brakes.* V+O

renewable /rɪ¹njuːəbəⁿl/. **1** If something is **renewable**, it is capable of replacing itself after it has been used, destroyed, or lost. EG *...renewable energy systems... ...alternative approaches based on renewable resources.* ADJ CLASSIF

2 Contracts, legal documents, licences, etc that are **renewable** can be renewed when their original date of expiry has been reached. ADJ CLASSIF

renewal /rɪ¹njuːəl/, **renewals**. **1** When there is a **renewal** of an activity or situation, it starts again after a period of inactivity. EG *...renewal of hostility with neighbouring countries... ...a renewal of civil disorders.* N UNCOUNT : USU +*of* = resumption

2 Renewal is **2.1** the process of improving or replacing old buildings, especially over a fairly large area in the centre of a town, in order to provide new shops, offices, flats, etc. EG *The Group put forward an imaginative urban renewal scheme.* N UNCOUNT ⇑ improvement **2.2** a spiritual experience that many Christians believe can happen to them, which causes them to feel closer to God. EG *All the local clergy are involved in the renewal movement.* N UNCOUNT

3 The **renewal** of a legal or official document such as a licence or contract is the official process of extending the time for which it remains valid. EG *Some licences need yearly renewal... The office dealt with visa renewals.* N UNCOUNT/ COUNT

rennet /rɛnɪ²t/ is a substance which causes milk to become thick and sour, and which is used in making yoghurt, cheese, or junket. N UNCOUNT

renounce /rɪ¹naʊns/, **renounces, renouncing, renounced**; a formal word. **1** If you **renounce** something such as a belief, a way of life, or a way of doing something, you decide to stop believing in it or acting in that way. EG *...their determination to renounce the materialism of society... We have renounced the use of force to settle our disputes.* V+O

2 If you **renounce** an official title, rank, or job, you formally give it up. EG *The Earl of Sandwich wanted to renounce his peerage... A clergyman may renounce his holy orders.* V+O

3 If you **renounce** someone, you say that you no longer support them; an old-fashioned use. EG *The candidate has been publicly renounced by the leader of his party.* V+O = disown

renovate /rɛnəveɪt/, **renovates, renovating, renovated**. If someone **renovates** an old building or a machine, they repair and improve it and get it back into good condition. EG *The house had been renovated three years earlier.* ◊ **renovation** /rɛnəveɪʃəⁿn/, **renovations**. EG *...the renovation of old industrial and commercial buildings.* V+O = restore, do up ◊ N UNCOUNT/ COUNT = restoration

renown /rɪ¹naʊn/ is the state of being well known, usually for something good; a rather formal or literary word. EG *His renown as a soldier spread throughout the country.* N UNCOUNT = fame

renowned /rɪ¹naʊnd/; a rather formal or literary word. If someone or something is **renowned** for a particular quality or thing, they are well-known or admired because of it. EG *The city is renowned for its magnificent abbey... The locals are renowned for their hospitality.* ADJ QUALIT : IF+ PREP THEN USU *for* = famed

rent /rɛnt/, **rents, renting, rented**. **1** If you **rent** something, you pay its owner a certain amount of money every week or every month in order to be able to have it and use it yourself. EG *They had rented a villa not far from Rome... He rented a colour TV soon after moving in.* ◊ **rented**. EG *...a rented flat.* V+O ◊ ADJ CLASSIF

2 The **rent** is the amount of money that you pay regularly to rent a house, flat, or piece of land. EG *He made enough money to pay the monthly rent punctually... Some families withheld rent and were evicted... 40% of his income goes on rent.* N UNCOUNT, OR N SING : *the*/POSS+ N ⇑ fee

3 If a house or flat is **for rent**, it is not occupied at the moment, and is available for someone to rent it. PHR : USED AS AN A

4 Rent is also the past tense and past participle of **rend**.

rent out. If someone **rents out** something such as a room or a car, they allow it to be used for a period of time in return for payment. EG *They had to rent out the upstairs room for years.* PHRASAL VB : V+ O+ADV = let

rental /rɛntəⁿl/, **rentals**. **1 Rental** companies, charges, etc are involved in the business of renting out goods and services. EG *...its highly profitable computer rental service.* ADJ CLASSIF : ATTRIB = hire

2 The **rental** is the amount of money that you have to pay when you rent something such as a television set or a car. EG *The quarterly rental will be £35.* N COUNT ⇑ fee

3 A **rental** is the agreement and process involved when someone rents something. EG *The rise of car rentals.* N COUNT

rent book, rent books. A **rent book** is a small book which is used to record the date and amount of rent paid by a tenant. N COUNT

rent-free. Accommodation that is **rent-free** is available for use without paying any rent. EG *...rent-free housing.* ▸ used as an adverb. EG *The other three houses were given rent-free to retired friends.* ADJ CLASSIF ≠ paying ▸ ADV WITH VB

renunciation /rɪ¹nʌnsieɪʃəⁿn/; a formal word. **1** The **renunciation** of a belief, a way of life, or a way of doing something is the act of rejecting it when you decide to stop having that belief or living in that way. EG *...the renunciation of human vanity... There is no need for renunciation or sacrifice.* N UNCOUNT : IF+ PREP THEN *of* ⇑ rejection

2 The **renunciation** of an official post, rank, or title is the formal act of giving it up. EG *Legislation allowing the renunciation of titles.* N UNCOUNT : IF+ PREP THEN *of*

3 The **renunciation** of a person involves saying that you no longer regard them as your friend or that you will no longer support them. EG *The public renunciation by the Party leader of the prospective candidate.* N UNCOUNT : IF+ PREP THEN *of* ≠ acceptance

reopen /riːəʊpəⁿn/, **reopens, reopening, reopened**. **1** If you **reopen** a shop, bar, restaurant, etc, or if it **reopens**, you open it again after it has been closed for some time. EG *When the pub reopened, everything was new and gleaming.* V-ERG

2 If someone **reopens** a discussion, a legal case, etc, they try and start it again after it has stopped or V-ERG ⇑ begin been closed. EG *A clear commitment to reopen disarmament talks... We can reopen the case and make a new decision.*

3 To **reopen** a border or a route means to allow people and goods to cross it or go along it after a period during which it has been closed. EG *They hoped to secure the reopening of the oil route.* V+O ⇑ open

4 When a wound **reopens**, it breaks open again after the skin has begun to heal. V-ERG

reorganization /riːɔːgənaɪzeɪʃəⁿn/, **reorganizations**; also spelled **reorganisation. Reorganization** involves changing the way something is organized, usually with the intention of making it more efficient or acceptable. EG *Recently there has been a reorganisation of the Health Service... There had been fewer reorganizations in the interests of economy.* N UNCOUNT, OR N COUNT : USU + *of* ⇑ organization

reorganize /riˈɔːgənaɪz/, **reorganizes, reorganizing, reorganized**; also spelled **reorganise**. If you **reorganize** something, you organize it in a new way that is intended to make it more efficient or acceptable. EG *The manufacturers were reorganising the soap industry.* V OR V+O ⇑ change

rep /rɛp/, **reps**; an informal word. **1** In informal English, a **rep** is **1.1** a person whose job is to sell a company's products or services, especially by travelling round and visiting other companies and organizations. EG *I've been working as a sales rep.* N COUNT : USU + SUPP ⇑ employee **1.2** someone who is elected as a representative for a group of people. EG *...the union rep.* N COUNT : USU + SUPP

2 If an actor or an actress is working in **rep**, he or she is working with a repertory company. EG *He spent 5 years in rep in Nottingham and Sheffield.* N UNCOUNT

Rep. is **1** an abbreviation for 'Representative'; written in front of someone's name to indicate that they are a member of the House of Representatives in the USA. EG *...Rep. Barber B. Conable.* **2** an abbreviation for 'Republican' or 'Republic'. N IN TITLES

repaid /riˈpeɪd/ is the past tense and past participle of **repay**.

repair /rɪˈpɛə/, **repairs, repairing, repaired**.

1 A **repair** is something that you do to mend a machine, piece of clothing, or other thing that has been damaged or is not working properly. EG *He had left his car for repairs in some garage or other... We negotiated with the landlord to carry out the repairs... ...curtains badly in need of repair.* N COUNT/ UNCOUNT

2 If something is **beyond repair**, it is in such bad condition that it cannot be repaired. EG *I have to tell you that the machine is beyond repair.* PHR : USED AS AN A ⇑ irreparable

3 When you say that something such as a building is **in good repair, in bad repair**, etc, you are referring to how good or bad its condition is; a rather formal use. EG *Some of the sheds were clearly in bad repair.* PHR : USED AS AN A

4 If you **repair** something that has been damaged or is not working properly, you mend it. EG *No one knew how to repair the engine... He was good at anything practical like repairing a washing machine.* V+O = fix

5 If you **repair** something wrong or harmful that someone has done, you do something in order to correct it or make it less serious; a formal use. EG *Can you see any way in which we can repair these two very major omissions?* V+O = rectify

reparation /rɛpəreɪʃəⁿn/, **reparations**. **1 Reparation** is the act of giving someone money or doing something for them because you have caused them to suffer in the past; a formal use. EG *They are still trying to make some sort of atonement and reparation.* N UNCOUNT = restitution

2 Reparations are sums of money that are paid after a war by the defeated country for damage and injuries it caused. EG *...war reparations... ...reparation debts.* N COUNT : USU PL = compensation

repartee /rɛpɑːtiː/, **repartees**. **1 Repartee** is conversation that consists of a lot of quick, witty comments and replies. EG *...his constant chatter and repartee with the spectators.* N UNCOUNT = banter

2 A **repartee** is a witty reply or comment. EG *...her witticisms and quick repartees.* N COUNT = riposte

repast /rɪˈpɑːst/, **repasts**. A **repast** is the same as a meal; a literary word. N COUNT

repatriate /riːpætriˈeɪt/, **repatriates, repatriating, repatriated**; a formal word. **1** If someone **is repatriated**, they are sent back to the country which they are citizens of. EG *The poor lad would be repatriated to Italy.* V+O : USU PASS = return ◇ **repatriation** /riːpætriˈeɪʃəⁿn/. EG *...emergency repatriation flights for summer tourists.* ◇ N UNCOUNT = return

2 If a company **repatriates** profits that it has made in another country, it brings them back to its own country. EG *The government encouraged foreign companies to invest and repatriate profits.* V+O ◇ **repatriation.** ◇ N UNCOUNT

repay /riˈpeɪ/, **repays, repaying, repaid**. **1** If you **repay** money, you give it back to the person who you borrowed or took it from. EG *He ordered the former Vice President to repay the money to the State.* V+O, V+O+O, OR V+O+A *(to)* = pay back

2 If you **repay** a favour that someone did for you, you do or give them something in return. EG *He had repaid as far as he could his debt of gratitude... We only hope we can repay you for the pleasure you have given us.* V+O : IF + PREP THEN *for* = pay back

3 If something **repays** your attention or interest, it is worth giving your attention or interest to; a rather formal use. EG *His operas repay much closer listening than his concertos.* V+O = reward

repayable /riˈpeɪəbəⁿl/. A loan that is **repayable** within a particular period of time must be paid back within that time. EG *The loan is repayable in ten years.* ADJ CLASSIF : PRED ⇑ payable

repayment /riˈpeɪməⁿnt/, **repayments**. **1 Repayments** are small amounts of money which you pay at regular intervals to a person or organization in order to repay a debt over a period of time. EG *...mortgage repayments... The country faced the burden of interest and loan repayments.* N COUNT : USU PL ⇑ payment

2 The **repayment** of money is the process of paying it back to the person you owe it to. EG *...repayment of international debts.* N UNCOUNT : USU + SUPP ⇑ payment

repeal /rɪˈpiːl/, **repeals, repealing, repealed**. If the government **repeals** a law, it officially puts an end to that law; a technical term. EG *The Labour Party said that they would repeal the whole Act once they got into power... Nine countries repealed their anti-discrimination laws last year.* V+O ⇑ cancel = revoke ▸ used as a noun. EG *...a campaign for the repeal of incomes legislation.* ▸ N UNCOUNT : USU + *of*

repeat /rɪˈpiːt/, **repeats, repeating, repeated**.

1 If you **repeat** something, you say or write it again. EG *Haldane repeated his statement in the presence of the Prime Minister... 'We need half a million dollars,' Monty kept repeating. 'Half a million dollars.'... There is, I repeat, a contradiction here which I would like to discuss.* V+O/QUOTE/ REPORT-CL = reiterate

2 If you **repeat** something that someone else has said or written, you say or write the same thing as they do. EG *The couple repeated after the rabbi the traditional phrases... Ballin repeated what he had been told by Haldane.* V+O/QUOTE/ REPORT-CL

3 If you **repeat** something secret or confidential that you have heard, you tell it to someone else. EG *Be careful or somebody will overhear what you say and may repeat it afterwards.* V+O/REPORT-CL

4 If you **repeat** something that you have memorized, you say it aloud. EG *I find myself frequently repeating a short prayer which I learnt when I was a child.* V+O = recite

5 If you **repeat** an action, you do it again. EG *I decided not to repeat the mistake of my first marriage... Jenny's blood test was repeated three times.* V+O

6 If you **repeat** yourself, you say or do something which you have said or done before. EG *People tend to repeat themselves when they are speaking spontaneously... History often repeats itself.* V+O (REFL)

7 If a television or radio programme **is repeated**, it is broadcast again. EG *'How Many Miles to Babylon' is being repeated on Radio 4 next Sunday afternoon.* V+O : USU PASS

8 A **repeat** is **8.1** something which is done or which happens again. EG *The events of that day were an exact repeat of those of the previous year... They agreed to put on a repeat performance of the play.* N COUNT, OR N BEFORE N = repetition **8.2** a broadcast of a radio or television programme which has already been heard or seen. EG *'Any Answers' can first be heard tomorrow night at 8, with a repeat on Monday afternoon.* N COUNT ⇑ transmission

9 If food **repeats** on you, you continue to taste it for some time after you have eaten it; mainly used in informal British English. EG *She said that she didn't like onions because they repeated on her.* V : IF + PREP THEN *on*

repeated /rɪˈpiːtɪ²d/. **Repeated** actions or events are ones which happen many times. EG *After repeated attempts, the manager finally managed to call the police... Anxious patients require repeated reassurance that they are getting better... His plans have suffered repeated delays.* ADJ CLASSIF : ATTRIB = frequent

repeatedly /rɪˈpiːtɪdliˈ/. If you do something **repeatedly**, you do it many times. EG *The child learns to read by seeing the words repeatedly.*
ADV WITH VB ⇑ often

repeater /rɪˈpiːtə/, **repeaters**. A **repeater** is a gun which can be fired several times without being reloaded.
N COUNT

repeating /rɪˈpiːtɪŋ/. A **repeating** gun is one which can be fired several times without being reloaded.
ADJ CLASSIF : ATTRIB

repel /rɪˈpel/, **repels, repelling, repelled**. 1 If something **repels** you, you find it so horrible and disgusting that you want to keep away from it or avoid even thinking about it. EG *Any deformity frightened and repelled her.*
V+O = revolt

2 When an army or other group **repels** attackers or invaders, they successfully fight them and drive them back; a formal use. EG *A country must have the will to overthrow a dictator or repel an invader.*
V+O = repulse

3 When a magnetic pole **repels** an opposite magnetic pole, it exerts a force which tends to push the opposite pole away; a technical use. EG *Opposite poles attract, like poles repel.*
V OR V+O : RECIP

repellent /rɪˈpelənt/, **repellents**. 1 If you find something **repellent**, you find it disgusting and extremely unpleasant; a rather formal use. EG *The idea of eating meat has become repellent to me... Some of his views are repellent.*
ADJ QUALIT : IF+PREP THEN *to* = repugnant

2 A **repellent** is a chemical which is used to keep insects or other creatures away from an area. EG *...a bottle of insect repellent.*
N MASS

repent /rɪˈpent/, **repents, repenting, repented**. If you **repent**, you feel sorry for something bad that you have done in the past; a formal word or a technical term in religion. EG *He has every prospect of living long enough to repent of his sins... He lived to repent his early love.*
V : IF+PREP THEN *of/for*, OR V+O = regret

repentance /rɪˈpentəns/ is sorrow and regret that you feel for something bad that you have done in the past; a formal word or a technical term in religion. EG *From confession flows repentance and from repentance forgiveness.*
N UNCOUNT = remorse

repentant /rɪˈpentənt/. Someone who is **repentant** feels or shows sorrow and regret for something bad that they have done in the past; a formal word or a technical term in religion. EG *I'm not repentant... ...a handful of repentant sinners.*
ADJ QUALIT = penitent

repercussion /riːpəkʌʃəⁿn/, **repercussions**. A **repercussion** is the effect or result of an event, action, or decision which takes place some time afterwards and which is usually unexpected; a rather formal word. EG *They cannot foresee the complex repercussions of the changes they seek to introduce... Years afterwards there were still repercussions from his fateful decision.*
N COUNT : USU PL = consequence

repertoire /repətwɑː/; a formal word or technical term. 1 A performer's **repertoire** is all the pieces of music, plays, etc that he or she has learnt and is able to perform. EG *She has an extraordinarily wide repertoire... It was wonderful to be able to extend my song repertoire... This play is now in their repertoire.*
N SING WITH DET +SUPP ⇑ range

2 The **repertoire** of a composer or writer is all the pieces of music, plays, etc that he or she has written. EG *We intend to perform the entire Haydn-Mozart-Beethoven repertoire.*
N SING WITH DET +SUPP

3 The **repertoire** of a particular musical instrument is all the pieces of music that have been written for that instrument. EG *...a concert of neglected music from the repertoire of the oboe.*
N SING WITH DET +SUPP

4 The **repertoire** of a person or thing is the total number of things that the person or thing is capable of doing. EG *All humanity shares a large repertoire of common movements and expressions... This computer is capable of only a limited repertoire of activities.*
N SING WITH DET +SUPP = range

repertory /repətəⁿriˈ/. 1 **Repertory** is the practice of performing a small number of plays in a theatre for a fairly short time, using the same actors in every play; a technical term in the theatre. EG *After leaving drama school I joined a repertory company.... I went to Oxford to play six or seven parts in a repertory season there.* ● If plays are being performed **in repertory**, the same group of actors and actresses is performing the plays, which are usually performed on alternating nights. EG *We were performing three plays in repertory... 'Hamlet' is in repertory at the National Theatre.*
N UNCOUNT, OR N BEFORE N = rep
● PHR : USED AS AN A

2 **Repertory** also means the same as repertoire; a formal use.
N SING WITH DET

repetition /repɪtɪʃəⁿn/, **repetitions**. A **repetition** is something that you say or do that you have already said or done before. EG *He didn't want a repetition of the scene with his mother.* ▸ used as an uncount noun. EG *Casual conversation tends to be filled with repetition and pauses.*
N COUNT = recurrence, repeat
▸ N UNCOUNT = duplication

repetitious /repɪtɪʃəs/. Something that is **repetitious** contains unnecessary repetition and so is boring; a formal word. EG *Much of the content of his book is devoted to repetitious accounts of his schooldays.*
ADJ QUALIT = repetitive

repetitive /rɪˈpetɪtɪv/. Something that is **repetitive** contains unnecessary repetition and so is boring. EG *Mr Starke asked endless repetitive questions about my childhood... His job consists of dull, repetitive work.*
ADJ QUALIT

rephrase /riːfreɪz/, **rephrases, rephrasing, rephrased**. If you **rephrase** a question or statement, you ask or say it in a different way.
V+O

replace /rɪˈpleɪs/, **replaces, replacing, replaced**. 1 If something **replaces** something else, it takes its place. EG *Thomas bought a new sweater to replace the one he lost... Arabic script was replaced with the Roman alphabet in official documents... The panic on the chief's face was replaced by relief.*
V+O, OR V+O+A *(with/by)*

2 If you **replace** something or someone, you put something else or someone else in their place to do their job. EG *The airline is currently replacing its DC10s with Boeing 747s... ...the cost of replacing window frames.*
V+O, OR V+O+A *(with)* ⇑ change

3 If you **replace** something that is broken, damaged, lost, etc, you get a new one or another one which will perform the same function. EG *The books that have been stolen will have to be replaced.*
V+O ⇑ provide

4 If you replace something, you put it back where it was before. EG *She replaced the receiver.*
V+O

replaceable /rɪˈpleɪsəbəˈl/. Something or someone that is **replaceable** can be replaced by something or someone else. EG *All members of staff are entirely replaceable.*
ADJ CLASSIF : USU PRED

replacement /rɪˈpleɪsməˀnt/, **replacements**. 1 **Replacement** is the act of putting a person or a thing in place of one that has left, stopped working, or is no longer suitable. EG *...the resignation of Jo Grimond and his replacement by Jeremy Thorpe.... ...the replacement of steam by diesel.*
N UNCOUNT = substitution

2 A **replacement** is a person or thing that takes the place of another. EG *We got him as a replacement for Elliott... The Colonel's replacement was due at the base any day now.*
N COUNT = substitute

replay /riːpleɪ/, **replays, replaying, replayed**. 1 A **replay** is a match, especially a football match, that is played between two teams in a knockout competition after the previous match or matches between them were drawn. EG *United beat Brighton after a replay.*
N COUNT

2 If two football teams **replay** a match in a knockout competition, they play it again because the previous match between them was drawn. EG *The final will be replayed on Thursday.*
V+O

3 If you **replay** something you have recorded on tape or film, you play it to see what it sounds or looks like. EG *He rewound the tape and replayed a few bits and pieces.*
V+O

replenish /rɪˈplenɪʃ/, **replenishes, replenishing, replenished**. To **replenish** something means to make it full or complete again by adding a quantity of the substance or material that has been lost or removed; a formal word. EG *We have to import an extra 4 million tons of wheat to replenish our reserves... My glass needs replenishing.*
V+O = top up, refill

replete /rɪˈpliːt/; a formal and rather old-fashioned word. 1 If you are **replete**, you are pleasantly full of food and drink so that you do not want to eat or drink anything else. EG *No more for me, thanks. I'm quite replete... Replete and drowsy, Gretchen lay on the couch.*
ADJ QUALIT = full up

2 If something is **replete** with something, it is fully supplied with it. EG *The battleships of the US North Atlantic Squadron were replete with fuel and ammunition.*
ADJ CLASSIF + *with* ⇑ full

replica /replɪkə/, **replicas**. A **replica** is 1 an accurate copy of a statue, machine, building, etc. EG *...a plaster replica of the Venus di Milo... He had installed a replica of a traffic light in his office.* 2
N COUNT : IF+PREP THEN *of* = model
N COUNT : IF+

someone or something that closely resembles someone else or something else. EG *She was a chubby blonde replica of Shirley Temple.* PREP THEN *of* = double

replicate /rɛplɪkeɪt/, **replicates, replicating, replicated.** To **replicate** something means to make an exact copy of it; a formal word. EG *DNA has the capacity to replicate itself.* V+O (NG/REFL) = duplicate

reply /rɪˈplaɪ/, **replies, replying, replied.** 1 When you **reply**, you say or write something as an answer to something that someone has said or written to you. EG *'Did you have a nice journey?'–'Yes,' Jenny replied, 'nice and quick'... If I am asked to dinner with them, I shall simply reply that I have to finish my essay... He gave me no chance to reply to his question... I have sent you a lot of letters, and you have never replied.* V: IF+PREP THEN *to*, OR V+QUOTE/REPORT-CL

2 If you **reply** to something that someone has done, you do something in answer to it. EG *We replied to the enemy's attack by bombing their navy.* V: IF+PREP THEN *to* = respond

3 A **reply** is something which you say or do as an answer to something which has been said or done. EG *He called 'Sarah', but there was no reply... The stranger made no reply to my greeting... I had only about a dozen replies to my request for information... Her reply to his bad behaviour was simply to walk away.* N COUNT: IF+PREP THEN *to* = response

4 If you do something **in reply** to something that someone else has said or done, you do it as an answer to their words or actions. EG *I have nothing to say in reply to your question.* PHR: USED AS AN A, IF+PREP THEN *to*

repoint /riːpɔɪnt/, **repoints, repointing, repointed.** If you **repoint** brickwork, you put new mortar between the bricks. V+O

report /rɪˈpɔːt/, **reports, reporting, reported.**
1 If you **report** something that has happened, you tell people about it. EG *He was unable to report that everything was going well... No casualties were reported following the bomb explosion... I have nothing else to report... The last reported position of the hurricane was 500 miles from the island.* V+O/REPORT-CL/QUOTE = record

2 If committees or other groups of people **report** on a particular subject, they present an official document which contains their ideas on that subject and the conclusions that they have reached. EG *The results were foreseen by the Deighton Committee when they reported in 1968.* V: IF+PREP THEN *on/upon*

3 If you **report** to someone on an event or subject, you tell them about it. EG *On his return from the Summit Meeting the Prime Minister reported to the Cabinet... He was summoned to report on the accident to his supervisor.* V+A (*to*): IF+PREP THEN *on/upon* ⇑ state

4 If a newspaper or the television **reports** something that has happened, it gives an account of it. EG *The newspapers reported the latest pop star's views on everything under the sun... The French press reported that she was engaged to a wealthy industrialist.* V+O/REPORT-CL/QUOTE, OR V: IF+PREP THEN *on* ⇑ describe

5 If you **report** something serious that has happened, you tell someone in authority that it has happened. EG *Accidents have to be reported to the police within twenty-four hours... He reported his father's death to the registrar... He reported the theft of his passport.* V+O: IF+PREP THEN *to*

6 If you **report** someone to a person in authority, you make a complaint about them. EG *He reported his friend to the Inland Revenue for not paying his taxes.* V+O: IF+PREP THEN *to*

7 If you **report** to someone or to a place, you go to that person or place and say that you are ready to start work. EG *On the first morning in his new job he reported for duty at Jack Starke's office... He was told to report to General Information when he arrived for his interview.* V: IF+PREP THEN *to/for*

8 If you **report** to someone, you are responsible to them in your work and must do as they tell you; a formal use. EG *You'll be reporting to Mr Harland.* V+A (*to*)

9 If you **report** sick, you tell your place of work that you are sick and unable to work. If you **report** fit for work, you tell your place of work that you are better after an illness and able to work. EG *He reported fit for work after six weeks' illness... When reported cured by doctors, she resumed her normal life.* V-ERG+C (ADJ)

10 If something **is reported** to be true, people say that it is true although there is no absolute proof of it. EG *She was reported to have ordered the murder of her husband... It is reported that all steel mills in Britain will be shut by 1989.* V+O+*to*-INF OR V+REPORT-CL: USU PASS = they say

11 A **report** is 11.1 a written or spoken account of something that has happened. EG *When you get back, write a report on everything that was said and done at the Conference... Have you had any reports about a lion walking the streets of Birmingham?... I placed a folder of intelligence reports and photographs on his desk.* N COUNT 11.2 an official document which is prepared by a committee or other group of people who have been working on a particular subject. EG *The committee published its final report, recommending legislation against racism.* N COUNT: ALSO IN NAMES 11.3 an account of something which is published in a newspaper or magazine or on radio or television. EG *He said that he always read the foreign reports in The Times... Press reports indicated that the price of bread would rise the following week.* N COUNT 11.4 a story or a piece of news for which there is no absolute proof. EG *There have been many reports of gas used in the war, but no-one knows whether they are true... Report has it that our professor is going to resign.* N COUNT/UNCOUNT = rumour, talk 11.5 a piece of paper on which teachers say how well or how badly a pupil has done at school that term; a British use. EG *My daughter got a very bad report last term.* N COUNT ⇑ review 11.6 the sound of a shot or an explosion; a formal use. EG *There came a violent report as the lock of the door was shot to pieces.* N COUNT

report back. 1 If you **report back** to someone, you give them an account of something that has happened and that it was your job to find out about. EG *She was sent to attend the meeting and then to report back on its discussions.* PHRASAL VB: V+ADV+REPORT-CL, OR V+ADV, IF+PREP THEN *to/on* ⇑ communicate

2 If you **report back**, you tell someone that you have returned after being away for a time. EG *Why don't you go away for a few days? You don't need to report back until Monday.* PHRASAL VB: V+ADV, IF+PREP THEN *to* ⇑ go back

reportage /rɪˈpɔːtɪdʒ, rɛpɔːtɑːʒ/ is the act or the technique of reporting news; a formal word. EG *...the rules of parliamentary reportage.* N UNCOUNT

> **REPORT-CL** □ In this dictionary REPORT-CL is used in the grammar notes beside verbs to indicate that the verb is followed by a clause which is typically introduced by *that*, although often *that* can be omitted. Questions are reported by *wh* words in a similar way to the questions themselves, and yes/no questions are reported by *if* or *whether*. Clauses of this type are known as reported clauses. This includes those clauses often called reported speech or indirect speech. The wording of the clause following the verb is similar to what someone has said or thought. Examples of verbs where the grammar notes include the notation REPORT-CL are **think**, **tell**, and **ask**. EG *He **thought** that he had missed the train... She had been **told** she could leave hospital... They **asked** you why you changed your mind... I **asked** him if he would finish decorating the room at the weekend.*

reportedly /rɪˈpɔːtɪdli[1]/. If something is **reportedly** true, it is said to be true; a formal word. EG *Tests reportedly showed that the island would be uninhabitable for one hundred years... He has reportedly instructed his family not to interfere if he tries to kill himself.* ADV WITH VB, OR ADV SEN ⇑ allegedly

reported speech gives an account of something that someone has said, but without quoting the actual words that are used. **Reported speech** is usually introduced by a verb such as 'say' or 'tell' followed by the word 'that'. See □ at QUOTE. N UNCOUNT = indirect speech

reporter /rɪˈpɔːtə/, **reporters.** A **reporter** is someone whose job is to find out and write what is happening in the world for a newspaper or magazine or for radio or television. EG *He told his story to a reporter from a Chicago newspaper... The prince was interviewed by his favourite television reporter.* N COUNT ⇑ worker

reporting /rɪˈpɔːtɪŋ/ is the presentation of news for newspapers and magazines or for radio and television. EG *I am constantly amazed by the enthusiasm that accompanies sports reporting... The magazine was asked to be less selective in its reporting.* N UNCOUNT

repose /rɪˈpəuz/, **reposes, reposing, reposed**; a formal word. 1 **Repose** is a state in which both your body and your mind are resting, for example when you are asleep or sitting comfortably. EG *Her mouth seemed always to be smiling, even in repose.* N UNCOUNT

2 If something **reposes** somewhere, it is there. EG *His battered leather case now reposed on the carpet at their feet... His rifle reposed safely inside an unobtrusive suitcase.* V+A = lie, rest

3 If someone **reposes** somewhere, they are resting there. EG *The streets were emptying, though in the square people still reposed on benches.* V+A

4 If you say that someone **reposes** in a particular V+A

place, you mean that they are dead and buried there. EG *All his uncles were now reposing with suitable memorial stones over them in the local churchyard.*
5 If you **repose** your trust in someone, you trust them. EG *...the trust I reposed in him.* V+O+A *(in)* ⇑ place

repository /rɪ¹pɒzɪtə⁰ri¹/, **repositories**; a formal word. A **repository** is 1 a person or a group of people who you can rely on to look after something important, especially information. EG *The Foreign Office was regarded as the repository of all wise and relevant information... They act as repositories and disseminators of specialist knowledge.* N COUNT+SUPP : USU+*of* ⇑ store = receptacle 2 a place where you keep objects of a particular kind. EG *The cupboard had become a repository for his growing collection of seashells.* N COUNT ⇑ store

repossess /riːpəzɛs/, **repossess, repossessing, repossessed**. If someone **repossesses** something, especially goods that have not been paid for, they take it back; a formal word. EG *They wanted to repossess the building.* V+O ⇑ reclaim

repot /riːpɒt/, **repots, repotting, repotted**. If you **repot** a plant, you plant it in a bigger pot because it has grown too big for the one that it is in. V+O

reprehensible /rɛprɪhɛnsə¹bə⁰l/. Behaviour that is **reprehensible** is very bad and morally wrong; a formal word. EG *He insisted that adultery was as reprehensible for a husband as for a wife... She put forward the idea that it is morally reprehensible not to be working hard all the time.* ADJ QUALIT = blameworthy

represent /rɛprɪ²zɛnt/, **represents, representing, represented**. 1 If you **represent** someone, you have the right to act on their behalf, for example to express their opinions in a parliament or committee or to state their case in a law court. EG *Shop stewards representing 56,500 workers are meeting the management for pay talks... Lawyers representing relatives of the victims are suing the government for thousands of pounds.* V+O (NG/REFL) ⇑ act
2 If a person or organization **is represented** at a meeting or event, someone is there who can make decisions and act on their behalf. EG *31 nations are now represented at the Geneva Disarmament Conference... The Queen cannot attend the funeral but will be represented by the Duke of Edinburgh.* V+O : USU PASS, USU+A
3 If a group of people is **well represented, strongly represented**, etc at a particular place, there are a lot of them present or a lot of examples of their work. EG *All these artists are well represented at the exhibition... All these nationalities were strongly represented amongst the immigrant population.* PHR : USED AS C
4 If something **represents** something else, it is a sign or symbol for that thing. EG *They use an omega with a dot over the top to represent angular acceleration... The word 'love' was represented by a small heart.* V+O : NO CONT = stand for, symbolize
5 If something **represents** an idea or quality, it is thought of as being a symbol or expression of it. EG *To many of the local people these castles represent a hundred years of domination.* V+O : NO PASS, NO CONT = embody
6 You can say that an action or event **represents** something as a way of saying that it is that thing; a formal use. EG *Does the budget represent a departure from stated government policy?... It represented a major advance in the treatment of malaria.* V+C : NO CONT ⇑ be = constitute, amount to
7 If you say that someone's ideas **represent** the ideas or views of a group of people, you mean that they are typical of those ideas or views. EG *These views don't represent the real thinking of the American people.* ▸ used also of the people themselves. EG *I think they represent a fair cross section of women in this country.* V+O : NO CONT = embody, typify
8 If you **represent** something as a particular thing or as having a particular quality, you describe it as that thing or as having that quality. EG *The evacuation of all our forces was glowingly represented as a triumphant success.* V+O+A *(as)* = depict, portray
9 To **represent** facts or a situation means to give a clear explanation or description of them. EG *The report tries truthfully to represent the results of our researches.* V+O = convey, present
10 If you say that a picture **represents** something, you mean that it shows that thing; a formal use. EG *...a photograph in a silver frame, representing a young woman in academic dress.* V+O = depict

representation /rɛprɪ²zɛnteɪʃə⁰n/, **representations**. 1 **Representation** is the state of having one or more representatives, for example on a committee or in a parliament, who can vote or make decisions on your behalf. EG *They're campaigning for student representation on the university's governing bodies... The party increased its representation from 20 to 38 delegates...* ● See also **proportional representation.** N UNCOUNT
2 A **representation** of a person, thing, or event is something that shows or describes them in an artistic form, for example in a painting or a play. EG *Her work is a subjective representation of the external world... It was a brilliant theatrical representation of the events leading up to the war.* N COUNT : IF+ PREP THEN *of* = portrayal
3 **Representations** are formal statements that are made to a government or other official body, in which you explain your opinion on a particular matter, usually in order to make a complaint or request a change; used in formal English. EG *The regulations may now be changed in the light of representations received from overseas governments... The committee's enquiry arose from representations made by a group of local residents.* N PLURAL

representational /rɛprɪ²zɛnteɪʃə⁰nəl, -ʃənə⁰l/. **Representational** art attempts to show things as they actually look; a formal word. EG *...representational images... ...representational styles of medieval manuscript illumination.* ADJ CLASSIF ⇑ realistic = figurative

representative /rɛprɪ²zɛntətɪv/, **representatives**. 1 A **representative** is 1.1 a person who has been chosen to act or make decisions on behalf of another person or a group of people. EG *They're demanding to have a representative of the workers on the board... The committee included representatives from the police and fire brigade.... We're currently talking to the union representatives about the scheme.* N COUNT = delegate 1.2 a person whose job is to sell a company's products or services, especially by travelling round to other companies or organizations; a formal use. EG *One of our representatives will be calling on you next week.* N COUNT ⇑ employee = rep, salesperson
2 **Representative** means belonging to a system of government or decision-making in which a small group of people is chosen to make decisions on behalf of a larger group. EG *The government consists of two representative assemblies... She's on the Students' Representative Council.* ADJ CLASSIF : ATTRIB
3 Something that is **representative** has qualities or characteristics that are typical of the group to which it belongs. EG *We questioned a representative cross-section of economic and occupational groups... We wondered if this case was in any way representative of the attitudes of the police.* ADJ QUALIT : IF+ PREP THEN *of*

repress /ri¹prɛs/, **represses, repressing, repressed**. 1 If you **repress** a feeling, 1.1 you manage not to show it to other people. EG *It was all I could do to repress my laughter... I could not repress a shiver whenever I thought about what had happened to him... She repressed the desire to mention his name.* V+O = suppress, hold back 1.2 you do not think about it and pretend to yourself that it does not exist so that after a period of time you are no longer aware of it; a technical term in psychology. EG *...a series of fantasies induced by repressed sexuality.* V+O
2 If a group of people **represses** another group, for example the inhabitants of a country, they control them by force. EG *The military officers would help to exploit and repress their own people... Whenever the workers openly began to organise they would be swiftly repressed.* V+O = subjugate, keep down

repressed /ri¹prɛst/. Someone who is **repressed** has many feelings and desires, especially sexual ones, that are not fulfilled. EG *In this play she played the part of a repressed governess.* ADJ QUALIT = frustrated

repression /ri¹prɛʃə⁰n/ is 1 the use of force to control the way of life of a group of people, especially the inhabitants of a country. EG *They wanted to fight all forms of injustice and repression... The government set out on a wholesale, deliberate policy of repression.* N UNCOUNT ⇑ oppression 2 the act of repressing your feelings and desires, especially sexual ones. EG *He felt that much unhappiness was due to sexual repression.* N UNCOUNT

repressive /ri¹prɛsɪv/. A government that is **repressive** uses force to control the way of life of the inhabitants of a country. EG *It was a repressive and authoritarian country... ...the repressive forces of the police state.* ADJ QUALIT ⇑ oppressive

reprieve /ri¹priːv/, **reprieves, reprieving, reprieved**. 1 If someone **is reprieved** after they have V+O : USU PASS been sentenced to death, their punishment is officially cancelled or postponed. EG *Dr Henesey was reprieved in 1758.*

2 A **reprieve** is **2.1** an official order cancelling or postponing a person's punishment, especially when they have been condemned to death. EG *He was unexpectedly granted a reprieve.* N COUNT = pardon **2.2** a temporary relief from difficulty or pain. EG *The finding of oil represents a colossal reprieve for the islanders.* N COUNT : USU SING ⇑ deliverance

reprimand /rɛprɪmɑːnd/, **reprimands, reprimanding, reprimanded. 1** If you **reprimand** someone, you speak or write to them officially, criticizing them severely for something that they have said or done. EG *He was called to the office of a superior to be reprimanded... The teacher reprimanded him for sulking.* V+O ⇑ scold = admonish

2 A **reprimand** is something that a person in authority writes or says to someone, criticizing them severely for something that they have said or done. EG *Continual reprimands lead to a feeling of resentment.* N COUNT/UNCOUNT ⇑ scolding = rebuke

reprint, reprints, reprinting, reprinted. The word **reprint** is pronounced /riːprɪnt/ when it is a noun and /riːprɪnt/ when it is a verb. **1** If a book **is reprinted**, a lot of new copies of it are printed because all the other ones have been sold. EG *The article was reprinted and used as propaganda.* V+O : USU PASS ⇑ print

2 A **reprint** is a copy of a book which has been reprinted. EG *...the 1959 reprint of his book.* N COUNT

reprisal /rɪˈpraɪzəˡl/, **reprisals. 1 Reprisals** are violent actions that are taken by one group of people against another, as punishment or revenge for similar actions carried out on the first group by the second group. EG *The occupying forces took bloody reprisals against the nationalist leaders.* N COUNT : USU PL ⇑ retaliation

2 Reprisal is act of carrying out reprisals; used in formal English. EG *There have been threats of reprisal.* N UNCOUNT = retaliation

reproach /rɪˈprəʊtʃ/, **reproaches, reproaching, reproached**; a formal word. **1 Reproach** is criticism of someone, usually expressed in a polite or gentle way, for something that they have said or done. EG *She was astonished at the look of reproach on his face... She wrote a long letter of reproach to Sarah on the subject... His behaviour throughout has been beyond reproach.* N UNCOUNT = reprimand

2 A **reproach** is something that you say to someone, usually in a polite or gentle way, in order to tell them that they have done something wrong or harmful. EG *His reply sounded to me like a reproach... She responded submissively to his reproaches.* N COUNT = rebuke

3 If you **reproach** someone for something, you tell them, usually in a polite or gentle way, that they have done something wrong or harmful. EG *Father reproached him, saying, 'This really won't do, you know.'... They are in no position to reproach the local people for their behaviour.* V+O : IF+PREP THEN *for/with* = rebuke, upbraid

4 If you **reproach** yourself, you think with regret about something that you have said or done that was wrong or harmful. EG *I've nothing to reproach myself with... He had bitterly reproached himself for his complacency.* V+O (REFL) : IF +PREP THEN *for/with* = blame

reproachful /rɪˈprəʊtʃfʊl/ looks, glances, remarks, etc show that you are criticizing someone for something wrong that they have done. EG *This remark earned a reproachful glance from Peterson... She was looking at me with rather reproachful brown eyes.* ADJ QUALIT ⇑ resentful ◊ **reproachfully**. EG *Morris looked at her reproachfully.* ◊ ADV WITH VB ⇑ resentfully

reprobate /rɛprəˢbeɪt/, **reprobates.** A **reprobate** is a person who behaves in a way that you do not approve of, for example by getting drunk regularly or by losing a lot of money through gambling; a rather old-fashioned word. EG *It is time this reprobate was removed from office.* N COUNT = libertine, rake ▸ used as an adjective. EG *...that reprobate, gambling aristocrat.* ▸ ADJ QUALIT = immoral

reproduce /riːprədjuːs/, **reproduces, reproducing, reproduced. 1** To **reproduce** something means to make a fairly accurate copy of it. EG *Each leaf on the tree had been faithfully reproduced... She tried to reproduce his accent... This superb recording reproduces all the immense power of this magnificent symphony.* V+O = duplicate, imitate

2 To **reproduce** a picture, speech, or piece of writing means to make a photograph or printed copy of it. EG *This painting has never been reproduced anywhere... On 17 October 1914 The Times reproduced a letter written by a Munich academic... I reproduce her words here.* V+O

3 If you **reproduce** an action or achievement, you repeat an action or achievement that you or someone else has already done. EG *I've never been able to reproduce the success of my first book.* V+O

4 If people, animals, or plants **reproduce**, they produce young. EG *Bacteria reproduce by splitting into two.* V OR V+O (REFL) = procreate

reproduction /riːprədʌkʃəⁿn/, **reproductions. 1 Reproduction** is **1.1** the copying of sound, writing, pictures, etc, so that these things can be heard or seen by a large number of people. EG *The sound reproduction is poor on my stereo... My art reaches an increased audience through reproduction... The Controller has no objection to the reproduction of the Report.* N UNCOUNT **1.2** the processes by which an animal or plant produces its young. EG *Today's lesson is about plant reproduction... ...human reproduction.* N UNCOUNT ⇑ propagation = procreation

2 A **reproduction** is a modern copy of a painting, a piece of furniture, an antique, etc. EG *I would rather have a good reproduction than a bad original... I first became interested in art through reproductions of Impressionist paintings... ...reproduction Colonial furniture.* N COUNT, OR N BEFORE N = facsimile

reproductive /riːprədʌktɪv/ means concerned with the reproduction of animals and other creatures or plants. EG *...a tapeworm's digestive and reproductive systems... ...the reproductive organs.* ADJ CLASSIF : USU ATTRIB

reproof /rɪˈpruːf/, **reproofs. Reproof** is a way of speaking or acting which shows that you disapprove of something that someone has done; a formal word. EG *Miss Head looked at me with reproof.* N UNCOUNT ⇑ criticism ▸ used as a count noun. EG *Before he left he gave Michael a mild reproof.* ▸ N COUNT = rebuke

reprove /rɪˈpruːv/, **reproves, reproving, reproved.** If you **reprove** someone, you tell them that they have behaved wrongly or foolishly; a formal word. V+O : IF+PREP THEN *for* ⇑ criticize = rebuke ◊ **reproving**. EG *All she got was a reproving letter from her Aunt Agnes.* ◊ ADJ CLASSIF

reptile /rɛptaɪl/, **reptiles.** A **reptile** is a cold-blooded animal which has a scaly skin and lays eggs. Tortoises, snakes, lizards, and crocodiles are all reptiles. N COUNT ⇑ vertebrate

reptilian /rɛptɪlɪən/ means characteristic of reptiles or like a reptile. ADJ CLASSIF : ATTRIB

republic /rɪˈpʌblɪk/, **republics.** A **republic** is a country whose system of government is based on the idea that every citizen has equal status, so that there is no king or queen and no aristocracy. The government is usually elected by the people. EG *Cuba became an independent republic after three years of US military rule.* N COUNT ⇑ state ▸ used as the official title of some republics. EG *...the Republic of Ireland... ...the Irish Republic.* ▸ ADJ CLASSIF ● See also **banana republic**.

Republican /rɪˈpʌblɪkən/, **Republicans.** A **Republican** is **1** a member or supporter of the Republican Party, one of the two main political parties in the United States of America. N COUNT ▸ used as an adjective. ▸ ADJ CLASSIF

2 a person from Northern Ireland who believes that Northern Ireland should not be ruled by Britain but should become part of the Republic of Ireland.. N COUNT ▸ used as an adjective. ▸ ADJ CLASSIF

republicanism /rɪˈpʌblɪkənɪzəⁿm/ is **1** the belief that the best system of government for a country is a republic. N UNCOUNT **2** support for the idea that Northern Ireland should become part of the Republic of Ireland. EG *He was particularly touchy about Irish republicanism and the Ulster question.* N UNCOUNT **3** membership of the Republican Party in the United States. EG *He was converted from his respectable Republicanism by President Roosevelt.* N UNCOUNT

repudiate /rɪˈpjuːdɪeɪt/, **repudiates, repudiating, repudiated**; a formal word. **1** If you **repudiate** a state of affairs or something that has been said, you say that you will have nothing to do with it. EG *He declined to repudiate violence... I repudiate everything you have said.* V+O = reject ≠ accept ◊ **repudiation** /rɪˈpjuːdɪeɪʃəⁿn/. EG *...his repudiation of the evidence.* ◊ N UNCOUNT

2 If you **repudiate** someone, you state publicly that you no longer have a connection with them, especially when it is someone who you have previously been married to or friendly with. EG *In this society a man was allowed to repudiate a wife who was barren.* V+O = cast off

repugnance /rɪˈpʌgnəns/ is a feeling of very strong dislike and disgust that you feel towards N UNCOUNT = revulsion someone or something. EG *He screwed up his face in an expression of utter repugnance.*

repugnant /rɪˈpʌgnənt/. If you feel that something is **repugnant**, you find it horrible and disgusting and you dislike it a lot. EG *The idea of kissing him is to me wholly repugnant... Brody found his father's attitudes both repugnant and silly.* — ADJ QUALIT: IF + PREP THEN *to* = distasteful

repulse /rɪˈpʌls/, **repulses, repulsing, repulsed.** 1 If something **repulses** you, you find it horrible and disgusting and you want to avoid it. EG *Like all the great war photographers he is at once repulsed by what he sees and drawn to it.* — V+O: USU PASS = repel

2 If an army or other group of people **repulses** an enemy force, they fight it and cause it to retreat. EG *The raid was swiftly repulsed.* — V+O = drive back

repulsion /rɪˈpʌlʃəⁿn/ is 1 a strong feeling of dislike and disgust that you feel towards something so that you want to avoid it. EG *She shivered with repulsion... I can't help feeling repulsion... My first movement was one of repulsion.* 2 a force which tends to push two objects apart, such as the force between two magnetic poles. EG *...magnetic repulsion.* — N UNCOUNT = revulsion; N UNCOUNT

repulsive /rɪˈpʌlsɪv/. If you say that something is **repulsive**, you mean that you find it horrible and disgusting and you want to avoid it. EG *His behaviour was repulsive... ...his slightly repulsive appearance... ...a rather repulsive child.* ◊ **repulsively**. EG *...a plump, sallow, repulsively plain girl of at least fifteen.* — ADJ QUALIT ⇑ unpleasant = revolting; ◊ ADV = revoltingly

reputable /rɛpjəⁱtəbəⁿl/. Something or someone that is **reputable** is known to produce a good standard of work and service or to be of good quality. EG *All reputable companies give a guarantee... Luxembourg produces six reputable and relatively inexpensive white wines.* ◊ **reputably**. EG *He is reputably established in the business world.* — ADJ QUALIT = respectable; ◊ ADV ⇑ well

reputation /rɛpjəⁱteɪʃəⁿn/, **reputations.** 1 The **reputation** that someone has is the opinion that other people have about them as a result of what they do and the way that they behave. EG *She acquired a reputation as a very good writer... Our doctor had a reputation for being good with children... He had earned the reputation of being a formidable opponent.* — N COUNT: USU + SUPP = name

2 The **reputation** that an institution has is is the opinion that people have about how good it is. EG *The school has a good reputation for exam results.* — N COUNT: USU + SUPP = name

repute /rɪˈpjuːt/; a formal word. 1 Something or someone **of repute** is respected and known to be honest and trustworthy. EG *This story was published by two journals of repute... There was an unsuccessful search for a witness of repute.* — PHR: USED AS C

2 If something is held **in repute**, it is respected and considered to be of high quality. EG *Her work was held in high repute by many critics... ...the task of bringing football back into repute.* — PHR: USED AS AN A

reputed /rɪˈpjuːtɪᵈd/. 1 If something is **reputed** to be true or to have happened, some people say that it is true or that it happened. EG *The buildings were reputed to be haunted... ...a man reputed to have worked miracles.* — ADJ CLASSIF: PRED + *to*-INF = rumoured

2 **Reputed** means generally believed to be true or to have existed. EG *...their reputed beauty.* — ADJ CLASSIF: ATTRIB

reputedly /rɪˈpjuːtɪdliᴵ/. If something is **reputedly** true, it is generally believed to be true. EG *...events that reputedly took place thousands of years ago.* — ADV = supposedly

request /rɪˈkwɛst/, **requests, requesting, requested**; a fairly formal word. 1 If you **request** something, you ask very politely for it. EG *The President requested an emergency session of the United Nations... Visitors are requested not to pick the flowers... Mr and Mrs Oliver Barrett request the pleasure of your company at a dinner to celebrate their fiftieth wedding anniversary.* — V+O, OR V+ REPORT-CL

2 A **request** is 2.1 a very polite demand for something. EG *We have received thousands of requests for our fact sheets... The Government rejected the Opposition's request to debate unemployment... I made repeated requests for money from my father.* 2.2 something which has been asked for, especially a piece of music played on the radio. EG *I'm playing this request for Mary Jones who lives in Cardiff.* — N COUNT = appeal; N COUNT

3 If someone will do something **on request** or if something is available **on request**, they will do it or it is available whenever you ask for it. EG *Your doctor will give, on request, a letter confirming that you are too ill to work.* — PHR: USED AS AN A

4 If you do something **at someone's request**, you do it because they have asked you to. EG *I offered to put him up temporarily at the request of his girl friend... At my personal request, a group of MPs will meet with your leaders.* — PHR + NG: USED AS AN A

request stop, request stops. A **request stop** is a bus stop at which a bus will stop only if someone signals it to do so. — N COUNT

requiem /rɛkwɪɛm/, **requiems.** 1 A **requiem** or a **requiem mass** is a mass celebrated in remembrance of someone who has recently died. EG *There will be a requiem mass for him at St Joseph's Church on the 15th.* — N COUNT = service

2 A **requiem** is a piece of music for singers and musicians that can be performed either as a celebration of a requiem mass or as part of a concert. EG *The concert will end with a performance of Verdi's Requiem.* — N COUNT

require /rɪˈkwaɪə/, **requires, requiring, required**; a formal word. 1 If you **require** something, or if something **is required**, you need it or it is necessary. EG *Is there anything you require, Mr Heissman?... Parliamentary approval would be required for any scheme.* — V+O: IF + PREP THEN *for*, OR V+ *to*-INF ⇑ want

2 If you **are required** to do something, or if someone **requires** you to do it, you have to do it because it is a rule or because someone insists that you do it. EG *The course requires you to be bilingual... The work isn't up to the standard I require.* ◊ **required**. EG *Check that the machines meet required standards.* — V+O: USU PASS + *to*-INF/REPORT-CL/*of* ⇑ demand; ◊ ADJ CLASSIF = necessary

requirement /rɪˈkwaɪəməᵊnt/, **requirements.** A **requirement** is 1 something that you must do, achieve, or possess in order to be allowed to do some other thing or to be suitable for a particular purpose. EG *Maths is no longer a prime requirement for a career in accounting... The applicant meets our general entrance requirements.* 2 something that is necessary. EG *Mexico imported half her grain requirements in 1940... As technology has advanced, the requirement for back-breaking toil has diminished... ...the particular requirements of radio acting.* — N COUNT: USU + SUPP ⇑ condition; N COUNT: USU + SUPP = need

requisite /rɛkwɪzɪt/, **requisites**; a formal word. 1 **Requisite** means necessary for a particular purpose. EG *She expected to achieve the requisite two-thirds majority for nomination... You do have to give the requisite amount of notice to get your money back.* — ADJ CLASSIF: ATTRIB = required

2 A **requisite** is something which is necessary for a particular purpose. EG *...the requisites of modern building.* — N COUNT = requirement

requisition /rɛkwɪzɪʃəⁿn/, **requisitions, requisitioning, requisitioned.** 1 If someone **requisitions** something such as a vehicle, building, or food, they formally demand the use of it, especially for the army. EG *I requisitioned a couple of vans.* — V+O = commandeer

2 A **requisition** is a formal demand for the use of a vehicle, building, supplies, etc, especially by the army. EG *He presented a list of requisitions to the depot commander.* ▸ used as an uncount noun. EG *We obtained petrol by requisition.* — N COUNT; ▸ N UNCOUNT

requite /rɪˈkwaɪt/, **requites, requiting, requited.** If a desire or feeling **is requited**, it is satisfied; a formal word. EG *No matter what desires are requited, they are always replaced by others... He had seen her flushed with requited love.* — V+O: USU PASS

re-route /riːruːt/, **re-routes, re-routing, re-routed.** If traffic **is re-routed**, it is directed along different roads, for example because there has been an accident and some roads are blocked. — V+O: USU + A = redirect

re-run, re-runs, re-running, re-ran. The word **re-run** is pronounced /riːrʌn/ in paragraph 1 and /riːrʌn/ in paragraph 2. The form **re-run** is used in the present tense and also as the past participle of the verb. 1 A **re-run** is a film, play, programme, etc that is broadcast or put on again. EG *They put on a re-run of 'The Government Inspector' with Alan Howard.* — N COUNT: IF + PREP THEN *of* = repeat

2 If a theatre company or cinema **re-runs** a play or a film, it shows or puts it on again. — V+O = repeat

rescind /rɪˈsɪnd/, **rescinds, rescinding, rescinded.** If a government or group of people in power **rescind** a law or agreement, they officially withdraw it and state that it is no longer valid; a formal word. EG *This law was later rescinded... They had to summon a second conference and rescind the previous motion.* — V+O: USU PASS = repeal

rescue /rɛskjuː/, **rescues, rescuing, rescued.** 1 If you **rescue** someone or something, you take — V+O action to help them get away from a dangerous or harmful situation. EG *All my attempts to rescue him were in vain... He was rescued from the sinking aircraft... The Cabinet decided on 3 February not to rescue the company.*

2 **Rescue** is help which is given to someone or something which saves them from a dangerous or unpleasant situation. EG *Rescue was at hand... You might dream of rescue, but it's useless.* N UNCOUNT = deliverance

3 If you **go** or **come to the rescue** of someone or something, you help them when they are in danger or difficulty. EG *It was William who came to the rescue... Toby came to my rescue.* PHR : VB INFLECTS

3 A **rescue** is a successful attempt to save someone or something from a difficult or dangerous situation. EG *The coastguard may be working on as many as 20 rescues at any one time.* N COUNT ⇑ recovery

rescuer /rɛskju:ə/, **rescuers**. A **rescuer** is a person who rescues or tries to rescue someone else. EG *Rescuers found her dead... The man's shouts could not be heard by the rescuers.* N COUNT ⇑ helper

research /rɪˈsɜ:tʃ/, **researches, researching, researched**. 1 **Research** is a detailed study of a subject or an aspect of a subject. When you do research, you collect and analyse facts and information and try to gain new knowledge or new understanding. EG *...scientific research... I had come to India to do some research on Anglo-Indian literature... Thank you for talking to us about your research.* ▸ used also as a plural noun. EG *He began his researches into electricity.* N UNCOUNT ⇑ investigation ▸ N PLURAL

2 If you **research** a subject, you study it in detail by collecting and analysing facts and information in order to try to gain new knowledge or new understanding. EG *The historical background to the play had been very carefully researched... I spent some time researching abroad.* V OR V+O ⇑ investigate

researcher /rɪˈsɜ:tʃə/, **researchers**. A **researcher** is someone who does research into a subject. N COUNT

reseat /ri:si:t/, **reseats, reseating, reseated**. If you **reseat** yourself, you sit down again; used in formal English. EG *Mary and Sam came slowly back and reseated themselves by his side.* V+O (REFL) ⇑ seat

resell /ri:sɛl/, **resells, reselling, resold**. If you **resell** something, you sell it again after you have bought it. EG *If they build at the back of the house we might not be able to resell it.* V OR V+O

resemblance /rɪˈzɛmbləns/ is similarity between two or more people or things, often in physical appearance. EG *She bore a striking resemblance to his wife... You can see the family resemblance... They were both in their early forties, but that was the only resemblance.* N SING WITH DET/ N UNCOUNT : IF + PREP THEN *to/between*

resemble /rɪˈzɛmbəˀl/, **resembles, resembling, resembled**. If one thing or person **resembles** another, they are similar to each other, for example in appearance or behaviour. EG *Both you and your father resemble him very much physically... The situation resembles that of Europe in 1940... She would never get anything that more closely resembled what she wanted.* V+O, NO CONT/ IMPER = be like

resent /rɪˈzɛnt/, **resents, resenting, resented**. If you **resent** something, you feel bitter or indignant about it and often express this in what you say or how you behave. EG *He seems to know his material very well, but resents questions and discussion... They resent being treated as common criminals... Cath said she felt we resented her.* V+O ⇑ dislike

resentful /rɪˈzɛntfʊl/. If you are **resentful**, you feel or show in your behaviour how much you resent someone or something. EG *Ralph watched them, envious and resentful... He was resentful at the way he had been treated... I felt resentful about having to see him again so soon.* ▸ used of people's gestures or behaviour. EG *...her sullen, resentful air.* ◊ **resentfully**. EG *They raised their heads, looking at him resentfully.* ADJ QUALIT = aggrieved, angry ▸ = grudging ◊ ADV WITH VB = grudgingly

resentment /rɪˈzɛntməˀnt/, **resentments**. **Resentment** is bitterness, indignation, or anger that you feel about a person, event, or situation. EG *He was filled with resentment... Brody sensed his own resentment at the intrusion.* ▸ used as a count noun. EG *They had to suppress all their natural resentments.* N UNCOUNT = rancour ▸ N COUNT = grudge

reservation /rɛzəveɪʃəˀn/, **reservations**. 1 A **reservation** is a doubt that you have about something or someone and that stops you from accepting them or approving of them completely. EG *This is the one big reservation I've got about the book... He shared his assistant's reservations.* N COUNT

2 If you do something **with reservation** or **with reservations**, you do it even though you are not completely sure that you want to do it or that it is the best thing to do. EG *With reservation, I would recommend this second film.* PHR : USED AS AN A

3 If you do something **without reservation**, you do it without any doubts or hesitation at all. EG *They accepted the plan without reservation.* PHR : USED AS AN A = unconditionally

4 A **reservation** is also 4.1 an arrangement that something such as a table in a restaurant, a seat in the theatre, or a room in a hotel will be kept for you. EG *I will make the reservation for seven thirty.* N COUNT = booking **4.2** an area of land that is kept separate for a particular group of people to live in. For example, there are reservations in the USA and Canada for tribes of American Indians. EG *...the Navaho reservation... ...a reservation for Xhosa tribes.* N COUNT = reserve

reserve /rɪˈzɜ:v/, **reserves, reserving, reserved**. 1 If something **is reserved** for a particular person or purpose, it is kept specially for that person or purpose. EG *The garden is private, its lawn reserved for those who work in the museum... Baldwin's reply was reserved for a public occasion... He gave me a look of the sort usually reserved for naughty schoolchildren.* V+O : USU PASS = set aside

2 If you **reserve** a table in a restaurant, a seat in a theatre, etc, you arrange for it to be kept for you. EG *He was busy adjusting his accounts and reserving an aeroplane ticket for himself.* V+O = book

3 If you say that you **reserve the right** to do something, you mean that you want to be allowed to do it if you feel that it is necessary. EG *The French reserved absolutely the right to decide their own agricultural policy... The management reserves the right to refuse admission.* PHR : VB INFLECTS

4 **Reserves** are military forces which are not permanently ready for action but which can be used in emergencies. EG *...the strategic deployment of naval reserves.* N PLURAL

5 A **reserve** is **5.1** a supply or stock of something that is not actually being used at the present but that is available for use when needed. EG *We have large coal reserves... They do not have the reserve funds needed to make these investments.... He was able to draw on vast reserves of talent and enthusiasm.* N COUNT ⇑ resource **5.2** someone who has not been chosen for a sports team, but who will be asked to play in it if one of its members cannot play. EG *He's first reserve for Liverpool.* N COUNT ⇑ substitute **5.3** an area of land that is kept separate or private in order to protect the animals, birds, or people living there. EG *...the Caucasus nature reserve... The government set up Aboriginal reserves on land that neither the cattlemen nor anyone else wanted.* N COUNT : USU MOD+N

6 If you have something **in reserve**, you have it ready or available to use when it is needed. EG *You will find a little stack of candles in reserve... I kept some tranquillizers in reserve in case I became agitated.* PHR : USED AS AN A ⇑ stored

7 **Reserve** is the quality of keeping your feelings hidden and not liking to show other people what you are really thinking. EG *She lacked all judgement, all reserve: her emotions swung violently... His tone had lost the cautious reserve it had previously had.* N UNCOUNT = restraint

8 A **reserve** price is the lowest sum of money that the owners will agree to accept for something being sold at an auction; used in British English. EG *The portrait sold for almost three times the reserve price.* N COUNT : USU BEFORE N ⇑ minimum

reserved /rɪˈzɜ:vd/. 1 Someone who is **reserved** keeps their feelings hidden and does not like to show other people what they are really thinking. EG *An Englishman is very reserved, quiet, always discreet... ...their cold and reserved little letters.* ADJ QUALIT

2 A table in a restaurant, a seat in a theatre, etc that is **reserved** is being kept for someone because they have asked for it to be kept for them. EG *Did you have a reserved seat?... I had a place reserved at the Youth Hostel in Stockholm.* ADJ CLASSIF = booked

reservist /rɪˈzɜ:vɪst/, **reservists**. A **reservist** is a soldier who belongs to a country's reserve army. N COUNT

reservoir /rɛzəvwɑ:/, **reservoirs**. A **reservoir** is 1 a natural or artificial lake that is used for storing water before it is supplied to a city or other area. EG N COUNT

Rivers and reservoirs overflowed.* **2** a large quantity of something that is not in use but that can be used when needed. EG *Industry must have a reservoir of cheap labour... History is a reservoir of human experience.*
N COUNT+*of* ⇑ store

reset /riːˈset/, **resets, resetting**. The form **reset** is used in the present tense and also as the past participle. **1** If you **reset** a machine or device, you set it again so that it is ready to work again or ready to perform a particular function. EG *He reset the alarm and climbed back into bed.*
V+O

2 If someone **resets** a bone, they put it back into its correct position after it has been broken. EG *His nose had been broken and reset.*
V+O ⇑ set

resettle /riːˈsetəˀl/, **resettles, resettling, resettled**. If people **resettle** or if a government or other organization **resettles** them, they move to a different place to live because they are no longer allowed to stay in the area where they are living. EG *The refugees themselves do not want to be resettled... These people began to resettle in London.*
V-ERG ⇑ settle

◊ **resettlement**. EG *...a massive programme of resettlement.*
◊ N UNCOUNT ⇑ settlement

reshuffle /riːˈʃʌfəˀl/, **reshuffles, reshuffling, reshuffled**. A **reshuffle** is a reorganization of people or things, especially of jobs within a government. EG *The Prime Minister announced a reshuffle of her Cabinet.* ▸ used as a verb. EG *He felt it was time to reshuffle the team.*
N COUNT : USU SING
▸ V OR V+O

reside /rɪˈzaɪd/, **resides, residing, resided**; a formal word. **1** If you **reside** somewhere, you live there and it is your home. EG *She decided to stay, despite the obvious cost of residing in such an exclusive area... It was said that a great poet had resided here.*
V+A : NO IMPER ⇑ stay = dwell

2 If something **resides** in a place or thing, it is present in that place or thing. EG *Strength resides in the gun... Real power resides in the workshop and on the office floor... Memory has been shown to reside in many different organisms.*
V+A : USU A *(in)*, NO CONT, NO IMPER ⇑ be

residence /ˈrezɪdəns/, **residences**; a formal word.
1 Your **residence** is your home. EG *...the prime minister's official residence... Years ago these houses had been very smart residences.*
N COUNT ⇑ house = dwelling

2 Your **residence** in a place is **2.1** the fact that you live there. EG *Shanty towns are places of work as well as of residence... Residence among the poor is suggested as a way of understanding their problems... ...a residence permit.*
N UNCOUNT ⇑ habitation
2.2 the period of time during which you live there. EG *In New York, average residence in one place is less than four years.*
N UNCOUNT ⇑ habitation

3 If you **take up residence** somewhere, you go and live there. EG *They had taken up residence together on the top floor of a hotel.*
PHR+A : VB INFLECTS

4 If a particular person is **in residence** in a particular place, they are living there. EG *None of the royal family are in residence at the palace at the moment.*
PHR : USED AS AN A = resident

5 An artist or writer **in residence** is one who works and teaches in an institution such as a school. EG *The school is providing money for an artist in residence.*
PHR AFTER N

6 See also **hall of residence**.

resident /ˈrezɪdənt/, **residents**. **1** The **residents** of a country, area, or house are the people who live in it. EG *The local residents complained about the noise from the disco... She became a permanent resident of California.*
N COUNT ⇑ inhabitant

2 Someone who is **resident** in a country, town, or building lives in that country, town, or building. EG *She is aged fifty-three, born at Lyons and resident in Paris... Since 1947 she has been resident abroad.*
ADJ CLASSIF : USU PRED+A *(in)*

3 Someone who is **resident** at the place where they work lives there. EG *They engaged a resident tutor... If the landlord is resident, the student may have less rights.*
ADJ CLASSIF = live-in

4 If an institution has a **resident** specialist of some kind, that specialist works for the institution. EG *She was their resident expert on the history of the town... ...the company's resident dramatist.*
ADJ CLASSIF : ATTRIB ⇑ attached

5 If a bird or animal is a **resident** in a region, it lives permanently in that region and does not move or fly to another place for part of the year.
N COUNT

residential /ˌrezɪˈdenʃəˀl/. **1** A **residential** area of a town consists mainly of people's houses and has very few offices and factories in it. EG *The school was in a residential part of town... ...separate residential and industrial areas.*
ADJ CLASSIF : ATTRIB ≠ industrial

2 A **residential** job is one in which you live in the place where you work or study. EG *...a weekend residential course at the college.* ▸ used of people who work in these jobs. EG *...residential staff in a children's home.*
ADJ CLASSIF : USU ATTRIB

residents' association, residents' associations. A **residents' association** is a group of residents in an area who try to encourage their local authority to make their area more pleasant to live in and who oppose undesirable developments.
N COUNT : IF SING, VB CAN BE SING OR PL

residual /rɪˈzɪdjuəl/ means remaining when the main part of something has disappeared or has been removed; a formal word. EG *She scraped off the residual cement... ...irrational and residual prejudices of a dark past.*
ADJ CLASSIF : USU ATTRIB

residue /ˈrezɪdjuː/, **residues**. A **residue** of something is a small amount of it that remains after most of it has disappeared or has been removed; a formal word. EG *Residues of pesticides can build up in the soil... The fuel shortage was so acute that even crop residues and stubble were uprooted and burned... The incident left Barbara with a residue of guilt.*
N COUNT : USU+SUPP

resign /rɪˈzaɪn/, **resigns, resigning, resigned**.
1 If you **resign** from a job or position, you state that you do not want to continue doing it and so you leave it. EG *She resigned from the Government... Lloyd George was threatening to resign... Robert Bignold resigned the Chairmanship.*
V OR V+O : USU V, IF+PREP THEN *from/as* = quit

2 If you **resign** yourself to something unpleasant, you accept it because you realize that you cannot change it or prevent it. EG *You're a widow now, Mrs Pearl. I think you must resign yourself to that fact.*
V+O (REFL)+A *(to)*

3 See also **resigned**.

resignation /ˌrezɪgˈneɪʃəˀn/, **resignations**. **1** A **resignation** is a formal statement of your intention to leave a job, position, or organization. EG *Mr McPherson has accepted my resignation... He threatened resignation from the company.*
N COUNT/UNCOUNT ⇑ departure

2 An attitude of **resignation** is acceptance of an unpleasant situation or the unpleasant circumstances of life without complaining or worrying about them or trying to change them. EG *...an expression of saintly resignation... She spoke with quiet resignation.*
N UNCOUNT ⇑ surrender

resigned /rɪˈzaɪnd/. If you are **resigned** to something unpleasant, you accept it without complaining because you realize that you cannot change it or prevent it. EG *They feel resigned to losing their money... He considered it his duty, in a resigned sort of way, to stand by her.* ◊ **resignedly**. EG *'He will come,' said Joe resignedly.*
ADJ CLASSIF : IF+PREP THEN *to* = reconciled
◊ ADV WITH VB

resilience /rɪˈzɪljəns/ is **1** the ability that a person or institution has to recover quickly from a setback or misfortune, such as an illness. EG *The chairman has shown remarkable resilience... Democratic political structures have a remarkable resilience... Signs of resilience in the economy abound.*
N UNCOUNT, OR N SING WITH DET ⇑ strength
2 the quality that something has of being strong and not damaged easily by being hit, stretched, or squeezed. EG *He was bouncing on the mattress to demonstrate its resilience.*
N UNCOUNT, OR N SING WITH DET ⇑ elasticity

resilient /rɪˈzɪljənt/. **1** Something that is **resilient** is strong and is not damaged easily by being hit, stretched, or squeezed. EG *We try to make things so that they are tough and resilient and lasting.*
ADJ QUALIT

2 Someone who is **resilient** is able to recover quickly from an illness or a misfortune. EG *Among all of us she had been the most resilient.*
ADJ QUALIT ⇑ strong

resin /ˈrezɪn/, **resins**. **Resin** is **1** a sticky substance that is produced by some trees, for example pines and firs. It is used in medicine and in making varnishes. EG *The trees protect their trunks from insect attack with a special gummy substance, resin.*
N UNCOUNT = natural resin

2 a substance resembling pine resin that is produced chemically. It is used especially in making plastics. EG *They are made of a common plastic resin.*
N MASS

resinous /ˈrezɪnəs/ means like resin or containing resin. EG *...their sweet, resinous smell.*
ADJ CLASSIF : ATTRIB

resist /rɪˈzɪst/, **resists, resisting, resisted**. **1** If you **resist** something such as a change, you refuse to accept it and to try to prevent it from happening. EG *Our trade union has resisted the introduction of automation... He resisted demands for a public enquiry... They are doing things they would have bitterly resisted only two years ago.*
V+O = oppose, withstand

2 If you **resist** someone or if you **resist** an attack by them, you fight against them in order to avoid being defeated by them. EG *They tried to resist the rob-*
V+O = oppose, withstand

bers... ...the last people who had resisted the Romans... Any attack will be resisted with force if necessary.

3 If you **resist** doing something or **resist** the temptation to do something, you stop yourself from doing it although you know that you would like to do it. EG *I can't resist teasing him... She resisted an urge to scream... I resisted the temptation to get very drunk.* V+O/-ING : USU WITH BROAD NEG = refrain from

4 If you **resist** arrest, you try to prevent someone from arresting you. Resisting arrest is a crime. EG *You will also be charged with resisting arrest.* V+O

5 If something **resists** damage of a particular kind, it remains unharmed or undamaged by it; a fairly formal use. EG *This special coating is designed to resist rust.* V+O = withstand

resistance /rɪˈzɪstəns/, **resistances**. 1 **Resistance** to something such as a change or a new idea is a refusal to accept it. EG *There will be fierce resistance to these proposals... We did a marketing study for yellow telephone boxes and found the resistance too strong... I have a resistance to innovation.* N UNCOUNT : IF+PREP THEN *to* = opposition

2 **Resistance** to an enemy or an attacker is fighting or other action that people take in order to keep their freedom or avoid being defeated or forced to do something. EG *The advancing army had met with no resistance... ...one small group of resistance fighters.* N UNCOUNT = opposition

3 The **resistance** of your body to germs or diseases is its power to remain unharmed or unaffected by those germs or diseases. EG *She has good resistance to most germs... ...bodily resistance to infection.* N UNCOUNT : IF+PREP THEN *to* = immunity

4 The **resistance** of a machine or a material to a particular problem is its ability to remain undamaged or unaffected by that problem. EG *...the missile's resistance to electronic jamming.* N UNCOUNT : IF+PREP THEN *to*

5 Wind or air **resistance** is a force which slows down an object or vehicle which is moving. EG *We have tried to reduce the weight and air resistance which slow the car down.* N UNCOUNT : USU AFTER N

6 **Resistance** is also the capacity of a substance or an electrical circuit to resist the flow of an electric current through it; a technical term in electrical engineering and physics. N UNCOUNT/COUNT

7 **The line of least resistance** is the course of action which is the easiest for you to take although you might not think that it is the right thing to do. EG *I took the line of least resistance and apologized.* PHR : USU USED AS O

-resistant is used to form adjectives that describe something as being not harmed or affected by the thing mentioned. EG *...penicillin-resistant strains of bacteria... ...water-resistant lotion.* COMB : FORMS ADJS = -proof

resistant /rɪˈzɪstənt/. 1 Someone who is **resistant** to something is opposed to it and wants to prevent it from happening. EG *They are extremely resistant to change... My country is strongly resistant to any foreign interference... They imposed their government by force on a resistant population.* ADJ QUALIT : IF+PREP THEN *to*

2 If something is **resistant** to a particular thing, it is not damaged or affected by that thing. EG *This type of plastic is highly resistant to steam and water... Bacteria become resistant to antibiotics over a period of time.* ADJ QUALIT : PRED+*to* = immune

resistor /rɪˈzɪstə/, **resistors**. A **resistor** is a device which is designed to increase the resistance in an electrical circuit; a technical term. N COUNT

resolute /rɛzəljᵒuːt/. Someone who is **resolute** shows great determination not to change their mind about something or not to do something that they do not want to do; a formal word. EG *We urged him to be resolute.* ▸ used of people's ideas and actions. EG *...a resolute and unshakeable faith... They were faced with resolute opposition... ...their resolute refusal to make any real concessions.* ◊ **resolutely**. EG *She resolutely refused to look at me or speak to me.* ADJ QUALIT = steadfast ◊ ADV

resolution /rɛzəljᵒuːʃᵊn/, **resolutions**. 1 **Resolution** is a firm determination to do something or not do something. EG *She shook her head with great resolution... A note of resolution entered the bishop's voice.* N UNCOUNT

2 If you make a **resolution**, you make a decision to do something or to stop doing something. EG *I'm always making resolutions, like giving up smoking... I came away full of good resolutions.* N COUNT, OR N COUNT+*to*-INF ⇑ intention

3 A **resolution** is a formal decision, usually by means of a vote, taken by a group of people at a meeting, conference, etc. EG *Congress passed a resolution accepting the services of the Attorney General as mediator... The French government supported the resolution and Britain abstained.* N COUNT, OR N COUNT+*to*-INF/REPORT-CL

4 The **resolution** of a problem or difficulty is the final solving of it; a formal use. EG *I longed for the resolution of the agonizing dilemma.* N UNCOUNT, OR N SING WITH DET+SUPP ⇑ settlement

resolve /rɪˈzɒlv/, **resolves, resolving, resolved**; a formal word. 1 If you **resolve** to do something, you make a definite decision to do it. EG *I resolved to tell the truth... He had already resolved that Kitchener should be appointed... The teachers resolved to take over the school.* V+*to*-INF/REPORT-CL ⇑ avow

2 **Resolve** is absolute determination to do what you have decided to do. EG *...the government's weakening resolve... We must be firm in our resolve to oppose them.* N UNCOUNT/COUNT = resolution

3 To **resolve** a problem, argument, or difficulty means to find or provide a solution to it. EG *There are a number of ways of resolving the problem... The Cabinet met to resolve the crisis... The controversy was not resolved when McKinley was assassinated... The difficult situation resolved itself much more easily than I had expected.* V+O (NG/REFL) ⇑ solve = remedy

4 To **resolve** something also means to break it down into its different parts. EG *What I did was resolve this force into its components.* V+O (NG/REFL) : IF+PREP THEN *into* ⇑ separate

resolved /rɪˈzɒlvd/. If you are **resolved** to do something, you are determined to do it. EG *I was firmly resolved to speak to her.* ADJ QUALIT : PRED, USU+*to*-INF = intent

resonance /rɛzənəns/, **resonances**; a formal word. 1 **Resonance** is the quality that a sound has of being deep, clear, and echoing. EG *His voice suddenly took on a new resonance.* N UNCOUNT

2 A **resonance** is the sound which is produced in one object by sound waves coming from another object. N COUNT/UNCOUNT

resonant /rɛzənənt/; a formal word. 1 A sound that is **resonant** is deep, clear, and echoing. EG *She could hear her father's resonant voice repeating The Lord's Prayer.* ADJ QUALIT = resounding

2 A place or thing that is **resonant** causes sound to echo in it or round it. EG *...the resonant open-air pulpit.* ADJ CLASSIF

resonate /rɛzəneɪt/, **resonates, resonating, resonated**; a formal word. 1 If something **resonates**, it makes a long, clear, echoing sound. EG *His laughter resonated among the hollow rocks.* V

2 If a place **resonates**, it is filled with a long, clear, echoing sound. EG *The hall resonated with the notes of the trumpet solo.* V = reverberate

resort /rɪˈzɔːt/, **resorts, resorting, resorted**. 1 If you **resort** to an unpleasant or unpopular course of action, you adopt it because you cannot see any other way of achieving what you want to achieve. EG *You must never resort to violence... The party's officials resorted to more drastic action... Some factions have resorted to terrorism.* ▸ used as a noun. EG *He was the first man to explain the universe without resort to gods or demons.* V+A (*to*) = turn to ▸ N UNCOUNT+*to* = recourse

2 If you do something **as a last resort**, you do it to help you in a difficult situation when you have tried a lot of other things and they have all failed. EG *As a last resort he tried the Lost Property Office... Children arrive in care as a last resort when family life breaks down.* PHR : USED AS AN A

3 **In the last resort** means after all other possibilities have been considered. EG *We must have prisons in the last resort to contain people who break the law frequently... The difference was in the last resort no more than a matter of emphasis.* PHR : USED AS AN A = ultimately

4 A **resort** is 4.1 a place that a lot of people go to for a holiday. EG *...a mountain resort... ...the growth of seaside resort towns during the last century.* 4.2 a place that a person or a particular group of people often visits. EG *This café happened to be a favourite resort of artists and writers.* N COUNT : USU MOD+N; N COUNT+SUPP = haunt

resound /rɪˈzaʊnd/, **resounds, resounding, resounded**. 1 When a sound or noise **resounds**, it continues in a long, loud way. EG *The drums resounded again through the camp.* V = resonate

2 When a place **resounds** with noise, it is filled with a loud, long sound. EG *The room began to resound with that powerful voice.* V : IF+PREP THEN *with* = reverberate

3 If a person's actions **resound** over an area, they are talked about a great deal; a formal or literary use. EG *Stories of his heroism resounded through the country.* V : USU+A

resounding /rɪˈzaʊndɪŋ/. 1 A **resounding** sound is loud and echoing. EG *'Dick, this is my dad!' cried* ADJ CLASSIF : ATTRIB

Dolly in a resounding voice... The tile sprang from the wall with a resounding crack. ◊ **resoundingly**. EG *He let his heavy bag drop resoundingly onto the floor.* ◊ ADV WITH VB ⇑ loudly

2 A **resounding** success, victory, etc, is one that is considered to be very great and emphatic. EG *It was a resounding victory for the party.* ADJ CLASSIF : ATTRIB

resource /rɪˈzɔːs, -sɔːs/, **resources**. 1 A **resource** is something useful, such as coal, oil, or land, that a country has and that it can use to increase its wealth. EG *The sea-bed is rich in buried minerals–a new resource for the future... ...Britain's energy resources... ...a great nation strong in natural resources.* N COUNT : USU PL ⇑ asset

2 **Resources** are the money that is available to a person, business, or government to use for the things they want to do or buy. EG *Julius had invested all his resources in an unsuccessful restaurant.* N PLURAL ⇑ wealth

3 A **resource** is also something or someone that you can use or refer to, especially when you need information on a particular subject. EG *We shared a resources room with the language teachers... ...the resource centre.* N COUNT : USU PL

4 Someone's **resource** is their ability to solve problems and difficulties quickly, efficiently, and with initiative. N UNCOUNT

resourceful /rɪˈzɔːsful, -sɔːs-/. Someone who is **resourceful** is good at finding ways of dealing with problems and difficulties quickly and efficiently; used showing approval. EG *...an able, keen, resourceful politician... ...the most resourceful and well-supplied cook in the town.* ◊ **resourcefulness**. EG *...people who faced misfortune with resourcefulness and courage.* ADJ QUALIT ⇑ capable; ◊ N UNCOUNT = resource

respect /rɪspɛkt/, **respects, respecting, respected**. 1 If you **respect** someone, you have a good opinion of their character or of their ideas, judgements, etc. EG *I had begun to respect Steve... He was particularly respected for his integrity.* V+O = esteem

2 If you **respect** someone's opinion, judgement, etc, you consider that it is interesting or important, although you may not agree with it. EG *I respect the other point of view... All sincere opinions should therefore be respected.* V+O = value

3 If you **respect** someone's wishes, you do something in the way that they want or need it to be done. EG *There is no particular need to respect their wishes.* V+O = honour, fulfil

4 If you **respect** something such as a custom or tradition, you do not interfere with it or disturb anything because you do not want to offend anyone. EG *We mean to respect the cultural peculiarities of each country.* V+O ⇑ honour

5 **Respect** is 5.1 the belief that a person and their opinions and feelings are important, and your behaviour towards the person. EG *I had an enormous respect and admiration for him... It is up to you to gain her respect... They treat one another's wives with extreme respect.* See also **self-respect**. N UNCOUNT : IF+ PREP THEN *for* = regard, reverence **5.2** a way of behaving in which you deliberately do not interfere with something such as a custom or a person's wish to be alone. EG *...respect for the rights of the minority... ...respect for privacy.* N UNCOUNT : IF+ PREP THEN *for* = regard

6 Your **respects** are a formal expression of respect for someone, which you usually send through another person. EG *Give my respects to His Lordship.* N PLURAL : USU POSS+N+*to* = regards

7 If you **pay** your **respects** to someone, you go to see or speak to them, not necessarily because you want to but because you feel you should; a fairly formal expression. EG *I though it only proper to stop for a moment and pay my respects.* PHR : VB INFLECTS

8 If you **pay** your **last respects** to someone who has just died, you express your feelings of respect for them, for example by standing quietly by their body or by their grave. EG *His tearful family came to pay their last respects.* PHR : VB INFLECTS

9 The word **respect** is used in expressions such as 'with respect' and 'with all respect to' when you want to politely disagree with someone or criticize them; a fairly formal use. EG *But Mr Hume, with respect, that wouldn't work... With the utmost respect to Blakemore, the report doesn't show any such thing.* N UNCOUNT : *with*+N, OR *with* +MOD+N

10 If you **treat** something **with respect**, you are very careful in the way that you treat it, because it is capable of harming you. EG *Electricity is potentially dangerous, so treat it with respect.* PHR : VB INFLECTS

11 You use the expressions **in this respect**, **in one respect**, **in many respects**, etc, when you are referring to one particular feature or detail, or to one group of features or details. EG *...we are lagging behind in this respect... He is different from the people around him in many respects... In one important respect, history does not seem to be repeating itself.* PHR : USED AS AN A

12 You say **with respect to** or **in respect of** a subject when you are giving information which is directly connected with it. EG *He informed me about my rights with respect to the forthcoming extradition... It's going to raise a lot of problems in respect of atmosphere pollution.* PREP

respectable /rɪˈspɛktəbəˈl/. 1 Places, activities, etc, that are **respectable** are approved of in the society where they exist or happen because they are considered to be fair, honest, or reasonable. EG *...young people from respectable homes... This change had made it respectable to be on the Left... It was an unusually respectable bookshop.* ◊ **respectability** /rɪˈspɛktəbɪlɪti/. EG *...middle class respectability.* ADJ QUALIT = reputable; ◊ N UNCOUNT ⇑ decency

2 Someone who is **respectable** behaves in a way that is approved of in the society where they live. EG *The teacher was a respectable woman who did her best.* ◊ **respectably**. EG *He is respectably married.* ◊ **respectability**. EG *A statesman of great eminence and respectability.* ADJ QUALIT = worthy; ◊ ADV; ◊ N UNCOUNT = repute

3 Something that is described as **respectable** is considered to be quite adequate or acceptable for its purposes; an informal use. EG *He had begun to earn a very respectable income... This is a primitive but thoroughly respectable bit of computing.* ADJ QUALIT = decent

respected /rɪˈspɛktɪˈd/. Someone or something that is **respected** is admired and considered to be important by many people. EG *...a highly respected scholar... ...one of Hollywood's most enduring and respected actors.* ADJ QUALIT : USU ADV+ADJ = distinguished, eminent

respecter /rɪˈspɛktə/, **respecters**. If you say that someone is a **respecter** of something such as a belief or idea, you mean that they behave in a way which shows that they have a high opinion of it. EG *The President is pre-eminently a respecter of this tradition.* N COUNT+*of*

respectful /rɪˈspɛktful/. If a person or their behaviour is **respectful**, they show respect for other people. EG *Allen was very apologetic, very respectful... 'My relatives, Mr Geard,' said Owen Evans, with a respectful glance at Cordelia... The woman kept a respectful silence.* ◊ **respectfully**. EG *He expected them to stand respectfully when he entered the room.* ADJ QUALIT = deferential; ◊ ADV WITH VB

respective /rɪˈspɛktɪv/. If you refer to **respective** things or places, you mean that they belong or relate separately to the people you have just mentioned. EG *He drove them both to their respective homes... ...the respective failures of Pollock and Coldstream.* ADJ CLASSIF : ATTRIB, USU WITH POSS+N IN PLURAL ⇑ various

respectively /rɪˈspɛktɪvliˈ/. **Respectively** means in the same order as the items that have just been mentioned. EG *Harvard University and MIT are respectively the fourth and fifth largest employers in the area... France and Britain lie third and fourth respectively.* ADV WITH VB

respiration /rɛspəreɪʃəˈn/. Your **respiration** is your breathing; a formal word. EG *I tried to gauge the depth of her sleep by the rate of her respiration... ...a uniform airless warmth which could not be good for anyone's respiration.* ● See also **artificial respiration**. N UNCOUNT

respirator /rɛspəreɪtə/, **respirators**. A **respirator** is 1 a device you can wear over your mouth and nose in order to be able to breathe when you are surrounded by smoke or poisonous gas. N COUNT 2 a device that allows people to breathe when they cannot breathe naturally, for example because they are ill or have been injured. N COUNT

respiratory /rɛspəˈrətriˈ/ means relating to the way people breathe; a technical term in medicine. EG *This can be harmful to the respiratory system... Death was caused by cardiac and respiratory failure.* ADJ CLASSIF : ATTRIB

respire /rɪˈspaɪə/, **respires, respiring, respired**. To **respire** means to breathe; a formal word. EG *You respire approximately 21,666 times a day.* V

respite /rɛspɪˈt/; a formal word. **Respite** is 1 a time of relief or rest from something such as pain, worry, or hard work. EG *She had got a job in town primarily as a respite from her husband... ...there was absolute-* N UNCOUNT, OR N SING : a+N, USU+ *from* = lull *ly no respite from the noise.* **2** a short delay before you have to do something unpleasant such as paying a bill, suffering punishment, etc. EG *They decided to sell the stock off bit by bit to buy a temporary respite.* N UNCOUNT, OR N SING : a+N = reprieve

resplendent /rɪˈsplendənt/. If you say that someone or something is **resplendent**, you mean that their appearance is brilliant and striking; a formal or literary word. EG *Ted, Mr Annett's brother, was resplendent in his best grey suit... Her husband sported a resplendent moustache.* ◇ **resplendently**. ADJ QUALIT : IF+PREP THEN in = dazzling ◇ ADV WITH VB

respond /rɪˈspɒnd/, **responds, responding, responded**. When you **respond**, **1** you react to what someone has said or done, either by saying something or doing something. EG *The pupil sat in front of the screen responding to questions by pushing either of the two buttons... The council responded by calling the raid 'deplorable'... The crowd waved and the liner responded with a blast on its siren.* V : IF+PREP THEN to/with, OR V+by+-ING = answer, reply **2** you say something in order to answer what someone has said to you; a fairly formal use. EG *When the murder charges were read to him, Sutcliffe responded very softly: 'not guilty to murder'.* V+REPORT-CL/QUOTE = reply **3** you react in a favourable way to what someone has said to you or asked you to do. EG *The government has responded to pressure and dropped the proposal... This case proves the importance of adults responding to children's needs as and when they arise.* V : IF+PREP THEN to

respondent /rɪˈspɒndənt/, **respondents**. A **respondent** is a person who answers a questionnaire or a request for information of some kind. EG *In 1959, 43 per cent of Gallup's respondents thought the trade unions 'too powerful'.* N COUNT

response /rɪˈspɒns/, **responses**. **1** A **response** is **1.1** a spoken or written answer to a question or statement; a fairly formal use. EG *His response was 'No!... That was the initial response to my question... Please write your responses in the appropriate place.* N COUNT, OR in+N = reply **1.2** an action which is done as an answer to a request, event, or situation. EG *The Government response to the recent riots was firm... As an immediate response the university has cut admissions by 20 per cent... Will waved his hand in response.* N COUNT, OR in+N = reply **1.3** a reaction to a particular situation or emotion. EG *Hate is an automatic response to fear... What truly shocked me was my own response to the tragedy.* N COUNT, OR in+N

2 If you do or say something **in response to** a person or event, you do or say it as an answer to the person or as a reaction to what has happened. EG *Clearly, they did it in response to external pressures.* PREP

3 The **response** to an event, especially an event of national importance, is the way that the public reacts to it. EG *The response throughout West Germany has been swift and uncompromising... The proposal has produced a united response from the French people.* N SING WITH DET

4 In some Christian church services, the **responses** are short sentences or phrases which are said or sung by the choir or congregation in answer to the priest. N COUNT : USU PL

responsibility /rɪˈspɒnsəbɪlɪti¹/, **responsibilities**. **1** If you have **responsibility** for someone or something, you have control and authority over them, and it is your duty to make sure that necessary tasks are carried out. EG *Wives still take most of the responsibility for the children... She herself took over the responsibility for the project.* N UNCOUNT : IF+PREP THEN for ⇑ liability

2 If you accept or assume **responsibility** for a particular event or situation, you agree that you caused it or that you were to blame for it. EG *I made a mistake and I will assume responsibility for it.* N UNCOUNT : IF+PREP THEN for = liability

3 Responsibility is **3.1** the ability to behave properly and to make the right decisions without needing to be watched or controlled by someone else. EG *...positions of public responsibility... ...men in positions of responsibility and power.* N UNCOUNT ⇑ authority **3.2** the right or opportunity to make important decisions or to take action without permission from anyone else. EG *Children in large families are often given responsibility when they are young.* N UNCOUNT

4 A **responsibility** is **4.1** a particular task that you have because of your job or position. EG *We have general responsibilities regarding the cleanliness of the environment... The handling of the vessel remained his responsibility... ...the responsibilities of her full time job at the NAACP.* N COUNT **4.2** an obligation that you have towards someone who is in a position of authority over you. EG *The Corporate Treasurer has a responsibility to his Board of Directors.* N COUNT

responsible /rɪˈspɒnsəbᵊl/. **1** If you are **responsible** for something or someone, you have control and authority over them, and it is your duty to make sure that necessary tasks are carried out. EG *...the junior minister responsible for civil defence... Men and women must become equally responsible for bringing up children... The children were responsible for cleaning their own rooms.* ADJ CLASSIF : PRED, USU+for/to

2 If someone or something is **responsible** for a particular event or situation, they are the cause of it or can be blamed for it. EG *I hold you personally responsible for all this... ...patients who aren't really responsible for their own behaviour.* ADJ CLASSIF : PRED : IF+PREP THEN for = answerable

3 If you are **responsible** to a person or group, you are controlled by them and have to report to them to explain what you have done. EG *We're responsible to a development committee... The senior members of the department are responsible to me.* ADJ CLASSIF : PRED, IF+PREP THEN to = answerable

4 A person who is **responsible** is able to behave properly and make the right decisions without needing to be watched or controlled by anyone else. EG *...responsible members of the local community... We must make multinational companies more socially responsible.* ▸ used of people's actions and behaviour. EG *I thought it was a very responsible decision.* ◇ **responsibly**. EG *You are doing your job conscientiously and responsibly.* ADJ QUALIT ⇑ trustworthy ▸ ⇑ wise ◇ ADV WITH VB ⇑ wisely

5 Responsible duties and activities involve making important decisions or carrying out important actions. EG *It's a terribly responsible job... Life is harder for women in less responsible and less flexible jobs.* ADJ QUALIT

responsive /rɪˈspɒnsɪv/. **1** Someone who is **responsive** is quick to react to people or events and to show emotions such as pleasure, sympathy, and affection. EG *The children there proved to be the quickest and most responsive members of the audience.* ◇ **responsiveness**. EG *The most essential thing is responsiveness between parent and child.* ADJ QUALIT ⇑ sensitive ◇ N UNCOUNT ⇑ sensitivity

2 If someone or something is **responsive**, they react quickly and favourably. EG *In many areas local police are responsive to the local community and its needs.* ADJ QUALIT : PRED, IF+PREP THEN to ⇑ sensitive

3 A **responsive** action is made as an answer to something that has just been said or done. EG *I gave her a responsive smile back and affectionately pressed her hand.* ADJ CLASSIF : ATTRIB = answering

rest /rest/, **rests, resting, rested**. **1** The **rest** is used to refer to all the parts of something or all the things in a group that remain or that you have not already mentioned. EG *He spent the rest of his life in prison... It was happening not only in America but also throughout the rest of the world... It was just another grave like all the rest... I thought you knew something the rest of us didn't.* N SING : the+N, IF+PREP THEN of, VB CAN BE SING OR PL = remainder

2 When you introduce a sentence by saying **for the rest**, you mean that you have already dealt with the important part of what you are saying and that you now want to say something briefly about the less important parts. EG *For the rest, he gave himself over to enjoying his surroundings... For the rest, she enjoyed being there.* PHR : USED AS ADV SEN

3 You say **and the rest** or **and all the rest of it** at the end of a statement or list to indicate that there are other items, events, or situations which you could mention if you had enough time and space; an informal expression. EG *She was a well-born girl–presented at Court and all the rest of it... You have to read up on the theory and the method and all the rest.* PHR

4 Rest is the state that you are in when you are sitting or lying or when you are not doing anything active, for example when you are asleep. EG *Try to get some rest... Today is a day of rest... It was several weeks before I got a decent night's rest... They had to work twelve hours a day without a rest break.* N UNCOUNT = repose

5 When you **rest**, you do not do anything active for a period of time. EG *'Try to rest,' the doctor said... Go back to bed and rest... The boy stopped for a moment to rest.* V ⇑ pause

6 A **rest** is a period of time during which you do not do anything active. EG *I need a rest... I always tell my patients that a change is as good as a rest.* N COUNT ⇑ pause

7 If you **rest** your body, muscles, legs, etc, you stop being active for a while and relax, for example after you have had some exercise. EG *She badly needed to* V+O *rest her body... Get comfortable so that you can relax and rest your muscles.*

8 At rest. 8.1 When you are **at rest**, you are not doing anything active and not worrying about anything. EG *They smoked for a while, contented and at rest.* **8.2** When an object is **at rest**, it is not moving. **8.3** If you say that someone is **at rest**, you mean that they are dead; a euphemistic expression.
PHR : USED AS C / PHR : USED AS C / PHR : USED AS C

9 When an object that has been moving **comes to rest**, it finally stops; a fairly formal expression. EG *It would drop thousands of feet before coming to rest.*
PHR : VB INFLECTS = halt

10 To **lay** someone **to rest** means to bury them after they have died; a euphemistic expression. EG *She's just been laid to rest in the same place as her husband.* • to **rest in peace**: see **peace**.
PHR : VB INFLECTS = inter

11 If you **put** or **set** someone's **mind at rest**, you say something to them that causes them to stop worrying about something. EG *I think we had better put their minds at rest... It would put our minds at rest if you would tell us what is really happening.*
PHR : VB AND N INFLECT ⇑ reassure

12 If someone tells you to **give** something **a rest**, they want you to stop doing it for a period of time because they think it is harming you, or because it annoys them; an informal expression. EG *I think you ought to give football a rest for a time... Give it a rest, will you? We're trying to get some sleep.*
PHR : VB INFLECTS = lay off

13 If you **let** a subject **rest**, you stop talking about it, especially after you have been talking about it for a long time. EG *She rather hoped that they would let the topic rest... He would never let it rest.*
PHR : VB INFLECTS = drop

14 If something such as an idea **rests** on a particular person or thing, it depends on them in order to exist or be valid. EG *Hopes rested on the new light aircraft.*
V+A *(on/upon)* = hang

15 If a responsibility, duty, etc, **rests** with a person, that person has the responsibility or must do the duty. EG *The responsibility rests with the Committee of Council... The decision was not his, but rested with the House.*
V+A *(with)* ⇑ depend = reside

16 When something **rests** somewhere or when you **rest** it there, you leave it there so that its weight can be supported. EG *He let her shoulders rest against his knees... Her hands rested on the table... ...a plastic tub with a wide edge to rest your arm on.*
V-ERG+A = lay, lie

17 If you **rest** on something or someone, you lean on them so that they support the weight of your body. EG *Joseph stopped and rested on his broom... He sang mockingly, resting on his oars.* • to **rest on** your **laurels**: see **laurel**.
V+A *(on)* = slump

18 A **rest** is also an object that is used to support something, especially your head or feet. EG *...a foot rest... He took the bottle across to its wrought-iron rest.*
N COUNT : USU MOD+N

19 Your eyes **rest** on a particular object or person when you stop looking round you and stare more fixedly at that object or person; a formal or literary use. EG *Her eyes travelled slowly upward and rested on his hands.*
V+A *(on/upon)* = alight, settle

20 If you tell someone to **rest** assured or to **rest** easy, you are telling them that a situation is as you say it is, and that they need not worry that it is dangerous or harmful. EG *Rest assured that everything's under control.*
V+C : USU+ REPORT-CL ⇑ be = remain

21 If someone **lays** or **puts** an idea **to rest**, they succeed in proving that it is not true. EG *Mr Casey vowed to stay on and to lay to rest allegations of improper business dealings... It should put to rest any lingering notion that his art is primitive.*
PHR : VB INFLECTS

22 If you say **I rest my case**, you mean that you have finished presenting your argument, and that you believe that it is convincing.
CONVENTION

23 See also **rested**.

restate /riːsteɪt/, **restates, restating, restated**. If you **restate** something, you say it again, usually in a new way; a fairly formal word. EG *I restated our readiness to resume negotiations... The government took the opportunity to restate its basic policies.*
V+O ⇑ repeat = reiterate

restatement /riːsteɪtmə2nt/, **restatements**. When someone makes a **restatement** of something, they repeat what they have already said, usually in a new way. EG *It was time for healthy self-criticism and a restatement of objectives.*
N COUNT/ UNCOUNT = reiteration

restaurant /rɛstə0rɒnt, -rɒŋ/, **restaurants**. A **restaurant** is a place where you can go to buy and eat a meal.
N COUNT = café

restaurateur /rɛstərətɜː/, **restaurateurs**. A **restaurateur** is a person who owns and runs a restaurant; a formal word.
N COUNT

rested /rɛstɪ2d/. If you feel **rested**, you feel more healthy and energetic because you have just had a period of rest. EG *Try it again in a few days, when you feel more rested.*
ADJ QUALIT = refreshed

restful /rɛstful/. Something that is **restful** helps you to feel calm and relaxed. EG *The lighting is restful... ...a restful Connecticut town.*
ADJ QUALIT = soothing, peaceful

rest-home, rest-homes. A **rest-home** is a place in which old people live and are looked after. EG *Bob finally had her sent off to a rest-home in Bournemouth.*
N COUNT

resting place, resting places; also spelled with a hyphen. A **resting place** is **1** a place where you can stay or rest, usually for a short period of time. EG *At least for the moment they have a resting place and a home.* **2** someone's grave. EG *...his final, private resting-place in a shaded corner of the churchyard.*
N COUNT / N COUNT

restitution /rɛstɪtjuːʃə0n/ is the act of giving back to a person something that was lost or stolen, or of paying them money for the loss; a formal word.
N UNCOUNT ⇑ compensation

restive /rɛstɪv/. If you are **restive**, you are impatient or disobedient because you are bored or because you are not satisfied with the way something is being done. EG *The crew were restive and mutinous.*
ADJ QUALIT ⇑ discontent

◊ **restiveness**. EG *There were already signs of restiveness among the men.*
◊ N UNCOUNT ⇑ discontent

restless /rɛstlɪ2s/. If you are **restless**, **1** you are bored or dissatisfied and want to do something else. EG *I knew that within a fortnight I should feel restless again.* ◊ **restlessness**. EG *They are showing some signs of restlessness.* **2** you are always moving, because you find it difficult to stay still. EG *My mother thought her restless and fidgety.* ◊ **restlessly**. EG *He walked restlessly around the room.* ◊ **restlessnesss**. EG *It was just the restlessness and fidgets that my mother complained of.*
ADJ QUALIT / ◊ N UNCOUNT / ADJ QUALIT = fidgety / ◊ ADV WITH VB / ◊ N UNCOUNT

restock /riːstɒk/, **restocks, restocking, restocked**. **1** When you **restock**, you buy a lot of food or other goods to replace things that you have used or sold. EG *I have to restock the freezer.*
V OR V+O ⇑ refill

2 To **restock** a park or a lake means to put an additional number of animals or fish in it because there are very few left.
V OR V+O ⇑ refill

restoration /rɛstəreɪʃə0n/. **Restoration** is **1** the process of returning something to its original state or condition, by cleaning it, decorating it, etc.
N UNCOUNT ⇑ renovation

2 The **restoration** of something is the act of returning it to its previous state, position, or owner. EG *The restoration of law and order... They demanded the restoration of all their lost lands... I owe the restoration of my hearing to this remarkable new technique.*
N UNCOUNT : IF PREP THEN *of* = recovery

3 The **restoration** of a law or tax is its reintroduction after it has been withdrawn. EG *...this inevitably led to the restoration of cuts in the public sector.*
N UNCOUNT : IF PREP THEN *of*

4 The **Restoration** was the event in 1660 when Charles the Second became King of England after a period when there had been no King or Queen.
N PROPER : *the*-N

5 Restoration is also used to refer to the style of architecture, drama, etc that was popular during and just after the reign of Charles the Second in England. EG *...a Restoration comedy.*
ADJ CLASSIF : ATTRIB

restorative /rɪ2stɒrətɪv/. **1** Something that is **restorative** is likely to make you feel better or more cheerful after you have been feeling tired or miserable. EG *...a hot bath scented with restorative powders.*
ADJ QUALIT = curative

2 A **restorative** is a drink, especially an alcoholic one, that you feel you need in order to feel better or more refreshed; a humorous use. EG *Captain Imrie poured himself his first restorative of the morning.*
N COUNT = pick-me-up

restore /rɪ1stɔː/, **restores, restoring, restored**. **1** If you **restore** something to someone, you return it to them after they have lost it or after it has been stolen from them. EG *The lost child was restored at last to his parents... The territories were restored to their former owners.*
V+O : IF+PREP THEN *to* = give back, hand back

2 When something **restores** a quality or ability of yours, you recover that quality or ability after you have not had it for some time. EG *He had his vision restored by surgical operation... This generous action restored my faith in human beings.*
V+O ⇑ bring back

3 To **restore** someone or something to a state or condition that they have been in earlier means to
V+O+A *(to)* ⇑ bring back

cause them to return to that state or condition. EG *...a Charter which we feel will restore pensioners to a position of equality... He succeeded in restoring the Post Office to high profits.*

4 If someone **restores** a particular feature or quality to a situation, they reintroduce it after it has been absent for some time. EG *He was sent in to try to restore calm... ...a national effort to restore confidence in the pound.* V+O ⇑ bring back

5 When someone **restores** something such as an old building, painting, etc, they repair it, clean it, and decorate it, so that it returns to its original condition. EG *I asked whether the pictures could be restored.* V+O ⇑ change

6 When a government **restores** a law, tax, etc, it brings it back after it has been withdrawn for a period of time. V+O ⇑ bring back

7 If someone such as a president or king **is restored**, they are asked to come back to their original position after they have been deposed. V+O : IF+PREP THEN *to* : USU PASS

restorer /rɪˈstɔːrə/, **restorers**. A **restorer** is someone whose job is to repair houses, pictures, or furniture which have got into a bad condition because they are very old. N COUNT

restrain /rɪˈstreɪn/, **restrains, restraining, restrained**. 1 If someone or something **restrains** you, they control your behaviour and stop you from doing what you had intended or wanted to do. EG *She was raising a cautionary finger as if to restrain Morris from speaking... The young girls had difficulty in restraining themselves from laughter.* V+O (NG/REFL) : IF+PREP THEN *from* = hold back

2 When someone or something **restrains** the power of a force or the speed of a process, they control it in order to prevent it from becoming too great or uncontrolled. EG *...the efforts of governments to restrain inflation... ...measures adopted to restrain prices and profits.* V+O = curb, curtail

restrained /rɪˈstreɪnd/. People who are **restrained** behave in a very calm and unemotional manner. EG *Christopher was wise and restrained and disciplined... We ate with chopsticks in restrained silence.* ADJ QUALIT ⇑ inhibited

restraint /rɪˈstreɪnt/, **restraints**. 1 A **restraint** is 1.1 a rule or condition that limits your freedom and stops you from doing what you had intended or wanted to do. EG *...the restraint imposed by lack of funds... In practice the king suffered few restraints on his freedom of action.* N COUNT : USU PL, OR N UNCOUNT = restriction, constraint 1.2 something that controls the power of a force or the speed of a process in order to prevent it from becoming too great or uncontrollable. EG *...an agreed policy of income and price restraint... ...one of the key restraints in holding back economic development.* N COUNT : USU PL, OR N UNCOUNT : USU MOD+N = restriction

2 **Restraint** is 2.1 behaviour or activity which deliberately prevents someone from doing what they had intended to do. EG *He believes that continued peace requires not just restraint of armed encroachment.* N UNCOUNT ⇑ control
2.2 calm, controlled, and unemotional behaviour. EG *They all spoke with restraint, shyness and delicacy... 'Dear me,' he said with splendid restraint.* N UNCOUNT ⇑ moderation

restrict /rɪˈstrɪkt/, **restricts, restricting, restricted**. 1 If you **restrict** something, you put a limit on it in order to prevent it being as large as it would otherwise be or to reduce its original size. EG *They restricted the number of students joining these faculties... A third possible line of attack would be to restrict wage increases.* V+O ⇑ confine ◇ **restricted**. EG *...the restricted field of vision provided by the camera... They spend their day in a restricted space.* ◇ ADJ QUALIT ⇑ confined

2 If you **restrict** a person, animal, or organization, you put a limit on their possible movements or actions, often in order to prevent them from doing something that you think is undesirable. EG *...to tether an animal or restrict its movement... Some food manufacturers were not prepared to restrict themselves voluntarily.* V+O (NG/REFL) ⇑ hinder ◇ **restricted**. EG *I very rarely wear corsets because I feel too restricted in them.* ◇ ADJ QUALIT ⇑ hindered

3 If you **restrict** someone or something to a particular activity or subject, you make sure that they only deal with or are involved in that one activity or subject. EG *The State should restrict its activities to the maintenance of law and order... I'd like to start by restricting myself to countries where English is the main language... Membership is restricted to men.* V+O (NG/REFL) +A *(to)* ⇑ limit = confine

restricted /rɪˈstrɪktɪ²d/. 1 Something, especially an abstract thing, that is **restricted** is quite small or limited. EG *Many of these are of restricted importance... The range of choices, fortunately, is not as restricted as this.* ADJ QUALIT

2 A **restricted** document is one that the authorities wish to keep secret. Only people with special permission are allowed to read a restricted document. ADJ CLASSIF ⇑ private = classified

3 A **restricted** place or area is one that is very dangerous or that the authorities wish to keep secret. Only people with special permission are allowed to visit a restricted place. ADJ CLASSIF ⇑ private

restriction /rɪˈstrɪkʃəⁿn/, **restrictions**. 1 A **restriction** is 1.1 a rule or order that limits what you can do or that limits the amount or size of something. EG *The government placed restrictions on sales of weapons.* N COUNT : IF+PREP THEN *of/on* 1.2 a fact or situation that limits what you can do or prevents you from doing what you want to do. EG *...the restrictions of ageing... ...small salaries which placed restrictions on our social life.* N COUNT : IF+PREP THEN *of/on* = restraint

2 **Restriction** involves 2.1 preventing something from being as large as it might be, or reducing its size. EG *There has been some restriction of entry into medical schools.* N UNCOUNT 2.2 limiting the movement or action of people, animals, or organizations. EG *This practice imposed such physical restriction on women that they could not walk properly.* N UNCOUNT

restrictive /rɪˈstrɪktɪv/. Something that is **restrictive** prevents you from doing something, usually in a way that you find unacceptable. EG *...teenagers eager to escape restrictive home environments.* ADJ QUALIT ⇑ confining

rest room, rest rooms; also spelled with a hyphen. A **rest room** is a toilet in a public place such as a restaurant or theatre; used in American English. N COUNT ⇑ lavatory

restructure /riːstrʌktʃə/, **restructures, restructuring, restructured**. To **restructure** an organization means to change the way it is organized so that it has a different structure, usually in order to make it work more effectively. EG *A start has been made in stimulating labour productivity and restructuring industry.* V+O

result /rɪzʌlt/, **results, resulting, resulted**. 1 A **result** is something that happens or exists because of something else that has happened. EG *The result was further victimisation... I nearly missed the first night as a result of going to Havana... His new politics were the direct result of his experience as Minister of Technology... Twice he followed his own advice, with disastrous results.* N COUNT/ UNCOUNT = consequence, effect

2 If something **results** in a particular situation, it causes that situation to happen or to exist. EG *The use of such techniques could result in disastrous ecological changes... Such behaviour may result in the executive being asked to leave.* V+A *(in)* = bring about

3 If something **results** from a particular event or action, it is caused by that event or action. EG *Four-fifths of the fire damage resulted from incendiary bombing... Inflation results from an excess of demand over supply... A saving in cost would result.* V : IF+PREP THEN *from* = ensue, stem

4 A **result** is also 4.1 the final situation that exists after a public event, such as an election or a sporting contest, in which two or more people or groups compete against each other. EG *...the result of the Warrington by-election... ...the latest football results.* N COUNT = outcome
4.2 the number that you get when you do a calculation or solve a mathematical problem. EG *The result should be calculated to three decimal places.* N COUNT = answer, solution

5 Your **results** are the marks, grades, etc that you get after you have taken an examination. EG *We already have their examination results... You need good A-level results.* N COUNT : USU PL

resultant /rɪzʌltənt/. A **resultant** state or situation has been caused by something which you have just referred to; a formal word. EG *If the whole of industry installed such equipment, the resultant saving of coal would be of considerable significance.* ADJ CLASSIF : ATTRIB = consequent, ensuing

resume /rɪˈzjᵒuːm/, **resumes, resuming, resumed**. 1 If an activity **resumes** or if you **resume** it, it begins again after a period when it has not been happening. EG *She was ready to resume her duties... They felt secure enough to resume their normal lives... The music would stop at intervals, then resume after a while.* V-ERG

2 If you **resume** a place or position that you were once in, you return to it after something had caused you to leave it. EG *The two passengers resumed their normal position... He resumed his seat with only a mild protest.* V+O ⇑ take up

3 If you **resume**, you begin doing something such as V

speaking again after you have stopped for a short time. EG *He broke off, only to resume almost at once.*

résumé /rɛzju:meɪ/, **résumés**; also spelled **resumé**. A **résumé** is a short account of something that somebody has said or written. EG *Later we received further résumés of what she had said.* N COUNT = summary

resumption /rɪ'zʌmpʃə⁰n/. The **resumption** of an activity is its beginning again after it has stopped for a while. EG *...the resumption of commercial whaling... ...the resumption of land sales.* N UNCOUNT

resurface /ri:sɜ:fɪs/, **resurfaces, resurfacing, resurfaced**. 1 To **resurface** something such as a road means to put a new surface on it. V+O

2 If someone or something that has been under water **resurfaces**, they come back to the surface of the water again. V

3 If someone **resurfaces** after they have been absent or busy for a time, they start to become socially active again; an informal use. EG *I had resurfaced in Harvard.* V = reappear

resurgence /rɪ'sɜ:dʒəns/ is the reappearance and growth of a particular attitude or activity among a group of people, especially one which has been forgotten for some time; a formal or literary word. EG *...a resurgence of small scale guerrilla activity.* N UNCOUNT+*of*, OR N SING WITH DET = revival

resurgent /rɪ'sɜ:dʒənt/. Something that is **resurgent** is becoming stronger and more popular again after a period of decline; a formal or literary word. EG *...the resurgent African states.* ADJ CLASSIF : USU ATTRIB

resurrect /rɛzərɛkt/, **resurrects, resurrecting, resurrected**. If someone **resurrects** something such as an attitude or activity, they cause it to exist again after it had disappeared. EG *A furious argument ensued in which both sides resurrected all their old differences.* ◊ **resurrection** /rɛzərɛkʃə⁰n/. EG *...a resurrection of the Jazz Festival.* V+O = reactivate; ◊ N UNCOUNT

Resurrection /rɛzərɛkʃə⁰n/. In Christian belief, the **Resurrection** is the event in which Jesus Christ came back to life three days after he had been killed. N PROPER : *the*+N

resuscitate /rɪ'sʌsɪteɪt/, **resuscitates, resuscitating, resuscitated**. If you **resuscitate** someone, you make them become conscious again, especially after they have become unconscious as a result of an accident or a sudden illness. EG *We have been trying to resuscitate him for over half an hour.* ◊ **resuscitation** /rɪ'sʌsɪteɪʃə⁰n/. EG *All their attempts at resuscitation were unsuccessful.* V+O = bring round, revive; ◊ N UNCOUNT = revival

retail /ri:teɪl/, **retails, retailing, retailed**. 1 **Retail** is the activity of selling goods to the public, usually in small amounts or quantities. EG *...small retail shops... Recommended retail price £1.75... He makes them himself and then sells them by retail.* N UNCOUNT : USU BEFORE N ⇑ trade ≠ wholesale

2 **Retail** goods are sold in ordinary shops to the public. EG *...a retail carpet and textile business.* ▸ used as an adverb. EG *I only wanted one, but nobody seemed to sell them retail.* ADJ CLASSIF : ATTRIB; ▸ ADV WITH VB

3 If someone **retails** goods, they sell them in small numbers or as single items to the public, usually in a shop. EG *He intended to retail bakery goods.* V+O ⇑ trade = trade in

4 If an item in a shop **retails** at a particular price, it is on sale at that price. EG *These shoes normally retail at £18.50.* V+A *(at)*

5 If you **retail** a story or event, you tell it to someone, often in detail; a formal or old-fashioned use. EG *He overheard two parents discussing the project heatedly and retailed it to me.* V+O : IF+PREP THEN *to* = relate

retailer /ri:teɪlə/, **retailers**. A **retailer** is a person or business that sells goods by retail. EG *A lot of money is spent by retailers on advertising.* N COUNT ⇑ trader

retail price index. In Britain, the **retail price index** is a list of prices of typical goods which shows how much the cost of living changes from one month to the next. EG *The retail price index announced on Friday showed inflation up by 0.6% in September.* N SING : *the*+N

retain /rɪ'teɪn/, **retains, retaining, retained**. 1 If you **retain** something, you continue to keep it, especially when it is something desirable or useful. EG *We are fighting to retain some independence... In her private life she managed to retain a certain reserve and dignity... The few remaining stone axes were retained by old men as keepsakes.* V+O = preserve

2 If an object or substance **retains** something, it continues to contain it. EG *Water retains heat much longer than air... The soil becomes porous and good at retaining moisture.* V+O ⇑ keep = hold

3 If you **retain** a lawyer, you pay him or her a fee to make sure that he or she will represent you when your case comes before the court; a technical use. V+O

retainer /rɪ'teɪnə/, **retainers**. A **retainer** is 1 a fee that you pay someone in order to make sure that they will be available to do work for you if you need them to. EG *...a one hundred dollar retainer agreement.* N COUNT ⇑ payment 2 a small amount of rent that you pay for a rented room, flat, etc, in order to make sure that you can use it in the future. EG *A retainer may be charged for keeping the student's room over the vacation.* N COUNT ⇑ rent 3 a servant who has been with one family for a long time. EG *Her arrival had just been announced by the faithful retainer.* N COUNT ⇑ employee

retake /ri:teɪk/, **retakes, retaking, retook, retaken**. 1 When a military force **retakes** a place or building which it has lost in a war or battle, it captures it again. EG *The last village had just been retaken.* V+O = recapture

2 A **retake** is a scene in a film that has been photographed again because it needed to be changed or improved. N COUNT

3 If you **retake** an exam, you take it again because you failed it the first time. ▸ used as a noun. EG *...'A' level and 'O' level retakes.* V+O; ▸ N COUNT

retaliate /rɪ'tælieɪt/, **retaliates, retaliating, retaliated**. If you **retaliate**, you do something which will cause someone harm or damage because they have acted in a similar way against you. EG *...the ability to retaliate during or after an attack... They retaliated by changing the venue for the meeting.* ◊ **retaliation** /rɪ'tælieɪʃə⁰n/. EG *It was agreed that immediate retaliation was necessary... They staged these attacks in retaliation for attacks on their own civilians.* V : USU+A ⇑ respond = reciprocate; ◊ N UNCOUNT = reprisal, revenge, retribution

retaliatory /rɪ'tæljətə⁰tri¹/. 1 **Retaliatory** actions are aggressive ones which you carry out against someone because they have done something harmful to you. EG *...a retaliatory attack against an opponent's cities.* ADJ CLASSIF : USU ATTRIB ⇑ reciprocal

2 **Retaliatory** weapons are intended to be used for attacking an enemy who has just attacked you. ADJ CLASSIF

retard /rɪ'tɑ:d/, **retards, retarding, retarded**. If something **retards** a process or development, it causes it to happen more slowly. EG *The children's emotional development had been retarded by traumatic experiences.* V+O = hinder, delay

retardation /ri:tɑ:deɪʃə⁰n/ is the process of making something happen or develop more slowly; a formal word. EG *...the risk of mental retardation and disturbed behaviour.* N UNCOUNT = backwardness

retarded /rɪ'tɑ:dɪ²d/. Someone who is **retarded** has made very little progress in their mental development compared with normal people of their age. EG *Her younger daughter was mentally retarded.* ▸ The **retarded** is also used to refer to people who are retarded. EG *...a secure and sometimes happy life for the retarded.* ADJ CLASSIF = backward; ▸ N PLURAL : *th*[e]+N

retch /retʃ, ri:tʃ/, **retches, retching, retched**. If you **retch**, your stomach reacts and moves in an uncontrolled way as if you are vomiting. EG *The thought made him retch.* ▸ used as a noun. EG *The laugh turned to a screech, and then a retch.* V ⇑ heave; ▸ N COUNT

retd is a written abbreviation for 'retired'; used after someone's name to indicate that they have retired from the army, navy, or air force. EG *Maj Gen George Grantham, retd.* ADJ AFTER N

retell /ri:tɛl/, **retells, retelling, retold**. If you **retell** a story, you write it, tell it, or present it again, often in a different way from its original form. EG *Why did Pinter choose this very curious way of retelling John Fowles's novel?* V+O

retention /rɪ'tɛnʃə⁰n/. 1 **Retention** is 1.1 the continued existence of something such as a tradition, an organization, or an institution. EG *He pleaded for the retention of the Industrial Liaison Centre.* N UNCOUNT = preservation 1.2 the continued possession of something such as land, especially when someone else is trying to take it from you. EG *Retention of these territories became a sacred national cause.* N UNCOUNT 1.3 your ability to remember facts or details and keep them in your memory. EG *...the two aspects involved are retention and recall.* N UNCOUNT ⇑ storage

2 The **retention** of something such as heat or water in your body is the continued presence of it in your body. EG *I suffer from fluid retention.* N UNCOUNT+SUPP ⇑ holding

retentive /rɪ'tɛntɪv/. If you have a **retentive** memory or mind, you are able to remember things very well and keep a lot of facts in your mind. ADJ QUALIT : U[SU] ATTRIB

rethink /ri:θɪŋk/, **rethinks, rethinking, rethought**. When you **rethink**, you think again about a situation or plan and come to a different decision about what you should do. EG *They had to rethink fast in order to survive... This forced us to rethink all of our plans.* — V OR V+O = reconsider

reticence /rɛtɪsəns/. **Reticence** is unwillingness to talk about what you know or what you feel; a fairly formal word. EG *He broke out of his normal reticence and told me the whole story.* — N UNCOUNT = taciturnity

reticent /rɛtɪsənt/. **1** Someone who is **reticent** does not say very much about what they know or about what they feel. EG *Their mother was a reticent woman, even with her children.* — ADJ QUALIT ⇑ quiet = taciturn

2 If someone is **reticent** about a particular subject, they are unwilling to say very much about it. EG *She was always extremely reticent about her colleagues.* — ADJ QUALIT : PRED, IF+PREP THEN *about* = reserved

reticule /rɛtɪkju:l/, **reticules**. A **reticule** is a type of small handbag; an old-fashioned word. — N COUNT = bag

retina /rɛtɪnə/, **retinae, retinas**. The plural can be either **retinae** or **retinas**. Your **retina** is the part of your eye at the back of your eyeball, which receives the image that you see. It then sends the image to your brain. — N COUNT

retinal /rɛtɪnə⁰l/ is used to refer to the condition, treatment, and function of a person's or animal's retina; a technical term. EG *...the retinal image... Many of them suffered retinal burns.* — ADJ CLASSIF : ATTRIB

retinue /rɛtɪnju:/, **retinues**. A **retinue** of people is the group of servants, friends, assistants, etc, who travel with an important or powerful person. EG *He strode past with his retinue of aides.* — N COUNT : ALSO N +*of*+N IN PL

retire /rɪ¹taɪə/, **retires, retiring, retired**. **1** When someone **retires**, they stop doing their job, usually because they have reached the age when they can get a pension. In Britain, women usually retire at the age of 60, and men at the age of 65. EG *Gladys retired at the age of sixty-eight... They had decided to retire from farming... Women and men will be able to retire five years earlier.* — V : USU+A

2 When an employer **retires** someone, they dismiss the person and give them a pension, especially when the person would not normally be old enough to have a pension. — V+O

3 If you **retire**, **3.1** you leave a group of people, usually because you want to be on your own; a fairly formal use. EG *I retired to my study upstairs... He consented to dance for us and retired to put on his costume.* — V : USU+A ⇑ go = retreat, withdraw **3.2** you go to bed; a formal use. EG *She retired early with a good book.* — V

retired /rɪ¹taɪəd/. Someone who is **retired** has left their job, usually because they have reached the age when they can get a pension. EG *...the daughter of a retired Army officer.* — ADJ CLASSIF

retirement /rɪ¹taɪəmə²nt/. **Retirement** is **1** the particular time in a person's life when they stop working, usually because they have reached the age at which they can get a pension. EG *He is on the verge of retirement... She was well under retirement age... You should give notice of your retirement in writing.* — N UNCOUNT **2** the period in a person's life during which they are no longer employed because they have retired. EG *...the house that his father had bought for his retirement... You should get a full retirement pension.* — N UNCOUNT

retiring /rɪ¹taɪərɪŋ/. **1** Someone who is **retiring** is very quiet and shy and avoids having to meet other people; a fairly formal use. EG *She was a shy, retiring girl.* — ADJ QUALIT = reserved

2 A **retiring** representative, official, employee, etc, is one who is going to retire very soon. EG *...Jim Dacre, the retiring Labour MP.* — ADJ CLASSIF : ATTRIB

retort /rɪ¹tɔ:t/, **retorts, retorting, retorted**. If you **retort**, you make a short and rather angry reply to someone who has said something that annoys you. EG *'No swifter than you, Father,' I retorted... Lady Sackville retorted that if they came, she would leave.* — V OR V+QUOTE/ REPORT-CL = rejoin

▸ used as a noun. EG *'Mind your own business,' was the quick retort.* — ▸ N COUNT = rejoinder

retouch /ri:tʌtʃ/, **retouches, retouching, retouched**. If you **retouch** a painting, photograph, etc, you restore or improve it by painting over parts of it. — V+O = touch up

retrace /ri:treɪs/, **retraces, retracing, retraced**. If you **retrace** your steps or your way somewhere, you go back by following exactly the same path or route that you took originally. EG *Stella retraced her steps toward the entrance.* — V+O : USU+A ⇑ turn back

retract /rɪ¹trækt/, **retracts, retracting, retracted**. **1** If you **retract** something that you have said or written, you say that you did not mean it. For example, if you retract a promise, you say that you do not intend to keep it; a fairly formal use. EG *I had just retracted some silly promise she had forced me to make... At his trial, he retracted his confession.* — V OR V+O = take back, withdraw

2 When a part of a machine or animal **retracts** or when something **retracts** it, it moves back to a different place or position. EG *The frog's eyes retract when its tongue shoots out.* — V-ERG = draw in, draw back

retractable /rɪ¹træktəbə⁰l/. **Retractable** parts of a machine can be moved back into a different place or position. EG *All the planes had retractable undercarriages.* — ADJ CLASSIF

retraction /rɪ¹trækʃə⁰n/, **retractions**. A **retraction** is a statement that you make when you want to say that you no longer mean what you said earlier. EG *His retraction was published in several newspapers.* — N COUNT = withdrawal

retraining /ri:treɪnɪŋ/ is education that is given to adults to teach them new skills, especially in order to help them get a new job. EG *...government job centres and retraining programmes.* — N UNCOUNT

retread /ri:trɛd/, **retreads**. A **retread** is a tyre that is made from an old tyre which has been given a new outer surface. — N COUNT

retreat /rɪ¹tri:t/, **retreats, retreating, retreated**. **1** If you **retreat**, **1.1** you move away from something or someone, for example because you are afraid or embarrassed. EG *Betsy and I retreated to the edge of the field... I nearly tripped and fell as I retreated from a gentleman who rushed up to me.* — V : USU+A = withdraw, draw back

1.2 you go to a quiet or private place in order to rest or in order to concentrate on a particular problem or task. EG *I retreated to the country for a long weekend.* — V+A *(to)* = retire, withdraw

2 When an army **retreats**, it moves away from opposing forces in order to avoid fighting them. EG *They retreated a few kilometres, then sent in aircraft.* — V ⇑ withdraw = turn tail

3 If you **retreat** from something such as a promise or a belief, you decide that it has become too difficult or too embarrassing, and try to change what you believe or what you have to do. EG *The Government had run out of steam and was retreating from its commitments.* — V : IF+PREP THEN *from* ⇑ abandon = renege

4 If you **retreat** into a different attitude, you begin to limit your activities and interests, often because you have had an unhappy experience; a fairly formal use. EG *Some people retreat into positions of hard irony and cynicism.* — V : IF+PREP THEN *into* = withdraw

5 A **retreat** is **5.1** a movement that you make away from something or someone, for example when you are afraid or embarrassed; a fairly formal use. EG *His retreat, walking backwards, had taken him three or four yards away from her.* — N COUNT **5.2** a quiet or private place that you go to in order to rest or in order to concentrate on a particular problem or task. EG *They met at a woodland retreat near the Canadian capital.* — N COUNT = hideaway

5.3 a withdrawal by an army when it is faced with a stronger force which it does not want to fight. EG *...the winter retreat of Napoleon's army from Moscow... They can be starved into retreat, but not into submission.* — N COUNT/ UNCOUNT **5.4** a change in your position when you have decided that you do not want to do what you have agreed or promised to do, usually because it has become too difficult, too expensive, or too embarrassing. EG *Some critics might say that this is almost a retreat from basic education.* — N COUNT/ UNCOUNT : IF+ PREP THEN *from* ⇑ abandonment

6 **Retreat** is **6.1** withdrawal to a quiet or private place in order to rest or in order to concentrate on a particular problem or task; a fairly formal use. EG *Every year, he goes into retreat for three weeks.* — N UNCOUNT = retirement **6.2** the limitation of your activities and interests, for example after you have had an unhappy experience; a fairly formal use. EG *He may think that difficulties can be evaded by retreat into a dream world.* — N UNCOUNT/ COUNT : IF+ PREP THEN *into* = withdrawal

7 If you **beat a retreat**, you run away from something such as a task that you do not want to do or a situation that you are afraid of; a fairly informal expression. EG *We beat a hasty retreat when we heard the car.* — PHR : VB INFLECTS

retrenchment /rɪ¹trɛntʃmə²nt/ is the process of reducing the amount of money that a person, organi- — N UNCOUNT/ COUNT zation, or government spends; a formal word. EG ...*an atmosphere of cutbacks and retrenchment.*

retrial /riːtraɪəl/, **retrials**. A **retrial** is a second trial that someone has, because the jury at the first trial could not reach a decision or because the first trial was not properly conducted. N COUNT

retribution /re̲trɪbju̲ːʃə⁰n/ is punishment which cannot be avoided and which some people believe comes from non-human sources, such as God or Fate; a formal word. EG ...*the fear of retribution*... ...*the swiftness of divine retribution.* N UNCOUNT = vengeance

retributive /rɪ²trɪbjə⁴tɪv/. **Retributive** actions or powers are involved in dealing out punishment that is just and unavoidable; a formal word. EG ...*a lifelong retributive vendetta.* ADJ CLASSIF: ATTRIB ⇑ vengeful

retrieval /rɪ¹triːvə⁰l/ is **1** the process of getting information back from a computer system; a technical term. EG ...*data inspection and retrieval*... ...*computer-based information storage and retrieval systems.* N UNCOUNT = recovery **2** the act of getting something back from a particular place, especially from a place where it should not be. N UNCOUNT = recovery

retrieve /rɪ¹triːv/, **retrieves, retrieving, retrieved**; a fairly formal word. **1** If you **retrieve** something, you succeed in getting it back from somewhere, especially from a place where you have hidden it or where it should not be. EG *I ran back to my room and retrieved my bag*... *He retrieved his rifle and strolled back to the car.* V+O = recoup

2 If you **retrieve** a situation, you succeed in bringing it back into a state which you feel is more satisfactory or suitable. EG *Henry did his best to retrieve the situation, amidst some laughter.* V+O = save

3 If you **retrieve** information, you get it back from a computer system or from your own memory; a technical term. V+O = recover

retriever /rɪ¹triːvə/, **retrievers**. A **retriever** is a large dog that is often used by hunters to bring back birds and animals which have been shot. N COUNT

retroactive /re̲trəuæktɪv/. If a decision or action is **retroactive**, it is intended to take effect from a date in the past; a formal word. EG ...*a fifty per cent increase in salaries retroactive to the beginning of August.* ADJ CLASSIF: IF+PREP THEN *to* ⇑ operative = backdated

retrograde /re̲trə⁶greɪd/. If an action or attitude is described as **retrograde**, it is considered to be undesirable because it involves old ideas or beliefs; a formal word. EG *The move was held to be an economically retrograde step.* ADJ CLASSIF ⇑ backward

retrogress /re̲trə⁶gre̲s/, **retrogresses, retrogressing, retrogressed**. If an organization or process **retrogresses**, it goes back to an earlier and less efficient stage in its development; a formal word. EG ...*civilization remained static or retrogressed instead of sustaining the original impetus.* V: IF+PREP THEN *to* ⇑ worsen = regress
◊ **retrogression** /re̲trə⁶gre̲ʃə⁰n/. ◊ N UNCOUNT

retrogressive /re̲trə⁶gre̲sɪv/. If an action or idea is **retrogressive**, it returns to old ideas or beliefs and does not take advantage of recent progress; a fairly formal word. EG ...*a fundamental and retrogressive change in the whole basis of industrial relations.* ADJ CLASSIF ⇑ backward = reactionary

retrospect /re̲trə⁶spɛkt/. When you form an opinion about something **in retrospect**, you look back on it and base your opinion on what actually happened, because you have had time to think about it and understand it more clearly. EG *There are some things that you only become totally conscious of in retrospect*... *It was, in retrospect, one of the worst mistakes I ever made*... *In retrospect we may deplore the methods used.* PHR: USED AS AN A OR ADV SEN

retrospective /re̲trə⁶spe̲ktɪv/, **retrospectives**.
1 A **retrospective** is an exhibition of the work of a famous artist or group of artists, which displays work from every period in their life. N COUNT = overview

2 Retrospective feelings, views, opinions, etc, involve looking back on the past or are influenced by something that happened in the past. EG ...*a kind of retrospective fear followed me everywhere*... *I had only a retrospective, academic interest in the subject.* ◊ **retrospectively**. EG *Her father was described retrospectively as 'reserved and taciturn'.* ADJ CLASSIF ◊ ADV WITH VB, OR ADV SEN

3 Retrospective laws or legal actions take effect from a date before the date when they are officially approved or begun; a formal use. ◊ **retrospectively**. EG *After I had recovered from the accident I thought of suing the town council retrospectively.* ADJ CLASSIF = retroactive ◊ ADV WITH VB

return /rɪ¹tɜːn/, **returns, returning, returned**. **1** When you **return** somewhere, you come or go back there after you have been away. EG *I returned to my hotel*... *I returned from the Middle East in 1956*... *He returned home several hours later*... *Her husband left for work one morning and did not return.* V: USU+A

2 Your **return** is the journey you make and your arrival back at a place where you had been before. EG *On his return Haldane reported to the Cabinet*... *He described his return to his home village*... *Julie had been tired since her return from New York.* N UNCOUNT: WITH POSS = homecoming

3 If you **return** something to someone, you give it back to them after you have taken it or borrowed it from them. EG *Will you be so good as to return the drawing to me*... *He borrowed my best suit and didn't return it.* V+O: IF+PREP THEN *to* = hand back

4 The **return** of something to someone involves giving it back to them after it has been taken or borrowed from them. EG *Greece will be offered the return of these treasures as a goodwill gift.* N UNCOUNT

5 If you send a reply to someone **by return** or **by return of post**, you send it to them in the next collection of mail that is taken by the post office after you have received their letter. EG *They'll send you the tickets by return of post.* PHR: USED AS AN A

6 If you **return** something to its previous place, you put it back there after it has been removed from there for a time. EG *He returned the gun to its holster*... *We returned the books to the shelf.* V+O+A *(to)* = replace

7 If you do something **in return**, you do it in exchange for something else, especially something that is thought to be of equal value or importance. EG *They had nothing to give in return*... *You get the following benefits in return for paying contributions and taxes.* PHR: USED AS AN A

8 If you **return** an action or sentiment, you repeat the same action or express the same sentiment as someone else has just done. EG *He didn't return their spoken greetings*... *She was looking for somebody to return her affection*... *Meadow paused and looked at Brody, who returned his gaze silently.* V+O = reciprocate

9 If you **return** a ball during a game, you hit it or throw it back in the direction it came from. EG *He would catch the ball on the bounce and return it with a single reflex.* ▸ used as a noun. EG *Miss Evert reached to lob a return of Miss Wade's.* V+O ⇑ send back ▸ N COUNT

10 When soldiers **return fire**, they shoot at an enemy who has already begun firing at them. PHR: VB INFLECTS

11 If a feeling or situation **returns**, it comes back or happens again after a period of absence. EG *If the pain returns, the rest treatment is repeated*... *After nine months, the rains at last returned.* ▸ used as a noun. EG ...*the return of better times*... *I think I detect a return in the popularity of scientific subjects.* V ⇑ reappear ▸ N SING WITH DET+SUPP = recurrence

12 If you **return** to a subject that you have mentioned before, you begin talking about it again, for example during a lecture or in a book. EG *Now let me return to the question of inflation*... *We shall return to this central theme in Chapter 7.* V+A *(to)* = go back, revert

13 If you **return** to an activity that you have been doing before, you start doing it again or continue doing it after a break. EG *After lunch, Edward returned to his gardening*... ...*his need to return to his old life.* ▸ used as a noun. EG *William Morris advocated a return to hand spinning.* V+A *(to)* = resume ▸ N SING WITH DET+*to*

14 You say that someone **returns** to a particular state when they have been in that state before and are now going back into it. EG *The Social Democratic Party seems poised to return to power at the first opportunity*... ...*the groans of wounded men returning to consciousness.* ▸ used as a noun. EG *He referred to the Party's hopes for a return to power*... *His return to office was widely approved of.* V+A *(to)* ⇑ resume ▸ N SING WITH DET+*to* = resumption

15 A **return** is a profit that you get from an investment. EG *Companies seek higher returns by investing in other corporations*... *They guarantee little by way of return for the money invested*... *The average return gradually rises to just over 10%.* ● The **law of diminishing returns** is the principle that for equal increases in a factor of production such as the number of workers you have, there will be smaller and smaller increases in what you produce. N COUNT/UNCOUNT = yield ● PHR: USED S/O/C

16 When electors **return** someone, they elect him or her as their member of parliament. EG *Benn was returned by a majority of 15,479.* V+O

17 Returns are the results of something such as an N PLURAL election after the votes have been counted and made public. EG *Early returns in the ballot indicate a considerable vote for strike action.*

18 When a judge or jury **returns** a verdict, they announce their decision as to whether the person on trial is guilty or not; a technical term in law. EG *The jury returned a verdict of guilty but insane.* — V+O ⇑ give

19 A **return** is also **19.1** a form on which a detailed statement is made, usually for some official purpose such as declaring your income before paying tax. EG *They have departments which will prepare tax returns for sole traders and partnerships.* — N COUNT **19.2** a ticket for a train, bus, or aeroplane that allows you to travel to a particular place and then back again. EG *The first-class return is about £74.* ● See also **day return**. — N COUNT

20 You say **many happy returns** or **many happy returns of the day** as a way of wishing someone a happy birthday. — CONVENTION

21 The **point of no return** is a particular stage that you reach, for example when you are trying to perform a task. Before you reach this stage, you do not have to continue with the task, but afterwards you must continue with it. EG *We have passed a point of no return... The point of no return may have been passed already.* — PHR : USU USED AS O

returnable /rɪˈtɜːnəbəᵊl/. Something that is **returnable** is intended to be taken back or given back to the people who provided it, usually after you have used it. EG *...returnable glass containers.* — ADJ CLASSIF

returning officer, returning officers. In Britain, a **returning officer** is the official who is responsible for arranging an election in a particular town or district and who formally announces the result. EG *Apply for nomination papers to your local returning officer.* — N COUNT

return match, return matches. A **return match** is the second of two matches that are played between two sports teams. — N COUNT

return ticket, return tickets. A **return ticket** is a ticket for a train, bus, or aeroplane that allows you to travel to a particular place and then back again. EG *He exchanged his return ticket to Vienna for one to Dusseldorf.* — N COUNT

reunion /riˈjuːnjəᵊn/, **reunions.** A **reunion** is 1 a party or dinner attended by relatives, friends, members of the same school, etc who have not seen each other for some time. EG *I've been dreaming about our family reunion for 23 years.* — N COUNT ⇑ gathering **2** a meeting between two people who have been separated for some time. EG *...there is obviously no chance of a reunion between parents and child... ...a happy, confused reunion with Jim.* ▸ used as an uncount noun. EG *...her hope of reunion with her father.* — N COUNT; ▸ N UNCOUNT

reunite /riːjuːnaɪt/, **reunites, reuniting, reunited. 1** If two people **are reunited** or if one person **reunites** with another, the two people meet each other again after they have been separated for some time. EG *They had laboured and sweated to be reunited, both of them. Her attempts to reunite with her father may end very unhappily...* — V+O : USU PASS, OR V+A *(with)* ⇑ unite

2 If you **reunite** something that has been divided, you bring its parts together to make it complete and united again. EG *During 1979-80 he also worked to reunite the Labour movement.* — V+O

re-use, re-uses, re-using, re-used; also spelled as one word. The word **re-use** is pronounced /riː juːs/ when it is a noun, and /riː juːz/ when it is a verb. **1** The **re-use** of materials involves using them again after they have already been used once, rather than throwing them away. — N UNCOUNT ⇑ recycle

2 When you **re-use** something, you use it again instead of throwing it away. EG *Much of the stone has been re-used in rebuilding.* — V+O ⇑ recycle

rev /rev/, **revs, revving, revved**; an informal word. **1** When a car or engine **revs** or when you **rev** it, you increase the engine speed by pressing on the accelerator. EG *The engines revved behind me... He revved the motor and then roared off.* — V-ERG

2 If you talk about the **revs** of an engine, you are referring to its speed, which is measured in revolutions per minute. EG *Keep it going at a steady 3,000 revs.* — N PLURAL

rev up. When a car or engine **revs up** or when you **rev it up**, you increase the engine speed by pressing on the accelerator. EG *Ginny revved up the jeep again and pulled out.* — PHRASAL VB : V-ERG+ADV

Rev. is an abbreviation for 'Reverend'; used as part of the title of a member of the clergy. **Rev.** can be written in formal English, but is always informal if it is spoken. EG *The director is the Rev. Colin Urquhart.* — N IN TITLES

revalue /riːvæljuː/, **revalues, revaluing, revalued. 1** To **revalue** a price or payment means to increase its amount so that its value stays roughly the same even if there is inflation. EG *Your earnings are revalued to keep pace with the general rise in earnings nationally.* ◊ **revaluation** /riːvæljuːeɪʃəᵊn/. EG *...the consolidation and revaluation of their holdings.* — V+O : USU PASS ⇑ value = reassess; ◊ N UNCOUNT = reassessment

2 When a country **revalues** its currency, it increases its value so that it can buy more foreign currency than before. ◊ **revaluation.** EG *...the progressive revaluation of the dollar.* — V+O : USU PASS; ◊ N UNCOUNT + SUPP

3 If you **revalue** something, you examine it again and decide what you think is good or bad about it. EG *...an inability to revalue what one sees because of commitment to previous methods.* ◊ **revaluation.** EG *...the cultural revaluation of decorative arts.* — V+O ⇑ evaluate; ◊ N UNCOUNT + SUPP

revamp /riːvæmp/, **revamps, revamping, revamped.** If someone **revamps** a system, group, or organization, they make changes to it in order to try and improve it and hide its faults; often used showing disapproval. EG *The system has been revamped considerably.* ◊ **revamped.** EG *The revamped management has been trying to sort out the mess.* ◊ **revamping.** EG *They were concerned with the revamping of their social frameworks.* — V+O = amend; ◊ ADJ CLASSIF = modified; ◊ N SING WITH DET+SUPP

Revd is a formal written abbreviation for 'Reverend'; used as part of the title of a member of the clergy. — N IN TITLES

reveal /rɪˈviːl/, **reveals, revealing, revealed.**

1 If you **reveal** something that has been unknown or secret until now, you make it known. EG *They were not ready to reveal any details of the arrest... A Sunday newspaper had once revealed that he'd wanted to marry his cousin... Howard now revealed a certain talent for fixing things.* — V+O/REPORT-CL = disclose, divulge

2 If you **reveal** something that has been out of sight, you uncover it so that people can now see it. EG *She drew the curtains aside to reveal beautiful gardens... Now he revealed himself, complete with multi-coloured hat.* — V+O (NG/REFL) ⇑ show = expose, display

3 If you **reveal** your feelings, you tell people what they are or show them in your expression or behaviour. EG *He still did not reveal what he had felt about me... The slant of his eyes and the line of his lips reveal his contempt for the critics.* — V+O/REPORT-CL

4 If something **reveals** itself as being in a particular state, it shows by its actions or appearance that it has reached that state, especially when people had not already realized this. EG *His gaiety had revealed itself as a manic fear of solitude.* — V+O (REFL)+as/to-INF

revealing /rɪˈviːlɪŋ/. **1** An action, statement, or experience that is **revealing** teaches you something that you did not know, especially about another person and their attitudes or feelings. EG *He had nothing very revealing to say... ...a very revealing experience.* ◊ **revealingly.** EG *Tyndall revealingly remarked that he'd never read the book.* — ADJ QUALIT = telling; ◊ ADV WITH VB, OR ADV SEN

2 Women's clothes that are **revealing** allow more of their body to be seen than is usual. EG *...an outfit that was scanty and revealing.* ◊ **revealingly.** EG *...the blouse was revealingly tight.* — ADJ QUALIT; ◊ ADV

reveille /rɪˈvæliⁱ/ is the time when soldiers have to get up in the morning. In military camps, a short tune is played on trumpets or drums to wake them up. EG *Several minutes before the usual five-thirty reveille, the whistle sounded... ...the drummer had sounded the reveille.* — N UNCOUNT, OR N SING : *the*+N ⇑ signal

revel /revəᵊl/, **revels, revelling, revelled**; also spelled **reveling** and **reveled** in American English. **1** If you **revel** in a situation or activity, you enjoy it enormously, for example because it is very pleasant or because you are very popular or very powerful. EG *She seemed to revel in her success... ...schoolchildren revelling in the bright sunshine.* — V : USU+A *(in)* = bask, glory

2 A **revel** is an occasion on which people meet together in order to enjoy themselves in a noisy and active way; a fairly old-fashioned use. EG *The revels are now beginning, she told herself.* — N COUNT : USU PL

revelation /revəleɪʃəᵊn/, **revelations. 1 Revelation** is the act of making known something which is true, but which was previously secret or unknown. EG *It was a revelation of the splendour of the times...* — N UNCOUNT/COUNT : IF+PREP THEN *of* ⇑ disclosure

How will her revelation affect the sensitive image of professional tennis?

2 A **revelation** is something true that is made known to people, especially in a dramatic or unexpected way. EG *His book offers no illuminating personal revelations... ...the Watergate revelations.* N COUNT: USU PL ⇑ disclosure

3 If you say that something was a **revelation** to you, you mean that when you experienced it you found it very surprising because it was not at all what you expected. EG *The whole episode was a revelation to him of how poor the family had been... Dali's show was a revelation.* N SING: *a*+N, IF +PREP THEN *to*

4 Divine **revelation** is a sign or explanation from God about His nature or purpose. EG *They were taught that the scriptures are divine revelations from God.* N UNCOUNT/COUNT ⇑ disclosure

reveller /rɛvəˀlə/, **revellers**; also spelled **reveler** in American English. **Revellers** are people who are enjoying themselves in a noisy and often drunken way; a fairly old-fashioned word. EG *The town stays packed with revellers most of the night.* N COUNT: USU PL

revelry /rɛvəˀlri¹/, **revelries**. **Revelry** is noisy and often drunken enjoyment. EG *The sound of good-natured revelry filled London's Savoy Hotel yesterday.* N UNCOUNT/N PLURAL

revenge /rɪ¹vɛndʒ/, **revenges, revenging, revenged**. **1 Revenge** is something that you do to hurt or punish someone who has hurt or harmed you, that gives you a great deal of satisfaction. EG *They were eager for revenge... They had taken their revenge by blowing up his house... ...an act of revenge... He did it in revenge for the loss of his job... They exacted one last revenge on their enemies.* N UNCOUNT = retaliation, vengeance

2 If you **revenge** yourself for a harm or wrong that has been done to you, you hurt or punish the person who has done the wrong or harm; a formal use. EG *She will revenge herself on those who helped him to escape.* V+O (REFL/NG): IF+PREP THEN *on*

revengeful /rɪ¹vɛndʒfʊl/. Someone who is **revengeful** wants to take their revenge on someone who has hurt or harmed them. EG *He looked angry now, almost revengeful.* ◊ **revengefully**. EG *He tore up her photograph savagely, revengefully.* ADJ QUALIT ⇑ vengeful ◊ ADV WITH VB

revenue /rɛvɪ²nju:/, **revenues**. **1 Revenue** is **1.1** the money that a company or organization receives over a fixed period of time. EG *The editor was concerned at the drop in advertising revenue... We need to channel oil revenues into other areas.* **1.2** the money that a government receives through taxation. EG *The loss of tax revenues in many towns is as high as 70%... Roads should be provided out of public revenue.* N UNCOUNT/N PLURAL = income; N UNCOUNT/N PLURAL ⇑ income

2 **Revenue** departments, officials, etc, are concerned with gathering taxes for the government. EG *The company's tax situation was rigorously probed by revenue officials.* ● See also **Inland Revenue**. N BEFORE N

reverberate /rɪ¹vɜːbəreɪt/, **reverberates, reverberating, reverberated**; a formal or literary word. **1** When a loud sound **reverberates**, it echoes around you and seems to shake the building you are in. EG *A clap of thunder reverberated throughout the house.* V: USU+A = resonate, resound

2 If a place **reverberates** with sound, it seems to shake because the sound is extremely loud and lasts a long time. EG *A second later the interior of the car reverberated with the report of a gun.* V+A (*with*)

3 If actions, ideas, theories, etc, **reverberate**, they have a powerful effect which lasts a long time. EG *Her determination gave him a shock which was to reverberate through the whole of his married life... His brave words reverberated through the silent room.* V: USU+A ⇑ influence = resonate

reverberation /rɪ¹vɜːbəreɪʃəˀn/, **reverberations**; a formal or literary word. A **reverberation** is **1** a serious effect that follows a sudden, dramatic event. EG *His action was not a self-contained incident; its reverberations would affect us all... ...the enormous reverberation of his downfall.* **2** the shaking and echoing effect that you hear after a loud sound has been made. EG *The reverberations could be heard for miles.* N COUNT: USU PL ⇑ influence; N COUNT: USU PL, OR N UNCOUNT = echo

revere /rɪ¹vɪə/, **reveres, revering, revered**. If you **revere** someone, you respect and admire them greatly; a formal word. EG *Why had she imagined that they loved and revered him so much?* ◊ **revered**. EG *He was a revered figure with a national reputation.* V+O = venerate ◊ ADJ QUALIT

reverence /rɛvəˀrəns/ is a feeling of great respect, admiration, and awe for someone or something. EG *'Sir,' he said with reverence, 'it is a work of genius.'... Such a philosophy teaches reverence for all life.* N UNCOUNT = veneration

reverend /rɛvəˀrənd/. **1 Reverend** is a title used before the name or rank of a member of the clergy. EG *...the Reverend John Lamb... ...Reverend and Mrs Mellish... ...the Reverend Dr Colin Thompson.* N IN TITLES

2 Someone who is **reverend** is considered to be worthy of respect; an old-fashioned use. EG *Even the most reverend judges can make a bad decision.* ADJ QUALIT ⇑ respected

reverent /rɛvəˀrənt/. If you say that someone's actions or behaviour are **reverent**, you mean that they express respect, admiration, or awe for someone or something; a formal word. EG *We were required to file past the tomb in a reverent manner.* ◊ **reverently**. EG *He was proud to hear his own grandfather spoken of so reverently.* ADJ QUALIT ⇑ respectful ◊ ADV WITH VB ⇑ respectfully

reverential /rɛvərɛnʃəˀl/. Something that is **reverential** has the quality of respect, admiration, and awe; a formal word. EG *...a reverential atmosphere... He uttered the name with the most reverential respect.* ADJ QUALIT ⇑ respectful

reverie /rɛvəri:/, **reveries**. A **reverie** is a kind of daydream in which you think about pleasant things or events; a formal word. EG *The Colonel snapped out of his reverie... I lapsed into a reverie of my own.* N COUNT/UNCOUNT

reversal /rɪ¹vɜːsəˀl/, **reversals**. **1** The **reversal** of a situation or process involves changing it so that it becomes the opposite of what it was before. EG *Fortunately there was a reversal of this suicidal tendency... They were pressing for a reversal of British policy.* N COUNT: USU SING+SUPP ⇑ change = turn round

2 If two people or things are involved in a **reversal**, they change over completely so that each acquires the other's position or function; a formal use. EG *Events in this present century have produced a complete reversal of roles.* N COUNT: USU SING+SUPP = exchange

reverse /rɪ¹vɜːs/, **reverses, reversing, reversed**. **1** If you **reverse** a process, you cause it to change so that it begins to have the opposite effect to the one it was having before. EG *They were determined to reverse their country's decline... Loving care and a good home can reverse the effects of early disadvantages... The newcomers to farming want to see this trend reversed.* V+O

2 If a government or other authority **reverses** a decision that has been made, they reject it and replace it with a decision that will have a different effect; a fairly formal use. EG *The Bill enabled the House of Commons to reverse any decision taken by the House of Lords... A judgement may be revised or reversed in the light of some particular action.* V+O ⇑ change = overturn

3 If you **reverse** an object or list, you turn it round so that it stands or is arranged in the opposite way. EG *He took the chair, reversed it, and drew it towards the fire... The order of the items had been reversed.* V+O

4 If you **reverse** the positions or functions of two things, you change them so that each thing has the position or function that the other one had. EG *In this play the traditional sex roles are reversed... The next stage was to reverse the positions of the two pictures.* V+O = exchange swop

5 When a car **reverses** or when you **reverse** it, you drive it backwards. EG *She reversed the car into the garage... The street was so narrow that cars which entered it had to reverse out again.* V-ERG = back

6 If your car is in **reverse** or if you have put it into **reverse**, you have engaged the reverse gear so that you can drive it backwards. EG *I threw the truck into reverse... Reverse is to the left of fourth gear, just here.* N UNCOUNT

7 **Reverse** means opposite to what is usual or to what has just been described. EG *In the past ten years I think we've seen the reverse process... I'll give you the names of the winners in reverse order.* ADJ CLASSIF: ATTRIB = contrary

8 The **reverse** is the exact opposite of a situation that has just been mentioned. EG *I don't believe so at all–I believe quite the reverse... You may think we have been making a profit, but in fact the reverse is true... I warn you they may do the reverse of what you want.* N SING: *the*+ = contrary

9 If a process happens **in reverse** or goes **into reverse**, things happen in the opposite way to what was usual or intended. EG *He seemed to be going through his daily routine, but in reverse... At this point the Party's fortunes went into reverse.* PHR: USED AS A

10 A **reverse** is a serious failure or setback in a process or attempt to achieve something; a formal use. EG *They suffered severe military reverses in North Africa... These reverses came after a long period of moderate success.* N COUNT ⇑ defeat

11 The **reverse** of an object that has two sides is the less important side of it. EG *...the figure of Mercury which appears on the reverse... On the reverse side of this coin you will see a Latin inscription.* N SING : *the*+N, IF+PREP THEN *of*, OR N BEFORE N ⇑ back

12 If you **reverse the charges** when you are making a telephone call, the person who you are calling receives the bill and not you; used in British English. EG *Ring me up when you get there–reverse the charges, if you like.* PHR : VB INFLECTS = call collect

13 A **reverse charge** telephone call is one which you do not pay for but which is paid for by the person who receives it. PHR BEFORE N = transfer charge

reverse gear, reverse gears. The **reverse gear** of a vehicle is the gear which you use in order to make the vehicle go backwards. EG *I found it difficult to get into reverse gear... The van had two reverse gears.* N COUNT/UNCOUNT

reversible /rɪˈvɜːsəbəˀl/. **1** If a process or decision is **reversible**, it can be stopped or changed at any time. EG *These decisions are reversible under favourable circumstances... Is vasectomy reversible?* ADJ CLASSIF

2 Clothing that is **reversible** has been made so that it can be worn with either side on the outside. EG *I was wearing a reversible winter jacket.* ADJ CLASSIF

reversing light, reversing lights. A **reversing light** is a white light on the back of a motor vehicle which shines when the vehicle is being driven backwards. EG *Very few cars had reversing lights in those days.* N COUNT

reversion /rɪˈvɜːʃəˀn/, **reversions. Reversion** is **1** the process of changing back to an earlier way of living or of making something; a fairly formal use. EG *...a reversion to the life she had so hated... ...the economic and social causes of this reversion to barbarism.* N UNCOUNT+*to* = regression **2** the process in which a species of animal begins to behave in a way that its ancestors behaved during a much earlier historical period; a technical term in zoology. EG *Some salamanders have taken this reversion to a fishlike existence even further.* N UNCOUNT/COUNT : IF+PREP THEN *to* = throwback

revert /rɪˈvɜːt/, **reverts, reverting, reverted.**
1 When people **revert** to a former state or condition, they change their present way of life or methods of work and go back to the way of life or methods of work that they had before; a formal use. EG *He was reverting rapidly to adolescence... ...a growing tendency to revert to earlier methods of production.* V+A *(to)* = return

2 When a situation **reverts** to a former state or condition, it goes back to that state or condition; a formal use. EG *Things will now revert to a healthy state of business.* V+A *(to)* = return

3 When a species of animal **reverts** to a former state, all the animals of that species go back to behaving as their ancestors behaved during an earlier historical period; a technical term in zoology. EG *This creature has reverted permanently to the aquatic life of its ancestors.* V+A *(to)*

4 When you **revert** to something that you have mentioned or discussed earlier, you begin talking about it again; a fairly formal use. EG *At this point in the discussion I reverted to money matters... Can I revert to one other point before you continue?* V+A *(to)* = go back, return

5 When money or property **reverts** to someone, it becomes their possession because they owned it before or because they are a descendant of the previous owner; a technical term in law. EG *The properties will either revert to the original owners or else be sold at auction.* V+A *(to)* ⇑ pass = return

review /rɪˈvjuː/, **reviews, reviewing, reviewed. 1** A **review** is **1.1** an article in a newspaper or magazine, or a programme on television or radio, in which someone gives their opinion of a new book, play, art exhibition, etc. EG *...a review of Lord Harewood's autobiography... ...a closely printed journal bursting with book reviews.* N COUNT ⇑ criticism = critique **1.2** a magazine, or a regular television or radio programme, that consists mainly of reviews of new books, plays, art exhibitions, etc. EG *...The New York Review of Books.* N COUNT : ALSO IN NAMES **1.3** a study of the way in which something is done or managed, which is made by a group of people in authority in order to decide whether any changes should be made. EG *A stringent review of public expenditure began immediately... Scotland has local review committees which deal with parole... These arrangements are subject to periodic review.* N COUNT/UNCOUNT = reassessment **1.4** a formal inspection of a large group of soldiers, sailors, ships, etc. N COUNT/UNCOUNT

2 When situations, methods, procedures, etc are **under review**, they are being examined in order to decide whether changes are needed. EG *They had the situation under review... Arrangements for mobilization will, of course, be kept under constant review.* PHR : USED AS AN A

3 When a situation, method, or procedure **comes up for review**, it reaches a time when a regular examination of it is carried out by a group of people in authority. EG *All your joint financial obligations and partnerships now come up for review.* PHR : VB INFLECTS

4 If you **review** a book, play, art exhibition, etc, you write an article in a newspaper or a magazine, or give a talk on television or radio, in which you express your opinion of it. EG *Tomorrow night, I will review two new plays by Michael Abbensett.* V+O ⇑ criticise

5 When someone **reviews** a situation, method, or procedure, they examine it in order to decide whether to make any changes in it. EG *It is a simple matter to review the contract... By law, state pensions must be reviewed once a year.* V+O = reassess

6 If you **review** a situation or series of events, you think about them or talk about them, often in order to understand them better. EG *At 6.30 each morning, the partners meet to review the previous day... This is not the place to review the history of colonial rule.* V+O = go over

7 When someone such as a president or queen **reviews** a large group of soldiers, sailors, ships, etc, they formally inspect them. EG *Elizabeth I reviewed her troops there.* V+O

reviewer /rɪˈvjuːə/, **reviewers.** A **reviewer** is a person who reviews books, plays, art exhibitions, etc. EG *Maeve Binchy was our reviewer of 'The Temptation of Eileen Hughes'.* N COUNT = critic

revile /rɪˈvaɪl/, **reviles, reviling, reviled.** If you **revile** someone or something, you insult them because you hate or despise them very much; a formal word. EG *They had been reviled and misunderstood by almost everyone.* V+O ⇑ curse

revise /rɪˈvaɪz/, **revises, revising, revised. 1** If you **revise** the way you do something or the way you think about something, you change your actions or beliefs, usually in order to try and improve them. EG *The judges may revise their selection process... You must revise your attitude to life.* V+O = alter, amend

2 If you **revise** an amount, price, estimate, etc, you alter it or correct it to make it more accurate. EG *The farm has already revised downward its crop estimate.* V+O ⇑ change = amend ◊ **revised.** EG *...revised figures... ...a revised offer of £92 a share.* ◊ ADJ CLASSIF = amended

3 If you **revise** something that has been written such as a book, a law, or a piece of music, you change its form in some way, usually in order to improve it. EG *This book has sold a half-million copies since it was revised last year.* V+O = alter, amend

4 When you **revise**, you read something again, usually several times, in order to learn it so that you can answer questions about it in an examination. EG *I've been revising for the last three days... I was revising Dickens last night.* V OR V+O ⇑ study = cram, swot

revision /rɪˈvɪʒəˀn/, **revisions. 1** A **revision** of something such as a law, book, or piece of music is an alteration that is made to it in order to improve it. EG *They're discussing a complete revision of the timetable.* N COUNT : IF+PREP THEN *of* ⇑ change = amendment ▸ used as an uncount noun. EG *The Shops Act is in need of revision... I sent the contract back for revision.* ▸ N UNCOUNT : IF+PREP THEN *of*

2 Revision is the activity of reading something again, usually several times, in order to learn it before you take an examination. EG *You may want to use them for revision during the holiday period.* N UNCOUNT ⇑ study

revisionism /rɪˈvɪʒənɪzəˀm/. **Revisionism** is a theory of socialism that is more moderate than orthodox Marxist theory, and is therefore considered to be wrong and dangerous by orthodox Marxists; a technical term. EG *...the struggle against imperialism and revisionism.* N UNCOUNT

revisionist /rɪˈvɪʒənɪst/, **revisionists. 1** Socialist ideas or groups that are **revisionist** are more moderate than orthodox Marxist theory, and are therefore considered to be wrong and dangerous by orthodox Marxists; a technical term. EG *...revisionist economic* ADJ CLASSIF *theory... The Party had grown increasingly revisionist.*

2 A **revisionist** is a socialist whose actions or opinions are more moderate than orthodox Marxist theory allows, and who is therefore considered to be wrong and dangerous by orthodox Marxists; a technical term. EG *Both defeats strengthened the position of the revisionists.* N COUNT

revisit /riːvɪzɪt/ **revisits, revisiting, revisited**. If you **revisit** a place, you go back there after you have been away for a long time, often after the place has changed a lot. EG *I have never revisited it for fear of spoiling my memories.* V OR V+O

revitalize /riːvaɪtəlaɪz/, **revitalizes, revitalizing, revitalized**; also spelled **revitalise**. To **revitalize** a situation, event, or activity means to cause it to become more active, lively, or efficient. EG *There was an attempt to revitalize the society later in the year... ...the Liverpool poets who revitalized poetry in England in the 1960s.* V+O = revivify

revival /rɪˈvaɪvəˡl/, **revivals**. 1 **Revival** is a process in which something that has been inactive begins again or becomes active again. EG *Inflation may start to rise again with the revival of trade... Why is there such a revival of interest in the supernatural?... Our main chance of economic revival.* N UNCOUNT : USU +SUPP = resumption, resurgence

2 A **revival** is 2.1 a sudden increase in the popularity and influence of a religion. EG *...the late nineteenth-century Catholic revival in England.* N COUNT/UNCOUNT 2.2 a new production of a play, opera, ballet, etc that has been performed previously. EG *...a revival of 'The Beggars' Opera'.* N COUNT

revivalism /rɪˈvaɪvəlɪzəˡm/ is a movement that tries to make a particular religion more popular and more influential. EG *By this time, militant Hindu revivalism had become more than a creed.* N UNCOUNT

revivalist /rɪˈvaɪvəlɪst/, **revivalists**. 1 A **revivalist** is a person who tries to make a particular religion more popular and more influential. N COUNT

2 **Revivalist** people or activities are involved in trying to make a particular religion more popular and more influential. EG *The religious revivalist movements.* ADJ CLASSIF : ATTRIB

revive /rɪˈvaɪv/, **revives, reviving, revived**. 1 When something such as a feeling, an attitude, or a practice **revives** or when you **revive** it, it begins again or becomes active again after a period of inactivity. EG *They failed to fulfil their promises to revive the economy... Her interest revived at the appearance of one of her neighbours... He called for a concerted international effort to revive the disarmament movement.* V-ERG

2 When you **revive** someone or when they **revive**, they become conscious again after they have fainted or been unconscious. EG *He was being revived by the rest of the household staff... He slowly began to revive.* V-ERG ⇑ resuscitate

3 When someone **revives** a play, opera, ballet, etc, they present a new production of it. EG *'The Dresser' is already being revived.* V+O ⇑ stage

revivify /riːvɪvɪfaɪ/, **revivifies, revivifying, revivified**. To **revivify** a situation, event, or activity means to cause it to become more active, lively, or efficient; a formal word. EG *Sport would play a major role in helping to revivify the nation.* V+O = revitalize

revocation /rɛvəkeɪʃəⁿn/ is the cancelling of an agreement, law, or title so that it is no longer legal or official; a technical term. N UNCOUNT ⇑ withdrawal = annulment

revoke /rɪˈvəʊk/, **revokes, revoking, revoked**. If someone **revokes** an agreement, law, or title, they cancel it so that it is no longer legal or official; a formal or technical word. EG *He may revoke my diploma.* V+O ⇑ withdraw = rescind

revolt /rɪˈvəʊlt/, **revolts, revolting, revolted**. 1 **Revolt** is violent action taken by a large group of people against the rulers of their country because they want a different system of government. EG *The country is still years away from open revolt... The settlers rose in revolt in 1960.* N UNCOUNT/COUNT = insurrection, uprising

2 When people **revolt**, they take violent action against the rulers of their country because they want a different system of government. EG *These latest injustices reinforced the urge to revolt... Large sections of the army revolted against the civil government.* V : IF+PREP THEN *against* = rebel

3 A **revolt** is a series of actions taken by a group of people within an organization in order to try and change its aims or policies. EG *He was facing a revolt in his own party... Morale was low and several backbench revolts had occurred.* N COUNT/UNCOUNT = rebellion

4 If something **revolts** you, it makes you feel disgust for it. EG *The image still revolts us irrationally... He was revolted by what he saw.* V+O = repel, sicken

5 When someone or something **revolts**, they refuse to continue to work properly because they are being badly treated. EG *...his stomach revolted.* V : IF+PREP THEN *against* = rebel

revolting /rɪˈvəʊltɪŋ/. Something that is **revolting** is so unpleasant to see or smell that you feel disgusted by it. EG *The smell was quite revolting.* ADJ QUALIT = abhorrent

◇ **revoltingly**. EG *...a revoltingly full ashtray.* ◇ ADV

revolution /rɛvəljˈuːʃəⁿn/, **revolutions**. 1 A **revolution** is a successful attempt by a large group of people, often using violent methods, to change the political system of their country. EG *...the fiftieth anniversary of the Russian revolution... ...in the years after the Revolution... Her grandparents had lost everything during the revolution.* ▸ used as an uncount noun. EG *France seemed to be on the verge of revolution.* N COUNT : ALSO IN NAMES ▸ N UNCOUNT

2 **Revolution** is a process which Marxists believe will happen in all societies. In this process, the system by which goods are made, bought, sold, etc will change until it finally becomes a socialist system. EG *Socialist revolution can never be achieved without a struggle.* N UNCOUNT

3 A **revolution** is also 3.1 an important change in a particular kind of human activity, for example in the way goods are made or in education or in the way people spend their spare time. EG *...the potentialities of the revolution in communications that has taken place... ...the significance of the Computer Revolution... ...the current revolutions in social behaviour.* N COUNT 3.2 the movement that takes place when something turns in a complete circle around a central point or line. EG *The needle turned through a tenth of a revolution... They spin at 400-500 revolutions per minute.* N COUNT = rotation, re

revolutionary /rɛvəljˈuːʃənəˡriˡ/, **revolutionaries**. 1 People or actions that are **revolutionary** are attempting to carry out a political revolution. EG *They had fled America as a result of their revolutionary activities... ...a revolutionary leader.* ADJ CLASSIF ⇑ rebellious

2 A **revolutionary** is a person who tries to cause a revolution or who takes part in one. EG *Many revolutionaries reject this point of view.* N COUNT ⇑ insurgent

3 Events or ideas that are **revolutionary** cause a great change in the way something is done or made. EG *The invention of writing was the most revolutionary of all human inventions... ...a revolutionary change in the way cars are manufactured.* ADJ QUALIT ⇑ innovatory

revolutionize /rɛvəljˈuːʃənaɪz/, **revolutionizes, revolutionizing, revolutionized**; also spelled **revolutionise**. If someone or something **revolutionizes** an activity, they make great changes in the way that it is done. EG *Our ideas will revolutionize the film industry... He revolutionized jazz saxophone playing... These time-saving techniques could revolutionise your working life.* V+O ⇑ overturn ◇ **revolutionizing**. EG *...a revolutionizing and modernizing force.* ◇ ADJ CLASSIF ATTRIB

revolve /rɪˈvɒlv/, **revolves, revolving, revolved**. 1 When something **revolves**, it moves or turns in a circle around a central point or line. EG *The earth revolves around the sun. ...The propellar began to revolve.* V : IF+PREP THEN *around/round* ◇ **revolving**. EG *They were watering the ground with big revolving sprinklers.* ◇ ADJ CLASSIF ATTRIB

2 If a debate or discussion **revolves** around a particular subject, it is entirely concerned with that subject. EG *The discussion revolved round three topics... The argument would revolve around what was considered 'reasonable'.* V+A *(around/round)* = centre on

revolver /rɪˈvɒlvə/, **revolvers**. A **revolver** is a kind of gun that you hold in your hand and that can fire several bullets quickly. N COUNT ⇑ pistol

revolving door, revolving doors. A **revolving door** is an entrance which some large buildings have instead of an ordinary door. It consists of four glass doors which turn together in a circle around a vertical post. N COUNT : SING=PL

revue /rɪˈvjuː/, **revues**. A **revue** is a light theatrical entertainment consisting of songs, dances, and jokes about recent events. EG *I was asked to arrange a Christmas revue.* N COUNT ⇑ show

revulsion /rɪˈvʌlʃəⁿn/. **Revulsion** is 1 strong dislike or disapproval that you feel towards something such N UNCOUNT = disgust as an activity or a habit. EG *Germ warfare has always been regarded with revulsion.* **2** a strong and sudden feeling of disgust for something you see or hear. EG *She started back in revulsion and terror.* N UNCOUNT ⇑ dislike = loathing

reward /rɪˈwɔːd/, **rewards, rewarding, rewarded. 1** A **reward** is **1.1** something that you are given, for example because you have behaved well, worked hard, or provided a service to the community. EG *There were never any rewards for being good at games... ...the emotional rewards of parenthood.* N COUNT ⇑ recompense ▸ used as an uncount noun. EG *There was rarely punishment and rarely reward in our school.* ▸ N UNCOUNT **1.2** a sum of money offered to anyone who can give information about stolen property or about someone who is wanted by the police. EG *Hearst announced a reward of £50,000 for information.* N COUNT : USU SING

2 To **reward** someone means to give them something because they have behaved well, worked hard, or provided a service to the community. EG *People should be rewarded for special effort... They rewarded the winners with gifts of fruit and flowers... He was rewarded by becoming the first man to walk on the moon.* V+O : USU PASS ⇑ recompense

3 If something **rewards** your attention, it becomes so interesting that you realize that it is worth spending some time or effort on it; a fairly formal use. EG *As well as the stained glass, the carvings on the roof also reward attention... He's a strange person with a very obscure past that might reward investigation.* V+O

rewarding /rɪˈwɔːdɪŋ/. Something that is **rewarding** gives you a lot of personal satisfaction and pleasure. EG *A much longer, but I think more rewarding, novel is 'Middlemarch.'.. It's been hard work but the climb has been immensely rewarding.* ADJ QUALIT ⇑ worthwhile

rewind /riːwaɪnd/, **rewinds, rewinding, rewound.** If you **rewind** the tape on a tape recorder, you make it go backwards towards the beginning, for example so that you can hear a recording for a second time. EG *...play the first phrase, stop, rewind, then play the first phrase again.* V OR V+O

rewire /riːwaɪə/, **rewires, rewiring, rewired.** To **rewire** a building or electrical device means to put a new system of electrical wiring into it. EG *Since the place had to be rewired, they took out all the central lights... To change a program, one literally had to rewire part of the machine.* V+O

rework /riːwɜːk/, **reworks, reworking, reworked.** If you **rework** something such as an idea or a piece of writing, you think about it again and make changes to it in order to improve it or bring it up to date. EG *He reworked the income schedules.* V+O ⇑ revise

rewrite, rewrites, rewriting, rewrote, rewritten. The word **rewrite** is pronounced /riːraɪt/ when it is a verb, and /riːraɪt/ when it is a noun.

1 If you **rewrite** something that you have written, you make significant changes to it in order to improve it. EG *...a junior reporter writing and rewriting every paragraph of a routine news item.* V+O ⇑ alter = revise

2 If you **rewrite** an account of something, you change it because new facts or information are available, or because you do not accept that a previous account is true. EG *He had had to rewrite his history so as to obliterate her from it.* V+O

3 A **rewrite** is the process of changing something that you have written in order to improve it, or the piece of writing that results from this process. EG *I had to spend some time doing last-minute rewrites... The last rewrite of 'Goodbye Mr Chips'.* N COUNT

rhapsodic /ræpsɒdɪk/ is used to describe statements or language which express great delight or enthusiasm about something. EG *He also wrote a rhapsodic description of a railway engine.* ADJ QUALIT = glowing, fulsome

rhapsodize /ræpsədaɪz/, **rhapsodizes, rhapsodizing, rhapsodized**; also spelled **rhapsodise**; a fairly formal word. If you **rhapsodize** about someone or something, you express great delight or enthusiasm about them. EG *'You've got wonderful hair,' he kept rhapsodizing.* V : IF+PREP THEN *about*, OR V +QUOTE ⇑ enthuse = eulogize

rhapsody /ræpsədiˡ/, **rhapsodies.** A **rhapsody** is a piece of music which is irregular in form, but very passionate and flowing. EG *Liszt's Second Hungarian Rhapsody.* N COUNT : ALSO IN NAMES ⇑ composition

rheostat /riəstæt/, **rheostats.** A **rheostat** is a device in an electrical machine which controls the flow of current. N COUNT

rhesus /riːsəs/, **rhesuses.** A **rhesus** or **rhesus monkey** is a small short-tailed monkey from Northern India which is often used in scientific experiments. N COUNT

rhetoric /retərɪk/. **Rhetoric** is **1** speech or writing that is presented in a forceful and dramatic way which appears to be clever and important; often used showing disapproval. EG *She simply ignored his bluster as empty rhetoric... The liberalism of their rulers was a rhetoric masking vicious exploitation.* N UNCOUNT ⇑ oratory **2** a grand, poetic way of speaking which once used to be practised as an art. EG *...the sombre rhetoric of Hamlet and Othello... ...the art of rhetoric.* N UNCOUNT = oratory

rhetorical /rɪˀtɒrɪkəºl/. **1** Actions or speech that are **rhetorical** are intended to be grand and impressive. EG *...a rhetorical flourish.* ADJ CLASSIF ⇑ dramatic = poetic

2 A question that is **rhetorical** is one which is asked in order to make a statement rather than to get an answer. EG *The question was purely rhetorical... It seemed to be a rhetorical question, so I countered it with another.* ◇ **rhetorically.** EG *'What have I done?' he demanded rhetorically, throwing his arms about.* ADJ CLASSIF ⇑ stylistic ◇ ADV WITH VB

rhetorician /retərɪʃəºn/, **rhetoricians.** A **rhetorician** is a person who is good at public speaking or who is trained in the art of rhetoric. EG *He was an ancient Greek–a rhetorician.* N COUNT ⇑ speaker = orator

rheumatic /ruːmætɪk/, **rheumatics. 1** A **rheumatic** pain is caused by rheumatism. EG *She had been up the whole night with rheumatic aches.* ADJ CLASSIF

2 Someone who is **rheumatic** suffers from rheumatism. EG *She was as yet neither blind, deaf, nor rheumatic...* ▸ used of parts of someone's body in which they suffer from rheumatism. EG *...her shaky, grey, rheumatic fingers.* ADJ CLASSIF = rheumaticky

3 A **rheumatic** is someone who suffers from rheumatism. N COUNT ⇑ person

rheumatic fever is a serious disease which causes fever, a sore throat, and swelling and pain in your joints. EG *He had been seriously ill with rheumatic fever and could no longer travel easily.* N UNCOUNT ⇑ illness

rheumaticky /ruːmætɪkiˡ/. Someone who is **rheumaticky** suffers from rheumatism; an informal word. EG *Only now he realized how rheumaticky he was becoming.* ▸ used of parts of someone's body that are affected by rheumatism or of pains that are caused by rheumatism. EG *...his rheumaticky fingers.* ADJ QUALIT = rheumatic

rheumatism /ruːmətɪzəºm/ is an illness that makes your joints or muscles stiff and painful. EG *She had suffered from rheumatism all her life... How's your rheumatism?* N UNCOUNT

rheumatoid arthritis /ruːmətɔɪd ɑːθraɪtəs/ is a chronic disease that causes your joints, for example your hands, wrists, or knees, to swell up and become painful. N UNCOUNT ⇑ illness

rheumy /ruːmiˡ/. If someone has **rheumy** eyes, their eyes are moist and watery, usually because they are very ill or old; a literary word. ADJ CLASSIF : USU ATTRIB ⇑ wet

rhinestone /raɪnstəʊn/, **rhinestones.** A **rhinestone** is a very bright, colourless jewel that is used in cheap jewellery and ornaments. EG *She wore dark glasses that had rhinestones on their frame... ...rhinestone earrings.* N COUNT

rhino /raɪnəʊ/, **rhinos.** A **rhino** is the same as a rhinoceros. N COUNT ⇑ mammal

rhinoceros /raɪnɒsəºrəs/, **rhinoceroses.** A **rhinoceros** is a big animal with a very thick skin and one or two horns on its nose. Rhinoceroses live in Africa and Asia and eat plants. N COUNT ⇑ mammal = rhino

rhododendron /rəʊdədendrən/, **rhododendrons.** A **rhododendron** is a bush with large pink or purple flowers and leaves which do not fall off in the winter. EG *The rhododendrons were massed in great banks of pink.* N COUNT : USU PL ⇑ shrub

rhombus /rɒmbəs/, **rhombuses.** A **rhombus** is a geometrical shape which has four equal sides but is not a square; a technical term in geometry. N COUNT ⇑ parallelogram = diamond

rhubarb /ruːbɑːb/. **1 Rhubarb** is a plant with long red stems which is cooked in puddings and can be used to make jam or wine. EG *I had rhubarb tart with a lot of cream.* N UNCOUNT

2 People sometimes repeat the word **rhubarb** several times in order to make the sound of a conversation when the meaning of the words is not important. For example, film actors pretending to be a noisy crowd may say, 'rhubarb, rhubarb, rhubarb.' CONVENTION ⇑ nonsense

rhyme /raɪm/, **rhymes, rhyming, rhymed. 1** If one word **rhymes** with another or if two words **rhyme**, they have a very similar sound. People often use words that rhyme with each other at the ends of V OR V+A *(with)* : RECIP

the lines in poems. EG *She called him Guppy, to rhyme with puppy... She could not see how he got the words to rhyme properly.* ◇ **rhyming**. EG *...rhyming couplets.* ◇ ADJ CLASSIF : ATTRIB

2 A **rhyme** is 2.1 a set of words or lines which rhyme, or one word which rhymes with another. EG *None of the rhymes were quite right... Can you think of a rhyme for 'seven'?* 2.2 a short poem, especially one that is used by children. EG *Do you enjoy songs, poems, rhymes, and jokes?* N COUNT; N COUNT = verse

3 **Rhyme** is the use of rhymes as a technique in poetry. EG *She had a gift for rhythm and rhyme.* N UNCOUNT = verse

4 If something is written **in rhyme**, it is written as a poem in which the lines rhyme. EG *Tennyson's work was mostly in rhyme.* PHR : USED AS AN A = in verse

5 If you say that someone does something **without rhyme or reason**, you mean that they do it although there is no logical reason for them to do it. EG *They left without rhyme or reason... Love happens irrationally, without the slightest rhyme or reason.* PHR : USED AS AN A ⇑ irrationally = illogically

6 See also **nursery rhyme**.

rhymed /raɪmd/. **Rhymed** poems or pieces of text contain lines or words which rhyme with each other. EG *...an enormous poem in rhymed couplets... ...rhymed sayings.* ADJ CLASSIF : ATTRIB = rhyming

rhyming slang is a colloquial form of language in which you do not use the normal word for something, but say a word that rhymes with it instead. In Cockney rhyming slang, for example, you say 'apple and pears' when you mean 'stairs'. N UNCOUNT

rhythm /rɪðəm/, **rhythms**. 1 A **rhythm** is 1.1 a regular movement or beat. EG *She rocked with the boat's rhythm, up and down, up and down... The marchers were all stepping to the swift rhythm of the drums... He was humming tunelessly and tapping an annoying rhythm on his glass with his fork.* 1.2 a regular pattern of change such as the changes in your body, the passing of the seasons, the cycle of the moon, or the movement of sea tides. EG *Human biological rhythms are related to the natural cycle of day and night... The fish sensed a change in the sea's rhythm.* N COUNT ⇑ regularity; N COUNT ⇑ regularity

2 **Rhythm** is a strong pattern of sound or movement that is used in music, poetry, or dancing. EG *J.J. Cale uses rhythm to create a lot of different effects.* N UNCOUNT = beat

rhythm and blues is a popular musical style developed in the 1940s from blues music, but using electrically amplified instruments. N UNCOUNT

rhythmic /rɪðmɪk/. If a movement or sound is **rhythmic** or **rhythmical**, it is repeated at regular intervals, forming a regular pattern or beat. EG *The machine made a soft rhythmic pulsing sound... ...rhythmic dancing... Her breathing became more rhythmical.* ◇ **rhythmically**. EG *The cradle rocked rhythmically to and fro.* ADJ QUALIT ⇑ repetitive; ◇ ADV WITH VB

rib /rɪb/, **ribs, ribbing, ribbed**. 1 Your **ribs** are the curved bones that go from your backbone to your chest. People and animals have twelve ribs on either side of their bodies. EG *He had a broken rib... Claud was grinning and nudging me in the ribs.* N COUNT

2 A **rib** of beef is a piece of beef that has been cut from the animal's body and includes one of its ribs. EG *He was dreaming of the fine rib of beef roasting in the oven for his lunch.* ● See also **spare ribs**. N COUNT

3 A **rib** is a long, curved piece of wood or metal that is part of the structure of a roof or a boat and that makes the structure strong. EG *...a big arched roof of steel ribs.* N COUNT ⇑ member

4 **Rib** is a method of knitting that makes a raised pattern of parallel lines. You use rib, for example, on the cuffs and round the bottom of jumpers. EG *Knit two inches in rib.* N UNCOUNT = ribbing

5 If you **rib** someone, you tease them in a friendly way; used in informal English. EG *I had been ribbing him about something he had written for our local newspaper.* V+O = chaff, kid

6 See also **ribbed, ribbing**.

ribald /rɪbəld/. When someone is **ribald**, they say things which are humorous but impolite because they refer to sex; an old-fashioned word. EG *After the fourth whisky the president became ribald.* ▸ used of the things people say or do. EG *All I could hear were exclamations of ribald encouragement... ...ribald laughter.* ADJ QUALIT = coarse, vulgar

ribaldry /rɪbəldri/ is humour that is considered to be impolite because it refers to sex; an old-fashioned word. EG *He was roused to laughter by her ribaldry.* N UNCOUNT

riband /rɪbənd/, **ribands**; also spelled **ribband**. A **riband** is the same as a ribbon; an old-fashioned word. N COUNT

ribbed /rɪbd/. Something that is **ribbed** has a raised pattern of parallel lines on it. EG *...ribbed black stockings... ...ribbed jumpers.* ADJ CLASSIF

ribbing /rɪbɪŋ/ is a method of knitting that makes a raised pattern of parallel lines. You use ribbing, for example, on the cuffs and round the bottom of jumpers. N UNCOUNT = rib

ribbon /rɪbən/, **ribbons**. 1 A **ribbon** is a long narrow piece of cloth that is used for tying things together or as a decoration. Ribbons are often brightly coloured. EG *There was a white ribbon in her black hair... She wore a grey wool frock and a black hat with a ribbon.* ▸ used as an uncount noun. EG *...a length of silk ribbon... He got a special parchment tied with red ribbon.* N COUNT ⇑ strip, trimming; ▸ N UNCOUNT

2 A **ribbon** is also 2.1 a long, narrow piece of cloth that contains a special ink and that you put into a typewriter. When the typewriter is used, the ink in the ribbon is pressed on to a piece of paper, where it makes marks in the form of letters, numbers, etc. EG *This typewriter needs a new ribbon.* 2.2 a small piece of coloured cloth that is given to someone, especially a member of the armed forces, to show appreciation of something that they have done. They may then wear the ribbon attached to a coat, jacket, shirt, etc. EG *He was wearing a military greatcoat with a single row of campaign ribbons.* N COUNT/UNCOUNT ⇑ band; N COUNT ⇑ decoration

3 You can also describe something that is in the shape of a long thin line as a **ribbon**. EG *He looked idly at the ribbon of road ahead of them... ...a ribbon of smoke... Stretching out along the highway is a ribbon of fast-food places and antique shops.* N COUNT : USU+SUPP

4 If something is **cut, torn,** or **slashed to ribbons**, it is cut or torn many times until it is very badly damaged. EG *They came home to find their rooms ransacked and their clothes slashed to ribbons... ...claws ready to scratch his bare chest to ribbons.* PHR : VB INFLECTS ⇑ shred

rib-cage, rib-cages; also spelled without a hyphen. Your **rib-cage** is the structure of ribs that protects your lungs and other internal organs in your chest. EG *The blow caught him in the top of his solar plexus, just under the centre of the rib cage.* N COUNT ⇑ bones

riboflavin /raɪbəʊfleɪvɪn/ is a vitamin that occurs in green vegetables, milk, fish, eggs, liver, and kidney; a technical word. N UNCOUNT ⇑ vitamin B

rib-tickler, rib-ticklers. A **rib-tickler** is a very funny joke or story; an old-fashioned informal word. N COUNT

rice /raɪs/ is a food consisting of white grains which you boil in water and eat, usually with meat or vegetables. Rice is eaten as the staple food in many countries. EG *He eats barely one pound of rice a day... She cooked a dish of rice and chicken... I put some long-grain rice into a saucepan.* ▸ used of the plants that rice is taken from, especially when they are grown as a crop. EG *He grows rice and timber and employs 8,000 workers... They started to wade into the soggy rice paddies.* N UNCOUNT

rice paper is a thin paper made from the straw of rice plants. Cakes can be baked on it and it can also be eaten. N UNCOUNT

rice pudding, rice puddings. **Rice pudding** is a food made by baking rice in milk and sugar. It is usually eaten as a dessert. N UNCOUNT/COUNT

rich /rɪtʃ/, **richer, richest**. 1 Someone who is **rich** has a lot of money or valuable possessions. EG *She was extremely rich... She told me that our father was a very rich man... There is an enormous difference in living standards between the rich and the poor countries... The richer he becomes, the unhappier he is.* ▸ **The rich** is used to refer to people who are rich. EG *Only the rich could afford his firm's products... You can tell the very rich by their evening dress.* ◇ **richness**. EG *For all its richness and all its progress, it is not an ideal society.* ADJ QUALIT = affluent, wealthy; ▸ N PLURAL : +N = well off; ◇ N UNCOUNT = wealth

2 **Riches** are valuable possessions or large amounts of money when they are owned by someone. EG *...young men in search of adventure and riches... We do not see education as merely the road to riches.* N PLURAL = wealth

3 Natural **riches** are things that exist naturally in large quantities and that are valuable or useful to human beings, for example minerals, wood, and oil. EG *...the exploitation of the earth's riches.* N PLURAL ⇑ resources

4 If something is **rich** in a desirable substance or quality, it contains a lot of that substance or quality. ADJ QUALIT : PRED+in/with

EG *The seabed is rich in buried powdered minerals... The story is rich in comic and dramatic detail... This land is known to be rich with oil, gas, coal, and diamonds.*

5 A **rich** deposit of a mineral or other substance is one that contains a large amount of that mineral or substance. EG *...the rich guano deposits of the Chincha islands... ...the world's richest vein of copper.* ADJ QUALIT : ATTRIB = abundant, plentiful

6 A **rich** life or history is one which is full of incidents and events and therefore very interesting. EG *It is done in the interests of a wider and richer life for all... The town has a rich social history... ...out of the depths of your rich experience.* ◊ **richness.** EG *...the richness of Asian culture... ...the richness and diversity of Christian experience.* ADJ QUALIT : USU ATTRIB ◊ N UNCOUNT

7 If you say that a story or situation is **rich**, you mean that it is very amusing; used in old-fashioned English. EG *...the rich humour of his dialect stories... Rich tales about him circulated at the Travellers' Club.* ADJ QUALIT ⇑ funny

8 Soil that is **rich** contains a lot of nutrients and so is good for growing crops or flowers in. EG *The area was noted for its rich black soils.* ◊ **richness.** EG *The soil had lost its richness.* ADJ QUALIT = fertile ◊ N UNCOUNT = fertility

9 Food that is **rich** contains a lot of fat, eggs, sugar, etc and is therefore unhealthy if eaten in large quantities; usually used showing disapproval. EG *He was prone to indigestion after rich restaurant meals... They kept gorging themselves on rich food.* ADJ QUALIT

10 Colours that are **rich** are strong and attractive. EG *There was a touch of blue in it, a deep rich blue.* ◊ **richness.** EG *...the richness of their colouring.* ADJ QUALIT = vivid ◊ N UNCOUNT

11 Voices and musical sounds that are **rich** are full and strong in a pleasing way. EG *...a cultivated man with a soft, rich voice... ...the rich sound of the brass instruments.* ◊ **richness.** EG *...a brilliant actress with a voice of great richness and range.* ADJ QUALIT = mellow ◊ N UNCOUNT

12 Smells that are **rich** are strong in a pleasing way. EG *He could smell the rich fragrance of bamboo freshly chopped... Never in my life have I smelled anything as rich and wonderful as this.* ADJ QUALIT ⇑ powerful

13 Clothes and fabrics that are **rich** are beautiful and valuable. EG *Rich tapestries billowed over holes in the walls.* ◊ **richness.** EG *I was struck by the richness of the costumes.* ADJ QUALIT = gorgeous ◊ N UNCOUNT ⇑ splendour

-rich combines with nouns like 'protein' and 'mineral' in order to form adjectives which indicate that something contains a lot of a particular substance. EG *This is a good environment for natural protein-rich plants... ...the refining of sulphur-rich crude oil.* COMB : FORMS ADJ CLASSIFS

richly /rɪtʃli¹/. 1 If someone is rewarded **richly** for something, they are rewarded well by being given something very valuable or desirable. EG *I will reward you richly... They benefited richly, if briefly, from the results.* ADV WITH VB = handsomely

2 You say that something is **richly** deserved or **richly** earned when you strongly believe that someone deserves it or has earned it. EG *It was a richly deserved honour... The judge said the man had 'richly earned a sentence of incarceration.'* ADV WITH VB = thoroughly

3 If a place is **richly** provided with a particular thing, it has a lot of that thing. EG *These libraries are richly equipped with games and books.* ADV = abundantly

4 If something is **richly** decorated, it has a lot of elaborate and beautiful decoration on it. EG *...a richly decorated staircase... The pulpit was very richly carved.* ADV = ornately

5 If something is **richly** coloured, it is of a strong and attractive colour. EG *...crystal, marble, granite and other richly coloured substances.* ADV = vividly

Richter scale /rɪktə skeɪl/. The **Richter scale** is a scale which is used for measuring how severe earthquakes are. N SING : the+N

rick /rɪk/, **ricks, ricking, ricked.** 1 A **rick** is a large pile of hay or straw that is built in a regular shape and usually has a thatched top. EG *Some ricks were nine yards long by five yards wide.* N COUNT ⇑ stack

2 If you **rick** your neck or your back, you hurt it by pulling or twisting it in an unusual way; used in informal English. EG *I ricked my neck and missed a game.* V+O = sprain, wrench

rickets /rɪkɪts/ is a disease that children sometimes get when their food does not contain enough Vitamin D. It makes their bones soft and causes their liver and spleen to become too large. EG *...a child who is suffering from rickets.* N UNCOUNT

rickety /rɪkɪti¹/. A **rickety** building or piece of furniture is not made well or strongly, and therefore likely to collapse or break. EG *I was working at a rickety table... She started off down the rickety stairs with me behind her... I had built a rather rickety hut.* ADJ QUALIT = ramshackle, shaky

rickshaw /rɪkʃɔː/, **rickshaws.** A **rickshaw** is a vehicle that is used for carrying passengers. Usually it has two wheels and is pulled by a man who walks in front of it, or it has three wheels and is driven by a man who sits on it and pedals it like a bicycle. Rickshaws are used in some parts of Asia. N COUNT ⇑ conveyance

ricochet /rɪkəʃeɪ, rɪkəʃɛt/, **ricochets, ricocheting, ricocheted**; also spelled **ricochetting, ricochetted.** If a bullet **ricochets**, it hits a surface such as a wall and bounces away from it again at an angle. EG *The bullet ricocheted back at my car.* ▸ used as a noun. EG *The bullet had been sent back across the street in a ricochet.* V : USU+A ⇑ rebound ▸ N COUNT ⇑ rebound

rid /rɪd/, **rids, ridding, rid.** The form **rid** is used in the present tense and is the past tense and past participle of the verb. The form **ridded** is also sometimes used as the past tense and past participle.

1 **Rid** is used in the expression **get rid of**, which has the following meanings. 1.1 When you **get rid of** something that you do not want, you remove it, dispose of it, or throw it away. EG *She bathed thoroughly to get rid of the last traces of make-up... There were pails and pails of muck to be got rid of... The body gets rid of excess water through the urine... How do they get rid of rats and mice?* PHR : get INFLECTS 1.2 If you **get rid of** someone who is causing you problems, you encourage them to leave or arrange for them to be sent somewhere else. EG *Gwyneth started to worry about how to get rid of her guests... Do your best to get rid of the children... We had to get rid of the director.* PHR : get INFLECTS 1.3 If you **get rid of** your car or your house, you sell it; used in informal English. EG *By this time Christopher had got rid of the van and bought himself a car... We can't get rid of the house.* PHR : get INFLECTS 1.4 If you **get rid of** a feeling, a situation, or an idea, you change or destroy it so that it no longer exists. EG *You should try to get rid of your inhibitions... We can get rid of imperialism.* PHR : get INFLECTS ⇑ remove

2 If you **rid** a place or object of something unpleasant or annoying, you succeed in removing the annoying or unpleasant thing completely; a fairly formal use. EG *It is difficult to rid clothes of cooking smells... We must rid the country of this wickedness.* V+O+A *(of)*

3 If you **rid** yourself of something unpleasant or worrying, you remove it or change it so that it is no longer a problem; a fairly formal use. EG *I had still not rid myself of the burden of my relations... He had rid himself of his illusions.* V+O (REFL)+A *(of)*

4 If you are **rid** of something or someone that had been worrying or upsetting you, they are no longer there and so you no longer feel worried or upset. EG *Eric was glad to be rid of him.* ADJ CLASSIF : PRED+*of*

riddance /rɪdəns/. You say **good riddance** or **good riddance to bad rubbish** to indicate that you are glad that someone has left; an informal expression. EG *You'll be glad to see me go. 'Good riddance to bad rubbish,' you'll say.* CONVENTION

ridden /rɪdə⁰n/ is the past participle of **ride.**

riddle /rɪdə⁰l/, **riddles, riddling, riddled.** 1 A **riddle** is a puzzle in which you ask a question that seems to be nonsense but which has a clever or amusing answer. N COUNT = conundrum

2 If you say that someone **is speaking** or **talking in riddles**, you mean that they are not talking in a simple and straightforward way and that they are saying things which do not seem to make sense. EG *I wish you would stop this talking in riddles.* PHR : VB INFLECTS = be cryptic

3 If you describe something as a **riddle**, you mean that you find it confusing and are unable to understand it. EG *There was a curious riddle about Uncle Charlie's early life... He thought he had solved a huge riddle of the universe.* N COUNT ⇑ problem = conundrum

4 To **riddle** something means to make a lot of holes in it. V+O ⇑ pierce

riddled /rɪdə⁰ld/. 1 If something is **riddled** with holes, it is full of holes. EG *They had left the whole building riddled with holes... The cliffs are riddled with caves.* ADJ QUALIT : PRED+*with*

2 If something is **riddled** with undesirable qualities or features, it is full of them. EG *His own arguments were riddled with false assumptions and errors of* ADJ QUALIT : PRED+*with* = rife with

fact... He fought for reform in cities riddled with corruption.

ride /raɪd/, **rides, riding, rode, ridden.** 1 When you **ride** or when you **ride** a horse, you sit on a horse and control its movements, especially as a form of sport or a means of transport. EG *He arrived later, riding on his large white horse... I put my pillow on the saddle so that I could ride comfortably... He saddled his horse and rode to town... Every morning he used to ride his mare across the fields.* ◊ **riding.** EG *All our family are very keen on riding... She goes riding every weekend with her cousin... Esmeralda was wearing her riding boots.*
V OR V+O; ◊ N UNCOUNT OR ADJ CLASSIF

2 When you **ride** a bicycle or motorcycle, you sit on it, control it, and travel along on it. EG *...a gang of youths riding motorbikes... He rode round the campus on a bicycle.*
V+O, OR V+A

3 When you **ride** in a vehicle such as a car, you travel in it. EG *That afternoon he rode in a jeep... It's a marvellous car, very comfortable to ride in.*
V+A

4 You also say that someone **is riding** something or **is riding** on it when they are helped or supported by it. EG *He returned to power after the election, riding an extraordinary surge of personal popularity.*
V+O, OR V+A

5 A **ride** is 5.1 a journey on a horse or bicycle, or a journey in a vehicle. EG *We decided to go for a ride... ...a ten-minute bus ride... It's an easy day's ride to the bottom of the canyon.* 5.2 a free trip in a vehicle that someone else is driving, especially a car. EG *Could you give me a ride to the station?*
N COUNT; N COUNT ⇑ journey = a lift

6 If someone **takes** you **for a ride**, they deceive you or cheat you in some way; an informal expression. EG *I'm afraid we've been taken for a ride.*
PHR : VB INFLECTS = swindle, con

7 You say that a ship or boat **rides** when it floats on the sea or a river and moves gently along. EG *We let the boat go with the current and then ride on the water close to the shore. ...a ship riding at anchor.*
V+A = be carried, float

ride out. If you **ride out** a period of difficulty or danger, you come successfully through it. EG *We were confident that we would be able to ride out the storm... The company managed to ride out the recession and is now doing well again.*
PHRASAL VB : ORDER V+ADV+O

ride up. If a skirt or dress **rides up**, it moves upwards, out of its proper position. EG *This skirt always rides up when I'm sitting down.*
PHRASAL VB : V+ADV

rider /raɪdə/, **riders.** A **rider** is 1 a person who rides a horse, a bicycle, a motorcycle, etc. EG *A horse and rider were racing towards them... ...the dare-devil motorcycle rider.* 2 a statement that is added to something that has already been said or decided, often in a way that produces some change in meaning or emphasis; a fairly formal use. EG *I only wanted to add one little rider to what you were saying.*
N COUNT; N COUNT = condition, proviso, qualification

ridge /rɪdʒ/, **ridges.** 1 A **ridge** is 1.1 a long, narrow piece of raised land. EG *We drove up a hillside and finally stopped on a high ridge... Way off in the distance on top of a ridge she could see her home.* 1.2 a raised line on a flat surface. EG *He was counting the ridges in the wet sand... ...the muscular ridges of his back.*
N COUNT; N COUNT

2 The **ridge** on the roof of a building is the part at the top where the two sloping sides meet.
N COUNT

3 A **ridge** of high pressure is an area of high pressure in the atmosphere; a technical term in meteorology. EG *Today's weather map shows a ridge of high pressure to the west.*
N COUNT : USU + *of*

ridged /rɪdʒd/. Something that is **ridged** has raised lines on its surface. EG *His forehead was ridged in concentration... ...muscles ridged like rope.*
ADJ CLASSIF

ridicule /rɪdɪkjuːl/, **ridicules, ridiculing, ridiculed.** 1 **Ridicule** is unkind laughter at someone or something that you consider foolish and not worthy of respect. EG *The official attitude is usually one of ridicule... He was the object of lively ridicule... His prophesy which was greeted with a good deal of ridicule.*
N UNCOUNT ⇑ criticism = derision, scorn

2 If you **ridicule** something or someone, you make fun of them in an unkind way. EG *Her own stupidity was publicly ridiculed in the classroom... He is liable to be teased and ridiculed.*
V+O ⇑ criticize = deride, mock

ridiculous /rɪdɪkjəˈləs/. 1 If you say that something or someone is **ridiculous**, you mean 1.1 that they are very foolish and unreasonable. EG *It was ridiculous, scientists used to argue, to talk of computers as brains... All his money will go, as a result of this ridiculous gambling... Don't be so ridiculous... They charge you a ridiculous price.* ◊ **ridiculously.** EG *He let out his house at a ridiculously low rent.* 1.2 that they are very funny and comical. EG *He jumped around on all fours like a pantomime bear and was perfectly ridiculous.*
ADJ QUALIT = ludicrous; ◊ ADV; ADJ QUALIT = foolish

2 **from the sublime to the ridiculous**: see **sublime.**

riding habit, riding habits. A **riding habit** is a long dress with a full skirt, or a jacket and long skirt, that women used to wear when they were riding horses.
N COUNT ⇑ clothing

rife /raɪf/; a formal word. 1 If you say that something bad or unpleasant is **rife**, you mean that it occurs very frequently. EG *Bribery and corruption in the government service were rife... Graduate unemployment is rife.*
ADJ QUALIT : PRED ⇑ common = widespread

2 If a place is **rife** with something bad or unpleasant, it contains a lot of it. EG *'The academic world,' he said bitterly, 'is rife with jealousy, treachery, and ingratitude.'*
ADJ QUALIT : PRED + *with*

riffle /ræfəˈl/, **riffles, riffling, riffled.** If you **riffle** through the pages of a book, or **riffle** them, you turn them over quickly, without reading all that is written on them. EG *He opened the book at random and riffled through the pages... I riffled through four or five newspapers, trying to find the article... He opened a volume of Hamilton's work and riffled the pages.*
V+A *(through)*, OR V+O = flick

riffraff /rɪf ræf/; also spelled with a hyphen. When someone refers to a group of people as **riffraff**, they are saying that they are worthless and disreputable; an old-fashioned word. EG *...poets, painters, and other such riffraff.*
N UNCOUNT, OR SING : *the*+N

rifle /raɪfəˈl/, **rifles, rifling, rifled.** 1 A **rifle** is a gun with a long barrel that you can use for shooting things that are a long way away. You fire it with the handle pressed against your shoulder. EG *He pointed the rifle at her head... He retrieved his rifle and strolled back to the car... ...a high velocity bullet fired from a modern rifle.*
N COUNT

2 If you **rifle** through a collection of things, you make a quick search among them. EG *The doctor rifled through the papers.*
V+A *(through)* = riffle

3 If you **rifle** something, you steal everything from it. EG *He rifled the dead man's wallet.*
V+O = clean out

rifleman /raɪfəˈlməˈn/, **riflemen.** A **rifleman** is a soldier of the lowest rank in a large unit of soldiers who are especially trained to use rifles. EG *The photograph shows a lone rifleman racing out of an open door... ...the Cape Mounted Riflemen.*
N COUNT

rifle range, rifle ranges; also spelled with a hyphen. A **rifle range** is a place where you can practise shooting with a rifle.
N COUNT

rift /rɪft/, **rifts.** A **rift** is 1 something that prevents friendship between two people, or two groups of people, who used to be friends. EG *A deep rift had started in their family life... It had been nine years since she had seen her brother, as a result of a rift between them... ...the rift between the government and the trade unions.* 2 a split that appears in something solid, for example in the ground. EG *Tiny blue flowers were growing in the rifts in the rock.*
N COUNT : IF + PREP THEN *between/in* = division; N COUNT = crack, fissure

rig /rɪg/, **rigs, rigging, rigged.** 1 If someone **rigs** an election or job appointment, they arrange the result of it so that they achieve the result that they want. EG *He rigged political appointments unashamedly... No one knows better how to rig an election.*
V+O = engineer, fix

2 If someone **rigs** a game, they change something in advance so that they have more chance of winning the game. EG *These darts are rigged. Some of them don't stick in the board... She had rigged the cards.*
V+O = fix

3 If you **rig** a device or piece of equipment or **rig** it **up**, you make it and fix it in place using materials that are available to you but are not necessarily the right materials. EG *A screen or curtain can be rigged to prevent her seeing them... We had to rig a string netting over the cot... He had rigged up a listening device... Some of the men had rigged up tents.*
V+O OR PHRA[SAL] VB : V+O+AD[V] ⇑ assemble = improvis[e]

4 When a ship **is rigged**, it is equipped with sails, rigging, etc. EG *The ship was rigged for sail.*
V+O

5 A **rig** is a large structure that is used for looking for oil and gas and for taking them out of the ground or sea bed. EG *...a drilling rig.*
N COUNT ⇑ installati[on]

6 Someone's **rig** is the clothes that they are wearing; a rather old-fashioned informal word. EG *Andrew was wearing his usual rig... ...football players in full rig.*
N UNCOUNT : POSS/MOD+N ⇑ costume = get up, t[...]

rig out. If you **rig** yourself **out** or **are rigged out** in a particular way, you wear a particular kind of clothes; an informal expression. EG *He had rigged*
PHRASAL VB : O (REFL)+A[DV] USU+A = get up

himself out like a Red Indian... He was rigged out in a policeman's uniform... She was rigged out as a First World War nurse.

rigging /rɪgɪŋ/ is all the ropes which are used to support a ship's masts and sails. EG *...the high pitched sound of the wind in the rigging.* N UNCOUNT

right /raɪt/, **rights, righting, righted.** 1 If something is **right**, it is correct and in accordance with the facts. EG *You've got the pronunciation right... Are you sure that clock's right?... Is that the right time?... I think that's probably right... You get full marks for getting the right answer... You are French, is that right?* ADJ CLASSIF ⇑ true ▸ used as an adverb. EG *Some of the pupils remembered right and some remembered wrong.* ▸ ADV WITH VB = correctly

2 If a choice, action, or decision is **right**, it is clearly the best or most appropriate one out of a number of alternatives. EG *Looking back on it, are you sure that was the right decision?... You must do things in the right order... ...being in the right place at the right time... Clare is obviously the right person to talk to about it.* ADJ CLASSIF = correct ◊ **rightly**. EG *He can be very good at acting when he is rightly cast.* ◊ ADV WITH VB = aptly

3 If an action is **right**, it is considered to be morally good and morally acceptable. EG *I don't think it's right to leave children alone in a house... It would not have been right to convict him... You certainly know whether what you are doing is right or wrong... It was right and proper that I should be present.* ADJ CLASSIF : USU PRED ≠ wrong

4 If something such as a machine or a situation is not **right**, it is not working or continuing smoothly and is therefore causing problems. EG *The engineer has been but it's still not right... She sensed that things weren't right between us.* ADJ CLASSIF : PRED, WITH BROAD NEG ≠ wrong

5 If someone is **right** about something, they are correct in their statements, judgement, or opinions. EG *Lally was right about the repairs which the cottage needed... You're absolutely right... I think I'm right in saying that the entire play lacks a central theme.* ADJ CLASSIF : PRED ≠ wrong ◊ **rightly**. EG *The arts in general are, as Geoffrey rightly said, underfinanced... I have the feeling, rightly or wrongly, that I shall regret my decision.* ◊ ADV WITH VB, OR ADV SEN = correctly

6 If you say that someone is **right** to do something, you mean that you think that they are morally justified in doing it. EG *We were right to insist on certain reforms... I think he was absolutely right in doing this.* ADJ CLASSIF : PRED, USU + to-INF ◊ **rightly**. EG *Many people are rightly indignant... We have, very rightly and properly, strong moral objections to abortion on demand.* ◊ ADV WITH VB

7 If you feel **right**, you feel healthy and well; used in informal English. EG *He doesn't feel right... I'm not right these days.* ADJ CLASSIF : PRED ≠ ill

8 If you refer to the **right** people or the **right** places, you are referring to people or places that are thought to be socially desirable. EG *He knew all the right people... Of course he was at the right school, Eton... She liked to be seen in all the right places.* ADJ CLASSIF : ATTRIB ≠ wrong

9 The **right** side of a piece of material is the side that is intended to be seen and that faces outwards when it is made into clothes. ADJ CLASSIF : ATTRIB ≠ wrong

10 People say **'Right'** in order to attract your attention, especially when they want to begin something. EG *Right, let's have you sitting at your desks... Right, open your mouth, let's have a look.* ADV SEN, USU + IMPER

11 If something is a **right**, you are morally or legally entitled to do it or to have it. EG *People in positions of influence have a right to comment on political issues... 'I know my rights,' he said... ...equal rights for women... ...basic civil and political rights... ...the right to strike... Both parents have an equal right to a career if they want one... ...whaling and mining rights... Authors should be protected over their rights.* N COUNT, OR N + to-INF ⇑ entitlement

12 **Right** is behaviour and ideas that are considered to be morally good and acceptable. EG *They began to ask difficult questions about right and wrong... One must have some principles, some sense of right and wrong.* N UNCOUNT ≠ wrong

13 **Right** means **13.1** on or towards the side which, in English writing, has the last letter of a word, or the side of the body which for most people has the hand they write with. EG *Turn right off Broadway into Caxton Street... Her right hand was covered in blood... They forced David into a room on the right side of the corridor... I had the impression that the car was going to swerve right.* ADV, OR ADJ CLASSIF : ATTRIB ≠ left **13.2** worn, or intended to be worn, on the right foot, hand, etc. EG *...his right shoe.* ADJ CLASSIF : ATTRIB ≠ left

14 The **right** is the right side, direction, or position. EG *He was firing high and slightly to the right... On my left was Tony Heard and on my right Allister Sparks... They turned their heads slowly from left to right... Take the second right off Walnut Street.* N SING : WITH the/POSS ≠ left

15 A **right** is also your right hand when you punch someone with it or a punch given with your right hand; a boxing term. EG *...a hard right to the jaw... I want to see you use your right a lot more in this round.* N COUNT : USU a/POSS + N IN SING ≠ left

16 The **Right** or the **right** is **16.1** the people or groups of people who support the political ideals of capitalism and conservatism rather than socialism. EG *The Left are said to be better organised than the Right... There's a considerable division between left and right in the British Labour Party.* N SING : the + N, VB CAN BE SING OR PL ≠ left **16.2** the political ideals, groups, and activities which are closer to conservatism than socialism or communism. Some people think of political ideals as being like a line with communism on the left and fascism on the right. EG *He began to move slowly away from the Right... Politically, she's further to the right than her predecessor.* N SING : the + N ≠ left

17 **Right** is used **17.1** to emphasize the precise place that you are talking about. EG *Our hotel was right on the beach... Stay right here... The pistol's right there by the bed.* ADV + ADV/PREP = exactly, precisely **17.2** to emphasize how far something moves or extends, or how long something continues. EG *We took the lift right down to the basement... The train takes you right through to London... I worked right on till four o'clock in the morning.* ADV + ADV/PREP **17.3** to emphasize the particular qualities, either good or bad, of the noun it goes with. EG *They've made a right mess of that, haven't they?... He's a right idiot.* ADJ CLASSIF : ATTRIB

18 **Right** is also used in some British titles to indicate the high rank or status of the person concerned. EG *...the Right Reverend Anselm Thatcher... There is not a Right Honourable or Honourable Gentleman on either side of the House who would disagree with this.* ADV + ADJ : USED IN TITLES = Very, most

19 **Right** also means immediately and without delay. EG *I'll be right back... The Music Hall is going to close down right after Easter.* ADV + ADV/PREP

20 To **right** something means **20.1** to put it back into its correct or proper state. EG *He was there to right the balance... The situation should right itself in time.* V + O (NG/REFL) ⇑ adjust **20.2** to return it to a normal upright position. EG *The ship righted itself.* V + O (NG/REFL)

21 To **right** a wrong means to correct it or compensate for it in some way. EG *Wrongs should be righted by the vote and not by violence.* V + O = redress

22 The word **right** is also used in the following expressions. **22.1** If a plan or situation **goes right**, it happens or progresses in the way that you hope or expect, so that you are pleased or happy. EG *Here's an example of plans not going quite right.* PHR : VB INFLECTS **22.2** If you feel **as right as rain**, you feel very well; used especially of someone who has just recovered from an illness. EG *I'm feeling right as rain now, thank you.* PHR : USED AS C **22.3** If you say that someone is **not right in the head**, you mean that they are a little mad; used in informal English. EG *Do you think he's right in the head?* PHR : USED AS C **22.4** If you do something **when the time is right**, you do it at the most appropriate time, when you think that you are most likely to succeed. EG *Elections will be held when the time is right.* PHR : USED AS A **22.5** If you **put** or **set** something **right**, you correct something that was wrong or that was causing problems in some way. EG *This has got to be put right... The only way we can really put things right is by borrowing even more money.* PHR : VB INFLECTS **22.6** **Right now** means at this very moment; an informal expression. EG *Things must be difficult for you right now... I can't let you out right now... I have no time right now to discuss your problems.* PHR : USED AS A ⇑ now = just now **22.7** **Right away** means immediately and without any unnecessary delay. EG *He had written down a list of things to do right away... He didn't answer right away.* PHR : USED AS A = at once **22.8** If you are **in the right**, you are behaving in a way which is morally or legally correct. EG *He had put himself in the right by his generous apology... No-one could argue that he is in the right in this dispute.* PHR : USED AS A **22.9** If you say that something should be true **by rights**, you are emphasizing that it should be true or saying that people would normally expect it to be true. EG *I should by rights speak German, my* PHR : USED AS A

mother's German, but I only know a few words. **22.10** If you are **within** your **rights** to do something, you are morally or legally entitled to do it. EG *You'd be within your rights to complain about those shoes, you know.* PHR : USED AS AN A

22.11 If you have a position, title, or claim to something **in** your **own right**, you have it because of what you are yourself rather than because of other people. EG *He had emerged as a leader in his own right.* PHR : USED AS AN A

22.12 If you say that you **would give** your **right arm** to do something, you mean that you would like very much to do it and would be willing to make some sacrifices in order to do it. EG *A dramatist would give his right arm to write a scene like that.* PHR : VB INFLECTS

22.13 If someone is **at a person's right hand**, they are near that person so that they can encourage or advise them. EG *George was always at his right hand to encourage him.* • See also **right-hand man.** PHR : USED AS AN A

22.14 • **on the right side of** someone: see **side.** • to **reserve the right to** do something: see **reserve.** • to **serve** someone **right**: see **serve.** • See also **civil right, Bill of Rights, human rights, all right.**

right-about turn, right-about turns. A **right-about turn** is a movement that you make that leaves you facing in the opposite direction to the one you started from. N COUNT

right angle, right angles. A **right angle** is an angle of 90°. A square has four right angles. N COUNT • If one thing is **at right angles** to another, or if the two things are **at right angles**, they are situated so that they touch each other forming an angle of 90°. EG *...four straight corridors at right angles to each other.* • PHR : USED AS AN A = perpendicular

right-angled. **1** A **right-angled** triangle has one angle which is a right angle. ADJ CLASSIF

2 A **right-angled** bend is a sharp bend that turns through approximately ninety degrees. ADJ CLASSIF

righteous /raɪtʃəs/. Someone who is **righteous** behaves in a way that is morally good, religious, and praiseworthy. EG *...a righteous and wise man.* ADJ QUALIT = virtuous ▸ used of people's feelings. EG *There was an outburst of righteous indignation.* ▸ = just ◇ **righteousness.** EG *Some of us strive for righteousness.* ◇ N UNCOUNT = justice

rightful /raɪtfʊl/. A **rightful** possession or action is one which you have a legal or moral right to have or do; a fairly formal word. EG *He denied his children of their rightful inheritance... They had been deprived of their rightful share of the property... They had no rightful role in the civil war... He can now take his rightful place as president.* ADJ CLASSIF : ATTRIB = due, just ▸ used of people who have a legal or moral right to have or do something. EG *She is the rightful heir to the estate... The rightful owner could not be traced.* ▸ = lawful ◇ **rightfully.** EG *They must give us what is rightfully ours.* ◇ ADV WITH VB = legally

right-hand describes the position of something when it is on the right side. EG *...a biggish house on the right-hand side of the road.* ADJ CLASSIF : ATTRIB ≠ left-hand

right-hand drive. A **right-hand drive** car, van, or lorry has the steering wheel on the right side, and is designed to be used in countries such as Britain where people drive on the left side of the road. ADJ CLASSIF : ATTRIB

right-handed. Someone who is **right-handed** uses their right hand rather than their left hand for activities such as writing and painting. EG *Are you sure Henry is right-handed?... My brother used to play tennis right-handed until he was fifteen.* ADJ CLASSIF, OR ADV ≠ left-handed

right-hander, right-handers. A **right-hander** is someone who uses their right hand rather than their left hand for activities such as writing and painting. N COUNT ⇑ person

right-hand man, right-hand men. Someone's **right-hand man** is a person who acts as their chief assistant and who helps and supports them a lot in their work. EG *...the Attorney General's right-hand man... I'm counting on you being my right-hand man.* N COUNT : USU WITH POSS ⇑ assistant

rightism /ræɪtɪzm/ refers to the beliefs and behaviour of people who support the ideals of conservatism and capitalism. EG *There was a strong tradition of rightism in the area.* N UNCOUNT ≠ leftism

rightist /raɪtɪst/, **rightists.** **1** A **rightist** is someone who is politically conservative and traditional and supports the ideas of capitalism. EG *He was able to bring back some of the rightists who had been dismissed.* N COUNT = right winger

2 **Rightist** ideals, activities, and people are politically conservative and traditional and support or believe in the ideas of capitalism. EG *The main opposition group is the rightist movement.* ADJ CLASSIF : ATTRIB = right-wing

right-minded. You describe someone as **right-minded** when you think that their opinions or beliefs are correct; used showing approval. EG *This is something perfectly forgivable by any right-minded person.* ADJ CLASSIF ⇑ reasonable

righto /raɪtəʊ/. You say **righto** or **right-ho** to show that you have heard what someone has said and are willing to do what they want or to do something to please them; an informal word. EG *'Drive on,' Mary cried. 'Righto,' he said... 'I'm bored stiff.'–'Righto,' I said cheerfully. 'What do you want to do?'* CONVENTION = okay

right-of-centre people or political parties support political ideas which are closer to conservatism and capitalism than socialism. EG *Some of its nominees suffered clear defeats against right-of-centre candidates.* ADJ CLASSIF

right of way, rights of way. **1** When a car or other vehicle has **right of way** or the **right of way**, it has the right to cross a road or continue round a roundabout, and other traffic must stop for it. EG *Who has right of way here?* N UNCOUNT

2 If people have a **right of way**, they have the right to use a path which goes across private property. N COUNT ▸ used of the path or road that people have the right to use. EG *Are there any rights of way across the property?*

right-thinking. A **right-thinking** person is the same as a right-minded one. EG *Every right-thinking young person is going to agree.* ADJ QUALIT : ATTRIB = right-minded

right-wing; also spelled without a hyphen. **1** **Right wing** means having or supporting political ideas that are close to conservatism and capitalism. EG *His politics are clearly right wing... ...the election of a right-wing government.* ADJ QUALIT = reactionary

2 The **right-wing** of a group of people, especially a political party, consists of the members of it whose beliefs are closer to conservatism and capitalism than are those of its other members. EG *He succeeded in uniting both the left and right wings of the party.* N COUNT : IF SING the+N ≠ left-wing

right-winger, right-wingers. A **right-winger** is a person whose political beliefs are close to conservatism and capitalism, or closer to them than most of the other people in the same group or party. EG *...Alain Bougrenet, an extreme right-winger from a family of landed gentry.* N COUNT ≠ left-winger

rigid /rɪdʒɪd/. **1** Laws or systems that are **rigid** are not able to be changed or varied, and are therefore sometimes considered to be rather severe. EG *Some mothers resented the rigid controls... ...a rigid censorship of the material... Child-raising methods were much more rigid than they are today.* ADJ QUALIT ⇑ firm = fixed, inflexible

2 People who are **rigid** are not able or not willing to change their way of thinking or behaving; used showing disapproval. EG *Some of the older nannies are extremely rigid.* ▸ used of people's beliefs and opinions. EG *...the rigid attitude of the Foreign Secretary.* ADJ QUALIT = inflexible

3 A substance or material that is **rigid** is very stiff and does not bend, stretch, or twist easily. EG *The structure became quite rigid.* ADJ QUALIT = firm

4 If you say that something **shook** you **rigid**, you mean that it gave you a serious shock; an informal expression. PHR : VB INFLECTS = shatter

rigidity /rɪdʒɪdɪti[1]/, **rigidities.** **Rigidity** is **1** the quality of stiffness that something has when it is rigid. EG *The function of bones is largely to give rigidity.* N UNCOUNT **2** inflexibility of attitudes, customs, beliefs, etc that prevents any change in the way that things are done; used showing disapproval. EG *...the rigidity of Victorian marriage.* N UNCOUNT/COUNT

rigidly /rɪdʒɪdli[1]/. **1** If something is held **rigidly**, it is held very firmly so that it cannot or does not move. EG *He found his hand shaking from holding the glass too rigidly... My features stayed rigidly fixed in the same expression.* ADV WITH VB = tightly

2 If something is done **rigidly**, it is done in a very strict way with no possibility of variation or change. EG *These suggestions must not be interpreted too rigidly... My correspondence happens to be rigidly controlled.* ADV WITH VB = closely

rigmarole /rɪgmərəʊl/, **rigmaroles**; an informal word. A **rigmarole** is **1** a complicated series of actions that have to be done in a particular activity. EG *I don't imagine you want to go through all that rigmarole.* N COUNT ⇑ procedure **2** a series of pointless or misleading N COUNT statements; a rather old-fashioned use. EG *She told me some rigmarole about the insurance.*

rigor. See **rigour**.

rigor mortis /rɪgə mɔ:tɪs/ is stiffness of the joints and muscles in the body of a dead person or animal. EG *Within a few hours rigor mortis would set in.* N UNCOUNT

rigorous /rɪgəʳrəs/. **1** Something that is **rigorous** is done or applied in a very thorough and strict way. EG *...rigorous controls... ...a series of gruelling courses and rigorous assessments.* ◊ **rigorously**. EG *These methods have been rigorously tested over many years.* ADJ QUALIT : USU ATTRIB = tight; ◊ ADV WITH VB = scrupulously, thoroughly

2 If you are **rigorous** in the way that you do something, you are very careful and thorough in the way that you do it. EG *I hope this will illustrate what I mean by being rigorous in record-keeping.* ADJ QUALIT : PRED, USU+A = scrupulous

rigour /rɪgə/, **rigours**; also spelled **rigor** in American English. **1** The **rigours** of a particular situation or way of life are the features that make it unpleasant and hard to bear; a rather formal use. EG *Even the rigours of Kurt's company seemed bearable... ...the rigours of a city winter.* N PLURAL : the+N+of = hardships

2 Rigour is strictness in something such as a law or a punishment; a formal use in British English. N UNCOUNT = severity

rig-out, **rig-outs**. A **rig-out** is a set of clothes, especially clothes that you would not usually wear; an old-fashioned informal word. EG *She'd got herself a whole new rig-out for the trip.* N COUNT = get-up, outfit

rile /raɪl/, **riles, riling, riled**. If someone **riles** you or if something that they do **riles** you, they make you angry; an informal word. EG *There are some things he does that really rile me... I don't see any reason why either of us should get riled.* V+O ⇑ annoy = irritate

rim /rɪm/, **rims**. **1** The **rim** of a container such as a cup or glass is the edge that goes all the way round the top. EG *The water spilled onto the floor over the rim of the bath... Whisky splashed over the rim of his glass... ...cups with broken rims.* N COUNT

2 The **rim** of a place or of a circular object such as a wheel or a pair of spectacles is the outside edge of it. EG *...the rims of the wheels... He glanced humorously at her, from above the rim of his spectacles.* N COUNT

3 A **rim** of dirt, grime, etc is a mark that goes all round the edge of something, especially something circular. EG *...a glass that still had a rim of foam around it.* N COUNT+of

rimless /rɪmlɪ²s/. **Rimless** spectacles or glasses do not have frames around the lenses. ADJ CLASSIF : ATTRIB

rimmed /rɪmd/. If something is **rimmed** with a particular colour, it has a border or edge of that colour; a rather literary word. EG *I saw my father's thick finger, its nail rimmed with black... They stood there exhausted, their eyes rimmed with red from the fatigue.* ADJ QUALIT : PRED+with ⇑ edged

-rimmed is added to nouns or adjectives to form adjectives which describe what sort of edge something has. EG *She wears gold-rimmed glasses.* COMB : FORMS ADJ CLASSIFS ⇑ edged

rind /raɪnd/, **rinds**. **1** The **rind** of a fruit such as a lemon or an orange is its thick outer skin. EG *...grated lemon rind... ...fruits with tough rinds.* N UNCOUNT/COUNT = peel

2 The **rind** of cheese or bacon is the hard outer edge which you do not usually eat. EG *He never cut the rinds off the rashers... ...bacon rind.* N UNCOUNT/COUNT ⇑ skin

ring /rɪŋ/, **rings, ringing**. The forms **rang** and **rung** are used as the past tense and past participle for the verbs in paragraphs 1 to 9 and in the expressions in paragraphs 14, 15, 17, and 18, and for the phrasal verbs. The form **ringed** is used as the past tense and past participle for the verbs in paragraphs 10 to 13. **1** If you **ring** someone, you call them on the telephone. EG *You must ring the hospital at once... 'Hello,' she said. 'I was hoping you might ring.'... I believe Louis rang you earlier about the tickets.* V OR V+O = phone

2 When you **ring** a bell or when it **rings**, it makes a metallic sound. EG *In the distance a church bell was ringing... He had to ring the bell several times before the door was opened... The alarm clock rings on the bedside table every morning at 6 o'clock.* ◊ **ringing**. EG *The discussion was stopped by the ringing of the doorbell.* V-ERG; ◊ N UNCOUNT

3 When a telephone **rings**, the bell inside it makes a sound to let you know that someone is telephoning you. EG *I waited for the phone to ring... The telephone's rung twice since midnight.* V

4 If you **ring** for someone or something, you ring a bell to call them or to announce that something is about to begin. EG *He rang for Tracy and asked, 'What's wrong with Davis?'... Tidy yourself up now, Mary. Sally will be ringing the bell for tea in a minute or two.* V OR V+O : IF+PREP THEN for

5 If a place **rings** with sound, it is completely filled with it; a literary use. EG *We went into a barn that rang with the cries of geese and turkeys... The boys took up the cry till the mountain rang.* V : IF+PREP THEN with

6 People also say that someone **rings** when they ring church bells or hand bells as a hobby. EG *I have been ringing all my life.* ◊ **ringing**. EG *The parson had two daughters who did a bit of ringing.* V OR V+O; ◊ N UNCOUNT

7 If a statement **rings** true, hollow, false, etc, it seems to have the particular quality that is mentioned. EG *The bishop's answers so often ring true... I was afraid that a mere 'yes' would ring hollow.* V+C

8 A **ring** is the sound made by a bell. EG *There was a ring at the door... The first ring of the phone failed to wake him... It was Julie's voice that answered, after two rings.* N COUNT

9 If something has a particular **ring**, it gives you the impression of having the quality that is mentioned. EG *The argument had a plausible ring when computers were very big, but not now... The books he mentioned had a familiar ring about them.* N SING : a+N+SUPP = feel

10 A **ring** is also **10.1** a small circle made of gold, silver, or another metal that you wear on your finger as an ornament or to show that you are engaged or married. EG *...an engagement ring... She wore many rings on her left hand.* N COUNT ⇑ band **10.2** an object that has the shape of a circle. EG *James unlocked the door from a key on his ring... I like to blow smoke rings.* N COUNT **10.3** a group of people or things standing or arranged in a circle. EG *They formed a ring round him... He was prevented from entering the building by a ring of campus policemen... Ralph looked for confirmation round the ring of faces.* N COUNT : USU+of **10.4** a small gas or electric plate that heats up and that is used for cooking. EG *Mrs Hockstadt brewed tea on a little electric ring.* N COUNT : USU MOD+N **10.5** an enclosed space with seats all round it that it used for boxing matches, show jumping, circus performances, etc. EG *Both wrestlers leaped into the ring and began to crouch and spring about... ...the show ring.* N COUNT : USU the+N ⇑ arena **10.6** a dark mark under a person's eyes that is caused by tiredness or anxiety. EG *There were dark rings of fatigue beneath his eyes.* N COUNT : USU PL **10.7** a group of people who work together, often illegally, to control the market in antiques, drugs, pornography, etc. EG *The police exposed a fairly large drug ring operating in the area.* N COUNT+SUPP

11 If you **ring** something, you put, draw, or make a ring round it. EG *I got a map and ringed all the likely villages where I might find a house for sale.* V+O = encircle

12 If something **is ringed**, it has a circle or the shape of a circle all around it. EG *His eyes were ringed with fatigue... ...a crater ringed with a low mud wall.* V+O : PASS, USU+with = be encircled

13 If you **ring** a bird, you put a ring round its leg so that you can identify it easily and study its movements and habits. EG *A blackbird was ringed in the wood here in 1963.* V+O ⇑ mark

14 The word **ring** is also used in the following expressions. **14.1** If you say that something **rings a bell**, you mean that it is familiar to you, but you cannot remember exactly why; an informal expression. EG *The name rings a bell.* PHR : VB INFLECTS **14.2** If you **ring the changes**, you make alterations in the way something is organized or done. EG *The time has come to ring the changes and get this country back on its feet.* PHR : VB INFLECTS

14.3 If you **give** someone **a ring**, you call them on the telephone; an informal expression. EG *You could give me a ring if you need me... Can we give you a ring to let you know when they're here?* PHR : VB INFLECTS = phone **14.4** If a sound or statement **rings in** your **head** or **ears**, it makes a great impression on you and you remember it for a long time. EG *His father's words rang in his head... He left the platform with the cheers still ringing in his ears.* PHR : VB AND N INFLECTS **14.5** If you talk about people **ringing in the New Year** or **ringing out the Old Year**, you are referring to the celebrations people have on New Year's Eve to mark the beginning of a New Year. PHR : VB INFLECTS ⇑ celebrate

14.6 If someone **runs rings round** you, they are much better or more successful than you in a particular activity; an informal expression. EG *She runs rings round all the other students... The government's confidence has allowed them to run rings round the opposition.* PHR : VB INFLECTS

ring around. To **ring around** means the same as to ring round. PHRASAL VB : V+ADV/PREP

ring back. If you **ring** someone **back**, you telephone them, either because they telephoned you earlier and you were not there, or because you did not finish an earlier conversation on the telephone. EG *He asked if you'd ring him back when you got in... I'm teaching at the moment, can I ring you back?* PHRASAL VB : V+ADV, OR V+O+ADV = call back, phone back

ring in. If you **ring in**, you report to someone at your place of work by telephoning them. EG *I rang in to say I was ill.* PHRASAL VB : V+ADV = phone in

ring off. If you **ring off**, you put down your telephone receiver at the end of a telephone call. EG *The girl laughed and rang off... With a last 'Fine,' Hogan had rung off.* PHRASAL VB : V+ADV ⇑ hang up

ring out. If sounds **ring out**, they are heard loudly and clearly. EG *Her voice rang out... The old stable clock rings out ten o'clock.* PHRASAL VB : V+ADV, OR V+O+ADV

ring round. If you **ring round** or **ring around**, you telephone several people, for example when you are trying to organize something or get a particular piece of information. EG *I got out the telephone book and began ringing round to heating contractors for estimates.* PHRASAL VB : V+ADV/PREP

ring up. 1 If you **ring** someone **up**, you telephone them; an informal use. EG *She had rung up Emily and had told her all about it... He was rung up in the night and asked if he'd come down.* PHRASAL VB : V+ADV, OR V+O+ADV

2 If you **ring up** an amount on a cash register, you press the levers or push the buttons in order to record the amount that is being put into the till. EG *She rang up £10.47 and gave me the receipt... He rang up the sale on the register.* PHRASAL VB : V+O+ADV ⇑ charge

ring binder, ring binders. A **ring binder** is a notebook with loose pages which are held together by metal rings on a bar that is attached to the cover. N COUNT ⇑ notepad

ringer /rɪŋə/, **ringers**. 1 A **ringer** is a person who rings church bells or hand bells, especially as a hobby. N COUNT

2 If you say that someone is a **dead ringer** for someone else, you mean that he or she looks exactly like the other person; an informal expression. PHR : USED AS C, USU *for*

ring finger, ring fingers. Your **ring finger** is the third finger of either your left or your right hand. It is the finger on which people wear a wedding ring or engagement ring. EG *Charlotte rapped on the door with her ring finger.* N COUNT

ringing /rɪŋɪŋ/. A **ringing** sound or noise is one that can be heard clearly and that is very impressive. EG *...clear ringing tones... ...powerful images and ringing phrases.* ADJ CLASSIF : ATTRIB ⇑ clear

ringleader /rɪŋliːdə/, **ringleaders**. The **ringleader** of a group of people is the person who appears to be leading them when they are rioting or causing trouble. EG *The six ringleaders were arrested and charged.* N COUNT ⇑ leader

ringlet /rɪŋlɪ²t/, **ringlets**. **Ringlets** are long, loose curls of hair that hang down. N COUNT

ringmaster /rɪŋmɑːstə/, **ringmasters**. The **ringmaster** in a circus is the person who introduces the different animals and performers. N COUNT

ring road, ring roads; also spelled with a hyphen. A **ring road** is a road that goes all the way round the edge of a town so that traffic does not have to go through the town centre. N COUNT

ringside /rɪŋsaɪd/. 1 The **ringside** is the area immediately around the edge of a circus ring, boxing ring, etc. EG *An usher led them to their seats three rows from the ringside.* N SING WITH DET

2 If you have a **ringside** seat or a **ringside** view, you have a clear and uninterrupted view of an event. EG *We got a ringside view of the procession.* ADJ CLASSIF : ATTRIB

ringway /rɪŋweɪ/, **ringways**. A **ringway** is the same as a ring road. N COUNT

ringworm /rɪŋwɜːm/ is a disease that causes red patches on a person's or animal's skin. N UNCOUNT

rink /rɪŋk/, **rinks**. A **rink** is a large area, usually indoors, with a floor made of ice or some other smooth surface, where people go in order to ice-skate or roller-skate. EG *There's a good ice rink in Leeds... ...a skating rink.* N COUNT

rinse /rɪns/, **rinses, rinsing, rinsed**. 1 When you **rinse** something that you have washed or **rinse** it **out**, you get rid of the soap by using clean water. EG *Gordon was washing the glasses in a bowl of soapy water and rinsing them at the sink... She left them in detergent overnight, then rinsed them out the next morning.* ▸ used as a noun. EG *With this machine an average wash and rinse uses 6 gallons of water.* V+O OR PHRASAL VB : V+O+ADV ▸ N COUNT : IF SING USU a+N

2 If you **rinse** something or **rinse** it **out**, you wash it quickly, often without using soap. EG *He rinsed his hands under the tap... She rinsed out the glass.* ▸ used as a noun. EG *I'll just give these a quick rinse under the tap, then I'll be off.* V+O OR PHRASAL VB : V+O+ADV ▸ N COUNT : IF SING USU a+N

3 If you **rinse** your mouth or **rinse** it **out**, you wash it by holding a mouthful of liquid in it, for example to get rid of an unpleasant taste. EG *Scott went into the bathroom and rinsed his mouth... He rinsed his mouth out with disinfectant.* V+O OR PHRASAL VB : V+O+ADV

riot /raɪət/, **riots, rioting, rioted**. 1 A **riot** is 1.1 a crowd of people shouting, fighting, throwing stones, etc and so causing injury to people and damage to buildings and vehicles. EG *The police drew praise for their handling of the riots... In May 1968 there was a massive wave of student riots.* N COUNT ⇑ disturbance 1.2 a lively occasion which people enjoy very much; a rather old-fashioned informal word. EG *How had the party been? Oh, it had been a riot.* N SING : a+N

2 If people **riot**, they behave violently in a public place or in an institution, for example by injuring people and damaging buildings and vehicles. EG *If food prices are put up too far, the people will riot.* V ◇ **rioting**. EG *The Army was called in to quell the rioting.* ◇ N UNCOUNT

3 If you say that a place is a **riot** of colour or colours, you mean that it is extremely colourful. EG *The desert was a riot of colours.* N SING WITH DET +*of* ⇑ display

4 If you **read** someone **the riot act**, you tell them they will be punished unless they stop behaving badly; an informal expression. EG *Father came in and read us the riot act, and we quietened down and went to sleep.* PHR : VB INFLECTS ⇑ warn

5 If people or things **run riot**, they behave in a wild and uncontrolled manner. EG *After the match their supporters ran riot in the streets near the ground.* PHR : VB INFLECTS

rioter /raɪətə/, **rioters**. A **rioter** is a person who takes part in a riot. EG *Courts dealt with rioters quickly and harshly.* N COUNT : USU P

riotous /raɪətəs/. 1 If someone has a **riotous** life style, they frequently take part in activities involving alcoholic drinks or sex and behave in a wild and uncontrolled way. EG *His early death was blamed on drink and riotous living... He was nineteen when he began his three riotous years at Harvard.* ADJ QUALIT = debauched

2 **Riotous** behaviour is 2.1 violent and uncontrolled, for example when people damage vehicles and buildings and fight in public; a formal or legal use. EG *He was found guilty of riotous behaviour.* ▸ used of people. EG *...a riotous mob.* ADJ CLASSIF : ATTRIB ⇑ rebellious 2.2 very enthusiastic and energetic. EG *Both children would come rushing out in a riotous welcome.* ADJ QUALIT = wild, exuberant

rip /rɪp/, **rips, ripping, ripped**. 1 When something **rips** or when you **rip** it, you tear it violently with your hands or with a knife. EG *The poster had been ripped to pieces... Two of the canvas bags had ripped because I had not thought of reinforcing them... I ripped open the envelope containing the money.* V-ERG : USU+A

2 If you **rip** something away from the place where it is held or fixed, you tear it away quickly and violently with your hands. EG *I ripped the phone from her hand... He ripped his shirt off... They ripped out all floors to make one huge space.* V+O+A ⇑ remove = snatch

3 A **rip** is a long cut or split in something made of cloth or paper. EG *He had seen the rip in the book.* N COUNT = tear

4 If you say **'let it rip'** or **'let her rip'**, you mean that you want someone to make a car or boat go at its fastest speed; an informal expression. CONVENTION

rip off. 1 If someone **rips** you **off**, they cheat you by charging you too much money for something; an informal expression. EG *The local shopkeepers were all trying to rip off the tourists.* ● See also **rip-off**. PHRASAL VB : O+ADV = fleece, swindle

2 To **rip** something **off** also means to steal it; an informal expression. PHRASAL VB : O+ADV

rip through. If something **rips through** a place or object, it moves through it very quickly and violently. EG *A roaring explosion ripped through the house.* PHRASAL VB : PREP = sweep, te

rip up. If you **rip** something **up**, you tear it into small pieces. EG *I wanted to rip up my schedule and fill out a new one.* PHRASAL VB : O+ADV = tear up

R.I.P. is often written on gravestones. It is an abbreviation for the Latin 'requiescat in pace' or 'requiescant in pace', which indicates a wish that the dead person or dead people may rest in peace. CONVENTION

ripcord /rɪpkɔ:d/, **ripcords**. A **ripcord** is the cord that you pull in order to open a parachute. N COUNT

ripe /raɪp/, **riper, ripest**. 1 When fruit or grain are **ripe**, they are fully grown and ready to be harvested or eaten. EG *The pears are heavy and ripe... ...ripe fruit.* ◊ **ripeness**. EG *It is important to test for ripeness.* ADJ QUALIT = mature ◊ N UNCOUNT ⇑ maturity

2 When cheese is **ripe**, it has developed a strong flavour and is ready to be eaten. ADJ QUALIT = mature

3 **Ripe** smells are strong and rather unpleasant; a fairly informal use. EG *He smelled rather ripe, and Thomas moved away from him.* ADJ QUALIT = pungent

4 **Ripe** language is rather crude and vulgar, often using swear words and making references to sex; a fairly informal use. EG *His language is a bit ripe at times... ...ripe humour.* ADJ QUALIT

5 If you say that something is **ripe** for a change of some kind, you mean that the change is likely to happen soon. EG *...another oil company ripe for takeover... The nation was ripe for collapse.* ● If you say **the time is ripe**, you mean that the moment has now arrived when it is suitable to do something that you have been thinking about or planning for some time. EG *The time is ripe for revolution... Colin decided that the time was ripe to change his job.* ADJ CLASSIF : PRED+*for* ● PHR : VB INFLECTS, USU+ *for/to-INF*

6 If someone lives to a **ripe old age**, they live to be very old and are admired because of this. EG *He lived to a ripe old age... Aunt Edna lived to the ripe old age of eighty.* PHR : USED AS O/C

ripen /raɪpəⁿn/, **ripens, ripening, ripened**. 1 When crops **ripen** or when the sun **ripens** them, they become ripe. EG *We're waiting for the first crops to ripen... It needs a good hot summer to ripen it... His gaze turned to the ripening asparagus field below.* V-ERG ⇑ grow = mature

2 When people's feelings or relationships **ripen**, they become fully developed and mature, so that they are more certain about them; a formal use. EG *His love for her had ripened over the years.* V ⇑ grow

rip-off, rip-offs; also spelled as one word. If you say that something that you bought was a **rip-off**, you mean that the person who sold it to you cheated you by charging too much for it; an informal word. N COUNT = swindle

riposte /rɪpɒst, rɪpəʊst/, **ripostes, riposting, riposted**; a literary word. 1 A **riposte** is a quick and clever reply to something that someone has said to you. EG *Edward's riposte was a neat one.* N COUNT = rejoinder

2 If you **riposte**, you make a quick and clever reply to something that someone has said to you. V, OR V+QUOTE = rejoin, retort

ripper /rɪpə/, **rippers**. A **ripper** is a person who kills people and mutilates their bodies for pleasure; an informal word. EG *...the case of the Yorkshire Ripper.* N COUNT ⇑ murderer

ripple /rɪpəˡl/, **ripples, rippling, rippled**. 1 A **ripple** is 1.1 a little wave on the surface of water caused by the wind or by a stone or other object dropping into the water. EG *A twig made tiny ripples on the water... ...a gleaming circle of ripples... Mary slid into the water, leaving not even a ripple.* N COUNT : USU PL 1.2 a little curved shape or movement on the surface of something such as fabric or hair. N COUNT ⇑ wave 1.3 a continuous sound which gently rises and falls. EG *There was a ripple of amused applause from the newsmen.* N SING WITH DET +*of* 1.4 an increase in interest, activity, or feeling which gradually develops in a person or which spreads through a group of people in response to something that has been done or said. EG *The ripples created by her entrance had not yet subsided... It is a thought which sends ripples through the mind... A sudden ripple of energy went through her.* N COUNT+SUPP : USU PL = reverberation

2 When the surface of water **ripples** or when something **ripples** it, there are a number of little waves on it. EG *I love to paint the light reflected off water when it ripples... A gentle breeze rippled the surface of the sea... The river was low, the light of the fair rippling faintly on the surface.* V-ERG ⇑ move

3 If something **ripples**, it has little wave-like movements on its surface. EG *Long shadows rippled across the courtyard... The muscles rippled under the skin of his arm.* V : USU+A

4 If the effects of an event or speech **ripple** somewhere, they spread gradually outwards through a group of people or over an area. EG *...pressures which must ripple across Europe in the next three years.* V+A

5 Raspberry **ripple**, chocolate **ripple**, etc is vanilla ice-cream with stripes of raspberry or chocolate flavour ice-cream in it. N MASS : MOD+N

rise /raɪz/, **rises, rising, rose, risen**. 1 If something **rises**, 1.1 it moves or travels upwards. EG *Hot air rises... We saw the black smoke rising over the barbed wire... Clouds of birds rose from the treetops... Her eyes rose to meet mine.* V : USU+A 1.2 it moves upwards from a flat position to an upright position, and stands up or sticks out. EG *She felt her hair rise on the back of her neck.* V : USU+A ⇑ stand 1.3 it appears as a large tall shape. EG *...the woods that rise from the long meadow... I stared out at Manhattan rising in the distance... St Paul's rose majestically from the trees.* V : USU+A = reach

2 If you **rise**, 2.1 you stand up after you have been sitting, kneeling, or lying down; a formal use. EG *Dr Willoughby rose to greet him... She rose from her knees... Poirot had risen to his feet... The Prime Minister rose to reply.* V : USU+A 2.2 you get out of bed, usually in the morning after you have slept at night; a formal use. EG *They had risen at dawn... Morris is energetic, rising at 6 am.* V : USU+A ≠ retire

3 When the sun or moon **rises**, it appears from below the horizon. EG *...the place where the sun would rise... An orange moon rose behind the rustling pine trees.* ◊ **rising**. EG *...the rising of the sun.* V ≠ set ◊ N UNCOUNT

4 When buildings are being built, you say that they **rise**. EG *In 1872, Chicago was burned to the ground and a new city rose out of the ashes... After his death in 1861, his Memorial rose first, and then trees were planted around it.* V ⇑ emerge

5 If land **rises**, it slopes upwards. EG *He followed Jack towards the castle where the ground rose slightly.* ◊ **rising**. EG *The house was built on rising ground.* V ◊ ADJ CLASSIF

6 If the level of something such as the water in a river **rises**, it becomes higher. EG *The level of the lake continues to rise... The rivers often overflow their banks and rise above the dykes.* V ≠ drop

7 When dough swells while you are making bread, you say that it **rises**. EG *Put the dough in a warm place to rise for about an hour.* V

8 If a sound **rises** or if someone's voice **rises**, it becomes louder in volume or higher in pitch. EG *His voice rose to a shriek... ...the tone rose higher and higher.* ▸ used as a noun. EG *...the sound of an oboe, a rise and descent of scales.* ◊ **rising**. EG *...the rising din of traffic from beyond the walls.* V : USU+A ⇑ increase ▸ N UNCOUNT ◊ ADJ CLASSIF : ATTRIB

9 If a sound or noise **rises** from a person or group of people, it comes from them. EG *A loud gasp rose from the boys... Laughter rose from the crowd... Great cheers rose from the people outside.* V : USU+A *(from)*

10 If an amount, cost or quantity **rises**, it increases. EG *Prices rose by more than 10% per annum... The temperature began to rise... Unemployment was rising.* ◊ **rising**. EG *...rising prices... ...the rising rate of inflation.* V ≠ fall ◊ ADJ CLASSIF : ATTRIB

11 If a feeling or atmosphere **rises**, it becomes more intense. EG *Tension is rising in the streets of the capital.* ◊ **rising**. EG *Ralph sighed, sensing the rising antagonism.* V = increase ◊ ADJ CLASSIF : ATTRIB

12 If someone's colour **rises** or if a blush **rises** to their cheeks, they blush as a result of something that has happened or been said. EG *She could feel the blush rising furiously to her cheeks.* V+A

13 If strong emotions **rise** in you, you begin to feel them and they affect your thoughts and behaviour. EG *A feeling of panic was rising in him... A mounting wave of dislike and anger rose within me.* V : USU+A ⇑ come = well

14 If something **rises** to a particular level or state, it achieves this level or state. EG *There's nothing in the play which rises to the level of character analysis... Mr Mitgang's script never rises above the level of historical summary.* V+A

15 If you **rise** to a challenge or remark, you respond to it in some way, rather than ignoring it. ● **to rise to the occasion**: see **occasion**. V+A *(to)* ⇑ respond

16 When the people in a country or region **rise**, they start fighting the group of people who are in authority there. EG *The settlers rose in revolt.* V : USU+A = rebel, revolt

17 If someone **rises** to a higher position or status, they become important, successful, or more powerful. EG *Alan Travers had risen to prominence in a matter of weeks... Men of his age rose gradually in rank and responsibility with each passing year... If Bergson rose rapidly to fame, it was because he had the talent.* V+A ≠ fall

18 If a court of law, parliament, or other official body **rises**, it stops its work at the end of a day or at the end of a formal session. EG *The light only goes off at night when the House rises... The court rose at 3pm.* V ⇑ adjourn = leave, retire

19 If you say that someone **rose** from the dead, **rose** from the grave, etc, you mean that they came back to life after they had been dead. EG *Did Christ really rise from the dead?... Tell the people the Saviour has risen.* V: USU+A

20 If the wind **rises**, it becomes stronger. EG *The sun was low above the gorse bushes and the wind was rising.* V ⇑ increase = get up

21 The place where a river starts is where it **rises**. EG *The Guadalquivir rises in the Sierra de Cazorla and flows south.* V: USU+A ⇑ begin

22 A **rise** is **22.1** an area of ground that slopes upwards. EG *The bunkers were situated on a rise that ran up from the river bank... There is a slight rise in the road after the bridge.* N COUNT ⇑ slope = incline **22.2** an increase in wages or salary. EG *He went to ask for a rise... ...a pay rise of about £20 a week... ...a 15 per cent wage rise.* N COUNT = raise **22.3** an increase in amount, cost or quantity. EG *...the big rise in fuel prices... ...price rises... ...the rise in crime.* N COUNT: IF+PREP THEN *in* ● If a figure or amount is **on the rise**, it is increasing steadily. EG *This figure, according to Monique Viot, is on the rise... The figures for marriage, far from falling, are on the rise again.* ● PHR: USED AS AN A

23 Someone's **rise is** the process by which they become more important, more successful, or more powerful. EG *...the decline of the Liberal Party and the rise of Labour... ...the rise and fall of the anti-war movement... ...his meteoric rise to fame.* N SING: WITH POSS

24 The **rise** of a particular state or quality occurs when more and more people begin to achieve that state or have that quality. EG *With the rise of affluence has come a new willingness to take risks.* N SING: *the*+N+*of*

25 If something **gives rise to** an event or situation, it causes the event or situation to happen. EG *The hope is that stimulation will give rise to new ideas... The central issues have not given rise to a lot of political discussion... ...the primitive molecules believed to have given rise to life on earth.* PHR: VB INFLECTS ⇑ create

26 See also **rising**.

rise above. If you **rise above** a difficulty or problem, you manage to succeed in what you are doing without being affected by it. EG *A woman who can rise above such disadvantages is clearly exceptional... She was in continual pain, but rose above it.* PHRASAL VB: V+PREP ⇑ overcome

rise up. **1** If emotions or feelings **rise up** in you, you begin to feel them strongly. EG *Old humiliations and terrors rose up within him.* PHRASAL VB: V+ADV = well up

2 If people **rise up**, they start to fight against their government and begin a revolution. EG *They will rise up and overthrow your imperialist government.* PHRASAL VB: V+ADV ⇑ rebel

risen /rɪzᵊn/ is the past participle of **rise**.

riser /raɪzə/, **risers**. **1** An early **riser** is someone who likes to get up early in the morning. A late **riser** is someone who likes to get up late. EG *I've been an early riser all my life.* N COUNT: ADJ+N ⇑ person

2 A **riser** is the flat vertical part of a step or stair; a technical term. N COUNT ⇑ surface

risible /rɪzɪbᵊl/. Something that is **risible** makes you want to laugh because it is ridiculous or funny; a formal word, used showing disapproval. EG *We found the whole ceremony quite risible.* ADJ QUALIT = laughable, ludicrous

rising /raɪzɪŋ/, **risings**. **1** A **rising** is an occasion when a lot of people in a country or region protest violently against the people who rule them. EG *...the Boxer Rising and the Revolution of 1911... A big peasant rising in the West of France was quelled quickly and brutally.* N COUNT = rebellion, revolt

2 Other meanings of **rising** can be found in the entry for **rise**.

rising damp. If a building has **rising damp**, moisture is getting into the bricks from the outside and is moving upwards, causing damage to the wall. EG *The basement is badly afflicted by rising damp.* N UNCOUNT

risk /rɪsk/, **risks, risking, risked**. **1** A **risk** is **1.1** a possibility that something unpleasant or undesirable might happen. EG *I sank to my knees to reduce the risk of detection... ...a life made thrilling by risk and confrontation... ...the risk that technical progress won't be very fast.* N COUNT/UNCOUNT = danger **1.2** something that you do which might have unpleasant or undesirable results. EG *To commit so much to a single project was an appalling risk... Such a response would be an irrational risk... It was a risk and it paid off.* N SING WITH DET ⇑ venture ● **calculated risk**: see **calculated**. **1.3** someone or something that is likely to cause danger. EG *Your television is a fire risk if left plugged in overnight... If something isn't done about that tip soon, it's going to be a health risk.* N SING WITH DET ● See also **security risk**.

2 If someone is **at risk**, they are in a dangerous situation where something unpleasant might happen to them. EG *The sick and lonely are most at risk... The children most at risk need educational day care... The economy will fall further, putting more jobs at risk.* PHR: USED AS AN A ⇑ exposed = vulnerable

3 If you do something **at the risk of** something unpleasant happening, you do it despite the fact that you know there might be an unpleasant result. EG *At the risk of seeming callous, I propose that we go straight on to the football match after the funeral... ...demands which can only be ignored at the risk of widespread condemnation.* PHR+NG/-ING: USED AS AN A

4 If you do an action **at your own risk**, it is entirely your responsibility if anything goes wrong, and you have been warned that nobody else will accept the responsibility. EG *If you go into the cave without waiting for the guide, you do it at your own risk... Light luggage may be left at the owner's risk.* PHR: USED AS AN A

5 If you **run** the **risk** of something unpleasant happening, you do something even though you know that it might have unpleasant or undesirable consequences. EG *These soldiers run little risk of death... He wanted to know what risks we were prepared to run.* PHR: VB INFLECTS

6 If you **take a risk**, you do something which you know might be dangerous or have unpleasant consequences. EG *I am taking a tremendous risk... This is a risk you have to take... There is no limit to the risks they are prepared to take.* PHR: VB INFLECTS

7 If you **risk** something unpleasant happening, you do something which makes it likely to happen, often in order to achieve something that is important to you. EG *They were willing to risk losing their jobs... To go out after curfew was to risk death... We can't risk a prolonged disruption of campus activities... They did not want to risk being blamed for the heavy casualties.* V+O/-ING

8 If you **risk** an action, you do it, even though you know it might have unpleasant consequences. EG *Knowing that the lines were tapped, I had not risked a phone call... If you have an expensive rug, don't risk washing it yourself... Risking another trip might be dangerous.* V+O/-ING = chance, hazard

9 If you **risk** someone or something, you put them in a dangerous position where they might be killed or destroyed EG *He was not willing to risk a single soldier in such a foolhardy cause... She had risked her life to help save mine... She guarded the reputation of her friends while risking her own.* V+O ⇑ expose = endanger

risk-taking involves doing something which you know might have unpleasant consequences, but which you believe is necessary in order to achieve your aim. EG *How can we create incentives for innovation and risk-taking?* N UNCOUNT ⇑ calculation

risky /rɪskiʹ/, **riskier, riskiest**. Activities that are **risky** are slightly dangerous because they might have unpleasant consequences. EG *The whole thing has become too risky... An attorney's life was drab compared with the riskier but more exciting career of a barrister.* ADJ QUALIT = chancy, hazardous

risotto /rɪzɒtəʊ/, **risottos**. **Risotto** is an Italian dish of rice cooked with tomatoes, cheese, chicken, etc. EG *I've made a risotto... Would you like some risotto?* N MASS

risqué /riˈskeɪ/. Jokes or stories that are **risqué** are considered to be slightly rude or offensive because they refer to sex. ADJ QUALIT = dirty, smutty

rissole /rɪsəʊl/, **rissoles**. **Rissoles** are round flat pieces of chopped meat or vegetables which are cooked in hot fat. N COUNT: USU PL ⇑ burger

rite /raɪt/, **rites**. A **rite** is **1** a series of words and actions which has a fixed order and which is used for a special religious purpose. EG *I don't know much about the rites and customs of other churches... ...a holy rite... ...the initiation rites used by ancient men upon their sons.* N COUNT ⇑ procedure = ritual ● See also **last rites**. **2** a tradition or custom that is carried out within a particular group or society. EG *...the rite of circumcision... ...fertility rites.* N COUNT+SUPP ⇑ habit = ritual

ritual /rɪtjuᵊl/, **rituals**. **1** A **ritual** is **1.1** a religious service or other ceremony which involves a series of actions usually performed in a fixed order. EG *I miss the old Latin Mass and its ritual... Water has often been used in ritual... Rituals of purification were* N COUNT/UNCOUNT *performed.* 1.2 a way of behaving or of doing something which people or animals regularly follow when they are in a particular situation. EG *Our society has many rituals of greeting, farewell, and celebration... Ritual is an important feature of sport... I've wound up the clock so many times it's become a ritual... ...the courtship ritual of frogs.* N COUNT/UNCOUNT

2 **Ritual** activities happen as part of a ritual or tradition. EG *I was once allowed to watch a ritual circumcision ceremony... ...the practice of ritual murder.* ◊ **ritually**. EG *...bodies washed ritually three times.* ADJ CLASSIF: ATTRIB ◊ ADV WITH VB

3 **Ritual** actions are always done in exactly the same way whenever a particular situation arises; a slightly humorous use. EG *Everyone makes ritual comments about the hardship of moving house... On Sunday we make our ritual visit to the pub at lunchtime.* ADJ CLASSIF: ATTRIB ⇑ usual = customary

ritualism /rɪtjʊ^{0}əlɪzə^{0}m/. **Ritualism** is the practice of using ritual during a religious service or other ceremony. N UNCOUNT

ritualistic /rɪtjə^{4}lɪstɪk/. **Ritualistic** activities or words 1 follow the same pattern every time they are used. EG *He came out with some ritualistic nonsense about 'the challenge of change'.* 2 are a regular and fixed part of a religious service or other ceremony. EG *...ritualistic words of prayer.* ADJ QUALIT; ADJ QUALIT = ritual

rival /raɪvə^{0}l/, **rivals, rivalling, rivalled**; also spelled **rivaling, rivaled** in American English. 1 Your **rival** is 1.1 a person, business, or organization that you are competing with in the same field or for the same aim. EG *The defeats left him with only one rival for the top party post... His popular newspaper outstripped its rivals in circulation.* ▸ used as an adjective. EG *I'm thinking of starting a rival paper... Fighting broke out between rival groups.* 1.2 someone or something that reaches the same standard as another person or thing. EG *This collection of paintings has few rivals in the world.* N COUNT = competitor; ▸ ADJ CLASSIF: ATTRIB; N COUNT: USU WITH BROAD NEG = equal

2 If something **rivals** something else, it is considered to be of the same standard or quality as the other thing. EG *Of all the flowers in the garden few can rival the lily... His stupidity is rivalled only by his meanness... The waterfall rivals skiing as the park's greatest attraction... Nothing he did in office could rival in importance his achievements in opposition.* V+O ⇑ equal = match

rivalry /raɪvəlri^1/, **rivalries**. **Rivalry** is active competition between people, businesses, or organizations. EG *Rivalry with other schools is encouraged... The focus on money and position tends to foster rivalry between workers... ...the intense rivalries between groups and personalities... The paper was launched in 1919 in direct rivalry to Hearst's 'American'.* N COUNT/UNCOUNT

riven /rɪvə^{0}n/. Something that is **riven** has been divided or split and is therefore weaker than it was; an old-fashioned or formal word. EG *...a country riven by deep divisions of race and ideology.* ADJ CLASSIF = torn apart

river /rɪvə/, **rivers**. 1 A **river** is a large amount of fresh water flowing continuously in a long curving line across the land. Rivers flow into the sea, into a lake, or into another river. EG *...the far side of the river... We fished in the river after lunch... He took her for a ride on the river... ...the River Thames... ...the Hudson River.* • to **sell** someone **down the river**: see **sell**. N COUNT: ALSO IN NAMES ⇑ watercourse

2 You can also refer to something that flows like a river as a **river**; a rather literary use. EG *The hut was a river of mud inside... Philip stared across the gleaming, throbbing river of cars to the Modern Times Bookshop.* N COUNT: ALSO N +of+N UNCOUNT/N IN PL = stream

river bank, river banks; also spelled with a hyphen. A **river bank** is the land along the edge of a river. EG *We walked along the river bank... They followed the river bank downstream.* N COUNT

river bed, river beds; also spelled with a hyphen. A **river bed** is the ground which a river flows over. N COUNT

riverside /rɪvəsaɪd/. The **riverside** is the area of land which is on or next to the banks of a river. EG *We had a lovely day by the riverside... ...a riverside swamp.* N SING: *the*+N

rivet /rɪvɪt/, **rivets, riveting, riveted**. 1 When people or things **rivet** you or **rivet** your attention, they fascinate you and hold your interest firmly and completely. EG *I was riveted by his words... She riveted her audiences with her superb authority and dynamic energy.* ◊ **riveted**. EG *Millions of people found themselves riveted to their television sets by the sight of a man walking on the moon... My eyes were riveted on the gun she was holding.* V+O: USU PASS = engross, transfix; ◊ ADJ CLASSIF: PRED

2 A **rivet** is a short thick pin with a flat head which is used to fasten flat pieces of metal together. N COUNT

3 If you **rivet** two pieces of metal together, you fasten them using rivets. V+O ⇑ join

riveting /rɪvɪtɪŋ/. Something that is **riveting** is extremely interesting and exciting. EG *James Joyce's letters are absolutely riveting... It is one of the most riveting films I've ever seen.* ADJ QUALIT = engrossing, gripping

rivulet /rɪvje^{4}ɪ^{2}t/, **rivulets**. A **rivulet** is a small stream; a formal word. N COUNT

RN is a written abbreviation for 'Royal Navy'; the navy of the United Kingdom. EG *...the HQ of the RN Flag Officer... ...Captain Andrew Waugh, RN.*

roach /rəʊtʃ/, **roaches**. In paragraph 1, **roach** is both the singular and the plural form. A **roach** is 1 a fish that lives in rivers and lakes in Europe. EG *The River Witham has a fine stock of healthy roach.* 2 the same as a cockroach; an informal use. EG *Roaches swarmed on the floor.* N COUNT; N COUNT ⇑ insect

road /rəʊd/, **roads**. 1 A **road** is 1.1 a long, smooth, hard piece of ground which is built between two places, for example between two towns, so that you can walk or drive easily from one place to the other. EG *Cross the main road, then go on down the lane to the village... They took the road that led up the hill... ...the road from Belfast to Londonderry... She was studying a road map when I got back into the car... By road Luxembourg is about 225 miles from the ferry... The ancient ruins were accessible by road.* N COUNT, OR *by*+N ⇑ way

1.2 a street in a town or city, which is built for people or cars to use, but which also has houses along it. EG *There is an antique shop at the top of my road... ...the quiet Edgbaston road where he had lived for some thirty years... The museum was in a side street leading off from a road of shops.* ▸ used in the name of a road or street. EG *...Tottenham Court Road... ...the Portobello Road.* N COUNT; ▸ N IN NAMES

2 You can use **road** when you are referring to places, people, or buildings that are a short distance from where you are or from where you live, and that are in the same road; an informal use in British English. EG *The hotel was just a little farther along the road... There are shops just down the road... ...her cousins from across the road... I was talking to Mr Marks from along the road... ...Janet from down your road.* N SING WITH DET: PREP+N ⇑ nearby

3 The London **Road**, the Bristol **road**, etc is a main road that leads to London, Bristol, etc. EG *...159, London Road... This is the Oxford road, and the Watford road turns off to the right... They crossed the Yugoslav border on the Budapest-Zagreb road.* N COUNT: N PROPER+N, USU SING

4 A **road** accident is an accident that involves motor vehicles. EG *The number of road accidents was greatly reduced.* ADJ CLASSIF: ATTRIB

5 **On the road**. If you are **on the road**, 5.1 you are travelling in a vehicle or going on a journey by road. EG *I was again on the road, again at the wheel of the old blue sedan... I was stiff after seven hours on the road.* 5.2 If a car or other vehicle is said to be **on the road**, it is still in working order and being used. EG *It could well be the only one of its type still on the road.* PHR: USED AS AN A; PHR: USED AS AN A = in use

5.3 If a circus or theatrical company is **on the road**, it is travelling around the country giving performances in several different places. EG *We'll take the play for a few weeks on the road before it opens in London.* 5.4 If you say that someone is **on the road** to a particular state or condition, you mean that they are likely to achieve that state or condition. EG *She was well on the road to recovery... Surely you're on the road to recognition, even if it's only as head of department.* PHR: USED AS AN A = on tour, touring; PHR: USED AS AN A = on the way

6 The **road** to a particular result is a course of action which you think is likely to achieve that result. EG *New information is probably the surest road to new ideas... We have science and technology to help us along the road to peace and plenty... This is the first step on the road to victory.* N COUNT: USU SING+*to* ⇑ method = route, path

7 If someone offers you **one for the road**, they are offering you a final alcoholic drink before you leave somewhere such as a party or a pub; an informal expression. EG *Let's have one for the road before we go.* PHR: USED AS O

8 If you say that an organization or relationship has come to **the end of the road**, you mean that it cannot continue any longer because it has failed. PHR: USED AS O/C

roadblock /rəʊdblɒk/, **roadblocks**. When the police put a **roadblock** across the road, they stop all the traffic going through, for example if they are looking for a criminal or an escaped prisoner. EG *A police roadblock stopped a private car containing four people... Emergency committees established roadblocks at many places throughout the towns.*
N COUNT ⇑ barricade

roadhog /rəʊdhɒg/, **roadhogs**. You say that the drivers of vehicles are **roadhogs** when they drive in the middle of the road so that nobody can overtake them; used showing disapproval in informal English.
N COUNT

roadhouse /rəʊdhaʊs/, **roadhouses**. A **roadhouse** is a pub or restaurant on a road outside a city, whose customers are usually people who are on a long journey; a rather old-fashioned word. EG *We had a few drinks in a roadhouse off the main highway.*
N COUNT ⇑ inn

road sense is the ability to make good judgements and decisions about how you walk or drive through traffic, so that you do not cause any accidents for yourself or for others.
N UNCOUNT ⇑ sense

roadside /rəʊdsaɪd/, **roadsides**. **1** The **roadside** is the edge of a road, especially a road in the country. EG *I sat down by the roadside and cried... The woman walked along the roadside.*
N COUNT : IF SING *the*+N, USU SING

2 A **roadside** building, sign, or verge is one that is by the side of a road, especially a road in the country. EG *We had stopped for coffee at a roadside cafe.*
ADJ CLASSIF : ATTRIB = wayside

roadster /rəʊdstə/, **roadsters**. A **roadster** is a car with no roof and only two seats; a rather old-fashioned word.
N COUNT = sports car

roadway /rəʊdweɪ/, **roadways**. The **roadway** is the part of a road that is used by traffic. EG *He began to cross the roadway towards me.*
N COUNT; USU *the*+N IN SING

road works; also spelled as one word. **Road works** are repairs or other work being done on the road. You often see a sign saying 'roadworks' to warn motorists that there are people working in the road.
N PLURAL ⇑ works

roadworthy /rəʊdwɜːðiˡ/. If a car is considered to be **roadworthy**, it is considered to be generally in quite good condition and unlikely to have any sudden mechanical problems or breakdowns. EG *I will only drive the car after he has made it roadworthy.*
ADJ CLASSIF : PRED

roam /rəʊm/, **roams, roaming, roamed**. If you **roam** an area or **roam** around it, you wander or travel around it without having a particular purpose. EG *They roam over the hills and plains... He roamed the streets at night... They enjoyed the freedom to roam.*
V : USU+A, OR V+O = rove

roan /rəʊn/, **roans**. A **roan** is a horse that is brown or black in colour with some white hairs mixed in.
N COUNT

roar /rɔː/, **roars, roaring, roared**. **1** If something **roars**, it makes a very loud noise. EG *The wind roared in the forest... The sea roared along the length of the shore.*
V

2 A **roar** is a very loud noise. EG *I could hear the roar of traffic outside... The barrel exploded with a thunderous roar... ...the confused roar from a football stadium.*
N COUNT

3 If someone **roars** with laughter or **roars**, **3.1** they laugh in a very noisy way. EG *He put back his head and roared with laughter... She roared when I told her what had happened to her father's false teeth.*
V : IF+PREP THEN *with* = howl
▸ used as a noun. EG *A roar of laughter followed this ridiculous remark.*
▸ N COUNT+*of*
3.2 they shout something in a very loud and deep voice. EG *'I'm not wavering!' he roared... 'Forward with the Revolution,' the crowd roared back... He used to kick and scream and roar if he didn't get what he wanted.*
V OR V+QUOTE ⇑ say = bellow, thunder
▸ used as a noun. EG *He stood with his spread-eagled arms acknowledging the roars of twenty thousand people.*
▸ N COUNT

4 When a lion utters a loud noise, it **roars**. EG *The lion was roaring triumphantly... The animals roared and fought.*
V
▸ used as a noun. EG *The wounded animal's roar could still be heard in the distance.*
▸ N COUNT = bellow

roaring /rɔːrɪŋ/. **1 Roaring** means making a very loud noise. EG *He sat on the terrace a few feet from the roaring traffic... A roaring explosion ripped through his home.*
ADJ CLASSIF : ATTRIB ⇑ noisy

2 A **roaring** fire is one which is burning with large flames and sending out a lot of heat. EG *Christmas pudding was set on the table by the roaring fire.*
ADJ CLASSIF : ATTRIB ⇑ fierce = blazing

3 If someone **does a roaring trade** in a particular type of goods, they sell a lot of them; an informal expression. EG *He was doing a roaring trade in T-shirts.*
PHR : VB INFLECTS, IF+PREP THEN *in*

4 If someone is **roaring** drunk, they are very drunk indeed and making a lot of noise; an informal use. EG *He was staggering along the Bristol Road, roaring drunk.*
ADV+ADJ

5 If something such as the production of a play is a **roaring** success, it is very successful indeed; an informal use. EG *The show was a roaring success.*
ADJ CLASSIF : ATTRIB

roast /rəʊst/, **roasts, roasting, roasted**. **1** When you **roast** meat or when it **roasts**, you cook it by dry heat in an oven or over a fire. EG *We got ourselves two fine chickens and roasted them... While the bird roasted he built a rough bush shelter... ...a feast of roasted ox-meat.*
V-ERG

2 If you **roast** things like nuts or beans, you dry them by using heat so that they turn brown. EG *...roasted peanuts... ...roasted coffee beans.*
V+O : USU PAST PART

3 Roast meat is meat that has been cooked by roasting. EG *I ordered roast beef.*
ADJ CLASSIF : ATTRIB

4 A **roast** is a piece of meat that has been cooked by roasting. EG *I thought I'd do a roast for dinner... We're having roast and Yorkshire pudding.*
N COUNT/ UNCOUNT = joint

5 If you say that you **are roasting**, you mean that you feel very hot indeed. EG *I started to roast sitting by his blazing fire... Can't we open a window? I'm roasting.*
V = boil

roasting /rəʊstɪŋ/, **roastings**. If someone gives you a **roasting**, they criticize you severely about something in a way that shows that they are very annoyed with you; an informal word. EG *The boss gave me a real roasting this morning.*
N COUNT : USU SING ⇑ telling-off = rocket

rob /rɒb/, **robs, robbing, robbed**. **1** If someone **robs** a person or institution, they steal money or property from them. EG *He tried to rob her of her share of her father's estate... The only way I can get the money is to rob a few banks... I've been robbed.*
V+O : IF+PREP THEN *of* ⇑ take from

2 If you **rob** someone of something that they deserve, need, or want, you take it away from them. EG *You robbed me of my moment of glory... I'm trying to give my life a little dignity without robbing anyone else of theirs... As these trees grow tall, they rob the grass of light.*
V+O+A *(of)* = deprive

3 If you say that you **were robbed** in a sport or game, you mean that you were beaten unfairly; used in informal English.
V+O : ONLY PA

robber /rɒbə/, **robbers**. A **robber** is a person who steals money or property from a bank, shop, train, etc, often by using force or threats. EG *...bank robbers... ...train robbers... The robbers escaped with the jewels.*
N COUNT ⇑ thief

robbery /rɒbəºriˡ/, **robberies**. **1 Robbery** is the crime of stealing money or property from a bank, shop, train, etc, often by using force or threats. EG *He was arrested on charges of armed robbery... My last offence was robbery with violence.*
N UNCOUNT ⇑ theft

2 A **robbery** is a crime in which someone steals money or property from a bank, shop, train, etc. EG *There have been a great number of robberies recently.*
N COUNT ⇑ theft

3 See also **daylight robbery**.

robe /rəʊb/, **robes, robing, robed**. **1** A **robe** is a loose piece of clothing which covers all of your body and goes down to the ground; used in formal English. EG *...his shapeless white gown, draped like a robe... ...women in long flowing robes.*
N COUNT ⇑ garment
▸ used as a plural noun. EG *There she sat, in her robes, smiling.*
▸ N PLURAL ⇑ clothes

2 A **robe** is also a dressing gown or other piece of clothing that you wrap around your body or wear over your nightclothes. EG *She was wearing a short robe over her bathing suit.*
N COUNT ⇑ garment

3 If you **robe** yourself, you get dressed; a formal use. EG *She washed and robed herself for the evening meal.*
V+O (REFL)

4 If you **are robed** in a particular way, you are dressed in that way; used in formal English.
V+O : ONLY P

robin /rɒbɪn/, **robins**. A **robin** is a small bird with a red neck and breast. There are different kinds of robin.
N COUNT

robot /rəʊbɒt/, **robots**. **1** A **robot** is **1.1** a machine which is programmed to automatically perform a number of mechanical tasks, especially dangerous or repetitive tasks in a factory. EG *Japanese industry is making increasing use of robots.*
N COUNT
1.2 a machine which looks like a human being, can walk and talk, but does not have feelings. Robots often appear in science fiction stories or films. EG *The robot thrust out its antennas.*
N COUNT

2 If you describe someone as a **robot**, you mean that they work or behave without thought or feeling, as if they were a machine; used showing disapproval. EG *I*
N COUNT ⇑ person = automat

was a robot designed for washing nappies and housework.

robotic /rəʊbɒtɪk/, **robotics**. **Robotic** is an adjective and **robotics** is an uncount noun. 1 If you describe someone's movements or parts of their body as **robotic**, you mean that they move in a quick and jerky way, like a robot. ADJ QUALIT

2 **Robotics** is is the science of designing and building robots. N UNCOUNT

robust /rə⁶bʌst, rəʊbə⁹st/. 1 Someone or something that is **robust** is very strong and healthy. EG *She has four robust daughters... I'm in robust health, I'm glad to say... The once robust economy now lies in ruins.* ADJ QUALIT = sturdy

◊ **robustness**. EG *...the robustness of her spirit.* ◊ N UNCOUNT

2 An activity that is **robust** needs a lot of strength and energy. EG *The children played robust games in the park or garden... He enjoyed more robust recreations, like rock climbing.* ADJ QUALIT

3 If you describe something that someone says as **robust**, you mean that it shows their strength of character or determination. EG *Applause greeted this robust statement... The President's speech was short but robust.* ◊ **robustly**. EG *'Not me,' said Frederica robustly.* ADJ QUALIT; ◊ ADV

rock /rɒk/, **rocks, rocking, rocked**. 1 **Rock** is the substance that forms the hardest parts of the surface of the earth. Cliffs and mountains are made of rock. EG *Large masses of rock are constantly falling into the sea... ...a cliff of naked red earth and rock... It was almost like a gorge, with very sheer rock sides.* N UNCOUNT

2 A **rock** is 2.1 a very large piece of rock that is higher than the land that surrounds it and that can therefore be seen from a long way away. EG *We arranged to meet again at Ayers Rock... The magazine had insisted that he get new and exciting shots of the rock.* N COUNT: ALSO IN NAMES AFTER N 2.2 a piece of rock that sticks up out of the ground or the sea or that has broken away from a mountain or a cliff. EG *I sat down on a rock... Hercule Poirot stood on the cliff overlooking the rocks below.* N COUNT = boulder, stone 2.3 a small stone that you can pick up with your hand; used in American English. EG *She started putting the rocks in his shirt pocket... The crowd howls and screams, rocks are thrown, and the police come running.* N COUNT = pebble

3 When something **rocks** or when you **rock** it, you make it move slowly and regularly backwards and forwards or from side to side. EG *I snatched away the stool she was rocking with her heel... Our parents cuddle and hug us, and rock us gently back and forth... She sat there, rocking gently backwards and forwards.* V-ERG = sway

4 If a building or tree **rocks** or if an explosion or blow **rocks** it, it shakes. EG *They heard him blunder against the trunk which rocked violently.* V-ERG

5 If something **rocks** a country or society, it causes feelings of shock, horror, or fear in that country or society. EG *Wars, plagues, earthquakes, and famine rocked many an earlier social order... France was rocked by an outbreak of violent crime.* V+O = shake

6 If you say that you do not want to **rock the boat**, you mean that you do not want to do anything that might cause problems or upset people; an informal expression. EG *We all keep very quiet and do nothing to rock the boat... He refuses to meddle with anything that might rock the boat.* PHR WITH BROAD NEG: VB INFLECTS

7 If you **rock with laughter**, you laugh a lot and for a long time. PHR: VB INFLECTS

8 **Rock** is also 8.1 music with simple tunes and a very strong beat that is played and sung, usually loudly, by a small group of people with electric guitars and drums. EG *The boy's been playing very loud rock for an hour in the bathroom... ...a rock concert... He has had success with rock groups... ...rock stars.* N UNCOUNT, OR N BEFORE N ⇑ pop music 8.2 a sweet made in long, hard sticks and sold at popular tourist places. EG *I got a stick of rock.* N UNCOUNT

9 If you have an alcoholic drink such as whisky **on the rocks**, you have it with lumps of ice. EG *I think I'll just have some vermouth on the rocks.* PHR AFTER N = with ice

10 If someone's marriage or relationship is **on the rocks**, it is unsuccessful and about to break up. PHR: USED AS AN A

rock and roll; spelled with a hyphen when used before another noun. **Rock and roll** is a kind of music with a strong beat that was sung and played by small groups of people, especially in the 1950s. It was very popular with young people, who often danced to it. EG *The car radio was tuned to a rock-and-roll station.* N UNCOUNT ⇑ rock

rock-bottom. 1 A **rock-bottom** price or level is a very low one. EG *You can get black-and-white television sets at rock-bottom prices.* ADJ CLASSIF: ATTRIB

2 If someone reaches **rock-bottom**, they become extremely poor or extremely depressed. EG *Until they reach rock-bottom, it is difficult for people to get financial help.* N UNCOUNT

rock bun, rock buns. A **rock bun** is the same as a rock cake. N COUNT

rock cake, rock cakes. A **rock cake** is a small cake that usually has dried fruit in it. It has a rough surface so that it looks like a rock. EG *Florrie handed round the rock cakes.* N COUNT = rock bun

rock-climber, rock-climbers; also spelled without a hyphen. A **rock-climber** is a person whose hobby or sport is climbing rocks, cliffs, or mountains. N COUNT

rock climbing is the activity of climbing rocks, cliffs, or mountains as a sport or hobby. N UNCOUNT

rocker /rɒkə/, **rockers**. 1 A **rocker** is a chair that is built on two curved pieces of wood so that you can rock yourself backwards and forwards when you are sitting in it. EG *Harry Truman loved to sit in an old rocker in the evenings.* N COUNT = rocking chair

2 **Rockers** are the two curved pieces of wood on which something such as a cradle or rocking-chair is built, and which allows you to rock it. N COUNT: USU PL

3 **Rockers** were groups of young people who in the 1960s wore leather jackets, rode motorcycles, and listened to rock-and-roll music. EG *...the mods and rockers who go down to Brighton and smash the windows.* N COUNT

4 If you say that someone is **off** their **rocker**, you mean that they are insane or very foolish; used in informal English. EG *Are you all off your rockers?... His landlady appeared to be slightly off her rocker.* PHR: N INFLECTS, USED AS AN A ⇑ mad = crazy

rockery /rɒkə⁰ri¹/, **rockeries**. A **rockery** is a raised part of a garden which is built of stones and soil and on which small plants are grown. EG *Outside there was a little front garden with a rockery.* N COUNT

rocket /rɒkɪt/, **rockets, rocketing, rocketed**.

1 A **rocket** is 1.1 a missile that contains an explosive and that drives itself through the air by sending out burning gas after it has been fired. EG *Rebels fired anti-tank rockets for three consecutive nights... No rocket attack was experienced for more than a fortnight.* N COUNT 1.2 the part of a space vehicle that sends out burning gas and so causes the vehicle to leave the earth, to move through space, and to return to the earth; sometimes used of the whole vehicle. EG *We do not have a very strong rocket development programme... It seemed that the country simply could not get a rocket off the ground.* N COUNT 1.3 a firework that is attached to a stick and that is driven high into the air when the gunpowder inside it explodes. EG *Thomas and Charlie could see the rockets and Roman candles that arched into the night sky over the river.* N COUNT

2 If things such as prices and profits **rocket**, they get bigger very quickly and suddenly; an informal use. EG *His profits rocketed... Land sales rocketed.* V ⇑ rise = soar

3 If someone gives you a **rocket**, they criticize you very severely and angrily; an informal use. EG *The judge gave him a most almighty rocket... The manufacturer gave her a rocket down the phone and she didn't care a bit.* N SING: a+N = reprimand, scolding

rocket launcher, rocket launchers. A **rocket launcher** is a device shaped like a tube that can be carried and used by soldiers for firing rockets. EG *He carried an antitank rocket launcher.* N COUNT ⇑ weapon = bazooka

rock garden, rock gardens; also spelled with a hyphen. A **rock garden** is a garden of rocks and soil, in which small plants are grown. EG *It's a big rock garden enclosed by skyscrapers.* N COUNT

rock-hard. Something that is **rock-hard** is very hard indeed. EG *It made absolutely no impression on the rock-hard earth.* ADJ CLASSIF

rocking chair, rocking chairs; also spelled with a hyphen. A **rocking chair** is a chair that is built on two curved pieces of wood so that you can rock yourself backwards and forwards when you are sitting in it. EG *He got up from the table, lit his pipe again, and settled himself in his rocking chair.* N COUNT = rocker

rocking horse, rocking horses; also spelled with a hyphen. A **rocking horse** is a toy horse which a child can sit on and which can be made to rock N COUNT backwards and forwards so that the child can pretend to be riding a real horse.

rock-like. Something that is **rock-like** is very strong or firm and unlikely to change. EG *...the rock-like quality of the old religion.* — ADJ QUALIT

rock music is a kind of music with simple tunes and a very strong beat that is played and sung, usually loudly, by a small group of people with electric guitars and drums. EG *...a new album by a superstar of rock music.* — N UNCOUNT ⇑ pop music = rock

rock'n'roll /rɒkə^{0}nrəʊl/ is the same as rock and roll. — N UNCOUNT ⇑ pop music

rock pool, rock pools; also spelled with a hyphen. A **rock pool** is a small pool between rocks on the seashore. EG *The rock-pools which so fascinated him were covered by the tide.* — N COUNT

rock salt is salt that is formed in the ground and that is removed by mining. — N UNCOUNT

rocky /rɒki^1/, **rockier, rockiest**. **1** A place that is **rocky** is covered with rocks. EG *The seabed where the wreck lies is rocky... She drives carefully up the rocky lane.* — ADJ QUALIT

2 Something such as a marriage that is **rocky** is in a bad state or condition, and therefore not likely to last very long; an informal use. — ADJ QUALIT = unstable

rococo /rə^{7}kəʊkəʊ/; also spelled with a capital letter. **Rococo** buildings, furniture, works of art, etc are in the style that existed in Europe in the eighteenth century. The rococo style is characterized by complicated curly decoration. EG *...a rococo shop front that dates from 1760.* — ADJ CLASSIF : USU ATTRIB

rod /rɒd/, **rods**. A **rod** is a long thin straight pole or bar made of metal, wood, or some other hard substance. EG *The aluminium rod that held the seats broke... ...rods of steel.* — N COUNT

rode /rəʊd/ is the past tense of **ride**.

rodent /rəʊdənt/, **rodents**. A **rodent** is a small mammal which has sharp front teeth that are used for gnawing. Rats, mice, rabbits, and squirrels are all rodents. EG *The plains of North America are colonized by rodents... Some of the crop may be eaten up by insects, rodents, and microbes.* — N COUNT

rodeo /rəʊdi^{1}əʊ/, **rodeos**. A **rodeo** is a public entertainment in North America in which cowboys show different skills, including riding wild horses and catching calves with ropes. EG *He used to be a rodeo rider in Iowa.* — N COUNT

roe /rəʊ/ is the eggs or sperm of a fish, which is eaten as food. EG *...fried cod's roe.* — N UNCOUNT : USU MOD+N

rogue /rəʊg/, **rogues**. **1** A **rogue** is **1.1** a man who has behaved in a way that you do not approve of, but who you nevertheless like and therefore find it difficult to be really critical of; often used showing slight approval. EG *My dear Howard, you really are an awful rogue... The old rogue lived for another thirty years... Fancy your meeting that rogue Charles Boon on the plane.* — N COUNT : ALSO VOC = scoundrel, rascal **1.2** a man who has a bad character and behaves in a dishonest or criminal way. EG *You're all cheats and rogues... He would slit the throat of any other rogue staking a rival claim.* — N COUNT : ALSO VOC = villain

2 A **rogues' gallery** is a group of people or things that you think of as dishonest, undesirable, or having unpleasant qualities; often used humorously. EG *It was quite a party. You've never seen such a rogues' gallery in your life.* — PHR : USED AS O/C

3 Rogue describes **3.1** a very fierce and often dangerous animal that lives apart from the main group of animals of the same type. EG *...a rogue elephant.* — ADJ CLASSIF : ATTRIB **3.2** someone who works alone, in a way that is different from the way that most people work and that is usually disapproved of. EG *...rogue policemen.* — ADJ CLASSIF : ATTRIB = maverick

roguery /rəʊgəri^1/ is behaviour that is dishonest, immoral, or against the law; a rather old-fashioned word. EG *There's corruption and roguery everywhere!* — N UNCOUNT = villainy

roguish /rəʊgɪʃ/. A **roguish** expression on your face shows that you are amused, especially because you are about to do something mischievous; used showing approval. EG *...a roguish smile... He has a most disconcerting, roguish laugh.* — ADJ QUALIT ⇑ playful ◊ **roguishly**. EG *He winked at me roguishly.* — ◊ ADV WITH VB

role /rəʊl/, **roles**; also spelled **rôle**; a formal word. **1** The **role** of a country, organization, etc is the position that it has in a particular situation, which determines how much it is involved in the situation or how much responsibility it has. EG *What is the role of the University in modern society?... He saw a role for government in stimulating industrial expansion... America is no longer prepared to play its role as world policeman... He had played a major role in the formation of the United Nations.* — N COUNT+SUPP = place, part

2 A **role** is also **2.1** a position in a social situation which has particular functions and behaviour associated with it. You take on a particular role because other people expect you to or because you think it is your duty. EG *Social roles are culturally induced... ...advertisements with women in a submissive role... ...an aunt who had assumed the mother role.* — N COUNT+SUPP ⇑ function **2.2** one of the characters that actors or singers can play in a film, play, opera, etc. EG *...the great Shakespearean roles... Jean Franval plays the title role of the highwayman... What would you think is your most successful role in opera so far?* — N COUNT : USU+SUPP = part

role-playing is the act of imitating the character and behaviour of a type of person who is very different from yourself, either deliberately, for example as a training exercise, or without knowing it. EG *I've got a general idea of using role-playing in the course... We all indulge in unconscious role-playing.* — N UNCOUNT

roll /rəʊl/, **rolls, rolling, rolled**. **1** When a round object **rolls** or when you **roll** it, it moves along a surface, turning over and over many times. EG *The bucket rolled and clattered down the path... We heard rumbling noises of barrels being rolled under the house.* — V-ERG : USU+A

2 If you **roll** something such as a long object or a long piece of material, you wrap it several times around itself until it is shaped like a cylinder or a ball, usually so that you can store it or carry it. EG *She went on sorting the socks, rolling them into neat little bundles.* — V+O ◊ **rolled**. EG *They carried rolled prayer rugs under their arms.* — ◊ ADJ CLASSIF ● You use the expression **rolled into one** when you want to emphasize that someone or something has all the best qualities of the people or things that you have just mentioned. EG *A good musical is a new play, a new opera and a new ballet all rolled into one... She sings a little better than Galli Curci and Deanna Durbin rolled into one.* — ● PHR

3 If you **roll** a part of your clothing, you fold the edge of it several times, in order to make it shorter. — V+O ◊ **rolled**. EG *She had her trousers rolled above her knees.* — ◊ ADJ CLASSIF

4 If you **roll** a cigarette, you make it by wrapping a piece of paper round some tobacco. EG *He came strolling out, rolling a cigarette... I rolled a joint... 'Have one of my cigarettes.'-'No, thanks. I roll my own.'* — V+O

5 If you **roll** somewhere, you move along a surface in a lying position by turning your body over and over so that you are sometimes on your back, sometimes on your side, and sometimes on your stomach. EG *Sometimes we used to roll on the floor... She rolled off the sofa... He rolled back to his side of the bed.* — V+A ● If a theatre audience is **rolling in the aisles**, they are so amused at something that they find it hard to stop laughing; an informal expression. EG *...helpless audiences rolling in the aisles.* — ● PHR : VB INFLECTS, USU CONT

6 If vehicles **roll** along a road or towards a place, they move there. EG *Trucks with loudspeakers rolled through the streets... The bus rolled to a stop.* — V+A

7 When ships or aircraft **roll**, they keep leaning in a regular way first to one side and then to the other side, because of the wind or waves. EG *The 'Morning Rose' was still rolling and pitching.* — V ⇑ sway = rock ▸ used as a noun. EG *The boat settled into a slow roll.* — ▸ N SING WITH DET

8 If a machine is **rolling**, it is operating. EG *Our three printing machines were rolling twenty-four hours a day... With the hidden cameras rolling, Williams boasted of his influence.* — V = working

9 If drops of liquid **roll** down a surface, they move quickly down that surface. EG *He stood in a corner with tears rolling down his face... The sweat rolled down my neck.* — V+A (down) = run, trick[le]

10 If a drum or thunder **rolls**, it makes a continuous loud noise. EG *The drums are faintly rolling... The thunder rolled in the distance.* — V ▸ used as a noun. EG *There was a roll of drums.* — ▸ N COUNT

11 If you **roll** your eyes or if your eyes **roll**, they move in a circle, especially as a result of a strong feeling such as fear; a literary use. EG *Lynn glanced at Marsha, who rolled her eyes hopelessly... His eyes rolled wildly.* — V-ERG

12 If you describe an area of land as **rolling** away or **rolling** into the distance, you mean that it extends a — V+A = undulat[e]

long way in a series of small hills and valleys. EG *...the countryside which rolled away for miles and miles.*

13 A **roll** of paper, cloth, etc is a long piece of it wrapped several times around itself or around something else. EG *...a roll of adhesive plaster... He produced several rolls of hessian sacking.* N COUNT: N+*of* +N UNCOUNT

14 A **roll** is a very small loaf of bread eaten by one person, usually with butter and sometimes with a filling of meat, cheese, etc. EG *...a roll and butter... ...a dozen rolls.* N COUNT

15 A **roll** is also a list of people's names, especially one that has been prepared for an official purpose. EG *He attends church and is on the parish roll... ...a book kept for the roll of members... ...membership rolls.* ● If someone **is struck off the roll**, they are expelled from a professional organization so that they can no longer do their professional work. EG *We can be struck off the roll for that!* N COUNT+SUPP ⇑ register ● PHR : VB INFLECTS

16 If you say that someone has **rolls** of flesh or **rolls** of fat on their body, you mean that they are very fat. N PLURAL : IF+ PREP THEN *of*

17 ● to **start the ball rolling**: see **ball**. ● See also **bedroll, rock and roll, sausage roll, toilet roll.** ● See also **rolling.**

roll about. If you **roll about** or **roll around**, you move along a surface in a lying position by turning your body over and over so that you are sometimes on your back, sometimes on your side, and sometimes on your stomach. EG *Next moment they were rolling about the floor... Two smallish children were rolling around fighting.* PHRASAL VB : V+ ADV

roll down. 1 If you **roll** something **down**, you cause it to move downwards by turning a handle. EG *Will you roll the blind down for me?* PHRASAL VB : V+ O+ADV ⇑ lower = wind down

2 If you **roll** a folded piece of clothing **down**, you unfold the edge of it, in order to make it longer. EG *He rolled his sleeves down.* PHRASAL VB : V+ O+ADV

roll in. If something such as money **is rolling in**, it is being received in large numbers or quantities; an informal expression. EG *Orders roll in... Once we get there the money will just start rolling in.* PHRASAL VB : V+ ADV, OR V+O+ ADV ⇑ come in

roll on. If you say **roll on** something, you mean that you want it to happen sooner, because you are looking forward to it; an informal expression. EG *Roll on four o'clock... Roll on the Republic.* PHR+NG ⇑ hurry

roll over. If you **roll over**, you turn your body so that you change from lying in one position to lying in a different position. EG *I rolled over on my stomach... He rolled over and peered into Jack's face.* PHRASAL VB : V+ ADV ⇑ turn over

roll up. 1 If you **roll up** something such as a long piece of material or if it **rolls up**, it is wrapped several times around itself until it is shaped like a cylinder or a ball. EG *The blind of the buffet rolls up.* PHRASAL VB : V-ERG+ADV

2 If you **roll up** a piece of clothing, you fold the edge of it several times, in order to make it shorter. EG *He rolled up his sleeves.* PHRASAL VB : V+ O+ADV

3 When people **roll up**, they arrive in large numbers in order to see something unusual. EG *Curious sightseers rolled up in their hundreds... Roll up! Roll up! Come and see the Elephant Man!* PHRASAL VB : V+ ADV = turn up

4 See also **rolled-up.**

roll-call, roll-calls; also spelled without a hyphen. A **roll-call** is the act of checking which of the members of a group are present by reading aloud a list of their names. EG *Take the roll call.* N COUNT

rolled-up describes 1 things that are folded or wrapped into a shape like a cylinder, for example a newspaper. EG *He lunged at the wasp with a rolled-up newspaper... Another man carries a rolled-up stretcher.* 2 pieces of clothing that are made shorter by being folded over at the edge. EG *...her rolled-up jeans... His father had his sleeves rolled up.* ADJ CLASSIF : ATTRIB; ADJ CLASSIF : ATTRIB

roller /rəʊlə/, **rollers.** 1 A **roller** is 1.1 a rotating cylinder inside a machine or device used for crushing, pressing, printing, etc. 1.2 a cylinder that an object stands on and that acts as a wheel when the object is moved. ● See also **steam roller.** N COUNT; N COUNT

2 **Rollers** are hollow tubes that you heat up and roll your hair round, in order to make it curly. EG *Her hair was wound round outsize pink plastic rollers.* N COUNT : USU PLURAL ⇑ curler

roller-coaster /rəʊlə kəʊstə/, **roller-coasters**; also spelled as two words. A **roller-coaster** is a small railway that goes up and down steep slopes and that people ride on for pleasure and excitement at fairs and in amusement parks. EG *We liked to ride the roller coaster... ...a roller coaster ride.* N COUNT = big dipper

roller-skate /rəʊlə skeɪt/, **roller-skates, roller-skating, roller-skated**; also spelled as two words. 1 A **roller-skate** is a type of shoe with four small wheels on the bottom. People wear roller-skates for pleasure, when they want to move quickly and smoothly over flat surfaces. EG *This is the appeal of roller-skates, ice-skates, trampolines, and swings... She tightened the strap of her roller skate.* N COUNT : USU PL

2 If you **roller-skate**, you move over a flat surface wearing roller-skates. EG *Christopher taught the children to roller skate... I once roller-skated down the Mall.* V

rolling /rəʊlɪŋ/. 1 A **rolling** walk is slow and swaying, especially because the person is very fat or drunk. ADJ CLASSIF : ATTRIB

2 If you say that someone is **rolling in money** or **rolling in it**, you mean that they are rich; an informal expression. EG *Now that their kids are working as well, they must be rolling in it.* PHR = loaded

3 **Rolling** hills are fairly small with gentle slopes and extend a long way into the distance. EG *...an estate of trees, lakes, lawns, and rolling hills.* ADJ CLASSIF : ATTRIB ⇑ undulating

rolling pin, rolling pins; also spelled with a hyphen. A **rolling pin** is a hard wooden, glass, or plastic cylinder that is used for spreading pastry before you bake it. N COUNT

rolling stock; also spelled with a hyphen. **Rolling stock** is the engines, carriages, and wagons that are used on a railway. N UNCOUNT

roll of honour, rolls of honour. A **roll of honour** is a list of the names of people who are admired or respected for something that they have done, for example the people who have died while they were fighting for their country. EG *The names of the dead women were inscribed in the journal's Roll of Honour... You won't find him in the encyclopedias or the Nobel roll of honour.* N COUNT

roly-poly /rəʊli[1] pəʊli[1]/. **Roly-poly** people are pleasantly fat and round. EG *...a roly-poly toddler.* ADJ QUALIT : ATTRIB = plump

Roman /rəʊmə[3]n/, **Romans.** 1 Something that is **Roman** is 1.1 related to or connected with Rome and its empire in ancient times. EG *...the Roman Empire... ...the type of building found in a Roman town... ...a Roman centurion.* 1.2 related to or connected with modern Rome. EG *...Roman hotels.* ADJ CLASSIF; ADJ CLASSIF

2 A **Roman** was a citizen of Rome or the Roman Empire in ancient times. EG *The Romans left Britain in 410.* N COUNT

3 A **Roman** is also someone who lives or was born in the city of Rome. EG *...Dr Carlo Spagnolli, a 32-year-old Roman.* N COUNT ⇑ person

4 **Roman** is the most common style of printing in books, magazines, etc. It consists of small upright letters. The definitions in this dictionary are printed in roman type. EG *Typeset this column in roman.* N UNCOUNT ⇑ print

Roman alphabet. The **Roman alphabet** is the alphabet which was used by the Romans in ancient times and which is used for writing most western European languages, including English. EG *Arabic script was replaced by the Roman alphabet in official documents.* N SING : *the*+N

Roman Catholic, Roman Catholics. A **Roman Catholic** is someone who belongs to the Catholic Church. EG *Caroline is a Roman Catholic.* ▸ used as an adjective. EG *...a Roman Catholic priest.* N COUNT ⇑ Christian ▸ ADJ CLASSIF

Roman Catholicism is the same as **Catholicism.** N UNCOUNT ⇑ belief

romance, romances, romancing, romanced. The word **romance** can be pronounced either /rəʊmæns/ or /rəmæns/. 1 A **romance** is 1.1 a relationship between two people who love each other but who are not married to each other. EG *...a wartime romance... Shipboard romances flourished more swiftly than those on land... ...holiday romance.* N COUNT/ UNCOUNT = love affair

2 **Romance** is 2.1 the pleasure and excitement that you feel when you are with the person who you love. EG *Suppose you fall in love with someone who, once the romance has worn off, is unsuitable?... Harold fell short of her idea of romance.* 2.2 the feeling of excitement and adventure that you get from a particular experience or from a way of life. EG *There is romance to be found in life on the river... The audiences liked the romance and colour of his films.* N UNCOUNT; N UNCOUNT

3 A **romance** is also 3.1 a short novel about a romantic relationship or love affair between a man and a woman. EG *...historical romances.* 3.2 a story that is full of strange and exciting adventures, espe- N COUNT; N COUNT/ UNCOUNT

cially one written in the Middle Ages. EG *...heroes of medieval epic and romance.*

4 To **romance** means to tell stories that are not true or that are only partly true. EG *There she goes-romancing about the past again.* [V: IF+PREP THEN *about* ⇑ invent]

5 **Romance** languages are languages such as French, Spanish, and Italian, which are derived from Latin; a technical term in linguistics. [ADJ CLASSIF: ATTRIB]

Romanian /ruːmeɪnɪən/, **Romanians**; also spelled **Roumanian**. 1 Something that is **Romanian** relates or belongs to Romania or to its people. EG *...the Romanian Government.* [ADJ CLASSIF]

2 **Romanian** is the language spoken by people who live in Romania. [N UNCOUNT]

3 A **Romanian** is someone who comes from Romania. [N COUNT ⇑ person]

Roman law is the system of laws which was used in Rome in ancient times and which is the basis of many western legal systems. EG *Concepts of private property derived from Roman law.* [N UNCOUNT]

Roman numeral, Roman numerals. A **Roman numeral** is one of the letters or groups of letters used by Romans in ancient times to write numbers, for example I(=1), IV(=4), VIII(=8), XL(=40). Roman numerals are sometimes used now. [N COUNT: USU PL ⇑ number]

romantic /rə⁶mæntɪk/. 1 Someone who is **romantic** has a lot of ideas that are not related to real life, for example about love or about ways of changing society. EG *She's as romantic as a child of sixteen... Your sister has a romantic disregard of the advantages of money.* ▸ used as a noun. EG *Deep down they are romantics... Cedric's a great romantic.* [ADJ QUALIT ⇑ unrealistic; ▸ N COUNT ⇑ idealist]

2 **Romantic** means connected with love or with a love affair. EG *A woman needs a romantic attachment... ...a romantic assignation.* [ADJ CLASSIF: ATTRIB = amorous]

3 A **romantic** play, film, story, etc describes or represents love or a love affair. EG *...a charming romantic comedy starring Audrey Hepburn.* [ADJ CLASSIF: ATTRIB]

4 Something that is **romantic** is beautiful in a way that strongly affects your thoughts or feelings. EG *The setting is romantic... ...a romantic moonlight ride.* ◇ **romantically**. EG *Her long hair was spread romantically over the pillow.* [ADJ QUALIT; ◇ ADV WITH VB]

5 **Romantic** also describes the artistic movement of the eighteenth and nineteenth centuries which was concerned with expressing feelings and emotions, rather than with simply making things in a perfect form; a technical term in art, literature, and music. EG *...the Romantic artists.* [ADJ CLASSIF: ATTRIB]

romanticism /rə⁶mæntɪsɪzə⁰m/ refers to 1 thoughts and feelings which are idealistic and romantic, rather than realistic. EG *This kind of romanticism is everywhere in Buchan's books... ...the romanticism of the women's magazines.* [N UNCOUNT ⇑ idealism] 2 the romantic movement in art, music, and literature in the late eighteenth century and early nineteenth century. EG *...an early writer on Romanticism.* [N UNCOUNT]

romanticize /rə⁶mæntɪsaɪz/, **romanticizes, romanticizing, romanticized**; also spelled **romanticise**. If you **romanticize** someone or something, you think or talk about them in a way that is not at all realistic, so that they seem more interesting or exciting than they really are. EG *I do not want to romanticize him... ...romanticized notions about marriage.* [V+O ⇑ distort = idealize]

Romany /rɒməni¹, rəʊ-/, **Romanies**. 1 A **Romany** is a gypsy. [N COUNT]

2 **Romany** is the language spoken by many gypsies. [N UNCOUNT]

romp /rɒmp/, **romps, romping, romped**. 1 When people **romp**, especially children, they play and move around in a noisy, happy way. EG *The smaller children romped... ...elegant Edwardian ladies romping about in fancy dress.* [V: USU+A = frolic, disport]

2 A **romp** is a lively and enjoyable activity which is usually noisy and amusing, especially a game or a play. [N SING: *a*+N = frolic]

romp through. If you **romp through** something, you do it quickly and easily without having any problems; an informal expression. EG *This is easy stuff, we'll romp through this.* [PHRASAL VB: V+PREP, HAS PASS = sail through]

rompers /rɒmpəz/ are a piece of clothing worn by a baby or a young child, which consists of loose trousers and a top that are joined together. EG *Doesn't he look sweet in those rompers?* [N PLURAL: ALSO *a pair of*+N]

rondo /rɒndəʊ/, **rondos**. A **rondo** is a piece of classical music in which the main tune is repeated several times. A rondo is often part of a sonata or concerto. [N COUNT]

roof /ruːf/, **roofs, roofing, roofed**. The plural form can be pronounced either /ruːvz/ or /ruːfs/. 1 A **roof** is the covering on top of a building which protects people and their possessions from the weather. EG *...a yellow brick house with a slate roof... I fixed a small leak in the roof of her woodshed... Smoke rose above the station roof... ...snow-covered roofs and towers.* [N COUNT]

2 When a house **is roofed**, it has a new roof put on it. EG *I'm having the house roofed in the spring.* ◇ **roofed**. EG *...a wooden shack roofed with polythene.* [V+O: USU PASS; ◇ ADJ CLASSIF]

3 The **roof** of a car or other vehicle is the covering on top of it which protects passengers or goods from the weather. EG *Topson looked up at the roof of the truck... Loud bangs were heard on the van roof.* [N COUNT]

4 The **roof** of your mouth is the highest part of it. EG *His tongue seemed stuck to the roof of his mouth.* [N COUNT: USU+*of*]

5 The **roof** of an underground space such as a cave or mine is the highest part of it. [N COUNT = ceiling]

6 The word **roof** is also used in the following expressions. 6.1 **A roof over your head** is a place that you can live in as your home. EG *It's worth it just to have a roof over your head... She was without money and with no real roof over her head.* [PHR: USU USED AS O ⇑ home] 6.2 If something happens **under** your **roof**, it happens in your home. EG *Are we prepared to let this happen under our own roofs?... You can't do that sort of thing when you're sleeping under someone else's roof.* [PHR: USED AS A] 6.3 If a number of things or people are **under one roof** or **under the same roof**, they are in the same building. EG *We must try and get them all under one roof... She refused to live under the same roof as her mother any longer.* [PHR: USED AS A] 6.4 If a group of people **raise** or **lift the roof**, they make a very loud noise inside a building by singing, shouting, cheering, etc. EG *Right, we'll do that song again. Let's see if we can really raise the roof this time... Another group raised the roof in enthusiasm when I brought up the same issue.* [PHR: VB INFLECTS] 6.5 If someone **hits the roof**, they are very angry indeed about something; an informal expression. EG *It's a good job he never found out. He'd have hit the roof.* [PHR: VB INFLECTS] 6.6 If someone **goes through the roof**, they are extremely angry and show their anger by shouting at someone; an informal expression. EG *When he hears about this, my old man is going to go right through the roof.* [PHR: VB INFLECTS] 6.7 If a particular type of goods or a service **is going through the roof**, the price of it is increasing very rapidly and in an unexpected way; an informal expression. EG *Train fares are going through the roof... At that time sugar was going through the roof.* [PHR: VB INFLECTS ⇑ go up = rocket]

-roofed is combined with words in order to form adjectives which are used to describe a building that has a roof of a particular kind. EG *...the slate-roofed rows of houses.* [COMB: FORMS ADJS]

roofing /ruːfɪŋ/. The materials used for making or covering roofs are referred to as **roofing**. EG *He sells bundles of rushes for roofing... Slate is the very best roofing material.* [N UNCOUNT]

roofless /ruːflɪ²s/. A **roofless** building has no roof, for example because the building has been damaged or not used for a long time. EG *...the roofless warehouses on the east bank... The chapel, now roofless, has trees growing out of it.* [ADJ CLASSIF]

roof-rack, roof-racks; also spelled as one word. A **roof-rack** is a metal frame that is fixed on top of a car roof and used for carrying large objects. [N COUNT]

rooftop /ruːftɒp/, **rooftops**; also spelled with a hyphen. A **rooftop** is the outside part of the roof of a building. EG *I never knew that the silhouettes of rooftops and chimneys could look so beautiful.* ● If you **shout** or **proclaim** something **from the rooftops**, you say it or announce it in a very public way. EG *We shall proclaim it from the roof tops that the armed struggle of the working people has begun... All right, all right-there's no need to shout it from the rooftops.* [N COUNT: USU; ● PHR: VB INFLECTS ⇑ broadcast]

rook /rʊk/, **rooks, rooking, rooked**. 1 A **rook** is 1.1 a large black bird very like a crow. [N COUNT] 1.2 one of the two chess pieces which stand in the corners of the board at the beginning of a game of chess, and which can be moved in straight lines across the board in any direction except diagonally. [N COUNT = castle]

2 If you **rook** someone, you cheat them, especially of money; an informal and rather old-fashioned use. [V+O]

rookery /rʊkəºri¹/, **rookeries**. A **rookery** is a place, usually a group of trees, where a lot of rooks have their nests. N COUNT

rookie /rʊki¹/, **rookies**. A **rookie** is a new recruit without much experience, especially in the army, police force, etc; an informal word, used in American English. EG *He was a rookie policeman.* N COUNT

room /ruːm/, **rooms, rooming, roomed**. **1** A **room** is **1.1** one of the separate sections in a house or other building, which has its own walls, ceiling, floor, and door, and is used for a particular kind of activity. Entrance halls and corridors are never called rooms. EG *The room contained a couch and a glass cabinet... Boylan came back into the room... You are to go straight up to Room 64... She's in the music room.* N COUNT ⇑ place ▸ also used to refer to the people who are in a room. EG *'Ladies and Gentlemen,' the Captain said to the room at large.* ▸ N COUNT : USU SING **1.2** someone's private room, especially their bedroom at home or their office at work. EG *I lay on my bed in my room at the top of the house... He wants you to come and see him now, in his room.* N COUNT : USU POSS+N **1.3** a bedroom in a hotel. EG *I'll just get myself a room somewhere for the night... ...hotel rooms.* N COUNT **1.4** a room which you rent from someone and which you live in. EG *I want to find a room in the country.* N COUNT ⇑ accommodation **1.5** See also **classroom, common room, men's room, ladies' room, spare room.**

2 If you **room** with someone, you share a rented room with them; used mainly in American English. EG *At first I roomed with Jill... I had hoped that we could room together.* V+A *(with/together)*

3 Room is **3.1** enough empty space in a place for people to be able to move freely or do what they want to, or for things to be fitted in. EG *There wasn't enough room for everybody... Just keep the crowd back so I have room to move... ...in the hall, where there's plenty of room... He waited impatiently for the crowd to give him more room.* N UNCOUNT ⇑ area ● to **give** something **houseroom**: see **houseroom**. ● See also **elbow room, leg-room, standing room**. **3.2** the opportunity that someone has to act or to take part in a particular situation, system, or society. EG *They should retire to make room for younger men... In a progressive economy, there is no room for loss-makers.* N UNCOUNT : USU +*for* ⇑ chance = opening, scope ● **room for manoeuvre**: see **manoeuvre**. **3.3** the freedom in a particular situation for people to be able to think or behave in the way that they want to. EG *There ought to be room for differences of opinion... It leaves room for a variety of interpretations.* N UNCOUNT : USU +*for* = scope

-roomed is combined with words in order to form adjectives which describe buildings as having a particular number of rooms or type of room. EG *...my two-roomed flat.* COMB : FORMS ADJS

roomful /ruːmful/, **roomfuls**. If you talk about a **roomful** of things or people, you mean a room that is full of them. EG *...a roomful of old ladies... ...a roomful of furniture.* N PART+N IN PL/ N UNCOUNT ⇑ crowd

rooming house, rooming houses; also spelled with a hyphen. A **rooming house** is a building that is divided into small flats or single rooms which people rent to live in; used in American English. EG *The big old homes were now rooming houses.* N COUNT = lodging house, boarding house

roommate /ruːmmeɪt/, **roommates**; also spelled with a hyphen. Your **roommate** is someone who you are sharing a rented room with. EG *...a college roommate of mine... ...my roommate, Ray Stratton.* N COUNT

room service; also spelled with a hyphen. **Room service** is a service in a hotel by which meals or drinks are provided for guests in their rooms. N UNCOUNT ⇑ facility

roomy /ruːmi¹/, **roomier, roomiest**. A place that is **roomy** is large inside, so that you can move around freely and comfortably; used showing approval. EG *...a ground floor apartment which was roomy but sparsely furnished.* ADJ QUALIT = spacious

roost /ruːst/, **roosts, roosting, roosted**. **1** A **roost** is **1.1** a place, such as the branch of a tree, where birds rest or build their nests. EG *...hundreds of crows bullying the blackbirds from their roost... The gulls were returning to their roosts among the rocks.* N COUNT : USU POSS+N **1.2** a place specially made for farm birds to rest at night. N COUNT = coop

2 When birds **roost**, they settle in a particular place for the night. EG *The chickens roost there all winter.* V

3 You say that someone's past actions **have come home to roost** or that their **chickens have come home to roost** when these actions are having bad effects in the present. EG *Mother's secret extravagance comes home to roost... What's the matter? Are your chickens coming home to roost?* PHR : VB INFLECTS

4 Someone who **rules the roost** in a particular place has complete control over the other people there; an informal expression. EG *...a woman of iron character who had ruled the roost for years.* PHR : VB INFLECTS = dominate

rooster /ruːstə/, **roosters**. A **rooster** is an adult male chicken; used mainly in American English. N COUNT = cockerel

root /ruːt/, **roots, rooting, rooted**. **1** A **root** is the part of a plant that grows completely or partly under the ground. Many kinds of root can be eaten. EG *These trees have large, spreading roots... They dug up roots and gathered berries, nuts, and fruit.* N COUNT

2 If you **root** a plant or cutting or if it **roots**, it grows roots on its stem and begins to grow. EG *Geraniums root very easily.* V-ERG

3 The **root** of a hair, tooth, or nail is the part that you cannot see because it is inside your body or covered with skin. EG *They pulled her hair out by the roots.* N COUNT

4 Your **roots** are the connection that you have with a particular place or culture, because you or your family were born there or grew up there. EG *...a people without roots in this land... People are searching again for their roots... They are now utterly cut off from their peasant roots.* N PLURAL ● If you **put down roots** in a particular place, you become connected with it, for example by taking part in activities there or by making a lot of friends, so that eventually you think of the place as your home and do not want to leave it. EG *They have no time to put down roots in the community.* ● PHR : VB INFLECTS = settle

5 If you talk about the **root** or the **roots** of something, especially something unpleasant or undesirable, you are talking about its original cause. EG *Perhaps the root of the tragedy was here... Many diseases have their roots in the genetic make-up of the individual.* N COUNT : USU WITH POSS, SING=PL = origin, source

6 The **root** of something such as a belief, attitude, or problem is the most important part of it. EG *...the metaphysical truths which lay at the root of human belief... Surveys show that 60 to 80 per cent of illnesses have at their root emotional problems.* N COUNT : USU WITH POSS, SING=PL = core, heart

7 The **root** cause of something is its most important cause. EG *I tried to find the root cause of this meanness in me... ...the root causes of poverty.* ADJ CLASSIF : ATTRIB = basic, fundamental

8 The **root** of a word is the part that contains its meaning and that remains after all the extra parts have been removed. For example, the root of the word 'situation' is the Latin word 'situ', meaning 'place'. This is a technical use of 'root'. N COUNT = stem

9 Take root. 9.1 If plants **take root**, they succeed in growing in a particular place. EG *The seedlings of bushes and trees might take root there.* PHR : VB INFLECTS **9.2** If ideas, beliefs, or customs **take root**, they become established among a group of people. EG *Modern mass nationalism took root, and drove out the older liberal nationalism... ...the ideas that were to take root in a new land.* PHR : VB INFLECTS = catch on, take hold

10 If you say that something has been removed or destroyed **root and branch**, you mean that it has been removed or destroyed completely; a fairly formal expression. EG *We intend to destroy these practices root and branch.* PHR : USED AS AN A ⇑ totally

11 If you **root** through or **root** among things, you search among them by moving them with your hands, usually because you are trying to find a particular object. EG *He opened a drawer, and rooted through it until he found Ellen's jewellery.* V+A ⇑ hunt = sift

12 When animals **root**, they dig up the earth looking for food. EG *Wild pigs often came rooting in herds right through the village.* V

13 ● See also **cube root, square root, grass roots**. ● See also **rooted**.

root about. If you **root about** or **root around** for something, you search for it in a particular place by moving a lot of things around. EG *My sister was rooting about in the cupboard, looking for a tin-opener... Smith rooted around in a large brown paper bag.* PHRASAL VB : V+ADV, USU+A = hunt

root for. If you are **rooting for** someone, you are giving them your support while they are doing something difficult; an informal expression. EG *Our friends were all rooting for us... Good luck in the interview–I'll be rooting for you.* PHRASAL VB : V+PREP ⇑ cheer on

root out. If you **root** someone or something **out**, you remove them by force from a particular place, organization, etc. EG *He was determined to root out* PHRASAL VB : V+O+ADV ⇑ eject *corruption in his department... He's in the library somewhere. Let's go and root him out.*

root up. If you **root up** a plant, you dig it up from the ground. EG *I had to root up all the plants and burn them.* PHRASAL VB : V+ ADV OR V+O+ ADV ⇑ extract

root crop, root crops. Root crops are plants such as potatoes or turnips that are grown in large quantities so that their roots can be eaten; a technical term in farming. N COUNT

rooted /ruːtɪ²d/. 1 If something is **rooted** in a particular tradition or belief, it is caused by or originates in that tradition or belief. EG *These sentiments were rooted in the tradition of radicalism... ...attitudes deeply rooted in class and history.* ADJ QUALIT : PRED+*in* ⇑ based = grounded

2 Opinions and beliefs that are **rooted** are very strongly held and therefore difficult to change or remove. EG *...deeply rooted impulses... These sort of feelings may be more deeply rooted than you suspect.* ● See also **deep-rooted**. ADJ QUALIT = embedded, seated

3 If you are **rooted** or you stand **rooted**, you are unable to move from the place where you are standing because you are very afraid or surprised. EG *They stood rooted in astonishment and stared.* ● You say that someone is **rooted to the spot** when you want to emphasize that they are very surprised or afraid and so are unable to move. EG *He became absolutely rooted to the spot.* ADJ CLASSIF : PRED, USU+*in* = immobile, frozen ● PHR : USED AS C ⇑ immobile

rootless /ruːtlɪ²s/. Someone who is **rootless** has no place that they regard as their home. EG *He became a rootless vagabond... He had joined the band of rootless unskilled labourers.* ADJ CLASSIF ⇑ transient

rope /rəʊp/, **ropes, roping, roped.** 1 A **rope** is a piece of very thick, strong string, usually made of several strands of hemp, nylon, or wire which have been twisted together. Ropes are used for jobs such as towing cars, mooring ships, or tying large things together. EG *One of the characters in the play hangs herself with a rope... She picked up the end of the rope, and pulled with all her might... ...a piece of rope.* N COUNT/ UNCOUNT ⇑ cord

2 The **ropes** refers to the fence made of ropes that surrounds a boxing ring or a wrestling ring. N PLURAL : *the*+ N

3 If you **rope** one thing to another thing, or if you **rope** two things together, you tie the things together with a rope. EG *The wagons were roped together.* V+O : USU+*to/together* ⇑ fasten

4 The word **rope** is also used in the following informal expressions. 4.1 If you **give** someone **plenty of rope** or **enough rope**, you give them a lot of freedom to do a task in their own way, often because you want their attempts to fail or you want the person to look foolish. EG *He said he would give her all the rope she wanted.* PHR : VB INFLECTS 4.2 If you describe a payment as **money for old rope**, you mean that it is earned very easily, for very little effort. PHR : USED AS O/C 4.3 If you say that someone is **on the ropes**, you mean that they are very near to giving up or being defeated. PHR : USED AS C
4.4 If you **know** or **learn the ropes**, you know or learn how to deal with a particular kind of task, job, or problem. EG *They've got a friend here who knows the ropes, who can show them around... She knew the ropes and the ways to get round the rules.* PHR : VB INFLECTS 4.5 If you **show** or **teach** someone **the ropes**, you show or teach them how to do a particular kind of work. PHR : VB INFLECTS

rope in. If you **rope** someone **in**, you persuade them to help you with a particular task, usually because you need the help of extra people in order to be able to finish it; an informal expression. EG *Some amazing people were roped in to work on these books.* PHRASAL VB : V+ O+ADV

rope off. If you **rope off** an area, you separate it from another area by surrounding it with a rope. EG *The track was roped off from the rest of the field.* PHRASAL VB : V+ O+ADV

rope ladder, rope ladders; also spelled with a hyphen. A **rope ladder** is a ladder made of two long ropes connected by short pieces of rope or by pieces of wood or metal. N COUNT

ropey /rəʊpi¹/, **ropier, ropiest**; an informal word. 1 If you say that something is **ropey**, you mean that it is not very good quality and so is unsatisfactory. EG *The food was a bit ropey... I thought it was a ropey performance.* ADJ QUALIT = crummy

2 If you feel **ropey**, you feel ill. ADJ QUALIT

rosary /rəʊzəri¹/, **rosaries.** A **rosary** is a string of beads that is used for counting prayers by members of various religions, especially, in Christianity, by Roman Catholics. EG *She clicked the beads of her rosary.* ▸ used of the series of prayers that are counted using the beads on a rosary. N COUNT ▸ ⇑ prayer

rose /rəʊz/, **roses.** 1 A **rose** is a garden flower which has a lot of petals and a pleasant smell. Roses grow on bushes that have thorny stems. They are usually red, white, or pink in colour. EG *Eleanor was holding an armful of red roses.* ▸ used of the bushes on which roses grow. EG *I have to prune the roses.* N COUNT

2 Something that is **rose** is reddish-pink or brownish-pink in colour. EG *The house was built of pale rose brick.* ADJ COLOUR

3 A **rose** is also a device with very small holes in it that fits onto the end of a hose or the spout of a watering can. The water comes out of the rose in a fine spray so that you can water plants. N COUNT ⇑ sprinkler

4 **Rose** is also the past tense of **rise**.

5 The word **rose** is also used in the following expressions. 5.1 If you say that a situation is not a **bed of roses** or is not **all roses**, you mean that it is not all pleasant, and there are unpleasant aspects to it as well. EG *Life isn't all roses* PHR : USED AS C 5.2 If you say that something **puts the roses back in** someone's **cheeks**, you mean that it makes them look healthier because it makes their cheeks pink. EG *The fresh air will soon put the roses back in your cheeks.* PHR : VB INFLECTS 5.3 If you say that someone **sees** things **through rose-coloured spectacles** or **rose-tinted spectacles**, you mean that they only notice the pleasant aspects of life and not the unpleasant ones. PHR : VB INFLECTS

rosé /rəʊzeɪ/ is wine which is pink in colour. N UNCOUNT

roseate /rəʊzi¹eɪt/. Something that is **roseate** is reddish-pink in colour; a formal word. EG *Alexander sipped tea from roseate china.* ADJ COLOUR

rosebud /rəʊzbʌd/, **rosebuds.** A **rosebud** is a young rose that is still rolled up and has not yet opened out fully. N COUNT ⇑ flower

rose hip, rose hips; also spelled with a hyphen. A **rose hip** is a bright red or orange fruit that grows on some kinds of rose bushes. N COUNT

rosemary /rəʊzmə⁰ri¹/ is a plant with small spiky greyish-green leaves that are used as a herb in cooking; used also to refer to the actual leaves or to the herb. N UNCOUNT

rosette /rəʊzet/, **rosettes.** A **rosette** is 1 a badge that is made from bright-coloured ribbons arranged in circles. You wear a rosette, for example, to show your support for a particular team or political party. N COUNT

2 an ornament or design that looks like a rose. N COUNT

rosewood /rəʊzwʊd/ is a hard, dark-coloured wood from a species of tropical tree. It is used for making furniture. EG *...a rosewood table.* N UNCOUNT

roster /rɒstə/, **rosters.** A **roster** is a list of people who must all take it in turn to do a particular job. EG *They supplied us with a roster of soloists.* N COUNT = register, rota

rostrum /rɒstrəm/, **rostrums** or **rostra.** The plural form **rostra** is used in formal English. A **rostrum** is a raised platform on which someone stands in front of a large group of people, usually in order to speak to them. EG *Inside, there is a high rostrum for preaching.* N COUNT = dais, podium

rosy /rəʊzi¹/, **rosier, rosiest.** 1 Something that is **rosy** is reddish-pink in colour. EG *...the dim, rosy light... ...a lamp with a rosy silk shade.* ADJ COLOUR

2 If you describe someone or their face as **rosy**, you mean that they look very healthy and their cheeks are pink. EG *He had five children, all rosy and handsome... Her rosy face was suddenly mischievous... ...her bright eyes and rosy cheeks.* ADJ QUALIT

3 If you say that a situation seems **rosy**, you mean that it seems likely to be satisfactory and very successful or enjoyable. EG *...the rosy world that lay ahead of them... Nothing was rosy, wherever you looked.* ADJ QUALIT = hopeful

rot /rɒt/, **rots, rotting, rotted.** 1 When things such as fruit, vegetables, wood, or eggs **rot**, they decay. EG *A week's supply of vegetables and fruit rotted... ...a piece of rotted linen.* ▸ used as a noun. EG *You should destroy any bulb with rot.* ● See also **dry rot**. V = decompos ▸ N UNCOUNT

2 When something **rots** an object or a substance, it causes it to decay. EG *...enough confectionery to rot one hundred thousand sets of teeth... A strong household bleach might rot the fibres.* V+O ⇑ disintegra

3 If you say that someone **is rotting** in a particular place, especially in a prison, you mean that they are slowly but steadily getting into a poor mental and physical condition because they are unable to leave V : USU+A ⇑ deteriora = languish

that place. EG *You will rot in jail... You think I'm going to let myself rot in this hole?*

4 If you say that **the rot set in**, you mean that a situation reached a stage where it began to slowly get worse without anyone being able to stop this happening. PHR : VB INFLECTS

5 If you say that what someone is saying is **rot**, you mean that they are saying very stupid things. EG *You're talking absolute rot, and you know it... What are you telling them all that rot for?... That's a lot of rot.* N UNCOUNT ⇑ nonsense = rubbish

rot away. When something **rots away**, it gradually decays and so disappears or falls to pieces. EG *His body is rotting away... The shack rotted away.* PHRASAL VB : V+ADV = decompose

rota /rəʊtə/, **rotas**. A **rota** is a list of people who must all take it in turn to do a particular job. EG *We have a cooking rota... The office work was shared on a rota system.* N COUNT = roster

rotary /rəʊtə⁰ri¹/ means moving or able to move in a circular direction round a fixed point. EG *...turning linear into rotary motion... ...rotary cutters.* ADJ CLASSIF : ATTRIB = rotating

rotate /rəʊteɪt/, **rotates, rotating, rotated**. 1 When something **rotates** or when you **rotate** it, it turns with a circular movement. EG *The capsule rotated anticlockwise... The string rotates the drum.* V-ERG : USU+A = spin, revolve

2 If you **rotate** crops, you plant a different crop on a particular piece of land each year, in order to keep the soil fertile. V+O

3 If people **rotate** jobs, they take it in turn to do different jobs, so that each person does each job in a regular order. EG *They avoid specialisation and hierarchy by rotating the jobs so that everyone works at the more creative ones.* V+O ⇑ distribute = share

rotation /rəʊteɪʃə⁰n/, **rotations**. 1 A **rotation** is a complete circular movement. EG *...the earth's rotation.* N COUNT/UNCOUNT ⇑ turn = revolution

2 **Rotation** of crops is a technique in farming or gardening in which a different crop is planted on a particular piece of land each year, in order to keep the soil fertile. EG *...the annual rotation of crops... We must establish crop rotations which will help to minimize disease.* N UNCOUNT/COUNT

3 The **rotation** of jobs is the sharing of them by a group of people. They take it in turns to do different jobs and each person does each job in a regular order. EG *We have a system of job rotation and sharing among staff.* N UNCOUNT/COUNT

4 If you do things **in rotation**, you do them in order, one after the other, and when you have done the last one you start again on the first one. EG *She did everything in strict rotation.* PHR : USED AS AN A = in sequence

rote /rəʊt/. 1 **Rote** means arrived at by routine or habit rather than by careful thought. EG *The company sought nothing more than rote agreement... ...rote learning.* ADJ CLASSIF : ATTRIB

2 If you learn something **by rote**, you learn it by memorizing it and not by thinking about it or trying to understand it. EG *He learned the work by rote.* PHR : USED AS AN A

rotor /rəʊtə/, **rotors**. The **rotor** or the **rotor** blades on a helicopter are the blades on the top of it which go round and lift it off the ground. EG *The rotor overhead begins turning slowly.* N COUNT

rotten /rɒtə⁰n/. 1 Fruit, vegetables, wood, eggs, etc that are **rotten** are decayed. EG *Most of the wood was so rotten that when they pulled it broke up... A dreadful odour of rotten vegetation came from the room.* ADJ QUALIT = decomposed

2 If you describe something as **rotten**, you mean that it is very poor quality; an informal use.. EG *...a rotten novel about a war-time romance... He is a rotten performer on television.* ADJ QUALIT = lousy

3 If you say that a situation is **rotten**, you mean that it is unpleasant and causes unhappiness; an informal use. EG *They're having a rotten deal... Rotten about poor Nigel, wasn't it?* ADJ QUALIT = dreadful

4 If you describe someone as **rotten**, you mean that they are very unpleasant or unkind; an informal use. EG *He was a rotten bastard, like all men.* ▸ used of people's actions. EG *That was a rotten thing to do.* ADJ QUALIT = lousy, beastly
◊ **rottenly**. EG *I think he behaved rottenly to her.* ◊ ADV WITH VB

5 If you feel or look **rotten**, you feel or look ill; used an informal use. EG *They were looking very white and rotten... When he woke up the next morning, he felt rotten.* ADJ QUALIT : PRED = seedy, fragile

6 You use **rotten** to emphasize that you do not like something or feel angry or frustrated about it; an informal use. EG *She was mumbling away about her rotten old sugar.* ADJ CLASSIF : ATTRIB

rotter /rɒtə/, **rotters**. If you call someone a **rotter**, you mean that they have behaved in a very unkind or selfish way; an old-fashioned informal use. N COUNT/VOC = bounder

rotund /rəʊtʌnd/. Something or someone that is **rotund** is round and fat; a formal word. EG *He turned and patted his rotund stomach.* ADJ QUALIT

rotunda /rə⁶tʌndə/, **rotundas**. A **rotunda** is a round building or room, especially one with a dome. EG *...the huge rotunda of the Albert Hall.* N COUNT

rouble /ruːbə⁰l/, **roubles**. A **rouble** is a unit of money that is used in the Soviet Union. N COUNT ⇑ currency

roué /ruːeɪ/, **roués**. A **roué** is a man who is regarded as behaving in a rather immoral way, for example by gambling, drinking, or having sexual relationships with many women; an old-fashioned word. EG *Anyone can see that he is nothing but a roué and not to be trusted.* N COUNT = rake

rouge /ruːʒ/, **rouges, rougeing, rouged**. 1 **Rouge** is a red powder which people, especially women and actors, put on their cheeks in order to give them more colour. EG *They wore lipstick and rouge.* N UNCOUNT ⇑ make-up

2 When people, especially women and actors, **rouge** their cheeks, they put rouge on them. EG *...an elderly lady with rouged cheeks and heavily mascaraed eyelashes.* V+O ⇑ make up

rough /rʌf/, **rougher, roughest; roughs, roughing, roughed**. 1 If something is **rough** or if it has a **rough** surface, its surface is uneven and not smooth. EG *They journeyed for several weeks over rough roads. ...the rough surface of the stone.* ADJ QUALIT = rugged
◊ **roughness**. EG *Roughness of the skin can be caused by bad diet.* ◊ N UNCOUNT ≠ smoothness

2 If an action is **rough**, it is done with too much force and without enough care or gentleness, with the result that people or things are likely to be hurt or damaged. EG *There were complaints of rough handling, especially by younger policemen.* ▸ used of people. EG *I grabbed her by the shoulders. Maybe I was too rough.* ◊ **roughly**. EG *His wrists were grabbed and roughly he was snatched up from the stool... She went to the window and roughly pulled back the curtain... He answered her roughly and in a greater hurry than he intended.* ADJ QUALIT ⇑ violent, harsh; ◊ ADV WITH VB = brusquely

3 If a situation is **rough**, it is unpleasant and difficult to bear because there are so many problems; an informal use. EG *I knew they were having a rough time and I felt sorry for them... Such a life is hazardous and rough... Having to cope with their parents' divorce can be really rough on children... Why is it that the Arts are getting such a rough deal?* ADJ QUALIT : IF+PREP THEN *on* ⇑ bad = hard
◊ **roughly**. EG *Life has treated him roughly.* ◊ ADV WITH VB

4 If you make a **rough** calculation or guess, it is more or less correct but is not exact or accurate. EG *Multiply the weekly cost by fifty two to get the rough annual cost... As a rough guide, 1 cubic foot stores 25lb frozen food.* ◊ **roughly**. EG *Are there roughly equal numbers of men and women in your group?... ...a section of road lying roughly on a north-south axis... ...a woman of roughly her own age.* ADJ QUALIT ⇑ near = approximate; ◊ ADV ⇑ almost = approximately

5 A **rough** description or drawing does not contain very much detail and is not very accurate, but shows only the most important features of something. EG *Mr Boggis drew a rough sketch on his pad showing the position of each building... The Russian visitor gave a rough outline of the proposals.* ◊ **roughly**. EG *She described roughly their planned course of action.* ADJ QUALIT ⇑ basic; ◊ ADV WITH VB ⇑ basically

6 Something that is **rough** is not made very well and is not very good quality. EG *They had built themselves a rough shelter of branches and leaves. ...rough red wine... The equipment taken from the prisoners was found to be rougher, clumsier, and worse fitting than our own. They were dressed in thick rough clothes.* ◊ **roughly**. EG *The buildings were roughly constructed using virtually anything that was available.* ADJ QUALIT ⇑ basic = crude; ◊ ADV WITH VB = crudely

7 If you say that the weather, the sea, or a journey across the sea is **rough**, you mean that the weather is windy or stormy and so there are very big waves. EG *The sea was really rough, swirling and crashing round the rocks... ...a rough Channel crossing.* ADJ QUALIT ⇑ stormy

8 **Rough** land is land which is not cultivated or looked after, or that is not used for a particular purpose. EG *The only place for the kids to play is on* ADJ CLASSIF : ATTRIB

the rough ground behind the factory... He had rented one acre of rough pasture.

9 If a machine sounds **rough**, it is making an unpleasant harsh or grating noise that suggests that it is not working properly or that it has been made badly; an informal use. EG *That engine sounds a bit rough!* ADJ QUALIT ⇑ bad

10 A part of a city or town that is **rough** is unpleasant because there is a lot of violence or crime there. EG *It's a very rough area, you mustn't go there alone at night!* ADJ QUALIT = seedy

11 The word **rough** is also used in the following expressions. **11.1** If you describe something as **rough justice**, you mean that the punishment that someone has received is harsh but fits the crime well. PHR : USED AS C **11.2** If you describe someone as a **rough diamond**, you mean that they are good and kind but do not have good manners and do not behave politely all the time. EG *Mayor Hyland was what they used to call a rough diamond.* PHR : USU USED AS C ⇑ person **11.3** If you write or draw something **in rough**, you write or draw it on a spare piece of paper so that you can change or improve it later. EG *When you've got the best layout in rough you can start to draw out your good one.* PHR : USED AS AN A **11.4** If someone **cuts up rough**, they become angry and violent; an informal expression. EG *I was just standing talking to him and he suddenly cut up rough.* PHR : VB INFLECTS **11.5** If you say that you must **take the rough with the smooth**, you mean that you must accept the unpleasant and difficult things that happen as well as the good things. PHR : VB INFLECTS **11.6** If you **sleep rough**, you sleep out of doors, for example on a park bench. EG *We had great fun sleeping rough on the beaches and washing in the sea for two weeks.* PHR : VB INFLECTS **11.7** If you **rough it**, you live in a very simple way for a while without all the normal comforts of life. EG *I'll have to rough it for a bit.* PHR : VB INFLECTS

rough out. If you **rough out** a drawing, painting, or idea, you draw or write out the main features of it before you do it properly and in detail. EG *I've roughed out a scene for my new play... I roughed out a sketch of the harbour.* PHRASAL VB : V+O+ADV ⇑ outline

rough up; an informal expression. **1** If you **rough** someone **up**, you attack them by hitting or beating them. EG *By now they were really roughing me up, the fight had turned into a free-for-all.* PHRASAL VB : V+O+ADV

2 If you **rough** something **up**, you make it untidy or uneven. EG *Don't rough up my hair–I've just combed it!* PHRASAL VB : V+O+ADV = ruffle up, mess up

roughage /rʌfɪdʒ/ refers to substances in food such as bran or fibre that make digestion easier and help your bowels to work properly. N UNCOUNT

rough and ready; also spelled with hyphens. If you describe something as **rough and ready**, you mean that it is very simple, usually because it has been made, done, or arranged in a hurry. EG *...a rough-and-ready motel... The accommodation was a bit rough and ready, but most people didn't seem to mind.* ADJ QUALIT

rough and tumble; also spelled with hyphens. **1** **Rough and tumble** is noisy and slightly violent behaviour, for example a playful fight. EG *The teacher rushed in to put an end to the rough-and-tumble.* N UNCOUNT ⇑ fighting

2 If you describe a situation as **rough and tumble**, you mean that you have to be strong and look after yourself, because people are acting for their own advantage and not to help others. EG *...the rough and tumble of world politics.* N UNCOUNT

roughcast /rʌfkɑːst/ is a mixture of plaster and small stones used for covering the outside walls of buildings. N UNCOUNT ⇑ substance

roughen /rʌfəⁿn/, **roughens, roughening, roughened.** To **roughen** something or to **roughen** its surface means to make its surface less smooth. EG *The harsh climate had roughened her skin.* V+O

rough-hewn /rʌf hjuːn/. Wood or stone that is **rough-hewn** has been cut into a shape but has not yet been smoothed or finished off. EG *...a wall of rough-hewn blocks of grey stone.* ADJ CLASSIF

roughshod /rʌfʃɒd/. If you **ride roughshod over** someone or something, you completely ignore their ideas or suggestions and use your authority to act in the way that you want to act. EG *The government has ridden roughshod over the recommendations made by the committee of enquiry.* PHR : VB INFLECTS

roulette /ruːlet/ is a gambling game in which a wheel with holes in it is spun round and a ball is dropped into the wheel. Players bet on which hole the ball will fall into when the wheel has stopped spinning. EG *We play roulette and blackjack.* • See also **Russian roulette.** N UNCOUNT

Roumanian /ruːmeɪnɪən/. See **Romanian.**

round /raʊnd/, **rounder, roundest; rounds, rounding, rounded.** The form **around** is also used for the meanings in paragraphs 4 to 17. **1** Something that is **round** is **1.1** shaped like a ball. EG *The earth is round... ...heavy round stones.* ◊ **roundness.** EG *...the roundness of the earth.* ADJ QUALIT = spherical **1.2** shaped like a circle. EG *...thatched round huts... Shanti had a round, middle-aged face.* ADJ QUALIT = circular **1.3** curved in shape, like the letter 'c', for example. EG *She admired the church's antiquated round arches... ...the clear round bulge of the girl's belly.* ◊ **roundness.** EG *Her body lost its roundness.* ADJ QUALIT = rounded ◊ N UNCOUNT

2 If your eyes are **round**, they are open very wide, usually because you are excited or surprised. EG *He looked up at me, his eyes round... Her face was bright, her eyes round and bright as two diamonds.* ADJ CLASSIF

3 If you say that something is a **round** number or a **round** figure, you mean that it is an easy number to remember because it is a whole number, probably ending with '0'. EG *That's a nice round figure.* ADJ CLASSIF : ATTRIB

4 **Round** or **around** is used in some phrasal verbs, for example 'look round' and 'hand round.' See the individual phrasal verb entries for such words, which are not explained here. PREP OR ADV

5 You use **round** or **around** **5.1** to indicate that something is positioned or arranged on all the sides of someone or something, or that it forms a circle on the outside of them. EG *We were sitting round a table eating... ...a cluster of four-storey buildings set around a courtyard... There was a wall all the way round... She picked up some toast and cut off the crusts all round.* PREP OR ADV **5.2** in measurements to indicate the circumference of an object. EG *It measures fifteen feet round the trunk... It's six feet high and five feet round.* PREP OR ADV **5.3** to indicate that something is very near a particular person or thing. EG *We waited for them to gather round... There was a flurry of people round a meat shop...* PREP, OR ADV AFTER VB **5.4** to indicate that something is situated on the other side of something. EG *The dustbins are round the back of the house... There are a couple of shops just around the corner.* PREP **5.5** to indicate that something happens or exists in a particular area or part of the country. EG *We were the first farmers round here to use the new fertilizers.* PREP OR ADV

6 A piece of clothing or jewellery that is **round** or **around** a particular part of your body is covering it. EG *She was wearing a scarf round her head... She had an old sack round her shoulders.* PREP

7 If you put your arm **round** or **around** someone, you are touching or holding them. EG *He put his arms round her... Heissman now had an arm around Mary Stuart's shoulders.* PREP

8 If something happens **round** or **around** the world, the country, etc, it happens all over the place that is mentioned. EG *Think of what's happening politically round the world... We have collected a lot of information from around the country... He now has five shops scattered around the town.* PREP = all over, throughout

9 If someone or something is moving **round** or **around an object or a person,** they are moving in the shape of a circle on the outside of that object or person. EG *The earth moves round the sun... The agitated youth danced around her in his pyjamas.* PREP AFTER VB OR ADV AFTER VB

10 If you move **round** or **around** something, you move to the other side of it. EG *Ralph jumped up and ran swiftly round the fire... Hogan walked round to the driver's side and unlocked the door... The boys had disappeared around a corner.* PREP AFTER VB OR ADV AFTER VB

11 If you turn or look **round** or **around**, you turn so that you are facing in a different direction. EG *He stood still for a second and then swung round and faced the window... Everybody turned around and looked at Jack... We've got to turn this thing round... He paused and looked round at me.* ADV AFTER VB

12 If you go or travel **round** or **around** a country, town, etc, you go to different parts of it. EG *Going round Italy, one is struck by the vast number of churches everywhere... ...a relay race round London... I wandered around the orchard.* PREP, OR ADV AFTER VB

13 If you hand or pass something **round** or **around**, it is passed from one person to another. EG *The book was handed round from one to the other... I've got a couple of pictures you might like to pass around... There were a lot of rumours going round.* PREP AFTER VB OR ADV AFTER VB

14 If you ask someone to come **round** or **around**, you are asking them to visit you, usually in your house or the place where you work. EG *Her friend Emily came round... They invited the public health inspector round... She came around a half-hour later.* ADV AFTER VB

15 If you move things **round** or **around**, you put them in different places. EG *We spent the afternoon moving the furniture round.* PREP AFTER VB, OR ADV AFTER VB

16 If there is a way **round** or **around** a problem or difficulty, there is a solution to it. EG *There are several ways round this... She knew the ropes and the ways to get round the limited rules.* PREP

17 When you are talking about time or numbers, **round** or **around** means approximately. EG *We should get there round four o'clock... The project was designed to irrigate around 200 acres... The computer burst upon the scene around 1950.* PREP : USU + NUM = about, roughly

18 If a conversation, a piece of music, etc is going **round and round in your head,** you cannot stop thinking about it. EG *I went over the dialogue in my head. Over and over and round and round... The same songs have been going round and round in my head all morning.* PHR : USED AS AN A

19 If someone or something is going **round and round**, they are going round in small circles. to say that something is spinning or moving in small circles. EG *The bee was flying in a panic round and round beneath the ceiling... He twirled round and round.* PHR : USED AS AN A

20 Round about means **20.1** very near a particular place. EG *She knew all the people in the houses round about... Have any of the shepherds who live round about here ever seen a sea gull?* **20.2** approximately. EG *He arrived at round about half past four or five... I've been here for round about ten years.* PREP, OR PHR : USED AS AN A; PREP = about, roughly

21 If you **round** something, you move or travel past it, rather than through it, over it, or under it, by turning a corner and changing your direction; a formal use. EG *We rounded Cape Horn and came north again... We traversed the lawns and rounded the silent lake... He rounded the corner at the top of the stairs.* V+O

22 A **round** of talks, discussions, etc is one of a series of groups of discussions, talks, or legal processes. EG *Turkey is eager for a further round of talks with Greece... They will testify at the second round of hearings.* N COUNT + SUPP

23 A **round** of events is a large number of these events that all occur soon after each other. EG *He scheduled a round of rallies around the country... Vita was whirled away from him by another round of parties... We were on our final round of visits.* N COUNT + SUPP ⇑ series

24 If you have a **round** or you go on your **rounds**, you make a series of visits to a lot of different people or places as part of your job, for example when you are delivering goods. EG *She does a paper round to earn a bit of extra cash... The doctor's on his rounds.* N COUNT

25 If someone **does the rounds** or **makes the rounds** of a place, they go from one person to another in that place, usually as part of their job or in order to ask for work. EG *A priest did the rounds of the ward, talking to each woman in turn... She had been making the rounds of theatrical offices, looking for a job.* PHR : VB INFLECTS

26 If something **goes the rounds**, it is passed from one person to another in a particular group of people. EG *McKellen recalls a joke that went the rounds of the office... There are three theories going the rounds... Flu was going the rounds.* PHR : VB INFLECTS

27 A **round** of golf is a game of golf, which consists usually of playing eighteen holes. EG *He won the US Open Championship with four rounds each under 70.* N COUNT

28 A **round** in a boxing or wrestling match is a period of time in which the boxers or wrestlers fight. EG *The coach was there to dust him down and sponge him off between rounds.* N COUNT

29 In sport, a **round** is a set of games in a particular competition. The winners of each round go on to play in the next round, and so on until one team wins the final. EG *York City managed to get to the third round of the F.A. Cup.* N COUNT

30 If you buy a **round** of drinks, you buy a drink for each member of the group of people that you are with. EG *He would have liked to pay for a round himself but he didn't have any money on him... Whose round is it?* N COUNT

31 A **round** of ammunition is a bullet or other form of ammunition. EG *These cannon can fire up to 250 rounds per minute... His men carried 100 rounds each.* N COUNT

32 In music, a **round** is a simple song sung by several people in which one person starts singing and the others join in one after the other, so that they are then all singing different parts of the song at the same time. EG *We could sing it as a round.* N COUNT

round off. If you **round** something **off**, you end it in a satisfactory or pleasant way; an informal expression. EG *How about a nice quiet drink to round off the evening?.* PHRASAL VB : V + O + ADV

round on. If you **round on** someone, you suddenly attack them, either physically or with unpleasant and aggressive words; an informal expression. EG *He rounded on his attacker... She rounded on a housing official and told him exactly what she thought.* PHRASAL VB : V + PREP, HAS PASS = lay into

round up. If you **round up** animals or people, you gather them together. EG *We sent in dogs to round up the sheep... They had rounded up people at gunpoint.* PHRASAL VB : V + O + ADV

roundabout /raʊndəbaʊt/, **roundabouts**; used in British English. **1** A **roundabout** is **1.1** a large rotating mechanical device that you often see at funfairs. It has plastic or wooden animals, cars, etc on it which children sit on and which then go round and round. EG *...old fairground roundabouts.* N COUNT = merry-go-round **1.2** a device which consists of a large round platform, usually in playgrounds. Children sit on the platform, which can be turned round by being pushed. EG *Children were playing on the roundabouts.* N COUNT

2 A **roundabout** is also a large stone or grass circle in the middle of the road at a place where several roads meet. You must drive round the roundabout in one particular direction until you come to the road that you want to go along. EG *Drive on 4 miles to the next roundabout.* N COUNT = traffic island

3 If you say something in a **roundabout** way, you are not saying directly and openly what you really think or want. EG *I suggested it in a very roundabout way... His answer was roundabout, but unequivocal.* ADJ QUALIT ⇑ circuitous

rounded /raʊndɪ²d/ is used to describe something which is round or curved in shape, and not flat, pointed, or straight. EG *...rounded hills... Her legs were long and rounded.* ADJ CLASSIF

rounders /raʊndəz/ is a game played by two teams, in which you score points by hitting a ball thrown by a member of the other team and running round all four sides of a square. EG *I hated playing rounders at school.* N UNCOUNT

round-eyed is used to describe someone whose eyes are open very wide, usually because they are surprised or afraid. EG *Suddenly they looked like twins, both of them round-eyed.* ADJ CLASSIF

roundly /raʊndli¹/. If you are **roundly** criticized for something, you are very severely criticized; a fairly formal word. EG *They could be roundly blamed for failing to negotiate successfully... His lack of experience was roundly criticized.* ADV WITH VB = soundly

round-shouldered. Someone who is **round-shouldered** bends forward when they sit or stand, and their shoulders are curved rather than straight; used showing disapproval. EG *He's very round-shouldered.* ADJ QUALIT

round-the-clock; also spelled as three words. Something that is **round-the-clock** happens or is available all day and all night. EG *The hotel was kept under round-the-clock surveillance... They are offering free round the clock legal advice.* ADJ CLASSIF : ATTRIB

round trip, round trips; also spelled with a hyphen. A **round trip** is a journey to a particular place and back again, using either the same route or a different one. EG *He got into his car, made the eighty mile round-trip, and returned before supper.* N COUNT

roundup /raʊndʌp/, **roundups**; also spelled with a hyphen. A **roundup** is **1** a summary of news or information, especially on television or radio. EG *...a news roundup... We'll end with a roundup of the day's sport.* N COUNT + SUPP : USU SING **2** the act of gathering together animals or people, often when they do not want to be gathered together. EG *...a cattle roundup... He gave the order in February 1942 authorizing the roundup.* N COUNT : USU SING

rouse /raʊz/, **rouses, rousing, roused. 1** If someone **rouses** or you **rouse** them, they wake from their sleep; a fairly formal use. EG *I was worried when I couldn't rouse her.* V-ERG = awaken, wake up

2 If you **rouse** yourself to do something, you make yourself get up and do it. EG *There was no need to* V + O (REFL) = stir *rouse himself, heavy with Sunday lunch... After a moment he roused himself to talk to Christine.*

3 If something **rouses** you, it makes you very emotional or excited and ready to take action. EG *He roused the troops with his oratory... He could move quickly when roused to anger.* — V+O: USU+*to* = provoke, stir

4 If something **rouses** particular emotions or reactions in you, it makes you feel these emotions very strongly. EG *The proposal roused fears among the public of nuclear devastation.* — V+O: USU+A ⇑ excite = arouse

rousing /rauzɪŋ/. Something that is **rousing** makes you feel very emotional or excited and ready to take action. EG *...a rousing speech... ...a final rousing cheer from the audience.* — ADJ QUALIT = provoking, stirring

rout /raut/, **routs, routing, routed**. 1 If an army or a sports team **routs** its opponents, it defeats them completely and easily. EG *Spain could not muster sufficient resources to rout the Cubans.* — V+O

2 A **rout** is a complete defeat, often resulting in the losers fleeing in confusion. EG *The retreat turned into a rout... The terrified army finally fled in rout.* — N COUNT/UNCOUNT

rout out. If you **rout** someone or something **out**, 1 you make them come out from where they are. EG *The boys would rout out little squirrels and chase them.* 2 you search for them and find them. EG *We finally routed them out at an address in Derby.* — PHRASAL VB: V+O+ADV ⇑ find; PHRASAL VB: V+O+ADV

route /ru:t/, **routes, routing, routed**. 1 A **route** is 1.1 a way from one place to another which is well known to people, either because it has been used before or because it is shown on a map. EG *This morning I took the route through Beechwood... ...the main route out of London to the west... ...my normal Wednesday route.* ● See also **en route**. 1.2 the fixed path that is followed by ships, aeroplanes, buses, or trains when they travel between two places. EG *Standard shipping routes have been established through the North Sea... ...the Southern route around South Africa and the Indian Ocean... ...bus routes into the city centre... ...international business routes... ...the route to New York.* 1.3 the particular path that is planned in advance for a public event such as a march, race, or procession. EG *...the wedding procession route... A million people were lining the route... The boys and girls along the route cheered and waved flags.* 1.4 a method that you use to make changes and developments, or to achieve a particular aim. EG *Her book came to the screen by a somewhat circuitous route... They were looking for a route back to reality.* — N COUNT: USU+SUPP = path, road; N COUNT: USU+SUPP = lane, way, track; N SING: *the*+N ⇑ course; N COUNT+SUPP ⇑ way

2 If you **route** someone or something somewhere, you plan the route that they should follow and send them in that direction. EG *The convoys were routed individually to a rendezvous point.* — V+O: USU PASS+A ⇑ direct = assign

3 In the United States, **Route** is used before a number in the names of main roads between major cities. EG *You can't ignore the traffic signals on Route 1, can you?... We headed southward on Route 95.* — N+NUM: IN NAMES = road

route march, route marches; also spelled with a hyphen. A **route march** is a long, difficult, and tiring walk, especially one done by soldiers as a training exercise. — N COUNT = trek

routine /ru:ti:n/, **routines**. 1 **Routine** tasks and activities 1.1 typically happen as part of a normal job or of normal procedure. EG *As is so often the case with police work, it was a routine check that brought results... She reported to the committee on routine operational matters... ...routine filing, sorting, and paperwork.* ◊ **routinely**. EG *Corporations today will routinely test a product to make sure it performs adequately.* 1.2 happen so often that you consider them to be ordinary, uninteresting, and predictable. EG *Faced by relatively routine problems, he was encouraged to seek routine answers... The men at the bar began some routine banter about their wives.* — ADJ CLASSIF ⇑ regular = conventional, procedural; ◊ ADV WITH VB; ADJ QUALIT

2 A **routine** is 2.1 a way of planning your time in which you do a regular set of jobs in a fixed order so that you can organize your work efficiently. EG *That was the monthly routine... My routine was built around my children's needs... They reorganised their routines... I'm an erratic person. I don't seem to have any routine at all, really.* 2.2 the boring repetition of a set of jobs which you have to keep doing but which seem to have no purpose. EG *...the drudgery of the assembly line, with its mindless routine... ...the awesome grind of the daily routine.* 2.3 a short rehearsed sequence which forms part of a performance on stage. — N COUNT/UNCOUNT ⇑ habit = organization; N UNCOUNT+SUPP = drudgery; N COUNT

3 In informal English, if you describe someone's behaviour as being a particular **routine**, you mean that they are behaving in a way which is prepared, rehearsed, or insincere. EG *Don't give me that 'helpless stare' routine.... He launched into a whole routine.* — N SING WITH DET+SUPP ⇑ pretence = act

rove /rəuv/, **roves, roving, roved**; a literary word. 1 If you **rove** around an area or **rove** an area, you go all around without going in any particular direction. EG *No longer could they rove at will... ...the thugs who rove the streets at night.* ◊ **roving**. EG *...roving bands of gypsies.* — V+A, OR V+O = range, roam, wander; ◊ ADJ CLASSIF: ATTRIB

2 If your eyes **rove** a place or **rove** around a place, you look around there to see what you find interesting. EG *Her eyes roved the cathedral... His eyes roved happily round the countryside.* — V+O, OR V+A ⇑ move = scan

3 If someone has a **roving eye**, they always pay attention to the things that might be of benefit to them. EG *He had a roving eye for other people's property.* — PHR: USED AS O

row, rows, rowing, rowed. The word **row** is pronounced /rəu/ for paragraphs 1 to 5, and /rau/ for paragraphs 6 and 7. 1 A **row** is 1.1 a number of people or things that are arranged in a line, especially a line that goes from side to side rather than from front to back. EG *The exam took place in a large hall filled with rows of desks... He dried the cups and arranged them carefully in a row... The seeds have to be carefully planted in straight rows.* 1.2 a line of seats in a cinema, theatre, etc. EG *We were sitting in the back row... Their seats were a few rows in front of ours.* — N PART+N IN PLURAL; N COUNT

2 If an event happens a certain number of times **in a row**, it is repeated that number of times and is not interrupted by a gap or by anything happening differently. EG *She has now won the championship three times in a row... For the fifth night in a row, the temperature has fallen below zero.* — PHR: USED AS A = in succession

3 **Row** is used in the names of some streets which have an unbroken line of similar buildings on one or both sides. EG *...Savile Row... ...Southampton Row.* — N IN NAMES = terrace

4 If you **row** or you **row** a boat, you make it move through the water by using oars. EG *We rowed slowly out towards the centre of the river... One night, we rowed the four miles to the village pub... When the motor broke down, we rowed the boat back to the shore.* ▸ used as a noun. EG *We went for a row after dark.* — V: USU+A, OR V+O ⇑ propel; ▸ N SING WITH DET ⇑ trip

5 If you **row** people or goods somewhere, you transport them there in a boat, using oars. EG *They rowed us across to the other side of the lake... I rowed them there and set them ashore.* — V+O: USU+A

6 A **row** is 6.1 a noisy argument, especially between people in the same family or people who know each other very well; an informal use. EG *They were always having terrible rows... ...a family row.* 6.2 a serious disagreement or dispute about a public matter such as a government policy, especially when it is described in newspapers and on television and radio; an informal use. EG *This was basically a political row... A new row has broken out over the government's plans to cut spending on the health service.* 6.3 a very loud and unpleasant noise, for example one made by a group of people shouting; an informal use. EG *What a row they're making next door!* — N COUNT = quarrel, squabble; N COUNT = furore, storm; N COUNT = commotion, din, racket

7 If people **row**, they have a noisy argument; an informal use. EG *He never rowed with her mother, at least not in front of her.* — V OR V+A (*with*): RECIP ⇑ argue = bicker

rowboat /rəubəut/, **rowboats**. A **rowboat** is a rowing boat; used in American English. — N COUNT ⇑ boat

rowdy /raudi[1]/, **rowdier, rowdiest; rowdies**. 1 If people, their behaviour, or events are **rowdy**, they are noisy and rough and are likely to cause trouble or arguments. EG *Not all teenage boys are noisy, rowdy and active. ...a rowdy party.* ◊ **rowdiness**. EG *Their public playfulness and rowdiness suddenly cease to amuse.* — ADJ QUALIT; ◊ N UNCOUNT

2 **Rowdies** are people who are rough and noisy and are likely to cause trouble; used showing disapproval. EG *...a bunch of young rowdies making a disturbance on a street corner.* — N COUNT: USU = thug, hooligan, yob

rower /rəuə/, **rowers**. A **rower** is a person who rows a boat, especially in the sport of rowing. EG *...long-distance rowers.* — N COUNT

rowing /rəʊɪŋ/ is a sport in which people or teams race against each other in specially built rowing boats. EG *Rowing is her favourite sport.* — N UNCOUNT

rowing boat, rowing boats; also spelled with a hyphen. A **rowing boat** is a small boat that you move through the water by using oars; used in British English. EG *He climbed into the rowing boat and took the oars.* — N COUNT = rowboat

rowlock /rɒlək/, **rowlocks**. **Rowlocks** are the U-shaped pieces of metal on the sides of a rowing boat that are used to hold the oars in position as you move them backwards and forwards. EG *He took the oars from the rowlocks and laid them side by side.* — N COUNT : USU PL ⇑ device

royal /rɔɪəl/, **royals**. 1 Someone or something that is **royal** is, belongs to, or is connected with a king, a queen, or a member of their family. EG *...the royal palace... He's going to Gibraltar on the royal yacht... We had to get into our seats fifteen minutes before the royal party arrived.* • **Royal Assent**: see **assent**. — ADJ CLASSIF

2 **Royal** is used in the titles of organizations, regiments, societies, etc that are supported by or appointed by the king or queen of a country or by a member of their family. EG *...the Royal Navy... ...the Royal Academy... ...the Astronomer Royal.* — ADJ IN NAMES/TITLES

2 In informal English, the **royals** are the members of the royal family. EG *The royals hadn't put in an appearance yet.* — N COUNT : USU PL = royalty

3 **Royal** treatment or gestures are very grand or impressive. EG *On his return he was given a royal welcome.* ◊ **royally**. EG *...a private home where we were royally entertained.* — ADJ QUALIT : ATTRIB; ◊ ADV WITH VB

royal blue. Something that is **royal blue** is deep blue in colour. EG *I brought back some royal blue ones for one of my sisters.* ▸ used as a noun. — ADJ COLOUR; ▸ N UNCOUNT

royal family, royal families. The **royal family** of a country is the king or queen and the members of their family. EG *The consecration service was restricted to the royal family and their immediate entourage... There are no members of the Royal Family staying at Buckingham Palace at present.* — N COUNT : the+N : IF SING, VB CAN BE SING OR PL

Royal Highness, Royal Highnesses. You say **Your Royal Highness, His Royal Highness, Her Royal Highness**, etc when you address or refer to a member of the royal family other than the king or queen. Compare **majesty**. EG *...Her Royal Highness Princess Alexandra... Their Royal Highnesses, The Prince and Princess of Wales.* — N COUNT : DETPOSS+N, USED IN TITLES

royalist /rɔɪəlɪst/, **royalists**. A **royalist** is someone who supports a king or queen, for example in a war, or who believes that their country should have a king or queen as head of state. EG *Most royalists rejected the idea.* ▸ used as an adjective. EG *He was born in 1847 into a royalist bourgeois family in Normandy... ...an Anglican and Royalist martyr, Archbishop Laud.* — N COUNT ≠ Republican; ▸ ADJ CLASSIF

royalty /rɔɪəlti¹/, **royalties**. 1 **Royalty** 1.1 are the people who belong to a royal family. EG *...two small thrones where the old Annamese royalty had sat... It was not an official visit by royalty... After the Stuarts, royalty moved from Whitehall.* — N UNCOUNT : VB CAN BE SING OR PL **1.2** is the state or quality of having royal rank. — N UNCOUNT

2 **Royalties** are **2.1** payments made to authors, playwrights, musicians, etc who are given a fixed percentage of the profits from the sale of their books or records. Musicians, playwrights, and performers also receive royalties when their work is performed on television and radio, or in a theatre. EG *His income was founded on the royalties from his first play... He used to insist on his royalties... Howard got a large royalty cheque for his book.* — N COUNT : USU PL ⇑ revenue **2.2** payments made to someone whose invention or property is used by a commercial company. — N COUNT : USU PL ⇑ revenue

R.P. is an abbreviation for 'received pronunciation'; it is a way of pronouncing English that some people believe is correct because it is neutral and has no regional distinction. — N UNCOUNT

rpm is an abbreviation for 'revolutions per minute'; used to indicate the speed of something by saying how many times it will go round in a circle in one minute. EG *Electricity generation requires speeds of several thousand rpm.* — N COUNT : NUM+N

RSVP is an abbreviation for 'répondez s'il vous plaît', which means 'please reply'; used at the end of an invitation to a party or other meeting. — CONVENTION

Rt. Hon. is a written abbreviation for 'Right Honourable'; used in Britain as part of the formal title of members of the Privy Council and some judges. EG *...the Rt. Hon. Roy Jenkins.*

rub /rʌb/, **rubs, rubbing, rubbed**. 1 If you **rub** a part of your body, you move your hand back and forward continuously over it while pressing firmly. EG *He groaned and rubbed his eyes... He rubbed his chin thoughtfully... He coughed and rubbed at his throat.* — V+O, OR V+A = stroke

2 If you **rub** a part of your body against a surface, you move it back and forward while pressing it against the surface. EG *The cats went on crying and rubbing their legs against the caravan steps... She rubbed her cheek against my temple... Each one would rub his thumb on the back of his head.* — V+O+A = brush

3 If you **rub** a surface, you move a cloth backward and forward over it in order to clean it or dry it. EG *Peter rubbed his glasses slowly and thought... His servant was squatting by the tap, cleaning pots by rubbing them with ash... Wipe enamel parts with a damp cloth and rub them dry.* ▸ used as a noun. EG *I'll just give this a quick rub.* — V+O ⇑ polish; ▸ N COUNT : IF SING a+N

4 If you **rub** a substance into or over a surface, you press the substance into it by continuously moving something such as your hand or a cloth over it. EG *The soothing paste his father rubbed into the wound made it feel better... Jack grabbed Maurice and rubbed the stuff over his cheeks.* — V+O+A ⇑ apply

5 If you **rub** two things or if they **rub** together, you press them against each other and move them continuously backward and forward. EG *He rubbed his hands and laughed... Claude spat on the palms of his hands and rubbed them together... His massive thighs rubbed together as he walked... It sounded as if two pieces of metal were being rubbed hard together.* — V-ERG : USU+ADV *(together)*

6 If something you are wearing or sitting on **rubs**, it makes you sore because it continuously presses against you. EG *He wanted to know whether the saddles would rub, and how the camels handled the work.* — V = chafe

7 The **rub** is a particular difficulty that makes it very hard or even impossible to achieve something; an old-fashioned literary use. EG *But here was the rub: if you haven't got a work permit, you can't get a residence permit.* — N SING : the+N = obstacle, snag

8 See also **rubbing**. • to **not have two pennies to rub together**: see **penny**. • to **rub shoulders with** someone: see **shoulder**. • to **rub salt into** someone's wounds: see **salt**.

rub along. If two people **rub along** together, they are able to live or work together in a reasonably friendly way; an informal expression. — PHRASAL VB : V+ADV, USU+ADV *(together)* = get along

rub down. 1 If you **rub down** a rough surface, you make it smooth by rubbing it with something such as sandpaper. EG *Rub it down with fine steel wool or glass paper... Layers of paint dissolved in spirit have been rubbed down to get the gleaming finish of French polish.* — PHRASAL VB : V+O+ADV = sand

2 If you **rub down** a person or animal, you make them dry by rubbing them with something such as a towel or a cloth. — PHRASAL VB : V+O+ADV

rub in. 1 If someone **rubs** it **in**, they remind you of something that you do not want to be reminded of, usually because it makes you embarrassed; an informal use. EG *All right, no need to rub it in... As if to rub it in, they gave the new men only what they felt was the appearance of respect... He told us what had happened without rubbing in how wrong we had been.* — PHRASAL VB : V+O+ADV = harp on

2 If you **rub** a substance **in**, you press it into an object by continuously moving something over the surface of the object. EG *Rub in linseed oil to darken it.* — PHRASAL VB : V+O+ADV ⇑ apply

rub off. 1 If you **rub** something **off** a surface, you remove it by rubbing the surface with something such as a cloth. EG *She dipped it in the water and rubbed off the dirt with her hand.* — PHRASAL VB : V+O+ADV

2 If someone's habits or characteristics **have rubbed off** on you, you have developed the same habits or characteristics that they have, usually because you have seen them and admired them; an informal use. EG *They hoped that some of his prowess might rub off on them... Something intangible but magical for myself which had rubbed off a little on to other people.* — PHR : VB INFLECTS ⇑ spread

rub on. If you **rub** a substance **on**, you cover a surface with it by spreading it over the surface and — PHRASAL VB : V+O+ADV by rubbing with your hand or with a cloth. EG *Try a little methylated spirit rubbed on with a soft cloth.*

rub out. If you **rub out** something that you have written, you remove it by rubbing it with something such as a cloth or a rubber. PHRASAL VB : V+O+ADV = erase

rub up. If someone **rubs** you **up the wrong way**, they unintentionally make you angry or hostile by saying or doing something that offends you or annoys you. EG *She did have a way of rubbing people up the wrong way.* PHR : VB INFLECTS ⇑ annoy

rubber /rʌbə/, **rubbers**. 1 **Rubber** is a strong, waterproof, elastic substance that is made from the sap of a tropical tree or is produced chemically. Rubber is used for making tyres, boots, etc. EG *...raw rubber from Malaysia...* • See also **foam rubber**. N UNCOUNT

2 **Rubber** things are made of rubber. EG *...a man in rubber boots... ...a rubber ball... ...rubber tubing.* ADJ CLASSIF

3 A **rubber** is 3.1 a small piece of rubber that you use to rub out mistakes that you have made while writing, drawing, or typing. EG *...pencils, rubbers, and paper clips.* N COUNT = eraser 3.2 a contraceptive device worn by men; a very informal use. N COUNT = condom

4 A **rubber** is also a series of games played between the same two people or teams, for example in cricket or bridge. EG *We won the final Test and drew the rubber against Australia.* N COUNT

rubber band, rubber bands. A **rubber band** is a thin circle of very elastic rubber that you put around papers in order to hold them together. EG *Keep it in position with a rubber band or a piece of string.* N COUNT = elastic band

rubber plant, rubber plants. A **rubber plant** or **rubber tree** is a type of plant with shiny leaves that grows naturally in Asia, but is also grown in pots indoors in other parts of the world. N COUNT

rubber-stamp, rubber-stamps, rubber-stamping, rubber-stamped; also spelled as two words when used as a noun. 1 A **rubber stamp** is a small device that you use to print information such as the name of a department, the date, etc on a document such as a passport or a letter in order to show that it has been officially approved or dealt with. ▸ used to refer to the mark made by such a device. EG *Their initials were still legible on the box-shaped rubber stamp at the top of the page.* N COUNT

2 If an official body **rubber-stamp** something, they approve it or agree to it, often without thinking about it or discussing it; used showing disapproval. EG *He used the Council to rubber-stamp decisions taken by himself and his office.* V+O

rubbery /rʌbə⁰ri¹/. 1 Something that is **rubbery** looks or feels soft or elastic like rubber. EG *My legs felt rubbery from disuse... ...a long, rubbery piece of seaweed.* ADJ QUALIT

2 Meat or other food that is **rubbery** is difficult to chew. ADJ QUALIT

rubbing /rʌbɪŋ/, **rubbings**. A **rubbing** is a picture that you make by putting a piece of paper over a carved surface and rubbing wax, charcoal, etc over it. EG *...rubbings of the tombstones.* • See also **rub**. N COUNT = brass rubbing

rubbish /rʌbɪʃ/, **rubbishes, rubbishing, rubbished**. 1 **Rubbish** is unwanted things or waste material such as used paper, empty tins and bottles, waste food, and dead plants. EG *That old shed is full of rubbish... ...the basement, where the rubbish is kept... ...a local rubbish dump.* N UNCOUNT = refuse, trash

2 If you refer to something as **rubbish**, you mean that you think it is very poor quality. EG *There is so much rubbish on TV... The films she makes are never rubbish.* N UNCOUNT = trash

3 If you refer to an idea or a statement as **rubbish**, you mean that you think it is very foolish or wrong; used mainly in informal, spoken English. EG *'Don't talk rubbish'... 'Rubbish! You don't even know him!'... How can you believe such rubbish?* N UNCOUNT, OR CONVENTION ⇑ nonsense = codswallop

4 If you **rubbish** a person, their ideas, or their work, you say that they are of little value; an informal use. EG *He is often rubbished for his opinions.* V+O ⇑ criticize = run down, decry

rubbishy /rʌbɪʃi¹/. If you describe something as **rubbishy**, you mean that you think it is very poor quality; an informal word. EG *...food that they believe to be rubbishy... ...rooms which he thought rubbishy.* ADJ QUALIT = trashy

rubble /rʌbə⁰l/ **Rubble** consists of 1 the bits of brick, wood, glass, etc that remain when a building is destroyed or falls down. EG *Every building was reduced to rubble... Injured people still lay amongst the rubble.* N UNCOUNT = debris 2 small pieces of rock or stone that are used in building houses, roads, etc. EG *...a dam of sand, rubble, and rock, faced with concrete.* N UNCOUNT

rubella /ru:bɛlə/ is a disease that causes you to have a cough, a sore throat, and red spots on your skin; a medical term. EG *Girls between 11 and 13 are given rubella vaccine.* N UNCOUNT = German measles

rubicund /ru:bɪkənd/. Someone who is **rubicund** has a red face; an old-fashioned and literary word. EG *Crowe smiled, benign and rubicund... ...a rubicund sea-captain.* ADJ QUALIT

ruble /ru:bə⁰l/. See **rouble**. ⇑ money

rubric /ru:brɪk/, **rubrics**. A **rubric** is a group of words, especially a title, explanation, or rule in an official document; a formal word. EG *...the rubric about not tearing out pages... ...under the rubric, 'Art: Duties and Freedoms'.* N COUNT

ruby /ru:bi¹/, **rubies**. 1 A **ruby** is a jewel that is dark red in colour. EG *...a small ruby earring.* N COUNT ⇑ gem

2 Something that is **ruby** is dark red in colour. EG *...a light of brilliant ruby.* ADJ COLOUR OR N UNCOUNT

ruck /rʌk/, **rucks, rucking, rucked**. 1 A **ruck** is 1.1 a group of struggling people, for example in a fight or a game such as rugby; an old-fashioned or technical use. EG *...when a player has been tackled and a ruck has been formed.* N COUNT = scrum 1.2 a fold or crease in cloth or clothing. EG *...a ruck of grey blanket... His sleeves were pushed back to the elbows in heavy rucks.* N COUNT

2 The **ruck** is used to refer to ordinary people or things when you are talking about a person or thing that is much better than they are. EG *Byron lifted him out of the ruck.* N SING : *the*+N

ruck up. If cloth or a person's clothing **rucks up**, it forms folds and covers a smaller area than it did before. EG *Her dress rucked up over her thighs.* PHRASAL VB : V+ADV = crease up, bunch up

rucksack /rʌksæk/, **rucksacks**. A **rucksack** is a bag in which you can carry things on your back, for example when you are walking or climbing. It has straps that go over your shoulders. N COUNT = haversack

ruction /rʌkʃə⁰n/, **ructions**. **Ructions** are strong protests, quarrels, or other trouble; an informal word. EG *There'll be ructions when your mother hears about that!* N COUNT : USU PL ⇑ argument = row

rudder /rʌdə/, **rudders**. A **rudder** is 1 a vertical piece of wood or metal at the back of a boat which is used to steer the boat. EG *Mary pulled her left rudder string... ...using the pole as a rudder.* N COUNT 2 a vertical piece of metal at the back of an aeroplane which is used to make it turn in a sideways direction. EG *At takeoff, he had his feet braced on the rudder pedal.* N COUNT

ruddy /rʌdi¹/, **ruddier, ruddiest**. 1 If you describe someone as **ruddy**, you mean that their skin or face is reddish in colour, usually because of good health, embarrassment, anger, or hard work. EG *Barber's normally ruddy face was white with tension... His cheeks were ruddy and gleamed with sweat.* ADJ COLOUR ⇑ red

2 Something that is **ruddy** is reddish in colour; a rather literary use. EG *The craft still burned, throwing a ruddy glare into the night sky.* ADJ COLOUR ⇑ red

3 **Ruddy** is used as a swear word in order to emphasize what you are saying or to express anger; a rather old-fashioned use. ADJ CLASSIF, OR ADV

rude /ru:d/, **ruder, rudest**. 1 If someone is **rude**, they are not polite in their behaviour towards other people. EG *I was rather rude to a young nurse... It's rude to stare... ...making rude remarks about me.* ADJ QUALIT = impolite ◇ **rudely**. EG *The President cannot rudely ignore a head of state.* ◇ ADV WITH V ◇ **rudeness**. EG *He seemed not to notice their rudeness.* ◇ N UNCOUNT = disrespect

2 **Rude** is used to describe words or behaviour that are likely to embarrass or offend other people, usually words or behaviour relating to sex or other bodily functions. EG *...a rude gesture... ...a rude joke... ...a rude noise.* ADJ QUALIT = dirty, naughty

3 A **rude** event is one that is unexpected and unpleasant; a rather literary use. EG *...a rude awakening to the realization that he had been robbed.* ADJ QUALIT : ATTRIB ⇑ harsh ◇ **rudely**. EG *My belief in the future was rudely shattered.* ◇ ADV WITH V ⇑ harshly

4 A **rude** object or building is one that is very simply and roughly made; a literary use. EG *I sat on the edge of one of the rude tables... ...a rude shelter facing the sea.* ADJ QUALIT : ATTRIB = crude

rudimentary /ru:dɪmɛntə⁰ri¹/; a formal word. 1 Something that is **rudimentary** is very basic or undeveloped and therefore unsatisfactory. EG ...a ADJ QUALIT = crude, primitive *rather rudimentary planning system... ...a handful of workers using rudimentary equipment.*

2 Knowledge that is **rudimentary** includes only the simplest and most important facts. EG *I had gathered only the most rudimentary information... ...rudimentary mathematics.* ADJ QUALIT = elementary

rudiments /ruːdɪmə²nts/. The **rudiments** of a subject or activity are the simplest and most important things about it which you need to know in order to understand it or to do it. EG *I had time to pick up the rudiments of driving... He was teaching them the rudiments of Christianity.* N PLURAL: the+N, USU+of = basics, fundamentals

rue /ruː/, **rues, ruing, rued.** If you **rue** an action, event, or decision, you regret it because it has unpleasant results; an old-fashioned or literary word. EG *I said, 'Sure, I'll drive you over,' words I was to rue before sunset... Karen rued the day she had opened that secret door.* V+O

rueful /ruːfʊl/. If someone is **rueful**, they feel or express regret or sorrow in a quiet and gentle way; a literary word. EG *She managed a rueful little smile... ...rueful contemplation of a life full of errors.* ADJ QUALIT = doleful
◇ **ruefully.** EG *He said ruefully, 'I fear it will be Fanny.'* ◇ ADV WITH VB = dolefully

ruff /rʌf/, **ruffs.** A **ruff** is 1 a stiff strip of cloth or other material with many small folds in it, which was worn round the neck in former times. EG *...a ruff of lace.* N COUNT ⇑ collar 2 a thick band of feathers or fur round the neck of a bird or animal. EG *...a deep brown ruff beneath the beak.* N COUNT ⇑ ring

ruffian /rʌfɪən/, **ruffians.** A **ruffian** is a person who is violent and often involved in criminal activity; an old-fashioned word. EG *...thieves, ruffians, murderers... Some local ruffians are responsible for this.* N COUNT = brute, villain, thug

ruffle /rʌfə⁰l/, **ruffles, ruffling, ruffled.** 1 If you **ruffle** someone's hair, you move your hand quickly and fairly roughly over their head as a way of showing affection. EG *...hugging him, kissing him, ruffling his hair.* V+O ⇑ disarrange

2 If you **ruffle** the pages of a book, newspaper, etc, you turn them over quickly. EG *She ruffled the pages of the notebook, searching for extracts.* V+O = riffle

3 When a bird **ruffles** its feathers, it causes them to stand out stiffly on its body, for example when it is afraid or is cleaning itself. EG *The bird will squat on its nest with feathers ruffled.* V+O

4 When something **ruffles** the sea, the grass, etc, it causes the surface to become uneven and wavy; a literary use. EG *...a stiff breeze ruffling the surface of the sea... ...the surface ruffled by flurries of mackerel.* V+O = ripple

5 **Ruffles** are small folds made in a piece of material or sewn onto it in order to decorate it. EG *...a dress adorned with ruffles and ribbons.* N COUNT: USU PL ⇑ decoration = frills

ruffled /rʌfə⁰ld/. 1 If someone is **ruffled**, they are surprised, confused, or annoyed. EG *He was not easily ruffled... 'Why don't you come back later?' said Alex, mildly ruffled.* ADJ QUALIT = flustered, perturbed

2 Something that is **ruffled** is no longer smooth or neat. EG *...the ruffled bed-clothes... She emerged, her hair ruffled and her face red... ...the black, ruffled waters.* ADJ QUALIT = rumpled, dishevelled

3 **Ruffled** clothes are decorated with small folds of material. EG *...a ruffled white blouse.* ADJ CLASSIF

rug /rʌg/, **rugs.** 1 A **rug** is a piece of thick material like a carpet but covering only a small area. Rugs are usually made of wool. EG *...kneeling on the hearth rug... The floor was covered with rugs and cushions.* N COUNT = mat
● to **sweep** something **under the rug**: see **sweep**. 2 A **rug** is also a small blanket which you use to cover your shoulders or your knees. EG *...her hands clasped together tight under the rug... She took a tartan rug out of her case.* N COUNT

rugby /rʌgbi¹/ is a game in which two teams try to score points by carrying an oval ball across a line at the end of a grass pitch, or by kicking the ball over a bar fixed between two goalposts. N UNCOUNT = rugger, rugby football

rugged /rʌgɪ²d/; a rather literary word. 1 A **rugged** area of land is rocky, uneven, and difficult to travel over or find shelter in. EG *The coastline is wild and rugged.* ADJ QUALIT ⇑ rough

2 If you describe a man as **rugged**, you mean that he has strong features, almost as if they have been carved out of stone. EG *He was rugged and handsome... ...rugged faces.* ADJ QUALIT = craggy

3 If you describe someone's character as **rugged**, you mean that they are honest, determined, and not easily upset, but may sometimes seem impolite. EG *They were a rugged and friendly lot of people... ...the tradition of rugged independence... ...Harry's rugged personality.* ADJ QUALIT

4 A **rugged** piece of equipment is made of strong material and is designed not to break easily or stop working even in severe conditions. EG *The projector was of unusually rugged construction... The batteries are rugged and reliable.* ADJ QUALIT = heavy-duty

rugger /rʌgə/ is rugby; a rather old-fashioned word. N UNCOUNT

ruin /ruːɪn/, **ruins, ruining, ruined.** 1 To **ruin** something means to severely damage or spoil it. EG *You are ruining your health... India's textile industry was ruined... ...ruining their relations with the unions... Villages had been burned and ruined.* V+O ⇑ harm = destroy
◇ **ruined.** EG *...the ruined patch of garden... ...my ruined career.* ◇ ADJ CLASSIF = wrecked

2 To **ruin** someone means to cause them to spend or lose all their money. EG *The contract would certainly have ruined him...* ◇ **ruined.** EG *...a ruined man.* V+O (NG/REFL) ⇑ impoverish ◇ ADJ CLASSIF

3 **Ruin** is 3.1 the state of being severely damaged or spoiled, or the process of reaching this state. EG *The villages are crumbling into ruin... The regime collapsed in total ruin.* ● to **go to rack and ruin**: see **rack**. N UNCOUNT = destruction 3.2 the state of no longer having any money. EG *Crow was heading for ruin... ...the idiots who had once more led us to ruin.* N UNCOUNT = penury, bankruptcy

4 The **ruins** of a building are the parts of it that remain after the rest has been destroyed or allowed to fall down. EG *...the ruins of a castle... Some of the houses were no more than ruins... It was very splendid once, but it is a ruin now.* N COUNT: USU PL, SING=PL = remains, shell

5 The **ruins** of something are the parts of it that remain after it has been severely damaged or spoiled. EG *The Progressive Party was founded on the ruins of our Federal Party... ...the ruins of my professional reputation.* N COUNT: USU PL, SING=PL

6 If a building or place is **in ruins**, it has been very badly damaged or neglected, and only parts of it remain. EG *...the splendid medieval castle, partly in ruins, stands on a crag... Bremen was in ruins.* PHR: USED AS AN A

7 If something is **in ruins**, it is completely spoiled. EG *Their once robust economy still lies in ruins... ...a civilization that was in ruins... Their friendship was in ruins.* PHR: USED AS AN A = destroyed, devastated

ruination /ruːɪneɪʃə⁰n/ is the act of ruining something or the process of being ruined. EG *...the ruination of fields and crops by chemical sprays... He muttered wildly about the ruination of his life.* N UNCOUNT = destruction, spoiling

ruined /ruːɪnd/. A **ruined** building has been partly destroyed or has gradually fallen down because of neglect. EG *...a ruined castle.* ADJ CLASSIF: ATTRIB

ruinous /ruːɪnəs/. 1 If something is **ruinous**, it costs far more money than you can afford or than is reasonable. EG *...the ruinous expense of a funeral... You went to the banks and paid ruinous interest.* ADJ CLASSIF ⇑ expensive
◇ **ruinously.** EG *...a long and ruinously expensive visit.* ◇ ADV+ADJ/ADV

2 A **ruinous** process or course of action is one that is likely to lead you to ruin. ADJ CLASSIF = disastrous

rule /ruːl/, **rules, ruling, ruled.** 1 **Rules** are official instructions, often written down, which tell you what you are allowed to do and what you are not allowed to do in a game or in a particular place or situation. EG *...the rules of chess... It is against the rules to keep pets... This is forbidden under rule 7(c)... Anyone who breaks the rules will be punished... ...the rules and regulations governing safety at work.* N COUNT: USU PL = regulation

2 A **rule** is 2.1 the course of action that you should take in order to do something properly or to achieve a particular goal. EG *The rule is: if in doubt, dry clean... The most important rule is to consult the doctor promptly... There are two important rules to follow.* N COUNT = guideline 2.2 a statement that describes the way that things usually happen in a system, for example in a language. EG *There are rules for relating English spelling and pronunciation... A computer's behaviour follows rules.* N COUNT 2.3 the way of behaving or taking part in something that most people agree is right and acceptable. EG *...the rules of conduct of the society in which they live... We adhered to the rule of only using chemical weapons in retaliation... He broke the rule that family discord should never reach the ears of outsiders.* N COUNT = convention

3 If something is **the rule**, it is the normal state of N SING: the+N = norm

affairs. EG *Short haircuts became the rule... Breast feeding is the exception rather than the rule... One-room dwellings are the rule in these areas.*

4 If you say that something is true or happens **as a rule** or **as a general rule**, you mean that it is usually true or normally happens. EG *The traffic consisted as a rule of nothing faster than bullock carts... Doctors are not as a rule trained in child rearing... As a general rule, the less important an executive is, the more status-conscious he is likely to be.* PHR : USED AS ADV SEN = generally, ordinarily

5 If you **make a rule** or **make it a rule** to do something, you try always to do that thing in a particular situation. EG *Make a rule never to take a decision if you are upset... You should make it a rule always to keep check of who has what.* PHR : VB INFLECTS, USU + *to*-INF

6 If someone in authority **bends the rules** or **stretches the rules**, they allow someone to do something, even though it is against the rules, because they think that it is justifiable in the particular circumstances. EG *Couldn't you bend the rules slightly?* PHR : VB INFLECTS

7 To **rule** a country or group of people means to have the power to control their affairs, and to use that power. EG *...feudal states, ruled by autocratic kings... The military government went on ruling the country... Computers might rule the world one day.* V+O, OR V+A (*over*) = govern

8 **Rule** is **8.1** the government of a country by a group or by a foreign country. EG *...the dangers of one-party rule... ...the days of British rule.* N UNCOUNT+SUPP **8.2** the power of control or the system of control over a group of people. EG *Rule by intimidation proved the best method in the classroom.* N UNCOUNT+SUPP

9 If something **rules**, it is the most powerful and influential feature of a particular situation. EG *Love did indeed seem to rule... Obviously economic forces rule.* V = prevail, reign

10 You sometimes see **United rules OK**, **Baz rules OK**, etc written on a wall or public place as a claim that the team, person, etc that is named is better than any other. CONVENTION

11 If an idea or feeling **rules** someone, it controls or strongly influences what they think or do. EG *Her love life is ruled by fear of pregnancy.* V+O

12 If someone in authority **rules** on a particular situation or problem, they give an official decision about it. EG *I was asked to rule on the case of a British seaman... The resolution was ruled out of order... The Supreme Court ruled that there was no federal offence involved.* V+A, OR V+REPORT-CL ⇑ decide = judge

13 A **rule** is also a piece of wood, plastic, or metal with straight edges marked in inches or centimetres, which you use for measuring things or drawing straight lines. N COUNT = ruler

14 If you **rule** straight lines, you draw them using something that has a straight edge. EG *I carefully ruled a margin.* V+O

15 See also **golden rule**, **ground rule**, **ruled**, **ruling**, **slide rule**, and **work-to-rule**. • **rule of thumb**: see **thumb**.

rule off. If you **rule off** a section on a piece of paper, you draw a straight line below it on the paper to divide it from the next section. PHRASAL VB : V+O+ADV

rule out. 1 If you **rule out** an idea, solution, or course of action, you decide that it is impossible, unsuitable, or not worth considering. EG *Washington need not rule out a selective military aid program... Police have ruled out murder but are still holding several people for questioning.* PHRASAL VB : V+O+ADV = dismiss, exclude

2 If one thing **rules out** another, it prevents it from happening or being possible. EG *A search had ruled out the possibility of further bombs... The radio was on, effectively ruling out conversation.* PHRASAL VB : V+O+ADV = eliminate, preclude

rule book, rule books. A **rule book** contains the official rules for a particular job, organization, etc. EG *He relied on his own initiative, instead of on the rule book... The rule book said he should be provided with protective clothing.* N COUNT : USU *the*+N IN SING • If someone does something **by the rule book**, they do it in the way that is considered to be correct or reasonable in a particular situation; an informal expression. EG *They aren't fighting by the rule book, so why should we?* • PHR : USED AS AN A

ruled /ru:ld/. **Ruled** paper has thin, straight lines printed across it. EG *She began to write on the ruled paper.* ADJ CLASSIF : ATTRIB = lined

rule of law. The **rule of law** refers to a situation in which the people in a society obey its laws and enable it to function properly; a formal expression. EG *A free society depends on the rule of law... It was essential to uphold the rule of law.* N SING : *the*+N

ruler /ru:lə/, **rulers**. 1 A **ruler** is a person such as a king, queen, or prime minister, who rules or governs a country or other area. EG *Caesar was then ruler of Persia... ...the world's rulers.* N COUNT

2 A **ruler** is also a long flat piece of wood, metal, or plastic with straight edges and marked in inches or centimetres, which you use to measure things or to draw straight lines. EG *...a six-inch ruler.* N COUNT = rule

ruling /ru:lɪŋ/. 1 The **ruling** group of people in an organization or country is the group in it that controls its affairs. EG *...the Church's ruling body... The ruling class will not surrender its wealth and power.* ADJ CLASSIF : ATTRIB = in power

2 A **ruling** idea or feeling is one that controls or strongly influences what a person thinks or does. EG *The threat of violent death is their ruling fear.* ADJ CLASSIF : ATTRIB = predominant

3 A **ruling** is an official decision made by a judge or court. EG *The Supreme Court ruling still stands... The judge gave his ruling... ...the ruling on the Rhondda case.* N COUNT ⇑ judgement

rum /rʌm/, **rums**. 1 **Rum** is an alcoholic drink made from sugar cane juice. EG *He sipped his rum... ...a bottle of rum.* N MASS

2 If you describe someone or something as **rum**, you mean that they are rather unusual, strange, or puzzling; used mainly in informal old-fashioned British English. EG *They were rum old boys... ...rum ideas... In a rum sort of way, Charles had helped enormously.* ADJ QUALIT = peculiar

Rumanian. See **Romanian**.

rumble /rʌmbəºl/, **rumbles, rumbling, rumbled**. 1 A **rumble** is **1.1** a low, continuous, throbbing sound. EG *...a menacing rumble of distant thunder... ...the rumble of a passing truck.* N COUNT **1.2** a low noise made by a lot of people speaking. EG *...the rumble of masculine voices in the smoky room.* N COUNT+*of* ⇑ murmur

2 If something **rumbles**, **2.1** it makes a low, continuous, throbbing sound. EG *His stomach was already rumbling for breakfast... ...the rumbling noises of barrels being rolled down the ramp.* V **2.2** it moves slowly, making a low, continuous, throbbing sound. EG *The bus rumbled into Lerwick at ten.* V+A

3 If someone **rumbles** or **rumbles on**, they continue to talk for a long time in a boring way. EG *He rumbled on in this vein for some time.* ▸ used of a conversation or discussion. EG *The argument rumbled on.* V, OR PHRASAL VB : V+ADV ▸ = drone

4 If you **rumble** someone or something, you find out their real character, intention, or purpose, which was being deliberately concealed; an informal use. EG *I rumbled her all right... You've rumbled that already, surely.* V+O ⇑ discover = twig

rumbling /rʌmblɪŋ/, **rumblings**. 1 A **rumbling** is a low, continuous, throbbing sound. EG *There was a distant rumbling and the air-conditioning came on... ...the rumbling of thunder.* N COUNT = rumble

2 **Rumblings** are signs that people are becoming dissatisfied or that a bad situation is developing. EG *There were rumblings of discontent... ...the first rumblings of World War II.* N COUNT : USU PLURAL

ruminate /ru:mɪneɪt/, **ruminates, ruminating, ruminated**. 1 If you **ruminate**, you think about something very carefully; a formal use. EG *The electorate ruminated over its choice of government... She ruminated a bit longer and then said, 'Older, I think.'* V : USU+A = ponder, deliberate

2 When animals such as cows, sheep, or deer **ruminate**, they bring food back from their stomach into their mouth and chew it again; a technical use. EG *...a ruminating ox.* V = chew the cud

rumination /ru:mɪneɪʃəºn/, **ruminations**. Your **ruminations** are your careful thoughts about something; a literary word. EG *...their inspector's ruminations... ...the ruminations of my disciples.* N COUNT : USU WITH POSS

ruminative /ru:mɪnətɪv/. If you are **ruminative**, you are thinking very deeply and carefully about something; a literary word. ▸ used to describe periods of time or situations. EG *...a ruminative twenty minutes.* ◊ **ruminatively**. EG *He stares into it ruminatively... He drove back ruminatively to the school.* ADJ QUALIT ⇑ thoughtful = contemplative ◊ ADV WITH V = pensively

rummage /rʌmɪdʒ/, **rummages, rummaging, rummaged**. 1 If you **rummage** in a particular place or among a group of things, you search for something by moving things around in a hurried or careless way. EG *He rummaged around in his draw-* V+A = scour, ransack

er... ...rummaging among the books and magazines... She rummaged until she found a tiny key. ▸ used as a noun. EG *He had a good rummage inside the sofa.* ▸ N SING : a+N ⇑ hunt

2 Rummage is old or unwanted things that people give away, especially to a charity, to be sold; used in American English. EG *She sorted through the clothes–this for rummage, that for mending and cleaning... ...rummage sales and church bazaars.* N UNCOUNT = jumble

rummy /rʌmi¹/ is a card game in which players try to collect cards of the same value or cards in a sequence in the same suit. N UNCOUNT

rumour /ru:mə/, **rumours, rumouring, rumoured**; also spelled **rumor** in American English. **1** A **rumour** is a story or piece of information that may or may not be true, but that people are talking about. EG *There's a rumour that Mangel is coming here to speak... A number of rumours were circulating in Fleet Street... ...rumours of street fighting and violence.* N COUNT : IF + PREP THEN *of*, OR + REPORT-CL

2 You use the word **rumour** to refer to information or sources of information that are considered to be unreliable. EG *Rumour has it that she's pregnant... There is nothing against him but rumour... ...the wave of rumour and alarm.* N UNCOUNT ⇑ talk = gossip, hearsay

3 If something **is rumoured**, people are suggesting that it is true, but do not know for certain. EG *It was rumoured that the body had been removed from the coffin... He was rumored to be living in Detroit.* V+O : ONLY PASS ⇑ be said

rump /rʌmp/, **rumps. 1** Someone's **rump** is their buttocks; used mainly in a humorous way. EG *He rubbed his rump.* N COUNT = bottom

2 The **rump** of an animal or bird is its rear end. EG *He sent the horse forward with a slap on its rump.* N COUNT

3 Rump or **rump steak** is meat which is cut from the rear end of a cow. EG *Rump and topside are the best pieces of beef for roasting.* N UNCOUNT

4 The **rump** of a group or organization, especially a political party, consists of the few members who remain in it or who are loyal to it after the rest have left it or lost their power. EG *The party has dwindled to a disorganized rump... The rump assembly came together in March.* N COUNT : USU SING+SUPP ⇑ remnant

rumple /rʌmpəᵒl/, **rumples, rumpling, rumpled.** If you **rumple** something, you cause it to be untidy, creased, or disordered; an informal word. EG *...rumpling the papers on her desk... He rumpled her hair.* ◇ **rumpled.** EG *Melanie answered the door looking flushed and rumpled... ...a large bed, rumpled and unmade... ...a rumpled grey suit.* V+O = ruffle ◇ ADJ QUALIT = crumpled

rumpus /rʌmpəs/. A **rumpus** is a lot of noise or a strong protest or argument; an informal word. EG *Only Arthur raised a rumpus... They caused a rumpus in the House of Commons... He heard the rumpus and came to the rescue... ...the rumpus about the cover.* N SING WITH DET ⇑ disturbance = commotion, furore

run /rʌn/, **runs, running, ran.** The form **run** is used in the present tense of the verb and is also the past participle. **1** When you **run**, you move faster than when you walk, by taking long strides and lifting both feet off the ground during each stride. EG *I ran downstairs to open the door... He jumped to the ground and ran... He went running to meet them... A dog was running around in the yard.* ▸ used as a noun. EG *He found himself breaking into a run.* V : USU+A, OR V +*to*-INF ▸ N SING : a+N

2 If you **run** or you **run** a particular distance, you run for pleasure or as a sport, for example in a race. EG *He has been running for 12 years... He ran the mile... Coe ran in the 1500 metres last night... The girls were in the field running races.* ▸ used as a noun. EG *Let the children have a run outside before settling down to work... He goes for a five-mile run every morning.* V : USU+A, OR V +O ▸ N COUNT : USU SING

3 If you **run** from a particular place or situation, you escape from it by going away quickly. EG *'Let's run,' he said. 'Let's stay and fight,' I said... We'll look very foolish if we turn and run now.* V : USU+A = flee

4 If you **run** around, about, or all over, you hurry from one place to another. EG *He had been running all over New York trying to find me.* V+A

5 If you **run** to someone, you go to them for help, advice, protection, etc. EG *He was always trying to run home to his mother... I didn't think he'd run to you with the story.* V : USU+A *(to)*

6 In games such as cricket and baseball, if you **run**, you hurry between marked places in order to score points or to stay in the game. EG *They ran three.* V+O (NG/NUM), OR V

7 If you **run** in an election, you are a candidate trying to get elected to an official post. EG *He ran for Governor... McGovern started to run against Nixon... Foot will not be running in the next election.* V+A ⇑ stand

8 If you **run** a horse or dog in a race or if it **runs** in it, it competes against other horses or dogs in the race. EG *...a horse running in the Derby... We shall run Red Rum against him at Roxburgh.* V-ERG : USU+A

9 If someone **runs** people or things into a country or area, they take them there secretly and illegally. EG *...running agents into enemy territory... ...a smuggler running diamonds from a lonely fishing village.* ▸ used as a noun. EG *If we need more, we can make a run across the border.* V+O+A = smuggle ▸ N COUNT : USU SING

10 If you **run** an object or your hand over something, you make the object or your hand touch it and move over it. EG *He ran his hand over her hair... She ran her finger down a list of names.* V+O+A = pass

11 If you **run** something such as a shop, business, organization, etc, you are in charge of it. EG *She ran the office as a captain runs a ship... He's just running it while the owner's away... ...a sloppily run hospital.* V+O ⇑ manage

12 If you **run** a service, an academic course, etc, you make it available to people or you teach it. EG *They run a library service... We've run a course for local teachers.* V+O ⇑ operate = provide

13 If you **run** an experiment, computer program, or other process, you start it and continue it until it finishes or until you achieve the results that you wanted. EG *Check everything and run the whole test again... We've run it through the computer a dozen times... ...the battle he was running with the council.* V+O

14 If you **run** a machine, you operate it or make it work properly. EG *You don't need a degree in mathematics to run a computer.* V+O

15 If you **run** a car or piece of equipment, you have it and use it. EG *My mother runs her own car... A freezer doesn't cost much to run.* V+O

16 When a machine **is running**, it is switched on and operating. EG *The engine was running.* V ⇑ go

17 If you **run** a machine on or off a particular source of energy, or if it **runs** on or off it, you use that source of energy to make it work. EG *You can run the entire system off a mains plug... The heater ran on half-price electricity.* V-ERG+A

18 If you **run** somewhere in a car, you make a short trip in it. EG *Why don't we run down to Worcester for the afternoon?* ▸ used as a noun. EG *I was taking her for a run in the car... We did runs further north.* V+A ⇑ visit ▸ N COUNT : USU SING

19 If you **run** someone somewhere in a car, you drive them there. EG *Would you mind running me to the station?* V+O+A

20 If you **run** a vehicle somewhere or it **runs** there, it moves to a particular place or in a particular direction. EG *Run the car into the garage before you go... The cart ran down the road out of control.* V-ERG+A

21 If a train, bus, etc **runs** somewhere, it travels on a regular route at set times. EG *...the ferry that runs to Spain... The buses run every hour.* ▸ used as a noun. EG *For years it was the fastest boat on the run... He does the West Africa run.* V-ERG+A ⇑ go ▸ N COUNT : USU SING+SUPP

22 If an object such as a ball **runs** somewhere, it moves smoothly and quickly over the ground. EG *The ball ran to the boundary.* V+A

23 If a liquid **runs** somewhere, it flows in a particular place or direction. EG *Tears were running down the side of his face... The water ran into a bucket.* V+A

24 If you **run** water using a piece of equipment such as a tap or a hose, you cause water to flow from it. EG *She was running hot water into the tub... Uncle Ted ran the hose over the lawn.* V+O : USU+A

25 If you **run** a bath, you fill it with water. V+O

26 If a river, the sea, or the water in it **runs** in a particular way, it flows or becomes the way that is mentioned. EG *The river was running clear... The waters of the sea ran a milky white.* V+C

27 If the tide **is running**, it causes the water in a river or sea to rise higher or flow faster. V : USU CONT

28 If your nose **is running**, mucus is flowing out of it, usually because you have a cold. V : USU CONT ⇑ discharge

29 If a fabric or piece of clothing **runs** or if the colour in it **runs**, the colour in it dissolves in the water when you wash it, and the fabric becomes a lighter shade. EG *You can tell whether the colour will run by wetting a corner of it in hot water.* V = bleed

30 If butter, wax, or a similar substance **runs**, it melts and begins to flow, usually because it is too hot. EG *It was such a hot day that the butter ran.* V

31 If plants **run** in a particular place or a particular V+A way, they grow and spread there or in that way. EG ...*with ivy running wild all over the walls... Bindweed ran up the stems of the corn.*

32 If your life or an activity **runs** in a particular way, it develops or progresses in that way. EG *Life is running smoothly for them... Our careers seemed to run on parallel lines.* V+A

33 If a feeling **runs** through your body, it passes through it quickly and strongly. EG *A sharp tingling sensation ran through her... A thrill ran down her spine.* V+A ⇑ move

34 If people or their emotions **are running** in a particular way, they are experiencing a strong emotion. EG *Public indignation was running high... Tempers were running thin... The chiefs were running scared.* V+C: USU CONT ⇑ be

35 If your thoughts **run** to something or if a thought **runs** in your mind, you start thinking about it and concentrating on it. EG *Her thoughts ran to her dead father... A warm bed ran in his mind.* V+A *(to/in)*

36 If newspapers or magazines **run** a particular item or story, they publish it. EG *The local newspaper ran a feature on Liverpool... We ran articles in Afrikaans in the paper.* V+O

37 You use the word **run** to indicate that you are quoting words or ideas that are not your own. EG *'Attack on mother-to-be' ran the Evening News headline... Social differentiation, the argument runs, will produce democracy.* V+QUOTE/REPORT-CL

38 If you say that something long, such as a road, **runs** in a particular place or direction, you are describing its position in relation to other places. EG *The reef runs parallel to the coast... ...a tunnel running from the Mediterranean into the Dead Sea... The road ran between the hills... Black iron railings ran around the garden.* V+A ⇑ go

39 If a feature **runs** from one end of a list, process, or system to the other, it exists in every item on the list or in all parts of the process or system. EG *...the nations of Africa running alphabetically from Algeria to Zaire... ...a chain of command running from the boss down to the lowliest worker...* V+A *(from...to)* ⇑ go

40 If something **is running** at a particular amount or rate, it regularly reaches that amount or rate over a period of time; a formal or technical use. EG *Urban unemployment is running at 20 per cent... ...grants running at 85,000 pounds... ...industry running at 75 per cent of capacity.* V+O+A *(at)*: USU CONT

41 If an event **runs** for a particular period of time, it continues to take place during that time before it finishes. EG *The class runs over three years... The monsoons had six weeks more to run... The campaign runs for four or five months.* V+A ⇑ last

42 If a production of a play, opera, or ballet **runs** for a particular period of time, it continues to be performed during that period. EG *Chu-Chin-Chow ran for years... The play ran a long time and did good business.* V+A

43 If someone or something **runs** early, late, on time, etc, they are taking less time, more time, or exactly the same time as had been planned or expected. EG *I'm running a bit over time, I'm afraid... Our programmes are running a few minutes late this evening.* V+A

44 If a legal document or contract **runs** for a particular period of time, it remains valid only for that time. EG *...summer tenants whose leases ran from 15 June to 15 September... My insurance policy's only got another week to run.* V+A

45 If you say that a particular characteristic **runs** in someone's family, you mean that most of the members of that family have it. EG *Twins run in my family.* V+A

46 If you say that a situation, especially a game, **runs** for a person or team or in their favour, or that it **runs** against them, you mean that it develops in a way that makes them more likely to win or lose, usually because of luck and not because of skill or effort. EG *The game was running against his side.* V+A = go

47 If stockings or tights **run**, they become damaged and gaps appear in a vertical line affecting several rows of stitches. ▸ used as a noun. EG *Bother! I've got a run in my new tights.* V = ladder ▸ N COUNT = ladder

48 A **run** is also **48.1** a particular long-distance running race. EG *Bernie won the Cardiff run in 2 hrs 26 mins.* N COUNT: *the*+MOD+N **48.2** a course or route which has been specially designed for a sport such as skiing. EG *The ski run had been closed to beginners... ...the Cresta Run.* N COUNT: USU MOD+N **48.3** a flight in an aeroplane during a war in order to drop bombs on the enemy. EG *We made three runs before we saw the target.* N COUNT = raid, mission

49 A **run** for something is an attempt to win or gain something, especially to get elected to a political post. EG *McGovern's run for the presidency... ...an open run for power.* N SING WITH DET +SUPP = bid

50 In the theatre, a **run** is the period of time during which a production of a play, opera, or ballet is performed. EG *...after the long run of 'Hamlet'... ...during its thirteen-week run at the Apollo Theatre.* N COUNT+SUPP

51 A **run** of good luck, bad luck, success, or failure is a continuous period of it. EG *This policy has had an unending run of success in Africa... They've had a good run without illness... Leeds United had a run of wins about December.* N COUNT+SUPP: USU SING

52 If there is a **run** on a bank, everybody wants to withdraw their money from it because they have lost confidence in it. N SING: *a*+N+*on*

53 If there is a **run** on a particular product or item which is for sale, there is a great demand for it, so that it soon becomes difficult to obtain. EG *There's been a run on tickets for the opera this week.* N SING: *a*+N+*on*

54 In a company or factory, a **run** is the amount of a particular type of product that the company or factory decides to produce at one time or over a particular period of time; a technical use. EG *The longer the production run of a product, the lower the unit cost... ...a trial run of 50,000.* N COUNT: USU SING

55 In games such as cricket and baseball, a **run** is a score of one, which is made by players running between marked places on the pitch after hitting the ball. EG *They had beaten England by seventeen runs to win the fifth Test.* N COUNT

56 In music, a **run** is a sequence of musical notes that are played quickly one after the other; a technical use. N COUNT

57 The average, usual, or common **run** of people or things means all the ordinary ones, when you are saying that a particular person or thing is different from or better than they are; an informal or literary use. EG *Politicians seem to be more fallible than the average run of mankind... The rioters were not the usual run of urban malcontents but men of responsibility... He and his family were all out of the common run, vital and clever.* N SING: *the*+N+SUPP ⇑ type

58 The **run** of a situation, especially a game, is the general way in which it develops, especially when it seems more likely to end in victory or advantage for a particular person or team. EG *They scored against the run of play.* N SING: *the*+N+SUPP

59 If someone has **the runs**, they have diarrhoea; a very informal use. N PLURAL: *the*+N

60 If someone is **on the run**, **60.1** they are trying to escape or hide from someone such as the police or an enemy. EG *Al was an ex-convict, on the run from his probation officer... If anything should go wrong, you might have to go on the run.* PHR: USED AS A **60.2** they are being severely defeated in a contest or competition. EG *The Conservatives are on the run throughout Wales.* PHR: USED AS A **60.3** they are always busy or in a hurry; an informal use. EG *She's always on the run.* PHR: USED AS A

61 If an army is **on the run** or if you have them **on the run**, they are retreating fast. PHR: USED AS A

62 If you do something **at a run**, you do it quickly, by running. EG *The stretchers were carried at a run from the helicopter to the medical tent.* PHR: USED AS A

63 If a river, well, etc **runs dry**, it ceases to have any water in it. EG *That year, even our well ran dry.* PHR: VB INFLECTS

64 If something **runs dry**, it comes to an end. EG *The stream of enquiries never ran dry.* PHR: VB INFLECTS

65 The word **run** is also used in the following expressions. **65.1** If you **give** someone **a run for** their **money**, you try hard to beat them in a contest or competition and you force them to use all their strength or skill before they can succeed in winning. EG *I'm sure he'll give McEnroe a good run for his money.* PHR: VB INFLECTS ⇑ tax **65.2** If someone **has had a good run for** their **money**, they have had a reasonable period of success or power. EG *The Government have had a good long run for their money, it's time for a change.* PHR: VB INFLECTS **65.3** If you talk about a situation **in the long run**, you are saying what you think is possible or will happen over a long period of time in the future. If you talk about a situation **in the short run**, you are saying what you think is possible or will happen in the near future. EG PHR: USED AS A

Computers can, in the long run, be made more secure than any bank... Their policy would prove very costly in the long run... Money will get you what you want-but only in the short run. **65.4** If you **make a run for it** or if you **run for it**, you go somewhere quickly in order to escape from a place or situation. EG *It was still raining hard, but we made a run for it... We'll just have to run for it.* PHR : VB INFLECTS ⇑ flee **65.5** If you say that someone will **run a mile** if something happens, you mean that they do their best to avoid a particular situation. EG *If he saw your dog, any burglar would run a mile.* PHR : VB INFLECTS **65.6** If you **run a temperature** or **run a fever**, your body's temperature is higher than normal because you are ill. EG *Nancy began to run a fever.* PHR : VB INFLECTS, USU CONT **65.7** If you give someone **the run of** a place such as a house or garden, or if they have **the run of** it, they have permission to use it as they wish. EG *My sister gave me the run of her house whilst she was away.* PHR + NG : USED AS O ⇑ use

66 The word **run** is also used in the following expressions, which are explained at other places in this dictionary. • to **run amok**: see **amok**. • to **make your blood run cold**: see **blood** . • to **run its course**: see **course**. • to **cut and run**: see **cut**. • to **run to earth**: see **earth**. • to **run an errand**: see **errand**. • to **run** your **eye over** something: see **eye**. • to **run the gamut** of something: see **gamut**. • to **run to ground**: see **ground**. • to **run riot**: see **riot**. • to **run the risk**: see **risk**. • to **run short**: see **short**. • to **run wild**: see **wild**. • See also **dummy run**, **trial run**.

67 See also **runner**, **running**.

run about. **1** If you **run about**, you visit several people or places in order to obtain information or to achieve something, often for someone else. EG *I have not run about, but I have had a few consultations with my colleagues.* PHRASAL VB : V + ADV/PREP = run around **2** See also **runabout**.

run across. If you **run across** someone, you meet them unexpectedly. EG *I keep running across my old students.* PHRASAL VB : V + PREP = bump into

run after. **1** If you **run after** someone or something, you chase them in order to catch them or stop them. EG *She ran after me and coaxed me to come back.* PHRASAL VB : V + PREP ⇑ pursue

2 If you **run after** something, you keep trying very hard to obtain it or to achieve it. EG *He's always been the same-always running after something, hoping for something.* PHRASAL VB : V + PREP ⇑ strive

3 If someone **runs after** another person, they find that person attractive and try to have a romantic or sexual relationship with them; an informal use. PHRASAL VB : V + PREP ⇑ pursue

run along. If you tell someone, especially a child, to **run along**, you mean that you want them to go away and leave you alone; an informal expression. EG *Run along now, my dear... Run along up to bed now, Sam.* PHRASAL VB : V + ADV, USU IMPER = run away

run around. **1** If you **run around**, you visit several people or places in order to obtain information or to achieve something, often for someone else. EG *He had done enough running around... You must be weary, running around for us the way you do.* PHRASAL VB : V + ADV/PREP = run about

2 If you **run around** with a particular person or group of people, you spend a lot of time with them socially. EG *He runs around with a rather odd crowd.* PHRASAL VB : V + ADV + A *(with/together)* ⇑ associate

3 See also **runaround**.

run away. **1** If you **run away** from a place or a person, you suddenly and secretly leave that place or person, often because you are unhappy. EG *He had run away from home at the age of thirteen... Why did you run away from me?* PHRASAL VB : V + ADV, USU + A *(from)*

2 If someone who is held a prisoner **runs away**, they escape. PHRASAL VB : V + ADV

3 If you **run away** with someone, you secretly go away with them in order to live with them or marry them. EG *They ran away and got married... She deserted her family and ran away with him.* PHRASAL VB : V + ADV, ALSO + A *(with)* : RECIP = elope, run off

4 If you tell someone, especially a child, to **run away**, you mean that you want them to go away and leave you alone; an informal use. EG *'I'll join you in a minute. Don't run away!'... Now you run away and play, I'm going to have a nap.* PHRASAL VB : V + ADV, USU IMPER = run along

5 If you **run away** from something difficult, unpleasant, or new, you try to avoid having to do it or having to deal with it, often by ignoring it, because you think that you will not be able to cope with it. EG *I can't run away from the horrors of the war... ...people running away from technology.* PHRASAL VB : V + ADV, USU + A *(from)* ⇑ escape

6 See also **runaway**.

run away with. **1** If a feeling **runs away with** you, it becomes so strong that you can no longer control it, and you cannot think clearly or sensibly. EG *They let their emotions run away with them.* PHRASAL VB : V + ADV + PREP

2 If you **run away with** a race, competition, or prize, you win it very easily. EG *Her sister ran away with every prize at school.* PHRASAL VB : V + ADV + PREP

3 If you **run away with** an idea or opinion, you wrongly accept it or decide on it very quickly, without thinking carefully about it. EG *Don't run away with the idea that this is the end of the matter!* PHRASAL VB : V + ADV + PREP = get

4 If a thief **runs away with** something, he or she steals it. PHRASAL VB : V + ADV + PREP

run down. **1** If you **run down** an idea, a person, or an experience, you criticize it or them strongly. EG *She was not used to people running down their own families... I'm not going to run down University education.* PHRASAL VB : V + O + ADV ⇑ criticize = decry

2 If someone **runs down** an industry, a company, etc, they deliberately reduce its importance, efficiency, etc, usually by reducing the money that is spent on it. EG *The air force had been run down... The government has been running down the coal industry.* PHRASAL VB : V + O + ADV

3 If a machine or device **runs down** , it gradually loses power or works more slowly. EG *The batteries in your radio are running down.* PHRASAL VB : V + ADV ⇑ stop

4 If a vehicle or its driver **runs** someone **down**, the vehicle hits and injures. EG *She was run down just outside the office.* PHRASAL VB : V + O + ADV = knock down, run over

5 If you **run down** something that you are looking for, you eventually find it, usually after a lot of difficulty. EG *I finally ran the article down in the university library.* PHRASAL VB : V + O + ADV = track down

6 If you **run down** a list of items, you read or mention them quickly, often without taking much interest. EG *He ran down their list of complaints.* PHRASAL VB : V + PREP

7 See also **run-down**.

run in. **1** If someone is **run in** by the police, they are arrested; an informal use. EG *Shortly afterwards Mascall was run in.* PHRASAL VB : V + O + ADV ⇑ catch

2 See also **run-in**.

run into. **1** If you **run into** problems or difficulties, you unexpectedly begin to experience them. EG *He ran into trouble with his economic policies... The firm ran into foreign exchange problems.* PHRASAL VB : V + PREP ⇑ encounter

2 If you **run into** someone, you meet them unexpectedly. EG *You might run into him one of these days... I first ran into him at the library.* PHRASAL VB : V + PREP = bump into

3 If something **runs into** a particular number or amount of money, it reaches the number or amount of money that is mentioned. EG *If you include dams used for power, it runs into the thousands... ...exports running into billions of dollars.* PHRASAL VB : V + PREP ⇑ amount to

4 If a vehicle or its driver **runs into** another vehicle, one vehicle hits the other. EG *He ran into a bus at the zebra crossing.* PHRASAL VB : V + PREP, HAS PASS = bump into

5 If one thing **runs into** another, it is very similar to it or becomes part of it, so that it is difficult to see the division between them. EG *...a streak of red running into purple... The words run into each other.* PHRASAL VB : V + PREP = merge, overlap

run off. **1** If someone **runs off**, they leave a place quickly and secretly, often because they have done something wrong. EG *He'd no right making all those promises and then running off.* PHRASAL VB : V + ADV ⇑ depart = abscond

2 If you **run off** with someone, you secretly go away with them in order to live with them or marry them. EG *His wife ran off with another man.* PHRASAL VB : V + ADV, ALSO + A *(with)* : RECIP = run away

3 If you **run off** copies of a piece of writing, you produce them by using a machine; an informal use. EG *Could you run me off five copies of this article, please.* PHRASAL VB : V + O + ADV = photocopy

4 If you tell someone, especially a child, to **run off**, you mean that you want them to go away and leave you alone. EG *They were told to run off and play... Run off now and stop being a nuisance.* PHRASAL VB : V + ADV, USU IMPER = run along

5 If you **run off** a liquid or if it **runs off**, it drains out of a container, often into another one. PHRASAL VB : V-ERG + ADV

6 See also **run-off**.

run off with. If someone **runs off with** something, they steal it. EG *He ran off with a book from the library.* PHRASAL VB : V + ADV + PREP = run away with

run on. **1** If someone **runs on**, they continue talking for a long time, often in a boring way; an informal use. EG *'How I run on, don't I?' Percival said... You do run on rather, don't you?* PHRASAL VB : V + ADV, USU + A = go on

2 If something **runs on**, it continues to exist or operate longer than expected. EG *Donleavy tends to* PHRASAL VB : V + ADV, USU + A *let his jokes run on too long... This project seems to be running on for ever!*

run out. 1 If you **run out** of something, you have no more of it left. EG *We were rapidly running out of money... Mankind is running out of time... Can I use your lighter? I've run out of matches.* ● to **run out of steam**: see **steam**. PHRASAL VB : V + ADV, IF + PREP THEN *of*

2 If something **runs out**, it becomes used up so that there is no more left. EG *Time is running out fast... My luck seemed to have run out... Their money ran out... It looks as if oil will run out faster than coal.* PHRASAL VB : V + ADV

3 If a legal document or contract **runs out**, it is no longer valid. EG *My passport's run out.* PHRASAL VB : V + ADV

4 If someone **runs out** on another person, they abandon them, especially when they have a duty towards them or were having a relationship with them. EG *I'm seeing her tonight, if she doesn't run out on me.* PHRASAL VB : V + ADV, USU + A *(on)* ⇑ desert = walk out

run over. 1 If a vehicle or its driver **runs over** someone or something, the vehicle knocks them down. EG *We almost ran over a fox that was crossing the road... Rosamund nearly got run over last night.* PHRASAL VB : V + PREP, HAS PASS

2 If a container of liquid **runs over**, it is too full and the liquid flows over its sides. EG *The sink's running over.* PHRASAL VB : V + ADV/PREP = overflow

3 If you **run over** something, **3.1** you rehearse or practise it before a performance or test. EG *He asked her to come into his room to run over some lines.* **3.2** you check through it quickly. EG *Let me run over the main points again.* PHRASAL VB : V + PREP; PHRASAL VB : V + PREP = go over

run through. 1 If an idea, piece of news, or emotion **runs through** a group of people, it spreads through them quickly, so that they all know it or feel it. EG *A kind of shock-wave ran through the room... ...the discontent that runs through America today.* PHRASAL VB : V + PREP

2 If something **runs through** the whole of a group of things or people, an activity, etc, it is present in every item or person in the group, or at every stage of the activity. EG *...the deep-rooted prejudice that runs through our society... Complaints of higher costs and lower standards of service run through recent reports.* PHRASAL VB : V + PREP = pervade

3 If you **run through** something, you rehearse or practise it before a performance or test. EG *You could hear the performers running through the whole programme in the background... I'll just run through it rather briefly.* PHRASAL VB : V + PREP, HAS PASS = run over

4 If you **run through** a list of items, you read or mention them quickly, often without taking much interest. EG *He ran through the list of men.* PHRASAL VB : V + PREP = run down

5 If you **run through** a large amount of money, you spend it quickly and often in a wasteful way. EG *How he managed to run through £100,000 so quickly I will never understand!* PHRASAL VB : V + PREP = squander

6 If you **run** someone or something **through** with a sharp tool or weapon, you pierce them with it; an old-fashioned use. EG *As he turned I ran him through with my sword.* PHRASAL VB : V + O + ADV

run to. 1 If something **runs to** a particular amount or size, it reaches it. EG *A housewife's work can run to ten or twelve hours a day if she has small children... The transcript runs to 1,200 pages... Applications to study English here run to about fifteen hundred a year.* PHRASAL VB : V + PREP, USU + NUM = amount to

2 If someone's taste **runs to** things of a particular kind, they like that kind very much. EG *O'Shea's tastes in TV ran to situation comedy and sentimental serials.* PHRASAL VB : V + PREP, HAS PASS

3 If someone or their salary **runs to** a particular thing, they are able to afford it. EG *He doesn't even run to a car.* PHRASAL VB : V + PREP

run up. 1 If someone **runs up** bills or debts, they allow them to accumulate. EG *He ran up a thousand dollars worth of bills... They would run up a few debts, and then go elsewhere.* PHRASAL VB : ORDER V + ADV + O = incur

2 If you **run up** something such as a dress or a skirt, you make or sew it quickly and often not very carefully. EG *She ran up a new blouse in a couple of evenings.* PHRASAL VB : V + ADV

3 See also **run-up**.

run up against. If you **run up against** problems or difficulties, you suddenly and unexpectedly begin to experience them. EG *You never know what you're liable to run up against... Economic growth would sooner or later run up against insurmountable problems.* PHRASAL VB : V + ADV + PREP ⇑ encounter = run into

runabout /rʌnəbaʊt/, **runabouts**. A **runabout** is a small car used mainly for short journeys; an informal word. EG *Sabine pulled up in her little runabout.* N COUNT

runaround /rʌnəraʊnd/. If someone **gives** you **the runaround**, they deliberately do not give you all the information or help that you want, and send you to another person or place to get it; an informal expression. EG *Everybody I ask gives me the runaround.* PHR : VB INFLECTS

runaway /rʌnəweɪ/, **runaways**. 1 A **runaway** is a person, especially a child, who suddenly goes away from a place without permission. EG *They failed to find any trace of the runaways... ...runaway slaves.* N COUNT ⇑ fugitive

2 A **runaway** animal or vehicle is one that is no longer under the control of its rider or driver. EG *...her attempt to stop a runaway horse... ...a runaway bulldozer.* ADJ CLASSIF : ATTRIB

3 A **runaway** situation happens very rapidly or forcefully and cannot be controlled. EG *...the runaway success of 'Nicholas Nickleby'... ...the runaway inflation after the war.* ADJ CLASSIF : ATTRIB = roaring

run-down; also spelled without a hyphen. 1 If someone is **run-down**, they are tired or ill, especially after working too hard; an informal use. EG *'You're probably run down,' Clarissa said. 'You need a holiday.'* ADJ QUALIT : PRED

2 A building or area that is **run-down** is in a very poor condition, because it has not been repaired or looked after. EG *...two small rooms in a run-down building... This neighbourhood is getting run down.* ADJ QUALIT = shabby, dilapidated

3 The **run-down** of an industry, company, etc is the reduction of its importance or efficiency, often as a deliberate policy. EG *...the run-down of the coal industry.* ▸ used as an adjective. EG *...run-down public services... ...the most run-down and old-fashioned industry in the land.* ● See also **run down**. N SING WITH DET + SUPP ⇑ decline; ▸ ADJ QUALIT ⇑ inefficient

4 A **run-down** on a particular situation or subject is a brief summary of the important events or information involved; an informal use. EG *Let me give you the rundown on the Ritz Hotel situation... We've had a rundown on everyone connected with Olympus.* N COUNT : USU SING + *on* ⇑ report

rung /rʌŋ/, **rungs**. 1 **Rung** is the past participle of **ring**.

2 A **rung** is a wooden or metal bar that forms a step on a ladder. EG *...the bottom rung of the ladder... I had my foot on the first rung when she grabbed my arm.* N COUNT

3 A **rung** in the structure of a society, organization, or career is a particular rank or level of importance in it. EG *...staff on the lower rungs of the ladder... ...the lower rungs of management... ...the bottom rung of the pay scale.* N COUNT : *the* + ADJ + N, IF + PREP THEN *of*

run-in, run-ins. 1 A **run-in** is **1.1** an argument or quarrel with someone; an informal use. EG *He's probably had a run-in at work with Ted... ...a minor run-in with Eldridge over the money.* **1.2** a rehearsal which takes place just before the actual performance or just before a more important performance. EG *We'd done it for two weeks in Birmingham as a run-in for the main season.* N COUNT; N COUNT = run-up

2 The **run-in** to an event is the period of time or the journey before it. EG *He quoted it to his men on the run-in... Poole had been wounded in the thigh on the run-in.* N COUNT : USU *the* + N IN SING = approach

runner /rʌnə/, **runners**. 1 A **runner** is **1.1** a person who runs, especially for sport or pleasure. EG *...a long-distance runner... Not being a fast runner, I was glad I had parked close to the hall.* **1.2** a person whose job is to take messages, collect money, or do other small errands for a person or company. EG *...a bookmaker's runner... The local runner for the A.B.C. noticed Rick's cameras... I became his runner, delivering legal papers.* **1.3** a person who takes people or things secretly and illegally into or out of a country or area. EG *...a gun runner.* N COUNT ⇑ athlete; N COUNT + SUPP ⇑ employee; N COUNT + SUPP ⇑ smuggler

2 A **runner** on something such as a piece of furniture is a thin strip of wood or metal underneath it which helps it to move smoothly. EG *Push the driving seat back on its runners... ...children cut by their sledge runners.* N COUNT

3 On a plant, a **runner** is a long shoot that grows from the main stem and puts down roots to form a new plant. EG *...strawberry runners... ...a low, creeping plant with hairy runners and stalks.* N COUNT

runner bean, runner beans. A **runner bean** is a vegetable in the form of a long green pod; used also of the climbing plant on which it grows. N COUNT

runner-up, runners-up. A **runner-up** is a person or team that finishes in second place in a race or N COUNT ⇑ finalist competition. In some competitions, many people can be runners-up. EG *He had once been runner-up for the King's Cup... One hundred runners-up will each receive a sweatshirt.*

running /rʌnɪŋ/. 1 **Running** is the activity of running, especially as a sport. EG *He started professional running only eight years ago... Running was not allowed in the school corridors... ...running tracks... ...running shoes.* N UNCOUNT ⇑ athletics

2 The **running** of an organization, company, etc is the activity of managing or organizing it. EG *...the day-to-day running of the school.* N UNCOUNT + SUPP = management

3 The **running** of a machine is the activity of operating it and looking after it so that it works properly. EG *...an expensive instrument to buy, but its running costs were low.* N UNCOUNT : USU BEFORE N ⇑ maintenance

4 **Running** is used to describe an activity that continues over a period of time, especially without any pause or lessening. EG *...a running battle between architects and planners... ...the running barrage of press criticism.* ADJ CLASSIF : USU ATTRIB = continuous, incessant

5 If you describe a play, TV series, etc as long-running or record running, you mean that it has been performed or shown regularly over a long period of time. EG *...a long-running play... ...films like the record running Star Wars.* ADJ CLASSIF : USU ATTRIB

6 If something happens for two weeks **running**, for the third day **running**, etc, it happens during each of the periods of time mentioned. EG *For three days running he had left the sandwiches at home... For the fourth year running, the weather was awful.* ADJ AFTER N = consecutively

7 **Running** water is **7.1** flowing rather than standing still in a container or pond. EG *...the sound of running water... ...a running stream... Never wash up under a running hot water tap.* ADJ CLASSIF : ATTRIB **7.2** supplied to a house or room through pipes and taps. EG *...with hot and cold running water in all rooms.* ADJ CLASSIF : ATTRIB

8 If you have a **running** nose, mucus is flowing out of it, usually because you have a cold. EG *Some were coughing. Others had running noses.* ADJ CLASSIF : ATTRIB

9 A **running** sore has pus flowing out of it, because it is infected. EG *...the dirt and disease, the children with running sores.* ADJ CLASSIF : ATTRIB = suppurating

10 If someone **makes the running** in a situation, especially in a race or contest, they do things faster, better, or more forcefully than the other people involved and so gain an advantage or lead over them. EG *The terrorist gunmen are making the running now... The early leaders drop back and allow others to make the running... Women made all the running in demands for change.* PHR : VB INFLECTS

11 If someone is **in the running** or **out of the running** for something, they have a good chance or little chance of winning or obtaining it. EG *She's in the running for promotion... He's still in the running for the leadership of the Labour Party... If you're over the age of 45, you're out of the running.* PHR : USED AS AN A

12 If you think someone will **come running**, you think they will be eager to do whatever you want. EG *They think they can snap their fingers and you will come running.* PHR : VB INFLECTS ⇑ obey

running commentary, running commentaries. A **running commentary** is a detailed, continuous description of an event, especially a sporting event, that is spoken or broadcast while the event is taking place. EG *...a running commentary on the match against Brazil... She gave him an exhaustive tour of the shrine and a running commentary.* N COUNT

running mate, running mates. Someone's **running mate** is the person that they choose to be the candidate for a political post that is the next lower in rank to the post for which they are trying to be elected; used mainly in American English. EG *...McGovern's vice presidential running mate... Wallace had asked him to be his running mate.* N COUNT : USU POSS + N IN SING

runny /rʌni¹/, **runnier, runniest**. 1 If something is **runny**, it is more liquid than usual or than was intended. EG *They had runny eggs for breakfast... If it looks thin and runny, add more breadcrumbs.* ADJ QUALIT

2 If someone's nose or eyes are **runny**, mucus or water is flowing from them, often because they have a cold. EG *...Kunta's runny eyes... His nose will be runny, he may cough a little.* ADJ QUALIT

run-off, run-offs. A **run-off** is an extra race or contest which is held at the end of a competition in order to decide the winner, because two people or teams have got the same number of points, votes, etc. EG *...school memories of run-off races which I always lost... ...in run-off elections in 1912.* N COUNT

run-of-the-mill. If you describe someone or something as **run-of-the-mill**, you mean that they are very ordinary in ability or quality and have no special or interesting features. EG *...a run-of-the-mill engineer... ...a run-of-the-mill product.* ADJ QUALIT

runt /rʌnt/, **runts**. 1 The **runt** of a group of animals born of the same mother at the same time is the smallest and weakest of them. EG *...the runt of the litter.* N SING : *the* + N ⇑ animal

2 If you refer to a person as a **runt**, you are expressing contempt for them, often because they are small, weak, or unimportant. EG *Pegler was a skinny little runt... I don't want to waste a prize on some little runt.* N COUNT : ALSO VOC

run-through, run-throughs. A **run-through** is a rehearsal or practice before a performance or test. EG *The director disdains straight run-throughs as time-consuming and irrelevant... He agreed to come to a run-through on condition that there were no outsiders present.* N COUNT

run-up, run-ups. 1 The **run-up** to an event is the period of time and the events that happen just before it. EG *The run-up to the election has been a time of confrontation... ...in the run-up to the Windscale Inquiry... ...during the run-up to the formation of a new party.* N SING : *the* + N, USU + *to* = build-up

2 In sport, a **run-up** is the running approach made by an athlete or player before jumping, throwing a javelin, kicking a ball, etc. EG *...the run-up and the position of the non-kicking foot... ...combining this spring with a sprinting run-up... He had no rhythm or speed in his run-up.* N COUNT : USU SING

runway /rʌnweɪ/, **runways**. A **runway** is a long, narrow strip of ground with a hard, level surface which is used by aeroplanes when they are taking off or landing. EG *The plane sped down the runway... ...the main runways at Heathrow Airport... ...the runway lights.* N COUNT

rupee /ruːpiː/, **rupees**. A **rupee** is a unit of money used in India, Pakistan, and some other countries; used also of a coin or banknote which is worth one rupee. EG *They are only three rupees a dozen... He borrowed 300 rupees... The bill was paid in one hundred rupee notes.* N COUNT : USU NUM + N ⇑ currency

rupture /rʌptʃə/, **ruptures, rupturing, ruptured**. 1 A **rupture** between people or groups is the severe worsening or ending of relationships between them; a formal use. EG *There were ruptures and divisions within the movement... ...a disagreement on strategy and not a fundamental rupture between us.* N COUNT ⇑ parting = breach

2 A **rupture** is also a severe injury to a person's or an animal's body in which a part of it tears or bursts open, especially the wall between the bowel and the abdomen. EG *...if you can open it without suffering a rupture... Strong contractions could lead to rupture of the uterus.* N COUNT ⇑ tear = hernia

3 If someone or something **ruptures** a relationship, a system, etc, they cause it to become worse or to end; a formal use. EG *...even at the risk of rupturing relations with the British... ...the economy, ruptured by war.* V + O = damage, sever

4 If you **rupture** a part of your body or if it **ruptures**, it tears or bursts open. EG *They saw the uterus rupturing.* ◇ **ruptured**. EG *...the Mayor's ruptured appendix.* V-ERG ⇑ injure ◇ ADJ CLASSIF = burst

5 If you **rupture** yourself, you cause the wall between your bowel and abdomen to burst, usually by lifting something heavy. EG *He ruptured himself playing football... My friend couldn't help, because he was ruptured.* V OR V + O (REFL) ⇑ injure

rural /rʊərəl/ means 1 living, existing, or happening in an area of a country that is far away from large towns or cities. EG *...a rural postmaster... Rural crime has increased... ...poverty in the rural areas... ...rural France.* ADJ CLASSIF : ATTRIB ≠ urban 2 having features that are typical of areas that are far away from large towns or cities. EG *India is still an overwhelmingly rural country... ...the rural beauty of Vermont... She spoke in a very rural accent.* ADJ QUALIT : USU ATTRIB ≠ urban

ruse /ruːz/, **ruses**. A **ruse** is an action or plan which is intended to deceive someone; a formal word. EG *They dismissed the offer as a ruse to gain time... ...a ruse for getting out of his house... His ruse had failed.* N COUNT/ UNCOUNT = stratagem, device, play

rush /rʌʃ/, **rushes, rushing, rushed.** 1 If you **rush** somewhere, you go there quickly. EG *Please don't rush off... I'll rush over on Monday morning... I'm late, I have to rush.* V : USU + A = dash, hurry

2 If you **rush** to do something, you do it without delay because it is exciting or important. EG *People were rushing to buy the newspaper... She rushed to book a seat on the next plane... Industrialised nations rush to the aid of regions devastated by natural disasters.* V + *to*-INF/*to* = hurry

3 If you **rush** something or **rush** at it, you do it in a hurry, often too quickly or without enough care. EG *I rushed my lunch... Stop rushing it... You tend to rush at things.* ◇ **rushed.** EG *...a rushed job.* V + O, OR V + A (*at*) ◇ ADJ QUALIT

4 If you **rush** someone or something or **rush** at them, you move quickly and forcefully towards them, often in order to attack them. EG *Protesters rushed the platform during his speech... He rushed at me... Don't rush the house.* ▸ used as a noun. EG *Robert made mock rushes at the dog.* V + O, OR V + A (*at*) ⇑ approach = storm ▸ N COUNT = charge

5 If you **rush** someone somewhere, you take them there quickly. EG *Barnett was rushed to hospital... They rushed him to the hut.* V + O + A = whisk

6 If you **rush** something to a person or place, you send it or take it to them without delay. EG *My suppliers will rush round some more... Please rush details in your next dispatch.* V + O : USU + A, OR V + O + O

7 If you **rush** someone into doing something, you influence them to do it without allowing them enough time to think or make their own decisions. EG *Do not be rushed into parting with goods before taking legal advice.* V + O : IF + PREP THEN *into* = pressurize

8 If air or liquid **rushes** somewhere, it flows there suddenly and quickly, often making a noise. EG *The water rushed in over the top of his boots... ...a river which rushed over smooth boulders.* ◇ **rushing.** EG *...a rushing stream... ...a rushing sound.* V : USU + A = surge ◇ ADJ CLASSIF : ATTRIB

9 If there is a **rush**, you need to go somewhere quickly or do something in a hurry. EG *He's in no rush... 'What's the rush?'... There was no rush... It was a bit of a rush to get here on time.* N SING WITH DET = haste

10 The **rush** is a busy period during a day, week, etc when many people go somewhere or do something. EG *...the Saturday afternoon rush... ...the five o'clock rush... We'll get there before the rush.* N SING WITH DET

11 If there is a **rush** for something, there is a sudden increase in people's attempts to buy or achieve it. EG *...the rush for small, fuel-efficient cars... ...a rush for tickets... ...a rush for quick profits.* N SING WITH DET + *for*/*to*-INF = stampede

12 If there is a **rush** in someone's physical feelings or emotions, there is a sudden increase in the strength of their feelings or emotions. EG *He felt a rush of nausea and dizziness... The memory came back with a painful rush.* N SING WITH DET : USU + SUPP ⇑ flow = surge

13 A **rush** of air or water is the sound or sensation of air or water moving quickly, or of something moving quickly through them. EG *...a little rush of air... ...the forward rush of the bullet... She shouted above the rush of water.* N SING WITH DET : USU + SUPP

14 The **rushes** of a film are the parts of it that have been filmed but have not yet been edited; a technical use. EG *On screen, in the rushes, she looked magnificent... We showed rushes from the documentary to the Press.* N PLURAL : *the* + N ⇑ prints

15 **Rushes** are plants that grow near water and have long, thin stems with no leaves. The stems can be dried and used to make mats, baskets, etc. EG *...the reeds and rushes along the banks of the river... ...baskets made from rushes... ...rush matting on the floor.* N COUNT

16 The word **rush** is also used in the following expressions. **16.1** If you do something **in a rush**, you do it quickly, often too quickly and without enough care. PHR : USED AS AN A **16.2** If the **blood rushes to** your **head** , or you **have a rush of blood to the head**, you lose control of yourself and do something daring or foolish. EG *I felt the blood rush to my head... Every so often the Duke does have a rush of blood to the head.* PHR : VB INFLECTS **16.3** If you are **rushed** or **rushed off** your **feet**, you are very busy. EG *He's so rushed these days, you can't get near him... I've been rushed off my feet all day.* ADJ QUALIT : PRED, OR PHR : USED AS C

rush in. If you **rush in** or **rush into** a situation, you get involved in it without thinking about it carefully enough. EG *...the fool who rushes in... Don't rush into marriage... We should not rush into the armed struggle.* PHRASAL VB : V + ADV/PREP

rush out. If someone **rushes out** a product, they produce it very quickly, because people are very interested in it at the time but may lose interest soon. EG *Three books on the General Election were rushed out within a couple of weeks.* PHRASAL VB : V + O + ADV

rush through. If you **rush** something **through**, you deal with it quickly so that it is ready in a shorter time than usual. EG *The government rushed the legislation through before the summer recess... Could you rush this application through?* PHRASAL VB : V + O + ADV

rush-hour, rush-hours; also spelled without a hyphen. A **rush-hour** is the period in the morning and evening when many people are travelling to and from work, so that the roads are full of traffic and trains and buses are crowded. EG *It's a real strain in the rush-hours... ...Victoria Station at rush hours, teeming with commuters... ...a drive through rush-hour traffic to find the house.* N COUNT

rusk /rʌsk/, **rusks.** A **rusk** is a hard, dry biscuit, especially one that is given to babies. EG *At six months, they can hold their own rusk... ...salads and slimming rusks.* N COUNT

russet /rʌsɪt/ means reddish-brown in colour; a rather literary word. EG *She had russet curls... ...golden-brown and russet leaves.* ADJ COLOUR

Russian /rʌʃəⁿn/, **Russians.** 1 A **Russian** person or thing is someone or something that belongs or relates to the Soviet Union. EG *...Russian dancers... ...the Russian Embassy.* ADJ CLASSIF

2 A **Russian** is a person who comes from the Soviet Union. EG *His father is a Russian.* N COUNT

3 **Russian** is the official language of the Soviet Union. EG *He had learnt to speak some Russian.* N UNCOUNT

rust /rʌst/, **rusts, rusting, rusted.** 1 **Rust** is **1.1** a reddish-brown substance that forms on metals such as iron and steel as a result of contact with water and gradually destroys them; used also of the process involved. EG *There's no rust on it... The chrome had been eaten away by rust... The car looked free of rust.* N UNCOUNT = iron oxide **1.2** a reddish-brown colour; a literary use. EG *...rust-coloured leaves... ...its pattern of rust and green designs.* ADJ COLOUR

2 When a metal or a metal object **rusts** or **rusts away**, it becomes affected by rust and gradually loses its strength. EG *The fittings had rusted... The ploughs were not in use and were rusting away... ...the rusting steel.* ◇ **rusted.** EG *...kicking some rusted tins.* V, OR PHRASAL VB : V + ADV ⇑ disintegrate = oxidize ◇ ADJ CLASSIF

rustic /rʌstɪk/ means 1 simple and unsophisticated in a way that is typical of places far away from large towns and cities or of people who live in such places. EG *...his healthy, rustic physique... ...rustic comfort and good food... ...Mary Webb's rustic novels.* ADJ QUALIT = bucolic, rural 2 made very simply and roughly, using materials found in the countryside. EG *...rustic benches... ...the rustic stone wall.* ADJ CLASSIF : ATTRIB

rustle /rʌsəᵒl/, **rustles, rustling, rustled.** 1 When something **rustles** or when you **rustle** it, it makes soft sounds as it moves gently. EG *...a cold wind rustling the leaves... She stepped out, skirts rustling... He rustled his papers... ...mice rustling about.* ◇ **rustling, rustlings.** EG *She made a rustling noise with the paper... Jim heard some furtive rustlings among the bushes.* V-ERG ◇ ADJ CLASSIF : ATTRIB, OR N COUNT/UNCOUNT

2 A **rustle** is a soft sound made by something moving gently. EG *She heard a rustle behind her and turned... ...the rustle of chocolate wrappers.* N COUNT, OR N UNCOUNT + *of*

rustle up. If you **rustle up** a meal, you cook it quickly, using whatever food you have available at the time. EG *I'll rustle something up... We could rustle up an omelette.* PHRASAL VB : V + O + ADV ⇑ prepare

rusty /rʌstiˡ/, **rustier, rustiest.** 1 Something that is **rusty** is **1.1** affected by rust. EG *...a heap of rusty tins... He drove them there in a rusty old truck... Can you get that rusty machinery working again?* ADJ QUALIT **1.2** reddish-brown in colour. EG *...a tinge of rusty brown... ...a rusty black dress.* ADJ COLOUR : ATTRIB

2 If someone's ability or knowledge of a particular subject or topic is **rusty**, it is poor because they have not used it for a long time. EG *My German's pretty rusty... Dilley looked rusty through lack of bowling... ...your rusty reflexes.* ADJ QUALIT ⇑ imperfect

rut /rʌt/, **ruts, rutting, rutted.** 1 A **rut** is a deep, narrow mark made in the ground by the wheels of vehicles. EG *...the ruts made by tractors... ...the ruts in the road surface... We bumped over the ruts.* N COUNT ⇑ groove

2 If someone is in a **rut**, they have fixed ways of thinking and doing things, which cause them to be dissatisfied or prevent them from making any pro- N COUNT : USU PREP + N ⇑ habit

gress. EG *He is in a real rut... Old firms get into a rut sometimes... Some people never get out of their ruts.*
3 The **rut** is the period of the year when some animals such as deer are sexually active, and males fight each other before mating with the females. EG *...a bison bull bellowing in the autumn rut... During the rut the males may not feed for many weeks.* N SING: *the*+N ⇑ season

ruthless /ru:θlɪ²s/. **1** Someone who is **ruthless** is very harsh or cruel towards their enemies, opponents, or inferiors. EG *...the most ruthless dictator... His adversary was ruthless... Political power was in the hands of a few ruthless men.* ◊ **ruthlessly**. EG *The government punishes resistance ruthlessly.* ◊ **ruthlessness**. EG *...the ruthlessness of union leaders when their power is threatened.* ADJ QUALIT = merciless, pitiless; ◊ ADV WITH VB = mercilessly; ◊ N UNCOUNT
2 A **ruthless action or activity is** done forcefully, thoroughly, and completely, without much concern for its effects on other people. EG *...a ruthless investigation... ...a ruthless determination to carry the policy through.* ◊ **ruthlessly**. EG *I pushed this advantage ruthlessly.* ◊ **ruthlessness**. EG *Francis has all the ruthlessness of the artist.* ADJ CLASSIF ⇑ determined = relentless; ◊ N UNCOUNT

rutted /rʌtɪ²d/. A road or surface that is **rutted** is very uneven because it has a lot of ruts in it. EG *We turned off down a little rutted lane... The road was narrow and deeply rutted by the passage of numerous heavy vehicles.* ADJ QUALIT ⇑ furrowed

rye /raɪ/ is a cereal grown in cold countries; used also of the grain of this cereal which you can grind into flour to make bread. EG *...one advantage of rye as a winter-sown crop... ...wheat, barley, rye, and oats.* N UNCOUNT

rye bread is dark brown bread made with rye flour. EG *...fresh, thinly cut rye bread.* N UNCOUNT

rye grass; also spelled as one word. **Rye grass** is a type of grass grown especially for animals such as cows to eat. EG *My sheep are put on to rye grass... ...fodder crops like ryegrass, red clover, and lucerne.* N UNCOUNT

rye whiskey is whiskey made from rye. EG *...several barrels of rye whiskey.* N UNCOUNT

Ss

S, s /ɛs/, **S's, s's** /ɛsɪz/. **1 S** is the nineteenth letter of the English alphabet.
2 S or **s** is also an abbreviation for various words beginning with s, such as 'seconds', 'shillings', 'son', and 'south'.

> **S** □ In this dictionary **s** is used in the grammar notes beside entries to refer to the subject of a clause. The subject of a clause is usually a noun group. In ordinary statements in English, the subject comes first, and announces the topic of the rest of the clause. In questions in English, the subject is normally placed after an auxiliary verb such as 'do' or after a modal verb.

-s; also spelled **-es**. **1 -s** or **-es** is added to a noun in order to form a plural. EG *...cat→cats... ...farmer→farmers... ...hand→hands... ...palace→palaces... ...boss→bosses... ...potato→potatoes.*
2 -s or **-es** is added to a verb in order to form the third person singular present tense. EG *...stop→stops... ...take→takes... ...stand→stands... ...realize→realizes... ...go→goes... ...push→pushes.*

's. **1 's** is added to singular nouns, especially nouns that refer to a person or an animal, in order to form possessives. It can also be added to the pronouns 'one', 'another', 'other', 'either', and 'neither'. You just add **'** to plural nouns ending in 's' in order to form the possessive. EG *...Ralph's voice... ...the President's conduct... ...friends of the wife's... ...one's self-esteem... ...my colleagues' offices.*
2 's is also added to plural nouns that do not end in **s** to form possessives. EG *...women's rights... ...children's games.*
3 's is the shortened form of 'is' in spoken English. It is added to the end of the pronoun or noun which is the subject of the verb. For example, **he is** can be shortened to **he's**. EG *He's a novelist... She's charming... It's fantastic... There's no hurry... Mary's going to look after you.*
4 's is also the shortened form of 'has' in spoken English, especially where 'has' is an auxiliary verb. It is added to the end of the pronoun or noun which is the subject of the verb. For example, **it has gone** can be shortened to **it's gone**. EG *He's got a problem... She's gone home... It's got to be done... Anne's got a scientific mind.*
5 's is the shortened form of 'us' that is used in informal English with the word 'let', so that you can say or write **let's** instead of **let us**. EG *Let's move on... Let's not talk about that.*
6 's is added to letters, numbers, abbreviations, and acronyms to form plurals. EG *...a row of q's... ...the 1870's... The temperature was in the low 50's.*

Sabbath /sæbəθ/. The **Sabbath** is the day of the week when members of some religious groups do not work and do not take part in certain other activities. For example, the Jewish Sabbath is Saturday and the Christian Sabbath is Sunday. EG *Observe the Sabbath and keep it holy... Do not even light a fire in your homes on the Sabbath... No amount of arguing could make them break the Sabbath.* N PROPER: *the*+N

sabbatical /səbætɪkə⁰l/, **sabbaticals**. A **sabbatical** is a period of time during which a teacher or university lecturer can leave their normal teaching duties so that they can travel or study. EG *The contract allows you to take a sabbatical every seven years... Professor Steel, currently on sabbatical in London, is doing research for a new book.* N COUNT, OR *on*+N = study leave

saber /seɪbə/. See **sabre**.

sable /seɪbə⁰l/, **sables**; **sable** can also be used as the plural form. **1 Sable** is a very expensive fur that is used to make coats, hats, etc. EG *The only furs I like are sable and mink... ...a sable jacket.* N UNCOUNT
2 A **sable** is a wild animal that lives in northern Europe and northern Asia, from which sable is obtained. N COUNT ⇑ mammal

sabotage /sæbətɑːʒ/, **sabotages, sabotaging, sabotaged**. **1 Sabotage** is the deliberate damaging or destruction of machines, railway lines, bridges, etc, usually by small groups of people. It is done as a way of weakening an enemy or as a protest. EG *...widespread sabotage and the disruption of rail communications... Demonstrations, strikes, and sabotage led to frequent clashes with the police.* N UNCOUNT
2 If a machine, railway line, bridge, etc **is sabotaged**, it is deliberately damaged or destroyed, for example in order to weaken an enemy or as a protest. EG *Railways and roads were sabotaged... The power station had been sabotaged by anti-government guerrillas.* V+O: USU PASS
3 To **sabotage** something such as a plan or a meeting means to deliberately prevent it from having a successful result. EG *Crumhorn had deliberately mislaid a file in order to sabotage the negotiations... I don't wish to be accused of sabotaging the President's programme.* V+O ⇑ spoil = disrupt

saboteur /sæbətɜː/, **saboteurs**. A **saboteur** is a person who deliberately damages or destroys machines, railway lines, bridges, etc in order to weaken an enemy or as a protest. EG *Orders were given to root out the saboteurs.* N COUNT = wrecker

sabre /seɪbə/, **sabres**; also spelled **saber** in American English. A **sabre** is **1** a heavy sword with a curved blade that was formerly used by soldiers on horseback. EG *A soldier came up to her with a drawn sabre.* N COUNT ⇑ weapon **2** a light sword used in fencing. N COUNT

sac /sæk/, **sacs**. A **sac** is a small part of an animal's body, shaped like a little bag. It contains air, liquid or some other substance; a technical word. EG *...the nectar that a bee can bring back in its honey sac... ...an extra amount of fluid in the sac that surrounds the testicle.* N COUNT

saccharine /sækəraɪn, -riːn/; also spelled **saccharin** for the meaning in paragraph 1. **1 Saccharine** is a very sweet chemical substance that some people N UNCOUNT use instead of sugar, especially when they are trying to lose weight.

2 You describe something as **saccharine** when you find it exaggeratedly sweet or sentimental; used showing disapproval. EG *We need something to keep the story from being too saccharine... ...saccharine sentimentality.* ADJ QUALIT = mawkish, sickly

sachet /sæʃeɪ/, **sachets**. A **sachet** is, 1 in British English, a small closed plastic bag or paper packet. It contains a very small quantity of sugar, shampoo, etc, usually enough for one occasion. 2 a small cloth bag containing something such as lavender which you use to make clothes, sheets, etc smell pleasant while they are being stored. N COUNT: ALSO N PART ⇑ container; N COUNT

sack /sæk/, **sacks, sacking, sacked**. 1 A **sack** is a large bag made of rough woven material. Sacks are used to carry or store goods such as potatoes, coal, etc. EG *...a large sack containing oranges...* ▸ used to refer to the sack and its contents. EG *A man arrived with a sack of sweet potatoes... ...a truck loaded with sacks of flour.* N COUNT; ▸ N PART

2 If your employer **sacks** you or **gives** you **the sack**, they say that you can no longer work for them, usually because you have done something that they do not like or because your work is not good enough; an informal expression. EG *The General had found him out and was going to sack him... Three railwaymen were sacked because they would not join a union.* ● If you **get the sack**, your employer sacks you. EG *Years ago he would have got the sack for something like that.* V+O, OR PHR : VB INFLECTS ⇑ dismiss = fire; ● PHR : VB INFLECTS = get the push

3 When an army **sacks** a town or city, they destroy it, taking away all the valuable things; an old-fashioned word. EG *Constantinople was sacked by the Turks in 1453.* V+O = lay waste

4 In informal American English, some people refer to bed as the **sack**. EG *Boon and Melanie had been in the sack together that afternoon.* N SING : *the*+N

sackcloth /sæklɒθ/. 1 **Sackcloth** is rough woven material that is used to make sacks. EG *...saris wrapped in sackcloth to protect them.* N UNCOUNT = sacking

2 If you talk about **sackcloth** or **sackcloth and ashes**, you are referring to someone's behaviour when they realize they have done something wrong and are making an exaggerated attempt to apologize or to compensate for it; an old-fashioned use. EG *They would long ago have repented in sackcloth and ashes.* N UNCOUNT

sacking /sækɪŋ/, **sackings**. 1 **Sacking** is rough woven material that is used to make sacks. EG *...a piece of old sacking... ...Mrs Pringle's sacking apron... He drew his rifle from its sacking cover.* N UNCOUNT ⇑ fabric = hessian

2 A **sacking** is the dismissal of a person from their job. EG *He promised that there would be no more sackings.* N COUNT : USU PL

sackload /sækləʊd/, **sackloads**. A **sackload** is the amount of something that can be carried in one sack. EG *The stamps were delivered to the warehouse in sackloads.* N COUNT : ALSO N PART = sack

sacrament /sækrəmə²nt/, **sacraments**. A **sacrament** is, in the Christian church, an important religious ceremony such as communion, baptism, or marriage. EG *...the Holy Sacrament of Baptism.* N COUNT

sacred /seɪkrɪ²d/. Something that is **sacred** is 1 believed to be holy and to have a special connection with a god or gods. EG *They entered the sacred mosque.... ...a group of magnificent sacred elephants... ...a sacred hill in the Transvaal.* ◊ **sacredness**. EG *...the sacredness of the shrine had been violated.* 2 connected with religion or used in religious ceremonies. EG *He is a favourite subject of sacred art... ...sacred music.* 3 regarded as too important to be changed or interfered with. EG *She saw motherhood as woman's sacred calling... No way of looking at things is too sacred to be reconsidered... In their search for a good news story, nothing was sacred.* ◊ **sacredness**. EG *...the sacredness of tradition... All civilizations have rested upon the sacredness of private property.* ADJ QUALIT; ◊ N UNCOUNT; ADJ CLASSIF : ATTRIB; ADJ QUALIT = sacrosanct; ◊ N UNCOUNT = inviolability

sacred cow, sacred cows. You describe a belief, custom, or institution as a **sacred cow** when you think that people regard it with too much respect and never criticize it or question it; used showing disapproval. EG *The need for secrecy has become a kind of sacred cow.* N COUNT = idol

sacrifice /sækrɪfaɪs/, **sacrifices, sacrificing, sacrificed**. 1 **Sacrifice** or a **sacrifice** is the offering of something valuable to a god or gods, especially by killing an animal or human being in a religious ceremony. EG *...a law banning the sacrifice of animals... ...a ritual sacrifice... Let them go and offer sacrifices to their God.* N UNCOUNT/COUNT

2 To **sacrifice** an animal or person means to kill them as a sacrifice. EG *They sacrificed two goats and a bullock every day.* V+O

3 To **sacrifice** something that is valuable or important means to give it up, often in order to obtain something for yourself or for someone else. EG *They will not readily sacrifice their freedom of choice... ...women who have sacrificed career and marriage to care for elderly relatives.* ▸ used as a noun. EG *Our citizens are being asked to make great sacrifices... ...a mother's day-to-day sacrifices for her children.* V+O (NG/REFL) = forfeit, renounce; ▸ N COUNT/UNCOUNT

sacrificial /sækrɪfɪʃə⁰l/ means connected with or used in a religious sacrifice. EG *...sacrificial victims.* ADJ CLASSIF : USU ATTRIB

sacrilege /sækrɪlɪdʒ/. 1 If you commit **sacrilege**, you behave in a way that shows great disrespect for a holy place or object. EG *He might have to be punished for his sacrilege.* N UNCOUNT ⇑ irreverence

2 **Sacrilege** is also the showing of disrespect for someone who is widely admired or for a belief that is widely accepted; a rather humorous use. EG *Criticism of Woolley is sacrilege... The idea of genes influencing cultural behaviour is sacrilege.* N UNCOUNT

sacrilegious /sækrɪlɪdʒəs/. If your behaviour is **sacrilegious**, you show great disrespect towards something holy or towards something that people think should be respected. EG *It would have been sacrilegious to speak... That practice was soon banned as sacrilegious.* ADJ QUALIT ⇑ irreverent

sacristy /sækrɪsti¹/, **sacristies**. A **sacristy** is a room in a church where the priest or minister changes into official clothes and where sacred objects are kept. EG *...the sacristy of the Church of Saint Mary.* N COUNT : USU *the*+N IN SING

sacrosanct /sækrə⁶sæŋkt/. If you describe something as **sacrosanct**, you mean that people are very unwilling to criticize it or change it. EG *Most of these ideas have been considered sacrosanct until quite recently... He seems to think there's something sacrosanct about his annual fishing trip.* ADJ CLASSIF : USU PRED = inviolable

sad /sæd/, **sadder, saddest**. 1 If you are **sad**, you are not happy, usually because something has happened that you do not like. EG *He was sad to see her go... I enjoyed the film even though it made me feel sad... The more he thought about it, the sadder he became... I thought she looked sad.* ▸ used of a person's appearance or expression. EG *A rather sad smile flickered across her face... Valentina made a sad face.* ◊ **sadly**. EG *He shook his head sadly... 'That,' she said sadly and anxiously, 'is what I had always been afraid of.'* ◊ **sadness**. EG *The news filled him with sadness. ...a sort of unexplained sadness that comes each afternoon.* ADJ QUALIT ⇑ unhappy = sorry, miserable; ◊ ADV WITH VB = sorrowfully; ◊ N UNCOUNT = sorrow

2 **Sad** stories, **sad** news, etc make you feel sad. EG *She told Susan there was some sad news for her... It seems rather sad that something like this should happen to such a nice person.* ◊ **sadness**. EG *...the indescribable sadness of those final pages.* ADJ QUALIT = distressing; ◊ N UNCOUNT = pathos

3 You also use **sad** in order to express regret about an unfortunate situation that you are describing. EG *The sad fact is that full employment may never be regained... This is a very sad comment on what is happening to our cities... It's a sad state of affairs when people are afraid to go out at night.* ◊ **sadly**. EG *One aspect of education today has been sadly neglected... The schools were sadly in need of new books... Sadly, we don't appear to have much chance of getting the contract.* ADJ QUALIT : USU ATTRIB = regrettable; ◊ ADV OR ADV SEN = regrettably

sadden /sædə⁰n/, **saddens, saddening, saddened**. If something **saddens** you, it makes you feel sad. EG *I'm saddened by the fact that so many people died for nothing... This is one of the things that saddens me most... It saddened her to think of the opportunity she had missed.* ◊ **saddened**. EG *She has a drained and saddened look.* ◊ **saddening**. EG *It was saddening to think that a whole way of life was about to vanish.* V+O = grieve; ◊ ADJ QUALIT; ◊ ADJ QUALIT

saddle /sædə⁰l/, **saddles, saddling, saddled**. 1 A **saddle** is 1.1 a leather seat that you put on the back of an animal so that you can sit on it and ride the animal. EG *He lifted the saddle from the horse's back... Jennifer swung herself into the saddle.* ● See also **side-saddle**. 1.2 a seat on a bicycle or motor- N COUNT; N COUNT

cycle. EG *He put a leg across the bicycle, and sat upon the high saddle.* **1.3** a large joint of meat, especially lamb or venison, from the middle part of the animal's back. EG *...saddle of lamb.*
N UNCOUNT + *of*

2 To be **in the saddle** means **2.1** to be riding a horse. EG *Doctor Ford was in the saddle... She was hardly in the saddle before she called out 'race you to the bridge'.* **2.2** to be in a position of power or control. EG *New groups of leaders establish themselves in the saddle... The chairman was determined to stay in the saddle at all costs.*
PHR : USED AS AN A
PHR : USED AS AN A = in charge

3 If you **saddle** a horse, pony, etc, you put a saddle on it so that you can ride it. EG *He saddled his horse and rode off.*
V+O

4 To **saddle** someone with a problem, responsibility, etc means to put them in the position where they have to deal with it. EG *They were in danger of being saddled with more responsibility than power... The last thing I want is to saddle myself with a second mortgage.* **saddle up.** If you **saddle up**, you put a saddle on a horse, pony, etc so that you can ride it. EG *I saddled up and rode off... Tell him to catch the ponies and saddle up.*
V+O (NG/REFL) + A *(with)* = lumber
PHRASAL VB : V + ADV, OR V + O + ADV

saddlebag /sædə[0]lbæg/, **saddlebags.** A **saddlebag** is a bag fastened to the saddle of a horse, bicycle, or motorcycle. EG *The letter is in my saddlebag... His riding clothes were packed in the saddlebags.*
N COUNT

saddler /sædlə/, **saddlers.** A **saddler** is a person who makes, repairs, or sells saddles and other equipment for horses. EG *The saddlers were at work in the back room... There was a customer at the saddler's.*
N COUNT ⇑ worker

sadism /seɪdɪzə[0]m, sæ-/ is the obtaining of pleasure from making people suffer physically or mentally, sometimes the obtaining of sexual pleasure. EG *The result is a rise in crime and sadism... He teased her with malicious sadism.* ◊ **sadist, sadists.** EG *Cruelty protects the sadist from realizing that his own nature is perverted... ...the sexual perversity of the sadist.*
N UNCOUNT ⇑ cruelty
◊ N COUNT

sadistic /sədɪstɪk/. When someone's behaviour is **sadistic**, they obtain pleasure from making someone suffer physically or mentally. EG *That was when the most sadistic beatings occurred... ...scenes of sadistic cruelty.* ▸ used of people. EG *He was nothing but a sadistic drunkard.* ◊ **sadistically.** EG *All its members were massacred sadistically... He was sadistically cruel in his interrogations.*
ADJ QUALIT ⇑ cruel = vicious
▸ ADJ QUALIT
◊ ADV WITH VB

s.a.e. is an abbreviation for 'stamped addressed envelope'; used to indicate that when you write to a person or organization you should enclose an envelope with a stamp and your name and address on it so that they do not have to pay to send you a reply. EG *Please include s.a.e. for return of material.*

safari /səfɑːri[1]/, **safaris.** A **safari** is an expedition for hunting or observing wild animals, especially in East Africa. EG *...a month's safari... We're going on safari.*
N COUNT, OR *on* + N

safari park, safari parks. A **safari park** is a large enclosed area of land where wild animals, such as lions and elephants, live and move around freely. The animals can be watched by people who drive through the area. EG *They preferred to see wild animals in safari parks, where they felt safer.*
N COUNT ⇑ game reserve

safe /seɪf/, **safes, safer, safest. 1** You describe something as **safe** when it cannot cause physical harm. EG *Is nuclear power safe?... This powder is not considered safe for babies... He asked me if I was sure it was safe to let my friend go out alone.*
ADJ QUALIT = harmless, innocuous

2 You are **safe** from something when you cannot be harmed by it. EG *We're safe now. They've gone... They were safe from attack.* ● You say that someone is **safe and sound** when they are still alive or unharmed after being in a dangerous situation. EG *I'm glad to see you home safe and sound... Fortunately, my wife was safe and sound after her ordeal.*
ADJ QUALIT
● PHR : USED AS C

3 If you have a **safe** journey or arrival, you reach your destination without being harmed. ◊ **safely.** EG *Just give me a ring to let me know you got home safely.*
ADJ CLASSIF
◊ ADV WITH VB

4 If there is a **safe** delivery of goods, equipment, etc, they reach their destination without being damaged, harmed, or lost. EG *We are relying on the safe delivery of essential equipment.* ◊ **safely.**
ADJ CLASSIF : ATTRIB ⇑ successful
◊ ADV WITH VB

5 A **safe** place is a place where you cannot be harmed, or from which something cannot be lost or stolen. EG *You should remain somewhere safe... Keep your passport in a safe place.* ◊ **safely.** EG *It was not possible to keep him hidden at home safely.*
ADJ QUALIT ⇑ secure
◊ ADV WITH VB

6 A **safe** is a strong metal container or cupboard with special locks where you keep money and valuable things. EG *I suppose he left it in the safe.*
N COUNT

7 A **safe** course of action is one in which you do not have to take any risks. EG *There's only one safe way to deal with this problem.*
ADJ QUALIT ⇑ unexciting

8 If it is **safe** to say something, you can say it with very little risk of being wrong or of getting into trouble for saying it. EG *These practices, it is safe to say, are no longer common... It is a safe assumption that she was very disappointed.* ◊ **safely.** EG *The number of people captured cannot be safely stated... These creatures, we can safely say, have been dead a long time.*
ADJ QUALIT : IF + PREP THEN + *to*-INF
◊ ADV WITH VB ⇑ reliably

9 If you **play safe** or **play it safe** in a particular situation, you do not take unnecessary risks; an informal expression. EG *Playing safe, I kept away... Play safe and always wear goggles.*
PHR : VB INFLECTS ⇑ be cautious

10 If you say that you are doing something **to be on the safe side**, you mean that you are doing it as a precaution, in case something unexpected or unpleasant happens. EG *I'll take a few extra groceries, just to be on the safe side.*
PHR : USED AS AN A

11 If you say that something or someone is **in safe hands**, you mean that they are being looked after by a reliable person and will not be harmed. EG *Don't worry, she's in safe hands at the hospital.*
PHR : USED AS AN A

12 If a secret is **safe** with you, you will not tell it to anyone who is not supposed to know it. EG *They knew their secrets would be safe with him.*
ADJ QUALIT PRED : IF + PREP THEN *with*

13 In Britain and some other countries, a parliamentary seat is described as a **safe seat** when it is unlikely to be lost by a particular party or candidate in an election. EG *It was a safe Conservative seat.*
PHR = secure

14 See also **safely, fail-safe.**

safe-conduct, safe-conducts; also spelled as two words. **Safe-conduct** or a **safe-conduct** is official permission to travel through a place, for example during a war, with an assurance that you will not be harmed or arrested while you are travelling. EG *They were issued with certificates guaranteeing safe conduct.* ▸ used also of the document on which the permission is written. EG *Both journalists were issued with a safe-conduct valid for thirty six hours.*
N UNCOUNT/ COUNT
▸ N COUNT

safeguard /seɪfgɑːd/, **safeguards, safeguarding, safeguarded. 1** To **safeguard** something means to prevent it from being harmed or destroyed. EG *The Bureau's purpose was to safeguard human life... They were mostly concerned with safeguarding the interests of the landowners... They have to fight to safeguard their future.*
V+O ⇑ protect

2 A **safeguard** is a law, rule, etc that is intended to prevent someone or something from being harmed. EG *This clause was inserted as a safeguard against possible exploitation... The French are likely to insist on tighter safeguards.*
N COUNT : IF + PREP THEN *against* ⇑ measure

safekeeping /seɪfkiːpɪŋ/. If something is given to you for **safekeeping**, it is given to you so that you will look after it properly and make sure that it is not harmed or stolen. EG *Valuable paintings had been removed for safekeeping... ...the people entrusted with its safekeeping.*
N UNCOUNT ⇑ protection

safely /seɪfli[1]/. **1** If something is done **safely**, it is done in a way that makes it unlikely that anyone will be harmed. EG *She checked that both rear doors were safely shut... Most food can safely be frozen for months.*
ADV WITH VB ⇑ securely

2 You also use **safely** to say that there is no possibility of a situation being changed. EG *The fire was safely alight... We're safely married now.*
ADV + ADJ/ADV ⇑ certainly = firmly

3 Other meanings of **safely** can be found in the entry for **safe.**

safety /seɪfti[1]/. **1 Safety** is **1.1** the state of being safe. EG *He was assured of his daughter's safety.* **1.2** the possibility of your being harmed in a particular situation. EG *Many worried about the safety of their children.* **1.3** a place where you are safe from a particular danger. EG *They were busy helping survivors to safety... They swim to the safety of a small, rocky island.*
N UNCOUNT
N UNCOUNT
N UNCOUNT ⇑ shelter

2 If you are concerned about the **safety** of a product, course of action, etc, you are concerned that it might be harmful or dangerous. EG *People worry about the safety of nuclear energy.*
N UNCOUNT

3 Safety features, **safety** measures, etc are intended
N BEFORE N

to make something less dangerous. EG *Every car will come with built-in safety features... Heating was by oil stoves without proper safety measures.*

safety belt, safety belts; also spelled with a hyphen. A **safety belt** is a belt or strap attached to a seat in a car, aeroplane, etc. You fasten it round your body, and it stops you being thrown forward if there is an accident. EG *He would have been killed if he hadn't been wearing a safety belt.* N COUNT = seat-belt

safety catch, safety catches; also spelled with a hyphen. 1 The **safety catch** on a gun stops you firing it accidentally. EG *Charles slipped on the safety catch and pocketed the gun.* N COUNT ⇑ lock

2 The **safety catch** on a window or door stops it being opened too far, or being opened by a thief. N COUNT

safety net, safety nets; also spelled with a hyphen. 1 In a circus, a **safety net** is a large net that performers on trapezes or high wires can fall into if they make a mistake. EG *His most dangerous stunt was walking the tightrope without a safety net.* N COUNT

2 A **safety net** is also something that you can rely on to help you if you get into a difficult situation. EG *The Fund is our safety net if anything should go wrong.* N COUNT ⇑ safeguard

safety pin, safety pins; also spelled with a hyphen. A **safety pin** is 1 a bent metal pin that is used for fastening two things together. It is designed so that the point of the pin is covered and does not stick into you. EG *My trousers were fastened with a safety-pin... Do it up with a safety pin.* N COUNT ⇑ fastener 2 a short piece of metal in a grenade, bomb, etc that has to be removed before the device can explode. N COUNT

safety-valve, safety-valves; also spelled as two words. 1 A **safety-valve** allows liquids or gases to escape from a steam engine or other machine when the pressure inside the machine becomes too great. N COUNT ⇑ valve

2 A **safety-valve** is also anything that allows you to express strong feelings without harming other people. EG *She needed a safety-valve, that was all... ...a safety-valve for the harmless release of rebellious feelings.* N COUNT ⇑ outlet

saffron /sæfrəˀn/. **Saffron** is 1 a yellowish-orange substance that is obtained from a flower. It is used to add flavour and colouring to some foods. EG *Toss a pinch of saffron into the rice while it is cooking.* N UNCOUNT 2 a yellowish-orange colour. EG *Desiree's red plaits flamed against the saffron pillows of the huge bed... ...a saffron robe.* ADJ COLOUR ⇑ yellow

sag /sæg/, **sags, sagging, sagged**. 1 When something **sags**, it hangs down loosely or sinks downwards in the middle. EG *The canvas tops of the jeeps sagged with the weight of the water... The bed sagged in the middle when he sat on it... She hated its low narrow rooms and sagging ceilings.* ▸ used as a noun. EG *The chair seat had a slight sag.* V = droop ▸ N COUNT : USU SING

2 To **sag** also means to become weaker. EG *Our spirits sagged... Interest rates were raised to brace up the sagging dollar.* V ⇑ decline = flag, sink

saga /sɑːgə/, **sagas**. A **saga** is 1 a long story composed in medieval times in Iceland or Norway. EG *As a child he loved to read the Norse sagas.* N COUNT ⇑ legend 2 any long story, account, or sequence of events. EG *I related some of the episodes of my domestic saga... The company's collapse was a saga of financial mismanagement.* N COUNT : USU+SUPP = tale

sagacious /səgeɪʃəs/. A **sagacious** person is intelligent and has the ability to make good judgements and decisions; a formal word. EG *...one of the more sagacious commentators... ...the most sagacious member of the committee.* ▸ used of people's actions and behaviour. EG *They nodded wisely to each other and exchanged sagacious remarks.* ◇ **sagaciously**. ADJ QUALIT ⇑ wise = discerning ◇ ADV WITH VB

sagacity /səgæsɪti¹/ is the quality of being sagacious; a formal word. EG *...their invariable sagacity and rectitude.* N UNCOUNT ⇑ wisdom

sage /seɪdʒ/, **sages**. 1 A **sage** is a person, especially an old man, who is regarded as being very wise; a rather literary use. EG *Homage was paid to the great sages buried in the city... ...the Sage of Chelsea, Thomas Carlyle.* N COUNT = guru

2 A **sage** person is wise and knowledgeable, especially as a result of age and experience; a rather literary use. EG *They became sage parents anxious to dispense their wisdom.* ◇ **sagely**. EG *He nodded his head sagely, a smile of amusement appearing on his face.* ADJ QUALIT ◇ ADV WITH VB

3 **Sage** is a small plant. Its leaves are used in cooking as a flavouring. EG *...wild sage and thistles.* ▸ used of the leaves. EG *Flavour the meat with a little powdered sage.* N UNCOUNT ⇑ herb

sago /seɪgəʊ/ is a white starchy substance that is obtained from the trunks of some palm trees. It is used for making sweet puddings and for thickening sauces. N UNCOUNT ⇑ starch

sahib /sɑːhɪb/, **sahibs**. Some people in India use **sahib** when they are referring to a man in a position of authority or influence, especially a white government official during the period of British rule. EG *She remembered the old race of British Sahibs and Memsahibs.* ▸ **Sahib** is also a form of address. EG *Dinner for tonight, Sahib... ...Cameron Sahib.* N COUNT ≠ memsahib ▸ N IN TITLES AFTER N ⇑ sir

said /sed/ is the past tense and past participle of **say**.

sail /seɪl/, **sails, sailing, sailed**. 1 A **sail** is a large piece of material attached to the mast of a boat or ship. The wind blows against the sail and pushes the boat or ship along. EG *...the white sails of the yacht.* ● If you cross the sea **under sail**, you cross it in a ship that has sails rather than an engine. EG *...the mariners who battled under sail round Cape Horn.* N COUNT ● PHR : USED AS AN A

2 When a ship moves over the sea, it **sails**. EG *The ship sailed down the east coast of South America.* ▸ used of the people who travel on the ship. EG *We were shortly to sail for New York... Churchill asked Luce to sail back to England with him... They sailed the Atlantic Ocean.* V+A ▸ V OR V+O : USU +A

3 To **sail** a boat means to make it move across water using its sails. EG *I sailed a thirty-six-foot catamaran... I spent two weeks swimming and sailing in New Hampshire.* ▸ used as a noun. EG *We went for a sail along the coast.* V OR V+O ▸ N SING WITH DET

4 When a ship **sets sail**, it leaves a port. EG *The Beagle set sail on 27 December 1831... The Empire Renown will set sail for Toulon at once.* ▸ used of people travelling on the ship. EG *Dubois set sail for Sumatra.* PHR : VB INFLECTS, IF+PREP THEN from/for

5 A **sail** is also one of the large flat pieces of wood on the top of a windmill which are driven round by the wind. N COUNT ⇑ blade

6 You describe a person or thing as **sailing** somewhere when they are moving there steadily and fairly quickly. EG *Miss Pulteney came sailing past her down the corridor... I watched the ball as it went sailing over the bushes.* V+A = glide

7 ● **to sail close to the wind**: see **wind**. ● **to take the wind out of** someone's **sails**: see **wind**.

sail through. If you **sail through** an experience, you get through it without difficulty. EG *How did she do in her exams?–She absolutely sailed through.* PHRASAL VB : V+ADV/PREP

sailcloth /seɪlklɒθ/ is 1 a strong heavy cloth that is used for making sails, tents, etc. N UNCOUNT 2 a light canvas material that is used for making clothes. N UNCOUNT

sailing /seɪlɪŋ/, **sailings**. 1 A **sailing** is a voyage made by a ship when it takes passengers from one place to another. EG *...regular sailings from Portsmouth... A summary of sailings is shown below... ...sailing times.* N COUNT

2 **Sailing** is the activity or sport of sailing boats. EG *Sailing is becoming very popular... ...the traditional Royal sailing week.* N UNCOUNT

3 If you describe a task as **plain sailing**, you mean that it is easy and will cause you no difficulty. EG *Once we've fixed the computer, it will be plain sailing.* PHR : USED AS C

sailing boat, sailing boats; also spelled with a hyphen. A **sailing boat** is a boat with sails. EG *The sunshine was sparkling on the white sailing boats.* N COUNT

sailing ship, sailing ships. A **sailing ship** is a large ship with sails, especially of the kind that were used to carry passengers or cargo. N COUNT

sailor /seɪlə/, **sailors**. A **sailor** is a person who works on a ship as a member of its crew. EG *He had been a sailor in the Italian navy.* ● If you are **a good sailor**, you are able to travel on a boat in rough weather without being seasick. EG *I thought you were a good sailor.* N COUNT ● PHR : USED AS

saint /seɪnt/, **saints**. 1 A **saint** is a dead person who has been officially recognized by a Christian church as deserving special honour, because their life was very good or holy. EG *Figures of saints line the nave of the church... ...the church of Saint Francis.* N COUNT : ALSO IN TITLES = St.

2 If you refer to a living person as a **saint**, you mean that they are extremely kind, patient, and unselfish; N COUNT = angel

used showing approval. EG *You would need to be a saint to put up with her children.*

sainted /seɪntɪ²d/. A **sainted** person has the qualities of a saint; an old-fashioned word, sometimes used humorously. EG *Your sainted father would agree.* ADJ CLASSIF : ATTRIB

sainthood /seɪnthʊd/ is the state of being a saint. N UNCOUNT

saintly /seɪntli¹/, **saintlier, saintliest**. A **saintly** person behaves in a very good or very holy way. EG *He was not at all a religious or saintly man.* ▸ used of people's behaviour and qualities. EG *He had a saintly concern for his fellow men... ...saintly virtues.* ADJ QUALIT = angelic ▸ = godly

◇ **saintliness**. ◇ N UNCOUNT

sake /seɪk/, **sakes**. 1 If you do something **for the sake of** something, you do it for a particular purpose or in order to achieve a particular result. EG *I usually check from time to time, just for safety's sake... The company might well decide, for efficiency's sake, to consolidate certain operations... You're just arguing for the sake of arguing... Let us assume, for the sake of argument, that the level of unemployment does not fall.* PHR : USED AS AN A

2 If you do something **for** its **own sake**, you do it simply because you are interested in it or enjoy it, and not for any other reason. EG *I'm studying the subject for its own sake... ...the pursuit of knowledge for its own sake.* PHR : USED AS AN A

3 When you do something **for** someone's **sake**, you do it in order to help them or to give them an advantage. EG *She was prepared to work all hours of the night for the sake of the company... We moved out to the country for the children's sake... For both our sakes, stay with me a little longer.* PHR : N INFLECTS, USED AS AN A

4 Some people say **for God's sake, for heaven's sake**, etc in order to express annoyance or impatience, or to add force to a question or request; an informal expression. EG *For God's sake don't tell anyone... What are you staring at for heaven's sake?... For pity's sake leave me alone!* CONVENTION

salaam /səlɑːm/, **salaams, salaaming, salaamed**. 1 To **salaam** means to bow with your right hand on your forehead as a formal and respectful way of greeting someone. People sometimes greet each other like this in India and in Muslim countries. EG *He looked from one to the other of them, then salaamed and left.* ▸ used as a noun. EG *She finally left with many salaams and apologies.* V ▸ N COUNT

2 Muslims also say **'Salaam'** as a way of greeting people. CONVENTION

salable /seɪləbə⁰l/. See **saleable**.

salacious /səleɪʃəs/. If you describe a book, joke, etc as **salacious**, you mean that you think it deals with sexual matters in an unnecessarily detailed way; used showing disapproval. EG *...a salacious novel... It is a theme which commonly gets salacious treatment in the media... ...Sheila's salacious wit.* ADJ QUALIT = obscene, smutty

◇ **salaciousness**. ◇ N UNCOUNT

salad /sæləd/, **salads**. 1 A **salad** is 1.1 a mixture of uncooked vegetables, for example lettuce, cucumber, and tomatoes. It is usually eaten with other foods as part of a meal. EG *I am not fond of salad... I haven't finished my salad... ...ham and salad... ...a salad bowl.* ● See also **fruit salad**. N MASS ⇑ dish 1.2 a dish consisting of a cold food, for example meat or fish, served with a salad of uncooked vegetables. EG *...chicken salad... ...cold lobster salad.* N MASS : MOD+N

2 Your **salad days** are the period in your life when you are young and inexperienced; a literary expression. EG *...the restrictions on our social life in our salad days... ...feelings of nostalgia for their salad days.* PHR : POSS+N ⇑ youth

salad dressing, salad dressings. **Salad dressing** is a mixture of oil, vinegar or lemon juice, and other flavourings, which you pour on salads. N MASS

salamander /sæləmændə/, **salamanders**. A **salamander** is an animal that looks rather like a lizard, and that can live on land and in water. N COUNT

salami /səlɑːmi¹/, **salamis**. **Salami** is a type of strong-flavoured sausage made from chopped meat and spices, which is usually sliced and eaten cold. N MASS

salaried /sælərɪd/. Someone who is **salaried** receives a salary from their job, and is usually paid monthly rather than weekly. EG *The report listed the names of all salaried employees who had been with the firm less than three years.* ADJ CLASSIF : USU ATTRIB ⇑ paid

salary /sæləri¹/, **salaries**. A **salary** is the money that someone is paid for their job each month, especially when they have a professional or other non-manual job. Salaries are usually paid directly into their bank account, or by cheque: compare **wage**. EG *She earns a high salary as an accountant... ...living on a teacher's salary... I've asked for an increase in salary.* N COUNT/ UNCOUNT

sale /seɪl/, **sales**. 1 The **sale** of goods or property is the selling of them for money. EG *They're trying to reduce their total dependence on the sale of cocoa.... ...new laws to control the sale of guns... We've just made our first sale... Any number of things could lead to a sale falling through... The object of the show was to stimulate sales of my new novel.* N COUNT : USU+SUPP ⇑ exchange

2 Something that is **for sale** or **up for sale** is being offered to people to buy; used especially of something that a private owner wants to sell, such as a house or car. EG *Their house is up for sale... ...a 'For Sale' sign.* PHR : USED AS AN A = on the market

3 Products that are **on sale** are available for buying in shops. EG *The first of the new computers may be on sale in the new year.* PHR : USED AS AN A

4 The **sales** of a product are the quantity that a particular company sells, or the quantity that is sold generally throughout a country. EG *Data General's sales grew by 140% a year in the first five years... Car sales are 5 per cent down on a year ago... She congratulated the department on meeting its sales target.* N PLURAL : PL FORM WHEN MOD ⇑ amount

5 The part of a company that deals with **sales** deals with selling the company's products. EG *Who's in charge of sales?... ...a sales executive... ...the area sales manager.* N PLURAL : PL FORM WHEN MOD

6 A **sale** is 6.1 an occasion when a shop sells things at less than their normal price. Many shops have a sale for a short period twice a year. EG *They're having a clearance sale... The sale price is only £9.95.* N COUNT 6.2 an event when goods are sold to the person who offers the highest price. EG *These farmers always came to the quarterly cattle sale... Lot No. 359 in the sale was a collection of original designs by William Morris.* N COUNT = auction ● See also **jumble sale**.

saleable /seɪləbə⁰l/; also spelled **salable**. Something that is **saleable** is easy to sell or suitable for being sold. EG *Smaller cars are more saleable than big ones at the moment.* ADJ QUALIT

sale room, sale rooms; also spelled with a hyphen. A **Sale room** is a place where things are sold by auction. N COUNT = auction house

sales clerk, sales clerks; also spelled with a hyphen. A **sales clerk** is a shop assistant; used in American English. N COUNT ⇑ employee

salesgirl /seɪlzgɜːl/, **salesgirls**. A **salesgirl** is a young woman who serves customers in a shop. N COUNT

salesman /seɪlzmə³n/, **salesmen**. A **salesman** is a man whose job is selling things, especially one who sells his company's products directly to shops or other businesses. EG *...a travelling salesman... ...an insurance salesman.* N COUNT ⇑ employee

salesmanship /seɪlzmənʃɪp/ is skill that a person has in persuading people to buy things. EG *...a two-day course on methods of salesmanship.* N UNCOUNT

salesperson /seɪlzpɜːsə⁰n/, **salespeople, salespersons**. The plural can be either **salespeople** or **salespersons**. A **salesperson** is a person whose job is to sell things, either in a shop or directly to customers. EG *We have a vacancy for an experienced salesperson.* N COUNT ⇑ employee

sales talk is all the things that a salesperson says when they are trying to persuade a customer to buy something. EG *I didn't believe all that sales talk about it cutting your heating bills in half.* N UNCOUNT ⇑ talk

saleswoman /seɪlzwʊ¹mə⁰n/, **saleswomen**. A **saleswoman** is a woman whose job is to sell things, especially in a shop. N COUNT ⇑ employee

salient /seɪlɪənt/, **salients**; a formal word. 1 The **salient** points or facts of a situation are the most important ones. EG *The paper reported the salient points of the prime minister's speech... What, after all, were the salient features of that society?... In this whole series of events, one salient fact commands attention.* ADJ QUALIT : USU ATTRIB = striking, noticeable

2 A **salient** is a narrow area where an army has pushed its front line forward into enemy territory. EG *Further enemy attacks had opened a salient on the left of our Corps.* N COUNT

saline /seɪlaɪn/. A **saline** substance contains salt or consists of salt; a formal word. EG *...saline deposits* ADJ CLASSIF : ATTRIB *from a mineral spring... ...a saline solution.* ◇ **salinity** /səlɪnɪti¹/. EG *...land that has been damaged by salinity... They are monitoring ocean currents, salinity and other factors.* ◇ N UNCOUNT

saliva /səlaɪvə/ is the watery liquid that forms in your mouth and helps you to chew and digest food. N UNCOUNT = spit, spittle

salivary gland /səlaɪvəri¹ glænd/, **salivary glands**. Your **salivary glands** are the glands that produce saliva in your mouth. N COUNT

salivate /sælɪveɪt/, **salivates, salivating, salivated**. If you **salivate**, you produce a lot of saliva in your mouth, often as a result of seeing or smelling food; used in formal English. EG *The mere thought of food made me start to salivate.* V

sallow /sæləʊ/, **sallower, sallowest**. If a person's skin is **sallow**, it has a pale yellowish colour and looks unhealthy. EG *...her sallow face... ...his naturally sallow complexion.* ADJ QUALIT

sally /sæli¹/, **sallies, sallying, sallied**. 1 If an army makes a **sally**, they make a sudden brief attack on an enemy; an old-fashioned use. EG *They made a successful sally at dawn.* N COUNT = sortie

2 A **sally** is a clever and amusing remark; a literary use. EG *The laughter with which his sallies were greeted excited him.* N COUNT = quip, witticism

sally forth. If a person or group **sallies forth** or **sallies out** somewhere, they go there quickly or energetically in order to make an attack or go on a journey; an old-fashioned use. EG *Boldly they sallied forth to meet them... He sallied out into the raw London night.* PHRASAL VB : V+ADV ⇑ set out

salmon /sæmən/. **Salmon** is both the singular and the plural form. A **salmon** is a large silvery fish which is highly valued as food. Salmon live in the sea but swim up rivers to lay their eggs. EG *We saw a few salmon jumping in the waterfall there.* ▸ used of the pink flesh of the fish, which you can eat. EG *...tinned salmon... ...smoked salmon.* N COUNT ▸ N UNCOUNT

salmonella /sælmənelə/ is a kind of bacteria which can cause severe food poisoning. EG *...an outbreak of salmonella poisoning.* N UNCOUNT

salon /sælɒn/, **salons**. A **salon** is 1 a place where hairdressers or beauticians have their business. EG *...a good beauty salon... I went to a hairdressing salon and had a new hair-do.* N COUNT ⇑ establishment = parlour 2 a shop where smart, expensive clothes are sold. EG *She is dressed by Dior, whose salon is located across the street.* N COUNT 3 a reception room in a large, grand house or other building. N COUNT 4 an informal meeting of fashionable writers or artists, which is held at the house of someone important or well-known. Salons were especially common in France in the eighteenth century. EG *...the salons where the brightest intellects of France were assembled.* N COUNT ⇑ gathering

saloon /səlu:n/, **saloons**. A **saloon** is 1 a car with seats for four or more people, a fixed roof, and a boot that is separate from the seating part of the car. EG *...Ford Cortina saloons... ...a family saloon car.* N COUNT = sedan 2 a large room on a passenger ship where the passengers can sit or eat. N COUNT 3 in the United States, a place where alcoholic drinks are sold and drunk. EG *There were nine saloons in those days, and they just stayed open all the time.* N COUNT ⇑ establishment = bar

saloon bar, saloon bars. In Britain, a **saloon bar** is a comfortably furnished bar in a pub or hotel where the prices of drinks are higher than in the other bars. N COUNT = lounge, lounge bar

salt /sɒlt/, **salts, salting, salted**. 1 **Salt** is a bitter-tasting substance, in the form of white powder or crystals, which is used mainly to improve the flavour of food or to preserve it. Salt occurs naturally in sea water. ● See also **rock salt**. N UNCOUNT = sodium chloride

2 Something that is **salt** contains salt or tastes of salt. EG *...water and salt porridge for breakfast.* ADJ CLASSIF

3 When you **salt** food, you add salt to it in order to improve the taste of it or to preserve it. EG *The potatoes should be lightly salted... The fish are cut up and salted.* ◇ **salted**. EG *Cook them in a little boiling salted water... ...salted peanuts.* V+O ◇ ADJ CLASSIF

4 When workmen **salt** roads or paths in cold weather, they put salt on them so that water or snow will not freeze on them. EG *Only the main roads have been salted.* V+O

5 The word **salt** is also used in the following expressions. 5.1 If you think that a person or group is **the salt of the earth**, you think that they are more admirable or valuable than any other person or group. EG *They think of themselves as the salt of the earth, and quite rightly too.* PHR : USU USED AS C 5.2 If something **rubs salt into** someone's **wounds** it makes an unpleasant situation that they are in even worse. EG *The proposed ten per cent cut in wages is really rubbing salt into the wound.* PHR : VB INFLECTS ⇑ exacerbate 5.3 If you **take** something that someone says **with a pinch** or **grain of salt**, you do not believe it to be completely accurate or true; an informal expression. EG *This calculation has to be taken with a pinch of salt.* PHR : VB INFLECTS ⇑ doubt

6 **Salts** are mineral salts that are used as a medicine. EG *...a dose of salts... ...liver salts.* ● See also **bath salts, Epsom salts, smelling salts.** N PLURAL

salt away. If you **salt away** money, you do not spend it, but keep it somewhere for the future; an informal use. EG *He was said to have salted away £4 million.* PHRASAL VB : V+O+ADV ⇑ hoard

SALT /sɒlt/ is an abbreviation for 'Strategic Arms Limitation Talks'; a series of discussions between the United States and the Soviet Union on how the number of nuclear weapons they possess could be limited or reduced. EG *I hoped the American Congress would ratify Salt II... ...the beginning of the SALT talks.* N PROPER

salt cellar, salt cellars; also spelled with a hyphen. A **salt cellar** is a small container for salt with one or more holes at the top for shaking out the salt onto savoury food. N COUNT ⇑ cruet

saltpetre /sɒltpi:tə/; also spelled **saltpeter** in American English. **Saltpetre** is potassium nitrate, a substance that is used in making gunpowder, matches, and fertilizers, and in preserving meat. N UNCOUNT

salt water; also spelled as one word, especially when used as an adjective. **Salt water** is water from the sea, which has salt in it. EG *Ralph wiped the salt water from his lips.* ▸ used as an adjective to describe animals that live in the sea. EG *...the saltwater crocodile.* N UNCOUNT ▸ ADJ CLASSIF : ATTRIB

salty /sɒlti¹/, **saltier, saltiest**. Something that is **salty** contains salt or tastes of salt. EG *We washed them in salty water... Sea salt may taste saltier than the stuff you usually buy in shops.* ◇ **saltiness**. EG *Wash the fish in water to remove some of the saltiness.* ADJ QUALIT ◇ N UNCOUNT

salubrious /səlu:briəs/. A place that is **salubrious** is pleasant and healthy; a formal word. EG *It wasn't the most salubrious of camp-sites... ...one of the less salubrious suburbs of London.* ADJ QUALIT = wholesome

salutary /sæljə⁴tə⁰ri¹/. A **salutary** experience is good for you or helps you, even though it may seem unpleasant at first. EG *The defeat was a deserved punishment, but also a salutary shock... It is salutary to consider that perhaps in future we will not have such easy access to coal and petrol.* ADJ QUALIT = beneficial

salutation /sæljə⁴teɪʃə⁰n/, **salutations**; an old-fashioned or formal word. 1 **Salutation** or a **salutation** is a greeting to someone. EG *They heard her voice raised in lively salutation... She threw a kiss as a salutation.* N UNCOUNT/COUNT

2 A **salutation** in a letter is the phrase that is used at the beginning of the letter, for example 'Dear Sir' or 'Dear Jim'. N COUNT ⇑ opening

salute /səlu:t/, **salutes, saluting, saluted**. 1 A **salute** is a formal sign of greeting or respect used especially in the armed forces. The commonest form of salute is when soldiers raise their right hand so that their fingers touch their forehead. At some ceremonial occasions, guns are fired into the air as a salute. EG *He greeted King Edward VIII with the customary salute... I saw the hand raised stiffly in salute... ...a ten gun salute.* ● If an important person such as a President or Queen **takes the salute** at a ceremonial occasion, he or she stands while soldiers march past and salute as a sign of respect. N COUNT, OR *in*+N ⇑ acknowledgement ● PHR : VB INFLECTS

2 When you **salute** someone, you greet them or show your respect with a formal sign. EG *Don't you know that you should salute officers?... He stood as if he were saluting the flag.* V OR V+O

3 If you **salute** a person or an achievement, you publicly show or state your admiration for them; a fairly formal use. EG *He saluted the decisive historic achievement of the government... ...festivals in Spain that salute the independence of the Spanish character.* ▸ used as a noun. EG *The monument was intended as a salute to the greatest Londoner of the twentieth century.* V+O ⇑ acknowledge ▸ N COUNT : USU +*to* ⇑ tribute

salvage /sælvɪdʒ/, **salvages, salvaging, salvaged.** 1 When you **salvage** things, you manage to save them, for example from a ship that has sunk or been wrecked, or from a building that has been burnt or destroyed. EG *He did all he could to salvage something from the wreck... A finely decorated window salvaged from an old chemist's shop.* ▸ used as a noun to refer to this activity. EG *...a salvage operation.* — V+O : IF+PREP THEN *from* ⇑ rescue; ▸ N UNCOUNT ⇑ rescue

2 The **salvage** from wrecked or sunken ships, burnt-down buildings, etc is the things that are saved from them. EG *They were arguing about who was entitled to a share in the salvage.* — N UNCOUNT

3 If you **salvage** a difficult situation, you manage to get something useful from it so that it is not a complete failure. EG *They were salvaging what they could from the present unhappy state of affairs.* — V+O ⇑ rescue

salvation /sælveɪʃəⁿn/. 1 In Christianity, the **salvation** of a person or of their soul is the condition in which they are saved from evil. EG *Through Christ and his death they found salvation.* — N UNCOUNT ⇑ deliverance

2 The **salvation** of a person, thing, or situation is the condition in which they are saved from serious harm or unpleasant effects. EG *Salvation lay in political reform... The country's salvation was of immense importance to the British.* — N UNCOUNT ⇑ rescue

3 If someone or something is your **salvation**, they save you from serious harm or an extremely unpleasant situation. EG *Their anti-tank defences had been their salvation... Small industries will be the salvation of many areas now in decline.* — N SING WITH DET : WITH POSS ⇑ deliverance

salve /sælv/, **salves, salving, salved.** 1 If you do something that **salves** your **conscience**, it makes you feel less guilty or worried; a formal expression. EG *We give money to charities, and thus salve our consciences.* — PHR : VB INFLECTS

2 **Salve** is an ointment or other substance that is put on sore skin or a wound to help it heal. EG *He could feel the nurse's hands smearing salve on his back again... ...lip salve.* — N UNCOUNT ⇑ application

salver /sælvə/, **salvers.** A **salver** is a tray or large plate, usually made of silver and finely decorated. — N COUNT

salvo /sælvəʊ/, **salvoes.** A **salvo** is 1 the firing of several guns or missiles at the same time in a battle or as part of a ceremony. EG *...two attacks, each consisting of salvoes of four missiles... The centre of London resounded with the triumphant salvoes.* — N COUNT ⇑ burst 2 a sudden outburst of clapping, laughing, or other activity. EG *...salvoes of raucous laughter... ...his wish to avoid a further salvo of intimate questions.* — N COUNT : USU+ *of*

Samaritan /səˈmærɪtən/, **Samaritans.** You refer to someone as a **Samaritan** if they help you when you are in difficulty. EG *This good Samaritan took me all the way there in his car.* — N COUNT

samba /sæmbə/, **sambas.** A **samba** is a lively Brazilian dance. — N COUNT

same /seɪm/. **Same** is usually preceded by the determiner 'the', except for the meaning explained in paragraph 4 and some of the expressions in paragraph 7. When **same** is used as an adjective, it usually occurs immediately after the determiner. 1 If two things or actions are the **same** or if one thing or action is the **same** as another, the two are exactly like each other in some way. EG *They both wore the same heavy tweed overcoats... Look! They're exactly the same... It is really just the same as any other police work... He did exactly the same as John did... Most of us in those circumstances would have done the same.* — ADJ CLASSIF : ATTRIB, OR PRON : *the*+ADJ/PRON, IF+PREP THEN *as* ⇑ alike = identical

2 If two things have the **same** quality or if one thing has the **same** quality as another, they have this quality in common, for example they both have a particular age, colour, or shape. EG *He and Tom were exactly the same age... It was the same colour as the wall... This fish is twice as big but the same shape.* — ADJ CLASSIF : ATTRIB, *the*+ADJ, IF+PREP THEN *as* = identical

3 You use **same** 3.1 to say that you are referring to only one thing, time, place, etc, and not different ones. EG *We come from the same place... They found it was possible to work while watching TV at the same time... I found she was staying in the same small hotel as I was... ...two different photographs of the same man.* — ADJ CLASSIF : ATTRIB, *the*+ADJ **3.2** to refer to a person, thing, quality, etc that has already been mentioned or suggested. EG *For the same reason, the United States lodged a formal protest... The same is true of the arts... It's the same with teenage fashions.* — ADJ CLASSIF : ATTRIB, OR PRON : *the*+ADJ/PRON = this

4 You use **same** in formal written English to refer to the exact thing that has already been mentioned in a document, especially one relating to work that has been done or that is going to be done. EG *Estimate for repairs to ceiling and re-painting of same: £100.* — PRON

5 Something that is still the **same** has not changed in any way. EG *The village stayed the same... He will never be the same again... It wouldn't improve me, I'd be the same person I was before I saw it.* — ADJ CLASSIF : ATTRIB, OR PRON : *the*+ADJ/PRON = unchanged

6 If you say that something is happening **the same as** something else, you mean that the two things are happening in a similar or identical way to each other; an informal use. EG *Here in Scotland the tradition is dying out the same as it's dying out everywhere else... Try to act the same as the person you are teaching.* — CONJ SUBORD, OR PREP = like

7 The word **same** is also used in the following expressions. **7.1** You say **all the same** or **just the same** when you want to say that a situation or your opinion has not changed, in spite of something that has happened or been said. EG *All the same, the courses are very popular... She knew he wasn't listening, but she went on all the same... Yes, you're a nuisance sometimes, but we love you just the same.* — PHR : USED AS ADV SEN = nevertheless, still, even so

7.2 If you say **'it's all the same to me'**, you mean that you do not care which of several things happens or is chosen; an informal expression. EG *Do whatever you want, it's all the same to me... 'Tea or coffee?'–'Tea, if it's all the same to you.'* — CONVENTION **7.3** You say **'thanks all the same'** when you are thanking someone for an offer that you are refusing. EG *'Do you want a lift?'–'No, but thanks all the same.'* — CONVENTION ⇑ thank you **7.4** If you say that something **is not the same**, you mean that it is not as pleasant or as good as something that you would prefer. EG *We started out again by car. But it wasn't the same... You can have frozen chicken but it's not the same as fresh.* — PHR : VB INFLECTS, IF+PREP THEN *as* **7.5** When two or more people or things are thought to be distinct or separate and you say that they are **one and the same**, you mean that they are in fact one single person or thing. EG *We're at cross purposes here; I think the articles we're talking about are one and the same.* — PHR : USED AS C **7.6** You say **the same** or **the very same** in reply to someone's question when you are saying that they have identified a person or thing correctly; a fairly formal expression. EG *'Is he that artist from New Orleans?'–'The same.'* — CONVENTION ⇑ yes **7.7** You say **'Same again'** when you want to order another drink of the same kind as the one you have just had; used in informal English. EG *Same again please, John.* — CONVENTION

7.8 If you say **'Same difference'** when someone has just corrected a statement that you made, you mean that you agree it was not completely accurate but that this is not important; an informal expression. EG *'They're both doctors.'–'Actually, one of them's a vet.'–'Same difference.'* — CONVENTION = so what **7.9** You say **'Same here'** in order to suggest that you feel the same way about something as the person who has just spoken, or that you have done the same thing; an informal expression. EG *'The adverts on television really annoy me.'–'Same here.'* — CONVENTION = ditto, me too **7.10** If someone says something insulting to you, you can reply **'same to you'** in order to insult them in return; a very informal expression, used mainly by children. EG *'You're a twit.'–'Same to you.'* — CONVENTION

8 The word **same** is also used in the following expressions, which are explained at other places in this dictionary. ● **in the same boat**: see **boat.** ● **in the same breath**: see **breath.** ● **the same old story**: see **story.** ● **at the same time**: see **time.** ● **by the same token**: see **token.** ● **in the same way**: see **way.**

sameness /seɪmnɪˀs/. The **sameness** of something is its lack of variety; used showing disapproval. EG *I was struck by the sameness of clothing among the villagers.* — N UNCOUNT : USU +SUPP ⇑ dullness = monotony

samovar /sæməvɑː, sæməvɑː/, **samovars.** A **samovar** is a large decorated metal container that was traditionally used in Russia for making tea. — N COUNT ⇑ urn

sampan /sæmpæn/, **sampans.** A **sampan** is a small boat with oars that is used especially in China. — N COUNT

sample /sɑːmpəˀl/, **samples, sampling, sampled.** 1 A **sample** of something is 1.1 an example or small quantity of it that shows you what the whole of it is like. EG *You could get samples of the colours of the wool... ...free samples of shampoo.... I ran through a sample exercise to check the procedure.* — N COUNT

1.2 a small amount of it that is examined and analysed scientifically. EG *I'll take water samples* — N COUNT = specimen *here and in East Hampton... None of the sample fragments picked up was radioactive.*

2 A **sample** of people or things is a number of them that are chosen at random out of a larger group and then used to test ideas or to provide information about the whole group. EG *Isn't your conclusion based on rather a small sample?... I asked a wide sample of people about it.* N COUNT

3 If you **sample** food or drink, you taste a small amount of it in order to find out if you like it. EG *Next he sampled the roast beef.* V+O ⇑ test

4 If you **sample** something such as a place or activity, you find out about it by experiencing it for a short time. EG *They can learn the language and sample the British way of life.* V+O ⇑ test

sampler /sɑːmplə/, **samplers**. A **sampler** is a piece of cloth embroidered with various patterns, which is intended to show the skill of the person who made it. N COUNT ⇑ embroidery

samurai /sæmjᵒʊraɪ/; **samurai** is both the singular and the plural form. A **samurai** was a member of a powerful class of warriors in Japan in former times. EG *...a samurai sword.* N COUNT ⇑ warrior

sanatorium /sænətɔːrɪəm/, **sanatoriums, sanatoria**. The plural can be either **sanatoriums** or **sanatoria**. It is also spelled **sanitarium** in American English. A **sanatorium** is an institution that provides medical treatment and rest, often in a specially healthy climate, for people who have been ill for a long time. EG *A dreadful breakdown sent me to a sanatorium for more than a year.* N COUNT ⇑ hospital

sanctify /sæŋktɪfaɪ/, **sanctifies, sanctifying, sanctified**. 1 If a priest or other holy person **sanctifies** something, they make it holy. EG *...the sanctified coffin... St Francis wanted to sanctify poverty, not to abolish it.* V+O

2 If something such as an activity **is sanctified**, it is permitted and given official approval, especially by the Church. EG *These practices were ordained by the state and sanctified by the Church.* V+O : USU PASS ⇑ approve

sanctimonious /sæŋktɪməʊnɪəs/. Someone who is **sanctimonious** tries to appear to be deeply religious and virtuous; used showing disapproval. EG *...a sanctimonious hypocrite.* ADJ QUALIT ⇑ pious

sanction /sæŋkᵒʃəᵒn/, **sanctions, sanctioning, sanctioned**. 1 If an institution or a person with authority **sanctions** an action or practice, they give their approval of it so that it can officially be done. EG *...the law of 1856 which sanctioned the remarriage of widows.* ▸ used as a noun. EG *It had the sanction of religion and therefore went unchallenged for many years... Some months later our proposal was given official sanction.* V+O ⇑ authorize = approve ▸ N UNCOUNT + SUPP

2 A **sanction** is a severe course of action or way of behaving which is intended to make people obey laws or customs. EG *The ultimate sanction of the central government is still the withdrawal of funds... ...the first legal sanction available for controlling the press, the law of 1819.* N COUNT ⇑ measure = weapon

3 **Sanctions** are measures taken by countries to restrict or prohibit trade and official contact with a country that has broken international law. EG *The UN would try to impose very serious economic sanctions against the offending nation... ...political sanctions.* N PLURAL : IF + PREP THEN *against/on*

sanctity /sæŋkᵒtɪti¹/. The **sanctity** of something is its quality of being considered so holy or important that it must always be respected totally. EG *The sanctity of marriage... Do you not believe in the sanctity of human life?... ...the sanctity of other people's property.* N UNCOUNT : IF + PREP THEN *of*

sanctuary /sæŋkᵒtjᵒʊəri¹/, **sanctuaries**. A **sanctuary** is 1 a place of safety for someone, often someone who is being chased or hunted. EG *Missions were undertaken to force the enemy out of his sanctuary... It was Clement's island and his sanctuary.* ▸ used as an uncount noun to refer to the safety that the place provides. EG *He staggered from his room and took sanctuary in his study... I was glad to climb into the sanctuary of my bed.* 2 a place where birds or animals are protected and allowed to live freely. EG *She wants to turn her orchard into a bird sanctuary.* N COUNT ⇑ shelter = refuge ▸ N UNCOUNT = refuge N COUNT : USU MOD + N

sand /sænd/, **sands, sanding, sanded**. 1 **Sand** is a powdery substance that consists of extremely small fine pieces of rock or other material. Most deserts and beaches are made of sand. EG *The little children played in the sand at the water's edge... ...grains of sand.* N UNCOUNT ⇑ substance

2 **Sands** are a large area of sand, for example a beach or a desert. EG *We went down to the beach, to miles of empty sands.* N PLURAL ⇑ stretch

3 If you **sand** a wood or metal surface, you rub sandpaper or a sander over it in order to make it smooth or to remove layers of paint or dirt from it. EG *A scratched item of furniture can be professionally sanded... The nickel had been finely sanded away to expose the lead inside.* V+O

sand down. If you **sand down** a wood or metal surface, you sand it until it is completely smooth. EG *Sand down that bit before you start painting it.* PHRASAL VB : V + O + ADV

sandal /sændəl/, **sandals**. **Sandals** are light shoes for wearing in warm weather, which have straps instead of a solid part over the top of your foot. N COUNT

sandalwood /sændəᵒlwʊd/ is 1 the sweet-smelling wood of a tree that is found in South Asia and Australia; also used of the tree itself. 2 an oil that is extracted from sandalwood and used to make perfume. N UNCOUNT N UNCOUNT

sandbag /sændbæg/, **sandbags, sandbagging, sandbagged**. 1 A **sandbag** is a sack filled with sand which is used, for example, to build walls as a protection against floods or explosions. N COUNT

2 To **sandbag** something means to protect or strengthen it by means of sandbags. EG *The water tank had been sandbagged.* V+O

sandbank /sændbæŋk/, **sandbanks**. A **sandbank** is a bank of sand below the surface of the sea or a river. N COUNT

sand castle, sand castles. A **sand castle** is a heap of sand in the shape of a castle, which children make when playing on the beach. N COUNT ⇑ mound

sander /sændə/, **sanders**. A **sander** is a machine that is used for removing layers of paint from wood or metal surfaces, or for making the surfaces smoother. N COUNT

sandpaper /sændpeɪpə/, **sandpapers, sandpapering, sandpapered**. 1 **Sandpaper** is strong paper that has a coating of sand or a similar rough substance, which is used for rubbing wood or metal surfaces to make them smoother. N UNCOUNT ⇑ abrasive

2 If you **sandpaper** a surface, you rub sandpaper over it to make it smooth. EG *Let it dry and sandpaper it smooth.* V+O ⇑ sand

sandpit /sændpɪt/, **sandpits**. A **sandpit** is, a shallow hole or box in the ground with sand in it where small children can play; used in British English. N COUNT

sandstone /sændstəʊn/ is a type of rock which contains a lot of sand and is often used in building. EG *...a long sandstone cliff.* N UNCOUNT

sandstorm /sændstɔːm/, **sandstorms**. A **sandstorm** is a strong wind that causes large clouds of sand in deserts and other sandy places. N COUNT ⇑ storm

sandwich /sænwɪdʒ, -wɪtʃ/, **sandwiches, sandwiching, sandwiched**. 1 A **sandwich** is 1.1 two or more slices of bread with a layer of food between them, for example meat, cheese, or jam. EG *...eating sandwiches in the office for lunch... ...a bacon, lettuce, and tomato sandwich.* 1.2 a cake that consists of two thinner cakes with a layer of jam or cream between them; used in British English. EG *...a recipe for a Victoria sandwich.* 1.3 something that consists of a layer of one thing between two layers of something else. EG *Much modern furniture is not solid but uses a sandwich of wood veneer on plywood.* N COUNT ⇑ snack N COUNT + SUPP N COUNT + *of*

2 When one thing **is sandwiched** between two other things, it is squashed between them. EG *Wooden shacks are sandwiched between modern blocks of flats... I was sandwiched in between two fat men.* V + O + A : USU PASS

3 If you **sandwich** two things together, you put them together with a layer of something different between them. EG *I sandwiched the cakes together with some cream.* V+O

sandwich board, sandwich boards; also spelled with a hyphen. A **sandwich board** is a pair of two connected boards which are hung over a person's shoulders, and which display advertisements in front and behind. N COUNT ⇑ display boar

sandwich course, sandwich courses; also spelled with a hyphen. A **sandwich course** is an educational course in which you have alternate periods of study and periods of work in industry or N COUNT business; used in British English. EG *...a four-year sandwich course in civil engineering.*

sandwich man, sandwich men; also spelled with a hyphen. A **sandwich man** is a man who carries a sandwich board through a busy shopping area in order to advertise things. N COUNT

sandy /sændi¹/, **sandier, sandiest**. 1 A **sandy** area is covered with sand. EG *...the long sandy beach.* ADJ QUALIT
2 **Sandy** hair is light orange-brown in colour. ADJ COLOUR

sane /seɪn/, **saner, sanest**. 1 Someone who is **sane** is is normal and healthy in mind. EG *She appeared to be completely sane... It's a wonder I keep sane with this lot around me.* ADJ QUALIT ≠ insane, mad
2 A **sane** action, system, etc is based on good sense and judgement. EG *...the campaign for a sane nuclear policy.* ADJ QUALIT = sensible, reasonable

sang /sæŋ/ is the past tense of **sing**.

sang-froid /sɑː frwɑː/. A person's **sang-froid** is their ability to remain calm in a dangerous or difficult situation; a formal word. EG *He faced the attack with amazing sang-froid.* N UNCOUNT ⇑ self-control = composure

sanguinary /sæŋgwɪnə⁰ri¹/; a formal word. 1 A **sanguinary** fight, battle, etc is very violent and involves a lot of blood being shed. EG *I was horrified by the senseless and sanguinary violence.* ADJ QUALIT = bloody
2 Someone who has a **sanguinary** nature is eager to use violence or to see violence. ADJ QUALIT

sanguine /sæŋgwɪn/; a formal word. If you are **sanguine** about something, you are cheerful and confident that things will happen as you want them to. EG *The commander was sanguine about the superiority of his airmen.* ▸ used of people's attitudes. EG *His private expectations were not so sanguine.* ADJ QUALIT : IF + PREP THEN *about/of* = optimistic ▸ ADJ QUALIT = optimistic

sanitarium /sænɪtɛərɪəm/, **sanitariums**. See **sanatorium**.

sanitary /sænɪtə⁰ri¹/. 1 If you say that a place is not **sanitary**, you mean that it is not very clean. EG *I sat in a small and not very sanitary café in Soho.* ADJ QUALIT = hygienic
2 **Sanitary** also means concerned with keeping things clean and healthy, especially with keeping buildings free from dirt and disease. EG *Sanitary conditions in the hospitals had deteriorated rapidly... There were no sanitary facilities of any kind... ...a sanitary inspector.* ADJ CLASSIF : ATTRIB ⇑ health

sanitary napkin, sanitary napkins. A **sanitary napkin** is the same as a sanitary towel; used mainly in American English. N COUNT

sanitary towel, sanitary towels. A **sanitary towel** is a pad of thick soft material which women wear to absorb the blood when they have a period. N COUNT

sanitation /sænɪteɪʃə⁰n/ is the business of keeping places clean and healthy, especially keeping buildings free from dirt and disease. EG *They live in conditions of appalling sanitation.* N UNCOUNT

sanity /sænɪti¹/. 1 A person's **sanity** is their state of being normal and healthy in mind. EG *He wanted to save his strength and his sanity.* N UNCOUNT ≠ insanity
2 **Sanity** is also good sense and judgement. EG *They give some point and sanity to daily life.* N UNCOUNT = reason

sank /sæŋk/is the past tense of **sink**.

Sanskrit /sænskrɪt/ is a very old language which used to be spoken in India and which is now used only in religious writings and ceremonies. N UNCOUNT

Santa Claus /sæntə klɔːz/ is another name for Father Christmas. N PROPER

sap /sæp/, **saps, sapping, sapped**. 1 Something that **saps** your strength, confidence, etc slowly weakens or destroys it over a long period of time. EG *The constant tension at work was sapping my energy... Everyone was sapped of strength by the sun's heat.* V+O = drain
2 **Sap** is the watery liquid that carries food through plants and trees. EG *The weather was warming up and the sap was rising in the maples.* N UNCOUNT

sapling /sæplɪŋ/, **saplings**. A **sapling** is a young tree. EG *The dead elms have been replaced by a row of saplings.* N COUNT

sapphire /sæfaɪə/, **sapphires**. A **sapphire** is a precious stone which is usually bright blue in colour. EG *He left a sapphire and diamond ring to Violet.* N COUNT ⇑ gem

sarcasm /sɑːkæzə⁰m/ is speech or writing which actually means the opposite of what it seems to say and which is usually intended to mock or insult someone. EG *'Oh yeah,' said Jenny with broad sarcasm, 'I notice how you hate doing well in exams.'* N UNCOUNT ⇑ satire

sarcastic /sɑːkæstɪk/. Someone who is **sarcastic** uses words to mean the opposite of what they seem to say in order to mock or insult someone. EG *Although she had been crying earlier, she seemed her usual sarcastic self at dinner.* ▸ used of a person's speech or actions. EG *Her remarks can at times be bitterly sarcastic... He turned to me with a superior and sarcastic smile.* ◇ **sarcastically**. EG *'Do you mind if I take notes?' said Stuart sarcastically.* ADJ QUALIT ⇑ ironic ◇ ADV : USU WITH VB

sarcophagus /sɑːkɒfəgəs/, **sarcophagi, sarcophaguses**. The plural can be either **sarcophagi** or **sarcophaguses**. A **sarcophagus** is a large decorated stone coffin that was used in ancient times. EG *...a Roman sarcophagus with a Saxon lid.* N COUNT ⇑ tomb

sardine /sɑːdiːn/, **sardines**. 1 A **sardine** is a small sea fish which is eaten as food. Sardines are often preserved and sold in tins. EG *He opened two tins of sardines for his supper.* N COUNT
2 If a crowd of people are **packed like sardines**, they are standing or sitting so close together that they cannot move easily; an informal expression. EG *We were packed like sardines all the way home on the bus.* PHR : USED AS C

sardonic /sɑːdɒnɪk/. If you describe someone or their behaviour as **sardonic**, you mean that they are mocking or scornful, for example because they feel that they are too important to take a particular person or problem seriously. EG *He uttered a sardonic chuckle... ...a sardonic young man who never joined in the fun.* ◇ **sardonically**. EG *She said nothing, although she smiled sardonically as she opened the door for me.* ADJ QUALIT = derisive ◇ ADV WITH VB = derisively

sari /sɑːri¹/, **saris**. A **sari** is a piece of clothing that is worn especially by Indian women. It consists of a long piece of thin material wrapped around the body. N COUNT ⇑ garment

sarong /sərɒŋ/, **sarongs**. A **sarong** is a piece of clothing that is worn especially by Malaysian men and women. It consists of a long piece of cloth attached around the waist or under the armpit. N COUNT ⇑ skirt

sartorial /sɑːtɔːrɪəl/ means relating to the making of clothes, especially men's clothes, or to the way they are worn; a formal word. EG *He was famous for his sartorial elegance.* ADJ CLASSIF : ATTRIB ⇑ tailored

SAS /ɛs eɪ ɛs/. The **SAS** is a group of highly trained British soldiers who work on secret or very difficult military operations; an abbreviation for 'Special Air Service'. EG *...a brilliantly successful SAS attack.* N PROPER : *the* + N

sash /sæʃ/, **sashes**. A **sash** is 1 a long piece of cloth which people wear either round the waist as a belt or over one shoulder, usually as a badge of honour. EG *Her dress had a bright blue sash which she tied in a bow... The President's sash of office was broad and colourful.* 2 a frame which is fitted with panes of glass and which forms part of a door or a window. N COUNT / N COUNT

sash cord, sash cords. A **sash cord** is a strong piece of thin rope which connects a weight to the sliding half of a sash window. EG *He tried to raise the window, but the sash cord was broken.* N COUNT

sash window, sash windows. A **sash window** is a window which consists of two frames that are placed one above the other so that the window can be opened by sliding one frame over the front of the other. N COUNT

sat /sæt/ is the past tense and past participle of **sit**.

Sat. is an abbreviation for 'Saturday'.

Satan /seɪtə⁰n/; usually spelled **Shaitan** by Muslims. In Judaism, Christianity and Islam, **Satan** is the Devil, especially when he is thought of as being the chief opponent of God. N PROPER

satanic /sətænɪk/. Something that is **satanic** is 1 considered to be caused by or typical of Satan. EG *...a satanic cult... ...the viciously satanic enemies of man and God.* 2 extremely wicked and evil. EG *The Colonel's reputation is now more satanic than before.* ADJ QUALIT / ADJ QUALIT

satchel /sætʃə⁰l/, **satchels**. A **satchel** is a bag, usually with a shoulder strap, that schoolchildren use for carrying books. EG *He went off to school with a satchel over his shoulder.* N COUNT

sated /seɪtɪ²d/. If you are **sated**, you have had more of something, for example food or pleasure, than you can enjoy at one time; a formal word. EG *There was so much food that even my father's appetite was sated... I was sated with opera after listening to it for a whole weekend.* ADJ CLASSIF : USU PRED, IF + PREP THEN *with* ⇑ satisfied

satellite /sætəlaɪt/, **satellites**. A **satellite** is 1 an object that is sent into space and travels round the earth or around another planet in space. It is used, N COUNT, OR *by* + N for example, in communications or to collect information. EG *The United States and Soviet Union have hundreds of satellites overhead... The pictures were transmitted by satellite throughout the world.* **2** a natural object in space that moves round a larger object, for example a moon that moves round a planet or a planet that moves round a star. EG *Astronomers were excited to discover a small, oddly shaped satellite, Jupiter's 14th known moon.* **3** a country or organization which has no real power of its own, but which is dependent on another larger and more powerful country or organization. EG *The party consolidates its power by building up satellite organizations.*

N COUNT
N COUNT

satiate /seɪʃieɪt/, **satiates, satiating, satiated.** If something such as food or pleasure **satiates** you, you have so much of it that you become tired of it; a formal word. EG *There is usually enough fruit on one apple tree to satiate several children... During the week of the royal wedding there were enough festivities to satiate most people.*

V+O ⇑ satisfy = pall

satiety /sətaɪɪti¹/ is the state of having had too much of something such as food; a very formal word. EG *...the feeling of satiety after a meal, which discourages further eating.*

N UNCOUNT ⇑ satisfaction

satin /sætɪn/ is a kind of cloth, often made from silk, which is smooth and shiny on the front and dull on the back. EG *The bride was dressed in white satin.*
▸ used as an adjective. EG *The bed was spread with a pink satin cover.*

N UNCOUNT ⇑ material
▸ ADJ CLASSIF : ATTRIB

satire /sætaɪə/, **satires. 1 Satire** is ridicule or irony that is used, especially in plays and novels, to show how foolish or wicked some people's behaviour or ideas are. EG *He made his speeches more powerful with exquisite touches of irony and satire.*

N UNCOUNT

2 A **satire** is a play or novel written in this style. EG *It is a satire on the administration of justice... ...a brilliant political satire.*

N COUNT

satirical /sətɪrɪkə⁰l/. A piece of writing that is **satirical** uses a lot of satire. EG *...a persistent campaign of mockery by the satirical fortnightly magazine... A local newspaper had printed a satirical article I had written about the flats.*

ADJ QUALIT ⇑ ironical

satirist /sætə¹rɪst/, **satirists.** A **satirist** is a person who uses satire in their writing in order to express their feelings about people or society.

N COUNT ⇑ writer

satirize /sætə¹raɪz/, **satirizes, satirizing, satirized**; also spelled **satirise.** If you **satirize** a person or group of people, you criticize them or make fun of them through the use of satire in a play, novel, poem, etc. EG *They satirized the way wealthy capitalists behaved... These characteristics were often used by caricaturists to satirize feminists.*

V+O ⇑ deride

satisfaction /sætɪsfækʃə⁰n/. **1 Satisfaction** is **1.1** the pleasure that you feel when you are doing or have done something that you wanted or needed to do. EG *She stopped writing and read what she had written with satisfaction... She gave a sigh which expressed her pleasure and satisfaction at being there... The women need jobs and job satisfaction... To see the task finished gives them a sense of satisfaction, a sense of pride.* **1.2** something, for example money or an apology, which you get because of some harm or injustice which has been done to you. EG *Consumers who have been unable to get satisfaction from their local branch should write direct to the Chairman of the Board.*

N UNCOUNT = contentment
N UNCOUNT = compensation

2 If you do something **to** someone's **satisfaction**, they are happy with the way you have done it. EG *He explained everything to his own satisfaction... Every detail was worked out to everyone's satisfaction.*

PHR : USED AS AN A ⇑ contentment

satisfactory /sætɪsfæktə⁰ri¹/. Something that is **satisfactory** is good enough to be acceptable or to fulfil a particular need or purpose. EG *He considered the answers to these questions, and found them satisfactory... His doctor described his general state of health as fairly satisfactory... It will be much more satisfactory from your point of view if you are given more responsibility in your job.* ◇ **satisfactorily.** EG *She was not recovering very satisfactorily from the accident... They voted to strike if the dispute was not satisfactorily settled by 1 October.*

ADJ QUALIT ⇑ adequate
◇ ADV : USU WITH VB

satisfied /sætɪsfaɪd/. Someone who is **satisfied** is **1** happy because they have got what they wanted. EG *He was well satisfied with the success of the aircraft... I talked to one or two satisfied customers who had bought the same car... My husband and I are very satisfied here in this small village.* **2** convinced that something is true or settled. EG *He turned to me and nodded, satisfied... Now we can be satisfied that we've missed nothing important... I'm satisfied that her death was accidental.*

ADJ QUALIT = content
ADJ QUALIT : PRED, USU + REPORT-CL ⇑ certain

satisfy /sætɪsfaɪ/, **satisfies, satisfying, satisfied. 1** Someone or something that **satisfies** you **1.1** gives you enough of what you want to make you pleased or contented. EG *More frequent feeding will usually help to satisfy a baby... Your curiosity must be well satisfied if you have no more questions to ask... The firm has been unable to satisfy demand for its new small car.* **1.2** convinces you of the truth of something, especially of something that you had doubted. EG *He would need to satisfy the authorities that he had paid tax for the previous three years... This court is satisfied that all of the defendants were proved innocent... I glanced around, satisfied myself that the last diner had left, and turned off the lights.*

V+O = fulfil, content
V+O (NG/REFL), OR V+O (NG/REFL) + REPORT-CL ⇑ persuade

2 If you **satisfy** the requirements for something, you are good enough or suitable to fulfil these requirements. EG *There is some doubt whether they can satisfy our general entrance requirements for a Physics degree... Are all these conditions satisfied?*

V+O = meet

satisfying /sætɪsfaɪɪŋ/. Something that is **satisfying** gives you a feeling of pleasure and fulfilment. EG *There's nothing more satisfying than doing the work you love... They found themselves in the most satisfying agreement on absolutely everything.*

ADJ QUALIT

satsuma /sætsuːmə/, **satsumas.** A **satsuma** is a citrus fruit that looks like a small orange and is easy to peel.

N COUNT

saturate /sætʃəreɪt/, **saturates, saturating, saturated. 1** If people or things **saturate** a place or an object, they fill it so completely that no more can be added. EG *The police saturated the area where the boy was killed with photographs of the wanted man... This area of the moon is completely saturated with craters.*

V+O : USU PASS, IF + PREP THEN *with/in* = swamp

2 If someone or something **is saturated**, they are extremely wet. EG *After cycling up the hill, his shirt was saturated with sweat.*

V+O : USU PASS, IF + PREP THEN *with* = drench

3 If a solid substance **is saturated** in a chemical solution, the maximum amount of the substance is dissolved in the solution; a technical term in chemistry.

V+O : USU PASS, IF + PREP THEN *in/into*

saturation /sætʃəreɪʃə⁰n/. **1 Saturation** is the process or state that occurs when one thing is filled so full of another thing that no more can be added. EG *The new perfume came onto the market to the accompaniment of a saturation marketing and advertising campaign.* ● If something reaches **saturation point**, it is so full of something that no more can be added to it. EG *The market for new houses seemed to be reaching saturation point.*

N UNCOUNT ⇑ limit
● PHR

2 The **saturation** of a chemical compound is the state that it is in when it is saturated.

N UNCOUNT

3 The **saturation** of an area is the use of very heavy military force there against the enemy. EG *Hundreds were killed in the saturation bombing of the capital.*

N UNCOUNT

Saturday /sætədi¹/, **Saturdays. Saturday** is one of the seven days of the week. It is the day after Friday and before Sunday. EG *I've never worked on a Saturday in my life... I'm busy on Saturdays.*

N UNCOUNT/COUNT

saturnine /sætənaɪn/. Someone who is **saturnine** is gloomy and unfriendly; a formal word. EG *A saturnine customs officer looked through our baggage.*

ADJ QUALIT = dour

satyr /sætə/, **satyrs.** A **satyr** is a man with strong sexual desires; a literary word.

N COUNT

sauce /sɔːs/, **sauces. 1** A **sauce** is a thick liquid, often made from vegetables or fruit, which is served with other food to improve the flavour. EG *...tomato sauce... You should always check the seasoning in a sauce before serving it.*

N MASS

2 If you say that someone has a **sauce**, you mean that they are capable of saying something something rude or cheeky without worrying about offending other people; an informal use. EG *She had the sauce to say that she'd never been there... You've got a sauce, telling me I'm too old.*

N SING WITH DE = cheek

sauce-boat, sauce-boats; also spelled without a hyphen. A **sauce-boat** is a long shallow jug in which sauce is served.

N COUNT ⇑ container

saucepan /sɔːspən/, **saucepans.** A **saucepan** is a deep metal cooking pot, often with a long handle and usually with a lid. EG *The milk was warming in a saucepan on the cooker.*

N COUNT

saucer /sɔːsə/, **saucers**. A **saucer** is 1 a small curved plate on which you stand a cup. EG *She offered me tea in her best cup and saucer.* 2 anything that is shaped like a saucer, especially the disc of a radio telescope. ● See also **flying saucer**. — N COUNT; N COUNT ⇑ dish

saucy /sɔːsi¹/, **saucier, sauciest**. Someone who is **saucy** is rather rude in a light-hearted, amusing way; an informal word. EG *Don't be saucy with me.* — ADJ QUALIT = impertinent

Saudi /saudi¹, sɔː-/, **Saudis**. 1 Something that is **Saudi** belongs or relates to Saudi Arabia or to its people. — ADJ CLASSIF

2 A **Saudi** is a person who comes from Saudi Arabia. — N COUNT

Saudi Arabian, Saudi Arabians. 1 Something that is **Saudi Arabian** belongs or relates to Saudi Arabia or to its people. EG *...the Saudi Arabian desert.* — ADJ CLASSIF

2 A **Saudi Arabian** is someone who comes from Saudi Arabia. — N COUNT ⇑ person

sauerkraut /sauəkraut/ is cabbage that has been cut into very small slices and pickled. It is eaten mainly in Germany. — N UNCOUNT ⇑ vegetable

sauna /sɔːnə/, **saunas**. A **sauna** is 1 a hot steam bath, often followed by a bath or a swim in cold water. 2 the room or building where you have a sauna. — N COUNT; N COUNT

saunter /sɔːntə/, **saunters, sauntering, sauntered**. If you **saunter** somewhere, you walk there in a casual and unhurried way. EG *All afternoon he sauntered up and down, looking at the shops and the people... A policeman sauntered over from across the road to find out what the crowd was doing.* ▸ used as a noun. EG *Let's go for a saunter in the park.* — V+A = stroll; ▸ N COUNT

sausage /sɒsɪdʒ/, **sausages**. 1 **Sausage** is finely minced meat, especially pork or beef, which is mixed with other ingredients such as herbs and fat and then put into a thin casing like a tube. There are different kinds of sausage: some are sliced and eaten cold, and some are cooked and eaten hot. EG *We lunched on garlic sausage and some bread... ...a kilo of sausage meat.* — N UNCOUNT

2 A **sausage** is a tube-shaped piece of sausage meat. EG *...bacon, eggs, and sausages for breakfast.* — N COUNT

sausage dog, sausage dogs. A **sausage dog** is the same as a dachshund; used in informal English. — N COUNT

sausage roll, sausage rolls. A **sausage roll** is a small amount of sausage meat which is covered with pastry and cooked. Sausage rolls are often eaten as snacks in Britain. — N COUNT

sauté /səuteɪ/, **sautés, sautéing, sautéed**. If you **sauté** food, you fry it quickly in hot oil or butter. EG *Sauté the chicken breasts until they are golden brown.* ◊ **sautéed**. EG *...sautéed potatoes.* — V+O ⇑ cook; ◊ ADJ CLASSIF

savage /sævɪdʒ/, **savages, savaging, savaged**. 1 Someone or something that is **savage** is cruel, vicious, and violent. EG *His voice was loud and savage, and struck them into silence... His decision to resign is being attacked with savage ferocity by the newspapers.* ◊ **savagely**. EG *He grabbed Claude by the hair and jerked him savagely to his feet.* — ADJ QUALIT = ferocious; ◊ ADV = ferociously

2 If you refer to someone as a **savage**, you mean that they behave in a rude, cruel, or violent way. — N COUNT ⇑ person

3 A **savage** animal is wild and fierce. EG *...savage tigers.* — ADJ CLASSIF

4 If an animal **savages** someone, it attacks them violently and causes serious injury to them. — V+O

5 If you **savage** someone or something they have done, you criticize them extremely severely. EG *An opposition spokesman savaged the Government's housing investment programme.* — V+O

6 Some people refer to members of primitive or uncivilized tribes as **savages**; an offensive use. — N COUNT

savagery /sævɪdʒri¹/ is violent cruelty. EG *I was appalled by the savagery of the attack... She recoiled from the savagery in his voice.* — N UNCOUNT ⇑ violence

savannah /səvænə/, **savannahs**; also spelled **savanna**. A **savannah** is an open, flat stretch of grassland, usually in Africa. — N COUNT/UNCOUNT ⇑ plain

save /seɪv/, **saves, saving, saved**. 1 If you **save** someone or something, you help them to avoid harm or failure or to escape from a dangerous or unpleasant situation. EG *An artificial heart could save his life... They prayed for rain to save the starving village... She saved him from drowning... They were trying to save their marriage.* ● If you say that you cannot do something **to save** your **life**, you mean that you cannot do it at all, no matter how hard you try; an informal expression. EG *I couldn't write a novel to save my life... He can't sing to save his life.* — V+O : IF+PREP THEN *from* ⇑ rescue; ● PHR : USED AS AN A

2 If you **save** money, you gradually collect it by not spending everything you earn, especially so that you can buy something that you want. EG *It's not easy to save... They had managed to save enough to buy a house... I've been saving for three years to get a new car... She's saved three hundred pounds since last Christmas... We're saving for a new cooker.* — V, V+O, OR V+A ⇑ keep

3 To **save** time, money, or some other useful commodity means to prevent or avoid the loss or waste of it. EG *You could save up to 75 per cent of your heat loss by efficient insulation... This measure would save the government £185 million... It saved us so much time and effort... They've reorganized the office in an attempt to save on labour costs... This makes the product cheaper because the manufacturers save money on promotion.* — V+O, V+O+O, V+O+A *(on)*, OR V+A *(on)*

4 If you **save** something that you think might be useful at a later time, you keep it so that it will be available when you need it. EG *It's always a good idea to save business letters, bills, and receipts... I decided I'd save the wine for later... Will you save him a place at your table?* — V+O, OR V+O+O

5 If someone **saves** you the trouble or **saves** you doing something, they help you by making a particular task unnecessary, especially a task that involves effort or difficulty. EG *He resigned immediately to save them the trouble of sacking him... I'll bring it round on my bike to save putting it through the post... If you do it tonight, it'll save you from having to get up early... You could save yourself a lot of work if you used a computer.* — V+O/-ING, OR V+O (NG/REFL)+O/-ING/A *(from)*

6 If a goalkeeper in a game of football or hockey **saves** or **saves** a shot, he or she succeeds in preventing the ball from going into the goal after an opposing player has made a shot. EG *Shilton saved the penalty.* — V OR V+O

7 A **save** is an action by the goalkeeper, in a game of football or hockey, that prevents the other team from scoring a goal. EG *He made a brilliant save.* — N COUNT ⇑ movement

8 In the Christian Church, to **save** means to free people from the power of sin. EG *Jesus saves.* — V OR V+O = redeem

9 You can use **save** in order to introduce the only things, people, or ideas that your main statement does not apply to; a very formal use. EG *No visitors are allowed save in the most exceptional cases.* — PREP = except

● You use **save for** to introduce the only things, people, or ideas that prevent your main statement from being completely true. EG *The curtained stage was empty save for a few pieces of furniture.* — ● PREP = except for

save up. If you **save up** money, you collect it by not spending everything you earn, usually in order to be able to buy something with it when you have got enough. EG *He had some money saved up... It took me a year to save up for a new coat.* — PHRASAL VB : V+PREP = save

saver /seɪvə/, **savers**. A **saver** is a person who regularly saves money, especially by paying it into a bank account or a building society. EG *The building societies are offering high-interest accounts to tempt new savers.* — N COUNT

-saver, -savers. **-saver** combines with words such as 'time' and 'energy' to indicate that something prevents the thing mentioned from being wasted. EG *This turned out to be a great time-saver.* — COMB : FORMS N COUNTS

saving /seɪvɪŋ/, **savings**. 1 A **saving** is a reduction in the amount of time or money that is used or needed. EG *The whole operation was computerized, thereby effecting a considerable saving in time and money... The new management had achieved even bigger savings... The day return fare is only £12–a saving of £8 on the full fare.* — N COUNT : ALSO SING=PL

2 Your **savings** consist of the money that you have saved, especially in an account at a bank or similar institution. EG *She went to the bank and drew out all her savings... ...a savings account.* — N PLURAL : PL FORM WHEN MOD

-saving combines with words like 'time' and 'labour' to describe something which prevents the thing mentioned from being wasted. EG *It made sense to adopt labour-saving technology... ...energy-saving gadgets.* — COMB : FORMS ADJS

saving grace. A **saving grace** is a good quality in a person or thing that prevents them from being completely bad or worthless. EG *The play's only saving grace was the high standard of acting.* — N SING WITH DET ⇑ virtue

saviour /seɪvɪə/, **saviours**. 1 A **saviour** is person who saves people from danger or loss. EG *Many people regarded Churchill as the saviour of the country.* — N COUNT

2 In the Christian Church, Jesus Christ is sometimes referred to as the **Saviour**. N PROPER WITH DET

savoir-faire /sævwɑ: fɛə/ is the confidence to say and do the appropriate thing in a social situation; a fairly formal word. EG *I was impressed with her savoir-faire and social skills.* N UNCOUNT ⇑ knowledge

savour /seɪvə/, **savours, savouring, savoured**; also spelled **savor** in American English. 1 If you **savour** food or drink, you enjoy and appreciate it by eating or drinking it slowly to taste its full flavour. EG *I savoured every mouthful of breakfast, reluctant to let it end.* V+O = relish

2 A **savour** is particular smell or taste of food, which you find very pleasant. EG *Marjoram gives a fine savour to casseroles.* N COUNT/ UNCOUNT : USU SING ⇑ flavour

3 If you **savour** an experience, you take great pleasure and delight in it, enjoying it as much and for as long as you can. EG *He leaned back into his seat and relaxed, savouring the comfort... He savoured the word as he said it.* V+O = relish

savour of. If something **savours of** something else, it has certain characteristics or qualities that are not very obvious but that make people think of something which they disapprove of. EG *To do a good deed a day consciously savours of priggishness... He had an aversion to anything that savoured of the supernatural.* PHRASAL VB : V+ PREP = smack

savoury /seɪvəⁿri¹/, **savouries**. 1 **Savoury** food has a salty or spicy flavour rather than a sweet one. ADJ QUALIT : USU ATTRIB

2 **Savouries** are small portions of savoury food that are usually served at the end of a meal. N COUNT : USU PL

3 If you say that something is not **savoury**, you mean that it is not pleasant, respectable, or morally acceptable. EG *...the less savoury episodes in her past.* ADJ QUALIT : USU ATTRIB, USU WITH BROAD NEG

saw /sɔ:/, **saws, sawing, sawed, sawn**. 1 **Saw** is the past tense of **see**.

2 A **saw** is a tool for cutting wood and other materials, which has a blade with sharp teeth along one edge. Saws can be pushed by hand backwards and forwards across a piece of wood, or they can be powered by electricity. N COUNT

3 To **saw** something means to cut it with a saw. EG *He sawed the branch in half... We'll have to saw through the tree.* V OR V+O

4 To **saw** means to move something such as your arm or a violin bow from side to side as if you were using a saw. EG *In the hotel lounge an awful chamber orchestra was sawing away under a lot of imitation palm leaves.* V : USU+A *(away)*

5 A **saw** is also a short, well-known saying or proverb; an old-fashioned use. N COUNT

saw off. To **saw** something **off** means to cut a piece from something by using a saw. EG *Jack had sawn off the broken ash bough... I started sawing the branches off the main trunk.* PHRASAL VB : V+ O+ADV/PREP

saw up. To **saw** something **up** means to cut it into pieces by using a saw. EG *He spent all day sawing up the dead wood.* PHRASAL VB : V+ O+ADV

sawdust /sɔ:dʌst/ is dust and very small pieces of wood which are produced when you saw wood or when you sand it. EG *Sawdust was scattered on the floor.* N UNCOUNT

sawmill /sɔ:mɪl/, **sawmills**. A **sawmill** is a factory in which wood is sawn up into planks, using a power-driven saw. N COUNT

sawn /sɔ:n/ is the past participle of **saw**.

sawn-off shotgun, sawn-off shotguns. A **sawn-off shotgun** is a shotgun on which the barrel has been cut short. Criminals use sawn-off shotguns because they can hide them more easily than complete shotguns. N COUNT

sax /sæks/, **saxes**. A **sax** is the same as a saxophone; an informal word. EG *Bobby played sax in a band.* N COUNT/ UNCOUNT

Saxon /sæksəⁿn/. Something that is **Saxon** relates to, or is characteristic of, the ancient Saxons, the Anglo-Saxons, or their descendants. ADJ CLASSIF

saxophone /sæksəfəʊn/, **saxophones**. A **saxophone** is a musical instrument that you play by blowing and pressing keys. It is made of metal in a curved shape, and is often played in jazz bands. N COUNT

saxophonist /sə³ksɒfənɪst/, **saxophonists**. A **saxophonist** is someone who plays a saxophone. N COUNT ⇑ musician

say /seɪ/, **says, saying, said**. 1 When you **say** something, you speak words. You use **say 1.1** for direct speech when you give the actual words that someone uses: see also □ at QUOTE. EG *'Please come in,' she said... 'What did you say?'–'I said, What about meeting tomorrow at 3?'... I said to him 'I'd never do anything like that, and you know it'... She kept saying to me 'don't forget, will you.'* V+QUOTE **1.2** for indirect speech when you do not give the exact words that someone uses: see also □ at REPORT-CL. EG *He says he wants to go to Bombay... He said it was an accident... I said that I would like to teach English... I was saying to John this morning that I was thinking of going to London for the weekend.* V+REPORT-CL

2 He **said** thank you, he **said** no, etc means that he thanked you, refused something, etc either by using the actual words 'thank you', 'no', etc, or by using a different form of words, for example 'I'm very grateful', 'I'd rather not', etc. EG *He said thank you... At the worst, they can only say no... He said sorry... People kept coming up to us to say hello... Don't forget to say thank you before you leave.* V+CONVENTION ⇑ express

3 To **say** something means to express an idea, fact, or opinion aloud in words. EG *I couldn't think of a single thing to say... I could never understand what they were saying... If they don't agree with me they say so... He had said nothing to me about his meeting... I'd like to say a few words.* V+O/REPORT-CL

4 You also use **say** in expressions like 'it is said' and 'they say' when you are giving an opinion that a lot of people have, especially when this supports your opinion. EG *It is commonly said that people get the government they deserve... You know what they say, better late than never.* PHR+O/REPORT-CL

5 You sometimes use **say** as a way of introducing a comment that you think is important, or a point of view that you have. EG *I just want to say how pleased I am to be here... I think I can safely say that we have all learnt a great deal this evening... I think it's fair to say we do the work because we're interested in it... I wouldn't really say London was a good place for children to grow up in... This is not to say that children can't grow up to be normal there... Most linguists would say they were concerned primarily with the structure of language.* V+REPORT-CL

6 If you must **say** something, you must admit that it is true. EG *I must say, though, it's a very sexist play... One thing you have to say about Americans: they love drama.* V+O/REPORT-CL

7 You also use **say** in expressions like 'just say' and 'let's say' when you want to discuss something that might possibly happen in the future or might possibly be true. EG *Just say you found buried treasure in your garden. Would you sell it?... Say the car breaks down on the journey. Have you enough money to catch a train?... Let's say you won £1,000. What would you do with it?* V+REPORT-CL ⇑ assume = suppose

8 You also use **say** in expressions like 'as you say' to indicate that you agree with someone else's view or to repeat your own view. EG *These books are designed, as you say, to appeal to children... So, as I say, this is a political judgement... She was not fussy. She was, one would say, almost the opposite... The play was directed, as we said, by Ron Daniels.* CONVENTION

9 To **say** words you have learned, such as the lines of a play or prayers means to repeat them aloud. EG *He said his lines perfectly... He knelt down and said his prayers.* V+O = recite • If you **say** something **to** yourself, you think it. EG *I began to say to myself, 'What about becoming an actor?'* • PHR : VB INFLECTS

10 If a letter, notice, poster, badge, etc **says** something, it expresses it in written words. EG *'Weekend in London' say the posters... There were stickers all over the crate, saying: 'Glass–Handle with Care'... She wrote to say she wanted to meet me in London.* V+QUOTE/ REPORT-CL

11 If something such as a clock, dial, map, etc **says** something, it gives you information which you can understand when you look at it or read it. EG *The clock says that it is six o'clock... The road was not exactly where the map said it should be.* V+O/REPORT-CL

12 If someone's face, behaviour, action, etc **says** something, it is a sign of that thing. EG *His face said that he was unhappy.* V+REPORT-CL ⇑ express

13 If artists, writers, composers, etc **say** something, they communicate ideas which they think are important through a work of art. EG *The composer had nothing to say in his second symphony.* V+O/REPORT-CL = express

14 **Say** is used, especially in American English, to attract someone's attention or to express surprise, pleasure or admiration. EG *Say, that's a good idea!* EXCLAM = I say

15 **I say** is used, in old-fashioned British English, to EXCLAM

express surprise or admiration. EG *I say, sir, that's a remarkably attractive girl.*

16 You also use **say** 16.1 when you give something as an example. EG *Compare, say, a Michelangelo painting with a Van Gogh... Is it possible to book the ferry, say, on Saturday and get there on Saturday?* = for example 16.2 when you give an approximate amount or time. EG *You seem to look forward to the next, say, ten years with great enthusiasm... Come for dinner at, say, eight o'clock.* = roughly

17 If you have a **say** in something, you have the right or the opportunity to give your opinion, especially when there is a decision to be taken. EG *Teachers have had very little say in the new curriculum... People want a much greater say in how the country should be governed.* N SING WITH DET : IF + PREP THEN *in* ● If you **have** your **say**, you give your opinion. EG *The workmen are to have their say about the new factory.* ● PHR : VB INFLECTS

18 The word **say** is also used in the following expressions. 18.1 You use **'say what you like'** when you are about to make a comment that you know the person you are speaking to is likely to disagree with. EG *Say what you like, but I think he was an excellent Hamlet.* CONVENTION 18.2 You use **'well said!'** to emphasize your agreement with an opinion that someone has just expressed. EG *'This meeting is a complete waste of time.'–'Well said! I couldn't agree more.'* CONVENTION 18.3 You use **'enough said'** or **'say no more'** to tell someone that you completely understand what they mean and that there is no need for them to add anything more; an informal expression. EG *'I'd be grateful if this could be kept quiet.'–'Enough said.'* CONVENTION 18.4 You use **not to say** when a word you have just used could have been replaced by a word which is even greater in degree or even more surprising. EG *It would be pleasant to live in a warm, not to say hot, climate... It was an interesting, not to say shocking, film.* PHR 18.5 You use **'say the word'** in order to tell someone that if they ask you to do something, you will do it willingly. EG *Just say the word and I'll come with you.* PHR 18.6 You use **to say the least** to indicate that you are definitely not exaggerating, and that what you are describing is in fact a lot more serious than you have suggested. EG *Her comment was tactless, to say the least.* PHR : USED AS ADV SEN 18.7 **That is to say** is used to indicate that you are about to express the same idea more clearly. EG *The Romans left Britain in 410 AD–that is to say, England was a Roman dependency for nearly 500 years... She took the case to court. But she lost. That is to say, she lost her main argument.* PHR : USED AS ADV SEN 18.8 You use **to say nothing of** when you add something which gives even more strength to the point you are making. EG *There is no time to do all the work, to say nothing of the cost.* PHR + NG = let alone 18.9 You use **'you can say that again!'** or **'you said it!'** when you completely agree with an opinion that someone has just expressed; an informal expression. EG *'I need a new suit.'–'You can say that again!'* CONVENTION 18.10 You use **you don't say** to express surprise at what someone has just told you, sometimes in a sarcastic way; an informal expression. EG *'I don't think your mother likes me.'–'You don't say!'* CONVENTION

18.11 You use **needless to say** when you state something that is exactly what the person you are speaking to would expect. EG *Needless to say, he was late for the meeting... This new social awareness will, needless to say, bring big changes in its wake.* PHR : USED AS ADV SEN = of course

18.12 If something **goes without saying**, it is so obvious that you do not need to explain it. EG *It goes without saying that I am grateful for all your help.* PHR : VB INFLECTS, USU *It* + PHR + REPORT-CL

18.13 **There is no saying** means it is not possible to know. EG *There is no saying what time he will come home.* PHR + REPORT-CL 18.14 You use expressions like **'what would you say to a cup of tea?'** in order to make a suggestion or an offer; an informal expression. EG *What would you say to a trip to Paris?* PHR 18.15 You use **'I wouldn't say no'** to indicate that you would like something, especially something that has just been offered to you; an informal expression. EG *I wouldn't say no to a cup of tea.* CONVENTION : IF + PREP THEN *to* 18.16 You use the expression **'I will say this for** him, her', etc before you mention a quality that you admire in a particular person, especially when you have been criticizing that person. EG *I will say this for her–she's brave.* PHR : USED AS ADV SEN 18.17 If something **has a lot to be said for it**, it has a lot of advantages or good qualities. EG *As a description it has a lot to be said for it.* PHR : *have* INFLECTS 18.18 If something **says a lot for** something else, it is an indication that this other thing has a lot of admirable qualities. EG *All these letters say a lot for your popularity... It says something for linguistics that so many interesting people study it.* PHR : VB INFLECTS 18.19 If something **says a lot about** another thing, or if it **says something about** it, it is very revealing about this other thing. EG *Your clothes say a lot about you... The condition of the roads says something about the Government's attitude to public spending.* PHR : VB INFLECTS 18.20 If you **have** something **to say for** yourself, you give an explanation for something wrong you have done. EG *What have you got to say for yourself?* PHR : *have* INFLECTS

saying /seɪɪŋ/, **sayings.** A **saying** is a statement which is often made and which is therefore usually well-known to native speakers of the language. EG *There is a saying that 'man shall not live by bread alone'... ...the sayings of Chairman Mao... He played it, as the saying goes, for real.* N COUNT ⇑ expression

say-so. If you do something on someone's **say-so,** they tell you to do it or they give you permission to do it; used in informal English. EG *Daniel had already left, on his father's say-so... No luggage can go into the aircraft without his say-so.* N SING : WITH POSS ⇑ command, authority

scab /skæb/, **scabs.** A **scab** is 1 a hard, dry covering that forms over the surface of a wound while it is healing. EG *A great scab had formed on his right knee.* N COUNT 2 someone who refuses to support a trade union's actions, and who continues to work when the people that he or she works with are on strike; used showing disapproval. EG *People have to be organised to stop lorries or scabs going in or out of the factories.* N COUNT = blackleg

scabbard /skæbəd/, **scabbards.** A **scabbard** is a holder for a sword, especially one that hangs from a belt. N COUNT ⇑ sheath

scabby /skæbi[1]/, **scabbier, scabbiest.** If your skin is **scabby**, it is covered with scabs. EG *...the freckled, scabby hands of the old men.* ADJ QUALIT

scabies /skeɪbi:z/ is a very infectious skin disease caused by a parasite, which makes you want to scratch a lot; a medical term. N UNCOUNT

scads /skædz/. If you have **scads** of something, you have a lot of it; used in very informal American English. EG *...glancing at the scads of notes they were holding.* PART = heaps, masses

scaffold /skæfə[ʊ]ld/, **scaffolds.** A **scaffold** is 1 a kind of platform on which criminals used to be hanged or beheaded. EG *Guy Fawkes died on the scaffold.* N COUNT : USU SING ⇑ structure 2 the same as scaffolding. EG *The builders promised to take the scaffold down on Friday.* N COUNT

scaffolding /skæfə[ʊ]ldɪŋ/ consists of metal poles and wooden boards that are made into a framework next to a high wall in order to support people who are building, repairing, or painting the wall. EG *He led me straight back past the scaffolding in the main hall.* N UNCOUNT

scald /skɔ:ld/, **scalds, scalding, scalded.** 1 If you **scald** yourself or **scald** a part of your body, you burn yourself with very hot liquid or steam. EG *Don't scald yourself: the water's very hot... When it was cool enough not to scald my lips, I swallowed the coffee and asked for more.* V + O (NG/REFL) ⇑ wound

2 A **scald** is a burn that has been caused by very hot liquid or steam. EG *This ointment is excellent for cuts and scalds.* N COUNT ⇑ wound

3 If you **scald** something, you put it into boiling water or steam for a short time, in order to clean or sterilize it. EG *When the needles have been rinsed, they are scalded in boiling water for about ten minutes.* V + O

4 If you **scald** milk, you heat it until it is almost boiling; often used in recipes. V + O

scalding /skɔ:ldɪŋ/. Something that is **scalding** is extremely hot. EG *...scalding coffee... ...a bath of scalding water... The tea is usually tasteless though always scalding.* ADJ CLASSIF : USU ATTRIB = boiling ▸ used as an adverb. EG *Her skin was scalding hot.* ▸ ADV + ADJ ⇑ very

scale /skeɪl/, **scales, scaling, scaled.** 1 The **scale** of something is the size and range of it; used especially of something that cannot be counted or physically measured. EG *The scale of change is so enormous... The scale of industry was the crucial factor... ...the sheer scale of the United States.* N SING WITH DET + SUPP = dimensions

2 You use **scale** in expressions such as **large scale**, **on a large scale**, and **large in scale** to mean the degree or extent to which something is made, done, or happens. EG *There's no possibility of jobs being* N UNCOUNT OR N SING WITH DET + SUPP

created on the scale needed... The district grew peas on a large scale... Their plan was never very grand in scale... ...small scale alternative methods of getting energy... It's her first full scale novel.

3 A **scale** is **3.1** a set of numbers which are used in a particular system of measuring something or of showing the standard or level of something in comparison with other things of the same kind. EG *Richter invented the scale by which we measure the severity of earthquakes... ...a temperature scale... ...a five-point scale.* **3.2** a series of marks on something that is used for measuring, for example on a thermometer, ruler, or measuring jug. **3.3** a list of amounts of money, which is used in deciding how much money a person should pay or receive, for example how much workers should be paid in relation to their ages, experience, and qualifications. EG *The salary for someone on the bottom rung of the pay scale would be £500 a month.*
N COUNT : USU + SUPP; N COUNT = gradations; N COUNT : USU + SUPP

4 You also use the word **scale** when you are considering all the different levels, degrees, or forms of something as if they were arranged in a neat, logical order. EG *It happened everywhere, through the social scale... What happens when we go down the evolutionary scale to the level of bacteria, viruses and other organisms?... They came to accept their guards' scale of values... At the other end of the scale there are simple actions such as blinking.*
N SING WITH DET + SUPP ⇑ hierarchy = range

5 The **scale** of a map, plan, drawing, or model is the relationship between the measurements of something in the real world and the measurements of it as shown by the map, plan, drawing, or model. EG *What's the scale of that map?... ...a scale of 1:50,000.* ▸ used as an adjective. EG *I used to collect scale models of well-known Navy ships... ...a large-scale map.* ● If a map, plan, drawing, or model is **to scale**, it is accurately drawn or made according to the particular scale that is being used. EG *Draw it out to scale neatly on graph paper.* ● If something is **out of scale**, the relationships between the measurements of its different parts are wrong. EG *Its parts look somehow out of scale, all lopsided.*
N COUNT/UNCOUNT ⇑ ratio; ▸ ADJ CLASSIF; ● PHR : USED AS AN A; ● PHR : USED AS AN A

6 A **scale** is also a sequence of musical notes that are played or sung in an upward or downward order. Musicians often practise scales to help them to play or sing better. EG *I dutifully played my scales... She told me to practise the scale of C.*
N COUNT

7 The **scales** of fish, snakes, or other reptiles are the small, flat pieces of skin that cover their body. EG *Wash the fish and take off the scales with a knife.*
N COUNT : USU PL

8 **Scales** are a device or a machine for weighing things or people. EG *You want me to get the scales, Mabel, so you can weigh her?... ...a pair of scales.*
N PLURAL : ALSO *a pair of*+N

9 **Scale** is **9.1** a hard layer of food and other substances that forms on teeth, especially when they have not been cleaned properly. **9.2** a layer of a substance such as calcium that forms on the inside of kettles, pipes, and other things that contain hot water.
N UNCOUNT ⇑ deposit; N UNCOUNT = fur, lime

10 If you **scale** something such as a mountain that is steep or difficult, you climb up or over it. EG *She scaled the barrier like a Commando... We had to penetrate dense scrub and scale rocks.*
V+O ⇑ ascend, mount

scale down. If something **is scaled down**, it has been made smaller in size, amount, or extent than it used to be, although it has the same proportions that it had before. EG *The operations were scaled down... ...a scaled-down version.*
PHRASAL VB : V+O+ADV, USU PASS ⇑ reduce

scallop /skɒləp, skæl-/, **scallops**. **1** **Scallops** are shellfish with two flat fan-shaped shells, which can be eaten.
N COUNT : USU PL

2 **Scallops** are also a series of small curves that form an ornamental border on things such as clothes, tablecloths, or handkerchiefs.
N COUNT : USU PL ⇑ edging

scalloped /skɒləpt, skæl-/. **Scalloped** objects are decorated with a series of small curves along the edges. EG *...scalloped skirts... ...a blue and green scalloped design.*
ADJ CLASSIF : ATTRIB ⇑ notched

scallywag /skæli^{1}wæg/, **scallywags**. If you call someone a **scallywag**, you mean that they have behaved badly but you like them, so you find it difficult to be really angry with them; an informal word.
N COUNT = rascal

scalp /skælp/, **scalps, scalping, scalped**. **1** Your **scalp** is the skin that is under the hair on your head. EG *...rubbing his sore scalp.*
N COUNT

2 To **scalp** someone who has just been killed means to remove the mass of skin and hair from the top part of their head. This was sometimes done by North American Indians as a sign of victory. EG *The whole family had been scalped.*
V+O

3 A **scalp** is also the piece of skin and hair that is removed when someone is scalped. Scalps were sometimes collected as symbols of victory. EG *...offering reward money for the scalps of their enemies.*
N COUNT

scalpel /skælpə°l/, **scalpels**. A **scalpel** is **1** a knife with a short, thin, and very sharp blade, which is used by surgeons during operations. **2** a tool with a sharp point, which is used by artists for carving wood.
N COUNT; N COUNT

scaly /skeɪli^{1}/, **scalier, scaliest**. **Scaly** means covered in small stiff patches of hard skin. EG *...round patches of scaly skin in which the hair is broken off short.*
ADJ QUALIT ⇑ layered

scamp /skæmp/, **scamps**. If you call a child a **scamp**, you mean that they are very naughty but you like them, so you find it difficult to be angry with them; an informal word. EG *What have you been up to, you young scamp?*
N COUNT/VOC = scallywag

scamper /skæmpə/, **scampers, scampering, scampered**. When people or small animals **scamper**, they move with small, quick, bouncing steps. EG *The squirrels scamper along the twigs... I saw him scamper away.*
V+A = scuttle, scurry

scampi /skæmpi^{1}/ is a dish of large prawns which have been fried in batter; used in British English.
N UNCOUNT

scan /skæn/, **scans, scanning, scanned**. **1** When you **scan** written material, you look through it quickly in order to find important or interesting information. EG *The other letter which I opened and scanned rapidly was from John... I scan the papers for all presidential news.*
V+O, OR V+A ⇑ survey

2 When you **scan** something, you look at it very carefully, usually because you are looking for something in particular. EG *Anxiously Carol scanned their faces to see who she might know... ...lifeguards scanning the sea for shark-fins... I was scanning the rows with binoculars.*
V+O, OR V+A ⇑ examine = scrutinize

3 If a machine **scans** something, **3.1** it reads or examines it quickly, often by moving a beam of light or electrons over it. EG *...a photo-electric reader capable of scanning characters at the rate of two thousand a second.* **3.2** it examines or searches a particular area or region by sending radar or sonar beams over it. EG *The reconnaissance plane's job was to scan the oceans with its radar.* ▸ used as a noun. EG *The next scan of the radar confirmed the ship's location.*
V+O ⇑ survey; V+O = comb; ▸ N COUNT : USU SING

4 If the words of a poem **scan**, they fit into a regular, rhythmical pattern.
V OR V+O

scandal /skændə°l/, **scandals**. **1** If something is a **scandal**, a lot of people know about it and think that it is very shocking and immoral. EG *We can't afford another scandal in the firm... It became known as the Marconi scandal.... There were no scandals about her or anything.*
N COUNT = outrage

2 **Scandal** is talk that emphasizes the shocking and immoral qualities of someone's behaviour or of something that has happened. EG *Someone must have been spreading scandal... They are really wanting information and not scandal.*
N UNCOUNT ⇑ rumour

3 If you say that something is a **scandal**, you are angry about it and think that the people responsible for it should be ashamed. EG *The defences were a scandal... In time, the president's meanness got to be a national scandal.*
N SING : a+N = disgrace, outrage

scandalize /skændə°laɪz/, **scandalizes, scandalizing, scandalized**; also spelled **scandalise**. If someone **is scandalized**, they are shocked and offended. EG *He was uncertain whether to laugh or be scandalized... It scandalized me that not even the children were fed properly.*
V+O : USU PASS = outrage

scandalmonger /skændə°lmʌŋgə/, **scandalmongers**. A **scandalmonger** is someone who deliberately spreads stories that emphasize the shocking or immoral qualities of particular people; used showing disapproval.
N COUNT ⇑ stirrer

scandalous /skændə°ləs/. If something is **scandalous**, **1** it is thought to be immoral and so is likely to shock people. EG *There were some scandalous stories about her... ...scandalous scenes of ladies with bare breasts.* ◇ **scandalously**. EG *Her fifteen-year-old sister had, scandalously, run off and married a nephew of the president.* **2** it makes you very angry and you
ADJ QUALIT ⇑ outrageous; ◇ ADV WITH V; ADJ QUALIT

think that the people responsible for it should be ashamed. EG *...a scandalous waste of brain power... Bribery and corruption reached scandalous proportions... It is scandalous that the public should be treated in this way.* ◊ **scandalously**. EG *...offering scandalously large tax advantages.* ◊ ADV+ADJ/ADV

Scandinavian /skændɪneɪvɪən/, **Scandinavians**. 1 Something that is **Scandinavian** belongs or relates to Scandinavia, or to its countries, peoples, or languages. EG *...The Netherlands, Austria and the Scandinavian countries.* ADJ CLASSIF

2 A **Scandinavian** is a person who comes from Scandinavia. EG *At the present time we have five Scandinavians and one German in our class.* N COUNT

scanner /skænə/, **scanners**. A **scanner** is 1 a device which uses ultrasonic waves for medical examinations. N COUNT 2 an aerial which is used to send out or to receive radar signals. N COUNT

scant /skænt/, **scanter, scantest**. If you say that something receives **scant** attention, you mean that it receives only a little attention, and certainly less than you think it should receive. EG *The ailments of the world's poor receive scant attention compared to the diseases of the rich... The campaign was conducted with scant regard for truth and less for justice...* ADJ QUALIT : : USU ATTRIB ⇑ meagre

scanty /skænti¹/, **scantier, scantiest**. Something that is **scanty** is smaller in quantity or size than you think it should be. EG *...a rather scanty but enthusiastic audience... ...scanty information about their pupils... ...subjects on which he had the scantiest knowledge.* ◊ **scantily**. EG *The bedroom was scantily furnished... ...a scantily cut blouse.* ADJ QUALIT = sparse ◊ ADV WITH VB

scapegoat /skeɪpgəʊt/, **scapegoats**. If someone is made a **scapegoat**, they are blamed publicly for something that has happened, although it may not be their fault, because other people are very angry about it and need to have someone they can blame and punish. EG *In their search for a scapegoat, the government found an easy target in the unions.* N COUNT

scapula /skæpjə⁴lə/, **scapulas**. Your **scapula** is your shoulder blade; a medical word. N COUNT ⇑ bone

scar /skɑː/, **scars, scarring, scarred**. 1 A **scar** is 1.1 a line or mark on the skin which is left after a wound has healed. EG *There was a scar on her right arm... ...deep knife scars across his face.* N COUNT 1.2 a mark on something, where it has been damaged. EG *The paint had been stripped away revealing scars of bare wood.* N COUNT ⇑ trace

2 If your skin **is scarred**, it is badly marked as a result of a wound. EG *If the victims survive initial burns, they will be badly scarred for life... ...combing her hair with scarred hands.* V OR V+O : USU PASS ⇑ blemish

3 If an object **is scarred**, it is damaged and there are ugly marks on it. EG *...the scarred trunk of the tree.* V+O : USU PASS ⇑ blemish

4 A **scar** is also a permanent effect on someone's mind that results from a very unpleasant physical or emotional experience. EG *The scars of poverty have undoubtedly left their mark... The first years of the eighties had left their scars.* N COUNT ⇑ damage

5 If an unpleasant experience **scars** you or your mind, it has a permanent effect on your mind, and influences the way you think and behave. EG *It wasn't the violence of the attack that scarred my mind.* V+O : USU PASS ⇑ damage

scarce /skeəs/, **scarcer, scarcest**. 1 If something is **scarce**, there is not very much of it, and there may not be enough for those who want or need it. EG *...an environment where water is still scarce... Potatoes became scarce.* ADJ QUALIT ⇑ uncommon = rare

2 If you **make** yourself **scarce**, you leave the place you are in, usually in order to avoid a difficult or embarrassing situation; an informal expression. PHR : VB INFLECTS = disappear

scarcely /skeəsli¹/. 1 **Scarcely** adds a negative quality to what you are saying, and so means that the thing you are talking about is only just true or is only just the case. EG *The landscape scarcely altered for hundreds of thousands of years... I can scarcely remember what we ate... They were scarcely ever apart... There was scarcely a moment they could call their own... It was a very young man who had said this, scarcely more than a boy... ...side-alleys scarcely wide enough for a cat to turn round.* ADV BRD NEG = barely, hardly

2 You can use **scarcely** in a slightly ironic way to mean not at all, or certainly not. By using 'scarcely' you emphasize that the opposite of what you are saying is actually true. EG *There could scarcely be a less promising environment for children... I need scarcely say... That is scarcely the point... The national newspaper industry is scarcely an advertisement for technological progress... It is scarcely conceivable that the plan can have remained a secret.* ADV BRD NEG = hardly

3 If you say **scarcely** had one thing happened when something else happened, or one thing had **scarcely** happened when something else happened, you mean that the first event was followed immediately by the second. EG *Scarcely had the car drawn to a halt when armed police surrounded it... The noise had scarcely died away when someone started to laugh again.* ADV BRD NEG = hardly, no sooner

scarcity /skeəsɪti¹/. If there is a **scarcity** of something, there is not enough of it for those who want or need it. EG *...the scarcity of food... ...problems of expense and scarcity.* N UNCOUNT ⇑ shortage = paucity

scare /skeə/, **scares, scaring, scared**. 1 Someone or something that **scares** you makes you feel frightened or alarmed. EG *There was nothing these creatures could do that scared me... I didn't mean to scare you.* ● If something **scares the life out of** you, **scares the hell out of** you, etc, it shocks you and makes you feel very frightened; an informal expression. EG *He scared the life out of her... Some of the talk we hear scares the hell out of us.* V+O = startle ● PHR : VB INFLECTS = terrify

2 If you **scare** easily, you are a nervous kind of person who gets frightened easily. V : USU+A, NO CONT

3 If you have a **scare**, you have a sudden unpleasant experience that makes you frightened or alarmed. EG *The first attack gave me a scare because I wasn't ready for it... That night I had an even worse scare.* N COUNT : USU SING = fright

4 A **scare** is a situation where people are afraid because they think that something very unpleasant or dangerous is happening which will affect them all. This thing often does not happen at all, or is less serious than people thought. EG *Since none of the sample fragments picked up was radioactive the scare died down... ...There was a rabies scare.* N COUNT : USU MOD+N ⇑ affair

scare away. If you **scare** someone **away** or if you **scare** them **off**, 1 you frighten them so that they go away. EG *The least shadow or movement would scare the fish away... The boys made enough noise to scare off any animals.* PHRASAL VB : V+O+ADV ⇑ drive away 2 you make them so nervous that they decide not to do something that they were planning to do. EG *The dispute there has scared away potential investors... He named a price he thought would scare me off.* ● See also **scared**. PHRASAL VB : V+O+ADV ⇑ drive away

scarecrow /skeəkrəʊ/, **scarecrows**. A **scarecrow** is an object in the shape of a person, which is put in a field where crops are growing in order to frighten birds away. It is usually made by hanging old clothes on sticks. N COUNT ⇑ effigy

scared /skeəd/. 1 If you are **scared**, you are very frightened of someone or something, and therefore unable to behave calmly. EG *He was terribly scared... ...too shocked and scared to move... Everybody's scared of him... I'm scared to answer the phone.* ADJ QUALIT : USU PRED, IF+PREP/VB THEN *of/to*-INF ⇑ afraid

● Someone who is **scared to death** or **scared stiff** is very scared indeed; an informal expression. ● PHR : USED AS C

2 If you are **scared** that something unpleasant may happen, you are very nervous and worried that it may happen. EG *I'm scared that these will turn out to be the wrong ones... They're scared of making a fool of themselves.* ADJ QUALIT : PRED+REPORT-CL/*of*+-ING = apprehensive

scaremonger /skeəmʌŋgə/, **scaremongers**. A **scaremonger** is someone who deliberately spreads worrying stories to try and frighten people. N COUNT ⇑ alarmist = stirrer

scare story, scare stories. A **scare story** is something that is said or written to make people feel frightened and think that a situation is much more unpleasant or dangerous than it really is. EG *...early scare stories, suggesting that a nuclear explosion had taken place.* N COUNT ⇑ rumour

scarf /skɑːf/, **scarfs, scarves**. The plural can be either **scarfs** or **scarves**. A **scarf** is a piece of cloth that you wear round your neck, shoulders, or head to keep yourself warm or to make yourself look attractive. Scarves are often long and narrow, but sometimes they are square or triangular in shape. EG *The east wind made the girl pull her black woollen scarf tightly round her neck.* N COUNT ⇑ accessory

scarlatina /skɑːlətiːnə/ is scarlet fever; a medical term. N UNCOUNT ⇑ illness

scarlet /skɑːlə¹t/, **scarlets**. Something that is **scarlet** is bright red in colour. ▸ used as a noun. EG *...silky glowing materials in brilliant scarlets, blues, and greens.* ADJ COLOUR ▸ N COUNT

scarlet fever is an infectious disease which causes you to have a painful throat, a high temperature, and a red rash on your body. N UNCOUNT ⇑ illness = scarlatina

scarper /skɑːpə/, **scarpers, scarpering, scarpered.** If someone **scarpers**, they go away from a place quickly; a very informal word used in British English. EG *Go on, scarper!... I had to scarper when I heard you at the door.* V: NO CONT ⇑ leave

scarves /skɑːvz/ is a plural of **scarf**. N COUNT

scary /skeəri[1]/, **scarier, scariest.** Something that is **scary** makes you feel a little bit frightened; a fairly informal word. EG *'Is it fun?'–'Not at first. It's scary.'... It was a scary moment.* ADJ QUALIT ⇑ frightening

scathing /skeɪðɪŋ/. Someone who is **scathing** about something criticizes it very harshly and scornfully. EG *She had written a rather scathing article about silly lady novelists... Miss Jackson was scathing about our efforts.* ◇ **scathingly.** EG *He refers scathingly to these superstitions.* ADJ QUALIT: IF+PREP THEN *about* = caustic ◇ ADV

scatter /skætə/, **scatters, scattering, scattered.** 1 If you **scatter** things over a large area of ground, you throw or drop a lot of them so that they are spread all over the area, often in an irregular or untidy way. EG *...raising the first crops from the seeds she scattered... The books had been snatched from the shelves and scattered all over the floor... David's possessions were scattered on the desk... ...a room with bowls of fruit and flowers scattered everywhere.* V+O (N IN PL/UNCOUNT): USU +A = strew

2 If a group of people or things **scatter**, they suddenly separate and move in different directions. EG *The boys scattered, squealing in horror... The pile of books fell down and scattered all over the floor... The noise scattered the dogs and chickens.* V-ERG ⇑ disperse

3 A **scatter** of things is a small number of things that are spread over a small area in an irregular way. EG *We went past a scatter of gas lit shops... I couldn't distinguish him among the scatter of distant faces.* N SING WITH DET +*of*+N IN PL/UNCOUNT ⇑ group = sprinkle

● See also **scattered, scattering.**

scatterbrain /skætəbreɪn/, **scatterbrains**; also spelled with a hyphen. Someone who is a **scatterbrain** often forgets things and seems unable to think sensibly about anything; an informal word. N COUNT

scatterbrained /skætəbreɪnd/. Someone who is **scatterbrained** often forgets things and seems unable to think sensibly about anything; an informal word. ADJ QUALIT ⇑ forgetful

scattered /skætəd/. 1 Things that are **scattered** in a particular area are situated throughout the area, but separate or far from each other. EG *Thousands of missiles are scattered across the planet... The old people could not travel to visit their scattered families and old friends.* ADJ QUALIT ⇑ dispersed

2 A surface that is **scattered** with a lot of small things has them spread over the whole of the surface but separate from each other. EG *Her hair was scattered with pollen... ...a piano scattered with photographs.* ADJ CLASSIF: PRED+*with* ⇑ cover = strew

3 **Scattered** things are far apart and few in number. EG *He crept down a slope to rocks and scattered trees by the sea... ...a number of small scattered riots.* ADJ QUALIT = isolated

scattering /skætə[0]rɪŋ/, **scatterings.** A **scattering** of things or people is a small number of them that are spread over a large area. EG *The Union can claim only a scattering of health service workers... ...the cold blue night with its scattering of stars.* N PART+N IN PL/UNCOUNT = handful, sprinkling

scatty /skæti[1]/, **scattier, scattiest.** Someone who is **scatty** often forgets things and behaves in a silly way; an informal word used in British English. EG *She's a scatty but charming girl.* ADJ QUALIT ⇑ foolish

scavenge /skævɪndʒ/, **scavenges, scavenging, scavenged.** 1 If you **scavenge** food or other things that you can use, you collect them by searching among waste and unwanted objects. EG *I had no resources at all, except what I could scavenge or beg.* V OR V+O: IF+PREP THEN *for* ⇑ search

2 If a bird or other animal **scavenges** for food, it gets food by searching for and eating the meat of dead creatures and other waste food. EG *...fish and crabs scavenging for decaying tissue and waste products.* V OR V+O: IF+PREP THEN *for*

scavenger /skævɪndʒə/, **scavengers.** A **scavenger** is a person, bird, or animal that collects food or other things by searching among waste and unwanted objects. EG *...a scavenger living from the dustbins behind restaurants... ...scavengers like the vulture.* N COUNT ⇑ collector

scenario /sɪnɑːrɪəʊ/, **scenarios.** A **scenario** is 1 a series of related events that form a pattern, with one event causing the next; a formal word, often used to refer to the way in which you expect or hope a particular situation will develop. EG *The death of democracy becomes quite a likely scenario... ...deeply involved in the scenario of suffering and loss.* N COUNT ⇑ outline 2 a piece of writing that gives the story of a film, with details of the characters and what they will say. EG *...a scenario in which the Indians beat the Cowboys.* N COUNT ⇑ plot

scene /siːn/, **scenes.** 1 A **scene** is 1.1 a part of a play, film, novel, etc, in which there is a single series of events or actions, all happening in the same place and without a break in the time sequence. EG *All we saw was about three scenes from a much bigger play... Act III, scene ii... ...the balcony scene from Romeo and Juliet... The book culminates in a terrible scene when this woman is killed.* N COUNT 1.2 the place where the action in a play, film, book, etc is happening. EG *...the play, with its scenes of Victorian London.* N COUNT = setting 1.3 the scenery that is used as the background for a particular part of a play, film, etc. EG *Wait while the other scene is being moved off the stage... She talked about becoming a scene designer as a profession.* N COUNT: USU SING = set

2 A **scene** of a particular kind mentioned is 2.1 a picture of a particular place or activity. EG *...the landscapes and harbour scenes that he drew as a teenager... ...cloth printed over with scenes from Indian village life.* N COUNT+SUPP 2.2 a particular impression that you get of a situation or activity as you look at it or think about it. EG *The moon rose over a scene of extraordinary destruction... ...a scene of domestic tranquillity.* N COUNT+SUPP ⇑ sight 2.3 a particular activity or aspect of life, and all the things that are associated with it. EG *This is a growing feature of the business scene in all advanced industrial countries... ...the German political scene.* N SING: *the*+MOD+N ⇑ area = front 2.4 an event or series of events that involves people's emotions and that is usually a very unpleasant or difficult experience for them. EG *There followed the most ridiculous scene... This scene unfolded before me in all its horror.* N COUNT: USU SING ⇑ episode

3 The **scene** around you is your surroundings, considered especially in relation to the way they look. EG *...commenting on the beauty of the scene... She was excited by the thought of a journey and a change of scene.* N COUNT/UNCOUNT ⇑ place

4 The **scene** of a particular event is the place where it happened. EG *...the scene of an automobile accident... ...the scene of the crime.* N COUNT: USU SING

5 If you make a **scene**, you loudly show your anger or other strong emotions that you feel about something. EG *There was a scene, and Father called Christopher a lot of rude names... Clarissa dear, please don't make a nasty scene... I expect we're going to have one of his little scenes.* N COUNT ⇑ outburst = display

6 Something that happens **behind the scenes** 6.1 happens at the back of the stage or in a part of the theatre that the audience cannot see. EG *Her voice was suddenly heard behind the scenes just before her entrance.* PHR: USED AS AN A = off-stage 6.2 is kept secret from other people. EG *Officials working behind the scenes urged them to avoid further confrontation.* PHR: USED AS AN A

7 If someone or something appears or arrives **on the scene**, they appear and often make an impact on the existing situation. If they disappear or depart **from the scene**, they disappear from the existing situation. EG *Relatives suddenly appear on the scene after years of neglect... The computer burst upon the scene around 1950.* PHR: USED AS AN A ⇑ there

8 If you say that something **is not** your **scene**, you mean that it is not the sort of thing you like; an informal expression. EG *That's not my scene... Jazz isn't really his scene.* PHR: VB INFLECTS = thing

9 **set the scene.** 9.1 If you **set the scene** for someone, you give them the information that they need in order to understand what is going to happen or be said next. EG *First of all let's set the scene: in 1900 the population of the world was much smaller.* PHR: VB INFLECTS, IF+PREP THEN *for* ⇑ describe 9.2 Something that **sets the scene** for a particular event to happen creates the conditions in which the event is likely to happen. EG *The realignment of 1963 set the scene for the decline of the organization's real power.* PHR: VB INFLECTS, IF+PREP THEN *for* ⇑ allow

scenery /siːnə[0]ri[1]/ is 1 the general appearance of a place, especially a part of the countryside with beautiful views and natural features. EG *As we neared the border the scenery became lush and spectacu-* N UNCOUNT *lar... ...time to admire the scenery... ...picturesque scenery.* 2 all the cloths and boards that are used as the background for the stage in a theatre to give an impression of the place where the play, opera, or ballet is supposed to be happening. EG *Who designed the scenery?... This production uses a minimum of scenery and lighting.* N UNCOUNT ↑ furnishings = set

scene-shifter, scene-shifters. A **scene-shifter** is a person who works in a theatre and moves scenery on and off the stage. N COUNT

scenic /si̲:nɪk/. 1 A place or journey that is **scenic** is attractive because it has beautiful views and natural features. EG *...all the best scenic locations in the country... ...a scenic drive.* ADJ QUALIT ↑ picturesque

2 **Scenic** is used to relate to scenery in the theatre. EG *...scenic design.* ADJ CLASSIF : ATTRIB

scent /se̲nt/, **scents, scenting, scented.** 1 A **scent** is a pleasant smell. EG *...the overpowering scent of English garden flowers.* N COUNT = fragrance, perfume

2 **Scent** is a liquid that you can put on your skin to make you smell nice. EG *She walked in smelling of French scent.* N MASS = perfume

3 The **scent** of an animal is a smell that it leaves and that people or other animals sometimes follow when hunting it. EG *The dog sniffed the air, trying to pick up their scent.* N UNCOUNT/COUNT ↑ secretion

4 A **scent** is also a series of signs or clues that helps you to find something out, for example where someone is or what something is. EG *He picked up a private scent that led him to Chicago... We are on the scent of something big.* N COUNT : USU SING = track, trail

5 If an animal or person **scents** something, it becomes aware of it by smelling it; used especially of animals that hunt. EG *If it scents its prey, it swings its head from side to side.* V+O ↑ smell

6 If you **scent** something, you begin to feel that it is going to happen. EG *Those who scent danger must not let themselves be deceived.* V+O ↑ sense

scented /se̲ntɪ²d/. Something that is **scented** has a pleasant smell, either naturally or because perfume has been added to it. EG *...a sweet scented variety of rose... ...scented soap... ...a scented handkerchief.* ADJ CLASSIF = fragrant, perfumed

scepter /se̲ptə/, **scepters.** See **sceptre.**

sceptic /ske̲ptɪk/, **sceptics**; also spelled **skeptic** in American English. A **sceptic** is a person who has a lot of doubts about things that other people believe. EG *The sceptic may argue that there are no grounds for such optimism.* N COUNT ↑ doubter

sceptical /ske̲ptɪkə⁰l/; also spelled **skeptical** in American English. Someone who is **sceptical** about something has a lot of doubts about it, for example about how useful, true, or likely it is. EG *Many were skeptical about this solution... ...intelligent, sceptical remarks.* ◊ **sceptically.** EG *I had listened sceptically to the broadcast.* ADJ QUALIT : USU PRED, IF+PREP THEN *about/of* ↑ doubtful ◊ ADV WITH VB

scepticism /ske̲ptɪsɪsə⁰m/; also spelled **skepticism** in American English. **Scepticism** is doubt that someone has about something, for example about how useful, true, or likely it is. EG *He listened with growing scepticism... ...scepticism about this idea.* N UNCOUNT : IF+PREP THEN *about/of* ↑ disbelief

sceptre /se̲ptə/, **sceptres**; also spelled **scepter** in American English. A **sceptre** is an ornamental rod that a king or queen carries as a symbol of his or her power on some ceremonial occasions. N COUNT ↑ mace

schedule /ʃe̲dju⁴l/, **schedules, scheduling, scheduled**; also pronounced /ske̲dju⁴l/, especially in American English. 1 A **schedule** is a plan that gives a list of events, jobs, etc, together with the times at which each thing should happen or be done. EG *...the next place on his busy schedule... ...the launch schedules for the space shuttle.* N COUNT ↑ schema = programme ● If you do something **to schedule** or **according to schedule**, you do it at the times and in the ways that have been planned in advance. EG *These operations have been carried out according to schedule.* ● PHR : USED AS AN A ● Something that happens **ahead of schedule** happens earlier than the time planned. EG *We arrived several hours ahead of schedule.* ● PHR : USED AS AN A ↑ early ● If you are **behind schedule**, you are doing things later than the time planned. EG *The project is behind schedule again.* ● PHR : USED AS AN A ● Something that happens **on schedule** happens at the time that was planned. EG *Three days later, on schedule, I met with Sheldon in his office.* ● PHR : USED AS AN A ↑ on time

2 A **schedule** is also 2.1 a list of the times when trains, boats, buses, or aircraft are supposed to arrive at or depart from a particular place. EG *...a bus schedule.* N COUNT = timetable 2.2 a list of things in a document, for example a list of prices, details, or conditions. N COUNT

3 If something **is scheduled** to happen, arrangements have been made for it to happen. EG *He was scheduled to leave Plymouth yesterday... The talks are scheduled for this weekend... Food supplies were scheduled to be a main item on the agenda.* V+O+*to*-INF, V+O, OR V+O+A *(for)* : USU PASS ↑ plan

schema /ski̲:mə/, **schemata.** A **schema** is an outline of a plan or theory; a technical word. EG *I condensed this into the following schema... This is, of course, a highly simplified schema.* N COUNT ↑ framework

schematic /ski¹mæ̲tɪk/. A **schematic** representation, diagram, etc shows how something works in a simplified way; a technical term. EG *...our schematic representation of the design process... ...a schematic diagram of a hydraulic ram.* ◊ **schematically.** EG *Here I can do no more than indicate the process schematically.* ADJ CLASSIF ◊ ADV WITH VB

scheme /ski̲:m/, **schemes, scheming, schemed.** 1 A **scheme** is 1.1 a plan produced by one person as a way of achieving something; often used showing disapproval. EG *He had a crazy scheme to corner the champagne market... ...some scheme for perfecting the world... To Mr Boggis's surprise, the scheme worked.* N COUNT = design 1.2 a large-scale plan produced by a government or other organization. EG *...the State pension scheme... ...training schemes... ...a 5.6 million pound scheme to build 63 houses and a motel.* N COUNT : USU MOD+N = project

2 If someone **schemes**, they make secret plans in order to gain something for themselves or for someone else; used showing disapproval. EG *He did not want her to suspect how he schemed against her... She frequently schemed on her daughter's behalf.* ◊ **scheming.** EG *...ignorant, scheming people... In those days scheming and plotting were the norm in such dealings.* V ↑ plan = plot ◊ ADJ CLASSIF : USU ATTRIB, OR N UNCOUNT

3 Someone's **scheme of things** is the way in which they want things to be organized. EG *There was an important place for the State in their scheme of things... Innovations that had no place in the traditional scheme of things.* ● **The scheme of things** is the way that everything in the world seems to have been organized, as if by a plan. EG *Man needed to understand his place in the scheme of things.* PHR : USU AFTER PREP ● PHR : AFTER PREP ↑ pattern

4 See also **colour scheme.**

schemer /ski̲:mə/, **schemers.** A **schemer** is a person who schemes. N COUNT = plotter

schism /sɪ̲zə⁰m, skɪ̲z-/, **schisms.** When **schism** or a **schism** happens, a group or organization divides into two groups as a result of differences in thinking and beliefs. EG *The problems are not those of class war, but of schism and separatism... ...ideological schisms.* N UNCOUNT/COUNT ↑ division = split

schizophrenia /skɪtsə⁴fri̲:nɪə/. 1 **Schizophrenia** is a serious mental illness in which someone is unable to relate their thoughts and feelings to what is happening around them. There are several kinds of schizophrenia. EG *There were no grounds for a diagnosis of schizophrenia... Few therapists agree on how you treat schizophrenia.* N UNCOUNT ↑ psychosis

2 **Schizophrenia** is also used informally to refer to a person's behaviour when they seem to have very different purposes or opinions at different times. EG *Most officials exhibit a degree of schizophrenia in what they say in public and what they tell their friends.* N UNCOUNT ↑ inconsistency

schizophrenic /skɪtsə⁴fre̲nɪk/, **schizophrenics.** 1 A **schizophrenic** person suffers from schizophrenia. EG *...a schizophrenic patient.* ▸ used of thoughts and behaviour. EG *...a schizophrenic delusion.* ADJ CLASSIF ↑ psychotic

2 A **schizophrenic** is a person who is suffering from schizophrenia. EG *The doctors diagnosed him as a paranoid schizophrenic.* N COUNT ↑ psychotic

3 A person's behaviour is described informally as **schizophrenic** when they seem to have very different purposes or opinions at different times. EG *The movement can't make up its mind on this–it's schizophrenic.* ADJ CLASSIF ↑ inconsistent

schnapps /ʃnæ̲ps/ is a strong alcoholic drink. EG *The bottle of schnapps had no label.* N UNCOUNT ↑ spirit

scholar /skɒ̲lə/, **scholars.** 1 A **scholar** is 1.1 a person who has acquired a great knowledge of a particular academic subject. EG *...a meeting of scientists and scholars... ...Benjamin Jowett, the theologian and Greek scholar.* N COUNT ↑ expert 1.2 a child or student who has obtained a scholarship. EG *...an Eton scholar... ...a Rhodes scholar.* N COUNT : MOD+N

2 A good **scholar**, poor **scholar**, etc is a person who is good at learning, bad at learning, etc; an old-fashioned use. EG *I wish I was a good scholar like you... Phaedrus was a poor scholar... ...a hopeless scholar... She's no scholar.*
N COUNT+SUPP : USU MOD+N

scholarly /skɒləli[1]/. 1 A **scholarly** person spends a lot of time studying and knows a lot about academic subjects. EG *He was a precise, scholarly man.* ▸ used of behaviour. EG *I've tried to be as scholarly as possible.* ▸ used of books. EG *...a scholarly volume on Stonehenge.*
ADJ QUALIT = learned

2 **Scholarly** matters, activities, etc involve or relate to scholars or their work. EG *...a topic of scholarly dispute... ...my scholarly exertions... His name is known in scholarly circles throughout the world.*
ADJ CLASSIF : ATTRIB ⇑ academic

scholarship /skɒləʃɪp/, **scholarships**. 1 If you obtain a **scholarship** to a school or university, your studies are paid for by the school or university or by some other organization. EG *He had won a scholarship to this school... I applied for a scholarship to study philosophy at Oxford.*
N COUNT : IF+PREP THEN *to* OR +*to*-INF ⇑ award

2 **Scholarship** is serious academic study, and the knowledge that is obtained as a result of it. EG *...the Islamic tradition of scholarship.*
N UNCOUNT = erudition, learning

scholastic /skə[7]læstɪk/. 1 Your **scholastic** ability is your ability to study while you are at school. EG *...the scholastic levels of sixteen-year-olds... He was more involved in sports than scholastic achievements.*
ADJ CLASSIF : ATTRIB ⇑ educational = academic

2 **Scholastic** arguments take place among scholars. EG *...scholastic controversy... ...scholastic squabbling.*
ADJ CLASSIF : ATTRIB

school /sku:l/, **schools, schooling, schooled**. 1 **School** or a **school** is a place where children are educated. EG *...a school with more than 1300 pupils... I went to school here... He was doing badly at school... They built the school in 1899... What do you want to do when you leave school?... ...the school holidays.* ▸ used to refer to the pupils or teachers at a school. EG *She gave a talk to the school... ...a good relationship between the school and the parent.* ▸ used to refer to the part of the day when you are at school. EG *We met every day after school.*
N COUNT/UNCOUNT ⇑ institution; ▸ N COUNT : USU PREP+N; ▸ N UNCOUNT

2 **School** or a **school** is also **2.1** an institution or university department where you can learn a particular skill or subject. EG *I went to an art school... She had recently graduated from law school... ...drama school... ...medical school... ...one of the best secretarial schools in Britain.* **2.2** a part of a university that teaches a group of closely-related subjects. EG *...the School of African and Asian Studies... ...the School of Physical Sciences.*
N COUNT/UNCOUNT : MOD+N = college; N COUNT+SUPP : ALSO IN NAMES ⇑ faculty

3 In informal American English, **school** is university.
N UNCOUNT

4 A **school** is also **4.1** a short educational course for adults, usually in a single subject. EG *...the one-day schools that we run for teachers.* **4.2** a group of artists, writers, thinkers, etc whose work, opinions, or theories are similar. EG *There is another school of economists whose views need to be taken into account... ...painters of the Veronese school.* **4.3** a large group of fish, whales, dolphins, etc. EG *...a school of tiny, glittering fish.*
N COUNT : USU MOD+N; N COUNT+SUPP; N PART+N IN PL

5 When you **are schooled** in something, you learn about it, as a result of training or experience. EG *She was schooled in charm by her mama... They were professionals, schooled in social research.*
V+O (NG/REFL) +A (*in*)/*to*-INF

6 A **school of thought** is a theory or an opinion shared by a group of people. EG *One school of thought argues that the enterprise should be abandoned... There seemed to be two schools of thought.*
PHR : *school* INFLECTS ⇑ view

7 If you describe someone as **of the old school**, you mean that they have good qualities that are no longer common; used showing approval. EG *...a gentleman of the old school.*
PHR : USED AS C OR AFTER N = traditional

8 When people talk about **the old school tie**, they are referring to the belief that people who go to the same public school try to help each other after they have left, especially in business; used showing disapproval. EG *An old school tie doesn't necessarily help profits.*
PHR

9 See also **schooling, boarding school, comprehensive school, day school, finishing school, first school, grammar school, high school, junior school, middle school, night school, nursery school, prep school, preparatory school, primary school, public school, summer school, Sunday school.**

school age. When a child reaches **school age**, he or she is old enough to go to school. EG *...children under school age.* ▸ used as an adjective. EG *...a school-age child.*
N UNCOUNT; ▸ ADJ CLASSIF

schoolboy /sku:lbɔɪ/, **schoolboys**. 1 A **schoolboy** is a boy who goes to school. EG *I was still a schoolboy... Schoolboys had made holes in the fences.*
N COUNT ⇑ schoolchild

2 **Schoolboy** behaviour is behaviour by an adult man that seems like that of a schoolboy; used showing disapproval. EG *...a schoolboy sense of humour.*
ADJ CLASSIF : ATTRIB ⇑ boyish = immature

schoolchild /sku:ltʃaɪld/, **schoolchildren**; also spelled as two words. **Schoolchildren** are children who go to school. EG *The schoolchildren performed their play... The hall was rapidly filling with schoolchildren.*
N COUNT ⇑ child = pupil

schooldays /sku:ldeɪz/; also spelled as two words. Your **schooldays** are the period in your life when you go to school. EG *I enjoyed my schooldays... His schooldays were a torment.*
N PLURAL : USU POSS+N ⇑ childhood

school friend, school friends; also spelled with a hyphen and as one word. Your **school friends** are the children who are your friends while you are at school. EG *They were used to bringing schoolfriends home... ...a postcard sent to me by an old schoolfriend.*
N COUNT = schoolmate

schoolgirl /sku:lgɜ:l/, **schoolgirls**. A **schoolgirl** is a girl who goes to school. EG *...a twelve-year-old schoolgirl... ...a dumpy schoolgirl in jodhpurs.*
N COUNT ⇑ schoolchild

schoolhouse /sku:lhaʊs/, **schoolhouses**. A **schoolhouse** is a small building that is used as a school, especially in a village. EG *...a new roof for the schoolhouse.*
N COUNT

schooling /sku:lɪŋ/. Your **schooling** is the education that you receive at school; an old-fashioned informal word. EG *Many of the workers had no schooling at all... Her schooling had been highly irregular.*
N UNCOUNT

school-leaver, school-leavers; also spelled without a hyphen. A **school-leaver** is a young person who has just left school and who is looking for a job or doing their first job. EG *...the growth of unemployment among school-leavers.*
N COUNT

schoolmaster /sku:lmɑ:stə/, **schoolmasters**. A **schoolmaster** is a man who teaches children in a school; a rather old-fashioned word. EG *He was village schoolmaster for several years... ...a retired schoolmaster.*
N COUNT ⇑ teacher = master

schoolmate /sku:lmeɪt/, **schoolmates**. Your **schoolmates** are your school friends; an old-fashioned word. EG *He met an old schoolmate of his from Umtata.*
N COUNT

schoolmistress /sku:lmɪstrɪ[2]s/, **schoolmistresses**. A **schoolmistress** is a woman who teaches children in a school; a rather old-fashioned word. EG *... the village schoolmistress.*
N COUNT ⇑ teacher = mistress

schoolroom /sku:lru[4]m/, **schoolrooms**. A **schoolroom** is a classroom, especially the only classroom in a small school.
N COUNT ⇑ room

schoolteacher /sku:lti:tʃə/, **schoolteachers**. A **schoolteacher** is a teacher in a school.
N COUNT

schoolteaching /sku:lti:tʃɪŋ/ is the work that schoolteachers do; a fairly old-fashioned word. EG *I was thinking of going in for schoolteaching.*
N UNCOUNT ⇑ teaching

schoolwork /sku:lwɜ:k/; also spelled as two words. **Schoolwork** is the work that a child does at school or as homework. EG *I was also worrying about school work.*
N UNCOUNT

schooner /sku:nə/, **schooners**. A **schooner** is 1 a sailing ship. 2 a large glass which you use for sherry; used mainly in British English. ▸ used to refer to the amount which can be held by a schooner. EG *You've already drunk three schooners of sherry.*
N COUNT; N COUNT; ▸

sciatica /saɪætɪkə/ is a severe pain in the nerve in your legs or the lower part of your back; a medical term.
N UNCOUNT ⇑ neuralgia

science /saɪəns/, **sciences**. 1 **Science** is the study of the nature and behaviour of natural things and the knowledge that we obtain about them through observation and experiments. EG *...advanced training and research in science... ...every new fact discovered by science... ...the importance of mathematics to science... Why don't many girls go into science?*
N UNCOUNT

2 A **science** is **2.1** a particular branch of science, for example physics, biology, or chemistry. EG *...one of the medical sciences... ...the science of genetics has developed rapidly.* **2.2** the study of some aspect of human behaviour, for example psychology, sociology, or anthropology. EG *For the first time man may develop a true science of education.*
N UNCOUNT/COUNT : USU+SUPP, ALSO SING=PL; N COUNT/UNCOUNT : USU+SUPP ⇑ subject

3 See **domestic science**, **political science**, **social science**.

science fiction consists of stories in books, comics, and films about events that take place in the future or in other parts of the universe. EG *...a science fiction story entitled 'The Weather Man'... ...science fiction films involving space travel.* N UNCOUNT ⇑ fiction = sci-fi

scientific /saɪəntɪfɪk/. 1 **Scientific** matters, activities, etc relate to science or to a particular science. EG *...scientific research... ...scientific discoveries... ...scientific instruments.* ◇ **scientifically**. EG *...a scientifically advanced civilization.* ADJ CLASSIF : USU ATTRIB ◇ ADV OR ADV SEN

2 If you do something in a **scientific** way, you do it carefully and systematically, carrying out proper experiments or tests. EG *...a scientific study of a language... ...scientific method... This study is not scientific.* ◇ **scientifically**. EG *Our relationship to apes has been confirmed scientifically.* ADJ QUALIT ⇑ methodical ◇ ADV

scientist /saɪəntɪst/, **scientists**. A **scientist** is an expert in one of the sciences who does work, especially research work, in connection with it. EG *...a distinguished medical scientist... This will keep the scientists busy for years.* • See also **political scientist**, **social scientist**. N COUNT

sci-fi /saɪ faɪ/ is science fiction; an informal word. EG *...sci-fi novels.* N UNCOUNT : USU BEFORE N

scimitar /sɪmɪtə/, **scimitars**. A **scimitar** is a sword with a curved blade that was used in former times in some Eastern countries. N COUNT

scintillating /sɪntɪleɪtɪŋ/. Conversation or humour that is **scintillating** is very lively and amusing. EG *...her scintillating wit... ...scintillating personalities.* ADJ QUALIT = sparkling

scion /saɪən/, **scions**. A **scion** of a rich or famous family is one of its younger or more recent members; a literary word. EG *...the scion of a distinguished family... ...the scions of the wealthy.* N COUNT + SUPP : USU + *of* ⇑ descendant

scissor /sɪzə/, **scissors**. A pair of **scissors** is a small tool that you use for cutting paper or cloth. It consists of two sharp blades and two rings in which you put your thumb and two or three of your fingers. You move your thumb and fingers so that the blades move together and cut something. EG *She took a pair of scissors and cut his hair... I wish I'd brought some scissors.* N PLURAL : ALSO *a pair of* + N

sclerosis /sklɔˀrəʊsɪs/ is a disease in which the tissue in a part of your body becomes abnormally hard; a medical term. • See also **multiple sclerosis**. N UNCOUNT

scoff /skɒf/, **scoffs, scoffing, scoffed**. 1 If you **scoff**, you speak in a scornful, mocking way to show that you disagree with something that someone has said. EG *They scoff at the idea that he will retire next year... Marco Polo was scoffed at... Don't scoff, Marnie.* V OR V + QUOTE : IF + PREP THEN *at* ⇑ ridicule = jeer, sneer

2 If someone **scoffs** food, they eat it quickly and greedily; an informal word used mainly in British English. EG *By the time I got there, they'd scoffed the lot.* V + O, OR V + O + A *(down)* = devour

scold /skəʊld/, **scolds, scolding, scolded**. If you **scold** someone, you speak angrily to them because they have done something wrong. EG *Mother scolded me this morning for being rude to you... 'Where have you been?' scolded Mary.* V + O : IF O + PREP THEN *for*, V, OR V + QUOTE ⇑ rebuke = chide

scolding /skəʊldɪŋ/, **scoldings**. A **scolding** consists of stern, angry words which are spoken to someone, often because they have done something wrong. EG *I sometimes get a scolding from my parents.* N COUNT = rebuke

scone /skəʊn, skɒn/, **scones**. A **scone** is a small cake made from flour and fat. Scones are usually eaten at teatime with butter. N COUNT

scoop /sku:p/, **scoops, scooping, scooped**. 1 A **scoop** is 1.1 a tool with a handle and a hollow part like a spoon which is used for holding or serving food such as flour, sugar, or ice cream. EG *...an ice-cream scoop.* ▸ used to refer to the amount which can be held by a scoop. EG *I sold ice-cream, at 20p a scoop.* N COUNT ⇑ ladle ▸ = scoopful

1.2 a large bucket on an machine that is used to move earth. N COUNT

2 If you **scoop** something or **scoop it up**, 2.1 you pick it up with a scoop. EG *He scooped some instant coffee into a cup.* 2.2 you pick it up by putting your hands or arms under it and lifting it in a quick movement. EG *The boys fell to their knees and began to scoop up handfuls of water... I scooped the child in my arms and carried her up the stairs.* V + O OR PHRASAL VB : V + O + ADV / V + O : USU + A, OR V + O + A *(up)* ⇑ gather up

3 A **scoop** is also a news story, especially an exciting one, which is reported in one newspaper or magazine before it appears anywhere else. EG *He got all the big scoops for the paper... They flew back to Perth with a scoop.* N COUNT ⇑ report

4 If one newspaper or magazine **scoops** all the others, it prints a news story before the story appears anywhere else. V + O

scoop out. If you **scoop** something **out**, you make it hollow by removing part of it with a scoop or as if you were using a scoop. EG *Scoop out the flesh of the melon with a teaspoon... ...a scooped-out pineapple.* PHRASAL VB : V + O + ADV

scoopful /sku:pful/, **scoopfuls**. A **scoopful** is the amount which can be held by a scoop. EG *Each of them had a scoopful of water.* N PART + N UNCOUNT/N IN PL

scoot /sku:t/, **scoots, scooting, scooted**. If you **scoot**, you leave quickly; an informal word. EG *I'd better scoot. Bye.* V ⇑ go

scooter /sku:tə/, **scooters**. A **scooter** is 1 a small, light motorcycle which has a low seat. 2 a type of child's bicycle which has two wheels joined by a wooden board and a handle on a long pole attached to the front wheel. The child makes it move by having one foot on the board and the other pushing against the ground. N COUNT / N COUNT ⇑ toy

scope /skəʊp/, **scopes**. 1 If you have the **scope** to do something, you have the opportunity to think or act freely and to use your abilities as well as you can. EG *There is not much scope for originality... A committee was set up and given scope to take instant decisions.* N UNCOUNT : USU + SUPP = room

2 The **scope** of an activity, topic, or piece of work is the whole area which it deals with or includes. EG *Lack of time limited the scope of the course... That question is beyond the scope of this book... The difference between the programmes is a difference in scope.* N UNCOUNT : USU WITH POSS = range

scorch /skɔ:tʃ/, **scorches, scorching, scorched**. 1 If you **scorch** something such as a piece of clothing, you burn it slightly, for example while you are ironing it. EG *I once scorched a beautiful pink suit.* V + O ⇑ damage

2 A **scorch** or **scorch mark** is a mark which is made by burning something slightly while you are ironing it. N COUNT

3 To **scorch** something also means to mark or discolour it by the use of too much heat or by a corrosive fluid. EG *The brutal afternoon sun scorched my face... The corner of the desk has been scorched with acid.* V + O ⇑ burn

4 If a plant or area of land **is scorched**, it is made dry and almost lifeless because of very hot sun. EG *The earth was scorched and bare... Most years there is a long dry season that shrivels and scorches plants.* V + O : USU PASS = wither

5 To **scorch** means to drive or travel very fast; an informal use, used mainly in British English. EG *It can scorch from 0-60 mph in just 10.1 seconds.* V ⇑ speed

scorched-earth policy, scorched-earth policies. A **scorched-earth policy** is the deliberate burning, destruction, and removal by an army of everything, especially food, shelter, and animals, that could be useful to an enemy who might invade the area. N COUNT : USU SING ⇑ strategy

scorcher /skɔ:tʃə/, **scorchers**. A **scorcher** is, a very hot day; an informal word. EG *Today's going to be a scorcher.* N COUNT

scorching /skɔ:tʃɪŋ/ is used to describe very hot weather; an informal word. EG *...a scorching day... ...scorching weather.* ADJ QUALIT

score /skɔ:/, **scores, scoring, scored**. 1 If someone **scores**, they get a goal, run, or other point in a game. EG *Barnes scored from a distance of twenty feet... Mexico scored a lovely goal... It was a good pitch for scoring runs.* V OR V + O

2 If someone **scores** a particular number of goals, runs, or points, that is the total they get in a game. EG *India scored 170... We scored more than a hundred runs between us.* V + O = make

3 The **score** in a game is the total number of goals, runs, or points made by the two teams or players. EG *What's the score?... At the end of the match the score was 2-2.* N COUNT : USU SING

4 If there is a **score** in a game, one or both of the teams or players have scored. EG *So at the end of the first half there's no score.* N SING WITH DET

5 The person who **scores** during a game keeps an official record of the number of goals, runs, or points which are made. EG *I was asked to score at the school cricket match.* V

6 If you **score** a particular mark, you get that mark in an examination or test. EG *In the last three tests he had scored 100... If a student is found to score very badly on the first test, then we can arrange extra lessons for her.* V+O, OR V+A ⇑ obtain

7 Your **score** in an examination or test is the mark which you get. EG *His score on the reading test last year was very disappointing.* N COUNT

8 If you **score** a success, victory, hit, etc, you are successful in what you are doing. EG *The Royal Shakespeare Company scored a runaway success with 'Richard III'... The Liberals have scored a dramatic victory in this by-election.* V OR V+O : USU V +O

9 If you **score** or **score** points, you gain an advantage over someone else, especially by saying something clever or by making a better argument. EG *Without realizing it, I had scored again... Gareth grinned to himself, as if he had scored an important point... The Government was anxious to score over the opposition in the education debate.* V OR V+O : IF+ PREP THEN *over*

10 If something sharp **scores** a surface, it cuts or marks it, usually with a line or a scratch. EG *There were lines scored on the wall... The bullet had scored its path across the skin of my arm.* ▸ used as a noun. EG *There were scores all over the kitchen table.* V+O ▸ N COUNT

11 If you **score** a piece of music, you write it or arrange it for specific instruments or voices. EG *The piece was scored for two pianos and a baritone.* V+O : USU PASS

12 The **score** of a piece of music is the written version of it, showing all the notes that must be played or sung. EG *I've got the scores of all his sonatas.* N COUNT

13 The **score** of a film, play, or other production is the music which is written or used for it. EG *'Sinfonietta', set to a score by Janacek, is a very successful ballet... He writes his own scripts and composes the scores.* N COUNT

14 If you **score**, you succeed in having sex with someone; an informal use. EG *He certainly looks as if he's going to score tonight!* V

15 If you **know the score**, you know what the real facts of the situation are, however unpleasant they might be. PHR : VB INFLECTS ⇑ understand

16 **On this score** or **on that score** means for the reason which has been given. EG *I'm perfectly capable of looking after myself, so please don't worry about me on that score.* PHR : USED AS AN A

17 If you **settle a score** or **settle old scores**, you take revenge on someone for something they have done in the past. EG *She was looking for a chance to settle old scores with her brother.* PHR : VB INFLECTS

18 A **score** is also twenty; a slightly old-fashioned use. EG *There were well over a score of policemen waiting outside the house... Even in my two score years the world has changed.* N COUNT : USED AS NUM

19 If things happen or exist **by the score**, they happen or exist in great numbers. EG *Cars were breaking down by the score.* PHR : USED AS AN A

20 If you talk about **scores of** things, you mean very many of them. EG *We've received scores of letters.* PHR+N IN PL

score off 1 If you **score off** someone, you make a clever or insulting reply to something they have said, usually because you want to make them appear foolish. EG *They spent the whole evening scoring off each other.* PHRASAL VB : V+ PREP, HAS PASS

2 If you **score off** a word, name etc, or if you **score** it **out**, or **score** it **through**, you draw a line through it to show that you do not want it to be read. EG *I asked him to score my name off the list of players next Saturday... The article was just too long, so I had to score out twenty words.* PHRASAL VB : V+ O+ADV = cross out

scoreboard /skɔ:bɔ:d/, **scoreboards**. A **scoreboard** is a large board which shows how many goals, runs, or points have been made in a match or competition. EG *We were standing around looking up at the scoreboard, trying to see who was winning.* N COUNT

scorecard /skɔ:kɑ:d/, **scorecards**. A **scorecard** is 1 a printed card which tells you who is playing in a match or race, and on which you can record the scores the players make. 2 a card on which players record the scores they make in various games, especially golf. N COUNT N COUNT

scorer /skɔ:rə/, **scorers**. A **scorer** is 1 a player who scores a goal, run, or points in a match. EG *Who were the scorers?... Gower was the highest scorer in the match.* 2 the official who writes down the score of a match or competition as it is being played. N COUNT N COUNT

scorn /skɔ:n/, **scorns, scorning, scorned**. 1 **Scorn** is a strong feeling of contempt for someone or something. EG *This suggestion was greeted with scorn... She had nothing but scorn for those who got themselves into debt.* N UNCOUNT

2 If you **heap** or **pour scorn on** something, you say that you think it is stupid and worthless. EG *She poured scorn on my ideas... Burgin heaped scorn on painting and sculpture which he described as pointless pastimes.* ● If you **laugh** something **to scorn**, you laugh at it to show your contempt for it. EG *I had laughed him to scorn.* PHR : VB INFLECTS = deride ● PHR : VB INFLECTS = ridicule

3 If you **scorn** a person or thing, you feel or show contempt for them. EG *As a teenager, she scorned the girls who worshipped football heroes... What is now admired as art was then scorned as vulgar extravagance.* V+O, OR V+O+A (AS) ⇑ despise

4 If you **scorn** something, you refuse to have or do it because you feel it is wrong or unsuitable for you. EG *You will find youths in all countries who scorn traditional dress and wear denims.* V+O ⇑ reject

5 If you **scorn** to do something, you refuse to do it because you feel it is wrong or unsuitable for you; a formal use. V+*to*-INF

scornful /skɔ:nfʊl/. Someone or something that is **scornful** is filled with, and often shows, great contempt for someone or something. EG *She is openly scornful of the idea that girls are in any way weaker than men... ...scornful laughter.* ◇ **scornfully**. EG *She looked at him scornfully.* ADJ QUALIT : IF+ PREP THEN *of* ⇑ contemptuous ◇ ADV WITH VB

scorpion /skɔ:piən/, **scorpions**. A **scorpion** is a small tropical animal which looks like a large insect. It has a long, pointed, curving tail with a poisonous sting on the end. N COUNT

Scot /skɒt/, **Scots**. 1 A **Scot** is a person who comes from Scotland. N COUNT

2 **Scots** is a dialect of the English language that is spoken in Scotland. EG *He speaks broad Scots.* N UNCOUNT

3 **Scots** also means the same as Scottish. EG *He chose to call his daughter the Scots name Catriona... Our professor has a strong Scots accent... ...Scots law.* ADJ CLASSIF : USU ATTRIB = Scotch

scotch /skɒtʃ/, **scotches, scotching, scotched**. 1 If you **scotch** a plan, idea, rumour, etc, you put an end to it before it can develop any further. EG *I think that proposal had better be scotched straightaway... Let me first scotch one or two rumours.* V+O = foil

2 **Scotch** or **Scotch whisky** is whisky made in Scotland. EG *...a bottle of Scotch.* ▸ used to refer to a glass of Scotch. EG *How about a Scotch before dinner?* N UNCOUNT ▸ N COUNT ⇑ drink

3 **Scotch** also means the same as Scottish. This use is considered incorrect by many people. ADJ CLASSIF

Scotch broth is a thick soup made mainly with beef or lamb and vegetables; used mainly in British English. N UNCOUNT

Scotch egg, Scotch eggs. A **Scotch egg** is, a hard-boiled egg which is covered with sausage meat and then fried in oil; used mainly in British English. N COUNT

Scotch tape is a trademark for transparent sticky tape that is sold in rolls and that is used for sticking together things such as paper and cardboard; used in American English. N UNCOUNT

scot-free. If you get away **scot-free**, you get away without being punished at all. EG *Davies managed to get off scot-free... I'm not letting you off scot-free.* ADV WITH VB

Scotsman /skɒtsmə[3]n/, **Scotsmen**. A **Scotsman** is a man who comes from Scotland. N COUNT

Scotswoman /skɒtswʊ[1]mə[0]n/, **Scotswomen**. A **Scotswoman** is a woman who comes from Scotland. N COUNT

Scotticism /skɒtɪsɪzə[0]m/, **Scotticisms**. A **Scotticism** is a Scottish word or expression. EG *His speech was full of Scotticisms.* N COUNT

Scottish /skɒtɪʃ/. Something that is **Scottish** concerns Scotland, its people and its language. EG *We spent a wonderful holiday in the Scottish mountains... ...Scottish football.* ▸ used as a noun to refer to the Scottish people. EG *The English are rather different from the Scottish in many ways.* ADJ CLASSIF = Scots ▸ N PLURAL : *the* +N = the Scots

scoundrel /skaʊndrə[0]l/, **scoundrels**. A **scoundrel** is a person, usually a man, who behaves badly towards other people, by cheating and deceiving them; a rather old-fashioned word. EG *Her husband was described in court as a lecherous scoundrel... He looked such a scoundrel.* N COUNT ⇑ villain = rogue

scour /skaʊə/, **scours, scouring, scoured**. 1 If you **scour** an area, book, etc, you make a thorough search of it because you are looking for someone or V+O ⇑ ransack something. EG *Traders were scouring the villages for family treasures... We have scoured the State archives.*

2 To **scour** a floor, pan, etc means to clean its surface by rubbing it hard with something rough. EG *She insisted on scouring her kitchen floor every week.* ▸ used as a noun. EG *Those tiles of yours could do with a good scour.* V+O ⇑ scrub ▸ N SING : *a*+N ⇑ scrub

3 If water **scours** a channel, passage, etc or **scours** something away, it washes away soil or other material by flowing over it. EG *Rainwater had scoured away the hillsides.* V+O, OR V+O+A *(away)* ⇑ clean

scourer /skaʊərə/, **scourers**. A **scourer** is a small, rough ball made of plastic or wire net which is used for cleaning kitchen pans. N COUNT

scourge /skɜːdʒ/, **scourges, scourging, scourged**. 1 If you describe something as the **scourge** of a place or group of people, you mean that it causes a lot of suffering or trouble to people. EG *Smallpox was the scourge of the Western world.* N SING WITH DET : IF+PREP THEN *of* = bane, plague

2 If something **scourges** a place or group of people, it causes great pain and suffering to people. EG *For fifty years the country was scourged by war.* V+O = bedevil

3 A **scourge** is also a whip, usually made of pieces of leather, which in former times was used to punish people. N COUNT

4 If you **scourge** someone, you beat them with a scourge. V+O = flog, whip

scouring powder is a rough, powdery mixture which is used for cleaning sinks, baths, etc. N UNCOUNT

scout /skaʊt/, **scouts, scouting, scouted**. 1 A **scout** or **boy scout** is a boy who is a member of the Scout Association. Scouts go camping and spend a lot of time out of doors. They learn how to look after themselves, and also do things to help other people. EG *He joined the boy scouts... He's going off to scout camp... ...the 15th Finchley Scouts.* N COUNT

2 A **scout** is also a person who is sent to an area of countryside in order to get information about the position of an enemy army. EG *The commanders sent scouts ahead to look for the enemy... The footpath was invisible, except to an Indian scout.* ▸ used as a verb. EG *...a platoon that had been chosen to scout the trail... The army began enlisting warriors to do their scouting for them.* ● See also **talent scout**. N COUNT ▸ V+O, V+O+A *(out)*, OR V+A

scout around. If you **scout around** or **scout round** for something, you go to different places looking for it. EG *I spend most of my time scouting around for books... We decided to scout around to see if we could find a decent restaurant.* PHRASAL VB : V+ADV, IF+PREP THEN *for* = hunt round

scoutmaster /skaʊtmɑːstə/, **scoutmasters**. A **scoutmaster** is a man who is in charge of a troop of boy scouts. N COUNT ⇑ leader

scowl /skaʊl/, **scowls, scowling, scowled**. When someone **scowls**, they show that they are angry or displeased by frowning. EG *I scowled at him... Jack stood up, scowling.* ▸ used as a noun. EG *Her grin changed to a scowl.* V : IF+PREP THEN *at* = glower ▸ N COUNT = glower

scrabble /skræbə°l/, **scrabbles, scrabbling, scrabbled**. 1 If you **scrabble** at something or **scrabble** against it, you scrape at it with your fingers or feet. EG *I scrabbled weakly at the sanded floor... She would scrabble at someone's hair... I hung there, scrabbling with my feet to find a foothold.* V+A : USU A *(against/at)* = claw

2 If you **scrabble** or **scrabble around**, you move your hands about in order to try to find something that you cannot see. EG *She scrabbled in her large handbag... Kate scrabbled around, looking for stones... I scrabbled around on the floor and eventually found my ring.* V OR V+A *(about/around)* : USU+A ⇑ search

3 **Scrabble** is a trademark for a game played on a board. Each player scores points by forming words from letters of the alphabet. When the game is finished, the board looks rather like a crossword. N PROPER

scraggy /skrægi[1]/, **scraggier, scraggiest**. **Scraggy** necks, wrists, etc are unpleasantly thin and bony. EG *He had a scraggy neck... He examined the large watch which ornamented his scraggy wrist.* ▸ used of people. EG *The vest made Pa look even scraggier.* ADJ QUALIT = scrawny ▸ = skinny

scram /skræm/, **scrams**. If you **scram**, you leave a place quickly; an informal word. EG *Maybe we both should scram... Scram!* V : NO COUNT ⇑ go away = scoot

scramble /skræmbə°l/, **scrambles, scrambling, scrambled**. 1 If you **scramble** over rough or difficult ground, you move quickly over it using your hands to help you. EG *John scrambled up the bank... They scrambled away over the rocks and fled.* ▸ used as a noun. EG *...a short scramble to the top of the hill.* V : USU+A = clamber ▸ N COUNT : USU SING

2 To **scramble** also means to move to a different position or place in a hurried, undignified way. EG *He scrambled to his feet... The smaller boys were trying to scramble out of the way.* ▸ used as a noun. EG *I hope we aren't going to have one of those awful scrambles to get to the airport.* V+A = clamber ▸ N COUNT : USU SING ⇑ rush

3 If a number of people **scramble** for something, they compete with each other for it in a rough and undignified way. EG *Sightseers had scrambled for the best position... The reporters scrambled for the phones.* ▸ used as a noun. EG *There was a mad scramble for the back seat... Many trees are left needlessly damaged in the scramble for profits.* V+A *(for)*, OR V+*to*-INF ⇑ struggle ▸ N COUNT : USU SING, IF+PREP THEN *for* ⇑ struggle

4 If you **scramble** eggs, you mix the whites and the yolks of the eggs, then cook the mixture by stirring and heating it in a pan. EG *Intending to scramble the eggs, I cracked one on the rim of a bowl.* V+O

5 If you **scramble** a radio or telephone message, you interfere with the sound so that the message can only be understood by someone who has special equipment; a technical word. EG *These devices can be used to scramble conversation.* V+O

6 When pilots **scramble** fighter aeroplanes, they get them into the air quickly in order to attack enemy aeroplanes; a technical military use. EG *Aircraft were already being scrambled.* V OR V+O

7 A **scramble** is a motorcycle race over very rough land. ◊ **scrambling**. N COUNT ◊ N UNCOUNT

scrambled egg, scrambled eggs. **Scrambled egg** or **scrambled eggs** is a food consisting of eggs mixed together and then cooked in a pan. N UNCOUNT ⇑ dish

scrambler /skræmblə/, **scramblers**. A **scrambler** is an electronic device which alters the sound of a radio or telephone message so that it can only be understood by someone who has special equipment; a technical word. EG *...the nearest phone with a scrambler.* N COUNT

scrap /skræp/, **scraps, scrapping, scrapped**. 1 A **scrap** of cloth, paper, etc is a very small piece of it. EG *...a scrap of old silk which I was using for a doll's dress... He found a scrap of paper and a pencil... There was just one rug made of scraps of old clothes.* N COUNT : USU N+*of*+N UNCOUNT ⇑ fragment = remnant

2 **Scraps** are pieces of food which have not been eaten and which are thrown away or given to animals. EG *Dogs would be gathering in the hope of scraps... Underneath small fish wait for food scraps to fall through the planking... She used to make soup from whatever scraps she could find.* N PLURAL ⇑ remains

3 If there is **not a scrap** of something, there is absolutely none of it. EG *There was not a scrap of direct evidence against him... I don't do a scrap of work... It never made a scrap of difference to his feelings for her.* PHR : USU+*of*+N UNCOUNT = not a jot, not a shred

4 To **scrap** something means to get rid of it or give it up, because it is useless or because you no longer need it; a fairly informal use. EG *The whole existing system should be completely scrapped... In the past three years plans have been scrapped for four nuclear power stations.* V+O = discard

5 **Scrap** or **scrap metal** is metal from old or damaged machinery, cars, etc that is melted down so that it can be used again. EG *All he could do was sell it for scrap... Her father had made a fortune in scrap metal.* ▸ used as a verb. EG *...a gunboat about to be scrapped.* N UNCOUNT ▸ V+O

6 A **scrap** is also a fight or quarrel, especially one that is not very serious; an informal use. EG *Mr Roberts dearly loved a scrap.* ▸ used as a verb. EG *She got very tired of her children scrapping all the time.* N COUNT ▸ V

scrapbook /skræpbʊk/, **scrapbooks**. A **scrapbook** is a book with blank pages into which you stick pictures, newspaper articles, etc in order to make a collection. EG *...scrapbooks filled with clippings... He was always wanting to show people his scrapbooks.* N COUNT

scrape /skreɪp/, **scrapes, scraping, scraped**. 1 If you **scrape** something, you remove its top skin or surface by passing the blade of a knife over it. EG *The nuts can be eaten raw once they have been scraped... You never even scraped a carrot for dinner.* V+O

2 If you **scrape** something from a surface or **scrape** it **off** or **scrape** it **away**, you remove it from the surface by passing the blade of a knife over it. EG V+O+A

Before eating, scrape the mould from the surface... She scraped the mud off her boots... I scraped away an inch of the lead.

3 If you **scrape** something against something else, you rub it against it, causing slight injury or damage. EG *He scraped his hand painfully on a rock.* V-ERG+A (against/on)

4 If something **scrapes**, it makes a harsh, unpleasant noise by rubbing against something else. EG *Gertrude's chair scraped... The lift doors scraped back.* ▸ used as a noun. EG *...the clink and scrape of knives and forks... ...the scrape of a shovel moving the chippings.* ◊ **scraping**. EG *There was a scraping of chairs.* V = grate ▸ N SING WITH DET ◊ N UNCOUNT

5 When people **scrape**, they go without things that they need or buy things cheaply, in order to save money. EG *It amazed me how many people scraped and saved to get their boys into boarding schools... They have pinched and scraped to get themselves to Mecca.* V : USU+A/to-INF ⇑ economize

6 If you are in a **scrape**, you are in a difficult situation that you have caused yourself; a slightly old-fashioned use. EG *He soon got into scrapes... Her ungovernable temper led her into all sorts of scrapes.* N COUNT : AFTER in/into, USU PL ⇑ predicament

7 If you **bow and scrape** to someone, you do everything that they tell you to do and behave in a humble way towards them; used showing disapproval. PHR : VBS INFLECT

8 to **scrape the bottom of the barrel**: see **barrel**.

scrape through. If you **scrape through** an examination, difficult situation, you just succeed in passing it or dealing with it. EG *I just scraped through my exams this summer... It began to look as though he would scrape through the crisis.* PHRASAL VB : V+ ADV/PREP

scrape together. If you **scrape together** or **scrape up** an amount of money, number of people, etc, you manage with some difficulty to get the amount of money, number of people, etc that you need in order to do something. EG *He scraped up the money to start his Hollywood restaurant... If we could scrape together a dozen people, we could hire a minibus.* PHRASAL VB : V+ O+ADV ⇑ acquire

scrap-heap, scrap-heaps. If you **throw** someone or something **on the scrap-heap**, you dismiss them or get rid of them completely because they are no longer of any use to you. EG *He found himself thrown on the political scrap-heap... The aircraft was ingloriously consigned to the scrap-heap in the mid-1970s.* PHR : VB INFLECTS

scrappy /skræpi[1]/, **scrappier, scrappiest**. You describe something as **scrappy** when it is does not seem to be well organized. EG *...a scrappy education... ...the play's somewhat scrappy structure.* ADJ QUALIT = disjointed

scratch /skrætʃ/, **scratches, scratching, scratched**. 1 If a sharp object **scratches** you or **scratches** a part of your body, it rubs against your skin, cutting you slightly. EG *I got scratched by a rose bush... His knees were scratched by thorns.* V+O ⇑ injure

2 A **scratch** is a small cut on your body. EG *You haven't cut yourself badly, it's only a scratch... ...a few bruises and scratches... The minister escaped without a scratch.* N COUNT ⇑ wound

3 If you **scratch** or **scratch** yourself or **scratch** a part of your body, you rub your fingernails against your skin. EG *We are scratching because we itch... Jackson was sleepily scratching himself... The cook began scratching the rash on his neck.* ● If something makes you **scratch** your **head**, it makes you very puzzled. EG *That will make him scratch his head... In the 1860s everyone was scratching their heads about that.* V OR V+O (NG/REFL) ● PHR : VB INFLECTS

4 If you **scratch** something, you make small cuts on it which spoil its appearance. EG *Don't use a scourer on a metal sink or you may scratch it... Your bike's hardly scratched.* ▸ **Scratches** are marks made by scratching. EG *White shoe polish can hide scratches on white woodwork.* ● If you say that an article, report, etc only **scratches the surface**, you mean that it deals with a subject in a superficial way; used showing disapproval. V+O ⇑ mark ▸ N COUNT ⇑ mark ● PHR : VB INFLECTS

5 If you make or organize something **from scratch**, you do it without making use of anything that has been made or done before. EG *Now we have to start again from scratch... Isaacs is building it from scratch... ...great data banks planned from scratch.* PHR : USED AS AN A

6 If something **is up to scratch** or **comes up to scratch**, it is of a satisfactory standard. EG *My Economics and English aren't likely to be up to scratch... It doesn't come up to scratch.* PHR : VB INFLECTS

scrawl /skrɔːl/, **scrawls, scrawling, scrawled**. 1 If you **scrawl** something, you write it in a careless or untidy way. EG *Their anger was summed up by this single word scrawled across the wall... Someone had scrawled 'What does it all mean?' across the cover... I tried to read his notes scrawled on a piece of paper.* V+O, V+A

2 A **scrawl** is a careless, untidy way of writing, or something that has been written carelessly and untidily. EG *I did my best to write neatly instead of with my usual scrawl... ...all manner of pencil scrawls.* N COUNT = scribble

scrawny /skrɔːni[1]/, **scrawnier, scrawniest**. A **scrawny** person or animal is unpleasantly thin and bony. EG *She was a scrawny little thing... ...a scrawny youth... ...scrawny cattle.* ▸ used of a part of someone's body. EG *His T-shirt clung to his scrawny back... He had a long, thin, scrawny neck.* ADJ QUALIT = scraggy

scream /skriːm/, **screams, screaming, screamed**. 1 When someone **screams**, they make a very loud, high-pitched cry, usually because they are in pain or very frightened. People also sometimes scream with excitement. EG *Kunta screamed as a whip seared across his back... He screamed in terror... ...screaming fans.* ▸ used as a noun. EG *He was awakened by the sound of screams.* V = shriek ▸ N COUNT = shriek

2 If something **screams**, it makes a very loud high-pitched noise. EG *The jets screamed overhead... We heard a siren screaming behind us... The birds screamed up in the trees.* ▸ used as a noun. EG *The car roared round the corner with a scream of tyres... The baboon's growling turned into a scream.* V ▸ N COUNT = screech

3 If someone **screams** something, they shout it in a very loud high-pitched voice. EG *'Get out of there,' I screamed... She stood there screaming abuse at me.* V+O/REPORT-CL. QUOTE = shriek

4 You describe someone or something as a **scream** when you think that they are very funny; an informal use. EG *Do you know Sheila? She's a scream.* N SING WITH DET = hoot

5 People also say that something **screams** when it is unpleasantly conspicuous. EG *The newspaper placards screamed the news of the election... He wore bright-coloured shirts and screaming ties.* V OR V+O

scree /skriː/, **screes**. **Scree** or a **scree** is a mass of loose stones on the side of a mountain. EG *...boulders and scree washed down by the floods... They made their way over screes of sharp stone.* N UNCOUNT/COUNT

screech /skriːtʃ/, **screeches, screeching, screeched**. 1 If a person or an animal **screeches**, they make an unpleasant, loud, high-pitched cry. EG *The parrots screeched in the trees above their heads... 'You'll be sorry you did that!' she screeched.* ▸ used as a noun. EG *The mongoose wrinkles his nose and gives a loud screech.* V OR V+O/QUOTE/REPORT-CL = shriek ▸ N COUNT : USU SING

2 If a vehicle **screeches** or if its tyres **screech**, its tyres make an unpleasant high-pitched noise on the road. EG *The bus came screeching to a stop... Sirens whooped and tyres screeched.* ▸ used as a noun. EG *I heard a screech of tyres.* V ▸ N UNCOUNT

screen /skriːn/, **screens, screening, screened**. 1 A **screen** is a flat, vertical surface on which a picture is shown. Television sets and computer terminals have screens, and films are shown on a screen in a cinema. EG *A picture would flash onto the screen... The television screen remained the centre of attention... The plane appeared as a dot on the radar screen.* ● See also **small screen**. N COUNT

2 The **screen** refers to the films that are shown in cinemas. EG *Greta Garbo and other stars of the screen... How on earth can it be dramatized for the screen?* N SING : the+N

3 When a film or a television programme **is screened**, it is shown in the cinema or broadcast on television. EG *His earlier films were only screened in France... They tried to prevent the programme being screened.* V+O

4 A **screen** is also 4.1 a vertical panel or frame which can be moved around in a room. It is used to keep cold air away from part of the room, or to create a smaller area within the room. EG *He got up and walked behind the screen... A little kitchenette was concealed by a screen from the living-room.* 4.2 something which prevents sunlight from reaching a place or prevents a building from being seen. EG *Beyond the screen of leaves the sunlight shone brightly.* N COUNT N COUNT : USU+SUPP ⇑ barrier

5 If you **screen** someone, 5.1 you stand in front of them or place a screen in front of them, in order to V+O ⇑ hide

prevent them from being seen or hurt. EG *I moved in front of her trying to screen her.* **5.2** you question or examine them carefully in order to make sure that they are not a security risk or do not have a particular disease. EG *The Secret Service screens several hundred people every week... ...women screened for breast cancer... In hospitals and clinics computers will screen patients before they see a doctor.* V+O ⇑ check

screen off. If you **screen off** a part of a room, you use a screen in order to make the part into a separate or private area. EG *It was one long room that had a sleeping area screened off.* PHRASAL VB : V+O+ADV ⇑ partition off

screening /skri:nɪŋ/, **screenings. Screening** or a **screening** is **1** the process of screening someone for security or health reasons. EG *There is no national policy concerning such screening... ...a screening at a London medical centre.* N UNCOUNT/COUNT ⇑ check = vetting **2** the showing of a film or television programme. EG *...the screening of information programmes... There was an attempt by descendants of the Captain to stop the screening.* N UNCOUNT/COUNT

screenplay /skri:nplei/, **screenplays.** A **screenplay** is the script for a film. EG *'The French Lieutenant's Woman' has a screenplay by Harold Pinter... There's only one copy of the screenplay.* N COUNT

screenwriter /skri:nraɪtə/, **screenwriters.** A **screenwriter** is a person who writes screenplays. N COUNT ⇑ scriptwriter

screw /skru:/, **screws, screwing, screwed. 1** A **screw** is a small sharp piece of metal, similar to a nail, which is used to fasten one thing to another. It has a spiral groove going round it from one end to the other, and it is fixed into wood, metal, or other materials by being firmly twisted, usually with a screwdriver. EG *Tighten the tiny screw on the side of the tap... I removed the last of the screws and took the back off the machine.* N COUNT

2 If you **screw** something into a particular position, **2.1** you fasten it, tighten it, or fix it there by means of a screw or screws. EG *Squeaking floorboards should be screwed down... I'm going to screw some handles onto the new bathroom cabinet... Screw the two pieces together at each end... The curtains are attached to special clips which screw to the window-frame.* V-ERG+A **2.2** you fasten it, tighten it, or fix it there by twisting it round and round. EG *He screwed the lid tightly onto the top of the jar... Slide the plug in, then screw in the screw... ...hollow tubes which screw together.* V-ERG+A

3 If you **screw** something or **screw** something **up** into a particular shape, you twist it or squeeze it tightly so that it is creased and no longer in its natural shape. EG *Etta painfully screwed her face into an expression of disgust... She screwed up her eyes as she faced the sun... She screwed up the paper and tossed it in the bin.* • See also **screwed-up.** V+O, OR PHRASAL VB : V+O+ADV ⇑ distort = scrunch up

4 If you **screw** something out of someone, you get it from them by means of strong persuasion; a very informal use. EG *I managed to screw a bit more money out of him.* V+O+A *(out of)* = squeeze

5 If someone says that they **have been screwed,** they mean that someone else has cheated them, especially by getting money from them dishonestly; a very informal use. EG *But suppose it is valuable, why should I get screwed?* V+O : USU PASS = swindle

6 If someone **screws** another person, they have sex with that person; a very informal use which many people consider to be rude and offensive. V OR V+O : RECIP

7 Someone might say **screw** something to say that they are not concerned about something, for example about the consequences of doing something; a very informal use. EG *'It could cost quite a lot,' he said. 'Screw the cost,' I said.* V+O : ONLY IMPER

8 A **screw** is also a guard in a prison; a very informal use. EG *I asked how he was treated by the screws.* N COUNT = warder

9 If you say that someone **has got a screw loose,** you mean that they are slightly mad; an informal expression. PHR : VB INFLECTS

10 If you **put the screws on** someone, you use force or threats on them; an informal expression. EG *I'll have to put the screws on if he won't pay.* PHR : VB INFLECTS

11 If you say that someone **has** their **head screwed on,** you mean that they are very sensible; an informal expression. EG *She's clearly got her head screwed on the right way.* PHR : VB AND N INFLECT

screw up. 1 If you **screw** something **up,** you make it fail or get it badly wrong and cause disorder; a very informal expression. EG *He can't do that; that screws up all my arrangements... They were using procedures that were all screwed up in the first place... The car broke down, so that screwed up our holiday.* PHRASAL VB : V+O+ADV

2 Something that **screws** you **up** makes you nervous, worried, or confused; a very informal expression. EG *Her mother's screwed her up and given her values she despises.* • See also **screwed-up.** PHRASAL VB : V+O+ADV, USU PASS

3 If you **screw up** your **courage,** you force yourself to be brave in order to do something unpleasant. EG *I screwed up my courage to ask for help.* PHR : VB INFLECTS = steel yourself

screwdriver /skru:draɪvə/, **screwdrivers.** A **screwdriver** is a tool that is used for turning screws, consisting of a long thin metal rod with a thin flattened end that fits into the slot in the head of a screw. EG *With the aid of a screwdriver, loosen the two screws at each end.* N COUNT

screwed-up. 1 A **screwed-up** piece of paper, face, etc has been twisted or squeezed tightly so that it is creased and no longer in its natural shape. EG *...a ball of screwed-up paper... Snow blew into our screwed-up eyes.* ADJ CLASSIF : ATTRIB

2 Someone who is **screwed-up** is very confused or worried and not at all relaxed. EG *He's really screwed up about these exams.* ADJ QUALIT

screw-top, screw-tops; also spelled as one word. A **screw-top** bottle, jar, etc has a lid or top that is fastened by being tightly twisted; also used of the lid itself. EG *It will keep for one week in a screwtop jar in the fridge.* ▸ used as a noun. EG *...bottles with screw-tops.* ADJ CLASSIF : ATTRIB ▸ N COUNT

screwy /skru:i¹/, **screwier, screwiest.** If you say that someone is **screwy,** you mean that they are crazy or eccentric; an informal word. ▸ used of people's attitudes and behaviour. EG *He's got some pretty screwy ideas.* ADJ QUALIT = dotty

scribble /skrɪbə⁰l/, **scribbles, scribbling, scribbled. 1** If you **scribble** something or if you **scribble, 1.1** you write quickly and roughly, often with the result that what you have written is hard to read. EG *She was scribbling a letter to her mother... ...a report with 'personal' scribbled in one corner... You can scribble your own ideas in the blank areas provided... We were scribbling away furiously, trying to finish the exam.* V OR V+O : USU+A = scrawl **1.2** you make meaningless marks or drawings, for example on paper or walls, using a pencil or pen. EG *Someone's scribbled all over the wall.* V+A = doodle

2 Your **scribble** is something that you have written or drawn quickly, roughly, or untidily. EG *She was looking at my scribble, trying to work out what it said... There are scribbles on the lift wall.* N UNCOUNT/COUNT = scrawl

scribe /skraɪb/, **scribes.** A **scribe** is a person who writes copies of things such as letters or documents; used especially of people who copied manuscripts before printing was invented. EG *These palace records were copied out three and a half thousand years ago by an Egyptian scribe.* N COUNT

scrimmage /skrɪmɪdʒ/, **scrimmages.** A **scrimmage** is a rough, disorganized fight or struggle. EG *There were howls and screams, rocks were thrown, and out of the scrimmage the police came running.* N COUNT = fray

scrimp /skrɪmp/, **scrimps, scrimping, scrimped.** Someone who **scrimps** on things lives cheaply and spends as little money as possible. EG *I was still broke, still scrimping and saving to buy necessities... ...the scrimping life of the peasants.* V : IF+PREP/VB THEN *on/to*-INF = skimp

script /skrɪpt/, **scripts. 1** A **script** is **1.1** the written version of something that is spoken or performed, such as a play, film, or television programme. EG *You can't have good acting without a decent script... ...a film script.* N COUNT **1.2** a particular system of writing. EG *...the Arabic script... It was written in a script I had never seen before.* N COUNT/UNCOUNT **1.3** a examination candidate's answer paper in an examination. N COUNT

2 Script is writing done by hand, or a particular way of writing by hand, especially when this is neat and regular. EG *It was written on blue paper in impressive italic script... Nobody could decipher my microscopic script.* N UNCOUNT = handwriting

scripted /skrɪptɪ²d/. A **scripted** speech or conversation is one in which you use a script that has been prepared beforehand. EG *...a carefully scripted interview... The programme started off with scripted dialogue on tape.* ADJ CLASSIF : USU ATTRIB ⇑ written

scriptural /skrɪptʃə⁰rəl/ is used to describe things that are written in or based on the Christian Bible. EG ADJ CLASSIF : ATTRIB

The belief has no scriptural basis... ...the scriptural account of the origins of the world.

scripture /skrɪptʃə/, **scriptures**. 1 **Scripture** or a **scripture** of a particular kind is a collection of writings that is regarded as sacred in a particular religion, especially a non-Christian religion. EG *They invoked Hindu scripture to justify their position... ...Buddhist scriptures.* — N UNCOUNT/COUNT

2 The **Scripture** or the **Scriptures** refers to the Christian Bible. EG *The scripture says, 'Man cannot live on bread alone.'... According to the Scriptures, Christ was born in Bethlehem.* — N COUNT: IF SING the+N, SING=PL ▸ **Scripture** is sometimes used to refer to a school subject which involves the study of the Bible. EG *After prayers we have a Scripture lesson.* — ▸ N UNCOUNT

scriptwriter /skrɪptraɪtə/, **scriptwriters**. A **scriptwriter** is a person who writes scripts, especially for films or radio and television programmes. EG *She's one of the scriptwriters on a popular TV detective series.* — N COUNT ⇑ writer

scroll /skrəʊl/, **scrolls**. A **scroll** is 1 a long roll of paper, parchment, or other material with writing on it, often one that was used as a book in ancient times. EG *...an ancient Chinese scroll.* — N COUNT 2 an ornamental carving in stone or wood made to look like a scroll. It is used for example to decorate buildings or furniture. EG *...intricate carvings of festoons and scrolls and clusters.* — N COUNT ⇑ decoration

scrotum /skrəʊtəm/, **scrotums, scrota**. The plural can be either **scrotums** or **scrota**. A man's **scrotum** is the bag of skin that contains his testicles; a technical term in biology or medicine. — N COUNT

scrounge /skraʊnd⁰ʒ/, **scrounges, scrounging, scrounged**; an informal word. 1 If you **scrounge** something such as money or food off someone, you get it by asking them for it, rather than by buying it or working for it. EG *He tried to scrounge some money off me for his bus fare... Could I scrounge a cigarette please?* — V OR V+O: USU+A = cadge

2 Someone who is **on the scrounge** is trying to get something by asking other people for it, rather than by paying for it. EG *They had gone out on the scrounge and come back with some things to eat... I'm afraid I'm on the scrounge–could you lend me a couple of pounds?* — PHR: USED AS AN A

scrounger /skraʊnd⁰ʒə/, **scroungers**. A **scrounger** is a person who tries to get money, food, etc without working for it; an informal word used showing disapproval. EG *You're a parasite, a scrounger, living off other people's efforts.* — N COUNT = sponger

scrub /skrʌb/, **scrubs, scrubbing, scrubbed**. 1 If you **scrub** something, you rub it hard in order to clean it, often using a stiff brush and water or another liquid. EG *The restaurant staff scrub the kitchen floor every day... ...a scrubbed pine table... Her face had a freshly scrubbed look about it.* — V OR V+O ⇑ wash = scour ▸ used as a noun. EG *That floor needs a good scrub.* — ▸ N COUNT: IF SING a+N

2 If you **scrub** dirt or stains off something, you remove them by rubbing hard. EG *There was a stain on the collar and he tried to scrub it off... ...scrubbing the dirty marks off the wall.* — V+O+A

3 If you **scrub** something that has been planned or suggested, you decide not to do it; an informal use. EG *The project had apparently been scrubbed or postponed.* — V+O = scrap

4 **Scrub** consists of low trees and bushes growing in an area that has very little rain. EG *The country is flat, grassy, and covered in scrub... It is so dry that only isolated trees and low scrub can survive there.* — N UNCOUNT ⇑ vegetation

scrubby /skrʌbi¹/, **scrubbier, scrubbiest**. **Scrubby** land is rough and dry and covered with scrub. EG *...the scrubby slopes of the hills.* — ADJ QUALIT

scrubland /skrʌblə³nd/. **Scrubland** is land that is covered with low trees and bushes. EG *Most of the country is desert and scrubland.* — N UNCOUNT

scruff /skrʌf/, **scruffs**. If someone holds you **by the scruff of the neck**, they hold the back of your neck or collar. EG *He was holding the girl by the scruff of the neck... Don't pick up a puppy by the scruff of its neck.* — PHR: USED AS AN A

scruffy /skrʌfi¹/, **scruffier, scruffiest**. Someone or something that is **scruffy** is dirty and untidy in appearance. EG *The child looked neglected, scruffy, unloved... ...a Harvard scientist who, despite his scruffy appearance, was once an adviser to the President.* — ADJ QUALIT = tatty, unkempt ◇ **scruffily**. EG *Everyone was scruffily dressed.* — ◇ ADV WITH VB = shabbily

scrum /skrʌm/, **scrums**. A **scrum** in the game of rugby is a formation in which players from each side form a tight pack and push against each other with their heads down in an attempt to get the ball. — N COUNT

scrumptious /skrʌmp⁰ʃəs/. If you describe food as **scrumptious**, you mean that it is extremely delicious or pleasing; an informal word. EG *Her cakes are scrumptious.* — ADJ QUALIT

scrunch /skrʌntʃ/, **scrunches, scrunching, scrunched**. 1 If you **scrunch** something or if it **scrunches**, you press it or crush it noisily. EG *...scrunching the pebbles as we walked across the beach... ...slow footsteps scrunched on the gravel.* — V-ERG = crunch

2 A **scrunch** is a noise made by pressing or crushing something, for example when you are walking or driving over loose stones. EG *And with a scrunch and a skid we drove off.* — N COUNT: USU SING = crunch

scrunch up. If you **scrunch** something **up**, you squeeze it or bend it so that it is no longer in its natural shape and is often crushed. EG *She started to read it, then scrunched it up and threw it in the bin.* — PHRASAL VB: V+O+ADV

scruple /skru:pə⁰l/, **scruples**. Your **scruples** are moral principles or beliefs that make you unwilling to do something that seems wrong, or uncertain about whether a course of action is right. EG *He wondered if Gwen had any religious scruples about abortion... Blind love had overcome a lifetime's scruples... Live fish are fried and boiled without scruple.* — N COUNT: USU PL = qualm

scrupulous /skru:pjə⁴ləs/. Someone or something who is **scrupulous** 1 takes great care to do what is fair, honest, or morally right. EG *The paper was not entirely scrupulous in setting out its assumptions.* — ADJ QUALIT ⇑ careful = conscientious ◇ **scrupulously**. EG *There's a lot of pressure on manufacturers to behave scrupulously... The judge's summary was scrupulously fair to both parties.* — ◇ ADV = honourably 2 is thorough, exact, and pays careful attention to detail. EG *...a historian with a reputation for scrupulous scholarship... The kitchen staff are scrupulous about hygiene.* — ADJ QUALIT = punctilious ◇ **scrupulously**. EG *The old church has been beautifully and scrupulously maintained... Everything was scrupulously clean.* — ◇ ADV = meticulously

scrutinize /skru:tɪnaɪz/, **scrutinizes, scrutinizing, scrutinized**; also spelled **scrutinise**. If you **scrutinize** something, you look at it very carefully, often in order to find out some information about it or from it. EG *Federal bank examiners scrutinized the books of 600 financial institutions... He began to scrutinize the faces in the compartment.* — V+O = examine

scrutiny /skru:tɪni¹/. **Scrutiny** of someone or something is very careful study or observation of them. EG *Some scrutiny of Britain's position in the world was needed.* — N UNCOUNT ⇑ examination ● Someone or something that is **under scrutiny** is being carefully studied or observed. EG *Their defence policy did not stand up under scrutiny... The chief kept the prisoners under close scrutiny.* — ● PHR: USED AS AN A

scuba diving /sku:bə daɪvɪŋ/ is the activity of swimming under water using a special type of breathing equipment. The equipment consists of cylinders of compressed air that you carry on your back connected to your mouth by a rubber tube. — N UNCOUNT

scud /skʌd/, **scuds, scudding, scudded**. To **scud** means to move quickly and smoothly along; often used of clouds; a fairly literary word. EG *...clouds scudding across the sky... ...children scudding downhill on their sledges.* — V+A = sail

scuff /skʌf/, **scuffs, scuffing, scuffed**. 1 If you **scuff** your feet, you drag them along the ground by walking without lifting them. EG *My sister was scuffing her feet as we walked down the road.* — V+O

2 If you **scuff** something such as your shoes, you mark or wear away the surface of them by rubbing or scraping. — V+O ◇ **scuffed**. EG *...a poor man in a baggy suit and scuffed shoes... ...a scuffed leather holdall.* — ◇ ADJ QUALIT

scuffle /skʌfə⁰l/, **scuffles, scuffling, scuffled**.
1 A **scuffle** is a rough fight or struggle, usually one that starts suddenly and ends quickly. EG *Two police officers were injured in a scuffle between pro- and anti-government demonstrators... There was a brief scuffle before they got the handcuffs on him.* — N COUNT = set-to

2 If people **scuffle**, they fight or struggle in a rough way, usually for a very short time. EG *The girls climbed into the bus and scuffled for the window seats.* — V = tussle

3 If you **scuffle** or if you **scuffle** something, you make a noise walking or moving something. EG *We* — V OR V+O = shuffle

scuffled our way down the lane. ◇ **scuffling**. EG *...a scuffling and crashing of furniture... ...the scuffling of their feet.* ◇ N UNCOUNT

scull /skʌl/, **sculls, sculling, sculled. 1 Sculls** are small oars which are held by one person and are used to move a boat, especially a racing boat, through water. N COUNT : USU PL

2 To **scull** means to move a boat through water using sculls. EG *We went sculling on the river.* V OR V+O ⇑ row

scullery /skʌləri¹/, **sculleries**. A **scullery** is a small room next to the kitchen, especially in an old house, where washing, cleaning, and other household work is done. N COUNT

sculpt /skʌlpt/, **sculpts, sculpting, sculpted**. If you **sculpt** something, you make it as a sculpture. EG *...a nude woman, sculpted in marble... Desert winds have sculpted the sands into long, low red-topped dunes.* V+O : USU PASS ⇑ form

sculptor /skʌlptə/, **sculptors**. A **sculptor** is someone who makes sculptures from stone, wood, clay, etc. EG *She is one of the best known British sculptors since Henry Moore.* N COUNT ⇑ artist

sculptural /skʌlptʃəᵒrəl/. Something that is **sculptural** consists of or is connected with sculpture. EG *...sculptural forms.* ADJ CLASSIF

sculpture /skʌlptʃə/, **sculptures, sculpturing, sculptured**. **1 Sculpture** is **1.1** the art of making objects or figures using solid materials, for example by carving stone or shaping clay. EG *The college offers classes in sculpture... Everyone agrees that she made a serious contribution to modern sculpture.* N UNCOUNT **1.2** objects that have been produced by someone working in this form of art. EG *I did some sculpture... ...an exhibition of 20th century sculpture.* N UNCOUNT

2 A **sculpture** is an object that has been produced by someone working in this form of art. EG *...an enormous iron sculpture... ...Aztec sculptures.* N COUNT

3 If you **sculpture** an object, you make it by carving stone, shaping clay, or a similar process. EG *...sculptured heads of civic dignitaries.* V+O : USU PASS ⇑ form = sculpt

4 Something that **is sculptured** has a distinct shape, as if it has been carved by a sculptor. EG *...the stiff, sculptured folds of her skirt.* V+O : USU PASS

scum /skʌm/, **scums. 1** A **scum** is a layer of dirty or unpleasant-looking substance that forms on the surface of a liquid. EG *In some areas, a limestone scum will form in the bath when you use soap... There was green scum over the pond.* N UNCOUNT/COUNT = film

2 If you refer to people as **scum**, you mean that they are the worst and most worthless type of people; an informal use. EG *These so-called football supporters are scum... It's time we were treated like human beings, instead of being treated like scum.* N PLURAL = trash

scupper /skʌpə/, **scuppers, scuppering, scuppered**. **1** To **scupper** something means to completely spoil a plan or attempt, or to make someone fail or get into difficulties; an informal use, used in British English. EG *This is an arrangement that could solve the problem, if its opponents do not scupper it before it's tried out... Any chance of a compromise was scuppered... We'll be scuppered if they won't lend us the money.* V+O : USU PASS = ruin

2 A **scupper** is an opening in the side of a boat that allows water to flow off the deck into the sea. N COUNT : USU PL

scurrility /skərɪlɪti¹/ is the practice of being scurrilous; a fairly literary word. EG *As a political satirist, scurrility was his trade, you might say.* N UNCOUNT ⇑ defamation

scurrilous /skʌrɪləs/. If something that you say or write is **scurrilous**, it uses lies, unfair criticism, and insulting language, usually in order to damage someone's reputation. EG *...the book is full of scurrilous gossip... ...a scurrilous weekly magazine.* ADJ QUALIT

scurry /skʌri¹/, **scurries, scurrying, scurried. 1** To **scurry** somewhere means to run quickly like small animals do when they are frightened or trying to escape. EG *The pig scurried into the undergrowth... Everyone scurried for cover when the police started firing.* V+A ⇑ hurry = scuttle

2 A **scurry** is a quick, hurrying movement or the sound of this movement. EG *I heard a scurry of footsteps.* N SING WITH DET

scurvy /skɜːvi¹/ is a disease that is caused by a lack of vitamin C through not eating enough fresh fruit and vegetables. People who have scurvy suffer from bleeding gums and extreme weakness. N UNCOUNT

scuttle /skʌtəᵒl/, **scuttles, scuttling, scuttled**. **1** To **scuttle** somewhere means to run with short, quick steps. EG *Sometimes a porcupine scuttled across the road... Ted scuttled after his brother.* V+A

2 To **scuttle** a ship means to sink it by making holes in the bottom, especially when this is done deliberately in order to prevent someone else from capturing it. EG *The captain gave orders that the ship should be scuttled... The Danish fleet had scuttled itself.* V+O

3 A **scuttle** is the same as a coal scuttle. N COUNT

scythe /saɪð/, **scythes, scything, scythed. 1** A **scythe** is a tool with a long curved blade fixed at right angles to the bottom of a long handle. It is used with a swinging movement to cut long grass or grain. N COUNT

2 If you **scythe** grass, a field, etc, you cut it with a scythe. EG *He'd scythed half the orchard.* V OR V+O = mow

3 If something **scythes**, it makes a wide, swinging movement through the air. EG *The ball scythed through the air.* V+A = arc

SDP is an abbreviation for 'Social Democratic Party'. The SDP is a British political party. N PROPER : the+N

SE; pronounced as 'south east' or /ɛs iː/. **SE** is an abbreviation for 'south-east'; used on a compass or in descriptions of where a particular place is situated. EG *...London SE11.*

sea /siː/, **seas. 1** The **sea** is **1.1** the salty water that covers about three quarters of the earth's surface. EG *I watched the children running into the sea again for a swim... ...a wrecked ship lying at the bottom of the sea... A gentle breeze rippled the surface of the sea... These fish are found in the seas along the North Atlantic coast of America... We were steaming through the calmest seas that we had encountered since leaving port.* ▸ used as an adjective. EG *...the sea floor... ...sea travel.* N COUNT : the+N, SING=PL ▸ N BEFORE N **1.2** the area on or close to the edge of the sea, especially as a place where people go on holiday. EG *...a pleasant weekend by the sea... ...Southend-on-Sea.* N SING : the+N **1.3** the career of being a sailor and all the activities connected with ships and navies. EG *He would often reminisce about his first experience of the sea... He ran away to sea when he was 15.* N SING : the+N, OR PREP+N

2 A **sea** is a large area of water that is smaller than an ocean and that is sometimes partly or completely surrounded by land. EG *...an inland sea... ...the North Sea... ...the Caspian Sea.* N COUNT : ALSO IN NAMES AFTER N

3 A **sea** of people or things is a very large number of them. EG *...a sea of white faces... ...a sea of troubles.* N SING+of+N IN PL/N UNCOUNT

4 at sea. 4.1 Something that is **at sea** is on the sea, far away from land. EG *...a storm at sea... Submarines can stay at sea for weeks.* PHR : USED AS AN A **4.2** Life **at sea** is life on a ship or on ships, especially working as a sailor. EG *He had seen a great deal during his lifetime at sea.* PHR : USED AS AN A **4.3** If you are **at sea**, you are in a state of confusion or uncertainty. EG *I'm afraid I'm rather at sea–could you explain that again?* PHR : USED AS AN A = baffled

5 If you travel, send something, etc **by sea**, you travel, send it, etc in a ship or using ships as a means of transport. EG *They sent all the heavy equipment by sea.* PHR : USED AS AN A

6 If you go or look **out to sea**, you go or look away from land and in the direction of the horizon where the sea meets the sky. EG *The little boat was swept out to sea... We turned and headed out to sea... He stared out to sea.* PHR : USED AS AN A = seawards

7 If something happens **on the high seas**, it happens far away from land, and outside those areas of the sea that belong to particular countries. EG *...piracy on the high seas.* PHR : USED AS AN A

sea air; also spelled with a hyphen. The **sea air** is the air at the seaside, which is regarded as being good for people's health. EG *She took a deep breath of sea air.* N UNCOUNT

seabed /siːbɛd/; also spelled with a hyphen and as two words. The **seabed** is the floor of the sea. N SING : the+N

seabird /siːbɜːd/, **seabirds**; also spelled with a hyphen and as two words. **Seabirds** are birds that live near the sea and get their food from the sea, such as seagulls or albatrosses. N COUNT

seaboard /siːbɔːd/, **seaboards**. The **seaboard** of a country is the land along its coastline, close to the sea; used especially of the coast in North America. EG *...the eastern seaboard of the United States.* N COUNT : USU SING ⇑ region

seaborne /siːbɔːn/. Something that is **seaborne** is carried on the sea in ships. EG *The timely arrival of seaborne reinforcements saved us from defeat... ...seaborne supplies.* ADJ CLASSIF : USU ATTRIB ⇑ transported

sea breeze, sea breezes. A **sea breeze** is a light wind blowing from the sea towards the land. N COUNT

sea dog, sea dogs; also spelled with a hyphen and as one word. A **sea dog** is a sailor, especially one who has spent many years at sea; sometimes used humorously. N COUNT

seafaring /siːfeərɪŋ/ means working as a sailor or travelling regularly on the sea. EG *...the seafaring life... Britain has always been a seafaring nation.* ADJ CLASSIF : ATTRIB = maritime

seafood /siːfuːd/, **seafoods**; also spelled with a hyphen and as two words. **Seafood** is used to refer to sea creatures that are used as food, especially shellfish such as lobsters, mussels, or crabs. EG *Do you like seafood?... ...a seafood restaurant.* N MASS

seafront /siːfrʌnt/, **seafronts**; also spelled with a hyphen. The **seafront** is the part of a seaside town that is next to the beach, and usually consists of a road or wide path, with buildings facing the sea. EG *...a walk along the seafront... ...a seafront café.* N COUNT : USU *the*+N IN SING = promenade

sea-going. **Sea-going** boats, ships, etc are designed for travelling on the sea, rather than on lakes or along the coast. ADJ CLASSIF : ATTRIB = ocean-going

seagull /siːgʌl/, **seagulls**. A **seagull** is a common medium-sized bird with short legs and white and grey or black feathers that lives near the sea and gets its food from the sea. EG *Our boat was followed by a whole flock of seagulls.* N COUNT = gull

seahorse /siːhɔːs/, **seahorses**. A **seahorse** is a type of small fish which swims in an upright position and whose head looks a little bit like the head of a horse. N COUNT

seal /siːl/, **seals, sealing, sealed**. 1 A **seal** is 1.1 a special design that is the official mark of a person or organization. Seals are sometimes fixed to documents, certificates, etc to show that they are legal or genuine. The design is usually pressed onto a piece of hot wax, soft metal, or coloured paper. EG *...a great parchment document with its official red seals... ...the presidential seal... ...the minister's seal of office.* N COUNT = insignia
1.2 a tool used for marking things with a design of this kind. N COUNT 1.3 something, such as thin paper, wire, or a piece of wax, that is fixed to the opening of a container, letter, etc and must be broken before the container, letter, etc can be opened. EG *I noticed that the seals of the packet had been broken.* N COUNT 1.4 something, such as part of a machine or system, that closes an opening tightly so that air, gas, or liquid cannot get in or out. EG *Worn oil seals can cause leakage of oil... This type of cork forms a tight seal and keeps the wine fresh.* N COUNT

2 If you **seal** a letter, box, etc, you close it firmly so that people cannot see what is inside. EG *The solicitor took a sealed envelope from the folder on his desk... The transcript of grand jury hearings is sealed.* V+O : USU PASS

3 If you **seal** something, you block the holes or openings in it in order to prevent air, gas, or liquid getting in or out. EG *...a thin rubber tube sealed at one end... Small cracks can be sealed with glue.* V+O : USU PASS

4 A **seal** is also a large, animal that eats fish and lives partly on land and partly in the sea, usually in cold parts of the world. N COUNT ⇑ mammal

5 If you say **'my lips are sealed'**, you are promising not to talk about a secret matter that you have just been told about. CONVENTION

6 If something **seals** your **fate** or **doom**, it makes it certain that you will die or fail. EG *This disaster sealed the fate of the expedition.* PHR : VB INFLECTS

7 If something **puts** or **sets the seal on** something, it makes it definite or confirms how it is going to be. EG *The experience set the seal on their friendship... The recent floods finally put the seal on a disappointing summer.* PHR : VB INFLECTS

8 If you **give** something your **seal of approval**, you officially say that you approve of it or like it. EG *The police have given this burglar alarm their seal of approval... The scheme certainly has my seal of approval.* PHR : VB INFLECTS

9 See also **sealing**.

seal in. If you **seal in** a smell or liquid, you prevent it from getting out. EG *Fry quickly to seal in the flavour of the meat.* PHRASAL VB : V+O+ADV ⇑ shut in

seal off. If you **seal** a place **off**, you keep it separate by tightly closing all the entrances or openings. EG *Police sealed off the area to try and control the riot.* PHRASAL VB : V+O+ADV ⇑ isolate

sea lane, sea lanes. A **sea lane** is a particular route that is regularly used by ships when crossing a sea or ocean. EG *It was vital for America to keep these sea lanes open.* N COUNT

sea legs. If you **get** or **find** your **sea legs**, you became used to the movement of a ship at sea, so that you do not feel seasick and are able to walk normally. PHR : VB INFLECTS

sea level is the average level of the surface of the sea, in relation to the land; often used in giving measurements. EG *Changes in sea level may cause the low-lying areas to be flooded... ...5,000 feet above sea level.* N UNCOUNT

sealing /siːlɪŋ/ is the hunting of seals. N UNCOUNT

sealing wax; also spelled with a hyphen. **Sealing wax** is a hard, usually red, substance that melts quickly and is used for putting seals on documents, certificates, letters, etc. N UNCOUNT ⇑ wax

sea lion, sea lions; also spelled with a hyphen and as one word. A **sea lion** is a type of large seal that lives on the shores of the northern Pacific Ocean. N COUNT

sealskin /siːlskɪn/ is the fur of a seal, used to make coats and other clothing. EG *...a sealskin coat.* N UNCOUNT

seam /siːm/, **seams**. 1 A **seam** is 1.1 a line of stitches which joins two pieces of cloth or other material together, usually close to their edges. EG *The seam has split.* N COUNT 1.2 the line formed where two things are joined together at their edges. EG *The work was done so neatly that you can scarcely see the seam between the old and the new building.* N COUNT = join 1.3 a long, narrow layer of coal, marble, etc formed under the ground between layers of other rocks. N COUNT

2 If something is **bursting** or **bulging at the seams**, it is very full. EG *My small flat is bursting at the seams... Our schools and universities are bulging at the seams.* PHR : USED AS C = overflow

3 If something is **coming apart** or **falling apart at the seams**, it is not in a good condition and needs to be repaired. EG *Our relationship is falling apart at the seams.* PHR : USED AS C = disintegrate

seaman /siːmə³n/, **seamen**. A **seaman** is a sailor, especially one who is not an officer. EG *...the National Union of Seamen.* N COUNT

seamanship /siːmə³nʃɪp/ is skill in managing a boat and controlling its movement through the sea. EG *The journey round Cape Horn demanded a high degree of seamanship.* N UNCOUNT

seamed /siːmd/. Something that is **seamed** has many long, thin lines on its surface. EG *His brown face was seamed and wrinkled.* ADJ QUALIT = lined

seamless /siːmlɪ²s/. 1 A **seamless** piece of clothing has no seams. ADJ CLASSIF

2 If you describe something as **seamless**, you mean that you cannot see where the different parts of it join together. EG *The gardens make a seamless whole with Hyde Park on the east.* ADJ CLASSIF

seamstress /semstrɪ²s/, **seamstresses**. A **seamstress** is a woman who sews and makes clothes as her job. N COUNT ⇑ needlewoman

seamy /siːmi¹/, **seamier, seamiest**. Something that is **seamy** is unpleasant, especially because it involves aspects of life such as crime, sex, poverty, or violence. EG *He was involved in a particularly seamy divorce case... ...the seamy side of life.* ADJ QUALIT = sordid

séance /seɪɑːns/, **séances**; also spelled **seance**. A **séance** is a meeting in which people try to speak to or get messages from people who are dead. N COUNT ⇑ gathering

seaplane /siːpleɪn/, **seaplanes**. A **seaplane** is a type of aeroplane that can take off or land on water. N COUNT ⇑ aircraft

seaport /siːpɔːt/, **seaports**. A **seaport** is a town with a harbour that is used by large ships. N COUNT = port

sea power, sea powers. 1 **Sea power** is the size and strength of a country's navy. EG *Sea power still plays a vital role in defence.* N UNCOUNT

2 A **sea power** is a country that has a large navy. N COUNT

sear /sɪə/, **sears, searing, seared**. 1 To **sear** something means to burn its surface with a sudden intense heat. EG *Sear the meat for one minute, then reduce the heat and cook slowly.* V+O = fry

2 If something **sears** a part of your body, it causes a painful burning feeling there. EG *The pungent, choking smell of sulphur and burnt sand seared our nostrils.* V+O = scorch

3 See also **searing**.

search /sɜːtʃ/, **searches, searching, searched**. 1 If you **search** for something or **search** a place for something, you look carefully in a place because you are trying to find something. EG *He glanced around the small room, searching for a* V OR V+O : USU+*for* *place to sit... Army patrols are still searching for survivors of the plane crash... He searched through a drawer and eventually found the photo... I searched everywhere but couldn't find your book... Police searched the building for clues.*

2 If you **search** or **search** your mind for something, you try to think of something that you need or want. EG *I'm searching for inspiration... She searched her mind for some words of comfort.* V OR V+O : USU+ *for*

3 A **search** is an attempt to find something by looking somewhere. EG *We eventually found the keys after a long search... A huge search for the missing documents was mounted... The company has spent millions in the search for oil... We went round the town in search of a place to stay.* N COUNT : IF+ PREP THEN *for*, OR *in*+N UNCOUNT+*of* = hunt

4 If someone such as the police **searches** a person, room, bag, etc, they examine the person, room, bag, etc because they are trying to find something that has been hidden. EG *We were stopped by the police and searched... Everyone's luggage was thoroughly searched.* ▸ used as a noun. EG *The police questioned the youth, and then a search revealed a pistol.* V+O ▸ N COUNT : USU SING

5 If someone asks you something and you say **'Search me'**, you mean that you have no idea what the answer is. EG *'Where has your father gone?'–'Search me.'* CONVENTION

search out. If you **search** something **out**, you find it after searching for it. EG *The library staff eventually searched out the book I wanted.* PHRASAL VB : V+O+ADV = uncover

searching /sɜ:tʃɪŋ/. A **searching** question, look, etc is one that is intended to discover the truth about what someone is thinking or about something that has happened. EG *She gave him a searching look... ...a searching inquiry.* ◇ **searchingly.** EG *She was looking at me searchingly.* ADJ QUALIT : USU ATTRIB = penetrating, probing ◇ ADV WITH VB

searchlight /sɜ:tʃlaɪt/, **searchlights.** A **searchlight** is a large powerful light that can be turned to shine in any direction. Searchlights are sometimes used to show the movements of enemy aeroplanes at night or in prison camps etc. N COUNT

search party, search parties; also spelled with a hyphen. A **search party** is an organized group of people searching for someone who is lost or missing. EG *Eventually a search party was sent out.* N COUNT

search warrant, search warrants; also spelled with a hyphen. A **search warrant** is an official document that gives the police permission to search a house or other building, for example when they are looking for drugs or stolen goods. N COUNT ⇑ permit

searing /sɪərɪŋ/. 1 **Searing** pain is very sharp and causes a burning feeling. EG *He felt a searing pain in his left arm.* ADJ QUALIT : ATTRIB ⇑ strong

2 A **searing** speech or piece of writing uses strong language, usually when criticizing someone or describing something unpleasant. EG *She wrote a searing attack on the government... ...a searing TV documentary.* ADJ QUALIT : USU ATTRIB ⇑ forceful = scorching

seascape /si:skeɪp/, **seascapes.** A **seascape** is a painting or photograph of a scene at sea. N COUNT ⇑ picture

seashell /si:ʃɛl/, **seashells.** A **seashell** is the shell of a small sea creature, often found empty lying on the shore. EG *We walked along the beach collecting seashells.* N COUNT

seashore /si:ʃɔ:/, **seashores.** The **seashore** is the part of a coast where the land slopes down into the sea. EG *We found some old boxes that had been washed up on the seashore... ...a walk along the seashore.* N COUNT : USU *the*+N IN SING = beach

seasick /si:sɪk/. Someone who is **seasick** when travelling in a boat on the sea feels sick and often vomits because of the movement of the boat. EG *The sea was so rough that nearly everybody was seasick.* ◇ **seasickness.** EG *He suffers from seasickness.* ADJ QUALIT = nauseous ◇ N UNCOUNT

seaside /si:saɪd/. The **seaside** is a place by the sea, especially one where people go for their holidays. EG *We spent the weekend at the seaside... During the holidays I went to the seaside.* ▸ used as an adjective. EG *...a Yorkshire seaside resort... ...a seaside cottage.* N SING : *the*+N ⇑ resort ▸ ADJ CLASSIF : ATTRIB

season /si:zə°n/, **seasons, seasoning, seasoned.** 1 A **season** is 1.1 one of the main periods into which each year can be divided, and which each have their own typical weather conditions. Most areas of the world have four distinct seasons, spring, summer, autumn, and winter. EG *Autumn is my favourite season... Most tropical areas have rainy and dry seasons... In the dry season, the stream disappears completely.* N COUNT ⇑ division 1.2 the period during each year that is the usual or proper time for a particular activity involving plants or animals, for example the time when a particular crop is ready to be harvested. EG *The strawberry season only lasts a few weeks... The female turtle, every breeding season, has to forsake the open ocean... ...the planting season.* N COUNT : MOD+N 1.3 a fixed period during each year that is officially reserved for a sporting activity, such as playing a particular game or hunting a particular kind of animal. EG *Have you seen any of the cricket this season?... When does the football season end?... ...the deer season.* N COUNT 1.4 any period during which a play or show, or a series of plays or shows, is performed in one place. EG *The show ran for a brief season at the Palladium... Of the three productions that season, it was the only one that lost money.* N COUNT 1.5 a series of films which are shown during a particular period and which are connected in some way, for example because they have the same director or the same subject. EG *...a new season of late-night horror films on television.* N COUNT+SUPP

2 The holiday **season** is the busiest, most popular time of year in a place where people go for their holidays. EG *...the tourist season... Hotel rooms are available even at the height of the season.* N COUNT ⇑ period

3 If you **season** food, you add salt, pepper, or spices to it in order to improve the flavour. EG *Season the soup with plenty of salt... ...a delicately seasoned French casserole.* V+O : IF+PREP THEN *with*

4 Wood that **has been seasoned** has been made suitable for making into furniture or for burning, usually by letting it dry out gradually. EG *Make sure the timber is well seasoned.* V+O : USU PASS ⇑ treat

5 The expressions **in season** and **out of season** are used in the following ways. 5.1 If a fruit or vegetable is **in season**, it is the time of year when it is ready for eating and easily available. If it is **out of season**, it is the time of year when it is not ready for eating and not easily available. EG *Raspberries are in season now... If you buy them out of season, they're rather expensive.* PHR : USED AS AN A 5.2 If a particular kind of animal is **in season**, it is the time of year when you are allowed to hunt it and kill it. If it is **out of season**, it is the time of year when you are not allowed to kill it. EG *Are pheasants in season now?... They were fined for salmon fishing out of season.* PHR : USED AS AN A 5.3 If an animal is **in season**, it is in a state when it is ready for mating. EG *...those uncontrollable urges of a bull in season.* PHR : USED AS AN A, OR AFTER N 5.4 If you go to a place **in season**, you go there during the busy holiday period. If you go there **out of season**, you go there when it is not the busy holiday period. EG *It's expensive if you go there in season... We've often been up there out of season, and it's much quieter.* PHR : USED AS AN A

6 ● See also **close season, high season, low season, seasoned, seasoning**.

seasonable /si:zə°nəbə°l/. 1 **Seasonable** weather conditions are of a kind that is expected or usual at a particular time of year. EG *...seasonable March winds.* ADJ QUALIT ⇑ normal

2 Something that is **seasonable** comes or happens at just the right time. EG *This seasonable advice was just what we needed.* ADJ QUALIT ⇑ appropriate = timely

seasonal /si:zənə°l/. Something that is **seasonal** is affected by conditions that depend on the seasons of the year, for example only happening in a certain season. EG *People found casual or seasonal work on farms.* ◇ **seasonally.** EG *...desperate men who migrate seasonally from flooded areas.* ADJ CLASSIF ⇑ periodic ◇ ADV WITH VB

seasoned /si:zə°nd/ is used to describe a person who has a lot of experience in a particular activity or situation. EG *...a seasoned election campaigner... It could turn your holiday into a nightmare if you're not a seasoned Greek traveller.* ADJ QUALIT : USU ATTRIB ⇑ experienced = hardened

seasoning /si:zə°nɪŋ/, **seasonings. Seasoning** is salt, pepper, or spices that are added to food to improve its flavour. EG *There wasn't enough seasoning in the soup... ...garlic, pepper, and other seasonings.* N MASS = condiment

season ticket, season tickets. A **season ticket** is a ticket for which you pay more and which you can then use repeatedly over a certain period. EG *...a monthly season ticket... This entrance is reserved for season ticket holders.* N COUNT

seat /si:t/, **seats, seating, seated.** 1 A **seat** is a place where you can sit, for example a chair or something that is used as a chair. EG *Roger sat down carefully, using the edge of the crate as a seat...* N COUNT ⇑ rest

'Come in, take a seat,' Muller told Castle... There was some beer in the back seat of the car... I rang the theatre to see if I could get seats for the show.

2 The **seat** of a chair or other piece of furniture is the part that you sit on. EG *There was a cushion on the seat of the chair.*
N COUNT

3 If you **seat** yourself somewhere, you sit down on a chair or a seat of some kind. EG *'Thank you,' she said, seating herself on the sofa.* ◊ **seated**. EG *General Tomkins was seated behind his desk.*
V+O (REFL): USU+A
◊ ADJ CLASSIF: PRED

4 A building or vehicle that **seats** a particular number of people has enough seats or sitting space for that number. EG *The hall seats four hundred.*
V+O: NO CONT ⇑ hold

5 The **seat** of a piece of clothing is the part of it that covers your bottom. EG *Her jeans had a gaping hole in the seat.*
N SING: *the*+N, USU+*of* ⇑ back

6 A person who has a **seat** in parliament or on an official committee has a place as a member of parliament or of the committee, often as a result of gaining the most votes in an election. EG *His party failed to win a single seat... The Tories had a 42-seat majority in the House of Commons.*
N COUNT ⇑ position

7 The **seat** of an organization or a wealthy family is the place where they are based. EG *The Earl rarely visited his country seat in Shropshire... In the eleventh century the seat of government shifted to London from Winchester.*
N COUNT+SUPP ⇑ centre

8 If you **take a back seat**, you take a position where you do not have much responsibility or power so that someone else is in charge and makes decisions. EG *I prefer to take a back seat in this matter.*
PHR: VB INFLECTS

9 If you do something **by the seat of** your **pants**, you do it by relying on your instinct and experience instead of using elaborate equipment or following a carefully prepared plan. EG *Pilots in the early days of aviation flew 'by the seat of their pants'.*
PHR: USED AS AN A

seat-belt, seat-belts; also spelled without a hyphen. A **seat-belt** is a strap attached to a car or aeroplane seat which you fasten across your body in order to prevent yourself being thrown out of the seat if there is a sudden violent movement. EG *He sat beside me and fastened his seat-belt.*
N COUNT ⇑ restraint = safety belt

-seater, -seaters. -seater is used after numbers to refer to cars, aeroplanes, and pieces of furniture that have seats for the number of people stated. EG *...a three-seater settee... A few sports cars are two-seaters.*
COMB: FORMS ADJ CLASSIFS OR NOUNS

seating /siːtɪŋ/. **1 Seating** is seats which are provided somewhere, especially in a public place. EG *The plastic seating was uncomfortable.*
N UNCOUNT

2 The **seating** in a theatre or at a formal meal is the arrangement of the seats in the theatre or of the guests at the meal. EG *Here's a seating plan of the concert hall.*
N UNCOUNT

sea urchin, sea urchins. A **sea urchin** is a small round sea creature that has a hard shell covered with sharp points.
N COUNT

seaward /siːwəd/, **seawards**. Something that moves **seaward** or **seawards** moves in the direction of the sea or further out to sea. EG *We left the harbour and sailed seawards... ...the seaward facing wall of the house.*
ADV WITH VB, OR ADJ CLASSIF: ATTRIB ≠ landward

seaweed /siːwiːd/, **seaweeds**. **Seaweed** is a plant that grows in the sea. There are many kinds of seaweed. EG *The rocks had green seaweed growing on them... The smell of seaweed drifts far inland on the breeze.*
N MASS

sec /sɛk/, **secs**. A **sec** is a very short period of time; an informal use, used mainly in spoken English. EG *Just a sec and I'll be with you.*
N COUNT: USU SING ⇑ second = tick

sec., secs. Sec. is **1** a written abbreviation for 'second'; written after a number to indicate a period of time. EG *He won the Cardiff run in 2 hrs 26 mins 4 secs.* **2** a written abbreviation for 'Secretary'; used as part of a person's title. EG *Yours sincerely, A. P. Handley, Gen. Sec.* **3** a written abbreviation for 'secondary'.
N COUNT
N IN TITLE
ADJ CLASSIF: ATTRIB

secateurs /sɛkətəz, sɛkətɜːz/. A pair of **secateurs** is a gardening tool that looks like a pair of strong, heavy scissors and is used for cutting the stems of plants. EG *Secateurs are very useful for pruning.*
N PLURAL: ALSO *a pair of*+N

secede /sɪ^{2}siːd/, **secedes, seceding, seceded**. If a group or region **secedes** from a larger group or country to which it belongs, it formally ends its membership of the group and forms a separate group or country; a fairly formal word. EG *Some would like the South to secede from France, to be an independent country.*
V: IF+PREP THEN *from* ⇑ withdraw = break away

secession /sɪ^{2}sɛʃə^{0}n/. The **secession** of a group or region from a larger group or country to which it belongs is its formal separation from the group or country; a fairly formal word. EG *The constitution provided for the secession of the constituent republics... ...the secession of a small group of MPs to form a new party.*
N UNCOUNT: IF+PREP THEN *from* ⇑ withdrawal

seclude /sɪ^{1}kluːd/, **secludes, secluding, secluded**. If you **seclude** someone from other people, you keep them away from any contact with other people. EG *The boys are secluded for three months in a special camp... The rich secluded themselves from contact with the poor.*
V+O: USU PASS, OR V+O (REFL): IF+PREP THEN *from* ⇑ isolate = segregate

secluded /sɪ^{1}kluːdɪ^{2}d/. A **secluded** place is quiet, private, and undisturbed. EG *...a secluded romantic spot... This is the quietest and most secluded area of the city.*
ADJ QUALIT ⇑ insulated

seclusion /sɪ^{1}kluːʒə^{0}n/. Someone who is in **seclusion** is in a private place away from all disturbance and apart from other people. EG *She was reared in seclusion... You'd probably feel more at home in the seclusion of Flint Street.*
N UNCOUNT = isolation

second, seconds, seconding, seconded. The word **second** is pronounced /sɛkənd/ except for paragraph 13 when it is pronounced /sɪ^{2}kɒnd/. **1** A **second** is **1.1** one of the sixty parts that a minute is divided into. EG *She looked up at me for a few seconds... The whole thing hadn't taken more than thirty seconds... The rocket was rising upwards at the rate of about 300 feet per second.* **1.2** a very short period of time, especially one that is surprisingly short. EG *Could I see your book for a second? Seconds later they were outside... In seconds the building had gone up in flames... Within seconds the letter was on its way.*
N COUNT: USU PL ⇑ period
N COUNT: IF SING *a*+N, SING=PL

2 The **second** item in a series is the one that you count as number two: see □ at NUMBER, AGE, and DATE. EG *...his father's second marriage... He had just finished his second cup of coffee when the phone rang... I stopped smoking the second day I was there... Your birthday is the second of February, isn't it?*
ORDINAL

3 You use **second** in speech or writing when you want to make a second point or give a second reason that is connected to the first point or reason that you have already given. EG *And second, this kind of policy doesn't help to create jobs.*
ADV SEN ⇑ next = secondly

4 Second is also used to describe a car, house, etc that you consider to be less important than another car or house that you have, especially because it is smaller and less expensive, and because you use it less often. EG *The Chevrolet was the Zapps' second car.*
ADJ CLASSIF: ATTRIB ⇑ subordinate

5 If you experience or learn something **at second hand**, you are told about it by other people rather than learning it directly. EG *I knew nothing about Judith except what I'd heard at second hand.* • See also **second-hand**.
PHR: USED AS AN A

6 If you say that someone is **second to none**, you mean that they do their job better than anyone else with the same job. EG *As a physician he is second to none.*
PHR: USED AS C ⇑ the best

7 If you say that something is **second only to** one other thing, you mean that this other thing is the only one better or more important than it. EG *San Francisco is second only to New York as the tourist city of the States.*
PREP

8 A **second** is also **8.1** something that is sold cheaply in the shops because it has a fault and is therefore not of a high enough quality. EG *Some of the articles you see are seconds.* **8.2** someone who supports and encourages a person who is fighting another person, for example in a boxing match or a duel. EG *The seconds were sent out of the ring and the fight began.* **8.3** a good or average honours degree that is obtained from a British University. EG *He had been awarded a low Upper Second.* **8.4** the interval between two notes in a musical scale when there is one tone or one semitone separating them.
N COUNT: USU PL
N COUNT ⇑ supporter
N COUNT: USU SING
N COUNT

9 If you have **seconds**, you have a second helping of food or a pudding that follows the main course of a meal; an informal use. EG *Is there any seconds, Mum?*
N PLURAL: VB CAN BE SING OR PL

10 Second is the second gear in a series of gears in a car or other vehicle. EG *He tried to drive off in second.*
N UNCOUNT

11 If you **second** a proposal or nomination in a meeting or debate, you formally agree with it so that the proposal or nomination can then be discussed and voted on. EG *'Does anyone second the motion?'–'I second it, Mr Chairman'... Since no one important had come, she had to second the vote of thanks herself.* — V+O

12 If you **second** something that someone has said, you say that you completely agree with them; a fairly informal use. EG *'I think some of us could do with a coffee.'–'I'll second that'... He says he and Sylvia have needed a holiday for years. Sylvia seconds this.* — V+O

13 If someone **is seconded**, they are moved from their usual job to do special duties somewhere else for a short time or to take an educational course. EG *He was for a time seconded to the army as a mortar expert.* — V+O: USU PASS ⇑ transfer

secondary /sekəndə^{0}ri^{1}/, **secondaries**. **1** Something that is **secondary** **1.1** is less important than something else: compare **primary**. EG *Many older people still believe that men's careers come first and women's careers are secondary.* — ADJ QUALIT: IF+PREP THEN *to* ⇑ unimportant **1.2** happens as a result of something else that has already happened. EG *Some ointments don't cure anything but set up a secondary irritant to make you forget the first.* — ADJ CLASSIF

2 Secondary education is the education of pupils who are between approximately eleven and eighteen years old: compare **primary**. EG *Both exams are taken after five years of secondary education.* — ADJ CLASSIF: ATTRIB

3 A **secondary** or a **secondary school** is a school for students between the ages of eleven or twelve and eighteen. EG *Virtually all secondary schools are in towns.* — N COUNT

secondary modern, secondary moderns. A **secondary modern** is a school which existed until recently in Britain for pupils aged between about eleven and eighteen, where more attention was paid to practical skills and less to academic study than in a grammar school. EG *If they didn't get through the exam they went to Framlingham Secondary Modern.* — N COUNT: ALSO IN NAMES

second-best is used **1** to refer to a situation that you have to accept even though you would rather have a different situation if you could choose. EG *Hiring professionals for the job is impractical, so as a second-best, we will use unpaid amateurs... Don't compromise. Don't settle for second best.* — ADJ CLASSIF, OR N SING WITH DET **2** to describe things that are of good quality, but not quite as good as the best. EG *I stayed in the second-best bedroom.* — ADJ CLASSIF

second childhood. If you say that an old person is in their **second childhood**, you mean that they find it difficult to remember things and have become similar to a very young child in some of their behaviour. EG *The poor old dear's in her second childhood and doesn't know what she's saying.* — N SING: USU POSS+N

second-class. **1** If you describe someone or something as **second-class**, you mean that they are of poor quality or not as important or valuable as something else. EG *There can be no second-class citizens in a free society.* — ADJ QUALIT: USU ATTRIB ⇑ inferior = second-rate

2 A **second-class** ticket allows you to travel in the ordinary type of accommodation on a train, aircraft, or ship. EG *He sat in a second-class carriage reading a local newspaper.* — N UNCOUNT

3 Second-class postage is the cheaper type of postage by which letters and parcels take slightly longer to arrive than those that are sent first-class. EG *...second-class mail... Six second-class stamps, please.* — ADJ CLASSIF ▸ used as an adverb. EG *Unfortunately I sent it second-class and it still hasn't arrived.* — ▸ ADV WITH VB

4 A **second class** or a **second-class** degree is a good or average honours degree that is obtained from a British university. EG *She says it wasn't a very good second class. She says I didn't work.* — N COUNT: USU SING

second cousin, second cousins. Someone's **second cousin** is the child of their father's or mother's first cousin. — N COUNT ⇑ relation

seconder /sekəndə/, **seconders**. A **seconder** is a person in a meeting or debate who formally agrees with a proposal or nomination so that it can then be discussed and voted on. EG *Does that motion have a seconder?* — N COUNT

second hand, second hands. A **second hand** is the hand that marks the seconds on a clock or watch. — N COUNT

second-hand; also spelled as one word. **1** Something that is **second-hand** is not new and has been owned by someone else before. EG *...buying secondhand clothing from jumble sales... My car was a second-hand Morris Minor.* — ADJ CLASSIF ⇑ used ▸ used as an adverb. EG *It's a book he bought second-hand, years ago, off a sixpenny stall.* — ▸ ADV WITH VB

2 A **second-hand** shop sells things that are not new and that have been owned by other people. EG *He went to a reputable second-hand salesman in Bath.* — ADJ CLASSIF: ATTRIB

3 Second-hand news, events, etc are those that you learn about from other people rather than directly or from your own experience. EG *...a second-hand report.* — ADJ CLASSIF ⇑ vicarious ▸ used as an adverb. EG *I heard about it secondhand.* — ▸ ADV WITH VB

second-in-command, seconds-in-command. A **second-in-command** is someone who is next in rank to the leader of a group, and who has the authority to give orders when the leader is not there. EG *This is Sheila, my second-in-command.* — N COUNT, OR ADJ CLASSIF: PRED ⇑ deputy

second language, second languages. Someone's **second language** is a language which is not their native language but which they use at work, school, or for business purposes. EG *...learners of English as a second language... English is the second language of Nigeria.* — N COUNT

secondly /sekəndli^{1}/ is used in speech or writing when you want to make a second point or give a second reason that is connected to the first point or reason that you have already given. EG *He was first of all an absolute idiot; secondly he was pretty dishonest.* — ADV SEN ⇑ next

secondment /sɪ^{2}kɒndmə^{2}nt/, **secondments**. If you are sent on **secondment**, you are sent away from your job for a short time to do a particular job or special duties somewhere else. EG *He's on secondment to the Ministry of Defence.* — N UNCOUNT/COUNT

second nature. If something is **second nature** to you, you have done it so much that you no longer think about it, and it seems as if it is part of your character. EG *Diplomacy was second nature to Jonathan.* — N UNCOUNT ⇑ habit

second person. In grammar, the **second person** is the person who is addressed in speech or writing. In modern English it is the word 'you'. — N SING: *the*+N

second-rate. If you describe something or someone as **second-rate**, you mean that they are of a poor quality or standard. EG *...a second-rate department store... ...second-rate ideas.* — ADJ QUALIT = mediocre, inferior

second sight. If you say that someone has **second sight**, you mean that they seem to be able to know or see things that are going to happen in the future, or that are happening in another place. — N UNCOUNT = clairvoyance

second thought, second thoughts. **1** If you do something without a **second thought**, you do not consider it at all carefully, usually because you do not have enough time or are not interested enough. EG *She had too many other worries to give him a second thought.* — N SING: *a*+N, WITH BROAD NEG

2 You say **on second thoughts** when you suddenly change your mind about something that you are saying or that you have decided to do. EG *Tell me more about America. No, on second thoughts, tell me more about your family.* — PHR: USED AS AN A

3 If you **have second thoughts** about a decision that you have made, you have doubts about it so that you are no longer sure if it is a wise decision. EG *They were having second thoughts about the tax program... He is not likely to have second thoughts at the last minute.* — PHR: VB INFLECTS, IF+PREP THEN *about*

second wind. If you get a **second wind**, you become able to continue doing a difficult or strenuous exercise after you were tired or out of breath. — N SING WITH DET

secrecy /siːkrɪsi^{1}/ is the act of keeping something secret, or the state of being kept secret. EG *She stressed the necessity of absolute secrecy... I'd like to tell you more, but I'm sworn to secrecy... The operation was being conducted in secrecy.* — N UNCOUNT

secret /siːkrɪt/, **secrets**. **1** Something that is **secret** is known about by only a small number of people, and not told or shown to anyone else. EG *The envelope was marked 'very secret'... We arrived through a secret back entrance... We had to promise to keep the information secret... ...secret negotiations.* — ADJ QUALIT = hush-hush ◇ **secretly**. EG *They met secretly to discuss the invasion plans.* — ◇ ADV WITH VB = in secret ● See also **top secret**.

2 If you do something **in secret**, you do it privately — PHR: USED AS AN and without anyone else knowing. EG *I arranged to meet him in secret.* A = secretly

3 If someone is a **secret** admirer, drinker, etc, they do not admit this to other people. EG *She had become a secret drinker... I'm a secret admirer of her novels.* ADJ CLASSIF : ATTRIB ⇑ private
◊ **secretly**. EG *He secretly hoped I would one day change my mind.* ◊ ADV WITH VB, OR ADV SEN

4 A **secret** is a fact or piece of information that is known about by only a small number of people, and is not told to anyone else. EG *The results of these experiments remain a secret... I'll tell you a secret... She has made no secret of the fact that she wants to get another job.* N COUNT

5 If you can **keep a secret**, you are not likely to tell other people a secret you have been told. PHR : VB INFLECTS

6 If you say that a particular way of doing things is the **secret** of achieving something, you mean that it is the best or only way to achieve it. EG *If you want to get the job done quickly, the secret is not to involve too many other people... Think big! This is the secret of success.* N SING : *the*+N, IF+PREP THEN *of* ⇑ factor = key

7 A **secret** is also something that has never been explained or understood. EG *...the secrets of nature.* N COUNT : USU PL = mystery

secret agent, secret agents. A **secret agent** is a person who is employed by a government to find out the military and political secrets of other governments. N COUNT = spy

secretarial /sɛkrətɛəriəl/. **Secretarial** work or training involves the work or skills of a secretary. EG *...a secretarial course... ...a member of the secretarial staff... His duties are mostly secretarial.* ADJ CLASSIF : USU ATTRIB

secretariat /sɛkrətɛəriət/, **secretariats**. A **secretariat** is an office or department responsible for the administration of an international political organization. EG *...a senior member of the U.N. Secretariat.* N COUNT

secretary /sɛkrətə^{0}ri^1/, **secretaries**. 1 A **secretary** is a person who is employed to do office work, such as typing letters, answering phone calls, and arranging meetings. N COUNT ⇑ employee

2 The **secretary** of a club, committee, etc is the person whose job is keeping records, writing letters, arranging events, etc. EG *If you want to join the cricket club write to the secretary.* N COUNT ⇑ official

3 The **secretary** of a company is a person who has the legal duty of keeping the company's records. N COUNT ⇑ official

4 **Secretary** is used in Britain in the titles of ministers who are in charge of one of the main government departments, such as foreign affairs, or defence. EG *...the new Social Services Secretary... ...one of the best Foreign Secretaries since the war.* N COUNT : MOD+N, ALSO IN TITLES ⇑ politician

5 **Secretary** is used in the USA in the titles of the heads of the main government departments, appointed by the president. EG *...the Secretary of Defense... ...the Treasury Secretary.* N COUNT+SUPP : ALSO IN TITLES = minister

secretary-general, secretary-generals; also spelled as two words. A **secretary-general** is the person in charge of the administration of an international political organization. N COUNT ⇑ official

Secretary of State, Secretaries of State. 1 A **Secretary of State** is a government minister in Britain. EG *...the Secretary of State for Northern Ireland... ...a meeting with the Secretary of State.* N COUNT : IF+ PREP THEN *for*

2 In the USA, the **Secretary of State** is the head of the government department that deals with foreign affairs. N COUNT = Foreign Secretary

secrete /si^{1}kri:t/, **secretes, secreting, secreted**. 1 If part of a plant, animal, or human **secretes** a liquid, it produces it. For example, glands in the stomach secrete juices that help in digesting food. V+O

2 If you **secrete** something somewhere, you put it in a secret place where nobody will find it. EG *He was looking for a bag of sweets he had secreted somewhere... She secreted herself behind the curtains.* V+O (NG/REFL) : USU+A = conceal

secretion /si^{1}kri:ʃə^{0}n/, **secretions**. 1 **Secretion** is the process by which certain kinds of liquid substance are secreted by parts of plants or parts of the body. EG *Hormone secretion is controlled by the pituitary gland.* N UNCOUNT

2 A **secretion** is a liquid substance that has been secreted. EG *...skin secretions.* N COUNT ⇑ fluid

secretive /si:krətiv, si^{1}kri:tiv/. If you are **secretive**, you like to have secrets and to keep your knowledge, feelings, or intentions hidden. EG *She's very secretive about money matters... ...secretive bureaucrats.* ADJ QUALIT
◊ **secretively**. EG *Howard wrote the book secretively late at night.* ◊ ADV : USU WITH VB

secret police. The **secret police** is a police force, especially in a non-democratic country, that works secretly and is concerned with political crimes. N PLURAL : USU WITH DET

secret service. A country's **secret service** is a secret government department whose job is to find out enemy secrets and to prevent its own government's secrets from being discovered. EG *She used to work for the Secret Service.* N COUNT

sect /sɛkt/, **sects**. A **sect** is a group of people that has separated from a larger group and has a particular set of religious or political beliefs, especially when these beliefs are strongly held or regarded by others as extreme. EG *Two religious sects came into being, one of which was the Quakers.* N COUNT

sectarian /sɛktɛəriən/; a formal word. 1 Something that is **sectarian** is caused by or results from the differences between sects. EG *The conference had collapsed in sectarian squabbles... ...a sectarian killing.* ADJ CLASSIF : USU ATTRIB

2 Someone who is **sectarian** strongly supports a particular sect and its beliefs. EG *This group is frequently attacked as sectarian and fanatical.* ADJ QUALIT = partisan

sectarianism /sɛktɛəriənizə^{0}m/ is strong support for a particular sect and its beliefs, often in a narrow-minded way. EG *The political scene there is dominated by uncompromising sectarianism.* N UNCOUNT

section /sɛkʃə^{0}n/, **sections**. 1 A **section** of something is one of the separate parts into which it is divided or from which it is formed. EG *I passed the written part easily but failed the oral section... ...the first-class section of the train... She works in the company's finance section... The meeting was attended by well-known people from all sections of public life.* N COUNT : USU+ SUPP ▸ used to refer to one of the parts that an official piece of writing such as a report or a law is divided into. EG *The lawyer referred to a section in the 1938 Food and Drugs Act... ...Section 5, Appendix 2A.* ▸ N COUNT, OR N +NUM

2 A **section** is also a picture or diagram of something, such as a building or a part of the body, showing how it would look if it were cut from top to bottom and looked at from the side. EG *The illustration on page 84 is a section of the human brain... They found the oil by looking at maps and geological sections.* ● **See also cross-section.** N COUNT ⇑ representation

3 See also **Caesarian**.

sectional /sɛkʃə^{0}nəl, -ʃənə^{0}l/. **Sectional** interests, objectives, etc are those of a particular group within a community or country. EG *Broadcasting must not become an instrument of narrow sectional interests.* ADJ CLASSIF : USU ATTRIB ⇑ limited

sector /sɛktə/, **sectors**. A **sector** is 1 a part of a country's economy. A particular sector consists of all the companies which are involved in a particular area of work or all the companies which are run according to a particular system of ownership or financial control. EG *...the manufacturing sector... ...Government support for the voluntary sector.* ● See also **private sector, public sector**. N COUNT : USU MOD+N ⇑ section **2** a group which is part of a larger group. EG *Among significant sectors of the population this trend is now declining... ...a very narrow sector of the Labour Party.* N COUNT+SUPP = section **3** an area of a town, country, etc, which is under military control. EG *The British pipeline runs south of the Norwegian sector.* N COUNT ⇑ section = zone **4** a part of a circle which is formed when you draw two straight lines from the centre of the circle to the edge; a technical term in mathematics. N COUNT ⇑ portion

secular /sɛkjə^{4}lə/. 1 **Secular** is used to describe something which has no connection with religion or churches. EG *...secular education... The choir sings both sacred and secular music.* ADJ CLASSIF ≠ religious

2 **Secular** priests live among ordinary people rather than in monasteries. ADJ CLASSIF : ATTRIB

secularise /sɛkjə^{4}ləraiz/. See **secularize**.

secularism /sɛkjə^{4}lərizə^{0}m/ is a system of social organization and education which believes that religion has no part to play in the problems and events of everyday life. N UNCOUNT

secularize /sɛkjə^{4}ləraiz/, **secularizes, secularizing, secularized**; also spelled **secularise**. To **secularize** society, education, etc means to change it so it is no longer under the control or influence of religion. V+O

secure /si^{2}kjʊə/, **secures, securing, secured**.
1 If you **secure** something, **1.1** you get it after a lot of effort. EG *He secured only 526 votes... I spent the morning securing their agreement... I did everything* V+O, V+O+O, OR V+O+A *(for)* = obtain

possible to secure him a posting. **1.2** you make it safe from attack, harm, or loss. EG *They endeavoured to secure the bridge from the threat of further attack.* **1.3** you fasten it firmly to another object or tie it together tightly. EG *A plastic box was secured to the wall by screws... They secured the bundles with twine.* V+O : IF+PREP THEN *against/from* ; V+O = make fast

2 If something is **secure**, **2.1** it is certain to remain and not to be lost. EG *You've got a secure job... It was a time when authority was secure and unchallenged.* ◇ **securely**. EG *The strike there was securely under the union's control.* **2.2** it is tightly locked or well protected, so that people cannot enter, leave, or use it. EG *Try and make your house as secure as you possibly can... Computers can be made far more secure than any bank vault.* **2.3** it is fixed firmly in position or tied firmly. EG *Check that the leads to the battery are in good condition and secure.* ◇ **securely**. EG *The chain seemed to be securely fastened.* ADJ QUALIT ⇑ safe ; ◇ ADV ; ADJ QUALIT : USU PRED ⇑ safe = impregnable ; ADJ QUALIT : USU PRED ⇑ fastened ; ◇ ADV WITH VB

3 If you feel **secure**, you feel safe and are not worried about life. EG *We feel financially secure... Boys grow up secure in the knowledge that they can go anywhere they want to.* ADJ QUALIT : USU PRED = confident

4 A **secure** base, foundation, etc is strong and reliable. EG *You need a secure base for the business... For the first time in the discussion I found myself on secure ground.* ADJ QUALIT = solid

security /sɪ²kjʊ̲ərɪti¹/, **securities**. **1 Security** is used to refer to all the precautions that are taken to protect a country from spying, to protect people from being attacked, to prevent prisoners from escaping, etc. EG *Security forces were patrolling the streets... The Queen's visit has been marked by tight security... ...a top security prison... ...the minister responsible for national security.* N UNCOUNT

2 Security is **2.1** safety from possible harm or loss. EG *He hasn't got security of employment... We are all concerned for the security of the passengers on the aircraft.* **2.2** a feeling of being safe and not having fears or worries. EG *Children count on their parents for love and security... It gave me a feeling of security.* **2.3** something valuable which you promise to give a person who lends you money, if you do not pay the money back in the proper time. EG *The bank may ask for security if you want an overdraft.* N UNCOUNT ; N UNCOUNT ⇑ safety ≠ anxiety ; N UNCOUNT/COUNT ⇑ guarantee

3 A **security** is a stock, bond, or some other document, which you have paid money for and which gives you the right to some property. N COUNT ⇑ investment

4 See also **social security**.

security risk, security risks. If you describe someone or something as a **security risk**, you mean that they may be a threat to the safety of a country or organization. N COUNT ⇑ danger

sedan /sɛdæ̲n/, **sedans**. A **sedan** is the same as a saloon car; used in American English. N COUNT

sedan chair, sedan chairs. A **sedan chair** is a closed chair for one person carried on two poles by two men, one in front and one behind. Sedan chairs were used in the 17th and 18th centuries. N COUNT ⇑ conveyance

sedate /sɪ²de̲ɪt/, **sedates, sedating, sedated**. **1** Someone who is **sedate** is quiet, calm, and rather dignified. EG *All his life he would remain the dull, sedate and reliable person he had always been.* ▸ used of people's behaviour and actions. EG *His university education led to a sedate career as a diplomat.* ◇ **sedately**. EG *He walked sedately off down the lane.* ADJ QUALIT ⇑ serious = staid ≠ frivolous ; ▸ ADV WITH VB = sober ; ◇ ADV ⇑ decorously

2 Something that is **sedate** is slow or peaceful instead of being full of activity. EG *The car moved off at a sedate speed.* ADJ QUALIT = staid

3 To **sedate** someone means to give them a medicine or drug in order to calm them or make them sleep. EG *She's been sedated.* V+O

sedation /sɪ²de̲ɪʃə⁰n/ is the use of medicine or drugs in order to calm someone or make them sleep. EG *Juliet was under sedation.* N UNCOUNT

sedative /sɛ̲dətɪv/, **sedatives**. **1** A **sedative** is a medicine or drug that calms you or makes you sleep. EG *The doctor prescribed a sedative.* N COUNT

2 Something that is **sedative** has the effect of calming you or making you sleep. EG *This drink has been recognized to have sedative properties.* ADJ CLASSIF

sedentary /sɛ̲dəntə⁰ri¹/. **1** A **sedentary** occupation, life, existence, etc is one in which you sit down a lot of the time and so do not have much exercise. EG *I'm bored with sedentary work.* ADJ QUALIT ⇑ inactive

2 Sedentary people are settled and do not travel from place to place. EG *...a sedentary community.* ADJ CLASSIF : ATTRIB

sedge /sɛ̲dʒ/, **sedges**. **Sedge** is a grass-like plant that grows in wet, marshy ground. N MASS

sediment /sɛ̲dɪmə³nt/, **sediments**. **Sediment** is **1** the solid material that settles at the bottom of a liquid. EG *Most of the sediment has sunk to the bottom... She scooped out the yeasty sediments.* **2** the material such as earth and rocks which has been carried along and then left somewhere by water, ice, or wind. EG *Rivers are bringing lots of sediment down to the sea.* N UNCOUNT/COUNT ; N UNCOUNT/COUNT ⇑ deposit

sedimentary /sɛdɪmɛ̲ntə⁰ri¹/. **Sedimentary** rocks, deposits, etc are formed from sediment left by water, ice, or wind. ADJ CLASSIF

sedition /sɪ²dɪ̲ʃə⁰n/ is speech, writing, or behaviour intended to encourage rebellion or resistance against the government. EG *They were charged with sedition... He went round the country preaching sedition.* N UNCOUNT

seditious /sɪ²dɪ̲ʃəs/. Something that is **seditious** encourages rebellion or resistance against the government. EG *They published pamphlets conveying instructions on seditious activities... ...seditious publications.* ADJ CLASSIF = subversive

seduce /si¹dju̲:s/, **seduces, seducing, seduced**. **1** If something **seduces** you, it is so attractive that it tempts you to do something that you would not normally approve of or think sensible. EG *He was seduced into saying that he would do it... Both he and his partner had been seduced by the grandeur of the scheme.* V+O : IF+PREP THEN *into* = beguile

2 If you **seduce** someone, you persuade them to have sex with you, especially when they are young and do not have much sexual experience. V+O

seduction /si¹dʌ̲kʃə⁰n/, **seductions**. A **seduction** is **1** the act of persuading someone to have sex, especially when they are young and do not have much sexual experience. EG *She knew he was not planning any seduction... The girl's seduction is an important part of the story.* **2** something which is very tempting. EG *...the seductions of life in television.* N COUNT/UNCOUNT ; N COUNT : USU PL = lure

seductive /si¹dʌ̲ktɪv/. **1** Something that is **seductive** is very attractive or tempting in some way. EG *These are seductive arguments... The trips were free and the destinations were seductive.* ◇ **seductively**. EG *My bed called me seductively.* ADJ QUALIT = beguiling ; ◇ ADV = invitingly

2 If someone, especially a woman, is **seductive**, they are very attractive sexually. EG *...the seductive softness of Mary's long limbs.* ◇ **seductively**. EG *She was seductively shaped.* ADJ QUALIT = alluring ; ◇ ADV

see /si̲:/, **sees, seeing, saw, seen**. **1** When you **see**, you use your eyes in order to recognize things or to look at them. EG *I can hardly see without my glasses... Some animals have the ability to see in very dim light.* V : USU+A, NO IMPER, NO CONT

2 When you **see** something, **2.1** you become aware of it or recognize it, using your eyes. EG *We suddenly saw a vessel through a gap in the fog... On Anthony's desk I saw a flower in a jamjar... He saw the tears come to her eyes... I could see Jenny in the kitchen.* **2.2** you look at it, because you are interested in it. EG *Mr Haswell can demand to see all the Insurance Company's files... They all expected to go in and see the treasures... Could I see your book for a second?* V+O : USU+A, NO IMPER, NO CONT ⇑ perceive ; V+O : NO IMPER = view

3 When a traveller or tourist **sees** a country, a famous building, etc, they visit it in order to look at it or to look at things that are there. EG *I have always wanted to see America... He went to India to see the Taj Mahal... We saw all the sights.* V+O

4 When you **see** a performance of a play, a television programme, etc, you watch it. EG *Sue went to Stratford to see three historical plays... We all went to see 'Bitter Sweet'.* V+O

5 You also talk about someone **seeing** something when they imagine that they can see it, because they are frightened. EG *I began to see a man behind every tree.* ● If someone says that they have seen something, and you say that they **are seeing things**, you mean that they imagined that they saw it, and that it was not really there. EG *Go on! You're seeing things.* V+O, NO IMPER ; ● PHR : VB INFLECTS

6 You talk about **seeing** someone when you have arranged to meet them beforehand. For example, you talk about 'seeing' a friend when you have arranged to visit them, or 'seeing' a doctor or lawyer when you are going to them for help or advice. EG V+O

Perhaps she did not wish to come and see me... It would be a good idea for you to see a doctor for a checkup... 'Are you seeing Stratton today?' she asked... We only see each other at weekends... They still saw quite a lot of Anthony and Jane.

7 If you **see** someone to a particular place, you accompany them to the place to make sure that they get there safely. EG *I went down to see her safely to her car... He saw her home... He saw me into a taxi.* V+O+A = escort

8 If you **see** that something is happening or that something is true, **8.1** you notice it or are aware of it. EG *Etta could see that he wasn't listening very much... I can see you're interested in the idea, Mr Dekker... I see your sense of humour hasn't changed, Professor... You play the oboe, I see... As you can see, I don't know what I'm talking about.* V OR V+REPORT-CL, NO IMPER, NO CONT **8.2** you find out about it by reading about it, especially in a newspaper. EG *I opened the paper and saw that the Prime Minister had resigned... I see in the evening papers that there's going to be a new law on drinking and driving... I see that Hitchcock film was actually shot in Canada.* V+REPORT-CL, NO IMPER, NO CONT ⇑ learn

9 If you **see** some aspect of a situation, you notice it or are aware of it. EG *He saw how crafty their question was... I was trying not to let the jailers see my agitation... He was depressed, for he saw something ominous in this dinner party... He saw the opportunity of being a renegade yet again.* V+O : NO IMPER, NO CONT = detect

10 If you **see** a particular quality in someone, you believe that they have this quality, and you find it attractive. EG *He saw in her a tender fragility... No one had understood what she saw in Dave... What can she see in him?* V+O+A *(in)*, NO IMPER, NO CONT ⇑ perceive

11 **You see** is used to say that a particular kind of person or thing exists in a place or situation. EG *Occasionally you see exceptionally big babies... You don't see any untidy people working there.* PHR : VB INFLECTS = you get

12 If you say that you will **see** what is happening, **see** if something is possible, etc, you mean that you intend to find out about it. EG *Shall I look and see who's there?... I must phone her up and see if she can come over tonight.* V+REPORT-CL, NO CONT ⇑ discover

13 If you say that you will **see if** you can do something, you mean that you will try to do it. EG *See if you can find my birthday book somewhere... Let me see if I can help you.* PHR : VB INFLECTS, NO PAST ● If, when someone asks you for help, you say that you will **see what you can do** or **see what can be done**, you mean that you will try to help them. EG *I'll see what I can do about this... He promised to see what could be done.* ● PHR : VB INFLECTS, NO PAST

14 If you **see** that something is done or **see to it** that it is done, you make sure that it is done, by getting someone else to do it or by doing it yourself. EG *The sergeant would have to see that something was done about this situation... See that everything is marked with your initials... We took care of his wounds and saw to it that he got home... I'll see to it that there is some action.* V+REPORT-CL, OR PHR+REPORT-CL ⇑ arrange = ensure

15 If someone says something and you **see** what they mean, you understand what they mean. EG *'Yes,' she said. 'I see what you mean.'.. I could see his point.* V+O/REPORT-CL : NO CONT, NO IMPER

16 If you can **see** why something happens, **see** how it happens, or **see** what it is, you can understand why it happens, how it happens, or what it is. EG *I can see why Mr Smith is worried... I began to see that Elijah's power came from his single-mindedness.... Somebody got killed and I don't see how... Now I could see more clearly what loneliness was.* V+O/REPORT-CL : NO CONT, NO IMPER ⇑ appreciate

17 You say **I see** **17.1** to indicate that you understand what someone is telling you. EG *'Monsieur Hercule Poirot asked me to come.'-'I see.'.. 'Humbert is Dolly's real father'-'I see.'* CONVENTION **17.2** to indicate that you are displeased about something. EG *'So you're satisfied?'-'Perfectly satisfied.'-'I see.'* CONVENTION

18 You say **you see** when you are telling someone something and you are very concerned that they should understand it. EG *That's very nice of you but, you see, Kurt, I have no money... You see, there is no alternative... Yes, I know, but, you see, computers might rule the world one day.* PHR : USED AS ADV SEN

19 People say **see?** in a fairly aggressive way after they have made a statement, to emphasize that what they have said is true and that they do not want anyone to disagree with them. EG *I'm tough, see?... When they come at me, then I'm upset. See?* ADV SEN = right?

20 If you **see** a situation, someone's behaviour, etc in a particular way, you regard it in that way. EG *I did not see his determination as a defect... How do you see yourself as an artist?... The problem, as I see it, is not advice but direct help... As far as I can see, it's not convenient to believe in an afterlife.* V+O+A, NO CONT/FUTURE/IMPER ⇑ consider

21 If you **see** an important change or development in society, technology, etc, you are alive at the time that it happens. EG *How would you like to see education changed?... It would be a tremendous achievement to see man flying under his own power... In recent times we have seen a huge split develop between rich and poor nations.* V+O = witness

22 If you **have seen** a particular kind of experience, you have had this experience. EG *He'd seen a lot of action... She seemed to think that she'd seen it all.* V+O : USU PAST

23 If you talk about a particular year, decade, etc **seeing** an event or change, you mean that the event or change happened or will happen during that year, decade, etc. EG *The Sixties saw an old world die and a new one come to birth... Last week saw a drop in the bond markets... The 90s will see great changes... The next four or five years are likely to see more industrial production.* V+O, NO IMPER = witness

24 If someone **sees** something happening in the future, they imagine it, or predict that it will happen. EG *She saw herself seated behind the cash register, smiling.... It is perfectly possible to see a situation in which war would break out... Can you see women going into combat carrying forty-pound guns?* V+O : USU+A, NO IMPER, NO FUTURE = picture

25 If you disagree with someone about what will happen in the future and they say **'You'll see'**, they mean that things will happen in the way that they have described. EG *Kwezi only smiled. 'You'll see,' he said.* CONVENTION

26 People say **'I'll see'** or **'We'll see'** to indicate that they do not intend to make a decision immediately, and will make it later. EG *'Will you write to me?' she asked. 'I'll see,' he said.* CONVENTION = perhaps

27 Writers often refer to things they are describing or explaining as being **seen** by their readers. EG *It has already been seen how rocks can be dated by the fossils they contain... We saw in the last chapter some of the risks inherent in these policies... As we shall see later, this is an attractive idea.* V+A, OR V+O/REPORT-CL = show

28 **See** is also used in books to indicate to readers that they should read another section, chapter, or page of the book, or another book, because more information is given there. 'See' is used in this dictionary to tell you that you can look up another word in order to find more information. EG *Reference to this problem is made elsewhere (see Chapter 14)... How to change a fuse (see also p 21)... See Figure 2... For more details see Part 2.* V+O : ONLY IMPER

29 People say **'let me see'** or **'let's see'** when they are trying to remember something, or trying to find something. EG *His address was, let me see, 10 Killer Street... Your husband is–let's see–a lawyer... 'I think I've got her address somewhere. Now let me see.' There was a long pause while she looked.* PHR : USED AS ADV SEN

30 If you say **seeing as** or **seeing that** one thing is true another thing is true or possible, you mean that because the first thing is true the second thing is true or possible; an informal expression. EG *Seeing that you're the guest on this little trip, you can decide where we're going... Seeing as you're coming down to my place later, we'll talk about it then.* CONJ SUBORD = since

31 **See you**, **see you later**, and **be seeing you** are informal ways of saying goodbye to someone when you expect to meet them again soon. CONVENTION

32 If you **see the Old Year out** or **see the New Year in**, you celebrate the New Year at midnight on December 31st, often by having a drink with friends or relations. EG *We must stay up to see the New Year in.* PHR : VB INFLECTS

33 A **see** is a diocese; a technical word. N COUNT

34 ● **be seen dead**: see **dead**. **see eye to eye**: see **eye**. **see fit**: see **fit**. **see life**: see **life**. **see the light**: see **light**. **see the light of day**: see **light**. **see red**: see **red**. **It remains to be seen**: see **remain**. **wait and see**: see **wait**.

see about. When you **see about** something, you arrange for it to be done, made, provided, etc. EG *Rudolph went into the station to see about Thomas's ticket... She realized it was time to get in touch with the office to see about an increase.* PHRASAL VB : V+PREP = fix up ● If someone says that they will do something, and you say **'We'll see about that'**, you mean that you intend to prevent ● CONVENTION them from doing it. EG *We're not moving–We'll see about that.*

see off. When you **see** someone **off**, you go with them to the station, airport, etc that they are leaving from, and say goodbye to them there. EG *She saw him off at the station.* PHRASAL VB : ORDER V+O+ ADV

see through. 1 If you **see through** a person or **see through** what they are doing, you realize what their intentions are, although they are trying to conceal them. EG *She had learned to see through him... The jailers saw through my scheme.* PHRASAL VB : V+ PREP, HAS PASS = be wise to

2 If someone or something **sees** you **through** a difficult time in your life, they give you help during this time. EG *He was a great friend of mine and saw me through all the hard times.* PHRASAL VB : V+ O+ADV/PREP = support

3 See also **see-through**.

see to. If you **see to** something that needs attention, you attend to it. EG *Don't you worry about that. I'll see to that... A man was there to see to our luggage... She really appreciates the way you stepped in and saw to things... He went out to see to the chickens.* PHRASAL VB : V+ PREP : HAS PASS = look after

seed /si:d/, **seeds, seeding, seeded**. 1 A **seed** is the small hard part of a plant from which a new plant grows. EG *I'm taking these seeds home to plant... ...sunflower seeds.* N COUNT

2 **Seed** is a quantity of seeds of a particular kind that you put in the ground in order to grow plants. EG *...a packet of carrot seed... All these trees were grown from seed.* N UNCOUNT ● If lettuces, cauliflowers, etc **go to seed** or **run to seed**, they produce flowers and seeds as well as leaves. EG *My lettuces have gone to seed.* ● PHR : VB INFLECTS ● If a person **goes to seed**, they become less physically fit or less mentally efficient; an informal expression. EG *He's really gone to seed.* ● PHR : VB INFLECTS = go downhill

3 If you **seed** a piece of land, you plant seeds in it. EG *One rancher has seeded his land with maize... Several coppice plantations have been seeded with poplar, willow, and alder.* V+O : IF+PREP THEN *with* = sow

4 The **seeds** of something are its small beginnings, from which it grows into something big and powerful. EG *The seeds of doubt had been sown... National revolt was a long way off but the seeds of it were already being sown.* N PLURAL : *the*+ N+*of* = germ

5 A **seed** is also a tennis player who is ranked according to his or her ability to play the game; a technical term. EG *...the number two seed.* N COUNT : USU *the*+*number*+ NUM+N

6 When tennis players **are seeded**, they are ranked according to their ability to play the game; a technical term. EG *He was seeded number 2.* V+O : USU PASS

seedbed /si:dbɛd/, **seedbeds**; also spelled with a hyphen. 1 A **seedbed** is an area of ground, usually with specially prepared earth, where young plants are grown from seed. EG *Before we could stop him, he had trampled the seedbeds.* N COUNT

2 A **seedbed** is also a place or situation in which something, for example rebellion or conflict, develops easily. EG *This household has been a seed-bed of ill-will and strife for five years... Education should be a seedbed in which to plant real ideas about life.* N COUNT : USU+ SUPP ⇑ environment

seedcake /si:dkeɪk/, **seedcakes**. **Seedcake** is a cake flavoured with caraway seeds. EG *...a large piece of seedcake.* N UNCOUNT/ COUNT

seedless /si:dlɪ²s/. A **seedless** fruit has no seeds in it. EG *...seedless grapes... ...seedless oranges.* ADJ CLASSIF

seedling /si:dlɪŋ/, **seedlings**. A **seedling** is a young plant that has been grown from a seed. EG *I prepared the earth carefully for my seedlings and cuttings.* N COUNT

seedy /si:di¹/, **seedier, seediest**. 1 A **seedy** person or place looks shabby and untidy. EG *...a seedy character with a cigarette butt jammed between his lips... ...a seedy and rundown photographer's studio.* ADJ QUALIT = down at heel

2 If you feel **seedy**, you feel slightly unwell; a rather old-fashioned expression. EG *I'm feeling a bit seedy this morning.* ADJ QUALIT : USU PRED = poorly

seek /si:k/, **seeks, seeking, sought**; a slightly formal word. 1 When someone **seeks** something such as a job or a place to live, they try to find one. EG *They moved to London to seek jobs... Thousands of people were seeking food and shelter.* V+O, OR V+A *(for)* ⇑ look for ● When someone **seeks** their **fortune**, they go to a different place in order to try to become rich; an old-fashioned expression. EG *He had decided to leave his village to seek his fortune.* ● PHR : VB INFLECTS

2 When someone **seeks** peace, revenge, etc, they try to obtain it. EG *Both the Russians and the Americans are seeking peace... The bombing could have been done by someone seeking revenge... They are seeking a 10 per cent a year reduction in their work force.* V+O ⇑ look for

3 If you **seek** an answer or solution to a problem, you try to find one. EG *I keep thinking about it, seeking a solution to my problem... The answers they seek are not forthcoming.* V+O, OR V+A *(for)* = search for

4 When you **seek** someone's help or advice, you go to them and ask them for it. EG *I was seeking the help of someone who spoke French... His views on the war were sought by the American press... My insomnia was bad enough for me to seek the advice of a psychiatrist.* V+O, OR V+A *(for)* ⇑ request

5 If you **seek** to do something, you try to do it. EG *Power stations are seeking to reduce their use of oil... Teachers are using the very teaching methods our parents had sought to reject.* V+*to*-INF = endeavour

6 See **hide-and-seek**.

seek out. If you **seek out** someone or something, you keep looking for them until you find them. EG *It was unusual for anyone to seek out her husband unnecessarily.* PHRASAL VB : V+ O+ADV = hunt down

seem /si:m/, **seems, seeming, seemed**. 1 If something **seems** to have a particular quality or feature, it gives the impression of having that quality or feature. EG *Even minor problems seem important... It seemed like a good idea.* V+C, OR V+ *to*-INF = appear

2 If someone **seems** to have a particular attitude or opinion, they give the impression of having that attitude or opinion. EG *He seemed nice enough... You seem to be very interested.* V+C, OR V+ *to*-INF = appear

3 If something **seems** to happen or if a particular state of affairs **seems** to exist, you get the impression that it happens or exists. EG *After what seemed like hours he came out with a wry smile... There don't seem to be many people on campus today... It seemed as though I had known them for a very long time.* V+C, OR V+ *to*-INF

4 **Seem** is used **4.1** when you are making a statement to indicate that you are not completely certain about the truth of what you are saying. EG *The experiments seem to prove that sugar is not very good for you.* V+C, OR V+ *to*-INF **4.2** when you are describing something in the past to indicate that you are not sure that you remember it correctly. EG *I seem to remember that he was a fiction writer.* V+*to*-INF **4.3** when you are giving your opinion about something or asking someone else's opinion. EG *It did seem to me that she was far too romantic... Does that seem nonsense to you?... That would seem a sensible thing to do.* V+C/REPORT-CL/ *to*, V+*to*-INF **4.4** when you are criticizing or questioning someone's attitude towards something. EG *You seem to think that these rules are made for your benefit... You seem to think I despise everything.* V+C, OR V+ *to*-INF

5 **Seem** is also used after 'cannot' and 'could not' to indicate that you have tried to do something and were unable to do it. EG *I just couldn't seem to take it in somehow... He could never seem to find the time for any serious thinking... I can't seem to get to sleep at night.* V : MODAL+ BROAD NEG+V+ *to*-INF

seeming /si:mɪŋ/. You talk about someone's **seeming** willingness, **seeming** interest, etc when they appear to you to be willing, interested, etc but you are not absolutely sure that they are; a rather formal word. EG *...his seeming willingness to participate... ...the seeming acceptance of the changes... The old woman's seeming inattention provoked her.* ADJ CLASSIF : ATTRIB = apparent

seemingly /si:mɪŋli¹/. 1 If something is **seemingly** large, **seemingly** important, etc, it seems to be large, important, etc even though it may not really be so. EG *...the seemingly limitless resources of the United States... ...the seemingly imminent collapse of the pier.* ADV+ADJ/ADV = apparently

2 **Seemingly** is also used when you want to say that something seems to be true; used mainly in spoken English. EG *They seemingly don't have any problems... They all have to be down at a certain time for lunch but seemingly it all depends on the warden.* ADV SEN = apparently

seemly /si:mli¹/. **Seemly** behaviour, dress, etc is appropriate in the particular circumstances; an old-fashioned word. EG *A seemly silence seemed indicated... ...seemly conduct.* ADJ QUALIT = suitable

seen /si:n/ is the past participle of **see**.

seep /si:p/, **seeps, seeping, seeped**. 1 When a liquid **seeps** through something, it flows through it very slowly and in small amounts. EG *I used to lie awake at night watching the rain seep through the* V+A = trickle, ooze

cracks... *Instead of draining away, water seeps down into the ground.* ▸ used of gases, smoke, smells, etc. EG *The petrol fumes seeped into the cab... Smoke was seeping through the branches... ...the faint smell of dirty socks seeping from the cupboard.* ▸ = ooze

2 If information **seeps** out of a place, it comes out very slowly, a little at a time. EG *Atrocity stories began to seep out of the Congo... Reports which seeped out made this clear.* V+A = filter

seer /sɪə/, **seers.** A **seer** is a person who tells people what will happen in the future; an old-fashioned or literary word. EG *He was considered a seer and a prophet... Ignatius sees himself as a seer and philosopher.* N COUNT

seesaw /siːsɔː/, **seesaws.** A **seesaw** is a long board which is balanced on a fixed part in the middle. If you sit on one end of the board, the other end goes up in the air. Children play on seesaws by making the plank tilt up and down when one child sits on each end. EG *There is a paddling pool, a sand pit, a seesaw, and swings.* N COUNT

seethe /siːð/, **seethes, seething, seethed.** 1 When you **seethe**, you are very angry or indignant about something but do not show or express your feelings about it. EG *I seethed with secret rage one night... By now David was seething.* V: NO IMPER = fume

2 If a place **seethes** with people, insects, etc, it is very full of them and they are all moving about in a busy way. EG *The streets of London seethed with a marching, cheering, flag-waving crowd... The ships seethed with noise and activity... ...a seething mass of maggots.* V+A *(with)*: NO IMPER = swarm

see-through. See-through clothes are made of fairly thin cloth, so that you can see a person's body or their underclothes through them. EG *...a see-through blouse.* ADJ CLASSIF: ATTRIB = transparent

segment /sɛgmə²nt/, **segments.** 1 A **segment** of something is one part of it, considered separately from the rest. EG *A much larger segment of the population might be affected... Different segments of the panel are painted different colours.* N PART = section

2 A **segment** of an orange, grapefruit, etc is one of the sections into which it is easily divided. EG *...grapefruit segments.* N COUNT ⇑ part

3 A **segment** of a circle is one of the two parts into which it is divided when you draw a straight line through it. N COUNT/PART

segmentation /sɛgmə²nteɪʃə⁰n/ is the dividing of something into loosely-connected parts; a technical word. N UNCOUNT ⇑ division

segmented /sɛgmɛntɪ²d/. If something is **segmented**, it is divided into parts that are loosely connected to each other. EG *...insects with segmented bodies.* ADJ CLASSIF: ATTRIB

segregate /sɛgrɪgeɪt/, **segregates, segregating, segregated.** To **segregate** two groups of people or things means to keep them physically apart from each other. EG *They tried to segregate pedestrians and vehicles... Little effort was made to segregate the sexes.* V+O ⇑ separate

segregated /sɛgrɪgeɪtɪ²d/. 1 A **segregated** group of people is kept apart from other people belonging to a different sex, race, or religion. EG *He refused to play before segregated audiences... None of the opposing teams was segregated.* ADJ CLASSIF

2 **Segregated** buses, schools, etc are provided for the use of one group of people who are of the same sex, race, or religion, and no other group is allowed to use them. EG *English language universities were not yet segregated... She had to walk two miles to a segregated school... ...segregated toilets.* ADJ CLASSIF

segregation /sɛgrɪgeɪʃə⁰n/ is the practice of officially keeping apart people of different sexes, or different racial or religious groups. EG *...a Supreme Court decision outlawing segregation in the schools... They imprisoned more than eight thousand people for defying segregation laws.* N UNCOUNT ⇑ separation

seismic /saɪzmɪk/. **Seismic** events happen as part of an earthquake, or as the result of an earthquake; a technical term. EG *A seismic shock caused the formation of a huge tidal wave... ...seismic activity.* ADJ CLASSIF: ATTRIB

seismograph /saɪzməgrɑːf, -græf/, **seismographs.** A **seismograph** is an instrument for recording and measuring the strength of earthquakes. N COUNT

seismology /saɪzmɒləʤi¹/ is the scientific study of earthquakes. N UNCOUNT ⇑ science

seize /siːz/, **seizes, seizing, seized.** 1 If you **seize** something, you take hold of it quickly and firmly. EG *Clarissa seized her arm and dragged her into the kitchen... The policeman seized him by the collar... Seizing the bowl, he ran off through the door.* V+O = grab

2 When a group of people **seize** a place or **seize** control of it, they take control of it quickly and suddenly, using force. EG *The airfield had been seized by US airborne troops... They planned to seize complete control of the Persian Gulf... ...plots to seize power in Britain.* V+O

3 When a government or other authority **seizes** someone's property, they take it from them by force, often because the person has broken the law or owes a lot of money. EG *The man was jailed, and his cattle and house were seized.* V+O = impound

4 When a person **is seized**, they are arrested or captured. EG *He was seized in the garage of his home in a Naples suburb... ...a university professor seized on Wednesday by 16 armed men.* V+O: USU PASS

5 When you **seize** an opportunity, you quickly take advantage of it, and do something that you want to do. EG *Derrick seized the chance and went to Spain... I always seize the opportunity to go to the opera.* V+O = grab

6 If you **are seized** with a desire to do something, you suddenly want to do it very much. EG *She was seized with the desire to play jazz piano.* V+O: USU PASS = overwhelmed

seize on. If someone **seizes on** something or **seizes upon** it, they show great interest in it, because they think that they will get an advantage from it. EG *The press were the next to seize upon his cause and champion it.* PHRASAL VB: V+PREP, HAS PASS

seize up. 1 If a part of your body **seizes up**, it suddenly stops working, because you have exerted it too much. EG *Your back may seize up... He felt a muscle in his calf seizing up... I had done enough to prevent my heart and lungs seizing up.* PHRASAL VB: V+ADV

2 If an engine **seizes up**, it stops working, because of overheating or lack of oil. PHRASAL VB: V+ADV

3 If the traffic in a city **seizes up**, it stops moving, because there is too much of it. PHRASAL VB: V+ADV

seizure /siːʒə/, **seizures.** 1 If someone has a **seizure**, they have a sudden violent attack of an illness, especially a heart attack or an epileptic fit. EG *It is conceivable that he had a seizure of some kind and then drowned... During the screening of the film, he had an epileptic seizure.* N COUNT

2 When there is a **seizure** of power or the **seizure** of a place, a group of people suddenly take control of a place, using force. EG *...the Nazi seizure of power in Germany. ...the seizure of factories by the workers.* N UNCOUNT: USU +of = capture

seldom /sɛldə⁰m/. If something **seldom** happens, it happens only occasionally. EG *He seldom bathed... It seldom rains there... 'How often do you manage to get these?'–'Very seldom.'.. The waiting time was seldom less than four hours... Seldom did a week pass without a request for information.* ADV BRD NEG = rarely

select /sɪ²lɛkt/, **selects, selecting, selected.** 1 When you **select** something or someone, you choose them in preference to other things or people of the same kind. EG *They select books that seem to them important... There was a large number of people from whom she could select friends... The delegates voted to select a new committee.* ◇ **selected.** EG *We were being shown carefully selected places during our visit... It has been distributed to selected bookshops in Britain.* V+O = pick; ◇ ADJ CLASSIF: ATTRIB ⇑ chosen

2 A **select** group of people or things is a very small group of some of the best people or things of a their kind. EG *They are members of a select band of professional athletes.* ADJ CLASSIF: ATTRIB = elite

3 A **select** school, housing area, etc has many desirable features, and is available only to people with a lot of money. EG *He went to a select New England school.* ADJ QUALIT = exclusive

selection /sɪ²lɛkʃə⁰n/, **selections.** 1 **Selection** is the selecting of one or more people or things from a group. EG *According to all the rules, she stood little chance of selection... The judges may revise their selection process.* ● See also **natural selection.** N UNCOUNT ⇑ choosing

2 A **selection** is 2.1 a set of people or things that have been selected from a group. EG *The orchestra was playing a selection of tunes from the Merry Widow.* N PART = medley

2.2 a collection of goods of a particular kind in a shop. EG *We have London's largest selection of new and second-hand office furniture.* N PART = range

selective /sɪ²lɛktɪv/. 1 A **selective** process applies only to a few things or people. EG *He is against the selective protection of declining industries... ...the* ADJ CLASSIF: ATTRIB ⇑ limited

selective breeding of stock animals... ...the selective education of the most talented children.
◊ **selectively**. EG *Trees are felled selectively.* ◊ ADV WITH VB
◊ **selectivity** /sɪlɛktɪvɪti¹/. EG *We are now introducing an element of selectivity.* ◊ N UNCOUNT

2 When someone is **selective**, they choose carefully the things that they buy, the entertainments that they go to, etc. EG *They are particularly selective in their television watching habits... The reporters were asked to be less selective in their reporting.* ADJ QUALIT = discriminating
◊ **selectively**. EG *We must aim to import more selectively.* ◊ ADV WITH VB

selector /sɪ²lɛktə/, **selectors**. A **selector** is 1 one of a group of people who choose the members of a sports team. EG *The selectors chose to leave him out... I consulted the other selectors for their views.* N COUNT : USU PL ⇑ person
2 a device that enables you to choose something, or that chooses it for you. EG *In Germany, TV sets have selectors for thirteen different channels.* N COUNT

self /sɛlf/, **selves**. 1 Your **self** is your basic personality or nature, considered especially in terms of what you are really like as a person or what you are really like at a particular time in your life. EG *She was her normal self again... He was his usual imperturbable self... Once dressed, they became their own decisive selves again.* N COUNT : USU DETPOSS + MOD + N IN SING
2 A person's **self** is the essential part of their nature which makes them different from everyone and everything else; a formal use. EG *Without a self one cannot give.* N COUNT : USU SING, OR N UNCOUNT ⇑ individuality
3 **Self** is your own pleasure, happiness, needs, or wants, when you consider them to be more important than anyone else's. EG *She's never understood anything except self, self, self.* N UNCOUNT = number one

self- 1 combines with adjectives and nouns to refer to something that you do by yourself or to yourself. For example, if you are self-admiring, you admire yourself. EG *...self-induced catastrophes... ...self-improvement.* PREFIX 2 combines with adjectives to describe something such as a device that does something automatically by itself. EG *...a self-locking door... ...self-fulfilling prophecies.* PREFIX

self-absorbed. If you are **self-absorbed**, you think so much about things concerning yourself that you do not notice other people or the things around you. EG *Single children are always intensely self-absorbed.* ADJ QUALIT = narcissistic

self-addressed. A **self-addressed** envelope is one that you write your address on and send to someone in another envelope with your letter so that they can send something back to you. EG *I enclose a stamped self-addressed envelope for your reply.* ADJ CLASSIF : USU ATTRIB

self-adhesive. Something that is **self-adhesive** is covered on one side with a sticky substance like glue, so that it will stick to surfaces. ADJ CLASSIF : USU ATTRIB

self-appointed. If you are a **self-appointed** leader, ruler, etc, you have given yourself this position of leader or ruler without anyone else asking you or choosing you to have it. EG *...Jackie Felt, our trainer and self-appointed spiritual guide... The revolutionary's mission was a self-appointed role.* ADJ CLASSIF : USU ATTRIB ≠ elected

self-assertion is confidence that you have in speaking firmly about your opinions and demanding the rights that you believe you should have. EG *The child has reached the stage of vigorous self-assertion... He became worried by the increasing self-assertion of surrounding countries.* N UNCOUNT

self-assertive. Someone who is **self-assertive** acts in an aggressively confident way, speaking firmly about their opinions and demanding the rights that they believe they should have. EG *Regular encouragement can help make them more self-assertive and confident.* ADJ QUALIT ⇑ assured

self-assurance. Someone who has **self-assurance** shows confidence in the things that they say and do because they are sure of their abilities and they are not afraid. EG *His monumental self-assurance was based upon his complete faith in his own ability.* N UNCOUNT = self-confidence

self-assured. Someone who is **self-assured** shows confidence in the things that they say and do because they are sure of their abilities and they are not afraid. EG *He states everything in a self-assured way... Personally, I'm more self-assured now.* ADJ QUALIT = self-confident

self-catering. **Self-catering** accommodation is intended for people who provide their own food. EG *...self-catering flats for students.* N UNCOUNT : BEFORE N

self-centred; also spelled **self-centered** in American English. Someone who is **self-centred** is always concerned with their own wants and needs and never thinks about other people. EG *He was much too self-centred to notice her... ...an increasingly self-centred society.* ADJ QUALIT = egotistic

self-confessed is used to describe someone who admits openly that they have a particular characteristic, often a characteristic that is considered to be bad. EG *You are a self-confessed liar, aren't you?... He was a self-confessed racialist.* ADJ CLASSIF : ATTRIB ⇑ admitted

self-confidence. If you have **self-confidence**, you behave confidently and assertively because you feel sure of your abilities or worth. EG *He can only develop self-confidence if he is told he is good and clever... We began to lose our self-confidence.* N UNCOUNT = self-assurance

self-confident. Someone who is **self-confident** behaves confidently and assertively because they feel sure of their abilities or worth. EG *She's a strong, self-confident woman... Because they are self-confident, they are not so likely to regard you as a threat.* ADJ QUALIT = self-assured

self-congratulation is the behaviour of someone who keeps emphasizing how well they have done or how good they are. EG *After his recent promotion his self-congratulation has really reached unbearable heights.* N UNCOUNT = smugness

self-conscious. 1 Someone who is **self-conscious** is shy and easily embarrassed, and feels that everyone is looking at them and judging them. EG *I stood there, feeling self-conscious. Was my hair out of place?... At first I was self-conscious about being a movie star.* ADJ QUALIT = uncomfortable, awkward
◊ **self-consciously**. EG *They posed somewhat self-consciously in front of the statue.* ◊ ADV WITH VB ◊ **self-consciousness**. EG *His self-consciousness was acute and distressing.* ◊ N UNCOUNT
2 A person or group that is **self-conscious** is strongly aware of who or what they are. EG *The proletarian movement is the self-conscious, independent movement of the oppressed classes.* ADJ CLASSIF

self-contained. 1 Something that is **self-contained** is complete and separate and does not need help or resources from outside. EG *The university campus is like a self-contained city with shops and all amenities... The intelligentsia often see themselves as a self-contained group outside the class system.* ADJ CLASSIF = self-sufficient
2 A **self-contained** flat has all its own facilities, so that a person living there does not have to share anything such as a kitchen or bathroom with other people. EG *She has a self-contained three-roomed flat with a garden.* ADJ CLASSIF

self-contradictory. If you say or write something that is **self-contradictory**, you make two statements which cannot both be true. ADJ CLASSIF ⇑ conflicting

self-control. A person's **self-control** is their ability to control their feelings so that they appear calm, even when they feel very angry or afraid. EG *He lost his self-control and cried aloud... Clive's calmness and self-control was very impressive.* N UNCOUNT = self-discipline

self-controlled. Someone who is **self-controlled** is able to control their feelings so that they appear calm, even when they feel very angry or afraid. EG *She appeared calm and self-controlled in the face of the disaster.* ADJ QUALIT = composed

self-defeating. A plan or action that is **self-defeating** is likely to cause problems or difficulties instead of producing any useful results. EG *It is self-defeating and ultimately suicidal to ignore the progress of events... ...a self-defeating policy.* ADJ CLASSIF ⇑ useless

self-defence; also spelled **self-defense** in American English. 1 **Self-defence** is 1.1 physical violence or particular physical skills that you use in order to protect yourself against someone who is trying to hurt you. EG *He had struck her only in self-defence... They carry knives as instruments of self-defense.* N UNCOUNT ⇑ protection 1.2 the use of particular actions by a person, group, country, etc in order to protect themselves from another one that is threatening them. EG *They were calling for revolution and self-defence against 'fascist and racialist brutality.'* N UNCOUNT
2 If you say something **in self-defence**, you give reasons or excuses for your behaviour to someone who thinks that you have behaved wrongly. EG *'I didn't want to go anyway,' he grumbled in self-defence.* PHR : USED AS AN A

self-denial is the habit of refusing to do or have things that you would like, either because you cannot afford them or because you believe it is morally good for you not to do them or have them. EG *The mission required total self-denial.* N UNCOUNT = self-sacrifice

self-determination is 1 the right of a country to be independent instead of being controlled by a foreign country, and to choose its own form of government. EG *Only national self-determination within a framework of parliamentary democracy would be acceptable.* 2 the power of individuals to make important decisions themselves without being influenced by others. EG *He believed in the self-determination, natural equality and freedom of individuals.* — N UNCOUNT ⇑ independence; N UNCOUNT ⇑ independence

self-discipline is the ability to control yourself and to make yourself work hard or behave in a particular way without needing anyone else to tell you what to do. EG *They approve of the independence and self-discipline which develops within a large family.* — N UNCOUNT = self-control

self-drive. A **self-drive** car or van is one which you hire and drive yourself. EG *He called in to order a self-drive hire car for the following morning.* — ADJ CLASSIF: ATTRIB

self-educated. People who are **self-educated** have learnt a skill by themselves rather than being taught it formally by someone else such as a teacher at school. EG *For a self-educated writer I think his work shows remarkable talent.* — ADJ CLASSIF = self-taught

self-effacing. If you are **self-effacing**, you feel that you are not important and do not like talking about yourself or drawing attention to yourself. EG *People here are rather self-effacing... He has shown a self-effacing charm.* — ADJ QUALIT = diffident

self-employed. Someone who is **self-employed** organizes their own work or business rather than being employed and paid by another person. EG *...his job as a self-employed builder and decorator.* — ADJ CLASSIF

self-esteem. If you have **self-esteem**, you feel that you are a good, worthwhile person, and for that reason you behave confidently. EG *He wanted to regain his self-esteem... Being right usually adds to one's self-esteem.* — N UNCOUNT = self-respect

self-evident. A fact or situation that is **self-evident** is so obvious that there is no need for further proof or explanation. EG *The need for reform was self-evident... The answers to moral problems are not self-evident.* ◊ **self-evidently.** EG *Self-evidently, this is a disastrous course.* — ADJ CLASSIF: USU PRED ⇑ apparent = clear; ◊ ADV SEN

self-examination is thought that you give to your own character and actions in order to judge whether you have been behaving in a way that is acceptable to your own set of values. — N UNCOUNT ⇑ analysis

self-explanatory. Something that is **self-explanatory** is clear and easy to understand without needing any extra information or explanation. EG *That phrase is self-explanatory.* — ADJ CLASSIF = self-evident

self-expression. A person's **self-expression** is the expression of their own personality, feelings, or opinions, for example through a creative activity such as drawing or dancing. EG *I do so admire your superb gift of self-expression... ...opportunities for political self-expression.* — N UNCOUNT

self-governing. A **self-governing** country, organization, etc is governed or run by its own members rather than by another country, organization, etc. EG *Summerhill is a self-governing school, democratic in form... ...members of a self-governing, co-operative group.* — ADJ CLASSIF = independent

self-government is government or control of a country, organization etc by its own people rather than by others. EG *In Parliament he called for the democratic self-government of the colonies... They really believe in and want self-government.* — N UNCOUNT = independence

self-help consists of doing things yourself to try and solve your own problems without depending on other people. EG *Single parents join self-help groups for social life and mutual help.* — N UNCOUNT

self-importance is the attitude of believing that you are more important than other people. — N UNCOUNT: USU WITH POSS

self-important. Someone who is **self-important** behaves in a way which shows that they believe they are more important than other people. EG *He coughed and hummed in a self-important way.* — ADJ QUALIT = conceited

self-imposed. A **self-imposed** task, condition, or responsibility is one that you have deliberately created or accepted for yourself. EG *...troubles that were largely self-imposed... ...self-imposed restrictions.* — ADJ CLASSIF

self-indulgence is the act of allowing yourself to have or do things that you enjoy. EG *Temptations to self-indulgence should be resisted.* — N UNCOUNT ⇑ selfishness

self-indulgent. If you are **self-indulgent**, you allow yourself to have or do things that you enjoy. EG *He continued to be self-indulgent, as he had been indulged when he was a little boy.* — ADJ QUALIT ⇑ selfish

self-inflicted. A **self-inflicted** wound or injury is one that you cause to yourself deliberately. — ADJ CLASSIF

self-interest is the attitude of always wanting to do what is best for yourself rather than for anyone else. EG *It depends which parties make the broadest appeal to the voter's self-interest.* — N UNCOUNT = egotism

self-interested. If you are **self-interested**, you always want to do what is best for yourself rather than for anyone else. EG *It is not enough to protect animals for self-interested reasons alone.* — ADJ CLASSIF = selfish

selfish /s̲elfɪʃ/. If you are **selfish**, you care only about yourself, and not about other people. EG *I didn't realize you were so selfish.* ▸ used of people's behaviour and attitudes. EG *...a totally selfish attitude... ...a selfish argument.* ◊ **selfishly.** EG *Why are you acting so selfishly?* ◊ **selfishness.** EG *Wherever you look, all you see is selfishness and dishonesty.* — ADJ QUALIT = egotistic ≠ considerate; ◊ ADV; ◊ N UNCOUNT = egotism

selfless /s̲elflɪ²s/. If you are **selfless**, you care about other people and their needs rather than considering yourself and your own needs. EG *...a brave, sincere and selfless person.* ▸ used of people's behaviour and attitudes. EG *...the selfless tenderness of his mother.* ◊ **selflessly.** EG *Christianity tells us we must love selflessly.* ◊ **selflessness.** — ADJ QUALIT ⇑ considerate = unselfish; ◊ ADV; ◊ N UNCOUNT

self-made is used to describe someone who is successful and rich and has achieved this through their own efforts, especially when they started life without money, education, or social status. EG *My father was a self-made man... ...a self-made millionaire.* — ADJ CLASSIF: USU ATTRIB

self-opinionated. Someone who is **self-opinionated** believes firmly that their own opinions and ideas are always right, and refuses to admit that they might be wrong. — ADJ QUALIT = cocksure

self-pity is a feeling of unhappiness and depression that you have about yourself and your problems, which is often unnecessary or greatly exaggerated. EG *He could not fight off the self-pity that welled up inside him.* — N UNCOUNT

self-portrait, self-portraits. A **self-portrait** is a drawing, painting, or written description that you do of yourself. EG *...an exhibition of Rembrandt's self-portraits.* — N COUNT

self-possessed. If you are **self-possessed**, you are calm and confident and in control of your emotions. EG *Anne is a pleasant, self-possessed girl of eighteen.* — ADJ QUALIT = self-assured

self-possession is the quality of being self-possessed. EG *She acted with the most extraordinary self-possession.* — N UNCOUNT = composure

self-preservation is the instinctive behaviour that makes you keep yourself safe from injury or death in a dangerous situation. EG *I have a strong instinct for self-preservation.* — N UNCOUNT = survival

self-raising flour. **Self-raising flour** is flour that contains baking powder to make it rise easily. You use self-raising flour for baking cakes. — N UNCOUNT

self-reliance is the ability to do things and make decisions by yourself, without needing other people to help you. EG *One needed an unusual degree of self-reliance to cope.* — N UNCOUNT = independence

self-reliant. If you are **self-reliant**, you are able to do things and make decisions by yourself, without needing other people to help you. EG *The children were very self-reliant.* — ADJ QUALIT = independe[nt]

self-respect is a feeling of confidence and pride in your ability and worth, which you sometimes lose when something makes you ashamed of yourself. EG *Billy needs to have his self-respect restored.* — N UNCOUNT = self-esteem

self-respecting. 1 A **self-respecting** person has self-respect. EG *...a mature, self-respecting citizen.* 2 **Self-respecting** is used to describe a particular type of person when you are saying that something must definitely be done or owned by people who want to be considered as this type of person; used humorously. EG *All self-respecting feminists have seen this film... No self-respecting oil tycoon has fewer than two helicopters.* — ADJ CLASSIF: USU ATTRIB; ADJ CLASSIF: ATTRIB = genuine, proper

self-righteous. If you are **self-righteous**, you are convinced that you are right in your beliefs, attitudes, and ways of behaving and that other people are wrong. EG *She told me that Jason was a self-righteous prig... ...self-righteous indignation.* ◊ **self-righteousness.** EG *There was a strong note of self-righteousness in his voice.* — ADJ QUALIT = smug; ◊ N UNCOUNT = self-satisfaction

self-sacrifice is the giving up of what you want so that other people can get what they want or need. EG *The children's education demanded effort and self-sacrifice.* N UNCOUNT = selflessness

self-sacrificing. Someone or something that is **self-sacrificing** shows self-sacrifice. ADJ QUALIT = selfless

self-same. You use **self-same** when you want to emphasize that the person or thing mentioned is exactly the same as the one mentioned previously. EG *This was the self-same woman I'd met on the train.* ADJ CLASSIF: ATTRIB = very

self-satisfaction is the feeling you have when you are self-satisfied. EG *His expression of self-satisfaction was almost grotesque.* N UNCOUNT = complacency

self-satisfied. If you are **self-satisfied**, you are so pleased about your achievements or your situation that you do not feel there is any need for you to do anything more; used showing disapproval. EG *...my self-satisfied colleagues... Travers had gone into a self-satisfied retirement.* ADJ QUALIT = complacent

self-seeking. 1 If you are **self-seeking**, you are interested only in doing things which give you an advantage over other people. EG *Most of her colleagues are intolerant, self-seeking and shallow.* ADJ QUALIT = selfish

2 **Self-seeking** is behaviour which shows you are interested only in doing things which give you an advantage over other people. EG *He is driven by ambition and self-seeking.* N UNCOUNT = selfishness

self-service. A **self-service** shop, cafe, garage, etc is one where you serve yourself rather than being served by another person. ADJ CLASSIF

self-starter, self-starters. A **self-starter** is 1 an electric device that starts a car engine. 2 someone who is prepared to work hard without much supervision, especially in business or commerce. EG *Here's an advert for 'an ambitious young self-starter'.* N COUNT; N COUNT

self-styled is used to describe someone who claims to have a particular title but does not actually have any right to this title. EG *He is the self-styled President of the island.* ADJ CLASSIF: ATTRIB = so-called

self-sufficiency is the state of being self-sufficient. EG *We have achieved self-sufficiency in coal and gas.* N UNCOUNT

self-sufficient. 1 If a country or some other group of people is **self-sufficient**, it is able to produce or make everything that it needs, without needing to import goods. EG *The country aims to be self-sufficient in liquid fuels by 1990... In pre-colonial India, villages were largely self-sufficient.* ADJ QUALIT: IF + PREP THEN *in* ≠ dependent

2 Someone who is **self-sufficient** is able to live happily without anyone else. EG *She became more self-sufficient with success.* ADJ QUALIT = independent

self-supporting. A **self-supporting** company, scheme, etc earns enough money to continue without needing financial help from anyone else. EG *The plan was for British Rail to become self-supporting.* ADJ CLASSIF ⇑ independent

self-taught. If you are **self-taught**, you have learnt a skill by yourself rather than being taught it formally by someone else such as a teacher at school. EG *...a self-taught artist.* ADJ CLASSIF

self-willed. If you are **self-willed**, you are determined to do the things that you want to do and will not take advice from other people; used showing disapproval. EG *Young Tony, like so many children, was self-willed and quick to anger.* ADJ QUALIT = headstrong

sell /sɛl/, **sells, selling, sold**. 1 If you **sell** something, you let someone have it in return for an agreed sum of money. EG *He is going to sell me his car... I hope to sell the house for £30,000... Who are you going to sell to?* V, V+O: IF + PREP THEN *to*, OR V+O+O ⇑ trade

2 If a shop **sells** a particular thing, it has it in the shop for people to buy. EG *Do you sell flowers?* V+O: NO CONT = stock

3 If something **sells** for a particular price, it is offered for sale at that price. EG *These little books sell for 95p each.* V+A *(for/at)* = go

4 If something **sells**, it is bought by the public. EG *It's a nice design, but I'm not sure if it will sell... Our product sells in forty-seven countries... The Daily Mail that year was selling two million copies a day.* V: USU+A, OR V+O

5 If a person or thing **sells** something, they cause people to want to buy it. EG *Scandal and gossip is what sells newspapers... Her name on the book certainly helped to sell it.* V+O

6 If you **sell** an idea to someone or **sell** someone on an idea, you convince them that it is a good thing; an informal use. EG *Let's hear your proposal. You've got 10 minutes to sell it to me... Somehow, the man sold the mayor on the idea of a city golf course.* V+O+O, OR V+O+A *(on/to)*

7 If you **sell** yourself, you present yourself in a way which makes people have confidence in you and your abilities; an informal use. EG *You've got to sell yourself at the interview.* V+O *(REFL)* = promote

8 If you **sell** your honour, principles, etc, you give these things up in order to gain some personal profit or advantage. EG *He sold his principles for a successful career.* V+O = trade

9 If you **sell** yourself **short**, you present yourself in a way which makes people believe you are worth less than you are. PHR: VB INFLECTS

10 If you **sell** someone **down the river**, you betray them for some personal profit or advantage; an informal expression. EG *He was only too ready to sell his native country down the river.* PHR: VB INFLECTS

11 See also **hard sell, soft sell**.

12 See also **selling**.

sell off. If you **sell** something **off**, you sell it all, usually because you need the money. EG *He was forced to sell off his land... We'll be selling off these assets at bargain prices.* PHRASAL VB: V+O+ADV = sell up

sell out. 1 If a shop is **sold out** of something or has **sold out** of it, it has sold it all and there is none of it left in the shop. EG *That shop is never sold out of bread... 'Could I buy some sun cream?'–'Sorry, we've sold out'.* PHRASAL VB: V+ADV/PREP, ONLY PAST PART

2 If a performance of a play, film, or some other form of entertainment is **sold out**, all the tickets have been sold. EG *The first performance was sold out and the play became a tremendous hit.* • See also **sell-out**. PHRASAL VB: V+O+ADV, USU PASS

3 If you **sell out**, you betray someone, especially in order to gain an advantage or benefit for yourself; an informal use. EG *I believe the union has once again sold out to the management... They thought of him as one who had sold out and was no longer to be regarded as a friend.* PHRASAL VB: V+ADV, IF+PREP, THEN *to*

sell up. If you **sell up**, you sell everything you have, for example your house or your business, because you need the money. PHRASAL VB: V+ADV, OR V+O+ADV

seller /sɛlə/, **sellers**. 1 A **seller** is a person or business that sells something. EG *Umbrella sellers went out of business... ...a seller of second-hand books.* N COUNT ⇑ merchant

2 If you say that a product is a good **seller**, a poor **seller**, etc, you mean that it sells a lot, very few, etc. EG *This car's a good seller.* • See also **best seller**. N COUNT: ADJ+N ≠ flop

selling /sɛlɪŋ/ is the act, practice, or business of selling goods. EG *Would you like a career in selling?* N UNCOUNT ⇑ trading

selling point, selling points. A **selling point** is a quality or feature that something or someone has which makes it likely that people will want to buy it or employ them. EG *Your experience of teaching abroad is certainly a selling point.* N COUNT ⇑ asset

selling price, selling prices. The **selling price** of something is the price at which it is sold. N COUNT

Sellotape /sɛləteɪp/, **Sellotapes, Sellotaping, Sellotaped**. 1 **Sellotape** is a trademark for transparent sticky tape that is sold in rolls and that is used for sticking together things such as paper and cardboard. EG *I tried to stick the sign back on with Sellotape.* N UNCOUNT

2 If you **Sellotape** something, you mend, fasten, or stick it together using Sellotape. EG *I Sellotaped the note to his door.* V+O+A

sell-out, sell-outs. 1 If a play, sports event, etc is a **sell-out**, all the tickets for it have been sold. EG *The show was a sell-out.* N COUNT: USU SING, USU USED AS C ⇑ success

2 If you describe someone's behaviour as a **sell-out**, you mean that they have betrayed you, especially in order to gain an advantage or benefit; an informal use. EG *This meeting was just another sell-out to the management.* N COUNT, USU USED AS C ⇑ betrayal

selves /sɛlvz/ is the plural of **self**.

semantic /sɪmæntɪk/, **semantics**. **Semantic** is an adjective and **semantics** is an uncount noun. 1 **Semantic** is used to describe something which concerns the meaning of words and sentences; a fairly formal use. EG *...semantic confusions... This argument is largely a semantic one.* ADJ CLASSIF: USU ATTRIB

2 **Semantics** is the branch of linguistics that deals with meaning in language. EG *...a course in semantics.* N UNCOUNT ⇑ study

semaphore /sɛməfɔː/ is a system of sending messages by using two flags. One flag is held in each hand and the arms are moved to various positions N UNCOUNT representing different letters of the alphabet. EG *The information was sent by semaphore.*

semblance /sɛmbləns/. If there is a **semblance** of a particular condition or quality, it appears to exist, even though this may be a false impression. EG *By this time some semblance of order had been established... The trial was conducted without even a semblance of justice.* N SING WITH DET +of: USU+N UNCOUNT ⇑ appearance

semen /siːmɛn/ is the liquid containing sperm that is produced by the sex organs of men and male animals. N UNCOUNT

semester /sɪ'mɛstə/, **semesters**. A **semester** is one of the two periods into which the year is divided at American universities and colleges. N COUNT

semi /sɛmi'/, **semis**. A **semi** is a semi-detached house; an informal word used in British English. EG *We have a semi in Acton.* N COUNT

semi- is added to adjectives and nouns in order to form other adjectives and nouns that describe someone or something which is partly, but not completely, in a particular state or situation. EG *...skilled→semi-skilled... ...automatic→semi-automatic... ...darkness→semi-darkness.* PREFIX

semibreve /sɛmi'briːv/, **semibreves**. A **semibreve** is a musical note that has a time value equal to four crotchets; used mainly in British English. N COUNT

semicircle /sɛmi'sɜːkəl/, **semicircles**; also spelled with a hyphen. A **semicircle** is one half of a circle, or something having the shape or form of half a circle. EG *We sat in a big semi-circle round Bedford's desk.* N COUNT

semicircular /sɛmi'sɜːkjələ/; also spelled with a hyphen. Something that is **semicircular** has the shape of a semicircle. ADJ CLASSIF

semi-colon, semi-colons. A **semi-colon** is the punctuation mark (;) which is used in writing to separate different parts of a sentence or list or to indicate a pause. N COUNT

semiconductor /sɛmi'kəndʌktə/, **semiconductors**; also spelled with a hyphen. A **semiconductor** is a substance used in electronics whose ability to conduct electricity increases with greater heat. N COUNT

semi-conscious. If someone is **semi-conscious**, they are not fully conscious. EG *He tripped into a ditch and lay there, semi-conscious, for a few minutes.* ADJ CLASSIF

semi-detached, semi-detacheds. A **semi-detached** house is a house that is joined to the house next door by a shared wall; used in British English. EG *...his small semi-detached house in King's Road.* ADJ CLASSIF
▸ used as a noun. EG *They have a small semi-detached.* ▸ N COUNT: USU SING

semi-final, semi-finals; also spelled as one word. A **semi-final** is one of the two matches in a competition which decides which two players or teams will compete in the final. EG *Borg lost his semi-final.* N COUNT
▸ The **semi-finals** is the round of a competition in which these two matches are played. EG *We lost in the semi-finals.* ▸ N PLURAL: USU the+N

semi-finalist, semi-finalists; also spelled as one word. A **semi-finalist** is a player or team who is competing in a semi-final. N COUNT

> **SEMI-MODAL** □ In this dictionary SEMI-MODAL is used in the entries for **need**, **dare**, and **used**, to show that they behave like modals in some ways, but not in all. For detailed information about the different semi-modals, see □ at NEED, DARE, and USED.

seminal /sɛmɪnəl/. A **seminal** book, work, etc is one that has a great influence in a particular field; a formal word. EG *Anthony Crosland's 'The Future of Socialism' in 1956 was seminal... This experience was to have a seminal influence on his own political development.* ADJ QUALIT ⇑ important

seminar /sɛmɪnɑː/, **seminars**. A **seminar** is a class, usually at college or university, where the teacher and the students discuss a particular topic or subject. N COUNT

seminary /sɛmɪnəri'/, **seminaries**. A **seminary** is a college where priests are trained. N COUNT

semiotics /sɛmi'ɒtɪks/ is the study of human communication, especially communication using signs and symbols. N UNCOUNT

semi-precious; also spelled as one word. **Semi-precious** stones are stones that are used in making jewellery. They are less valuable than precious stones. Amethysts and garnets are semi-precious stones. EG *...handbags set with semi-precious stones.* ADJ CLASSIF: ATTRIB

semiquaver /sɛmi'kweɪvə/, **semiquavers**. A **semiquaver** is a musical note that has the time value of one quarter of a crotchet; used mainly in British English. N COUNT

Semitic /sɪ'mɪtɪk/. **1** The **Semitic** languages are a group of languages that include Arabic and Hebrew. EG *...the root structure of the Semitic languages... ...Comparative Semitic Grammar.* ADJ CLASSIF: ATTRIB
2 Semitic people belong to one of the groups of people who speak a Semitic language. EG *...people of Semitic origin... ...the Semitic Phoenicians.* ADJ CLASSIF
3 Semitic is sometimes used to mean Jewish. • See also **anti-Semitic**. ADJ CLASSIF

semitone /sɛmi'təʊn/, **semitones**. A **semitone** is the smallest interval between two notes in Western music, for example from C to C sharp, or from C sharp to D. Two semitones are equal to one tone. N COUNT

semolina /sɛməliːnə/ consists of small hard grains of wheat that are used for making foods such as spaghetti and macaroni and for making sweet puddings with milk. EG *...semolina pudding.* N UNCOUNT

SEN /ɛs iː ɛn/, **SEN's**. In Britain, **SEN** is an abbreviation for 'State Enrolled Nurse'. An SEN is a nurse who has successfully completed a two-year practical course in nursing; compare **SRN**. EG *...Rita Walker, SEN.* N COUNT: ALSO IN TITLE
▸ used of the qualification received at the end of the course. EG *She's got her SEN now.* ▸ N COUNT

Senate /sɛnɪ't/. **1** The **Senate** is the smaller and more important of the two councils that form the law-making part of the government in some countries, for example in Australia and the U.S.A. EG *This proposal was approved by both the House and the Senate... ...four of the leading conservatives in the Senate... ...the Senate Armed Services Committee.* N SING: the+N ⇑ legislature
2 Senate or the **Senate** is also the main governing council in some universities. EG *...interference from Senate in the affairs of the department.* N SING: the+N, OR N UNCOUNT ⇑ committee

senator /sɛnətə/, **senators**. A **senator** is a member of a law-making Senate, for example in Australia or the U.S.A. EG *...three of the senators who signed last week's resolution... ...Senator Edward Kennedy.* N COUNT: ALSO IN TITLE ⇑ politician

senatorial /sɛnətɔːrɪəl/ means belonging to or relating to a Senate; a formal word. EG *...a senatorial investigation.* ADJ CLASSIF: ATTRIB

send /sɛnd/, **sends, sending, sent**. **1** When you **send** something to someone, you arrange for it to be taken and delivered to them, for example by the postal service. EG *The children used to send me a card at Christmas... I promised I would send her the money... You will be sent a timetable of the election... I drafted a letter and sent it up to the President... You'd better send it round in the morning.* V+O+O, OR V+O+A
• If you **send word** about something, you send a message about it. EG *He sent word that he wouldn't be coming.* • PHR: VB INFLECTS, USU+about/REPORT-CL
2 If you **send** a radio signal or message, you cause it to be carried from one place to another by means of radio waves. EG *Marconi succeeded in sending a signal across the Atlantic... ...the pictures that the satellite was sending back.* V+O: USU+A = transmit
3 If you **send** someone somewhere, **3.1** you tell them to go there. EG *The doctor sent me to a specialist... Could you send someone round to fix the washing machine?... Immediate reinforcements were sent from North America.* V+O+A = dispatch **3.2** you arrange for them to stay there for a period of time. EG *The courts are now sending fewer offenders to prison... His parents couldn't afford to send him to university.* V+O+A
4 If you **send** someone **packing**, you tell them to go away; an informal expression. EG *If you carry on like that, you'll soon be sent packing.* PHR: send INFLECTS = dismiss
5 If something **sends** things or people in a particular direction, it causes them to move in that direction, often rapidly or suddenly. EG *The bomb exploded, sending lethal fragments flying in all directions... The stubble was burning in the fields, sending wisps of black smoke into the air... This product will send competitors scurrying to their labs.* V+O+A, OR V+O+-ING ⇑ drive
6 If something **sends** you into a particular state, it causes you to be in that state. EG *His lessons used to send me to sleep... This sent us all into fits of laughter.* V+O+A ⇑ put

send down. If a student **is sent down**, he or she is made to leave a university or college because of bad behaviour; used in British English. PHRASAL VB: V+O+ADV, USU PASS = expel

send for. **1** If you **send for** someone, you ask them PHRASAL VB:

to come and see you, by sending them a message. EG *She sent for a doctor... I think we'd better send for the police.* PREP, HAS PASS = summon

2 If you **send for** something or **send off for** it, you ask for it to be sent to you, by sending a request for it. EG *Do you remember where to send off for the replacements?... I'm going to send for their new catalogue.* PHRASAL VB : V+PREP, HAS PASS ⇑ order

send in. 1 If you **send in** something such as a report or an application, you send it to a place where it can be officially dealt with. EG *Don't forget to send in your entries for the competition... I was expected to send in a written report every two months.* PHRASAL VB : V+O+ADV = submit

2 When a group of people, especially soldiers or police, **are sent in**, they are sent to a place in order to deal with a dangerous or difficult situation. EG *We decided it was time to send in British troops... They sent in the riot police to break up the demonstration.* PHRASAL VB : V+O+ADV

send off. 1 If you **send off** a letter, parcel, etc, you send it somewhere using the postal system or a similar service. EG *You fill in both parts of the form, then send it off... From the city's main post office he sent off two angry telegrams... We sent a consignment off on this morning's train.* PHRASAL VB : V+O+ADV

2 If a football player **is sent off**, the player is made to leave the field during a game as a punishment for seriously breaking the rules. EG *Two players were involved in a violent incident, and the referee sent them both off.* PHRASAL VB : V+O+ADV ⇑ punish

send on. If your mail **is sent on** to you, it is sent to your new address after it has been delivered to your former address. EG *If they post the money to you here, I'll send it on to you... Shall we send your letters on or keep them till you get back?* PHRASAL VB : V+O+ADV = forward

send up. If you **send** someone or something **up**, you imitate them in a way that makes them appear foolish; an informal expression. ● See also **send-up**. PHRASAL VB : V+O+ADV ⇑ ridicule

sender /sendə/, **senders.** The **sender** of a letter, parcel, etc is the person who sends it. EG *The sender's name and address should be written on the back.* N COUNT

send-off, send-offs. A **send-off** is an occasion when people come together to say goodbye to someone who is starting a journey or going away to live in another place; an informal expression. EG *They certainly gave us a fine send-off.* N COUNT = farewell

send-up, send-ups. A **send-up** is a piece of writing or acting in which a person or practice is imitated in a way that makes them appear foolish in order to amuse other people; an informal expression. N COUNT = parody

Senegalese /senɪgəliːz/. **Senegalese** is both the singular and the plural form. 1 Something that is **Senegalese** belongs or relates to Senegal or to its people. EG *...the Senegalese Four-Year Plan.* ADJ CLASSIF

2 A **Senegalese** is a person who comes from Senegal. EG *One hundred and seven Senegalese were working in the foundry.* N COUNT

senile /siːnaɪl/. When old people become **senile**, they become confused, can no longer remember things, and are unable to look after themselves. EG *The old lady was half-blind and nearly senile... Mildred told him he was getting senile... He evidently regarded me as a senile old idiot.* ◊ **senility** /sənɪlɪti[1]/. EG *Sheila became increasingly affected by senility.* ADJ CLASSIF ◊ N UNCOUNT

senior /siːnjə/, **seniors.** 1 The **senior** people in an army or in another organization are the people who have the highest and most important jobs in it. EG *...an attempted coup in which senior officers were involved... There are separate dining rooms for staff, middle management, and senior management.* ▸ used of the posts these people hold. EG *The right wing now held nine out of twelve senior cabinet posts... Another post was advertised which was more senior, so I applied for that.* ADJ QUALIT

2 If someone is **senior** to you in an organization, **2.1** they have a higher and more important job than you. EG *Although he only joined the firm last year he's senior to me already.* ADJ QUALIT : IF+PREP THEN *to* ≠ junior **2.2** they have worked there longer than you and so are considered to be superior to you because or their greater experience. EG *He's senior to me in experience and length of service.* ADJ QUALIT : IF+PREP THEN *to* ⇑ superior

3 If someone is your **senior**, they are older than you are. EG *She was at least fifteen years his senior.* N SING : POSS+N ≠ junior

4 At a school or college, the **seniors** are the pupils or students who are older and have reached an advanced level in their studies. EG *Harland, who was now a senior at the school, was unfailingly kind to me... She gave civics lessons at high schools where the seniors were eligible to vote.* N COUNT

senior citizen, senior citizens. A **senior citizen** is an old person, especially someone who is old enough to receive an old-age pension.. EG *...free bus travel for senior citizens.* N COUNT

seniority /siːni[1]ɒrɪti[1]/. A person's **seniority** in an organization is their degree of importance and power compared to other people who work there. EG *The size of office will vary according to your seniority... Those with the least seniority do most of the routine work... The report listed their names in order of seniority.* N UNCOUNT ⇑ status

sensation /sɛnseɪʃə[0]n/, **sensations.** 1 **Sensation** is your ability to feel things physically, especially through your sense of touch. EG *He had no sensation in his right leg... Clearly, all sensation wasn't lost.* N UNCOUNT ⇑ faculty = feeling

2 A **sensation** is **2.1** a physical feeling. EG *This gave her a sharp tingling sensation that ran through her whole body... It produces a mild burning sensation in the mouth.* N COUNT **2.2** a general feeling or impression caused by a particular experience. EG *It was a strange sensation to return to the school again after so long... She had the sensation that she had done all this before.* N COUNT **2.3** an event or situation which causes great excitement or interest. EG *The film was an overnight sensation... The discovery was hailed as the scientific sensation of the century.* ▸ used also of the excitement or interest caused. EG *The news caused a sensation.* N COUNT ▸ N SING WITH DET = stir

sensational /sɛnseɪʃə[0]nəl, -ʃənə[0]l/. 1 Something that is **sensational** is so remarkable that it causes great excitement and public interest. EG *This is the most sensational result of any election since the war... ...a sensational discovery.* ◊ **sensationally.** EG *De Gaulle had just sensationally announced his recognition of Red China.* ADJ QUALIT ⇑ exciting = electrifying ◊ ADV WITH VB = dramatically

2 A **sensational** report in a newspaper presents the facts in a way that is intended to produce strong feelings of shock, anger, or excitement; used showing disapproval. EG *The newspapers carried sensational reports of a shark attack.* ◊ **sensationally.** EG *They complained that the story had been rather sensationally reported.* ADJ QUALIT ⇑ exaggerated ◊ ADV

3 You also describe something as **sensational** when you think that it is extremely good; an informal use. EG *I've discovered a sensational health-food store.* ◊ **sensationally.** EG *Edith Evans was sensationally good.* ADJ QUALIT = terrific ◊ ADV

sensationalism /sɛnseɪʃə[0]nəlɪzə[0]m/ is presentation of facts in a way that is intended to produce strong feelings of shock, anger, or excitement; used showing disapproval. EG *Many people were affronted by the Post's resort to sensationalism and scandal.* ◊ **sensationalist, sensationalists.** EG *He was a sensationalist and a showman... The Chronicle was criticized for being sensationalist.* N UNCOUNT ◊ N COUNT, OR ADJ QUALIT : USU PRED

sense /sɛns/, **senses, sensing, sensed.** 1 Your **senses** are the physical powers that make it possible for you to know about things outside your own mind and body. You have five senses. They are your senses of sight, smell, hearing, touch, and taste. EG *All knowledge comes to us through our senses... These dogs have an excellent sense of smell... For these men, sight was the most important sense.* ● See also **sixth sense**. N COUNT ⇑ faculty

2 If you **sense** something, you become aware of it or realize that it is going to happen, often in an unconscious way and without receiving any direct information. EG *Doctors often sense uneasiness in the people they deal with... He sensed that she did not want to talk to him... The assembly, sensing a crisis, was tensely expectant... He was at last beginning to sense what the trouble was.* V+O/REPORT-CL = feel

3 If you have a **sense** of something such as duty or justice, you believe that it is valuable or important. EG *She has a strong sense of justice... Surely one must have some sense of right and wrong... They seem to have an exaggerated sense of their own importance.* N SING WITH DET +SUPP = awareness

4 If you have a **sense** of something such as freedom or independence, you feel that you are free, independent, etc. EG *Living away from home had given her a sense of independence... I was overcome by a sense of failure.* N SING WITH DET +*of* = feeling

5 If you have a **sense** that something is happening or that something is true, you believe as a result of your experiences that it is happening or true. EG *His reply* N SING WITH DET +REPORT-CL ⇑ feeling

left me with the sense that we would never reach agreement.

6 A **sense** is also a natural ability or talent for something. EG *She had a wonderful sense of humour... A good sense of timing is important for an actor... He hasn't got much dress sense... She has very good business sense.* • **sense of direction**: see **direction**. N SING WITH DET + SUPP = appreciation

7 **Sense** is the ability to make good judgements and to behave in a practical and reasonable way. EG *She had the good sense to realize that the plan would never work... I thought he would have had more sense than to do a thing like that... Your friends have more money than sense.* N UNCOUNT = brains

8 If you say that there is **no sense** or **little sense** in doing something, you mean that nothing useful would be gained by doing it. EG *There's no sense in making people unhappy... There would be little sense in analysing the reasons for our defeat... I can't see much sense in what they're doing.* PHR + *in* : WITH BROAD NEG = no point

9 **make sense**. **9.1** If something **makes sense**, you can understand it. EG *A sentence must make sense... I looked at the printed page but the words made no sense.* PHR : VB INFLECTS **9.2** When you **make sense** of something, you succeed in understanding it. EG *You had to read it six times to make any sense of it... Children need to make sense of the world... He could not make sense of his parents' moods.* PHR : VB INFLECTS + *of* **9.3** If you say that someone **makes sense** or **talks sense**, you mean that they are saying wise or sensible things. EG *On defence matters he talked a great deal of sense.* PHR : VB INFLECTS **9.4** If a course of action **makes sense**, it seems reasonable and practical. EG *Under these conditions it made sense to adopt labour-saving methods... It often makes hard economic sense to borrow extra money.* PHR : VB INFLECTS

10 The **sense** of something spoken or written is its general meaning. EG *They talked rather fast, making it very difficult for her to grasp the sense of what they were saying... He didn't understand every word, but he got the sense of it.* N SING : *the* + N, IF + PREP THEN *of* = substance

11 A **sense** of a word or expression is one of its possible meanings. EG *He may not be lying in the strict sense of the word, but he is certainly hiding something from us.... I don't like the Washington climate–in all senses of the word.* N COUNT + *of*

12 The word **sense** is also used in the following expressions. **12.1** If you say that something is true **in a sense**, you mean that it is partly true, or that it is true according to one possible interpretation of the situation. EG *This may, in a sense, be true... We are, in a sense, being deceitful... In a sense, I still love him... In a sense, the whole book is a commentary on the sixties.* PHR : USED AS ADV SEN **12.2** You say **in a very real sense** in order to emphasize that something is true. EG *This is what we aimed to do, and in a very real sense we have succeeded.* PHR : USED AS ADV SEN **12.3** You say **in no sense** in order to emphasize that something is not true at all. EG *They have in no sense been elected to represent the nation.* PHR : USED AS ADV SEN

13 The word **senses** is used to refer to a person's normal state of mind, especially in the following expressions. **13.1** If you say that someone has **taken leave of** their **senses**, you mean that they are behaving as if they have gone mad; a rather old-fashioned expression. EG *Have you taken leave of your senses?* PHR : VB INFLECTS **13.2** If you say that someone has **come to** their **senses** or **been brought to** their **senses**, you mean that they have stopped behaving in a foolish way and are acting sensibly again. EG *They were waiting for me to come to my senses and realize that I was wrong... I hope this warning will bring him to his senses.* PHR : VB INFLECTS

14 See also **common sense**.

senseless /sɛnslɪ²s/. 1 You describe an action as **senseless** when it seems to have no meaning or purpose; used showing disapproval. EG *It was a senseless thing to do... He made senseless expeditions to India.... ...some senseless act of cruelty to a pet animal.* ◊ **senselessly**. EG *They had senselessly destroyed the original.* ◊ **senselessness**. EG *She condemned the sheer senselessness of the attack.* ADJ QUALIT = pointless, futile; ◊ ADV WITH VB; ◊ N UNCOUNT

2 When someone is **senseless**, they are unconscious. EG *He collapsed on the floor and lay there senseless... A heavy blow with a club knocked him senseless.* ADJ CLASSIF

sensibility /sɛnsɪbɪlɪti¹/, **sensibilities**. Someone's **sensibility** is 1 their ability to experience deep feelings and often to express their understanding of those feelings, for example in literature or art. EG *The film tells the story of her developing sensibility against the background of the war... ...a writer of high sensibility and intelligence.* N UNCOUNT + SUPP, OR N UNCOUNT : POSS + N **2** a tendency that they have to be easily influenced or offended by things that other people say or do. EG *...his sensibility to criticism... We have to be careful not to offend our readers' sensibilities.* N UNCOUNT/COUNT : USU + SUPP = sensitivity

sensible /sɛnsɪbə⁰l/. 1 A **sensible** person is able to make good decisions and judgements that are based on reasons rather than emotions. EG *She was far too sensible a person to believe these ridiculous lies.* ▸ used of actions and behaviour. EG *It seemed sensible to move to bigger premises when the company started expanding... I think that's the most sensible thing to do... ...sensible decisions.* ◊ **sensibly**. EG *They quite sensibly concluded that this wouldn't be a good idea... Try to use your time sensibly.* ADJ QUALIT ⇑ wise = rational; ◊ ADV WITH VB = intelligently

2 Clothes that are **sensible** are practical and strong rather than fashionable and attractive. EG *She invariably wore 'sensible' clothes and plain shoes... Those shoes aren't very sensible for walking.* ADJ QUALIT = functional

sensitise /sɛnsɪtaɪz/. See **sensitize**.

sensitive /sɛnsɪtɪv/. 1 If you are **sensitive** to things such as artistic ideas or other people's feelings and problems, you show a deep understanding and awareness of them. EG *We're trying to make people more sensitive to the problems faced by working mothers... ...if you are sensitive enough to realise your own shortcomings... ...a sensitive story about the problems of growing up.* ◊ **sensitively**. EG *...this well acted, sensitively directed play.* ◊ **sensitivity** /sɛnsɪtɪvɪti¹/. EG *Her remarks showed a lack of sensitivity to the problems of the unemployed... ...new sensitivities to colour and form.* ADJ QUALIT : IF + PREP THEN *to* = perceptive; ◊ ADV WITH VB; ◊ N COUNT/UNCOUNT

2 If you are **sensitive** about something, you are easily offended about it and often worried about it. EG *You really must stop being so sensitive about your accent... Some parents are sensitive about advice from their children's teachers... ...sensitive to criticism.* ◊ **sensitivity, sensitivities**. EG *I don't want to insult your sensitivities.* ADJ QUALIT : IF + PREP THEN *about/to* = touchy, open; ◊ N COUNT/UNCOUNT

3 A **sensitive** subject or issue involves difficult problems and is likely to cause deep disagreement or strong feelings. EG *This is one of the most sensitive issues that the government faces... The president has overriding authority only in a few politically sensitive areas... The conference debated the sensitive issue of race relations.* ◊ **sensitivity**. EG *...an issue of great sensitivity.* ADJ QUALIT = delicate, prickly; ◊ N UNCOUNT = delicacy

4 Something that is **sensitive** to a physical force, substance, or condition is easily affected by it and quickly shows its effect. EG *...people with sensitive skin... Children's bones and organs are very sensitive to radiation.* ◊ **sensitivity**. EG *This condition may affect the sensitivity of the lining of the nasal cavity.* ADJ QUALIT : IF + PREP THEN *to* = susceptible; ◊ N UNCOUNT ⇑ delicacy

5 A **sensitive** piece of scientific equipment is capable of measuring very small changes or of reacting to physical impressions that are difficult to detect, such as sounds or light rays. EG *...highly sensitive electronic cameras... We didn't have a sensitive enough receiver to pick up the signal... The thermometer is so sensitive that it responds to even the slightest rise in temperature.* ◊ **sensitivity**. EG *...the enormous sensitivity of these devices.* ADJ QUALIT = delicate, exact; ◊ N UNCOUNT = precision

sensitize /sɛnsɪtaɪz/, **sensitizes, sensitizing, sensitized**; also spelled **sensitise**. 1 If you **sensitize** people to a particular problem or situation, you make them aware of it; a formal use. EG *Hinkle has worked for years to sensitize the medical profession to the importance of this.* V + O : USU PASS IF + PREP THEN *to* ⇑ alert

2 If a material **is sensitized** to a physical effect such as light or touch, it is made sensitive to it. EG *...writing on a sensitised electronic pad.* V + O : USU PASS IF + PREP THEN *to*

sensor /sɛnsə/, **sensors**. A **sensor** is an instrument which reacts to certain physical conditions or impressions such as heat or light, and which is used to provide information. EG *Information gathered by sensors is transmitted to the control centre's computer.* N COUNT ⇑ device

sensory /sɛnsə⁰ri¹/ is used to describe things that relate to the five physical senses; a formal word. EG *All knowledge comes from sensory impressions... With these two highly developed sensory organs it hunts at night for insects.* ADJ CLASSIF : ATTRIB

sensual /sɛnsjʊ⁰əl/. 1 If someone or something is **sensual**, they show or suggest a great liking for pleasures that are experienced through the physical ADJ QUALIT ⇑ hedonistic senses, especially sexual pleasures. EG ...*an extravagantly sensual woman... He led a wickedly sensual life... ...plump sensual lips.* ◇ **sensuality** /sɛnsjuælɪti[1]/. EG *Cindy's anger was forgotten in a wave of sensuality which engulfed them.* ◇ N UNCOUNT

2 Something that is **sensual** gives pleasure to a person's physical senses and feelings rather than to their mind or soul. EG ...*the subtle, sensual rhythms of the drums.* ◇ **sensuality.** EG *They luxuriated in the sensuality of the silks and other materials.* ADJ QUALIT ◇ N UNCOUNT

sensuous /sɛnsjuəs/. Something that is **sensuous** gives pleasure to the mind or body through the senses. EG *Sculpture is a sensuous art... ...her deep red sensuous lips.* ◇ **sensuously.** EG *Her fingers sensuously stroked his neck.* ADJ QUALIT ◇ ADV WITH VB

sent /sɛnt/ is the past tense and past participle of **send.**

sentence /sɛntəns/, **sentences, sentencing, sentenced. 1** A **sentence** is a group of words which, when they are written down, begin with a capital letter and end with a full stop. EG *Most of them could read a simple sentence in English... The government's failure is admitted in the opening sentence of the report... He put the phone down before she could finish the sentence.* N COUNT ⇑ unit

2 In a law court, a **sentence** that a person receives is the punishment that they receive after being found guilty of a crime. EG *If they are found guilty they will face a sentence of ten years in prison... She had been found guilty but sentence had not yet been passed... He is at present serving a life sentence for murder... ...a death sentence.* N COUNT/UNCOUNT ⇑ penalty

3 When a judge **sentences** someone, he or she states in court what their punishment will be. EG *From 1861 to 1958, 431 women were sentenced to death in England and Wales... The judge sentenced him to ten years' imprisonment... They were sentenced to be hanged.* V+O : IF+PREP/VB THEN *to/to-INF* ⇑ condemn

4 If people **are sentenced** to a particular unpleasant condition, they are forced to suffer the condition. EG *It was the signal of hope to millions of people sentenced to suffer poverty in their home country... Are they going to be sentenced to a lifetime of unemployment?* V+O+A *(to)*: USU PASS = condemn, doom

sentence adverb, sentence adverbs. In grammar, a **sentence adverb** is an adverb which comments on the whole clause or sentence rather than on a single word. Sentence adverbs usually express the speaker's or writer's personal opinion. In this dictionary the abbreviation ADV SEN is used in the grammar notes beside entries to mean 'sentence adverb'. See □ at ADV SEN. N COUNT

sententious /sɛntɛnʃəs/. Someone who is **sententious** tries to say things that sound wise and often makes judgements about moral questions; a formal word. ▸ used of speech. EG ...*sententious remarks.* ◇ **sententiously.** EG *'Well, you must persevere,' said Fanny sententiously.* ADJ QUALIT = moralistic ◇ ADV WITH VB

sentient /sɛntɪənt/. Something that is **sentient** is capable of experiencing sensations through the physical senses; a formal word. EG ...*sentient creatures.* ADJ CLASSIF

sentiment /sɛntɪmə[2]nt/, **sentiments. 1** A particular **sentiment** that people have is an attitude that they have which is based on a mixture of thoughts and feelings. EG *These events led to a vast upsurge of anti-imperialist sentiment... The issue has aroused strong public sentiment... ...social conflicts out of which revolutionary sentiments have begun to grow.* N UNCOUNT/COUNT+SUPP = feeling

2 Someone's **sentiment** is an idea or feeling that they express in words. EG *These sentiments were generally echoed by other speakers at the meeting... ...an admirable and very shrewdly phrased sentiment.* N COUNT : PL=SING ⇑ meaning = opinion

3 Sentiment is an emotion such as tenderness, romance, or sadness, which influences a person's behaviour and is sometimes considered to be exaggerated to a foolish extent. EG *I'm worried that you might be doing it out of sentiment. Out of affection for me... He scorns sentiment and emotion.* N UNCOUNT ⇑ feeling

sentimental /sɛntɪmɛntə[0]l/. **1** Someone or something that is **sentimental** feels or arouses emotions such as tenderness, romance, or sadness, sometimes to an extent which is considered exaggerated and foolish. EG ...*sentimental songs... People have become sentimental about the passing of ways and customs... I got a bit sentimental remembering the old days.* ◇ **sentimentally.** EG *Romantic love and motherhood are sentimentally idealized.* ◇ **sentimentality** /sɛntɪmɛntælɪti[1]/. EG ...*sentimentality about animals... ...softened by charm and over-sweetened by sentimentality.* ADJ QUALIT = mawkish, soppy ◇ ADV WITH VB ◇ N UNCOUNT = sentiment

2 Sentimental is used to relate to something that affects or concerns a person's emotions. EG *The ring had been her mother's and she wore it for sentimental reasons.* ◇ **sentimentally.** EG *He had become sentimentally attached to a postgraduate student.* ADJ CLASSIF ◇ ADV WITH VB

sentimentalize /sɛntɪmɛntəlaɪz/, **sentimentalizes, sentimentalizing, sentimentalized;** also spelled **sentimentalise.** If you **sentimentalize** something or if you **sentimentalize,** you make something seem sentimental or think about it in a sentimental way; a formal word. EG *This image was distorted and sentimentalized by the press.* V OR V+O ⇑ romanticize

sentinel /sɛntɪnə[0]l/, **sentinels.** A **sentinel** is a sentry; a rather old-fashioned word. EG *Sentinels were placed at all the approaches to the farm... ...sentinel duties.* N COUNT ⇑ guard

sentry /sɛntri[1]/, **sentries.** A **sentry** is a soldier whose job is to guard a place such as a camp or building, especially one who stands at the entrance. EG ...*look-out posts where sentries kept watch... Who is on sentry duty tonight?* N COUNT

sentry box, sentry boxes. A **sentry box** is a narrow shelter with an open front in which a sentry can stand while on duty. EG *In the twin sentry boxes, the two troopers of the Household Regiment stand guard.* N COUNT

Sep. is an abbreviation for September.

separable /sɛpə[0]rəbə[0]l/. If things are **separable,** they can be separated from each other. EG *There may be some parts which seem separable from the whole.* ADJ CLASSIF : IF+PREP THEN *from* ⇑ divisible = distinct

separate, separates, separating, separated. The word **separate** is pronounced /sɛpə[0]rət/ when it is an adjective or a noun, and /sɛpəreɪt/ when it is a verb. **1** If one thing is **separate** from another, the two things are apart from each other rather than joined or connected to each other. EG *Rosa had remained separate from us, asking for a room by herself... Two masses can be kept separate inside the bomb casing... They left the party in 1963 to form the first separate Maoist group in Britain.* ◇ **separately.** EG *What we achieve together is more important than what we can do separately.* ◇ **separateness.** EG ...*the age of individualism, when separateness has become a playwright's cliché.* ADJ CLASSIF : IF+PREP THEN *from* ◇ ADV WITH VB ◇ N UNCOUNT

2 Things that are **separate** are distinct from each other; often used to show that you are considering each member of a group of things individually. EG *The sunlight caught each tiny separate hair and made it shine like gold... Babies feed eagerly for two separate reasons... There are three separate coverings around the brain itself.* ◇ **separately.** EG *I remember each one of them separately... Wash each pile separately.* ● If two or more people who are together in a group **go** their **separate ways,** they go to different places and do not see each other any more. EG *It is awful to think that when we graduate we shall all go our separate ways.* ADJ CLASSIF ⇑ individual = different ◇ ADV WITH VB ● PHR : VB INFLECTS ⇑ part = drift apart

3 Separates are clothes such as skirts, trousers, and shirts that only cover half your body, unlike a dress or suit. N PLURAL

4 If you **separate** two or more people or things, you move them or keep them apart from each other so that they are not connected or cannot communicate. EG *These three parts have always been separated... Even at dinner time we were separated; she ate in one place, and I ate in another... In any hot discussion he would separate the opponents and soothe them.* V+O, OR V+O+A *(from)* : RECIP ⇑ divide = move apart

5 If you **separate** two or more ideas from each other, you consider them or present them individually and show the distinction between them. EG *Faith and God to me are the same thing, I can't separate them... Myth and history cannot be separated... It is important to separate learning English orally from learning English by reading books.* V+O, OR V+O+A *(from)* : RECIP ⇑ divide

6 If one thing has a detail or aspect that **separates** it from another thing, this detail shows that it is different from the other thing. EG *Higher living standards separate the older generation from their children... It wasn't their talk which separated them from the gentry, it was their meanness.* V+O+A *(from)* = distinguish, divide

7 If a physical object, a period of time, or a stretch of V+O : USU+A space **separates** two people, groups, or things, it exists between them and prevents them from having contact with each other. EG *An old fence at the back of the garden separated us from the neighbours... ...the Great Lakes separating Canada from America... ...two equivalent groups separated by a mere century of technological advance.* (from) ⇑ divide

8 If you **separate** a group of things or if you **separate** the things **out**, you divide them so that each different part becomes separate. EG *Most schools decide to separate out their pupils into different groups according to age... ...separating out bits of paper, some white, some orange... Separate this up again into its bits.* V+O, OR PHRASAL VB : V+O+ADV

9 If a group of people or things **separate**, they move away from each other after being together or connected for a time. EG *The three of them separated at the corner... They talked by the gate, unwilling to separate... The two rods separated from each other.* V OR V+A (from) : RECIP ⇑ part = break away

10 If you **separate** from another person or group, you go away from them. EG *Carson separated from him at the door.* V+A (from) ⇑ leave = part from

11 If a couple who are married or living together **separate**, they begin to live apart. Couples usually separate before they get divorced. EG *Her parents separated when she was eleven... I'm separating from him.* V : IF+PREP THEN from ⇑ part = break up

12 When certain smooth liquids **separate**, they become a mixture of solid lumps and thin, watery liquid; used for example of milk that has been left for a few days. V

13 If you **separate** an egg, you break it over a bowl so that the white all goes into the bowl but the yolk stays in the shell, ready for you to use separately. V+O

separated /sɛpəreɪtɪ²d/. Someone who is **separated** from their wife or husband lives apart from them, but is not divorced. EG *My wife and I are separated.* ADJ CLASSIF : PRED

▸ The **separated** is used to refer to people who are separated. EG *The divorced and separated have the highest suicide rates among women.* ▸ N PLURAL : the+N

separation /sɛpəreɪʃə⁰n/, **separations**. 1 The **separation** of two or more people, things, or groups is their movement away from each other or their state of being kept apart from each other. EG *The bourgeoisie were simply cut off from the peasants by their physical separation in the towns. ...the separation of infant from mother.* N UNCOUNT : USU +of ⇑ partition, break

2 A **separation** between two or more people is a period of time that they spend apart from each other. EG *Children recover remarkably quickly from a brief separation from parents... Separation does not end all relationships.* N COUNT/UNCOUNT ⇑ break

3 If a couple who are married or living together have a **separation**, they begin to live apart. EG *Last night we talked about a separation.* N COUNT/UNCOUNT ⇑ parting

4 If you make a **separation** between two things, people, or groups, you consider them or present them individually and show the distinction between them. EG *I don't think that the separation of politics and religion is actually a valid process.* N UNCOUNT/COUNT : USU+ between/of ⇑ division

5 A **separation** is also a mark, object, period of time, or amount of space that separates things from each other. N COUNT ⇑ division

separatism /sɛpə⁰rətɪzə⁰m/ consists of the aims or beliefs of an ethnic or cultural group of people within a country who want to establish their own separate government instead of being ruled by the existing government of the country. EG *Ukrainian separatism was beginning to stir.* ◊ **separatist, separatists**. EG *...the Basque separatist movement... The central government took fright at this separatist trend.* N UNCOUNT = autonomy ◊ N COUNT : USU MOD

sepia /siːpɪə/. Something that is **sepia** is deep brown in colour, like the colour of very old photographs. EG *...a sepia print of Reynolds' 'Age of Innocence'... ...sepia photographs of Paignton.* ADJ COLOUR

Sept. is an abbreviation for September.

September /sɛptɛmbə/ is the ninth month of the year in the Western calendar. EG *Gladys died on September 27th, 1976.* N UNCOUNT

septic /sɛptɪk/. If a wound or a part of your body is **septic**, it is infected as a result of bacteria getting into your body through a cut or burn. EG *The scar showed no sign of going septic... ...a septic throat... ...septic poisoning.* ADJ CLASSIF

septic tank, septic tanks. A **septic tank** is an underground tank where faeces, urine, and other waste matter is made harmless using bacteria. N COUNT ⇑ cesspit

septuagenarian /sɛptjuᵒədʒɪnɛərɪən/, **septuagenarians**. A **septuagenarian** is a person who is between seventy and seventy-nine years old; a fairly formal word. N COUNT

sepulchral /sɪ²pʌlkrə⁰l/. Something that is **sepulchral** is gloomy and solemn; a literary word. EG *The man asked me, in a sepulchral tone, if I believed in the Lord... There was a rather sepulchral atmosphere in the room.* ADJ QUALIT = funereal, sombre

sepulchre /sɛpəlkə/, **sepulchres**; also spelled **sepulcher** in American English. A **sepulchre** is a large tomb in which a dead person is buried; a literary word. N COUNT

sequel /siːkwə⁰l/, **sequels**. 1 A **sequel** to a book, play, or film is one which continues the story that was told in an earlier book, play, or film. EG *The first book had been an enormous success, but the sequel was much less popular... He starred in 'The Godfather' and in its sequel, 'The Godfather II'.* N COUNT; IF+ PREP THEN to = follow-up

2 A **sequel** to something that has happened is an event or situation that happens after it, or as a result of it. EG *The fight for Irish independence had a grim sequel in the streets of Belfast... There was a strange sequel to these events.* N COUNT : IF+ PREP THEN to = consequence, development

sequence /siːkwə⁰ns/, **sequences**. 1 A **sequence** is 1.1 a number of things or events that come one after another in a fixed order or according to a definite pattern, usually moving in stages towards a particular result. EG *We discussed the strange sequence of events that led up to the murder... The book contains a sequence of carefully arranged lessons in computer programming.* 1.2 the particular order or pattern in which things or events follow one another. EG *I completed all the calculations in the correct sequence... The paintings are exhibited in a more or less chronological sequence.* N COUNT+of ⇑ series; N COUNT, OR in/out of+N

2 A film **sequence** is a part of a film that shows a single event or set of actions. EG *What did you think of that ghastly sequence at the end when she strangles him?* N COUNT = scene

sequential /sɪ¹kwɛnʃə⁰l/. Something that is **sequential** follows a fixed order and thus forms a pattern; a formal word. EG *...sequential mental processes... She wanted to find some sequential link.* ADJ CLASSIF

sequester /sɪ¹kwɛstə/, **sequesters, sequestering, sequestered**. When property **is sequestered**, it is taken officially from someone who has debts, usually after a judgement in a court of law. When the debts are paid off, the property is returned to its owner. EG *The Emperor's troops were disarmed and his mother's estate sequestered.* V+O : USU PASS = sequestrate

sequestered /sɪ¹kwɛstəd/. A **sequestered** place is quiet, undisturbed, and far away from other people or places; a literary word. EG *...a lonely, sequestered village in the hills.* ADJ QUALIT = isolated, secluded

sequestrate /sɪ¹kwɛstreɪt/, **sequestrates, sequestrating, sequestrated**. When property **is sequestrated**, it is taken officially from someone who has debts, usually after a decision in a court of law. When the debts are paid off, the property is returned to its owner. ◊ **sequestration** /siːkwɛstreɪʃə⁰n/. EG *...the forcible sequestration of large estates.* V+O : USU PASS ⇑ seize = sequester ◊ N UNCOUNT

sequin /siːkwɪn/, **sequins**. **Sequins** are small, flat, round pieces of shiny metal or plastic that are sewn on clothes to decorate them. EG *...a dress embroidered with thousands of tiny sequins.* N COUNT ⇑ ornament = spangle

sequinned /siːkwɪnd/; also spelled **sequined** in American English. Something that is **sequinned** is covered or decorated with sequins. EG *...a blue sequinned evening dress.* ADJ CLASSIF

seraph /sɛrəf/, **seraphs, seraphim**. The plural can be either **seraphs** or **seraphim**. A **seraph** is one of the angels that guard God's throne, according to the Bible. N COUNT

Serbo-Croat /sɜːbəʊ krəʊæt/ is one of the languages spoken by people who live in Yugoslavia. N UNCOUNT

serenade /sɛrɪneɪd/, **serenades, serenading, serenaded**. 1 If you **serenade** someone, you sing or play a piece of music for them. People sometimes do this outside the window of the person they love. EG *He serenaded her in the moonlight... We cuddled each other on the porch, serenaded by the dawn chorus of a thousand birds.* V+O

2 A **serenade** is 2.1 a song or piece of music that is performed outside in the evening, especially by a man under the window of a woman he loves. EG *He* N COUNT ⇑ tune

composed a serenade to a woman called Felicity. **2.2** a piece of classical music in several parts, written for a small orchestra. N COUNT ⇑ composition

serendipity /serendɪpɪti[1]/ is the natural talent that some people have for finding interesting or valuable things by chance; a formal word. EG *Friendship has got to be found, and it won't be found by serendipity. It has to be worked at.* N UNCOUNT

serene /sɪ'riːn/. Something that is **serene** is peaceful, quiet, and completely calm. EG *...a serene mountain landscape... There was a quiet, almost serene quality to the atmosphere.* ▸ used also of people and their expressions. EG *She had a naturally cheerful and serene expression... Her picture shows a face that is quite passive, almost serene.* ◊ **serenely**. EG *Her blue eyes gazed serenely into space.* ADJ QUALIT = tranquil ▸ ADJ QUALIT = composed ◊ ADV = placidly

serenity /sɪ'renɪti[1]/. If someone or something has the quality of **serenity**, they are peaceful, quiet, and calm. EG *She looked at the world with a detachment and a serenity that very few people have.* N UNCOUNT = tranquillity

serf /sɜːf/, **serfs**. **Serfs** were a class of people in medieval Europe who, although they were not slaves, had to work on their master's land and could not leave without his permission. EG *The nobles had oppressed and exploited their serfs.* N COUNT

serfdom /sɜːfdə[0]m/. **1** The system of **serfdom** was the social and economic system by which the land was cultivated by serfs. N UNCOUNT

2 If someone was in a state of **serfdom**, they were a serf. N UNCOUNT

serge /sɜːdʒ/ is a type of strong woollen cloth which is used to make coats, suits, trousers, or other clothes. EG *...a dark blue serge jacket.* N UNCOUNT

sergeant /sɑːdʒənt/, **sergeants**. **1** A **sergeant** in some military forces, such as the British army or air force, is a non-commissioned officer of middle rank. EG *...a group of four soldiers commanded by a sergeant... ...Sergeant Edwards... 'Is that clear, sergeant?' he asked.* N COUNT : ALSO IN TITLES ⇑ soldier

2 A **sergeant** in a police force is **2.1** in Britain, an officer with the rank above constable and below inspector. **2.2** in America, an officer with the rank above patrolman and below captain or lieutenant. N COUNT : ALSO IN TITLES N COUNT : ALSO IN TITLES

sergeant major, sergeant majors; also spelled with a hyphen. A **sergeant major** in some military forces, such as the British army, is a non-commissioned officer of the highest rank. N COUNT : ALSO IN TITLES

serial /sɪərɪəl/, **serials**. **1** A **serial** is a story on television or radio, or in a newspaper or magazine, which appears in a number of parts at regular times, such as once a week or once a day. EG *...one of the characters in Radio 4's endless serial about a farming family... The novel has recently been dramatized as a television serial... Many of Dickens' novels were published in serial form.* N COUNT

2 Serial means arranged in order or belonging to a series of things that come one after another. EG *Almost any machine that can be stolen has a serial number somewhere on it.* ADJ CLASSIF : ATTRIB ⇑ consecutive

serialization /sɪərɪəlaɪzeɪʃə[0]n/, **serializations**; also spelled **serialisation**. **1 Serialization** is the serializing of a book. N UNCOUNT

2 A **serialization** is a story, originally written as a book, which is being published or broadcast in a number of parts. EG *...a new serialization of a novel by Jane Austen.* N COUNT

serialize /sɪərɪəlaɪz/, **serializes, serializing, serialized**; also spelled **serialise**. If a book **is serialized**, it is published in a newspaper or magazine, or broadcast on the radio or television, in a number of parts. EG *His book 'Blood on the Snow' is currently being serialized on 'Woman's Hour'.* V+O : USU PASS

series /sɪəri[1]z/. **Series** is both the singular and the plural form. **1** A **series** of things or events is a number of things or events of the same kind that follow each other, often without any obvious pattern or order. EG *He was arrested in connection with a series of armed bank robberies... The region has suffered an unprecedented series of natural disasters.* N SING WITH DET : USU N+*of*+N IN PL = succession

2 A **series** of things or events, such as books, lectures, or concerts, is a group of them that are all related to each other or that are intended to form a complete set. EG *She was invited to deliver a series of lectures on American politics... He edits a sociology series for a paperback publisher.* N COUNT : ALSO N +*of*+N IN PL

3 A radio or television **series** is a set of programmes that deal with the same subject, especially a set of programmes that have the same characters but tell different stories. EG *He is the co-author of the popular television series, 'Yes, Minister'... ...a comedy series.* N COUNT

4 If parts of an electrical system are **in series**, they are connected in a single line, so that the current flows through each one in turn. EG *...a number of resistors in series.* PHR : USED AS AN A

serious /sɪərɪəs/. **1** Problems or situations that are **serious** are very bad and cause people to be worried or afraid. EG *Bad housing is one of the most serious problems in the inner cities... ...a serious illness... The situation is serious enough to warrant a special report.* ◊ **seriously**. EG *She was seriously ill... Cigarette smoking can seriously damage your health.* ◊ **seriousness**. EG *...the seriousness of the problem.* ADJ QUALIT = severe ◊ ADV = critically ◊ N UNCOUNT

2 Serious matters, suggestions, ideas, etc are important enough to deserve careful and thoughtful consideration. EG *I think this is a serious point... It's time to get down to the serious business of the meeting... They have become a serious political force... She is beginning to emerge as a serious candidate for the presidency.* ADJ QUALIT = earnest

3 When important matters are dealt with in a **serious** way, they are given a lot of thought and require concentration to understand or appreciate. EG *The programme is a forum for serious political discussion... ...a student of serious literature... ...a serious newspaper.* ◊ **seriously**. EG *...a play that deals seriously with the question of divorce.* ADJ CLASSIF : ATTRIB = earnest ◊ ADV WITH VB

4 When people and their behaviour are **serious**, they are sincere in what they say and do, and are not joking or pretending in any way. EG *They haven't really made a serious attempt to solve the problem... At first I thought he was continuing the joke, but he was serious... You can't be serious!* ◊ **seriously**. EG *We should begin to look seriously at the whole question of job sharing.* ◊ **seriousness**. EG *I see no reason, in all seriousness, why women should not become priests.* ADJ QUALIT : IF + PREP THEN *about* ⇑ sombre ◊ ADV ⇑ sombrely ◊ N UNCOUNT

5 People who are **serious** are thoughtful, quiet, and slightly humourless. EG *...a rather serious girl... She has a serious, thoughtful face... Don't look so serious!* ◊ **seriously**. EG *He talked very seriously and solemnly about theoretical matters.* ADJ QUALIT = earnest ◊ ADV WITH VB = solemnly

seriously /sɪərɪəsli[1]/. **1** You use the word **seriously** **1.1** when you want the person you are talking to to realize that you are not joking and that you mean what you say. EG *What I do think is important, quite seriously, is that people should know the facts.* **1.2** when you are surprised by what someone has said, as a way of asking them if they really mean it. EG *'I've given up my job.'–'Seriously?'* ADV SEN CONVENTION

2 If you **take** someone or something **seriously**, you believe that they are important and deserve to be treated with consideration and respect. EG *They have rarely been taken seriously as a political force in America... They take their responsibilities seriously... His work was not taken seriously.* PHR : VB INFLECTS

3 Other meanings of **seriously** can be found in the entry for **serious**.

sermon /sɜːmən/, **sermons**. A **sermon** is **1** a talk on a religious or moral subject that is given by a member of the clergy as part of a church service. EG *The vicar preached a sermon on the importance of humility.* **2** any long, serious talk in which someone tells other people how they should behave or what is right and wrong; usually used showing disapproval. EG *We have been overwhelmed by medical sermons preaching the lethal qualities of fats.* N COUNT ⇑ speech = homily N COUNT ⇑ speech = lecture

sermonize /sɜːmənaɪz/, **sermonizes, sermonizing, sermonized**; also spelled **sermonise**. If someone **is sermonizing**, they are giving people advice about how they should behave and what is right and wrong, although usually the people do not want the advice and are bored or annoyed by it; used showing disapproval. EG *He's always sermonizing.* ◊ **sermonizing**. EG *Why does she have to adopt this sermonising manner?... ...a piece of political sermonizing.* V = moralize, preach ◊ ADJ CLASSIF : ATTRIB, OR N UNCOUNT = moralizing

serpent /sɜːpənt/, **serpents**. A **serpent** is a snake; an old-fashioned or literary word. EG *...the serpent in the Garden of Eden.* N COUNT ⇑ reptile

serpentine /sɜːpəntaɪn/. Something that is **serpentine** is curving and winding in shape, like a snake when it moves; a literary word. EG *...a serpentine stream.* ADJ CLASSIF = coiling, sinuous

serrated /sɪ²reɪtɪ²d/. Something that is **serrated** has a row of V-shaped points along the edge, like a saw. EG *Serrated scissors grip what you are cutting... ...huge serrated leaves.* — ADJ CLASSIF : USU ATTRIB ⇑ notched

serried /sɛrɪd/ means closely crowded together in a regular arrangement; a fairly literary word. EG *The soldiers marched in serried ranks towards the depot... ...the serried red plumes of the Guards.* — ADJ CLASSIF : USU ATTRIB = dense, packed

serum /sɪərə⁰m/, **serums**. 1 **Serum** is the watery, pale yellow part of blood. — N UNCOUNT ⇑ liquid

2 A **serum** is a liquid that is taken from the blood of an animal which has become immune to a disease. The serum is injected into people's blood to prevent them from catching the disease. — N COUNT/ UNCOUNT = antitoxin

servant /sɜːvə⁰nt/, **servants**. 1 A **servant** is someone who is employed to work in another person's house, for example as a cleaner or gardener. EG *A servant came to the door and showed me in... She worked all her life as a domestic servant.* — N COUNT ⇑ employee = domestic

2 You can also use the word **servant** to refer to someone or something that can be used by people or that provides a service for them. EG *I feel that an MP is the servant of his constituents... Technology must become our servant, not our master.* ● See also **civil servant**. — N COUNT+SUPP

serve /sɜːv/, **serves, serving, served**. 1 If you **serve** something such as a company, community, or your country, you work for it or work in order to benefit it, usually for a long time. EG *We have been elected to serve the whole community, not just part of it... For over thirty years, she has served the company loyally and well... ...to organise the enquiry in a way to best serve the public interest.* — V+O

2 If you **serve** in a particular place, under a particular person, etc, you perform official duties of some kind, for example in the army or for the government. EG *He had served in France... The delegates serve for five years... ...the explorer Pinzon, who had served under Columbus... He served as an adviser to the Sultan of Oman.* — V+A

3 If one thing **serves** as or for something else, it is used for a particular purpose, often because nothing more satisfactory is available. EG *There was a long, grey building that served as a cafeteria... He was sitting at the plain table that served him for a desk.* — V+A *(as/for)*, OR V+O+A *(as/for)* ⇑ do

4 If something **serves** as a particular thing or **serves** to do something, it has the effect or result indicated. EG *This will serve as a valuable reminder of the dangers involved... This action merely serves as another example of the government's lack of compassion... His refusal to answer only serves to increase our suspicions.* — V+A *(as/for/ to-INF)*

5 If something **serves a purpose**, it helps achieve something useful. EG *I failed to see what purpose this could serve... It wasn't very good, but it would serve its purpose.* — PHR : VB INFLECTS

6 If something **serves** people or an area, it provides them with something that they need. EG *There were five water taps to serve all thirty camps... ...people who live or work in the area served by London Transport... She believes that we have been poorly served by the education system.* — V+O = cater for, supply

7 If you **serve** people or if you **serve** food and drink, you give them food and drink, for example in a restaurant, at a meal, or at a party. EG *When everybody had been served, the meal began... She drifted around serving drinks and engaging in casual conversation... She was served an elaborate ice-cream concoction.* — V, V+O, V+O+O, OR V+O+C (ADJ)

8 If a meal or recipe **serves** a particular number of people, it provides enough food for that number. EG *This recipe serves six.* — V+O : NO CONT

9 If someone **serves** customers in a shop, bar, etc, they help them and provide them with what they want to have or to buy. EG *The bartender refused to serve us because, he said, we looked too young... Are you being served?... She spent six months serving in a shop.* — V OR V+O = attend to

10 If you **serve** a legal document on someone or if you **serve** them with it, you deliver it to them. The document usually orders them to appear in a court of law or to do something that they have previously refused to do. EG *A House Committee tried to serve a subpoena on Harry Truman... The court served her with an enforcement notice.* — V+O+A *(on/ with)*

11 If you **serve** something such as a prison sentence or an apprenticeship, you spend a period of time doing it. EG *He is now serving a life sentence in an Italian jail... The pay increases after you have served a five-year apprenticeship... Does she want to serve another term as governor?* ● If someone **is serving time**, they are in prison; an informal expression. EG *She's serving time for terrorist offences.* — V+O = undergo; ● PHR : VB INFLECTS = do time

12 In tennis, badminton, and similar games, when you **serve**, you throw up the ball or shuttlecock and hit it as a way of starting play. EG *It's my turn to serve... She served an ace.* ▸ used as a noun. EG *Her second serve went into the net.* — V OR V+O; ▸ N COUNT/ UNCOUNT

13 If you say that someone has a good **serve**, a poor **serve**, etc, you mean that they serve well or badly when they are playing tennis, badminton, or a similar game. EG *He has a powerful serve.* — N SING WITH DET : ADJ+N = service

14 If you say that something **serves** someone **right**, you mean that what has happened is their own fault because they have behaved badly or stupidly. EG *'I feel terrible.'–'It serves you right for drinking so much last night.'... She said it served the boy right.* — PHR : VB INFLECTS, NO CONT

15 See also **serving**.

serve out. If you **serve out** food or **serve** it **up**, you give it to people during a meal. EG *Army kitchens serve up better fare than some hotels do... Shall I serve out the vegetables?* — PHRASAL VB : V+O+ADV = dish up

server /sɜːvə/, **servers**. A **server** is 1 a fork, spoon, or other tool used for serving food, especially food of a particular kind. EG *I banged the fish server against the side of the pan... ...salad servers.* 2 the player who is serving the ball or shuttlecock in a game of tennis, badminton, etc. — N COUNT : USU AFTER N ⇑ implement; N COUNT

service /sɜːvɪs/, **services, servicing, serviced**. 1 A **service** is 1.1 an organization or system that provides something which the public needs, especially transport, communications facilities, or information. EG *I think the train service is better than it used to be... We want to improve the productivity and profitability of the postal service... ...a local information service.* 1.2 an official organization or government department that does a particular job. EG *...the probation service... ...the diplomatic service... ...the intelligence services.* 1.3 a job or type of work that an organization or person can do for you if you want or need them to do it. EG *The post office can forward your letters; the fee for this service is 6 pounds... Customers will benefit from a new range of financial services... They provide a twenty-four-hour service... People often don't realize what services the library can offer.* 1.4 the army, navy, or air force. EG *The army is a voluntary service... He joined the Navy as a 16-year-old and spent 30 years in the service.* ▸ The **services** is used to refer to the army, the navy, and the air force, considered as a group. EG *Young people are being encouraged to join the services... ...service pay and conditions.* — N COUNT : MOD+N; N COUNT : MOD+N; N COUNT ⇑ provision; N COUNT; ▸ N PLURAL : the+N

2 **Services** are 2.1 things such as public transport, schools, hospitals, roads, etc that are paid for from people's rates and taxes and are controlled by the government. EG *The cuts to services were condemned by all delegates... ...social issues such as housing, rents and welfare services.* 2.2 all the jobs in which people are paid to do something for others rather than to make things. EG *The nation's economy is shifting increasingly to services and high-technology businesses... VAT will add 15 per cent to the total cost for goods and services... ...service industries.* — N PLURAL; N PLURAL ⇑ work

3 Someone's **services** are the things they do in their job, especially when these are regarded as special, useful, or important. EG *People skilled in these arts could command good fees for their services... They will be very happy to give their services free of charge... Sir Huw was knighted ten years ago for his services to television... Their services are no longer required.* — N PLURAL : WITH POSS ⇑ aid

4 **Service** is 4.1 the state or activity of working for a particular person or organization. EG *Conscription would be limited to a maximum of six months' service... He is keen to participate actively in any form of service to the community... He travelled from village to village in the service of Allah.* 4.2 the work or fighting that someone does in the army, navy, or air force. EG *He was too young for service in the Second World War... He had seen plenty of service in the armoured cavalry.* 4.3 the process of being served in a shop, restaurant, etc; used also in saying whether you are served well or badly. EG *He* — N UNCOUNT; N UNCOUNT = action; N UNCOUNT ⇑ attention

would pound the dining-room table for immediate service... ...an old hotel with traditional standards of individual service... Service is not included on the bill.

5 The **service** of someone or something is the period of time during which they work or are used. EG *Those with the shortest service have been quick to seize the payments on offer.* N SING WITH DET/ N UNCOUNT

6 If something such as a machine or type of vehicle is in **service**, it is being used or is able to be used. EG *We need to replace the submarines now in service... New weapons were now coming into service... Most of the vehicles had been withdrawn from service.* N UNCOUNT: PREP+N = operation

7 To **service** an engine, vehicle, or other machine means to examine, adjust, and clean it so that it will keep working efficiently and safely. EG *There was a pickup truck waiting to be serviced... Gas appliances should be serviced regularly.* ▸ used as a noun. EG *The car needs a service.* V+O ⇑ maintain ▸ N COUNT ⇑ inspection

8 A **service** is also a formal religious ceremony that is held on a particular occasion or at a particular time. EG *...the Sunday evening service... An hour before the service was due to begin there were queues outside the Abbey.* ▸ used to refer to what is supposed to be said or done during a service. EG *The new Communion Service was introduced in 1967.* N COUNT ▸ N COUNT: ALSO IN NAMES

9 A dinner **service** or a tea **service** is a complete set of dishes, plates, cups, saucers, etc. EG *...a porcelain tea service... ...a dinner service.* N COUNT: USU MOD+N

10 In tennis, badminton, and some other sports, it is your **service** when it is your turn to serve. EG *And it's McEnroe's service next.* N SING: USU POSS +N

11 To **service** an organization or group means to make sure that it has all the things it needs to function properly. EG *Our first priority is to make sure we service the university with its needs... The council is responsible for servicing these bodies and their sub-committees.* V+O ⇑ provide

12 **Service** is used to describe something which is used by people working in a place and not by the public. EG *...waiters kicking open service doors and whispering messages... There is a leak in the service pipe supplying the meter.* ADJ CLASSIF: ATTRIB

13 **Service** is also the work that servants do. EG *...a parlourmaid called Louise who had been in service since 1946.* N UNCOUNT

14 If you **do** someone **a service**, you do something that helps or benefits them. EG *The Government must be persuaded to do us all a service by banning such events... In one sense he did do a service to British journalists.* PHR: VB INFLECTS ⇑ assist

15 If something is **at the service of** a person, group, or thing, it is able to be used or controlled easily by them. EG *Nature had been put completely at the service of humanity.* PHR+NG: USED AS AN A

16 You say **'at your service'** after your name as a formal and perhaps humorous way of introducing yourself to someone and saying that you are willing to help in any way you can. EG *Good morning. Richard Soames at your service.* CONVENTION

17 If someone or something is **of service** to you, they help you do something, or are useful for a particular purpose. EG *In what way may I be of service to you?... A bird's feathers, which keep it warm and enable it to fly, are of service to it in a third way.* PHR: USED AS AN A

18 If you **press** someone or something **into service**, you use them or make them do something for you. EG *All possible techniques are pressed into service... If somebody does show interest, they press him into service.* PHR: VB INFLECTS ⇑ compel

19 See also **active service, Civil Service, community service, National Health Service, national service, room service, secret services, social services.**

serviceable /sɜːvɪsəbəˀl/. Something that is **serviceable 1** performs its function effectively. EG *Many amphibians, including the horned toad, have very serviceable rows of teeth... I wore serviceable boots... Our ideas of justice and fairness, serviceable enough for certain purposes, are broken down in a crisis.* **2** is able or ready to be used. EG *Those aircrew who had serviceable aircraft flew to Spain.* ADJ QUALIT ⇑ useful; ADJ CLASSIF ⇑ operative

service charge. A **service charge** is an amount that is added to a bill in a restaurant, hotel, etc to pay for the work of the waiter or waitress who serves you. EG *Coffee is 50p and the service charge is 10 per cent.* N SING WITH DET

service flat, service flats. A **service flat** is a flat in which you pay for cleaning, gardening, etc to be done as part of the rent. N COUNT

serviceman /sɜːvɪsməˀn/, **servicemen**. A **serviceman** is a man who is in the army, navy, or air force. EG *...a young American serviceman.* N COUNT

service road, service roads. A **service road** is a smaller road that runs parallel to a main road and which you use to reach shops, houses, offices, etc. N COUNT

service station, service stations. A **service station** is **1** a garage that sells petrol, oil, spare parts, etc. **2** a place where you can stop on the motorway and where there is a garage, restaurant, shop, toilets, etc. N COUNT; N COUNT

serviette /sɜːvɪɛt/, **serviettes**. A **serviette** is a small piece of cloth or paper that you use to protect your clothes or wipe your mouth when you are eating; used in British English. N COUNT = napkin

servile /sɜːvaɪl/. Someone who is **servile** is too eager to obey someone or do things for them and shows them too much respect; used showing disapproval. EG *...the incurably servile housekeeper.* ▸ used of the way people behave or speak. EG *He spoke in a servile tone.* ◇ **servility** /sɜːvɪlɪti[1]/. EG *James returned to work with a gratitude that verged on servility.* ADJ QUALIT ⇑ respectful = obsequious; ◇ N UNCOUNT

serving /sɜːvɪŋ/, **servings**. **1** A **serving** is an amount of food that is given to one person at a meal. EG *There should be enough for three servings.* N COUNT = helping, portion

2 A **serving** spoon, dish, etc is used for giving out food at a meal. EG *...a serving fork.* ADJ CLASSIF: ATTRIB

servitude /sɜːvɪtjuːd/ is the condition of being a slave or of being completely under the control of someone else. EG *...years of servitude.* ● See also **penal servitude**. N UNCOUNT = bondage, slavery

sesame /sɛsəmi[1]/. **1 Sesame** is a plant grown for its seeds and oil, which are used in cooking. EG *...sesame seeds... ...sesame crackers.* N UNCOUNT

2 If you describe something, especially a word or name, as an **open sesame**, you mean that it allows you to go into a place which you would not normally be allowed into. EG *The mention of her name became my open sesame to the most exclusive clubs in London.* PHR: USED AS S/ C/O, OR CONVENTION

session /sɛʃəˀn/, **sessions**. A **session** is **1** a meeting of an official group or organization, such as a law court, a parliament, or a city council. EG *...an emergency session of the United Nations Security Council... The court is still in session.* **2** a period during which such meetings are regularly held. EG *...the government's programme for the 1966-67 parliamentary session... The House is not in session during the summer months.* **3** a meeting or period of time used for a particular purpose or activity. EG *It seems certain to be a long and tough bargaining session... ...a recording session... In just one session of trading last week, the share index fell 30 points... ...an all-night drinking session.* **4** a university year or one of the terms into which it is divided; used especially in American English and Scottish English. EG *...the summer session... ...the 1984-5 session.* N COUNT, OR *in*+N = sitting; N COUNT, OR *in*+N = term; N COUNT: USU+SUPP ⇑ occasion; N COUNT: USU+SUPP ⇑ period = academic year

set /sɛt/, **sets, setting**. The form **set** is used in the present tense and is the past tense and past participle of the verb.

1 A **set** is **1.1** a number of things of the same kind that belong together or that are thought of as a group. EG *We lost our keys but fortunately there was a duplicate set... ...a set of encyclopaedias... You'll need a clean set of clothes for each child... We soon encountered a new set of problems.* **1.2** a number of objects or pieces of equipment that are used together for performing a particular activity, for example for playing a game. EG *...a child's printing set... ...a chess set.* **1.3** a group of mathematical quantities that have some characteristic in common; a technical term. EG *...the set of prime numbers.* N PART+N IN PL; N COUNT: MOD+N; N COUNT = class

2 If you **set** something somewhere, you put it there, especially in a careful or deliberate way. EG *He filled the kettle and set it on the stove... She took out a sheaf of papers which she set before him... Mary set down her glass on the side table.* V+O+A

3 If something, especially a building, **is set** in a particular place or position, it is in that place or position. EG *They live in a country house set in 1500 acres of forest and farmland... The house is set back from the road... His eyes were set close together.* V+O+A: ONLY PASS = be situated

4 If something **is set** into a surface or object, it is V+O+A *(in/*

fixed there and does not stick out. EG *There was one tiny window set into the stone wall... ...nine large panels set in a rich framework... A large drain was set into the pavement.* into): USU PASS = be sunk

5 If an object **is set** with jewels, it is decorated with jewels which are fixed into its surface. EG *The crown is set with diamonds and rubies.* V+O+A (*with*): ONLY PASS

6 Set is used in many expressions, for example 'to set free' and 'to set in motion', in which it means to cause something to be in a particular condition or situation. EG *Let me set your mind at rest on that point... The judge set her free on bail... The change was set in motion by President Carter... They claim that these measures will set us on the road to economic recovery... Because of its high temperature it sets alight any inflammable material.* V+O (NG/REFL) +A, OR V+O (NG/REFL)+C (ADJ) ⇑ put

7 If something **sets** you doing something, it causes you to start doing it. EG *Two further pieces of information set me questioning it all again... A gust of wind set all the candles spluttering.* V+O+-ING ⇑ cause

8 When the sun **sets**, it goes down below the horizon. EG *Our working day began when the sun rose and ended when it set... ...in the light of the setting sun.* V ⇑ go down ≠ rise

9 When someone **sets** a trap, **sets** the table, etc, they get it ready for use. EG *He had fallen into a trap set by one of the hunters... Shall I set the table for supper?* V+O ⇑ prepare = lay

10 When someone **sets** a clock, control, or instrument, they adjust it to a particular point or level. EG *Set the control to the coldest setting... I set the dial at 0.5... His alarm clock was set for four a.m.* V+O: USU+A

11 When someone **sets** a broken bone or when a broken bone **sets**, the bone is put back into its proper position so that it will heal. EG *The doctor set my broken arm.* V-ERG

12 When someone **sets** a person's hair, they arrange it while it is wet, for example using curlers, so that it will have a particular style when it dries. EG *She had her hair cut, washed, and set.* ▸ used as a noun. EG *How much do they charge for a shampoo and set?* V+O ▸ N SING WITH DET

13 If you **set** a time, price, level, etc, you decide what it will be. EG *They haven't yet set a firm date for the wedding... The government set a minimum price of £1.15... Official standards of quality or safety are set artificially high.* V+O ⇑ determine = fix

14 Set is used to describe something which is fixed beforehand, and does not change. EG *We paid a set amount for each part of the course... There are no set rules laid down for dealing with this kind of emergency... Meals are at set times.* ADJ CLASSIF: ATTRIB

15 A **set** meal is one that is offered by a restaurant at a fixed price. It is usually quite cheap, but you do not have much choice about what you can eat. EG *The set lunch is good value at £5.95... ...a set menu.* ADJ CLASSIF: ATTRIB

16 If you **set** a way of behaving or a level of achievement, you establish it for other people to copy or to try to achieve. EG *Try and set the younger children a good example... The government's ban has set a dangerous precedent... Their music set the fashion for a generation... A world record was set here tonight.* V+O, V+O+O, OR V+O+A (*for*)

17 If you **set** a target or aim, you establish it as something that you or other people must achieve. EG *It set a target for economic growth in excess of 4%... The new management set itself three aims.* V+O, V+O (NG/REFL)+O, OR V+O+A (*for*) ⇑ fix

18 If you **set** yourself to achieve something, you make a firm decision to achieve it. EG *They had set themselves to build a new nation.* V+O (REFL)+ to-INF

19 To **set** an examination means to invent the questions in it. EG *At that time all O and A levels were set and marked in London... I have to set an exam at the end of each term.* V+O

20 If someone **sets** you some work, a task, a problem, etc, they give it to you to do or to solve. EG *She had set a half-hour composition for her pupils... Let me set you a little problem.* V+O, V+O (NG/REFL)+O, OR V+O+A (*for*) = allot, assign

21 Set work or a **set** book must be done or studied by students taking a particular course or examination. EG *A number of exam boards now do set project work as part of the assessment for 'O' levels... What are your set books?* ADJ CLASSIF: ATTRIB = prescribed

22 If you are **set** to do something, you are ready to do it or the conditions are favourable for you to do it. EG *The left-wing parties seem set to do very well in the general election... We're all set to go... They're set for a world cruise.* ADJ CLASSIF: PRED, USU+*for*/ to-INF

23 If you are **set** on doing something, you are strongly determined to do it. EG *She is dead set on regaining her title.* ADJ QUALIT: PRED+*on* = intent

24 If you **set** your face, you fix it into a firm expression, in a way that shows determination or unwillingness to change your mind. EG *His square red face was set in grim determination... I suppose we've got to set our teeth and go through with it.* V+O

25 The **set** of someone's face or part of their body is the way that it is fixed in a particular expression or position, especially one that shows determination. EG *...the set of her jaw.* N SING: *the*+N+ *of*

26 Set is used to describe an expression or posture which is deliberately fixed and not natural. EG *She looked tired and faded under the set smile and the make-up... People in the palace gardens were standing in set attitudes.* ADJ CLASSIF: ATTRIB

27 Set is used to describe people's behaviour when it does not change at all, but is fixed as a result of habit. EG *Others had their set hours and set places and set friends... Her day usually followed a set pattern.* ADJ CLASSIF: ATTRIB = invariable

28 If you **are set in** your **ways**, your habits and ideas are fixed and not likely to change. EG *She's really set in her ways.* PHR: AUX INFLECTS ⇑ inflexible

29 When jelly, glue, cement, or some other soft or liquid substance **sets**, it becomes firm or hard. EG *Leave the jelly to cool and set... He held the veneer in place while the glue set... The cement had set hard.* V OR V+C ⇑ solidify

30 If you **set** a high value, a great deal, etc on something, you think it has great importance or value. EG *They set a high value on self-expression... He also sets a great deal on loyalty to the company.* V+O+A (*on*) = place

31 If someone **sets** a poem or prayer to music, they write or provide music for it, so that it can be sung. EG *It was set to music by Schubert.* V+O: USU PASS+ A (*to*)

32 A **set** is also **32.1** a television or piece of radio equipment. EG *There was a family photo on top of the T.V. set... I removed the protective grille at the back of the set.* N COUNT: USU MOD+N = receiver **32.2** a series of songs or tunes performed by a musician or group of musicians, especially as part of a concert of jazz or pop music. EG *Muddy Waters did a splendid set.* N COUNT: USU SING

33 The **set** of a play or film is the furniture, buildings, or scenery on the stage or in the studio, where the events of the play or film are shown as taking place. EG *He did some brilliantly inventive sets for 'The Three Sisters'... ...a set designer... ...a film set... He was always late on set.* N COUNT, OR *on*+ N

34 If a play, film, or story **is set** at a particular time or in a particular place, the events in it take place at that time or in that place. EG *The play is set in a small Midlands village... Set in the mid-eighteenth century, the story deals with intrigue at the French royal court.* V+O+A:

35 In tennis, a **set** is one of the groups of six or more games that form part of a tennis match. EG *He won the first set easily.* N COUNT

36 If you refer to a group of people as a **set**, you mean that they meet together socially or have the same social interests and the same life style; sometimes used showing disapproval. EG *His swimming pool is full of the yachting set... It's a satire on the jet set.* N SING WITH DET: MOD+N ⇑ clique

37 The word **set** is also used in the following expressions, which are explained at other places in this dictionary. ● to **set eyes on** someone or something: see **eye**. ● to **set** your **face against** something: see **face**. ● to **set fire to** something: see **fire**. ● to **set foot**: see **foot**. ● to **set** your **heart on** something: see **heart**. ● to **set** your **mind on** something: see **mind**. ● to **set sail**: see **sail**. ● to **set the stage for**: see **stage**. ● to **set great store by**: see **store**. ● to **set to work**: see **work**.

38 See also **setting**.

set about. If you **set about** doing something, you start doing it, especially in an energetic or purposeful way. EG *The next morning they awoke and set about cleaning and sweeping the house... How are we going to set about this?* PHRASAL VB: V PREP, HAS PASS, USU+-ING

set against. 1 If you **set** one fact or argument **against** another, you consider it in relation to the other one, and this often makes the first fact or argument seem less important. EG *This slight improvement has to be set against an enormous increase in crime.* PHRASAL VB: V O+PREP

2 If you **set** an amount of money **against** tax, you PHRASAL VB: V record the amount that you have spent in connection with your job or business, in order to reduce the amount of tax you have to pay. EG *It is usually possible to set against tax the costs of setting up a new business.* O+PREP

3 To **set** one person **against** another, especially a relative or friend, means to cause them to become enemies or rivals. EG *The last thing I wanted to do was to set her against me... As a result of this war, parent had been set against child and child against parent.* PHRASAL VB : V+O+PREP

set apart. 1 If something **is set apart** for a special use or purpose, it is kept for that use or purpose. EG *One day of the week should be set apart for relaxation... There are no rooms specifically set apart for quiet study.* PHRASAL VB : V+O+ADV, USU PASS = reserve

2 If something, especially a good characteristic, **sets** you **apart** from other people, it makes you recognizably different from the others. EG *His exceptional height set him apart from the rest of the men... These attributes set humans apart from even the highest primates.* PHRASAL VB : ORDER V+O+ADV, IF+PREP THEN *from* = distinguish

set aside. 1 If you **set aside** something such as time or money, you keep it for a special use or purpose. EG *Try and set aside time to do some mending jobs... The government set aside barely thirteen per cent of this money for health and education.* PHRASAL VB : V+O+ADV = reserve

2 If you **set aside** a belief, principle, or feeling, you decide that you will not be influenced by it since other things are more important. EG *...a coalition of patriots that would set aside party dogma and lead the nation towards recovery... We must try and set aside our past hostilities.* PHRASAL VB : V+O+ADV ⇑ disregard = discard

3 If a judge or court **sets** a decision or judgement **aside**, they state that it is not legally valid or has no legal force. EG *To set the committee's recommendations aside would be to create a serious precedent... The original verdict was eventually set aside by the Supreme Court.* PHRASAL VB : V+O+ADV = quash, overturn

set back. 1 If something **sets** you **back** or **sets back** a project, scheme, etc, it causes a delay. EG *Bad weather set us back by about three weeks... This has set back the whole programme of nuclear power in America.* PHRASAL VB : V+O+ADV ⇑ retard

2 If something **sets** you **back** a large amount of money, it costs you that much; used in informal English. EG *The legal costs of the case set him back something in the order of £10,000... It did set us back a bit.* PHRASAL VB : V+O+ADV+O = knock back

3 See also **setback**.

set down. 1 If a bus or train **sets** you **down**, it stops and lets you get out. EG *Can you set me down here?... The bus set us down outside the station.* PHRASAL VB : V+O+ADV, USU+A = drop

2 If you **set down** your thoughts, feelings, or a series of events, you write them all down because you want to keep a record of them. EG *They were asked to set down a summary of their views.* PHRASAL VB : V+O+ADV = put down

set forth. 1 If you **set forth** a number of facts, beliefs, or arguments, you give them in writing or speech in a clear, organized way; used in formal English. EG *The committee set forth their findings in a report published today.* PHRASAL VB : ORDER V+ADV+O = expound, present

2 When you **set forth**, you start a journey; a rather literary expression. EG *We set forth the next morning.* PHRASAL VB : V+ADV = set off, set out

set in. If something unpleasant **sets in**, it begins and seems likely to continue or develop. EG *A feeling of anti-climax set in... It must be treated quickly before infection sets in... The bad weather has set in for the winter.* PHRASAL VB : V+ADV take a hold

set off. 1 When you **set off**, you start a journey. EG *We set off on another four-hour trek through the swamps... Dan set off down the mountain to find help.* PHRASAL VB : V+ADV = set out

2 If you **set off** a bomb or firework, you cause it to explode. EG *Tear-gas bombs were set off to disperse the crowds.* PHRASAL VB : V+O+ADV ⇑ trigger

3 If something **sets off** a process or series of events, it causes it to start happening. EG *Most analysts expected that Mobil's offer would set off a new round of bidding for Conoco... The broadcast was to set off a train of thoughts and actions.* PHRASAL VB : ORDER V+ADV+O = prompt, spark off

4 If something **sets** someone **off**, it causes them to start doing something, such as laughing, complaining, or telling stories. EG *If you mention the war, it'll just set him off on one of his boring stories.* PHRASAL VB : ORDER V+O+ADV, IF+PREP THEN *on*

5 If one thing **sets** something else **off**, it provides a contrast that makes the other thing look more attractive or more noticeable than it would on its own. EG *She wore a blazing red dress that set off that miraculous complexion.* PHRASAL VB : V+O+ADV ⇑ enhance

set on. 1 To **set** animals or people **on** someone means to cause the animals or people to attack them. EG *We were afraid they might set the dogs on us.* PHRASAL VB : V+O+PREP

2 If you **are set on** by animals or people, they make a sudden and unexpected physical attack on you. PHRASAL VB : V+PREP, USU PASS

set out. 1 When you **set out**, you start a journey. EG *We set out along the beach... Mr Dekker and his son set out to walk to Whitelake River.* PHRASAL VB : V+ADV, USU+A = set off

2 If you **set out** to do something, you start taking action or making plans with the aim of achieving a particular result. EG *They had failed in what they had set out to do... They set out to recruit a team of the brightest minds available.* PHRASAL VB : V+ADV+*to*-INF ⇑ try

3 If you **set** things **out**, you arrange or display them so that they are ready to use. EG *There were plenty of chairs set out for the guests... The brushes and paints had been set out.* PHRASAL VB : V+O+ADV = lay out

4 If you **set out** a number of facts, beliefs, or arguments, you give them in writing or speech in a clear, organized way. EG *Darwin set out his theory in detail in 'The Origin of Species'... Speaking in the debate, he set out his views on the party system.* PHRASAL VB : V+O+ADV ⇑ present = set forth

set to. 1 If you **set to**, you start working or dealing with something busily and energetically. EG *We all set to and got the place cleaned up in no time.* PHRASAL VB : V+ADV = get cracking

2 See also **set-to**.

set up. 1 If you **set up** something such as a structure or monument, you place it or build it somewhere. EG *Police have set up roadblocks at all the exits to the motorway... A fund was launched to set up a monument in memory of the dead men.* PHRASAL VB : V+O+ADV = erect, raise

2 If you **set up** a piece of equipment or an experiment, you make the preparations that are necessary so that it is ready to work or be used. EG *Can you show me how to set up the video?... It took a long time to set up the experiment.* PHRASAL VB : V+O+ADV

3 If you **set up** a company, a course, an investigation, etc, you make the arrangements and preparations that are necessary to start it. EG *Try to set up a dialogue between the rival groups... The government announced that they were setting up an inquiry into the affair... An anti-terrorist squad was set up.* PHRASAL VB : V+O+ADV

◊ **setting up.** EG *...the setting up of a Northern Seas Environmental Control body.* ◊ N SING : *the*+N+*of*

4 If you **set up** somewhere or **set up** doing something, you establish yourself in a position or function, for example in a new business or in a new home. EG *She left her parents' home and set up on her own... He used the money to set himself up in business... After leaving art college she set up as an interior designer... I persuaded him to set me up in a photocopying shop.* PHRASAL VB : V+ADV+A, OR V+O (NG/REFL)+ADV+A ⇑ start

5 If you **set up home** or **set up house**, you start living in your own home, usually in a home you have bought, rather than living with your parents. EG *She talked about setting up home and getting a job... He had given them a lot of money to set up house.* PHR : VB INFLECTS

6 If you **set up shop**, you start working for yourself or running your own business. EG *He set up shop as an interior designer.* PHR : VB INFLECTS, IF+PREP THEN *as*

7 If something **sets** you **up**, it puts you in a satisfactory condition or position, for example by providing you with money or by making you feel healthy and energetic. EG *He insisted on a contract that would set him up for life... That holiday has really set me up.* PHRASAL VB : ORDER V+O+ADV

8 If something **sets up** a process or series of events, it causes it to begin and continue. EG *It may become possible to set up a nuclear chain reaction... These ointments don't cure anything, but set up a secondary irritant... As we approached the house, the dogs set up a terrific racket.* PHRASAL VB : ORDER V+ADV+O ⇑ produce

9 If someone **sets** you **up**, they make it seem that you have done something wrong when you have not, or they deceive you and get you into a situation in which you may be harmed; used in informal English. EG *I think I've been set up.* PHRASAL VB : V+O+ADV = fit up, frame

10 Someone who is **well set-up** has a strong-looking, well-developed body; a rather old-fashioned expression. EG *...a vigorous and well set-up man with a dark moustache.* PHR : USED AS A C, OR BEFORE N = well-built

11 See also **set-up**.

set upon. 1 To **set** animals or people **upon** someone means to cause the animals or people to attack them. PHRASAL VB : V+O+PREP = set on

2 If you are **set upon** by animals or people, they make a sudden and unexpected physical attack on you. EG *I was set upon by a gang of thugs.* PHRASAL VB : V+PREP, HAS PASS = set on

setback /sɛtbæk/, **setbacks.** A **setback** is an event that delays your progress or makes your position less favourable than it was before. EG *The by-election result is being interpreted as a serious setback for the government... They had to persevere and face up to innumerable setbacks before they achieved their goal.* N COUNT = reverse, hitch

set piece, set pieces. 1 A **set piece** is a part of a play, piece of music, etc which has a strong dramatic effect and which often is not an essential part of the main story. EG *There are some marvellous set pieces... He is at his best in the great set piece scenes, like the Hall of the Mountain King.* N COUNT ⇑ section 2 a military operation or a move in a football match, that has been carefully planned and is carried out in an ordered way. EG *Both cities were targets for a setpiece offensive.* N COUNT

set square, set squares. A **set square** is a flat piece of plastic or metal in the shape of a right-angled triangle, which is used, especially in geometry, for drawing angles and lines. N COUNT

settee /sɛtiː/, **settees.** A **settee** is a long seat with a back and usually with arms, which is covered in soft material and which two or more people can sit on. N COUNT = couch, sofa

setter /sɛtə/, **setters.** A **setter** is a long-haired dog that can be trained to show hunters where birds and animals are. N COUNT

set theory is the part of mathematics that deals with sets. N UNCOUNT

setting /sɛtɪŋ/, **settings.** A **setting** is 1 the surroundings in which an event or series of events takes place, especially in a story. EG *The old castle would have provided the perfect setting for a horror story... It was a lovely setting for a picnic.* N COUNT+SUPP = scene 2 a particular set of circumstances or conditions. EG *Working in a university setting, you can't ignore these things... The group setting has several distinct advantages for dealing with these problems.* N COUNT : MOD+N ⇑ situation = environment 3 one of the positions or levels to which the controls of a machine can be adjusted. EG *Set the control to the coldest setting... It has four different temperature settings.* N COUNT 4 the piece of metal, in a ring or other piece of jewellery, in which a precious stone is fixed. EG *The ring had three diamonds in a very plain gold setting.* N COUNT ⇑ framework = mounting 5 a complete set of equipment for eating, including knives, forks, spoons, and glasses, arranged on a table for the use of one person. EG *How many settings do we need?* N COUNT ⇑ place 6 a piece of music that has been written for the words of a poem, prayer, etc. N COUNT

settle /sɛtə⁰l/, **settles, settling, settled.** 1 If you **settle** or **settle** yourself, you sit or make yourself comfortable. EG *Casson took off his raincoat and settled before the fire... She settled herself down in the grass... He caught a taxi at the airport, gave the address, and settled back.* V OR V+O (REFL/NG) : USU+A

2 If something **settles** or if you **settle** it, it moves down slowly and easily into a particular place or position and stays there. EG *The hull of the boat slowly settled in the mud... He settled his briefcase comfortably in his lap... He took a sip of tea, and settled the cup into its saucer.* V-ERG : USU+A ⇑ sink

3 If something such as dust, sand, or mud **settles**, it sinks slowly and becomes still, covering somewhere evenly. EG *We must wait for the dust to settle before starting the painting... The sand was blowing into a fierce storm, settling over the entire area.* ● to **allow the dust to settle**: see **dust.** V

4 When your food **settles**, you have digested it properly. V = go down

5 If someone **settles** an argument or problem, they end it by making a decision about who is right or about what to do. EG *The strike went on for over a year before it was finally settled... To settle all these differences will take time... We have renounced the use of force to settle our disputes.* V+O ⇑ resolve

6 If you **settle**, you agree to end a disagreement or dispute without going to a court of law, for example by offering someone money, or by apologizing to them. EG *Isaacs was offering to settle outside the courts for £10,000.* V ⇑ bargain

7 If something **is settled**, it has all been decided and arranged. EG *Good, well, that's settled then... It's all settled... That settles it.* V+O : USU PASS

8 If you **settle** your affairs, you make the arrangements that are necessary to put everything in order. EG *Before leaving, I resolved to settle some affairs of mine in New York... These little details I leave behind for you to settle.* V+O ⇑ conclude

9 If you **settle** a bill or **settle** with someone, you pay an amount that you have been charged or that you owe. EG *I'll settle with you on Friday... He came out to settle the charge for the hire car.* V OR V+O : IF+PREP THEN *with*

10 If you **are settled** somewhere, you have become used to living in a particular house, town, area, etc. EG *Have a chat with the Branch Manager as soon as you've got yourself settled... When I'm settled, I'll write to you and let you know what's happening.* V+O : USU PASS ⇑ adapt

11 When people **settle**, they start living or working in one place, rather than moving around all the time. EG *Most newcomers settle close to relatives or acquaintances from home... He had settled in England.* V : USU+A ⇑ establish

12 When people **settle** a country or area where there are no people living, or no advanced people living, they go there and make their home there. EG *...the East Anglians who helped to settle New England... Their grandparents settled the land in 1856.* V+O = colonize

13 When birds, insects, snowflakes, etc **settle** on something, they land on it from above. EG *A bird settled on a beam near the top of the roof... Flies and other insects settle on plants growing on the banks.* V+A = alight

14 If your eyes **settle** on something or if you **settle** your eyes on something, you look at it for a period of time. EG *The woman's eyes settled on the baby... He settled his gaze on me.* V-ERG+A ⇑ rest

15 If an expression **settles** on your face, it appears there and stays there. EG *Gradually a lopsided smile settled on her face... A peculiar hardness settled itself upon her features.* V+A OR V+O (REFL)+A ⇑ descend

16 If a feeling or quality **settles** somewhere, it affects a person, group, or place. EG *A deep gloom has settled upon the party following the recent by-election... A calm settled over the forests.* V+A ⇑ fill

17 If you **settle a score** or **settle an account**, you take revenge on someone who has harmed you in the past. EG *There might be a chance to settle old scores.* PHR : VB AND N INFLECT

18 To **settle** money on someone means to formally give it to them, for example in a will. EG *Some money was settled on him when he was adopted.* V+O : USU+*on* ⇑ leave

19 A **settle** is a large wooden seat with a high back. EG *The women were sitting on the settles and talking excitedly.* N COUNT

20 See also **settled.**

settle down. 1 If you **settle down** to something, you prepare to do it, especially by getting rid of all distractions and giving serious attention to it. EG *...when they settle down to full-time study... He had settled down to watch a sports programme... At eight o'clock he settles down for supper.* PHRASAL VB : V+ADV, USU+*to/for/to*-INF ⇑ concentra

2 When someone **settles down,** they start living a life in which they need to stay in one place all the time because of the responsibilities they have, for example when they get married, get a job, buy a house, etc. EG *Al told her that after this, he would settle down and marry her... You have to get a job and settle down.* PHRASAL VB : V+ADV

3 If people **settle down** or if you **settle** them **down,** they stop talking or being worried and become calm, peaceful, or quiet. EG *It took her some time to settle down... Eddie's presence settled me down... Take it easy, she'll be all right, settle down.* PHRASAL VB : V-ERG+ADV = relax, calm down

settle for. If you **settle for** something, you choose or accept it, when it is not what you really want but there is nothing else available or it is the safest or easiest thing to do. EG *Don't settle for second best... When in doubt he settled for hamburgers.* PHRASAL VB : V+PREP, HAS PASS ⇑ comprom

settle in. If you **settle in** or you **are settled in,** you become used to living in a new house or town or doing a new job. EG *And how are you settling in, Mr Swallow?... There's plenty of time to get settled in.* PHRASAL VB : V+ADV ⇑ adapt

settle on. If you **settle on** a particular idea, suggestion, etc, you decide on it after thinking or talking about it. EG *A week ahead of the joint negotiations, exporters settled on a figure of 52.1 million... Have you settled on a name for him yet?* PHRASAL VB : V+PREP, HAS PA = decide o

settle up. When you **settle up,** you pay a bill or pay someone what you owe them. EG *As soon as the money arrived I was able to settle up with him.* PHRASAL VB : V+ADV, OR V+A+A (*with*) : RECIP

settled /sɛtəºld/. 1 Something that is **settled** 1.1 exists or happens in a particular place rather than travelling or moving all the time. EG *...the advent of settled civilization... They are practising settled agriculture... ...settled farmers.* 1.2 stays the same all the time rather than attempting to change. EG *...an easy, rich, peaceful and settled social order... ...a very settled, fairly traditional grammar school.* ADJ CLASSIF ⇑ fixed; ADJ QUALIT ⇑ fixed

2 If you are or feel **settled**, you have been living or working in a place long enough to feel comfortable there, rather than feeling like a stranger. EG *After a few days, I began to feel as settled and comfortable as I could in such circumstances... I don't feel entirely settled here.* ADJ QUALIT = at home

settlement /sɛtəºlməºnt/, **settlements**. 1 A **settlement** is 1.1 an official agreement between two sides in a disagreement. EG *The chance for a peaceful political settlement has disappeared... A speedy settlement of the strike by the new Labour government was inevitable... I believe the deal will now set a standard for other settlements.* 1.2 an agreement to end a disagreement or dispute without going to a court of law, for example by offering someone money, or by apologizing to them. EG *He paid £175,000 in the biggest libel settlement awarded up to that time... Casey was involved in an out-of-court settlement.* N COUNT/ UNCOUNT = compact; N COUNT ⇑ compact

2 The **settlement** of a debt is the act of paying back money that you owe. N UNCOUNT ⇑ payment

3 A **settlement** is also a place where people have come to live and have built homes. EG *He lives in the jungle, in a settlement by a river... ...an extensive Roman settlement in Northwest England.* N COUNT ⇑ territory

4 **Settlement** is also the process of settling in a place where previously there were no people living, or no advanced people living. EG *Civilization began with agriculture, which meant settlement... The settlement of the island is still under way.* N UNCOUNT ⇑ establishment

settler /sɛtlə/, **settlers**. A **settler** is someone who settles in a new country. EG *The first white settlers in South Africa had been Dutch.* N COUNT ⇑ person = colonist

set-to, set-tos. A **set-to** is a fight, especially one in which people use their fists. EG *There was a bit of a set-to outside the pub.* N COUNT = scuffle

set-up, set-ups. 1 A particular **set-up** is a particular system or way of organizing something. EG *I've only been here a couple of days and I don't quite know the set-up... ...the British political set-up.* N COUNT : USU SING

2 See also **set up**.

seven /sɛvəºn/, **sevens**. **Seven** is the number 7: see ☐ at NUMBER, AGE, DATE, MEASUREMENT, MONEY, and TIME. EG *I was seven years older than Wendy.* NUM

seventeen /sɛvəºntiːn/ is the number 17: see ☐ at NUMBER, AGE, DATE, MEASUREMENT, MONEY, and TIME. EG *Buxhall is seventeen miles from Akenfield.* NUM

seventeenth /sɛvəºntiːnθ/. The **seventeenth** item in a series is the one that you count as number seventeen: see ☐ at NUMBER, AGE, and DATE. EG *It was Rudolph's seventeenth birthday.* ORDINAL

seventh /sɛvəºnθ/, **sevenths**. 1 The **seventh** item in a series is the one that you count as number seven: see ☐ at NUMBER, AGE, and DATE. EG *She died giving birth to her seventh child.* ORDINAL

2 A **seventh** is 2.1 one of seven equal parts of something. EG *A seventh of the profits will be sent to charity.* 2.2 the interval between two notes in a musical scale when there are five whole notes separating them. N COUNT : USU + *of*; N COUNT : USU SING

seventieth /sɛvəºntiɪθ/. The **seventieth** item in a series is the one that you count as number seventy: see ☐ at NUMBER and AGE. EG *...her seventieth birthday.* ORDINAL

seventy /sɛvəºntiˡ/, **seventies**. **Seventy** is the number 70: see ☐ at NUMBER, AGE, DATE, MEASUREMENT, and MONEY. EG *...seventy acres of good irrigated land.* NUM

sever /sɛvə/, **severs, severing, severed**. 1 To **sever** something means to cut right through it so that one part is completely separated from the rest of it. EG *...a dog's head completely severed from the body... A bulldozer had severed a gas main... The boy's legs were severed at the hip.* V+O ⇑ divide

2 If you **sever** a relationship or connection that you have with someone, you end it suddenly, completely, and for ever. EG *She had to sever all ties with her parents... He had severed his connection with them.* V+O = break off

several /sɛvəºrəl/ is used to refer in an imprecise way to a number of things or people, when the number is not large but is more than two. EG *He returned home several hours later... There have been several hundred people killed in the North Sea... Several of us are married and have children... He burned several of the letters... I feel the burden of these worries and several I haven't mentioned.* QUANTIF + N IN PL

severance /sɛvəºrəns/. Your **severance** from other people or from a place is your separation from them so that you no longer have a relationship or connection with them; a formal word. EG *The real severance from my father came later... The ruling council announced the severance of their new relationship with Egypt.* N UNCOUNT : IF + PREP THEN *of/from* = break

severance pay is money that a firm pays its employees as compensation when it has to stop employing them. N UNCOUNT

severe /sɪ²vɪə/, **severer, severest**. 1 **Severe** is used of something bad or undesirable that is very great in degree. EG *The blast caused severe damage and heavy loss of life... ...a severe shortage of food... ...a period of severe wage restraint... We have been under severe pressure to cut costs.* ◊ **severely**. EG *A fire had severely damaged part of the school... Bad weather severely hampered the emergency services.* ◊ **severity** /sɪ²vɛrɪtiˡ/. EG *The price rise affected the Third World countries with special severity.* ADJ QUALIT = grave, grievous; ◊ ADV WITH VB = badly, gravely; ◊ N UNCOUNT = gravity

2 Someone who is **severe** 2.1 treats people harshly and is unwilling to forgive their mistakes, weaknesses, or crimes. EG *I hope the magistrate has not been too severe with him... I was his severest critic.* ▸ used of a person's actions and behaviour. EG *...severe penalties... She was a harsh mother and imposed severe discipline.* ◊ **severely**. EG *They were severely punished.* ◊ **severity**. EG *...prison sentences of excessive severity.* 2.2 is stern, unfriendly, and lacking in kindness or humour. EG *She wore a habitually severe expression... He spoke to her in a severe voice.* ◊ **severely**. EG *She sat in her chair, peering severely over her glasses.* ◊ **severity**. EG *She addressed the man with great severity.* ADJ QUALIT = strict; ◊ ADV WITH VB; ◊ N UNCOUNT; ADJ QUALIT = grim, serious; ◊ ADV WITH VB; ◊ N UNCOUNT

3 A style of appearance that is **severe** is plain and simple, with little or no decoration. EG *...a picture of a man in severe 17th-century costume... ...the lower arches, severe and clean-cut.* ◊ **severity**. EG *...the fine severity of this old church.* ADJ QUALIT = austere; ◊ N UNCOUNT = austerity

sew /səʊ/, **sews, sewing, sewed, sewn**. 1 When someone **sews**, they join pieces of cloth together, or attach things such as buttons to cloth, by passing thread through them with a needle. EG *You finish the dress by sewing the edges together... They teach the children to cook, sew, or knit... ...sewing buttons onto one of my shirts.* V, OR V+O : USU +A ⇑ stitch

2 When someone **sews** a piece of clothing, a bag, etc, they make it by sewing cloth together using a needle and thread. EG *The early humans used bone needles and sinew to sew clothes of skin and fur.* V+O = stitch

3 See also **sewing**.

sew up. 1 If you **sew up** two pieces of cloth, you join them together using a needle and thread. EG *You tore it so you can sew it up!* PHRASAL VB : V+O+ADV ⇑ close = mend

2 If you **sew up** something such as a business deal or an election, you arrange it in such a way that you can be sure of favourable results; a fairly informal use. EG *We thought that everything was sewn up so we were surprised when they didn't sign the contract.* PHRASAL VB : V+O+ADV, USU PASS ⇑ complete

sewage /suːɪdʒ/ is waste matter such as human faeces or water that has been used in homes and factories, which is carried away in sewers. N UNCOUNT

sewage farm, sewage farms. A **sewage farm** is a place where sewage is treated so that it can be used as manure or disposed of safely. N COUNT

sewer /suːə/, **sewers**. A **sewer** is a large underground channel or pipe that carries household and industrial waste matter, as well as rain water that drains from roads and buildings, to a place where it can be treated and made harmless. N COUNT

sewerage /suːərɪdʒ/ is the system by which waste matter is carried away in sewers and made harmless. EG *Investment is needed to improve the roads, sewerage, and electricity supply... ...drainage and sewerage facilities.* N UNCOUNT

sewing /səʊɪŋ/ is 1 the skill of making or mending clothes or other things using a needle and thread. EG *All the children are taught sewing... ...a pocket sewing kit... ...a sewing class.* 2 cloth or clothes that N UNCOUNT = needlework; N UNCOUNT are being sewn or that need to be sewn. EG *My aunt put aside her sewing... ...a basket full of sewing.*

sewing machine, sewing machines; also spelled with a hyphen. A **sewing machine** is a machine that you use for sewing, with a needle that is driven by an electric motor or by movements of your hand or foot. N COUNT

sewn /səʊn/ is the past participle of **sew**.

sex /sɛks/, **sexes, sexing, sexed**. 1 The two **sexes** are the two groups, male and female, into which people and other living things are divided according to the function they have in producing young. EG *The job is open to people of both sexes... ...a member of the opposite sex... ...inequalities between the sexes.* ● See also **fair sex**. N COUNT ⇑ category

2 The **sex** of a person or other living thing is their characteristic of being either male or female. EG *They did tests to ascertain the sex of the baby before it was born... The purpose of the law is to prevent discrimination on the grounds of sex... ...stereotyped sex roles.* N UNCOUNT ⇑ gender

3 **Sex** is the activity by which people and animals can produce young, involving the joining of the male and female sex organs. EG *We weren't taught anything about sex... He did not agree with his mother's views on premarital sex.* ● If two people **have sex**, they perform the act of sex or a similar activity that involves contact between each other's sex organs. EG *She said, 'I've never had sex with a man.'* N UNCOUNT ⇑ sexual; ● PHR OR PHR + A *(with)*: RECIP, VB INFLECTS = copulate

4 **Sex** is also all the feelings and activities that are connected with having sex or with the desire to have sex. EG *He talked non-stop about sex... The film contains no explicit sex or violence... ...his desire for a better sex life.* N UNCOUNT

5 If someone **sexes** a living thing, they find out whether it is male or female, often in order to sort a group into males and females; a technical term. EG *He went on sexing kittens.* V+O

sex appeal. If you say that someone has **sex appeal**, you mean that they are sexually attractive. N UNCOUNT ⇑ desirability

sex education is education in schools on the subject of sexual activity and sexual relationships. N UNCOUNT

sexism /sɛksɪzəºm/ is the idea or belief that the members of one sex are less intelligent or less capable than those of the other sex, and that certain jobs or activities are suitable for women and others are suitable for men; often used by women expressing disapproval. EG *Their aim is to eradicate the racism and sexism which occurs in all the major institutions.* N UNCOUNT

sexist /sɛksɪst/, **sexists**. 1 Something that is **sexist** is based on sexism or shows sexism; used showing disapproval. EG *...sexist attitudes... ...sexist toys like guns and dolls... Most of the advertising is really sexist.* ADJ QUALIT

2 If you refer to a person, especially a man, as a **sexist**, you mean that they have sexist attitudes; used showing disapproval. N COUNT

sexless /sɛksli²s/. 1 A living thing that is **sexless** is neither male nor female. EG *Angels are supposed to be sexless.* ADJ CLASSIF ⇑ neuter

2 If you describe a person as **sexless**, you mean that they are not sexually exciting or that they cannot experience sexual feelings. ADJ QUALIT ⇑ boring

sex object, sex objects; also spelled with a hyphen. If someone, especially a woman, is considered as a **sex object**, they are considered only in terms of their physical attractiveness and not their character or abilities. N COUNT

sex shop, sex shops. A **sex shop** is a shop that sells products that are connected with sexual pleasure, for example magazines, video films, and special clothing and equipment. N COUNT

sextant /sɛkstənt/, **sextants**. A **sextant** is an instrument used for measuring angles, for example between the sun and the horizon, so that the position of a ship or aeroplane can be calculated. N COUNT

sextet /sɛkstɛt/, **sextets**. A **sextet** is a group of six musicians or singers who play or sing together. EG *He plays the drums in a jazz sextet.* N COUNT

sexton /sɛkstən/, **sextons**. A **sexton** is a person whose job is to look after a church and its graveyard. N COUNT ⇑ worker

sexual /sɛksjuºəl/. 1 **Sexual** is used to describe feelings, activities, etc that are connected with the act of sex or with people's desire for sex. EG *...sexual attraction... ...the sexual behaviour of young people... They were not having a sexual relationship.* ◊ **sexually**. EG *I find her sexually attractive.* ADJ CLASSIF : USU ATTRIB ⇑ physical; ◊ ADV

2 **Sexual** also means 2.1 relating to the differences between male and female people or animals. EG *...campaigning for non-discrimination and sexual equality... ...sexual stereotyping.* ◊ **sexually**. EG *...sexually segregated groups.* 2.2 relating to the biological process by which people and animals produce young. EG *...the sexual cycle of the elephant... ...sexual reproduction.* ADJ CLASSIF : USU ATTRIB; ◊ ADV WITH VB; ADJ CLASSIF : USU ATTRIB

sexual intercourse is the physical act of sex between a man and a woman; a fairly formal expression. N UNCOUNT = coitus, copulation

sexuality /sɛksjuælɪti¹/. A person's **sexuality** is their ability to experience sexual feelings. EG *Victorian women were severely discouraged from any admission of sexuality.* N UNCOUNT

sexy /sɛksi¹/, **sexier, sexiest**. Someone or something that is **sexy** is sexually exciting or sexually attractive. EG *He is tremendously sexy... The evening wear is sexy and spectacular.* ◊ **sexiness**. EG *...the irresistible sexiness of his eyes.* ADJ QUALIT ⇑ attractive; ◊ N UNCOUNT

Sgt is the written abbreviation for 'sergeant' when it is part of someone's title. EG *...Sgt Kirby.* N IN TITLES : BEFORE NAME

sh is a noise that you make in order to tell someone to be quiet. EXCLAM = hush

shabby /ʃæbi¹/, **shabbier, shabbiest**. 1 Something that is **shabby** looks old and is in bad condition, because it has not been cared for properly. EG *...his shabby clothes... ...a shabby house with worn carpeting on the stairs.* ◊ **shabbily**. EG *They were shabbily dressed.* ◊ **shabbiness**. EG *I was struck by the shabbiness of the furnishings.* ADJ QUALIT = tatty; ◊ ADV WITH VB; ◊ N UNCOUNT

2 Someone who is **shabby** is wearing old, worn clothes. EG *...a shabby little man.* ADJ QUALIT = seedy

3 You describe someone's behaviour as **shabby** when they behave in an unfair or dishonest way, especially towards someone such as a friend, who they should treat better. EG *...a series of shabby compromises... What a shabby way to treat your friends!* ◊ **shabbily**. EG *Don't you think you've treated me a little shabbily?* ◊ **shabbiness**. EG *...the shabbiness of my motives.* ADJ QUALIT ⇑ dishonourable; ◊ ADV WITH VB; ◊ N UNCOUNT

shack /ʃæk/, **shacks, shacking, shacked**. A **shack** is a small hut built from tin, bits of wood, or other materials which are not very strong. N COUNT = shanty

shack up. When someone **shacks up** with someone else or when two people **shack up** together, they start living together as lovers; an informal expression. EG *He wants to shack up with me... If we'd been five years younger, we'd just have shacked up together.* PHRASAL VB : V + ADV, V + ADV + A *(together/with)*: RECIP

shackle /ʃækəºl/, **shackles, shackling, shackled**. 1 **Shackles** are two metal rings joined by a chain and fastened around someone's wrists or ankles in order to prevent them from moving or escaping. EG *They rattled their shackles frantically.* N PLURAL : ALSO *a pair of* + N ⇑ chains = fetters

2 To **shackle** someone means to put shackles on them. EG *The prisoners were shackled by their wrists... The guards shackled them together.* V+O ⇑ bind = fetter

3 If you **are shackled** by something, it prevents you from doing or saying what you want to do or say. EG *Industrialists cannot afford to be shackled by the ideologies of politicians... He thought of himself as too shackled by domestic responsibilities.* V+O : USU PASS ⇑ restrain = hamper

4 You can also use **shackles** to refer to conditions or circumstances that prevent you from doing or saying what you want to do or say. EG *There are a few who have managed to throw off the shackles of the past... At last they were freed from the shackles of colonial rule.* N PLURAL = constraints, trammels

shade /ʃeɪd/, **shades, shading, shaded**. 1 **Shade** is the darkness that is caused when sunlight does not reach a place because a tree or other object stands between the place and the sun. EG *There are no trees or bushes to give shade... Right now the air is cool in the shade... He led the way to the shade of a large banyan tree.* N UNCOUNT, OR SING : *the* + N ⇑ shadow

2 If a place **is shaded** by trees, the trees prevent the heat and brightness of the sun from reaching the place; used showing approval. EG *The broad fields and walks are shaded by chestnut trees.* V+O : USU PASS ⇑ screen

3 If you **shade your eyes**, you put your hand across your forehead in order to prevent a bright light from shining directly into your eyes. PHR : VB INFLECTS ⇑ shield

4 A **shade** is something that partly covers an electric light and prevents it from shining too brightly into your eyes. EG *...a series of small lamps with red glass* N COUNT ⇑ shield

shades... *None of our street lights have effective shades.* ● See also **lampshade**.

5 Shades are sunglasses; an informal use. N PLURAL

6 In American English, a **shade** or a **window shade** is a piece of stiff cloth, heavy paper, etc that you can pull down over a window in order to prevent sunlight from coming into a room. EG *In the room the yellow window shades were pulled down.* N COUNT : USU PL ⇑ screen = blind

7 Shade is also the darkness or shadows that are shown by an artist in a painting. EG *The painting is a dramatic pattern of light and shade.* N UNCOUNT

8 If you **shade** an area in a drawing or painting or **shade** it **in**, you make it appear dark, for example by filling it in with pencil lines or with a dark colour. V+O, OR V+O+A (in) = hatch

9 The **shades** of a particular colour are its different forms. For example, emerald green and olive green are shades of green. EG *They wore tight-fitting jackets in shades of pink, blue, and brown.* N COUNT : USU PL, IF+PREP THEN of ⇑ variety = tint

10 The **shades** of something abstract are its different forms. EG *The phrase has many shades of meaning... Various shades of radical and socialist opinion are found in the party.* N COUNT+SUPP : USU PL+of ⇑ variety

11 When something **shades** into something else, there is no clear division between the two things, so that you cannot tell where one thing ends and the other begins. EG *...reds shading into pinks... Professor Wilson now sees instinct and culture as shading into one another.* V+A (into) ⇑ merge

12 a shade. 12.1 If you move something or alter something **a shade**, you move it or alter it by a very small amount; an informal expression. EG *I was asked to turn the radio down a shade.* PHR : USED AS AN A = a fraction **12.2** If you say that something is **a shade** large, **a shade** bright, etc, you mean that it is a little too large, a little too bright, etc; an informal expression. EG *I find the food a shade rich... That dress is a shade big for you.* PHR+ADJ/ADV ⇑ slightly = a touch

13 A **shade** is also the spirit of a dead person; a literary use. N COUNT = ghost

14 If someone or something **puts** someone or something else **in the shade**, they are so impressive that they make the other person or thing seem unimportant by comparison. EG *An achievement like that would put Penkovsky in the shade.* PHR : VB INFLECTS ⇑ overshadow

15 If you say **shades of** someone or something, you mean that something that has just happened or just been said reminds you of that person or thing. For example, if you hear that someone has stolen money and given it to poor people, you might say 'Shades of Robin Hood', because the outlaw Robin Hood is supposed to have given stolen money to poor people. PHR+NG

shading /ʃeɪdɪŋ/, **shadings**. **1** The **shading** in a drawing or painting is the dark parts of it, which often make objects in the picture look three-dimensional rather than flat. N UNCOUNT

2 Shadings are very small changes or differences between things. EG *There are many fine shadings of status through the social hierarchy... The gardens, hedges and ground were all in muted shadings of grey, black and white.* N COUNT : USU PL, IF+PREP THEN of = gradation

shadow /ʃædəʊ/, **shadows, shadowing, shadowed**. **1** A **shadow** is a dark shape on a surface that is made when something stands between a light and the surface. EG *There was a car parked down the street in the shadow of a tree... The smoky fires cast dancing shadows upon the wide circle of faces.* N COUNT

2 Shadow is darkness in a place caused by something preventing light from reaching it. EG *The whole canyon is in shadow.* N UNCOUNT ⇑ shade

3 If something **shadows** a place, it covers it with a shadow; a literary use. EG *The lawn was shadowed by a linden tree.* V+O : USU PASS ⇑ shade

4 A **shadow** is also **4.1** someone, for example a child, who does not like being separated from someone else and follows them about. EG *Peter had become Nina's adoring shadow.* N COUNT : USU POSS+N ⇑ companion **4.2** someone, for example a detective, who follows someone secretly in order to find out what they are doing or where they are going. EG *When I returned to the highway, our shadow had disappeared.* N COUNT : USU POSS+N

5 If someone **shadows** you, they follow you very closely wherever you go. EG *They were already having him shadowed by a plain-clothes detective.* V+O = dog

6 A **shadow** of a doubt or a **shadow** of a suspicion is a very small doubt or suspicion. EG *I never had a shadow of a doubt that he was right.* N SING WITH DET +of: WITH BROAD NEG ⇑ bit

7 A British Member of Parliament who is a member of the **Shadow** Cabinet or who is the **Shadow** Home Secretary, the **Shadow** Foreign Secretary, etc belongs to the main opposition party in Parliament and is the person who is most likely to be Home Secretary, Foreign Secretary, etc if that political party forms the next government. EG *There was a meeting of the Shadow Cabinet yesterday... He is Shadow Secretary for Trade and Industry.* ADJ CLASSIF : ATTRIB

8 If you say that someone is **afraid** or **frightened of** their **own shadow**, you mean that they become afraid very easily. PHR : USED AS C

9 If you say that something or someone is **a shadow of** their **former self**, you mean that they are much less vigorous or less powerful than they used to be. EG *The organization is now no more than a shadow of its former self.* PHR : USED AS C

10 See also **five o'clock shadow**.

shadowy /ʃædəʊi[1]/. **1** A **shadowy** place is full of shadows or is made dark by shadows. EG *Her face was dark in this shadowy place... The rock receded into a shadowy alcove.* ADJ CLASSIF

2 A **shadowy** figure, shape, etc is someone or something that you can hardly see because it is dark or misty. EG *They began firing haphazardly at the shadowy figures who seemed to have appeared from nowhere... ...the shadowy musicians in the background.* ADJ CLASSIF : ATTRIB = dim

3 You describe people and activities as **shadowy** when very little is known about them. EG *...the shadowy world of espionage.* ADJ QUALIT ⇑ vague = mysterious

shady /ʃeɪdi[1]/, **shadier, shadiest**. **1** A **shady** place is sheltered from bright sunlight by buildings or trees. EG *He found a shady place where he had an early lunch... They walked off down the shady side of the street.* ADJ CLASSIF ⇑ dark = shaded

2 Shady trees produce a lot of shade. EG *It was a delightful walk, under cool and shady trees... ...shady hedgerows.* ADJ CLASSIF

3 You describe activities as **shady** when you think that they are dishonest or illegal. EG *He had been getting money out of the country in various rather shady ways.* ▸ used of people. EG *Shady financiers had no difficulty in finding gullible customers.* ADJ QUALIT = dubious, questionable

shaft /ʃɑːft/, **shafts**. **1** A **shaft** is **1.1** a long thin piece of wood or metal that forms part of a spear or arrow or is the handle of an axe, golf club, or other tool. EG *...the slender spear whose shaft was polished from so much use.* N COUNT ⇑ pole **1.2** a rod or bar in a machine, for example in a car engine, that turns round and round in order to transfer power or movement. EG *...the drive shaft... ...the propeller shaft.* N COUNT **1.3** a long, narrow, usually vertical passage, for example one that forms the entrance to a mine or one in which a lift goes up and down. EG *...a mine shaft... ...the lift shaft... The shaft was bricked off.* N COUNT

2 The **shafts** of a cart or carriage are the two wooden poles at the front between which an animal is fastened when it pulls the cart or carriage. N COUNT : USU PL

3 A **shaft** of light is a narrow ray of light, for example a ray of sunlight shining through an opening. EG *The hatch was opened, admitting a shaft of daylight.* N COUNT : IF+PREP THEN of = beam

4 A **shaft** of wit or humour is a clever or amusing remark, especially one made as an attack on someone or something; a rather literary use. EG *...Sheila's devastating shafts of wit.* N COUNT : IF+PREP THEN of = sally

shag /ʃæg/, **shags, shagging, shagged**. **1** A **shag** is a black seabird with a yellow beak. N COUNT

2 Shag is a strong tasting tobacco which has been cut into long thin pieces. N UNCOUNT

3 A **shag** carpet or rug is made of long thick woollen threads. ADJ CLASSIF : ATTRIB

4 To **shag** someone means to have sex with them; a rude and offensive use in very informal English. V+O

shagged /ʃægd/. If you are **shagged** or **shagged out**, you are very tired and have no energy left; a very informal expression which some people consider rude. ADJ QUALIT : PRED, USU+out

shaggy /ʃægi[1]/, **shaggier, shaggiest**. **1 Shaggy** hair or fur is long and very untidy. EG *He was craggily handsome with a shaggy, unkempt beard.* ▸ used of a person or animal with shaggy hair or fur. EG *...a shaggy elderly man smoking a little pipe... Shaggy sheep roamed on the higher slopes.* ADJ QUALIT

2 A **shaggy dog story** is a very long joke with a rather silly ending. PHR HAS PL

Shah /ʃɑː/, **Shahs**. The **Shah** of Iran was the ruler of Iran. N IN TITLES

shake /ʃeɪk/, **shakes, shaking, shook, shaken.** 1 If you **shake** someone or something, you make them move vigorously backwards and forwards or up and down, especially by pushing and pulling them quickly with your hands. EG *They collected the berries by shaking the bushes over cloths spread beneath... He awakened to find himself being shaken roughly by his father... Mix the oil and vinegar together and shake well before using.* ▸ used as a noun. EG *Screw the lid tightly onto the top of the jar and give it a good shake.* V+O OR V+A ▸ N COUNT : USU a+N

2 If you **shake** something from somewhere, you make it come out or fall off by vigorously moving the thing that it is in or on. EG *He shook from a bag a heap of dried leaves... The wind shook a little shower of white petals from the tree... Carefully he opened it and gently shook everything out... I turned and shook off the hand she had placed on my sleeve.* V+O+A ⇑ remove

3 If you **shake** something such as a piece of cloth or if you **shake it out**, you hold it by one of its edges and move it about vigorously, for example in order to open it out or to make it flat. EG *You have to shake the quilt to redistribute the filling... ...a napkin which she shook out and spread on the table... ...shaking out her umbrella... He pulled a handkerchief from his pocket and shook it open with a violent flourish.* V+O, OR PHRASAL VB : V+O+ADV

4 If something **shakes**, it moves from side to side or up and down with quick, small movements, because some force is acting on it. EG *The earth shook and the sky darkened... The table shook.* V = tremble

5 If your body **is shaking**, it is moving from side to side or up and down with quick, small movements that you cannot control, for example because you are cold or frightened. EG *Meg was so nervous that her knees were shaking... I was drenched in sweat and shaking like a leaf... I couldn't believe what was happening to me: shaking, I picked up the telephone... He was shaking with laughter.* V = quiver, tremble

6 If your voice **is shaking**, it is trembling because you are nervous or very angry. EG *His eyes were wild and his voice shook.* ▸ used as a noun. EG *Her voice was low and had a shake to it.* V ⇑ vibrate ▸ N SING WITH DET

7 If something bad, unexpected, or frightening **shakes** you, it makes you feel suddenly very shocked and upset, and unable to think calmly or clearly. EG *My mother's death had shaken him dreadfully... Every one of them was in favour of hanging. It shook me. You find some funny things out.* ◊ **shaken.** EG *I was badly shaken. I had never had a crash before... Shaken, he offered to resign.* V+O : NO CONT ◊ ADJ QUALIT : USU PRED

8 If something **shakes** your beliefs or ideas, it makes you less certain about them. EG *The lecture did little to shake his convictions... In China, some of my most basic beliefs were shaken.* V+O : NO CONT ⇑ affect

9 If you **shake hands** with someone, **shake** their **hand**, or **shake** them **by the hand**, you hold their right hand in your own for a few moments, sometimes moving it up and down slightly, when you are meeting them, saying goodbye to them, or congratulating them. EG *Elijah and I shook hands and said good night... Someone shook my hand and said, 'Goodbye, Mr Baldwin.'... He shook Lexington warmly by the hand and congratulated him.* PHR OR PHR+A *(with)* : RECIP, VB INFLECTS

10 If you **shake on** an arrangement or deal with someone or if you **shake hands on** it, you shake hands with them in order to show that you agree to the arrangement that you have made together. EG *We all shook hands on the deal.* PHR : VB INFLECTS

11 If you **shake** your **head**, you turn it from side to side in order to show that you mean 'no' or to show disbelief or sadness. EG *He offered her a cigarette. She shook her head. 'No thank you. I don't smoke.'... She put the phone down, sighed and shook her head sadly... He shook his head in disapproval.* PHR : VB INFLECTS

12 If you **shake** your **fist** at someone or something, you hold your fist up and move it vigorously backwards and forwards, to show that you are angry with them. EG *He shook his fist at Thomas. 'You young idiot!'* PHR : VB+N INFLECT, USU+A *(at)*

13 If you tell someone to **shake a leg**, you are telling them to hurry up and do something instead of sitting about lazily; an informal expression. EG *Come on, shake a leg! We've got loads to do today.* PHR : ONLY IMPER = move it

14 If you get **the shakes**, your body shakes uncontrollably because you are frightened or ill or because you have drunk too much alcohol. EG *I'll have to keep off the booze, can't afford to have the shakes.* N PLURAL : *the*+N = jitters

15 If you say that you will be somewhere **in a couple of shakes** or **in two shakes**, you mean that you will be there very soon indeed; an informal expression. PHR : USED AS AN A

16 If you say that someone or something **is no great shakes**, you mean that they are not very skilful or effective; an informal expression. EG *She's certainly no great shakes as a mother.* PHR : VB INFLECTS

shake down. If you **shake down** somewhere, for example on the floor or on a settee, you sleep there temporarily; an informal expression. EG *You can shake down at my place for tonight.* PHRASAL VB : V+ADV+A = crash

shake off. If you **shake off** someone or something that you do not want, you get rid of them or get away from them. EG *It had taken Franklin several hours to shake off the police... Such habits cannot be shaken off in the course of a few decades.* PHRASAL VB : V+ADV+O = elude

shake up. 1 If you **shake** two or more things **up**, you mix them together by shaking the container that they are in. EG *Here are the raffle tickets; shake them up well before you pick one.* PHRASAL VB : ORDER V ↕ O+ADV ⇑ agitate

2 If something bad, unexpected, or frightening **shakes** you **up**, it makes you feel suddenly very shocked and upset, and unable to think calmly or clearly. EG *Did that lightning shake you up?* PHRASAL VB : V+O+ADV : NO CONT

3 See also **shake-up**.

shaker /ʃeɪkə/, **shakers.** A **shaker** is 1 a container used for shaking liquids in order to mix them. EG *...a cocktail shaker.* N COUNT : USU MOD+N 2 a container used for shaking a powdered substance onto a surface. EG *...a salt shaker... ...a flour shaker.* N COUNT : USU MOD+N

shake-up, shake-ups. A **shake-up** is a change that affects the whole of something such as an organization, with the result that it becomes very different from before. EG *Many were eager for a shake-up in the two-party system... I felt my life needed a shake-up.* N COUNT ⇑ revolution

shaky /ʃeɪki[1]/, **shakier, shakiest.** 1 If you are **shaky**, you are shaking or feeling weak because you are frightened, shocked, or ill. EG *I was nervous and a bit shaky.* ◊ **shakily.** EG *The man stood up shakily.* ADJ QUALIT ⇑ unsteady = wobbly ◊ ADV WITH VB

2 Something that is **shaky** is uncertain, doubtful, or weak in a way that makes people think it is not going to be very successful. EG *After a shaky start the orchestra grew more confident and played well... ...a company with very shaky financial prospects... They are building their arguments on very shaky premises.* ADJ QUALIT = dubious

shale /ʃeɪl/ is smooth soft rock that breaks easily into thin layers. N UNCOUNT

shall /ʃə[3]l/. 1 You use **shall** 1.1 when you are referring to something that you are going to do or that will happen to you in the future. EG *I shall get angry in a moment... I shall be killed... That was a moment I shall never forget... If you do that I shall be very pleased... We probably shan't sleep much.* MODAL : *I/we*+MODAL 1.2 to emphasize that something will definitely happen. EG *It must be done and therefore it shall be done... I promise you shan't be made to dance this time.* MODAL : WITH *he/she/it/they, you* 1.3 to say that you intend to do something. EG *I shall kill you, without fail, if you ever mention his name again... We shall impose extreme penalties on them... Oh dear, I'm late. I shall have to go... I shan't let you go... I shall be leaving soon.* MODAL : *I/we*+MODAL = will 1.4 during a speech or piece of writing to say what you are going to discuss or explain later. EG *Their quest is still a hopeless one, as I shall explain... In a few minutes we shall be hearing about some of the research that is underway... We shall be discussing some of the implications of this.* MODAL : *I/we*+MODAL = will 1.5 before verbs such as 'hope' and 'look forward' to say that you are hoping to do something, looking forward to something, etc; a fairly formal use. EG *Whatever it is you produce next, we shall look forward to reading it... I also do my own personal experimental work there, and I shall hope to be able to continue it.* MODAL : *I/we*+MODAL = will 1.6 to give an order that something must be done or must happen; a formal use. EG *I am giving orders that these pages shall not be delivered to you until a week after I die... One of the school rules is that after ten o'clock at night there shall be quietness on the upper corridor... No more drink shall be drunk tonight... You're here to enjoy yourself, and enjoy yourself you shall.* MODAL : WITH *he/she/it/they, you* 1.7 when you are giving your permission for something to happen; a rather old-fashioned use. EG *Very well, my dear. You shall have the coat.* MODAL ⇑ may

2 You use **shall** in questions 2.1 when you are asking someone for advice or suggestions. EG *Whatever* MODAL : *I/we*+MODAL

shall I do?... What shall I give them for dinner?... Where shall we go for our drink? **2.2** when you are asking someone if they would like you to do something or if they would mind if you did something. EG *Shall I shut the door?... Shall I tell them to send the bill to you up here?* MODAL : I/we+ MODAL = should

3 You use **shall we** in questions **3.1** when you are suggesting to another person or group of people that you should do something together. EG *Shall we go and see a film?... Shall we talk about something different now?* **3.2** after you have suggested to another person or group of people that you should do something, in order to ask them whether they agree with your suggestion. EG *Let's try one out for size, shall we?... We'll go forward a little more, shall we, and you'll be able to see the whole thing at once.* PHR + INF; PHR : USED AS ADV SEN

shallot /ʃəlɒt/, **shallots**. A **shallot** is a small, round vegetable that grows underground and is similar to an onion. It has a strong taste and is used especially for flavouring other food. N COUNT

shallow /ʃæləʊ/, **shallower, shallowest; shallows**. **1** A **shallow** hole, container, or layer of material measures only a short distance from the top or surface to the bottom. EG *I could never tell whether I was in deep or shallow waters... Gradually the deep ravine became shallower... ...shallow graves... ...the shallow end of the bathing pool.* ADJ QUALIT

2 A **shallow** argument, idea, etc does not show any serious or careful thought. EG *His arguments seemed shallow and tedious... His art had grown steadily shallower as he grew older.* ▸ used of people. EG *I was too young and shallow to understand love.* ◇ **shallowness**. EG *...the shallowness of her social life.* ADJ QUALIT ⇑ worthless = trivial; ◇ N UNCOUNT

3 If your breathing is **shallow**, you only take a very small amount of air into your lungs at each breath. EG *His breathing became shallow and infrequent.* ◇ **shallowly**. EG *She inhaled shallowly and let the smoke out of her mouth.* ADJ QUALIT ⇑ weak; ◇ ADV WITH VB ⇑ weakly

4 **Shallows** are an area of shallow water. EG *Thousands of little fish swim in the shallows.* N PLURAL : the+ N

sham /ʃæm/, **shams, shamming, shammed**. **1** Something that is a **sham** is not real or is not really what it seems to be; used showing disapproval. EG *...those who dismiss the workings of democracy as a sham... Their independence is a sham.* ▸ used as an adjective. EG *...a sham fight.* N COUNT : USU USED AS C; ▸ ADJ CLASSIF : ATTRIB

2 Someone who is a **sham** pretends to have qualities that they do not have or pretends to be something they are not. N COUNT : USU USED AS C = fraud, cheat

3 If you **sham** a particular state, you pretend to be in that state when in fact you are not. EG *...a child shamming sleep... The bird shammed death... He's not really drunk, he's only shamming.* V OR V+O = fake, feign

shamble /ʃæmbə⁰l/, **shambles, shambling, shambled**. **1** If you **shamble**, you walk in a careless, heavy way, dragging your feet and bending forwards slightly. EG *He had a stoop and shambled apologetically when he walked... There was something pathetically animal-like about his shambling limbs.* V ⇑ hobble

2 If a situation, place, or event is a **shambles**, there is great disorder and confusion because things have not been organized or have not happened as they were planned. EG *The meeting ended in a complete shambles... The rehearsal was a shambles... The Party is in the biggest shambles it has ever been in.* N PLURAL : a/the +N ⇑ mess

shame /ʃeɪm/, **shames, shaming, shamed**. **1** **Shame** is **1.1** an uncomfortable feeling of guilt and failure that you have because you have not behaved in an acceptable way or because someone close to you has not behaved in an acceptable way. EG *The memory fills me with shame... I almost died of shame because of your behaviour... Simon lowered his face in shame.* **1.2** the loss of the good opinion and respect that other people have for you and the uncomfortable feeling that this loss causes you. EG *Don't bring shame on the family... Bankruptcy involves serious loss of face and lasting shame.* N UNCOUNT ⇑ remorse; N UNCOUNT = disgrace, dishonour

2 If you say that you have done something **to** your **shame**, you mean that you feel guilty about it because you know that it is wrong. EG *Something I have done, much to my shame, is to fiddle my expenses.* PHR : USED AS AN A

3 If you say that something has happened **to the shame of** a particular person, you mean that you think that this person ought to feel shame about it. EG *The only growth industry in this country, to the shame of the Government, is unemployment.* PHR + NG : USED AS AN A

4 If something **shames** you, it causes you to feel shame. EG *It shamed him to know that his father had behaved in such a way.* V+O ⇑ humiliate

5 If you **shame** someone close to you, you make other people lose the respect that they have for that person by behaving in an unacceptable way. EG *Will I shame you in front of your fine friends?* V+O ⇑ humiliate

6 If you **shame** someone into doing something, you force them to do it by making them feel shame. EG *Father was shamed into giving a donation to the church by the vicar's sermon... ...horrific living conditions that would shame councillors out of their complacency.* V+O+A (into/out of) ⇑ persuade = cajole

7 If you say that a situation is **a shame**, you are expressing your regret about it and indicating that you think it ought not to be as it is. EG *It's a real shame, these poor kids have nowhere they can call home... What a shame the pubs were closed... It's a shame to waste all this food.* N SING : a+N

8 If you say **'Shame on you'** to someone, you are indicating in a strong way that they ought to feel shame for something that they have said or done. EG *A woman shouted, 'Shame on you! What do you know about poverty?'* CONVENTION

9 If something **puts** you or what you have done to **shame**, it makes you feel ashamed of yourself because it is of much better quality than what you have done. EG *Your work puts me to shame... Your lovely, neat embroidery puts mine to shame!* PHR : VB INFLECTS

shamefaced /ʃeɪmfeɪst/. If you are **shamefaced**, you feel embarrassed or awkward because you have done or said something that you feel you should not have done. EG *Henry stared at Howard with a slightly shamefaced look.* ◇ **shamefacedly**. EG *Sally came back shamefacedly into the dining-room.* ADJ QUALIT = sheepish; ◇ ADV WITH VB = sheepishly

shameful /ʃeɪmfʊl/. An action, attitude, or experience that is **shameful** is so bad that the person who does it or has it ought to feel shame; used showing disapproval. EG *An experience of this kind need no longer be regarded as shameful or unmentionable... It shows a shameful lack of concern.* ◇ **shamefully**. EG *The government have shamefully neglected this sector... ...a shamefully high rent.* ADJ QUALIT = disgraceful; ◇ ADV = disgracefully

shameless /ʃeɪmlɪ²s/. Someone who is **shameless** does not try to hide their behaviour, which is unacceptable to other people; used showing disapproval. EG *...a shameless hussy.* ▸ used of people's behaviour and actions. EG *...the shameless way in which these ladies are now behaving... He had been gazing at Nell with a shameless glance of lechery.* ◇ **shamelessly**. EG *He is well aware of his gift, using it shamelessly on every possible occasion.* ADJ CLASSIF ⇑ disgusting = brazen; ◇ ADV brazenly

shampoo /ʃæmpuː/, **shampoos, shampooing, shampooed**. **1** **Shampoo** is **1.1** a soapy liquid that you use for washing your hair. EG *She poured some shampoo onto my hair... There are shampoos for babies that do not sting the eyes.* **1.2** a liquid or other substance that is used for cleaning carpets. EG *Use proper carpet shampoo.* N MASS ⇑ soap; N MASS ⇑ cleaner

2 When you **shampoo** your hair or someone else's hair, you wash it using shampoo. EG *I had a bath and shampooed my hair.* V+O

3 If you have a **shampoo** at a hairdresser's, your hair is washed using shampoo. EG *Would you like a shampoo before Paul cuts your hair?* N COUNT : USU+ SING

4 If you **shampoo** a carpet or rug, you clean it using carpet shampoo. V+O

shamrock /ʃæmrɒk/, **shamrocks**. A **shamrock** is a plant with three round leaves on each stem. The shamrock is the national emblem of Ireland. N COUNT

shandy /ʃændi¹/, **shandies**. **Shandy** is a drink which is made by mixing beer and lemonade. EG *I'll have a shandy.* N MASS

shank /ʃæŋk/, **shanks**. **1** The **shank** of an object is the long, thin, straight part that is usually fixed to the centre of the object. EG *...the shank of your screwdriver... ...the door-knob shanks.* N COUNT : USU+ SUPP

2 A **shank** is a long, firm piece of something such as metal or thread that is used for joining one thing to another, for example a button to a coat, or the heel of a shoe to the sole of the shoe. N COUNT : USU+ SUPP

3 Your **shanks** are the parts of your legs between your knees and your ankles. EG *His shanks were thin.* N COUNT : USU WITH POSS

shan't /ʃɑːnt/ is the usual spoken form of 'shall not'.

shanty /ʃænti^1/, **shanties**. A **shanty** is 1 a small rough hut which poor people live in, built from tin, cardboard, or another material that is not very strong. EG *...shanty dwellers.* 2 a song which sailors used to sing while they were doing work on a ship such as pulling in ropes. — N COUNT = shack; N COUNT

shanty town, shanty towns. A **shanty town** is a town that consists of shanties which poor people live in. — N COUNT

shape /ʃeɪp/, **shapes, shaping, shaped**. 1 The **shape** of a physical object or area is the way that its outside edges join each other, for example whether they are straight or curved. EG *If you look at its shape you'll see that it's slightly wider at the bottom... Great Britain is roughly triangular in shape... ...a huge animal the size and shape of a rhinoceros... You can spin-dry this sweater and it will still retain its shape... ...pieces of wood of different sizes and shapes.* — N COUNT/UNCOUNT ⇑ outline

2 A **shape** is 2.1 something that you can see has its outside edges joining each other in a particular way, for example a circle, square, or triangle. EG *...patterns created from geometric shapes... ...a huge rectangular shape.* **2.2** an object or a person that you cannot identify because it is too dark or too far away to see clearly. EG *One could just distinguish a slim shape in a short white dress.* — N COUNT ⇑ figure; N COUNT ⇑ outline

3 The **shape** of something such as a plan or an organization is the way in which its various sections fit together to form a distinctive structure. EG *Organizations now change their internal shape with alarming frequency... He outlined his ideas about the manifesto's shape... ...developments which may alter the future course and shape of industry.* — N SING : WITH POSS = framework

4 If you **shape** an object, you give it a particular shape, especially using your hands. EG *Cut the paper in half and shape each piece to make rounded edges... He began to shape the dough into rolls.* — V+O : IF+PREP THEN *into* = fashion, form

5 Something that **shapes** a particular situation or activity is the most important factor in causing it to develop in the way it does. EG *It was the Greeks who shaped the thinking of Western man... ...Pascal's idea that history is shaped by trivial accidents.* — V+O ⇑ determine

6 The word **shape** is used in the following expressions. **6.1** You use the expression **in the shape of** after mentioning something using a general word, in order to introduce more specific information about it. EG *...large-scale enterprise in the shape of mines or plantations... There was entertainment too, in the shape of a couple of songs from Bill.* — PREP **6.2** If you are **in shape**, you are healthy and able to do a lot of physical activity without getting tired. If you are **out of shape**, you are unhealthy and unable to do a lot of physical activity without getting tired. EG *I ought to do something about getting into shape for this walking tour... You must be out of shape if you're puffed already.* — PHR : USED AS AN A **6.3** If someone or something is **in good shape, in bad shape**, etc, they are in a good or bad condition or state of health. EG *He kept his house in absolutely tip-top shape... Mrs Humbert's car was in respectable shape... The State Department was in poor shape.* — PHR : USED AS AN A **6.4** If you say, for example, that you will not accept something **in any shape or form**, you are emphasizing that you will not accept any form of it whatsoever. EG *I'm strongly opposed to violence in any shape or form... There never was and never will be magic in any shape or form.* — PHR AFTER N : WITH BROAD NEG **6.5** If you describe something as **the shape of things to come**, you mean that it is the start of a new trend or development, and in future things will be like this. — PHR : USED AS C/O **6.6** If something **takes shape**, it develops to an extent where it becomes fairly clear what the final result will be like. EG *As Robin's plan took shape we could appreciate the brilliance of its simplicity... Miss Lenaut's face took shape under his pen.* — PHR : VB INFLECTS **6.7** If you say that something **comes in all shapes and sizes**, you mean that there are many different types of it, and some types are very different from other types. EG *Murderers, I knew, came in all shapes and sizes... Queries to workers at a Citizens Advice Bureau come in all shapes and sizes.* — PHR : VB INFLECTS **6.8** If someone **licks** you **into shape** or **knocks** you **into shape**, they make you think, work, or behave in the way that they expect people to; a fairly informal expression. EG *We'll soon lick them into shape... ...bullying their children into shape.* — PHR : VB INFLECTS

shape up; used in fairly informal English. 1 If someone or something **shapes up** well, they develop or progress well. EG *The new recruits are shaping up quite well... Things are shaping up quite nicely on the South American contract... This campaign is shaping up as one of the most intensive sales campaigns ever.* — PHRASAL VB : V+ADV, USU+A

2 If someone tells you to **shape up**, they are telling you to start behaving or working satisfactorily. EG *You'd better shape up or you'll be out on your ear!* — PHRASAL VB : V+ADV

shaped /ʃeɪpt/. Something that is **shaped** like a particular object or in a particular way has the kind of shape indicated. EG *...a chair shaped like a saddle... ...oddly shaped rocks.* — ADJ CLASSIF ⇑ fashioned

-shaped combines with nouns to describe the shape of an object. EG *...an egg-shaped face... ...a star-shaped card.* — COMB : FORMS ADJS

shapeless /ʃeɪplɪ^{2}s/. 1 A person or object that is **shapeless** does not have a distinctive or attractive shape. EG *...shapeless lumps... ...shapeless striped pyjamas.* — ADJ QUALIT

2 Something such as a plan or an emotion that is **shapeless** has no distinct features or structure. EG *The final monologue seems to me quite shapeless... The apprehension she had felt had been shapeless, completely lacking in detail.* — ADJ QUALIT ⇑ amorphous

shapely /ʃeɪpli^1/, **shapelier, shapeliest**. A **shapely** person, especially a woman, has a well-proportioned body and an attractive shape. EG *She was well groomed and shapely... She had a slim waist and shapely legs.* — ADJ QUALIT

shard /ʃɑːd/, **shards**. A **shard** is a piece of broken pottery, glass, metal, etc; a formal word. EG *...white porcelain shards from the early Yung Cheng period... It bounced twice and exploded, sending white-hot shards of shrapnel flying through the air.* — N COUNT ⇑ fragment

share /ʃɛə/, **shares, sharing, shared**. 1 If you **share** something with another person, you both have the use of it. EG *Ralph went upstairs to the room he shared with his brother... The children had shared the same bed for years... Are you going to share my taxi?... ...all the other living creatures with whom we share the earth.* — V, V+O, OR V+O +A (with) : ALSO RECIP

2 If two or more people **share** a task or duty, they do it together in such a way that they each do a part of it. EG *We share the washing up... We all share the decision making... Let's share the petrol costs... Both partners share in preparing for and rearing their family.* — V+O, OR V+A (in) ⇑ divide

3 If you **share** in an activity that someone else is doing, you take part in it with them. EG *She should encourage her husband to share in the care of the baby... ...the principle of sharing in decision making by the electorate... There are a growing number of women who want to share some of the traditional male roles.* — V+A (in), OR V+O = participate

4 If you **share** an experience that someone else has, you are with them and so you experience it as well. EG *Old age was something they would never be able to share... The boy had been given the honour of sharing the elder's journey.* — V+O, OR V+O+(with) : ALSO RECIP

5 If you **share** something or **share** something **out** between a group of people, you divide the total amount into separate parts and give each part to a person in the group. EG *Share the sweets between the children... ...sharing out the money and possessions.* ● See also **share-out**. — V+O OR V+O+(out) : IF+PREP THEN among/betwe[en] ⇑ allocate = apportion

6 If you **share** something that you have with someone, you give part of it to them or let them use it. EG *I shared my tea and blankets... The children were being taught to share.* — V, V+O OR V+O+A (with) : ALSO RECIP

7 If you **share** something personal such as a thought or a piece of news with someone, you tell them about it. EG *He was so excited about his idea that he felt he had to share it with someone.* — V+O OR V+O+(with) : RECIP

8 If someone or something **shares** the same idea, quality, etc as someone or something else, the two people or things both have the same idea, quality, etc. EG *I share your concern... China and Japan share many characteristics... Victoria was called Vicky to distinguish her from her mother who shared the same name.* — V+O

9 If you have or do a **share** of something which a group of people are sharing, you have or do part of it. EG *A steadily increasing share of the work is handed over to computers... ...a campaign for foster parents to have a share in discussing fostering* — N SING WITH DET : IF+PREP THEN in/of ⇑ proportion

policy... You have increased your share of the vote among the population.

10 If you have or do your **share** of something, you have the amount that you are entitled to or do the amount that you are expected to do or ought to do. EG *It does help when a father does his share at home... He tried to rob her of her share in her father's estate... ...if one man seizes more than his fair share of the food available.* N SING : WITH POSS, IF+PREP THEN *in/of* ⇑ quota

11 A **share** in a company is one of the many equal parts into which the ownership of the company can be divided. Shares can be bought by people as an investment. EG *A week ago, the firm's shares jumped 10p to 114p... I wonder how many companies he has shares in?* N COUNT : USU PL

12 If you say that you **have** your **share of** bad things, disasters, etc, you mean that so many bad things happen to you that it seems unfair. EG *Well, we've certainly had our share of disasters... ...families with more than their fair share of tensions.* PHR : VB INFLECTS ⇑ proportion

13 The idea of **share and share alike** is the idea that people should each have or contribute an equal or fair part of something. EG *The twins had an easy-going family spirit of share and share alike... Come on, share and share alike, it's David's turn to choose the programmes today.* PHR

shareholder /ʃeəhəʊldə/, **shareholders**. A **shareholder** is a person who owns one or more shares in a company. N COUNT = investor

share-out, share-outs. If there is a **share-out** of something, several people are given equal or fair parts of it. EG *Children get lowest priority in the share-out of family food supplies... ...a share-out of the profits.* N COUNT : USU SING, IF+PREP THEN *of* ⇑ division

shark /ʃɑːk/, **sharks**. **1** A **shark** is a very large fish that has sharp teeth and lives in the sea. Several types of shark attack people, often killing them. EG *They were killed by a man-eating shark.* N COUNT

2 You might refer to a person as a **shark** if they persuade people to pay too much money for something or to sell something at too low a price; used showing disapproval. ● See also **loan shark**. N COUNT ⇑ crook

sharp /ʃɑːp/, **sharper, sharpest; sharps**. **1** A **sharp** object **1.1** has a very thin edge that is good for cutting things; used especially of knives. EG *Cut it away with a sharp knife... They could cut it open using the sharp edge of a stone.* ◊ **sharpness**. EG *She first satisfied herself as to the sharpness of her blade.* **1.2** has a very finely pointed end. EG *Use a sharp pencil... ...small, sharp teeth... ...sharp-thorned bushes.* ◊ **sharply**. EG *He had on sharply pointed brown shoes.* ◊ **sharpness**. EG *...feeling the sharpness of his claws.* ADJ QUALIT; ◊ N UNCOUNT; ADJ QUALIT; ◊ ADV; ◊ N UNCOUNT

2 A **sharp** picture, outline, or distinction is very clear and easy to see or understand. EG *The pictures were so sharp and detailed that you could see the weave of the fabric... ...sharp, fresh footprints in the snow... Although we try hard to draw a sharp dividing line between Civil Service and Government the distinction can often become blurred.* ◊ **sharply**. EG *The memory remains sharply engraved on my mind... His optimism contrasted sharply with the low morale of his supporters.* ADJ QUALIT; ◊ ADV

3 Someone who is **sharp** is quick to notice, hear, or understand things in detail; used showing approval. EG *You've got to be sharp to get ahead... His sharp eyes would never miss it... There seems to be a sharper awareness of the threat to peace.* ◊ **sharply**. EG *Her ears were sharply attuned to anything coming from that direction.* ADJ QUALIT = keen; ◊ ADV WITH VB = keenly

4 A **sharp** change happens suddenly and is great in amount or degree. EG *...sharp food-price increases... ...a sharp growth in the number of registered child-minders... The British two party system encourages sharp fluctuations in policy.* ◊ **sharply**. EG *Sales of the car have risen sharply in recent weeks... My opinion of Smithy had fallen sharply.* ADJ QUALIT; ◊ ADV WITH VB

5 A **sharp** hit, blow, or other action is done quickly and firmly with a strong effect. EG *She received a sharp clout on the head... With his finger and thumb he gave it a sharp turn anti-clockwise... He brought them into sharp and brutal contact.* ◊ **sharply**. EG *Daintry put his glass sharply down and spilt some sherry... Both birds turned their heads sharply at the sound.* ADJ QUALIT; ◊ ADV WITH VB

6 A **sharp** bend or turn is one that changes direction suddenly. EG *Careful, this is a sharp bend.* ▸ used as an adverb. EG *You go over the bridge and the road turns sharp left.* ◊ **sharply**. EG *It measures how sharply the curve bends round.* ADJ QUALIT; ▸ ADV; ◊ ADV WITH VB

7 If someone's face has **sharp** features, their features are pointed and hard rather than rounded and gentle. EG *He has dark hair, blue eyes, and a sharp nose.* ◊ **sharpness**. EG *...a pleasant, friendly smile that softened the sharpness of his features.* ADJ QUALIT = angular; ◊ N UNCOUNT

8 Sharp pain or cold affects you deeply and suddenly in a way that hurts. EG *His blistered foot at that moment caused him a sharp pang... This gave her a sharp, tingling sensation... ...a sharp, buffeting wind.* ADJ QUALIT ⇑ acute

9 A **sharp** sound is very short and sudden and quite loud. EG *...the sharp crack of a twig.* ADJ QUALIT ⇑ clear

10 Food that has a **sharp** taste is slightly bitter and sour but also clear and fresh. EG *...the sharp, pure taste of red gooseberries.* ◊ **sharpness**. EG *The fruit is sometimes cooked with sugar to mellow its sharpness.* ADJ QUALIT; ◊ N UNCOUNT

11 Sharp actions or statements are said or done in a quick, hard, and direct way, often showing slight anger, disagreement, or warning. EG *A sharp order came through his radio headphones.* ◊ **sharply**. EG *...sharply worded attacks on ministers... 'Don't talk nonsense,' she said sharply... He looked at me sharply over the top of his glasses.* ADJ QUALIT ⇑ fierce; ◊ ADV WITH VB ⇑ fiercely

12 Sharp is used after stating a particular time in order to say that something happens at exactly that time. EG *His train came in at eight sharp.* ADJ AFTER NUM = precisely ADV WITH VB

13 If you tell someone to **look sharp**, you tell them to do something quickly or to move faster. EG *Come on, look sharp!... We'll have to look sharp or we'll never get there in time.* PHR : VB INFLECTS, USU IMPER = hurry up

14 A **sharp** in music is a note that is a semitone higher than the note which is described by the same letter. It can be represented by the symbol ♯ after the letter. EG *I have to play four sharps in this piece... ...the C sharp minor Prelude, Opus 45.* N COUNT, OR ADJ AFTER N ≠ flat

15 A **sharp** note or a musical instrument that is **sharp** is slightly higher in pitch than it should be. EG *The violin sounds a bit sharp–can you come down a little?* ▸ used as an adverb. EG *She sang sharp all the way through.* ADJ QUALIT ⇑ high ≠ flat; ▸ ADV ≠ flat

sharpen /ʃɑːpə⁰n/, **sharpens, sharpening, sharpened**. When you **sharpen** something or when it **sharpens**, it is made sharp or sharper than it was. EG *...neatly sharpened pencils... Roger sharpened a stick at both ends... He felt a pang of alarm, which sharpened when he saw the crowd outside.* V-ERG

sharpen up. If you **sharpen** something **up**, you make it sharper than it was. EG *I was practical enough to sharpen up my knives... It sharpened up her hearing.* PHRASAL VB : V+O+ADV

sharpener /ʃɑːpə⁰nə/, **sharpeners**. A **sharpener** is a tool or machine used for sharpening a particular type of object, especially pencils. EG *...a pencil sharpener... ...an electric knife sharpener.* N COUNT : USU AFTER N ⇑ device

sharp-eyed. Someone who is **sharp-eyed** is observant and quick to notice things. EG *...sharp-eyed newsmen.* ADJ QUALIT ⇑ vigilant

sharpish /ʃɑːpɪʃ/ means quickly, without any delay; an informal word. EG *I've no doubt she'll want her supper sharpish after that long journey.* ADV WITH VB

sharp practice. If you describe something that someone does as **sharp practice**, you mean that it is clever but dishonest. EG *There's been some sharp practice going on here.* N UNCOUNT

shatter /ʃætə/, **shatters, shattering, shattered**. **1** If something **shatters** or if you **shatter** something, it breaks suddenly into lots of small pieces. EG *The vase fell from her hand and shattered on the floor... I shattered the glass.* V-ERG = smash

2 If something **shatters** something such as a person's beliefs or hopes or confidence, it destroys or badly damages it. EG *A row in 1932 shattered his allegiance to the Democrats... My dreams have been shattered... His composure was shattered, his eloquence gone.* V OR V+O : USU V+O ⇑ break

3 If someone **is shattered**, **3.1** they are badly affected emotionally by something unexpected that has happened. EG *When Harris died, Dean was shattered... The girl looked shattered by this attack.* **3.2** they feel very tired and have no energy left; an informal use. EG *I feel absolutely shattered!... The week at summer school completely shattered me.* V+O : ONLY PASS ⇑ upset; V+O = exhaust

shattering /ʃætə⁰rɪŋ/. Something that is **shattering** **1** badly affects you emotionally, especially because ADJ QUALIT you have learned something that shocks you. EG *This conversation had a shattering effect on me... ...a shattering experience.* **2** makes you very tired indeed. EG *Sunday had been a shattering day.* ADJ QUALIT = exhausting

shave /ʃeɪv/, **shaves, shaving, shaved. 1** When a man **shaves**, he cuts hair from his face, very close to the skin, using a razor or shaver. EG *When he had shaved and dressed, he went down to the kitchen... He had shaved off his beard... I cut myself shaving.* V, V+O OR V+O+A *(off)*

2 A **shave** is the removal of hair from the face by shaving. EG *He had a shave and a bath... I need a shave.* N COUNT : IF SING a+N

3 If you **shave** a man, you cut hair from his face, very close to the skin, using a razor or shaver. V+O

4 If someone **shaves** a part of their body, they cut all the hair from it using a razor or shaver. EG *To enter the convent she would have to have her head shaved... She shaved her legs and under her arms... A small patch of his hair was shaved off.* V+O, OR V+O+A *(off)*

5 If you **shave** something off a piece of wood or other material, you cut very thin pieces from it. EG *Use a plane to shave off a small amount from the bottom of the door.* V+O+A *(off)*

6 If you **shave** something by a small amount or **shave** a small amount off it, you reduce it by that amount. EG *Georges Marchais's winning margin was shaved by 8 per cent... We could shave prices a little.* V+O, OR V+O+A *(off)*

7 If something is a **close shave**, it is very near to being an accident or disaster but you just manage to avoid this; used in informal English. PHR : USED AS C/O

8 See also **shaving**.

shaven /ʃeɪvəⁿn/. Something that is **shaven** has been shaved. EG *His hair was very short and the back of his neck shaven.* ● See also **clean-shaven**. ADJ CLASSIF

shaver /ʃeɪvə/, **shavers**. A **shaver** is an electric tool, used for shaving hair from the face and body. EG *...an electric shaver... Does the room have a shaver point?* N COUNT ⇑ razor

shaving /ʃeɪvɪŋ/, **shavings. 1 Shaving** is used to describe something that you use when you shave. EG *He put his shaving things into a plastic bag... ...a shaving brush... ...shaving cream.* N BEFORE N

2 Shavings are small, very thin pieces of something such as wood which have been shaved from a larger piece. N COUNT : USU PL = sliver

shawl /ʃɔːl/, **shawls**. A **shawl** is a large piece of woollen cloth which is worn by women over their shoulders or head, or which is wrapped around a baby to keep it warm. N COUNT ⇑ garment

she /ʃiː/ is used as the subject of a verb. **1** You use **she** to refer to a woman or girl who has already been mentioned or named, or whose identity is known. EG *'So long,' Mary said as she passed Miss Saunders... Ask her if she can do something with them.* ▸ used also to refer to a female animal. EG *I patted the dog and she wagged her tail.* PRON : SING, USED AS S

2 You also use **she 2.1** to refer to a nation. EG *Britain is a poor nation now, and she would do well to remember this.* PRON : SING, USED AS S **2.2** to refer to a ship, car, or other vehicle, machine, or structure; sometimes used to show affection for the thing you are talking about. EG *See how sweetly she moves through the water!... She does 0 to 60 in 10 seconds.* PRON : SING, USED AS S = it

sheaf /ʃiːf/, **sheaves**. A **sheaf** is **1** a small bundle of papers lying one on top of the other. EG *He drew a sheaf of papers from his breast pocket... ...a thick sheaf of letters.* N COUNT : ALSO N PART+N IN PLURAL = bunch **2** a bundle of corn or other grain plants that are tied together after they have been cut, so that they can stand in the field to dry. EG *A machine was invented that mowed, threshed, tied straw into sheaves and poured grain into sacks... ...a sheaf of corn.* N COUNT : ALSO N PART+N UNCOUNT

shear /ʃɪə/, **shears, shearing, sheared, shorn**. The past participle can be either **sheared** or **shorn**. **1** To **shear** a sheep means to cut the wool off it. EG *I sheared 500 ewes this summer.* V+O ◊ **shearing**. EG *I start shearing at the beginning of July.* ◊ N UNCOUNT

2 To **shear** hair means to cut it off; a fairly literary use. EG *Her hair had been shorn when she had a fever.* V+O : USU PASS

3 Shears are **3.1** a large pair of scissors, like the kind used for shearing sheep. EG *He handled the shears with skill and speed.* N PLURAL : ALSO a pair of+N **3.2** a tool like a very large pair of scissors with long cutting blades, used especially for cutting garden hedges. N PLURAL : ALSO a pair of+N

shear off. If something such as a piece of metal **shears off**, it breaks because of pressure from something heavy or a twisting force or because of old age; used especially of metal machine parts. EG *Another bolt has sheared off.* PHRASAL VB : V+ADV

sheath /ʃiːθ/, **sheaths**. A **sheath** is **1** a covering for the blade of a knife, usually made of leather. EG *He wiped the knife and put it back in the sheath.* N COUNT ⇑ case **2** a protective covering for something. EG *Their claws are kept sharp by being retracted into sheaths... The dress was a strapless sheath which clung to her body.* N COUNT **3** a rubber covering that fits closely over a man's penis and is used as a contraceptive during sexual intercourse. N COUNT = condom ▸ used to refer to this method of contraception. EG *The sheath is not 100% reliable.* ▸ N SING : the+N

sheathe /ʃiːð/, **sheathes, sheathing, sheathed. 1** If you **sheathe** a knife, you put it in a sheath. V+O

2 If you **sheathe** something, you put it or enclose it in a protective covering. EG *Trees, sheathed in ice, glittered in the sun.* V+O : IF+PREP THEN in/with ⇑ cover

sheath knife, sheath knives. A **sheath knife** is a knife that has a blade that is sharp on one side and has a heavy handle. Sheath knives are used outdoors, especially for cutting sticks or rope. N COUNT

sheaves /ʃiːvz/ is the plural of **sheaf**.

shed /ʃed/, **sheds, shedding**. The form **shed** is used in the present tense and is the past tense and past participle of the verb. **1** A **shed** is **1.1** a small, roughly-made building of wood or metal that is used for storing things such as garden tools. EG *She went to find her wellingtons in the shed... ...a garden shed.* N COUNT

1.2 a large shelter or building, for example one found at a railway station, port, or factory, that is used for a particular activity. EG *You have to go through the customs shed... ...a bicycle shed.* N COUNT : USU MOD+N

2 To **shed** hair or skin or leaves means to go through a natural process which causes the skin or hair or leaves to come off. EG *Many trees shed their leaves in winter... Have you ever seen a snake shedding its skin?* V+O = lose, slough

3 To **shed** something also means to get rid of it or let it fall off. EG *We shed our clothes and jumped into the water... The house has been shedding tiles... 2,600 workers are due to be shed by the company... I shed all my restraint.* V+O = cast off, discard

4 If a lorry or van **sheds its load**, it accidentally drops on to the road all the goods that are being transported. EG *A lorry has shed its load on the M1 north of Watford.* PHR : VB INFLECTS ⇑ lose

5 If you **shed** tears, you cry. EG *...a child shedding tears over a broken toy.* V+O = weep

6 To **shed blood** means to kill people by violence or war. EG *They called for an end to the shedding of blood.* ● See also **bloodshed**. PHR : VB INFLECTS

7 If something **sheds** water, it causes water to run off its surface instead of soaking through it. EG *These birds build nests with flat roofs which shed water.* V+O : NO CONT ⇑ repel

8 If something **sheds light on** a problem or situation, it makes it easier to understand by providing more information. EG *Can you shed any light on the problem?... He talked for an hour without shedding any light on what was happening.* PHR : VB INFLECTS = elucidate

she'd /ʃiːd/ is **1** the usual spoken form of 'she had', especially when 'had' is an auxiliary verb. EG *It was too late. She'd done it... She'd been on holiday in June.* **2** a spoken form of 'she would'. EG *She said she'd come by train... She'd like to earn some money.*

sheen /ʃiːn/, **sheens**. A **sheen** is a smooth and gentle brightness on the surface of something, usually because it is in good condition; used showing approval. EG *...beautiful, long hair with a silky sheen... Her face glowed with a healthy red sheen... ...a silvery metallic sheen.* N COUNT+SUPP USU SING = lustre

sheep /ʃiːp/. **Sheep** is both the singular and the plural form. **1** A **sheep** is a farm animal with a thick woolly coat, especially a white one. Sheep are usually kept either for their wool or for their meat. EG *There wasn't a sheep in sight... ...six hundred sheep... ...a flock of sheep... We heard the sheep bleating.* ● See also **black sheep**. N COUNT

2 If you say that a group of people are **like sheep**, you mean that if one person does something, all the others do it as well rather than making their own decisions about what to do. PHR : USED AS A

3 If you **make sheep's eyes** at someone, you look at them in a loving and adoring way. PHR : VB INFLECTS

4 If you **separate the sheep from the goats**, you select from a group of people those who are consid- PHR : VB INFLECTS ered to be better in some way than the others. EG *This test should separate the sheep from the goats!*

5 ● **a wolf in sheep's clothing**: see **wolf**.

sheepdip /ʃi:pdɪp/, **sheepdips**. 1 **Sheepdip** is a liquid which is used to kill harmful insects in a sheep's coat. N UNCOUNT = dip

2 A **sheepdip** is the trough which contains this liquid and in which the sheep are treated. N COUNT ⇑ container

sheepdog /ʃi:pdɒg/, **sheepdogs**. A **sheepdog** is a dog that was bred originally for its skill in working with and controlling large numbers of sheep. N COUNT

sheepfold /ʃi:pfəʊld/, **sheepfolds**. A **sheepfold** is a small area of land that is surrounded by a fence or low wall. It is used for keeping sheep safely together for short periods of time. N COUNT ⇑ enclosure = pen

sheepish /ʃi:pɪʃ/. If you look **sheepish**, you look a bit embarrassed because you feel foolish or have done something silly. EG *He gave me a sheepish grin.* ADJ QUALIT
◇ **sheepishly**. EG *He smiled sheepishly.* ◇ ADV WITH VB

sheepskin /ʃi:pskɪn/, **sheepskins**. **Sheepskin** is the skin of a sheep with the wool still attached to it, used especially for coats and rugs. EG *...a sheepskin jacket... ...a coat made of sheepskin.* N UNCOUNT/COUNT

sheer /ʃɪə/, **sheers, sheering, sheered**. 1 **Sheer** means complete and not involving or mixed with anything else; often used simply to emphasize the word it describes. EG *The eighth floor of the hotel was sheer luxury... By sheer coincidence, Michael was there too... Many of the audience walked out through sheer boredom.* ADJ CLASSIF: ATTRIB ⇑ absolute = pure

2 **Sheer** is used to describe silk or other material which is very fine, light, and delicate. EG *...sheer silk... ...sheer stockings.* ADJ QUALIT

3 A **sheer** cliff or drop is so steep that it is almost vertical. EG *He peered over the sheer drop... ...a sheer rock face.* ▸ used as an adverb. EG *The great cliffs drop sheer for over 1400 feet.* ADJ QUALIT ▸ ADV AFTER VB

4 If something **sheers** in a particular direction, it suddenly changes direction, for example to avoid hitting something. EG *The car was heading straight towards us but sheered away at the last minute... The wind had sheered round to due south... The argument sheered off, bringing up fresh, unpleasant matters.* V+A ⇑ deviate = veer off

sheet /ʃi:t/, **sheets, sheeting, sheeted**. 1 A **sheet** is 1.1 a rectangular piece of cloth, usually made of cotton and often one of a pair, which is put either under you or over you in bed. EG *It was bliss to sleep in a soft bed with clean sheets again.* ● **as white as a sheet**: see **white**. N COUNT ⇑ cover 1.2 a large, flat, square or rectangular piece of a solid material. EG *...the aluminium sheets of which the shelter was constructed... ...a single sheet of glass... Expanded foam polystyrene also comes in sheet form.* N COUNT: ALSO N PART 1.3 a rectangular piece of paper, for example from a writing pad or for wrapping up a parcel. EG *He started off by writing his name at the top of a blank sheet of paper... Each sheet was covered with small, neat handwriting... ...a couple of sheets of wrapping paper.* N COUNT: ALSO N PART+N UNCOUNT ▸ used to refer to a sheet of paper that has been printed to make postage stamps, with rows of small holes between the stamps so that they can be torn off individually. EG *...a sheet of stamps.* ▸ N PART+N IN PLURAL 1.4 a sheet of paper which gives information about something. EG *He himself kept daily time sheets of how he spent every hour... ...a fact sheet.* ● See also **balance sheet**. N COUNT: USU MOD+N

1.5 a line or rope used for controlling the position of a sail on a boat. N COUNT

2 A **sheet** of something thin is a wide expanse of it which forms a thin layer covering the surface of something else. EG *Flowering sheets of water lilies stretched across the lake... Watch how you go, the pavement's like a sheet of ice.* N PART+N UNCOUNT

3 A **sheet** is also a fast-moving mass of fire or water that you cannot easily see through. EG *A sheet of flame shot up into the air... The rain was coming down in sheets.* N COUNT: ALSO N PART+N UNCOUNT

4 See also **sheeting**.

sheet down. If it **is sheeting down**, it is raining very heavily indeed. EG *It's absolutely sheeting down outside... The rain was sheeting down now.* PHRASAL VB: V+ADV, USU CONT = bucket down, pour down

sheet anchor, sheet anchors. A **sheet anchor** is 1 an anchor which is much larger and stronger than an ordinary anchor and which is only used when a boat is in difficulties. N COUNT 2 the thing that helps you more than anything else when problems or difficulties occur. EG *People nowadays put much more stress on friendship as the sheet anchor of marriage.* N SING WITH DET = mainstay

sheet ice is a solid layer of ice over a road or path. EG *The pavement was covered in sheet ice.* N UNCOUNT

sheeting /ʃi:tɪŋ/ is 1 metal, plastic, polythene, etc, that is made in the form of sheets. EG *Why was tin sheeting so popular as a roof material in Africa?* N UNCOUNT ⇑ material 2 cloth that is used for making sheets. N UNCOUNT

sheet lightning is lightning that appears to flash across a large area of the sky at once. N UNCOUNT

sheet metal is metal which is made into thin sheets rather than being made into solid bars or cast in moulds. EG *...the sheet metal workers' union.* N UNCOUNT

sheet music is printed music on single sheets of paper or on sheets that are fastened together without a hard cover. N UNCOUNT

sheikh /ʃeɪk/, **sheikhs**; also spelled **sheik**. A **sheikh** is an Arab chief or ruler. N COUNT: ALSO IN TITLES

sheikhdom /ʃeɪkdəm/, **sheikhdoms**; also spelled **sheikdom**. A **sheikhdom** is the area of land that is ruled by or controlled by a sheikh. N COUNT

shekels /ʃekə⁰lz/ is money; used in informal English, usually humorously. EG *You look well, Tom. Still gathering in the shekels, eh?* N PLURAL

shelf /ʃelf/, **shelves**. 1 A **shelf** is 1.1 a flat piece of a hard material, for example wood, metal, or glass, which is attached to a wall or to the sides of a cupboard. Shelves are used for keeping things on. EG *There were a lot of books on the shelves along the walls... He returned the silver teapot to its shelf... Most of these artificial sweeteners have disappeared from supermarket shelves.* ● See also **bookshelf**. N COUNT ⇑ ledge 1.2 a section of rock on a cliff or mountain or underwater, that sticks out like a shelf. N COUNT = ledge

2 If you **leave** something **on the shelf**, you take no action at all about it. EG *The report will be left on the shelf as so many reports have been left in the past.* PHR: VB INFLECTS

3 If you say that someone, especially a woman, **is left on the shelf**, you mean that they did not get married while they were young, and are now too old to find anyone to marry; a rather old-fashioned expression. PHR: VB INFLECTS, USU PASS

4 If something is sold **off the shelf**, it is sold in shops as a standard product which does not have to be specially made or ordered. EG *You can buy a computer off the shelf... ...cheap 'off the shelf' mechanical components.* PHR: USED AS AN A, OR BEFORE N

shelf life; also spelled with a hyphen. The **shelf life** of a product, especially food, is the length of time that it can be kept in a shop before it becomes too old to sell. EG *This process should give butter a longer shelf life.* N SING WITH DET +SUPP

shell /ʃel/, **shells, shelling, shelled**. 1 The **shell** of an egg or nut is the hard covering which surrounds it. EG *Three of these eggs have got cracked shells... ...coconut shells.* N COUNT/UNCOUNT

2 The **shell** of a tortoise, snail, or other animal is the hard, protective covering that it has on its back. N COUNT/UNCOUNT

3 A **shell** is the hard covering, often white or pink in colour, in which certain kinds of small sea animals live. Shells are found in many different sizes and shapes. EG *I used to spend hours collecting shells on the beach... ...a crab shell.* N COUNT/UNCOUNT

4 If you **shell** peas, nuts, eggs, etc, you remove the natural covering from them, before or after cooking them. EG *Can you help me shell these peas?* V+O

5 If you say that someone has **come** or **crawled out of** their **shell**, or that they have **been brought out of** their **shell**, you mean that are beginning to be friendly and more interested in other people and less shy, quiet, and reserved. PHR: VB INFLECTS

6 If you say that someone **retires** or **crawls into** their **shell**, you mean that they become very quiet and shy and not at all interested in other people. EG *He's useless at parties. He retires into his shell and won't speak to anybody.* PHR: VB INFLECTS

7 A **shell** is also 7.1 the outside frame of something such as a building, boat, or car, especially when it is being made or built, or when the completed object has been damaged for example by fire. EG *Beyond, shells of hotels, office blocks, and flats are rising fast... ...the burned-out shell of thatch and mud that had once been the farmhouse.* N COUNT ⇑ structure 7.2 a metal container filled with explosives that can be fired from a large gun over long distances. EG *Arnold had his leg smashed when a shell hit the truck he was driving.* N COUNT ⇑ missile

8 To **shell** something means to fire shells at it. EG *They continued to shell towns on the northern coast.* V+O
◇ **shelling**. EG *There had been some heavy shelling.* ◇ N UNCOUNT

shell out. If you **shell out** for something, you spend an amount of money on it, especially when you do not really want to; an informal expression. EG *How much did you have to shell out?* PHRASAL VB : V+ADV, OR V+O+ADV ⇑ pay = fork out

she'll /ʃiːl/ is the usual spoken form of 'she will'. EG *I hope she'll be all right... She'll remember me if I go back, won't she?*

shellfish /ʃelfɪʃ/. **Shellfish** is both the singular and the plural form. A **shellfish** is a small creature that lives in the sea and has a shell. Prawns, crabs, and lobsters are all types of shellfish that people eat. N COUNT/UNCOUNT = crustacean

shell shock is an illness affecting the mind or the nerves, caused by the frightening experiences that happen to soldiers during a war. N UNCOUNT

shell-shocked. 1 A soldier who is **shell-shocked** is suffering from shell shock. ADJ CLASSIF

2 If you feel **shell-shocked**, you feel very tired and under stress because of something you have just experienced. EG *I was feeling shell-shocked after the interview.* ADJ CLASSIF

shelter /ʃeltə/, **shelters, sheltering, sheltered.** 1 A **shelter** is a small building or covered place which is made to protect people from something such as bad weather or bomb attacks. EG *That shelter might fall down if the rain comes back... ...a bus shelter.* N COUNT ⇑ structure

2 If a place provides **shelter**, it provides protection from bad weather or danger. EG *There was no shelter anywhere from the rain... I stopped in the shelter of the trees... He found shelter in caves... They are glad to take shelter in a barn.* N UNCOUNT = refuge

3 If you **shelter** in a place, you stay there and are protected from bad weather or danger. EG *You can find these creatures hiding beneath stones or sheltering in damp mossy places... It is natural to shelter from a storm.* V : USU+A = take refuge

4 If a place or thing **is sheltered** by something, the place or thing is protected by it from wind and rain. EG *This wide alley is sheltered by plane trees.* V+O : USU PASS = shield

5 If you **shelter** someone, 5.1 you provide them with a place to stay or live. EG *Can those being sheltered be adequately fed?* V+O 5.2 you help them by hiding them somewhere when they are being hunted by the police or other people. EG *...revolutionary colleagues whom he sheltered in the monastery... Some villagers are prepared to help to shelter wanted men.* V+O : IF+PREP THEN *from* = harbour

6 If you have **shelter**, you have a place where you can stay or live. EG *The basic necessities of life are food, shelter and clothing.* N UNCOUNT

sheltered /ʃeltəd/. 1 A place that is **sheltered** is protected from wind and rain. EG *Scrabster has a sheltered harbour... I lay down in the warmest and most sheltered spot I could find.* ADJ QUALIT

2 If you have a **sheltered** life, you are protected and kept away from things which could upset you or harm you. EG *They had led a sheltered life.* ADJ QUALIT

3 **Sheltered** work or accommodation is designed for old or handicapped people, and allows them to be independent, while also giving them supervision when they need it. EG *...sheltered work for the disabled... ...a sheltered housing scheme.* ADJ CLASSIF : ATTRIB ⇑ supervised

shelve /ʃelv/, **shelves, shelving, shelved.** 1 If you **shelve** a plan, you decide not to continue with it for a while. EG *The project seems to have been shelved for the moment... I had simply shelved this awkward problem.* V+O ⇑ postpone = put aside

2 If a stretch of land **shelves**, it slopes downwards, especially on a seashore. EG *...long, gently shelving sands.* V

3 **Shelves** is the plural of **shelf**.

shelving /ʃelvɪŋ/ is a set of shelves, or material for making shelves. EG *Thousands of books are stocked on more than 8 miles of shelving in this library.* N UNCOUNT

shepherd /ʃepəd/, **shepherds, shepherding, shepherded.** 1 A **shepherd** is a person whose job is looking after sheep. EG *My best friend is a Dorset shepherd.* N COUNT

2 If you **shepherd** someone, you accompany them to make sure that they go to the right place, sometimes also giving them help and advice so that they behave in the correct way. EG *I was glad Dan was going to be there to shepherd me in the morning... I shepherded them towards the lobby... I'm just shepherding her through her first experience of Hollywood.* V+O : USU+A

shepherdess /ʃepədes/, **shepherdesses.** A **shepherdess** is a woman or girl whose job is looking after sheep. N COUNT ⇑ worker

shepherd's pie, shepherd's pies. Shepherd's pie is a dish eaten in Britain, consisting of a layer of minced meat covered with a layer of mashed potato. N UNCOUNT/COUNT ⇑ food

sherbet /ʃɜːbət/, **sherbets. Sherbet** is 1 a sweet dry powder that tastes fizzy and is eaten as a sweet or used to make a drink. N UNCOUNT 2 the same as sorbet; used in American English. N UNCOUNT/COUNT

sheriff /ʃerɪf/, **sheriffs.** A **sheriff** is 1 a person who is elected in America to make sure that the law is obeyed in a particular county. EG *He was appointed Sheriff of New York.* N COUNT : ALSO IN TITLES ⇑ officer 2 the senior judge of a county or district in Scotland. EG *...charges of murder and robbery in the Sheriff Court at Ayr.* N COUNT : ALSO IN TITLES 3 a person in England or Wales appointed by the Queen or King, mainly to carry out ceremonial duties in a particular county. N COUNT : ALSO IN TITLES ⇑ official

sherry /ʃeri[1]/, **sherries. Sherry** is a pale or dark brown alcoholic drink that is made from grapes and is usually drunk in small glasses, especially before a meal. EG *...a glass of sherry... Would you like a sherry?* N MASS

she's /ʃiːz/ is the usual spoken form of 'she is' or 'she has', especially when 'has' is an auxiliary verb. EG *She's Swedish... She's a sweet person... She's going to be busy till about Friday. She's gone back to Montrose this morning... She's got a very good job there.*

shibboleth /ʃɪbəleθ/, **shibboleths.** A **shibboleth** is an old idea or practice which is no longer thought to be important; a formal word. EG *He has never sought to hide his contempt for 'outworn shibboleths' like discipline and examinations.* N COUNT

shield /ʃiːld/, **shields, shielding, shielded.** 1 A **shield** is 1.1 a large piece of metal or leather, which soldiers carried in former times to protect their bodies from injury while they were fighting. N COUNT 1.2 a sports trophy or a badge that is shaped in the same way that many shields were made. EG *Our school won the sports shield last year.* N COUNT

2 Something which is a **shield** against particular danger or damage provides protection from it. EG *Dark pigment in the skin provides an effective shield against the sun... He must pile more sand on top as a shield... ...a wind shield.* N COUNT : IF+PREP THEN *against*

3 If someone or something **shields** a person or thing from particular danger or damage, they protect them from it, especially by putting a barrier between them. EG *Her parasol was propped up behind her to shield her from the sun... She intended to shield the child from this information.* V+O (NG/REFL) : USU+A (*from*)

shift /ʃɪft/, **shifts, shifting, shifted.** 1 If you **shift** something or if it **shifts**, you move it or change its direction slightly from one place or position to another. EG *He shifted the chair closer to the bed... Muller's eyes shifted to the telephone... The doctor shifted his feet uneasily on the bare floor... The edge of the battle area shifted westward.* V-ERG : USU+A

2 A **shift** is a slight change from one position or direction to another. EG *There was a shift in the wind.* N COUNT : USU+SUPP

3 A **shift** in something such as a belief or activity is a slight change that occurs in it. EG *The late seventies had seen something of a shift in attitudes to East-West relations... You may detect a shift of emphasis... ...emotional shifts.* N COUNT+SUPP ⇑ alteration

4 If you **shift** your attitude or belief about something, you change it slightly. EG *'I don't know,' Margaret said, shifting from her earlier attitude... The balance has to be shifted towards developing agriculture.* V OR V-ERG : IF V USU+A ⇑ alter

5 If you **shift** responsibility or blame onto someone else, you transfer it to them. EG *She could no longer shift to her husband the responsibility of amusing the kids... Don't try to shift the blame onto me!* V+O : USU+A

6 If you **shift** a stain or mark or if it **shifts**, you remove it. EG *How are we going to shift these stains?... If the stain still doesn't shift, try this.* V-ERG

7 If you **shift** gears in a car, you change gears; used in American English. V OR V+O

8 A **shift** is also 8.1 a group of workers who work for a period of time during the day or night, and are then replaced by another group who continue their work. EG *They waited for the day shift to appear... Despite double shifts in some of its car assembly plants, the company failed to meet the targets.* N COUNT : IF SING, VB CAN BE SING OR PL ▸ used of the period of time during which one of these groups of people is at work. EG *He had chosen the midnight to 8 shift... Industrial workers can arrange to work different shifts.* ▸ N COUNT 8.2 a loose-fitting N COUNT

piece of clothing, especially one worn by a woman under a dress in former times.

shifting /ʃɪftɪŋ/ is used to describe something which is made up of parts that are continuously moving and changing position in relation to other parts. EG *He drifted into the shifting crowd... The Congo still remains divided between shifting coalitions of the various political parties.* — ADJ CLASSIF : ATTRIB

shift key, shift keys. A **shift key** on a typewriter is the button which you press so that the next letter that you type is a capital. — N COUNT

shiftless /ʃɪftlɪ²s/. Someone who is **shiftless** has no interest in doing anything and no desire to achieve anything. EG *He's lazy and shiftless.* — ADJ QUALIT ⇑ lazy

shifty /ʃɪfti¹/, **shiftier, shiftiest**. Someone who looks **shifty** gives the impression of being deceitful and not to be trusted. EG *...a man with a wide mouth and small shifty eyes... He gave me a shifty look.* — ADJ QUALIT ⇑ dishonest
◇ **shiftiness**. EG *...a disturbing shiftiness in his eyes.* — ◇ N UNCOUNT

shilling /ʃɪlɪŋ/, **shillings**. A **shilling** is 1 a unit of money which was used in Britain until 1971 and which was the equivalent of 5p. There were twenty shillings in an English pound. ▸ also used of a coin with this value. EG *You had to put a shilling in the meter every now and again.* 2 a unit of money which is used in the African countries of Kenya, Somalia, Tanzania, and Uganda. — N COUNT; N COUNT ⇑ currency

shilly-shally /ʃɪli¹ ʃæli¹/, **shilly-shallies, shilly-shallying, shilly-shallied**. If someone is **shilly-shallying**, they are hesitating a great deal when they should be making a decision; an informal word. EG *For goodness sake stop shilly-shallying and get a move on!* — V ⇑ delay

shimmer /ʃɪmə/, **shimmers, shimmering, shimmered**. If something **shimmers**, it shines with a faint unsteady light, for example as the moon does on water. EG *I sat looking at the sea shimmering in the moonlight... The heat haze shimmered through wisps of smoke... ...velvet curtains shimmering with gold embroidery.* ▸ used as a noun. EG *He stood still, a dark figure against the shimmer of the lake.* — V = glisten; ▸ N SING WITH DET

shin /ʃɪn/, **shins, shinning, shinned**. 1 Your **shin** is the front part of your leg between your knee and your ankle. EG *I got kicked on the shins while playing football.* — N COUNT
2 A **shin** of beef is a joint from the lower foreleg of a cow. — N COUNT/UNCOUNT

shin up. If you **shin up** something such as a tree or a pole, you climb it quickly and easily by using both hands and legs to grip it. EG *I shinned up a lamp post to get a better view of the procession.* — PHRASAL VB : V+PREP/ADV

shindig /ʃɪndɪg/, **shindigs**. A **shindig** is a large, noisy, enjoyable party; an informal word. EG *'When are you planning this shindig for?'–'I was thinking about tomorrow night.'* — N COUNT

shine /ʃaɪn/, **shines, shining, shone, shined**. The past tense and past participle of the verb is **shone**, except for paragraph 5 when it is **shined**. 1 When the sun or a light **shines**, it gives out bright light. EG *The sun came up brightly at dawn and shone all day... I was woken by a bright light shining in my face... She moved the lamp and made it shine upwards at the ceiling.* — V
2 If you **shine** a light such as a torch or a lamp somewhere, you point it there, usually so that you can see something when it is dark. EG *We shone our torches on the snowman... I asked him to shine the headlight on the door.* — V+O+A ⇑ focus
3 Something that **shines** is very bright and clear, usually because it is reflecting light. EG *His eyes shone like stars... Sunlight caught each hair and made it shine like gold... The guns shone with oil... Her whole face was shining with excitement now.* — V = gleam
4 Something that has a **shine** is bright because it reflects light, often when it has been well polished. EG *Your floors had such a fantastic shine... ...the shine of the handles on the doors... There's a little smile on his face and a shine of glory in his eyes.* — N SING WITH DET ⇑ brightness = gleam
5 If you **shine** an object, you make it bright by rubbing it or polishing it so that it reflects light. EG *I had to shine my father's shoes every morning.* ▸ used as a noun. EG *He gave his shoes a good shine.* — V+O ⇑ polish; ▸ N SING : a+N ⇑ polish
6 If a quality or feeling **shines** from someone, it can be seen clearly and obviously by other people. EG *Happiness shone on his face... Her influence for good shone from her like a beacon.* — V+A
7 Someone who **shines** at a skill or activity does it extremely well. EG *He shines at amateur theatricals... Here at last is your chance to shine.* — V : IF+PREP THEN at = excel
8 If you **take a shine to** someone, you like them very much as soon as you meet them; an informal expression. EG *I think Richard has taken a bit of a shine to you.* — PHR : VB INFLECTS
9 See also **shining**.

shiner /ʃaɪnə/, **shiners**. A **shiner** is a black eye, usually caused by someone hitting you; an informal word. EG *That's a real shiner you've got there!* — N COUNT

shingle /ʃɪŋgə⁰l/, **shingles**. 1 **Shingle** consists of small rough pieces of stone which you find on the shore by a sea or a river. EG *...shingle beaches.* — N UNCOUNT
2 A **shingle** is a small thin tile, especially one made of wood, which is laid in overlapping rows to cover a roof or a wall. EG *Armadillos have an armour of horny scales that overlap like shingles on a roof... We listened to the rain on the shingle roof.* — N COUNT
3 **Shingles** is a disease that causes a rash of painful red spots which spread in bands over a person's body, especially around their waist. — N UNCOUNT

shining /ʃaɪnɪŋ/. 1 Something that is **shining** is very bright and clear, usually because it is reflecting light. EG *Ralph turned with shining eyes to the others... ...rows of shining glasses... He fixed a shining new name plate on the wall of the building.* — ADJ CLASSIF = gleaming
2 A **shining** achievement, quality, etc, is a very good one which should be greatly admired. EG *She was a shining example to people everywhere... She was obviously a shining success.* — ADJ CLASSIF : ATTRIB ⇑ outstanding

shiny /ʃaɪni¹/, **shinier, shiniest**. Something that is **shiny** is bright and looks as if it has been polished; used especially of things with smooth surfaces. EG *...shiny black shoes... The street was shiny with rain... He wore a shiny suit.* — ADJ QUALIT

ship /ʃɪp/, **ships, shipping, shipped**. 1 A **ship** is a large boat which carries passengers or cargo on sea journeys. EG *The ship was due to sail the following morning... ...merchant ships... They were sent home by ship.* — N COUNT, OR by+N ⇑ vessel
2 If people or things **are shipped** somewhere far away, they are sent there on a ship or by some other means of transport. EG *They had their luggage shipped to Nigeria... The cattle were shipped out by rail... The troops were shipped off to Germany.* ● See also **shipping**. — V+O : USU+A, USU PASS = transport

-ship is 1 added to nouns in order to form other nouns that refer to a person's position, status, or office. EG *...member→membership... ...apprentice→apprenticeship... ...lord→lordship... ...partner→partnership.* 2 added to nouns in order to form other nouns that refer to relations between people or things. EG *...relation→relationship... ...friend→friendship... ...fellow→fellowship.* 3 added to nouns in order to form nouns that refer to people's skills or abilities. EG *...craftsman→craftsmanship... ...statesman→statesmanship... ...marksman→marksmanship.* — SUFFIX : FORMS NOUNS

shipboard /ʃɪpbɔːd/. Something that happens on **shipboard** happens on a ship. EG *A sailor has to perform thousands of shipboard tasks... ...crowded conditions that prevailed on shipboard.* — ADJ CLASSIF : ATTRIB, OR on+N = on board

shipbuilder /ʃɪpbɪldə/, **shipbuilders**. A **shipbuilder** is a person or company that builds ships. EG *...a firm of ship-builders on the Clyde.* — N COUNT : USU PL

shipbuilding /ʃɪpbɪldɪŋ/ is the industry of building ships. EG *We are relaunching British shipbuilding with this new Bill.* — N UNCOUNT

shipmate /ʃɪpmeɪt/, **shipmates**. Sailors who are **shipmates** work together on the same ship. EG *We were shipmates on our first voyage.* — N COUNT

shipment /ʃɪpmə²nt/, **shipments**. 1 A **shipment** is an amount of a particular kind of cargo that is sent to a place in another country on a ship, train, aeroplane, or other vehicle. EG *They sent him a shipment of tobacco... The blockade prevented shipments of foreign food from reaching our shores.* — N COUNT : IF+PREP THEN from/to/of
2 The **shipment** of a cargo somewhere is the sending of it there by ship, train, aeroplane, or some other vehicle. EG *...food supplies for shipment to the Third World.* — N UNCOUNT : IF+PREP THEN from/to

shipping /ʃɪpɪŋ/ is 1 the transport of cargo, especially on ships, when it is done as a business. EG *...the boom in world shipping... ...a rich shipping magnate... It was sent at a cost, including shipping, of only £35.* — N UNCOUNT
2 ships considered as a group. EG *Nearly a fifth of the shipping had been sunk.* — N UNCOUNT

shipshape /ʃɪpʃeɪp/. Something that is **shipshape** is tidy and neat with everything in its proper place. EG *I got the house all shipshape while she was away.* ADJ QUALIT : USU PRED

shipwreck /ʃɪprɛk/, **shipwrecks, shipwrecked.** 1 A **shipwreck** is 1.1 the destruction of a ship in an accident at sea, for example in a storm or by hitting rocks. EG *They heard the news of the shipwreck on the radio... The whole family perished in a shipwreck.* N COUNT/UNCOUNT 1.2 a ship which has been destroyed in an accident at sea. EG *Treasure has sometimes been found in shipwrecks.* N COUNT

2 If someone **is shipwrecked**, their ship is destroyed in a shipwreck and they survive, especially by swimming to an island. EG *He was shipwrecked off the lonely island of Iona.* V+O : ONLY PASS ◊ **shipwrecked.** EG *...shipwrecked sailors.* ◊ ADJ CLASSIF

shipyard /ʃɪpjɑːd/, **shipyards.** A **shipyard** is a place where ships are built and repaired. EG *Many shipyards will have to close... ...shipyard workers.* N COUNT = dockyard

shire /ʃaɪə/, **shires.** 1 A **shire** is a county; an old-fashioned word. N COUNT

2 The **Shires** or **shire counties** are the counties in the central part of England, for example Leicestershire, which are mainly rural. EG *He spent his time in the Shires riding, hunting, and shooting... This proposal should go down well in the shire counties.* N PLURAL : the+N

3 A **shire** or **shire horse** is a large heavy horse used for pulling loads. N COUNT

shirk /ʃɜːk/, **shirks, shirking, shirked.** If someone **shirks** something such as a job or task, they avoid doing it; used showing disapproval. EG *It was a job everyone shirked whenever possible... He never shirked his duty.* V OR V+O

shirt /ʃɜːt/, **shirts.** 1 A **shirt** is a piece of clothing worn on the upper part of your body. Shirts are worn especially by men. They are made of a light material and have a collar, sleeves, and buttons down the front. EG *He was wearing a suit and a shirt and tie... They were spotless in their white shirts and jeans... I folded the letter carefully and put it into my shirt pocket.* ● See also **dress shirt, stuffed shirt, sweatshirt, T-shirt.** N COUNT ⇑ garment

2 If you **put** your **shirt on** something, you risk all your money, your reputation, etc in doing it or supporting it; an informal expression. EG *The union put its shirt on the success of the venture.* PHR : VB INFLECTS

shirtfront /ʃɜːtfrʌnt/, **shirtfronts**; also spelled with a hyphen. A man's **shirtfront** is the front part of his shirt, especially the starched front of a shirt he wears on formal occasions. EG *The coffee stained a fair proportion of his shirt-front.* N COUNT

shirtsleeves /ʃɜːtsliːvz/; also spelled with a hyphen. If a man is **in shirtsleeves** or **in** his **shirtsleeves**, he is wearing a shirt but not a jacket, usually because it is hot or because he is working hard. EG *I started coming to work in shirtsleeves... I lay on the bed in my shirt-sleeves.* PHR : USED AS AN A

shirttail /ʃɜːt teɪl/, **shirttails**; also spelled with a hyphen. A man's **shirttails** are the long parts of his shirt below the waist, which are normally tucked into his trousers. EG *His shirttails were hanging out at the back.* N COUNT : USU PL

shirty /ʃɜːti[1]/. If someone is **shirty**, they are behaving in a bad-tempered and rude way, often because they are annoyed about something; an informal word. EG *Sorry if I was a little shirty just now.* ADJ QUALIT

shish kebab /ʃiːʃ kəbæb/, **shish kebabs. Shish kebab** is a dish consisting of small pieces of meat and sometimes vegetables that are put on a long thin metal rod and grilled. N UNCOUNT/COUNT

shit /ʃɪt/, **shits, shitting, shat**; a rude word used in very informal English. 1 **Shit** is waste matter from the body of a human being or an animal. N UNCOUNT = faeces

2 To **shit** means to get rid of faeces from the body. V ▸ used as a noun to refer to this process. ▸ N SING

3 People sometimes refer to things that they do not like as **shit**; an offensive use. N UNCOUNT

4 People sometimes refer to someone who they do not like as a **shit**; an offensive use. N COUNT : ALSO VOC

5 **Shit** is used to express anger, impatience or disgust. EXCLAM

6 The **shits** is diarrhoea. N UNCOUNT

7 The word **shit** is used informally in the following expressions, all of which are rude. 7.1 **'Tough shit'** is used as a way of saying to someone that they will have to put up with a situation that they do not like because they have no choice. EXCLAM 7.2 If someone is **in the shit**, they are in trouble. PHR 7.3 If people **are shitting themselves**, they are very afraid. PHR 7.4 If someone says that they do not **give a shit** about something, they mean that it does not matter to them and they do not care about it. PHR : VB INFLECTS, WITH BROAD NEG 7.5 To **beat, kick,** or **knock the shit out of** someone means to beat or kick them so violently that they are badly injured. PHR : VB INFLECTS

shitty /ʃɪti[1]/. People describe something or someone as **shitty** when they dislike them or think they are nasty; a very informal rude word. ADJ QUALIT = lousy

shiver /ʃɪvə/, **shivers, shivering, shivered.** When you **are shivering**, your body shakes slightly because you are cold or frightened. EG *I stood shivering with cold on the doorstep.* V : NO IMPER = tremble, quiver ▸ used as a noun. EG *I could not repress a shiver whenever I thought of him... A shiver of excitement ran through the audience.* ▸ N COUNT = shudder ● If something **gives** you **the shivers**, it makes you feel very frightened; an informal expression. EG *That place gives me the shivers.* ● PHR : VB INFLECTS ⇑ frighten

shivery /ʃɪvəri[1]/. If you are **shivery**, you cannot stop shivering, because you are cold or frightened; a rather informal word. ADJ QUALIT : USU PRED ⇑ shaky

shoal /ʃəʊl/, **shoals.** A **shoal** is 1 a large group of fish swimming together. EG *...a shoal of fish... ...shoals of whiting.* N PART+N IN PLURAL 2 a large group of people arriving somewhere together. EG *Emigration had carried to its shores shoals of men and women.* N PART+N IN PLURAL = crowd

shock /ʃɒk/, **shocks, shocking, shocked.** 1 A **shock** is a strong feeling of fear or distress that you get when something unpleasant suddenly happens to you. EG *I slapped her hand and she got such a shock that she dropped the milk... I recovered very gradually from the shock of her death... Frankly, this has all come as a bit of a shock.* N COUNT ⇑ reaction

2 **Shock** is 2.1 a person's emotional and physical condition when something very frightening or distressing has happened to them. EG *Numb with shock, she stood watching as they took his body away.* N UNCOUNT 2.2 a serious physical condition in which your blood cannot circulate properly, for example because you have had a bad injury; a medical term. EG *She was taken to hospital suffering from shock... Annie was by then in shock.* N UNCOUNT

3 A **shock** is also 3.1 something sudden and unexpected that threatens the beliefs, traditions, or way of life of a group of people. EG *Let us hope that these shocks and upheavals to the social order can be contained... It was the greatest shock to the English establishment in decades.* N COUNT : IF + PREP THEN *to* = jolt 3.2 a slight movement in something when it is hit or jerked by something else. EG *This padding should absorb any sudden shocks.* N COUNT/UNCOUNT 3.3 the same as an electric shock; an informal use. EG *I got a nasty shock from the electric iron.* N COUNT

4 If something **shocks** you, 4.1 it makes you feel very upset, because it involves death or suffering and because you had not expected it. EG *She was deeply shocked by her husband's death.* V+O : NO CONT, NO IMPER = shake up ◊ **shocked.** EG *A shocked parliament was told that an airliner had been shot down.* ◊ ADJ CLASSIF : ATTRIB 4.2 it upsets or offends you because you think it is rude or morally wrong. EG *This film is not intended to shock... I often deliberately shock him... I'm not easily shocked.* V OR V+O ◊ **shocked.** EG *Don't look so shocked, John.* ◊ ADJ QUALIT

5 A **shock** of hair is a very thick mass of hair on a person's head. EG *He was tall and handsome with a shock of hair falling over his forehead.* N PART = mop

6 See also **shocking.** ● See also **culture shock, electric shock, shell shock.**

shock absorber, shock absorbers. A **shock absorber** is a device fitted near the wheels of a car or other vehicle to reduce the effects of travelling over bumpy surfaces. EG *...front and rear shock absorbers.* N COUNT

shocker /ʃɒkə/, **shockers.** A **shocker** is something, for example a story, a piece of news, or a film, that shocks people or that is intended to shock them; an informal word, often used humorously. EG *We watched a late-night shocker called 'Tales of Terror'... The last shocker was the discovery that the judge had been taking bribes.* N COUNT

shocking /ʃɒkɪŋ/. Something that is **shocking** 1 is very bad; an informal use. EG *The paintwork was really shocking... His liver was in a shocking state... I'm shocking at spelling... ...The furniture was shockingly scratched.* ADJ QUALIT = appalling, dreadful ◊ **shockingly.** EG *You're shockingly late, you know.* ◊ ADV + ADJ/ADV 2 makes people feel upset or angry, because they think that it is morally wrong. EG *It was* ADJ QUALIT = outrageo…

shocking how badly paid these young girls were... ...the most shocking act of callous irresponsibility... ...the most shocking book of its time. ◊ **shockingly.** EG *Most of them behaved shockingly last week.* ◊ ADV WITH VB

shocking pink. Something that is **shocking pink** is very bright pink. ADJ COLOUR

shockproof /ʃɒkpru:f/. A **shockproof** watch is not easily damaged if you knock it or drop it. ADJ CLASSIF ⇑ tough

shock tactics are a way of carrying out a plan, especially in a war, in which you use surprise in order to defeat your opponent. N PLURAL

shock therapy is the same as shock treatment. N UNCOUNT

shock treatment is a way of treating mental illness by passing an electric current through a patient's brain. EG *She had to undergo shock treatment.* N UNCOUNT

shock wave, shock waves; also spelled with a hyphen. **1** A **shock wave** is an area of intense heat and high pressure moving through the air. It is caused by an explosion, earthquake, or by an object travelling faster than sound. EG *The shock wave from a one megaton bomb could devastate a whole city.* N COUNT

2 A **shock wave** is also the effect of something such as a piece of news or a new type of activity that causes strong reactions when it spreads through a place. EG *When the news was broadcast, shock waves spread through voters from Land's End to John o' Groats... ...the difficulties of absorbing the shock waves of change.* N COUNT

shod /ʃɒd/. **1** You can use **shod** when you are describing the kind of shoes that a person is wearing; a fairly formal use. EG *Andrew was shod in sneakers... She was not, however, shod for church.* ADJ CLASSIF : PRED

2 Shod is also the past tense and past participle of **shoe**.

shoddy /ʃɒdi[1]/, **shoddier, shoddiest.** Something that is **shoddy** has been done or made carelessly or badly; used showing disapproval. EG *It is up to the teacher not to accept shoddy work... ...tiny shoddy houses... They are the result of shoddy workmanship.* ADJ QUALIT ⇑ bad = trashy

◊ **shoddily.** EG *The place was shoddily built.* ◊ ADV WITH VB

◊ **shoddiness.** EG *There was shoddiness and dirt everywhere.* ◊ N UNCOUNT

shoe /ʃu:/, **shoes, shoeing, shod. 1 Shoes** are objects which you wear on your feet when you are out of doors. They cover all of your foot and are worn over your socks or stockings. Shoes are usually made of leather or another strong material. EG *I took off my shoes... She needs ten pounds for a new pair of shoes... The sole of my left shoe is worn through... ...high-heeled shoes... ...shoe polish.* N COUNT ⇑ footwear

2 A **shoe** is the same as a horseshoe. N COUNT

3 If someone **shoes** a horse, they fix horseshoes onto its hooves. EG *I was shoeing an average of eight horses a day.* V+O

4 The word **shoe** is also used in the following expressions. **4.1** If you talk about being **in** someone's **shoes**, you are imagining what you would do or how you would feel if you were in the situation that they are in. EG *I would have done it sooner in his shoes... Put yourself in my shoes for a minute. What would you do?* PHR : USED AS AN A **4.2** If you **fill** someone's **shoes** or **step into** their **shoes**, you take their place by doing the job that they were doing. EG *You'll never be able to fill your father's shoes.* PHR : VB INFLECTS ⇑ replace

5 See also **shod**.

shoehorn /ʃu:hɔ:n/, **shoehorns.** A **shoehorn** is a piece of metal or plastic with a slight curve that you put in the back of your shoe so that your heel will go into the shoe easily. N COUNT

shoelace /ʃu:leɪs/, **shoelaces.** A **shoelace** is a long narrow piece of material like a piece of string that is used to fasten a shoe; used in British English. EG *He stopped to tie up his shoelace.* N COUNT : USU PL ⇑ cord = shoestring

shoemaker /ʃu:meɪkə/, **shoemakers.** A **shoemaker** is a person whose job is making shoes and boots. N COUNT = cobbler

shoestring /ʃu:strɪŋ/, **shoestrings. 1** If you do something or make something **on a shoestring**, you do it using very little money; an informal expression. EG *The film was made on a shoestring at Teddington... ...cookery on a shoestring.* PHR : USED AS AN A ⇑ cheaply

2 A **shoestring** budget is one where you have very little money to spend. EG *She made the film on a shoestring budget.* ADJ CLASSIF : ATTRIB

3 A **shoestring** is a shoelace; used in American English. N COUNT : USU PL

shoetree /ʃu:tri:/, **shoetrees.** A **shoetree** is a long piece of metal, plastic, or wood which is put into a shoe or boot so that the shoe or boot will keep its shape when it is not being worn. N COUNT

shone /ʃɒn/ is the past tense and past participle of **shine**.

shoo /ʃu:/, **shoos, shooing, shooed. 1** If you **shoo** an animal or person, you make them go somewhere else by telling them to go there and often by waving your hands or arms at them. EG *She shooed the birds in the direction of the open window... The visitors were politely shooed away... She shooed her daughters out of the room.* V+O+A = drive

2 You say or shout **shoo** at an animal in order to make it go away. EG *'Go away!' we shouted. 'Shoo!'* EXCLAM

shook /ʃʊk/ is the past tense of **shake**.

shoot /ʃu:t/, **shoots, shooting, shot. 1** To **shoot** means to fire a bullet from a gun. EG *The men were armed and ready to shoot... 'Don't shoot', he shouted... We were told to shoot first and ask questions later... We suddenly realized we were being shot at.* V : IF+PREP THEN at

2 If you **shoot** a person or an animal, you kill them or injure them by firing a gun at them. EG *He shot his wife and then in a fit of remorse shot himself... The judge was shot and critically wounded as he left the court... One of the policemen was shot in the back... We heard on the news that she had been shot dead.* V+O (NG/REFL), OR V+O+C (ADJ)

3 To **shoot** also means to hunt birds or animals with a gun as a form of sport or recreation; used in British English. EG *They used to fish in the summer and shoot in the winter... He went to Scotland at the weekend to shoot pheasants... Do you shoot, Rudolph?* V OR V+O

4 A **shoot** is an occasion when people hunt birds or animals with guns as a form of sport or recreation; used in British English. EG *They often take part in the local shoot.* N COUNT

5 If you **shoot** an arrow, you fire it from a bow. EG *He shot an arrow into the air... I couldn't even shoot a bow and arrow.* V+O

6 If a person or vehicle **shoots** in a particular direction, the person or vehicle moves in that direction quickly and suddenly. EG *The cars will shoot off at a terrific speed... The boat shot forward... The sports car shot past the entrance... She shot back into the room.* V+A = hurtle

7 If you **shoot** something somewhere, you send or move it there quickly and suddenly. EG *He shot out his hand and stopped the child from falling... She was shot through the windscreen when the car hit a tree.* V+O+A

8 If you **shoot** a glance or look at someone or something, you look at them quickly and briefly. EG *She shot me a sideways glance... The girl shot a look at Judy... He shot a suspicious glare at me.* V+O+O, OR V+O +A (at) = dart

9 When a film **is shot**, it is photographed using film cameras. EG *Most of the film was shot in Spain... We rehearse five or six times before the scene is shot... Her next project was cancelled after eight weeks of shooting.* V OR V+O

10 When someone **shoots** in a game of football, hockey, etc, they try to score by suddenly sending the ball towards the goal. EG *He missed a great opportunity to shoot at goal... 'Shoot!' yelled the crowd.* V

11 A **shoot** is also a plant that is beginning to grow, or a new part growing from a plant or tree. EG *...bamboo shoots... A few tender shoots of green had started to appear.* N COUNT

12 If a car **shoots the lights**, it drives very fast past traffic lights although they are signalling it to stop. PHR : VB INFLECTS

13 If someone **shoots** their **mouth off**, they talk carelessly, especially about things which should be kept secret; an informal expression. EG *How are you going to stop them shooting their mouths off to the newspapers?* PHR : VB INFLECTS = blab

14 See also **shot**.

shoot down. 1 If someone **shoots down** an aeroplane or helicopter, they make it fall to the ground by hitting it with a bullet or missile. EG *The enemy claimed to have shot down 22 of our planes... Their helicopter was shot down in flames.* PHRASAL VB : V+O+ADV = bring down

2 If someone **shoots down** a person, especially an unarmed person, they shoot them with a gun, so that they fall to the ground. EG *A firing squad will shoot him down... I will shoot him down like a dog.* PHRASAL VB : V+O+ADV = gun down

3 If you **shoot** someone **down** or **shoot down** their PHRASAL VB : V+

proposals or ideas, you show that their proposals or ideas are wrong or foolish; an informal expression. EG *No doubt you could shoot me down by all kinds of quotations... My suggestion was immediately shot down by everyone else at the meeting.* O+ADV ⇑ disprove

shoot up. If something **shoots up**, it grows or increases very quickly. EG *In a single year the inflation rate shot up from 30% to 48%... The number of people owning videos has shot up in the last five years... Your children have really shot up since the last time I saw them.* PHRASAL VB: V+ADV

shooting /ʃu:tɪŋ/, **shootings**. 1 A **shooting** is an occasion when someone is killed or injured by being shot with a gun. EG *The police arrived fifteen minutes after the shooting... There was almost a riot after the shootings.* N COUNT/UNCOUNT

2 **Shooting** is the hunting of birds or animals with a gun as a form of sport or recreation; used in British English. EG *He had concentrated on his racehorses, his shooting, and his mistresses.* ▸ used as an adjective. EG *He went off somewhere for a shooting weekend... ...the shooting season.* N UNCOUNT; ▸ N BEFORE N

shooting gallery, shooting galleries. A **shooting gallery** is a place where people use rifles to shoot at targets, especially in order to win prizes. N COUNT

shooting star, shooting stars. A **shooting star** is a piece of rock or metal that burns very brightly when it enters the earth's atmosphere from space, and is seen from earth as a bright star travelling very fast across the sky. N COUNT = meteor

shooting stick, shooting sticks. A **shooting stick** is a strong stick with a sharp point at one end and a flat piece at the other end. You stick the point into the ground and sit on the flat end, for example when you are trying to shoot birds that are flying past you. N COUNT ⇑ seat

shoot-out, shoot-outs. A **shoot-out** is a fight in which people shoot at each other with guns, usually until all the people on one side are dead or injured or until they surrender. EG *He was wounded during a shoot-out with the police.* N COUNT

shop /ʃɒp/, **shops, shopping, shopped**. 1 A **shop** is 1.1 a building or part of a building where things are sold. EG *Two customers came into the shop... ...a butcher's shop... ...a shoe shop... I'm just going out to the shops.* 1.2 a place where things are made, especially in a factory. EG *...metalwork shops... ...the repair shop.* N COUNT = store; N COUNT: MOD+N

2 If you **shop**, you go to shops and buy things. EG *I usually shop on Saturdays... I like shopping for clothes.* V: USU+A = go shopping

3 When a shop, office, or firm **shuts up shop**, it stops doing business or selling things and closes, either at the end of the day or permanently. EG *I'll have to shut up shop early tonight... Most offices shut up shop over Christmas and New Year.* PHR: VB INFLECTS

4 If you **set up shop**, you start up a business. EG *Two years ago she set up shop as a freelance photographer.* PHR: VB INFLECTS, IF+PREP THEN *as*

5 If people who do the same work **talk shop**, they talk to each other about their work. EG *If we go to dinner with your boss, you're not to talk shop.* PHR: VB INFLECTS

6 If you say that there are things **all over the shop**, you mean that they are scattered round different parts of a place, usually in an untidy manner; an informal expression. EG *You've left your clothes all over the shop.* PHR: USED AS AN A ⇑ everywhere

7 If you **shop** someone, you inform on them; used in very informal English, expressing disapproval. EG *We all heard about how you shopped your brother.* V+O ⇑ betray

8 See also **shopping**.

shop around. If you **shop around**, 1 you go to different shops in order to compare the prices and quality of something before you decide to buy it. EG *The prices are variable so shop around by all means.* PHRASAL VB: V+ADV

2 you compare the value and quality of several similar deals or contracts before you decide which one to accept. EG *We'll shop around the building societies to find the best terms... Those two companies may be shopping around for merger partners.* PHRASAL VB: V+ADV/PREP

shop assistant, shop assistants. A **shop assistant** is a person who works in a shop selling things to customers and helping them to find what they are looking for. N COUNT

shop floor; also spelled with a hyphen and as one word. The **shop floor** is used to refer to the workers in a factory, especially in contrast to the management. EG *There should be participation in decisions made on the shop floor... ...trade union affairs at shop-floor level.* N SING: USU *the*+N

shop front, shop fronts; also spelled with a hyphen. A **shop front** is the outside part of a shop which faces the street, including the door and windows. EG *Quite a few of the shop-fronts were still boarded up.* N COUNT ⇑ facade

shopkeeper /ʃɒpki:pə/, **shopkeepers**. A **shopkeeper** is a person who owns or manages a small shop. N COUNT = storekeeper

shoplifter /ʃɒplɪftə/, **shoplifters**. A **shoplifter** is a person who steals things from a shop by shoplifting. N COUNT ⇑ thief

shoplifting /ʃɒplɪftɪŋ/ is stealing from a shop by walking round the shop and hiding things in your bag or in your clothes. N UNCOUNT ⇑ theft

shopper /ʃɒpə/, **shoppers**. A **shopper** is a person who is shopping. EG *The city centre was crowded with shoppers.* N COUNT: USU PL

shopping /ʃɒpɪŋ/. 1 **Shopping** is the activity of going to shops and buying things. EG *I was in the West End doing a bit of shopping... Who's going to do the shopping?... They went shopping after lunch... I don't like shopping... ...a shopping bag.* N UNCOUNT

2 Your **shopping** is the things that you have bought from shops, especially food and groceries. EG *She put her shopping away in the kitchen.* N SING: *the*/POSS+N = purchases

shopping centre, shopping centres. A **shopping centre** is an area in a town where a lot of shops have been built close together. N COUNT

shopping list, shopping lists. A **shopping list** is a list of the things that you want to buy when you go shopping, which you write on a piece of paper. EG *Make a shopping list and try to keep to it.* N COUNT

shop-soiled. Goods that are **shop-soiled** are slightly dirty or damaged, because they have been displayed in a shop for a long time or have been touched a lot by customers. EG *...a shop-soiled dress.* ADJ QUALIT = shopworn

shop steward, shop stewards. A **shop steward** is a trade union member who is elected by members of a union in their place of work to speak for them at meetings and to deal with other union business. EG *He became a prominent shop steward in the Engineering Union.* N COUNT ⇑ representative

shopworn /ʃɒpwɔ:n/. Goods that are **shopworn** are slightly dirty or damaged, because they have been displayed in a shop for a long time or have been touched a lot by customers; used in American English. ADJ QUALIT = shop-soiled

shore /ʃɔ:/, **shores, shoring, shored**. 1 The **shore** of a sea, lake, or wide river is the land along the edge of it. EG *We could see the trees on the other shore... ...the eastern shores of Lake Tangyanika... We were now a few hundred yards from shore.* N COUNT: PL=SING

2 Someone who is **on shore** is on the land rather than on a ship. EG *The ship's cinema was empty because everyone was on shore.* PHR: USED AS AN A = ashore

3 A particular country with a coastline is sometimes referred to in literary English as the **shores** of the country. EG *And so he left the shores of England... ...one of the first Americans to arrive on these shores.* N PLURAL+SUPP ⇑ land

shore up. 1 If you **shore up** something such as a wall, you put a wooden board or other strong support next to it or under it in order to stop it from falling down. EG *The villagers shored up sagging huts.* PHRASAL VB: V+O+ADV = prop up

2 If you **shore up** something that is weak or about to fail, you support it or strengthen it in some way. EG *Action is needed to shore up economic links with American suppliers.* PHRASAL VB: V+O+ADV = reinforce

shoreline /ʃɔ:laɪn/, **shorelines**. A **shoreline** is the edge of a sea, lake, or wide river. EG *The shark was moving parallel to the shoreline.* N COUNT

shorn /ʃɔ:n/. 1 If something is **shorn**, it is cut very short. EG *...shorn blades of grass... ...his shorn head.* ADJ CLASSIF

2 If you are **shorn of** something that is an important part of you, it is removed from you. EG *She had been shorn of her power... Shorn of his protective clothing, he looked rather small.* PHR+NG: USED AS C

3 **Shorn** is the past participle of **shear**.

short /ʃɔ:t/, **shorter, shortest; shorts**. 1 If something lasts for a **short** time, it does not last for very long. EG *They left for a short holiday in Venice... He recently had a short stay in hospital... It's a job that can be done over a very short period... The war was far shorter than they expected.* ADJ QUALIT = brief ≠ long

2 A **short** hour, day, year, etc is one that seems to pass very quickly. EG *In the two short decades between now and the twenty-first century, we have to find a way of preventing nuclear war... In a couple of short years she has destroyed all our hopes.*
ADJ CLASSIF : ATTRIB = brief ≠ long

3 Movements and sounds that are **short** occur suddenly and quickly, and are often repeated several times. EG *She spoke in short bursts... He uttered a short cry of surprise... He listened to himself breathing in short gasps... She gave a short laugh, which didn't sound in the least amused.*
ADJ CLASSIF : USU ATTRIB = abrupt

4 Someone who is **short** is not tall, or is not as tall as most people are. EG *Montclair was short and stocky... Without his shoes on, he seemed much shorter.*
ADJ QUALIT ⇑ small ≠ tall

5 Something that is **short** is not long, or is not as long as most things of that type are. EG *Her hair was cut short... She held a short bamboo stick... She led the way through a passage down a short flight of steps.*
ADJ QUALIT ⇑ small ≠ long

6 Speeches, letters, books, etc that are **short** do not have many words or pages in them. EG *She spoke in short, economical sentences... That book has extremely short chapters... He made the shortest speech I've ever heard.*
ADJ QUALIT = brief

7 Distances that are **short** are not long and so you can, for example, easily walk or drive them. EG *They moved on for a short distance... The property is a short walk from the shops... She showed us the shortest way home.*
ADJ QUALIT

8 If you are **short** with someone, you are rude to them, saying as little as possible to them, usually because you are impatient or angry. EG *I'm sorry I was so short with you.*
ADJ QUALIT : PRED + *with* = abrupt, curt

9 If you have a **short** temper, you get angry very easily and quickly. EG *Her temper was even shorter than usual.*
ADJ QUALIT = quick

10 Short pastry or dough is made with a lot of fat so that it crumbles easily.
ADJ CLASSIF : ATTRIB

11 Shorts are **11.1** short trousers that cover your bottom and sometimes also the tops of your legs. EG *I tucked my shirt into my shorts.*
N PLURAL : ALSO *a pair of*+N
11.2 men's underpants; used especially in American English. EG *Tom just stripped to his shorts for sleeping.*
N PLURAL : ALSO *a pair of*+N ⇑ pants

12 A **short** is **12.1** a short film that is shown before the main film at a cinema.
N COUNT : USU PL
12.2 an alcoholic drink of a spirit such as brandy, whisky, or vodka, as opposed to drinks such as beer or wine that you can drink in larger quantities.
N COUNT : USU PL
12.3 a short-circuit; an informal use.
N COUNT ⇑ fault

13 If you are **short** of something or if it is **short**, you do not have enough of it or there is not enough of it. EG *We're dreadfully short of staff at present... He looked short of sleep... When money is short, we need a very careful budget... If there is one thing that is short in the Middle East, it's water.*
ADJ CLASSIF : PRED : IF + PREP THEN *of*
● If you are **short of breath**, you cannot breathe in enough air, usually because you have just run very fast, climbed a steep flight of stairs, etc.
● PHR : USED AS C ⇑ breathless

14 If you **go short** of something, you do not have as much of it as you want or need. EG *We had to go short of meat that week.*
PHR : VB INFLECTS

15 If something **is running short** or if you **are running short of** it, you have almost used up your supply of it and you are beginning to need more of it. EG *Water was running short... I'm afraid time is running short... We were running short of food.*
PHR : VB INFLECTS = run out

16 If something is **in short supply**, there is not enough of it. EG *In her country, meat is in constant short supply... Petrol is in desperately short supply here.*
PHR : USED AS AN A

17 If a name **is short for** another name, it is the short version of that name. EG *Fred is short for Frederick.*
PHR + N PROPER : VB INFLECTS
● If a person or thing is called something else **for short**, that is the short version of their name. EG *Her name was Madeline and Celia always called her 'Maddy' for short... It is called deoxyribonucleic acid, or DNA for short.*
● PHR : USED AS AN A

18 If one thing or number is **short** of another, it almost reaches or includes it, but not quite. EG *He drove up the hill and stopped the car just short of the summit... He was only a year short of fifty when I was born... The number of college students was one short of 5,000...*
PREP ⇑ before

19 You use **short of** to mean except for something or without actually doing something. EG *Short of dynamiting his door open, how do I attract his attention?... You should do anything you feel like doing in public, short of assault or robbery.*
CONJ SUBORD = bar

20 If you say that one thing is **little short of** or **nothing short of** something else, you are emphasizing that it is equal to that other thing, and not less in achievement, degree, importance, etc. EG *Her action is truly nothing short of heroic... He would settle for nothing short of total independence.*
PHR + ADJ/N

21 If someone is **short on** a particular quality or emotion, they do not have as much of it as they should have. EG *She looked intelligent but was a bit short on wisdom... Margaret was short on neither humour, creativity nor vitality.*
PHR : USED AS C + N ⇑ lacking

22 If something **brings** or **pulls** you **up short**, it causes you to suddenly stop doing what you were doing. EG *We were brought up short by the news... 'I must stop this,' he said sharply, pulling himself up short.*
PHR : VB INFLECTS

23 If something **is cut short**, it is forced to stop before it has finished. EG *He cut the discussion short by clapping loudly... The war had cut short his education... If rains are late, the growing season is cut short.*
PHR : VB INFLECTS = curtail

24 stop short. 24.1 If you **stop short** or if something **stops** you **short**, you suddenly stop walking, speaking, or doing something and become very still, for example because you have suddenly realized something or been surprised. EG *The soldier took a few steps and then stopped short... I started to laugh and then stopped short... His disapproval stopped her short.*
PHR : VB INFLECTS
24.2 If someone **stops short of** doing something, they come close to doing it but do not actually do it, often because they do not have the courage. EG *He just stopped short of calling her a murderer... They still stopped short of severe action against newspapers.*
PHR : VB INFLECTS
24.3 If something **stops short** of a particular level or amount, it does not quite reach that level or amount. EG *She could earn only a certain maximum, which stopped short of the general level of wages paid to men.*
PHR : VB INFLECTS

25 The word **short** is also used in the following expressions. **25.1** You use the expression **in short** when you have been listing or giving a lot of details about facts, events, feelings, situations, etc and you want to show a final conclusion or to summarize things quickly. EG *I was packing, arranging the trip, cleaning the house, and saying countless goodbyes. In short, it was a hectic week... The single-minded pursuit of wealth–in short, materialism–does not fit into my way of life.*
PHR : USED AS ADV SEN = in brief
25.2 If you have to do something **at short notice**, you do not have as much time as usual in which to prepare yourself or to make the necessary arrangements. EG *My visit was arranged at rather short notice... It'll be almost impossible to get the visa at such short notice.*
PHR : USED AS AN A
25.3 If you do something **in short order**, you do it very quickly and without any difficulty. EG *In short order they tried, condemned and hanged all the prisoners.*
PHR
25.4 If something such as a conversation is **short and sweet**, it does not last for long because it is deliberately dealt with very quickly.
PHR : USED AS C
25.5 If you **are taken short** or **are caught short**, you feel a sudden strong need to urinate, especially when you cannot easily find a toilet; an informal expression. EG *He was taken short on his way to the interview.*
PHR : VB INFLECTS
25.6 If shopkeepers **give** you **short weight**, they cheat you by pretending that the weight of the goods that they are selling to you is greater than it really is. You then get less than you have paid for.
PHR : VB INFLECTS
25.7 If you say that you would like **a short word** or **a few short words** with someone, you mean that you would like a brief talk with them. EG *I'd like a short word with you if I may.*
PHR : USED AS S/O
25.8 If you **make short work of** someone or something, you deal with them or defeat them very quickly; an informal expression. EG *She certainly made short work of her next two opponents.*
PHR : VB INFLECTS ⇑ overcome

26 The word **short** is also used in the following expressions, which are explained at other places in this dictionary. ● **the long and the short of it**: see **long**. ● **short shrift**: see **shrift**. ● **to cut a long story short**: see **story**. ● **to draw** or **get the short straw**: see **straw**. ● **in the short term: see term.**

shortage /ʃɔːtɪdʒ/, **shortages**. A **shortage** is a situation where there is not enough of something or where the supply of something begins to decrease. EG *There's a world shortage of fuel... Up to the early sixties there was no shortage at all of good students... Bungalows were built in 1946 to ease the housing shortage after the last war.*
N COUNT : USU + SUPP = dearth ≠ surplus

short back-and-sides. A **short back-and-sides** is a man's haircut in which the hair is cut very short at the back and sides with slightly thicker, longer hair on the top of the head. Men in the armed forces often have this kind of haircut. N SING WITH DET

shortbread /ʃɔːtbrɛd/ is a hard, sweet cake, rather like a biscuit, which is made from flour, sugar, and butter. N UNCOUNT

shortcake /ʃɔːtkeɪk/ is the same as shortbread. N UNCOUNT

short-change, short-changes, short-changing, short-changed. If someone **short-changes** you, 1 they cheat you by not giving you enough change when you have bought something from them. EG *That's the second time I've been short-changed in that shop.* V+O : USU PASS 2 they behave unfairly or dishonestly towards you, for example by treating you badly or giving you less than they should; an informal use. EG *We have been short-changed by the government.* V+O : USU PASS ⇑ cheat

short-circuit, short-circuits, short-circuiting, short-circuited. 1 A **short-circuit** happens when there is a wrong connection or damaged wires in an electric circuit so that the current travels across the connection or wires at the wrong place. At this point the electric circuit usually fails and electricity stops flowing along the wires. EG *The lamp-post was heating up from an electrical short-circuit inside.* N COUNT ▸ used as a verb. EG *Then the whole thing short-circuited and there was a mighty explosion.* ▸ V-ERG

2 If someone or something **short-circuits** a plan or process, **2.1** they avoid long, difficult, or complicated methods and achieve something by a quicker, simpler method. EG *Using these models we can short-circuit this process completely.* V+O = bypass **2.2** they cause it to fail by damaging it in its early stages. EG *I found myself disregarding anything that could short-circuit the realization of my dream.* V+O

shortcoming /ʃɔːtkʌmɪŋ/, **shortcomings. Shortcomings**, especially in a person's character or personality, are faults or defects which spoil it. EG *You've got to realize your own shortcomings... ...whatever shortcomings the airport might have... We cannot be held responsible for any defects or shortcomings of properties on our lists of houses for sale.* N COUNT : USU PL = failing

shortcrust /ʃɔːtkrʌst/. **Shortcrust** pastry is made with a lot of fat and crumbles very easily. ADJ CLASSIF : ATTRIB = short

short-cut, short-cuts; also spelled without a hyphen. A **short-cut** is 1 a quicker way of getting somewhere than the more usual, acceptable route. EG *Will you show me that short cut to Wirral Hill?... We were in a quiet street, taking a short cut.* N COUNT 2 a method of achieving something more quickly than if you use the usual or more acceptable methods. EG *There is continuing proof about risky short-cuts in the manufacture of automobiles... Parents of twins simply have to find short-cuts in housework.* N COUNT

shorten /ʃɔːtᵊn/, **shortens, shortening, shortened.** When you **shorten** something or when it **shortens**, you make it shorter than it was or would otherwise be. EG *Once I met a colonel who had a plan to shorten the war... Bleaching shortens the life of any fabric... Gradually the animal's intestine shortens to adjust to a carnivorous diet.* V-ERG ≠ lengthen

shortening /ʃɔːtəᵊnɪŋ/ is cooking fat that you use with flour in order to make pastry or dough; used especially in British English. N UNCOUNT

shortfall /ʃɔːtfɔːl/, **shortfalls.** A **shortfall** in something is the amount that is still needed in order to make up the required amount. EG *A shortfall of energy supplies seems inevitable in the near future.* N COUNT : USU SING+SUPP

shorthand /ʃɔːthᵊænd/. **Shorthand** is 1 a way of writing which uses signs instead of letters or words and so makes it easier to write down what someone is saying at the same speed as they are talking. EG *He took the notes in shorthand... Why not enrol in a shorthand and typing course?* N UNCOUNT = stenography 2 a quick and simple way of referring to something longer or more complicated. EG *'Rep' is often used in knitting patterns as shorthand for 'repeat'... I'm using the term Catholic just as a sort of shorthand term.* N UNCOUNT

short-handed. If a firm or company is **short-handed**, it does not have enough people to work on a particular job. ADJ QUALIT = short-staffed

shorthand typist, shorthand typists. A **shorthand typist** is a person whose job is to type and do shorthand, usually in an office. N COUNT

short-haul is used to describe something that is concerned with transporting goods or passengers over short distances. EG *Her family owned three small trucks and did a short-haul business... The employees prepare meals for short-haul jets.* ADJ CLASSIF : ATTRIB

shortie /ʃɔːti¹/, **shorties**; also spelled **shorty**. If you call someone who is small a **shortie**, you are being either rude or affectionate. EG *Hey, shortie! Come over here!* N COUNT : USU VOC

shortish /ʃɔːtɪʃ/. Someone or something that is **shortish** is fairly short. EG *He was a shortish fat man.* ADJ CLASSIF

short-list, short-lists, short-listing, short-listed; also spelled as one word. 1 If someone or something is on a **short-list**, they are one of a smaller number of people or things that have been selected from a larger group. From this smaller group a final decision or judgement is then made about which of them is the best or most suitable. EG *Doris Lessing's new novel is on the short list for the Booker Prize... We've drawn up a short-list of candidates.* N COUNT : USU SING

2 If someone or something **is short-listed** for something, they are put on a short-list. EG *I've been short-listed for the job.* V+O : USU PASS ⇑ select

short-lived. Something that is **short-lived** does not last for a long time. EG *The alliance was short-lived... But his joy and relief were short-lived.* ADJ QUALIT = temporary

shortly /ʃɔːtli¹/. 1 If something is going to happen **shortly**, it is going to happen soon. If something happened **shortly** after something else, it happened soon after it or a short time later. EG *She's going to London shortly... Very shortly after I joined the church, I became a preacher... She died in an accident shortly afterwards... The movie was over shortly before six.* ADV WITH VB, OR ADV+PREP

2 If you speak to someone **shortly**, you speak to them crossly or impatiently. EG *'You ought to be in bed,' I said shortly... He told me shortly to get on with it.* ADV WITH VB ⇑ sharply = brusquely

short-range. Something that is **short-range** reaches or covers only a short distance or time. EG *Short-range weapons were carried on smaller missiles.* ADJ CLASSIF

short-sighted. If you are **short-sighted**, 1 you cannot see things properly when they are far away, although you can see things when they are near to you. EG *He finally realized that he was short-sighted and went to the optician.* ADJ QUALIT = myopic, near-sighted ≠ long-sighted ◊ **short-sightedness.** EG *Is my short-sightedness likely to get worse?* ◊ N UNCOUNT 2 you do not make proper or careful judgements about the future; used showing disapproval. EG *He's being very short-sighted about this.* ADJ QUALIT ≠ far-sighted ▸ used also of the decisions or judgements that a person makes. EG *Until this short-sighted policy is reversed we shall never make any progress.*

short-staffed. If a company is **short-staffed**, it does not have enough people working for it, and so it is not as efficient as it might be. EG *They're rather short-staffed at the moment.* ADJ QUALIT : USU PRED = short-handed

short story, short stories. A **short story** is a piece of prose fiction that is only a few pages long. EG *...a collection of Scott Fitzgerald's short stories... Bierce was a journalist, poet, and writer of short stories.* N COUNT

short-tempered. Someone who is **short-tempered** gets angry very quickly and easily. EG *I was short-tempered all day.* ADJ QUALIT = irascible, fiery

short-term. 1 Effects or developments that are **short-term** are those that will happen soon, rather than those that will happen more gradually over a longer period of time. EG *The effects of the Computer Revolution will be felt in the short-term future... This one is a good bet, even on a short-term view... Decisions are taken short-term.* ADJ QUALIT : USU PRED, OR ADV WITH VB ⇑ near

2 Something such as a problem or a solution that is **short-term** lasts for only a short time. EG *The artificial heart is designed only for short-term use... That's the difference between a lasting settlement and a short-term solution... We can't reduce the number of children needing short-term foster homes.* ADJ QUALIT : USU PRED

short-wave is used to describe radio transmissions which use wavelengths that are less than 60 metres long. EG *The only communication with the mainland was by short-wave radio.* ADJ CLASSIF

short-weight, short-weights, short-weighting, short-weighted. If shopkeepers **short-weight** you, they cheat you by pretending that the weight of the goods that they are selling to you is greater than it really is. You then get less than you have paid for. EG *The factory was using inferior fish-oils and short-weighting the public.* V+O

shorty /ʃɔːti¹/, **shorties**. See **shortie**.

shot /ʃɒt/, **shots**. 1 **Shot** is the past tense and past participle of **shoot**.

2 A **shot** is an act of firing a gun or other weapon. EG *Someone had fired a shot... One of the neighbours says she heard a shot.* N COUNT

3 In sports such as football, golf, or cricket, a **shot** is an act of hitting or kicking the ball, especially in an attempt to score a point. EG *A defender deflected the shot... Try to hit the green with your first shot... Oh, good shot... Nicklaus is now just one shot behind the leaders.* N COUNT ⇑ blow

4 Someone who is a good **shot**, a poor **shot**, etc can shoot with a particular degree of skill. EG *I'm not really a good shot but I enjoy shooting... By now they were crack shots with their catapults.* N COUNT : ADJ+N = marksman

5 **Shot** is a mass of small metal balls that is fired from a shotgun. N UNCOUNT

6 A **shot** is also 6.1 a heavy metal ball that is thrown by contestants in the shot put. N COUNT 6.2 the sending of a rocket or spacecraft into space. EG *...the Sputnik shots... ...a moon shot.* N COUNT : AFTER N 6.3 a photograph. EG *She had taken some very good close-up shots of the children.* N COUNT = snap 6.4 a single picture or uninterrupted sequence in a film. EG *The film contained some shots of children playing... ...a long shot of thousands of dead men on open ground.* N COUNT

7 If you have a **shot** at something, you attempt to do it or win it. EG *I decided to have a shot at fixing the car myself... He's next in line for a shot at the title.* N COUNT : IF+ PREP THEN *at* = try, go

8 A **shot** of a drug is an injection of it. EG *The doctor gave her a shot of morphine to kill the pain.* N COUNT ● If you describe something as **a shot in the arm**, you mean that it provides help and encouragement, and is likely to produce an improvement. EG *The latest fall in interest rates has given industry a shot in the arm.* ● PHR : USED AS O/C = boost

9 A **shot** of a strong alcoholic drink is a small glass of it. EG *He poured me a shot of whisky.* N PART = tot

10 **Shot** is used to describe material, especially silk, which is made by a special process so that it shows different colours depending on the angle from which you look at it. EG *...a dress of shot silk.* ADJ CLASSIF : ATTRIB ⇑ iridescent

11 If something is **shot** through with another element or feature, it contains a lot of that element or feature, which produces a contrasting effect. EG *...a comic novel shot through with sadness... The upper air is shot with sunlight.* ADJ CLASSIF : PRED+*through/with* = suffused

12 If you describe an attempt or guess as **a long shot**, you mean that it is unlikely to succeed or be correct, but is nevertheless worth trying. EG *It's a long shot, but let's ask.* PHR : USED AS O/C = gamble

13 If you describe a guess as a **shot in the dark**, you mean that it is a complete guess because you really have no idea what the answer is. EG *It was a complete shot in the dark but it turned out to be the right answer.* PHR : USED AS O/C = gamble

14 If you do something **like a shot**, you do it without any delay or hesitation; used in informal English. EG *If they offered me the job I'd take it like a shot.* PHR : USED AS AN A = like a flash

15 If you **get shot of** something, you get rid of it; used in informal English. EG *We were glad to get shot of that old car.* PHR : VB INFLECTS

shotgun /ʃɒtgʌn/, **shotguns**. A **shotgun** is a gun that fires cartridges containing shot and is used for shooting birds and animals. N COUNT

shot put. The **shot put** is an athletic competition in which the contestants throw a heavy metal ball, called a shot, as far as possible. N SING : *the*+N

shot putter, shot putters. A **shot putter** is an athlete who takes part in the shot put. N COUNT

should /ʃəᵈd/. 1 You say **should** 1.1 to say that you think that an action or someone's behaviour is morally right. If you say **should not**, you think it is morally wrong. EG *Crimes should be punished... These birds shouldn't be in a cage... Should a doctor tell a patient he is going to die?* MODAL = ought to 1.2 to say that you think it is a good idea and important for you or someone else to do a particular thing, and that it would be slightly wrong of you or them not to do it. EG *A man shouldn't be a parson until he's in his forties... We should be going back to wind-power... Should we remain in the Common Market?... Shouldn't you switch it off first?* MODAL = ought to 1.3 to criticize someone's attitude or behaviour. EG *You should be ashamed of yourself... You really shouldn't tell such obvious lies.* MODAL = ought to

2 You use **should** in questions when you are asking someone for advice, permission, information, etc. EG *Where should I meet you tonight?... Should I turn the light on?... Who should I see about my teaching programme?* MODAL = shall

3 You use **should** to give advice about what needs to be done. EG *Carbon steel knives should be wiped clean after use... That tooth should be extracted at once... You should write all this down.* MODAL = ought to

4 You use **'I should'** when you are giving someone advice in an informal way. EG *If you have anything really confidential I should install a safe... I shouldn't bother to copy these down.* PHR+INF = I would

5 You also use **should** 5.1 to say that a particular feeling or attitude is reasonable or appropriate in the circumstances, even if you do not actually have it. EG *I suppose we should be glad... 'Oh, Cyril, I'm so excited.'–'So you should be'... I should hate him for all the trouble he's caused me.* MODAL = ought to 5.2 to indicate the correct way to do something or the correct position for something. EG *We can't be certain how an unfamiliar word should be pronounced... Those brackets should be there and not how you've got them.* MODAL = ought to 5.3 to say that something is probably true or is likely to happen in the way mentioned. EG *We should be there by dinner time... 'Where's the butter?'–'It should be in the fridge'... There shouldn't be any difficulties.* MODAL = ought to 5.4 to say that you think it is the right point in a piece of writing or speech to explain something or add new information, because it is important or relevant. EG *At this point, I should explain that when I use the word 'church' I am only referring to the building... I think I should point out that you may get criticism for these ideas.* MODAL = ought to 5.5 to say that something would be true under certain conditions or circumstances; used especially in formal English. EG *I should be very unhappy on the continent... I should be grateful if you could do it by Monday... I shouldn't be surprised if the flight's cancelled.* MODAL 5.6 in conditional sentences in which you talk about an event or situation which might happen, in order to consider what the likely consequences might be. EG *He remarked that if we should be seen arriving together at the stage door people would jump to conclusions... Should you have an accident, synthetic quilts are quite easy to wash... I did maths in case I should fail in one of the other subjects... Suppose he should fail?* MODAL = were to 5.7 in a 'that' clause, after some adjectives and after verbs such as 'agree', 'decide', 'intend', etc. EG *It's strange you should come today... He was anxious that I should be there... I have agreed that he should do it... It was arranged that Celia should come to Switzerland.* MODAL 5.8 with verbs expressing opinions to show that you are not absolutely certain about something but are guessing. EG *I should think it was about twelve years ago... He weighs, I should say, about 140 pounds... 'Will Nick come?'–'No, I shouldn't think so.'* MODAL = would 5.9 to express a wish about what you would like to be doing rather than what you are actually doing. EG *We should be out in the garden in this weather... That's the kind of job I should be doing.* MODAL = ought to 5.10 to tell someone that you must do something, for example leave; a polite use. EG *I should be on my way, too.* MODAL 5.11 after 'why' to emphasize that there is no reason for something. EG *Why should I be angry with you?... Why shouldn't he go to college?... I couldn't imagine why she should want to know.* MODAL : *why*+ MODAL 5.12 when you do not want to do something or do not know something and want to show that you are angry that someone expects you to do it or know it. EG *'Will you come?'–'No, why should I?'... How the hell should I know?* MODAL : *why/how*+MODAL

6 **'You should'** and **'you should have'** are used when you are telling someone that something is or was very surprising, unusual, amusing, etc and that it is a pity that they did not witness it. EG *You should hear the way she talks to me... You should have seen it.* PHR

7 **Should** is used in structures like 'who should I meet but' when you are emphasizing that something is very surprising. EG *'Who should I meet on the plane but Colin Harper.'–'Gosh, really?'*

8 Should have is used, usually in front of a past participle, **8.1** to say that something was expected or intended to happen but did not happen. EG *Muskie should have won by a huge margin... I should have felt annoyed with her for interrupting... Yesterday should have been the start of the soccer season.* MODAL = ought to have **8.2** to say that it is likely that something has happened by now or will happen before some time in the future. EG *Dear Mom, you should have heard by now that I'm O.K.* MODAL **8.3** to say that something would have happened under certain conditions or circumstances; used especially in formal English. EG *I thought it was best just to go, otherwise we should have been there all day... If the exam had been yesterday, I should have failed.* MODAL **8.4** when you realize that you or someone else has made a mistake and you are suggesting how it could have been avoided. EG *I should have bought a bigger chicken... You should have thought about that before you invited her... I shouldn't have trusted that man.* MODAL = ought to have

shoulder /ʃəʊldə/, **shoulders, shouldering, shouldered.** 1 Your **shoulders** are the two parts of your body between the neck and the top of the arm. EG *She rubbed her left shoulder... She wept in silence, her shoulders shaking... Two buckets hung from a bamboo pole across his shoulders.* N COUNT

2 The word **shoulder** is used in a number of expressions that are related to this part of the body. **2.1** If you look **over** your **shoulder**, you look behind you by turning your neck. EG *He stopped and looked over his shoulder.* PHR : USED AS AN A **2.2** If two people are **shoulder to shoulder**, they are side by side, close together. EG *They were standing shoulder to shoulder.* PHR : USED AS AN A **2.3** If a group of people work **shoulder to shoulder**, they work together, co-operating with one another, in order to achieve a common aim. PHR : USED AS AN A **2.4** If someone needs a **shoulder to cry on**, they need a person who will listen sympathetically to all their troubles and will try to comfort them. EG *I think I was only a shoulder to cry on that evening.* PHR : USED AS O ⇑ comforter **2.5** If you **rub shoulders with** people, especially famous people, you meet and talk to them; an informal expression. EG *It was a rare opportunity to rub shoulders with the rich and famous.* PHR : VB INFLECTS ⇑ associate with

3 The **shoulders** of a piece of clothing are the parts that cover your shoulders. EG *Her dress had padded shoulders.* N COUNT : USU PL

4 If you **shoulder** something heavy, you put it across one of your shoulders or across the top part of your back, so that you can carry it more easily. EG *The soldiers shouldered their kit and moved on.* V+O = hoist

5 If you **shoulder** someone, you push them roughly with your shoulders. EG *I shouldered the guard aside and went in.* V+O = thrust

6 If you **shoulder** your **way** somewhere, you get there by pushing people out of their way with your shoulders. EG *They shouldered their way through the crowd.* PHR : VB INFLECTS ⇑ push

7 If you **shoulder** the responsibility or blame for something, you accept it yourself and so have to deal with it. EG *Many of us would rather someone else shouldered the responsibility. ... I had decided to tell nobody, to shoulder the entire burden myself.* V+O = bear

8 When you are talking about burdens or responsibilities, you sometimes say that they are on someone's **shoulders**. EG *They laid an even heavier burden on her shoulders... Responsibility for the task was lifted from his shoulders.* N PLURAL

9 A **shoulder** is also **9.1** part of a hill or mountain where the slope changes and makes a shape like a person's shoulder. N COUNT : IF + PREP THEN *of* **9.2** a joint of meat from the upper part of the front leg of an animal. EG *...a shoulder of lamb.* N COUNT/ UNCOUNT **9.3** an unpaved strip of ground along the sides of a road; used in American English. EG *I sat in the grass at the shoulder of the road.* ● See also **hard shoulder.** N COUNT ⇑ edge

10 If something is or stands **head and shoulders** above other things, it is **10.1** a lot taller than them. EG *The poplars tower head and shoulders above the other trees.* PHR + A *(above)* **10.2** a lot better than them. EG *They are head and shoulders above other orchestras.* PHR + A *(above)* = way

11 If you **put** your **shoulder to the wheel**, you start work at a difficult task. PHR : VB INFLECTS

12 See also **cold-shoulder.**

shoulder-bag, shoulder-bags. A **shoulder-bag** is a bag, especially a handbag, that has a long strap so that it can be carried on a person's shoulder. N COUNT

shoulder blade, shoulder blades; also spelled with a hyphen. Your **shoulder blades** are the two large, flat, triangular bones that you have, one on each side, in the upper part of your back. N COUNT = scapula

shoulder-high. If something is **shoulder-high**, it is as high as your shoulders. ▸ used as an adverb. EG *They carried him shoulder-high.* ADJ CLASSIF ▸ ADV WITH VB

shoulder-length. Shoulder-length hair is long enough to reach your shoulders. ADJ CLASSIF

shoulder-strap, shoulder-straps. 1 The **shoulder-straps** on a piece of clothing such as a dress are the two narrow straps that go over the shoulders to prevent the piece of clothing from falling down. N COUNT

2 A **shoulder-strap** on a bag is a long strap that you put over you shoulder to carry the bag. N COUNT

shouldn't /ʃʊdənt/ is the usual spoken form of 'should not'.

should've /ʃʊdəv/ is the usual spoken form of 'should have', especially when 'have' is an auxiliary verb.

shout /ʃaʊt/, **shouts, shouting, shouted. 1** A **shout** is a loud call or cry, for example made by children when they are playing or by a person who is ordering someone to do something. EG *'Stop it!' Jim's shout was a command that was instantly obeyed... His news was greeted with shouts of joy... Excited shouts and laughter could be heard from the garden.* N COUNT = yell, shriek

2 If you **shout**, you say words as loudly as you can, so that you can be heard from a long distance away. EG *There was lots of wind, and we had to shout to be heard... She was ready to shout for help... The children on the sand were shouting with excitement.* V = yell

3 If you **shout** at someone, you talk angrily to them in a loud voice. EG *She shouted at us for spoiling her lovely evening... Calm down, there's no need to shout.* V : IF + PREP THEN *at*

4 If you **shout** something, you say it in a very loud voice. EG *'Stop it!' he shouted... He shouted an order and they halted... The crowd marched down the road shouting slogans.* V+O/QUOTE/ REPORT-CL = yell

5 If it is your **shout**, it is your turn to buy a drink for someone else; an informal expression. EG *'What are you having? It's my shout.'* N SING : POSS+N = round

6 If you say that it is **all over bar the shouting**, you mean that something is nearly finished, the important actions or decisions have been taken, and so there is no doubt about the result. EG *A goal in the final minutes made the score 3-0. It was all over bar the shouting.* PHR : USED AS C

7 If you **shout** yourself **hoarse**, you shout so much that you can hardly speak. PHR : VB INFLECTS

shout down. If people **shout** a person **down**, they prevent the person from being heard by speaking very loudly. EG *The crowd shouted the speaker down... Mr Healey was shouted down at a meeting in Birmingham.* PHRASAL VB : V+O+ADV

shout out. If you **shout** something **out**, you suddenly shout it. EG *I just had time to shout out and warn them not to cross the road... Little Billy shouted out the answer.* PHRASAL VB : V+ADV, OR V+ADV+O/QUOTE/ REPORT-CL = call out

shove /ʃʌv/, **shoves, shoving, shoved. 1** If you **shove** someone or something, you push them with a quick, rather violent movement. EG *He dragged her out to the door and shoved her into the street... She grabbed a trolley and shoved it along... Her hand jerked up to shove him away.* ▸ used as a noun. EG *He pushed the child forward with a hard shove on her shoulders... The car won't start. Can you give it a shove?* V+O+A ▸ N COUNT : USU SING

2 If people **are shoving**, they are pushing with their bodies, especially in a crowd of people, with quick, rather violent movements. EG *Everyone was pushing and shoving towards the stage... Stop shoving, Sebastian.* V OR V+O (DETPOSS+wa +A = jostle

3 If you **shove** something somewhere, you push it quickly and carelessly into a particular place. EG *He started shoving clothes into drawers... She shoved the letter under the door... We'll shove an extra paragraph in here.* V+O+A = stuff, stick

shove off. If you tell someone to **shove off**, you are telling them angrily to go away; used in very informal English. EG *Shove off!–I'm trying to read.* PHRASAL VB : ADV = buzz off

shove-halfpenny /ʃʌv heɪpni[1]/ is a British game in which players try to push coins onto a wooden board with their hands. It is usually played on a table in pubs. N UNCOUNT

shovel /ʃʌvəᵒl/, **shovels, shovelling, shovelled**; also spelled **shoveling** and **shoveled** in American English. **1** A **shovel** is a tool like a spade, with a rounded blade attached to a long handle, used for lifting and moving earth, coal, or snow. EG *He was working with a pick and shovel... ...a coal shovel.* N COUNT

2 If you **shovel** earth, coal, snow, etc, you lift and move it with a shovel. EG *She helped us stack the wood and shovel the snow off the front path... He was shovelling earth into the grave.* V+O ⇑ dig

3 If you **shovel** something somewhere, you push a lot of it quickly into that place. EG *They were shovelling food into their mouths... She shovelled the vegetable peelings into the bag.* V+O+A ⇑ put

4 A **shovel** is also a machine or a part of a machine used for digging or moving earth. N COUNT = digger

shovelful /ʃʌvəᵒlfʌl/, **shovelfuls**. A **shovelful** is the amount of earth, coal, snow, etc that you can carry on a shovel. EG *...a shovelful of snow.* N PART

show /ʃəʊ/, **shows, showing, showed, shown.**

1 If something **shows** that a state of affairs exists, it gives information or evidence that proves it or makes it clear to people. EG *These figures show an 8.5% increase in exports... The post-mortem shows that death was due to natural causes... Public opinion polls showed Giscard trailing Mitterand by as much as 3%... The new plane was subsequently shown to be capable of flight... A few questions show whether they have understood the story.* V+O/REPORT-CL, OR V+O+-ING/ to-INF/REPORT-CL ⇑ indicate = demonstrate

2 If a picture, diagram, table, piece of writing, etc **shows** something, it represents it or expresses information. EG *...a snapshot which showed Annabel and her parents... An early vase painting shows four athletes bathing outside a gymnasium... A statement showing how much you need to pay is sent each month... She accepted his visiting card showing him to be a partner in a firm of solicitors.* V+O/REPORT-CL, OR V+O+-ING/ to-INF (be+C)

3 If an instrument **shows** a level or measurement, it indicates it. EG *Last winter my wall thermometer showed an average temperature of around 57°F... The digital clock showed the wrong time.* V+O = register

4 If you **show** something to someone, you give it to them or take them to it in order that they can see it and examine it. EG *Could you show me some identification?... I showed William what I had written... Let me show you the garden... Fetch that lovely drawing you did and show it to the parson.* V+O, V+O+O, OR V+O+A (to)

5 If you **show** someone something or **show** them where something is, you point to it or take them there so that they know where it is or which one you mean. EG *She showed me where to park the car... Show me who you mean... Let me show you the way.* V+O+O/REPORT-CL, OR V+O+A (to)

6 If you **show** someone to a room, seat, table, etc, you lead them there. EG *She showed us to our rooms... I was shown into a large apartment... Will you show Miss Nester out please?* V+O+A ⇑ take = escort

7 If you **show** someone something or **show** them how to do something, you do it yourself so that they can watch you and learn how to do it. EG *The woman took the gun and showed how the cylinder slotted into the barrel. Can you show me that again?... Mom would play the piano or show us a card game.* V+O/REPORT-CL (how), V+O+O/ REPORT-CL (how), OR V+O+A (to) = demonstrate

8 If you **show** something or if it **shows**, it becomes visible, especially because something that was covering it has been removed. EG *He had a strange fierce way of grinning that showed his teeth... Her face was covered by a scarf, only her eyes showing... The edge of the moon is just showing... Holes in the walls showed daylight.* V OR V-ERG ≠ cover, hide

9 If something **shows**, it becomes noticeable. EG *The stitching is very fine and it doesn't show at all... Her pregnancy was beginning to show.* V

10 If something **shows** dirt, it is a colour or made of a material that allows dirt to be easily seen. EG *They're cheap, tough, and don't show dirt.* V+O

11 If you **show** yourself, you move into a position or go somewhere where you can be seen by other people. EG *Come out from there and show yourself.* • to **show** your **face**: see **face**. V+O (REFL) = reveal ≠ hide

12 If something **shows** a quality, characteristic, or feature, there is evidence of it which can be observed. EG *A majority of babies show a preference for a 5-hour feeding interval... The sketch shows a lot of talent... Prices levelled off and began to show some signs of decline in 1974.* V+O ⇑ have = display

13 If a company **shows** a profit, loss, etc, its accounts indicate that it has made a profit, loss, etc. EG *Only one in four of the companies actually showed any profit at all.* V+O ⇑ have

14 If you **have** something **to show for** your efforts or time, you have produced something as a result of it. EG *Rodin's search was over and what he had to show for it was three slim dossiers... Each evening they returned with nothing to show for their day but tired feet.* PHR : VB INFLECTS

15 If something **shows** itself or **shows**, it is obvious to other people. EG *His radicalism showed itself in his belief that abolition was the only course... You've put hardly any effort into this and it shows.* V, OR V+O (REFL) : USU+A

16 If you **show** a particular characteristic or feature, you behave in a way that makes it clear to other people. EG *Can't you fellows show a bit more consideration?... This is a way in which Britain can show a readiness to help... He showed himself reluctant... Every state in New England has shown itself prepared to take risks.* V+O, OR V+O (REFL)+C/to-INF (be+C)

17 If you **show** someone affection, mercy, respect, etc, you behave towards them with that quality or feeling. EG *He would be shown no mercy... She often showed me kindness... I had been taught to show respect towards my elders.* V+O, V+O+O, OR V+O+A (to/ towards)

18 When you **show** your feelings or intentions or when they **show**, you reveal them by the expression on your face or by your actions. EG *She was feeling sad too, and didn't want to show it... Hooper let the surprise show in his eyes for only an instant... Her face must have shown her disappointment... He nodded to show her that she had his attention.* V-ERG, V+ REPORT-CL, OR V +O+REPORT-CL ⇑ display

19 If you say to someone **'I'll show you'**, you mean that you will prove to them that you can do something or that they are wrong; used especially as a threat or to express your determination. EG *Just you wait. I'll show you.* CONVENTION

20 You say **'it just goes to show'** or **'it just shows'** when you want to emphasize a point that you are making and to say that it is an obvious or expected conclusion from what has just been said or done. EG *You got there eventually. It only goes to show what you can do if you try.* PHR

21 If you describe something as a **show**, you mean that it is done in order to give someone a particular impression, especially an impression that is false. EG *She put on a good show of looking interested... Maybe the killings are going to be announced as a show of strength, or a warning... Those who had made the most open shows of defiance.* N COUNT ⇑ act

22 If something is done **for show**, it has no real purpose or justification apart from giving people a good impression. EG *These regulations are just for show.* PHR

23 A **show** is a form of entertainment at the theatre or on television that consists usually of various comedy scenes and popular songs. EG *Joy Leomine has been appearing in a show in London... He was giving three shows a day... ...The Morecambe and Wise show.* ▸ used sometimes to refer to any play at a theatre, especially a musical. EG *Let's go to a show.* N COUNT

24 If someone **steals the show**, they unexpectedly get most of the admiration or attention in a performance or some other event. EG *Little Jennie stole the show.* PHR : VB INFLECTS

25 To **show** a film or television programme means to put it on or present it so that people can watch it. EG *One evening the school showed a cowboy film... The ceremony was also shown on BBC 1... What film was showing?* V-ERG : IF V, THEN ONLY CONT

26 A **show** is also **26.1** a television or radio broadcast. EG *I've been watching all the news shows.* • See also **chat show**. N COUNT = programme **26.2** an exhibition of things often involving competitions to judge which are of the highest standard. EG *I have been judging village flower shows for nearly ten years... ...a trade show... ...an air show.* N COUNT : USU MOD+N ⇑ display

27 If something is **on show**, it is in an exhibition or place where it can be seen by the public. EG *The photographs are on show at the Museum until October... All there was on show were a dozen cases of apples.* PHR : USED AS AN A ⇑ displayed

28 To **show** a painting or other work of art means to put it in an exhibition so that people can see it. EG *James hopes to show his canvas at the Academy... The exhibition contains some of her sketches. These have never been shown.* V OR V+O : USU V +O ⇑ display = exhibit

29 In a vote, when people raise their hands in order V

to vote, you sometimes say that they **show**. EG *All those in favour please show.*

30 A **show of hands** is a method of voting in which people raise their hands. EG *...a winning vote by a show of hands.*
PHR

31 If you **put up a good show** or **a poor show**, you make a good or poor attempt at something. EG *They put up quite a good show, but never looked like winning.*
PHR : VB INFLECTS

32 Show is used as an informal way of referring to something that is being organized or that is happening. EG *...the way in which the Foreign Office ran the show... It's your show, Colonel.*
N SING WITH DET
⇑ affair

33 If you say **'Let's get this show on the road'**, you are telling people that it is time to start something, especially to start working.
PHR

34 Good show or **jolly good show** are rather old-fashioned expressions of approval. EG *'They've accepted.'–'Oh, good show.'*
CONVENTION
= great

35 If someone **shows**, they arrive at a place where they are expected by someone else; used in American English. EG *When nobody showed, he didn't know what to do.*
V
= turn up

36 • to **show** your **hand**: see **hand**. • to **show** someone **the ropes**: see **rope**.

show around. If you **show** someone **around**, you go with them to show them all the interesting, useful, or important features of a place when they first visit it. EG *Could you spare an afternoon to show the new students around?*
PHRASAL VB : V+O+ADV/PREP
= show round

show off. **1** If you **show off**, you behave in a way that makes your skills, abilities, or good qualities too obvious in order to impress people; used showing disapproval. EG *Don't show off... Kids showing off on the diving board.*
PHRASAL VB : V+ADV

2 If you **show off** something special, beautiful, or valuable, you show it to as many people as possible because you are proud of it. EG *He was eager to show off the new car... ...tossing their heads and arms, showing off their jewellery.*
PHRASAL VB : V+O+ADV
⇑ display
= parade

3 If one thing **shows** something else **off**, it makes the other thing look especially attractive or effective because it emphasizes the good qualities or features of this other thing. EG *A plain pale green background shows the plants off to good effect.*
PHRASAL VB : V+O+ADV
⇑ complement
= set off

4 See also **show-off**.

show round. If you **show** someone **round**, you go with them to show them all the interesting, useful, or important features of a place when they first visit it.
PHRASAL VB : V+O+ADV/PREP
= show around

show up. **1** If you **show up**, you appear at a place where you are expected by someone; an informal use. EG *Over a hundred people showed up at the meeting... I waited for an hour but he didn't show up.*
PHRASAL VB : V+ADV
= turn up

2 When one thing **shows** something else **up**, it makes the other thing visible, especially when previously it has been difficult to see it. EG *...occasional flashes of light that show up the house in the gathering dusk... Dark colours will not show up against a similar background.*
PHRASAL VB : V-ERG+ADV

3 If something **shows up**, it is able to be noticed or appears on a measuring instrument. EG *Small differences in temperament are bound to show up.*
PHRASAL VB : V+ADV

4 If you are with someone and you **show** them **up**, you make them feel embarrassed and ashamed of you by behaving in an unacceptable way. EG *Behave yourself! You're showing me up!*
PHRASAL VB : ORDER V+O+ADV
⇑ embarrass

showbiz /ʃəʊbɪz/ is show business; an informal word. EG *We do get some remarkable glimpses of showbiz life.*
N UNCOUNT

show business; also spelled with a hyphen, especially when used before another noun. **Show business** is the popular entertainment industry of film, theatre, and television, especially in relation to the work and life of actors, directors, and producers. EG *Then he went into show business... ...show-business gossip.*
N UNCOUNT
= showbiz

showcase /ʃəʊkeɪs/, **showcases**. A **showcase** is **1** a glass container with valuable objects inside that people can look at, for example at an exhibition. EG *...the Ottoman palace in Istanbul where a sequence of showcases display the costumes worn by each successive generation... ...showcases of gold artefacts.* **2** a situation or setting in which something is displayed or presented to its best advantage. EG *The tournament ought to be a showcase of European football... This opera is a stunning showcase for the company.*
N COUNT ⇑ cabinet
N COUNT+SUPP

showdown /ʃəʊdaʊn/, **showdowns**. A **showdown** is a big argument or conflict which is intended to settle a dispute that has lasted for a long time. EG *It's time for a showdown with your boss... They were seeking a final showdown.*
N COUNT : USU SING, IF+PREP THEN *with*

shower /ʃaʊə/, **showers, showering, showered**. **1** A **shower** is a device, usually in a bathroom, used for washing yourself. It consists of a pipe attached to a wall with a flat piece across one end and a lot of holes in it so that water comes out in a spray. EG *All rooms have got a bath, shower and toilet... She turned on the shower... ...a shower curtain.*
N COUNT

2 If you have a **shower**, you wash yourself by standing under a spray of water from a shower. EG *A hot shower and a change of clothes would be wonderful... I want to brush my teeth and take a shower.*
N COUNT
▸ used as a verb. EG *I'll shave and shower and then have some coffee.*
▸ V

3 A **shower** is also **3.1** a short period of light rain. EG *Between the showers the children would dash about in the yard... ...a week of scattered showers.* **3.2** a falling movement of lots of light things. EG *...a shower of falling leaves... ...a shower of sparks from the fire.*
N COUNT
N PART
= stream

4 If you **are showered** with a lot of small light things or if they **shower** on you, they are scattered onto you from above. EG *They showered the bride with paper rose petals... Suddenly the lid came off and showered him with flakes of rust... Dust, dirt and concrete splinters showered about him.*
V+O+A (*with/on/upon*)
= sprinkle

5 If you **shower** someone with things, especially presents or kisses, you give them a lot of them in a very generous and extravagant way. EG *They showered each other with gifts at Christmas... ...holidays and salary rises were showered on staff... They have all been showering us with affection.*
V+O+A (*with/on/upon*)
= heap

showerproof /ʃaʊəpruːf/. A **showerproof** coat is one that will keep you dry in a small amount of rain but not in a lot of rain.
ADJ CLASSIF
⇑ waterproof

showery /ʃaʊəri[1]/. If the weather is **showery**, there are showers of rain but it is not raining all the time. EG *A raincoat will keep you dry in showery weather.*
ADJ QUALIT
⇑ rainy

showing /ʃəʊɪŋ/, **showings**. A **showing** of a film or exhibition is a presentation of it somewhere so that people can see it. EG *He had just been to a private showing of the film... ...Kung Fu films, now shown at special late night showings.*
N COUNT

show jumping is a sport in which horses are ridden in competitions to demonstrate skill in jumping over walls and fences without knocking them over.
N UNCOUNT

showman /ʃəʊmə[3]n/, **showmen**. A **showman** is a person who is skilful at presenting or expressing something in an effective and entertaining way. EG *Mr Perkins, always the showman, arrived on the back of an elephant.*
N COUNT

showmanship /ʃəʊmə[3]nʃɪp/ is a person's skill at presenting or expressing something in an effective and entertaining way. EG *This was a piece of calculated showmanship.*
N UNCOUNT

shown /ʃəʊn/ is the past participle of **show**.

show-off, show-offs. If you refer to someone as a **show-off**, you mean that they behave in a way that makes their skills, abilities, or good qualities too obvious in order to impress people; an informal word used showing disapproval.
N COUNT

showpiece /ʃəʊpiːs/, **showpieces**. A **showpiece** is **1** something that is displayed, usually in an exhibition. **2** something that is admired as a fine example of its type.
N COUNT
N COUNT

showplace /ʃəʊpleɪs/, **showplaces**. A **showplace** is a place or building that is very impressive, for example because it is beautifully designed or well equipped. EG *The factory was a showplace... Too much was spent on showplace terminals.*
N COUNT

showroom /ʃəʊru[4]m/, **showrooms**. A **showroom** is a shop or a room in which goods are displayed for sale, especially cars or electrical or gas appliances. EG *The new model will be in the showrooms in a fortnight's time... ...your local gas or electricity showroom.*
N COUNT

showy /ʃəʊi[1]/, **showier, showiest**. Something that is **showy** is colourful or bright in appearance and therefore very noticeable; often used showing disapproval. EG *The wild rose has a simpler and less showy blossom... ...a showy bracelet and earrings.*
ADJ QUALIT
= flamboy

◊ **showily.** EG *The women tend to dress more elegantly or more showily.* ◊ ADV WITH VB

shrank /ʃræŋk/ is the past tense of **shrink**.

shrapnel /ʃræpnəºl/ is small pieces of metal which are scattered from exploding bombs and shells. EG *He'd been caught in the knee by a large piece of shrapnel... Most injuries resulted from shrapnel wounds.* N UNCOUNT

shred /ʃred/, **shreds, shredding, shredded. 1** If you **shred** something such as food or paper, you cut it or tear it into very small pieces. EG *Mice will shred things such as newspapers and make a terrible mess... Her new food processor has five slicing and shredding discs for various foods... Carrots taste delicious shredded in salad... The judge ordered that some evidence be shredded.* V+O

2 A **shred** of material is a small narrow piece which is torn or cut from a larger piece. EG *Two of the rioters had shirts torn almost into shreds... ...a shred of tobacco... She took the letter and ripped it to shreds.* N COUNT : USU PL, ALSO N PART+N UNCOUNT ⇑ bit

3 A **shred** of something is a very small amount of it. EG *There is no shred of evidence to support the theory that Emily was murdered... Without a shred of proof, he accused them of drinking beer... There are shreds of truth in most of their stories.* N PART = scrap

shredder /ʃredə/, **shredders.** A **shredder** is a machine which slices paper into very small pieces. EG *He picked up the agenda sheets and fed them into a shredder.* N COUNT

shrew /ʃruː/, **shrews. 1** A **shrew** is a small brown animal like a mouse with a long pointed nose. N COUNT

2 If you refer to a woman as a **shrew**, you mean that she is very bad-tempered or mean; an offensive use. EG *He found himself married to a vulgar shrew.* N COUNT

shrewd /ʃruːd/, **shrewder, shrewdest.** Someone who is **shrewd** is able to understand and judge a situation quickly and to use this understanding to their own advantage. EG *He is a shrewd and sometimes ruthless adversary... His keen, shrewd eyes looked across at his wife.* ▸ used of people's actions and judgements. EG *I have a shrewd suspicion she's had an anonymous letter too... It was a shrewd assessment and probably pretty close to the truth... I think you've made a shrew investment there.* ADJ QUALIT ⇑ clever = astute

◊ **shrewdly.** EG *She looked at him shrewdly and he could only shake his head.* ◊ ADV ◊ **shrewdness.** EG *With great shrewdness, Jane decided not to repeat the news she had heard that morning.* ◊ N UNCOUNT

shrewish /ʃruːɪʃ/. A **shrewish** woman is very bad-tempered or mean; an offensive word. ADJ QUALIT

shriek /ʃriːk/, **shrieks, shrieking, shrieked. 1** If you **shriek**, you give a sudden sharp scream of pain, terror, or high-pitched laughter. EG *She shrieked in alarm... One of the prisoners started shrieking with terror... Ralph shrieked with laughter... ...the shrieking of the wind.* V : IF+PREP THEN *with/in* = screech

2 A **shriek** is a sudden sharp scream of pain, terror, or high-pitched laughter. EG *She let out a shriek of laughter... My sister gave a shriek of delight... ...shrieks of pain... In the darkness he heard the shrieks of some forest creature.* N COUNT : IF+PREP THEN *of* = howl, screech

3 If you **shriek** something, you shout it in a loud, high-pitched voice. EG *Outside the courtroom girls shrieked abuse at the lawyers... I went stiff with terror. 'No!' I shrieked. 'Don't!'* V+O/REPORT-CL/QUOTE

shrift /ʃrɪft/. If you **give** someone or something **short shrift**, you pay very little attention to them. EG *The Secretary gave short shrift to criticisms of Government policy... Meanwhile, a host of real problems are given short shrift.* PHR : VB INFLECTS

shrill /ʃrɪl/, **shriller, shrillest; shrills, shrilling, shrilled. 1** A **shrill** sound such as a cry is high-pitched, piercing, and unpleasant to listen to. EG *The boys broke into shrill, excited cheering... By shrill blasts on his whistle he stopped all the traffic... ...the shrill screaming of jet engines... Her voice was shriller now. 'Where is he?'* ◊ **shrilly.** EG *Lewis whistled shrilly... 'Jump!' she cried shrilly.* ADJ QUALIT ◊ ADV WITH VB

2 A **shrill** demand, protest, etc is a strong one that someone makes repeatedly to complain about something or to demand that something should be done. EG *Shrill protests about the new taxes filled the newspapers.* ◊ **shrillness.** EG *The shrillness and extremism of the revolutionaries is likely to alienate people.* ADJ CLASSIF : ATTRIB = fierce ◊ N UNCOUNT

3 If something **shrills**, it makes a high-pitched, unpleasant sound. EG *Telephones shrill uselessly in deserted offices.* V

4 If someone **shrills** something, they say it in a high-pitched voice. EG *'Stop!' she shrilled... His voice shrilled again. 'I didn't steal it!'* V+O/QUOTE/REPORT-CL

shrimp /ʃrɪmp/, **shrimps. 1** A **shrimp** is a small shellfish with a long tail and a pair of pincers. There are many different kinds of shrimp, some of which can be eaten. EG *I caught about a dozen shrimps... ...a shrimp cocktail.* N COUNT

2 If you refer to someone as a **shrimp**, you mean that they are smaller and weaker than they should be for their age. EG *He was a shrimp of a boy, about six years old.* N COUNT

shrimping /ʃrɪmpɪŋ/ is the activity of fishing for shrimps. EG *We all went shrimping... ...shrimping nets.* N UNCOUNT

shrine /ʃraɪn/, **shrines.** A **shrine** is **1** a place of worship which people think is holy because it is associated with a sacred person or object. EG *To your left, you will find yourself in the Shrine of Edward the Confessor.* **2** a decorated container in which holy objects, such as the bones or clothes of a saint, are kept. EG *...the shrine containing the Turin Shroud.* **3** the tomb of a saint or other person who is thought to be holy. **4** a place which people visit and treat with respect because it is associated with a famous person or event. EG *...the shrine of the Renaissance – Florence.* N COUNT N COUNT N COUNT N COUNT

shrink /ʃrɪŋk/, **shrinks, shrinking, shrank, shrunk. 1** If cloth or a piece of clothing **shrinks** or if you **shrink** it, it becomes smaller in size, usually as a result of being washed. EG *You should dry-clean curtains if possible, as they are less likely to shrink... Do not allow your washing to boil, or you may shrink it.* V-ERG

2 If something **shrinks** or if you **shrink** it, it becomes smaller. EG *He commented on the amazing way in which computers have recently shrunk in size... The economy is shrinking instead of expanding... The world's forests are shrinking at an alarming rate.* V-ERG ⇑ contract

3 If you **shrink** away from something, you move away from it because you are frightened, horrified, or disgusted by it. EG *The boys shrank away in horror... She suddenly shrank from him crying, 'Oh! You terrify me.'* V+A = recoil

4 If you **shrink** from something such as a task or duty, you are reluctant to do it because you find it unpleasant. EG *They shrank from what was to come.* V+A *(from)* = recoil

5 A **shrink** is a psychiatrist; used in informal English. N COUNT

shrinkage /ʃrɪŋkɪdʒ/ is a decrease in the size, weight, or amount of something. EG *When buying materials allow 10 per cent extra length for shrinkage... There has been a twenty per cent shrinkage in the steel industry in the past few years.* N UNCOUNT ⇑ reduction

shrivel /ʃrɪvəºl/, **shrivels, shrivelling, shrivelled**; also spelled **shriveling** and **shriveled** in American English. When something **shrivels** or **shrivels up**, it becomes dry and wrinkled, usually because it loses moisture in the heat. EG *The seedlings had shrivelled up a bit in the hot sun... Every year we have a long dry season that shrivels and scorches plants.* ◊ **shrivelled.** EG *...shrivelled tomatoes... Although he's only in his late thirties, he looks shrivelled and ill.* V-ERG, OR PHRASAL VB : V+ADV = wither ◊ ADJ QUALIT = withered

shroud /ʃraʊd/, **shrouds, shrouding, shrouded. 1** A **shroud** is **1.1** a cloth which is used for wrapping a dead body in. EG *The doctor wanted to use the sheet for a shroud.* **1.2** something which hides things and keeps them secret or mysterious. EG *His past is enveloped in a shroud of mystery.* N COUNT N COUNT+SUPP : USU+*of* = veil

2 If something **is shrouded, 2.1** it is hidden by darkness, fog, etc. EG *Everything was shrouded in mist and raindrops... The entire jail was shrouded in darkness.* **2.2** very little is known about it, for example because it is kept secret. EG *The group shrouded its communications with every possible secrecy... Later events are shrouded in mystery.* V+O : USU PASS, IF+PREP THEN *in* V+O : USU PASS, IF+PREP THEN *in* = cloak

shrub /ʃrʌb/, **shrubs.** A **shrub** is a low plant like a small tree with several woody stems instead of a trunk. There are many different kinds of shrub. EG *...the pale lilac of flowering shrubs.* N COUNT

shrubbery /ʃrʌbəºriˡ/, **shrubberies. Shrubbery** or a **shrubbery** is a place where a lot of shrubs are growing, which is sometimes part of a garden. EG *The voice seemed to be coming from the shrubbery... Branches of shrubbery concealed the car from view.* N UNCOUNT/COUNT

shrug /ʃrʌg/, **shrugs, shrugging, shrugged.** If you **shrug** your shoulders or if you **shrug**, you raise your shoulders in order to show that you are not interested in something or that you do not know or care about it. EG *'Do you mind if I wait?' I asked. Melanie shrugged. 'Please yourself.'... Don't just shrug your shoulders. Say something!* ▸ used as a noun. EG *'Come then,' Chang said with a shrug... The man nodded with a faint shrug of his shoulders.* V OR V+O ⇑ move ▸ N COUNT : USU SING ⇑ movement

shrug off. If you **shrug** something **off**, you ignore it or treat it as if it is not really important or serious. EG *I admire the way she can just shrug off all her problems... ...criticism which she can just about shrug off but which he takes painfully to heart... He shrugged off the rejection as 'a matter of academic jealousy.'* PHRASAL VB : V+O+ADV

shrunk /ʃrʌŋk/ is the past participle of **shrink**.

shrunken /ʃrʌŋkəᵊn/. Something that is **shrunken** has become smaller. EG *...a shrunken old man.* ADJ QUALIT

shucks /ʃʌks/. You can say **shucks** to express disappointment, annoyance, or embarrassment; used especially in American English. EG *'You made a fine speech.'–'Shucks, it was nothing really.'* EXCLAM

shudder /ʃʌdə/, **shudders, shuddering, shuddered.** 1 If you **shudder**, you tremble with fear, horror, or disgust. EG *Robert shuddered with fear... He touched Ralph's shoulder and Ralph shuddered at the human contact.* ▸ used as a noun. EG *The invasion of the island sent a shudder of horror through the people.* ● If something **gives** you **the shudders**, it terrifies you; an informal expression. EG *It gave him the shudders just to go inside the door.* V : IF+PREP THEN *at/in/with* = quake, shiver ▸ N COUNT : USU SING ● PHR : VB INFLECTS

2 If you say that you **shudder to think** of something, you mean that you expect it to be so awful or disastrous that you do not really want to think about it. EG *I shudder to think of the consequences... 'What will happen now?'–'I shudder to think.'* PHR

3 If something such as a machine or vehicle **shudders**, it shakes suddenly in a very violent manner. EG *The tank braked and shuddered to a violent halt... The plane was shuddering and lurching in the most terrifying manner.* ▸ used as a noun. EG *It takes only a momentary shudder, some deep earth movement, to destroy hundreds of homes... The tank came to a halt with a shudder.* V ▸ N COUNT : USU SING ⇑ movement

shuffle /ʃʌfəᵊl/, **shuffles, shuffling, shuffled.** 1 If you **shuffle**, 1.1 you walk without lifting your feet properly off the ground. EG *He slipped on his shoes and shuffled out of the room... ...a fat woman shuffling along with a pushchair.* ▸ used as a noun. EG *We recognized him by his distinctive walk, a kind of shuffle in which he scarcely bothered to lift his feet.* V : USU+A ▸ N SING WITH DET

1.2 you move your feet about while standing or move your bottom about while sitting, often because you feel uncomfortable or embarrassed. EG *I looked at the ground, shuffled my feet and mumbled something defensive... I was shuffling in my seat.* V OR V-ERG = fidget

2 If you **shuffle** a pack of cards, you mix them up before you begin a game so that their order is changed and nobody knows where individual cards are. EG *He took out the cards, shuffled them loudly, and put them down on the table... Whose turn is it to shuffle?* ▸ used as a noun. EG *Give the cards a good shuffle.* V OR V+O ▸ N SING : *a*+N

3 If you **shuffle** things, you change their order or move them from one place to another, sometimes causing a muddle or confusion. EG *He was bent over a number of shells which he was shuffling and reshuffling on a mat... He shuffled the papers back into their folder.* V+O : USU+A

shuffle off. If you **shuffle** something **off**, you avoid talking or thinking about it because you decide that it is not very important. EG *He shuffled the question off and changed the topic.* PHRASAL VB : V+O+ADV = evade

shuffle out. If you **shuffle out** or **shuffle out of** something such as an unpleasant task, you try to avoid it by acting dishonestly. EG *I mistrust the way in which they shuffle out of any sustained effort.* PHRASAL VB : V+ADV, OR V+ADV+PREP = dodge out

shun /ʃʌn/, **shuns, shunning, shunned.** If you **shun** someone or something, you deliberately avoid becoming involved with them. EG *His later writings reveal his contempt for the critics who shunned him... Most medical graduates shun posts in geriatric medicine.* V+O ⇑ reject = eschew

shunt /ʃʌnt/, **shunts, shunting, shunted.** 1 If you **shunt** objects or people, you move them to a different place, especially one that is more suitable or convenient. EG *...the groaning of heavy desks being shunted across the room... His intention had been to shunt the immigrants back where they came from.* V+O : USU+A ⇑ transfer

2 When railway engines **shunt**, they push or pull wagons or carriages from one railway line to another. EG *I used to hear the trains shunting in Newbury station... ...a shunting engine.* V OR V+O ⇑ transfer

shush /ʃʊʃ, ʃʌʃ/, **shushes, shushing, shushed.** 1 You say **shush** when you are telling someone, especially a child, to be quiet. EG *Shush, I know he's back... Shush shush darling, don't cry.* EXCLAM = hush, sh

2 If you **shush** someone, you tell them to be quiet by saying shush or sh. EG *Piggy snivelled and Simon shushed him.* V OR V+O ⇑ silence

shut /ʃʌt/, **shuts, shutting.** The form **'shut** is used in the present tense and is the past tense and past participle of the verb. 1 If you **shut** something or if it **shuts**, its position is changed so that it fills a hole or gap. EG *I shut the door quietly... When the ferret goes in, the door shuts behind him.* ▸ used as an adjective. EG *The windows were all shut... She slammed the drawer shut.* V-ERG = close ▸ ADJ CLASSIF : PRED = closed

2 If you **shut** your eyes, you lower the lids of your eyes so that you cannot see anything. EG *Mrs Kaul shut her eyes for a moment.* ▸ used as an adjective. EG *He lay with his eyes shut.* ● If someone **shuts** their **eyes** to something, they deliberately ignore it; used showing disapproval. EG *It is foolish to shut our eyes to the social cost of such a policy... What are the facts that so many of our citizens shut their eyes to?* V+O = close ▸ ADJ CLASSIF ● PHR : VB INFLECTS, USU+*to*

3 If you **shut** your mouth, you place your lips together so that nothing can get into your mouth or out of it. EG *Mr Boggis opened his mouth, then quickly shut it again.* ● If someone tells you to **shut** your **mouth**, **shut** your **face**, etc, they are telling you very rudely to stop talking. EG *Shut your big mouth!... Shut your gob, Kingston.* ● If someone tells you to **keep** your **mouth shut**, **keep** your **trap shut**, etc, they are telling you rather rudely to keep quiet and not say anything, especially about something that they want to be kept a secret. EG *Do as you are told and keep your mouth shut!... He warned me to keep my mouth shut about his visit.* V+O = close ≠ open ● CONVENTION = be quiet, shut up ● PHR : VB INFLECTS, OR CONVENTION = keep silent, keep mum

4 If a shop, pub, etc **shuts** or if someone **shuts** it, it is closed and you cannot go into it until the next day or until the next time that it is open. EG *'What time do the shops shut?'–'Half past five.'... They decided to shut the library at 6 o'clock.* ▸ used as an adjective. EG *I'm afraid all the pubs will be shut.* V-ERG = close ≠ open ▸ ADJ CLASSIF : PRED

shut away. If you **shut** something **away**, you keep it in a special room or cupboard where people cannot see it. EG *We have a small number of books which are shut away.* PHRASAL VB : V+O+ADV = put away

shut down. If a factory, business, etc **shuts down** or if someone **shuts it down**, it stops working, either for a short time or for ever. EG *His department was shut down for lack of funds... That year my grandfather had to shut down the forge.* ● See also **shutdown**. PHRASAL VB : V-ERG+ADV = close down

shut in. 1 If someone **shuts** you **in** a room, you cannot get out of it. EG *He was shut in with an assortment of strangers.* PHRASAL VB : V+O+ADV/PREP = imprison

2 If you **shut** yourself **in** a room, you stay in there and make sure nobody else can get in. EG *She shut herself in the bathroom and wept.* PHRASAL VB : V+O (REFL)+ADV/PREP

shut off. 1 If someone **shuts off** the supply of a particular commodity or kind of goods, they stop sending the commodity or goods to the people who normally use them. EG *The OPEC nations threatened to shut off oil supplies... They might shut off supplies of labour power one day.* PHRASAL VB : V+O+ADV ⇑ cease

2 If you **shut off** an engine, water supply, etc, you turn it off to stop it working. EG *I stopped the car and shut off the engine.* PHRASAL VB : V+O+ADV

3 If something **shuts off** a view, it stands between you and the view so that you cannot see the view. EG *A row of trees shut off the view.* PHRASAL VB : V+O+ADV = block

shut out. 1 If you **shut** something or someone **out**, you prevent them from getting into a place, such as a building, for example by closing the doors. EG *They had covered the holes to shut out the water.* PHRASAL VB : V+O+ADV ⇑ exclude

2 If you **shut out** a thought or a sensation, you prevent yourself from thinking or feeling it. EG *He shut out the thought... She found it impossible to shut out the pain.* PHRASAL VB : V+O+ADV = keep out

shut up. 1 If you **shut up**, you stop talking; an informal use. EG *She was always telling him to shut* PHRASAL VB : V+ADV

up... *I tried to shut up about him.* • **Shut up** is a rude way of telling someone to stop talking. EG *Shut up and listen... Why don't you shut up?*
• CONVENTION = be quiet

2 If someone **shuts** you **up**, **2.1** they keep you in a room or building from which you cannot get out. EG *They wanted to shut Sarah up in a mental hospital... He was shut up for life as a dangerous criminal.*
PHRASAL VB : V+O+ADV = imprison, confine
2.2 they prevent you from talking; an informal use. EG *Turn the television on. That usually shuts them up.*
PHRASAL VB : V+O+ADV = silence

shutdown /ʃʌtdaʊn/, **shutdowns**. A **shutdown** is the closing of a factory, shop, or other business, either for a short time or for ever. EG *Irish bar proprietors called for a shutdown between 3 and 5 pm... Refinery owners have already resorted to temporary shutdowns.*
N COUNT = closure

shut-eye is sleep; an informal word. EG *You'd better get some shut-eye.*
N UNCOUNT

shutter /ʃʌtə/, **shutters**. 1 **Shutters** are wooden or metal covers fitted in pairs on the outside of a window. They can be opened to let in the light or shut to keep out the sun, the cold, or for privacy or security. EG *I'll close the shutters... He got up and opened one of the big wooden shutters.*
N COUNT : USU PL

2 A **shutter** is **2.1** the part of a camera which opens to allow light through the lens when a photograph is taken. EG *He rotated the focus ring slightly and pressed the shutter.*
N COUNT ⇑ cover
2.2 a device that closes something. There are many kinds of shutter. EG *An automatic door shutter prevents draughts.*
N COUNT

shuttered /ʃʌtəd/. A **shuttered** window 1 has shutters fitted to it. EG *A few houses in the village had shuttered windows.*
ADJ CLASSIF
2 has its shutters closed. EG *All doors were locked and the windows closed and shuttered... The townspeople watched from behind their shuttered windows.* ▸ used of rooms and buildings with shuttered windows. EG *Smells issued from dim, shuttered rooms... We turned back into the dark, shuttered house.*
ADJ CLASSIF

shuttle /ʃʌtəl/, **shuttles, shuttling, shuttled**.
1 A **shuttle** service is an air, bus, or train service which makes frequent journeys between two places which are fairly near to each other. EG *The university was a mile away from the halls of residence and a shuttle bus service was employed.*
N COUNT : USU BEFORE N

2 A **shuttle** is a plane used in a shuttle service. EG *He caught the nine o'clock shuttle to New York.*
N COUNT ⇑ plane

3 If you **shuttle** between two places, you make frequent journeys between them. EG *He shuttles back and forth some 50,000 miles a year... A little tram shuttles between the piers.*
V+A ⇑ travel

4 If you **shuttle** a lot of people or things to a place, you take them there using a shuttle service. EG *Troops were shuttled down to the battle area.*
V+O ⇑ transport

5 A **shuttle** is also **5.1** a piece of equipment used in weaving. It takes a thread backwards and forwards over the other threads in order to make a piece of material. EG *The shuttle moves backwards and forwards through the warp.*
N COUNT ⇑ device
5.2 a small piece of equipment on a sewing machine. It carries the lower thread to form a loop with the upper thread in order to make a stitch.
N COUNT ⇑ device
5.3 a shuttlecock. EG *Don't let the shuttle drop, Samantha.*
N COUNT = cock

6 See also **space shuttle**.

shuttlecock /ʃʌtəlkɒk/, **shuttlecocks**. A **shuttlecock** is the object that you hit over the net in a game of badminton. It is small, rounded at one end, and has real or artificial feathers fixed in the other end.
N COUNT = shuttle, cock

shy /ʃaɪ/, **shyer, shyest; shies, shying, shied**.
1 A **shy** person is nervous and uncomfortable in the company of other people, especially people who he or she does not know. EG *I've always been a bit shy... He was too shy to talk to anyone at the party.*
ADJ QUALIT = retiring, diffident
▸ used of people's behaviour. EG *She lowered her head and eyes in a shy reaction... ...a shy smile.*
▸ ADJ QUALIT : ATTRIB
◊ **shyly**. EG *She smiled shyly at him.*
◊ ADV WITH VB
◊ **shyness**. EG *I tried to overcome my shyness.*
◊ N UNCOUNT = diffidence

2 If you are **shy** of doing something, you are unwilling to do it because you are afraid of what might happen. EG *Don't be shy of telling them what you think.*
ADJ QUALIT : PRED+OF = wary, hesitant
• If you **fight shy** of something, you try hard to avoid it. EG *All the children fight shy of lessons.*
• PHR : VB INFLECTS+*of*

3 Animals that are **shy** avoid humans and are easily frightened by them. EG *The brook was muddy and the trout were shy... They are shy birds that normally live unobtrusive lives.*
ADJ QUALIT ⇑ timid

4 When a horse **shies**, it moves back or turns aside suddenly, because something has frightened it. EG *You must have complete control of him should he decide to shy.*
V

5 If you **shy** something such as a ball or a stone, you throw it, usually with a sideways movement of your arm; an old-fashioned use. EG *The youths were shying rocks at the police.*
V+O : USU+A
▸ used as a noun. EG *He had a shy at the wicket but missed.*
▸ N COUNT : USU SING

6 See also **camera-shy, coconut shy, work-shy**.

shy away from. If you **shy away from** doing something, you avoid doing it, often because you are afraid to do it or not confident enough. EG *Are you going to grasp these opportunities or shy away from them?*
PHRASAL VB : V+ADV+PREP = shrink from

SI /ɛs aɪ/is a system of metric units.
N UNCOUNT

Siamese /saɪəmiːz/. **Siamese** is both the singular and the plural form. 1 **Siamese** means relating or belonging to Thailand or to its people; an old-fashioned use. EG *...the Siamese delegate.*
ADJ CLASSIF = Thai

2 A **Siamese** is **2.1** a person who comes from Thailand; an old-fashioned use.
N COUNT
2.2 a Siamese cat; an informal use.
N COUNT

Siamese cat, Siamese cats. A **Siamese cat** is a type of cat with short cream or brown fur, blue eyes, dark ears, and a dark tail. EG *She was cradling two Siamese cats.*
N COUNT

Siamese twins are twins who were born joined to each other by a part of their bodies, for example by their hips.
N COUNT : USU PL

sibilant /sɪbɪlənt/. Something that is **sibilant** makes a hissing sound, like the sound a snake makes. EG *There was a little sibilant whispering.*
ADJ CLASSIF : USU ATTRIB

sibling /sɪblɪŋ/, **siblings**. Your **siblings** are your brothers and sisters; a formal or technical word. EG *Probably the optimum number of siblings is four... ...sibling rivalry.*
N COUNT

sic /sɪk/. You write **sic** in brackets after a word or expression when you are quoting something that someone else has written. You do it because the word or expression may look odd or wrong to a reader and you want to indicate that it really was spelled or written in the way that you are spelling or writing it. EG *...No Smokeing (sic)... ...February Fun Raising (sic).*

Sicilian /sɪsɪljən/, **Sicilians**. 1 Something that is **Sicilian** belongs or relates to Sicily or to its people. EG *...the Sicilian shore.*
ADJ CLASSIF

2 A **Sicilian** is a person who comes from Sicily. EG *...a quarrel between two Sicilians.*
N COUNT ⇑ Italian

sick /sɪk/, **sicker, sickest**. 1 If you are **sick**, you are ill. **Sick** usually means physically ill, but it can sometimes be used to mean mentally ill. EG *Your uncle is very sick... ...a sick child... I remembered how sick she had been.*
ADJ QUALIT = poorly, unwell
▸ The **sick** are people who are sick. EG *The sick and the lonely are most at risk.*
▸ N PLURAL : *the*+N
• If someone **falls sick**, they become ill; a fairly literary expression. EG *The two girls fell sick and died.*
• PHR : VB INFLECTS
• If you are **off sick**, you are absent from work or school because of illness or injury. EG *He smashed his nose and was off sick for some time.*
• PHR : USED AS AN A

2 If you feel **sick**, you feel ill in your stomach, and food that you have eaten is likely to be sent out through your mouth. EG *Flying always makes me feel sick... You'll make yourself sick if you eat all those sweets.*
ADJ QUALIT : PRED = nauseous
• If you **are sick**, food that you have eaten is sent out through your mouth. EG *I think I'm going to be sick... He was kneeling by the lavatory being violently sick.*
• PHR : VB INFLECTS = vomit, throw up

3 **Sick** is the substance that comes out of your mouth when you are sick; an informal use in British English. EG *...a fat baby, who smelled of sick.*
N UNCOUNT = vomit

4 If you feel **sick** about something, you feel annoyed, unhappy, or disappointed about it. EG *I feel sick about the way she was treated.*
ADJ QUALIT : PRED
• If you say that something that has happened **makes** you **sick**, you mean that you feel angry or disgusted about it. EG *It makes me sick the way they waste our money.*
• PHR : VB INFLECTS ⇑ displease = sicken

5 If you are **sick** of something or **sick and tired** of it, you are very annoyed by it and want it to stop, because it has happened too often or continued for too long. EG *We're sick of sitting around waiting for something to happen... Europe was sick of war... She must have got sick and tired of hearing people say that.*
ADJ QUALIT : PRED+*of*, OR PHR+*of* : USED AS C ⇑ dissatisfied = fed up

6 You describe acts, stories, or jokes as **sick** when they deal with death, cruelty, or suffering in a frivolous or tasteless way; used showing disapproval.
ADJ QUALIT ⇑ offensive

EG *Who would be so sick as to do such a thing?... She made a rather sick joke... It was the sickest thing Jane had ever heard of.*

7 If you are **worried sick**, you are extremely worried; an informal expression. EG *He was worried sick that the factory might close.* PHR : USED AS C

sick bay, sick bays. A **sick bay** is an area, for example on a ship, where medical treatment is given and where beds are provided for people who are ill. EG *The sick bay was generally empty.* N COUNT ⇑ infirmary

sickbed /sɪkbɛd/, **sickbeds**; also spelled with a hyphen. Your **sickbed** is the bed that you lie in when you are ill. EG *I was able to watch television from my sickbed... He was forced to rise from his sickbed.* N COUNT : USU SING

sicken /sɪkə^{0}n/, **sickens, sickening, sickened.**

1 If something **sickens** you, it makes you feel disgusted. EG *The roar of the crowd when they saw the blood sickened her... The young officers were sickened by the greed of their generals... My uncle left in the middle of the play thoroughly sickened.* V+O = repulse

2 If you **sicken**, you become ill; a rather old-fashioned use. EG *In these conditions a child could sicken and die in a year.* V = fall ill

sickening /sɪkə^{0}nɪŋ/. You describe something as **sickening** 1 when it gives you feelings of horror or disgust, or makes you feel sick in your stomach. EG *The car crashed with a sickening crunch into a tree... The food smelled sickening... That's the most sickening thing I ever heard.* ◊ **sickeningly**. EG *The canoe plunged sickeningly downward.* 2 when it annoys you very much; an informal use. EG *We're going to be late again. How sickening.* ADJ QUALIT ⇑ unpleasant; ◊ ADV WITH VB; ADJ QUALIT = infuriating

sickle /sɪkə^{0}l/, **sickles.** A **sickle** is a tool that is used for cutting grass and grain crops. It has a short handle and a blade shaped like a hook. N COUNT

sick leave is the time that a person is officially allowed to spend away from work because of illness of injury. EG *...a job with paid holidays and sick leave... She's on sick leave at the moment.* N UNCOUNT ⇑ leave

sickly /sɪkli^1/, **sicklier, sickliest.** 1 A **sickly** person is weak, unhealthy, and often ill. EG *He was a sickly and ineffective man... New babies were stunted and sickly.* ADJ QUALIT ≠ strong, healthy

2 If someone's face is **sickly**, they look pale and ill. EG *...his sickly pallor.* ▸ used as an adverb. EG *Bill went sickly pale... His colour was sickly grey.* ADJ QUALIT; ▸ ADV+ADJ

3 You describe things as **sickly** when they are very unpleasant to smell or look at. EG *There was a musty, sickly smell of droppings... ...a sickly fragrance... He was wearing a sickly brown shirt... Hogan responded with a sickly smile.* ADJ QUALIT = nauseous

sickness /sɪknɪ^{2}s/, **sicknesses.** 1 **Sickness** is 1.1 the state of being ill or unhealthy. EG *...people who are not working because of sickness or unemployment.* 1.2 a condition in which you feel ill in your stomach and in which food that you have eaten is sent out through your mouth. EG *The disease causes sickness and diarrhoea.* • See also **morning sickness.** N UNCOUNT ⇑ illness; N UNCOUNT = nausea

2 A **sickness** is a particular illness. EG *Her sickness was so far advanced that the doctors could not save her... ...the first signs of radiation sickness.* N COUNT/ UNCOUNT

sickness benefit is money that you receive regularly from the government when you are unable to work because of illness. EG *Are you qualified for sickness benefit?* N UNCOUNT

sickroom /sɪkru^{4}m/, **sickrooms**; also spelled as two words. A **sickroom** is a room in which a sick person is lying in bed. EG *They hustled him out of the sickroom.* N COUNT : USU SING

side /saɪd/, **sides, siding, sided.** When 'side' is used as a noun in the singular, you do not normally use 'a' before it, you say 'one side', except in paragraphs 15, 21, 24, and 25. 1 You use **side** to refer to a position that is to the left or right of something or someone, rather than in front of them or behind them. EG *He had brown hair combed to the side... A taxi bumped into us from the side... They sat each side of a small table... Standing on either side of him were two younger men... She reached across to the table at her side... I sat down by her side.* N COUNT : USU PREP+N

2 The word **side** is used in the following expressions referring to the position of things or people. 2.1 If something is **on every side** or **on all sides** of you, you are surrounded by it. EG *The sea lay on every side... There were children ten deep on every side.* 2.2 If something is **to one side** of something else or **on one side** of it, it is either to its left or to its right. EG *Boylan stood to one side of the hearth... Her wig tipped slightly to one side.* 2.3 If you move or are moved **to one side**, you get out of someone's way. EG *He shrank to one side... Ralph elbowed him to one side... 'Get out of my way,' she cried, pushing Tom to one side.* 2.4 If you **take** someone **on one side**, you speak to them privately away from other people in order to give them advice or a warning. EG *I was taken on one side by a man I knew vaguely and told to get out of town.* 2.5 If you put something **to one side** or **on one side**, you keep it separate from other things, so that you can deal with it later. EG *She put the unfinished letter to one side.* 2.6 If two people are **side by side**, they are sitting or walking next to each other. EG *They sat side by side... He was walking side by side with Ralph.* 2.7 If people work **side by side**, they work closely together. EG *We have worked together side by side for many years... Student and tutor learn side by side... More and more women are taking their place side by side with men.* 2.8 If two things develop or exist **side by side**, they do it in the same place at the same time. EG *Two interdependent communities evolved side by side... All these virtues exist side by side with the real vices.* 2.9 If something moves **from side to side**, it moves repeatedly to the left and to the right. EG *Her head tilted rhythmically from side to side... The ship was swaying from side to side.* ▸ used as an adjective, usually with hyphens. EG *The boat settled into a slow side-to-side roll.* PHR : USED AS AN A; PHR : USED AS AN A, IF+PREP; THEN *of*; PHR : USED AS AN A; PHR : VB INFLECTS ⇑ buttonhole = collar; PHR : USED AS AN A = aside; PHR : USED AS AN A; PHR : USED AS AN A; PHR : USED AS AN A; PHR : USED AS AN A ⇑ sideways; ▸ ADJ CLASSIF : ATTRIB ⇑ sideways

3 Your **sides** are the parts of your body under your arms from your armpits down to your hips. EG *I've got a pain in my side... She lay on her side with her back to me... Her fists were clenched at her sides.* N COUNT : USU DETPOSS+N

4 If someone is at your **side**, by your **side**, etc, they stay near you and give you comfort, support, or loyalty. EG *All night she never left her mother's side... I'm eager to be at the President's side... He wanted to live forever by her side.* N COUNT : USU SING WITH POSS

5 The **sides** of an area or surface are 5.1 its two halves considered as if the area or surface was divided by a central line. EG *Blood was streaming from one side of her face... He rolled back to his side of the bed.* 5.2 the parts that are not in its centre but are near to its left or right hand edges. EG *She cleared a space by pushing piles of mail to the sides and back of the desk.* 5.3 its edges. EG *A hedge surrounds my garden on three sides.* N COUNT : USU+SUPP ⇑ part; N COUNT : IF SING THEN USU *one/the*+N ⇑ position; N COUNT

6 The **sides** of an object such as a box are its flat outside surfaces. EG *The box opens on this side... The parcel was marked 'this side up'.* N COUNT

7 The **sides** of something such as a building or a vehicle are the vertical outer parts which are not its front or its back. EG *He noticed a ladder against the side of the house... Hogan walked round to the driver's side and unlocked the car door.* ▸ used as an adjective. EG *Smithy left the side door open.* N COUNT; ▸ ADJ CLASSIF : ATTRIB

8 The **sides** of a long rectangular object such as a table or a bed are its two long edges. EG *The table was set for six, two at each side and one at each end... She was kneeling by the side of the bed.* N COUNT

9 The **sides** of a road or street are 9.1 its two parts along which vehicles drive in opposite directions. EG *She was driving on the wrong side of the road.* 9.2 the parts which are next to its edges rather than in its centre. EG *There was an ambulance behind us, so we got into the side to let it pass.* 9.3 the grass, pavement, or other land that is immediately next to it. EG *She crossed Elm Road and walked back on the other side... She stood on the side of the empty road... The streets had houses on both sides.* N COUNT; N COUNT : USU SING; N COUNT

10 A **side** road or **side** street is a less important road or street leading off an important one. EG *I slipped away down a side street.* ADJ CLASSIF : ATTRIB ≠ main

11 The **sides** of a river or lake are its banks. N COUNT

12 The **sides** of a hill or valley are the sloping parts between its top and bottom. EG *We were driving up the side of a mountain... The sides of the valley were white with snow.* N COUNT : USU+*of* ⇑ slope = incline

13 The two **sides** of something that acts as a boundary are the areas of land on each side of the boundary. EG *We were told of threatening developments on the other side of the border... We live on the English side of the river Wye.* N COUNT : USU SING+SUPP

14 When you talk about **the other side** of a town or country, you mean the part of it that is furthest away PHR : USED AS O, USU PREP+PHR

from you. When you talk about **the other side** of the world, you mean a part of the world that is a very long way away. EG *That restaurant's right over at the other side of town... The ship has come from far away, from the other side of the world... I'm going on a trip to the other side of the earth.*
+of
⇑ far away
= distant

15 A **side** of meat is the meat of a dead animal which has been cut in half along its backbone. EG *We bought half a side of pork and half a side of beef.*
N COUNT+of

16 The **sides** of a piece of paper or cloth are its front and its back. EG *What does the leaflet say on the other side?*
N COUNT

17 If you write a certain number of **sides**, you cover that number of pages with writing, for example when you are writing an essay or taking an examination. EG *She wrote about twenty sides for the last exam... My essay is only three sides long.*
N COUNT : USU NUM+N

18 A **side** of a cassette or tape is the amount of tape or taped material that is available when you play the cassette or tape from beginning to end without turning it over. EG *Which side did you use to tape the Tina Turner album?... ...Tape 70 Side B.*
N COUNT
⇑ track

19 The two **sides** in a war, debate, or argument are the two groups of people who are fighting each other or debating or arguing with each other. EG *The threat of attack from the Confederate side was a very real one... They made a fortune by selling arms to both sides... He was one of the more liberal spokesmen on the Opposition side... The argument was settled to the satisfaction of both sides.*
N COUNT
= party, participant

20 The **sides** of an argument are the different points of view of the people who are arguing. EG *Parents and children are on opposing sides of most arguments... She only ever hears his side of things.*
N COUNT
⇑ aspect
= viewpoint

21 The two **sides** in a game or match are the two teams who are playing against each other. EG *We beat the Scottish First Division side.*
N COUNT : USU+SUPP

22 The word **side** is used in the following expressions connected either with wars, quarrels, or arguments or with attempts to achieve something. **22.1** If you **take sides** or **take** someone's **side**, you support one of the two sides in an argument or a quarrel. EG *I'm not going to take sides. They're both my friends... I wouldn't want anyone to take my side against Tom.*
PHR : VB INFLECTS

22.2 If you are **on** someone's **side**, you are supporting them in an argument, a quarrel, or a war. EG *Whose side are you on?... Do everything you can to win people on to your side... We brought the majority of the staff over to our side... His country never intervened on the side of one state against another.*
PHR : USED AS AN A
⇑ for

22.3 If you are **on the side of** something that someone is trying to achieve, you are in favour of it and support the people who are trying to achieve it. EG *They're on the side of justice... They know who's on the side of law and order around here.*
PREP

22.4 If something is **on** your **side**, it gives you an advantage when you are trying to achieve something. EG *Luck was on our side... She had both money and time on her side, being both wealthy and in her twenties... He has got the system on his side and he is determined to use it.*
PHR : USED AS AN A

23 The two **sides** in something such as an agreement or a partnership are two people or groups of people who are dealing with each other. EG *Both sides were confident that they would benefit from the partnership.*
N COUNT
⇑ party
= half

24 The **sides** of something such as a play, a film, or a situation are its different aspects. EG *The producers wanted to emphasize the political side of the play... One has to think of the practical side of things.*
N COUNT : USU+SUPP
⇑ facet

● When you talk about one **side of the story** or one **side of the picture**, you are referring to one aspect of a situation which can only be understood properly when all its aspects are known. EG *Though undeniable, this is only one side of the story... This is, of course, only one side of the picture... They were punished immediately, without ever having their side of the story told.*
● PHR : USU USED AS C/O
⇑ point of view

25 A **side** of someone's character or personality is one aspect of it. EG *There is something distasteful about this side of her character... Yevtushenko reveals an unexpected side of himself in his first book of photographs.*
N COUNT
⇑ facet

26 The two **sides** of your family are your mother's family and your father's family. EG *She was Giovanna's grandmother on her mother's side... My grandparents on my father's side were both Polish.*
N COUNT : USU WITH POSS IN SING

27 If you do something **on the side**, you do it **27.1** in addition to your main work. EG *If we get good profits from the farm, maybe we could start a little business on the side.*
PHR : USED AS AN A

27.2 secretly and dishonestly in connection with your job. EG *She manages to sell some of the goods on the side.*
PHR : USED AS AN A

28 The word **side** is also used in the following expressions. **28.1** If you say that something is **on the** large **side**, **on the** small **side**, etc, you mean that it is slightly too large, slightly too small, etc. EG *Maybe her dress is a little on the small side... The inhabitants tended to be on the conservative side... The food is excellent though on the expensive side.*
PHR : USED AS AN A
⇑ rather
= quite, somewhat

28.2 If you say that someone has **let the side down**, you mean that they have embarrassed their family or friends by behaving in a way that is not socially acceptable.
PHR : VB INFLECTS
⇑ betray
= embarrass, discredit

28.3 If you keep **on the right side of** someone, you try to please them and avoid annoying them. If you get **on the wrong side of** someone, you annoy them and make them dislike you. EG *It pays to keep on the right side of him at all times... He can be really angry if you get on the wrong side of him.*
PHR

28.4 If you say that something will happen **this side of** a particular time, you mean that it will happen before that time; an informal expression. EG *We have no prospect of another holiday this side of Christmas.*
PHR+NG : USED AS AN A

28.5 If you say that someone is **the wrong side of** a particular age, you mean that they are older than that age. EG *It wouldn't be too easy to get a job now that she was the wrong side of thirty-five.*
PHR+NG : USED AS C

28.6 You use the expression **leaving to one side** when you are saying that you want to ignore a particular fact or detail in order to make a general statement. EG *Leaving to one side the loss of the Venezuelan contract, I think I can say that we have had a good year.*
PHR+NG
= apart from

29 The word **side** is also used in the following expressions, which are explained at other places in this dictionary. ● to **be on the safe side**: see **safe**. ● to **be on the side of the angels**: see **angel**. ● to **err on the side of** something: see **err**. ● to **get out of bed on the wrong side**: see **bed**. ● to **know which side** your **bread is buttered on**: see **bread**. ● to **look on the bright side**: see **bright**. ● **the other side of the coin**: see **coin**.

side against. If people **side against** you, they join together in order to defeat you, for example in a quarrel or an argument. EG *Her supporters sided against me.*
PHRASAL VB : V+PREP

side with. If you **side with** someone, you support them in a quarrel or argument. EG *The daughters sided with their mothers.*
PHRASAL VB : V+PREP

sideboard /saɪdbɔːd/, **sideboards**. **1** A **sideboard** is a long cupboard which is about the same height as a table. Sideboards are usually used in dining rooms to hold plates, glasses, bottles, etc. EG *Castle went to the sideboard and poured himself a whisky.*
N COUNT

2 If a man has **sideboards**, he has two strips of hair growing down the sides of his cheeks which he deliberately does not shave off. EG *He had a moustache and sideboards.*
N PLURAL
= whiskers

sidecar /saɪdkɑː/, **sidecars**. A **sidecar** is a kind of box with a seat in it and a wheel on the bottom. You attach a sidecar to the side of a motorcycle so that it can carry a passenger.
N COUNT

side-effect, side-effects; also spelled as two words. **1** The **side-effects** of a drug are the effects that the drug has on you in addition to its intended function such as curing a particular illness or pain. Side-effects may be considered unimportant in comparison with the cure, and can vary greatly in how serious they are. EG *This type of aspirin can have appalling side-effects... Reported side effects of the drug are heightened blood pressure and headaches.*
N COUNT : USU PL
⇑ result

2 The **side-effects** of a situation are the unplanned things that happen in addition to the main results or effects that are expected to happen. EG *Britain suffered the side-effects of early industrial development more than France did... One side-effect of the crisis could be that she loses her seat in Parliament.*
N COUNT : USU PL, IF+PREP THEN of
= by-product

side issue, side issues. A **side issue** is an issue or subject that is not considered to be as important as the main one. EG *I think that's rather a side issue, don't you?*
N COUNT
= red herring

sidekick /saɪdkɪk/, **sidekicks**. If you say that someone is another person's **sidekick**, you mean that they work with that person who is more important than they are, so that they only help with the routine things that have to be done; an informal word. EG
N COUNT+SUPP : USU SING
⇑ assistant

When you were at the Home Office, I was your sidekick.

sidelight /saɪdlaɪt/, **sidelights**. The **sidelights** on a car are the small lights on the outside of each headlight.
N COUNT

sideline /saɪdlaɪn/, **sidelines**. 1 A **sideline** is something that you do in addition to your main job in order to earn some extra money. EG *He has several sidelines, none of which pay very much... Fishing is both a relaxing hobby and a money-producing sideline.*
N COUNT ↑ occupation

2 The **sidelines** are the lines around the edge of a playing field or sports pitch. During the game the players and ball should remain inside these lines.
N COUNT : USU PL

3 If you are waiting **on the sidelines**, you are waiting eagerly to take an active part in something. EG *There is at least one group of sure winners waiting on the sidelines.*
PHR : USED AS AN A = in the wings

4 If you are standing **on the sidelines**, you are in a situation in which you are not personally involved and have no power to influence events directly. EG *I prefer to stand on the sidelines and watch. I really find it much safer... Solidarity leaders kept to the political sidelines.*
PHR : USED AS AN A

sidelong /saɪdlɒŋ/. If you look at someone or something **sidelong** or if you give them **sidelong** looks, you look at them out of the corner of your eyes, usually because they are to one side rather than directly in front of you. You sometimes use **sidelong** to describe a look that involves a feeling of secrecy, which is caused perhaps by shyness or dishonesty. EG *Terry and I exchanged sidelong glances... Ralph looked at him sidelong and said nothing.*
ADV WITH VB, OR ADJ CLASSIF : ATTRIB ↑ indirect = sideways

side-saddle. When you ride a horse **side-saddle**, you sit on a special saddle with both your legs on one side rather than one leg on either side of the horse. EG *The Queen rode out side-saddle in uniform.*
ADV WITH VB, OR ADJ CLASSIF : ATTRIB ↑ sideways

sideshow /saɪdʃəʊ/, **sideshows**. **Sideshows** are the stalls at a fairground or circus where you can do things such as shooting at moving targets and throwing darts, or where people perform short plays, puppet shows, etc.
N COUNT

side-splitting. Something that is **side-splitting** is very funny and makes you laugh so much that you ache all over; an informal word.
ADJ QUALIT = hilarious

sidestep /saɪdstɛp/, **sidesteps, sidestepping, sidestepped**. 1 If you **sidestep** a problem or a question, you manage to avoid discussing or solving it. EG *...a book that does not sidestep essential questions... In the end, the question was side-stepped.*
V OR V+O = evade

◇ **sidestepping**. EG *The decision was reversed after some adept ministerial side-stepping.*
◇ N UNCOUNT = evasion

2 If you **sidestep**, you step sideways in order to avoid something or someone that is coming towards you or going to hit you. EG *It is hard to side-step a tackle.*
V OR V+O = dodge

sideswipe /saɪdswaɪp/, **sideswipes**. If you take a **sideswipe** at something, you make an unexpected attack on it while you are discussing something else.
N COUNT

sidetrack /saɪdtræk/, **sidetracks, sidetracking, sidetracked**. If someone or something **sidetracks** you, they cause you to forget what you are supposed to be doing or thinking, usually by introducing a new topic of conversation. EG *I told him how I'd been sidetracked by Mr Starke.*
V+O = distract, divert

sidewalk /saɪdwɔːk/, **sidewalks**. A **sidewalk** is a path with a hard surface at the edge of a street in a town; used in American English. EG *He avoided stepping on a crack in the sidewalk... ...a sidewalk cafe.*
N COUNT = pavement

sideways /saɪdweɪz/. 1 **Sideways** means from or to the side of something or someone. EG *Flames blew out sideways from the fire... He rubbed his chin thoughtfully, and shot me a sideways glance.*
ADV WITH VB, OR ADJ CLASSIF : ATTRIB

2 **Sideways** is used to describe something or someone that is lying, standing, or moving with one side (rather than the front, back, top, or bottom) facing forwards or upwards. EG *She sat leaning sideways a little... The picture showed her car slightly sideways on.*
ADV WITH VB, OR ADJ CLASSIF : ATTRIB

3 If something **knocks** you **sideways**, it makes you feel amazed, stunned, or very upset; an informal expression. EG *Her news just knocked me sideways.*
PHR : VB INFLECTS = floor

4 If you say that something such as your career is developing **sideways**, you mean that it is developing in such a way that you are making no progress but simply staying at the same level. EG *You may find that in your career you have to move sideways for a start, rather than upwards.*
ADV WITH VB, OR ADJ CLASSIF : ATTRIB

siding /saɪdɪŋ/, **sidings**. A **siding** is a short railway track, off the main track, where trains stand when they are not being used.
N COUNT

sidle /saɪdəl/, **sidles, sidling, sidled**. If you **sidle** somewhere, you walk there uncertainly or cautiously, as if you do not want anyone to notice you. EG *She stammered some apology as she sidled towards the door... A man sidled up to me and asked if I wanted a ticket for the match.*
V+A = edge, slink

siege /siːdʒ/, **sieges**. 1 A **siege** is 1.1 a military operation in which an army tries to capture a town or other place by surrounding it and preventing food or help from reaching the people inside. EG *This famous castle withstood a siege by Prince John of France... ...the siege of Mafeking... The town was under siege for six months.*
N COUNT/UNCOUNT ↑ attack

1.2 any situation in which a place is surrounded for a long period of time, for example by police, in order to force the people inside to come out. EG *The terrorists gave themselves up after a 48-hour siege.*
N COUNT/UNCOUNT ↑ attack

2 If soldiers **lay siege** to a place, they surround it in order to force the people inside to surrender. ▸ used also to describe what people other than soldiers do in order to see or question someone as they come out of a place where they are living or hiding. EG *Dozens of journalists laid siege to his flat.*
PHR : VB INFLECTS, IF + PREP THEN *to* = besiege

siesta /siˈɛstə/, **siestas**. A **siesta** is a short sleep or rest which you have in the early afternoon, usually because the weather is too hot to work in at that time of day. EG *Most people here take a siesta after lunch.*
N COUNT/UNCOUNT = nap

sieve /sɪv/, **sieves, sieving, sieved**. 1 A **sieve** is a tool used for separating liquids from solids or larger pieces from smaller pieces. It consists of a ring with a round plastic or wire net attached underneath, through which liquids and smaller pieces pass, leaving the solids or larger pieces in the net.
N COUNT ↑ utensil

2 When you **sieve** a liquid or powdery substance, you put it through a sieve. EG *Sieve the flour into a basin to remove all the lumps.*
V+O = sift

3 If you say that someone has **a memory like a sieve**, you mean that they forget things very easily.
PHR : USED AS O

sift /sɪft/, **sifts, sifting, sifted**. 1 If you **sift** a loose or powdery substance such as flour or sand, you put it through a sieve in order to remove large pieces or lumps. EG *Always sift icing sugar through a fine sieve.*
V+O

2 If you **sift** something such as evidence or if you **sift** through it, you examine it carefully and thoroughly, especially in order to separate what is important or useful from what is not. EG *He was accustomed to sifting evidence and assessing the difference between fact and fiction... There are archives and documents to be sifted through.*
V+O, OR V+A *(through)* ↑ sort

sigh /saɪ/, **sighs, sighing, sighed**. 1 When you **sigh**, you let out a deep breath that is loud enough to be heard, as a way of expressing certain feelings, such as disappointment, tiredness, relief, or pleasure. EG *She put down the phone, sighed, and shook her head sadly... Sighing with relief, she put the money back in her pocket... He sighed a deep sigh.*
V OR V+O *(sigh)* ↑ exhale

2 A **sigh** is the sound that someone makes when they sigh, or the action of sighing. EG *With a sigh, he rose and walked slowly away... They had breathed a great sigh of relief at the ending of the war... The news was greeted with deep sighs.*
N COUNT ↑ exhalation

● If you **heave a sigh**, you sigh.
● PHR : VB INFLECTS

3 When something such as the wind or a tree **sighs**, it makes a noise that sounds like someone sighing. EG *The trees of the forest sighed in the wind.*
V = whisper

sight /saɪt/, **sights, sighting, sighted**. 1 **Sight** is the ability to see. EG *For the ape, sight was the most important sense... Her sight is failing... ...loss of sight.*
N UNCOUNT ↑ faculty = vision

2 The **sight** of something is the act of seeing it or an occasion of seeing it. EG *I had my first sight of home for two years... He was reduced to tears at the sight of the hundreds of dead bodies.*
N SING WITH DET : IF + PREP THEN *of* = view

3 **Sight**, especially in the expressions **in sight** and **out of sight**, means the distance or area within which it is possible to see someone or something. EG *As soon as the car was out of sight, we relaxed... She waited until the departing figures had vanished from sight... At last a bus came into sight.*
N UNCOUNT : PREP + N ↑ range = view

4 A **sight** is something that is seen. EG *This was the*
N COUNT + SUPP

most encouraging sight I'd seen all day... Few sights have become more familiar in recent times... It was an awe-inspiring sight.

5 If you say that someone is a **sight** or looks a **sight**, you mean that you think they look untidy or ridiculous. EG *What a sight you are!... His clothes looked a sight.* N SING: a+N, USED AS C = fright

6 The **sights** are the places, especially in a city, that are interesting to see, and so are often visited by tourists. EG *You can get a guide to take you round the sights... ...the sights of London.* N PLURAL

7 The **sight** or the **sights** of a gun or other weapon is that part of it which helps the person who is using it to aim more accurately. EG *You can hit the target easily from a hundred and thirty metres using a telescopic sight... ...adjusting the sights and firing some practice shots.* N COUNT: ALSO SING=PL ⇑ device

8 If you say that something is **a sight** better, **a sight** worse, etc, you mean that it is very much better, very much worse, etc; a very informal use. EG *It's a damn sight better than most of the places we've stayed in... You'll get there a sight quicker if you take the train.* PHR+COMPAR = far, miles

9 If you **sight** someone or something, you see them, often briefly or suddenly. EG *The missing woman has been sighted in the Birmingham area... At last they sight a zebra and the hunt begins.* V+O = spot

10 The word **sight** is also used in the following expressions. **10.1** If you say that something or someone seems to have certain characteristics **at first sight**, you mean that when you first see or consider them that is how they appear, although they may not actually be like that when you know more about them. EG *The problem is not as simple as it might seem at first sight... She's actually very nice but at first sight seems terribly bossy.* PHR: USED AS AN A = initially **10.2** If someone or something is **in sight** or **within sight**, they can be seen. EG *There wasn't a policeman in sight.* PHR: USED AS AN A **10.3** If something such as a result or a decision is **in sight** or **within sight**, it is likely to happen or to be reached within a short time. EG *It seemed that an end to his agony was in sight... The minister said that single figure inflation was now within sight.* PHR: USED AS AN A = approaching **10.4** If someone is ordered to do something **on sight**, they have to do it without delay, as soon as a person or thing is seen. EG *They were told to shoot on sight.* PHR: USED AS AN A **10.5** If you **catch sight of** someone, you see them, either suddenly or just for a moment or two. EG *I caught sight of an old friend of mine in the middle of the crowd.* PHR: VB INFLECTS = spot **10.6** If you **lose sight of** something, you get into a situation where you no longer pay attention to the things that are important and start worrying about things that do not really matter. EG *We mustn't get so bogged down by detail that we lose sight of our main objectives... Unfortunately this may gradually be lost sight of.* PHR: VB INFLECTS = forget **10.7** If you **know** someone **by sight**, you recognize them when you see them, although you have never actually been introduced to them. PHR: VB INFLECTS **10.8** If you **set** your **sights on** something, you decide that you want it and try very hard to get it. EG *We have set our sights on a bigger house... They may have to set their sights on something less ambitious.* PHR: VB INFLECTS ⇑ desire **10.9** If you agree to buy something **sight unseen**, you agree to buy it, even though you have not seen it and do not know what condition it is in. EG *I bought the manuscript sight unseen.* PHR: USED AS AN A

sighted /sa̲ɪtɪ²d/. People who are **sighted** are able to see; used especially when you are contrasting them with people who are blind. EG *This is more of a problem for blind people than for those who are sighted.* ● See also **clear-sighted, far-sighted, long-sighted, short-sighted.** ADJ CLASSIF ≠ sightless

sighting /sa̲ɪtɪŋ/, **sightings**. A **sighting** is an occasion on which something is seen, especially something unusual or unexpected. EG *There had been four reports of shark sightings... This was the first sighting of a bird of this type outside Australia.* N COUNT: USU+SUPP ⇑ discovery

sightless /sa̲ɪtlɪ²s/. Someone who is **sightless** is blind and therefore unable to see. ADJ CLASSIF ≠ sighted

sight-read, sight-reads, sight-reading. Someone who can **sight-read** can play or sing music from a printed sheet the first time they see it, without practising it beforehand. V OR V+O ⇑ read

sightseeing /sa̲ɪtsiːɪŋ/. If you go **sightseeing** or do some **sightseeing**, you travel around, usually in a city, in order to see the interesting places that tourists usually visit. EG *...a two-week tour, allowing some time in all the major cities for sightseeing.* N UNCOUNT

sightseer /sa̲ɪtsiːə/, **sightseers**. A **sightseer** is someone who is travelling around, usually in a city, in order to visit places of interest. EG *The Changing of the Guard is normally watched by a large crowd of sightseers.* N COUNT = tourist

sign /sa̲ɪn/, **signs, signing, signed**. **1** A **sign** is **1.1** a mark or shape that always has a particular meaning, for example in mathematics or music. EG *...a minus sign... Look at the figures on either side of the equals sign.* N COUNT ⇑ symbol **1.2** a movement of your arms, hands, or head which is intended to have a particular meaning. EG *Through signs she communicated that she wanted the women to bring their children to the hospital... At the end of his speech the workers would applaud and give the thumbs-up sign of approval.* N COUNT = gesture

2 When Christians **make the sign of the cross**, they make the shape of a cross over the top half of their body by moving their hand. EG *Angelica had made the sign of the cross and was already sitting down in the pew.* PHR: VB INFLECTS = cross yourself

3 A **sign** is also a piece of wood, metal, or other firm material with words or pictures on it. Signs tell you where or what a particular place is, or give you a warning, an instruction, or some other information. EG *The exit sign is marked with an arrow... A sign saying 'Women's Centre' hung over the door... Every so often along the road a sign proclaimed the name of another village.* N COUNT ⇑ notice

4 If there is a **sign** of something, **4.1** a characteristic feature of it is present, which makes you realize that it is actually happening. EG *How pleasant to see a sign or two of summer once again... Wood dust beneath a piece of furniture is a sure sign of woodworm... I catch myself thinking like this more often these days–a sign of age, no doubt.* N COUNT+*of* ⇑ indication **4.2** you can actually see something which makes it clear that the particular thing is present or is felt by someone. EG *She's supposed to have a terrible temper but I never saw a sign of it myself... Poirot greeted her with every sign of pleasure... The Englishman showed no signs of his annoyance.* N COUNT+*of* ⇑ manifestation **4.3** there is something which makes you think that the particular thing is developing or is going to happen. EG *His sores had begun to show signs of healing... There is no sign that the economy is on the upturn... All the signs are that this increase will continue.* N COUNT+SUPP = indication

5 If you say that something is **a sign of the times**, you mean that it is typical of the way people behave nowadays; used especially when you want to indicate that you disapprove of something. EG *Kids nowadays are lazy: it's a sign of the times.* PHR: USU USED AS C

6 If you say that there is **no sign of** someone, you mean that they have not yet arrived, although you are expecting them to come. EG *There's no sign of her yet.* PHR+NG: USED AS C/O

7 The **signs** of the zodiac are the twelve areas into which the heavens are divided in astrology, each of which has a special symbol. EG *'I'm a Capricorn,' said Melissa, 'what's your sign?'* N COUNT ⇑ division

8 If you **sign** something or **sign** your name on something, you write your name on it, usually either at the end or in a special space. You do this to show, for example, that you have written the document, that you agree with what is written, or that you have been present on a particular occasion. EG *I was in the act of signing a travellers' cheque... Sign your name in the book each time you use the photocopier... There are four letters here for you to sign... He presented her with a signed copy of his latest novel.* V OR V+O

9 If you say that something is **signed and sealed**, you mean that it is absolutely definite because everyone involved has signed all the legal documents. EG *As soon as everything's signed and sealed we can start thinking about the actual removal.* PHR: USED AS C = finalized

sign away. If you **sign** something **away**, you sign official documents that mean that you no longer own it or have any right to it. EG *Chiefs were encouraged to sign away land that appeared to be unoccupied... She felt she was being asked to sign away her independence.* PHRASAL VB: V+O+ADV ⇑ relinquish

sign for. If you **sign for** something, **1** you sign an official form or book as proof that you have received it. EG *When signing for any parcel, always add 'not inspected'.* PHRASAL VB: V+PREP, HAS PASS ⇑ accept **2** you sign a form, list, or contract, by which you agree to do something. EG *It was in the same week that he signed for his second film.* PHRASAL VB: V+PREP, HAS PASS

sign in. **1** If you **sign in**, you sign your name in a PHRASAL VB: V+

book or on a special form when you arrive at a hotel or club. EG *They signed in at the reception desk.* ADV ⇑ register

2 If you **sign** someone **in** at a club, institution, etc of which you are a member, you sign your name in a special book in order to allow them to be there as your visitor since they are not a member. EG *Just get someone who's on the staff to sign you in.* PHRASAL VB: V+O+ADV ⇑ admit

sign off. If you **sign off**, you write a final message and your name at the end of a letter. EG *It's just about tea time so I'll sign off now–with love from us both, Wendy.* PHRASAL VB: V+ADV = finish, close

sign on. If you **sign on**, 1 you sign a contract, form, or other document which states that you will work for a particular organization, study on a particular course, etc. EG *He signed on the next morning with the RAF... You could sign on for a full-time course in word processing.* PHRASAL VB: V+ADV, OR V+O+ADV ⇑ register = sign up 2 you go to your local social security office and confirm that you are unemployed, so that you can get state benefit, especially unemployment benefit. EG *You have to sign on every fortnight while you are getting supplementary benefit.* PHRASAL VB: V+ADV ⇑ register

sign out. If you **sign out**, 1 you sign your name in a book or on a special form when you leave a hotel, club, office etc, to show officially that you have left. EG *Upon signing out, I left my baggage at the station and went off to Tim's.* PHRASAL VB: V+ADV 2 you sign your name in a book or on a card, to say that you have borrowed a book, journal, or magazine from a library. EG *You can keep them as long as you want, as long as you've signed them out.* PHRASAL VB: V+O+ADV ⇑ register

sign over. If you **sign** something **over**, you sign documents that give someone else property, possessions, or rights that were previously yours. EG *One way of avoiding death duties might be to sign the house over to your son now.* PHRASAL VB: V+O+ADV = make over

sign up. 1 If you **sign up**, you sign forms or documents saying that you will do a particular job or study on a particular course. EG *He signed up as a painter on the Federal Art Project... What made you decide to sign up for that art course?* PHRASAL VB: V+ADV ⇑ register = sign on

2 If you **sign** someone **up**, they sign a contract stating that they will work for you. EG *Southall police division has failed to sign up one Asian.* PHRASAL VB: V+O+ADV ⇑ recruit

signal /sɪgnəºl/, **signals, signalling, signalled**; also spelled **signaling** and **signaled** in American English. 1 A **signal** is a gesture, movement, sound, or action which is intended to give a particular message to the person who sees or hears it. EG *My signal will be three knocks, a pause, then two more knocks... He sat in the studio and waited for the signal to speak... Waving the newspaper would give the signal to Serge.* N COUNT ⇑ sign

2 If you **signal** something or if you **signal** to someone, you make a gesture, movement, sound, or action which is intended to give a particular message to the person who sees or hears it. EG *If you're going to stop you're supposed to signal... All of a sudden John passed me, his palm down, signalling a stop... Milk left in the breast is nature's method of signalling to the glands, 'make less'... Signal the driver to move off.* V, V+O/REPORT-CL, V+A *(to)*, OR V+O+A *(to)/to*-INF ⇑ indicate

3 If an event or action is a **signal** of something, it seems to suggest that this thing probably exists or is likely to happen. EG *This was the first signal that an attack was brewing... These initiatives were intended to send warning signals to Moscow.* ▸ used as a verb. EG *The decision to publish these articles seemed to signal a switch in the paper's editorial policy... Although it lacks delicacy, this method does signal considerable determination on her part.* N COUNT+SUPP ⇑ indication = sign ▸ V+O/REPORT-CL ⇑ indicate

4 A **signal** is also 4.1 a piece of equipment beside a railway track, which shows train drivers if it is safe for them to go on or if they should stop. EG *We were held up for ages at a signal just outside Waterloo.* N COUNT 4.2 a series of radio waves, light waves, electrical impulses, etc, which carry information of some kind. EG *Marconi finally succeeded in sending a signal across the Atlantic.* N COUNT ⇑ message

5 A **signal** triumph, failure, etc is one that is significant and considerable in degree. EG *The year has seen one signal triumph for the Labour Party–victory in the Darlington by-election.* ADJ CLASSIF: ATTRIB = notable ≠ minor ◊ **signally**. EG *Despite much advice I had failed signally to devise a satisfactory trap.* ◊ ADV WITH VB

signal box, signal boxes; also spelled with a hyphen. A **signal box** is a small building near a railway track, which contains all the switches and buttons used to control the signals on that section of the railway. EG *The signalman had already left the signal box when the collision occurred.* N COUNT

signalman /sɪgnəºlməˢn/, **signalmen**. A **signalman** is a person whose job is to control the signals on a particular section of a railway. N COUNT ⇑ worker

signatory /sɪgnətəºri¹/, **signatories**. A **signatory** is a person, organization, or country that has signed a contract or other official document as a way of showing that they agree to something. EG *As a signatory to the North Atlantic Treaty, France was also expected to send a peace-keeping force... The fifteen signatory states each sent a representative.* N COUNT: IF+PREP THEN *to/of* ⇑ party

signature /sɪgnə¹tʃə/, **signatures**. 1 Your **signature** is your name which you write in your own characteristic way, often at the end of a piece of writing as a way of officially identifying the writing as yours or of showing that you agree with what it says. EG *He underlined his signature with a little flourish... The vicar's signature was forged in thin ink... Petitions bearing nearly a half-million signatures were sent to the White House.* N COUNT ● If you **put** your **signature to** a piece of writing, you sign it as a way of officially showing that you agree with what is written. EG *Only put your signature to paper once you've been given the go-ahead by your accountant.* ● PHR: VB INFLECTS

2 A **signature** of a particular animal or person is a strong feature or characteristic that it has, which shows that it has been present somewhere or that it has been involved in something. EG *The male cat uses scent not only as a signature but as a means of offence... We all have our own pattern; it is our signature.* N COUNT ⇑ mark

signature tune, signature tunes. A **signature tune** is a tune which is always played at the beginning or end of a particular television or radio programme or which a band plays every time they perform. N COUNT

signboard /saɪnbɔːd/, **signboards**. A **signboard** is a piece of wood which has been painted with pictures or words and which gives some information about a particular building or place. EG *The railway authority has labelled the station signboard 'Shimla'.* N COUNT ⇑ sign

signet ring /sɪgnə¹t rɪŋ/, **signet rings**. A **signet ring** is a ring which has a flat oval or circular section at the front with a pattern, a drawing, or letters carved into it. EG *His signet ring bore the emblem of a dagger.* N COUNT

significance /sɪgnɪfɪkəns/. The **significance** of something is 1 its importance in terms of the effect that it has had or is likely to have on other things or people. EG *The meeting was of no significance... The repeal of this law was of vast historical significance to the whole of Europe... ...a fiery discussion about the significance of Marxism for the movement.* N UNCOUNT = consequence 2 a fundamental meaning or importance that it has, which is not necessarily obvious at first but which you are aware of if you think more carefully. EG *A year later I found out the true significance of the name... They failed to appreciate the significance of the precautions... This has deeper significance than one first realizes.* N UNCOUNT = implication

significant /sɪgnɪfɪkənt/. 1 Something that is **significant** 1.1 has an important effect on other things or people, usually because it is large in quantity or degree. EG *Exports reached 232m, making a significant contribution to the balance of payments... Lack of insulation can result in a significant amount of heat being lost... In ceasing to publish cigarette advertisements, Metropolitan made a small but significant gesture.* ADJ QUALIT = marked, appreciable ◊ **significantly**. EG *...wage increases which are significantly below those in Germany... Most varieties of hyacinths don't differ significantly from each other.* ◊ ADV = markedly, considerably 1.2 seems to have a fundamental meaning or importance, which is not necessarily obvious at first but which you are aware of if you think more carefully. EG *It is significant that this is the only door that is ever locked... In that respect, what is happening in sculpture is more significant than what is happening in painting.* ADJ QUALIT = noteworthy ◊ **significantly**. EG *...a book significantly called Now It Can Be Told... Significantly, we have not as yet a special term for this phenomenon.* ◊ ADV WITH VB, OR ADV SEN

2 A **significant** action or gesture is intended to have a special meaning that is not obvious but that should be understood by someone present. EG *With a last* ADJ QUALIT = meaningful

significant look at her husband, Mrs Hochstadt went to answer the door. ◇ **significantly**. EG *He cleared his throat significantly a few times.* ◇ ADV WITH VB = meaningfully

signify /sɪgnɪfaɪ/, **signifies, signifying, signified.** 1 A sign, symbol, or gesture that **signifies** something has a particular meaning mentioned. EG *A P in a circle signifies a multi-storey car park... ...the orange robes that signify a follower of Hare Krishna.* V+O/REPORT-CL ⇑ denote = indicate

2 If you **signify** something, you make a sign or gesture in order to convey a particular meaning. EG *She was in complete disagreement, and signified this fact immediately... I sighed and closed the file as if to signify that this chapter of my life had ended.* V+O/REPORT-CL ⇑ show = indicate

sign language, sign languages. Sign language is a method of communicating by using movements of your hands and arms. There are several formal systems of sign language, used for example by deaf people, as well as informal methods that you might invent when you talk to a foreigner. EG *He told the Bomvanas by sign language that he had fallen from an aircraft... ...the Deaf-and-Dumb sign language of hand signals.* N UNCOUNT/COUNT

signpost /saɪnpəʊst/, **signposts, signposting, signposted.** 1 A **signpost** is 1.1 a sign with information written on it, such as the name of a town, which is fixed to a pole at a road junction, often so that it points along the road that leads to the town written on it. EG *Out in the country again we drove past a signpost I couldn't read... ...a signpost marked 'Fairford 8 miles'.* N COUNT **1.2** something which helps you to know how a situation or a course of action will develop, or which may help you to decide what to do next in a particular situation. EG *I have tried to provide some signposts which will set you on your way... ...signposts to the future.* N COUNT : USU+SUPP ⇑ indication

2 If you **signpost** the way or the path for someone, you give an indication of how a situation or a course of action is likely to develop, or of what would be the best thing to do next in a particular situation; a fairly literary use. EG *We hope this book will have signposted a way into starting your public life... He appointed himself a political sage, signposting the path for future generations.* V+O ⇑ show

signposted /saɪnpəʊstɪ²d/. A road or route that is **signposted** has signposts beside the road to show you the way. EG *It is well signposted so you shouldn't get lost.* ADJ QUALIT : PRED ⇑ indicated = signed

Sikh /siːk/, **Sikhs.** 1 A **Sikh** is a person who believes in the Indian religion of Sikhism and follows its teachings. EG *...the Golden Temple in Amritsar, the holy town of the Sikhs.* N COUNT

2 Something that is **Sikh** belongs or relates to the Sikhs or to their religious beliefs and customs. EG *...a Sikh province.* ADJ CLASSIF

Sikhism /siːkɪzm/ is an Indian religion which separated from Hinduism in the sixteenth century and which teaches that there is only one God. N UNCOUNT

silage /saɪlɪdʒ/ is a crop that is harvested when it is green, and partially fermented in order to make fodder for animals. EG *This grassland is best cut for silage and fed to animals kept indoors in the winter.* N UNCOUNT

silence /saɪləns/, **silences, silencing, silenced.** 1 If there is **silence**, it is quiet because nobody is speaking. EG *He sat down in the usual chair and the usual silence fell between them... We walked on in silence... 'Silence!' A hush fell on the crowd... There was a shocked silence... ...the long silences between words.* N UNCOUNT/COUNT ≠ noise

2 The **silence** of a place is the complete quiet that exists when there is no sound at all. EG *...walking into the heavy silence of a shuttered room... He had to escape from his noisy surroundings into the silence of the high mountains... A sudden shot broke the silence.* N UNCOUNT ≠ noise

3 Someone's **silence** about a particular subject is the absence of any communication of information from them about it, for example in order to keep it secret. EG *We review her new book, published after a ten year silence from this author... Levy's silence on the subject was unnerving... My silence costs a thousand pounds.* N UNCOUNT+SUPP

4 If you **silence** someone or something, you stop them speaking or making a noise. EG *All the bells of England were silenced... Rodin silenced him with a gesture.* V+O

5 If someone **silences** you, they stop you expressing opinions that they do not agree with. EG *Butler's firm speech failed to silence opposition.* V+O

silencer /saɪlənsə/, **silencers.** A **silencer** is 1 a special metal box or tube that is attached to a petrol engine to make it quieter; used in British English. N COUNT = muffler **2** a device that is attached to a gun to make it very quiet when it is fired. N COUNT

silent /saɪlənt/. 1 Someone who is **silent** 1.1 is not speaking. EG *The woman was silent for a moment, letting the words register in her mind.* ◇ **silently**. EG *We finished breakfast silently.* ADJ CLASSIF; ◇ ADV WITH VB **1.2** does not talk to people very much and may therefore give an impression of being unfriendly. EG *He seems to be a rather silent and stand-offish person... She was a silent girl, cool and aloof.* ADJ QUALIT ⇑ quiet = taciturn **1.3** does not provide any statement or information about a particular subject. EG *He has remained absolutely silent on his plans for using the money... The law is silent on this point.* ADJ CLASSIF : PRED

2 A **silent** emotion or action is one that exists or happens but is not expressed in words to other people. EG *...a stern-faced warrior dwelling with silent emotion upon his dear one... ...a silent prayer.* ◇ **silently**. EG *We were all silently nervous.* ADJ CLASSIF : ATTRIB ⇑ quiet; ◇ ADV

3 Something that is **silent** makes no sound at all. EG *The guns have fallen silent... The organ breathed a last note and fell silent.* ◇ **silently**. EG *It appeared suddenly and silently out of the dusk.* ADJ CLASSIF ⇑ quiet; ◇ ADV WITH VB

4 A **silent** film has no sound or speech; used of films that were made a long time ago. EG *In 1924 I did my first silent film... ...the silent screen.* ADJ CLASSIF : ATTRIB ≠ talking

5 A **silent** letter in a word is one that is written but not pronounced. EG *The 'k' is silent in the word 'knock'.* ADJ CLASSIF

silhouette /sɪluːɛt/, **silhouettes.** 1 A **silhouette** is the outline of a dark shape with a bright light or pale background behind it. EG *...the silhouettes of rooftops and chimneys against a February sky... The figure turned towards the sunrise, a tiny silhouette with uplifted arms.* N COUNT = contour, profile ● If you see something **in silhouette**, you see it as a dark shape with no detail except for the outline. EG *A low building could just be made out in silhouette.* ● PHR : USED AS AN A = in outline

2 The **silhouette** of something is the outline that it has, which often helps you to recognize it. EG *The silhouette of bats is quite unlike that of birds... ...the new tank with a low silhouette and special armour.* N COUNT ⇑ shape

silhouetted /sɪluːɛtɪ²d/. If something is **silhouetted** against a background, it can be seen in silhouette. EG *There was a line of bare trees silhouetted against the horizon... ...hills silhouetted against a pale blue sky.* ADJ CLASSIF : PRED, USU+*against* ⇑ be visible

silica /sɪlɪkə/ is a substance which is found in sand, quartz, and flint, and which is used to make glass. It contains silicon. EG *...crystals of silica.* N UNCOUNT = silicon dioxide

silicon /sɪlɪkən/ is an element that is used to make parts of computers and other electronic equipment. It is also used to make glass and is found in sand and minerals such as quartz and granite. EG *...minicomputers mounted on tiny silicon chips... A computer book is merely a slice of silicon holding information in machine code.* N UNCOUNT

silicone /sɪlɪkəʊn/ is a tough artificial substance made from silicon, which is used to make several things such as paints and protective sprays. EG *...the silicone spray used on furniture.* N UNCOUNT

silk /sɪlk/, **silks.** 1 **Silk** is a substance that is produced by silkworms and made into smooth, fine cloth and sewing thread of high quality. ▸ also used of the cloth and sewing thread that is made from this substance. EG *...a white silk scarf... ...making something fragile in threads and silks... ...embroidery silks.* N UNCOUNT ⇑ fibre; ▸ N MASS

2 **Silks** are clothes made from silk. EG *...the wearing or selling of silks and cottons from India.* N PLURAL ⇑ garments

3 **Silk** is also 3.1 a substance similar to silk that is produced by some insects and small creatures. EG *The spider catches an insect and carefully parcels it up in silk.* N UNCOUNT **3.2** long brown threads that grow on the end of sweetcorn or maize. N UNCOUNT

silken /sɪlkə⁰n/. 1 **Silken** is used to describe something that is smooth and soft in a luxurious way; used showing approval. EG *...his large deep black eyes amid their silken lashes.* ADJ CLASSIF : USU ATTRIB

2 **Silken** material is made of silk. EG *...silken ribbon.* ADJ CLASSIF

silk-screen. Silk-screen printing is a method of printing patterns on to cloth by forcing paint or dyes through silk or similar material. EG *...silk-screen posters.* ADJ CLASSIF : ATTRIB

silkworm /sɪlkwɜːm/, **silkworms**. A **silkworm** is a type of caterpillar that produces silk. N COUNT

silky /sɪlki¹/, **silkier, silkiest**. Something that is **silky** is soft, smooth, and shiny, like silk; used showing approval. EG *Her hair was very long and silky... ...fine silky skin.* ◊ **silkiness**. EG *She nuzzled into the thick silkiness of his hair.* ADJ QUALIT; ◊ N UNCOUNT

sill /sɪl/, **sills**. A **sill** is 1 a ledge at the bottom of a window, either inside or outside a building. EG *She sat with one elbow resting on the sill of the open window.* 2 a ledge on a car body, extending under the doors from the front of the car to the back. EG *The saloon door sill is three inches wide.* N COUNT = window-sill; N COUNT ⇑ frame

silly /sɪli¹/, **sillier, silliest**. 1 If you say that someone is **silly**, you mean that they are behaving in a foolish or childish way. EG *You're a silly little boy... The enemy commanders were even sillier than ours... You silly fool! I've lost the hooks now.* ▸ used of people's behaviour and actions. EG *I'm sorry. It was a silly thing to say... It was silly to worry... This may sound like a silly question, but how do the women conceive?* ◊ **silliness**. EG *No amount of dialogue improvement could hide the basic silliness of the story.* ADJ QUALIT ⇑ stupid; ▸ = ridiculous; ◊ N UNCOUNT ⇑ stupidity

2 If you **drink** yourself **silly** or if you **laugh** yourself **silly**, you drink or laugh so much that you become unable to think or behave sensibly; used in informal English. PHR : VB INFLECTS

silo /saɪləʊ/, **silos**. A **silo** is 1 a tall round metal tower on a farm, in which silage is stored. 2 a specially built place underground where a nuclear missile is kept ready to be launched. N COUNT; N COUNT

silt /sɪlt/, **silts, silting, silted**. **Silt** is fine sand, soil, or mud which is carried along by a river. EG *The main problem is keeping the harbours free of silt.* N UNCOUNT ⇑ deposit

silt up. If a river, lake, etc **silts up** or **is silted up**, it becomes blocked with silt. EG *The lake silted up... The channels have been silted up.* PHRASAL VB : V-ERG+ADV

silting /sɪltɪŋ/ is the process by which a river, lake, etc becomes gradually blocked with silt. EG *...the ever-present problem of silting.* N UNCOUNT

silver /sɪlvə/, **silvers**. 1 **Silver** is a valuable greyish-white metal that is used for making jewellery and ornaments. EG *...a little box made of solid silver.* ▸ used as an adjective. EG *...beautiful silver coffee pots.* N UNCOUNT; ▸ ADJ CLASSIF : ATTRIB

2 **Silver** is also coins that are made from silver or that look like silver. EG *Can you give me a pound in silver and the rest in notes please?* N UNCOUNT ⇑ money

3 In a house, **silver** or **the silver** is the things there that are made from silver, especially the cutlery and dishes. EG *The silver and the glasses sparkled in the candlelight... ...Ellen's wedding silver... Never let bleach get near silver.* N UNCOUNT = silverware

4 You describe something as **silver** when 4.1 it looks as if it is made from silver. EG *...sparkling silver paint... ...a cap with two silver bars and the officer's braid.* 4.2 it is greyish-white in colour. EG *He was a tall old man with long silver hair... ...a big silver motor car.* ▸ used as a noun. EG *...the subtle greys and silvers of the rococo interior.* ADJ CLASSIF ⇑ shiny; ADJ COLOUR; ▸ N UNCOUNT/COUNT

5 If you say that someone **was born with a silver spoon in** their **mouth**, you mean that their family was rich and aristocratic. PHR : be/mouth INFLECT

silver birch, silver birches. **Silver birch** can also be used as the plural form. A **silver birch** is a tree with a silvery-white trunk and branches. N COUNT

silvered /sɪlvəd/. You describe something as **silvered** when it has become silver in colour; a literary word. EG *...his silvered beard... ...the moonlit silvered country.* ADJ COLOUR

silverfish /sɪlvəfɪʃ/. **Silverfish** is both the singular and the plural form. A **silverfish** is a small silvery-coloured insect without wings, which you find in houses. N COUNT

silver jubilee, silver jubilees. A **silver jubilee** is the 25th anniversary of an important event. EG *It's the College's Silver Jubilee year... ...the Queen's Silver Jubilee.* N COUNT

silver lining. A **silver lining** is a reason for thinking that a bad situation will not continue. EG *There's usually a silver lining if you look hard enough.* N SING WITH DET

silver medal, silver medals. A **silver medal** is a small, circular piece of silver that is given to the person who wins the second place in a competition, especially a sporting competition. N COUNT ⇑ prize

silver paper is thin paper covered with silver-coloured foil. It is used for wrapping things. EG *...a piece of silver paper.* N UNCOUNT

silver-plated. **Silver-plated** objects are metal objects coated with silver. EG *...a silver-plated sauceboat... ...silver-plated forks.* ADJ CLASSIF

silversmith /sɪlvəsmɪθ/, **silversmiths**. A **silversmith** is a person who makes things out of silver. N COUNT ⇑ craftsman

silverware /sɪlvəweə/ is knives, forks, dishes, and other things for the table that are made from silver or from a metal that looks like silver. N UNCOUNT

silver wedding, silver weddings. A married couple's **silver wedding** is the 25th anniversary of their wedding. N COUNT

silvery /sɪlvəᵒri¹/. Something that is **silvery** 1 looks like silver. EG *...a silvery dress... His hair is silvery now.* 2 has a pleasant, light, tinkling sound; used showing approval. EG *...a silvery voice... ...the silvery chime of the old clock.* ADJ COLOUR ⇑ white; ADJ QUALIT

simian /sɪmɪən/ is used to describe 1 someone who looks like a monkey or ape. EG *The man in the lift was a small simian creature... ...an ugly, simian face.* 2 things relating to monkeys or apes; a formal or technical use. ADJ QUALIT; ADJ CLASSIF ⇑ animal

similar /sɪmɪlə/. 1 If something is **similar** to something else or if two or more things are **similar**, the things are almost alike, or they have features that are the same. EG *My problems are very similar to yours... Some shares have gone up 50%, some down a similar amount... Burmese and Siamese cats are very similar in appearance and size... The four restaurants were all serving similar food at similar prices.* ADJ QUALIT : IF+PREP THEN *to* ⇑ like ≠ different

2 **Similar** triangles are different in size but have exactly the same shape; a technical term in geometry. ADJ CLASSIF ⇑ alike

similarity /sɪmɪlærɪti¹/, **similarities**. 1 If there is a **similarity** between two or more things, they are similar to each other. EG *There were points of similarity between them... Liverpool has a certain similarity to Marseilles... Any similarity with your routine is purely coincidental.* N UNCOUNT : USU +*between/in/of/with* ⇑ resemblance

2 **Similarities** are features that things have which make them similar to each other. EG *We are going to explore some of the similarities and differences between British and American English... Many species have close similarities with one another... These compounds have structural similarities to penicillin.* N COUNT : IF+PREP THEN *between/of/with* ⇑ resemblance

similarly /sɪmɪləli¹/. 1 You use **similarly** to say that an action or event is similar to one that you have just mentioned, or that something has a similar feature to one that you have just described. EG *This wasn't an isolated occurrence–other members of our group were similarly threatened... We sipped our Martinis under a red and white striped umbrella on the lawn. Other guests sat under similarly striped umbrellas.* ADV ≠ differently

2 You also use **similarly** to say that there is a correspondence or similarity between the way two things happen, are done, or should be done. EG *You should notify any change of address to the Bonds and Stock Office. Similarly, savings certificates should be re-registered with the Post Office.* ADV SEN = likewise

simile /sɪmɪli¹/, **similes**. A **simile** is an expression which describes a person or thing as being similar to someone or something else. For example, the sentences 'She runs like a deer' and 'He's as white as a sheet' contain similes. Similes usually start with 'like' or 'as'. N COUNT ⇑ comparison

simmer /sɪmə/, **simmers, simmering, simmered**. 1 When you **simmer** food or when it **simmers**, you cook it by keeping it at boiling point or just below boiling point. EG *Simmer the beans for four hours until tender.* V-ERG

2 When violence or a quarrel **simmers**, during a period of time it seems likely to happen, but it doesn't actually happen. EG *Violence simmered in various centres... ...a simmering quarrel... The potential for chaos lies simmering beneath the surface.* V

3 If you **simmer**, you are very hot because the weather is hot; an informal use. EG *...seats where pensioners simmer on warm days... The city of London simmered.* V = roast

simmer down. If you **simmer down**, you stop being angry about something; an informal expression. EG *I thought the trip might give me time to simmer down... Simmer down!* PHRASAL VB : V+ADV = calm down

simper /sɪmpə/, **simpers, simpering, simpered**. When someone **simpers**, they smile in a rather silly way. EG *The maid lowered her chin and simpered.* ▸ used as a noun. EG *'Thank you, doctor,' said the nurse with a simper.* ◊ **simpering**. EG *...two portraits of simpering girls.*
V = smirk
▸ N COUNT
◊ ADJ CLASSIF : ATTRIB

simple /sɪmpəºl/, **simpler, simplest**. **1** If something is **simple**, **1.1** it is not complicated, and is therefore easy to understand. EG *The point I am making is a very simple one... It's useful to have a simple guide for money matters... What we have been describing is a very simple mechanical calculator... He had gone into trading for the simple reason that he could find no other work.* **1.2** it consists only of things that are necessary without any extra features. EG *...a tall woman in a simple brown dress... ...simple but effective lighting.*
ADJ QUALIT = straightforward ≠ complicated
ADJ QUALIT ≠ elaborate

2 If a problem is **simple** or if its solution is **simple**, the problem can be solved easily. EG *At lower levels the problem was simple... The solution is very simple.*
ADJ QUALIT = easy ≠ complicated

3 A **simple** task is easy to do. EG *It's a simple operation, you can do it in a lunch hour... Electromechanical devices are relatively simple to design.*
ADJ QUALIT ≠ difficult

4 A **simple** way of doing something is an easy way of doing it. EG *Deep freezing is the simplest natural way of preserving food... Wouldn't it be simpler to chop the tree down?*
ADJ QUALIT ≠ difficult

5 Simple people have an uncomplicated way of life, especially in a country district; used showing approval. EG *I want to live here among these simple people... They are only simple farmers.* ▸ used of people's way of life. EG *Nature, the simple life, that's what I need desperately.*
ADJ QUALIT = unsophisticated

6 A **simple** person behaves in an honest and straightforward way; used showing approval. EG *Ellen found him delightful: strong, simple, and sincere.* ▸ used of people's behaviour. EG *How simple and good her gesture seemed in the clear light of day.*
ADJ QUALIT = genuine
▸ = innocent

7 A person who is **simple** is mentally retarded. EG *Noreen despised Joyce's mother and said she was simple.*
ADJ QUALIT = backward

8 You use **simple** to emphasize that one particular thing is responsible for something happening. EG *Simple fear of death is often what turns people to religion... Was it a simple difference in national characteristics?*
ADJ CLASSIF : ATTRIB = plain

9 If you say that something is a particular thing **pure and simple**, you mean that it is that thing and nothing else. EG *Family allowance is a matter of investment, pure and simple.*
PHR AFTER N

10 See also **simplicity, simply**.

simple interest is interest that is calculated on the sum of money that you originally invest and not on any interest that is added to it later: compare **compound interest**.
N UNCOUNT

simple-minded. Someone who is **simple-minded** interprets everything in a way that is too simple, because they do not understand how complicated things are; used showing disapproval. EG *She was regarded by everyone as simple-minded... ...simple-minded flower people.* ▸ used of people's attitudes and behaviour. EG *...the simple-minded view people have about robots.* ◊ **simple-mindedness**. EG *He scoffed at such simple-mindedness.*
ADJ QUALIT = naive ≠ subtle, sophisticated
◊ N UNCOUNT = naivety

simpleton /sɪmpəºltən/, **simpletons**. A **simpleton** is a person with very low intelligence; an old fashioned word. EG *The other inhabitants took him for a simpleton... He had a simpleton for a sister.*
N COUNT = idiot

simplicity /sɪmplɪsɪti¹/, **simplicities**. **1** The **simplicity** of something is the fact that is it is uncomplicated and can be understood easily. EG *...the stunning simplicity of the Foucault pendulum... The advantage of the idea was its simplicity... The major considerations were simplicity and effectiveness.*
N UNCOUNT ≠ complexity

2 A **simplicity** is something that can be understood easily; a fairly literary use. EG *He focussed his mind upon these simplicities... ...the simplicities of propaganda.*
N COUNT : USU PL ≠ subtlety, complexity

3 If you say that there is **simplicity** in the way that someone behaves or dresses, you mean that they behave or dress in a simple way that is very attractive; used showing approval. EG *I think of Jenny, her simplicity and careless grace... He dressed with elegant simplicity.*
N UNCOUNT ≠ fussiness

simplification /sɪmplɪfɪkeɪʃəºn/, **simplifications**. A **simplification** is the thing that you produce when you make something simpler. EG *The V-sign is a simplification of an obscene gesture... I regard this proposal as a long overdue simplification.*
N COUNT/ UNCOUNT

simplify /sɪmplɪfaɪ/, **simplifies, simplifying, simplified**. If you **simplify** something, you make it easier to understand or do. EG *It would be a good idea if British Rail started simplifying their timetables... The subject is immensely complex, and hard to simplify... Continental quilts simplify bed-making.* ◊ **simplified**. EG *The account given so far is a simplified one... A useful, if somewhat simplified, classification can be drawn up as follows.*
V+O ⇑ modify
◊ ADJ QUALIT : ATTRIB ⇑ modified

simplistic /sɪmplɪstɪk/. A **simplistic** view or interpretation of something makes it seem much simpler than it really is; used showing disapproval. EG *...a simplistic view of human evolution... The Department has based its policies on a rather simplistic analysis of the situation.*
ADJ QUALIT = oversimplified

simply /sɪmpli¹/. **1** You use **simply** to emphasize that something consists only of one particular thing, happens for one particular reason, or is done in one particular way. EG *The job of a caterpillar is simply to eat... It's simply a question of hard work... There were women who spent months in jail simply because they didn't have fifty dollars... A good deal can be done simply by suggestion.*
ADV = just, merely

2 You also use **simply** to give emphasis to something that you are saying. EG *Wouldn't it be simply awful with no Christmas!... I simply can't believe it... I was happy, there is simply no other word for it... We simply must face facts.*
ADV = just

3 You use **simply** or **quite simply** to emphasize that what you are saying is correct. EG *There is, simply, no reason to go out of the house... It will be, quite simply, the longest tunnel in the world... The Drawing Room is, quite simply and beyond argument, magnificent.*
ADV SEN = without question

4 You use **simply** before giving the informal name of someone or something, in order to draw attention to how short the name is. EG *The Duke has been called simply 'Master' since he was a boy... The anti-riot squads became known simply as the CRS.*
ADV+as/NG ⇑ just

5 If you say or write something **simply**, you do it in a way that makes it easy to understand. EG *This puts the matter somewhat too simply... It's difficult to get interesting teaching materials simply written.*
ADV WITH VB

6 If you live **simply**, you have an uncomplicated, inexpensive way of life. EG *My grandmother lived very simply.*
ADV WITH VB = modestly

simulate /sɪmjə⁴leɪt/, **simulates, simulating, simulated**. **1** If you **simulate** a feeling or an action, you pretend that you are feeling it or doing it. EG *We used to use this trick in the Army to simulate illness... Actors and actresses simulate everything for our amusement... He simulated a mopping of his brow.* ◊ **simulated**. EG *He began rubbing his hands in simulated pleasure.*
V+O ⇑ imitate = feign, fake
◊ ADJ CLASSIF = feigned

2 If you **simulate** an object, a substance, or a noise, you produce something that looks or sounds like it. EG *The wood underneath is carved to simulate hair... His face was reddened with paint to simulate the blood of sacrificial victims... Nutshells were used to simulate the sound of galloping hooves.* ◊ **simulated**. EG *I gave her a new purse of simulated calf.*
V+O ⇑ imitate = suggest
◊ ADJ CLASSIF = imitation

3 If you **simulate** a set of conditions, you reproduce these conditions, for example in order to conduct an experiment; a technical use. EG *They had often practised under simulated conditions... ...a machine designed to simulate the effects of zero gravity.*
V+O ⇑ model

simulation /sɪmjə⁴leɪʃəºn/, **simulations**. **1 Simulation** or a **simulation** is the process of simulating something or the result of simulating it. EG *Spectators are entertained by the simulation of fighting... The viewer was unable to distinguish reality from simulation.*
N UNCOUNT/ COUNT = pretence

2 A **simulation** is also an attempt to solve a problem or to work out the consequences of doing something by representing the problem or possible course of events mathematically, often using a computer; a technical use. EG *Computer modelling and simulation have been used as an aid to battle tactics... The task was to program the computer to play a moon-landing simulation.*
N COUNT/ UNCOUNT

simulator /sɪmjə⁴leɪtə/, **simulators**. A **simulator** is a device which is designed to reproduce actual conditions, for example in order to train pilots or astronauts. EG *I spent months on the simulator flying*
N COUNT ⇑ machine

the Mig-31... We were reviewing information on our mission simulator.

simultaneous /sɪmə⁴lteɪnɪəs/. Things which are **simultaneous** happen or exist at the same time. EG *...the simultaneous failure of all the lifts in the building... ...a simultaneous broadcast on Radio 3 and BBC 2.* ◊ **simultaneously**. EG *Perhaps she held both views simultaneously... He is simultaneously conservative and militant.*
ADJ CLASSIF: IF + PREP THEN *with*
◊ ADV WITH VB

sin /sɪn/, **sins, sinning, sinned**. 1 **Sin** or a **sin** is an action or type of behaviour which is believed to break the laws of God. EG *They believed they were being punished for their sins... ...the sin of greed... They have no sense of sin.*
N UNCOUNT/COUNT ↑ transgression

2 If you **sin**, you do something that is believed to break the laws of God; an old-fashioned use. EG *You have sinned against the Lord.*
V: IF + PREP THEN *against* ↑ transgress

3 A **sin** is also any action or behaviour that someone disapproves of because it offends their moral principles. EG *A workers' paradise would emerge once the sin of ownership was extinguished.*
N COUNT: USU SING = evil

4 If you say that a man and a woman **are living in sin**, you mean that they are living together as if they are married although they are not married; an old-fashioned expression, now often used humorously. EG *I had always wondered what living in sin would be like.*
PHR: VB INFLECTS ↑ cohabit

5 See also **cardinal sin, mortal sin, original sin.** ● to **cover** or **hide a multitude of sins**: see **multitude**.

since /sɪns/. **Since** is usually used with perfect tenses for the meanings explained in paragraphs 1, 2, 3, and 5. 1 **Since** means **1.1** from the time or event you are mentioning until now or until a specified later time. EG *Since 1974, Marilyn has lived in Paris... I've been wearing glasses since I was three... He had been up since 4 am... Ever since you arrived you've been causing trouble... It's two weeks now since I wrote to you... For the first time since leaving home she is without a boyfriend... It rose very rapidly in 1973-4, but since then the price has risen very little.*
PREP, OR CONJ SUBORD

1.2 from the time when you were living or working in a particular place until now or until a specified later time. EG *We hadn't seen each other since Oxford.*
PREP

2 **Since** or **ever since** means from a time or event that you have already mentioned until now or until a specified later time. EG *She got her first acting job in 1952. She has rarely been out of work since... I came here in 1972 and I have lived here ever since... We met ten years ago and we have been friends ever since.*
ADV WITH VB

3 If you say that something has happened **since** a particular time or event, you mean that it happened at some stage between that time and now or between that time and a specified later time. EG *When I met him he was a philosophy student. He has since become a chartered accountant... I wrote this last year, but I've since revised it... Originally called 'Having a Ball', the play has since been retitled 'Private Practices'.*
ADV WITH VB = subsequently

4 If you say that something is the best, biggest, first, etc thing of a particular kind **since** another thing of the same kind, you mean that it is the best, biggest, first, etc thing of that kind that has occurred or existed from the time of the other thing. EG *He was by common agreement the best War Minister since Cardwell... It was the largest rally since the demonstrations of the 'thirties.*
PREP: SUPERL + PREP + NG

5 If something has **long since** happened, it happened a long time ago. EG *The time for talking has long since passed... The truth had long since become apparent.*
PHR: USED AS AN A

6 You use **since** to introduce a reason for something, especially when this reason is something that is already known to the person you are talking to. EG *Aircraft noise is a particular problem here since we're close to Heathrow Airport... Since it was Saturday, he stayed in bed an extra hour... He looked round for a chair and, since there wasn't one, he shared Mary's... Since you're on your feet, hand me down the tin of peaches, will you?*
CONJ SUBORD ↑ because = as

sincere /sɪnsɪə/. **Sincere** people say things that they really mean or believe. EG *He was decent, sincere, a good man.* ▸ used of behaviour and beliefs. EG *The apology was sincere... I am really sincere about giving you my allegiance... Please accept it with my sincere good wishes.* ◊ **sincerity** /sɪnserɪti¹/. EG *The Head Master is a man of deep conviction and sincerity... The film was made with sincerity.*
ADJ QUALIT ↑ honest = genuine, open
◊ N UNCOUNT

sincerely /sɪnsɪəli¹/. 1 If you say something **sincerely**, you mean what you say, and are not joking or being dishonest. EG *'I owe you an awful lot,' I said sincerely... The question was put to me quite sincerely.*
ADV WITH VB = honestly

2 If you feel or believe something **sincerely**, you really feel it or believe it and are not just pretending to. EG *He loves you very sincerely... She urged Judy to come, sincerely believing that it would do her good... I sincerely hope you'll come with us... I am sincerely delighted to hear you say that.*
ADV = genuinely

3 You write **Yours sincerely, Yours very sincerely, Sincerely**, etc before your signature at the end of a formal letter, usually when you have addressed it to someone by their name. For example, if you begin a letter 'Dear Mrs Smith', you can end it 'Yours sincerely'. EG *Yours sincerely, Winston S. Churchill... Yours very sincerely, Vita Sackville-West.*
CONVENTION

sinecure /saɪnɪkjʊə/, **sinecures**. A **sinecure** is a job for which you receive payment but which does not involve much work or responsibility. EG *This job's no sinecure, believe me.*
N COUNT

sine qua non /saɪnɪ kwɑ: nɒn/. A **sine qua non** is something that is essential if you want to achieve something or take part in something; a fairly formal expression. EG *Affection and love–each is a sine qua non of parenting... Tracing history was a sine qua non when addressing this group of academics.*
N SING WITH DET = must

sinew /sɪnju:/, **sinews**. 1 A **sinew** is the cord in your body that connects a muscle to a bone. EG *The sinews of his arm were tense... ...bags made from animal sinews.*
N COUNT/UNCOUNT = tendon

2 **Sinew** is physical strength or toughness; a fairly literary use. EG *We will fight with all our mind and heart and sinew.*
N UNCOUNT = muscle

3 **The sinews of war** consist of the money that is available for weapons and supplies during a war. EG *They continue to supply the sinews of war to our beloved country.*
PHR: USED AS O ↑ funding

sinewy /sɪnju:i¹/. Someone who is **sinewy** or has a **sinewy** body has a lean body with strong muscles. EG *...a broad, sinewy man of forty-nine... ...his sinewy body... ...a sinewy neck.*
ADJ QUALIT = muscular

sinful /sɪnfʊl/. 1 Someone who is **sinful** has a tendency to commit sins. EG *Good women have always saved sinful men in stories... ...the sinful world.*
ADJ QUALIT ↑ bad = erring

2 Something that is **sinful** is wicked because it is a sin. EG *She believed that eye-shadow was sinful.*
ADJ QUALIT ↑ bad

sing /sɪŋ/, **sings, singing, sang, sung**. 1 If you **sing**, or if you **sing** a song, verse, etc, you make musical sounds with your voice, usually producing words that fit a tune. EG *I started to sing... My sister was singing happily... Will you sing to me?... They sang the next line of the hymn... The title song is sung by Romy Blakeley.*
V OR V + O/QUOTE

2 If you **sing** someone a song, you sing it to them so that they can listen to it. EG *Would you like me to sing you a song?*
V + O + O, OR V + O + A *(for/to)*

3 If you **sing** someone to sleep, **sing** a worry away, etc, you make the person go to sleep, make the worry disappear, etc by singing. EG *She bent over their cradles, singing them to sleep... Why don't you just sing your troubles away?*
V + O + A

4 If someone **sings** a particular type of music or a particular musical role, they perform it as a singer, especially as a professional. EG *For five years I didn't sing opera on stage at all... I enjoy singing a part like this very much.*
V + O

5 If you **sing** of something, you tell a story of it in the form of a poem or song, especially a story that praises someone; an old-fashioned or literary use. EG *The old man was singing of a green hill far away... One of the women had sung of being a prisoner.*
V + A *(of)*, OR V + REPORT-CL

6 If you **sing** someone's **praises**, you enthusiastically praise them. EG *He was always singing his daughter's praises... Sociologists frequently sing the praises of the village society.*
PHR: VB INFLECTS = laud ≠ criticize

7 When birds, insects, etc **sing**, they make noises that sound like music. EG *I could hear birds singing in the trees... We still do not know why whales sing.*
V OR V + O

8 If something such as the wind, a kettle, or a bullet **sings**, it makes a whistling, buzzing, or ringing sound.
V: USU + A, NO IMPER

EG *I lay there listening to the wind singing through the trees... A bullet sang past the top of his head.*

9 If your ears **are singing**, they are filled with a continuous humming or ringing sound. EG *Ralph continued to blow till his ears were singing with the effort.* V : USU CONT, NO IMPER

10 See also **singing**.

sing up. If you **sing up**, you sing more loudly, so that people can hear you better. EG *You boys at the back! Can you sing up?* PHRASAL VB : V+ADV

sing. is an abbreviation for 'singular'. ADJ CLASSIF

Singaporean /sɪŋəpɔːrɪən/, **Singaporeans**. **1** Something that is **Singaporean** belongs or relates to Singapore or to its people. ADJ CLASSIF

2 A **Singaporean** is a person who comes from Singapore. N COUNT

singe /sɪndʒ/, **singes, singeing, singed**. **1** If you **singe** something such as cloth or hair or if it **singes**, you burn it very slightly so that it changes colour but does not catch fire. EG *I'm afraid I've singed the collar of your shirt... A grey cat nearly got its coat singed by the bonfire... ...the smell of singeing hair.* V-ERG = scorch

2 A **singe** is a slight burn, especially on cloth or hair. N COUNT

singer /sɪŋə/, **singers**. A **singer** is **1** a person who sings, especially one who earns a living by singing. EG *His mother was an actress and a singer... ...an opera singer... ...a pop singer.* N COUNT

2 a bird or animal that produces musical sounds. EG *Frogs and toads are most impressive singers.* N COUNT

Singhalese /sɪŋhəliːz/. See **Sinhalese**.

singing /sɪŋɪŋ/. **1 Singing** is **1.1** the making of musical sounds with your voice. EG *The dancing and singing ended at midnight... A piper led the singing... ...folk singing.* N UNCOUNT **1.2** the art of being a singer. EG *I studied singing with a wonderful teacher... ...singing lessons.* N UNCOUNT **1.3** the making of musical sounds by birds and animals. EG *...the singing of the blackbirds.* N UNCOUNT **1.4** a buzzing, whistling, or ringing sound. EG *I realized that the buzz I had thought was a singing in my ear was really a medley of voices.* N SING WITH DET

2 Your **singing** voice is the quality of your voice when you are singing. EG *He had a fine singing voice.* ADJ CLASSIF : ATTRIB

single /sɪŋgəl/, **singles, singling, singled**. **1** If you refer to a **single** thing, you mean only one, and not more. EG *In the distance a single bird cries... We heard a single shot... She had screamed for half an hour and not a single person had come to her aid... I just couldn't think of a single thing to say.* ADJ CLASSIF : ATTRIB = solitary

2 Single is used to describe something that has only one part or feature, rather than having two or more of them. EG *Single thicknesses of material will not be enough... He was fined £15 for parking on a single yellow line... ...a single-sex school.* ADJ CLASSIF : USU ATTRIB • If a number or score is **in single figures**, it is not more than 9. EG *England are still only in single figures.* • PHR : USED AS AN A

3 You use **single** to indicate that you are considering something on its own and separately from the other things like it or the other things in a group. EG *We are dealing not only with single cells but with groups of cells... This is the most important single invention since the wheel... We went there every single day.* ADJ CLASSIF : ATTRIB = individual

4 If you are **single**, you are not married, or no longer married. EG *She shared a room with another single woman... 'Marital status?'–'Single.'* ADJ CLASSIF ⇑ unmarried

5 A **single** bed, room, etc is one that is intended to be used by only one person. EG *Do you have two single rooms?... ...a single bed.* ADJ CLASSIF : USU ATTRIB

6 A **single** is a bedroom for one person in a hotel or guest house. N COUNT

7 A **single** ticket is a ticket for a journey that is made from one place to another but not back again; used in British English. EG *How much is the single fare to London?* ▸ used as a noun. EG *A single to Edinburgh, please.* ADJ CLASSIF = one-way ≠ return ▸ N COUNT ≠ return

8 A **single** is also a gramophone record which has one short song on each side. Singles are usually played at 45 rpm. EG *Last week two of the best-selling singles in America were by Australians.* N COUNT

9 In cricket, a **single** is a hit from which one run is scored. EG *They ran a quick single.* N COUNT

10 If an amount of money is **singles**, it is in the form of $1 notes or £1 coins, rather than fives, tens, etc. EG *'How would you like the money?'–'Three fives, and the rest in singles please.'... ...two hundred dollars in singles.* N COUNT : USU PL = one

11 Singles is a game or a competition of tennis, badminton, etc in which one player plays another player. EG *The high serve is used a lot in singles... Who will be the men's singles champion?* N PLURAL ≠ doubles

12 If a group of people walk or move **in single file**, they walk or move in a line, one behind the other. EG *We were crossing the bridge now, in single file... The boys came downstairs single file.* PHR : USED AS AN A

13 See also **singly**.

single out. If you **single** someone **out**, you choose them from a group for special attention or treatment. EG *Three other people were singled out for special praise... She singled him out at once as a possible victim... Why have badgers been singled out as culprits?* PHRASAL VB : V+O+ADV, IF+PREP THEN as/for ⇑ select = pick out

single-breasted. A **single-breasted** coat, jacket, or suit has coat fronts that meet in the centre of the chest and only one row of buttons. ADJ CLASSIF

single cream is thin cream that does not have a lot of fat in it; used in British English. N UNCOUNT

single-decker, single-deckers. A **single-decker** or a **single-decker bus** is a bus that has only one deck. N COUNT ≠ double-decker

single-handed. If you do something **single-handed**, you do it on your own, without help from anyone else. EG *Her job six nights a week on top of caring single-handed for seven children left her exhausted... He used to dream of rowing across the Pacific single-handed.* ▸ used as an adjective. EG *...a single-handed yachtsman... ...a single-handed achievement.* ADV WITH VB ⇑ alone ▸ ADJ CLASSIF : ATTRIB ◊ **single-handedly**. EG *He created a world fashion almost single-handedly.* ◊ ADV WITH VB

single honours. A **single honours** degree course is one in which only one main subject is studied. N UNCOUNT

single-minded. If someone is **single-minded**, they have only one aim or purpose and are determined to achieve it. EG *He was obsessively single-minded... ...the single-minded pursuit of wealth.* ADJ QUALIT = dogged, unswerving ◊ **single-mindedly**. EG *She is single-mindedly determined to preserve this policy.* ◊ ADV ◊ **single-mindedness**. EG *I admire your single-mindedness.*

singles bar, singles bars. A **singles bar** is a bar in the United States where single people can go in order to drink and meet other single people. N COUNT

singlet /sɪŋglɪt/, **singlets**; used in British English. A **singlet** is **1** a sleeveless sports shirt with no front opening, worn by athletes, boxers, etc. N COUNT **2** a sleeveless piece of underwear that is worn by a man on the top half of his body. N COUNT = vest

singly /sɪŋgli/. If people do something **singly**, they do it on their own or one by one. EG *I am prepared to see a husband and wife singly or together... A vitamin bottle should dispense pills singly.* ADV WITH VB = individually

sing-song, sing-songs. **1** A **sing-song** voice repeatedly rises and falls in pitch, and so sometimes sounds rather boring. EG *The dialect of the area has a sing-song intonation.* ADJ CLASSIF : ATTRIB

2 A **sing-song** is an occasion when a group of people sing songs together for pleasure. EG *After a few beers, John said, 'How about a sing-song?'* N COUNT

singular /sɪŋgjələ/. **1** In grammar, the **singular** of a noun is the form of it that refers to one person or thing, and not more. EG *The singular of 'lice' is 'louse'.* ▸ used as an adjective. EG *What is the singular form of 'media'?* N SING WITH DET ≠ plural ▸ ADJ CLASSIF ≠ plural

2 In formal English, something that is **singular** is **2.1** of an unusually high quality or standard. EG *...a lady of singular beauty. It was a campaign of singular scheming.* ADJ QUALIT : USU ATTRIB = outstanding ◊ **singularity** /sɪŋgjəlærɪti/. EG *They were convinced of the singularity of their good taste.* ◊ N UNCOUNT = uniqueness **2.2** strange and unusual. EG *...his singular manner of dress... How very singular!* ADJ QUALIT ◊ **singularity**. ◊ N UNCOUNT

singularly /sɪŋgjələli/ means to a remarkable or extraordinary degree; a formal word. EG *There was a singularly successful agreement on pay... Then we did some singularly boring experiments.* ADV+ADJ/ADV

Sinhalese /sɪnhəliːz/; also spelled **Singhalese**. **1** Something that is **Sinhalese** belongs or relates to a group of people who live mainly in Sri Lanka, or to their language. EG *This region in central Sri Lanka is the heartland of the dominant Sinhalese culture.* ADJ CLASSIF

2 Sinhalese is one of the languages that is spoken by people who live in Sri Lanka. N PROPER

sinister /sɪnɪstə/. Something that is **sinister** makes you afraid that something evil or harmful will happen. EG *A rather sinister figure was walking about behind the bushes... ...an evil and sinister place... ...certain sinister political implications.* ADJ QUALIT = ominous

sink /sɪŋk/, **sinks, sinking, sank, sunk.** 1 A **sink** is 1.1 a large basin in a kitchen, with taps that supply water, used especially for washing plates, pans, cups, etc. EG *There was a stack of dirty dishes in the sink... ...the kitchen sink.* 1.2 the same as a wash-basin. EG *He has gold faucets on his sinks and bath tubs.* — N COUNT; N COUNT

2 If something **sinks**, it moves slowly downwards and disappears from sight, especially below the surface of water. EG *The torpedo hit one of the aircraft carriers, which blew up and sank at once... The body sank to the bottom of the lake... Bread yeast sinks to the bottom in beer... The sun had just sunk below the horizon.* ◊ **sinking.** EG *She was rescued from the sinking aircraft by a passing ship.* — V : USU+A, NO IMPER ⇑ descend; ◊ ADJ CLASSIF : ATTRIB = foundering

3 If people **sink** a ship, they cause it to sink, usually by attacking it with bombs, torpedoes, or other weapons. EG *They were ordered to trail the damaged US intelligence ship and sink her by torpedo.* — V+O

4 If something **sinks**, it moves slowly down to a lower level. EG *Slowly the flood waters sank and life got back to normal... It's possible that the building may be sinking a little.* — V : NO IMPER = subside

5 If you **sink** somewhere, you move or fall into a lower position, for example by sitting down in a chair, usually because you are tired or weak or because you are getting comfortable. EG *I sank luxuriously into his biggest armchair... She sank back in her chair and sipped her drink... His head seemed to sink helplessly down... She couldn't walk any further and she sank to her knees in exhaustion.* — V+A = slump

6 If an amount or value **sinks**, it becomes lower or less. EG *Wages have sunk so low in relation to the cost of living... The pound has sunk to its lowest level against the dollar.* — V+A : NO IMPER = fall

7 If your voice **sinks**, it becomes quieter. EG *His voice had sunk to a whisper.* — V : NO IMPER = fall

8 If you **sink** into a particular state or situation, you pass gradually into it, especially one that is unpleasant or one in which you are less active. EG *My father sank further into debt... After the busy Christmas period he was glad to sink back into his customary torpor... I sank into a deep sleep.* — V+A *(into)* ⇑ decline = slip

9 If someone who is very ill **is sinking**, they are becoming weaker and weaker in health. EG *The patient was sinking fast and was not expected to live much longer.* — V : USU CONT, NO IMPER = fail

10 If your heart **sinks** or your spirits **sink**, you become depressed or lose hope. EG *His heart sank at the thought that the exams were only a week away... My spirits sank when I looked at all the bills I had to pay.* — V : NO IMPER

11 If you **are sunk**, you have no hope of avoiding trouble or failure; an informal expression. EG *We would've been completely sunk if they hadn't lent us the money... You have to have a map with you–otherwise you're sunk.* — V+O : ONLY PASS

12 If you **sink** something sharp into something solid, you make it go deeply into it. EG *He sank his teeth into a juicy steak... I sank my knife into the cheese.* — V-ERG+A *(into)* ⇑ dig

13 If you **sink** something into the ground, you make a hole for it or force it into the ground. EG *There was an old tin bath which they had sunk into the ground to make a little pond... The houses have to be built on poles which are sunk down into the bed of the lake.* — V+O+A *(into)* ⇑ put

14 When people **sink** a well or mine shaft, they make a deep hole in the ground by digging or drilling. EG *To boost meat production, the government sank wells and built watering places.* — V+O

15 If you **sink** money into a business or project, you spend money on it in the hope of making more money. EG *We sank nearly all our money into the new company.* — V+O+A *(in/into)* ⇑ invest = plough

16 If you **sink** a number of alcoholic drinks, you drink them; used in informal British English. EG *We usually sink a couple of pints in the pub after work.* — V+O = down

17 In games such as golf or snooker, if you **sink** a putt or **sink** the ball, you successfully hit the ball into a hole or pocket. EG *Try to reach the green with your first shot and then sink the ball with two puts.* — V+O

18 When you refer to **that sinking feeling**, you are referring to the uncomfortable feeling you get when you realize that something unpleasant has happened or is going to happen. EG *I experienced that sinking feeling you get when you know you have made a dreadful mistake.* — PHR : USED AS O

19 If you say that someone will have to **sink or swim**, you mean that they will have to succeed or fail through their own efforts, without being helped by anyone else. EG *She criticized those people who leave their teenage children to sink or swim... It's a case of sink or swim.* — PHR : INF/*to*-INF

20 See also **sunken**.

sink in. If something **sinks in**, it becomes fully understood or realized. EG *It took a moment or two for her words to sink in... The implications of this did not at first sink in.* — PHRASAL VB : V+ADV = penetrate

sinker /sɪŋkə/, **sinkers**. A **sinker** is a weight attached to a fishing line or net to keep it under the water. — N COUNT

sinner /sɪnə/, **sinners**. A **sinner** is someone who has committed a sin. EG *Christ is inviting sinners to repentance.* — N COUNT = wrongdoer

sinuous /sɪnjuəs/. Something that is **sinuous** 1 moves with smooth twists and turns, like a snake. EG *...a long sinuous snake... Women danced sinuous dances in the middle of the room.* 2 has many smooth wavy turns and curves; a rather literary use. EG *...a sinuous trail of slime.* — ADJ QUALIT = undulating; ADJ QUALIT = winding

sinus /saɪnəs/, **sinuses**. A **sinus** is a hollow space in a bone, especially one of the spaces in the bones of your skull just behind your nose. EG *Scent affects my sinuses... ...a sinus infection.* — N COUNT : USU PL

sip /sɪp/, **sips, sipping, sipped**. 1 If you **sip** a drink, you drink by taking just a small amount at a time. EG *The guests were sipping their drinks... He sipped at the wine.* — V OR V+O ≠ gulp

2 A **sip** is a small amount of drink that you take into your mouth. EG *She took another sip from her glass.* — N COUNT/PART ⇑ swallow

siphon /saɪfəⁿn/, **siphons, siphoning, siphoned**; also spelled **syphon**. 1 If you **siphon** a liquid or **siphon it off**, you draw it out of a container through a tube using atmospheric pressure. EG *You siphon the water off like this... Claude siphoned off a little petrol from his father's car.* — V+O, OR PHRASAL VB : V+O+ADV ⇑ remove

2 A **siphon** is 2.1 a tube that you use for siphoning liquid. 2.2 a soda siphon; an informal use. EG *She splashed soda from a siphon into the glasses.* — N COUNT; N COUNT

3 If you **siphon** money or resources or **siphon** them **off**, you cause them to be used for a purpose for which they were not intended. EG *Much of the trade surplus is siphoned off by the few industrial cities... This scheme involved siphoning colossal sums of money into public transport.* — V+O, OR PHRASAL VB : V+O+ADV ⇑ take away

sir /sɜː/, **sirs**. 1 People sometimes address a man as **sir** when they are being formal and polite. 'Dear Sir' is often used at the beginning of official letters. 'Sir' is most commonly used by shop assistants and waiters, by schoolchildren when they address their male teachers, and by soldiers when they address their officers. It is not a normal form of address in English. In spoken English, the plural of 'sir' is 'gentlemen'. EG *Dear Sir, I am writing in response to your letter of the 25th... What would you like, sir?... Sir, where did you put my book?... Brigadier Tomlinson wants to see you, sir.* — N VOC

2 **Sir** is the title used in front of the name of a knight or baronet. EG *He had invited Sir John Hargreaves to lunch with him at his club... Sir Oswald was immaculately dressed.* — N IN TITLES

sire /saɪə/, **sires, siring, sired**. 1 When a man **sires** a child, the child is born and the man is its father; an old-fashioned use. EG *The old man had sired a healthy boy child at the age of ninety.* — V+O ⇑ beget

2 Your **sire** is your father; an old-fashioned use. — N COUNT

3 An animal's **sire** is its father; a technical term, used especially of farm animals and racehorses. — N COUNT : POSS+N

siren /saɪərəⁿn/, **sirens**. 1 A **siren** is a device which makes a long, loud, wailing noise, and which is used to give a warning. Most fire engines, ambulances, and police cars have sirens. EG *...the distant wail of police sirens... We heard a siren screaming behind us.* — N COUNT ⇑ signal

2 You refer to something as a **siren** when it is very attractive, but also harmful or dangerous. EG *Chic, flash Abidjan has become the siren of West Africa.* — N COUNT ⇑ attraction

● A **siren call** or **siren song** is the appeal that something has when it is very attractive but also harmful or dangerous. EG *As a politician he was not deaf to the siren call of public popularity.* — ● N COUNT

3 A woman is described as a **siren** when she is attractive and dangerous to men. EG *One of the women, another of those sirens, haughtily regarded us as we talked.* — N COUNT ⇑ beauty

sirloin /sɜːlɔɪn/, **sirloins**. A **sirloin** is a piece of beef which is cut from the lower part of a cow's back. EG ...*a sirloin of Scotch beef.* N MASS ⇑ steak

sisal /saɪsəºl/ is a plant which is cultivated so that the fibre from its leaves can be used to make rope. Sisal is grown in the West Indies, South America, and Africa. EG *Long fibres are picked carefully from the sisal leaves.* ▸ used of the fibre. EG *Tanzania is one of the world's biggest producers of sisal.* N UNCOUNT

sissy /sɪsiˈ/, **sissies**; also spelled **cissy**; an informal word used showing disapproval. 1 A boy is described as a **sissy**, especially by other boys, if he does not like sport and is afraid to do things that are slightly dangerous. EG *You're a lot of cry-babies and sissies... ...Mummy's little sissy boy.* N COUNT : ALSO VOC = coward

2 A girl or young woman is described as a **sissy**, especially by other girls, if she is weak and cowardly. EG *I thought she was stuck up, a sissy, and soft in the head.* N COUNT = weed

sister /sɪstə/, **sisters**. 1 Your **sister** is a girl or woman who has the same parents as you. EG *My sister Jane married a farmer... Have you got any brothers and sisters?... Aunt Mabel was the youngest of my mother's three sisters.* ● A child's **big sister** is his or her older sister. A child's **little sister** is his or her younger sister. EG *She cheated her little sister out of some money.* ● See also **half-sister**. N COUNT ⇑ sibling ● PHR : USED AS S/O/C

2 A **sister** is 2.1 a woman who is a member of a religious order. Sisters sometimes work at schools or hospitals that are run by their order. EG *The Sisters taught her a love of religion.* ▸ used as part of a title or as a form of address. EG *Sister Catherine had given her a book.* 2.2 a senior nurse who supervises a hospital ward; used in British English. EG *If death occurs in hospital the ward sister will tell the nearest relative.* ▸ used as part of a title or as a form of address. EG *...Sister Manning... Sister, when is the doctor coming to see me?* N COUNT ⇑ nun ▸ N IN TITLES : ALSO VOC N COUNT ▸ N IN TITLES : ALSO VOC

3 A woman sometimes refers to other women as her **sisters** when she feels very close to them because they work for the same organization or have the same aims or beliefs. EG *They would go to Paris and stay with feminist sisters there... We called down to them that a sister had just been beaten.* N COUNT : USU PL

4 The **sister** of something is another thing of the same type that has the same function or that was built at the same time. EG *The city shows every sign of outgrowing its sister.* ▸ used as an adjective. EG *...Fylingdales and its sister stations in Alaska and Greenland... Her sister ship was sunk by a torpedo.* N COUNT : USU POSS+N ▸ ADJ CLASSIF : ATTRIB

sisterhood /sɪstəhʊd/ is a strong feeling of companionship between women who work for the same organization or who have the same aims or beliefs. N UNCOUNT

sister-in-law, sisters-in-law. Your **sister-in-law** is the sister of your husband or wife, or the wife of your brother. Some people also refer to a woman as their **sister-in-law** when she is married to their wife's or husband's brother. N COUNT ⇑ relative

sisterly /sɪstəliˈ/. A woman's **sisterly** feelings are the feelings of warmth and affection that she has towards her sister or brother or towards a man who she likes very much but does not love. EG *I had no nice sisterly feelings at all.* ▸ used of behaviour. EG *She treated him in a cordial, sisterly way.* ADJ CLASSIF : ATTRIB ⇑ affectionate

sit /sɪt/, **sits, sitting, sat**. 1 If you **are sitting** somewhere, for example in a chair or on the floor, the weight of your body is resting on your buttocks, rather than on your feet, and the upper part of your body is upright. EG *She was sitting on the edge of the bed... I was sitting at my desk reading... We sat by the fire and chatted... She found it hard to sit still.* V : USU+A = be seated

2 If you **sit** somewhere, you lower your body until you are sitting on something. EG *He came into the room and sat in his usual chair... A strange woman came and sat next to her.* V : USU+A = sit down

3 If you **sit** someone somewhere or **sit** them **down**, you persuade or force them to sit, or put them into a sitting position when you have been carrying them. EG *I sat him down and gave him a drink.* V+O+A, OR PHRASAL VB : V+O+ADV

4 If you say in a disapproving way that someone **is sitting** and doing something, you mean that they are continuing to do it when they should be doing something else. EG *It's no good sitting and waiting for success to come.* V : ONLY CONT, USU+*and*+-ING

5 If you **sit tight**, you remain in the same place or situation and do not take any action. EG *All they have to do is sit tight until the Republic recognises their claims... Just sit tight and wait for them to make the first move.* PHR : VB INFLECTS ⇑ wait

6 If you **sit** for an artist or a photographer, you place yourself in a sitting position so that the artist can paint you or the photographer can take a photograph of you. EG *She had sat for famous painters like Rossetti.* V+A *(for)* ⇑ pose

7 If you **sit** an examination, you take it; used in British English. EG *After the third term we'll be sitting the exam.* V+O

8 If you **sit** on something such as a committee, you are a member of it. EG *She sits on a lot of committees... Representatives of the workers should sit on the board of directors... He was elected to sit in the House of Commons.* V+A ⇑ belong

9 When a parliament, law court, or other official body **sits**, it officially carries out its work; a formal use. EG *Visitors are only allowed in on days when the Houses are not sitting... The House sat until after midnight.* V = be convened, be in session

10 If a building or other object **sits** in a particular place or position, it is in that place or position; a literary use. EG *The little parish church sits cosily in the middle of the village... She looked at the telephone sitting on the table beside her.* V+A = lie, stand

11 If an animal **sits** in a place or position, it remains there with its body resting on the ground or on some other object, usually with the upper part of its body upright. EG *There was a cat sitting on the sofa.* V : USU+A ⇑ rest

12 When a bird **sits** on its eggs, it covers them with its body in order to hatch them. V+A *(on)*

13 See also **sitting, baby-sit**. ● **to sit on the fence**: see **fence**.

sit around. If you **sit around** or **sit about**, you spend a lot of time doing nothing except sit; a fairly informal expression. EG *He often sat around in his bathrobe all day... We were tired of sitting about waiting for something to happen.* PHRASAL VB : V+ADV, USU+-ING/A

sit back. If you **sit back** while something is happening, you relax and do not become actively involved in it; a fairly informal expression. EG *He believes he has the right to sit back while others do the hard work... All you have to do is sit back and enjoy the fun.* PHRASAL VB : V+ADV PHRASAL VB :

sit by. If you **sit by** while something wrong or illegal is happening, you allow it to happen and do not do anything about it. EG *We can't just sit by while these people break the law... I for one am not going to sit by and see everybody quietly forget about it.* PHRASAL VB : V+ADV = stand by

sit down. 1 If you **sit down** or **sit** yourself **down**, you lower your body until you are sitting on something. EG *I was looking for a place to sit down... He sat down on the edge of the bed... She placed the cat on the sofa and sat herself down beside it.* PHRASAL VB : V+ADV, OR V+O (REFL)+ADV

2 If you **sit down** and do something, you spend time and effort doing it in order to try to achieve something. EG *The parties in the dispute have decided to sit down together and hammer out an agreement... The Party has decided to sit down and try to work out a compromise.* PHRASAL VB : V+ADV+*and*+VB

3 See also **sit-down**.

sit in on. If you **sit in on** a meeting or discussion, you are present while it is taking place but do not take part in it. EG *I was allowed to sit in on the deliberations of the board.* PHRASAL VB : V+ADV+PREP ⇑ attend

sit on. If you say that someone **is sitting on** something, you mean that they are delaying dealing with it; an informal expression, used showing disapproval. EG *She's been sitting on those application forms for weeks.* PHRASAL VB : V+PREP, HAS PASS ⇑ hold

sit out. If you **sit** something **out**, you wait patiently for it to finish, without taking any action. EG *They would retire to their caves to sit out the winter... The union decided to down tools, organize picket lines and sit it out.* PHRASAL VB : V+O+ADV = endure

sit through. If you **sit through** something such as a concert or a lecture, you stay until it is finished although you are not enjoying it. EG *I sat through all three performances but none of them was any good.* PHRASAL VB : V+PREP, HAS PASS

sit up. 1 If you **sit up**, 1.1 you bring yourself into a sitting position when you have been leaning back or lying down. EG *She sat up in bed when she saw him coming... The baby was struggling to sit up.* 1.2 you do not go to bed although it is very late. EG *Sometimes I sit up reading until three or four in the morning.* PHRASAL VB : V+ADV PHRASAL VB : V+ADV ⇑ stay up

2 If something makes you **sit up**, it makes you PHRASAL VB : V+

suddenly pay attention to what is happening. EG *Why don't you threaten to resign–that would make them sit up... At this point the audience began to sit up and take notice.* ADV

sitar /sɪtɑ:, sɪtɑ:/, **sitars**. A **sitar** is an Indian musical instrument with two layers of strings, a long neck, and a round body. N COUNT

sitcom /sɪtkɒm/, **sitcoms**. A **sitcom** is a television comedy series which shows the same set of characters in each episode in amusing situations that are similar to everyday life. EG *This is the stuff most standard TV sitcoms are made of.* N COUNT = situation comedy

sit-down, sit-downs. 1 If you have a **sit-down**, you sit down and rest for a short time; an informal use. EG *When we got to the top we had a bit of a sit-down... I could do with a sit-down.* N SING: a+N

2 A **sit-down** meal is served to people sitting at tables. EG *...sit-down dinners.* ADJ CLASSIF: ATTRIB

3 A **sit-down** strike is a strike in which workers refuse to leave the place where they work until they get what they are asking for. EG *They staged a number of sit-down strikes.* ADJ CLASSIF: ATTRIB

site /saɪt/, **sites, siting, sited**. 1 A **site** is 1.1 a piece of ground that is used or will be used for a particular purpose. EG *The city is full of dusty building sites... Immigrants are provided with sites on which to build their own houses... ...a caravan site.* N COUNT ⇑ area

1.2 a piece of ground where a building, statue, or monument stands or used to stand. EG *It is the third cathedral to stand on the site... It is built on the site of the old Lion Tower.* N COUNT = location 1.3 the place where a particular event happened. EG *The Bloody Tower is said to be the site of the murder of the little princes in 1483.* N COUNT = location

2 If something **is sited** in a particular place or position, it is put there or built there. EG *They refused to have cruise missiles sited on their soil... The observation post couldn't have been better sited.* V+O+A: USU PASS = locate

sit-in, sit-ins. A **sit-in** is a protest in which people go into a public place and stay sitting there for a long time. EG *She arranged sit-ins at employment agencies... The students voted to continue the sit-in.* N COUNT

sitter /sɪtə/, **sitters**. A **sitter** is the same as a babysitter. EG *We can get a sitter for Roger... It's important for the sitter to be someone the children know and like.* N COUNT

sitting /sɪtɪŋ/, **sittings**. 1 A **sitting** is 1.1 one of the times when a meal is served, for example in a school, when there is not enough space for everyone to eat at the same time. EG *The first sitting for breakfast is at 7.30... We have to have two sittings for lunch.* N COUNT ⇑ mealtime 1.2 one of the occasions when an official body, such as a parliament or law court, meets in order to carry out its work. EG *It was the first sitting of the Senate since the election.* N COUNT = session

2 If you do something **at one sitting**, you do it in one continuous session without getting up from your chair. EG *It was so interesting I read it at a single sitting.* PHR: USED AS AN A

3 If someone is in a **sitting** position, they are in a position where they are sitting or appear to be sitting, although they may be ill, unconscious, or dead. EG *I levered Smithy into a sitting position... I propped her up to a sitting position.* ADJ CLASSIF: ATTRIB

4 A **sitting** member is the present member of parliament for a particular place, rather than a past or future member. EG *The sitting member is a leading left-winger... Some candidates and sitting members have been dismissed.* ADJ CLASSIF: ATTRIB

5 If you say that someone or something that is a **sitting duck**, you mean that they are very easy to attack or harm. EG *Even the fastest merchant ships were sitting ducks... They became sitting ducks for the extortions of corrupt officials.* N COUNT ⇑ victim = easy prey

6 If you are **sitting pretty**, you are in a very favourable position; an informal expression. EG *We'll be sitting pretty once the new product comes out.* PHR: USED AS C = in clover

sitting-room, sitting-rooms; also spelled as two words. A **sitting-room** is a room in a house where people sit and relax. EG *Castle went back into the sitting-room... I spent the night on the sitting-room sofa.* N COUNT ⇑ living-room = lounge

sitting tenant, sitting tenants. A **sitting tenant** is a person who rents a house or flat as their home. EG *If you're a sitting tenant, then you're protected by a number of laws.* N COUNT

situate /sɪtjʊeɪt/, **situates, situating, situated**. If you **situate** something such as an idea or fact, you relate it to a particular context, especially in order to understand it better; a formal word. EG *The dangers which press upon us must be situated in this context... This approach situates fads and fashions in terms of symbolic behaviour.* V+O+A = locate, set

situated /sɪtjʊeɪtɪ²d/. 1 If something is **situated** in a particular place or position, it is in that place or position; a fairly formal use. EG *...Clervaux, a small town situated picturesquely in a deep, narrow, wooded valley... The control centre is situated many miles away... He had gone to the back of the cafe where the telephone was situated... ...the building in which Morris's office was situated... The nursery is situated well away from the rest of the house.* ADJ CLASSIF: PRED, VB (be)+ ADJ+A = located, positioned

2 If your house or flat is pleasantly **situated**, conveniently **situated**, etc, it is in a pleasant area, a convenient position, etc. EG *Their flat on Broad Street was most conveniently situated.* ADJ CLASSIF: ADV +ADJ = located

situation /sɪtjʊeɪʃə⁰n/, **situations**. 1 You use the word **situation** 1.1 to refer generally to what is happening in a particular place at a particular time. EG *The situation was beginning to frighten me... She felt pleased with herself at coping with the situation... It's an impossible situation... Social problems are mounting with consequent loss of morale. Surely this situation calls for urgent planning... The situation in Georgia, USA, is radically different... We have to consider what to do in situations where there are many people involved.* N COUNT: USU SING+SUPP 1.2 to refer to a particular aspect of what is happening in a place. EG *...the Greek economic situation... They were indignant about the housing situation... ...the oil and energy situations.* N COUNT: MOD+ N, USU SING ⇑ state = circumstances 1.3 to refer to what is happening or likely to happen in connection with a particular matter. EG *The situation is that our legal advisers are happy... I explained the situation, and we talked about Anthony.* N COUNT: USU the+N IN SING ⇑ state = circumstances

2 A **situation** is 2.1 the set of circumstances on a particular occasion. EG *Rules governed every situation. And each man knew exactly where he stood... One has to know how to handle oneself in social situations.* N COUNT ⇑ event 2.2 something difficult, dangerous, or unpleasant that is happening. EG *One sits back and just watches a situation develop which is really a confrontation... That's quite a situation. You might say there's a little problem.* N COUNT ⇑ crisis

3 Your **situation** is the things that are happening to you or that are likely to happen to you at a particular time. EG *...girls in your situation, hard-working girls with family responsibilities... He knew a lot about my father's situation... ...the situation of the Irish a hundred years ago... After the Napoleonic wars, the situation for farm labourers worsened further.* N COUNT: USU WITH POSS IN SING ⇑ state = position

4 If someone says, for example, that they are in a holiday **situation**, they mean that they are on holiday. If someone says that there is a crisis **situation**, they mean that there is a crisis. This sense is used mainly in spoken English and is considered by some people to be bad style. EG *This was in an overseas situation... A crisis situation had erupted... We must beware of drawing too many parallels between the serious music situation and the pop situation.* N COUNT: MOD+ N, USU SING

5 The **situation** of a building or town is the kind of place where it is, for example the kind of surroundings that it has or its distance from other buildings or towns; a rather formal use. EG *The city is in a beautiful situation... The best situations for windmills are where the wind is blowing strongest.* N COUNT: USU+ SUPP = location, spot

6 A **situation** is also a job or post, especially a professional job, a clerical job, or a job as a servant; a formal or old-fashioned use. EG *It's not so easy to find another situation.* N COUNT = position ● **Situations Vacant** is the title of a column or page in a newspaper where jobs of all kinds are advertised. EG *She studied the 'Situations Vacant' columns in the newspapers.* ● PHR = vacancies

situation comedy, situation comedies. A **situation comedy** is a type of comedy, especially on television or radio, which shows the characters in amusing situations that are similar to everyday life. EG *O'Shea's tastes in TV ran to situation comedy and sentimental serials.* N COUNT/ UNCOUNT

six /sɪks/, **sixes**. 1 **Six** is the number 6: see □ at NUMBER, AGE, DATE, MEASUREMENT, MONEY, and TIME. EG *The attack occurred about six days ago.* NUM

2 **at sixes and sevens**; an informal expression. 2.1 If PHR: USED AS AN

a place or event is **at sixes and sevens**, it is disorganized. EG *The household is at sixes and sevens at the moment... We had a few odd meetings but they were all at sixes and sevens.* **2.2** If you are **at sixes and sevens**, your thoughts and feelings are confused. EG *I was worried. Everything seemed at sixes and sevens.* — A; PHR : USED AS AN A

3 You use the expression **six of one and half a dozen of the other** when you want to say that there is really no difference between two alternatives; used in informal English. EG *'Which is preferable?'–'I don't think it matters, it's six of one and half a dozen of the other.'* — PHR : USED AS C

4 A **six** is a score of six runs in cricket. It is gained by hitting the ball so that it crosses the boundary before it touches the ground. — N COUNT : USU SING

sixpence /sɪkspə²ns/, **sixpences**. A **sixpence** is a small silver coin which was used in Britain before the decimal money system was introduced in 1971. It was worth six old pence. — N COUNT

sixteen /sɪkstiːn/ is the number 16: see □ at NUMBER, AGE, DATE, MEASUREMENT, MONEY, and TIME. EG *...a young woman of sixteen.* — NUM

sixteenth /sɪkstiːnθ/, **sixteenths**. **1** The **sixteenth** item in a series is the one that you count as number sixteen: see □ at NUMBER, AGE, and DATE. EG *...a furnished room on the sixteenth floor.* — ORDINAL

2 A **sixteenth** is one of sixteen equal parts of something. — N COUNT : USU + of ⇑ fraction

sixteenth note, sixteenth notes. A **sixteenth note** is a semiquaver; used in American English. — N COUNT

sixth /sɪksθ/, **sixths**. **1** The **sixth** item in a series is the one that you count as number six: see □ at NUMBER, AGE, and DATE. EG *On the sixth day we went on an excursion.* — ORDINAL

2 A **sixth** is one of six equal parts of something. EG *...one sixth of an acre of land.* — N COUNT : USU + of

sixth form, sixth forms; also spelled with a hyphen, especially when used before another noun. A **sixth form** in a British school is the class that students go into at the age of sixteen or seventeen, usually in order to study for 'A' Levels and after passing 'O' levels. EG *What subjects are you taking in the sixth form?... ...a group of sixth-form pupils.* — N COUNT

sixth former, sixth formers; also spelled with a hyphen. A **sixth former** is a student who is in the sixth form at school. EG *This course is for sixth formers and teachers.* — N COUNT

sixth sense. Someone who has a **sixth sense** seems to know things or see things without using the five senses of sight, hearing, touch, smell, and taste. EG *He was an unusually able detective with a sort of sixth sense for tracking down burglary suspects.* — N SING : USU *a*+N

sixtieth /sɪkstɪə²θ/. The **sixtieth** item in a series is the one that you count as number sixty: see □ at NUMBER and AGE. EG *The dinner was in celebration of Mr Barrett's sixtieth birthday.* — ORDINAL

sixty /sɪksti¹/, **sixties**. **Sixty** is the number 60: see □ at NUMBER, AGE, DATE, MEASUREMENT, MONEY, and TIME. EG *She was being paid sixty dollars a week.* — NUM

sizable /saɪzəbə⁰l/. See **sizeable**.

size /saɪz/, **sizes, sizing, sized**. **1** The **size** of something is **1.1** how big or small it is, or how great it is in amount. You can find the size of things by comparing them, measuring them, or counting them. EG *The lemur is about the size of a rabbit... The company doubled its size in nine years... The population of the country has increased in size... ...a block of ice one cubic foot in size.* **1.2** the fact that it is very large. EG *The Grand was the only hotel of any size in the town... The main concern is the size of the Government's budget deficit.* — N UNCOUNT; N UNCOUNT ⇑ magnitude

2 A **size** is one of a series of graded measurements used as units for things such as clothes, so that you can tell whether they are big enough or small enough. EG *'What size do you take?'–'Ten.'... ...a size 9 shoe... ...a jacket three sizes too big... They are made in several sizes.* — N COUNT

3 If you try on a piece of clothing **for size**, you try it on to see if it is the right size. EG *She tried it on for size.* — PHR : USED AS AN A

4 If you alter something **to size**, you alter it to make it the right size. EG *Glass can be pre-cut to size by a glass merchant.* — PHR : USED AS AN A

5 If you **cut** someone **down to size**, you make them realize that they are not as important as they think they are, usually by embarrassing them or humiliating them. EG *Your boss isn't just trying to cut you down to size, but actually to get rid of you.* — PHR : VB INFLECTS

size up. If you **size up** a person or situation, you carefully look at the person or think about the situation, so that you can decide what to do next, or how to deal with the person; an informal expression. EG *He glanced back constantly, to size up the situation... ...people sizing each other up as if for a fight.* — PHRASAL VB : V+O+ADV ⇑ examine = weigh up

-size or **-sized** **1** combines with nouns to say that something is the same size as the noun mentioned. EG *...a city-size population... ...egg-sized lumps of white clay.* **2** combines with adjectives to describe the size of something. EG *...75 average-size Japanese farms... ...a decent-sized single portion.* **3** combines with nouns to say that something is big enough to be suitable for a particular job or purpose. EG *...park-size mowers and other machines... Cut the meat into bite-sized chunks and fry it.* — COMB : FORMS ADJ CLASSIFS; COMB : FORMS ADJS; COMB : FORMS ADJ CLASSIFS

sizeable /saɪzəbə⁰l/; also spelled **sizable**. Something that is **sizeable** is fairly large in amount. EG *...a sizeable sum of money... The conference voted, by a sizeable majority, against the motion.* — ADJ QUALIT

-sized. See **-size**.

sizzle /sɪzə⁰l/, **sizzles, sizzling, sizzled**. If something **sizzles**, it makes a hissing sound like the sound made by frying food. EG *When I put a wet finger on it, the rock sizzled like a hot iron... The steak and kidney pudding sizzled deliciously on the stove.* — V ⇑ hiss

skate /skeɪt/, **skates, skating, skated**. **1** A **skate** is **1.1** an **ice-skate**. **1.2** a **roller skate**. — N COUNT; N COUNT

2 If you **skate**, **2.1** you move about on ice wearing ice-skates. EG *...skating across the frozen pond.* **2.2** you move about over a flat surface wearing roller skates. — V; V

3 A **skate** is also a very flat sea fish which has two large fins like wings and can be eaten. — N COUNT

4 If someone tells you to **get your skates on**, they are telling you to hurry; an informal expression. EG *We'll have to get our skates on or we'll miss the train.* — PHR : VB INFLECTS

5 If you **skate round** a difficult subject or problem, or **skate around** or **over** it, you avoid discussing it or dealing fully with it. EG *He skated warily round the subject once or twice... The book skates over the technicalities of adult life... They prefer to skate around the issue of sex.* — PHRASAL VB : V+PREP, HAS PASS = skirt, evade

skateboard /skeɪtbɔːd/, **skateboards**. A **skateboard** is a narrow board with a set of small wheels at each end, which you can stand on and ride for sport or pleasure. — N COUNT

skateboarding /skeɪtbɔːdɪŋ/ is the activity of riding on a skateboard. — N UNCOUNT

skater /skeɪtə/, **skaters**. A **skater** is someone who ice-skates or roller-skates, especially in races or competitions. — N COUNT

skein /skeɪn/, **skeins**. A **skein** is **1** a loosely coiled length of thread, especially wool or silk. EG *...a skein of wool.* **2** a group of geese flying in a long line. EG *Long skeins of geese were flying over the rooftops.* — N COUNT ⇑ bundle; N PART

skeletal /skelɪ²tə⁰l/. **1** **Skeletal** is used to describe things relating to the skeleton of a person or an animal. EG *Girls are born with slightly more mature skeletal and nervous systems... Skeletal muscle contains about 70 per cent water.* — ADJ CLASSIF : ATTRIB ⇑ structural

2 A **skeletal** person is extremely thin because of hunger or illness. EG *...harrowing photographs of skeletal children in the desert.* — ADJ CLASSIF = emaciated

3 The **skeletal** structure of something is the basic framework around which it is built up; a formal use. EG *The following skeletal timetable emerged.* — ADJ CLASSIF

skeleton /skelɪ²tə⁰n/, **skeletons**. **1** The **skeleton** of a person or an animal is the framework of bones which supports and protects the organs and muscles of their body. EG *The ground floor of the museum is taken up by the skeleton of a gigantic whale... ...a human skeleton.* — N COUNT

2 If you refer to someone as a **skeleton**, you mean that they are extremely thin, usually because of hunger or illness. EG *She was worrying herself into a skeleton.* — N COUNT

3 The **skeleton** of a building or other construction is its basic framework which supports its shape and structure. EG *He centres his constructions around reinforced concrete or steel skeletons.* — N COUNT

4 The **skeleton** of an essay, report, contract, etc is the basic plan for it, to which details may be added later. EG *I only submitted a skeleton draft–Patrick will have to fill in the details himself.* — N COUNT = outline

5 A **skeleton** staff is the smallest amount of staff necessary in order to run an organization or service. EG *They only employ a skeleton staff of fulltime workers at weekends.* N BEFORE N ⇑ minimum

6 If you have **a skeleton in the cupboard** or **a skeleton in the closet**, you are keeping an unpleasant fact about yourself secret. EG *I'd be obliged if you'd keep this other skeleton in the cupboard quiet.* PHR : USU USED AS O

skeleton key, skeleton keys. A **skeleton key** is a key which has been specially made so that it will open many different locks. EG *My father has a skeleton key to all the classrooms.* N COUNT = master key, pass key

skeptic /skeptɪk/. See **sceptic**.

skeptical /skeptɪkəᵒl/. See **sceptical**.

sketch /sketʃ/, **sketches, sketching, sketched**. 1 A **sketch** is a drawing that is done quickly without a lot of details. EG *He drew a rough sketch on his pad showing the position of the entrances to the camp... He writes all his own scripts and even makes sketches for the costumes and sets.* N COUNT

2 If you **sketch** something, you draw it quickly without a lot of details. EG *She began to sketch on a piece of paper... These little drawings were sketched by a seventeenth century botanist.* V OR V+O

3 If you **sketch** or **sketch out** a situation or an incident, you give a short description of it, including only the most important facts or details. EG *His rise to power is briefly sketched in the first two chapters... He sketched out his plan for the new sales campaign.* ▸ used as a noun. EG *The first section is a brief sketch of the school's early history.* V+O, OR PHRASAL VB : V+ADV ⇑ describe = outline ▸ N COUNT : USU SING

4 A **sketch** is also a short humorous piece of acting, usually forming part of a comedy show on television or radio or in the theatre. EG *I loved the sketch about the dead parrot.* N COUNT ⇑ scene = skit

sketch in. If you **sketch in** a point or detail about something, you give it as extra information. EG *In this programme I'm going to sketch in a bit of the background to the current crisis.* PHRASAL VB : V+O+ADV ⇑ supply = fill in

sketchbook /sketʃbʊk/, **sketchbooks**; also spelled with a hyphen. A **sketchbook** is a book of blank pages for drawing on. N COUNT = sketchpad

sketchpad /sketʃpæd/, **sketchpads**; also spelled with a hyphen. A **sketchpad** is a pad of blank pages for drawing on. N COUNT = sketchbook

sketchy /sketʃi¹/, **sketchier, sketchiest**. Something that is **sketchy** does not have many details and is therefore incomplete or inadequate. EG *Her sketchy account of the incident hasn't really helped us much... I had only the sketchiest notion of what it was all about... The details of the plan remain sketchy.* ◇ **sketchily**. EG *The animal's behaviour was only sketchily understood.* ADJ QUALIT = patchy ◇ ADV WITH VB

skew /skjuː/, **skews, skewing, skewed**. 1 If something is **skewed**, its position or shape is distorted, usually because it is placed in a slanting or crooked position when you would normally expect it to be straight. EG *There was a pink cliff surmounted by a skewed block of white limestone... Their vision is skewed by the distorting lenses.* V+O : ONLY PASS ⇑ twist = slant

2 Something that is **skew** is in a slanting position when it should be vertical or horizontal. EG *The picture was skew.* ▸ used as an adverb. EG *The cupboard my father had fixed was hanging a bit skew.* ADJ QUALIT ⇑ crooked ▸ ADV WITH VB = skew-whiff

3 If a vehicle **skews** in a particular direction, it turns aside sharply from the direction in which it should be going. EG *At that moment the boat skewed off course, heading straight for the rocks.* V+A = veer, swerve

skewed /skjuːd/. If an idea that you have is **skewed**, it is distorted or prejudiced, usually because you do not know all the facts. EG *Their conception of religion is heavily skewed.* ADJ QUALIT = biased

skewer /skjuːə/, **skewers, skewering, skewered**. 1 A **skewer** is a long metal or wooden pin which is used to hold pieces of meat or other food together or in a particular shape during cooking. N COUNT

2 If you **skewer** something, you push a skewer or other long, thin, pointed object through it. EG *They skewered bits of meat on branches and held them in the flames.* V+O ⇑ impale

skew-whiff /skjuː wɪf/. Something that is **skew-whiff** is in a slanting position when it should be vertical or horizontal; an informal word. EG *Your hat's skew-whiff.* ADJ QUALIT : PRED ⇑ crooked

ski /skiː/, **skis, skiing, skied**. 1 A **ski** is one of a pair of long, flat, narrow pieces of wood, metal, or plastic that can be fastened to boots so that the person wearing them can move easily on snow. EG *...a pair of skis... You can hire skis here if you haven't got your own.* N COUNT ⇑ equipment

2 When people **ski**, they move on snow wearing skis and using a pair of long sticks to push themselves along, especially as a sport or a holiday activity. EG *You need a good instructor if you're learning to ski... They go skiing in Switzerland every winter.* V

3 **Ski** is used to describe things used for skiing or concerned with skiing. EG *...ski boots... ...a ski resort... ...a ski instructor.* ADJ CLASSIF : ATTRIB

skid /skɪd/, **skids, skidding, skidded**. If a vehicle **skids**, it slides sideways while moving, for example if you are trying to stop it suddenly on a wet or icy road. EG *I heard a screech of tyres skidding on the road surface... I tried to brake and we skidded into the ditch.* ▸ used as a noun. EG *With a scrunch and a skid we drove off at high speed... ...skid marks on every corner... The car went into a skid and ended up on the wrong side of the road.* V : USU+A ▸ N COUNT ⇑ movement

skier /skiːə/, **skiers**. A **skier** is a person who skis. N COUNT

skiff /skɪf/, **skiffs**. A **skiff** is a small, light rowing-boat or sailing-boat, usually with room for only one person. N COUNT

ski jump, ski jumps. A **ski jump** is a specially-built steep slope covered in snow with one end curving upwards. People ski down it and jump into the air at the end. ▸ used of the sporting event in which people ski down this slope and try to travel as far as possible through the air at the end. EG *He did well in the downhill race, but badly in the ski jump.* N COUNT ▸ N SING : the+N

skilful /skɪlfʊl/; also spelled **skillful** in American English. Someone who is **skilful** at something does it very well. EG *Telemann was a lesser-known but similarly skilful composer... The girl had grown more skilful with the sewing-machine.* ▸ used of a person's actions and abilities. EG *This authentic effect had been achieved by skilful retouching.* ◇ **skilfully**. EG *...a skilfully organized campaign.* ADJ QUALIT ⇑ able = accomplished ◇ ADV WITH VB

ski lift, ski lifts. A **ski lift** is a machine for taking people to the top of a slope so that they can ski down it. It consists of a series of seats hanging down from a moving wire. N COUNT ⇑ conveyance

skill /skɪl/, **skills**. 1 **Skill** is the knowledge and ability that enables you to do something such as a job, game, or sport very well. EG *Organized games involve skill, competition and teamwork... Nowadays teachers use more imagination and skill in explaining things to children... The carving shows remarkable technical skill... They acted with great skill and conviction.* N UNCOUNT = expertise

2 A **skill** is a type of work or an art or craft which requires special training and knowledge. EG *If you want to learn a new skill, ask at the careers office... ...the skills of painting, sculpture, and drawing... Where are the traditional skills of village craftsmen today?* N COUNT ⇑ ability

skilled /skɪld/. 1 Someone who is **skilled** has the knowledge and ability needed to do something well. EG *A skilled engineer takes four years to train.* ADJ QUALIT ⇑ able = skilful

2 **Skilled** work involves or requires a certain level of trained ability; used especially of manual and industrial work. EG *There is still a shortage of skilled labour in some industries... ...skilled and semi-skilled work.* ADJ CLASSIF

skillet /skɪlɪt/, **skillets**. A **skillet** is a shallow cast-iron pan for cooking. EG *Fry for twenty-five seconds each side in a very hot skillet.* N COUNT

skillful /skɪlfʊl/. See **skilful**.

skim /skɪm/, **skims, skimming, skimmed**. 1 If you **skim** something from the surface of a liquid, you remove it. EG *Skim off the cream... Strain the sauce and skim away any fat that rises to the surface.* V+ADV+O, OR V+O+A

2 If something **skims** a surface, it moves fast just above it. EG *The birds swoop in a breathtaking arc to skim the pond surface... Fish passed beneath him, skimming the sandy bottom of the sea.* V+O

3 If you **skim** a newspaper or other piece of writing, you read through it quickly without looking at the details. EG *Just skimming the paper, I saw a headline about the Pope's visit... I thought I would skim through a few of the letters.* V+O, OR V+A *(through)* = glance through

4 If you **skim** flat stones, you throw them across water so that they touch the surface and bounce off it several times. EG *A boy was skimming stones out into the water.* V+O

skimmed milk or **skim milk** is milk from which the cream has been removed. EG *She can drink skimmed milk but should keep off butter.* N UNCOUNT

skimp /skɪmp/, **skimps, skimping, skimped.** If you **skimp** on something, you use less time, money, material, etc, for it than you really need, so that the result is unsatisfactory. EG *Never skimp on your warm-up exercises... When people get harassed work is skimped or rushed.* V, V+A (on), OR V+O ⇑ economize

skimpy /skɪmpi¹/, **skimpier, skimpiest.** Something that is **skimpy** is small in size or quantity and therefore often inadequate. EG *Sneaking off to buy hamburgers was the only way they could supplement the skimpy meals... ...little girls in skimpy cotton frocks.* ADJ QUALIT = scant

skin /skɪn/, **skins, skinning, skinned.** 1 Your **skin** is the natural covering of your body. EG *They had light skin and blue eyes... The poison may be absorbed through the skin... Wear rubber gloves if your skin is sensitive to washing powders... The sun's rays can be very harmful beating on an unprotected fair skin... The Lapps of Scandinavia have fair skins... ...skin cancer.* N UNCOUNT/COUNT ⇑ substance

2 An animal **skin** is the natural covering of the animal's dead body together with its fur or hair, when it is separated from the animal's body and used to make things such as coats or rugs. EG *They used bone needles and sinew to sew clothes of skin and fur... A few coats hung in the closet, one of leopard skin... ...a polar bear skin on the floor... ...a ban on the wearing of anything made from animal skins.* N COUNT/UNCOUNT = pelt

3 The **skin** of a type of food, usually a fruit or vegetable, is its outer layer or covering. EG *Cook the potatoes quickly with their skins on... ...a banana skin... ...sausage skins.* N COUNT/UNCOUNT

4 A **skin** on the surface of some liquids, for example paint or warm milk, is a fairly solid layer that sometimes forms on it. EG *Stir the paint well to get rid of any skin... The custard had a thick skin on it.* N COUNT/UNCOUNT

5 If you **skin** a dead animal, you remove the skin from it, usually in order to cook the animal. EG *The boys skinned and cleaned the day's game... The fish should be skinned and filleted.* V+O

6 If you **skin** part of your body, you injure it by scraping some of the skin off. EG *She skinned her knee... His elbows were quite badly skinned.* V+O = graze

7 The word **skin** is used in the following informal expressions. 7.1 If you describe someone as **skin and bone** or **skin and bones**, you mean that they are extremely thin. EG *She's nothing but skin and bones!* PHR : USED AS C = emaciated
7.2 If you do something **by the skin of** your **teeth**, you just manage to do it but very nearly fail. EG *I only passed by the skin of my teeth.* PHR : USED AS AN A 7.3 If you say that something made you **jump out of** your **skin** or **leap out of** your **skin**, you are emphasizing how much it surprised or shocked you. EG *He nearly jumped out of his skin when he saw her face at the window.* PHR : VB AND N INFLECT ⇑ react = start 7.4 If you do something to **save** your **skin** or to **protect** your **own skin**, you do it to save yourself from something dangerous or unpleasant, often without caring what happens to anyone else. EG *My first thought was to protect my own skin... When they heard the police cars, they all set about saving their own skins.* PHR : VB AND N INFLECT 7.5 If you say that someone **gets under** your **skin**, you mean that they irritate you; an informal expression. EG *He really gets under my skin sometimes.* PHR : VB INFLECTS ⇑ affect 7.6 If you say **'It's no skin off my nose'**, you mean that it doesn't matter to you at all if a particular thing mentioned happens; an informal expression. EG *It's no skin off my nose if she decides not to come.* CONVENTION, OR PHR : VB INFLECTS

skin-deep. If you say that something is **skin-deep**, you mean that it has no real importance when it is thought about deeply, although it may often seem important. EG *Beauty is only skin-deep.* ADJ CLASSIF : USU PRED ⇑ apparent = superficial

skin-diver, skin-divers. A **skin-diver** is someone who does skin-diving. N COUNT

skin-diving is the sport or activity of swimming underwater using only light breathing apparatus and without a special diving suit. N UNCOUNT

skinflint /skɪnflɪnt/, **skinflints**. A **skinflint** is a very mean person who hates spending money; an informal word. N COUNT = miser

skinhead /skɪnhɛd/, **skinheads**. A **skinhead** is a young person whose hair is shaved or cut very short. Most skinheads in Britain wear tight trousers and heavy boots and are usually regarded as violent and aggressive. N COUNT ⇑ youth

-skinned combines with adjectives to indicate that someone has skin of the kind mentioned. EG *...soft-skinned babies... Most of them are fair-skinned.* COMB : FORMS ADJS

skinny /skɪni¹/, **skinnier, skinniest**. Someone who is **skinny** is very thin, especially in an unattractive way. EG *He's tall and skinny... One of the wrinkled old women waved her skinny arms.* ADJ QUALIT = scrawny

skint /skɪnt/. If you are **skint**, you have no money; an informal word, usually used when you are temporarily without money but are not really worried about it. EG *I could do with £10, I'm skint.* ADJ QUALIT : PRED ⇑ poor = broke

skin-tight clothes fit very tightly so that they show the shape of a person's body. ADJ CLASSIF ⇑ tight

skip /skɪp/, **skips, skipping, skipped.** 1 When you **skip**, 1.1 you move almost as if you are dancing, with a series of little jumps from one foot to the other. EG *They ran back to the house, skipping over the grass and singing all the way... He skipped around the room.* ▸ used as a noun. EG *...taking little skips as they walked.* V : USU+A ⇑ run ▸ N COUNT 1.2 you play by jumping up and down to step over a rope which you or two other people are holding at each end and turning round and round; often done by children. EG *The children chant the same rhymes when they're skipping that I used to do at school... Three energetic little girls were skipping in the playground.* V

2 If you **skip** something that you usually do or that you ought to go to, you deliberately do not do it or go to it; an informal use. EG *I could skip every lecture for a month and still graduate... I'm skipping breakfast this morning.* V+O ⇑ miss

3 If you **skip** something such as a section of a book that you are reading, you miss it out or pass quickly over it. EG *I'd skip this chapter if I were you.* V OR V+O ⇑ omit

4 If you **skip** from one subject to another, you move from one to the other when there is no obvious or direct connection between them. EG *The narrative skips from one episode of history to another in a very confusing manner.* V+A = jump, flit

5 A **skip** is a large metal container for holding rubbish, old bricks, pieces of stone, etc which need to be taken away from a place; used in British English. EG *Debris was being loaded into skips.* N COUNT

skipper /skɪpə/, **skippers**; an informal word. A **skipper** is 1 the captain of a ship or boat. EG *I had to pass the signals to the skipper.* N COUNT 2 the captain of a team in a sport such as football. N COUNT

skipping rope, skipping ropes; also spelled with a hyphen. A **skipping rope** is a rope, usually with a handle at each end, that is used for skipping. N COUNT

skirmish /skɜːmɪʃ/, **skirmishes, skirmishing, skirmished.** A **skirmish** is 1 a minor battle which is usually short and is not part of a planned war strategy. EG *There had been a bitter skirmish in the half light of dawn... He was shot in a skirmish with a loyalist Army unit.* N COUNT ⇑ fight ▸ used as a verb. EG *The expedition spent two years crossing deserts and skirmishing with tribesmen.* ▸ V ⇑ fight 2 a short, sharp argument, often one of many that take place before agreement is finally reached. EG *Her eyes shone when she described the early skirmishes in the campaign for equality for women... This is just a preliminary skirmish. The meeting will warm up later.* N COUNT ⇑ disagreement = brush ▸ used as a verb. EG *The headmaster and teachers skirmished for a term over the question of corporal punishment... Political skirmishing was resumed after the vacation.* ▸ V ⇑ argue

skirt /skɜːt/, **skirts, skirting, skirted.** 1 A **skirt** is a piece of clothing worn by women and girls, which fastens at the waist and hangs down from the waist to above or below the knees. EG *She was dressed in a very short skirt.* N COUNT ⇑ garment

2 The **skirt** of a dress or coat is the part which hangs below the waist. EG *She danced about, making the skirt of her dress flare out... There always seemed to be a child clutching at her skirts.* N COUNT, SING=PL

3 A **skirt** is also a cover which is put onto a machine in order to prevent accidents when the machine is working. EG *...a radiation-proof lead skirt covered the moving parts.* N COUNT = guard

4 Something that **skirts** an area is situated around the edge or the outside of it. EG *A flagged path skirted the house... ...a new road skirting the northern suburbs.* V+O ⇑ pass = border

5 If you **skirt** something, you go around the edge or V+O, OR V+A

the outside of it. EG *As I walked through the lobby, I had to skirt a group of ladies... They skirted round a bus.* [*(round/around)* ⇑ pass]

6 If you **skirt** a subject or question, you avoid dealing with it, usually because it is difficult or controversial. EG *He was skirting the issue. 'Get to the point!' I said.* [V+O, OR V+A *(round/around)* ⇑ bypass]

7 Skirt is an offensive term used by some men to refer to a woman when they are thinking of her in a sexual way. [N UNCOUNT]

skirting /skɜːtɪŋ/, **skirtings**. A **skirting** or a **skirting board** is a narrow length of wood which goes along the bottom of a wall in a room and makes a border between the walls and the floor; used in British English. EG *Gaps between floorboards and skirting should be filled.* [N COUNT/UNCOUNT]

skit /skɪt/, **skits**. A **skit** is a short performance in which actors make fun of people, events, types of literature, etc by imitating them. EG *Shaw wrote it as a skit on her real character.* [N COUNT = sketch]

skitter /skɪtə/, **skitters, skittering, skittered**. To **skitter** means to move about very lightly and quickly; used especially of insects and small animals. EG *The canary skittered about... Colourful leaves skittered around on the pavement... A small white dog came skittering out of the bushes.* [V+A]

skittish /skɪtɪʃ/. **1** Someone who is **skittish** is lively and does not concentrate for a long time on anything or take life very seriously. EG *I was too skittish to study it closely... Profits remain so low that skittish investors are cancelling their plans.* [ADJ QUALIT]

2 An animal that is **skittish** is very excitable and easily frightened. EG *...a skittish filly.* [ADJ QUALIT]

skittle /skɪtəl/, **skittles**. **1** A **skittle** is a wooden bottle-shaped object that is used as a target in the game of skittles. [N COUNT = pin]

2 Skittles is a game in which players try to knock over as many skittles as they can out of a group of nine by throwing a ball at them. EG *They play skittles and ten-pin bowling.* [N UNCOUNT]

skive /skaɪv/, **skives, skiving, skived**. If you **skive**, you avoid doing work that you should be doing, especially by staying away from the place where you should be working; an informal word used in British English. EG *Were you skiving or were you really ill?... You got out of the washing up again, you skiving devil!* [V: USU+A *(off)*]

skulduggery /skʌldʌgəri¹/ is behaviour in which someone acts secretly in a dishonest way in order to achieve their aim; an old-fashioned word. EG *Living in Washington he became accustomed to intrigue and political skulduggery.* [N UNCOUNT ⇑ trickery]

skulk /skʌlk/, **skulks, skulking, skulked**. If you **skulk** somewhere, you sit or move about there in such a way that you seem to be trying to avoid being seen. EG *There were half a dozen foxes skulking in the undergrowth... They were skulking in a corner.* [V+A: USU CONT ⇑ hide = lurk]

skull /skʌl/, **skulls**. **1** Your **skull** is the bony casing of your head which encloses your brain. EG *Leakey discovered the skull of a woman who lived a million years ago... He had two broken ribs and a fractured skull.* [N COUNT]

2 The word **skull** is used informally, sometimes in an offensive way, to refer to someone's brain and their ability to understand something. EG *Can't you get it into that thick skull of yours?* [N COUNT: USU WITH POSS ⇑ head = mind]

skull and crossbones /skʌl ənd⁰ krɒsbəʊns/. A **skull and crossbones** is a picture of a human skull above a pair of crossed bones, used to indicate death or danger. It used to be found on the flags flown on pirate ships and is now sometimes found as a warning on bottles of poison. [N COUNT]

skullcap /skʌlkæp/, **skullcaps**. A **skullcap** is a close-fitting cap worn on the top of the head by some people, for example by Catholic priests and Jewish men. [N COUNT]

skunk /skʌŋk/, **skunks**. **1** A **skunk** is a small black and white animal which gives off an unpleasant smell if it is frightened or attacked. [N COUNT ⇑ mammal]

2 Skunk is an offensive name used by someone for a person that they think is unpleasant or unfair. EG *That was a rotten thing to do, you skunk!* [N COUNT/VOC]

sky /skaɪ/, **skies**. **1** The **sky** is the space around the earth which you can see when you stand outside and look upwards, and where you can see the sun, the moon, and the stars. EG *There were little white clouds high in the blue sky... It'll warm up as soon as the sun gets higher in the sky... There seemed to be only hills, grass, and sky... We drove under a gloomy sky... The night skies of London flare with rockets.* [N SING: *the*+N, OR N COUNT+SUPP = firmament, heavens]

2 If you **praise** someone **to the skies**, you praise them very strongly and extravagantly. ● **pie in the sky**: see **pie**. [PHR: VB INFLECTS = laud]

sky-blue. Something that is **sky-blue** is very pale blue in colour. EG *...sky-blue uniforms.* [ADJ COLOUR]

skydiver /skaɪdaɪvə/, **skydivers**. A **skydiver** is someone who does skydiving. [N COUNT]

skydiving /skaɪdaɪvɪŋ/ is the sport of jumping out of an aeroplane and falling freely through the air for a period of time before opening your parachute. [N UNCOUNT ⇑ parachute jumping]

sky-high. **1** Prices, wages, etc that reach **sky-high** reach a very high level. EG *Land value has gone sky-high.* [ADV, OR ADJ CLASSIF]

2 A structure that is **sky-high** reaches very high up in the air. EG *...towering trees eight feet wide and sky-high.* [ADJ CLASSIF, OR ADV]

3 If you **blow** something **sky-high**, you destroy it completely. EG *His argument has just been blown sky-high.* [PHR: VB INFLECTS]

skylark /skaɪlɑːk/, **skylarks**. A **skylark** is a small brown bird that has a pleasant song, which it usually sings while it is hovering high above the ground. [N COUNT = lark]

skylight /skaɪlaɪt/, **skylights**. A **skylight** is a window that has been built into a roof in order to let in light. EG *They converted the attic into a bedroom and put in a skylight.* [N COUNT]

skyline /skaɪlaɪn/, **skylines**. The **skyline** is the line where the sky and the earth meet, especially in a city where you can see the shape of buildings against the sky. EG *...the impressive Manhattan skyline... ...a church silhouetted against the skyline.* [N COUNT: *the*+N OR N+SUPP ⇑ horizon]

skyscraper /skaɪskreɪpə/, **skyscrapers**. A **skyscraper** is a very tall building with lots of storeys, usually in a city. EG *The view was blocked by new skyscrapers.* [N COUNT]

skyward /skaɪwəd/. If you look **skyward** or **skywards**, you look up in the direction of the sky; a literary word. EG *He had a habit of looking skyward each time he made a pronouncement.* [ADV AFTER VB ⇑ up]

slab /slæb/, **slabs**. A **slab** of material such as stone, wood, or meat is a thick, flat piece of it which is usually square or rectangular in shape. EG *...a great rough slab 20 feet high and 50 feet long... Their toilet is no more than a hole in a concrete slab with an earthen pit underneath.* [N COUNT OR N PART]

slack /slæk/, **slacker, slackest; slacks, slacking, slacked**. **1** Something that is **slack** is loose and not firmly stretched or tightly in position. EG *...a slack soft rope... ...his slack and wrinkled skin... His grimacing face began to go slack.* [ADJ QUALIT ≠ taut]

2 A **slack** period of business is one in which there is not much work being done or activity taking place. EG *Very few hotels offered work for the slack season.* [ADJ QUALIT ≠ busy]

3 If you are **slack** in work that you do, you do not take enough care in making sure that it is done properly. EG *Security's got a bit slack.* ◊ **slackly**. EG *The theory was inadequately researched and slackly argued.* ◊ **slackness**. EG *She was dismissed for slackness in her duties as secretary.* [ADJ QUALIT ⇑ careless; ◊ ADV WITH VB; ◊ N UNCOUNT = negligence]

4 If you **slack** at your work, you do not take enough care in making sure that it is done properly. EG *The instructors were slacking on the job.* [V: IF+PREP THEN *at/on*]

5 Slacks are trousers, especially casual ones; a rather old-fashioned use. EG *I put on a pair of golfing slacks and a blazer.* [N PLURAL: ALSO *a pair of*+N]

6 The **slack** in a rope, thread, or wire is a part of it that hangs loose. [N UNCOUNT]

7 Slack is a period of inactivity or recession in an industry. EG *There's a certain amount of slack in the car industry at the moment.* [N UNCOUNT]

8 take up the slack. **8.1** If you **take up the slack** in a rope, you pull it so that it becomes tight. EG *As soon as the slack in the rope was taken up the boat heeled hard to the left.* [PHR: VB INFLECTS ⇑ tighten] **8.2** To **take up the slack** in an industry means to regulate it so that activity and production increases. EG *...increasing construction to take up slack in a depressed private building industry.* [PHR: VB INFLECTS]

slacken /slækən/, **slackens, slackening, slackened**. **1** If something **slackens** or you **slacken** it, or if it **slackens off**, it becomes slower, less active, or less intense. EG *Simon allowed his pace to slacken... The rain began to slacken... Mrs Kaul did not slacken in her efforts to get her daughter a job... The Depression slackened off and prosperity was return-* [V-ERG, OR PHRASAL VB: V+ADV = slow down] *ing... There has been a slackening of the arms race recently.*

2 If a tight grip or hold **slackens** or if you **slacken** it, it becomes looser. EG *The grip on Casson's right wrist did not slacken... Slacken your legs and slowly lie back.* V-ERG = loosen

slacker /slækə/, **slackers**. A **slacker** is someone who is lazy and does much less work than they should; an informal word. N COUNT: ALSO VOC ⇑ idler

slag /slæg/, **slags, slagging, slagged**. 1 **Slag** is the waste material which is left when ore has been melted down to remove the metal. EG *Black tides of lava lie spilt over the ground like slag from a furnace.* N UNCOUNT

2 A **slag** is a very offensive term for a woman whose appearance and behaviour are considered to be very unacceptable, especially one who is thought to be very immoral in her sexual behaviour. N COUNT: ALSO VOC

slag off. If you **slag** someone **off**, you criticize them in an unpleasant way; an informal expression. EG *Mark's always slagging off his friends behind their backs.* PHRASAL VB: V+O+ADV

slag heap, slag heaps; also spelled as one word. A **slag heap** is a hill made of slag. Slag heaps are usually found near mines. N COUNT

slain /sleɪn/ is the past participle of **slay**.

slake /sleɪk/, **slakes, slaking, slaked**. 1 If you **slake** your thirst, you drink something which takes your thirst away. EG *We returned to the barn and slaked our thirst with tea.* V+O ⇑ satisfy = quench

2 To **slake** lime means to add water to it and so change it chemically. EG *...slaked lime.* V+O

slalom /slɑːləm/, **slaloms**. A **slalom** is a race, on skis or in canoes, in which the competitors have to avoid a series of obstacles in a very twisting, difficult course. N COUNT

slam /slæm/, **slams, slamming, slammed**. 1 If you **slam** a door or window or if it **slams**, you shut it noisily and with great force. EG *She went out, slamming the door behind her... Out in the street a car door slammed... The commissionaire opened the taxi door and slammed it shut after me.* V-ERG, OR V-ERG +*shut/to* = bang

2 A **slam** is the act of slamming a door or the sound of a door being slammed. EG *Our conversation was terminated by the slam of her car door... The door shut with a loud slam.* N SING WITH DET = bang

3 If you **slam** something down or into a particular position, you put it there quickly and with great force. EG *He slammed the money on the table... I was so annoyed I just slammed the phone down... He slammed on his brakes.* V+O+A, OR V+A

4 If someone **slams** a person, action, proposal, etc, they criticize the person or thing very severely; used especially in newspapers. EG *The new proposals have been slammed by all the opposition parties.* V+O = slate

slammer /slæmə/. The **slammer** is prison; an informal word. EG *I was thrown in the slammer.* N SING: *the*+N

slander /slɑːndə/, **slanders, slandering, slandered**. 1 A **slander** is an untrue spoken statement about someone which is intended to damage their reputation. EG *The article is a slander on ordinary working people.* N COUNT = smear

2 **Slander** is the act of making slanders about someone, especially as an offence for which you can be tried in a court of law. EG *I'll sue her for slander.* N UNCOUNT ⇑ defamation

3 If someone **slanders** you, they make untrue spoken statements about you with the intention of damaging your reputation. EG *She slandered him behind his back.* V+O = malign

slanderous /slɑːndəᵒrəs/. A spoken statement that is **slanderous** is untrue and intended to damage the reputation of the person that it refers to. EG *This is a slanderous misrepresentation of our policy... ...slanderous allegations.* ADJ QUALIT = scurrilous

slang /slæŋ/ consists of words, expressions, and meanings that are informal and are used by people who know each other very well or who have the same job or the same interests. Slang is not considered suitable for formal social situations or serious writing. EG *Their conversation was full of slang... ...the Dictionary of American Slang... ...military slang.* ▸ used as an adjective. EG *'Porridge' is a slang term for 'prison'.* N UNCOUNT ⇑ language; ▸ ADJ CLASSIF: ATTRIB

slanging match /slæŋɪŋ mætʃ/, **slanging matches**. A **slanging match** is an angry quarrel in which people attack each other with rude and insulting remarks; used in British English. EG *We had a full-scale slanging match.* N COUNT = row

slangy /slæŋiˡ/, **slangier, slangiest**. **Slangy** speech or writing has a lot of slang in it. EG *I found it hard to understand the slangy colloquial passages in the book.* ADJ QUALIT ⇑ informal

slant /slɑːnt/, **slants, slanting, slanted**. 1 If something **slants**, it lies along a line that is neither horizontal nor vertical. EG *The old wooden floor slanted a little... Her handwriting tends to slant from right to left... Rain slanted sharply in the chill grey morning.* ◇ **slanting**. EG *...a slanting roof... The lunar module begins a slanting descent to the moon's surface.* V: NO IMPER = slope; ◇ ADJ CLASSIF: ATTRIB = sloping

2 A **slant** is a slanting line or position. EG *At the back of the house, the floors have a noticeable slant... The title is written at a slant on the cover... For some reason the shelf was set on a slant.* N SING WITH DET

3 If someone **slants** news, information, etc, they present it in a way that shows favour towards a particular group or opinion. EG *No matter how he slanted the facts, he could not convince us that there had been no cover-up.* ◇ **slanted**. EG *I thought the programme was rather slanted.* V+O = angle, weight; ◇ ADJ QUALIT = biased

4 A **slant** on a subject is a way of thinking about it or presenting it that shows favour towards a particular group or opinion. EG *These two papers give a completely different slant on the events of the last week... I was furious at the slant that had been put on the evidence... ...a leftist political slant.* N SING WITH DET +SUPP

slap /slæp/, **slaps, slapping, slapped**. 1 If you **slap** someone, you hit them with the palm of your hand. EG *He slapped her across the face.* ▸ used as a noun. EG *Give him a slap if he is too much of a pest.* V+O = smack; ▸ N COUNT = clout

2 If you **slap** someone on the back, you hit them in a friendly manner on their back. EG *I slapped him on the back.* ▸ used as a noun. EG *I was nearly knocked down by a hefty slap on the back.* V+O = clap; ▸ N COUNT

3 If something that someone does is **a slap in the face**, it upsets and shocks you because it shows that they do not support you, respect you, or wish to be helped by you. EG *Their refusal was like a slap in the face.* PHR: USED AS O/C = rebuff

4 A **slap on the wrist** is a warning or punishment that is not very severe. EG *The warning amounted to little more than a slap on the wrist.* PHR: USED AS O/C = ticking-off

5 If you **slap** something onto a surface, you put it or spread it there quickly or carelessly. EG *We slapped some paint on the wall to brighten up the room... All you have to do is slap a bit of Sellotape horizontally across it.* V+O+A = plaster

6 If you **slap** something down, you bring it forcefully down onto a surface, making a noise like the sound of a slap. EG *He slapped the report down on the table... They were vigorously slapping and pounding wet clothes on the stone floor.* V+O+A *(down/on)*

7 If you walk or drive **slap** into someone or something, you walk or drive into them suddenly and with great force. EG *We rounded the corner and drove slap into a parked car.* ADV+PREP: AFTER VB ⇑ straight = smack

8 If something is **slap** in a particular place, it is in exactly that place; usually used showing disapproval. EG *A hotel had been built slap in the middle of the beach.* ADV+PREP: AFTER VB ⇑ right = bang

slap around. If you **slap** someone **around**, you hit them a few times. EG *I'll just slap him around a little.* PHRASAL VB: V+O+ADV

slap-bang; used mainly in spoken English. 1 If you walk or drive **slap-bang** into someone or something, you walk or drive into them suddenly and with great force. ADV+PREP = smack

2 If something is **slap-bang** in a particular place, it is in exactly that place. ADV+PREP: AFTER VB

slapdash /slæpdæʃ/. Something that is **slapdash** is done quickly and carelessly, without much thinking or planning. EG *My cooking is rather slapdash.* ADJ QUALIT = haphazard

slapstick /slæpstɪk/ is a simple type of comedy in which the actors make people laugh by behaving in a rough and foolish way, falling over a lot, etc. EG *It was quite funny, but there was a bit too much slapstick... ...slapstick comedy.* N UNCOUNT: USU BEFORE N

slap-up. A **slap-up** meal is a large enjoyable meal, especially one that costs a lot of money at a restaurant; used in informal English. ADJ CLASSIF: ATTRIB ⇑ extravagant

slash /slæʃ/, **slashes, slashing, slashed**. 1 If you **slash** something, you make a long, deep cut in it with something sharp like a knife or a piece of glass. EG *Jack's face had been slashed with broken glass... I* V+O *just don't understand people who slash seats on buses.*

2 To **slash** at something means to swing at it with a quick cutting movement. EG *Jo slashed at the ball and missed it... ...children slashing at each other with plastic swords.* V : IF+PREP THEN *at* = swipe

3 A **slash** is a mark or line in a colour which shows very strongly against its background. EG *The bonfire left a thick slash of black soot on the washing.* N COUNT = splodge

4 To **slash** something such as an amount of money or time means to reduce it by a large amount. EG *...a plan to slash taxes... Sixty per cent has been slashed from the average time needed.* V+O = cut

5 In spoken English, **slash** is used to refer to a diagonal line that separates letters, words or numbers, in a number like 340/21/K. EG *Three four zero, slash two one, slash K.* N COUNT/UNCOUNT = stroke

6 To **go for a slash** means to go to the toilet in order to urinate; a very informal expression, usually used by men. PHR : VB INFLECTS

slat /slæt/, **slats**. A **slat** is one of the flat narrow pieces of wood, metal, or plastic set in things like Venetian blinds or cupboard doors. N COUNT : USU PL ⇑ strip

slate /sleɪt/, **slates, slating, slated**. **1 Slate** is a dark grey rock that can be easily split into thin layers, and that is often used for covering roofs. EG *In the mid-nineteenth century slate was exploited commercially... ...a slate quarry.* N UNCOUNT

2 A **slate** is **2.1** one of the small flat pieces of slate that are used for covering roofs. EG *The roofs are covered with the beautiful stone slates of the district... ...a yellow brick house with a peaked slate roof.* N COUNT **2.2** a small piece of slate in a wooden frame, used for writing on by schoolchildren in former times. N COUNT

3 If critics, reviews, newspapers, etc **slate** something such as a play, film, or book, they criticize it severely and say that it is very bad; used in British English. EG *The critics slated it, but it has turned into one of the most successful films of the year.* V+O

4 If something **is slated** to happen, it is planned to happen at a particular time; used in American English. EG *The first killing is slated for October 16th... Mr Miller is slated to become chairman next month.* V+O+*to*-INF, OR V+O+A *(for)* : USU PASS = scheduled

5 If you want to **start with a clean slate**, you want other people to forget about your previous mistakes, debts, or failures and allow you to make a fresh start in life. EG *He's trying to start again with a clean slate after two years in jail.* PHR : VB INFLECTS

6 If you **wipe the slate clean**, you decide that your previous mistakes, debts, or failures no longer matter and that you are going to make a fresh start. PHR : VB INFLECTS

7 If something is put **on the slate**, it is bought on credit; used in British English. PHR : USED AS AN A

slatted /slætɪ²d/. Something that is **slatted** is made with slats. EG *...white slatted Venetian blinds... ...slatted cupboard doors.* ADJ CLASSIF

slattern /slætə⁵n/, **slatterns**. A **slattern** is a dirty untidy woman; an old-fashioned word. N COUNT = slut

slatternly /slætə⁵nli¹/. A **slatternly** woman is dirty and untidy. EG *...slatternly Mrs Coggs next door.* ADJ QUALIT = slovenly

slaughter /slɔːtə/, **slaughters, slaughtering, slaughtered**. **1** To **slaughter** a large number of people means to kill them in a way that is cruel, unjust, or unnecessary. EG *Opponents of the regime were systematically slaughtered... On the Western Front, men were being uselessly slaughtered in hundreds of thousands.* V+O = butcher, massacre

2 Slaughter is the cruel, unjust, or unnecessary killing of large numbers of people. EG *Wholesale slaughter was carried out in the name of progress... ...the needless annual slaughter on our roads.* N UNCOUNT = carnage

3 To **slaughter** animals such as cows and sheep means to kill them for their meat. EG *...a freshly slaughtered bullock.* V+O = butcher

4 Slaughter is also the killing of farm animals for their meat. EG *...animals going away to slaughter.* N UNCOUNT

5 If you **slaughter** someone, you defeat them in a game very easily and very thoroughly; an informal use. EG *We were slaughtered.* V+O = thrash

slaughterhouse /slɔːtəhaʊs/, **slaughterhouses**. A **slaughterhouse** is a place where animals are killed for their meat. N COUNT = abattoir

Slav /slɑːv/, **Slavs**. A **Slav** is a member of any of the peoples of Eastern Europe who speak a Slavonic language. EG *He had something of the Slav temperament.* N COUNT

slave /sleɪv/, **slaves, slaving, slaved**. **1** A **slave** is **1.1** a person who belongs to someone else as their property and has to work for them. EG *...a story about a slave who escapes and becomes a free man... ...a slave ship... You will have to work like a slave if you take that job.* N COUNT ⇑ servant **1.2** a person who is completely under the control of another person or of a powerful feeling or influence. EG *He's just become a slave to possessions and money.... You are the slave of guilt feelings.... We have to make the technology work for us, and not become its slaves.* N COUNT+SUPP : IF+PREP THEN *of/to* = prisoner

2 If someone **slaves**, they work hard and continuously, especially for the benefit of someone else. EG *They just sit idly by while you slave over a hot stove... Why am I slaving away, running a house and family single-handed?* V : IF+PREP THEN *away* = slog

slave driver, slave drivers; also spelled with a hyphen. A **slave driver** is someone who makes their employees or students work very hard; used in informal English. N COUNT = taskmaster

slave labour; also spelled **slave labor** in American English. **Slave labour** refers to **1** slaves or very badly-paid people who are used for doing very hard, unpleasant work. EG *The pyramids were mostly built by slave labour... These are volunteer workers–they're not slave labour.* N UNCOUNT **2** work done by slaves or by people who have to work very hard for little money. EG *I'm not working there any more–it's just slave labour.* N UNCOUNT

slaver /slævə/, **slavers, slavering, slavered**. To **slaver** means to let saliva drip from the mouth; used especially of animals. EG *Slavering at the mouth, the dogs rushed at me.* V = drool

slavery /sleɪvə⁰ri¹/ is **1** the system by which people can be owned by other people as slaves. EG *He campaigned for the abolition of slavery.* N UNCOUNT **2** the condition of belonging to someone else as their slave. EG *All those who were captured were sold into slavery.* N UNCOUNT = bondage **3** the state of not being free because you have to work very hard or because you are strongly influenced by something. EG *I had at last been freed from the slavery of a 9 to 5 job... ...his slavery to ambition.* N UNCOUNT+SUPP

slave trade. The **slave trade** is the buying and selling of slaves; used especially to refer to the transportation of Black Africans to America and the Caribbean from the 16th to the 19th centuries. N SING : *the*+N

slavish /sleɪvɪʃ/. **1** A **slavish** copy or imitation is one that copies or imitates something exactly, without any attempt to be original; used showing disapproval. EG *Traditionalism does not necessarily mean a slavish adherence to things of the past... It's just a slavish remake of Hitchcock's 1942 classic.* ADJ QUALIT ⇑ imitative ◊ **slavishly**. EG *I don't expect you to slavishly copy this.* ◊ ADV WITH VB

2 Someone who is **slavish** is like a slave, for example in showing complete obedience to someone else; used showing disapproval. ADJ QUALIT = servile

Slavonic /sləvɒnɪk/. Something that is **Slavonic** **1** relates to the group of languages, including Polish, Czech, and Russian, which are spoken in Eastern Europe. ADJ CLASSIF **2** relates to the people who speak these languages. EG *He had broad, Slavonic cheekbones.* ADJ CLASSIF

slay /sleɪ/, **slays, slaying, slew, slain**. **1** If someone **slays** someone else, they kill them in a violent way; a formal or literary word. EG *...a painting entitled 'Saint George slaying the Dragon'... Two visitors were brutally slain yesterday.* V+O

2 If you say that something **slays** you, you mean that you find it very amusing; used in fairly old-fashioned, informal English. EG *You slay me, you really do.* V+O = kill

sleazy /sliːzi¹/, **sleazier, sleaziest**. A place that is **sleazy** looks dirty and badly cared for, and does not look like a place where respectable people would go. EG *Her studio was in a sleazy attic... ...a sleazy cafe.* ADJ QUALIT = squalid

sled /slɛd/, **sleds, sledding, sledded**. **1** A **sled** is the same as a sledge; used in American English. N COUNT

2 To **sled** means the same as to sledge; used in American English. EG *We went sledding.* V

sledge /slɛdʒ/, **sledges, sledging, sledged**. **1** A **sledge** is a vehicle designed for travelling on snow, either for sport and pleasure or as a form of transport. It consists of a framework that is fixed onto two N COUNT = sled long narrow pieces of wood or metal which slide over the snow.

2 If you **sledge**, you ride on a sledge, especially as a sport or amusement. EG *After it had stopped snowing, we all went sledging.* V = sled

3 A **sledge** is also a sledge-hammer; an informal use. N COUNT

sledgehammer /slɛdʒhæmə/, **sledgehammers**; also spelled with a hyphen. A **sledgehammer** is a large heavy hammer with a long handle, used for smashing concrete. N COUNT

sleek /sliːk/, **sleeker, sleekest**. 1 Hair or fur that is **sleek** is smooth, shiny, and healthy-looking. EG *...her sleek black hair.* ADJ QUALIT = glossy

2 Someone who is **sleek** has a very stylish and prosperous appearance; usually used showing disapproval. EG *They were all too fat and sleek and too pleased with themselves.* ADJ QUALIT

3 Something such as a vehicle that is **sleek** has a smooth, graceful shape. EG *...sleek, black limousines... The sleek ship slid from the harbour.* ADJ QUALIT ⇑ elegant

sleep /sliːp/, **sleeps, sleeping, slept**. 1 **Sleep** is the natural state of rest in which your eyes are closed and your mind and body are inactive and unconscious, usually for several hours every night. EG *I haven't been getting enough sleep recently... She fell into a dreamless sleep... Suddenly the girl gave a cry in her sleep.... Now go to sleep and stop worrying about it... I soon went back to sleep... I brought him a hot drink, hoping it would send him to sleep.* N UNCOUNT

2 If you cannot **get to sleep**, you are unable to sleep, especially because there is too much noise or because you are worried or excited. EG *Could you turn that radio down–I'm trying to get to sleep... I didn't get to sleep until six in the morning.* PHR : VB INFLECTS

3 A **sleep** is a period of sleeping. EG *You'll feel better if you have a little sleep... He hadn't had a proper night's sleep for a month.* N SING : a+N

4 When you **sleep**, you rest in a state of sleep. EG *She slept till ten in the morning... The baby slept peacefully in her lap... I slept all day... He was so excited he could hardly sleep.* ◊ **sleeping**. EG *I glanced down at the sleeping figure.* V; ◊ ADJ CLASSIF : ATTRIB

5 If you say that a house, caravan, etc **sleeps** a particular number of people, you mean that it has beds or sleeping space for that number. EG *...a holiday cottage that sleeps six.* V+O (NUM) : NO CONT/PASS ⇑ accommodate

6 **Sleep** is also the substance that you sometimes get in the corners of your eyes after you have been sleeping; used in informal English. EG *Our eyes were clogged with sleep.* N UNCOUNT

7 If you are trying to make a decision and you say you will **sleep on it**, you mean that you will delay making a decision about it until the following day, in order to give yourself more time to think. EG *I think I'll sleep on it.* PHR : VB INFLECTS

8 If you **lose sleep over** something, you worry about it a lot. EG *Don't lose any sleep over it... He says he's been losing sleep over the project.* PHR : VB INFLECTS, USU WITH BROAD NEG

9 If an animal, especially a sick or injured animal, is **put to sleep**, it is painlessly killed, usually by an injection. EG *Sheba had to be put to sleep.* PHR : VB INFLECTS = put down

10 If your foot or some other part of your body **goes to sleep**, it becomes numb and you cannot feel it. EG *His foot had gone to sleep.* PHR : VB INFLECTS

11 See also **sleeping**.

sleep around. If someone **sleeps around**, they have sex with several different people rather than having a sexual relationship with only one person; an informal expression used showing disapproval. EG *I did everything I could to hurt her, including sleeping around.* PHRASAL VB : V+ADV = be promiscuous

sleep in. If you **sleep in**, you stay asleep in the morning for longer than you usually do; used in British English. EG *We usually sleep in for a bit on Sundays.* PHRASAL VB : V+ADV

sleep off. If you **sleep** something **off**, especially the effects of eating or drinking too much, you recover from it by sleeping. EG *He's sleeping off his hangover... We went back to our room to sleep it off.* PHRASAL VB : V+O+ADV

sleep out. If you **sleep out**, you sleep outdoors. EG *It's getting a bit cold to sleep out.* PHRASAL VB : V+ADV

sleep through. If you **sleep through** a noise or disturbance, you fail to wake up in spite of it. EG *The alarm clock went off, but I just slept through it.* PHRASAL VB : V+PREP, HAS PASS

sleep together. If two people **sleep together**, they have a sexual relationship, but are not usually married to each other. EG *Do you think they're sleeping together?* PHRASAL VB : V+ADV

sleep with. If you **sleep with** someone, you have sex with them, especially when you are not married to them. EG *I heard all the gossip about who was sleeping with whom.* PHRASAL VB : V+PREP, HAS PASS

sleeper /sliːpə/, **sleepers**. A **sleeper** is 1 someone who has the habit of sleeping in a particular way. EG *I'm a light sleeper... She was a late sleeper and hated getting up before 10.* 2 someone who is asleep. EG *Modern studies of sleepers reveal that we are actively dreaming most of the night.* 3 a bed on a train, usually in its own compartment, in which a passenger can sleep during an overnight journey. EG *I booked a first-class sleeper.* 4 a train whose carriages are equipped with beds for passengers on overnight journeys. EG *I usually go up to London on the sleeper.* 5 one of the large heavy beams, usually of wood or concrete, that supports the rails of a railway track; used in British English. N COUNT : ADJ+N; N COUNT; N COUNT ⇑ berth; N COUNT; N COUNT

sleeping /sliːpɪŋ/. **Sleeping** is used to describe something which is concerned with where people will sleep. EG *The sleeping accommodation is somewhat primitive... Let's sort out the sleeping arrangements.* ● See also **sleep**. ADJ CLASSIF : ATTRIB

sleeping bag, sleeping bags; also spelled with a hyphen. A **sleeping bag** is a large deep bag with a warm lining, used for sleeping in, especially when you are camping. N COUNT

sleeping car, sleeping cars. A **sleeping car** is a railway carriage that provides beds for passengers to sleep in. N COUNT

sleeping partner, sleeping partners. A **sleeping partner** is a person who provides some of the capital for a business but who does not take an active part in managing the business; used in British English. N COUNT

sleeping pill, sleeping pills. A **sleeping pill** or a **sleeping tablet** is a pill that you can take to help you sleep. N COUNT

sleepless /sliːplɪ²s/. 1 A **sleepless** night is one during which you do not sleep. EG *He'd had a sleepless night... I had to sit by his bed and keep a sleepless vigil until the morning came.* ADJ QUALIT

2 Someone who is **sleepless** is unable to get to sleep. EG *Late in the night, sleepless and troubled, he got up and went for a walk.* ◊ **sleeplessness**. EG *I began to suffer from sleeplessness.* ADJ QUALIT = restless; ◊ N UNCOUNT = insomnia

sleepwalk /sliːpwɔːk/, **sleepwalks, sleepwalking, sleepwalked**. If someone **is sleepwalking**, they are walking around while they are asleep. EG *She must have been sleepwalking.* V : USU CONT

sleepwalker /sliːpwɔːkə/, **sleepwalkers**. A **sleepwalker** is someone who walks around while they are asleep. N COUNT = somnambulist

sleepy /sliːpi¹/, **sleepier, sleepiest**. 1 If you are **sleepy**, you are very tired and ready to go to sleep. EG *I am so sleepy I can hardly keep my eyes open... She suddenly started to feel very sleepy... ...a sleepy yawn.* ◊ **sleepily**. EG *'Where have you been?' Rudolph asked sleepily.* ADJ QUALIT = drowsy; ◊ ADV WITH VB

2 A **sleepy** place is one which is quiet and where there is not much activity or excitement. EG *It was one of those sleepy rural towns in the southwest of the country.* ADJ QUALIT : ATTRIB ≠ bustling

sleepyhead /sliːpi¹hɛd/, **sleepyheads**. If you call someone, especially a child, a **sleepyhead**, you mean that they look sleepy or are not paying attention. EG *Wake up you sleepyheads!* N COUNT : ALSO VOC

sleet /sliːt/, **sleets, sleeting, sleeted**. **Sleet** is rain that is partly frozen as it falls. EG *An icy sleet was beginning to fall... It was a wild night, with sleet threatening to turn to snow.* ▸ used as a verb. EG *Look, it's sleeting outside.* N UNCOUNT; ▸ V : it+V

sleeve /sliːv/, **sleeves**. 1 The **sleeves** of a coat, shirt, or other piece of clothing are the parts that cover your arms. EG *He took a handkerchief from his sleeve and wiped his nose... His father had his sleeves rolled up and was working with great care.* ● See also **shirt-sleeves**. N COUNT

2 A **sleeve** is 2.1 a tube that completely surrounds something such as a machine part; a technical use. 2.2 the stiff envelope in which you keep a gramophone record. EG *...the photograph of the conductor on the record sleeve.* N COUNT; N COUNT = cover

3 The word **sleeve** is also used in the following informal expressions. 3.1 If you **have** something **up** PHR : VB

your **sleeve**, you have an idea or plan in your mind which you have not told anyone about and which you intend to use later. EG *She thought the old man had some clever trick up his sleeve.* INFLECTS **3.2** If you **are laughing up** your **sleeve**, you are secretly amused because you know that you have an advantage that other people do not know about. EG *She must have been laughing up her sleeve all the time.* PHR : VB INFLECTS **3.3** If someone **wears** their **heart on** their **sleeve**, they behave in a way that makes their feelings obvious, especially when they are in love with someone. PHR : VB INFLECTS

sleeveless /sliːvlɪ²s/. A **sleeveless** dress, jacket, etc has no sleeves. EG *Denise was dressed in a light-blue sleeveless dress.* ADJ CLASSIF : USU ATTRIB

sleigh /sleɪ/, **sleighs**. A **sleigh** is the same as a sledge. N COUNT

sleight of hand /sleɪt əv hænd/. **1** If someone does something by **sleight of hand**, they do it using quick skilful movements of their hands which other people cannot see. Someone might use **sleight of hand** if they are stealing something or performing a trick. EG *He switched the watches by sleight of hand.* N UNCOUNT ⇑ movement

2 Sleight of hand is also a skilful piece of deception. EG *With a little statistical sleight of hand we could make things look all right.* N UNCOUNT : USU MOD+N = manipulation

slender /slendə/. **1** A **slender** person is attractively thin and graceful; used showing approval. EG *She was slender and had long dark hair.* ▸ used of part of someone's body. EG *...his long, slender, sensitive hands... ...the tall girl's slender waist.* ADJ QUALIT = slim

2 If something is **slender**, it is hardly enough to enable you to achieve what you want. EG *With such slender resources they cannot hope to achieve their aims... There were now slender prospects of promotion... That is the case, however slender, for nationalization.* ADJ QUALIT = poor

slept /slept/ is the past tense and past participle of **sleep**.

sleuth /sluːθ/, **sleuths**. A **sleuth** is a detective; an old-fashioned informal word, often used humorously. N COUNT

slew /slj⁰uː/, **slews, slewing, slewed**. **1** If a vehicle **slews**, it slides or skids. EG *A double-decker bus slewed across the road.* V : USU+A = veer

2 Slew is the past tense of **slay**.

slewed /slj⁰uːd/. If someone is **slewed**, they are drunk; an informal word. EG *I was somewhat slewed by this time.* ADJ QUALIT : PRED

slice /slaɪs/, **slices, slicing, sliced**. **1** A **slice** is a piece of food that has been cut from a larger piece. A slice of bread is a flat piece of bread cut from a loaf. EG *She cut him three large slices of bread... ...slices of cold chicken pie.* N COUNT OR N PART ⇑ portion

2 If you **slice** a piece of food or **slice it up**, you cut it into thin pieces of the same size. EG *I saw her slicing an apple.* V+O, OR V+O+A *(+up)*

3 A **slice** of something is a part of it. EG *Rents provided a large slice of his income... These groups form only a relatively small slice of the total population... They conquered a sizeable slice of territory.* N PART = proportion

4 If you **slice** a ball in tennis or golf, you hit the edge of the ball rather than the centre, so that it travels at an angle away from your racket or club. EG *He sliced a drive to Gower.* ▸ used as a noun. *...a slice through the slips.* V+O ▸ N COUNT ⇑ stroke

5 If something **slices** air, water, etc, or **slices** through it, it cuts through it like a knife; a literary use. EG *They sliced the air with their knives... The shark's fin sliced through the water.* V+O, OR V+A *(through)* = carve

6 See also **fish slice**.

sliced /slaɪst/. A **sliced** loaf is a loaf of bread that has been cut into slices before being wrapped up and sold. EG *I'll have a sliced white loaf... ...sliced bread.* ADJ CLASSIF : USU ATTRIB

● If you describe someone or something as **the best thing since sliced bread**, you mean that you approve of them very strongly; an informal expression. EG *She thinks he's the best thing since sliced bread.* ● PHR : USED AS C ⇑ excellent

slick /slɪk/, **slicker, slickest; slicks, slicking, slicked**. **1** If you describe something such as a book or film as **slick**, you mean that it is well-made and attractive, but has little artistic quality or intellectual honesty; used showing disapproval. EG *Some people thought the broadcasts too slick.* ◊ **slickness**. EG *The slickness of the programmes became tedious.* ADJ QUALIT = glib, superficial ◊ N UNCOUNT

2 You describe an action as **slick** when it is done with speed and smoothness and without any obvious effort. EG *...a relay race round London, with slick baton-changing.* ADJ QUALIT

3 A **slick** person speaks easily and persuasively without being sincere; used showing disapproval. EG *...one of those slick salesmen.* ▸ used of behaviour. EG *...a slick, evasive answer.* ADJ QUALIT = glib

4 A **slick** is the same as an **oil slick**. N COUNT

slick down. If you **slick down** your hair, you make it smooth and shiny by putting water or hair oil on it. PHRASAL VB : V+O+ADV

slide /slaɪd/, **slides, sliding, slid**. **1** When something **slides** or when you **slide** it, it moves smoothly over or against something else. EG *Susan stared at the drops sliding down the glass... The gate slid open at the push of a button... She slid the key into the keyhole.* V-ERG : USU+A = slip

2 If someone **slides** somewhere, they move there smoothly and quietly. EG *I had seen him sliding quietly out of his caravan... An elderly lady slid into the seat.* ▸ used of vehicles. EG *The black Mercedes slid away.* V : USU+A = slip ▸ = glide

3 If you **slide** into a particular attitude or kind of behaviour, you change to it so gradually and smoothly that people do not notice the change. EG *He could slide smoothly into whichever mood suited the client.* V+A = slip

4 If currencies or prices **slide**, they gradually change to a worse state or condition. EG *The pound is sliding... With prices sliding fast, small computers are becoming popular.* ▸ used as a noun. EG *...a slow but steady slide.* V = fall ▸ N SING WITH DET

5 If you **let** something **slide**, you allow it to change to a worse state or condition by not attending to it. EG *I've just let things slide, I'm afraid.* PHR : VB INFLECTS

6 A **slide** is **6.1** a small piece of photographic film with a frame around it which can be projected on to a screen so that you can see the picture. EG *...colour slides showing rice fields in Bangkok... ...a slide show.* N COUNT = transparency **6.2** a structure, often found in playgrounds, that has a steep slope for children to slide down. EG *There were a few slides and climbing frames.* N COUNT **6.3** an area of ice, for example on a path or a pavement, that children enjoy sliding on in winter. N COUNT **6.4** a small piece of glass on which you put something such as a sample of blood so that you can examine it through a microscope; a technical use. N COUNT **6.5** a **hair slide**; used in British English. EG *She wore glasses and a slide in her hair.* N COUNT

slide rule, slide rules; also spelled with a hyphen. A **slide rule** is an instrument that you use for calculating numbers. It looks like a ruler and has a middle part which you slide backwards and forwards. EG *You've got to learn to use a slide rule.* N COUNT

sliding scale, sliding scales. A **sliding scale** is a system for calculating something such as wages or taxes, in which the amounts paid vary because other things vary; a technical term. N COUNT

slight /slaɪt/, **slighter, slightest; slights, slighting, slighted**. **1** Something that is **slight** is very small in degree or quantity. EG *He had a slight German accent... 'Not at the moment,' she said after a slight hesitation... The differences between us are really quite slight... He'd had a slight stroke... The slightest noise startled him... I haven't the slightest idea what you're talking about.* ◊ **slightly**. EG *White wine should be slightly chilled... I hope you can see slightly more clearly what is going on... Her husband was slightly shorter than she was... 'Do you know him?'–'Slightly.'* ● **in the slightest** is used to intensify a negative statement. EG *My tennis hadn't improved in the slightest... Your father's not suffering in the slightest... 'Do you mind?'–'Not in the slightest.'* ADJ QUALIT : USU ATTRIB ≠ considerable, significant ◊ ADV = a bit ● PHR : WITH BROAD NEG, USED AS AN A = at all

2 A **slight** person has a slim and delicate body. EG *...a lean, slight, young teenage girl... He is slight and dark.* ▸ used of a person's body. EG *I watched her slight figure cross the street.* ◊ **slightly**. EG *Graham is rather slightly built.* ADJ QUALIT ▸ = slim ◊ ADV WITH VB

3 If you describe a book, piece of music, etc as **slight**, you mean that it is not important, especially when compared to other works by the same person. EG *In my opinion this is a very slight book indeed.* ADJ QUALIT = insignificant

4 If you **slight** someone, you insult them by ignoring them or by treating them as if they were unimportant. EG *He had a chronic fear of being slighted... He'll live to rue the day he slighted Maria Fox.* ▸ used as a noun. EG *She takes offence at certain kinds of slight... It was a slight on a past award-winner, Stevenson.* ◊ **slighted**. EG *Mrs Pringle will feel slighted.* ◊ **slighting**. EG *The speech was full of slighting remarks about the Labour Party.* V+O = snub ▸ N COUNT : IF+PREP THEN *on* ◊ ADJ QUALIT ◊ ADJ QUALIT

◊ **slightingly**. EG *Christine had referred slightingly to him at breakfast.* ◊ ADV WITH VB

slim /slɪm/, **slims, slimming, slimmed; slimmer, slimmest**. **1** A **slim** person has an attractively thin and well-shaped body; used showing approval. EG *...a tall, slim girl with long, straight hair... Regular exercise will make you slimmer.* ▸ used of a part of someone's body. EG *Her waist was slim.* ◊ **slimness**. EG *She envied her cousin's slimness, youth and glamour.* ADJ QUALIT = slender ◊ N UNCOUNT

2 If you **slim**, you deliberately make yourself thinner and lighter by dieting or by taking exercise. EG *I may be slimming but I've no intentions of starving myself.* ◊ **slimming**. EG *I mean to take slimming a little more seriously... ...slimming magazines.* V = diet ◊ N UNCOUNT

3 You describe an object as **slim** when it is thinner than usual. EG *She took a slim book out of her pocket... ...his slim lizard-skin wallet.* ADJ QUALIT

4 If the chance of something happening is **slim** or if people's expectations of it happening are **slim**, it is unlikely to happen. EG *The chance of American intervention is slim... You have little political support and even slimmer expectations of political survival.* ADJ QUALIT ⇑ small = faint

slime /slaɪm/ is **1** any thick, slippery substance which covers a surface and which looks or smells unpleasant. EG *There was a green slime around the edges of the tub.* **2** a thick, sticky substance which comes from the bodies of snails, fish, and other creatures. EG *Their skin produces a slime that helps to keep it moist... ...a trail of slime.* N UNCOUNT = ooze; N UNCOUNT

slimmer /slɪmə/, **slimmers**. A **slimmer** is someone who is trying to lose weight by dieting and exercising. EG *...clubs for slimmers.* N COUNT

slimy /slaɪmi¹/, **slimier, slimiest**. **1** Something that is **slimy** is covered in slime. EG *They breed near stagnant water, such as a slimy pond... ...the slimy green walls of the piers... ...crawling, slimy creatures.* ADJ QUALIT

2 People are described as **slimy** when they are friendly towards people who they do not really like, and flatter them; used showing disapproval. EG *...a slimy politician... You slimy bastard.* ADJ QUALIT = oily

sling /slɪŋ/, **slings, slinging, slung**. **1** If you **sling** something somewhere, you throw it carelessly and with a lot of force. EG *She slung the book across the room... They slung a whole lot of crates aboard.* V+O+A = fling

2 If you **sling** something over your shoulder or over your back, you hang it there loosely so that you can carry it. EG *He handed the bag to Boylan, who slung it over his shoulder... ...men with bows and arrows slung on their backs.* V+O+A

3 If you **sling** something over a hook, over the back of a chair, etc, you put it over it quickly and carelessly. EG *His few bits of clothing were slung over a string on the wall.* V+O+A ⇑ hang = fling

4 If you **sling** something such as a rope between two points, you attach it to them so that it hangs loosely between them. EG *...two tall piers and, slung between them, a catwalk... Pieces of meat were hanging to dry over a rope slung on the wall.* V+O+A : USU PASS = suspend

5 If someone **slings** their **hook**, they leave a place suddenly; an informal expression. EG *I reckon he'll sling his hook... Go on, sling your hook.* PHR : VB INFLECTS = scarper

6 A **sling** is **6.1** a device made of ropes or straps that is used for lifting and carrying heavy loads. EG *Food was flown up in a sling load and dropped into the village.* **6.2** a piece of cloth which you hang from your neck in order to support a broken or injured arm. EG *His arm was in a sling.* **6.3** a device in which you carry a baby on your back or across the front of your body. EG *Mothers carry their babies around with them in slings.* N COUNT; N COUNT; N COUNT

7 Slings and arrows are unpleasant things that happen to you and that are not your fault; a literary expression. EG *In every profession there are slings and arrows to contend with... Hunger is the worst of all the many slings and arrows suffered by the poor inhabitants.* PHR = tribulations

slink /slɪŋk/, **slinks, slinking, slunk**. If you **slink** somewhere, you move there in a slow and secretive way because you do not want to be seen, for example because you are ashamed of something that you have done. EG *I slunk away to my room, to brood in front of the fire... I thought you'd come slinking back.* V+A = sneak

slinky /slɪŋki¹/, **slinkier, slinkiest**. **Slinky** clothes fit closely to a woman's body in a way that makes her sexually attractive. EG *She browbeat her parents into letting her wear a slinky dress.* ADJ QUALIT = clinging

slip /slɪp/, **slips, slipping, slipped**. **1** If you **slip**, you accidentally slide and lose your balance when you are walking or running. EG *I slipped on the snow and sprained my ankle.* ▸ used as a noun. EG *A slip on the ice can cause a nasty injury.* V = slither ▸ N SING WITH DET

2 If something **slips**, it slides out of place or out of your hands in a way that you do not intend. EG *It slipped from his fingers and fell with a bump... The knife slipped and I cut my hand... She pulled up her sock which had slipped down.* V : USU+A

3 If you **slip** somewhere, you go there quickly, usually without being noticed. EG *I hope we can slip away before she notices... She's just slipped out for a packet of fags.* V+A = sneak

4 If you **slip** something somewhere, you put it there quickly in a way that does not attract attention. EG *I saw him slip a note into her hand... He slipped it quickly into his pocket.* V+O+A = slide

5 If you **slip** something to someone, you give it to them secretly. EG *She slipped him a ten dollar bill.* V+O+O

6 If someone **slips** into a particular state or activity, they change to it in a way that is hardly noticed. EG *Grandma had slipped into a coma... Take care not to slip back into your bad habits.* V+A = slide

7 If something **slips** to a lower level or standard, it falls to that level or standard. EG *Industrial production has slipped by 12 per cent in a year.* V : USU+A = drop

8 If something **slips** your **memory** or **slips** your **mind**, you forget about it or forget to do it. EG *I'm sorry–it just slipped my memory... It must have slipped his mind.* PHR : VB INFLECTS

9 If you **let** something **slip**, you say it without intending to, especially when you had wanted to keep it a secret. EG *He carelessly let slip this information in conversation with a journalist... She let slip that she was looking for another job.* PHR : *let* INFLECTS ⇑ disclose = let out

10 If you **slip into** clothes or **slip** them **on**, you put them on quickly or easily. If you **slip out of** clothes or **slip** them **off**, you take them off quickly or easily. EG *I slipped into my pyjamas... He slipped on his shoes and went out... She slips out of her working clothes... She slipped off her dress.* V+A *(into/out of)*, OR V+O+A *(off/on)*

11 If you **give** someone **the slip**, you succeed in escaping from them; an informal expression. EG *I tried to follow her but she gave me the slip.* PHR : VB INFLECTS = elude

12 A **slip** is **12.1** a mistake, especially a small or unimportant one. EG *I must have made a slip somewhere.* ● See also **Freudian slip**. **12.2** a small piece of paper, for example one that records the details of a payment in a bank or shop. EG *It is used as a payment slip and a receipt... He handed me a slip of paper.* N COUNT = slip-up; N COUNT

13 A **slip** is also a piece of clothing without sleeves that a woman wears under her dress. EG *She was wearing a black nylon slip with a lace top.* ● See also **gym-slip**. N COUNT = petticoat

slip up. If you **slip up**, you make a mistake. EG *We must have slipped up somewhere.* ● See also **slip-up**. PHRASAL VB : V+ADV

slipcover /slɪpkʌvə/, **slipcovers**. A **slipcover** is a cloth cover for a chair or sofa which can easily be removed; used in American English. N COUNT

slipknot /slɪpnɒt/, **slipknots**. A **slipknot** is a knot that slips along the string or rope around which it is tied, so that you can tighten a loop in the string or rope. N COUNT

slip-on shoes or clothes have no laces or buttons and so can be be put on or taken off easily. ADJ CLASSIF : ATTRIB

slipover, slipovers. A **slipover** is a pullover without sleeves. N COUNT

slipped disc, slipped discs. A **slipped disc** is a painful condition in which one of the discs that connect the bones in your spine has moved out of its proper position. EG *I've got a slipped disc.* N COUNT : USU SING

slipper /slɪpə/, **slippers**. **Slippers** are loose soft shoes that you wear in the house. EG *...a pair of slippers.* N COUNT : USU PL, ALSO *a pair of*+N IN PL

slippery /slɪpəºri¹/. **1** Something that is **slippery** is smooth, wet, or greasy and therefore difficult for you to keep hold of or walk on without sliding. EG *The soap was smooth and slippery... ...a slippery pavement.* ADJ QUALIT

2 Someone who is **slippery** behaves in a cleverly ADJ QUALIT dishonest way and cannot be trusted. EG *He's rather a slippery character.*

3 If you say that someone is **on the slippery slope** or is going **down the slippery slope**, you mean that they are involved in a course of action that cannot be stopped and that will lead eventually to failure or serious trouble. EG *The economy is steadily sliding down the slippery slope.* PHR : USED AS AN A

slippy /slɪpi¹/. A **slippy** surface is smooth, wet, or greasy and therefore difficult for you to walk on without sliding; used in informal spoken English. EG *Be careful. It's a bit slippy.* ADJ QUALIT = slippery

slip road, slip roads. A **slip road** is a road which cars use to drive onto or off a motorway; used in British English. N COUNT

slipshod /slɪpʃɒd/. Something that is **slipshod** is done without care or thoroughness. EG *...a slipshod and inaccurate piece of research... ...slipshod spelling.* ADJ QUALIT ⇑ careless = sloppy

slipstream /slɪpstri:m/. The **slipstream** of a fast-moving object, especially a car or plane, is the flow of air directly behind it. EG *Police on motorcycles were riding in the slipstream of the official cars.* N SING WITH DET ⇑ current

slip-up /slɪpʌp, slɪpʌp/, **slip-ups**. A **slip-up** is a mistake, especially one that is small or unimportant; an informal expression. N COUNT

slipway /slɪpweɪ/, **slipways**. A **slipway** is a large platform that slopes down into the water, on which ships are built or repaired and from which they are launched. EG *The ship was already beginning to move down the slipway.* N COUNT

slit /slɪt/, **slits, slitting**. The form **slit** is used in the present tense and is the past tense and past participle of the verb. **1** If you **slit** something, you make a long narrow cut in it. EG *She got her paper-knife and slit the envelope... He slit open the packet with his thumb nail... She wore a black skirt slit at one side.* V+O, OR V+O+A *(open)*

2 A **slit** is **2.1** a long narrow cut. EG *We make a tiny slit in one side of it with a razor blade.* N COUNT **2.2** a long narrow opening in something. EG *...neon light came through the slits in the blind... Her eyes narrowed to slits.* N COUNT

3 If you **slit** your eyes, you make them nearly closed so that you can only just see. EG *Dolly slit her pale eyes at us.* V+O ⇑ narrow

4 Slit eyes are nearly closed so that you can only just see. EG *I opened slit eyes.* ADJ CLASSIF : ATTRIB

slither /slɪðə/, **slithers, slithering, slithered**. **1** If you **slither**, you slide in an uneven way. EG *We slithered down the steep slope to Itford Farm... There was no sound except our feet slithering among the roots.* V : USU+A ▸ used as a noun. EG *The air was filled with the slither and stomp of infant feet.* ▸ N COUNT : USU SING

2 If something **slithers**, it moves along in a twisting way, like a snake. EG *I saw Diggity about to pounce on a huge snake slithering under my bed.* V : USU+A ⇑ slide

slithery /slɪðəri¹/. Something that is **slithery** is slippery and moves in a twisting way, like a snake. EG *...a bucketful of wet, slithery eels.* ADJ QUALIT = undulating

sliver /slɪvə/, **slivers**. A **sliver** of something is a small thin piece of it. EG *...a sliver of soap... He picked slivers of glass out of his hand.* N COUNT/PART = fragment

slob /slɒb/, **slobs**. A **slob** is someone who is very lazy and untidy. EG *You're a slob.* N COUNT

slobber /slɒbə/, **slobbers, slobbering, slobbered**. If someone **slobbers**, they let liquid fall from their mouth, like babies do. EG *Sally was happily slobbering in her pram.* V = dribble

slobber over. If you **slobber over** something or someone, you keep saying that you are very fond of them in a way that is considered excessive and too sentimental. EG *Did you come here to slobber over me?* PHRASAL VB : V+PREP, HAS PASS = drool over

slobbery /slɒbəri¹/. A **slobbery** mouth, kiss, etc is very wet. ADJ QUALIT

sloe /sləʊ/, **sloes**. A **sloe** is a small sour fruit that has a dark purple skin. EG *Sloes make marvellous fruit wine.* N COUNT

slog /slɒg/, **slogs, slogging, slogged**; an informal word. **1** If you **slog** at something or if you **slog** your **way** through it, you work hard and steadily at it. EG *The children are slogging away at revision... Each night she has to slog through long lists of spelling.* V+A, OR PHR+A : VB INFLECTS = plough

2 If you **slog** somewhere, you make a long and difficult journey there, especially on foot. EG *Many of the early settlers had slogged their way to the west over this pass.* V = trek

3 A **slog** is **3.1** a difficult piece of work which needs a lot of effort. EG *It's a hard slog.* N SING WITH DET **3.2** a long and difficult walk somewhere. EG *...his long slog home.* N SING WITH DET

4 If two people **slog it out**, they fight each other by punching each other hard, like boxers. EG *We left them to slog it out.* PHR : VB INFLECTS

slogan /sləʊgə⁰n/, **slogans**. A **slogan** is a short, easily-remembered phrase which is used in advertising and by political parties and other groups who want people to remember what they are saying or selling. EG *I read with horror the racist slogans scratched on walls throughout the city... E F Schumacher coined the slogan 'small is beautiful'.* N COUNT

sloop /slu:p/, **sloops**. A **sloop** is a small sailing ship with one mast. N COUNT ⇑ boat

slop /slɒp/, **slops, slopping, slopped**. **1** If liquid **slops** or if you **slop** it, it spills over the edge of a container in a messy way. EG *We carried the buckets, slopping water, back to the kitchen... She was trying to pour out cups of tea without slopping them too much.* V-ERG : USU+A

2 Liquid waste containing the remains of food, used to feed animals, is called **slop** or **slops**. EG *I gathered the eggs and fed the slop to the pigs.* N UNCOUNT/PLURAL : SING=PL = swill

3 Slop is writing or part of a play or film that is extremely sentimental and romantic; used showing disapproval. N UNCOUNT = slush

slope /sləʊp/, **slopes, sloping, sloped**. **1** A **slope** is **1.1** the side of a mountain, hill, or valley. EG *She rode up a grassy slope... ...a tiny cottage high up on the slopes of the Blue Ridge Mountains.* N COUNT **1.2** a surface that is flat and at an angle so that one end is higher than the other. EG *They were now reaching a little upward slope of the road.* N COUNT : USU SING ⇑ incline ● **the slippery slope**: see **slippery**.

2 If a surface **slopes**, it is at an angle, so that one end is higher than the other. EG *The roof sloped down at the back.* V : USU+A ⇑ slant ◊ **sloping**. EG *...a long pale green room with a sloping ceiling... ...gently sloping hills.* ◊ ADJ CLASSIF ATTRIB

3 If something **slopes**, it leans to the right or to the left rather than standing upright. EG *My handwriting slopes to the left.* V : USU+A ⇑ slant ◊ **sloping**. EG *...long sloping handwriting.* ◊ ADJ CLASSIF ATTRIB

4 The **slope** of something is the angle at which it slopes. EG *The slope increases as you go up the curve... ...a slope of ten degrees.* N COUNT : USU SING = gradient

slope off. If you **slope off**, you go away quickly and quietly, as if you are trying to escape or avoid something; an informal expression, used showing disapproval. EG *I have a feeling that most of them have sloped off.* PHRASAL VB : V+ADV = slink off

sloppy /slɒpi¹/, **sloppier, sloppiest**. Something that is **sloppy** is **1** messy, careless, or muddled; an informal word showing disapproval. EG *...sloppy workmanship.* ADJ QUALIT = slipshod ◊ **sloppily**. EG *...a sloppily run hospital... The dolls were sloppily made.* ◊ ADV ◊ **sloppiness**. EG *I hate sloppiness of thinking.* ◊ N UNCOUNT **2** extremely sentimental and romantic; used showing disapproval. EG *You'll write me sloppy letters... I got very bored with all his sloppy clichés.* ADJ QUALIT = slushy

slosh /slɒʃ/, **sloshes, sloshing, sloshed**. **1** If a liquid **sloshes**, it splashes or moves around messily, especially within a container. EG *The whiskey sloshed over from his glass on to his hand... There was a lot of petrol sloshing around.* V : USU+A = slop

2 If you **slosh** liquid, you drop or pour it carelessly so that it splashes around. EG *They sat out on the decks laughing and sloshing water everywhere.* V+O : USU+A = slop

slosh about. If you **slosh about** or **slosh around**, you move around in a lot of liquid, such as water or mud, so that you cause it to splash; used in informal English. EG *I sloshed around in the tub, adding more hot water every so often... I sloshed about in muddy wellingtons all day.* PHRASAL VB : V+ADV

sloshed /slɒʃt/. Someone who is **sloshed** is drunk; used in informal English. EG *Everyone is totally sloshed.* ADJ QUALIT : USU PRED

slot /slɒt/, **slots, slotting, slotted**. **1** A **slot** is a narrow opening in a machine or container, for example the hole in a public telephone where you put coins in. EG *He put money in the slot and the music started again... The mailman dropped the letters through a slot.* N COUNT ⇑ slit

2 When something **slots** into something or when you **slot** it in, you put it through a narrow opening into a V-ERG+A *(in/into)*

machine or other object. EG *His hands slotted into the back pockets of his jeans... The cylinder just slots into the barrel... I slotted my money in.*

3 A **slot** is also a place in a schedule, scheme, or organization, especially one that is kept for a particular purpose. EG *There should be better TV programmes to fill the time slots just before prime viewing time... Students get only two timetabled slots in the week for private study.* N COUNT

4 If you **slot** someone or something into a schedule, scheme, or organization, you find a place for them within it. EG *I could slot him in on Friday morning.* V-ERG+A *(in/into)* = fit

sloth /sləʊθ/, **sloths.** 1 **Sloth** is laziness, especially with regard to work; a formal word showing disapproval. EG *Mrs Humbert would have to overcome her habitual sloth and write to Miss Phalen's sister.* N UNCOUNT = idleness

2 A **sloth** is an animal from Central and South America. Sloths live in trees, move very slowly, and hang upside down from branches with their long legs. N COUNT

slothful /sləʊθfʊl/. Someone who is **slothful** is lazy and unwilling to make an effort to work; a formal word showing disapproval. EG *...a life of slothful ease.* ADJ QUALIT = indolent

slot machine, slot machines. A **slot machine** is a machine from which you can get food or cigarettes or on which you can gamble. You work it by putting coins into a slot in the machine. N COUNT

slouch /slaʊtʃ/, **slouches, slouching, slouched.** 1 If you **slouch**, you sit or walk in a lazy or tired way with your shoulders and head drooping down. EG *There was a man slouched in one of the armchairs... Many children slouch because of lack of self-confidence... She slouched about in slacks.* ▸ used as a noun. EG *Brad straightened out of his usual slouch.* V ⇑ droop ▸ N SING WITH DET ⇑ droop

2 If you **are no slouch** at a particular activity, you are skilful at it or willing to work hard at it; an informal expression, used showing approval. EG *You're certainly no slouch in the kitchen... I was no slouch when it came to doing the housework.* PHR : VB INFLECTS

slough, sloughs, sloughing, sloughed. The word **slough** is pronounced /slaʊ/ when it is a noun and /slʌf/ when it is a verb. A **slough** of despair, self-pity, etc is a bad emotional state that you find it difficult to get rid of; an old-fashioned use. N SING WITH DET *+of* = well

slough off. 1 If an animal such as a snake **sloughs off** its outer skin, it goes through a natural process which causes this skin to come off. PHRASAL VB : V+O+ADV = shed

2 If you **slough off** something that you no longer need, you get rid of it. EG *Women are less willing than their husbands to slough off a friendship after a move.* PHRASAL VB : V+O+ADV = abandon

slovenly /slʌvənli¹/. Someone who is **slovenly** is careless, untidy, and inefficient in their appearance or behaviour. EG *His appearance was even more slovenly than usual... Try not to speak slovenly English at your interview.* ADJ QUALIT = scruffy, sloppy ≠ neat, smart

slow /sləʊ/, **slower, slowest; slows, slowing, slowed.** 1 Something that is **slow** 1.1 moves along or does something without very much speed. EG *His steps were slow as he went up the path... They played the slow movement superbly... It was a long, slow drive in the taxi.* ◊ **slowly.** EG *Ralph said they were going too slowly... He nodded slowly.* ◊ **slowness.** EG *Helen is touchy about her slowness with the needle.* 1.2 takes a long time, especially more time than is usual or expected. EG *Don't worry if your child is slow to learn to walk... I was slow in reacting to her news... The economy showed a slow but steady growth.* ◊ **slowly.** EG *He slowly began to realize what she meant.* ◊ **slowness.** EG *The slowness of your progress should not discourage you.* ● **slowly but surely**: see **surely**. ADJ QUALIT ≠ fast, speedy ◊ ADV WITH VB ◊ N UNCOUNT ADJ QUALIT = sluggish ≠ fast, quick ◊ ADV WITH VB ◊ N UNCOUNT ≠ speed

2 If something goes **slow**, it goes or moves at a low speed. EG *You're going too slow... How slow would you like me to play?... ...slow-moving traffic... ...a slow-burning fire.* ● to **go slow**: see **go**. ADV = slowly ≠ fast

3 If something **slows** or if you **slow** it, it starts to move or happen more slowly. EG *He slowed to a walk... We slowed our speed to thirty miles an hour... Her breathing had slowed.* V OR V-ERG ⇑ decrease

4 Someone who is **slow** takes a long time to understand something, especially because they are not clever. EG *He may be a bit slow in picking things up.* ● If you say someone is **slow off the mark** or **slow on the uptake**, you mean that they are slow to understand something, for example a joke. EG *You were a bit slow off the mark there.* ADJ QUALIT : PRED+*in/to*-INF ● PHR : USED AS C

5 If you describe an activity or form of entertainment as **slow**, you mean that it is progressing slowly and is not very busy or interesting. EG *Business will be slow in the shop for another hour... Have you found the series slow?* ADJ QUALIT : PRED ≠ brisk, exciting

6 If a clock or watch is **slow**, it shows a time that is earlier than the correct time. EG *The clock's half an hour slow.* ADJ CLASSIF : PRED

7 The **slow** lane on a motorway is the lane designed for vehicles which are moving more slowly than other vehicles. ADJ CLASSIF : ATTRIB

slow down. 1 If something **slows down** or if you **slow** it **down**, it starts to move or happen more slowly. EG *Economic growth has slowed down dramatically... Harold slowed the car down.* PHRASAL VB : V-ERG+ADV

2 If someone **slows down**, they become less active, when they have been working very hard or have been very energetic. EG *He needs to slow down a little or he'll get an ulcer.* PHRASAL VB : V+ADV, OR V+O (REFL)+ADV = relax

3 See also **slowdown.**

slow up. If something **slows up** or if you **slow** it **up**, it starts to move or happen more slowly. EG *The extra weight would have slowed me up considerably... She slowed up a little.* PHRASAL VB : V-ERG+ADV

slowcoach /sləʊkəʊtʃ/, **slowcoaches.** If you call someone a **slowcoach**, you mean that they are moving or doing something too slowly; used in informal British English. N COUNT = slowpoke

slowdown /sləʊdaʊn/, **slowdowns.** A **slowdown** is 1 a reduction in speed or activity. EG *He projects a slowdown in the rate of expansion of world trade.* 2 a protest by workers in which they deliberately work slowly and cause problems for their employers; used in American English. N COUNT N COUNT = go-slow

slow-motion; also spelled as two words. **Slow-motion** is movement which is much slower than normal speed, especially when used in a film or television programme. EG *I dreamt I was falling off a cliff in slow motion... We're using slow-motion to record these subtle changes.* N UNCOUNT

slowpoke /sləʊpəʊk/, **slowpokes.** If you call someone a **slowpoke**, you mean that they are moving or doing something too slowly; used in informal American English. N COUNT = slowcoach

slow-witted. Someone who is **slow-witted** is slow to understand things. ADJ QUALIT ⇑ stupid

slowworm /sləʊwɜːm/, **slowworms.** A **slowworm** is a small lizard with no legs that moves along like a snake. N COUNT

sludge /slʌdʒ/ is 1 thick mud. EG *I was covered in sludge and weeds.* 2 sewage. EG *...a protest about the disposal of sludge at sea.* N UNCOUNT N UNCOUNT

slug /slʌg/, **slugs, slugging, slugged.** 1 A **slug** is 1.1 a small slow-moving creature with a long slimy body, like a snail but without a shell. Slugs are usually found in damp places and are regarded as pests in the garden. 1.2 a large mouthful of drink that you are going to swallow; an informal use. EG *Ken took a long slug of scotch... He poured a slug into both glasses.* 1.3 a bullet; used especially in informal American English. N COUNT ⇑ mollusc N COUNT : ALSO N PART = shot N COUNT

2 If you **slug** someone, you hit them hard with your fist. EG *I raised a fist to slug Eddie.* V+O = sock

3 If two people **slug it out**, they fight each other by punching each other hard, like boxers. EG *They slugged it out in the street.* PHR : VB INFLECTS

sluggish /slʌgɪʃ/. Something that is **sluggish** moves or works at a very slow rate, much slower than normal or than other things of its kind. EG *I feel very sluggish... ...the black sluggish waters of East Canal... ...even the most sluggish of today's computers.* ◊ **sluggishly.** EG *I could feel the blood thumping sluggishly in my temples.* ADJ QUALIT = lethargic ≠ fast ◊ ADV WITH VB

sluice /sluːs/, **sluices, sluicing, sluiced.** 1 A **sluice** is a passage that carries a current of water and has an opening, called a sluice gate, which can be opened and closed to control the flow of water. N COUNT

2 If you **sluice** something, you wash it with a stream of water or some other liquid. EG *We sluiced out the trough... Excellent food should be sluiced down with shrewdly chosen wines.* V+O, OR V+O+A *(down/out)*

slum /slʌm/, **slums, slumming, slummed.** 1 A **slum** is 1.1 an area of a city where living conditions are very bad and where all the houses are overcrowded and need to be repaired. EG *I grew up in a* N COUNT *slum... ...children from a slum area... ...slum-clearance programmes.* 1.2 a room or house which is very untidy and dirty; an informal use. EG *I'm not staying in that slum.* N COUNT : USU SING = tip

2 If you say that you **are slumming** or **slumming it**, you mean that you are spending time in a place or in conditions that are at a much lower social level than is usual for you; used in informal English, often humorously. EG *We're slumming tonight... On Saturday nights they're usually out slumming it in the East End.* V, OR V+O *(it)* : USU CONT = rough it

slumber /slʌmbə/, **slumbers, slumbering, slumbered.** Slumber is sleep; a literary word. EG *She fell into a heavy slumber and slept long and late... Roused from his slumbers, O'Shea departed.* ▸ used as a verb. EG *One old man slumbered over his newspaper... She gazed with affection at his slumbering form.* N UNCOUNT/ COUNT : ALSO SING=PL ▸ V

slummy /slʌmi¹/, **slummier, slummiest.** A **slummy** area of a town is one where the houses are in very bad condition and a large number of poor people live. EG *That part was once very slummy but is now very smart.* ADJ QUALIT = run-down

slump /slʌmp/, **slumps, slumping, slumped.** 1 If something such as demand for a particular product or the price or value of a product **slumps**, it falls suddenly and sharply. EG *Circulation slumped and the magazine closed... Profits last year slumped from $40 million to $26 million.* ▸ used as a noun. EG *...the continuing slump in world oil demand... The slump in commercial vehicle sales is showing no sign of improving.* V ⇑ decline = drop ▸ N COUNT : USU SING, IF+PREP THEN *in* = drop

2 A **slump** is also a time when the activity of a country's industry or economy slows down greatly, causing high unemployment and poverty. EG *The slump set in during the summer of 1921... The slump certainly had some impact on inflation.* N COUNT : USU SING ⇑ decline = depression

3 If you **slump** somewhere, you fall or sink down there heavily, for example because you are very tired or you have fainted. EG *He slumped into his chair... Sarah slumped against the wall... They both slumped back in exhaustion.* ◊ **slumped.** EG *He sat slumped forward... A passer-by noticed me slumped over the wheel and called an ambulance.* V+A ⇑ collapse ◊ ADJ CLASSIF = hunched

slung /slʌŋ/ is the past tense and past participle of **sling.**

slunk /slʌŋk/ is the past tense and past participle of **slink.**

slur /slɜː/, **slurs, slurring, slurred.** 1 A **slur** is an insulting remark or action which is intended to damage the reputation of a person or group. EG *He got angry whenever anyone cast the slightest slur on the regiment... There were complaints of racial slurs and rough manhandling.* N COUNT ⇑ insult

2 If you **slur** your speech or if your speech **slurs**, you pronounce words in a way which is not clear or distinct, often when you have drunk a lot of alcohol. EG *'I'll sing for you,' he said, his voice slurring so that he could barely be understood... ...words that slur into one another.* ◊ **slurred.** EG *His words were slurred and his breath smelled of wine.* V-ERG, OR V+ QUOTE ◊ ADJ QUALIT

3 If you **slur** a number of notes in a piece of music, you play them or sing them smoothly by moving from one note to the next without a break. ◊ **slurred.** EG *Those quavers should be played slurred, not separate.* V+O ◊ ADJ CLASSIF

4 A **slur** in music is a curved line drawn above or below a group of notes to indicate that the notes should be played or sung smoothly without a break. N COUNT ⇑ symbol

slurp /slɜːp/, **slurps, slurping, slurped.** 1 If you **slurp** a liquid, you drink it noisily. EG *He slurped the soup greedily.* V OR V+O

2 A **slurp** is a noise that you make with your mouth when you drink noisily. EG *Gill drank her tea with loud slurps.* N COUNT

slurry /slʌri¹/ is a watery mixture of something such as mud, cement, or clay. EG *It rained–how it rained! The farm turned into slurry.* N UNCOUNT

slush /slʌʃ/ is 1 snow which has begun to melt and is therefore very wet and dirty. EG *You couldn't walk anywhere without getting slush over the top of your boots.* 2 romantic, sentimental love stories which cannot be taken seriously. N UNCOUNT / N UNCOUNT = mush

slushy /slʌʃi¹/, **slushier, slushiest.** 1 Ground that is **slushy** is covered in wet, dirty, melting snow. EG *A thaw had set in and the streets were slushy.* ADJ QUALIT

2 A **slushy** story or idea is so romantic and sentimental that it cannot be taken seriously. EG *I've been put off romance after seeing that slushy film last night.* ADJ QUALIT

slut /slʌt/, **sluts**; a very offensive word. A **slut** is 1 a woman who is dirty and untidy. 2 a woman who is considered to be very immoral in her sexual behaviour. N COUNT / N COUNT = whore

sly /slaɪ/, **slyer, slyest.** The forms **slier** and **sliest** are also used.

1 If you give a **sly** look, gesture, or remark, you show that you know something that other people present might not know. EG *A slow sly smile was creeping around the corners of his mouth... ...making sly remarks about her strange taste in clothes.* ◊ **slyly.** EG *She glanced slyly at Madeleine... 'Must've been reading the papers,' Pam said slyly, digging Marsha in the ribs.* ADJ QUALIT = knowing ◊ ADV WITH VB = knowingly

2 Someone who is **sly** is rather secretive and clever at deceiving people. EG *They are suspicious and wary and sly... ...the slyest trickster of our time.* ◊ **slyly.** EG *He was lurking slyly in the background.* ADJ QUALIT = cunning ◊ ADV WITH VB

3 If someone does something **on the sly**, they do it in a secretive way, often because it is something that they should not be doing; an informal expression. EG *...sitting in the toilets smoking on the sly, just like kids do in school.* PHR : USED AS AN A ⇑ secretly

smack /smæk/, **smacks, smacking, smacked.**

1 If you **smack** someone, you hit them sharply with your hand. A parent, for example, may smack a child who has behaved badly. EG *He smacked her on the bottom.* ▸ used as a noun. EG *He was rude, so I gave him a smack in the face.* V+O = slap ▸ N COUNT = slap

2 If you **smack** something somewhere, you push it, hit it, or throw it there so that it makes a loud, sharp noise as it hits something else. EG *He laughed, smacking the flat of his hand on the steering wheel... The boat took the waves roughly, smacking its wooden prow into each one.* ▸ used as a noun. EG *We heard the hard smack of tennis balls from behind the wall... She gave out the books, dropping them with a satisfying smack on each desk.* V+O+A = slap ▸ N SING WITH DET ⇑ sound

3 If you **smack** a kiss on someone's face, you kiss them noisily. EG *She smacked a kiss on his forehead.* V+O

4 If you **smack** your **lips**, you open and close your mouth noisily in order to express how much you have enjoyed eating some food or how much you are looking forward to eating it. EG *He looked at the plate and smacked his lips... He tasted the wine.'Ah!' he said, smacking his lips.* PHR : VB INFLECTS

5 If something **smacks** of something else, it is slightly similar and it reminds you of it. EG *Any literature other than romantic novels smacked to her of school... Their room had square leather sofas, smacking more of the airport lounge than a middle-class home.* ▸ used as a noun. EG *Their strange morality is portrayed with that smack of truth which comes off the pages of all good novels... Her lightness of touch gave her actions that smack of humour which annoyed her mother.* V+A *(of)* = be reminiscent ▸ N SING WITH DET+*of*

6 Something that is **smack** in a particular place is exactly in that place; an informal use. EG *The office was right smack in the middle of town... I parked smack in front of the building.* ADV+PREP : AFTER VB ⇑ exactly = bang

7 If one thing moves **smack** into or onto another thing, it moves directly into it or onto it with a great deal of force; an informal use. EG *The bus ran smack into a car in St Andrew's Square.* ADV+PREP : AFTER VB = slap

8 A **smack** is also a small fishing boat. N COUNT

9 **Smack** is heroin; used in informal English. N UNCOUNT

10 See also **smacking.**

smacking /smækɪŋ/. Something that moves at a **smacking** pace moves very quickly; an informal word. ADJ QUALIT : ATTRIB = spanking

small /smɔːl/, **smaller, smallest; smalls.** 1 Something or someone that is **small** is not large in physical size compared with other things of the same kind or with other people. EG *She was rather small in stature... ...a number of small sharp teeth... The male is smaller than the female... This is the smallest church in England.* ◊ **smallness.** EG *The smallness of the courtroom exaggerated its height.* ADJ QUALIT ≠ big ◊ N UNCOUNT

2 A **small** group contains only a few people or things or not much of something. EG *...children in small families, with no more than one brother or sister... ...a relatively small number of people... She divided them into smaller groups... ...a small amount of milk.* ADJ QUALIT ≠ large, great

3 A **small** child is young and therefore not very big ADJ QUALIT

physically. EG *She had two small children... I was very small at the time, only about eight.*

4 A **small** action or effect is not very strong and therefore not significant or effective. EG *The cumulative result of such small changes is a massive shift... His words were small comfort... I felt strongly about this, even though my contribution to the discussion was small... Why did he never make the smallest effort to reach my father?* ADJ QUALIT = insignificant ≠ considerable, great

5 If something is given **small** attention, is of **small** importance, etc, it is given very little attention or is of very little importance; a formal use. EG *They paid small attention to the Vatican's offer of mediation... ...a matter of small importance.* ADJ CLASSIF : ATTRIB+N UNCOUNT = scant

6 A **small** task, problem, etc is fairly unimportant and easy to do or deal with. EG *That's a very small problem... He made a lot of small mistakes... ...small jobs, such as mending electrical plugs.* ADJ QUALIT = minor

7 A **small** business or occupation involves doing only a small amount of business or activity, rather than trying to operate on a large scale. EG *...a city of small businesses... He is a small farmer, a very poor farmer, barely making a living.* ADJ CLASSIF : ATTRIB = small-scale

8 A **small** voice is quiet, soft, and not powerful. EG *'He knows us,' she said in a small voice.* ADJ QUALIT

9 **Small** letters are letters that are not written or printed as capitals. For example, 'a' is a small letter but 'A' is a capital. ADJ CLASSIF : ATTRIB

10 The **small of** your **back** is the narrow part of your back where it curves inwards slightly. EG *She had a pain in the small of her back.* PHR WITH DET

11 If you say that something has a particular effect **in** its **small way**, you mean that the effect is only limited or on a small scale. EG *They are good in their small way... This was, in its small way, a crisis... She started business in a small way with her own private nursery at home.* PHR : USED AS AN A

12 If something makes you **feel small** or **look small**, it makes you feel or look ridiculous so that you are ashamed and humiliated. EG *Feeling small and childish, she crossed back over the bridge... She had been made to look very small.* PHR : VB INFLECTS

13 **Smalls** are pieces of personal clothing, usually underwear; used in old-fashioned British English. N PLURAL

14 • **the small hours**: see **hour**. • **small wonder**: see **wonder**.

small ad, small ads. A **small ad** in a newspaper or journal is a short advertisement in which you can advertise something, for example an object for sale, a room to let, or something that you want to buy. EG *The best place to look for accommodation is in the small ads section of your local newspaper.* N COUNT : USU PL

small arms are guns that are light and have a small calibre. EG *They became experts in fighting with small arms.* N PLURAL ⇑ weapons

small change is coins of low value. EG *I need some small change to make a phone call.* N UNCOUNT ⇑ money

small fry is used to refer to people who are considered to be unimportant. EG *Being small fry they had done what they were told... Yu Soong Kwong is small fry compared to Deng.* N UNCOUNT

smallholder /smɔ̲ːlhəʊldə/, **smallholders**. A **smallholder** is someone who has a smallholding. EG *All over Asia smallholders are being pauperized.* N COUNT ⇑ farmer

smallholding /smɔ̲ːlhəʊldɪŋ/, **smallholdings**. A **smallholding** is a piece of land used for farming that is smaller than a small farm. EG *...smallholdings of one acre or less.* N COUNT

smallish /smɔ̲ːlɪʃ/. Something that is **smallish** is fairly small in size or amount. EG *He was a smallish man... I only want a smallish amount.* ADJ QUALIT

small-minded. Someone who is **small-minded** has fixed opinions and is unwilling to change them or to think about more general subjects; used showing disapproval. EG *This is a very small-minded old-fashioned attitude.* ADJ QUALIT = narrow-minded, petty

smallpox /smɔ̲ːlpɒks/ is a serious infectious disease in which a person has a high fever and develops a rash and scabs that leave deep scars on the skin. N UNCOUNT

small-scale. A **small-scale** activity, organization, etc is small in size and has a limited extent. EG *Small-scale confrontations occur almost daily... ...small-scale industry.* ADJ CLASSIF : USU ATTRIB ≠ large-scale

small screen. The **small screen** is television, especially considered in contrast to the cinema. EG *Despite his film successes, he has achieved little on the small screen.* N SING : *the*+N

small talk is light conversation that people make at social occasions about unimportant things. EG *We stood around making small talk.* N UNCOUNT

small-time workers or businesses are not very important, because they operate only on a small scale. EG *...the small-time farmers and traders of the region.* ADJ CLASSIF : ATTRIB ⇑ minor

smarmy /smɑ̲ːmi[1]/, **smarmier, smarmiest**. Someone who is **smarmy** is unpleasantly polite and flattering, usually because they want you to like them; an informal word. EG *...a nasty little man, smarmy and obsequious.* ADJ QUALIT = oily

smart /smɑ̲ːt/, **smarter, smartest; smarts, smarting, smarted**. 1 Someone who is **smart** is 1.1 pleasantly neat and clean in appearance. EG *The boys looked smart in their school uniforms.* ADJ QUALIT = spruce ◊ **smartly**. EG *...a smartly dressed executive... ...her smartly arranged hair.* ◊ ADV WITH VB ◊ **smartness**. EG *He seemed impressed by my smartness.* ◊ N UNCOUNT 1.2 clever and able to understand and judge things quickly; used especially in American English. EG *She's one of the smartest students in the whole school... It wasn't very smart of you to tell him your name.* ▸ used of people's actions and ideas. EG *...a smart idea.* ADJ QUALIT = bright

2 A **smart** place or event is connected with people who are wealthy and fashionable. EG *We met at a very smart lunch party... ...the smart areas of town, where the diplomatic corps have their houses.* ADJ QUALIT = chic

3 A **smart** movement or action is sharp and quick; a fairly literary use. EG *I heard the smart crack of a whip... ...walking along at a smart pace.* ADJ QUALIT : ATTRIB ◊ **smartly**. EG *Grabbing the empty lemonade bottle, she hit him smartly on the head... Elaine noticed how smartly Helen leapt to his defence.* ◊ ADV WITH VB

4 If a part of your body or a wound **smarts**, you feel a sharp stinging pain in it. EG *His eyes smarted from the smoke of the fire.* V = sting

5 If you **smart** from something that has happened, you feel upset about it, for example because someone has been unkind to you or criticized you. EG *Brody smarted under Quint's derision... She was smarting from a guilty conscience.* V : IF+PREP THEN *from/under* ⇑ suffer

smarten /smɑ̲ːtə[0]n/, **smartens, smartening, smartened**. If you **smarten** yourself, or if you **smarten** yourself or a place **up**, you make yourself or the place look neater and tidier. EG *I'll just smarten up a bit, then we can go... He had attempted to smarten himself... The New Electric Cinema has been smartened up.* V+O (REFL), OR V+O (NG/REFL) +A *(up)* ⇑ improve = spruce up

smash /smæʃ/, **smashes, smashing, smashed**. 1 If you **smash** something, you hit it, throw it, or drop it so that it breaks into many pieces and makes a loud sound like breaking glass. EG *Smash the bottles with a hammer... Some windows have been smashed... When I heard about that I nearly smashed the TV set... The ornament was smashed to pieces.* V+O

2 If something **smashes**, it falls and hits the ground, breaking into many pieces and making a loud sound. EG *A plate dropped from his fingers and smashed on the kitchen floor.* ▸ used as a noun. EG *There was a smash of breaking china.* V : NO CONT, NO IMPER = shatter ▸ N SING WITH DET

3 If you **smash** through something such as a wall or **smash** your way through it, you move forwards by hitting it and breaking it. EG *The police smashed their way into eleven homes... They smashed through the plate-glass wall.* V+A, OR V+O+A ⇑ burst

4 If something **smashes** or **is smashed** against something solid, it moves very fast and with great force against it. EG *The waves smashed onto the shore... The sea smashed the boat against the rocks.* V+A, OR V-ERG+A = pound

5 If people **smash** something such as a political system or a person's career, they deliberately ruin it. EG *We are interested in transforming the system rather than smashing it... Smash the capitalist state!* V+O ⇑ destroy

6 A comedy, musical play, or other piece of entertainment that is a **smash** or a **smash hit** is very successful and popular with the public. EG *The show was a smash hit in London and New York... It looks like being the comedy smash of the season.* N COUNT : USU SING ⇑ success

7 A **smash** is also 7.1 a car crash. EG *She had a serious motor smash on the way to Scotland.* N COUNT 7.2 a way of hitting the ball in tennis, in which you bring the racquet over your head from behind and hit the ball forwards and downwards very hard. EG *Her overhead smash went out of the court.* N COUNT : USU SING ⇑ stroke

8 If someone **smashes** your **head in** or **smashes** your PHR : VB

face in, they hit you hard on the head or face so that you are very badly hurt; an informal expression used in British English, mainly in making threats. EG *If you don't let me go, my mates will smash your head in.* INFLECTS ⇑ attack

9 • See also **smashed, smashing.**

smash down. If you **smash down** something such as a door, you hit it and break it so that it falls onto the ground. EG *King Kong lurched around smashing down skyscrapers... I'm going to smash this door down if you don't come out!* PHRASAL VB : V+O+ADV = knock down

smash up. If you **smash** something **up**, you hit it so that it breaks into many pieces and is completely destroyed. EG *He started smashing up all the furniture... They smashed the place up... Six students smashed up a car.* • See also **smash-up.** PHRASAL VB : V+O+ADV

smash-and-grab. A **smash-and-grab** robbery is a quick way of stealing from a shop, in which a person smashes the shop window, seizes the things that are on display there, and rushes away with them. EG *...smash-and-grab raids at jewellers' shops.* ADJ CLASSIF : ATTRIB

smashed /smæʃt/. **1** Someone who is **smashed** is extremely drunk or under the influence of drugs such as hashish; an informal use. EG *I spent that evening smashed out of my mind.* ADJ QUALIT : PRED = stoned

2 A **smashed** object is one that has been broken into many pieces. EG *The floor was covered with smashed machinery.* ADJ CLASSIF = wrecked

smasher /smæʃə/, **smashers.** If you refer to someone as a **smasher**, you mean that you find them very pleasant or attractive; an informal word. EG *She's a real smasher.* N COUNT = cracker

smashing /smæʃɪŋ/. If you say that something is **smashing**, you mean that you like it very much; an informal word. EG *We had a smashing time... We had smashing food in Paris.* ADJ QUALIT = terrific

smash-up, smash-ups. A **smash-up** is a bad car crash; an informal word. EG *We saw a terrible smash-up on the way home.* N COUNT = pile-up

smattering /smætəʳrɪŋ/. A **smattering** of something such as knowledge or information is a very small amount of it. EG *Jane spoke English, Spanish, and a smattering of Greek.* N PART : SING = modicum

smear /smɪə/, **smears, smearing, smeared. 1** A **smear** is a dirty or greasy mark that has been left on something when a person or thing has rubbed against it. EG *There were still lipstick smears on her chin... ...a smear of blue paint.* N COUNT = smudge

2 If something **smears** something else, it leaves a dirty or greasy mark by rubbing against it. EG *Soot smeared our faces... The plate glass windows were all smeared... Her pasty face was smeared with orange make-up.* V+O = streak

3 If you **smear** a surface with a greasy or sticky substance or **smear** the substance onto the surface, you spread a layer of the substance over the surface, without being very careful how you do it. EG *Smear the baking tin all around the inside with butter... My lipstick was smeared around my mouth... ...thick slices of bread, smeared with butter.* V+O+A ⇑ coat

4 If you **smear** someone or something, you try to damage their reputation by starting unpleasant rumours about them and telling people things that are not true. EG *...their zeal to smear all opponents as traitors or subversives.* V+O = malign

5 A **smear** is also an unpleasant and untrue rumour or accusation that is intended to damage the reputation of someone or something. EG *Party leaders denounced the allegation as a right-wing smear... These are simply smear tactics.* N COUNT ⇑ defamation

6 A **smear** or a **smear test** is a medical test in which a very small amount of the coating of a woman's cervix is removed and analysed to see if any cancer cells are present. N COUNT

smear campaign, smear campaigns. A **smear campaign** is an attempt made by a group of people over a period of time to damage the reputation of someone or something by starting unpleasant rumours and telling untrue stories about them. N COUNT ⇑ defamation

smell /smel/, **smells, smelling, smelled, smelt.** The forms **smelled** and **smelt** are both used as the past participle and past tense of the verb.

1 The **smell** of something is the effect it has on your nose. If you do not say what kind of smell it is, you usually mean it is unpleasant. EG *What's that smell?... Antonio unlocked the door. The smell was revolting... ...the smell of fresh bread... The air had a sweet smell... ...cooking smells.* N COUNT = odour

2 If something **smells**, it has an effect on your nose. You usually mean it is unpleasant, unless you say something else about it. EG *The fridge is beginning to smell... The room smelled of cigars... The papers smelt musty and stale... He smelt like a distillery... Dinner sure smells good.* • to **smell to high heaven**: see **heaven.** V : IF+PREP THEN *like/of*, NO CONT

3 If you **smell** something, **3.1** you become aware of it because of the effect it has on your nose. EG *Don't strike a match if you smell gas... Sharks can smell blood in the water at a distance of many miles... He had a smell I'd never smelt before.* V+O : NO CONT ⇑ notice **3.2** you put your nose near it and breathe in, in order to discover its smell. EG *She picked up the soap and smelled it.* V+O ⇑ test = sniff ▸ used as a noun. EG *Here, have a smell–do you think there's too much garlic?* ▸ N SING WITH DET

4 **Smell** is the physical ability that is related to the nose. EG *He has no sight, no hearing, no touch, no smell, no taste–nothing... They all have an excellent sense of smell.* N UNCOUNT ⇑ sense

5 If you **smell** danger, trouble, etc, you feel instinctively that it is likely to happen or be true. EG *I smell danger... He's shrewd and can smell a successful, well-conceived project.* V+O : NO CONT ⇑ sense = scent • If you **smell a rat**, you become suspicious that there is something wrong with a situation. EG *I accepted with suspicious gratitude. I could smell a rat.* • PHR : VB INFLECTS

6 If someone's behaviour or action **smells** a particular way, it seems to be a sign of an undesirable quality or attitude. EG *Such an action would have smelt, to her, of defeat.* V : IF+PREP THEN *of* = smack

smell out. 1 To **smell** something **out** means to find where something is by following its smell; used especially of animals. EG *We'll take the dog–she'll smell those rabbits out.* PHRASAL VB : V+O+ADV ⇑ track

2 If you **smell** someone **out**, you discover where they are or what they are doing, by making a determined effort. EG *...the usual rhetoric about smelling out the traitor in our midst.* PHRASAL VB : V+O+ADV = root out

-smelling combines with words such as 'sweet' or 'foul' to indicate that something has a particular type of smell. EG *...sweet-smelling roses.* COMB : FORMS ADJ QUALITS

smelling salts are a chemical with a strong smell, kept in a small bottle and held under someone's nose if they faint. Smelling salts are not used very much nowadays. N PLURAL

smelly /smeli¹/, **smellier, smelliest.** Something that is **smelly** has an unpleasant smell. EG *...some rather smelly cheese... ...a smelly room.* ADJ QUALIT

smelt /smelt/, **smelts, smelting, smelted. 1** **Smelt** is the past tense and past participle of **smell.**

2 To **smelt** a substance containing metal means to process it by heating it until it melts, so that the metal is extracted and changed chemically. EG *Fire provided a means of smelting ores.* V+O

smelter /smeltə/, **smelters.** A **smelter** is a furnace used for smelting metal. N COUNT

smile /smaɪl/, **smiles, smiling, smiled. 1** A **smile** is an expression on your face in which the corners of your mouth curve upwards and you sometimes show your teeth. A smile usually shows that you are happy, pleased, or amused, but can sometimes also express other feelings such as bitterness or resignation. EG *Barber welcomed me with a smile... 'How nice to see you.' He gave a smile... ...a mocking, unpleasant smile.* N COUNT = grin

2 When you **smile**, you have a smile on your face. EG *Hooper smiled and leaned back in his chair... The girl was smiling at me... He smiled coldly... She smiled a broad smile.* V OR V+O

3 If you say that you **smile** at something, you mean that you are amused by it, usually without showing that you are amused. EG *She smiled at her nervousness.* V+A *(at)*

4 If you **smile** something, you say it with a smile or express it by a smile. EG *'That remains to be seen,' smiled Mrs Barrett... She smiled her approval.* V+O/QUOTE

5 If someone is **all smiles**, they look very happy, especially when earlier they were worried about something. EG *His reputation was saved. He was all smiles... She bustled about all smiles.* PHR : USED AS C

smile on. If luck, fate, the weather, etc **smiles on** you or **smiles upon** you, you are very fortunate; a formal or literary expression. EG *Fortune has smiled on us today.* PHRASAL VB : V+PREP, HAS PASS = favour

smiling /smaɪlɪŋ/. **1** Someone who is **smiling** has a smile on their face. EG *...thousands of smiling young* ADJ CLASSIF = beaming *people.* ▸ used of a person's face, expression, eyes, etc. EG *...a room of smiling faces.* ▸ ADJ CLASSIF : ATTRIB

2 Smiling is used to describe something which is done with a smile. EG *I was given a smiling demonstration of the way to bath a baby.* ◇ **smilingly.** EG *Smilingly, he assured me that he would keep his promise.* ADJ CLASSIF : ATTRIB ◇ ADV WITH VB

smirk /smɜːk/, **smirks, smirking, smirked.** If you **smirk**, you smile in an unpleasant and superior way, usually because you have gained an advantage over someone else or you know something that they do not know. EG *'That's where you're wrong,' Ellen said smirking.* ▸ used as a noun. EG *Mark detected a smirk on the clerk's face.* V = sneer ▸ N COUNT = sneer

smite /smaɪt/, **smites, smiting, smote, smitten.** If you **smite** something, you hit it hard; an old-fashioned word. EG *He smote the ball over my head... The sun smote their faces.* ● See also **smitten.** V+O

smithereens /smɪðəriːnz/. If something is smashed **to smithereens**, it is smashed into many small pieces so that it is completely destroyed. EG *She dropped the vase and smashed it to smithereens.* PHR : USED AS AN A

smithy /smɪði[1]/, **smithies.** A **smithy** is a place where a blacksmith works. N COUNT = forge

smitten /smɪtə[a]n/. **1** If you are **smitten**, you find someone so attractive that you are or seem to be in love with them. EG *I was smitten with her... I was quite smitten by her luminous green eyes and gold curls.* ADJ QUALIT : PRED, IF+PREP THEN *by/with* = besotted, captivated

2 If you are **smitten** by something, you are very impressed and enthusiastic about it. EG *After his first visit to France he was smitten by the French.* ADJ QUALIT : PRED, IF+PREP THEN *by/with* = captivated

3 Smitten is the past participle of **smite.**

smock /smɒk/, **smocks.** A **smock** is **1** a loose garment, rather like a long blouse, usually worn by women. **2** a loose garment which is worn by artists, doctors, technicians etc to protect their ordinary clothes. N COUNT; N COUNT ⇑ overall

smog /smɒg/, **smogs. Smog** is a mixture of fog and smoke, only found in busy industrial centres. EG *Black smog reduced visibility to about fifty yards.* N MASS

smoke /sməʊk/, **smokes, smoking, smoked. 1 Smoke** consists of the clouds of gas and small bits of solid material that are sent into the air when something is burning. EG *The room was full of smoke... ...cigarette smoke... ...a cloud of smoke.* N UNCOUNT

2 If something **is smoking**, it is sending smoke into the air, especially a large amount of smoke. EG *Down below in the valleys the chimneys were smoking.* ◇ **smoking.** EG *...a smoking fireplace.* V : USU CONT ⇑ emit ◇ ADJ CLASSIF

3 If you **smoke** a cigarette, pipe, etc, you have it in your mouth, sucking the smoke into your mouth and blowing it out again. EG *I hadn't smoked a cigarette in five weeks... He was sitting quietly in his armchair, smoking a pipe... He sat and smoked and stared out of the window.* ▸ used as a noun. EG *I'm dying for a smoke... We went outside to have a smoke.* V OR V+O ▸ N SING : a+N = puff

4 If you **smoke**, you have the habit of smoking cigarettes. EG *Do you smoke?* V

5 A **smoke** is a cigarette; an informal use. EG *He smiled and offered me a smoke.* N COUNT = fag

6 To **smoke** fish or meat means to hang it over burning wood so that the smoke will preserve it and give it a special flavour. ◇ **smoked.** EG *...smoked salmon... ...smoked bacon.* V+O ⇑ treat ◇ ADJ CLASSIF : ATTRIB

7 If something **goes up in smoke, 7.1** it is destroyed by fire. EG *Hundreds of valuable books had gone up in smoke.* **7.2** it fails or ends without anything being achieved. EG *Because of one stupid remark, his whole campaign went up in smoke.* PHR : VB INFLECTS; PHR : VB INFLECTS = come to nothing

8 If you say that **there's no smoke without fire**, you mean that if there are rumours or other signs that something bad is happening, then they must be at least partly true. CONVENTION

9 See also **smoked, smoking.**

smoke out. 1 If you **smoke out** a person or animal, you force the person or animal to come out of a place by filling it with smoke. PHRASAL VB : V+O+ADV

2 If you **smoke out** someone who is hiding, you discover them and make them publicly known. EG *They finally smoked out the group that had been passing secrets to the papers.* PHRASAL VB : V+O+ADV ⇑ expose

smoked /sməʊkt/. **Smoked** glass is glass that has been made darker by being treated with smoke. ● See also **smoke.** ADJ CLASSIF : ATTRIB

smokeless /sməʊklɪ[2]s/. **Smokeless** fuel burns without producing smoke. ADJ CLASSIF : ATTRIB

smokeless zone, smokeless zones. A **smokeless zone** is an area, especially in a big city, in which the burning of any fuel that produces smoke is forbidden by law. N COUNT

smoker /sməʊkə/, **smokers.** A **smoker** is **1** someone who smokes cigarettes or other forms of tobacco. EG *One smoker in 20 will give up the habit permanently... ...a pipe smoker.* **2** a carriage in a train in which passengers are allowed to smoke. N COUNT; N COUNT

smokescreen /sməʊkskriːn/. If something that you do or say is a **smokescreen**, it is intended to hide the truth about your activities or intentions. EG *Working at the embassy was just a smokescreen for his work as a spy.* N SING WITH DET = cover

smokestack /sməʊkstæk/, **smokestacks.** A **smokestack** is a tall chimney that carries smoke away from a factory. N COUNT

smoking /sməʊkɪŋ/. **1 Smoking** is the act or habit of smoking cigarettes or other forms of tobacco. EG *Does smoking cause cancer?... I'm trying to give up smoking... ...a 'No smoking' sign.* N UNCOUNT

2 A **smoking** section, compartment, etc, is intended for people who want to smoke. EG *Do you want to go in the smoking or non-smoking section?* ADJ CLASSIF : ATTRIB

3 See also **smoke.**

smoky /sməʊki[1]/, **smokier, smokiest. 1** A place that is **smoky** has a lot of smoke in the air. EG *...a smoky pub... ...a smoky industrial scene of the 1930's.* ADJ QUALIT

2 A **smoky** fire or chimney sends out a lot of smoke. ADJ QUALIT

3 Smoky food has the taste or smell of smoke. EG *It has a smoky taste... ...smoky bacon crisps.* ADJ QUALIT : ATTRIB

4 Something that is **smoky** looks like smoke, for example because it is a bit bluish or greyish in colour or because it appears cloudy or misty. EG *...a smoky-blue scarf... ...the orange, smoky twilight.* ADJ CLASSIF : ATTRIB = dusty

smolder /sməʊldə/. See **smoulder.**

smooch /smuːtʃ/, **smooches, smooching, smooched;** an informal word. If two people **smooch, 1** they kiss and hold each other closely. EG *He was smooching with her in the car. ...They were smooching on the sofa.* ▸ used as a noun. EG *We had yet another long smooch during the film.* **2** they dance very slowly and closely together with their arms around each other. EG *The room was full of couples smooching around the floor... ...a good record to smooch to.* V OR V+A (*with*) : RECIP ▸ N SING; V OR V+A (*with*) : RECIP

smoochy /smuːtʃi[1]/. A **smoochy** record or piece of music is slow and suitable for people to smooch to; an informal word. EG *Put on a smoochy record.* ADJ QUALIT ⇑ romantic

smooth /smuːð/, **smoother, smoothest; smooths, smoothing, smoothed. 1** A **smooth** surface or object has no roughness, lumps, or holes. EG *Your skin looks so smooth... The boulders were so smooth and slippery I couldn't get a grip.* ▸ used as an adverb. EG *Squeeze the filler into the crack, let it dry and sandpaper it smooth.* ADJ QUALIT ≠ rough, lumpy ▸ ADV AFTER VB

2 A **smooth** liquid or mixture has been mixed well and so is without lumps and has the same thickness throughout. EG *Beat the cream with the eggs and cheese until the mixture is smooth. ...a smooth paste.* ADJ QUALIT ⇑ even ≠ lumpy

3 If you **smooth** something or **smooth** it out, you remove the creases or roughness from it and make it flat, especially by moving your hands over its surface. EG *I started smoothing out the tablecloth... Don't iron pyjamas or night clothes. Just smooth and fold them... He turned his head and smoothed back the hair over one temple.* V+O, OR V+O+A ⇑ flatten

4 If you **smooth** wood, clay, or some other material, you make its surface smooth, for example by using sandpaper on wood. EG *She smoothed the clay with her fingers.* V+O

5 Something that is **smooth** happens or continues evenly and steadily with no sudden changes or breaks. EG *He walked with a long, smooth stride... James lit his pipe without interrupting the smooth flow of his speech.* ▸ used as an adverb. EG *...a smooth-running engine.* ◇ **smoothly.** EG *The snake glides smoothly towards it.* ◇ **smoothness.** ADJ QUALIT ⇑ even = flowing ≠ erratic ▸ ADV WITH VB ◇ ADV WITH VB ◇ N UNCOUNT

6 To **smooth** something also means to make it happen or continue more evenly or regularly with fewer sudden changes or breaks. EG *We are reducing the cost of night-time supply to smooth the demand for electricity.* V+O ⇑ regulate

7 A **smooth** ride, flight, etc is one that is very comfortable because there are no bumps or jolts. EG *Did you have a smooth crossing?* ADJ QUALIT = calm

8 A **smooth** situation, start, operation, etc is one that ADJ QUALIT

goes well and is free of problems or trouble. EG *Cooperation is essential if you are going to lead a reasonably smooth existence in the office.*
◊ **smoothly**. EG *HQ was able to put the plans into effect quickly and smoothly... Life is running smoothly for them.* ◊ ADV WITH VB ⇑ easily

9 A man who is **smooth** behaves so politely and looks so smart and confident that you feel suspicious that he may be doing this simply to impress you; used showing disapproval. ADJ QUALIT = slick

10 If you **smooth the path** or **smooth the way** to something, you make it easier or more likely to happen. EG *Goodwill and cooperation can go a long way towards smoothing your way to the top... MPs agreed to smooth the path of the bill through Parliament.* PHR : VB INFLECTS ⇑ facilitate

11 • to **take the rough with the smooth**: see **rough**.

smooth over. **1** If you **smooth over** a problem or difficulty, you make it seem less serious and easier to deal with, especially by talking to the people concerned. EG *I tried to smooth over the awkwardness of this first meeting.* PHRASAL VB : ORDER V+ADV+O

2 If you **smooth over** a surface, you make it smooth, for example by using sandpaper on wood. PHRASAL VB : ORDER V+ADV+O

smoothie /smuːðiˡ/, **smoothies**; also spelled **smoothy**. A **smoothie** is a man who behaves so politely and looks so smart and confident that you feel suspicious that he may be doing this simply to impress you; an informal word, used showing disapproval. EG *He's a real smoothie!* N COUNT = poser

smooth-talking. Someone who is **smooth-talking** is very confident and persuasive in the way they talk, but is perhaps not sincere or honest. EG *...a smooth-talking salesman.* ADJ QUALIT

smoothy /smuːðiˡ/. See **smoothie**.

smote /sməʊt/ is the past tense of **smite**.

smother /smʌðə/, **smothers, smothering, smothered**. **1** If you **smother** a fire, you cover it with something in order to put it out. EG *She grabbed a blanket to smother the flames.* V+O ⇑ extinguish

2 To **smother** someone means to cover their face with something so that they cannot breathe, sometimes with the result that they die. EG *The babies had been smothered to death.* V+O = suffocate

3 If a lot of things **smother** something, they cover it all over. EG *If you leave sugar all over the place, we'll be smothered in ants... White roses smothered the apple tree.* ◊ **smothered**. EG *...bonnets smothered with sequins.* V+O : IF+PREP THEN *in* ◊ ADJ CLASSIF : PRED

4 If you **smother** someone with something such as love or attention, you give them so much of it that they are overwhelmed or have more than is good for them. EG *She smothered him with kisses... She should love them without smothering them with attention... A lot of married couples smother each other with needs and demands.* V+O : USU+A *(with)*

5 If you **smother** an emotion or the expression of an emotion, you control it so that people do not notice it. EG *I turned into the pillows and tried to smother my sobs... He smothered his feelings as best he could... ...smothered laughter.* V+O = suppress, stifle

6 If someone **smothers** an activity or process, they prevent it from continuing and developing, for example by forbidding people to speak freely about what they think; used showing disapproval. EG *He maintains power by smothering all opposition... Direct action and dissent had been smothered by consensus politics.* V+O = suppress, stifle

smoulder /sməʊldə/, **smoulders, smouldering, smouldered**; also spelled **smolder** in American English. **1** If something **smoulders**, it burns slowly without any flames, but sometimes with a lot of smoke. EG *A small fire was smouldering in the grate... The ruins are still smouldering.* V

2 If you have a feeling of anger or hatred that **is smouldering**, you are keeping the feeling inside you so that it only shows occasionally. EG *His hatred for his brother still smoulders after twenty years... And yet there is always the smoldering resentment against the public he serves... Inside me was growing a smouldering anger.* V ⇑ lurk

smudge /smʌdʒ/, **smudges, smudging, smudged**. **1** A **smudge** is **1.1** a dirty mark, often caused by rubbing your hand over something wet, dirty, or greasy. EG *He wiped his mouth with the back of his hand, leaving a smudge of flour across his face... The wallpaper had smudges all over it.* **1.2** an unclear, blurred shape or area; a rather literary use. EG *There was a long green smudge half-way up the rock... The lagoon lay below them and beyond that a long white smudge that was the reef.* N COUNT = smear; N COUNT : USU+SUPP = blur

2 If you **smudge** something, you make it blurred so that it is messy and its outline or details are no longer clear. EG *I'm not allowed to kiss her in case I smudge her lipstick... The smudged pictures showed a terrified little girl.* V+O

3 If you **smudge** something or **smudge** a mark onto it, you make a mark on it roughly, usually by rubbing it. EG *Jack smudged blood over his forehead... Her cheeks were smudged with tears... His small black moustache looked as if it had been smudged on with coal.* V+O : USU+A = smear

smudgy /smʌdʒiˡ/, **smudgier, smudgiest**. Something that is **smudgy** is **1** covered with dirty marks. EG *Her face was smudgy with tears.* **2** blurred so that it is messy and its outline or details are no longer clear. EG *...old smudgy photos.* ADJ QUALIT; ADJ QUALIT

smug /smʌg/, **smugger, smuggest**. Someone who is **smug** is very pleased with how good or clever they are; used showing disapproval. EG *...looks of smug satisfaction.* ◊ **smugly**. EG *'Just look at me,' she said smugly.* ◊ **smugness**. EG *There was smugness in Marsha's eyes.* ADJ QUALIT = self-satisfied; ◊ ADV; ◊ N UNCOUNT

smuggle /smʌgəˡl/, **smuggles, smuggling, smuggled**. **1** If someone **smuggles** goods or people into or out of a country, they take them there illegally, for example without paying tax or without valid passports or entry permits. EG *She smuggled these diamond bracelets out... Illegal smuggling of timber is already common... ...smuggling refugees into the country.* V+O : USU+A ⇑ convey

2 If you **smuggle** someone or something to a place where they should not be, you take them there secretly. EG *She agreed to smuggle me into their meeting... ...smuggling letters out of prison.* V+O+A ⇑ convey = sneak

smuggler /smʌglə/, **smugglers**. A **smuggler** is a person who takes goods into or out of a country illegally. EG *...hunting drug smugglers.* N COUNT ⇑ criminal

smut /smʌt/, **smuts**. **1 Smut** refers to words or pictures that shock and offend some people because they are related to nudity, sex, or body functions. EG *I find the media's growing obsession with smut and sensation deplorable.* N UNCOUNT = filth

2 Smut or **smuts** refers to dirt such as soot which makes a dark mark on something. N UNCOUNT/COUNT : USU PL

smutty /smʌtiˡ/, **smuttier, smuttiest**. **1** Words or pictures that are **smutty** shock and offend some people because they are related to nudity, sex, or bodily functions. EG *My daughter would never read smutty books.* ADJ QUALIT ⇑ rude = dirty, filthy

2 Something that is **smutty** is marked with dark smudges of dirt such as soot. EG *...smutty seats.* ADJ QUALIT ⇑ dirty

snack /snæk/, **snacks**. **1** A **snack** is a light, quick meal which you eat instead of a main meal or between main meals. EG *Sardines can be piled on toast and served as a delicious snack... He felt like a midnight snack... We made a snack supper out of the rest of the bread and salad.* N COUNT

2 Snacks are small, light things to eat, which are often served with drinks. EG *She brings from the kitchen delicious snacks–sausages rolled in bacon, crisps, and cheese.* N PLURAL

snack bar, snack bars. A **snack bar** is a café or other place where you can buy light meals, sandwiches, drinks, etc. EG *She had an omelette in a brightly lit snack bar.* N COUNT

snag /snæg/, **snags, snagging, snagged**. **1** A **snag** is a small difficulty, disadvantage, or problem. EG *This stuff is really good. The only snag is that it dissolves plastics... Look for the snags in the arguments and face them.* N COUNT

2 If you **snag** part of your clothing on something sharp, you damage it by catching it on the sharp thing as you move. EG *I snagged my best skirt on a bramble... Baskets take up too much room and snag your tights.* V+O : IF+PREP THEN *on/with* = catch

snail /sneɪl/, **snails**. **1** A **snail** is a small, slow-moving creature with a long, slimy body and a spiral-shaped shell on its back. N COUNT ⇑ mollusc

2 If you move or do something **at a snail's pace**, you move or do it very slowly. EG *Negotiations have been proceeding at a snail's pace.* PHR : USED AS A

snake /sneɪk/, **snakes, snaking, snaked.** 1 A **snake** is a long, thin reptile that has scales on its skin and no legs. EG *He was bitten by a poisonous snake.* N COUNT

2 Something that **snakes** in a particular direction moves in long winding curves; a literary use. EG *The musicians led them out in a snaking line beyond the village... A train snaked into sight.* V+A ⇑ wind

3 If you refer to someone such as a business colleague or a friend as **a snake in the grass**, you mean that they are secretly acting against you, for example by saying things which are harmful to you. PHR : USED AS C/S/O

snakebite /sneɪkbaɪt/; also spelled with a hyphen. **Snakebite** is the poisonous bite of a snake. EG *It was reputedly used to cure snakebite.* N UNCOUNT

snake charmer, snake charmers; also spelled with a hyphen. A **snake charmer** is a person who entertains people by controlling the behaviour of a snake, for example by playing music and causing the snake to rise out of a basket and drop back again. N COUNT ⇑ entertainer

snakes and ladders is a children's game played with dice on a board which has squares, some of which are connected by drawings of snakes and ladders. As you play, you move up the board where there is a ladder and down it where there is a snake. The first player to get to the finishing square at the top of the board is the winner. N UNCOUNT ⇑ board game

snaky /sneɪki¹/, **snakier, snakiest.** Something that is **snaky** moves or lies in long curves. EG *...thick snaky wires.* ADJ QUALIT ⇑ winding

snap /snæp/, **snaps, snapping, snapped.** 1 If something **snaps** or if you **snap** it, it breaks suddenly, usually with a sharp cracking noise. EG *The rope snapped... I grabbed a branch and tried to snap it off... The wind snapped the mast in half.* ▸ used as a noun. EG *The snap of a twig broke the silence.* V-ERG ▸ N SING WITH DET

2 If you **snap** something into a particular position or if it **snaps** into that position, it moves quickly into this position and makes a sharp sound, for example when it shuts. EG *She snapped the silver chain around her neck... ...pulling on her gloves and snapping her handbag shut... The lid snapped shut.* ▸ used as a noun. EG *The trap closes with a sudden snap.* V-ERG+A ⇑ jerk ▸ N SING WITH DET

3 If you **snap** your **fingers** or give **a snap of** your **fingers**, you make a sharp sound by moving your middle finger quickly across your thumb, often in order to attract someone's attention. EG *He snapped his fingers in time to the music... I could obtain with a snap of my fingers anything I chose.* PHR : *snap* INFLECTS ⇑ click

4 If a dog or other animal **snaps**, it closes its jaws with a sudden quick biting movement. EG *The dogs ran snapping and barking at his heels... She had seen the fox snap its jaws at her.* V OR V+O : IF+PREP THEN *at*

5 If someone **snaps** at you, they speak to you in a sharp, unfriendly way. EG *She would often snap at her younger son... 'Don't do that!' she snapped.* V+A *(at)*, OR V+QUOTE/REPORT-CL

6 If someone **snaps**, they are suddenly unable to remain calm and unworried any longer, because the situation they are in has become too difficult or tense. EG *He may snap at any minute... Before long, something in us snaps and we have to look away.* V = crack

7 A **snap** decision or action is one that you make suddenly and without thinking about it carefully. EG *It was a snap decision... The snap reaction of the press was favourable.* ADJ CLASSIF : ATTRIB

8 A **snap** is a photograph that is taken casually, for example of your family or of a place you have visited on holiday; an informal use. EG *We had to look through all her holiday snaps... ...taking snaps of the children at the beach.* N COUNT = snapshot

9 If you **snap** someone or something, you take a photograph of them. EG *Our photographer snapped a nice photograph of him.* V+O

10 **Snap** is a simple card game in which the players take turns to put cards down on a pile, and try to be the first to shout 'snap' when two cards with the same number or picture are put down. The first player to do this wins all the cards in the pile. EG *The children are playing snap.* N UNCOUNT

11 You say **'Snap!'** as an expression of surprise when you realize that two things are similar, for example if you meet a friend wearing the same shirt as you; an informal expression used in British English. EXCLAM

12 • See also **cold snap**.

snap out of. If you **snap out of** a sad mood that you are in, or if you **snap out of it**, you quickly change by forcing yourself to act more cheerfully; an informal expression. EG *I snapped out of this melancholy the moment a friend called... Come on, snap out of it!* PHRASAL VB : V+ADV+PREP = throw off

snap up. If you **snap up** something such as a bargain or an opportunity, you quickly buy the bargain or make use of the opportunity in order to gain an advantage; an informal expression. EG *All these houses were snapped up as soon as they were offered for sale... I would have snapped up a chance like that.* PHRASAL VB : V+O+ADV = grab, seize

snapdragon /snæpdrægəⁿn/, **snapdragons.** A **snapdragon** is a common garden plant with small colourful flowers that can open and shut like a mouth. N COUNT

snappish /snæpɪʃ/. Someone who is **snappish** speaks to people in a sharp, unfriendly manner. EG *When she was rushed she became snappish.* ADJ QUALIT ⇑ irritable

snappy /snæpi¹/, **snappier, snappiest.** 1 Someone who is **snappy** 1.1 wears smart, fashionable clothes. EG *He's such a snappy dresser.* 1.2 speaks to people in a sharp, unfriendly manner. EG *It was run by a peculiarly snappy and short-tempered woman.* ADJ QUALIT; ADJ QUALIT = testy

2 Something that is **snappy** is lively and energetic in style or performance. EG *The mood of the show is spirited, snappy, and young.* ADJ QUALIT = brisk

3 If you tell someone to **make it snappy**, you tell them to do something quickly; an informal expression. EG *Look at the pamphlets and make it snappy.* PHR : USU IMPER ⇑ hurry up

snapshot /snæpʃɒt/, **snapshots.** A **snapshot** is a photograph that is taken casually, for example of your family or of a place you have visited on holiday; an informal word. EG *...family snapshots.* N COUNT = snap

snare /snɛə/, **snares, snaring, snared.** 1 A **snare** is a trap for catching birds or small animals, usually consisting of a loop of wire or rope which pulls tight around the animal. EG *...rabbit snares.* N COUNT

2 If you **snare** an animal or bird, you catch it using a snare. EG *They are worried about the way in which badgers are being snared.* V+O ⇑ trap

3 A **snare** is also a plan which is designed to deceive someone and lead them into a difficult situation from which they cannot escape; a formal use. EG *They are creating wealth through political agencies as a snare and a delusion... She had been warned of the snares of the world.* N COUNT = trap

4 If someone **snares** you, they deceive you with a plan and lead you into a difficult situation from which you cannot escape; a formal use. V+O = trap

snarl /snɑːl/, **snarls, snarling, snarled.** 1 When an animal **snarls**, it makes a fierce, rough sound in its throat while showing its teeth. EG *...dogs snarling and snapping at the heels of sheep.* ▸ used as a noun. EG *The lion would bare his teeth in a furious snarl.* V ⇑ growl ▸ N COUNT

2 If you **snarl** something, you say it in a fierce, angry way. EG *'Let me alone,' I snarled.* V+QUOTE/REPORT-CL/O

3 A **snarl** is a disorganized situation in which things are unable to move or work as normal. EG *Perfect societies have no snarls and flaws.* N COUNT ⇑ problem = hitch

snarl up. When traffic or a system or process **is snarled up**, it becomes blocked, disorganized, and unable to move or continue. EG *The traffic was snarled up due to riots on the campus... The distributors are snarled up.* PHRASAL VB : V+O+ADV, USU PASS = block, hold up

snarl-up, snarl-ups. A **snarl-up** is a confused, disorganized situation such as a traffic jam, in which things are unable to move or work as normal. N COUNT ⇑ blockage

snatch /snætʃ/, **snatches, snatching, snatched.** 1 If you **snatch** something or **snatch** at something, you take it quickly by making a very fast movement. EG *He snatched the letter from the man's hand... ...children fighting, snatching each other's sweets... He snatched his hands away... He remembered snatching at his gun.* V+O, OR V+A *(at)* = grab

2 If you **snatch** an opportunity or a small amount of time, you quickly make use of it to do what you want. EG *I packed, then snatched four hours' sleep... She snatched a brief time alone with him... They struggled on, snatching happiness where they could.* V+O = grab

3 If someone **snatches** something from you, they steal it from you, usually outside in the street and using force. EG *He snatched my wallet and a bag.* V+O = grab

4 A **snatch** of a conversation or a song is a very small piece of it. EG *Sometimes I overheard snatches of their talk... He sang a snatch of his song.* N COUNT/PART ⇑ fragment = snippet

snatch up. If you **snatch** something **up**, you pick it up very quickly. EG *I snatched up Otto's glass just as it began to topple off the table.* PHRASAL VB : V+O+ADV = grab

snazzy /snæzi[1]/, **snazzier, snazziest**. Something that is **snazzy** is stylish and attractive, sometimes in a rather bright or showy way; an informal word. EG *I like your outfit-very snazzy!... It was one of those snazzy adverts.* ADJ QUALIT ⇑ smart = neat, trendy

sneak /sni:k/, **sneaks, sneaking, sneaked. 1** If you **sneak** somewhere, you go there very quietly on foot, trying to be careful that other people do not see you or hear you. EG *That night I sneaked out of my dormitory and crept down the drive... I didn't notice Bob sneaking up behind me... He's going to sneak off alone with Nell.* V+A ⇑ move = steal

2 If you **sneak** something somewhere, you take it there secretly, trying to be careful that other people do not catch you taking it. EG *I tried to sneak her some turkey, but the nurse stopped me... ...sneaking spies over the river.* V+O+O, OR V+O +A = smuggle

3 If you **sneak** a look, comment, etc, you give the look, comment, etc secretly, trying to be careful that other people do not realize that you are doing it. EG *He sneaked a look at her as she was passing by... He might sneak in a few minutes' sleep on the job.* V+O ⇑ have = steal

4 If someone, especially a child, **sneaks** on you, they tell a teacher, parent, or other adult in authority that you have done something naughty or wrong. EG *You won't sneak on us, will you?... I suppose you'll go sneaking to teacher.* ▸ used as a noun to refer to a person who does this. EG *I heard what that stinking sneak did.* V: IF+PREP THEN *on* ⇑ betray = split ▸ N COUNT

5 ● See also **sneaking**.

sneaker /sni:kə/, **sneakers. Sneakers** are light, casual shoes with rubber soles and soft canvas or leather that covers your feet. N COUNT: USU PL

sneaking /sni:kɪŋ/. If you have a **sneaking** feeling about something or someone, the feeling embarrasses you, for example because it is caused by the realization that someone else was right and you were wrong, or because it is the opposite of what you normally feel about them. EG *His book leaves one with a sneaking admiration for his shameless commercialism... I couldn't help a sneaking regard for them... I've a sneaking feeling she's right.* ADJ CLASSIF: ATTRIB ⇑ suppressed = grudging

sneak preview, sneak previews. A **sneak preview** of something is an unofficial opportunity to look at it before it is officially published or shown to the public. EG *He showed me his latest masterpiece in a sneak preview.* N COUNT

sneaky /sni:ki[1]/, **sneakier, sneakiest**. A **sneaky** action is done secretly, in the hope that other people will not notice. EG *I have just had a sneaky glimpse of the new list... But they gained a sneaky advantage.* ▸ used of people who do things in this way. EG *So that's what goes on here when I leave, you sneaky devil!* ADJ QUALIT ⇑ secret

sneer /snɪə/, **sneers, sneering, sneered. 1** If you **sneer** at someone or something, you express your contempt for their inferiority or stupidity, often by putting an expression of superiority or distaste on your face. EG *She was afraid he would sneer at the idea... ...sneering out of the window at people.* V: IF+PREP THEN *at*, OR V+QUOTE ⇑ ridicule = scoff

2 A **sneer** is an expression on a person's face, or something that they say, which indicates their contempt for someone or something that they think is inferior or stupid. EG *'Oh yes,' said McFee, a sneer flitting over his face... Etta smiled, part smile, part sneer... ...the sort who drew sneers about feminism.* N COUNT

sneeze /sni:z/, **sneezes, sneezing, sneezed. 1** When you **sneeze**, you suddenly take in your breath and then blow it down your nose noisily. You cannot help sneezing when there is a tickling feeling in your nose or when you have a cold. EG *We sneezed a lot with hay fever.* ▸ used as a noun. EG *They worry about every sneeze and rash... ...no coughs, no sneezes.* V ▸ N COUNT

2 If you say that something **is not to be sneezed at**, you mean that it is quite important or worth having and should not be ignored or rejected without careful thought; an informal expression. EG *The pension from the university was small but not to be sneezed at.* PHR: AUX INFLECTS

snick /snɪk/, **snicks, snicking, snicked**. If you **snick** something, you make a small cut in it. EG *I snicked my forefinger with a bread knife.* V+O = nick

snicker /snɪkə/, **snickers, snickering, snickered**. If you **snicker**, you laugh quietly and disrespectfully, for example at something rude or at someone's misfortune. EG *They all snickered and giggled.* ▸ used as a noun. EG *She gave a short snicker.* V = titter, snigger ▸ N COUNT

snide /snaɪd/. A **snide** comment or remark is one which criticizes someone in a malicious and often contemptuous way, especially using sarcastic humour. EG *There were one or two snide comments about my family... He may become a target for snide innuendoes.* ADJ QUALIT ⇑ disparaging

sniff /snɪf/, **sniffs, sniffing, sniffed. 1** If you **sniff**, you draw in air though your nose hard enough to make a sound, especially when you have a cold or are trying not to cry. EG *Felicity said, sniffing, 'I'll be so lonely without you. When will you see me again?'... For goodness sake, stop sniffing.* V ⇑ inhale

2 A **sniff** is the sound you make when you sniff. EG *Mary gave a sniff and said 'Don't worry, I'm not going to cry.'* N COUNT

3 If you **sniff** something, you smell it by sniffing. EG *'What a revolting smell,' he said, sniffing the air... The dog sniffed at Marsha's bags.* ▸ used as a noun. EG *A fox came along and gave the stone a good sniff.* V+O, OR V+A ▸ N COUNT

4 You can use **sniff** to indicate that someone is saying something in a superior or contemptuous way. EG *'The judge seems to suggest,' sniffed the professor, 'that I do not know my subject.'* V+QUOTE/ REPORT-CL

5 If you say that something **is not to be sniffed at**, you mean that it is quite important or worth having and should not be ignored or rejected without careful thought; an informal expression used mainly in British English. EG *Such an offer is not to be sniffed at.* PHR: AUX INFLECTS

6 If you **sniff** something such as glue, you deliberately inhale it into your body as a drug. EG *A lot of children are sniffing glue these days.* V+O

7 If you do not **get a sniff of** something, you do not succeed in obtaining any of it; an informal expression. EG *He is never going to get a sniff of any real money.* PHR: VB INFLECTS

sniff out. If you **sniff** something **out**, you discover or find it after some searching; used in informal English. EG *Gordon and his two friends sniffed out some lovely little quiet beaches.* PHRASAL VB: V+O+ADV = nose out

sniffer dog, sniffer dogs. A **sniffer dog** is a dog used by the police or army to find explosives or drugs by sniffing. N COUNT

sniffle /snɪfə[0]l/, **sniffles, sniffling, sniffled. 1** If you **sniffle**, you sniff repeatedly, as you do when you have got a cold or when you are crying. EG *I seem to have been sniffling for weeks.* V = snuffle

2 If you **have got the sniffles**, you have a slight cold; used in informal English. PHR: VB INFLECTS

sniffy /snɪfi[1]/, **sniffier, sniffiest**. Someone who is **sniffy** has a scornful and contemptuous attitude about something; an informal word. EG *James got sniffy at what Bill had said.* ADJ QUALIT = superior

snifter /snɪftə/, **snifters**. A **snifter** is **1** a small amount of an alcoholic drink; an informal use. EG *Will you join me in a snifter?* **2** a bowl-shaped glass for brandy; used in American English. N COUNT/PART: USU SING N COUNT

snigger /snɪgə/, **sniggers, sniggering, sniggered**. If you **snigger**, you laugh quietly and disrespectfully, for example at something rude or at someone's misfortune. EG *What are you sniggering at?* ▸ used as a noun. EG *There were sniggers from the children when the lady fell over.* V OR V+QUOTE = snicker ▸ N COUNT

snip /snɪp/, **snips, snipping, snipped. 1** If you **snip** or **snip** something, you cut it, usually with scissors or shears, in a single quick action or a number of short quick movements. EG *He took out a cigar and, after snipping off the end, lit it... Brian snipped energetically at the hedge.* ▸ used as a noun. EG *Linda cut the cotton with a satisfying snip of the scissors.* V: USU+A, OR V+O = clip ▸ N COUNT

2 If you describe something that is for sale as a **snip**, you mean that it is cheap and good value for the money; used in informal British English. EG *The ring was a snip at twenty-five pounds.* N SING: a+N = bargain

snipe /snaɪp/, **snipes, sniping, sniped. Snipe** is both the singular and plural form of the noun. **1** If you **snipe** at someone, **1.1** you criticize or attack them in speech or writing, especially when they do not have the opportunity to reply. EG *The unions are an easy target to snipe at... His sniping has irritated the chairman.* **1.2** you shoot at them from a hidden position. EG *Just then someone started sniping at us.* V: IF+PREP THEN *at* = sneer, dig V: USU+*at* = fire

2 A **snipe** is a bird with a very long beak, which usually lives in marshy areas. N COUNT

sniper /snaɪpə/, **snipers**. A **sniper** is a person such as a soldier who shoots at people from a hidden position. EG *A sniper's bullet tore up a wall two inches above his head.* — N COUNT ⇑ rifleman

snippet /snɪpɪt/, **snippets**. A **snippet** of something such as information, news, or gossip is a small piece of it. EG *Occasionally children come out with absolutely fascinating snippets of information... On the bus I heard this interesting snippet of conversation.* — N COUNT/PART = scrap, snatch

snitch /snɪtʃ/, **snitches, snitching, snitched**. If you **snitch** or **snitch** on someone, you tell someone in authority that another person has done something naughty or wrong; an informal word. — V : IF+PREP THEN *on* = rat, sneak

snivel /snɪvəˀl/, **snivels, snivelling, snivelled**; also spelled **sniveling, sniveled** in American English. If someone **is snivelling**, they are crying and sniffing in a way that irritates you. EG *They started to snivel, and after that, to cry... I know you're tired, but do stop snivelling!* — V = whimper ▸ used as a noun. EG *All I could hear was Robert's frightened snivels.* — ▸ N COUNT = sniffle

snob /snɒb/, **snobs**. A **snob** is 1 someone who belongs to or admires the higher social class in society, and despises people of a lower social class; used showing disapproval. EG *Like both her parents she was a snob.* — N COUNT 2 someone who believes that their own special tastes, interests, and abilities are superior to those of other people. EG *He is a dreadful intellectual snob.* — N COUNT : MOD+N

snobbery /snɒbəˀri¹/ is 1 the attitude of someone who belongs to or admires the higher social class of society, and despises people of a lower social class; used showing disapproval. EG *The Public Schools of England are said to be the breeding ground of snobbery.* — N UNCOUNT ⇑ condescension 2 the attitude of someone who believes that their own special tastes, interests, and abilities are superior to those of other people. EG *At the beginning of the Sixties there was a kind of snobbery in England about Central European writing.* — N UNCOUNT ⇑ superiority

snobbish /snɒbɪʃ/. Someone who is **snobbish** is too proud of their social status, intelligence, or special knowledge. EG *Because she was too shy and too snobbish to mix with her neighbours, she had few friends... She had a slightly snobbish attitude towards the theatre.* — ADJ QUALIT = snobby, superior, pretentious

snobby /snɒbi¹/, **snobbier, snobbiest**. **Snobby** means the same as snobbish. — ADJ QUALIT

snog /snɒg/, **snogs, snogging, snogged**. If two people **snog**, they kiss and cuddle each other continuously for a period of time; used in informal English, especially by teenagers. EG *...a couple snogging in the doorway... She was snogging with him throughout the party.* — V OR V+A (*with*) : RECIP = neck ▸ used as a noun. EG *We had a lovely snog during the film.* — ▸ N COUNT : USU SING

snook /snu:k/. If you **cock a snook at** someone in authority, you do something which they cannot punish you for, but which insults them or expresses your contempt for them. EG *Whenever he had the chance he cocked a snook at the headmaster.* — PHR : VB INFLECTS

snooker /snu:kə/, **snookers, snookering, snookered**. 1 **Snooker** is a game played on a large table covered with smooth, green cloth. The players use a long stick called a cue to hit a white ball and score points by knocking coloured balls into the pockets at the sides of the table. EG *...a game of snooker... Do you play snooker?* — N UNCOUNT

2 If something **snookers** you, it makes it difficult or impossible for you to take action or do what you want to do; used in informal British English. — V+O : USU PASS = stymie

snoop /snu:p/, **snoops, snooping, snooped**. If someone **snoops**, they secretly look round a place in order to find something out about the place or about other people. EG *It's good to be alone with nobody around to snoop or make a fuss... He might have been killed simply for snooping around.* — V : USU+A = pry

snooper /snu:pə/, **snoopers**. A **snooper** is someone who secretly looks round a place in order to find something out about the place or about other people. EG *We caught a snooper outside.* — N COUNT

snooty /snu:ti¹/, **snootier, snootiest**. Someone who is **snooty** behaves and talks as if they are very important and everyone else is inferior to them; used showing disapproval. EG *Don't be so snooty.* — ADJ QUALIT = snotty, superior ▸ used to describe something that is said or written. EG *...a snooty letter.*

snooze /snu:z/, **snoozes, snoozing, snoozed**; an informal word. A **snooze** is a short, light sleep, especially during the day. EG *I've just had a nice snooze.* — N SING : *a*+N = nap, doze ▸ used as a verb. EG *Tom is snoozing upstairs.* — ▸ V

snore /snɔ:/, **snores, snoring, snored**. 1 If you **snore**, you breathe very noisily when you are sleeping, usually because you have got your mouth open. EG *Ellen's mouth fell open and she began to snore... He's fast asleep, snoring.* — V

2 A **snore** is the noise that you make when you snore. — N COUNT

snorkel /snɔ:kəˀl/, **snorkels, snorkelling, snorkelled**; also spelled **snorkeling, snorkeled** in American English. 1 A **snorkel** is an air tube of which one end stays above the surface of the water so that a person swimming under water can breathe or so that a submarine can receive air. — N COUNT

2 If you **snorkel**, you swim under water using a snorkel. EG *We went snorkelling today.* — V : USU CONT

snort /snɔ:t/, **snorts, snorting, snorted**. 1 When animals **snort**, they breathe air noisily in through their noses. EG *The pigs grunted and snorted.* — V ⇑ exhale

2 If you **snort**, you breathe air noisily through your nose in order to express anger, disapproval, contempt, or amusement. EG *She began to show signs of impatience and snorted audibly... My sister snorted with laughter.* — V ⇑ exhale

3 A **snort** is a loud sound you make by breathing air through your nose, in order to express anger, disapproval, contempt, or amusement. EG *Clarissa gave a snort of disgust... Their suppressed chokes and snorts of amusement.* — N COUNT = hoot

4 You can use **snort** to indicate that someone is saying something with a snort. EG *'I'm bored!'–'For heaven's sake, read a book,' Posy snorted.* — V+QUOTE

5 A **snort** is also a glass of an alcoholic drink, which you drink in one mouthful; an informal use. — N COUNT/PART = snifter

snot /snɒt/ is the slimy substance that is produced inside your nose; a very informal word. — N UNCOUNT = mucus

snotty /snɒti¹/, **snottier, snottiest**. 1 Something that is **snotty** is covered with snot; a very informal use. EG *...a snotty handkerchief.* — ADJ QUALIT

2 Someone who is **snotty** has a very proud and superior attitude to other people; an informal use showing disapproval. — ADJ QUALIT = snooty

snout /snaʊt/, **snouts**. 1 The **snout** of an animal such as a pig or dog is its long nose. — N COUNT

2 Your **snout** is your nose; used in very informal English, often humorously. — N COUNT : USU POSS+N

3 The **snout** of something is a long, pointed part of it that is usually hollow. EG *He moved towards the gun whose snout had not quivered a millimetre in the hand that held it.* — N COUNT = muzzle

snow /snəʊ/, **snows, snowing, snowed**. 1 **Snow** consists of a lot of soft white bits of frozen water, called snowflakes, that fall from the sky in cold weather. EG *The entire country was covered in snow... Two inches of snow fell on London a day or two ago.* — N UNCOUNT

2 You sometimes use **the snows** to refer to a long period during which there are frequent falls of snow. EG *Remember how bad it was during the snows?* — N PLURAL : *the*+N

3 If it **snows**, snow falls from the sky. EG *It's snowing outside.* — V : *it*+V

4 If you **are snowed in** or if you **are snowed up**, you are prevented from leaving your house or travelling anywhere because there is so much snow on the ground. EG *I hope we don't get snowed in... We were snowed up for a week.* — PHR : AUX INFLECTS ⇑ be cut off

5 **Snow** is also cocaine; used in very informal English. — N UNCOUNT

6 If you **snow** someone, you talk in a flattering and insincere way in order to deceive or influence them; used in American English. — V+O

snow under. If you **are snowed under**, you have a large amount of work, especially paperwork, to deal with. EG *I've been snowed under by reports from over 200 organisations... At present we are snowed under with work.* — PHRASAL VB : V+ADV, ONLY PASS : IF+PREP THEN *by/with* = be inundated

snowball /snəʊbɔ:l/, **snowballs, snowballing, snowballed**. 1 A **snowball** is a ball made from snow for throwing at other people, especially by children when they are playing. EG *This snow's perfect for snowballs... ...a snowball fight.* — N COUNT

2 If something such as a project or business **snowballs**, it grows at a rapidly increasing rate. EG *Once the business starts to snowball we should be able to take on more staff.* — V ⇑ escalate ◊ **snowballing**. EG *...a snowballing effect.* — ◊ ADJ CLASSIF ⇑ escalating

snowbound /snəʊbaʊnd/. If people or vehicles are **snowbound**, they are prevented from going anywhere because of heavy snow. EG *Half the country was snowbound.* [ADJ CLASSIF = snowed in]

snow-capped. A **snow-capped** mountain is covered with snow at the top; a fairly literary word. EG *...a wonderful view of the snow-capped peaks.* [ADJ CLASSIF]

snowdrift /snəʊdrɪft/, **snowdrifts**. A **snowdrift** is a deep pile of snow which is made by the wind blowing a lot of snow into one place. EG *My car's stuck in a snowdrift.* [N COUNT = drift]

snowdrop /snəʊdrɒp/, **snowdrops**. A **snowdrop** is a small white flower which appears in the early spring. EG *The snowdrops are out now.* [N COUNT]

snowfall /snəʊfɔ:l/, **snowfalls**. **1** The **snowfall** in an area or country is the amount of snow that falls there during a particular period. EG *What's the average snowfall in San Moritz?* [N UNCOUNT]

2 A **snowfall** is a fall of snow. [N COUNT]

snowfield /snəʊfi:ld/, **snowfields**. A **snowfield** is a large area which is always covered in snow. EG *...the mountain lakes and snowfields below.* [N COUNT ⇑ region]

snowflake /snəʊfleɪk/, **snowflakes**. A **snowflake** is one of the soft, white bits of frozen water that fall as snow. EG *Snowflakes were melting in her hair.* [N COUNT]

snowline /snəʊlaɪn/. The **snowline** is the height on a mountain or group of mountains above which there is snow all the time. [N SING : the+N]

snowman /snəʊmæn/, **snowmen**. A **snowman** is a pile of snow that is made to look like a human figure, especially by children. EG *Let's build a snowman.* [N COUNT]

snowplough /snəʊplaʊ/, **snowploughs**; also spelled **snowplow** in American English. A **snowplough** is a vehicle which is used to remove snow from roads or railway lines by pushing it to the side. [N COUNT]

snowshoe /snəʊʃu:/, **snowshoes**. **Snowshoes** are oval frames which have a strong net stretched across them and which you fasten to your feet so that you can walk on deep snow. [N COUNT : USU PL]

snowstorm /snəʊstɔ:m/, **snowstorms**. A **snowstorm** is a very heavy fall of snow, usually when there is a lot of wind blowing at the same time. EG *She rushed out of the house into a whirling snowstorm.* [N COUNT = blizzard]

snow-white. Something that is **snow-white** is of a brilliant white colour. EG *...his snow-white hair.* [ADJ COLOUR]

snowy /snəʊi[1]/, **snowier, snowiest**. Something that is **snowy 1** has a lot of snow. EG *I went to see him one snowy day in London... ...a ridge between two high snowy peaks.* [ADJ QUALIT] **2** is like snow in appearance; used especially to describe something which is white. EG *...snowy hair.* [ADJ COLOUR]

Snr is a written abbreviation for 'Senior'; used especially in American English after someone's name to distinguish them from a younger member of the family who has the same name. EG *...Charles Parker, Snr.* [ADJ AFTER NAME]

snub /snʌb/, **snubs, snubbing, snubbed**. **1** If you **snub** someone, you insult them deliberately, either by ignoring them or by behaving rudely towards them. EG *She was always snubbing her old friends by pretending not to see them.* [V+O = slight]

2 A **snub** is a deliberately insulting remark or piece of behaviour. EG *Her comments were clearly intended as a snub.* [N COUNT ⇑ insult]

3 A **snub** nose is short and slightly turned up at the end. EG *She had an interesting face with a snub nose and large appealing eyes.* [ADJ CLASSIF : ATTRIB]

snub-nosed. A person, animal, or face that is **snub-nosed** has a short nose which points slightly upwards. [ADJ CLASSIF]

snuff /snʌf/, **snuffs, snuffing, snuffed**. **1** **Snuff** is powdered tobacco which is taken by sniffing it up your nose. EG *My father used to take snuff... ...a snuff box.* [N UNCOUNT]

2 If an animal **snuffs**, it breathes air or a smell in through the nose, often rather noisily. EG *A male badger came out of its den and snuffed the air.* [V OR V+O = sniff]

3 If you **snuff** a candle, you stop its flame burning or cut off the burnt end of the wick. [V+O]

4 When someone **snuffs it**, they die; used in informal British English. EG *Their cat snuffed it last Friday.* [PHR : VB INFLECTS]

snuff out. **1** If you **snuff out** a flame, you put it out, usually by using your fingers or by putting a cover over it for a few seconds. [PHRASAL VB : V+O+ADV = extinguish]

2 If someone **snuffs out** something such as a rebellion or disagreement, they put an end to it. EG *In the past the voice of dissension has been quickly snuffed out.* [PHRASAL VB : V+O+ADV = crush]

snuffle /snʌfə[0]l/, **snuffles, snuffling, snuffled**. If you **snuffle**, you make sniffing noises, usually because you have a cold or are trying not to cry. EG *Angela snuffled and buried her face in her hands.* [V = sniffle]

snug /snʌg/, **snugger, snuggest; snugs**. **1** If you feel **snug**, you are very warm and comfortable, especially when you are protected from the cold weather. EG *We lit a big fire which made us feel very snug and safe.* ◊ **snugly**. EG *Jamie was snugly wrapped in a white woollen scarf.* [ADJ QUALIT = cosy, comfy; ◊ ADV WITH VB]

2 Something such as a piece of clothing that is **snug** fits very closely or tightly. ◊ **snugly**. EG *You can save heat by making sure that doors close snugly.* [ADJ QUALIT; ◊ ADV WITH VB]

3 A **snug** is a small room in a pub; used in British English. [N COUNT : USU SING]

snuggle /snʌgə[0]l/, **snuggles, snuggling, snuggled**. If you **snuggle** somewhere, you settle yourself into a very warm, comfortable position, especially by lying very near to another person. EG *He stirred and turned over to snuggle close to her... She pulled the quilt over her and snuggled down.* [V+A = nestle]

so /səʊ/. **1** You use **so** in the following ways to refer to something that has already been said: **1.1** when you are simply referring back to something that has just been mentioned. **So** can be used as a substitute for a single word, a group of words, or a clause. EG *He went to close the door, tripping, as he did so, over a pair of boots... Do you enjoy romantic films? If so, you should watch the film on ITV tonight... 'Is it raining?'–'I'm afraid so.'... 'You're not allowed to do that.'–'Who says so?'... 'Is there anything else you want to tell me about?'–'I don't think so.'... People can write to me personally if they so desire... The issue is unresolved, and will remain so until the next SDP Congress... Society was cruel to bastards and even more so to their mothers.* [ADV] **1.2** when you are agreeing with a statement that has just been made or confirming that it is true. EG *'It's raining.'–'Yes, so it is.'... 'The phone isn't working.'–'So I see.'... 'He's very sorry.'–'So he ought to be.'* [ADV SEN] **1.3** when you are saying that something which has just been said about one person or thing is also true of another one. EG *His shoes are brightly polished; so is his briefcase... 'You were different then.'–'So were you.'... Etta laughed heartily and so did he... 'He looks very hot and dry.'–'So would you if you had a temperature of 103.'* [ADV SEN] **1.4** to disagree and to emphasize a statement; used especially by children. EG *'You weren't there!'–'I was so!'* [ADV SEN = too]

2 If you say that a state of affairs **is so**, you mean that it is the way that it has been described. EG *If you tell me that something is so, I believe you... It is worth knowing just why this is so... 'I think you are being silly.'–'Is that so?'* [PHR : VB INFLECTS = be true]

3 You use **so** and **so that** to introduce the result or consequence of something that you have just mentioned. EG *He speaks very little English, so I talked to him through an interpreter... He was the only person she knew in England, so she'd turned to him for help... The door was often open, so that anyone passing could look in... This call's costing you a fortune, so listen... I don't think there's any more news so I'll finish.* [CONJ SUBORD, OR ADV SEN = then, therefore]

4 You also use **so that** and **so as** to introduce the reason for something that you have just mentioned. EG *Any holes and openings should be fenced so that people can't fall down them... He has to earn lots of money so that he can buy his children nice food and clothes... You take some of the honey and replace it with sugar so that the bees have something to eat... He zig-zagged across the field so as to provide a difficult target... They went on foot, so as not to be heard.* [CONJ SUBORD]

5 You say **'So?'** and **'So what?'** to indicate that you think that something that someone has said is unimportant and therefore not worth mentioning or worrying about; an informal use. EG *'Illegal means it was smuggled in?'–'Yes–so?'... 'We can never go out with each other.'–'So?'... 'Someone will see us.'–'So what?'* [CONVENTION]

6 You can also use **so** **6.1** when you are checking that you have correctly understood something that has just been said or when you are summarizing something. EG *'This is my second year, yes.'–'So you've done two years.'... So it wasn't just an accident?... So I* [ADV SEN ⇑ then] *won't see you tonight then?... So that's how we know from day to day what is happening.* **6.2** when you are asking a question about something that has just been discussed. EG *So how much is the dole now, 20 quid?... So what are the advantages of nuclear energy?... So do you want to be a barrister or not?* **6.3** when you are accepting what someone has just said but are showing that you do not think that it is important; an informal use. EG *So I'm a slob. Why all the fuss?... 'What do you know about life in England?'–'Okay, so I wasn't born here. But I've spent a lot of time here.'* ADV SEN ⇑ then; ADV SEN = okay, all right

6.4 when you are commenting on a statement that you are making and saying where you got the information from. EG *Life is a jolly affair, so they tell me... Etta–so she herself kept insisting–had been bullied into coming... There were–or so they argued–economic reasons.* **6.5** when you are saying that something is done or arranged in the way that you are about to describe. EG *The majority of them have the eyes so located as to give panoramic vision... Alternatively you can so colour it as to break up the contours... The machine is so designed that you only need one hand to operate it.* **6.6** when you are drawing attention to what you are about to say. EG *And so for now, goodnight... So to the winners, and in third place we have Rita Walker... So this is America... So here we have two equations.* ADV SEN; ADV+VB+*as*+*to*-INF, OR ADV+VB+CONJ *(that)*; ADV SEN

7 When you are telling or giving an account of something, you can use **so** in the following ways: **7.1** when you are introducing the next event in a series of events. EG *This mother has twins and so she sets off one day to take her twins to the zoo... We shook hands on the deal and so a whole new era began... Last thing at night I have a cup of cocoa. And so to bed.* **7.2** when you want to say that a situation continued for some time. EG *And so it dragged on, that gradual decaying of my life... They met again in the same place, and so it had continued.* ADV SEN = then; ADV SEN

8 You can also use **so** in the structures 'as...so' and 'just as...so' when you want to indicate that two events or situations are alike in some way. EG *Just as one gesture can have many different meanings, so many different gestures can have the same meaning... As with the railways, so with coal.* CONJ SUBORD

9 You use **and so on** or **and so forth** at the end of a list to indicate that there are other items that you could mention in addition to the ones that you have already mentioned. EG *You can program a computer to paint, play chess and so on... He can talk for hours about realism, naturalism, surrealism and so forth... The university pays for the cleaners, and porters and so on and so forth.* PHR = etcetera

10 You use **or so** when you are giving an approximate amount or period of time. EG *I only have an hour or so... We arrived a month or so ago.* PHR : NG+PHR ⇑ about or two

11 You can also use **so** in the following ways to describe or emphasize the degree or extent of something. **11.1 So** can mean to a great degree or extent. It can be used to emphasize adjectives, adverbs, or verbs. EG *I'm so glad you could come... I had never felt so alone in my life... What's so funny?... We had not expected so overwhelming a response... Don't go so fast... I don't think that one can so easily dismiss so serious a subject... I don't know why you must always fuss so... There's so much work to be done... They were privileged in so many ways... I do so love you.* **11.2 Oh so** means to a very great degree or extent; a literary expression. EG *The flames spread quickly, oh so quickly.* **11.3** You can use the structures **so...that** and **so...as** to emphasize the degree of something by mentioning the result or consequence of it. EG *The objection is so fundamental and so widely accepted that it needs to be answered in detail... 'Never,' she said, so firmly that it closed the subject... So critical is the shortage that some villagers will soon be completely without water... ...a loss so vast as to be almost incomprehensible... Mountaineering is now very popular, so much so that there's been talk of restricting access to Mount Snowdon.* **11.4 Not so** means to a less great or less serious degree than you would expect or than has previously been stated or suggested. EG *It wasn't so very long ago... Carrying the weight was not so difficult.* ADV; PHR+ADJ/ADV; ADV...CONJ *(that)*, OR ADV...*as*+*to*-INF; PHR+ADJ/ADV = not that

12 So is used in combination with actions and gestures in the following ways: **12.1** when you are using a gesture to show the size, height, or length of something. EG *'How tall was he?'–'About so tall.'* **12.2** when you are showing someone how to do something by doing it yourself. EG *Fold the paper over, like so... You read off the top, so.* ADV+ADJ/ADV = this; ADV = thus

13 You can use the expressions **so much** and **so many** in the following two ways: **13.1** when you are saying that there is a definite limit to something but are not saying what this limit is. EG *We will only pay so much, no more... I can only take so much, and then I get annoyed... There are only so many ways of cooking an egg.* **13.2** when you are comparing a number or amount of something to an identical number or amount of something else, especially something inferior. EG *They just sat there like so many dummies.* PHR; PHR+NG

14 You use the structures **not so much** and **not so much...as** to say that something is one kind of thing rather than another kind. EG *It isn't the money so much, it's the chase... ...a cry not so much of pain as of amazement... He did not walk so much as trot.* PHR

15 You use the structure **not...so much as** to emphasize that something does not exist or happen even in the smallest amount or degree. EG *I didn't have so much as the price of a cup of tea on me... I didn't allow anyone to so much as breathe on my car.* PHR = not even

16 The word **so** is also used in the following expressions, which are explained at other places in this dictionary. • **so much the better**: see **better.** • **ever so**: see **ever.** • **so far as, in so far as**: see **far.** • **so far so good**: see **far.** • **so help me**: see **help.** • **just so**: see **just.** • **so long**: see **long.** • **so long as**: see **long.** • **so much for**: see **much.** • **every so often**: see **often.** • **so to speak**: see **speak.** • **so there**: see **there.** • **not in so many words**: see **word.**

soak /səʊk/, **soaks, soaking, soaked. 1** When you **soak** something or leave it to **soak**, you put it into a liquid and leave it there, usually in order to clean it. EG *'Can I help you with the dishes?'–'Oh, I'll just leave them to soak.'... Soak the material for several hours in cold water.* V-ERG = steep

2 When a liquid **soaks** something, it makes it very wet. EG *Water came in the tent and soaked both sleeping bags... The sun dried the sweat that had soaked their clothes.* V+O = saturate

3 When a liquid **soaks** through something, it passes through it. EG *The blood had soaked through his bandage... The rain water soaks away, and the desert becomes dry again.* V+A ⇑ permeate = seep

4 When someone **soaks**, they spend a long time in a hot bath, because they enjoy it; an informal use. EG *...the hot bath in which she liked to soak before dinner.* ▸ used as a noun. EG *...my lunchtime soak.* V ⇑ bathe; ▸ N COUNT

5 If someone **soaks** you, they take a lot of money from you by making you buy something expensive or by making you pay heavy taxes; an informal use. EG *The new government set out to soak the rich.* V+O = milk

6 A **soak** is a person who drinks too much alcohol and who is often drunk; an informal use. EG *...that old soak Matthews.* N COUNT = drunkard

7 See also **soaked, soaking.**

soak up. 1 If something **soaks up** a liquid, it absorbs it. EG *The soil soaked up a huge volume of water very rapidly.* **2** If you **soak up** sunshine, you sit or lie for a long time in the sun, because you enjoy it; an informal use. EG *She sat on the edge of her seat, leaning back to soak up the sun... She liked to soak up the Mediterranean sunshine.* PHRASAL VB : V+O+ADV; PHRASAL VB : ORDER V+ADV+O

soaked /səʊkt/. **1** If something made of cloth is **soaked** or **soaked through**, it is extremely wet with water or some other liquid. EG *His beret was soaked... Fortunately her clothes weren't soaked through.* ADJ CLASSIF : PRED = drenched, sopping

2 If you get **soaked**, you get very wet, usually because you have been outdoors in the rain. EG *Go on indoors, you'll get soaked... It was teeming down and we all got soaked... His feet were soaked.* • If you are **soaked to the skin**, you are very wet indeed, so that you need to change all your clothes. EG *We were soaked to the skin but very happy.* ADJ CLASSIF : PRED = drenched, saturated; • PHR : USED AS C = drenched, saturated

3 If you are **soaked** in something, you have studied it, know a great deal about it, and are strongly influenced by it. EG *She became soaked in Portuguese literature.* ADJ QUALIT : PRED+*in* = steeped

soaking /səʊkɪŋ/. If your clothes or shoes are **soaking** or **soaking wet**, they are very wet. EG *Her clothes were soaking and her hair was in a terrible mess... She sat down, clutching her soaking sandals... My boots were soaking wet inside.* ADJ CLASSIF = drenched

so-and-so, so-and-sos; used in informal English. 1 You use **so-and-so** instead of a name, title, word, etc when you are talking about a class of things or people, rather than a particular member of the class. EG *If you say my name's Dr so-and-so, people always think that you are a medical doctor... People ask me: 'As a woman, what do you think of so-and-so?'* N UNCOUNT

2 You call someone a **so-and-so** or refer to them as a **so-and-so** when you are annoyed with them or think that they are foolish. You say **so-and-so** in order to avoid using a swear word. EG *I'll get you for that, you so-and-so... A bloke got on the bus today and–silly so-and-so–he didn't know what to do.* N COUNT: ALSO VOC

soap /sәʊp/, **soaps, soaping, soaped**. 1 **Soap** is a substance that you use with water for washing yourself or for washing clothes. It is made from oil or fats and alkali and is sold in small hard pieces, as a liquid, or as a powder. EG *Wash your hands with soap and water before preparing food... ...a bar of yellow soap... ...soap powder.* ● See also **toilet soap**. N MASS

2 If you **soap** yourself, you rub soap on your body in order to wash yourself. EG *She soaped herself all over... She soaped between her toes.* ● See also **soft-soap**. V+O

3 A **soap** is the same as a soap opera; an informal use. EG *She has appeared in a few soaps.* N COUNT

soapbox /sәʊpbɒks/, **soapboxes**. A **soapbox** is 1 a small temporary platform on which a person stands when he or she is making a speech outdoors to passers-by. EG *He was equally at home in a pulpit or on a soapbox... ...a soapbox orator.* 2 a box or crate for packing soap in. EG *I had made a cage for my pigeons out of a soapbox.* N COUNT; N COUNT ⇑ container

soapflakes /sәʊpfleɪks/; also spelled with a hyphen. **Soapflakes** are very small, thin pieces of soap used for washing clothes. N PLURAL

soap opera, soap operas; also spelled with a hyphen. A **soap opera** is a popular television drama serial about the daily lives and problems of the same group of people. Soap operas do not have a fixed number of episodes. EG *We were so bored we were ready to watch even a soap opera... They spend their time gaping at Western soap operas.* N COUNT

soapsuds /sәʊpsʌdz/; also spelled with a hyphen. **Soapsuds** are the same as suds. EG *...a soft cloth dipped in warm soapsuds.* N PLURAL

soapy /sәʊpi¹/, **soapier, soapiest**. Something that is **soapy** 1 is full of, or covered with, soap. EG *Wash your brushes in warm soapy water, then rinse them thoroughly... She slipped on the soapy floor.* 2 looks, smells, or tastes like soap; usually used showing disapproval. EG *It was a dull, soapy colour... ...a soapy smell... The cheese had a soapy taste.* ADJ QUALIT; ADJ QUALIT = waxy

soar /sɔː/, **soars, soaring, soared**. 1 If something connected with money or business **soars**, it suddenly increases or becomes more valuable. EG *They watched the value of their shares soar from less than £50 to £87... The development costs of the RB211 engine had soared... Rice production soared from 694,000 tons to 913,000.* V: IF+PREP THEN *from/to* ⇑ increase = rocket

2 If something **soars** into the air, it goes quickly up into it. EG *The second missile soared into space... Flames were soaring into the sky.* V: USU+A ⇑ rise = shoot up

3 If trees or buildings **soar**, they are extremely tall or high. EG *Great trees soar above to cut out most of the light.* ◊ **soaring**. EG *...the soaring skyscrapers of New York.* V: USU+A = tower; ◊ ADJ CLASSIF: ATTRIB

4 If music **soars**, it rises in volume or pitch. EG *...the soaring, triumphant horn notes... The voices of the singers blended and soared.* V ⇑ rise

sob /sɒb/, **sobs, sobbing, sobbed**. 1 When someone **sobs**, they cry in a noisy way, breathing in short breaths. EG *She put her head on her friend's shoulder and began to sob... He sat down at the table, sobbing.* ◊ **sobbing**. EG *The sobbing began again.* V = weep; ◊ N UNCOUNT

2 If you **sob** something, you say it at the same time as you are crying. EG *'Oh, Albert, I'm tired,' she sobbed... He sobbed that he wanted to go home.* V+REPORT-CL/QUOTE/O

3 A **sob** is one of the noises that you make when you are crying. EG *She began to weep in gasping, choking sobs... A sob welled up in his throat.* N COUNT

sober /sәʊbә/, **soberer, soberest; sobers, sobering, sobered**. 1 When you are **sober**, you are not drunk. EG *Rudolph knew he had to stay sober to drive home.* ● If you describe someone as being **as sober as a judge**, you mean that they are completely sober. ADJ QUALIT ≠ drunk; ● PHR: USED AS C ≠ drunk

2 A **sober** person is serious and thoughtful. EG *...the soberest and most respected of astronomers.* ▸ used of behaviour and attitudes. EG *...a sober pattern of living... ...sober and sensible attitudes.* ◊ **soberly**. EG *'I don't know what I'd call it,' Smithy said soberly.* ADJ QUALIT; ◊ ADV WITH VB

3 **Sober** colours and clothes are plain and rather dull. EG *...a pair of sober black walking shoes... ...jackets of sober charcoal grey... ...sober-suited office workers.* ◊ **soberly**. EG *...the soberly clad villagers.* ADJ QUALIT: ATTRIB = sombre, staid; ◊ ADV WITH VB

sober up. When someone **sobers up**, they cease to be drunk. EG *When you sober up you may be ashamed of what you've done.* PHRASAL VB: V+ADV

sobering /sәʊbә⁰rɪŋ/. **Sobering** words, actions, ideas, etc make you serious and thoughtful. EG *His words had a sobering effect... There was a more sobering thought: perhaps we should not succeed.* ADJ QUALIT: ATTRIB

sobriety /sә⁶braɪәti¹/ is serious and thoughtful behaviour; a formal word. EG *Jane's new sobriety surprised her friends.* N UNCOUNT ⇑ seriousness

sob story, sob stories. If someone tells you a **sob story**, they tell you about something that has happened to them in a way that is intended to make you feel sorry for them; used showing disapproval. EG *She'll tell you a sob story about the hours she had to work.* N COUNT

Soc. is a written abbreviation for 'Society'; used when it is part of a name.

so-called. 1 You use **so-called** to indicate that you think the name or description of something is incorrect or misleading. EG *Father was in his so-called study... ...the so-called 'developed' countries... He is a Minister of Religion, so called.* ADJ CLASSIF: US ATTRIB

2 If you say that someone or something is **so called** for a particular reason, you mean that is the reason why they have their name; usually written as two words in this sense. EG *...the 'Red' people (so called from their custom of smearing their bodies with a red dye)... Why are disc jockeys so called?* PHR

soccer /sɒkә/ is the same as football; used especially to distinguish this kind of football from other kinds such as Rugby or American football. EG *...the start of the soccer season... ...the best soccer player in the school.* N UNCOUNT

sociable /sәʊʃәbә⁰l/. **Sociable** people are friendly and enjoy talking to other people. EG *Adler was an outgoing, sociable kind of man.* ▸ used of behaviour. EG *They eat together because it's sociable... Kitty had tried to be sociable to everyone.* ◊ **sociability** /sәʊʃәbɪlɪti¹/. EG *There was no doubt about his sociability.* ADJ QUALIT; ◊ N UNCOUNT

social /sәʊʃә⁰l/, **socials**. 1 **Social** means 1.1 relating to society and the way it is organized, and to the way that the various groups within society depend on each other. EG *...a social system based on private ownership... ...a particular culture and social structure... ...government social and economic policy... ...demands for modernisation and social change... ...educational and social benefits... There's repression and social injustice everywhere... ...the social problems of industrialised societies.* ◊ **socially**. EG *...a socially oriented market economy.* 1.2 relating to the position that particular people have in the structure of society. EG *...children from a number of different social backgrounds... This is more important than their age, income, or social class... ...his privileged social position... He is compelled by social pressures to seek advancement.* ◊ **socially**. EG *They must behave in a way which will be socially acceptable... If you couldn't spell, you were considered inferior both socially and educationally.* 1.3 relating to leisure activities that involve meeting other people. EG *In those pre-war days life seemed a bustle of social activity... We've met at social and business functions... It's a social rather than an artistic occasion... It is a way to broaden their circle of social contacts.* ◊ **socially**. EG *...the only people my father ever visited socially... Socially, it had been a memorable occasion.* ADJ CLASSIF: ATTRIB ⇑ communal; ◊ ADV; ADJ CLASSIF: ATTRIB; ◊ ADV; ADJ CLASSIF: ATTRIB; ◊ ADV

2 A **social** is a party, dance, or informal gathering organized for the members of a club or institution. EG *Judy had met Bill at an International Youth social in London.* N COUNT = do

3 **Social** animals live in groups and co-operate regularly with other members of the group. EG *...social insects such as ants... Human beings are social animals, gregarious by nature.* ADJ CLASSIF: ATTRIB

social climber, social climbers. A **social climber** is a person who tries to have friends and acquaintances who belong to a higher social class, so that he or she will also be regarded as belonging to that class; used showing disapproval. EG *The social climbers started to mimic their dress and behaviour.* — N COUNT ⇑ snob

social democracy, social democracies. 1 **Social democracy** is a kind of socialism in which people are allowed a relatively large amount of freedom. — N UNCOUNT ⇑ system

2 A **social democracy** is a country which has a social democratic form of government. — N COUNT

social democrat, social democrats. A **social democrat** is a person who is a member or supporter of a social democratic party. — N COUNT

social democratic party, social democratic parties. A **social democratic party** is a political party whose principles are based on social democracy. There are social democratic parties in many countries and their principles are not always the same. EG *...the special relationship which trade unions tend to have with socialist or social democratic parties... ...the alliance between the Social Democratic Party and the Liberal Party.* — N PROPER : *the*+ N, OR N COUNT

social drinker, social drinkers. If you say that you are a **social drinker**, you mean that you drink alcohol on social occasions and with friends rather than when you are on your own. — N COUNT

social drinking is the practice of drinking alcohol on social occasions and with friends rather than when you are on your own. — N UNCOUNT

socialise /səuʃəlaɪz/. See **socialize**.

socialism /səuʃəlɪzə⁰m/ is a set of political beliefs and principles whose general aim is to create a system in which everyone has an equal opportunity to benefit from the country's wealth, usually by having the country's main industries owned by the state. There are many kinds of socialism. EG *...the road to socialism in an industrial society... They equated socialism with the welfare state.* — N UNCOUNT ⇑ ideology

socialist /səuʃəlɪst/, **socialists**; often spelled with a capital letter. 1 **Socialist** means relating to or based on socialism. EG *...the return of a Labour government with socialist policies... ...the Pan-Hellenic Socialist Party... ...members and sympathisers of the International Socialist movement.* — ADJ CLASSIF : USU ATTRIB ⇑ political

2 A **socialist** country has a political system based on some kind of socialism, especially a Marxist kind. EG *...Poland and other Eastern European socialist states... ...the countries of the socialist bloc.* — ADJ CLASSIF : USU ATTRIB

3 A **socialist** is a person who believes in socialism or who is a member of a socialist party. In Britain, members of the Labour Party are often referred to as Socialists. EG *It doesn't matter whether he's a Conservative, a Socialist, or what... Unlike the socialists, the Communists have been able to gather some support.* — N COUNT

socialistic /səuʃəlɪstɪk/. If you describe something as **socialistic**, you mean that it has some of the features of socialism. EG *This is in many respects more socialistic than the nationalization policies proposed by Labour... The less socialistic countries adopt a different approach.* — ADJ QUALIT

socialite /səuʃəlaɪt/, **socialites**. A **socialite** is a person who attends many fashionable upper-class social events and who is well known because of this. EG *Sir Oswald was generally regarded as a socialite.* — N COUNT

socialization /səuʃəlaɪzeɪʃə⁰n/; also spelled **socialisation**. **Socialization** is a technical word. **Socialization** is 1 the process by which people, especially children, are made to behave in ways that are acceptable in their culture or society. EG *Girls experience different patterns of socialization from boys... ...the early socialisation of children.* — N UNCOUNT ⇑ development — 2 the process by which something is made to operate on socialist principles. EG *...socialization of the means of production.* — N UNCOUNT

socialize /səuʃəlaɪz/, **socializes, socializing, socialized**; also spelled **socialise**. 1 If you **socialize**, you meet other people socially, for example at parties. EG *I socialized with the philosophy students... He seems to find it difficult to socialize.* — V : IF+PREP THEN *with* ⇑ mix

◊ **socializing**. EG *There was very little socialising between staff and students.* — ◊ N UNCOUNT

2 When people **are socialized**, they are made to behave in a way that is acceptable in their culture or society; a technical use. EG *Women have been socialized into stereotyped role-expectations... He claimed that television socialized children much more effectively than their parents could.* — V+O : USU PASS ⇑ condition

3 When something **is socialized**, it is made to operate on socialist principles; a technical use. EG *Once the means of production is fully socialized, more advanced technology can be introduced.* — V+O : USU PASS ⇑ control

social life, social lives. Your **social life** consists of the activities in which you meet your friends and acquaintances, for example in their houses or at dances or parties. EG *Much of Dad's social life was with local friends from the bowling club... ...busy, competent people, with active social lives... I stayed out of the social life of the school.* — N COUNT : USU WITH POSS, OR N UNCOUNT

social order, social orders. The **social order** in a place is the way that society is organized there. EG *...acquiescence in the established social order... They have striven to create a new social order.* — N COUNT : USU SING = regime

social science, social sciences. **Social science** is the scientific study of society. Sociology, anthropology, politics, and economics are all branches of social science. EG *He left his firm to study social science... ...a social science degree.* — N UNCOUNT

▸ The **social sciences** are the various branches of social science. EG *In the sixties the social sciences were enormously popular... Economics is the oldest of the social sciences.* — ▸ N COUNT : USU PL

social scientist, social scientist. A **social scientist** is a person whose job is to teach, study, or do research in social science. — N COUNT ⇑ scholar

social security is a system by which the government pays money regularly to people who have no other income or only a very small income; used mainly in British English. EG *He gets more on social security than he did when he was working... ...social security benefits... ...the social security system.* — N UNCOUNT ⇑ welfare

social services. The **social services** in a town or district are the facilities and services provided by the local authorities to help people who have particular social problems and needs. EG *The tax cuts would have required major cuts in social services... ...the new Social Services Secretary... ...the local social services department.* — N PLURAL : PL FORM WHEN MOD

social studies is a subject taught in British schools and colleges. It includes sociology, politics, and economics. — N PLURAL

social work is work which involves giving help and advice to people who have serious problems of many kinds, for example to people who are very poor or who live in bad conditions. EG *I really want to go into some kind of social work... ...professional training in social work.* — N UNCOUNT = service

social worker, social workers. A **social worker** is a person whose job is to do social work. EG *She's going to be a social worker... He needs help from a psychiatrist or a social worker.* — N COUNT

society /səsaɪəti¹/, **societies**. 1 **Society** is people in general, thought of as a large organized group. EG *People who are growing up have to adapt to society... Women must have equal status in society... We are going to have to change the whole structure of society.* — N UNCOUNT ⇑ organization

2 A **society** is 2.1 the people who live in a country or region, their organizations, and their way of life. EG *...the deep-rooted prejudice that runs through our society... ...the increasing complexities of industrial societies... We live in a multi-racial society... ...the role of large businesses in Western society.* — N COUNT : USU+ SUPP — 2.2 an organization for people who have the same interests or aims. EG *I'm on the committee of the local film society.* — N COUNT = group ▸ used as part of a name. EG *...the Royal Horticultural Society... ...the Society of African Culture.* — ▸ N IN NAMES

3 If you are in someone's **society**, you are in their company; a formal use. EG *They found contentment in each other's society.* — N COUNT : WITH POSS = presence

4 **Society** is also the rich, upper-class, fashionable people in a particular place who meet at dinners, parties, and other entertainments. EG *He was good in society and a perfect gentleman... To get extra money Sargent would paint some society lady.* — N UNCOUNT

5 See also **building society, co-operative society, friendly society**.

socio- is added to some adjectives and nouns in order to form other adjectives and nouns. Words formed in this way are technical terms in the social — PREFIX sciences. EG *...economic→socioeconomic... ...political→socio-political... ...biology→sociobiology.*

sociologist /sǝʊsɪɒlǝdʒɪst/, **sociologists**. A **sociologist** is someone who studies or teaches sociology. EG *There are plenty of other causes which the sociologist has not been able to measure... This only bears out what sociologists have been saying for years.* N COUNT ↑ social scientist

sociology /sǝʊsɪɒlǝdʒi¹/ is the study of human societies and of the relationships between groups in these societies. EG *A few years ago, sociology was the most popular subject for undergraduates... ...a sociology lecturer.* ◊ **sociological**. EG *...sociological studies of criminals... ...sociological research on housing associations.* ◊ **sociologically**. EG *This report was statistically sophisticated and sociologically informative.* N UNCOUNT ↑ social science; ◊ ADJ CLASSIF : ATTRIB; ◊ ADV

sock /sɒk/, **socks, socking, socked. 1** A **sock** is a piece of clothing which covers your foot and ankle and is made of wool, nylon, or some other soft material. Socks are often worn inside shoes. EG *...a pair of socks.* N COUNT

2 If you tell someone to **pull** their **socks up**, you mean that they should improve their behaviour and their work; used in informal British English. EG *You'd better pull your socks up, young man!* PHR : VB INFLECTS

3 If you tell someone to **put a sock in it**, you are telling them in an angry and rude way to stop talking; used in informal British English. CONVENTION = belt up

4 If you **sock** someone, you hit them very hard with your fist; an informal use. EG *He socked Brady in the mouth.* ▸ used as a noun. EG *...a sock on the jaw.* V+O : IF+PREP THEN *in/on*; ▸ N COUNT

socket /sɒkɪt/, **sockets**. A **socket** is **1** a place on a wall that you can put an electric plug into, or a place on a piece of electrical apparatus that you put a light bulb or other fitment into. EG *Never put a finger or anything wet into a light bulb socket or wall socket.* N COUNT

2 any hollow part or opening in a structure which another part fits into. EG *She feared her eyes might actually pop out of their sockets... ...the hip socket.* N COUNT : USU MOD+N ↑ cavity

sod /sɒd/, **sods**. **Sod** is a swear word in all the following paragraphs except paragraph 6. It is used mainly to express anger, annoyance, or contempt. **1** Some people call someone a **sod 1.1** when they are angry with them or think that they are unpleasant. N COUNT : ALSO VOC

1.2 when they feel sympathy for them or are jealous of them. EG *He doesn't need any more bad luck, poor sod.* N COUNT : ADJ+N, ALSO VOC

2 Some people say that a task or job is a **sod** when it is very difficult to do. N COUNT : USU a +N IN SING

3 Some people use **sod** before a word or expression in order to indicate that they think that it is not important or that they do not care about it. V+O : ONLY IMPER

4 Sod all is used to mean 'nothing at all'. People use this expression when they are angry or annoyed about something. PHR : USED AS O

5 Some people say **sod it** when they are angry because something has gone wrong or when they want to indicate that something is unimportant. EXCLAM

6 The **sod** is the surface of the ground, together with the grass and roots that are growing in it; a literary word. EG *...the heavy plough that slices through the sod.* N SING : *the*+N ↑ ground

sod off. **Sod off** is an insulting and offensive way of telling someone to go away. PHRASAL VB : V+ADV : USU IMPER

soda /sǝʊdǝ/, **sodas. 1 Soda** is **1.1** sodium in the form of crystals or a powder which is used for cooking or cleaning. EG *...caustic soda... ...baking soda... ...washing soda.* ● See also **bicarbonate of soda. 1.2** fizzy water used for mixing with whisky, fruit juice, etc. EG *...a whisky and soda.* N UNCOUNT : ADJ CLASSIF+N; N MASS

2 A **soda** is a sweet fizzy drink; used in American English. EG *...an ice-cream soda... ...soda pop.* N COUNT

soda fountain, soda fountains. In America, a **soda fountain** is a cafe or bar where sweet drinks and food, for example ice cream, are sold. N COUNT

soda siphon, soda siphons; also spelled **soda syphon**, or with a hyphen. A **soda siphon** is a bottle with soda water in it. It is made so that when you press a lever, the soda water comes quickly and forcefully out of a tube on the top of the bottle. N COUNT

soda water, soda waters; also spelled with a hyphen. **Soda water** is a drink which is fizzy water, used for mixing with whisky, fruit juice, etc. N MASS = soda

sodden /sɒdǝⁿn/. Something that is **sodden** has absorbed a lot of water or other liquid, and is very wet. EG *Ida dropped her blanket onto the sodden ground... My shirt was sodden with sweat.* ADJ QUALIT : IF+PREP THEN *with*

sodding /sɒdɪŋ/ is a swear word used by people who are very angry about something. ADJ CLASSIF : ATTRIB, OR ADV WITH VB

sodium /sǝʊdɪǝm/. **1 Sodium** is a silvery-white chemical element which combines with other chemicals. Salt is a sodium compound. EG *...sodium bicarbonate... ...sodium chloride.* N UNCOUNT ↑ element

2 Sodium lighting gives out a strong orange light. EG *Out over the town the sodium lights were lit... ...a sodium streetlamp.* N BEFORE N

sodomy /sɒdǝmi¹/ is anal sexual intercourse, especially between males. N UNCOUNT

sofa /sǝʊfǝ/, **sofas**. A **sofa** is a long, comfortable seat with a back and usually with arms, which is intended for more than one person. N COUNT = settee

sofa-bed, sofa-beds. A **sofa-bed** is a sofa which is made with a folding seat so that it can also be used as a bed. N COUNT

soft /sɒft/, **softer, softest. 1** Something that is **soft 1.1** changes shape or bends easily when you touch it or press it. EG *...a soft bed... Add the remaining flour to make a soft dough... His feet left prints in the soft soil.* ◊ **softness**. EG *...the comfort and softness of leather armchairs.* ADJ QUALIT; ◊ N UNCOUNT **1.2** is less hard than average. EG *...a soft pencil... ...soft cheese... ...soft metals.* ADJ CLASSIF **1.3** is very smooth and pleasant to touch. EG *Her skin was soft and white... ...soft auburn hair... ...the soft black fur of the coat.* ◊ **softness**. EG *...the softness of her arms.* ADJ QUALIT; ◊ N UNCOUNT **1.4** is very gentle and has no force or violence. EG *...a soft breeze... ...fine, soft rain... A moment later, there was the softest of bumps.* ◊ **softly**. EG *I closed the door softly... Mike softly placed his hand on her shoulder.* ADJ QUALIT ↑ light; ◊ ADV WITH VB = gently

2 A **soft** sound or voice is quiet and not too harsh. EG *She had a soft German accent... Her voice grew softer.* ◊ **softly**. EG *'Listen,' she said softly... Someone began to play softly on the organ.* ADJ QUALIT = faint; ◊ ADV WITH VB

3 A **soft** light or colour is pleasant and restful to look at because it is not too bright. EG *...the soft glow of the evening light... ...walls in soft pink stone.* ◊ **softly**. EG *The lamp glowed softly.* ADJ QUALIT = mellow; ◊ ADV WITH VB

4 If the appearance of something is **soft**, it has smooth curves rather than sharp or distinct edges. EG *...the soft folds of her dress.* ◊ **softness**. EG *There was a softness about her good looks.* ADJ CLASSIF = gentle; ◊ N UNCOUNT

5 Someone who is **soft** is **5.1** kind and cares about other people's feelings. EG *Phyllis was a soft, caring person... Her clear, brown eyes seemed soft and considerate.* ADJ QUALIT = gentle N UNCOUNT **5.2** easily upset or made to feel sympathy for someone. EG *I was in tears by the end of the film–I'm awfully soft at times... He's got a very soft heart.* ADJ QUALIT ↑ sensitive **5.3** easily persuaded, weak, and not strict enough; used showing disapproval. EG *I think your teachers are too soft.* ADJ QUALIT = lenient

6 If you **are soft on** someone, **6.1** you treat them in a way that is too generous rather than criticizing them or dealing harshly with them. EG *You're far too soft on those kids... It seemed that the President was going soft on tax evasion.* PHR : VB INFLECTS **6.2** you like them a great deal and feel attracted to them; a fairly informal expression. EG *In fact she was quite soft on him.* PHR : VB INFLECTS ● If you **have a soft spot for** someone, you are especially fond of them. ● PHR : VB INFLECTS

7 If you say that someone is **soft in the head**, you mean that they are rather stupid or mad; an informal expression. EG *My cousin Jimmy was a bit soft in the head.* PHR : USED AS C = dim

8 A **soft** life, **soft** job, etc is easy and involves very little work. EG *Some of them have a soft life, nothing but champagne and receptions... ...a soft option.* ADJ QUALIT : ATTRIB ≠ tough

9 Water that is **soft** does not contain much lime in it and so makes bubbles easily when you use soap to wash things. ADJ QUALIT ≠ hard

10 Soft drugs are drugs, such as marijuana, which are illegal but which are not considered to be very strong, harmful, or addictive. ADJ CLASSIF ↑ weak ≠ hard

softball /sɒftbɔːl/, **softballs. 1 Softball** is a game similar to baseball, played with a larger, softer ball. N UNCOUNT

2 A **softball** is the ball used in this game. N COUNT

soft-boiled. A **soft-boiled** egg is one that has been boiled for only a few minutes, so that the yolk is still soft. ADJ CLASSIF ≠ hard-boiled

soft drink, soft drinks. A **soft drink** is a cold, non-alcoholic drink such as lemonade, cola, or orange juice. N COUNT

soften /sɒfəⁿn/, **softens, softening, softened.** 1 If something **softens** or if something else **softens** it, it becomes less hard, stiff, or firm. EG *I'm waiting for the ice-cream to soften... Fry the onions for about 10 minutes to soften them.* V-ERG

2 If something **softens** the impact or shock of something else, it makes it less severe. EG *The shock had been softened a little by Mary's kind words.* ● to **soften the blow**: see **blow**. V+O = cushion

3 If you **soften** or if your attitude **softens**, you become more sympathetic and less hostile or critical. EG *'I'm sorry about your mother,' Ira said, softening... Grady was beginning to soften towards the project... Attitudes to the soldiers had softened... We tried to get her to soften her attitude.* V-ERG ⇑ weaken

4 If your expression **softens** or if something **softens** it, it becomes much more gentle and friendly. EG *His mother's face softened a little... Her mouth softened as she stood up... The memory of their initial meeting softened her face.* V-ERG ⇑ relax

5 If you **soften** light, a colour, or a sound, you make it less bright or harsh. EG *You need to soften the lighting.* V+O = subdue

6 If something **softens** your skin, it makes it very smooth and pleasant to touch. V+O

soften up. If you **soften** someone **up**, you put them into a good mood or prepare them before asking them a favour or persuading them to do something; used in informal English. EG *I wondered if there was any hope of softening him up.* PHRASAL VB : V+O+ADV = butter up

softener /sɒfəⁿnə/, **softeners.** A **softener** is a chemical substance that you add to water when you wash clothes in order to make the clothes feel softer. EG *...a fabric softener.* ● See also **water softener**. N COUNT

soft focus. If something in a photograph or film is in **soft focus**, it has been made to look slightly blurred to give it a more romantic effect. EG *In the background, in soft focus, we see his smiling wife... ...soft-focus photographs.* N UNCOUNT : USU *in*+N

soft furnishings are cushions, curtains, lampshades, and furniture covers. N PLURAL

soft-headed. If you say that someone's opinions or beliefs are **soft-headed**, you mean that they are too simple and do not reflect an understanding of the real world. EG *They regarded our hopes as ridiculously soft-headed.* ADJ QUALIT = naive

soft-hearted. Someone who is **soft-hearted** has a very sympathetic and kind nature. ADJ QUALIT

softie /sɒfti¹/, **softies.** See **softy**.

softly-softly. A **softly-softly** approach to something is one which is cautious and patient and avoids direct action or force. ADJ CLASSIF : ATTRIB, OR ADV WITH VB ⇑ careful

soft palate, soft palates. Your **soft palate** is the soft top part of the inside of your mouth, near your throat. N COUNT

soft-pedal, soft-pedals, soft-pedalling, soft-pedalled; also spelled **soft-pedaling, soft-pedaled** in American English. If you **soft-pedal**, you deliberately reduce the amount of activity or pressure that you have been using to get something done. EG *I think we'd better soft-pedal on that contract for a while.* V = go easy

soft porn is pornography that shows or mentions sexual acts, but not in a very explicit or violent way. N UNCOUNT

soft science, soft sciences. A **soft science** is a field of study, such as sociology or psychology, which involves studying things that cannot be measured as accurately as things in the physical world. N COUNT = social science

soft sell. A **soft sell** is a method of selling or advertising that involves gentle persuasion rather than putting a lot of pressure on people. N SING : DET+N

soft-soap, soft-soaps, soft-soaping, soft-soaped. If you **soft-soap** someone, you flatter them in order to try to persuade them to do something; an informal word. V+O

soft-spoken. Someone who is **soft-spoken** has a quiet, gentle voice. EG *Rose was soft-spoken and introverted.* ADJ QUALIT

soft touch. If you describe someone as a **soft touch**, you mean that they can easily be persuaded to lend you money or to do things for you; used in informal English. N SING : *a*+N = sucker

software /sɒftweə/ consists of the programs that control a computer as opposed to the actual machinery of the computer. EG *My job is writing the software... ...advances in computer software.* N UNCOUNT ⇑ programming

softwood /sɒftwʊd/, **softwoods. Softwood** is wood from trees, such as pines, that grow quickly and produce wood which can be easily sawn. N MASS

softy /sɒfti¹/, **softies**; also spelled **softie**. You call someone a **softy** 1 if they react to being hurt by crying too easily or making too much fuss; used showing disapproval. EG *Get up, you big softy! You haven't really hurt yourself.* N COUNT : ALSO VOC = cry baby **2** if they are easily made to feel sympathy or sadness, for example by a sad film or story. EG *I'm really a softie, you know.* N COUNT : ALSO VOC

soggy /sɒgi¹/, **soggier, soggiest.** Someone or something that is **soggy** is unpleasantly wet or full of water. EG *...a soggy dishcloth... When we got home, we were soggy and depressed.* ADJ QUALIT = sodden

soil /sɔɪl/, **soils, soiling, soiled.** 1 **Soil** is the top layer of earth, which plants can grow in. EG *Plant it so that there are 4 or 5 inches of soil above the bulb... The soil here is very fertile.* N UNCOUNT

2 A **soil** is soil of a particular kind or quality. EG *The heavy clay soils of the region were unworkable.* N COUNT : ADJ+N

3 You use **soil** in expressions like 'British soil' to refer to a particular country or territory. EG *...my native soil... It was the first time I had set foot on British soil* N UNCOUNT : USU MOD+N = land

4 If you **soil** something, you make it dirty or stained. EG *He began to play with earth and slightly soiled his clothes... She never soils her dainty fingers with a washing up mop.* ◊ **soiled.** EG *...a soiled handkerchief... ...soiled nappies... The book was thin and rather soiled.* V+O = sully ◊ ADJ QUALIT = grubby

soiree /swɑːreɪ/, **soirees**; also spelled **soirée**. A **soiree** is a social gathering in the evening; a formal, rather old-fashioned word. EG *I was usually invited to the musical soirees they regularly held.* N COUNT ⇑ party

sojourn /sɒdʒɜːn, sʌdʒ/, **sojourns.** A **sojourn** is a stay for a short time in a place that is not your home; a literary word. EG *His sojourn in France had provided him with a number of stories.* N COUNT : USU SING, USU+A = visit

solace /sɒlɪs/; a fairly formal word. 1 **Solace** is a feeling of comfort that makes you less upset, sad, or disappointed. EG *He began to find solace in prayer.* N UNCOUNT = consolation

2 If something is a **solace** to you, it gives you comfort and makes you less upset, sad, or disappointed. EG *Her poetry has always been a solace to me in times of unusual stress.* N SING WITH DET = consolation

solar /səʊlə/. 1 **Solar** is used to describe something that relates to or belongs to the sun. EG *They accurately predicted solar eclipses.* ADJ CLASSIF : USU ATTRIB

2 **Solar** energy, heating, etc uses the sun's light and heat as a source of energy. EG *...the potential of solar energy... ...solar-heated walls... ...solar panels.* ADJ CLASSIF : USU ATTRIB

solar cell, solar cells. A **solar cell** is a device that produces electricity from the sun's rays. N COUNT

solarium /səᶜleərɪəm/; **solariums.** A **solarium** is a place equipped with sun-lamps, where you can go to get an artificial suntan. N COUNT

solar plexus. Your **solar plexus** is the part of your stomach, below your ribs, where it is painful if you are hit hard. N SING : *the*/POSS +N

solar system. The **solar system** is the sun and all the planets, comets, and asteroids that go round it. EG *The solar system was formed 4.5 billion years ago.* N SING : *the*/POSS +N

sold /səʊld/ is the past tense and past participle of **sell**.

solder /sɒldə/, **solders, soldering, soldered.** 1 If you **solder** two pieces of metal together, you join them by melting a small piece of soft metal and putting it between them, so that it holds them together after it has cooled. V+O

2 **Solder** is the soft metal used for soldering. N UNCOUNT

soldering iron, soldering irons. A **soldering iron** is a tool used to solder things together. N COUNT

soldier /səʊldʒə/, **soldiers, soldiering, soldiered.** A **soldier** is a person who works in an army, especially a person who is not an officer. EG *These exits are guarded by soldiers.* N COUNT

soldier on. If you **soldier on** at something, you continue to do it and to work hard at it, even though it is difficult and unpleasant. EG *You have to admire them as they soldier on smiling in the face of adversity.* PHRASAL VB : V+ADV = keep going

soldierly /səʊldʒəli¹/ is used to describe someone or something that is worthy of or like a good soldier; a formal word. EG *...a soldierly English retired officer... ...their soldierly abilities.* ADJ QUALIT : USU ATTRIB ⇑ courageous

sole /səʊl/, **soles, soling, soled. Sole** can also be used as the plural form for paragraph 4. 1 You use

sole 1.1 to describe the only example of something, when there are no others at all. EG *In some families, the woman is the sole wage earner... They went with the sole purpose of making a nuisance of themselves.* ADJ CLASSIF: ATTRIB ⇑ single

1.2 to describe someone or something that is not shared with anyone else. EG *She has the sole responsibility for bringing up the child... He had acquired sole control of the newspaper in 1914.* ADJ CLASSIF: ATTRIB ⇑ exclusive

2 The **sole** of your foot or of a shoe or sock is the underneath surface of it. EG *She softly scratched the sole of her foot... ...a hole in the sole of his shoe.* N COUNT

3 When cobblers **sole** shoes or boots, they put new soles on them. EG *Get your shoes heeled and soled here.* V+O

4 A **sole** is a flat fish which you can eat. There are several kinds of sole. EG *The restaurant is reported to provide excellent sole... We're having the Dover sole with lemon butter.* N COUNT/UNCOUNT

solecism /sɒləsɪzəᵒm/, **solecisms**. A **solecism** is a minor grammatical mistake in speech or writing; a formal word. N COUNT

-soled combines with nouns and adjectives to form other adjectives which describe shoes or feet that have soles of a particular kind. EG *...rubber-soled shoes.* COMB: FORMS ADJS

solely /səʊlli¹/. If something involves **solely** one thing, it involves this thing only and no others. EG *I do not believe that this is solely a matter of money... We can't rely solely on the television for news... He had made these false declarations simply and solely to save her reputation.* ADV ⇑ exclusively

solemn /sɒləm/. 1 Someone or something that is **solemn** is very serious rather than cheerful or humorous. EG *...a special opera with a solemn social message... The service of burial is done with solemn and mournful music... ...the solemn tones of Winston Churchill.* ◊ **solemnly**. EG *Ralph nodded solemnly.* ◊ **solemnity** /sə⁷lemnɪti¹/. EG *He preserved his mask of solemnity even with acquaintances.* ADJ QUALIT = grave, sombre ◊ ADV WITH VB ◊ N UNCOUNT

2 A **solemn** promise, agreement, etc is one that you make in a very formal, committed way. EG *The government has solemn commitments and must honour them.* ◊ **solemnly**. EG *He vowed quite solemnly that he would carry out his promise.* ADJ QUALIT ◊ ADV WITH VB

solicit /səlɪsɪt/, **solicits, soliciting, solicited**. 1 If you **solicit** something such as money or information from someone, you ask them for it; a formal use. EG *We had to open a fund and solicit contributions to pay off her debts... Roy solicited aid from a number of influential members... He sent cards to all his constituents to solicit their views about his action.* V+O = request

2 When a prostitute **solicits**, he or she offers to have sex with someone in return for money. ◊ **soliciting**. EG *...public soliciting by prostitutes in the streets... She's been fined £35 for soliciting.* V OR V+O: USU V ◊ N UNCOUNT

solicitor /səlɪsɪtə/, **solicitors**. A **solicitor** is a lawyer who gives legal advice to clients and prepares legal documents and cases. EG *He was a partner in a firm of solicitors... I was advised to put the matter into the hands of a solicitor.* N COUNT

Solicitor General, Solicitors General. In Britain, the **Solicitor General** is the second most important legal officer, next in rank to the attorney general. EG *...the Solicitor General of Scotland, Mr Ewan Stewart, Q.C.* N COUNT

solicitous /səlɪsɪtəs/. Someone who is **solicitous** shows an anxious or eager concern for someone else; a fairly formal word. EG *The desk clerk was most solicitous, promising that I would be called as soon as my visitors arrived.* ◊ **solicitously**. EG *'Now, Mr Gerran, you must take it easy,' I said solicitously.* ADJ QUALIT ⇑ concerned ◊ ADV WITH VB

solicitude /səlɪsɪtju:d/. Your **solicitude** for someone is anxious concern that you show for them; a fairly formal word. EG *I was moved by their genuine kindness and solicitude for Karin.* N UNCOUNT

solid /sɒlɪd/, **solids**. 1 A **solid** substance or object stays the same shape whether it is in a container or not. Things that are solid are usually also firm or hard, and other objects cannot get through them without leaving a hole. EG *The canoe bumped hard against something solid and unyielding... It froze and became one solid block... Even the sea around them is frozen solid.* ADJ CLASSIF ⇑ material

2 A **solid** is 2.1 a substance that stays the same shape whether it is in a container or not. EG *You must at least know whether it's a solid or a liquid or a gas.* N COUNT

2.2 a three-dimensional shape in geometry. N COUNT

3 **Solids** are 3.1 types of food that consist of solid substances, as opposed to liquids such as milk or soup. EG *How old was your baby when you started her on solids?* 3.2 particles of solid matter that are present in a liquid and that would remain behind if the liquid was evaporated; a technical term in chemistry. EG *Ingredients: Non-fat milk solids, soya flour, whole milk solids, corn oil.* N PLURAL; N PLURAL: USU MOD+N

4 A **solid** material is made of the same substance all the way through with no holes inside. EG *...shapes carved into the solid rock... Is that bracelet really solid gold like it looks?... Much modern furniture is not solid but uses a sandwich of wood veneer on plywood... ...a solid oak desk.* ADJ CLASSIF ≠ hollow

5 Something that is **solid** 5.1 has all its individual pieces very close together so that there is no space between them. EG *Press the peat down firmly so it forms a solid layer... The crowd, though still thick, is less solid and one can make out individual human beings... We were packed solid from eight o'clock.* ADJ QUALIT ⇑ thick = dense, compact

5.2 has no gaps and no areas of a different colour. EG *...the solid blue of the sky... What's the significance of a solid yellow line down the edge of a road?... The police linked arms to form a solid line in front of the entrance.* ADJ CLASSIF: ATTRIB = continuous, unbroken

6 If you do something for a **solid** period of time, you do it without any pause or interruption throughout that time. EG *I waited a solid hour... ...fifteen minutes' solid conversation... I read for two hours solid.* ◊ **solidly**. EG *If you work for ten weeks solidly you might stand more of a chance.* ADJ CLASSIF: ATTRIB, OR ADV ⇑ unbroken ◊ ADV WITH VB

7 A **solid** grip, push, etc is very strong and firm. EG *He found himself held in a solid, vice-like grip... She was persuaded out of that nonsense with a few solid clouts round the ear.* ADJ QUALIT = powerful

8 A structure that is **solid** is strong and sturdy, and not likely to collapse or fall over. EG *They walked between the lines of solid Victorian houses.* ◊ **solidly**. EG *...large houses built solidly of rough wooden planks.* ◊ **solidity** /səlɪdɪti¹/. EG *In spite of their appearance of massive solidity, many of these buildings are in need of major repairs.* ADJ QUALIT ◊ ADV WITH VB ◊ N UNCOUNT

9 A person who is **solid** is very respectable and reliable. EG *She regarded them as solid, good, dull people... They have solid faces which say, 'We will do what teacher wants.'* ◊ **solidly**. EG *...a solidly respectable family.* ◊ **solidity**. EG *He and his staff would testify to the solidity of their characters.* ADJ QUALIT = worthy ◊ ADV ◊ N UNCOUNT = worthiness

10 Work, advice, etc that is **solid** is practical and useful or reliable. EG *Jane was at least able to give me some solid advice... ...a veteran British Council worker, with solid experience in Asia and Africa... She has done some very solid and important work on eighteenth-century architecture... He was put off by the vagueness of these prospects compared to a solid career in a country law practice.* ADJ QUALIT ⇑ worthwhile

11 **Solid** evidence or information is real or definite because it is based on facts rather than promises or assumptions. EG *He'd be a fool to settle out of court without some fairly solid compensation to show for it... Solid empirical evidence is needed... They went ahead on the strength of nothing more solid than Lee's optimism.* ADJ QUALIT = concrete, tangible

12 If something such as a basis for an idea or a situation is **solid**, it is strong because it has been developed slowly and carefully, and therefore cannot easily be disproved, destroyed, or changed. EG *It is important that he has a really firm, solid foundation of scientific knowledge on which to build... There is a solid mathematical basis for this observation... ...a solid understanding of Newton's Laws... A solid relationship and mutual trust are established only over a period of years.* ◊ **solidity**. EG *...giving an added dimension of strength and solidity to the nation-state.* ADJ QUALIT = firm, soun[d] ◊ N UNCOUNT ⇑ substance

13 If someone's control over something or support for something is **solid**, it is strong and unlikely to change or be removed. EG *Glasgow Central has always been a solid Labour stronghold.* ◊ **solidly**. EG *They are solidly behind the proposal.* ADJ QUALIT = firm ◊ ADV = firmly

solidarity /sɒlɪdærɪti¹/. If a group of people show **solidarity**, they show complete unity and agreement with each other, especially in supporting the same aims or actions. EG *Their spontaneous show of solidarity had saved us from a real massacre... ...working-class solidarity... The strike spread throughout the jail in solidarity with my action.* N UNCOUNT

solid fuel is fuel that is a solid rather than a liquid or gas, for example coal, wood, or peat. EG *The basic choice is gas, electricity, or solid fuel... ...a solid fuel cooker.* N UNCOUNT

solidify /səlɪdɪfaɪ/, **solidifies, solidifying, solidified.** 1 When a liquid or a semi-liquid **solidifies** or **is solidified**, it changes into a solid. EG *Pour the fat into a basin and when it has solidified take it out of the basin... The silica melts and solidifies on cooling to form a coating of glass.* V-ERG = harden

2 If something such as a system or an opinion **solidifies** or **is solidified**, it becomes firmer and more definite and unlikely to change; a fairly formal use. EG *Increasingly this arrangement became solidified and it has in fact proved permanent... These modes of conduct are calculated to solidify and stabilize his rule... This had an immense effect in solidifying the allegiance of our followers.* V-ERG ⇑ consolidate

solid-state. **Solid-state** electronic equipment is made using transistors, silicon chips, or other semiconductors, instead of valves or mechanical parts; a technical term in physics. EG *...solid-state microelectronics.* ADJ CLASSIF : ATTRIB

soliloquy /səlɪləkwi¹/, **soliloquies**. A **soliloquy** is 1 a speech in a play in which an actor or actress speaks to himself or herself and to the audience, rather than to another actor in the play. EG *He comes centre stage and begins a soliloquy, unburdening his heart and mind to the audience.* N COUNT 2 something that you say to yourself; a formal use. EG *I again held my ritual soliloquy.* N COUNT ⇑ speech = monologue

solitaire /sɒlɪtɛə/, **solitaires**. 1 **Solitaire** is 1.1 a game that one person plays alone by moving pegs to different positions on a board, with the aim of having one peg left at the end of the game. N UNCOUNT 1.2 a card game for only one player; used in American English. N UNCOUNT = patience

2 A **solitaire** is a diamond or other jewel that is set on its own in a ring or other piece of jewellery. EG *...a solitaire diamond of immense value.* N COUNT

solitary /sɒlɪtə⁰rɪ¹/. 1 A **solitary** activity is one that you do alone without any companions. EG *He formed the habit of taking long solitary walks through the streets... Few people live entirely solitary lives... ...my solitary boyhood.* ADJ CLASSIF : ATTRIB ⇑ lonely ◇ **solitariness**. EG *...the solitariness of a task meant to be shared.* ◇ N UNCOUNT ⇑ loneliness

2 Someone who is **solitary** spends a lot of time alone. EG *For the first few years of his life he was a solitary child... Thank you for joining me. I'm not a solitary drinker.* ADJ QUALIT

3 A place that is **solitary** has no people there. EG *One night I came across Mary on a solitary street.* ADJ QUALIT = empty

4 A **solitary** person or object is alone and has no others nearby. EG *I remember that solitary ash tree by the lake... Madeleine walked over to the solitary figure.* ADJ CLASSIF : ATTRIB ⇑ lone = single, sole

solitary confinement is a condition in which a prisoner is kept on his or her own, usually in a special prison cell, and is not allowed to see or speak to anyone else. EG *The jailers insisted that he had been placed in solitary confinement for his own protection.* N UNCOUNT ⇑ seclusion

solitude /sɒlɪtju:d/ is the state of being alone without other people, especially when this is calm and pleasant. EG *He began to like these moments of solitude... They searched for a place where they could live in solitude.* N UNCOUNT

solo /səʊləʊ/, **solos**. 1 A **solo** is a performance, especially of a piece of music, done by one person. ▸ used of a piece of music for one person to play. EG *...a clarinet solo by Donizetti.* N COUNT

2 A **solo** performance or activity is one that is done by one person alone. EG *All the musicians had long solo passages of their own... The morning of Will Kent's solo flight was fine and clear... We want an assurance that you won't make any more solo decisions.* ▸ used as an adverb. EG *The greatest challenge was to perform solo in the Shakespeare recital... Will you be flying solo?* ADJ CLASSIF : ATTRIB ⇑ lone ▸ ADV AFTER VB

soloist /səʊləʊɪst/, **soloists**. A **soloist** is a person who performs a solo, usually a piece of music. EG *Jenny was a harpsichord soloist... They have professional soloists and an amateur chorus.* N COUNT ⇑ performer

solstice /sɒlstɪs/, **solstices**. A **solstice** is one of the two times in the year when the sun is farthest away from the equator. In the northern hemisphere, the summer solstice is on June 21 or 22, and the winter solstice is on December 21 or 22. In the southern hemisphere, the winter solstice is in June, and the summer solstice is in December. N COUNT

soluble /sɒljə⁴bə⁰l/. 1 Something that is **soluble** will dissolve in a liquid. EG *The soil which remains loses most of its soluble minerals... The powder is soluble in water.* ADJ CLASSIF

2 A problem that is **soluble** can be solved; a formal use. ADJ CLASSIF

solution /səlu:ʃə⁰n/, **solutions**. 1 A **solution** is a way of dealing with a difficult situation so that the difficulty is removed. EG *It seemed that devaluation was the only solution... This is the latest attempt to find a peaceful solution to the troubles in the area... The loan was only a temporary solution to the country's financial difficulties.* N COUNT : IF + PREP THEN to = remedy

2 The **solution** to a question or a puzzle is the answer or explanation to it. EG *...the solution to a riddle... The solution to yesterday's crossword is on page 12.* N COUNT : IF + PREP THEN to

3 The **solution** of a question or a problem is the process of finding the answer to the question or a satisfactory way of dealing with the problem. EG *These methods can be applied to the solution of problems... We should be working together on the solution of our national problems... There was simply no solution for Sylvia.* N UNCOUNT : IF + PREP THEN of/for = resolution

4 A **solution** is also a liquid in which a solid substance or a gas has been dissolved; a technical term. EG *Immerse it in a solution of peroxide and water... A mild household bleach solution will often get rid of these stains.* N COUNT/UNCOUNT : IF + PREP THEN of ● A substance **in solution** is one that is dissolved in a liquid. EG *The sugar is held in solution.* ● PHR : USED AS AN A

solvable /sɒlvəbə⁰l/. A problem that is **solvable** can be solved. EG *You must realize that the problems of the world may not be solvable by human intellects alone.* ADJ CLASSIF = soluble

solve /sɒlv/, **solves, solving, solved**. If you **solve** a question or a problem, you find an answer to the question or a satisfactory solution to the problem. EG *I think this would create more problems than it would solve... ...the failure of successive Government policies to solve Britain's economic problems... ...a new way of solving differential equations... ...a notorious murder case which has never been solved.* V+O = remedy, resolve

solvency /sɒlvənsi¹/ is a state in which you are able to pay all your debts; a fairly formal word. EG *...moving suddenly from hopeless bankruptcy to total solvency.* N UNCOUNT ⇑ condition ≠ insolvency

solvent /sɒlvənt/, **solvents**; a fairly formal word. 1 If you are **solvent**, you have enough money to pay all your debts. EG *They have low reserves and need the money to stay solvent.* ADJ QUALIT : USU PRED ⇑ in credit

2 A **solvent** is a liquid that can dissolve other substances. EG *The grey dye was washed out with the aid of a solvent.* N COUNT/UNCOUNT

Somali /sə⁶mɑ:li¹/, **Somalis**. 1 **Somali** means belonging or relating to Somalia or to its people. ADJ CLASSIF

2 A **Somali** is a person who comes from Somalia. EG *The Somalis had no difficulty in establishing themselves in the area.* N COUNT

sombre /sɒmbə/; also spelled **somber** in American English. 1 **Sombre** colours are dark and dull. EG *...two women identically dressed in sombre black... ...a background of somber dark green.* ADJ QUALIT : ATTRIB = sober

2 You describe a place as **sombre** when it is dark or has no bright colours. EG *Calderwood led him into the sombre oak-panelled room.* ADJ QUALIT = gloomy

3 If a person looks or sounds **sombre**, they give an impression of sadness or seriousness. EG *I noticed he looked unusually sombre.* ▸ used of someone's expression or the sound of their voice. EG *Her face grew sombre... His voice was sombre.* ADJ QUALIT ⇑ serious = grave ◇ **sombrely**. EG *Mercer shook his head sombrely... 'I shot it myself,' he added sombrely.* ◇ ADV WITH VB = gravely

4 In a **sombre** statement or remark, someone gives sad news or expresses doubts about the future. EG *His report was sombre... They awaited each sombre bulletin... Mr Morris took a more sombre view.* ADJ QUALIT = grim ≠ optimistic

sombrero /sɒmbrɛərəʊ/, **sombreros**. A **sombrero** is a man's hat with a very wide brim which is worn especially in Mexico. EG *...an Indian in a sombrero.* N COUNT

some /sʌm/. **Some** is not usually used with negatives. When **some** is a quantifier, it is used mainly in statements, rather than questions. 1 You use **some** to refer to a quantity of something or to a number of people or things, when you are not stating the quantity or number precisely. You can use **some** like this in three ways: **1.1** when you are referring to the quantity or number without saying whether it is large or small, because this is not important. EG *She had a piece of pie and some coffee... My brother got some more good news this week... I've got some friends coming over... I have some important things to tell them... 'You'll need graph paper.'–'Yeah, I've got some at home.'* QUANTIF+N IN PL/UNCOUNT **1.2** when you are saying that the quantity or number is fairly large. EG *I did not meet her again for some years... She was moving around some distance away... They were having some difficulty in following the plot... He will take some convincing on this.* DET **1.3** when you are saying that the quantity or number is fairly small, but that it is nevertheless greater than none. EG *There's at least some chance that it will work... I was gratified to find that I'd had some effect... That is still true to some extent.* DET ⇑ slight ≠ no

2 You also use **some** to refer to a part of something, or to a part of a group of people or things, when you are not stating the size of the part precisely. EG *She took some of the meat from her bag... They spread out and some of them went up north... Some activities are very dangerous and some are not so dangerous.* QUANTIF+N IN PL/UNCOUNT ≠ all

3 You also use **some** to refer to a particular thing or person without saying exactly which thing or person you mean. EG *We found it lying in some ditch in the middle of the desert... Some grinning stranger shouted at us.* DET

4 You also use **some** in front of a number to say that it is approximate. EG *...Buzaruto, some 150 miles south of Beira... ...a single layer of stone, some four metres thick.* ADV+NUM ⇑ about

5 You also use **some** in spoken English **5.1** to express scorn at what someone has just said, and to suggest that a word or expression that they have used does not describe something accurately. EG *'And then we had a little discussion about everything.'–'Some discussion.'* DET **5.2** to express irritation or impatience. EG *Some people!* DET : USU+N IN PL

6 **Some** is used informally, especially in American English, to express approval or admiration. EG *That was some meal we had last night... Boy, wouldn't that be some sport.* DET

7 In American English, **some** also means to a small extent or degree. EG *And then we waited some... I guess I like him some.* ADV AFTER VB = a bit

somebody /sʌmbə⁷di¹/. See **someone**.

some day; also spelled as one word. **Some day** means at a date in the future that is unknown or that has not yet been fixed. EG *I'd like to see it some day... I hope someday we'll have enough money to get those pictures.* ADV WITH VB = one day

somehow /sʌmhaʊ/. You use **somehow** **1** to say that you do not know how something was done or will be done. EG *...a boy who'd somehow broken his thumb... We'll manage somehow.* ADV **2** to say that you do not know the reason for something. EG *I couldn't get to sleep, somehow... Somehow it didn't seem very important to him any more... To hear her talking this way was somehow shocking.* ADV SEN, OR ADV +ADJ

someone /sʌmwə⁰n/. The form **somebody** is also used. **Someone** and **somebody** are not usually used with negatives. You use **someone** and **somebody** when you are talking about people rather than things. Compare **something**. **1** You use **someone** or **somebody** to refer to a person without saying exactly who you mean. EG *There's someone coming upstairs... Carson sent someone to see me... There was an accident and somebody got killed... She wrote a book on somebody famous but I can't remember who... It belongs to somebody else... We were seeking the help of someone who spoke French.* PRON INDEF : SING

2 If you say that a person is **someone** or **somebody** in a particular kind of work, you mean that they are considered to be important in that kind of work. EG *His sister is someone in television.* PRON INDEF : SING, USU USED AS C

someplace /sʌmpleɪs/ means the same as somewhere; an informal word used in American English. EG *Why don't you boys sit someplace else?* ADV

somersault /sʌməsɒ:lt/, **somersaults, somersaulting, somersaulted**. **1** A **somersault** is a rolling movement that you perform by putting your head on the ground and bringing the rest of your body over it. EG *My sister turned a somersault.* N COUNT ⇑ roll

2 If you **somersault**, you perform a somersault once or several times. EG *She somersaulted across the room... ...somersaulting circus clowns.* V

something /sʌmθɪŋ/. **Something** is not usually used with negatives. You mainly use **something** when you are talking about things, events, ideas, etc. **1** You use **something** to refer to an object, action, activity, situation, remark, idea, etc without saying exactly what you mean. EG *Hendricks saw something ahead of him... We have something rather strange to show you... He started talking about something else... It's something that has often puzzled me... I've got something to do tonight... I knew I'd forgotten something.* PRON INDEF : SING

2 You also use **something** as a contrast to 'nothing', for example when you are referring to the taking of an action rather than to doing nothing at all. EG *Do something–anything–just do something... Of course I've got my savings now, that's something.* PRON INDEF : SING ≠ nothing

3 If you say that there is **something** strange, **something** surprising, etc about a situation, person, or thing, you mean that you feel that the situation, person, or thing has an aspect which is strange, surprising, etc although you are not sure what this aspect is. EG *Don't you find something odd, something strange about the people?... I knew there was something wrong when I got that answer... The grin lingered, but I sensed something troubled underneath.* PRON INDEF : SING, PRON+AD ≠ nothing

4 You also use **something** **4.1** to say that the description or account that you are giving is not exact. EG *I can't remember the details, but it was something like this.* PRON INDEF : SING, PRON+A = roughly **4.2** to state an amount, number, time, etc approximately or to say that it is within a particular range, rather than saying what it is exactly. EG *Profits have fallen by something over 35%... Something between one and a half and three million people are affected.* ADV+PREP ≠ exactly **4.3** instead of a word that you do not know or cannot remember, especially when the word is the second part of a name or number; used in spoken English. EG *His name is Victor something... It's been here since eighteen hundred and something... The bag was 6 pounds something.* PRON INDEF : SING

5 You use the expression **something of** in the following ways. **5.1** If you say that a person or thing has **something of** a particular quality, feeling, etc, you mean that they have it to some extent. EG *He had something of the Slav temperament... I confess I had something of the raw-recruit feeling when I went in.* PHR+NG ⇑ a bit **5.2** If you say that a person is **something of** an actor, **something of** a poet, etc, you mean that the person can act, write poetry, etc to some extent. EG *...Dr Mitra, a scholar and something of a philosopher.* PHR+NG (a/an N) = a bit of **5.3** If you say that a situation is **something of** a mystery, **something of** a surprise, etc, you mean that it is slightly mysterious, slightly surprising, etc. EG *It is something of a mystery why the party should continue to support this policy.* PHR+NG (a/an N) = a bit of

6 You use the expression **or something** to express uncertainty about what you have just said; an informal use. EG *I mean, she had cancer or something... Would you like another biscuit or something?... They turned green or yellow or something... And then he died or something.* PHR

7 You also use the word **something** in the following expressions. **7.1** If you say that **there is something in** a story or account, you mean that it is partly true. EG *There must be something in the legend of the curse... Of course, there was something in Vita's version of the story.* PHR : VB INFLECTS **7.2** If you say that **there is something in** an idea or suggestion, you mean that it may be worthwhile and should be considered seriously. EG *I believe that there is something in having ballots in trade unions.* PHR : VB INFLECTS **7.3** If you say that **there is something about** a place, person, etc, you mean that the place, person, etc has a quality which you cannot describe or do not understand, but which affects you in some way. EG *There is something about places like this that raises your spirits... There was something about the man's tone that raised the girl's suspicions.* PHR+NG+REPORT-CL : INFLECTS **7.4** If you say that someone **has got something there**, you mean that they have said something interesting or important. EG *You've got something there.* PHR : VB INFLECTS **7.5** If you say that a situation, object, or place **is something** or **is really something**, you mean that you are very impressed by it; an informal use. EG *These swords are something... That's really something.* PHR : VB INFLECTS ⇑ be impressive

8 ● **something like**: see **like**. ● **something for nothing**: see **nothing**.

sometime /sʌmtaɪm/. 1 **Sometime** means at a time in the future or the past that is unknown or that has not yet been fixed. EG *Can I come and see you sometime?... All summers have to end sometime, you know... He saw Frieda Maloney sometime last week... It was sometime in the early fifties.* ADV WITH VB

2 You also use **sometime** to say that a person had a particular job or role at some time in the past. EG *Sir Alfred Munnings, sometime President of the Royal Academy.* ADJ CLASSIF : ATTRIB = former

sometimes /sʌmtaɪmz/. You use **sometimes** to say that something happens on certain occasions rather than all the time, or in certain cases rather than in every case. EG *'Do you hear from your sister?'–'Sometimes.'... Sometimes I wish I was back in Africa... Sometimes they just come for a term, sometimes six months.* ADV = at times

somewhat /sʌmwɒt/ means to a fairly large extent or degree; a rather formal word. EG *My own part was fascinating, if somewhat alarming... Communication has altered things somewhat... I found, somewhat to my surprise, that I enjoyed myself.* ADV : USU+ADJ/ADV

somewhere /sʌmweə/. **Somewhere** is not usually used with negatives. 1 You use **somewhere 1.1** to refer to a place without saying exactly where you mean. EG *I was somewhere in Greenwich Village... They lived somewhere near Bournemouth... He had to go off somewhere else for an appointment... There's an ashtray somewhere... I read somewhere that they cost about £200 each to make.* ADV = someplace **1.2** to refer to a particular point or stage in a situation, without saying what point or stage you mean. EG *A line has to be drawn somewhere. And what happens then is up to you.* ADV ≠ nowhere **1.3** to say that an amount, number, time, etc that you are mentioning is approximate. EG *...somewhere between 55,000 and 60,000 men... This is part of the original Saxon church built somewhere around 700 AD... He was somewhere in his sixties.* ADV+ADV/PREP = roughly

2 If you **are getting somewhere**, you are making progress towards achieving something. EG *If we had that sort of reaction, then I think we'd be getting somewhere.* PHR : VB INFLECTS = make headway

somnambulist /sɒmnæmbjə⁴lɪst/, **somnambulists**. A **somnambulist** is a sleepwalker; a formal word. EG *He was walking more like a somnambulist than a person fully awake.* N COUNT

somnolent /sɒmnələ⁰nt/. If you are **somnolent**, you are sleepy; a formal word. EG *'Have a glass of wine,' I said, feeling somnolent... I returned to collect my somnolent children.* ADJ QUALIT = DROWSY

son /sʌn/, **sons**. 1 Someone's **son** is their male child. EG *He was the son of the local vicar... She was carrying her baby son in her arms... They had lost a son in the war... Tony was the second of four sons.* N COUNT ⇑ offspring

2 Some people use **son** as a form of address when they are showing kindness or affection to a boy or man who is younger than them. EG *'Don't worry son,' he said. 'It'll turn up soon.'* N AS VOC

3 A man is described as a **son** of a place, when he comes from that place; a formal use. EG *...a large photograph of Poland's most famous living son.* N COUNT+SUPP

sonar /səʊnɑː/ is equipment on a ship which calculates the depth of the sea or the position of an underwater object using sound waves. EG *Passive sonar listens for noises emanating from a submarine... We were able to start sonar soundings.* N UNCOUNT, OR N BEFORE N

sonata /sənɑːtə/, **sonatas**. A **sonata** is a piece of classical music, especially one written for the piano, or for a piano and one other instrument. EG *...Chopin's Sonata number 2 in B flat minor.* N COUNT ⇑ composition

son et lumière /sɒn eɪ luːmɪeə/ is an entertainment which is held at night in an old building such as a castle. A person describes the history of the place, and at the same time different parts of the building are brightly lit and music is played. N SING WITH DET

song /sɒŋ/, **songs**. 1 A **song** is a piece of music with words that are sung to the music. EG *Would you like me to sing you a song?... ...a love song... ...a Beatles song... ...Mussorgsky's Song of the Flea.* N COUNT ⇑ composition

2 **Song** is **2.1** a number of songs regarded as a group. EG *...a concert entitled 'A Pageant of British Song'... It was wonderful to be able to extend my song repertoire.* N UNCOUNT **2.2** the act of singing. EG *Our group had all burst into song... The church is alive with prayer and song.* N UNCOUNT

3 A bird's **song** is a sound that it makes which is pleasant and musical. EG *...the sweet song of the skylark.* N COUNT/UNCOUNT = voice

4 If you buy something **for a song**, you buy it for much less than its real value; an informal expression. EG *I was wearing a dress that I had bought for a song in India.* PHR : USED AS AN A = cheap

5 See also **swan song**.

song and dance. 1 A **song and dance** act is an act performed in a theatre in which a person or group of people both sing and dance. N UNCOUNT

2 If you say that someone is making a **song and dance** about something, you mean that they are making an unnecessary fuss about it; an informal expression. EG *Her father made a great song and dance about her being late home.* N UNCOUNT = to-do

songbird /sɒŋbɜːd/, **songbirds**. A **songbird** is a bird that produces musical sounds which are like singing. There are many different kinds of songbird. N COUNT

sonic /sɒnɪk/ is used to describe things related to sound; a technical word. EG *...sonic probes.* ADJ CLASSIF : ATTRIB

sonic boom, sonic booms. A **sonic boom** is the loud noise caused by something such as an aircraft when it travels faster than the speed of sound. EG *...popular anxiety about Concorde's sonic boom.* N COUNT/UNCOUNT

son-in-law, sons-in-law. Someone's **son-in-law** is the husband of their daughter. N COUNT ⇑ relative

sonnet /sɒnɪt/, **sonnets**. A **sonnet** is a poem with 14 lines, in which some lines rhyme with others according to certain fixed patterns. EG *...Shakespeare's sonnets.* N COUNT

sonny /sʌni¹/ is an informal word sometimes used to address a young boy. EG *Hallo, sonny.* N AS VOC

son of a bitch, sons of bitches; also spelled with hyphens. If you call someone a **son of a bitch**, you are referring to them in a very offensive way, usually because they have made you angry or upset; used especially in American English. EG *What's that son of a bitch done this time?.* N COUNT/VOC

sonority /sə⁷nɒrə¹ti¹/. The **sonority** of a sound is its deep resonance; a formal word. EG *They sing in a harmony given added sonority on a still and frosty night.* N UNCOUNT

sonorous /sənɔːrəs, sɒnərəs/; a formal word. 1 A sound that is **sonorous** is deep and rich. EG *...his deep sonorous voice... ...from the piping choirboys to the sonorous bass.* ADJ QUALIT

2 Words that are **sonorous** sound important and impressive. EG *...the sonorous names of Betelgeuse and Aldebaum.* ADJ QUALIT = high-sounding, imposing

soon /suːn/, **sooner, soonest**. 1 You use **soon 1.1** to say that something will happen in a very short time from now, or that something happened a short time after the time that you are talking about. EG *It will soon be Christmas... Soon she would have to retire... Write soon... 'When are you going to do the dishes?'–'Soon.'... I soon forgot about our conversation... He rented a TV soon after moving into his apartment.* ADV WITH VB, OR ADV+PREP/ADV = before long **1.2** to ask how long it will be before something happens in the future, or to talk about how early something happens in the course of events. EG *How soon are you returning to Paris?... It's too soon to talk about stopping... I should finish within a few years, perhaps sooner... I swore I'd get out the soonest.* ADV WITH VB

2 If you say that a second thing will happen **as soon as** a first thing happens, you mean that the second thing will happen immediately after the first thing happens. EG *As soon as we get the tickets we'll send them to you... As soon as she got out of bed the telephone stopped ringing... My legs cramped up as soon as I stopped walking.* CONJ SUBORD ⇑ when

3 If you ask someone to do something **as soon as possible, as soon as** they **can**, etc, you ask them to do it quickly and with as little delay as possible. EG *Contact the police as soon as possible... Let us know as soon as you can.* PHR : USED AS AN A

4 If you say that you **would just as soon** do something different from a thing mentioned previously, you mean that you would prefer to do this; a fairly informal expression. EG *I really don't want to go there. I'd just as soon turn around and go back... I'd just as soon not, to tell you the truth.* PHR+INF : = rather, sooner

sooner /suːnə/. 1 If you say that you would **sooner** do something different from a thing mentioned previously, you mean that you would prefer to do this. EG ADV COMPAR : *would*+ADV+INF = rather

I would sooner read than watch television... I'd sooner not trouble Mr Lane.

2 If you say that **no sooner** has a first thing happened **than** a second thing happens, you mean that the second thing happens immediately after the first thing has happened. EG *No sooner had he closed his eyes than he fell asleep... You no sooner pour your aperitif than the bell goes.* ● You use the expression **no sooner said than done** to say that something just mentioned is done or will be done immediately. EG *'Can you put the kettle on?'-'No sooner said than done.'* CONJ SUBORD = hardly, scarcely ● CONVENTION

3 If you say that something will happen **sooner or later**, you mean that it will definitely happen at some time in the future, even though it might take a long time. EG *Everyone tells everything to me sooner or later... Sooner or later, it was bound to happen.* PHR : USED AS AN A = eventually

4 You use the expression **the sooner the better** to say that you think something should be done as soon as possible. EG *The sooner we get out the better... You need a holiday and the sooner the better.* CONVENTION

soot /sʊt/ is black powder which is carried into the air in the smoke from a fire, and which is left on the sides of chimneys and on other surfaces. N UNCOUNT

soothe /suːð/, **soothes, soothing, soothed.** 1 If you **soothe** someone who is angry, worried, or upset about something, you make them feel calmer. EG *He tried to soothe her by making conversation... Her sympathetic manner seemed to soothe their hurt feelings.* ◊ **soothing**. EG *...soothing music... It has a most soothing effect on the nerves.* ◊ **soothingly**. EG *'There's nothing to worry about,' she said soothingly.* V+O = placate, quieten ◊ ADJ QUALIT ◊ ADV WITH VB

2 Something such as ointment that **soothes** pain makes the pain less severe. EG *...cream she put on to soothe her sunburn.* ◊ **soothing**. EG *...the soothing paste his father rubbed into the wound.* V+O = alleviate ◊ ADJ QUALIT ↑ relieving

sooty /sʊti¹/. Something that is **sooty** is covered with soot. EG *...his sooty hands... We looked out through the sooty windows.* ADJ QUALIT ↑ dirty

sop /sɒp/, **sops, sopping, sopped.** 1 A **sop** is something small or unimportant that you offer to someone who is dissatisfied or discontented in order to prevent them from getting angry or causing trouble. EG *The only sop they throw in the direction of the OAPs is their free bus passes.* N COUNT : USU SING ↑ offering

2 See also **sopping**.

sop up. Material that **sops** a liquid **up** soaks it up like a sponge; a fairly informal expression. EG *My bandage would sop the blood up all right.* PHRASAL VB : V+O+ADV ↑ absorb = soak up

sophisticated /səfɪstɪkeɪtɪ²d/. 1 A **sophisticated** person 1.1 shows experience in social situations and knowledge about culture, fashion, and other matters that are considered socially important. EG *...a glossy magazine designed for today's sophisticated woman.* ▸ used of people's behaviour. EG *Vidal was a picture of sophisticated detachment... ...a sophisticated lifestyle.* 1.2 is intelligent, well-informed, and shows an ability to understand complicated matters. EG *...a politically sophisticated electorate.* ▸ used of people's behaviour. EG *They're trying to find a more sophisticated approach to East-West relations.* ADJ QUALIT = refined ▸ = cultured ADJ QUALIT = aware

2 A **sophisticated** machine or device is made using advanced and complex methods. EG *These planes are among the most sophisticated aircraft now being manufactured.* ▸ used of the methods used to make such machines or devices. EG *...sophisticated computer search methods... ...sophisticated techniques.* ADJ QUALIT

sophistication /səfɪstɪkeɪʃəⁿn/. The **sophistication** of people, methods, machines, etc is their quality of being sophisticated. EG *Their elegantly cut suits projected sophistication... ...TV games of startling sophistication... The military machinery will grow in sophistication and destructive power.* N UNCOUNT

sophistry /sɒfɪstri¹/, **sophistries**. **Sophistry** is the practice of using clever arguments that sound convincing but are in fact false; a formal word. EG *...Iago's satanic sophistry.* ▸ used to refer to such an argument. EG *...the complex falsities and sophistries of an unwise age.* N UNCOUNT ▸ N COUNT

soporific /sɒpərɪfɪk/. Something that is **soporific** makes you feel sleepy. EG *I had to fight the soporific effect of the drug all day... I found his style of lecturing rather soporific.* ADJ QUALIT

sopping /sɒpɪŋ/. Something that is **sopping** or **sopping** wet is extremely wet; an informal word. EG *I was sopping wet when I got back... He held out a sopping handful of clothes.* ADJ CLASSIF, OR ADV+ADJ = drenched, soaked

soppy /sɒpi¹/, **soppier, soppiest**. If you describe someone or something as **soppy**, you mean that they are foolishly sentimental; an informal word. EG *I was determined not to get soppy about it... A drawing of a cat will always sell if it is soppy enough.* ADJ QUALIT = mawkish, daft

soprano /səprɑːnəʊ/, **sopranos**. 1 A **soprano** is a woman, girl, or young boy with a singing voice in the highest range of musical notes. EG *His mother had been a soprano with the Berlin State Opera.* ▸ used to refer to this range of musical notes. EG *She had a high, thin soprano voice.* N COUNT ↑ singer ▸ N BEFORE N

2 A woman, girl, or young boy who sings **soprano** sings a part written for a soprano voice in a piece of music such as an opera. EG *Who is going to sing soprano?* N UNCOUNT

sorbet /sɔːbeɪ/, **sorbets**. **Sorbet** is water ice that is usually made from fruit. EG *...orange sorbet.* N MASS ↑ dessert

sorcerer /sɔːsərə/, **sorcerers**. A **sorcerer** is a person who performs magic by using the power of evil spirits. N COUNT ↑ magician

sorceress /sɔːsərɛs/, **sorceresses**. A **sorceress** is a woman who performs magic by using the power of evil spirits. N COUNT ↑ magician

sorcery /sɔːsəri¹/ is the practice of performing magic by using the power of evil spirits. EG *At that time most people believed in sorcery and witchcraft.* N UNCOUNT

sordid /sɔːdɪd/. Something that is **sordid** 1 involves dishonest or immoral behaviour that is often caused by a desire to gain money or some other advantage. EG *Their decision seems to have been dictated by sordid material interests... ...a rather sordid affair... I hope you don't mind my mentioning the sordid subject of finance.* 2 is dirty, unpleasant, and depressing, usually because of poverty or lack of care. EG *...sordid back streets in the poorest part of town... During her research she witnessed the most sordid effects of heroin.* ADJ QUALIT ↑ dishonourable = shabby ADJ QUALIT = squalid, wretched

sore /sɔː/, **sores**. 1 If part of your body is **sore**, it causes you pain and discomfort, for example because of a wound or infection or because your muscles have been used too much. EG *Her throat was so sore she could not talk... I've got sore feet after all that walking... He was sore all over.* ADJ QUALIT ↑ painful = aching

2 A **sore** is a painful place on the body where the skin is infected. EG *She had a big open sore on her leg... After infection sets in, sores break out around the lips.* N COUNT ↑ wound

3 If you are **sore** about something, you are angry and upset, often because someone has done something to offend you; used especially in American English. EG *Nobody believed him of course, and this made him sore as hell... I tried to persuade her not to be sore about it.* ADJ QUALIT : PRED, IF+PREP THEN *about* = aggrieved

4 **Sore** is used to describe something that is causing great difficulty, worry, or suffering; a literary use. EG *The man is in sore need of new standards... I was a sore trial to him because I seemed unable to learn.* ◊ **sorely**. EG *They were both sorely in need of rest... We shall miss her sorely.* ADJ CLASSIF : ATTRIB ◊ ADV = badly

5 If a particular subject is a **sore point** with someone, it is likely to make them angry or embarrassed if you mention it or try to discuss it. EG *Don't say anything about his driving test-it's become a bit of a sore point.* PHR : USED AS ↑ issue

6 If something **sticks out like a sore thumb**, it is very obvious or noticeable, usually because it is strange or inappropriate; an informal expression. EG *You'll stick out like a sore thumb with that hat on.* PHR : VB INFLECTS

sorrel /sɒrəl/ is a plant with arrow-shaped leaves that have a bitter taste and are sometimes used in salads and sauces. N UNCOUNT = dock

sorrow /sɒrəʊ/, **sorrows, sorrowing, sorrowed.** 1 **Sorrow** is a feeling of deep sadness or regret, caused for example by the death of someone you love or because of your sympathy for the sufferings of someone else. EG *She wrote to express her sorrow at the tragic death of their son... Their feelings about the murder are expressed more in terms of sorrow than of anger.* N UNCOUNT = grief

2 Someone who **sorrows** about something feels or shows sorrow about it; a fairly literary use. EG *He made a face of sympathy to show he sorrowed for the dead son.* V : USU+A = grieve

3 A **sorrow** is an event or situation that causes deep sadness. EG *After all these sorrows and trials, she had become a very embittered person... ...enjoying the pleasures and suffering the sorrows that life brings.* N COUNT = affliction, trouble

4 If you **drown** your **sorrows**, you drink alcohol to try and forget your troubles or your disappointment about something. EG *The losing team went to drown their sorrows in the pub.* — PHR : VB INFLECTS

sorrowful /sɒrə[6]fʊl/. Someone or something that is **sorrowful** shows or causes deep sadness; a fairly literary word. EG *It was a sorrowful day in that town when the orders came to close down the mine... She was giving me sorrowful looks.* ◊ **sorrowfully**. EG *He shook his head sorrowfully.* — ADJ QUALIT ⇑ unhappy; ◊ ADV WITH VB

sorry /sɒri[1]/, **sorrier, sorriest**. **1** **'Sorry', 'I'm sorry', 'I really am sorry'**, etc are ways of apologizing to someone for something that you have done which has upset them or caused them difficulties. EG *'You're giving me a headache with all that noise.'–'Sorry,' Thomas said... I'm sorry I'm so late... I'm sorry to have been such a nuisance... Sorry about the coffee on your bedspread... I'm sorry if I worried you... I'm sorry for all this confusion.* — CONVENTION, OR PHR + about/for/ REPORT-CL/ to-INF

2 If you are **sorry** about a situation, you feel sadness, regret, or disappointment about it. EG *He was sorry he had agreed to stay for dinner... He knew he had behaved badly. He seemed truly sorry... He didn't know whether to feel glad or sorry at his dismissal... No one seemed very sorry to see me go... I now feel even sorrier about leaving school.* — ADJ QUALIT : PRED, USU + about/for/ to-INF/REPORT-CL ⇑ regretful

3 You use **sorry** as a polite introduction when you are saying that you are unable to help someone or when you are giving someone bad news. EG *I'm sorry but there's no-one here called Nikki... 'Could I speak to Mr Duff, please?'–'Oh I'm sorry, he's busy at the moment.'... He left no forwarding address. Sorry... I'm sorry to tell you this, but the Board have decided to make you redundant... The manager had said he was sorry, there was nothing he could do about it.* — CONVENTION, OR ADJ QUALIT : PRED, ALSO + to-INF/REPORT-CL

● You use the expression **'I'm sorry to say'** to express regret together with disappointment or disapproval. EG *This treatment doesn't help them if they've got a bad heart, I'm sorry to say... I'm sorry to say that the experiment has not been a success.* — ● PHR + REPORT-CL, OR PHR : USED AS ADV SEN = I fear, I regret

4 You also say **'I'm sorry'** to give a genuine expression of regret and sadness when you hear sad or unpleasant news. EG *'Jenny's dead,' I told him. 'I'm sorry,' he said in a stunned whisper... 'I'm seriously thinking of retiring.'–'I'm sorry to hear that.'* — CONVENTION, OR PHR + to-INF

5 If you **are sorry for** or **feel sorry for** someone who is unhappy or in an unpleasant situation, you feel sympathy and sadness for them. EG *I knew they were having a rough time and I felt sorry for them... He felt extremely sorry for the little boy.* — PHR : VB INFLECTS ⇑ pity

6 If you **are sorry for** yourself or **feel sorry for** yourself, you are miserable and feel pity for yourself, often because you think that life is unfair or that people do not like you; usually used showing disapproval. EG *He appeared to be permanently sorry for himself... How dare you feel sorry for yourself? It was your own fault!* — PHR + REFL : VB INFLECTS

7 You also use **sorry 7.1** when you haven't heard something that someone has said and you want them to repeat it. EG *'Have you seen the health guide book anywhere?'–'Sorry?'–'Seen the health guide book?'* — CONVENTION = pardon, excuse me

7.2 as a polite introduction when you are disagreeing with someone or refusing to do something for them. EG *I'm sorry, I wouldn't agree with that at all, Brian... I'm very sorry but I feel I cannot oblige you in this matter.* — CONVENTION, OR ADJ QUALIT : PRED

7.3 as a polite introduction when you want to interrupt other people who are having a discussion. EG *Sorry, we're getting away from the point... I'm sorry, I don't actually get your meaning... Sorry, may I just add something here?* — CONVENTION, OR ADJ QUALIT : PRED = excuse me, forgive me

7.4 to correct yourself when you have said something incorrect. EG *It's in the southeast, sorry, southwest corner of the USA... The other three suggestions–sorry–I should have said the other two suggestions, were very helpful.* — ADV SEN = I mean, rather

8 **Sorry** is also used to describe people and things that are in a bad physical or mental state. EG *He glared at them as if he had never seen such a sorry lot... ...a sorry remnant of besotted, ragged hangers-on... 'We are in a sorry state,' she lamented.* — ADJ QUALIT : ATTRIB = sad

sort /sɔːt/, **sorts, sorting, sorted**. **1** If you talk about a particular **sort** of something, **1.1** you are referring to a class of things that have particular features in common and that belong to a larger group of related things. EG *'What sort of iron did she get?'–'A steam iron.'... They are a sort of chocolate... There were five different sorts of biscuits... We had a good run without illness or upset of that sort... ...a rock plant of some sort... I need a new typewriter. The electronic sort are easier to use, but more expensive.* — N COUNT + SUPP : USU SING = kind, type, variety

1.2 you are referring to a particular thing or person in relation to other things or people that have similar natures or qualities, or in relation to something else that has just been mentioned. EG *There is an unnecessary amount of this sort of crime... I know you're interested in this sort of thing... The changes are of a rather high level sort.* — N COUNT + SUPP : USU SING = kind, type

2 **All sorts** of things or people means a large number of different things or people. EG *When you are young you dream about all sorts of things... There are all sorts of reasons why this is true... ...suspicion and distrust and evil imaginings of all sorts.* — PHR : USU + of + N IN PL ⇑ many = all kinds PREP

3 In informal English, you use **sort of 3.1** to describe or refer to something that you are uncertain about but that is roughly like the thing mentioned or has the qualities mentioned. EG *She was wearing a sort of velvet dress... I heard a strangling sort of noise... ...a dark thing, a beast, some sort of animal... She gave us the most exotic sort of creamy thing for dessert.* — PHR + NG : WITH DET = kind of, type of

3.2 to say that something is partly true or partly the case, but does not fully describe the actual situation. EG *'Blue hair?'–'Well, sort of mauve really.'... I'm sort of fond him... 'Is it a literary thing?'–'Well sort of.'... I've sort of heard of him but I don't know who he is.* — PHR : USU + ADJ/ PAST PART = kind of

3.3 if you are uncertain about what you are saying and wondering if you are using the right word. EG *Mike had it sort of behind him on the window sill... He was sort of banging his head against a window... It had sort of rather substantial walls... ...I mean sort of recently, like, you know, the last 5 or 7 years.* — PHR + VB/ADV/ PREP = kind of

4 If you describe something as a thing **of sorts** or **of a sort**, you add uncertainty and vagueness to the description, and sometimes suggest that the thing is of a rather poor quality or standard. EG *Farlow was a lawyer of sorts... I did carry a medical library of sorts around with me.* — PHR AFTER N ⇑ sort of

5 A particular **sort** of person has the character that is mentioned or suggested. EG *She was a good sort... What sort of fellow is he? Did you like him?* — N SING WITH DET + SUPP

6 If you feel **out of sorts**, you feel slightly unwell, discontented, or annoyed. EG *She sighed too and complained of being out of sorts... ...when you are out of sorts with the group.* — PHR : USED AS AN A

7 If you say **'It takes all sorts'**, you express mild scorn or disapproval of someone's individuality or unconventional behaviour. EG *She wants sardine and banana sandwiches? Oh well, I suppose it takes all sorts.* ● **nothing of the sort**: see **nothing**. ● **sort of thing**: see **thing**. — CONVENTION

8 If you **sort** things, you separate them into different classes, groups, places, etc, so that you can arrange them in a useful or sensible order. EG *Minnie was alone in the post office, sorting mail... They had got thoroughly mixed up and needed to be sorted into three complete sets... He was sorting through a pile of clean socks.* — V + O, OR V + A

sort out. **1** If you **sort out** a group of things that are not in order or not ready for use, you organize them or tidy them. EG *It took quite a while to sort out all our luggage... The remaining girls were collecting and sorting out the balls... Mrs Kirk and I got everything sorted out.* ● See also **sort-out**. — PHRASAL VB : V + O + ADV

2 If you **sort out** a problem or misunderstanding, you deal with it and find a solution to it. EG *I need to get my own problems sorted out... We have to sort things out between us... He sat down to sort out the meaning of these changes in his life.* — PHRASAL VB : V + O (NG/REFL) + ADV ⇑ solve

3 If you **sort** someone **out**, you make them realize how wrongly they have behaved, for example by talking to them or punishing them; used in informal British English. EG *I'll soon sort him out for you.* — PHRASAL VB : V + O + ADV ⇑ reprove

sortie /sɔːti[1]/, **sorties**. **1** A **sortie** is a brief trip away from your home or base, especially a trip to an unfamiliar place. EG *Apart from his occasional sorties to Exeter he hardly ever left the farm... The maid kept darting out on little sorties.* — N COUNT = foray

2 If a military force makes a **sortie**, it makes an attack or raid by leaving its own position and going briefly into enemy territory. EG *The counter-revolutionaries made guerrilla sorties into the border regions.* — N COUNT = foray

sorting office, sorting offices. A **sorting office** is a place where letters, packages, etc are taken after posting and are sorted according to their delivery addresses. — N COUNT

sort-out, sort-outs. If you have a **sort-out**, you tidy something such as a room or house and put everything in the right place; an informal word. EG *I gave the bedroom a good sort-out.* N COUNT : USU SING

SOS /ɛs əu ɛs/. An **SOS** is a signal which indicates to other people that you are in danger and need help quickly. The signal consists of the letters SOS which you transmit in morse code. EG *No SOS messages were received from the plane.* ▸ used to refer to any urgent request for help. EG *He was tempted to make an urgent SOS.* N SING WITH DET = mayday

so-so. If you say that something is **so-so**, you mean that it is average in quality, rather than being either very good or very bad; an informal word. EG *Some of the food is very good, some of it's so-so, and some of it's plain ordinary... ...a so-so golfer... 'How did the meeting go?'-'So-so.'... 'How are you feeling?'-'So-so.'* ADJ CLASSIF, OR ADV WITH VB = fair, okay

sot /sɒt/, **sots**. If you describe someone as a **sot**, you mean that they often get drunk; an old-fashioned word. N COUNT ⇑ drunkard

sotto voce /sɒtəu vəutʃi¹/. If you say something **sotto voce**, you say it in a soft voice so that nobody else will hear what you are saying; a literary expression. EG *'I'm glad,' I said sotto voce, 'I'm not married to you.'* ADV AFTER VB ⇑ quietly

souffle /suːfleɪ/, **souffles**; also spelled **soufflé**. A **souffle** is a light airy food made from beaten egg whites that are mixed with other ingredients and baked in the oven. EG *...a cheese soufflé... Would you like some chocolate soufflé?* N COUNT/ UNCOUNT

sough /sau/, **soughs, soughing, soughed**. When the wind **soughs**, it makes a whispering sound in the trees; a literary word. EG *There was no sound but the soughing of the breeze in the pine trees.* V : USU+A = sigh

sought /sɔːt/ is the past tense and past participle of **seek**.

sought-after. Something that is **sought-after** is in great demand, usually because it is rare or is of very good quality. EG *The most sought-after item was an early painting by Picasso... She became quite sought-after as an after-dinner speaker.* ADJ QUALIT ⇑ wanted

soul /səul/, **souls**. 1 A person's **soul** is 1.1 the spiritual part of that person that is believed to continue existing after the body is dead. EG *They said a prayer for the souls of the men who had been drowned in the storm.* N COUNT : USU WITH POSS = spirit 1.2 the non-physical part of that person, where the person's true nature and deepest thoughts and feelings are believed to be. EG *Only someone with the soul of a poet can really understand this... His soul was in turmoil.* N COUNT : USU WITH POSS

2 The **soul** of a nation or a political movement is the special quality it has that represents its true and basic nature. EG *...the soul of the American people.* N SING WITH DET = essence

3 **Soul** is the quality in a person, work of art, etc of feeling, expressing, or producing deep and sincere emotions. EG *It's quite an attractive building, but somehow it hasn't got much soul.* N UNCOUNT = character

4 A **soul** is 4.1 a person of a particular kind, especially someone that you like or feel sorry for. EG *She was a kind and generous soul... Some poor soul will be looking for these keys.* N SING WITH DET : ADJ+N = creature 4.2 any person at all; only used in negative statements like 'not a soul'. EG *When I first went there I didn't know a single soul... I swear I will never tell a soul.* N SING : a+N, WITH BROAD NEG

5 **Souls** are people; used in formal or pompous English, especially when talking about the number of people who live in a place. EG *...this vast country of 200 million souls.* N PLURAL : NUM +N = inhabitant

6 If you say that someone is **the soul of** good manners, discretion, etc, you mean that their behaviour is a perfect example of this good quality. EG *She was the soul of good nature.* PHR+NG

7 **Soul** is also the same as soul music. EG *...a soul band.* N UNCOUNT

8 If you **bare** your **soul**, you tell someone your most secret thoughts and feelings. PHR : VB INFLECTS

9 If you **keep body and soul together**, you have enough money to provide what you need to live. EG *I was earning just enough to keep body and soul together.* ● **the life and soul of the party**: see **life**. PHR : VB INFLECTS = make ends meet

soul-destroying. Something that is **soul-destroying** is very boring and so makes you extremely depressed. EG *...a soul-destroying job.* ADJ QUALIT = stultifying

soulful /səulful/. Something that is **soulful** expresses deep and sincere emotions. EG *...a soulful performance... ...big, soulful eyes.* ADJ QUALIT = expressive

soulless /səulli²s/. Something that is **soulless** lacks human qualities and lacks the ability to feel or produce deep and sincere emotions. EG *The place seemed soulless... ...a soulless routine job.* ADJ QUALIT = sterile

soul music is a type of pop music performed mainly by black American musicians. It developed from gospel and blues music and often expresses deep emotions. N UNCOUNT

soul-searching is long and careful examination of your thoughts and feelings, especially when you are trying to make a difficult moral decision. EG *After much soul-searching the union called off the strike.* N UNCOUNT = deliberation

sound /saund/, **sounds, sounding, sounded; sounder, soundest**. 1 A **sound** is something that you hear. EG *He heard the sound of footsteps in the hall... He opened the door without a sound... I was uncertain whether it was a 'sh' or a 'ch' sound... We have identified twenty different sounds that dolphins make.* N COUNT

2 **Sound** is what you hear as a result of vibrations travelling through the air, water, etc. EG *Sound travels better in water than in air... ...the speed of sound.* N UNCOUNT

3 If something **sounds** or if you **sound** it, it makes a particular noise. EG *The intercom buzzer sounded... A motor car passed him at top speed, sounding its horn.* V-ERG

4 If you **sound** a particular letter or sound, you pronounce it or say it clearly. EG *He couldn't sound his aitches.* V+O = enunciate

5 If a word **sounds** a particular way, it is pronounced that way. EG *You just spell it as it sounds.* V+A

6 If you **sound** a warning, you announce a message to everyone which warns them about something. ● to **sound the alarm**: see **alarm**. ● to **sound the death knell**: see **death knell**. V+O ⇑ broadcast

7 If you **sound** a particular way, you suggest a particular feeling or quality in your voice or in the way you speak. EG *Miss Lenaut sounded as though she had just run all the way from the station... 'Ah,' Piper said. He sounded a little discouraged... You know, you sound just like an insurance salesman.* V+C (ADJ), OR V +A (as/like) ⇑ seem

8 If something **sounds** a particular way, it makes that kind of sound. EG *The stiff rustling of the woman's dress sounded alarmingly loud.* V+A ⇑ seem

9 The **sound** of a singer, band, orchestra, etc is the distinctive quality of the music. EG *The group have their own unique sound... The Beatles were just part of the Liverpool sound.* N COUNT

10 **Sound** is the business of recording and broadcasting sound, especially in television and cinema. EG *The three young sound assistants worked all night to get everything finished.* N UNCOUNT

11 The **sound** is what you hear on a television; used especially to talk about how loud it is or how well you can hear it. EG *When the news had finished Morris would turn down the sound and get out a book.* N SING : the+N = volume

12 If something that you hear or read **sounds** a particular way, it produces a particular feeling or reaction in you. EG *'They've got a small farm down in Devon.'-'That sounds nice.'... It all sounded so crazy that I laughed out loud... It sounds to me as though he's just doing it to be awkward.* V+C (ADJ), OR V +A (as/like) ⇑ seem

13 The **sound** of something that you hear about or read about is the impression that you get from what you know about it. EG *I don't like the sound of linguistics... She had a rather off-putting manner by the sound of it.* N SING : the+N

14 If a word, expression, or way of speaking **sounds** like something, it suggests a particular thing to you. EG *We considered calling it an allowance-but that sounded like pocket money... I remember everybody called me Matt. I thought it sounded grown-up.* V+C (ADJ), OR V +A (like) ⇑ seem

15 If someone **sounds** something deep such as a well or the sea, they measure how deep it is by the use of a weighted line or by sonar. V+O = fathom

16 A building or structure that is **sound** is firm and not broken or damaged in any way. EG *The house was surprisingly sound... The aluminium body was perfectly sound.* ● **safe and sound**: see **safe**. ADJ QUALIT = sturdy

17 If part of your body or your mind is **sound**, it is healthy or well. EG *My heart is basically sound... These people are mentally sound.* ● If you are **of sound mind**, you are sane. ADJ CLASSIF ≠ ill ● PHR : USED AS AN A

18 A **sound** argument, judgement, piece of advice, etc is sensible and based on reason. EG *Cook met every objection with sound arguments... We need to* ADJ QUALIT ⇑ good ≠ unreliable

develop a sound theoretical foundation... Is this sound advice?

19 If you say that someone or something is **sound**, you mean that you approve of them and think they are correct. EG *I don't think Hawkins is sound on foreign affairs... He had a sound grasp of tactics... I believe that it's sound for boys and girls to have basically the same education.* — ADJ QUALIT ⇑ good ≠ poor

20 A **sound** business, investment, etc can be relied on to make money successfully. EG *Industrial expansion was a sound investment... He has a sound business instinct.* — ADJ QUALIT ⇑ good = reliable

21 A **sound** defeat, beating, or punishment is severe and thorough. ◊ **soundly**. EG *They submitted a number of candidates, all of whom were soundly defeated... He was grabbed and soundly whipped.* — ADJ QUALIT; ◊ ADV WITH VB = thoroughly

22 A **sound** sleep is deep, peaceful, and continuous. ▸ used of people. EG *He seems to be a sound sleeper.* ◊ **soundly**. EG *I slept soundly that night.* — ADJ QUALIT ≠ light; ◊ ADV

23 If you are **sound asleep**, you are sleeping deeply and peacefully. EG *Chris is still sound asleep.* — PHR : USED AS C = fast asleep

24 See also **sounding**.

sound off. If you **sound off**, you express your opinions strongly or loudly to everyone without being asked; a fairly informal expression. EG *On most matters she's quite prepared to sound off without inhibition.* — PHRASAL VB : V+ADV ⇑ speak = hold forth

sound out. If you **sound** someone **out**, you question them in order to find out what their opinion is about something. EG *Standard Oil's officials were sounded out by Conoco's investment banker.* — PHRASAL VB : V+O+ADV = probe

sound barrier. The **sound barrier** is the sudden increase in the force of the air against an aircraft that occurs as it passes the speed of sound. EG *In a few minutes, ladies and gentlemen, we will be breaking the sound barrier.* — N SING : the+N

sound effect, sound effects. **Sound effects** are the sounds that are created artificially to make a play more realistic, especially a radio play. — N COUNT : USU PL

-sounding combines with adjectives to indicate a quality that a name, word, or expression seems to have. EG *Mr Death is a rather sinister-sounding name, isn't it?* — COMB : FORMS ADJ QUALITS

sounding /saʊndɪŋ/, **soundings**. **1** The **sounding** of something such as a bell or a horn is the act of causing it to make a sound. — N SING WITH DET = ringing

2 Soundings are **2.1** measurements of the depth of something such as a well or a sea, by the use of a weighted line or by sonar. EG *Once they suspect that a submarine is in the area they start sonar soundings over a wide area.* — N COUNT : USU PL **2.2** questions that you ask someone in order to find out what their opinion is about something. EG *Mr Ford's soundings about a campaign of his own provided little encouragement.* — N COUNT : USU PL ⇑ investigation

sounding board, sounding boards. If you use someone as a **sounding board**, you discuss your ideas with them while you are working them out. — N COUNT ⇑ test

soundless /saʊndlɪ^{2}s/. Something that is **soundless** does not make a sound. EG *...a dry, soundless laugh... ...the soundless flight of the long-eared owl.* ◊ **soundlessly**. EG *Three times he vanished soundlessly beneath the surface of the sea.* — ADJ CLASSIF ⇑ quiet; ◊ ADV WITH VB

soundproof /saʊndpru:f/, **soundproofs, soundproofing, soundproofed**; also spelled with a hyphen. **1** Something such as a room that is **soundproof** is able to stop all sound from getting in or from escaping. EG *The studio was sound-proof.* — ADJ CLASSIF ⇑ sealed

2 If you **soundproof** something, especially a room, you make it soundproof. EG *...his small sound-proofed office.* — V+O ⇑ seal

soundtrack /saʊndtræk/, **soundtracks**; also spelled with a hyphen. The **soundtrack** of a film is its sound, speech, and music; used especially to refer to the music. EG *The movie was a Western and the noisy soundtrack had given him a headache... I've got the record of the sound-track from 'The Graduate'.* — N COUNT

sound wave, sound waves. A **sound wave** is a wave on which sound is carried. EG *Radar employs radio waves whereas sonar uses sound waves.* — N COUNT

soup /su:p/, **soups, souping, souped**. **1 Soup** is liquid food made by boiling meat, fish, or vegetables in water. EG *...a bowl of soup... ...chicken soup.* — N MASS

2 If you are **in the soup**, you are in a difficult or unpleasant position; a rather old-fashioned informal expression. EG *We'll really be in the soup if the car won't start.* — PHR : USED AS AN A = in trouble

soup up. If you **soup up** a car, you make it more powerful, for example by adjusting the engine or adding special parts; an informal expression. ◊ **souped-up**. EG *...a souped-up mini.* — PHRASAL VB : V+O+ADV; ◊ ADJ CLASSIF

soupçon /su:psɒŋ/. A **soupçon** of something is a very small amount of it that is not easy to notice. EG *...a soupçon of coriander... ...a favourable review, but with just a soupçon of sarcasm.* — N SING : a+N, IF +PREP THEN of ⇑ bit = dash

soup kitchen, soup kitchens. A **soup kitchen** is a place that provides free food for people who are very poor or for people who have become homeless because of a war or a natural disaster. — N COUNT

sour /saʊə/, **sours, souring, soured**. **1** Something that is **sour** has a sharp taste like the taste of a lemon or of an apple that is not yet ripe. EG *These plums taste sour... His face screwed up as if on a sour taste.* — ADJ QUALIT = bitter

2 Sour milk has an unpleasant taste because it is no longer fresh. EG *This milk's gone sour.* — ADJ CLASSIF = off

3 Someone who is **sour** is bad-tempered and unfriendly. ▸ used of people's expressions and behaviour. EG *I received a sour look every time I passed her house.* ◊ **sourly**. EG *'What are you laughing at?' he said sourly.* — ADJ QUALIT ⇑ disagreeable; ◊ ADV WITH VB

4 If something **goes sour** or **turns sour**, it becomes less enjoyable or less satisfactory. EG *After a promising start, things began to turn sour.* — PHR : VB INFLECTS = go wrong

5 If a relationship, friendship, or attitude **sours** or if something **sours** it, it becomes less friendly, enjoyable, or hopeful. EG *These latest cuts might sour relations between the government and the military... Their bitter personal experience has soured their whole view of the medical profession... By this time détente had soured for the United States.* — V-ERG ⇑ worsen

6 Sour grapes is the attitude that you have if you say that something is worthless or undesirable when you secretly want it but cannot have it. EG *She said that the hat made me look silly, but perhaps that was sour grapes.* — PHR : USED AS C ⇑ jealousy

source /sɔ:s/, **sources**. **1** The **source** of something is **1.1** the person, place, or thing which you get it from. EG *...one of the world's main sources of uranium... Candidates are required to publish the sources of their campaign funds... Because of the war, the oil was cut off at source... ...the development of new energy sources.* — N COUNT : USU+SUPP, OR at+N **1.2** the place where it starts from or the thing which causes it. EG *They're trying to trace the source of the trouble... Have they found the source of the gas leak?... 13% of those questioned gave bad housing as their main source of worry... ...a heat source.* — N COUNT : USU SING, USU+SUPP ⇑ origin

2 A **source** is a person, book, etc that provides information for a news story or for a piece of research. EG *Western diplomatic sources confirmed reports of fighting in the capital... The story was based on information from a 'reliable source'... The author has examined all the relevant source material.* — N COUNT

3 The **source** of a river or stream is the place where it begins. EG *We are following the creek to its source.* — N SING : USU SING

sour cream. **Sour cream** or **soured cream** is cream that has been artificially made sour by being mixed with bacteria. It is used in cooking. — N UNCOUNT

south /saʊθ/; often spelled with a capital letter when used to refer to a region. **1** The **south** is **1.1** the direction which is on your right when you are looking towards the direction where the sun rises. EG *We want to find a quiet place in the hills to the south of the little town... The island is a mile in length from north to south... Which way is south?* — N SING : the+N, OR N UNCOUNT **1.2** the part of a place, country, or region which is towards the south. EG *...the South of France... She's from the South.* — N SING : the+N, IF+PREP THEN of

2 South means towards the south or to the south of a place or thing. EG *I then travelled south by Greyhound bus through Philadelphia... The cattle are gathered for the exhausting trip south... I was living in a house just south of Market Street... The youngest was sent to a boys' home somewhere down south.* — ADV WITH VB : USU AFTER VB

3 The **south** part of a place, country, or region is the part which is towards the south. EG *At least 300,000 people took to the streets in South Wales... She owned a detached boarding house on the bleak south coast... ...William Wilson, Labour MP for Coventry South.* — ADJ CLASSIF : ATTRIB, OR IN NAMES = southern

4 A **south** wind blows from the south. — ADJ CLASSIF

southbound /saʊθbaʊnd/. **Southbound** roads, cars, trains, etc lead or are travelling towards the south. — ADJ CLASSIF

EG *Southbound traffic is being diverted via Northampton... ...the southbound carriageway of the M1.*

south-east; also spelled without a hyphen, and often spelled with a capital letter or capital letters when used to refer to a region. 1 The **south-east** is 1.1 the direction which is halfway between south and east. EG *To the south-east there is a dense date plantation... We peered into the dark doorway while the sun was still in the south-east.* N SING : the+N, OR N UNCOUNT 1.2 the part of a place, country, or region which is towards the south-east. EG *...the south-east of England... There are seventy branches in London and the South East.* N SING : the+N, IF+PREP THEN of

2 **South-east** means towards the south-east or to the south-east of a place or thing. EG *...a forest somewhere south-east of Berlin... If we proceed south-east we come to Eaton Place.* ADV WITH VB : USU AFTER VB

3 The **south-east** part of a place, country, or region is the part which is towards the south-east. EG *I got it from a bookshop in the Old Kent Road in south-east London.* ADJ CLASSIF : ATTRIB

4 A **south-east** wind blows from the south-east. ADJ CLASSIF

south-easterly; also spelled without a hyphen. 1 A **south-easterly** point, area, or direction is to the south-east or towards the south-east. EG *All the yachts took a south-easterly course at 5 minute intervals.* ADJ QUALIT

2 A **south-easterly** wind blows from the south-east. ADJ CLASSIF

south-eastern; also spelled without a hyphen. **South-eastern** means in or from the south-east of a region or country. EG *We were staying in Beaumont, in southeastern Kansas.* ADJ CLASSIF : ATTRIB

southerly /sʌðəli[1]/. 1 A **southerly** point, area, or direction is to the south or towards the south. EG *Peter headed in a southerly direction... ...the most southerly tip of Bear Island.* ADJ QUALIT = southern

2 A **southerly** wind blows from the south. ADJ CLASSIF

southern /sʌðə[5]n/ means in or from the south of a region or country. EG *From Florida they crossed the southern States in very easy stages... ...the southern edge of the Sahara... ...a Southern English accent.* ADJ CLASSIF : ATTRIB

southerner /sʌðə[5]nə/, **southerners**. A **southerner** is a person who was born in or who lives in the south of a place or country. N COUNT

southernmost /sʌðə[5]nməʊst/. The **southernmost** part of an area or the **southernmost** thing in a line is the one that is farther towards the south than any other. EG *There's a 100-mile string of islands stretching from the southernmost tip of Florida.* ADJ CLASSIF : ATTRIB

South Pole. The **South Pole** is the place on the surface of the earth which is farthest towards the south. EG *...an expedition to the South Pole.* N PROPER : the+N

southward /saʊθwəd/ or **southwards** means towards the south. EG *A level expanse of low-lying country extended southward... He took the road southwards into the hills.* ADV WITH VB ▸ used as an adjective. EG *The shore was badly eaten away on its southward side.* ▸ ADJ CLASSIF

south-west; also spelled without a hyphen, and often spelled with a capital letter or capital letters when used to refer to a region. 1 The **south-west** is 1.1 the direction which is halfway between south and west. EG *To the south-west lay the city. ...You should head towartds the south-west.* N SING : the+N, OR N UNCOUNT 1.2 the part of a place, country, or region which is towards the south-west. EG *...the south-west of England... We then moved on to Houston and Dallas in the South-West.* N SING : the+N, IF+PREP THEN of

2 **South-west** means towards the south-west or to the south-west of a place or thing. EG *It flows south-west to the Atlantic Ocean... Down the mountain road southwest of Sappora is a lake as blue as the sea.* ADV WITH VB : USU AFTER VB

3 The **south-west** part of a place, country, or region is the part which is towards the south-west. EG *He works as full-time Conservative Party agent for Southwest Staffordshire.* ADJ CLASSIF : ATTRIB

4 A **south-west** wind blows from the south-west. ADJ CLASSIF

south-westerly; also spelled without a hyphen. 1 A **south-westerly** point, area, or direction is to the south-west or towards the south-west. ADJ QUALIT

2 A **south-westerly** wind blows from the south-west. ADJ CLASSIF

south-western; also spelled without a hyphen. **South-western** means in or from the south-west of a region or country. EG *This type of pine grows in the dry mountains of the southwestern United States.* ADJ CLASSIF

souvenir /suːvənɪə, suːvənɪə/, **souvenirs**. A **souvenir** is something which you acquire and then keep to remind you of a holiday, place, or event. EG *She spent the morning buying souvenirs... He had kept a spoon as a souvenir of his journey... ...a souvenir shop.* N COUNT ⇑ keepsake

sou'wester /saʊwestə/, **sou'westers**. A **sou'wester** is a waterproof hat that is worn especially by sailors in stormy weather. It has a wide brim at the back to keep your neck dry. N COUNT

sovereign /sɒvrɪn/, **sovereigns**. 1 A **sovereign** is a king or queen, regarded as the person who has the highest level of authority in a country. EG *The guard gets changed at 10.30 when the sovereign is not at Buckingham Palace... ...the Sovereign's effective power of veto.* N COUNT = monarch

2 A **sovereign** state or country is independent and not under the authority of any other country. EG *The Punjab was the last sovereign independent Indian state... Embassies are regarded as extensions of sovereign territory.* ADJ CLASSIF : ATTRIB

3 **Sovereign** is used to describe someone who has the highest power in a country. EG *Parliament is sovereign... He will be given vast new sovereign powers.* ADJ CLASSIF ⇑ supreme

4 A **sovereign** remedy is one that is able to cure or solve anything without any difficulty at all; a formal use. EG *Military force no longer provided a sovereign remedy for political dissent.* ADJ CLASSIF : ATTRIB ⇑ excellent

5 A **sovereign** is also an old British coin that was worth £1. Sovereigns are only made nowadays to commemorate special royal occasions. N COUNT

sovereignty /sɒvrə[1]nti[1]/ is 1 complete political power that a country possesses to govern itself or another country or state. EG *...a threat to national sovereignty... They refuse to give up sovereignty over the island.* N UNCOUNT ⇑ domination 2 the power to act completely freely, without interference. EG *...the sovereignty of parliament.* N UNCOUNT ⇑ supremacy

Soviet /səʊvɪət, sɒv-/, **Soviets**. 1 **Soviet** is used to describe something that belongs or relates to the Soviet Union, or to its people. EG *...the Soviet bloc.* ADJ CLASSIF : USU ATTRIB

2 A **Soviet** is a person who comes from the Soviet Union. EG *In 1957 the Soviets had put an astronaut into space.* N COUNT : USU P

3 A **soviet** is an elected local, regional, or national council in the Soviet Union. N COUNT

sow, sows, sowing, sowed, sown. The word **sow** is pronounced /səʊ/ when it is a verb, and /saʊ/ when it is a noun. 1 If you **sow** seeds, you plant them in the ground in order to grow something. EG *It's time to sow the winter wheat.* V+O, OR V

2 If you **sow** an area of land, you plant seeds in order to grow a particular crop. EG *The land was cleared of weeds and sown with guinea grass.* V+O+A (with)

3 If you **sow** an undesirable feeling or situation, you cause it to begin and develop; a fairly literary use. EG *She attacked those who sow dismay and division in the party.* V+O = stir up

4 If one thing **sows the seeds of** something else, it starts the process which leads eventually to that other thing. EG *These medical advances sowed the seeds of the population explosion... ...sowing the seeds of the Second World War.* PHR : VB INFLECTS ⇑ begin

5 A **sow** is an adult female pig. N COUNT

sown /səʊn/ is the past participle of **sow**.

soya /sɔɪj[0]ə/. **Soya** flour, butter, etc is made from soya beans. N UNCOUNT : U BEFORE N

soya bean, soya beans. A **soya bean** is a type of bean that can be eaten or used to make flour, oil, or soy sauce; used in British English. N COUNT = soybean

soybean /sɔɪbiːn/, **soybeans**. A **soybean** is the same as a soya bean; used in American English. N COUNT

soy sauce /sɔɪ sɔːs/ is a dark brown liquid made from soya beans and used as a flavouring, especially in Chinese cooking. N UNCOUNT

sozzled /sɒzə[0]ld/. Someone who is **sozzled** is very drunk; a rather old-fashioned informal word. EG *He was sozzled when he arrived at the party.* ADJ QUALIT : PRED = plastered

spa /spɑː/, **spas**. A **spa** is a place where water which has minerals in it bubbles out of the ground. People sometimes drink the water to improve their health. EG *Cheltenham is still a spa town.* N COUNT ⇑ spring

space /speɪs/, **spaces, spacing, spaced**. 1 **Space** is 1.1 the amount of the area in a place, building, container, cupboard, etc, that is empty or unblocked. EG *There was just enough space for a bed and a table... I did not have the space to store the bricks... There should be more space between the houses... Belongings take up space.* N UNCOUNT = room 1.2 the space that is used for a particular kind of activity or for storing a particular kind of thing. EG *...a tiny area of* N UNCOUNT : +N living space... ...the luggage space at the back of the car. **1.3** the area without boundaries or limits that lies beyond our planet's atmosphere. Space is usually thought of as the empty place that surrounds or lies between the stars and planets. EG *The missile soared out of the atmosphere into space... ...the first human being to travel in space... ...space research.* **1.4** the whole area without boundaries or limits in which everything that exists is found. EG *I exist at a particular point in space and time.* **1.5** the amount of a talk, programme, or piece of writing that is available for something to be discussed. EG *There is no space in this book to argue in detail the alternative viewpoint... I shall devote some space to describing my own experiences.* **1.6** the impression that a place is large, open, and light, rather than being too small and enclosed. EG *The low hills give a feeling of great, intense space... A mirror can add space to a room.* N UNCOUNT; N UNCOUNT; N UNCOUNT; N UNCOUNT = spaciousness

2 If you **make space for** someone or something, you move or rearrange things in a place, so that there is enough empty space for them to fit in. EG *Can you make space round the table for two extra people?* PHR : VB INFLECTS

3 If you are looking or staring **into space**, you are looking straight in front of you, without actually looking at anything in particular, usually because you are thinking or daydreaming. EG *She was just staring into space.* PHR : USED AS AN A ↑ ahead

4 A **space** is **4.1** a gap or empty place in something solid or crowded. EG *The door had spaces at the top and bottom... He had spaces between his teeth... ...an open space in the jungle.* **4.2** a place or area that is blank or is available for people to use or fill. EG *There is no official space for this information on the form... There were two spaces on the morning plane to Canton... We spent half an hour looking for a parking space.* **4.3** a gap between words or sequences of letters or numbers. EG *Leave two spaces after a full stop.* N COUNT ↑ hole; N COUNT; N COUNT

5 If you **space** a series of things, you arrange them so that they are not all together but have gaps or periods of time between them. EG *The lines were parallel and spaced well apart... I had to space my inquiries carefully.* V+O : USU PASS, USU+A ↑ position

6 A **space** is also a room or some other enclosed place, often considered in relation to its size. EG *...in a darkened cinema or other closed space... Tomorrow's computers will bring you a whole library in a space about the size of one of today's paperbacks.* N COUNT ↑ area

7 A **space** of time is a period of time. EG *It happened three times in the space of five months... He should arrive in a very short space of time.* N SING WITH DET +of ↑ interval

8 See also **spacing, outer space**.

space out. 1 If you **space** things **out**, you arrange them so that they are not all together but have gaps or periods of time between them. EG *Could you space yourselves out, please... These books should have large print well spaced out on the page.* PHRASAL VB : V+O (NG/REFL)+ ADV, USU PASS ↑ position

2 See also **spaced out**.

space age; spelled with a hyphen when used before another noun. **1** The **space age** is the present period in the history of the world, when travel in space has become possible. N SING : the+N ↑ era

2 You use **space-age** to describe something which is very modern and makes you think of the technology of the space age. EG *...a space-age kitchen.* ADJ CLASSIF : ATTRIB = futuristic

space capsule, space capsules. A **space capsule** is the part of a spacecraft in which people travel in space and in which they return to earth. N COUNT

spacecraft /speɪskrɑːft/. **Spacecraft** is both the singular and the plural form. A **spacecraft** is a rocket or other vehicle that can travel in space. N COUNT

-spaced combines with words such as 'closely' or 'widely' to indicate the width of the space between things. EG *The eyes are large and widely-spaced... The typing was single-spaced.* COMB : FORMS ADJS

spaced out; also spelled with a hyphen. Someone who is **spaced out** has taken drugs that make them feel as if nothing around them is real; an informal expression. EG *Most of them were spaced out on drugs.* ADJ QUALIT : PRED = high

Space Invaders is the name of a computer game in which players try to defend themselves against a fleet of enemy spaceships shown moving on a screen. EG *The college was not allowed to have Space Invaders machines.* N UNCOUNT

spaceman /speɪsmæ³n/, **spacemen**. A **spaceman** is someone who travels in space, for example an astronaut. N COUNT ↑ traveller

space probe, space probes. A **space probe** is a small spacecraft that is sent into space in order to transmit information about what space is like. N COUNT

spaceship /speɪsʃɪp/, **spaceships**. A **spaceship** is a spacecraft that carries people through space. N COUNT

space shuttle, space shuttles. A **space shuttle** is a spacecraft that is designed to be used many times for travelling into space and returning again to earth. EG *...launch schedules for the space shuttle Orbiter vehicles.* N COUNT

space station, space stations. A **space station** is an object which is sent into space and then goes round the earth, and which is used as a base by people travelling in space or doing research into space. N COUNT ↑ satellite

spacesuit /speɪssjᵘuːt/, **spacesuits**. A **spacesuit** is a special protective suit that is worn by an astronaut and that covers the whole of the body. N COUNT ↑ outfit

spacing /speɪsɪŋ/ refers to the way that typing or printing is arranged on a page, especially in relation to the amount of space that is left between words or lines of printing and typing. EG *With its even spacing and equal margins it was a work of art... The document should be typed in double spacing.* N UNCOUNT ↑ arrangement

spacious /speɪʃəs/. A room or other place that is **spacious** is large in size or area inside, so that you can usually move around freely in it. EG *...a spacious dining-room... ...spacious parks.* ◊ **spaciousness**. EG *...seemingly endless rooms, all that spaciousness and graciousness.* ADJ QUALIT ↑ roomy; ◊ N UNCOUNT ↑ expanse

spade /speɪd/, **spades**. **1** A **spade** is a tool used for digging, with a flat metal blade and a long handle. EG *...a garden spade... ...children carrying their buckets and spades to the beach.* N COUNT ↑ shovel

2 Spades is one of the four suits in a pack of playing cards. Each card in the suit is marked with one or more black symbols in the shape of a heart-shaped leaf with a stem. N UNCOUNT/ COUNT

3 Spade is used in offensive English to refer to a black person, especially a Negro. N COUNT

4 If you **call a spade a spade**, you speak frankly and directly, often about an embarrassing or unpleasant subject. EG *He's not afraid to call a spade a spade.* PHR : VB INFLECTS

spadework /speɪdwɜːk/ is uninteresting work that has to be done as preparation before you can start a project or activity. EG *Writing this sort of article always involves a certain amount of preliminary spadework.* N UNCOUNT = groundwork

spaghetti /spəgeti¹/ is a type of food made from pasta, which looks like long pieces of string and is usually served with a sauce. N UNCOUNT

spaghetti western, spaghetti westerns. A **spaghetti western** is a film made in Europe by an Italian director about life in the American Wild West, in which there is usually a great deal of violence and very little story. N COUNT

spake /speɪk/ is a very old-fashioned form of the past tense of **speak**. It is usually only used humorously nowadays. EG *Thus spake Zapp in his seminar.* V+O/QUOTE, OR V+A

span /spæn/, **spans, spanning, spanned**. **1** A **span** is **1.1** the period of time between two dates or events or during which something exists or functions. EG *...during the forty-year span from 1913 to 1953... ...in the short span that man has been on earth... ...the public's span of interest in a book... ...experiments designed to test memory span.* **1.2** the range of things that are included in a subject, task, etc. EG *Each manager has a manageable span of responsibility.* N COUNT : USU+ SUPP; N SING WITH DET : USU+SUPP ↑ extent

2 Something that **spans** a particular length of time lasts throughout that time. EG *At 79, Dame Flora can look back at a career spanning more than half a century.* V+O ↑ cover = stretch over

3 A **span** is also **3.1** the distance from one end of something right across to the other end, especially when it is stretched out as far as possible; often used to refer to the distance between your thumb and your little finger when you stretch your hand as widely as possible. EG *Some eagles have a wing span of one and a half metres... Lamis–though still a hand's span shorter than her–was growing fast.* **3.2** a bridge or part of a bridge that stretches right across a river or valley, or between two pillars. EG *...that* N COUNT : USU+ MOD ↑ stretch; N COUNT breathtaking modern span of which Brunel would have rightly approved.*

4 A bridge that **spans** something such as a river or a valley stretches right across it. EG *...a long tree-bordered lake spanned by a high, graceful, arching iron bridge.*
V+O ⇑ cross

5 See also **spick-and-span**.

spangle /spæŋgəºl/, **spangles, spangling, spangled**. 1 Small bright objects that **spangle** something are scattered over it and make it sparkle. EG *Starfish of an intense blue spangled the sand.* ◊ **spangled**. EG *...a crown spangled with glitter... ...the spangled scarves of the dancers... He gazed out at the star-spangled night sky.*
V+O
◊ ADJ CLASSIF: IF+PREP THEN *with* ⇑ decorated

2 A **spangle** is a small piece of metal or plastic which sparkles brightly and is used to decorate clothing or hair.
N COUNT

Spaniard /spænjəd/, **Spaniards**. A **Spaniard** is a person who comes from Spain.
N COUNT

spaniel /spænjəl/, **spaniels**. A **spaniel** is a type of dog with long ears that hang down.
N COUNT

Spanish /spænɪʃ/. 1 Something that is **Spanish** belongs or relates to Spain, its people, or their language. EG *Are you Spanish?... ...the Spanish government.*
ADJ CLASSIF

2 **Spanish** is the language that is spoken by people who live in Spain, and in many countries in Central and South America.
N UNCOUNT

3 The **Spanish** are the people who live in Spain. EG *They inherited much of their land from the Spanish.*
N PLURAL: *the*+N

spank /spæŋk/, **spanks, spanking, spanked**. If you **spank** a child, you punish it by hitting it sharply with your hand, usually on its bottom several times. EG *The only way to keep Johnny out of the street is to spank him.* ▸ used as a noun. EG *I gave him a spank for being so rude.*
V+O ⇑ slap = smack
▸ N COUNT = smack

spanking /spæŋkɪŋ/, **spankings**. 1 A **spanking** is a series of slaps that you give to a child with your hand, usually on its bottom, as a way of punishing it. EG *Andrea gave her son a sound spanking.*
N COUNT ⇑ punishment

2 You use **spanking** in informal English 2.1 to describe something that is clean, bright, and in excellent condition. EG *A coat of enamel paint will give your bath a spanking new look... The skins were in spanking condition.* 2.2 to describe something that is moving quickly. EG *Despite its spanking pace, the ball was quite easy to return.*
ADJ CLASSIF: ATTRIB ⇑ pristine
ADJ CLASSIF: ATTRIB ⇑ brisk

spanner /spænə/, **spanners**. 1 A **spanner** is a metal tool with a specially shaped end that fits over or round a nut so that it can be loosened or tightened. EG *Take your spanner, and tighten the nut about a quarter of a turn.*
N COUNT = wrench

2 If someone **throws a spanner in the works**, they prevent something happening smoothly in the way that it was planned, by causing a problem or difficulty; used in British English. EG *That would really throw a spanner in the works.*
PHR: VB INFLECTS ⇑ spoil

spar /spɑː/, **spars, sparring, sparred**. 1 If you **spar** with someone, 1.1 you box using fairly gentle blows instead of hitting your opponent hard, either when you are training or when you want to test how quickly your opponent reacts. EG *The aim was to spar, to feint and to strike mock blows rather than to fight in earnest.* 1.2 you argue with them, but not in an unpleasant or very serious way. EG *After some initial sparring about who would take the minutes, the discussion eventually got underway.*
V OR V+A (*with*): RECIP ⇑ fight
V OR V+A (*with*): RECIP

2 A **spar** is a strong pole, especially one that a sail is attached to on a sailing ship. EG *...sails rigged to rigid wooden spars.*
N COUNT

spare /speə/, **spares, sparing, spared**. 1 You use **spare** 1.1 to describe something that is of the same kind as things that you are already using, but that you do not need yet and are keeping ready in case another one is needed. EG *Keep a spare fuse handy by the fuse box... All you need to take is a spare shirt and a spare set of underwear.* ▸ used as a noun. EG *There are some spares at the back if anyone wants more.* 1.2 to describe something that is not planned to be used or not being used at present, and is therefore available for the purpose you want. EG *Within a few minutes we had found a spare parking meter... Every piece of spare ground has been built on... There were no chairs spare.*
ADJ CLASSIF ⇑ extra = reserve
▸ N COUNT ⇑ extra
ADJ CLASSIF = free

2 If you have something such as time or money **to spare**, you have it as extra time or money that is not needed for a particular purpose. EG *He often had money to spare nowadays... I don't have the time or energy to spare... She caught her plane with a few minutes to spare.*
PHR AFTER N ⇑ surplus

3 If you **spare** something for a particular purpose, you make it available for that purpose, for example for someone else's use. EG *Nowadays more land is needed to grow food and less can be spared to graze cattle... I got to my feet, thanking him for sparing time to see me... Do sign the book when you can spare a minute... Spare a thought for me working here while you're enjoying the sun.*
V+O: USU+ *to*-INF/*for* ⇑ give, take

4 If someone **spares** a person or a place, they do not harm or destroy them although they may have threatened to or they are harming or destroying other people or places. EG *Everyone prayed that Allah might spare the village from starvation... The great cities of the Rhineland had not been spared.*
V+O: IF+PREP THEN *from* ⇑ exempt

5 If you **spare** someone an unpleasant experience, you prevent them from suffering it. EG *His intervention may have spared me a bloody nose... We telephoned, wishing to spare poor Charlotte two or three hours of suspense... At least I am spared the shame of the children knowing... I could have spared myself the trouble.*
V+O (NG/REFL) +O = save

6 If someone **spares** you the unpleasant aspects of a story or incident, they do not tell them to you. EG *Morris shuddered. 'Spare me the details,' he begged... They had it printed in the Palace News, sparing no detail of what was going on.*
V+O, OR V+O+O ⇑ keep quiet = leave out

7 Someone who is **spare** is tall but has little or no excess fat anywhere on their body; a literary use. EG *The captain of the boat was a tall, spare man.*
ADJ QUALIT ⇑ thin = lean

8 Something that is **spare** is very plain with no unnecessary features, details, or decoration; a literary use. EG *...the spare but elegant precision of his performance.*
ADJ QUALIT = austere, stark

9 If you **go spare** or if something **drives** you **spare**, you become frantic with anger, irritation, or worry; used in very informal English. EG *Mum'd go spare if she knew... She drove me spare with her moaning.*
PHR: VB INFLECTS = go crazy, g mad

10 If you **spare no expense** in doing something, you do it without any attempt to reduce the amount of money spent. EG *The Agency has spared no expense with the best system for storage... ...made out of real ships' timbers, no expense spared.* • to **spare** someone's **blushes**: see **blush**.
PHR: VB INFLECTS

11 See also **sparing**.

spare part, spare parts. A **spare part** is a replacement for any of the individual components in a piece of equipment, especially mechanical or electrical equipment such as a car. EG *Does the guarantee include the cost of spare parts and labour?... One of his friends made a radio from spare parts.*
N COUNT: USU P

spare ribs are the ribs of a pig which are served as a cut of meat with most of the meat trimmed off.
N PLURAL ⇑ pork

spare room, spare rooms. A **spare room** is a bedroom which is kept especially for visitors to sleep in. EG *They can both sleep in the spare room.*
N COUNT

spare time; often used before another noun and spelled with a hyphen. Your **spare time** is the time during which you do not have to work and you can do what you want. EG *I did a lot of drawing in my spare time... ...a spare-time occupation.*
N UNCOUNT: US +SUPP = free time, leisure

spare tyre, spare tyres. 1 A **spare tyre** is the same as a spare wheel.
N COUNT

2 If you describe someone as having a **spare tyre**, you mean that they have a bulging ring of fat round their waist; used humorously in British English.
N SING WITH DE

spare wheel, spare wheels. A **spare wheel** is a complete wheel with a tyre already on it, which is kept in a vehicle in case one of the tyres is punctured. EG *Is the spare wheel in this car under the bonnet?*
N COUNT = spare tyre

sparing /speərɪŋ/. Someone who is **sparing** uses or gives something only in very small quantities. EG *She was sparing with heat and light.* ▸ used of people's actions and behaviour. EG *...the designer's sparing use of colour.* ◊ **sparingly**. EG *Use hot water sparingly.*
ADJ QUALIT: U +*with* = meagre, f gal
◊ ADV WITH V

spark /spɑːk/, **sparks, sparking, sparked**. 1 A **spark** is 1.1 a tiny piece of very bright burning material that flies up from something burning or that is caused, for example, by two hard things rubbing against each other. EG *The fire sent smoke and sparks over the top of the fence... ...a spray of orange sparks.* 1.2 a flash of light that is caused by an electrical discharge and often makes a crackling
N COUNT
N COUNT

sound. EG *Watch the gap for a blue spark. If there isn't one, check the points in the circuit.* **1.3** a tiny area of bright reflected light. EG *...large eyes with a little spark of excitement dancing slowly in each.* N COUNT+of ⇑ flash

2 A **spark** of a particular quality is a small but noticeable amount of the quality that might get stronger. EG *I told her a little about my life at her age, and I saw a spark of interest... The spark of resistance in them is all too easily crushed.* N COUNT+of ⇑ trace

3 If something **sparks**, it makes sparks of fire or light. EG *Something sparked white against the wall.* V ⇑ flash

4 If one thing **sparks** or **sparks off** something else happening, it is the direct cause of it starting although it was probably not deliberately intended. EG *There was a risk that the decision would spark off a conflict... The letter sparked off a friendship between the two men... What first sparked my interest was a comment of Simon's.* V, OR PHRASAL VB : V+ADV OR V +O+ADV ⇑ instigate = prompt, trigger

5 If **sparks fly** between people, they have a lively argument or heated discussion with each other. EG *The sparks fly whenever they meet... We ought to invite the critics as well as the cast. That'd soon get the sparks flying!* PHR : VB INFLECTS

6 If two people **strike sparks off each other**, they are stimulated mentally by each other, so that together they have a lot of good ideas. EG *This particular couple seemed to strike sparks off each other.* PHR : VB INFLECTS

7 See also **bright spark**.

sparking plug, sparking plugs. A **sparking plug** is the same as a spark plug. N COUNT

sparkle /spɑːkəºl/, **sparkles, sparkling, sparkled**. **1** If something **sparkles**, it is clear and bright and often shines with a lot of very small points of light that look like flashes of silver or gold being reflected all over the surface. EG *They looked down to the sea, sparkling in the sun... The lawn outside was sparkling with frost.* ▸ used as a noun. EG *It cleans windows, mirrors, and adds sparkle to silver.* ◇ **sparkling**. EG *...inquisitive sparkling eyes... ...sparkling white tile walls... The sky outside is sparkling and clear... ...a sparkling October day.* V = glitter, glisten ▸ N UNCOUNT = twinkle ◇ ADJ QUALIT ⇑ brilliant

2 Someone who **sparkles** shows a quality of lively intelligence or wit that makes them seem special. EG *He's quite different at parties–witty, outgoing, he really sparkles.* ◇ **sparkling**. EG *She felt electric, sparkling, and irresistible.* ▸ used of people's actions and behaviour. EG *He gave a sparkling performance.* V = shine ◇ ADJ CLASSIF ⇑ animated = scintillating

3 **Sparkle** is a quality of lively intelligence or interest that makes someone or something seem special. EG *They played it quite well, but the whole thing lacked sparkle somehow... These prosaic details take all the sparkle out of the conversation.* N UNCOUNT ⇑ spirit = verve

sparkler /spɑːklə/, **sparklers**. A **sparkler** is a small firework that you can hold alight in your hand. It looks like a piece of thick wire and burns with a lot of small, bright sparks. N COUNT

sparkling wine, sparkling wines. **Sparkling wine** is wine which is slightly fizzy and is sold in bottles where the cork is held in place with wire. N MASS = bubbly

spark plug, spark plugs. A **spark plug** is a device in the engine of a motor vehicle that is used to make an electric spark so that the fuel is ignited. It is made of porcelain and has a metal rod running through it and bent over at the top. EG *Replace the spark plugs every 10,000 miles.* N COUNT ⇑ component = sparking plug

sparring match, sparring matches. A **sparring match** is a good-humoured argument or fight that is not meant very seriously. N COUNT

sparring partner, sparring partners. A **sparring partner** is **1** a person who a boxer fights with regularly when he is training. N COUNT **2** a person with whom you regularly have good-humoured arguments. N COUNT

sparrow /spærəʊ/, **sparrows**. A **sparrow** is a small brown bird that is very common in Britain and many other countries. N COUNT = house sparrow

sparse /spɑːs/, **sparser, sparsest**. Something that is **sparse** is small in number or amount and spread out over an area. EG *The population was sparse... His sparse white hair was ruffled.* ◇ **sparsely**. EG *...a sparsely populated region... ...his sparsely furnished room.* ADJ QUALIT ⇑ scarce = meagre ◇ ADV WITH VB = scantily

spartan /spɑːtəºn/. A **spartan** way of life is very simple or strict, with no luxuries. EG *...the spartan lives of the islanders... We prepared for a more spartan existence.* ▸ used of places where people live and the food that they eat. EG *...spartan accommodation... ...spartan living quarters... ...the spartan diet of the poor.* ADJ QUALIT ⇑ severe = austere

spasm /spæzəºm/, **spasms**. **1 Spasm** or a **spasm** is a sudden tightening of your muscles which you cannot control. EG *The soreness is due to muscular spasm... Spasms shook her lungs and chest.* N UNCOUNT/N COUNT ⇑ convulsion

2 A **spasm** is also a sudden strong pain or unpleasant emotion which lasts for a short period of time. EG *His whole body was one spasm of pain... ...a spasm of anger.* N SING WITH DET +of ⇑ burst

spasmodic /spæzmɒdɪk/. Something that is **spasmodic** happens suddenly for short periods of time at irregular intervals. EG *As she talked, she kept making spasmodic dashes to the window.* ◇ **spasmodically**. EG *The orchestra continued to play spasmodically.* ADJ QUALIT ⇑ intermittent = occasional ◇ ADV WITH VB

spastic /spæstɪk/, **spastics**. **1** Someone who is **spastic** is born with a disability which makes it difficult for them to control their muscles, especially their arm and leg muscles. It can also affect their brain. EG *The child may be born deformed, spastic, or crippled in some way.* ▸ used as a noun. EG *She works with spastics... ...the Spastics Society.* ADJ CLASSIF ⇑ handicapped ▸ N COUNT

2 Someone might describe a person who they think is very clumsy or incompetent as **spastic**; a very offensive use. ADJ QUALIT

spat /spæt/, **spats**. **1 Spat** is the past tense and past participle of **spit**.

2 **Spats** are specially shaped pieces of cloth or leather which button down one side and which were worn in former times by men over their ankles and part of their shoes. N COUNT : USU PL = gaiter

spate /speɪt/, **spates**. **1** A **spate** of things is a large number of them, happening within a short period of time. EG *The incident caused another spate of protests... We turned on our television to hear about the day's spate of bans and detentions... We had a spate of bad luck.* N SING WITH DET +of = run, series

2 When a river is **in spate**, it contains a lot more water than usual and is flowing very fast. EG *On our left there was a big river running in spate... The brook came down in roaring spate.* PHR : USED AS AN A ⇑ in flood

3 When someone is **in full spate**, they are talking about something and seem to be intending to talk about it for a long time. EG *Already the boss was in full spate.* PHR : USED AS AN A = in full flow

spatial /speɪʃəºl/. **1 Spatial** is used to describe things relating to size, area, or position rather than, for example, to time. EG *The first dimension to concentrate on is the spatial one... ...spatial and temporal variations.* ADJ CLASSIF : ATTRIB ⇑ physical

2 Your **spatial** ability is your ability to see and understand the relationships between shapes, spaces, or areas. EG *...the child's spatial ability... None of us had the right kind of spatial awareness.* ADJ CLASSIF : ATTRIB

spatter /spætə/, **spatters, spattering, spattered**. **1** If something **spatters** an object or a surface or **spatters** a liquid or substance over it, it covers the object or surface with drops of the liquid or with small pieces of the substance. EG *He picked up his spoon so hurriedly that it spattered milk over his cardigan.* ◇ **spattered**. EG *My goggles were spattered with mud... The verandah was spattered with broken glass... ...a blood-spattered room.* V+O : USU+A = sprinkle, spot ◇ ADJ CLASSIF = spotted, sprinkled

2 A **spatter** of something such as a liquid, a substance, or a noise is a small amount of it in drops, tiny pieces, short sounds, etc. EG *There was a spatter of rain... ...a spatter of applause... There was a sudden spatter of small explosions.* N SING WITH DET +of ⇑ scatter = sprinkling

spatula /spætjəᵘlə/, **spatulas**. A **spatula** is an object like a knife with a wide, flat blade, which is used in cooking and by doctors. EG *Smooth the icing over the cake with a spatula... ...the spatula that the doctor used when inspecting throats.* N COUNT

spawn /spɔːn/, **spawns, spawning, spawned**.
1 Spawn is a soft, jelly-like substance containing the eggs of fish, frogs, or other amphibians. EG *...frog spawn.* N UNCOUNT

2 When fish, frogs, and other amphibians **spawn**, they lay their eggs. EG *The salmon fight their way back up the river to spawn.* V

3 If something **spawns** something else, it causes it to happen, exist, or be created; a literary use. EG *Poverty had spawned numerous religious movements... ...the electronic movement and the devices it has spawned.* V+O = bring about

spay /speɪ/, **spays, spaying, spayed**. When a female animal, especially a cat or a dog, **is spayed**, it V+O : USU PASS ⇑ sterilize has its ovaries removed so that it cannot become pregnant. EG *All stray bitches are spayed before being found new homes.* ◇ **spaying**. EG *Many people are against spaying and neutering.* ◇ N UNCOUNT ⇑ sterilization

speak /spiːk/, **speaks, speaking, spoke, spoken**. 1 When you **speak**, you use your voice in order to say words. EG *Simon opened his mouth to speak... He drove without speaking for a while... She spoke with an Irish accent... I speak the way my parents spoke... He picked up the telephone. 'Leslie speaking. Leslie Thomson.'* V = talk

2 If you **speak** a word or expression, you say it. EG *It was the first time the baby's name had ever been spoken.* V+O

3 When you **speak** to someone or **speak** with them, you have a conversation with them. EG *Mary turned her head to speak to him... When he spoke with his friends, he told them what had happened... Hello. Could I speak to Sue, please?... 'Did you ever see her again?'–'Not to speak to.'* V+A = chat, converse, talk

4 If you **speak** a foreign language, you know the language and are able to have a conversation in it. EG *The men at the airport spoke fluent English... He does not speak English very well... How many languages can you speak?* V+O

5 If you do not **speak a word**, you do not or cannot say anything at all. EG *We didn't speak a word while the children were in the room... They passed one another without a single word being spoken... He doesn't speak a word of English.* PHR : VB INFLECTS

6 If you **speak the truth**, you tell someone the correct facts about something. EG *Howard felt the need to speak the truth.* PHR : VB INFLECTS

7 If you **speak** to someone about something that they have done, you discuss it with them, often telling them that they should not have done it and that they must not do it again. EG *'Mary hasn't done her homework again.'–'I know. But I've spoken to her about it and I think she will do it in future.'* V+*to*+O+A *(about)*

8 If you **are speaking** to someone or are **on speaking terms** with them, you are on friendly terms with them, often after having quarrelled with them and been unfriendly previously. EG *She's speaking to her neighbour again at last... I haven't been on speaking terms with my sister for three years... They were rarely on speaking terms.* V+A : ONLY CONT, OR PHR : USED AS AN A, USU WITH BROAD NEG

9 If you **speak** about someone or something or **speak** of them, they are the subject of conversation when you are talking to other people. EG *These were things that she didn't want to speak about to other people... They began to speak about him with respect... They seemed to be speaking of someone whom he hardly knew... He hadn't been able to speak until now of what had happened.* V+A *(about/of)* ⇑ discuss

10 If you **speak** well of someone or **speak** badly of them, you say good or bad things about them. EG *He spoke well of me to his parents... The students spoke highly of their history lecturer... Bill, it was said, never spoke ill of other people.* V+ADV+A *(of)*

11 If you **speak** for a group of people, you act as their spokesperson. EG *I think I can speak for everyone here when I say that we deplore this violence... He spoke for a whole generation in his poetry... I'm only speaking for myself, not for my colleagues.* V+A *(for)* ⇑ represent

12 If you **speak** your **mind** about something, you say exactly what you think about it. PHR : VB INFLECTS

13 When actors **speak** the lines of a play, they recite them from memory when they are acting in the play. EG *In the last act I had only four lines to speak... People seemed to want to hear modern verse spoken on the stage... My first speaking part was in 'Henry V'.* V+O ⇑ say

14 When someone **speaks** to a group of people, they make a speech. EG *It was announced that the Prime Minister would speak to the nation on television... Speaking in the debate, he set out his views on abortion... He declined to speak at the Labour Party rally.* V : USU+A

15 If you say that something **speaks** to you, you mean that it makes you realize or understand something, or that it gives you the same feelings that you would have if it had said actual words to you. EG *Looks sometimes speak louder than words... The music spoke more deeply to me than ever before... ...the past of which these ancient stones speak.* ● If you say that something **speaks volumes**, you mean that it expresses or suggests a great deal to you. EG *That one photograph speaks volumes.* V+A, OR V+O ● PHR : VB INFLECTS

16 If you say that something **speaks for itself**, you mean that 16.1 it is so obvious that it does not need any special explanation. EG *His writing speaks for itself.* 16.2 it makes it obvious that a particular fact is true. EG *The fact that you never see them around together speaks for itself.* PHR : VB INFLECTS PHR : VB INFLECTS

17 The word **speak** is also used in the following expressions. 17.1 You say **so to speak** when you are speaking in metaphors, puns, or other figures of speech and you want to make it clear that what you are saying is not literally true. EG *He goes to work early; before the office is awake, so to speak... These were creatures thrown up, so to speak, from the depths.* PHR : USED AS ADV SEN = as it were 17.2 **Nobody to speak of** or **nothing to speak of** means hardly anyone or anything, or only unimportant people or things. EG *Christmas is the one time when there is nobody to speak of on campus... 'Did you find anything?'–'No, nothing to speak of.'* PHR : USED AS S/O

17.3 You say **not to speak of** when you are including something or someone else in what you have already said. EG *His friends and colleagues will be very upset. Not to speak of his parents.* PREP 17.4 If you say **speak for yourself** when someone has said something, you mean that what they have said is only their opinion or applies only to them; an informal expression, often used humorously. EG *'Posy, we're ridiculous.' – 'Speak for yourself.'* CONVENTION 17.5 If something or someone **is spoken for**, you cannot have them, because they have already been promised to someone else. EG *I'm afraid you can't have that car. It is already spoken for... You can't marry Mary. She's spoken for.* PHR : VB INFLECTS = reserved

18 See also **speaking**.

speak up. 1 If you **speak up** or **speak out** about something, you say publicly what you believe, even though it might be dangerous or difficult for you to do so. EG *Never be frightened of speaking up for your beliefs... Why do women not speak up for themselves?... The cricketers themselves should speak up in favour of non-racial cricket... He spoke out against racial discrimination many times... She did not speak out in condemnation of the massacre.* PHRASAL VB : V+ADV, USU+A 2 If you **speak up**, you speak more loudly. EG *Could you please speak up, We can't hear you at the back.* PHRASAL VB : V+ADV

-speak can be added to the end of a person's name in order to form a noun referring to the person's characteristic way of speaking, especially to their use of particular words. EG *...Haigspeak... ...the flourishing of a new language–Thatcher speak.* COMB : FORMS N UNCOUNTS

speaker /spiːkə/, **speakers**. 1 A **speaker** is 1.1 the person who is speaking at a particular time. EG *When a speaker emphasises something, he often speaks more loudly... Sometimes the listener takes over the talk and becomes the speaker.* N COUNT = talker 1.2 a person who is making a speech or giving a talk to a group of people. EG *The chairman got up to introduce the speaker... Only a few of us can ever become really good speakers... 'Forward with the revolution!' cried the speaker.* N COUNT

2 A **speaker** of a particular language is a person who can speak that language. EG *Some sounds are very difficult for French speakers of English.* ● See also **native speaker**. N COUNT : USU MOD+N

3 A **speaker** is also a loudspeaker. EG *The left-hand speaker doesn't seem to be working.* N COUNT

4 The **Speaker** is the person who presides over meetings of law-making bodies in many countries, for example in Britain, America, and Australia. EG *There were rumours that he would resign as Speaker after 1982... Mr Speaker, the Honourable Member seems to have missed the point... ...Tip O'Neill, Speaker of the House of Representatives.* N PROPER : IF VOC THEN *Mr/Madam*+N ⇑ chairman

-speaking is added to the names of languages in order to form adjectives. These adjectives describe someone either as able to speak a language or as speaking it every day as their normal language. EG *...English-speaking South Africans.* COMB : FORMS ADJ CLASSIFS

speaking /spiːkɪŋ/. 1 You use **speaking** with an adverb when you are defining the way that you are describing something. EG *America is still the dominant arms producer and, generally speaking, the most technologically advanced... Luke was a village boy, and we weren't, strictly speaking, allowed to play with him... Roughly speaking, there are two possibilities... He's not a doctor–technically speaking,* PHR : USED AS ADV SEN he's a medical practitioner. • **broadly speaking**: see **broadly**.

2 You also use **speaking 2.1** to indicate what your position or viewpoint is in what you are saying. EG *Speaking as a married woman, I consider it important to provide nursery schools for all children who need them... Speaking as a Conservative–the best thing would be to privatize the industry.* V+*as*+C : ONLY CONT, USED AS ADV SEN **2.2** to introduce a new topic, by repeating words that have just been used, but putting them in a different context. EG *'We had a wonderful holiday in Spain last year.'–'Speaking of holidays, I must book mine.'* V+*of*+NG

3 **Speaking** is the activity of giving speeches and talks. EG *...public speaking... He went on a speaking tour of the United States.* N UNCOUNT : USU MOD+N

4 **Speaking** machines give you information by reproducing or simulating a human voice. EG *It is now possible to get speaking bathroom scales.* ADJ CLASSIF : ATTRIB = talking

spear /spɪə/, **spears, spearing, speared**. 1 A **spear** is a weapon consisting of a long pole with a sharp point, usually made of metal, at one end. Spears are either thrown or used with a stabbing movement. EG *He snatched up his spear... They sprang about brandishing their spears.* N COUNT

2 If you **spear** someone or something, you push or throw a spear into them. EG *The warriors clubbed and speared each other.* V+O ⇑ impale

3 If you **spear** a fish, piece of food, etc, you push a pointed object such as a stick or a fork into it so that you can lift it up. EG *Lally took her fork and speared an oyster from its shell.* V+O ⇑ impale

4 A **spear** is also **4.1** a long, thin, pointed leaf. EG *...spears of green, with white flowers.* N COUNT **4.2** an individual stalk of asparagus or broccoli. EG *...spears of asparagus... ...broccoli spears.* N COUNT+SUPP, OR N PART+N UNCOUNT

spearhead /spɪəhɛd/, **spearheads, spearheading, spearheaded**. 1 If you **spearhead** something such as a campaign, you are the person who leads it. EG *In India, Mrs Gandhi's son Sanjay spearheaded a 'moral crusade' against slums... IBM spearheaded the recruitment drive.* V+O ⇑ lead

2 If soldiers **spearhead** an attack, they lead other troops into it. ▸ A **spearhead** is a group of soldiers doing this. EG *German spearheads were at the gates of Paris.* V+O ▸ N COUNT ⇑ vanguard

spearmint /spɪəmɪnt/, **spearmints**. **Spearmint** is a strong flavour that is used especially to flavour sweets; also used to refer to the plant from which this flavouring is obtained. ▸ A **spearmint** is a sweet which has this flavour. EG *...the smell of the spearmint she was chewing.* N UNCOUNT ▸ N COUNT ⇑ mint

spec /spɛk/, **specs**; an informal word. 1 Someone's **specs** are their glasses. EG *I've been wearing specs since I was three.* N PLURAL : ALSO *a pair of*+N

2 If you do something **on spec**, you do it hoping to get something that you want as a result, but without any certainty that you will get it. EG *They just turned up on spec.* PHR : USED AS AN A

special /spɛʃəºl/, **specials**. 1 Something that is **special** is **1.1** more important or better than other things of its kind. EG *Would she be prepared to undertake a special job for the organization?... ...china that was reserved for special occasions... Is there anything special about this sort of computer?... What is so special about the year 2000?... I had no special reason to confide in him.* ADJ CLASSIF : ATTRIB ≠ ordinary **1.2** different from normal and therefore set apart from other things of its kind in a particular way. EG *We treat them as a special case... What's special about the new form of polymer plastic?* ADJ CLASSIF : PRED+*about* ⇑ different

2 **Special** is used **2.1** to describe someone or something that is officially appointed or done for a particular purpose. EG *He was a special adviser to Mrs Judith Hart at the Ministry... Congress passed a special bill forbidding the army to waste any more money on this project... ...a report from its special correspondent... To marry a foreigner, special permission had to be obtained... A special meeting of the Soviet Politburo was called.* ADJ CLASSIF : ATTRIB ⇑ specific **2.2** to describe products that are designed and made for a specific purpose. EG *My Hoover has special attachments for curtains and upholstery... The scientists dived down in special suits to walk on the bed of the sea.* ADJ CLASSIF : ATTRIB = specialized **2.3** to describe something that belongs to only one particular person, group of people, place, etc. EG *He spoke his own special variety of German... Britain had its own special problems... Hospital food seldom caters for the special needs of the aged.* ADJ CLASSIF : ATTRIB = unique

3 You also use **special 3.1** to describe someone's attitude or behaviour towards others when it is greater than normal, especially in relation to their helping or caring for others. EG *She made a special effort to be helpful and polite... The Party paid special attention to the role of women... This law provides special assistance to those with large families... She asked whether I would consider, as a special favour, letting her rent a room.* ADJ CLASSIF : ATTRIB = extra, particular **3.2** to describe something of very high quality or something that you like or enjoy very much. EG *...the very delicate, very special French perfume... Is there anything special you would like for dinner, dear?... ...a visit to the cinema followed by tea at Lyons Corner House as a special treat.* ADJ QUALIT ⇑ particular **3.3** to describe products, services, or performances which are being offered, often at a reduced price, in addition to the normal ones. EG *Some places do special offers in May... When we finish early there's a special bus... He will be appearing in a special Sunday night show at the Duke of York's.* ADJ CLASSIF : ATTRIB

4 A **special** is a product, programme, etc which is only available or shown at a certain time, or which is made for a special purpose. EG *Monday's special was chicken, Tuesday's lamb, and so forth... I had seen his production of a TV special called 'The Male of the Species.'... ...the third in the new season of National Geographic Specials to be shown on television.* N COUNT

5 **Special** is also used **5.1** to describe a particular part of an academic subject that someone has studied in great detail and knows a lot about. EG *...an historian with a special interest in the French Revolution... My special period was Trojan and Hadrian.* ADJ CLASSIF : ATTRIB ⇑ specific **5.2** in British English, to describe institutions such as schools or hospitals which are for people who have particular problems such as physical or mental handicaps. EG *...special schools for maladjusted children... ...special hospitals such as Broadmoor.* ADJ CLASSIF : ATTRIB ⇑ specialized

6 See also **speciality, specially**.

Special Branch. The **Special Branch** is the department of the British police that is concerned with political security and deals with problems such as terrorism, visits by foreign leaders, political refugees, etc. EG *...members of the Special Branch... ...a maximum security check with the help of Special Branch.* N PROPER : IF WITH DET THEN *the*+N

special delivery is a service offered by the Post Office by which, for an extra amount of money, letters or parcels are delivered at a time which is not a usual delivery time. EG *I'll have it sent down by special delivery.* N UNCOUNT ⇑ post

special effect, special effects. A **special effect** is an unusual result in the scenery or sound track of a film that is achieved using special techniques. EG *There are some very unusual special effects.* N COUNT : USU PL

specialise /spɛʃəlaɪz/. See **specialize**.

specialism /spɛʃəlɪzəºm/, **specialisms**. 1 Someone's **specialism** is a particular subject or skill which they study and know a lot about. EG *He may get too committed to his specialism.* N COUNT = speciality

2 **Specialism** in a particular subject is specialization in it. EG *...medical specialism.* N UNCOUNT

specialist /spɛʃəlɪst/, **specialists**. 1 A **specialist** is **1.1** a person who studies a particular subject or skill and knows a lot about it. EG *She is a specialist in Eastern European affairs... It's a good thing for a specialist to have to explain his or her subject.* N COUNT = expert **1.2** a doctor who treats one particular kind of disease or does one particular kind of treatment. EG *I went to a specialist who found I had too little sugar in my blood... ...an eye specialist.* N COUNT

2 Someone who has **specialist** skills or knowledge has skills or knowledge in one particular subject or area of work. EG *...a specialist teacher of mathematics... I have acquired a great deal of specialist knowledge.* ADJ CLASSIF : ATTRIB

speciality /spɛʃiælɪti¹/, **specialities**. 1 Someone's **speciality** is a particular area of work that they do or a subject that they know a lot about. EG *Work with children is their speciality... They enjoy talking about their own specialities.* N COUNT = field

2 A **speciality** of a particular place is a special product that is always very good there, for example a kind of food that is especially good in a restaurant. N COUNT+SUPP

EG *Chocolate gateau was a speciality of the Café de Montmartre.*

specialize /spɛʃəlaɪz/, **specializes, specializing, specialized**; also spelled **specialise**. If you **specialize** in one thing, you concentrate most of your time and resources on this thing, especially in your work or when you are studying or training. EG *...a shop specializing in camping equipment... I'm hoping to specialize in a literary field in the final year.* ◊ **specialization** /spɛʃəlaɪzeɪʃəⁿn/, **specializations**. EG *...the increasing specialisation of working life... Her lectures are meaningless to anyone outside her specialization.* — V: IF + PREP THEN *in*; ◊ N UNCOUNT/COUNT

specialized /spɛʃəlaɪzd/; also spelled **specialised**. Someone or something that is **specialized** is trained or developed for a particular purpose or area of knowledge. EG *...highly specialised staff... ...radar and specialised television systems... ...specialised interest such as the 'Women's lib' movement.* — ADJ QUALIT ⇑ special

specially /spɛʃəli¹/. 1 If you say that something has been done **specially** for a particular person or purpose, you emphasize that it has been done only for that person or purpose. EG *...free hotels run by the state specially for tourists... I'm going to alter my programme specially for you... The rules were specially designed to protect the traveller... A couple of experts had come specially.* — ADV ⇑ particularly

2 You use **specially** 2.1 to say that something has a particular quality more than average or normal; an informal use. EG *...a pub where the beer was specially good... Was she a brilliant teacher? Not specially.* — ADV + ADJ/ADV = particularly **2.2** to emphasize that you are choosing or referring to one particular person, thing, or group out of a larger group. EG *They were pro-Nazi during the war, specially Malan and Verwoerd... I was thinking specially of motorists and cyclists.* — ADV WITH VB = particularly

specialty /spɛʃəlti¹/, **specialties**. A **specialty** is the same as a speciality; used mainly in American English. EG *...suitable people to practise a specialty in a hospital... The old boundaries between specialties are collapsing.* — N COUNT = specialization

species /spiːʃiːz/. **Species** is both the singular and the plural form. A **species** is a class of plants or animals, or a variety of that class, whose members have the same main characteristics and are therefore able to breed with each other. EG *There are more than two hundred and fifty species of shark... This evergreen species will keep its berries until March.* — N COUNT ⇑ group

specific /spɪ²sɪfɪk/, **specifics**. 1 You use **specific** to refer to a particular fixed area, subject, etc. EG *Education should not be restricted to any one specific age group... ...the serious and specific charge of 'obstruction of justice'... On certain specific issues there may be changes of emphasis... Let us look at a specific area of public policy.* — ADJ CLASSIF : ATTRIB = specified

2 If a description is **specific**, it is precise with clearly defined limits. EG *It was a tooth, a tiger-shark tooth, to be more specific... The play is specific in time and place... Let me be more specific.* — ADJ QUALIT ⇑ exact ≠ vague

3 Something that is **specific** to a particular thing is connected with that thing only. EG *It's the program that's specific to this problem.* — ADJ QUALIT : PRED = peculiar

4 The **specifics** of a subject are the particular details of it that need to be considered. EG *Let us focus on the specifics of Bengal's life... When are we going to get down to specifics?* — N PLURAL = particulars

specifically /spɪ²sɪfɪkəⁿli¹/. You use **specifically** 1 to emphasize that a particular subject is being given special attention and being considered separately from other things of the same kind. EG *...a programme specifically for teenagers... It is Christianity with which we are specifically concerned... I haven't come across anything specifically to do with religion.* — ADV ⇑ specially ≠ broadly **2** to say that you are concentrating on a particular aspect of a subject. EG *Specifically these records show the following.* — ADV SEN **3** to indicate that you are stating or describing something precisely and clearly. EG *...the peasant rising in the West of France, in Brittany specifically... ...from Manhattan Island, more specifically from West Fifty-Third Street... The point is specifically made in the following passage... Can you define 'reasonable force' more specifically, please?* — ADV WITH VB ⇑ exactly ≠ ambiguously **4** to emphasize a particular way of describing something, often when you are contrasting this with other ways of describing it. EG *I don't think it's a specifically medical problem... He could be described as radical, more than specifically socialist... Nor is the pursuit of specifically political aims anything new.* — ADV + ADJ ⇑ particularly

specification /spɛsɪfɪkeɪʃəⁿn/, **specifications**. A **specification** is 1 a detailed description of features in the design or composition of a machine, building, material, etc. EG *...ships built to merchant ship specifications... ...the specification of a power amplifier... We make them to specification.* — N COUNT, OR *to* + N **2** a requirement or piece of information which is clearly stated. EG *Was there no specification of the experience required?... The only specification was that the women should be unemployed.* — N COUNT + SUPP = stipulation

specific gravity, specific gravities. The **specific gravity** of a substance is the ratio of the density of the substance to the density of water; a technical term in physics. EG *The specific gravity is 0.84.* — N COUNT

specify /spɛsɪfaɪ/, **specifies, specifying, specified**. If you **specify** something, 1 you state it or describe it precisely, so that it is clear which of several things you mean. EG *Government hospital contracts generally specify ICI's Terylene P3... The report specified seven areas where the Government had a responsibility.* — V + O **2** you clearly state a certain requirement or condition. EG *Our instructions specify that we tell no one about this.* ◊ **specified**. EG *Do you have to eat at a specified time?* — V + O/REPORT-C; ◊ ADJ CLASSIF = particular

specimen /spɛsɪmɪ²n/, **specimens**. 1 A **specimen** is a single plant, animal, rock, etc, which is an example of a particular species or type and is examined or analysed by scientists. EG *The fins of fossil specimens are carefully dissected... ...specimens of the atlas moth... Occasionally gigantic specimens are found with stems twenty metres long.* — N COUNT

2 A **specimen** of something is an example or small amount of it which shows you or gives an idea of what the whole of it is like. EG *For a detailed character analysis, just send a specimen of your handwriting to this address... Over a hundred teachers will receive specimen copies of the dictionary.* — N COUNT = sample

3 A **specimen** is also a small quantity of someone's urine, blood, etc which is examined in a medical laboratory, usually in order to discover whether they are ill. EG *You'll be asked to provide a urine specimen.* — N COUNT = sample

4 You can refer to a person, animal, or thing as a **specimen** when you are describing it as having a quality of a particular kind; an informal use. EG *I stood looking at an unfortunate specimen of a man... ...a perfect specimen of womanhood.* — N COUNT + SUPP ⇑ example

specious /spiːʃəs/. Something that is **specious** appears to exist or to be true, but is in fact false or an illusion; a formal word. EG *Ralph had been deceived by the specious appearance of depth in a beach pool... The argument is a specious one.* — ADJ QUALIT = misleadir

speck /spɛk/, **specks**. A **speck** is 1 a very small stain, mark, or shape. EG *There was a speck or two of blood upon his collar... Looking up between the leaves you could just see little specks of blue sky... The boat was two miles away, a mere speck.* — N COUNT ⇑ spot **2** a very small piece of a powdery substance. EG *...a tiny speck of dust.* — N PART + N UNCOUNT **3** a very small amount of a quality or an emotion. EG *...every speck of information imaginable... There's not a speck of truth in it.* — N PART + N UNCOUNT ⇑ bit = scrap

speckle /spɛkəⁿl/, **speckles, speckling, speckled**. If something **speckles** a surface, it covers it with very small marks or spots of a different colour. EG *I stood watching the rain speckling the asphalt.* ◊ **speckled**. EG *The beach in front of the hotel was speckled with people... ...villages speckled around the sides of the valleys... ...speckled eggs.* — V + O = fleck; ◊ ADJ CLASSI IF + PREP THE *with* = dotted

spectacle /spɛktəkəⁿl/, **spectacles**. 1 Someone's **spectacles** are their glasses; a formal use. EG *...a schoolteacher in horn-rimmed spectacles.* — N PLURAL : A *a pair of* + N

2 A **spectacle** is 2.1 a strange or interesting display or scene. EG *She stood at the head of the stairs and surveyed the spectacle... ...the tragic spectacle of a deaf and dumb person trying to talk.* — N COUNT **2.2** something such as a large theatrical event which is very dramatic or beautiful to look at. EG *It was a grand seven-hour spectacle consisting of songs, comedy acts, and acrobatics... She had a sensitive feeling for poetry and spectacle and romantic theatre.* — N COUNT/UNCOUNT ⇑ sight

3 If you **make a spectacle of** yourself, you do something which draws attention to yourself, often something which makes you look ridiculous in front of other people. EG *She wasn't going to make a* — PHR : VB INFLECTS = embarra

spectacle of herself by bursting into tears in the street.

spectacular /spɛktækjə⁴lə/, **spectaculars**. 1 Something that is **spectacular** is very impressive or dramatic. EG *The most spectacular of these extraordinary fossils can be seen in the museum... It was a spectacular jump... ...a spectacular rise in house prices.* ◊ **spectacularly**. EG *It is Vienna's most spectacularly illuminated church... They were running in different directions and leaping spectacularly into the air.* ADJ CLASSIF = breathtaking; ◊ ADV = breathtakingly

2 A **spectacular** is a show or a performance which is very grand and impressive. EG *They are to hold a fashion spectacular on Friday night with 100 models.* N COUNT : MOD+N = extravaganza

spectator /spɛkteɪtə/, **spectators**. A **spectator** is a person who watches something, especially a sporting event. EG *Thousands of spectators came to their feet to pay tribute to an outstanding performance... British soccer used to be a spectator sport for all the family.* N COUNT ⇑ viewer

spectra /spɛktrə/ is a plural form for **spectrum**.

spectral /spɛktrə⁰l/ is used to describe something that is like a ghost or relates to a ghost; a literary word. EG *What spectral shape was brushing against his shoulder?... ...the spectral voices of drowned sailors.* ADJ CLASSIF : ATTRIB = ghostly

spectre /spɛktə/, **spectres**; also spelled **specter** in American English. A **spectre** is 1 a ghost; a literary use. EG *My spectre shall come at him, like black smoke.* N COUNT 2 a frightening image or idea which you have in your mind. EG *...the spectre of the murderer stalking her imagination.* N SING : *the*+N+*of*

spectrum /spɛktrəm/, **spectra**, **spectrums**. The plural can be either **spectra** or **spectrums**. 1 The **spectrum** is the range of different colours in the order of their wavelengths, which is produced when light passes through a prism or a drop of water. A rainbow shows the colours in the spectrum. EG *Many insects can perceive colours of the spectrum that are invisible to us.* N SING : *the*+N

2 A **spectrum** is an ordered range of different sized waves, for example light waves, radio waves, or sound waves. EG *...the electromagnetic spectrum... They could look at the spectra of the light the moons reflected.* N COUNT

3 A **spectrum** of opinions, emotions, skills, etc is a range of different ones, especially when one end of the range is considered as opposite to the other end. EG *They have considerable support at both ends of the political spectrum... We have experienced together the whole spectrum of emotion... The questionnaire covered an extremely broad spectrum of topics.* N COUNT : USU SING, USU+SUPP

speculate /spɛkjə⁴leɪt/, **speculates**, **speculating**, **speculated**. 1 If you **speculate** about something, you think about what all its possible aspects, effects, or consequences might be, although you realize that you cannot know for certain. EG *It is natural for us to speculate about the reasons for their visits... Do not speculate on what he would have done had he lived... Industry sources speculated that the least expensive model will be priced at £7000.* ◊ **speculation** /spɛkjə⁴leɪʃə⁰n/, **speculations**. EG *The papers are full of speculation about who is likely to be the next prime minister... Such speculations no longer belong to the realm of science.* V+REPORT-CL, OR V : IF+PREP THEN *about/on* = conjecture; ◊ N UNCOUNT/COUNT : IF+PREP THEN *about* = conjecture

2 If someone **speculates** financially, they buy property, stocks, shares, etc, especially on a large scale or as a business, in the hope of being able to sell them again at a higher price and make a profit. EG *She speculated successfully on the stock exchange... Members of the government had speculated in Marconi shares.* ◊ **speculation**. EG *...speculation on the gold markets of Zurich... ...intense international speculation against the pound.* V ⇑ gamble; ◊ N UNCOUNT

speculative /spɛkjə⁴lətɪv/. 1 A prediction or piece of information that is **speculative** is based on speculation rather than knowledge. EG *Much of our information is always speculative... Budgets and profit forecasts were equally speculative.* ADJ QUALIT ⇑ guesswork

2 Someone who has a **speculative** expression seems to be trying to guess what a person, thing, or situation is like. EG *He looked at me with an oddly speculative glint in his eyes.* ◊ **speculatively**. EG *She looked round speculatively.* ADJ QUALIT : ATTRIB = contemplative; ◊ ADV WITH VB = inquiringly

3 **Speculative** is used to describe people or their activities which involve buying goods, shares, etc in the hope of being able to sell them again at a higher price and make a profit. EG *...speculative builders... ...speculative aircraft projects... Land could no longer be subject to speculative hoarding and selling.* ADJ CLASSIF : USU ATTRIB

speculator /spɛkjə⁴leɪtə/, **speculators**. A **speculator** is a person who speculates financially. EG *His case was financed by speculators who hoped to profit from his victory.* N COUNT ⇑ merchant

sped /spɛd/ is the past tense and past participle of **speed 3**.

speech /spiːtʃ/, **speeches**. 1 **Speech** is 1.1 the ability to speak or the act of speaking. EG *Although he was born two months early, that part of the brain that controls speech was fully developed... These children have achieved speech but struggle over reading and writing... She was so shocked that she lost her powers of speech... Mr Baily has a speech impediment, which makes him difficult to understand.* N UNCOUNT ⇑ language 1.2 spoken language. EG *In ordinary speech we often shorten the word 'cannot' to 'can't'... We had to do a lot of work which required very little speech... His classes concentrated on verbal communication through writing and speech... We condemn them for denying the right of free speech.* N UNCOUNT ≠ writing

2 A **speech** is 2.1 a formal talk which someone gives to an audience, and which they have usually prepared in advance. EG *Mr Macmillan presented the prizes and made a speech on the importance of education... He gave a very amusing speech at her wedding... We listened to an excellent speech by the president.* N COUNT = address 2.2 a group of lines spoken by an actor or actress in a play. EG *She recited a speech from 'As You Like It'.* N COUNT

3 Your **speech** is the characteristic way in which you speak. EG *I detected a slight Brooklyn accent in her speech... After three large whiskies her speech was not as clear as it had been.* N SING : POSS+N ⇑ dialect

4 The **speech** of a particular country or region is the language or dialect spoken in that country or region. EG *He can mimic Cockney speech quite well... A person unfamiliar with French speech finds it difficult to understand the way in which the words are run into each other... She found it difficult to acquire the speech sounds of Portuguese.* N UNCOUNT+SUPP

speech day, **speech days**. A **speech day** is a day each year in a school when prizes are presented to pupils and speeches are made by guest speakers, the head teacher, etc. N COUNT

speechless /spiːtʃlɪ²s/. If you are **speechless**, you are temporarily unable to speak, usually because something that you have heard or seen has shocked or amazed you. EG *She was speechless with astonishment... Fanny gazed at him, totally speechless.* ▸ used of people's emotions which they are unable to express in words. EG *...staring from face to face in speechless horror... After the first reaction of speechless fury, I agreed.* ADJ CLASSIF : USU PRED, IF+PREP THEN *with* ⇑ silent = dumb

speech therapist, **speech therapists**. A **speech therapist** is a person whose job is to help people to overcome speech and language problems. N COUNT

speech therapy is the treatment of people who have speech and language problems. N UNCOUNT ⇑ therapy

speed /spiːd/, **speeds**, **speeding**, **sped**, **speeded**. The form of the past tense and past participle is **sped** in paragraph 3, but **speeded** for the phrasal verb. 1 The **speed** of something is 1.1 the rate at which it moves or travels. EG *I drove at great speed to West Bank... My speed slowed down now as I was in stonier country... ...capable of reaching speeds of over 110kph... ...wind speed and direction... ...a heavy disc which can rotate at a high speed.* N UNCOUNT : MOD+N, OR N COUNT 1.2 the rate at which it happens or is done. EG *None of us grows at the same speed... The funeral march when played at high speed becomes a merry tinkle of sounds... Read this at a sensible speed... Computer processing speeds have increased astronomically.* N UNCOUNT/COUNT+SUPP ⇑ pace

2 **Speed** is 2.1 very fast movement or travel. EG *...that pleasure associated with speed... The train gathered speed... The car is travelling at speed.* N UNCOUNT 2.2 a very fast rate at which something happens or is done. EG *...a room of busy journalists typing at speed... He prepared the dinner with remarkable speed and efficiency... We can't add up with the speed and accuracy of a computer.* N UNCOUNT

3 If you **speed** somewhere, you move or travel there very quickly, usually when you are in a vehicle. EG *I* V+A

watched her speed away in her jeep... They sped along Main Street towards the highway... They drove through Port Philip and sped on down south.

4 Someone who **is speeding** is driving a car or other vehicle faster than the legal speed limit. ◊ **speeding**. EG *His driver's licence was suspended for speeding.* — V : ONLY CONT; ◊ N UNCOUNT

5 **Speed** is also an illegal drug which some people take to increase their energy and make them feel excited or have unusual sensations in their mind; used in informal English. EG *...roaming the night spots, getting high on speed or heroin.* — N UNCOUNT = amphetamine

speed up. 1 When something **speeds up** or when you **speed** it **up**, its speed increases so that it moves or travels faster. EG *They're way ahead of us. Speed up!... Tom speeded up and overtook them.* — PHRASAL VB : V-ERG+ADV

2 When a process or activity **speeds up** or when something **speeds** it **up**, it happens at a faster rate. EG *Africa's population growth speeded up... Warmth speeds up chemical reactions... Bad housing and poverty speed up the breakdown of family life.* — PHRASAL VB : V-ERG+ADV ⇑ increase

-speed combines with numbers to say that a bicycle, car, etc has a particular number of gears. EG *...a five-speed car... ...a ten-speed racer.* — COMB : FORMS ADJ CLASSIFS

speedboat /spiːdbəʊt/, **speedboats**. A **speedboat** is a boat that is propelled by an engine and can travel at high speed. — N COUNT ⇑ motorboat

speed limit, speed limits. The **speed limit** on a road is the maximum speed at which you are legally allowed to drive a vehicle on the road. EG *A motorist was trapped exceeding the speed limit... ...a speed limit of 40 mph.* — N COUNT

speedometer /spi¹dɒmɪtə/, **speedometers**. A **speedometer** is an instrument in a vehicle which shows how fast the vehicle is moving. EG *The car's speedometer read only up to 85 miles per hour.* — N COUNT

speed trap, speed traps. A **speed trap** is a section of a road along which the police are checking whether vehicles are going faster than the speed limit allows. — N COUNT

speedway /spiːdweɪ/ is the sport of racing lightweight motorcycles on special tracks. — N UNCOUNT

speedwell /spiːdwel/, **speedwells**. A **speedwell** is a small blue wild flower. — N COUNT

speedy /spiːdi¹/, **speedier, speediest**. 1 A **speedy** action happens or is done very quickly. EG *A speedy settlement of the strike is essential... They will be capable of speedier, more accurate diagnoses.* ◊ **speedily**. EG *Such doubts were now speedily removed... It would be dealt with very speedily by the government.* — ADJ QUALIT = quick, rapid; ◊ ADV WITH VB = rapidly

2 A **speedy** vehicle can move very quickly; an informal use. EG *...a speedy little car.* — ADJ QUALIT = fast

spell /spel/, **spells, spelling, spelled, spelt**. The forms **spelled** and **spelt** are both used as the past tense and past participle of the verb. 1 When you **spell** a word, you write or speak the individual letters of the word in the correct order. EG *'My name is Khulaifi. Shall I spell that for you?'... Bauxite is spelt B A U X I T E... He was given two hundred words to learn how to spell every night... Ninety per cent of the words were spelt wrong.* — V+O

2 When letters in a sequence **spell** a particular word, they form that word when placed together in that sequence. EG *C A T spells cat.* — V+O

3 Someone who can **spell** knows the correct order of letters in most words, and can write words in this way. EG *Just because a person can't spell doesn't mean they are stupid.* — V OR V+O : USU V

4 If something **spells** a particular result, often an unpleasant one, it suggests that this will be the result. EG *Nuclear conflict would spell the end of life as we know it... Something in his very presence spelled danger... Any discussions of politics and programmes would spell disaster.* — V+O : NO PASS, NO CONT = mean, signify

5 A **spell** of a particular activity, type of weather, etc is a period of time that is usually short, during which this activity, type of weather, etc occurs. EG *At that time there was a frightful cold spell in Britain... ...a spell of good summer weather... She had a spell as editorial page director.* — N COUNT : USU+SUPP

6 A **spell** is also 6.1 a condition in which you or the events which occur are controlled by some magical power. EG *Maggie could 'smell out' evildoers and cast spells on them... The spell of the wicked fairy was broken.* — N COUNT ⇑ trance = charm 6.2 a sequence of words used to perform magic. EG *He whispered a spell: 'Blood of bats and teeth of rats, turn this girl into a cat!'* — N COUNT ⇑ incantation = charm

7 If you are **under** someone's **spell**, you are so fascinated by them that you cannot think about anything else. EG *The people on the stage were completely under his spell.* — PHR : USED AS AN A = captivated

8 See also **spelling**.

spell out. 1 If you **spell** something **out**, you explain it in detail or in a very clear way. EG *Let me try and spell out what I mean by that... This is spelled out in the critical writings of the American art world.* — PHRASAL VB : V+O+ADV = explicate

2 If you **spell out** a word, you write or speak each letter in the word one after the other. EG *We had to spell out the words we heard... To communicate with her you have to spell words out on her hand.* — PHRASAL VB : V+O+ADV

spellbinding /spelbaɪndɪŋ/. If you find something **spellbinding**, you find it so fascinating that you cannot think about anything else. EG *It was a spellbinding experience... I found his description of life in Ancient Rome absolutely spellbinding.* — ADJ QUALIT = enthralling, riveting

spellbound /spelbaʊnd/. If you are **spellbound**, you are so fascinated by something that you cannot think about anything else. EG *We were all spellbound as we listened to her... He held his audience spellbound.* — ADJ CLASSIF : US PRED = enchanted, enthralled

speller /spelə/, **spellers**. If you describe someone as either a good or a bad **speller**, you mean that they spell words either correctly or badly. EG *Most poor spellers improve with care and encouragement.* — N COUNT : ADJ+

spelling /spelɪŋ/, **spellings**. 1 A **spelling** is the correct order of the letters in a word. EG *...alternative spellings in a dictionary... I always get the spellings wrong... They were given twenty spellings to learn.* — N COUNT ⇑ orthograph

2 **Spelling** is the ability to spell words in the correct way, or the way that words are spelt. EG *I'm terrible at spelling... In this language the pronunciation has changed over the centuries but the spelling has not... That piece of writing was full of spelling mistakes.* — N UNCOUNT

spelt /spelt/ is a form of the past tense and past participle of **spell**.

spend /spend/, **spends, spending, spent**. 1 When you **spend** money, you pay out the money for things that you want. EG *We always spend a lot of money on parties... Whenever I go there I get the urge to spend... The buildings need a lot of money spent on them.* ● to **spend a penny**: see **penny**. — V+O, OR V

2 If you **spend** time somewhere or energy doing something, you pass the time there or use your energy doing it. EG *He spent most of his time in the library... She woke early, meaning to spend all day writing... What a way to spend a weekend!... We found a hotel where we could spend the night... I have spent all my life in this town... He spent a lot of effort organizing that trip.* — V+O+A

3 See also **spending, spent**.

spender /spendə/, **spenders**. A **spender** is a person or organization that spends money. EG *Though a compulsive collector of wealth, he was a spender as well... This council is one of the big spenders.* — N COUNT

spending /spendɪŋ/ is payment of large amounts of money for public services, the armed forces, etc by a government or other organization. EG *City departments must reduce their spending by £35 million before July 1st... ...demanding a reduction in defence spending by one third... We need to counter the effects of government spending cuts.* — N UNCOUNT : MOD+N = expendit

spending money is money that you have or that you are given to spend on personal things for pleasure, for example when you are on holiday. EG *They indulged all three children with plentiful spending money.* — N UNCOUNT ⇑ allowanc = pocket m ey

spendthrift /spendθrɪft/, **spendthrifts**. A **spendthrift** is a person who spends money in a wasteful or extravagant way. EG *What a spendthrift! All the money he makes goes on new cars.* ▸ used as an adjective. EG *This confirmed all his worst fears about her spendthrift habits.* — N COUNT; ▸ ADJ QUALIT

spent /spent/. 1 **Spent** is the past tense and past participle of **spend**.

2 **Spent** is used to describe something that has already been used so that all its fuel, energy, etc has been burnt up. EG *It will take several seconds to extract the spent cartridge and insert a fresh one... ...spent matches... I think they are a spent force already.* — ADJ CLASSIF : ATTRIB ⇑ consume = burnt ou

3 If you are **spent**, you are exhausted and have no energy left; a literary use. EG *I was spent, and I cried for a long time... We lay spent, breathless, giggling.* — ADJ CLASSIF PRED = worn ou

sperm /spɜːm/, **sperms**. **Sperm** can also be used as the plural form. A **sperm** is a cell which is — N COUNT produced in the sex organs of a male animal and can enter a female animal's egg and fertilize it. A sperm is usually in a liquid with lots of other sperms. EG *During fertilization the sperm and the egg fuse... Jelly fish reproduce by releasing eggs and sperm into the sea.* ▸ also used of the liquid that contains sperm when it is produced. ▸ N UNCOUNT = semen

spermatozoon /spɜːmətəʊzəʊɒn/, **spermatozoa**. A **spermatozoon** is a sperm; a technical biological term. N UNCOUNT : USU PL

sperm whale, sperm whales. A **sperm whale** is a large whale which has a cavity in its head that contains a large amount of oil. N COUNT

spew /spjuː/, **spews, spewing, spewed**. 1 When something **spews** things or **spews** them **out**, the things flow out in large quantities like a stream. EG *Coal-burning factories spewed dense dirty smoke... Volcanoes were abundant, spewing ash and lava... This river spewed forth its waters upon the sea... Another burst spewed from the soldier's gun.* V OR V+O : USU+A ⇑ eject = gush

2 If someone **spews** or **spews up**, they vomit; a very informal use. V OR V+A *(up)*

sphere /sfɪə/, **spheres**. 1 A **sphere** is an object or figure that has the shape of a perfectly round ball. N COUNT

2 A **sphere** of activity, interest, etc is a particular area of activity, interest, etc. EG *Apart from photography, he has several other spheres of interest... Students also need advice outside the academic sphere... He works in the sphere of race relations.* N COUNT+SUPP = field

3 A **sphere** of people is a particular group of people, for example with the same rank in society or with the same interests. EG *She's used to mixing in an altogether different sphere.* N COUNT ⇑ environment = circle

spherical /sfɛrɪkəl/. Something that is **spherical** has the shape of a sphere. EG *The earth is spherical and moves around the sun.* ADJ CLASSIF ⇑ round

sphinx /sfɪŋks/, **sphinxes**. A **sphinx** is one of the huge statues of a monster with a person's head and a lion's body which stand near the pyramids in Egypt and were built by the ancient Egyptians. The sphinxes in mythology were supposed to set riddles, and so a person who seems mysterious or puzzling is sometimes referred to as a sphinx. EG *She gave the radiant but ambiguous smile of an ecstatic sphinx.* N COUNT

spice /spaɪs/, **spices, spicing, spiced**. 1 A **spice** is the powder or seeds from a particular plant, which you put in food while you are cooking it in order to give it flavour. Cinnamon, ginger, and cumin are examples of spices. EG *...a collection of herbs, spices, and sauce ingredients... This is a good spice to enhance your cooking.* N COUNT/UNCOUNT ⇑ seasoning

2 When you **spice** food, you add spice to it while you are preparing it. EG *Take peas and butter and spice gently with nutmeg.* ◊ **spiced**. EG *The soup was heavily peppered and spiced to improve the taste... I gave her a sip of hot spiced wine.* V+O : IF+PREP THEN *with* ◊ ADJ CLASSIF ⇑ seasoned

3 If you **spice** something that you do or say, or if you **spice** it **up**, you add excitement or liveliness to it. EG *His speech was spiced with anti-imperialist sentiment.* V+O, OR V+O+A *(up)* : IF+PREP THEN *with*

4 **Spice** is something which makes life more exciting and interesting. EG *Variety is the spice of life... We'll have to add a bit of spice to our relationship.* N UNCOUNT ⇑ excitement = zest

spick-and-span /spɪk ənd spæn/. A place that is **spick-and-span** is very clean and tidy; an informal expression. EG *I must make everything spick-and-span before they arrive.* ADJ CLASSIF : PRED ⇑ neat

spicy /spaɪsi[1]/, **spicier, spiciest**. **Spicy** food is strongly flavoured with spices. EG *...a red-hot spicy sauce.* ADJ QUALIT ⇑ pungent

spider /spaɪdə/, **spiders**. A **spider** is a small creature with eight legs that looks like an insect. Most types of spider make webs in which they catch insects for food. EG *The spider shot sideways into its hole... I hate spiders.* N COUNT

spidery /spaɪdəri[1]/. You describe something as **spidery** when it consists of dark, angular lines or strands that remind you of a spider's legs. EG *...spidery writing... ...the spidery ironwork of the Orange River bridge.* ADJ QUALIT : USU ATTRIB

spiel /ʃpiːl/. Someone's **spiel** is a speech that they make, usually one that they have made many times before and often one in which they try to persuade someone to do something or buy something; an informal use showing disapproval. EG *Has he delivered his spiel yet?... I didn't think that you'd fall for the spiel... I know that spiel. I've heard it often.* N UNCOUNT : USU *the*/POSS+N ⇑ talk = patter

spike /spaɪk/, **spikes, spiking, spiked**. 1 A **spike** is 1.1 a long piece of metal with a sharp point at one end. EG *...an asphalted playground surrounded by high iron spikes... Their heads were cut off and impaled on spikes.* N COUNT 1.2 something long and pointed. EG *It bears spikes of greenish flowers... ...with my three inches of hair standing up in spikes.* N COUNT

2 **Spikes** are also pointed pieces of metal attached to the soles of sport shoes. They help your feet to grip the ground when you are running. N COUNT : USU PL

3 If someone **spikes** you, they force a spike or a sharp stick into your body. EG *...his horror of being spiked on a stick.* V+O ⇑ impale

4 If someone **spikes** a drink, they add alcohol to it; an informal use. EG *He had made them hot tea spiked with rum.* V+O : USU PASS+*with* = lace

5 If you **spike** someone's **guns**, you prevent them from doing what they want to. PHR : VB INFLECTS

spiked /spaɪkt/. Something that is **spiked** has a spike or spikes on it. EG *...a spiked stick... ...spiked shoes.* ADJ CLASSIF

spiky /spaɪki[1]/, **spikier, spikiest**. 1 Something that is **spiky** has a sharp point or points. EG *...spiky hair... The shrub has spiky green leaves.* ADJ QUALIT : USU ATTRIB ⇑ pointed

2 A **spiky** person is bad-tempered and easily irritated. EG *She is a rather spiky child.* ▸ used of behaviour. EG *He was typing with spiky malice.* ADJ QUALIT = touchy

spill /spɪl/, **spills, spilling, spilled, spilt**. The forms **spilled** and **spilt** are both used as the past participle and past tense of the verb. 1 If you **spill** a liquid or if it **spills**, it accidentally flows over the edge of a container. EG *She carried the bucket without spilling a drop... Make sure the water doesn't spill over the floor.* V-ERG ⇑ pour

2 If people or things **spill** out of a place, they come out of it in large numbers. EG *Near midnight crowds started spilling out of bars.* V+A ⇑ flow

3 If you **spill** someone's **blood**, you kill them or wound them, especially with a knife or a sword; a literary use. EG *Cut his throat! Spill his blood!... He did not want to see any American blood spilt.* PHR : VB INFLECTS

4 A **spill** is 4.1 an amount of liquid that has spilled out of a container onto something. EG *Wipe any spills immediately.* N COUNT : USU PL ⇑ splash 4.2 a fall from a motor cycle, bicycle, or horse, especially during a sports competition. EG *Quite a spill you took, Oliver... ...the thrills and spills of the racing circuit.* N COUNT = tumble

5 A **spill** is also a thin piece of wood or twisted paper used for lighting pipes, cigarettes, or fires. EG *He offered her a cigarette and lit a spill.* N COUNT

6 • to **spill the beans**: see **bean**. • to **cry over spilt milk**: see **milk**.

spill out. If you **spill out** information or if it **spills out**, you tell it to someone in a hurried way, because you cannot or do not want to keep it secret. EG *He will talk to anyone and spill out his life story to a total stranger... He was tempted to spill out everything he had been thinking.* PHRASAL VB : V-ERG+ADV ⇑ reveal = divulge

spillage /spɪlɪdʒ/, **spillages**. **Spillage** or a **spillage** is the spilling of oil into the sea from a ship. EG *...the spillage of oil... ...the danger of spillage.* N UNCOUNT/COUNT ⇑ discharge

spilt /spɪlt/ is a past tense and past participle form of **spill**.

spin /spɪn/, **spins, spinning, spun**. 1 If something **spins** or if you **spin** it, it turns round quickly once or several times, around a central point. EG *He spun the chair round to face the desk... My sister gave a shriek and spun on one foot... Spin the wheel to the left... Small rotors can spin at 400-500 rpm... The football went spinning into the canal.* ▸ used as a noun. EG *...the rapid spin of the wheel.* V-ERG : USU+A ⇑ rotate ▸ N UNCOUNT ⇑ rotation

2 If you **spin** clothes, sheets, etc after you have washed them, you get water out of them using a spin drier or a washing machine. EG *I haven't spun them yet.* ▸ used as a noun. EG *Give the dressing-gowns another spin.* V+O ▸ N COUNT : USU SING

3 When someone **spins**, they make thread from a natural fibre such as cotton or wool by pulling out pieces of the fibre and twisting them together very quickly, using a device or machine. EG *My mother taught me to spin.* ◊ **spinning**. EG *...the spinning of flax and wool... ...a spinning machine.* V OR V+O ◊ N UNCOUNT

4 When a spider **spins** its web, it makes it from a silky thread that comes out of its body. V+O

5 If your head **is spinning**, you feel dizzy because you are excited or slightly drunk. EG *His head was* V : IF+PREP THEN *from/with*

spinning from wine and liqueurs... My mind was spinning with all the ideas I could introduce.

6 If you are **in a spin** or **in a flat spin**, you are confused and unable to act sensibly because of something that has happened; used in informal English. EG *Margery was thrown into a flat spin by this unexpected visit.* PHR : USED AS AN A

7 If you go for a **spin**, you make a short journey in a car or other vehicle just to enjoy yourself; a rather old-fashioned use. EG *We took an hour's spin around the city... Care for a spin?* N SING : a+N ⇑ trip

8 If a plane goes into a **spin**, it falls very rapidly towards the ground in a spiral movement. N SING WITH DET ⇑ plunge

9 If you put **spin** on a ball, you deliberately make it spin rapidly when you hit it or throw it in tennis, cricket, or some other game, in order to affect the way it bounces or its path through the air. N UNCOUNT

10 If someone **spins a story** or **spins a yarn**, they give you an account of something that is untrue or only partly true. EG *He's always got some sad story to spin... He's spinning one of his yarns again.* PHR : VB AND N INFLECT

spin out. **1** If you **spin out** something such as a task or a talk, you make it last longer than is necessary or natural. EG *He'll spin out this lecture until lunchtime... I might even be able to spin it out to three-quarters of an hour.* PHRASAL VB : V+O+ADV ⇑ extend = prolong

2 If you **spin out** money, you make it last as long as possible by spending it very carefully. EG *I'll have to spin out these last few pounds.* PHRASAL VB : V+O+ADV ⇑ extend

spina bifida /spaɪnə bɪfɪdə/ is a condition of the spine that some people are born with. It often causes paralysis. EG *...victims of spina bifida.* N UNCOUNT

spinach /spɪnɪdʒ, -ɪtʃ/ is a plant with large green leaves that is eaten as a vegetable. EG *Either you eat your spinach or you go without ice cream.* N UNCOUNT

spinal /spaɪnəºl/ means relating to someone's spine. EG *...spinal fluid... ...spinal damage.* ADJ CLASSIF : ATTRIB

spinal column, spinal columns. Your **spinal column** is your spine; a formal or technical expression. N COUNT = backbone

spinal cord, spinal cords. Your **spinal cord** is a thick cord of nerves inside your spine which connects your brain to nerves in all parts of your body. N COUNT

spindle /spɪndəºl/, **spindles**. A **spindle** is **1** a rod in a machine, around which another part of the machine turns. N COUNT **2** a pointed rod which you use when you are spinning wool by hand. You twist the wool round the spindle and form it into a long thread. N COUNT ⇑ tool

spindly /spɪndli¹/, **spindlier, spindliest**. Something that is **spindly** is long and thin and looks very weak. EG *...spindly legs... There are two spindly trees there.* ADJ QUALIT = skinny

spin drier, spin driers; also spelled **spin dryer**. It can also be spelled with a hyphen. A **spin drier** is a machine that gets water out of clothes, sheets, etc after you have washed them. You put the clothes inside it and it spins them round very rapidly. N COUNT

spin-dry, spin-dries, spin-drying, spin-dried, spun dry. **Spin-dried** and **spun dry** are both used as the past participle. **Spin-dried** is also the past tense. If you **spin-dry** clothes, sheets, etc after you have washed them, you get water out of them using a spin drier or a washing machine. EG *You can spin-dry this jumper and it'll keep its shape... You can use your machine to rinse and spin-dry... After the clothes had been washed, they had to be spun dry.* V OR V+O

spine /spaɪn/, **spines**. **1** Your **spine** is the row of bones down your back that supports your body and that has your spinal cord inside it. EG *His spine developed a slight curve.* N COUNT = backbone

2 The **spine** of a book is the narrow stiff part which the pages and covers are attached to. The title and author's name are usually printed on the spine as well as on the front cover. N COUNT

3 Spines are also long, sharp points on an animal's body or on the leaves or stalk of a plant. EG *...a cactus with red spines.* N COUNT = spike, prickle

spine-chilling. A **spine-chilling** film or story makes you feel very frightened. ADJ QUALIT ⇑ terrifying

spineless /spaɪnlɪ²s/. **1** A **spineless** person behaves in a cowardly way. EG *He was a weak and spineless creature.* ADJ QUALIT ⇑ weak = feeble

2 A **spineless** animal has no spine. ADJ CLASSIF

spinet /spɪnɪt/, **spinets**. A **spinet** is a small harpsichord. N COUNT

spinner /spɪnə/, **spinners**. A **spinner** is **1** a person who makes thread by spinning. EG *...a cotton-spinner from Lancashire.* N COUNT **2** a cricketer who makes the ball spin when he or she bowls it so that it changes direction when it hits the ground or the batsman's bat. EG *...the left-arm spinner Stephen Boock.* N COUNT ⇑ bowler ▸ used also to refer to a ball that is bowled like this. EG *He plays the spinners competently.* ▸ ⇑ ball

spinney /spɪni¹/, **spinneys**. A **spinney** is a small wood. N COUNT = copse

spinning wheel, spinning wheels; also spelled with a hyphen. A **spinning wheel** is a wooden spinning machine used in people's homes, mainly in former times. It has a wheel which makes the spindle turn round. EG *...the whirr of the spinning-wheel.* N COUNT

spin-off, spin-offs. **1 Spin-off** or a **spin-off** is something useful that happens unexpectedly as a result of activities that were designed to achieve something else. EG *The search for knowledge frequently has beneficial spin-offs for mankind... ...spin-off from military and space research.* N COUNT/UNCOUNT : IF+PREP THEN *from/of* = by-product

2 A **spin-off** is also a book, film, or television series that is derived from a similar book, film, or television series which has been very successful. N COUNT : IF+PREP THEN *from/of*

spinster /spɪnstə/, **spinsters**. A **spinster** is a woman who is not married, especially an old or middle-aged woman; a formal or old-fashioned word. EG *...a forty-year-old spinster.* N COUNT

spinsterhood /spɪnstəhʊd/ is the state of being a spinster. N UNCOUNT

spiny /spaɪni¹/. A **spiny** animal or plant is covered with long, sharp points. EG *...the spiny ant-eater... ...a spiny shrub... ...creatures with spiny skins.* ADJ CLASSIF : USU ATTRIB = prickly

spiral /spaɪərəºl/, **spirals, spiralling, spiralled**; also spelled **spiraling** and **spiraled** in American English. **1** A **spiral** is a curved shape which winds round and round, with each curve above the previous one or outside it. EG *...a right-handed spiral.* N COUNT ⇑ curve ▸ used as an adjective. EG *...a spiral staircase... ...an antelope with spiral horns.* ▸ ADJ CLASSIF : ATTRIB

2 If something **spirals**, it moves up or down, especially up, in a spiral curve. EG *A small bird shot up, spiralling into the sky... The aircraft began spiralling downwards.* V+A ⇑ wind ▸ used as a noun. EG *...the gliding spiral of a gull's flight.* ▸ N COUNT

3 If an amount, especially an amount of money, **spirals**, it rises quickly and at an increasing rate. EG *Military budgets had continued to spiral.* V ▸ used as a noun. EG *...a wage and price spiral.* ▸ N SING WITH DET : MOD+N

4 If an amount, especially an amount of money, **spirals downwards**, it falls quickly and at an increasing rate. EG *Costs started to spiral downwards.* PHR : VB INFLECTS ▸ used as a noun. EG *Industry entered a spiral of decline.* ▸ N SING WITH DET+SUPP

spire /spaɪə/, **spires**. A **spire** is a tall cone-shaped structure on the top of a building such as a church. EG *...the glorious spire of a medieval cathedral... He could see grimy roofs, factory chimneys and church spires.* N COUNT = steeple

spirit /spɪrɪt/, **spirits, spiriting, spirited**. **1** Your **spirit** is the part of you that is not physical and that is concerned with your deepest thoughts and feelings. EG *Fulfilment must be sought through the spirit, not the body or the mind.* N SING : the/POSS+N = soul

2 The **spirit** of a dead person is a non-physical part of them that is believed to remain alive after their body has died. EG *They believe that his spirit lives on... ...prayers to our dead ancestors' spirits.* N COUNT : USU WITH POSS = soul

3 A **spirit** is also a ghost or other supernatural power, especially one that is believed to take control of people's minds. EG *The charm is worn to ward off evil spirits.* N COUNT ⇑ being

4 Spirit is **4.1** liveliness and energy that is shown in what someone does. EG *...a performance full of spirit and originality.* N UNCOUNT = vigour **4.2** courage and determination that helps people to survive in difficult times and to keep their way of life and their beliefs. EG *...a policy of covert terror designed to break their spirit.* N UNCOUNT = will

5 A particular kind of **spirit** is **5.1** a feeling of loyalty to a group that is shared by the people who belong to the group. EG *There's a strong community spirit.* N UNCOUNT+SUPP **5.2** a set of ideas, beliefs, and aims that is typical of a group of people in the same place or in similar circumstances. EG *...the American spirit of optimistic materialism... ...the pioneering spirit.* N SING WITH DET+SUPP ⇑ mood ● **The spirit of the age** or **the spirit of the times** is the set of ideas, beliefs, and aims that is typical of people at a ● PHR : USED AS O particular period in history. EG *It is not easy to stand out against the spirit of the age... More than any other politician he embodied the spirit of the times.*

6 The **spirit** in which you do something is the attitude that you show when you are doing it. EG *We're seeing a welcome spirit of realism in their approach to the problem... They did it more in a spirit of moral rectitude than of brotherly love... She approaches most of life's challenges in the same positive spirit.* N SING WITH DET +SUPP

7 Your **spirits** are your feelings at a particular time, especially your feelings of happiness or unhappiness. EG *The children lifted my spirits with their laughter.* N PLURAL+SUPP ⇑ mood

8 The **spirit** of something such as a law or an agreement is the way that it was intended to be interpreted or applied. EG *I think we'd be breaking the spirit of the agreement if we went ahead.* N SING : *the*+N+*of* ⇑ intention

9 Spirits are strong alcoholic drinks, such as whisky or gin, that are made by distillation. EG *Beer costs only 33p a pint here and spirits are 27p.* N PLURAL ⇑ liquor

10 Spirit or **spirits** is an alcoholic liquid that is used as a fuel, for cleaning things, or for other purposes. There are many kinds of spirit. EG *...two pints of white spirit.* • See also **methylated spirits, surgical spirit.** N UNCOUNT+SUPP

11 If you **spirit** something or someone into or out of a place, you get them into it or out of it quickly and secretly, without anyone noticing. EG *They had worked out a way to spirit the assassin and his gun into the conference hall... To avoid angry demonstrators, the minister was spirited through the back entrance.* V+O+A ⇑ move

12 The word **spirit** is also used in the following expressions. **12.1** If you say that you are with someone **in spirit** or are taking part in something **in spirit**, you mean that you feel as if you were with the person or taking part in the activity, although you are actually in a different place. EG *We'll be there in spirit.* PHR : USED AS AN A **12.2** If you **enter into the spirit of** something, you take part in it in an enthusiastic way. EG *They didn't really enter into the spirit of it at all.* PHR : VB INFLECTS **12.3** You say **'That's the spirit!'** in order to encourage someone in something that they are doing. EG *Keep it up! That's the spirit!* CONVENTION **12.4** • **high spirits**: see **high.** • See also **free spirit, Holy Spirit, kindred spirit, team spirit.**

spirited /spɪrɪtɪ²d/. **1** A **spirited** action shows great energy and determination; used showing approval. EG *Despite spirited resistance by Republican forces, the town fell to the Nationalists... She put up a spirited defence of her government's policies.* ADJ QUALIT ⇑ determined

2 See also **high-spirited, low-spirited, public-spirited.**

spirit level, spirit levels; also spelled with a hyphen. A **spirit level** is a device for testing a surface to see if it is level. It consists of a piece of wood or metal containing a tube of liquid with a bubble of air in it. When the bubble is in the middle of the tube, the surface that the spirit level is on is level. N COUNT

spiritual /spɪrɪtʃʊ⁰əl/, **spirituals. 1 Spiritual** means **1.1** relating to people's deepest thoughts and beliefs, rather than to their bodies and physical surroundings. EG *...the modern world's pursuit of material ends to the neglect of its spiritual needs.* ADJ CLASSIF ◊ **spiritually.** EG *...a spiritually sick society.* ◊ ADV ◊ **spirituality** /spɪrɪtjʊælɪti¹/. EG *...the decline of spirituality in our time.* ◊ N UNCOUNT **1.2** relating to people's religious beliefs. EG *...the spiritual authority of the Christian Church... ...a Muslim book of spiritual instruction.* ADJ CLASSIF = religious

2 Your **spiritual home** is the place where you feel that you belong, for example because you have ideas and attitudes in common with the people who live there. EG *Germany is his spiritual home.* PHR : USED AS O/C, USU POSS+N

3 A **spiritual** is a religious song of a type originally sung by Negro slaves in America. N COUNT

spiritualism /spɪrɪtʃʊ⁰əlɪzə⁰m/ is the belief that the spirits of people who are dead can communicate with people who are still alive. EG *He decided that spiritualism might have something to be said for it.* N UNCOUNT ◊ **spiritualist.** EG *My mother's a spiritualist.* ◊ N COUNT

spit /spɪt/, **spits, spitting, spat. Spat** is the usual form of the past tense of the verb, but **spit** is also used sometimes. **1 Spit** is the watery liquid which is produced in the mouth; used especially of small amounts of this liquid which have been forced out of the mouth. EG *Rhoda's spit flew as she shouted.* N UNCOUNT ⇑ saliva

2 If you **spit**, you force an amount of spit out of your mouth, sometimes in order to show hatred or scorn. EG *The driver spat contemptuously... Claud spat on the palms of his hands and rubbed them together.* V

3 If you **spit** liquid or food somewhere, you force a small amount of it out of your mouth. EG *If I don't like it I can always spit it out... Dave spat tobacco juice into the tin can on the floor.* V+O : USU+A ⇑ eject

4 If something such as a machine or fire **spits**, it makes a series of short, sharp, hissing noises as bits are shot out. EG *The fire crackled and spat... The fat began to spit.* V ⇑ sound = splutter

5 If you **spit** something or **spit it out**, you say it in an angry way so that it seems that you are forcing the words out of your mouth. EG *He spat out his answer... She turned round and almost spat: 'Oh get on with it!'* V+O/QUOTE, OR V+O+A *(out)*

6 You can say **'spit it out!'** to someone as a way of telling them to say something which they seem reluctant to say; used in informal English. CONVENTION

7 If it **is spitting** or if it **is spitting** with rain, it is raining very lightly. EG *It's only spitting. We don't need an umbrella.* V : *it*+V, ONLY CONT

8 A **spit** is **8.1** a long stick made of metal or wood which is pushed through a piece of meat and hung over an open fire or in an oven so that the meat is roasted. EG *There was still food left on the wooden spits.* N COUNT ⇑ skewer **8.2** a long, flat, narrow piece of land which sticks out from the beach into the sea. EG *There was a spit of dry land beyond the edge of the village.* N COUNT ⇑ promontory = spur

9 If you say that someone is **the spitting image of** someone, **the spit and image of** someone or **the dead spit of** someone, you mean that they look very like that person. EG *She was the spitting image of her mother.* PHR+NG ⇑ resemble

10 If something is **within spitting distance**, it is very close; an informal expression. EG *We lived within spitting distance of the river.* PHR : USED AS AN A

spit and polish is very thorough cleaning and polishing; a fairly informal expression. EG *That table needs a bit of spit and polish.* N UNCOUNT

spite /spaɪt/. **1 In spite of** is used to introduce a fact which makes the other part of the sentence extremely surprising. EG *The morning air was still clear and fresh, in spite of all the traffic and the crowd... In spite of poor health, my father was always cheerful... It was a life which, in spite of my Aunt and Uncle's warmth and affection, made me unhappy.* PREP = despite, notwithstanding

2 If you do something **in spite of** yourself, you do it although you did not really intend or expect to. EG *Jane became edgy in spite of herself.* PREP+REFL ⇑ unwillingly = despite

3 Spite is a feeling that makes you behave in a deliberately nasty way towards someone, either because they have hurt or annoyed you or because you dislike them. EG *He wrote that review out of pure spite... He misbehaved from simple spite.* N UNCOUNT ⇑ malice

4 If you do something nasty to **spite** someone, you do it deliberately in order to annoy or upset them. EG *They are being provocative and controversial just to spite us.* V+O (NG/REFL) : ONLY INF ⇑ get at

5 If you **cut off** your **nose to spite** your **face**, you deliberately do something that you think will harm or upset someone, without realizing or caring that it will harm or upset you as well. PHR : VB INFLECTS

spiteful /spaɪtful/. Someone who is **spiteful** does nasty things to people they dislike. EG *You're destructive and spiteful.* ▸ used of actions and behaviour. EG *They proceeded to tell spiteful stories about the fat lady.* ADJ QUALIT ⇑ malicious ◊ **spitefully.** EG *They both laughed spitefully.* ◊ ADV

spitfire /spɪtfaɪə/, **spitfires.** A **spitfire** is a woman or girl who gets angry very easily. EG *She can be a real spitfire sometimes.* N COUNT

spittle /spɪtə⁰l/ is the watery liquid which is produced in the mouth. EG *The dog left a trail of spittle on my trousers.* N UNCOUNT = saliva

spittoon /spɪtu:n/, **spittoons.** A **spittoon** is a bowl that is intended for people to spit into. N COUNT

splash /splæʃ/, **splashes, splashing, splashed. 1** If you **splash** or if you **splash** something, you cause an amount of water to fly up into the air with a loud noise by hitting or disturbing the water. EG *They wanted to splash in the surf, giggling and shouting... Ralph started to run, splashing through the shallow water... Neil was bending over the basin and splashing his face.* V : USU+A, OR V+O

2 If water **splashes** or if it **splashes** something, it hits V+A, OR V+O against something and scatters in a lot of small drops. EG *The rain splashes on the windows... Drenching spray splashed over the deck... I got splashed by the waves.*

3 If you **splash** a liquid somewhere, you pour or throw it into or onto something rather carelessly. EG *I put down my things and splashed some cold water on my face... Otto splashed some brandy into a glass... Not every child who can splash colour about is artistic.* V+O+A

4 A **splash** is 4.1 the sound made when an amount of water flies up into the air because it has been hit by something. EG *She disappeared into the water with a splash... There were loud splashes and giggles coming from the bathroom.* N COUNT **4.2** a drop or small quantity of a liquid that has been spilt on something or scattered over it. EG *He wiped away the splash of gasoline on the near fender.* N COUNT/PART ⇑ mark

5 A **splash** of water, soda water, gin, etc, is a small amount of it added to a drink. EG *He poured in a generous splash of rye... 'Soda?'–'Just a splash, please.'* N PART : USU SING+N UNCOUNT ⇑ quantity = drop

6 If you **make a splash**, you are the centre of everybody's attention on a particular occasion because you are a famous person or because of the way you act or dress. EG *The Princess made quite a splash in Australia.* PHR : VB INFLECTS

7 If a newspaper or magazine **splashes** a story, it prints it in such a way that it is very noticeable. EG *The Dispatch splashed the story all over the front page.* V+O ⇑ display

8 A **splash** of colour or light is an area which contrasts strongly with everything that surrounds it. EG *A large bouquet of tulips made a brilliant splash of yellow on the table.* N PART : USU SING+N UNCOUNT ⇑ patch

9 If something **is splashed** with colour or light, it has patches of contrasting colour or light in various places on it. EG *The garden is like an impressionist painting, splashed with colour... ...thousands of square miles of water splashed with white foam.* V+O+A *(with)* : ONLY PASS

splash down. When a space vehicle **splashes down**, it lands in the sea at the end of a space flight. EG *The three astronauts splashed down safely at nine o'clock this morning.* ● See also **splashdown**. PHRASAL VB : V+ADV

splash out. If you **splash out** on something, especially on a luxury, you spend a lot of money on it; an informal expression. EG *We splashed out on a colour television... I really splashed out and bought a new coat.* PHRASAL VB : V+ADV, IF+PREP THEN *on* = splurge

splashdown /splæʃdaʊn/, **splashdowns.** A **splashdown** is the landing of a space vehicle in the sea after a flight. N COUNT

splat /splæt/ is used to describe the sound of something wet hitting a surface with a lot of force. EG *The egg landed on my cheek with a splat.* N SING WITH DET, OR EXCLAM ⇑ noise

splatter /splætə/, **splatters, splattering, splattered.** 1 If a thick wet substance such as paint or mud **splatters** or **is splattered** on something, it is dropped or splashed so that small amounts of it are spread out over a wide area. EG *Food was splattered all over the kitchen wall... She was wearing an apron splattered with blood... We were too tired to wipe off the mud that splattered onto us.* V-ERG : USU+A = spatter, splash

2 A **splatter** is the sound something makes when it splatters. EG *She could hear an occasional splatter of snow on the window.* N COUNT : IF+PREP THEN *of*

splay /spleɪ/, **splays, splaying, splayed.** If two or more things **are splayed** or **splay out**, their ends are spread out away from each other. EG *He pressed the mattress with splayed fingers... The bristles on this toothbrush are beginning to splay out already.* V-ERG, OR PHRASAL VB : V+ADV

spleen /spliːn/, **spleens.** 1 Your **spleen** is an organ near your stomach. It controls the quality of the blood. N COUNT

2 **Spleen** is violent and spiteful anger; a formal use. EG *In an unusual burst of spleen, Rob wrote me a furious letter... He had to vent his spleen on someone.* N UNCOUNT

splendid /splendɪd/. 1 Something that is **splendid** is excellent and of very good quality. EG *She wrote splendid detective novels... You do such a lot of splendid work here... ...a splendid idea.* ◊ **splendidly.** EG *She was caring for him splendidly... The infantry did splendidly but the conditions were too hard.* ADJ QUALIT = marvellous ◊ ADV WITH VB = marvellously

2 Something such as a building, dress, or work of art that is **splendid**, is beautiful and impressive. EG *This collection includes splendid paintings by Reynolds and Gainsborough... In the middle of Hull stands a splendid Victorian building.* ◊ **splendidly.** EG *The old woman dressed even more splendidly... ...a splendidly furnished room.* ADJ QUALIT ⇑ excellent = magnificent ◊ ADV = magnificently

3 You say **'splendid'** in a conversation to indicate that you think a certain situation is good or that you approve of something that has been said. EG *'We've been helping out in the old people's home over the Christmas holidays.'–'Splendid.'* CONVENTION = marvellous, super

splendiferous /splendɪfəʳrəs/. Something that is **splendiferous** is very grand and wonderful; a rather old-fashioned, humorous word. ADJ QUALIT

splendour /splendə/, **splendours**; also spelled **splendor** in American English. 1 **Splendour** is great beauty and magnificence which is very impressive. EG *The draped curtains add to the effect of decaying splendour... ...the splendour and beauty of nature.* N UNCOUNT

2 The **splendours** of something are the features or elements it has which are very beautiful and which cause it to be admired. EG *...the Elizabethan splendours of Watermouth Hall... ...the finest splendours of the natural world.* N PLURAL+SUPP : USU+*of*

splenetic /splɪ²netɪk/. Someone who is **splenetic** is bad-tempered and irritable; a formal word. ADJ CLASSIF

splice /splaɪs/, **splices, splicing, spliced.** 1 If you **splice** two pieces of rope, film, or tape together, you join them together neatly at the ends so that they make one long continuous piece. V+O

2 When two people **get spliced**, they get married; an informal expression, often used humorously. EG *John and Mary are getting spliced on Saturday.* PHR : VB INFLECTS ⇑ marry

splint /splɪnt/, **splints.** A **splint** is a long flat piece of wood or metal that is fastened to a broken arm, leg, or some other bone. The splint keeps the bone still so that it will heal. EG *She wore a metal splint on one leg.* N COUNT ⇑ support

splinter /splɪntə/, **splinters, splintering, splintered.** 1 A **splinter** is a very thin, sharp piece of wood, glass, metal, etc, which has been broken off from a larger piece; used especially to refer to a small piece of wood which has accidentally got stuck in your skin. EG *...splinters of coloured glass... Sue was worried about splinters in her bare feet.* N COUNT ⇑ sliver

2 If something **splinters** or **is splintered**, it breaks into long, thin, sharp pieces. EG *When feeding dogs, avoid chicken, rabbit or fish bones which can splinter... This wood needs to be splintered into kindling for the fire.* V-ERG ⇑ fragment

splinter group, splinter groups. A **splinter group** is a group of people who decide to break away from a larger group and form a separate organization of their own because they no longer agree with the views of the larger group. N COUNT ⇑ faction

splintery /splɪntəʳri¹/. A wooden surface that is **splintery** is rough and not polished, and splinters break off it easily. EG *...beneath the splintery planking.* ADJ QUALIT

split /splɪt/, **splits, splitting.** The form **split** is used in the present tense and is the past tense and past participle of the verb. 1 If something **splits** or if something else **splits** it, it is divided into two or more parts. EG *Three people died when their car split in two after hitting a tree... When an atom is split, it releases neutrons... Main roads like motorways can split communities in half... The profits are to be split fifty-fifty between the two of them... The children were split into two groups.* V-ERG

2 If a group **splits** or if something **splits** it, one group of members disagree strongly with the other members, and may form a group of their own. EG *The council split down the middle over the issue... The government is split on how to deal with the situation.* V-ERG

3 A **split** is 3.1 a division between two or more things or groups of people, especially between things which are opposite to each other. EG *...the split between the 'rich' and the 'poor'... They avoided the traditional split into students, faculty and administration.* N COUNT : USU SING+*between into* = gap **3.2** a division of a group into two groups of people who disagree very strongly about something. EG *The last thing he wanted was a split in the party under his leadership. ...splits in our society.* N COUNT : USU *in*

4 If something such as wood or a piece of clothing **splits**, a long crack or tear appears in it, especially because there is pressure on it. EG *It was a very poor quality wood which had already split in many places... The jeans split the first time she wore them... The bag split open.* V-ERG

5 A **split** is also a long crack or tear. N COUNT

6 If you **split** someone's head or lip, you make a long wound in it. EG *I saw a boy with his head split open.* V+O+C ⇑ cut

◇ **split**. EG *...a split lip.* ◇ ADJ CLASSIF

7 If you **split**, you leave a place; an informal use. EG *This is boring. Let's split.* V ⇑ go

8 A **split** is also a dessert made from a banana or other fruit that is cut in two, together with ice cream and cream. EG *...a banana split.* N COUNT/UNCOUNT : USU AFTER N

9 When someone does the **splits**, they sit on the floor with their legs straight out on either side of them, or with one leg straight out behind them and the other straight out in front of them. N PLURAL : *the*+N ⇑ posture

10 If you **split** your **sides**, you laugh a great deal. EG *I nearly split my sides, it was so funny.* PHR : VB INFLECTS

11 If you **split the difference**, you agree on a figure which is halfway between the two different figures that have been mentioned. EG *Okay, we'll split the difference and call it £10.* PHR : VB INFLECTS ⇑ compromise

12 If you **split hairs** when you are discussing something, you make small, subtle distinctions unnecessarily. EG *Am I splitting hairs here?* PHR : VB INFLECTS

13 See also **splitting**.

split off. 1 If you **split** part of something **off** or if it **splits off**, it is cut or broken off, or breaks off. EG *A block had been split off from the main rock.* PHRASAL VB : V-ERG+ADV, IF+PREP THEN *from* = break off

2 If people **split off** from a group, they stop being part of the group and become separated from it. EG *The Marxist wing split off to form a separate faction.* PHRASAL VB : V+ADV, IF+PREP THEN *from* = break away

split on. If you **split on** someone, you betray them by telling other people something you ought to keep secret; used in informal British English. EG *Don't split on me.* PHRASAL VB : V+PREP, HAS PASS = tell on

split up. 1 If you **split** something **up**, you divide it so that it is in a number of smaller separate sections or parts. EG *Texas was split up into three geographical zones... You might achieve more by splitting them up into small groups.* PHRASAL VB : V+O+ADV, USU+*into*

2 If a group of people **split up**, they go away in different directions. EG *In Hamburg the girls split up.* PHRASAL VB : V+ADV

3 If two people **split up**, they end their relationship or marriage. EG *After he split up with his wife he went to Arizona... I think we should split up.* PHRASAL VB : V+ADV, ALSO+A *(with)* : RECIP

split infinitive, split infinitives. A **split infinitive** is a construction in English in which an adverb or adjunct is put between the infinitive marker 'to' and the infinitive verb itself. An example of a split infinitive is 'to boldly go'. People used to think that split infinitives were incorrect grammar, but nowadays they are much more acceptable. N COUNT

split-level. A **split-level** house or room has part of the ground floor at a different level from another part, usually because the house has been built on ground that slopes. ADJ CLASSIF : USU ATTRIB

split pea, split peas. A **split pea** is a dried pea which has been split into two halves and which is cooked before eating, for example in soups. N COUNT : USU PL

split personality. If you say that someone has a **split personality**, you mean that their moods can change so much that they seem to have two different, separate personalities. N SING WITH DET

split-screen. **Split-screen** is used to describe 1 a technique in making films and television programmes in which two different pieces of film are shown at the same time, one on the left half of the screen and one on the right. EG *There has been an obsession recently with split-screen movies.* ADJ CLASSIF : ATTRIB 2 a technique of using a screen with a computer or word-processor in which two different sets of information are shown at the same time, one at the top of the screen and one at the bottom. ADJ CLASSIF : ATTRIB

split second; also spelled with a hyphen, especially when used before another noun. A **split second** is an extremely short period of time, shorter than the time it would take you to blink your eye. EG *For a split second nothing happened... She has to make split-second decisions.* N SING WITH DET

splitting /splɪtɪŋ/. A **splitting** headache is very severe or painful. ADJ CLASSIF : ATTRIB

splodge /splɒdʒ/, **splodges**. A **splodge** is a large uneven mark or stain, especially one that has been caused by a liquid. EG *The painting consisted of two red and green splodges in a blue circle.* N COUNT = blotch

splotch /splɒtʃ/, **splotches**. A **splotch** is the same as a splodge. EG *His face is tanned and there are pink splotches on his nose.* N COUNT

splurge /splɜːdʒ/, **splurges, splurging, splurged**; an informal word. 1 If you **splurge** on something, you spend a lot of money extravagantly, especially on things that you do not need. EG *We used to have lunch in a restaurant and then perhaps splurge on a movie... I splurged the extra money on a silver cigarette box.* V OR V+O : IF+PREP THEN *on* = splash out

2 If you have a **splurge**, you spend a lot of money, usually on things that you do not need. EG *We had a bit of a splurge and bought a video.* N COUNT

splutter /splʌtə/, **splutters, spluttering, spluttered**. 1 If something **splutters**, it makes a series of short spitting sounds, usually caused by small amounts of liquid being forced out. EG *Smoke makes you cough and splutter if you breathe it in... Ink spluttered out of my pen and made a terrible blot on the page.* ▸ used as a noun. EG *The engine gave a splutter and went dead.* V ⇑ spit = sputter ▸ N COUNT : USU SING

2 If someone **splutters**, they have difficulty speaking clearly and make spitting sounds as they are talking because they are angry, embarrassed, or surprised. EG *'I know them. They're my friends,' I was spluttering in embarrassment.* ▸ used as a noun. EG *'Of course not,' she said with a splutter of mirth.* V OR V+QUOTE ⇑ speak = stutter ▸ N COUNT : USU SING, IF+PREP THEN *of*

spoil /spɔɪl/, **spoils, spoiling, spoiled, spoilt**. The past participle can be either **spoiled** or **spoilt**. 1 If you **spoil** something, 1.1 you make it less enjoyable, attractive, or interesting than it would otherwise have been. EG *She shouted at him for spoiling her lovely evening... You've spoilt everything by your rudeness!... The presence of the woman spoiled his enjoyment of the view.* V+O = mar, ruin 1.2 you damage it so that it loses part of its value, beauty, or usefulness. EG *Always complain immediately if dry cleaners spoil your clothes... That new fence has spoilt the garden.* V+O = mar, ruin

2 If food **spoils** or if it **is spoilt**, it is no longer good enough to eat. EG *Dinner's ready and it'll spoil if you don't come straight away!... I really must be getting home. My meal will be spoilt.* V-ERG = ruin

3 If you **spoil** someone, especially a child, you give them everything they want or ask for. By doing this, you make their behaviour and character worse than they would otherwise have been. EG *His children are being spoiled by their grandparents... She thinks you shouldn't pick up a baby all the time because you might spoil him.* ◇ **spoilt** or **spoiled**. EG *I think he's just a spoilt child... He's terribly spoiled.* V+O ◇ ADJ QUALIT

4 If you **spoil** yourself or if you **spoil** someone you love, you pay a lot of attention to your or their comfort or desires. EG *Go on, spoil yourself. Buy a nice dress... 'Oh you are spoiling me, aren't you,' Clarissa said. 'First chocolates and now flowers!'* V+O (NG/REFL) = coddle

5 The **spoils** are the rewards, profits, land, etc that you get from something that you have done or from having political power. EG *We had many bitter battles over the division of the spoils... ...the spoils of war.* N PLURAL : *the*+N = booty, loot

spoil for. If you **are spoiling for** something such as trouble or a fight, you are very eager for it to happen. EG *The unions are spoiling for a fight about pay and conditions once again.* PHRASAL VB : V+PREP, ONLY CONT

spoilsport /spɔɪlspɔːt/, **spoilsports**. If you say that someone is a **spoilsport**, you mean that they are behaving in a way that ruins other people's pleasure or enjoyment; an informal word. EG *'Oh, Don, don't be a jealous spoilsport,' said Dolly.* N COUNT

spoke /spəʊk/, **spokes**. 1 **Spoke** is the past tense of **speak**.

2 **Spokes** are the bars that connect the outer ring of a wheel such as a bicycle wheel to the centre of it. EG *Her baby caught his fingers in the spokes of the pram wheel.* N COUNT : USU PL

3 If you **put a spoke in** someone's **wheel**, you deliberately make it difficult for them to do what they were planning to do. PHR : VB INFLECTS

spoken /spəʊkə[ə]n/. 1 **Spoken** is the past participle of **speak**.

2 **Spoken** means produced by speaking. EG *She is a master of both the written and the spoken word... Their understanding of spoken English is largely based on films and television... He built a robot capable of understanding spoken commands.* ADJ CLASSIF : ATTRIB

-spoken combines with words such as 'well' or 'attractively' to indicate that someone speaks in that way or that something is said in that way. EG *She was very well-spoken... ...a badly-spoken speech.* COMB : FORMS ADJ QUALITS

spokesman /spəʊksmə^{3}n/, **spokesmen**. A **spokesman** is a person who is asked to speak as the representative of other people, for example of the government or a trade union. EG *Common Market spokesmen claim that more than 800,000 jobs have been lost recently.* — N COUNT : IF+ PREP THEN *for/of*

spokesperson /spəʊkspɜːsə^{0}n/, **spokespersons**. A **spokesperson** is the same as a spokesman. The word **spokesperson** is sometimes used by people when it is not relevant whether the person is male or female. — N COUNT : IF+ PREP THEN *for/of*

spokeswoman /spəʊksw^{1}u^{1}mə^{0}n/, **spokeswomen**. A **spokeswoman** is the female equivalent of a spokesman. The word **spokeswoman** is sometimes used by people who object to the word 'spokesman' being used to mean both 'man' and 'woman'. — N COUNT : IF+ PREP THEN *for/of*

sponge /spʌndʒ/, **sponges, sponging, sponged**. 1 **Sponge** is a very soft, very light substance that is full of tiny holes and can therefore absorb a lot of water. Sponge can be either man-made or natural. EG *...a mop made of sponge.* — N UNCOUNT

2 A **sponge** is 2.1 a piece of sponge that you hold in your hand and use for washing or cleaning. EG *There was a pink sponge in the bath... Wipe the surface with a clean sponge.* — N COUNT 2.2 a sea animal with a soft round body made of natural sponge. EG *Sponges can grow to a very considerable size.* — N COUNT

3 If you **sponge** something or **sponge** it **down**, you clean it by wiping or rubbing it gently with a wet sponge or cloth. EG *Don't immerse it in water; just sponge it lightly... Sponge down the work surface with a wet cloth.* — V+O, OR PHRASAL VB : V+O+ADV ▸ used as a noun. EG *Give it a quick sponge.* — ▸ N SING : a+N

4 A **sponge** is also a light cake or pudding made from flour, eggs, sugar, and sometimes fat. EG *I made a sponge for my party... ...baked apple with a layer of sponge on top.* — N COUNT/UNCOUNT

5 If someone **throws in the sponge**, they admit that they have failed or been defeated in something they are trying to do and so they stop doing it. — PHR : VB INFLECTS

sponge off. Someone who **sponges off** or **sponges on** other people takes advantage of their generosity by getting money and other things from them, without giving them anything back in return; an informal expression, used showing disapproval. EG *The young unemployed are not simply layabouts who sponge off the Welfare State... She found it distasteful the way Clarissa sponged on them.* — PHRASAL VB : V+PREP = scrounge off

spongebag /spʌnd^{0}ʒbæg/, **spongebags**; also spelled with a hyphen. A **spongebag** is a small bag, usually one made of a waterproof material, in which you keep things such as soap, a face cloth, and a toothbrush when you are travelling; used in British English. — N COUNT = toilet bag

sponge cake, sponge cakes; also spelled with a hyphen. A **sponge cake** is a very light cake made from flour, eggs, sugar, and sometimes fat. EG *Mr Geard had his mouth full of sponge cake, of which he was particularly fond.* — N COUNT/UNCOUNT

sponger /spʌndʒə/, **spongers**. A **sponger** is a person who sponges off other people or sponges off organizations; an informal word, used showing disapproval. EG *Unlike that sponger Charles, she never once asked him to lend her a penny.* — N COUNT ⇑ parasite = scrounger

spongy /spʌndʒi^{1}/, **spongier, spongiest**. Something that is **spongy** is soft and feels like sponge. EG *Her flesh was spongy to the touch.* — ADJ QUALIT

sponsor /spɒnsə/, **sponsors, sponsoring, sponsored**. 1 If people or commercial organizations **sponsor** something such as an event, a theatre production, or someone's training, they pay some or all of the expenses connected with it. They often do this in order to get publicity for themselves. EG *My trip was sponsored by the Metal Box Company... The conference, which ended on Saturday, was sponsored by the Guardian.* — V+O = back, finance, fund

2 If you **sponsor** someone who is doing something such as running a marathon or swimming ten kilometres, you agree to give them a certain sum of money if they succeed in doing it. They then give this money to charity. EG *Would you sponsor Karen in her swim for cancer research next week? ... ...a sponsored walk.* — V+O

3 If you **sponsor** a particular proposal or suggestion, you officially support it and accept some responsibility for persuading other people to agree to it. EG *Two Liberal MPs sponsored the Bill.* — V+O ⇑ promote = back

4 A **sponsor** is 4.1 a person or organization that pays some or all of the expenses connected with something such as an event, a theatrical production, or an athletics meeting. EG *...Virginia Slims, sponsors of the first professional women's tennis tour... The newspaper lasted less than a year, and its sponsors lost a lot of money.* — N COUNT ⇑ financier = backer 4.2 a person who agrees to give a certain sum of money to someone who does something special for charity. EG *I managed to get 31 sponsors for my 24-hour non-stop piano playing in aid of Relief for Ethiopia.* — N COUNT 4.3 an important person or organization that supports the actions and beliefs of another person or organization in order to make them more popular, more powerful, or better known. EG *The professor agreed to act as the group's sponsor.* — N COUNT ⇑ backer = patron

sponsorship /spɒnsəʃɪp/ is the financial support that is given to someone by a sponsor. EG *She talked me into writing to National Geographic for sponsorship for my trip... ...industrial sponsorship.* — N UNCOUNT ⇑ backing = funding

spontaneity /spɒntəniːɪti^{1}, -neɪ-/ is the quality of acting or behaving in a spontaneous, natural way. EG *She acted with an extraordinary spontaneity... ...the spontaneity and vigour of American schools.* — N UNCOUNT ⇑ naturalness

spontaneous /spɒnteɪnɪəs/. 1 Something that is **spontaneous** 1.1 is not planned or arranged, but is done because someone suddenly wants to do it. EG *I waved, and the applause grew, a spontaneous display of friendship and affection... There's very little spontaneous music-making among the pupils... ...spontaneous peasant rebellions.* — ADJ QUALIT = impulsive ◇ **spontaneously**. EG *Flo and I decided spontaneously to board a train for Geneva.* — ◇ ADV WITH VB = impulsively 1.2 happens because of what is happening within something rather than because of the effect of something else outside it. EG *...spontaneous generation of new life... ...spontaneous combustion.* — ADJ QUALIT ⇑ independent ◇ **spontaneously**. EG *The fuel ignites spontaneously from the heat created by the compression.* — ◇ ADV WITH VB

2 People who are **spontaneous** are lively and natural, and do and say things as they occur to them, rather than planning them. EG *The Kirks are very fresh and spontaneous people... Their Irish ebullience made them outgoing and spontaneous.* — ADJ QUALIT = unaffected

spoof /spuːf/, **spoofs, spoofing, spoofed**; a fairly informal word. 1 A **spoof** is 1.1 a very amusing imitation of a book, play, piece of music, etc, which exaggerates and mocks the most noticeable features of the original. EG *The weather forecast seemed to be some kind of spoof, predicting every possible combination of weather... Stephen Potter's well known spoof on the subject makes good reading.* — N COUNT : IF+ PREP THEN *of/o[n]* ⇑ parody 1.2 a type of joke in which someone is tricked into believing that something is true when it is actually not true. EG *He finally realized that the whole thing was a spoof.* — N COUNT ⇑ trick

2 If you **spoof** or if you **spoof** someone, you tease them, especially by making them believe that something is true when it is not true. EG *We thought they might be spoofing... He was just spoofing you.* — V OR V+O = kid

spook /spuːk/, **spooks, spooking, spooked**; an informal word. 1 A **spook** is 1.1 a ghost, especially one that is thought to appear and haunt a place. — N COUNT 1.2 a person whom you find strange and rather frightening. — N COUNT = weirdo 1.3 in American English, a spy. EG *I asked a spook what that message meant and he just smiled.* — N COUNT

2 When something or someone **spooks** people, they are scared; used especially in American English. EG *We were getting more and more spooked as the search went on... He used to enjoy spooking everyone.* — V+O ⇑ frighten

spooky /spuːki^{1}/, **spookier, spookiest**. A place that is **spooky** has a frightening atmosphere, and makes you feel that there are ghosts around; an informal word. EG *The whole place has a slightly spooky atmosphere.* — ADJ QUALIT = scary

spool /spuːl/, **spools**. A **spool** is an object shaped like a cylinder which has a larger, round, flat part at each end so that a long piece of thread, film, tape, etc, can be wound round it without coming off. Different types of spool are used in sewing machines, tape recorders, film projectors, etc. — N COUNT = reel

spoon /spuːn/, **spoons, spooning, spooned**. 1 A **spoon** is an object shaped like a small shallow bowl with a long handle, which is used for eating, mixing, stirring, and serving food. EG *...knife, fork, and spoon... ...a wooden spoon.* — N COUNT ▸ used also of the amount that a spoon can hold. EG *He takes six spoons of sugar in his tea.* — ▸ N PART

2 If you **spoon** food onto or into something or **spoon it up**, you pick it up in a spoon and put it somewhere else. EG *She stood spooning the juice over the chicken... He spooned the vegetables onto the plates... Spoon up all you can of the gravy.* V+O: USU+A = scoop

3 If you say that someone **was born with a silver spoon in** their **mouth**, you mean that they were born into a very wealthy family. PHR: VB INFLECTS

spoonerism /spuːnərɪzəᵒm/, **spoonerisms**. A **spoonerism** is a mistake made by a speaker in which the first sounds of two words are changed over, often with a humorous result. A well-known example of a spoonerism is 'You have hissed all my mystery lectures', when the speaker actually intended to say 'You have missed all my history lectures'. N COUNT

spoon-feed, spoon-feeds, spoon-feeding, spoon-fed. 1 If you **spoon-feed** someone, you do everything for them or tell them everything that they need to know, thus preventing them from having to think or act for themselves. EG *There is a tendency to spoon-feed your pupils when you're teaching because it is quicker and easier.* V+O, OR V+O+O

2 If you **spoon-feed** a baby, you feed it using a spoon. V+O, OR V+O+O

spoonful /spuːnfʊl/, **spoonfuls, spoonsful**. The plural can be either **spoonfuls** or **spoonsful**. A **spoonful** is the amount that a spoon can hold. EG *She put a spoonful of milk in each of the two cups.* N PART

spoor /spʊə, spɔː/. The **spoor** of an animal is the visible trail that it leaves as it moves along, especially its footprints. EG *They were amazed to notice that the elephant spoor had vanished from the path.* N SING WITH DET

sporadic /spəʳrædɪk/. Something that is **sporadic** happens at irregular intervals. EG *Sporadic attacks continued throughout the night... In most wars there have been sporadic civilian riots.* ◊ **sporadically**. EG *Instead of sniping at me sporadically from far away, they suddenly swooped down on me.* ADJ QUALIT; ◊ ADV WITH VB

spore /spɔː/, **spores**. A **spore** is a small reproductive cell, produced mainly by bacteria, ferns, and grasses, which develops into a new individual, often after a long period of inactivity. EG *The seed pod suddenly snaps apart, throwing the spores into the air to be distributed by the wind.* N COUNT

sporran /spɒrəᵒn/, **sporrans**. A **sporran** is a large purse, usually made of leather or fur, which is worn on a belt around their waists by Scotsmen when they are wearing a kilt. N COUNT ⇑ bag

sport /spɔːt/, **sports, sporting, sported. 1 Sports** are games such as football and cricket and other activities which need physical effort and skill. Sport is often organized competitively and as a form of entertainment for people to watch or to take part in. EG *My favourite sport is football... We should use our free time for more creative leisure, active sports and hobbies... I was good in the classroom and bad at sport... The new sports centre will open soon.* N UNCOUNT/COUNT: USU PL FORM WHEN MOD, ALSO UNCOUNT = PL

2 Sport is **2.1** any kind of enjoyable activity for which you need physical or mental skill. EG *He was obviously chasing rabbits for sport rather than for food... Science is their own special sport.* **2.2** fun or amusement, especially of a kind that ridicules someone or something and makes them look silly or stupid. EG *We used to tease Johnny, just for the sport of it.* ● If you **make sport of** someone, you ridicule and mock them. EG *He likes to make sport of British bureaucrats.* N UNCOUNT; N UNCOUNT; ● PHR: VB INFLECTS

3 If you say that someone is a **sport** or a good **sport**, you mean that they are fun to be with and react well and cheerfully whatever happens. EG *She was so kind, was Rita, such a good sport.* N COUNT: USED AS C

4 If you **sport** a piece of clothing, jewellery, etc, you wear it proudly, so that everyone can see it. EG *He was a bit of a show-off, sporting an earring in his left ear and an enormous moustache.* V+O ⇑ display

sporting /spɔːtɪŋ/. **1 Sporting** means relating to or used for sport. EG *It was his 29th international sporting event.* ADJ CLASSIF: ATTRIB

2 If you behave in a **sporting** way, **2.1** you behave with fairness and decency, as you should if you are playing a game and obeying all its rules. EG *'Have one of mine.'–'Thank you. That's a very sporting gesture.'* **2.2** you behave cheerfully in spite of the difficult situation you are in, in order not to spoil other people's enjoyment. EG *He smiled, in a sporting way.* ADJ QUALIT; ADJ QUALIT = brave

3 If there is **a sporting chance** that something will happen, it is quite likely that it will happen. EG *He's got a sporting chance of passing his exams.* PHR: USED AS O/C

sports car, sports cars. A **sports car** is a low, fast car, usually with room for only two people. EG *He's bought a flashy sports car.* N COUNT

sports day, sports days. In a school, a **sports day** is a day or afternoon on which pupils compete in activities such as races, the high jump, throwing the javelin, etc. Often parents are invited to come and watch the events. N COUNT

sports jacket, sports jackets. A **sports jacket** is a man's jacket, usually made of tweed. It is worn on informal occasions with trousers which are a different colour or made of a different material. N COUNT

sportsman /spɔːtsməᵌn/, **sportsmen**. A **sportsman** is **1** a man who takes part in and is good at sports. EG *...a professional sportsman.* **2** someone who, when they are playing games, is fair, obeys the rules, and is a good loser. N COUNT; N COUNT: USU SING

sportsmanlike /spɔːtsməᵌnlaɪk/. Behaviour that is **sportsmanlike** is fair and decent, as it should be when you are playing a game. ADJ QUALIT

sportsmanship /spɔːtsməᵌnʃɪp/ is the behaviour and attitudes that a good sportsman is expected to have. EG *He believed in manners and decency and sportsmanship.* N UNCOUNT

sportswear /spɔːtswɛə/ is the special clothing that is worn for playing sports, or for informal leisure activities. N UNCOUNT

sportswoman /spɔːtswʊᶦməᵒn/, **sportswomen**. A **sportswoman** is a woman who takes part in and is good at sports. N COUNT

sporty /spɔːtiᶦ/; a fairly informal word. **1** If a small car is **sporty**, it is fast. EG *I like the car's sporty performance.* ADJ QUALIT

2 Someone who is **sporty** likes playing sports. ADJ QUALIT

spot /spɒt/, **spots, spotting, spotted. 1** A **spot** is **1.1** a round area or shape on a surface, which is of a different colour from the background and which often forms part of a pattern. EG *She was wearing a white blouse with red spots... ...spots of light on a dark background.* **1.2** a small dirty or unwanted mark or patch of something. EG *There's a damp spot on the wall... This may damage the chrome and start small rust spots.* **1.3** a small raised area or mark on a person's skin, for example one that is caused by a disease. EG *Their bites leave itching red spots on the skin... I was covered with spots for a week.* **1.4** a place that has a particular quality or that is connected with a particular event or activity. EG *It's a lovely spot for a picnic... ...a popular beauty spot... She showed us the exact spot where the king was executed... ...journalists who hop from one trouble spot to another.* **1.5** a part or feature of something that has the quality mentioned. EG *The one bright spot in Louisa's life was her latest boyfriend... The trip to the Pyramids was the high spot of the tour.* N COUNT, OR N PART+N UNCOUNT ⇑ dot; N COUNT, OR N PART+N UNCOUNT; N COUNT ⇑ blemish = pimple; N COUNT: USU MOD+N; N COUNT: USU MOD+N = aspect

2 A **spot** of liquid, especially rain, is a very small drop of it. EG *I felt a few spots of rain.* N PART+N UNCOUNT

3 If you do or have a **spot** of something, you do or have a small amount of it; an informal use. EG *I think I'll do a spot of gardening... He's having a spot of girl trouble... What about a spot of lunch?* N PART+N UNCOUNT = bit

4 A **spot** in a show, television programme, etc is a part of the show or programme that is regularly reserved for a particular performer or type of entertainment. EG *They're doing the guest spot on the Muppet Show tonight.* N COUNT: USU MOD+N = slot

5 If you **spot** something, you notice it, often when this is difficult to do. EG *We suddenly spotted another boat about a mile away... You soon get good at spotting where they are under the sand... Well spotted!* V+O

6 If you are **in a spot**, you are in a difficult situation and do not know what to do; an informal expression. EG *He was in a bit of a spot because he'd lost his car keys.* PHR: USED AS AN A

7 on the spot. 7.1 If you are **on the spot**, you are actually at the place where something is happening. EG *They know what's going on because they're on the spot... Certain decisions had to be taken by the man on the spot.* **7.2** If you do something **on the spot**, you do it immediately, without any delay. EG *We thought they were going to shoot us down on the spot... I would have resigned on the spot if she'd said that to me.* **7.3** If someone is **on the spot**, they are in a difficult or embarrassing position, especially one in which they have to answer a difficult question or PHR: USED AS AN A ⇑ there; PHR: USED AS AN A = there and then; PHR: USED AS AN A

make a difficult decision. EG *I think you've really put him on the spot.*
8 If you say that someone **knocks spots off** another person, you mean that they are much better than the other person; used in informal British English. EG *There's one student who knocks spots off all the others.* PHR : VB INFLECTS ⇑ surpass
9 ● **rooted to the spot**: see **rooted.** ● to **have a soft spot for** someone: see **soft.** ● See also **black spot, blind spot, spotted.**

spot check, spot checks; also spelled with a hyphen. A **spot check** is a quick random inspection of one thing among a group of things. EG *Spot checks revealed a number of minor faults.* N COUNT

spotless /spɒtlɪ²s/. 1 Something that is **spotless** is perfectly clean. EG *...a spotless white shirt.* ADJ QUALIT
◊ **spotlessly.** EG *The room was spotlessly clean.* ◊ ADV+ADJ
2 If someone has a **spotless** character or reputation, they are known to be completely honest and respectable. ADJ QUALIT = flawless

spotlight /spɒtlaɪt/, **spotlights, spotlighting, spotlighted.** 1 A **spotlight** is a powerful light, often in a theatre, which can be directed so that it lights up a small area. EG *...standing on stage under the bright spotlights... I switched on the spotlight over the bed.* N COUNT
2 Someone who is in the **spotlight** is getting a great deal of public attention. EG *He's tired of being in the spotlight... ...one of a number of bands currently competing for the spotlight.* N SING : *the*+N = limelight
3 If something **spotlights** a particular situation or problem, it causes public attention to be directed towards it. EG *The event is intended to spotlight the plight of the mentally handicapped... It spotlighted the deficiencies of current appeal procedures.* V+O ⇑ show = highlight

spotlit /spɒtlɪt/. A **spotlit** stage, building, etc is brightly lit up by one or more spotlights. EG *...the spotlit spires of Notre Dame.* ADJ CLASSIF ⇑ illuminated

spot-on; also spelled as two words. If you say that someone is **spot-on**, you mean that they are exactly right or accurate; used in informal British English. EG *Her analysis of the situation is absolutely spot-on... Spot on, Ted!* ADJ CLASSIF : PRED

spotted /spɒtɪ²d/. Something that is **spotted** 1 has a pattern of spots on it. EG *...a red and white spotted handkerchief.* ADJ CLASSIF ⇑ dotted 2 is marked with small dirty or unwanted stains. EG *The inside may be spotted with nasty green mould.* ADJ CLASSIF : PRED+*with*

spotter /spɒtə/, **spotters.** A **spotter** of things of a particular type is a person whose hobby is looking out for those things. EG *...a train spotter... He's a compulsive spotter of oddities.* N COUNT+SUPP

spotty /spɒti¹/, **spottier, spottiest.** Someone who is **spotty** has spots or pimples on their skin, especially on their face. EG *...spotty adolescents... I've never seen so many freckles, you're like a spotty dog!* ADJ QUALIT

spouse /spaʊs, spaʊz/, **spouses.** Someone's **spouse** is the person they are married to; a formal word. EG *They receive free membership for themselves and their spouses.* N COUNT ⇑ partner

spout /spaʊt/, **spouts, spouting, spouted.** 1 When a liquid or flame **spouts** out of something, it comes out very fast in a long stream, with quite a lot of force. EG *...jets of water spouting up from the basins below... ...a fountain which spouted water into a basin... The blood spouted over his hands... Their tanks came on in hordes, spouting flames and thunder.* V-ERG : USU+A ⇑ flow = gush, spurt
2 A **spout** of liquid is a long stream of it which is coming out of something very fast. EG *The pipe burst and a spout of water shot out... It shot up in the air as though lifted by a water spout.* N COUNT : USU+SUPP jet, stream
3 If someone **spouts** or **spouts out** words, they say something in a way which is often boring and which gives people the impression that they are not thinking about what they are saying. EG *You were always spouting some theory to us at the table... The answer was mechanically spouted out to us: 'obstructing pedestrian traffic'... What about all the garbage you're always spouting about mingling with the people?... Everything we've been so glibly spouting may well be true.* V+O, V+A (*about*), OR PHRASAL VB : V+O+ADV ⇑ speak = churn out
4 A **spout** is a specially shaped opening or tube which allows liquids to be poured easily out of a container. EG *This teapot's got a broken spout.* N COUNT
5 **up the spout**; an informal expression. 5.1 If you say that something is **up the spout**, you mean that it is completely wrong. EG *If you ask me, your figures are completely up the spout.* PHR : USED AS AN A 5.2 If you say that something has gone **up the spout**, you mean that it is completely wasted. EG *That's another ten pounds up the spout... Their lives have gone up the spout.* PHR : USED AS AN A 5.3 If you say that someone is **up the spout**, you mean that they are in great difficulty. EG *I'm really up the spout now.* PHR : USED AS AN A

sprain /spreɪn/, **sprains, spraining, sprained.** 1 If you **sprain** your ankle, wrist, knee, etc, you accidentally hurt it by a sudden, violent twisting motion, which usually causes it to swell. EG *Rosa fell and sprained her ankle.* V+O ⇑ injure
2 A **sprain** is the injury caused by spraining a joint. EG *Don't worry, it's only a slight sprain.* N COUNT

sprang /spræŋ/ is the past tense of **spring.**

sprat /spræt/, **sprats.** A **sprat** is a very small European sea fish that is related to the herring and can be eaten. N COUNT

sprawl /sprɔːl/, **sprawls, sprawling, sprawled.** 1 If you **sprawl** or **sprawl out** somewhere, you sit or lie down and spread your legs and arms out in a careless manner. EG *Segal sprawled out on the couch... I tried to pick it up, but I overbalanced in the process and fell sprawling.* V OR V+O, OR PHRASAL VB : V+ADV OR V+O+ADV, USU+A ⇑ stretch out
2 A place that **sprawls** covers a large area, with various parts extending untidily in different directions; usually used showing disapproval. EG *The village sprawled all over the side of the mountain.* V+A
◊ **sprawling.** EG *The house was large and sprawling... The shopping area gradually gave way to sprawling suburbia.* ◊ ADJ QUALIT ⇑ extensive = rambling
3 **Sprawl** is used to refer to part of a city where houses or factories have been built untidily over a large area without any overall plan; used showing disapproval. EG *...the monstrous sprawl of the city... The new towns were to bring an end to London's urban sprawl... They find a refreshing absence of industrial sprawl.* N UNCOUNT+SUPP ⇑ spread

sprawled /sprɔːld/. If you are **sprawled** somewhere, you are sitting or lying with your legs and arms spread out in a careless manner. EG *He lay sprawled in the chair with his legs stretched out... The boy was sprawled out on the bed.* ADJ CLASSIF : PRED+A ⇑ stretched

spray /spreɪ/, **sprays, spraying, sprayed.** 1 **Spray** is 1.1 a lot of small drops of water or other liquid which are being forced upwards and scattered, for example by the wind or from a hose. EG *The fountain threw up clouds of spray... A spray of salt water hit her in the face.* N UNCOUNT/PART 1.2 a liquid under pressure in a spray can, which is forced out in very fine drops. EG *...paint spray... ...hair spray... ...a spray insecticide.* N MASS = aerosol, atomizer
2 If you **spray** a liquid over something or if you **spray** something with a liquid, 2.1 you scatter a lot of small drops of the liquid on it, for example using a hose. EG *We saw a huge vehicle spraying water on the road... David leapt to his feet, spraying his neighbours with cold coffee.* V+O : USU+A ⇑ shower 2.2 you cover it with very fine drops of the liquid from a spray can or a similar container. EG *He sprayed a little eau-de-cologne over himself... Spray the shelves with insecticide.* V OR V+O : USU+A ⇑ shower
3 If a lot of small things **spray** somewhere or if you **spray** something with them, they are scattered with quite a lot of force, often in a fan shape. EG *A fine red dust sprayed out from the edge of the saw... Sand blew across the stage, spraying the orchestra... They sprayed the enemy with bullets.* V+A, OR V+O : USU+A ⇑ shower
4 A **spray** is 4.1 a piece of equipment for spraying water or other liquid, especially over growing plants. EG *An ordinary garden spray might not reach to the far fence.* N COUNT 4.2 a lot of small things that are being scattered in a group, often in a fan shape. EG *...a spray of orange sparks... ...a spray of bullets.* N COUNT+SUPP = shower
5 A **spray** of flowers or leaves is a number of flowers or leaves on one stem or branch. EG *...a spray of chrysanthemums.* N PART

spray can, spray cans; also spelled with a hyphen. A **spray can** is a can which contains liquid under pressure, used for spraying. N COUNT ⇑ container

sprayer /spreɪə/, **sprayers.** A **sprayer** is 1 an apparatus for spraying a liquid. EG *...a pressure sprayer which releases a fine mist.* N COUNT 2 a person who uses a sprayer. EG *Sprayers are instructed to wear special clothes.* N COUNT

spread /spred/, **spreads, spreading**. The form **spread** is used in the present tense and is the past tense and past participle of the verb. **1** If you **spread** something, you open it out or arrange it over a place or surface, in order that all of it can be seen or used easily. EG *He took the envelope, tipped it open and spread the contents on the table... Their clothing was spread across low bushes to dry.* V+O : USU+A = lay

2 If you **spread** your fingers, arms, etc, you stretch them out until they are far apart. EG *He just shrugged and spread his hands... Jack lay with his arms spread.* V+O ↑ open = extend

3 If you **spread** a substance, especially something soft or sticky, on a surface or if you **spread** the surface with the substance, you put a thin layer of the substance over the surface. EG *Liz was spreading marmalade on a piece of toast... I love biscuits spread with butter.* V+O : USU+A

4 A **spread** is a soft food made from something such as meat or cheese, which is usually put on bread. EG *...cheese spread.* N MASS = paste

5 If something such as liquid, smoke, or gas **spreads** or if you **spread** it, it moves outwards in all directions so that it covers a larger area. EG *A stain was spreading on the bathroom ceiling... Rose trod with care, in order not to spread the dirt.* V-ERG : USU+A ↑ cover = disperse

6 If something such as fire or disease **spreads**, it starts affecting more and more of an area or more and more people. EG *We had to stop the fire getting out of control and spreading... Disease might be spread very easily.* V-ERG ↑ grow ▸ used as a noun. EG *Many people died as a result of the spread of fire.* ▸ N SING : USU the+N+of

7 If something such as news or an idea or feeling **spreads** or if people **spread** it, it becomes known or shared by more and more people. EG *News of the wreck spread quickly... Hinduism spread far beyond India... People seem to love spreading gossip.* V-ERG = be disseminated ▸ used as a noun. EG *Girls have benefited more than boys from the spread of higher education.* ▸ N SING : USU the+N+of = expansion

8 If people **spread** somewhere, they travel further in a particular direction and begin to live in areas that they have not lived in before. EG *They spread south and colonised the plains of Africa.* V : USU+A

9 If things **spread** over an area, they become more and more common. EG *Big glass-framed buildings were now beginning to spread across the site... Tractors are spreading faster in Asia than in any other continent.* V ↑ appear

10 If something such as a city or forest **spreads** or **is spread**, it covers a large area. EG *The city spreads for miles to the north... I drove out through the spreading suburbs west of Chicago.* V OR V+O : USU PASS ↑ extend

11 The **spread** of something is **11.1** the area it covers, or a large area of it. EG *We topped the rise and saw a new spread of land before us.* N SING WITH DET : USU+of **11.2** the greatest distance that it can be spread. EG *The wing has a spread of 2 metres.* N SING WITH DET = span

12 If something **spreads** over a period of time, it takes place regularly or continuously over that period. EG *They had experience spreading over twenty years... The job losses may not seem catastrophic when spread over a period... The breeding season is a very long one, spread over five months.* V+A (over), OR V+O+A (over) ↑ extend = distribute

13 If you **spread** something such as wealth or work, you divide it so that it is distributed evenly or equally. EG *The challenge to the government is to spread the wealth it creates more widely... Public investment in agriculture has not been evenly spread... You are advised to spread the work load.* V+O = distribute

14 A **spread** of ideas, subjects, products, etc is a wide variety of them. EG *The IBA wants to have a broad spread of interest and opinion represented on its board.* N SING WITH DET +of = range

15 A **spread** is also **15.1** two pages of a book or magazine that are opposite each other when you open it at a particular place. EG *...a double-page spread.* N COUNT **15.2** a large meal, especially one that has been prepared for a special occasion. EG *The farmhouse puts on quite a decent spread.* N COUNT : USU ADJ+N **15.3** a large area of land, especially a farm or ranch; used in American English. EG *We were on our way to visit his spread in Kansas.* N COUNT = place

spread out. 1 If people, animals, vehicles, etc **spread out** or **are spread out**, they move away from each other or are positioned away from each other so that they fill a large area and are far apart. EG *They followed him and spread out, nervously, in the forest... There in the harbour was a line of dark battleships spread out under the night sky... My family were spread out all over the countryside.* PHRASAL VB : V-ERG+ADV, IF V+O THEN USU PASS = disperse

2 If something such as a city or forest **spreads out** or **is spread out**, it covers a large area. EG *At the foot of the mountain the city spread out to the bay... The country was spread out around us, wild and harsh.* PHRASAL VB : V-ERG+ADV, IF V+O THEN USU PASS ↑ extend

3 If you **spread** something **out**, you open it out or arrange it over a place or surface, in order that all of it can be seen or used easily. EG *I removed the tool kit and spread it out on the seat... They took seats directly opposite me and spread out their newspapers.* PHRASAL VB : V+O+ADV = lay

4 If you **spread out** your fingers, arms, etc or if they **spread out**, you stretch them out until they are far apart. EG *He lifted up a hand and held it there, the fingers spread out.* PHRASAL VB : V-ERG+ADV

spread-eagled /spred iːgəᵊld/. Someone who is **spread-eagled** is lying with their arms and legs spread out. EG *Buller was found spread-eagled outside the bedroom door.* ADJ CLASSIF : USU PRED

spree /spriː/, **sprees**. A **spree** is a fairly short period of doing something enjoyable with a lot of energy, especially in an excessive way. EG *Tim was away on a shopping spree... He went on a drinking spree.* N COUNT

sprig /sprɪg/, **sprigs**. A **sprig** is a small twig or stem with leaves on it which has been picked from a bush or plant, especially so that it can be used in cooking or as a decoration. EG *...a sprig of holly... ...a sprig of thyme.* N PART+N UNCOUNT

sprightly /spraɪtli[1]/, **sprightlier, sprightliest**. Someone who is **sprightly** is lively and full of energy; used especially to describe people who are old. EG *She was as sprightly as a woman half her age... Jimmy McGregor is a sprightly 71-year old.* ADJ QUALIT = spry

spring /sprɪŋ/, **springs, springing, sprang, sprung**. **Sprang** is the usual form of the past tense of the verb, but **sprung** is sometimes used. **Sprung** is the past participle of the verb. **1 Spring** is the season between winter and summer. In the spring the weather begins to get warmer and leaves and plants start to grow again. EG *It would have been better to have waited until the spring... Each spring an immense migration begins... He left in the spring of 1956.* N UNCOUNT/COUNT

2 A **spring** is **2.1** a coiled piece of wire which returns to its original shape when it is pressed or twisted. EG *One day they would get a real sofa, with springs... ...a watch spring.* N COUNT ↑ coil **2.2** a pool that is formed where water comes up through the ground. EG *...a mountain spring... ...hot volcanic springs.* N COUNT

3 When a person or animal **springs**, they jump upwards or forwards suddenly and quickly. EG *She sprang to her feet and faced him... She sprung at him, and aimed a wild blow at his face... The panther crouched, ready to spring... They sprang to attention.* V : USU+A

4 If something **springs** in a particular direction, it moves suddenly and quickly. EG *Hands sprang up... The door of the safe had sprung open.* V+A = fly

5 Spring is used in expressions such as 'spring into action' and 'spring to life' when you are saying that something starts or comes into existence very quickly and suddenly. EG *A computer will not spring into action without something powering it... At last factories sprang to life again.* V+A

6 If one thing **springs** from something else, it is the result of the other thing or it started there. EG *These problems spring from different causes... This is a strong indication that the two groups sprang from common stock... Her hostility to him sprang out of sheer envy.* V+A (from/out of) ↑ come

7 If you ask someone where they have **sprung** from, you are asking them where they have come from in a rather surprised way, because they have appeared unexpectedly. V+A (from)

8 If a boat, container, etc **springs a leak**, it starts to let water or some other liquid in or out through a hole or crack. EG *The water tank had sprung several leaks.* PHR : VB AND N INFLECT

9 If you **spring** some news or a surprise on someone, you tell them some unexpected news or ask them to do something that surprises them. EG *It was then that I sprang my surprise... She couldn't understand why this should be sprung on her at such short notice.* V+O : IF+PREP THEN on

10 If you **spring** someone from prison or some other form of captivity, you help them escape; an informal V+O : IF+PREP THEN from/out

use. EG *Eighteen months later Blake was sprung from prison.* — of ⇑ free

11 If you walk **with a spring in** your **step**, you walk in a bouncy way that shows that you are cheerful and enthusiastic. — PHR : USED AS AN A

12 See also **sprung**.

spring up. If something **springs up**, it appears or comes into existence quickly. EG *Computer stores are springing up all over the place... These friendships spring up and very often don't last... A fresh wind had sprung up.* — PHRASAL VB : V+ADV

springboard /sprɪŋbɔːd/, **springboards**. 1 A **springboard** is a flexible board on which you jump in order to give you more height to perform a dive or a gymnastic movement. — N COUNT ⇑ equipment

2 Something that acts as a **springboard** for an action or enterprise is something that it can start from or that can be used as a source of strength or ideas. EG *The campaign might well be the springboard for the launching of a new party.* — N COUNT : USU+ for/to

springbok /sprɪŋbɒk/, **springboks**. **Springbok** can also be used as the plural form. A **springbok** is an antelope that lives in southern Africa. — N COUNT

spring-clean, spring-cleans, spring-cleaning, spring-cleaned; also spelled as two words. When you **spring-clean** a house, you thoroughly clean everything in it, including things that you do not clean very often. ◊ **spring-cleaning**. EG *Mrs Pringle came to give me a hand with the spring-cleaning.* — V OR V+O; ◊ N UNCOUNT

spring onion, spring onions. A **spring onion** is a small onion with long green leaves that is often eaten raw in salads. — N COUNT ⇑ vegetable

spring roll, spring rolls. A **spring roll** is a Chinese item of food consisting of a small roll of thin pastry filled with vegetables and sometimes meat, and cooked in oil. — N COUNT

springtime /sprɪŋtaɪm/ is the period of time during which it is spring. EG *The Greek Islands are lovely in springtime.* — N UNCOUNT

springy /sprɪŋi[1]/, **springier, springiest**. If something is **springy**, it returns easily and quickly to its original shape when you press it. EG *...a springy mattress... The grass was short and springy.* — ADJ QUALIT ⇑ soft = bouncy

sprinkle /sprɪŋkə[0]l/, **sprinkles, sprinkling, sprinkled**. 1 If you **sprinkle** a substance such as water or sugar over something, you scatter it in small drops or pieces over that thing. EG *Never sprinkle washing powder on clothes, dissolve it separately first... A little cinnamon sprinkled over cooked cabbage is delicious... She sprinkled the cakes with sugar.* — V+O : USU+A

2 If things **are sprinkled** over a place, they are found all over it, but are quite far apart. EG *Booksellers are sprinkled all over the city.* — V+O : ONLY PASS ⇑ be spread = be dotted

3 See also **sprinkling**.

sprinkler /sprɪŋklə/, **sprinklers**. A **sprinkler** is a device with small holes which is used to spray water. Sprinklers are used to water plants or lawns or to put out a fire in a building. — N COUNT

sprinkling /sprɪŋklɪŋ/, **sprinklings**. A **sprinkling** of something is a small quantity or amount of it, especially one that is spread out or scattered. EG *There is always a sprinkling of sightseers outside the palace... ...a sprinkling of grey hairs.* — N PART : USU SING

sprint /sprɪnt/, **sprints, sprinting, sprinted**. 1 A **sprint** is 1.1 a short race, for example the 100 metres race, in which the runners run very fast. — N COUNT 1.2 a very fast run that someone does, either at the end of a longer race or when they are in a hurry. EG *I'm really a long-distance runner, but I do my best in the final sprint... Bessie had suddenly broken into a sprint.* — N SING WITH DET

2 If you **sprint**, you run as fast as you can over a short distance, either in a race or because you are in a hurry. EG *She sprinted to her car... He sprinted for the finishing line.* — V : USU+A

sprinter /sprɪntə/, **sprinters**. A **sprinter** is a person who can run very fast over short distances. — N COUNT ⇑ runner

sprite /spraɪt/, **sprites**. A **sprite** is a type of fairy; a literary word. — N COUNT

sprocket /sprɒkɪt/, **sprockets**. A **sprocket** or **sprocket wheel** is a wheel with one or more rows of teeth that fit into the holes in a chain, reel of film or tape, etc in order to turn it. — N COUNT

sprout /spraʊt/, **sprouts, sprouting, sprouted**. 1 When plants or vegetables **sprout**, they produce new leaves or shoots. EG *If you leave onions long enough they will generally sprout.* — V OR V+O

2 When leaves or shoots **sprout**, they begin to grow from a plant or vegetable. EG *Everywhere, leaves sprouted.* — V

3 When hairs, feathers, horns, etc **sprout** or when a person or animal **sprouts** them, they start to grow. EG *At last the essential feathers of the young eagles sprout... Bob's beginning to sprout a beard.* — V-ERG

4 If things **sprout** up or if something **sprouts** them, they appear or spread rapidly. EG *Caravans had suddenly sprouted up in the fields... San Francisco and other cities have sprouted a rash of little theatres.* — V-ERG : IF V THE USU+A (up)

5 **Sprouts** or **brussels sprouts** are small green vegetables which look like very small cabbages. — N COUNT : USU PL

6 A **sprout** is a new shoot on a plant. EG *Even in frost roots are usually unharmed and they produce new sprouts.* — N COUNT

spruce /spruːs/, **spruces, sprucing, spruced**. **Spruce** is both the singular and the plural form of the noun. 1 A **spruce** is an evergreen tree which grows in the shape of a pyramid and has needle-like leaves. EG *...a forest of spruce and fir.* — N COUNT ▸ used to refer to the wood of this tree. EG *...a log of spruce.* — ▸ N UNCOUNT

2 Someone who is **spruce** is very neat and smart in appearance. EG *You're looking very spruce in your new suit.* — ADJ QUALIT = dapper

spruce up. If you **spruce** yourself **up** or **spruce** something **up**, you make yourself or it neat and smart. EG *Spruce yourself up a bit–you look a mess!... If you spruce the bodywork up and the interior, you'll have no trouble selling it.* — PHRASAL VB : V O (NG/REFL)+ADV ⇑ tidy up

sprung /sprʌŋ/. 1 A **sprung** mattress has springs, in order to make it more comfortable. — ADJ CLASSIF : ATTRIB

2 **Sprung** is the past participle or alternative past tense of **spring**.

spry /spraɪ/, **spryer, spryest**. Someone who is **spry** is very lively and active; used especially of elderly people. EG *My father's eighty, but he's remarkably spry for his age.* — ADJ QUALIT ⇑ agile = sprightly

spud /spʌd/, **spuds**. A **spud** is a potato; an informal word. EG *Will you peel the spuds, please?* — N COUNT ⇑ vegetable

spume /spjuːm/ is the white foam on top of waves when the sea is very rough; a literary word. EG *...the white and icy spume hissing into the sea.* — N UNCOUNT = froth, surf

spun /spʌn/ is the past tense and past participle of **spin**.

spunk /spʌŋk/ is courage; an informal, rather old-fashioned word. EG *You've got to admire her spunk.* — N UNCOUNT = pluck

spunky /spʌŋki[1]/, **spunkier, spunkiest**. Someone who is **spunky** shows courage; an informal, rather old-fashioned word. EG *She's a spunky kid.* — ADJ QUALIT ⇑ brave = plucky

spur /spɜː/, **spurs, spurring, spurred**. 1 If someone or something **spurs** you or **spurs** you **on**, they give you encouragement to do something. EG *Her approval spurred him to enter a poetry contest... You need someone to spur you on... I am not conceited about my achievement but I am spurred on by it.* — V+O OR PHRAS VB : V+O+ADV USU+to-INF/A ⇑ encourage = urge

2 If something **spurs** an improvement or change, it makes it happen faster. EG *...a period of extremely rapid growth, spurred by the advent of the microprocessor.* — V+O ⇑ stimulate

3 Something that acts as a **spur** gives encouragement to a person to do something or makes an improvement or change happen faster. EG *Unfortunately there is no spur to efficiency or improvement of technology... The shortage of labour acts as a powerful spur to more economical methods of production.* — N COUNT : USU SING+to = incentive, stimulus

4 A **spur** is also 4.1 a small metal wheel with sharp points which is attached to the heel of a rider's boot and used to urge a horse to go faster. EG *He clapped his spurs to the horse's flanks.* — N COUNT : USU 4.2 a high piece of land which sticks out from the side of a mountain or hill. — N COUNT ⇑ ridge

5 If you do something **on the spur of the moment**, you do it suddenly and without any preparation. EG *I just took the bus on the spur of the moment.* ● See also **spur-of-the-moment**. — PHR : USED AS A = on impulse

6 If you **win** your **spurs**, you earn a particular status or right, for example by passing some kind of test. — PHR : VB INFLECTS

spurious /spjʊərɪəs/. 1 Something that is **spurious** has the appearance of something else but is not genuine. EG *...the spurious attractions of modernity...* — ADJ QUALIT = phoney, fake, bogus

His display of emotion on that occasion had been spurious.

2 A **spurious** argument or statement is based on faulty reasoning and is therefore probably not correct. EG *The whole argument was spurious... It would be spurious to claim that redundancies alone will solve our problems.* ADJ QUALIT = false

spurn /spɜːn/, **spurns, spurning, spurned.** If you **spurn** something, you refuse to accept it; a formal word. EG *...fears that they will spurn disarmament talks... I can't help feeling spurned... ...his spurned gift.* V+O = reject

spur-of-the-moment. A **spur-of-the-moment** action or decision is sudden and has not been planned. EG *...spur-of-the-moment impulses.* ADJ CLASSIF: ATTRIB = snap

spurt /spɜːt/, **spurts, spurting, spurted.** 1 When a liquid or flame **spurts** out of something, it comes out quickly and suddenly in a thin, powerful stream. EG *...a blow that sent blood spurting from his mouth... The water spurted out... My arm began to spurt blood.* ▸ used as a noun. EG *...a small, clear spurt of flame... Water came out of the tap in spurts.* V-ERG: USU+A = gush, spray ▸ N PART+N UNCOUNT

2 A **spurt** of activity, effort, or emotion is a sudden, brief period of activity, effort, or emotion. EG *Her feelings varied from tenderness to sudden spurts of genuine love... ...the technological spurt caused by the threat of war.* N COUNT: USU+SUPP, OR N PART+N UNCOUNT = burst

3 If you **spurt** somewhere, you suddenly start to move much faster, especially for only a short while. EG *The deer spurted with her last strength... With Claude driving they spurted through back streets.* ▸ used as a noun. EG *I put on a spurt and caught them up... He drove fast, passing cars in racing-driver spurts.* V: USU+A ▸ N COUNT

sputter /spʌtə/, **sputters, sputtering, sputtered.** If something, for example an engine, **sputters**, it makes soft hissing and popping sounds. EG *Then the engine began coughing and popping and sputtering... The fire sputtered quietly.* ▸ used as a noun. EG *The engine gave a sputter and died.* V = splutter ▸ N COUNT = splutter

spy /spaɪ/, **spies, spying, spied.** 1 A **spy** is a person whose job is to find out secret information about another country, business, or organization, by becoming involved in their work without them realizing. EG *A member of his staff was discovered to be a foreign spy... A police spy infiltrated his rooms and sent back a detailed report... ...a spy satellite.* N COUNT = mole

2 Someone who **spies** tries to find out secret information about another country, business, or organization. EG *Three of its embassy officials have been expelled for spying.* V

3 If you **spy** on someone, you watch them secretly. EG *They could spy on me through a porthole window... ...girls spying on their unfaithful lovers.* V+A *(on)*

4 If you **spy** someone or something, you notice them, especially when they are not obvious; a fairly formal use. EG *Suddenly Quint spied the triangular fin of a shark coming towards them.* V+O

spy out. If you **spy** something **out**, you try to find out information about it secretly or while pretending to do something else. EG *You've probably been sent here to spy out my latest designs.* ● If you **spy out the land** before doing something, you try to find out about the things that you are going to be dealing with. EG *I suggest that you spy out the land a bit before you go ahead.* PHRASAL VB: V+O+ADV ⇑ investigate ● PHR: VB INFLECTS

sq. 1 **sq** is a written abbreviation for 'square'; used in measurements. EG *...280,000 sq. ft. of office space.*

2 **Sq** is a written abbreviation for 'Square'; used in addresses and on maps or signs. EG *...Hanover Sq, London W1.*

squabble /skwɒbəºl/, **squabbles, squabbling, squabbled.** If people **squabble**, they quarrel noisily, usually about something that is not really important. EG *They're always squabbling over little details.* ▸ used as a noun. EG *I had to sort out all the squabbles between the children.* V: USU CONT = bicker ▸ N COUNT ⇑ argument

squad /skwɒd/, **squads.** When **squad** is used in the singular, it can be used with a singular or a plural verb. A **squad** is 1 a section of a police force that is responsible for dealing with a particular type of crime. EG *...the drugs squad... Anti-riot squads were called out to deal with the situation.* 2 a group of players from which a sports team will be chosen. EG *The England World Cup squad was named today.* 3 a small group of soldiers which form a unit working together. EG *The sergeant had just brought his squad in from a long patrol.* N COUNT: MOD+N ⇑ division N COUNT+SUPP N COUNT

squad car, squad cars. A **squad car** is a car used by the police. EG *They had several squad cars strategically positioned in the area.* N COUNT = patrol car, police car

squadron /skwɒdrəºn/, **squadrons.** When **squadron** is used in the singular, it can be used with a singular or a plural verb. A **squadron** is a section of one of the armed forces, especially the air force. EG *...a squadron of US Air Force Phantoms.* N COUNT ⇑ division

squadron leader, squadron leaders. A **squadron leader** is an officer in the British air force who has a rank above that of flight lieutenant. EG *...Squadron Leader Philips.* N COUNT: ALSO IN TITLES

squalid /skwɒlɪd/. 1 A place that is **squalid** is dirty, untidy, and in bad condition, usually because of poverty. EG *...a squalid, overcrowded flat in the poorest part of town.* ADJ QUALIT ⇑ filthy = nasty

2 **Squalid** activities involve a lack of honesty and moral principles. EG *They're involved in a rather squalid battle as to who controls the party... ...a squalid political deal.* ADJ QUALIT = sordid, wretched

squall /skwɔːl/, **squalls, squalling, squalled.** 1 A **squall** is a sudden strong wind, often causing a brief, violent storm. EG *I was flying my plane and ran into a squall over San Francisco Bay.* N COUNT

2 If a person or animal **squalls**, they make a loud unpleasant noise like the noise made by a crying baby. EG *He squalled like a wildcat this morning... ...housewives confronted with squalling children.* ▸ used as a noun. EG *There was an angry squall from the bedroom.* V ⇑ cry ▸ N COUNT

squalor /skwɒlə/ is the quality of being physically squalid, or squalid conditions or surroundings. EG *...poor people living in conditions of squalor and privation... It's my duty to rescue you from this squalor.* N UNCOUNT ⇑ filth = wretchedness

squander /skwɒndə/, **squanders, squandering, squandered.** If you **squander** money or resources, you use them all up in a foolish and wasteful way. EG *If we squander our fossil fuels, we threaten civilisation... I've known you to squander half the week's housekeeping in half an hour.* V+O ⇑ spend = waste

square /skweə/, **squares, squaring, squared.**

1 A **square** is 1.1 a shape with four sides of the same length and four corners that are all right angles. EG *I folded the newspaper neatly into a square and put it away... The courtyard was paved in black and white marble squares.* ▸ used of anything that has this shape. EG *He filled in a crossword puzzle, leaving one square blank... He dabbed the cuts with disinfectant and taped a gauze square over them.* 1.2 a flat open place in a town or city, sometimes in the shape of a square. EG *...the town square... ...Trafalgar Square... ...St James's and Mayfair, with their great squares.* N COUNT ⇑ quadrilateral ▸ ⇑ object N COUNT: ALSO IN NAMES

2 Something that is **square** has a shape the same as a square or similar to a square, for example with straight sides and corners, or flat surfaces rather than curves. EG *The post office was a small, square building... ...little square holes in the ground... He had a square ruddy face.* ADJ QUALIT

3 **Square** is used 3.1 before units of length when referring to how large the area of something is. For example, a square metre is one metre long and one metre wide. EG *...hundreds of square miles of pine forest... ...an area of approximately thirty square kilometres.* 3.2 after units of length when referring to the length of each side of something that has the shape of a square. EG *The main area of the site measured roughly 35 feet square... ...a silicon chip less than a centimetre square and a millimetre thick.* ADJ CLASSIF: ATTRIB ADJ AFTER N

4 If you hit something **square**, you hit it directly, firmly, and in the middle rather than indirectly or at an angle. EG *The wave was going to crash down square on the deck of the trawler... For once in her life, Jenny couldn't look me square in the eye.* ADV AFTER VB: USU+PREP ⇑ straight

5 If you place something **square**, you place it so that it is parallel with something else. EG *He put the chart on the coffee table and set it square with the edges.* ADV AFTER VB, OR ADJ CLASSIF: PRED

6 If you **square** things, you make them parallel or straight. EG *He squared the papers before him and studied them.* ◊ **squared.** EG *He walked in an easy gliding motion with his shoulders squared.* V+O ⇑ straighten ◊ ADJ CLASSIF

7 If two people are **square**, they are even, level, or equal with each other, for example they no longer owe each other any money; a fairly informal use. ADJ CLASSIF: PRED = straight

8 If you **square** a situation, you make it even, level, or equal. EG *He scored seventeen runs to win the Fifth Test and square the 1957 series.* V+O

9 When you **square** two situations or ideas with each other or when they **square** with each other, you enable them to be considered or accepted together even though they seem different. EG *How do you square being a Lord with being a Marxist?... How does this work square with the other plays he was writing?* V-ERG: ALSO V OR V+A (with): RECIP ⇑ balance = accord

10 Someone who is **square** is boring, unfashionable, or out of date; a rather old-fashioned, informal use. EG *They were square, but nice to know.* ▸ used as a noun. EG *Don't be such a square.* ADJ QUALIT ⇑ old-fashioned ▸ N COUNT ⇑ person

11 The **square** of a number is the number produced when you multiply that number by itself. For example, the square of 3 is 9. N COUNT: IF+ PREP THEN *of* ⇑ product

12 If you **square** a number, you multiply it by itself. For example, 3 squared is 3 x 3, or 9. 3 squared is usually written as 3^2. EG *We take two, we square it, and we get four.* V+O

13 If you describe someone as **a square peg in a round hole**, you mean that they do not seem to be suitable or successful in a particular situation; an informal expression. PHR: USED AS C = misfit

14 If you go **back to square one** or if you start again **from square one**, you start to consider or deal with a situation from the beginning again, because one line of thought or course of action has failed; an informal expression. EG *I would have to start again from square one, and rely on my own judgement... You are back to square one again.* PHR: USED AS AN A

15 • **fair and square**: see **fair**. • See also **squarely**.

square up. 1 If you **square up** with someone, you pay the bills or debts that you owe them; an informal use. EG *Do you want to square up now or later?* PHRASAL VB: V+ ADV, ALSO+A (with): RECIP = settle up

2 If you **square up** to a problem, person, or situation, you accept that you have to deal with it and take action to do so. EG *But she had squared up to him all right.* PHRASAL VB: V+ ADV, USU+*to/for* ⇑ confront

square bracket, square brackets. A **square bracket** is a bracket that is shaped like half a square rather than being round. N COUNT

square deal, square deals. If you are given a **square deal**, you are treated fairly and honestly. EG *We've got to give them a square deal.* N COUNT = good

squarely /skwɛəli¹/. 1 **Squarely** means directly and in the middle rather than indirectly or at an angle. EG *He limped down the street, his cloth cap squarely on top of his head... The television mast fell squarely onto a Methodist chapel.* ADV WITH VB: USU+PREP ⇑ right

2 If you look at or face something **squarely**, you look at it or face it directly, without trying to avoid looking at it. EG *...one of the few feature films that looks squarely at social problems... This difficulty will have to be squarely faced.* ADV WITH VB

square meal, square meals. A **square meal** is a meal that is big enough to make you feel full. EG *He had gone without a square meal for nearly three days.* N COUNT = decent

square root, square roots. The **square root** of a number is the number that produces the first number when it is multiplied by itself. For example, the square root of 16 is 4. N COUNT

squash /skwɒʃ/, **squashes, squashing, squashed**. 1 If you **squash** something, you press it or crush it, often with great force, so that it becomes flat or loses its shape. EG *I sat on my bag and squashed the tomatoes... We saw a car squashed between two heavy lorries on the motorway... My hand got caught in the door and my fingers were squashed.* V+O: USU PASS = flatten, squeeze

2 If there is a **squash** in a place or vehicle, there are a lot of people pressed against each other so that there is very little room to move. EG *The children sat in the back so there wasn't a squash.* N SING WITH DET = squeeze

3 If you **squash** something that is causing you trouble, you put a stop to it, often by means of force. EG *They stayed in power by squashing any attempts to organize an opposition party... Her speech squashed all the rumours of an early election.* V+O ⇑ end = quash, suppress

4 **Squash** is a game played between two players in a square court surrounded by walls. The players hit a small rubber ball against the walls using long-handled rackets. N UNCOUNT

5 In British English, **squash** is also a drink made from fruit juice, sugar, and water. It is usually sold in bottles in a concentrated form to which you add more water. EG *We gave all the children a glass of lemon squash.* N MASS = cordial

6 A **squash** is any vegetable belonging to the marrow family; used especially in American English. N COUNT

squashy /skwɒʃi¹/, **squashier, squashiest**. Something that is **squashy** is soft and able to be squashed easily. EG *...squashy tomatoes.* ADJ QUALIT = squidgy

squat /skwɒt/, **squats, squatting, squatted**. 1 If you **squat** or **squat down**, you sit close to the ground, balancing on your feet with your legs bent under your body. EG *He told the boys to squat in a semicircle around him... We squatted down under the tree.* V OR PHRASAL VB: V+ADV, USU +A

2 Someone or something that is **squat** is short and thick, often in an unattractive way. EG *...a squat, bald, plump man... ...the little church with its squat tower.* ADJ QUALIT = stocky

3 A person who **squats** in an unused building lives there without having a legal right to do so and without paying any rent. EG *There were two young men squatting in one of the empty houses.* V

4 A **squat** is an unused building that people are living in without having a legal right to do so and without paying rent; used in British English. EG *They live in a squat in Camden Town.* N COUNT ⇑ house

squatter /skwɒtə/, **squatters**. A **squatter** is 1 a person who lives in an unused building without having a legal right to do so and without paying any rent. EG *The police evicted squatters who had occupied some empty council flats.* N COUNT ⇑ occupant 2 a person who occupies unused land, either to farm it or to build a house on it, without having a legal right to do so. EG *...squatter settlements on the outskirts of the city.* N COUNT

squaw /skwɔː/, **squaws**. A **squaw** is a North American Indian woman. N COUNT

squawk /skwɔːk/, **squawks, squawking, squawked**. 1 When a bird **squawks**, it makes a loud sharp noise, for example when it is frightened or excited. EG *Scrawny chickens ran squawking around the village.* V

2 A **squawk** is 2.1 a loud sharp noise that some birds make. EG *I listened to the sad squawks of the peacocks.* N COUNT 2.2 a loud angry complaint. EG *His latest proposal has raised squawks of protest in Congress.* N COUNT

squeak /skwiːk/, **squeaks, squeaking, squeaked**. If an animal, person, or thing **squeaks**, it makes a short, high-pitched sound or cry. EG *A door squeaked open nearby... When its mouth is filled by an insect, a bat cannot squeak in the normal way.* ▸ used as a noun. EG *You could hear the tiny squeaks of voles and mice... She let out a squeak.* V ▸ N COUNT

squeaky /skwiːki¹/, **squeakier, squeakiest**. Something that is **squeaky** makes squeaking noises. EG *...a wooden fence with a squeaky iron gate... His voice was squeaky with fear.* ADJ QUALIT

squeal /skwiːl/, **squeals, squealing, squealed**. 1 If an animal, person, or thing **squeals**, it makes a long, high-pitched sound. EG *The boys scattered, squealing in horror.* ▸ used as a noun. EG *The pig gave a gasping squeal... There was a squeal of brakes.* V ▸ N COUNT ⇑ noise

2 If you **squeal** to the police, you give them information about someone who has committed a crime, usually when you are a friend or partner of the criminal; used in very informal English. EG *He squealed on his mates.* V: USU+A ⇑ inform = grass

squeamish /skwiːmɪʃ/. If you are **squeamish**, you are easily shocked or upset by unpleasant sights or situations. EG *I was too squeamish to look.* ADJ QUALIT ⇑ sensitive

squeeze /skwiːz/, **squeezes, squeezing, squeezed**. 1 When you **squeeze** something, you press it firmly from all sides, usually with your hands, often so that its shape changes or it becomes smaller. EG *The children were squeezing the packets to find out what was inside... He was holding her hands and squeezing them between his.* ▸ used as a noun. EG *He gave her hand a squeeze.* V+O ▸ N COUNT

2 When you **squeeze** a liquid or a soft substance out of an object, you get the liquid or substance out by pressing the object. EG *Squeeze all the surplus water out of the cloth... ...squeezing out the last bit of toothpaste from the tube... ...freshly squeezed orange juice.* V+O: USU+A

3 When you **squeeze** a fruit such as a lemon or an orange, you get juice out of it by cutting it in half and pressing each half, usually against a special object. EG *I watched Bernard squeeze the limes.* V+O

4 A **squeeze** of a liquid is a small amount of it that N PART+N

you get by squeezing something, for example juice from a lemon. EG *Add a squeeze of lemon just before serving.* UNCOUNT

4 If you **squeeze** through a small space, you manage to get through it, often with great effort. EG *We squeezed under the wire and into the garden... She squeezed in beside me on the seat... He squeezed himself carefully into the back.* V+A, OR V+O (REFL)+A ⇑ move

5 If there is a **squeeze**, there are a lot of people crowded into a small space; a fairly informal use. EG *We all got in the lift but it was a bit of a squeeze.* N SING : a+N = jam, squash

6 If you **squeeze** an object or activity into a small amount of space or time, you manage to fit the object into the space or to do the activity in the time, often with great difficulty. EG *By this time thousands of components were being squeezed onto a single microchip... Do you think you can squeeze in your lunch break between the two meetings?* V+O+A = cram

7 If you **squeeze** something out of someone, especially something that you need, you get it from them by means of force, persuasion, or great effort. EG *He's hoping to squeeze the extra cash out of his bank manager... It's not clear how much extra output they could squeeze from the existing machinery.* V+O+A = extract

8 A **squeeze** is also a situation in which it is difficult to borrow money because of strict controls, usually imposed by the government. EG *...a credit squeeze... ...another squeeze on borrowing.* N SING WITH DET +SUPP

squelch /skweltʃ/, **squelches, squelching, squelched.** To **squelch** means to make a wet, sucking sound like the sound that your shoes make when you are walking on soft muddy ground. EG *I squelched along by the water's edge... He heard a squelching sound in his ears.* ▸ used as a noun. EG *...a satisfying squelch.* V : USU+A ▸ N COUNT ⇑ noise

squib /skwɪb/, **squibs. 1** A **squib** is a small firework that makes a loud bang. EG *Little boys were throwing home-made squibs.* N COUNT = banger

2 You can describe something such as an event or a performance as a **damp squib** when it is expected to be interesting, exciting, or impressive, but fails to be any of these things; used showing disapproval. EG *The party turned out to be a bit of a damp squib.* PHR : USED AS C ⇑ disappointment = non-event

squid /skwɪd/, **squids. Squid** can also be used as the plural form. A **squid** is a sea creature with a long body and many arms around its mouth. Some squid are very small and some are very large. EG *Squids can grow to an immense size... Sperm whales frequently dive to search for squid.* N COUNT ⇑ mollusc

squiffy /skwɪfi¹/. If someone is **squiffy**, they are slightly drunk; an old-fashioned informal word. EG *She had come from cocktails at the Hogans' and was a bit squiffy already.* ADJ QUALIT : PRED = tiddly

squiggle /skwɪgəºl/, **squiggles.** A **squiggle** is a line, especially one that someone has written or drawn, that twists and curls in an irregular way. EG *Her signature looked like a series of inky squiggles.* N COUNT = scribble

squint /skwɪnt/, **squints, squinting, squinted.**

1 If you **squint** at something, you look at it with your eyes partly closed, in order to try to see it better. EG *He squinted at the brightly coloured figures... He held up the rifle and squinted as he took aim.* V : USU+A (at)

2 A **squint** is an eye disorder in which someone's eyes look in different directions from one another. EG *She told me how she'd got her squint.* N COUNT : USU SING

3 If you **have a squint** or **take a squint** at something, you look at it; an informal expression. EG *One of the men said, 'Take a squint at this, Taylor.'* PHR : VB INFLECTS = have a peek

squire /skwaɪə/, **squires. 1** The **squire** was the man who owned most of the land around an English village in former times. EG *Like many Devon villages, we had no real squire... Things hadn't been the same since the old Squire died.* N COUNT : ALSO IN TITLES ⇑ landowner

2 Some English men address other men in a friendly way as **squire**. EG *Now squire, what can I get you?* N VOC

squirm /skwɜːm/, **squirms, squirming, squirmed.** If you **squirm**, 1 you move your body from side to side, often because you are nervous or uncomfortable. EG *Poppy squirmed and wriggled her shoulders... The child can't squirm out of this position very easily.* V : USU+A ⇑ twist = wriggle

2 you are very embarrassed or ashamed. EG *I still squirm when I think of how stupidly I behaved... He squirmed with embarrassment.* V : IF+PREP THEN with = wince

squirrel /skwɪrəºl/, **squirrels.** A **squirrel** is a small furry animal with a long bushy tail. It eats nuts and usually lives in trees. There are many kinds of squirrel. EG *She was staring out of the window at a red squirrel in the elm tree.* N COUNT ⇑ rodent

squirt /skwɜːt/, **squirts, squirting, squirted. 1** If a liquid **squirts** or if you **squirt** it, it comes out of a narrow opening in a thin fast stream. EG *Squirt a little oil into the keyhole... Water squirted out of a hole in the pipe.* ▸ used as a noun. EG *Give it a quick squirt.* V-ERG : USU+A = spurt ▸ N COUNT

2 If you **squirt** an area or an object, you make it wet by squirting a liquid at it. EG *It won't smell much if you squirt the area with soda water... The children squirted each other with water from the hose.* V+O : USU+A (with)

3 If you call someone a **squirt**, you dislike them strongly and want to say how unimportant you think that they are; an offensive use. EG *Clear off then, you squirt!... They're all cheeky young squirts.* N COUNT : ALSO VOC

Sr is a written abbreviation for 'Senior', and is written after a man's name. It is used, especially in America, in order to distinguish the man from his son when they both have the same name. EG *...Charles Parker, Sr.* N IN TITLES

Sri Lankan /srɪ læŋkən/, **Sri Lankans. 1** Something that is **Sri Lankan** belongs or relates to Sri Lanka or to its people. EG *...Sri Lankan tea estates.* ADJ CLASSIF

2 A **Sri Lankan** is a person who comes from Sri Lanka. EG *The Sri Lankans forbade the practice.* N COUNT

SRN, SRNs. SRN is an abbreviation for 'State Registered Nurse'. An SRN is someone who is fully qualified as a nurse in the United Kingdom. EG *...Jane Wilson SRN.* ▸ used of the qualification that you must obtain in order to be an SRN. EG *He got his SRN last year.* N COUNT : ALSO IN TITLES ▸ N COUNT : USU SING

SS. See **St.**

ST, STs. ST is an abbreviation for 'sanitary towel'.

St. SS is the plural in paragraph 2. **1 St** is a written abbreviation for 'Street' when it is part of the name of a street in an address. EG *...22 Harley St, London W1.* N IN NAMES

2 **St** is also a written abbreviation for 'Saint' when it is part of the name of a saint. EG *...St Anselm... ...SS Peter and Paul.* N COUNT : IN TITLES

st is a written abbreviation for 'stone'. EG *She weighs 8st 6lb.* N COUNT : NUM+N

-st (pronounced as 'first') is added to numbers that end in 1 and that are written in figures, in order to form ordinal numbers or fractions. EG *...1st... ...21st... ...101st.* SUFFIX : FORMS ORDINALS

stab /stæb/, **stabs, stabbing, stabbed. 1** If someone **stabs** you, they push a knife into your body. EG *One risk is that you'll get stabbed... A man was stabbed to death as he left a London library... The young man stabbed himself and died in his mother's arms.* V+O ⇑ injure

2 If you say that someone **has stabbed** you **in the back**, you mean that they have done something very harmful to you when you thought that you could trust them; an informal expression. EG *The first opportunity she gets she stabs me in the back... This kind of stabbing in the back gives journalism a bad name.* PHR : VB INFLECTS ⇑ betray

3 If you **stab** something or **stab** at it, you push at it with your fingers or with something that you are holding in your hand. EG *She was typing in a fury, her fingers stabbing at the keys... He stabbed down at the ground with his finger... Sheila stabbed the air with her fork.* V+O, OR V+A = jab

4 If you have a **stab** at something, you try to do it, especially when you have not done it before; an informal use. EG *I'd like to have a stab at tap dancing... I took this to be a stab at humour.* N COUNT : IF+ PREP THEN at ⇑ attempt = crack

5 A **stab** of pain, alarm, etc is a sudden feeling of pain, alarm, etc. EG *I saw it with a stab of surprise and alarm.* N PART+N UNCOUNT = twinge

stabbing /stæbɪŋ/, **stabbings. 1** A **stabbing** is an incident in which someone stabs someone else. EG *There have been one or two stabbings in this street.* N COUNT ⇑ attack

2 A **stabbing** pain is a sudden sharp pain. EG *I get these stabbing pains in my back.* ADJ CLASSIF : ATTRIB

stability /stəbɪlɪti¹/ is the state of being stable. EG *Internal arguments had threatened the stability of the government.... ...a period of economic growth and stability.* N UNCOUNT ⇑ strength

stabilize /steɪbɪlaɪz/, **stabilizes, stabilizing, stabilized**; also spelled **stabilise.** If something **stabilizes** or **is stabilized**, it becomes stable. EG *After 24 hours the patient's condition began to stabilize... This will help to stabilize prices... The family is seen as one of the great stabilizing elements in society.* V-ERG = normalize, steady

◇ **stabilization** /steɪbɪlaɪzeɪʃəⁿn/. EG *There has recently been some stabilization in world population.* ◇ N UNCOUNT = levelling out

stabilizer /steɪbɪlaɪzə/, **stabilizers**; also spelled **stabiliser**. A **stabilizer** is a device that helps a ship, plane, or racing car to remain stable. EG *He managed to complete his first lap without stabilisers.* N COUNT

stable /steɪbəⁿl/; **stables, stabling, stabled**. **1** If something is **stable**, **1.1** it is not likely to experience any sudden changes. EG *Oil prices are stable for the first time in years... ...a stable marriage... ...the most politically stable country in the region.* ADJ QUALIT ⇑ unchanging **1.2** it is firmly fixed in position and is not likely to move or fall. EG *That ladder's not very stable... ...a stable structure.* ADJ QUALIT ⇑ steady = secure

2 If someone has a **stable** personality or character, they are calm and reasonable and do not have frequent changes of mood. ADJ QUALIT = steady ≠ moody

3 Chemical substances are described as **stable** when they tend to remain in the same chemical or atomic state; a technical term. EG *...one of the most stable of all organic substances.* ADJ QUALIT ≠ volatile

4 A **stable** or **stables** is a building in which horses are kept. EG *He went to the stables to fetch his horse.* N COUNT : USU SING = PL

● If you say that someone has **shut** or **closed the stable door after the horse has bolted**, you mean that they have taken a precaution when it is too late, because the harm has already been done. ● PHR : VB INFLECTS

5 If you **stable** a horse, you put it into a stable. EG *I was attending to the stabling of the horses.* V+O : USU+A

6 A **stable** or **stables** is also an organization that breeds and trains racehorses. EG *The winner was a horse from the Queen's stables.* N COUNT : USU SING = PL ⇑ establishment

stable-boy, stable-boys; also spelled as one word. A **stable-boy** or **stable-lad** is a young man who works in a stable looking after the horses. EG *She was always kind to the stableboy or the chauffeur... He got a job as a stable-lad in a Long Island mansion.* N COUNT

stab wound, stab wounds. A **stab wound** is a wound that is caused by stabbing with a knife. N COUNT

staccato /stəkɑːtəʊ/. **1** If you play or sing a piece of music **staccato**, you play or sing the individual notes very briefly with gaps between them. EG *She played three quick chords, very firm and staccato.* ▸ used as an adjective. EG *...a rapid staccato passage.* ADV WITH VB ▸ ADJ CLASSIF : ATTRIB

2 A **staccato** noise consists of a series of short separate sounds. EG *Our breath began to take the form of staccato gasps... ...the staccato sound of the guns.* ADJ CLASSIF : ATTRIB = broken, abrupt

stack /stæk/, **stacks, stacking, stacked**. **1** A **stack** is a number of things arranged in a neat pile. EG *On the sideboard was a stack of plates... ...the long table with its neat stacks of journals.* N PART

2 If you **stack** a number of things or **stack** them **up**, you arrange them in neat piles. EG *I started stacking the chairs... We stacked up the plates and carried them to the sink.* V+O, OR PHRASAL VB : V+O+ADV = pile up

3 If an area or space **is stacked** with objects, it is filled with them, arranged in piles. EG *The room was stacked with old boxes... The shelves were stacked with empty bottles.* V+O : USU PASS+with = be piled

4 A **stack** of something is a very large amount of it; an informal use. EG *I got a stack of different job offers... They've got stacks of money.* N PART = mass

5 A **stack** is also **5.1** a chimney stack. EG *We could see several smoking stacks in the distance.* N COUNT **5.2** a haystack. EG *The grain had gone mouldy in the stack.* N COUNT

6 If you say that **the odds** or **the cards are stacked against** someone, you mean that conditions or circumstances are unfavourable for them in what they want to do, and that it is unlikely that they will succeed. EG *Any new political party in Britain starts with the odds heavily stacked against it... The cards are stacked against girl school leavers.* PHR : VB INFLECTS

stadium /steɪdɪəm/, **stadiums, stadia**. The plural can be either **stadiums** or **stadia**. A **stadium** is a large sports ground with rows of seats all round it. EG *Professional soccer is now being played in modern stadiums... ...the lecture rooms, stadia and laboratories of the university... ...Wembley Stadium.* N COUNT : ALSO IN NAMES ⇑ arena

staff /stɑːf/, **staffs, staffing, staffed**. **1** The **staff** of an organization are the people who work for it. EG *She was invited to join the staff of the BBC... We've got a staff of about forty... ...a major error of judgement by one of his staff... There are two students to every member of staff... ...airline staffs.* ● See also **Chief of Staff**. N COUNT : USU SING + SUPP, IF SING USU WITH VB IN PL, OR N UNCOUNT ⇑ employees

2 If an organization **is staffed** by particular people, they are the people who work for it. EG *It was staffed and run by engineers... ...one of the army officers who staff the emergency government.* ● See also **short-staffed**. V+O : USU PASS

3 A **staff** is also a strong stick or pole; an old-fashioned use. EG *...a very old man, walking with the help of a wooden staff.* N COUNT

staffing /stɑːfɪŋ/ is the appointing of the workers who are needed to do the jobs within an organization. EG *Progress is slow because of restrictions on staffing... ...staffing problems.* N UNCOUNT

staff nurse, staff nurses. A **staff nurse** is a hospital nurse whose rank is just below that of a sister or charge nurse. N COUNT : ALSO IN TITLES

stag /stæg/, **stags**. A **stag** is an adult male deer belonging to one of the larger species of deer. Stags usually have large branch-like horns called antlers. EG *...a fine stag going through the heather... ...the velvet on a young stag's antlers.* N COUNT

stage /steɪdʒ/, **stages, staging, staged**. **1** A **stage** is **1.1** a particular point in a continuous process. EG *There are many intermediate stages in this degenerative process... Short cuts at this stage can be costly... Women who wish to re-enter the job market at a later stage can do so.* N COUNT ⇑ period **1.2** one part in a process of development that consists of several parts. EG *The next major stage in computer technology is the so-called fifth generation... I believe in national independence as the first stage of responsible self-government.* N COUNT + SUPP = phase ● If you carry out a process **stage by stage**, you do it progressing gradually and logically from one part of the process to the next. EG *The means of bringing about disarmament stage by stage ought to be possible... It's very tedious to work out if one goes through it stage by stage.* ● PHR : USED AS AN A = step by step

2 A **stage** of a journey is one part of it, when you are making it in several parts. EG *...the first stage of an 800 mile expedition.* N COUNT + SUPP = leg

3 A **stage** is also a raised platform in a theatre where actors or other entertainers perform. EG *I walked out on the stage and started to sing... She stood alone on the enormous stage... ...a stage set.* N COUNT ● When an actor is **on stage** or **on the stage**, he or she is performing on a stage before an audience. EG *She has been accused of being too flamboyant on stage... I had seen Ralph quite often on the stage before I got to know him.* ● PHR : USED AS AN A

4 The **stage** is **4.1** the profession and career of an actor or actress who works in the theatre. EG *I got to like the whole idea of the stage... My Aunt Mabel went on the stage... She retired from the stage some years ago.* N SING : *the*+N **4.2** all the activities connected with producing plays and other entertainments in the theatre. EG *He's adapted one of his novels for the stage... I had seen most of what was interesting on the stage in Paris.* N SING : *the*+N ▸ used as an adjective. EG *I have, of course, used music in many of my stage productions... ...another of Houdini's stage tricks.* ▸ N BEFORE N = theatrical

5 If you **stage** a play, ballet, etc, you organize and present a performance of it. EG *My aunt decided to stage a series of performances of a one-act play... I thought of staging the play as if it were a rehearsal.* V+O = put on

6 If you **stage** an event or ceremony, you plan and organize it. EG *He staged the solemn ceremony in the East Room of the White House... The union kept plans alive to stage new strikes.* V+O = hold

7 If you **set the stage** for something, you make preparations so that it can happen. EG *We have set the stage for a completely new society... The stage was set for a massive publicity drive.* PHR : VB INFLECTS ⇑ prepare

8 A **stage** is also a particular area of activity. EG *This may not appear as a major factor on the stage of world events... ...a quick survey of the European political stage... The Republic appears on the international trading stage mainly as a supplier of raw materials.* N SING : *the*+N SUPP

stagecoach /steɪdʒkəʊtʃ/, **stagecoaches**. A **stagecoach** is a large carriage pulled by horses. In former times, stagecoaches used to carry passengers and mail. EG *The journey took two days by stagecoach.* N COUNT, OR *by*+N ⇑ conveyance

stage door, stage doors. The **stage door** of a theatre is the entrance used by actors and actresses and by employees of the theatre. EG *Crowds mobbed me at the stage door.* N COUNT : USU *the*+SING

stage fright; also spelled with a hyphen. **Stage fright** is a feeling of fear or nervousness that some N UNCOUNT ⇑ nerves people have just before they appear in front of an audience. EG *What he experienced was intense stage fright.*

stagehand /steɪdʒhænd/, **stagehands**; also spelled as two words. A **stagehand** is a person whose job is to move the scenery and equipment on the stage in a theatre. EG *One of the stagehands was kind enough to compliment me after the performance.* N COUNT ⇑ worker

stage-manage, stage-manages, stage-managing, stage-managed. If someone **stage-manages** an event, they organize it, especially secretly. EG *Who was to say that the attacks were not stage-managed?* V+O ⇑ arrange = orchestrate

stage-manager, stage-managers; also spelled as two words. A **stage manager** is the person who is responsible for the scenery and for the way that actors or other performers move about and use the stage during a performance in the theatre. EG *'Miss Jordache,' the stage manager said. 'We're ready when you are.'... She asked me to go on tour with her, as assistant stage manager.* N COUNT ⇑ supervisor

stage-struck. Someone who is **stage-struck** is fascinated by the theatre and wants to become an actor or actress. EG *He's been stage-struck ever since we took him to 'Peter Pan'.* ADJ QUALIT ⇑ obsessed

stage whisper, stage whispers; also spelled with a hyphen. A **stage whisper** is a loud whisper that is meant to be heard by several people. EG *'That was terrific,' she told him in a stage-whisper.* N COUNT

stagger /stægə/, **staggers, staggering, staggered.** 1 If you **stagger**, you walk or stand very unsteadily, as if you are about to fall. EG *I staggered to the nearest chair... We managed to stagger back up to the deck.* V: USU+A = lurch

2 If something **staggers** you, it makes you feel surprised and shocked, usually because it is so unexpected that you can hardly believe it; an informal use. EG *...an event that staggered the world.* V+O ⇑ amaze = astound

◊ **staggered.** EG *We were staggered to learn they would be closing down the college.* ◊ ADJ QUALIT ◊ **staggering.** EG *Its estimated cost has climbed to a staggering £35 billion... The effects are staggering.* ◊ ADJ QUALIT = stunning ◊ **staggeringly.** EG *...staggeringly high prices.* ◊ ADV+ADJ/ADV

3 If things such as people's holidays or hours of work **are staggered**, they are arranged so that they do not all happen at the same time. EG *The summer holidays are staggered so that we can keep the factory running... They staggered their church-going hours.* V+O: USU PASS

stagnant /stægnənt/. 1 If something such as a situation is **stagnant**, it is unsuccessful or dull because it is not changing or developing in any way. EG *...a stagnant society... British shipbuilding output remained stagnant at around one million tons a year.* ADJ CLASSIF = sluggish, stale

2 **Stagnant** water is not flowing or moving, and therefore often smells unpleasant. EG *The White Volta dries up into a string of stagnant pools in the summer.* ADJ CLASSIF ⇑ still = brackish, stale

stagnate /stægneɪt, stægneɪt/, **stagnates, stagnating, stagnated.** If a situation **stagnates**, it is unsuccessful or dull because it is not changing or developing in any way. EG *The economy stagnated as a result of these tax measures... The party's membership has stagnated and its electoral performance has declined.* V ◊ **stagnation** /stægneɪʃəⁿn/. EG *Industrial stagnation inevitably leads to the loss of jobs.* ◊ N UNCOUNT

stag party, stag parties. A **stag party** is a party for a man who is getting married the next day, to which only men are invited. N COUNT

stagy /steɪdʒi¹/, **stagier, stagiest.** A **stagy** action or gesture is done in a deliberately exaggerated way, as if you were performing on a stage. EG *With a rather stagy flourish he left the room.* ADJ QUALIT ⇑ theatrical = showy

staid /steɪd/. Someone or something that is **staid** is serious, dull, and rather old-fashioned in appearance or behaviour. EG *...two middle-aged gentlemen of staid and learned appearance... ...the staid office.* ADJ QUALIT = sober, stolid

stain /steɪn/, **stains, staining, stained.** 1 If a substance **stains** something, it leaves a mark which is difficult or impossible to remove. EG *There were bodies in the street and blood stained the pavements.* V+O = discolour ◊ **stained.** EG *...a little man with stained teeth.* ◊ ADJ CLASSIF

2 A **stain** is a mark which is difficult or impossible to remove, often made by something being spilt. EG *There was a dark oval stain on the chair where his head had rested... If cold water doesn't remove a stain, try using lukewarm water and soap.* N COUNT

3 If something **stains**, it becomes marked with something which is difficult or impossible to remove. EG *These carpets don't stain, they're impregnated with a special chemical.* V

4 **Stain** is a dye used to colour the surface of wooden things such as furniture or floors. EG *I sanded the shelves and put teak stain on them.* N MASS

5 If you **stain** something made of wood such as a piece of furniture or a floor, you change its colour by using a special dye. EG *She stained the table black to match her new chairs.* V+O

6 A **stain** on someone's character or reputation is a trace of disgrace that they have; a literary use. EG *She left the court without a stain on her character.* N COUNT = blemish, flaw, taint

7 If you **stain** someone's character or reputation, you bring disgrace on them; a literary use. EG *His reputation had been stained for life.* V+O = tarnish

-stained combines with nouns to describe something that is marked with a particular substance. EG *...a blood-stained cloth... Tom was ashamed seeing his grease-stained hands.* COMB: FORMS ADJ CLASSIFS

stained glass; spelled with a hyphen when used before another noun. **Stained glass** is glass which is coloured in various ways when it is made and is then used for artistic purposes, especially for creating pictures in church windows. EG *St Nicholas's has a fine set of Victorian stained-glass windows.* N UNCOUNT

stainless steel; sometimes spelled with a hyphen when used before another noun. **Stainless steel** is a metal made from steel and chromium, which does not rust or corrode and is used to make household items such as cutlery. EG *...a kitchen fitted with a stainless steel sink.* N UNCOUNT

stair /steə/, **stairs.** 1 **Stairs** are a set of steps, usually inside a building, which go from one level to another. EG *I was running up and down the stairs most of the time... I did not relish the prospect of climbing another flight of stairs... Bill stood at the foot of the stairs... ...the stair carpet.* N PLURAL

2 A **stair** is 2.1 one of the steps in a set of stairs. EG *A stair creaked as she made her way downstairs.* N COUNT 2.2 one of the floors of a block of flats or other building with rooms in which people live. EG *I phoned an old lady on the next stair.* N COUNT 2.3 a staircase; a literary or old-fashioned use. EG *He went carefully up the winding stair.* N COUNT

staircase /steəkeɪs/, **staircases.** A **staircase** is a set of stairs inside a building, usually with a rail that you can hold on to. EG *Tom came down the staircase... There was a large hall with a big staircase winding up from it.* N COUNT

stairway /steəweɪ/, **stairways.** A **stairway** is a staircase or a flight of steps. EG *He stood halfway up the wooden stairway.* N COUNT

stairwell /steəwel/, **stairwells.** A **stairwell** is the part of a building that contains a staircase. EG *He leaned over the balcony above the stairwell.* N COUNT

stake /steɪk/, **stakes, staking, staked.** 1 If you **stake** something that you value such as your money or your reputation on the result of a race, contest, argument, etc, you risk your money or reputation on the result. EG *Sums large and small were staked upon the fortunes of a rolling wheel... I've heard that she's good at swimming but I wouldn't like to stake my life on that.* V+O: IF+PREP THEN *on/upon* = bet

2 **Stakes** are something, especially money, which you risk on the result of a race, contest, argument, etc. EG *I'm playing for high stakes... They were embarking on a tense struggle for enormous stakes.* N PLURAL

3 If something that you value such as your money or your reputation is **at stake**, it is being risked and is in danger of being lost or damaged, depending on the result of something that is happening. EG *There's a great deal of money at stake... He admits that his political life is at stake... Basic issues of health and safety are at stake.* PHR: USED AS AN A = at risk

4 A **stake** is the amount of money which a gambler bets on a horse in a race, on a throw of a dice, etc. EG *This bar was the scene of poker games with stakes of many hundreds of dollars.* N COUNT = bet

5 **Stakes** is used 5.1 in the name of a horse race in which the prize money comes from the owners of all the horses in the race. EG *The Newmarket Stakes is run in June.* N IN NAMES 5.2 to refer to something that you are considering in terms of a race or a competition which it is possible to win or lose. EG *This gives you a competitive advantage in the promotion stakes...* N PLURAL: the+N

This minority group has at last achieved parity in the media stakes.

6 A **stake** is also a pointed piece of wood or metal which is pushed into the ground and used for example to support a young tree or as part of a fence. EG *His boat was fastened by a chain to a stake in the ground.* ● When people **were burned at the stake** in former times, they were tied to a wooden post over a bonfire and burned to death. EG *A number of English Catholics were burned at the stake.*
N COUNT ↑ post; ● PHR : VB INFLECTS ↑ kill

7 If you **stake** something, you fasten it to a wooden post in the ground. EG *After the storm he had to stake all his roses.*
V+O

8 If you have a **stake** in something such as a business, property, or idea, you have a share or an interest in it, usually of a financial kind. EG *The Government owned a large stake in the oil industry.*
N COUNT : USU SING+*in* = investment

9 If someone **stakes** a business or company, they support it by supplying it with money or other financial help. EG *The Government said they would stake the airbus industry for 200 million pounds.*
V+O

10 If you **stake a claim** to something, you say that you have a right to it and so it belongs to you or should belong to you. EG *Each group had staked its claim to its own territory... Once the older boys had staked a claim to the grass, no others dared go on it.*
PHR : VB INFLECTS, USU+*to*

stake out. If you **stake out** a position that you are stating or a claim that you are making, you are defining the boundaries or limits of the position or the claim. EG *The committee's report stakes out the new frontiers of acceptable advance.*
PHRASAL VB : V+O+ADV

stalactite /stæləktaɪt/, **stalactites.** A **stalactite** is a piece of rock which looks like a large icicle and which hangs down from the roof of a cave. It is formed by the dripping of water containing lime. EG *These caves are famous because of the beauty of their stalactite formations.*
N COUNT ≠ stalagmite

stalagmite /stæləgmaɪt/, **stalagmites.** A **stalagmite** is a long piece of rock which sticks up from the floor of a cave and is formed by water containing lime dripping from the roof.
N COUNT ≠ stalactite

stale /steɪl/, **staler, stalest. 1** Food, tobacco, etc that is **stale** is old and no longer fresh. EG *...stale bread... The box smelled of stale tobacco... ...the sour odour of stale urine.* ◇ **staleness.** EG *...the staleness of the chocolates.*
ADJ QUALIT ↑ old; ◇ N UNCOUNT ↑ age

2 Air, smoke, etc that is **stale** has an unpleasant smell, for example because no windows have been opened or because people have been smoking in a place for a long time. EG *Inside the flat was a musty smell of stale air... ...stale cigarette smoke.*
ADJ QUALIT ≠ fresh

3 If you feel **stale**, you are no longer as full of enthusiasm or as full of interesting ideas as you used to be, because you have been doing the same job for too long. EG *You need a break, a change. You're getting stale here.*
ADJ QUALIT = jaded

4 If something such as a place or an activity is **stale**, it is no longer interesting or exciting because you have already seen it or done it too many times. EG *The phony glamour of night clubs soon became stale and boring.*
ADJ QUALIT ↑ boring = tedious

stalemate /steɪlmeɪt/, **stalemates.** A **stalemate** is **1** a situation in which neither side in an argument or contest can win or gain any advantage. EG *He hoped that the nuclear stalemate would lead to disarmament... A stalemate had been reached.* **2** a position in chess in which one player can only move the king into check and out of check, so that neither player can win the game.
N UNCOUNT/COUNT : USU SING = deadlock; N UNCOUNT/COUNT : USU SING

stalk /stɔːk/, **stalks, stalking, stalked. 1** A **stalk** is **1.1** the main stem of a plant, usually one that is fairly thick and strong. EG *After the harvest, the stalks were brown and bare... He pushed away the stalk from which he had stripped the fruit.* **1.2** the part of a plant that joins the flowers, fruit, or leaves to the main stem. EG *In the angles formed between the leaf stalk and the stem, buds develop.*
N COUNT; N COUNT

2 If you **stalk** a person or a wild animal, you move gradually and quietly as close as possible to them, so that you can kill them, capture them, or observe them carefully. EG *At dawn I was already stalking, gun loaded and ready... He moved like a tiger stalking its prey... ...a rapist stalking every female in Amity.*
V+O, OR V : USU +A ↑ hunt

3 If a ghost or a bad person or thing **stalks** a place, it moves menacingly through the place, causing death or disaster; a rather literary word. EG *Drought and famine stalked the land... The murderer stalked the streets for hours.*
V OR V+O

4 If you **stalk** somewhere, you walk there in a stiff, proud, or angry way. EG *Florrie stalked out, her head high.*
V+A

stall /stɔːl/, **stalls, stalling, stalled. 1** A **stall** is a large table on which you put goods that you want to sell, for example in a market, or information that you want to give to people. EG *Tim was looking at the purchase he had made the previous evening from a market stall... They run such projects as manning counselling stalls at pop festivals.*
N COUNT = booth, stand

2 The **stalls** in a theatre or concert hall are the seats on the ground floor directly in front of the stage. EG *I suddenly noticed her in the front row of the stalls... I could only get four seats together in the stalls.*
N PLURAL : *the*+N

3 The **stalls** in a church are the rows of seats where members of the clergy or the choir sit. There are usually several rows of stalls facing each other across the aisle.
N COUNT : USU PL = choir stall

4 When a vehicle **stalls** or when you **stall** it, the engine stops suddenly. EG *The jeep stalled... I stalled at the traffic lights and then had to wait for ages.*
V-ERG

5 If you **stall**, you wait for a period of time before you act, because you are not sure what to do, or because you think that you will gain some advantage if you wait. EG *The new union had stalled before accomplishing its full purpose... There was exasperation over the government's stalling tactics on a settlement.*
V = delay, hesitate

6 If you **stall** a person or an event, you prevent the person from doing something or prevent the event from happening for a short period of time, for example so that you have more time to think or to do something else. EG *Perhaps I can stall him till Thursday or Friday... Difficulties in arranging financing had temporarily stalled the award.*
V+O ↑ delay = postpone, put off

7 A **stall** is also **7.1** a small area of a shed where one cow or horse is kept. There are usually several stalls in a shed, separated from each other by a wall or fence. **7.2** a small area of a room which is partially separated from the rest of the room by a wall or curtain; used especially to refer to an area of a room where there is a toilet or shower. EG *Eddie pulled me into the shower stall... We went to look at the black-and-white marble stalls in a Roman urinal.*
N COUNT ↑ compartment; N COUNT ↑ compartment = booth, cubicle

stallholder /stɔːlhəʊldə/, **stallholders.** A **stallholder** is a person who sells goods at a stall in a market.
N COUNT ↑ trader

stallion /stæljən/, **stallions.** A **stallion** is a fully grown male horse, usually kept for breeding.
N COUNT = stud

stalwart /stɔːlwət/, **stalwarts. 1** A **stalwart** person is **1.1** loyal, steady, and completely reliable over a period of time. ▸ used of work that a person does. EG *She has done stalwart voluntary work.* **1.2** strong and firm in appearance. EG *...three tall, stalwart sons.*
ADJ QUALIT; ▸ = sterling; ADJ QUALIT = sturdy

2 A **stalwart** is a loyal and hard-working supporter, especially of a political party. EG *They were all Government stalwarts.*
N COUNT

stamen /steɪmɛ²n/, **stamens.** The **stamens** of a flower are the small, delicate stalks which grow inside the blossom and produce pollen.
N COUNT

stamina /stæmɪnə/ is the energy and the physical, mental, or emotional strength that you need in order to continue with an activity for a long period of time. EG *I did not have the physical stamina needed for digging... Circuit training has done wonders for your speed and stamina.*
N UNCOUNT = endurance, resilience

stammer /stæmə/, **stammers, stammering, stammered. 1** If you **stammer**, you speak with difficulty, hesitating and repeating words or sounds, because you are afraid, nervous, etc, or because you have a speech defect. EG *'But...but...that's impossible,' the youth stammered... I used to stammer quite badly when I was young.*
V OR V+O/QUOTE = stutter

2 Someone who has a **stammer** has a difficulty in speaking in which they hesitate and repeat words or sounds. EG *His stammer was troublesome for him.*
N COUNT : USU SING = stutter

stammer out. If you **stammer** something **out**, you say it with difficulty, hesitating and repeating words or sounds, because you are afraid, nervous, etc. EG *Before he could stammer out his thanks, she walked away.*
PHRASAL VB : V+O+ADV, OR ORDER V+ADV+QUOTE

stamp /stæmp/, **stamps, stamping, stamped. 1** A **stamp** is **1.1** a small piece of gummed paper, usually with a picture or pattern on it, which you buy in a post office and have to stick onto an envelope or
N COUNT ↑ token = postage stamp

parcel before you post it. EG *She licked the stamp and stuck it on the letter... They rushed to the counter and bought stamps and postcards to send home... His interests were drawing and stamp collecting.* **1.2** a small gummed piece of paper which represents a particular amount of money, and which you buy as a way of saving money for the future, or as a way of paying for something expensive over a period of time. EG *I don't buy savings stamps... ...television licence stamps... When you're self-employed you have to allow for tax and national insurance stamps when budgeting.* **1.3** a small gummed piece of paper that some shops give to their customers when they buy goods. Customers can exchange a number of these stamps for goods.

N COUNT: USU MOD+N ⇑ token / N COUNT ⇑ token

2 If you **stamp** an envelope or a postcard, you stick a postage stamp on it before you post it to someone. EG *Do you have to stamp all the letters?... Two letters in stamped envelopes were already laid out on the desk.* — V+O

3 A **stamp** is also a small block of wood or metal which has a pattern or a group of letters on one side. You press it onto a pad of ink, and then onto a piece of paper in order to produce a mark on the paper. EG *From the printing set he made up a stamp reading: 'St Mark's Parish Church.'* ▸ used of the mark left on a piece of paper by this block. EG *They had German passports with Brazilian entrance stamps.* — N COUNT

4 If you **stamp** a mark, word, etc on an object, you put the mark or word on it using a special tool or machine, usually in order to identify it, to make it valid, or to tell people how to use it. EG *Articles that conform with the relevant British Standards are stamped with a kite-shaped mark... Unless they are stamped 'ovenproof' assume they are not... They stamp the card and send it back to you.* — V+O+O/C

5 If you **stamp** your foot, you lift your foot and put it down very hard and very quickly on the ground so that you make a loud noise, for example because you are angry. EG *'Damn you, Edward!' she shouted, stamping her foot... The crew were stamping their feet to keep warm.* ▸ used as a noun. EG *There is a brick courtyard, where the stamp of the guards echoes.* — V OR V+O ⇑ move; ▸ N COUNT: USU SING ⇑ walk

6 If you **stamp** somewhere, you walk there quickly and noisily because you are angry about something. EG *We reluctantly stamped into the principal's office... I set my face into stiff grimaces as I stamped along.* — V+A = stomp

7 If you **stamp** on an object, animal, etc, you put your foot down on it very hard, usually in order to damage it or hurt it. EG *...boys who stamped on fledglings when they fell out of the nest... I stamped heavily on her foot and muttered, 'Shut up.'* — V+A *(on)* ⇑ tread = trample

8 **Stamp** is used when mentioning a quality that someone or something clearly has, or a quality in someone's work or achievement that shows that it is theirs. EG *His work hardly bore the stamp of maturity... He is a designer who has left his stamp on 20th century industry.* — N SING WITH DET +SUPP = hallmark, mark

9 A quality, feature, or action that **stamps** someone or something as a particular type shows clearly that they are of this type. EG *His achievement stamps him as one of the masterminds of our era... The shield stamps it as Norman in style.* — V+O+A *(as)* ⇑ identify = brand, mark

10 If you **stamp** yourself on something, you have a strong effect on it, for example by giving it your qualities or by influencing it. EG *Britain was to stamp itself upon India in a way that was to shape history for many years... He had already stamped his presence on the face of science... These concepts have strongly stamped the societies they have been applied to.* — V+O: USU+A *(on/upon)* ⇑ impress = mark

stamp down. If you **stamp** something **down**, you lift your feet one after the other and put them down very hard on it in order to make it flatter or firmer. EG *He put dirt around the base of the cross, and stamped it down hard with his feet... He put the cardboard boxes in a heap and stamped them down.* — PHRASAL VB: V+O+ADV ⇑ press down = trample

stamp out. If you **stamp** something **out**, you put an end to it or destroy it completely. EG *They are determined to stamp out political extremism... The rail strike was stamped out with particular brutality... To stamp out woodworm thoroughly they will have to heave up floorboards.* — PHRASAL VB: V+O+ADV = eliminate, eradicate

stamped addressed envelope, stamped addressed envelopes. A **stamped addressed envelope** is an envelope on which you stick a stamp and write your own name and address. You send it to an organization or person so that they can send you something such as information in it, and do not have to pay the cost of posting the information to you. EG *Write to them enclosing a stamped addressed envelope.* — N COUNT

stampede /stæmpiːd/, **stampedes, stampeding, stampeded.** **1** When animals in a herd **stampede** or **are stampeded**, they rush away suddenly and wildly in a large group, usually because they are frightened. EG *The horses were frightened by the gunfire and stampeded... Indians set fires to stampede game.* — V-ERG: USU PASS

2 A **stampede** is **2.1** a sudden, wild rush of animals stampeding. **2.2** a sudden rush by a lot of people who all want to do the same thing or go to the same place. EG *The gold stampede turned it from a shanty town into a bustling city... ...a stampede for tickets.* — N COUNT / N COUNT: USU SING+SUPP ⇑ demand

3 If someone **stampedes** you into doing something, they put a lot of pressure on you in order to make you do it, when you have not yet decided or do not want to do it so quickly; used showing disapproval. EG *They were stampeded into errors in strategy.* — V+O: IF+PREP THEN *into* ⇑ influence = pressurize

stamping ground, stamping grounds. Someone's **stamping ground** is a favourite place where they like to go often. — N COUNT: WITH POSS = haunt

stance /stæns, stɑːns/, **stances.** Your **stance** is **1** the way you are standing at a particular time. EG *He altered his stance slightly and leaned against a tree... She was standing in a fighting stance.* **2** your attitude about a particular matter. EG *They criticized Martin Luther King for his rigid stance on non-violence... The newspaper defended its unpopular editorial stance.* — N COUNT: USU POSS/MOD+N = posture / N COUNT: USU POSS/MOD+N, IF +PREP THEN *on* = position, standpoint

stanchion /stænʃən/, **stanchions.** A **stanchion** is a pole or bar that stands upright and is used as a support. — N COUNT

stand /stænd/, **stands, standing, stood.** **1** If you **are standing**, you are in a position in which your body is upright and your legs are straight, and the weight of your body is supported by your feet. EG *She was standing at the bus-stop... He was so drunk that he could barely stand... I decided to stand at the back of the hall... I stood very still, hoping they wouldn't see me.* — V: USU+A

2 If you **stand** or **stand up**, you raise your body until you are standing when you have been sitting or lying. EG *The judge asked us all to stand... I put down my glass and stood up.* — V, OR PHRASAL VB: V+ADV = get up, rise

3 If you **stand** somewhere, you move to that position and remain standing there. EG *She told the girls to stand aside and let her pass... He stood back and surveyed his handiwork.* — V+A

4 If something such as a building or piece of furniture **stands** somewhere, it is situated there. EG *The town hall stood at the end of Main Street... In the middle of the town stands a splendid Victorian building... An old piano stood in the corner of the room.* — V+A ⇑ be

5 You sometimes say that a building **is standing** when it remains after other buildings have fallen down or been destroyed. EG *Very few buildings were left standing after the earthquake... Most of the houses that still stand are unoccupied.* — V ⇑ remain

6 If you **stand** something somewhere, you put it there, in an upright position. EG *He stood the bottle on the bench beside him... The empty wine bottles stand in a neat row against the wall.* — V-ERG+A

7 A **stand** is **7.1** a small shop or stall with an open front, usually outdoors or in a large public building, which provides various services such as selling food or newspapers or giving information. EG *There was a hamburger stand at the entrance to the station... ...a news stand... ...an information stand.* **7.2** a large structure at a sports ground or race track, where people sit or stand in rows in order to watch what is happening. EG *I managed to get a seat in the Members' Stand.* **7.3** the place in a law court where a witness stands when he or she is answering questions; used in American English. EG *Hearne had not yet taken the stand.* **7.4** a framework, piece of furniture, or other object that is designed for holding or storing a particular kind of thing. EG *A number of hats hung from a stand on the left of the door... ...an umbrella stand.* ● See also **music stand.** — N COUNT: MOD+N / N COUNT / N SING: *the*+N = witness box / N COUNT ⇑ structure

8 If something **is standing** in a particular place or — V+A, OR V+C state, it is not moving or not being used. EG *The train stands at the platform for several minutes... Keep the mixture warm and leave it standing for at least seven hours... Millions are unemployed while machines stand idle... A lot of these houses are standing empty at the moment.*

9 If a decision, offer, etc **stands**, it continues to be effective or be valid. EG *Fifty years later, this Supreme Court ruling still stands... Our original offer stands.*
V : NO CONT ⇑ exist = endure

10 If a value, level, score, etc **stands** at a particular amount, it is that amount. EG *Unemployment in the North Wales town of Flint now stands at 38 per cent... With the score standing at 4-1, Liverpool seemed certain to win.*
V+A *(at)*

11 When you are saying how tall someone is, you sometimes say that they **stand** a particular height. EG *The visitor stood about six feet tall... These are the tallest birds that have ever existed, standing over three metres high.*
V+C : NO CONT = measure

12 If something **stands** in a particular condition or situation, it is in that condition or situation. EG *Their obvious honesty stands in total contrast to the deceitfulness of their opponents... His real intentions now stand revealed... Lack of investment stood in the way of industrial development... As things stand, the rural areas bear most of the cost of local transport services... They are dissatisfied with the law as it stands.*
V+A, OR V+C : NO CONT ⇑ be

13 If you **stand** in a particular way, you take a particular attitude or course of action as a way of dealing with a situation. EG *We can't just stand on the side lines and watch our competitors gaining a bigger share of the market... I suppose I shouldn't stand in the way of progress... It is important that the government should stand firm against these kind of threats.*
V+A, OR V+C

14 If you ask someone **how** or **where** they **stand** on a particular issue or question, you are asking them what their attitude or policy is. EG *There was never any doubt about where he stood on the racial issue... People can help by letting their MP's know how they stand on the nuclear question.*
PHR : VB INFLECTS, IF + PREP THEN *on*

15 If you **take a stand** on an issue, you publicly state the strongly held attitude that you have about it. EG *It's an important issue and you must be prepared to take a stand on it... The family agreed to take a stand for what they believed in.*
PHR : VB INFLECTS

16 A **stand** is also a strong effort to prevent the success of an enemy or of a policy or belief which you oppose. EG *They are making a determined stand against the introduction of the new law... This river bank was the scene of Custer's last stand.*
N SING WITH DET

17 If something can **stand** a difficult situation or a serious test, it is good enough or strong enough to survive or withstand it. EG *In its present state, the economy couldn't stand another rise in interest rates... Her arguments could hardly stand close inspection... Do you think their music will stand the test of time?... I don't think anybody can really stand comparison with her.*
V+O : USU WITH MODAL + BROAD NEG ⇑ undergo = endure

18 If you cannot **stand** something or someone, you **18.1** find it or them very difficult to bear or tolerate. EG *He kept on nagging until I couldn't stand it any longer... I've had as much as I can stand of your constant complaining... I don't think my nerves will stand much more of this.* **18.2** dislike it or them very strongly. EG *She said she couldn't stand him... I can't stand jazz... She can't stand the sight of him.*
V+O : USU WITH MODAL + BROAD NEG
V+O : USU WITH MODAL + BROAD NEG = loathe

19 If you **stand** to gain something, lose something, etc, you are in a position in which you are likely either to gain something or lose something. EG *They are the only people who stand to make a profit out of it... Few people are yet aware of how much we stand to lose by this agreement.*
V+*to*-INF

20 If you **stand** in an election, you are a candidate. EG *She was invited to stand as the Liberal candidate... Do you think he'll win if he decides to stand again?... I'm going to stand for election.*
V : USU+A = run

21 If you **stand** someone a meal or a drink, you buy it for them; used mainly in spoken English. EG *I'll stand you a drink.*
V+O+O = treat to

22 If you **stand a chance** of doing something, there is a possibility that you will be successful. EG *She doesn't stand a chance... I think we stand a good chance of defeating them... ...plans which stand little chance of being carried out.*
PHR : VB INFLECTS IF + PREP THEN *of*

23 If you say that you can do something **standing on** your **head**, you mean that you can do it without any difficulty or effort. EG *He could have done the job standing on his head.*
PHR : USED AS AN A, N INFLECTS

24 If you say **'it stands to reason'**, you mean that it is obvious that something is true or likely to happen; a fairly informal expression. EG *If they keep doing that, it stands to reason that the police are going to get suspicious... It must have been him that did it–it stands to reason.*
PHR, OR PHR + REPORT-CL

25 If someone **stands trial**, they are tried in a court of law. EG *He is going to stand trial on a murder charge.*
PHR : VB INFLECTS

26 • to **stand on ceremony**: see **ceremony**. • to **stand on** your **own two feet**: see **foot**. • to **stand** your **ground**: see **ground**. • to **stand** someone **in good stead**: see **stead**.

27 See also **standing**.

stand back. If you **stand back** from a situation, you put yourself in a position in which you are not too closely involved in it, so that you can understand the situation better. EG *She has a remarkable ability to stand back and look critically at what the company is doing.*
PHRASAL VB : V+ ADV, USU+A/*and*

stand by. **1** If you **stand by**, you **1.1** let something bad happen without doing anything to stop it. EG *We cannot stand by and watch while our allies are attacked.* **1.2** are ready to provide help or take action if it becomes necessary. EG *Government engineers were standing by to provide emergency repairs in the event of a breakdown... Stand by with lots of water in case a fire breaks out.*
PHRASAL VB : V+ ADV = sit by
PHRASAL VB : V+ ADV

2 If you **stand by** someone, you continue to give them help or support, especially when they are in a difficult position. EG *If they try to make you resign, we'll stand by you.*
PHRASAL VB : V+ PREP = stick by

3 If you **stand by** an earlier decision, promise, or agreement, you continue to support or agree with it. EG *I said I would do it and I stand by my promise... He confirmed that his Government would stand by the NATO decision.*
PHRASAL VB : V+ PREP = abide by, adhere to

stand down. If someone **stands down**, they resign from an important position, often in order to let someone else take their place. EG *She was asked if she was prepared to stand down in favour of a younger candidate.*
PHRASAL VB : V+ ADV = step down

stand for. **1** If you say that a letter or initial **stands for** a particular word or name, you mean that it is an abbreviation for that word or name. EG *What does CSE stand for?... T.E.C. stands for Technical Education Certificate.*
PHRASAL VB : V+ PREP, NO CONT

2 If someone or something **stands for** an idea, belief, or quality, they support it and are thought of as being a symbol of it. EG *I disagreed so fundamentally with what the party stood for... They oppose capitalism and all that it stands for.*
PHRASAL VB : V+ PREP, NO CONT = represent

3 If you will not **stand for** something, you will not allow it to happen or continue. EG *He warned that the Army would not stand for it much longer... I won't stand for any more of your disobedience.*
PHRASAL VB : V+ PREP, WITH BROAD NEG, HAS PASS = tolerate

stand in. **1** If you **stand in** for someone, you take their place or do their job for a short time, for example if they are ill or away. EG *Will you stand in for me at today's meeting?*
PHRASAL VB : V+ ADV, USU+*for* = deputize

2 See also **stand-in**.

stand out. **1** If something **stands out**, **1.1** it can be seen very clearly because of its colour, size, or shape. EG *The name on the van stood out clearly.* **1.2** it is much better or much more important than other things of the same kind. EG *This is one of the things that stand out in my memory... One single issue stood out as more important than any other... One article in this collection stands out from all the others.*
PHRASAL VB : V+ ADV, NO CONT
PHRASAL VB : V+ ADV, NO CONT = stick out

2 If you **stand out** for or against something, you continue with a particular attitude or policy and do not give up, even though this is an unpopular or difficult thing for you to do. EG *The union decided to stand out for its original claim... They're standing out against any change in the law.*
PHRASAL VB : V+ ADV+A *(for/against)* = hold out, stick out

stand up. **1** If you **stand up**, you raise your body until you are standing when you have been sitting or lying. EG *I put down my glass and stood up.*
PHRASAL VB : V+ ADV = stand

2 If something **stands up** to a lot of use, pressure, etc, it remains unharmed or in good condition after being severely tested in this way. EG *This carpet stands up to the wear and tear of continual use... The economy would not stand up to wartime pressures...*
PHRASAL VB : V+ ADV, USU+A *(to, under)* ⇑ resist

...*a faith that will stand up to some very testing questions.*

3 If you **stand up** to someone, especially someone more powerful than you are, you defend yourself against their attacks or demands. EG *He's too weak to stand up to her.* PHRASAL VB : V+ ADV+A (to)

4 If you **stand up** for a person or principle that is being attacked or criticized, you take forceful action in order to defend that person or principle. EG *I'm glad to see that he's standing up for himself... Don't be afraid to stand up for your rights.* PHRASAL VB : V+ ADV+A (for) ⇑ support

5 If something such as a claim or piece of evidence **stands up**, it is accepted as true or satisfactory after being carefully examined. EG *The prosecution had no evidence which would stand up in a court of law... I'm afraid these claims just don't stand up.* PHRASAL VB : V+ ADV

6 If you **stand** someone **up**, especially someone you are just beginning a romantic or sexual relationship with, you fail to keep an arrangement to meet them; an informal expression. EG *He said he'd meet her outside the station, but he stood her up... I think I've been stood up.* PHRASAL VB : ORDER V+O+ ADV

7 See also **stand-up**.

standard /stændəd/, **standards**. 1 A **standard** is 1.1 a level of quality or achievement, especially a level that is thought to be acceptable. EG *The acting ability of the pupils is of a high standard... The course was very varied in standard... I'll never reach that standard... You're way below the standard required... They don't have the same standard of hygiene as we have.* N COUNT : USU+ SUPP, OR in+N 1.2 something used to measure or estimate the quality or degree of something, for example how good a piece of work is. EG *These families would be classified as rich by Asian standards... By any standard the work was good... Here was a standard against which its performance could be classified... We belong to a civilization whose standard of success is money.* N COUNT : USU+ SUPP ⇑ principle = criterion 1.3 a moral principle which affects people's attitudes and behaviour. EG *Another public figure is found to have private standards that do not accord with the nation's expectations... There has been a corruption of moral standards.* • See also **double standard**. N COUNT : USU PL +SUPP = precept

2 **Standard** is used to describe something which is 2.1 usual and normal, rather than being special or extra. EG *There is a standard procedure for recording drugs given to patients... The stereo radio is now a standard feature... Metallic finish is standard.* ADJ CLASSIF 2.2 of a normal, basic size, quality, or amount. EG ...*a standard brick... ...a standard grant... You can use a standard wax polish.* ADJ CLASSIF : ATTRIB = ordinary, regular

3 **Standard** is used to describe spelling, pronunciation, grammar, etc which is generally regarded as correct or acceptable. EG *Most people regard this dialect as 'standard' English.* ADJ CLASSIF = orthodox

4 If a book is described as a **standard** work or text, it is the one most widely read and recommended in a field or the best about a particular subject. EG *This is the standard work on British moths... My tutor wrote all the standard textbooks.* ADJ CLASSIF : ATTRIB

5 A **standard** is also 5.1 a flag which is associated with a particular person or group of people. Some standards have two long points on one side. EG *If the standard is flying, the Queen is in residence.* N COUNT 5.2 an upright pole or post which is used to support something, for example a flag or light. EG ...*a lamp standard.* N COUNT

standard bearer, standard bearers; also spelled with a hyphen. A **standard bearer** is a person who acts as the leader of a group of people who have common aims or interests. EG *He was a standard-bearer of the Right.* N COUNT

standardize /stændədaɪz/, **standardizes, standardizing, standardized**; also spelled **standardise**. If you **standardize** things, you cause them to be all the same or to have the same features. EG *Some people have criticized television for standardizing speech, habits, and tastes.* V+O
◊ **standardized**. EG *Equipment is going to become more standardized.* ◊ ADJ QUALIT
◊ **standardization** /stændədaɪzeɪʃəⁿn/. EG *Standardization of order forms reduces delivery time.* ◊ N UNCOUNT

standard lamp, standard lamps. A **standard lamp** is an electric light which stands on the floor in a room. It consists of a bulb and shade fixed to the top of a tall wooden or metal pole on a base. N COUNT

standard of living, standards of living. A **standard of living** is the level of comfort and wealth which people have in a particular society or country. EG *There will have to be a painful adjustment to a lower standard of living... North Sea oil contributed to some recovery in the standard of living in Britain.* N COUNT : USU the/ADJ/POSS+N IN SING = lifestyle

standby /stændᵊbaɪ/, **standbys**; also spelled with a hyphen. 1 A **standby** is something that is always ready to be used if it is needed, especially in an emergency. EG *Eggs are a great standby in the kitchen.* N COUNT

2 If someone or something is **on standby**, they are ready to be used if they are needed. EG *We have a crew on stand-by.* PHR : USED AS AN A

3 A **standby** ticket for something such as the theatre or a plane journey is a cheap ticket that you buy just before the performance starts or the plane takes off, provided that there are still some seats left. EG *I got a standby booking.* N BEFORE N

stand-in, stand-ins. A **stand-in** is a person who takes someone else's place or does someone else's job for a short time, for example if the other person is ill or away. EG *She couldn't get to the meeting so she sent me as her stand-in.* ▸ used as an adjective. EG *I'm trying to arrange a stand-in lecturer.* N COUNT ⇑ substitute ▸ N BEFORE N

standing /stændɪŋ/. 1 **Standing** is used to describe something which is 1.1 done from a position of standing or not moving. EG *He got the longest standing ovation I have ever seen... The car can reach 60 mph in 6 seconds from a standing start.* ADJ CLASSIF : ATTRIB 1.2 permanently in existence, rather than being formed or made only when it becomes necessary. EG ...*a standing army... ...a standing committee... Remember that you have a standing invitation to stay with us whenever you're in New York.* ADJ CLASSIF : ATTRIB ⇑ permanent

2 Someone's **standing** is their status or reputation in a particular area of activity. EG *She was an economist of considerable standing... ...people of a slightly higher social standing... They're making enquiries into his financial standing.* N UNCOUNT : POSS/ADJ+N

3 A person or thing **of long standing, of five years' standing**, etc has lasted or existed for the length of time mentioned. EG *The present unrest has its origins in social and economic ills of long standing... A member of twenty-five years' standing told us she had never seen anything like it.* PHR : USED AS AN A ⇑ duration

standing order, standing orders. A **standing order** is 1 an instruction to your bank to pay a fixed amount of money to a person or organization at regular times. EG *I get paid by standing order.* N COUNT, OR by+ N 2 a rule or order that remains permanently in existence, for example concerning the way a court or council should deal with its business. EG *Can I ask whether, under standing orders of the Senate, we are required to finish this debate today?* N COUNT : USU PL

standing room is space in a room, theatre, bus, etc where people can stand when all the seats have been taken. EG *The hall was packed, with standing room only.* N UNCOUNT

stand-offish. You say that someone is **stand-offish** if they are rather unfriendly and behave in a formal or distant way to other people; an informal word used showing disapproval. ADJ QUALIT = aloof, reserved

standpipe /stændpaɪp/, **standpipes**. A **standpipe** is a vertical pipe that is connected to a water supply and stands in a street or other public place. EG *They have to queue for water at standpipes serving a thousand people.* N COUNT

standpoint /stændpɔɪnt/, **standpoints**. A **standpoint** is a particular way of looking at or thinking about an event, situation, or idea. EG *Up to now, we have only discussed the issue from a western standpoint... We need to consider the problem from the standpoint of Africa and Asia.* N COUNT+SUPP ⇑ position = viewpoint

standstill /stændstɪl/ is used in expressions such as 'come to a standstill' or 'bring to a standstill' when you are saying that all movement and activity has stopped. EG *The traffic had come to a standstill... The negotiations are at a standstill.* N SING : a+N ⇑ condition = halt

stand-up. 1 **Stand-up** comedy is comedy in which a comedian stands up alone in front of an audience and tells jokes. EG ...*a stand-up comedian.* ADJ CLASSIF : ATTRIB

2 A **stand-up** fight or argument is one in which people stand up and hit or shout at each other in an unrestrained way. EG *It started as a quarrel but turned into a stand-up fight... These proposals caused a stand-up row in Parliament.* ADJ CLASSIF : ATTRIB

stank /stæŋk/ is the past tense of **stink**.

stanza /stænzə/, **stanzas**. A **stanza** is a verse of a poem; a technical term. EG *Read the last stanza aloud.* N COUNT

staple /steɪpə⁰l/, **staples, stapling, stapled**. 1 A **staple** is 1.1 a small piece of wire used for holding sheets of paper together firmly. You push the staple through the sheets of paper using a special device called a stapler. N COUNT ⇑ clip 1.2 a U-shaped piece of stiff wire used for holding things in place. Its ends are pushed into wood or brick by using a hammer or other tool. N COUNT ⇑ fastener

2 If you **staple** something, you fasten it to something else or fix it in place using staples. EG *The letter was stapled to the other documents in the file... Various notices had been stapled on the board.* V+O+A

3 A **staple** meal or food is one that forms a regular and basic part of your everyday life. EG *...their staple meals of fish and rice.* ADJ CLASSIF: ATTRIB ⇑ normal = standard

4 A **staple** is also 4.1 a type of food or crop that forms a regular and basic part of the diet of a group of people or of a species of animal. EG *Insects are a staple for most frogs.* N COUNT = necessity, essential 4.2 an important product in a particular region or in a particular industry. EG *Cloth is still a main staple of business in this part of Soho... Prices for staples came down in real terms.* N COUNT = mainstay 4.3 something that forms an important or regular part of something else. EG *The theme of insanity has recently become a staple in drama and film.* N COUNT

staple diet. The **staple diet** of a person or animal is the type of food that is the regular and basic part of the person's or animal's diet. EG *...the dry bread which is their staple diet.* N SING: USU WITH POSS ⇑ standard

staple gun, staple guns. A **staple gun** is a small machine used for forcing staples into wood or brick. N COUNT ⇑ tool

stapler /steɪplə/, **staplers**. A **stapler** is a special device used for putting staples into sheets of paper. N COUNT ⇑ machine

star /stɑː/, **stars, starring, starred**. 1 A **star** is 1.1 a large ball of burning gas in space. The sun is a star, but usually we think of stars as the very distant things which appear as small points of light in the sky on clear nights. EG *The sky was full of stars... They slept under the stars... One day Man may travel to the stars.* N COUNT ⇑ body = astral body 1.2 any of the small points of light, including planets or meteors, that are seen in the sky at night. ● See also **evening star, shooting star**. N COUNT 1.3 a shape or object that has four, five, or more points sticking out of it in a regular pattern. There are stars on the American flag. EG *...little star-shaped flowers... The man with the two gold stars on his uniform shouted an order to the sentry.* N COUNT ⇑ figure 1.4 a mark that is given to something to indicate that it is of high quality. Often the mark is indicated by a star-shaped symbol or sign. EG *This restaurant won a star in the 1981 Michelin guide... She had received the greatest number of gold stars for her Sunday School lessons.* N COUNT

1.5 the same as an asterisk. N COUNT

2 If you **star** something, you mark it with an asterisk or star-shaped symbol. EG *The starred items on the list are things you will need to buy every week.* V+O: USU PASS

3 If a large number of brightly-coloured or sparkling things **star** an area, they are scattered over it, like stars in the sky; a literary use. EG *Autumn crocuses star the grass under the trees... The ponds were starred with water-lilies.* V+O: USU PASS+ *with*

4 A **star** is also a very successful and famous actor, actress, musician, or sports player. EG *I will make you a star... ...a tennis star... ...film stars... ...rock stars.* N COUNT ⇑ celebrity

5 If an actor or actress **stars** in a play or film, he or she has one of the most important parts in it. EG *She'll be starring in a new play by Alan Bleasdale... Robert Powell is starring as Philip Marlowe.* V: USU+A

6 If a play or film **stars** a famous actor or actress, he or she has one of the most important parts in it. EG *The last version of the movie starred John Garfield and Lana Turner.* V+O ⇑ feature

7 The **star** of a group is the most important, successful, or skilful person in it. EG *They're my star pupils... ...the star witness... Michael is the star of the class.* N BEFORE N, OR COUNT: USU+ SUPP

8 The horoscope in a newspaper or magazine is sometimes referred to as the **stars**; an informal use. EG *I'm just reading my stars.* N PLURAL

9 The word **star** is also used in the following expressions. 9.1 If you say that someone **is born under a lucky** or **unlucky star**, you mean that they have a lot of good luck or bad luck in their life, because of fate. PHR: VB INFLECTS

9.2 If you **see stars**, you see flashes of light, as a result of being hit hard on the head; an informal expression. PHR: VB INFLECTS 9.3 If you **thank** your **lucky stars** for something, you are grateful for your good luck; an informal expression. EG *I thank my lucky stars that I met you when I did.* PHR: VB INFLECTS

-star. 1 A **two-star, three-star**, etc hotel or restaurant is one that has been awarded a particular number of stars because of its high quality. COMB: FORMS ADJ CLASSIFS

2 Petrol is described as **two-star, four-star**, etc to show what grade it is. Four-star petrol has a higher octane content than two-star. EG *The price of 4-star is rapidly approaching 2 pounds a gallon.* COMB: FORMS ADJ CLASSIFS, OR N UNCOUNTS

starboard /stɑːbəˢd/. The **starboard** side of a ship or aircraft is the right side when you are facing towards the front end of it; a technical term. EG *White, icily-cold water foamed over the starboard side... ...the starboard door of the saloon.* ▸ used as a noun. EG *...a few hundred yards to starboard.* ADJ CLASSIF ≠ port ▸ N UNCOUNT

starch /stɑːtʃ/, **starches, starching, starched**.

1 **Starch** is a substance that is used for stiffening cloth, especially cotton and linen. N UNCOUNT ⇑ stiffener

2 If you **starch** cloth, you stiffen it by using starch. ◊ **starched**. EG *They wore starched caps and white gloves.* V+O ◊ ADJ CLASSIF

3 **Starch** is also a white substance that is found in quite large amounts in bread, potatoes, pasta, rice, etc. EG *Your doctor may recommend limiting the amount of fat and starch in your diet.* N MASS ⇑ carbohydrate

starchy /stɑːtʃi¹/, **starchier, starchiest**. 1 **Starchy** food contains a lot of starch and not much protein. ADJ QUALIT ⇑ fattening

2 You describe a person as **starchy** when he or she behaves in a very formal way and does not show a sense of humour; a rather old-fashioned word, used showing disapproval. EG *Don't be so starchy.* ADJ QUALIT = stuffy

stardom /stɑːdəm/ is the state of being a film star, rock star, etc. EG *It's difficult to explain her rise to stardom.* N UNCOUNT ⇑ fame

stare /steə/, **stares, staring, stared**. 1 If you **stare**, you look at something or someone for a long time with wide open eyes. You may do this when you are amazed, afraid, or deep in thought. EG *He stared at us in disbelief... He sat there quietly, staring out of the window.* ▸ used as a noun. EG *She gave him a dreamy stare.* V: USU+A ⇑ gaze ▸ N COUNT

2 If an answer or solution **is staring** you **in the face**, it is so obvious that you should have seen it long ago; an informal expression. PHR: VB INFLECTS

stare out. If you **stare** someone **out**, you look steadily into their eyes for such a long time that they feel that they have to turn their eyes away from you. PHRASAL VB: V+O+ADV

starfish /stɑːfɪʃ/. **Starfish** is both the singular and the plural form. A **starfish** is a flat, star-shaped creature with five arms that lives in the sea. N COUNT

stark /stɑːk/, **starker, starkest**. 1 Something that is **stark** is very bare and plain in appearance, with nothing that makes it pleasant to look at. EG *We then passed through a much starker landscape... ...the stark black rocks and deserted beaches... The names were written in stark black print.* ◊ **starkly**. EG *The bare black trees stood out starkly against their grey background.* ◊ **starkness**. EG *...the starkness of the American desert.* ADJ QUALIT = austere ◊ ADV WITH VB ◊ N UNCOUNT = bareness

2 A **stark** fact, statement, description, etc is unpleasantly clear and simple, with no inessential words or explanations. EG *Those are the stark facts of the matter... The problem, in its starkest form, is just this.* ◊ **starkly**. EG *He put the choice starkly.* ADJ QUALIT: USU ATTRIB = bald, bare ◊ ADV WITH VB

3 **Stark** is used to emphasize that something is quite considerable in degree, and very obvious. EG *...grim stark poverty... The slump in commercial vehicles is in stark contrast to the boom in private car sales.* ◊ **starkly**. EG *One thing becomes starkly clear... This is more starkly evident than ever.* ADJ QUALIT: ATTRIB = total, utter ◊ ADV+ADJ/ADV

4 You say that someone is **stark naked** when you want to emphasize that they are completely naked; a fairly informal expression. EG *He came out of the bathroom stark naked.* PHR: USED AS C

5 If you say that someone is **stark staring mad** or **stark raving mad**, you mean that they behave as if they were completely mad; an informal expression. EG *All writers are stark raving mad.* PHR: USED AS C

starkers /stɑːkəz/. If someone is **starkers**, they are completely naked; an informal word, often used humorously. EG *One of the girls was starkers.* ADJ QUALIT: PRED

starlet /stɑ:lɪ²t/, **starlets**. A **starlet** is a young actress who, it is claimed, will be a film star in the future. N COUNT

starlight /stɑ:laɪt/ is the light that comes from the stars at night. EG *I enjoyed the view of the bay in the starlight.* N UNCOUNT

starling /stɑ:lɪŋ/, **starlings**. A **starling** is a very common European bird with greenish-black feathers. Starlings are found in large numbers, often in cities. N COUNT

starlit /stɑ:lɪt/. A **starlit** night, sky, sea, etc is made lighter or brighter by the stars. ADJ CLASSIF : ATTRIB

starry /stɑ:ri¹/. A **starry** night or sky is full of stars. EG *It was a cold, starry night.* ADJ CLASSIF : ATTRIB

starry-eyed. If you are **starry-eyed**, you are so full of dreams or hopes or idealistic thoughts that you do not see how things really are. EG *We were all starry-eyed about visiting London.* ADJ QUALIT ⇑ naive

Stars and Stripes. The **Stars and Stripes** is the name of the national flag of the United States of America. EG *The ship was flying the Stars and Stripes.* N SING : *the*+N

star sign, star signs. Your **star sign** is the sign of the Zodiac under which you were born. N COUNT = birth sign

star-studded. A **star-studded** show, film, cast, etc is one that includes a large number of famous performers. EG *Don't miss Sunday's star-studded performance.* ADJ CLASSIF : ATTRIB = glittering

start /stɑ:t/, **starts, starting, started**. 1 If you **start** to do or feel something, you begin doing or feeling it from a particular time, when you were not doing or feeling it before. EG *Ralph started to run... He started laughing... My father started work when he was ten... He'd hate me to start feeling independent... Now we have to start again almost from scratch.* V, V+O, OR V+ *to*-INF/-ING = commence

2 When something **starts** or when you **start** it, it takes place from a particular time; used of something that has not been taking place before that time. EG *His meeting starts at 7... I was only five when World War II started... I heard the beat of a drum start up fairly close by... We didn't want to start a panic... I started a fire.* V-ERG = begin, commence

3 The **start** of something is **3.1** the first part of it. EG *I was terribly lonely at the start.* N SING WITH DET **3.2** the time at which it begins. EG *...the start of the tax year... The project was doomed to failure from the start... You were awful from start to finish.* N SING WITH DET = beginning **3.3** the act of beginning it. EG *...the start of police enquiries... We need a fresh start... My career had been one long series of stops and starts.* N COUNT

4 If you **get off to a good start, get off to a bad start**, etc, you begin doing something well, badly, etc. EG *It isn't going to get off to a very good start... Treatment sometimes gets off to a bad start.* • to **get off to a flying start**: see **flying**. PHR : VB INFLECTS

5 If something has a **false start**, it is begun incorrectly or unsuccessfully, so that it has to be begun again. EG *There were a few false starts caused by over-enthusiasm.* • **in fits and starts**: see **fit**. PHR : USED AS O/ C/S, N INFLECTS

6 If you **start** with something or **start** by doing something, you begin an activity, process, etc by doing the thing mentioned as the first part of it. EG *I started with a joke... He had started his scientific career by playing around with pins and threads... The students started off with scripted dialogue on tape... We have to start out by understanding managers.* V+A, OR V+O+A = commence

7 If you **started** or **started out** as something, you began your career by doing a particular job or kind of work. EG *She started as a secretary ... I started off as a bookseller in Bristol... He started out in vaudeville.* V OR PHRASAL VB : V+ADV, USU +A

8 If you **start** something such as a new business or **start** it **up**, you establish it. EG *He scraped up the money to start his Hollywood restaurant... I thought of starting a home for old ladies... She wanted to start up a little country pub.* V OR PHRASAL VB : V+O+ADV = found, open

9 If you **start** an engine, motor, car, etc, or **start** it **up**, you make it begin to work. EG *He couldn't get his engine started... The driver started up the car... There's no reason why it shouldn't start.* V-ERG, OR PHRASAL VB : V-ERG+ADV

10 If you **start** somewhere, you begin going in a particular direction. EG *Ralph started back to the shelters... They started across the hotel's cobbled forecourt... They started down the street together.* V+A = set off

11 If you have a **start** on someone, you are ahead of them when you begin a race or when they begin to chase you. EG *You must give me fifty yards start.* • See also **headstart**. N SING : *a*+N

12 If you **start** a race, you cause it to begin, for example by firing a pistol. V+O

13 Where a region, place, type of countryside, etc **starts** is where its boundary begins. EG *The moors start a little further to the north.* V+A

14 A **start** is also a quick uncontrolled movement of your body, caused by surprise or fear. EG *Andrew gave a start... He awakened with a start.* N COUNT : USU SING ⇑ twitch

15 If you **start**, you quickly move your body, or a part of your body, as a result of surprise or fear. EG *'Oh no!' she cried, starting up suddenly from the pillow... It might cause her to start back in revulsion and terror.* V : USU+A

16 When a man and woman **start a family**, they have their first child. EG *We're hoping to start a family soon.* PHR : VB INFLECTS

17 **to start with**. **17.1** You use **to start with** to introduce the first of a number of things that you want to say, especially when you want to correct something that someone else has just said. EG *'Why do you call her a witch?'–'Well, she looks like a witch to start with.'. 'Why are you so cross with me, Trevor?'–'Well, to start with, my name isn't Trevor.'* PHR : USED AS ADV SEN

17.2 To start with also means at the very first stage of an event, process, etc. EG *To start with, United looked the stronger team... He was an engineer to start with, then a designer.* PHR : USED AS AN A

18 You use **for a start** to indicate that what you are saying is only one of a number of things that you could say, for example only one of a number of reasons for doing or for not doing something. EG *We can't afford this house for a start... For a start, you're too young.* PHR : USED AS ADV SEN

start off. 1 When someone **starts off**, they begin going in a particular direction. EG *Before we could stop him, he had started off across the desert.* PHRASAL VB : V+ADV

2 If you **start** someone **off**, you cause them to begin doing something. EG *I'll start you off with a few ideas... Don't start her off on that again!* PHRASAL VB : V+O+ADV

start on. If you **start on** something that needs to be done, you begin dealing with it. EG *She put the forks in a neat pile and started on the knives.* PHRASAL VB : V+PREP, HAS PASS = tackle

start out. If you **start out**, you begin going somewhere. EG *They started out to church.* PHRASAL VB : V+ADV

starter /stɑ:tə/, **starters**. 1 A **starter** is **1.1** a small quantity of food that is served as the first part of a meal. EG *Serve noodles tossed in butter or cream as a starter.* N COUNT : ALSO SING=PL = hors d'oeuvres **1.2** a device for starting an internal combustion engine. N COUNT **1.3** a person who causes a race to start, for example by firing a gun. N COUNT **1.4** a person or animal that is about to take part in a race. • See also **non-starter**. N COUNT ⇑ entrant

2 You use **for starters** when you mention something, to indicate that it is the first item or point in a series; an informal expression. EG *You will find that ten thousand dollars has been transferred into your bank account. That's for starters.* PHR : USED AS AN A OR ADV SEN

starting point, starting points; also spelled with a hyphen. A **starting point** is 1 something, for example an idea, statement, or belief, that can be used to begin something such as a discussion or an argument. EG *The starting point of the discussion is a recognition of the nature of inflation... I think that's actually quite a good starting point.* N COUNT : IF+ PREP THEN *of/ for* = basis 2 a place from which you can start a particular journey. EG *This makes a good starting point for a car tour around the Grand Duchy.* N COUNT : IF+ PREP THEN *of/ for*

startle /stɑ:tə⁰l/, **startles, startling, startled**. If you **startle** someone, you surprise and often slightly frighten or worry them by doing something that they do not expect you to do, for example by making a sudden movement or loud noise. EG *Goodness, you startled me–I thought you were in the garden... He was startled by the fevered look of his patient... The sound of machine-gun fire startled the pigeons.* V+O = alarm ◇ **startled**. EG *We laughed at the startled expressions on their faces.* ◇ ADJ QUALIT

startling /stɑ:tlɪŋ/. Something that is **startling** is so different, unexpected, or remarkable that people react with surprise. EG *...Sydney's startling new Opera House... The results were quite startling–a 77% increase in six months.* ADJ QUALIT = dramatic ◇ **startlingly**. EG *She was startlingly dressed.* ◇ ADV

starvation /stɑːveɪʃəⁿn/ is death or extreme suffering caused by lack of food. EG *Many thousands of people die from starvation every year... Society condemns human beings to starvation, disease and poverty... She lived on a starvation diet of bread and beans.*
N UNCOUNT ⇑ hunger

starve /stɑːv/, **starves, starving, starved.** 1 When people or animals **starve**, they suffer greatly from lack of food and sometimes die. EG *People are starving in the Third World because of inefficient farming methods... Reptiles can often live in deserts where other animals would starve... When the rescuers arrived, the survivors were starving.*
V ⇑ go hungry

2 If you **starve** someone, you do not give them any food at all. EG *The prison guards starved their prisoners... Ten men starved themselves to death in prison last year.*
V+O (NG/REFL)

3 If someone **starves** you into doing something, they force you to do it by depriving you of food. EG *They will never be starved into submission... The alternative to starving the prisoners out is to set fire to the building.*
V+O+A

4 If you say that you **are starving**, you mean that you are very hungry; an informal use. EG *I've got to have something to eat. I'm starving... The children were starving after their game of football.*
V : ONLY CONT

5 If someone or something **is starved** of something that they need, they are suffering because they are being deprived of it. EG *They seem to be starved of attention from adults... The children were starved for affection... The plant was starved of light and died... The coal industry had been starved of capital investment by previous governments.*
V+O : USU PASS+ *of/for*

stash /stæʃ/, **stashes, stashing, stashed.** If you **stash** something valuable such as a quantity of money in a secret place, you store it there to keep it safe; an informal word. EG *They had all that money stashed away in the loft.*
V+O+A ⇑ hide

state /steɪt/, **states, stating, stated.** 1 When you talk about the **state** of someone or something, you refer to an aspect of them, for example to what they are generally like or what form they are in at a particular time. EG *They are very concerned about the state of the churchyard... His general state of health is fairly satisfactory... ...the state of relations between the two countries... According to Hindus, a being may pass through numberless states of existence... ...the bullfighter's emotional state... We will restore the house wherever possible to its original state.*
N COUNT : USU SING+SUPP ⇑ shape = condition

2 If you say that someone or something is in a particular **state**, you describe an aspect of them such as their physical appearance, their behaviour or feelings, or the way that they are functioning. EG *She returned to the meeting in a cheerful state... The telephone service was in a precarious state... Scattered crowds wandered about in a state of shock... My office is in a constant state of change.*
N SING WITH DET +SUPP = condition

3 If you say that someone **is not in a fit state** to do something, you mean that they are not capable of doing it, for example because of their lack of experience, their state of health, or their mental attitude. EG *A young childminder left with the children is often in no fit state to help them at a time of crisis... I don't think you're in a state to understand anything that's being said... His father, had he been in a fit state to approve of anything, would have approved.*
PHR : VB INFLECTS, USU+ *to*-INF

4 If you are **in a state** or if you have got **into a state**, you have become very upset or nervous about something and are therefore behaving in an excited and perhaps foolish way; an informal expression. EG *He used to get into an awful state as exams approached... Get your facts right before you get into such a state.*
PHR : USED AS AN A ⇑ in a panic

5 If there is a **state** of war, **state** of emergency, etc in a country, the government has formally announced that the country is at war, that there is an emergency, etc, so that appropriate action can be taken. This can result in a restriction of people's freedom. EG *France was now in a state of war... The Government proclaimed a state of emergency.*
N SING WITH DET +*of* ⇑ situation

6 A **state** is **6.1** a country, usually when it is considered in terms of its political organization and structure. EG *The Latin American states maintained their independence... ...the State of Israel... It is now a one-party state... Many heads of state are here.* ● See also **nation-state, police state, welfare state. 6.2** one of the areas or divisions in a country such as the USA or Australia which is made up of a number of areas or divisions that each have control over many of their own affairs. EG *Haryana and Punjab were the fastest-developing states in India... ...the state of Washington... Minnesota introduced state laws restricting unnecessary lighting... ...San Diego State College.*
N COUNT, OR *of*+ N : ALSO IN NAMES / N COUNT : ALSO IN NAMES

7 When you talk about the **state**, you refer to a particular country in terms of its government, civil service, armed forces, and other organizations that control it, sometimes in contrast to the individuals who live in it or to independent organizations within it. EG *...the freedom of the individual and the security of the state... ...the political machinery of the state... ...state institutions for the mentally handicapped... ...state secrets... ...a state-owned oil firm.*
N SING : *the*+N

8 The USA is sometimes referred to informally as **the States.** EG *He had at one time lived in the States... ...our extensive travels all over the States.*
N PROPER : *the*+ N = US, USA

9 **State** is also used **9.1** in referring to ceremonies, events, buildings, etc which are very grand and which are celebrated, organized, or used on special occasions that are supposed to be of national significance. EG *...the state visit of a European monarch... They were suitably dressed for State occasions... ...the London palace with its splendid apartments of state.* **9.2** in names and titles, to refer to the part of the government of the USA that deals with foreign affairs. EG *...the State Department.* ● See also **Secretary of State.**
N UNCOUNT : USU BEFORE N ⇑ ceremonial / N IN NAMES/ TITLES

10 Something that is done **in state** is done as part of a special ceremony which is supposed to be of national significance. EG *Then the keys proceed in state to safety for the night.*
PHR : USED AS AN A = ceremonially

11 When a king, queen, or other leader who has died **lies in state**, his or her body is displayed before it is buried, so that people can visit it and pay their respects.
PHR : VB INFLECTS

12 If you **state** something, you say it in words or writing, usually in a fairly formal and definite way, for example to give information, a conclusion, or an opinion. EG *The government have stated quite categorically that we're going to see changes... As the pamphlet states: 'the electoral fight is of enormous importance'.... The police were called, but the man refused to state his business... ...achieving the goals stated in the initial contract.*
V+O/REPORT-CL/ QUOTE = declare

13 If you **state** a particular problem, attitude, argument, etc, you explain it so that other people understand it and can react to it. EG *The General Assembly will allow the Republic to state its case on the dispute... A letter had come from Miss Pollard, stating the situation... The newspaper defiantly stated its position.*
V+O = articulate, enunciate

State Enrolled Nurse. See **SEN.**

stateless /steɪtlɪ²s/. A person who is **stateless** is not a citizen of any country and therefore has no nationality. EG *...people who have been made stateless.*
ADJ CLASSIF

stately /steɪtli¹/, **statelier, stateliest.** Something that is **stately** is impressive because it looks very graceful and dignified. EG *...portraits of landowners and their stately mansions.* ◊ **stateliness.** EG *She had stateliness and dignity even in death.*
ADJ QUALIT = imposing / ◊ N UNCOUNT = majesty

stately home, stately homes. A **stately home** is a large old house in large grounds or gardens, especially one which has been owned by a particular family for a long time and which can be visited by the public.
N COUNT = mansion

statement /steɪtmə²nt/, **statements.** 1 A **statement** is **1.1** something that you say in a fairly formal and definite way, rather than just suggesting it. EG *I could not deny the truth of this statement... I thought at first that she said it as a statement, but it was a question.* **1.2** an official or formal announcement that has been specially prepared for a particular occasion or situation. EG *The announcement was made in a statement immediately after the meeting... Russell put out a statement denouncing the commission's conclusions... Soon afterwards he made his first public statement about the affair.*
N COUNT = declaration / N COUNT

2 The **statement** of a policy, theory, etc is the expression of it in words in a fairly formal and definite way. EG *The very statement of these aims demonstrated the weakness of their policies... This isn't a list of complaints, merely a statement of fact.*
N SING WITH DET +*of* = affirmation

3 A **statement** is also **3.1** something which you do or
N COUNT

make in a way that clearly expresses a particular opinion or idea that you have. EG *His sculpture can be seen as a positive statement of general relevance to modern society.* **3.2** a printed document that your bank sends you at regular intervals, which lists all the sums of money that you have paid in or taken out, and also shows how much money you currently have. EG *I get a bank statement at the start of every month.* N COUNT ⇑ list **3.3** a specially prepared list of costs and bills for something, showing the total that needs to be paid. N COUNT ⇑ document

state of affairs. A **state of affairs** is the general situation and circumstances connected with a particular thing, person, event, etc. EG *What our present state of affairs demands is a firm leader... Any relief to this unjust state of affairs is welcome.* N SING WITH DET

state of mind, states of mind. 1 Your **state of mind** is your mood at a particular time, especially in connection with the way it affects your attitude and behaviour. EG *My sister was in a happier state of mind... ...words that in no way reflected my state of mind.* N COUNT : USU SING

2 If you say that a particular feeling, condition, etc is a **state of mind**, you mean that it is only the result of a mood or an idea in someone's mind rather than existing in the real world or being determined by facts and events. EG *Illiteracy is as much a state of mind as a deficiency in skills... Happiness is just a state of mind.* N COUNT : USU SING, USED AS C

State Registered Nurse. See **SRN.**

stateroom /steɪtruːm/, **staterooms.** A **stateroom** is 1 a private room on a passenger ship; an old-fashioned word. EG *We called on him in his stateroom.* N COUNT 2 a large room in a palace or other building, for use on formal occasions. N COUNT

statesman /steɪtsmən/, **statesmen.** A **statesman** is an important and experienced politician, especially one who is widely known and respected. EG *...a Tory statesman of great eminence... Terrorism could threaten any visiting statesman.* • See also **elder statesman.** N COUNT

statesmanship /steɪtsmənʃɪp/ is the skill and activities of a statesman. EG *Stanley Baldwin was the symbol of statesmanship... ...an act of supreme statesmanship.* N UNCOUNT

static /stætɪk/, **statics.** 1 Something that is **static** stays in the same position and does not move at all. EG *...a series of static images.* ADJ CLASSIF = stationary

2 If a situation, atmosphere, etc is **static**, there is very little action or liveliness; often used showing disapproval. EG *...the static quality in all village life... ...the static scene at the lunch table.* ADJ QUALIT ⇑ changeless

3 A **static** idea, opinion, etc does not change or develop at all. EG *The mother's role has remained static and constant throughout the ages... Your model of society is static.* ADJ QUALIT ⇑ unchanging

4 A quantity that is **static** remains at the same level instead of increasing or decreasing. EG *Manufacturing output has remained virtually static for twenty years... Even with static population, consumption rose steeply.* ADJ QUALIT ⇑ unchanging = fixed, frozen

5 **Static** or **static electricity** is electricity which is caused by friction and which collects in your body or hair, in metal objects, etc. N UNCOUNT

6 If there is **static** on the radio or television, you hear a series of loud crackling noises which are caused by electricity that has collected in the air. EG *I switched on and got nothing but static.* N UNCOUNT ⇑ interference

7 **Statics** is the part of mechanics concerned with the forces that produce a state of equilibrium; a technical term in physics. N UNCOUNT

station /steɪʃən/, **stations, stationing, stationed.** 1 A **station** is **1.1** a building by a railway line or bus route where a train or a bus stops to pick up passengers and goods. EG *The train stopped at a small station... We sat down in the railway station... ...the hotel at Victoria Station... ...a London tube station... ...station platforms.* N COUNT : ALSO USED IN NAMES **1.2** a building which is the headquarters of a service, for example the police or the fire brigade, or where there is equipment for a particular purpose. EG *Go to your local police station... ...the fire station... ...a nuclear power station.* N COUNT : AFTER N **1.3** a small military camp or headquarters. EG *He's returning from the Air Force station.* N COUNT **1.4** a large sheep or cattle farm in Australia. EG *...the flat desert land of a cattle station in Northwestern Australia.* N COUNT : MOD + N

• See also **gas station, petrol station, service station, tracking station, weather station.**

2 A radio **station** is **2.1** a building with equipment for broadcasting programmes that is used by a radio company. EG *...the new local radio station.* N COUNT **2.2** a channel on the radio waves which is used by a radio company. EG *The radio was tuned permanently to his favourite station.* N COUNT

3 If you refer to someone's **station**, you refer to their position or rank in society; a rather old-fashioned use. EG *She had been educated above her station.* N SING : POSS+N = class, standing

4 If someone **is stationed** in a particular place, **4.1** they are sent there while working for the Army, Navy or Air Force. EG *...the British forces stationed in Germany.* V+O+A : USU PASS = be posted **4.2** they are told to stay there, usually so that they can watch people or be ready to prevent trouble. EG *Two guards were stationed at the top of the stairs.* V+O+A : USU PASS ⇑ position = post

stationary /steɪʃənəri/. Something that is **stationary** is not moving. EG *Only use the handbrake when your vehicle is stationary.* ADJ CLASSIF = immobile

stationer /steɪʃənə/, **stationers.** A **stationer** is a person who sells paper, envelopes, pens, and other equipment used for writing. ▸ The **stationer** or **stationer's** is used to refer to a shop where these things are sold. EG *...a stationer's in Islington.* N COUNT ⇑ shopkeeper ▸ N SING : DET+N

stationery /steɪʃənəri/ is paper, envelopes, pens, and other equipment used for writing. EG *We buy things like stationery and toilet rolls in bulk... ...the office stationery cupboard.* N UNCOUNT

stationmaster /steɪʃənmɑːstə/, **stationmasters**; also spelled with a hyphen. A **stationmaster** is the official who is in charge of a railway station. N COUNT

station wagon, station wagons; also spelled with a hyphen. A **station wagon** is the same as an estate car; used in American English. N COUNT

statistic /stətɪstɪk/, **statistics.** 1 **Statistics** are facts which are obtained from analysing information expressed in numbers, for example information about the number of times that something happens. EG *Statistics never prove anything... I happen to have the official statistics with me.* • See also **vital statistics.** N COUNT : USU PL = figure

2 **Statistics** is a branch of mathematics concerned with the study of such information. EG *I teach mathematics and statistics... ...a Professor of Statistics.* N UNCOUNT

statistical /stətɪstɪkəl/. **Statistical** means relating to the use of statistics. EG *Statistical techniques are regularly employed... ...the Central Statistical Office.* ADJ CLASSIF ◊ **statistically.** EG *Statistically you have a one in six chance of succeeding.* ◊ ADV

statistician /stætɪstɪʃən/, **statisticians.** A **statistician** is a person who studies statistics or who works using statistics. EG *...a statistician in the Civil Service... A test run would be useful to the statisticians.* N COUNT ⇑ expert

statuary /stætjuəri/. If you talk about the **statuary** in a place, you are referring to all the statues and sculpture there. EG *...some magnificent Roman statuary.* N UNCOUNT

statue /stætjuː/, **statues.** A **statue** is a large lifelike sculpture of a person or an animal, made of stone, marble, bronze, or some other hard material. Statues are usually found in public places such as parks and churches. EG *...a bronze statue of Charles I.* N COUNT

statuesque /stætjuesk/. A woman who is **statuesque** is big and tall and looks rather like a Greek statue of a woman. EG *She was a beautiful, statuesque creature with pale blue eyes.* ADJ QUALIT = stately

statuette /stætjuet/, **statuettes.** A **statuette** is a very small statue which is often displayed on a shelf or stand. N COUNT

stature /stætʃə/. 1 Someone's **stature** is their height and general size. EG *She was rather small in stature.* N UNCOUNT : USU +SUPP

2 The **stature** of a person or of their achievements is the importance and reputation that they have. EG *...a new English achievement of international stature... I can't tell you how pleased we are to have someone of your stature here.* N UNCOUNT : USU +SUPP = prominence

status /steɪtəs/. 1 Your **status** is **1.1** your position in society, especially the position that other people think that you have. EG *...people of roughly equal status... ...the changing status of women... ...citizens who wish to enhance their social status.* N UNCOUNT **1.2** the prestige or importance that you have in the eyes of N UNCOUNT other people. EG *He came in search of wealth, status, and power... Age has status in the villages.*

2 **Status** is also an official classification that a person, organization, country, etc receives, which gives them the rights or advantages of being classified in that particular way. EG *...Malaysia's non-aligned status... They appeared to have dropped their demand for status as political prisoners.* N UNCOUNT+SUPP ⇑ categorization

3 The **status** of something such as a dispute or a discussion between people is how important it is and how seriously it should be taken. EG *They are meeting to discuss the status of the dispute with club owners over free membership.* N UNCOUNT+SUPP ⇑ importance

status quo. The **status quo** is the situation that exists at a particular time without any changes being made to it. EG *...talks on maintaining the status quo... They will quickly retreat and the status quo will be restored.* N SING WITH DET

status symbol, status symbols. A **status symbol** is something that a person has or owns that shows they have prestige and importance in the society in which they live. EG *A personal chauffeur is undoubtedly a status symbol... A lot of sons remained an important status symbol for the men.* N COUNT

statute /stætju:t/, **statutes**. A **statute** is 1 a law which has been made by a government and which has been formally written down. EG *There have been more than twenty statutes governing what can be published in newspapers... Working hours were limited by statute.* 2 a formal rule which is made by a company or other institution about how the institution must operate. EG *The Union's statutes forbade party members from holding high office.* N COUNT, OR *by*+N; N COUNT = regulation

statute book. The **statute book** is a collection of all the laws made by a government. EG *This legislation is not on the statute book.* N SING : *the*+N

statutory /stætjə[4]tə[0]ri[1]/. 1 **Statutory** means consisting of, or done because of, laws which have been formally written down. EG *...the IBA's statutory code of advertising standards... The conference opposed all incomes policies, whether statutory or voluntary.* ◊ **statutorily**. EG *Elementary education began statutorily in 1870.* ADJ CLASSIF : USU ATTRIB ⇑ legal; ◊ ADV ⇑ legally

2 **Statutory** is also used to indicate that someone has been selected as a member of something such as a committee not because of their merits but because of some other characteristic that is thought to be important; used showing disapproval. EG *I was the statutory woman on the committee.* ADJ CLASSIF : ATTRIB = token

staunch /stɔːnt[0]ʃ/, **stauncher, staunchest; staunches, staunching, staunched**. 1 A **staunch** supporter or believer is very loyal to a person, an organization, or a set of beliefs, and supports them strongly. EG *Both are staunch supporters of Manchester United... ...Benny's staunchest ally... We don't understand politics, but we're staunch Tories.* ◊ **staunchly**. EG *They moved to a staunchly Republican area.* ADJ QUALIT : USU ATTRIB = faithful, steadfast; ◊ ADV

2 When you **staunch** blood, you stop it from flowing out of a person's or animal's body. EG *Sophia staunched the blood with a cloth.* V+O = stem

stave /steɪv/, **staves, staving, staved**. A **stave** is 1 the five lines that music is written on. 2 a thick stick which people carry to show that they have a certain job or position. EG *...the white staves of the officers of the Queen.* N COUNT; N COUNT = staff

stave off. If you **stave** something **off**, you delay it happening, although you know that it will happen eventually. EG *They want to stave off any attempt to intervene.* PHRASAL VB : V+O+ADV = hold off

stay /steɪ/, **stays, staying, stayed**. 1 If you **stay** in a place, 1.1 you continue to be there and do not move away. EG *Fewer women these days stay at home to look after their children... You go ahead, we'll stay behind.* 1.2 you live there for a short time as a guest or a visitor. EG *She was staying in the same hotel as I was... How long can you stay in Brussels?... She had Ellen Terry to stay for a week.* V+A = remain; V : USU+A

2 If someone or something **stays** in a particular condition or situation, they continue to be in it, so that their condition or situation does not change. EG *Last night I stayed awake until the whole house was sleeping... The unemployment rate stayed below 4 per cent... We'll work till eight if it stays light.* V+C, OR V+A ⇑ remain

3 If you **stay** in a job, at school, etc or if you **stay on** there, you remain there and do not leave. EG *I could do a better job by staying in politics... Do you intend to stay with London Transport?... Pupils have to stay on at school till they are 16.* V+A, OR PHRASAL VB : V+ADV, USU+A ≠ leave

4 If you **stay** away from a place or **stay** out of it, you do not go there. EG *This town is unsafe: stay away from here.* ▸ used also to warn people not to become involved in arguments, discussions, etc. EG *Stay out of this; it's my problem, not yours.* V+A = keep

5 If you **stay put**, you remain in a place, job, etc and do not try to move from it. EG *Those kinds of people stay put in one job all their lives.* PHR : VB INFLECTS = stop

6 If you say that something **is here to stay** or **has come to stay**, you mean that people have accepted it and it will continue to be used, thought, believed, etc. EG *The microchip is here to stay.* PHR : VB INFLECTS ⇑ be established

7 A **stay** is a short time that you spend somewhere as a guest, visitor, etc. EG *We want to make your stay as pleasant and enjoyable as possible... ...an overnight stay in hospital.* N COUNT : USU+SUPP = sojourn

stay in. If you **stay in**, you remain at home rather than go out and enjoy yourself. EG *She had to stay in and do the dishes.* PHRASAL VB : V+ADV ≠ go out

stay out. 1 If you **stay out**, you remain away from home, especially when you are expected to be there. EG *She stayed out all night.* PHRASAL VB : V+ADV = stop out

2 If workers **stay out**, they remain on strike. EG *The men stayed out for nearly a year.* PHRASAL VB : V+ADV

stay up. If you **stay up**, you remain out of bed rather than go to bed. EG *Nobody stayed up to give us our supper.* PHRASAL VB : V+ADV

stay-at-home, stay-at-homes. A **stay-at-home** is a person who prefers to remain quietly at home rather than to go out or to travel; usually used showing disapproval. EG *He's always been a bit of a stay-at-home.* N COUNT

staying power; also spelled with a hyphen. If you have **staying power**, you have the strength and stamina to keep going until you reach the end of what you are doing. EG *They do not have much staying-power.* N UNCOUNT ⇑ endurance

stay of execution, stays of execution. If you are given a **stay of execution**, you are legally permitted to delay obeying an order of a court of law; a legal expression. N COUNT : USU SING = reprieve

STD is an abbreviation for 'subscriber trunk dialling'; a system of making a telephone call in which you dial a number yourself and do not have to ask the operator to get the number for you. N UNCOUNT

stead /stɛd/. 1 If you say that something **will stand** someone **in good stead**, you mean that it will be very useful to them in the future. You sometimes use this expression to reassure children at school that what they are learning is not a waste of time. EG *My school theatrical performances stood me in good stead in later years.* PHR : VB INFLECTS

2 If you do something **in** someone's **stead**, you replace them and do it instead of them; a formal expression. EG *She implored me to go to the meeting in her stead.* PHR : USED AS AN A

steadfast /stɛdfəst, -fɑ:st/. If you are **steadfast** in something that you do, you are determined that what you are doing is right and you refuse to change or to give up; used showing approval. EG *He was steadfast in his praise of the Prime Minister... ...steadfast dedication.* ◊ **steadfastly**. EG *Her father has steadfastly refused to take part in such activities... He is now moving steadfastly in the wrong direction.* ◊ **steadfastness**. EG *She believed in self-respect, courtesy, kindness, integrity, steadfastness of principle.* ADJ QUALIT ⇑ persistent; ◊ ADV WITH VB; ◊ N UNCOUNT ⇑ resolution

steady /stɛdi[1]/, **steadier, steadiest; steadies, steadying, steadied**. 1 Something that is **steady** 1.1 continues or develops gradually and without any interruptions. EG *There has been a steady stream of programmes about India... This year we've seen a steady rise in prices... ...slow but steady progress.* ◊ **steadily**. EG *Unemployment has risen steadily... ...the steadily increasing level of misery and discomfort.* 1.2 stays at about the same level or value with not much change or variation. EG *These bulky vehicles are reasonably economical at a steady 56 mph... Membership of the committee stayed steady at twenty-nine... ...the steady monotone of his voice.* ◊ **steadily**. EG *The bats' huge wings beat steadily... He could hear Rudolph breathing steadily.* ADJ QUALIT = constant; ◊ ADV WITH VB; ADJ QUALIT = constant ≠ variable; ◊ ADV WITH VB = regularly

2 If something such as a ladder is **steady**, it is firm and does not shake or move about. EG *His hand was* ADJ QUALIT

not quite steady... Try to hold the tray steady. ◊ **steadiness**. EG *...his steadiness of hand.* ◊ N UNCOUNT

3 If you look at someone or speak to them in a **steady** way, you look or speak in a calm, controlled way which indicates that you are not nervous. EG *Her voice was faint but steady.* ◊ **steadily**. EG *Foster looked steadily at me for some moments.* ADJ QUALIT = composed; ◊ ADV WITH VB

4 Work or payment that is **steady** is certain to continue for a long period of time. EG *My son has a steady job... I wanted a steady income.* ADJ CLASSIF = stable

5 If you describe a person as **steady**, you mean that they are sensible and reliable. EG *I like Simon very much–he's a very steady boy.* ADJ QUALIT = dependable

6 If you have a **steady** girlfriend or boyfriend, you like her or him very much and spend as much time as possible together; a rather old-fashioned word. EG *She has become Charles Boon's steady girlfriend... What you need is a steady relationship with someone.* ▸ used as a noun. EG *I don't have a steady at the moment.* ADJ CLASSIF: ATTRIB = regular; ▸ N COUNT

7 If you **are going steady** with someone, you are having a romantic or sexual relationship with them and you spend as much time as possible with them; a rather old-fashioned expression. EG *Are you and Kevin going steady?* PHR OR PHR + A *(with)*: RECIP, VB INFLECTS = date

8 You say **'Steady!'** or **'Steady on!'** to someone **8.1** to warn them to be careful. EG *Steady! You're rocking the boat.* **8.2** to tell them to calm down or to be careful about what they are saying; used especially in British English. EG *Steady on! There's no need to lose your temper... I say, steady!* EXCLAM = watch it; EXCLAM = cool it

9 When you **steady** something or when it **steadies**, you stop it shaking or moving about. EG *His elbows were resting on his knees to steady the binoculars... The boat moved slightly, and he steadied himself with his right hand.* V-ERG, OR V+O (REFL) ⇑ support = stabilize

10 When you **steady** yourself or **steady** your voice, your expression, etc, you control your voice, expression, etc, so that people will think that you are calm and not nervous. EG *He drew a deep breath to steady himself... I need a drink to steady my nerves.* V-ERG, OR V+O (REFL) = compose

steak /steɪk/, **steaks**. **1 Steak** is **1.1** beef without much fat on it that you cook by grilling or frying. EG *There's steak for dinner... Do you want your steak rare, medium, or well done?* **1.2** beef that you use for making stews and casseroles. EG *...stewing steak... ...steak-and-kidney pie.* N MASS; N UNCOUNT

2 A **steak** can also be a firm piece of fish taken from a large fish, such as a cod. EG *...four halibut steaks.* N COUNT: AFTER N

steal /stiːl/, **steals, stealing, stole, stolen**. **1** If you **steal** something from someone, you take it away from them without their permission and without intending to return it. EG *My first offence was stealing a pair of binoculars... Children often steal.* ◊ **stealing**. EG *He had been expelled from his previous school for stealing.* V OR V+O = pilfer; ◊ N UNCOUNT = thieving

2 If you **steal** something such as the attention of an audience from someone, you do something which takes it from them. EG *...an expert in stealing scenes by putting in extra unrehearsed movements.* • to **steal the show**: see **show**. V+O

3 If you **steal** somewhere, you move there quietly and cautiously so that nobody notices you. EG *Simon came stealing out of the shadows... We could steal up on her.* V+A = creep

4 If you **steal a glance** at someone or something, you look at them so quickly that nobody sees you looking. EG *He stole a glance over his shoulder.* PHR: VB INFLECTS = peek

stealth /stɛlθ/. If you use **stealth** when you do something, you do it in such a slow, quiet, and secretive way that other people do not notice what you are doing. EG *They achieved their original dominance by stealth... Sometimes tigers rely on stealth, creeping towards their victims.* N UNCOUNT ≠ openness

stealthy /stɛlθiˈ/, **stealthier, stealthiest**. **Stealthy** actions or movements are performed quietly and secretively, so that no one will notice what you are doing. EG *I managed to get there by a series of stealthy movements.* ◊ **stealthily**. EG *I heard my landlady creeping stealthily up to my door.* ADJ QUALIT = furtive ≠ overt; ◊ ADV WITH VB

steam /stiːm/, **steams, steaming, steamed**. **1 Steam** is **1.1** the hot mist that water turns into when it boils. EG *The room was filled with steam... Steam hissed between the blocks of lava.* **1.2** the mist that is formed when water in the air becomes cool. EG *That morning his breath turned to steam.* N UNCOUNT ⇑ vapour; N UNCOUNT ⇑ vapour

2 Steam vehicles and machines are operated using steam as a means of power. EG *The first steam locomotive was introduced in 1825.* ADJ CLASSIF: ATTRIB

3 If something **steams**, it gives off steam. EG *The kettle was steaming away on the stove... The old train creaked and steamed as it gathered speed... Lynn brought her a steaming cup of tea.* V

4 If a vehicle **steams** somewhere, it moves along, giving out steam. EG *A British ship was steaming into Valetta Harbour... The train started to steam out of the station.* V+A = chug

5 If you **steam** food, you cook it in steam rather than in water. EG *Steam vegetables or cook them quickly with their skins on... ...steamed rice.* V+O

6 If you **steam** something open or off, you use steam in order to open it or remove it. EG *I'll have to steam open this letter.* V+O+C, OR V+O +A

7 The word **steam** is also used in the following expressions. **7.1** If a vehicle **gets up steam** or **picks up steam**, it slowly increases its speed. EG *The train pulled away and gradually picked up steam.* **7.2** If plans, projects, beliefs, etc **get up steam** or **pick up steam**, they become more important and more and more people become involved in them. EG *The race to sell arms to the Third World picked up steam in the early 1950's.* **7.3** If you **let off steam**, you get rid of your energy, anger, or strong emotions by behaving in a noisy or violent way in order to make yourself feel better; an informal expression. EG *They can let off steam in pubs where nobody knows them.* PHR: VB INFLECTS; PHR: VB INFLECTS = gather momentum; PHR: VB INFLECTS

7.4 If you **run out of steam**, you stop doing something because you are tired and have no more energy or enthusiasm left; an informal expression. EG *She would let me ramble on until I ran out of steam.* **7.5** If you do something or go somewhere **under** your **own steam**, you do it on your own or using your own effort, power, transport, etc; an informal expression. EG *Nobody's offered me a lift so I'm going under my own steam.* PHR: VB INFLECTS; PHR: USED AS AN A

steam up. **1** If a window, glass, etc **steams up**, it becomes covered with steam or mist. EG *My glasses steamed up as soon as I walked into the room... The windows always get steamed up when I'm cooking.* PHRASAL VB: V+ ADV = mist up

2 If someone is **steamed up**, they are very annoyed, angry, or excited about something; an informal expression. EG *My friend was very steamed up about this project.* PHR: USED AS C = het up

steamer /stiːmə/, **steamers**. A **steamer** is **1** a boat or ship that has an engine powered by steam. EG *He put her aboard the steamer Seneca bound for New York... ...a pleasure steamer.* **2** a container with small holes in the bottom which you place over boiling water so that you can cook food in the steam. N COUNT; N COUNT

steam iron, steam irons. A **steam iron** is an electric iron that produces steam from water that you put into it. The steam makes it easier to get the creases out of your clothes when you iron them. N COUNT

steamroller /stiːmrəʊlə/, **steamrollers, steamrollering, steamrollered**. **1** A **steamroller** is a large heavy vehicle with wide solid wheels or rollers, which is used to flatten the surface of a road. In the past, steamrollers had engines which were powered by steam. N COUNT

2 If you **steamroller** someone who disagrees with you, you force them to do what you want by using your power or by putting a lot of pressure on them; an informal use. EG *He had made up his mind that Johnson was guilty, and he steamrollered anyone who disagreed with him.* V+O = bulldoze

steamy /stiːmiˈ/, **steamier, steamiest**. **1** A place that is **steamy** is very hot and humid, usually because it is full of steam. EG *The corridor opened into a steamy and noisy kitchen... She sat in a bare, steamy cellar.* ADJ QUALIT

2 Books, films, or plays that are **steamy** are erotic; an informal use. ADJ QUALIT

steed /stiːd/, **steeds**. A **steed** is a large strong horse used for riding; a literary word. EG *He rode in on a white Arab steed.* N COUNT

steel /stiːl/, **steels, steeling, steeled**. **1 Steel** is a very strong metal which is made mainly from iron but also contains carbon and other elements. Steel is used for making many things, for example bridges, buildings, vehicles, and household things such as cutlery. EG *...a modern tower made of concrete and steel... ...built on steel girders... ...carbon steel knives.* ▸ also used to refer to the steel industry and the production of steel. EG *...the subject of nationalising* N UNCOUNT; ▸ N UNCOUNT: USU BEFORE N steel... ...*a working men's club in the heart of the steel area of Sheffield... ...the steel strike... ...plans for new steel mills in Lanarkshire.* • See also **stainless steel.**

2 A **steel** is a long rod made of steel with a handle at one end, which is used for sharpening knives. N COUNT ⇑ tool

3 **Steel** is used 3.1 to refer to great strength or courage. EG *She had nerves of steel... He held my arm with a grip of steel.* 3.2 to describe colours, especially shades of blue or grey, that have a hard greyish tone. EG *...steel blue eyes... The darkness had turned to steel-grey mist.* N UNCOUNT : USU *of*+N / ADJ+ADJ COLOUR

4 If you **steel** yourself, you prepare to deal with something unpleasant by making yourself feel stronger so that you will not be too hurt or upset. EG *If you don't know the news you had better steel yourself for a shock... I had steeled myself to manage without it.* V+O (REFL) : USU+*for/to*-INF = nerve

steel band, steel bands. A **steel band** is a band of people who play music on metal drums. The top surface of the drums produce different notes when different areas are hit. Steel bands are especially popular in the West Indies. N COUNT

steel wool is a mass of fine steel threads that are twisted together into a small ball and used for cleaning surfaces or removing paint, especially on metal surfaces. EG *Carefully remove stubborn stains with fine steel wool.* N UNCOUNT ⇑ abrasive

steelworker /stiːlwɜːkə/, **steelworkers.** A **steelworker** is a person who works in a steelworks. N COUNT ⇑ worker

steelworks /stiːlwɜːks/. **Steelworks** is both the singular and the plural form. A **steelworks** is a factory where steel is made. N COUNT

steely /stiːli¹/. You use **steely** 1 to describe something that has a hard, greyish colour like steel. EG *The blue sky had changed to a steely grey... Her steely eyes glinted.* 2 to emphasize that a person is hard, strong, and determined. EG *There was shy modesty behind that steely determination.* ADJ COLOUR, OR ADJ+ADJ COLOUR : ATTRIB / ADJ CLASSIF : ATTRIB = grim

steep /stiːp/, **steeper, steepest; steeps, steeping, steeped.** 1 A road, hillside, etc that is **steep** slopes at an angle so that it rises or falls sharply. EG *The street was not very steep... ...an old house with steep stairs and dark corridors... He reached the steepest part of the mountain.* ▸ used of a line of movement. EG *An aircraft was making a very steep descent.* ◇ **steeply.** EG *...mountains rising steeply on three sides.* ◇ **steepness.** EG *The steepness of the climb soon left me out of breath.* ADJ QUALIT / ◇ ADV WITH VB / ◇ N UNCOUNT : USU+*of*

2 A **steep** increase in something is a very big increase. EG *There's likely to be a steep increase in the cost of petrol.* ◇ **steeply.** EG *The costs of public services have risen steeply... ...a time of steeply rising prices.* ADJ QUALIT = sharp / ◇ ADV WITH VB = sharply

3 If you say that a price is **steep**, you mean that it is expensive; an informal use. EG *The price is a bit steep... Your fees are pretty steep.* ADJ QUALIT : PRED = high

4 If you say that an action, demand, or request is a **bit steep**, you mean that it is an unreasonable thing to do or ask and you feel rather angry about it; an informal expression. EG *It's a bit steep to expect us to do that!* PHR : USED AS C = a bit much

5 When food **is steeped** in a particular liquid, it is immersed in it, for example so that it will soften or absorb the flavour of the liquid. EG *The olives are steeped in flavoured oil.* V+O+A *(in)* : USU PASS = marinate

steeped /stiːpt/. If something is **steeped** in a particular characteristic, it has so much of the characteristic that it seems as if it is surrounded by it or covered in it. EG *The house is centuries old and steeped in history... The more steeped in violence our environment became, the more unhappy we were... He was steeped in thought.* ADJ QUALIT : PRED+*in* = submerged

steeple /stiːpə⁰l/, **steeples.** A **steeple** is a tall pointed structure on top of the tower of a church. N COUNT = spire

steeplechase /stiːpə⁰ltʃeɪs/, **steeplechases.** A **steeplechase** is 1 a long horse race in which the horses have to jump over different obstacles such as hedges and water jumps. 2 a long race in which people jump over hurdles and water jumps round an athletics track. N COUNT / N COUNT

steeplejack /stiːpə⁰ldʒæk/, **steeplejacks.** A **steeplejack** is a person who climbs up high parts of buildings, for example church steeples, in order to repair them, paint them, etc. N COUNT

steer /stɪə/, **steers, steering, steered.** 1 When you **steer** a car, boat, plane, etc, you operate it so that it goes in the direction that you want. EG *They set off with no idea how to steer a boat... He steered the car through the broad entrance... The freighter steered out of Santiago Bay that evening.* V ERG OR V ⇑ guide

2 If you **steer** someone in a particular direction, you guide them there, for example by putting your hand on their arm or back and pushing them very gently. EG *He steered me to a table and sat me down in a chair.* V+O : USU+A = propel

3 If you **steer** people towards a particular course of action or way of behaving, you change their behaviour, especially without them noticing, by guiding them into this course of action or way of behaving. EG *The leader had steered the party away from communism... He steers the conversation towards more general topics.* V+O : USU+A ⇑ guide

4 If you **steer** a particular course, you take a particular line of action. EG *The course he steered was perilous... The panel finally steered a judicious middle course.* V+O = follow

5 A **steer** is a bull or an ox that has been castrated. N COUNT

steering /stɪərɪŋ/. The **steering** in a car or other vehicle is the mechanical parts of it which make it possible to steer. EG *They had terrible troubles with the steering and transmission.* N UNCOUNT : USU *the*+N

steering wheel, steering wheels. The **steering wheel** in a car, lorry, etc is the wheel which the driver holds when he is steering the vehicle. EG *He was sitting there with his hands on the steering wheel.* N COUNT

stellar /stelə/ is used to describe things connected with stars; a formal word. EG *...beyond the earth's atmosphere, beyond the whole stellar system.* ADJ CLASSIF : ATTRIB

stem /stem/, **stems, stemming, stemmed.** 1 The **stem** of a plant is the long thin central part above the ground, or any smaller parts growing off the central part, from which the leaves and flowers grow. EG *Bindweed ran up the stems of the corn... They were removing every shoot, leaf, and stem.* N COUNT = stalk

2 The **stem** of a glass or vase is the long thin part of it which connects the bowl to the base. N COUNT

3 The **stem** of a pipe is the long thin part of it through which you suck the smoke into your mouth. EG *He bit on the stem of his pipe.* N COUNT

4 The **stem** of a word is the main part of it which remains unchanged when the ending changes, for example when it is in the plural or in a particular tense. N COUNT

5 If you **stem** something that is passing or spreading from one place to another, you put a stop to it. EG *...stemming the flow of illegal drugs... Officials tried to stem the tide of refugees... They believed that they had a duty to stem the advance of Communism.* V+O = check, halt

6 If a condition, problem, etc **stems** from a particular past situation, it started originally because of this situation. EG *...customs which stemmed from circumstances that have long since changed... Their aggressiveness stemmed from fear.* V+A *(from)* = arise

-stemmed combines with adjectives to describe something as having a stem of the length or type mentioned. EG *...a long-stemmed pipe.* COMB : FORMS ADJS

stench /stentʃ/, **stenches.** A **stench** is a strong and very unpleasant smell. EG *...the unmistakable stench of rotting eggs.* N COUNT : USU+*of* = stink

stencil /stensə⁰l/, **stencils, stencilling, stencilled**; also spelled **stenciling, stenciled** in American English. 1 A **stencil** is 1.1 a piece of paper, plastic, metal, etc which has a design cut out of it. The design is printed onto a surface by rolling or pressing ink or paint across the stencil, allowing it to come through the holes onto the surface below. 1.2 a piece of paper with a waxed coating that can be used in a typewriter to make a stencil for printing letters, memos, etc. N COUNT / N COUNT

2 If you **stencil** letters or designs, you print them using a stencil. EG *...large dustbins bearing the stencilled word LITTER.* V OR V+O

stenographer /stə²nɒgrəfə/, **stenographers.** A **stenographer** is a shorthand typist; used in American English. N COUNT

stentorian /stentɔːrɪən/. A **stentorian** voice is very loud and strong; a formal word. EG *...the stentorian voices of the guides.* ADJ QUALIT = strident

step /step/, **steps, stepping, stepped.** 1 A **step** is the movement that you make when you lift your foot and put it down in a different place, for example when you are walking. EG *She took a step back... I* N COUNT = pace *walked on with quick steps.* ▸ used of the distance you move when you take a step. EG *I'll be a few steps behind... Twenty steps away was the border bridge.* [▸ = footstep] ▸ also used of the sound that you make when you take a step. EG *I heard the steps cross the ceiling from the room above.*

2 If you **step** on something or **step** in a particular direction, you put your foot on the thing or move your foot in that direction. EG *He had stepped on a thorn... She must have stepped in something wet... Step over the wire... Tom stepped back... She stepped into the corridor... The captain stepped close to my side.* ● to **step into** someone's **shoes**: see **shoe**. ● to **step out of line**: see **line**. [V+A]

3 If someone tells you to **watch** your **step**, **3.1** they are telling you to walk carefully so that you don't fall over or have an accident. EG *Watch your step–it's a bit dark down here.* [PHR : VB INFLECTS ⇑ be careful] **3.2** they are telling you to be careful about how you behave or what you say so that you don't get into trouble. EG *I'm cleverer than you are, so watch your step.* [PHR : VB INFLECTS = watch it]

4 A **step** is also one of a series of actions that you take in order to achieve a particular goal. EG *Today's announcement is a step in the right direction... ...the first step on the road to victory.* [N COUNT : USU+SUPP = move] ● If you **take steps** to achieve a particular goal, you do the things that are necessary to achieve it. EG *If elected president, he would take steps to tighten up the administration... Have you taken steps to protect your home?* [● PHR : VB INFLECTS, USU+*to*-INF]

5 A **step** in an explanation, process, method, etc is one of a series of stages in its procedure. EG *Simmel carried this idea one step further... Brody was several steps ahead of Cassidy... We can miss out the next few steps if you like.* [N COUNT = stage] ● If you do something **step by step**, you do it by progressing gradually from one stage to the next. EG *The proof is set out, step by step, on the blackboard... ...a step by step guide to oil painting.* [● PHR : USED AS AN A = stage by stage]

6 A **step** is also a raised flat surface that usually looks like a block, on which you put your feet in order to walk up or down to a different level. Steps are usually built in a series, especially outside a building. EG *She was sitting on the top step... Mind the step... ...a flight of concrete steps.* ● See also **doorstep**. [N COUNT = stair]

7 Steps are the same as a stepladder. [N PLURAL]

8 If you talk about someone's **step**, you are describing the way that they walk, which often gives an idea of their feelings; a literary use. EG *Her step was without its usual spring... She moved from stall to stall, firm of step and dedicated of purpose.* [N UNCOUNT]

9 A **step** in a dance is a short sequence of foot movements which are performed as part of the dance. EG *We knew all the steps.* [N COUNT]

10 in step. 10.1 If a group of people are walking or marching **in step**, they are walking or marching with their feet going forward at exactly the same time as each other. EG *They marched in step.* [PHR : USED AS AN A] **10.2** If your ideas or opinions are **in step** with those of other people, usually the majority of people, they are the same as other people's. EG *I hope I'm in step with public opinion.* [PHR : USED AS AN A, IF+PREP THEN *with* = in line]

11 out of step. 11.1 If a group of people are walking **out of step**, they are walking with their feet going forward at different times, so that some people are putting their left feet forward at the same time that others are putting their right feet forward. [PHR : USED AS AN A ≠ in step] **11.2** If your ideas or opinions are **out of step** with those of other people, usually the majority of people, they are different from other people's. EG *His public statements are so obviously out of step with the majority of the party.* [PHR : USED AS AN A, IF+PREP THEN *with* ≠ in line]

12 If you **break step**, you change the way that you are walking so that you are no longer putting your left foot and right foot forward at the same time as the left foot and right foot of the people you are walking with. EG *The soldiers passed without breaking step.* [PHR : VB INFLECTS]

13 If you **fall into step**, you begin to walk so that you are putting your left foot and right foot forward at the same time as the left foot and right foot of the people you are walking with. EG *The three of them fell into step.* [PHR : VB INFLECTS]

step aside. To **step aside** means the same as to step down. [PHRASAL VB : V+ADV]

step back. If you **step back** and think about a problem or situation, you think about it in a fresh way as if you were not involved in it or influenced by your personal feelings. EG *It is tempting to step back and ask whether it is worth all the trouble.* [PHRASAL VB : V+ADV]

step down. If you **step down** or **step aside** from an important job or position, you resign from it, often in order to let someone else take your place. EG *He stepped down last month because of illness... The committee asked Mr Casey to step aside.* [PHRASAL VB : V+ADV ⇑ leave]

step in. If you **step in** on a difficult situation or argument that people are unable to deal with, you get involved in it so that you can help to find a solution. EG *She really appreciates the way you stepped in and saw to things... We step in and protect children from injury.* [PHRASAL VB : V+ADV = intervene]

step on. 1 If you **step on** someone who has a less important or less powerful position than you, you treat them badly or harshly; an informal expression. EG *Stephens didn't care whether he stepped on anyone or not.* [PHRASAL VB : V+PREP, HAS PASS = trample on]

2 If you tell the driver of a car to **step on it**, you are telling him or her to drive fast, because you are in a hurry; an informal expression. EG *Step on it, we're late.* [PHR : USU IMPER = hurry]

step up. If you **step up** something, you increase the speed, amount, or extent of it. EG *The government is stepping up its efforts... The pace of exploration for fossil fuels has been stepped up enormously... ...a sudden stepping up of the conflict.* ● See also **stepped-up**. [PHRASAL VB : V+O+ADV = intensify]

stepbrother /stɛpbrʌðə/, **stepbrothers**; also spelled with a hyphen. Someone's **stepbrother** is the son of their stepfather or stepmother. [N COUNT]

stepchild /stɛptʃaɪld/, **stepchildren**; also spelled with a hyphen. Someone's **stepchild** is the child of their husband or wife by an earlier marriage. [N COUNT]

stepdaughter /stɛpdɔːtə/, **stepdaughters**; also spelled with a hyphen. Someone's **stepdaughter** is the daughter of their husband or wife by an earlier marriage. [N COUNT]

stepfather /stɛpfɑːðə/, **stepfathers**; also spelled with a hyphen. Someone's **stepfather** is the man who has married their mother after the death or divorce of their father. EG *The children spent the holiday with their mother and stepfather.* [N COUNT]

stepladder /stɛplædə/, **stepladders**; also spelled with a hyphen. A **stepladder** is a ladder which you can carry around, consisting of two sloping parts that are hinged together at the top so that it will stand up on its own. EG *He got down off the stepladder.* [N COUNT = steps]

stepmother /stɛpmʌðə/, **stepmothers**; also spelled with a hyphen. Someone's **stepmother** is the woman who has married their father after the death or divorce of their mother. EG *He eventually married her and she became my stepmother.* [N COUNT]

stepparent /stɛppɛərənt/, **stepparents**; also spelled with a hyphen. Someone's **stepparent** is their stepfather or stepmother; a formal word. [N COUNT]

steppe /stɛp/, **steppes**. A **steppe** is a large area of land with grass but no trees. It is often used to refer specifically to the area that stretches from Eastern Europe across the south of the USSR to Siberia. EG *...the harshness of their nomadic life on the steppes.* [N COUNT : USU PL, SING=PL ⇑ grassland]

stepped-up is used to describe something which is done at a faster rate or to a greater extent than before. EG *They are already caught up in a new, stepped-up pace of life.* [ADJ CLASSIF : ATTRIB = intensified]

stepping stone, stepping stones; also spelled with a hyphen. **1** A **stepping stone** is a job or event that helps you to make progress, often in your career. EG *I regard my present job as a useful stepping stone to something better... That film was a big stepping-stone in my career.* [N COUNT ⇑ aid]

2 Stepping stones are a line of large stones which you can walk on in order to cross a shallow stream or river. EG *...the stepping stones at Ebchester.* [N COUNT : USU PL]

stepsister /stɛpsɪstə/, **stepsisters**; also spelled with a hyphen. Someone's **stepsister** is the daughter of their stepfather or stepmother. [N COUNT]

stepson /stɛpsʌn/, **stepsons**; also spelled with a hyphen. Someone's **stepson** is the son of their husband or wife by an earlier marriage. [N COUNT ⇑ relation]

stereo /stɛriəʊ/, **stereos**. **Stereo** is used to describe a record or a system of playing music in which the sound is directed through two different speakers. EG *...a stereo hi-fi... It sounds much better in stereo.* [ADJ CLASSIF, OR N UNCOUNT] ▸ used of a hi-fi or record player with two [▸ N COUNT] speakers; a fairly informal use. EG *He turned on the stereo.*

stereophonic /stɛri¹ə⁶fɒnɪk/. Stereophonic sound is the same as stereo sound. ADJ CLASSIF

stereotype /stɛri¹ə⁶taɪp/, **stereotypes, stereotyping, stereotyped.** 1 A **stereotype** is a fixed general image, characteristic, etc that a lot of people believe to represent a particular type of person or thing. EG *The song perpetuates two racist stereotypes... His training will have taught him certain stereotypes.* N COUNT

2 If you **stereotype** someone, you form a fixed general idea or image of them, so that you assume that they will behave in a particular way. EG *...sexual stereotyping... These images confine women to stereotyped roles.* V+O = typecast

sterile /stɛraɪl/. 1 Something that is **sterile** is completely clean and free from germs. EG *...rolls of sterile bandage... Conditions for a premature baby should be as sterile as possible.* ADJ CLASSIF = aseptic

2 A person or animal that is **sterile** is unable to reproduce. EG *He had learnt early in his marriage that he was sterile.* ◇ **sterility** /stə²rɪlɪti¹/. EG *...physical degeneration leading to sterility and cancer of the cervix.* ADJ CLASSIF = infertile; ◇ N UNCOUNT = infertility

3 A situation that is **sterile** is lacking in energy and new ideas; used showing disapproval. EG *The meeting degenerated into a sterile debate... Its ideology is sterile and lacking in originality.* ◇ **sterility.** EG *...the sterility of urban life.* ADJ QUALIT ⇑ unproductive; ◇ N UNCOUNT

sterilize /stɛrɪ¹laɪz/, **sterilizes, sterilizing, sterilized**; also spelled **sterilise.** 1 If you **sterilize** a thing or a place, you make it completely clean and free from germs. EG *All nearby brickwork must be sterilized with a blowlamp, then treated with fungicide.* ◇ **sterilized.** EG *Transfer the milk to a sterilized bottle.* V+O; ◇ ADJ CLASSIF

2 If a person or an animal **is sterilized**, something is done to them that makes it physically impossible for them to reproduce. EG *By 1950, 16 per cent of women over twenty had been sterilized... He bombards male insects with radioactive particles to sterilise them.* ◇ **sterilization** /stɛrɪ¹laɪzeɪʃ⁰n/. EG *Women were approached about sterilization immediately after giving birth.* V+O : USU PASS; ◇ N UNCOUNT

sterling /stɜːlɪŋ/. 1 **Sterling** is the money system of Great Britain. EG *Sterling has once again become one of the stronger currencies... ...a hundred and fifty pounds sterling.* N UNCOUNT ⇑ currency

2 **Sterling** means excellent in quality; used rather formally to describe someone's character or work. EG *...a man of sterling character.* ADJ CLASSIF : ATTRIB = first-class

stern /stɜːn/, **sterner, sternest; sterns.** 1 Someone who is **stern** is very serious and expects to be obeyed. EG *Sylvia had a stern father who never praised her... Don't get too stern with them.* ▸ used to describe something that is said. EG *...a stern warning.* ◇ **sternly.** EG *He walked over to the boy and said to him very sternly, 'Give that to me'.* ADJ QUALIT = strict, harsh; ▸ = severe; ◇ ADV WITH VB = severely

2 A **stern** look or expression shows disapproval. EG *She was looking really stern all the time.* ◇ **sternly.** EG *Her husband looked at her sternly.* ADJ QUALIT; ◇ ADV WITH VB

3 **Stern** is used to describe something that is very strict and severe. EG *Many people are beginning to call for sterner measures.* ADJ QUALIT = harsh

4 A **stern** job or task is unpleasant and difficult. EG *...a stern task... We just had time for a rest before the sterner business began.* ADJ QUALIT : USU ATTRIB ⇑ hard

5 If you say that someone **is made of sterner stuff**, you mean that they have a strong personality and are capable of overcoming difficulties and problems. PHR : VB INFLECTS

6 The **stern** of a boat is the back part of it. EG *She seated herself in the stern.* N COUNT ≠ prow, bow

sternum /stɜːnə⁰m/, **sternums, sterna.** The plural can be either **sternums** or **sterna.** Your **sternum** is the long flat bone which goes from your throat to the bottom of your ribs and to which your ribs are attached; a formal or technical word. N COUNT = breastbone

steroid /stɛrɔɪd, stɪə-/, **steroids.** A **steroid** is a type of chemical substance found in your body. Steroids can be artificially introduced into the bodies of sportsmen to improve their strength. EG *He was disqualified when it was found that he was taking steroids.* N COUNT

stertorous /stɜːtə⁰rəs/. **Stertorous** breathing is very noisy, like snoring; a formal word. EG *Her breathing became loud and stertorous.* ADJ QUALIT = rasping

stethoscope /stɛθəskəʊp/, **stethoscopes.** A **stethoscope** is an instrument that a doctor uses to listen to your heart and other sounds inside your body. It consists of a small disc that the doctor places on your body and a hollow tube that connects the disc to earpieces. N COUNT

stetson /stɛtsən/, **stetsons.** A **stetson** is a hat with a wide brim that is worn especially by cowboys. N COUNT

stevedore /stiːvədɔː/, **stevedores.** A **stevedore** is a person who loads and unloads ships; used especially in American English. N COUNT = docker

stew /stjuː/, **stews, stewing, stewed.** 1 A **stew** is a meal which you make by cooking meat, vegetables, etc in liquid at a low temperature. EG *We've got lamb stew tonight.* N MASS ⇑ food

2 If you **stew** meat, vegetables, fruit, etc, you cook the food slowly in liquid in a closed dish. EG *...stewed fruit.* V+O

3 If you **let** someone **stew** or **let** them **stew in** their **own juice**, you deliberately leave them to worry about something for a while, rather than telling them something which would make them feel better; an informal expression. EG *He let her stew for a day or two... Let Margaret stew in her own juice.* PHR : VB INFLECTS

4 If someone is **in a stew**, they feel very worried or upset; an old-fashioned informal expression. EG *The farmer was in a terrible stew.* PHR : USED AS AN A

steward /stjʊəd/, **stewards.** A **steward** is 1 a man who works on a ship, plane, train, etc looking after passengers and serving meals to them. EG *He went round the world as a ship's steward.* 2 someone who has the responsibility of looking after property. EG *Estate business was now conducted by a steward.* 3 someone who helps to organize a race, march, or some other public event. ● See also **shop steward.** N COUNT ⇑ employee; N COUNT = custodian; N COUNT

stewardess /stjʊədɛs/, **stewardesses.** A **stewardess** is a woman who works on a ship, train, etc looking after passengers and serving meals to them. N COUNT = air hostess

stewardship /stjuːədʃɪp/ is the responsibility of looking after property; a formal word. EG *The man gave an account of his stewardship.* N UNCOUNT : IF + PREP THEN *of*

stewing steak is beef which is suitable for cooking slowly in a stew. N UNCOUNT ⇑ meat

stick /stɪk/, **sticks, sticking, stuck.** 1 A **stick** is 1.1 a small thin piece of dead wood from a tree. EG *I gathered some sticks to start the fire.* 1.2 a long thin piece of wood. EG *They tried to break through police cordons, using sticks and assorted missiles... ...hockey sticks.* 1.3 the same as a walking-stick. EG *She handed him his hat and stick.* N COUNT; N COUNT; N COUNT

2 A **stick** of something is a long thin piece of it. EG *...a stick of rock... ...a stick of rhubarb... ...sticks of dynamite.* N PART+N UNCOUNT ⇑ rod

3 If a pointed object **sticks** in something or if you **stick** it in something, you push it in. EG *He stuck the knife right in... The pig had two spears sticking in her side... He stuck a cigar in his mouth.* V-ERG+A

4 If you **stick** one thing to something else, you attach it to it using glue, Sellotape, or some other sticky substance. EG *They went round sticking posters on walls and lamp-posts... Stick a numbered label on each case.* V+O+A = paste

5 If a substance or object **sticks** to a surface, it becomes attached to it and is difficult to remove. EG *...powdered sand that sticks to your hair and skin... Knead the dough until it no longer sticks to your hands.* V : USU+A *(to)* = adhere

6 If something which can usually be moved **sticks**, it becomes fixed in position so that it can no longer be moved. EG *The car horn has stuck... This drawer is always sticking.* V = jam

7 If something **sticks** in your mind, it makes such an impression on you that you remember it for a long time. EG *That thought stuck in my mind.* V : USU+A ⇑ stay = persist

8 If you think of a name or term for someone or something and the name or term **sticks**, it becomes the name or term which most people use for the person or thing. EG *I nicknamed him 'Fingers', a name which stuck.* V = remain

9 If you **stick** something somewhere, you put it there in a rather casual, careless way; an informal use. EG *She closed the bag and stuck it back on the shelf... I just stuck it in an envelope and sent it off.* V+O+A ⇑ shove

10 If you **stick** a difficult or unpleasant situation, you continue to the end of it, rather than give up; a fairly informal use. EG *I don't know how I've stuck it. It's been hell... We stuck the full course.* V+O = stand

11 If you cannot **stick** something, you dislike it very much; an informal use. EG *I can't stick anybody sitting next to me when I'm reading.* V+O : USU WITH MODAL+BROAD NEG

12 Sticks of furniture are pieces of furniture, especially ones of little value. EG *Here and there were sticks of furniture, but mostly the house was bare.* N PLURAL : IF+ PREP THEN *of*

13 If you **stick**, you stop what you are doing and do not go any further; often used in card games when you decide not to play any more cards. EG *I'm sticking.* V

14 If you **stick at nothing**, you are prepared to do things that you know are wrong, in order to achieve what you want. PHR : VB INFLECTS

15 If you **give** someone **stick**, you severely criticize or tease them. If you **get** or **take stick**, you receive a lot of criticism or teasing; an informal expression. EG *They gave me a lot of stick at work... The President has taken a lot of stick in his time.* PHR : VB INFLECTS

16 If you live in the **sticks**, you live in a quiet region in the countryside far from a city; a fairly informal use. EG *We used to live out in the sticks.* N PLURAL : *the*+ N = the backwoods

17 If someone **gets** or **gets hold of the wrong end of the stick**, they completely misunderstand a situation or something that is said; used in informal English. EG *How on earth could you get the wrong end of the stick?* PHR : VB INFLECTS ⇑ misinterpret

18 Stick is used in expressions such as 'a dull old stick' and 'not a bad old stick' as a way of referring to a person, especially someone rather uninteresting; a fairly old-fashioned use. EG *Johnny isn't a bad old stick, but he simply isn't aware.* PHR : USED AS C = chap

19 • to **stick** your **neck out**: see **neck**. • to **stick in** your **throat**: see **throat**.

stick around. If you **stick around**, you stay where you are, often because you are waiting for something; an informal expression. EG *I'll stick around and keep an eye on the food.* PHRASAL VB : V+ ADV = hang around

stick at. If you **stick at** something, you continue working at it or trying as hard as you can, even if it is very difficult or unpleasant. EG *You must stick at it if you want to succeed.* PHRASAL VB : V+ PREP = keep at

stick by. **1** If you **stick by** someone, you continue to give them help or support, especially when they are in difficulty. EG *I shall stick by you as long as I live... He was a good commanding officer who stuck by his men when they got into trouble.* PHRASAL VB : V+ PREP = stand by

2 If you **stick by** something, you do what you have promised, decided, or agreed to do and do not change your mind. EG *I'm sticking by my principles on this matter.* PHRASAL VB : V+ PREP ≠ desert

stick down. If you **stick** something **down**, you attach it firmly to a surface using glue or paste and then pressing it. EG *Stick it down round the edge.* PHRASAL VB : V+ O+ADV ⇑ affix

stick on. If you **stick** something **on**, you attach it to a surface using glue, Sellotape, or some other sticky substance. EG *I stuck the stamp on and ran to the post-box.* PHRASAL VB : V+ O+ADV ⇑ affix

stick out. **1** If you **stick** something **out**, you push it so that it appears from inside or behind something else. EG *Lally stuck her head out of a window... Lynn stuck out her tongue.* PHRASAL VB : V+ O+ADV = poke out

2 If something **sticks out**, **2.1** it extends beyond something else, because of its length or because of the direction in which it is pointing. EG *There was a little chimney sticking out of the roof... She sat on the hard beach, her bony legs sticking straight out in front of her... A few grey hairs stuck out from under her hat... A champagne bottle was sticking out of an ice bucket.* PHRASAL VB : V+ ADV, USU+A = protrude, poke out **2.2** it is very obvious or noticeable because of some unusual quality. EG *His country accent made him stick out.* • to **stick out like a sore thumb**: see **thumb**. PHRASAL VB : V+ ADV = stand out

3 If you **stick out** a difficult or unpleasant situation, you continue to the end of it, rather than give up. EG *I promised myself I'd stick it out even if it killed me.* PHRASAL VB : V+ O+ADV

stick out for. If you **stick out for** something, you keep demanding it until you get what you want. EG *He stuck out for twice the usual salary, and got it.* PHRASAL VB : V+ ADV+PREP = hold out for

stick to. **1** If you **stick to** a promise, decision, agreement, etc, you do what you have promised, decided, or agreed to do and do not change your mind. EG *He insisted on sticking to his original idea... Make sure that everyone sticks to the agreement.* PHR : V+PREP, HAS PASS = keep to

2 If you **stick to** an activity or subject, you keep doing the same activity or talking about the same subject, and do not change to something else. EG *I think I'll just stick to painting... Will you please stick to the facts.* PHRASAL VB : V+ PREP, HAS PASS = stick with

3 If you **stick to** a law, instruction, rule, etc, you behave in the way that it tells you to. EG *We'd better stick to the rules... It is always advisable to stick as close to the truth as possible.* PHRASAL VB : V+ PREP, HAS PASS = keep to

4 If you **stick to** someone, you keep supporting and trusting them, especially when they are in a difficult situation. EG *She is sticking to her husband through thick and thin.* PHRASAL VB : V+ PREP = stand by

5 If you **stick to** someone or something when you are travelling somewhere, you stay close to them. EG *I went over the hill instead of sticking to the river... Stick to your group leader at all times.* PHRASAL VB : V+ PREP, HAS PASS ⇑ follow

6 If you **stick to** your **guns**, you do what you originally decided and do not give up or change your mind; a fairly informal expression. PHR : VB INFLECTS

stick together. If people **stick together**, they stay with each other and support each other. PHRASAL VB : V+ ADV

stick up. **1** If you **stick up** something such as a picture or notice, you attach it to a wall so that it can be seen. EG *I've got posters stuck up all round my room.* PHRASAL VB : V+ O+ADV ⇑ affix

2 If something long **sticks up**, it points upwards in an upright position. EG *These plants stick up vertically from the seabed.* PHRASAL VB : V+ ADV

3 If someone with a gun says **'stick 'em up'**, they mean that you must raise your hands; used especially in rather old films and books. EG *'Stick 'em up!' the cops shouted.* PHR : USED AS IMPER

4 See also **stick-up**.

stick up for. If you **stick up for** a person, principle, right, etc, you take forceful action in order to defend that person, principle, right, etc. EG *He should have thanked his father for sticking up for him that way... I was too small to stick up for my rights.* PHRASAL VB : V+ ADV+PREP = stand up for

stick with. **1** If you **stick with** an activity or subject, you keep doing the same activity or talking about the same subject, and do not change to something else. EG *I stuck with what was to be my staple diet: brown rice.* PHRASAL VB : V+ PREP = stick to

2 If you **stick with** someone, you stay close to them. EG *Stick with me and you'll be okay.* PHRASAL VB : V+ PREP

sticker /stɪkə/, **stickers**. A **sticker** is a small piece of paper or plastic that you can stick onto a surface. It has writing or a picture on one side and adhesive material on the other side. EG *On the rear window was a sticker saying 'Save the Whales'.* N COUNT ⇑ notice

sticking plaster, sticking plasters; also spelled with a hyphen. **Sticking plaster** is material that you can stick over a cut, blister, etc in order to protect it. N UNCOUNT/ COUNT ⇑ bandage

stick insect, stick insects; also spelled with a hyphen. A **stick insect** is an insect with a long thin body and legs. It looks like a small stick. N COUNT

stick-in-the-mud, stick-in-the-muds. If you describe someone as a **stick-in-the-mud**, you mean that they do not like doing anything that is new or fun; an informal word, used showing disapproval. EG *Don't be such a stick-in-the-mud.* N COUNT : USU SING = fuddy-duddy

stickleback /stɪkə⁰lbæk/, **sticklebacks**. A **stickleback** is a small fish which has spikes along its back. N COUNT

stickler /stɪklə/. If you **are a stickler for** something, you always insist on it. EG *Kitty was a stickler for routine.* PHR : VB/N INFLECT

stick-on is used to describe something such as a label which has an adhesive material on one side so that it will stick to surfaces. EG *...stick-on labels.* ADJ CLASSIF : USU ATTRIB

stickpin /stɪkpɪn/, **stickpins**. A **stickpin** is the same as a tie-pin; used in American English. EG *He wore a pearl stickpin and a white carnation in his buttonhole.* N COUNT

stick-up, stick-ups. A **stick-up** is a robbery of a shop, bank, etc, in which the thieves use guns; an old-fashioned informal word. N COUNT = hold-up

sticky /stɪki¹/, **stickier, stickiest**. **1** Something that is **sticky** **1.1** is covered with a substance that can stick to other things and leave unpleasant marks. EG *Anne wiped her hands, which were sticky from the lollipop, on her skirt... ...a sticky bottle of fruit juice.* ADJ QUALIT

◊ **stickiness**. EG *To remove stickiness use a damp cloth.* ◊ N UNCOUNT **1.2** has glue on one side so that you can stick it to surfaces. EG *...sticky labels... ...sticky tape.* ADJ CLASSIF : ATTRIB

2 If you describe a situation as **sticky**, you mean that it is is very difficult for you because you find it complicated or embarrassing; an informal use. EG ADJ QUALIT = awkward

Conversation was very sticky... We had a very sticky first day together in London.

3 **Sticky** weather is unpleasantly hot and damp. EG *...a hot, sticky, July afternoon.* ADJ QUALIT = muggy

4 If someone **comes to a sticky end** or **meets a sticky end**, they get killed or suffer something very unpleasant or disastrous in their life; an informal expression. PHR : VB INFLECTS

5 If someone **has sticky fingers**, they have a strong tendency to steal things; an informal expression. PHR : VB INFLECTS

6 If someone is **on a sticky wicket**, they are in a situation where there may be a lot of problems; an informal expression. PHR : USED AS AN A

stiff /stɪf/, **stiffer, stiffest; stiffs.** 1 Something that is **stiff** is quite hard or firm, and therefore not likely to bend very much if it is pressed. EG *...a stiff brush... ...a new pair of stiff climbing boots... ...stiff brown paper... I went stiff with terror.* ◊ **stiffly.** EG *...stiffly starched shirts.* ADJ QUALIT ⇑ rigid ≠ flexible, pliable ◊ ADV WITH VB

2 A **stiff** mixture is thick and difficult to stir. EG *The furniture is treated with beeswax made into a stiff paste with turpentine.* ADJ QUALIT = firm

3 Something such as a door or drawer that is **stiff** does not move as easily as it should. EG *The door was rather stiff... ...a stiff latch.* ADJ QUALIT

4 If you or your muscles or joints are **stiff**, your muscles or joints hurt when you move, for example because of arthritis or because you have had too much exercise. EG *I'm too stiff to move after that yoga last night.* ◊ **stiffly.** EG *He got out of bed stiffly.* ◊ **stiffness.** EG *She complained of stiffness in her knees.* ADJ QUALIT = sore ≠ nimble ◊ ADV WITH VB ◊ N UNCOUNT

5 **Stiff** behaviour is rather formal and not very friendly or relaxed. EG *...a stiff smile... The letter was stiff and formal.* ◊ **stiffly.** EG *'No, I haven't,' Rudolph said stiffly... The three officials waved stiffly.* ◊ **stiffness.** EG *Their stiffness and self-consciousness soon disappeared.* ADJ QUALIT = chilly ◊ ADV WITH VB ◊ N UNCOUNT

6 Something that is **stiff** is difficult or severe. EG *Competition is so stiff that he'll be lucky to get a place at all... ...a stiff warning... There will be stiffer penalties for drunken drivers.* ADJ QUALIT = tough

7 A **stiff** drink is a large strong drink such as gin or whisky which does not have much water, soda, lemonade, etc, added. EG *Morris fixed himself a stiff drink... ...a stiff whisky.* ADJ QUALIT : ATTRIB

8 A **stiff** breeze is one that is blowing quite strongly. EG *There was a stiff breeze blowing up from the estuary.* ADJ QUALIT ≠ gentle

9 If you are bored **stiff**, worried **stiff**, or scared **stiff**, you are extremely bored, worried, or scared; an informal use. ADV AFTER ADJ

10 A **stiff** is a dead body; an informal use in American English. N COUNT = corpse

11 If you show or keep a **stiff upper lip**, you do not show that you are nervous, upset, or frightened. EG *We must try to keep a stiff upper lip.* PHR : USED AS O

stiffen /stɪfəᵒn/, **stiffens, stiffening, stiffened.** 1 If you **stiffen** something, you make it hard or firm so that it is not likely to bend very much if it is pressed. V+O ⇑ harden

2 If your muscles or joints **stiffen**, they become difficult to bend or move. EG *You are unlikely to be troubled with stiffening joints.* V-ERG

3 If you **stiffen**, you stop moving and stand or sit with muscles that are suddenly tense, for example because you feel afraid or angry. EG *Tom suddenly stiffened with alarm... Her whole body stiffened.* V

4 If attitudes or behaviour **stiffen**, they become stronger or more severe, and less likely to be overcome or changed. EG *Resistance stiffened even further last week... You will only stiffen his resolve.* V-ERG = strengthen

stiffener /stɪfəᵒnə/, **stiffeners.** A **stiffener** is something used to make something less likely to bend if it is pressed. EG *...collar stiffeners.* N COUNT

stiffening /stɪfəᵒnɪŋ/ is cloth which is stuck or sewn into a piece of clothing in order to make the piece of clothing more stiff. N UNCOUNT

stiff-necked. Someone who is **stiff-necked** is proud and stubborn; used showing disapproval. ADJ QUALIT = obstinate

stifle /staɪfəᵒl/, **stifles, stifling, stifled.** 1 If someone **stifles** something that is happening they stop it from continuing. EG *Its strategy seemed to stifle progress... An authoritarian leadership stifled internal debate.* V+O ⇑ suppress = repress

2 If you **stifle** a cry, a yawn, etc, you stop yourself from expressing it aloud. EG *She placed a hand over her mouth to stifle a shriek of laughter... She reacted with a few stifled sobs.* V+O ⇑ suppress

3 If you **stifle** your natural way of behaving, you prevent yourself from behaving like this. EG *She stifled her impulses in favour of planned actions... ...an unsuccessful attempt to stifle their scruples.* V+O ⇑ suppress = quell

4 If the air or the atmosphere **stifles** you, it makes you feel as if you cannot breathe properly. EG *The air stifled and suffocated us... She was stifled with its scent.* ◊ **stifling.** EG *It was stifling inside... ...the stifling atmosphere.* V+O = suffocate ◊ ADJ QUALIT = stuffy

stigma /stɪgmə/, **stigmas, stigmata** /stɪgmɑːtə/. The plural can be either **stigmas** or **stigmata.** 1 A **stigma** is a shameful reputation that a particular action or way of behaving has because so many people disapprove of it. EG *Illegitimacy is no longer the social stigma that it was... He will be shunned by his friends, and the stigma could last a lifetime.* N COUNT : USU SING = disgrace

2 The **stigma** of a flower is the top of the centre part which takes in pollen; a technical term in botany. N COUNT

3 **Stigmata** are marks that appear on a person's body in the same places that Christ was wounded when he was crucified. Some Christians believe that this is a sign of holiness. EG *...Francis's assumption of the stigmata following a vision of Christ.* N COUNT : USU PL

stigmatize /stɪgmətaɪz/, **stigmatizes, stigmatizing, stigmatized**; also spelled **stigmatise.** If something **is stigmatized**, a lot of people regard it as shameful in some way. EG *Minorities everywhere have been stigmatized as being mentally inferior.* V+O : USU PASS, IF+PREP THEN as = brand

stile /staɪl/, **stiles.** A **stile** is an entrance to a field or path that consists of a step on either side of a fence or wall. This allows you to get to the field or path, without letting animals through. EG *I set off again along the path, over the stile, and up the lane.* N COUNT

stiletto /stɪletəʊ/, **stilettos.** A **stiletto** or a **stiletto shoe** is a woman's shoe with a very narrow high heel. EG *Stilettoes are out of fashion.* ▸ used to describe the heel of this kind of shoe. EG *I heard her stiletto heels move quickly across the room.* N COUNT : USU PL ▸ N BEFORE N

still /stɪl/, **stills, stilling, stilled; stiller, stillest.** 1 You use **still** 1.1 to say that a situation, state, or action which began at an earlier time has continued right up to the present. 'Still' sometimes expresses surprise that something has continued for such a long time. EG *She was still beautiful... She still lives in London... I was very greedy then, as I still am... I still don't understand.* ADV WITH VB 1.2 to say that, although something has not yet happened, it is possible or probable that it will happen in the future. EG *She could still change her mind... Even if he doesn't hurt himself, he could still get into serious trouble... There is still a chance that a few might survive... Bombs had fallen, and were still to fall, on other cities.* ADV WITH VB 1.3 to emphasize an amount of something that is left, especially an amount of time. EG *Tomorrow is still to come... There are ten whole weeks of term still to go... I've still got three left.* ADV 1.4 to emphasize that something is the case in spite of what you have just said. EG *His mother was Canadian: Irish-Canadian but still Canadian... This might be their best but that still did not make it good enough for her... Whatever they have done, they are still your parents... I didn't win. Still, it's been a good experience.* ADV, OR ADV SEN = nonetheless 1.5 when you are dismissing a problem or difficulty as not really worth worrying about; used mainly in spoken English. EG *It's been a terrible day. Still... Just as I reached the bus-stop the bus went off. Still, that's life, isn't it?... I've got to find the money from somewhere. Still, that's my problem.* ADV SEN = however

2 You also use **still** 2.1 with comparative adjectives and adverbs to say that the degree is even greater than what you have just mentioned. EG *To the astonishment of his friends, he ran for Governor of New York. More astonishing still, he won... How about some Bach to begin with? Or, better still, Vivaldi... He is unsuited to be leader of a great party and still less suited to be Prime Minister of a great country... He was forced to deflate the economy still further.* ADV : WITH COMPAR 2.2 with words such as 'another', 'other', 'further', and 'more' to emphasize the quantity of something. EG *They stared at him, hoping for still more secrets... On the other side of the room was still another portrait of the Chairman... There is,* ADV+NG = yet

however, still another even more powerful reason for staying.

3 If you are **still**, sit **still**, etc, you stay in the same position and do not move. EG *Stand still!... We had to keep still for about four minutes... His hands were never still... The cat stayed quite still.* ◊ **stillness.** EG *A breath of wind stirred the stillness of the robes.* — ADJ QUALIT : PRED, OR ADV AFTER VB; ⇑ motionless; ◊ N UNCOUNT

4 Something that is **still** is quiet and shows no sign of activity. EG *Except for the approaching engines, everything was still... The forest was very still.* ◊ **stillness.** EG *The stillness of the fields was broken by the sound of a gunshot.* — ADJ QUALIT : USU PRED; = tranquil, silent; ◊ N UNCOUNT

5 If something **stills** you or **stills** your voice, it makes you quiet or calm; a literary use. EG *By the Sixties such voices were all stilled.* — V+O; = silence

6 If something **stills** a doubt or fear that someone has, it puts a stop to it. EG *His statement was a way of stilling doubts and silencing rumours.* — V+O; = allay

7 **Still** water is calm and not flowing. EG *...the still water of the lagoon... I heard the bait plop into the still water.* — ADJ QUALIT; ⇑ motionless

8 When the air is **still**, there is no wind at all. EG *Everyone was sweltering in the still air... His handkerchief dangled from his pocket like a flag on a still day.* — ADJ QUALIT; ≠ windy

9 Soft drinks which are **still** are not fizzy. EG *A still orange juice, please.* — ADJ CLASSIF : ATTRIB

10 A **still** is 10.1 a photograph taken from a cinema film which is used for publicity purposes. EG *...striking black-and-white stills... ...John Halliday, the stills photographer.* **10.2** an apparatus used for distilling alcoholic drinks. — N COUNT; N COUNT

stillbirth /stɪlbɜːθ/, **stillbirths.** A **stillbirth** is the birth of a dead baby. — N COUNT/ UNCOUNT

stillborn /stɪlbɔːn/. 1 A baby that is **stillborn** is dead when it is born. — ADJ CLASSIF

2 If an idea, attempt, or action is **stillborn**, it is completely ineffective or unsuccessful. EG *Her apology rendered stillborn any cutting remarks I'd been about to make... The outcry against the minister was stillborn.* — ADJ CLASSIF; ⇑ useless

still life, still lifes. A **still life** is a painting or drawing of an arrangement of objects such as flowers or fruit. EG *He's done some lovely still lifes.* ▸ used to refer to this type of painting or drawing. EG *Still life is much harder... ...Ben Nicholson's early still-life paintings.* — N COUNT; ▸ N UNCOUNT

stilt /stɪlt/, **stilts. Stilts** are 1 long pieces of wood or metal which are sunk into the ground, especially when the ground is wet or boggy, and which are used to support buildings. EG *Thatched huts were raised high above the paddy fields on stilts... ...a city built on stilts out over the ocean.* **2** two long pieces of wood with small ledges high up on the sides. People such as circus clowns stand on the ledges, hold onto the stilts, and walk with them high up above the ground. — N COUNT : USU PL, USU *on*+N; ⇑ posts; N COUNT : USU PL, USU *on*+N; ⇑ poles

stilted /stɪltɪ²d/. If someone's behaviour or conversation is **stilted**, they behave or speak in an unnatural, jerky, and self-conscious way, rather than smoothly and with confidence. EG *This made my actions stilted and unnatural... After some stilted efforts at conversation, he gave up and left... He speaks a slightly stilted French suitable for foreigners.* — ADJ QUALIT; ⇑ stiff; = laboured; ≠ fluent

stimulant /stɪmjə⁴lənt/, **stimulants.** A **stimulant** is a drug, medicine, or food that makes your body work faster, often increasing your heart rate and making you less likely to sleep. EG *...coffee in which the drug caffeine acts as a stimulant.* — N COUNT

stimulate /stɪmjə⁴leɪt/, **stimulates, stimulating, stimulated.** 1 To **stimulate** something means to encourage it to begin or to develop further. EG *The fighting has greatly stimulated weapons technology... Rising prices will stimulate demands for higher incomes... An outsider who can offer a fresh point of view may stimulate new ideas.* — V+O; = provoke

2 If something **stimulates** you, it makes you feel full of ideas and enthusiasm. EG *The art course stimulated me.* ◊ **stimulating.** EG *...a conversation which I found both stimulating and exciting... She's brilliant and stimulating.* ◊ **stimulation** /stɪmjə⁴leɪʃə⁰n/. EG *Young children need stimulation... I find great intellectual stimulation in these surroundings.* — V OR V+O; = inspire; ◊ ADJ QUALIT; = inspiring; ◊ N UNCOUNT; = stimulus

3 If something **stimulates** a part of a person's or animal's body, it causes it to move or function, usually automatically by a natural reflex; a technical use. EG *The optical system of the eye stimulates cells in the retina.* ◊ **stimulation, stimulations.** EG *Illusions may be produced by stimulation of the temporal cortex.* — V+O; = trigger off; ◊ N UNCOUNT/ COUNT

stimulus /stɪmjə⁴ləs/, **stimuli.** 1 **Stimulus** or a **stimulus** is 1.1 something that makes a process develop more quickly, for example because people have new ideas on the subject. EG *There would not have been the same stimulus to mechanize production so rapidly... ...the stimulus of commercial competition.* **1.2** something which causes people to feel energetic and enthusiastic. EG *...all the stimulus and excitement that battle brought.* — N UNCOUNT/ COUNT; = incentive; N UNCOUNT; = stimulation

2 A **stimulus** is something that causes a part of a person's or animal's body to move or function, usually automatically by a natural reflex; a technical use. EG *They change automatically in response to stimuli... ...auditory stimuli.* — N COUNT

sting /stɪŋ/, **stings, stinging, stung.** 1 If an insect, animal, or plant **stings** you, it causes you to feel a sharp pain and sometimes get a wound or rash, usually by pricking your skin with poison or brushing your skin with poisoned hairs. EG *Bees do not normally sting without being provoked... The wet grasses were stinging my legs.* — V OR V+O; ⇑ hurt

2 The **sting** of an insect, animal, or plant is the part that can be used to prick through a person's or animal's skin like a sharp needle and leave poison behind. EG *This is not a worker bee, it has no sting.* — N SING WITH DET

3 If you feel a **sting**, you feel a sharp pain in your skin, for example because an insect has stung you. EG *He felt a sting on his elbow as the spider jumped away.* — N COUNT

4 If part of your skin **stings** or if something that you put on it **stings**, you feel a sharp pain there. EG *He felt the iodine stinging like a needle thrust into his leg... My eyes were stinging.* — V OR V-ERG; ⇑ hurt; = smart

5 If someone's remarks **sting** you, they make you feel hurt and annoyed, often because they are very critical. EG *I was bitterly stung by what she said.* ◊ **stinging.** EG *I remember the stinging things I said about them... The peer came out with a stinging remark.* ◊ **stung.** EG *'You English are strange.' Stung, Judy retorted that the Scots could be pretty strange, too.* — V+O : USU PASS, NO IMPER, NO CONT; ◊ ADJ QUALIT; = cutting; ◊ ADJ QUALIT; = nettled

6 If someone **stings** you for something, they make you spend a surprisingly large amount of money for it when it is not worth that much; an informal use. EG *He has stung me for £25!* — V+O+A *(for)*; = rip off

7 If something that is spoken or written, for example a joke, has **a sting in the tail**, it contains a critical or bitter part, usually at the end. EG *There's always a sting in the tail when she tells a story.* — PHR : USED AS O/C

8 If something **takes the sting out** of a situation, it removes the aspect of it which makes someone feel pain or unhappiness. EG *This was bound to take the sting out of nationalist resentment... He smiled to take the sting out of his words.* — PHR : VB INFLECTS

stingray /stɪŋreɪ/, **stingrays.** A **stingray** is a round, flat fish with a long tail which it can use as a weapon. — N COUNT

stingy /stɪndʒi¹/, **stingier, stingiest.** Someone who is **stingy** uses or gives away very little of something because they want to keep it or because they want to save money; used showing disapproval. EG *Go on, give me a really large drink. Don't be stingy.* ◊ **stinginess.** EG *Such stinginess came from my side of the family.* — ADJ QUALIT; = mingy, mean; ≠ generous; ◊ N UNCOUNT; = meanness

stink /stɪŋk/, **stinks, stinking, stank, stunk.** 1 Something that **stinks** smells extremely unpleasant. EG *The butcher's shop stank in hot weather... ...a foul, stinking lavatory.* ▸ used as a noun. EG *The stink of vomit reached Brody almost instantly.* — V; = reek; ▸ N SING WITH DET

2 If you say that something **stinks**, you mean that you think it is extremely bad or unpleasant; used in informal English. EG *'What do you think of the town so far?' she asked. 'I think it stinks,' I replied.* — V : NO CONT; = be disgusting

3 If you **make a stink** or **create a stink** about a situation, you publicly show your anger about it so that people have to take notice; an informal expression. EG *She created a terrible stink about the new motorway.* — PHR : VB INFLECTS; ⇑ complain

stink bomb, stink bombs; also spelled with a hyphen. A **stink bomb** is a small round object which can be easily broken and which contains a gas or liquid with a very unpleasant smell like rotten eggs. Children like to release the gas as a joke. — N COUNT

stinking /stɪŋkɪŋ/. 1 You use **stinking** to describe something as extremely unpleasant; an informal word. EG *I've got a stinking cold coming on... You couldn't hide anything in this stinking little town.* ADJ CLASSIF : ATTRIB = rotten
2 If you say that someone is **stinking rich**, you mean that they are very rich indeed; an informal expression. PHR : USED AS C

stint /stɪnt/, **stints**. A **stint** is a period of time which you spend doing a particular job or activity or working in a particular place. EG *I had first met her during my stint in Washington... I'm having a rest now; I've done my stint... I arrived at the University for a three month stint as a lecturer.* N COUNT+SUPP = stretch

stipend /staɪpɛnd/, **stipends**. A **stipend** is a sum of money paid regularly to a person, especially a clergyman, as a salary or as living expenses. EG *This sum was nearly a third of his total stipend.* N COUNT = allowance

stipendiary /staɪpɛndɪəri[1]/, **stipendiaries**. A **stipendiary** is a person, usually a clergyman or a magistrate, who receives a stipend. EG *The trend is towards more stipendiaries.* ▸ used as an adjective. EG *...stipendiary magistrates... ...the full-time stipendiary parish priest.* N COUNT; ▸ ADJ CLASSIF : ATTRIB ⇑ paid

stippled /stɪpəld/. A surface that is **stippled** is covered with dots. EG *...a stippled glaze on earthenware... The green moss is stippled with bright toadstools.* ADJ CLASSIF : IF+PREP THEN *with* = flecked

stipulate /stɪpjəleɪt/, **stipulates, stipulating, stipulated**. If you **stipulate** a condition, you state it clearly and precisely so that it has the force of a rule which must be followed. EG *The document stipulated nine criteria as the basis for any reform... I won't stipulate that it must be a story or a poem, just that it should be a written piece.* ◊ **stipulation** /stɪpjəleɪʃən/, **stipulations**. EG *His only stipulation was that Hearst might not ask him any questions concerning his private life.* V+O/REPORT-CL/QUOTE = specify; ◊ N COUNT/UNCOUNT

stir /stɜː/, **stirs, stirring, stirred**. 1 When you **stir** a liquid, you mix it inside a container by moving something such as a spoon around in it with a circular motion. EG *The sauce should be stirred constantly with a wooden spoon.* ▸ used as a noun. EG *I think the soup needs a stir.* V+O ⇑ move; ▸ N COUNT : USU a+SING
2 If you **stir**, you move slightly, for example because you are restless, uncomfortable, or beginning to wake up. EG *The boys stirred uneasily, as though something indecent had happened... Etta didn't stir, pretending to be asleep... I read it through to the end without stirring from the table.* V = shift
3 If something, especially the wind, **stirs** an object, it makes it move gently. EG *A stray breath of wind stirred the stillness of the robes.* V+O = disturb
4 If you **stir** yourself or **stir** someone else, you move yourself in order to do something, or make someone else start doing something. EG *I just couldn't stir myself enough to get out of bed... Stir yourself, or we'll never get this finished!... The committee found another issue to stir it back into action.* ● If someone tells you to **stir** your **stumps**, they are telling you to move and start to do something; an old-fashioned informal expression. EG *Come on, stir your stumps, there's lots to do!* V+O (NG/REFL) = shift; ● PHR : USU IMPER = look lively
5 If something beautiful or terrible **stirs** you, it makes you react with a strong emotion. EG *There was a particular passage which always stirred him profoundly... ...stirred by the beauties of nature... He was deeply stirred by the appalling conditions.* V+O = move, affect
6 If something such as an event causes a **stir**, it causes great excitement, shock, or anger among a number of people. EG *Her speech created a huge stir... We made a bit of a stir–it was quite exciting... They wanted to avoid anything that would cause a stir.* N SING WITH DET = commotion
7 If a particular mood, feeling, or idea **stirs** in someone, they begin to feel it or think about it. EG *The political debate was reopened and a new mood was stirring... Something seemed to stir within her.* V : USU+A = awaken
8 If you say that someone **is stirring**, you mean that they are deliberately trying to cause trouble in an unpleasant way; used informally showing disapproval. EG *Just ignore him, he's only stirring!* V OR V+O : USU CONT
9 ● See also **stirring**.

stir in. If you **stir** a substance **into** a liquid or if you **stir** it **in**, you put it into the liquid and mix it by moving something such as a spoon around in it with a circular motion. EG *When the yeast is dissolved, stir the flour in gradually.* PHRASAL VB : V+O+ADV, OR V+O+PREP, HAS PASS ⇑ add

stir up. 1 If a force **stirs up** something such as dust on the ground or mud on the bottom of a river, it causes it to rise up and move around, making the air or water cloudy. EG *Some gentle winds stirred up the dust... His movements stirred up the mud and sand, blinding him as he swam along the river bottom.* PHRASAL VB : V+O+ADV = disturb
2 If you **stir up** trouble or a particular feeling, you cause trouble or cause people to have this feeling, by doing things such as talking in public or writing letters which people react to in a strong way. EG *He was prevented from speaking on the grounds that it would 'stir up trouble'... ...a rally called to stir up popular support for nuclear disarmament... Being back in the hospital stirred up unpleasant memories... She was one of those people who likes stirring things up.* PHRASAL VB : V+O+ADV ⇑ encourage

stir-fry, stir-fries, stir-frying, stir-fried. If you **stir-fry** vegetables, meat, etc, you cook small pieces of them quickly by stirring them in a small quantity of very hot oil. This method is often used in Chinese cookery. ▸ used as an adjective to describe food cooked in this way. EG *...stir-fry vegetables.* V OR V+O; ▸ ADJ CLASSIF : ATTRIB

stirrer /stɜːrə/, **stirrers**. If you refer to someone as a **stirrer**, you mean that they deliberately cause trouble whenever they can. N COUNT

stirring /stɜːrɪŋ/, **stirrings**. 1 A **stirring** speech, occasion, etc, produces strong feelings of admiration or excitement. EG *You made a very stirring speech... They must have been stirring times.* ADJ QUALIT = rousing, inspiring
2 The **stirring** of a feeling or thought is the beginning and growth of one. EG *There was a slight stirring of interest among them now... ...deep stirrings of unease... ...stirrings of nationalist revolt.* N COUNT/UNCOUNT : USU+*of* ⇑ development

stirrup /stɪrəp/, **stirrups**. **Stirrups** are a pair of metal loops which are attached to either side of a horse's saddle by a long piece of leather and which you put your feet through when riding the horse. N COUNT

stitch /stɪtʃ/, **stitches, stitching, stitched**. 1 If you **stitch** material, you push a needle and thread in and out through it in order to join two pieces together or to make a decoration. EG *They were cut out and stitched together rather than pinned... She picked up her embroidery and started stitching... ...finely stitched collars.* V OR V+O ⇑ sew
2 A **stitch** is 2.1 one of the short pieces of thread that can be seen on a piece of material when it has been stitched. EG *...all marvellously hand-sewn with ten or twelve stitches to the inch.* **2.2** a loop made by one turn of the wool around a knitting needle or crochet hook. EG *Oh dear! I've dropped a stitch... You should now have 57 stitches on the needle.* **2.3** a particular way of doing stitches when you are sewing or knitting, which produces a particular pattern. EG *Moss stitch is done by alternating groups of plain and purl stitches... ...a cloth embroidered in chain stitch.* N COUNT; N COUNT; N MASS : MOD+N
3 When a doctor **stitches** or **stitches up** a deep cut in someone's skin, he or she uses a special needle and thread to join the edges of it together so that it will heal. EG *You'll have to go to the casualty department and have this stitched... The doctor stitched up the finger.* V+O, OR PHRASAL VB : V+O+ADV = suture
4 A **stitch** is also one turn of a special piece of thread that a doctor uses to join the edges of a deep cut together. EG *He had to go to hospital and have twenty stitches in his face.* N COUNT = suture
5 If you have a **stitch** or if you have the **stitch**, you feel a sharp pain in your side, usually as a result of running very fast or laughing a lot. EG *I can't run any more, I've got a stitch.* N SING WITH DET
6 If you are **in stitches**, you are laughing uncontrollably; an informal expression. EG *We were in stitches–we could hardly stand up it was so funny!* PHR : USED AS A
7 Someone who **does not have a stitch on, has not got a stitch on**, etc is not wearing any clothes at all; an informal expression. PHR : VB INFLECTS ⇑ naked
8 **'A stitch in time'** or **'A stitch in time saves nine'** is a saying that you use to suggest that someone should do something about a problem as soon as it appears because it will only get worse if it is left until later. PHR

stitching /stɪtʃɪŋ/ is a row of stitches that have been sewn in a piece of material. EG *It pulled his suit with enough force to break the stitching.* N UNCOUNT ⇑ sewing

stoat /stəʊt/, **stoats**. A **stoat** is a small wild animal that has brown fur and is similar to a weasel. Some stoats that live in northern Europe have fur that turns white in winter. N COUNT

stock /stɒk/, **stocks, stocking, stocked.** 1 **Stocks** are shares which are large parts of the ownership of a company or industry and which can be bought as an investment. EG *Heavy bidding for oil company stocks may be just beginning... You may be able to offer stocks and shares as security.* N COUNT : USU PL

2 The **stock** of a company is the amount of money which the company has through selling shares to people. EG *They had acquired 48.5 per cent of Continental's stock... ...seeking about 51 per cent of the stock for £85 a share... Companies deposited a controlling slice of their stock with trustees.* N UNCOUNT ⇑ capital

3 A shop, library, factory, etc that **stocks** particular goods keeps a supply of these goods ready to sell or to lend to customers. EG *Several shops in London stock or deal exclusively in large fittings... The library didn't stock zoology textbooks... It's the only shop I know round here that stocks pure silk.* V+O : NO CONT ⇑ store

4 The **stock** that a shop has is the total amount of goods which are available to be sold in the shop. EG *...selling out a week's worth of stock in a single day of panic buying.* N UNCOUNT • Goods that are **in stock** are stored in a shop, factory, etc and available to be sold to customers. EG *I hope we've got some more of those in stock.* • PHR : USED AS AN A • Goods that are **out of stock** are not available to be sold to customers because the supplies have all been sold already. EG *You can't buy it because it's out of stock.* • PHR : USED AS AN A

5 If you **stock** or **stock up** a container such as a cupboard, freezer, or shelf, you fill it with food or other appropriate goods. EG *Buying and stocking a deep freeze is a major expense... His toolbox was always stocked with a quantity of cheap brass screws... The fridge was carefully stocked up with food... ...part-time work stocking shelves in supermarkets.* V+O, OR PHRASAL VB : V+O+ADV

6 If a stream or lake **is stocked**, it is filled with fish so that people can go fishing. EG *We have quite a good stream on the property. It's stocked every year.* V+O : USU PASS

7 If you have a **stock** of particular things, you have a supply of them stored and ready to be used. EG *Keep a stock of plug fuses... He was smoking a cigar (one of the last of the stock he had brought with him)... They want to conserve coal stocks during the miners' strike... This required the destruction of existing stocks of weapons.* N COUNT+SUPP : SING=PL

8 The **stock** of something is the total amount of it which is available in a particular area. EG *You have to have a look at the whole of the housing stock... ...the progressive destruction of the Third World's stock of trees.* N SING WITH DET +SUPP ⇑ supply

9 The **stock** that a person or animal is from is the original group of people or animals of a particular type from which they have descended. EG *You come from sturdy, peasant stock... They were of European stock... The two groups sprang from common stock... Marsupials were developing from the early mammal stock.* N UNCOUNT/COUNT : USU MOD +N ⇑ descent

10 **Stock** are animals, especially cattle, sheep, or pigs, which are kept by a farmer; often used when considering the quality of a herd which has been specially bred. EG *There was a sale of dairy stock at Bishop's Stortford... The boar soon improved our stock.* N PLURAL ⇑ livestock

11 The **stock** of a rifle or air gun is the triangular-shaped handle which you hold against your shoulder in order to steady the gun when you are firing it. EG *...two sawn-off gun stocks... The rifle had been cut down and fitted with a special stock.* N COUNT = butt

12 **Stock** is a liquid which you make by boiling meat, bones, or vegetables in water, and which is used to give soups and sauces a stronger flavour. EG *...beef stock.* N MASS

13 A **stock** is a plant which has lots of small pink, white, or mauve flowers with a strong sweet scent. There are several kinds of stocks. N COUNT

14 Someone's **stock** is the degree of status and popularity that they have; a rather old-fashioned use. EG *I told him that his stock was now so high in this town he couldn't lose.* N UNCOUNT : POSS +N

15 In former times, the **stocks** were used as an instrument of punishment. The victim's hands and legs were locked into holes in a wooden frame, and they were forced to sit in public like this, often while people threw things at them. N PLURAL : USU *the*+N

16 A **stock** idea, expression, or way of behaving is one that is very common or typical of a particular person or group because they have used it or done it so much. EG *'Wild and wanton' was a stock undergraduate phrase of the time... It was quite out of keeping with the stock character she was supposed to impersonate... ...the stock pastimes, the 'things that are done'.* ADJ CLASSIF : ATTRIB

17 If you **take stock**, you think about all the aspects of something that has happened and what it means, often so that you can decide what to do about it. EG *The emergency committees had a chance to take stock of the situation... This gave him time to take stock of what he had overheard.* PHR : VB INFLECTS, USU+*of* ⇑ appraise = consider

18 If you **put stock** in something such as a person's work, you have a high opinion of it. EG *Do you put a lot of stock in language lab work?* PHR : VB INFLECTS ⇑ value

19 See also **laughing stock.** • **lock, stock, and barrel**: see **lock.**

stock up. If you **stock up** with things, you buy a lot of them so that you have them available, often because there is going to be a shortage or because you will not be able to go shopping very often. EG *Stock up now on alternative methods of lighting... Stock up with groceries and canned foods.* PHRASAL VB : V+ADV

stockade /stɒkeɪd/, **stockades.** A **stockade** is a wall of large wooden posts built round an area to keep out enemies or wild animals. EG *...huts protected by an enormous high stockade of wood interlaced with branches.* N COUNT ⇑ fence

stockbroker /stɒkbrəʊkə/, **stockbrokers.** A **stockbroker** is a person whose job is to buy and sell stocks and shares for people who want to invest money. N COUNT ⇑ broker

stock-car, stock-cars. A **stock-car** is an old car which has had changes made to it to make it suitable for races on a small track, in which the cars often collide. N COUNT

stock cube, stock cubes. A **stock cube** is a solid cube made from dried meat or vegetable juices and other flavourings. Stock cubes are used for adding flavour to stews, soups, etc. N COUNT ⇑ seasoning

stock exchange, stock exchanges. A **stock exchange** is a place where an organization of professional people buy and sell stocks and shares; also used of the organization itself and the trading activity that goes on there. EG *Prices on the New York Stock Exchange staged a rally... She speculated successfully on the stock exchange.* N COUNT/PROPER : USU *the* +N = stock market

stockholder /stɒkhəʊldə/, **stockholders.** A **stockholder** is 1 a shareholder; used mainly in American English. EG *Her father is the majority stockholder in an oil company... This would have realized more than $60 a share for stockholders.* N COUNT 2 a person who owns some of a company's stock. N COUNT

stocking /stɒkɪŋ/, **stockings. Stockings** are two pieces of clothing, worn by women and made of a thin stretchy material such as nylon, which fit closely round each foot and leg up to the top part of the thigh. They are usually held in place by suspenders. EG *...a woman in a flowered skirt and black stockings and shoes.* • See also **body stocking.** N COUNT : USU PL ⇑ hosiery

stockinged /stɒkɪŋd/. Someone who is in their **stockinged** feet is wearing socks, stockings, or tights, but no shoes. EG *I stood five and a half feet tall in my stockinged feet.* ADJ CLASSIF : ATTRIB ⇑ clothed

stock-in-trade; also spelled without hyphens. Someone's **stock-in-trade** is the way in which they typically behave, or a job which they typically have to do. EG *Tony was the master of eloquent cynicism; it was his stock in trade... Complaints were a stock-in-trade of an airport manager's job.* N SING : WITH POSS ⇑ routine

stockist /stɒkɪst/, **stockists.** A **stockist** of a particular brand or type of goods is someone who sells this brand or type in their shop; used in British English. EG *Try your nearest Moulinex stockist.* N COUNT ⇑ retailer

stock market, stock markets. A **stock market** is an organization of professional people who buy and sell stocks and shares; also used of the trading activity of these people and the place where they work. EG *Prices have risen sharply on the stock market... ...the Financial Times's list of stock-market prices.* N COUNT : USU *the*+N = stock exchange

stockpile /stɒkpaɪl/, **stockpiles, stockpiling, stockpiled.** 1 If people **stockpile** things such as food or weapons, they store large quantities of them so that they can use them whenever they are needed. EG *...equipment stockpiled by local author-* V+O = accumulate *ities... ...a convention banning the development, production and stockpiling of biological weapons.*

2 A **stockpile** is a large quantity of things such as food or weapons, which are stored so that they can be used whenever they are needed. EG *...a stockpile of canned food and first aid supplies.* — N COUNT: USU+SUPP ⇑ store

stockroom /stɒkru[4]m/, **stockrooms**; also spelled with a hyphen. A **stockroom** is a room, for example in a shop or factory, where a stock of goods is kept. — N COUNT

stock-still; also spelled as two words. A person or animal that is standing **stock-still** is not moving at all. EG *He stood stock-still and stared at the approaching tank.* — ADV AFTER VB = motionless

stocktaking /stɒkteɪkɪŋ/; also spelled with a hyphen. **Stocktaking** is 1 a thorough check made on all the goods in a shop in order to count them and make sure the records are correct. EG *We're closed for stocktaking on Thursday.* — N UNCOUNT ⇑ checking 2 thinking about your situation and the things you have done, in order to help you consider what to do in the future. EG *It will be a time of stocktaking and good resolutions.* — N UNCOUNT ⇑ review

stocky /stɒki[1]/, **stockier, stockiest**. Someone who is **stocky** is broad and solid in appearance. EG *He was short and stocky... He was stockier and more muscular than his father.* — ADJ QUALIT = thickset

stodge /stɒdʒ/ is food which contains a lot of starch and makes you feel very full, for example potatoes, rice, and suet pudding; used showing disapproval. EG *It's pure stodge, that's why I'm putting on pounds.* — N UNCOUNT

stodgy /stɒdʒi[1]/, **stodgier, stodgiest**. 1 **Stodgy** food is full of starch and makes you feel very full; used showing disapproval. EG *...drowsiness induced by a stodgy meal.* — ADJ QUALIT ⇑ starchy

2 Someone or something that is **stodgy** is serious and boring; used showing disapproval. EG *The fellow was stodgy and solemn.* — ADJ QUALIT = dreary

stoic /stəʊɪk/ or **stoical** /stəʊɪkə[0]l/, **stoics**; a fairly formal word. The form **stoical** can only be used for the meaning in paragraph 1. 1 If you behave in a **stoic** or **stoical** way, you suffer hardship without showing your emotions. EG *I admired her stoic patience... I saw passengers staring out with stoic resignation... Ali was the sad and stoic clown... He knew how brave and stoical an explorer had to be... She was brave, independent, and sometimes stoical.* — ADJ QUALIT ⇑ stolid

◊ **stoically**. EG *They seem stoically resigned to their fate.* — ◊ ADV WITH VB ⇑ impassively

2 A **stoic** is someone who suffers hardship without showing their emotions. — N COUNT

stoicism /stəʊɪsɪzə[0]m/ is a way of behaving in which you are steady and unchanging and do not show your emotions when you are suffering hardship; a fairly formal word. EG *He endured this treatment with stoicism... ...an incredible stoicism displayed in the face of economic difficulties.* — N UNCOUNT

stoke /stəʊk/, **stokes, stoking, stoked**. 1 If you **stoke** a fire or if you **stoke** it **up**, you add coal or wood to it or you make it burn faster and hotter by moving the coal or wood with a stick or a poker. EG *...it was the caretaker's job to stoke the furnace... The servants were there to stoke up coal fires.* — V+O, OR PHRASAL VB: V+O+ADV ⇑ heat up

2 If you **stoke** a particular feeling or idea, or if you **stoke** it **up**, you encourage people to feel more excited, angry, or enthusiastic about it. EG *...but Philip was still stoking his anger... ...stoking up popular prejudice.* — V+O, OR PHRASAL VB: V+O+ADV ⇑ stir = fuel

stole /stəʊl/, **stoles**. 1 **Stole** is the past tense of **steal**.

2 A **stole** is a long scarf or shawl worn by women. — N COUNT

stolen /stəʊlə[0]n/ is the past participle of **steal**.

stolid /stɒlɪd/. Someone who is **stolid** is rather solemn and does not show any emotion or interest in anything. EG *He was a rather stolid, serious type.* — ADJ QUALIT ⇑ solid = phlegmatic ▸ used of a person's actions or behaviour. EG *Every step he took was stolid and careful.* ◊ **stolidly**. EG *Vita was stolidly and uncompromisingly British.* — ◊ ADV WITH VB

stomach /stʌmək/, **stomachs, stomaching, stomached**. 1 The **stomach** of a person or an animal is an organ inside the body where food is digested before it moves into the intestines. In humans it is situated inside the ribs and underneath the lungs. EG *Cows have seven stomachs... In this country an animal has to wander far to fill its stomach... His stomach started to growl with hunger.* — N COUNT = belly, insides ▸ also used to refer to this part of your body when it feels uncomfortable because you are afraid or worried. EG *His stomach knotted with fright... ...the worry in the pit of your stomach.*

2 Your **stomach** is also the part of the front of your body below your waist. EG *He folded his arms on his rather large stomach.* — N COUNT ⇑ abdomen = belly

3 If you are able to **stomach** something, you are able to accept it without feeling disapproval or strong dislike. EG *I just couldn't stomach his childishness... You never could stomach the idea of living in Hull, could you?* — V+O: USU AFTER MODAL ⇑ tolerate = abide, bear

4 If you **have no stomach for** something such as a type of food or an activity, you find it very unpleasant and have no desire or appetite for it. EG *I've no stomach for boxing... I'm afraid I've no stomach for seafood.* — PHR: VB INFLECTS ⇑ dislike

5 If something **turns** your **stomach** or **makes** your **stomach turn**, it is so horrible or unpleasant that it makes you feel as if you are going to be sick. EG *It turned my stomach to see the corpses all laid out.* — PHR: VB INFLECTS

● **butterflies in** your **stomach**: see **butterfly**.

stomach-ache, stomach-aches. If you have a **stomach-ache**, you have a pain in your stomach, for example because you have eaten too quickly or because you have eaten something bad. EG *Then Tanya got a stomach-ache and asked to be excused.* — N COUNT

stomach pump, stomach pumps. A **stomach pump** is a pump with a long tube that is pushed down someone's throat into their stomach so that the contents can be removed. Doctors use it when people have eaten poisonous substances or taken an overdose of pills. — N COUNT

stomp /stɒmp/, **stomps, stomping, stomped**. 1 If you **stomp** somewhere, you walk with very heavy steps, for example when you are annoyed about something. EG *Michael stomped off home... Who's stomping around up there?* — V+A ▸ used as a noun. EG *I heard the stomp of infant feet coming downstairs.* — ▸ N SING WITH DET

2 To **stomp** your foot means the same as to stamp it; used in American English. — V+O

stone /stəʊn/, **stones, stoning, stoned**. The form **stone** can also be used as a plural in paragraph 5 if you are stating a weight or if the noun is in modifier position. 1 **Stone** is a hard, dry substance which is dug out of the ground, and which is often used for building houses and walls. EG *...houses of grey stone... You have to wonder at the fantastic accuracy with which they worked the stone... ...a stone wall... ...stone steps.* — N MASS ⇑ rock

2 A **stone** is 2.1 a small piece of rock which you find on the surface of the ground. EG *I stubbed my toe against a stone... Roger picked up a stone and threw it at Henry.* — N COUNT = pebble 2.2 a large piece of stone specially put somewhere in memory of a person or event, or as a religious symbol. Some stones have writing on them. EG *I sat on one of the stones and peeled some moss off the inscription... These two square carved stones are pieces of Saxon crosses.* — N COUNT 2.3 a jewel, especially one in a ring or necklace. EG *...a ring with a white stone in it.* — N COUNT = gem 2.4 a small hard ball consisting of minerals and other substances which sometimes forms in a person's kidneys or gall bladder, and which is very painful. — N COUNT 2.5 a large, hard seed which is in the middle of some types of fruit, such as cherries, dates, and apricots. — N COUNT ⇑ pip

3 If you **stone** a piece of fruit, you remove the stone from it. EG *I didn't have time to stone the dates.* — V+O

4 If people **stone** someone, they throw a lot of stones at them, for example as a punishment. EG *Widows were forbidden to remarry and were stoned to death if they did... Cars were being stoned and fired on.* — V+O

5 A **stone** is also a measurement of weight which is equal to 14 pounds, or 6.35 kilograms; used especially to say how heavy a person is. EG *She weighed twelve stone... She had put on over a stone.* — N COUNT/PART: a/NUM+N

6 You use **stone** in expressions such as 'to be made of stone' or 'a heart of stone' when you are describing someone who does not show their feelings or someone who shows no pity or sympathy. EG *I was just getting near to accepting the fact that my father was made of stone... She must have a heart of stone to refuse them like that.* — N UNCOUNT

7 **Stone** pottery is made of very hard clay. EG *...a stone marmalade jar.* — ADJ CLASSIF: ATTRIB

8 If you **leave no stone unturned**, you try every way you can think of in order to achieve what you want. EG *They left no stone unturned in their search for the money.* — PHR: VB INFLECTS

9 If you say that a distance is a **stone's throw** or that something is a **stone's throw** away, you mean that it is not very far. EG *They live within a stone's throw of the school... The hospital is only a stone's throw away.* PHR : USED AS O

10 See also **stoned, cornerstone, foundation stone, paving stone, precious stone, stepping stone.**

11 • **to kill two birds with one stone**: see **bird.** • **to get blood from a stone**: see **blood.** • **a rolling stone gathers no moss**: see **moss.**

Stone Age. The **Stone Age** is the earliest known period of human history when people used tools and weapons made of stone. N PROPER : the+N ⇑ epoch

stonebreaker /stəʊnbreɪkə/, **stonebreakers**. A **stonebreaker** is a machine which breaks large pieces of stone into smaller pieces so that they can be used for making roads. N COUNT

stone-cold. **1** Something that is **stone-cold** is very cold indeed. EG *...stone-cold coffee.* ADJ CLASSIF

2 If someone is **stone-cold sober**, they are completely sober; an informal expression. PHR : USED AS C

stoned /stəʊnd/; a very informal word. If someone is **stoned**, **1** they are very drunk. **2** heavily affected by drugs. ADJ CLASSIF / ADJ CLASSIF

stone deaf; also spelled with a hyphen. Someone who is **stone deaf** is completely deaf. EG *I had an infection of the ears that made me stone deaf for some time.* ADJ CLASSIF

stone-ground; also spelled as one word. **Stone-ground** grain has been crushed between two large, heavy pieces of stone. EG *...stone-ground wheat.* ▸ used to describe flour or bread which has been made with this grain. EG *Make your own stone-ground, wholewheat bread.* ADJ CLASSIF

stonemason /stəʊnmeɪsəⁿn/, **stonemasons**. A **stonemason** is a person who is skilled at cutting and preparing stone so that it can be used for building walls and buildings. N COUNT ⇑ craftsman = mason

stonewall /stəʊnwɔːl/, **stonewalls, stonewalling, stonewalled**. If you **stonewall**, you talk for a long time or ask a lot of questions in order to prevent other people from giving their opinions, or to make a discussion last for a long time. EG *He was stonewalling and everybody knew it.* V OR V+O = filibuster

stoneware /stəʊnweə/. **Stoneware** is very hard earthenware pottery which is baked at a high temperature. N UNCOUNT

stonework /stəʊnwɜːk/ consists of pieces of stone which have been skilfully shaped and joined together as part of a wall or building. EG *A few pillars of stonework still remained.* N UNCOUNT : IF DET THEN the+N = masonry

stony /stəʊni¹/, **stonier, stoniest**. **1 Stony** ground is rough and contains a lot of stones. EG *The ground here had always been too steep and stony for the plough... ...a stony lane.* ADJ QUALIT

2 A **stony** voice, face, attitude, etc shows no pity, sympathy, or friendliness. EG *Her voice was stony... Kurt was shocked into stony silence... She considered throwing herself upon his stony mercy.* ADJ QUALIT ⇑ cold = icy

3 Something that is **stony** is like stone in hardness or colour. EG *These corals secrete lime, forming stony cushions... ...a stony greyness.* ADJ QUALIT ⇑ hard

stony-broke. If you are **stony-broke**, you have no money at all; used in informal English. ADJ CLASSIF : PRED = penniless

stood /stʊd/ is the past tense and past participle of **stand**.

stooge /stuːdʒ/, **stooges**. A **stooge** is **1** a person who is used by someone in a superior position to do jobs which are unpleasant or dishonest; used in informal English. EG *I think he hopes to use me as one of his stooges.* **2** a person who takes part in a comedy act and gives other performers the opportunity to make jokes at his or her expense. EG *His stage stooge changed from year to year.* N COUNT ⇑ subordinate / N COUNT ⇑ entertainer = straight man

stool /stuːl/, **stools**. A **stool** is a seat with legs but no support for your arms or back. EG *He was sitting on a stool in the kitchen.* N COUNT

stoolpigeon /stuːlpɪdʒɪn/, **stoolpigeons**. A **stoolpigeon** is a criminal who gives the police information about other criminals. N COUNT ⇑ informer = grass

stoop /stuːp/, **stoops, stooping, stooped**. **1** If you **stoop**, **1.1** you stand or walk with your back and shoulders bent forward and downward. EG *If your ironing board is too low you have to stoop over it... Tall people often stoop in order to make themselves look shorter.* ▸ used as a noun. EG *Bradshaw had a kind of literary stoop... My aunt walks with a stoop.* V : USU+A (over) = hunch ▸ N COUNT : USU SING

◇ **stooping**. EG *...his gaunt, slightly stooping figure.*

1.2 you bend your body down from the waist or from the knees, usually so that you can pick something up from the ground or avoid a low roof. EG *Then he stooped, picked up his case, and waited... The girl stooped down to pick up the two pebbles.* V : USU+A (down)

2 If you **stoop** to doing something, you lower your usual standards of behaviour in order to do it; used showing disapproval. EG *...his refusal to stoop to insulting his political enemies... The depths to which newspapers will stoop to get a story never fails to astound me... Only once did he stoop to the tactics of his opponents... I honestly think he would stoop to anything.* V+to+-ING, OR V+to-INF, ORDER TO V+O = condescend, lower yourself

3 When a bird of prey **stoops**, it flies down quickly and steeply. V = swoop

4 A **stoop** is also a small platform at the door of a building, with steps leading up to it; used in American English. EG *An imposing house with two marble pillars and a marble stoop.* N COUNT = porch

stop /stɒp/, **stops, stopping, stopped**. **1** If you have been doing something and then you **stop** doing it, you no longer do it. EG *We all stopped talking... He couldn't stop crying... She put the key in the keyhole, began turning it, and then she stopped... Writing is a continual process of stopping and starting... She shouted to us to stop all the noise... She stopped work to have her baby.* V, V+-ING, OR V+O = cease, finish, quit

2 If you **stop** someone or something, you prevent someone from doing something or prevent something from happening. EG *You're trying to stop my trip to London... Does putting people in prison stop crime?... How do I stop a tap dripping?... Did any of them try to stop you coming?... Nothing was going to stop Sandy from being a writer... He broke two plates before I could stop him... He was about to say something, but stopped himself.* V+O (NG/REFL), OR V+O (NG/REFL)+-ING/A (from)

3 You tell someone to **stop** when you want them not to continue doing something. EG *'Stop,' I said. 'It makes me nervous.'... Ow! Stop it! You're hurting!... Stop that, you kids.* EXCLAM = don't

4 If something such as an activity or process **stops**, it comes to an end. EG *The music stopped abruptly... They were waiting for the rain to stop... My breathing almost stopped as I listened.* V = cease, finish

5 If a machine or device **stops** or if you **stop** it, it no longer works or it is switched off. EG *My watch has stopped... Can you stop the engine?... It might be a good idea to stop the recording now... When your heart stops they call it cardiac arrest.* V-ERG OR V

6 If you are walking or moving somewhere and then you **stop**, you no longer walk or move but stand still. EG *He followed them for a few yards, and then stopped... She stopped and stared at the poster.* V : NO CONT = halt, pause

7 If a vehicle **stops** or if you **stop** it, it comes to rest after moving along. EG *The lorry couldn't stop... The train stopped at Watford... Stop the car and let me out... I can't stop here, it's on a corner.* V OR V-ERG

8 If you **stop** a vehicle, you signal for it to stop or force it to stop. EG *I raised my hand and stopped another cab... A police roadblock stopped a private car containing four men.* V+O

9 If you **stop** someone, **9.1** you go up to them and speak to them. EG *Stop a thousand people in Oxford Street and ask them to fill in the questionnaire.* **9.2** you prevent them from continuing their journey, for example because you suspect that they may have done something wrong. EG *Somebody had been stopped at London airport with 50,000 pounds worth of heroin.* V+O ⇑ approach / V+O ⇑ arrest

10 A **stop** is **10.1** a place where buses, trains, etc regularly stop so that people can get on and off. EG *Turn left at the bus stop... We'll get off at the next stop.* **10.2** a time or place at which you stop during a journey. EG *We wondered where the next stop would be... The first stop in our itinerary was a hotel outside Paris.* N COUNT / N COUNT = break, rest

11 A **stop** is also the state of no longer moving; used in expressions like 'come to a stop' and 'bring to a stop'. EG *The elevator came to a stop on the main floor... The bus rolled to a stop... Harris brought the plane to a stop.* N SING : a+N = halt, standstill

12 If you **put a stop to** something, you prevent it from happening or continuing. EG *I am going to put a stop to this once and for all... Let's put a stop to all this nonsense.* PHR : VB INFLECTS

13 If you **stop** somewhere, you stay there for a short V : USU+A while in order to see someone or to do something, often while you are on a journey to somewhere else. EG *On my way home I stopped at the shop... We had to find somewhere to stop for lunch... I can go and stop with my brother for a couple of days... 'Won't you take off your coat?'–'Thanks, but I can't stop.'*

14 If a road, sea, region, etc, **stops** somewhere, it goes no further than that place. EG *At Norwich the road stops.* — V : IF+PREP THEN *at* ⇑ end = finish

15 If you say that a quality or state **stops** somewhere, you mean that it is true or exists up to that point, and no further. EG *Heroism began where politics stopped.* — V : IF+PREP THEN *at* = end

16 If someone **stops** something such as money, gas, electricity, etc, they prevent it from being paid or received. EG *The farmer stopped my pay because it was raining... She stopped the cheque before I had managed to cash it... If you don't deal with that bill quickly, they might stop your electricity.* — V+O

17 If you **stop** or if something **stops** you, you no longer continue talking or reading something aloud. EG *I read it to her without stopping... Stop there a second, will you?... A commotion out in the hall stopped Meadows in mid-sentence.* — V-ERG ⇑ wait = pause, halt

18 You can use **stop** with other verbs in expressions like 'stop to think' and 'stop and listen', in order to indicate that someone is taking time to think, listen, etc and giving their attention to something. EG *I didn't stop to think where the money was coming from... We seldom stop to consider how few of the friends we have really do care... It might have made people stop and listen.* — V+*to*-INF, OR V+*and*+V ⇑ wait = pause

19 A **stop** is also the same as a full stop. EG *She does not always see what makes a sentence, and puts stops in the wrong place.* — N COUNT = period

20 The **stops** on an organ are the knobs at the side, which you pull or push to control the type of musical sound that comes out of the organ pipes. — N COUNT

21 To **stop** a tooth means to fill it, for example when it is decaying and has a hole in it. — V+O

22 The word **stop** is also used in the following expressions. **22.1** If you **stop dead** or **stop in** your **tracks**, you stop walking suddenly, as if you are shocked or frightened. EG *Mr Boggis saw it at once, and he stopped dead... He stopped in his tracks and glared at me... It can stop you in your tracks.* — PHR : VB INFLECTS **22.2** If someone **knows where** or **when to stop**, they are in control of their behaviour so that they are able to stop behaving in a way that offends, upsets, or irritates people. EG *He doesn't know when to stop... Like most sensible people, they know where to stop.* — PHR : VB INFLECTS
22.3 If you would **stop at nothing**, you are prepared to take any risks and even do things that are wrong, in order to get or achieve what you want. — PHR **22.4** If you **pull all the stops out**, you do everything possible to make something happen successfully; an informal expression. EG *We pulled all the stops out for our daughter's 21st birthday party.* — PHR : VB INFLECTS

23 • to **stop short**: see **short**.

stop by. If you **stop by**, you visit somewhere for a short time; an informal use. EG *Are you feeling better now, or shall I ask the doctor to stop by on her way home?... She stopped by my place the other day.* — PHRASAL VB : V+ADV/PREP = drop by

stop in. If you **stop in**, you stay at home rather than going out; used in informal British English. — PHRASAL VB : V+ADV

stop off. If you **stop off** somewhere, you stop there for a short time in the middle of a journey. EG *On the way home I stopped off in London to attend a conference.* — PHRASAL VB : V+ADV

stop out. If you **stop out**, you stay out late rather than coming home; used in informal British English. EG *Billie stopped out all night last Saturday.* — PHRASAL VB : V+ADV

stop over. If you **stop over** somewhere, you stay there for one or more nights in between two parts of a journey, especially a plane journey. • See also **stopover**. — PHRASAL VB : V+ADV ⇑ wait

stop up. **1** If you **stop** something **up**, you cover or fill a hole or gap in it. EG *Stop up each breach as it occurs... I need to have a couple of teeth stopped up.* — PHRASAL VB : V+O+ADV = block

2 If you **stop up**, you go to bed much later than usual, for example because there is something you want to do; used in informal British English. EG *I stopped up to watch the match.* — PHRASAL VB : V+ADV

stopcock /stɒpkɒk/, **stopcocks**. A **stopcock** is a tap on a pipe, which you turn in order to allow something to pass through the pipe or to stop it from passing through. EG *I turned the stopcock on the tank for a little gas.* — N COUNT = valve

stopgap /stɒpgæp/, **stopgaps**; also spelled with a hyphen. Someone or something that acts as a **stopgap** fills a particular job, position, or need for a short time, but is replaced as soon as possible. EG *After her death the committee appointed her deputy as a stopgap... ...a stop-gap measure.* — N COUNT, USU SING = temporary

stopover /stɒpəʊvə/, **stopovers**. A **stopover** is a short stay in a particular place between parts of a long journey. EG *...a five-week tour abroad with a three-day stopover in the United States.* — N COUNT : USU SING = stop

stoppage /stɒpɪdʒ/, **stoppages**. **1** **Stoppages** are **1.1** strikes in which people either stop working or prevent goods from being delivered, transport from being used, etc. EG *There was a nationwide eruption of strikes and industrial stoppages.* — N COUNT : USU PL = action **1.2** amounts of money that your employer takes from your wages or salary to pay your tax, national insurance, pension, etc. EG *How much do you get after stoppages?* — N COUNT : USU PL = deduction

2 **Stoppage** is the act of preventing something from moving or the state of being prevented from moving; a formal use. EG *...the stoppage of the flow of oil from the North Sea.* — N UNCOUNT+SUPP = blocking

stopper /stɒpə/, **stoppers**. The **stopper** of a bottle or jar is the thing that fits into the top of it to prevent the contents from spilling. EG *She lifted the stopper from the carafe.* — N COUNT

stop press; also spelled with a hyphen. The **stop press** is the most recent news, which is inserted into a special space on the front or back page of a newspaper after the rest of the newspaper has been printed. — N SING : *the*+N ⇑ report

stopwatch /stɒpwɒtʃ/, **stopwatches**. A **stopwatch** is a watch that you use to measure the time that passes during a particular event such as a race. You press buttons to start and stop the watch whenever you want to. — N COUNT ⇑ timer

storage /stɔːrɪdʒ/. **1** Something that is in **storage** is being kept in a special place until it is needed. EG *A quarter of the crop may be lost in storage... If you haven't much storage space, stack shoes on plastic racks.* — N UNCOUNT

2 **Storage** is also **2.1** the keeping of something in store until it is needed. EG *Storage so far has proved rather expensive... Ask in advance what the cost of storage and insurance will be.* — N UNCOUNT **2.2** the process of storing facts, knowledge, data, etc in a computer. EG *Computers have a storage capacity greater than the human memory.* — N UNCOUNT : USU BEFORE N

store /stɔː/, **stores, storing, stored**. **1** A **store** is **1.1** a shop; used especially in American English, although you can use 'store' in British English, particularly if you say what kind of shop it is. EG *She came out of the store and sat down on the bench... I've discovered a marvellous health-food store in Birmingham.* — N COUNT **1.2** a very large shop which sells a lot of different types of goods. EG *...the largest department store... ...smart stores like Harrods.* • See also **chain store**. — N COUNT

2 When you **store** things or **store** them **away**, you put them away and keep them until they are needed. EG *I did not have the space to store the bricks... The goods were stored away at the back of the warehouse... One could store all the energy from the sun during the summer months.* — V+O, OR PHRASAL VB : V+O+ADV

3 When you **store** facts, knowledge, data, etc, you keep them in your brain or in a computer. EG *He stored the knowledge somewhere in his fearsome memory... A computer can store and remember a great deal of information.* — V+O ⇑ retain

4 A **store** is also **4.1** a quantity of things or an amount of something that you keep together in a place ready for when you want to use them. EG *...the cupboard where Captain Imrie kept his private store of tobacco... Mary made tea from her special store... ...the store cupboard.* — N COUNT = supply, stock **4.2** a place where things are kept while they are not being used. EG *It is held in a temporary store... Goods in store will be covered for loss or damage... We take them out of store every April, ready for the summer.* — N COUNT, OR *in/out of*+N = storehouse

5 If you have a **store** of a particular emotion or of facts, knowledge, etc, you have a large amount of it ready to be used. EG *...their considerable store of forbearance and understanding... ...unlimited stores of love... Each new fact discovered by science adds to the universal store of human knowledge.* — N COUNT+*of*+N UNCOUNT = reserve

6 **Stores** are food and other essentials which are needed for a journey, such as an expedition or a — N PLURAL = provisions military exercise. EG *Villagers were recruited to carry stores and tents... They uncovered box after box of weapons and stores.*

7 If something is **in store** for you, it is going to happen at some time in the future. EG *Think of all the travel and adventures in store for her... You never know what the next few months have got in store.* PHR : USED AS AN A ↑ waiting

8 If you **set great store** on or by something, you think that it is extremely important and care a great deal about it. EG *He set the greatest store on carrying out his decision... A mother who has set great store by breast-feeding may feel mildly let down by the experience.* PHR : VB INFLECTS ↑ value

store up. If you **store** something **up**, you keep it until there is an appropriate occasion when you can use it. EG *She had some sausage carefully stored up for the occasion... Jane had noticed what he said, and stored it up as a weapon.* PHRASAL VB : V+O+ADV = save up

storefront /stɔ:frʌnt/, **storefronts.** A **storefront** is a shop front; used especially in American English. N COUNT ↑ facade

storehouse /stɔ:haus/, **storehouses.** 1 A **storehouse** is a warehouse; used especially in American English. EG *Food was still plentiful in the storehouses.* N COUNT

2 A **storehouse** of things or ideas is a collection of them in which there are a number of very good and interesting examples. EG *...a storehouse of memories.* N PART+N IN PLURAL = treasury

storekeeper /stɔ:ki:pə/, **storekeepers.** A **storekeeper** is a shopkeeper; used especially in American English. N COUNT

storeroom /stɔ:ru⁴m/, **storerooms.** A **storeroom** is a room in which you can put things away and keep them until they are needed. EG *The storeroom held the trunks and other household stuff.* N COUNT ↑ store

storey /stɔ:ri¹/, **storeys**; also spelled **story** in American English. The **storeys** of a house or building are its different floors or levels. EG *...a house with four storeys... ...a single storey building... ...the multi-storey car park.* N COUNT : USU ADJ/NUM+N

stork /stɔ:k/, **storks.** A **stork** is a large bird with a long beak and long legs, which usually lives near water. There is a traditional story that storks bring new babies to the parents' home. EG *Waves of cranes, storks, and pelicans rose from the lake.* N COUNT

storm /stɔ:m/, **storms, storming, stormed.** 1 A **storm** is 1.1 very bad weather in which there is heavy rain, strong wind, and often thunder and lightning. EG *I think we should wait until the storm passes over... A tremendous storm broke... Electrical storms raged in the clouds.* N COUNT = tempest 1.2 a large amount of comment and criticism made by people who are very angry, indignant, or excited about a particular subject. EG *Derrida's theories touched off a storm in intellectual communities from France to America... A theological storm of huge proportions broke during the decade... The decision provoked a storm of criticism from Conservative MPs.* N COUNT : ALSO N+of+N UNCOUNT/N IN PL = furore 1.3 a sudden loud expression of people's feelings, which they show by laughing, shouting, clapping, etc. EG *A storm of laughter arose... ...the storm of applause that greeted the actors.* N COUNT : ALSO N+of+N UNCOUNT/N IN PL = roar

2 If you **storm** into or out of a place, you move quickly and noisily in a way that shows that you are very angry about something. EG *I stormed into the room in a rage... Her mother went storming off.* V+A = charge

3 If you **storm**, you shout because you are extremely angry. EG *'What the hell are you doing in my house?' stormed my father... No matter how I pleaded or stormed, I could never make her understand.* V OR V+QUOTE = rage

4 When people **storm** a place that is being defended, they suddenly attack it, usually in order to get inside it. EG *They decided to storm the aircraft... Two days later the infantry stormed through the walls of the Imperial Palace.* V+O, OR V+A = rush, invade ◊ **storming.** EG *...July 14–the anniversary of the storming of the Bastille.* ◊ N UNCOUNT+of

5 If soldiers or the police **take** a place **by storm**, large numbers of them attack it and capture it. EG *The army took the capital by storm.* PHR : VB INFLECTS = seize

6 If someone or something **takes** a place **by storm**, they are very successful indeed; an informal expression. EG *'Nicholas Nickleby' took London by storm a year ago.* PHR : VB INFLECTS = conquer

stormbound /stɔ:mbaʊnd/. Ships, aeroplanes, or passengers that are **stormbound** are prevented from travelling because of stormy weather. EG *Our ferry is stormbound at Holyhead.* ADJ CLASSIF ↑ stuck

storm cloud, storm clouds; also spelled with a hyphen and as one word. 1 **Storm clouds** the dark clouds which are seen before a storm. EG *I looked up at the storm clouds.* N COUNT : USU PL

2 You also use **storm clouds** to mean a sign that something violent is going to happen; a formal use. EG *The storm clouds of war gathered over Europe.* N COUNT : USU PL ↑ indication

storm trooper, storm troopers. **Storm troopers** were members of a force of soldiers in Nazi Germany, who were specially trained to be violent and ruthless. EG *Columns of storm troopers marched past.* N COUNT

stormy /stɔ:mi¹/, **stormier, stormiest.** 1 When the weather is **stormy**, there are strong winds, heavy rain, and dark clouds. EG *...a stormy sky.* ADJ QUALIT = turbulent

2 If something such as a relationship or a discussion is **stormy**, it is full of strong emotions, especially anger. EG *...a stormy debate full of interruptions... His parliamentary career was stormy... She had several affairs, all stormy.* ADJ QUALIT = tempestuous

story /stɔ:ri¹/, **stories.** 1 A **story** is 1.1 a description of a series of events, either real or imaginary, that is written or told in order to entertain people. EG *Do you know any good ghost stories?... Tell me a story, Daddy!... ...Tolstoy's story about the death of Ivan Ilich.* N COUNT = tale 1.2 the series of events about which a book, film, or play is written. EG *There's not much of a story to it, but the acting is wonderful.* N COUNT = plot 1.3 a description of an event or incident that has happened to someone, especially a spoken description of it. EG *My children love to hear stories about when they were babies... Even his approaching execution did not change his story... ...appalling stories of hatred and violence.* N COUNT = account 1.4 a description of the main events that have happened during a person's life or in the history of, for example, an organization or a country. EG *The story of the firm began in 1820... I told her the story of my life.* N COUNT 1.5 an explanation or an account of an event that has been deliberately invented. People sometimes make up a story in order to provide themselves with an excuse or to discredit other people. EG *What a story! I don't believe a word of it... You seem to have invented a few stories against your opponents.* N COUNT ↑ lie = fiction 1.6 a newspaper article or an item that is part of a news broadcast. EG *I thought it was the best story in that day's newspaper... I planned to run a story on the opening of the new arts centre.* N COUNT

2 You say **'but that's another story'** when you have mentioned a subject that you are not going to talk about or explain in detail. EG *Actually, I divorced him three years later, but that's another story.* CONVENTION, OR PHR : VB INFLECTS

3 You might say that something is **the same old story** or **the old old story** when you are talking about something, especially something bad, that has often happened in the same way in the past. EG *It's the same old story, people will never learn!* PHR : USED AS C/O

4 If you say that something is **only part of the story** or is **not the whole story**, you mean that there are more details that need to be known in order to understand the situation properly. EG *One suspects this was only part of the story... This is not the whole story nor anything like the whole story.* PHR : USED AS C/O

5 If you add **so the story goes** to something that you are saying, you mean that that is what other people say, although you do not know whether or not it is true. EG *And even worse, so the story goes, the most highly qualified candidate was rejected.* PHR : USED AS ADV SEN ↑ apparently

6 You say **to cut a long story short** to indicate that you are only going to describe the final result of an event and not all the details that led up to it. EG *Well, to cut a long story short, I decided to turn down the job.* PHR : USED AS ADV SEN ↑ briefly

7 A **story** is also the same as a storey; used in American English. N COUNT : USU ADJ/NUM+N

8 See also **short story, sob story, tall story.**

storybook /stɔ:ri¹bʊk/, **storybooks.** 1 A **storybook** is a book of stories, usually for children; a literary use. N COUNT

2 A **storybook** relationship, love, life, etc is one that is perfect and ends happily, just as many fairy stories do. EG *...a storybook romance.* N BEFORE N = fairy story

stout /staʊt/, **stouter, stoutest.** 1 Someone who is **stout** is rather fat. EG *My father was short and rather stout... My teacher was a stout old lady.* ADJ QUALIT = portly

2 Things such as arms and legs, branches and sticks, etc that are **stout** are thick and strong. EG *He held onto a stout branch... I wish I didn't have such stout legs.* ADJ QUALIT = sturdy

3 If your belief in something or your determination to achieve something is **stout**, it is firm and strong. EG *...the determination of our forces to offer the stoutest possible resistance on land.* ◊ **stoutly**. EG *Martin stoutly maintained that he was right.* ADJ QUALIT : ATTRIB = tough, bold; ◊ ADV WITH VB

4 **Stout** is also a strong dark beer. EG *A pint of stout, please.* N MASS

stout-hearted. Someone who is **stout-hearted** is brave and determined; a literary word. EG *...a loyal and stout-hearted servant.* ADJ QUALIT = stalwart

stove /stəʊv/, **stoves**. A **stove** is an apparatus which provides heat, either for cooking or for heating a room. EG *...a gas stove... She left the Doctor's sausages on the stove to keep warm.* N COUNT

stow /stəʊ/, **stows, stowing, stowed**. If you **stow** something somewhere or **stow it away**, you put it neatly away in a place where it can be kept until it is needed. EG *We stowed all the boxes in the attic... His baggage was safely stowed away in the plane.* V+O+A, OR PHRASAL VB : V+O+ADV = store, stash

stow away. If someone **stows away**, they hide in a ship, aeroplane, or other vehicle in order to make the journey secretly or without paying the fare. PHRASAL VB : V+ADV

stowaway /stəʊəweɪ/, **stowaways**. A **stowaway** is a person who hides in a ship, aeroplane, or other vehicle in order to make a journey secretly or without paying the fare. N COUNT ⇑ passenger

straddle /strædəᵒl/, **straddles, straddling, straddled**. To **straddle** something means **1** to sit or stand with one leg or supporting part on each side of it. EG *He stepped over the fallen figure, straddling her back... An enormous viaduct straddles the river Wye.* V+O

2 to extend widely in space or time, so as to form a connection between different places or different periods of time. EG *The Roman roads stretched out from London and straddled the country.* V+O = span

strafe /streɪf, strɑːf/, **strafes, strafing, strafed**. To **strafe** an enemy means to attack them by scattering bullets or bombs on them from a low-flying aircraft. EG *They strafed the invasion beaches and headlands.* V+O ⇑ bombard

straggle /strægəᵒl/, **straggles, straggling, straggled**. **1** If something such as a town or village **straggles**, it spreads out untidily in different directions. EG *The houses straggled down the hillside... ...straggling branches.* V = sprawl

2 If someone **straggles**, they wander away from the path when they are walking along with a group of people. EG *Keep up with the rest of us and don't straggle.* V = dawdle

straggly /strægliˡ/, **stragglier, straggliest**. Something that is **straggly** grows or hangs untidily and spreads out in different directions. EG *...straggly hair.* ADJ QUALIT ⇑ untidy

straight /streɪt/, **straighter, straightest**. **1** Something such as a line that is **straight** continues in the same direction and does not bend or curve. EG *...a long straight road... ...a high ridge which ran in a straight line down to the sea.* ▸ used as an adverb. EG *I saw the car coming straight at me... She was staring straight ahead... They can't shoot straight.* ADJ QUALIT ≠ bent, crooked; ▸ ADV+VB/PREP/ADV

2 If the position of something is **straight**, it is upright or level, rather than sloping or bent. EG *Keep your knees bent and your back straight... Check that all the pictures hang straight... They were all standing up straight.* ADV AFTER VB, OR ADJ CLASSIF

3 If you do something such as going **straight** home or coming **straight back,** you do it immediately and without delay. EG *The doctor told me to go straight to bed... I may as well come straight to the point.* ADV+A : AFTER VB = directly

4 You use **straight** to describe an action that you do or that happens without any break or interruption. EG *...youngsters who move straight from school onto the dole queue... We finished the season with four straight wins... Her own track record is one of straight success... We worked on the harvest for three days straight.* ADV WITH VB/PREP/ADV, ADJ CLASSIF : ATTRIB, OR ADJ AFTER N ⇑ nonstop

5 If you **put the record straight** or **get something straight**, you give a correct account of facts or events, or you make sure that you understand them properly. EG *There's been a misunderstanding and I'd like to put the record straight... Let me get this straight–you claim that the other driver pulled out in front of you.* PHR : VB INFLECTS

6 If you give someone a **straight** answer or if you tell them something **straight**, you are honest and frank and do not try to hide the truth. EG *I just want a straight answer to the question... Don't be afraid to tell them–they appreciate straight talk... I don't think she's being completely straight with us.* ● If you tell someone something **straight out**, you speak plainly and directly, without trying to hide your meaning. EG *I shall tell him straight out that I'm not going to do it.* ADJ, OR ADV AFTER VB = straightforward ≠ evasive; ● PHR : USED AS AN A = point-blank

7 If someone's hair is **straight** it has no curls or waves in it. EG *...a tall slim girl with long straight hair.* ADJ QUALIT ≠ curly

8 If a room or house is **straight**, it is clean and tidy, with everything in its proper place; a fairly informal use. EG *I'll have to get the house straight and send the kids off to school.* ADJ CLASSIF : PRED ⇑ orderly

9 A **straight** choice, a **straight** fight, etc involves only two people or things. EG *The voters have a straight choice between two candidates... It was a straight fight between Labour and Conservative.* ADJ CLASSIF : ATTRIB ⇑ simple

10 To drink alcohol **straight** means to drink it by itself and not mix it with water or anything else. EG *...straight vodka... I like my whisky straight.* ADJ CLASSIF : OR ADV AFTER VB = neat

11 **Straight** theatre consists of serious plays, rather than comedy or musical drama. EG *She wants to get back to straight theatre... ...a straight play.* ADJ CLASSIF : ATTRIB

12 If someone who has been involved in crime is **going straight**, he or she is now no longer involved in criminal activities but is living an honest, decent life. PHR : VB INFLECTS

13 If something keeps people **on the straight and narrow**, it helps to keep them living an honest, decent life and prevents them getting involved in criminal or immoral activities. EG *The threat of jail helps to keep them on the straight and narrow.* PHR : USED AS AN A ⇑ law-abiding

14 If you keep **a straight face**, you manage to look serious while you tell someone something that is untrue or amusing. EG *I found it hard to keep a straight face... She said this with a completely straight face.* PHR : USED AS O

15 In informal English, if you describe someone as **straight**, you mean that they are **15.1** normal and conventional, for example in their opinions, in the way they live, or in the clothes they wear. EG *She's a nice person, but awfully straight.* **15.2** heterosexual. ADJ QUALIT = conservative; ADJ CLASSIF

straightaway /streɪtəweɪ/. If you do something **straightaway**, you do it immediately and without any delay. EG *We went to work straightaway.* ADV WITH VB = at once

straighten /streɪtəᵒn/, **straightens, straightening, straightened**. **1** When you **straighten** something or when it **straightens**, it becomes straight. EG *Her hair is being straightened at the hairdresser... The curtains will straighten after a few days.* V-ERG

2 If you **straighten** something, you arrange or adjust it so that it is in the proper position or is neat and tidy. EG *I'll just straighten the bed... Straightening his tie, he knocked on the door.* V+O

3 When you **straighten** or **straighten up**, you make your back or body straight and upright, especially after you have been bending or stooping. EG *The man straightened and looked him in the face... He straightens up, combs his hair, and walks into the meeting.* V, OR PHRASAL VB : V+ADV

straighten out. If you **straighten out** a situation that is full of disorder or confusion, you succeed in getting it organized and tidied up. EG *It'll take six weeks to get things straightened out... A legal contract does help to straighten out the mess when things go wrong.* PHRASAL VB : V+O+ADV = sort out, clear up

straight-faced. Someone who is **straight-faced** shows no sign of amusement in a funny situation, even though they really think that it is very amusing. EG *It was a brilliant joke and she told it completely straight-faced.* ADJ QUALIT, OR ADV AFTER VB

straightforward /streɪtfɔːwəd/. **1** Something that is **straightforward** is clear and simple, without any special difficulties or complications. EG *...a very straightforward set of instructions in simple English... The issue is not quite as straightforward as it seems.* ADJ QUALIT = clear-cut ≠ complex

2 Someone who is **straightforward** is honest and frank and does not attempt to hide their feelings. EG *He has a nice straightforward manner.* ADJ QUALIT = candid

straightlaced /streɪtleɪst/. See **straitlaced**.

straightway /streɪtweɪ/ means the same as straightaway; a rather old-fashioned word. ADV WITH VB

strain /streɪn/, **strains, straining, strained. 1** **Strain** is a force or pressure that pushes, pulls, or stretches something tightly, often causing it to break or to move out of place. EG *The bridge collapsed* N UNCOUNT = weight *under the strain of all the extra traffic... The additional supports will help to take some of the strain off the original structure.*

2 A **strain** is **2.1** a difficulty that is caused for something when its powers or resources are severely tested or used to an extent that goes beyond normal or reasonable limits. EG *This policy puts a greater strain on the economic system that it can bear... Police and civil defence forces were under heavy strain... The system could not cope with the strain caused by all the extra work.* **2.2** a state of worry and tension caused by a situation that severely tests your mental and physical powers. EG *Many people doing this sort of job suffer from strain... ...nervous strain... Overcrowding imposes severe mental strains.* — N COUNT/UNCOUNT = pressure; N COUNT/UNCOUNT = stress

3 If you refer to a situation as being a **strain**, you mean that it causes you to feel worried and tense. EG *I found it a strain being totally responsible for the child.* — N SING: a+N ⇑ worry

4 Strain is also injury to a part of your body that is caused by using it too much or by twisting it awkwardly. EG *Both of us were suffering from back strain.* — N UNCOUNT: USU AFTER N

5 If you say that someone has a **strain** of a particular quality, you mean that they have that quality in their character. EG *There's a certain strain of ruthlessness in that family... Perhaps it was the romantic strain in me which made me do it.* — N SING WITH DET +SUPP = streak

6 A **strain** of a plant or animal is a particular type that has some special characteristic. EG *...high-yielding strains of wheat... ...penicillin-resistant strains of bacteria.* — N COUNT+SUPP = variety

7 If you hear the **strains** of music, you hear music being played. EG *The strains of Chopin drifted in from the music room.* — N PLURAL+SUPP ⇑ sound

8 To **strain** something means to cause it to be used or tested to an extent that goes beyond normal or reasonable limits. EG *These increases have strained the resources of the poorer countries... That noise is really straining my patience.* — V+O = tax, stretch

9 If you **strain** to do something, you make a great effort to do it, using all your strength or all the power of your mind or senses. EG *He was straining to hear what the speaker was saying... People would strain and push to see the procession... He strained his eyes to catch a glimpse of the President.* — V+*to*-INF, OR V+O+*to*-INF ⇑ try

10 If you **strain** a part of your body, especially one of your muscles, you injure it, by using it too much or by stretching it awkwardly. EG *She's strained her back.* — V+O ⇑ damage

11 If you **strain** something such as food, you remove the liquid from it, by pouring it into a device with many small holes at the bottom, such as a colander or strainer. EG *I'll just strain the potatoes.* — V+O = drain

12 If you **strain** at something such as a rope, you pull on it using all your strength. — V+A *(at)* = heave

strained /streɪnd/. **1** Someone who is **strained** is worried and nervous in their manner or appearance. EG *She looked strained and tired... Her voice was decidedly strained as she asked the next question.* — ADJ QUALIT = tense

2 If your behaviour is **strained**, it shows a lack of naturalness or sincerity. EG *'And what's your name, dear?' he asked with strained jollity... She gave a strained laugh.* — ADJ QUALIT = forced

3 If relations between people are **strained**, they are unfriendly and there is distrust and suspicion between them. EG *Relations between the two families had become increasingly strained.* — ADJ QUALIT = awkward, uneasy

strainer /streɪnə/, **strainers**. A **strainer** is a tool used for separating liquids from solids. It has a lot of small holes at the bottom through which liquid can pass but solid substances cannot. EG *...a tea strainer.* — N COUNT ⇑ device

strait /streɪt/, **straits**. **1** A narrow strip of sea which joins two large areas of sea is sometimes called the **strait** or the **straits**. EG *...the Strait of Gibraltar... ...the Turkish Straits... The waves in the straits were 8 feet high.* — N COUNT: USED IN NAMES, *the*+N, SING=PL

2 If someone is **in desperate straits, in financial straits**, etc, they are in serious trouble, usually because they do not have much money. EG *My parents were in such difficult straits they were living off welfare... He found the organization in serious financial straits.* — PHR: USED AS AN A

straitened /streɪtəᵒnd/. If someone is living **in straitened circumstances**, they do not have as much money as they used to, and are finding it very hard to buy all the food and other things that they need. EG *How long have they been in such straitened circumstances?* — PHR: USED AS AN A ≠ well-off

straitjacket /streɪtdʒækɪt/, **straitjackets**. **1** A **straitjacket** is a special piece of clothing which is used to bind the arms of the person who is wearing it in order to prevent them from moving. Mental patients and criminals are sometimes put into straitjackets to prevent them from harming themselves or other people. EG *What Anthony requires is a gag, a straitjacket, and a nursemaid, in that order.* — N COUNT ⇑ garment

2 You can also use the word **straitjacket** to refer to anything which prevents or restricts growth, development, or freedom. EG *The government has forced the economy into an over-centralized, undemocratic straitjacket... The attempt to save money placed the company in a straitjacket that stifled its natural development.* — N COUNT ⇑ constraint

straitlaced /streɪtleɪst/; also spelled **straightlaced**, and also spelled with a hyphen. If you describe someone who **straitlaced**, you mean that they have a very strict and severe attitude towards questions of morality. EG *Aunt Josephine is very straitlaced–she doesn't approve of Martin at all.* — ADJ QUALIT = puritanical

strand /strænd/, **strands, stranding, stranded**. **1** A **strand** of thread, wire, wool, etc is a single piece of it which is often twisted with others to make rope, string, or similar materials. EG *When changing a plug, make sure that there are no loose strands of wire... A strand of hair fell over her eyes.* — N PART+N UNCOUNT

2 A **strand** of something is one of a number of parts or factors that form it into a whole. EG *They ran a campaign that drew together these various strands... His financial plight is only one of several strands in his present difficulties.* — N COUNT ⇑ element

3 If a ship, whale, fish, etc **is stranded**, it goes out of the sea onto the shore and is unable to get back to the sea. EG *The boat was stranded in the mud... ...the marks left by jellyfish stranded on the beach.* — V+O: USU PASS = be beached

4 If you **are stranded** somewhere, you are left helpless there and unable to get away, often because you have no money. EG *He was stranded in Paris... I was left stranded on the ice.* ◊ **stranded**. EG *...the stranded holidaymakers.* — V+O: USU PASS+A = be stuck; ◊ ADJ CLASSIF = marooned

5 A **strand** is also a shore or beach; a rather literary use. — N SING: *the*+N

strange /streɪndᵒʒ/, **stranger, strangest**. **1** Something that is **strange** is odd, unfamiliar, or unexpected, often with the result that you feel uneasy or afraid. EG *I had a strange dream last night... He behaved in a very strange way... Truth may well be stranger than fiction... It was strange to hear her voice again... It's strange you should come today... The strange thing is that this teacher didn't even know us... Her husband has become strange and distant...* ◊ **strangeness**. EG *I was overwhelmed with a sense of strangeness.* — ADJ QUALIT ⇑ different = bizarre, peculiar ≠ normal; ◊ N UNCOUNT = weirdness

2 A **strange** place or person is one you have never visited before or met before. EG *I don't like strange people coming into my house... Culture shock is the effect that immersion in a strange culture has on the unprepared visitor... Never get in a strange car... Ipswich is really quite strange to me.* — ADJ QUALIT = unknown ≠ familiar

3 If you feel **strange**, you have unpleasant or uncomfortable feelings, either physical or emotional. EG *Can I sit down? I feel a bit strange.* — ADJ QUALIT: USU PRED ⇑ unwell

strangely /streɪndᵒʒliⁱ/. **1** If you do something **strangely**, you do it in an odd or unexpected way, which people think is not normal. EG *They had acted strangely as he went by... He laughed strangely.* — ADV WITH VB = oddly

2 If you say that something is **strangely** familiar, **strangely** enjoyable, etc, you mean that it has that quality, even though you did not expect it to, or cannot understand why. EG *Your face is strangely familiar... He answered in a strangely calm voice.* — ADV+ADJ/ADV = oddly

3 You use **strangely** or **strangely enough** in order to emphasize that what you are saying is surprising and interesting. EG *It has, strangely, only recently been discovered... 'Are students interested in religion these days?'–'Strangely enough, they are.'* — ADV SEN OR PHR: USED AS ADV SEN = surprisingly

stranger /streɪndᵒʒə/, **strangers**. **1** A **stranger** is **1.1** a person you do not know or have never met before. EG *A stranger appeared... Her mother didn't trust strangers... Antonio was a total stranger to all of us.* **1.2** a person who does not know a place very well, for example because they have only just arrived there or because they do not live there. EG — N COUNT ≠ acquaintance, friend; N COUNT ≠ local

They know they are regarded as strangers in the village and they cannot bear it.

2 If two people **are strangers**, they do not know each other. PHR : VB INFLECTS

3 If you are a **stranger** to something, you do not understand it or have not had any experience of it. N COUNT : IF+ PREP THEN *to* EG *I was not a stranger to visiting arrangements in jails... Martin, himself no stranger to controversy, began the debate.*

strangle /stræŋgə[0]l/, **strangles, strangling, strangled.** 1 To **strangle** someone means to kill them by putting pressure on their throat, and so preventing them from breathing. V+O = throttle EG *He was strangled in his bed... I was so angry I could have strangled you.*

2 If something **strangles** something else, it prevents its growth or development by putting some kind of pressure on it, usually of an economic or political kind. V+O = stifle EG *Creativity is being strangled by financial pressures... Greed is beginning to strangle this country.*

strangled /stræŋgə[0]ld/. A **strangled** voice, laugh, cry, etc sounds unclear and partly suppressed, as if someone is being strangled. ADJ CLASSIF : ATTRIB = stifled EG *...a high strangled cry of stunned amazement... ...a little strangled laugh.*

stranglehold /stræŋgə[0]lhəuld/, **strangleholds.** A **stranglehold** is 1 a position, sometimes used in wrestling, in which your arm is pressed tightly against someone else's throat, so that they have difficulty in breathing. N COUNT ⇑ hold 2 a powerful control over something which prevents freedom or development or growth. N COUNT : USU SING EG *...reforms which loosened the stranglehold of the upper classes.*

strangler /stræŋglə/, **stranglers.** A **strangler** is a criminal who has killed one or more people by strangling them. N COUNT ⇑ murderer

strangulation /stræŋgjə[1]leɪʃə[0]n/ is 1 the act of killing someone by putting pressure on their throat, and so preventing them from breathing. N UNCOUNT EG *She died by strangulation.* 2 the prevention of the growth or development of something by means of pressure, usually of an economic or political kind. N UNCOUNT : USU +SUPP ⇑ suppression EG *...the strangulation of economic freedom.*

strap /stræp/, **straps, strapping, strapped.** 1 A **strap** is 1.1 a narrow band of leather, cloth, or other material, which is used to carry something or to hold a piece of clothing in place. N COUNT EG *He had a bag from an airline, on a strap... ...high-heeled shoes, with straps above the ankle.* 1.2 a strong narrow band of leather, cloth, or other material, which is used with a buckle to fasten something, such as a suitcase or a wristwatch. N COUNT ⇑ fastening EG *I unstrapped the straps, and opened the case.* 1.3 a strong narrow piece of leather which is used for hitting people as a punishment, especially in schools in former times. N COUNT EG *My form teacher was always using the strap.* ▸ used to refer to this punishment. ▸ N SING : *the*+N EG *The headmaster gave us both the strap... We got the strap.* 1.4 a loop of leather, rubber, or other material, which hangs down from the roof of a bus or train so that passengers who are standing can hold on to it. N COUNT ⇑ handle EG *She couldn't reach the strap.*

2 If you **strap** something somewhere, you fasten it in place with a strap. V+O+A ⇑ attach EG *A small child should be strapped into a special car seat... All the time he was fingering the holster strapped to his waist... He straps on his watch.*

strapless /stræplɪ[2]s/. A **strapless** dress, bra, etc does not have the usual narrow bands of material over the shoulders. ADJ CLASSIF

strapping /stræpɪŋ/. 1 You describe someone as **strapping** if they are tall, strong, and healthy-looking. ADJ QUALIT = well-built EG *...the eldest son, a tall strapping boy of eighteen.*

2 **Strapping** is a collection of straps used to fasten things in place. N UNCOUNT

strata /strɑːtə/ is the plural of **stratum.**

stratagem /strætə[1]dʒəm/, **stratagems.** A **stratagem** is a clever plan which you use to deceive someone so that you can achieve a particular goal. N COUNT : USU+ SUPP = ploy EG *They used every stratagem to acquire the company.*

strategic /strətiːdʒɪk/. 1 Something that is **strategic** is done or planned to put you in a situation in which you can achieve what you want or in which you can get an advantage over other people. ADJ CLASSIF ⇑ advantageous = tactical EG *I took up a strategic position near the exit... The police made a strategic withdrawal against overwhelming odds.* ◇ **strategically.** ◇ ADV WITH VB, OR ADV SEN EG *We brought the rocks down by using a number of strategically placed explosions... I felt it was a mistake, strategically and in principle.*

2 You use **strategic** to describe something which relates to the distribution and placement of armies and weapons for military advantage. ADJ CLASSIF EG *The islands are of fundamental strategic importance... Britain's large oil and strategic interests in the area.* ◇ **strategically.** ◇ ADV EG *...these strategically important places.*

3 **Strategic** weapons, are aimed at places of military or economic importance, for example air bases or docks, and are ready to be fired if a war starts; used especially to describe nuclear weapons. ADJ CLASSIF : ATTRIB

strategist /strætə[1]dʒɪst/, **strategists.** A **strategist** is a person who is skilled in planning the best way to gain an advantage or to achieve success, especially military advantage or success. N COUNT ⇑ planner = tactician EG *To many Western European strategists these weapons are crucial... She was the family's strategist.*

strategy /strætə[1]dʒi[1]/, **strategies.** 1 A **strategy** is a plan you adopt in order to get something done, especially in politics, economics, or business. N COUNT : USU+ SUPP = policy EG *...the Government's economic strategy... He adopted a strategy of massive deflation... What strategies do you use to teach a child to read?*

2 **Strategy** is 2.1 the art of planning where to place armies and weapons in order to gain the best military advantage. N UNCOUNT = tactics EG *...the debate over strategy and the allocation of resources... ...an expert in military strategy.* 2.2 the art of planning the best way to achieve something or to be successful in a particular field. N UNCOUNT = tactics EG *...a master of chess strategy... I would like to have seen the expression on her face, but strategy forbade my looking back.*

stratification /strætɪfɪkeɪʃə[0]n/ is the division of something, especially society, into different classes or layers. N UNCOUNT EG *...the existing class stratification in this country.*

stratified /strætɪfaɪd/. 1 A **stratified** society is one that is divided into different classes or social layers. ADJ CLASSIF EG *...a rigidly stratified society.*

2 **Stratified** rock is formed in horizontal layers of different materials. ADJ CLASSIF ⇑ layered EG *...stratified escarpments.*

stratosphere /strætəsfɪə/. The **stratosphere** is the layer of the earth's atmosphere which lies between 10 and 50 kilometres above the earth. N SING : *the*+N

stratum /strɑːtəm/, **strata.** A **stratum** is 1 a group of people in society who have similar features of class, education, power, etc. N COUNT : USU+ SUPP = echelon EG *Our political leaders have always been drawn from the upper strata of society... Let us choose a particular social stratum.* 2 a horizontal layer of rock, earth, or other material, which lies between layers of other kinds of material. N COUNT EG *We can follow the history of life through the strata.*

straw /strɔː/, **straws.** 1 **Straw** is dried yellowish stalks of wheat, barley, oats, etc. Straw is used as a material for making mats and baskets, for packaging, and for other purposes. N UNCOUNT EG *They make the roofs out of straw... ...a white straw hat... The eggs were packed in straw... Her hair was the colour of straw.*

2 A **straw** is 2.1 a single stalk of straw. 2.2 a thin tube made of paper or plastic, which you use to suck a drink into your mouth. N COUNT EG *Fiona was drinking a frothy milk shake through a straw.*

3 The word **straw** is also used in the following expressions. 3.1 If you say that someone is being forced to **make bricks without straw**, you mean that they are forced to try to do something without having everything that they need to do it properly. PHR : VB INFLECTS = skimp EG *I feel that they are having to make bricks without straw.* 3.2 If you **do not care a straw** or **do not care two straws**, you think that something is so unimportant that you do not care about it at all; a rather old-fashioned informal expression. PHR : VB INFLECTS EG *I don't care two straws about your problems.* 3.3 If you **clutch at straws**, you are so desperate that you put your hopes in something which is very unlikely to succeed. PHR : VB INFLECTS 3.4 If you say that an event is **the last straw** or **the straw that broke the camel's back**, you mean that although it is not important in itself, it happens after a series of similar unpleasant or annoying events, and makes you angry or makes you want to give up what you are doing. PHR : USED AS C[illegible] EG *The sight of Peter complaining*

about the food was the last straw. **3.5** If you **draw** or **get the short straw**, you are chosen from a number of people to perform a job or duty that you will not enjoy. EG *I'm afraid you've drawn the short straw-you're sitting next to Richard.* **3.6** If you say that an incident or piece of information is a **straw in the wind**, you mean that it gives you an indication of what might happen in the future. PHR : VB INFLECTS; PHR : USED AS C/O = hint

strawberry /strɔːbəʳri¹/, **strawberries**. A **strawberry** is a small red fruit which is soft and juicy and has tiny yellow seeds on its skin. Strawberries are usually eaten as a dessert or made into jam. EG *...strawberry jam.* N COUNT

strawberry mark, strawberry marks. A **strawberry mark** is a reddish mark on someone's skin which has been there since birth. N COUNT ⇑ birthmark

straw-coloured. Something that is **straw-coloured** is pale yellow; used especially of hair. ADJ COLOUR

straw poll, straw polls. A **straw poll** or **straw vote** is the unofficial questioning of a group of people to find out their opinion about something, especially during an election. EG *We took a straw poll of voters outside the polling stations.* N COUNT ⇑ survey

stray /streɪ/, **strays, straying, strayed**. **1** If something **strays**, it wanders away from where it is supposed to be. EG *I put up a fence so that my animals wouldn't stray too far... I'll make sure that he doesn't stray off on his own... Children had strayed on to an airport runway... Her eyes kept straying away from the page.* V : USU+A = rove, roam

2 A **stray** dog, cat, or other domestic animal is one that has wandered away from home and is lost. EG *There are four million stray cats in this country.* ▸ used as a noun. EG *...the rescue of trapped animals and strays.* ADJ CLASSIF : ATTRIB; ▸ N COUNT

3 If you or your thoughts **stray**, you do not concentrate on one particular topic or thought, but start thinking or talking about something else. EG *He let his thoughts stray for five minutes... Her mind had strayed back to her childhood... She would stray away from the point of what she was saying.* V = wander

4 You also use **stray** to describe things which occur alone or separately from a main group. EG *Stray pieces of information came my way... A hen was pecking around for stray grains of corn... ...a stray bullet.* ADJ CLASSIF : ATTRIB ⇑ random = odd

streak /striːk/, **streaks, streaking, streaked**.
1 A **streak** is a long stripe or mark on a surface which contrasts with the surface because it is a different colour. EG *The carpet was smeared with white streaks of paint.... Her hair had a very pretty grey streak in it... I noticed a long streak of a tear on her cheek.* N COUNT : USU+*of* ⇑ line

2 If something **streaks** a surface, it leaves long stripes or marks of a different colour on the surface. EG *His moustache was streaked with grey... The sun is streaking the sea with long lines of gold... On a clear night scores of meteors streak the sky.* V+O : IF+PREP THEN *with*

3 A **streak** in someone's character is a part of their character which sometimes makes them behave in a particular way. EG *Children have a streak of cruelty... I had been always aware of the possessive streak in her.* N COUNT : ADJ+N, OR N+*of* ⇑ element

4 If something **streaks** somewhere, it moves there very quickly in a straight line. EG *We saw Sputnik streak across the sky... Twice the fish was nearly his and twice it streaked away.* V+A = dart

5 A **lucky streak**, an **unlucky streak**, a **winning streak**, etc is a continuous series of successes or failures, for example in sport or gambling. EG *I seem to be having a lucky streak... A defeat in the Cup broke our winning streak.* N COUNT

6 If someone **streaks**, they run quickly through a public place without any clothes on. EG *Do you think people streak just to get on television?* ▸ used as a noun. EG *...the man who did a streak during the Cup Final.* V; ▸ N COUNT : USU SING

7 If light **streaks** somewhere, it appears in as streaks of light. V+A

streaker /striːkə/, **streakers**. A **streaker** is a person who runs quickly through a public place without any clothes on. EG *The game was interrupted when a streaker ran across the pitch.* N COUNT

streaky /striːki¹/, **streakier, streakiest**. Something that is **streaky** is marked with streaks. EG *...horrible streaky wallpaper... The light made a streaky pattern on the carpet.* ADJ QUALIT

streaky bacon is bacon which has stripes of fat between stripes of meat. N UNCOUNT

stream /striːm/, **streams, streaming, streamed**. **1** A **stream** is **1.1** a small river. EG *He led us along the bank of the stream... The hills abound with streams and waterfalls.* **1.2** a part of a liquid or gas that flows or is forced to move in a different direction from the rest of the liquid or gas. EG *...powerful tidal streams... Fallout can be carried thousands of miles by the wind stream.* **1.3** a narrow and continuous movement of liquid or smoke. EG *A sponge feeds by filtering particles from the stream of water passing through its body... Horace blew out a stream of smoke.* ● See also **bloodstream**. N COUNT = brook; N COUNT = current; N COUNT : ALSO N+*of*+N UNCOUNT = trickle

2 A **stream** of people, animals, vehicles, etc is a long or continuous line of them travelling in the same direction, or to or from the same place. EG *A steady stream of workers came in looking for jobs... Local airfields had been receiving a continuous stream of reinforcements.* N COUNT, OR N PART+N UNCOUNT

3 A **stream** is also a long, continuous series of things. EG *He sat dumb for several minutes while the stream of insults continued... ...a steady stream of questions... These ideas have been hammered into their heads by a stream of movies, plays and books.* N COUNT, N PART+N UNCOUNT = flood

4 If something such as tears, blood, or sweat **streams** it pours out or down in large amounts. EG *She stood in the doorway, tears streaming down her face... Blood was streaming from her arm... His back was streaming with sweat... Streaming sweat, the farmers trudged wearily home.* V-ERG ⇑ flow

5 If people, animals, vehicles, etc **stream**, they move together in the same direction, in a long line or in large numbers. EG *The doors opened and the audience began to stream out... The herds stream across the valley onto the plateau... On the main road the cars are streaming by at sixty miles an hour.* V+A = rush

6 If something such as a flag or someone's hair **is streaming** in the wind, it is moving about quickly and freely. EG *...a pigtail with a ragged red ribbon streaming in the wind... ...the flags streaming in the breeze.* V : USU+A, USU CONT = flutter

7 If light **streams**, it shines strongly through or between things. EG *The sun was streaming in through the windows... As she climbed the stairs, she saw the light streaming from the open door.* V+A = flood

8 In a school, a **stream** is a group of children who have been put together because they have the same ability as each other. EG *...pupils who ended up in the B streams and C streams... These are low stream children in a secondary modern school.* N COUNT+SUPP

9 If a school **streams** its students, it puts them into groups according to their ability. EG *...streamed and mixed ability classes.* ◊ **streaming**. EG *Presumably the case for streaming gets stronger as you get higher up the school.* V+O; ◊ N UNCOUNT

streamer /striːmə/, **streamers**. A **streamer** is **1** a long roll of coloured paper that unrolls when you throw it. Streamers are thrown at parties, parades, and other celebrations. **2** a long narrow flag. N COUNT; N COUNT

streamline /striːmlaɪn/, **streamlines, streamlining, streamlined**. **1** If you **streamline** the shape of something, you make it streamlined. V+O

2 If you **streamline** something such as an organization or piece of writing, you make it more efficient or effective by reducing or removing parts of it which you do not think are useful. EG *He aimed to streamline the Post Office... All movie scripts are carefully pre-edited and streamlined.* V+O ⇑ reduce

streamlined /striːmlaɪnd/. Something that is **streamlined 1** has a long, narrow, smooth shape and so can move quickly and easily through the air or through water. EG *Mackerel have most marvellously streamlined bodies... His car has remote-control headlights and streamlined wing mirrors.* **2** has been made smaller or shorter in order to be more effective, useful, or efficient. EG *The account given here is of necessity extremely streamlined and oversimplified.* ADJ QUALIT; ADJ QUALIT ⇑ reduced

street /striːt/, **streets**. **1** A **street** is a road in a town or village which has houses or other buildings along it and which usually has a pavement on each side of it. EG *The two men walked slowly down the street... She spent the morning strolling through the narrow streets of Ghent... They went into the café across the street... ...a street map of Paris.* ▸ used in N COUNT; ▸ N IN NAMES the name of a street. EG *She lives in Seyer Street... The post office was on Teal Street.*

2 You can also use **street** to refer to something that happens out of doors in a town or to someone who is out of doors rather than inside a building. EG *We've got to keep youngsters off the streets... We are called reserved because we don't embrace friends in the street... ...street theatre... There were riots in the streets... They are likely to find themselves turned out on the streets.*

N COUNT : the+N, USU off/on+N
⇑ outside

3 The word **street** is also used in the following expressions. **3.1** If you talk about **the man in the street, the man or woman in the street**, etc, you are referring to ordinary people in general. EG *In the city the man in the street was unlikely ever to have seen an Aborigine... It doesn't affect the immediate interests of the ordinary man or woman in the street.*

PHR : USED AS S/O

3.2 If you say that someone is **streets ahead** of you, you mean that they are much better at something than you are or that they have progressed much further; a fairly informal expression. EG *The Germans are streets ahead of us with metal designing.*

PHR : USED AS AN A, USU+of
= way ahead

3.3 If you say that two people or things are **streets apart**, you are emphasizing that they are very different from each other; a fairly informal expression.

PHR : USED AS AN A
= poles apart

3.4 If a particular subject or activity is **up** your **street** or **right up** your **street**, you are very interested in it or know a lot about it. EG *Shakespeare and Congreve were not really up his street... If you ever need a hand with the repairs, ask Ted next door; that sort of thing's right up his street.*

PHR : USED AS AN A

3.5 If a woman is **on the streets**, she is earning money as a prostitute.

PHR : USED AS AN A

3.6 Someone who is **walking the streets** has nowhere to live.

PHR : VB INFLECTS

4 See also **back street, civvy street, Downing Street, Fleet Street, high street, Wall Street.**

streetcar /striːtkɑː/, **streetcars.** A **streetcar** is a tram; used in American English. EG *He caught the streetcar to his home in the Bronx.*

N COUNT

street credibility. If someone says that you have **street credibility** or **street cred**, they mean that ordinary young people would approve of you and consider you to be part of their culture, usually because you are modern or fashionable rather than old-fashioned; an informal expression made popular in the 1980s. EG *Wearing that will do nothing for your street credibility!... When the band became more successful, I felt they rather lost their street credibility.*

N UNCOUNT
⇑ image

streetlamp /striːtlæmp/, **streetlamps**; also spelled with a hyphen. A **streetlamp** is the same as a streetlight. EG *The streetlamps were out.*

N COUNT

streetlight /striːtlaɪt/, **streetlights**; also spelled with a hyphen. A **streetlight** is a light at the top of a tall post which stands by the side of a road to light it up, usually in a town.

N COUNT

street value. The **street value** of a drug such as heroin is the price that is paid for it when it is sold illegally to drug users. EG *Police at Heathrow Airport have seized drugs with a street value of half a million pounds.*

N SING WITH DET

streetwalker /striːtwɔːkə/, **streetwalkers.** A **streetwalker** is a prostitute who stands or walks in the streets in order to get customers.

N COUNT

streetwise /striːtwaɪz/; also spelled with a hyphen. Someone who is **streetwise** knows how to deal with rough people or dangerous situations, especially in big cities; an informal word.

ADJ QUALIT
⇑ knowledgeable

strength /strɛŋθ/, **strengths. 1** Your **strength** is the physical energy that you have to move your body or to do a particular activity. EG *I admired his immense physical strength... ...recovering their strength before setting off on another ten mile stage of the journey... It started to rain on the way but I had not the strength to go back for a mackintosh... Everyone was sapped of strength by the sun's heat.*

N UNCOUNT
= stamina

● If you do something **with all** your **strength**, you do it using as much physical effort as you can. EG *He looped the rope over the branch and pulled with all his strength... He punched the pillow with all his strength.*

● PHR : USED AS AN A
= hard

2 The **strength** of a machine or other object is its ability to withstand rough physical treatment, such as supporting heavy weights, without being damaged or destroyed. EG *The car is tested to establish bodywork strength... The decaying core has lost much of its strength.*

N UNCOUNT
= toughness

3 The **strength** of a wind or a water current is its force and speed of movement.

N UNCOUNT

4 The **strength** of a light or sound produced by a device is the amount of light or sound that it produces. EG *Make a list of the different strength light bulbs used in the house.*

N UNCOUNT+SUPP
⇑ intensity

5 The **strength** of a person, organization, etc is **5.1** the influence and power that they have, which is often based on the number of people who support their opinions or on the amount of money they have. EG *They fully recognized the enormous strength and influence of the unions... The SDP cannot afford to shirk an opportunity to try its strength against Labour... Pacifist movements gathered strength in Norway.*

N UNCOUNT

5.2 their success as a result of earning or being worth a lot of money. EG *IBM's economic strength is phenomenal... Those imbalances have led to the strength of the German Mark.*

N UNCOUNT
⇑ greatness

● If a person or organization **goes from strength to strength**, they gradually become more confident or successful. EG *His company went from strength to strength, and in 1911 merged with a number of other companies.*

● PHR : VB INFLECTS
= prosper

6 A **strength** that a person, organization, etc has is **6.1** a quality or ability which is thought to be an advantage. EG *Diversity is Labour's greatest strength... Each firm has its particular strengths and weaknesses... It is often said that the strength of Tyneside is the family.*

N COUNT/UNCOUNT : USU WITH POSS
⇑ asset

6.2 their ability to do something well and succeed at it. EG *Basic wages are determined by overall bargaining strength and skill... Their chess-playing strength is rising.*

N COUNT/UNCOUNT : USU+SUPP
= capability

7 If you show **strength** in a situation, you show confidence in yourself and determination or courage to do something that is difficult or frightening. EG *This gave us the strength to resist further temptation... With unshakeable strength of character she stayed on after the crisis... She answered with great strength: 'No. There is no other way.'*

N UNCOUNT
= resolution

8 The **strength** of a particular feeling or opinion that you have is the degree to which you have it, usually a large degree. EG *The strength of the writer's convictions is evident... The Government had clearly underestimated the strength of popular feeling about this.*

N UNCOUNT : USU+of
⇑ intensity

9 The **strength** of a particular opinion, argument, or story is the extent to which it influences people or is likely to be true in view of the evidence which supports it. EG *He continued to deny it, despite the growing strength of the argument... John said he himself had seen the man, so giving further strength to the story... This lent some strength to the complaint.*

N UNCOUNT
= credibility, force

● If you do one thing **on the strength of** a second thing, the second thing influences you and makes you decide to do the first thing. EG *They persuaded the Cabinet to agree to a grant of £4m on the strength of the Company's own projections of sales... Fergus ordered one on the strength of seeing mine.*

● PREP
= on the basis of

10 The **strength** of a relationship that you have with a person or group is the degree of closeness that it has. EG *This leads to bonds of deceptive strength being formed with the company.*

N UNCOUNT

11 The **strength** of a performance or a work of art is how well it expresses a particular subject or emotion; a fairly formal use. EG *The carol has the primitive strength and haunting simplicity of those early folk tunes... I tried to inject more strength into the part.*

N UNCOUNT
= force

12 The **strength** of a group of people, often a group of workers, is the total number of people in the group. EG *The workforce has seen its strength cut down from 5,000 to under 3,000 in two years... Their forces in the south were growing in strength and now numbered about 25,000.*

N COUNT/UNCOUNT
= numbers

13 The word **strength** is also used in the following expressions. **13.1** A group that exists **in strength, in great strength**, etc consists of a large number of people. EG *By Easter, the tourists were arriving in strength.*

PHR : USED AS A

13.2 A group of people that is **at full strength, up to full strength**, etc has all its members present. EG *The company is at last working at full strength... Supporting troops were now up to full strength.*

PHR : USED AS A

13.3 A group of people that is **below strength** or **under strength** does not have enough people or does not have all its members present. EG *The local police force is considerably below strength.*

PHR : USED AS A

strengthen /strɛŋθəᵊn/, **strengthens, strengthening, strengthened**. 1 If a number of people **strengthen** a group, they are brought in to increase the size of the group, usually to make it more powerful. EG *The new peers are designed to strengthen the Labour Party in the Upper House... The regiment was moving eastwards to strengthen the southern flank... ...a Post Office Users' Council strengthening the representation of consumers' interests.* V+O = reinforce

2 If something **strengthens** a particular argument or opinion, it supports the argument or opinion by providing more reasons or evidence for it to be true. EG *Additional reasons can be thrown in to strengthen the point... The uncertainty surrounding the future of the railways strengthened the argument for planning.* V+O = reinforce

3 If a feeling or attitude **strengthens**, or if someone **strengthens** it, it becomes more intense so that it has greater influence on people's behaviour. EG *He performed countless little cruelties that only strengthened my resolve not to give in... Such tendencies were enormously strengthened and accelerated by the social pressure... During the prolonged depression of the seventies, racialism strengthened.* V-ERG = increase

4 If you **strengthen** an organization, industry, country, etc, you make it stronger and more successful or influential, for example by increasing the range of its activities or the amount of work it does. EG *He stressed the need to strengthen the Party's organisation... He saw the potential of the Post Office for strengthening other industries, such as computers... India should welcome the strengthening of Pakistan... It is a systematic attempt to strengthen our competitive ability.* V+O ⇑ improve = boost

5 If a particular currency **strengthens** or **is strengthened**, it increases in value in relation to the currency of other countries. EG *It would surprise me if sterling strengthened much more... High US interest rates and a strengthening US dollar have depressed their economy.* V-ERG

6 If someone or something **strengthens** the financial state of a person, country, or organization, they improve it so that the person, country, or organization makes more profit or owes less money to others. EG *He had struck at the root of Labour's strategy for strengthening the balance of payments... The sale of his aunt's house considerably strengthened his financial position.* V+O = boost

7 When a relationship between two people or groups **strengthens**, or when you **strengthen** it, it becomes closer, often by an increase in the number of ideas or activities they have in common. EG *We want to strengthen our ties with the United States... ...cooperation strengthening the bond between members of the group... Its importation is yet another sign of China's strengthening links with the West.* V-ERG ⇑ develop

8 If something **strengthens** you, it increases your confidence in yourself so that you have determination or courage to deal with difficult or frightening situations. EG *It is designed to strengthen you against the loveless world... She had strengthened herself on those hard years... This greatly strengthened him in resisting any further pressure.* V+O (NG/REFL) = fortify

9 If someone or something **strengthens** something such a custom or a tradition, they make it more widely known or used. EG *The Welsh language must be revived and strengthened, and taught in the schools... Its function is to strengthen tradition.* V+O = encourage

10 Something that **strengthens** an object or a structure makes it physically strong so that it is able to withstand rough treatment, such as supporting heavy weights, without being damaged or destroyed. EG *The bridge is being strengthened... ...struts designed to strengthen the wings of aeroplanes.* V+O = reinforce

11 If a wind or a water current **strengthens**, it increases in force and speed. EG *The wind was now a few degrees south of east, and strengthening.* V

strenuous /strɛnuːəs/. A **strenuous** activity involves or requires a lot of effort or energy. EG *It is a strenuous twenty minute walk... Backs may be injured by strenuous and prolonged leg-raising exercises... Alf made strenuous efforts to improve his reading.* ◇ **strenuously**. EG *He strenuously denied that his airline was in any serious danger.* ADJ QUALIT : USU ATTRIB ⇑ energetic; ◇ ADV WITH VB

stress /strɛs/, **stresses, stressing, stressed**. 1 If you **stress** a point, argument, subject, etc, you put extra emphasis on it because you think it is important and you want other people to consider it carefully. EG *I ought to stress that this was not a trial but an enquiry... He stressed the importance of better public relations... They stress brotherly community in their rhetoric.* ▸ used as a noun. EG *This stress on community values is not so apparent in the east of the country.* V+O/REPORT-CL/QUOTE; ▸ N UNCOUNT + on

2 If you feel **stress** or if you are under **stress**, you feel tension and anxiety because of difficulties in your life. EG *Some young people are completely struck down by the stress of examinations... They were away from home, and in times of stress they felt it strongly... The family cannot cope under stress... The rationale for the divorce rate is that too many stresses are being placed on the modern family.* N UNCOUNT/N COUNT ⇑ strain = pressure

3 A **stress** is a strong physical pressure applied to an object. EG *...the stress due to bending... Earthquakes can result from stresses in the earth's crust.* N COUNT/UNCOUNT ⇑ force

4 **Stress** is emphasis that you put on a word or a part of a word when you pronounce it, so that it sounds slightly louder. EG *...the importance of stress and intonation... My father read English verse with the emphatic stress of his own classical schooldays.* ▸ used as a verb. EG *You should stress the second syllable in 'computer'.* N UNCOUNT; ▸ V+O = accent

stressed /strɛst/. 1 If you are **stressed**, you feel tension and anxiety because of difficulties in your life. EG *This has not stopped adults feeling stressed and anxious.* ADJ QUALIT : USU PRED = pressured

2 An object that is **stressed** is affected because strong physical pressure has been applied to it; a technical term in physics. ADJ QUALIT : USU PRED

stressful /strɛsful/. A situation or experience that is **stressful** causes a person to feel stress. EG *Life with several children is hard and stressful... Working parents often feel guilty at stressful times.* ADJ QUALIT ⇑ tense

stretch /strɛtʃ/, **stretches, stretching, stretched**. 1 A large area of land that **stretches** over a particular distance extends over this distance. EG *The countryside stretched far and wide into the darkness... The road stretched over two hundred miles through the heart of the country... The dry region stretches across the southern edge of the Sahara.* V+A = spread

2 A **stretch** of land or water is an area or distance of land or water, usually one that is fairly large. EG *...the stretch of water that separates Asia from Europe... ...seeing nothing but the small stretch of road immediately ahead... They were planning to go the whole stretch across country this way.* ● See also **home stretch**. N COUNT + SUPP = expanse

3 If you **stretch**, or if you **stretch** yourself, you push your arms or legs stiffly away from your body. People often stretch when they have just woken up, just got out of bed, or when they are feeling tired. EG *Thomas yawned and stretched... The men began to get up and stretch themselves... I just grunted and stretched my limbs non-committally.* ▸ used as a noun. EG *He had another lazy, luxurious stretch and then he said, 'I'll think about it.'* V OR V+O (NG/REFL); ▸ N COUNT : USU SING

4 A **stretch** of time is a period of time. EG *It was awful, that stretch of time before I knew the worst... Any job carries with it daily stretches of boredom.* N COUNT = spell

● If you do an activity for a particular length of time **at a stretch**, you do it for this length of time without stopping. EG *It was impossible to work for more than an hour or so at a stretch.* ● PHR : USED AS AN A = non-stop

5 A **stretch** is also a period of time that someone spends in prison; an informal use. EG *He did a five year stretch in Dartmoor.* N COUNT : USU SING = stint

6 If an activity **stretches** into a longer period of time, it lasts over this period of time. EG *The process often stretches out to years, even decades... The minutes had now stretched into hours.* V+A = lengthen

7 When you **stretch** something soft or elastic, or when it **stretches**, it is pulled until it becomes very tight or firm. EG *Stretch elastic between two drawing pins to hold it in place... The skin stretched tight over her fine facial bones.* V-ERG

8 **Stretch** material becomes longer or wider when you pull it and returns to its normal length or width when you let it go. EG *...a wide selection of stretch fabrics... ...stretch covers on armchairs.* ADJ CLASSIF : ATTRIB

9 If you **stretch** an amount of something such as food or money, you make it last longer than it usually V+O = eke out

does by being extremely careful and not wasting anything. EG *I had enough supplies for six months which I could stretch to eight if needs be... We simply can't stretch the budget enough to buy a car.*

10 If a person's or company's money or resources **are stretched**, they have hardly enough money or resources. EG *The nation's diplomatic resources were already stretched to their limits... Today many women are stretched economically.* V+O : USU PASS

11 If something such as your job **stretches** you, it makes you work hard and use all your energy or skills. EG *I think it's great to have to stretch oneself... I'm worried he's not being stretched enough at school.* V+O (NG/REFL) = push

12 If you **stretch** a rule, you adapt it or extend it slightly in order to be able to do something that you would not otherwise be able to do. EG *Protocol can only be stretched so far... Anyone can win if they stretch the rules like that.* V+O = bend

13 If you are **at full stretch**, 13.1 you have your arm extended straight as far as possible, usually when you are trying to reach something which is almost too far away. PHR : USED AS AN A 13.2 you are using the maximum amount of power or energy. EG *...running at full stretch towards the finishing line.* PHR : USED AS AN A = flat out

14 If you go to **stretch** your **legs**, you go for a short walk, often after you have been sitting down for a long time. EG *They left the boat for a time to stretch their legs on the land.* PHR : VB INFLECTS ⇑ exercise

15 If you **stretch** your **wings**, you do something new and rather difficult or move to a new place, because you want to gain wider experience. EG *You need to stretch your wings a bit.* PHR : VB INFLECTS ⇑ experiment

16 If someone in authority **stretches a point**, they allow another person to break the rules, because there are special reasons for doing so. EG *One might even stretch a point and say let her off this time.* PHR : VB INFLECTS

17 If you say that something is not true or possible etc **by any stretch of the imagination**, you are emphasizing that you think it is completely untrue or absolutely impossible. EG *It could by no stretch of the imagination be seen as a victory... Not by the wildest stretch of the imagination could he have conceived of such a plan.* PHR : USED AS AN A

stretch out. 1 If you **stretch out** or if you **stretch** yourself **out** somewhere, you lie there in a comfortable position with your legs and body in a straight line. EG *I just want to stretch out in my own bed... She groaned and stretched herself out flat on the sofa.* PHRASAL VB : V+O, OR V+O (REFL)+ADV

2 If you **stretch out** a part of your body, you extend it, usually in order to reach something or in order to see something better. EG *He stretched out a thin arm and took our hands... By stretching her neck out, she could see the sign.* PHRASAL VB : V+O+ADV

stretcher /stretʃə/, **stretchers**. A **stretcher** is a long piece of canvas with a pole along each side which is used to carry an injured or sick person, often into an ambulance. EG *He lay out on the stretcher while the doctor explained what he was going to do.* N COUNT ⇑ conveyance

stretcher-bearer, stretcher-bearers; also spelled as one word. A **stretcher-bearer** is a person who helps to carry a stretcher. EG *An ambulance pulled up and two stretcher-bearers jumped out.* N COUNT ⇑ attendant

stretchy /stretʃi[1]/, **stretchier, stretchiest**. **Stretchy** material is slightly elastic and able to stretch easily. EG *That material's a bit stretchy for a shirt* ADJ QUALIT

strew /stru:/, **strews, strewing, strewed, strewn**. 1 If things **are strewn** over a floor or other surface, they are scattered untidily over it. EG *His clothes were strewn all over the room... The carpet is strewn with broken glass... ...a piano with a lot of music strewn on it... They continued to strew cans and wrappers all across the fields.* V+O : USU PASS+A

2 If things **strew** a floor or other surface, they lie scattered over it. EG *Books and cushions strewed the floor.* V+O = litter

strewth /stru:θ/. Some people say **'strewth!'** when they are surprised or alarmed by something that has happened or that they have heard; a very informal word. EXCLAM

stricken /strɪkə[0]n/. If someone is **stricken**, they are badly affected by illness, trouble, unhappiness, etc. EG *Madeleine was stricken by fear... He seemed bewildered and stricken by the dreadful news... Stricken with crippling arthritis, she lay bed-ridden for many years... More than 800,000 jobs have been lost in the stricken industry in less than a decade.* ADJ QUALIT : IF+PREP THEN *with/by* ⇑ afflicted

-stricken is combined with some uncount nouns in order to form adjectives which describe negative emotions or unpleasant conditions. EG *...the poverty-stricken National Health Service... His wife was horror-stricken at what he'd done.* COMB : FORMS ADJS

strict /strɪkt/, **stricter, strictest**. 1 Someone who is **strict** does not tolerate behaviour which they consider to be impolite or disobedient, and is very firm in the way that they bring up their children. EG *Parents were strict in Victorian times... She was very strict with the children... ...a boarding school with strict discipline... ...Betty's strict upbringing.* ADJ QUALIT = rigorous, firm

◇ **strictly**. EG *Tony was brought up strictly but fairly.* ◇ ADV WITH VB

◇ **strictness**. EG *Strictness can be harmful when the parents are totally inflexible.* ◇ N UNCOUNT

2 A **strict** rule, law, order, etc is very precise and must be obeyed absolutely. EG *I doubt that stricter laws on guns would do anything at all to curb violence... Strict instructions were issued... I trust you will treat what I say in the strictest confidence... The Opposition demanded stricter control of prices.* ADJ QUALIT ⇑ absolute = stringent

◇ **strictly**. EG *This arrangement is to be kept strictly confidential... Smoking is strictly prohibited.* ◇ ADV WITH VB = rigidly

◇ **strictness**. EG *The curfew began early in the afternoon and was strictly enforced.* ◇ N COUNT

3 You use **strict** to describe the most basic and precise meaning of a word or piece of writing, rather than its more vague or general meanings. EG *He may not be lying in the strict sense of the word, but he's certainly not telling the whole truth... ...a strict interpretation of the law.* ◇ **strictly**. EG *That's not strictly true.* ADJ CLASSIF : ATTRIB = exact ◇ ADV+ADJ/ADV

4 You also use **strict** to describe someone who follows carefully and exactly the principles, rules, conventions, etc of a particular group, religion, or belief. EG *His family were strict Methodists... She was a strict vegetarian.* ADJ QUALIT : ATTRIB = faithful

strictly /strɪktli[1]/. 1 If something is **strictly** for a particular thing or person, it is to be used or done only by that thing or person and by nothing or nobody else. EG *The car park is strictly for the use of residents... Discussion was strictly for members.* ADV+*for* = solely

2 You use **strictly** to emphasize that someone keeps to a particular subject, relationship, etc and does not change it at all. EG *Everything he said was strictly to the point... This is a strictly doctor-patient relationship.* ADV+ADJ/ADV/PREP = scrupulously

3 You say **strictly speaking** when you want to correct a fact or to give more precise information about it. EG *Paul's a friend of mine. Well, strictly speaking my sister's friend... I think, strictly speaking, you are wrong there.* PHR : USED AS ADV SEN

4 Other meanings of **strictly** can be found in the entry for **strict**.

stricture /strɪktʃə/, **strictures**. A **stricture** is a severe criticism or disapproval of something; a formal word. EG *Throughout history the strictures of society have weighed more heavily upon women than upon men... His administration of the company was even more deserving of stricture than it appeared.* N COUNT : USU PL OR N UNCOUNT ≠ approval

stridden /strɪdə[0]n/ is the past participle of **stride**.

stride /straɪd/, **strides, striding, strode, stridden**. 1 If you **stride**, you walk with long steps, often because you are in a hurry. EG *Louisa watched him striding across the lawn towards his bonfire... He had turned and was striding out of the entrance.* V : USU+A = march

2 If you **stride** over or across something, you cross over it with just one long step. EG *The river was so narrow that he could easily stride over it.* V+A

3 A **stride** is 3.1 a long step which you take when you are walking or running. EG *When you run, take good strides and not dainty little steps.* N COUNT 3.2 a way of walking with long steps. EG *She walked ahead with her purposeful stride.* N SING WITH DET ⇑ gait

4 If you make **strides** in something such as scientific research or negotiations, you make rapid progress in that field. EG *This is a great stride forward... On the question of pay, giant strides have been made.* N COUNT : USU PL = advance

5 If you **get into** your **stride**, you start to do something confidently and fluently, whereas before you were a bit slow or uncertain. EG *He's really getting into his stride–he'll talk for hours.* PHR : VB INFLECTS = get going

6 If you **take** something **in** your **stride**, you accept it and deal with it calmly and sensibly without consid- PHR : VB INFLECTS

ering it to be a problem. EG *She takes examinations in her stride.*

stridency /straɪdənsi[1]/ is the quality of being strident. N UNCOUNT

strident /straɪdənt/. 1 A **strident** voice or sound is loud, harsh, and unpleasant to listen to. EG *He could not help overhearing the conversation, so strident was her tone... The note on the trumpet became a strident blare.* ◇ **stridently**. EG *The telephone rang stridently.* ADJ QUALIT; ◇ ADV WITH VB

2 If you are **strident** or if what you say is **strident**, you make your feelings or beliefs known in a very harsh, persistent manner. EG *There have been strident demands that more should be done for one-parent families.* ◇ **stridently**. EG *Once again he was stridently proclaiming that he had never been wrong.* ADJ QUALIT ⇑ loud = clamorous; ◇ ADV

strife /straɪf/ is trouble and fighting between people or groups caused by conflict or disagreement. EG *He used the opportunity to exaggerate the strife between the two organizations.* N UNCOUNT

strike /straɪk/, **strikes, striking, struck**. 1 A **strike** is a refusal by workers to continue working, usually because they are demanding more pay or better conditions, or because they are protesting about something. EG *...the miners' strike... The union leaders called a strike... Workers went on strike for better pay... They've been on strike for nearly three weeks now... The print workers came out on strike yesterday... We will not be involved in strike action.* N COUNT, OR *on*+N ⇑ dispute

2 If workers **strike**, they refuse to continue working, usually because they are demanding more pay or better conditions, or because they are protesting about something. EG *Airline pilots are threatening to strike... We are striking for more pay.* V ⇑ protest

3 A hunger **strike**, rent **strike**, etc is a refusal to eat anything, pay your rent, etc as a protest about something. EG *They decided to organize a rent strike... He went on a nine-week hunger strike.* N COUNT : MOD+N

4 If you **strike** someone or something, you hit them with your hand, a stick, or something else, usually because you are angry with them. EG *The young man struck his father... He was striking his dog with his whip.* V+O

5 If you **strike** an object such as a ball, you hit it hard, so that it goes in a particular direction. EG *He struck the ball beautifully.* V+O

6 If something **strikes** against something else or if you **strike** it against something, it knocks or bumps against the other thing. EG *He struck his hand against the wood of the door... The trawler struck heavily against the jetty.* V-ERG+A = bang

7 If something **is struck** by a missile, bomb, lightning, etc, it is hit by it, usually causing damage. EG *A frigate was struck by a torpedo... The house was struck by lightning.* V+O : USU PASS

8 If an illness, disaster, etc **strikes**, it has a sudden harmful effect on a person or an area. EG *When personal disaster strikes, you need sympathy and practical advice... The earthquake that struck Fiji last Tuesday caused 150 deaths... Illness struck once again.* V OR V+O ⇑ attack

9 If you **strike** at someone or something, you do or say something which attacks them. EG *The opposition had struck at the root of Labour's strategy.* V+A *(at)*

10 If a blow, force, or impact **strikes home**, it hits its target exactly. EG *Her blow struck home... She stopped for ten seconds to allow the full impact of what she had said to strike home.* PHR : VB INFLECTS

11 If you **strike a blow for** a particular cause, belief, or ideal, you do something significant on behalf of it or in support of it. EG *He struck a blow for democracy.* PHR : VB INFLECTS

12 To **strike** means to attack someone or something quickly and violently. EG *Raising herself slightly, the snake strikes... When will the killer strike again?* ▸ used as a noun. EG *Its soundless flight makes the long-eared owl's strike a sudden and fatal surprise.* V; ▸ N COUNT : USU SING

13 A **strike** is also a military attack, especially an attack from the air which succeeds in hitting the target. EG *The Air Force carried out air strikes as a result of information received.* N COUNT : USU MOD+N = raid

14 If an idea or thought **strikes** you, it comes into your mind suddenly. EG *The usual thought struck him-what to do for money?... It struck him how foolish her behaviour was... The next morning it struck me that there was no shower in the flat.* V+O : USU+REPORT-CL = occur to

15 If something **strikes** you in a particular way, it gives you a particular impression, usually a strong one. EG *Gertie strikes me as a very silly girl... How did London strike you?* V+O : USU+A *(as)* ⇑ impress

16 If you are **struck** by something, you are very impressed by it. EG *I was immediately struck by the idea... I was very much struck by London.* V+O : USU PASS+*with/by* ⇑ be taken

17 If something **strikes the eye**, it is noticeable. EG *What strikes the eye in Hyde Park are the flowers.* PHR : VB INFLECTS

18 When a clock **strikes**, its bells or chimes make a sound to indicate what the time is. EG *The church clock struck eleven... It is just striking six on the grandfather clock.* V OR V+O

19 If you **strike** a note, chord, etc on a musical instrument, you play that note, chord, etc on it. EG *He struck a few notes on the piano... She struck the last chord and looked up.* V+O

20 If someone says something which **strikes a** particular **note**, it gives you a particular impression about them or about their attitude. EG *His words struck a slightly false note for me.* PHR : VB INFLECTS

21 If someone says something which **strikes a chord**, other people sympathize or identify with it in some way. EG *It was obvious that his speech was striking a chord among the group.* PHR : VB INFLECTS

22 If you **strike** a bargain or deal with someone, you come to an agreement, especially after a lot of discussion or argument. EG *The bargain we struck with them last year has already been broken... The city council hoped to strike a deal that would give the council more power.* V+O ⇑ agree

23 If you **strike a balance**, you reach a sensible middle point between two extremes. EG *It is not easy to strike a balance between too much and too little freedom.* PHR : VB INFLECTS

24 If something **strikes** fear or terror **into people** or their **hearts**, it causes sudden, strong feelings of fear or terror. EG *The enormous metal tanks struck terror into the hearts of the peasants.* PHR : VB INFLECTS

25 If you **are struck dumb** or **are struck blind**, you suddenly become unable to speak or to see. EG *We were struck dumb with horror.* PHR : AUX INFLECTS

26 If you **strike** a match or a light, you produce a flame or sparks with a match. EG *Don't strike a match if you smell gas... He struck a light.* V+O ⇑ ignite

27 If you **strike** oil, gold, or some other valuable substance, you discover it, usually as a result of mining or drilling for it. EG *They struck oil in the North Sea... Finding a flat you can afford is like striking gold in your garden.* V+O ⇑ find

28 If you **strike lucky** or **strike oil**, you have good luck; used in informal English. EG *He had struck lucky in having someone who was so sensitive to look after him... She struck oil when she met John.* PHR : VB INFLECTS

● If you **strike it rich**, you make a lot of money, especially very suddenly or unexpectedly. ● PHR : VB INFLECTS

29 An oil **strike**, gold **strike**, etc is the discovery of oil, gold, or some other mineral, by mining or drilling for it. N COUNT : USU MOD+N ⇑ find

30 If you **strike** a particular posture, pose, attitude, etc, you put your body into that position and hold it there. EG *He was reluctant to strike such an undignified pose before his girlfriend.* V+O ⇑ adopt

31 To **strike** something such as a coin or medal means to produce it. EG *The government decided that a one pound coin should be struck.* V+O = mint

32 To **strike camp** means to take down the tents in a camp. PHR : VB INFLECTS

33 See also **striking**. ● to **strike while the iron is hot**: see **iron**.

strike back. If you **strike back**, you attempt to harm someone in return for some injury they have done you. PHRASAL VB : V+ADV

strike down. If something **strikes** someone **down**, it is the cause of death, injury, or serious disability. EG *Kennedy was struck down by an assassin's bullet... Polio struck him down.* PHRASAL VB : V+O+ADV ⇑ afflict

strike off. If someone such as a doctor, lawyer, or other professional person **is struck off**, their name is taken off an official list or register and they are not allowed to practise any more. This is usually because they have done something criminal or unethical. PHRASAL VB : V+O+ADV, USU PASS ⇑ remove

strike on. 1 If you **strike on** a solution, answer, plan, etc, you unexpectedly think of it. EG *He had for once struck on a quite shrewd judgement.* PHRASAL VB : V+PREP, HAS PASS = hit on

2 If you **are struck on** an idea, you are impressed with it. PHRASAL VB : V+PREP

strike out. 1 If you **strike out**, you begin to do something different, often because you want to become more independent. EG *He decided to strike out on his own... The company was striking out in new directions in the field of drama.* PHRASAL VB : V+ADV, USU+A = start out

2 If you **strike out** somewhere, you **2.1** set out in a particular direction. EG *He decided to leave the path and strike out across the grass.* PHRASAL VB : V+ADV, USU+A **2.2** swim strongly in order to get there. EG *He struck out for the island.* PHRASAL VB : V+ADV, USU+A

3 If you **strike out** at someone, you aim a blow or punch at them. PHRASAL VB : V+ADV, USU+A

4 If you **strike out** something you have written, you put a line through it because it is a mistake or because you do not want it to be seen. EG *She read through her essay and struck out a few words here and there.* PHRASAL VB : V+O+ADV = cross out

strike up. 1 When you **strike up** a conversation or friendship with someone you have just met, you begin it. EG *Alice and I struck up a friendship immediately... I struck up conversations with a number of women in the school playground.* PHRASAL VB : ORDER V+ADV+O ↑ start

2 When musicians **strike up**, they begin to play music. EG *The orchestra struck up the national anthem... The band strikes up at noon.* PHRASAL VB : V+ADV, OR ORDER V+ADV+O

strikebound /straɪkbaʊnd/. If a place is **strikebound**, people are unable to work or move around freely because other people are on strike. EG *The whole country was strikebound.* ADJ CLASSIF : USU PRED ↑ restricted

strike-breaker, strike-breakers; also spelled without a hyphen. A **strike-breaker** is a person who continues to work during a strike, or someone who takes over the work of a person who is on strike. EG *Clashes would break out between strikers and strike breakers.* N COUNT = scab

strike pay; also spelled with a hyphen. **Strike pay** is money which is paid by a trade union to workers who are on strike. N UNCOUNT

striker /straɪkə/, **strikers**. A **striker** is 1 someone who refuses to continue working, usually because they are demanding more pay or better conditions. N COUNT ↑ worker

2 a football player whose main purpose is to attack rather than defend. N COUNT

striking /straɪkɪŋ/. 1 Something that is **striking** is so remarkable that it cannot be ignored. EG *Patients are often willing to chat to a computer, in striking contrast to their reluctance to talk to their doctors... The most striking thing about Piccadilly Circus is the statue of Eros in the centre.* ◊ **strikingly**. EG *The two women appeared strikingly different.* ADJ QUALIT = conspicuous, marked ◊ ADV+ADJ/ADV

2 Someone who is **striking** attracts attention, usually because of their attractive appearance. EG *She was a striking redhead... His striking good looks and charm made him very popular.* ◊ **strikingly**. EG *...a strikingly pretty girl.* ADJ QUALIT = stunning ◊ ADV+ADJ/ADV

3 If you are **within striking distance** of something, you are very near to it. EG *The enemy were within striking distance... She never came within striking distance of passing a Latin exam!* PHR : USED AS AN A

string /strɪŋ/, **strings, stringing, strung**. 1 **String** is thin cord made of twisted threads. It is used, for example, for tying things together or for tying up parcels. EG *She took the parcel and started to undo the string... ...a ball of string... ...a vast bunch of balloons on a string.* N UNCOUNT/COUNT

2 A **string** of similar objects is a number of them that have been connected together on a thread or wire. EG *...strings of beads round her neck... The only lights were a distant string of bulbs.* N COUNT : ALSO N+*of*+N IN PL = row

3 A **string** of events, objects, etc is a series of them that happen or are found one after the other. EG *...a 100 mile string of islands... It was the latest in a string of hotel disasters.* N COUNT OR N PART+N IN PL = chain

4 On a musical instrument, a **string** is a thin length of wire, nylon, or other material that is stretched tightly across it. You make sounds by plucking the strings or by passing a bow across them. EG *...a violin string... ...a guitar with only one string.* N COUNT

5 The section of an orchestra which consists of stringed instruments that are played with a bow is called the **strings**. EG *Gradually, as the frenzied strings take over, the hall fills with a crescendo of sound... The orchestra has brilliant wind players but not such good string players.* N PLURAL

6 If you **string** a musical instrument, you put the strings on it. EG *I've always had trouble stringing my violin.* V+O

7 If you **string** something somewhere or **string it up**, you hang or tie a long line of it high in the air between two or more objects. EG *Lights had been strung in the trees of the big gardens... She had strung up new curtains against the window.* V+O+A, OR PHRASAL VB : V+O+ADV = put up

8 The word **string** is also used in the following expressions. **8.1** If you **have got** someone **on a string**, you can make them do what you want them to do, whether they really want to or not. EG *She's really got him on a string!* PHR : AUX INFLECTS ↑ dominate **8.2** If you **have two strings to** your **bow, more than one string to** your **bow**, etc, you have at least one more idea, job, or ability which you can use if your first one is not successful. EG *The recession won't hit him–he's got more than one string to his bow!* PHR : VB INFLECTS **8.3** If you **pull strings** to get something, you use the influence that you have with other people in order to get it; often used showing disapproval. EG *Jane took up Derek's offer to pull a few strings and get her at least a year at university.* PHR : VB INFLECTS

8.4 If something is offered to you **with no strings attached**, it is offered to you without any conditions or restrictions. EG *We will pay you ten and a quarter per cent with no strings attached... They offered medical aid without strings attached.* PHR : USED AS AN A ↑ unconditionally

string along. 1 If you **string along** with someone, you stay with them rather casually for the time being and do what they are doing; an informal expression. EG *I'll string along with you... He'll string along if he gets bored.* PHRASAL VB : V+ADV = tag along 2 If you **string** someone **along**, you deceive them by encouraging them to believe that you both have the same desires, beliefs, hopes, etc; used in informal English showing disapproval. EG *He'll never marry her, he's just stringing her along!* PHRASAL VB : V+O+ADV

string out. If something **is strung out**, it is spread out in a line, as if it were on a string. EG *...boom towns strung out along dirt roads.* PHRASAL VB : V-ERG+ADV

string together. If you **string together** several things, you join them together, so that they follow one another. EG *I sang her a wistful ballad and strung together some rhymes to amuse her.* PHRASAL VB : V+O+ADV = put together

string up. 1 To **string** someone **up** means to kill them by hanging them; an informal expression. PHRASAL VB : V+O+ADV

string bean, string beans. A **string bean** is the same as a runner bean. N COUNT

stringed instrument /strɪŋd¹ ɪnstrə⁴mə²nt/, **stringed instruments**. A **stringed instrument** is a musical instrument which has strings, such as a violin or a guitar. N COUNT

stringency /strɪndʒənsi¹/. **Stringency** is 1 shortage of money, either for spending or for investing. EG *They suffered a year of appalling financial stringency.* N UNCOUNT 2 severity in the application of rules, laws, and other things which should be obeyed. N UNCOUNT

stringent /strɪndʒənt/. Laws, rules, or conditions that are **stringent** are very strictly controlled or enforced because they must be obeyed. EG *There were no stringent rules applied to the hunting of deer in the forest... He gave his sister one hundred dollars per month under the stringent condition that she would never enter his house again... It may be that we need to introduce stringent controls.* ◊ **stringently**. EG *Information from the trial was treated much less stringently than in previous similar cases.* ADJ QUALIT = strict ◊ ADV WITH VB

stringy /strɪŋi¹/, **stringier, stringiest**. 1 Meat or other food that is **stringy** is unpleasant and tough and difficult to chew. EG *The meat was brownish-grey and stringy.* ADJ QUALIT = chewy

2 Something such as hair that is **stringy** is thin and coarse, and looks rather like string. EG *...her stringy hair, the colour of straw.* ADJ QUALIT = ratty

strip /strɪp/, **strips, stripping, stripped**. 1 A **strip** of paper, cloth, or other material is a long, narrow piece of it. EG *...a thin strip of paper... The room was bare, apart from a strip of carpet.* N COUNT : ALSO N+*of*+N UNCOUNT = shred

2 A **strip** of land or water is a long narrow area of it. EG *There was only a narrow strip of firm beach... Between Grosvenor Road and the river is a strip of green called Pimlico Gardens.* N COUNT : ALSO N+*of*+N UNCOUNT = belt

3 A **strip** or an **airstrip** is a stretch of land which has been cleared so that aircraft can take off and land, but which is not part of a commercial airport. EG *We watched the planes taking off from his private landing strip... A bunch of marines appeared on the edge of the strip and ran to the chopper.* N COUNT ↑ runway

4 When you **strip** or **strip off** your clothes, **4.1** you take off your clothes. EG *They told her to strip...* V OR PHRASAL VB : V+ADV, OR

Casson stripped off his raincoat... ...all those housewives, stripped to their leotards... ...stripped to the waist. +O+ADV ⇑ undress **4.2** you take off your clothes in a slow and sexy way in order to give pleasure and excitement to other people. EG *She wasn't willing to strip for such a small audience.* ▸ used as a noun. EG *...a strip show.* V ⇑ undress ▸ N UNCOUNT/ COUNT

5 If you **strip** someone or **strip off** their clothes, you take off their clothes, sometimes rather carelessly or brutally. EG *The other one stripped off my waistcoat and threw it in the corner... Before the ship sailed they were stripped to their skins by the captain, who suspected they were smuggling.* V+O, OR PHRASAL VB : V+O+ADV ⇑ undress

6 To **strip** something means to remove everything that is covering its surface, in order to expose the basic structure. EG *The wind stripped the tree of all its leaves. Someone got up on the roof and stripped away all the lead... The paint could easily be stripped off.* V+O, OR V+ADV +O

7 If you **strip** a building or ship, you take all the furniture, etc out of it so that only the basic structure remains. EG *Thieves stripped all the furniture out of the house... They stripped the house of everything of value... The company had had the 'Morning Rose' completely stripped and re-fitted for passenger accommodation.* V+O : USU+A ⇑ empty

8 If you **strip** an engine or a piece of equipment, or if you **strip** it **down**, you take it to pieces, usually in order to clean it or because it is not working properly. V+O, OR PHRASAL VB : V+O+ADV

9 To **strip** people or society of habits, customs, etc or to **strip** these habits etc **away** means to get rid of them. EG *The individual must strip himself of old habits... This is the pretence that is to be stripped away on the Day of Judgement.* V+O (NG/REFL) +*of*, OR PHRASAL VB : V+O+ADV

10 If you **strip** someone of their property, rights, or titles or if you **strip** these things **away**, you take them away from them. EG *She was discarded by her husband and automatically stripped of all her property and possessions... The company went through the final process of stripping away my remaining pension rights.* V+O+*of*, OR PHRASAL VB : V+O+ADV ⇑ deprive

11 In a newspaper or magazine, a **strip** or a **strip cartoon** is a row of separate drawings which together tell a story, often a funny or satirical one. The words spoken by the characters are often written on the drawings. EG *...the American comic strip, the Katzenjammer kids.... Every morning she read the adventures of her favourite strip characters in the Daily Express.* N COUNT

12 When you play a sport, especially football, your **strip** is the clothing you wear. N COUNT : USU SING

13 If you **tear a strip off** someone or if you **tear** them **off a strip**, you are very angry with them and tell them so very clearly indeed. EG *His father really tore him off a strip.* PHR : VB INFLECTS ⇑ reprimand

strip club, strip clubs; also spelled with a hyphen. A **strip club** is a club which people go to in order to see striptease. N COUNT

stripe /straɪp/, **stripes**. **1** A **stripe** is a long line which is usually a different colour or texture from the parts which are next to it. EG *...a pram-cover in stripes of white and blue... ...a white shirt with a thin grey stripe.* N COUNT

2 In the police or the armed forces, **stripes** are narrow bands of material sewn onto a uniform to indicate someone's rank. EG *She was very proud when at last he received his stripes.* N COUNT

striped /straɪpt/. Something that is **striped** is made up of a number of stripes. EG *...a gentleman in a black coat and striped trousers... Ralph pointed fearfully at Eric's face, which was striped with scars where the bushes had torn him.* ADJ CLASSIF ⇑ lined

strip joint, strip joints; also spelled with a hyphen. A **strip joint** is the same as a strip club; used especially in informal American English. N COUNT

strip lighting; also spelled with a hyphen. **Strip lighting** is a method of lighting which uses long tubes rather than electric light bulbs. N UNCOUNT

stripling /strɪplɪŋ/, **striplings**. A **stripling** is a young man who is no longer a boy but is not yet really a man; often used humorously. EG *He was a stripling, a boy of nineteen.* N COUNT = youngster

stripper /strɪpə/, **strippers**. A **stripper** is a woman who earns money doing striptease in clubs or at parties. N COUNT

striptease /strɪpti:z/, **stripteases**; also spelled with a hyphen. **Striptease** is a form of entertainment in which someone takes off their clothes slowly and sexily to music in order to give pleasure and excitement to other people. EG *I'd like to see some striptease... He's never been to a striptease in his life... The strip-tease clubs were all closed.* N COUNT/ UNCOUNT = strip

stripy /straɪpi¹/, **stripier, stripiest**. Something that is **stripy** is made up of a lot of stripes. EG *...a very French shirt all stripy like a sailor's.* ADJ QUALIT = striped

strive /straɪv/, **strives, striving, strove, striven**. If you **strive** for something or **strive** to do something, you make a very great effort, usually over a long period of time, to get it or to do it. EG *The history of train transport has partly been a history of striving for greater efficiency... The Russians strove to give the impression that they were going to land on the moon... Historians should strive after objectivity... They have striven for freedom to create a new social order.* ◇ **striving**. EG *The rebellious striving to get free from the parents does not arise with all children.* V+*to*-INF/A ⇑ struggle ◇ N UNCOUNT ⇑ struggle

strobe /strəʊb/. **Strobe** or **strobe lighting** is very bright lighting which flashes on and off very quickly. N UNCOUNT

strode /strəʊd/ is the past tense of **stride**.

stroke /strəʊk/, **strokes, stroking, stroked**. **1** If you **stroke** someone or something, you move your hand slowly over them, touching them in a gentle, loving way. EG *She put out a hand and stroked the cat softly... He stroked her hair affectionately.* ▸ used as a noun. EG *I gave the kitten a little stroke, but it kept on mewing.* V+O = caress ▸ N COUNT : USU SING = caress

2 A **stroke** is a sudden illness like a heart attack, but which can cause brain damage or paralysis in part of your body. EG *She had a stroke and was unable to walk for the rest of her life... The stroke paralysed half his face.* N COUNT : USU SING ⇑ seizure

3 The **strokes** of a pen or brush are the movements you make with it when you are writing or painting. EG *She began to paint with bold, defiant strokes.* ▸ used also of the lines that you make with these movements. EG *...a piece of paper covered in illegible strokes.* N COUNT = sweep ▸ N COUNT = mark

4 When you are swimming or rowing, your **strokes** are your repeated action of pushing your arms out and pulling them back. EG *She swam with steady strokes... He kicked only every third or fourth stroke.* N COUNT ⇑ move

5 A swimming **stroke** is a particular style or method of swimming. EG *Which stroke do you prefer-butterfly or crawl?* N COUNT : USU SING+SUPP

6 A **stroke** is also one action of hitting somebody with a stick or other weapon; a rather old-fashioned use. EG *I received twelve strokes of the cane as punishment.* N COUNT ⇑ blow

7 The **strokes** of a clock are the sounds that it makes when it strikes or chimes. You count the strokes in order to find out what time it is. EG *The clock stopped after six strokes... At the twelfth stroke, we welcomed in the New Year.* N COUNT = peal

8 In speech, **stroke** means the same as oblique. You say 'stroke' between two words when you want to indicate that there is a choice or connection between them which would not be as clear if you used a linking word such as 'and' or 'or'. When you say 'stroke', you are deliberately reminding people of the oblique punctuation mark that is used to indicate this connection in writing. EG *If somebody comes up to you, ask what he stroke she wants... Bette Midler is the greatest singer stroke comedian in the world.* = slash

9 A **stroke** of luck, a **stroke** of genius, etc is something, usually a good thing, that happens or occurs to you quickly, suddenly, and unexpectedly. EG *It was a stroke of luck-nothing could have been more suited to our needs... Her idea was a stroke of genius.* N SING : *a*+N+*of* ⇑ occurrence

10 If you say that something happens **at a single stroke, in one stroke**, etc, you mean that it happens by one single, sudden, strong action. EG *He was determined at a stroke to remove those distinctions between senior and junior pupils in the school.* PHR : USED AS AN A = at one go

11 If you say that someone **does not do a stroke** or **does not do a stroke of work**, you mean that they are very lazy and never do any work; an informal expression. EG *We haven't done a stroke tonight.* PHR : VB INFLECTS

12 If you say that something **puts** someone **off** their **stroke**, you mean that it prevents them from concentrating on what they are doing, so that they do not do it as well as usual. EG *I wish you wouldn't stare like that, you know it puts her off her stroke.* PHR : VB INFLECTS ⇑ distract

stroll /strəʊl/, **strolls, strolling, strolled.** If you **stroll** somewhere, you walk in a slow, relaxed way. EG *They strolled along the beach.* ▸ used as a noun. EG *She decided to take a stroll in the garden.* [V+A = ramble; ▸ N COUNT = turn]

stroller /strəʊlə/, **strollers.** A **stroller** is a baby's pushchair; used especially in American English. [N COUNT]

strong /strɒŋ/, **stronger, strongest.** 1 People or animals that are **strong** have well-developed muscles and great physical ability so that, for example, they can work hard, carry heavy objects, or hold things very tightly. EG *She was small and frail-looking, but deceptively strong... His strong arms were around me, pinning me down.* [ADJ QUALIT = powerful ≠ weak]

2 Objects that are **strong** are made of a material which is not easily broken so that they are able to support a considerable weight. EG *They buried writings in steel cylinders strong enough to survive even a nuclear catastrophe... Check that your ladder is strong and firm.* [ADJ QUALIT = sturdy, tough] ◊ **strongly.** EG *A few of the smaller and more strongly constructed buildings remained standing after the earthquake.* [◊ ADV WITH VB = solidly]

3 You use **strong 3.1** to describe something such as an influence which affects you very much, and which causes you to feel a particular emotion or to have a particular opinion. EG *His teachings still exert a strong influence... The compulsion to return may be strong... All these factors combined add up to a strong incentive to buy more machines and employ more people.* [ADJ QUALIT ⇑ great = considerable] ◊ **strongly.** EG *His mother will strongly influence his choice of a wife when he grows up.* [◊ ADV WITH VB] **3.2** to describe an attitude or situation which is very intense or serious or which you cannot easily ignore. EG *There is strong criticism of certain particular aspects of the case... It had the strong support of the General Council... I don't have any very strong views on the subject at all.* [ADJ QUALIT = passionate, fervent] ◊ **strongly.** EG *I feel very strongly about the price of petrol... I would strongly advise you against such an action... Sir Samuel's summing-up was strongly in Sackville's favour.* [◊ ADV WITH VB = firmly] **3.3** to describe opinions and actions which other people may think are unpleasant or severe, but which you believe are necessary in order to improve a difficult situation. EG *Their action would necessitate strong measures... They came to power in 1968 with a strong anti-inflation programme.* [ADJ QUALIT = tough]

4 If the arguments for something are **strong**, they are supported by a lot of evidence and are likely to succeed in convincing people that something is true or that a particular course of action is right. EG *There is a strong case for an Act of Parliament... He certainly would need strong arguments before he would divert significant funds to the project.* [ADJ QUALIT ⇑ good] ◊ **strongly.** EG *Gibson argues, and argues very strongly indeed, for this proposal.* [◊ ADV WITH VB]

5 If someone is **strong** in their beliefs, attitudes, etc. they are not easily influenced by other people and are confident that they can deal with a particular situation or problem. EG *I felt suddenly very strong and serene in the knowledge of my own innocence... He has the rare power of being a strong personality without dominating.* [ADJ QUALIT = powerful]

6 If you say that someone is a **strong** supporter or believer in something, you mean that they support it or believe in it very much. EG *An old lady, a strong Labour supporter, grabbed me by the arm... I'm a strong believer in the chemistry of love.* [ADJ QUALIT : USU ATTRIB = staunch, fervent] ◊ **strongly.** EG *They were strongly anti-war.* [◊ ADV = fervently]

7 If individuals or groups are **strong**, they are important and have great influence or power. EG *On that committee there's a very strong student representation... The police were strong enough to keep such movements in check...* [ADJ QUALIT = powerful] ◊ **strongly.** EG *The cordon was strongly manned by police and military units.* [◊ ADV WITH VB]

8 If you describe a particular group as **strong**, you mean that it includes a lot of people who are very good at a particular activity or job. EG *It's the strongest cast of actors we have seen on their main stage for a long time.* [ADJ QUALIT ⇑ competent]

9 Someone who is **strong** on something is very good at it. EG *Comedy is where I'm strong... All the lecturers are very strong on practical coaching.* [ADJ QUALIT : USU +on]

10 Your **strong** points or your **strong** subjects are things which you are good at or which are likely to make you popular or successful. EG *Diplomacy and an eye for publicity are your strong points... Maths was always his strong subject.* [ADJ QUALIT : USU ATTRIB = best]

11 You can also use **strong** to indicate how successful a person was or is likely to be in a competition. EG *I always thought she was a very strong candidate... He surprised everyone by finishing a strong second.* [ADJ QUALIT : ATTRIB ⇑ good]

12 You describe people who have been ill as **strong** when they are well again. EG *Next week you may travel, when you are a little stronger... Swearing that he was strong enough to cook again, he sent me off with a shopping list.* [ADJ QUALIT : USU PRED = fit]

13 If you describe someone's face as **strong**, you mean that it has very distinct features. EG *It was one of those strong, firm faces which have a permanent tan... The glance was strong and steady in its challenge.* [ADJ QUALIT = firm, hard]

14 If you say that someone has **strong** nerves or a **strong** head or stomach, you mean that that they have sufficient character and personality to succeed in or to overcome a difficult situation. EG *His success was based on inner calm, strong nerves and an acute memory for dates... It was an unpleasant world and one that required a strong stomach.* [ADJ QUALIT ≠ weak]

15 Someone who has a **strong** accent has one which is very distinct and which indicates where they live or what their native language is. EG *They still spoke the language with a strong German accent... Most of them have strong local accents.* [ADJ QUALIT = pronounced ≠ faint] ◊ **strongly.** EG *Their accents sounded strongly northern.* [◊ ADV+ADJ = markedly]

16 Relationships that are **strong** are firm and are likely to last for a long time. EG *Links with the trade unions were in any case strong... The family in China today is as strong a unit as anywhere else in the world.* [ADJ QUALIT]

17 If there is a **strong** chance, likelihood, probability, etc of something happening, it is very likely to happen. EG *The strong possibility is that he will be told to try again next year.* [ADJ QUALIT = definite]

18 Winds, currents, or earthquakes that are **strong** move very fast or with great force. EG *He only felt the cold strong wind in the reeds... These local volcanic tremors are usually not strong.* [ADJ QUALIT ≠ gentle]

19 Industries, economies, currencies, etc that are **strong** are financially successful. EG *Sterling has once again become one of the stronger currencies... This harmony might not last for long if the economy stays strong... It also has a very strong chemical industry.* [ADJ QUALIT = prosperous]

20 Drinks such as coffee or tea that are **strong** are dark in colour and have a very distinct flavour, because they are made using a lot of coffee or tea. EG *She made him a cup of tea so strong that he could hardly drink it.* [ADJ QUALIT = concentrated]

21 Alcoholic drinks that are **strong** contain a lot of alcohol. EG *The drink wasn't strong enough for him and he added more whisky... She never drank anything stronger than Coke.* [ADJ QUALIT = alcoholic]

22 Chemicals, drugs, etc that are **strong** are very effective for a particular purpose and contain a large amount of a particular substance in proportion to the amount of water and other substances. EG *...a strong household bleach... I take some very strong tranquillisers which keep me dazed all day.* [ADJ QUALIT = powerful ≠ mild]

23 Smells and tastes that are **strong** are very distinct and easily noticed. EG *The smell of the gas grew stronger; she began to feel giddy... It had a bad taste, strong and salty.* [ADJ QUALIT ⇑ noticeable ≠ faint] ◊ **strongly.** EG *The kitchen smelled strongly of fish.* [◊ ADV WITH VB]

24 Light that is **strong** is very bright and clear so that you can see well. EG *The light of the moon was so strong that I could read the small print along the base of the form... There was a pitch-dark stage with very strong lights shining on the actors.* [ADJ QUALIT ⇑ intense ≠ faint]

25 Colours that are **strong** are very bright and intense. EG *In dyeing patterned material, the strongest colour in the pattern should be used as the test-piece.* [ADJ QUALIT = vivid, bold]

26 Sounds or voices that are **strong** are very loud or clear. EG *The choir from the nearby training school were in strong voice that evening.* [ADJ QUALIT = good] ◊ **strongly.** EG *'Hands up,' said Jack strongly, 'whoever wants Ralph to be chief?'* [◊ ADV WITH VB = powerfully]

27 A **strong** lens helps you to see very small objects more clearly by making them appear much larger. EG *The egg would barely be visible through a strong lens.* [ADJ QUALIT = powerful]

28 If you say that a group of people is twenty **strong**, forty **strong**, etc, you mean that there are twenty or forty people in it. EG *Some army troops nearly 50,000* [ADJ CLASSIF : ONLY NUM+AD]

strong continued to be stationed in Germany... ...the forty-two strong executive committee.

29 If someone **comes on strong**, **29.1** they indicate clearly by their behaviour that they are sexually attracted to another person; an informal expression used showing disapproval. EG *She comes on very strong indeed whenever he's in the room.* PHR : VB INFLECTS **29.2** they speak or act towards another person in a way which other people think is too severe; an informal expression. EG *Don't you think you came on a bit strong there?* PHR : VB INFLECTS = go too far

30 If something is still **going strong**, it has existed for a long time but is still popular, successful, or working well now; an informal expression. EG *The station started in 1904, it's still going strong and it currently produces 405 megawatts of electricity.* PHR : USED AS C = flourishing

31 If someone is still **going strong**, they are very old but are still alive and healthy. EG *He's nearly ninety and still going strong.* PHR : USED AS C

strong-arm people or tactics rely on threats or force in order to persuade other people to behave in a particular way; used showing disapproval. EG *He brought along two strong-arm men from his private guard... They began by offering protection against the gang's strong-arm tactics.* ADJ CLASSIF : ATTRIB ↑ bullying

stronghold /strɒŋhəuld/, **strongholds**. **1** If you say that a place or region is a **stronghold** of a particular attitude or belief, you mean that most people there share that attitude or belief. EG *It is a solid Labour stronghold with only negligible Liberal strength... They were resuming their air raids on guerrilla strongholds in the south of the country.* N COUNT+SUPP = bastion

2 A **stronghold** is also a fortress; an old-fashioned use. N COUNT

strong-minded. Someone who is **strong-minded** has their own attitudes and opinions and is not easily influenced by other people. EG *...a strong-minded local girl named Katharine.* ADJ QUALIT = independent, determined

strong-willed. Someone who is **strong-willed** is determined to behave in a particular way although other people may advise them not to; sometimes used showing disapproval. ADJ QUALIT = headstrong

stroppy /strɒpi¹/, **stroppier, stroppiest**. Someone who is **stroppy** is bad-tempered and obstinate; an informal word used in British English. EG *She threatened to get stroppy.* ADJ QUALIT = obstreperous

strove /strəuv/ is the past tense of **strive**.

struck /strʌk/ is the past tense and past participle of **strike**.

structural /strʌktʃəᵒrəl/ is used to describe an aspect of the structure of something. EG *We plastered over the major structural faults in the walls... I was shocked at the structural damage... These compounds have structural similarities to penicillin... The film would require some major structural changes.* ADJ CLASSIF : USU ATTRIB ◇ **structurally**. EG *Gaps between walls and ceilings are structurally rarely serious.* ◇ ADV

structuralism /strʌktʃəᵒrəlɪzəᵒm/ is a theory of the method of analysing a subject such as literature, language, or society, in which the different and changing aspects of the subject are considered as being caused and organized by a hidden set of rules and patterns which form an important basic structure to the subject. N UNCOUNT ◇ **structuralist, structuralists**. EG *...Levi-Strauss, the great French structuralist anthropologist... New theories about language and writing have supplanted the structuralist movement of the 1950s.* ◇ N COUNT

structure /strʌktʃə/, **structures, structuring, structured**. **1** The **structure** of something is the way in which it is made, built, or organized, with all its different parts or aspects forming a particular shape, pattern, or system. EG *We know a lot about the structure of genes now... She analysed the structure of its skull in great detail... The whole structure of the film was rather simplistic... Mozart and Haydn changed the whole structure of opera... Linguistics is the study of the structure of language... ...the elaborate structure of the Party... You're going to have to change the whole structure of society.* N UNCOUNT : USU +SUPP = make-up

2 A **structure** is **2.1** something that has been formed or arranged in a particular way; used especially in discussing chemistry, physics, geometry, etc. EG *Ice is a solid, relatively ordered structure... Her face has a fine bone structure.* N COUNT/ UNCOUNT : USU+ SUPP ↑ formation **2.2** something that has been built or constructed, especially a large building. EG *We visited the Children's Palace, a great sprawling structure... The walkway was a steel and cement structure weighing 65,000 pounds.* N COUNT : USU+ SUPP ↑ construction

3 The **structure** of a group of people such as a family, an organization, or a society is the pattern of their relationships with each other and the way their various roles, powers, laws, etc are arranged. EG *...a pyramidal structure of authority, with power concentrated at the top... The company developed a career structure that would attract able engineers... The class structures of England and America are quite different... The family is seen as the primary social structure for meeting the emotional needs of children.* N COUNT : USU SING+SUPP = framework

4 A **structure** of thinking, working, or behaving is a method of thinking, working, or behaving that will help you to plan or organize activities, relationships, information, etc in an orderly and useful way. EG *What we must do is create structures where we can work together in harmony... She is able to give a structure to his world... The trouble with this teaching is that there isn't a built-in structure that you can follow.* N COUNT : USU SING ↑ system = framework

5 A system, activity, etc that has **structure** has things well arranged and neatly organized and is therefore efficient. EG *She loved the sense of structure, organization and enthusiasm... Structure, regimentation, order–these are what you lack.* N UNCOUNT ↑ order

6 If you **structure** something, you arrange it in a careful, organized pattern or system. EG *They structure their communication to meet the needs of the client... They could never achieve anything because they wouldn't structure the group and have effective leadership... Kingdoms, empires, churches, armies have all been structured into hierarchies.* V+O = organize, design ◇ **structured**. EG *Let us look at the way in which these elements are structured to make up a whole... He's been used to a fairly structured situation at school.* ◇ ADJ QUALIT

struggle /strʌgəᵒl/, **struggles, struggling, struggled**. **1** If you **struggle** to do something, you try very hard to do it, although it is difficult for you and other people may be trying to prevent you from doing it. EG *We should give moral support to them as they struggle to build a more democratic society... ...a nationalist movement that has had to struggle for independence... He'd rather watch TV than pick up a paper and struggle through it.* V : IF+PREP THEN *for/ through*, OR V+ *to*-INF = battle, strive ▸ used as a noun. EG *...the day-to-day struggle for survival... She feels that she will have to give up the struggle... ...the bitter power struggles between Left and Right for control of the Party... He had lost his struggle to keep his job.* ▸ N COUNT : USU SING = battle

2 If you **struggle** when you are being held by a person, caught in a trap, etc, you twist, kick, and move violently in order to get free. EG *The guard was standing hitting him whenever he struggled... She struggled in his embrace... Even the smallest animals struggle a little when they feel themselves trapped... She made a valiant attempt to rescue the struggling victim.* V : IF+PREP THEN *in*, OR V+ *to*-INF ↑ fight

3 If two people **struggle** with each other, they fight with each other, often because one person wants to get something from the other. EG *We struggled for the revolver, until at last it went off... We fell into a struggling heap, laughing and howling.* V OR V+A *(with)* : RECIP = scuffle ▸ used as a noun. EG *There was a moment's struggle and the gun fell to the ground..* ▸ N COUNT = tussle

4 A **struggle** is also a violent attempt to get something or to defeat a group of people who are trying to take away your freedom. EG *The country had endured centuries of invasion or struggles to resist invasion... ...the armed struggle of the working people of England.* N COUNT/ UNCOUNT ↑ fight

5 If you **struggle** to move yourself or to move a heavy object, you manage to do it with great difficulty. EG *He struggled to his feet... He struggled forward for about half a mile... She struggled to unload a case of wine from the car.* V+*to*-INF, OR V+ A ↑ strain

6 An action or activity that is a **struggle** is very difficult for you to do, so that you have to try very hard. EG *Reading was a struggle for him... That school has always had a bit of a struggle to keep going.* N SING : *a*+N ↑ effort

struggle on. If you **struggle on**, you manage with great difficulty to continue doing something, for example walking or working. EG *Some struggled on, but those who couldn't were left for dead... He has agreed to struggle on, even though he was hoping to* PHRASAL VB : V+ ADV = battle on retire... Fifteen years older than Gladys, he struggled on manfully only for a few years longer.*

strum /strʌm/, **strums, strumming, strummed.** If you **strum** a stringed instrument such as a guitar, you play it by moving your thumb or a small piece of plastic up and down across the strings. EG *The guitar player started strumming softly.*
V OR V+O

strumpet /strʌmpɪt/, **strumpets.** A **strumpet** is a prostitute; an old-fashioned word, used showing disapproval. EG *...a throng of beggarly strumpets.*
N COUNT ⇑ woman

strung /strʌŋ/ is the past tense and past participle of **string**.

strut /strʌt/, **struts, strutting, strutted. 1** Someone who **struts** walks in a proud way, with their head held high and their chest out, as if they are very important. EG *Eddie turned around and strutted back to them... This honour entitled her to strut in front of the marching band at football games... ...a peacock strutting on the lawn.*
V: USU+A = parade

2 A **strut** is a piece of wood or metal which holds the weight of other pieces in a building. EG *Beyond the shingle, supported on struts, rose the flat-topped houses.*
N COUNT ⇑ bar

strychnine /strɪkni:n/ is a very poisonous drug which is sometimes used in very small amounts as a medicine.
N UNCOUNT ⇑ poison

stub /stʌb/, **stubs, stubbing, stubbed. 1** The **stub** of a long thin object such as a cigarette or a pencil is the last short piece of it which remains after the cigarette, pencil, etc has been used. EG *...an ashtray full of old cigarette stubs.*
N COUNT+SUPP = butt

2 The **stub** of a cheque is the part of the cheque which you keep so that you know how much you have paid for something. EG *She always kept her cheque books up-to-date, with stubs properly filled in.*
N COUNT = counterfoil

3 The **stub** of a ticket for a performance in a theatre, cinema, etc is the part of the ticket which you keep when you have gone in to watch the performance. Sometimes it indicates the number of the seat where you should sit. EG *I couldn't find my ticket stub anywhere.*
N COUNT

4 If you **stub** your toe or your foot on a hard surface, you accidentally hit or kick the surface and hurt your toe or foot. EG *I stubbed my toe against a stone.*
V+O = knock

stub out. When someone **stubs out** a cigarette or cigar, they put it out by pressing the burning end against something hard. EG *He stubbed his cigarette out in an ash tray.*
PHRASAL VB: V+O+ADV = extinguish

stubble /stʌbə^{0}l/. **1** The short stalks which are left standing in the fields after the corn, wheat, etc, has been harvested are referred to as **stubble**. EG *The stubble was burning on the harvested fields.*
N UNCOUNT

2 The very short coarse hairs which can be seen on a man's face if he has not shaved recently are also referred to as **stubble**. EG *There was a hint of stubble round the chin... I shaved away my four days' growth of stubble.*
N UNCOUNT

stubborn /stʌbə^{0}n/. **1** Someone who is **stubborn** is determined to do what they want and very unwilling to change their mind; used showing disapproval. EG *She is stern, insistent and stubborn.* ▸ used of people's actions and behaviour. EG *...their stubborn resolve to win political independence.* ◊ **stubbornly.** EG *'It was an accident,' said Piggy stubbornly, 'and that's that.'* ◊ **stubbornness.** EG *She had a streak of stubbornness.*
ADJ QUALIT = obstinate; ◊ ADV WITH VB; ◊ N UNCOUNT

2 A **stubborn** stain, unpleasant condition, etc is difficult to remove or deal with. EG *Remove stubborn marks on tiles with a wire brush... He treated a twenty-one-year-old with a stubborn case of acne.* ◊ **stubbornly.** EG *Inflation remains stubbornly in double figures.*
ADJ QUALIT = persistent; ◊ ADV WITH VB

stubby /stʌbi^{1}/, **stubbier, stubbiest.** An object that is **stubby** is shorter and thicker than normal. EG *She was making marks in a book with a stubby pencil... He drew a map using his stubby finger on the table top... The bird was frantically beating its stubby wings.*
ADJ QUALIT ⇑ short = stumpy

stucco /stʌkəʊ/ is a type of plaster used for covering walls, decorating ceilings, and making ornaments. EG *The house was red brick without a covering of stucco... ...a grey stucco house.*
N UNCOUNT

stuck /stʌk/. **1 Stuck** is the past tense and past participle of **stick**.

2 If something is **stuck** in a particular position, for example in a gap between two things, it is fixed tightly in this position and unable to move. EG *The lift seems to be stuck between the second and third floors... The door was stuck... The mouse got stuck in a hole.*
ADJ CLASSIF: PRED, USU+A

3 If you are **stuck** when you are trying to do something, you are unable to continue doing it because it is too difficult or because there is something you do not understand. EG *Ask for help the minute you're stuck... They used the dictionary when they got stuck on words... I was stuck for an answer.*
ADJ CLASSIF: PRED = stumped

4 If you are **stuck** in a place, you are helpless and unable to get away from the place. EG *I got stuck in the lift... A little boy got stuck on a sinking ship in a storm... The boss rang to explain that he was stuck in Milan.*
ADJ CLASSIF: PRED, USU+A = stranded

5 If you are **stuck** in an unpleasant situation, you are in this situation and unable to change it. EG *They are stuck in boring jobs... I can see myself being stuck here for 5 or 6 years.*
ADJ CLASSIF: PRED, USU+A = trapped

6 If you are **stuck** with something that you do not want, you are burdened with it and cannot get rid of it. EG *Remember, if you choose a coloured oven you will be stuck with that colour.*
ADJ CLASSIF: PRED+*with* = lumbered

7 If you are **stuck** on a person or an idea, you feel a strong attraction to the person or a strong liking for the idea; an informal use. EG *I'm stuck on you... They were absolutely stuck on it–very, very keen.*
ADJ QUALIT: PRED+*on* = mad

8 If you **get stuck in**, you start what you are going to do with enthusiasm and determination; an informal expression. EG *Come on, let's get stuck in.*
PHR: VB INFLECTS

stuck-up. Someone who is **stuck-up** has too high an opinion of their own importance and is very proud and unfriendly; an informal word used showing disapproval.
ADJ QUALIT = snooty

stud /stʌd/, **studs. 1** A **stud** is **1.1** a small piece of metal which is attached to a surface for decoration. EG *...the black leatherette bar with gold studs.*
N COUNT ⇑ ornament
1.2 an earring which consists of one very small piece of jewellery attached to a bar which goes through your ear. EG *Some women wore jade studs in their ears.*
N COUNT
1.3 one of the small round objects which are attached to the bottom of a football boot so that your foot can grip the ground better.
N COUNT
1.4 a fastener on a shirt or a pair of trousers which consists of two small round flat objects joined together by a small bar. EG *I had lost my stud, so I put through a large safety pin... ...cufflinks, collar studs and detachable collars.*
N COUNT

2 Male animals, especially horses, that are kept for **stud** purposes are kept to be used for breeding. EG *I'm not going to race him, I'm going to put him to stud... ...stud horses.*
N UNCOUNT

3 A **stud** or a **stud farm** is a place where horses are bred.
N COUNT

4 A **stud** is also a man who is thought to be very active sexually and good at satisfying women's sexual desires; an informal use. EG *...the film star and her stud.*
N COUNT

studded /stʌdɪ^{2}d/. Something that is **studded** is decorated with studs or things that look like studs. EG *...enamel bracelets studded with precious stones... ...quilted and studded satin seats.*
ADJ CLASSIF: IF+PREP THEN *with* ⇑ ornamented

student /stju:dənt/, **students. 1** A **student** is **1.1** a person who is studying or training at a university or college. EG *...a part-time student at King's College, London... ...a medical student... ...student nurses.*
N COUNT ⇑ learner
1.2 a person who is studying in a secondary school; used especially in American English. EG *He had been a disinterested student in high school.* ● See also **mature student**.
N COUNT = pupil

2 Someone who is a **student** of a particular subject studies this subject. EG *She was a student of serious literature... It is our treatment of the old which most shocks students of our culture.*
N COUNT+*of* = scholar

studentship /stju:dəntʃɪp/, **studentships.** A **studentship** is a scholarship to study at a university or other educational institute.
N COUNT

students' union, students' unions. A **students' union** or a **student union** is the students' organization in a British university or college which organizes leisure activities, provides welfare services, and represents students' political interests. EG *...the secretary of the student union.* ▸ also used of the building where the students' union has its offices and which usually has a shop, a coffee bar, and a meeting place. EG *They went to the coffee bar in the Students' Union.*
N COUNT: ALSO IN NAMES; ▸ N SING: *the*+

studied /stʌdɪd/. A **studied** action or way of behaving is done in a way which has been carefully
ADJ CLASSIF: ATTRIB

thought about or planned and so is not spontaneous or natural. EG *With studied casualness he mentioned his departure to Hilary... She gave him a studied look over the tops of her dark glasses.*

studio /stjuːdɪəʊ/, **studios.** 1 A **studio** is 1.1 a room where an artist such as a painter or photographer works. EG *Upstairs he had a studio where he painted a little... ...a run-down photographer's studio.* 1.2 a room where radio or television programmes are recorded, records are produced, or films are made. EG *I went up to the big recording studio in Maida Vale... In the studio with me is film-maker and critic, Iain Johnson.* — N COUNT = workshop; N COUNT

2 The **studios** of a film, radio, television, or record company are the buildings where the company produces films, programmes, or records and has its main offices. EG *...Hollywood Studios... ...the recording studios of EMI.* — N PLURAL: ALSO IN NAMES

3 A **studio**, a **studio flat**, or a **studio apartment** is a small flat, usually with one room for living and sleeping in and a small kitchen and bathroom. — N COUNT ⇑ dwelling

studio audience, studio audiences. A **studio audience** is a group of people who are in a television or radio studio watching while a programme is being made, so that their clapping, laughter, and talking are recorded on the programme. — N COUNT: IF SING, VB CAN BE SING OR PL ⇑ gathering

studious /stjuːdɪəs/. Someone who is **studious** spends a lot of time reading and studying books and is quiet. EG *Jones was very quiet, a studious boy.* — ADJ QUALIT = bookish

studiously /stjuːdɪəsli[1]/. If you **studiously** do something, you do it carefully and deliberately. EG *The Colonel studiously examined his folders... They had studiously avoided treating me in any way differently... Even legal limits to exploitation are studiously ignored.* — ADV WITH VB = diligently

study /stʌdi[1]/, **studies, studying, studied.** 1 If you **study** or **study** a particular subject, you spend time learning about it, especially by reading books and doing a course at a university or college. EG *He'd studied chemistry at university... She's studying for a law degree... He was studying all evening in his room.* — V OR V+O

2 **Study** is the activity of studying a subject. EG *There are no rooms specifically set aside for quiet study.* ▸ used as a plural noun. EG *I'm not surprised your studies are suffering.* — N UNCOUNT; ▸ N PLURAL

3 **Studies** are subjects which are studied, especially ones which deal with different aspects of one particular area of interest or one particular theme. EG *...the School of European Studies... ...the introduction of new studies into the curriculum.* — N PLURAL

4 If you **study** something, 4.1 you observe it carefully over a period of time and analyse what you see. EG *Several groups of gorillas have been studied for many years.* 4.2 you look at it very carefully and slowly because you are trying to find something out. EG *He looked at her hard, studying her face... I studied a map.* — V+O = examine; V+O = scrutinize

5 A **study** is a piece of research on a particular subject. EG *She has made a close study of male executives and their drinking habits.* ▸ used to refer to the written form of this research. EG *Studies have shown that 30% of all households are headed by women.* ● See also **case study**. — N COUNT ⇑ investigation

6 A **study** is also 6.1 a drawing which is done by an artist in preparation for a larger picture. 6.2 a piece of classical music which is composed in order to help you practise a particular technique. 6.3 a piece of writing, a film, or some other artistic work which describes and examines closely a particular theme. EG *Tarkovsky's film was a study in past and present.* 6.5 a room in a house which used for reading, writing, and studying. — N COUNT; N COUNT; N COUNT: USU *a* +N IN SING+*in/of*; N COUNT

stuff /stʌf/, **stuffs, stuffing, stuffed.** 1 The word **stuff** is often used in informal English instead of a more precise word. It is used 1.1 to refer to a substance or material. EG *Tar is sticky black stuff... What's that stuff in the bucket?... 'Do you want some beetroot?'–'No, I hate the stuff.' Have you got any more of that varnish stuff?* 1.2 to refer to a collection of things, for example your belongings or clothes or the things for sale in a shop. EG *There's some very good stuff in the sale... Quite a lot of stuff had been stolen... They moved all their stuff down to Watermouth.* 1.3 to refer to the content of something, for example writing, talk, music, or ideas. EG *It was a boring lecture. It was all stuff I'd heard before... She was reading the travel stuff in the colour supplement... Most of my poetry is very poor stuff... What's all this apology stuff?* ● See also **hot stuff.** 1.4 in lists and descriptions when giving examples or showing the range of what you are referring to. EG *They visited churches and stuff like that... We had an awfully jolly time at Christmas-tree, carols and all that stuff... He was putting the compost and stuff round his roses.* — N UNCOUNT: USU +SUPP; N UNCOUNT: USU +SUPP; N UNCOUNT: USU +SUPP; N UNCOUNT = things

2 If you **stuff** something somewhere, you put or push it quickly and roughly into a container, hole, opening, etc. EG *Willie gathered up the bills and stuffed them carelessly into his pocket... Nora stuffed a cigarette into her mouth... She could stuff quite a lot of things under the bed.* — V+O+A = shove

3 If a place or container **is stuffed** with something, it is filled with it so that there is not much room left. EG *The cupboard was stuffed with old fishing tackle... He'd got a big rucksack, stuffed with notes, on his back.* — V+O: USU PASS+*with* = cram

4 If you **stuff** yourself or **stuff** your mouth, stomach, etc, you eat a large amount of food; an informal use. EG *They were too busy stuffing themselves to notice anything... I was stuffing my face with ice-cream.* — V+O (NG/REFL)

5 If you **stuff** something, you fill it with material until it is full and solid. EG *We made felt animals and stuffed them with kapok.* ◇ **stuffed.** EG *...stuffed toys.* — V+O: USU PASS+*with*; ◇ ADJ CLASSIF

6 If you **stuff** a chicken, turkey, tomatoes, etc, you put a mixture of food inside it before cooking. ◇ **stuffed.** EG *...stuffed cabbage.* — V+O: USU PASS; ◇ ADJ CLASSIF

7 If you **stuff** a dead animal, bird, of fish, you fill the skin with material so that it can be preserved and displayed. ◇ **stuffed.** EG *...a stuffed parrot.* — V+O: USU PASS; ◇ ADJ CLASSIF

8 The **stuff** of something is the most important or characteristic part of it; a fairly formal use. EG *Shoddy, shabby compromises are the very stuff of politics.* — N SING: *the*+N+*of* = essence

9 **Stuff** is also used to refer to the qualities in someone's character that are needed for them to do something. EG *We aren't the stuff of secret agents, you and me... He was made of less heroic stuff.* — N UNCOUNT+SUPP

10 If you **stuff** someone in a game, you beat them easily; a very informal use. — V+O = thrash

11 Some people say a man **stuffs** a woman when they mean that he has sex with her; a rude and offensive use in very informal English. — V+O

12 **'Get stuffed!'** is used to express anger or annoyance at what someone has said or done; a very rude expression. — EXCLAM

13 The word **stuff** is also used in the following expressions in informal English. 13.1 If you say that someone **knows** their **stuff**, you mean that they are good at doing something because they are experienced at it and know a lot about it. EG *These union negotiators know their stuff.* 13.2 If you **do** your **stuff**, you perform an activity in the way that people expect. EG *Go on, Jim, do your stuff! Let's see a goal!* 13.3 If you say **'that's the stuff'**, you mean that something is exactly what is needed or wanted. — PHR: VB INFLECTS = know your onions; PHR: VB INFLECTS; CONVENTION

14 You say **'stuff and nonsense'** to express your scorn and disbelief of what someone has just said; a fairly old-fashioned expression. EG *'I want to show Angelica where the witch lives,' I said. 'Stuff and nonsense!' said Lally.* — CONVENTION = rot, rubbish

15 See also **stuffing.**

stuffed shirt, stuffed shirts. If you describe someone as a **stuffed shirt**, you mean that they are extremely formal, old-fashioned, and pompous; an informal expression. EG *...all those stuffed shirts at the Ministry.* — N COUNT = dullard ≠ live wire

stuffed-up. If you are **stuffed-up**, you have the passages of your nose blocked with mucus so that you cannot breathe properly through it. EG *I'm all stuffed-up today.* — ADJ QUALIT = bunged up

stuffing /stʌfɪŋ/. 1 **Stuffing** is 1.1 a mixture of food that is put inside chicken, turkey, tomatoes, etc before cooking them together. EG *We had a chicken and stuffing, and new potatoes from the garden.* 1.2 material that is put inside furniture, pillows, cushions, toys, etc in order to fill the object and make it firm or solid. EG *There's hardly any stuffing left in the sofa.* — N MASS ⇑ filling; N UNCOUNT = padding

2 If something **knocks the stuffing out of** you, it makes you feel very weak; an informal expression. EG *Then I caught flu, which really knocked the stuffing out of me.* — PHR: VB INFLECTS = lay you low

stuffy /stʌfi¹/, **stuffier, stuffiest. 1 Stuffy** people and institutions are formal and old-fashioned. EG *Lloyd's isn't as stuffy as most people think.*
ADJ QUALIT = staid ≠ lively

2 If it is **stuffy** in a place, it is unpleasantly warm and there is not enough fresh air. EG *It's a bit stuffy in here, I'm afraid... ...a stuffy room.*
ADJ QUALIT = airless, stale

stultify /stʌltɪfaɪ/, **stultifies, stultifying, stultified**. If something **stultifies** you, it makes you feel empty or dull in your mind, usually because it is so boring or repetitive. EG *The regular use of calculators could stultify a child's capacity to do basic mental operations.* ◇ **stultifying**. EG *This work is absolutely stultifying.*
V+O ⇑ deaden ≠ stimulate; ◇ ADJ QUALIT

stumble /stʌmbə⁰l/, **stumbles, stumbling, stumbled**. If you **stumble**, **1** you put your foot down awkwardly while you are walking or running and nearly fall over or start to fall over. EG *The man was drunk and he stumbled on the bottom step... He stumbled and fell, exhausted.* ▸ used as a noun. EG *Ralph made a sudden movement that became a stumble.* **2** you walk in a very unsteady way, so that you nearly fall over. EG *He stumbled into his cabin and sat heavily on his bed... He stumbled about drunkenly.* **3** you make a mistake while you are reading aloud or speaking, so that you have to stop for a short time. EG *I don't rush and stumble now that I can read better... The waiter stumbled several times over our order.*
V: NO IMPER = trip; ▸ N COUNT = trip; V+A: NO IMPER = lurch; V: NO IMPER ⇑ hesitate

stumble across. If you **stumble across** something or someone, you discover or meet them unexpectedly. EG *In the course of their search they may stumble across something quite different.*
PHRASAL VB: V+PREP, HAS PASS = come across

stumble on. If you **stumble on** or **stumble upon** something or someone, you discover or meet them unexpectedly. EG *Sir Alexander Fleming stumbled on his great discovery of penicillin quite by accident.*
PHRASAL VB: V+PREP, HAS PASS ⇑ discover = come across

stumbling block, stumbling blocks; also spelled with a hyphen. A **stumbling block** is something which stops you from doing or getting what you want. EG *Perhaps the biggest stumbling block to disarmament is the deterrent theory.*
N COUNT ⇑ impediment = obstacle

stump /stʌmp/, **stumps, stumping, stumped**.
1 A **stump** is **1.1** the small part of something such as a limb, tooth, or blade, that remains when most of it has been removed or broken off. EG *Its tail is reduced to a tiny stump... ...a broad grin, displaying twin stumps of teeth.* **1.2** the part of a tree trunk that remains standing upright in the ground when the rest of the tree has fallen down or been cut down. EG *We left him sitting on the stump of an old felled oak.* **1.3** one of the three wooden poles that are stuck in the ground to form the wicket in a game of cricket.
N COUNT; N COUNT; N COUNT

2 To **stump** a batsman in a game of cricket means to get him out by knocking the bails off the stumps of the wicket. Only the wicket keeper can stump people.
V+O

3 If something **stumps** you, you cannot think of any solution or answer for it. EG *...the question that has stumped philosophers since the beginning of time... It's unusual for Jeremy to be stumped for an answer... You've got me stumped there.*
V+O = confound, puzzle

4 If politicians **stump** or **stump** an area, they travel around an area making campaign speeches before an election; used in American English.
V OR V+O

5 If politicians are **on the stump**, they are campaigning for an election; used in American English. EG *...a gruelling, two-month stint on the stump for Ronald Reagan.*
PHR: USED AS AN A

6 If you **stump** somewhere, you walk with heavy steps. EG *My cousin stumped around in the mud... She stumped back into the house.*
V+A = stomp

stump up. If you **stump up** a sum of money, you pay the money that is required for something, but only reluctantly because it seems a lot of money; an informal use. EG *The government is being asked to stump up the rest of the cash.*
PHRASAL VB: V+ADV+O = cough up, pay up

stumpy /stʌmpi¹/, **stumpier, stumpiest**. **Stumpy** legs, fingers, etc are short and thick, often with fairly flat ends. EG *...a short stumpy tail.*
ADJ QUALIT ⇑ squat = stubby

stun /stʌn/, **stuns, stunning, stunned**. **1** If you **are stunned** by something, you are shocked or astonished by it and often are therefore unable to speak or do anything. EG *We were all stunned by the news... I was stunned to hear it... This film stunned the movie world in 1955.* ◇ **stunned**. EG *We, in the audience, all sat stunned... Stunned scientists had found not one but at least three viruses... I sat in stunned silence.*
V+O: USU PASS = amaze, bowl over; ◇ ADJ QUALIT

2 If something such as a blow on the head **stuns** you, it makes you unconscious or not really aware of where you are. EG *The fall had stunned me... ...a partially stunned stag.*
V+O = daze

3 See also **stunning**.

stung /stʌŋ/ is the past tense and past participle of **sting**.

stunk /stʌŋk/ is the past participle of **stink**.

stunner /stʌnə/, **stunners**. A **stunner** is an extremely attractive woman; an informal use. EG *I didn't know your sister was such a stunner.*
N COUNT ⇑ beauty

stunning /stʌnɪŋ/. Something that is **stunning 1** is extremely beautiful or impressive. EG *The film is visually stunning... Her dress was simply stunning... There's one absolutely stunning poet.* ◇ **stunningly**. EG *...a stunningly brilliant and original piece of orchestration.* **2** is so unusual or unexpected that people are astonished by it. EG *The remark was so stunning that Marsha fell back into her seat... ...a stunning victory in the general election.* ◇ **stunningly**. EG *The bronze medal for Oakes was the day's stunningly unexpected event.*
ADJ QUALIT = fabulous ≠ ghastly; ◇ ADV; ADJ QUALIT = amazing ≠ predictable; ◇ ADV

stunt /stʌnt/, **stunts, stunting, stunted**. **1** A **stunt** is **1.1** something that is done in order to attract attention and get publicity for the person or company responsible for it. EG *Meanwhile the promotion department drummed up obvious stunts... Climbing up the church tower was a fine publicity stunt.* **1.2** an exciting, often dangerous, piece of action in a film. EG *Steve McQueen did most of his own stunts.* **1.3** a skilful and dangerous trick in a car, plane, etc which is performed in public. EG *...the stunt rider, Evel Knievel... ...stunt flying.*
N COUNT; N COUNT; N COUNT

2 If someone **pulls a stunt**, they do something silly or risky. EG *Only an idiot would pull such a stunt.*
PHR: VB INFLECTS

3 If something **stunts** the growth or development of something, it prevents it from growing or developing as much as it should. EG *These insecticides can stunt plant growth.*
V+O ⇑ impede ≠ encourage

stunted /stʌntɪ²d/. Something that is **stunted** has been prevented from growing to its full height. EG *They were cowslips, but so stunted that they were barely recognizable... ...old, stunted, thorn trees.*
ADJ QUALIT ⇑ deformed

stunt man, stunt men; also spelled as one word. A **stunt man** is a man whose job is to do dangerous things in a film, often on behalf of an actor so that the actor does not have to risk being injured.
N COUNT

stunt woman, stunt women; also spelled as one word. A **stunt woman** is a woman whose job is to do dangerous things in a film, often on behalf of an anctress so that the actress does not have to risk being injured.
N COUNT

stupefaction /stjuːpɪfækʃə⁰n/ is **1** the state of feeling so tired or bored that you are unable to think clearly. EG *...an expression of glazed stupefaction.* **2** great surprise. EG *He had all the drawers open, to Steve's stupefaction.*
N UNCOUNT ⇑ bewilderment; N UNCOUNT = amazement

stupefy /stjuːpɪfaɪ/, **stupefies, stupefying, stupefied**. If something **stupefies** you, **1** it makes you feel so tired or bored that you are unable to think clearly. EG *I felt stupefied by the heavy meal.* **2** it surprises you very much. EG *He was too stupefied to answer her.*
V+O ⇑ bewilder; V+O = amaze

stupendous /stjuːpendəs/. Something that is **stupendous** is surprisingly large or impressive. EG *The roar of the explosion was stupendous... ...stupendous sums of money.* ◇ **stupendously**. EG *The computer's memory banks have been increased stupendously.*
ADJ QUALIT ⇑ great = staggering; ◇ ADV

stupid /stjuːpɪd/, **stupider, stupidest**. **1** Something or someone that is **stupid** shows a lack of good judgement or intelligence and is not at all sensible. EG *I turned the job down, which was stupid of me... ...a stupid question... It's stupid to leave something lying around like that... Are you trying to make us look stupid?... I have been extremely stupid... These people may be ignorant, but they are not stupid.* ◇ **stupidly**. I once stupidly asked him why he smiled so often... EG *He shook his head stupidly.*
ADJ QUALIT = foolish ≠ sensible, wise; ◇ ADV WITH VB

2 You say that something is **stupid** to indicate that **2.1** you think it is very silly or childish. EG *It was stupid to be frightened... I think it's a stupid game.* **2.2** you do not like it or it annoys you. EG *I hate these stupid black shoes... I don't know why he worked for the stupid company in the first place.*
ADJ QUALIT = foolish; ADJ CLASSIF ⇑ awful = wretched

3 If you are **stupid** with sleep, tiredness, etc, you are
ADJ QUALIT:

so sleepy, tired, etc, that you cannot think clearly. EG *We were stupid with exhaustion.* PRED+*with*

stupidity /stju:pɪdɪti¹/, **stupidities. Stupidity** is 1 behaviour that lacks good judgement and is not at all sensible. EG *It was an unpardonable stupidity to tell Mary... I used to find her occasional stupidities amusing... That decision was sheer stupidity.* N COUNT/UNCOUNT = idiocy 2 the quality of being stupid. EG *...the stupidity of their error... He is paying a big price for his stupidity.* N UNCOUNT = foolishness

stupor /stju:pə/, **stupors**. Someone who is in a **stupor** is almost unconscious and is unable to think or behave normally, especially as a result of drugs, drink, shock, or illness. EG *He collapsed in a drunken stupor... Sue was overcome by a kind of stupor.* N COUNT : USU SING ↑ state = daze

sturdy /stɜ:di¹/, **sturdier, sturdiest**. 1 Someone who is **sturdy** 1.1 looks strong and is unlikely to be easily tired or injured. EG *He is short and sturdy... ...Barbara Burke, a sturdy blonde.* ADJ QUALIT = robust ◊ **sturdily**. EG *She was sturdily built.* ◊ ADV WITH VB 1.2 is very loyal to their friends, beliefs, and opinions, and is determined to keep to them, although it would sometimes be easier not to do so. EG *With the help of sturdy friends like Robert Benchley he set about rebuilding his life.* ADJ QUALIT : USU ATTRIB ↑ dependable = steadfast ◊ **sturdily**. EG *He replied sturdily that he had only followed her orders.* ◊ ADV WITH VB

2 Something that is **sturdy** looks strong and is unlikely to be easily damaged or knocked over. EG *...sturdy oak tables... ...a sturdy branch.* ADJ QUALIT = tough

sturgeon /stɜ:dʒən/. **Sturgeon** is both the singular and the plural form. A **sturgeon** is a fish which lives in the northern hemisphere. You can eat sturgeon, but they are usually caught especially for their eggs, which are known as caviar. N COUNT

stutter /stʌtə/, **stutters, stuttering, stuttered**. 1 If someone has a **stutter**, they find it difficult to say the first sound of a word, and so they often hesitate or repeat it two or three times: compare **stammer**. EG *She has a slight stutter, but you only notice it when she's tired or upset.* N COUNT : USU SING ↑ impediment

2 If someone **stutters**, they have difficulty speaking because they find it hard to say the first sound of a word. EG *He was stuttering with rage... Maria turned bright red and stuttered a few words of apology.* V OR V+O/QUOTE ↑ speak ◊ **stuttering**. EG *The Greek orator Demosthenes overcame stuttering by practising speaking on the seashore.* ◊ N UNCOUNT

sty /staɪ/, **sties**. A **sty** is 1 the same as a pigsty. 2 the same as a stye. N COUNT

stye /staɪ/, **styes**. A **stye** is an infection of the skin at the bottom of an eyelash, which makes the eyelid red and swollen. N COUNT

style /staɪl/, **styles, styling, styled**. 1 The **style** of something is the general way in which it is done or presented, which often shows the attitudes of the people involved. EG *Some people find our leisurely style of decision-making rather frustrating... Drama schools nowadays are favouring a more realistic acting style... Management has become much more democratic in style... ...western styles of education.* N COUNT+SUPP, OR *in*+MOD+N = technique

2 The **style** of a particular person or group is all the general attitudes, likes, dislikes, and ways of behaving that are characteristic of them. EG *A real local style is emerging... ...a consciously national style... In characteristic style, he peered over his glasses and cleared his throat... Purple is not my style.* ● to **cramp** someone's **style**: see **cramp**. N COUNT+SUPP, OR *in*+MOD+N

3 If people or places have **style**, they have a combination of smartness, elegance, and distinctiveness which impresses people. EG *Both were rather short and plump, but they had style... Baker brings a touch of style to an otherwise dowdy provincial group... Here you can eat in style.* N UNCOUNT

4 A particular **style** of painting, writing, composing music, etc is the way that is characteristic of a particular period or group of people. EG *...this ancient and decorative lettering style... There's something here for lovers of every style of jazz... ...a large, square building in the neoclassical style... Every room is different. It's a jumble of styles, but it doesn't seem to matter.* N COUNT : IF SING, USU+SUPP, OR *in*+N ↑ type

5 Someone's **style** of writing is their choice of words and the way in which they structure sentences, use punctuation, etc. EG *...the style and vocabulary of new writers like himself... I have managed to tune my style to the style of the journal.* N UNCOUNT

6 The **style** of a product is its design, especially with regard to its shape or the main characteristic that makes it different from other similar things. EG *Babies' plastic pants come in several styles... The clothes I wore weren't different in style or appearance from those of the other children... ...the latest spring styles.* ● See also **hairstyle**. N COUNT : IF SING, USU+SUPP, OR *in*+N

7 If you **style** something such as a piece of clothing or someone's hair, you design the garment or do their hair in such a way that it has a smart and distinctive shape. EG *'You've had your hair styled. I like it.'... Her hair was styled in a short cropped pony tail.* V+O : USU PASS = cut

8 If you **style** yourself a particular name or title, you refer to yourself by it and expect other people to call you it. EG *...a group of Africans who collectively style themselves the West African National Conference... It styled itself merely as 'political party of Afghanistan'.* V+O (REFL)+C/A = label

stylised /staɪlaɪzd/. See **stylized**.

stylish /staɪlɪʃ/. Someone or something that is **stylish** is smart, elegant, and fashionable in a distinctive way that attracts people's attention and impresses them. EG *He is a little less posh, but every bit as stylish as Lord Peter Wimsey... Rosa Luz Algeria, Mexico's stylish Secretary of Tourism... ...the stylish Swizz resort of Gstaad.* ADJ QUALIT = chic, classy ◊ **stylishly**. EG *She is always stylishly dressed.* ◊ ADV WITH VB

stylist /staɪlɪst/, **stylists**. A **stylist** is 1 a hairdresser. EG *It's a very small salon with only one stylist.* N COUNT 2 someone who pays a lot of attention to their choice of words and the way in which they structure sentences, use punctuation, etc when they are writing. EG *Henry James was a great stylist.* N COUNT

stylistic /staɪlɪstɪk/, **stylistics. Stylistic** is an adjective and **stylistics** is an uncount noun. 1 **Stylistic** relates to the methods and techniques used in creating a piece of writing, music, or art which enable it to produce a particular effect. EG *...the use of representational elements as stylistic devices.* ADJ CLASSIF : USU ATTRIB ◊ **stylistically**. EG *Stylistically, Bomberg's late work was backward-looking.* ◊ ADV

2 **Stylistics** is the study of the methods and techniques used by writers to create particular effects with language. N UNCOUNT

stylized /staɪlaɪzd/; also spelled **stylised**. Something that is **stylized** uses various artistic or literary conventions in order to create an effect, instead of being natural, spontaneous, or true to life. EG *...a stylised picture of a Japanese garden... In the past, acting performances were usually highly stylized.* ADJ QUALIT ↑ artificial

stylus /staɪləs/, **styluses**. A **stylus** is the small pointed instrument on a record player that picks up the sound signals on the records. N COUNT = needle

stymie /staɪmi¹/, **stymies, stymieing, stymied**. If something **stymies** you, it makes it difficult or impossible for you to take action or to do what you want to do; an informal word. EG *That's really stymied me.* V+O : USU PASS = foil

suave /swɑ:v/, **suaver, suavest**. Someone who is **suave** is charming and polite in social situations, especially in a way that seems rather insincere. EG *...a suave young man.* ADJ QUALIT = smooth, urbane ▸ used also of people's behaviour, expressions, etc. EG *...suave manners... I had difficulty answering his suave questions.* ▸ = polished ◊ **suavely**. EG *'We all have our limitations,' said Dr Mayfield suavely.* ◊ ADV WITH VB = smoothly

sub /sʌb/, **subs**; an informal word. 1 In a game such as football, a **sub** is a player who comes onto the field to play instead of someone who was playing. EG *Liverpool brought on their sub at half-time.* N COUNT = substitute

2 A **sub** is also a submarine. N COUNT

3 A fixed amount of money that you pay regularly in order to be a member of a club or society is called your **subs**. EG *Have you paid your subs this week?* N PLURAL = subscription

sub-. 1 **Sub-** is used at the beginning of words that have 'under' as part of their meaning. EG *...submerge... ...submarine... ...subway... ...subsoil.* PREFIX

2 **Sub-** is added 2.1 to the beginning of nouns in order to form other nouns that refer to things which are part of a larger thing. EG *...committee→subcommittee... ...division→subdivision... ...species→subspecies.* PREFIX 2.2 to the beginning of adjectives in order to form other adjectives that describe someone or something as inferior, for example inferior to normal people or to normal things of the same kind. EG *...human→subhuman... ...normal→subnormal... ...standard→substandard.* PREFIX

subaltern /sʌbəᵒltən/, **subalterns**. A **subaltern** is any commissioned officer in the army below the rank of a captain. N COUNT

subatomic /sʌbətɒmɪk/; also spelled with a hyphen. A **subatomic** particle is a particle which is part of an atom, for example an electron, a proton, or a neutron; a technical term in nuclear physics. ADJ CLASSIF

subcommittee /sʌbkəmɪti[1]/, **subcommittees**; also spelled with a hyphen. A **subcommittee** is a small committee made up of members of a larger committee. The task of a subcommittee is to consider a particular subject in detail and then report what they find to their main committee. EG *...the security and terrorism subcommittee of the Senate judiciary committee.* N COUNT : IF SING, VB CAN BE SING OR PL ⇑ group

subconscious /sʌbkɒnʃəs/; also spelled with a hyphen. 1 Your **subconscious** or your **subconscious** mind is the part of your mind that is active and can influence you or affect your behaviour even though you are not aware of it. EG *The knowledge was there somewhere in the depths of his subconscious... My answer seemed to come almost directly from the subconscious... Once the subconscious mind has been called in, the results tend to be unpredictable.* N SING WITH DET

2 Something that is **subconscious** happens or exists in the part of your mind that can influence you or affect your behaviour even though you are not aware of it. EG *...a subconscious wish not to perjure herself... ...the subconscious information an expert draws on without having to think about it.* ADJ CLASSIF = unconscious ≠ conscious

◊ **subconsciously**. EG *She had created a fictional character with whom millions could subconsciously identify.* ◊ ADV WITH VB ≠ consciously

subcontinent /sʌbkɒntɪnənt/, **subcontinents**; also spelled with a hyphen. A **subcontinent** is part of a larger continent, made up of a number of countries that form one large mass of land. 'The subcontinent' is often used to refer to the area that contains India, Pakistan, and Bangladesh. EG *...immigrants from the Indian subcontinent.* N COUNT ⇑ area

subcontract, subcontracts, subcontracting, subcontracted; also spelled with a hyphen. The verb in paragraph 1 is pronounced /sʌbkə⁷ntrækt/, and the noun in paragraph 2 is pronounced /sʌbkɒntrækt/. 1 If one firm **subcontracts** work to another firm, they pay that other firm to do part of a job that they are being employed to do. EG *They had subcontracted some of the work to an electrician.* V+O : IF+PREP THEN *to* ⇑ pass on

◊ **subcontracting**. EG *...hundreds of subcontracting firms.* ◊ ADJ CLASSIF : ATTRIB

2 A **subcontract** is a contract between a firm which is being employed to do a certain job and another firm which agrees to do part of that job. EG *We managed to get the subcontract for that job in Edinburgh.* N COUNT ⇑ agreement

subcontractor /sʌbkə⁷ntræktə/, **subcontractors**; also spelled with a hyphen. A **subcontractor** is a person or firm that has a contract to do part of a job which another firm is responsible for. EG *The Corporation was a publicly-owned company and a sub-contractor for private industry.* N COUNT

subculture /sʌbkʌltʃə/, **subcultures**; also spelled with a hyphen. A **subculture** is the ideas, art, and way of life of a group of people within a society who have different ideas, art, etc from the rest of that society. EG *...an extremist political subculture... ...the posters and poetry of the hippie and post-hippie subcultures.* N COUNT

subdivide /sʌbdɪvaɪd/, **subdivides, subdividing, subdivided**; also spelled with a hyphen. If something **is subdivided**, it is made into several smaller areas, parts, or sections. EG *The site had been subdivided but not developed... Inside the perimeter, the compound was subdivided into living areas for each of the five groups.* V+O : USU PASS+ *into* = be split

subdivision /sʌbdɪvɪʒᵊn/, **subdivisions**; also spelled with a hyphen. A **subdivision** is an area, part, or section of something that is itself a part of something larger. EG *Officials are willing to take over all but two subdivisions... ...one of the Department's most important sub-divisions.* N COUNT

subdue /səbdjuː/, **subdues, subduing, subdued**. 1 If soldiers **subdue** a group of people who are causing trouble, they defeat them or bring them under control, especially by using force. EG *Troops were sent to subdue the rebels.* V+O = crush

2 If something **subdues** a person's emotions, it reduces them so that they become less lively or violent. EG *This thought subdued my initial delight at the news... Surely she could have subdued her fears?* V+O

3 If something **subdues** the brightness of a light or of a colour, it reduces it, and therefore makes it softer. EG *The lamp's brightness was subdued by a thick silk shade.* V+O = soften

subdued /səbdjuːd/. 1 Someone who is **subdued** is very quiet and shows little energy or excitement, often because they are sad about something. EG *They were subdued and silent.* ADJ QUALIT = downcast

2 **Subdued** feelings, sounds, or qualities are ones that are deliberately kept quiet or not very noticeable. EG *The assembly murmured in subdued agreement... I heard a subdued, delicate wailing.* ADJ QUALIT = hushed

3 **Subdued** lights or colours are not very bright. EG *...subdued lights and soft music.* ADJ QUALIT = dim

subeditor /sʌbɛdɪtə/, **subeditors**; also spelled with a hyphen. A **subeditor** is a person whose job is to check and correct articles in newspapers or magazines before they are printed; used especially in British English. N COUNT ⇑ journalist

subgroup /sʌbgruːp/, **subgroups**; also spelled with a hyphen. A **subgroup** is a group that is part of another, larger group. EG *They are members of a small sub-group, an elite.* N COUNT ⇑ subdivision

subheading /sʌbhɛdɪŋ/, **subheadings**; also spelled with a hyphen. A **subheading** is a heading to a piece of writing, which is less important than another heading, and which divides the writing into shorter sections. EG *You can make 'PROBLEMS' your third sub-heading.* N COUNT

subhuman /sʌbhjuːmən/; also spelled with a hyphen. If you describe someone as **subhuman**, you mean that they behave in a way that people consider to be disgusting and not worthy of a civilized person; used showing disapproval. EG *...this subhuman trickster... I closed my door on another wave of subhuman noises.* ADJ CLASSIF = monstrous

subject, subjects, subjecting, subjected. The word **subject** is pronounced /sʌbdʒɪ²kt/ in paragraphs 1 to 10 where it is a noun or adjective, and /səbdʒɛkt/ in paragraphs 11 and 12 where it is a verb. 1 The **subject** of a discussion, letter, book, etc is the thing, person, idea, issue, or event that is being discussed, written about, or considered. EG *I don't have any strong views on the subject... I simply did not know which subjects I could acceptably talk about.* N COUNT = topic

● If you **change the subject**, you deliberately talk about something different, usually because the thing that you were discussing was embarrassing or awkward for some reason. EG *Ralph was glad of the chance to change the subject... However much you try to change the subject, the conversation invariably returns to politics.* ● PHR : VB INFLECTS

2 The **subject** of a work of art is the person, thing, event, or idea that is represented, expressed, or considered. EG *The sky is often the true subject of his paintings... The Ulster Question is the subject of a new feature film, 'The Outsider'.* N COUNT : USU SING = theme

3 In grammar, the **subject** of a sentence or clause is the word or words that represent the person or thing that is doing the action expressed by the verb. The verb agrees grammatically with the subject. In the sentence 'My cat keeps catching birds', 'my cat' is the subject. N COUNT

4 A **subject** is also a branch of knowledge, especially one studied in a school, college, or university. EG *I enjoyed maths and that was my best subject... If you don't pass in your subsidiary subject you can't get a degree... ...an arts subject.* N COUNT

5 In an experiment or a piece of research, the **subject** is the person or animal whose behaviour or reaction is studied and tested. EG *This is a rather nice way to present a visual stimulus to your subjects... Using the same method I tried to get a subject to hallucinate a square circle.* N COUNT

6 The **subjects** of a country are the people who live there or who have the right to live there. EG *All British subjects are eligible to enter the country at all times.* N COUNT = citizen

7 **Subject** peoples and countries are under the strict rule or control of the government of another country, which means that they do not have an acceptable degree of freedom. EG *...the hopes of freedom in the subject peoples of the world... ...subject territories.* ADJ CLASSIF : ATTRIB ⇑ subordinat ≠ independe

8 If someone or something is **subject** to something else, **8.1** they are affected by it or are made to experience it. EG *...a quiet situation where they are not going to be subject to outside noises... Your gift will be subject to tax.* **8.2** they are likely to be affected by it, especially when it is unpleasant. EG *The area is subject to drought and floods and earthquakes... He is highly strung and, therefore, subject to heart attacks.*
ADJ CLASSIF : PRED+*to*
ADJ QUALIT : PRED+*to* = prone

9 If people are **subject to** the rules or laws of a particular authority, they have to obey those laws because they are under the control of that authority. EG *The police are–like the rest of us–subject to the law... He is not subject to the orders of any court.*
ADJ CLASSIF : PRED+*to* = bound by

10 If you say that one thing will happen **subject to** another, you mean that the first thing will happen or be successful only if the second thing happens. EG *They have authority to decide, subject to the minister's approval... The property is sold and will be conveyed subject to the following conditions.*
PREP = depending on

11 If you **subject** someone to something, you make them experience it, especially when it is unpleasant. EG *Every single member of the crew had been subjected to a rigorous medical... The air bases were subjected to intense air attack.*
V+O+A *(to)* = expose

12 If rulers, governments, etc **subject** their people or their country, they put them under strict control and take away a lot of their freedom. EG *He began to pass statute laws to subject every area of the country... ...a law designed to keep them permanently subjected to Government-paid chiefs.* ◊ **subjection** /səbˈdʒɛkʃən/. EG *...the protracted subjection of the enemy... Women ought not to be in complete financial subjection to their husbands.*
V+O
◊ N UNCOUNT = subjugation

subjective /səbˈdʒɛktɪv/. Something that is **subjective** is influenced by or based on personal opinion and feelings rather than on facts. EG *He knew his arguments were subjective, based on intuition... The experience of colour is wholly subjective.* ◊ **subjectively**. EG *I'm too subjectively bound up with the work.*
ADJ QUALIT ⇑ emotional ≠ objective
◊ ADV WITH VB ≠ objectively

subject matter; also spelled with a hyphen. The **subject matter** of a discussion, book, film, etc is the subject that is being considered or discussed.
N UNCOUNT

sub judice /sʌb ˈdʒuːdɪsi/. When something is **sub judice**, people are not allowed to comment about it in newspapers, on television, etc, because it is the subject of a trial in a court of law; a legal term. EG *This matter is now sub judice.*
ADJ CLASSIF : PRED

subjugate /ˈsʌbdʒəgeɪt/, **subjugates, subjugating, subjugated**. **1** When someone **subjugates** a group of people, they take complete control of them, especially by defeating them in a war. EG *They wondered where Hitler would turn when he had subjugated Europe.* ◊ **subjugation** /sʌbdʒəˈgeɪʃən/. EG *These people are resisting attempted subjugation by armed minorities.*
V+O = conquer, overpower
◊ N UNCOUNT : USU+*of*

2 If wishes, desires, etc **are subjugated** to something else, they are treated as less important than the other thing. EG *She's subjugated her own desires to those of her husband.* ◊ **subjugation**. EG *...the subjugation of the interests of the working class.*
V+O : USU PASS = subordinate
◊ N UNCOUNT

subjunctive /səbˈdʒʌŋktɪv/. The **subjunctive** or **subjunctive mood** is one of the moods that a verb can take in some languages such as French and Latin. In contrast with the indicative and imperative moods, the subjunctive is usually used to express wishes, hopes, doubt, etc.
N SING : *the*+N

sublet /sʌbˈlɛt/, **sublets, subletting**; also spelled with a hyphen. The form **sublet** is used in the present tense and is also the past tense and past participle of the verb. If you **sublet** a building or part of a building, you allow someone to use it and you take rent from them, although you are not the owner and pay rent for it yourself. EG *They've sublet the flat to the Countess.*
V OR V+O ⇑ let

sub-lieutenant, sub-lieutenants. A **sub-lieutenant** is a naval officer of the lowest rank.
N COUNT : ALSO IN TITLES

sublimate /ˈsʌblɪmeɪt/, **sublimates, sublimating, sublimated**. If you **sublimate** a strong desire or feeling, you express it in a way that is socially acceptable; a technical term in psychology. EG *She had been conditioned to sublimate her own desires in nurturing others... Romance contains a large portion of sublimated sex.* ◊ **sublimation** /sʌblɪˈmeɪʃən/. EG *...the sublimation of sexuality.*
V+O
◊ N UNCOUNT

sublime /səˈblaɪm/. **1** If you describe something as **sublime**, you mean that it has a wonderful quality that affects you deeply; a fairly literary word. EG *She paid me a sublime compliment which I shall always cherish... ...the author of this sublime document.* ▸ The **sublime** is this quality. EG *Their best approximated very closely to the sublime.* ● You describe something as going **from the sublime to the ridiculous** when it changes from being of high quality to being silly or trivial. EG *Films easily go from the sublime to the ridiculous.*
ADJ QUALIT = magnificent, heavenly
▸ N SING : *the*+N
● PHR : USED AS AN A

2 You describe someone's behaviour or attitude as **sublime** when they seem surprisingly ignorant or unaware of something. EG *She carried on with a sublime disregard for the organist's accompaniment.* ◊ **sublimely**. EG *Caro was sublimely ignorant of Freud.*
ADJ CLASSIF : ATTRIB ⇑ total = blissful
◊ ADV+ADJ/ADV

subliminal /səbˈlɪmɪnəl/. Something that is **subliminal** affects your mind without your being aware of it. EG *...subliminal memories... ...subliminal advertising.*
ADJ CLASSIF = subconscious

sub-machine gun, sub-machine guns; also spelled **submachine gun**. A **sub-machine gun** is a light portable type of machine-gun.
N COUNT

submarine /sʌbməˈriːn/, **submarines**. **1** A **submarine** is a naval vessel that can travel below the surface of the sea as well as on top of it. Submarines are used in war because they cannot be seen easily. EG *...a giant nuclear submarine... ...a strong force of submarines.*
N COUNT = sub

2 Submarine means existing below the surface of the sea; a formal or technical use. EG *...submarine plants.*
ADJ CLASSIF : ATTRIB

submerge /səbˈmɜːdʒ/, **submerges, submerging, submerged**. **1** If something **submerges** or if you **submerge** it, it goes below the surface of the sea or of a lake, river, etc. EG *The alligator showed its snout before submerging... The animals were submerged experimentally.*
V-ERG : USU+A

2 If you **submerge** yourself in an activity, you give all your attention to it and do not think about anything else. EG *He submerged himself in company reports... I was eager to submerge myself in the feminist movement.*
V+O (REFL)+A *(in)* = immerse

submerged /səbˈmɜːdʒd/. If something is **submerged**, it is below the surface of the sea or of a lake, river, etc. EG *The boat was driven on to a line of submerged rocks... The submarine can remain submerged for eight weeks at a time.*
ADJ CLASSIF ⇑ underwater

submission /səbˈmɪʃən/, **submissions**. **1 Submission** is a state in which people can no longer do what they want to do because they are under the control of someone else. EG *The trade unions were brought into submission... He hated the idea of a God who required submission... ...the submission of the press to the military.*
N UNCOUNT = subjection, capitulation

2 The **submission** of something such as a proposal or an application is the act of sending it to someone so that they can decide whether to accept it or not. EG *...the submission of these plans to the local authority... We try to encourage the widest possible submission of applications.* ▸ A **submission** is something that is sent in this way. EG *We can send up these submissions together with our own plans.*
N UNCOUNT ⇑ presentation
▸ N COUNT = entry

submissive /səbˈmɪsɪv/. If your behaviour is **submissive**, you behave in a quiet, obedient way, doing whatever someone wants you to do. EG *She became submissive and subservient... Men show dominant and submissive behaviour to each other in work situations.* ◊ **submissively**. EG *He submissively lowered his eyes.* ◊ **submissiveness**. EG *They are trying to encourage obedience and submissiveness.*
ADJ QUALIT = meek, passive
◊ ADV
◊ N UNCOUNT

submit /səbˈmɪt/, **submits, submitting, submitted**. **1** If you **submit** to something, you accept it, because you are are not powerful enough to resist it. EG *They were forced to submit to military discipline... They had to submit to a thorough body search at the airport... We are merely submitting to the inevitable.*
V : IF+PREP THEN *to* = give in, yield

2 If you **submit** something such as a proposal or an application to someone, you send it to them so that they can decide whether to accept it or not. EG *I submitted my resignation... Every company must by law submit accounts annually.*
V+O ⇑ present

subnormal /sʌbˈnɔːməl/; also spelled with a hyphen. If someone is **subnormal**, they have less ability or intelligence than a normal person of their age. EG *...a woman who was clearly educationally subnormal... The antisocial youth is often subnormal in*
ADJ CLASSIF = retarded

intelligence. ▸ used as a noun to refer to people who are subnormal. EG ...*schools for the educationally subnormal.* ▸ N PLURAL : the +N

subordinate, subordinates, subordinating, subordinated. The word **subordinate** is pronounced /səbɔ:dɪnət/ when it is a noun or an adjective, and /səbɔ:dɪneɪt/ when it is a verb. **1** If someone is your **subordinate**, they have a less important position than you in the organization that you both work for. EG *His immediate subordinate was the commander of our group... He humiliated his senior staff before their subordinates.* ▸ used as an adjective. EG *We were hindered by our subordinate position... There was pressure on the Supreme Allied Commander from subordinate commanders to release troops.* N COUNT WITH POSS = junior ▸ ADJ CLASSIF : IF +PREP THEN to

2 If something is **subordinate** to another thing, it is less important than the other thing. EG *All other questions are subordinate to this one.* ADJ CLASSIF : IF + PREP THEN to = secondary

3 If you **subordinate** one thing to another thing, you regard or treat it as less important than the other thing. EG *To keep his job, he willingly subordinated his own interests and convictions to the objectives of the company.* ◊ **subordination** /səbɔ:dɪneɪʃəⁿn/. EG *...the subordination of materialism to other ideals.* V+O+A (to) = subjugate ◊ N UNCOUNT + of/to

subordinate clause, subordinate clauses. A **subordinate clause** is a clause which adds some details to the main clause of a sentence. The details are such things as time and conditions in adverbial clauses, reports in reporting clauses, and descriptive matter in relative clauses. N COUNT

subpoena /səbpi:nə/, **subpoenas, subpoenaing, subpoenaed**. **1** A **subpoena** is a legal document telling someone that they must attend a court of law and give evidence as a witness. EG *A House committee tried to serve a subpoena on Harry Truman.* N COUNT = summons

2 To **subpoena** someone means to issue them with a subpoena telling them that they must attend a court of law and give evidence as a witness. EG *Our head of personnel was subpoenaed as a witness.* V+O ⇑ summon

subscribe /səbskraɪb/, **subscribes, subscribing, subscribed**. **1** If you **subscribe** to something such as an opinion or a belief, you are one of a number of people who have this opinion or belief. EG *A large number of them now subscribe to the Mohammedan faith... They find they cannot subscribe to the values of an older generation... The rest of us do not subscribe to this theory.* V : USU+A (to)

2 If you **subscribe** to a magazine or a newspaper, you pay to receive copies of it regularly. EG *She subscribed to Reader's Digest and TV Guide... I started subscribing to a morning newspaper.* V : USU+A (to)

3 If you **subscribe** money to something such as a charity or a campaign, you send money regularly to its organizers, as a way of supporting it. EG *They subscribed to local charities... Substantial sums were subscribed towards the work... Can we afford to subscribe 5,000 pounds a year to such an institution?* V+O+A (to) ⇑ give = donate

subscriber /səbskraɪbə/, **subscribers**. **1** A magazine's or newspaper's **subscribers** are the people who pay to receive copies of it regularly. EG *The number of individual subscribers rose by an annual rate of 2.7 per cent... My publisher tells me that many subscribers are asking for their money back.* N COUNT

2 Subscribers to a service are the people who pay to receive the service. EG *...telephone subscribers... Prestel relies on subscribers buying expensive equipment.* N COUNT : USU PL

3 The **subscribers** to something such as a charity or a campaign are the people who support it by sending money regularly to its organizers. EG *The campaign now has sixty thousand members and subscribers.* N COUNT : USU PL, IF+PREP THEN to ⇑ supporter

subscription /səbskrɪpʃəⁿn/, **subscriptions**. **1** A **subscription** is an amount of money that you pay regularly to a society, charity, or campaign in order to belong to the society or to help the charity or campaign. EG *When I was fifteen my father took out my first year's subscription to the National Union of Agricultural Workers... How much are the subscription fees?... I might send a subscription to the Friends of the Earth.* N COUNT ⇑ payment

2 A **subscription** is also an amount of money that you pay regularly in order to receive copies of a magazine or a newspaper. EG *Please send your subscription now if you wish to receive further copies.* ▸ used also to refer to the arrangement by which people do this. EG *You can take out a subscription direct from our publishing office... I have a life subscription to the Guardian.* N COUNT ⇑ payment ▸ N COUNT : USU SING

subsection /sʌbsɛktᵊʃəⁿn/, **subsections**; also spelled with a hyphen. A **subsection** of a text or a document such as a law is one of the smaller parts into which its main parts are divided. EG *...under subsection 2 of section 13 of the Act.* N COUNT

subsequent /sʌbsɪkwənt/ means happening or existing at a later time than something else. EG *This incident was not without importance in the subsequent development of events... Subsequent research has produced even better results... It is a hint of what might be expected from subsequent generations.* ◊ **subsequently**. EG *Brooke was arrested and subsequently sentenced to five years' imprisonment... The business was forced to close down for a period but was subsequently revived.* ADJ CLASSIF : ATTRIB = following ◊ ADV WITH VB = afterwards

subservience /səbsɜ:vɪəns/ is a state in which you do whatever someone else wants you to do. EG *They became conditioned to subservience... How long would they keep us in subservience?* ▸ used to refer to behaviour. EG *I cultivated an air of politeness bordering on subservience.* N UNCOUNT = subordination, servility ▸ = servility

subservient /səbsɜ:vɪənt/. **1** If your behaviour is **subservient**, you do whatever someone wants you to do. EG *She has become submissive and subservient... She has thought more for herself and is less subservient to the priests.* ADJ QUALIT : IF+ PREP THEN to ⇑ obedient = servile

2 If you treat something as **subservient** to something else, you treat it as less important than the other thing. EG *Economic systems became subservient to social objectives... Man was subservient to the organization.* ADJ CLASSIF : PRED+to ⇑ inferior = subordinate

subside /səbsaɪd/, **subsides, subsiding, subsided**. **1** If a feeling **subsides**, it becomes less violent or intense. EG *By now his terror had subsided enough for him to think... She stopped and waited until the pain subsided.* V ⇑ decrease = recede

2 If a noise **subsides**, it becomes much quieter. EG *His voice subsided to a mutter.* V = die down

3 If water **subsides** or if the ground **subsides**, it sinks to a lower level. EG *The flooded river was subsiding rapidly... The earth subsided under foundations and buildings began to crack.* V

subsidence /səbsaɪdəns, sʌbsɪdəns/. When there is **subsidence** in a place, the ground there sinks to a lower level. EG *The cracks in your house are due to subsidence... The ground on which the house is built suffers from subsidence.* N UNCOUNT ⇑ sinking

subsidiary /səbsɪdjəri¹/, **subsidiaries**. **1** If something is **subsidiary**, it is less important than something else with which it is connected. EG *I tried to discuss this and some subsidiary questions... Public transport played a strictly subsidiary role... The Department offers a course in Opera Studies as a subsidiary subject.* ADJ CLASSIF = secondary, supplementary

2 A **subsidiary** or **subsidiary company** is a company which is part of a larger and more important company. EG *The British company is Racal Datacomm, a subsidiary of Racal Electronics... ...a big group with a number of divisions and subsidiaries... One of our subsidiary companies was a security company.* N COUNT

subsidize /sʌbsɪdaɪz/, **subsidizes, subsidizing, subsidized**; also spelled **subsidise**. **1** If a government or other authority **subsidizes** a public service, they make it cheaper for the public by paying part of the cost. EG *In every western country the State subsidizes education, housing and health provision... School meals are subsidized.* ◊ **subsidized**. EG *...subsidized housing.* V+O ⇑ finance ◊ ADJ CLASSIF ⇑ financed

2 If a government **subsidizes** an industry, they provide money in order to enable the industry to continue. EG *Every government since the last war has subsidized upland farming.* V+O ⇑ finance

subsidy /sʌbsɪdi¹/, **subsidies**. A **subsidy** is money that is paid by a government or other authority in order to help a company financially or to make something cheaper for the public. EG *The government has had to provide massive subsidies to cover deficits.* N COUNT/ UNCOUNT ⇑ grant

subsist /səbsɪst/, **subsists, subsisting, subsisted**. When people **subsist**, they are just able to obtain the food that they need in order to stay alive. EG *To feed their huge families, most families subsist on cassava flour... In some places the settlers were subsisting on potato peelings and olives.* V : IF+PREP THEN on ⇑ live = survive

subsistence /səbsɪstəns/ is the condition of just having enough food to stay alive. EG *The Indians do not have access to sufficient land for subsistence... Thousands of pensioners live out their lives at subsistence level... They are dependent on local government for a subsistence existence.* — N UNCOUNT ⇑ survival

subsoil /sʌbsɔɪl/. The **subsoil** is a layer of soil that is just below the surface soil but above hard rock. EG *These herbs send their roots right down into the subsoil.* — N SING : *the*+N

subsonic /sʌbsɒnɪk/. **Subsonic** speeds are very fast but lower than the speed of sound. EG *They had flown at a high subsonic speed.* ▸ used of planes that fly at these speeds. EG *...the first generation of subsonic jets.* — ADJ CLASSIF : ATTRIB ≠ supersonic

subspecies /sʌbspi:ʃi:z/; also spelled with a hyphen. The form **subspecies** is used for both the singular and the plural. A **subspecies** of a plant or animal is is a subdivision of a species. EG *...a pale subspecies, the western long-eared owl... ...one of nine subspecies or races of seaside sparrow.* — N COUNT = race

substance /sʌbstəns/, **substances**. 1 A **substance** is a solid, powder, or liquid with particular properties. EG *He discovered a substance called phosphotase... Olney claimed that the substance caused brain damage... An ash-like substance fell from the sky... They were trying to remove harmful substances from cigarettes.* — N COUNT = stuff, material

2 **Substance** is something that you can touch and feel, as opposed to something that you can only see, hear, or imagine. EG *They had no more substance than shadows.* — N UNCOUNT

3 The **substance** of what someone says or writes is the main thing that they are trying to say. EG *The substance of their talk is condensed into a paragraph.* — N SING : *the*+N+*of* = gist, essence ● You use **in substance** when you are drawing attention to the main thing that someone is trying to say. EG *What he is saying in substance is that the present system cannot continue indefinitely.* — ● PHR : USED AS AN A = essentially

4 **Substance** is also the quality of being real, important, or significant. EG *There isn't anything of real substance in her book... There is some substance to this critique... Practical experience gives substance to the more abstract descriptions.* — N UNCOUNT ⇑ significance

5 A **man of substance**, **woman of substance**, etc is a man or woman who has a lot of money, power, and influence. EG *Maggie was a woman of substance... He intended to become a man of substance by the time he reached twenty-five.* — PHR : USED AS C ⇑ person

substandard /sʌbstændəd/; also spelled with a hyphen. If something is **substandard**, it is below a required standard, and therefore unacceptable. EG *The materials are substandard and will soon wear out... ...substandard housing.* — ADJ QUALIT = second-rate

substantial /səbstænʃəl/. 1 **Substantial** means 1.1 very large in amount or degree. EG *She will come into a substantial amount of money... They were given a substantial supper... Many factories suffered substantial damage... Government policy has created a very substantial change in attitudes towards work.* — ADJ QUALIT = considerable 1.2 able to be touched and felt, and not just seen or imagined; a formal use. — ADJ CLASSIF = tangible

2 A **substantial** building is large and strongly built. EG *On the site were a number of substantial timber buildings.* — ADJ CLASSIF = massive

substantially /səbstænʃəli/. 1 If something increases or decreases **substantially**, it increases or decreases by a significant amount. EG *The number of successful students has increased substantially in recent years... The price may go up quite substantially.* — ADV WITH VB = considerably

2 If you say that something is **substantially** true, you mean that it is generally true. EG *Society has remained substantially unchanged for many years... Steed always maintained that the story was substantially true.* — ADV+ADJ/ADV = largely

substantiate /səbstænʃieɪt/, **substantiates, substantiating, substantiated**. To **substantiate** a statement or a story means to show that it is true. EG *It was the one piece of evidence that could substantiate my statement... Your report might be difficult to substantiate... I suppose she can substantiate your story?* — V+O = verify, confirm

substantive /sʌbstəntɪv/ means concerned with real issues or real effects; a formal word. EG *Hattersley argued that more substantive measures were needed... He promised that there would be substantive arms control talks... Conflicts may not always be over substantive issues.* — ADJ QUALIT : USU ATTRIB = meaningful

substitute /sʌbstɪtju:t/, **substitutes, substituting, substituted**. 1 If you **substitute** something for something else, you use it instead of the other thing, or put it in the place where the other thing was. EG *Force and the display of force were substituted for argument... Cattle dung is substituted as a fuel when no wood is available... A stretch of piano wire was substituted for one of the ordinary strings.* — V+O : IF+PREP THEN *for* ⇑ exchange ◊ **substitution** /sʌbstɪtju:ʃən/, **substitutions**. EG *...the substitution of local goods for those previously imported... Some of these substitutions were successful.* — ◊ N UNCOUNT/COUNT ⇑ replacement

2 If something or someone **substitutes** for something or someone else, they take the place or perform the function of the other thing or person. EG *In the past, oil has substituted for certain natural materials... A neighbour may be able to substitute until one of the parents comes home.* — V : IF+PREP THEN *for* = stand in

3 A **substitute** is something that you have or use instead of something that you had previously or instead of something that you would have liked to have. EG *Their dog was a substitute for the children they had never had... It may replace saccharin as a sugar substitute... They prepared a synthetic rubber as a substitute for the natural rubber which they could no longer obtain.* — N COUNT : IF+PREP THEN *for* ⇑ replacement ▸ used as an adjective. EG *She had become attached to her substitute parents.* — ▸ ADJ CLASSIF

4 If you say that something is **no substitute** for another thing or that it is **a poor substitute** for it, you mean that it is does not have certain desirable features that the other thing has, and is therefore unsatisfactory. EG *This was no substitute for a proper communications system... The pub was no substitute for a luxury hotel... Text and pictures are poor substitutes for personal tuition.* — PHR : USED AS C

substructure /sʌbstrʌktʃə/, **substructures**; also spelled with a hyphen. A **substructure** is a structure that forms part of another, larger structure. EG *...the organization and its substructures.* — N COUNT

subsume /səbsju:m/, **subsumes, subsuming, subsumed**. If something **is subsumed** within a larger group or class, it is included within it, rather than being considered as something separate; a formal word. EG *Their efforts cannot easily be subsumed under a few headings... Feudalism was itself subsumed within a wider concept of divine order.* — V+O+A *(within/under)* : USU PASS

subsystem /sʌbsɪstəm/, **subsystems.** A **subsystem** is a system that forms part of a larger system. EG *...political and social subsystems.* — N COUNT ⇑ subdivision

subterfuge /sʌbtəfju:dʒ/, **subterfuges**. A **subterfuge** is a trick or deceitful way of getting what you want. EG *Paul wasn't really ill–it was a subterfuge... Resistance will be possible only through cheating, subterfuge and sabotage.* — N COUNT/UNCOUNT = deception

subterranean /sʌbtəreɪniən/; a formal word. 1 A **subterranean** river, building, etc, is one that is underground. EG *We wandered through winding subterranean passages.* — ADJ CLASSIF : USU ATTRIB

2 **Subterranean** is used to describe something which works in a mysterious and hidden way. EG *The subterranean forces governing her behaviour gradually led her to change her life.* — ADJ CLASSIF : ATTRIB

subtitles /sʌbtaɪtəlz/ are the printed translation that you can read at the bottom of the screen when you are watching a foreign film. EG *...an Italian film with English subtitles.* — N PLURAL

subtle /sʌtəl/, **subtler, subtlest**. 1 Something that is **subtle** is not immediately obvious or noticeable, and therefore a little difficult to explain or describe. EG *His whole attitude had undergone a subtle change... There's a subtle distinction between these two words... ...subtle forms of racism... The problem is more subtle than that.* — ADJ QUALIT ⇑ slight ≠ blatant ◊ **subtly**. EG *The tastes are subtly different... Their attitude to me altered subtly.* — ◊ ADV = faintly

2 Someone who is **subtle** uses indirect and clever methods to achieve something, rather than doing something that is obvious. EG *Hughes was a nice man, but not a subtle one... You must be more subtle... ...the subtlest of our politicians.* — ADJ QUALIT ≠ crude ▸ used to describe something that a person does. EG *That doesn't sound terribly subtle... My plan was subtler.* ◊ **subtly**. EG *He subtly criticized me.* — ◊ ADV WITH VB

3 A **subtle** smell, taste, or colour is pleasantly — ADJ QUALIT

delicate and faint. EG *...a very subtle perfume... ...some new subtle pastels.*

subtlety /sʌtəᵒlti¹/, **subtleties**. 1 A **subtlety** is a detail or distinction which is important in a particular situation or subject, but which is almost hidden and therefore difficult for you to notice. EG *...the subtleties of middle-class English intonation... He was aware of the subtleties of Elaine's moods.* N COUNT : USU + *of* = intricacy

2 **Subtlety** is 2.1 the quality of being not immediately obvious or noticeable, and therefore a little difficult to explain or describe; often used showing approval. EG *In your cooking remember that subtlety is everything... It has none of the delicate subtlety of character that Chekhov's plays have.* N UNCOUNT ⇑ delicacy = understatement 2.2 the ability to notice and recognize things which are not obvious, especially small differences between things. EG *They can sense each other's intentions with great subtlety.* N UNCOUNT = sensitivity

2.3 the ability to use indirect and clever methods to achieve something, rather than doing something that is obvious. N UNCOUNT

subtract /səbtrækt/, **subtracts, subtracting, subtracted**. 1 If you **subtract** one number from another, you are doing a calculation in which you take away one number from another number. For example, if you subtract 3 from 5 you get 2. EG *A week later, read the meter again and subtract the first reading from the second.* V+O (NUM) : IF + PREP THEN *from* = deduct

2 If you can **subtract**, you have the ability to do calculations in which you subtract numbers from each other. EG *I am very slow at adding and subtracting.* V ⇑ calculate

subtraction /səbtrækʃəᵒn/, **subtractions**. **Subtraction** is the act or skill or subtracting numbers from each other. N UNCOUNT/COUNT ⇑ calculation

subtropical /sʌbtrɒpɪkəᵒl/; also spelled with a hyphen. **subtropical** means relating to the areas of the world that lie between the tropical and temperate regions. EG *...miles and miles of sub-tropical forests.* ADJ CLASSIF : ATTRIB

suburb /sʌbɜːb/, **suburbs**. A **suburb** is an area of a town or city which is not close to the centre of the town or city and where people who work in the town or city often live. EG *...the London suburb of Surbiton... ...people who live in the suburbs.* N COUNT

suburban /səbɜːbəᵒn/. 1 If you describe something as **suburban**, you mean that it has qualities associated with life in a suburb. You usually mean that it is dull, conventional, and lacks change or excitement. EG *...a suburban lifestyle.* ADJ QUALIT ⇑ ordinary

2 **Suburban** is also used to describe something which relates to a suburb. EG *...suburban areas.* ADJ CLASSIF

suburbia /səbɜːbɪə/ is the suburbs of towns and cities considered as a whole. EG *I come from suburbia... ...the gardens of London suburbia.* N UNCOUNT

subversion /səbvɜːʃəᵒn/ is the attempt to weaken or destroy a political system, government, religion, etc by secretly saying or doing things from inside that system, government, religion, etc. EG *She was arrested for subversion... ...fears of extremist subversion.* N UNCOUNT ⇑ treachery

subversive /səbvɜːsɪv/, **subversives**. 1 If something that is said or done is **subversive**, it is intended to weaken or destroy a political system, government, religion, etc from inside that system, government, religion, etc. EG *The new regime regarded teaching as a subversive activity... ...subversive literature.* ▸ used of people. EG *Some people, simply by existing, struck him as subversive.* ADJ QUALIT ⇑ treacherous = propagandist

2 A **subversive** is a person who attempts to weaken or destroy a political system, government, religion, etc, often by secretly saying or doing things from inside that system, government, religion, etc. N COUNT

subvert /səbvɜːt/, **subverts, subverting, subverted**. To **subvert** something means to destroy its power and influence. EG *Conflict and division subvert the foundations of society... The best intentions can be subverted by an overpowering commercial atmosphere.* V+O = undermine

subway /sʌbweɪ/, **subways**. A **subway** is 1 a passage for pedestrians underneath a busy road. N COUNT 2 an underground railway; used in American English. EG *...a subway station.* N COUNT, OR *by* + N = tube

succeed /səksiːd/, **succeeds, succeeding, succeeded**. 1 If you **succeed**, you manage to do something or to gain something. EG *She tried to smile but did not succeed... I succeeded in getting the job.* V : IF + PREP THEN *in* ≠ fail

2 If something **succeeds**, it 2.1 has the result that is intended. EG *Nobody expected that strike to succeed.* V : IF + PREP THEN *in* 2.2 works in a satisfactory way. EG *Do you think their marriage will succeed?* V : IF + PREP THEN *in*

3 Someone who **succeeds** gains a high position in what they do, for example in business or politics. EG *He's too nice to succeed in business... She is determined to succeed.* V : IF + PREP THEN *in* = get on

4 If you **succeed** another person, you are the next person to have their job or position. EG *Somebody's got to succeed Murray as editor... He was succeeded by his son... Elizabeth succeeded to the throne in 1952.* V, OR V+O : IF + PREP THEN *to*

5 If something **succeeds** something else, it comes next in time; a formal use. EG *The dry weather was succeeded by a month of rain.* V+O = follow ◊ **succeeding**. EG *During the succeeding weeks, the situation became more serious. ...the values we hope to pass on to succeeding generations.* ◊ ADJ CLASSIF : ATTRIB = subsequent

success /səksɛs/, **successes**. 1 **Success** is 1.1 the achievement of something that you have been trying to do. EG *His attempt to shoot the president came very close to success... Her speech praised the government for their success in reducing inflation... I tried to distract him but without success... ...his immense success in making money.* N UNCOUNT ≠ failure 1.2 the achievement of a high position in a particular field, for example in business or politics. EG *Confidence is the key to success.* N UNCOUNT = prosperity

2 A **success** is someone or something that achieves a high position, makes a lot of money, or is popular. EG *His next film–'Jaws'–was a tremendous success... The plane would never be a commercial success... They've just opened a new restaurant and they're determined to make a success of it.* N COUNT = triumph

successful /səksɛsful/. 1 Something that is **successful** 1.1 achieves what it was intended to achieve. EG *...a successful attempt to land on the moon.* ADJ QUALIT = victorious ◊ **successfully**. EG *The day ended successfully... ...with their objective successfully achieved.* ◊ ADV WITH VB 1.2 is popular or makes a lot of money. EG *...a very successful film.* ADJ QUALIT

2 Someone who is **successful** achieves a high position in what they do, for example in business or politics. EG *Do you think she'll be successful?... ...a successful writer... Men are still under strong pressure to be successful and competitive.* ADJ QUALIT = prosperous

succession /səksɛʃəᵒn/, **successions**. 1 A **succession** of things of the same kind is a number of them coming one after the other. EG *The holiday was spoiled by a succession of rainy days.* N COUNT + *of* + N IN PL = string

2 **Succession** is the act, process, or right of being the next person to have an important job or position. EG *...his succession to the peerage.* N UNCOUNT : IF PREP THEN *to*/...

3 If something happens a number of weeks, years, etc **in succession**, it happens for that number of weeks, years, etc, with one following the other without a break. EG *They won the European cup three years in succession.* PHR : USED AS A A = running

successive /səksɛsɪv/ is used to describe things which come one after another without a break. EG *We have had three successive years of low rainfall... Successive British governments have tried to solve this problem.* ADJ CLASSIF : ATTRIB = consecutive ◊ **successively**. EG *...the public image upon which Labour Prime Ministers have successively gained office.* ◊ ADV WITH VB

successor /səksɛsə/, **successors**. A **successor** is someone or something that comes directly after and takes the place of another person or thing, especially in an important job or position. EG *Who will be Brearley's successor?... Miller appointed me to be his successor.* N COUNT : USU WITH POSS = replacement

success story, success stories. A **success story** is someone or something that is very successful, often unexpectedly or in spite of unfavourable conditions. EG *The new car is one of the company's few success stories in recent years.* N COUNT

succinct /səksɪŋkt/. Something that is **succinct** expresses facts or ideas clearly and in few words. EG *...an accurate and succinct account of their policies.* ADJ QUALIT = concise ≠ rambling ◊ **succinctly**. EG *She puts the case very succinctly.* ◊ ADV WITH VB = concisely

succour /sʌkə/, **succours, succouring, succoured**; also spelled **succor** in American English. **Succour** is a fairly formal and old-fashioned word. 1 **Succour** is help given to someone who is suffering or in difficulties. EG *They were busy providing succour to the injured.* N UNCOUNT = assistance

2 If you **succour** someone, you help them when they V+O

are suffering or in difficulties. EG *He strove to succour the oppressed.*

succulence /sʌkjəˈləns/. If you refer to the **succulence** of food, you are referring to the fact that it is juicy and delicious. N UNCOUNT

succulent /sʌkjəˈlənt/, **succulents**. 1 Food, especially fruit and meat, that is **succulent** is juicy and delicious. EG *...a succulent mango.* ADJ QUALIT = mouth-watering

2 A **succulent** is a type of plant that has a thick stem or thick leaves which are full of moisture, for example a cactus. N COUNT

succumb /səkʌm/, **succumbs, succumbing, succumbed**. 1 If you **succumb** to something such as persuasion or desire, you are unable to stop yourself being influenced by it. EG *He finally succumbs to the temptation to have another drink.* V: IF+PREP THEN *to* = yield

2 If you **succumb** to a disease, you become affected by it so that you die or become seriously ill. V: IF+PREP THEN *to*

such /sʌtʃ/. When **such** is used as a predeterminer, it is usually followed by 'a' and a count noun in the singular. When it is used as a determiner, it is usually followed by a count noun in the plural or by an uncount noun. **Such** can also be used as a pronoun. 1 **Such** is used to refer back to something which has already been mentioned or to introduce something which you are going to talk about. **Such** is slightly more emphatic or formal than 'the', 'this', 'that', or 'it'. EG *They lasted for hundreds of thousands of years. On a human time scale, such a period seems an eternity... 60% of the state's electricity comes from burning imported oil, the highest use of such fuel in the country... We have been asked to consider radical alternatives. Many such have been proposed in the last few years... In any case I don't believe in magic, there is no such thing.* ▸ **Such** can be followed by a structure introduced with 'as'. EG *There they had been given shelter and such medical help as existing facilities allowed.* PREDET/DET/PRON

2 **Such** means of the kind which you have previously mentioned or which you are about to mention. EG *New businesses provide the great majority of new jobs. By their nature such businesses take risks... A psychiatrist can be of great assistance and comfort at such a time... The nobility held tournaments, but peasants had no time to spare for such frivolity.* ▸ **Such** can be followed by a structure introduced with 'as'. EG *Much has been contributed to modern liberal and working-class movements by men such as these... ...a general prolonged rise in prices such as occurred in the late 1960s.* PREDET/DET/PRON

3 **Such as** or **such...as** is used to introduce examples of something. EG *...countries such as France, Germany, and Italy... ...a game of chance such as roulette... ...such things as pork pies, sausage rolls, and plum cake... We talked about such subjects as the weather.*

4 You say **or some such** place, **or some such** animal, etc to indicate that something is like the other things mentioned. EG *It was in Brighton or Bournemouth or some such place... I saw the name JIM on it, or TIM, or PIM, or some such word... A bird, a raven or some such, peered out.* PHR: USU+NG

5 You say **and such** to indicate that you are also talking about other things that are like or associated with the ones already mentioned; an informal expression. EG *It's morbid to think about cemeteries and such.* PHR ⇑ etc

6 You say **such** a place, **such** a time, etc to refer to something in the situation around you, especially something that seems uncommon or surprising in some way. EG *What an amazing restaurant to find in such a place... I have been waiting for just such an occasion.* PREDET/DET

7 **Such** also means to a very great degree or extent; used to emphasize an adjective or noun. EG *It was such a lovely day... Lonnie's such a nice man... It was strange that such elegant creatures made such ugly sounds... My life is such a mess.* PREDET/DET

8 You use **such...that** in order to emphasize the degree of something by mentioning the result or consequence of it. EG *I slapped her hand and she got such a shock that she dropped the milk-can... The extent of the disaster was such that the local authorities were quite unable to cope... There are such great differences that close parallels cannot be drawn.* PREDET/DET/PRON: *such*+CONJ *(that)*

9 You also use **such...that** or **such...as** in order to introduce the result or consequence of something that you have just mentioned. EG *They have to charge in such a way that they don't make a loss... The system can be allowed to operate in such a way as to meet these three fundamental objectives... Previously their diet was such that they weren't getting the necessary vitamins.* PREDET/DET/PRON: *such*+CONJ *(that)*, OR *such*+*as*+*to*-INF

10 You use **such as it is** or **such as there is** to say that something is not very valuable, important, useful, great, numerous, etc. EG *Dinner's on the table, such as it is... She had two unhappy marriages, and her love affairs, such as they were, were not very successful... He read the documents, such as there were.* PHR: USED AS ADV SEN

11 You use **as such** to say that you are considering a particular subject only from a theoretical point of view, rather than taking into account its practical aspects or its relevance to a particular situation. EG *He is not terribly interested in politics as such... The ministers are not necessarily hostile to growth as such.* PHR AFTER N = per se

such and such; also spelled with hyphens. You use **such and such** to refer to a particular thing or person when you do not want to be exct or precise. EG *He'd like to give a course of lectures on such and such a topic... John will always tell me that I have not taken such and such into account.* PREDET+a+N IN SING: ALSO PRON

suchlike /sʌtʃlaɪk/ is used to refer to another thing or other things like the one or ones already mentioned. EG *...mills, threshing machines and such like... ...artichokes, smoked fish, and suchlike delicacies.* DET+N IN PL/N UNCOUNT: ALSO PRON = similar

suck /sʌk/, **sucks, sucking, sucked**. 1 If you **suck** something, you draw liquid from it into your mouth by holding it between your lips and tensing and moving the muscles in your cheeks. EG *The baby went on sucking the bottle... Ken was sucking on an orange.* V OR V+O

2 If you **suck** a liquid or some other substance from something, you take liquid into the mouth with sucking movements or by drawing it through a narrow opening. EG *Billy was sucking lemonade through a straw... It uses its long beak to suck nectar from the Andean flowers... You bite open the fruit and suck out the soft sweet flesh.* V+O+A

3 If you **suck** a cigarette, a pencil, your thumb, etc, you hold it between your lips and make sucking movements. EG *He sucked his bruised fist... Stop sucking your thumb... He sucked at a cigarette.* ▸ used as a noun. EG *She put the cigarette between her lips and took a long suck.* V+O, OR V+A ▸ N COUNT: USU a+SING

4 If you **suck** something such as a sweet, you eat it by putting it in your mouth and making it dissolve with sucking movements of the muscles in your cheeks. EG *If you suck one of these your throat won't feel so sore.* V+O

5 If something **sucks** an object in a particular direction, it draws it there with a powerful force. EG *The water is sucked upwards through the roots... They were sucked down into the mud.* V+O+A ⇑ pull

6 If you **are sucked** into a situation, you are unable to prevent yourself from becoming involved in it. EG *They are becoming sucked into the world market-system rapidly... They found themselves sucked into an East-West quarrel.* V+O: USU PASS+*into* = draw

suck up. If you **suck up** to someone in a position of authority, you try to please them by flattering them or by doing things to help them; an informal expression, used showing disapproval. EG *He's been sucking up like mad to the boss.* PHRASAL VB: V+ADV, USU+*to* = crawl

sucker /sʌkə/, **suckers**. 1 If you call someone a **sucker**, you mean that it is very easy to cheat them, because they believe anything they are told. EG *He'd believe anything–he's such a sucker!... He was no sucker.* N COUNT: ALSO VOC = mug

2 If someone is a **sucker** for something, they find it very difficult to resist it. EG *Christopher was a real sucker for flattery.* N COUNT+*for* = pushover

3 The **suckers** of some animals and insects are the parts of their body which they use in order to stick to a surface. EG *Newly hatched tadpoles hang with specialized suckers from the underside of a pad for protection.* N COUNT ⇑ organ

4 A **sucker** is also a small device used for attaching things to surfaces. It consists of a cup-shaped piece of rubber that sticks to a surface when it is pressed flat. EG *...toy arrows with suckers on the end.* N COUNT

5 On a plant, a **sucker** is the new growth that is sent out from the base of the plant or from its root. This N COUNT ⇑ shoot

may produce its own roots and develop as a separate plant.

suckle /sʌkəºl/, **suckles, suckling, suckled.** 1 If a mother **suckles** a baby or a young animal, she feeds it by letting it suck milk from her breast or from a similar milk-producing part. EG *Hardly any cows in dairy herds are allowed to suckle their calves for more than three days.* V+O

2 If a baby or young animal **suckles**, it takes milk by sucking it from its mother's breast or from a similar milk-producing part. EG *When it is a little older it grazes but still comes back to the mother to suckle.* V ⇑ feed

suction /sʌkʃəºn/. **Suction** is 1 the process by which liquids, gases, or other substances are drawn from one space to another, in the way that a drink is sucked through a straw, or dust is sucked into a vacuum cleaner. Suction involves the removal of air from one space so that something from another space can be drawn in to fill that empty space. EG *The vertical distance that water can be lifted by suction is limited to about ten metres... ...a suction pump.* N UNCOUNT 2 a similar process by which two surfaces stick together when the air between them is removed. EG *...suction pads.* N UNCOUNT

Sudanese /suːdəniːz/. **Sudanese** is both the singular and the plural form. 1 Something that is **Sudanese** belongs to or relates to the Sudan or to its people. EG *...the development of Sudanese nationalism.* ADJ CLASSIF

2 A **Sudanese** is a person who comes from the Sudan. N COUNT

sudden /sʌdəºn/. 1 Something that is **sudden** happens quickly and unexpectedly. EG *...a sudden drop in the temperature... I felt a sudden twinge of regret... Her marriage was all rather sudden.* ◊ **suddenly.** EG *Suddenly, the door opened and in walked the boss... It suddenly occurred to me that we would need a visa... Her voice and manner changed suddenly.* ADJ QUALIT ◊ ADV WITH VB, OR ADV SEN ⇑ unexpected = swift

◊ **suddenness.** EG *America's allies were rather taken aback by the suddenness of this announcement.* ◊ N UNCOUNT = abruptness

2 If something happens **all of a sudden**, it happens so quickly and unexpectedly that you are surprised by it. EG *All of a sudden I noticed that someone was following me.* PHR : USED AS AN A = suddenly

suds /sʌdz/ are the bubbles that are produced when soap or washing-up liquid is mixed with water. N PLURAL = soapsuds

sue /suː/, **sues, suing, sued.** If you **sue** or you **sue** someone, you start a legal case against them, usually in order to claim money from them because they have harmed you in some way. EG *He let it be known that he would sue if these allegations were published... He couldn't even sue them for wrongful arrest.* V OR V+O : IF+ PREP THEN *for*

suede /sweɪd/ is leather with a surface that is soft and slightly rough rather than smooth and shiny. EG *...a coat made of suede... ...suede shoes.* N UNCOUNT

suet /sjºuːɪt/ is hard animal fat used in cooking, especially for making puddings or pastry. EG *...puddings with plenty of suet and lemon peel in them.* N UNCOUNT

suffer /sʌfə/, **suffers, suffering, suffered.** 1 If you **suffer** pain, you feel it in your body or mind, either because of an illness or injury, or because something has made you unhappy. EG *She was admitted to hospital suffering violent abdominal pains... They had suffered a lot of nervous strain and shock... With a dose of that new drug he'll hardly suffer at all.* V OR V+O ⇑ experience

◊ **suffering.** EG *...a message of hope for suffering humanity.* ◊ ADJ CLASSIF : ATTRIB

2 If you **suffer** from an illness, shock, etc, you are badly affected by it. EG *Seventy-five percent of its population suffers from malnutrition... They had to be taken to hospital suffering from shock.* V+A *(from)*

3 If you **suffer** something bad, you are in a situation in which something painful, harmful, or very unpleasant happens to you. EG *Three days later Nagasaki suffered the same terrible fate... Her campaign had suffered a staggering setback... We were warned to agree with the government or suffer the consequences.* V+O ⇑ experience = endure

4 If you **suffer**, you are badly affected by an unfavourable event or situation. EG *The only people that'll suffer are the vehicle owners... They would be the first to suffer if these proposals were ever carried out.* V

5 If something **suffers**, it becomes worse in quality or condition because it has been neglected or because there have been a number of unfavourable circumstances. EG *In these circumstances relationships tend to suffer... I'm not surprised that your studies are suffering.* V ⇑ deteriorate

6 If you do not **suffer fools gladly**, you do not have much patience with people who are stupid. EG *I suffer fools less gladly than I used to do.* PHR : VB INFLECTS

sufferance /sʌfəºrəns/. If you are allowed to do something **on sufferance**, you can do it, although you know that the person who gave you permission would prefer that you did not do it. EG *He felt himself to be there on sufferance.* PHR : USED AS AN A

sufferer /sʌfərə/, **sufferers.** A **sufferer** is a person who is affected by a particular illness or other painful condition. EG *This treatment has proved effective for slipped disc sufferers... ...sufferers of chronic disease.* N COUNT+SUPP

suffering /sʌfəºrɪŋ/, **sufferings.** 1 **Suffering** is serious pain which a person feels in their body or their mind. EG *I was unable to bear the sight of so much suffering... This would cause great hardship and suffering.* N UNCOUNT = torment

2 Someone's **sufferings** are the things that cause them pain or unhappiness. EG *...facing their losses or sufferings as though these things were inevitable.* N COUNT : USU PL = affliction

suffice /səfaɪs/, **suffices, sufficing, sufficed**; a formal word. 1 If something **suffices**, it is enough to achieve a purpose or to fulfil a need. EG *They made her have an operation when a mere prescription of rest would have sufficed... Any one of these arguments suffices to make my case.* V : NO CONT

2 **Suffice it to say** is used at the beginning of a statement to indicate that what you are saying is enough to explain your meaning or to prove your argument, even though you could say much more. EG *Suffice it to say that it was a complete failure.* PHR : USED AS ADV SEN + REPORT-CL

sufficiency /səfɪʃənsiˡ/. If there is a **sufficiency** of something, there is an amount or a supply that is large enough to achieve a purpose or to fulfil a need; a formal word. EG *In 1957 we had some 600 jet fighters and a sufficiency of airfields to support them.* N SING WITH DET : IF+PREP THEN *of*

sufficient /səfɪʃənt/. If something is **sufficient** for a particular purpose, there is as much of it as you need or as is necessary. EG *Japan had a reserve of oil sufficient for its needs... If the matter is of sufficient importance it will be referred to the directors... Sales were not sufficient to make it a profitable proposition... It is sufficient to say here that it worked very well.* ◊ **sufficiently.** EG *It turned out that he had not insured the house sufficiently... The mammals had not yet developed into forms sufficiently powerful to dominate the land.* ADJ CLASSIF ⇑ enough ◊ ADV WITH VB = adequately

suffix /sʌfɪks/, **suffixes.** A **suffix** is a letter or group of letters which is added to the end of a word in order to form a new word, often of a different word class. The suffix 'ist' can be added to 'sex' to form the word 'sexist'. N COUNT ⇑ addition

> **SUFFIX** □ In this dictionary SUFFIX is used in the grammar notes beside entries to describe a unit of language which cannot normally be used on its own, but which is placed after another word, so that a new word is formed. The suffix decides which word class the new word belongs to. Examples are **-ness** and **-ly**. ***Goodness*** is a noun, made up of the adjective *good* + the noun suffix *-ness*. ***Quickly*** is an adverb, made up of the adjective *quick* + the adverb suffix *-ly*.

suffocate /sʌfəkeɪt/, **suffocates, suffocating, suffocated.** 1 When someone **suffocates** or when something **suffocates** them, they die because there is no air for them to breathe. EG *If we had arrived a minute later they would have suffocated... The smoke and fumes almost suffocated me.* ◊ **suffocation** /sʌfəkeɪʃəºn/. EG *Over nine million slaves died of heat and suffocation on their way from Africa to America.* V-ERG = choke ◊ N UNCOUNT = asphyxiation

2 If you say that you **are suffocating**, you mean that you feel very uncomfortable because there is not enough fresh air and it is difficult to breathe, as it is, for example, in a hot crowded room. EG *Can you open the window–we're all suffocating.* ◊ **suffocating.** EG *Inside the hall it was hot and airless, even more suffocating than before.* V-ERG ◊ ADJ QUALIT = stifling

3 If something **suffocates** a company, an enterprise, a movement, etc, it prevents that thing from developing properly. EG *They inherited an enfeebled economy, suffocating from enormous wage settlements... The merger threatens to suffocate the very* V-ERG

qualities that make the company so successful. ◇ **suffocating.** EG *...a suffocating dictatorship.* ◇ ADJ QUALIT

suffrage /sʌfrɪdʒ/ is the right that people have to vote in order to choose a government or a national leader. EG *...the introduction of universal adult suffrage.* ● If someone is elected to a position **by suffrage**, they are voted into that position; a formal expression. EG *The President is elected directly by adult suffrage.* N UNCOUNT ● PHR : USED AS AN A

suffragette /sʌfrədʒet/, **suffragettes.** In Britain in the early twentieth century, a **suffragette** was a woman who was involved in the campaign for women to be given the right to vote. N COUNT

suffuse /səfju:z/, **suffuses, suffusing, suffused.** If something **is suffused** with light or colour, light or colour spreads gradually over or through it; a fairly literary word. EG *It was nearly dawn, and the room was already suffused with light.* V+O : USU PASS+ *with/in* = be bathed

sugar /ʃʊgə/, **sugars, sugaring, sugared.** 1 **Sugar** is a sweet substance, often in the form of white or brown crystals, which is used to sweeten food and drink. Sugar occurs naturally in plants and is obtained especially from sugar beet and sugar cane. EG *Lally poured us all a cup of tea and helped herself to sugar.* N MASS ⇑ sweetener

2 When you **sugar** food or drink, you add sugar to it in order to make it sweet. EG *Is this my tea? Did you sugar it?* V+O ⇑ sweeten

3 If you say or do something to **sugar the pill**, you try to make an order, suggestion, activity, etc seem more attractive because you know that people will not like what you are saying or what you are asking them to do. EG *They're not going to like it, you know–we'll have to think of some way of sugaring the pill.* PHR : VB INFLECTS

4 You sometimes call someone **sugar** if you are very fond of them. EG *Come over here, sugar, and let mummy look at your new dress.* N VOC = darling

5 You sometimes say **'Oh sugar!'** when you are annoyed about something silly or clumsy that you have done or when something goes wrong; an informal expression. EXCLAM = bother

6 See also **sugared.**

sugar beet; also spelled with a hyphen. **Sugar beet** is a plant which is cultivated for the sugar that can be obtained from its root. N UNCOUNT

sugar cane; also spelled with a hyphen. **Sugar cane** is a tall tropical plant which is cultivated because of the sugar that can be obtained from its thick stems. N UNCOUNT

sugar-coated. 1 Something that is **sugar-coated** is covered with a sweet substance which is usually made of sugar. EG *Most pills these days are sugar-coated, so be careful that children don't mistake them for sweets.* ADJ CLASSIF

2 Promises, words, etc that are **sugar-coated** are superficially attractive, but actually conceal something unpleasant. EG *She was not deceived by his sugar-coated promises.* ADJ CLASSIF ⇑ deceptive

sugar daddy, sugar daddies. A **sugar daddy** is a rich old man who gives money and presents to a young woman, usually in return for her company, affection, and often sexual intercourse; an old-fashioned informal expression. N COUNT ⇑ lover

sugared /ʃʊgəd/. If you describe what people say and how they say it as **sugared**, you mean that it is pleasant and attractive, but not always to be trusted. EG *The proposition was couched in sugared terms... She spoke in sugared tones.* ADJ CLASSIF = honeyed

sugared almond, sugared almonds. A **sugared almond** is an almond with a hard white or pink sugar coating which is eaten as a sweet. N COUNT

sugar lump, sugar lumps; also spelled with a hyphen. A **sugar lump** is a small cube of white sugar, which you use for sweetening hot drinks. N COUNT

sugary /ʃʊgəᵒriʲ/. 1 Something that is **sugary** contains a lot of sugar. EG *...sugary breakfast cereal.* ADJ QUALIT ⇑ sweet

2 Language or behaviour that is **sugary** seems to be very pleasant and attractive, but is probably insincere. EG *...a sugary phrase, that didn't manage to conceal his dislike of her... She gave a sweet sugary smile that made my blood run cold.* ADJ QUALIT = saccharine

suggest /sədʒest/, **suggests, suggesting, suggested.** 1 If you **suggest** something or **suggest** that someone should do something, you put forward a plan or an idea for them to think about. EG *We have to suggest a list of possible topics for next term's seminars... Various techniques can be used and these are suggested in other chapters... Might I suggest that you offer your manuscript to Collins?* V+O/REPORT-CL/ QUOTE ⇑ say = propose

2 If you **suggest** the name of a person or place, you recommend them for something such as a job or as being an interesting place to visit. EG *Helen has suggested Richard as the next chairman of the society... Can you suggest somewhere for a short holiday?* V+O : USU+A = propose

3 If you **suggest** something to someone, you say something to them which then puts an idea into their mind. EG *I'm not suggesting that the accident was your fault... It would be foolish to suggest that everyone in Britain is rich... No one would dream of suggesting retirement to him.* V+O/REPORT-CL = imply

4 You sometimes use **I suggest** in the middle of a sentence to say that, although nobody is likely to disagree with the first part of the sentence, they might not agree with the second part. EG *Her husband is a very dignified man with, I suggest, a very obscure past.* PHR : USED AS ADV SEN

5 If one thing **suggests** another, **5.1** it implies it or makes you think that it is the case. EG *His expression suggested some pleasure at the fact that I had come... It is ridiculous to increase public spending at a time when all the evidence suggests it should be cut.* **5.2** it brings it to someone's mind through an association of ideas. EG *We used swaying green curtains to suggest the wood in the play.* V+O/REPORT-CL = indicate; V+O/REPORT-CL = evoke

suggestible /sədʒestɪbəᵒl/. Someone who is **suggestible** can be easily influenced by other people. EG *He was a strange man: shy, eager to please, and very suggestible.* ADJ QUALIT

suggestion /sədʒestʃəᵒn/, **suggestions.** 1 A **suggestion** is **1.1** an idea or a plan which is put forward for people to think about. EG *I made a few suggestions about how we could spend the afternoon... The other governments greeted the suggestion with caution.* **1.2** a recommendation that you make. EG *His golf club recruits mostly on suggestions from present members.* N COUNT; N COUNT

2 If there is a **suggestion** of something, there is a slight indication or sign of it. EG *He replied to her question with the merest suggestion of a smile... Her hands had about them no suggestion of age.* N COUNT : USU SING+*of* = hint

3 **Suggestion is 3.1** the act of mentioning something which you or other people might do. EG *Books can be built from work-cards to the children's suggestion... She was always clear and incise in practical suggestion.* **3.2** giving people a particular idea by associating it with other ideas. EG *Such is the power of suggestion that within two minutes the patient is asleep.* N UNCOUNT; N UNCOUNT

suggestive /sədʒestɪv/. 1 Remarks, looks, etc that are **suggestive** cause people to think about sex. EG *The girls stood around, exchanging gossip and calling out suggestive remarks... If she said something that I considered suggestive, I would make a sharp retort.* ◇ **suggestively.** ADJ QUALIT = improper; ◇ ADV

2 Something that is **suggestive** of something else, gives a hint of it or reminds you of it. EG *His behaviour was suggestive of a cultured man.* ADJ QUALIT : PRED+*of*

suicidal /sjᵒu:ɪsaɪdəᵒl/. 1 People who are **suicidal** want to kill themselves. EG *What should you do if you or your friend feels suicidal?... Counsellors are used to dealing with suicidal people.* ▸ used also of people's moods and feelings. EG *...an unsuccessful struggle against depression and suicidal despair.* ADJ CLASSIF ⇑ depressed

2 Behaviour that is **suicidal 2.1** leads to great danger or death. EG *He made a suicidal attempt to rescue his wife... ...suicidal violence.* **2.2** leads to the destruction of things that you value, such as your career, wealth, or position. EG *It is self-defeating and ultimately suicidal to ignore such warnings by your superiors.* ADJ CLASSIF ⇑ dangerous; ADJ CLASSIF ⇑ ruinous

suicide /sjᵒu:ɪsaɪd/, **suicides.** 1 People who commit **suicide** deliberately kill themselves because they do not want to continue living. EG *The founder of British India, Clive, committed suicide in 1774... Deep depression is typical of so many young women who attempt suicide... There is a connection between a rising rate of unemployment and a rising suicide rate.* ▸ used of people who kill themselves. EG *A typical suicide is a late middle-aged or elderly man.* N UNCOUNT/ COUNT ⇑ killing; ▸ N COUNT

2 You also say that people commit **suicide** when they deliberately do something which ruins their career, position in society, or other things that they value. EG *People had told me it was suicide to admit* N UNCOUNT ⇑ ruin

to my past... By refusing to accept the decision, he had committed professional suicide.

suicide pact, suicide pact. A **suicide pact** is an agreement made between two or more people that they will deliberately kill themselves together at a particular time and place. EG *The teenagers were said to have killed themselves in a suicide pact.*
N COUNT ⇑ arrangement

suit /sj^{0}u:t/, **suits, suiting, suited.** 1 A man's **suit** is an outfit which consists of a jacket, trousers, and sometimes a waistcoat, all made from the same fabric. EG *He always wore an expensive grey suit and dark tie.*
N COUNT

2 A woman's **suit** is an outfit which consists of a jacket and skirt made from the same fabric. EG *She wore a black suit and a tiny black hat with a yellow feather.*
N COUNT = costume

3 A **suit** can also be a piece of clothing that you wear for a particular activity. EG *They dived down in special suits to walk on the bed of the sea... She was wearing a short robe over her bathing suit.*
N COUNT : USU MOD+N ⇑ garment

4 If something **suits** you, **4.1** it is the best thing for you in the circumstances. EG *All this suits my purpose very well... You should do what the doctor thinks will suit you and the baby best.* **4.2** it makes you look attractive. EG *That colour didn't suit them. ...I love you in that dress, it really suits you.* **4.3** it is convenient for you. EG *Would Monday suit you?... ...It suits me fine, but what about Robin?* **4.4** you like it. EG *A job where I was inside all day wouldn't suit me.*
V+O : NO PASS; V+O : NO PASS, NO CONT; V+O : NO PASS, NO CONT; V+O : NO PASS, NO CONT

5 If you **suit** yourself, you do something just because you want to do it, and do not bother to consider other people or other factors in the situation. EG *'I don't care what you say, I'm still going.'–'Suit yourself: but don't expect me to feel sorry for you tomorrow.'*
V+O (REFL) : USU IMPER = please

6 If people **follow suit**, they do the same thing that someone else has just done. EG *He bowed his head. Mother and Jenny followed suit.*
PHR : VB INFLECTS ⇑ copy

7 In a court of law a **suit** is a case in which a person tries to get justice for some wrong that has been done to them. They might, for example, try to get back from someone money that they are owed. EG *We discussed the progress of the suit and the legal fight to prevent my extradition.*
N COUNT = lawsuit

8 If you **file a suit** against someone or **bring a suit** against them, you start legal proceedings against them. EG *The airline fears there will be hundreds of negligence suits filed by relatives of passengers.*
PHR : VB INFLECTS

9 A **suit** is also one of the four types of card in a set of playing cards. These are hearts, diamonds, clubs, and spades.
N COUNT

suitable /sj^{0}u:təbə^{0}l/. Someone or something that is **suitable** for a particular purpose or occasion has qualities that are right or appropriate for that purpose or occasion. EG *He was just not suitable for the job... These flats are not really suitable for families with children... It takes years to turn suitable young men into fighter-pilots.* ◊ **suitability** /sj^{0}u:təbɪlɪti^1/. EG *The second requirement is suitability for every day use.*
ADJ QUALIT : IF+PREP THEN *for/as*; ◊ N UNCOUNT : USU+SUPP

suitably /sj^{0}u:təbli^1/. 1 If you are **suitably** dressed, equipped, etc, you are dressed, equipped, etc in a way that is right and appropriate for a particular purpose or occasion. EG *I'm not really suitably dressed.*
ADV = appropriately

2 **Suitably** means to a degree that you would expect in the circumstances. EG *I told them the news. They were all suitably amazed... Mary thanked him, looking suitably grateful, and left.*
ADV = appropriately

suitcase /sj^{0}u:tkeɪs/, **suitcases.** A **suitcase** is a case, with a handle, in which you can carry your clothes when you are travelling.
N COUNT ⇑ container

suite /swi:t/, **suites.** A **suite** is 1 a set of rooms, especially in a hotel. EG *In London they always stayed in a suite at the Ritz... On the first floor a long suite of state-rooms is open to the public.* 2 a set of matching furniture, for example for a sitting room or a bathroom. EG *I need a three-piece suite for the lounge... ...a bathroom suite.* 3 a piece of music which is written for instruments and consists of several short parts, usually all in the same key. EG *...Bach's Suite for Lute... The concert ended with a Janacek suite.*
N COUNT; N COUNT; N COUNT : ALSO IN NAMES

suited /sj^{0}u:tɪ^{2}d/. 1 If something is **suited** to a particular purpose, it has qualities that are right or appropriate for that purpose. EG *The climate there was more suited to her health... He considered himself ideally suited for the job of Prime Minister.*
ADJ QUALIT : PRED, USU ADV+ADJ+*to/to*-INF/FOR

2 If two people, especially a man and a woman, are **suited**, they have similar personalities, interests, etc and so are likely to have a successful relationship. EG *They are well suited, I think.*
ADJ QUALIT : PRED, USU ADV+ADJ = matched

suiting /sj^{0}u:tɪŋ/ is cloth from which trousers, jackets, skirts, and men's suits are made. EG *He was dressed in sober black suiting.*
N UNCOUNT ⇑ fabric

suitor /sj^{0}u:tə/, **suitors.** A woman's **suitor** is a man who wants to marry her and is trying to persuade her to marry him; an old-fashioned word. EG *She has many suitors.*
N COUNT = wooer

sulfur /sʌlfə/. See **sulphur.**

sulk /sʌlk/, **sulks, sulking, sulked.** 1 If you **sulk**, you are silent and bad-tempered for a while because you are annoyed or resentful about something. EG *They used to fight and then cry and then sulk if they could not get their own way... She had sulked all weekend.* ▸ used as a noun. EG *Richard's having a bit of a sulk upstairs... She was in one of her sulks.*
V; ▸ N COUNT ⇑ mood

2 If you are having **the sulks**, you are in a bad-tempered mood, shown especially by a refusal to talk to other people. EG *...a brief fit of the sulks.*
N PLURAL : *the*+N

sulky /sʌlki^1/, **sulkier, sulkiest.** Someone who is **sulky** is silent and bad-tempered for a while because they are annoyed or resentful about something. EG *He was very sulky about it indeed... ...a sulky boy.* ▸ used to describe someone's behaviour or appearance. EG *Sam glowered at him in sulky silence... ...her sulky face.* ◊ **sulkily.** EG *'That's all I'm telling you,' said Joe sulkily.* ◊ **sulkiness.**
ADJ QUALIT = sullen, surly; ◊ ADV WITH VB; ◊ N UNCOUNT

sullen /sʌlən/. 1 Someone who is **sullen** is silent and not at all cheerful or pleasant to people. EG *I never laughed and became very sullen... ...a sullen boy.* ▸ used to describe someone's appearance, behaviour, or attitude. EG *He had a heavy, sullen face... A bitter and sullen obstinacy arose in her.* ◊ **sullenly.** EG *'So what?' Thomas said sullenly.* ◊ **sullenness.** EG *Victoria tolerated her husband's sullenness.*
ADJ QUALIT ⇑ moody = surly; ◊ ADV WITH VB; ◊ N UNCOUNT

2 Something that is **sullen** is dull and unpleasant to look at. EG *He drew the curtains and looked out at the sullen sky.*
ADJ QUALIT = leaden

sully /sʌli^1/, **sullies, sullying, sullied.** If you **sully** something, 1 you make it dirty. EG *He could not sully that pure water with his sweat.* 2 you spoil it so that it is no longer pure or of such high value. EG *Nothing had ever happened to sully her reputation.*
V+O; V+O = tarnish

sulphur /sʌlfə/; also spelled **sulfur** in American English. **Sulphur** is 1 a light yellow substance which burns brightly and has a strong choking smell. Sulphur is used to make things like matches and gunpowder and is used in industry and medicine. 2 a light yellow colour.
N UNCOUNT ⇑ element; ADJ COLOUR

sultan /sʌltə^{0}n/, **sultans.** A **sultan** is a ruler in some Muslim countries. EG *...the Sultan of Oman.*
N COUNT : ALSO IN TITLES

sultana /sʌltɑ:nə/, **sultanas.** A **sultana** is 1 a dried white grape which is used in cooking, especially in making cakes. 2 the wife or female relative of a sultan.
N COUNT; N COUNT : ALSO IN TITLES

sultry /sʌltri^1/. 1 **Sultry** weather is unpleasantly hot and humid. EG *It was so hot and sultry that day.*
ADJ QUALIT = muggy

2 A **sultry** woman is attractive in a way that suggests hidden passion. EG *She gave him a sultry look.*
ADJ QUALIT = seductive

sum /sʌm/, **sums, summing, summed.** 1 A **sum** is **1.1** an amount of money. EG *...the staggering sum of 212,000 million pounds... Manufacturers spend huge sums of money on advertising their product... Industrial organizations often raise large sums for charity.* ● See also **lump sum.** **1.2** a simple calculation in arithmetic. EG *Invest in a pocket calculator, and let it do the sum for you... He couldn't do his sums.* **1.3** the result obtained when two or more numbers are added together. EG *What is the sum of 14, 17, and 23?*
N PART+N UNCOUNT ⇑ quantity; N COUNT; N SING : *the*+N USU+*of* = total

2 The **sum** of something is all of it, when you are suggesting that it is not very much or not very good. EG *If that's the sum of the Chancellor's proposals, we shouldn't be too badly affected... This seems to be the entire sum of our achievement.*
N SING : *the*+N *of* ⇑ total

3 You use **in sum** to introduce a statement that contains the most important information about something and that can therefore be considered as a summary of the whole subject. EG *But in sum it was a good year for all of them.*
PHR : USED AS ADV SEN = in short

4 If you say that something is **greater** or **more than the sum of its parts**, you mean that it is better or more effective than you would expect from the individual parts, because the way they combine with
PHR : USED AS

each other adds a different quality. EG *A good team is always greater than the sum of its parts... When they're playing together, of course, they add up to more than the sum of their own instruments.*

sum up. 1 If you **sum** something **up**, you express as briefly as possible all the important aspects of something, and by doing this describe the whole thing. EG *She was searching for the words that would sum it up... My mood could be summed up by the single word 'boredom'... I can't sum up his whole philosophy in one sentence.* PHRASAL VB : V+O+ADV = encapsulate

2 If you **sum up** a person or situation, you make an accurate judgement of the person's character or the situation. EG *He was able to sum us up in a very short time.* PHRASAL VB : V+O+ADV = size up

3 If you **sum up**, you state briefly and clearly the main points of a speech, argument, etc, as a conclusion. EG *At the end of the discussion, he summed up, and added a few points... To sum up: within our society there still exist rampant inequalities.* PHRASAL VB : V+ADV ⇑ summarize

4 When a judge **sums up**, he or she makes a speech to the jury at the end of a trial reminding them of the evidence and the main arguments of the case they have heard. PHRASAL VB : V+ADV ⇑ summarize

5 See also **summing-up**.

summarize /sʌməraɪz/, **summarizes, summarizing, summarized**; also spelled **summarise**. If you **summarize** something, you give a summary of it. EG *I will summarize these opinions here, adding my own comments... The seven categories can be briefly summarized as follows... The argument might be summarised in a few words.* V OR V+O = outline

summary /sʌməri¹/, **summaries**. 1 A **summary** is a short written or spoken account of something, which gives the important points but not the details. EG *A summary of the findings was published in 1948... Here is a summary of the plot.* N COUNT = outline

2 You use **in summary** to indicate that what you are going to say next is a summary of what has just been said. EG *In summary, all government departments are administered rather differently... So your advice would in summary be to look rather carefully at the small print of contracts.* PHR : USED AS ADV SEN

3 Something that is **summary** is done quickly and without delay, with very little attention paid to detail or to formalities. EG *The summary justice meted out was harsh... ...summary executions.* ◊ **summarily**. EG *He summarily dismissed our problem as being unimportant... They were summarily evicted.* ADJ CLASSIF : USU ATTRIB = unceremonious ◊ ADV WITH VB = promptly

summat /sʌmət/ is used in nonstandard English in some parts of Britain to mean the same as the word 'something'. EG *I've summat on my mind.*

summation /sʌmeɪʃəⁿn/, **summations**; a formal word. 1 A **summation** is a summary of what someone has said or done. EG *Let me give a final summation of what they've achieved.* N COUNT = summing-up

2 The **summation** of two or more numbers or amounts is the result obtained when they are added together. N COUNT : IF+PREP THEN *of* ⇑ total

summer /sʌmə/, **summers**. **Summer** is the season between spring and autumn. In the summer the weather is usually warm or hot and drier than it is during other seasons. EG *I am going to Greece this summer... She's spending the summer in Europe... I went there two summers ago... ...summer holidays... ...a warm summer afternoon.* • See also **Indian summer**. N COUNT/UNCOUNT

summerhouse /sʌməhaʊs/, **summerhouses**; also spelled with a hyphen. A **summerhouse** is a small building in a garden. It contains seats, and people can sit there in the summer. N COUNT

summer school, summer school. A **summer school** is an educational course that is held during the summer to teach people a particular subject. People usually stay at the place where the course is being held, and the course usually lasts for a week or more. N COUNT/UNCOUNT

summertime /sʌmətaɪm/ is the period of time during which summer lasts. EG *The dust from the roads in the summertime was enough to blind you.* N UNCOUNT

summer time is a period of time in the summer in some countries during which the clocks are put forward, in order that people can have extra daylight in the evening. In Britain summer time lasts from the end of March to the end of October, and the clocks are put forward one hour. N UNCOUNT

summery /sʌməri¹/. Something that is **summery** is suitable for or characteristic of summer. EG *...a summery dress... ...a summery day.* ADJ CLASSIF

summing-up, summings-up; also spelled without a hyphen. In a trial the judge's **summing-up** is the speech he or she makes to the jury at the end of a trial to remind them of the evidence and the main arguments of the case they have heard. EG *In his summing up, the judge again returned to the part played by the doctor in the case.* N COUNT ⇑ summary

summit /sʌmɪt/, **summits**. 1 A **summit** is a meeting at which world leaders, or the leaders of a particular group of countries, discuss important matters such as trade, the world economy, peace, etc. EG *Western leaders are gathering for this week's Ottawa summit... ...a summit meeting... ...summit talks.* N COUNT

2 The **summit** of a mountain or hill is the highest point or part of it. EG *From here you can see the summit of Snowdon... Did anyone reach the summit?* N COUNT ⇑ top

3 The **summit** of your career, achievements, etc is the greatest thing that you have achieved or hope to achieve. EG *He had attained the summit of realizable ambition... The summit of his career came when he was made managing director.* N SING : *the*+N+*of* = peak

summon /sʌmən/, **summons, summoning, summoned**. 1 If you **summon** someone, you order them to come to you. EG *He summoned his secretary... He was summoned to report on the accident.* V+O = send for

2 If you **summon** a meeting, you tell people that they must come to it. EG *They had to summon a second conference and change the previous decision.* V+O = call

3 If someone **is summoned**, they are officially ordered to appear in court. EG *A few weeks later I was summoned before the magistrate.* V+O : USU PASS

4 If you **summon** your strength, energy, or some other quality, you make a great effort and bring it out from within yourself in order to be able to do something. EG *She could not summon the strength even to sit up... I replied in as neutral a voice as I could summon.* V+O = muster

summon up. 1 If you **summon up** your strength, energy, or some other quality, you make a great effort and bring it out from within yourself in order to be able to do something. EG *I couldn't summon up the energy... He eventually summoned up the courage to ask them if Melanie was all right.* PHRASAL VB : V+O+ADV = muster

2 If you **summon up** support, help, resources, etc, you persuade people to give you support or help in some way. EG *He was hoping to summon up support for his measures.* PHRASAL VB : V+O+ADV = raise

3 If something **summons up** a memory or thought, it causes you to have it. EG *The odour summoned up memories of my childhood.* PHRASAL VB : V+O+ADV = awake

summons /sʌmənz/, **summonses, summonsing, summonsed**. 1 A **summons** is **1.1** an order to go to a particular place and see the person who gave the order. EG *I waited in my office for a summons from the boss.* N COUNT **1.2** an official order to appear in court. EG *You parked in a no parking space, then ignored the summons.* N COUNT

2 If someone **is summonsed**, they are officially ordered to appear in court. EG *He was summonsed, and fined fifty pounds.* V+O

sump /sʌmp/, **sumps**. The **sump** is the place under an engine which holds the engine oil. N COUNT

sumptuous /sʌmptjuəs/. Something that is **sumptuous** is luxurious or magnificent, and obviously very expensive. EG *They were ushered into a sumptuous dining hall... ...a sumptuous lunch, with bottles of champagne.* ADJ QUALIT = opulent, lavish

sum total. The **sum total** of something is the entire amount of it when all the various parts or aspects are considered together. EG *A few laboriously handwritten books contained the sum total of men's thoughts in the Middle Ages... Prisons make a significant contribution to the sum total of human misery.* N SING : *the*+N, USU+*of* ⇑ whole

sun /sʌn/, **suns, sunning, sunned**. 1 The **sun** is the ball of fire in the sky that the Earth goes round, and that gives us heat and light. N SING : *the*+N ⇑ star

2 You also use **sun** to mean **2.1** the light and heat that reach us from the sun. EG *His face was healthily tanned by the sun... ...on a sandy beach under a hot sun. You need plenty of sun and fresh air.* N UNCOUNT, OR N SING+SUPP **2.2** somewhere that is bright and warm, because the sun is shining on it. EG *We all sat in the sun.* N UNCOUNT : USU *the*+N = sunshine

3 You say **everything under the sun** to emphasize that you are talking about a very great number of PHR : USED AS O/S

things. EG *She's tried everything under the sun... He shouted at Kurt, calling him every name under the sun.* ● **Nothing under the sun** means nothing at all. EG *Nothing under the sun lasts for long... There's no reason under the sun why you shouldn't go.* ● PHR : USED AS O/S

4 If you **catch the sun**, you get a slight suntan. EG *You've really caught the sun.* PHR : VB INFLECTS

5 If a place **catches the sun**, it gets a lot of sunshine. EG *This room certainly catches the sun.* PHR : VB INFLECTS

6 If you **sun** yourself, you sit or lie somewhere where the sun shines on you in order to get a suntan. EG *He spent Saturday sunning himself on the beach.* V+O (NG/REFL) : USU+A = tan

7 A **sun** is also any star which has planets revolving round it. N COUNT

Sun. is an abbreviation for 'Sunday'.

sun-baked. Land, earth, etc that is **sun-baked** has been made hard and dry by the sun shining on it. EG *...the silence of the sunbaked countryside.* ADJ CLASSIF = parched

sunbathe /sʌnbeɪθ/, **sunbathes, sunbathing, sunbathed**. If you **sunbathe**, you sit or lie in a place where the sun shines strongly on you, so that you get a suntan. EG *I spent my afternoons sunbathing instead of doing my work.* ◊ **sunbathing**. EG *I had a day off to do some sunbathing.* V = bask ◊ N UNCOUNT

sunbather /sʌnbeɪθə/, **sunbathers**. A **sunbather** is someone who lies or sits in the sun in order to get a suntan. EG *The park was full of sunbathers.* N COUNT

sunbeam /sʌnbi:m/, **sunbeams**. A **sunbeam** is a ray of light from the sun. N COUNT

sunbonnet /sʌnbɒnɪt/, **sunbonnets**. A **sunbonnet** is a cloth hat with a soft brim. It covers most of your head and protects your face and neck from the sun. Sunbonnets are now worn mainly by babies, although they used to be worn also by women and girls. N COUNT

sunburn /sʌnbɜ:n/. If someone with white skin has **sunburn**, they have sore red patches on their skin as a result of having spent too much time in hot sunshine. EG *She put on some cream to soothe her sunburn.* N UNCOUNT ⇑ burn

sunburnt /sʌnbɜ:nt/; also spelled **sunburned**. Someone who is **sunburnt** 1 has sore red skin because they have spent too much time in hot sunshine. EG *...sunburnt bright pink legs.* 2 has attractively brown skin because they have spent some time in the sunshine; used especially in British English. EG *The skiing instructor was a tall, sunburnt man.* ADJ QUALIT ⇑ burnt; ADJ QUALIT = bronzed

sundae /sʌndi:, -deɪ/, **sundaes**. A **sundae** is a dish of ice cream, with nuts, whipped cream, and fruit on top. N COUNT : USU AFTER N

Sunday /sʌndi[1]/, **Sundays**. **Sunday** is one of the seven days of the week. It is the day after Saturday and before Monday. In many Western and Christian countries, Sunday is a special day, when shops are closed and some people go to church. EG *Sunday was Rudolph's seventeenth birthday... I never eat breakfast on Sundays.* ● **month of Sundays**: see **month**. N UNCOUNT/COUNT

Sunday school, Sunday schools. If children go to **Sunday school**, they go to a special class on Sundays in order to learn about Christianity. EG *She insisted that John go to Sunday school every single week... My wife became a Sunday-school teacher.* N UNCOUNT/COUNT

sundeck /sʌndek/, **sundecks**. A **sundeck** is a platform or other flat, open space outside, for example near a house or on a large ship, where you can sit or lie in the sun. EG *The sundeck was crowded with holidaymakers.* N COUNT

sundial /sʌndaɪəl/, **sundials**. A **sundial** is a device which uses the sun to show you what time it is. During the day, when the sun is shining, a pointer makes a shadow on a flat surface that is marked with numbers. If the shadow falls on the number 2, you know that it is two o'clock. N COUNT

sundown /sʌndaʊn/ is sunset; used especially in American English. EG *It was about an hour before sundown.* N UNCOUNT

sun-drenched; also spelled as one word. Places that are **sun-drenched** have a lot of hot sunshine. EG *...the sundrenched beaches in the south of France.* ADJ CLASSIF ⇑ sunny

sundry /sʌndri[1]/, **sundries**. 1 **Sundry** is used to refer to several things which are all different from each other and which you do not want to describe individually. EG *Sundry judges have serious doubts about the new law... ...stools, wicker mats, food bowls, and sundry other objects.* ● **All and sundry** means everyone; an informal expression. EG *She was fondly known to all and sundry as 'Little Madge'... ...a man so genial to all and sundry.* ADJ CLASSIF : ATTRIB = various; ● PHR : USED AS S/O

2 The items on a list or bill which are not important enough to be mentioned individually are sometimes all put together under the word **sundries**. N PLURAL = miscellaneous

sunflower /sʌnflaʊə/, **sunflowers**. 1 A **sunflower** is a very tall plant that has large flat flowers with yellow petals and brown centres. EG *We passed through wheat fields and golden plots of sunflowers.* N COUNT

2 **Sunflower** is used to describe something that uses or is made from the oil from the seeds of sunflowers. EG *...sunflower margarine.* N BEFORE N

sung /sʌŋ/ is the past participle of **sing**.

sunglasses /sʌnglɑ:sɪz/; also spelled with a hyphen. **Sunglasses** are spectacles which have dark-coloured glass in them. You wear sunglasses to protect your eyes from bright sunlight. EG *To stop squinting I put on some sunglasses... ...two pairs of sunglasses.* N PLURAL : ALSO *a pair of*+N = dark glasses

sunhat /sʌnhæt/, **sunhats**; also spelled with a hyphen. A **sunhat** is a hat that protects your head from the sun. N COUNT

sunk /sʌŋk/ is the past participle of **sink**.

sunken /sʌŋkə[0]n/. 1 **Sunken** is used to describe 1.1 things that are lying at the bottom of a river, lake, or sea, especially if they have been wrecked or hidden there; a fairly literary use. EG *...the remains of a sunken battleship... The oceans of the world are full of sunken treasure.* 1.2 things that are made or constructed below the level of the surrounding area. EG *...a sunken garden.* ADJ CLASSIF : ATTRIB ⇑ submerged; ADJ CLASSIF : ATTRIB

2 A person's face or body that is **sunken** seems to sink or curve inwards, especially because of illness or old age. EG *His cheeks were sunken... ...her sunken eyes.* ADJ CLASSIF = hollow

sun lamp, sun lamps; also spelled with a hyphen and as one word. A **sun lamp** is a lamp that produces ultraviolet rays. People use sun lamps to make their skins look suntanned. N COUNT

sunless /sʌnlɪ[2]s/. Days or places that are **sunless** have no sunshine. EG *The street was grim and sunless.* ADJ CLASSIF ≠ sunny

sunlight /sʌnlaɪt/ is the light that comes from the sun during the day. EG *The sea sparkled in the brilliant sunlight... A patch of sunlight fell on his face.* N UNCOUNT = sunshine

sunlit /sʌnlɪt/. Places that are **sunlit** are made light and bright by the sun. EG *...the sunlit slopes of the canyon... ...fish that live in clear sunlit waters.* ADJ CLASSIF ⇑ illuminated

sun lounge, sun lounges; also spelled with a hyphen. A **sun lounge** is a sitting-room with walls that are mostly made of glass, so that a lot of sunlight gets into the room. N COUNT = sun parlor

sunny /sʌni[1]/, **sunnier, sunniest**. 1 When the weather is **sunny**, the sun is shining brightly. EG *It was a sunny day.* ADJ QUALIT ⇑ bright

2 Places that are **sunny** are made very bright by sunlight. EG *...a lovely, sunny region of green hills and valleys.* ADJ QUALIT ⇑ sunlit

3 People who are **sunny** are always happy and cheerful. EG *He had a sunny disposition.* ADJ QUALIT = cheery

sun parlor, sun parlors. A **sun parlor** is the same as a sun lounge; used in American English. N COUNT

sunrise /sʌnraɪz/, **sunrises**. 1 **Sunrise** is the time in the morning when the sun is first seen in the sky. EG *They left their camp at sunrise.* N UNCOUNT = sun-up

2 A **sunrise** is the part of the sky where the sun first appears in the morning, particularly with regard to the colours that it has at that time. EG *The figure turned towards the sunrise.* N COUNT/UNCOUNT = dawn

sunroof /sʌnru[4]f/, **sunroofs**. A **sunroof** is an opening part in the roof of a car which lets sunshine or air into the car. N COUNT

sunset /sʌnset/, **sunsets**. 1 **Sunset** is the time in the evening when the sun disappears out of sight from the sky. EG *I hate the time just after sunset.* N UNCOUNT = sundown

2 A **sunset** is the part of the sky where the sun disappears out of sight in the evening, particularly with regard to the colours that it has at that time. EG *You must really see some beautiful sunsets here.* N COUNT/UNCOUNT

sunshade /sʌnʃeɪd/, **sunshades**. A **sunshade** is a thing like an umbrella that you use to protect yourself from strong sunshine. N COUNT = parasol

sunshine /sʌnʃaɪn/. **Sunshine** is the light and heat that reach us from the sun. EG *Families were scattered along the beach enjoying the sunshine... ...a day of brilliant sunshine... We went down to the harbour and sat in the sunshine.* N UNCOUNT

sunstroke /sʌnstrəuk/ is an illness that is caused by spending too much time in hot sunshine. People with sunstroke develop very high temperatures, and sometimes lose consciousness and die. EG *Lally was sure that we would get sunstroke while we were fishing.* N UNCOUNT

suntan /sʌntæn/, **suntans**. If you have a **suntan**, the sun has turned your skin an attractive brown colour. EG *They sat there, admiring each other's suntans.* N COUNT = tan

sun-tanned. Someone who is **sun-tanned** has attractively brown skin because they have been in the sunshine. EG *He looked fit, and his face was sun-tanned.* ADJ QUALIT = bronzed

suntrap /sʌntræp/, **suntraps**. A **suntrap** is a very sunny, sheltered place. EG *That corner of the garden is a real suntrap.* N COUNT

sun-up is the same as sunrise; used especially in American English. EG *I worked sun-up to sun-down and sometimes long after.* N UNCOUNT

sup /sʌp/, **sups, supping, supped**; a rather old-fashioned word. 1 If you **sup** something, you drink it, especially in fairly small sips. EG *She supped the hot tea Delia had brought her.* V+O = sip

2 If you **sup**, you eat dinner in the evening. EG *You must sup with me tonight to celebrate your engagement.* V = dine

super /sj⁰u:pə/. 1 If you say that someone or something is **super**, you like them and are pleased or excited by them; an informal, slightly old-fashioned use. EG *His new car's rather expensive, but it's super... I'll be a super secretary for you.* ADJ CLASSIF = fantastic

2 **Super** is also used to describe objects or substances that are better, larger, or more efficient than similar objects or substances. EG *It's made of a super plastic that is resistant to high temperatures... ...the building of new super warships.* ADJ CLASSIF : ATTRIB = superior

super- can be added to nouns and adjectives in order to form other nouns and adjectives. Words formed in this way refer to things that are larger or more powerful than other things of the same kind. PREFIX

superabundance /sj⁰u:pə⁰rəbʌndəns/. If there is a **superabundance** of something, there is a very large amount of it, often more than you need or want; a formal word. EG *Once, there had been a superabundance of leaves to make compost.* N PART+N IN PL/N UNCOUNT = plethora

superabundant /sj⁰u:pə⁰rəbʌndənt/. Something that is **superabundant** exists in very large quantities or amounts; a formal word. EG *This species is famous for its neat foliage and superabundant flowers and fruits.* ADJ CLASSIF = plentiful

superannuated /sj⁰u:pər⁰ænjueɪtɪ²d/. Something that is **superannuated** is old and no longer used for its original purpose; a formal word. EG *We found ourselves aboard a superannuated trawler.* ADJ CLASSIF = antiquated

superannuation /sj⁰u:pər⁰ænjueɪʃə⁰n/ is money which people pay regularly into a special fund so that when they retire from their job they will receive money regularly as a pension; used especially in Britain. EG *Are you paying superannuation at the moment?... Teachers now have to come under the State Superannuation Scheme.* N UNCOUNT ⇑ contribution

superb /sj⁰upɜ:b/. 1 If something is **superb**, its quality is very good indeed. EG *The children's library is superb... Now this gives you, I think, a superb indication of his capabilities.* ◊ **superbly**. EG *...a small but superbly equipped workshop.* ADJ CLASSIF = excellent ◊ ADV

2 If you say that a person has **superb** control, **superb** confidence, etc, you mean that they have very great control or confidence. EG *She was basking in superb confidence of achievement... She amazed her audiences with her superb authority and vocal power.* ADJ CLASSIF = splendid

supercilious /sj⁰u:pəsɪlɪəs/. If you are **supercilious**, you are unfriendly towards other people and scornful of them because you think that your position or achievements are superior to theirs; a formal word, used showing disapproval. EG *Teachers sometimes show cruelty by being supercilious and sarcastic.* ▸ used also of people's attitudes and expressions. EG *She retained her slightly hurt and supercilious air.* ◊ **superciliously**. EG *He stood, superciliously looking down at her.* ◊ **superciliousness**. EG *In comparison with Rosa's superciliousness, Jeremy was a paragon of humility.* ADJ QUALIT ⇑ proud = condescending ▸ = disdainful ◊ ADV WITH VB ◊ N UNCOUNT

super-ego, super-egos; also spelled as one word. Your **super-ego** is the part of your mind which makes you aware of what is right and wrong, and which causes you to feel guilt when you have done something wrong. EG *He challenged the idea of woman's lack of a super-ego, her dependence upon the approval of others.* N COUNT = conscience

superficial /sj⁰u:pəfɪʃə⁰l/. 1 Something that is **superficial** involves only the most obvious or easily understood features or aspects of it, and not those which require more effort to understand or accomplish, although these may be more important than the others. EG *They've only got a superficial knowledge of linguistics... ...the inadequacies of a superficial education.* ADJ QUALIT = sketchy ≠ profound

2 **Superficial** is also used to describe the appearance of something or the impression that it gives when you first look at it or think about it, especially when this does not reflect what it is actually like. EG *The new scheme has superficial similarities with the old one.* ◊ **superficially**. EG *Superficially it looks rather harmless.* ADJ QUALIT = apparent ◊ ADV, OR ADV SEN

3 People who are **superficial** do not care very deeply about anything or are not interested in anything serious or important; used showing disapproval. EG *I suddenly realized how superficial she was.* ADJ QUALIT = shallow

4 If injuries, bruises, etc are **superficial**, they are close to the surface of your skin. EG *Most of the wounds were only superficial.* ADJ QUALIT = slight

superficiality /sj⁰u:pəfɪʃiælɪti¹/ is concern for only the most obvious or easily understood features or aspects of something and not for those which require more effort to understand or accomplish, although these are usually more important than the others. EG *He exaggerates the superficiality of their current affairs programmes.* N UNCOUNT : USU +of ≠ depth, profundity

superfluity /sj⁰u:pəflu:ɪti¹/. If there is a **superfluity** of something, there is more of it than is needed; a formal word. EG *Do not be misled by the superfluity of allegedly scientific advice.* N UNCOUNT/N SING WITH DET : USU+of

superfluous /sj⁰u:pɜ:fluəs/. Something that is **superfluous** is unnecessary or is no longer needed. EG *Certain parts of our religion have become superfluous... I had not been using maps at all, they were superfluous with Eddie around.* ADJ CLASSIF = redundant

superhuman /sj⁰u:pəhju:mən/; also spelled with a hyphen. Something that is **superhuman** is extraordinary and beyond the powers or experience of an ordinary person. EG *You can't control wild horses with just a halter, unless you have super-human strength... There is something superhuman, even magical and alien, about the Pyramids.* ADJ CLASSIF = miraculous

superimpose /sj⁰u:pə⁰rɪmpəuz/, **superimposes, superimposing, superimposed**. 1 If you **superimpose** a word, drawing, painting, etc on something else, you write, draw, or paint on top of it in such a way that the thing underneath can still be seen. EG *Three photos were superimposed one on top of the other... ...a superimposed slogan.* V+O : IF+PREP THEN on/with = overlay

2 If you **superimpose** features or characteristics from one situation on to another situation, you add them, and thus lose the clarity and individuality of that situation. EG *It would be wrong to superimpose the pattern of the East-West conflict on the present problems.* V+O : IF+PREP THEN on/with

superintend /sj⁰u:pə⁰rɪntend/, **superintends, superintending, superintended**. If you **superintend** something or someone, you have responsibility for particular items or equipment or for ensuring that a person does something correctly or properly; a formal word. EG *The children were dressing in the lobby, superintended by Mrs Moffatt.* V+O = supervise

superintendent /sj⁰u:pə⁰rɪntendənt/, **superintendents**. A **superintendent** is 1 a person who has a high rank in the police force. EG *'What intrigued me,' said Superintendent Garroway, 'is the way you jumped from the train.'* 2 a person who is responsible for the work done in a particular department or office, or for ensuring that something is kept in good condition. EG *His late brother had been attached to the College as Superintendent of Buildings and Grounds... ...the superintendent of the security force.* N COUNT : ALSO IN TITLES; N COUNT : ALSO IN TITLES ⇑ manager

superior /sj⁰u:pɪərɪə/, **superiors**. 1 Something that is **superior** to something else which is similar or which has a similar function is better, more useful, or more effective. EG *The school prided itself upon its policy of providing a superior education... The computer is vastly superior to the book.* ◊ **superiority** /sj⁰u:pɪərɒrɪti¹/. EG *Their vast superiority in speed* ADJ QUALIT : IF+PREP THEN to ◊ N UNCOUNT = advantage *would be easily outweighed by the extortionate running costs.*

2 Someone who is **superior** to someone else is more important or has more authority in a particular situation. EG *He was in a state of depression because of a warning from a superior civil servant... These matters are better left to someone superior to you.* ADJ CLASSIF : IF+ PREP THEN *to* = senior
◊ **superiority.** EG *It affords visible proof of the master's superiority.* ◊ N UNCOUNT = seniority

3 If you feel **superior** to other people, you believe that you are better than they are. You often make people aware of your attitude by your expression or tone of voice or by the way you treat them. EG *Who did Boylan think he was to be so superior?... I'm always feeling superior about all sorts of things.* ADJ QUALIT : IF+ PREP THEN *to*
▸ used also of people's behaviour. EG *He turned to me with a superior and sarcastic smile... 'You wouldn't understand,' Clarissa said in a superior way.* ▸ = patronizing
◊ **superiority.** EG *Quite often, his sense of superiority makes him deride her opinions.* ◊ N UNCOUNT = supremacy

4 Superior, in expressions such as 'superior race' or 'superior class', means having a higher position and more respect in society than another person or group of people, and considered to be better. EG *He was from a caste so superior to their own... They counted themselves the most superior race in the world.* ADJ QUALIT : IF+ PREP THEN *to*
◊ **superiority.** EG *The so-called superiority of any human being or race or class is hereby called into question.* ◊ N UNCOUNT = ascendancy

5 A **superior** is **5.1** a person who has a higher position and more respect in society than another person or group of people. EG *Myra was his social superior... Don't go giving yourself airs as if you were her superior.* N COUNT : USU POSS+N = better
5.2 a person who holds a higher position than you or has authority over you in the organization for which you work. EG *He was called to the office of a superior to be reprimanded... He was extra polite to his superiors lest something adverse might be written about him.* N COUNT ⇑ colleague = senior
● See also **mother superior**.

6 If one group of people or things has **superior** numbers to another group of people or things, there are more of them. EG *These factors did much to offset the enemy's superior numbers.* ADJ CLASSIF = greater
◊ **superiority.** EG *There was a significant increase in Soviet numerical superiority in the air.* ◊ N UNCOUNT = advantage

7 If someone or something is on a **superior** surface or in a **superior** position, they are on the upper side or surface or are in a position immediately above someone or something else; a formal use. EG *...a point on the superior surface of the leaf.* ADJ CLASSIF

> **SUPERL** □ In this dictionary SUPERL is used in the grammar notes beside an entry to mean that the headword is an adjective in the superlative form. A few adverbs also have an inflected superlative form. Superlatives are typically used to indicate that you are picking out an extreme instance of something. As a rule, superlatives are formed by placing *the most* in front of an adjective. However, superlatives of fairly short adjectives are formed by adding *-est* to the ordinary form of an adjective, preceded usually by *the*. There are a few irregularly formed superlatives in English, such as *the best* from *good* and *the worst* from *bad*. If a superlative form is not given in this dictionary after the entry word for an adjective, it means that you form the superlative by placing the words *the most* in front of the entry word. Examples of superlatives are **the most interesting**, **the heaviest**, and **the worst**. EG *These are* ***the most interesting*** *years of my life... This is* ***the heaviest*** *load of all... An anxious mother imagines* ***the worst***.

superlative /sj^{0}u:pɜ:lətɪv/, **superlatives. 1** If you describe someone's abilities or achievements as **superlative**, you mean that they are very good indeed. EG *He has superlative technical skills.* ADJ CLASSIF ⇑ excellent = superb
▸ used of people. EG *She is a versatile and superlative actress... He was a superlative examiner of undergraduates.* ▸ = outstanding
◊ **superlatively.** EG *...a superlatively good candidate... The fans come to see a game superlatively played.* ◊ ADV = outstandingly

2 In grammar, a **superlative** is the form of an adjective which indicates that the person or object being described has more of a particular quality or character than anyone or anything else in a group. EG *The Coronation commentaries lavished superlatives on the English genius for ceremonial.* N COUNT

superman /sj^{0}u:pəmæn/, **supermen.** A **superman** is a man who has extraordinarily great physical or mental powers. EG *To succeed in that task you need to be a superman.* N COUNT

supermarket /sj^{0}u:pəmɑ:kɪt/, **supermarkets.** A **supermarket** is a large shop which sells all kinds of food and household goods. You walk round the shop and take items off the shelf yourself, and pay for them all together before you leave. EG *...the girl at the check-out counter at the supermarket... ...the weekly supermarket bill.* N COUNT

supernatural /sj^{0}u:pənætʃrəl/. **1 Supernatural** things and creatures are believed by some people to exist and to have magical properties or powers. EG *Feathered serpents and owl-monkeys were among the supernatural beings of many South American cultures.* ADJ CLASSIF

2 Supernatural events are believed by some people to happen although they involve things which are not physically possible, such as the re-appearance of dead people. ADJ CLASSIF

3 The **supernatural** is the existence of supernatural things and creatures and the occurrence of supernatural events. EG *Do you believe in the supernatural?* N SING : *the*+N = occult

superpower /sj^{0}u:pəpaʊə/, **superpowers**; also spelled with a hyphen. A **superpower** is a state which has very great economic and military strength. When people talk about 'the superpowers', they usually mean the USA and the USSR. EG *...the two superpowers that currently dominate the world... ...the destructive capacity of the superpowers' strategic weapons.* N COUNT

supersede /sj^{0}u:pəsi:d/, **supersedes, superseding, superseded.** If something **supersedes** something else, it takes its place, often because the other thing has become unacceptable or old-fashioned; a slightly formal word. EG *Steam locomotives were superseded by diesel... New ways of thinking superseded older ones.* V+O : USU PASS = replace

supersonic /sj^{0}u:pəsɒnɪk/. **Supersonic** speeds are greater than the speed of sound. EG *...the hazards of flying aircraft at supersonic speeds.* ADJ CLASSIF ⇑ fast
▸ used of planes that fly at these speeds and of the journeys that they make. EG *In 1958 only four Third World countries had supersonic aircraft... ...the demand for supersonic travel.*

superstar /sj^{0}u:pəstɑ:/, **superstars.** A **superstar** is a very famous entertainer, sportsman or sportswoman; an informal word. EG *The press built me up into a superstar... ...superstar golfers.* N COUNT ⇑ celebrity

superstition /sj^{0}u:pəstɪʃə^{0}n/, **superstitions. Superstition** is belief in magic, ghosts, devils, fairies, etc. EG *They were filled with ignorance and superstition... Like all such tales, it is part superstition, part fact... Coincidences have often given rise to superstitions.* N UNCOUNT/ COUNT

superstitious /sj^{0}u:pəstɪʃəs/. **Superstitious** people believe in magic, ghosts, fairies, etc, or they believe that certain things are signs of bad luck, and that other things are signs of good luck. EG *Surely you are not superstitious?... He was a superstitious man with an unnatural fear of the dark... Many people are superstitious about death at sea.* ADJ QUALIT ⇑ irrational ≠ rational
▸ used of feelings and beliefs. EG *She felt a vague superstitious uneasiness... There is still a good deal of superstitious belief about.* ▸ ⇑ irrational

superstructure /sj^{0}u:pəstrʌktʃə/, **superstructures.** The **superstructure** of a ship is the part of it that is above its main deck. EG *In the heavy seas her superstructure was almost awash.* N COUNT

supervise /sj^{0}u:pəvaɪz/, **supervises, supervising, supervised. 1** If you **supervise** someone, you ensure that they behave correctly or that they do a task properly. EG *Jenny was supervising her children in a game of rounders... One evening, when there were no staff to supervise her, she walked out of the hospital.* V OR V+O ⇑ watch over

2 If you **supervise** an activity or process, you ensure that it is done correctly or legally. EG *Miss Young had three netball games to supervise... Dieting should be supervised by a doctor... A Gambling Board was set up to control and supervise the activities of the casinos.* V OR V+O ⇑ control = superinten[d]

3 If you **supervise** a place where work is done, you ensure that the work there is done properly. EG *Gwyneth supervised the launderette... Grandma herself had supervised the organisation... He is quite capable of supervising the ship.* V OR V+O = run

supervision /sjᵘu̲:pəvɪʒəⁿn/ is the supervising of people, activities, or places. EG *I was principally concerned with staff supervision... It is forbidden to bathe in the sea without the supervision of life-guards.* • If someone does something **under supervision**, someone else supervises them while they do it. EG *She'll be working under the supervision of qualified social workers... It was translated from the German under the personal supervision of the author.* — N UNCOUNT; • PHR : USED AS AN A

supervisor /sjᵘu̲:pəvaɪzə/, **supervisors**. A **supervisor** is a person who supervises people, activities, or places, especially an employee who supervises other workers or a tutor who supervises students. EG *The maintenance supervisor would dispatch a crew to repair the damage... My supervisor said he would strongly recommend me for the course.* — N COUNT ⇑ overseer

supervisory /sjᵘu̲:pəvaɪzəri¹/ means concerned with the supervision of people, activities, or places. EG *Supervisory control was carried out by officials... ...supervisory staff... ...technologists in supervisory positions.* — ADJ CLASSIF : ATTRIB = managerial

supine /sjᵘu̲:paɪn/. If you are **supine**, you are lying flat on your back; a literary word. EG *She was relaxing, supine, on the beach... He lay supine on the couch, arms folded.* — ADJ CLASSIF, OR ADV WITH VB = prostrate

> **SUPP** □ In this dictionary SUPP is used in the grammar notes beside a noun to indicate that the noun is not normally used on its own, but occurs with a supporting word, phrase, or clause which gives further information about the noun. The supporting element may come before or after the noun. If it comes before the noun, it is usually an adjective or another noun used as a modifier. If it comes after the noun, it is usually in the form of a relative clause or a prepositional group, often one that starts with *of*. The supporting element need not always be present because it can be referred to by the determiner *the*, indicating that information has already been given in the preceding discourse or text. Examples of nouns which are given the extra notation SUPP in the grammar notes are **hunting 3** and **state 1**. EG *I spent all weekend house* ***hunting****... Job* ***hunting*** *can be very depressing... Her emotional* ***state*** *is very worrying... ...the* ***state*** *of the economy... Just look at the* ***state*** *of your room!*

supper /sʌ̲pə/, **suppers**. 1 **Supper** or a **supper** is a large meal eaten in the early part of the evening, especially by members of a family eating together. EG *I've got to make the supper for the kids coming home from school... I'm tired and hungry and I want some supper.* — N UNCOUNT/COUNT = dinner

2 **Supper** or a **supper** is also a small meal eaten just before you go to bed at night. EG *He returned to his hotel in time for a late supper.* — N UNCOUNT/COUNT ⇑ snack

supplant /səplɑ̲:nt/, **supplants, supplanting, supplanted**. If something or someone **supplants** something or someone else, they take the place of the other thing or person; a slightly formal word. EG *Electric cars may one day supplant petrol-driven ones... Soon afterwards he began his campaign to supplant Mendoza as leader of the Party.... My panic and fear had been supplanted by happiness.* — V+O = replace

supple /sʌ̲pəⁿl/. 1 A **supple** person moves and bends easily and gracefully. EG *She had once been slim and supple.* ▸ used of someone's body or of a part of their body. EG *If you run frequently, your body becomes more supple... He keeps his fingers supple with regular exercises.* ▸ used of someone's movements. EG *She dances with a supple grace that is amazing.* ◊ **suppleness**. EG *She tried to recover her lost fitness and suppleness.* — ADJ QUALIT = lissom ≠ stiff; ▸ = flexible; ▸ = fluid; ◊ N UNCOUNT = elasticity

2 If an object or material is **supple**, it is soft and bends easily without cracking or breaking. EG *The leather straps were worn supple with use... Polish it regularly to keep it supple and prevent cracks.* ◊ **suppleness**. EG *...the pleasing suppleness of old leather.* — ADJ QUALIT ⇑ flexible ≠ stiff; ◊ N UNCOUNT ≠ stiffness

supplement /sʌ̲plɪməˀnt/, **supplements, supplementing, supplemented**. 1 A **supplement** is something that is added to something else, usually in order to make it more adequate. EG *The money they get from fruit-picking is often a supplement to incomes earned in the town... They will sometimes eat fish as a supplement to their natural diet... ...vitamin supplements.* — N COUNT : IF + PREP THEN *to* ⇑ addition

2 If you **supplement** something, you add something to it, usually in order to make it more adequate. EG *They had to get a job to supplement the family income... I supplemented my diet with vitamin pills.* — V+O : IF + PREP THEN *with/by*

3 A **supplement** is also 3.1 an extra amount of money that you pay in order to obtain special facilities or services, for example when you are travelling or staying at a hotel. EG *Passengers holding second class tickets may travel in first class accommodation for a £1 supplement... ...a single room supplement.* **3.2** an amount of money that the government gives regularly to certain people who have difficulty affording things that they and their families need. EG *...Family Income Supplement.* — N COUNT ⇑ payment; N COUNT : MOD + N ⇑ allowance

4 A magazine or newspaper **supplement** is a separate part of a magazine or newspaper. Some supplements deal with particular subjects. EG *...the Times Literary Supplement.* • See also **colour supplement**. — N COUNT ⇑ publication

5 A **supplement** to a book is an additional section, written some time after the main text and published either at the end of the book or as a separate volume. EG *...A Supplement to the Oxford English Dictionary.* — N COUNT ⇑ addition

supplementary /sʌplɪme̲ntəⁿri¹/. Something that is **supplementary** is added to something else in order to make it more adequate. EG *...a supplementary pension... ...supplementary navigation satellites.* — ADJ CLASSIF : ATTRIB ⇑ additional

supplementary benefit is an amount of money that the government in Britain gives regularly to people with very low incomes, so that they can buy the things that they and their families need. EG *You can always claim supplementary benefit... You may be able to get supplementary benefit while you are looking for work... They asked if I was on Supplementary Benefit.* — N UNCOUNT ⇑ allowance

supplicant /sʌ̲plɪkənt/, **supplicants**. A **supplicant** is a person who humbly asks God or an important person to help them or to give them something that they want very much; a formal word. EG *I come as a supplicant begging a favour.* — N COUNT = petitioner

supplication /sʌplɪke̲ɪʃəⁿn/, **supplications**. **Supplication** or a **supplication** is a prayer or humble request made to God or to someone in authority; a formal word. EG *Maria was crouching on the abbey floor in supplication.* — N UNCOUNT/COUNT = entreaty

supplier /sʌpla̲ɪə/, **suppliers**. A **supplier** is a person or firm that provides you with something such as goods or equipment. EG *Check with your supplier which adhesive to use... ...textile suppliers... I asked my suppliers to send more toys.* — N COUNT

supply /səpla̲ɪ/, **supplies, supplying, supplied**. 1 If you **supply** someone with something, you provide them with it. EG *Germany is supplying much of the steel for the new pipeline... Most large towns are supplied with electricity... Much of the material supplied to the army was faulty.* — V+O, USU+A *(with/to)*

2 **Supply** of something is the act of providing someone with it. EG *Supply of the first 850 tractors was soon arranged.* — N UNCOUNT ⇑ provision

3 **Supply** is also the amount of a commodity that can be produced and made available for people to buy. EG *Economic stability can only be reached if demand and supply are in approximate balance.* — N UNCOUNT

4 If something is **in short supply**, there is very little of it and it is therefore hard to obtain. EG *Many materials are now in short supply... Petrol is in desperately short supply.* — PHR : USED AS AN A = scarce

5 A **supply** of something is an amount of it which someone has or which is available for them to use. EG *Bill had his own supply of whisky... There are very large supplies of oil in the North Sea... ...the world's food supply... Most houses now have indoor lavatories and a hot water supply.* — N COUNT

6 **Supplies** are food, equipment, and other things needed by a group of people, for example by an army, or by people living in remote places or going on an expedition. EG *They tried to stop supplies reaching the guerrillas.* — N PLURAL = provisions

supply teacher, supply teachers. A **supply teacher** is a teacher whose job is to take the place of other teachers at different schools when they are absent. EG *She worked as a supply teacher after the birth of her son.* — N COUNT

support /səˀpɔ̲:t/, **supports, supporting, supported**. 1 If you **support** a politician or political party or if you **support** their policies, you show that you want them to succeed, especially by voting for them. EG *I've always supported her and I still do...* — V+O = back

The policies which he supports are ultra-Left policies... A lot of building workers supported the campaign. ▸ used as a noun. EG *They offered unconditional support to the Christian Democrats... They have continued to attract some support from outside the party... They had failed to mobilize trade union support.*
▸ N UNCOUNT = allegiance, backing

2 The **support** that something such as a political party or an idea has is the people who support it. EG *The party's support is so scattered that it is quite powerless.*
N UNCOUNT = supporters

3 If you **support** someone who is trying to do something or **support** what they are trying to do, you help them in a practical way. EG *His work colleagues refused to support him... They supported the war effort.* ▸ used as a noun. EG *Women wanted support in setting up a creche... They had set up a mutual support scheme.* ● If you do something **in support of** something that someone is trying to achieve, you do it in order to help them to achieve it. EG *...the Navy's capacity to act in support of their political objectives... They left their children at the office in support of their pay claim.*
V+O/REPORT-CL = back
▸ N UNCOUNT = assistance
● PREP

4 If you give **support** to someone during a difficult or unhappy time in their life, you help them by spending time with them and by being kind to them. EG *They find it hard to give their children emotional support.* ▸ A **support** is someone who does this. EG *She was a practical support to her mother... His one support is the art teacher.* ● **moral support**: see **moral**.
N UNCOUNT = comfort
▸ N COUNT : USU SING = prop

5 If you **support** a sports team, especially a football team, you go regularly to their games and encourage them to win, for example by cheering them.
V+O

6 If something **supports** an object, it holds it firmly from below, so that it does not drop downwards. EG *...the girders that supported the walkway... He had to sit down, because his knees wouldn't support him any more.* ▸ A **support** is something that supports something else. EG *Most large scale buildings now have steel supports.*
V+O = hold up, carry
▸ N COUNT = underpinning

7 If you **support** yourself, you prevent yourself from falling by holding on to something or by leaning on something. EG *I clung to the outside edge of the door to support myself.* ▸ used as a noun. EG *She was standing behind the ladder and holding on to it for support.*
V+O (REFL)
▸ N UNCOUNT

8 Financial **support** is money provided by someone, especially a government or local authority, in order to enable a firm or organization to continue. EG *We are dependent on them for financial support... It is voluntarily run, with local authority support.*
N UNCOUNT = funding

9 If you **support** someone, especially members of your family, you earn the money that is needed to buy their food, clothing, etc. EG *She supports a family of three... He has a wife and three children to support.*
V+O = keep

10 If the land in a place **supports** the people who live there, it is fertile enough to provide the food that they need. EG *The valley had a vast population to support... ...land so poor that it cannot support a small family.*
V+O = sustain

11 If something **supports** something such as a statement or a theory, it helps to show that it is true or correct. EG *You can be medically examined to support your statement... There was simply no visible evidence to support such a theory.* ▸ used as a noun. EG *Scholars have found little support for this interpretation... In support of this view, Rose cites Pollock's own evidence.* ◊ **supporting**. EG *There seems to be little supporting evidence.*
V+O = substantiate
▸ N UNCOUNT = evidence
◊ ADJ CLASSIF : ATTRIB

supporter /sə'pɔːtə/, **supporters**. A **supporter** is someone who supports someone or something, for example a political leader, a political party, or a sports team. EG *The Minister's supporters did not desert him in his hour of need... ...an Everton supporter.*
N COUNT+SUPP ⇑ follower

supportive /sə'pɔːtɪv/. If you are **supportive**, you help someone by being kind to them at a difficult or unhappy time in their life. EG *When I became a student he was supportive... She was helping them in a strongly supportive way... ...the supportive network of the family.*
ADJ QUALIT ⇑ helpful

suppose /sə'pəʊz/, **supposes, supposing, supposed**. **1** If you **suppose** that something is true, you think that it is likely that it is true, because of other things that you know. EG *It was quite reasonable to suppose that he wanted the money too... No one supposes that nuclear weapons are going to be swept away overnight... The situation was even worse than was supposed... It's not simply a drop in the temperature as one might suppose.*
V+REPORT-CL, OR V+O (NG/REFL)+C = assume

2 The expression **I suppose** is used in the following ways. **2.1** in order to introduce an idea or thought you have had that concerns a possible explanation or reason for something. EG *I suppose the answer is that he wasn't trying hard enough... I suppose I felt slightly jealous.* **2.2** in order to say that you are only guessing something such as a number or a size, because you do not know it exactly or cannot remember it exactly. EG *He was an elderly man, sixty I suppose, very amusing... I suppose I saw twelve takes of this scene.* **2.3** in order to say that you think that something is true, and that you are angry or upset about it. EG *I suppose you'll want half of that, won't you.?... You know what you've done, I suppose, by your silly talk? You've spoilt everything!* **2.4** in order to say that you think that something is true, although you hope that it might not be true and would be glad if someone contradicted you. EG *I suppose it's too late to see the doctor now... I don't suppose you would be prepared to stay in Edinburgh?* **2.5** in order to indicate that you do not really want to do something or to agree with someone, and that you are doing so reluctantly. EG *We could take Davis with us, I suppose... 'So it was worth doing?'–'I suppose so.'... He did his best, I suppose.*
PHR+REPORT-CL OR PHR : USED AS ADV SEN ⇑ perhaps
PHR+REPORT-CL OR PHR : USED AS ADV SEN = perhaps
PHR+REPORT-CL OR PHR : USED AS ADV SEN = I presume
PHR+REPORT-CL OR PHR : USED AS ADV SEN
PHR+REPORT-CL OR PHR : USED AS ADV SEN = I guess

3 The word **suppose** is also used in the following expressions. **3.1 You don't suppose** is used to introduce an idea or thought which you want someone else to give their opinion about. EG *You don't suppose he'll get lost out there?* **3.2 Who do you suppose** and **what do you suppose** are used when you are telling a story or describing an event in order to create suspense by making people imagine several possible answers to your question before you tell them the correct one. EG *Then we went back to the bar, and who do you suppose was the only other chap there? His father.* **3.3 Suppose** and **supposing** are used when you are considering a possible situation or course of action and trying to decide what results or effects it would have. EG *Suppose we don't say a word, and somebody else finds out about it... Supposing something should go wrong, what would you do then?*
PHR+REPORT-CL
PHR
CONJ COORD = what if

supposed /sə'pəʊzd/. **1** The expression **be supposed** is used in the following ways. **1.1** If you say that something **is supposed** to be done or **is not supposed** to be done, you mean that it should be done or should not be done because of a law, rule, or custom. EG *You are supposed to report it to the police as soon as possible... Aren't you supposed to be at work?... I'm not supposed to talk to you about this... You're not supposed to abandon your car on the motorway.* **1.2** If you say that something **was supposed** to happen, you mean that it was planned or intended that it should happen; used especially when the particular thing does not happen. EG *I was supposed to go last summer... She was supposed to be in Cuba... A machine at the entrance is supposed to issue and check the tickets.* **1.3** You say that something **is supposed** to be true when people think that it is true but you do not know for certain that it is true. EG *The hill was supposed to be haunted by the ghost of a leper... The original inhabitants are supposed, according to legend, to have been black... She was supposed to be very good as an actress.* **1.4** People say **What's that supposed to mean?** when they are puzzled or angry by something that you have just said.
PHR : VB INFLECTS+to-INF
PHR : VB INFLECTS+to-INF = be meant
PHR : VB INFLECTS+to-INF = be reputed
CONVENTION

2 Supposed is used when you are referring to a statement or to a way of describing something and when you want to express doubt about the truth of the statement or about how appropriate it is. EG *...his supposed ancestor, the pirate Henry Morgan... ...the supposed benefits of a progressive welfare state.* ◊ **supposedly**. EG *...a robot supposedly capable of understanding spoken commands... It supposedly tied up with her interest in dance... ...a supposedly inferior form of life such as the reptile.*
ADJ CLASSIF : ATTRIB = alleged
◊ ADV = allegedly

supposition /sʌpəzɪʃə'n/, **suppositions**. A **supposition** is an idea or statement which is thought to be true or correct, or one which people assume to be true or correct in order to discuss what its conse-
N COUNT = hypothesis, assumption

quences would be; a formal word. EG *That he resigned on political grounds is a not very unreasonable supposition... These facts, surmises and plain guesses rest on a central supposition–that equality between men and women is possible.*

suppress /səprɛs/, **suppresses, suppressing, suppressed.** 1 If an army or government **suppresses** an activity, it prevents it from continuing, by using force or by making it illegal. EG *The army soon suppressed the revolt... All religious activities were suppressed.*
V+O = crush

2 If someone **suppresses** a piece of information, they prevent it from becoming known to the general public. EG *Morgan was careful to suppress such information... The working party's report has been suppressed.*
V+O = withhold

3 If you **suppress** your feelings or **suppress** your way of expressing them, you prevent yourself from expressing them. EG *Men are required by society to suppress a large proportion of their feelings... She was struggling to suppress her sobs... His eyes were no longer mild but glittered with a suppressed fury.*
V+O = repress, restrain

4 If you **suppress** a form of life or **suppress** its growth or development, you prevent it from growing or developing. EG *You put it on the land to suppress weeds.*
V+O = inhibit

suppression /səprɛʃəⁿn/. 1 When there is **suppression** of rights or activities, people lose these rights or are prevented from continuing with their activities as a result of action by a government or army. EG *The suppression of freedom in one European country would have repercussions in others... ...the suppression of competition... ...the suppression of rebellions.*
N UNCOUNT : USU +SUPP = crushing

2 When there is **suppression** of a piece of information, someone prevents it from becoming known by other people.
N UNCOUNT : USU +SUPP

3 When there is **suppression** of a person's feelings or of their way of expressing them, the person prevents himself or herself from expressing these feelings. EG *There will be a deliberate suppression of personal likes and dislikes... Do I sense the first polite suppression of a yawn?*
N UNCOUNT : USU +SUPP = smothering

4 When there is **suppression** of a form of life or **suppression** of its growth or development, it is prevented from growing or developing; a formal use. EG *...the answer to weed suppression.*
N UNCOUNT : USU +SUPP = elimination

suppurate /sʌpjʌ⁴reɪt/, **suppurates, suppurating, suppurated.** If a wound or a part of your body **suppurates**, pus forms inside it or comes out of it, because it is infected; a medical term. EG *Her little boy has an infected ear that suppurates.*
V = fester
◊ **suppurating.** EG *...suppurating flesh.*
◊ ADJ CLASSIF

supremacy /sjᵒuprɛməsɪ/. 1 If one group of people has **supremacy** over another group, they are stronger or more powerful militarily, economically, or politically. EG *...the struggle to maintain white supremacy... Their political supremacy continued.*
N UNCOUNT = dominance

2 If one kind of thing has **supremacy** over another kind, it is better than the other kind; a formal use. EG *They were convinced of the supremacy of European medicines and science.*
N UNCOUNT = superiority

supreme /sjᵒupriːm, -prɛm/. 1 When **Supreme** is part of a person's title or part of the title of an official body, it indicates that the person or body is at the highest level in a particular organization or system. EG *The Supreme Commander ordered the release of four divisions... ...the Supreme Soviet... ...the Supreme Court.*
ADJ CLASSIF : IN NAME/TITLES BEFORE N ⇑ chief

2 **Supreme** also means the greatest possible. EG *...one of this century's supreme achievements... ...tasks of supreme importance... ...an act of supreme heroism.*
ADJ CLASSIF : ATTRIB ⇑ outstanding
◊ **supremely.** EG *The ascent was supremely difficult... ...a supremely important moment.*
◊ ADV+ADJ/ADV

3 If you talk about someone's **supreme** skill, artistry, etc you mean that they are very skilful indeed. EG *She can do certain things with supreme skill... ...an act of supreme statesmanship.* ▸ used of people. EG *These people are supreme artists of dance and theatre.*
ADJ CLASSIF : USU ATTRIB ⇑ great
▸ = brilliant

Supt is an abbreviation for 'superintendent' when it is part of someone's title in the police force. EG *...Chief Supt Walker of Scotland Yard.*
N IN TITLES

surcharge /sɜːtʃɑːdʒ/, **surcharges.** A **surcharge** is an extra amount of money in addition to the usual payment. It is charged by a government or other authority as a tax or as a penalty. EG *The Government is imposing a 15% import surcharge.*
N COUNT

sure /ʃʊə, ʃɔː/, **surer, surest.** 1 If you are **sure** that something is true, you believe that it is true and feel fairly certain that it is true. EG *I'm sure she's right... I feel fairly sure that the work can be done... How could he be so sure?... Her basic decision I'm quite sure was right... Something had gone wrong, he was sure of it... I'm not quite sure but I think it's about half past five.*
ADJ QUALIT : PRED, USU+REPORT-CL ≠ doubtful

2 If you are **sure** about your feelings, wishes, or intentions, you believe that you know exactly what you feel, want, or intend to do. EG *Jane wasn't sure how she felt about being married... He wasn't quite sure what it reminded him of... I'm not sure that I'd like to do that... Are you sure you won't have another drink?*
ADJ QUALIT : PRED, USU+REPORT-CL = certain, positive

3 If you say that you are **sure** about a person or are **sure** of them, you mean that you can trust them or rely on them. EG *I'm not sure about Rossiter... He was never quite sure of Flora.*
ADJ QUALIT : PRED, USU+about/of = confident

4 If you say that someone is **sure** of himself or herself, you mean that they are very confident of their own abilities or opinions. EG *Bal was so confident, so sure of himself... She's not so sure of herself these days.*
ADJ QUALIT : PRED+of+PRON REFL = cocksure

5 If you say that someone is **sure** of getting something or of achieving something, you mean that they will certainly get it or achieve it. EG *We can be sure of success... He was always sure of sympathy from his mother-in-law... You could not be sure of winning that time.*
ADJ QUALIT : PRED+of+-ING/N = certain

6 If you say that something is **sure** to happen, you mean that it will certainly happen. EG *He was sure to see her again... The telephone stopped ringing. 'It's sure to ring again,' Sarah said.*
ADJ CLASSIF : PRED+to-INF = bound

7 The expression **make sure** is used in the following ways. **7.1** If you **make sure** that something is the way that you want it to be or expect it to be, you confirm that it is that way, especially by looking. EG *We watched the baby to make sure she was really asleep... He glanced over his shoulder to make sure that there was nobody listening... He sent the boy off to make sure no one was in the house... She looked over her shoulder to make sure her dress wasn't wrinkled at the back.*
PHR : VB INFLECTS, USU+REPORT-CL = check, ascertain
7.2 If you **make sure** that you do something or **make sure** that it is done, you do it or get someone else to do it, and do not allow it to be forgotten or overlooked. EG *Ask for a receipt and make sure that you get it... We try and make sure that they see each other's work... Brody made sure to warn the driver that the roads were flooded.*
PHR : VB INFLECTS, USU+REPORT-CL/to-INF = make certain

8 If you tell someone to **be sure** to do something, you mean that they must not forget to do it. EG *Be sure to remind your uncle. You know how forgetful he is... Be sure not to take any weapons.*
PHR+to-INF/and

9 You describe something as **sure** when it can be relied on to have a particular result or to indicate what is happening. EG *Going to places is a sure way of getting to know them... New information is the surest road to new ideas... Wood dust beneath a piece of furniture is a sure sign of woodworm.*
ADJ QUALIT : USU ATTRIB ⇑ reliable = certain

10 If you have a **sure** knowledge or understanding of something, you know or understand it very well; a formal use. EG *She had a sure grasp of the subject... Anthony had a much surer knowledge of who he was than before.*
ADJ QUALIT : USU ATTRIB = firm

11 **Sure** and **sure thing** are informal ways of saying 'yes' in reply to a question; used especially in American English. EG *'Can I go with you?'–'Sure.'... 'Did you like it?'–'Sure thing.'*
CONVENTION = of course

12 You can also use **sure** in order to emphasize your feelings or reactions; an informal use, used in American English. EG *He sure is cute... I sure am bored... I don't know what they're made of, but they sure smell good... 'Know what I mean?'–'Sure do.'*
ADV = certainly

13 The word **sure** is also used in the following expressions. **13.1 Sure as** and **as sure as** are used before various expressions to emphasize the fact that you are absolutely sure that something is true or that it has happened or will happen. EG *As sure as heat rises, their time was over... They'll be boiled like a couple of eggs, sure as sure... Claude sure as hell wouldn't take the blame alone.*
PHR ⇑ certainly
13.2 If you say that something is **for sure** or that you know it **for sure**, you mean that it is definitely true or will definitely happen; an informal expression. EG *One*
PHR : USED AS AN A = for certain

thing was for sure, there was nothing wrong with Allen's eyesight... He assured us that tomorrow we would get it for sure... She said that her mother was Irish, but nobody knew for sure... He could not say for sure how effective it had been. **13.3 Sure enough** is used, especially in stories, to confirm that something is really true or is actually happening. EG *He cried, 'She's eating it!' And sure enough, the head of the baby rabbit was disappearing down her throat.* PHR : USED AS ADV SEN

13.4 You use **to be sure** when you are admitting that something is true, although it seems to contradict a more general statement that you are making; a fairly formal use. EG *To be sure, such people do not commit these crimes often.* PHR : USED AS ADV SEN = of course

sure-fire means certain to succeed or win; a fairly informal word. EG *There are no sure-fire techniques for guaranteeing equal representation... ...sure-fire winners.* ADJ CLASSIF : ATTRIB = guaranteed

sure-footed. A **sure-footed** person or animal can move easily over steep or uneven ground without falling. EG *You had to be sure-footed and ready to make a fast getaway.* ADJ QUALIT ⇑ nimble

surely /ʃʊəli¹, -ʃɔː/. **1** You use **surely** **1.1** in order to emphasize that you think something is true and to express surprise that other people do not necessarily agree with you. EG *She was surely one of the rarest women of our time.* ADV SEN **1.2** in order to express surprise at something that seems to contradict what you are saying. EG *Ivan must surely have known... Surely they'll get in.* ADV SEN **1.3** in order to contradict something that someone else has said. EG *'The woman's approaching ninety.'–'Eighty-five, Mother, surely?'... Was he a Minister? Surely not.* ADV SEN

2 Some people use **surely to God** and **surely to goodness** when they want to express disbelief that anyone could disagree with what they are saying; an informal expression. EG *Surely to God that itself is reason enough to call the police.* PHR : USED AS ADV SEN OR CONVENTION

3 You also use **surely** when you are asking someone a question about something that they have just said and are trying to get them to admit something. EG *Well, you don't mind that surely?... But there must be more to it than that, surely?... Good heavens! Surely you are not suggesting she did it on purpose?* ADV SEN

4 Surely is an informal way of saying 'yes' in reply to a question; used in American English. EG *'Will you excuse me just a second?'–'Surely.'* ADV SEN = certainly

5 If someone says that something will **surely** happen, they mean that it will definitely happen; an old-fashioned use. EG *Please send them money or they will surely die.* ADV WITH VB = undoubtedly

6 If you say that something changes or progresses **slowly but surely**, you mean that it changes or progresses gradually but in a way that is significant and noticeable. EG *Slowly but surely Stephen's hair was dropping out.* PHR : USED AS AN A **surety** /ʃʊərɪ⁰ti¹/, **sureties**. A **surety** is **1** a person who accepts responsibility for another person's debt or for their behaviour. EG *There are some parents who are not prepared to act as sureties for the future good behaviour of their children.* N COUNT/ UNCOUNT = guarantor **2** something valuable which you give to someone to show that you will do what you have promised. EG *He gave me a gold watch as surety.* N COUNT/ UNCOUNT = insurance

surf /sɜːf/, **surfs, surfing, surfed**. **1 Surf** is the mass of white foam that is formed by waves as they fall upon the shore or crash against rocks. EG *We watched the children play in the surf.* N UNCOUNT : USU *the*+N ⇑ froth

2 If you **surf**, you ride towards the shore on the top of a big wave while standing or lying on a surfboard. EG *Where's the best place to go surfing?* V : USU CONT ◇ **surfing**. EG *Surfing is popular here.* ◇ N UNCOUNT

surface /sɜːfɪs/, **surfaces, surfacing, surfaced**. **1** The **surface** of a solid object is the outside or top part of it. EG *He wiped the lock and all outer surfaces of the trunk to remove any fingerprints... ...a network of tiny red veins running over the whole surface of the eyeball.* N COUNT : USU WITH POSS ⇑ exterior

2 A **surface** is **2.1** a flat area, for example the top of a table, desk, or cupboard, on which you can work or do a particular job. EG *The jumble which covers the surface of my desk... Knead the dough on a well-floured surface for five to ten minutes.* N COUNT **2.2** a thin layer of a particular substance that covers the outside or top part of something. EG *If you use scourers you may remove the non-stick surface of the pan... ...holes in the road surface.* N COUNT : USU MOD+N ⇑ covering

3 The **surface** of an area of land or water is the top part of it, especially the part on which you stand or on which things float. EG *A gentle breeze rippled the surface of the sea... Three-quarters of the world's surface is covered by water.* N COUNT

4 Surface is used to describe the part of the army, navy, or air force which travels in ships or by land rather than underwater or in the air. EG *The strength of our surface fleet was about to be further reduced.* N BEFORE N

5 If something **surfaces**, it comes to the surface of a river, the sea, etc. EG *Bobby surfaced twenty feet in front of the boat.* V : USU+A

6 The **surface** of a situation is what can be seen easily rather than what is hidden or not immediately obvious. EG *The film, despite its tough surface, is not without sentimentality... ...its implicit as opposed to its surface meaning... His job was not as enviable as it appeared on the surface.* N COUNT ⇑ appearance = exterior

7 If a quality, feeling, etc **comes** or **rises to the surface**, it appears or becomes obvious after being hidden. EG *At the meeting, all the inconsistencies which haunt the party came to the surface... This dispute first came to the surface in 1962.* PHR : VB INFLECTS = come to light

8 If a quality, feeling, etc is **below** or **beneath the surface**, it is hidden rather than obvious. EG *You don't have to look far to encounter the tensions beneath the surface... Prejudice against old age is never far below the surface.* PHR : USED AS AN A ⇑ concealed

9 If a quality, feeling, piece of news, etc **surfaces**, it appears or becomes obvious or known. EG *Such rumours have surfaced several times over the past ten years... Concern for the children never took long to surface.* V = emerge

10 If someone **surfaces**, they appear after being in bed; an informal use. EG *He didn't surface today until after eleven.* V : USU+A = get up

surface-to-air. **Surface-to-air** missiles are fired from the land or sea at aircraft or at other missiles. ADJ CLASSIF : ATTRIB

surfboard /sɜːfbɔːd/, **surfboards**. A **surfboard** is a long narrow board made of plastic or wood that is used for riding on the waves in the sport of surfing. N COUNT

surfeit /sɜːfɪt/. A **surfeit** of something is an amount which is too large; a formal word. EG *Recently there has been a surfeit of cricket on the television.* N SING : a+N+of = excess

surfer /sɜːfə/, **surfers**. A **surfer** is a person who rides on a surfboard. N COUNT

surge /sɜːdʒ/, **surges, surging, surged**. **1** A **surge** is **1.1** a sudden and great increase in something that has previously been steady or only increases or develops slowly. EG *It failed to stimulate a surge of investment in the industry... ...an unprecedented surge in demand.* N COUNT : USU SING+*of/in* = rise, growth **1.2** a sudden and powerful increase in an emotion or feeling. EG *She felt a surge of affection for him... With a surge of pity , I picked the child up.* N COUNT : USU SING+*of* = upsurge **1.3** a sudden, powerful movement forward, especially of water in a large wave. EG *...the surge of the tide... ...a surge of people.* N COUNT : USU SING+*of* = rush

2 If an emotion or sensation **surges** in you, or **surges up** in you, you feel it suddenly and powerfully. EG *Hope surged in Peter... His true feelings keep surging up inside him.* V+A, OR PHRASAL VB : V ADV+A = well up

3 If people, animals, vehicles, etc **surge**, they move forward suddenly and powerfully. EG *Every time a bus came, the crowd surged forward... After a momentary loss of power the car surged forward again.* V+A = rush, lunge ◇ **surging**. EG *Police fired bullets into surging crowds of demonstrators, many of whom fled.* ◇ ADJ CLASSIF ATTRIB

4 If water **surges**, it moves forwards suddenly and powerfully, especially in the form of large waves. EG *...the tides surging over the rocks.* V : USU+A = rush ◇ **surging**. EG *She clung to the rocks among the surging waves.* ◇ ADJ CLASSIF ATTRIB

surgeon /sɜːdʒən/, **surgeons**. A **surgeon** is a medical doctor who is specially trained to perform surgery. EG *...a brain surgeon.* N COUNT

surgery /sɜːdʒə⁰ri¹/, **surgeries**. **1 Surgery** is medical treatment in which the body of a person or animal is cut open so that a surgeon can repair or remove the part which is causing the problem. EG *The patient had suffered a heart attack while undergoing surgery... ...brain surgery.* ● See also **plastic surgery**. N UNCOUNT = operation

2 A **surgery** is **2.1** the room or house where a doctor or dentist works and where people go to receive advice or minor treatment. EG *He saw the poster in the doctor's surgery.* N COUNT = consulting room **2.2** a fixed period of time each day when patients can see their doctor at his or her surgery; used in British English. EG *Which doctor is taking surgery this morning?... Outside surgery* N UNCOUNT/ COUNT ⇑ session *hours, please phone the emergency number.* **2.3** a regular period of time when people can visit their member of parliament in order to discuss their problems; used in British English. N COUNT ⇑ session

surgical /sɜ͟ːdʒɪkəºl/. **1 Surgical** is used to describe something which is used in surgery. EG *...surgical instruments... ...a surgical mask.* ADJ CLASSIF : ATTRIB ⇑ medical

2 Surgical treatment involves surgery. EG *Some people can have their vision restored by a surgical operation.* ◊ **surgically**. EG *The cataract can then be removed surgically.* ADJ CLASSIF : ATTRIB ◊ ADV WITH VB

3 Surgical boots, stockings, etc are specially designed for people with particular illnesses, injuries, or disabilities, usually to strengthen a part of the body and reduce pain. ADJ CLASSIF : ATTRIB

surgical spirit is a liquid which is used in first-aid or medical treatment to clean wounds or sterilize instruments. It consists mainly of alcohol. N UNCOUNT

surly /sɜ͟ːliˡ/, **surlier, surliest**. Someone who is **surly** behaves in a rude and bad-tempered way. EG *Salesmen in stores and shops are now often surly... He had a surly manner.* ADJ QUALIT = churlish

surmise /səma͟ɪz/, **surmises, surmising, surmised**; a formal word. **1** If you **surmise** that something is true, you guess it from the available evidence, although you do not know for certain. EG *I can only surmise that this happened last week... The last question, Turing surmised, was the key one... All kinds of influences had been surmised.* V+REPORT-CL/O = infer, suspect

2 If you say that a particular conclusion is **surmise**, you mean that it is a guess and you do not know for certain that it is true. EG *I think I am right, only this is pure surmise on my part... Of course, that's just a surmise.* N UNCOUNT/ COUNT = conjecture

surmount /səma͟ʊnt/, **surmounts, surmounting, surmounted**. **1** If you **surmount** a problem or difficulty, you deal successfully with it. EG *She managed to surmount every obstacle that came her way... ...a hairdresser who specialized in surmounting the problems of gentlemen's baldness.* V+O = overcome, conquer

2 If something **surmounts** something such as a wall or hill, it is situated on the highest part of it; a fairly formal use. EG *The column is surmounted by a statue.* V+O = crown

surmountable /səma͟ʊntəbəºl/. A **surmountable** difficulty or problem is one that can be dealt with successfully. EG *Those barriers that do exist are mostly surmountable.* ADJ CLASSIF ≠ insuperable

surname /sɜ͟ːneɪm/, **surnames**. Your **surname** is the name you share with other members of your family. It is usually your last name. EG *What's your surname?... They assumed I was Welsh from my surname.* N COUNT : USU POSS+N

surpass /səpɑ͟ːs/, **surpasses, surpassing, surpassed**; a formal word. **1** If one thing **surpasses** another thing, it is better than that other thing or shows more of a particular quality than the other thing. EG *It was a gesture that no one could have surpassed for dignity and grace... The modesty of this approach was surpassed only by its success.* V+O = outshine

2 If something **surpasses** expectations or understanding, it goes beyond the limit of what could have been expected or what can be understood. EG *His performance surpassed all expectations... Your behaviour surpasses understanding.* V+O = exceed

surpassing /səpɑ͟ːsɪŋ/ is used to describe something which is greater in degree than anything else; a formal word. EG *What a surpassing piece of good fortune!* ADJ CLASSIF : ATTRIB = exceptional

surplice /sɜ͟ːplɪs/, **surplices**. A **surplice** is a loose white knee-length garment which is worn over a long robe by priests and members of the choir in some churches. N COUNT

surplus /sɜ͟ːpləs/, **surpluses**. **1** A **surplus** is a quantity of something that is extra or more than is needed. EG *...the recent worldwide surplus of crude oil... ...a time of overall labour surplus.* N COUNT/ UNCOUNT ⇑ excess

2 Surplus is used to describe something which is extra or more than is needed. EG *We have no surplus grain to sell... The amount of surplus capacity in the economy was about 16 per cent... I'm afraid your job is surplus to requirements.* ADJ CLASSIF = superfluous

3 Surplus refers to clothes and other goods that were originally intended to be used by the armed forces but are sold because they are not needed by them. EG *He was dressed in US Army surplus.* N UNCOUNT

surprise /səpra͟ɪz/, **surprises, surprising, surprised**. **1** A **surprise** is **1.1** an unexpected event. EG *This ruling came as a surprise to everyone... As always on these occasions, there are one or two surprises, some pleasant, some less so.* **1.2** a gift or some other pleasant experience which is unexpected. EG *What a lovely surprise!... I have a surprise for you... 'Why don't you tell me?'–'Because I want it to be a surprise.'* N COUNT; N COUNT

2 Surprise is **2.1** the feeling you have when something unexpected happens. EG *Boylan looked at her in surprise... To my surprise, he nodded and agreed... There was some surprise at his return, but no one said anything.* **2.2** the act of attacking or capturing someone when they are not ready. EG *Surprise would be an essential element in any such offensive.* N UNCOUNT; N UNCOUNT

3 If something **takes** you **by surprise**, it happens to you suddenly or unexpectedly and you are not expecting it. EG *The click of Florrie's camera took her by surprise... The storm, when it broke, took them entirely by surprise.* PHR : VB INFLECTS = catch unawares

4 If you **take** someone **by surprise**, you attack or capture them when they are not ready. EG *It is usually impossible for a hunter to take the herd by surprise.* PHR : VB INFLECTS

5 A **surprise** attack, announcement, etc is one that happens or is made suddenly or unexpectedly. EG *We were the victims of a surprise attack... The minister made the surprise announcement in a statement that evening.* N BEFORE N ⇑ unexpected

6 If something **surprises** you, it gives you a feeling of surprise. EG *The meal was very cheap, which surprised me... It would not surprise me if he ends up in jail.* V+O

7 If you **surprise** someone, you find, catch, or attack them when they are not expecting it. EG *They were surprised by a unit of US marines during the night... She feared her parents would return and surprise them.* V+O

surprised /səpra͟ɪzd/. If you are **surprised** by something, you have a feeling of surprise, because it is unexpected or unusual. EG *The twins were very surprised to see Ralph... I was surprised at the number of bicycles... Gretchen stood up, surprised that Miss Saunders remembered her name... Don't be surprised if she bursts into tears.* ADJ QUALIT : USU PRED = astonished, amazed

surprising /səpra͟ɪzɪŋ/. Something that is **surprising** is unexpected or unusual and makes you feel surprised. EG *He leapt out of the car, with surprising agility... It was surprising how much money she managed to earn.* ADJ QUALIT = remarkable, amazing

surprisingly /səpra͟ɪzɪŋliˡ/ is used to emphasize that a particular statement or idea is surprising. EG *Surprisingly, this tendency has declined in recent years... Not surprisingly the proposal met with hostile reactions... It was surprisingly cheap.* ADV SEN, OR ADV +ADJ/ADV

surreal /sərɪ͟əl/. If you describe a situation as **surreal**, you mean that it is very strange because ideas, images, or objects are combined in it which you would not normally expect to find together, like in a dream. EG *It was surreal meeting her at the abattoir.* ADJ QUALIT = bizarre, weird

Surrealism /sərɪ͟əlɪzəºm/ is a modern style in art and literature in which ideas, images, or objects are combined which you would not normally expect to find together, like in a dream. N UNCOUNT

surrealist /sərɪ͟əlɪst/, **surrealists**. **1 Surrealist** means related to or in the style of Surrealism. EG *...a surrealist painter.* ADJ CLASSIF : ATTRIB

2 A **surrealist** is an artist or writer whose work has the weird dreamlike qualities characteristic of Surrealism. N COUNT

surrealistic /sərɪ͟əlɪstɪk/. **1** If you describe a situation as **surrealistic**, you mean that it is very strange because ideas, images, or objects are combined in it which you would not normally expect to find together, like in a dream. EG *The whole scene was getting more and more surrealistic.* ADJ QUALIT = surreal, bizarre

2 Surrealistic means related to or in the style of Surrealism. EG *...books of surrealistic paintings.* ADJ CLASSIF = surrealist

surrender /səre͟ndə/, **surrenders, surrendering, surrendered**. **1** If you **surrender**, you stop fighting or resisting someone and agree that you have been beaten, often by formally signing a document. EG *We will never surrender... The protesters surrendered to the police after about an hour.* ▸ used as a noun. EG *They tried to starve us into surrender.* V = give in, capitulate ▸ N UNCOUNT

2 If you **surrender** to a force, temptation, feeling, etc, you are unable to resist it any longer and so you V : IF+PREP THEN *to*

allow it to gain control of you or influence you. EG *A nation of nature-lovers seemed to have surrendered to technology... He must decide either to curb his appetites or surrender to them.* ▸ used as a noun. EG *...their surrender to the demands of the students.* ▸ N UNCOUNT : IF +PREP THEN *to*

3 If you **surrender** something to someone, you give away something that is valuable or important to you. EG *The United States would never surrender this territory... The ruling class will not easily surrender wealth and power.* ▸ used as a noun. EG *Any surrender of civil liberties could be irrevocable.* V+O : IF+PREP THEN *to* = relinquish, give up ▸ N UNCOUNT+ *of*

4 If you **surrender** a ticket, passport, or some other document, you give it to someone in authority when you are told to do so. EG *Surrender your ticket at the barrier.* V+O = hand in

surreptitious /sʌrə²ptɪʃəs/. Something that is **surreptitious** is done or enjoyed secretly, because you do not want people to know what you are doing or what your feelings are. EG *Mr Dekker began to take a little surreptitious pleasure in their excursion.* ◇ **surreptitiously**. EG *Rudolph looked surreptitiously at his watch... I surreptitiously made an extra copy.* ADJ QUALIT ⇑ secret = furtive ◇ ADV WITH VB ≠ openly

surrogate /sʌrəgət/, **surrogates**. A **surrogate** is a person or thing that acts as a substitute for someone or something else; a formal word. EG *Art is a surrogate for the individual imaginations of its audience.* ▸ used as an adjective. EG *Uncle Paul has become a surrogate father to me.* N COUNT ⇑ replacement ▸ ADJ CLASSIF

surrogate mother, surrogate mothers. A **surrogate mother** is a woman who agrees to give birth to a baby on behalf of another woman, who cannot have babies herself because she is infertile. N COUNT

surround /sərau̲nd/, **surrounds, surrounding, surrounded**. 1 If something **surrounds** something else, it is positioned all around it or covers it completely. EG *Muscles surround blood vessels in the body... The house was surrounded by high walls... The whole cake is surrounded by a thick coat of jelly.* V+O : USU PASS ⇑ enclose

2 If people, especially soldiers or police, **surround** someone or **surround** a place, they spread out so that they are positioned all the way round. EG *Don't get near him. Just surround him and keep him there... The village was surrounded by troops.* V+O = encircle, hem in

3 If problems, dangers, temptations, etc **surround** something, they exist all around it or are closely associated with it. EG *Let me explain some of the dangers which surround us... There is much controversy surrounding this new law... ...the uncertainty surrounding the future of the railways.* V+O : USU CONT = concern

4 If you **surround** yourself with something, you make sure that you have a lot of it near you all the time. EG *The only way to stay a winner is to surround yourself with losers.* V+O (REFL)+A (*with*)

5 A **surround** is a border around the edge of something, especially the area of floor between the edge of a carpet and the walls in a room. N COUNT

surrounding /sərau̲ndɪŋ/, **surroundings**. 1 **Surrounding** is used to describe the area which is near a particular place and all round it. EG *Foxes started coming in from the surrounding countryside... They could see into the courtyard from the roofs of the surrounding buildings.* ADJ CLASSIF : ATTRIB = neighbouring

2 Your **surroundings** consist of the place where you live and the conditions in which you live. EG *We used to live in much nicer surroundings... He didn't pay much attention to his surroundings.* N PLURAL = environment

surtax /sɜ̲ːtæks/ is an additional tax on incomes higher than a particular level. N UNCOUNT

surveillance /səve̲ɪləns/ is the careful watching of someone, especially someone suspected of being a criminal, spy, etc; a formal word EG *I have been subjected to continuous surveillance... Everyone we knew was under surveillance... ...a surveillance team.* N UNCOUNT ⇑ observation

survey, surveys, surveying, surveyed. The word **survey** is pronounced /səve̲ɪ/ when it is a verb, and /sɜ̲ːveɪ/ when it is a noun. 1 If you **survey** something, you look carefully at the whole of it. EG *He surveyed the bookshelves... She stepped back and surveyed her work.* V+O = contemplate

2 If you **survey** a group of people, you find out about their opinions or behaviour, usually by asking them detailed questions. EG *In five of the villages that were surveyed, non-farm work provided one quarter of their income.* V+O : USU PASS = study

3 To **survey** an area of land means to make an examination of it in order to measure it and make a map of it. EG *He had had the land surveyed from a helicopter.* V+O

4 To **survey** a house means to examine it carefully and report on any problems with its structure, often in order to give advice to someone who is considering buying it. EG *I'll have to get the house surveyed first, before I can make you an offer.* V+O ⇑ inspect

5 A **survey** is 5.1 a detailed investigation of something, for example people's behaviour or their opinions. EG *A recent survey of 450 advertising companies found that art schools are providing most of their new recruits... This chapter includes a brief survey of the more commonly used drugs.* **5.2** an examination of an area of land in order to measure it and to make a map of it. EG *They took preliminary surveys and then started drilling... ...aerial surveys.* **5.3** a careful examination of the condition of a house in order to say what the price of the house should be. EG *After I saw the results of the survey, I decided not to buy it.* N COUNT = study; N COUNT; N COUNT ⇑ inspection

surveyor /səve̲ɪə/, **surveyors**. A **surveyor** is a person whose job is to survey houses or land. • See also **quantity surveyor**. N COUNT

survival /səva̲ɪvə⁰l/, **survivals**. 1 **Survival** is the state of continuing to live in spite of nearly dying or being destroyed or having to deal with very difficult circumstances. EG *Our chances of survival were negligible... The day-to-day struggle for survival drained her energy.* N UNCOUNT ⇑ living

2 A **survival** is something which continues to exist in spite of being nearly destroyed or made extinct; a fairly formal use. EG *The tool was a survival from the pre-machine age.* N COUNT = relic

survival kit, survival kits. A **survival kit** is a pack of objects that you need in order to stay alive if you get hurt or lost in a dangerous place out of doors. N COUNT

survive /səva̲ɪv/, **survives, surviving, survived**. 1 If someone **survives**, they continue to live in spite of being in situation in which they came close to death. EG *Four of his brothers had died as babies: the fifth survived... Only two people survived the fire... She is Britain's longest surviving transplant patient.* V OR V+O : NO PASS, NO IMPER

2 If you **survive** someone, you continue to live after their death. EG *She will probably survive me by many years.* V+O : NO PASS, NO IMPER = outlive

3 If something **survives**, it continues to exist in spite of being nearly destroyed or made extinct. EG *There are three main types of reptile that survive today from the period of the dinosaurs... I doubt whether the National Health Service will survive to the end of the century... The project survived three changes of government.* V OR V+O : NO PASS, NO IMPER ⇑ remain

4 If you **survive** a difficult situation or experience, you have the qualities that are necessary to cope with it, without allowing it to affect you too badly. EG *She seems to have survived the divorce pretty well... You'll have to learn to make difficult decisions if you are to survive in business.* V OR V+O : NO PASS, NO IMPER ⇑ endure

survive on. If you **survive on** something, you earn just enough money to buy the necessities of life, or you have just enough food to live. EG *My salary's only just enough to survive on.* PHRASAL VB : V+PREP = subsist on

survivor /səva̲ɪvə/, **survivors**. A **survivor** is 1 someone who continues to live in spite of being in a situation in which they came close to death. EG *I talked to one of the survivors of the crash... There are no reports of any survivors.* 2 someone who is able to carry on with their life even though they experience many difficulties or hardships. EG *He sounds like one of life's survivors.* N COUNT; N COUNT = winner

susceptibility /səse̲ptɪbɪlɪti¹/, **susceptibilities**. 1 If you have a **susceptibility** to something, you are likely to be affected by it. EG *...his susceptibility to infection.* N UNCOUNT/COUNT : USU+*to*

2 **Susceptibilities** are feelings you have which are especially likely to be hurt. EG *This is a concession to your susceptibilities... He decided to spare no susceptibilities.* N PLURAL = sensibilities

susceptible /səse̲ptɪbə⁰l/. 1 If you are **susceptible** to something, you are likely to be influenced by it. EG *We are all susceptible to advertising... These organizations are susceptible to Government pressure.* ADJ QUALIT : PRED+*to* = vulnerable

2 If you are **susceptible** to a disease or injury, you are likely to be affected by it. EG *Many people were lightly dressed and therefore susceptible to burn* ADJ QUALIT : IF PREP THEN *to* = vulnerable

injuries on their skin... Some types of animal hair cause allergy in a susceptible child.

3 Someone who is **susceptible** is easily affected emotionally by other people. EG *...a susceptible young man.* ADJ QUALIT: ATTRIB ⇑ impressionable

suspect, suspects, suspecting, suspected. The word **suspect** is pronounced /səspekt/ when it is a verb, and /sʌspekt/ when it is a noun or adjective. 1 If you **suspect** something, you 1.1 think that it is likely or is probably true. EG *There is reason to suspect that the death occurred between 6.30 and 7 o'clock last night... I suspect the boy is in love... What is shattered, I suspect, is morale... He suspected a plot against his life.* V+O/REPORT-CL: NO CONT, NO IMPER ⇑ believe 1.2 doubt that it can be trusted or that it is reliable. EG *I had many reasons for suspecting this approach... She suspected her husband's honesty.* V+O: NO CONT, NO IMPER = mistrust

2 If you **suspect** someone of something such as a crime, you have a feeling that they are guilty of it. EG *He was suspected of treason... My friends told me that I was crazy to suspect her.* V+O: IF+PREP THEN *of*: USU NO CONT, USU NO IMPER

3 A **suspect** is a person who is thought to be guilty of something, especially a crime. EG *Last week police finally had a suspect for the murder.* N COUNT

4 If something is **suspect**, it cannot be trusted or regarded as genuine. EG *The man who always keeps his office door shut is suspect, because he might be doing no work... The notion of freedom was suddenly suspect... His story was told with suspect enthusiasm.* ADJ QUALIT = questionable, dubious

suspend /səspend/, **suspends, suspending, suspended.** 1 If something **is suspended** from a high place, it is hanging from there, usually so that it can swing or move about. EG *A model aeroplane was suspended above the stage... Dozens of balloons were suspended from the ceiling.* V+O+A: USU PASS = dangle

2 If small bits of solid material **are suspended** in air or a liquid, they float there and remain still. EG *A cloud of smoke was suspended in the air.* V+O+A: ONLY PASS = hang

3 If you **suspend** something, you delay it or stop it from being in effect for a while. EG *There were demands that trial by jury be temporarily suspended... Both governments are refusing to suspend hostilities... Her friends had to suspend their normal judgements and allow her to go ahead with her plans.* V+O ⇑ discontinue

4 If someone **is suspended**, they are prevented from continuing to be a member of a team or continuing to hold a particular job or position, usually as a punishment for a specific period of time. EG *The people involved in the incident have been suspended from their duties... He was the third member to be suspended from the party... Morgan is still suspended and will miss the semi-final.* V+O: USU PASS ⇑ be removed

suspended animation is a state which resembles death but which can be reversed, in which the important body functions of an animal are slowed right down for a period of time. This is done by freezing or because the animal hibernates. N UNCOUNT

suspended sentence, suspended sentences. A **suspended sentence** is a sentence to go to prison, which a criminal does not serve unless he or she commits another crime within a specified period of time. EG *He got a two-year suspended sentence.* N COUNT

suspender /səspendə/, **suspenders.** 1 A **suspender** is one of the fastenings hanging down from a belt or girdle which holds a woman's stockings up. N COUNT: USU PL

2 **Suspenders** are a pair of straps that go over someone's shoulders and are fastened to their trousers at the front and at the back to prevent their trousers from falling down; used in American English. N PLURAL: ALSO *a pair of*+N = braces

suspender belt, suspender belts; also spelled with a hyphen. A **suspender belt** is a piece of underwear for women that has suspenders attached to it. N COUNT

suspense /səspens/. 1 **Suspense** is a state of excitement or anxiety about something that is going to happen very soon, for example when you are waiting for some news. EG *Waiting for bells to ring is a torment. The suspense claws at my heart... I try to add an element of suspense and mystery to my novels.* N UNCOUNT = anticipation

2 If you **keep** someone **in suspense**, you delay telling them something that they are very eager to know about. EG *I did not leave him in suspense, but quickly informed him that he d misjudged the position.* PHR: VB INFLECTS

suspension /səspenʃəⁿn/, **suspensions.** 1 **Suspension** is 1.1 the act of delaying something or stopping it from being in effect for a while. EG *...the suspension of all social security payments.... ...defence programmes whose suspension would increase domestic unemployment.* N UNCOUNT: IF+PREP THEN *of* = postponement 1.2 the removal of a person from a team, job, or position for a specific period of time, usually as a punishment. EG *If he is found guilty, he could face suspension from duty.* N UNCOUNT/COUNT: IF+PREP THEN *from*

2 A vehicle's **suspension** consists of the springs and shock absorbers attached to the wheels, which give a smooth ride in spite of bumps in the road. EG *You are liable to harm the suspension and the steering if you drive regularly over rough roads at high speed.* N UNCOUNT

3 **Suspension** is also a structure of wires or springs that support something, or that something is hung from. EG *The mattress has independent suspension... ...the suspension cables of the Silver Span bridge.* N UNCOUNT

4 A **suspension** is a liquid mixture in which very small bits of a solid material are contained and are not dissolved. EG *...the amount of solid matter in suspension in the water.* N COUNT, OR *in*+N

suspension bridge, suspension bridges. A **suspension bridge** is a bridge which is hung from strong steel ropes that are attached to towers at both ends of the bridge. N COUNT

suspicion /səspɪʃəⁿn/, **suspicions.** 1 **Suspicion** is the feeling that you do not trust someone or that something is wrong in some way, although you have no evidence for this. EG *Derek had always shared Lynn's suspicion of Michael... I had aroused his suspicions last week... Their friendship is regarded with suspicion by their teachers.* N UNCOUNT/COUNT ⇑ doubt

2 If someone is **under suspicion**, they are suspected of being guilty of something such as a crime. EG *He felt that he was possibly under suspicion.* PHR: USED AS AN A

3 If you say that someone is **above** or **beyond suspicion**, you mean that they could not possibly be guilty of something, because of their good character. PHR: USED AS AN A = unimpeachable

4 A **suspicion** is a feeling that something is probably true or is likely to happen. EG *The suspicion grew in Darwin's mind that species were closely related to each other... Did he intend to leave her penniless? She had her suspicions.* N COUNT: USU+REPORT-CL = hunch, idea

5 A **suspicion** of something is a small amount or trace of it. EG *My dog barks at the slightest suspicion of danger.* N SING WITH DET +*of* = hint

suspicious /səspɪʃəs/. 1 If you are **suspicious** of someone, you feel or show that you do not trust them. EG *The policeman on duty became suspicious of the youth and asked him why he was standing there... I am suspicious of the government's intentions.... He shot a suspicious glance at me.* ADJ QUALIT = distrustful, wary ◇ **suspiciously.** EG *'Why are you laughing?' Rachel asked suspiciously.* ◇ ADV WITH VB ◇ **suspiciousness.** EG *I admire the scepticism of the press, and their suspiciousness.* ◇ N UNCOUNT

2 If something is **suspicious**, it causes people to feel that something is wrong in some way, so that they are not sure what to believe. EG *There were suspicious circumstances about his death... Several suspicious aircraft and ships were spotted.* ADJ QUALIT = dubious, fishy ◇ **suspiciously.** EG *His remarks sounded suspiciously close to treason... I wasn't sure it had been an accident. The hit was suspiciously clean.* ◇ ADV+ADJ/ADV

suss /sʌs/, **susses, sussing, sussed**; an informal word. 1 If you **suss** something **out**, you discover how it works or how to do it. PHRASAL VB: V+O+ADV

2 If you **suss** someone **out**, you discover what their true character is. EG *She had me sussed out in ten minutes.* PHRASAL VB: V+O+ADV

sustain /səsteɪn/, **sustains, sustaining, sustained.** 1 If you **sustain** something, you maintain it or keep it going for a period of time. EG *They do not have enough money to sustain a strike... The problem was how to create and sustain public interest.* V+O = keep up

2 If you **sustain** a sound or note, you hold it for a long time. V+O

3 If food or drink **sustains** you, it gives you energy and strength. EG *They had nothing to sustain them all day except two cups of coffee.* V+O = nourish

4 If something **sustains** you, it supports you, by giving you help, strength, or encouragement. EG *It is his belief in God that sustains him... She was sustained by pride in her family.* V+O = keep you going

5 If you **sustain** something such as a defeat, loss, or injury, you suffer it; a formal use. EG *He sustained a* V+O = receive

serious wound in the battle... He's not capable of sustaining shocks.

6 If something **sustains** the weight of something, it supports it; a formal use. EG *The foundations were not strong enough to sustain the weight of the house.* V+O = carry

sustained /səsteɪnd/. Something that is **sustained** is kept up for a long time; used of things which require effort. EG *We had a long, sustained discussion on the problems of young people... The enemy mounted a sustained attack on the castle.* ADJ QUALIT = prolonged

sustenance /sʌstənəns/ is food and drink which helps to keep a person, animal, or plant strong and healthy; a formal word. EG *We derive our sustenance from the land... In coniferous woodlands goats will find very little sustenance.* N UNCOUNT = nourishment

suture /suːtʃə/, **sutures**. A **suture** is a stitch made to join together the open parts of a wound, especially one made after a patient has been operated upon; a technical word used in surgery. N COUNT

svelte /svɛlt, sfɛlt/. Someone who is **svelte** is attractively slim, elegant, and stylish. ADJ QUALIT = slender

SW is 1 an abbreviation for 'south-west'; used on a compass or in descriptions of where a particular place is situated. EG *...London SW7.* 2 an abbreviation for 'short wave'.

swab /swɒb/, **swabs, swabbing, swabbed**. 1 A **swab** is a small piece of cotton wool used by a doctor or a nurse for cleaning a wound or for taking a small amount of liquid from a patient's body. N COUNT

2 If you **swab** something, you clean it using a wet cloth or mop. V+O ↑ wipe

swaddle /swɒdəºl/, **swaddles, swaddling, swaddled**. If you **swaddle** a baby, you wrap cloth round it in order to keep it warm or to prevent it from moving; an old-fashioned word. EG *Try swaddling the baby snugly in a blanket.* ◊ **swaddled**. EG *She produced the damp swaddled bundle, wriggling and crying.* ◊ **swaddling**. EG *The baby was wrapped in swaddling clothes.* V+O = wind, roll up ◊ ADJ CLASSIF = swathed ◊ ADJ CLASSIF : ATTRIB

swagger /swægə/, **swaggers, swaggering, swaggered**. If you **swagger**, you walk in a proud way, holding your body upright and swinging your hips. EG *The lord and his lady got up and swaggered out... She swaggered back to her place.* ▸ used as a noun. EG *Bernard left the room with a swagger.* V : USU+A = strut ▸ N SING WITH DET

swain /sweɪn/, **swains**. A **swain** is a young man in a village, especially one who is in love with a girl; an old-fashioned word. EG *...a love-sick swain.* N COUNT ↑ youth

swallow /swɒləʊ/, **swallows, swallowing, swallowed**. 1 If you **swallow** something, you cause it to go from your mouth down into your stomach. EG *He swallowed more pills... ...the only food and drink she was still able to swallow.* ▸ used as a noun. EG *He finished off the whisky with a swallow... The man took a long swallow of his beer.* V+O ▸ N COUNT = gulp

2 To **swallow** also means to make a movement in your throat as if you were swallowing something, often because you are nervous or because you are about to say something. EG *He swallowed and closed his eyes... Ellen swallowed and said, 'Hi. It's me.'* V = gulp

3 If someone **swallows** a story, statement, etc, they believe it completely, without thinking that it might not be true. EG *I trusted her so much that I would have swallowed any story she told me.* V+O = accept

4 If you **swallow** something such as an insult or an unkind remark, you accept it patiently and do not protest. EG *She swallowed the sarcasm and got on with her work.* V+O ↑ endure

5 If you **swallow** your feelings, you stop yourself from showing them. EG *He swallowed his rage and said 'Forget it.'* ● to **swallow** your **pride**: see **pride**. V+O = choke back

6 If something **is swallowed** by something else or **is swallowed up** by it, it becomes a part of it and no longer has a separate identity of its own. EG *The members would not tolerate the Liberal Party being swallowed by the SDP... He did not want his firm to be swallowed up by a multinational giant.* V+O, OR PHRASAL VB : V+O+ADV, USU PASS ↑ be absorbed

7 A **swallow** is also a small bird with long pointed wings and a forked tail. It catches insects while it is flying. There are different kinds of swallow. N COUNT

swam /swæm/ is the past tense of **swim**.

swamp /swɒmp/, **swamps, swamping, swamped**. 1 A **swamp** is an area of very wet land with wild plants growing in it. EG *...wading for hours in a cold swamp... They grow by the edges of marshes, swamps, and shallow fresh water... There must have been a time when the country was all forest and swamp.* N COUNT/UNCOUNT = marsh

2 If something **swamps** a ship or boat, it fills it with water and causes it to sink. EG *Sudden heavy seas swamped the ship.* V+O ↑ flood

3 If you **are swamped** by things or people, you have more of them than you can deal with. EG *Dance halls and pubs were suddenly swamped by a flood of troops... The switchboard was being swamped with bitterly complaining calls.* V+O : USU PASS+ *with/by* = be inundated

swampy /swɒmpiˡ/, **swampier, swampiest**. A **swampy** area of land consists mainly of swamps. EG *The river's swampy banks couldn't be seen... More could be done to clear these swampy areas.* ADJ QUALIT = marshy

swan /swɒn/, **swans**. A **swan** is a large bird with a long neck which often lives on rivers and lakes on which it swims. There are different kinds of swan. Most swans are white. N COUNT

swank /swæŋk/, **swanks, swanking, swanked**; an informal word. 1 If someone **is swanking**, they are speaking in a boastful way in order to try to impress other people; used showing disapproval. EG *Stop swanking!* ▸ used as a noun. EG *It's all a lot of swank.* V : USU CONT = show off ▸ N UNCOUNT = posturing

2 People describe something as **swank** or **swanky** when it is smart, fashionable, and expensive. EG *...the swank Hotel Princess... She goes to a swanky private school.* ADJ QUALIT = swish

swan song; also spelled with a hyphen. A person's **swan song** is the last time that they do something for which they are famous, for example the last time that an actor gives a performance in the theatre. EG *It was said that Baldwin's speech that day would be his swan song.* N SING : WITH POSS

swap /swɒp/, **swaps, swapping, swapped**; also spelled **swop**; an informal word. 1 If you **swap** something for something else, 1.1 you give it to someone and receive something else in exchange for it. EG *He swapped a dozen goats for a female calf... Try swapping homes with a friend.... I would not swap my career for anyone else's.* ▸ used as a noun. EG *Let's do a swap... He regarded a silver vase for an ivory ornament as a fair swap.* 1.2 you remove it and replace it by something else. EG *I swapped my cap for a large black waterproof hat.* V OR V+O : IF+ PREP THEN *for/with* ↑ change = trade ▸ N COUNT ↑ deal V+O+A *(for)* = substitute

3 If you **swap** stories or opinions with someone, you tell each other stories or give each other your opinions. EG *They swap amusing stories about the place... One of the most interesting aspects was swopping views with the other people.* V+O : IF+PREP THEN *with* = exchange

swap over. If you **swap** two things **over** or **swap** them **round**, you remove them and put each one in the place where the other one was before. EG *See if you can swap them over... I swapped them round when he wasn't looking.* PHRASAL VB : V+O+ADV = switch

swarm /swɔːm/, **swarms, swarming, swarmed**. 1 A **swarm** is a large group of bees or other insects flying together. EG *The showers brought swarms of flying insects to torment them.* N PART

2 When bees or other insects **swarm**, they move or fly in a large group, usually in order to find a new place to live. EG *When the bees swarmed we used to all rush out into the garden.* V

3 When people **swarm** somewhere, they move about quickly in a large group. EG *They swarmed across the bridge and began climbing up the bank... She was in the yard, her numerous children swarming round her.* ▸ A **swarm** is a group of people moving about like this. EG *She left amid a swarm of photographers.* V+A = flock ▸ N PART = horde

4 If a place **swarms** with people or animals, it is full of people or animals moving about in a busy way. EG *The White House rose garden was swarming with security men... The Great Barrier Reef swarms with life.* V+A *(with)* = teem

swarthy /swɔːðiˡ/, **swarthier, swarthiest**. A **swarthy** person has a dark complexion. EG *The photographer was dark, swarthy, and unsmiling.* ▸ used of someone's complexion. EG *...people with swarthy complexions... There was a knowing expression on his swarthy face.* ADJ QUALIT

swashbuckling /swɒʃbʌklɪŋ/ is used to describe the exciting appearance or behaviour of pirates, especially in films. You can also use it to describe someone's appearance or behaviour if it reminds you of pirates. EG *...a fashionable version of the swashbuckling pirate look... She adopted a slightly* ADJ QUALIT : ATTRIB ↑ adventurous = daredevil *swashbuckling stance.* ▸ used of people. EG *...a swashbuckling rock musician.*

swastika /swɒstɪkə/, **swastikas**. A **swastika** is a symbol in the shape of a cross with each arm bent over at right angles. It is used in India as a good luck sign, but in the 1920's to the 1940's it was also used by the Nazis in Germany as their official symbol. EG *In its centre was painted a huge Nazi swastika.* — N COUNT

swat /swɒt/, **swats, swatting, swatted**. If you **swat** something such as an insect, you hit it with a quick, swinging movement, using either your hand or an object such as a folded newspaper. EG *He lay awake all night, swatting mosquitoes.* — V+O ▸ used as a noun. EG *He took a swat at the wasp and missed.* — ▸ N COUNT = swipe

swathe /sweɪð/, **swathes, swathing, swathed**. The form **swath** /swɔːθ/ is also used for the noun. 1 A **swathe** or **swath** is 1.1 a long strip of cloth, especially when it is wrapped round someone or something. EG *...balconies strewn with swathes of silk.* — N COUNT: ALSO N PART 1.2 a strip of crops cut by a machine or by people moving from one end of a field to the other. EG *They were scything the first swathe round the hedges... The wheat is six or seven swathes in breadth.* — N COUNT: ALSO N PART 1.3 a long strip of land that is different in some way from the land on either side of it, for example because it is higher, or has no vegetation, or is controlled by a different country. EG *He limped on, dragging one leg and leaving a swathe through the underbrush... ...new roads cutting swathes through our countryside... The army now holds a swathe of land some 30 kilometres wide.* — N COUNT: ALSO N PART

2 If you **swathe** something, you wrap strips of cloth around it so that it is almost completely covered. EG *...the blankets that swathe his disabled limbs.* — V+O = bind up

swathed /sweɪðd/. If someone is **swathed** in something, it is wrapped around them, almost completely covering their body. EG *She was swathed in bandages from head to foot. ...an ancient lady swathed in violet veils.* — ADJ CLASSIF: PRED+*in* = enveloped ▸ used of a part of someone's body. EG *Her face was swathed in a scarf.* — ▸ = muffled up

sway /sweɪ/, **sways, swaying, swayed**. 1 When people or things **sway**, they lean or swing slowly first to one side and then to the other side, usually several times. EG *He didn't fall, but swayed a little... She clapped her hands in time to the music and swayed from side to side... He could see the trees swaying in the wind.* — V = rock ▸ used as a noun. EG *The sway of the coach lulled her to sleep.* — ▸ N SING WITH DET

2 If you **are swayed** by something that you hear or read, it influences you, especially by making you decide to do one thing rather than another thing. EG *A jury is more likely to be swayed by eloquent arguments... Do not be swayed by glamorous advertisements.* — V+O: USU PASS = be persuaded

3 **Sway** is the power that someone or something has to influence people. EG *Laing was coming increasingly under the sway of new ideas.* — N UNCOUNT = dominion ● If someone or something **holds sway**, they have great power or influence in a particular place or field of activity. EG *For forty years John Dryden held sway as the arbiter of literary England... The beliefs which now hold sway may one day be rejected.* — ● PHR: VB INFLECTS = rule

swear /sweə/, **swears, swearing, swore, sworn**. 1 When someone **swears**, they use language that is considered to be rude or blasphemous. People often swear when they are angry. EG *Glenys leant out of the car window and swore at the other driver... Stop swearing, Marcus! I don't like to hear you talking like that... He could hear them shouting and swearing at each other.* — V: IF+PREP THEN *at* = curse

2 If you **swear** to do something, you solemnly promise that you will do it. EG *I swear I will never tell anyone.* — V+REPORT-CL/*to*-INF = vow

3 If you **swear** in a court of law, you solemnly promise that everything that you say to the court will be true. EG *Do you swear to tell the truth, the whole truth, and nothing but the truth?... They refused to swear on a Bible.* — V OR V+O: USU+A, OR V+*to*-INF

4 If you say that you **swear** that something is true or that you can **swear** to it, you are saying very firmly that it is true. EG *She did not know a thing, she swore... I'm not prepared to swear to it, but I thought I saw him in Exeter once.* — V+REPORT-CL, OR V+A *(to)* = insist ● to **swear blind**: see **blind**.

5 See also **sworn**.

swear by. If you **swear by** something, you believe that it can be relied on to have a particular effect; an informal expression. EG *When the children are ill, I swear by hot lemon and honey.* — PHRASAL VB: V+PREP, HAS PASS

swear in. When someone **is sworn in**, they are made to make a solemn promise or promises, either at the beginning of a trial in a court of law or when they are starting a new official appointment. EG *The jury was sworn in on March 14... The new President of the United States will be sworn in next January.* — PHRASAL VB: V+O+ADV, USU PASS

swear-word, swear-words; also spelled as two words. A **swear-word** is a word which is considered to be rude or blasphemous, which people use when they are angry. EG *Dixon reeled off a long string of swear-words... I must ask you to leave out the swear words.* — N COUNT = obscenity

sweat /swet/, **sweats, sweating, sweated**. 1 **Sweat** is the salty, colourless liquid which comes through your skin in drops to cool your body, for example when the weather is hot or when you are working hard or are ill, afraid, or very worried. EG *Jack paused, wiping the sweat from his face... His entire body poured with sweat.* — N UNCOUNT = perspiration

2 When you **sweat**, sweat comes through your skin because you are hot, ill, afraid, or working very hard. EG *The heat was nearly unbearable, but the sweating people danced and cheered... Tom thought of Clothilde sweating over the stove in the kitchen... He was sweating like a bullock.* — V = perspire

3 If someone is **in a sweat** or **in a cold sweat**, 3.1 they are sweating a lot, especially because of fear or illness. EG *He awoke trembling and in a cold sweat.* — PHR: USED AS C 3.2 they are very worried or very frightened. — PHR: USED AS C

4 **Sweat** is also hard work or effort, especially when it is unpleasant or exhausting. EG *...the money he makes out of the labouring man's sweat... Machines have increasingly replaced human sweat.* — N UNCOUNT = toil

5 If someone says **'No sweat'** when you ask them about a job or task, they mean that it can be done easily without causing problems or effort; an informal expression. EG *'May we proceed?' George smiled and said, 'Sure–no sweat.'* — CONVENTION = no problem

6 If you **sweat it out**, you endure something unpleasant in the hope that when it ends the situation will have improved; an informal expression. EG *There's nothing we can do, we'll just have to sweat it out.* — PHR: VB INFLECTS

sweatband /swetbænd/, **sweatbands**. A **sweatband** is a thin strip of towelling or other material which someone such as an athlete wears around their head to keep sweat from running into their eyes, or around their wrist to keep sweat from running onto their hand. — N COUNT

sweater /swetə/, **sweaters**. A **sweater** is a warm knitted garment covering the upper part of your body and your arms, which you put on by pulling it over your head. EG *The girl had come out wearing blue jeans and a sweater... She had bought some wool to knit a sweater... ...the young man in the turtle-neck sweater.* — N COUNT = pullover

sweat gland, sweat glands. Your **sweat glands** are the organs under your skin which produce sweat. — N COUNT: USU PL

sweatshirt /swetʃɜːt/, **sweatshirts**; also spelled with a hyphen. A **sweatshirt** is a piece of leisure clothing, usually made from thick cotton, which covers the upper part of your body and your arms. You put it on by pulling it over your head. EG *The students dress casually, in jeans and sweatshirts.* — N COUNT ⇑ garment

sweatshop /swetʃɒp/, **sweatshops**. A **sweatshop** is a small factory or workshop where many people work together in poor conditions for low pay; used showing disapproval. EG *...the horrifying conditions in the sweatshops of the nineteenth century.* — N COUNT

sweaty /sweti[1]/. 1 You describe a place, the weather, or an activity as **sweaty** when it makes you sweat because it is hot or tiring. EG *...the dust-filled sweaty inferno that central London had become... ...a sweaty August... ...the sweaty march along the blazing beach.* — ADJ QUALIT = sticky

2 If your clothes or parts of your body are **sweaty**, they are soaked with sweat or covered in sweat. EG *...American correspondents in sweaty sports shirts... I grabbed the rope with cold sweaty shaking hands.* — ADJ QUALIT ⇑ damp = clammy ▸ used of people. EG *...dirty, sweaty men.* — ▸ = perspiring

swede /swiːd/, **swedes**; spelled with a capital letter for paragraph 2. 1 A **swede** is a round root vegetable with a thick brown or purple skin. — N COUNT

2 A **Swede** is a person who comes from Sweden. EG *Over 20% of Swedes own a vacation cottage in the country.* — N COUNT ⇑ Scandinavian

Swedish /swiːdɪʃ/. 1 Someone or something that is **Swedish** comes from, belongs to, or is concerned with Sweden, its people, or their language. ADJ CLASSIF

2 **Swedish** is the language used in Sweden. N UNCOUNT

sweep /swiːp/, **sweeps, sweeping, swept**. 1 If you **sweep** a floor or other surface, you clean it by pushing a brush over it in order to collect the dirt in one place. EG *I cleaned the windows and I swept the floor... They set about cleaning and sweeping the house... He found a broom and a dustpan and he swept away the broken glass... He started sweeping out the hut.* ▸ used as a noun. EG *The floor could do with a sweep.* V+O, OR V+A; ▸ N SING: a+N

2 If you **sweep** things away or into a particular place, you push them with a quick, smooth movement of your hand in order to move them to a different place. EG *She swept the bottles from her bedside table... He went into the study and swept some books and papers off the couch... Dr Hochstadt swept all his coins back into the cigar-box.* V+O+A ⇑ move

3 If your hand or arm **sweeps** in a particular direction, it moves quickly and smoothly in that direction. EG *Their hands sweep down through the air... One of the dogs was flung aside by the panther's sweeping paw.* ▸ used as a noun. EG *With a great sweep of the arm he flung the whole handful high in the air.* V-ERG+A ⇑ move; ▸ N COUNT ⇑ movement

4 If a strong force such as the wind or a rough sea **sweeps** you along, it moves you violently and quickly in a particular direction. EG *She was swept out to sea by the currents... The crowd surged again and she let herself be swept forward by it.* V+O+A

5 If a natural force such the wind **sweeps** from one place to another, it moves across it very quickly indeed. EG *Cold winds sweep over the barren, treeless plains... A great fire swept across the brush land.* ▸ used also of other things or people that move in this way. EG *He stared out at the traffic sweeping along the road towards Cleveland... The Muslim Arabs swept in from the east in the eighth century... The ruling National Party swept back into office.* V+A ⇑ rush; ▸ V+A

6 If things such as ideas, beliefs, or statements **sweep** a place or **sweep** through it, they spread quickly through it. EG *Rumours of a prospective settlement swept the building... The camping craze is currently sweeping America... Have you noticed how pocket calculators have swept through the school system?* V+O, OR V+A ⇑ spread through

7 If you **sweep** about, you walk in a proud, confident manner, often because you are wearing splendid clothes. EG *Mrs Kaul came sweeping in wearing a beautiful batik skirt.* V+A = glide

8 If one thing **sweeps** something else away or aside, it removes the other thing completely. EG *The matter was soon swept from his mind... All these restrictions were swept aside... The economic crisis has drowned these initiatives by sweeping away the premise on which they have all been based.* V+O+A = get rid of

9 If land, water, etc **sweeps** away, down, etc, it stretches out in a long, wide curved shape. EG *...a flight of steps sweeping down from the house.* V: USU+A

10 If you **sweep** an area around you, you look round it. EG *The expert lecturer will sweep the audience slowly with his eyes... One of the submarines grasped the handles of the periscope and began to sweep another sector of the horizon... We began rushing around madly in the dark, sweeping the ground with our flashlights.* ▸ used as a noun. EG *His eyes made a sweep of the people who were waiting to see him.* V+O ⇑ survey = pan; ▸ N COUNT: USU SING

11 If people **sweep** something such as an election, they win it very easily indeed. EG *The 'progressives' swept all the seats in city council contests.* ● to **sweep the board**: see **board**. V+O = run away with

12 If someone **sweeps** you **off** your **feet**, you fall in love with them almost as soon as you meet them, because you find them dashing and exciting. EG *She was swept off her feet by this fun-loving youth.* PHR: VB INFLECTS

13 If you **sweep** something **under the rug** or **under the carpet**, you keep silent about it so that nobody else finds out about it, usually because you are rather ashamed of it. PHR: VB INFLECTS ⇑ hide = keep secret

14 A **sweep** is the same as a chimney sweep. EG *If you still use open fires, get a sweep to call regularly.* N COUNT ⇑ cleaner

15 A **sweep** of land, water, etc forms a long, wide, curved shape. EG *...a high ridge overlooking a great sweep of country... ...the sweep of the hills.* N COUNT+*of*: USU SING

16 A **sweep** of a place is also a search of a wide area, especially by the police when they are looking for criminals or illegal activities. EG *Yesterday the police made a sweep through the campus.* N COUNT: USU SING

17 A **sweep** of qualities, opinions, etc is the wide variety of them which something contains. EG *It was the historical event of a lifetime, just in its scale and sweep... ...representatives from a broad sweep of left-wing opinion.* N SING WITH DET +SUPP = range

18 If you **make a clean sweep** of something such as a series of matches or tournaments, you win them all. PHR: VB INFLECTS, IF+ PREP THEN *of*

19 See also **sweeping**.

sweeper /swiːpə/, **sweepers**. A **sweeper** is the same as a carpet sweeper. N COUNT

sweeping /swiːpɪŋ/, **sweepings**. 1 A **sweeping** curve is long, wide, and stretched out. EG *...a place where the stream made a sweeping curve.* ADJ QUALIT: ATTRIB = broad

2 A **sweeping** statement or generalization is a very general one one that you assume is true, without considering specific facts or details carefully; used showing disapproval. EG *That's rather a sweeping statement... It is too easy to go and make sweeping generalizations about someone else's problems... In order to construct his theories he must make a number of very sweeping assumptions.* ADJ QUALIT: USU ATTRIB = broad ≠ specific

3 **Sweeping** is also used to describe amounts that are very large and therefore significant. EG *...sweeping public expenditure cuts... The swing of the pendulum will bring Labour sweeping gains in the next election.* ADJ QUALIT: ATTRIB = huge ≠ small

4 If something has **sweeping** effects or **sweeping** consequences, the effects or consequences are great and therefore very important. EG *They had already embarked on a course which might have quite sweeping effects... ...one of the most sweeping and far-reaching pieces of child legislation.* ADJ QUALIT: ATTRIB ⇑ extensive = far-reaching, wide-ranging

5 **Sweepings** are the bits of rubbish or dirt that you collect together when you sweep the floor. EG *Put the sweepings in the dustbin.* N PLURAL

sweepstake /swiːpsteɪk/, **sweepstakes**. A **sweepstake** is a method of gambling in which each person is given the name of a horse in a race and pays a small amount of money into a kitty. After the race has taken place, the person who has the name of the winning horse receives all the money in the kitty. EG *We had a sweepstake in the office on the Grand National.* N COUNT

sweet /swiːt/, **sweets; sweeter, sweetest**. 1 Food or drink that is **sweet** contains, or tastes as if it contains, a lot of sugar. EG *I had some horribly sweet chocolate gateau... ...a cup of sweet tea.* ◊ **sweetness**. EG *Sugar substitutes tend to lose their sweetness over long periods of storage.* ADJ QUALIT ⇑ sugary; ◊ N UNCOUNT

2 In British English, **sweets** are sweet things such as toffees, chocolates, and mints which people eat purely for pleasure and not as part of a meal. Sweets are eaten especially by children. EG *If you have too many sweets and ice-creams, you won't want your dinner!* N COUNT: USU PL ⇑ confectionery = hard candy

3 In British English, a **sweet** is the same as a dessert. EG *We get a good meal in our canteen; soup and a main meal and a sweet.* N COUNT = afters, pudding

4 If you describe an emotion or a feeling as **sweet**, you mean that it gives you intense pleasure, satisfaction, and reward. EG *However sweet love is, when it goes there is always bitterness... It is this dream, this sweet possibility, that keeps him going... Success in medicine may be sweet but it brings new responsibilities.* ◊ **sweetness**. EG *...the sweetness of freedom.* ADJ QUALIT ⇑ pleasant ≠ bitter; ◊ N UNCOUNT

5 If you describe something such as air or water as **sweet**, you mean that it smells or tastes pleasantly fresh, clear, and clean. EG *She stood on the beach watching the waves crash in and smelling the sweet air... No other well has such sweet water... The room was cool and sweet-smelling.* ADJ QUALIT ≠ foul

6 A **sweet** smell is pleasant, fragrant, and slightly sugary. EG *This rose is a handsome and sweet scented variety... The air was filled with the sweet smell of ripe blackberry bushes.* ADJ QUALIT ≠ foul

7 A **sweet** sound is pleasant, smooth, and gentle. EG *...the sweet song of the skylark... ...a very sweet violin solo.* ◊ **sweetly**. EG *...a piper who played sweetly on his pipes.* ADJ QUALIT ≠ harsh; ◊ ADV WITH VB

8 People who are **sweet** are kind, gentle, and generous towards other people. EG *My grandparents were very sweet to me... She's a sweet person, awfully nice.* ◊ **sweetness**. EG *He had the most entrancing generosity and sweetness.* ● If you say that someone is **all sweetness and light**, you mean that they are ADJ QUALIT ⇑ nice ≠ horrible; ◊ N UNCOUNT; ● PHR: USED AS

behaving unusually well, generously, or with extra kindness, although you suspect that it will not last. EG *That child is so naughty, yet the moment you arrive, she's all sweetness and light.*

9 If you describe someone or something that is small as **sweet**, you mean that they are pretty, attractive, and delightful. EG *Oh! Look at that kitten! How sweet!... It's a very sweet little place... She has a really sweet face.* ◊ **sweetly.** EG *She remembered him sitting so sweetly on the cot, looking up at her.* ADJ QUALIT ⇑ lovely = cute ◊ ADV WITH VB

10 If you **are sweet on** someone, you are very fond of them and are romantically or sexually attracted to them; an old-fashioned informal expression. EG *He's sweet on Mrs Pennington. Do you think they are having an affair?* PHR : VB INFLECTS ⇑ like = fancy

11 You might call someone **my sweet** if you are very fond of them. EG *Give me the flask, my sweet.* N VOC = darling

12 If someone has a **sweet tooth**, they have a great liking for things that taste sweet. PHR : USED AS O

13 If you use an expression such as **go your own sweet way** or **her own sweet self**, you are criticizing the fact that the person you are talking about is determined to do just what they want to do without considering other people's actions or feelings. EG *It won't make any difference talking to her, she'll go her own sweet way... She'll just please her own sweet self.* PHR : VB INFLECTS, OR PHR : USED AS O

14 If you do something to **keep** someone **sweet**, you do something to please them in order to prevent them from becoming annoyed or dissatisfied; an informal expression. EG *They're campaigning for higher prices simply to keep their farmers sweet.* PHR : VB INFLECTS = keep someone happy

sweet-and-sour is used to describe food, especially a sauce or a meat dish in Chinese cookery, that contains both a sweet flavour and something sharp or sour such as lemon or vinegar. EG *...sweet-and-sour pork with bamboo shoots.* ADJ CLASSIF : ATTRIB

sweetbread /swi:tbrɛd/, **sweetbreads.** **Sweetbreads** are meat obtained from the pancreas of a calf or a lamb. N COUNT

sweet corn; also spelled as one word. **1 Sweet corn** is a vegetable which comes from the maize plant. It is a cob covered with small round yellow seeds which taste fairly sweet and are the only part that you eat. ▸ used also of the plant on which sweet corn grows. N UNCOUNT

2 You also use **sweet corn** to mean the round yellow pieces of corn after they have been removed from the husk. These are then eaten as a vegetable. N UNCOUNT = maize

sweeten /swi:tə⁰n/, **sweetens, sweetening, sweetened.** **1** If you **sweeten** food or drink, you add sugar, honey, or another sweet substance to it. EG *...tea sweetened with honey.* V+O

2 If you **sweeten** something such as an offer or a business deal, you make it more attractive by improving it or by raising the amount of money that you are willing to pay. EG *They sweetened their offer to £95 a share.* ● **to sweeten the pill**: see **pill.** V+O ⇑ improve

3 If you **sweeten** someone or **sweeten** them **up**, you give them a gift or do something nice for them, in order to prepare them for something unpleasant or to get them to do something that you want them to do. EG *He bought her lunch to sweeten her before telling her the bad news... They sweetened him up by offering him another £1000 a year.* V+O, OR PHRASAL VB : V+O+ADV ⇑ bribe

sweetener /swi:tə⁰nə/, **sweeteners.** A **sweetener** is **1** an artificial substance that you use in drinks to make them taste as if they have sugar in them. Sweeteners are usually non-fattening. N MASS **2** something that you give to someone or offer them in order to persuade them to do something that they do not want to do or do not have to do; an informal use. EG *They offered him a company car as a sweetener.* N COUNT ⇑ bribe

sweetheart /swi:thɑ:t/, **sweethearts.** **1** You call someone **sweetheart** if you are very fond of them. EG *'Mary's leaving now, sweetheart.'* N VOC = dear, love

2 Your **sweetheart** is your boyfriend or your girlfriend. You use the word 'sweetheart' especially for boyfriends or girlfriends whom you have when you are young. EG *Then he left her and married his childhood sweetheart.* N COUNT

sweetie /swi:ti¹/. **1** You might call someone **sweetie** if you are fond of them, especially if they are younger than you are; an informal word sometimes used in a rather patronising way. N VOC ⇑ darling

2 If you say that someone is a **sweetie**, you mean that they are kind, pleasant, and loveable. EG *Isn't she a sweetie!* N COUNT

3 Children or adults speaking to children sometimes call sweets **sweeties.** N COUNT

sweetish /swi:tɪʃ/. Smells, tastes, etc that are **sweetish** are fairly sweet, sometimes unpleasantly so. EG *...a sweetish breakfast cereal... There was a sweetish smell, vaguely reminiscent of coffee.* ADJ CLASSIF

sweetly /swi:tli¹/. **1** If you behave **sweetly**, you are pleasant and show gentleness and affection. EG *He looked at Daisy who was smiling sweetly at him.* ADV WITH VB ⇑ pleasantly

2 If an engine or machine is running **sweetly**, it is working well, smoothly, and efficiently. EG *The wheels of my bicycle were spinning as sweetly as the cogs of a Swiss watch.* ADV WITH VB ⇑ nicely

3 If you kick or hit a ball **sweetly**, you kick or hit it in the very middle of it so that it goes firmly and accurately to the place you are aiming for. ADV WITH VB ⇑ well

4 Other meanings of **sweetly** can be found in the entry for **sweet.**

sweetmeat /swi:tmi:t/, **sweetmeats.** **Sweetmeats** are food made from or preserved in sugar, especially delicacies that are considered to be rather special; an old-fashioned word. EG *...a glass of pink champagne and a few sweetmeats on a plate.* N COUNT ⇑ sweet

sweet nothings. If someone whispers **sweet nothings** in your ear, they quietly say nice, loving, and rather flattering things to you. N PLURAL

sweet pea, sweet peas; also spelled as one word. A **sweet pea** is a climbing plant which has delicate, light-coloured flowers with a nice smell. Sweet peas are usually grown in gardens. N COUNT

sweet pepper, sweet peppers. A **sweet pepper** is the same as a green pepper or a red pepper. N COUNT = capsicum

sweet potato, sweet potatoes. A **sweet potato** is a root vegetable that looks rather like an ordinary potato. Sweet potatoes have pinkish brown skin and yellow flesh. EG *A man arrived with a sack of sweet potatoes.* ▸ used to refer to the climbing plant that produces sweet potatoes. It grows in hot countries. N COUNT = yam

sweet shop, sweet shops; also spelled with a hyphen and as one word. A **sweetshop** is a small shop that sells sweets and cigarettes, and sometimes newspapers and magazines; used in British English. N COUNT

swell /swɛl/, **swells, swelling, swelled, swollen.** The past participle can be either **swelled** or **swollen.** **1** If parts of your body **swell** or **swell up**, they become larger and rounder than normal, usually as a result of an injury or an illness. EG *The left side of Thomas's face began to swell... A mosquito had bitten her and her whole arm had swollen up.* V OR PHRASAL VB : V+ADV ⇑ expand = puff up

2 When something **swells** or **swells up**, it becomes larger and rounder by being filled with air or liquid. EG *The insect inflates her lungs so that they swell into her abdomen... Take a raisin and soak it till it swells up.* V OR PHRASAL VB : V+ADV ⇑ expand ≠ shrink

3 If numbers or amounts **swell**, they increase in amount by more and more being added. EG *It took another twenty years for the population to swell to twice its size... The army had its ranks swollen by new recruits... Craftsmen were engulfed by the demands of the swelling numbers of customers.* V-ERG = grow, expand ≠ decrease

4 If emotions or feelings **swell**, they very quickly grow much stronger than they were. EG *His guilt swelled, but he quashed it... All at once hope would swell again.* V ≠ die down

5 When the sea **swells**, it moves suddenly and powerfully upwards and forwards. EG *The tide swelled in over the sand.* V : USU+A ⇑ rise = surge

6 If sounds **swell**, they suddenly get louder. EG *The murmur swelled and then died away... The music swelled and quickened into an exciting rhythm.* V ≠ die away

7 A **swell** is **7.1** the regular up-and-down movement of waves in the open sea. EG *A swell caught the raft and lifted it... The waves had taken on a deep swell... Brody could see the boat bobbing gently in the swells.* N COUNT **7.2** a sudden increase in sound produced by a musical instrument. EG *...the loud swell of the organ.* N SING WITH DET ⇑ surge **7.3** the curved shape of something round, for example a part of the body. EG *Power lay in the brown swell of his forearms.* N SING WITH DET ⇑ curve

8 You might describe someone or something as **swell** if you think that they are really nice; used in informal American English. EG *She's a swell kid.* ADJ QUALIT ⇑ good = great, super ≠ awful

9 See also **swollen.**

swelling /swɛlɪŋ/, **swellings.** A **swelling** is a raised, curved shape on the surface of your body, N COUNT/UNCOUNT that appears as a result of an injury or an illness. EG *I had a nasty swelling on my leg... She had a lot of pain in her feet, although there was little swelling.*

swelter /swe̲ltə/, **swelters, sweltering, sweltered.** If you **swelter** or **are sweltering**, you are very uncomfortable because the weather is extremely hot and you cannot find a way of becoming cool. EG *On the deck everyone was sweltering in the still air.* V : USU CONT = bake, boil

sweltering /swe̲ltəᵒrɪŋ/. If you describe the weather as **sweltering**, you mean that it is extremely hot and that people are very uncomfortable because of it. EG *Hot? It was sweltering... ...a good place to go on a sweltering August day.* ADJ CLASSIF = scorching, boiling

swept /swe̲pt/ is the past tense and past participle of **sweep**.

swerve /swɜ̲:v/, **swerves, swerving, swerved. 1** If something that is moving **swerves**, it suddenly changes direction, usually in order to avoid colliding with something else. EG *The car almost swerved off the road and into the river... As we swerved towards them, the nuns leapt back onto the pavement... A charging shark cannot stop, it can only swerve away to one side.* V : USU+A ⇑ turn = veer ▸ used as a noun. EG *...the swerve which the car made to avoid hitting her.* ▸ N COUNT ⇑ turn

2 If a ball **swerves**, for example when it has been kicked, it moves in a slight curve. EG *The ball swerved towards him, and he headed it into the net.* V : USU+A = swing

swift /swɪ̲ft/, **swifter, swiftest; swifts. 1** A **swift** event or process happens very quickly. EG *...the swift descent from gentility to near-poverty... ...never making a swift decision about anything.* ADJ QUALIT ⇑ quick = rapid, abrupt ◇ **swiftly.** EG *His basic lack of intelligence was swiftly exposed... ...a puppy which swiftly grew to the size of a small sofa.* ◇ ADV WITH VB = rapidly ◇ **swiftness.** EG *The country was occupied with dramatic swiftness.* ◇ N UNCOUNT ⇑ speed

2 A **swift** vehicle or animal is able to move very quickly. EG *The president's swift fleet would reach Dover around 10 a.m... The bull became so swift and savage that it killed two picadors and a matador.* ADJ QUALIT ⇑ quick ◇ **swiftly.** EG *He walked swiftly towards home down the dark street.* ◇ ADV WITH VB = rapidly

3 A **swift** river, stream, or current flows very quickly. EG *Marigolds reflected their bright cups in the swift water.* ADJ QUALIT ◇ **swiftly.** EG *...the river flowing swiftly by in the darkness.* ◇ ADV WITH VB

4 If you are **swift** to do something, you do it quickly in response to something else, very soon after it has happened or arisen. EG *He was swift to publicise the potentialities of motoring... She was swift in pointing out that she was a member of a trade union.* ADJ QUALIT : PRED+*to*-INF/A = quick, prompt ▸ used to describe such a response. EG *The response throughout West Germany was swift and intense.* ▸ ADJ QUALIT = quick ◇ **swiftly.** EG *...the capacity to respond swiftly to market changes... No one volunteered very swiftly.* ◇ ADV WITH VB = promptly

5 A **swift** is a small bird with crescent-shaped wings. Swifts fly very quickly and catch insects while they are flying. They make a loud noise like a scream. EG *Above the glaring lights of the fairground the swifts swung and screamed.* N COUNT

swig /swɪ̲g/, **swigs, swigging, swigged**; an informal word. If you **swig** a drink, you drink it from a bottle, cup, etc quickly and in large amounts. EG *They used to sit and swig local gin from tiny metal cups... When her back was turned I swigged two cupfuls from the tub.* V+O, OR V+A = knock back ▸ used of an amount of drink that is drunk like this. EG *She wants another swig at that bottle... He took a long swig of whiskey.* ▸ N COUNT ⇑ swallow

swill /swɪ̲l/, **swills, swilling, swilled. 1** If you **swill** an alcoholic drink, you drink a lot of it; an informal use. EG *He sits there swilling his gin-and-tonics without a care in the world.* V+O = guzzle

2 To **swill** something also means to clean it by pouring a large amount of water over it. EG *I'll just go and swill this out under the tap.* V+O+A = rinse

3 Swill is a liquid mixture containing waste food such as vegetable peelings, that is given to pigs to eat. EG *He was on his way to the sty with a bucket of swill.* N UNCOUNT = slops

swim /swɪ̲m/, **swims, swimming, swam, swum. 1** When you **swim**, you move through water by making movements with your arms and legs. EG *The children are learning to swim... It's too cold to swim today... When the boat capsized, we managed to swim ashore... I used to go swimming two or three times a week.* V ▸ used as a noun. EG *We decided to go for a swim.* ▸ N SING WITH DET

2 When a fish **swims**, it moves through water by making movements with its tail and fins. EG *At this time of year, the salmon swim upstream.* V

3 If you **swim** a stretch of water or **swim** a particular distance, you keep swimming until you have crossed the stretch of water or completed the distance. EG *We swam the river again, starting from the other bank... Once I swam eight kilometres.* V+O ⇑ cross

4 If objects seem to you to **swim**, they seem to be moving backwards and forwards, because you are ill or because there is smoke or vapour in the air. EG *The room swam and darkened before his eyes... The oasis swam in the rising air currents.* V = shimmer

5 If your head **is swimming**, you feel dizzy. EG *All that dancing has made my head swim.* V = spin

swimmer /swɪ̲mə/, **swimmers.** A **swimmer** is a person who is swimming or who knows how to swim. EG *He went to the aid of a swimmer in difficulty... Are they all good swimmers?* N COUNT

swimming /swɪ̲mɪŋ/ is the activity of swimming, especially when it is done as a sport or recreation. EG *Her father had encouraged her to take up swimming again... Boating and swimming were popular... ...swimming lessons.* N UNCOUNT

swimming bath, swimming baths; also spelled with a hyphen. A **swimming bath** is a public swimming pool, especially an indoor one; used in British English. N COUNT : SING=PL

swimming costume, swimming costumes; also spelled with a hyphen. A **swimming costume** is the same as a swimsuit; used in British English. EG *She looked slightly plump in her one-piece swimming costume.* N COUNT = bathing costume, swimsuit

swimmingly /swɪ̲mɪŋli¹/. If something **goes swimmingly**, it proceeds in a very satisfactory way, without any problems; a slightly informal word. EG *Everything seems to be going swimmingly.* PHR : VB INFLECTS = go like clockwork

swimming pool, swimming pools; also spelled with a hyphen. A **swimming pool** is a place built for people to swim in, usually consisting of a large hole in the ground that has been paved or tiled and filled with water. EG *Each house had its own swimming pool... We spent the afternoon at the swimming pool.* N COUNT

swimming trunks; also spelled with a hyphen. **Swimming trunks** are a piece of clothing worn by men and boys for swimming. Swimming trunks are similar to a pair of shorts or underpants. EG *He bought a pair of swimming trunks.* N PLURAL : ALSO *a pair of*+N ⇑ garment

swimsuit /swɪ̲msjᵒu:t/, **swimsuits.** A **swimsuit** is a piece of clothing that is worn for swimming, especially by women and girls. EG *...a girl in a two-piece swimsuit.* N COUNT = swimming costume

swindle /swɪ̲ndəᵒl/, **swindles, swindling, swindled.** If someone **swindles** a person or an organization, they deceive them in order to get something valuable from them, especially money. EG *He tried to swindle the railway company... I'm sure they swindled you out of that money.* V OR V+O = fiddle, diddle ▸ used as a noun. EG *I'm afraid we have been the victims of a monumental swindle.* ▸ N COUNT ⇑ deception

swindler /swɪ̲ndlə/, **swindlers.** A **swindler** is someone who swindles other people or an organization. EG *They are the biggest swindlers on earth... He was a known swindler and bankrupt.* N COUNT = fiddler, cheat

swine /swa̲ɪn/, **swines.** The form **swines** is used as the plural for paragraph 1, and the form **swine** is used as both the singular and the plural for paragraph 2. **1** People call a man a **swine** or refer to him as a **swine** when he has caused trouble or unhappiness and does not seem to care about it. EG *'You're a cynical swine,' she said... He realised what a swine he had been.* N COUNT : ALSO VOC

2 A **swine** is a pig; an old-fashioned or literary use. EG *...a squealing, filthy swine.* ● to **cast pearls before swine**: see **pearl**. N COUNT ⇑ animal

swing /swɪ̲ŋ/, **swings, swinging, swung. 1** If something **swings** or if you **swing** it, it moves repeatedly backwards and forwards or from side to side from a fixed point. EG *The chandelier started to swing... Sides of beef and pork swung from steel hooks... He sat there swinging his legs... Jane walked ahead, swinging the shopping bag.* V-ERG ▸ used as a noun. EG *She walked like a model, with an exaggerated swing of the hips... Arresting the swing of the door with one hand, he stepped forward.* ▸ N SING WITH DET ⇑ movement

2 If something **swings** in a particular direction or if you **swing** it in that direction, it moves in that V-ERG+A

direction with a smooth curving movement. EG *I pushed the front door and it swung open... Boylan swung the bag on to the back seat.* ▸ used as a noun. EG *He swept all she said aside with a grand, impatient swing of his arm.*
▸ N COUNT = wave

3 If a moving vehicle **swings** in a particular direction or if you **swing** it in that direction, it turns suddenly and sharply in that direction. EG *The taxi turned left and swung in through the gates of the vicarage... He swung his car out of the side road.*
V-ERG+A

4 If someone **swings** in a particular direction, they turn suddenly and face that direction. EG *He swung round in his chair and smiled... He swung round to search the horizon.*
V+A = swivel

5 If you **swing** at something or **swing** a blow at it, you try and hit it using the strength of your arms and shoulders. EG *The soldier swung a slow, heavy right hand at Tom.* ▸ used as a noun. EG *I took a swing at him, and he punched me hard in the stomach.*
V+A OR V+O+A ⇑ aim; ▸ N COUNT = swipe

6 A **swing** is a seat hanging by two ropes or chains from a metal frame or from the branch of a tree. A child can sit on the seat and move forwards and backwards through the air. EG *The children have a sand pit, a seesaw and swings.*
N COUNT

7 A **swing** is also a sudden or extreme change, especially in people's attitudes, beliefs, or political opinions. EG *There was a 16.2% swing to the Social Democrats.* ▸ used as a verb. EG *The balance of power on the Executive had swung decisively in favour of the moderates.*
N COUNT : USU+A ⇑ move, switch; ▸ V+A = shift

8 Swing was a style of dance music that was popular in the 1930's. It was played by big bands.
N UNCOUNT

9 If someone says that a piece of music, party, etc **swings**, they mean that it is lively and exciting; a rather old-fashioned informal expression, used showing approval. EG *The party's beginning to swing.*
V ⇑ succeed

10 The word **swing** is also used in the following expressions: **10.1** If you say that something **is going with a swing**, you mean that it is happening in a lively and exciting way; used informally showing approval. EG *This will make your party go with a swing.* **10.2** If something is **in full swing**, it is operating fully and no longer in its early stages. EG *By the 1980's the Computer Revolution was in full swing.* **10.3** If you **get into the swing** of something, you become very involved in it and enjoy what you are doing; an informal expression. EG *Dr Stein had got into the swing of his speech and was enthusiastically quoting classical authors.* **10.4** The saying **'What you lose on the swings you gain on the roundabouts'** means that although you may have some losses or failures in a particular situation, you will also have a similar number of gains or benefits. ▸ **Swings and roundabouts** is used to describe a situation in which there are both gains and losses. EG *Well, it's swings and roundabouts, isn't it?*
PHR : VB INFLECTS ⇑ succeed; PHR : USED AS AN A = under way; PHR : VB INFLECTS; PHR; ▸ PHR : USED AS C

swing door, swing doors; also spelled with a hyphen. A **swing door** is a door that can open both towards you and away from you, and which closes by itself after you have gone through it. EG *He went down a short flight of steps and pushed through the swing door at the bottom of it.*
N COUNT

swingeing /swɪndʒɪŋ/. Something that is **swingeing** causes serious harm or hardship. EG *...a swingeing indictment of her policies... ...swingeing tax increases.*
ADJ CLASSIF : ATTRIB = devastating

swinger /swɪŋə/, **swingers**. A **swinger** is a person who is lively and fashionable; a rather old-fashioned informal word. EG *Forty years ago Feldstein was a swinger... I'm not really a swinger like most of the girls here.*
N COUNT = raver

swinging /swɪŋɪŋ/. If you describe something or someone as **swinging**, you mean that they are lively and fashionable; a rather old-fashioned informal word. EG *...swinging London... He fancied himself as a swinging chic dresser.*
ADJ CLASSIF = dynamic, trendy

swipe /swaɪp/, **swipes, swiping, swiped**. **1** If you **swipe** at something, you try to hit it with a stick or some other object, making a swinging movement with your arm. EG *He swiped at the wasp with a rolled-up newspaper.* ▸ used as a noun. EG *He missed the ball with his first swipe... She took a casual swipe at the nettles.*
V+A (at) = strike, lunge; ▸ N COUNT : IF+PREP THEN *at* = swing

2 If you **swipe** something, you steal it by removing it quickly; an informal use. EG *Somebody has swiped Sir George's silver... The boss has swiped my pen again.*
V+O = whip, pinch

swirl /swɜːl/, **swirls, swirling, swirled**. If something **swirls**, it moves round and round quickly. EG *The sea was swirling and crashing round the breakwaters... Dust swirled in small circles around me... ...a swirling pool.* ▸ used as a noun. EG *...the slow swirl of the stream.*
V-ERG+A = whirl, eddy; ▸ N COUNT = eddying

swish /swɪʃ/, **swishes, swishing, swished**. **1** If something **swishes** or if you **swish** it, it moves quickly through the air making a soft sound. EG *The curtains swished open... The horses stood together swishing their tails because of the flies.* ▸ used as a noun. EG *...the swish of a horse's tail.* ◊ **swishing**. EG *There was a soft swishing sound as he pulled out a garment from the drawer.*
V-ERG; ▸ N COUNT; ◊ ADJ CLASSIF : ATTRIB ⇑ rustling

2 If you describe something as **swish**, you mean that it is smart and fashionable; a rather old-fashioned informal use. EG *...the swish discos and nightclubs around Corfu.*
ADJ QUALIT = plush

Swiss /swɪs/. **Swiss** is both the singular and the plural form. **1** Something that is **Swiss** belongs or relates to Switzerland or to its people. EG *He lives in the French Alps near the Swiss border.*
ADJ CLASSIF

2 A **Swiss** is a person who comes from Switzerland. EG *...a Swiss from Geneva... The Swiss have been neutral for centuries.*
N COUNT

switch /swɪtʃ/, **switches, switching, switched**. **1** A **switch** is a small control for an electrical device such as a light, a radio, or a heater. You move the switch up or down or press the top or bottom part of it in order to turn the device on or off. EG *Somebody pressed the wrong switch... ...electric light switches.*
N COUNT

2 If you **switch** to something different, for example to a different task or a different subject of conversation, you change to it suddenly from what you were doing or saying before. EG *I would like now to switch to quite a different subject... ...the difficulty of suddenly switching from Afrikaans to English.* ▸ used as a noun. EG *...the switch from planned to impromptu tactics... The campaign seemed to signal a switch in the paper's editorial policy.*
V : IF+PREP THEN *to/from* = shift; ▸ N COUNT = changeover

3 If you **switch** your attention from one thing to another, you stop paying attention to the first thing and start paying attention to the other. EG *He switched his attention back to the magazine.*
V+O : IF+PREP THEN *to* = transfer

4 If you **switch** something, you remove it and replace it with something else. EG *The plane switched loads and took off.* ▸ used as a noun. EG *I asked him why he'd made the switch.*
V+O = exchange; ▸ N COUNT = exchange

5 If you **switch** with someone else, you change places with them; an informal use. EG *I'm on duty on Saturday but I'll switch with one of the other men.*
V+A (with) = swap

switch off. **1** If you **switch off** an electrical device, you stop it working by pressing a switch. EG *He switched the radio off... He switched off the light.*
PHRASAL VB : V+O+ADV = turn off

2 If you **switch off**, you stop paying attention to something, because you are no longer interested in it; an informal use. EG *The lecture was so boring I just switched off half-way through.*
PHRASAL VB : V+ADV = turn off

switch on. **1** If you **switch on** an electrical device, you make it begin working by pressing a switch. EG *He switched on the TV... Would you switch the light on, please?*
PHRASAL VB : V+O+ADV = turn on

2 If you **switch on** a particular kind of behaviour, you suddenly and deliberately start behaving in that way; often used showing disapproval. EG *He had the ability to switch on the concentration when necessary... He was good at switching on the charm.*
PHRASAL VB : V+O+ADV = turn on

switchback /swɪtʃbæk/, **switchbacks**. A **switchback** is something, such as a mountain road, which rises and falls sharply many times or which has many sharp bends.
N COUNT

switchboard /swɪtʃbɔːd/, **switchboards**. A **switchboard** is the place in a large office or business where all the telephone calls are connected. EG *The girl on the switchboard told me there was a phone call for me... ...the switchboard operator.*
N COUNT : USU SING

swivel /swɪvəl/, **swivels, swivelling, swivelled**; also spelled **swiveling, swiveled** in American English. **1** If something **swivels** or if you **swivel** it, it turns on a central pivot or axle so that it is facing in a different direction. EG *Mellors slowly swivelled his chair round.*
V-ERG : USU+A = spin

2 If you **swivel** or **swivel round**, you turn round quickly, especially when you are in a sitting position. EG *I swivelled right round in my chair.*
V OR PHRASAL VB : V+ADV = spin round

3 If you **swivel** your head or eyes in a particular
V-ERG : USU+A

direction, you turn your head or eyes in that direction, so that you can look at something. EG *His blond head swivelled toward her.*

4 A **swivel** chair, lamp, etc is made so that you can revolve the main part of it while its base remains in the same position. EG *Sonny leaned back in the swivel chair.* ADJ CLASSIF : ATTRIB = revolving

swizzle stick /swɪzə⁰l stɪk/, **swizzle sticks**. A **swizzle stick** is a small ornamental stick that you use for stirring cocktails. N COUNT ↑ stirrer

swollen /swəʊlə⁰n/. 1 **Swollen** is the past participle of **swell**.

2 Something that is **swollen** has grown outwards until it is broader or wider than usual. EG *Her fingers were badly swollen with arthritis... I could not sleep for the pain in my swollen, infected feet... The raisins were plump and soft and swollen from being soaked in water.* ADJ QUALIT ↑ enlarged = distended

swollen-headed. You say that someone has become **swollen-headed** when they behave as if they think that they are very clever or important, often because someone has praised them; used showing disapproval. EG *She was growing ever more swollen-headed and arbitrary.* ADJ QUALIT ↑ conceited = big-headed

swoon /swuːn/, **swoons, swooning, swooned**. If you **swoon**, 1 you are strongly affected by your feelings for someone who you admire very much. EG *We fell in love, and swooned in each other's arms.* V : USU+A 2 you collapse because you are fainting; a rather old-fashioned use. EG *She cried as the tension in herself grew, and began to swoon.* ▸ used as a noun. EG *Miss Archer fell off her chair in a swoon.* V = faint ▸ N COUNT = faint

swoop /swuːp/, **swoops, swooping, swooped**. 1 When a bird or an aeroplane **swoops**, it suddenly moves downwards through the air in a smooth, curving movement. EG *We saw a distant eagle swoop down from the sky... Air Force planes swooped low over the target.* ▸ used as a noun. EG *The swallow made another dazzling swoop through the air.* V : USU+A ↑ drop = dive ▸ N COUNT

2 If soldiers or police **swoop** on a place, they move towards it suddenly and quickly, usually in order to attack or arrest the people there. EG *British troops swooped down twice in pre-dawn raids... A band of raiders would swoop down to capture horses or cattle.* ▸ used as a noun. EG *The police made a swoop on the headquarters.* V+A = pounce ▸ N COUNT = raid

3 If you achieve something **in one fell swoop**, you do it on a single occasion or by means of a single action. EG *All our problems solved in one fell swoop... They enclosed over 1,000 acres in one fell swoop.* PHR : USED AS AN A ↑ together

swop /swɒp/. See **swap**.

sword /sɔːd/, **swords**. 1 A **sword** is a weapon with a long blade, and a handle at one end. EG *He cut off the Duke's head with this sword... They were armed with sticks, swords, and guns.* N COUNT

2 If you **cross swords** with someone, you disagree with them about something and argue with them about it. EG *That was where I crossed swords with Wolfit... It was then that Miss Clare and Arthur crossed swords.* PHR OR PHR+A *(with)* : RECIP, VB INFLECTS

swordfish /sɔːdfɪʃ/, **swordfishes**. **Swordfish** can also be used as the plural form. A **swordfish** is a large sea fish with a very long upper jaw. N COUNT

swordplay /sɔːdpleɪ/ is the activity and skill of fighting with swords. EG *I taught him all I know of marksmanship and swordplay.* N UNCOUNT

swore /swɔː/ is the past tense of **swear**.

sworn /swɔːn/. 1 **Sworn** is the past participle of **swear**.

2 If two people are **sworn enemies**, they dislike each other very much and do not wish to become friendly towards each other. EG *They had been sworn enemies since their schooldays... He was Clem's sworn enemy.* PHR : USED AS C

3 If you make a **sworn** statement, declaration, etc, you swear that everything that you have said in it is true. EG *The American made a sworn statement to the police... The girl made a sworn complaint against her attacker.* ADJ CLASSIF : ATTRIB

swot /swɒt/, **swots, swotting, swotted**; an informal word. 1 If you **swot**, you study very hard, especially when you are preparing for an examination. EG *How do you find time to swot for exams?* V OR V+O = cram

2 A **swot** is a student who works extremely hard and who takes little interest in other things apart from his or her studies; used showing disapproval. EG *I was looked on as a swot.* N COUNT

swot up. If you **swot up** a subject or **swot up** on it, you read as much as you can about it, usually because you are going to be asked questions about it or because you have to take an examination. EG *She swotted up American history... I was swotting up on my transformational grammar.* PHRASAL VB : V+O+ADV, OR V+ADV+A = mug up

swum /swʌm/ is the past participle of **swim**.

swung /swʌŋ/ is the past tense and past participle of **swing**.

sycamore /sɪkəmɔː/, **sycamores**. **Sycamore** can also be used as the plural form. A **sycamore** is a tree that has leaves with five points and seeds with winged cases which spin as they fall to the ground. EG *...a few sycamores and elms... ...woods of oak and sycamore.* N COUNT ↑ maple

sycophant /sɪkəfə³nt/, **sycophants**. A **sycophant** is a person who behaves in a sycophantic way; a formal word. EG *He's a coward, a traitor, and a sycophant.* N COUNT = toady

sycophantic /sɪkəfæntɪk/. **Sycophantic** behaviour is behaviour in which someone flatters and praises important and powerful people and always agrees with what they say, in order to get some advantage from them; a formal word, used showing disapproval. EG *They would break into peals of sycophantic laughter.* ▸ used of people. EG *He hadn't expected an assistant as sycophantic as this one... ...sycophantic courtiers.* ADJ QUALIT = obsequious, ingratiating

syllable /sɪləbə⁰l/, **syllables**. A **syllable** is a part of a word that contains a single vowel-sound and that is pronounced as a unit. So, for example, 'book' has one syllable, and 'reading' has two syllables. ● If you state or explain something **in words of one syllable**, you do it very simply and clearly. EG *He told Mr Nixon in words of one syllable that his party would not consider this option... You'll have to explain it in words of one syllable.* N COUNT ● PHR : USED AS AN A

syllabus /sɪləbəs/, **syllabuses**. A **syllabus** is the subjects to be studied in a particular course. EG *They've got to cover a very wide syllabus... ...the new physics syllabus.* ▸ used also to refer to a written outline of these subjects. EG *I've got some copies of the syllabus here.* N COUNT = curriculum

sylvan /sɪlvə⁰n/ means full of trees, or belonging to woods and trees; an old-fashioned literary word. EG *The foliage lent a certain sylvan charm to the place... ...a sylvan setting.* ADJ CLASSIF : ATTRIB = wooded

symbiosis /sɪmbɪəʊsɪs/. **Symbiosis** is 1 a close relationship between two organisms of different kinds which benefits both organisms; a technical term in life sciences. EG *...the bacteria that live in the soil, sometimes in symbiosis with higher plants.* N UNCOUNT ↑ association 2 any relationship between different things, people, or groups that benefits all the things or people concerned. EG *The first steps toward some form of man-machine symbiosis are already being taken.* N UNCOUNT ↑ association

symbiotic /sɪmbaɪɒtɪk/. A **symbiotic** relationship is one in which organisms, people, or things exist together in a way that benefits them all. EG *...a symbiotic relationship between algae and fungi... In the modern state there is a deeply symbiotic relationship based on shared power.* ADJ QUALIT ↑ beneficial

symbol /sɪmbə⁰l/, **symbols**. 1 A **symbol** is 1.1 a shape or design that is used to represent something such as an idea. EG *Picasso painted a red circle as a symbol of the Revolution... She had a silver peace symbol hanging on a chain around her neck.* N COUNT = emblem 1.2 something that seems to represent a society or aspect of life, because it is very typical of it. EG *Perhaps the most glittering symbol of the new Britain was London's Post Office Tower... It was a mysterious place, a symbol of the unreachable and the remote.* N COUNT 1.3 a number, letter, or shape that represents an item in a calculation or formula. EG *...the symbol for angular acceleration... I use my own symbol for 'very approximately'.* N COUNT ↑ sign

2 See also **status symbol**.

symbolic /sɪmbɒlɪk/. Something that is **symbolic** 1 is regarded or used as a symbol of someone or something else. EG *The crescent moon is symbolic of Allah... ...gold, with its rich symbolic significance.* ◊ **symbolically**. EG *To put on someone else's clothes is symbolically to take on their personality.* ADJ CLASSIF : US+*of* ↑ representative ◊ ADV 2 involves or relates to symbols. EG *Water is full of symbolic associations... ...a symbolic play... ...the symbolic content of Abstract Expressionism.* ADJ QUALIT

symbolise /sɪmbəlaɪz/. See **symbolize**.

symbolism /sɪmbəlɪzəᵒm/ is the use of symbols in order to represent something. EG *...the widespread and increasing use of symbolism... ...the Rosebud symbolism in Welles' 'Citizen Kane'... ...ballets that scream with symbolism.* — N UNCOUNT = imagery

symbolize /sɪmbəlaɪz/, **symbolizes, symbolizing, symbolized**; also spelled **symbolise**. If something **symbolizes** something else, it is used or regarded as a symbol of it. EG *He wore a flame-red robe symbolizing the sun... The final division of Germany was symbolised by the completion of the Berlin Wall.* — V+O = represent

symmetrical /sɪmetrɪkəᵒl/. If something is **symmetrical**, it has two halves which are exactly the same, except that one half is the mirror image of the other. EG *A new house of any size was now almost invariably symmetrical... ...pleasingly symmetrical designs.* — ADJ CLASSIF ↑ balanced
◇ **symmetrically**. EG *Smaller rooms were arranged symmetrically to either side.* — ◇ ADV WITH VB

symmetry /sɪmɪ²tri¹/, **symmetries**. 1 **Symmetry** is the state of being symmetrical. EG *The need to incorporate a staircase prevented perfect symmetry... ...the symmetry of the Square.* — N UNCOUNT ↑ balance
2 A **symmetry** is a particular symmetrical arrangement; a formal use. EG *...the Arab exploration of the subtleties and symmetries of space... They could not have anything but symmetries in their designs.* — N COUNT

sympathetic /sɪmpəθetɪk/. 1 If you are **sympathetic** to someone who has had a misfortune, you are kind to them and show that you understand their feelings. EG *My boyfriend was very sympathetic and it did make me feel better... I found her immensely sympathetic and understanding... He was obviously sympathetic over what had happened.* — ADJ QUALIT = understanding, concerned
◇ **sympathetically**. EG *She put a hand sympathetically on his arm... 'Of course not, dear,' Sarah said sympathetically.* — ◇ ADV WITH VB
2 If you are **sympathetic** to a proposal, action, or cause, you approve of it and are willing to support it. EG *He is sympathetic to our cause... The university is not particularly sympathetic to this problem... Public opinion seemed sympathetic.* — ADJ QUALIT : PRED, IF + PREP THEN *to* = well-disposed ◇ **sympathetically**. EG *His campaign was reported sympathetically in the local papers.* — ◇ ADV WITH VB
3 You describe someone as **sympathetic** when you like them and approve of the way that they behave. EG *Isaac Bassett is altogether a more sympathetic figure... I was beginning to find Sandy a less than sympathetic character.* — ADJ QUALIT ↑ likeable = appealing

sympathize /sɪmpəθaɪz/, **sympathizes, sympathizing, sympathized**; also spelled **sympathise**. 1 If you **sympathize** with someone who has had a misfortune, you are sorry for them, and show this in the way that you behave towards them. EG *I sympathise with Delia... Everyone sympathized with Bruce.* — V : IF + PREP THEN *with* = commiserate
2 If you **sympathize** with someone's feelings, you understand them and are not critical of them, because you think that you would have the same feelings in the same circumstances. EG *We understand such feelings and sympathise with them... He could neither understand nor sympathize with Isobel's eagerness.* — V + A *(with)* = identify
3 If you **sympathize** with a proposal, action, or cause, you approve of it and are willing to support it. EG *Everyone sympathised with the anti-colonial cause... Many people might sympathize with and even condone my deception.* — V + A *(with)* = side

sympathizer /sɪmpəθaɪzə/, **sympathizers**; also spelled **sympathiser**. The **sympathizers** of a particular organization or cause are the people who approve of it and support it. EG *White was an ardent Communist sympathiser... ...members and sympathisers of such organisations.* — N COUNT = supporters

sympathy /sɪmpəθi¹/, **sympathies**. 1 If you feel or show **sympathy** for someone who has had a misfortune, you are sorry for them and show it in the way that you behave towards them, especially by being kind to them. EG *People feel immediate sympathy for a man left alone with his children... These people need our help and sympathy.* — N UNCOUNT : IF + PREP THEN *for* = compassion
2 If you have **sympathy** with a person or with an idea or opinion that they have expressed, you agree with their idea or opinion. EG *On that point I'm in sympathy with Mr McCabe... Do you have sympathy with that viewpoint?* — N UNCOUNT + *with* ↑ agreement
3 Your **sympathies** are your feelings of approval and support for a particular proposal, action, or cause. EG *Her sympathies lay with what we were doing... His sympathies had been with the Liberals... He knows I have strong left-wing sympathies.* — N PLURAL
4 If you take some action **in sympathy** with someone else or **in sympathy** with what they are doing, you do it in order to show that you support them. EG *They were carrying out a hunger strike in sympathy with mine... Workers downed tools and came out in sympathy with their colleagues in other shipyards.* — PHR : USED AS AN A
5 If there is **sympathy** between different people or between people and animals, they seem to understand each other and are able to live together in a peaceful and harmonious way. EG *There was a peculiar bond of sympathy and understanding between them... Clearly there was some some strange sympathy between this boy and the bees.* — N UNCOUNT : IF + PREP THEN *between* = affinity

symphonic /sɪmfɒnɪk/ means relating to or like a symphony. EG *The work combines symphonic, choral, and operatic elements... The first movement is a conventional symphonic Allegro.* — ADJ CLASSIF : ATTRIB ↑ orchestral

symphony /sɪmfəni¹/, **symphonies**. 1 A **symphony** is a piece of music written to be played by an orchestra. Symphonies are usually in four parts, called movements. EG *...Sibelius's Second Symphony.* — N COUNT
2 A **symphony** is also a pleasing arrangement of colours and shapes; a literary use. EG *It was a symphony in teak furniture and wine-coloured carpets.* — N COUNT + SUPP = vision

symphony orchestra, symphony orchestras. A **symphony orchestra** is a large orchestra that plays classical music. EG *...the City of Birmingham Symphony Orchestra.* — N COUNT : ALSO IN NAMES

symposium /sɪmpəʊzɪəm/, **symposia, symposiums**. The plural can be either **symposia** or **symposiums**. A **symposium** is 1 a conference in which experts or scholars discuss a particular subject. EG *He took part in a symposium on Arab-Jewish relations... They have held many symposia on animal-welfare issues.* — N COUNT ↑ meeting 2 a collection of essays by experts or scholars on a particular subject. EG *His views were included in a symposium published in 1974.* — N COUNT ↑ anthology

symptom /sɪmpᵒtəm/, **symptoms**. 1 A **symptom** is something wrong with your body or with the way that it works, that is taken as a sign of illness. EG *Most infections are contagious before any symptoms are noticed... ...the symptoms of flu.* — N COUNT ↑ indication
2 A **symptom** is also something that happens in a society and that is taken as a sign of something seriously wrong with that society. EG *Migration is a symptom of rural poverty and of urban over-privilege... ...the symptoms of social breakdown.* — N COUNT : IF + PREP THEN *of* = indication

symptomatic /sɪmpᵒtəmætɪk/. If something is **symptomatic** of something else, especially something more important or serious, it is a sign of it. EG *The irritation seems symptomatic of something deeper... The proliferation of candidates was symptomatic of the increasing fragmentation of British politics.* — ADJ QUALIT : PRED, USU + *of* = indicative

synagogue /sɪnəgɒg/, **synagogues**. A **synagogue** is a building where Jewish people meet to worship or to study their religion. — N COUNT : ALSO IN NAMES

sync /sɪŋk/. If two things are **out of sync**, they are not synchronized with each other; an informal expression. EG *Our watches are out of sync.* — PHR : USED AS AN A

synchronize /sɪŋkrənaɪz/, **synchronizes, synchronizing, synchronized**; also spelled **synchronise**. 1 If two people **synchronize** something that they do, they do it at the same time and speed as each other. EG *They frequently synchronize their movements as they talk... The rhythm was not synchronized with the steps.* — V+O : IF + PREP THEN *with* ↑ match
◇ **synchronization** /sɪŋkrənaɪzeɪʃəᵒn/. EG *Each operation demanded minute-to-minute synchronisation.* — ◇ N UNCOUNT ↑ matching
2 If you **synchronize** two watches or clocks, you adjust them so that they say exactly the same time. EG *His watch has been accurately synchronized with the church clock.* — V+O : IF + PREP THEN *with*
3 If someone **synchronizes** a film, they fit the sound track and the pictures of the film together so that the sounds are heard at exactly the right moment. — V+O ↑ align

syncopate /sɪŋkəpeɪt/, **syncopates, syncopating, syncopated**. If notes in a piece of music **are syncopated**, weak beats in the bar are stressed instead of the strong beats that are usually stressed. EG *...a natural syncopated rhythm.* — V+O : USU PASS
◇ **syncopation** /sɪŋkəpeɪʃəᵒn/, **syncopations**. EG *...masterly syncopation.* — ◇ N UNCOUNT/COUNT

syncope /sɪŋkəpi[1]/ is **1** a temporary loss of consciousness when someone faints; a technical term in medicine. EG *Motionless standing is a classic physical cause of syncope.* [N UNCOUNT = fainting] **2** the omission of sounds or letters from the middle of a word, for example changing 'is not' to 'isn't'; a technical linguistic term. [N UNCOUNT]

syndicate /sɪndɪki[3]t/, **syndicates, syndicating, syndicated. 1** A **syndicate** is **1.1** an association of people or organizations that is formed for business purposes or in order to carry out a project together. EG *...a syndicate of German industrialists... ...organised crime syndicates.* [N COUNT: ALSO IN NAMES ⇑ alliance] **1.2** a news agency that sells articles, cartoons, photographs, etc to several newspapers or journals for publication in all of them. EG *...American News Syndicate.* [N COUNT: ALSO IN NAMES]

2 When articles, cartoons, photographs, etc **are syndicated**, they are sold to several newspapers or journals for publication in all of them. EG *The news was syndicated in papers around the world.* [V+O: USU PASS ⇑ circulate]

3 If a group or organization **syndicates** something, it produces it or agrees to it through a syndicate. EG *We didn't syndicate the deal with them... The bank often syndicates large loans among other banks.* [V+O]

syndrome /sɪndrəʊm/, **syndromes.** A **syndrome** is **1** a medical condition that is characterized by a particular group of signs and symptoms. Different syndromes are often called by the name of the person who first discovered or described them. EG *...children with Down's syndrome.* [N COUNT+SUPP: USU SING] **2** a condition that is characterized by a particular type of activity, behaviour, or feeling. The condition is usually unpleasant or undesirable. EG *...the capitalist syndrome of growth, profits, competition... They demonstrated the 'I'm no good' syndrome in varying degrees... ...the big spender syndrome.* [N COUNT+SUPP: USU SING ⇑ phenomenon]

synod /sɪnə[7]d/, **synods.** A **synod** is a special council of members of a Church, which meets regularly to discuss religious issues. EG *...the General Synod of the Church of England.* [N COUNT: ALSO IN NAMES ⇑ committee]

synonym /sɪnənɪm/, **synonyms.** A **synonym** is a word or expression which means the same as another word or expression. EG *They loved the word 'storm' as a synonym for energy... The term 'National Front' is in use as a virtual synonym of 'fascist'.* [N COUNT: IF+PREP THEN *for/of*]

synonymous /sɪnɒnɪməs/. **1** Two words or expressions that are **synonymous** have the same meaning as each other. EG *The terms are really synonymous... For these economists 'development' seems to be synonymous with 'growth'.* [ADJ CLASSIF: IF+PREP THEN *with* ⇑ equivalent]

2 If you say that one thing, group, idea, etc is **synonymous** with another, you suggest that the two things are very closely associated with each other so that one implies the other or one cannot exist without the other. EG *Government early developed the belief that it was synonymous with the country... ...the natural cork stopper that is synonymous with a quality wine.* [ADJ CLASSIF: PRED, IF+PREP THEN *with* ⇑ identified]

synopsis /sɪnɒpsɪs/, **synopses.** A **synopsis** is a summary of a longer piece of writing or work. EG *...a memo containing a synopsis of a dispatch from their office in Geneva.* [N COUNT = outline]

syntactic /sɪntæktɪk/ is used to describe something relating to syntax; a technical term in linguistics. EG *...a program capable of syntactic and semantic analysis.* [ADJ CLASSIF = grammatical] ◇ **syntactical.** EG *...the syntactical relationships between words.* [◇ ADJ CLASSIF = syntactic]

syntax /sɪntæks/ is the grammatical arrangement of words or grammatical rules in a language; a technical term in linguistics. [N UNCOUNT = grammar]

synthesis /sɪnθə[1]sɪs/, **syntheses** /sɪnθə[1]siːz/. **1** A **synthesis** of different ideas, styles, etc is a mixture or combination of these ideas, styles, etc, in which they blend together. EG *...a synthesis of Jewish theology and Greek philosophy... It was all stuff I'd heard before, a synthesis of everything Prager had already told me.* [N COUNT: USU+*of* = amalgamation]

2 The **synthesis** of a substance is the production of it by means of chemicals and chemical reactions, or by a natural biological process. EG *...methanol synthesis... Humans need some sunlight for the synthesis of vitamin D which takes place in the skin.* [N UNCOUNT+SUPP = manufacture]

3 The **synthesis** of sounds such as speech or music is the electronic production of them using a synthesizer. EG *The company started experimenting with speech synthesis to help the blind.* [N UNCOUNT+SUPP]

synthesize /sɪnθɪsaɪz/, **synthesizes, synthesizing, synthesized** also spelled **synthesise. 1** If you **synthesize** a substance, you produce it by means of chemicals and chemical reactions, or by a natural biological process. EG *...trying to synthesize products chemically... There are eight proteins which the body is unable to synthesise for itself from other proteins.* [V+O = manufacture]

2 If you **synthesize** different ideas, experiences, etc, you combine them to develop a single idea, impression, etc. EG *He synthesizes data from a variety of disparate sources... They synthesise their experience into principles and theories.* [V+O = fuse]

3 If you **synthesize** a sound such as speech or music, you produce it electronically using a synthesizer. [V+O]

synthesizer /sɪnθɪsaɪzə/, **synthesizers**; also spelled **synthesiser.** A **synthesizer** is an electronic machine that produces speech, music, or other sounds by using its computer to combine individual syllables or sounds that have been previously recorded and are stored by it. EG *..a voice synthesizer.* [N COUNT]

synthetic /sɪnθetɪk/, **synthetics. 1** A **synthetic** material is made from chemicals or artificial substances rather than from natural ones. EG *...curtains made of synthetic fibres... ...a synthetic rubber that would act as a substitute for natural rubber.* [ADJ CLASSIF: USU ATTRIB = man-made] ▸ used as a noun to refer to synthetic clothing and materials. EG *Use hand-hot water for washing synthetics.* [▸ N COUNT ⇑ fabric]

2 Synthetic sounds such as speech or music are produced electronically using a synthesizer. EG *...a matter of producing synthetic speech.* [ADJ CLASSIF: ATTRIB ⇑ electronic]

3 If you describe someone's action or way of behaving as **synthetic**, you mean that it is not sincere or genuine; used showing disapproval. EG *...a synthetic skin-deep smile.* [ADJ QUALIT ⇑ false = plastic] ▸ used of people. EG *Dan found her synthetic and stupid.* [▸ = artificial]

4 If you describe food as **synthetic**, you mean that it does not have a natural taste or appearance and is therefore unpleasant. EG *...a frightful synthetic fruit omelette.* [ADJ QUALIT]

syphilis /sɪfɪlɪs/ is a type of venereal disease that produces sores first on a person's sex organs and, if it is not treated, on their whole body. [N UNCOUNT]

syphon /saɪfə[0]n/, **syphons.** See **siphon.**

Syrian /sɪrɪən/, **Syrians. 1** Something that is **Syrian** belongs or relates to Syria or to its people or language. [ADJ CLASSIF]

2 A **Syrian** is a person who comes from Syria. EG *The Syrians need some oil for their own eastern cities.* [N COUNT]

syringe /sɪrɪnd[0]ʒ, sɪrɪnd[0]ʒ/, **syringes, syringing, syringed. 1** A **syringe** is a small tube with a suction device such as a plunger at one end and a fine hollow needle with a tiny hole in it at the other. Syringes are used for putting liquids into something and for taking liquids out, for example for injecting drugs into a person's body or for taking blood samples from them. EG *I attached the syringe and injected 10cc of the stuff... ...a hypodermic syringe.* [N COUNT]

2 If a doctor **syringes** your ear or nose or a wound, he or she cleans it out or cleans the wound using a syringe to suck substances out. EG *I went to the doctor to have my ears syringed.* [V+O = wash out]

syrup /sɪrəp/, **syrups. Syrup** is **1** a sweet, fairly thick liquid made by cooking sugar with water, sometimes with fruit juice as well, used for example to sweeten fruit. EG *...peaches in syrup... ...syrup of figs.* [N MASS] **2** a very sweet thick liquid food made from sugar. EG *...hot cakes and maple syrup... ...bread spread with golden syrup.* [N UNCOUNT ⇑ sauce]

syrupy /sɪrəpi[1]/. **1** Liquid that is **syrupy** is sweet or thick like syrup. [ADJ QUALIT]

2 A **syrupy** quality of behaviour is sentimental in an irritating way. EG *She admired everything she saw in a tone of syrupy earnestness... ...the syrupy glorification of home.* [ADJ QUALIT = cloying]

system /sɪstə[0]m/, **systems. 1** A **system** is **1.1** a way of working, organizing, or doing something in which you follow a fixed plan or set of rules. EG *Now that the new system has been running for a number of years, we can evaluate its success... They have developed a remarkably efficient system for gathering food... They don't have any system of collective child care... The simplest filing system might just be an alphabetical index.* [N COUNT: USU+SUPP = method, scheme] **1.2** a particular set of rules, especially one in mathematics or science which is used to count, measure, or calculate things. EG *...Egyptian or Roman number systems... In modern* [N COUNT+SUPP ⇑ method] *maths we often use the binary system... Gestures are part of a formal system of signals.*

2 If a situation or activity has some **system**, it has a sense of orderliness or good organization. EG *There's got to be some sort of system around here or we won't be able to function properly.*
N UNCOUNT ⇑ order = routine

3 A **system** is also the way that a whole institution or aspect of society has been organized and arranged. EG *Our first task was to create a new administrative system... The class system is often based on land ownership... There's a difference between the Scottish legal system and the English one... ...a new centre party which will break the two-party system.*
N COUNT+SUPP ⇑ organization = structure

4 People sometimes talk about the **system** to refer to the government or administration of a country when they think that it is too strong and has too many rules. EG *They are out to break the system... ...the revolutionary overthrow of the system... ...those who had opted to work 'within the system'.*
N SING : *the*+N = regime

5 The **system** of something is the way in which it is arranged so that all its parts fit together or work together. EG *...the phonological systems of language... The earth's weather system is an integrated whole.*
N COUNT+SUPP ⇑ structure

6 A **system** of a particular kind is **6.1** a set of roads, railways, canals, etc that are linked together so that people or vehicles can travel from one place to another. EG *In these towns the outline of the road system was still visible... ...the need to modernise Britain's transport system... There's a complex system of canals connecting the Texas ports.* **6.2** a set of equipment or parts such as water pipes or electrical wiring, which is used in processes such as supplying water or heat or providing electrical power. EG *Have you thought of installing your own central heating system?... What is wrong with the electrical system?* **6.3** a device or set of devices powered by electricity, for example a hi-fi or a computer. EG *They stole the stereo system and the television set... It has a sophisticated new sound system... Any words stored in the system can be inspected by the computer at any time.* **6.4** all the organs or parts of a person's or animal's body that together perform a particular function. EG *...a diagram of the digestive system... He has a very delicate nervous system... The way in which the human visual system can pick up movement is astonishing.*
6.1 N COUNT+SUPP = network; 6.2 N COUNT+SUPP; 6.3 N COUNT+SUPP; 6.4 N COUNT+SUPP

7 You might refer to your body as your **system** when considering it as a whole set of physical organs, with all the feelings and functions that they have. EG *The strenuous exercise made great demands on her system.*
N COUNT : POSS+N, USU SING

8 If you **get** something **out of** your **system**, you do something that you have a strong urge to do, for example express fully the feelings of anger or anxiety that you have about a situation, so that you feel better afterwards; an informal expression. EG *I think he's got it out of his system... Getting it out of my system made me relax a bit.*
PHR : VB INFLECTS = let off steam

systematic /sɪstɪmætɪk/. Activity or behaviour that is **systematic** follows a fixed plan or system, so that things are done in a thorough and efficient way. EG *These skills are developed in a formal and systematic way... Their economic foundations rest on the systematic cultivation of greed and envy.* ▸ used of people. EG *He was very systematic in his approach to his work.* ◊ **systematically**. EG *I wish they'd organise themselves more systematically... Her old house was being systematically demolished by bulldozers.*
ADJ QUALIT = methodical, consistent; ◊ ADV WITH VB = efficiently

systematize /sɪstɪmətaɪz/, **systematizes, systematizing, systematized**; also spelled **systematise**. If you **systematize** things such as facts or ideas, you arrange them in a well-organized pattern or system; a formal word. EG *...the method of systematizing the information derived.*
V+O = organize, order

Tt

T, t /tiː/ **Ts, t's**. 1 **T** is the twentieth letter of the English alphabet.
N COUNT

2 You use the expression **to a T** to say that something resembles a person exactly, is exactly typical of them, or is exactly right for them; used in informal English. EG *That's her to a T... That dress suits you to a T.*
PHR : USED AS AN A

3 **T** or **t** is an abbreviation for various words beginning with 't', such as 'temperature', 'tense', 'ton', 'transitive', etc.

ta /tɑː/ is an informal way of saying thank you; used in British English. EG *He passed it over to Myra, who smiled at him and said 'Ta'.*
CONVENTION = thanks

tab /tæb/, **tabs**. 1 A **tab** is **1.1** a small piece of cloth or paper that is attached to something, usually with information on it about the thing that it is attached to. EG *It had the maker's name on a small cloth tab inside.* **1.2** a metal strip that you pull off the top of a can of drink in order to open it; used in American English. **1.3** a tabulator; an informal use.
1.1 N COUNT = label; 1.2 N COUNT; 1.3 N COUNT

3 If you **pick up the tab**, you pay a bill on behalf of a group of people or provide the money that is needed for something; an informal expression. EG *Who's picking up the tab for the research?*
PHR : VB INFLECTS = foot the bill

4 If you **keep tabs on** someone, you make sure that you always know where they are and what they are doing, usually so that you can control them; an informal expression. EG *The President himself approved of burglary to keep tabs on radicals.*
PHR : VB INFLECTS ⇑ watch

Tabasco /təˈbæskəʊ/ is a trademark for a hot spicy sauce made from peppers.
N UNCOUNT

tabby /tæbiˡ/, **tabbies**. A **tabby** or a **tabby cat** is a cat whose fur has grey, brown, orange, or black markings, usually in stripes.
N COUNT

tabernacle /tæbənækəˡl/, **tabernacles**. 1 The **Tabernacle** was a small tent which contained the most sacred writings of the ancient Jews and which they took with them when they travelled.
N PROPER : *the*+N

2 **Tabernacle** is used as part of the name of some churches by certain Christian Protestant groups and by Mormons. EG *...a cross-shaped sign with the words 'Gospel Tabernacle' printed on it.*
N IN NAMES AFTER N

table /teɪbəˡl/, **tables, tabling, tabled**. 1 A **table** is a piece of furniture with a flat top, used for putting things on. EG *The book is there on the table... She kept his picture on her bedside table... ...the kitchen table... ...a billiard table.* ▸ also used to refer to the people sitting round a table. EG *The whole table laughed.*
N COUNT; ▸ N COUNT : IF SING, VB CAN BE SING OR PL

2 If you **table** something such as a proposal, **2.1** you say formally that you want it to be discussed at a meeting. EG *...a set of parliamentary questions tabled by Frank Field.* **2.2** you leave it to be discussed at a later time; used in American English. EG *The investigation was temporarily tabled due to more pressing business.*
2.1 V+O = propose; 2.2 V+O = shelve

3 If you put something **on the table**, **3.1** you present it at a meeting for it to be discussed; a British use. EG *There's not much point in a meeting until he has something definite to put on the table.* **3.2** you leave it to be discussed at a later time; an American use.
3.1 PHR : USED AS AN A; 3.2 PHR : USED AS AN A

4 A **table** is also **4.1** a chart of facts and figures which are shown in rows going across the page and columns going down the page. EG *The tables and graphs on p.43 show the turnover rate.* **4.2** a list of the multiplications of numbers between one and twelve, which children have to learn at school. EG *You could teach him to repeat the eleven times table... She knows her tables already.*
4.1 N COUNT; 4.2 N COUNT

5 If you **turn the tables on** someone, you change the situation completely, so that they now have the same problems that they were causing, or were going to cause, for you. EG *He completely turned the tables on his dreadful wife.*
PHR : VB INFLECTS

tableau /tæbləʊ/, **tableaux, tableaus**. The plural can be either **tableaux** or **tableaus**. A **tableau** is 1
N COUNT

a scene from history or a legend, represented by people in costumes standing on a stage, often as part of a procession; a formal use. **2** a moment when a group of people happen to be completely still and silent, and are arranged in an interesting or dramatic way, almost as if they were in a painting. EG *The children remained crouching in a motionless tableau, as if frozen into stone.* *N COUNT*

tablecloth /teɪbə[0]lklɒθ/, **tablecloths**; also spelled with a hyphen. A **tablecloth** is a cloth used to cover a table and keep it clean, for example while you are eating a meal. *N COUNT*

table lamp, table lamps; also spelled with a hyphen. A **table lamp** is a small electric lamp which stands on a table or other piece of furniture. *N COUNT*

table manners. Your **table manners** are the way you behave when you are eating a meal at a table. EG *He had to be most careful about his table manners.* *N PLURAL: USU POSS/MOD+N*

tablespoon /teɪbə[0]lspu:n/, **tablespoons**. A **tablespoon** is a large spoon used for serving food onto a plate. ▸ also used to refer to the amount that a tablespoon contains. EG *Use a solution of 1 tablespoon of vinegar to 1 pint of warm water.* *N COUNT; ▸ N PART+N UNCOUNT*

tablespoonful /teɪbə[0]lspu:nfʊl/, **tablespoonfuls, tablespoonsful**. The plural can be either **tablespoonfuls** or **tablespoonsful**. A **tablespoonful** is the amount that a tablespoon contains. EG *...two level tablespoonfuls of sugar.* *N COUNT: ALSO N PART+N UNCOUNT*

tablet /tæblɪ[2]t/, **tablets**. A **tablet** is **1** a small, hard piece of medicine, which you swallow. EG *Take three tablets after each meal... The drug is available in tablet form... ...a bottle of aspirin tablets.* *N COUNT = pill* **2** a flat solid piece of soap; a formal use. EG *...a tablet of soap.* *N COUNT+of = cake* **3** a flat piece of clay, stone, etc, which people used to write on before paper was invented. EG *...archaeologists labouring to decipher clay tablets.* *N COUNT* **4** a piece of stone, wood, etc, with words cut into it, which is fixed to a wall, especially the wall of a public building, so that a person or event will be remembered for a long time. EG *There is a tablet in memory of those who died.* *N COUNT ⇑ memorial = plaque*

table tennis; also spelled with a hyphen. **Table tennis** is a game played indoors by two or four people. They stand at each end of a long table which has a low net across its middle and hit a small, light ball to each other, using small bats. *N UNCOUNT = ping-pong*

tableware /teɪbə[0]lwɛə/ consists of the objects used on the table at meals, such as plates, glasses, cutlery, etc. *N UNCOUNT*

table wine, table wines. **Table wine** is fairly cheap wine that is drunk with meals. *N MASS = plonk*

tabloid /tæblɔɪd/, **tabloids**. A **tabloid** is a small-sized newspaper in which the news stories and articles are short, usually with a lot of photographs. EG *...the kind of sensational headlines typical of the tabloids.* *N COUNT*

taboo /təbu:/, **taboos**. A **taboo** is **1** a religious custom that forbids people to touch, say, or do something, because they believe that they will be punished by God or the gods. EG *Tribal taboos forbade the Mandinkas to eat the monkeys and baboons.* *N COUNT ⇑ belief* ▸ used as an adjective. EG *The priest's hut was taboo for women.* *▸ ADJ CLASSIF* **2** a social custom that certain words, subjects, or actions must be avoided because people think they are embarrassing or offensive. EG *...the old taboo on kissing in public.* *N COUNT = prohibition* ▸ used as an adjective. EG *For most people, birth control is no longer such a taboo subject.* *▸ ADJ CLASSIF*

tabular /tæbjə[4]lə/ is used to describe an arrangement of information in lists and columns; a fairly formal word. EG *The results are given in tabular form in Appendix III.* *ADJ CLASSIF: ATTRIB ⇑ chart*

tabulate /tæbjə[4]leɪt/, **tabulates, tabulating, tabulated**. To **tabulate** information means to arrange it in columns on a page. EG *It took twenty hours for officials to tabulate the results.* *V+O ⇑ order* ◊ **tabulation** /tæbjə[4]leɪʃə[0]n/. EG *The figures are ready for tabulation.* *◊ N UNCOUNT*

tabulator /tæbjə[4]leɪtə/, **tabulators**. A **tabulator** is a device on a typewriter that enables a typist to move the carriage quickly to a particular place in the line. *N COUNT = tab*

tacit /tæsɪt/ means understood or implied without actually being spoken. EG *They had by tacit agreement not renewed the contract... My attitude was taken as a tacit admission of guilt.* *ADJ CLASSIF: USU ATTRIB = unspoken* ◊ **tacitly**. EG *Is she tacitly admitting that her place is in the home?* *◊ ADV WITH VB*

taciturn /tæsɪtɜ:n/. Someone who is **taciturn** does not say very much and so sometimes seems unfriendly. EG *He was described as reserved and taciturn.* *ADJ QUALIT = reticent* ◊ **taciturnity** /tæsɪtɜ:nɪti[1]/. EG *...a man of legendary taciturnity.* *◊ N UNCOUNT*

tack /tæk/, **tacks, tacking, tacked**. **1** A **tack** is a short nail with a broad, flat head, used especially for fastening carpets to the floor. EG *I fixed it with cardboard and tacks.* ● to **get down to brass tacks**: see **brass tacks**. *N COUNT = thumbtack*

2 If you **tack** something to a surface, you nail it there with tacks. EG *Gretchen had tacked some prints and travel posters on the wall... The carpet needs to be tacked down.* *V+O: USU+A ⇑ attach*

3 If you change **tack** or try a different **tack**, you try a different method for dealing with a situation. EG *I changed tack: I smiled at her... They didn't seem convinced so I tried another tack.* *N UNCOUNT, N SING WITH DET = approach*

4 If a sailing boat **is tacking**, it is sailing towards a particular point in a series of diagonal movements rather than in a straight line, because the wind is coming from the wrong direction. *V: USU+A*

5 If you **tack** pieces of material together, you sew them together with big, loose stitches before sewing them properly; used in British English. EG *Tack up the hem and I'll sew it later.* *V+O, OR V+ADV +O = baste*

tack on. If you **tack** something **on**, you add an extra part to something else that is already complete, often in a way that seems unsatisfactory. EG *They've tacked a couple of new clauses on to the end of the contract... It's got a sort of conservatory tacked on at the back.* *PHRASAL VB: V+O+ADV ⇑ append*

tackle /tækə[0]l/, **tackles, tackling, tackled**. **1** If you **tackle** a difficult task or problem, you deal with it in a very determined or efficient way. EG *The computer can be programmed to tackle a whole variety of tasks... Is the government serious about tackling its spending problem?* *V+O = attend to*

2 If you **tackle** someone in a game such as football or hockey, you try to take the ball away from them. EG *He was tackled before he had a chance to shoot.* *V+O* ▸ used as a noun. EG *The tackle looked fair but a free kick was awarded.* *▸ N COUNT ⇑ challenge*

3 If you **tackle** a person, animal, etc, you attack and fight them, especially when they are bigger than you. EG *Some pythons can tackle creatures as big as goats.* *V+O = take on*

4 If you **tackle** someone about something, you speak to them frankly about it, especially in order to tell them off or to try and persuade them to change their mind. EG *He tackled me about several editorials I had written... I intend to tackle both management and union on the issue.* *V+O: USU+A (about/on) = confront*

5 Tackle is **5.1** the equipment that you need for a sport or activity, especially fishing. EG *The tackle was already in the car... ...fishing tackle.* *N UNCOUNT = gear* **5.2** the equipment, usually consisting of ropes and pulleys, needed for lifting or pulling something. *N UNCOUNT*

tacky /tæki[1]/, **tackier, tackiest**. Something that is **tacky** is **1** slightly sticky and not yet dry. EG *Press the two parts together while the glue is tacky.* *ADJ QUALIT* **2** badly made and unpleasant to look at; an informal use. EG *...tacky jewellery... ...the tacky shopfronts that line the main streets.* *ADJ QUALIT = tatty*

tact /tækt/ is the ability to avoid upsetting or offending people by being careful not to say or do things that would hurt their feelings. EG *With great tact, Lily said that it was time for her to go... Phil had the tact to leave a moment's respectful silence.* *N UNCOUNT = diplomacy, thoughtfulnes*

tactful /tæktfʊl/. Someone who is **tactful** is careful not to say or do something which would hurt other people's feelings or would offend or upset them. EG *Uncle Nick was tactful enough not to shatter this illusion... The tactful thing would have been not to say anything.* *ADJ QUALIT = diplomatic* ◊ **tactfully**. EG *The topic was tactfully dropped.* *◊ ADV WITH VB*

tactic /tæktɪk/, **tactics**. **Tactics** are **1** the methods that you use in order to achieve what you want when you are dealing with other people. EG *They use delaying tactics... Different circumstances involve adopting different tactics... This is a fairly common tactic among junior executives.* *N COUNT: USU = stratagem ploy* **2** the ways in which troops and military equipment are positioned and used in order to try to win a battle. EG *...a general with a sound grasp of tactics.* *N COUNT: USU*

tactical /tæktɪkə[0]l/ is used to describe **1** something that you do in order to be successful in a particular *ADJ CLASSIF = strategic* situation, usually something which you would not normally do. EG *This was simply a tactical move by De Gaulle.* ◊ **tactically.** EG *Tactically, I think we can be faulted for not voting against the strike.* ◊ ADV **2** weapons that have a short range, or military actions that take place over a short distance. EG *...a vast arsenal of tactical nuclear weapons designed for limited purposes.* ADJ CLASSIF : ATTRIB **3** something that relates to military tactics. EG *Our generals may have to revise their tactical thinking.* ADJ CLASSIF : ATTRIB

tactical voting is the act of voting for a particular person or political party in order to prevent someone else from winning, rather than because you agree with that person or party. N UNCOUNT

tactician /tæktɪʃəⁿn/, **tacticians.** A **tactician** is **1** an expert in military tactics. EG *He is a tactician unrivalled since Napoleon.* N COUNT = strategist **2** someone who is very good at choosing the best methods in order to achieve what they want. EG *An airport manager needed to be a tactician as well as a versatile administrator.* N COUNT

tactile /tæktaɪl/ is used to describe things which you know about, understand, or experience by touching them; a formal word. EG *...the sights, sounds, odours, flavours, and tactile qualities of the physical world... His paintings had tactile appeal... ...the tactile sense.* ADJ CLASSIF

tactless /tæktlɪ²s/. Someone who is **tactless** behaves or speaks in a way that is likely to upset or offend other people. EG *I suppose it was rather tactless of me to ask... Tilly's tactless outburst had really upset her.* ADJ QUALIT = insensitive, indiscreet ◊ **tactlessly.** EG *She behaved very tactlessly in reminding him of their love affair.* ◊ ADV WITH VB ◊ **tactlessness.** EG *She aggravated an already difficult situation by her tactlessness.* ◊ N UNCOUNT

tadpole /tædpəʊl/, **tadpoles. Tadpoles** are small water creatures which grow into frogs or toads. They have long tails and round black heads. N COUNT

taffeta /tæfɪ²tə/ is shiny stiff material made of silk or nylon that is used mainly for making women's clothes. N UNCOUNT ⇑ fabric

tag /tæg/, **tags, tagging, tagged. 1** A **tag** is **1.1** a small piece of cloth or paper which is attached to an object such as a piece of clothing or a suitcase and which has information on it about the object or its owner. EG *Have you tied the airline tags on the luggage?... Where's the price tag?* N COUNT = label **1.2** a small piece of metal or plastic that is attached to an animal so that it can be identified. EG *The pigs had metal tags in their ears bearing a number.* N COUNT ⇑ marker

2 If you **tag** animals, you attach tags to them so that they can be identified later. EG *We were tagging sharks to study their movements.* V+O ⇑ mark

3 A **tag** is also a short quotation or saying; a fairly formal use. EG *Her speech was full of boring tags... ...Biblical tags.* N COUNT = quote

4 A **tag** or **tag question** is a very short clause at the end of a statement which changes the statement into a question. In *'She said half price, didn't she?'*, the words *'didn't she'* are a tag. N COUNT

5 Tag is a game in which one child chases other children in order to try to touch one of them. After a child has been touched, he or she becomes the one who chases the others. EG *The kids spent the morning chasing one another up trees and playing tag.* N UNCOUNT

tag along. If you **tag along** with someone, you go with them, especially when they have not asked you to. EG *Our younger sisters always wanted to tag along when we went somewhere with our friends.* PHRASAL VB : V+ADV

tag on. If you **tag on** something such as a remark, you add it to the end of something that you have said or written. EG *This information was revealed in a throwaway line, tagged on to the end of a casual conversation.* PHRASAL VB : V+O+ADV = tack on

tail /teɪl/, **tails, tailing, tailed. 1** A **tail** is **1.1** the part of an animal, bird, or fish that grows out from the end of its body furthest from its head. EG *The dog was wagging his tail... It has a long furry tail.* N COUNT **1.2** a long part of something which sticks out from the back of it like a tail. EG *He ran into the street, the tails of his crumpled shirt flying... ...the tail of a falling star... ...the tail of the bus queue.* N COUNT : USU+SUPP **1.3** the back part of an aeroplane. EG *...the stairway descending from the tail of the old freight plane.* N COUNT : USU+SUPP = rear

2 If a man is wearing **tails**, he is wearing a formal jacket which has two long pieces hanging down at the back. Tails are worn only on very formal occasions. EG *The duke wore white tie and tails.* N PLURAL

3 To **tail** someone means to follow close behind them and watch where they go and what they do; an informal use. EG *All day he was tailed by police cars.* V+O = shadow

4 A **tail** is also someone who is paid to watch and to follow another person, such as a criminal; an informal use. N COUNT

5 When you are tossing a coin and it comes down **tails**, you can see the side of the coin which does not have a picture of a head on it: compare **head.** ● **heads or tails:** see **head.** ADV AFTER VB

6 The word **tail** is also used in the following expressions. **6.1** If you say that **the tail is wagging the dog**, you mean that a small or unimportant part of something is becoming too important and is controlling the whole thing. PHR **6.2** If you have your **tail between** your **legs**, you feel defeated and humiliated. EG *She left the kitchen with her tail between her legs.* PHR : USED AS O **6.3** If you **turn tail**, you turn and run away. EG *There was nothing for it but to turn tail.* PHR : VB INFLECTS **6.4** ● **can't make head or tail of** something: see **head.** ● **nose to tail:** see **nose.** ● to **top and tail** something: see **top.**

tail away. When a person's voice **tails away**, it gradually becomes quieter and then silent. EG *As I walked in her voice tailed away.* PHRASAL VB : V+ADV = tail off

tail back. Traffic that **tails back** stretches back along the road, moving very slowly or not at all, from something which is blocking the way, for example road works or a road accident. EG *Traffic tailed back from the roundabout to the M4 junction.* ● See also **tailback.** PHRASAL VB : V+ADV ⇑ extend

tail off. 1 When something **tails off**, it gradually becomes less in amount or value, often before coming to an end completely. EG *The rains tail off in September... The average figure has tailed off in the last few years.* ● See also **tail-off.** PHRASAL VB : V+ADV

2 When a person's voice **tails off**, it gradually becomes quieter and then silent. PHRASAL VB : V+ADV

tailback, tailbacks. A **tailback** is a long queue of traffic stretching back along a road, moving very slowly or not at all, for example because of road works or an accident. EG *...a two-mile tailback on the M6.* N COUNT ⇑ traffic jam

-tailed is used to describe the type of tail that an animal has. EG *...long-tailed monkeys... ...white-tailed deer.* COMB : FORMS ADJS

tailgate /teɪlgeɪt/, **tailgates.** A **tailgate** is the door at the back of a hatchback car, hinged at the top so that it opens upwards. EG *Paul slammed the tailgate of the Volvo.* N COUNT

tail light, tail lights; also spelled with a hyphen and as one word. The **tail lights** on a car or other vehicle are the two red lights at the back. EG *Rudolph watched the red tail lights speeding off... ...headlight and taillight bulbs.* N COUNT = rear light

tail-off. A **tail-off** in something is a gradual decrease in its amount or value. EG *There's been a slight tail-off in profits this month.* N SING : a+N = drop

tailor /teɪlə/, **tailors, tailoring, tailored. 1** A **tailor** is a person who makes men's clothes for people who have ordered them specially to be made to fit their particular measurements. EG *...gentlemen's tailors of the highest quality... ...new suits made by their local tailors.* N COUNT

2 If you **tailor** something such as a plan or system, you make it suitable for a particular purpose by changing the details of it. EG *...factories and equipment tailored to meet the needs of the 20th century.* V+O ⇑ adjust

tailored. Tailored clothes are made to fit close to a particular person's body. EG *...a tight-fitting tailored dress.* ADJ CLASSIF : ATTRIB = fitted

tailor-made. 1 Something that is **tailor-made** has been specially designed for a particular purpose or is very well suited to a particular purpose or need. EG *It may be best to have your golf-clubs tailor-made to your build and swing... Both the play and the role were tailor-made for her.* ADJ CLASSIF : IF+PREP THEN *for/to* = custom-made

2 Tailor-made clothes have been specially made by a tailor to fit a particular person. EG *He was wearing a tailor-made jacket... Who is buying tailor-made suits these days?* ADJ CLASSIF : IF+PREP THEN *for* = made to measure

tailwind /teɪlwɪnd/, **tailwinds.** A **tailwind** is a wind that is blowing from behind an aeroplane, boat, or other vehicle and that helps it to move forward. EG *It's faster coming back across the Atlantic because of tailwinds.* N COUNT

taint /teɪnt/, **taints, tainting, tainted.** 1 To **taint** something means to spoil it by introducing an undesirable or corrupt quality into it. EG *He feared that this would taint the scheme with some element of commercialism... There has not been a man elected to office yet that has not been tainted in some way.*
V+O = contaminate

2 A **taint** is an undesirable quality which spoils a person's reputation or the way that you think about something. EG *His career was never free of the taint of corruption... ...the taint of cowardice.*
N SING WITH DET +SUPP

tainted /teɪntɪ²d/. Something that is **tainted** is spoiled because it contains an undesirable quality. EG *The report was heavily tainted with racism... The system is tainted with corruption.*
ADJ QUALIT : IF + PREP THEN *with* = contaminated

take /teɪk/, **takes, taking, took, taken.** The most frequent use of **take** is in expressions where it does not have a very distinct meaning of its own, but where most of the meaning is in the noun that follows it (i.e. its direct object). The first paragraph gives examples of some of the main nouns which follow **take**, grouped as clearly as possible into different senses. **1 Take** is used **1.1** with nouns that refer to physical actions. There is often an equivalent verb, but using 'take' shows that the action is a separate and deliberate one, and not something that goes on indefinitely. So, for example, 'to take a look' means almost the same as 'to look', although it may suggest that the action is more deliberate. It also means that you can give more information about the action, as in the final two examples here. EG *He took a step towards Jack... Willie had taken a nap after lunch... She took a shower... He took a very deep breath... He formed the habit of taking long solitary walks.* V+O **1.2** with nouns that mean 'photograph'. EG *I took a magnificent photo of him... He'd been out all day taking pictures of the fighting.* V+O **1.3** with nouns that refer to a particular role, especially one of power or leadership. EG *The new government took office in July... The military regime took power in 1964... He asked me to take charge... Davis took the lead in blaming the pilots.* V+O **1.4** with nouns that refer to decisions or choices. EG *Certain decisions had to be taken... They were prepared to take risks... He was taking no chances.* V+O **1.5** with nouns that refer to the effort or care with which you do something. EG *Not enough time or trouble is taken in introducing foster children to their new families... ...the dress she had taken so much care to choose.* V+O **1.6** with nouns that refer to a time when you are not working, for example when you are on holiday. EG *She talked me into taking a week's holiday... Let's take a break... She's taken the day off.* V+O ⇑ have **1.7** with nouns that refer to an attitude or opinion that you have or are expressing. EG *That is a very foolish attitude to take... The public was beginning to take a positive interest in defence... Mrs Hall is always quick to take offence.* V+O
1.8 with nouns to form expressions that mean that you agree to accept the responsibility or blame for something. EG *She doesn't expect you to take the blame... I would be perfectly willing to take the consequences.* V+O **1.9** with nouns referring to formal declarations such as oaths and vows. EG *He stood there frowning, resembling a man taking the oath in court... Nuns still take vows of poverty and celibacy and obedience.* V+O **1.10** with a large number of other nouns to form expressions referring to actions, activities, or events of some kind. EG *Flo, Harriet, and I took turns sleeping on the bed... Mr Coby took his leave... A pattern began to take shape... Such aggression may simply take the form of bad language.* V+O

2 Take is also used in some some very common idiomatic expressions where most of the meaning is derived from the following noun. For other explanations of 'take' used in idiomatic expressions, see paragraph 46. **2.1** If you **take account of** something or **take** something **into account**, you include it in your thinking about a problem or topic because you feel that it is important. EG *If governments want growth, they have to take account of the needs of the business community... You have to take into account the additional costs that a baby will incur.* PHR : VB INFLECTS **2.2** If you **take care**, you are very careful. EG *I felt I should take care not to mention her name... Take care, darling, don't have another accident.* PHR : VB INFLECTS = be careful **2.3** If you **take care** of someone or something, you look after them well. EG *I knew he would take care of her for me... Take care of yourself... My job was to take care of any problems that arose.* PHR : VB INFLECTS **2.4** If you **take part** in something, you join in it, often as a member of a team or group. EG *I wanted to take part in a modern play... She took part in local government most of her life.* PHR : VB INFLECTS **2.5** If something **takes place**, it happens. EG *I want to tell you about the activities that take place at university... The killings took place over a period of about five years.* PHR : VB INFLECTS

3 If something **takes** a certain amount of time, you need that amount of time in order to do it. EG *You should take time to explain fully... How long will it take?... By all means take a day or two to think about it... It can take ten years for a new plane to be developed. It took her eyes only a few seconds to adjust.*
V+O, OR *it*+V+O +O : USU+*to*-INF/*for*

4 If you **take** something, you reach out for it and hold it in your hand or hands. EG *Let me take your coat... She took the menu from him.*
V+O ≠ give

5 If you **take** a person by a part of his or her body, you hold the person by it. EG *He took Sam by the hand... Bill took her in his arms... He walked round the car to take his wife's arm.*
V+O+A, OR V+O

6 If you **take** something with you when you go somewhere, you carry it or have it with you. EG *She gave me some books to take home... He has to take the boxes to the office every morning... Don't forget to take your umbrella.*
V+O : USU+A ≠ bring

7 If you **take** someone somewhere, they go there with you, especially when you are driving or you are leading them there. EG *Where are you taking me for dinner?... He took her to Edinburgh... He offered to take her home in a taxi... It's his turn to take the children to school.*
V+O : USU+A = bring

8 If you **take** something from a place, you remove it from there. EG *She took the car out of the garage... He walked over and took a cigarette from the box on the table.*
V+O : USU+A ≠ put back, return

9 You use **take**, often in the imperative, to introduce an example of the point that you are making. EG *Some men change the world. Take Alfred Adler. There was a man who revolutionized our understanding of ourselves... Poverty in Africa is appalling. Let's take Namibia. It's the most immediate case... If we take wage-earning as a whole, then women come a long way below average.*
V+O : USU IMPER = consider

10 If you **take** something that is given or offered to you, you accept it and get some benefit or disadvantage from it. EG *She took a job in publishing... We've just had to take a pay cut.*
V+O ≠ refuse

11 If you **take** something from among a number of things, **11.1** you choose it. EG *I'll take that yellow one, please.* V+O **11.2** you buy it. EG *I'll take a dozen eggs.* V+O

12 If you **take** a house or flat, you rent it, usually for only a short time. EG *He had taken a small flat in Brussels.*
V+O

13 If you **take** something such as a newspaper or milk, you buy it on a regular basis. EG *We take about two and a half thousand periodicals in this section of the library... We take two pints of milk a day.*
V+O ⇑ get

14 If you **take** something from someone who owns it, you steal it or go away with it without their permission. EG *In the crowd a pickpocket took Barry's wallet and passport... Someone's taken my pen... Parts of her book are taken from my own notebooks.*
V+O = pinch

15 If you can **take** something such as pain, suffering, or loneliness, you endure it without trying to avoid it or without weakening or giving in to it. EG *OK, mate, you win. I can't take any more... Some people find it easier to take hostility than others... I just used to listen and take it.*
V+O : NO CONT = bear, stand

16 If soldiers or terrorists **take** people or places, they seize or capture them, usually by force. EG *We took the village without a shot being fired... We were lucky to be taken alive.*
V+O, OR V+O+C A

17 If you **take** something such as damage or loss, you suffer it, especially in war or in a battle. EG *He withdrew VII Corps which had taken very heavy punishment in the past few days... The camp was rocketed heavily, but took no serious casualties.*
V+O

18 If something **takes** a particular quality or thing, it requires it. EG *It took a lot of courage to admit his mistake... It takes a great deal of money to fight a general election... You took a bit of persuading... One gentle movement of the wrist was all it took.*
V+O, OR V+O+C = need

19 If you **take** a subject or course at school or
V+O : USU+A

university, you study it. EG *She took Greek at university... I took a course in marine biology.*

20 If you **take** a test or examination, you do it in order to obtain a certificate, diploma, or other qualification. EG *She's not yet taken her driving test... She took her degree last year.* V+O = sit

21 If you **take** someone in or for a subject, you give them lessons in that subject. EG *He took us in maths... She took them for geography.* V+O : USU+A

22 If you **take** patients, clients, etc, you accept them as your patient, clients, etc. EG *Some of the doctors here take only paying patients... We never take problem children in this school.* V+O

23 If you **take** food or drink, you eat or drink it. EG *I invited her to take a cup of coffee.* V+O = have

24 If you **take** drugs, pills, or other medicine, you swallow them. EG *I took a couple of aspirins... Alice took an overdose after a row with her mother.* V+O

25 If you **take** something such as tea or coffee in a particular state, you usually drink it with or without something else added, such as milk or sugar. EG *I take it black with no sugar... Do you take sugar?* V+O : USU+C/A = have

26 If you **take** something such as a letter or a note, you listen to what someone is saying and write it down. EG *Would you be willing to take notes of our meeting?... She hated being asked to take letters.* V+O

27 If you **take** something such as a person's temperature, you find out what it is by measuring it. EG *I took her temperature... Let me take your pulse.* V+O

28 If a place or thing **takes** a particular amount or number, there is enough space for that amount or number. EG *The new stadium can take about 8,000 people... I don't think that case will take any more.* V+O = hold

29 If a shop, restaurant, etc **takes** a certain amount of money, they get that amount from the things that they sell. EG *The Jubilee Club took $2,700 one night... I only take about £5 a week.* V+O ⇑ receive

30 If you **take** a particular size in shoes or clothes, you wear that size. EG *She asked what size of shoes he took.* V+O

31 If you **take** a car, train, etc, you use it to go from one place to another. EG *She said she'd take a taxi from the station... I think we ought to take the car.* V+O : USU+A

32 If a car, bus, etc **takes** you from one place to another, it transports you there. EG *I have a car waiting outside to take me there.* V+O : USU+A

33 If something such as a job or interest **takes** you to a place, it is the reason for you going there. EG *His first war assignment took him to Cyprus in 1964... His job takes him all over the world.* V+O+A

34 If you **take** something such as a problem to someone, you discuss it with them because you want their help or advice in solving it. EG *Andrew said that he always took his problems to his mother... They were going to take their case before the council.* V+O+A

35 If you **take** someone's advice or **take** notice of what they say, you accept what they say you should do and you do it. EG *I didn't have the heart to take the vet's advice... I took no notice of his warning.* V+O

36 If you **take** one number or amount from another, you subtract it or deduct it. EG *Take 6 from 9 and the answer is 3... They've taken $3.50 off the price of all their skirts.* V+O+A

37 If you **take** a telephone call, you speak to someone who is telephoning you. EG *It's difficult to take a private phone call in my office... Can I take it in your room?* V+O : USU+A

38 If you **take** a road or route, you choose to travel along it. EG *He took the road southwards into the hills... Take the second road on the left.* V+O : USU+A = follow

39 If you **take** something in a particular way, **39.1** you react in the way mentioned to a situation or to someone's beliefs or behaviour. EG *He would never take her fears seriously... Mother took the news very badly.* V+O+A **39.2** you think about things or deal with problems in the way mentioned. EG *You mustn't take these things in isolation... Let's take one thing at a time.* V+O+A

40 If you **take** someone's meaning, you understand and accept what they are saying. EG *He took my meaning perfectly... I take the point that anything nuclear is potentially dangerous... Don't take that too literally... They took what I said as a kind of rebuke.* V+O+A ⇑ interpret

41 If one thing **takes** another to a particular point, it causes it to reach a new level, condition, or state. EG *The TV production took the book to the top of the best-seller lists... What will the increase take your salary to?* V+O+A

42 If you **take** something beyond the point that it has reached, you continue it or develop it even further. EG *His parents are keen to take the matter further.* V+O+A

43 If something such as a drug or a dye **takes**, it has the effect or result that is intended. EG *You need a few minutes for cortisone to take... I'm afraid the dye hasn't taken on your shoes.* V = work ⇑ react

44 If plants **take**, they start growing properly. EG *It was so cold that hardly any of the seedlings took.* V ≠ fail

45 A take is a short piece of action which is filmed in one continuous session for a cinema or television film. Sometimes one scene needs several takes. EG *We had a talk between takes.* N COUNT

46 The word **take** is also used in the following expressions. **46.1** Something that is **hard to take** is difficult to accept without arguing or protesting about it. EG *Ordinary people find his arrogance hard to take.* PHR : USED AS C = too much **46.2** You can say **'I take it'** to check that the person you are speaking to knows something, understands what you are saying, or is giving you correct information. EG *I take it you know what a stethoscope is?... I take it that you've been quite candid with me.* PHR+REPORT-CL : VB INFLECTS = I presume

46.3 You can say **'take my word', 'take my word for it'**, or **'take it from me'** to tell someone that you are absolutely sure that what you are saying is correct, and that they should believe you. EG *Take my word, it's a good deal... You can take it from me that Patrick's worried.* PHR : USED AS ADV SEN, OR PHR +REPORT-CL = believe me **46.4** If something **takes a lot out of** you or **takes it out of** you, it makes you feel very tired and weak because you have used a lot of energy. EG *Talking in a foreign language all day takes a lot out of you.* PHR : VB INFLECTS **46.5** If something **takes** you **out of** yourself, it makes you feel better and so you forget all your worries and unhappiness. EG *Her magnificent poetry took him out of himself.* PHR : VB INFLECTS **46.6** If you **take** something **as read**, you accept that it is correct or is agreed, without discussing it or trying to prove it. EG *His sincerity must be taken as read... I took it as read that the program would need changing.* PHR : VB INFLECTS **46.7** If you **take** something **seriously,** you believe that it is important and needs to be thought about or discussed. EG *Good tutors are people who take seriously the importance of helping their students... She took life far too seriously.* PHR : VB INFLECTS **46.8** If something **takes** you **by surprise,** you do not expect it and so you are amazed by it. EG *Since Poirot knew she was coming, he was not taken by surprise when she burst through the door... The announcement really took me by surprise.* PHR : VB INFLECTS

take aback. If you **are taken aback**, you are so surprised or shocked that you have to pause for a moment and cannot think or do anything. EG *I was momentarily taken aback... Jenny was taken aback by some of the portraits.* PHRASAL VB : V+ADV, USU PASS ⇑ startle

take after. If you **take after** a member of your family, you resemble them in your appearance, your behaviour, or your character. EG *You don't take after your sister... He'd got a way of his own and I tend to take after him.* PHRASAL VB : V+PREP

take against. If you **take against** someone or something, you develop a dislike for them, often for no good reason. EG *William III took against the castle and built Kensington Palace instead.* PHRASAL VB : V+PREP ≠ take to

take apart. 1 If you **take** something **apart**, you separate it into the different parts that it is made of. EG *We encouraged them to explore, invent, take things apart, and put them together... I'll have to take the bike apart.* PHRASAL VB : V+O+ADV = dismantle

2 If you **take apart** something such as an argument or an essay, you analyse it critically and carefully and show what its weaknesses are. EG *She simply took apart my chapter with the same techniques that I had used to take apart her essay.* PHRASAL VB : V+O+ADV

take away. 1 If you **take** something **away** from someone, you remove it from them, so that they no longer have it. EG *A maid came to take away the tray... Nothing seems to take away your appetite... ...people from whom everything has been taken away.* PHRASAL VB : V+O++A

2 If you **take** one number or amount **away** from another, you subtract one number from the other. EG *This last amount is then taken away from each annual figure of earnings.* PHRASAL VB : V+O+ADV, USU+*from* ≠ add

3 If something **takes away** from an achievement, success, quality, etc, it has the effect of making the PHRASAL VB : V+O+ADV, USU+

achievement, success, quality, etc seem lower in value or worth than it should be. EG *Whatever he may have been like as a person, nothing can take away from his achievements as a scientist.*
from = detract

4 If you **take** someone **away**, you make them go with you to prison or to a mental hospital; a rather informal use. EG *His parents were taken away in a dark van... They'll take me away and they'll say I'm guilty of murder.*
PHRASAL VB : V+O+ADV

5 See also **takeaway**.

take back. 1 If you **take** something **back**, 1.1 you return it to the place where you borrowed it from or where you bought it, either because you have finished with it or because it is broken or unsuitable. EG *He wouldn't take the scratched records back to the shop... Don't forget to take your books back to the library.*
PHRASAL VB : V+O+ADV
1.2 you agree to accept it again after you have sold it or got rid of it, and to give back any money that was paid for it, usually because it is unsuitable or does not work. EG *Shopkeepers are often reluctant to take back unsatisfactory goods.*
PHRASAL VB : V+O+ADV
1.3 you admit that something that you said or thought is wrong. EG *I'm going to have to take back all those things I said about you.*
PHRASAL VB : V+O+ADV = withdraw

2 If you **take** someone **back**, you allow them to come home again, after they have gone away because of a quarrel. EG *She said she would be willing to take him back if he promised to behave.*
PHRASAL VB : V+O+ADV

3 If you say that something **takes** you **back**, you mean that it reminds you of a period of your past life and makes you think about it again. EG *The jive, eh?–That takes me back a bit.*
PHRASAL VB : V+O+ADV

take down. If you **take** something **down**, 1 you reach up and get it from a high place such as a shelf. EG *Expert removal men will take down curtains for you... He took down a volume of verse.*
PHRASAL VB : V+O+ADV
2 you remove each piece of a temporary structure, such as scaffolding or a stage, when it is no longer needed. EG *The scaffolding won't be taken down until next year.*
PHRASAL VB : V+O+ADV = dismantle ≠ put up
3 you listen to what someone is saying and write it down. EG *The postmistress began to take down the message... Anything you say may be taken down and used in evidence against you.*
PHRASAL VB : V+O+ADV

take in. 1 If you **take** someone **in**, 1.1 you allow them to stay in your house with you, especially if they are homeless or are in trouble. EG *It was kind of her to take me in.*
PHRASAL VB : V+O+ADV ≠ turn out
1.2 you allow them to live in a part of your house in exchange for payment. EG *She takes in lodgers in the summer.*
PHRASAL VB : V+O+ADV
1.3 you deceive them, often by pretending that your character or feelings are different from what they really are. EG *I was sure I wasn't going to be taken in by this kind of sentimentality... Even after years of close acquaintance he could take you in.*
PHRASAL VB : V+O+ADV ⇑ trick

2 If you **take** something **in**, 2.1 you understand it when you hear it or read it. EG *People never take in new facts very easily when they're unhappy.*
PHRASAL VB : V+O+ADV
2.2 you see all of it at the same time or with just one glance. EG *One might take in at a glance the whole scene.*
PHRASAL VB : V+O+ADV

3 If you **take in** something such as a film or a museum, you go to see it, usually while you are spending time in a place that you are visiting. EG *We spent lots of weekends in London, where we would always take in a show or two.*
PHRASAL VB : V+O+ADV = do

4 If people, animals, etc **take in** air, drink, or food, they allow it to enter their body, usually by breathing or swallowing. EG *Sharks take in water through the mouth.*
PHRASAL VB : V+O+ADV

5 If something big **takes in** something smaller, it is big enough to include the smaller thing within it. EG *The area was stretched to take in some parts of Wales too... The truth takes in both extremes.*
PHRASAL VB : V+O+ADV

6 If you **take in** a dress, jacket, or other item of clothing, you make it smaller and tighter by altering its seams. EG *He lost so much weight that he had to take in all his trousers.*
PHRASAL VB : V+O+ADV ⇑ alter ≠ let out

take off. 1 When an aeroplane **takes off**, it leaves the ground and starts flying. EG *The pilot turned the plane into the wind to take off... We took off in a cloud of dust.*
PHRASAL VB : V+ADV ≠ land

2 If something such as a product, a film, or a sport **takes off**, it suddenly becomes very successful and popular. EG *Do-it-yourself began seriously to take off in the 1930s... I bought a computer a couple of years before computers really began to take off.*
PHRASAL VB : V+ADV ≠ flop

3 If you **take off** or **take** yourself **off**, you go away, often suddenly and unexpectedly. EG *They took off for a weekend in the country... She took herself off to Amsterdam.*
PHRASAL VB : V+ADV, OR V+O (REFL)+ADV : USU+A

4 If you **take** something **off**, you remove it. EG *'Good afternoon,' Mr Tinker said, taking off his hat... He took off his glasses and blinked... Use towels to take off greasy makeup.*
PHRASAL VB : V+O+ADV ≠ put on

5 If you **take off** something such as money or a mark, you deduct it from the total. EG *Your employer will take off some of your wages to pay your national insurance contribution.*
PHRASAL VB : V+O+ADV ≠ add on

6 If you **take** someone **off**, 6.1 you make them go with you to a particular place, especially when they do not want to go there. EG *She came down with pneumonia and was taken off to hospital... Dickens finally was caught and taken off to prison.*
PHRASAL VB : ORDER V+O+ADV
6.2 you imitate them and the things that they do and say, in such a way that you make other people laugh; an informal use. EG *Mike can take off his father to perfection.*
PHRASAL VB : V+O+ADV = mimic

7 If a bus, train, or plane service is **taken off**, it is withdrawn so that it is no longer available for people to use. EG *The 7.18 London train was taken off for the winter.*
PHRASAL VB : V+O+ADV, USU PASS = cancel

8 If a play is **taken off**, it is withdrawn from a theatre, so that there are no more performances of it. EG *'My Fair Lady' was taken off when it was at the peak of its success.*
PHRASAL VB : V+O+ADV, USU PASS ≠ put on

9 See also **takeoff**.

take on. 1 If you **take on** a job or responsibility, you accept it. EG *She takes on more work than is good for her... With promotion, he had taken on greater responsibilities.*
PHRASAL VB : V+O+ADV

2 If something **takes on** a new appearance or quality, it develops that appearance or quality. EG *His voice took on a new note of uncertainty... Her face took on a haunted quality... The word 'profession' is taking on a new meaning.*
PHRASAL VB : ORDER V+ADV+O = assume ≠ lose

3 If buses, ships, etc **take on** passengers, goods, or fuel, they stop in order to allow them to get on or to be loaded on. EG *Buses stopped by request to take on more passengers... We're only stopping briefly to take on fuel.*
PHRASAL VB : V+O+ADV

4 If you **take** someone **on**, 4.1 you employ them to do a job. EG *They took me on because I was a good mathematician.*
PHRASAL VB : V+O+ADV
4.2 you fight them or compete against them, especially when they are bigger or more powerful than you are. EG *British Leyland plans to take on the competition at home and abroad... I'll take you all on, one by one.*
PHRASAL VB : V+O+ADV ⇑ challenge

5 If you **take** something **on** or **upon** yourself, you decide to do it without asking anyone for permission or approval. EG *Mrs Kaul took it upon herself to turn round and say 'Sh'... I took it upon myself to phone your parents.*
PHRASAL VB : V+O+PREP ⇑ presume

6 If you tell someone **not to take on**, you are telling them not to get angry or upset about something and not to make a fuss about it; an informal use. EG *There's no need to take on so; I'm only going out for a couple of hours!*
PHRASAL VB : V+ADV, USU WITH BROAD NEG

take out. 1 If you **take** something **out**, 1.1 you remove it from its usual place for a short time. EG *Emma opened her bag and took out her comb.*
PHRASAL VB : V+O+ADV
1.2 you remove it for ever from its place. EG *Why don't we just take this sentence out?... Ian's having three teeth taken out tomorrow.*
PHRASAL VB : V+O+ADV = extract

2 If you **take out** something such as a licence or an insurance policy, you arrange to get it from somewhere such as a court of law, an insurance company, or a bank. EG *I want to take out a mortgage... Court orders were taken out in the name of the landlords.*
PHRASAL VB : V+O+ADV

3 If you **take** someone **out**, 3.1 they go with you to a restaurant, theatre, park, etc, and you pay for them as well as for yourself. EG *He offered to take her out for a meal... Why don't you take the children out?... You used to take me out to shows.*
PHRASAL VB : V+O+ADV ⇑ accompany
3.2 you kill them, or injure them so badly that they are put out of action completely; an informal use. EG *He and his brother have taken out 58 enemy soldiers between them.*
PHRASAL VB : V+O+ADV

4 If you **take** something **out on** someone, you behave in an unpleasant way towards them, because you feel angry, disappointed, or frustrated, even though it is not their fault that you feel so upset. EG *She took out most of her unhappiness on her husband.*
PHRASAL VB : V+O+ADV+PREP = vent

take over. 1 If you **take over** a company, you get or are given control of it, for example by buying its
PHRASAL VB : V+O+ADV

shares. EG *The agency has advised its clients to take over or merge with another company.*

2 If someone **takes over** a country, they get control of it, usually with the help of the army, and replace the government with a new one. EG *Once again the military had taken over.* PHRASAL VB : V+O, OR V+O+ADV

3 If someone **takes over** a building, they occupy it and prevent it from being used for its normal purposes. EG *The television station was taken over and held for some hours.* PHRASAL VB : V+O+ADV

4 If you **take over** a job or you **take over**, you become responsible for the job after someone else has stopped doing it. EG *They want me to take over as editor when Harold Evans leaves... You'll probably be taking over my tutorial groups... You can take over now.* PHRASAL VB : V+O+ADV, OR V+ADV

5 If one thing **takes over** from something else, it becomes more important, successful, or powerful than the other thing, and eventually replaces it. EG *Microfilms might even take over from libraries one day.* PHRASAL VB : V+ADV ⇑ replace

6 See also **takeover**.

take to. **1** If you **take to** someone or something, you are attracted to them and like them, especially after knowing them or thinking about them for only a short time. EG *It was impossible to tell whether he had taken to Rose or not... We asked him if the Russians would take to golf.* PHRASAL VB : V+PREP ≠ take against

2 If you **take to** doing something, you begin to do it as a regular habit. EG *He took to wearing black leather jackets... As they grow larger, they take to eating fish.* PHRASAL VB : V+PREP+-ing

take up. **1** If you **take up** an activity or a subject, you become interested in it and spend time doing it, either as a hobby or as a career. EG *I thought I'd take up fishing... He decided to take up medicine as a career.* PHRASAL VB : V+O+ADV ≠ drop

2 If you **take up** a point, idea, or suggestion that has been raised, you discuss it further, either agreeing or disagreeing with what has already been said. EG *I'd like to take that up. I think there's a lot of truth in what you say, but you don't go far enough... The committee is expected to take up the question of the government's role in the arts.* PHRASAL VB : V+O+ADV = pursue

3 If you **take up** a job, you begin to work at it. EG *My assistant left to take up another post.* PHRASAL VB : V+O+ADV

4 If you **take up** an offer or a challenge, you accept it, so that you get the benefit or problems that come with it. EG *She wished Jane would take up Derek's offer to decorate the house.* PHRASAL VB : V+O+ADV ≠ refuse

5 If something **takes up** a particular amount of time, space, or effort, it uses that amount. EG *I won't take up any more of your time... The baby took up all her energy and attention... Much of the day was taken up with classes or study.* PHRASAL VB : ORDER V+ADV+O ⇑ occupy

6 If you **take up** a particular position, you get into a particular place in relation to something else, either so that you can see better or so that you are better placed for what you think is going to happen. EG *The fire engines had taken up position by the runway... The two motor-cycle outriders dropped back to take up their stations at the rear of the convoy.* PHRASAL VB : V+O+ADV ⇑ adopt

7 If you **take up** a particular attitude or belief, you adopt it and make it your own, as a standard for what you say and do. EG *He hated to see her taking up this hard, uncompromising attitude.* PHRASAL VB : ORDER V+O+ADV

8 If you **take up** something such as a task or a story, you begin again doing something that has been interrupted or that was begun by someone else. EG *David was taking up where he had left off... Sam took up the story.* PHRASAL VB : V+O, OR V+O+ADV ⇑ continue

9 If you **take up residence** in a particular place, you begin to live there; a formal or humorous use. EG *She's virtually taken up residence at the doctor's surgery.* PHR : VB INFLECTS

10 See also **take-up**.

take up on. If you **take** someone **up on** something, **1** you accept an offer or invitation that they have made. EG *She paused a while, in case he might care to take her up on her offer.* PHRASAL VB : V+O+ADV+PREP **2** you ask them to explain or justify something that they have just said, because you think that they are wrong. EG *I think I would like to take Tony up on something that he said.* PHRASAL VB : V+O+ADV+PREP = challenge

take upon. To **take** something **upon** yourself means the same as to take it on yourself. PHRASAL VB : V+O+PREP

take up with. **1** If you **take up with** someone, you begin to be friendly with them and spend a lot of time with them. EG *For a little time after she took up with Mr Marvin she went on singing in public.* PHRASAL VB : V+ADV+PREP ⇑ befriend

2 If you **are taken up with** something, it keeps you busy or fully occupied. EG *Their sessions were taken up with talk about all sorts of subjects... She was too taken up with her own feelings to pay much attention to his.* PHRASAL VB : V+ADV+PREP, ONLY PASS

takeaway /teɪkəweɪ/, **takeaways**. A **takeaway** is **1** a shop or restaurant which sells cooked food that you eat somewhere else, such as at home; used in British English. EG *...the man behind the counter at the Chinese takeaway.* N COUNT : USU MOD+N **2** hot cooked food that is sold to be eaten somewhere else. EG *I really fancy an Indian takeaway... ...takeaway pizzas.* N COUNT

take-home pay. Your **take-home pay** is the amount of your wages or salary that is left after income tax, national insurance, and all other official deductions have been made. EG *His pension amounts to about 75% of his take-home pay before he retired.* N UNCOUNT = net pay ≠ gross pay

taken /teɪkəⁿn/. **1 Taken** is the past participle of **take**.

2 If you are **taken** with something, you find it attractive and interesting. EG *Philip had been rather taken with the idea... We were all very taken with Mrs Wilkins.* ADJ QUALIT : PRED+*with*

takeoff /teɪkɒf/, **takeoffs**; also spelled with a hyphen. **1 Takeoff** is **1.1** the beginning of a flight, when an aircraft leaves the ground. EG *...about fifty minutes after takeoff... Ninety per cent of all aircraft accidents occur at either take-off or landing.* N UNCOUNT/COUNT **1.2** the time or stage in the development of a company, business, product, etc when it begins to be successful. EG *The government had already provided the groundwork for economic take-off by creating almost full employment.* N UNCOUNT

2 A **takeoff** of someone is an imitation of the way in which they walk, talk, or behave, that is done in order to make people laugh. EG *He did a very amusing take-off of the headmaster.* N COUNT : USU+*of*

takeover /teɪkəʊvə/, **takeovers**; also spelled with a hyphen. A **takeover** is **1** the act of getting control of a company by buying a large number of its shares. EG *All middle-size oil companies are likely candidates for takeover... The trend towards takeovers has intensified... ...the latest take-over battle.* N COUNT/UNCOUNT **2** the act of taking control of a country, political party or movement, etc, usually by force rather than by democratic procedures. EG *He may be ousted by a military take-over... ...against the liberal takeover of the women's liberation movement.* N COUNT/UNCOUNT **3** the act of taking control of an organization or building so as to prevent it being used for its normal purposes. EG *The student takeover was just the beginning.* N COUNT/UNCOUNT

taker /teɪkə/, **takers**. A **taker** is a person who agrees to accept something that is offered, especially a bet or a challenge. EG *The bookmakers were offering 4 to 1 on, but there were no takers.* N COUNT

take-up is the rate at which people apply for or buy something which is offered, for example financial help from the government or shares in a company. EG *Initially, there wasn't much take-up of the home improvement offers... ...the take-up rate for Social Security benefits.* N UNCOUNT+*of*

takings /teɪkɪŋz/ are the amount of money that a shop, theatre, cinema, etc gets from selling its goods or tickets. EG *The manager said that takings were as high as ever.* N PLURAL = receipts

talc /tælk/ is the same as talcum powder; an informal word. N UNCOUNT

talcum powder /tælkəm paʊdə/ is a soft, fine, perfumed powder which people put on their bodies after they have had a bath. N UNCOUNT = talc

tale /teɪl/, **tales**. **1** A **tale** is **1.1** a story, especially one involving adventure or magic. EG *He was a good story-teller and used to make up tales about farmers and animals... They acted out tales of princes and magic birds and wars... ...a book called 'Tales from Mozambique'.* N COUNT : ALSO IN TITLES ⇑ narrative **1.2** a spoken or written account of things that have happened, especially one that is very interesting or exciting. EG *Everyone had some tale to tell about the very cold winter... Since childhood he had heard tales of the rebellion... Tony grew up on tales of London politics.* N COUNT ⇑ report ● See also **old wives' tale**.

2 If you **live to tell the tale**, you survive a very dangerous or frightening experience and so are able PHR : VB INFLECTS to tell people about it afterwards. EG *Still, we all lived to tell the tale... It's amazing that I'm still alive to tell the tale.*

3 If you say that something **tells a tale**, you mean that it reveals something important. EG *The lack of evidence tells a tale.* ● If you say that something **tells its own tale**, you mean that what has happened should be obvious to anyone. — PHR : VB INFLECTS; ● PHR : VB INFLECTS = speak for itself

4 If a child **tells tales**, it tells a parent, teacher, or some other person in authority about something naughty that another child has done, because it wants the other child to be punished. EG *Teachers hate children who tell tales about their friends.* — PHR : VB INFLECTS = splits

5 To **tell tales** also means to tell lies. EG *David's mother was worried because he was always telling her tales.* — PHR : VB INFLECTS

talent /tæləⁿnt/, **talents**. 1 **Talent** is 1.1 the natural ability that a person has to do something well. EG *She's a pianist of absolutely phenomenal talent... I did not have much confidence in my talent as a film actor... Rudolph had a talent for music and played the trumpet... This sort of work calls for special talents.* 1.2 people who have a natural ability to do something well. EG *There's such a lot of acting talent about... We risk a major loss of talent to overseas jobs... She's an exciting new swimming talent.* — N UNCOUNT/COUNT ⇑ aptitude = gift; N UNCOUNT/COUNT

2 Some men use the word **talent** to refer to women who they find sexually attractive; a very informal use. EG *There's not much talent about tonight... We all went to the disco to eye up the local talent.* — N UNCOUNT

talented /tæləntɪ²d/. Someone who is **talented** has a natural ability to do something well. EG *She's independent, talented, courageous, and politically active.* — ADJ QUALIT = gifted

talent scout, talent scouts. A **talent scout** is someone whose job is to go around looking for people who have talent as actors, dancers, footballers, comedians, etc so that they can be offered work. — N COUNT

talisman /tælɪzmən/, **talismans**. A **talisman** is an object which you believe has magic powers to protect you or bring you luck. EG *Those icons are sacred talismans for him... With the other talismans of his youth it had been discarded.* — N COUNT = charm

talk /tɔːk/, **talks, talking, talked**. 1 If you can **talk**, you have the ability to use spoken words to express your thoughts, ideas, or feelings. EG *Imagine not being able to see or hear or talk... Your dolly can't talk... Is your baby talking yet?... Nancy's throat was so sore that she could not talk... Talk, dear, don't grunt.* — V ⇑ communicate

2 If something can **talk**, it produces noises which sound like a human being talking. EG *He spent years teaching his parrot to talk... How about a talking watch? One will shortly be on the market.* — V = speak

3 When you **talk**, you use spoken language to express your thoughts, ideas, or feelings. EG *I listened as she talked... We sat down together and talked for hours... All the boys were talking at once... What on earth are you talking about?* ▸ used as a noun. EG *Here everything was laughter and talk... I will not have that kind of talk at my breakfast table!* ● See also **small talk**. — V = speak; ▸ N UNCOUNT = speech

4 If you **talk** to someone about something, 4.1 you have a conversation with them about something that interests you. EG *They talked about old times... She liked hearing him talk about his children... Thank you very much for talking to me about your new book.* 4.2 you tell them about the things that are worrying you. EG *He was the only one in the family she could talk to... He could have come to the office if he wanted to talk.* ▸ used as a noun. EG *I want to have a long talk with her... I think it's time we had a serious talk.* — V : USU+A = chat; V : USU+A ⇑ confide; ▸ N COUNT ⇑ discussion

5 If someone **talks**, they give other people important or secret information, usually unwillingly. EG *Start talking, Castle. Or I'll shoot.* — V

6 If people **are talking** or **are talking** about someone, they are discussing other people and gossiping about them. EG *We must be careful. We don't want the neighbours to talk... Give me a kiss. Let's give Mrs Smith something to talk about.* ▸ used as a noun. EG *There was a lot of talk about his divorce... There is talk that the president may be deposed.* — V = gossip; ▸ N UNCOUNT : USU WITH SUPP

7 If you **talk** a particular way, you use spoken language with a particular accent or type of voice. EG *They listened to records that taught them to talk properly... She talks with an Edinburgh accent.* — V+A/ADV = speak

8 To **talk** a language means to use it in conversation. EG *There were a lot of people on the boat talking French... It's one thing to read a language, it's quite different when you have to talk it.* — V+O

9 If you **talk** something such as politics or sport, you discuss it. EG *We used to sit and talk politics all evening... Let's talk a little business, shall we?* ● to **talk shop**: see **shop**. — V+O

10 If you **talk** on or about something, you make an informal speech about it, for example in a college or on the radio, often with some discussion or questions afterwards. EG *I talked yesterday about the problems facing young people in today's society... He has an ability to talk on almost any topic you mention.* ▸ used as a noun. EG *Angus Wilson came here and gave a talk last week... This term we are having talks on careers overseas.* — V+A *(on/about)* ⇑ speak; ▸ N COUNT

11 To **talk** of or about a particular word means to use the word that most clearly or appropriately expresses what you mean. EG *One shouldn't talk of an agreement but rather of a possible compromise... When you talk about prose and poems do you mean literature?* — V+A *(of/about)* = speak

12 If you **talk** yourself hoarse, **talk** yourself into trouble, etc, you get yourself into a particular condition or state of mind by talking. EG *She talked herself hoarse... She talked herself into a state of righteous indignation.* — V+O (REFL)+C/A ⇑ become

13 If someone is **talking sense**, they are expressing opinions that you think are sensible. EG *He was talking sense for once.* — PHR : VB INFLECTS

14 If someone is **talking nonsense** or **talking rubbish**, they are expressing opinions that are stupid or not based on facts. EG *'I'll get another job! I'll move away!'–'Don't talk nonsense.'* — PHR : VB INFLECTS

15 If you say **'talk about ...'**, you mean that the thing that you mention is or was very noticeable; an informal expression. EG *Did you see the film last night? Talk about laugh! I've never laughed so much in my life.* — PHR+C

16 If you say **'talking of ...'**, you are introducing the thing that you mention as a new topic that you want to discuss, after it has already been mentioned in another context. EG *Talking of marriage, did you know that Jill's getting married again ?... Talking of cleaning, it's about time you did the windows, isn't it?* — PHR+O = speaking of

17 **Talks** are formal discussions intended to produce a new agreement or a change in policy, usually between different countries or between employers and employees. EG *Talks in London last week produced no hint of a settlement... Further arms talks are to be held.* ▸ used as a verb. EG *At least the superpowers are talking to one another.* — N PLURAL = negotiations; ▸ V+A = negotiate

18 **Talk** is things that people say that do not have any real meaning or that are exaggerated. EG *She says she's a millionaire, but I think it's just talk... She's all talk.* — N UNCOUNT = hot air

19 If you say to someone **'you can talk'**, you mean that they are just as guilty of some fault as someone else they have been talking about. EG *'And she's so untidy around the house.'–'You can talk!'* — CONVENTION

20 If you say to someone **'now you're talking'**, you mean that they are at last saying something that you want to hear, for example they have just made a good suggestion or offer. — CONVENTION

21 to **talk through** your **hat**: see **hat**.

talk back. If you **talk back** to someone, you answer them in a rude way, especially someone such as a parent or teacher. EG *Don't you dare talk back to me like that!* — PHRASAL VB : V+ADV = answer back

talk down. 1 If someone **talks** you **down**, they talk longer and louder than you do and so make you stop talking. EG *Mr Smith talked down all the other members of the committee.* — PHRASAL VB : V+O+ADV ⇑ silence

2 To **talk down** the pilot of an aircraft means to give him or her instructions over the radio on how to land the aircraft, in bad weather or in an emergency. EG *The pilot was talked down through the fog and made a perfect landing.* — PHRASAL VB : V+O+ADV ⇑ instruct

3 If someone **talks down to** you, they talk to you in a way that shows that they think that they are more important or clever than you. EG *Children always sense immediately when you are talking down to them.* — PHRASAL VB : V+ADV+PREP ⇑ patronize

talk into. If you **talk** someone **into** doing something, you persuade them to do it by continually telling them why they should do it; an informal — PHRASAL VB : V+O+PREP+-ING/ ≠ talk out of

zoology, Edinburgh is the place to go to... The library didn't have any zoology textbooks. ◊ **zoological** /zu:ə⁷lɒdʒə¹kə⁰l/. EG *...the Zoological Society... ...zoological specimens.* ◊ **zoologist, zoologists.** EG *Many zoologists in Europe regarded her ideas as being ridiculous.* ◊ ADJ CLASSIF : ATTRIB ◊ N COUNT ⇑ scientist

zoom /zu:m/, **zooms, zooming, zoomed.** 1 To **zoom** somewhere means to go there very quickly indeed. EG *They zoomed down to Folkestone on their bikes... He's always zooming off to New York or somewhere... Vast dragonflies zoom over the blue water.* ▸ used as a noun. EG *...the zoom of motorbikes on the night air.* V : USU+A = speed ▸ N UNCOUNT

2 If prices or sales **zoom**, they increase very rapidly. EG *By the end of the month sales had zoomed to 33 million.* V : USU+A = shoot up

zoom in. If a camera **zooms in** on the person or thing being photographed, it gives a close-up picture of them. PHRASAL VB : V+ADV

zoom out. If a camera **zooms** out, it draws back from the person or thing being photographed and shows the things that surround them. PHRASAL VB : V+ADV

zoom lens, zoom lenses. A **zoom lens** is a lens that is attached to the front of a camera in order to allow you to make the detail larger or smaller while always keeping the picture clear. N COUNT

zucchini /zʊki:ni:/. **Zucchini** is both the singular and the plural form. **Zucchini** are small vegetable marrows; used mainly in American English. N COUNT : USU PLURAL

Zulu /zu:lu:/, **Zulus.** 1 A **Zulu** is a member of a race of black people who live in Southern Africa. N COUNT

2 **Zulu** is a language, spoken by Zulus and also by many other black South Africans. N UNCOUNT

expression. EG *She talked me into taking a week's holiday.*

talk out. If you **talk out** something such as a problem, you discuss it thoroughly in order to settle it. EG *The trade unions and the management began talking things out between them.* PHRASAL VB : V+O+ADV

talk out of. If you **talk** someone **out of** doing something, you persuade them not to do it by continually telling them why they should not do it. EG *He tried to talk me out of buying such a big car.* PHRASAL VB : V+O+ADV+PREP+-ING/O ≠ talk into

talk over. If you **talk** something **over**, you think about it and discuss it thoroughly. EG *I agreed to go home and talk things over with my father... We all met in Pat's room, to talk over what we had seen.* PHRASAL VB : V+O+ADV

talk round. 1 If you **talk** someone **round**, you persuade them to change their mind and agree with you or agree to do what you want them to do. EG *He didn't really want to go to France, but I managed to talk him round.* PHRASAL VB : V+O+ADV

2 If people **talk round** a subject or problem, they discuss it in a general way, often failing to deal with the central points. PHRASAL VB : V+PREP

talkative /tɔ:kətɪv/. Someone who is **talkative** talks a lot. EG *Shy students are sometimes discouraged by the more talkative members of the class... John wasn't very talkative, but he was pleasant to be with.* ADJ QUALIT = chatty ≠ quiet

talker /tɔ:kə/, **talkers**. A **talker** is a person who can talk in the way mentioned, usually well, persuasively, or quickly. EG *He is very much at ease in life and is a good talker... He is the best talker in the village.* N COUNT+SUPP

talkie /tɔ:ki[1]/, **talkies**. A **talkie** is a cinema film made with sound as well as pictures; a very old-fashioned word. EG *...in the days of the silent film and the early talkies.* N COUNT : USU PL ≠ silent film

talking book, talking books. A **talking book** is a tape or cassette recording of a book, made especially for use by people who are blind. N COUNT

talking point, talking points; also spelled with a hyphen. A **talking point** is an interesting subject for discussion or argument. EG *His own prospects were still a talking point.* N COUNT ⇑ topic

talking-to. If you give someone a **talking-to**, you tell them that you are angry about something that they have done. EG *My teacher gave me a real talking-to for not doing my homework... I got a hell of a talking-to when I got home.* N SING : *a*+N = telling-off, scolding

talk show, talk shows. A **talk show** is a television or radio show in which an interviewer and his or her guests talk in a friendly, informal way about different topics. N COUNT = chat show

tall /tɔ:l/, **taller, tallest**. 1 Someone or something that is **tall** has a greater height than is normal or average. EG *He was a tall, dark and undeniably handsome man... In the background is a tall cypress tree... ...two tall glasses of pineapple juice.* ADJ QUALIT ⇑ big

2 **Tall** is used when you are asking what height someone or something is, when you are describing how high they are, or when you are comparing the height of one person or thing with another. EG *How tall is he?... He was about six feet tall... ...a six-foot tall fifteen-year-old... She is starting to put on weight and grow taller.* ADJ QUALIT

3 If you say that someone **walks tall**, you mean that they behave in a way that shows they have pride in themselves and in what they are doing. EG *The British policeman can still walk tall.* PHR : VB INFLECTS

4 If you say that a task is a **tall order**, you mean that it is going to be difficult to succeed in it, but that you have to try anyway; an informal expression. EG *It was a bit of a tall order to expect us to do the whole job in three days.* PHR : *a*+PHR, USED AS C

tallish /tɔ:lɪʃ/. If you describe someone as **tallish**, you mean that they are fairly tall; an informal word. EG *The door was opened by a thin, tallish woman with a lined face.* ADJ CLASSIF

tallow /tæləʊ/ is hard animal fat used for making candles and soap. N UNCOUNT

tall story, tall stories. A **tall story** is a story or statement that is difficult to believe, usually because it is so exaggerated or unlikely. EG *He was full of tall stories.* N COUNT

tally /tæli[1]/, **tallies, tallying, tallied**. 1 A **tally** is a record of amounts, such as how much you spend or how many points you score during a game, which you can keep adding to as you go along. EG *Can you keep a tally of your own marks, please?... The tally had now reached thirty-six.* N COUNT : USU SING, IF+PREP THEN *of*

2 If two or more numbers or statements of events **tally**, they are the same as each other or are consistent with each other. EG *We've checked their stories and they don't quite tally... The amount she said she had received failed to tally with the figure shown in the records.* V OR V+A (*with*) : RECIP = correspond

Talmud /tælmʊd/. The **Talmud** is the collection of ancient Jewish laws which governs the religious and non-religious life of Orthodox Jews. N PROPER : *the*+N

talon /tælən/, **talons**. The **talons** of a bird of prey, such as an eagle, are its hooked claws. EG *The owls' formidable talons can carry birds up to the size of a chicken.* N COUNT : USU PL

tamarind /tæmərɪnd/, **tamarinds**. A **tamarind** is a tropical evergreen tree which has pleasant-smelling flowers and edible fruit. N COUNT

tamarisk /tæmərɪsk/, **tamarisks**. A **tamarisk** is a bush or small tree which grows mainly around the Mediterranean and in Asia, and which has feathery pink or white flowers. N COUNT

tambourine /tæmbəri:n/, **tambourines**. A **tambourine** is a musical instrument which you shake or hit with your hand. It consists of a drum skin on a circular frame and small round pieces of metal all around the edge. N COUNT

tame /teɪm/, **tames, taming, tamed; tamer, tamest**. 1 A **tame** animal or bird is one that is not afraid of humans or violent towards them, because it is used to being with them. EG *We decided to let it go because it would never have got tame; wild birds never do in cages... ...a tame monkey.* ◊ **tameness**. EG *We fed them for a while, amazed at their tameness.* ADJ QUALIT = domesticated ≠ wild ◊ N UNCOUNT

2 If you describe someone as **tame**, you mean that they tend to do what they are told without questioning or criticizing it. EG *...the urbane societies of the West, with their tame populations made gentle by decades of prosperity.* ◊ **tamely**. EG *These measures are unlikely to be accepted as tamely as the government hopes.* ADJ QUALIT = compliant ◊ ADV WITH VB = meekly

3 An activity that is **tame** is considered to be uninteresting because it does not involve any excitement or risk. EG *It sounded like a rather tame party.* ADJ QUALIT = flat, dull

4 If someone **tames** a wild animal or bird, they train it not to be afraid of humans and to be obedient. EG *He made quite a name for himself taming hawks.* V+O

5 If people **tame** something such as land, they change it from a wild or unmanageable state to a neat or manageable one. EG *Within two years they had tamed this inhospitable landscape.* V+O = conquer

6 If you **tame** someone or something that is dangerous or likely to cause trouble, you bring them under control. EG *This urge to take revenge is something that we have to tame.* V+O

tammy /tæmi[1]/, **tammies**. A **tammy** is a soft woollen hat, similar to a beret but with a bobble in the centre, worn especially by women. N COUNT

tam o'shanter /tæm əʃæntə/, **tam o'shanters**. A **tam o'shanter** is a soft woollen hat with a bobble in the centre, worn especially by Scots. N COUNT

tamp /tæmp/, **tamps, tamping, tamped**. If you **tamp** something **down**, you press it down by tapping it several times so that it becomes more solid and compact. EG *One man shovelled tarmac into the hole, the other tamped it down.* PHRASAL VB : V+O+ADV = pack down

Tampax /tæmpæks/. **Tampax** is both the singular and the plural form. **Tampax** is a trademark for a particular make of tampon. N COUNT/UNCOUNT

tamper /tæmpə/, **tampers, tampering, tampered**. If you **tamper with** something, you interfere with it or try to change it when you have no right to do so. EG *Someone had tampered with the register of the church and changed the christening records... He claimed that his briefcase had been tampered with on the flight.* PHRASAL VB : V+PREP, HAS PASS

tampon /tæmpɒn/, **tampons**. A **tampon** is a firm, specially shaped piece of cotton wool that a woman puts inside her vagina to absorb the blood when she has a period. N COUNT

tan /tæn/, **tans, tanning, tanned**. 1 If someone has a **tan**, their skin has become darker than it usually is as a result of spending a lot of time in the sun. EG *Her bare legs and arms had lost all their tan.* N SING : *a*+N = suntan

2 If you **tan**, your skin turns darker because you have spent a lot of time in the sun. EG *He was never going* V-ERG = go brown

to tan, no matter how many months he spent in the sun. ◊ **tanned**. EG *Everybody was so tanned. I don't think there was any rain all summer... ...the tanned, slim young men.* ◊ ADJ QUALIT = suntanned

3 Something that is **tan** is of a light yellowish-brown colour. EG *I bought a pair of tan shoes.* ADJ COLOUR

4 To **tan** an animal's skin means to make it into leather by treating it with tannin or other chemicals. EG *...a large piece of tanned hide.* V+O

5 If you **tan** someone's **hide**, you punish them by hitting them hard or repeatedly; an old-fashioned use. EG *He'll tan your hide if you do that again.* PHR : VB INFLECTS = wallop

tandem /tændəᵒm/, **tandems**. 1 A **tandem** is a bicycle designed for two riders, with one rider sitting behind the other. EG *We travelled round Cornwall on a tandem.* N COUNT

2 When two people are riding **tandem**, they are riding one behind the other. EG *Tom and Ruth arrived, riding tandem.* ADV AFTER VB

3 **in tandem**. 3.1 If something happens or is done **in tandem with** something else, or if two things happen **in tandem**, they happen at the same time. EG *In tandem with these changes must come a change in our attitudes to work and leisure.* PREP, OR PHR : USED AS AN A ⇑ together 3.2 If someone does something **in tandem with** someone else, or if they do it **in tandem**, they do it by working together. EG *...a new play we had written in tandem.* PREP, OR PHR : USED AS AN A

tandoori /tændʊəri¹/ is an Indian method of cooking meat in a clay oven. N UNCOUNT

tang /tæŋ/, **tangs**. A **tang** is a strong sharp smell or taste. EG *...the tang of an expensive perfume... The cologne gave a tang to the air around him.* N COUNT : USU SING

tangent /tændʒənt/, **tangents**. 1 A **tangent** is a line that touches the edge of a curve or circle at one point, but does not cross it. N COUNT

2 If you **go off at a tangent**, you start saying or thinking something that does not seem to be connected with what you had been saying or thinking before. PHR : VB INFLECTS

tangential /tændʒenʃəl/. A remark, method, etc that is **tangential** has only a slight or indirect connection with something else; a fairly formal word. EG *My remark was considered somewhat tangential.* ◊ **tangentially**. EG *You can either confront a problem directly or approach it tangentially.* ADJ QUALIT ≠ central ◊ ADV WITH VB

tangerine /tændʒəriːn/, **tangerines**. A **tangerine** is a small, sweet orange with a loose skin which you can easily remove. N COUNT

tangible /tændʒəˈbəᵒl/. Something that is **tangible** is clear enough or definite enough to be easily seen, felt, or noticed. EG *His brief rule as Prime Minister brought few tangible benefits to the poor... Then there are less tangible factors like job satisfaction.* ◊ **tangibly**. EG *The only available evidence tangibly supports his claim.* ADJ QUALIT = concrete ◊ ADV WITH VB

tangle /tæŋgəᵒl/, **tangles, tangling, tangled**. 1 A **tangle** is 1.1 a mass of things such as string, wire, or hair that are twisted together in an untidy way so that they are difficult to unravel or smooth out. EG *On their left was an impenetrable tangle of creepers and trees... There were tangles of barbed wire on the wall.* N COUNT : IF + PREP THEN *of* = knot 1.2 a state of disorder and confusion. EG *My tax affairs were in a complete tangle.* N SING WITH DET 1.3 a complicated problem or situation. EG *A legal contract does help to straighten out the tangles when the relationship breaks up.* N COUNT 1.4 a quarrel, fight, or small battle. EG *...messy tangles across a militarily open border.* N COUNT = skirmish

2 If something **tangles** or if you **tangle** it, it becomes twisted together in an untidy way so that it is difficult to unravel or smooth out. EG *He shouldn't have allowed the strings of the parachute to tangle.* V-ERG

3 If you **are tangled** in something such as a mass of wires or ropes or if you **are tangled up** in them, you are caught or trapped in them so that it is difficult to get free. EG *His leg may have got tangled in a harpoon line.* V+O+A, OR PHRASAL VB : V+O+ADV+A : ONLY PASS

tangle up. If you **tangle** something **up**, you twist it into an untidy mass so that it is difficult to unravel or smooth out. EG *Don't do that, you're tangling them up!* PHRASAL VB : V+O+ADV

tangle with. If you **tangle with** someone, you get involved in a fight or quarrel with them, especially one that you are unlikely to win. EG *I wouldn't tangle with him if I were you.* PHRASAL VB : V+PREP, HAS PASS

tangled /tæŋgəᵒld/. Something that is **tangled** is 1 twisted together in an untidy way so that it is difficult to unravel or smooth out. EG *She pushed the tangled hair back from her face... ...tangled string... The wires got all tangled.* ADJ QUALIT = matted 2 complicated in a confused and disorderly way. EG *The negotiations became hopelessly tangled and confused.* ADJ QUALIT

tango /tæŋgəʊ/, **tangos, tangoing, tangoed**. 1 A **tango** is a South American dance for two people that has an unusual, very strong rhythm. EG *Can you do the tango?* N COUNT

2 When you **tango**, you dance the tango. V

tangy /tæŋi¹/, **tangier, tangiest**. A **tangy** flavour or smell is one that is sharp, especially a flavour like lemon juice or a smell like that of sea air. ADJ QUALIT = piquant

tank /tæŋk/, **tanks**. A **tank** is 1 a large container, usually made of metal or glass, which is designed to store or hold liquid or gas. EG *The tank will only hold three gallons... There's a leak in the cold water tank... ...a petrol tank.* N COUNT ▸ You also use **tank** to refer to the liquid or gas inside a tank or the amount of liquid or gas it contains. EG *It will go over 500 miles on a single tank of petrol.* ▸ N COUNT : ALSO N PART+N UNCOUNT ● See also **septic tank**. 2 a military vehicle covered with strong metal armour to protect the soldiers inside it, which is equipped with guns or rockets, and which moves along on metal tracks fitted over the wheels. EG *Their equipment included more than 2,000 tanks... ...a tank battalion.* N COUNT

tankard /tæŋkəd/, **tankards**. A **tankard** is a large mug with a handle, usually made of metal, which you can drink beer from. EG *Imagine that you are in an oak-beamed country pub with your tankard of ale.* N COUNT : ALSO N PART+N UNCOUNT

tanked up. Someone who is **tanked up** is very drunk; a very informal use. EG *They were pretty well tanked up before they even got to the party.* ADJ QUALIT : PRED = sozzled

tanker /tæŋkə/, **tankers**. A **tanker** is a ship, truck, or railway vehicle used for transporting large quantities of gas or liquid, especially oil. N COUNT, OR *by*+N

tanner /tænə/, **tanners**. A **tanner** is 1 someone whose job is making leather from animal skins. N COUNT 2 a coin that is no longer used which was worth six pence in old British currency; an informal use. N COUNT

tannery /tænəri¹/, **tanneries**. A **tannery** is a place where animal skins are made into leather. EG *Our leather was bought from a tannery in Ipswich.* N COUNT

tannic acid /tænɪk æsɪd/ is the same as tannin. N UNCOUNT

tannin /tænɪn/ is a yellow or brown chemical found in plants such as tea, which is used in the process of making leather and in dyeing. N UNCOUNT

Tannoy /tænɔɪ/; a trademark. The **Tannoy** is a system of loudspeakers used to make public announcements, for example at a fete or at a sports stadium. EG *Could you make an announcement over the Tannoy?* N SING WITH DET = PA

tantalize /tæntəlaɪz/, **tantalizes, tantalizing, tantalized**; also spelled **tantalise**. If you **tantalize** someone, you make them feel hopeful and excited, and then disappoint them, for example by showing or offering them something that they want and then not letting them have it. EG *They've been tantalizing him with vague hints about what's happening.* V+O ⇑ tease ◊ **tantalizing**. EG *This raises the tantalizing possibility that there may be life on other stars.* ◊ ADJ QUALIT ◊ **tantalizingly**. EG *Sometimes a new idea may be tantalizingly close.* ◊ ADV

tantamount /tæntəmaʊnt/. If you say that an action, event, or state of affairs is **tantamount** to something else, you mean that its real effect or value is in fact the same as the other thing it is being compared to. EG *His statement was tantamount to an admission of responsibility... His bail was so low that it was tantamount to no bail at all.* ADJ CLASSIF : PRED+*to* ⇑ equal = as good as

tantrum /tæntrəm/, **tantrums**. A **tantrum** is a sudden noisy outburst of bad temper, especially by a child or by someone behaving in a childish way. EG *...children who act out their frustration in temper tantrums... He was warned that one more tantrum like that and he would be thrown out of the team.* N COUNT = scene, fit

Taoism /taʊɪzəᵒm/ is a Chinese religion which believes that people should lead a simple, honest life and not interfere with the course of natural events. N UNCOUNT

tap /tæp/, **taps, tapping, tapped**. 1 A **tap** is a device that controls the flow of a liquid or gas from a pipe or container. Taps are often attached to a sink or bath. EG *Someone left the tap running... Turn on the hot tap... ...a gas tap.* N COUNT = faucet

2 **on tap**. 2.1 Beer or other alcoholic drink that is **on tap** is in a barrel with a tap on it, rather than in a bottle. EG *They have several well-known real ales on tap.* PHR : USED AS AN A 2.2 If something such as information or advice is PHR : USED AS AN

on tap, it is available and ready for immediate use. EG *We've got all the information permanently on tap on a computer.* A

3 If you **tap** something, you hit it with a quick light blow or a series of quick light blows. EG *It will come loose if you tap it sharply with a hammer... I tapped him on the shoulder... She tapped on the glass partition and the car stopped... Others tap away at their typewriters.* ▸ used as a noun. EG *She gave him a little tap on the arm... I heard a soft tap at the front door.*
V OR V+O : USU+A = rap
▸ N COUNT = rap

4 If you **tap** a sound or if you **tap it out**, you produce it by hitting a surface lightly and repeatedly. EG *He was humming tunelessly and tapping an annoying rhythm on his glass... I could hear the telegraph instrument tapping out morse.*
V+O, OR PHRASAL VB : V+O+ADV = rap, beat

5 If you **tap** your fingers or feet, you make a rhythmic sound because you hit a surface lightly and repeatedly with them. EG *She was tapping one foot to the music.* V+O

6 If you **tap** a resource or situation, you make use of it by getting from it something that you need or want. EG *...a new way of tapping the sun's energy... ...commercial interests seeking to tap the expanding 'leisure' industry.*
V+O = draw on, exploit

7 If you **tap** someone for something, you persuade them to give you something that you want, especially money or information; an informal use. EG *They've been trying to tap me for information about the exam.*
V+O+A *(for)* = pump

8 If someone **taps** your telephone, they attach a special device to the line so that they can secretly listen to your conversations. EG *I think my phone has been tapped.*
V+O = bug

9 If you **tap** a tree such as a rubber tree, you get liquid out of it by making a hole in its trunk. V+O

10 Tap is also the same as tap dancing. N UNCOUNT

tap dancer, tap dancers; also spelled with a hyphen. A **tap dancer** is a dancer who does tap dancing. N COUNT

tap dancing; also spelled with a hyphen. **Tap dancing** is a style of dancing in which the dancers wear special shoes with pieces of metal on the heels and toes. The shoes make clicking noises as the dancers move their feet.
N UNCOUNT = tap

tape /teɪp/, **tapes, taping, taped**. **1 Tape** is plastic in the form of a long thin strip covered with a magnetic substance. It is used to record sounds such as speech or music, images such as television pictures, or numbers and other symbols for use in a computer. EG *We wanted to get all the conversation down on tape... ...a conversation recorded on tape... ...blank tape.* • See also **magnetic tape, video tape**. N UNCOUNT

2 A **tape** is **2.1** a cassette or spool with magnetic tape wound round it, used for recording or replaying sounds on a tape recorder, pictures and sounds on a video recorder, or information on a computer. EG *Do you want to put on a tape?... I returned his tapes with a short letter.* **2.2** the music, conversation, or pictures that have been recorded or stored on a particular length of magnetic tape. EG *His manager persuaded him to make a tape of the song... ...transcripts of tapes... This tape is in German.*
N COUNT
N COUNT = recording

3 If you **tape** speech, music, or pictures, you record them using a tape recorder or video recorder. EG *I'm having to tape this talk several days in advance... ...a taped commentary... You're not taping now are you?*
V+O = tape-record

4 A **tape** is also **4.1** a long narrow strip of cloth which is sewn onto a piece of clothing or some other piece of material. Tapes are used to tie things together or to identify who a piece of clothing belongs to. EG *Use the tapes that are sewn inside the tent flap to tie it back... You have to sew name tapes into everything when your child first goes to school... ...three metres of white tape.* **4.2** a ribbon that is stretched across the finishing line of a race. EG *The crowd cheered loudly as the local runner broke the tape.*
N COUNT/ UNCOUNT
N COUNT : IF SING *the*+N

5 Tape is also plastic in the form of a narrow strip which has one sticky side, and which you use to stick things such as pieces of paper together. EG *...a bit of adhesive tape... ...attached by sticky tape to a cardboard tube.* • See also **masking tape**.
N MASS : USU MOD +N

6 If you **tape** something to something else, you attach it or fix it there using adhesive tape. EG *I tape lists to the fridge door... Anne dabbed the cuts with disinfectant and taped a gauze square over them.*
V+O+A ⇑ stick

7 If you **have** someone or something **taped**, you understand them completely and know how to deal with them; an informal expression. EG *She thinks she's got him taped.*
PHR : AUX INFLECTS

8 See also **red tape**.

tape deck, tape decks. A **tape deck** is a machine which can play or record tapes of speech or music. N COUNT

tape drive, tape drives. A **tape drive** is a machine which can be used to transfer information from a tape onto a computer, or to store information from a computer; a technical term. N COUNT

tape measure, tape measures; also spelled with a hyphen. A **tape measure** is a long, narrow strip of plastic or cloth that has centimetres or inches marked on it so that you can use it for measuring things such as material or the size of your body. N COUNT

taper /teɪpə/, **tapers, tapering, tapered**. **1** If something **tapers**, it becomes gradually thinner at one end. EG *...long tapering fingers... Most jeans these days taper towards the ankle.* ◊ **tapered**. EG *The trousers should have tapered legs.*
V
◊ ADJ QUALIT

2 A **taper** is a long, thin, fast-burning candle, used mainly for lighting gas fires. N COUNT

taper off. If something **tapers off**, it becomes greatly reduced in size or quantity. EG *...in the 1970s, as the economic boom tapered off... The wailing of the sirens tapered off.*
PHRASAL VB : V+ADV ⇑ reduce = die down

tape-record, tape-records, tape-recording, tape-recorded. If you **tape-record** speech, music, etc, you use a tape recorder to record it on tape. EG *If I could tape-record half an hour or more of the conversation, that would be fine.* V+O

tape recorder, tape recorders; also spelled with a hyphen. A **tape recorder** is a machine used for recording and playing music, speech, or other sounds on tape. N COUNT

tape recording, tape recordings; also spelled with a hyphen. A **tape recording** is music, speech, or other sounds that have been recorded onto tape. EG *This tape recording demonstrates some of the features of the Norfolk dialect.* N COUNT

tapestry /tæpɪstri[1]/, **tapestries**. A **tapestry** is **1** a large piece of heavy cloth which has a picture sewn on it using coloured threads. Large tapestries were made in former times as decorative coverings for walls. EG *...the famous Bayeux tapestry.* **2** a piece of embroidery or needlework that is done by stitching canvas with wool to make a picture or pattern. EG *They're experts in stretching and framing tapestries.*
N COUNT/ UNCOUNT
N COUNT/ UNCOUNT

3 a situation or sequence of events that is considered to be colourful and complicated because it is made up of many different kinds of things or people. EG *The book presents a tapestry of teenage life in the provinces.*
N COUNT+*of* ⇑ picture

tapeworm /teɪpwɜ:m/, **tapeworms**. A **tapeworm** is a long flat creature which lives in the stomach and intestines of animals or people. Tapeworms are parasites and get their food from the body of the animal or person they live in. N COUNT

tapioca /tæpi[1]əʊkə/ is a food consisting of white grains, rather like rice, which come from the cassava plant.
N UNCOUNT ⇑ starch

tapir /teɪpə/, **tapirs**. A **tapir** is an animal similar to a pig, which has a long snout and lives in tropical America. N COUNT

tappet /tæpɪt/, **tappets**. A **tappet** is a lever in an engine that moves up and down, transferring movement from one part of the machine to another. N COUNT

tar /tɑ:/, **tars, tarring, tarred**. **1 Tar** is a thick black sticky substance that becomes hard when it is cold. Tar is used especially for making roads, and is also produced when tobacco burns. N UNCOUNT

2 To **tar and feather** someone means to punish them by smearing them with tar and then covering them with feathers.
PHR : VBS INFLECT

3 See also **tarred**.

taramasalata /təræ:məsəlɑ:tə/ is a pink, creamy food made from the eggs of fish such as cod or mullet. It is usually eaten at the beginning of a meal. N UNCOUNT

tarantula /tərænʧə[1]lə/, **tarantulas**. A **tarantula** is a large hairy spider which has a poisonous bite. N COUNT

tardy /tɑ:di[1]/, **tardier, tardiest**; a fairly literary word. Something that is **tardy** **1** happens or is done later than it should or than it was expected to. EG *I spent Monday morning writing tardy 'thank you' letters.* ◊ **tardily**. EG *He always replied rather tardily to my letters.* ◊ **tardiness**. EG *I apologize for my*
ADJ QUALIT ⇑ late
◊ ADV WITH VB
◊ N UNCOUNT

tardiness in getting here. 2 moves or happens slowly. EG *We made tardy progress across the ice.* ADJ QUALIT = sluggish
◊ **tardiness.** EG *...the tardiness of evolution.* ◊ N UNCOUNT

target /tɑːgɪt/, **targets, targeting, targeted.** 1 A **target** is 1.1 a town, building, or other place at which a weapon such as a missile or bomb is aimed. EG *The missile is capable of landing within a half-mile radius of its target... The station was an easy target for an air attack... The village is within the main target area.* N COUNT 1.2 an object at which you fire arrows or bullets when you are shooting for sport or practice. It usually consists of a board with circles marked on it. EG *My first two shots missed the target... Bad light and a target at twenty yards makes it difficult.* N COUNT 1.3 a person or thing that someone else is attacking, for example someone who is being criticized. EG *In their search for a scapegoat, the Government found an easy target in the unions... Her proposal has been the target of much criticism.* N COUNT : USU + *of/for* ⇑ object = butt 1.4 a result that you aim to achieve, for example an amount of profit that you hope to make or a quantity of goods that you hope to sell. EG *It set a target for economic growth in excess of 4% a year... The latest sales figures are dead on target.* N COUNT OR *on*+ N UNCOUNT ⇑ objective
2 If someone **targets** a missile or some other weapon on something, they aim it at that thing. EG *...weapons which they have targeted on inland airfields.* V+O+A : USU PASS

tariff /tærɪf/, **tariffs**. A **tariff** is 1 a tax that a government collects on goods coming into a country. EG *...a high tariff on all imports.* N COUNT 2 a list of fixed prices for services, especially the prices of rooms, meals, etc in a hotel. EG *May I see your tariff, please?* N COUNT 3 the rate at which you are charged for public services such as gas and electricity; used mainly in British English. EG *Check that you are on the correct tariff.* N COUNT : USU MOD+N

tarmac /tɑːmæk/. 1 **Tarmac** is a material used for making road surfaces, consisting of crushed stones mixed with tar. EG *...a tarmac road.* N UNCOUNT
2 The **tarmac** is an area that has a surface of tarmac, especially the part of an airport where planes stand before they take off or after they land. EG *We had to wait for an hour on the tarmac.* N SING : *the*+N

tarn /tɑːn/, **tarns**. A **tarn** is a small lake in an area of mountains. N COUNT : ALSO IN NAMES

tarnish /tɑːnɪʃ/, **tarnishes, tarnishing, tarnished.** 1 If something **tarnishes** metal or if metal **tarnishes**, it becomes stained and loses its brightness. EG *The damp atmosphere tends to tarnish the brass taps... Chrome doesn't tarnish easily.* V-ERG
◊ **tarnished.** EG *There was a photo in a silver frame, by now rather tarnished.* ◊ ADJ QUALIT
2 If something **tarnishes** someone's reputation, it causes people to have a worse opinion of them than they used to. EG *It turned into a witch-hunt that tarnished the names of many of the country's intellectuals.* V+O = taint ◊ **tarnished.** EG *...an attempt to restore some of their tarnished popularity.* ◊ ADJ QUALIT = tainted

tarot /tærəʊ/. The **tarot** is a pack of cards with pictures on them that is used to predict what will happen to people in the future. EG *It is not known who invented the tarot... He sat cross-legged on the floor laying out tarot cards.* N SING : USU *the*+N

tarpaulin /tɑːpɔːlɪn/, **tarpaulins.** 1 **Tarpaulin** is a fabric made of canvas or similar material coated with tar, wax, paint, or other waterproof substance. N UNCOUNT
2 A **tarpaulin** is a sheet of heavy waterproof material that is used to cover things in order to protect them against rain. EG *The deck cargo was covered with a large tarpaulin.* N COUNT ⇑ covering

tarragon /tærəgən/ is a small European herb with narrow leaves which are used to add flavour to food. EG *Season it with a teaspoon of chopped tarragon.* N UNCOUNT

tarred /tɑːd/. 1 A road that is **tarred** has a surface of tar. ADJ CLASSIF
2 If you say that two or more people are **tarred with the same brush**, you mean that they all have the same faults; an informal expression. EG *She does seem to be tarred with the same brush as Bertrand as far as ruthlessness is concerned.* PHR : USED AS C

tarry, tarries, tarrying, tarried. The word **tarry** is pronounced /tæri[1]/ when it is a verb, and /tɑːri[1]/ when it is an adjective. 1 If you **tarry** somewhere, you stay there longer than you meant to and delay leaving; an old-fashioned use. EG *Some stayed overnight, but most tarried only a few hours before moving on.* V : USU+A = linger
2 Something that is **tarry** is covered with tar or marked with tar. EG *...tarry stones from the garage roof.* ADJ QUALIT

tart /tɑːt/, **tarts, tarting, tarted; tarter, tartest.** 1 A **tart** is 1.1 a piece of pastry with an open filling of something sweet such as jam or custard. Tarts can be large and cut into slices, or small and intended for one person only. EG *...raspberry jam tarts... Have another slice of tart.* N COUNT/ UNCOUNT : USU MOD+N 1.2 a fruit pie, with a pastry covering on top. EG *...a plum tart.* N COUNT/ UNCOUNT : USU MOD+N
2 Something such as fruit that is **tart** has an unpleasantly sharp taste. EG *These apples are a bit tart.* ADJ QUALIT = sour
3 A **tart** remark or way of speaking is one that is sharp and unpleasant, often in a way that is rather cruel. EG *She spoke with tart contempt for the Opposition's objections.* ADJ QUALIT = acid, biting ◊ **tartly.** EG *She finished by tartly pointing out that he owed her some money.* ◊ ADV WITH VB
4 In very informal English, a **tart** is also 4.1 a woman or girl whose behaviour is considered to be sexually immoral or whose appearance is considered sexually attractive in an obvious and vulgar way; an offensive use. EG *She's a bit of a tart, but she'd do anything for you.* N COUNT 4.2 a prostitute; an offensive use. EG *They were thinking of picking up a couple of tarts.* N COUNT

tart up. 1 If a woman **tarts** herself **up**, she tries to make herself look especially smart and attractive; used in informal British English. EG *I didn't know whether to tart myself up or just go in my normal clothes.* PHRASAL VB : V+O (REFL)+ADV
2 If someone **tarts up** something such as a room or building, they try to improve its appearance by painting it, putting in new furniture, etc, often with the result that it looks vulgar; used in informal British English. EG *It was a nice old pub till they decided to tart it up.* PHRASAL VB : V+O+ADV ⇑ smarten up

tartan /tɑːtə[0]n/, **tartans.** 1 **Tartan** is woollen cloth with a pattern of lines of different widths and different colours which cross each other at right angles. There are many different designs of tartan, which is traditionally associated with Scotland. EG *...a skirt made of tartan... ...a tartan rug.* N UNCOUNT = plaid
2 A **tartan** is a tartan design that is associated with a particular Scottish clan. EG *...the Mackenzie tartan.* N COUNT+SUPP

tartar /tɑːtə/, **tartars.** 1 **Tartar** is a hard yellowish substance that forms on your teeth. N UNCOUNT
2 A **tartar** is a fierce, bad-tempered person, especially a woman, who is in a position of authority; an offensive use. EG *Their new boss is a bit of a tartar.* N COUNT = tyrant

tartar sauce; also spelled **tartare sauce**. **Tartar sauce** is is a thick cold sauce, usually eaten with fish, consisting of chopped onions and capers mixed with mayonnaise. N UNCOUNT

task /tɑːsk/, **tasks.** 1 A **task** is 1.1 a piece of work which has to be done as a duty or as part of a regular routine, and which may be difficult or unpleasant. EG *...the endless task of classifying and ordering the samples... Modern computers can be applied to a wide range of tasks.* N COUNT = chore 1.2 an important and often difficult piece of work which is undertaken for a particular reason, especially one which is part of a larger project. EG *Our first task is to set up a committee... We need thousands of workers for the task of reconstruction.* N COUNT : USU SING
2 If you **take** someone **to task**, you criticize them or reprimand them in a severe or angry way because of something bad or wrong that they have done. EG *He was taken to task over the poor quality of his work... I took myself to task for having indulged in self-pity.* PHR : VB INFLECTS = scold, rebuke

task force, task forces; also spelled with a hyphen. A **task force** is 1 a small section of an army, navy or air force that is sent to a particular place to deal with a military crisis. EG *...a naval task force of twenty warships.* N COUNT ⇑ group 2 a group of people assembled in order to do a particular piece of work. EG *A Cabinet level task force will visit Liverpool to study the cause of the riots.* N COUNT

taskmaster /tɑːskmɑːstə/, **taskmasters.** A **taskmaster** is a person who makes people work so hard that they feel he or she is unfair. EG *I shall prove a very hard taskmaster, I warn you.* N COUNT

tassel /tæsə[0]l/, **tassels.** A **tassel** is a bunch of short pieces of wool or other material tied together at one end and attached as a decoration to something such as a piece of clothing or a lampshade. EG *...boots with thick soles and leather tassels.* N COUNT

tasselled /tæsəld/. Something that is **tasselled** is decorated with tassels. EG *All the lamps in the room were tasselled.* ADJ CLASSIF

taste /teɪst/, **tastes, tasting, tasted**. **1** **Taste** is one of the five senses that people and animals have. When you have food or drink in your mouth, it is your sense of taste that makes it possible for you to recognize what it is. EG *Some animals have a better sense of taste than others.* N UNCOUNT

2 The **taste** of something that you eat or drink is the quality it has that makes it individual. Because of its taste, you can distinguish it when it is in your mouth from other things that you eat or drink, for example because it is sweet, bitter, or salty. EG *I don't like the taste of fresh fish... There was a sour taste in his mouth... The soup was heavily peppered and spiced to improve the taste.* N COUNT : USU + SUPP = flavour

3 If you have a **taste** of food or drink, you try a small amount of it in order to see what the flavour is like. EG *I opened one of the bottles and had a taste of the contents. Go on, have a little taste.* N SING WITH DET

4 If you have a **taste** of a particular way of life or activity, you have a brief experience of it. EG *The child may already have had a taste of street life.* N SING WITH DET + *of*

5 If you have a **taste** for something, you have a liking or preference for it. EG *These birds acquired a taste for fruit.* N COUNT + *for*

6 A person's **taste** is their choice in the things that they like or buy, for example their clothes, their possessions, or the music that they enjoy; often used with an adjective meaning 'good' or 'bad' that shows your opinion about their choice. EG *I think she has very good taste in clothes... The film wasn't entirely to my taste... Her novels are too violent for my taste.* N UNCOUNT : USU POSS + N

7 **in good taste, in bad taste**. **7.1** When you are discussing something such as a person's choice of clothes, or a piece of music or work of art, you can say that it is **in good taste** or **in bad taste** to indicate whether you think it is elegant and attractive or vulgar and unattractive. EG *I am sure you are going to find his house in very good taste.* PHR : USED AS AN A **7.2** If you say that something that is said or done is **in good taste, in bad taste**, etc, you are talking about how offensive you think it is. EG *That remark was in rather poor taste... Her jokes may be sharp, but they are always in the best possible taste.* PHR : USED AS AN A

8 If you **taste** something that you are eating or drinking, you are aware of its flavour, especially when this is very enjoyable. EG *Roger chewed and swallowed so fast that he hardly tasted the meat... I wish you were with me now so you could taste this remarkable dish.* V + O ⇑ savour

9 If you **taste** some food or drink, you eat or drink a small amount of it in order to try its flavour, for example to see if you like it or not. EG *He insisted on pouring the wine for a guest to taste... He offered the soup to Derek to taste.* V + O = sample

10 If you **taste** something such as a way of life or a pleasure, you experience it for a short period of time. EG *She didn't want to lose the freedom she had tasted.* V + O

11 If food or drink **tastes** of something, it has that particular flavour, which you notice when you eat or drink it. EG *The tea tasted faintly of bitter almonds... She ate a bit of meat which tasted like chicken... Cereal can taste good without sugar.* V + A/C : NO CONT, NO IMPER

taste bud, taste buds; also spelled with a hyphen. Your **taste buds** are the little points on the surface of your tongue which enable you to recognize the flavour of a food or drink. N COUNT : USU PL

tasteful /teɪstful/. Something that is **tasteful** is considered to be attractive, elegant, and of good quality; used showing approval. EG *The bedroom was simple but tasteful.* ◊ **tastefully** EG *Their house was tastefully furnished.* ADJ QUALIT ◊ ADV WITH VB

tasteless /teɪstlɪ[2]s/. Something that is **tasteless** is **1** not enjoyable to eat, because it has very little flavour. EG *The cafeteria serves cold, tasteless pizzas.* ADJ QUALIT = flavourless **2** considered to be unattractive, ugly, and vulgar, and often of poor quality. EG *The room was full of tasteless ornaments.* ◊ **tastelessly**. EG *...a cosy but tastelessly decorated room.* ADJ QUALIT ◊ ADV WITH VB **3** shocking and offensive to other people. EG *He could be very tasteless in his acting... Apart from a few tasteless remarks, he was reasonably well-behaved.* ADJ QUALIT = indelicate

taster /teɪstə/, **tasters**. A **taster** is someone whose job is to taste different wines, teas, or other foods or drinks, in order to test their quality. EG *...a wine taster.* N COUNT

tasty /teɪsti[1]/, **tastier, tastiest**. **1** Something that is **tasty** has a fairly strong and pleasant flavour when you eat it. EG *That meat was really tasty.* ADJ QUALIT

2 If you describe someone as **tasty**, you mean that you think they are very attractive and sexually desirable; used in very informal British English. EG *I met this really tasty bloke.* ADJ QUALIT

tat /tæt/. **1** **Tat** is ornaments, second-hand goods, cheap clothes, etc that are cheap and of bad quality; an informal word. EG *...antique shops full of Victorian tat.* N UNCOUNT

2 **tit for tat**: see **tit**.

tata /tætɑː/ is used in British English as an informal way of saying goodbye. EG *'Tata,' she said, 'Be seeing you.'* CONVENTION = cheerio

tattered /tætəd/. **1** Something such as clothing or paper that is **tattered** is damaged, torn, or crumpled, especially because it has been used a lot over a long period of time. EG *...a man in a tattered shirt... ...carrying some canvasses tied up in tattered brown paper.* ADJ QUALIT = ragged

2 A **tattered** person is one who is wearing clothes that look old and torn. EG *...a tattered, barefoot figure in a jacket three sizes too big.* ADJ QUALIT ⇑ shabby

3 A **tattered** idea, belief, hope, or situation is one that is sad and disappointing because it is has failed or been badly damaged. EG *...a symbol of my torn and tattered past... ...their tattered little secret.* ADJ QUALIT

tatters /tætəz/. **1** Clothes that are **in tatters** are badly torn in several places, so that pieces can easily come off. EG *He lived in a cave and his single robe was in tatters.* PHR : USED AS AN A = in rags

2 If something such as a plan or a person's state of mind is **in tatters**, it is weak, has suffered a lot of damage, and likely to fail completely. EG *Peter was dejected, his confidence in tatters.* PHR : USED AS AN A ⇑ damaged = shattered

tattle /tætə[ə]l/. See **tittle-tattle**.

tattoo /tætuː/, **tattoos, tattooing, tattooed**. **1** A **tattoo** is **1.1** a coloured picture or design on someone's body, made by pricking little holes in the skin and then filling them with small amounts of coloured dye. EG *He had a tattoo on the back of his hand.* N COUNT ⇑ decoration **1.2** a continuous beating on a drum; a military term. N COUNT **1.3** the sound that is made when you are hitting or tapping something quickly and continuously. EG *He beat a frantic tattoo with his hands on the door.* N COUNT : USU SING **1.4** a public display of exercises and music given by members of the army, navy, or air force. EG *He was guest of honour at the Marines' weekly tattoo.* N COUNT

2 If you **tattoo** something such as a design or picture onto a part of someone's body, you mark it there permanently by pricking little holes in the skin and filling them with coloured dye. EG *He had tattooed the name 'Marlene' on his upper arm.* V + O

3 To **tattoo** someone means to put a tattoo or tattoos onto their body. ◊ **tattooed**. EG *He saw the tattooed sailor about to attack the captain.* V + O ◊ ADJ CLASSIF

tattooist /tætuːɪst/, **tattooists**. A **tattooist** is a person who earns money by putting tattoos onto people's bodies. N COUNT

tatty /tæti[1]/, **tattier, tattiest**. Something that is **tatty** is untidy, rather dirty, and looks as if it has not been cared for. EG *...a tatty old peasant skirt.* ADJ QUALIT ⇑ shabby = scruffy

taught /tɔːt/ is the past tense and past participle of **teach**.

taunt /tɔːnt/, **taunts, taunting, taunted**. If you **taunt** someone, you say unkind or insulting things to them, especially about their weaknesses or failures, in order to upset or annoy them. EG *...street marchers taunting the police and fighting them... She had taunted him with not having the courage of his instincts.* ▸ used as a noun. EG *The children had been insulted by other pupils with taunts like 'You haven't got a Dad.'* V + O ⇑ tease ▸ N COUNT ⇑ insult

taut /tɔːt/, **tauter, tautest**. **1** Something that is **taut** is stretched very tight. EG *Wind it round the screws until the wire is taut.* ADJ QUALIT

2 A person who is **taut** is very worried and tense. EG *...his mother looking taut and anxious.* ADJ QUALIT

3 A piece of writing or a film that is **taut** is very concentrated and has no unnecessary or irrelevant details; used showing approval. EG *...his taut and provocative film 'Rough Treatment'.* ADJ QUALIT

tauten /tɔːtə[ə]n/, **tautens, tautening, tautened**. If something **tautens**, it becomes very tightly V stretched. EG *The rope tautened... The sinews in his neck tautened.* **tautological** /tɔ:təlɒdʒɪkə⁰l/. A **tautological** statement is one that uses different words to say the same thing twice. 'The money should be adequate enough' is an example of a tautological statement. ADJ QUALIT

tautology /tɔ:tɒlədʒi¹/, **tautologies**. A **tautology** is a statement which uses different words to say the same thing twice. ▸ used as an uncount noun. EG *...a speech full of tautology.* N COUNT ▸ N UNCOUNT

tavern /tævə⁰n/, **taverns**. 1 In British English, a **tavern** is the same as a pub; a very old-fashioned use. N COUNT: ALSO IN NAMES

2 In American English, a **tavern** is the same as a bar; a very old-fashioned use. N COUNT

tawdry /tɔ:dri¹/, **tawdrier, tawdriest**. Something that is **tawdry** is cheap and of bad quality, although at first sight it may seem attractive. EG *He was looking at some rather tawdry hats in a shop window.* ADJ QUALIT

tawny /tɔ:ni¹/, **tawnier, tawniest**. Something, especially fur or skin, that is **tawny** is yellowish-brown in colour. EG *...tawny cats... ...a tawny sunset.* ADJ COLOUR

tax /tæks/, **taxes, taxing, taxed**. 1 A **tax** is an amount of money that you have to pay to the government so that it can pay for public services. You usually pay a percentage of your income as tax, companies pay some of their profits as tax, and the price of most goods and services includes a certain amount of tax. EG *A cut in taxes will mean a cut in government spending... ...a tax on pensions... ...and you make a tax return to the Inland Revenue... The tax cuts take effect on July 1st.* ▸ used as an uncount noun. EG *...assets on which tax is payable.* ● See also **income tax, purchase tax**. N COUNT ▸ N UNCOUNT

2 If earnings or sums of money **are taxed**, a percentage of them has to be paid to the government. EG *Any money earned over that level is taxed at the rate of 59%.* V+O: USU PASS ⇑ levy

3 If goods **are taxed**, a percentage of their price has to be paid to the government. EG *Household goods are taxed at the rate of 15%.* V+O: USU PASS ⇑ levy

4 If a person or company **is taxed**, they have to pay a part of their income or profits to the government. EG *The government's policy is to tax the rich more heavily than the poor... Under that system, the wife was not taxed separately from her husband.* V+O: USU PASS ⇑ levy

5 When you **tax** your car or motorbike, you pay the government a fixed sum of money that is due every year in order to be allowed to drive it on the roads. EG *I haven't taxed my car yet.* V+O

6 If something **taxes** your strength, patience, resources, etc, it uses nearly all the energy, money, etc that you have, with the result that you have great difficulty in carrying out what you are trying to do. EG *A mountaineering course will really tax your powers of endurance... Hospitals, overloaded with battle casualties, were severely taxed.* V+O: USU WITH ADV ⇑ strain = stretch

7 If you **tax** someone **with** something, you show them evidence about something wrong which you believe that they have done, in order to try and make them admit their guilt. EG *I have decided not to tax Mr Hawkins with the information at this stage.* V+O+A *(with)* ⇑ confront

8 See also **taxing**.

taxable /tæksəbə⁰l/. If something is **taxable**, you have to pay tax on it. EG *No previous government had ever dared to make betting winnings taxable.* ADJ CLASSIF

taxation /tækseɪʃə⁰n/ is 1 the system by which a government takes money from the people and spends it on education, health, defence, etc. EG *He denied that the burden of taxation had wrecked the economy.* 2 the amount of money that people have to pay in taxes. EG *They said they would cease their pay demands if the government would reduce taxation.* N UNCOUNT N UNCOUNT

tax avoidance is the use of legal methods to pay the smallest amount of tax necessary. N UNCOUNT

tax-deductible. An expense that is **tax-deductible** is one that can be paid out of your untaxed income, so that the amount of tax that you have to pay is smaller. EG *Because I work at home, some of my heating and lighting is tax-deductible.* ADJ CLASSIF

tax disc, tax discs. In Britain, a **tax disc** is a small round piece of paper which you put on your car and which proves that you have paid the annual tax that is due in order to be allowed to drive on the roads. N COUNT

tax evasion is the crime of not paying the full amount of tax that you should. EG *Most crooked businesses rely on substantial tax evasion.* N UNCOUNT

tax-free. If goods or services are **tax-free**, you do not have to pay tax on them. EG *Father has been offered a tax-free lump sum of £4,000.* ADJ CLASSIF

tax haven, tax havens. A **tax haven** is a country or place which has a low rate of taxation, so that people choose to live there or register companies there in order to avoid paying higher tax in their own countries. EG *The Isle of Man is still a tax haven.* N COUNT

taxi /tæksi¹/, **taxis, taxiing, taxied**. 1 A **taxi** is a car driven by a person whose job is to take people where they want to go in return for money. Taxis usually have a meter inside the car which shows how much the journey is costing. EG *She said she'd come by train and take a taxi from the station... We'll get a taxi back to the office... ...a taxi driver.* N COUNT OR *by*+N = cab

2 When an aircraft **is taxiing**, it is moving slowly along a runway at an airport before taking off or after landing. EG *As the plane taxied to the runway, he made the mistake of looking out of the window.* V: USU+A

taxicab /tæksi¹kæb/, **taxicabs**; also spelled with a hyphen. A **taxicab** is the same as a taxi. N COUNT

taxidermist /tæksi¹dɜ:mɪst/, **taxidermists**. A **taxidermist** is a person whose job is to stuff dead animals and birds so that they look lifelike and can be displayed. N COUNT

taxidermy /tæksɪdɜ:mi¹/ is the art of stuffing dead animals and birds so that they look lifelike and can be displayed. N UNCOUNT

taxing /tæksɪŋ/. A **taxing** task or problem is one that requires a lot of mental or physical effort. EG *They faced new and taxing problems.* ADJ QUALIT ⇑ difficult

taxi rank, taxi ranks. A **taxi rank** is a place where taxis wait for passengers, for example at an airport or outside a station; used in British English. N COUNT

taxi stand, taxi stands. A **taxi stand** is the same as a taxi rank; used in American English. N COUNT

taxonomy /tæksɒnəmi¹/, **taxonomies**. **Taxonomy** is the classification and naming of things such as animals and plants in groups within a larger system, according to their similarities and differences; a technical term. N UNCOUNT/COUNT

taxpayer /tækspeɪə/, **taxpayers**; also spelled with a hyphen. A **taxpayer** is a person who pays income tax. N COUNT

tax relief is a reduction in the amount of tax that a person or company has to pay, for example because of expenses associated with their business, work, or house. EG *You can get tax relief on your mortgage.* N UNCOUNT

tax year, tax years. A **tax year** is a particular period of twelve months which is used by the government as a basis for calculating taxes and for organizing its own finances and accounts. In Britain, the tax year begins on April 6th and ends on April 5th. N COUNT = fiscal year

TB is an abbreviation for 'tuberculosis'. N UNCOUNT

tbs. is a written abbreviation for 'tablespoonful'; used especially in recipes. N PART+UNCOUNT

tbsp., tbsps. tbsp. is a written abbreviation for 'tablespoonful'; used especially in recipes. N PART+N UNCOUNT

tea /ti:/, **teas**. 1 **Tea** is 1.1 a drink made by pouring boiling water onto the dried leaves of the tea bush. In Britain it is usually drunk mixed with milk and often with sugar. EG *She poured herself another cup of tea... She went into the kitchen to make a fresh pot of tea... The day started early with tea at 6.15.* ▸ You can also use **tea** to refer to a cup of tea. EG *We'll have three teas and one coffee, please.* 1.2 a bush whose leaves are dried and chopped into small pieces which are used to make tea. Tea bushes are grown as a crop mainly in Asia. EG *He had always wanted to go to Ceylon and plant tea.* 1.3 the dried and chopped-up leaves of the tea bush which you use to make tea. EG *...shops selling the basics: tea, sugar, flour... ...a wealthy Chinese trader in teas.* 1.4 a drink made by pouring boiling water onto the dried leaves or flowers certain plants. EG *The old man was carrying a tray of mint tea and cakes.* N MASS ▸ N COUNT N MASS ⇑ plant N MASS N MASS: MOD+N

2 **Tea** is also 2.1 the main meal that a family has in the early evening. This meaning of **tea** is used in Britain especially by working-class people and in the north. EG *I always come back from work to find the tea ready... At tea we all sat round the table and talked about the day's events.* 2.2 a light meal taken in the afternoon, usually consisting of sandwiches and cakes, with tea to drink. This meaning of **tea** is N UNCOUNT/COUNT N UNCOUNT/COUNT

used in Britain mainly by middle-class people. EG *For tea they usually had bread and butter, home-made cakes, and tea... Mr Evans is coming to tea... Do you serve afternoon tea?*

3 If you say that something is **not** your **cup of tea**, you mean that you do not like it and so would not choose to do it, read it, etc. EG *Ballet isn't really my cup of tea, I'm afraid.* PHR : USED AS C, WITH BROAD NEG

tea bag, tea bags; also spelled with a hyphen. A **tea bag** is a small thin paper bag which has tea leaves inside it. You put it into a cup or a teapot and pour boiling water on it in order to make a cup of tea. N COUNT ⇑ sachet

tea break, tea breaks; also spelled with a hyphen. A **tea break** is a short time, usually in the morning and the afternoon, when you stop working and have a cup of tea or coffee. EG *She usually takes a fifteen-minute tea break at 3 o'clock.* N COUNT = coffee break

tea caddy, tea caddies; also spelled with a hyphen. A **tea caddy** is a small tin in which you keep tea. N COUNT

teacake /ti:keɪk/, **teacakes**. A **teacake** is a round, flat cake with raisins in it, usually toasted and eaten with butter. N COUNT ⇑ bun

teach /ti:tʃ/, **teaches, teaching, taught**. 1 If you **teach** someone something, 1.1 you give them instructions so that they know about it or how to do it. EG *Does your book teach us how to forecast foreign exchange rates?... I had no idea how to do this and Michael had to teach me every move... My mother taught me how to cook... I taught my little dog to sit up and beg.* V+O+O/REPORT-CL/to-INF, OR V+O+A (to) ⇑ instruct 1.2 you make them think, feel, or act in a new or different way. EG *Gandhi taught the world passive resistance... Boys are often taught that they mustn't show their feelings... Experience had taught him not to trust people... We've been taught to believe in the wisdom of those who govern us... We have not always been taught to think for ourselves.* V+O+O/REPORT-CL/to-INF, OR V+O+A (to) ⇑ educate

2 If you **teach** or **teach** a subject, you help students to learn about it by explaining it or showing them how to do it, usually as a job at a school, college, or university. EG *Mrs Barton teaches in a secondary modern school... I taught history for many years... I found a job teaching English to a group of adults in Paris... This is the sort of maths we should be teaching children in schools... I like teaching sixth-formers.* V, V+O, OR V+O+A (to) ⇑ instruct

3 If you **teach** someone **a lesson**, you do something unpleasant to them as a punishment for something that they have done and as a warning to them not to do it again; an informal expression. EG *I'll just give him a smack, to teach him a lesson.* PHR : VB INFLECTS

4 You say **'that'll teach you'** to someone who has ignored a warning you gave them and who has suffered something unpleasant as a result; an informal expression. EG *That'll teach you. I always told you not to stroke strange dogs.* CONVENTION

teachable /ti:tʃəbəᵊl/. 1 Someone who is **teachable** is capable of learning by being taught. EG *...a very teachable group of students.* ADJ QUALIT

2 A subject that is **teachable** is one that it is possible or easy to teach. EG *These skills are all teachable.* ADJ QUALIT

teacher /ti:tʃə/, **teachers**. A **teacher** is a person who teaches, usually as a job at a school or similar institution. EG *She's a school teacher... I am a qualified French teacher.* N COUNT

tea chest, tea chests; also spelled with a hyphen. A **tea chest** is a large wooden box in which tea is packed when it is exported. In Britain, people also use tea chests for putting things in when they move from one house to another. EG *I filled two and a half tea chests with my books.* N COUNT

teach-in, teach-ins. A **teach-in** is a meeting, usually between students and teachers, with talks and discussions on important or controversial topics. Teach-ins are not usually part of a formal academic course. EG *There were mass gatherings, demonstrations, and teach-ins.* N COUNT

teaching /ti:tʃɪŋ/, **teachings**. 1 **Teaching** is the work that a teacher does in helping students to learn. EG *Have you done any teaching lately?* N UNCOUNT

2 The **teachings** of a particular person, school of thought, or religion are all the ideas and principles that they teach. EG *Reverence for life is one of the main principles of Christian teaching... His teachings still exert a strong influence... ...the teachings of the Catholic Church.* N COUNT : USU PL

teaching hospital, teaching hospitals. A **teaching hospital** is a hospital that is linked with a medical school, where medical students and newly qualified doctors receive practical training. N COUNT

teaching practice is a period that a student teacher spends at a school doing practical teaching as part of his or her training. N UNCOUNT

teacloth /ti:klɒθ/, teacloths; also spelled with a hyphen. A **teacloth** is a cloth which you use to dry dishes, cutlery, etc, after they have been washed. EG *He rinsed the cups and wiped them on a decorated tea-cloth.* N COUNT = tea-towel

tea cosy, tea cosies; also spelled with a hyphen. A **tea cosy** is a soft cover of cloth or wool which you put over a teapot to keep the tea hot. N COUNT

teacup /ti:kʌp/, **teacups**; also spelled with a hyphen. 1 A **teacup** is a cup that you use for drinking tea. N COUNT

2 If you describe a situation as a **storm in a teacup**, you mean that a lot of fuss is being made about something that is not important; an informal expression. EG *Don't worry about this silly row. It's just a storm in a teacup.* PHR : USED AS C

teak /ti:k/. **Teak** is both the singular and the plural form. A **teak** is a tall tree with very hard wood which grows in South-East Asia. ▸ also used to refer to the hard wood that comes from this tree. EG *...teak furniture.* N COUNT ▸ N UNCOUNT

teal /ti:l/, **teals**. **Teal** can also be used as the plural form. A **teal** is a small duck found in Europe and Asia. The female has brown feathers and the male has a grey body and a red head. N COUNT

tea leaf, tea leaves; also spelled with a hyphen. **Tea leaves** are the small pieces of dried leaves that are left in a teapot or a cup after the tea has been drunk. N COUNT : USU PL

team /ti:m/, **teams, teaming, teamed**. A **team** is 1 a group of people who play a particular sport or game together against other similar groups of people. EG *He got into the New Zealand rugby team in 1978... I particularly loathed team games at school.* N COUNT : IF SING, VB CAN BE SING OR PL 2 a group of people who work together for a particular purpose. EG *...an international team of scientists... ...a group of 25 actors who work very well as a team.* N COUNT : IF SING, VB CAN BE SING OR PL 3 two or more animals which work together to pull a cart or a plough. EG *The sewer was so big you could drive teams of horses through it.* N COUNT : IF SING, VB CAN BE SING OR PL

team up. If you **team up** with someone, you join them in order to work together for a particular purpose. EG *I teamed up with Oliver on my next record... The two players teamed up perfectly.* PHRASAL VB : V+ADV, ALSO RECIP (with)

team-mate, team-mates. If people who play a sport or game are **team-mates**, they are members of the same team. N COUNT

team spirit is the feeling of pride and loyalty that exists among the members of a team and that makes them want their team to do well or to be the best. N UNCOUNT

teamster /ti:mstə/, **teamsters**. A **teamster** is a lorry driver; used in American English. N COUNT

teamwork /ti:mwɜ:k/ is the ability a group of people have to work well together. EG *Teamwork and communication were even more important in the later stages of the project.* N UNCOUNT ⇑ co-operation

tea party, tea parties; also spelled with a hyphen. A **tea party** is a social gathering in the afternoon at which tea is served. N COUNT

teapot /ti:pɒt/, **teapots**; also spelled with a hyphen. A **teapot** is a container with a lid, a handle, and a spout. You use it for making and serving tea. N COUNT ⇑ vessel

tear, tears, tearing, tore, torn. The word **tear** is pronounced /tɪə/ for paragraphs 1 to 3, and /teə/ for paragraphs 4 to 13 and the phrasal verbs. 1 **Tears** are the drops of salty liquid that come out of your eyes when you are crying. EG *He was sitting there with tears in his eyes... Tears were streaming down her face... I've never seen her shed a single tear.* N COUNT : USU PL

2 If someone is in **tears**, they are crying because they are upset or unhappy, or sometimes because they are very happy. EG *The next time he saw her, she was in tears... When Curzon heard the news, he burst into tears... She was close to tears.* N PLURAL

3 If you are **bored to tears**, you are very bored indeed; an informal expression. PHR : USED AS C = bored stiff

4 If you **tear** something such as your clothing or if it **tears**, it gets damaged by being pulled sharply or by being pierced by something sharp so that the material splits and a hole appears. EG *He tore my coat in* V-ERG = rip

the struggle... ...my filthy and torn sweater... This paper tears easily. ▸ If you **tear** a hole in something, you make a hole in it by tearing it. EG *I caught my trousers on the fence and tore a hole in them.* ▸ V+O+A

5 A **tear** in something such as a piece of clothing is a hole that has been made in it because the material has been pulled sharply or has been pierced by something sharp and has split. EG *There was a triangular tear at the knee of his trousers.* ● See also **wear and tear.** N COUNT = rip

6 If you **tear** something or **tear** it into pieces, you pull it or scratch it violently, often causing it to split into several pieces. EG *Regretfully, he tore both letters into small pieces... His arm was striped with scars where the bushes had torn him... He picked up his contract and tore it in half... Eagles have hooked and powerful beaks for tearing flesh.* V+O, OR V+O+A ⇑ destroy = rip

7 If you **tear** a page or piece of paper out of a book, you remove it by pulling it out sharply rather than by cutting it out. EG *She tore several sheets of paper out of the back of the book... He finished writing the cheque and tore it from the book.* V+O+A = rip

8 If a powerful force **tears** something from somewhere, it removes it roughly and violently. EG *The boat was washed up on this beach after being torn from its moorings by a storm... The water raced down the mountain and tore leaves and branches from the trees.* V+O+A

9 If you **tear** one of your muscles or ligaments, you injure it by moving it accidentally and violently in the wrong way. EG *Was it a broken bone or a torn ligament?* V+O

10 If you **tear** someone **to pieces** or **tear** them **to shreds,** you criticize them, their work, or their behaviour very severely and thoroughly. EG *It is not in our interest to tear one another to pieces.* PHR : VB INFLECTS

11 If someone or something **tears** somewhere, they move very quickly, often in an uncontrolled or dangerous way. EG *She came tearing out of the house... All kinds of thoughts tore through my mind.* V+A ⇑ go = rush

12 If you **are torn** between two or more things, you cannot decide which one to choose, and this makes you feel rather anxious or troubled. EG *The government is torn between principle and expediency.* V+O : USU PASS+A

13 If you say that a place **is torn** by particular events, you mean that the events are unpleasant and cause suffering and division among the people who live there. EG *An attempt to come to terms with a world torn by riots, revolution, and corruption.* V+O : USU PASS+A ⇑ divide

tear apart. 1 If you **tear** something **apart**, you split it into pieces by pulling at it roughly or violently. EG *I saw a flak jacket so torn apart that no one would ever want it again.* PHRASAL VB : V+O+ADV

2 If something **tears** people **apart**, it causes them to quarrel or to leave each other. EG *They have lived through so much together; what could possibly tear them apart?... He was fighting against the 'anarchy' which he insisted was tearing the Church apart.* PHRASAL VB : V+O+ADV = divide

3 If something **tears** you **apart**, it makes you feel very upset, worried, and unhappy, often because you cannot decide what is right or which of two demands on you is more important. EG *She is torn apart by conflicting pressures.* PHRASAL VB : V+O+ADV

tear at. If you **tear at** something, you pull it violently and try to break it into pieces. EG *The boys tore at the meat like hyenas.* PHRASAL VB : V+PREP

tear away. If you **tear** someone **away** from a place or activity, you force them to leave the place or stop doing the activity, even though they want to remain there or carry on. EG *What a shame it was to tear Dolly away from the play... Mourners often find it difficult to tear themselves away from a newly filled grave.* ● See also **tearaway.** PHRASAL VB : V+O (NG/REFL)+A, USU+*from* = drag away

tear down. If you **tear** something **down**, you destroy it or remove it completely. EG *It is often cheaper to tear down the ten-year-old buildings than to modify them... Men were breaking windows with canes, tearing posters down from the walls.* PHRASAL VB : V+O+ADV

tear into. If you **tear into** someone, you criticize them, their work, or their behaviour very strongly; an informal use. EG *He really tore into me about my work.* PHRASAL VB : V+PREP = lay into

tear loose. 1 If you **tear loose** or **tear** yourself **loose**, you escape from something that is holding you by struggling violently. EG *The piglet tore loose from the creepers and scurried into the undergrowth... John's answer to this was to tear himself loose and go down on his knees.* PHRASAL VB : V+ADV, OR V+O (REFL)+ADV = free yourself

2 If you **tear** something **loose**, you remove it by pulling it violently. PHRASAL VB : V+O+ADV

tear off. 1 If you **tear** your clothes **off**, you take them off in a rough and violent way. EG *I tore off my shirt and changed hurriedly.* PHRASAL VB : V+O+ADV ⇑ remove = strip off

2 If you **tear off** somewhere, you go there very quickly, often in an uncontrolled way. EG *He tore off home... I watched them tearing off into the distance.* PHRASAL VB : V+ADV, USU+A ⇑ depart = rush off

3 If you **tear** someone **off a strip**, you tell them off angrily because they have done something wrong; used in informal British English. PHR : VB INFLECTS = lay into

tear open. If you **tear** something **open**, you open it roughly and very quickly, by tearing it. EG *He tore open the envelope.* PHRASAL VB : V+O+ADV

tear up. If you **tear** something **up**, **1** you destroy it by pulling it quickly into a lot of small pieces. EG *She smiled and folded the letter, intending to tear it up and throw it out of the window.* PHRASAL VB : V+O+ADV **2** you destroy it by violently breaking it into pieces. EG *We do not yet have basketball and baseball crowds tearing up the grounds or breaking up trains... Parks, once bursting with flowers, were now being torn up in favour of factories.* PHRASAL VB : V+O+ADV

tearaway /tɛərəweɪ/, **tearaways.** A **tearaway** is a young person who behaves in a wild and uncontrolled way; used in British English. EG *He's a real young tearaway!* N COUNT

teardrop /tɪədrɒp/, **teardrops.** A **teardrop** is a large pear-shaped tear that comes from your eye when you are crying quietly. EG *A teardrop glistened on her cheek.* N COUNT

tearful /tɪəful/. If someone is **tearful,** their face or voice shows signs that they have been crying or that they want to cry. EG *His tearful family came to pay their last respects.* ▸ used also of the way people speak and behave. EG *She cried out to him in a tearful voice.* ◊ **tearfully.** EG *He looked at her tearfully.* ADJ QUALIT ⇑ sad; ◊ ADV WITH VB

tear gas /tɪə gæs/; also spelled with a hyphen. **Tear gas** is a gas that causes your eyes to sting and fill with tears so that you cannot see. It is sometimes used by the police or army to control crowds. EG *The police were granted permission to use tear gas, water cannons, and plastic bullets.* N UNCOUNT

tearing /tɛərɪŋ/. If you are in a **tearing** hurry, you are trying to go somewhere or do something as quickly as possible. EG *I'm in a tearing hurry this morning.* ADJ CLASSIF : ATTRIB = mad

tear-jerker, tear-jerkers; also spelled without a hyphen. A **tear-jerker** is a play, film, or book that is very sad or sentimental; an informal expression. N COUNT

tea-room, tea-rooms. A **tea-room** is the same as a tea-shop. N COUNT : ALSO IN NAMES

tease /tiːz/, **teases, teasing, teased. 1** If you **tease** someone, you make fun of them, for example by embarrassing them or by making them believe something that is not true. EG *She teased him about his girlfriends... I teased him for using such language... 'And you'll miss us, I hope?' she teased him mildly.* V+O/QUOTE, V+O+A, OR V+O+QUOTE = chaff, kid

2 If someone **is teasing**, they are pretending to offer you something that you want, especially sex, but then not giving it to you. EG *He suspected that Etta was teasing.* V : USU CONT ⇑ tantalize

3 A **tease** is **3.1** someone who makes fun of people in a gentle but slightly cruel way. EG *She's a big tease, but she doesn't mean anything by it.* N COUNT : USU SING **3.2** a person who pretends to offer someone something that they want, especially sex, but then does not give it to them. N COUNT : USU SING **3.3** a type of joking behaviour which makes fun of someone in a gentle but slightly cruel way. EG *Her remark held a tiny hint of a challenge, or of a tease.* N SING : a+N

tease out. 1 If you **tease** tangles and knots **out** of your hair, you remove them very carefully by using a brush or comb. PHRASAL VB : V+O+ADV

2 If you **tease** information **out of** someone, you persuade them to tell you something, even though they are reluctant to do so. EG *He didn't want to tell, but I teased it out of him.* PHRASAL VB : V+O+ADV+PREP ⇑ extract

teasel /tiːzəºl/, **teasels**; also spelled **teazel** or **teazle.** A **teasel** is a plant with dry prickly flowerheads and prickly leaves. N COUNT

teaser /tiːzə/, **teasers.** A **teaser** is **1** a difficult question, especially one in a quiz or competition; an N COUNT = poser informal use. 2 someone who makes fun of people in a gentle or slightly cruel way. N COUNT = tease

tea service, tea services; also spelled with a hyphen. A **tea service** is the same as a tea set. N COUNT

tea set, tea sets; also spelled with a hyphen. A **tea set** is a set of cups, saucers, and plates, with a milk jug, a sugar bowl and a teapot, used when tea is served. N COUNT = tea service

tea shop, tea shops; also spelled with a hyphen and as one word. A **tea shop** is a small restaurant or café where tea, coffee, cakes, sandwiches, and light meals are served; used in British English. N COUNT : ALSO IN NAMES

teasing /tiːzɪŋ/ is behaviour that is intended to make fun of someone, for example by embarrassing them or by making them believe something that is not true. EG *This form of teasing is nasty enough to be taken as an affront.* ▸ used as an adjective. EG *Be polite in a teasing, nonchalant manner.* ◊ **teasingly**. EG *'Who do you like today, Honey?' he said teasingly.* N UNCOUNT = kidding ▸ ADJ QUALIT ◊ ADV WITH VB ⇑ jokingly

Teasmaid /tiːzmeɪd/, **Teasmaids**; a trademark. A **Teasmaid** is a device consisting of a teapot and a kettle attached to a clock, which automatically makes tea at a pre-set time. People use Teasmaids in order to have a cup of tea ready when they wake up in the morning. N COUNT

teaspoon /tiːspuːn/, **teaspoons**. A **teaspoon** is a small spoon that you use to put sugar into tea or coffee. ▸ also used to refer to the amount that a teaspoon will hold. EG *Add one teaspoon of salt.* N COUNT ▸ N PART+N UNCOUNT

teaspoonful /tiːspuːnfʊl/, **teaspoonfuls** or **teaspoonsful**. A **teaspoonful** is the amount of powder or liquid that a teaspoon will hold; used especially in instructions for cooking and food preparation. EG *...two teaspoonfuls of sugar.* N COUNT : ALSO N PART+N UNCOUNT ⇑ spoonful

tea strainer, tea strainers; also spelled with a hyphen. A **tea strainer** is a small metal or plastic object with a lot of small holes in it, which catches tea leaves and stops them going into the cup when you are pouring tea. N COUNT ⇑ sieve

teat /tiːt/, **teats**. A **teat** is 1 a pointed part on the body of a female animal which her babies suck in order to get milk: compare **nipple**, **udder**. EG *...tiny naked pink creatures clinging to the teats with their mouths.* N COUNT 2 a piece of rubber or plastic that is shaped like a teat, especially one that is fitted to a bottle so that a baby can suck liquids from it. EG *The baby grabbed the teat and began to suck.* N COUNT

tea table; also spelled with a hyphen. The **tea table** is the table you are sitting at when you are eating tea. EG *They took their seats at the tea table.* N SING : the+N

teatime /tiːtaɪm/; also spelled with a hyphen and as two words. **Teatime** is the time in the afternoon when English people usually have tea. EG *At teatime there was much excited chatter around the table.* N UNCOUNT

tea-towel, tea-towels; also spelled without a hyphen. A **tea-towel** is a cloth which you use to dry dishes, cutlery, etc, after they have been washed; used in British English. N COUNT = tea cloth

teazel /tiːzəl/. See **teasel**. N COUNT

teazle /tiːzəl/. See **teasel**. N COUNT

tech /tek/, **techs**. A **tech** is a technical college; used in informal British English. N COUNT : ALSO IN NAMES

technical /teknɪkəl/. 1 **Technical** matters, activities, etc 1.1 involve detailed practical knowledge of scientific, technological, and industrial subjects. EG *...scientific and technical knowledge... ...technical advances that improve productivity... Technical experts also pointed out that the design was faulty.* ADJ QUALIT : USU ATTRIB 1.2 relate to the skills and methods needed to carry out a practical activity or process. EG *I don't really paint very well–I have technical problems... ...wood carving of remarkable technical skill.* ADJ QUALIT : USU ATTRIB 1.3 relate to arguments, requirements, or decisions that are based on a strict interpretation of the law or a set of rules. EG *It was a serious matter, more than a technical offence.* ADJ QUALIT : ATTRIB

2 **Technical** language or meanings involve using words in a very precise and specialized way in order to discuss and describe the details of a particular subject or activity. In this dictionary, language of this kind is indicated by the use of the word 'technical' in definitions. EG *The term was used in a fairly technical sense.* ADJ QUALIT : ATTRIB = specialist

technical college, technical colleges. In Britain, a **technical college** is a college of further education where you can go after leaving school in order to study arts and technical subjects to 'O' or 'A' level. N COUNT : ALSO IN NAMES

technicality /teknɪkælɪti/, **technicalities**. 1 The **technicalities** of a process or activity are the detailed methods used to do it or to carry it out. EG *I was quite interested in the technicalities of the recording.* N PLURAL = mechanics

2 A **technicality** is a point, especially a legal one, that is based on a strict interpretation of the law or of a set of rules. EG *On a technicality, the judge dismissed the case... ...a legal technicality.* N COUNT

technically /teknɪkəli/ means 1 according to a strict interpretation of facts, laws, rules, or the meaning of words. EG *He's not a doctor, technically speaking, he's a medical practitioner... He was technically in breach of contract.* ADV OR ADV SEN 2 in accordance with practical knowledge of and skill in scientific, technological, and industrial subjects. EG *It's quite clear that the electric car is technically feasible.* ADV 3 in accordance with the skills and methods needed for a practical activity, especially an artistic one. EG *Pollock was certainly a skilful artist technically.* ADV

technician /teknɪʃən/, **technicians**. A **technician** is 1 someone whose job involves skilled practical work with scientific equipment, for example in a laboratory. EG *...European scientists, engineers, and technicians... ...thousands of technicians were trained for this work.* N COUNT 2 someone who is very good at the detailed technical aspects of an activity. EG *The man who made this was not just a technician, but an artist.* N COUNT ⇑ craftsman

Technicolor /teknɪkʌlə/; a trademark. 1 **Technicolor** is a system of colour photography used in making cinema films. N UNCOUNT

2 You can use **Technicolor** to describe very colourful sights or scenes in films, especially when they seem exaggerated; an informal use. EG *The camera focused on the Technicolor sunset as the film ended.* N UNCOUNT

technique /tekniːk/, **techniques**. 1 A **technique** is a particular method of doing an activity, usually a method that involves practical skills. EG *...the techniques of film-making... ...modern management techniques.* N COUNT : IF+PREP THEN *of/for*

2 **Technique** is skill and ability in an artistic, sporting, or other practical activity that you develop through training and practice. EG *She owed her technique entirely to his teaching... They don't have the technique to express all that in written form.* N UNCOUNT

techno- is used at the beginning of words that refer to technology. EG *...techno-societies... ...technomania... ...technocrats.* PREFIX

technocracy /teknɒkrəsi/, **technocracies**; a formal word. A **technocracy** is 1 a group of scientists, engineers, and other experts who have political power as well as technical knowledge. EG *...the cream of the military technocracy.* N COUNT : IF SING, VB CAN BE SING OR PL ⇑ elite 2 a country or society that is controlled by scientists, engineers, and other experts. N COUNT

technocrat /teknəkræt/, **technocrats**; a formal word. A **technocrat** is a scientist, engineer, or other expert who is one of a group of similar people who have political power as well as technical knowledge. N COUNT

technological /teknəlɒdʒɪkəl/. **Technological** means relating to, resulting from, or associated with technology. EG *...modern scientific and technological knowledge... ...high-speed technological change.* ◊ **technologically**. EG *...the world's richest and most technologically advanced nations.* ADJ CLASSIF : ATTRIB ⇑ technical ◊ ADV ⇑ technically

technologist /teknɒlədʒɪst/, **technologists**. A **technologist** is a person who is an expert in a technology. EG *...a small group of distinguished scientists and technologists.* N COUNT ⇑ scientist

technology /teknɒlədʒi/, **technologies**. 1 **Technology** is the activity or study of using scientific knowledge for practical purposes in industry, farming, medicine, business, etc. EG *...advances in technology and science... ...our belief in the power of modern technology.* N UNCOUNT ⇑ applied science

2 A **technology** is a particular area of activity that requires scientific method and knowledge. EG *...changes in agricultural technology... ...computer technology... ...western technologies of housing, industry, health.* N COUNT/UNCOUNT+SUPP ⇑ applied science

Ted /ted/, **Teds**. A **Ted** is a Teddy boy; used in informal English. EG *My father insisted that we mustn't talk to the Teds.* N COUNT ⇑ youth

teddy /tedi¹/, **teddies**. A **teddy** is a teddy bear; used especially by children and by adults talking to children. Children often call their teddies 'Teddy' when they are talking to them. EG *I tucked in the moth-eaten teddy beside her... Teddy isn't very well today.* — N COUNT: ALSO VOC ⇑ toy

teddy bear, teddy bears; also spelled with a hyphen. A **teddy bear** is a children's soft toy which looks like a friendly bear. EG *She walked over to her parents still clutching her teddy bear.* — N COUNT

Teddy boy, Teddy boys; also spelled with a hyphen. A **Teddy boy** is a man who dresses in a style that became popular in the 1950's. Teddy boys in the 1950's were associated with early rock and roll music, and were often regarded as bad or violent. — N COUNT ⇑ youth

tedious /ti:dɪəs/. Something that is **tedious** is boring and uninteresting, and seems to last for a very long time. EG *The arguments were tedious and complicated... ...rather tedious lunch parties.* — ADJ QUALIT = tiresome ◊ **tediously**. EG *The experience of long-distance air travel is tediously familiar.* — ◊ ADV

tedium /ti:dɪəm/. The **tedium** of a situation is its quality of being boring and uninteresting; a fairly literary word. EG *The most notable quality of the meeting was its sheer tedium... ...the tedium of being young and broke.* — N UNCOUNT ⇑ boredom

tee /ti:/, **tees, teeing, teed**; a word used in golf. A **tee** is **1** a small piece of wood or plastic which is pushed into the ground and is used to support the golf ball before it is hit at the start of each hole. — N COUNT ⇑ peg **2** one of the small flat areas of ground on a golf course from which people start their attempts to get the ball into each of the holes. — N COUNT

tee off. If you **tee off**, you hit a golf ball from a tee at the start of a hole. — PHRASAL VB: V+ADV

tee up. If you **tee up** means you place a golf ball on a tee so that it is ready for you to hit it. — PHRASAL VB: V+ADV

teem /ti:m/, **teems, teeming, teemed**. **1** If a place **is teeming** with animals or people, it is very crowded and the animals or people are moving around a lot. EG *The desert is teeming with life in the good seasons... The water teems with thousands of organisms.* — V+A *(with)*: USU CONT = abound ◊ **teeming**. EG *...the teeming millions... ...this teeming, milling mass of sun worshippers.* — ◊ ADJ CLASSIF: ATTRIB

2 If it is **teeming** or **teeming down** with rain, it is raining very heavily. EG *It was teeming down and we all got soaked. ...When I came out it had stopped teeming down so I walked.* — V+A *(with)*, OR PHRASAL VB: V+ADV ◊ **teeming**. EG *...the teeming rain.* — ◊ ADJ CLASSIF

teenage /ti:neɪdʒ/. **1 Teenage** people are aged between thirteen and nineteen years. EG *...a divorced woman with two teenage children... ...a few teenage girls in brightly colored silk blouses.* — ADJ CLASSIF: ATTRIB ⇑ young

2 Teenage fashions and activities are considered to be typical of or suitable for young people aged between thirteen and nineteen years. EG *...the teenage culture of pop music and magazines... ...teenage fashions.* — ADJ CLASSIF: ATTRIB ⇑ youth

teenager /ti:neɪdʒə/, **teenagers**. A **teenager** is someone between thirteen and nineteen years of age. EG *...a highly intelligent teenager... Most of the volunteers are teenagers and young adults.* — N COUNT ⇑ adolescent

teens /ti:nz/. Your **teens** are the period of your life when you are between thirteen and nineteen years old. EG *She was short and young, maybe still in her teens.* — N PLURAL: USU PREP+DETPOSS+N ⇑ adolescence

teeny /ti:ni¹/, **teenier, teeniest**. **Teeny** means very small; an informal word, used especially by young children. EG *I must admit to a teeny touch of envy.* — ADJ QUALIT: ATTRIB = tiny

teeny-bopper /ti:ni¹ bɒpə/, **teeny-boppers**. A **teeny-bopper** is a teenager, usually a girl, who is very interested in pop music; a rather old-fashioned informal word. — N COUNT

tee-shirt. See **T-shirt**.

teeter /ti:tə/, **teeters, teetering, teetered**. **1** If someone or something **teeters**, they shake in an unsteady way, because they are about to lose their balance and fall over. EG *My last penny wobbled across the board, teetered about for a second, and then fell over.* — V: USU+A ⇑ wobble

2 The word **teeter** is also used in expressions like 'teeter on the brink' and 'teeter on the edge' to describe situations which are very close to becoming disastrous. EG *British theatre is in a perilous state, teetering on the brink of ruin.* — V+A *(on)* = totter

teeth /ti:θ/ is the plural of **tooth**.

teethe /ti:ð/, **teethes, teething, teethed**. When babies **are teething**, their teeth are starting to appear through their gums, often causing them some pain. EG *He's teething at the moment, poor little thing.* — V: USU CONT/INF ◊ **teething**. EG *...a painful stage of teething.* — ◊ N UNCOUNT

teething troubles are difficulties or problems which arise during the early stages of a project or when something new first becomes available. EG *They had terrible teething troubles with the steering on the four-wheel-drive model.* — N COUNT: USU PL

teetotal /ti:təʊtə⁰l/. Someone who is **teetotal** never drinks alcohol. EG *I happen to be teetotal, I'm afraid.* — ADJ CLASSIF

teetotaller /ti:təʊtə⁰lə/, **teetotallers**. A **teetotaller** is someone who never drinks alcohol. EG *They provided soft drinks for the teetotallers.* — N COUNT

TEFL /tefə⁰l/ is an abbreviation for 'teaching English as a foreign language'; the teaching of English to students whose first language is not English. — N UNCOUNT

tel. is an abbreviation for 'telephone number'. EG *Tel. 021-472-1301.*

telecommunications /telɪkəmju:nɪkeɪʃə⁰nz/ is the technology of sending signals and messages over long distances using electronic equipment, for example radio and telephone. EG *We hope that the Japanese can be persuaded to buy British telecommunications equipment.* — N UNCOUNT: USU BEFORE N

telegram /telɪgræm/, **telegrams**. A **telegram** is a message that is sent by telegraph and then printed and delivered to someone's home or office. EG *I sent a telegram to my mother saying I had arrived safely... You are not going to solve these problems by telegram.* — N COUNT, OR *by*+N = wire

telegraph /telɪgræf, -grɑ:f/, **telegraphs, telegraphing, telegraphed**. **1** The **telegraph is** a system of sending messages over a distance, either by means of electricity or by radio signals, and writing them or printing them out at the other end. EG *He wanted Federal ownership of the cable and telegraph services.* — N SING: *the*+N, OR *by*+N

2 If you **telegraph** someone, you send them a message by telegraph. EG *Harold had telegraphed him in France... He'd forgotten to telegraph condolences to the widow.* — V, V+O, OR V+O+O/A *(to)*/REPORT-CL

telegraphese /telɪgrɑ:fi:z/ is a style of language which uses the fewest number of words possible, often by leaving out words such as prepositions or pronouns. It is used in sending telegrams; for example, if you want to say 'I am arriving in London on Friday', you might send a telegram saying 'arriving London Friday'. — N UNCOUNT

telegraphic /telɪgræfɪk/. **1 Telegraphic** methods or systems are involved in sending information by telegraph. EG *...telegraphic equipment.* — ADJ CLASSIF: ATTRIB

2 Telegraphic messages or statements are written or spoken in a very concise style, using the smallest possible number of words. EG *Daniel delivered his message with telegraphic brevity.* — ADJ CLASSIF: ATTRIB ◊ **telegraphically**. EG *There was also a telegraphically short letter from Claude.* — ◊ ADV

telemetry /təlemə¹tri¹/ is the science of using automatic equipment to make scientific measurements and transmit them by radio to a receiving station; a technical word. EG *...a new industry supplying telemetry systems to the medical profession.* — N UNCOUNT

teleology /telɪɒlədʒi¹, ti:lɪ-/ is the theory or belief that all natural things are designed to fulfil a particular purpose; a technical word in philosophy. — N UNCOUNT

telepathic /telɪpæθɪk/. **1** Someone who is **telepathic** has mental powers which cannot be explained by scientists, such as being able to communicate with other people without using speech, writing, touch, or any other normal signal. EG *The experiment was to see whether either of us was telepathic.* — ADJ CLASSIF

2 Communications or powers that are **telepathic** involve communication between people's minds without using speech, writing, touch, or any other normal signal. EG *...the almost telepathic skills of the dog handlers.* — ADJ CLASSIF ◊ **telepathically**. EG *They were an enigmatic pair, communicating telepathically with each other.* — ◊ ADV

telepathy /tɪ²lepəθi¹/ is the direct communication of thoughts and feelings between people's minds, without the need to use speech, writing, touch, or any other normal signals. EG *We are particularly interested in phenomena such as telepathy and levitation.* — N UNCOUNT ⇑ ESP

telephone /tɛlɪfəʊn/, **telephones, telephoning, telephoned.** 1 The **telephone** is an electrical system of communication that makes it possible for you to talk directly to someone else in a different place, usually by dialling a number on a piece of equipment and speaking into it. EG *Reports came in by telephone... All telephone communication had been destroyed... I have to make a telephone call.* — N SING : *the*+N, OR *by*+N

2 A **telephone** is a piece of equipment that you use when you talk to someone by telephone. EG *She walked over to the office telephone... When the telephone rang he picked up the receiver... He put down the telephone.* — N COUNT

3 If you **telephone** someone, you dial their telephone number and speak to them by telephone; a fairly formal use. EG *I'll telephone her this evening... Brody telephoned to thank her... He telephoned a warning from London.* — V OR V+O

4 If you are **on the telephone**, 4.1 you are speaking to someone by telephone. EG *She was talking on the telephone... Somebody wants you on the telephone.* — PHR : USED AS AN A

4.2 you have a telephone in your house or office which is connected to the rest of the telephone system. EG *Are you on the telephone?* — PHR : USED AS AN A

telephone book, telephone books. A **telephone book** is a book that contains an alphabetical list of the names, addresses, and telephone numbers of the people in a particular town or area. EG *You can find me in the telephone book.* — N COUNT = telephone directory

telephone booth, telephone booths. A **telephone booth** is a place in a station, hotel, or other public building where there is a public telephone; a formal expression. — N COUNT = phone booth

telephone box, telephone boxes. A **telephone box** is a small shelter in the street in which there is a public telephone. EG *There is a telephone box about a mile away.* — N COUNT = call box

telephone directory, telephone directories. A **telephone directory** is the same as a telephone book. EG *Look them up in the telephone directory.* — N COUNT = phone book

telephone exchange, telephone exchanges. A **telephone exchange** is a central office or building where connections are made between telephone lines so that people can talk to each other by telephone. — N COUNT : USU SING

telephone number, telephone numbers. Your **telephone number** is the number that other people dial when they want to talk to you on the telephone. EG *He gave her his telephone number.* — N COUNT = phone number

telephonist /tɪ²lɛfənɪst/, **telephonists.** A **telephonist** is someone who works at a telephone exchange or whose job is to answer the telephone for a business or other organization; used in British English. EG *He was always being complimented on his interesting accent by anonymous telephonists.* — N COUNT ↑ operator = switchboard operator

telephoto lens, telephoto lenses. A **telephoto lens** is a long tube-shaped lens which can be fixed to a camera in order to take close-up pictures of something far away. EG *They came so close that a good telephoto lens would pick up the markings on the plane.* — N COUNT

teleprinter /tɛlɪprɪntə/, **teleprinters.** A **teleprinter** is an electronic printer which prints out messages that it receives from machines in other places. EG *They are connected with their London offices by teleprinters... Reports came in by telephone and teleprinter during the meeting.* — N COUNT, OR *by*+N

telescope /tɛlɪskəʊp/, **telescopes, telescoping, telescoped.** 1 A **telescope** is a long instrument that is shaped like a tube and has lenses inside it. You look through it with one eye in order to make distant things seem larger and nearer. EG *He squinted through the telescope... ...one of the furthest bodies in the solar system to be discovered by telescope.* • See also **radio telescope.** — N COUNT, OR *by*+N

2 If you **telescope** something such as a book or a report, you make it shorter by using fewer words but still keeping all the important points in. EG *I hope that I have given a fair, if telescoped, summary of the arguments.* — V+O ↑ shorten = condense

3 If a device **telescopes** or if you **telescope** it, it is able to become longer or shorter because it is made of movable sections which can slide inside each other. EG *He took out a white rod which he telescoped into a walking stick.* — V-ERG

telescopic /tɛlɪskɒpɪk/. 1 Instruments and lenses that are **telescopic** make things seem larger and nearer. EG *The telescopic sight fitted snugly along the top of the gun... ...a 400 mm telescopic lens.* — ADJ CLASSIF : USU ATTRIB

2 Something that is **telescopic** is made of sections that fit or slide into each other so that it can be made shorter when it is not being used. EG *I pulled out the telescopic aerial to its fullest extent.* — ADJ CLASSIF : USU ATTRIB

Teletype /tɛlɪtaɪp/, **Teletypes**; a trademark. A **Teletype** is a teleprinter. EG *Simultaneously all other branches were informed by teletype... ...assorted electronic gear and automatic teletypes.* — N COUNT, OR *by*+N

televise /tɛlɪvaɪz/, **televises, televising, televised.** To **televise** a programme means to broadcast it so that it can be seen on television. EG *The BBC agreed to televise a debate on the siting of nuclear missiles in Britain.* — V+O

television /tɛlɪvɪʒəⁿn/, **televisions.** 1 A **television** is a piece of electrical equipment that consists of a box containing a special electronic tube with a screen in front of it, on which you can watch programmes with pictures and sounds. EG *You don't have a television, do you?... I turned on the television to watch the news.* — N COUNT = TV, telly
• If something is **on television** or is shown **on television**, it is a programme or is in a programme that can be seen on a television. EG *His first film was shown on television this weekend... The Princess agreed to go on television.* — • PHR : USED AS AN A

2 **Television** is 2.1 a system of sending pictures and sounds by electrical signals over a distance so that people can receive them on a television in their home. EG *...television pictures transmitted from a camera on the other side of the world.* — N UNCOUNT
2.2 all the programmes, such as plays, films, news, etc, that are broadcast and that you can watch on a television. EG *The boys were watching television... Howard was away in London doing a television programme on the drugs problem.* — N UNCOUNT = telly
2.3 the business or industry concerned with making programmes and broadcasting them on television. EG *Television is an enormously competitive business... ...the most exciting job in television.* — N UNCOUNT

3 See also **breakfast television, cable television, closed circuit television.**

television set, television sets. A **television set** is a television. EG *Facing the sofa were three television sets, each tuned to a different station.* — N COUNT = TV, telly

telex /tɛlɛks/, **telexes, telexing, telexed.** 1 **Telex** is an international system of sending written messages immediately from one place to another. You type a message on to a machine, and the machine sends the message by telegraph to another machine, which prints it. EG *We had our own telex facilities.* — N UNCOUNT ↑ service

2 A **telex** is 2.1 a machine that transmits telex messages. EG *I asked the telex operator if he could get my stories off first.* — N COUNT
2.2 a message that you send or that has been received and printed by telex. EG *He burst in with an urgent telex.* — N COUNT

3 If you **telex** a message, you send it using the telex service. EG *The file on this man had been telexed to Paris.* — V+O/REPORT-CL : IF+PREP THEN *to*

tell /tɛl/, **tells, telling, told.** 1 If you **tell** someone something, 1.1 you give them information about it by speaking or writing to them. EG *He told me that he was a farmer... I told her what the doctor had said... 'Jenny's dead,' I told him... He told his friends of a party he had attended... I'm told you were at the meeting last week... Newspapers tell us about what is happening... My aunt wrote and told me all about it.* — V+O+O/REPORT-CL/QUOTE/ *about/of* ↑ inform
1.2 you give an account of it by describing it in words. EG *She told me the story of her life... I asked him to tell the story in his own words... She told him anecdotes about the hospital... It was not long before he was telling her his family history.* — V+O+O, V+O, OR V+O+A *(to)* ↑ narrate
1.3 you give them a precise piece of information by speaking or writing. EG *I wondered why I hadn't told Mary the truth... John refused to tell me her name... 'I'll tell you a secret,' he said... 'We told a lot of lies,' said Bill.* — V+O+O, V+O, OR V+O+A *(to)* ↑ utter

2 If you **tell** someone to do something, 2.1 you order or instruct them to do it. EG *I was furious and told them to get out of my house... Don't argue with me, George. Just do as you're told... 'I'm sorry I'm late but my aunt told me not to run,' he explained.* — V+O+*to*-INF/QUOTE/REPORT-CL
2.2 you advise them to do it or warn them not to do it. EG *My uncle smiled and told me not to worry... I told him to get a good lawyer.* — V+O+*to*-INF/QUOTE/REPORT-CL

3 If you **tell** yourself something, you think it out for yourself and put it into words in your own mind, because you think it is important for you to understand the situation properly. EG *He told himself it was only a game... Be careful, she told herself. Be very careful.*
V+O (REFL)+O/REPORT-CL/QUOTE ⇑ say

4 If you can **tell** what is happening or what is true, you are able to know or judge the truth about events. EG *I couldn't tell what they were thinking... It was impossible to tell which island they came from... So far as we can tell, it is still in perfect condition.*
V+O/REPORT-CL : WITH MODAL, NO CONT

5 If you can **tell the time**, you are able to find out what the time is, usually by looking at a clock or watch. EG *Can you tell the time yet?... They used to tell the time of day by the position of the sun.*
PHR : USU MODAL +PHR

6 If you **tell**, you reveal or give away a secret; an informal use. EG *Don't try and make me tell, because I never shall... He's won a lot, hasn't he? Or aren't you telling?*
V = talk, say

7 If facts or events **tell** you something, they reveal certain information to you through ways other than speech. EG *Every movement they make tells you that they are tired... My intuition told me to stay away.*
V+O+O/REPORT-CL/to-INF ⇑ make known

8 If something **tells** on you, it has a bad effect on you which you cannot resist. EG *The strain was beginning to tell... All these late nights were beginning to tell on my health.*
V : IF+PREP THEN *on* ⇑ affect

9 If you can **tell** one thing from another, you are able to recognize the difference between it and other similar things. EG *All cows look the same to me, I can never tell one from another.*
V+O : IF+PREP THEN *from*, NO CONT = distinguish

10 If you **tell** the votes in a ballot or election, you officially count them. EG *Two members of each party were there to tell the votes.*
V+O

11 The word **tell** is also used in the following expressions. **11.1** You say **'tell me another'** when you do not believe what someone is telling you because you think they are teasing you or are deliberately exaggerating; an informal expression. EG *'They came 300 miles just to see me!'–'Oh yeah, tell me another'.*
CONVENTION

11.2 You say **'I tell you', 'I can tell you'**, or **'I can't tell you'** to emphasize something that you are saying; an informal expression. EG *This country is bursting with energy, I tell you, energy and talent... I can't tell you how pleased we are to have you here today, Professor Sinclair... Some of your friends have some very funny ideas, I can tell you.*
CONVENTION

11.3 If you say **'you're telling me'**, you are emphasizing that you already know and agree with something that someone has just told you; an informal expression.
CONVENTION

11.4 If you say **'You never can tell'**, you mean that the future is always uncertain and it is never possible to know exactly what will happen.
CONVENTION

11.5 If someone disagrees with you or refuses to do what you suggest and you are eventually proved to be right, you can say **'I told you so'**; a very informal expression, especially used by children.
CONVENTION

11.6 If you say **'time will tell'**, you mean that the truth about something will not be known until some time in the future.
CONVENTION

tell against. If a feature or characteristic **tells against** someone, it spoils their chance of success when they are being considered for something, for example a job. EG *Her bad temper has always told against her.*
PHRASAL VB : V+PREP = count against

tell apart. If you can **tell** people or things **apart**, you are able to recognize the differences between them and can therefore identify them individually. EG *I've never been able to tell those two apart.*
PHRASAL VB : ORDER V+O+ADV, WITH MODAL, NO CONT = distinguish

tell off. If you **tell** someone **off**, you speak to them angrily or seriously as a way of punishing them for doing something wrong. EG *I don't like being told off by anybody... We don't want to get told off, do we?*
PHRASAL VB : V+O+ADV ⇑ rebuke = reprimand, scold

tell on. If you **tell on** someone, you give information about them to someone in authority, especially if they have done something wrong; an informal expression used especially by children. EG *'Don't tell on me for tearing my trousers'.*
PHRASAL VB : V+PREP ⇑ inform = grass on

teller /te̱lə/, **tellers.** A **teller** is **1** a person who has been appointed to count votes, for example at an election or in parliament. EG *Each party appointed two tellers to watch the vote counting... Tellers will collect the ballot forms and the result will be known at midnight.*
N COUNT ⇑ counter
2 a cashier in a bank.
N COUNT

telling /te̱lɪŋ/, **tellings. 1** The **telling** of a story or of something that has happened involves repeating it to other people, either by writing or speaking; a fairly formal use. EG *The story takes more than five hundred pages in the telling... The earlier tellings of the story had concentrated on the battle.*
N UNCOUNT/COUNT ⇑ recounting

2 If something that you say is **telling, 2.1** it is very important or sensible and has a great effect on the people who hear it. EG *The lawyer made a brief, telling speech to the magistrate.*
ADJ QUALIT ⇑ effective
2.2 it shows what you are feeling or thinking, although you might not intend it to. EG *He made a particularly telling remark.*
ADJ QUALIT = revealing

3 If you say **'there's no telling'**, you mean that it is impossible to know what will happen; an informal expression. EG *There was no telling what sort of trouble she might get into.*
CONVENTION

telling-off, tellings-off. If you give someone a **telling-off**, you tell them that you are very angry with them about something they have done. EG *When she got back she would give him such a telling-off about that doll.*
N COUNT = scolding

telltale /te̱lteɪl/, **telltales**; also spelled with a hyphen. **1** Something that is described as **telltale** gives away information, often about something that is meant to be secret. EG *His head was totally bald-not shaven, for there were no telltale black spots on his scalp... I was beginning to recognize the first tell-tale signs of panic.*
ADJ CLASSIF ⇑ revealing

2 A **telltale** is someone who tells things about other people in order to get them into trouble; used informally, especially by children. EG *'You little telltale', she shouted.*
N COUNT OR VOC

telly /te̱li[1]/, **tellies.** A **telly** is a television; an informal word. EG *Did you see The Doctor's Dilemma on telly last night?*
N COUNT/UNCOUNT

temerity /tɪ[2]me̱rɪti[1]/. If you have the **temerity** to do something, you do it in a very confident way that indicates that you are not modest or polite and that other people usually think is rude or inappropriate. EG *He had the temerity to suggest that a few changes might be needed.*
N UNCOUNT : USU *the*/POSS+N ⇑ boldness = rashness

temp /te̱mp/, **temps, temping. 1** A **temp** is a person, usually a secretary, who is employed by an agency that sends him or her to work in different offices for short periods of time, for example to replace someone who is ill or on holiday. EG *Being a temp gives you a chance to gain experience.*
N COUNT

2 If someone **is temping**, they are working as a temp. EG *I'm temping at the moment, until I can find a really interesting job.*
V : USU CONT

temper /te̱mpə/, **tempers, tempering, tempered. 1** Your **temper is 1.1** the tendency that you have to become angry or to stay calm. EG *He had a most violent temper... ...a quick temper... They could see he was having trouble controlling his temper... He was a man of surprisingly mild temper for an artist.*
N COUNT/UNCOUNT ⇑ mood
1.2 the state you are in when you are so angry that you cannot think clearly about what you are saying or doing. EG *One day the man attacked me in a temper... ...fits of temper.*
N SING : a+N, OR N UNCOUNT = rage
1.3 the way you are feeling at a particular time, especially how cheerful and happy or how angry you are. EG *He couldn't put up with her moods, her sulkiness, her bad temper... She might come home in a better temper.*
N COUNT/UNCOUNT+SUPP ⇑ mood

2 If you **lose** your **temper** or **fly into a temper**, you become so angry that you cannot think clearly about what you are saying or doing. EG *She suddenly lost her temper and left the room.*
PHR : VB INFLECTS

3 If you **temper** something that is difficult or unpleasant, you make it more acceptable and enjoyable; a formal use. EG *A romantic courtship serves to temper the harsh reality of daily life.*
V+O ⇑ moderate

temperament /te̱mpə[0]rəmə[2]nt/, **temperaments.** Your **temperament** is your basic nature, especially as it is shown in the way that you react to situations or to other people, for example whether you are calm, energetic, cheerful, or quiet. EG *The differences in temperament between the two brothers were striking.*
N COUNT/UNCOUNT ⇑ character = disposition

temperamental /te̱mpə[0]rəme̱ntə[0]l/. **1** Someone who is **temperamental** is not calm or quiet by nature, but has moods that change often and suddenly. EG *In her latest film she portrayed a temperamental Polish actress.*
ADJ QUALIT ⇑ changeable = volatile

2 Temperamental features are related to the natural temperament a person has, especially as this is shown in the way that they react to situations or to other people. EG *Many political and temperamental differences still exist between them.*
ADJ CLASSIF

◊ **temperamentally**. EG *He was a likeable man, temperamentally unsuited to politics.* ◊ ADV = by nature

3 Something, such as a car or a machine, that is **temperamental** sometimes works well but at other times works badly or does not work at all. EG *There was a temperamental gas stove which needed an endless supply of matches.* ADJ QUALIT = unpredictable

temperance /tɛmpə⁰rəns/ is **1** behaviour that is very self-controlled. For example, a person who shows temperance does not eat too much, drink too much, or do anything to excess; a formal use. EG *He believed in the value of work, of industry, of fidelity, and temperance in all things.* N UNCOUNT ⇑ moderation **2** the habit of not drinking alcohol because you believe that it is dangerous or morally wrong. EG *She didn't need temperance lectures from me.* N UNCOUNT

temperate /tɛmpə⁰rəˡt/. **1** A **temperate** place has weather that is never extremely hot or extremely cold. EG *...a temperate climate... ...the temperate woodlands of Tasmania.* ADJ QUALIT ⇑ moderate

2 If a person's behaviour is **temperate**, it is calm and self-controlled, so that they do not get angry or lose their temper easily; a formal or literary use. EG *If you had remained calm the discussion might have been a lot more temperate.* ADJ QUALIT ⇑ moderate

temperature /tɛmprəˡtʃə/, **temperatures**. **1** The **temperature** is the amount of heat that something has or that there is in a place. Temperatures can be felt or measured. EG *...a very high temperature... Temperatures fell by 26 degrees Centigrade... ...a sudden drop in temperature... ...a temperature of 10°C.* N COUNT/UNCOUNT

2 Your **temperature** is the temperature of your blood. If you are well, your temperature should be about 37° centigrade. If it is higher than that, you are probably ill. N COUNT : USU POSS/a+N

3 If you are **running a temperature** or if you **have got a temperature**, you are ill because the temperature of your body is higher than it usually is. PHR : VB INFLECTS

4 If you **take** someone's **temperature**, you use a thermometer to measure the temperature of their blood in order to see if they are ill. EG *I took her temperature and it was 40°C.* PHR : VB INFLECTS

5 You talk about the **temperature** of a group of people when you want to describe the way they are showing their feelings in a situation, especially strong feelings. If the temperature is raised, then people are usually excited and angry or violent, and if the temperature is cool, then they are usually calm and quiet or unfriendly. EG *He tried to cool the temperature by stating some obvious facts.* N COUNT

tempest /tɛmprˀst/, **tempests**. A **tempest** is a very violent storm; a literary word. EG *Fierce raged the tempest o'er the deep.* N COUNT

tempestuous /tɛmpɛstjuəs/. **1** Something or someone that is **tempestuous** is full of very strong and passionate emotions. EG *April could prove a tempestuous time in your private life... ...a tempestuous relationship.* ◊ **tempestuously**. EG *She stormed tempestuously out of the room.* ADJ QUALIT ⇑ violent = stormy; ◊ ADV WITH VB ⇑ violently

2 Tempestuous weather is very rough and stormy; a formal or literary use. EG *...a tempestuous night.* ADJ QUALIT

tempi /tɛmpiˡ/ is a plural of **tempo**.

template /tɛmpləˡt/, **templates**. A **template** is a thin piece of metal or plastic cut into a particular shape. It is used to help you cut wood, metal, etc accurately, or to reproduce the same shape many times. EG *There would on this model be a different template for each letter of the alphabet.* N COUNT ⇑ guide

temple /tɛmpə⁰l/, **temples**. **1** A **temple** is a building used for the worship of a god or gods, especially in the Buddhist and Hindu religions. EG *She had said her prayers and made her visits to the temple... ...a Roman temple.* N COUNT : ALSO IN NAMES

2 Your **temple** is the rather flat part on either side of your head above your ear and close to your eye. EG *He felt the vein throb in his temple where Thomas had hit him.* N COUNT

tempo /tɛmpəʊ/, **tempos, tempi**. The plural can be either **tempos** or **tempi**. **1** The **tempo** of an event is the speed at which it happens; a fairly formal use. EG *...the tempo of everyday life... Events had been moving at an equally dramatic tempo.* N SING WITH DET/UNCOUNT+SUPP = pace

2 The **tempo** of a piece of music is the speed at which it is played; a technical term. EG *We play the music of Mozart at a faster tempo than it was originally performed at.* N COUNT/UNCOUNT

temporal /tɛmpə⁰rəl/; a formal word. **1** If you describe processes or features as **temporal**, you are referring to how they change or endure over a period of time. EG *...the temporal and historical process... ...the temporal character of human bonds.* ADJ CLASSIF : USU ATTRIB

2 Temporal events or matters involve earthly existence and are limited by time. EG *...human institutions and temporal events.* ADJ CLASSIF : ATTRIB

3 Temporal powers or authorities are not controlled by a church and are not connected with the religious or spiritual lives of people. EG *...the temporal power of the state.* ADJ CLASSIF : ATTRIB = lay, secular

4 Temporal is also used to refer to the part of your brain that is near your temples; a technical use. EG *...the temporal cortex of the brain.* ADJ CLASSIF : ATTRIB

temporary /tɛmpə⁰rəriˡ/. Something that is **temporary** **1** lasts or is in a particular situation for only a short time. EG *She's a temporary resident... ...a temporary assistant lectureship.* ◊ **temporarily**. EG *Each person is alone, temporarily, with his own thoughts.* ADJ CLASSIF ≠ permanent; ◊ ADV

2 lasts for a short time until it is replaced by something better and more permanent. EG *It's a temporary arrangement which we'll have for the next few weeks.* ◊ **temporarily**. EG *I offered to put him up temporarily at the request of his girlfriend.* ADJ QUALIT = provisional; ◊ ADV

temporize /tɛmpəraɪz/, **temporizes, temporizing, temporized**; also spelled **temporise**. If you **temporize**, you keep talking about or keep doing something unimportant, in order to delay making a decision or stating your real opinion in a conversation, argument, etc; a formal word. EG *'Well,' I temporized, 'you'll have to ask your mother.'* V OR V+QUOTE

tempt /tɛmp⁰t/, **tempts, tempting, tempted**. **1** If you **tempt** someone, you offer them something that they want in order to encourage them to do something that you want them to do. EG *The new university of Watermouth had tempted him with two additional increments... The building societies are offering higher rates of interest to tempt new savers.* V+O = lure, entice

2 If something **tempts** you, it attracts you and makes you want it, often when it is something which you know you should avoid. EG *His success tempted many others to try the same route... She wasn't seriously tempted by the prospect of leaving.* V+O ⇑ persuade

3 If you say that you **are** or **feel tempted** to do something, you mean that you would like to do it, but you feel it might be wrong or inappropriate. EG *I was tempted to call you last night, but I thought you'd probably be asleep... I sat there sipping my drink, once more tempted to blame Nell for everything.* PHR : VB INFLECTS+to-INF ⇑ urge

4 If you say that someone is **tempting fate** or **tempting providence**, you mean that they are taking a rather foolish and unnecessary risk, which is likely to end badly for them. PHR : VB INFLECTS, USU CONT

temptation /tɛmp⁰teɪʃə⁰n/, **temptations**. **1** **Temptation** is the state you are in when you feel you want to do something or have something which you know you really ought to avoid. EG *If you can't resist buying things, shop by telephone to avoid temptation... He had the strength to resist further temptation.* N UNCOUNT

2 A **temptation** is something that attracts you a great deal, even though you know you ought to avoid it. EG *...the temptations to which he was continually exposed.* N COUNT

tempting /tɛmp⁰tɪŋ/. Something that is **tempting** attracts you a great deal, even though you know you do not need it or should avoid it. EG *...an extremely tempting price... ...spicy vegetable cutlets, the smell of which was so tempting that they became hungry again.* ◊ **temptingly**. EG *The sunlight streamed temptingly through the windows and made me restless.* ADJ QUALIT = alluring; ◊ ADV = invitingly

ten /tɛn/, **tens**. **1 Ten** is the number 10: see □ at NUMBER, AGE, DATE, MEASUREMENT, MONEY, and TIME. EG *It had been ten years since I left school.* NUM

2 If you say that it is **ten to one** that something will happen, you mean that it is extremely likely. EG *It's ten to one they miss their train... Ten to one he will end up in the pub.* ● See also **Number Ten**. ● **ten a penny**: see **penny**. PHR : USED AS C/A = odds-on

tenable /tɛnəbə⁰l/. **1** An argument or point of view that is **tenable** is reasonable and able to be successfully defended against criticism. EG *It seemed a tenable proposition.* ADJ QUALIT = plausible, defensible

2 A job or position that is **tenable** is intended to be held by someone for a particular length of time. EG ADJ CLASSIF+A

The position of Chairman is tenable for a maximum of three years.

tenacious /tɪ²neɪʃəs/. 1 If you are **tenacious**, you are very determined and do not give up easily. EG *He's pretty tenacious when it comes to standing up for his rights... They kept a tenacious grip on their possessions.* ◇ **tenaciously**. EG *People tenaciously hold on to old beliefs.* ADJ QUALIT = stubborn, resolute ◇ ADV WITH VB = stubbbornly

2 Something such as an idea that is **tenacious** has a strong influence on people and is difficult to change or get rid of. ADJ QUALIT = deep-rooted

tenacity /tɪ²næsɪti¹/. If you have **tenacity**, you are very determined and do not give up easily. EG *I don't like the man, but I admire his tenacity... He was trying with astonishing tenacity to preserve his self-respect.* N UNCOUNT = doggedness, obstinacy

tenancy /tenənsi¹/, **tenancies**. 1 **Tenancy** is the use that you have of land and property belonging to someone else, for which you pay rent. EG *Once they took up the tenancy they couldn't be evicted.* N UNCOUNT

2 A **tenancy** is the period of time during which a person pays rent for the use of land or property. EG *It's a three-year tenancy.* N COUNT ⇑ occupancy

tenant /tenənt/, **tenants**. A **tenant** is someone who pays rent to live in a house or flat or who pays rent for the use of land or buildings. EG *The landlord must give the tenant 'reasonable notice' of his intention to call.* ● **sitting tenant**: see **sitting**. N COUNT ⇑ occupant

tench /tentʃ/. **Tench** is both the singular and the plural form. A **tench** is a dark green European fish that lives in lakes and rivers. N COUNT

tend /tend/, **tends, tending, tended**. 1 If something **tends** to happen, it happens often and so it is what usually happens. EG *I tend to wake up early in the morning... Shopping lists on old envelopes tend to get lost.* V+*to*-INF = be apt

2 If something **tends** to or toward a particular feature or characteristic, it shows that feature or characteristic more strongly than others. EG *Our school dramas tend toward comedy and farce... Your own contemporaries tend to self-centredness.* V+A *(to/toward)* = incline

3 People sometimes say **'I tend'** when they want to appear modest about what they are saying or to reduce the force of a claim they are making. EG *I tend to think that's not a good solution... I tend to know Eastern European countries pretty well.* V+*to*-INF

4 If you **tend** someone or something, you look after them very carefully, especially in a loving way. EG *She'd tended four very sick men... He looked forward to tending his sheep again.* V+O = care for

5 If you **tend** a piece of land, you work on it so that plants or crops will grow there. EG *They tend both the rice fields and the vegetable garden.* V+O = cultivate

6 If you **tend** to someone or something, you pay attention to them and deal with their problems and needs. EG *Excuse me, I have to tend to the other guests... In his spare time he tends to the family business.* V+A *(to)* = attend

tendency /tendənsi¹/, **tendencies**. A **tendency** is 1 a habit, trend, or other piece of behaviour that keeps happening. EG *How can we combat this permanent tendency towards inflation?... There is a tendency to select some details and ignore others.* 2 a part of your character that makes you behave in a particular way. EG *The girl might have murderous tendencies... ...a magazine of anarchic tendencies.* N COUNT+SUPP = inclination; N COUNT+SUPP = inclination

tendentious /tendenʃəs/. Something that is **tendentious** expresses very strongly a particular opinion or point of view, especially one that many people disagree with; a formal word. EG *She's always raising tendentious issues.* ADJ QUALIT ⇑ biased = controversial

tender /tendə/, **tenderest; tenders, tendering, tendered**. 1 Someone or something that is **tender** has or expresses gentle and caring feelings. EG *He gave her a tender smile... What a child needs is tender, loving care.* ◇ **tenderly**. EG *She cradled the baby tenderly.* ◇ **tenderness**. EG *I have a feeling of great tenderness for you.* ADJ QUALIT ⇑ loving = fond ◇ ADV WITH VB ◇ N UNCOUNT ⇑ affection

2 If you say that someone is at a **tender** age or of **tender** years you mean that they are still young and inexperienced. ADJ QUALIT: ATTRIB ≠ mature

3 Meat or other food which is **tender** is very soft and easy to cut or chew. EG *The steak was so tender you could have eaten it with a spoon.* ◇ **tenderness**. ADJ QUALIT ≠ tough ◇ N UNCOUNT

4 Plants and trees are described as **tender** if they are young and easily damaged or broken. EG *This crop was at its most tender stage.* ADJ QUALIT ⇑ fragile

5 If part of your body is **tender**, it is sensitive and painful when it is touched, for example because you have injured it. EG *He touched the tender, swollen side of his jaw.* ADJ QUALIT = sore

6 A **tender** is a formal offer to supply goods or to do a particular job, and a statement of the price that you or your company will charge. EG *Tenders are to be submitted on 15 December at 10 a.m... The firm accepted the tender of the Marconi company.* N COUNT ⇑ proposal

7 If you **tender** something such as a suggestion, an apology, or your resignation, you formally offer it. EG *Dr Mayfield has tendered his resignation.* V+O ⇑ give

8 If you **tender** an amount of money, you offer it so that someone can take it, usually in order to pay for something; a formal use, especially on notices. EG *Tender the exact fare, please.* V+O ⇑ present

9 A **tender** is also a waggon behind the engine of a steam train. It is filled with coal and water for the engine. N COUNT

10 See also **legal tender**.

tender-hearted. If you are **tender-hearted**, you have a gentle and caring nature. ADJ QUALIT

tenderize /tendəraɪz/, **tenderizes, tenderizing, tenderized**; also spelled **tenderise**. If you **tenderize** food, you make it more tender by preparing it in a particular way. EG *The meat should be marinated overnight to tenderize and flavour it.* V+O ⇑ soften

tenderloin /tendəlɔɪn/ is pork from a part of the back of a pig where the meat is lean and tender. EG *...a tenderloin steak.* N UNCOUNT

tendon /tendə⁰n/, **tendons**. A **tendon** is a strong cord in a person's or animal's body which joins a muscle to a bone. N COUNT = sinew

tendril /tendrɪ⁰l/, **tendrils**. 1 **Tendrils** are the short stems which grow from the main stem of a climbing plant and which the plant uses to attach itself to a wall, tree, etc. N COUNT : USU PL

2 A **tendril** is also something thin and wispy, for example a piece of hair, which hangs loose away from the main part. EG *Ralph pushed the damp tendrils of hair out of his eyes.* N COUNT = wisp

tenement /tenəmənt/, **tenements**. A **tenement** is a large building, especially one in a poor part of a city, which is divided into a lot of small flats that can be rented cheaply. EG *They live in a tenement... ...the tenement area of the city.* N COUNT

tenet /tenɪt, tiːnɪt/, **tenets**. A **tenet** is one of the principles on which a theory or belief is based. EG *This is a basic tenet of capitalism.* N COUNT : USU+ *of* = precept

tenner /tenə/, **tenners**. A **tenner** is ten pounds or a ten-pound note; used in informal British English. EG *It's worth a tenner at least... Can you lend me a tenner?* N COUNT

tennis /tenɪs/ is a game played by two players or two pairs of players on a rectangular court. They use rackets to hit a ball over a net which is between them. EG *They've gone to play tennis in the park... ...a tennis player... ...a tennis court.* N UNCOUNT

tenon /tenən/, **tenons**. A **tenon** is a part of a piece of wood that has been cut in such a way that it fits into a rectangular slot in another piece of wood. The slot is called a mortise; a technical term in carpentry. N COUNT ⇑ projection

tenor /tenə/, **tenors**. 1 A **tenor** is a male singer whose voice is higher than that of a baritone and lower than that of an alto. EG *The tenors have to be all together on this side.* ▸ used as an adjective. EG *...his pleasant tenor voice.* N COUNT ▸ ADJ CLASSIF

2 The **tenor** in an opera or other piece of singing is the part for a man with a tenor voice. EG *Who's going to sing the tenor?* N SING WITH DET

3 A **tenor** recorder, saxophone, or other musical instrument has a range of notes that is similar to that of a tenor voice. ADJ CLASSIF: ATTRIB

4 The **tenor** of something written or spoken is the general meaning that is expressed by it; a formal use. EG *I forget the tenor of her reply.* N SING WITH DET +SUPP = drift

5 The **tenor** of something is its basic character and the way that it develops; a formal use. EG *There has been a shift in the whole tenor of the anti-nuclear campaign.* N SING WITH DET +SUPP ⇑ quality

tenpin /tenpɪn/, **tenpins**. 1 **Tenpins** are the wooden bottle-shaped objects that you try to knock down when you play tenpin bowling. N COUNT ⇑ skittle

2 **Tenpins** is the same as tenpin bowling; used in American English. N UNCOUNT

tenpin bowling is a game in which you try to knock down ten objects, called tenpins, by rolling a heavy ball towards them. Tenpin bowling is usually played in a bowling alley. N UNCOUNT = tenpins

tense /tens/, **tenser, tensest; tenses, tensing, tensed.** 1 If you are **tense**, you are worried and nervous, so that you are unable to relax. EG *They began to grow tense over the likelihood of a long delay... He's much too tense.* ◊ **tensely.** EG *Her fingers tensely twisted the handle of her bag.* ◊ **tenseness.** EG *Worries and tenseness can lead to insomnia.* ADJ QUALIT = edgy, anxious; ◊ ADV WITH VB = nervously; ◊ N UNCOUNT = tension

2 If your body or a part of your body is **tense**, your muscles are stretched tight and not at all relaxed. EG *With her body so tense, it seemed as though she were listening for something... Your neck is tense.* ADJ QUALIT ⇑ taut

3 If you or the muscles in your body **tense** or **tense up**, your muscles stiffen and stretch tight, usually because you are afraid or are preparing yourself to make a movement. EG *The man on the terrace tensed slightly... All the muscles of his body were tensed... 'Who are you?' I asked, the skin of my cheek-bones tensing up.* V-ERG, OR PHRASAL VB : V-ERG + ADV ⇑ tighten

4 A **tense** situation or period is one that makes people anxious, for example because they are afraid that it may suddenly become violent. EG *The situation was very tense... ...a long, tense silence.* ADJ QUALIT = strained, fraught

5 The **tense** of a verb is the form which shows whether you are referring to the past, the present, or the future. EG *The present tense is 'I swim' or 'I am swimming'.* N COUNT/UNCOUNT

tensed up. If you are **tensed up**, you are nervous and unable to relax, because of something that is about to happen or that you are afraid may happen. EG *Relax-you're all tensed up.* ADJ QUALIT : PRED = strung up

tensile /tensaɪl/. You use **tensile** when you are talking about the amount of stress that wire, rope, concrete, etc can take without breaking, especially when it is stretched; a technical term in engineering. EG *...the tensile strength of steel.* ADJ CLASSIF : ATTRIB

tension /tenʃə⁰n/, **tensions.** 1 **Tension** is 1.1 the feeling that is produced in a situation when people are anxious and do not trust each other, and when there is a possibility of sudden violence or conflict. EG *This latest spy affair has created a lot of tension... ...during a period of high tension in 1974... Family tensions are increasing.* N UNCOUNT/N IN PLURAL ⇑ uneasiness 1.2 a feeling of worry and nervousness which makes it difficult for you to relax. EG *She could feel her muscles tighten into hard lumps with tension and fear... With tension in his voice he said he wanted to tell me something..* N UNCOUNT = apprehension 1.3 the degree to which something is stretched tight. EG *The loss of tension in the cables is a problem.* N UNCOUNT ⇑ tautness

2 If you describe a situation as a **tension** between a number of different influences, forces, factors, etc, you mean that the situation is not very stable because they are all pulling in different directions. EG *So I think it's a tension between knowing yourself and knowing God... All these forces within society are in tension.* N SING : a+N, OR N UNCOUNT ⇑ conflict

tent /tent/, **tents.** A **tent** is a shelter made of canvas or nylon, which you sleep in when you are camping. It is held up by poles and ropes. EG *She pitched her tent in a field.* ● See also **oxygen tent.** N COUNT

tentacle /tentəkə⁰l/, **tentacles.** 1 The **tentacles** of an animal such as an octopus are the long thin parts that are used for feeling and holding things, for getting food, and for moving. N COUNT : USU PL ⇑ limb

2 The **tentacles** of an organization or of a political, religious, or social idea are the ways in which this organization or idea controls you, making it difficult for you to act or think without being influenced by it. EG *These men have cut loose from the tentacles of class background.* N PLURAL + SUPP = clutches

tentative /tentətɪv/. If something you do or say is **tentative**, it is cautious and not very confident because you are not sure you are right and you want to see what will happen. EG *A few tentative conclusions may be drawn... Each step he took was slightly tentative.* ◊ **tentatively.** EG *She raised her hand and waved, tentatively.* ADJ QUALIT ⇑ uncertain = experimental; ◊ ADV WITH VB = hesitantly

tenterhooks /tentəhʊks/. If you are **on tenterhooks** you are in a state of anxiety and excitement about something that is going to happen, especially when you do not know exactly what is going to happen. EG *He went in while we waited on tenterhooks in the car.* PHR : USED AS AN A ⇑ anxious

tenth /tenθ/, **tenths.** 1 The **tenth** item in a series is the one that you count as number ten: see ☐ at NUMBER, AGE, and DATE. EG *...the tenth day of the strike.* ORDINAL

2 A **tenth** is one of ten equal parts of something. EG *...a tenth of a second.* N COUNT : USU + of

tenuous /tenjuəs/. If you describe something such as evidence, a relationship, or a link, as **tenuous**, you mean that it is so weak or slight that it could easily be lost, broken, or destroyed. EG *There is only the most tenuous evidence for it... He struggled to maintain his tenuous hold on her.* ◊ **tenuously.** EG *He kept in contact with her, if only very tenuously and intermittently.* ADJ QUALIT = flimsy, insubstantial; ◊ ADV WITH VB ⇑ slightly

tenure /tenjʊ⁰ə/ is 1 the legal right to live in a particular building or to use a particular piece of land during a fixed period of time. EG *They get tenure under the Rent Act.* N UNCOUNT ⇑ entitlement 2 the holding of an important job in government or another organization; also used to refer to the period of time during which a person works in such a job. EG *His Government was doomed, and his tenure of Downing Street with it... ...the first week of his tenure of the Home Office.* N UNCOUNT + of = occupancy 3 the right to keep your job at a university until you retire. EG *A lecturer in the English Department has recently been refused tenure.* N UNCOUNT ⇑ security

tepee /tiːpiː/, **tepees.** A **tepee** is a tent made by North American Indians from animal skins. N COUNT = wigwam

tepid /tepɪd/. 1 Water or another liquid that is **tepid** is slightly warm. EG *The fish lay their eggs in the shallow tepid pools.* ADJ CLASSIF = lukewarm

2 If you describe something such as a feeling or reaction as **tepid**, you mean that it lacks enthusiasm or liveliness. EG *Tepid applause greeted her efforts.* ADJ QUALIT = lukewarm

tercentenary /tɜːsentiːnəri¹/, **tercentenaries.** A **tercentenary** is a day or a year which is exactly three hundred years after an important event such as the birth of a famous person. EG *...the tercentenary of the birth of Handel.* N COUNT : IF + PREP THEN of ⇑ anniversary

term /tɜːm/, **terms, terming, termed.** 1 If you talk about something **in** economic **terms, in** political **terms**, etc, you are specifying which aspect of a situation you are concerned with. EG *Life is going to be a little easier in economic terms... Of course he was talking in international terms.* PHR : USED AS AN A

2 You use **in terms of** 2.1 when you make a statement, to specify which particular aspect of a situation you are concerned with. EG *It has been a terrible year in terms of business... A computer is powerful in terms of capacity and speed... Do you have much work to do in terms of marking?* PREP = as regards 2.2 to say what is forming the basis for an explanation, description, attitude, etc. EG *These events are not to be explained in terms of what happened last week... Older men tended to see external problems more in terms of Europe.* PREP

3 If you are **thinking** or **talking in terms of** doing something, you are considering doing it. EG *You should be thinking in terms of paying off your debts... He's talking in terms of leaving.* PHR : VB INFLECTS ⇑ plan

4 If you say or express something **in** strong **terms, in** abstract **terms**, etc, you say or express it using a particular level or type of language or using language that shows clearly your attitude or feelings. EG *The report describes your work in glowing terms... She condemned the protest in strong terms... Try to explain it in terms a small boy might understand.* PHR : USED AS AN A

5 If you express an opinion **in no uncertain terms**, you express it strongly and clearly so that there is no doubt about what you mean. EG *She has been denouncing me in no uncertain terms.* PHR : USED AS AN A = vehemently

6 You use **in** someone's **terms, in** those **terms**, etc when you are referring to a particular point of view or way of thinking. EG *In Keynesian terms the issue was much more one of politics than economics... In your terms the situation's got worse.* PHR : USED AS AN A

7 A **term** is a word or expression with a specific meaning, especially one that is used in a particular variety of English or in relation to a particular subject. EG *He asked them what they understood by the term 'radical'... 'Habeas corpus' is a legal term... ...a term of abuse.* ● **contradiction in terms**: see **contradiction.** N COUNT : USU + SUPP

8 If you **term** something, you give it a name or describe it with a particular word or expression. EG *...recent breakthroughs in what might be termed 'birth technology'... The press termed the visit a triumph.* V+O+C = call

9 A **term** is also **9.1** one of the periods of time that a school, college, or university divides the year into. In Britain there are usually three terms in a year. EG *None of you have any lectures next term... ...the spring term... It was the first week of term.* **9.2** a period of time between two elections during which a particular party, prime minister, president, etc is in power. EG *...Baldwin's second term of office as Premier... ...a mid-term by-election.* **9.3** a period of time spent doing a particular job or in a particular place. EG *He has just been sentenced to a long prison term... ...a fifteen-month term of service.* **9.4** the period for which a legal contract, insurance policy, etc is valid. EG *The policy is near the end of its term.*
N COUNT/UNCOUNT = semester; N COUNT+SUPP = spell; N COUNT+SUPP = spell; N COUNT+SUPP ⇑ validity

10 A pregnant woman's **term** is the end of her pregnancy when the birth of her baby is expected. EG *...the reasons for not carrying this pregnancy to term.*
N UNCOUNT

11 **Term** is used in the expressions 'the long term', 'the medium term' and 'the short term' when you are talking about what happens over a particular period of time, in the future or after a particular event. EG *Such a policy would be economically–and in the long term, socially also–highly disadvantageous... What are your plans over the long term?... These are only short-term solutions.*
N SING : the+MOD+N

12 The **terms** of an agreement, treaty, or other arrangement are the conditions that must be accepted by the people involved in it. EG *We will not accept these terms... They would never surrender this territory, on any terms whatever.*
N PLURAL

13 **Terms of reference** are the limits given to someone when they are asked to consider or investigate a particular subject. These limits tell them what they must deal with and what they can ignore; used in formal or official English. EG *The question of finance was not within our terms of reference... The Opposition welcomed the inquiry, though called for wider terms of reference.*
PHR : USED AS S/O/C ⇑ range

14 **Terms** are also the conditions relating to the sale of something or to payment. EG *I'm prepared to sell it at highly favourable terms.* .
N PLURAL = rates

15 If two people or groups compete or are treated **on the same terms** or **on equal terms**, neither of them has an advantage over the other. If they compete or are treated **on unfair terms** or **on unequal terms**, one of them has an advantage over the other. EG *They decided to let women be conscripted on the same terms as men... They are trying to compete with us on unfair terms.*
PHR : USED AS AN A

16 If you do something **on** your **terms**, you do it under conditions that you decide because you are in a position of power. EG *She certainly wanted his money, but on her own terms... They finally agreed to the Bill on the President's terms.*
PHR : USED AS AN A

17 You say that two people or groups are **on** good **terms, on** friendly **terms**, etc when you are saying how friendly or how formal they are with one another. EG *You need to be on friendly terms with him... They lived on good terms... They were on Christian-name terms when they were alone.* • **on speaking terms**: see **speak**.
PHR : USED AS AN A

18 If you **come to terms with** something that is difficult or unpleasant, you learn to accept and deal with it. EG *He has come to terms with death.*
PHR : VB INFLECTS

19 A **term** in a mathematical equation, series, formula, etc is one of the numbers or quantities in it.
N COUNT ⇑ quantity

terminal /tɜ̲:mɪnəºl/, **terminals**. **1** A **terminal** illness or disease causes death, often slowly, and cannot be cured.
ADJ CLASSIF = fatal, incurable

2 A **terminal** patient is dying of a terminal illness or disease. ◇ **terminally**. EG *...a hospice for the terminally ill.*
ADJ CLASSIF; ◇ ADV+ADJ = fatally

3 A **terminal** is **3.1** a place where buses, planes, ships, etc begin or end their journeys and load or unload their passengers or goods. EG *...a bus terminal... Work has started on the construction of a container terminal.* **3.2** one of the parts of an electrical device through which electricity enters or leaves the device. EG *...the current flowing out of the output terminal.* **3.3** a device, especially one consisting of a keyboard and a VDU, which you use for obtaining information from a computer or for putting information into it. EG *The data will be fed into a computer terminal... The present plan is to charge a small rental for the terminal.*
N COUNT : USU MOD+N = terminus; N COUNT; N COUNT

terminate /tɜ̲:mɪneɪt/, **terminates, terminating, terminated**. **1** When you **terminate** something or when it **terminates**, it ends completely; a formal word. EG *I thought that he would terminate the discussion then and there.* ◇ **termination** /tɜ̲:mɪneɪ̲ʃəºn/. EG *...the termination of one's links with the organization.*
V-ERG ⇑ finish; ◇ N UNCOUNT ⇑ ending

2 When a train or bus **terminates**, it stops at a particular place and does not go any further; used especially in official announcements and timetables. EG *This train will terminate at Coventry.*
V+A

3 To **terminate** a pregnancy means to end it, especially in hospital, so that the child dies; a formal or medical use. ◇ **termination, terminations.** EG *In the end she had to have a termination, she was so ill.*
V+O; ◇ N COUNT = abortion

termini /tɜ̲:mɪnaɪ/ is a plural of **terminus.**

terminology /tɜ̲:mɪnɒ̲lədʒi¹/, **terminologies.** The **terminology** of a subject is the set of special words and expressions used in connection with it. EG *The critique uses Marxist terminology... This had for a long time been described in Western terminology as the 'encounter battle.'* ◇ **terminological** /tɜ̲:mɪnəlɒ̲dʒɪkəºl/. EG *...a few terminological differences.*
N UNCOUNT/COUNT : USU+SUPP ⇑ language; ◇ ADJ CLASSIF ⇑ linguistic

terminus /tɜ̲:mɪnəs/, **termini, terminuses**. The plural can be either **termini** or **terminuses.** A **terminus** is a large railway station or bus station where several routes begin and end. EG *...the great continental railway termini... How much to the terminus, please?*
N COUNT = terminal

termite /tɜ̲:maɪt/, **termites**. **Termites** are small white insects which live in hot countries in nests made of earth. They do a lot of damage by eating wood. EG *Flying termites poured out of the clefts... ...a colony of termites.*
N COUNT : USU PL = white ant

tern /tɜ̲:n/, **terns**. A **tern** is a small black and white seabird with long wings and a forked tail.
N COUNT

terrace /te̲rə¹s/, **terraces**. **1** A **terrace** is **1.1** a row of similar houses joined together by their side walls; used in British English. EG *...a house in a fashionable terrace... ...a tiny terrace house.* **1.2** a street that has rows of terraced houses in it; used in British English. EG *He turned the van into the terrace.* ▸ used as the name of a street. EG *...Adelphi Terrace.*
N COUNT; N COUNT; ▸ N IN NAMES AFTER N

2 A **terrace** is also **2.1** a flat area of stone or grass next to a house or other building where people can sit or eat meals. EG *He wandered out onto the terrace... ...the terrace of the Continental Hotel.* **2.2** one of a series of flat areas of ground built like steps on a hillside so that crops can be grown there.
N COUNT = patio; N COUNT : USU PL

3 The **terraces** at a football ground are wide steps that people can stand on when they are watching a game. EG *The noise from the terraces was deafening.*
N PLURAL : the+N

terraced /te̲rə¹st/. A **terraced** hillside has flat areas of ground like steps built on it so that people can grow crops there. EG *...a pretty terraced garden.*
ADJ CLASSIF ⇑ stepped

terraced house, terraced houses. A **terraced house** or **terrace house** is one of a row of similar houses joined together by their side walls; used in British English. EG *...a damp and draughty terraced house.*
N COUNT

terracotta /te̲rəkɒ̲tə/ is a brownish-red clay that has been baked but not glazed and that is used for making flower pots, small statues, etc. ▸ **Terracotta** is also the colour of terracotta.
N UNCOUNT ⇑ pottery; ▸ ADJ COLOUR

terra firma /te̲rə fɜ̲:mə/ is used to refer to the ground when you are contrasting it with the sea or air, especially because it seems safer. EG *He found himself on terra firma at last.*
N UNCOUNT

terrain /tereɪ̲n/ is used to refer to an area of land or type of land when you are considering its physical features. EG *The commander had made a detailed study of the terrain... ...hilly terrain... ...the rugged terrain of the Anatolian plateau.*
N UNCOUNT+SUPP

terrapin /te̲rəpɪn/, **terrapins**. A **terrapin** is a small turtle that lives in rivers or lakes, especially in North America.
N COUNT

terrestrial /tə¹re̲strɪəl/. **1** A **terrestrial** animal lives on land or on the ground rather than in the sea, in trees, or in the air; a technical use in zoology. EG *...terrestrial mammals, reptiles, and insects.*
ADJ CLASSIF : ATTRIB

2 **Terrestrial** means relating to the planet Earth rather than to some other part of the universe.
ADJ CLASSIF : ATTRIB

terrible /te̲rə¹bəºl/. **1** A **terrible** experience or situation is very serious and unpleasant. EG *Conditions in our country are terrible–there is hunger and*
ADJ QUALIT ⇑ bad = dreadful

disease everywhere... ...a terrible accident... It was a nightmare. It was terrible.

2 If you feel **terrible**, you have a very unpleasant feeling of some kind, for example you feel guilty, ashamed, or ill. EG *I feel terrible, I should never have told him... ...a terrible sense of guilt.* ADJ QUALIT ↑ bad = awful

3 You describe something as **terrible** when you think that it is very bad, unpleasant, or unsatisfactory. EG *I've had a terrible day at the office... ...terrible weather... The food was terrible... Goodness, you do look terrible!* ADJ QUALIT = dreadful

4 **Terrible** is also used to emphasize the great degree or extent of something, especially something undesirable. EG *I've been a terrible fool... It will be a terrible pity if this should happen... You're going to get in the most terrible muddle.* ADJ CLASSIF: ATTRIB = frightful

terribly /tɛrəˈbliˈ/ is used informally to emphasize the extent or degree of something. EG *I'm terribly sorry... It's terribly important... It wasn't a terribly good summer... They were terribly pleased to see you.* ADV ↑ very = frightfully

terrier /te̱rɪə/, **terriers**. A **terrier** is a small dog. There are several kinds of terrier. N COUNT

terrific /tərɪ̱fɪk/. 1 You describe something as **terrific** when you are very pleased with it or very impressed by it; an informal use. EG *Our new carpet looks terrific... 'I'll come and give you a hand tomorrow.'–'Terrific.'* ADJ CLASSIF ↑ excellent = great

2 **Terrific** also means very great in amount, degree, or intensity. EG *...a terrific thunderstorm... ...a terrific amount of money.* ◇ **terrifically**. EG *He's terrifically good-looking.* ADJ CLASSIF: ATTRIB ◇ ADV+ADV/ADJ

terrify /te̱rɪfaɪ/, **terrifies, terrifying, terrified**. If something **terrifies** you, it makes you feel extremely frightened. EG *Rats terrify me.* ◇ **terrified**. EG *My sister was too terrified to cry.* V+O ↑ frighten = petrify ◇ ADJ QUALIT

terrifying /te̱rɪfaɪɪŋ/. Something that is **terrifying** makes you very frightened. EG *The most terrifying aspect of nuclear bombing is radiation... ...a terrifying nightmare.* ◇ **terrifyingly**. EG *Catastrophe had seemed terrifyingly close.* ADJ QUALIT = horrifying ◇ ADV+ADJ/ADV

territorial /te̱rɪtɔ̱ːrɪəl/, **territorials**. 1 **Territorial** means concerned with the ownership of a particular area of land or water. EG *...territorial boundaries... ...territorial possessiveness.* ◇ **territoriality** /te̱rɪtɔ̱ːrɪæ̱lɪtiˈ/. EG *...a sense of territoriality.* ADJ CLASSIF: USU ATTRIB ◇ N UNCOUNT

2 A **territorial** is a member of the Territorial Army. EG *Jack is in the Territorials... ...a territorial officer.* N COUNT: USU PL ↑ soldier

Territorial Army. The **Territorial Army** is a British armed force whose members are not professional soldiers but train as soldiers in their spare times. EG *I've done 27 years in the Territorial Army.* N PROPER: *the*+N ↑ army = Territorials

territorial waters. A country's **territorial waters** are the parts of the sea close to its coast which it considers to be under its control, especially with regard to fishing rights. EG *They were caught violating territorial waters.* N PLURAL

territory /te̱rɪtəºriˈ/, **territories**. 1 **Territory** is land which is controlled by a particular country or ruler. EG *...British territory... ...enemy-occupied territory... This meeting is to be held on neutral territory.* N UNCOUNT: USU +SUPP ↑ domain

2 A **territory** is a country or region that is controlled by another country. EG *...the French territories on the Eastern coast... ...colonial territories.* N COUNT ↑ province

3 An animal's **territory** is an area which it regards as its own and which it defends when other animals try to enter it. EG *They stop along the boundary of their territory and refresh its markings with urine... ...an animal's impulse to fight for territory.* N UNCOUNT/COUNT ↑ land

4 **Territory** is also 4.1 land with a particular character. EG *We were passing through mountainous territory... Everyone had assumed that it was uninhabited territory.* 4.2 an area of knowledge or experience. EG *All this is familiar territory to readers of her recent novels... This of course brings us into rather difficult territory.* N UNCOUNT+SUPP = country, terrain N UNCOUNT+SUPP = terrain

terror /te̱rə/, **terrors**. 1 **Terror** is very great fear. EG *She awakened in terror as the flaming roof came crashing down... Eyes wide with terror, he watched the knife flash towards him.* N UNCOUNT ↑ panic

2 A **terror** is someone or something, especially a thought or an experience, that makes you very frightened. EG *They shrank back in fear at some unseen terror... They suffered untold terrors in the dark.* N COUNT = horror

3 People sometimes refer to a child as a **terror** when he or she is naughty and hard to control; an informal use. EG *That boy's a little terror.* N COUNT: ALSO VOC

4 The word **terror** is also used in the following expressions. 4.1 If you **go** or **live in terror of** something, you are very frightened of it. EG *Africans, equally, went in terror of the white man.* 4.2 If you **go** or **are in terror of** your **life**, you are very frightened that you will be killed. 4.3 If something **holds no terrors for** you, you are not at all frightened or worried by it. 4.4 ● a **reign of terror**: see **reign**. ● to **strike terror into someone's heart**: see **strike**. PHR: VB INFLECTS PHR: VB INFLECTS PHR: VB INFLECTS

terrorise /te̱rəraɪz/. See **terrorize**.

terrorism /te̱rərɪzəºm/ is the use of violence, especially murder, kidnapping, and bombing, in order to achieve political aims or to force a government to do something; used showing disapproval. EG *These measures failed to bring acts of terrorism to an end.* N UNCOUNT

terrorist /te̱rərɪst/, **terrorists**. A **terrorist** is a person who uses violence, especially murder, kidnapping, and bombing, in order to achieve his or her political aims or to force a government to do something; used showing disapproval. EG *They have given aid to terrorists.* ▸ used as an adjective. EG *She is in prison for terrorist activities... ...a new wave of terrorist bombing against civilian targets.* N COUNT ▸ ADJ CLASSIF: ATTRIB

terrorize /te̱rəraɪz/, **terrorizes, terrorizing, terrorized**; also spelled **terrorise**. If someone **terrorizes** you, they keep you in a state of fear by making it seem likely that they will attack you. EG *Lee was a bully who terrorized us all.* ◇ **terrorization** /te̱rəraɪzeɪ̱ʃəºn/. EG *...the terrorization of the young.* V+O ↑ frighten = terrify ◇ N UNCOUNT ↑ intimidation

terror-stricken. If someone is **terror-stricken** or **terror-struck**, they are extremely frightened. ADJ CLASSIF = petrified

terry /te̱riˈ/ is a type of cloth which has lots of very small loops covering both sides. It is used especially for making things like towels and babies' nappies. EG *The most popular materials for nappies are gauze and terry towelling.* N UNCOUNT

terse /tɜ̱ːs/, **terser, tersest**. People who are **terse** use very few words to express themselves and often seem harsh or unfriendly. EG *Sandra was terse in her answer.* ▸ used of things that people say or write. EG *The book was a collection of terse, powerful articles... They received a terse and unsympathetic reply.* ◇ **tersely**. EG *He had been tersely instructed not to be a young fool.* ADJ QUALIT = abrupt, curt ◇ ADV WITH VB = abruptly

tertiary /tɜ̱ːʃəºriˈ/. 1 **Tertiary** means third in order, third in importance, or at a third stage of development; a formal use. ADJ CLASSIF

2 **Tertiary** education is education at university or college level: compare **secondary, primary**. ADJ CLASSIF: ATTRIB

terylene /te̱rəˈliˈn/; a trademark. **Terylene** is a light and strong artificial cloth which is used especially for making clothes. EG *...a pair of drip-dry terylene trousers.* N UNCOUNT ↑ material

TESL /te̱səºl/ is an abbreviation for 'teaching English as a second language'; the teaching of English to students whose first language is not English. See also **second language**. N UNCOUNT

tessellated /te̱səleɪtɪ²d/. A **tessellated** floor or pavement is made of lots of small, flat, coloured pieces of stone arranged in a pattern; a formal word. EG *At the back of the church you will find a rough and battered patch of tessellated paving.* ADJ CLASSIF: USU ATTRIB

test /te̱st/, **tests, testing, tested**. 1 When you **test** something, 1.1 you use it for a short time in order to see how well it works. EG *Rick called the ranger at Ayers Rock, to test his radio... The drug is quite safe, we've tested it on gorillas... A number of new techniques were tested.* ▸ used as a noun. EG *They proved it by several tests... ...an underground nuclear test.* 1.2 you find out what it is like by touching, tasting, or smelling it. EG *The dog scampered over the ground, inquisitively testing everything with its pointed nose... The groundnuts had been pulled up to test for ripeness.* 1.3 you take part in it in order to find out how effective it is. EG *...an opportunity to try out and test new relationships.* V OR V+O: IF+PREP THEN *for* = try out ▸ N COUNT = trial V+O: IF+PREP THEN *for* ↑ examine V+O = prove

2 A **test** is also 2.1 an event or situation that makes clear the real nature of something, and proves how strong, effective, or true it is. EG *...the first major test of the President's policies... A good test of a relationship is supposed to be whether you can tell your partner anything.* 2.2 a series of questions that you must answer or actions that you must do in order to N COUNT: USU SING, IF+PREP THEN *of* ↑ trial N COUNT ↑ examination

indicate how much you know about a subject or how well you are able to do something. EG *...a mathematics test... ...an intelligence test... What would have happened if he hadn't passed the test?* ▸ used as a verb. EG *I will test you on your knowledge of French.* ▸ V+O : IF+PREP THEN *on*

2.3 a medical examination of a part of your body in order to check that you are healthy or to find out what is wrong with you. EG *Jenny's blood test had been repeated three times... They had rushed her to a hospital for tests.* ▸ used as a verb. EG *They tested your blood type... ...a simple device to test lung function.* N COUNT : USU MOD+N; ▸ V+O ⇑ examine **2.4** a test match; used in British English. EG *...the Third Test between England and Australia.* N COUNT : ALSO IN NAMES

3 put to the test. 3.1 If you **put** something **to the test**, you find out how useful or effective it is by using it. EG *The idea is being put to the test in a theatre in Paris.* PHR : VB INFLECTS = try out **3.2** If new circumstances or events **put** something **to the test**, they put strain on it and indicate how strong or stable it really is. EG *All your relationships are going to be put to the test.* PHR : VB INFLECTS = try

4 If you say that something will **stand the test of time**, you mean that it is strong or effective enough to last for a very long time. EG *If this romance is real, it can stand the test of time.* PHR : VB INFLECTS ⇑ endure

5 See also **testing, acid test, means test.** ● **to test the waters**: see **water.**

testament /tɛstəmə²nt/, **testaments. 1** A **testament** is a sign that provides strong evidence for a particular fact about someone or something; a formal or literary word. EG *The building is a testament to their success.* N COUNT : USU+*to* = testimony

2 Someone's **last will and testament** is the most recent will that they have made, especially the last will that they make before they die; a legal expression. PHR : USED AS S/O/C, WITH POSS ⇑ document

3 See also **New Testament, Old Testament.**

test case, test cases; also spelled with a hyphen. A **test case** is a case that is heard by a court of law and that establishes an important principle that can afterwards be applied to other cases. N COUNT

testicle /tɛstɪkə⁰l/, **testicles.** A man's **testicles** are the two sex glands that produce sperm and that are contained in his scrotum. N COUNT

testify /tɛstɪfaɪ/, **testifies, testifying, testified. 1** When someone **testifies**, they make a solemn statement, especially under oath in a court of law, about something that has happened. EG *None of the onlookers would appear in court to testify against him... Williams testified that he never actually promised to deliver the guns... Witnesses testify to his attempts at rape.* V : IF+PREP THEN *against/for/to*, OR V+REPORT-CL ⇑ state

2 If something **testifies** to something else or **testifies** that it is true, it supports the belief that it is true; a formal use. EG *All kinds of human experience testify to the close link between love and fear.* V : IF+PREP THEN *to*, OR V+REPORT-CL = attest

testimonial /tɛstɪməʊnɪəl/, **testimonials.** A **testimonial** is a written statement about a person's character and abilities, often written by their employer. EG *I sent them background details of my career and copies of testimonials.* N COUNT = reference

testimony /tɛstɪmənɪ¹/, **testimonies. 1** A person's **testimony** is a formal statement that they make about something, especially under oath in a court of law. EG *...the angry testimony of injured wives and husbands... ...witnesses whose testimony would be believed.* N UNCOUNT/COUNT = evidence

2 If something is a **testimony** to something else's qualities, it shows clearly that it has these qualities; a formal or literary use. EG *The seriousness of the questions posed by the film is a testimony to its virtues... This is spectacular testimony to the computer's creative powers.* N SING : *a*+N+*to*, OR N UNCOUNT+*to* ⇑ proof

testing /tɛstɪŋ/. **Testing** situations, problems, etc are very difficult to deal with and show a lot about the character of the person dealing with them. EG *...a testing situation... ...the very testing questions which are hurled at you in an exam.* ADJ QUALIT : USU ATTRIB = tricky

Test match, Test matches. A **Test match** is a match in a series of cricket or rugby matches played between two countries. EG *...the fourth Test match between Englnd and Australia.* N COUNT = test

test pilot, test pilots; also spelled with a hyphen. A **test pilot** is a pilot who flies aircraft of a new design in order to test their performance. N COUNT ⇑ flier

test tube, test tubes; also spelled with a hyphen. A **test tube** is a small glass tube-shaped container that is used in chemical experiments. N COUNT

test-tube baby, test-tube babies. A **test-tube baby** is a baby that develops from an egg which has been removed from the mother's body, fertilized, and then replaced in her womb so that it can continue developing. EG *...the world's first test-tube baby.* N COUNT

testy /tɛstɪ¹/, **testier, testiest.** You can describe someone as **testy** when they easily become impatient or angry; a slightly formal word. EG *...the testy impatience of the old General... ...testy comments about their leader.* ◇ **testily.** EG *I answered, perhaps a bit testily, that my wife was safe and sound.* ADJ QUALIT = crotchety, snappy; ◇ ADV WITH VB = irritably

tetanus /tɛtə⁰nəs/ is a serious, painful disease caused by bacteria getting into wounds. It makes your muscles, especially your jaw muscles, go stiff. EG *I was injected against tetanus.* N UNCOUNT

tetchy /tɛtʃɪ¹/. A **tetchy** person is likely to get cross and irritable suddenly without an obvious reason. EG *She started to get distinctly tetchy... ...a tetchy state of mind.* ADJ QUALIT = touchy

tether /tɛðə/, **tethers, tethering, tethered. 1** A **tether** is a rope or chain used to tie an animal to a post, fence, etc, so that it can only move around within a small area. EG *...a cow on a tether.* N COUNT ⇑ restraint

2 If you **tether** an animal, you tie it to a post, fence, etc using a tether. ◇ **tethered.** EG *The horse stood tethered to the gate.* V+O; ◇ ADJ CLASSIF = tied

3 If you say that you are **at the end of** your **tether**, you mean that you are so worried, tired, and unhappy because of your problems that you do not know what to do about them. PHR : USED AS AN A

text /tɛkst/, **texts. 1** The **text** of a book is the main part of it as opposed to things such as notes, pictures, the introduction, or the index. EG *The excellent photographs in this book did a lot to amplify the text... This idea is expressed not in the main body of the text but in a footnote.* N SING : *the*+N ⇑ writing

2 Text is any written material. EG *These machines have the capacity to 'read' printed text... This system is excellent for editing text... ...500 words of newspaper text.* N UNCOUNT ⇑ writing

3 The **text** of a speech, broadcast, or recording is the written version of it. EG *He released to the press the text of the speech.* N COUNT : USU SING+*of*

4 A **text** is **4.1** a book or other piece of writing, especially one connected with science or learning. EG *The bookshelves are filled with sociology texts... ...a text on oriental philosophy.* N COUNT ⇑ work **4.2** a written or spoken passage, especially one that is used in a school or university for discussion or in an examination. EG *'Listening comprehension text: Trade Unionism in Britain'... We're supposed to discuss a text we've been assigned.* N COUNT ⇑ extract **4.3** a short passage from the Bible that a Christian preacher chooses as the subject for a sermon. N COUNT ⇑ extract

textbook /tɛkstbʊk/, **textbooks**; also spelled with a hyphen. **1** A **textbook** is a book containing facts about a particular subject that is used by people studying that subject. EG *I think probably the best text book on projected geometry is Seidenberg... ...a history textbook.* N COUNT

2 A **textbook** action is done in exactly the way that it should be done according to an accepted standard or set of rules; used showing approval. EG *'It was a textbook arrest,' said the FBI agent.* N BEFORE N = copybook

textile /tɛkstaɪl/, **textiles. 1** A **textile** is a cloth or fabric, especially one that has been woven. EG *Islanders were engaged to collect and dry the textiles... The designers have created a new textile, spun thin like lace.* ▸ used as an adjective. EG *...textile workers... ...a new textile factory... ...the world textile market.* N COUNT; ▸ N BEFORE N

2 Textiles are the industries concerned with the manufacture of cloth. EG *There are still more people employed in textiles than in computers.* N PLURAL ⇑ industry

textual /tɛkstjʊ⁰əl/ means relating to the way a work of literature is written; a technical word. EG *...textual analysis... ...textual criticism.* ADJ CLASSIF : ATTRIB

texture /tɛkstʃə/, **textures. 1** The **texture** of something is **1.1** the way that it feels when you touch it, for example how smooth, rough, or lumpy it is. EG *I don't like the rough texture of this wallpaper... He was aware of the texture of the cotton material.* N UNCOUNT/COUNT : USU WITH POSS/SUPP = feel **1.2** its appearance, considered from the point of view of the quality and structure of the substance that it is made from. EG *...the house's rough brick, most satisfying in its texture... The leaves seemed to have a* N UNCOUNT/COUNT : USU WITH POSS/SUPP *glossy texture.* **1.3** its structure, for example whether it is light with lots of holes, or very heavy and dense; used especially of food and soil. N UNCOUNT/COUNT : USU WITH POSS/SUPP

2 The **texture** of a piece of music or a work of literature is the impression that it makes on you as a result of the way that its different elements are combined, so that it is often easy to identify it as being composed or written by a particular person; a technical use. EG *...the truly Dickensian sweep and texture of Nicholas Nickleby... ...orchestral texture.* N UNCOUNT : USU +SUPP = character

Thai /taɪ/, **Thais**. **1 Thai** means belonging or relating to Thailand or to its people. EG *...a Thai cabinet minister.* ADJ CLASSIF

2 Thai is the main language spoken by the people who live in Thailand. N UNCOUNT

3 A **Thai** is a person who comes from Thailand. N COUNT

Thalidomide /θəlɪdə⁶maɪd/; a trademark. **Thalidomide** is a drug which used to be given to pregnant women as a tranquilliser, and which was withdrawn from use after it was discovered to cause abnormalities in developing foetuses. EG *...thalidomide babies.* N UNCOUNT

than /ðæn/. **1** You use **than** in order to link two parts of a comparison. EG *She was older than I was... She was much older than me... You've got more money than me... I am happier than I have ever been... A shower uses less water than a bath... She was fatter than when he last saw her.* PREP/CONJ SUBORD : AFTER COMPAR

2 You use **than** when you are stating a number, quantity, or value approximately by saying that it is above or below another number, quantity, or value. EG *We talked for more than an hour... She was elected by more than 5,000 votes... James is more than twice Ovett's age... ...temperatures lower than 25 degrees.* PREP/CONJ SUBORD : AFTER COMPAR

3 You use **than** in expressions such as 'rather than' and 'other than' in order to link two parts of a contrast, where the second part is regarded as being different from or an exception to the first. EG *He chose the stairs rather than the lift... She likes to keep things rather than throw them away... There's no choice other than to reopen his case.* CONJ SUBORD/PREP

4 You use **than** with the words 'rather' and 'sooner' when you are saying which of two alternatives you prefer. 'Than' introduces the alternative that you do not like or do not want to do. EG *I'd rather starve than ask for a penny... I would sooner read than watch television.* CONJ SUBORD/PREP

5 The word **than** is also used in the following expressions, which are explained at other places in this dictionary. • **easier said than done**: see **easy**. • **less than**: see **less**. • **more than, no more than**: see **more**. • **more often than not**: see **often**. • **other than, no other than**: see **other**.

thank /θæŋk/, **thanks, thanking, thanked**. **1 Thanks, thank you, thanks a lot**, and **thank you very much** are all ways of expressing gratitude to someone for something they have given you or for something that they have done, suggested, or said. You use these expressions and the verb 'thank' in the following ways: **1.1** in a conversation or letter, especially at the beginning, in order to express gratitude to someone for something that they have given you or done for you. EG *Thank you very much indeed for coming to see me... Dear Grandmother, Thank you very much for the nice book you sent me... Many thanks for your long and interesting letter... Thanks for the hospitality... Thank you, Sydney. I knew I could depend on you... Don't forget to say thank you... Myra and I both want to say thank you very much indeed.* ▸ used as a verb. EG *He thanked me for bringing the books.* CONVENTION ▸ V+O **1.2** to politely accept or refuse something that has just been offered to you. EG *'How about a cup of tea?'–'Thank you. I'd love one.'... 'What'll you take, Castle? A whisky?'–'A small one, thank you.'... 'Shall I take you on down to town now?'–'Thank you.'... 'Do you want a biscuit?'–'No thanks.'... I'm not a bit hungry, thank you... No, thank you, I don't smoke... 'Won't you take off your coat?'–'Thanks, but I can't stop.'* CONVENTION **1.3** when you are answering a polite enquiry or acknowledging compliments, good wishes, the giving of information, etc. EG *'How are you?'–'Fine, thanks.'... 'All right then?'–'Yes, thanks a lot.'... 'Have a good flight?'–'Not at all bad, thank you.'... 'You are a beautiful woman.'–'Thank you.'... 'And your name, sir?'–'Hare.'–'Thank you. We'll see you tomorrow at 8, then.'* ▸ used as a verb. EG *'Have a good time,' he said. She smiled at him, thanked him, and drove off.* CONVENTION ▸ V+O **1.4** You use **thank you** or **thank you very much** in order to say firmly that you do not want someone's help or to tell them that you do not like the way that they are behaving towards you. EG *We know quite well what we have to do, thank you... We don't need your oil, thank you very much... Get your hands off. And don't call me 'love', thank you.* **1.5** See also **thankyou**. CONVENTION

2 Thanks are the things that you say when you are expressing gratitude for something that someone has given to you or done for you. EG *Before Alex could stammer out his thanks, Harvey walked away... He sent a letter of thanks to Haldane.* N PLURAL

3 The word **thank** is also used in the following expressions. **3.1** You use expressions like **thank God, thank goodness, thank heavens**, etc when you are very relieved about something. EG *We were finally driving back to Cambridge, thank God... Thank goodness it only lasts an hour... 'Yes, good news!'–'Thank God!'* CONVENTION **3.2** If you say that you **have** someone **to thank for** something or that it is **thanks to** that person that something has happened, you mean that that person is responsible for what has happened. EG *Thanks to him I began to learn to trust my feelings... Thanks to John we arrived 3 hours late... 'You got there in the end, didn't you?'–'No thanks to you.'... 'Who broke my window?'–'Oh, you've got David to thank for that.'* PHR **3.3** You also use the expression **thanks to** when you are saying that something is the cause of something else. EG *It was airy and light inside, thanks to the huge Tudor windows... The building became very well known, thanks to detective films... She's better now. Swears it was all thanks to ginseng.* PREP = due to **3.4** If you say that someone **won't thank** you for something that you have done, you mean that they will be very annoyed about what you have done. EG *He won't thank you for damaging his new car.* PHR : WITH BROAD NEG **3.5** When people **give thanks**, they thank God for something good that has happened. EG *They bowed their heads and gave thanks.* PHR : VB INFLECTS **3.6** • to **thank** your **lucky stars**: see **star**.

thankful /θæŋkful/. When you are **thankful**, you are very happy and relieved that something has happened. EG *We were thankful that it was all over... He is thankful for the survival of the official archives... Ralph walked in the rear, thankful to have escaped responsibility for a time.* ADJ QUALIT : USU PRED ⇑ pleased = grateful

thankfully /θæŋkfə⁴li¹/. **1** If you do something **thankfully**, you do it feeling happy and relieved that something is the case or that something has happened. EG *We sat down thankfully... 'It wasn't like that with Tony,' Alice said, thankfully.* ADV WITH VB = gratefully

2 You also use **thankfully** in order to express approval and relief about a statement that you are making. EG *The move was agreed and, thankfully, worked well... Thankfully, the memory of it soon faded.* ADV SEN = fortunately

thankless /θæŋklɪ²s/. A **thankless** job or task is one that is hard work and that nobody thanks you for doing. EG *She used to cheerfully take on thankless jobs like running school dances.* ADJ QUALIT : ATTRIB = unrewarding

thanksgiving /θæŋksgɪvɪŋ/. The word **thanksgiving** is always spelled with a capital for paragraph 2. **1 Thanksgiving** is an act of thanking God, especially in a religious ceremony. EG *The cross stood in the centre of the table throughout Easter as a symbol of thanksgiving... A thanksgiving ceremony was arranged for the following Sunday.* N UNCOUNT

2 Thanksgiving or **Thanksgiving Day** is a public holiday in the United States and Canada in the autumn. It was originally a day when people celebrated the end of the harvest and thanked God for it. EG *Robertson was released the week after Thanksgiving... We always had turkey for our Thanksgiving meal.* N UNCOUNT ⇑ celebration

thankyou /θæŋkju:/, **thankyous**; also spelled with a hyphen, especially when used before another noun. A **thankyou** is something that you say or do as a way of thanking someone. EG *I wanted to do the play just as a sort of thankyou... She went home and wrote Brody a thank-you note.* N COUNT

that /ðə³t/, **those** /ðəʊz/. The pronunciation /ðət/ can only be used for the meanings in paragraphs 5, 6, and 7. For the meanings in all the other paragraphs, the pronunciation is /ðæt/.

1 You use **that** to refer to things or people in the

following ways: **1.1** to refer back precisely to something which or someone who has already been mentioned. EG *That old woman saved my life... The institute was set up by France, Germany, and Britain and it was run jointly by people from each of those countries.* ▸ used as a pronoun. In the singular **that** can only refer to things. EG *What about other forms of energy? How about natural gas? Is that an alternative?* **1.2** to introduce more information about something already mentioned, instead of repeating the noun which refers to it. This use often sounds slightly formal. EG *It has a horny beak, shaped like that of a parrot... There had been only one set of footprints there, those which I'd made myself.* **1.3** to refer back to what has previously been said, mentioned, or suggested. **That** can be used as a pronoun to refer back to plurals. EG *'I didn't think you were so selfish.'–'That just shows you don't know me.'... You went to the farm show? Is that why you had a few days off?... What about fire precautions, does that form part of your duties?* ▸ used as a determiner. EG *They use their cars and help us that way... I'm not sure all crimes are committed for those reasons.*

DET — ▸ PRON — PRON+SUPP — PRON — ▸ DET

2 You also use **that** in front of other words or expressions in order to express agreement, responses, or reactions. EG *'It's a difficult area to get jobs in.'–'Yes, that's true.'... 'I can give you an appointment at 10.30.'–'That'll be fine.'... 'Did you see him?'–'No.'–'That's a pity.'* PHR+C

3 You can use **those** to refer to a particular group of people or things when you are going to give details or information about them. **That** can also be used in this way in formal English. EG *I want to thank those of you who've offered to help... The scheme was set up to help those concerned with the teaching of reading.* ▸ used as a determiner. EG *Students should write off to those bodies which provide awards.* PRON — ▸ DET

4 You use **that** and **those**, especially in spoken English, in the following ways when you are referring to people, things, events, or situations in the world around you: **4.1** when you refer to something which is a distance away from you in position or time, especially when you indicate or point to it. When there are two or more things near you, **that** refers to the more distant one. EG *Look at that bird!... Who are those men in the sitting-room?* ▸ used as a pronoun. EG *Hello. Is that Mrs Vassiliou? My name is Jones.* **4.2** when you refer to a situation, activity, or event which you have heard about or have recently been involved in. EG *That was a terrible air crash last week.* ▸ used as a determiner. EG *'What did you think of that?'–'Of what?'–'That spy business.'* **4.3** when you refer to something which you expect the hearer to know about or when you are checking that you are both thinking of the same person or thing. EG *I remember what you wore. That white dress with the red apples on the skirt... Think of all those comedies which run for years in London... 'I've just seen Roger.'–'That snob in the Treasury?'–'Yes.'*

DET — ▸ PRON — PRON — ▸ DET — DET

5 You use **that** after verbs like 'say', 'tell', and 'suggest' in order to introduce a clause in which you report what someone has said. EG *She suggested that I telephoned you... I informed her that I was unwell.* CONJ SUBORD

6 You use **that** after some verbs, nouns, and adjectives in order to introduce a clause in which you give information or details, or a reason, opinion, idea, feeling, result, etc. EG *He could prove that he had been in Aberystwyth on Saturday... It is important that you should know precisely what is needed... The noise became so great that he was asked to leave... Well, the reason for this is that cancer cells differ from normal cells.* CONJ SUBORD

7 You also use **that** to introduce a relative clause. EG *I reached the gate that opened onto the lake... He talked about windmills and other things that produce energy... For dessert there was ice cream that Mum had made herself.* PRON REL = which

8 If something is not **that** bad, funny, expensive, etc, it is not as bad, funny, expensive, etc as it might be or as has been suggested. EG *It isn't quite that bad.* ADV+ADJ/ADV: WITH BROAD NEG = so

9 You can use **that** to emphasize the degree of a feeling or quality; an informal use. EG *I was that annoyed, I could have screamed.* ADV+ADJ/ADV = so

10 The word **that** is also used in the following expressions. **10.1** You use **and all that** or **and that** to refer generally to everything else which is associated with what you have just mentioned; used in informal English. EG *Have you got the tickets and that?... ...ghosts and seances and all that... Everyone's very proud, and that.* **10.2** You use **at that** when you are modifying or limiting what you have previously said. EG *There is work for only 250 people, and a very specialized 250 at that.* **10.3** You also use **at that** to express agreement, acceptance, or approval of what has just been said; an informal use. EG *'You just like lying around doing nothing.'–'Perhaps I do, at that.'* **10.4** You use **that is** or **that is to say** when you are giving further details about something or explaining or correcting what you have just said. EG *It deals with matters of social policy; that is to say, everything from housing to education... There was one golf club, the building, that is, not the thing you hit balls with.*

PHR: USED AS AN A = and so on, etc — PHR: USED AS AN A = too — PHR: USED AS AN A — PHR: USED AS ADV SEN = i.e

11 You use **that's it** **11.1** to express agreement, approval, or confirmation of what has just been said or done. EG *'You want to know the cause of the problem?'–'Well, yes, that's it.'... Right, that's it, that's how I want it.* **11.2** to indicate that nothing more needs to be done or that the end has been reached. EG *They get a direct grant of a sum of money and that's it... 'I quit,' I said. 'That's it. Finish.'*

CONVENTION = exactly — PHR: VB INFLECTS

12 You use **that's that** to say there is nothing more you can do or say about a particular matter. EG *Well, that's that... It was an accident, and that's that... Then off he drove, and that was that.* PHR: VB INFLECTS, OR CONVENTION

13 this and that: see **this**.

thatch /θætʃ/, **thatches, thatching, thatched.**
1 To **thatch** a house or its roof means to make a roof with straw or reeds. EG *I can remember the first house I thatched on my own.* ◊ **thatched**. EG *...a three-hundred-year old thatched cottage... ...a thatched roof.* V OR V+O ⇑ cover — ◊ ADJ CLASSIF: ATTRIB ⇑ covered
2 **Thatch** is straw or reeds used to make a roof. EG *The best quality roofing thatch is required.* N UNCOUNT = thatching
3 A **thatch** is **3.1** a roof made from straw or reeds. EG *...sheltering under the thatch.* **3.2** a large amount of thick, untidy hair on a person's head. EG *He was ruggedly handsome, with a thatch of thick brown hair.* N COUNT — N SING WITH DET: IF+PREP THEN *of* = mop

thatcher /θætʃə/, **thatchers.** A **thatcher** is a person whose job is thatching roofs. N COUNT

thatching /θætʃɪŋ/ is straw or reeds used to make a roof. N UNCOUNT = thatch

that's /ðæts/ is a spoken form of 'that is'.

thaw /θɔː/, **thaws, thawing, thawed.** **1** When ice, snow, or something else that is frozen **thaws** or **is thawed**, it melts. EG *The snow thawed in early spring... The ice was thawed by the warm wind.* V-ERG
2 When it **thaws**, the weather becomes warmer and the snow and ice melt. EG *It was thawing fast.* V: *it*+V
3 A **thaw** is a period of warmer weather, usually at the end of winter, when the snow and ice melts. EG *A thaw had set in and the streets were slushy.* N COUNT
4 If you **thaw** frozen food, you leave it in a place where it can warm up so that it is ready for cooking or eating. EG *Unwrap the pastry and then thaw it overnight.* V+O = defrost
5 If someone **thaws** after they have been unfriendly, they become friendly again. EG *He'll thaw when it's time to go to church.* V
6 A **thaw** is also an increase in friendliness or co-operation. EG *A slight diplomatic thaw is just beginning.* N SING WITH DET

thaw out. When you **thaw out** frozen food, you thaw it completely. EG *Pre-cooked food can be thawed out quicker than a joint or poultry.* PHRASAL VB: V+O+ADV = defrost

the is the definite article. It is used at the beginning of noun groups. **The** is usually pronounced /ðə/ before a consonant and /ðɪ/ before a vowel, but it is pronounced /ðiː/ when you are emphasizing it. **1** You use **the** at the beginning of noun groups to refer to someone or something when a reader or hearer knows exactly who or what you are talking about, or when you go on to explain which particular person or thing you mean. EG *...the waiter with the droopy mustache... Her face was the colour of chalk... Another mineral was named by the scientist who first examined it... I think I'll keep the information to myself... I asked to see the manager... They continued walking on the opposite pavement.* DET
2 You use **the** in front of some nouns that refer to something in our general experience of the world. EG *The sea was really rough... They drove home* DET

through the darkness... ...at some distant point in the future.

3 You use **the** in front of nouns that refer to things, activities, or people that are associated with everyday life. EG *He turned the water off... She was talking on the telephone... He said that she ought to see the doctor.*
DET

4 You can use **the** instead of a possessive determiner, especially when you are talking about a part of someone's body or a member of their family. EG *He took Sam by the hand... How's the family?*
DET

5 You use **the** in front of a singular noun to refer to a whole class of people or things when you are describing their typical behaviour, characteristics, needs, etc. EG *When this happens, the baby will begin to sleep for longer and longer periods... The koala is a medium-sized creature that lives in trees.*
DET+N COUNT IN SING

6 You use **the** in front of a plural noun when you are referring generally to people or things in a particular group or of a particular kind. EG *The Germans have a word for this... This is never mentioned in the history books or even in the newspapers.*
DET+N COUNT IN PL

7 If you want to refer to a whole family or to a married couple, you can make their surname into a plural and use **the** in front of it. EG *...some friends of hers called the Hochstadts.*
DET+NAMES IN PL

8 You use **the** in front of an adjective to make it a noun **8.1** when you are referring to everyone or everything that can be described by that adjective. EG *...institutions for the mentally handicapped... ...the British and the French... The wounded were given first aid.*
DET+N PLURAL
8.2 when you are referring to a particular thing that is described by that adjective. EG *Don't you think that perhaps you're wanting the impossible?... I apologize for not returning the enclosed sooner.*
DET

9 You use **the** to indicate that you have enough of the thing mentioned for a particular purpose. EG *I wish you could manage the time to come in and talk with me... He hasn't got the money to do it.*
DET+NG+ to-INF/for
= sufficient

10 You use **the** with some titles, place-names, and other names. EG *...Her Majesty the Queen... ...the Foreign Secretary... ...the Soviet Union... ...the Atlantic Ocean.*
DET+N PROPER

11 You use **the** in front of nouns referring to musical instruments, dances, or sporting or physical movements when you are talking about them generally. EG *Do you play the violin?... We were dancing the can-can.*
DET+N COUNT IN SING

12 You use **the** in front of ordinal numbers, especially in spoken English. EG *...Tuesday, May the thirteenth... It was the first time she had seen him since Wednesday.*
DET+ORDINAL

13 You use **the** in front of numbers that are used to refer to decades. EG *...in Stockholm in the thirties... ...in the early 1960's.*
DET+NUM IN PL

14 You use **the** in front of superlative adjectives and adverbs. EG *This is one of the most difficult things that I have ever done... ...the smallest church in England... The least expensive model will be priced at £7,000.*
DET+ADJ/ADV SUPERL

15 You use **the** in front of each of two comparative adjectives or adverbs when you are describing how two amounts, qualities, etc increase or decrease in relation to each other. EG *The more I hear about him, the less I like him... The longer we look at it the more interesting we find it.*
DET+ADJ/ADV COMPAR

16 You can use **the** in front of a comparative adjective or adverb to add emphasis. EG *She looks the better for her holiday.*
DET+ADJ/ADV COMPAR

17 You use **the** in front of nouns that refer to illnesses or other physical conditions. EG *Our usual man has got the flu... I got the shakes today.*
DET+N UNCOUNT/N PLURAL

18 When you express rates, ratios, prices, and measurements, you can use **the** to say how many units apply to each of the items being measured, charged, etc. EG *It does thirty miles to the gallon... Potatoes are 10 pence the pound.*
DET+N COUNT IN SING
= per

19 You use **the** to indicate that something or someone is the most famous, important, or best thing of its kind or person with a particular name. When you use **the** in this way, you emphasize it. EG *It's the club in town... You don't mean the William Shakespeare?.*
DET
≠ any old

theatre /θɪətə/, **theatres**; also spelled **theater** in American English. 1 A **theatre** is **1.1** a building with a stage in it, on which plays, shows, and other entertainments are performed for people to go and watch. EG *...the new Arnold Wesker play at the National Theatre... ...a theatre audience... Her mother never went to the theatre.*
N COUNT: ALSO IN NAMES AFTER N
1.2 the same as an operating theatre.
N COUNT

2 The **theatre** is used to refer to work in the theatre, including acting in, producing, and writing plays. EG *She was only really happy when she was working in the theatre.*
N SING: the+N

3 **Theatre** is the presentation and performance of plays considered as an art form or as a form of entertainment. EG *Good theatre always nourishes the human spirit.*
N UNCOUNT
⇑ drama

4 The **theatre** of war or other conflict is the area or region in which the war or conflict is happening. EG *The Columbian countryside has turned into a theatre of the most terrible violence.*
N COUNT+SUPP
= arena

theatregoer /θɪətəgəʊə/, **theatregoers**. A **theatregoer** is a person who regularly goes to the theatre to see plays.
N COUNT

theatrical /θiˈætrɪkəºl/, **theatricals**. 1 A **theatrical** event or production is one performed in a theatre or relating to the theatre. EG *Posters advertising theatrical productions... It will be the theatrical event of a lifetime.* ◊ **theatrically**. EG *Theatrically, it works very well indeed.*
ADJ CLASSIF: ATTRIB
⇑ dramatic
◊ ADV WITH VB
⇑ dramatically

2 **Theatricals** are performances of plays and other entertainments, especially when they are done by amateur actors. EG *He shines at amateur theatricals.*
N PLURAL
= dramatics

3 **Theatrical** behaviour is exaggerated and unnatural, and done for effect. EG *He has a very theatrical style of speaking.* ◊ **theatrically**. EG *My friends clapped hands to foreheads and groaned theatrically.*
ADJ QUALIT: ATTRIB
◊ ADV WITH VB
= melodramatically

thee /ðiː/ is an old-fashioned, poetic, or religious word for 'you' when you are talking to only one person. It is used as the object of a verb or preposition. See **thou**. EG *If I should meet thee after long years, how should I greet thee?*
PRON: SING, USED AS O

theft /θɛft/, **thefts**. 1 A **theft** is the act of stealing something. EG *He reported the theft of his passport.*
N COUNT/ UNCOUNT

2 **Theft** is the crime of stealing. EG *The drop in petty crime and theft will mean less work for the police.*
N UNCOUNT

their /ðɛə/. 1 You use **their** to indicate that something belongs or relates to people, animals, or things that have just been mentioned or whose identity is clear. See **they**. EG *...the car companies and their workers... In a pre-industrial society most people spend their lives in their own village... Don't hope to change anyone or their attitudes.*
DETPOSS

2 **Their** is also used in some titles when you are referring to people with that title. EG *...Their Highnesses the Prince and Princess of Wales.*
DETPOSS: USED IN TITLES WITH N IN PL

theirs /ðɛəz/. You use **theirs** to indicate that something belongs or relates to people, animals, or things that have just been mentioned or whose identity is clear. See **they**. EG *It was his fault, not theirs... They were off to visit a friend of theirs.*
PRON POSS

theism /θiːɪzəºm/ is the belief in the existence of a god or gods.
N UNCOUNT

them /ðɛm/ is used as the object of a verb or preposition. You use **them** when you are referring to people, animals, or things that have already been mentioned or named, or whose identity is known. See **they**. EG *He took off his glasses and put them in his pocket... Smith harangued his fellow students and persuaded them that they must support the strike... Neither of them moved... We had our troubles, but this was not one of them... When they find out what my job is, people ask me to lend them money... If I think someone may attempt to take an overdose, I will spend hours talking to them.*
PRON: PL, USED AS O

thematic /θiˈmætɪk/. Something that is **thematic** is concerned with particular subjects or topics; a formal word. EG *...thematic teaching... ...a thematic approach.*
ADJ CLASSIF

theme /θiːm/, **themes**. 1 A **theme** is the main idea or subject in a discussion, conversation, lecture, etc. EG *...organised public meetings on the theme: 'Law not War'... Posy warmed to her theme... We shall return to this central theme in chapter 7.*
N COUNT
⇑ topic

2 A **theme** is also **2.1** an idea that an artist or writer develops or repeats in his or her work. EG *The main theme of the play was clear... One of the constant themes in Picasso's work is that of the outsider.*
N COUNT
= motif
2.2 a short simple tune, often one of a number of tunes, on which a piece of music is based. A theme may be repeated several times in the piece. EG *The order of the themes in a song can always be changed...*
N COUNT
⇑ melody

...variations on a theme. **2.3** a tune that is played at the beginning and end of a film or of a television or radio programme, and which is associated with that film or programme in people's minds. EG *...the theme from 'Dr Finlay's Casebook'.* N COUNT = signature tune

3 A **theme** song or **theme** tune is a song or tune which is played several times in a film or a musical and which expresses the mood of the show or is identified with a particular person or character. EG *...its unmistakable theme tune.* ADJ CLASSIF : ATTRIB = signature

themselves /ðəmselvz/. **1** You use **themselves** as the object of a verb or preposition in order to refer to the same people, animals, or things that are mentioned as the subject of the clause, or as a previous object in the clause. See **they**. EG *They are trying to educate themselves... Children gain trust in themselves from being respected... They had ceased to think of themselves as rebels... Other species feed themselves as much as they can.* ▸ You also use **themselves** to emphasize the subject or object of a clause, and to make it clear who or what you are referring to. It is usually used in addition to a subject or object, although it is sometimes used instead of 'them' as an object. EG *Let's turn to the books themselves... ...a cultural preference on the part of the Chinese themselves... The theory is that these people ill-treat their babies because they come from broken homes themselves.* PRON REFL : PL

2 If people do something **themselves,** they do it without any help or interference from anyone else. EG *They must settle it themselves and get their own solutions... They wouldn't have to do it themselves.* PRON REFL : PL ⇑ alone

then /ðen/. **1 Then** means at a particular time in the past or in the future. EG *I thought she was a phony then and I think she's a phony now... Mrs Kaul came in just then... 'Any Questions' next week goes to Northampton. Until then, goodbye.* ADV ≠ now

2 Then is used when you refer to something which was true at a particular time in the past but is not true now. EG *...the then Chancellor Mr. Barber... She was at that time much closer to the then unformulated ideas of women's liberation.* ADJ CLASSIF : ATTRIB ≠ current, present

3 Then is used when you are talking about what happens next, or what is done next in a procedure, or what the next thing is in a list. EG *He went to the village school, then to the grammar school, and then to the university... I am going to my room to read, and then I will have a sleep... It didn't hurt at first, but then I realized you could die from a cut like that... You then take the square root of this number.* ADV ⇑ afterwards

4 Then is used in conversation **4.1** when what you are saying refers to something that has just been said or to something that has been said in the past. **Then** is often added at the end of questions when you are asking a person for an explanation or opinion which you expect they will willingly give you. EG *'Are you a student?'–'No, I'm not'–'Well do you do then?'... 'I'm afraid we are sold out.'–'Well, then, could you tell me how long it'll be before you have some?'... 'Have some more cake.'–'Oh all right then.'* ADV SEN = in that case **4.2** at the end of a conversation or when you think that there is nothing more than can be usefully said about a particular topic. **Then** is often used when you are saying goodbye or confirming something that has been arranged. EG *Bye then... Until next week then, goodnight... Well, that's settled, then.* ADV SEN **4.3** with words like 'now', 'well' and 'okay', to draw attention to what you are about to say. EG *Now then, sleepyhead, it's time you went to bed... Right then, who'd like some more stew?* ADV SEN

5 You use **then** when you are introducing a conclusion that you are about to draw from what you have already said or written. EG *These then are some of the feelings which a pregnant woman may experience... The importance of education, then, has been infinitely greater than in previous centuries... That then is the basis for wheat bread.* ADV SEN = therefore

6 You can use **then** to introduce the second part of a sentence which begins with 'if'. EG *If we say y equals ax^2 then we get a curve like this... If any questions do occur to you, then don't hesitate to write.* ADV SEN

7 You use **then** at the beginning of a sentence or after 'and' or 'but' to add another remark or piece of information which is relevant to what you have been talking about. EG *Then there could be a tax problem... Iron would do the job much better. But then you can't weld iron so easily... I thought the questions were very easy, but then again I'm a genius.* ADV SEN ⇑ also

8 ● **now and then:** see **now.** ● **there and then:** see **there.**

thence /ðens/; a fairly formal and old-fashioned word. **1 Thence** means from a particular place, especially when you are giving directions about how to get somewhere. EG *He hitched south towards Italy, and thence into France... The way thence is through the Peers' Lobby.* ADV

2 Thence is used to say that something changes from one state or condition to another. EG *This feeling of dislike grew into a disgust, thence to a loathing.* ADV SEN

thenceforth /ðensfɔ:θ/ means from that time on; a formal or literary word. EG *...the man who would thenceforth be his master.* ADV = thereafter

theocracy /θi[1]ɒkrəsi[1]/, **theocracies.** A **theocracy** is a society which is ruled by priests who represent a god; a technical word. EG *These people were content, living in a kind of theocracy.* N COUNT

theocratic /θi[1]ə[6]krætɪk/. A **theocratic** society is ruled by priests who represent a god; a technical word. EG *...the ancient traditional societies, either theocratic or tribal.* ADJ CLASSIF ≠ secular

theodolite /θi[1]ɒdəlaɪt/, **theodolites.** A **theodolite** is an instrument used in surveying for measuring angles. N COUNT

theologian /θɪələʊdʒɪən/, **theologians.** A **theologian** is someone who studies the nature of God and his relationship with and influence on people. EG *...the German theologian Dietrich Bonhoeffer.* N COUNT ⇑ scholar

theological /θɪəlɒdʒɪkə[0]l/ is used to describe something which concerns the study of religion and of God. EG *...a theological college... The Sixties were a time of theological ferment.* ADJ CLASSIF : USU ATTRIB ⇑ religious

theology /θi[1]ɒlədʒi[1]/, **theologies. 1 Theology** is the study of the nature of God, of God's influence on people, and of religion and religious beliefs. EG *The argument from science quite drowned the argument from theology in the evolutionary debate... ...a diploma in theology.* N UNCOUNT ⇑ discipline

2 A **theology** is a particular set of religious beliefs and ideas. EG *Many theologies express the same ideas.* N COUNT ⇑ doctrine

theorem /θɪərə[0]m/, **theorems.** A **theorem** is a statement in mathematics or logic that can be proved to be true by reasoning. EG *...Godel's theorem.* N COUNT ⇑ proposition

theoretical /θɪəretɪkə[0]l/. **1** A **theoretical** study or explanation is based on or uses the ideas and abstract principles that relate to a particular subject, rather than the practical aspects or uses of it. EG *I think that Marxism is the only scientific theoretical explanation of the capitalist system... ...theoretical biology.* ADJ CLASSIF : USU ATTRIB

2 If you describe a situation as a **theoretical** one, you mean that it is supposed to be true or to exist in the way stated, but perhaps it is not true in reality. EG *The government and central bank were in theoretical harmony... ...the theoretical parity in powers between Lords and Commons.* ADJ CLASSIF : USU ATTRIB

theoretically /θɪəretɪkə[0]li[1]/. You use **theoretically** to say that although something is supposed to be true or to happen in the way stated, it may not in fact be true or happen in that way. EG *All actors were paid the same and theoretically they all got to play leading roles... Laws still theoretically controlled the availability of alcohol... ...the theoretically limitless powers of the machines.* ADV OR ADV SEN ⇑ supposedly = ostensibly

theoretician /θɪərətɪʃə[0]n/, **theoreticians.** A **theoretician** is someone who develops an idea or set of ideas about a particular subject in order to explain it. EG *...Marxist theoreticians.* N COUNT ⇑ thinker = theorist

theorist /θɪərɪst/, **theorists.** A **theorist** is someone who develops an abstract idea or set of ideas about a particular subject in order to explain it. EG *...the education theorist, John Jones.* N COUNT = theoretician

theorize /θɪəraɪz/, **theorizes, theorizing, theorized;** also spelled **theorise. 1** If you **theorize** about something or **theorize** that something is true, you develop an abstract idea or set of ideas about something in order to explain it. EG *Morris theorises that the female also had to adapt her behaviour... ...our theorizing about social and psychological change.* V+A (about), OR V+REPORT-CL ⇑ think

2 If you **theorize,** you think in an abstract way about things, instead of doing something practical or use- V ful. EG *I am not theorizing. I know that this problem exists.*

theory /θɪəri¹/, **theories.** 1 A **theory** is 1.1 an idea or set of ideas that is intended to explain something. It is based on evidence and careful reasoning but it cannot be completely proved. EG *Darwin spent more than twenty years working on his theory of evolution... ...the quantum theory... ...his theories about language and writing.* 1.2 an idea about something that is based on a lot of thinking but not on actual knowledge or evidence. EG *Mary is full of fascinating theories about men and women... The theory was that by Monday their tempers would have cooled... She had a theory that aniseed was good for their digestions.*
N COUNT : USU+SUPP = hypothesis
N COUNT : USU+SUPP = notion

2 **Theory** is 2.1 the set of ideas and abstract principles that relate to a particular subject or to a particular view of that subject. EG *...Marxist economic theory... A discipline is more firmly established when backed by theory.* 2.2 the set of rules and principles that form the basis for a particular practical subject or skill. EG *...musical theory... ...the theory and practice of inoculation.*
N UNCOUNT : USU +SUPP ↑ philosophy
N UNCOUNT : USU +SUPP

3 You use **in theory** to modify a statement and to say that although something is thought to be true or to happen in the way stated, in reality it may not be true or may not happen in that way. EG *In theory all British subjects are eligible for this... The meeting with the organizer should, in theory, have taken place at least six months earlier.*
PHR : USED AS ADV SEN = theoretically

therapeutic /θerəpjuːtɪk/. 1 If something is **therapeutic**, it helps you to relax or to feel better about things, especially about a situation that made you unhappy. EG *All that fresh air is very therapeutic... I believe more and more in the therapeutic effect of creative work.*
ADJ QUALIT ↑ beneficial

2 In medicine, **therapeutic** treatment is designed to treat a disease or to improve a person's health. EG *...therapeutic measures.*
ADJ CLASSIF ↑ beneficial

therapist /θerəpɪst/, **therapists.** A **therapist** is a person skilled in a particular type of therapy. EG *...a speech therapist... Few therapists agree on how to treat schizophrenia.*
N COUNT : USU MOD+N ↑ specialist

therapy /θerəpi¹/ is the treatment of mental or physical illness without the use of drugs or operations. EG *Therapy does not cure at once... ...a short course of heat therapy... There are units to provide group therapy and teaching.* • See also **occupational therapy, speech therapy**.
N UNCOUNT

there /ðeə/. 1 **There** is used as the subject of the verb 'be'. It is used when you want to say that something exists, or when you want to draw attention to a fact. EG *There was a new cushion on one of the settees... There are about forty of us, I think... There was not a tree in sight... What happens if there's a power cut?... There must be a reason... Are there any prospects for peace?... There is less complacency than there ever was... There's no kind of inspection service, is there?*
PRON : *there+be*

2 **There** is used in front of a verb in order to emphasize the meaning of the verb when you are speaking or writing formally. The subject of the verb is placed after the verb. EG *There follow below guidelines on two aspects of terminal connection... Beside them there curls up a twist of blue smoke... There still remains the point about creativity.*
PRON : *there*+VB +S

3 **There** is used after 'hello' or 'hi' when you are greeting someone. EG *Hallo there, Mike, how are you today?... Hi, there!*
ADV

4 Something that is **there** 4.1 actually exists in the world. EG *We talked about reality, about whether things are really there... I found a road that wasn't meant to be there... She's got to look after herself, the problem is still there.* 4.2 is available and ready for people to use. EG *We have a play group here which, of course, is there for the children of staff and students... If the techniques are there, someone's going to use them... We had better take the advantage while it's there.*
ADV *there* : USU AFTER *be* ↑ in existence
ADJ CLASSIF : PRED

5 **There** is also used in the following ways when you are referring to a place: 5.1 when you are referring to a place which has been mentioned. EG *My family still live in India. I still go there all the time... I must get home. Bill's there on his own... I walked two miles there and back for a couple of pails of water.* 5.2 after a verb when you are referring to a place where someone is just standing, sitting, etc without doing anything else. EG *Since she died he just sits there all day doing nothing... None of us said anything for some time. We just lay there... She looked up to find Tony standing there.* 5.3 when you are referring to the place where something is. For example you often say **there** when you are pointing at something to show where it is. EG *'Over there,' she said and pointed to the door... The book is there on the table... Where's the pointer gone to? Oh, there it is... Get out of there... Are you comfortable there?* 5.4 when you are telling a story, to give emphasis to the fact that a person was in a particular place or situation at the time you are talking about. EG *And there we were, as I say, producing material in a small dark room... So when the war ended, there we were, Germans, Poles, and Russians, all together.* 5.5 when you are on the telephone and you want to ask if someone is available or check that they are still listening to you. EG *Is Jane still there? Can I speak to her?... Hello, are you there?*
ADV AFTER VB
ADV AFTER VB
ADV
ADV WITH VB
ADV WITH VB

6 **There** is also used to refer to 6.1 the argument or ideas that someone has put forward or the general situation that has been discussed. EG *You're right there Howard... I think the panel would agree with me there... The source is reasonably accessible but the problem there is getting the energy ashore... They were gorgeous photos, no complaints there.* 6.2 a particular point that has been reached in an activity or procedure. EG *I'll write to the headmaster and then take the matter from there... Clean one room at a time because you can stop right there if time runs out or you get bored.* 6.3 the point that has just been made or is being made in a conversation or discussion. EG *Could I interrupt you just there?... Let's leave it there for the moment.*
ADV
ADV
ADV AFTER VB

7 You sometimes use **there** when you say that something has reached a point or level which is completely successful. EG *The man who wants to be president will do anything to get there... I like this essay–it's got some good points, but it's not quite there.*
ADV AFTER VB

8 If you say that someone is **not all there** or **not quite there**, you mean that they are rather stupid or are not mentally alert; used in informal English. EG *She spoke as if half asleep or drugged; somehow not quite there... He's a bit funny you know, I don't think he's all there.*
PHR : USED AS C

9 You use **there and then** or **then and there** to say that an action is performed at exactly the time that is being talked of and without any delay. EG *She took the clippers from her husband and there and then did an absolutely expert cut... He decided that he would terminate the discussion then and there.*
PHR : USED AS AN A = immediately

10 You say **there you are** or **there you go** 10.1 to say that the situation that has been described cannot be changed and whatever your views are you accept the situation as it is. EG *It wasn't what I'd call a very good reason for wanting to be a doctor, but there you are... I was hoping to get it all finished today but there you go.* 10.2 when something happens that confirms you were right. EG *There you are, Mabel! What did I tell you?* 10.3 when you are offering something to someone. EG *I had a quantity of cheap brass screws of various sizes. 'There you are' he said, handing the screwdriver over... 'There you are, sir.'–'Thanks'.*
CONVENTION
CONVENTION = you see
PHR

11 If you say to someone **'there you go again'**, you are reminding them that they are saying the same thing that they have said before, when you have already told them that they keep saying it. EG *There you go again. Insults!... 'I tell you, I'm just a failure.'–'You see? There you go again.'*
CONVENTION

12 You use **there again** to introduce an extra piece of information which gives either an explanation or an alternative explanation for what has been said. EG *I hadn't heard of it, but there again since I'm not interested in cars it's hardly surprising... I believe one of the servants was suspected. But there again there seemed no doubt that Mrs Jarrow had been guilty of the attack.*
PHR : USED AS ADV SEN = then again

13 **So there** is used to say that you are determined about something and will not change your mind; used especially by children. EG *Well, I won't give up, I just won't, so there.*
PHR : USED AS ADV SEN

14 You say **'there there'** to someone who is very upset, especially a small child, in order to comfort or soothe them. EG *There, there, it's not your fault.*
CONVENTION

thereabouts /ðɛərəbauts/ is used when you want to say that the number, year, place, etc that you have mentioned may not be exactly right but is nearly right. EG *Inflation could be down to 8 per cent or thereabouts... It was in 1982 or thereabouts.* ADV = approximately

thereafter /ðɛərɑ:ftə/ means during the time following the event that has been mentioned; a formal word. EG *The day started early with tea at 6.15. Thereafter it was punctuated by meals and hot drinks... This system, once learned, can thereafter be applied with great effectiveness.* ADV WITH VB = thenceforth, subsequently

thereby /ðɛəbaɪ/ is used to say that something will happen after another thing has happened as an inevitable consequence; a formal word. EG *He implied that the President had lied and thereby obstructed justice... The strike closed the ports, thereby adversely affecting the balance of payments.* ADV SEN = thus, as a result

therefore /ðɛəfɔ:/. You use **therefore** to indicate that what you are about to say is the result of something that has just been said, or to introduce a conclusion that you are about to make. EG *We have a growing population and therefore we need more and more food... The new car is smaller and therefore cheaper... I'm not a member of the Church of England myself, therefore it would be rather impertinent of me to express an opinion.* ADV SEN = consequently, hence

therein /ðɛərɪn/. 1 **Therein** means contained in the place that has been mentioned; an old-fashioned or literary use. EG *...the world and all that therein dwelt.* ADV WITH VB

2 When you say **therein lies** a situation or problem, you mean that an existing situation has caused that situation or problem; a formal or old-fashioned expression. EG *He was not a snob, you see. And therein lay his downfall.* PHR : VB INFLECTS

thereof /ðɛərɒv/ is used to refer back to a situation or thing that has previously been mentioned and to relate the word just used to that situation or thing; a formal word. EG *All persons born or naturalized in the United States, and subject to the jurisdiction thereof, are citizens of the United States... EEC Law entitles an individual to go before his own National Court and to claim the benefits thereof.* ADV AFTER NG

thereupon /ðɛərəpɒn/ means happening immediately after something else has happened and usually as a consequence of it; a formal word. EG *I flung a few copies of the report in his lap, which thereupon fell to the floor... The principal criticism was that these educational innovations were not ambitious enough. Local reformers thereupon sought to fill the gap themselves.* ADV ⇑ then

therm /θɜ:m/, **therms**. A **therm** is a measurement of heat; a technical word. N COUNT : NUM + N

thermal /θɜ:məºl/, **thermals**. 1 Thermal means relating to or caused by heat or by changes in temperature. EG *...the thermal efficiency of engines... ...thermal energy.* ADJ CLASSIF : ATTRIB

2 **Thermal** streams or baths contain water which is naturally hot or warm. ADJ CLASSIF : ATTRIB

3 **Thermal** clothes are specially designed to keep you warm in cold weather. EG *...thermal underwear.* ADJ CLASSIF : ATTRIB

4 A **thermal** is a movement of rising warm air which is used by gliders and birds in order to gain height. EG *Hawks circle at very slow speeds supported by a thermal.* N COUNT ⇑ current

thermodynamics /θɜ:məudaɪnæmɪks/ is the branch of physics that is concerned with the relationship between heat and other forms of energy. N UNCOUNT

thermometer /θəmɒmɪtə/, **thermometers**. A **thermometer** is an instrument for measuring the temperature of a room or a person's body. It usually consists of a narrow glass tube containing a thin column of mercury which rises and falls as the temperature rises and falls. EG *The thermometer reads 92 degrees... ...a clinical thermometer.* N COUNT

thermonuclear /θɜ:məunju:klɪə/. A **thermonuclear** weapon or device is one which uses the high temperatures that are generated in nuclear fission to detonate it. ADJ CLASSIF : ATTRIB ⇑ atomic

thermoplastic /θɜ:məuplæstɪk/, **thermoplastics**. A **thermoplastic** is a plastic which becomes soft when it is heated and hard when it cools down. N COUNT : USU BEFORE N

Thermos /θɜ:məs/, **Thermoses**; a trademark. A **Thermos** or a **Thermos flask** is a container which is used to keep hot drinks hot and cold drinks cold. A Thermos has two thin silvery glass walls with a vacuum between them. ▸ also used to refer to the liquid inside a Thermos or the amount of liquid it contains. EG *She brought them Thermoses of coffee.* N COUNT = vacuum flask ▸ N PART+N UNCOUNT

thermostat /θɜ:məstæt/, **thermostats**. A **thermostat** is a device that automatically keeps a heating system, for example central heating in a house, at a constant temperature by switching the system on or off when necessary. N COUNT ⇑ control

thesaurus /θɪ²sɔ:rəs/, **thesauruses**. A **thesaurus** is a reference book in which lists of words with similar meanings are grouped together. N COUNT

these /ði:z/ is the plural of **this**.

thesis /θi:sɪs/, **theses** /θi:si:z/. A **thesis** is 1 an idea or theory that is expressed as a statement and is discussed in a logical way. EG *The main thesis of the book was that human beings fall into three main types... It is my thesis that Australia underwent fundamental changes in the 1920s.* 2 a long piece of writing, based on your own ideas and research, that you do as part of a university degree, especially a Ph.D. EG *He is writing a thesis on the novels of Jane Austen... ...his doctoral thesis in electrical engineering.* N COUNT, ALSO N COUNT + REPORT-CL = argument; N COUNT = dissertation

thespian /θɛspɪən/, **thespians**; an old-fashioned or humorous word. 1 A **thespian** is an actor or actress. N COUNT

2 **Thespian** means relating to drama and the theatre. ADJ CLASSIF

they /ðeɪ/ is used as the subject of a verb. You use **they** 1 to refer to people, animals, or things that have already been mentioned or named, or whose identity is known. EG *All universities have chancellors. They are always rather senior persons... These steels are too strong. They cannot give. They just get fatigue and crack.* 2 to refer to people in general, or to a group of people whose identity is not actually stated. EG *I've had what they call writer's block... They found the body in a dustbin.* 3 instead of 'he' or 'she' to refer to a person whose sex is not known or stated, especially after pronouns such as 'someone' or 'nobody', or when you have used a singular noun to refer generally to a particular class or group of people. Some people dislike this use. EG *Nearly everybody thinks they're middle class... I was going to stay with a friend, but they were ill.* PRON : PL, USED AS S

they'd /ðeɪd/ is 1 a spoken form of 'they had', especially when 'had' is an auxiliary verb. EG *They said they'd read it all before.* 2 a spoken form of 'they would'. EG *I wish that they'd publish more books like this.*

they'll /ðeɪl/ is the usual spoken form of 'they will'. EG *They'll probably sell it cheaper.*

they're /ðɛə, ðeɪə/ is the usual spoken form of 'they are'. EG *They're not interested.*

they've /ðeɪv/ is the usual spoken form of 'they have', especially when 'have' is an auxiliary verb. EG *They've been studying very hard... They've got a new car.*

thick /θɪk/, **thicker, thickest**. 1 Something that is **thick** 1.1 has a larger distance between its two opposite surfaces than most other things of the same type. EG *...thick slices of bread... We were separated by thick concrete walls.* 1.2 has a particular width, depth, or distance between its two opposite surfaces. EG *The young tree was about fifteen feet high and one foot thick at the base... How thick is that plank of wood?* ◊ **thickness**. EG *Insert a new wire of the same thickness and wind it round the screws.* 1.3 is growing or is grouped very closely together and in large quantities. EG *The trees were so thick that the forests were as dark as night... She had white teeth and a lot of thick black hair.* ◊ **thickly**. EG *Plants and trees grew thickly on both sides of the river.* 1.4 is made up of a large number of things or people closely grouped together. EG *They were on the edge of the thick forest... ...a thick crowd.* ◊ **thickly**. EG *...a thickly populated area.* 1.5 is lying, or is put on top of something, in such a way that there is a lot of it. EG *Last winter the snow was very thick. ...She spread the jam thick.* ◊ **thickly**. EG *She buttered my bread thickly.* ADJ QUALIT ≠ thin; ADJ QUALIT; ◊ N UNCOUNT; ADJ QUALIT ≠ thin; ◊ ADV WITH VB; ADJ QUALIT = dense; ◊ ADV WITH VB; ADJ QUALIT ≠ thin; ◊ ADV WITH VB ≠ thinly

2 Someone who is **thick** is stupid and slow to understand things; an informal use. EG *He's a bit thick.* ● If you say that someone is **as thick as two short planks**, you mean that they are very stupid indeed and do not seem to understand anything; an informal expression. ADJ QUALIT; ● PHR : USED AS

3 Clothes that are **thick** are made from heavy cloth, ADJ QUALIT

so that they will keep you warm in cold weather. EG *...a thick sweater... She put on a pair of thick gloves.*
4 Liquids that are **thick** are fairly stiff and solid and do not flow easily. EG *The chef has made the sauce too thick.* ADJ QUALIT = viscous
5 Smoke, fog, or air that is **thick** is difficult to see through. EG *The smoke rose, yellow and thick... The fog seemed to be getting thicker as they went along.* ADJ QUALIT
6 If you say that the sky or the night is **thick,** you mean that it is very dark and cloudy. EG *...a thick damp sky... The night all around was thick and obscure.* ADJ QUALIT
7 If someone's voice is **thick**, it is indistinct and sounds as if they are unable to speak clearly, for example because they have a cold or have drunk too much. EG *His voice sounded blurred and thick.* ◊ **thickly**. EG *'Let's get out of here,' Tom said thickly.* ADJ QUALIT ⇑ unclear ◊ ADV WITH VB
8 An accent that is **thick** is one that is very obvious and so is easy to identify. EG *He asked, with a thick American accent, to see a pair of shoes.* ADJ QUALIT = pronounced, strong
9 Smells that are **thick** are very strong and unpleasant. EG *The smell of blood was rather thick and nauseating.* ADJ QUALIT
10 If people or things are **thick on the ground**, they are very common or are present in large numbers; an informal expression. EG *College graduates are thick on the ground.* PHR : USED AS C
11 You say **it's a bit thick** or **that's a bit thick** when you feel that something is unreasonable and unfair; used in informal English. EG *He wants you to work an extra five hours a week? That's a bit thick!.* CONVENTION ⇑ unacceptable
12 If your head is **thick**, you are unable to think quickly or clearly or you have a slight headache, usually because you are very tired or have drunk too much. EG *I woke up with a thick head.* ADJ QUALIT ≠ clear
13 If things happen **thick and fast**, they happen very quickly and in large numbers. EG *More discoveries followed thick and fast.* PHR : USED AS AN A
14 To be **thick with** something means to be full of it or be covered with it. EG *The river was thick with industrial waste... The windows were thick with grime.* PHR : USED AS C
15 If you are **in the thick of** an activity, situation, or event, it is happening at the time and you are very involved in it. EG *It won't be long before Amanda is in the thick of O level exams.* PREP
16 If you continue to do something **through thick and thin**, you do it however bad the conditions or circumstances might become. EG *She stayed with her husband through thick and thin.* PHR : USED AS AN A
17 A person who is **thick** with someone is very friendly with them; used showing disapproval in informal English. EG *Since when have you been so thick with him?* ● If you say that two people are **as thick as thieves**, you mean that they are very friendly indeed and don't seem to want other friends; used showing disapproval in informal English. ADJ QUALIT : PRED, IF+PREP THEN *with* ● PHR : USED AS C
18 If you threaten to give someone **a thick ear**, you mean that you will hit them hard, probably on the side of their head; an informal expression. EG *If you don't shut up I'll give you a thick ear!* PHR : USED AS O
19 See also **thickness**.

thicken /θɪkəⁿn/, **thickens, thickening, thickened**. 1 If something **thickens**, it becomes more closely grouped together than it has previously been. EG *Here the vegetation thickens into a jungle.* V ⇑ increase
2 If fog or smoke **thickens**, it becomes denser or darker and more difficult to see through. EG *The fog began to thicken and the car had to slow down.* V ⇑ increase
3 When you **thicken** a liquid or it **thickens,** you make it stiffer and more solid, so that it flows less easily. EG *You can use flour to thicken sauces.* V-ERG ≠ thin
4 **The plot thickens** is an expression that you use when the situation or series of events you are talking about is getting more and more complicated and mysterious. CONVENTION

thickener /θɪkəⁿnə/, **thickeners**. A **thickener** is a substance that is added to a liquid in order to make it stiffer and more solid. EG *You can use cornflour as a thickener for sauces, soups and stews.* N COUNT/UNCOUNT ≠ thinner

thicket /θɪkɪt/, **thickets**. A **thicket** is a small group of trees or bushes which are growing closely together. EG *They live in hidden valleys or dense thickets.* N COUNT

thickness /θɪknɪ²s/, **thicknesses**. A **thickness** of something is a layer of it. EG *Merion was wearing several thicknesses of clothing.* ● See also **thick**. N COUNT

thickset /θɪksɛt/; also spelled with a hyphen. Someone who is **thickset** is broad and heavy, with a solid-looking body. EG *...a big, thickset man with heavy shoulders.* ADJ QUALIT = stocky

thick-skinned. If you are **thick-skinned,** you are not easily hurt by what other people say to you or about you, especially when they criticize or insult you. EG *...a thick-skinned, brutal person.* ADJ QUALIT ⇑ insensitive

thief /θiːf/, **thieves**. A **thief** is a person who steals something from another person, especially without using violence. EG *If you catch a thief breaking open your door, shout like hell... ...jewel thieves.* N COUNT ⇑ criminal = burglar

thieving /θiːvɪŋ/. 1 **Thieving** is the act of stealing things from people; an old-fashioned use. EG *...the dreadful risks involved in thieving.* N UNCOUNT = robbery
2 **Thieving** means involved in stealing things or intending to steal something. EG *...those thieving village kids... Keep your thieving hands off!* ADJ CLASSIF : ATTRIB

thigh /θaɪ/, **thighs**. Your **thighs** are the top parts of your legs, between your knees and your hips. EG *I walked the last six miles in water up to my thighs.* N COUNT

thimble /θɪmbəⁿl/, **thimbles**. A **thimble** is a small metal or plastic object that you put on the end of your finger when you are sewing. The thimble protects your finger when you push the needle through the cloth. N COUNT

thimbleful /θɪmbəlfʊl/, **thimblefuls**. A **thimbleful** is a very small amount of liquid. EG *'More sherry?'-'Just a thimbleful please.'* N COUNT : ALSO N PART+N UNCOUNT = drop

thin /θɪn/, **thinner, thinnest; thins, thinning, thinned**. 1 Something that is **thin** is much narrower than it is long. EG *His nose was long and thin... ...their tall, thin house... ...a collarless shirt with a thin grey stripe.* ◊ **thinness**. EG *The thinness of the wire was a great problem.* ADJ QUALIT ≠ thick ◊ N UNCOUNT ≠ thickness
2 A person or animal that is **thin** has no extra fat on their body. EG *Angela was dreadfully thin... You are thinner. Are you ill?* ● If you say that someone is **as thin as a rake**, you mean that they are very thin indeed. ADJ QUALIT = skinny, lean ● PHR : USED AS C
3 Something such as paper or cloth that is **thin** is flat and has only a very small distance between its two opposite surfaces. EG *...thin slices of bread... ...thin cotton cloth... ...a thin layer of soil and coarse grass.* ◊ **thinly**. EG *...fresh, thinly cut rye bread... ...a grassed area now thinly covered with snow.* ◊ **thinness**. EG *...the thinness of the cord carpet.* ADJ QUALIT ≠ thick ◊ ADV WITH VB ◊ N UNCOUNT ≠ thickness
4 Liquids that are **thin** are weak and watery. EG *The liquid was thin and greyish brown... ...thin ink.* ADJ QUALIT ≠ thick
5 Smoke that is **thin** is very easy to see through because it is not dense. EG *The thin blue smoke went curling up.* ADJ QUALIT
6 A crowd, an audience, or a group that is **thin** is made up of only a small number of people or things, which are widely spread out, so that there is a lot of space between them. EG *The crowd seemed suddenly thinner... ...the unimaginable vastness of space with its thin population of burning stars.* ◊ **thinly**. EG *...a thinly populated region.* ADJ QUALIT = sparse ◊ ADV WITH VB = sparsely
7 Explanations, excuses, and arguments that are **thin** are not convincing, usually because they are not well thought out or are badly presented. EG *Your excuses are becoming thinner, I'm afraid... At best, this argument is thin, but it is often raised... The script is very thin at the best of times.* ◊ **thinly**. EG *...a thinly disguised piece of electioneering. ...a thinly veiled criticism.* ADJ QUALIT = weak ◊ ADV WITH VB = barely
8 A voice that is **thin** is high-pitched and not very loud. EG *'Come in,' he said in a thin, cracked voice.* ADJ QUALIT = reedy
9 When you **thin** something or it **thins,** it becomes less crowded because people or things have been removed. EG *I think the difficult years thinned the artists' ranks considerably.* V-ERG ⇑ lessen
10 To **thin** a sauce or liquid means to make it weaker and more watery by adding another liquid to it. EG *I think the gravy needs thinning a bit.* V+O = dilute
11 If your hair **is thinning** or you are getting **thin on top**, you are beginning to go bald. EG *His hair was thinning slightly... He ran a hand through his thinning hair.* V : ONLY CONT, OR PHR : USED AS C
12 People or businesses are having **a thin time** when they are not being very successful, often because economic conditions in general are not good. EG *The local papers are having a thin time.* PHR : USED AS C = lean time
13 When you say that people or things are **thin on the ground**, you mean that there are not very many PHR : USED AS C = scarce

of them and so they are hard to find. EG *Good new plays are still rather thin on the ground.*
14 When a joke or a story **is wearing thin**, it is beginning to lose its interest because it has been repeated too many times. EG *The joke had begun to wear very thin.* PHR : VB INFLECTS = pall
15 When your patience or your temper **is wearing thin**, you are beginning to become impatient or angry. EG *Her patience will probably have worn thin by the end of the day.* PHR : VB INFLECTS = run out
16 • **on thin ice**: see **ice**. • to **disappear** or **vanish into thin air**: see **air**.

thin down. When you **thin** something **down** you make it weaker or more watery than it was. EG *The paint has been thinned down too much.* PHRASAL VB : V+O+ADV

thin out. If an area **thins out**, it become less crowded because people are moving away. EG *Western cities are thinning out as people move to the suburbs... The inner-city neighbourhoods have thinned out.* PHRASAL VB : V+ADV

thine /ðaɪn/ is an old-fashioned, poetic, or religious word for 'yours' when you are talking to only one person. See **thou**. EG *Thine is the kingdom, the power, and the glory... I am thine for ever.* ▸ also used instead of 'thy' in front of a word that begins with a vowel. EG *Love thine enemy.* PRONPOSS : SING ▸ DETPOSS

thing /θɪŋ/, **things. Thing** is often used in English as a substitute for another word when you cannot or do not want to be more precise, especially when you are referring to an object or to an action, activity, situation, idea, etc. which has already been mentioned. **1 Thing** is used **1.1** instead of a more accurate word when the situation or context makes it fairly clear what you are talking about. EG *He needed a few things so we went to the store to purchase them... It's silly to train a group of people just to do one thing... A terrible thing happened to me on my way to work... When you are young you dream about all sorts of things.* N COUNT ⇑ something **1.2** when you want to avoid repeating a word, or in preference to a more accurate word. EG *Damp clothes are unhealthy. So air things after ironing them.* N COUNT **1.3** to refer to something, especially a physical object, when you want to express contempt, dislike, or irritation for it. EG *Do you know how to drive this thing?* N COUNT ⇑ it **1.4** in lists and descriptions to give examples or to widen the range of what you are referring to. EG *The fourth drawer holds family things such as photographs, letters and schools reports... You can have coffee and talk about books and things.* N COUNT : USU PL **1.5** to refer to something that you give as an example and then use as a basis for a remark or a general statement. EG *I've seen this sort of thing in South Africa so many times it just doesn't horrify me any more... Don't bother me with little things like that.* N COUNT : USU PL **1.6** to refer to something or someone and to the situation or activity connected with them; sometimes used also to suggest that they are not very important or serious. EG *When you did this discussion thing... He'd been photographing the Liverpool thing for seven or eight years now.* N COUNT : MOD+N = affair, business **1.7** to describe or refer to something that you are uncertain about but that is rather like the object mentioned. EG *He limped away up a long grassy path to a big box thing. Well, it looked like a box.* N COUNT : MOD+N
2 The word **thing** is also often used **2.1** instead of the pronouns 'anything,' 'nothing,' 'everything,' or 'something' in order to emphasize what you are saying. EG *I just couldn't think of a single thing to say... Don't worry about a thing. Everything'll be fine.* N SING WITH DET **2.2** after the word 'such' and instead of the pronouns 'it,' 'this,' or 'that,' especially in negative statements, in order to emphasize what you are referring back to. EG *He didn't want to let her know that he was even considering such a thing... I had said no such thing.* N COUNT : USU WITH BROAD NEG • **such a thing** and **no such thing** are used in making statements about whether something exists or not, or whether it is possible or likely. EG *There's no such thing as perfection... In fact, I think I'd have enjoyed it, if such a thing is possible.* • PHR : USED AS S/O **2.3** after an adjective for emphasis or for reasons of style. EG *Education isn't the same thing as intelligence... It was a lucky thing he would still be there tonight.* N COUNT : ADJ+N **2.4** to introduce and draw attention to a statement, explanation, opinion, question, etc. EG *One thing I want to ask you: have you found my book yet?... The first thing I did when I came back was clean the bathroom.* N COUNT : USU NUM/ORDINAL+N **2.5** as an introduction to a statement or comment in order to express your attitude towards the topic or to emphasize your opinion of it. EG *The awful thing is, we're going away... One of the odd things about her novels is that the leading character is usually male.* N COUNT : MOD+N • **The thing is...** is a way of introducing an explanation, objection, or opinion relating to something that has just been said; used in spoken English. EG *I can't come on Thursday. The thing is, I've already arranged to do something on Thursday.* • PHR : VB INFLECTS+REPORT-CL **2.6** to refer back to something that has just been mentioned, either to emphasize it or to give more information about it. EG *She sobbed last night, a thing she rarely does.* N COUNT
3 A **thing** is **3.1** a physical object that is considered as having no life of its own. EG *The ageing and decay of things and organisms... They become things and not people.* N COUNT ⇑ object **3.2** a monster or something else that is too frightening, strange, or horrible to describe clearly. EG *But my hunters sometimes talk of a thing, a dark thing, a beast, some sort of animal.* N COUNT
4 Your **things** are your clothes or possessions, especially the ones which you use for a particular activity or at a particular time. EG *She changed into her bathing things... I like my own things around me: my photos and my furniture.* N PLURAL : POSS+N
5 Things are the objects or equipment that are used for a particular purpose or activity. EG *Lally started washing up the breakfast things.* N PLURAL : MOD+N
6 Things can also refer to **6.1** actions, events, facts, stories, etc, when you want to suggest that they are too nasty to describe in detail. EG *The rain did things to the corpses... I've heard things about them.* N PLURAL **6.2** the situation or life in general, especially in relation to the way it is changing or the way it is affecting you. EG *All the time things are changing... Things are going very well for us at the moment... I hope I've not spoiled things... How are things?* N PLURAL ⇑ everything **6.3** a particular aspect of life, especially physical or spiritual matters. EG *...things of the flesh... ...spiritual things.* N PLURAL+SUPP
7 You call a person or an animal a **thing** when you want to indicate what your feelings are to the particular qualities that you mention. EG *She was turning blue with cold, poor thing... ...a funny little thing with glasses... You lucky thing!* N COUNT : ADJ+N, ALSO VOC = creature
8 If you say that something is **the thing**, you mean that it is fashionable or popular. EG *Dominoes is the current thing in our household... It became the thing to do: to scream whenever they appeared.* N SING : *the*+N, USU+SUPP ⇑ fashion • If something is **the done thing**, it is the socially acceptable way to behave. EG *It was quite the done thing to eat with your hands.* • PHR : USED AS C ⇑ correct
9 You start a sentence by saying **'It's one thing to...'** when you want to contrast two ideas, facts, etc, and to say that the second one makes the first seem unimportant or irrelevant. EG *It's one thing to play with a computer toy: quite another to understand how it works.* PHR : VB INFLECTS
10 You use **with one thing and another** when you mean that there are several reasons for something, but you are not going to explain what they are. EG *He sees a lot of her, you know, with one thing and another... We kept putting it off what with one thing and another.* PHR : USED AS AN A
11 You say **for one thing** when you are giving a reason that explains the statement or comment you have just made. EG *I prefer badminton to squash. It's not so tiring for one thing.* PHR : USED AS AN A
12 The word **thing** is also used in the following expressions. **12.1** If something is **a thing of the past**, it no longer exists or happens. EG *This was now a thing of the past.* PHR : USED AS C **12.2** If something is **the shape of things to come**, that is the way it is likely to develop in the future. EG *It is an indication of the shape of things to come.* PHR : USED AS C **12.3 In all things** means in every situation and at all times. EG *I believe in total honesty in all things.* PHR : USED AS AN A **12.4** If you say **it is just one of those things**, you mean that you cannot explain something because it seems to happen by chance. EG *It was just one of those things.* PHR : VB INFLECTS **12.5** If you try to **be all things to all men**, you try to behave towards everyone in ways that you think will please them. EG *He was so anxious for so long to be all things to all men.* PHR : VB INFLECTS **12.6** If you say that something is **just the thing** or is **the very thing**, you mean that it is exactly what you want. EG *A whisky would be the very thing.* PHR : USED AS C **12.7** If you **do the** decent **thing, do the** democratic **thing**, etc, you behave in the particular way mentioned. EG *...the* PHR : VB INFLECTS

British concept of doing 'the decent thing'. **12.8** If you **do** your **own thing**, you live, act, or behave in the way you want to, without paying attention to convention or depending on other people; an informal expression. EG *There's far less room in a society like that for people to do their own thing.* PHR : VB INFLECTS **12.9** If you **have a thing** about someone or something, you have very strong feelings about them; an informal expression. EG *He seems to have a thing about her... No wonder I've got a thing about drink.* PHR : VB INFLECTS + A *(about)* **12.10** If you **make a thing** of or out of something, you make it much more important than it really is; an informal expression. EG *He made a big thing of how he didn't like chilli... Don't let's make a thing out of this.* PHR : VB INFLECTS + A *(of/ out of)*

13 The word **thing** is also used in the following expressions, which are explained at other places in this dictionary. • **of all things**: see **all**. • **all** or **other things being equal**: see **equal**. • **first thing**: see **first**. • **to know a thing or two**: see **know**. • **last thing**: see **last**. • **one thing leads to another**: see **lead**. • **near thing**: see **near**. • **the real thing**: see **real**. • **to see things**: see **see**.

thingamabob /θɪŋəməbɒb/, **thingamabobs.** See **thingummy**. N COUNT

thingummy /θɪŋəmi¹/, **thingummies**. You refer to something or someone as **thingummy**, **thingummyjig**, or **thingamabob** when you cannot remember or do not know the proper word or name for them, or when you cannot be bothered to use the proper word or name for them; used in informal spoken English. EG *Can you pass me that thingummyjig over there?* N COUNT ⇑ thing

thingy /θɪŋi¹/, **thingies. Thingy** is used to refer to something such as a physical object or activity that you are uncertain about, a person whose name you have forgotten, or something that you do not want to name directly; used in informal spoken English. EG *Oh, I saw thingy the other day.* N COUNT ⇑ thing

think /θɪŋk/, **thinks, thinking, thought. 1** If you **think** that something is the case, you have the opinion that it is the case. EG *I think a woman has as much right to work as a man... I think that you should go... She's cleverer than I thought... What did you think of her?* V + REPORT-CL/*of*

2 If you say that you **think** that something is true or will happen, you mean that you have the impression that it is true or will happen, although you are not certain about it. EG *I think it's six thirty on Sundays... They are, I think, a good bit younger than Mary... 'Will she mind, do you think?'-'No, I shouldn't think so.'... How old do you think I am?... You're not free, you just think you are... At first I thought he was asleep... His job was to protect me, or so I thought... Who would ever have thought that he would become a monk?* V + REPORT-CL ⇑ believe = imagine

3 If you **think** of someone or something as having a particular quality or purpose, you regard them as having this quality or purpose. EG *She thought of Deirdre simply as an old chum... People think of computers as being devices that calculate... He was thought by the Conservatives to be an extreme radical... Milk was thought a luxury.* V + A *(of)*, OR V + O + C/*to*-INF : USU PASS ⇑ consider

4 If you **think** like someone else, you have the same general opinions as them. EG *You expect everyone to think like you... Her servants thought as she did.* V + A

5 If you **think** in a particular way, you consider things, solve problems, or make decisions in this way, for example because of your job or your background. EG *I think as a scientist... Twenty years ago, students simply didn't think this way... Unless you think like that, disaster will ensue... They thought primarily in terms of being good Christians.* V + A = reason

6 When you **think** about ideas, problems, etc, you make a mental effort to consider them. EG *He thought for a moment, looked us up and down, and still said nothing... Do we need language to think or to communicate?... That ought to make us all think hard about how we can make a safer product... ...the society in which most of us live without even thinking about it.* ▸ used as a noun. EG *We'll be in touch when we've had a think about what to do.* V : IF + PREP THEN *about*, OR V + QUOTE = reflect, ponder ▸ N SING : *a* + N

7 If you **think** of something, you remember it or it comes into your mind, when you have been trying to remember it. EG *I'm trying to think which other companies I can try for you... If you think of anything else, ask the lady here... I can never think of her name.* V : USU + *of*

8 If you **are thinking** of one particular part of a subject or problem, you are concentrating your attention on this part. EG *I'm thinking here particularly of doctors... One thinks particularly of the laws on divorce.* V : USU CONT + *of*

9 If you **are thinking** something at a particular moment, you have words or ideas in your mind without saying them out loud. EG *All the while I was thinking, 'What's happening here?'... What it was to have a friend, Deirdre thought... I lay there thinking how funny it was.* ▸ **Think** can also be used with 'thought' as an object. EG *...thinking beautiful thoughts.* V + QUOTE/ REPORT-CL = reflect, muse ▸ V + O

10 If you **think** of someone, you show consideration for them and pay attention to their needs. EG *It was very kind of you to think of him... I had my own survival to think of... You never think about anybody but yourself!* V + *of/about*

11 If you can **think** of something such as a fact or a reason for something, you know it and can therefore suggest it to other people. EG *I can think of at least two examples of this Government's stupidity... He can think of no reason for going on living.* V + A *(of)* : WITH MODAL

12 If you **think** of an idea, you make a mental effort and use your imagination and intelligence to create it or develop it. EG *...a method which, so far as he knew, had never even been thought of before... I kicked myself for not having thought of it earlier.* V + A *(of)* = conceive

13 If you **are thinking** of taking a particular course of action, you are considering it as a possible course of action. EG *Is he still thinking of going away to Italy for a month?... I thought about being a sports reporter... I keep thinking about getting a flat.* V : USU CONT + *of/ about* + -ING

14 You use **'I think' 14.1** as a way of being polite when you are explaining or suggesting to someone what you want to do, or when you are accepting or refusing an offer. EG *I think I ought to go, if you don't mind... I thought we'd go swimming tomorrow... Thank you, I don't think I will, if you don't mind.* PHR + REPORT-CL **14.2** in formal conversations or speeches to make your statements sound less forceful or rude. EG *I think you mean the eighteenth century rather than the nineteenth... I think that you will find my figures are correct... I think actually it might be a good idea to close the meeting at this point.* PHR + REPORT-CL

15 You use **think** in questions to express your anger or shock at someone's behaviour. You do not usually expect an answer to these questions. EG *Who do you think you are?... What do you think you're doing?* V + REPORT-CL : IN QUESTIONS

16 If you **think** a lot of someone or something, you admire them very much or think they are very good. EG *She thinks a lot of you... I didn't think much of his letter.* V + QUANTIF + *of/ about*

17 If you **think the best of** people, you expect that they will behave in the best possible way and will not do anything wrong. If you **think the worst of** people, you expect them to behave badly. EG *You always think the best of everyone... I suppose he can't help it, but I must say I thought better of you... Why do you always think the worst of me?* PHR : VB INFLECTS

18 If you are intending to do something but you **think better of it**, you decide not to do it because you realize that it would be a foolish thing to do. EG *She was on the point of waking Bal again, but then thought better of it.* PHR : VB INFLECTS ⇑ reconsider

19 If you **think nothing of** doing something that other people might consider difficult or strange, you consider it to be easy or normal, and you do it often or would be quite willing to do it. EG *We would think nothing of walking six or more miles just to post a letter.* PHR : VB INFLECTS

20 If you **think aloud**, you say all the thoughts that are in your head without organizing them in any way. EG *Don't take any notice, I'm just thinking aloud.* PHR : VB INFLECTS

21 If you **think twice** or **think again** about doing something, you consider it very carefully before you do it and sometimes change your mind and decide not to do it, often on the basis of new information that you learn. EG *You've got to think twice before you spend ten pounds on a book... I might have thought twice about staying there if I'd known how much it would cost... He may have to think again.* PHR : VB INFLECTS = reconsider

22 You use an expression such as **come to think of it**, **when you think about it**, or **thinking about it** when you suddenly remember or realize something that had not occurred to you before. EG *Come to think of it, I have seen her before... If you think about it, a* PHR : USED AS ADV SEN ⇑ actually *modern economy needs steel... I suppose it's obvious when you stop and think about it.*

23 If you ask **what** someone **is thinking of**, you are expressing your surprise at how foolish, careless, or forgetful they have been. EG *What were you thinking of?... Whatever could I have been thinking about?* PHR : AUX INFLECTS = what possessed you

24 If you say to someone **'I wasn't thinking'**, you are apologizing to them or explaining why you have been foolish, careless, or forgetful. EG *I'm terribly sorry, I just wasn't thinking.* CONVENTION

25 You use **think** when you are commenting on something which you did or experienced in the past and which now seems surprising, foolish, or strange to you. EG *To think that I trusted him!... When I think of how she went on about Hughie, I can see why he left her.* V+REPORT-CL/*of*

26 If you say **anybody would think** that a particular thing was true, **you would have thought** that it was true, etc, you are expressing your surprise or disapproval at someone's behaviour by suggesting that something that you know is untrue is true. EG *Anybody'd think you were our nanny... You would have thought they had never seen a man before... Anyone would think you weren't keen to go.* PHR+REPORT-CL

27 You say **just think** when you feel excited, fascinated, or shocked by something, and you want the person to whom you are talking to feel the same. EG *Judy, just think, what an opportunity!... Just think, we're nothing but masses of molecules... Just think how much it's going to cost us.* PHR : USED AS ADV SEN = imagine

28 If you say **'That's what you think'**, **'That's what he thinks'**, etc, you mean that you intend to prevent the person you are referring to from doing something that they are intending or expecting to do; a fairly informal expression. CONVENTION

29 If you say to someone who is expecting you to do a particular thing **'If you think that, you've got another think coming'**, you are telling them that you are not going to do it, because it is unreasonable; a fairly informal expression. EG *If you think I'm just going to wait here, you've got another think coming.* CONVENTION

30 • **can't hear** yourself **think**: see **hear**. • to **think big**: see **big**. • to **think the world of** someone: see **world**. • See also **thinking, thought**.

think back. If you **think back**, you make an effort to remember things that happened to you in the past. EG *Think back to some of your history lessons... I'm thinking back to my own experience as a teacher... It gives you an opportunity to think back over the year.* PHRASAL VB : V+ADV, USU+*to/over* = look back

think out. If you **think** something **out**, for example a plan or a piece of writing, you prepare it fully and consider all the details of it before doing anything. EG *You have to think out what you're going to say... He's a great believer in thinking things out.* PHRASAL VB : V+O+ADV

think over. If you **think** something **over**, you consider it carefully before making a decision. EG *I wanted to think over one or two business problems which we had discussed.* PHRASAL VB : V+O+ADV = weigh up

think through. If you **think** a situation **through**, you consider it thoroughly, together with all its possible effects or consequences. EG *I haven't really thought the whole business through in my own mind.* PHRASAL VB : ORDER V+O+ADV

think up. If you **think** something **up**, for example a clever idea, you invent it using mental effort. EG *I kept thinking up ways I could murder him without getting caught... He informed me of a new financial agreement he had thought up... ...examples that mathematicians think up.* PHRASAL VB : V+O+ADV = concoct, devise

thinker /θɪŋkə/, **thinkers**. A **thinker** is a person who spends a lot of time thinking deeply about important things, especially a philosopher who is famous for thinking of new ideas. EG *...Morris, another Marxist thinker... ...such thinkers as Plato, Rousseau, and Freud.* N COUNT ⇑ theorist

thinking /θɪŋkɪŋ/. 1 The general ideas or opinions of a person or group can be referred to as their **thinking**. EG *We are so alike in our thinking... ...the new direction of Tyler's thinking... He hoped we would come round to his way of thinking... ...a reluctance which dominated the thinking of a whole generation.* N UNCOUNT+SUPP ⇑ philosophy

2 You add **to my way of thinking, to their way of thinking**, etc to a statement to emphasize that it is your opinion or someone else's opinion, and not a fact. EG *...issues which, to my way of thinking, are some of the fundamental human issues.* PHR : USED AS ADV SEN = to my mind

3 **Thinking** is 3.1 the activity of using your brain by considering a problem or possibility or creating an idea. EG *I've done some thinking... That requires a great deal of serious thinking about... ...the thinking behind the campaign.* N UNCOUNT ⇑ considering 3.2 the condition of having thoughts and opinions, in contrast with seeing, hearing, feeling, or doing things. EG *...the power to subordinate thinking to feeling.* N UNCOUNT = reasoning

4 **Thinking** is also used to describe people who are intelligent and who take an interest in important events and issues; used showing approval. EG *...conditions which forced the thinking countryman to decide that changes must be made... ...the thinking woman's heart-throb.* ADJ CLASSIF : ATTRIB = reasoning

5 **wishful thinking**: see **wishful**.

think-tank, think-tanks; also spelled without a hyphen. A **think-tank** is a group of experts who are gathered together by an organization, especially by the government, in order to consider various problems and try and work out ways to solve them. EG *...last week's so-called secret Think-Tank report.* N COUNT : USU SING, IF SING VB CAN BE SING OR PL

thinner /θɪnə/, **thinners**. **Thinner** is a liquid which you add to another liquid, often paint, to make it less thick or easier to spread. EG *Try turpentine as a thinner.* N MASS = solvent

thin-skinned. Someone who is **thin-skinned** is easily upset by criticism or insults from other people. EG *Be careful, he's rather thin-skinned.* ADJ QUALIT = sensitive

third /θɜːd/, **thirds**. 1 The **third** item in a series is the one that you count as number three: see ☐ at NUMBER, AGE, and DATE. EG *This room was on the third floor.* ORDINAL

2 A **third** is one of three equal parts of something. EG *It covers a third of the world's surface.* N COUNT : USU+*of*

3 You use **third** or **thirdly** in speech or writing when you want to make a third point or give a third reason that is connected with the first two points or reasons that you have already given. EG *Third, the confused military set-up was causing problems... And thirdly, remember that they have supported you in the past.* ADV SEN ⇑ also

4 A **third** is also the lowest honours degree that can be obtained from a British university. EG *'You read History, I think?'–'Yes. I got a third.'* N COUNT : USU SING

5 **Third** is the third gear in a series of gears in a car or other vehicle. EG *The traffic was so slow I couldn't get above third.* N UNCOUNT

6 In music, a **third** is the interval between two notes on a musical scale when there are either two or three semitones separating them. N COUNT

third-class. 1 **Third class** is the cheapest and least comfortable section of accommodation on a ship or train. EG *I shall go third class... I saw her emerging from a third-class carriage of the train.* ADJ CLASSIF, OR ADV AFTER VB

2 A **third class** or a **third-class** degree is the lowest honours degree that can be obtained from a British university. EG *...a third class in history.* N COUNT : USU SING

third degree. If someone is given the **third degree**, they are bullied, tortured, etc, especially in order to make them confess or to make them give secret information; an informal expression. EG *He was probably being put through the third degree down there.* N SING : *the*+N ⇑ torture

thirdly /θɜːdli¹/. See **third**.

third party, third parties; spelled with a hyphen when used before another noun. 1 A **third party** is someone who is not one of the main people involved in a legal case, business agreement, etc, but is involved in it in a minor role or becomes involved by chance. EG *A third party from outside the village was brought in as a witness... Frequently governments become involved as third parties in major wage negotiations.* N COUNT

2 **Third-party** insurance is a type of insurance you have that gives financial compensation to people who are hurt or whose property is damaged as a result of something you have done. EG *A further 186 enquiries dealt with third party motor claims.* ADJ CLASSIF

third person. The **third person** refers to a person, thing, or group in speech or writing, and is expressed as 'he', 'she', 'it', or 'they' with the appropriate form of a verb. N SING : *the*+N

third-rate. Something that is **third-rate** is of a very poor quality or standard. EG *...the seedy world of third-rate theatricals... ...a third-rate Congress member.* ADJ QUALIT = inferior

Third World. The countries of Africa, Asia, and South America are sometimes referred to collectively as the **Third World**, especially those parts that are N PROPER : *the*+N poor, do not have much power, and are considered to be underdeveloped. EG *I had seen a good deal of the Third World before I visited Calcutta... In 1958 only four Third World countries had supersonic aircraft.*

thirst /θɜ:st/, **thirsts, thirsting, thirsted.** 1 A **thirst** is a feeling you have of wanting or needing to drink something. EG *He sat down at the stream to quench his thirst... All this gardening has given me a real thirst.*
N SING WITH DET ⇑ desire

2 **Thirst** is the condition of not having enough to drink. EG *She was dying of thirst.*
N UNCOUNT

3 A **thirst** for something is a very strong desire for that thing; a fairly literary use. EG *...the thirst for the absolute which is inherent in human nature... ...his thirst for knowledge.*
N SING WITH DET + for = passion

4 If you **thirst** for something, you want it very much; a literary use. EG *The story is so gripping; it makes you thirst for the next episode.*
V+A *(for/after)* = crave

thirsty /θɜ:sti[1]/, **thirstier, thirstiest.** 1 If you are **thirsty**, you feel that you want or need to drink something. EG *I felt thirsty and walked to the drinking fountain... 'Have you got any water? I'm thirsty.'*
ADJ QUALIT = dry, parched

◊ **thirstily.** EG *Jane drank thirstily.*
◊ ADV WITH VB

2 **Thirsty** is also used to describe things that make you feel thirsty. EG *Gardening is really thirsty work... We sat down on our towels in the thirsty sun.*
ADJ QUALIT : ATTRIB

3 If you are **thirsty** for something, you want it very much; a fairly literary use. EG *He was thirsty for adventure.*
ADJ QUALIT : PRED+*for* = eager

thirteen /θɜ:ti:n/ is the number 13: see □ at NUMBER, AGE, DATE, MEASUREMENT, MONEY, and TIME. EG *He hadn't even appeared in a film for thirteen years.*
NUM

thirteenth /θɜ:ti:nθ/. The **thirteenth** item in a series is the one that you count as number thirteen: see □ at NUMBER, AGE, and DATE. EG *...my thirteenth birthday.*
ORDINAL

thirtieth /θɜ:ti[1]ɪθ/. 1 The **thirtieth** item in a series is the one that you count as number thirty: see □ at NUMBER, AGE, and DATE. EG *...a parade to celebrate the thirtieth year of its use.*
ORDINAL

thirty /θɜ:ti[1]/, **thirties. Thirty** is the number 30: see □ at NUMBER, AGE, DATE, MEASUREMENT, MONEY, and TIME. EG *...thirty years of marriage.*
NUM

this /ðɪs/, **these** /ði:z/. 1 You use **this to refer to things or people in the following ways: 1.1** to refer back to a particular person or thing that has been mentioned, or to introduce someone or something that you are going to talk about. EG *These particular students are extremely bright... He's from the Institute of English Language in Bangkok, and this institute is set up to serve the language teachers in the area.* ▸ used as a pronoun. In the singular **this** can only refer to things. EG *Where steam is found underground, this can be trapped and used to drive electrical machinery.* **1.2** to refer to a statement, opinion, or explanation that has already been expressed, or that you are going to express. **This** can be used as a pronoun to refer to plurals. EG *New machines are of course more expensive and this is also something one has to consider... Well, you might not believe this, but I don't drink very much.* ▸ used as a determiner. EG *So, for all these reasons, my advice is to be very, very careful.* **1.3** to introduce a person or thing into a story or account and make the listener or reader feel interested and involved; used in informal spoken English. EG *I stopped at a junction and this bowler-hatted gent comes up... I was walking through this rather mountainous country.*
DET / ▸ PRON / PRON / ▸ DET / DET

2 You use **this** and **these**, especially in spoken English, in the following ways when you are referring to people, things, events, or situations in the world around you: **2.1** when you refer to a person or thing that is near you, especially when you touch them or point to them. When there are two or more people or things near you, **this** refers to the nearest one. EG *The colonel handed him the bag. 'This is for you.'* ▸ used as a determiner. EG *'Please show Mr Jordache where the office is.'–'This way, sir'... Get these kids out of here.* **2.2** when you refer to a situation, activity, or event which is happening or has just happened and which you feel involved in. EG *'My God,' I said. 'This is awful.'... I'm sorry to barge in on you like this.* ▸ used as a determiner. EG *This whole business has gone on far too long.* **2.3** when you refer to the present time or place. EG *...the prime minister of this country... Could I make an appointment to see the doctor this morning please?... The prices these days are absolutely astronomical.* **2.4** when you refer to the next occurrence in the future of a particular day, month, season, or festival. EG *Let's fix a time. This Sunday. Four o'clock... Any chance of you getting away this summer?.*
PRON / ▸ DET / PRON / ▸ DET / DET / DET ⇑ coming

3 You also use **this 3.1** when you are indicating the size or shape of something with your hands or with another object at the same time as you are speaking. EG *It was about this big.* **3.2** when you are going to specify how much you know or how much you can tell someone. EG *I can tell you this much: he won't try it again.*
ADV+ADJ/ADV = so / ADV+ADJ/ADV

4 If you say **this is it**, you are **4.1** agreeing with what someone else has just said. EG *'It's a difficult habit to break, isn't it?'–'This is it.'* **4.2** telling someone that you have made a firm decision, or that you have reached an important or exciting point in a situation or story. EG *Right. I'm going. This is it... This was it: the step forward into the blank space.*
CONVENTION = absolutely / PHR : VB INFLECTS

5 You say **this is 5.1** in order to introduce someone or to say what you are showing to someone. EG *This is Desiree, my father's second wife.* **5.2** in order to say who you are or what organization you are representing, when you are speaking on the telephone, radio, or television. EG *'This is BBC Radio Brighton'... He looked for her number, and dialled it. 'Sally? This is Martin Brody.'*
PHR+NAME/NG ⇑ here is / PHR+NAME

6 If you say that you are doing or talking about **this and that**, or **this, that, and the other**, you mean that you are doing or talking about a variety of things that you do not want to specify. EG *'What have you been up to ?'–'This and that.'... We sat talking about this, that and the other.*
PHR : USED AS O ⇑ something

thistle /θɪsə[0]l/, **thistles.** A **thistle** is a wild plant with prickly leaves and purple flowers.
N COUNT

thistledown /θɪsə[0]ldaʊn/ is a soft, white, fluffy substance attached to the seeds of thistles, that allows the seeds to be carried by the wind.
N UNCOUNT

thither /ðɪðə/ means to the place that has already been mentioned; an old-fashioned word. ● **hither and thither**: see **hither** .

tho /ðəʊ/. See **though.**

thong /θɒŋ/, **thongs.** A **thong** is a long thin strip of leather, plastic, or rubber.
N COUNT

thoracic /θɔ:ræsɪk/ means relating to or affecting your thorax; a medical term. EG *...an eminent thoracic surgeon.*
ADJ CLASSIF : ATTRIB

thorax /θɔ:ræks/, **thoraxes, thoraces.** The plural can be either **thoraxes** or **thoraces. 1** Your **thorax** is the part of your body between your neck and your waist, including the organs that are inside, for example your heart and lungs; a medical term.
N COUNT : USU SING = chest

2 An insect's **thorax** is the central part of its body, between the head and the abdomen, to which the legs and wings are attached; a technical term.
N COUNT : USU SING

thorn /θɔ:n/, **thorns. 1** A **thorn** is **1.1** one of the sharp points on the stem of a plant such as a rose bush, or on the branches of a tree such as a hawthorn. EG *He stepped on a sharp thorn.* **1.2** a tree or bush such as a hawthorn. EG *At the foot of that thorn there's a path... ...a huge thorn bush... ...thickets of thorn.*
N COUNT = prickle / N COUNT/ UNCOUNT

2 If you describe something as a **thorn in your flesh or side**, you mean that it is a constant problem or annoyance to you. EG *The biggest thorn in the Prime Minister's side is inflation... Howard is a well-known activist, a thorn in the flesh of the council.*
PHR : USU USED AS C

thorny /θɔ:ni[1]/, **thornier, thorniest. 1** A **thorny** plant or tree is one that is covered with thorns. EG *Few birds could eat such a thorny plant.*
ADJ QUALIT = prickly

2 A **thorny** problem or subject is one that is very complicated and difficult to solve or discuss. EG *...the thorny problem of what happens when the boss is absent.*
ADJ QUALIT : USU ATTRIB = knotty

thorough /θʌrə/. **1** A **thorough** action or activity is one that is done very carefully and methodically so that nothing is overlooked. EG *The vet gave the animals a thorough check-up... ...a thorough search.*
ADJ QUALIT = exhaustive, full

◊ **thoroughly.** EG *They had not studied the language very thoroughly.* ◊ **thoroughness.** EG *Hazel was reassured by the thoroughness of the training programme.*
◊ ADV WITH VB / ◊ N UNCOUNT

2 Someone who is **thorough** is always very careful and methodical in their work. EG *He is enormously thorough and full of inspiration.* ◊ **thoroughness.** EG *The President was impressed by his speed and thoroughness.*
ADJ QUALIT = meticulous / ◊ N UNCOUNT

3 **Thorough** is also used to emphasize the great degree or extent of something. EG *I'd enjoy giving him a thorough walloping... The narrow equatorial belt can rely on a thorough and regular soaking from the annual rains.* ◊ **thoroughly**. EG *...a thoroughly unreasonable person... I was thoroughly ashamed of myself... Yes, I thoroughly agree.* ADJ QUALIT : ATTRIB = proper ◊ ADV = utterly

thoroughbred /θʌrəbrɛd/, **thoroughbreds**. A **thoroughbred** is a horse that has parents that are of the same high quality breed. N COUNT

thoroughfare /θʌrəfɛə/, **thoroughfares**. 1 A **thoroughfare** is a main road in a town or city which usually has the main shops along it and a lot of traffic; a formal word. EG *We went back towards the main thoroughfare.* N COUNT = street, highway

2 **No thoroughfare** is used on road signs to tell people not to use a road or path, for example because it is private property. CONVENTION = no access

thoroughgoing /θʌrəgəʊɪŋ/; also spelled with a hyphen. A **thoroughgoing** action, quality, etc is complete and full. EG *More thorough-going analysis was needed... ...founded on a thoroughgoing radicalism.* ADJ QUALIT : USU ATTRIB

those /ðəʊz/ is the plural of **that**.

thou /θaʊ/ is an old-fashioned, poetic, or religious word for 'you' when you are talking to only one person. It is used as the subject of a verb. PRON : SING, USED AS S

though /ðəʊ/. The spellings **tho** and **tho'** are also used. 1 You use **though** 1.1 to introduce and emphasize a fact or comment which makes another part of the sentence rather surprising. EG *She wore a fur coat, even though it was a very hot day.... Though he hadn't stopped working all day, he wasn't tired.... He recognized his own name, badly pronounced though it was.* CONJ SUBORD = although 1.2 to add information to a statement when this information makes the statement less emphatic or points out exceptions to it. EG *It wasn't entirely my decision, though I think that generally I agree with it... She was, after all, quite sweet. Though annoying... She could not help thinking (though she could not be sure) that he did not trust her.* CONJ SUBORD = although 1.3 to add your opinion to a statement that you know is true and that your opinion cannot affect. EG *Sad though it is, that's the situation.* ADJ + *though* + NG + VB 1.4 to prevent someone thinking something that may follow logically from what you have just said, but is not true. EG *The classrooms are small, though not unsuitable... She resembled her mother physically, though not mentally.* CONJ SUBORD : WITH BROAD NEG = yet 1.5 to add a comment which seems to contradict what has just been said, or contrasts with it. EG *I can't stay. I'll have a coffee, though... 'It's not very useful.'-'It's pretty, though, isn't it?'* ADV SEN = however

2 You say **though I say it myself** or **though I say so myself** after praising yourself or something you have done, in order to sound less boastful. EG *It is a damn good photograph, though I say it myself.* PHR : USED AS ADV SEN

3 **as though**: see **as**.

thought /θɔːt/, **thoughts**. 1 **Thought** is the past tense and past participle of **think**.

2 A **thought** is 2.1 a single idea that you have in your mind. EG *The thought never crossed my mind... It's a very tempting thought... She felt some satisfaction at the thought that all her children were safe... He couldn't bear the thought of going home yet.* N SING WITH DET : USU + SUPP/REPORT-CL = notion 2.2 a feeling which is your immediate reaction to an event. EG *She was asked what her first thought was when her lover told her the news.* N COUNT : USU SING + SUPP = impulse 2.3 an intention, hope, or reason for doing something. EG *Her one thought was to get back to Derek... They will work with no thought of reward... I had vague thoughts of emigrating.* N COUNT : IF + PREP THEN *of* ⇑ aim = notion 2.4 an act of kindness or an offer of help; used especially when you are thanking someone. EG *It's a kind thought, sir. I'll tell him you called... Thanks for the thought, anyway..* N SING WITH DET = gesture

3 **Thought** is also 3.1 the activity of thinking, especially deeply, logically, or with concentration. EG *She frowned as though deep in thought... ...a pause for thought... I don't really understand his thought processes.* N UNCOUNT 3.2 the action of thinking carefully about something and considering all the problems or details. EG *...buying Western technology with little thought for its effect on employment... He's carefully avoiding giving any thought whatsoever to the subject... After giving our predicament some thought, he said he had a proposal.* N UNCOUNT = consideration 3.3 the group of ideas or way of thinking which belongs to a particular religion, philosopher, political party, academic subject, etc. EG *Such doctrine may seem foreign to our thought... ...two bitterly opposed schools of socialist thought... They paid allegiance to the thought of Karl Marx.* N UNCOUNT + SUPP = philosophy

4 A person's **thoughts** are 4.1 their mind, or all the ideas in their mind when they are concentrating on one particular thing. EG *They walked back, each deep in his own private thoughts... Posy had been in her thoughts a lot... My thoughts were still on that bottle... His mind was empty except for thoughts of her.* N PLURAL : USU POSS + N 4.2 their opinions on a particular subject. EG *Rothermere disclosed his thoughts on Britain... Do you have any thoughts about what happened?* N PLURAL : USU POSS + N = view

5 ● **a penny for your thoughts**: see **penny**. ● **second thoughts**: see **second**.

thoughtful /θɔːtful/. If you are **thoughtful**, 1 you are quiet and serious because you are thinking about something. EG *He looked thoughtful for a moment.* ▸ used of actions and moods. EG *That put us all in a thoughtful mood.* ◊ **thoughtfully**. EG *Stryker looked thoughtfully at the Count.* ADJ QUALIT = pensive ◊ ADV WITH VB 2 you remember what other people want, need, or feel, and try not to upset them. EG *That's very kind of you, Mr Zapp, very thoughtful.* ▸ used of actions. EG *I thanked him for his thoughtful gesture.* ◊ **thoughtfully**. EG *The book thoughtfully provides a clue on how to do this.* ◊ **thoughtfulness**. EG *I was very touched by his thoughtfulness.* ADJ QUALIT = considerate ◊ ADV WITH VB ◊ N UNCOUNT

thoughtless /θɔːtlɪ²s/. If you are **thoughtless**, you forget or ignore what other people want, need, or feel, for example because you are selfish or very busy. EG *I had to scold Vita severely for being so thoughtless... How thoughtless of you!* ◊ **thoughtlessly**. EG *Traditional sources of employment are thoughtlessly destroyed.* ADJ QUALIT = inconsiderate ◊ ADV WITH VB

thousand /θaʊzənd/, **thousands**. A **thousand** or one **thousand** is the number 1,000: see □ at NUMBER, AGE, MEASUREMENT, and MONEY. EG *...an annual income of twenty thousand dollars.* ▸ A **thousand** or **thousands** is often used to mean a very large number. EG *...prayers to God in a thousand languages... I've told him thousands of times.* ● **a thousand and one, one in a thousand**: see **one**. NUM : USU *a*/NUM + *thousand* ▸ NUM WITH PL : USED AS N PART

thousandth /θaʊzənθ/, **thousandths**. 1 The **thousandth** item in a series is the one that you count as number one thousand: see □ at NUMBER and AGE. ORDINAL

2 A **thousandth** is one of a thousand equal parts of something. EG *...a thousandth of a second.* N COUNT : USU + *of*

thrall /θrɔːl/. If you are **in thrall** to someone, you are completely in their power or are greatly influenced by them; an old-fashioned expression. EG *The poet was in thrall to the sophisticated woman... The story-teller held us all in thrall.* PHR : USED AS AN A, IF + PREP THEN *to*

thrash /θræʃ/, **thrashes, thrashing, thrashed**. 1 If you **thrash** someone, 1.1 you hit them several times, especially as a punishment. EG *We were thrashed a lot at school.* V + O = beat 1.2 you defeat them completely in a game, contest, or fight. EG *They had challenged and thrashed the enemy's navy.* V + O = trounce

2 If you **thrash** or if you **thrash** around, you twist and turn your body, or a part of it, quickly and violently because of fear or pain. EG *The boy was thrashing around, trying to get free.* ▸ used as a noun. EG *...the powerful thrash of their tails.* V : USU + A, OR V + O = writhe, toss ▸ N COUNT ⇑ movement

thrash out. If you **thrash out** a difficult problem or idea, you discuss it in detail until you reach agreement or arrive at a solution. EG *A new economic strategy is being thrashed out... We'll thrash this out after dinner.* PHRASAL VB : V + O + ADV = settle, resolve

thrashing /θræʃɪŋ/. If you give someone a **thrashing**, 1 you give them a severe beating, usually as a punishment. EG *He got such a thrashing from his father... Give him a good thrashing and he won't do it again.* N COUNT : USU *a* + N = hiding 2 you defeat them severely in a game, contest, or fight. EG *...the thrashing our team got at Southampton last week.* N COUNT : USU *a* + N = hammering

thread /θrɛd/, **threads, threading, threaded**.

1 **Thread** or a **thread** is a long, very thin piece of cotton, silk, nylon, wool, etc. Thread can be used for sewing pieces of cloth together or can be woven into cloth. EG *...a reel of thread.* ● If you say that someone's life or the survival or success of something **hangs by a thread**, you mean that it is very likely that they will not survive or succeed. EG *The survival of the coalition hung by a thread.* N UNCOUNT/COUNT ● PHR : VB INFLECTS ⇑ be uncertain

2 A **thread** of something is a long thin line or piece of it. EG *A thread of white smoke climbed up the sky.* N PART + N UNCOUNT

3 The **thread** on something such as a screw or a N COUNT

container whose top screws on is the raised spiral line of metal or plastic around it.

4 The **thread** of an argument or a set of ideas or events is a connection or theme that links the various parts of it. EG *He had lost his thread and didn't know what to say next... There have always been two basic threads running through socialist ideology.* N COUNT : USU DETPOSS/*the*+N = train of thought

5 The **threads** of something are the various parts or elements of it. EG *The threads of the problem were being gathered together.* N PART : PLURAL = strands

6 When you **thread** a needle, you put a piece of thread through a hole in the top of it in order to sew with it. V+O

7 If you **thread** objects such as beads onto a string or thread, you push the string through a hole in the objects. EG *...lavatory rolls threaded like beads on loops of string.* V+O : USU+A

8 If you **thread** a long thin piece of thread, ribbon, tape, etc through a hole or space, or a series of holes or spaces, you put it through the hole or space. EG *He threaded the film through the projector... ...a petticoat threaded with black ribbon.* V+O+A ⇑ insert

9 If you **thread** your way through a group of people or things or **thread** through it, you move through it, moving around and between the people or things in your way. EG *We turned and threaded our way through the fairground.* V+O+A, OR V+A = pick

threadbare /θredbɛə/. 1 **Threadbare** clothes, carpets, and other pieces of cloth are old and have been used so much that the cloth has become very thin. EG *O'Shea's suit was baggy and threadbare.* ADJ QUALIT = worn

2 **Threadbare** jokes, stories, excuses, etc have been said so often that they are no longer funny, interesting, or believable. ADJ QUALIT = stale

threat /θret/, **threats**. 1 A **threat** is 1.1 a statement that you will harm someone or do something that will upset them, especially if they do not do what you want them to do. EG *We mustn't give in to threats... Under threat of death, he confessed.* N COUNT, OR *under*+N ⇑ warning 1.2 something or someone that may harm a particular person or thing. EG *This was regarded by the Government as a possible threat to national security.* N COUNT : IF+PREP THEN *to* = menace

2 If there is a **threat** of something unpleasant, it is possible or likely that it will happen. EG *...the ever-growing threat of flooding... ...officers under threat of attack.* N COUNT, OR *under*+N, USU+*of* = risk

threaten /θretəᵒn/, **threatens, threatening, threatened**. 1 If you **threaten** to harm someone or to do something that will upset them, you say that you will do it. EG *He threatened to resign... The group's members were threatened with imprisonment... ...slogans threatening death to the oppressors... She threatened that she would leave home.* V+*to*-INF, V+O/REPORT-CL, OR V+O+A ⇑ warn

2 If someone or something **threatens** someone or something else, they are likely to harm or destroy them. EG *He said that the war threatened the peace of the whole world.* ◇ **threatened**. EG *He felt threatened.* V+O = endanger ◇ ADJ QUALIT : PRED

3 If something **threatens** to do something unpleasant or have an unpleasant result, it seems likely to do it. EG *The riots threatened to get out of hand.* V+*to*-INF

4 If something unpleasant **threatens** or if someone or something **is threatened** with it, it seems likely to happen or to be experienced. EG *Tortoises are able to withdraw their head and limbs should danger threaten... The whole country is threatened with starvation.* V, OR V+O : USU PASS+*with*

threatening /θretəᵒnɪŋ/. Something or someone that is **threatening** seems likely to cause harm. EG *The world faces dangers greater and more threatening than any known in the past... He became angry and threatening.* ◇ **threateningly**. EG *He advanced threateningly on the boy.* ADJ QUALIT = menacing ◇ ADV WITH VB = menacingly

three /θriː/, **threes**. **Three** is the number 3: see ☐ at NUMBER, AGE, DATE, MEASUREMENT, MONEY, and TIME. EG *We agreed to meet three days later.* NUM

three-cornered. A **three-cornered** object is triangular. EG *...three-cornered hats.* ADJ CLASSIF : USU ATTRIB

three-dimensional. The form **3-D** can also be used for paragraphs 1 and 2. 1 A **three-dimensional** picture, film, or image looks as if it is deep or solid rather than flat. ADJ CLASSIF

2 A **three-dimensional** object is solid rather than flat. ADJ CLASSIF

3 If you say that a character in a book, play, or film is **three-dimensional**, you mean that he or she seems real and lifelike. ADJ QUALIT

three-legged race, three-legged races. A **three-legged race** is a race in which pairs of people try to run with one leg tied to the other person's leg. N COUNT

three-line whip, three-line whips. A **three-line whip** is a notice sent out by an official of a political party which tells the members of parliament belonging to that party that they must vote in a particular way on a particular issue. N COUNT

three-ply. **Three-ply** wool, rope, wood, etc has three layers or strands. ADJ CLASSIF

three-point turn, three-point turns. When someone driving a vehicle does a **three-point turn**, they turn the vehicle around by driving the car forwards in a curve, then backwards in a curve, and then forwards in a curve. N COUNT

three-quarters is an amount that is three out of four equal parts of something. The form **three-quarter** is used when it is followed by a noun. EG *Three-quarters of the world's surface is covered by water... ...a play lasting one and three-quarter hours.* N COUNT ⇑ fraction
▸ used as an adverb or adjective. EG *The tank is three-quarters full... A bright three-quarter moon was coming up over the hills.* ▸ ADV OR ADJ CLASSIF

three Rs. When talking about children's education, you can refer to the basic skills of reading, writing, and arithmetic as the **three Rs**. N PLURAL : *the*+N

threesome /θriːsəm/, **threesomes**. A **threesome** is a group of three people. N COUNT

three-wheeler, three-wheelers. A **three-wheeler** is a light car with three wheels. N COUNT

thresh /θreʃ/, **threshes, threshing, threshed**. When people **thresh** corn, wheat, rice, etc, they beat it in order to separate the grains from the rest of the plant. V OR V+O = flail

threshold /θreʃhᵒəʊld/, **thresholds**; a fairly formal word. 1 The **threshold** of a building or perhaps a room is the floor in the doorway, or the doorway itself. EG *Suddenly the door opened and Madame stood on the threshold... Morris had never crossed the threshold of a public house before.* N COUNT : USU SING

2 A **threshold** is a particular significant amount, level, or limit, at which something begins to happen or take effect. EG *The tax threshold for a single pensioner is £445... I have a low pain threshold.* N COUNT : USU+SUPP

3 Someone who is **on the threshold of** a particular action, activity, or state is about to do it or experience it. EG *He was on the threshold of public life.* PREP

threw /θruː/ is the past tense of **throw**.

thrice /θraɪs/; a fairly formal or literary word. 1 Something that happens **thrice** or is done **thrice** happens or is done three times. EG *Joseph Chamberlain was thrice mayor of Birmingham.* ADV

2 If something is **thrice** as big, old, etc as something else or is **thrice** the size, age, etc of something else, it is three times as big, old, etc as that thing. EG *His vegetables were thrice the size of mine... Our products were seen by twice or thrice that number.* PREDET, OR ADV+*as*+ADJ/ADV

thrift /θrɪft/ is the quality and practice of being thrifty. EG *...the virtues of thrift, hard work, and punctuality.* N UNCOUNT ≠ extravagance

thrifty /θrɪftiˡ/, **thriftier, thriftiest**. Someone who is **thrifty** saves money, does not buy things they do not need, and does not waste things; used showing approval. EG *She was a thrifty housekeeper.* ADJ QUALIT ⇑ careful

thrill /θrɪl/, **thrills, thrilling, thrilled**. 1 A **thrill** is 1.1 a sudden feeling of great excitement, pleasure, or perhaps shock or fear. EG *The sound of the bell sent a thrill of anticipation through her... They get a considerable thrill out of it.* N COUNT : USU SING = frisson, buzz 1.2 an event or experience that gives you a thrill. EG *The thrill for me was finding the rare specimens... ...her search for fun and thrills.* N COUNT = excitement, kick

2 If something **thrills** you, or if you **thrill** to it, it gives you a feeling of great pleasure and excitement. EG *It's a sight that never fails to thrill me... ...the stories which David himself had thrilled to so often.* V-ERG : IF V THEN +*to* ⇑ excite

thrilled /θrɪld/. If someone is **thrilled**, they are extremely pleased about something. EG *I was thrilled to be sitting next to such a distinguished author.* ADJ QUALIT : PRED ● If you say that someone is **thrilled to bits**, you are saying and emphasizing that they are very pleased. ● PHR : USED AS C

thriller /θrɪlə/, **thrillers**. A **thriller** is a book, film, or play that tells an exciting story about dangerous, frightening, or mysterious events such as murder or kidnapping. EG *...a spy thriller.* N COUNT

thrilling /θrɪlɪŋ/. Something that is **thrilling** is very exciting and usually enjoyable. EG *She gave a thrilling performance.* ADJ QUALIT = electrifying

thrive /θraɪv/, **thrives, thriving, thrived, throve**. The forms **thrived** and **throve** are both used as the past tense but **throve** is used less often. If someone or something **thrives**, they do well and are healthy, happy, successful, or strong. EG *Are you the type of person who thrives on activity?... ...the hazel's ability to thrive in the British climate.* ◊ **thriving**. EG *...a thriving business.* V: USU+A; ◊ ADJ CLASSIF = flourishing

throat /θrəʊt/, **throats**. 1 Your **throat** is 1.1 the back of your mouth and the top part of the tubes that go down into your stomach and your lungs. EG *His throat was so dry that he could hardly swallow.* 1.2 the front part of your neck. EG *He grabbed the man by the throat... We have no wish to have our throats cut.* N COUNT ⇑ passage; N COUNT

2 The word **throat** is also used in the following expressions. 2.1 If two people or groups are **at each other's throats**, they are quarrelling or fighting violently with each other. EG *When the danger had passed they would again be at each other's throats.* PHR: USED AS AN A = at loggerheads

2.2 If you say that someone **is cutting** their **own throat**, you mean that they are doing something which will result in failure or disaster for them. PHR: VB INFLECTS 2.3 If you **ram** something such as an idea **down someone's throat, force** it **down their throat**, etc, you mention it very often and very emphatically in order to make them accept it, believe it, or learn it. EG *They have this viewpoint rammed down their throats every day.* PHR: VB INFLECTS 2.4 If an action, situation, remark, etc **sticks in** someone's **throat**, they find it unacceptable. EG *It was his arrogance which stuck in my throat.* PHR: VB INFLECTS 2.5 ● to **clear** your **throat**: see **clear**. ● to **jump down** someone's **throat**: see **jump**.

throaty /θrəʊti[1]/, **throatier, throatiest**. A **throaty** voice, whisper, laugh, etc is low and rather rough. ADJ QUALIT = hoarse

throb /θrɒb/, **throbs, throbbing, throbbed**. 1 If your heart or blood, or part of your body, **throbs**, you feel a series of strong beats or dull pains. EG *My heart is throbbing and I'm shaking... His head was throbbing.* ▸ used as a noun. EG *She felt her heart give a great throb.* V ⇑ beat; ▸ N COUNT

2 If something **throbs**, it vibrates and makes a loud, rhythmical noise. EG *The drums seemed to throb in his ears.* ▸ used as a noun. EG *...the throb of the engine.* V; ▸ N COUNT

3 A place that **is throbbing** is full of activity and noise; a literary use. EG *...throbbing factories.* V: USU CONT = pulsate

throes /θrəʊz/. 1 If you are **in the throes of** doing or experiencing something, especially something difficult, you are busy doing it or are deeply involved in it; a fairly formal expression. EG *The British Army was in the throes of reorganization... The country was in the throes of a passion for all things musical.* PREP

2 See also **death throes**.

thrombosis /θrɒmbəʊsɪs/, **thromboses**. **Thrombosis** or a **thrombosis** is the forming of a blood clot in a person's heart or in one of their blood vessels, which can cause death; a medical term. EG *There is an increased incidence of coronary thrombosis.* N COUNT/UNCOUNT

throne /θrəʊn/, **thrones**. 1 A **throne** is a special chair used by a king, queen, emperor, etc on important official occasions. EG *...a picture of the Queen seated on a rich throne.* N COUNT ⇑ seat

2 You can refer to the **throne** as a way of referring to the position of being king, queen, emperor, etc. EG *She came to the throne when she was a very small child... ...when Queen Victoria was on the throne... ...the heir to the throne.* N SING: *the*+N

throng /θrɒŋ/, **throngs, thronging, thronged**; a formal or literary word. 1 A **throng** is a large crowd of people. EG *A patient throng was waiting in silence... She slipped through the throngs of people, frantically searching for David.* N COUNT/PART = mass

2 If people **throng** somewhere, they go there in great numbers. EG *Mourners thronged to the funeral... The whole city thronged to hear him.* V+A/*to*-INF ⇑ gather

3 If people **throng** a place, they are present there in great numbers. EG *The lane was thronged with shoppers.* V+O ⇑ fill = crowd, pack

throttle /θrɒtə[0]l/, **throttles, throttling, throttled**. 1 If you **throttle** someone, you grasp them by the throat so that they cannot breathe, usually in order to kill them. EG *He would have liked to put his hands around her throat and throttle her.* V+O = strangle

2 The **throttle** of a motor vehicle or aircraft is a device that controls the quantity of fuel entering the engine and is used to control the vehicle's speed. EG *The throttle wide open, she shot down the hill... We were going at full throttle.* N COUNT/UNCOUNT

throttle back. If you **throttle back** or **throttle down** when driving a motor vehicle or aircraft, you make it go slower by reducing the quantity of fuel entering the engine. EG *I throttled the motor right back.* PHRASAL VB: V+ADV, OR V+O+ADV

through /θru:/; also spelled **thru** in informal American English. 1 To move **through** a space or hole means to move from one side or end of it to the other. EG *Go straight through that door and then turn right... The rain poured through a hole in the roof... She led the way through a passage and down a short flight of steps... She was lifting handfuls of fine sand and letting it pour through her fingers.* PREP, OR ADV AFTER VB

2 To cut or make a hole **through** an object means to cut it in two or to make a hole in it. EG *The fish must have chewed right through it... It went through like a knife through butter.* PREP, OR ADV AFTER VB

3 To go **through** a town, area, or country means to travel across it or in it. EG *We drove through London... We were travelling through some marshland... We decided to drive straight through to Birmingham.* PREP, OR ADV AFTER VB

4 To move **through** something means to be moving within it and be surrounded by it. EG *The fish swims through the water... They drove home through the darkness.* PREP ⇑ in

5 To get **through** a barrier or obstruction means to get from one side of it to the other. EG *They had to check the tickets and let passengers with valid tickets through... The traffic couldn't get through... We managed to get all the wine through customs.* PREP, OR ADV AFTER VB = past

6 If there is an object or hole **through** something, the object or hole is in it, from one side of it to the other. EG *The heating pipes pass through a series of tunnels... ...a hat with a feather stuck through it... ...a huge geological fault running through the entire state.* PREP, OR ADV AFTER VB

7 To go **through** a system means to move around it or to pass from one end of it to the other. EG *The current flows through this circuit... Don't send cash through the post.* PREP

8 If you see, hear, feel, or say something **through** something else, that thing is between you and what you are seeing, hearing, and feeling, or between you and the person you are speaking to. EG *Lonnie gazed out through a side window... He's looking at them through a magnifying glass... I can hear John snoring right through the motel partition... She could feel the gravel through the thin soles of her slippers.* PREP

9 If a feeling, attitude, quality, etc happens or exists **through** an area, organization, or a person's body, it happens or exists everywhere in it or affects all of it. EG *Discontent runs through the country today... A chill shot through him.* PREP ⇑ in = throughout

10 **Through** a period of time means from the beginning of it until the end. EG *I suddenly wished that I could stay through an entire English winter... We had no rain from March right through to October... All through 1970-71, he had travelled around the country.* PREP, OR ADV+PREP = throughout

11 From one date **through** another means from the first date until the second one; used in American English. EG *I was in college from 1927 through 1932... The museum is open every day, June through August.* PREP

12 If you go **through** a particular experience or event, you experience it, and if you behave in a particular way **through** it, you behave in that way while it is happening. EG *Both brothers lived through the decline of the Liberal Party... The girl slept through everything... Through it all, the prince kept his sense of humour... He didn't want to go through all that divorce hassle again.* PREP, OR ADV AFTER VB ⇑ during

13 If you are **through** with something or if it is **through**, you have finished doing it and will never do it again. EG *He was through with seminars and tutorials... His days of acting were through.* ADJ CLASSIF: PRED, IF+PREP THEN *with* ⇑ over

14 You also use **through** in expressions such as 'half-way through' and 'all the way through' to indicate to what extent an action or task is completed. EG *Harris tried to stop the operation half-way through... I'm* PREP, OR ADV AFTER VB

two thirds through number six... She played it all the way through... I do not think she ever saw a play right through.

15 You also use **through** when stating **15.1** the cause of a particular fact or situation. EG *Many people have difficulty in walking, for example through age or frailty... The discovery of adrenalin came about through a mistake.* **15.2** the means by which a particular thing is achieved. EG *They were opposed to terrorism or change through violence... Not all the artists' problems can be solved through funding... Through him, I was introduced to several high-up people.* PREP = because of; PREP

16 If you do something **through** someone else, they take the necessary action for you. EG *I talked to him through an interpreter... You should get in touch with a psychiatrist, through your regular doctor.* PREP = via

17 If a proposal, idea, etc goes **through**, it is accepted by people in authority and is made legal or official. EG *The President might not be able to get the bill through Congress... The adoption went through.* PREP, OR ADV AFTER VB

18 If someone gets **through** an examination or a round of a competition, they succeed or win. EG *She is now through to the next round... They even told me that I would get through my degree exams.* PREP OR ADV AFTER VB

19 When you get **through** while making a telephone call, the call is connected and you can speak to the person you are phoning. EG *I tried to phone him but I couldn't get through... She asked for my name before putting the call through.* ADV AFTER VB

20 If you go **through** or look **through** a lot of things of the same type, for example the pages of a book or a pile of objects, you touch them or look at them one after another. EG *'You can read it yourself,' he said, flipping through until he found the page he sought... I wanted to plough through as much information as possible... She was sorting through a pile of clean socks in her lap.* PREP, OR ADV AFTER VB

21 If something turns **through** a complete circle or part of a circle, it turns round as far as is indicated. EG *We've turned it round through a hundred and fourteen degrees... It can turn its head through a complete circle.* PREP

22 A **through** train goes directly to a particular place, so that the people who want to go there do not have to change trains. EG *The only through train to Landor is at 9 o'clock.* ADJ CLASSIF: ATTRIB = direct

23 If you say that someone is wet **through**, frozen **through**, etc, you are emphasizing how wet, cold, etc they are. ADV AFTER ADJ ⇑ extremely

24 **Through and through** means completely and to the greatest extent possible. EG *Those boards are rotten through and through... She had said to Crummie that she knew Mr Evans through and through.* PHR: USED AS AN A

throughout /θru:aʊt/. **1** If something happens **throughout** a particular event or period of time, it happens during the whole of that event or period of time. EG *This particular dream recurred throughout her life... Throughout the journey, Rosa had remained silent... The country has made the transition, while retaining throughout a truly democratic system.* PREP, OR ADV AFTER VB

2 If something happens or is present **throughout** a particular area or thing, it happens or is present in every part or area of it. EG *The pictures can be transmitted by satellite throughout the world... I could feel the tension throughout her body... This new idea is being instituted throughout industry... The house was carpeted throughout.* PREP, OR ADV AFTER VB ⇑ in

throughput /θru:pʊt/; also spelled with a hyphen. The **throughput** of an organization, system, etc is the amount of things it can do or deal with in a particular period of time. EG *It is sold and replaced more rapidly. The through-put is faster.* N SING WITH DET

throve /θrəʊv/ is a past tense of **thrive**.

throw /θrəʊ/, **throws, throwing, threw, thrown. 1** When you **throw** an object that you are holding, you move your hand or arm quickly upwards or forwards and let go of the object, so that it moves through the air. EG *Roger picked up a stone, aimed, and threw it at Henry... He threw the book in the air.* ▸ used as a noun. EG *That was a good throw.* V+O: USU+A = pitch; ▸ N COUNT

2 When something such as an explosion or a fierce wind **throws** someone or something through the air, it causes them to move violently through the air. EG *Langtry felt himself thrown into the air.* V+O+A = toss

3 If you **throw** something into a particular place or position, you put it there in a quick and careless way. EG *Tom undressed in the dark, throwing his clothes carelessly over a chair... She threw both letters in the bin... He threw the manuscript aside... I threw open the door of the closet.* V+O+A = chuck, fling

4 If someone or something **throws** someone into a particular place or position, they force them roughly into that place or position. EG *He threw Gladys to the floor... They were beaten up and thrown into police lorries... The train braked violently, throwing everyone to the floor.* V+O+A ⇑ push = fling

5 If the authorities **throw** someone into prison, they send them there immediately and without trial. EG *The cop threatened to throw all of us in jail.* V+O+A (in/into) = clap

6 If you **throw** part of your body, especially your arms or head, in a particular direction, you move it suddenly and with a lot of force. EG *She came up to him and threw her arms around his neck... He threw up his hands in horror.* V+O+A = fling

7 If you **throw** yourself somewhere, you move or jump suddenly and with a lot of force. EG *He threw himself on his bed... He threw himself in the Nile.* V+O (REFL)+A

8 When you **throw** a dice in a game or **throw** a particular number, you drop the dice out of your hand or a cup onto the surface you are playing on, with the result that a particular number is on the top of it. EG *I threw a six.* ▸ used as a noun. EG *I needed a throw of four to win.* V OR V+O; ▸ N COUNT

9 If someone who is wrestling with someone else **throws** them, they make them fall to the ground. ▸ used as a noun. V+O; ▸ N COUNT

10 If a horse or other animal **throws** its rider, it makes him or her fall off, by suddenly jumping or moving violently. V+O

11 If something **throws** a person or thing into a particular situation or state, especially an unpleasant one, it suddenly causes them to be in that situation or state. EG *She plays the part of a young girl whose world is thrown completely into disarray... The Depression had thrown almost everybody out of work... The thought of being late on occasions like these would throw her into a state of panic... The discussion was thrown open to all present.* V+O+A ⇑ put

12 If something **throws** light or a shadow on a particular thing or area, it causes that thing or area to have light or a shadow on it. EG *A spotlight threw a pool of violet light onto the stage.* V+O+A = cast, shed

13 If something **throws** something such as strain or weight on a person or thing, it causes it to affect them or be directed towards them. EG *The young men might be absent from the villages, throwing a heavy strain on the old men and women... This threw suspicion on all his colleagues.* V+O+A ⇑ direct = put

14 If you **throw** a question or remark at someone, you say it suddenly or in a casual or rather aggressive way. EG *This question has been thrown at me time and time again... I'm sorry about throwing all these random suggestions at you... He threw remarks at the silent Ralph.* V+O+A ⇑ direct

15 If you **throw** a look at someone or something, you look at them quickly and suddenly. EG *She threw nervous glances at him every now and again.* V+O+A ⇑ direct = cast

16 If you **throw** a lot of your energy, money, etc into a particular activity or enterprise, you work or help very actively and enthusiastically. EG *Many women throw all of their energies into a career... Both political parties threw considerable resources into the campaign.* V+O+A (into) = devote, pour

17 If you **throw** yourself into a particular activity, you begin it or do it with a lot of effort and energy. EG *Mrs Kaul threw herself into her work heart and soul... He threw himself into the battle against Chamberlain.* V+O (REFL)+A (into)

18 If you **throw** a fit, a tantrum, or a faint, you suddenly start to behave in an uncontrolled way. EG *She threw a fit of hysterics... He's always throwing tantrums.* V+O

19 If something, for example a remark or an experience, **throws** you, it makes you feel confused and bewildered because it is unexpected or strange; a fairly informal use. EG *It was the fact that she was married that threw me.* V+O ⇑ confuse

20 When someone **throws** their voice, they make it seem to be coming from somewhere else. V+O

21 If you **throw** a punch, you punch someone; a rather old-fashioned use. V+O

22 When someone **throws** a party or other social event, they have one; a fairly informal use. EG *I promised to throw a party at our house.* V+O = give

23 When someone **throws** a switch, they turn it on or off. EG *He threw the switch of the alarm system.* V+O

24 When someone **throws** a piece of pottery, they make it on a potter's wheel; a technical term. V+O

25 If you **throw** yourself **at** someone, you behave in a bold way that makes it obvious that you want them to begin a relationship with you; used showing disapproval. PHRASAL VB: V+O (REFL)+PREP

26 If you **throw overboard** something such as an idea or suggestion, you reject it completely. EG *The country threw his economic policies overboard.* PHR: VB INFLECTS

27 If things of a particular kind cost a particular amount of money **a throw**, they cost that amount each; an informal expression. EG *'How much are they, then?'–'Fifty quid a throw.'* PHR: USED AS AN A, NG+PHR

28 • **a stone's throw**: see **stone**. • **thrown in at the deep end**: see **deep**. • **to throw light on** something: see **light**. • **to throw** your **weight about**: see **weight**.

throw around. If you **throw** money **around** or **throw** it **about**, you spend it freely and in large amounts, especially on things that are not very useful or sensible. EG *She does not have money to throw around.* PHRASAL VB: V+O+ADV

throw away. 1 When you **throw away** something that you do not want, you get rid of it, for example by putting it in a dustbin. EG *She likes to keep things, even old things, rather than throw them away.* PHRASAL VB: V+O+ADV ⇑ discard = throw out

2 If you **throw away** something you have, you waste it rather than using it sensibly. EG *He is evidently prepared to throw his money away... Any votes for him will be votes thrown away... They threw away their advantage.* PHRASAL VB: V+O+ADV

3 See also **throwaway**.

throw back. 1 If you **throw back** at someone something they said or did in the past, you remind them of it in order to hurt them. EG *He threw back at me everything that I'd said the week before.* PHRASAL VB: V+O+ADV+A

2 If someone **is thrown back** on their own powers or resources, they have to use them, because there is nothing else they can use. EG *They were thrown back on their own and their neighbours' resources.* PHRASAL VB: V+O+ADV+A *(on)*

3 See also **throwback**.

throw in. 1 If you **throw in** a particular remark when having a conversation, you add it in a casual or unexpected way. EG *He said nothing more, except to throw in a warning about the possible consequences of their decision... 'It's simply disgraceful of you, Philip,' threw in Ann.* PHRASAL VB: V+O+ADV, OR ORDER QUOTE+V+ADV ⇑ say = interpolate

2 If someone who is selling something **throws in** something extra, they give it in addition and do not ask for any money for it, or for very much money. EG *We only had to pay £9 for bed and breakfast, with lunch thrown in.* PHRASAL VB: V+O+ADV = include

3 See also **throw-in**.

throw off. 1 If you **throw off** your clothes, you take them off quickly and carelessly. EG *She threw off the pink dress she was wearing.* PHRASAL VB: V+O+ADV

2 If you **throw off** something that limits your freedom, for example a system of laws or ideas, you get rid of it; a fairly literary use. EG *They tried to throw off the chains of tradition.* PHRASAL VB: V+O+ADV

throw on. If you **throw on** your clothes, you put them on quickly and carelessly. EG *He threw on his jacket and went out.* PHRASAL VB: V+O+ADV

throw out. 1 If you **throw** something **out**, 1.1 you get rid of it, for example by putting it in a dustbin, because you do not want it. EG *The broken cooking pots were thrown out.* PHRASAL VB: V+O+ADV ⇑ discard = throw away 1.2 you reject it. EG *He threw out the scripts for twenty-six planned episodes... The Land Reform Bill was thrown out by the House of Lords.* PHRASAL VB: V+O+ADV

2 If you **throw** someone **out**, you force them to leave their job or their home. EG *I knew that if I didn't do the work pretty quickly I'd be thrown out and replaced in a flash... Her parents threw her out when they found she was pregnant.* PHRASAL VB: V+O+ADV = turf out

3 If something **throws out** something such as smoke, heat, or a smell, it produces it from itself, usually in large quantities. EG *The chimneys were throwing out huge plumes of smoke.* PHRASAL VB: V+O+ADV ⇑ emit = give out

throw over. If you **throw over** someone you are having a romantic relationship with, you end the relationship; a rather old-fashioned expression. PHRASAL VB: V+O+ADV = chuck

throw together. 1 If you **throw** something **together**, for example a meal or a costume, you make it quickly and not very carefully; an informal use. EG *I suppose I could throw something together, or we could go out to eat.* PHRASAL VB: V+O+ADV ⇑ concoct

2 If a situation or event **throws** two or more people **together**, it causes them to meet each other and get to know each other. EG *...people whom circumstances have thrown together.* PHRASAL VB: V+O+ADV

throw up. 1 When someone **throws up**, food or drink in their stomach comes back up and out of their mouth, for example because they are ill; an informal use. EG *She got out of the car and threw up by the side of the road.* PHRASAL VB: V+ADV, OR V+O+ADV ⇑ vomit = spew

2 If something **throws up** dust, stones, water, etc as it moves over the ground or hits the ground, it causes it to rise up from the ground into the air. EG *Each passing car threw up a cloud of white dust.* PHRASAL VB: V+O+ADV ⇑ produce

3 If people **throw up** something, for example a building or structure, they build or make it very quickly. EG *I watched a troupe of travelling actors throw up a wooden stage.* PHRASAL VB: V+O+ADV

4 If you **throw up** your job, you leave it suddenly and unexpectedly. EG *Philip thought he had found the perfect excuse for throwing up his job and returning to England.* PHRASAL VB: V+O+ADV = give up

5 If an event, situation, or country **throws up** a particular person or thing, it produces them or causes them to become noticeable. EG *A lot of problems have been thrown up by the Revolution... Neither country has thrown up many good writers or poets.* PHRASAL VB: V+O+ADV

throwaway /θrəʊəweɪ/; also spelled with a hyphen. 1 A **throwaway** product is intended to be used only once, or only for a short time, and then to be got rid of. EG *...a throw-away toothbrush.* ▸ used of a society in which these products are common. EG *...the spread of the throw-away culture.* ADJ CLASSIF: ATTRIB ⇑ temporary = disposable

2 A **throwaway** remark or gesture is spoken or done in a way which suggests that the person making it does not expect a response. ADJ CLASSIF: ATTRIB

throwback /θrəʊbæk/, **throwbacks**. Something, for example an idea or an attitude, that is a **throwback** is like something that existed or was common a long time ago. EG *His sentiments were a throwback to the old colonial days.* N COUNT: USU SING+*to* ⇑ reminder

throw-in, throw-ins. When there is a **throw-in** in a football match, the ball is thrown back onto the field after it has been kicked off it. N COUNT

thrown /θrəʊn/ is the past participle of **throw**.

thru /θru:/. See **through**.

thrum /θrʌm/, **thrums, thrumming, thrummed**. When something, for example an engine, **thrums**, it makes a low, beating sound. EG *He could hear the thrumming of the traffic.* V: USU CONT = throb

thrush /θrʌʃ/, **thrushes**. 1 A **thrush** is a fairly small bird with a brown back and a spotted breast. N COUNT

2 **Thrush** is an infectious disease that most often occurs in the mouths of babies or in women's vaginas. N UNCOUNT

thrust /θrʌst/, **thrusts, thrusting**. The form **thrust** is used in the present tense and is the past tense and past participle of the verb. 1 If you **thrust** something somewhere, you push it or move it there quickly and using a lot of force. EG *The captain thrust his hands into his pockets... He thrust the bag at Buddy.* V+O+A = shove

2 A **thrust** is a sudden forceful movement, usually in a forwards direction. EG *With two quick thrusts of its tail, the shark was upon her... ...repeated sword thrusts.* N COUNT = lunge

3 If you **thrust** your way somewhere or **thrust** through a crowd, a forest, etc, you move along, pushing between people, branches, etc. EG *Edward thrust his way towards them.* V+O+A, OR V+A = jostle

4 If something **thrusts** up or out of something else, it sticks up or sticks out in a noticeable way; a literary use. EG *...an imposing rock needle thrusting up at least 250 feet.* V+A = poke

5 **Thrust** is the power or force that is required to make a plane, rocket, car, etc move in a particular direction. EG *The direction of thrust of the rockets and their power are controlled by computer.* N UNCOUNT = propulsion

6 The main **thrust** of an activity or idea, the broad **thrust**, the general **thrust**, etc is the main or most important part of it, or its general nature. EG *The main thrust of robot research in the '80s has been towards improving vision techniques... This has had* N SING: DET+MOD+N

a great influence on the broad thrust of government social and economic policy.

7 The **thrust** behind a particular activity or course of action is the aim which leads to that activity or course of action. EG *The thrust behind modern physics is an attempt to discover the basic nature of matter.*
N UNCOUNT = impetus

thrust upon. If you **thrust** something **upon** someone, you force them to have it. EG *The conquerors' religion was thrust upon the population by force.*
PHRASAL VB : V+O+PREP, HAS PASS

Thu. is an abbreviation for Thursday.

thud /θʌd/, **thuds, thudding, thudded.** 1 A **thud** is a dull sound, such as a heavy object makes when it falls onto a carpet. EG *He fell on the floor with a thud... There was a dull thud.*
N COUNT = thump

2 If something **thuds**, it makes a thud, especially when it falls onto something else or hits something else. EG *The mail bags thudded onto the platform... His feet came thudding up the stairs.*
V : USU+A = thunder

3 When your heart **thuds**, it beats strongly and rather quickly, for example because you are very frightened or happy. EG *She spoke slowly, with a thudding heart.*
V = pound

thug /θʌg/, **thugs.** A **thug** is a person who is very violent and rough, especially a criminal. EG *...a gang of thugs.*
N COUNT = tough

thuggery /θʌgəri[1]/ is rough, violent behaviour.
N UNCOUNT

thumb /θʌm/, **thumbs, thumbing, thumbed.** 1 Your **thumb** is the long jointed part on your hand which is nearer your wrist than your other four fingers. EG *I took her ear between my thumb and forefinger, and tugged it playfully.*
N COUNT ⇑ digit

2 The **thumb** of a glove or mitten is the part which a person's thumb fits into.
N COUNT

3 If you **thumb** a lift, or **thumb** your way somewhere, you stand by the side of the road holding out your thumb until a driver stops and gives you a lift. EG *Here they stand, waiting for buses and thumbing lifts... Jackie is a confirmed hitch-hiker, thumbing her way all over Europe.*
V+O, OR V+O+A = hitch

4 If you **thumb** through a book or magazine, you turn over the pages fairly quickly rather than reading each page carefully. EG *He went to the shelf, took down a book, thumbed through it quickly, and chose another.* ● See also **well-thumbed.**
V+A *(through)* = flick

5 The word **thumb** is also used in the following expressions. 5.1 If you say that you are **all fingers and thumbs** or **all thumbs**, you mean that you find it very difficult to do something delicate or detailed using your hands. EG *Can you do these buttons up for me? I'm all fingers and thumbs.* 5.2 If you do something by **rule of thumb**, you do it in the way that you judge is best at the time, rather than having a fixed set of rules to follow. 5.3 If you are **under** someone's **thumb**, you are under their control, or very heavily influenced by them. EG *Some teachers are very good at keeping their pupils under their thumbs.* 5.4 ● to **stick out like a sore thumb**: see **sore.** ● to **thumb** your **nose at** someone: see **nose.** ● to **twiddle** your **thumbs**: see **twiddle.**
PHR : USED AS C ⇑ clumsy; PHR : USED AS O; PHR : USED AS AN A

thumbnail /θʌmneɪl/, **thumbnails**; also spelled with a hyphen. 1 Your **thumbnail** is the nail on your thumb.
N COUNT

2 A **thumbnail** sketch or account is a very short description of an event, idea, plan, etc, which gives only the main details.
ADJ CLASSIF : ATTRIB = brief

thumbscrew /θʌmskru:/, **thumbscrews**; also spelled with a hyphen. A **thumbscrew** is an object that was used in the past to torture people by crushing their thumbs.
N COUNT

thumbs-down. If something, for example an idea or performance, receives a **thumbs-down**, people say that it is not good or not likely to be successful, or do not give their permission for it; an informal word.
N SING WITH DET, OR N UNCOUNT ⇑ disapproval

thumbs-up. 1 A **thumbs-up** sign or a **thumbs-up** is a sign that you make by holding up your thumb to show that you agree with someone, or that you are happy with an idea or situation. EG *The workers would applaud and give the thumbs-up sign of approval.*
N SING WITH DET ⇑ gesture

2 If something, for example an idea or performance, receives a **thumbs-up**, people say that it is good or likely to be successful, or give their permission for it; an informal use. EG *We've got the thumbs-up, so now we can get down to work... It's thumbs-up for the new project.*
N SING WITH DET, OR N UNCOUNT = go-ahead

thumbtack /θʌmtæk/, **thumbtacks.** A **thumbtack** is a short nail with a broad, flat top, which is used for fastening pieces of paper to a board, wall, or other surface; used in American English.
N COUNT = drawing pin

thump /θʌmp/, **thumps, thumping, thumped.** 1 If you **thump** someone or something, you hit them hard, usually with your fist. EG *I'll thump you, Tommy, if you don't get out of my way... Some fathers might have ranted and thumped the table.*
V+O ⇑ strike = clout

2 If you **thump** something onto something else or if it **thumps** onto something else, it hits the other thing with quite a lot of force. EG *He thumped a few shillings onto the table... Two rockets thumped into the ground by the roadside... ...with the bag thumping against his thigh at each step.*
V-ERG+A = smack

3 If something **thumps**, it makes a fairly loud but dull sound, such as a heavy object makes when it hits something. EG *The kitchen door opened, feet thumped up the stairs... I could hear the banging and thumping of people moving furniture.*
V = crash

4 When your heart **thumps**, it beats strongly and rather quickly, for example because you are very frightened or happy. EG *My heart was thumping.*
V = pound

5 A **thump** is 5.1 a hard blow that you give to someone or something, usually with your fist. EG *Ralph pushed between them and got a thump on the chest.* 5.2 a fairly loud but dull sound. EG *He heard the thump of a man's head against the floor... He sat down with a thump.*
N COUNT = wallop; N COUNT = thud

thump out. If you **thump out** a tune on the piano, you play it by hitting the keys very hard.
PHRASAL VB : V+O+ADV

thumping /θʌmpɪŋ/ is used to emphasize that something is very great or severe; an informal word. EG *She was elected with a thumping majority... She kept getting thumping colds.*
ADJ CLASSIF : ATTRIB = whopping

thunder /θʌndə/, **thunders, thundering, thundered.** 1 **Thunder** is the loud noise that you hear from the sky after a flash of lightning, especially during a storm. EG *Tnere's going to be thunder tonight... A clap of thunder shook the house... ...thunder and lightning.*
N UNCOUNT

2 When it **thunders**, a loud noise comes from the sky after a flash of lightning.
V : *it*+V

3 If you refer to the **thunder** of something, for example traffic or a drum, you are referring to the loud, deep noise it makes. EG *...the thunder of five hundred war drums.*
N UNCOUNT+*of* = crashing

3 If something **thunders**, it makes a very loud noise, usually continuously. EG *Loud crashing noises thundered from the next room... She took a bow to the thundering applause of the audience.*
V : USU+A = resound

4 If something, for example a lorry or a horse **thunders** along, it goes along quickly and with a lot of noise. EG *A truck thundered by.*
V+A = roar

5 If you **thunder** something, you say it loudly and forcefully, especially because you are angry; a literary word. EG *'Get out of my house!' he thundered.*
V+REPORT-CL/QUOTE = bellow

6 If you say that someone's face is **like thunder** or **as black as thunder**, you mean that they look as if they are very angry. EG *Robert walked in with a face like thunder.*
PHR : USED AS A/C

7 If you **steal** someone's **thunder**, you attract attention instead of them, especially by saying or doing what they had intended to say or do.
PHR : VB INFLECTS

8 See also **thundering.**

thunder against. If you **thunder against** someone or something, you criticize that person or thing very strongly and loudly; a fairly literary expression.
PHRASAL VB : V+PREP = rail against

thunderbolt /θʌndəbəult/, **thunderbolts.** A **thunderbolt** is a flash of lightning, accompanied by thunder, which strikes something such as a building or a tree. EG *The plane might be struck by a thunderbolt.*
N COUNT

thunderclap /θʌndəklæp/, **thunderclaps.** A **thunderclap** is a short, loud bang that you hear from the sky just after a flash of lightning.
N COUNT

thundercloud /θʌndəklaud/, **thunderclouds.** A **thundercloud** is a large, dark cloud that is likely to produce thunder and lightning.
N COUNT

thundering /θʌndə°rɪŋ/ is used to emphasize what you are saying; an informal, rather old-fashioned word. EG *It's a thundering good read... They get in here and make a thundering nuisance of themselves.*
ADV+ADJ/ADV, OR ADJ CLASSIF : ATTRIB = terrific

thunderous /θʌndə°rəs/. 1 A **thunderous** noise is very loud and deep. EG *The tree fell with a thunderous crash.*
ADJ CLASSIF = deafening

2 A **thunderous** statement is made with great force
ADJ CLASSIF

and intensity. EG *This gave the paper ammunition for a thunderous new attack on the government.*

thunderstorm /θʌndəstɔːm/, **thunderstorms**. A **thunderstorm** is a storm in which there is thunder and lightning and a lot of heavy rain. N COUNT

thunderstruck /θʌndəstrʌk/. If you are **thunderstruck**, you are very surprised or shocked; a formal or literary word. ADJ CLASSIF : PRED = stunned

thundery /θʌndəºriˈ/. When the weather is **thundery**, there is a lot of thunder, or there are heavy clouds which make you think that there will be thunder soon. EG *The night had been warm and thundery.* ADJ QUALIT ⇑ stormy

Thur. or **Thurs.** is an abbreviation for 'Thursday'.

Thursday /θɜːzdiˈ/, **Thursdays**. **Thursday** is one of the seven days of the week. It is the day after Wednesday and before Friday. EG *I got your postcard on Thursday... The question was raised at the meeting last Thursday.* N UNCOUNT/ COUNT

thus /ðʌs/; a fairly formal word. 1 You use **thus** to show that what you are about to mention is the result or consequence of something else that you have just mentioned. EG *...former miners who are now down to their last 2,000 pounds and thus qualify for social security benefits... If I am to accept certain limitations on my freedom, I must be assured that others are accepting the same restraints. Thus, an incomes policy has to be controlled if it is to be effective... A rise in incomes will create increased purchasing power, thus stimulating demand for goods and services.* ADV SEN = therefore, hence

2 If you say that something is **thus** or happens **thus**, you mean that it is, or happens, as you have just described or as you are just about to describe. EG *Her eyelids closed with weariness. It was thus that Robert Ford saw her from his bedroom window... There was a notice which said VISITORS WELCOME AT ANY TIME, and, thus encouraged, Lexington walked through the gate... It has always been thus and will continue to be so... In her diary her state of mind is simply recorded thus: 'I am fed up with everything.'* ADV WITH VB

3 **thus far**: see **far**.

thwack /θwæk/, **thwacks, thwacking, thwacked**. A **thwack** is a hard and noisy blow. EG *Davis raised his walking stick and with a tremendous thwack broke the man's nose.* ▸ used as a verb. EG *He thwacked his cane idly against his thigh.* N COUNT = whack; ▸ V+O = whack

thwart /θwɔːt/, **thwarts, thwarting, thwarted**. To **thwart** someone or their plans means to prevent them from doing or having something which they had been trying or hoping to do or get; a fairly formal word. EG *Here, too, I was thwarted... Expectations are disappointed and ambitions are thwarted.* V+O = frustrate

thy /ðaɪ/ is an old-fashioned, poetic, or religious word for 'your' when you are talking to only one person. See **thou**. EG *Do not covet thy neighbour's goods.* DET POSS

thyme /taɪm/ is a small plant with scented leaves that are used to flavour food. N UNCOUNT ⇑ herb

thyroid /θaɪrɔɪd/, **thyroids**. Your **thyroid** or your **thyroid gland** is a gland in your neck that produces substances which control the way your body grows and functions. N COUNT

thyself /ðaɪself/ is an old-fashioned, poetic, or religious word for 'yourself' when you are talking to only one person. See **thou**. EG *Defend thyself.* PRON REFL : SING

tiara /tiˈɑːrə/, **tiaras**. A **tiara** is a semicircular metal band decorated with jewels which a woman of very high social rank wears on her head at very formal social occasions. EG *...a diamond tiara.* N COUNT ⇑ crown

Tibetan /tɪbetəºn/, **Tibetans**. 1 A **Tibetan** person or thing comes from, belongs to, or relates to Tibet. ADJ CLASSIF

2 A **Tibetan** is a person who comes from Tibet. N COUNT

tibia /tɪbɪə/, **tibias**. Your **tibia** is one of the bones in your leg between your knee and your ankle. N COUNT

tic /tɪk/, **tics**. If someone has a **tic**, part of their body, especially part of their face, keeps making a twitching movement, for example because they are tired or have a nervous illness. EG *She seemed to have developed a tic in her neck.* N COUNT : USU SING ⇑ twitch

tick /tɪk/, **ticks, ticking, ticked**. 1 A **tick** is a written mark like a V with the right side extended. It is used to show that something is correct, wanted, or acceptable, or that it has been dealt with. EG *There was a nice red tick in the margin.* N COUNT

2 If you **tick** a piece of writing or a box on a form, you put a tick by it or in it. V+O ⇑ mark

3 When something such as a clock or watch **ticks**, it makes a regular series of short sounds as it works. EG *It was so quiet I could hear my wrist-watch ticking away.* ◇ **ticking**. EG *They eyed each other, the silence broken only by the ticking of the clock on the mantelpiece... She could hear a faint ticking.* V ⇑ click; ◇ N UNCOUNT ⇑ clicking

4 The **tick** of a clock or watch is the series of short sounds it makes when it is working, or one of those sounds. EG *The clock in the kitchen had a noisy tick... Each tick of the clock was bringing the fatal hour nearer.* N COUNT ⇑ click

5 A **tick** is a very short period of time; an informal use, mainly in British English. EG *Just hang on a tick while I get a pen.* N COUNT = mo, sec

6 If you refer to what makes someone **tick** or to how they **tick**, you are referring to the beliefs, wishes, and feelings they have which make them behave in the way that they do; an informal use. EG *What makes Patrick White tick?* V

7 A **tick** is also a small creature like a spider which lives on the bodies of people or animals and uses their blood as food. N COUNT ⇑ parasite

8 If you get something from a shop **on tick**, you do not pay for it straight away, but pay for it later; a rather old-fashioned, informal expression used in British English. PHR : USED AS AN A = on credit

tick by. If you say that the seconds, minutes, or hours **tick by** or **tick away**, you are emphasizing the fact that time is passing, especially when describing an occasion when someone is waiting for something to happen; a literary expression. EG *The seconds ticked by and still they heard no explosion... As the seconds before impact ticked away, Poole waited with mounting tension.* PHRASAL VB : V+ADV ⇑ pass

tick off. 1 If you **tick off** an item on a list, you put a tick or other mark by it, usually in order to show that it has been dealt with. ● If you **tick off** the items in a list **on your fingers**, you mention each one in turn, and touch your fingers in turn with another finger as you mention each item. EG *She ticked the items off on her fingers. 'Cutlery, plates, glasses, napkins.'* PHRASAL VB : V+O+ADV; ● PHR : VB INFLECTS

2 If you **tick** someone **off**, you speak rather angrily to them because they have done something wrong; an informal use. EG *David had ticked her off for being careless.* ● See also **ticking-off**. PHRASAL VB : V+O+ADV = scold

tick over; used mainly in British English. 1 An engine that **is ticking over** is running at a low speed, for example when you are not actually using it but it is switched on. PHRASAL VB : V+ADV, USU CONT = idle

2 A business, organization, etc that **is ticking over** is functioning steadily but is not doing or producing very much. EG *At this time, the country was ticking over under a rather uninspired President.* PHRASAL VB : V+ADV, USU CONT = chug along

ticker /tɪkə/, **tickers**. Your **ticker** is your heart; a rather old-fashioned, informal word. EG *I hear old Bill's died. It was his ticker, of course.* N COUNT

ticker tape; also spelled with a hyphen. **Ticker tape** is long narrow strips of paper on which information such as stock exchange prices is printed by a machine. People used to throw ticker tape from high windows to give a welcome to a famous person who was driving in a procession through their city, especially in the USA. EG *The city gave the royal couple a ticker-tape welcome.* N UNCOUNT

ticket /tɪkɪt/, **tickets**. 1 A **ticket** is 1.1 an official piece of paper or card which you are given so that you can prove that you have paid for a journey or for a visit to a theatre, museum, etc. EG *She bought two tickets for the opera... I'd like a return ticket to Vienna, please... The ticket office was closed.* N COUNT, OR *by* N; **1.2** a piece of paper or card, often with your name or a number on it, which shows that you are entitled to receive or use something. EG *...library tickets... The customers all clutched ration tickets.* N COUNT; **1.3** a piece of card which is attached to an item that is for sale, and which shows its price and size, instructions for its use, etc. N COUNT = tag; **1.4** an official piece of paper which orders you to pay a fine or to appear in court because you have committed a driving or parking offence. EG *There was a parking ticket under the windshield wiper.* N COUNT

2 The particular **ticket** on which a person fights an election is the party or the part of a party which that person represents, or the political policies that he or she supports. EG *He ran as Vice-President on the* N SING : *the*+MOD+N

Republican ticket... They fought the election on the pro-Common Market ticket.

3 If you say **'that's the ticket'** or **'that's just the ticket'**, you are saying that something is just what is needed; a rather old-fashioned informal expression. CONVENTION

4 See also **meal ticket, season ticket.**

ticking /tɪkɪŋ/ is a strong cotton material, often striped, which is used, for example, to cover mattresses and pillows. • See also **tick**. N UNCOUNT ⇑ fabric

ticking off, tickings off. If you give someone a **ticking off**, you speak rather angrily to them because they have done something wrong; an informal word. EG *Then Lally confessed and got a ticking off.* N COUNT : USU SING = scolding

tickle /tɪkəºl/, **tickles, tickling, tickled. 1** When you **tickle** someone, you move your fingers playfully and lightly on a sensitive part of their body, often in order to make them laugh. EG *Babies want to be tickled and hugged.* V+O

2 If something **tickles** you or **tickles**, it produces an irritating but sometimes pleasant feeling in a part of your body by touching it lightly. EG *He flicked away a strand of hair that was tickling Ellen's nose.* V OR V+O

3 If you give someone a **tickle**, you tickle them. N SING : a+N

4 A **tickle** is also an unpleasant irritation in your throat or somewhere on your body. N SING : a+N ⇑ sensation

5 If a situation, event, or idea **tickles** someone, it amuses them or gives them pleasure. EG *'Yes, sir,' she answered. The Colonel was tickled by that.* V+O = entertain

6 If something **tickles** your **fancy** or your **vanity**, it appeals to you and perhaps amuses you. EG *Somehow it rather tickled his fancy to be able to say, 'My friend the Ambassador.'* PHR : VB INFLECTS ⇑ please

7 If you **are tickled pink** or **are tickled to death**, you are really delighted by something that happens. EG *The vast majority of men are tickled pink at being wined, dined, and paid for by women.* PHR : AUX INFLECTS = be thrilled

ticklish /tɪklɪʃ/. **1** Someone who is **ticklish** is **1.1** sensitive to being tickled, and laughs as soon as you tickle them. **1.2** easily upset or offended; a fairly informal use. EG *He's a bit ticklish about people walking through his garden.* ADJ QUALIT : USU PRED / ADJ QUALIT : PRED = touchy

2 A **ticklish** problem, situation, or task is difficult and needs to be dealt with carefully; a fairly informal use. EG *It was a ticklish moment in the discussion.* ADJ QUALIT : USU ATTRIB = delicate

tidal /taɪdəºl/. **1** A **tidal** river, lake, or sea has regular currents that cause the level of the water to rise and fall each day. EG *...tidal estuaries.* ADJ CLASSIF : ATTRIB

2 Tidal also means relating to or produced by tides. EG *...tidal energy.* ADJ CLASSIF : ATTRIB

3 A **tidal** kind of activity is one which occurs only sometimes rather than being constant, or is intense only sometimes. EG *...tidal movements of human beings.* ADJ CLASSIF

tidal wave, tidal waves. 1 A **tidal wave** is a very large wave of the sea that comes over the land and destroys things. Tidal waves are often caused by earthquakes. N COUNT

2 You can refer to a very large number of people or things which all come at the same time as a **tidal wave** of them. EG *There was a tidal wave of new arrivals... ...a tidal wave of publications.* N PART = flood

tidbit /tɪdbɪt/, **tidbits.** A **tidbit** is the same as a titbit; used in American English. N COUNT

tiddler /tɪdlə/, **tiddlers.** A **tiddler** is a very small fish of any kind; used in informal British English. N COUNT

tiddly /tɪdli¹/, **tiddlier, tiddliest**; an informal word in British English. **1** Someone who is **tiddly** is rather drunk. ADJ QUALIT = tipsy

2 Something that is **tiddly** is very small. EG *They gave us tiddly little cups of coffee.* ADJ QUALIT = titchy

tiddlywink /tɪdli¹wɪŋk/, **tiddlywinks. 1 Tiddlywinks** is a game in which the players try to make small round pieces of plastic jump into a container, by pressing the edge of them with a larger piece of plastic. N UNCOUNT

2 A **tiddlywink** is a small round piece of plastic used in the game of tiddlywinks. N COUNT ⇑ counter

tide /taɪd/, **tides, tiding, tided. 1** When you refer to the **tide**, you are referring to the regular and continuous change in the level of the sea on the shore. When the tide is high, full, or in, it is at its highest level, and when the tide is low or out, it is at its lowest level. EG *The tide was coming in... The rocks were exposed at low tide.* N SING : the+N, OR at+MOD+N

2 A **tide** is a current in the sea that is caused by the regular and continuous movement of large areas of water towards and away from the shore. EG *...the strong northerly tides.* N COUNT

3 The **tide** of opinion or fashion is what the majority of people think or do at a particular time. EG *The film was effective in turning the tide of American opinion against the war... He's always gone against the tide of fashion.* N PART : SING+N UNCOUNT ⇑ tendency

4 A **tide** of things or of something is a large quantity of them or it, or a widespread occurrence of it. EG *...the tide of highly qualified academics who come looking for work... The company has been troubled by a rising tide of alcoholism and drug abuse.* N SING+SUPP = wave, flood

tide over. If you do something for someone, especially lend them money, to **tide** them **over**, you do it to help them through a period when they are having difficulties. EG *I only want to borrow enough to tide me over till Monday.* PHRASAL VB : ORDER V+O+ ADV/PREP

tideline /taɪdlaɪn/, **tidelines**; also spelled with a hyphen. The **tideline** is the highest point, or perhaps the lowest point, that the sea reaches on a shore. EG *The wind rustled the dead seaweed on the tideline.* N COUNT = tidemark

tidemark /taɪdmɑːk/, **tidemarks**; also spelled with a hyphen. A **tidemark** is **1** the same as a tideline. **2** a line of dirt that is left around the inside of a bath when the water is emptied out. N COUNT / N COUNT ⇑ mark

tidings /taɪdɪŋz/ are news that someone tells you; a formal, old-fashioned word. EG *He kissed her and told her the good tidings.* N PLURAL : USU+ SUPP ⇑ information

tidy /taɪdi¹/, **tidier, tidiest; tidies, tidying, tidied. 1** Something that is **tidy** is neat and arranged in an orderly way. EG *It is very difficult to keep a house tidy... ...a tidy desk... Please leave your books in a tidy pile.* ◊ **tidiness.** EG *...his parents' concern with tidiness and punctuality.* ADJ QUALIT ≠ messy / ◊ N UNCOUNT = neatness

2 Someone who is **tidy** likes everything to be neat and arranged in an orderly way. EG *I wish you were a little bit tidier!* ADJ QUALIT ≠ messy, untidy

3 When you **tidy** a room, cupboard, etc, you make it neat by putting things in their proper places. EG *You can't tidy a bedroom until you've made the beds.* V+O = straighten

4 If you **tidy** things into a particular place, you put them there so that they are not in the way. EG *I told you to tidy everything onto the trolley.* V+O+A

5 A sink **tidy**, a desk **tidy**, etc is a small container in which you put things to keep them out of the way. N COUNT : MOD+ N

6 A **tidy** amount of money is a large amount of money; a fairly informal use. EG *He managed to make quite a tidy income every year.* ADJ QUALIT : ATTRIB = sizeable

tidy away. When you **tidy** something **away**, you put it in something else so that it is not in the way. EG *She tidied the box away in her dressing-table.* PHRASAL VB : V+ O+ADV

tidy out. When you **tidy out** a room, cupboard, etc, you take everything out of it, throw away the things that you do not want, and put the rest back neatly. PHRASAL VB : V+ O+ADV = sort out

tidy up. When you **tidy up** or **tidy** a place or person **up**, you put things back in their proper places so that everything is neat again. EG *I wish that people would tidy up after themselves... You'd better tidy yourself up now.* PHRASAL VB : V+ ADV, OR V+O+ ADV = clean up

tie /taɪ/, **ties, tying, tied. 1** If you **tie** something to a particular thing or into a particular position, you fasten it to that thing or into that position using string, rope, etc. EG *We are going to tie this letter to a brick and throw it over the railings... ...one of those labels you tie onto the handle of your suitcase... Her thin hair was tied up in a bun.* V+O+A ⇑ attach

2 If you **tie** a piece of string, cloth, etc round something or **tie** something with a piece of string or cloth, you put the piece of string or cloth round it fairly tightly and fasten the ends together in a knot or bow. EG *...a little dog which had a ribbon tied round its neck... She was busy undoing a little newspaper parcel tied with string... The children had a blissful morning tying the straw into small bundles.* V+O+A

3 If you **tie** a knot or a bow in a piece of string, cloth, etc or **tie** the string or cloth into a knot or bow, you make a knot or bow in it. V+O : USU+A

4 When you **tie** shoelaces, a tie, a hair-ribbon, etc, you fasten the ends together in a bow or in the right sort of knot. EG *He was still tying his laces.* V+O = do up

5 A **tie** is **5.1** a long narrow piece of cloth that is worn round the neck under a shirt collar and tied in a knot at the front. Ties are worn mainly by men. EG *He took off his jacket and loosened his tie... I was wearing a jumper and sports jacket, not a suit and tie.* • See also **bow tie, old school tie. 5.2** a long narrow piece of cloth, plastic, wire, etc that is used N COUNT = necktie / N COUNT ⇑ fastening to attach one thing to another, or to close or fasten something such as a bag or a piece of clothing.

6 Something that **ties** people to each other unites them or makes them feel linked to each other. EG *In the past, kinship still tied the elite to the ordinary people.* V+O+A = bind

7 Something that **is tied** to or into something else is connected to it or linked closely with it. EG *...micro-computers tied into an information system... Canada is tightly tied into the American economy.* V+O+A (to/into) : USU PASS

8 If you **are tied** to a particular place, situation, way of life, or job, you are forced to remain in it or to have it. EG *Really, you're tied to your home when you have small children... She wasn't tied to a particular academic discipline.* V+O+A (to) : USU PASS ⇑ be restricted

9 A **tie** is also **9.1** a connection, relationship, or feeling that links a person with another person, a place, an organization, etc. EG *Family ties are often very strong... ...the magical tie between mother and child... They want to loosen their ties with Britain.* N COUNT : USU+SUPP = bond, link

9.2 something that limits your freedom because it forces you to remain in a particular place or situation, or to have a particular way of life or job. EG *Pets are as much of a tie as children.* N COUNT ⇑ restriction

10 If your **hands are tied**, you are prevented from acting in the way you want to. EG *We'd like to help, but our hands are tied.* PHR : VB INFLECTS

11 If you **tie** with someone in a competition or game, you do exactly as well as they do, for example you both have the same score. EG *Bill tied with Margaret for first place... Two actresses tied for the Best Actress award.* V OR V+A (with) : RECIP = draw

12 A **tie** is also **12.1** a result of a competition or game, in which two or more people do exactly as well as each other, especially when they beat everyone else. EG *In the event of a tie, the winner will be the contestant who took the shortest time.* N COUNT = draw **12.2** a sports match, for example a football match, that is played as part of a larger competition. The winner of the match plays in the next set of matches. EG *Peterborough haven't played their third round tie yet.* N COUNT

13 See also **tied**.

tie down. A person or thing that **ties** someone **down** restricts their freedom, for example by forcing them to keep to a particular way of life or to an agreement. EG *You're not tied down to a date... She doesn't want children because she says they tie you down.* PHRASAL VB : V+O+ADV

tie in with. An idea, fact, etc that **ties in with** something else fits in with it or agrees with it. EG *His beliefs didn't seem to tie in at all with reality.* PHRASAL VB : V+ADV+PREP = coincide with

tie up. 1 If you **tie** something **up**, you put string, rope, etc round it so that it is firm or secure. EG *Clarissa came in, carrying some canvases tied up in brown paper.* PHRASAL VB : V+O+ADV ⇑ fasten

2 If you **tie** someone **up**, you fasten ropes, chains, etc around them so that they cannot move or escape. PHRASAL VB : V+O+ADV

3 When you **tie up** laces, you fasten them in a bow. EG *He saw the man tying up his shoelace.* PHRASAL VB : V+O+ADV

4 When you **tie up** an animal such as a horse or a dog, you fasten it to a fixed object with a piece of rope or chain so that it cannot wander off. PHRASAL VB : V+O+ADV = tether

5 When a boat **ties up** or **is tied up**, it is attached to something on land with a rope or chain, for example in a harbour. EG *The ships made for port and tied up.* PHRASAL VB : V-ERG+ADV, OR V+ADV = moor

6 If someone or something **ties** something else **up**, they use it or do something with it, with the result that it is not available for other people or other purposes. EG *The big companies were tying up supplies of minerals in long-term contracts... People don't want to tie their money up for long periods.* PHRASAL VB : V+O+ADV

7 Something that **is tied up** with something else or **ties up** with it is closely linked with it. EG *The problem of unemployment is tied up with the development of new technology... It supposedly tied up with her interest in dance.* PHRASAL VB : V-ERG+ADV

8 If you **tie up** an issue or problem, you deal with it in a way that gives definite conclusions or answers. EG *Cobb ties it up in 100 pages of the book.* PHRASAL VB : V+O+ADV = wrap up

9 See also **tied up**.

tie-break, tie-breaks. A **tie-break** is a special extra game which is played in a tennis match when the score in a set is 6-6. The player who wins the tie-break wins the set. N COUNT

tie-breaker, tie-breakers. A **tie-breaker** is an extra question or round that decides the winner of a competition or game when two or more people have the same score at the end. N COUNT

tied /taɪd/. A **tied** cottage or house belongs to a farmer, factory owner, etc, and is rented to someone who works for him or her. ADJ CLASSIF : USU ATTRIB

tied up; a fairly informal word. 1 If you are **tied up**, you are busy, with the result that you are not free to do anything else. EG *I'm tied up right now, can you call me back later?* ADJ QUALIT : PRED = occupied

2 If you are **tied up** with someone, you are involved in a personal relationship with them. EG *He got tied up with some girl.* ADJ QUALIT : PRED+with = mixed up

tie-dye, tie-dyes, tie-dyeing, tie-dyed. When someone **tie-dyes** a piece of cloth, they colour it by tying it in knots and putting it in a coloured liquid, so that some parts become more deeply coloured than others. V OR V+O ⇑ dye

tie-pin, tie-pins. A **tie-pin** is a narrow brooch used to pin a person's tie to their shirt. N COUNT

tier /tɪə/, **tiers**. A **tier** is 1 a row or layer of something that has other layers above or below it. EG *The theatre had semicircular tiers of seats... ...a wedding cake with three tiers.* N COUNT 2 a level in an organization or system. EG *Tier 1 looks after education and highways.* N COUNT

tiff /tɪf/, **tiffs**. A **tiff** is a small, unimportant quarrel, especially between two lovers or between a husband and wife. N COUNT = squabble

tiger /taɪgə/, **tigers**. A **tiger** is a large, fierce animal that belongs to the cat family and is orange with black stripes. Tigers live in Asia. • See also **paper tiger**. N COUNT

tiger lily, tiger lilies. A **tiger lily** is a lily which has flowers that are orange with black spots. N COUNT

tight /taɪt/, **tighter, tightest; tights**. 1 Clothes or shoes that are **tight** fit closely to your body, often so closely that they feel uncomfortable. EG *He was wearing tight cream-coloured trousers... My shoes are too tight.* ◊ **tightly**. EG *...a tightly fitting suit.* ADJ QUALIT = close-fitting ≠ loose ◊ ADV WITH VB

2 If you hold something or someone **tight** or hold **tight**, you hold them firmly and securely. EG *She had to hold the boy tight, to keep him from falling... Ann was now clutching the letter tight in her hand... She held on tight.* ADV AFTER VB

3 A **tight** hold or grip is firm and secure. EG *He held Sandy with a grip tight enough to make the little man squeal with pain... His fingers were tight on Thomas's arm.* ◊ **tightly**. EG *She kissed him tenderly, and they clung together very tightly.* ADJ QUALIT ≠ loose ◊ ADV WITH VB = closely

4 Something that is **tight** is firmly in place or firmly fastened, and difficult to move. EG *The critical bolts are all tight enough... ...a tight knot.* ◊ **tightly**. EG *He screwed the caps tightly onto the bottles.* ADJ QUALIT ≠ loose ◊ ADV WITH VB ⇑ securely

5 Something that is shut **tight** is shut very firmly. EG *The windows were shut tight against the rain... He closed his eyes tight.* ADV AFTER VB

6 Skin, cloth, string, etc that is **tight** is stretched or pulled so that it is smooth or straight. EG *The skin was stretched tight over her fine facial bones.* ◊ **tightly**. EG *The skin on his face was drawn back tightly like stretched leather.* ADJ QUALIT = taut ≠ slack ◊ ADV WITH VB

7 **Tight** is also used to describe a group of things or an amount of something that is closely packed together, especially so that it takes up little space. EG *They stood in a tight group with their hands in their pockets... The pub was packed tight... Her hair was arranged in tight curls... ...tight little bundles.* ◊ **tightly**. EG *...clusters of houses tightly packed together.* ADJ QUALIT ◊ ADV WITH VB = compactly

8 If you make a sharp, **tight** turn or go round a **tight** bend, you make a sharp, narrow turn. ADJ QUALIT

9 If your voice or a part of your face is **tight**, it shows that you are feeling tense, worried, or angry. EG *Jack cleared his throat and spoke in a queer, tight voice... His mouth was tight and pale.* ADJ QUALIT

10 If your chest or stomach feels **tight**, it feels rather uncomfortable and painful, especially because you are feeling ill or anxious. EG *My chest feels rather tight.* ◊ **tightness**. EG *I went to the interview with the familiar tightness in my stomach.* ADJ QUALIT = constricted ◊ N UNCOUNT

11 A **tight** group of people is one whose members are closely linked by beliefs, feelings, etc. EG *The Common Market should be a tight federation of states.* ◊ **tightly**. EG *In the past individuals may have been more tightly bound to one another.* ADJ QUALIT ⇑ close = close-knit ◊ ADV WITH VB

12 A **tight** plan or arrangement allows only the minimum time or money for doing things. EG *We* ADJ QUALIT = strict

have a tight schedule... No matter how tight your budget there is room in it for economy.

13 A **tight** rule or form of control is fairly strict and restricts people quite a lot. EG *Security has become visibly tighter over the last year.* ◊ **tightly**. EG *We're talking about a society which is very tightly controlled.* ADJ QUALIT = rigorous ◊ ADV WITH VB = rigorously

14 If money is **tight** or if things are **tight**, you do not have very much money to spend; a fairly informal use. ADJ QUALIT : PRED

15 A **tight** situation is a difficult or dangerous one. EG *He could conceal his nervousness in tight situations.* ADJ QUALIT : ATTRIB

16 Someone who is **tight** is **16.1** rather drunk; an informal use. **16.2** unwilling to spend their money; an informal use. EG *He's really tight with his money.* ADJ QUALIT ADJ QUALIT = stingy

17 **Tights** are a piece of clothing made of a thin, stretchy material. They fit closely round a person's hips, legs, and feet, and are worn by women or performers such as dancers. EG *She had a ladder in her only pair of silk tights.* N PLURAL : ALSO *a pair of*+N

18 You can say **'sleep tight'** to someone when they are going to bed as a way of saying that you hope they will sleep well. CONVENTION

19 • to **keep a tight rein on** someone: see **rein**. • to **sit tight**: see **sit**. • See also **airtight, watertight**.

tighten /taɪtəⁿn/, **tightens, tightening, tightened**. 1 If you **tighten** your hold on something or if your hold **tightens**, you hold the thing more firmly or securely. EG *His fingers tightened like a vice around his rifle... He tightened his grip on the spear he was carrying.* V-ERG ⇑ strengthen

2 If you **tighten** a rope, chain, etc or if it **tightens**, it is stretched or pulled until it is straight. EG *The chain tightened and the pig's leg was pulled up and back.* V-ERG

3 When you **tighten** a fastening or **tighten it up**, you move it so that it is more firmly in place or holds something more firmly. EG *Smithy tightened the last screw... Tighten up the axle nut... She bent down to tighten the strap of her roller skate.* • to **tighten** your **belt**: see **belt**. V+O, OR PHRASAL VB : V+O+ADV ⇑ secure

4 If a part of your body **tightens**, it becomes tense and stiff, for example because you are angry or afraid. EG *His face and eyes tightened with hatred... I felt my stomach tighten.* V ⇑ harden

5 If someone **tightens** a rule or system or **tightens** it **up**, they make it stricter or more efficient. EG *The authorities tightened security around the embassy... He said he would take steps to tighten up the administration.* V+O, OR PHRASAL VB : V+O+ADV ⇑ improve

tight-fisted. Someone who is **tight-fisted** is unwilling to spend their money. EG *He was unable to squeeze the extra cash out of his tight-fisted employers.* ADJ QUALIT = stingy, mean

tightlipped /taɪtlɪpt/; also spelled with a hyphen. Someone who is **tightlipped** 1 is unwilling to give any information about something. EG *The government has been very tight-lipped about it.* 2 has their lips pressed tightly together, especially because they are angry. ADJ QUALIT ADJ QUALIT

tightrope /taɪtrəʊp/, **tightropes**. 1 A **tightrope** is a tightly-stretched piece of rope on which an acrobat balances and performs tricks. EG *...a tightrope walker.* N COUNT

2 Someone who is **on a tightrope** or **walking a tightrope** is in a difficult or delicate situation and has to be careful about what they say or do. EG *He recognized that he was walking a tightrope: one slip would mean political destruction.* PH : USED AS AN A, OR PHR : VB INFLECTS

tigress /taɪgrɪˀs/, **tigresses**. A **tigress** is a female tiger. N COUNT

tilde /tɪldə/, **tildes**. A **tilde** is a symbol that is sometimes written over the letter n in Spanish to change its pronunciation, for example in the word 'señor' which is pronounced as if it was written 'senyor'. N COUNT

tile /taɪl/, **tiles, tiling, tiled**. 1 A **tile** is **1.1** a flat square piece of baked clay, carpet, cork, etc. Tiles are put together edge to edge to cover surfaces such as floors or walls. EG *Avoid ceramic tiles, which are very hard on the feet... Polystyrene ceiling tiles help to insulate a room.* **1.2** a flat square or rectangular piece of baked clay which is used for covering roofs. EG *...brick houses roofed in reddish-brown tiles.* N COUNT ⇑ covering N COUNT

2 When someone **tiles** a roof, floor, etc, they cover it with tiles. ◊ **tiled**. EG *...yellow stone houses with red tiled roofs... He heard footsteps on the tiled floor.* V+O, OR V ◊ ADJ CLASSIF

till /tɪl/, **tills, tilling, tilled**. 1 **Till** means the same as until; not usually used in formal English. EG *Wait till I come back... He wrote from morning till night... Etta had not up till then taken a very active part in the discussion... We didn't get back till 2.* PREP

2 A **till** is a drawer or box in a shop where money is kept, usually in a cash register. EG *He put the money into the till... I've just been counting the till money.* N COUNT

• If someone **is caught with** their **fingers in the till**, they are caught stealing cash from the place where they work. • PHR : VB INFLECTS

3 When people **till** land, they prepare the earth and work on it in order to grow crops. EG *One man tilled the soil and produced vegetables... They worked hard tilling the fields.* V+O = cultivate

tiller /tɪlə/, **tillers**. The **tiller** of a boat is a handle that is fixed to the rudder and is used to turn the rudder and so steer the boat. N COUNT

tilt /tɪlt/, **tilts, tilting, tilted**. 1 If you **tilt** an object or if it **tilts**, it moves into a sloping position with one end or side higher than the other. EG *He tilted the flask and two or three drops trickled out... He sat down on the chair that was tilted against the wall... Sonny tilted back in his chair... The earth is tilted on its axis.* V-ERG : USU+A = incline

2 If you **tilt** part of your body, usually your head, or if it **tilts**, you move it slightly upwards or to one side. EG *She tilted her head to one side... Let your head gently tilt forwards... She looked on with disdain, tilting her nose in the air.* V-ERG : USU+A = incline

3 A **tilt** is a tilting movement or position. EG *She smiled with an upward tilt of her head... The table was at a tilt.* N COUNT ⇑ inclination

4 If something **tilts** an opinion, situation, etc towards a particular group, it influences the opinion, situation, etc in favour of that group. EG *He was making a major effort to tilt American policy towards Africa... These costs are significant enough to tilt the advantage in the opposite direction... Circumstances are tilted in its favour.* V+O+A = incline

5 If you go somewhere **at full tilt**, you go as fast as you can. EG *She was running at full tilt.* PHR : USED AS AN A

timber /tɪmbə/, **timbers**. 1 **Timber** is wood that is used for building houses, making furniture, etc. EG *Most of the region's building timber is imported from the south... We live in timber cabins... If your house timber has woodworm, get expert advice.* ▸ also used to refer to trees that are grown to be used for building houses, making furniture, etc. EG *They grow rice and timber.* N UNCOUNT ▸ ⇑ crop

2 A **timber** is a long, fairly wide piece of wood that is part of a ship, house, etc. EG *He could hear the ship's timbers creaking... ...the roof timbers of the houses.* N COUNT ⇑ support = beam

3 You shout **'Timber!'** to warn people when you have just cut a tree and it is about to fall. CONVENTION

timbered /tɪmbəd/. A **timbered** building has a wooden frame or wooden beams showing on the outside. EG *...an old timbered lodge.* ADJ CLASSIF : ATTRIB

timbre /tɪmbə, tæmbə/, **timbres**. The **timbre** of a particular voice or musical instrument is the quality of sound that it has. EG *The voice had an ugly timbre to it.* N UNCOUNT : USU +SUPP

time /taɪm/, **times, timing, timed**. 1 **Time** is what we measure in hours, days, years, etc. EG *...a period of time... More time passed, and finally Kunta fell asleep again... You're getting more and more depressed as time goes on... It has increased in size over time.* N UNCOUNT ⇑ continuum

2 **Time** is used **2.1** to refer to a specific point in time, which can be stated in hours, minutes, etc and is shown on clocks. EG *What's the time?... 'What time is it?'–'Almost six.'... What time did you get back to London?... Ask the times of planes from Rome to Vienna... I will see you at the same time next week.* N COUNT : USU *the/what*+N IN SING

2.2 to refer to the system of counting hours that is used in a particular time zone in the world. EG *It was 1035 hours Greenwich Mean Time, 0535 Eastern Standard Time... ...at 6 in the evening, local time.* N UNCOUNT : MOD +N

3 You use **time 3.1** to refer to the period of time that someone spends doing something or that is available for doing something. EG *How do you find time to write these books?... I didn't know if we'd have time for tea... She seems to be spending most of her time sunbathing... Unfortunately we've run out of time.* N UNCOUNT

3.2 to describe the length of time that something takes or that something has been happening. EG *The proposal would take quite a long time to discuss in* N SING WITH DET : USU+SUPP ⇑ duration

detail... ...the short time that I've been there... ...one of the best films I've seen for some time... They were very irritating a lot of the time. **3.3** to refer to a period of time or a point in time, when you are describing what is happening then. EG *It seemed a good time to invite my sister to stay... ...during my time in Toronto... It was winter time... ...in time of war... I had the idea of writing from the time that I was about 12... This time next year I'll be in America... ...at the time of his death... It is only a remote possibility at the present time... ...a minister in Prague at that time... By the time the waiter brought their coffee she was drunk.*
N UNCOUNT/COUNT : USU SING, USU+SUPP

4 A particular **time** in history is a particular period in the history of the world, of a society, etc. EG *...the history of modern times... The film begins at the time of the Roman Empire... ...in these very difficult times.*
N COUNT/UNCOUNT+SUPP

5 If you say it is **time** for something or **time** to do something, you mean that this thing ought to happen or be done now. EG *It is time to go... It was time for tea... I think it's time we stopped, children... Is it lunch time yet?*
N UNCOUNT+SUPP : USU *it*+VB+N ⇑ point

6 You use **time** when you are saying that a situation has reached a stage when you feel that action or change of a particular kind is needed. EG *They now feel the time has come to change things... It is time we realized that this is not always true... There comes a time when nothing more can be done... This is no time for her to stop.*
N SING WITH DET+SUPP ⇑ point

7 When you talk about a **time** when something happens, you are referring to a specific occasion when it happens. EG *Do you remember that time when Adrian phoned up?... He blushed each time she spoke to him... For the first time since he had left home he felt sad... Ask for something different next time... There were times when I didn't know what to do.*
N COUNT+SUPP : USU SING

8 If you say that something has been happening for a **time**, you mean that it has been happening for a fairly long period of time. EG *It's nice to be in London for a time after running around constantly... It became clear after a time that in fact he was very ill.*
N SING : *a*+N = spell

9 When you describe the **time** that you had on a particular occasion or during a particular part of your life, you are describing the sort of experience that you had then. EG *There were good times, when we laughed together... Our negotiators must expect a rather tough time... For the rest of the trip he had an easy time of it.*
N COUNT+SUPP

10 You use **time** after numbers to say how often something happens. EG *Ray and I play squash at least three times a week... How many times have you been to see them?... The telephone rang a second time.*
N COUNT : USU NUM/QUANTIF/ORDINAL+N

11 You use **times** after numbers when you are comparing two things, amounts, situations, etc to say how much bigger or smaller, better or worse, etc one of them is. EG *It would have cost me about ten times as much... I think it has become three times as difficult as it used to be... The rate was six times greater among old people.*
N PLURAL : NUM+N+COMPAR, OR NUM+N+*as*+ADJ/ADV

12 You use **times** in arithmetic to link numbers or amounts that are multiplied together to reach a total. EG *5 times 50–that's 250... Force equals mass times acceleration.* ▸ used as a verb instead of 'multiply', especially by children. EG *If you times 6 by 7 you get 42.*
= multiplied by
▸ V+NUM+*by/and*+NUM = multiply

13 The **time** of a piece of music is the number of beats that the piece has in each bar. EG *...music written in three time.*
N UNCOUNT : USU +SUPP

14 When a person in charge of a pub calls **time**, they call out the word 'Time!' to say that they are closing and everyone must finish their drinks. EG *Time now, please, ladies and gents!*
CONVENTION

15 If you **time** something for a particular time, you plan that it should happen at this time. EG *They timed the attack for six o'clock.* ◊ **timed.** EG *The boat was timed to leave at 8.30... The staff meeting was timed for 10 a.m.*
V+O+*for/to*-INF = schedule
◊ ADJ CLASSIF : PRED+*for/to*-INF

16 If you **time** something well or badly, you judge well or badly the moment at which to do it in a situation, activity, sports match, etc. EG *Keegan had timed the ball brilliantly.* ◊ **timed.** EG *His remarks were badly timed... ...ill timed remarks.*
V+O : USU PASS+ADV ⇑ calculate
◊ ADJ CLASSIF : USU WITH ADV

17 If you **time** an action, activity, etc, you measure how long someone takes to do it or how long it lasts. EG *This was repeated at intervals which he timed on his watch... They timed his rate of breathing.*
V+O

18 Time is used in a number of expressions with the preposition 'at'. **18.1** You use the expression **at a time** after an amount to say how many things or people there are together in a particular sequence, group, or action. EG *He used to abandon his work for many months at a time... I ran upstairs three steps at a time... There was only room for one person at a time.*
PHR : NG+PHR

18.2 If you say that something happens **at times**, you mean that it sometimes happens. EG *She's really rude at times.... At times I hardly knew what I was doing.*
PHR : USED AS AN A

18.3 If you say that something happens **at all times**, you mean that it happens always or on every occasion. EG *You should have control of your vehicle at all times... He tried to sound tough at all times.*
PHR : USED AS AN A

18.4 Something that may happen **at any time** will probably happen at a time which cannot be stated definitely, but which may be very soon. EG *Doctors said the baby could die at any time.*
PHR : USED AS AN A

18.5 At one time or **at any one time** means at a single point in time or during a single period of time. EG *That is a lot for anyone to possess at one time... The library has room for about six hundred readers at any one time.*
PHR : USED AS AN A = at once

18.6 If you say that something was the case **at one time**, you mean that it was the case once in the past. EG *You worked for them, didn't you, at one time?... At one time I resented this fact.*
PHR : USED AS AN A = formerly

18.7 You say **at the best of times** when you are making a negative or critical comment to emphasize that it is true even when the circumstances are as favourable as possible. EG *Puno province would not be rich at the best of times... I find cleaning tedious at the best of times.*
PHR : USED AS AN A

19 at the same time is used **19.1** when referring to two things that happen at the same moment as each other. EG *They started moving at the same time.*
PHR : USED AS AN A

19.2 when referring to two or more qualities or desires which someone or something possesses together but which seem to contradict one another. EG *It made us cautious but at the same time it made us willing to take a risk... They want to look at each other and at the same time they want to look away.*
PHR : USED AS AN A = yet

19.3 to introduce a statement that modifies or raises an objection to the previous statement. EG *Such a development would be welcome. At the same time, it is crucial to recognize the narrowness of the approach... This seems to penalize families unfairly. But at the same time, the State cannot go on as it has been doing.*
PHR : USED AS ADV SEN ⇑ yet

20 before your **time**. **20.1** If you say that something was **before** your **time**, you mean that it happened or existed before you were born or before you were old enough to remember it. EG *I wouldn't know, those songs were before my time.*
PHR : USED AS AN A

20.2 If someone has reached a particular stage in life **before** their **time**, they have reached it at a younger age than is normal. EG *...the huddle of grubby, nervous faces old before their time... The child growing up there is forced to mature before his time.*
PHR : USED AS AN A

21 in time. **21.1** If you say that something will happen **in time**, you mean that it will happen eventually, when a lot of time has passed. EG *No doubt in time the arguments will straighten themselves out.*
PHR : USED AS AN A

21.2 If you are **in time** for a particular event, you are not too late for it. EG *We're just in time... He returned to his hotel in time for a late supper.*
PHR : USED AS AN A

21.3 If you are **in time** with someone when playing a piece of music, you are following the rhythm and speed of the music correctly. If you are **out of time** with them, you are not following the rhythm and speed of the music correctly.
PHR : USED AS AN A

22 Time is used in a number of other expressions with the preposition 'in'. **22.1** If you say that something will happen **in a week's time, in two years' time**, etc, you mean that there will be a week, two years, etc between now and the time when it will happen. EG *Celia is coming along in about an hour's time... ...in three weeks' time.*
PHR : USED AS AN A

22.2 If you arrive somewhere **in good time**, you arrive early so that there is time to spare before a particular event. EG *She is in good time for the train... We got there in plenty of time.*
PHR : USED AS AN A

22.3 If you tell someone that something will happen **all in good time**, you are telling them to be patient because it will happen eventually.
PHR : USED AS AN A

22.4 If something happens **in no time, in next to no time**, etc, it happens almost immediately and very
PHR : USED AS AN A

quickly. EG *In no time at all the whole sky was lit up... She was back in next to no time.* **22.5** If you do work that is part of your job or course **in** your **own time**, you do it in your free time and not at work, school, etc. EG *They have finished the reading in their own time.* PHR : USED AS AN A

23 Time is used in a number of expressions which begin with other prepositions. **23.1** If you say it is **about time** that something was done, you are saying in an emphatic way that you think it should be done, because you do not like the situation as it is now. EG *It's about time that Members of Parliament concentrated on things that really matter... Stupid drinking laws. About time they were modified, isn't it?* PHR : USED AS C, USU + REPORT-CL, OR CONVENTION **23.2** If you say **about time too, not before time**, etc, after a statement has been made about something that has been done, you are saying in an emphatic way that you think it should have been done sooner. EG *She's finally written to me, and about time too... I shall soon be home, and not before time too.* PHR : USED AS A/C, OR CONVENTION **23.3** If you are **ahead of time**, you are earlier than you expected or needed to be. If you are **behind time**, you are later or slower than you expected or needed to be. EG *...arranging everything ahead of time.... She did the final year practical exam two years ahead of time... We're a bit behind time today.* PHR : USED AS AN A **23.4** Someone who is **ahead of** their **time**, **in advance of** their **time**, etc has new ideas a long time before other people start to think in the same way. EG *Diaghilev was brilliantly ahead of his time... His ideas were thrilling and before their time.* PHR : USED AS AN A **23.5** Someone who is **behind the times** is old-fashioned and apparently unaware of recent developments or changes. EG *The law is behind the times on a number of important issues.* PHR : USED AS AN A **23.6** If you say that something will be the case **for all time**, you mean that it will be the case forever. EG *No formula will be ideal for all time.* PHR : USED AS AN A **23.7** If you say that you will do something **for the time being**, you mean that you will do it now for a while, until it becomes possible to do something else. EG *For the time being, maybe we ought to stay with him... But for the time being there was little I can do.* PHR : USED AS AN A **23.8** If you do something **from time to time**, you do it occasionally but not at regular intervals. EG *He made me promise to write to him from time to time... From time to time she stopped and looked round.* PHR : USED AS AN A **23.9** If you say that someone or something is, for example, the best writer **of all time**, the most successful radio drama **of all time**, etc, you mean that they are the best or most successful that there has ever been. PHR : NG + PHR, WITH SUPERL **23.10** If you do something **on time**, you do it at the correct time. EG *We all caught the train and we all got here on time... I think you were almost on time.* PHR : USED AS AN A = punctual

24 keep time. 24.1 When you talk about how well a watch or clock **keeps time**, you are talking about how accurately it measures time. EG *My watch doesn't keep good time... This has kept perfect time since I got it back.* PHR : VB INFLECTS **24.2** If you **keep time** to a beat when playing a piece of music, you follow the beat to keep the correct tempo. EG *Keep time to the drum.* PHR : VB INFLECTS, USU + *to*

25 make time. 25.1 If you **make time** for a particular activity or person, you make sure that you have enough time free so that you can do the activity or spend time with the person. EG *...making time to talk over what had been done... He makes time for football, but not much else.* PHR : VB INFLECTS, USU + *for/to*-INF **25.2** If you say that you **made good time, made poor time**, etc on a journey, you are saying how long it took you compared to the length of time you expected it to take. EG *We made pretty good time on the journey up here.* PHR : VB INFLECTS

26 pass the time. 26.1 If you do something to **pass the time**, you do it because you have some time available and not because you really want to do it. EG *They read every page with no other purpose than just to pass the time.* PHR : VB INFLECTS **26.2** If you **pass the time of day** with someone, you have a short friendly conversation with them. PHR : VB INFLECTS, RECIP

27 take time. 27.1 If you say that something will **take time**, you mean that it will take a long time. EG *It would take time to get results... These things take time... It takes time for true democracy to work.* PHR : VB INFLECTS **27.2** If you **take** your **time** doing something, you do it quite slowly and do not hurry. EG *The steamer took its time... Oh, take your time, I'm in no hurry.* PHR : VB INFLECTS

28 Time is used in a number of expressions with other verbs. **28.1** Someone who **is doing time** is in prison; an informal expression. EG *He's doing time for manslaughter.* PHR : VB INFLECTS **28.2** If you say that you **have no time for** someone or something, you mean that you do not like them or approve of them; an informal expression. EG *I haven't got a lot of time for politicians.* PHR : VB INFLECTS **28.3** Someone who **moves with the times** changes in the same ways as society has changed or developed recently, and keeps up to date. EG *She should move with the times a little more.* PHR : VB INFLECTS

29 Time is also used in the following expressions. **29.1** If something happens or is done **all the time**, it happens or is done continually. EG *It rained all the time.* PHR : USED AS AN A **29.2** If you say that something has a particular quality **half the time**, you mean that it often has this quality; an informal expression. EG *He's drunk half the time... Half the time the computers were out of action.* PHR : USED AS AN A **29.3** If you talk about **old times** with someone, you talk about the past that you shared and that you both remember. EG *They talked about old times, about people they had known and what had happened to them... It's just like old times.* PHR : USED AS O/A **29.4** When you refer to **our time** or **our times**, you are referring to the present period in the history of the world. EG *...one of the great unsolved mysteries of our time... Such warfare is likely, in our times, to provide a history of defeats.* PHR : USED AS O = today **29.5** If you say that something happens **nine times out of ten** or **ninety-nine times** PHR : USED AS AN A

TIME □ This entry shows ways of referring to time in English. The following examples show how to ask or say what time it is. EG *'What time is it, Gordon?'–'Just after five.'... 'What's the time now?'–'It's quarter past.'... 'Can you tell me the time?'–'It's twenty-five past twelve.'... 'Have you got the time?'–'It is nearly one o'clock.'... 'What time does the boat leave from Weymouth?'–'At a quarter past three in the afternoon.'... The time is six forty-five... My watch says six thirty... It's five to eight and breakfast's at eight o'clock... The time was 1035 hours Greenwich Mean Time...* The following examples show other ways of mentioning time. EG *I'll be back at quarter past one... By eleven o'clock Brody was back in his office... At two o'clock in the morning Castle was still awake... You should be there no later than nine thirty... Office hours are from 9 a.m. to 6 p.m.*

four o'clock four 4 o'clock	four in the morning 4 a.m.	04:00
	four in the afternoon 4 p.m.	16:00
nine o'clock nine 9 o'clock	nine in the morning 9 a.m.	09:00
	nine in the evening nine at night 9 p.m.	21:00
twelve o'clock twelve 12 o'clock	twelve in the morning 12 a.m. midday noon	12:00
	twelve at night 12 p.m. midnight	00:00

a quarter past twelve quarter past twelve twelve fifteen a quarter after twelve	12:15 00:15
twenty-five past two twenty-five minutes past two two twenty-five twenty-five after two	02:25 14:25

half past eleven eleven-thirty half eleven half after eleven	11:30 23:30

a quarter to one quarter to one twelve forty-five a quarter of one	12:45 00:45
ten to eight ten minutes to eight seven-fifty ten of eight	07:50 19:50

…ndred, you mean that it happens on nearly …occasion. EG *Normally, nine times out of ten, …e happy to accept these results.* **29.6** If some-…ng happens **time after time, time and again**, or **time and time again**, it happens in a similar way on many occasions. EG *She had threatened time after time to leave him... Thousands of people have proved it time and time again.* PHR : USED AS AN A ⇑ often = repeatedly **29.7** If you have **the time of** your **life**, you enjoy yourself very much indeed. PHR : USED AS O **29.8** If there is **no time to lose, no time to be lost**, etc, you must hurry as fast as you can to do something. EG *We have no time to lose.* PHR : USED AS O **29.9** If you say that **it is only a matter of time** or **it is only a question of time** before something happens, you mean that it is unavoidable and will definitely happen at some future date. EG *There was nothing to worry about–it was just a matter of time... It is probably only a question of time before another crisis erupts.* CONVENTION **29.10** If you say that someone's **time is drawing near**, their **time is approaching**, their **time is up**, etc, you mean that they are going to die soon. EG *As my time draws near, it is natural that I begin to think of eternal things... ...an animal whose time is up.* PHR : VB INFLECTS ⇑ end **29.11** • **high time**: see **high**. • **once upon a time**: see **once**. • **time will tell**: see **tell**. • to **beat time**: see **beat**. • to **make the time up**: see **make up**. • to **make up for lost time**: see **make up**. • to **mark time**: see **mark**. • to **play for time**: see **play**. • to **tell the time**: see **tell**. • See also **timing, big time, small-time**.

-time combines with words such as 'part' and 'full' to refer to the proportion of a normal working week that someone is working or studying. EG *...a full-time job... 40 per cent of women work part-time... ...children on half-time schooling.* COMB : FORMS ADJ CLASSIFS OR ADVS

time and motion study, time and motion studies. A **time and motion study** is an analysis of industrial or work procedures to discover the most efficient methods of working. N COUNT

time bomb, time bombs; also spelled with a hyphen. A **time bomb** is **1** a bomb with a mechanism that causes it to explode at a particular time. N COUNT **2** something that will have a major effect on a situation or person at a later date, for example causing a lot of damage. EG *Such a shortsighted policy is a time bomb that will one day explode in America's face.* N COUNT : USU USED AS C

time-consuming. Something that is **time-consuming** takes a great deal of time. EG *...a difficult and time-consuming job.* ADJ QUALIT ⇑ lengthy

time-honoured. A **time-honoured** way of doing something is one that has been used and respected for a very long time. EG *...a time-honoured practice.* ADJ CLASSIF : ATTRIB = age-old

timekeeper /taɪmki:pə/, **timekeepers**. If you say that someone is a good **timekeeper**, a poor **timekeeper**, etc, you are saying how good or bad they are at arriving at work on time, rather than being late. N COUNT : MOD+N

time lag, time lags; also spelled with a hyphen. A **time lag** is an interval of time between one event and another related event that happens after it. EG *There is always a considerable time lag between the exam and results.* N COUNT = interim

timeless /taɪmlɪ[2]s/. Something that is **timeless** is unaffected by the passing of time or by changes in society, fashion, etc, especially with the result that it is always valued or admired; a formal word. EG *His art has something universal, something timeless and enduring from age to age.* ADJ CLASSIF = ageless, eternal

time limit, time limits; also spelled with a hyphen. A **time limit** is a date before which a particular task must be completed. EG *I had set myself a time limit of two years overseas... There is a time limit for paying the bonus.* N COUNT ⇑ maximum

timely /taɪmli[1]/. Something that is **timely** happens at just the right point in a situation, with the result that problems or difficulties are avoided or prevented. EG *...the safe and timely arrival in Europe of reinforcements.* ADJ QUALIT = opportune

time out is a break or a period of time when you do something different from the job or activity that you are involved in. EG *He took time out to chair a meeting of local officials.* N UNCOUNT = pause

timepiece /taɪmpi:s/, **timepieces**. A **timepiece** is a clock or watch or other device that measures and shows time; an old-fashioned or formal word. N COUNT

timer /taɪmə/, **timers**. A **timer** is a device that measures time, especially one that is part of a device or machine and causes it to start or stop working at specific times. EG *The timer on the cooker is broken.* • See also **egg-timer, old-timer**. N COUNT

-timer, -timers. **-timer** combines with words such as 'part' and 'full' to refer to someone who works or studies for the stated proportion of a normal working week. EG *Part-timers tend to be less well paid.* COMB : FORMS N COUNTS ⇑ worker

time scale, time scales; also spelled with a hyphen. The **time scale** of an event is the length of time during which it happens or develops. EG *...the time scale of technological development... ...the timescale over which these changes have occurred.* N COUNT ⇑ period

timeserver /taɪmsɜ:və/, **timeservers**; used showing disapproval. A **timeserver** is **1** someone who changes their opinions according to current fashion. N COUNT **2** someone who makes very little effort in their job and is just waiting until their retirement. N COUNT

time-share, time-shares. A **time-share** is the right to use holiday accommodation for a specific amount of time each year in a time-sharing system. N COUNT

time-sharing is **1** an arrangement in which different people each buy a share in a cottage or flat. Each person has the right to use that accommodation for a specific amount of time each year for their holidays. N UNCOUNT ⇑ system **2** a system by which many different people can use the same computer at the same time. N UNCOUNT

time sheet, time sheets; also spelled as one word. A **time sheet** is a card or sheet of paper that records how many hours an employee works. N COUNT ⇑ record

time signal, time signals. The **time signal** is a signal broadcast on the radio, usually consisting of six high-pitched sounds, which indicates that it is exactly one o'clock, two o'clock, etc. N COUNT = pips

time signature, time signatures. The **time signature** of a piece of music consists of two numbers written at the beginning that show how many beats in each bar there are. N COUNT

time switch, time switches. A **time switch** is a device that causes a machine to start or stop working at specific times. N COUNT

timetable /taɪmteɪbə[0]l/, **timetables, timetabling, timetabled**. **1** A **timetable** is **1.1** a plan of the times when particular activities, jobs, or parts of a larger piece of work should be done. EG *...a timetable of all events on Wednesday... ...infant feeding timetables.* N COUNT = programme **1.2** a chart in a school, college, etc that shows the times in the week at which particular subjects are taught; used also to refer to the range of subjects that a student learns or the classes that a teacher teaches. EG *...the timetable of a second year pupil at a comprehensive school... When I saw my timetable at the beginning of term I was horrified.* N COUNT ⇑ plan **1.3** a list of the times when trains, boats, buses, or aeroplanes are supposed to arrive at or depart from a particular place. EG *...railway timetables.* N COUNT = schedule

2 If you **timetable** something or **timetable** someone to do something, you write a timetable stating when something should happen or be done. EG *We were timetabled to have five hours of French a week.* V+O, OR V+O+to-INF = schedule

timeworn /taɪmwɔ:n/. Something that is **timeworn** is old or has been used a lot over a long period of time, and so is no longer interesting, in good condition, etc. EG *...a timeworn phrase.* ADJ QUALIT = hackneyed

time zone, time zones. A **time zone** is one of the areas into which the world is divided where the time is calculated as being a particular number of hours behind or ahead of Greenwich Mean Time. N COUNT ⇑ region

timid /tɪmɪd/. A person or animal that is **timid** is shy and shows no courage or self-confidence. EG *He was a tall, plump, very timid man... ...a timid young girl.* ADJ QUALIT = diffident, timorous ▸ used of actions or behaviour. EG *...a timid smile.* ◇ **timidly**. EG *I left the car and timidly rang the doorbell.* ◇ ADV WITH VB ◇ **timidity** /tɪmɪdɪti[1]/. EG *He had a terrible time in overcoming his timidity.* ◇ N UNCOUNT = shyness

timing /taɪmɪŋ/. **1 Timing** is **1.1** used to refer to the skill or action of judging the right moment in a situation, activity, sports match, etc at which to do something. EG *She displayed perfect timing and control... My timing was completely wrong.* N UNCOUNT ⇑ judgement **1.2** used to refer to the time at which something happens or is planned to happen, or to the length of time that something takes. EG *They met to consider the timing of elections... How is your timing on this job?* N UNCOUNT

2 The **timing** in a car engine is the way in which electricity is caused to reach the sparking plugs at the right time in relation to the speed of the engine. N SING : *the*+N

timorous /tɪm⁰ərəs/. A person who is **timorous** is frightened and nervous of other people, situations, etc; a fairly literary word. EG *The new occupants were too timorous to complain to the landlord about the high rent.* ADJ QUALIT = diffident, timid

timpani /tɪmpəni¹/ are kettledrums that are played in an orchestra. N PLURAL

timpanist /tɪmpənɪst/, **timpanists**. A **timpanist** is someone who plays the timpani in an orchestra. N COUNT ⇑ musician

tin /tɪn/, tins. 1 **Tin** is a soft silvery-white metal. EG *...a tin can... ...a tin kettle... Tin used to be mined throughout Cornwall.* N UNCOUNT

2 A **tin** is 2.1 a metal container which is filled with food and sealed in order to preserve the food for long periods of time; used mainly in British English. EG *Antonio would never eat anything out of a tin... ...a tin of sardines.... ...tins of tomatoes.* N COUNT/PART = can ▸ also used to refer to the food inside a tin or the amount it contains. EG *Add a tin of condensed milk.* ▸ N PART 2.2 a metal container with a lid in which things such as biscuits, cakes, or tobacco can be kept. EG *...a biscuit tin.* N COUNT ⇑ container ▸ also used to refer to the contents of a tin or the amount it contains. EG *I need another tin of paint.* ▸ N PART 2.3 a metal container used for baking things such as cakes and bread in an oven. EG *Put the dough into loaf tins... ...a cake tin.* N COUNT

tincture /tɪŋktʃə/, **tinctures**; a formal or old-fashioned word. A **tincture** is a medicine consisting of alcohol and a small amount of a drug. N COUNT

tinder /tɪndə/ is small pieces of something dry, especially wood or grass, that burns easily and can be used for lighting a fire. N UNCOUNT

tinderbox /tɪndəbɒks/, **tinderboxes**. A **tinderbox** was a box that was used for holding tinder, especially one with a flint and steel to help light the tinder. N COUNT

tine /taɪn/, **tines**. The **tines** of a fork, rake, or deer's antler are the long pointed parts; a formal or technical word. N COUNT = prong

tinfoil /tɪnfɔɪl/ is a shiny sheet of metal as thin as paper, which is used for wrapping food in. N UNCOUNT = baking foil

ting /tɪŋ/, **tings, tinging, tinged**. 1 A **ting** is a single high-pitched ringing sound like that which is made when you tap a small bell. EG *The clock struck a quarter. Ting, ting, ting.* N COUNT, OR EXCLAM = ping

2 When a bell **tings** or when you **ting** it, it makes a single high-pitched ringing sound. EG *The bell tinged once.* V-ERG ⇑ ring

ting-a-ling /tɪŋ ə lɪŋ/. When you want to describe in a childish way the sound a small bell makes, you say it goes **ting-a-ling**. ADV WITH VB, OR EXCLAM

tinge /tɪndʒ/, **tinges, tingeing, tinged**. 1 A **tinge** is 1.1 a small amount of a particular colour that you notice in something. EG *The sky had a greenish tinge... ...a tinge of brown.* N COUNT/PART 1.2 a small amount of a quality or feeling. EG *Her politics were conservative with a tinge of liberalism... This gave our romance a gloomy tinge.* N COUNT : MOD+N, OR N PART+N UNCOUNT = touch

2 To **tinge** something with a particular colour or to **tinge** something a particular colour means to colour it very slightly. EG *The sunset tinged the lake with pink... The moon's rays tinged the mountains silver.* V+O+A *(with)*, OR V+O+C (ADJ COLOUR)

tinged /tɪndʒd/. 1 If something is **tinged** with a particular colour, it has a small amount of that colour in it. EG *Her eyes were slightly tinged with red.* ADJ QUALIT : PRED+*with* = touched

2 Something that is **tinged** with a particular feeling or quality has or shows a small amount of that feeling or quality. EG *Her voice was tinged with regret.* ADJ QUALIT : PRED+*with* = touched

tingle /tɪŋg⁰əl/, **tingles, tingling, tingled**. 1 When a part of your body **tingles**, you feel a slight prickling or stinging feeling in it. EG *The side of my face was still tingling from the blow she'd given me.* V = smart ◇ **tingling**. EG *...a sharp tingling in her fingers.* ◇ N UNCOUNT

2 A **tingle** is a slight prickling or stinging feeling in a part of your body. N COUNT : USU SING

3 When you **tingle** with a feeling such as excitement or shock, you feel it very strongly but usually do not express or show it. EG *I was tingling with excitement.* V : USU+*with*

tin god, tin gods. If you describe someone as a **tin god**, you mean they are thought to be far more important than they really are; a fairly informal expression. N COUNT

tin hat, tin hats. A **tin hat** is a metal hat that soldiers sometimes wear to protect their heads. N COUNT ⇑ helmet

tinker /tɪŋkə/, **tinkers, tinkering, tinkered**. 1 A **tinker** is a person who travels from place to place mending metal pots and pans or doing other small repair jobs. N COUNT

2 If you call a small child a **tinker**, you mean that they have done something naughty but you are not really angry with them; an informal use. EG *You little tinker!–Look at the mess you've made!* N COUNT : ALSO VOC = scamp

3 If you **tinker** with something, you try to repair it by making a lot of small alterations and adjustments to it. EG *Who's been tinkering with my record player?* V : USU+A *(with)* = fiddle ▸ used as a noun. EG *I just want to have a tinker with my car.* ▸ N SING WITH DET

tinkle /tɪŋkə⁰l/, **tinkles, tinkling, tinkled**. 1 If something **tinkles**, it makes a sound like a small bell ringing or like thin glass breaking and falling to the ground. EG *I could hear bells tinkling... His glasses fell off and tinkled on the rocks.* V = clink ▸ used as a noun. EG *The telephone gave a tinkle... ...the tinkle of shattered glass.* ▸ N COUNT : USU +*of*

2 If you **give** someone **a tinkle**, you call them on the telephone; an informal expression. EG *I'll give you a tinkle later on tonight.* PHR : VB INFLECTS = phone

tinned /tɪnd/. **Tinned** food is food that has been preserved by being sealed in a tin. EG *...tinned peas... ...tinned salmon.* ADJ CLASSIF = canned

tinny /tɪni¹/, **tinnier, tinniest**. 1 A sound that is **tinny** has a high-pitched irritating quality like that of thin metal being shaken. EG *One hears bursts of tinny pop music from teenagers' handbags.* ADJ QUALIT ⇑ metallic

2 Something such as a cheap car that is **tinny** is made of thin metal and is of poor quality. ADJ QUALIT = shoddy

tin opener, tin openers; also spelled with a hyphen. A **tin opener** is a device that you use for opening tins of food. N COUNT = can opener

Tin Pan Alley is used to refer to the life and activities of song writers, performers, and agents who are involved in jazz, rock, and pop music; an informal expression. N UNCOUNT ⇑ show business

tinpot /tɪnpɒt/. A **tinpot** country or government is considered to be inferior and unimportant; used showing disapproval. EG *...a tinpot little dictatorship.* ADJ CLASSIF : ATTRIB = puny

tinsel /tɪnsəl/ consists of long pieces of thread with small pieces of shiny metallic material attached to them. It is used as a decoration, especially at Christmas. EG *We ran out of tinsel before we'd finished decorating the tree.* N UNCOUNT

tint /tɪnt/, **tints, tinted, tinting**. 1 A **tint** is 1.1 a small amount of a particular colour that you can see in something. EG *His eyes had a yellow tint... The soils have a rusty red tint.* N COUNT : WITH ADJ COLOUR = tinge 1.2 a colour that has some white mixed in it. EG *...pastel tints.* N COUNT 1.3 a weak dye used for changing the colour of your hair. EG *She gave me instructions on how to apply the tint.* N UNCOUNT/COUNT = rinse

2 If you **tint** your hair, you change its colour by adding a weak dye to it. EG *He acquired a preparation for tinting his hair chestnut brown.* V+O ▸ used as a noun. EG *I'm calling in at the hairdresser's for a tint.* ▸ N COUNT = rinse

tinted /tɪntɪ²d/. Something such as glass that is **tinted** is coloured, especially with a pale or weak colour. EG *...the suffused tinted light from the coloured glass of aisle windows... ...tinted lenses.* ADJ CLASSIF

tiny /taɪni¹/, **tinier, tiniest**. 1 Something that is **tiny** is extremely small. EG *...tiny shells, the size of your little finger nail... ...the tiny little room at the end of the flat... He was a tiny bit frightened of them.* ADJ QUALIT = teeny

2 A **tiny** child is very young and therefore very small. EG *Being a mother of tiny children is more exhausting than any other job.* ADJ CLASSIF ⇑ little

tip /tɪp/, **tips, tipping, tipped**. 1 The **tip** of something long and narrow is the end of it. EG *He was suspended by his finger tips from a window frame... The animal plucks fruit and leaves from the tips of branches... ...a chain of islands off the southern tip of South America.* N COUNT : IF+ PREP THEN *of*

2 If you **tip** an object, you move it so that it is leaning to one side and no longer standing up straight. EG *He tipped his soup bowl towards himself... He was sitting with his chair tipped back against the wall.* V+O+A

3 If you **tip** something somewhere, you pour it there quickly and in an uncontrolled way. EG *He tipped the contents of the rucksack out on to the floor... Claud pulled the bag out of his pocket and tipped a pile of raisins into her hand.* V+O+A

4 To **tip** rubbish or other things you do not want means to get rid of them by leaving them somewhere; used in British English. EG *The council is trying to stop people tipping rubbish in the canal... No tipping.* V OR V+O : USU+A = dump

5 If you **tip** someone such as a waiter, you give them an amount of money in order to thank them for their services. EG *A lot of people seem to panic when deciding how much to tip... I tipped the chauffeur.* V OR V+O ⇑ pay

6 If a person **is tipped** for success or for a particular job, someone who is considered to know about these things has suggested that they will be successful or that they will get the job. EG *Once again he was widely tipped for a ministerial post... He has been tipped to succeed Mrs Thatcher... These two men are widely tipped as future contestants for the leadership.* V+O : USU PASS+A/to-INF ⇑ consider

7 A **tip** is a place where rubbish is dumped, especially household rubbish or a large pile of waste from coal mining; used in British English. EG *You could see nothing but wrecked cars and rubbish tips.* N COUNT

8 If you refer to a building or room as a **tip**, you mean that it is very untidy; an informal British English use. EG *This place is a real tip!* N COUNT = pigsty

9 A **tip** is also **9.1** an amount of money that you give to someone such as a waiter or a taxi driver, in order to thank them for their services. EG *Most restaurants now include the tip in the price of the meal... The woman gave me a dollar tip.* N COUNT ⇑ gift **9.2** a small but useful piece of advice. EG *He consulted books by well-known tennis players for tips on basic techniques... The book gives some good central heating tips.* N COUNT **9.3** a piece of advice that you give to someone about the likely outcome of a horse race when they are going to bet money on the race. EG *What's your tip for the Derby?* N COUNT

10 If someone **tips the scales** at a particular weight, they weigh that amount; an informal expression. EG *He tipped the scales at a hundred and sixty pounds.* PHR : VB INFLECTS = weigh

11 If something **tips the scales** or **tips the balance**, it gives someone a slight advantage. EG *The scales could well be tipped towards the opposition by the time the election starts... The party can often find the balance tipped in its favour.* PHR : VB INFLECTS

12 If you **tip** someone **the wink**, you let them know quietly or secretly that something has happened, so that they can take some immediate action; an informal expression. EG *I'll tip you the wink when it's safe to come in.* PHR : VB INFLECTS ⇑ inform

13 If you say that **it is tipping** or that **it is tipping down**, you mean that it is raining very heavily; an informal expression. EG *It's really tipping down... It's tipping with rain.* PHR : AUX INFLECTS

14 If you say that a word, expression, etc is **on the tip of your tongue**, you mean that you cannot remember the word, expression, etc, but that you might suddenly remember it at any moment. EG *I'm just trying to remember his name. It's on the tip of my tongue.* PHR : USED AS AN A

15 If you say that something is **the tip of the iceberg**, you mean that it is the small part of a problem that is obvious, when the problem is much more serious and widespread than it seems to be. EG *But this, of course, is only the tip of the iceberg.* PHR : USED AS C

tip off. If you **tip** someone **off**, you tell them that something has happened or that it is going to happen. EG *The burglars were tipped off by a lookout and escaped.* ● See also **tip-off**. PHRASAL VB : V+O+ADV = forewarn

tip over. When you **tip** something **over** or when it **tips over**, it falls over or turns over. EG *The last of the glasses broke when Sean tipped over the sideboard... She tipped the pan over and a dozen fish flopped out... The boat transporting them had somehow tipped over.* PHRASAL VB : V-ERG+ADV = overturn

tip up. If you **tip** a bucket, glass, etc **up**, you make it lean to one side so that a liquid begins to pour out of it. EG *She tipped up the sherry glass... I had to hold the can to his mouth and tip it up as his head went back.* PHRASAL VB : V+O+ADV = tilt

tip-off, tip-offs. A **tip-off** is a piece of information that you give to someone, usually as a warning that something is going to happen. EG *The building was evacuated as the result of a tip-off.* N COUNT

tipped /tɪpt/. 1 Something that is **tipped** has a tip made of a particular substance or a tip covered with a particular material. EG *They hunted in the woods with spears tipped with stone blades... ...a gold tipped fountain pen.* ADJ CLASSIF : MOD+ADJ, OR ADJ+*with*

2 A tipped **cigarette** has a filter on the end which the smoke passes through when you breathe it in. ADJ CLASSIF

tippet /tɪpɪt/, **tippets**. A **tippet** is a long piece of fur, often made from the whole skin of a small animal, which a woman wears around her shoulders. N COUNT ⇑ cape

tipple /tɪpəl/, **tipples, tippling, tippled**. 1 In informal English, a person's **tipple** is the alcoholic drink that they usually drink. EG *'What's your tipple?' said Superintendent Garroway.* N COUNT

2 If you **tipple**, you drink alcoholic drinks quite often but not in large quantities. V : NO IMPER

tippler /tɪplə/, **tipplers**. A **tippler** is a person who drinks alcoholic drinks quite often but not in large quantities. EG *He's a bit of a tippler.* N COUNT ⇑ drinker

tipster /tɪpstə/, **tipsters**. A **tipster** is someone who tells you, usually in exchange for money, which horses they think will win particular races, so that you can bet money on the horses. N COUNT

tipsy /tɪpsi/, **tipsier, tipsiest**. Someone who is **tipsy** is slightly drunk. EG *The wine had made Barton a trifle tipsy.* ADJ QUALIT = tiddly

tiptoe /tɪptəʊ/, **tiptoes, tiptoeing, tiptoed**. 1 If you **tiptoe** somewhere, you walk there very quietly on your toes. EG *He knocked softly on the door and tiptoed into the room.* V : USU+A ⇑ creep

2 If you do something **on tiptoe**, you do it standing or walking on your toes. EG *They stretched their arms and stood on tiptoe... He was very careful and walked on tiptoe.* PHR : USED AS AN A

tip-top; also spelled as one word. If you say that something is in **tip-top** condition, order, etc, you mean that it is in excellent condition, order, etc. EG *My car is in tip-top condition at the moment... He kept his palace in tip-top shape.* ADJ CLASSIF : USU ATTRIB = perfect, first-rate

tirade /taɪreɪd/, **tirades**. A **tirade** is a long angry speech in which you criticize someone or something; a fairly formal word. EG *He launched into a familiar tirade against the new policies.* N COUNT = diatribe

tire /taɪə/, **tires, tiring, tired**. 1 If something **tires** you, it makes you use a lot of energy, with the result that you want to rest or sleep. EG *She was always rushing around, doing things that would tire women half her age... Most mothers tire easily the first few weeks at home with the baby.* V OR V-ERG = exhaust

2 If you **tire** of something, you become bored with it and no longer interested in it. EG *Father would simply stop talking when he tired of my questions.* V+A (*of*) = weary

3 See also **tyre**.

tire out. If something **tires** you **out**, it makes you exhausted. PHRASAL VB : V+O+ADV

tired /taɪəd/. 1 If you are **tired**, you feel that you want to rest or sleep. EG *I'm sure you must be tired after cycling all that distance... He was getting very tired... He looked old and tired... Edgar was too tired even to eat.* ADJ QUALIT = weary, fatigued ◇ **tiredness**. EG *Tiredness overwhelmed me.* ◇ N UNCOUNT ● If you are **tired out**, you are exhausted. EG *By the time we got there, we were tired out.* ● PHR : USED AS C = worn out

2 If you say that a person's voice, eyes, etc are **tired**, you mean that they show that the person needs rest or sleep. EG *'I'm hungry,' said the little boy in a tired voice... Her eyes were tired but resolute.* ADJ QUALIT = exhausted

3 If you are **tired** of something, you are bored with it and no longer interested in it. EG *Judy was tired of quarrelling with her husband... He was finally getting tired of the student Revolution.* ● **sick and tired**: see **sick**. ADJ QUALIT : PRED+*of* = sick

4 Something that is **tired** is **4.1** rather old and no longer functioning well, often because it has been used too much in the past. EG *...a tired, worn-out, elderly organization... ...our tired old car.* ADJ QUALIT : ATTRIB **4.2** very familiar and therefore no longer very interesting. EG *The tired topics of equality and birth-control came up yet again... ...her dull, tired, very ordinary marriage.* ADJ QUALIT : ATTRIB ⇑ boring = stale

tireless /taɪəlɪ²s/. A **tireless** person puts a lot of effort into something and seems to have no need of rest. EG *She is a tireless promoter of new causes.* ADJ CLASSIF = indefatigable ◇ **tirelessly**. EG *The organization works tirelessly to help solve the problems of local peasants.* ◇ ADV WITH VB

tiresome /taɪəsəm/. A person or thing that is **tiresome** makes you feel annoyed, irritated, or bored. EG *She can be a very tiresome child at times... ...a tiresome obstacle to be overcome... The arrival of the baby made his life complicated and tiresome.* ADJ QUALIT = irritating

tiring /taɪərɪŋ/. Something that is **tiring** makes you tired so that you want to rest or sleep. EG *We should have an early night after such a tiring day... Standing still for any length of time can be tiring.* ADJ QUALIT = fatiguing

tiro /taɪrəʊ/, **tiros**. see **tyro**.

tissue /tɪsju:, tɪʃu:/, **tissues**. 1 **Tissue** is a group of cells in an animal or plant that are similar to each other and that have the same function. EG *Nuclear* N MASS *radiation can attack the cells in living tissue... ...the scar tissue left by a wound... The organs and tissues of the body are extremely complex.*

2 Tissue or **tissue paper** is thin paper that is used especially for wrapping things that are easily damaged, such as objects made of glass or china. EG *The man wrapped them up for her carefully in tissue paper... ...a big bunch of flowers done up in white tissue.* N UNCOUNT

3 A **tissue** is a small square piece of thin soft paper that you can use as a handkerchief, kitchen cloth, etc. It can be thrown away after you have used it. EG *Have you got a tissue?... There was a box of tissues in the back window of the car... It's more hygienic to use disposable paper tissues.* N COUNT

4 A **tissue of lies** is a totally false story or series of false statements. EG *Their allegations were a tissue of lies and fabrication.* PHR : USED AS C/O ⇑ fabrication

tit /tɪt/, **tits**. **1** A **tit** is **1.1** a small European bird that eats insects and seeds. There are several kinds of tit. • See also **blue tit**. N COUNT **1.2** a person who you consider to be stupid; an informal use. N COUNT : ALSO VOC

2 A woman's **tits** are her breasts; an informal and rather rude use. N COUNT : USU PL

3 Something that is **tit for tat** is something unpleasant that you do to someone in return for something unpleasant that they have done to you. EG *I expect we'll get the usual tit for tat response... It was just tit for tat, after all.* ADJ CLASSIF ⇑ retaliation

titan /taɪtən/, **titans**. A **titan** is a person who is very big and strong or very important; a fairly formal word. EG *They stand up like titans against their oppressors... He was a titan among pygmies.* N COUNT ⇑ giant

titanic /taɪtænɪk/. Something that is **titanic** is very big or important. EG *He was a titanic force in the history of modernism.* ADJ CLASSIF = monumental

titanium /taɪteɪnɪəm/is a strong white metal used in making lightweight alloys for machine parts. N UNCOUNT

titbit /tɪtbɪt/, **titbits**. A **titbit** is **1** a small piece of gossip or scandal. EG *The letter was grasped by the National Review as a succulent titbit for its readers.* N COUNT

2 a small delicious piece of food. EG *What nice titbits have you got in your pockets for me?* N COUNT = delicacy

titchy /tɪtʃi^1/, **titchier, titchiest**. Something that is **titchy** is extremely small; an informal word. EG *You're not dying. It's only a titchy little scratch.* ADJ QUALIT = tiny

titfer /tɪtfə/, **titfers**. A **titfer** is a man's hat; an old-fashioned, informal word, used in British English. N COUNT

tithe /taɪð/, **tithes**. A **tithe** was a fixed amount of money or goods that people used to give regularly in order to support churches, priests, charities, etc. N COUNT ⇑ contribution

titillate /tɪtɪleɪt/, **titillates, titillating, titillated**. If something **titillates** someone, it pleases and excites them, especially in a sexual way. EG *The film is intended to inform, not to titillate.* V OR V+O = tease

◊ **titillation** /tɪtɪleɪʃə^{0}n/. EG *...every cliché, embellishment and titillation known to romantic fiction.* ◊ N UNCOUNT

title /taɪtə^{0}l/, **titles**. **1** The **title** of a book, play, piece of music, etc is the name given to it by the person who wrote it or composed it, or the name by which it is usually known. EG *He wrote a book with the title 'The Castle'... 'Walk under Ladders' is the title of her new play.* N COUNT

2 A **title** is also a book or periodical; used especially by publishers and booksellers. EG *He had a library of 100,000 titles... In the 1960s Europe was producing 120,000 titles a year.* N COUNT : USU PL ⇑ publication

3 Someone's **title** is **3.1** a name such as Lord, Lady, Sir, Princess, etc, used before their own name in order to show their social rank. See □ at TITLE. EG *There were a lot of gentlemen in tweed suits, some with titles and some merely rich.* N COUNT **3.2** a name such as Mr, Mrs, Doctor, Professor, etc, used before their own name in order to show their status or profession. See □ at TITLE. EG *A lot of academics carry the title of professor.* N COUNT **3.3** a name that describes their job or status in an organization. EG *The person in charge usually has a title of some sort like Administration Manager.* N COUNT = designation

4 A **title** is also the position of champion in a sports competition. Usually a person keeps a title until someone else defeats them. EG *He's next in line for a crack at the title... We had beaten Cornell and taken the title.* N COUNT

5 Title is the legal ownership of something, especially land or property. EG *The landlords had no title to the land, no right to be occupying it.* N UNCOUNT = entitlement

6 A **title** is also a document that gives you the legal ownership of something, especially land or property. EG *The land was divided into small private plots with negotiable freehold titles.* N COUNT = deeds

TITLE □ In this dictionary TITLE is used in the grammar notes beside entries to indicate that the word can be used as part of a person's title. A title is a word or phrase which refers to a person's place in a profession (for example, ***Dr.*** *Smith)* or in society (for example, ***Sir*** *John Smith* or ***Lord*** *Oakfield).* There are two ways in which TITLE is used in this dictionary. **1** Words which are only used when you are talking or writing to or about someone are described in the grammar notes as N IN TITLES. Examples are **Mr** and **Highness**. EG *...**Mr** Castle... I've invited **Mr** Jones to dinner this evening... ...Her Royal **Highness**, Princess Margaret... Greetings to Your Royal **Highness**.* When words such as *your, his,* and *her* are used in titles, they are described in the grammar notes as DET POSS: USED IN TITLES. **2** Words which can be used both as count nouns and as titles are described in the grammar notes as N COUNT: ALSO IN TITLES. Examples are **bishop** and **queen**. EG *How do **bishops** get chosen?... ...the **Bishop** of Lewes... ...**Bishop** John Robinson... The actors were dressed like kings and **queens**... ...**Queen** Victoria... ...a statue of **Queen** Anne.*

titled /taɪtə^{0}ld/. Someone who is **titled** has a name such as Lord, Lady, Sir, Princess, etc before their own name showing their high social rank. EG *...titled ladies.* ADJ CLASSIF

title-holder, title-holders. The **title-holder** is the person who holds the position of champion in a sports competition that is held regularly. EG *He's been the title-holder for the last three years.* N COUNT

title role, title roles. The **title role** or **title part** in a play or a film is the role referred to in the name of the play or film. EG *...an actor best known for the title role in 'The Eddie Cantor Story'.* N COUNT

titter /tɪtə/, **titters, tittering, tittered**. If you **titter**, you give a nervous little laugh, especially when you are embarrassed about something. EG *The audience tittered... Whenever a critic looked at it, he would stand and titter.* V OR V+QUOTE = giggle, snigger ▸ used as a noun. EG *He allowed himself a little titter at my expense.* ▸ N COUNT = snigger

tittle-tattle /tɪtə^{0}l tætə^{0}l/; also spelled as two words. **Tittle-tattle** is the gossip or unimportant things that a group of people talk about. EG *...the tittle-tattle about publishing.* N UNCOUNT = talk

titular /tɪtjə^{4}lə/. A **titular** job or position has a name that makes it seem important, although the person who has it is not really important or powerful. EG *...men who occupy the seats of titular power in these countries... ...the titular head of state.* ADJ CLASSIF : ATTRIB = so-called, nominal

tizzy /tɪzi^1/. If you **get in a tizzy** or **get into a tizzy**, you get excited, worried, or nervous about something, especially something that is not important; an informal expression. EG *He got in a tizzy because the car wouldn't start... Don't get into a tizzy.* PHR : VB INFLECTS

TM is an abbreviation for **1** 'trademark'. **2** 'transcendental meditation'.

TNT is a powerful explosive substance. N UNCOUNT

to /tə, tuː/. **To** is used as a preposition and adverb, and also as part of an infinitive. The prepositional and adverbial uses are given in paragraphs 1 to 18. The infinitive uses are given in paragraph 19. **1 To** is used indicating movement, direction, or position, in the following ways: **1.1** indicating the direction in which someone or something moves or the place where someone goes. EG *I'm going with her to Australia... We'll drive to the top of the next hill... The children have gone to school... He thought that he might go to a concert.* PREP **1.2** indicating the direction in which you are looking or pointing, or the direction in which something is facing. EG *He was pointing to an oil tanker somewhere on the horizon... He stood with his back to the wall.* PREP = towards **1.3** indicating that something is touching a part of your body, or that you are holding something against your body. EG *My friends clapped their hands to their foreheads and groaned theatrically... He clutched the parcel to his chest.* PREP **1.4** indicating where something is tied, attached, etc. EG *I was planning to tie him to a tree.* PREP **1.5** indicating the position of something or someone in relation to something or someone else. EG *My father was in the middle, with me to his left carrying the umbrella... To the west lies Gloucester... To one side, he could see the block of luxury flats.* PREP

2 If you say that something moves **to and fro** or that someone goes **to and fro**, you mean that **2.1** the thing PHR : USED AS AN or person moves repeatedly from one place to another and back again. EG *Armies marched to and fro across the great land mass... He spends his life going to and fro between his living quarters and his place of work.* A = back and forth **2.2** the thing or person moves repeatedly and continuously from side to side or from front to back. EG *She rocked herself to and fro in amusement.* PHR : USED AS AN A ● See also **to-ing and fro-ing**.

3 To is also used indicating **3.1** who an action, for example giving something or speaking, is directed towards. EG *I had to pay a pound a year to an old woman... He showed the letter to Barbara... She had given German lessons to a leading industrialist.* PREP **3.2** the thing towards which an action is directed, or the thing which is affected by an action. EG *We don't do repairs to farm machines... She gave a tiny sigh and did something to her smartly arranged hair... The bad weather resulted in severe frost damage to Brazil's coffee plantations.* PREP

4 To is also used in the following ways indicating a limit or the final point in a process, for example a change: **4.1** indicating what something or someone becomes or changes into. EG *It had almost turned to dust over the years... We have now switched over to computers... It is impossible to translate satisfactorily from one language to another... The vase was smashed to pieces... It drove me to distraction and despair.* PREP **4.2** indicating movement or development towards a particular state or condition. EG *...her rapid rise to fame... ...their return to reality... The settlement brought a radical government to power.* PREP : USU+N UNCOUNT **4.3** indicating an amount or level that is reached. EG *Unemployment in the town has risen to almost 20 per cent... The danger is that a conventional conflict might escalate to a nuclear confrontation... She had lived to a great age.* PREP **4.4** indicating that something happens until the time, date, amount, etc mentioned. EG *Breakfast was from 9 to 10 in the morning... The job will take anything from two to five weeks... This scale goes from zero to forty.* PREP : USU NUM +PREP+NUM

5 If you say that something is true **to** a particular person, you are saying what that person's opinion is or what their feelings are about something. EG *To an outsider, the financial dealings of the City are a mystery... To me it didn't seem necessary... It began to make sense to me.* PREP = for

6 If you say that something happens **to** someone's surprise, relief, horror, etc, you mean that feelings of surprise, relief, horror, etc are caused by what happens. EG *To his relief he heard Cynthia's voice... To his great surprise he was offered both jobs... To my horror, there was a most enormous laugh from the back of the room.* PREP : USU+POSS +N UNCOUNT

7 In expressions of time, if you say that it is a particular number of minutes **to** an hour, you mean that that number of minutes remain before it will be the hour mentioned: see ☐ at TIME. EG *It's five to eight and breakfast's at eight o'clock... We must leave at ten to.* PREP : NUM+ PREP+NUM, OR ADV : NUM+ADV

8 If you say that there is a particular amount of time **to** an event or date, you mean that that amount of time remains before that event or date. EG *Only ten shopping days to Christmas... It's two days to D-day.* PREP = until

9 If you say that someone works **to** someone, you mean that they work for them. EG *For nearly five years he was dresser to Donald Wolfit... She is ballet mistress to the Stroganov company... She had acted as interpreter to a group of Hungarian judges.* PREP

10 If you drink a toast **to** someone or dedicate something **to** someone, you do it in their honour. EG *'A toast. To absent friends.'... The statue is a memorial to Queen Victoria.* PREP

11 If you say that there are a particular number of units of measure **to** a larger unit of measure, you mean that that number of smaller units makes up the larger unit. EG *There are 1760 yards to the mile.* PREP = in

12 If you push or shut a door **to**, you close it, but do not shut it completely. ADV AFTER VB

13 If you say that something is **to** someone's advantage, liking, etc, you mean that it is in accordance with it. EG *It's to your own advantage... They are interested in harnessing the power of computers to their own ends... I hope the room is to your liking.* PREP : USU+POSS +N ⇑ for

14 If you say that something happens **to** music or **to** a particular reaction, you mean that the music or reaction accompanies or happens at the same time as the thing mentioned. EG *They danced to the regular beat of the drums... To a chorus of laughter the President left the room... He walked off to cheers and loud applause.* PREP

15 To is also used **15.1** with certain nouns and adjectives showing that a following noun is related to them as a subject or object. EG *She was an inspiration to all the world... Jim watched my reaction to all of this... The answer to your question is unexpectedly simple... Governments came and went, none sympathetic to his ideas... She made allegations similar to those made by Mr Overmeyer... He is heir to the throne.* PREP : N/ADJ+ PREP **15.2** with certain verbs to indicate that a following noun is related to them as a subject or object. EG *She compared the meetings to a campaign... I think we'd better stick to business... ...an office block devoted to administration... One thing leads to another... She listened to a flute being played.* PREP : VB+PREP **15.3** in phrasal verbs, for example 'see to', 'come to'. See individual verb and phrasal verb entries.

16 You use the expression **from** one thing **to** another thing when you are giving two extreme examples of something so that you can emphasize the scope or range of what you are saying. EG *I do everything, from washing up dishes to putting out the cat at night... We have branches in most of the cities of the world, from Yokohama to York.* PHR : USED AS AN A

17 If you say that someone moves **from** place **to** place, you mean that they move repeatedly from one of the places mentioned to another. EG *I've spent years going from town to town... She had gone round from place to place asking for a job... He's one of these journalists who hop from trouble-spot to trouble-spot on the globe.* PHR : USED AS AN A

18 If you say that there is **nothing to it** or **not much to it**, you are saying how simple or easy you think something is. EG *There's nothing to it... That was all there was to it.* PHR

19 To is used as part of the infinitive of a verb in the following ways. The verb part of the infinitive can be omitted in some cases when the context makes it clear what you are referring to. **19.1** indicating what the aim or intention of an action is. EG *To answer this question, we must look more closely at the facts... People would stroll down the path to admire the garden... They could use these bombs to destroy airfields and oil depots.* *to*+INF **19.2** indicating that one action leads to another action, which happens at the same time. For example, the first example means, 'when she looked up she found Tony standing there'. EG *She looked up to find Tony standing there... He pulled back the curtain to admit dull wet daylight.* *to*+INF **19.3** indicating that something must happen, or that it did happen. EG *I am to complete it by Monday... He was to become one of Europe's most famous writers.* *to*+INF **19.4** forming the subject or complement of another verb. EG *To exclude religion is to deny it... It was like medicine to be able to laugh like that again... It costs about 150 pounds a week to keep someone in prison.* *to*+INF **19.5** in exclamations, when you are emphasizing that you feel a very strong emotion, for example a desire or wish, or a regret or disappointment. EG *But then to be let down like that, oh it's so unfair... At home we both said, 'Oh, to get away from here!'* *to*+INF **19.6** after certain verbs. See individual verbs for detailed accounts of the way in which they are used. EG *The rocket soon begins to accelerate upwards... Harris tried to stop the operation half-way through... 'Let's be explicit.'–'I don't want to'... Barbara's asked me to come and stay here over the weekend.* VB+*to*+INF **19.7** after certain nouns. See individual nouns for detailed accounts of the way in which they are used. EG *The most difficult thing had been the decision to act... She actually pined away–lost her will to live.* N+*to*+INF **19.8** after words such as 'how', 'which', 'where', 'what', 'when', 'who', and 'whether', and the nouns which have these meanings, for example 'way' and 'place'. EG *I never know what to do with rotten cabbage... I can't even remember any English or how to divide or multiply... They wouldn't know who to ask... That's not the way to do it; why don't you turn it round?* WH+*to*+INF **19.9** relating a noun to a verb as the verb's subject or object. This construction can be replaced by a relative clause using 'that', 'which', or 'who'. EG *Some of us have got work to do... I haven't got money to throw around... We should have some milk to sell... He had no time to dread the meeting.* N+*to*+INF **19.10** to relate an adjective to ADJ+*to*+INF a following verb in order to show a particular quality that something or someone has. EG *These cars were simple to design, cheap to build, easy to assemble... You may find the claim form difficult to fill in... They were lovely to watch.* **19.11** in constructions with 'too' and 'enough' in order to say why it is easy or difficult for the action described by the verb to occur. EG *My fingers were too clumsy to handle it properly... He was too proud to apologize... It cannot produce enough heat to activate the electrons.* too/enough+ADJ/ADV+to+INF **19.12** showing the feeling that you have about the action that the following verb describes. EG *He was very happy to accept their invitation... In the past the US has been reluctant to accept their proposals... Scientists were excited to discover a small, potato-shaped satellite.* ADJ+to+INF **19.13** in polite greetings or apologies, where you are expressing how you feel about the action of the verb. EG *Pleased to meet you... Sorry to keep you waiting... It was lovely to hear from you.* ADJ+to+INF+you: CONVENTION **19.14** relating an adjective to the action of a following verb, in an impersonal construction. EG *It is dangerous for me to drink an entire cup of coffee... It was impossible not to admire her speed and accuracy... This is difficult for us to accept.* ADJ+to+INF **19.15** with superlatives, in the place of a relative clause. For example 'the first person to climb Everest' means the first person who climbed or who has climbed Everest. EG *He was their last representative to die on the hunger strike.* SUPERL+to+INF **19.16** when you are commenting on the statement that you are going to make, either to indicate that you are being honest, brief, etc or that you are summing up, concluding, giving an example, etc. EG *To be honest, we were glad that he was there... To tell you the truth, Phil, I don't have too much confidence in him... To sum up, my contention is that these people must be stopped... To take a very mundane example the horse has been replaced by the tractor.* to+INF **19.17** in newspaper headlines to indicate that an event is going to happen. EG *Miners to meet T.U.C. again in new search for negotiations.* to+INF ⇑ will

20 Compare 'in order to': see **order**.

toad /təʊd/, **toads**. A **toad** is a creature which is similar to a frog but which has a drier skin and lives less in the water. EG *All frogs and toads blink when they swallow.* N COUNT ⇑ amphibian

toad-in-the-hole is a cooked dish made with sausages. The sausages are baked in a mixture of beaten egg, milk, and flour; used in British English. N UNCOUNT

toadstool /təʊdstu:l/, **toadstools**. A **toadstool** is a fungus that you cannot eat because it is poisonous. EG *I learned at an early age to distinguish toadstools from mushrooms.* N COUNT

toady /təʊdi¹/, **toadies**. A **toady** is someone who flatters and is pleasant towards people who are important or in authority in the hope of being liked by them and of getting some advantage from them; used showing disapproval. N COUNT = crawler

toast /təʊst/, **toasts, toasting, toasted**. **1 Toast** is bread which has been cut into slices and made brown and crisp by cooking at a high temperature. EG *Lally was spreading marmalade on a piece of toast... I like baked beans on toast.* N UNCOUNT

2 When you **toast** bread, you cook it at a high temperature in a toaster or under a grill so that it becomes brown and crisp. EG *You can toast sliced bread while it's still frozen.* V+O

3 If you **toast** yourself or a part of your body, you sit in front of a fire so that you feel pleasantly warm. EG *There he was, toasting himself by the fire.* V+O (NG/REFL) = roast

4 When you drink a **toast** to someone, you wish them success or good health, and then drink some wine or another alcoholic drink as a symbolic gesture. EG *...a toast to the chef... It was an old fisherman's custom to drink a toast to the dead... He raised his glass in a toast.* N COUNT: USU a+N ⇑ tribute

5 When you **toast** someone, you show your respect for them or wish them success by saying their name, and then drinking some wine or other alcoholic drink. EG *As a diplomat he had often toasted the Kaiser... I was toasted by him most eloquently at the dinner.* V+O = drink to

6 If someone is the **toast** of a place, company, etc, they are very popular and greatly admired, for example because they have done something particularly useful or successful. EG *She's the toast of the town.* N SING: the+N+of

toaster /təʊstə/, **toasters**. A **toaster** is an electric device which is used toast slices of bread. N COUNT

toasting fork, toasting forks; also spelled with a hyphen. A **toasting fork** is a fork with a long handle that is used for toasting slices of bread by a fire. N COUNT ⇑ utensil

toastmaster /təʊstmɑ:stə/, **toastmasters**. A **toastmaster** is the person who proposes toasts and who introduces the speakers at formal receptions and dinners. N COUNT ⇑ official

toast rack, toast racks; also spelled with a hyphen. A **toast rack** is an object that is designed to hold pieces of toast in an upright position and separate from each other, ready for people to eat. N COUNT ⇑ holder

tobacco /təbækəʊ/, **tobaccos**, or **tobaccoes**. **Tobacco** is **1** a substance which people smoke in pipes, cigars, and cigarettes, or which is formed into a block for people to chew. EG *He took out his pipe and filled it with tobacco and lit it... The poacher was chewing on a wad of tobacco.* N UNCOUNT **2** the plant from which tobacco is obtained. N UNCOUNT

tobacconist /təbækənɪst/, **tobacconists**. A **tobacconist** is a person who runs a shop that sells tobacco, cigarettes, cigars, etc. ▸ A **tobacconist's** is a shop that sells tobacco, cigarettes, cigars, etc. N COUNT

toboggan /təbɒgən/, **toboggans, tobogganing, tobogganed**. **1** A **toboggan** is a vehicle for travelling on snow. It consists of a flat seat attached to two long narrow pieces of wood or metal that slide easily over the snow. N COUNT = sled, sledge

2 When you **toboggan**, you ride on a toboggan, especially for sport or amusement. EG *In the distance I could see the children tobogganing down the hill.* V: USU+A = sledge

toccata /təkɑ:tə/, **toccatas**. A **toccata** is a fast piece of music for the organ, piano, or harpsichord. N COUNT

tod /tɒd/. In informal British English, when you are **on your tod** you are alone. EG *I came here on my tod.* PHR: USED AS AN A

today /tədeɪ/ means **1** the day that is happening at the time when you are speaking or writing. EG *I hope you're feeling better today... I had a letter today from my solicitor...* ▸ **Today** can also be used like a noun. EG *Today is Thursday... Have you got today's paper?* ADV **2** the present period of time in the history of the world. EG *This is the best translation available today... Today we are threatened on all sides by financial and political crises...* ▸ **Today** can also be used like a noun. EG *...the modern world of today.* ADV ⇑ now

toddle /tɒdə⁰l/, **toddles, toddling, toddled**. When a child **toddles**, it walks unsteadily with short quick steps. EG *You could see his grandson toddling around in the garden.* V

toddler /tɒdlə/, **toddlers**. A **toddler** is a small child who has only just learnt to walk. N COUNT

toddy /tɒdi¹/, **toddies**. A **toddy** is a drink that is made by adding hot water and sugar to whisky, rum, or brandy. N COUNT/UNCOUNT

to-do /tə du:/. A **to-do** is a situation in which people are very agitated, confused, or annoyed about something. EG *There was an awful to-do about his being elected president.* N SING WITH DET+SUPP = fuss, palaver

toe /təʊ/, **toes, toeing, toed**. **1** Your **toes** are the five movable parts at the end of your foot. EG *I stubbed my toe against a stone.* ● to **tread on** someone's **toes**: see **tread**. N COUNT: USU PL ⇑ digit

2 The **toe** of a shoe or sock is the part that covers the end of your foot. EG *Maria's shoes had got holes in the toes.* N COUNT

3 If you **keep** someone **on** their **toes**, you make sure that they are paying attention to what they are doing or saying. EG *My weekly pep talks from Patrick certainly kept me on my toes.* PHR: VB INFLECTS

4 If you **toe the line**, or **toe the party line**, you behave in the way that people expect you to, especially by obeying orders, not breaking rules, and expressing opinions that are acceptable to people in authority. EG *She had always tried to toe the line in public.* PHR: VB INFLECTS ⇑ conform

toecap /təʊkæp/, **toecaps**; also spelled with a hyphen. A **toecap** is a piece of leather or metal which is fitted over the end of a shoe or boot in order to protect it. N COUNT

toehold /təʊhəʊld/, **toeholds**. A **toehold** is **1** a small place on a rock, mountain, etc, where there is just enough room for you to put the end of your foot when you are climbing. N COUNT = foothold **2** a first uncertain position in a job or area of work which you hope will give you the opportunity to go on to better things. EG *Starting* N COUNT = foothold *off as a secretary on a local paper may give you a toehold in journalism.*

toenail /təʊneɪl/, **toenails**; also spelled with a hyphen. Your **toenails** are the thin hard pale coverings that grow on the end of each of your toes.
N COUNT : USU PL
⇑ nail

toff /tɒf/, **toffs**. A **toff** is an upper-class or rich person; an old-fashioned, informal word used in British English.
N COUNT
= nob

toffee /tɒfi¹/, **toffees**. 1 A **toffee** is a sticky chewy sweet that is made by boiling sugar and butter together with water. EG *...a bag of toffees... ...a chunk of toffee.*
N COUNT/ UNCOUNT

2 If you say that someone **can't** do something **for toffee**, you mean that they are completely unable to do it; an informal expression. EG *He couldn't act for toffee.*
PHR : VB INFLECTS

toffee apple, toffee apples; also spelled with a hyphen. A **toffee apple** is an apple that is covered with a thin hard layer of toffee and is held with a stick.
N COUNT
⇑ food

toffee-nosed. If you say that someone is **toffee-nosed**, you mean that they have a high opinion of themselves and a low opinion of other people; used in informal English showing disapproval.
ADJ QUALIT
= snooty

tog /tɒg/, **togs**. 1 A **tog** is an official measurement that shows how warm a blanket or quilt is. EG *Down quilts vary between ten and fifteen togs.*
N COUNT : NUM+ N

2 Your **togs** are your clothes; an informal use. EG *I'll just get my swimming togs.*
N PLURAL
= gear

toga /təʊgə/, **togas**. A **toga** is a piece of clothing which was worn by citizens in ancient Rome.
N COUNT
⇑ garment

together /təgeðə/. 1 If people do something **together**, they do it with each other. EG *They flew back to London together... The two brothers used to go on fishing parties together... You all work together as a team in the office... We'll be dealing with those problems together.*
ADV WITH VB
≠ alone

2 If you do two things **together** or if two things happen **together**, you do the two things or the two things happen at the same time. EG *The reports will have to be seen and judged together before a decision can be taken... 'Of course not,' said Laing and the minister together.*
ADV WITH VB
= simultaneously
≠ separately

3 If things join or fix **together**, they join or fix with each other. EG *...a series of hollow aluminium tubes which screw together... Mix together equal parts of coarse salt and soda crystals... Her hands were clasped tightly together.*
ADV WITH VB
≠ apart

4 If things or people are situated **together**, they are very near to each other. EG *There were two metal plates lying close together on the floor... Antelope seek safety in numbers, gathering together in large herds... The fossils are packed densely together in display cases.*
ADV WITH VB
⇑ close

5 If people are held or bound **together**, they are united with each other in some way. EG *...a father who has left his job to keep the family together... And what bound it all together was faith.*
ADV WITH VB
≠ apart

6 If two people are **together**, they are married, living together, or having a sexual relationship with each other. EG *We're together now, we're happy... ...their eight years together.*
ADV
≠ apart, separated

7 **Together with** something else means as well as that other thing. EG *Mabel Lee proceeded to hand over the key to his room, together with a wad of forms and leaflets... Pop music is, together with football, the chief enthusiasm of these boys.*
CONJ COORD
= along with

8 If you say that things go **together**, you mean that they are compatible with each other or cannot be separated from each other. EG *Independence and equality went together... Nell feels marriage and studying don't go together.*
ADV WITH VB
= hand in hand

9 You use **together** when you are adding two or more things to each other in order to consider the total as a whole. EG *She was wiser than the other two put together... The two companies together spend more on research than the whole of the rest of the industry... Together these factors have brought about the disintegration of the local community.*
ADV
≠ individually

10 If you do something for days or hours **together**, you do it continuously and without stopping for the amount of time that is mentioned or specified. EG *I worked for nine hours together before I got it finished.*
ADV AFTER N
= nonstop

11 If you say that someone is **together**, you mean that they are very confident, self-assured, and organized, and know what they want; an informal use. EG *She's really together... ...a together sort of person.*
ADJ QUALIT

togetherness /təgeðənɪ²s/ is a warm happy feeling of affection and closeness to other people, especially your friends and family. EG *Grandma and Grandpa share the joys of togetherness made possible by a lifetime of giving.*
N UNCOUNT

togged /tɒgd/. If you are **togged up** or **togged out**, you are dressed in the right clothing for a particular activity. EG *She's all togged up to go climbing.*
PHR : USED AS C
= rigged out

toggle /tɒgəºl/, **toggles**. A **toggle** is a small rod of wood or plastic which is sewn to a coat, bag, tent flap, etc, and which is pushed through a loop or hole as a fastener.
N COUNT
⇑ fastener

toil /tɔɪl/, **toils, toiling, toiled**; a formal word. 1 If you **toil**, you work hard at something that is unpleasant and physically very tiring. EG *...factories where men toiled all through the night.*
V : USU+A
= slave, slog

2 If you **toil** up a slope or along a road, you move slowly and with difficulty, especially when you are very tired. EG *John toiled up that dusty ascent.*
V+A
⇑ go
= slog

3 **Toil** is unpleasant work that is very tiring physically. EG *The wealth of industrial society could only come from the toil of the masses.*
N UNCOUNT
= labour

toil away. If you **toil away**, you work hard at something continuously over a long period of time, especially something that is unpleasant and physically very tiring. EG *...the coalminer toiling away in the black deeps.*
PHRASAL VB : V+ ADV
= slave away

toilet /tɔɪlɪ²t/, **toilets**. 1 A **toilet** is 1.1 a large bowl that is connected to the plumbing of a building and that people use when they get rid of urine or faeces from their bodies. EG *She heard the toilet flush... ...a total lack of toilet facilities.* 1.2 a room containing a toilet, and sometimes also a wash-basin. EG *He opens the door of the toilet.* 1.3 a small building, or a large room in a hotel, office block, etc, that contains a lot of smaller rooms with toilets in them. EG *...public toilets.*
N COUNT
= lavatory, loo
N COUNT
= lavatory, loo
N COUNT : USU PL

2 When you **go to the toilet**, you get rid of urine or faeces from your body, especially by using a toilet. EG *He wants to go to the toilet.*
PHR : VB INFLECTS

3 Your **toilet** is the activity of washing and dressing yourself, and making yourself look tidy and attractive; an old-fashioned use. EG *She took a long time over her toilet.*
N SING : POSS+N

toilet bag, toilet bags; also spelled with a hyphen. A **toilet bag** is a small waterproof bag in which you put things such as your soap, shaving kit, make-up, etc, when you are travelling.
N COUNT
= sponge bag

toilet paper is thin absorbent paper that you use to clean yourself after you have got rid of urine or faeces from your body. EG *...a roll of toilet paper.*
N UNCOUNT
= loo paper

toiletries /tɔɪlɪ²trɪz/ are the things that you use when cleaning or taking care of your body, such as soap, deodorant, toothpaste, etc.
N PLURAL

toilet roll, toilet rolls. A **toilet roll** is a long narrow strip of toilet paper that is wound around a small cardboard tube. EG *Can you buy some toilet rolls when you go to the shops?*
N COUNT/ UNCOUNT
= loo roll

toilet soap, toilet soaps. **Toilet soap** is soap that you use for washing yourself with; used mainly on soap wrappers and in advertisements.
N MASS

toilet-train, toilet-trains, toilet-training, toilet-trained; also spelled as two words. When you **toilet-train** a child, you teach it to control itself so that it only passes urine or faeces when it is sitting on a potty or toilet. EG *Most of them were rigidly toilet-trained as babies... Parents often worry too much about toilet training.*
V+O
= potty train

toilet water is fairly weak and inexpensive perfume.
N MASS

***to*-INF** □ In this dictionary *to*-INF in the grammar notes beside entries refers to an infinitive with *to*. The *to*-infinitive can be the verb of a clause. Clauses with a *to*-infinitive can occur in several places in structure, as the examples show. EG *I wanted him* **to come back** *early...* **To avoid** *any accidents, we must take precautions... The most difficult thing had been the decision* **to act**... *This is difficult for us* **to accept**... **To exclude** *religion is* **to deny** *it.*

to-ing and fro-ing /tuːɪŋ ən frəʊɪŋ/ is a situation where the same action or the same movement between two places is repeated many times. EG *There was a lot of to-ing and fro-ing between London and the Potteries.*
PHR : USED AS O

token /tə͟ukəⁿn/, **tokens**. 1 A **token** is 1.1 a round flat piece of metal that is sometimes used instead of money. Some vending machines, for example, accept tokens instead of coins. N COUNT 1.2 a piece of paper or card that is worth a particular amount of money and that can be exchanged for goods in a particular shop or for a particular kind of goods. EG *I got three book tokens for my birthday.* N COUNT : USU MOD+N 1.3 a present that a person gives to someone else as a symbol of his or her love or in memory of a very happy or special occasion. EG *He gave her a gold watch as a token of his esteem.* N COUNT

2 **Token** also means small and unimportant, and not genuine and sincere or having much effect. EG *The union wanted to go beyond one-day token strikes and marches... We received a token wage.* ADJ CLASSIF : ATTRIB = nominal

3 You use **by the same token** to mean that a fact or statement is true for the same reasons and in the same way as something you have already mentioned. EG *We make people mentally old by retiring them, and we may even by the same token make them physically old.* PHR : USED AS ADV SEN

told /tə͟uld/. 1 **Told** is the past tense and past participle of **tell**.

2 You use **all told** when you want to emphasize that everything has been counted. EG *There are only four characters all told in Pinter's new play.* PHR : USED AS AN A = altogether

tolerable /tɒ͟ləⁿrəbəⁿl/. If something is **tolerable** it is 1 bearable, even though it is unpleasant or painful. EG *They never found the climate tolerable enough to settle.* ADJ QUALIT ≠ unbearable 2 fairly good and reasonably satisfactory, but not of the highest quality or standard. EG *I picked up a tolerable working knowledge of the language.* ADJ QUALIT ⇑ adequate = reasonable
◇ **tolerably**. EG *...emergency systems which were working tolerably well.* ◇ ADV+ADJ/ADV

tolerance /tɒ͟lərəns/, **tolerances**. 1 **Tolerance** is 1.1 the quality of allowing other people to have their own attitudes or beliefs, or to behave in a particular way, even if you do not agree or approve; used showing approval. EG *He has a sense of humour plus tolerance and patience.* N UNCOUNT = forbearance ≠ intolerance 1.2 the ability or readiness of a person to bear or endure something unpleasant or painful. EG *The stench was beyond tolerance, and the men began to choke and vomit.* N UNCOUNT = endurance

2 A **tolerance** is 2.1 the ability of a substance to endure heat, physical stress, treatment with chemicals, etc, without breaking or being damaged; a technical term in physics. EG *They are made to the highest possible tolerances.* N COUNT/UNCOUNT 2.2 an acceptable degree of variation in a measurement, value, or calculation; a technical term in mathematics, statistics, etc. N COUNT/UNCOUNT

tolerant /tɒ͟lərənt/. 1 If you are **tolerant**, you allow other people to have their own attitudes or beliefs, or to behave in a particular way, even if you do not agree or approve; used showing approval. EG *Michael is a remarkably tolerant person... We do well to be tolerant of 'superstition'.* ADJ QUALIT ≠ intolerant ◇ **tolerantly**. EG *Sheldon only smiled tolerantly.* ◇ ADV WITH VB

2 If a substance is **tolerant** of heat, physical stress, treatment with chemicals, etc, it is able to endure them without breaking or being damaged; a technical term in physics. EG *The new compound is tolerant of temperatures exceeding 180C.* ADJ QUALIT+*of*

tolerate /tɒ͟ləreɪt/, **tolerates, tolerating, tolerated**. If you **tolerate** something, 1 you allow it to exist or to happen in a particular way, even though you do not agree or approve. EG *They happily tolerated the existence of opinions contrary to their own.* V+O ⇑ accept
◇ **toleration** /tɒ͟ləre͟ɪʃəⁿn/. EG *This led to the greater toleration by the party organisation of such views.* ◇ N UNCOUNT 2 you are able or willing to bear something unpleasant or painful. EG *I was wondering how much longer I could tolerate isolation.* V+O = put up with

toll /tə͟ul/, **tolls, tolling, tolled**. 1 When a bell **tolls** or when you **toll** it, it rings slowly and repeatedly, especially at funerals or as a sign that someone has died. EG *The bell tolled for him.* V-ERG

2 A **toll** is the total number of deaths, accidents, or disasters that occur in a particular period of time. EG *The death toll rose from 270 in 1952 to 5000 in 1954.* N COUNT+SUPP : USU SING

3 If something **takes a heavy toll**, it causes a high number of deaths, injuries, or defeats. EG *...the snow that takes a heavy toll of lambs and calves.* PHR : VB INFLECTS

4 If you say that something **takes a toll** or **takes its toll**, you mean that it has a very serious effect on something or someone, and causes a lot of suffering. EG *The walking was beginning to take its toll on all of us... The pressures on the community take their toll.* PHR : VB INFLECTS ⇑ affect

5 A **toll** is also 5.1 a small sum of money that you sometimes have to pay in order to be allowed to cross a particular bridge or to use a particular stretch of road. EG *Anyone travelling across the Forth road bridge has to pay a toll.* N COUNT ⇑ fee 5.2 a place where you stop to pay a toll. N COUNT

tollhouse /tə͟ulhaus, tɒl-/, **tollhouses**. A **tollhouse** is a small house by a bridge or gate where people used to stop to pay a sum of money in order to be allowed to cross a particular bridge or to use a particular stretch of road. N COUNT

tom /tɒ͟m/, **toms**. A **tom** is a male cat. N COUNT

tomahawk /tɒ͟məhɔːk/, **tomahawks**. A **tomahawk** is a small light axe that is used by North American Indians. N COUNT ⇑ weapon

tomato /təmɑ͟ːtəu/, **tomatoes**. A **tomato** is a soft smallish red fruit that you can eat raw in salads, or cooked as a vegetable or in sauces. EG *'Please don't touch the tomatoes,' said the shop assistant... ...a bacon, lettuce, and tomato sandwich.* ▸ also used to refer to the plant that this fruit grows on. N COUNT

tomb /tu͟ːm/, **tombs**. A **tomb** is a large grave that is above ground and that usually has a sculpture or other decoration on it. EG *...the bronze tomb of Henry VII and Elizabeth of York.* N COUNT

tombola /tɒmbə͟ulə/, **tombolas**. **Tombola** is a game in which you buy a ticket with a number on it and can win a small prize if this number is chosen. N COUNT/UNCOUNT = draw

tomboy /tɒ͟mbɔɪ/, **tomboys**. A **tomboy** is a girl who likes playing rough or noisy games. N COUNT

tombstone /tu͟ːmstəun/, **tombstones**. A **tombstone** is a large flat piece of stone that is placed over someone's grave or tomb and on which their name, dates of birth and death, and sometimes other details, are written. N COUNT = gravestone

tomcat /tɒ͟mkæt/, **tomcats**. A **tomcat** is a male cat. N COUNT = tom

tome /tə͟um/, **tomes**. A **tome** is a very large, heavy book; a formal word. EG *...rows of bookshelves loaded with tomes devoted to the general topic of therapy.* N COUNT = volume

tomfoolery /tɒmfu͟ːləriˡ/ is playful behaviour, usually of a rather silly, noisy, or rough kind. EG *Right, that's enough of this tomfoolery, it's time you got on with some work.* N UNCOUNT ⇑ messing about

tommyrot /tɒ͟miˡrɒt/ means complete nonsense; an old-fashioned word used in informal English. N UNCOUNT = rubbish

tomorrow /təmɒ͟rəu/ means 1 the day after today. EG *They're coming tomorrow... 'Good night,' he said. 'See you tomorrow'.* ▸ **Tomorrow** can also be used like a noun. EG *...tomorrow's concert performance... ...Shall I come tomorrow night?* ADV 2 the future, especially the near future. EG *They live today as millions more will live tomorrow...* ▸ **Tomorrow** can also be used like a noun. EG *...You're always searching after a better tomorrow... ...a citizen of tomorrow's super-industrial world.* ADV

tomtit /tɒ͟mtɪt/, **tomtits**. a small European bird that eats insects and seeds. N COUNT ⇑ bird

tom-tom /tɒ͟m tɒm/, **tom-toms**. A **tom-tom** is a long narrow African or Asian drum that you play with your hands. EG *They heard the beat of a tom-tom start up fairly close by.* N COUNT

ton /tʌ͟n/, **tons**. 1 A **ton** is 1.1 a unit of weight that is equal to 2240 pounds in Britain and to 2000 pounds in the United States. EG *It's made of steel and weighs ten tons... The Japanese extract ten million tons of coal each year from underwater mines.* N COUNT : USU a/NUM+N 1.2 the same as a tonne. N COUNT : USU a/NUM+N

2 When you say that something **weighs a ton**, you mean that it is extremely heavy. EG *It'll need six of us to lift that piano–it weighs a ton.* PHR : VB INFLECTS

3 If you **come down on** someone **like a ton of bricks**, you are extremely angry with them and tell them off because of something wrong that they have done. This expression is used especially when talking about people who are in a position of authority or responsibility. EG *She came down on me like a ton of bricks when she found out.* PHR : VB INFLECTS ⇑ tell someone off

4 **Tons** means a very large amount of something; used in informal British English. EG *I've got tons of paper to draw on.* N PART : PLURAL = lots, heaps

5 If you **do a ton**, you travel at over 100 miles per hour, for example on a motorbike; an old-fashioned and informal expression. EG *My brother once did a ton down the motorway but he didn't get caught.* PHR : VB INFLECTS ⇑ speed

tonal /təʊnəºl/ means relating to the qualities or pitch of a sound or to the tonality of a piece of music. ADJ CLASSIF : ATTRIB

tonality /təʊnælɪti¹/ is the presence of a musical key in a piece of music; a technical term. N UNCOUNT

tone /təʊn/, **tones, toning, toned.** 1 Someone's **tone** is a quality in their voice which shows what they feel or think. EG *'Very good,' he said in an encouraging tone... She was speaking now in cold sarcastic tones... Her tone was defiant.* N COUNT : WITH SUPP/POSS = manner

2 A **tone** is also **2.1** a sound with a particular quality. EG *...the vibrant tones of Richard Burton... They spoke briefly in low tones... A clear tone cut the silence.* N COUNT : USU PL +SUPP **2.2** one of the sounds that you hear when you are using a telephone, for example the sound that tells you that a number is engaged. EG *Don't put your money in until you hear the pay tone.* N COUNT : MOD+N **2.3** a difference in pitch between two musical notes. A tone is twice as large as a semitone; a technical term in music. N COUNT ⇑ interval

3 The **tone** of a musical instrument or a singer's voice is the kind of sound it has, for example a rich sound or a thin sound. EG *I wish I had a piano with a better tone.* N COUNT/UNCOUNT+SUPP

4 The **tone** of something such as a piece of writing or an activity is its general nature or the qualities it has that tell you something about the attitudes of the person writing it or involved in it. EG *I was greatly offended by the tone of the article... ...countries where governments tend to be social democratic in tone... The critical tone was set by the committee in a preparatory report.* N UNCOUNT ⇑ character

5 The **tone** of something such as a place or a meeting is its degree of respectability. EG *He said the new people had lowered the tone of the neighbourhood... She thought that it lent a certain tone to a gathering to have a clergyman present.* N SING WITH DET +SUPP ⇑ quality

6 A **tone** is also one of several forms of a particular colour which are slightly lighter, darker, brighter, etc than each other. EG *The colours of the pigeons matched the tones of the sky... You need a blue that's slightly deeper in tone.* N COUNT/UNCOUNT = shade, hue

7 If something **tones** with something else or **tones in** with it, it looks nice with it because their colours are similar in quality or brightness. EG *I want the furniture to tone with the wallpaper... That carpet doesn't really tone in with the curtains.* V+A, OR PHRASAL VB : V+ADV, IF+PREP THEN *with* = harmonize

8 If something **tones** your muscles or **tones** them **up**, it makes them firm and strong. EG *Do the exercises and they will tone you up nicely.* V+O, OR PHRASAL VB : V+O+ADV

tone down. 1 If you **tone down** something that you have written, you make it less strong, severe, or offensive. EG *He advised me to tone down my article.* PHRASAL VB : V+O+ADV = moderate

2 If you **tone down** a colour, you make it less bright. EG *You will have to tone down the red a little.* PHRASAL VB : V+O+ADV

tone-deaf. Someone who is **tone-deaf** is unable to sing in tune or to recognize different tunes. ADJ CLASSIF

toneless /təʊnlɪ²s/. A **toneless** voice is dull and does not express any feeling. EG *He replied in a toneless mechanical voice.* ◇ **tonelessly.** EG *'You're back,' she said tonelessly.* ADJ QUALIT = lifeless ◇ ADV WITH VB

tongs /tɒŋz/. You use **tongs** to pick up objects that you do not want to touch. Tongs consist of two long narrow pieces of metal joined together at one end. You press the pieces together in order to grip the object and pick it up. EG *She was putting lumps of sugar into her tea with a pair of silver tongs.* ● See also **curling tongs.** ● **hammer and tongs**: see **hammer.** N PLURAL : ALSO *a pair of*+N

tongue /tʌŋ/, **tongues.** 1 Your **tongue** is the soft movable part inside your mouth which you use for tasting and licking and for speaking. EG *Lynn stuck out her tongue... He ran his tongue over his lips.* N COUNT ⇑ organ

2 You can use **tongue** to refer to the kind of things that a person says. EG *She had a sharp and hurtful tongue... He could use his eloquent tongue to stir them to greater savagery... She is too free with her tongue.* N COUNT : USU POSS/MOD+N ⇑ talk

3 A **tongue** is also a language; an old-fashioned or literary use. EG *I answered her in her own tongue.* N COUNT

4 **Tongue** is the cooked tongue of an ox or sheep. It is usually eaten cold. N UNCOUNT/COUNT

5 The **tongue** of a shoe or boot is the piece of leather which is underneath the laces. N COUNT ⇑ flap

6 A **tongue** of something, for example of fire or land, is a long thin piece of it that sticks or moves outwards; a rather literary use. EG *A tongue of flame leapt up the side of the building.* N COUNT+*of* = snake

7 The word **tongue** is also used in the following expressions. **7.1** If you **hold** your **tongue**, you do not say anything. EG *I just held my tongue and followed them... Hold your tongue!* PHR : VB INFLECTS **7.2** If you ask someone whether they **have lost** their **tongue** or whether **the cat has got** their **tongue**, you mean that you want them to say something and that you are annoyed because they have not been answering you. EG *Well? Lost your tongue?* PHR : VB INFLECTS = be dumb **7.3** If you **find** your **tongue**, you become able to say something after you have been too shy, frightened, or surprised to speak. EG *Oh, found your tongue, have you?* PHR : VB INFLECTS **7.4** If you tell someone to **keep a civil tongue in** their **head**, you are telling them not to be rude; an old-fashioned expression. PHR : VB INFLECTS **7.5** If you **give** someone **the rough side of** your **tongue** or if they **feel the rough side of** your **tongue**, you speak to them angrily or harshly; an old-fashioned expression. PHR : VB INFLECTS **7.6** If you can't **get** your **tongue round** a word or name, you find it difficult to pronounce. EG *I just can't get my tongue round his name.* PHR : VB INFLECTS **7.7** If a name or word **trips off the tongue**, it is easy to say. PHR : VB INFLECTS **7.8** If you **have** your **tongue in** your **cheek** when you say or do something, you are not being sincere or serious about it, although you may appear to be. EG *I suspect Dr Vidler had his tongue in his cheek when he wrote that.* ● See also **tongue-in-cheek.** PHR : VB INFLECTS = be facetious **7.9** A **slip of the tongue** is a small mistake that you make when you are saying something, for example when you say a different word from the one that you intend to say. EG *If I did say that, it was just a slip of the tongue.* PHR : USED AS C/O ⇑ error **7.10 on the tip of your tongue**: see **tip.**

tongue-in-cheek. A **tongue-in-cheek** remark is made as a joke, and is not serious or sincere. EG *He offered some tongue-in-cheek advice about keeping out of the rain.* ADJ QUALIT = flippant

tongue-tied. If someone is **tongue-tied**, they are unable to say anything because they feel shy or nervous. EG *He became completely tongue-tied.* ADJ QUALIT = speechless

tongue-twister, tongue-twisters. A **tongue-twister** is a sentence or expression which is very difficult to say properly, especially when you try saying it quickly a number of times. For example 'she sells seashells on the seashore' is an English tongue-twister. N COUNT

tonic /tɒnɪk/, **tonics.** 1 **Tonic** or **tonic water** is a colourless fizzy drink that has a slightly bitter flavour and is often mixed with alcoholic drinks, especially gin. EG *A gin and tonic, please.* N MASS

2 A **tonic** is **2.1** a medicine that makes you feel stronger, healthier, and less tired. N MASS **2.2** anything that makes you feel stronger or more cheerful. EG *She was so charming that it was a tonic to talk to her.* N COUNT = boost

3 Skin **tonic** or hair **tonic** is a liquid that you put on your skin or hair in order to improve it. N MASS : USU MOD +N

4 The **tonic** of a musical scale is its first note; a technical term in music. N COUNT

tonight /tənaɪt/ is used to refer to the evening of today or the night that follows today. EG *I think I'll go to bed early tonight... He is prepared to fly to Vienna tonight on the evening plane... You mustn't take the conversation tonight too seriously.* ▸ **Tonight** can also be used like a noun. EG *In tonight's programme we shall be explaining the history of the movement.* ADV

tonnage /tʌnɪdʒ/, **tonnages.** 1 The **tonnage** of a ship is its size or the amount of space that it has inside it for cargo; a technical term. EG *...8000 registered merchant ships with a gross tonnage of 20 million.* N UNCOUNT/COUNT : IF+PREP THEN *of* ⇑ weight

2 **Tonnage** is also the total number of tons that something weighs, or the total amount that there is of it. EG *This is far more than the total tonnage of TNT used by either side during the last war... Very large tonnages of fuel and munitions could not be handled.* N COUNT/UNCOUNT : IF+PREP THEN *of* ⇑ quantity

tonne /tʌn/, **tonnes.** A **tonne** is a metric unit of weight that is equal to 1000 kilograms. EG *The United States now imported 500 million tonnes of crude oil annually.* N COUNT : A/NUM +N

tonsil /tɒnsºəl/, **tonsils.** Your **tonsils** are the two small soft lumps in your throat at the back of your mouth. EG *I went to hospital to have my tonsils out.* N COUNT : USU PL

tonsillitis /tɒnsɪ¹laɪtɪ¹s/ is a painful swelling of your tonsils caused by an infection. N UNCOUNT ⇑ illness

tonsure /tɒnʃə/, **tonsures.** If a man has a **tonsure**, he has cut his hair so that there is a bald area on his head surrounded by hair. Some monks have their heads shaved to look like this. ▸ used also to refer to N COUNT the bald area or to the hair surrounding it. EG ...*a small round spot like a tonsure.*

too /tu:/. **1** You use **too** at the end of a sentence or after a word or phrase to say that what has just been said also applies to or includes the person or thing mentioned. EG *I'm on your side. Seibert is too... There were carrots too... I wondered whether I too would become one of its victims... Hey, where are you from? Brooklyn? Me too!... Physically, too, the peoples of the world are incredibly mixed.* ADV = as well

2 You also use **too** when you want to link two very different qualities or actions together and you know that the combination seems unlikely or surprising. **Too** is placed after the second quality or action. EG *It was a pretty play, and very sad too... He was always kind and helpful to me. But he could be alarming too.* ADV = as well

3 You also use **too** at the end of a sentence when you have just added an extra piece of information, especially something surprising or important. EG *I remember that quite well. It was a Tuesday too... You ought to see a doctor. And quickly, too.* ADV SEN = what's more

4 You also use **too** at the end of a sentence when you have added your opinion after a statement of fact made by you or by another person. EG *A lot of the films were American, and very good too... Quite right, too.* ADV

5 You also use **too** when you want to emphasize the anger, impatience, indignation, or hostility you feel, for example because someone is late or has agreed with you only after a long argument. EG *I should think so, too!... About time, too!* ADV SEN

6 You also use **too** in order to indicate that an amount or degree of something is more than is desirable, necessary, acceptable, or sensible, or that it is so great that it makes it impossible for a particular thing to happen. EG *Avoid using too much water... There were just too many people there... Philip decided it was not too far to walk... My sister's boots were a bit too small for her long feet... I realized my mistake too late... Don't leave it in too warm a place.* ADV+ADJ/ADV/QUANTIF

7 You use **all too** or **only too** before an adverb or adjective to indicate that something happens to a greater extent or degree than is pleasant or desirable. EG *I can remember only too well the disasters that followed... The suspicions had proved all too true... All too soon, the party was over.* PHR+ADJ/ADV = very

8 You also use **too** with a negative before an adjective when you really mean the opposite of the adjective but are being polite, sarcastic, or cautious. EG *That's probably not too far from the truth... He wasn't too keen on it... It's not too bad.* ADV+ADJ/ADV: WITH BROAD NEG ⇑ very = excessively

9 You also use **too** in order to emphasize in a fairly humorous or childish way your denial of what someone else has said or your refusal to obey them. EG *'You're not going.'–'I am too!'* ADV SEN = so

10 You also use **too** when you want to emphasize in a fairly formal way your thanks to someone for something that they have done for you. EG *You're too kind.* ADV+ADJ/ADV = extremely

11 • **too bad**: see **bad**. • **too clever, arrogant**, etc **by half**: see **half**. • **none too**: see **none**.

took /tʊk/ is the past tense of **take**.

tool /tu:l/, **tools**. **1** A **tool** is any instrument or piece of equipment that you hold in your hands in order to help you to do a particular kind of work. There are many kinds of tool. For example, spades, hammers, and knives are tools. EG *He used the knife because that was the only tool he had.* • When workers **down tools**, they stop working suddenly in order to strike or to make a protest of some kind; used in British English. EG *Workers downed tools in what soon became a general strike.* N COUNT = implement • PHR: VB INFLECTS

2 A **tool** is also any object, skill, idea, etc that you use in your work or that you need for a particular purpose. EG *Textbooks became the essential tools of the teacher... Goodwill towards others has always been a necessary tool of survival.* N COUNT+SUPP

3 The tools of your **trade or the tools of the trade** are the skills, instruments, and other equipment that you need in order to do your job properly. PHR: USED AS S/O/C

4 You call someone a **tool** or refer to them as a **tool** when they are in someone else's power and are used by them, especially to do unpleasant or dishonest things; used showing disapproval. EG *Many senior military leaders had become the tools of foreign governments.* N COUNT = puppet, hireling

tool box, tool boxes; also spelled with a hyphen. A **tool box** is a metal or plastic box which contains general tools that you need at home, for example in repairing your house or car. EG *Keep your tool box in your garage.* N COUNT ⇑ container

tool kit, tool kits; also spelled with a hyphen. A **tool kit** is a special set of tools that are kept together and that are often used for a particular purpose. EG *A standard tool kit comes with the bicycle.* N COUNT

tool shed, tool sheds; also spelled with a hyphen. A **tool shed** is a shed where you keep large tools and equipment that are used outside, for example the tools that you use for gardening. N COUNT ⇑ outhouse

toot /tu:t/, **toots, tooting, tooted**. If you **toot** your car horn or if it **toots**, you make it produce a short sound or series of sounds. EG *People wave and toot... He tooted his horn.* ▸ used as a noun. EG *'Look,' she said and gave a toot on the horn.* V-ERG OR V = hoot, beep ▸ N COUNT = hoot

tooth /tu:θ/, **teeth** /ti:θ/. **1** Your **teeth** are the hard white objects which grow in two rows in your mouth and which you use for biting and chewing food. EG ...*a loose tooth... He had very white, even teeth... Sweets are bad for your teeth.* • See also **eye tooth, wisdom tooth**. N COUNT

2 The **teeth** of a comb, saw, cog, zip, etc are the parts that stick out in a row on its edge. EG *Each of these cogs has ten teeth.* N COUNT ⇑ projection

3 If something such as an official group or a law has **teeth**, it has power and is able to be effective. EG *If the Commission is to be effective it must be given more teeth.* N PLURAL = authority

4 The words **tooth** and **teeth** are also used in the following expressions. **4.1** Someone who is **long in the tooth** is old or getting old; an informal expression. EG *She's getting a bit long in the tooth for this sort of thing.* PHR: USED AS C = aged **4.2** Someone who is **armed to the teeth** is carrying a lot of weapons or carrying very effective weapons. PHR: USED AS C **4.3** If you **fight** something **tooth and nail** or **fight** for it **tooth and nail**, you do everything you can in order to prevent it or achieve it. EG *They will fight tooth and nail for the right to vote... She will fight the idea tooth and nail.* PHR: VB INFLECTS **4.4** If you **get** your **teeth into** something, you become very involved in it and deal with it with a great deal of concentration or energy; an informal expression. EG *I like a job I can get my teeth into.* PHR: VB INFLECTS = get stuck into **4.5** If you are **fed up to the teeth** with something or **fed up to the back teeth** with it, you are very dissatisfied or bored with it; an informal expression. EG *I'm fed up to the back teeth with people complaining.* PHR: USED AS C **4.6** If you say that someone is **lying through** their **teeth** or **lying in** their **teeth**, you mean that they are deliberately telling lies; an informal expression. PHR: VB INFLECTS **4.7** If you do something **in the teeth of** a difficulty or danger, you do it in spite of the difficulty or danger. EG *They struggled on in the teeth of the gale... He managed it in the teeth of the most terrifying odds.* PREP = despite

5 The words **tooth** and **teeth** are also used in the following expressions, which are explained at other places in this dictionary. • to **get** or **take the bit between** your **teeth**: see **bit**. • to **set** your **teeth on edge**: see **edge**. • to **grind** your **teeth**: see **grind**. • to **grit** your **teeth**: see **grit**. • a **kick in the teeth**: see **kick**. • **by the skin of** your **teeth**: see **skin**. • a **sweet tooth**: see **sweet**.

toothache /tu:θeɪk/ is a feeling of pain in or near one of your teeth. N UNCOUNT

toothbrush /tu:θbrʌʃ/, **toothbrushes**. A **toothbrush** is a small brush with a long handle which you use for cleaning your teeth. N COUNT

toothcomb /tu:θkəʊm/. See **fine-tooth comb**.

toothless /tu:θlɪ²s/. **1** If someone is **toothless** or if their mouth is **toothless**, they have no teeth. EG ...*a toothless old woman.* ▸ used of a smile or other facial expression. EG ...*a sly toothless grin.* ADJ CLASSIF ▸ ≠ toothy

2 If an organization or official group is **toothless**, it has no real power and is not effective. ADJ QUALIT ⇑ powerless

toothpaste /tu:θpeɪst/, **toothpastes**. **Toothpaste** is a thick substance which you put on your toothbrush and use to clean your teeth. EG ...*a tube of toothpaste.* N MASS

toothpick /tu:θpɪk/, **toothpicks**. A **toothpick** is a very small wooden or plastic stick with pointed ends which you use to remove food that is stuck between your teeth. N COUNT

toothpowder /tu:θpaudə/, **toothpowders.** **Toothpowder** is a powder which you put on your toothbrush and use to clean your teeth.
N MASS

toothy /tu:θi¹/, **toothier, toothiest**. A **toothy** smile is one in which a person shows a lot of teeth. EG *...a toothy, comedian's grin.*
ADJ QUALIT : ATTRIB

tootle /tu:təᵒl/, **tootles, tootling, tootled**; an informal word. **1** If you **tootle** somewhere, you go there in a calm and unhurried way.
V+A = toddle

2 If you **tootle** on a musical instrument such as a recorder or flute, you play it in a not very serious way.
V+A

tootsie /tu:tsi¹/, **tootsies**. Someone's **tootsie** is their toe or foot; used by small children, or by adults when they are talking to small children.
N COUNT

top /tɒp/, **tops, topping, topped**. **1** The **top** of something is its highest point or part. EG *...at the top of the steps... He filled his glass almost to the top... ...over the tops of the houses... ...hill tops.*
N COUNT : USU the+N IN SING+SUPP ≠ bottom

2 The **top** thing of a series of things is the highest one. EG *She was sitting on the top step... ...a room on the top floor.*
ADJ CLASSIF : ATTRIB

3 The **top** of a page, piece of paper, etc is its highest part when you hold it in your hand to read it. EG *Let's look at the top of page 14.*
N COUNT : USU the+N IN SING+SUPP ≠ bottom

4 The **top** of a street, garden, field, long room, etc is one end of it, usually the end furthest away from you or from the entrance. EG *...a new building at the top of Victoria Street.* ▸ used as an adjective. EG *...the top end of the field... ...the patient in the top bed.*
N SING : the+N, IF+PREP THEN of = far end ▸ ADJ CLASSIF : ATTRIB

5 The **top** of something such as a box or a table is its flat upper surface. EG *...the rough wooden top of the bench... She slipped the paper over the table top to Marvin.*
N COUNT+SUPP

6 The **top** of something such as a bottle, jar, or tube is a cap, lid or other device that fits or screws onto one end of it. EG *He unscrewed the top and put the bottle to his mouth.*
N COUNT = cover

7 The **top** of a carrot, parsnip, turnip, etc is the leafy part at one end of it.
N COUNT

8 A **top** is also a piece of clothing that a woman wears on the upper half of her body, for example a blouse. EG *The top doesn't fit very well, but the skirt's all right.*
N COUNT

9 A **top** is also a toy which has a pointed base on which it spins.
N COUNT

10 The **top** of something such as a scale is the highest point on it. EG *This group is already near the top of the UK income scale.*
N COUNT : USU the+N IN SING+SUPP

11 **Top** is the highest gear used in a car or other vehicle; an informal use. EG *She changed into top.*
N UNCOUNT

12 You can also use **top** to refer to something which is at the highest level or which has reached the greatest extent possible. EG *The vehicle's top speed is just about 100... ...a matter of top priority... ...an Italian top security prison.*
ADJ CLASSIF : ATTRIB = maximum

13 **Top** people are more important or successful than other people. EG *...top executives... ...a top team of Chinese surgeons.* ▸ used of the jobs that these people do. EG *...these people who stand between you and the top jobs.*
ADJ CLASSIF : ATTRIB = leading

14 When someone is at the **top** in an organization, business, social system, etc they have reached the most powerful and important part of it. EG *Officials at the top make the decisions... He hasn't got the drive and ruthlessness to take him to the top.*
N SING : the+N

15 If someone **tops** a poll, popularity chart, etc, they do better than anyone else in it. EG *She topped a nationwide poll for 1981's most outstanding sportswoman.*
V+O = head

16 If something **tops** a particular amount, it is larger than that amount. EG *US investments here topped fifty million dollars.*
V+O = exceed

17 If you **top** a story, remark, action, etc, you follow it with a better or more impressive one. EG *Sudhir topped her story with one about an Indian princess.*
V+O : IF+PREP THEN with = cap

18 If you say that someone or something is **tops** or **the tops**, you mean that they are better than anyone or anything else; an old-fashioned informal expression. EG *Miss Millar is tops as far as I am concerned... She's the tops.*
ADJ CLASSIF : PRED = terrific

19 on top. 19.1 If something is **on top** of something else, it is placed over it or on its highest part. EG *She laid her hand on top of his... My sister started piling the hymn books on top of each other... ...a model of the Eiffel Tower with a little flag on top.*
PHR : USED AS AN A, IF+PREP THEN of

19.2 When something is painted, written, pasted, etc **on top** or **over the top** of something, it is put on it in a way that covers it completely. EG *You can paint on top with distemper... Something had been stamped over the top.*
PHR : USED AS AN A, IF+PREP THEN of

19.3 If something happens **on top** of something else, it happens in addition to it; used especially of unpleasant situations or events. EG *You don't want to give the poor man ulcers on top of all the problems he's already got.*
PHR : USED AS AN A, USU+of = besides

19.4 You say that someone is **on top** when they have reached the most important position in an organization or business. EG *You have to fight in order to stay on top.*
PHR : USED AS AN A

19.5 If a person, organization, country, etc **comes out on top**, they are more successful than the others that they have been competing with. EG *India would no doubt come out on top, given its tradition of excellence in this field.*
PHR : VB INFLECTS ⇑ win

19.6 If you **are on top of** something that you are doing, you are dealing with it successfully. EG *...jobs that they never really got on top of.... ...their hurry to be on top of things.*
PHR : VB INFLECTS = master

19.7 If you say that something such as an approaching vehicle is **on top of** you, you mean that it has suddenly come too close to you. EG *All at once it was right on top of me.*
PREP ⇑ near

19.8 You say that people are **on top of** each other or live **on top of** each other when they work or live in such a small space that they are in each other's way or find it difficult to have any privacy. EG *One of us would have to go out else we'd be on top of each other... The children are always on top of us.*
PREP

19.9 When something **gets on top of** you, it makes you feel depressed and helpless because it is very difficult or worrying, or because it involves more work than you can cope with. EG *You may find the housework is getting on top of you.*
PHR : VB INFLECTS = get you down

20 The word **top** is also used in the following expressions. **20.1** If you clean, tidy, or examine something **from top to bottom**, you do it completely and thoroughly. EG *She had the house clean from top to bottom.*
PHR : USED AS AN A = throughout

20.2 If you are covered with something **from top to toe**, you are covered with it completely. EG *He was covered in mud from top to toe..*
PHR : USED AS AN A

20.3 You describe something that someone does or says as **over the top** when you think that it is exaggerated, and therefore unacceptable; an informal expression. EG *Here I think Wenders goes right over the top.*
PHR : USED AS AN A

20.4 If you **top and tail** fruit such as gooseberries, you cut off the top and bottom of them when you are preparing them to be eaten. EG *Come and help me top and tail the blackcurrants.*
PHR : VB INFLECTS

20.5 If you say that someone does not have very much **up top**, you mean that you think they are not very intelligent; an informal expression.
PHR : USED AS AN A

20.6 If someone **blows** their **top**, they lose their temper and express their strong anger about something. EG *He'll blow his top if he finds out what you've done.*
PHR : VB INFLECTS

21 The word **top** is also used in the following expressions, which are explained at other places in this dictionary. ● **off the top of** your **head**: see **head**. ● **thin on top**: see **thin**. ● **top of the tree**: see **tree**. ● **at the top of** your **voice**: see **voice**. ● **on top of the world**: see **world**.

22 See also **topped, topping**.

top up. If you **top up** something such as a container or a drink, you fill it up again when it has been partly emptied. EG *The radiator will have to be topped up because of evaporation... Philip topped up his gin and tonic.* ● See also **top-up**.
PHRASAL VB : V+O+ADV = replenish

topaz /təʊpæz/, **topazes**. A **topaz** is a precious stone which is usually yellowish-brown in colour and which is used in making jewellery. EG *...a topaz ring.*
N COUNT ⇑ gem

topcoat /tɒpkəʊt/, **topcoats**. A **topcoat** is **1** the final coat of paint that is put on a surface. **2** an overcoat; an old-fashioned use.
N COUNT
N COUNT

top-drawer. Someone who is **top-drawer** is of a very high social class; an old-fashioned informal expression.
ADJ QUALIT = upper crust

top dressing, top dressings. A **top dressing** is a layer of something such as manure or fertilizer which is put on the surface of the ground.
N COUNT

top hat, top hats; also spelled with a hyphen. A **top hat** is a man's hat with a tall crown and a narrow brim. Top hats are now worn only on special occasions. EG *...silk top hats and tail coats.*
N COUNT = topper

top-heavy. **1** Something that is **top-heavy** is larger or bulkier at the top than at the bottom, and is therefore not stable.
ADJ QUALIT ⇑ unbalanced

2 A business or other organization that is **top-heavy** has too many senior people in relation to the number
ADJ QUALIT

of junior people or workers; used showing disapproval. EG ...*a top-heavy and inefficient bureaucracy.*

topiary /təʊpɪəri[1]/ is the art of cutting hedges and bushes into different shapes, for example into the shapes of birds or animals; a technical term. N UNCOUNT

topic /tɒpɪk/, **topics**. A **topic** is a particular subject that you write about or discuss. EG *It often seemed that the main topic of conversation was food... The Industrial Revolution will be the topic for our lecture next week.* N COUNT+SUPP = theme

topical /tɒpɪkᵊl/. Something that is **topical** concerns or relates to events that are happening at the present time. EG *We used to discuss topical issues... The question you ask is very topical.* ◊ **topicality** /tɒpɪkælɪti[1]/. EG *Everyone congratulated Alexander on the brilliance and topicality of his work.* ADJ QUALIT ≠ out-of-date; ◊ N UNCOUNT

top-knot, top-knots; also spelled as one word. A **top-knot** is a hairstyle, especially for women, in which a person's hair is arranged in a small neat pile on the top of his or her head, and is sometimes decorated with ribbons, feathers, etc. N COUNT

topless /tɒplɪˢs/. 1 When a woman is **topless** she is not wearing anything to cover her breasts. EG ...*a topless dancer.* ▸ used as an adverb. EG *I've never had the courage to sunbathe topless.* ADJ CLASSIF; ▸ ADV

2 A **topless** show or entertainment is one in which the women entertainers or staff are naked from the waist upwards. ADJ CLASSIF : ATTRIB

top-level. A **top-level** discussion or activity is one that involves the people with the greatest amount of power and authority in an organization, country, etc. EG ...*top-level negotiations between the two embassies.* ADJ CLASSIF : ATTRIB ⇑ important

topmost /tɒpməʊst/. The **topmost** thing in a number of things is the one that is highest or nearest the top. EG ...*the topmost branches of the lime trees.* ADJ CLASSIF : ATTRIB = uppermost

top-notch. If you describe a person or activity as **top-notch**, you mean that they are of a very high standard or quality; an informal word. EG ...*a top-notch footballer... ...absolutely top-notch tennis.* ADJ QUALIT : ATTRIB = first-rate

topographical /tɒpəgræfɪkᵊl/. A **topographical** survey or map relates to or shows the physical features of an area of land, for example its hills, valleys, or rivers. ADJ CLASSIF : USU ATTRIB ⇑ geographical

topography /təpɒgrəfi[1]/, **topographies**. 1 **Topography** is the study and description of the physical features of an area, for example its hills, valleys, or rivers; used also of the representation of these features on maps. N UNCOUNT ⇑ geography

2 The **topography** of a particular area is its physical shape, including its hills, valleys, rivers, etc. EG *The topography of this area is very interesting.* N UNCOUNT : USU WITH POSS ⇑ geography

topped /tɒpt/. If something is **topped** by or **topped** with another thing, the other thing covers it or is on top of it. EG ...*a heap of stones topped by a wooden cross... Mother served the vegetables topped with melted butter.* ADJ CLASSIF : PRED+NG

topper /tɒpə/, **toppers**. A **topper** is a top hat; an informal word. EG ...*a man in a ridiculous topper.* N COUNT

topping /tɒpɪŋ/, **toppings**. 1 A **topping** is food, such as cream or cheese, that is poured or put on top of other food in order to decorate it or add to the flavour. EG *Serve the mousse with a topping of whipped cream.* N MASS ⇑ garnish

2 If you say that something is **topping**, you mean that it is very good; an informal, old-fashioned British English use. ADJ QUALIT

topple /tɒpᵊl/, **topples, toppling, toppled**. 1 If something **topples** or if you **topple** it, it becomes unsteady or unstable and falls over. EG *He caught the glass just as it began to topple... He dragged the boulder up the rock and toppled it over the edge.* V-ERG = tumble

2 If something or someone **topples** a government or **topples** the leader of a country or organization, they cause them to be no longer in power. EG *This action threatens to topple the government.* V+O = overthrow

topple over. If something **topples over**, it becomes unsteady and falls over. EG *She looked at the young tree nervously, as if expecting it to topple over.* PHRASAL VB : V+ADV = keel over

top-ranking. A **top-ranking** person is one of the most important or powerful people in a country or organization. EG ...*a top-ranking agent.* ADJ CLASSIF : ATTRIB = leading

top-secret; also spelled as two words. Something that is **top-secret** is intended to be kept completely secret so that the enemies of your country do not know about it. EG ...*a period of top secret work for the British Navy... ...a top-secret experiment.* ADJ CLASSIF = classified

topside /tɒpsaɪd/ is a joint of beef cut from the upper part of the leg and usually cooked by roasting. N UNCOUNT

topsoil /tɒpsɔɪl/ is the layer of soil nearest the surface of the ground. EG *The topsoil has been almost completely washed away.* N UNCOUNT

topsy-turvy /tɒpsi[1] tɜːvi[1]/. Something that is **topsy-turvy** is in a confused state; used in informal English. EG ...*that's rather a topsy-turvy way of looking at things... The room was all topsy-turvy.* ADJ CLASSIF = upside-down

top-up, top-ups. A **top-up** is another serving of a drink in the same glass that you have just used. EG *Anyone ready for another top-up?* N COUNT

torch /tɔːtʃ/, **torches**. 1 A **torch** is 1.1 a small lamp which you carry in your hand and which gets its power from batteries inside it. EG *He took the torch and disappeared into the dark.* N COUNT = flashlight 1.2 a long stick with material that burns easily wrapped around one end. You set fire to the end in order to provide light. N COUNT ⇑ flame

2 If someone **carries a torch for** someone else, they secretly admire them or love them. PHR : VB INFLECTS

torchlight /tɔːtʃlaɪt/ is the light that is produced by a torch or torches. EG ...*men with pickaxes working by torchlight... ...a torchlight procession.* N UNCOUNT

tore /tɔː/ is the past tense of **tear**.

torment, torments, tormenting, tormented. The word **torment** is pronounced /tɔːməˀnt/ when it is a noun, and /tɔːment/ when it is a verb. 1 **Torment** is extreme physical or mental pain. EG ...*the scream of a man dying in torment... He has never suffered the torment of rejection.* N UNCOUNT = agony, anguish

2 A **torment** is something that causes extreme physical or mental pain. EG *His schooldays were a torment... He was subjected to a variety of psychological torments.* N COUNT = ordeal

3 To **torment** someone means to cause them to feel extreme physical or mental pain. EG *His emotional turmoil continues to torment him... He tormented himself with doubts about his ability... The central character is the tormented Bernard McAuley.* V+O (NG/REFL) = torture

4 To **torment** a person or an animal also means to annoy them in a playful, rather cruel way for your own amusement. EG *Stop tormenting that poor dog!* V+O = persecute

tormentor /tɔːmentə/, **tormentors**. A **tormentor** is someone who deliberately causes another person physical or mental pain. EG *The child eventually turned on his tormentors.* N COUNT : USU POSS+N

torn /tɔːn/ is the past participle of **tear**.

tornado /tɔːneɪdəʊ/, **tornadoes** or **tornados**. A **tornado** is a violent storm whose centre is a cloud in the shape of a funnel. Tornados are accompanied by very strong circular winds. EG *A tornado whirled into town.* N COUNT = cyclone

torpedo /tɔːpiːdəʊ/, **torpedoes, torpedoing, torpedoed**. 1 A **torpedo** is a narrow cylindrical weapon fired from ships, submarines, and aircraft. It travels underwater and explodes when it hits its target. EG *His ship was blown up by a torpedo.* N COUNT ⇑ missile

2 If a ship **is torpedoed**, it is hit, and usually sunk, by a torpedo or torpedoes. EG *Valuable ships had been torpedoed, or sunk by air attack.* V+O : USU PASS ⇑ attack

3 If someone **torpedoes** negotiations or plans, they deliberately prevent them from being completed or from being successful; an informal use. EG *He was accused of trying to torpedo the talks.* V+O = sabotage

torpid /tɔːpɪd/. If you are **torpid**, you are mentally or physically inactive, especially because you are feeling lazy or sleepy; a formal word. ADJ QUALIT = lethargic

torpor /tɔːpə/ is the state of being torpid; a formal word. EG *He was sunk in a dismal torpor.* N UNCOUNT = lethargy

torque /tɔːk/ is a force that causes something to spin around a central point such as an axle; a technical term in engineering. EG *What is the magnitude of the torque required?* N UNCOUNT

torrent /tɒrənt/, **torrents**. 1 A **torrent** is a lot of water falling or flowing rapidly or violently. EG ...*a stream which swelled to a raging torrent when the rains came... I was proceeding through torrents of rain.* N COUNT OR N PART = flood

2 A **torrent** of questions, abuse, etc is a lot of questions, abuse, etc directed continuously at someone. EG *He was answered with a torrent of French oaths.* N PART = hail

torrential /təˀrenʃᵊl/. **Torrential** rain pours down very rapidly and in great quantities. EG *Before the meeting could end, torrential rain began to pour.* ADJ CLASSIF : ATTRIB

torrid /tɒrɪd/; a literary word. 1 **Torrid** weather is very hot and dry in an unpleasant way. EG *She was sitting on the rocks in the torrid sun.* ADJ QUALIT = scorching

2 A **torrid** love affair is one in which people feel very strong emotions. ADJ QUALIT = passionate

torsion /tɔːʃəⁿn/ is a twisting effect on something such as a piece of metal when equal forces are applied at both its ends but in opposite directions; a technical term in engineering. N UNCOUNT

torso /tɔːsəʊ/, **torsos**. Your **torso** is the main part of your body, excluding your head, arms, and legs. N COUNT = trunk

tort /tɔːt/, **torts**. A **tort** is something that you do or fail to do which harms someone else and for which you can be sued for damages; a legal term. N COUNT/UNCOUNT

tortilla /tɔːtiːlə/, **tortillas**. A **tortilla** is a Mexican pancake made from corn and eggs. N COUNT

tortoise /tɔːtəs/, **tortoises**. A **tortoise** is a slow-moving animal that has a hard shell round its back. It can pull its legs and head inside the shell in order to protect itself. N COUNT ⇑ reptile

tortoiseshell /tɔːtəsʃel/, **tortoiseshells**. 1 **Tortoiseshell** is the hard shell of a kind of sea turtle. It is brown and yellow in colour and is often polished and used to make jewellery and ornaments. N UNCOUNT

2 A **tortoiseshell** is 2.1 a butterfly with brown and orange wings. N COUNT 2.2 a cat with brown, black, and yellow fur. N COUNT

tortuous /tɔːtjuəs/. 1 A **tortuous** road is full of bends and twists. EG *They walked through the narrow, tortuous streets of the old city centre.* ADJ QUALIT = winding

2 A **tortuous** piece of writing is long and complicated and does not give information clearly; used showing disapproval. EG *I wrote tortuous essays for obscure journals.* ADJ QUALIT = convoluted

torture /tɔːtʃə/, **tortures, torturing, tortured**. 1 **Torture** is great pain that is deliberately caused to someone, especially in order to punish them, to get information from them, or to make them confess to something. EG *...the constant threat of death and torture... ...instruments of torture... Many of the prisoners died under torture.* N UNCOUNT ⇑ cruelty ▸ used as a count noun. EG *Here floggings and tortures were carried out.* ▸ N COUNT ⇑ atrocity

2 To **torture** someone means 2.1 to deliberately cause them great pain, especially in order to punish them, to get information from them, or to make them confess to something. EG *...prisons where the inmates were tortured and murdered by the thousand.* V+O ⇑ hurt 2.2 to cause them to suffer mentally. EG *Why do we have to keep on torturing ourselves by talking about it?... He opened it slowly. Not to torture me, I don't think, but to stall for time.* V+O (NG/REFL) ⇑ hurt = torment ▸ used as a noun. EG *It was torture to be ill in bed while everyone was celebrating downstairs.* ▸ N UNCOUNT/COUNT

torturer /tɔːtʃərə/, **torturers**. A **torturer** is someone who tortures people. N COUNT

Tory /tɔːri¹/, **Tories**. In Britain, a **Tory** is a member or supporter of the Conservative Party; an informal word, often used by members and supporters of other parties. EG *The Tories were restored to power.* N COUNT ▸ used as an adjective. EG *...Mr Robin Squire, the Tory MP for Hornchurch.* ▸ N BEFORE N

toss /tɒs/, **tosses, tossing, tossed**. 1 If you **toss** something, you throw it lightly, often in a rather careless way. EG *He took the bag and tossed it into some nearby bushes... I tossed him ten pounds.* V+O : USU+A

2 If you **toss** food while you are preparing it, you put pieces of it into a liquid and lightly turn or shake them to cover them with the liquid. EG *Serve noodles tossed in butter or cream... ...a tossed salad.* V+O : IF+PREP THEN *in* ⇑ stir

3 If you **toss** pancakes, you throw them up in the air and then catch them again in a frying pan so that they are the other way round. V+O

4 If you **toss** your head, you move it suddenly backwards. EG *'That's the main thing, isn't it?' said Frederica, tossing her head.* V+O = shake ▸ used as a noun. EG *She gave a toss of her head.* ▸ N COUNT ⇑ movement

5 If you **toss, toss up**, or **toss a coin**, you make a decision about something by throwing a coin into the air and guessing which side of the coin will be on top when it falls. EG *We tossed up to decide who should pay the bill... We tossed for the last piece of chocolate... We'll toss a coin to see who does the washing up... I'll toss you for it.* V OR V+O, OR PHRASAL VB : V+ADV, USU+A ▸ used as a noun. EG *The decision was finally made by the toss of a coin.* ● See also **toss-up**. ▸ N COUNT

6 If something or someone **tosses** or **is tossed**, they move restlessly from side to side or up and down. EG *I tossed and turned all night... Ships were tossed at sea... Palm trees tossed like heads of hair.* V-ERG

7 If someone **argues the toss**, they argue for longer than is necessary about a point which is not very important. PHR : VB INFLECTS ⇑ dispute

8 If you **don't give a toss** about something, you do not care at all about it; an informal expression. PHR : VB INFLECTS

toss off. If you **toss off** something such as a letter or an article, you write it very quickly. PHRASAL VB : V+O+ADV

toss-up. A **toss-up** is a situation in which either of two results seems equally likely. EG *It was a toss-up who would get there first.* N SING : a+N ⇑ uncertainty

tot /tɒt/, **tots, totting, totted**. 1 A **tot** is a very young child; an informal use. EG *I'd wanted to come ever since I was a tot.* N COUNT = toddler

2 A **tot** of a strong alcoholic drink such as whisky or brandy is a small amount of it in a glass. N PART : +N UNCOUNT

tot up. To **tot up** means to add numbers together in order to get the total number or amount of something. EG *I'll just tot up what you owe me.* PHRASAL VB : V+O+ADV ⇑ calculate

total /təʊtəⁿl/, **totals, totalling, totalled**. 1 A **total** is the number that you get when you add a series of figures together or when you count how many things there are in a group. EG *The factory employed a total of forty workers.* N COUNT ▸ used as an adjective. EG *...the total number of students on campus... ...a total cost of over £3,000.* ● See also **sum total**. ▸ ADJ CLASSIF : ATTRIB = overall

2 If you say that there are a number of things **in total**, you mean that there are that many of them altogether. EG *A force containing in total over half a million men and 11,000 tanks... It was enlarged by less than 50 cubic metres in total.* PHR : USED AS AN A, OR AFTER N = in all

3 When you **total** a set of numbers or objects, you add them all together. EG *Votes cast for each candidate in each section will be totalled to get a result.* V+O = tot up

4 If several numbers or things **total** a certain figure, that figure is the total of all the numbers or all the things. EG *Conoco's 1980 revenues totalled £18.3 billion... Subsidies on basic commodities total 25 per cent of the budget.* V+C = come to

5 You also use **total** 5.1 to say that something is complete, or to emphasize its completeness. EG *The aircraft was blown up with total loss of life... ...a total eclipse of the sun... ...a total failure... She had been incredibly foolish to tell such things to a total stranger.* ADJ CLASSIF : USU ATTRIB ⇑ full ≠ partial ◇ **totally**. EG *He became almost totally blind... I totally disagree... A totally new situation arose.* ◇ ADV 5.2 to indicate that you are referring to everything that is included in a situation. EG *The total effect is intensely joyful... A total policy is being devised for the care of all.* ADJ CLASSIF : USU ATTRIB = overall

totalitarian /təʊtælɪteəriən/. A **totalitarian** political system is one in which there is only one political party, and this party controls everything and does not allow any opposition parties; used showing disapproval. EG *...the brutalities of the totalitarian regimes.* ADJ CLASSIF ⇑ authoritarian

totalitarianism /təʊtælɪteəriənɪzm/ is the ideas, principles, and practices of totalitarian political systems. EG *We are all opposed to apartheid and totalitarianism.* N UNCOUNT ⇑ authoritarianism

totality /təʊtælɪti¹/. The **totality** of something is the whole of it; a formal word. EG *...participation in the totality of French culture... ...truth in its totality, its variety of aspects.* N UNCOUNT : USU +SUPP

tote /təʊt/, **totes, toting, toted**. 1 The **tote** is a system of betting money on horses at a racetrack, in which all the money bet on a race is divided among the people who have bet on the winning horses; an informal British English use. EG *He always bets on the tote at the week-end.* N SING : *the*+N

2 Someone who **totes** a gun takes a gun with them, for example in their pocket, wherever they go; an old-fashioned use. EG *In some small towns they tote guns.* V+O ⇑ carry

totem /təʊtəⁿm/, **totems**. A **totem** is an object that is regarded as a symbol by a particular group of people who treat it with great respect. N COUNT

totem pole, totem poles; also spelled with a hyphen. A **totem pole** is a long wooden pole with symbols and pictures carved and painted on it. Totem poles are made by some North American Indians and placed outside their homes. N COUNT

totter /tɒtə/, **totters, tottering, tottered**. 1 If someone **totters**, they walk in an unsteady way, for example because they are ill or drunk. EG *Thelma tottered from the stage in search of the gin bottle.* V : USU+A

2 If something such as a government **totters**, it is weakened and likely to lose control. EG *The wartime Liberal Government was tottering.* V

toucan /tu:kən/, **toucans**. A **toucan** is a South American bird that eats fruit. It has a large brightly-coloured beak. N COUNT

touch /tʌtʃ/, **touches, touching, touched**. 1 If you **touch** something, 1.1 you put your hand onto it in order to feel it or to make contact with it. EG *The metal is so hot I can't touch it.* ▸ used as a noun. EG *The wood is so rotten that it crumbles at the touch... They collapse at the touch of a finger.* 1.2 you hit it very gently with hardly any force at all. EG *In fact I did just touch the car in front.* V+O = handle ▸ N COUNT : USU SING V+O = graze

2 If you **touch** someone or **touch** a part of their body, you put your hand on their hand, arm, or shoulder, or on another part of their body, in order to show friendship or affection. EG *Madeleine stretched out her hand to touch his... Mrs Travers' fingers touched the little girl's cheek.* ▸ used as a noun. EG *He remembered the touch of her hand.* V+O ⇑ contact ▸ N COUNT : USU SING

3 To **touch** someone also means to put your hand onto their body in an intimate way that is intended to give sexual pleasure. EG *I wouldn't let him touch me unless I was in the mood.* V+O ⇑ fondle

4 If you say that you did not **touch** someone, you are denying that you hit them or attacked them in any way; an informal use. EG *I never touched him!* V+O : WITH BROAD NEG

5 If someone **touches** you for something, they persuade you to give them or lend them money or to buy something for them; an informal use. EG *Harry was hoping to touch her for a sandwich and a glass of beer.* ● See also **soft touch**. V+O+A *(for)*

6 If something **touches** you, it affects you emotionally for a short time. EG *Something mysterious had touched all of us at the same moment... The play is certainly political in intent but hopefully it touches people personally too.* V+O = stir, move

7 If you **are touched** by something that someone has done, you are emotionally affected by it, because you realize that they have been very kind or unselfish. EG *I was very touched by his thoughtfulness.* V+O : USU PASS = be moved

8 If you do not **touch** something, you avoid picking it up, damaging it, or interfering with the way that it is arranged. EG *Put it down! Don't touch anything... This tomb was the only one that wasn't touched.* V+O : WITH BROAD NEG

9 If you do not **touch** a particular kind of food or drink, you never eat it or drink it. EG *Drink? No, she never touches the stuff.* V+O : WITH BROAD NEG

10 If you say that someone or something cannot **be touched**, you mean that the standard that they have achieved is so high that it cannot be equalled by any other person or thing. EG *The queen of Restoration comedy was Edith Evans. Nobody could touch her in parts like Millamant.* V+O : USU PASS, WITH BROAD NEG = rival, better

11 If two things **are touching**, they are in contact with one other. EG *Space the plants out so that the leaves are not touching... He stood close to me in the queue so that our bodies touched.* V OR V+O : RECIP

12 Your sense of **touch** is the sense that tells you how something feels, for example when you put your fingers on it. EG *I had to rely on my sense of smell and touch... The skin was fleshy and slightly waxy to the touch.* N UNCOUNT

13 A **touch** is 13.1 a detail which is added to something and which improves it. EG *The final touches were put to their report.* ● a **finishing touch**: see **finish**. 13.2 a particular manner of doing something. EG *In the play, religion is handled with quite a light, comic touch.* ● **the common touch**: see **common**. N COUNT : MOD+N N SING WITH DET +SUPP = approach

14 A **touch** of something is a very small amount of it. EG *There was a touch of frost this morning... 'What do you think?' asked Dave with a touch of anxiety.* N PART : a+N+N UNCOUNT

15 If something is **a touch** slow, **a touch** expensive, etc, it is slightly slow, slightly expensive, etc. EG *Just a touch slower... Richard's voice suddenly became important and even a touch official.* PHR+ADJ/ADV = fractionally

16 **in touch, out of touch**. 16.1 If you **get in touch** with someone, you contact them, especially by writing to them or telephoning them. EG *You should take your temperature and get in touch with your doctor... A man from the Organization got in touch with me.* 16.2 If you **put** someone **in touch** with someone else, you arrange for them to visit, telephone, or write to the other person. EG *If you write they will put you in touch with their local group.* 16.3 If someone says that they **will be in touch** with you, they mean that they will write to you or telephone you. EG *We'll be in touch when we've had a think about what to do.* PHR+*with* : VB INFLECTS ⇑ communicate PHR+*with* : VB INFLECTS PHR : VB INFLECTS, IF+PREP THEN *with*

16.4 If you **keep in touch** with someone, you write to them, telephone them, or visit them regularly so that you can exchange news. EG *Please drop in when you can. I'd like to keep in touch.* 16.5 If you are **in touch** with something or if you keep **in touch** with it, you have up-to-date information, knowledge, and understanding about it. If you are **out of touch** with it, you no longer have this information, knowledge, or understanding. EG *I am helping the Government to stay in touch with the feelings of the Black people... They seem incredibly out of touch with the reality of living in Britain.* PHR OR PHR+A *(with)* : RECIP, VB INFLECTS ≠ lose touch PHR : USED AS AN A, IF+PREP THEN *with*

17 **lose touch**. 17.1 If you **lose touch** with someone, you gradually stop writing, telephoning, or visiting them. EG *We finally lost touch after she moved to London.* 17.2 If you **lose touch** with something, you no longer have up-to-date knowledge, understanding, or information about it. EG *He claimed that party leaders had lost touch with the working class.* PHR OR PHR+A *(with)* : RECIP, VB INFLECTS PHR : VB INFLECTS, IF+PREP THEN *with*

18 **Touch** is also used in the following expressions. 18.1 **Touch wood** is a superstitious or humorous expression that is supposed to prevent bad luck. Often people actually touch a piece of wood when they say it. EG *'You've not had anything go wrong with your car yet?'–'No, touch wood.'* 18.2 If you say that something is **touch and go**, you mean that you are uncertain whether it will happen or succeed. EG *It was touch and go whether we'd arrive before we ran out of petrol.* PHR PHR : USED AS C = a near thing

19 See also **touched, touching**.

touch down. When an aircraft **touches down**, it lands. EG *He watched the plane as it touched down.* ● See also **touchdown**. PHRASAL VB : V+ADV ⇑ arrive

touch off. If something **touches off** a situation or series of events, it causes it to start happening. EG *The police action touched off another night of rioting.* PHRASAL VB : V+O+ADV = spark off

touch on. If you **touch on** something or **touch upon** it, you mention it or write briefly about it. EG *This is a topic which I touched on at the beginning of my talk.* PHRASAL VB : V+PREP, HAS PASS = allude to

touchdown /tʌtʃdaʊn/, **touchdowns**. **Touchdown** or a **touchdown** is the landing of an aircraft. EG *Failure of any mechanical system to function after touchdown could destroy human lives.* N COUNT/UNCOUNT ⇑ arrival

touché /tu:ʃeɪ/. You say **touché** when you want to admit that the other person in an argument has won a point, usually with a short and witty remark. CONVENTION

touched /tʌtʃt/. If you say that someone is **touched**, you mean that they are slightly mad. EG *We thought she was a bit touched.* ADJ QUALIT : PRED = batty

touching /tʌtʃɪŋ/. If something is **touching**, it causes feelings of sadness and sympathy. EG *'I've seen the photographs.'–'Touching, weren't they?'* ◊ **touchingly**. EG *He was touchingly proud of his son's gifts.* ADJ QUALIT = moving ◊ ADV

touch paper; also spelled with a hyphen. The **touch paper** on a firework is a small piece of dark blue paper on one end of it which you light in order to start it. N SING WITH DET ⇑ fuse

touchstone /tʌtʃstəʊn/, **touchstones**. A **touchstone** is a feature of something which is used as a test by which its quality can be judged. EG *Inventiveness has become the touchstone both of intelligence and excellence.* N COUNT ⇑ criterion

touch-type, touch-types, touch-typing, touch-typed. When someone **touch-types**, they type without looking at the keys on the typewriter. V

touchy /tʌtʃi[1]/, **touchier, touchiest**. 1 A **touchy** person is easily upset, offended, or irritated. EG *He always was a touchy and quick-tempered man... They are touchy about criticism.* ◊ **touchiness**. EG *She was amused by his touchiness.* ADJ QUALIT ◊ N UNCOUNT

2 A **touchy** subject is one that needs to be dealt with carefully and tactfully, because it might upset or offend people. EG *Security is a touchy subject among government officials at the moment.* ADJ QUALIT : USU ATTRIB = sensitive

tough /tʌf/, **tougher, toughest; toughs**. 1 Someone who is **tough** has a strong and independent character and is able to tolerate a lot of pain or hardship. EG *He's not hard-hearted but resolute and tough... He was mentally tough enough to keep going long after his body had given up.* ◊ **toughness**. EG *She had an unusual degree of self-reliance and mental* ADJ QUALIT = resilient ◊ N UNCOUNT ⇑ strength *toughness.* ● If you say that someone is **as tough as old boots**, you mean that they are very tough indeed. ● PHR : USED AS C

2 You also describe someone as **tough** when they are rough and violent rather than gentle and kind. EG *We have to keep tough law-breaking youngsters off the streets.* ▸ used as a noun. EG *They're a couple of young toughs.* ADJ QUALIT = vicious, hard-bitten ▸ N COUNT = thug

3 An animal or plant that is **tough** is able to survive in very difficult conditions. EG *Camels are tough and hardy creatures.* ADJ QUALIT = hardy

4 A **tough** substance is strong, and difficult to break, cut, or tear. EG *Some plastics are as tough as metal... He cut through the tough, orange-yellow skin of the mango.* ◊ **toughness**. EG *The mass and toughness of the stone created several problems.* ADJ QUALIT = sturdy, hard ◊ N UNCOUNT = strength

5 Meat or other food which is **tough** is difficult to cut and chew. EG *The meat was smelly and a little tough... Rattlesnake is just like chicken, only tougher.* ADJ QUALIT ≠ tender

6 A **tough** task, problem, way of life, etc is difficult or full of hardship. EG *It was to be one of the toughest by-elections for a long time... It was tough to get a cab... It was a tough life.* ADJ QUALIT = hard

7 **Tough** policies or actions are strict and firm, and show determination. EG *Many people are convinced that her tough economic policies will succeed... ...a very tough form of law and order.* ADJ QUALIT = harsh, stern

8 A place, for example a part of a town or city, that is **tough** is considered to have a lot of crime and violence. EG *...tough comprehensive schools.* ADJ QUALIT = rough

9 If you say **'tough'** or **'tough luck'** to someone, you are showing that you do not have any sympathy for their problems or difficulties and will not do anything to help them; an informal use. EG *If you can't get here in time, that's your tough luck.* PHR = hard cheese

toughen /tʌfəⁿn/, **toughens, toughening, toughened**. 1 If you **toughen** something, you make it stronger so that it will not break easily. ◊ **toughened**. EG *...toughened glass.* V+O ◊ ADJ CLASSIF

2 When someone **toughens** or when an experience **toughens** them, they become stronger and more independent in character, for example because they have experienced a lot of difficulties. EG *He has toughened a lot since his mother died.* V-ERG

toupee /tuːpeɪ/, **toupees**. A **toupee** is a small wig worn by a man. It covers a bald patch on his head. EG *In the shop was a collection of hair dyes, toupees, and wigs.* N COUNT = hairpiece

tour /tʊə, tɔː/, **tours, touring, toured**. 1 A **tour** is 1.1 a journey during which you visit several places that interest you. EG *I went on a tour of the North of Scotland during my vacation.* N COUNT = trip 1.2 a short trip that you make round a place, for example round a historical building, so that you can look at it. EG *The guests were given a tour of the castle... This way for the guided tours.* N COUNT 1.3 an official journey through several parts of a country, made for example by a sports team which stops in different places to play matches, or by a theatre company which gives performances in different places. EG *...the English cricket team's tour of Australia... ...a lecture tour in America... We went on tour for several weeks before opening in London.* N COUNT, OR on+N = circuit

2 If you **tour** a place, you go on a journey or trip round it. EG *He spent his vacation touring the highlands of Scotland... The Prime Minister toured the hardest hit area of Liverpool.* V+O : NO IMPER = travel round

3 When a theatre company **tours**, it goes on a tour, performing in different places. EG *He used to invite various touring companies to appear in his theatre.* ▸ used of actors and actresses. EG *I'd like to tour in companies that go round the country.* V : NO IMPER ⇑ travel ▸ ⇑ travel

tour de force /tɔː də¹ fɔːs/. A **tour de force** is a brilliant and skilful action or theatrical performance. EG *I thought her Lady Macbeth was a tour de force.* N SING : a+N = masterpiece

tourism /tʊərɪzəⁿm, tɔː-/ is the business of providing services for people on holiday, for example hotels, restaurants and sightseeing trips. EG *Tourism is a big industry in Spain.* N UNCOUNT

tourist /tʊərɪst, tɔː-/, **tourists**. A **tourist** is a person who visits places for pleasure and interest, especially when he or she is on holiday. EG *She showed a party of tourists round the museum... July is the height of the tourist season in England.* N COUNT ⇑ traveller

tourist class is the class on a ship or plane which is not as expensive or as high quality as first class. N UNCOUNT

touristy /tʊərɪsti¹, tɔː-/. If you describe a place as **touristy**, you mean that it is full of tourists or full of things for tourists to buy and do; an informal word, usually used showing disapproval. EG *One of the less touristy parts of Westminster Abbey.* ADJ QUALIT

tournament /tʊənəməⁿnt, tɔː-, tɜː-/, **tournaments**. A **tournament** is a sports competition in which players who win a match continue to play further matches in the competition until just one person or team is left. EG *He was the best boxer in the tournament... ...a table-tennis tournament.* N COUNT

tourniquet /tʊənɪkeɪ, tɔː-/, **tourniquets**. A **tourniquet** is a strip of cloth that you tie tightly round an injured arm or leg in order to stop it bleeding. N COUNT ⇑ bandage

tousled /taʊzəⁿld/. **Tousled** hair is untidy and looks as if it has not been combed. EG *Their teacher was an old man with tousled grey hair.* ADJ QUALIT = dishevelled

tout /taʊt/, **touts, touting, touted**. 1 If someone **touts** something that they are not officially allowed to sell, they try and sell it. For example some people tout tickets for sports matches and theatre performances when there are more people who want to go than there are tickets available. V OR V+O = peddle

2 A **tout** is someone who touts tickets outside a sports ground or theatre. Usually, they charge more than the original value of the ticket. N COUNT

3 If someone **touts** for business or custom, they try to obtain it in a very direct way. EG *He went from door to door touting for custom..* V+A (for)

tow /təʊ/, **tows, towing, towed**. 1 If a vehicle **tows** another vehicle, it pulls it along behind it. EG *If you leave your car there you might have it towed away by the police... The lifeboat towed them to safety.* ▸ used as a noun. EG *My car broke down but luckily someone gave me a tow.* ● If a vehicle is **on tow**, it is being towed by another vehicle. V+O = haul ▸ N SING : a+N ● PHR : USED AS AN A

2 If you have someone **in tow**, they are following closely behind you because you are looking after them; an informal expression. EG *He arrived on Sunday with his children in tow.* PHR : USED AS AN A

towards /təwɔːdz/. The form **toward** is also used. 1 If you move, look, or point **towards** something or someone, you move, look, or point in their direction. EG *He saw his mother running towards him... She turned towards John... She glanced towards the mirror... 'Turn in here,' he said, pointing toward a footpath.* PREP ⇑ to

2 You also use **towards** 2.1 to indicate that a situation or state is becoming closer or more likely. EG *There is a permanent tendency towards inflation... We are working towards a solution... We are drifting towards disaster... ...the advance toward accurate weather prediction.* PREP 2.2 to indicate that you have a particular attitude or way of behaving in relation to a subject or a person. EG *There has been a fundamental change of attitude towards science... He felt very friendly towards them... He recalled how peculiarly she had acted towards him... They were all hostile toward me.* PREP

3 If something happens **towards** a particular time or date, it happens just before that time. EG *Towards midnight the rain ceased... I went to a conference in London towards the end of 1977... He had made efforts towards the end to reassert his authority.* PREP

4 **Towards** a place or area can also mean near to it. EG *He was sitting towards the rear end of the room... It was pink and, towards the middle, almost red.* PREP

5 If you give a sum of money **towards** something, 5.1 you give it for a particular purpose or cause. EG *British Rail contributed 154,000 pounds towards improving safety... From 1967-70, only 54m pounds went towards capital investment.* PREP = on 5.2 you give it to help pay for that thing, although it is not a large enough sum to pay for it completely. EG *They may give you something towards your housing costs... They launched a public appeal towards the cost of the £19,000 special bus.* PREP

6 You can also use **towards** to indicate a particular result that you are trying to achieve. EG *The twins did a lot towards making Tom willing to stay... His goodwill and co-operation can go a long way towards smoothing your way to the top.* PREP

towel /taʊəl/, **towels, towelling, towelled**. 1 A **towel** is a piece of thick, soft cloth that you use to dry your body with, for example after you have had a bath. EG *He dried his feet with the towel... My hair* N COUNT *is wrapped up in a towel, because I'd just washed it when you rang.* • See also **tea towel**.

2 If you **throw in the towel** or **chuck in the towel**, you stop trying to do something because you realize that you cannot succeed; an informal expression. EG *I think it's time to throw in the towel.* PHR : VB INFLECTS = give in

towel down. If you **towel** yourself **down**, you rub your body with a towel in order to dry it. PHRASAL VB : V+O (REFL)+ADV

towelling /taʊəlɪŋ/ is a kind of fairly thick, soft cloth that is used especially for making towels. EG *She was dressed in a towelling bath-robe.* N UNCOUNT ⇑ fabric

tower /taʊə/, **towers, towering, towered**. 1 A **tower** is a tall, narrow building. Many churches and castles have towers attached to them. EG *...a church tower... ...the Eiffel Tower.* • See also **ivory tower**. N COUNT : ALSO IN NAMES

2 If you refer to someone as a **tower of strength**, you mean that they give you a lot of help, support, and encouragement when you have problems or are in a difficult situation. EG *You've been a tower of strength to me.* PHR : USED AS C = comfort

3 Someone or something that **towers** over surrounding people or things is a lot taller than they are. EG *Mary Jane stood up, towering over him... The dark high shape towering ominously on your left is Mount Etna.* V+A = loom

tower block, tower blocks. A **tower block** is a tall building divided into flats or offices; used in British English. EG *This was one of the last tower blocks to be built in the sixties.* N COUNT = skyscraper

towering /taʊərɪŋ/. A **towering** building, tree, etc is very tall and therefore rather impressive or frightening. EG *...a landscape of lush green meadows surrounded by towering trees.* ADJ CLASSIF : ATTRIB = lofty, gigantic

town /taʊn/, **towns**. 1 A **town** is a place with many streets and buildings where people live and work. Towns are larger than villages and have factories, shops, offices, and places of entertainment. EG *...the town of Pangbourne in England... He had a boring, badly-paid job in a northern town.* N COUNT ⇑ settlement ▸ used of the people who live in a town. EG *The whole town is furious about the new motorway.* ▸ N COUNT : USU SING

2 **Town** is 2.1 the town that you live in or the town that is closest to where you live. EG *...the finest and most expensive restaurant in town... We packed our stuff and left town on a bus... ...a week-end resort about twenty-five miles out of town.* N UNCOUNT **2.2** the central area of a town where most of the shops and offices are. EG *I had lunch in town... Can we give you a lift into town?* N UNCOUNT ⇑ centre • If you go **on the town** or **out on the town**, you visit some of the nightclubs, restaurants, etc that there are in a particular city or town, especially at night. EG *That night they took me out on the town.* • PHR : USED AS AN A

3 If you talk about the **town**, you are referring to town and city areas in general, as opposed to country areas. EG *In the last century there was a considerable migration from the country to the town... There is nothing I like about town life.* N SING : *the*+N

4 If you **go to town** on an activity you put a lot of effort and enthusiasm into doing it, especially by spending a lot of money. EG *They really went to town on the Christmas decorations this year.* PHR : VB INFLECTS

5 See also **county town, ghost town, new town**. • to **paint the town red**: see **paint**.

town council, town councils. A **town council** is a group of officials who have been elected to govern a town. EG *The town council, in theory, represents the people.* N COUNT : ALSO IN NAMES

town crier, town criers. A **town crier** was a man who used to walk through the streets of a town shouting out news and official announcements. N COUNT ⇑ announcer

town hall, town halls. A **town hall** is a large building in a town, often where the town council has its offices. Public meetings and concerts are also sometimes held in town halls. EG *The town hall stood at the head of Main Street.* ▸ also used of a town council that has its offices there. EG *Ask the town hall for full details.* N COUNT : ALSO IN NAMES

town house, town houses. 1 A **town house** is a modern house which is tall and narrow and which is built in a town, usually in a row of similar houses. N COUNT

2 The **town house** of a wealthy person or member of the aristocracy is the house that they own in a town or city, rather than another house that they own in the country. EG *Here, till 1874, stood the town house of the Dukes of Northumberland.* N COUNT ⇑ residence

townie /taʊni¹/, **townies**. A **townie** is someone who lives in a town or city; an informal word, often used showing disapproval of someone who does not know anything about country life. N COUNT

town planning is the planning and design of all the new buildings, roads, parks, etc in a place in order to make them attractive and convenient for the people who live there. EG *We held an architectural exhibition on town planning in our headquarters... ...the Town Planning Committee.* N UNCOUNT

townsfolk /taʊnzfəʊk/. The **townsfolk** of a town or city are the people who live there; an old-fashioned word. N PLURAL : USU *the*+N ⇑ inhabitants

township /taʊnʃɪp/, **townships**. A **township** is 1 a town in South Africa where only black people or coloured people are allowed to live. N COUNT 2 a small area of local government in the United States or Canada, especially a town and the land surrounding it. EG *...the Florida township of Ticklaw.* N COUNT

townspeople /taʊnzpiːpəºl/. The **townspeople** of a town or city are the people who live there; an old-fashioned word. EG *None of the townspeople had ever seen such weather.* N PLURAL : USU *the*+N = townsfolk

towpath /təʊpɑːθ/, **towpaths**. A **towpath** is a path along the side of a canal or river, which horses used to walk on when they towed boats. EG *Would you like a little stroll along the towpath?* N COUNT

towrope /təʊrəʊp/, towropes; also spelled with a hyphen. A **towrope** is a strong rope used for towing vehicles. N COUNT

toxic /tɒksɪk/. A **toxic** substance is poisonous. EG *Water became dangerously contaminated by toxic chemicals... Excessive vitamin D can be toxic.* ▸ used of the effects of poisonous substances. EG *Different forms of asbestos varied in their toxic effects.* ADJ QUALIT ⇑ harmful

toxicology /tɒksɪkɒlədʒi¹/ is the study of poisons. N UNCOUNT ◊ **toxicological**. EG *...the toxicological experts and their learned textbooks.* ◊ ADJ CLASSIF ◊ **toxicologist, toxicologists**. ◊ N COUNT

toxin /tɒksɪn/, **toxins**. A **toxin** is a poisonous substance that is produced by bacteria and is very harmful to plants, people, or other living creatures. EG *...the process of eliminating toxins... ...diphtheria toxin.* N COUNT/UNCOUNT ⇑ poison

toy /tɔɪ/, **toys, toying, toyed**. 1 A **toy** is an object that children play with, for example a doll or a model car. EG *The children could bring their own toys... My favourite toy was a rag doll... Boys are given toy cars and construction sets.* N COUNT = plaything

2 A **toy** is also an object that adults use for amusement rather than for a serious purpose. EG *In no sense are these toys–they are genuine computers... ...executive toys.* N COUNT ⇑ plaything

toy with. 1 If you **toy with** an idea, you consider it without being very serious about it or without making a definite decision on it. EG *I've been toying with the idea for some time.* PHRASAL VB : V+PREP, HAS PASS = play with

2 If you **toy with** an object, you keep moving it about with your fingers with small movements, especially while you are thinking about something else. EG *He withdrew the key from his pocket where he had been toying with it... She toyed with the one shrimp remaining on her plate.* PHRASAL VB : V+PREP, HAS PASS = play with

trace /treɪs/, **traces, tracing, traced**. 1 If you **trace** the cause of something, you find out what it is after looking for it. EG *The man traced the trouble to a faulty transformer... I think I've traced the source of the poison.* V+O = track down

2 If you **trace** the origins of something, for example of an idea, you find out how it first began. EG *British empiricism can be traced back to Hume, Locke, and Bacon... He came from an ancient, Catholic family which traced its origins to Anne of Cleves.* V+O ⇑ discover

3 If you **trace** the progress or development of something, you find out or describe how it progressed or developed. EG *Throughout the nineteenth century we can trace the gradual development of more complex machinery... The course of the battle for the Atlantic has been traced in Chapter 17.* V+O = map out

4 If you **trace** something that has disappeared, you find it by looking in all the places where you think that it could be. EG *We have been unable to trace your letter... They were trying to trace her missing husband.* V+O = track down

5 If you **trace** something such as a drawing or a map, you copy it by covering it with a piece of transparent V+O

paper and drawing over the lines underneath. EG *It is easier and quicker to trace a map than to draw it yourself.* ● See also **tracing**.

6 If you **trace** something such as a pattern or a shape, for example with your finger or toe, you mark its outline on a surface. EG *Hughie was tracing a pattern in the carpet with his finger.*
V+O = delineate

7 A **trace** is a sign which shows you that someone or something has been present in a particular place. EG *The vast majority of animals leave no trace of their existence after their passing... No trace was found of either the bag or its contents.* ● If someone or something disappears **without trace**, they disappear without leaving any signs of where they have gone or why they have disappeared. EG *Madeleine vanished without trace... The ship has sunk without trace.*
N COUNT = evidence; ● PHR : USED AS AN A

8 A **trace** is also 8.1 a very small amount of something that remains after most of it has disappeared or been removed. EG *I can still see the traces of the old paint on the wall... All traces of anger are gone.*
N PART : +N UNCOUNT = remnant

8.2 a very small amount of something that is hardly noticeable. EG *There wasn't the slightest trace of fear in my father... I anticipated a trace of jealousy in her.*
N PART : +N UNCOUNT = hint, bit

8.3 a pattern that is made on a screen or piece of paper by a machine that is recording an electrical signal; a technical use. EG *...a baffling radar trace.*
N COUNT

trace out. If you **trace** something **out**, you write it or mark it clearly and carefully. EG *The names were traced out in stark black print.*
PHRASAL VB : V+O+ADV = outline

trachea /trəkɪə/, **tracheae, tracheas.** The plural can be either **tracheae** or **tracheas**. Your **trachea** is your windpipe; a medical term.
N COUNT

tracing /treɪsɪŋ/, **tracings.** A **tracing** is a copy that has been made by covering a drawing or map with a piece of special transparent paper and drawing over the lines underneath. EG *...a tracing of a Union Jack.*
N COUNT

tracing paper is special transparent paper on which you can make tracings.
N UNCOUNT

track /træk/, **tracks, tracking, tracked. 1** A **track** is 1.1 a narrow road or path that has an uneven surface made of earth rather than of tarmac or gravel. EG *I remember riding along a dusty mountain track in Morocco... We covered the last five miles on a narrow bumpy track.*
N COUNT = trail

1.2 a narrow path that has been made by animals or people moving along it frequently. EG *...sheep tracks.*
N COUNT

1.3 a piece of ground, usually in the shape of a ring, that has been specially prepared for racing, especially for athletics. EG *The recreation ground had a proper cinder track... ...track events.*
N COUNT

1.4 a long, narrow strip of ground with rails on either side that a train travels along. EG *The train on the next track was moving.*
N COUNT

2 The **track** of a satellite, planet, rocket, etc is the course that it takes through the air. EG *The Earth crosses the tracks of certain comets.*
N COUNT : USU+*of* = path

3 **Tracks** are footprints or other marks which animals or people make on the ground and which show that they have been there. EG *The fox didn't leave any tracks.*
N PLURAL ⇑ imprints

4 If you **track** animals or people, you find them by following their footprints or by following other signs that show you where they have been. EG *I lost my camels, tracked them, and found them again... The sergeant tracked the wife to the constable's lodgings.*
V+O = trail

5 If someone **tracks** a vehicle such as an aircraft or a ship, they follow its movements by means of radar; a technical use. EG *...the greatly increased capacity to track and identify aircraft.*
V+O

6 A **track** is also one of the songs or pieces of music on a record or tape, when the record or tape has more than one song or piece of music on each side. EG *That's Sonny Rollins singing on that track... The title track is Bridge Over Troubled Water.*
N COUNT

7 The word **track** is also used in the following expressions. 7.1 A place that is **off the beaten track** is in a quiet and isolated area. EG *The village where Elaine lives is a bit off the beaten track.*
PHR : USED AS AN A

7.2 If you are **on the track of** a person or animal, you are searching for them or hunting them.
PHR : USED AS AN A

7.3 If you **hide** your **tracks** or **cover** your **tracks**, you are careful not to leave any signs or clues that could let people know what you have been doing, because you want to keep it secret.
PHR : VB INFLECTS

7.4 If you **stop dead in** your **tracks** or if someone or something **stops** you **dead in** your **tracks**, you stop walking somewhere or stop doing something, because something has surprised you. EG *He stopped dead in his tracks and gave a shrill gasp of shock... The sight of the two men stopped her dead in her tracks.*
PHR : VB INFLECTS = freeze

7.5 If you **make tracks**, you leave a place; a rather informal expression. EG *It's getting late. We must make tracks.*
PHR : VB INFLECTS

7.6 If you **keep track of** things or people, you pay attention to them so that you know where they are or what is happening. If you **lose track of** them, you no longer know where they are or what is happening. EG *We would never be able to keep track of the luggage on such a long journey... Gwyneth had lost all track of time.*
PHR : VB INFLECTS

7.7 If you are **on the right track**, you are reasoning in a way that is likely to give you the right answer to a question or problem. If you are **on the wrong track**, you are reasoning in a way that is mistaken and that will not give you the right answer. EG *The fellow was probably on the right track, but his pronouncements were extravagant... I'm sorry, but I think you're on the wrong track there.*
PHR : USED AS AN A

8 See also **one-track mind, racetrack, soundtrack**.

track down. If you **track down** someone or something, you find them by searching for them, especially by following signs or clues that show you where they have been or where they might be now. EG *...an able detective with a special skill for tracking down burglary suspects... You have to cover a wide area to have any hope of tracking down the submarine.*
PHRASAL VB : V+O+ADV = hunt down

tracker /trækə/, **trackers.** A **tracker** is a person or animal that finds other people or animals by following footprints or other signs that show where they have been. EG *...anti-terrorist trackers... ...a tracker dog.*
N COUNT ⇑ hunter

tracking station, tracking stations. A **tracking station** is a building from which the movement of spacecraft, satellites, etc can be followed by means of radar or radio. EG *...a guided missile tracking station.*
N COUNT

track record, track records. The **track record** of a person or a company is all the achievements or failures that they have had since they started in their job or business. EG *They have established a good track record of successful trading... He has the best track record in the business.*
N COUNT : WITH POSS/SUPP ⇑ history

tracksuit /træksj^{u}uːt/, **tracksuits.** A **tracksuit** is a loose suit of clothing, consisting of trousers and a jacket, that sportsmen and sportswomen sometimes wear during training to keep warm.
N COUNT

tract /trækt/, **tracts.** A **tract** is 1 a short article expressing a strong opinion on a religious, moral, or political subject in order to try to influence people's attitudes. EG *...the usual newspaper cuttings, campaign tracts, letters, et cetera.*
N COUNT = treatise, pamphlet

2 a very large area of land or forest. EG *...immense tracts of impenetrable jungle.*
N COUNT

3 a system of organs and tubes in an animal's or person's body that has a particular function, especially the function of processing a substance in the body. EG *...the digestive tract.*
N COUNT : USU MOD+N

tractable /træktəbə^{0}l/. A **tractable** person or problem is easily controlled or dealt with; a formal word. EG *Be good and tractable and you will be looked after... Airfields presented a less tractable problem.*
ADJ QUALIT = manageable

traction /trækʃə^{0}n/. **Traction** is 1 a form of medical treatment given to an injured limb which involves pulling it gently for long periods of time using a system of weights and pulleys. EG *His leg is in traction.*
N UNCOUNT

2 a particular form of power that makes a vehicle move. EG *...the increased use of electric traction.*
N UNCOUNT

3 the grip that the wheels of a vehicle have on the ground. EG *Four wheel drive gives greatly improved traction in rain, snow and ice.*
N UNCOUNT = purchase

traction engine, traction engines. A **traction engine** is a large, heavy vehicle powered by steam that was used in the past for pulling heavy loads along roads or rough ground.
N COUNT

tractor /træktə/, **tractors.** A **tractor** is a vehicle with large rear wheels that is used on a farm for ploughing fields, sowing crops, pulling trailers, etc.
N COUNT

trad /træd/ is a kind of jazz based on the jazz that was played in the 1920s; an informal word.
N UNCOUNT ⇑ music

trade /treɪd/, **trades, trading, traded. 1 Trade** is the activity of buying, selling, or exchanging goods or services between people, firms, or countries. EG *...the development of more intensive trade with Eastern Europe... France is heavily dependent on foreign trade... ...the lucrative trade in tea and porcelain.*
N UNCOUNT ⇑ business

2 When people, firms, or countries **trade**, they buy, sell, or exchange goods or services between themselves. EG *He had stopped trading in hardware... They specialized in trading with China... We increased our share of the market and traded at a profit.* ◊ **trading**. EG *...a record of successful trading.* — V: USU+A ⇑ deal; ◊ N UNCOUNT

3 The **trade** is the people or businesses involved in a particular kind of work. EG *There is no way the trade can employ so many people... ...a boom in the tourist trade... A friend of mine went into the antique trade.* — N COUNT: USU the+SING = business

● A **trick of the trade** is a clever technique or a quicker way of doing something that is only known by the people who work in a particular job. EG *These are standard tricks of the clothing trade.* — ● PHR: USED AS C/O

4 Someone's **trade** is the kind of work that they do, especially when they have been trained to do it over a period of time. EG *My dad has no skilled trade... His trade was welding... By trade he was a dealer in antique furniture.* ● See also **jack of all trades.** — N COUNT: USU POSS+N, OR *by*+N ⇑ job

5 If you **trade** or **trade off** one thing for another thing, you exchange it for the other thing. EG *Leah traded off a piece of her jewelry for food... He traded a job in New York City for the life of a cowboy... We traded stories about objects falling on people's heads.* — V+O, OR PHRASAL VB: V+O+ADV, USU+A = swap

trade in. If you **trade in** something such as your old car or TV set, you give it to a dealer when you buy a new one so that you get a reduction on the price. EG *You might trade the car in for a smaller one.* ● See also **trade-in.** — PHRASAL VB: V+O+ADV, USU+A ⇑ exchange

trade on. If you **trade on** something such as another person's weakness, you make use of it for your own advantage; often used showing disapproval. EG *...people who trade on the hopes of the desperately ill.* — PHRASAL VB: V+PREP, HAS PASS = exploit

trade fair, trade fairs. A **trade fair** is an exhibition where manufacturers show products that they want to sell to people from other industries. EG *...visitors returning from the Canton Trade Fair.* — N COUNT: ALSO IN NAMES

trade-in, trade-ins. A **trade-in** is a business deal in which someone buys a new car, washing machine, etc at a reduced price by giving an old car, washing machine, etc as well as money in payment. EG *What is the car's trade-in value?* — N COUNT ⇑ exchange

trademark /treɪdmɑːk/, **trademarks**; also spelled with a hyphen. **1** A **trademark** is a name or symbol that a manufacturer always uses on a product or a range of products. A trademark is usually registered and protected by law. EG *Precision tools are still in use bearing that famous trademark... ...information concerning patents, copyrights and trademarks.* — N COUNT

2 A **trademark** is also a feature which is considered to be a typical characteristic of a person or thing. EG *Beautiful homes and gardens are trademarks of the south... That wistfully regal expression which was her trademark.* — N COUNT: WITH POSS = hallmark

trade name, trade names; also spelled with a hyphen. A **trade name** is the name which manufacturers give to a product or to a range of products. EG *Some acrylic trade names are Courtelle, Acrilan, and Dralon... This drug is being marketed under one trade name only.* — N COUNT = brand name

trader /treɪdə/, **traders.** A **trader** is a person whose job is to trade in goods. EG *Traders sold basic commodities to the tribesmen... ...a wealthy trader in tea.* — N COUNT ⇑ merchant

trade route, trade routes. A **trade route** is a route, often covering long distances, that was regularly used by traders in the past. — N COUNT

trade secret, trade secrets. A **trade secret** is **1** a secret, for example about a particular method of production or a chemical formula, that is known and used by only one firm. **2** some knowledge that you have, for example about how to do something, that you are not willing to tell to other people. EG *'Where did you get this information from?'–'Sorry, mate–trade secret.'* — N COUNT; N COUNT

tradesman /treɪdzmə³n/, **tradesmen.** A **tradesman** is a person, for example a shopkeeper, whose job is to sell goods. — N COUNT ⇑ merchant

tradesmen's entrance, tradesmen's entrances. A **tradesmen's entrance** is a side or back entrance, for example to a large private house, which is used by tradesmen to deliver their goods. EG *We were sent round to the tradesmen's entrance.* — N COUNT

tradespeople /treɪdzpiːpə⁰l/ are people whose job is to trade goods. — N PLURAL ⇑ merchants

trades union, trades unions. See **trade union.**

Trades Union Congress. See **T.U.C.**.

trade union, trade unions; also written **trades union.** A **trade union** is an organization of workers that represents them and has the aim of improving such things as the working conditions, pay, and benefits of its members. EG *...a highly organized trade union.* ▸ used before another noun, often spelled with a hyphen. EG *The Secretary of State will meet the trade union leaders tomorrow... ...leaders of the free trade-union movement.* — N COUNT ⇑ association; ▸ N BEFORE N

trade unionism is the system, practices, and ideology of trade unions. — N UNCOUNT

trade unionist, trade unionists. A **trade unionist** is an active member of a trade union. EG *...militant trade unionists.... Labour retained the allegiance of the mass of trade unionists.* — N COUNT

trading estate, trading estates. A **trading estate** is the same as an industrial estate. — N COUNT: ALSO IN NAMES

trading stamp, trading stamps. A **trading stamp** is a stamp that some shops give to their customers when they buy goods. Customers can collect the stamps and exchange a number of them for certain goods. — N COUNT ⇑ token

tradition /trə³dɪʃə⁰n/, **traditions. 1** A **tradition** is a custom or belief that the people in a particular group or society have practised or held for a long time. EG *We ought to consider briefly the history and traditions of the movement... ...Britain's long tradition of political independence... I was not going to keep up the family tradition.* ▸ **Tradition** is all the customs and beliefs of a group or society. EG *We must have respect for tradition... ...Tagore's fusion of classical Indian tradition and Western liberal thought.* — N COUNT: IF+PREP THEN *of* ⇑ practice; ▸ N UNCOUNT = folklore

2 If you say that something or someone is **in the tradition of** something or someone else from the past, you mean that they have many features that remind you of the other person or thing. EG *...a play in the tradition of Macbeth and Hamlet... ...a political essayist in the tradition of Cobbett and Orwell.* — PHR: USED AS AN A ⇑ like

traditional /trə³dɪʃə⁰nəl, -ʃənə⁰l/. **1 Traditional** dress, customs, etc have existed in a place without changing for a long time. EG *The bride is dressed in traditional costume... Development in the Third World is rapidly destroying good and bad in traditional cultures... Women are questioning their traditional role in society, as wives and mothers.* ◊ **traditionally.** EG *Traditionally in this culture, there is no figurative art.* — ADJ CLASSIF: USU ATTRIB ⇑ established; ◊ ADV OR ADV SEN

2 Traditional beliefs and attitudes have existed in a place for a long time and are not expected to change. EG *I asked him whether the traditional East-West divisions still existed... She scored a surprising number of votes in traditional Nationalist strongholds.* ◊ **traditionally.** EG *Some of these groups were traditionally antagonistic.* — ADJ CLASSIF: USU ATTRIB = customary, standard; ◊ ADV OR ADV SEN

3 A **traditional** organization or institution is one in which older methods are used in preference to modern ones. EG *She went to a fairly traditional grammar school.* — ADJ QUALIT: USU ATTRIB = conventional

traditionalism /trə³dɪʃə⁰nəlɪzə⁰m/ is behaviour and ideas that support old customs and beliefs rather than modern ones. EG *The Royal Shakespeare Company is a bastion of traditionalism.* — N UNCOUNT

traditionalist /trə³dɪʃə⁰nəlɪst/, **traditionalists. 1** A **traditionalist** is a person who supports the established customs and beliefs of his or her society or group, and does not want to change them. EG *The fact that many mothers now work need not threaten the family, as so many traditionalists fear.* — N COUNT ≠ radical

2 A **traditionalist** idea, argument, etc supports the established customs and beliefs of a society. EG *This argument is too traditionalist and too boring to go into again.* — ADJ QUALIT = conservative

traduce /trə³djuːs/, **traduces, traducing, traduced.** If you **traduce** someone, you deliberately say unpleasant things about them that are untrue; a formal word. — V+O = defame, slander

traffic /træfɪk/, **traffics, trafficking, trafficked. 1 Traffic** is **1.1** the movement of cars and other vehicles on the roads, especially in towns and cities. EG *...a one-way traffic system... ...the dislocation of traffic caused by the construction work.* **1.2** all the cars, buses, trucks, and other vehicles that — N UNCOUNT; N UNCOUNT are moving along a road at any one time. EG *He eased the van out into the line of rush-hour traffic... ...the strain of getting to school through heavy traffic along crowded streets.* **1.3** the movement of ships or aircraft between one place and another. EG *...sea traffic between the UK and the Continent.* **1.4** the transporting of people or goods from one place to another by rail, road, sea, or air, especially when this is done for business reasons. EG *Passenger traffic has gone up by about 12 per cent.* — N UNCOUNT : MOD +N; N UNCOUNT+ SUPP ⇑ transportation

2 Traffic in something such as drugs or stolen goods is an illegal trade in it, involving buying and selling and transporting it from one place to another. EG *...an operation designed to uncover illegal traffic in protected animals.* — N UNCOUNT+ SUPP ⇑ business

3 Someone who **traffics** in something such as drugs or stolen goods buys and sells them even though it is illegal to do so. EG *...rumours that he trafficked in opium... ...illegal arms trafficking.* — V+A *(in)* = deal

4 Traffic is also used to refer to the exchange of ideas between people or organizations. EG *...an organization encouraging a two-way traffic in ideas.* — N UNCOUNT+ SUPP

traffic circle, traffic circles. A **traffic circle** is a roundabout in the road; used in American English. — N COUNT

traffic jam, traffic jams. A **traffic jam** is a long line of cars, buses, trucks, and other vehicles that cannot move forward because the road is blocked. EG *There were traffic jams, and police clearing people away.* — N COUNT ⇑ queue

trafficker /træfɪkə/, **traffickers.** A **trafficker** in particular goods, for example drugs, is a person who illegally buys or sells these goods. — N COUNT : USU MOD+N ⇑ trader

traffic light, traffic lights. **Traffic lights** are sets of red, green, and amber lights at a road junction for controlling the flow of traffic. A red light means stop, green means go. EG *He thought the traffic lights weren't working.* — N COUNT : USU PL

traffic warden, traffic wardens. A **traffic warden** is a person whose job is to make sure that cars are not parked where they should not be, and that they are not parked anywhere for longer than is allowed. — N COUNT

tragedy /trædʒɪ²di¹/, **tragedies.** **1** A **tragedy** is **1.1** a very sad event or situation, especially one that involves death, suffering, or disaster. EG *The change of flight plans was the principal cause of the tragedy... I know something of Dolly, the tragedy of her life, the sorrow, the unhappiness.* **1.2** a play, film, opera, etc, that is serious and sad, especially one that ends with the death of the main character. EG *I am a playwright. I have written tragedies, comedies, fantasies.* — N COUNT/ UNCOUNT ⇑ misfortune; N COUNT ⇑ work

2 Tragedy is a type of literature, especially drama, that is serious and sad and that often ends with the death of the main character. EG *Tragedy faces up to the horrors of life.* — N UNCOUNT ⇑ genre

tragic /trædʒɪk/. **1** Something that is **tragic** is very sad because it involves death, suffering, or disaster. EG *The most tragic sight of all was the very young addicts... ...the tragic death of his elder brother Michael.* ◊ **tragically.** EG *He was tragically killed in a car crash.* — ADJ QUALIT ⇑ distressing; ◊ ADV WITH VB, OR ADV SEN

2 Tragic is also used to refer to tragedy as a form of literature. EG *...the Greek tragic heroes... ...Scott Fitzgerald's tragic semi-autobiographical novel 'Tender is the Night'.* — ADJ CLASSIF : ATTRIB ≠ comic

tragicomedy /trædʒɪkɒmədi¹/, **tragicomedies**; also spelled with a hyphen. A **tragicomedy** is a play or other written work that is both sad and funny. — N COUNT

tragicomic /trædʒɪkɒmɪk/; also spelled with a hyphen. Something that is **tragicomic** is both sad and funny at the same time. — ADJ CLASSIF

trail /treɪl/, **trails.** **1** A **trail** is **1.1** a rough path across open country or through forests. EG *...walking along a trail in the forest... They set out on the trail once again.* **1.2** a route along a series of paths or roads, often one that has been specially planned for a particular purpose. EG *The trail follows the old Midland rail line from Buxton... ...a nature trail through the woods.* **1.3** the scent, footprints, and other marks that a person or animal leaves when moving along. Dogs, other animals, and some specially trained people can use this scent or these marks to follow a person or animal. EG *He followed their trails carefully... Eventually we lost the trail.* **1.4** something, for example smoke or a series of marks, which shows you that a person or thing is in a place or has been there a short time before. EG *She didn't want him to leave a trail of wet footprints all over the house... ...a thick trail of smoke from a village up ahead.* • to **blaze a trail**: see **blaze.** — N COUNT; N COUNT; N COUNT : USU SING; N COUNT : USU+ SUPP

2 If you are **on** someone's **trail**, you are gathering information about where they have been and what they have been doing, in order to find where they are now. EG *After her husband disappeared she put a private detective on his trail.* — PHR : USED AS AN A

3 If you **trail** someone or something, you follow them, usually secretly, by finding the tracks that they have left. — V+O = track

4 If you **trail** something behind you or if it **trails** behind you, it drags along the ground or flows through the air or water behind you as you go. EG *...with part of her sari trailing behind her on the floor... She trails the fingers of her right hand through the water.* — V-ERG : USU+A

5 If someone **is trailing** along or behind, they are moving slowly along, often following behind someone else, in a tired or rather disorganized way. EG *Everyone else came trailing behind, singing and applauding... I used to trail around after him like a small child.* — V+A

6 If a person or team in a contest or competition **is trailing**, they have a lower score than their rival. EG *Public opinion polls showed Giscard trailing Mitterand by as much as 3 points... United were trailing 2-0 at half-time.* — V OR V+O : USU CONT

7 See also **trailing.**

trail away or **trail off.** If a speaker's voice **trails away** or **trails off**, it gradually becomes quieter or less certain until it stops completely, often in the middle of a sentence, usually because the speaker feels uncertain or thinks that nobody is listening. EG *He didn't finish what he'd intended saying. His voice trailed away... 'You see, there are circumstances--' He trailed off.* — PHRASAL VB : V+ ADV ⇑ diminish = die away

trailer /treɪlə/, **trailers.** **1** A **trailer** is **1.1** a vehicle pulled by a car, used for carrying camping equipment, a boat, or other things. EG *...two Landrovers with trailers loaded with ammunition.* **1.2** the long rear section of an articulated lorry, in which the goods are carried. **1.3** in American English, a vehicle that can be pulled by a car, which people use as a home or an office. EG *The surgeon's wife and children were in a trailer nearby.* — N COUNT; N COUNT; N COUNT = caravan

2 A **trailer** for a film or a television or radio programme is a series of short extracts from the film or programme, which is shown or broadcast in order to advertise the film or programme. Cinemas often show trailers of the films that will be showing in the next few weeks. EG *...a trailer for the screenplay of his memoirs.* — N COUNT : IF+ PREP, THEN *for/ of* ⇑ advertisement

trailing /treɪlɪŋ/. **Trailing** plants have long stems that spread over the ground or hang down loosely. EG *...trailing geraniums.* — ADJ CLASSIF : ATTRIB

train /treɪn/, **trains, training, trained.** **1** A **train** is **1.1** a number of carriages or trucks which are all connected together and which are pulled by an engine along a railway. Trains carry people and goods from one place to another. EG *When the train stopped at a small station, he got off... I caught a train to Oxford... We are planning to go by train... ...express trains... ...the long train journey there and back.* **1.2** a long line of slowly moving vehicles, people, or animals travelling in the same direction. EG *...long trains of cars that had come in from another city... ...a wagon train.* — N COUNT, OR *by*+ N; N COUNT+SUPP = file

2 A **train** of thoughts, events, etc is a connected sequence, in which each thought or event seems to arise naturally or logically as a result of the previous one. EG *I felt annoyed with her for interrupting my train of thought... It sets off a whole train of events that ends in his suicide.* — N COUNT+*of*: USU SING = chain

3 If you say that one thing brings other things **in its train**, you mean that they occur naturally as a result of it. EG *This may be expected to bring in its train the most hideous consequences for the world.* — PHR : USED AS A[N] A ⇑ cause

4 If something is **in train**, it is actually happening or being done; a fairly formal expression. EG *Their modernization plan was in train... ...the era in which he put in train all his reforms.* — PHR : USED AS A[N] A = in operatio[n]

5 The **train** of a woman's formal gown or wedding dress is a long part at the back of it which flows along the floor behind her when she is wearing it. EG — N COUNT

The bride was wearing a dress with a long white train.

6 If someone **trains** you to do something, they teach you the skills that you need in order to do it. EG *The police are trained to keep calm.* ◊ **trained.** EG *...a lack of trained manpower... ...highly trained women who are involved in demanding careers.* — V+O, OR V+O+to-INF/A; ◊ ADJ CLASSIF ⇑ skilled

7 If you **train** as something, you learn the skills that you need for the particular job or activity mentioned, usually by taking a course of study. EG *She started to train as a nurse.* — V OR V+to-INF/A

8 If someone **trains** a particular ability that you have, for example your ability to reason well or to sing well, they help you to develop that ability. EG *...a general education which will train the mind.* ◊ **trained.** EG *She has a trained voice.* — V+O ⇑ educate; ◊ ADJ CLASSIF

9 If you **train** an animal or bird, you teach it a set of skills or tricks, so that, for example, it can work for you, perform in a circus, or be kept as a pet. EG *Dogs were trained to attack intruders... I wanted to get three wild camels and train them.* ◊ **trained.** EG *Trained pigeons are used for this purpose.* — V+O, OR V+O+to-INF; ◊ ADJ CLASSIF

10 If you **train** for an activity such as a sports match or a race, or if someone **trains** you for it, you prepare yourself for it by taking a lot of physical exercise and eating a special diet. EG *He was training for the London marathon... They were trained to a peak of physical fitness.* — V-ERG: IF+PREP THEN *for/to*

11 If you **train** something such as a gun, a camera, or a light on someone or something, you aim it at them and keep it pointing steadily towards them. EG *One gun was trained on Jo.* — V+O+A *(on)* ⇑ direct

12 If you **train** a tree, bush, or other plant, you tie it and prune it so that it grows in a particular way, for example up a pole or flat against a wall. — V+O: USU+A

13 See also **training**.

trainee /treɪniː/, **trainees**. A **trainee** is someone who is employed at a junior level in a particular job in order to learn the skills needed for that job. EG *The trainees are shown around each of the departments... ...a trainee chef.* — N COUNT ⇑ novice = apprentice

trainer /treɪnə/, **trainers**. **1** A **trainer** is **1.1** a person who trains animals, birds, etc to do things, for example to do work or to perform tricks that will entertain the public. EG *...the trainers from a nearby circus.* **1.2** a person who prepares race horses for races. **1.3** a person who coaches other people in sports such as boxing. — N COUNT; N COUNT; N COUNT = coach

2 Trainers are special shoes that people wear for running or jogging. — N COUNT: USU PL

training /treɪnɪŋ/. **1 Training** is **1.1** the process of learning the skills that you need for a particular job or activity. EG *I had a great training as a gardener... ...giving people training in computer programming.* — N UNCOUNT

1.2 physical exercise that you do regularly in order to keep fit or to prepare your body for an activity such as a sports match or a race. EG *There are no compulsory games or physical training at the school... He didn't turn up for training today.* ● If you are **in training**, you are preparing yourself for an activity such as a sports match or a race, by taking a lot of physical exercise and eating a special diet. EG *You are in training for a cross-country run?* — N UNCOUNT; ● PHR: USED AS AN A

2 If you say that something is **good training**, you mean that it will be useful to you later on in life. EG *I liked sleeping on the ground; it was good training... It's good training for their adult life.* — PHR: USED AS C

3 Training is often used before a noun to refer to the teaching and learning of skills that people need in a particular job, activity, or situation. EG *...a training course... ...a student at a teachers' training college.* — N BEFORE N ⇑ educational

training shoe, training shoes. **Training shoes** are special shoes that people wear for running or jogging. — N COUNT: USU PL = trainer

traipse /treɪps/, **traipses, traipsing, traipsed**. If you **traipse** around, you walk slowly and wearily for a long time over a long distance. EG *For eighteen weeks we traipsed around southern England... I've been traipsing round the shops all day looking for Christmas presents.* — V+A = trek, trudge

trait /treɪt⁰/, **traits**. A **trait** is a particular characteristic, quality, or tendency that someone or something has. EG *Certain personality traits had made her unpopular.* — N COUNT+SUPP

traitor /treɪtə/, **traitors**. A **traitor** is **1** a person who betrays his or her country or a group of which he or she is a member, for example by giving information to its enemies. EG *He was denounced as a traitor to France... ...traitors to the working class... You aren't suggesting he'd turn traitor, are you?* **2** a person who speaks against beliefs that he or she holds or used to hold. EG *He is a traitor to the faith into which he has been born.* — N COUNT: IF+PREP THEN *to*; N COUNT: IF+PREP THEN *to*

trajectory /trədʒɛktə⁰ri¹/, **trajectories**; a formal word. **1** The **trajectory** of an object moving through air is the curving path that it follows after it has been hit or thrown upwards and as it moves forwards and down again towards the ground. EG *It had come down, as footballs do, and under the trajectory of its descent there happened to be Henry.* — N COUNT+SUPP

2 The **trajectory** of something such as a marriage or a person's career is a pattern of development in which it seems to start by going up and end by coming down. EG *Each man's trajectory or career line will differ.* — N COUNT+SUPP

tram /træm/, **trams**. A **tram** is an electric vehicle for carrying people, which travels along rails laid in the surface of a street in a town or city. EG *The conductor blew his whistle, and the tram stopped... ...a tram driver.* — N COUNT, OR *by*+N = streetcar, tram car

tramline /træmlaɪn/, **tramlines**. **1** A **tramline** is one of the rails laid in the surface of a road that trams travel along. — N COUNT

2 In tennis or badminton, you say that a ball is in the **tramlines** when it is in the space between the two parallel lines on each side of the court. These lines mark an area which is only used when you are playing doubles. — N COUNT: USU PL

trammel /træmə⁰l/, **trammels, trammelling, trammelled**; also spelled **trammeling** and **trammeled** in American English. If you **are trammelled** by something, you are prevented from acting freely by something that is outside your control, especially something which you think is unjust or unfair; a formal word. EG *He had come to think of himself as trammelled and shackled by domestic responsibilities.* ▸ used as a noun. EG *...to free yourself from the trammels of the flesh.* — V+O: ONLY PASS ⇑ be restricted = shackled; ▸ N COUNT ⇑ restriction

tramp /træmp/, **tramps, tramping, tramped**. **1** A **tramp** is **1.1** a person who has no home or permanent job and very little money. Tramps go from place to place getting food and money by taking occasional jobs or begging. **1.2** a woman who is thought to have sex with a lot of men; an offensive use. EG *She's a tramp and a slut!* — N COUNT = vagrant, vagabond; N COUNT

2 A **tramp** is also a small cargo ship which does not have a regular route, but which is used to carry different cargoes to different ports. — N COUNT

3 If you **tramp** from one place to another, you walk heavily in a particular direction or along roads or streets. EG *She tramped slowly up the beach to where Amy was sitting... We tramped through the wood... ...a postman tramping the streets.* — V+A, OR V+O = trudge

4 The **tramp** of people is the sound of their heavy, regular walking. EG *We could hear the tramp of the marching soldiers.* — N UNCOUNT+SUPP

5 If you go for a **tramp**, you go for a long walk. EG *She wants to go for a long tramp over the downs.* — N COUNT: USU SING = trek

trample /træmpə⁰l/, **tramples, trampling, trampled**. **1** If people or animals **trample** on something or **trample** something, they tread heavily on it so that it is crushed and damaged or destroyed. EG *They don't want hundreds of tourists trampling over the grass... They had trampled his lovely rose garden.* ◊ **trampled.** EG *He slipped away over the trampled grass.* — V+A, OR V+O ⇑ crush = stamp on; ◊ ADJ QUALIT ⇑ crushed

2 If someone **is trampled** underfoot, they are injured or killed by being trodden on by animals or by other people. EG *One young woman was trampled under the hooves of the horses... In former days he would have been trampled to death by the Rajah's elephants.* — V+O+A: USU PASS ⇑ crush

3 If you **trample** on someone or on their rights, beliefs, hopes, etc, you indicate by the way in which you behave that you do not care about them. EG *Half the population trample on the rights of the other half.* — V+A *(on)* ⇑ ignore

trampoline /træmpə⁰liⁱn/, **trampolines**. A **trampoline** is a piece of gymnastic apparatus which consists of strong cloth held by springs in a large frame above the ground, so that people can do acrobatic jumps and somersaults on it. — N COUNT

tramway /træmweɪ/, **tramways**. A **tramway** is a set of rails laid in the surface of a road for trams to travel along. N COUNT ⇑ track = tramlines

trance /trɑːns/, **trances**. A **trance** is a state of mind in which someone seems to be asleep and to have no conscious control over their thoughts or actions, but in which they can see and hear things and respond to commands given by other people. EG *While in a trance a hypnotized person can be instructed to perform a variety of actions... She used to go into a trance and talk to the spirits... ...when she came out of the trance.* N COUNT: USU PREP+N ⇑ unconsciousness

tranquil /træŋkwɪl/; a fairly literary word. **1** Something that is **tranquil** is calm and peaceful, so that it has a soothing effect on you. EG *It's such a peaceful house, such a tranquil setting... ...a lake of tranquil blue water.* ADJ QUALIT = serene

2 People who feel **tranquil** are calm, peaceful, and relaxed. EG *There was a tranquil expression on his face.* ADJ QUALIT = serene, unruffled

3 If your breathing or your sleep is **tranquil**, it is steady and indicates that you are calm, peaceful, and relaxed. EG *...long, deep, dreamless, tranquil sleep.* ADJ QUALIT

tranquillity /træŋkwɪlɪti[1]/; also spelled **tranquility** in American English. **Tranquillity** is a situation of calmness and stability. EG *...relative political tranquillity... They all lived together to a great age in undisturbed tranquillity.* N UNCOUNT ⇑ peace

tranquillize /træŋkwɪlaɪz/, **tranquillizes, tranquillizing, tranquillized**; also spelled **tranquillise**. American English also uses the spelling **tranquilize**. **1** If you **tranquillize** a person or an animal, you make them become calm, sleepy, or unconscious by giving them a drug. EG *He chartered a plane, tranquillized the bears, and flew them 500 miles north.* V+O: USU PASS ⇑ sedate

2 If something has a **tranquillizing** effect on people, it has a soothing or calming effect on them. EG *Music has a tranquillizing effect and is astonishingly therapeutic.* ADJ QUALIT

tranquillizer /træŋkwɪlaɪzə/, **tranquillizers**; also spelled **tranquilliser**. American English also uses the spelling **tranquilizer**. A **tranquillizer** is a drug that makes people feel calmer and less anxious or nervous. In stronger doses tranquillizers can be used to make a person or animal unconscious. N COUNT ⇑ sedative

trans- is added **1** to adjectives formed from place names, to make words with the meaning 'across the place mentioned'. EG *...Atlantic→transatlantic... ...continental→transcontinental... ...Siberian→trans-Siberian.* PREFIX **2** to other words, to make words with the meaning 'moving from one container, group, or set of ideas to another'. EG *...shipment→transshipment... ...national→transnational.* PREFIX

trans. is used as an abbreviation for various words beginning with trans-, such as 'translated', 'transferred', and 'transitive'.

transact /trænzækt/, **transacts, transacting, transacted**. If you **transact** business, a deal, or some other arrangement that involves discussion or exchange, you start it and carry on with it until you finish it, usually by making an agreement with someone about it. EG *He told them not to transact any business without him.* V+O ⇑ carry out = execute

transaction /trænzækʃə⁰n/, **transactions**. A **transaction** is a piece of business or other activity that is carried out by two or more people negotiating about it, for example an act of buying or selling something. EG *...nervously awaiting the end of this transaction... ...a business transaction.* N COUNT

transatlantic /trænzə³tlæntɪk/ is used **1** to refer to something that travels or is transmitted across the Atlantic Ocean, usually between the United States and Britain. EG *...a transatlantic phone call... ...regular transatlantic crossings.* ADJ CLASSIF: ATTRIB **2** to describe something that happens or exists on the other side of the Atlantic, or that comes from the other side of the Atlantic; often used by British people to refer to the United States. EG *...a transatlantic television soap opera... He had had a transatlantic upbringing.* ADJ CLASSIF: ATTRIB

transcend /trænsɛnd/, **transcends, transcending, transcended**. Something that **transcends** a particular thing goes beyond it or above it, ignoring the normal limits or boundaries; a fairly formal word. EG *...a vital national issue that transcended party loyalties... ...the experience of drama transcends national boundaries.* V+O

transcendence /trænsɛndəns/ is the quality of being able to go beyond normal limits or boundaries or of existing outside them; a formal word. EG *...if love is a genuine transcendence of self... ...transcendence of time and death.* N UNCOUNT

transcendent /trænsɛndənt/. Something that is **transcendent** goes beyond or exists outside normal limits or boundaries; a formal word. EG *They believe in the transcendent unity of religions.* ADJ CLASSIF

transcendental /trænsə²ndɛntə⁰l/. A **transcendental** experience, idea, etc is based on things that lie beyond the practical experience of ordinary people, and cannot be discovered or understood by ordinary reasoning; a fairly formal word. EG *...a transcendental world view... ...eternal truths and transcendental values.* ADJ CLASSIF: USU ATTRIB ⇑ spiritual

transcendental meditation is a kind of meditation derived from Hinduism, in which people mentally relax by silently repeating over and over again a special formula of words. N UNCOUNT

transcribe /trænskraɪb/, **transcribes, transcribing, transcribed**. **1** If you **transcribe** a text, you write it out in a different form from the one in which it exists. You can transcribe a text by writing it out in full from notes or from a tape recording, or by changing the alphabet or set of symbols in which it is written. V+O: USU+A

2 If you **transcribe** a piece of music that was written for a particular instrument or group of instruments, you rewrite it so that it can be played by a different instrument or group of instruments. EG *...piano music which they transcribe for orchestra.* V+O: USU+A ⇑ arrange

transcript /trænskrɪpt/, **transcripts**. A **transcript** is a written text that has been made from a tape-recording, notes, etc. EG *...transcripts of tapes.* N COUNT: IF+PREP THEN *of*

transcription /trænskrɪpʃə⁰n/, **transcriptions**. **1** A **transcription** is a written text that has been made from a tape-recording, notes, etc. EG *...phonetic transcriptions of dialect speakers.* N COUNT ⇑ version = transcript

2 **Transcription** of a text or piece of music is the process of transcribing it. EG *Caxton liberated them from manual transcription of the holy word... ...musical transcription.* N UNCOUNT

transept /trænsɛpt/, **transepts**. The **transept** of a cathedral or church is a part which projects to the north or south of the main part of the building. EG *...the north transept.* N COUNT: USU MOD/*the*+N ⇑ wing

transfer, transfers, transferring, transferred. The word **transfer is pronounced** /trænsfɜ⁵/ when it is a noun and /trænsfɜː/ when it is a verb. **1** If you **transfer** something, you move it to a different place or position. EG *Perkins transferred the trout to a silver platter... The shop closed and the business was transferred somewhere else.* V+O: USU+A ▸ used as a noun. EG *There ought to be tighter control of the transfer of nuclear materials.* ▸ N UNCOUNT: USU+SUPP ⇑ movement

2 If money or something connected with money **is transferred**, it is moved from the control of one person or institution to another. EG *Ten thousand pounds has been transferred into your account... Your right to a guaranteed minimum pension may be transferred to your new employer's scheme... This ticket cannot be transferred to another airline.* V+O: USU+A ▸ used as a noun. EG *Many firms nowadays pay their employees' salaries by direct transfer into their bank accounts.* ▸ N UNCOUNT/COUNT: USU+SUPP

3 When information **is transferred**, it is copied from one type of storage to another. EG *The event was recorded on video tape and transferred to film.* V+O: USU+A

4 When property or land **is transferred**, it legally stops being owned by one person or institution and becomes owned by another; a technical use. EG *This is another method of transferring Aboriginal land to White ownership.* V+O: USU+A = make over, convey ▸ used as a noun. EG *...the transfer of property.* ▸ N UNCOUNT: USU+SUPP

5 When responsibility or power **is transferred**, it is taken from one person or institution and given to another. EG *Responsibility is lifted from individual shoulders and transferred to the State.* V+O+A = hand over ▸ used as a noun. EG *...the peaceful transfer of power from military to civil government.* ▸ N UNCOUNT: USU+SUPP = shift

6 If you **transfer** your loyalty or affection, you lose your feelings of loyalty and affection for one person and start to have these feelings about someone else. EG *Parents feared that the children might transfer to the school their loyalty toward home... Ravenscroft transferred his affections fairly soon to his secretary.* V+O+A *(to)* = shift

▸ used as a noun. EG *The situation provokes a transfer of feelings.* ▸ N UNCOUNT : USU + SUPP

7 If you **transfer** or **are transferred** to a different place or job, you move to a different place or job within the same organization. EG *She's been transferred to another department... What branch did you say you would like to transfer to?* ▸ used as a noun. EG *He got a transfer to the colonial paratroops... He initially resisted his transfer to the political section.* — V-ERG : USU + A (*to*), USU PASS; ▸ N COUNT : USU SING, OR N UNCOUNT + SUPP

8 A **transfer** is also a piece of paper with a design on one side. The design can be transferred by heat or pressure onto material, china, etc, for decoration. — N COUNT

transferable /trænsfɜːrəbəˈl/. If something such as a ticket is **transferable**, it can be passed to another person or organization and used by them. Often a ticket is marked 'Not transferable'. — ADJ CLASSIF : USU WITH BROAD NEG

transference /trænsfəˈrəns/ is the transferring of something to a different place, person, etc; a fairly formal word. EG *There has been no genuine transference of authority to local level.* — N UNCOUNT : USU + SUPP = transfer

transfigure /trænsfɪgə/, **transfigures, transfiguring, transfigured.** If something **transfigures** you or if you **are transfigured** or if your face or features **are transfigured**, the appearance of your face changes because something has made you very happy; a literary word. EG *Their faces became transfigured with joy.* — V + O : USU PASS ↑ transform

transfix /trænsfɪks/, **transfixes, transfixing, transfixed**; a fairly literary word. **1** If you **are transfixed** by something that you see, you are so impressed or frightened by it that you cannot move or do anything except look at it. EG *Millions stand transfixed as the countdown begins... I stood transfixed with terror.* — V + O : USU PASS = rivet

2 If you **transfix** a person or an animal, you stick a long pointed object in them or through them. EG *...a wild animal transfixed by a spear.* — V + O = impale

transform /trænsfɔːm/, **transforms, transforming, transformed.** If something or someone **is transformed**, **1** their appearance or function is completely changed. EG *An area of sandy pastureland can be transformed into a barren landscape in two or three years... They have transformed themselves into permanent city-dwellers.* ◊ **transformation** /trænsfəmeɪʃəˈn/, **transformations.** EG *...the social and political transformation of society.* **2** they are changed in a way that makes them much better or more attractive than they were before. EG *They claimed to be able to transform the lives of millions of people... By the time they got there, the situation had been transformed.* ◊ **transformation.** EG *There was a noticeable transformation in his appearance.* — V + O : IF + PREP THEN *from/into* ↑ alter; ◊ N COUNT/UNCOUNT; V + O ↑ alter; ◊ N COUNT/UNCOUNT

transformer /trænsfɔːmə/, **transformers.** A **transformer** is a piece of electrical equipment which changes the voltage of a current. — N COUNT ↑ device

transfusion /trænsfjuːʒəˈn/, **transfusions.** A **transfusion** or a **blood transfusion** is a process in which blood is injected into the body of a person who is badly injured or ill. EG *She had a transfusion this afternoon.* — N COUNT ↑ injection

transgress /trænzgres/, **transgresses, transgressing, transgressed.** When someone **transgresses**, they break a moral law or rule of behaviour; a formal word. ◊ **transgression** /trænzgreʃəˈn/, **transgressions.** EG *Apologize at once for your transgressions.* — V, V + O, OR V + A ↑ sin; ◊ N COUNT/UNCOUNT

transience /trænziˡəns/. When there is **transience** in a society, situation, etc, people's arrangements tend to last only a short time, because the society is changing rapidly; a fairly formal word. EG *Even babies soon become aware of the transience of human ties.* — N UNCOUNT ↑ brevity

transient /trænziˡənt/. **1** Something that is **transient** lasts only a short time and then changes, ends, or disappears. EG *Once again this will be a transient phase... She had a number of transient, casual relationships with fellow students.* — ADJ QUALIT ↑ brief = fleeting

2 Transient people stay in a place for only a short time and then move somewhere else; a fairly formal use. EG *Islamic Cairo is rarely explored by transient tourists.* ▸ used as a noun. EG *...a strange, drifting population of transients.* — ADJ CLASSIF ↑ temporary; ▸ N COUNT : USU PL

transistor /trænzɪstə/, **transistors. 1** A **transistor** is a very small device in something such as a television or radio. It is used for amplification, switching, etc. EG *...highly sophisticated transistors.* — N COUNT

2 A **transistor** or a **transistor radio** is a small portable radio containing transistors. EG *I would spend Saturdays with a transistor at my ear, listening to the sports broadcasts... From one of the rooms came the sound of a transistor radio.* — N COUNT

transit /trænzɪt/. **1 Transit** is the carrying of goods or people by vehicle from one place to another. EG *...the transit from London Airport to Paris... The worst part of the ocean transit was now over... Our transit time will be fifty-five minutes... ...a transit van.* — N UNCOUNT = conveyance

2 If people or things are **in transit**, they are travelling or being taken from one place to another. EG *Farm animals continue to suffer in transit... The tablets had been lost in transit... At the moment I have no address. I'm in transit.* — PHR : USED AS AN A

3 A **transit** area or building is an area or building where people wait or where goods are kept between different stages of a journey. EG *...the transit lounge... ...a typical transit area... ...the transit camp at Heaton Park.* — ADJ CLASSIF : ATTRIB

transition /trænzɪʃəˈn/, **transitions. Transition** or a **transition** is the process in which something changes from one state to another. EG *How do you think this made the transition from book to stage?... He was still a young intellectual in transition.* — N COUNT/UNCOUNT : USU + *from/to*

transitional /trænzɪʃəˈnəl, -ʃənəˈl/. **1** A **transitional** period, stage, etc is a period of time during which something or someone is changing from one state to another. EG *During this transitional period pensions should be increased... She was still in a transitional stage and was unable to feed herself.* — ADJ CLASSIF

2 Transitional is also used to describe something that happens or exists during a transitional period. EG *...a transitional economy... ...the transitional forms between species.* — ADJ CLASSIF

transitive /trænzɪtɪv/. In grammar, a **transitive** verb is a verb which has an object. In this dictionary O is used in the grammar notes beside entries to indicate that the verb is transitive. — ADJ CLASSIF

transitory /trænzɪtəˈriˡ/. If something is **transitory**, it lasts only for a short time; often used showing disapproval or regret. EG *Love is transitory, but art is eternal... ...the transitory nature of human ties in urban society.* — ADJ QUALIT ↑ temporary = passing

translate /trænsleɪt, trænz-/, **translates, translating, translated. 1** If you **translate** something that someone has said or written, **1.1** you say it or write it in a different language. EG *My books have been translated into many languages... ...an epic poem, translated from the Armenian... These jokes would be far too difficult to translate... 'Who are you?' she asked as Chang translated.* **1.2** you express it in a different way, using a different system, alphabet, etc. EG *The temperature is sixteen degrees Centigrade or, if we translate into Fahrenheit, sixty degrees.* — V OR V + O : IF + PREP THEN *from/into* ↑ change = render; V + A (*into*), OR V + O + A (*into*) ↑ convert

2 If you **translate** something such as an idea, you express it in a different way, for example by putting the idea into practice. EG *He started to translate into action the dreams of African unity.* — V + O + A (*into*) = transform, turn

3 If you **translate** a remark, gesture, action, etc in a particular way, you decide that this is what it means. EG *I gave him what I hoped would be translated as a thoughtful look.* — V OR V + O : IF + PREP THEN *as* ↑ take = interpret

translation /trænsleɪʃəˈn, trænz-/, **translations.**
1 A **translation** is a piece of writing or speech that has been translated from a different language. EG *...a new translation of the Bible... He made a translation into Hindi of Ibsen's 'Doll's House'... ...translations from Arabic... I read the Iliad in translation.* — N COUNT, OR *in* + N ↑ version = rendering

2 Translation is the translating of speech or writing from one language into another. EG *We did translation from English to Classical Arabic.* — N UNCOUNT ↑ exercise

3 Translation is also the expressing of something in a different way. EG *...the translation of potential violence into actual violence... The novel cannot survive translation to film.* — N UNCOUNT + *from/into/to*

translator /trænsleɪtə, trænz-/, **translators.** A **translator** is a person whose job is translating writing or speech from one language to another. EG *He was recruited as a translator for US military intelligence.* — N COUNT ↑ interpreter

translucent /trænzluːsəˈnt/. If something is **translucent**, light passes through it, so that it seems to glow. EG *The leaves of the beeches are translucent in the setting sun.* ▸ used of other things that seem to — ADJ QUALIT glow like this. EG *The skin on the baby's face had a pearly translucent quality.*

transmission /trænzmɪʃəⁿn/, **transmissions.** 1 **Transmission** is 1.1 the sending of something to a different place or person. EG *...the long-distance transmission and distribution of energy... ...data transmission... ...the transmission of diseases.* 1.2 the communicating of ideas, knowledge, etc to other people. EG *...the transmission of knowledge... He handled the transmission of presidential orders to the military.* 1.3 the broadcasting of television or radio programmes. EG *...a unique film record that was destroyed after transmission... ...transmission of last week's programme.* ▸ A **transmission** is a broadcast. EG *Millions would have heard that transmission.... ...sporting transmissions on BBC 1.* — N UNCOUNT; N UNCOUNT; N UNCOUNT; ▸ N COUNT

2 The **transmission** on a car or other motor vehicle is the system of gears and shafts by which the power from the engine reaches and turns the wheels. — N COUNT

transmit /trænzmɪt/, **transmits, transmitting, transmitted.** 1 When a message or electronic signal **is transmitted**, it is sent by means of radio waves, telegraph, or some other electronic system. EG *The material was transmitted by satellite throughout the world... Information gathered by sensors is transmitted to the control centre's computer... The cable office was reluctant to transmit the report.* — V OR V+O : USU PASS

2 If you **transmit** something to a different place or person, you pass it or send it to the place or person; a fairly formal use. EG *...a disease that is sometimes transmitted to humans... ...a superior way of storing and transmitting energy.* — V+O

3 If an object or substance **transmits** sound, vibrations, power, etc, the sound, vibrations, etc are able to pass through it or along it. EG *Water transmits sound better than air... ...the bone that transmits vibrations from an ear drum.* — V+O = conduct

4 If you **transmit** knowledge, ideas, etc to other people, you communicate them to the people; a fairly formal use. EG *There were many values transmitted to me during that conditioning process.* — V+O = convey

transmitter /trænzmɪtə/, **transmitters.** A **transmitter** is a piece of apparatus that is used for broadcasting television or radio programmes. EG *The BBC in Scotland wanted to test the range of their transmitters.* — N COUNT ⇑ device

transmute /trænzmjuːt/, **transmutes, transmuting, transmuted.** If something is **transmuted** into a different form, it is changed into that form; a formal word. EG *The drizzle had been transmuted into thin layers of mist... The agony of her loss had been transmuted into numb acceptance.* — V+O : IF+PREP THEN *into*

◊ **transmutation** /trænzmjəˈteɪʃəⁿn/, **transmutations.** EG *...the transmutation of matter.* — ◊ N UNCOUNT/COUNT

transparency /trænspærənsi¹/, **transparencies.** 1 A **transparency** is a small piece of photographic film with a frame around it which can be projected onto a screen so that you can see the picture. EG *...colour transparencies.* — N COUNT = slide

2 **Transparency** is the quality that an object or substance has when you can see through it. EG *The crystal lost its transparency.* — N UNCOUNT ≠ opacity

transparent /trænspærənt/. 1 If an object or substance is **transparent**, you can see through it. EG *...a transparent plastic lid... ...her transparent cotton nightgown... The plastic capsule was transparent all the way round.* — ADJ CLASSIF ⇑ clear

2 If something such as a situation or statement is **transparent**, it is easily understood or recognized. EG *It was transparent that he was hurt and resentful... We wanted our goals to be transparent.* — ADJ QUALIT ⇑ clear = plain

◊ **transparently.** EG *The true nature of liberty must have been transparently clear.* — ◊ ADV+ADJ/ADV

3 If a dishonest statement or action is **transparent**, people are not deceived by it. EG *...a transparent lie... No thinking person could believe such a transparent fabrication... The economies were made in the mid-seventies under the transparent guise of improved efficiency.* ▸ used also of people. EG *He's so transparent.* ◊ **transparently.** EG *...an attitude that was transparently false.* — ADJ QUALIT ⇑ clear = obvious; ◊ ADV+ADJ/ADV

transpire /trænspaɪə/, **transpires, transpiring, transpired.** 1 When it **transpires** that something has happened or that something is the case, people discover that it has happened or that it is the case; a formal use. EG *The man refused to state his business. It finally transpired that he was a special investigator for the CIA... These, it transpired, were forbidden under Saudi law..* — V : *it*+V+REPORT-CL ⇑ appear = turn out

2 When something **transpires**, it happens. This use is sometimes considered to be incorrect. EG *Nobody knows what transpired at the meeting.* — V : USU *what*+V

transplant, transplants, transplanting, transplanted. The word **transplant** is pronounced /trænsplɑːnt/ when it is a noun and /trænsplɑːnt/ when it is a verb. 1 A **transplant** is a surgical operation in which a diseased or missing part of a person's body, such as their kidney, their heart, or a part of their skin or hair, is replaced by a part from another person's body or from a different part of their own body. EG *Several of the patients had received kidney transplants... ...one of Britain's youngest heart transplant patients.* ▸ used as a verb. EG *Doctors hope to transplant a human heart into the patient within the next few days.* — N COUNT/UNCOUNT; ▸ V+O

2 When something or someone **is transplanted**, they are moved to a different environment. If they **transplant** well, the move is a successful one. EG *Imagine the law faculty being transplanted to the middle of Chelsea... Adults are not flexible; they do not transplant comfortably to another place.* — V-ERG : USU+A, IF V THEN+ADV = uproot

3 If a plant **is transplanted**, it is taken out of the ground and planted somewhere else. If it **transplants** well, it grows satisfactorily in the new place. EG *Tea was transplanted from China to India and Ceylon... These flowers don't transplant easily.* — V-ERG : USU+A, IF V THEN+ADV ⇑ move

transport, transports, transporting, transported. The word **transport** is pronounced /trænspɔːt/ when it is a noun and /trænspɔːt/ when it is a verb. 1 When goods or people **are transported**, they are moved from one place to another in a vehicle or vehicles. EG *Sculptures are often heavy and costly to transport... The goods were transported to East and South Africa... The boat that was transporting them tipped over and they fell into the water.* — V+O : USU+A = convey

2 **Transport** is 2.1 the moving of goods or people from one place to another by vehicle. EG *The goods were now ready for transport and distribution.* 2.2 a lorry, car, or other vehicle used for moving something or for travelling from one place to another. EG *It is easier to travel if you have your own transport... Many people spend a huge proportion of their wages on transport... Coach transport is provided.* 2.3 the system of trains, buses, coaches, etc that people can use in order to travel from one place to another, especially when these things are owned by the government or local authority. EG *He was interested in the planning of housing, transport, and the environment... Local authorities must ensure that transport facilities meet the needs of the population.* — N UNCOUNT; N UNCOUNT; N UNCOUNT

3 In former times, when a criminal **was transported**, he or she was sent to a distant country as a punishment. British prisoners used to be transported to Australia. — V+O : USU PASS

4 If you **are transported** to another place or time, for example when you are reading a book, you feel as though you were living in the other place or at the other time. EG *As he talked, I was transported back to a time when pirates used this harbour... Alone in her hotel room, a fever of longing transported her to her bedroom at home.* — V+O : USU PASS+A ⇑ take

transportation /trænspɔːˈteɪʃəⁿn/; used especially in American English. **Transportation** is 1 the moving of goods or people from one place to another in a vehicle or vehicles. EG *The boxes were ready for transportation.* 2 a lorry, car, or other vehicle used for moving something or for travelling from one place to another. EG *...the fastest transportation available to man.* 3 the system of trains, buses, coaches, etc that people can use in order to travel from one place to another. — N UNCOUNT = transport; N UNCOUNT = transport; N UNCOUNT = transport

transport cafe, transport cafes. A **transport cafe** is a cafe beside a main road that is used mainly by lorry drivers and that provides cheap food and drink. — N COUNT

transporter /trænspɔːtə/, **transporters.** A **transporter** is a large vehicle that is used for carrying very large or heavy objects, for example cars. EG *He swung the enormous transporter back on the road... ...tank transporters.* — N COUNT

transpose /trænspəʊz/, **transposes, transposing, transposed;** a formal word. 1 If you **transpose** something to a different place or position, you — V+O+A move it to that place or position. EG *He was unable to transpose himself to the cockpit.*

2 To **transpose** something also means to alter it to a different form, while keeping its essential features. EG *...a Jacobean drama transposed into modern dress.* V+O

transverse /trænzvɜːs/. **Transverse** is used to describe something that is in a direction or position at right angles to something else; a technical word. EG *...the transverse arches in the nave of the cathedral... ...the transverse acceleration.* ADJ CLASSIF : ATTRIB

transvestism /trænzvestɪzəᵊm/ is the practice of wearing clothes normally worn by a person of the opposite sex, especially for sexual pleasure; a formal word. N UNCOUNT

transvestite /trænzvestaɪt/, **transvestites**. A **transvestite** is a person, usually a man, who enjoys wearing clothes normally worn by people of the opposite sex. N COUNT

trap /træp/, **traps, trapping, trapped**. 1 A **trap** is a device or hole which has been placed or dug somewhere in order to catch animals or birds. EG *...an otter trap... The farmer was glad that he had set the traps.* N COUNT

2 Someone who **traps** animals catches them using traps. EG *My father doesn't like the idea of trapping otters.* V OR V+O

3 If you **trap** a person, you make them do something that they do not want to do by tricking them or deceiving them. EG *This wasn't the first time we had been trapped into a situation like this... You're not going to trap me.* ▸ used as a noun. EG *I knew perfectly well it was a trap, a deceit.* V+O ⇑ trick ▸ N COUNT

4 If you **are trapped** in a building or **are trapped** in a particular position, you cannot escape or cannot move because something is in your way or something is holding you down. EG *Many people trapped in buildings died before they could be rescued... I can't get up, I'm trapped here.* V+O : USU PASS ⇑ confine

5 If you **are trapped**, you are in an unpleasant situation that it is difficult to escape from. EG *She felt trapped... Many women are trapped in loveless marriages.* ▸ A **trap** is a situation like this. EG *To break out of the poverty trap they need help from the government.* V+O : USU PASS ⇑ confined ▸ N COUNT ⇑ state

6 When something **traps** gas, water, energy, etc, it retains it so that it can be used. EG *A building can be designed to trap and store radiation from the sun... Where steam is found underground this can be trapped and used to drive electrical generators.* V+O ⇑ catch

7 If you tell someone to **shut** their **trap** or **keep** their **trap shut**, you mean that they should be quiet and not say anything; a very rude expression. EG *Now get moving and keep your trap shut... Why don't they shut their traps and go fishing?* PHR : USU IMPER = shut up

8 A **trap** is also a light horse-drawn carriage with two wheels. EG *The farmer went ahead in his trap.* N COUNT

9 See also **booby trap, radar trap**.

trapdoor /træpdɔː/, trapdoors; also spelled with a hyphen. A **trapdoor** is a small horizontal door in a floor, a ceiling, or a stage. EG *The box was placed over a trapdoor in the stage.* N COUNT

trapeze /trəpiːz/, **trapezes**. A **trapeze** is a bar of wood or metal hung from a high place by a rope at each end. People swing and perform skilful movements on trapezes in circuses. EG *She hung from the trapeze by one leg.* N COUNT ⇑ apparatus

trapper /træpə/, **trappers**. A **trapper** is a person who traps animals, especially for their fur. N COUNT ⇑ hunter

trappings /træpɪŋz/ are extra things that you acquire as a result of having a particular job or status and which people therefore associate with that job or status. EG *...the trappings of power that have surrounded him since he took office.* N PLURAL : USU + *of* ⇑ additions = trimmings

trash /træʃ/. 1 **Trash** is rubbish; used especially in American English. EG *Trash is collected and disposed of in incinerators.* N UNCOUNT

2 If you say that something such as a book, painting, or film is **trash**, you mean that it is of poor quality and has no artistic merit; an informal use. EG *'I've told you not to read that trash,' he said... Abstract art can produce as much trash as representational art.* N UNCOUNT = rubbish

3 If you refer to people as **trash**, you mean that you think that they are worthless; an informal use. EG *...the assorted trendy trash who fill the wine bars and bistros.* N UNCOUNT

trashcan /træʃkæn/, **trashcans**. A **trashcan** is a dustbin; used in American English. EG *He disposed of the body in the trashcan.* N COUNT = rubbish bin

trashy /træʃiˡ/, **trashier, trashiest**. Something that is **trashy** is of very poor quality; an informal word. EG *I wouldn't call his book trashy but it wasn't very well written.* ADJ QUALIT ⇑ worthless = rubbishy

trauma /trɔːmə/, **traumas**. A **trauma** is 1 a very unpleasant and upsetting experience. EG *...the distressing trauma of family break-up... I look at my daughter and think of what traumas lie in store for her.* 2 an emotional shock that causes long-term psychological damage; a technical term in psychology. N COUNT/ UNCOUNT N COUNT/ UNCOUNT

traumatic /trɔːmætɪk/. 1 A **traumatic** experience is very unpleasant and upsetting. EG *...the traumatic experience of two world wars.* ▸ used of the effects of an experience like this. EG *The industrial revolution had traumatic effects on society.* ADJ QUALIT = distressing, painful

2 **Traumatic** also means relating to or resulting from a psychological trauma; a technical term in psychology. EG *...traumatic neurosis.* ADJ CLASSIF : ATTRIB

travel /trævəᵊl/, **travels, travelling, travelled**; also spelled **traveling** and **traveled** in American English. 1 If you **travel**, you go from one place to another or go to several places, especially in foreign countries. EG *I travelled to work by train... You have to have a passport to travel abroad... He has travelled widely... Margaret travelled alone around the United States.* ▸ used as a noun. EG *They arrived after 4 days of hard travel... ...air travel... ...space travel... ...travel writers.* ● If you **travel light**, you travel without taking much luggage. V : USU + A = journey ▸ N UNCOUNT ● PHR : VB INFLECTS

2 If you **travel** a particular distance or **travel** at a particular speed, you go that distance or move at that speed. EG *I travelled sixty miles to buy those books... The vehicle was travelling along at 30 mph.* V+O, OR V+A

3 When something such as light or sound gets from one place to another, you say that it **travels** there. EG *Nothing can travel faster than light... When an atom is split its neutrons travel outwards.* V+A ⇑ move

4 When news is carried to different places, you say that it **travels** to them. EG *News travels fast.* V : USU + A, NO CONT

5 In informal English, if you say that a vehicle really **travels**, certainly **travels**, etc, you mean that it is able to move very quickly; used showing approval. EG *That car certainly travels.* V : USU ADV + V = go, move

6 If you say that a particular kind of food **travels** well, you mean that it can be taken on a journey without decaying. If you say that it **travels** badly, you mean that it decays easily on a journey. EG *Cheese does not travel well.* V + A : NO CONT = transport

7 Someone's **travels** are the journeys that they make through places a long way from their home. EG *Marsha told us all about her travels.* N PLURAL : WITH POSS = wanderings

8 See also **travelled, travelling**.

travel agency, travel agencies. A **travel agency** is a business which makes arrangements for people's holidays and journeys, for example by booking their tickets or hotel accommodation for them. N COUNT = travel bureau

travel agent, travel agents. A **travel agent** is a person who manages or works in a travel agency. N COUNT

travel bureau, travel bureaux. A **travel bureau** is the same as a travel agency. N COUNT

travelled /trævəᵊld/; also spelled **traveled** in American English. A **travelled** person has travelled a lot in foreign countries; a fairly formal word. EG *I think of him as a travelled, educated man... They were all well-travelled people.* ADJ QUALIT : ATTRIB, USU *well* + ADJ

traveller /trævəᵊlə/, **travellers**; also spelled **traveler** in American English. A **traveller** is 1 a person who is making a journey or who travels a lot. EG *...a party of English travellers... ...tropical shells brought back by travellers.* 2 the same as a commercial traveller. 3 a gypsy. N COUNT = wanderer N COUNT N COUNT

traveller's cheque, traveller's cheques; also spelled **traveler's check** in American English. **Traveller's cheques** are cheques that you buy at a bank and take with you when you travel abroad so that you can exchange them for the currency of the country that you are in. EG *He changed the first of his traveller's cheques.* N COUNT : USU PL

travelling /trævəᵊlɪŋ/; also spelled **traveling** in American English. A **travelling** actor, musician, etc goes to different places as part of his or her work. EG *...travelling businessmen... ...a group of travelling actors.* ADJ CLASSIF : ATTRIB = itinerant

travelling expenses are money that you claim back from your employer when you have spent that amount of money on travelling as part of your work; used in British English. EG *They get travelling expenses and are also paid a fee.* N PLURAL

travelling salesman, travelling salesmen; also spelled **traveling salesman** in American English. A **travelling salesman** is a salesman who travels to different places and meets people in order to sell goods or take orders. N COUNT = commercial traveller

travelogue /træ̱vəlɒg/, **travelogues**; also spelled **travelog** in American English. A **travelogue** is a talk or film about travel or about a particular person's travels. N COUNT

travel-sick. If someone is **travel-sick**, they feel sick as a result of travelling in a vehicle. EG *My son always gets travel-sick on car journeys.* ◊ **travel sickness**. EG *Take one tablet before the start of your journey to prevent travel sickness occurring.* ADJ QUALIT ◊ N UNCOUNT

traverse /træ̱vɜːs, trəˀvɜ̱ːs/, **traverses, traversing, traversed**. If you **traverse** a river, area of land, etc, you go across it or over it; a formal word. EG *He once traversed San Francisco harbour in a balloon... ...a territory that a man on horseback could traverse in a single day.* V+O = cross

travesty /træ̱vəsti¹/, **travesties**. A **travesty** is a very bad representation or imitation of something; used showing disapproval. EG *His account of my essay was a travesty... ...the travesties of justice played out in their courts.* N COUNT : IF+ PREP THEN *of* = parody, farce

trawl /trɔ̱ːl/, **trawls, trawling, trawled**. 1 When fishermen **trawl**, they drag a wide net behind a ship in order to catch fish. EG *When trawling you may catch hermit crabs... ...the fishermen who trawl the offshore waters.* V OR V+O ⇑ fish

2 A **trawl** or **trawl net** is the wide net that fishermen use in trawling. N COUNT

3 If you **trawl** for something, you search among a large number of similar things in order to find the best or most suitable one. EG *She trawled the play for suitable quotations.* ▸ used as a noun. EG *As a result of a nation-wide trawl thirty actors were enlisted... ...a concerted trawl for new enthusiasts.* V+A, OR V+O+A = sift ▸ N COUNT

trawler /trɔ̱ːlə/, **trawlers**. A **trawler** is a ship that is used for trawling. EG *...the very first trawler ever to fish those waters.* N COUNT ⇑ boat

tray /treɪ̱/, **trays**. A **tray** is a flat piece of wood, plastic, or metal, which usually has raised edges and which is used for carrying things, especially food and drinks. EG *There were two champagne glasses on the tray... ...trays of tea and sandwiches.* N COUNT/PART

treacherous /tre̱tʃərəs/. 1 A **treacherous** person is likely to betray you and cannot be trusted. EG *He was cruel, treacherous and unscrupulous.* ADJ QUALIT ⇑ untrustworthy, disloyal

2 You describe the ground, the sea, etc as **treacherous** when it is dangerous to walk on, or to sail on or swim through, because it may suddenly change its character when you do not expect it. EG *...the horrible suck of treacherous sand beneath her feet... ...a rocky and treacherous coastline... The tides are treacherous and only strong swimmers can make it.* ADJ QUALIT ⇑ perilous

treachery /tre̱tʃəri¹/, **treacheries**. **Treachery** is behaviour in which someone betrays their country or betrays a person who trusts them. EG *...the treachery of Benedict Arnold... Clemenza was guilty of treachery.* ▸ A **treachery** is an act of treachery. EG *I would pay him back for his treacheries.* N UNCOUNT ⇑ disloyalty ▸ N COUNT ⇑ perfidy

treacle /tri̱ːkəᵊl/ is a thick, sweet, sticky liquid that is obtained when sugar is refined. It is used in making cakes and puddings. EG *...treacle tart... ...treacle pudding.* N UNCOUNT

treacly /tri̱ːkli¹/. 1 A **treacly** substance is thick and sticky. ADJ QUALIT

2 A **treacly** voice has a rich, deep sound. ADJ QUALIT

tread /tre̱d/, **treads, treading, trod, trodden**.

1 If you **tread** on something, you step on it or press your foot on it. EG *Oh, do be careful, don't tread on it, they cost 8 pounds each... He found himself treading more and more wildly on the brake.* V+A

2 If you **tread** something into the ground or into a carpet, rug, etc, you crush it into the ground, carpet, etc by stepping on it. EG *Damp chips had been trodden into the carpet.* V+O+A = trample

3 When people **tread** grapes, they crush them by stepping on them so that the juice can be made into wine. EG *...a painting of peasants treading grapes.* V+O ⇑ press = trample

4 If you **tread** in a particular way, you walk that way. EG *Rose trod with care... She trod heavily out of the room and into the courtyard.* V+A

5 A person's **tread** is the sound that they make with their feet as they walk. EG *They could hear his heavy limping tread.* N SING WITH DET : WITH POSS/ SUPP = step

6 If you **tread** a path, road, etc, you walk along it; a literary use. EG *There was a winding path, too narrow to be trodden by horses and cattle.* ● If you **tread** a particular **path**, you behave in a particular way. EG *Their leaders wished to tread the path of moderation.* V+O ● PHR : VB INFLECTS

7 If you **tread** carefully, **tread** warily, etc, you behave carefully in your dealings with someone. EG *Tread carefully, my instincts said... The government was treading warily.* V+A

8 If you **tread on** someone's **toes**, you offend them by criticizing the way that they do something or by interfering in something that is their responsibility; a fairly informal expression. EG *They are trying to force us out because we're treading on a few toes.* PHR : VB INFLECTS

9 If you **tread water**, for example when you are in the sea, you stay afloat in an upright position by moving your legs slightly. EG *She rested for a moment, treading water, and then started for shore.* PHR : VB INFLECTS ⇑ float

10 A **tread** is 10.1 the flat upper surface of a step or stair. EG *Madeleine, ascending, paused on each tread.* N COUNT ≠ riser

10.2 the pattern of grooves in the outer surface of a tyre that helps prevent slipping or skidding. EG *The back tyre tread is down a little... ...the minimum legal requirement of 1 millimetre of tread all round.* N COUNT/ UNCOUNT = grip

11 See also **trodden**.

treadle /tre̱dəᵊl/, **treadles**. The **treadle** on a spinning wheel, sewing machine, etc is a lever that you operate with your foot in order to turn a wheel in the machine. EG *...a treadle sewing machine.* N COUNT

treadmill /tre̱dmɪl/, **treadmills**. You refer to a task or a job as a **treadmill** when you must keep doing it although it is unpleasant and exhausting. EG *No woman should waste her life on the treadmill of housework.* N COUNT+SUPP ⇑ routine = grind

treason /tri̱ːzəᵊn/ is the crime of betraying your country, for example by helping its enemies or by trying to overthrow its government; a formal word. EG *He was suspected of treason... They have committed treason against the state.* N UNCOUNT ⇑ treachery

treasonable /tri̱ːzəᵊnəbəᵊl/. **Treasonable** acts or activities are intended to help your country's enemies or to overthrow its government. EG *We were warned that we would be committing a treasonable offence.* ADJ CLASSIF ⇑ treacherous

treasure /tre̱ʒə/, **treasures, treasuring, treasured**. 1 **Treasure** is a collection of gold or silver objects, jewels, etc, especially one that has been hidden. EG *...buried treasure... Patrick, you want to steal the treasure, don't you?* N UNCOUNT = cache, hoard

2 **Treasures** are valuable paintings, carvings, ornaments, etc, especially in a museum or private collection. EG *...the sale of art treasures.* N COUNT : USU PL

3 If you **treasure** something such as a possession or a memory, you are very pleased that you have it and regard it as very valuable. EG *...one of the memories which they would treasure.* ◊ **treasured**. EG *I kept one room locked, with my most treasured possessions inside.* V+O ⇑ value = cherish ◊ ADJ QUALIT : ATTRIB = precious

4 You refer to something that you possess as a **treasure** when it is valuable or important to you. EG *My solitude was a treasure which I guarded like a jewel.* N COUNT

5 You refer to someone as a **treasure** when they are very helpful and useful to you. EG *She was a treasure... He said with admiration, 'Gwyneth, you're a treasure.'* N COUNT/VOC = gem

treasurer /tre̱ʒərə/, **treasurers**. The **treasurer** of a society or organization is in charge of its finances and keeps its accounts. EG *They elected Benn as Treasurer... His father was treasurer of the club.* N COUNT : ALSO IN TITLES ⇑ official

treasure trove; also spelled with a hyphen. You refer to a large amount of money or to a collection of valuable objects as **treasure trove** when it has been found somewhere and nobody knows who it belongs to; a legal term. N UNCOUNT

treasury /tre̱ʒəri¹/, **treasuries**. 1 The **Treasury** is the government department in Britain and some other countries that deals with the country's finances. EG *The Treasury was opposed in principle to the proposals... ...a former Treasury official.* N PROPER : *the*+N, VB CAN BE SING OR PL = Exchequer

2 The **treasury** in a castle, cathedral, etc is a room where valuable objects are displayed or stored. EG *...the priceless collections that are put on show in cathedral treasuries.* [N COUNT]

treat /tri:t/, **treats, treating, treated.** 1 If you **treat** someone in a particular way, you behave that way towards them. EG *We were treated with respect... Their parents continue to treat them as children... Everybody treats you like a member of the family... ...badly treated children.* [V+O+A]

2 If you **treat** something in a particular way, you deal with it that way. EG *Electricity is potentially dangerous, so treat it with respect... Invalid care allowance is treated as income for tax purposes... Your problems will be treated as confidential.* [V+O+A; ⇑ handle]

3 If you **treat** an idea or statement in a particular way, you consider it or regard it in that way. EG *What does he expect me to do? Treat it as some sort of joke?... I think we must treat this as a serious question.* [V+O+A; ⇑ think]

4 If you **treat** an illness, injury, or disease or **treat** the person who has it, you give the person medical attention and try to make him or her well again. EG *There are only two doctors and eight nurses to treat more than 300 patients... The drug is prescribed to treat nasal congestion... ...a way to treat cancer.* [V+O]

5 If you **treat** something such as wood or cloth, you put a special substance on it to protect it from damage or decay, to clean it, or to give it special properties. EG *New timber should be treated with a preservative... ...children's pyjamas that are treated for resistance to fire.* [V+O : USU+A]

6 If you give someone a **treat**, you arrange a special event for them which you know that they will enjoy. EG *Granny took us for tea at Lyons Corner House as a special treat.* ▸ used as a verb. EG *She offered to treat them to dinner... I can't afford it but I think I'll treat myself.* [N COUNT; ▸ V+O]

7 If you say that something is your **treat**, you mean that you are paying for it as a treat for someone else. EG *'I'll pay.'–'Oh, no. This is my treat.'* [N SING : WITH POSS; ⇑ gift]

8 You also describe something as a **treat** when it is especially pleasant or enjoyable. EG *A meal in a restaurant came as a real treat after all the institutional food I'd been having.* [N SING : a+N; ⇑ pleasure = delight]

9 If you say that something looks **a treat**, works **a treat**, etc, you mean that it looks very good, works very well, etc; an informal expression. EG *It worked a treat... Everything will look a treat, you see.* [PHR : USED AS C]

treatise /tri:tɪz/, **treatises.** A **treatise** is a long, formal piece of writing about a particular subject. EG *Malthus published his treatise on population.... ...a technical scientific treatise.* [N COUNT : IF+ PREP THEN *on*; ⇑ article]

treatment /tri:tmə²nt/, **treatments. 1 Treatment** or a **treatment** is medical attention given to a sick or injured person or animal. EG *...free dental treatment... I tried every treatment the vet suggested.* [N UNCOUNT/ COUNT]

2 Your **treatment** of someone is the way that you behave towards them. EG *There should be special treatment for the smaller developing nations... The party felt that they should have fairer treatment in the press.* [N UNCOUNT]

3 **Treatment** of wood, cloth, etc involves putting a special substance on to it to preserve it from decay, to clean it, or to give it special properties. EG *Make sure the insecticide penetrates well into the surface: but be careful, as treatment may discolour light woods.* [N UNCOUNT; ⇑ process]

treaty /tri:ti¹/, **treaties.** A **treaty** is a written agreement between countries in which they agree to do something or to help each other. EG *...the Treaty of Versailles... The Government has signed a treaty with Moscow.* [N COUNT : ALSO IN NAMES]

treble /trɛbə⁰l/, **trebles, trebling, trebled. 1** When something **trebles** or when you **treble** it, it becomes three times as great in number, amount, or size. EG *The population has nearly trebled in thirty years... By 1966 the grain harvest had trebled.* [V-ERG; ⇑ increase = triple]

2 If you say that something is **treble** the amount, size, strength, etc of something else, you mean that it is three times as large or three times as strong as the other thing or amount. EG *It merited expanding to double if not treble its size... ...rents that were treble their current levels.* [PREDET]

3 You use **treble** when you are telling someone a number to indicate that a digit is repeated three times; for example you would say the number 61888 as 'six one treble eight'. [ADJ CLASSIF+ NUM]

4 A **treble** whisky, **treble** gin, etc has three measures in the same glass. EG *He shouted for the waitress and ordered three treble brandies.* ▸ used as a noun. EG *I asked for a treble.* [ADJ CLASSIF : ATTRIB; ▸ N COUNT = triple]

5 A **treble** is a boy with a singing voice in the highest range of musical notes. EG *...the tenors, basses, and trebles.* ▸ used as an adjective to refer to this range of musical notes. EG *Tony still had a fine treble voice.* [N COUNT; ⇑ singer; ▸ ADJ CLASSIF : ATTRIB]

tree /tri:/, **trees.** 1 A **tree** is a tall plant with a long trunk made of wood, which usually has leaves and branches, and which can live for many years. EG *In the middle of the lawn was a great cedar tree... The trees and shrubs were in full leaf.* [N COUNT]

2 If you say that someone is at **the top of the tree**, you mean that they have reached the highest or most successful point in their career or profession. [PHR : USED AS O]

3 See also **Christmas tree, family tree, shoetree.** ● **barking up the wrong tree**: see **bark.** ● **up a gum tree**: see **gum.**

treeless /tri:lɪ²s/. An area that is **treeless** has no trees on it. EG *...driving through the treeless mountains.* [ADJ CLASSIF]

tree-lined. Streets or roads that are **tree-lined** have trees on either side of them. EG *...a pleasant tree-lined avenue in Bristol.* [ADJ CLASSIF : USU ATTRIB]

treetop /tri:tɒp/, **treetops**; also spelled with a hyphen. The **treetops** are the top part of the trees in a wood or forest. EG *Monkeys were bounding away through the treetops... Clouds of birds rose from the tree-tops... ...planes flying at tree-top level.* [N COUNT : USU PL]

tree-trunk, tree-trunks; also spelled as two words. A **tree-trunk** is the tall central part of a tree, which the branches grow out from. [N COUNT]

trefoil /trɛfɔɪl/ is a plant such as clover whose leaves are each divided into three smaller leaves. ▸ used as an adjective to describe these leaves. EG *...looking for the trefoil leaves in the bracken.* [N UNCOUNT; ▸ ADJ CLASSIF : ATTRIB]

trek /trɛk/, **treks, trekking, trekked.** If you **trek** somewhere, you go on a long and difficult journey, especially on foot. EG *They trekked for three days along the banks of the Zambezi... I used to see the workers trekking every morning to the steel mills.* ▸ used as a noun. EG *We set off on another four hour trek through swamps and fields.* [V+A; ▸ N COUNT : USU +A]

trellis /trɛlɪs/, **trellises.** A **trellis** is a frame made of horizontal and vertical strips of wood, which is used to support climbing plants in a garden. [N COUNT/ UNCOUNT; ⇑ structure]

tremble /trɛmbə⁰l/, **trembles, trembling, trembled. 1** If you **tremble**, you shake slightly with movements that you cannot control, for example because you are frightened, upset, ill, or cold. EG *The room was cold, but that wasn't why he was trembling... Claude's hands trembled as he struck a match... Karen trembled with happiness.* ▸ used as a noun. EG *She was aware of the tremble of his hands.* ◇ **trembling.** EG *I put down my fork with trembling fingers.* [V = quiver, shiver; ▸ N COUNT; ◇ ADJ CLASSIF = quivering]

2 If something **trembles**, it shakes slightly, for example because it is being struck by something else. EG *The wind made the branches shake and tremble.* ▸ used as a noun. EG *He felt under him the tremble and hum of the bridge.* [V = quiver; ▸ N COUNT]

3 If your voice **trembles**, it sounds uncertain and unsteady, for example because you are in pain or because you are upset. EG *His voice trembled with theatrically controlled anger.* ▸ used as a noun. EG *Excitement and apprehension added a tremble to his voice.* [V ⇑ shake = quaver; ▸ N COUNT = quiver]

4 If you say that someone **is trembling**, you mean that they are worried or afraid of what is about to happen. EG *His father and mother trembled with apprehension about his future.* [V : USU+A; ⇑ shake]

tremendous /trɪ²mɛndəs/. If you say that something is **tremendous**, you mean that **1** it is very great, important, or impressive. EG *There was a tremendous feeling of urgency and excitement... The play became a tremendous hit.* ◇ **tremendously.** EG *There is a tremendously difficult struggle ahead of us... She envied and admired Judy tremendously.* **2** it is very large and impressive in size or amount. EG *The church was centuries old, with tremendous pillars... When we crossed the bridge over the Lauter, there was a tremendous flash... With tremendous noise, a plane took off... They cost a tremendous amount of money.* **3** you think it is very good and you like it [ADJ QUALIT : ATTRIB = immense; ◇ ADV = immensely; ADJ QUALIT ⇑ great = enormous, vast; ADJ QUALIT] very much or are pleased about it. EG *A tremendous tale of love and courage... A marvellous design and a tremendous crew.*

tremolo /trɛmələʊ/, **tremolos. Tremolo** is a technique used in playing a violin or other stringed instrument, in which a note is repeated several times rapidly; a technical term in music. N UNCOUNT/COUNT

tremor /trɛmə/, **tremors.** A **tremor** is 1 a shaking movement that you cannot control. EG *Warburton detected more than a tremor in the voice of his friend... Words cannot describe the tremor of pleasure that went through me.* N COUNT ⇑ shake 2 a small earthquake. EG *There had been a tremor so slight that I did not even feel it... There have been no earthquakes or tremors anywhere near here in living memory.* N COUNT 3 a minor change or event that shocks people or is considered to be threatening to the stability of a society or of a particular organization. EG *Organizational tremors are similarly felt in all the agencies... The education system has been a focal point for minor tremors of protest in the last few years.* N COUNT+SUPP

tremulous /trɛmjə⁴ləs/. If you or your actions are **tremulous**, you are shaking slightly, for example because you are afraid, nervous, or uncertain; a literary word. EG *She looked up: her mouth was tremulous... ...the first tremulous beginnings of a smile... Jack's voice went on, tremulous yet determined.* ADJ QUALIT = quivering, trembling ◇ **tremulously.** EG *The twins were holding tremulously to each other.* ◇ ADV WITH VB

trench /trɛntʃ/, **trenches.** A **trench** is 1 a long narrow channel cut into the ground, for example for drainage or in order to lay pipes. EG *I forgot to dig a trench around the tent... They're slightly larger than gas pipes, but the size of trench required is the same.* N COUNT ⇑ hole

2 a long narrow channel in the ground used by soldiers as a defensive position. EG *Twelve of them had come out of the trench, their arms raised high above their heads... ...the hideous conditions of trench warfare.* N COUNT ▸ The **trenches** is also used to refer to the battle grounds of the First World War in Northern France and Belgium. EG *Grandfather was in the trenches during the First War.* ▸ N PLURAL: *the* +N

trenchant /trɛntʃənt/. **Trenchant** writing or comments are bold, effective, and sincere; a formal word. EG *...another of Adam Smith's very trenchant observations.* ADJ QUALIT = forthright

trench coat, trench coats; also spelled with a hyphen and as one word. A **trench coat** is a type of raincoat with pockets and a belt, especially one that is similar in design to military coats. N COUNT

trend /trɛnd/, **trends.** A **trend** is a general and obvious movement or development of events, fashion, attitudes, etc. EG *There is a trend towards equal opportunities for men and women... The trend has been to stress more the artistic side of education... A more reliable indication of the trend of inflation will be provided by the latest figures.* N COUNT = tendency ● If someone **sets a trend**, they do something that becomes accepted or fashionable, and that is copied by a lot of other people. EG *In these negotiations, other traders tended to follow the trend set by the strong.* ● PHR: VB INFLECTS ⇑ pattern

trend-setter, trend-setters. A **trend-setter** is a person or institution that starts a new fashion or trend. N COUNT ⇑ leader

trendy /trɛndi¹/, **trendier, trendiest; trendies.** 1 **Trendy** things or people are very fashionable and modern. EG *...trendy clothes... ...London's trendiest night clubs... ...trendy intellectuals talking about life.* ADJ QUALIT

2 A **trendy** is a person who follows all the latest fashions, for example in their clothes or ideas, because they want to create a particular impression on other people; used in informal English, often showing disapproval. EG *Subtle propaganda has persuaded trendies that living in inner cities is the latest 'in-thing'.* N COUNT

trepidation /trɛpɪdeɪʃə⁰n/ is fear or anxiety about something that you are going to do or experience; a formal word. EG *'What do you mean?' I asked, with some trepidation... His interest was mixed with a certain amount of trepidation.* N UNCOUNT ⇑ alarm

trespass /trɛspəs/, **trespasses, trespassing, trespassed.** 1 If you **trespass**, you go onto someone else's land without their permission. EG *Don't come trespassing on my land again... No trespassing.* V ⇑ encroach ▸ used as a noun. EG *...She sued them for trespass... They began to organise a mass trespass.* ▸ N UNCOUNT/COUNT

2 A **trespass** is a sin; an old-fashioned, biblical use. N COUNT

trespass upon. If you **trespass upon** someone's generosity, friendship, etc, you take advantage of them by asking or expecting too much from them; a formal and old-fashioned use. EG *May I venture to trespass upon your sense of justice?* PHRASAL VB: V+PREP, HAS PASS ⇑ abuse

trespasser /trɛspəsə/, **trespassers.** A **trespasser** is a person who goes onto someone else's land without the owner's permission. EG *Trespassers will be prosecuted.* N COUNT

tress /trɛs/, **tresses.** A woman's **tresses** are her long flowing hair; an old-fashioned, literary word. N COUNT: USU PL = lock

trestle /trɛsə⁰l/, **trestles.** A **trestle** is a wooden or metal structure that is used as one of the supports for a table. It has two pairs of sloping legs which are joined by a flat piece across the top. N COUNT ⇑ support

trestle table, trestle tables. A **trestle table** is a table made of a long board that is supported on trestles. N COUNT

tri- is used at the beginning of some words that have 'three' as part of their meaning. EG *...triangle... ...tripartite.* PREFIX

triad /traɪæd/, **triads.** A **triad** is a group of three similar things; a fairly formal word. EG *Each of this sonorous triad of pleas was meant to be taken as of equal weight.* N PART+N IN PLURAL

trial /traɪəl/, **trials.** 1 A **trial** is 1.1 a formal legal process in which a judge and jury decide whether someone is guilty of a particular crime by questioning them and considering the evidence. EG *Bierce's name was not mentioned at the trial... He was committed for trial at Knightsbridge Crown Court... Huey was awaiting trial for murder... Putting people in jail without trial is not democratic.* N COUNT/UNCOUNT 1.2 an experiment in which you test something by using it or doing it for a short time to see how well it works. EG *We've completed a number of fairly successful trials with laboratory animals... ...clinical trials.* N COUNT/UNCOUNT 1.3 a test of whether someone is suitable for a particular job by letting them do it for a short time before deciding whether to employ them. EG *If you want the job I'm prepared to give you a trial... I was called into the editor's office and told that my trial period was over.* N SING WITH DET

2 **on trial.** 2.1 If someone is **on trial**, they have been accused of committing a crime and are going through the legal process in which a judge and jury will decide whether they are guilty or not. EG *We don't intend to put him on trial... The group went on trial in January 1963.* PHR: USED AS AN A ● to **stand trial**: see **stand.** 2.2 If something is **on trial**, it is being tested or closely examined to see if it is suitable for a particular purpose. EG *The Parliamentary system is on trial.* PHR: USED AS AN A

3 If you talk about the **trials** of a situation, you are referring to the difficulties and unpleasantness that it causes you. EG *...the trials of pregnancy and childbirth.* N COUNT+SUPP: USU PL

4 If you say that someone or something is a **trial** to you, you mean that they are annoying, worrying, or frustrating to you. EG *My uncle was unfailingly kind to me, but I was a sore trial to him.* N SING: *a*+N, USU +*to* ⇑ tribulation

5 **Trials** are a sporting competition that test a competitor's skill and ability. EG *She came first in the horse trials.* N COUNT: USU PL

trial and error. If you do something by **trial and error**, you try several different methods of doing it until you find the method that works properly. EG *The best solution can only be found by a process of trial and error.* N UNCOUNT

trial run, trial runs. A **trial run** is a first attempt at doing something in which you get practice and test yourself, ready for the time when you intend to do it properly or completely. EG *We planned a trial run there with the camels and gear.* N COUNT = dry run

triangle /traɪæŋgə⁰l/, **triangles.** 1 A **triangle** is 1.1 a flat shape which has three straight sides and three angles. EG *The angles of a triangle total 180... The pigeons had arranged themselves in a triangle.* N COUNT 1.2 a place or object which is shaped like a triangle. EG *I met friends in Plac Zamkowy, a cobbled triangle dominated by a statue of King Zigismund... The place of assembly in which he stood was roughly a triangle.* N COUNT

2 If you refer to a **triangle** of people, ideas, points of view, etc, you are referring to a situation in which three people, ideas, points of view, etc are equally involved but are usually opposed to each other. EG N COUNT: USU+SUPP

...the uneasy triangle of forces so accurately forecast for 1984. ● See also **eternal triangle**.

3 A **triangle** is also a musical instrument that consists of a piece of metal shaped like a triangle. You play it by hitting it with a short metal bar. N COUNT

triangular /traɪæŋgj^{ə}^{4}lə/. **1** Something that is **triangular** is in the shape of a triangle. EG *...a pretty little triangular garden... ...a splendid Victorian building, triangular in shape.* ADJ CLASSIF

2 A **triangular** situation or relationship involves three people or things. EG *A triangular relationship between Eileen and the two men.* ADJ CLASSIF

tribal /traɪbə^{0}l/ is used to describe things relating or belonging to tribes and to the way they are organized. EG *...political and tribal leaders... Her father had recently died in a tribal war.* ADJ CLASSIF : USU ATTRIB

tribalism /traɪbəlɪzə^{0}m/ is **1** the state of existing as a tribe. EG *...feudalism, tribalism, or slavery.* N UNCOUNT **2** the behaviour and attitudes shown by people in a particular group in society, especially with regard to the loyalty they feel for each other. EG *A nationalist movement opposed to 'tribalism' and devoted to national consolidation.* N UNCOUNT

tribe /traɪb/, **tribes**. When **tribe** is used in the singular, it can be used with a singular or plural verb. A **tribe** is **1** a group of people of the same race, who share the same customs, religion, language, or land, especially when they are not considered to have reached a very advanced level of civilization. EG *Mr Otunnu is a member of the Acholi tribe... This attitude still remains in some primitive tribes.* N COUNT, OR N PART+N IN PLURAL ⇑ society **2** a group of related animals, especially ones that live or hunt together. EG *...the tribe of cheetahs.* N PART+N IN PLURAL **3** a group of people who do the same activities or the same job. EG *There was a tribe of schoolchildren coming up the path.* N PART+N IN PLURAL **4** a family; an informal and humorous use. EG *Good to see you, John! How's the tribe?* N COUNT

tribesman /traɪbzmə^{3}n/, **tribesmen**. A **tribesman** is a man who belongs to a particular tribe. N COUNT

tribulation /trɪbjə^{4}leɪʃə^{0}n/, **tribulations**. **Tribulation** is difficulty or trouble that you experience in a particular situation; a formal word. EG *It should also teach you that life is uncertain and full of tribulation.* N UNCOUNT ⇑ trial ▸ used as a count noun. EG *A few of his tribulations were already common knowledge.* ▸ N COUNT : USU PL

tribunal /trɪ^{5}bju:nə^{0}l/, **tribunals**. A **tribunal** is a special court or committee that is appointed to deal with particular problems. EG *...an industrial tribunal which was hearing cases of unfair dismissal.* N COUNT : IF SING, VB CAN BE SING OR PL

tributary /trɪbjə^{4}tə^{0}ri^{1}/, **tributaries**. **1** A **tributary** is a stream or river that flows into a larger river. EG *...the Neander River, a tributary of the Rhine.* N COUNT

2 A **tributary** road, river, path, etc joins another more important road, river, or path. EG *There was one street, apart from a tributary road near the end of the village.* ADJ CLASSIF : ATTRIB

tribute /trɪbju:t/, **tributes**. **1** A **tribute** is a speech, gift, or action made in order to show your admiration and respect for someone and to praise or thank them. EG *On Johnson's death in 1922, Asquith paid tribute to his personal qualities... She accepted the tribute graciously.* N COUNT/ UNCOUNT : IF+ PREP THEN *to*

2 If you say that something is a **tribute** to a quality that someone or something has, you mean that it deserves praise or admiration because it is equally as good as the other quality. EG *The car's top speed is just about 100mph–a tribute to its low aerodynamic drag.* N SING : a+N, IF +PREP THEN *to*

3 Tribute is a payment of goods or money that a country is forced to give to another country or person in authority in return for peace or protection. N UNCOUNT/ COUNT

trice /traɪs/. If someone does something **in a trice**, they do it very quickly; a fairly informal expression. EG *He sized the situation up in a trice... I'll be back in a trice.* PHR : USED AS AN A = immediately

triceps /traɪseps/. **Triceps** is both the singular and the plural form. Your **triceps** is the muscle in the back part of your upper arm. N COUNT

trick /trɪk/, **tricks, tricking, tricked**. **1** If someone **tricks** you, they deceive you, especially in order to obtain something from you or to make you do something foolish. EG *He realized that the visitors had tricked him... She felt she had been tricked into marriage.* V+O : IF+PREP THEN *into* = dupe, cheat ▸ used as a noun or adjective. EG *The government dismissed the offer as a trick... He was willing to use any dirty trick to get what he wanted... ...a trick question.* ▸ N COUNT, OR ADJ CLASSIF : ATTRIB ⇑ deception

2 A **trick** is also **2.1** a clever or skilful action that someone does in order to entertain or amuse people. EG *Mr Poliakin was performing his popular trick of playing the bow with the violin.* N COUNT = stunt **2.2** a clever way of doing something, especially one that is only known by people who have been doing a particular activity regularly. EG *An old campers' trick is to use three thin blankets instead of one thick one... These are standard tricks of the trade.* N COUNT ⇑ technique **2.3** an expression, gesture, etc that you use very often, usually without realizing that you are doing it. EG *She had a trick of saying 'Oh dear'.* N COUNT+SUPP = habit **2.4** a group of playing cards that has been placed on the table during a card game and that is won by one player or team. EG *She won four tricks in a row.* N COUNT

3 Trick devices and methods make people see things in a strange or inaccurate way, often in order to amuse them. EG *...trick mirrors... ...trick photography.* ADJ CLASSIF : ATTRIB ⇑ joke

4 The word **trick** is also used in the following expressions. **4.1** If you say that something is a **trick of the light**, you mean that it is not really there or not the way that it appears and that what you are really seeing is an effect caused by the way that the light falls on things. PHR : USED AS C ⇑ illusion **4.2** If you say that someone is **up to their tricks**, you mean that they are behaving in a typically dishonest or deceitful way; an informal expression. EG *He's up to his tricks the minute my back's turned.* PHR : USED AS AN A **4.3** If you say that something **does the trick**, you mean that it is satisfactory for a particular purpose; an informal expression. EG *He thought that four colours would do the trick.* PHR : VB INFLECTS = work **4.4** If you say that someone **never misses a trick**, you mean that they always know about everything that is happening, even when it does not concern them; an informal expression, often used showing disapproval. EG *She never seemed to miss a trick.* PHR : VB INFLECTS

5 See also **confidence trick, conjuring trick**.

trick out. If someone or something **is tricked out** in a particular way, they are made to look that way. EG *...cupboards with sliding doors tricked out to look like Georgian cocktail cabinets.* PHRASAL VB : V+ O+ADV, USU PASS ⇑ decorated

trickery /trɪkəri^{1}/. If someone uses **trickery**, they try to deceive someone else, often in order to get money from them. EG *The old man suspected trickery... The case involved much violence and trickery.* N UNCOUNT ⇑ deception = chicanery

trickle /trɪkə^{0}l/, **trickles, trickling, trickled**. **1** When a liquid **trickles**, it flows slowly in very small amounts. EG *He tilted the flask and two or three drops trickled into his glass... The tears were beginning to trickle down her cheeks.* V : USU+A = drip, dribble ▸ used as a noun. EG *The flood subsided to a trickle... ...a thin trickle of blood.* ▸ N PART : USU SING+N UNCOUNT = dribble

2 When people or things **trickle** in a particular direction, they move there slowly in small groups or amounts, rather than all together. EG *The coach parties began trickling back to the buses.* V+A = straggle ▸ used as a noun. EG *The march became a trickle of dawdlers... Receipts are down to a trickle.* ▸ N PART : USU SING

trickster /trɪkstə/, **tricksters**. A **trickster** is a person who deceives or cheats people, usually in order to get money from them; a rather old-fashioned word. N COUNT = swindler

tricky /trɪki^{1}/, **trickier, trickiest**. **1** A **tricky** task or problem is difficult to do or deal with. EG *Dyeing patterned material is tricky and I personally wouldn't do it... Beaton had to face a tricky problem.* ADJ QUALIT = awkward, complicated

2 A **tricky** person is likely to deceive you or cheat you. EG *He's a bit of a tricky customer.* ADJ QUALIT : ATTRIB

tricolour /trɪkələ/, **tricolours**; also spelled **tricolor** in American English. A **tricolour** is a flag with three equal stripes in different colours; used especially to describe the French or Irish national flag. EG *...the Irish tricolour.* N COUNT

tricycle /traɪsɪkə^{0}l/, **tricycles**. A **tricycle** is a vehicle similar to a bicycle but with two wheels at the back instead of one. Children often ride small tricycles. EG *Her small son was riding his tricycle... ...invalid tricycles.* N COUNT

tried /traɪd/. **1 Tried** is the past tense and past participle of **try**.

2 You describe a product or a method as **tried** when it has already been used and has been found to be successful. EG *...tried and tested products.* ADJ CLASSIF

trier /traɪə/, **triers**. You describe someone as a **trier** when they try very hard at things that they do; N COUNT : USU USED AS C used showing approval. EG *Jack was always a trier... The others are tremendous triers.*

trifle /traɪfə⁰l/, **trifles, trifling, trifled.** 1 A **trifle** means to a small extent or degree; a fairly formal expression. EG *She was a trifle breathless... 'They seemed very nice men,' she added, a trifle wistfully.* PHR+ADJ/ADV = slightly

2 A **trifle** is something that is considered to have little importance, value, or significance. EG *He told her not to pester him with trifles... They worry over trifles.* N COUNT: USU PL = triviality

3 **Trifle** or a **trifle** is a cold pudding made of layers of sponge cake, fruit, jelly, custard, etc and often decorated with cream, nuts, or chocolate. EG *...sherry trifle... Would you like some more trifle?* N UNCOUNT/COUNT ⇑ dessert

trifle with. If you **trifle with** someone or something, you treat them in a frivolous or disrespectful way. EG *Mitchell was not someone to be trifled with... He was in no mood to be trifled with... One does not trifle with history.* PHRASAL VB: V+PREP, HAS PASS

trifling /traɪflɪŋ/. Something that is **trifling** is small and unimportant; used showing disapproval. EG *There was no need for you to come out here on such a trifling matter... ...a trifling misunderstanding... Such occupations were so trifling as to be unworthy of his full attention.* ADJ QUALIT = petty, trivial

trigger /trɪgə/, **triggers, triggering, triggered.** 1 A **trigger** is a small lever on a gun or machine. You press it in order to make the gun or machine work. EG *He aimed at the far wall and squeezed the trigger.* N COUNT

2 If something **triggers** an event or **triggers** it **off**, it causes it to happen. EG *There had been disagreements between them, triggered by his work... The Dispatch published a report which triggered off a parliamentary debate.* ▸ used as a noun. EG *The manifesto proved to be the trigger which set off the revolution.* V+O, OR PHRASAL VB: V+O+ADV = provoke, spark off ▸ N COUNT: USU SING = spark

trigger-happy. You describe someone as **trigger-happy** when they are too ready and willing to use violence and weapons, especially guns; an informal expression. EG *The national guard have been very trigger-happy lately... There are a number of trigger-happy soldiers in the area.* ADJ QUALIT ⇑ violent

trigonometry /trɪgənɒmɪ²tri¹/ is the branch of mathematics that is concerned with calculating the angles of triangles or the lengths of their sides. EG *I didn't do much trigonometry at school... ...a trigonometry problem.* N UNCOUNT

trike /traɪk/, **trikes.** A **trike** is a child's tricycle; an informal word. EG *...a back yard big enough for trike riding.* N COUNT

trilby /trɪlbi¹/, **trilbies.** A **trilby** or **trilby hat** is a man's hat made of felt with a dent along the top from front to back. EG *He crammed his trilby on his head... He was wearing a brown trilby hat.* N COUNT

trill /trɪl/, **trills, trilling, trilled.** 1 A **trill** is the playing of two musical notes repeatedly one after the other very quickly; a technical term in music. EG *...the famous orchestra trill at the end of the first act.* N COUNT ⇑ quiver

2 If a bird **trills**, it sings with sharp, high-pitched short repeated notes. ▸ used as a noun. EG *...the canary's high trills.* V ▸ N COUNT/UNCOUNT

3 If a woman **trills**, she talks or laughs in a high-pitched voice that sounds rather musical. EG *'It's only us,' trilled the girls... She gave a trilling laugh.* V OR V+QUOTE = shrill

trillion /trɪljən/, **trillions.** A **trillion** is a number representing a million million, or a million million million in rather old-fashioned British English: see ☐ at NUMBER. EG *We now use about 83 trillion kilowatt hours of energy per year.* ▸ **Trillions** is often used to mean an extremely large number. EG *There's trillions of places where we could go.* NUM: USU a/NUM+*trillion* ▸ NUM IN PL: USED AS N PART ⇑ many

trilogy /trɪlədʒi¹/, **trilogies.** A **trilogy** is a series of three books, plays, operas, etc that have the same subject or the same characters, but are each complete works in themselves. EG *He is best known for his trilogy on working-class life.* N COUNT

trim /trɪm/, **trimmer, trimmest; trims, trimming, trimmed.** 1 Something that is **trim** is neat, tidy, and attractive. EG *...the trim lawns and trees of suburbia... ...a small, trim housing estate.* ADJ QUALIT = spruce

2 If a person is **trim** or has a **trim** figure, they are slim and fit; used showing approval. EG *...a trim, balding man in his early sixties... ...a body kept trim by exercise.* ADJ QUALIT

3 When things or people are **in trim** or **in good trim**, they are in good physical condition. EG *Repair them regularly and keep them in good trim... He appeared healthy and untroubled, in good physical trim... I spent some time getting into trim.* PHR: USED AS AN A = in good shape

4 If you **trim** your hair or **trim** something such as a lawn or a hedge, you cut off small amounts of it in order to make it look neater and tidier. EG *He trimmed his hair carefully... His beard was freshly trimmed... The grass needed trimming.* ▸ used as a noun. EG *'How would you like it done, sir?'–'Just a trim, please.'... The hedge needs a trim.* V+O = clip ▸ N SING WITH DET

5 If a government **trims** something such as a plan or a policy, it alters it by removing parts that do not seem necessary. EG *The prospect of trimming welfare programmes is deeply unsettling... Sometimes it is necessary to trim those very policies in order to stay in office.* V+O = cut back

6 The **trim** of something that you make or buy is a decoration, for example along its edges, that is a different colour from the rest of it or made of a different substance. EG *...a velour suit with scarlet trim... ...cars with sunroofs or fabric trim.* UNCOUNT: USU+SUPP = trimming

7 See also **trimmed, trimming.**

trim off. If you **trim off** parts of something or **trim** them **away**, you cut them off, because they are not needed. EG *Most of the fat should be trimmed off meat... Her chicken sandwiches had the crusts trimmed off... Waste material has been trimmed away.* PHRASAL VB: V+O+ADV ⇑ remove

trimaran /traɪmərən/, **trimarans.** A **trimaran** is a fast sailing boat like a catamaran but with three hulls instead of two. N COUNT

trimmed /trɪmd/. If a dress is **trimmed** with a particular material or ornament, the material or ornament has been added to it in order to make it look more attractive. EG *All these garments were richly trimmed with lace... ...a pink dress trimmed with ostrich feathers.* ADJ CLASSIF: PRED ⇑ decorated

trimming /trɪmɪŋ/, **trimmings.** 1 The **trimming** or **trimmings** on an piece of clothing are extra parts added for decoration. They are usually of a different colour or different material from the rest of the article. EG *She was about to alter the trimming of the dress... ...a pink-coloured nightdress with nylon lace trimmings.* N MASS/N PLURAL

2 **Trimmings** are also 2.1 special sauces or other foods that are traditionally served with particular kinds of meat, puddings, etc. EG *Tonight it was turkey with all the trimmings.* 2.2 any extra things that are added to something as a decoration or as a luxury. EG *...a car with expensive trimmings... You fly into London–first class with all the trimmings–and check into this flashy hotel.* 2.3 the small pieces of a substance that you have left when you have cut something out of a large piece. EG *Re-roll any pastry trimmings and cut into thin strips.* N PLURAL = frills; N PLURAL ⇑ extras; N PLURAL ⇑ left-overs

trinity /trɪnɪti¹/. 1 In the Christian religion, **the Trinity** or **the Holy Trinity** is the union of Father, Son, and Holy Spirit in one God. EG *...a modern day account of the Holy Trinity.* N PROPER: *the*+N

2 A **trinity** is a group of three things or people; a literary use. EG *...the evil trinity of imperialism, capitalism and fascism... ...a trinity of quality, mind, and matter.* N PART: USU SING = trio

trinket /trɪŋkɪt/, **trinkets.** A **trinket** is a pretty piece of jewellery or small ornament that is worth very little money. EG *He bought her trinkets and took her to the theatre.* N COUNT = bauble

trio /tri:əʊ/, **trios.** 1 When **trio** is used in the singular, it can be used with a singular or plural verb. A **trio** is 1.1 a group of three people together or of three things that have something in common. EG *...a trio of ladies in the corner of the room... ...the traditional trio of finance, marketing, and production.* 1.2 a group of three musicians or singers. EG *...the Pump Room Trio... The violinist walked on stage and the duo became a trio.* N PART: USU SING+N IN PLURAL = threesome; N COUNT: ALSO IN NAMES

2 A **trio** is also a piece of music written for three musical instruments or three voices. EG *She wanted to play more duets and trios and fewer solo numbers.* N COUNT: ALSO IN NAMES

trip /trɪp/, **trips, tripping, tripped.** 1 A **trip** is a journey that you make to a place and back again. EG *He talked about his recent trip to Africa... They took a coach trip round the island... She often goes on business trips abroad... On that trip I travelled with Gregory Smith.* N COUNT = excursion

2 If you **trip** or **trip up** or if you **trip** over something, V: USU+A, OR

you knock your foot against something when you are walking and lose your balance so that you fall or nearly fall. EG *I tripped and fell... She tripped over a stone... He put each foot down carefully to avoid tripping up.* PHRASAL VB : V+ADV = stumble

3 If you **trip** someone or **trip** them **up**, **3.1** you put something in front of them, for example your foot, so that they knock their own foot against it and fall. EG *Somebody thrust out a foot and tripped him... She tripped up the steward as he passed.* V+O, OR PHRASAL VB : V+O+ADV ⇑ unbalance **3.2** you make them confused so that they say something that they did not intend to say. EG *The judges' questions tripped him up completely.* V+O, OR PHRASAL VB : V+O+ADV ⇑ confuse

4 If you **trip** somewhere or **trip along**, you walk lightly and quickly, so that you are almost dancing. EG *Her daughter tripped in, wearing white muslin and looking enchanting... I could see Amelia tripping along beside him.* V+A, OR PHRASAL VB : V+ADV/PREP = skip

5 A **trip** is also what a person sees and hears when they have taken a drug and are experiencing reality in a strange way; an informal use. EG *She had a bad trip.* N COUNT ⇑ experience

6 See also **ego trip**, **round trip**.

tripartite /traɪpɑːtaɪt/ means made of or involving three people or things; used especially of discussions or agreements between three people, groups, or countries. EG *The unions called for the holding of tripartite talks... ...a tripartite alliance of France, Russia, and England.* ADJ CLASSIF : ATTRIB

tripe /traɪp/. **1 Tripe** is the stomach of a pig, cow, or ox when it is cooked and eaten as food. EG *...tripe and onions.* N UNCOUNT

2 You refer to something that someone has said or written as **tripe** when you think that it is silly and worthless; an informal use. EG *You expect me to read tripe like that?* N UNCOUNT = garbage

triple /trɪpəᵒl/, **triples, tripling, tripled**. **1 Triple** means consisting of three things or three parts. EG *They were allies in a triple cause... I found myself in the middle of the triple front seat... He was present in his triple role of school manager, churchwarden and donor.* ADJ CLASSIF : USU ATTRIB

2 A **triple** whisky, **triple** brandy, etc is a glass of whisky, brandy, etc containing three times the usual amount. EG *He poured himself a triple whisky.* ▸ used as a noun. EG *Make it a triple.* ADJ CLASSIF : ATTRIB ▸ N COUNT = treble

3 If something **triples** or if you **triple** it, it becomes three times as big in size or number. EG *In three years the company had tripled its sales... During this period the Japanese national income has tripled.* V-ERG ⇑ increase = treble

triple jump. The **triple jump** is an athletic event in which competitors have to jump as far as they can, and are allowed to touch the ground once with each foot in the course of the jump. N SING : *the*+N

triplet /trɪplɪ²t/, **triplets**. **Triplets** are three children born at the same time to the same mother. N COUNT : USU PL

triplicate /trɪplɪkəˡt/. If you have a document **in triplicate**, you have three identical copies of it. EG *I had filled in the forms in triplicate.* PHR : USED AS AN A

tripod /traɪpɒd/, **tripods**. A **tripod** is a stand with three legs on which something, for example a camera, can be supported. N COUNT

tripper /trɪpə/, **trippers**. A **tripper** is a person who is on a trip or on holiday; an old-fashioned, fairly informal word. EG *We were paddling in the sea, like elderly trippers at Southend.* N COUNT ⇑ tourist

triptych /trɪptɪk/, **triptychs**. A **triptych** is a painting or a carving on three panels that are usually joined together by hinges. The subject of the painting is usually religious. N COUNT

tripwire /trɪpwaɪə/, **tripwires**; also spelled with a hyphen. A **tripwire** is a wire stretched just above the ground, which triggers a trap or an explosion if someone touches it. N COUNT

trite /traɪt/. Ideas, remarks, and stories that are **trite** are dull and not original because they have been told too many times. EG *Your alibi is pretty trite.* ADJ QUALIT = uninspired

triumph /traɪəmf/, **triumphs, triumphing, triumphed**. **1** A **triumph** is an outstanding success or achievement, often one that has been gained by great skill or effort. EG *The election result was a personal triumph for the party leader... This machine is a triumph of advanced technology.* N COUNT = feat, victory

2 Triumph is a feeling or state of great satisfaction and pride resulting from success or victory. EG *With an expression of triumph on her face, she watched the losers leave the field... It is evidence of a triumph over adversity.* N UNCOUNT

3 If you **triumph**, you gain complete success, control, or victory, often after a long or difficult struggle. EG *They had met the challenge and triumphed... She learned to triumph over her disabilities.* V : IF+PREP THEN *over* = prevail

triumphal /traɪʌmfəᵒl/ is used to describe things that are done or made to celebrate a victory or great success. EG *...his triumphal return to Peking... ...a triumphal arch.* ADJ CLASSIF : ATTRIB ⇑ celebratory

triumphant /traɪʌmfənt/. Someone who is **triumphant** has gained a victory or succeeded in something and feels very happy about it. EG *He felt triumphant... ...triumphant soldiers.* ▸ used of actions and gestures. EG *Her smile was triumphant... His comments were positively triumphant.* ▸ used of events that celebrate a victory or success. EG *...his triumphant entry into the city.* ◊ **triumphantly**. EG *I walked to the door triumphantly... Robert was looking at me triumphantly.* ADJ QUALIT = cock-a-hoop, exultant ▸ = exultant ▸ = victorious ◊ ADV = exultantly

triumvirate /traɪʌmvɪrəˡt/, **triumvirates**. When **triumvirate** is used in the singular, it can be used with a singular or plural verb. A **triumvirate** is a group of three people who together are in charge of something; a formal word. EG *...the artistic triumvirate of playwright, actor, and director.* N COUNT/PART ⇑ trio

trivia /trɪvɪə/. If you refer to things as **trivia**, you mean that they are unimportant and uninteresting. EG *She was not interested in the trivia of gossip... I can't understand why they show much emotion over trivia.* N UNCOUNT

trivial /trɪvɪəl/. Something that is **trivial** is unimportant and uninteresting. EG *Don't waste your strength on trivial things until you have done the important ones... You may consider this sort of information trivial.* ADJ QUALIT = insignificant, worthless

triviality /trɪvɪælɪti¹/, **trivialities**. If you refer to something as a **triviality**, you mean that it is unimportant and uninteresting. EG *...the daily trivialities which seem so important to men... One cannot criticize the book on the grounds of triviality.* N COUNT/UNCOUNT = pettiness

trivialize /trɪvɪəlaɪz/, **trivializes, trivializing, trivialized**; also spelled **trivialise**. If you **trivialize** something, you make it seem unimportant and uninteresting by removing or ignoring the complex and interesting parts of it. EG *Their political role is often trivialized.* V+O = belittle

trod /trɒd/ is the past tense of **tread**.

trodden /trɒdəᵒn/. **1** Ground that is **trodden** has been walked over by a lot of people or animals, and is therefore crushed, marked with footprints, etc. EG *The grass was trodden and muddy.* ADJ CLASSIF = beaten

2 Trodden is also the past participle of **tread**.

troglodyte /trɒglədaɪt/, **troglodytes**. A **troglodyte** is someone who lives in a cave; a technical word. EG *...the troglodytes of Stone Age Adriatic caverns.* N COUNT

Trojan /trəʊdʒəᵒn/, **Trojans**. If you **work like a Trojan**, you work very hard. PHR : VB INFLECTS

troll /trəʊl/, **trolls**. A **troll** is an imaginary creature in Scandinavian mythology. Trolls look like very ugly people, live in caves or mountains, and turn to stone at daybreak. N COUNT

trolley /trɒli¹/, **trolleys**. A **trolley** is **1** a small cart with two or four wheels that you pull or push and use to carry heavy things, for example shopping or luggage. EG *I wheeled the trolley down to where Caro had parked her mini.* N COUNT **2** a small table on wheels that is used for carrying food and drinks or for serving them to people. EG *You can get coffee from the coffee machine, or from the trolley which comes round the office twice a day.* N COUNT **3** a low truck or other vehicle that moves on railway lines and is operated by hand. N COUNT **4** a device, for example a wheel, that transmits the electric current from an overhead wire to the motor of an electric vehicle to make it move forward. N COUNT **5** a tram; used in American English. EG *Cars and trolleys filled the street.* N COUNT, OR *by*+N

trolley bus, trolley buses; also spelled with a hyphen. A **trolley bus** is an electric bus that is driven by electric power taken from cables above the street. N COUNT, OR *by*+N

trollop /trɒləp/, **trollops**. A **trollop** is a woman who is untidy or who seems to be sexually promiscuous; an old-fashioned and offensive word. N COUNT/VOC = harlot

trombone /trɒmbəʊn/, **trombones**. A **trombone** is a large musical instrument consisting of a long N COUNT oval tube of brass with a funnel at the end. You play it by blowing into the mouthpiece and sliding a rod backwards and forwards to vary the note.

trombonist /trɒmbəʊnɪst/, **trombonists**. A **trombonist** is a person who plays a trombone. N COUNT ⇑ musician

troop /truːp/, **troops, trooping, trooped**. 1 **Troops** are soldiers, especially when they are in a large controlled group and on a particular mission. EG *They have more than 11,000 troops in Northern Ireland... They waved their boys off on the troop trains.* N PLURAL ⇑ armed forces

2 A **troop** is 2.1 a group of soldiers within a cavalry or armoured regiment. N COUNT 2.2 a large group of scouts, guides, etc. EG *That summer our Brownie troop was at Camp Blossom Hill.* N COUNT ⇑ company

3 A **troop** of people or animals is a group of them. EG *A troop of strange children ran at his heels... These animals spend a lot of time on the ground in troops.* N PART+N IN PLURAL = pack

4 If people **troop** somewhere, they walk there in a group; an informal use. EG *The satisfied visitors trooped off home... The twelve men trooped downstairs.* V+A

5 When soldiers **troop the colour**, they carry a regiment's flag ceremonially in front of the regiment, especially as part of a parade. EG *He recalls being taken in 1930 to see the Trooping of the Colour.* PHR : VB INFLECTS ⇑ march

trooper /truːpə/, **troopers**. 1 A **trooper** is 1.1 a soldier of low rank in the cavalry or in an armoured regiment in the army. EG *He became a trooper in the Royal Tank Regiment... In the twin sentry boxes were two troopers of the Household Cavalry.* N COUNT : ALSO IN TITLES 1.2 a policeman in a state police force in the United States. N COUNT

2 If someone **swears like a trooper**, they swear a lot; an informal expression, used showing disapproval. PHR : VB INFLECTS

trophy /trəʊfi[1]/, **trophies**. A **trophy** is 1 a prize, for example a silver cup or shield, that is given to the winner of a competition or race. EG *The cup remains a cherished trophy of the company.* N COUNT ⇑ reward 2 something that you keep in order to remember or to show other people that you have done something very difficult. For example, if you kill an animal you might keep its head as a trophy. N COUNT ⇑ souvenir

tropical /trɒpɪkə[0]l/. 1 **Tropical** means belonging to or typical of the tropics. EG *Most tropical areas have rainy and dry seasons... ...tropical rain forests.* ADJ CLASSIF : ATTRIB

2 **Tropical** weather is weather that people consider to be typical of the tropics, for example very hot and very wet. EG *What began as an English summer, turned into a right tropical downpour.* ADJ QUALIT : ATTRIB

tropics /trɒpɪks/. The **tropics** are the hottest parts of the world, between two lines of latitude, the tropic of Cancer, 23½° north of the equator, and the tropic of Capricorn, 23½° south of the equator. EG *Twenty-five years ago, I went to the tropics for the first time.* N PLURAL : *the*+N ⇑ zone

trot /trɒt/, **trots, trotting, trotted**. 1 When an animal such as a horse **trots**, it moves fairly fast, lifting its feet quite high off the ground, at a speed which is faster than walking and slower than galloping. EG *He made the beast turn aside and trot away... Her heels were making a noise like a pony trotting.* V : USU+A ▸ used as a noun. EG *She urged her pony into an energetic trot... The brisk trot of Miss Vernon's pony was heard on the cobble stones.* ▸ N SING WITH DET

2 If you **trot** somewhere, you move fairly fast at a speed between walking and running, taking small quick steps. EG *The two men began to trot along the sand... He trotted around the room, showing an interest in everything.* V+A = jog ▸ used as a noun. EG *Busby had broken into a trot.* ▸ N SING WITH DET

3 If you say that you have been **on the trot** for a long time, you mean that you have been very busy for that time. EG *I've been on the trot all day.* PHR : USED AS AN A = on the go

4 If you say that several things have happened **on the trot**, you mean that they have happened soon after each other. EG *He's had three accidents on the trot.* PHR : USED AS AN A = in a row

trot out. If you **trot out** old information or ideas, you repeat them in a way that is not new or interesting; an informal expression. EG *This idea has been trotted out once more as an illustration of the horrors of civil war.* PHRASAL VB : V+O+ADV = drag up

troth /trəʊθ/. If lovers **plight** their **troth**, they promise their love to each other or promise to marry each other; a literary word. EG *They plighted their troth for the rest of their days.* PHR : VB INFLECTS ⇑ vow

Trotskyist /trɒtski[1]ɪst/, **Trotskyists**. A **Trotskyist** is the same as a **Trotskyite**. EG *...the newest Trotskyist group to appear in Britain.* N COUNT

Trotskyite /trɒtski[1]aɪt/, **Trotskyites**. A **Trotskyite** is someone who supports the left-wing ideas of Leon Trotsky, the twentieth-century Russian politician. Trotskyites believe that the working class should take control of every country. EG *Not all the members were Trotskyites.* N COUNT = Trotskyist

trotter /trɒtə/, **trotters**. A **trotter** is a pig's foot which you can cook and eat. N COUNT

troubadour /truːbədɔː/, **troubadours**. A **troubadour** is a poet and singer. Troubadours used to travel around and perform to noble families in Italy and Southern France in the twelfth and thirteenth centuries. EG *Troubadours sang of ladies fair.* N COUNT = minstrel

trouble /trʌb[0]əl/, **troubles, troubling, troubled**. 1 If you have **trouble** doing something, or if it causes you **trouble**, you have difficulties or problems doing it. EG *Did you have any trouble finding your way here?... I had the same trouble when I first bought my house... That might cause trouble... This would save everyone a lot of trouble.* N UNCOUNT = hassle, bother

2 If you say that a particular aspect of something is the **trouble**, you mean that this aspect is the one which is causing problems. EG *It's getting a bit expensive now, that's the trouble... The trouble with Clive is he's not old enough to understand... You know what your trouble is, you're too generous.* N SING WITH DET ⇑ disadvantage

3 If you refer to your **troubles**, you mean the problems in your life. EG *The old lady next door was telling me all her troubles... She thought that all her troubles were over now she had the insurance money.* N PLURAL : USU POSS+N = woe

4 If you refer to a particular **trouble** that you have, you mean a problem with a particular aspect of your health. EG *I have high blood pressure and heart trouble... Come in, Mrs Griffiths, take a seat. Now, what seems to be the trouble?* N UNCOUNT : MOD +N, OR N SING : *the*+N ⇑ disorder

5 If you are **in trouble**, 5.1 you have a serious problem which will be difficult to solve. EG *We are in trouble... It had been apparent for some time that the magazine was in trouble... She got into trouble with the repayments.* PHR : USED AS AN A 5.2 you are in a situation in which someone in authority is angry with you because of something you have done. EG *Often if a child is in trouble with the police, a social worker will visit the family... I don't want to get you into trouble.* PHR : USED AS AN A

6 If a woman is **in trouble**, she is pregnant when she does not want to be, for example because she is not married. EG *The girl from the post office is in trouble... He's got several girls into trouble.* PHR : USED AS AN A

7 If there is **trouble** between people, there is unpleasant or strongly felt disagreement between them. EG *He's the sort of person who always makes trouble... If there is trouble in the Birmingham factory, management might decide to move production elsewhere.* N UNCOUNT ⇑ conflict = unrest

8 If there is **trouble** somewhere, there is fighting or rioting there, usually in a public place. EG *The police had orders to intervene at the first sign of trouble.* N UNCOUNT = unrest, disturbance ▸ used as a plural noun. EG *More than a decade of student troubles have given the French police considerable experience in riot control... There's no mention of the actual troubles, as they're euphemistically called in Northern Ireland.* ▸ N PLURAL ⇑ conflict

9 **Trouble** is also a breakdown or fault in something mechanical. EG *Our flight was delayed because of engine trouble.* N UNCOUNT+SUPP = malfunction

10 If you say that someone or something is no **trouble**, you mean that they do not annoy you or disturb you. EG *She sat there quietly, making no fuss, a trouble to no one.* N UNCOUNT/N SING WITH DET : WITH BROAD NEG = inconvenience

11 If you say that it is no **trouble** to do something, you mean that you do not mind doing it because it does not require any special effort or is not inconvenient. EG *'It wouldn't be any trouble.'–'That's very kind of you.'* N UNCOUNT : WITH BROAD NEG = bother

12 If you say that something is **more trouble than it is worth**, you mean that it takes a lot of time and effort and you do not achieve or gain very much in return. EG *Baking their own bread, they decided, was more trouble than it was worth.* PHR : USED AS C, VB INFLECTS

13 If you **take the trouble** to do something, you do it although it requires quite a lot of your time or effort. EG *If you take the trouble to attend the meeting you should at least be allowed to vote.* PHR : VB INFLECTS+*to*-INF

14 If something **troubles** you, 14.1 it makes you feel a certain amount of worry, doubt or uneasiness. EG *What's troubling you?... He was deeply troubled by the thought that she might leave him.* ◊ **troubling**. EG *It was a new and troubling thought.* 14.2 it causes you physical pain or discomfort. EG *Is your knee still troubling you?* V+O = bother ◊ ADJ QUALIT V+O ⇑ hurt

15 If you do not **trouble** to do something, you do not do it because it requires requires a special effort or is inconvenient. EG *He dismissed the deeds as forgeries without even troubling to examine them.* V+to-INF : WITH BROAD NEG = bother

16 If you say that you are sorry to **trouble** someone, you mean that you are sorry to have to ask them to do something when you think that it may be inconvenient or a nuisance for them. EG *I'm sorry to trouble you, but I wondered if we could have a word some time... I do apologise for troubling you, especially on a Sunday.* V+O = bother, inconvenience

troubled /trʌbəˡld/. 1 Someone who is **troubled** is worried because they have problems. EG *He was deeply troubled.* ▸ used of people's appearance, actions, etc. EG *...Sam's troubled face... She seemed to lapse into a troubled sleep.* ADJ QUALIT = disquieted ▸ = uneasy

2 A situation that is **troubled** is full of problems, disagreements, and conflicts. EG *We live in vexed and troubled times... ...Britain's troubled car industry... Government of the troubled areas has been left too long with colonial administrators.* ADJ QUALIT

3 **Troubled** water has its surface disturbed by the wind; a literary use. ● If you **pour oil on troubled waters**, you try to calm down a difficult situation. EG *Is there a strike to settle? He can pour oil on troubled waters.* ADJ QUALIT ● PHR : VB INFLECTS ⇑ pacify

trouble-free. Something that is **trouble-free** does not cause any problems or difficulties. EG *Each submarine reported a trouble-free launch.* ADJ QUALIT ≠ problematic

troublemaker /trʌbəˡlmeɪkə/, **troublemakers**; also spelled with a hyphen. A **troublemaker** is someone who causes trouble, unpleasantness, or ill feeling, for example by encouraging people to rebel against authority; used showing disapproval. EG *The trouble-makers are a tiny minority.* N COUNT = agitator, rabble-rouser

troublemaking /trʌbəˡlmeɪkɪŋ/; also spelled with a hyphen. **Troublemaking** means tending to cause unpleasantness, quarrels, ill feeling, or rebellion; used showing disapproval. EG *...a quarrelsome, troublemaking wife... ...troublemaking influences.* N UNCOUNT : USU BEFORE N ⇑ disruptive

troubleshooter /trʌbəˡlʃu:tə/, **troubleshooters**; also spelled with a hyphen. A **troubleshooter** is a person whose job is to solve major problems or difficulties that occur in a company or in an aspect of the company's work. N COUNT

troublesome /trʌbəlsəm/. 1 Something or someone that is **troublesome** causes annoying problems or difficulties. EG *His stammer was troublesome for him... ...troublesome tenants.* ADJ QUALIT = bothersome

2 A situation that is **troublesome** is full of problems or difficulties which cannot easily be solved. EG *...the most troublesome issue facing the commission... We can't afford in these troublesome times to have a Prime Minister who is weak.* ADJ QUALIT = trying

trouble spot, trouble spots; also spelled with a hyphen. A **trouble spot** is a country or an area of a country where there is repeated fighting between two or more groups of people. N COUNT ⇑ region

trough /trɒf/, **troughs**. 1 A **trough** is 1.1 a long narrow container in which food or drink for farm animals is put. EG *They led the workhorses to the watering trough.* 1.2 a long, narrow, and shallow channel that is cut into a surface, such as the ground, along which water runs so that it drains away. EG *Sewage ran down troughs on either side of the road.* 1.3 the area between two big waves on the sea. EG *As the wave bore down on us, the trough to starboard deepened.* 1.4 a low point in a pattern that has regular high and low points, for example the way in which prices or the demand for particular goods rise and fall regularly over a period of time. EG *The trough in consumption of electricity occurs at night.* N COUNT; N COUNT = gutter; N COUNT ⇑ depression; N COUNT

2 A **trough** of low pressure is a long narrow area of low air pressure, especially an extension of a depression; a technical term in meteorology. EG *There's a trough of low pressure over the South West.* N COUNT

trounce /traʊns/, **trounces, trouncing, trounced**. If you **trounce** someone, you defeat them severely and completely; an informal word. EG *...the game in which the Boston Red Sox trounced the St Louis Browns by the score of 29-2.* V+O = thrash

troupe /tru:p/, **troupes**. A **troupe** is a group of actors, singers, or dancers that work together and often travel around together, performing in different places. EG *I watched a troupe of travelling actors.* N COUNT : IF + PREP THEN of; IF SING, VB CAN BE SING OR PL = company

trouper /tru:pə/, **troupers**. A **trouper** is a member of a troupe of dancers, actors, or singers. N COUNT ⇑ entertainer

trouser /traʊzə/, **trousers**. **Trousers** are a piece of clothing. Trousers cover your bottom and have two tubes of material to cover your legs. EG *Claud was dressed in a pair of black trousers... The waiter took a handkerchief from his trouser pocket.* N PLURAL : ALSO *a pair of*+N

trouser suit, trouser suits; also spelled with a hyphen. A **trouser suit** is a suit of clothes worn by women. It consists of a pair of trousers and a matching top or jacket; used mainly in British English. EG *Sue wears a blue trouser suit and a neat scarf.* N COUNT

trousseau /tru:səʊ/, **trousseaux, trousseaus**. The plural can either be **trousseaux** or **trousseaus**. A **trousseau** is the clothes, linen, and other possessions that a bride collects for her marriage; a rather old-fashioned word. N COUNT = bottom drawer

trout /traʊt/, **trouts**. The form **trout** can also be used as the plural in paragraph 1. 1 A **trout** is a fairly large fish that lives in rivers and streams. There are several kinds of trout, and many of them can be eaten as food. EG *His father used to have trout for breakfast... I caught seven trout in fifteen minutes.* N COUNT/UNCOUNT

2 If you call an old woman an old **trout**, you mean that she is stupid, ugly, or has a bad temper; an offensive use. EG *She's a real old trout.* N COUNT : ALSO VOC = bag

trove /trəʊv/. See **treasure trove**.

trowel /traʊəl/, **trowels**. A **trowel** is 1 a garden tool that is rather like a small curved and pointed spade. You hold it in one hand and use it for things such as digging small holes or removing weeds. EG *He was fiddling around in the garden with a small trowel.* 2 a small tool with a flat blade that you use for spreading things such as cement and plaster onto walls and other surfaces. EG *You apply the filler with a knife or small trowel.* N COUNT; N COUNT

truancy /tru:ənsi[1]/ is the practice by children of staying away from school when they should be there. EG *The schools were fighting endlessly to combat truancy.* N UNCOUNT ⇑ absence

truant /tru:ənt/, **truants**. 1 A **truant** is a pupil who stays away from school when he or she should be there. EG *I found the truant throwing stones in the river... Truant children ran wild.* N COUNT ⇑ absentee

2 If a child **plays truant**, he or she stays away from school without permission. EG *I don't play truant very often.* PHR : VB INFLECTS = bunk off

truce /tru:s/, **truces**. A **truce** is an agreement between two people or groups of people to stop fighting or quarrelling for a short time. EG *Before the announcement of the truce, the commandos made another raid.* N COUNT ⇑ arrangement

truck /trʌk/, **trucks, trucking, trucked**. 1 A **truck** is 1.1 a lorry; used in American English. EG *There was a big truck parked on the side of the road... A grocer's van came up behind the truck and began hooting to get by... We heard the occasional rumble of a passing truck.* 1.2 a large motor vehicle which is open at the back and is used for carrying goods, animals, or people, often on rough roads that are not suitable for cars. EG *The farmer drove them out to the orchard in a rusty old truck... He was carted away in the back of a truck full of other wounded men.* 1.3 an open vehicle used for carrying goods on a railway. EG *...a long truck loaded with bricks... ...timber trucks.* N COUNT OR *by*+N ⇑ vehicle; N COUNT; N COUNT = wagon

2 If you **truck** something somewhere, you drive it there in a lorry; used in American English. EG *Sallay offered to truck the camels as far as Glen Helen... The goods were trucked to a warehouse.* V+O+A ⇑ transport

3 If you say that you will **have no truck with** someone, you mean that you will refuse to be involved with them or do business with them. EG *The Transport and General Workers' Union said yesterday that it would have no truck with a future Labour government on pay policy.* PHR : VB INFLECTS ≠ deal with

trucker /trʌkə/, **truckers**. A **trucker** is someone who drives a lorry as their job; used mainly in American English. N COUNT ⇑ driver

truckle /trʌkəˡl/, **truckles, truckling, truckled**. If you **truckle** to someone, you behave in a V+A (to) humble way towards them and do whatever they tell you to do. EG *I am sick of having to truckle to the professors.*

truckle bed, truckle beds. A **truckle bed** is a low bed which is on wheels and which you can push under another bed when you are not using it. N COUNT

truckload /trʌkləʊd/, **truckloads**. A **truckload** of goods or people is the amount of them that a truck can carry. EG *There was a whole truckload of us.* N COUNT ⇑ quantity

truculence /trʌkjə⁴ləns/ is the quality or state of being bad-tempered and aggressive. EG *Sandy's brief moment of truculence had vanished.* N UNCOUNT = belligerence

truculent /trʌkjə⁴lənt/. Someone who is **truculent** is bad-tempered and aggressive. EG *He was a truculent and quarrelsome man.* ADJ QUALIT = sullen

trudge /trʌdʒ/, **trudges, trudging, trudged**. If you **trudge** somewhere, you walk there slowly and with heavy steps, especially because you are tired or unhappy. EG *There was a stream of refugees trudging up the valley towards the border... He trudged wearily along the path.* ▸ used as a noun. EG *They set off before dawn for the long trudge home.* V+A = tramp, trek ▸ N SING WITH DET

true /tru:/, **truer, truest**. 1 A story or account of something that is **true** is based on facts and on things that really happen and are not imagined or invented. EG *The story about the murder is true... She gave the true account of what had happened... Unfortunately it was true about the illness of little Sylvie.* ADJ QUALIT ⇑ factual

2 You sometimes say that something is **true** when you want to admit that a fact, piece of information, or opinion is true or valid, but then to indicate that it is not important or to give a different point of view. EG *She longed for Europe, it was true, and would do anything to get there, but she wasn't prepared to give up her job for just two weeks in the South of France... True, Halliday had not appeared for breakfast, but then I knew he liked to get up late, so I didn't worry.* ADV SEN

3 If a dream, wish, or prediction **comes true**, it actually happens. EG *My wish had come true... That prediction from Ola Balogun is coming true.* PHR : VB INFLECTS = come to pass

4 If you say that an argument or fact is **true** for a particular situation, you mean that it is relevant for that situation. EG *Two-thirds of the energy from power stations is wasted; the same is true of nuclear power stations... Research also shows that what is true for ability is also true for achievement.* ADJ QUALIT : PRED+*of/for* ⇑ applicable

5 **True** is used to describe people or things that have all the characteristics of a particular thing, or of a particular kind of person or animal. EG *He was a true American... I suppose it takes time for true democracy to work.* ADJ QUALIT : ATTRIB = real

6 **True** feelings are sincere and genuine. EG *We sometimes wish to hide our true feelings... She smiled with true amusement.* ADJ QUALIT : ATTRIB = real

7 If you are **true** to someone, you are faithful, loyal, and honest towards them; a formal use. EG *I wanted to find out if my lover was true to me.* ADJ QUALIT : PRED, IF+PREP THEN *to* ≠ false

8 If you are **true to** your **word** or **promise**, you do what you had promised to do. EG *She was always true to her word.* PHR : USED AS C ⇑ reliable

9 If your aim is **true**, it is precise. EG *He looked through the telescopic sight until he was convinced his aim was true.* ADJ CLASSIF ⇑ good = spot-on

10 If something is **true**, it is perfectly straight and level and has a regular and accurate shape. EG *The window frame isn't quite true.* ADJ CLASSIF : PRED

11 If something is **out of true**, it is not perfectly straight and level or does not have a regular and accurate shape. EG *The tower was at least a quarter-inch out of true.* PHR : USED AS AN A

true-blue. A **true-blue** person is conventional in his or her ideas, opinions, and behaviour, especially in a way that is associated with the Conservative Party in Britain. EG *He soon became a reliable true-blue country club conservative.* ADJ CLASSIF = confirmed

true north is the direction that is north according to the earth's geographical poles, rather than according to magnetic poles. N UNCOUNT

truffle /trʌfə⁰l/, **truffles**. A **truffle** is 1 a soft round sweet flavoured with chocolate or rum. EG *He gave her a box of truffles for Christmas.* N COUNT 2 a round mushroom-like fungus which is expensive and considered very pleasant to eat. Truffles grow underground, and people use pigs to search for them. EG *He would go after it like a pig after truffles.* N COUNT

trug /trʌg/, **trugs**. A **trug** is a wide, shallow, oval basket used for carrying garden tools, flowers, plants, etc. N COUNT

truism /tru:ɪzə⁰m/, **truisms**. A **truism** is a statement that is so clearly true and repeated so often that it is boring. EG *It is a trite and obvious truism that people act in accordance with their motives.* N COUNT = cliché

truly /tru:li¹/. 1 **Truly** means completely and genuinely. EG *He was now truly American... Some doctors believe the truly accidental pregnancy is rare... He alone truly appreciates its finer points.* ADV = really

2 If you feel something **truly**, you feel it in a sincere and genuine way. EG *He knew he had behaved badly and he seemed truly sorry... She didn't let anyone know what she truly felt.* ADV = really

3 **Truly** also means to a very great degree. EG *He possessed a truly remarkable talent... He had a truly alarming capacity for food... ...a truly awful book.* ● **well and truly**: see **well**. ADV+ADJ/ADV = really

4 You also use **truly** to emphasize or confirm that what you are saying is actually true. EG *And truly, coming home was about the nicest part of the evening.* ADV SEN = in fact

5 You write **Yours truly** at the end of a formal letter to someone you do not know very well. You write your signature after the words 'Yours truly'. EG *I would be very grateful if you could see me. Yours truly, Desmond Burton-Cox.* PHR+N PROPER

6 You can say **yours truly** as an informal and rather humorous way of referring to yourself. EG *Consider the case of yours truly.* PHR = myself

trump /trʌmp/, **trumps, trumping, trumped**.

1 **Trumps** is the suit in a game of cards which is chosen to have the highest value in one particular game. EG *Spades are trumps.* N PLURAL

2 A **trump** or a **trump card** is a playing card which belongs to the suit that is trumps in a particular game of cards. EG *She played a trump.* N COUNT

3 Your **trump card** is the most powerful thing that you can use or the most effective thing that you can do in order to gain an advantage over someone and beat them. EG *His trump card played, Captain Imrie rested his case... Spain has at last produced her trump card and sent on the field of battle her most deadly weapon.* PHR : USED AS S/O/C

4 If you **trump** a card in a game of cards, you beat it by playing a trump. EG *He trumped her king.* V+O

5 If you **trump** something that someone has said or done, you beat it by saying or doing something else that seems better; a rather old-fashioned use. EG *She trumped his news by announcing that she had been picked for the Olympic team.* V+O = cap

6 If you say that someone **turned up trumps** or **came up trumps**, you mean that they gave you a lot of help when you had a problem, especially when you did not expect them to; an informal expression. EG *I was really desperate, but Bill turned up trumps and lent me £200.* PHR : VB INFLECTS

trumped-up. **Trumped-up** charges are untrue, and made up in order to deceive someone. EG *He was hauled into a military court on trumped-up charges of selling secrets.* ADJ CLASSIF : USU ATTRIB = phoney, false

trumpet /trʌmpɪt/, **trumpets, trumpeting, trumpeted**. 1 A **trumpet** is a brass musical instrument that you play by blowing into it. It consists of a long curved metal tube ending in a bell-like shape, and has three buttons that you press to get different notes. EG *He put the trumpet to his lips... He's a trumpet player... I don't think I know of any duets for piano and trumpet.* N COUNT

2 If you **blow** your **own trumpet**, you boast about something; an informal expression. EG *I'm not blowing my own trumpet, but I do all the top jobs.* PHR : VB INFLECTS = brag

3 When an elephant makes a sound, it **trumpets**. EG *The two elephants stretch up their necks and trumpet a celebratory chorus.* ▸ used as a noun. EG *The elephant's trumpet was very loud and rather frightening.* V OR V+O = bellow ▸ N COUNT : USU SING

4 If you **trumpet** something, you state it publicly in a very forceful way, usually because you want other people to accept your opinions. EG *This ideology was being trumpeted very effectively by highly committed party members... The local newspaper had trumpeted for 'the useful vote'.* V OR V+O/QUOTE/REPORT-CL = noise abroad

trumpeter /trʌmpɪtə/, **trumpeters**. A **trumpeter** is someone who plays a trumpet. N COUNT ⇑ musician

truncate /trʌŋkeɪt/, **truncates, truncating, truncated.** If something **is truncated**, it is made shorter. EG *The truncated corpse was stuffed into a rubber bag.* V+O: USU PASS ⇑ shorten

truncheon /trʌntʃən/, **truncheons.** A **truncheon** is a short, thick stick that is carried by a British policeman. EG *Last night police with truncheons fought a pitched battle with about 40 pickets.* N COUNT

trundle /trʌndəl/, **trundles, trundling, trundled.** 1 If a vehicle **trundles** somewhere, it moves there slowly. EG *We watched the combine harvesters trundling through the ripening maize... The lorry turned the corner and trundled up the hill.* V+A ⇑ drive = lumber

2 If you **trundle** something somewhere, you push or pull it along slowly on its wheels. EG *She saw him every Saturday, trundling the push chair along in the nearby park.* V+O+A = wheel

3 If you **trundle** somewhere, you walk there without hurrying. EG *I trundled along to the enquiry office... The other two trundled off into the woods.* V+A = toddle

trunk /trʌŋk/, **trunks.** 1 The **trunk** of a tree is its large main stem from which the branches grow. EG *I sat down on a fallen tree trunk and thought deeply.* N COUNT

2 Your **trunk** is the main central part of your body, but not the neck, head, legs or arms. N COUNT: USU POSS+N

3 An elephant's **trunk** is the long cylindrical part of its head that it uses to lift food and water and bring them to its mouth. N COUNT: WITH POSS = proboscis

4 A **trunk** is also a large case or box with strong rigid sides. You use it to carry your belongings on a long journey or for storing things in. N COUNT ⇑ container

5 In American English, a **trunk** is also the part at the back of a car in which you put your luggage or other belongings. N COUNT = boot

6 **Trunks** are the same as swimming trunks. EG *We had to go and buy a new pair of trunks yesterday.* N PLURAL: ALSO *a pair of*+N

trunk call, trunk calls. A **trunk call** is a telephone call to a place which is a long way away but in the same country; a rather old-fashioned expression. N COUNT

truss /trʌs/, **trusses, trussing, trussed.** 1 If you **truss** someone or **truss** them **up**, you tie them up with ropes very tightly so that they cannot move; a rather old-fashioned use. EG *The bank robbers trussed up the manager and his staff and locked them in the vault.* V+O, OR PHRASAL VB: V+O+ADV = bind

2 If you **truss** a chicken, duck, turkey, etc, you tie its legs and wings before it is cooked, so that they will stay in place. EG *I plucked and trussed the chicken.* V+O

3 A **truss** is a special belt with a pad that a man wears when he has a hernia in order to prevent it from getting worse. N COUNT ⇑ support

trust /trʌst/, **trusts, trusting, trusted.** 1 If you **trust** someone, you believe that they are honest and sincere and that they will not deliberately do anything that will hurt you in any way. EG *Everybody liked and trusted him... You can never trust a man.* V+O = have faith in

2 If you **trust** someone to do something, you believe that they are able and willing to do what you want them to do or to act in the way that you want. EG *I trust you to find them... She didn't trust anyone to look after her child properly.* V+O+*to*-INF

3 If you **trust** someone with something that you consider to be very valuable or important, you give it or tell it to them. EG *She's not a person I can trust with this sort of secret... Next year I hope the company will trust me with a bigger budget.* V+O+A *(with)* = entrust

4 If you **trust** in someone or something, you believe deeply in them; a literary use. EG *I slowly found myself able again to hope and trust in the human race.* V+A *(in)* = have faith

5 If you **trust** a story or someone's account of something, you believe it. EG *I'm not sure I trust their story.* V+O = credit

6 If you do not **trust** something, you feel that it is not safe or not completely reliable. EG *I don't trust fancy gimmicks in cars... He wanted to get up and walk out to the kitchen, but he didn't trust his legs.* V+O: WITH BROAD NEG

7 If you **trust** your judgement or someone's advice, you believe that it is good or right, and therefore do what it suggests you should do. EG *Don't be afraid to trust your own common sense... Trust your own instincts... She seems to trust his advice about people.* V+O = have faith in

8 If you **trust** to someone or something, you rely on them to make decisions for you or look after you. EG *The people of England are discovering that it is no good trusting to the old politicians... I suppose we'll just have to trust to luck.* V+A *(to)*

9 If you say that you **trust** that something is true, you mean that you hope and expect that it is true. EG *They will give you a good pension, I trust?... I trust you all like coffee.* V+REPORT-CL = assume

10 If you say '**trust** someone **to do** something', you mean that it is typical of that person to do that foolish thing. EG *Trust Julia to get the name wrong.* PHR+NG

11 **Trust** is 11.1 confidence that you have in someone and the belief that they are honest and sincere and will not deliberately do anything that will hurt you in any way. EG *She was filled with a sense of trust and happiness... Adam could feel his father's trust in him.* N UNCOUNT: IF+PREP THEN *in* = reliance, faith

11.2 responsibility, for example in your job, with things or information that are very important or secret. EG *The judge took the view that to betray a position of trust in such a manner was disgraceful... Sometimes civil servants can be bribed to betray their trust.* N UNCOUNT

12 If you **take** something that someone tells you **on trust**, you accept that it is true, without questioning it and without asking for proof that it is true. EG *You take certain things on trust.* PHR: VB INFLECTS ⇑ believe

13 A **trust** is 13.1 a financial arrangement in which a group of people or an organization holds and invests money for someone, either until they reach a particular age, or so that they can receive a regular income from the investment. EG *...a lifetime interest trust.* N COUNT 13.2 a group of people or an organization that has control of and invests an amount of money, property, etc on behalf of other people or as a charity. EG *...charitable trusts... Local trusts often support local activities.* N COUNT: MOD+N 13.3 an amount of money, property, etc that someone owns, usually by inheriting it, and that is kept and invested for them by a group of people or an organization. EG *He wanted to secure the best deal for his trust.* N COUNT 13.4 a group of companies that join together in order to control the market for the particular thing that they produce. Trusts are illegal in the United States; used mainly in American English. EG *Newspaper combines were one thing, soap trusts another... ...anti-trust laws.* N COUNT ⇑ syndicate

14 If money is kept **in trust**, it is held and invested for someone by a a group of people or an organization. EG *Erich's money is in trust... His mother's money was left in trust for him to acquire at the age of twenty-five.* PHR: USED AS AN A

15 See also **trusting**.

trustee /trʌstiː/, **trustees.** A **trustee** is someone who has legal control of an amount of money, property, etc that they are keeping or investing for another person, or for a company or other organization. EG *Her request for money was turned down by the trustees.* N COUNT ⇑ guardian

trustful /trʌstful/. Someone who is **trustful** trusts other people easily; a rather old-fashioned word. ADJ QUALIT = trusting

trust fund, trust funds. A **trust fund** is an amount of money, property, etc that someone owns, usually by inheriting it, but which is kept and invested for them. EG *My money is all tied up in trust funds... She inherited part of a trust fund.* N COUNT

trusting /trʌstɪŋ/. If you are **trusting**, you always tend to believe that people are honest and sincere and that they do not intend to hurt you in any way. EG *Judy had an open and trusting nature.* ◊ **trustingly**. EG *In many villages back doors are still left trustingly open.* ADJ QUALIT = credulous ≠ suspicious ◊ ADV

trustworthy /trʌstwɜːðiˡ/. Someone who is **trustworthy** is reliable and responsible so that you can trust them completely. EG *He was an experienced and trustworthy travelling companion.* ADJ QUALIT = dependable

trusty /trʌstiˡ/, **trustier, trustiest. Trusty** things and animals are reliable because they have always worked well in the past; a rather old-fashioned word. EG *My trusty weapon was within reach at all times... I tied up my trusty horse.* ADJ QUALIT: ATTRIB = faithful

truth /truːθ/, **truths.** 1 The **truth** is all the real facts about a situation, event, or person, rather than things that are imagined or invented. EG *He learned the truth about Sam... He's probably telling the truth... This is not the whole truth... Two people knew the truth.* N SING: *the*+N

2 If you say that a statement or story contains **truth**, you mean that it is true, or at least partly true. EG *There is no truth in the story... There is of course an* N UNCOUNT = truthfulness ≠ fiction

element of truth in this argument... I could not deny the truth of this statement.

3 A **truth** is a fact, idea, or principle that is generally accepted to be true. EG *It's a book that contains important truths... The purpose of scientific method is to select a single truth from among many hypothetical truths... ...a universal truth.*
N COUNT ≠ falsehood

4 You say **in truth** or **in all truth** when you are giving your honest opinion about something. EG *In truth he remained intensely selfish... In all truth, the British people deserved something better than this.*
PHR : USED AS AN A = in all honesty

5 You say **to tell you the truth** or **truth to tell** when you want to emphasize the fact that you are telling someone something in an open and honest way, without trying to hide anything. EG *I can't remember his name, to tell you the truth... For, truth to tell, the situation was drifting towards a crisis... Well, to tell you the honest truth, I think it's all a bit too much trouble.*
PHR : USED AS ADV SEN = to be honest

truthful /tru:θfʊl/. **1** Someone who is **truthful** is honest and tells the truth. EG *Being truthful is a profoundly practical thing... Many patients are more truthful when they talk to the computer than when they talk to the doctor.* ◊ **truthfully**. EG *If I ask him a question he will answer it as truthfully as he can.* ◊ **truthfulness**. EG *I began to suspect his truthfulness.*
ADJ QUALIT ≠ untruthful; ◊ ADV WITH VB; ◊ N UNCOUNT

2 A statement, declaration, or account that is **truthful** is true and based on facts rather than on things that are imagined or invented.
ADJ QUALIT ≠ untrue

try /traɪ/, **tries, trying, tried**. **1** If you **try** to do something, you make an effort in order to be able to do it. EG *My sister tried to cheer me up... I tried again to explain... They tried but failed... You can do it if you try... I tried hard not to think about it... He was trying his best to understand.* ▸ used as a noun. EG *It was decided that we would go and have a try ourselves... After a few tries they gave up... It's certainly worth a try.*
V, V+*to*-INF, OR V+O+*to*-INF = attempt; ▸ N COUNT = attempt

2 To **try** and do something means to try to do it; an informal use. EG *We must try and understand... Angelica started to try and help her up.*
V (INF)+*and*+VB (INF)

3 If you **try** for something, you make an effort to get it or achieve it. EG *The Government tried for this two-thirds majority and failed... The school advised Mr Denby to let his son try for university.*
V+A *(for)* ⇑ aim for

4 If you **try** something, you use it, do it, or experience it in order to find out how useful, helpful, effective, or enjoyable it is. EG *So I tried a different approach to the problem... The fourth key he tried opened the lid... Have you ever tried painting, Humbert?... He tried his wine again.* ▸ used as a noun. EG *We can give it a try and see how it looks in the photo.*
V+O/-ING; ▸ N COUNT : USU SING = go

5 If you **try** your **luck** or **try** your **fortunes**, you do something in which risk or luck is involved in order to see how successful you can be. EG *Davis lingered in the bar to try his luck with a fruit machine... She wanted to come to England and try her fortunes on our stage.* ● to **try** your **hand at** something: see **hand**.
PHR : VB INFLECTS ⇑ have a go

6 If you **try** a particular place or person, you go to that place or person because you think that they may be able to provide you with a service or something else that you want. EG *I had a dreadful job in getting the book. I tried everywhere... We tried two or three hotels, but they were full.*
V+O ⇑ ask

7 If you **try** a door or window, you try to open it. EG *She tried the front door... I tried the handle, but it was locked.*
V+O

8 When a person **is tried**, he or she has to appear in a court of law and the judge and jury listen to the evidence about a particular case or crime, and decide if the person is guilty. EG *A youth was tried in the criminal courts for stealing... We tried and convicted Carleson.*
V+O : USU PASS = put on trial

9 If something **tries** your **patience**, it angers or annoys you and you have to make a great effort in order to remain patient and calm.
PHR : VB INFLECTS

10 A **try** is also the action in a game of rugby when a player puts the ball down behind the goal line of the opposing team, and scores three or four points.
N COUNT

try on. **1** If you **try on** a piece of clothing, you put it on to see if it fits you or if it looks nice. EG *She tried on her new party dress... She tried it on for size.*
PHRASAL VB : V+O+ADV

2 If you say that someone **is trying it on**, you mean that they are behaving in a deceitful, outrageous, or extreme way in order to see how far other people will tolerate their behaviour; an informal expression. EG *She is probably trying it on to see how far she can go with you.*
PHR : VB INFLECTS

try out. If you **try** something **out**, you test it in order to find out how useful or effective it is or what it is like. EG *Oxford is trying out another idea to help working parents... It's best to try this out first on a bit of spare fabric.* ● See also **try-out**.
PHRASAL VB : V+O+ADV

trying /traɪɪŋ/. Something or someone that is **trying** is difficult to deal with and likely to make you feel impatient or annoyed. EG *It had been a most trying experience for them... I find him very trying.*
ADJ QUALIT

try-out, try-outs; also spelled as one word. If you give something a **try-out**, you try it or test it so that you can find out how useful or effective it is or what it is like. EG *A neighbour had given the machine a good try-out.*
N COUNT = trial

tryst /trɪst, traɪst/, **trysts**. A **tryst** is a meeting between lovers in a quiet secret place; a literary word.
N COUNT = assignation

trysting place, trysting places. A **trysting place** is a quiet secret place where lovers meet; a literary expression. EG *It was a favourite trysting place of couples.*
N COUNT ⇑ rendezvous

tsar /zɑ:/, **tsars**; also spelled **czar** or **tzar**. A **tsar** was a king of Russia in former times. EG *...Tsar Nicholas II of Russia.*
N COUNT : ALSO IN TITLES = ruler

tsarina /zɑ:ri:nə/, **tsarinas**; also spelled **czarina** or **tzarina**. A **tsarina** was a queen of Russia or the wife of a king of Russia in former times.
N COUNT : ALSO IN TITLES = ruler

tsarist /zɑ:rɪst/; also spelled **czarist** or **tzarist**. **Tsarist** means belonging to or believing in the system of government by a tsar, especially in Russia before 1917. EG *...tsarist Russia... ...tsarist dreams of empire.*
ADJ CLASSIF : ATTRIB ⇑ royalist

tsetse fly /tsetsi[1] flaɪ/, **tsetse flies**; also spelled **tzetze fly**. A **tsetse fly** or a **tsetse** is an African fly that feeds on blood and can cause serious diseases in the people and animals that it bites. EG *Mosquitoes and tsetse flies plagued us... ...farming in the tsetse zones.*
N COUNT/UNCOUNT

T-shirt, T-shirts; also spelled **t-shirt**. A **T-shirt** is a piece of clothing that you wear on the top half of your body. It has short sleeves, no collar, and no buttons down the front.
N COUNT ⇑ garment

tsp., tsps. Tsp. is a written abbreviation for 'teaspoon'; used to give quantities of ingredients, especially in recipes.

TT is an abbreviation for 'teetotal'.

tub /tʌb/, **tubs**. **1** A **tub** is a wide circular container of any size, into which a liquid can be poured. EG *...a tub big enough to hold eighteen gallons... All the beer should now be in one tub.* ▸ **Tub** also refers to the things in a tub or the amount of something that it can hold. EG *...tubs of lard.*
N COUNT = barrel; ▸ N COUNT : ALSO N PART+N UNCOUNT

2 In American English, a **tub** is also a bath. EG *I splashed around in the tub.*
N COUNT = bath tub

3 A **tub** is also an old boat that is slow and uncomfortable. EG *I've been at sea for four lousy weeks in this tub.*
N COUNT = wreck

tuba /tju:bə/, **tubas**. A **tuba** is a large musical instrument consisting of a curved tube of brass with a very large funnel at the end. It is played in a similar way to a trumpet but produces very low notes.
N COUNT

tubby /tʌbi[1]/, **tubbier, tubbiest**. Someone who is **tubby** is rather fat; a fairly informal word. EG *She was a short, tubby woman.*
ADJ QUALIT = plump

tube /tju:b/, **tubes**. **1** A **tube** is **1.1** a long hollow object made of rubber, plastic, glass, etc, that is usually round, like a pipe. Tubes are often used for moving liquids along. EG *He proceeded to force into the prisoner's mouth a hollow tube and pour the gruel through it... He slipped the telescope into the steel tube designed for it.* **1.2** a hollow organ in your body that is long and round in shape, like a pipe. EG *...fallopian tubes... ...bronchial tubes.* **1.3** a long thin container for thick liquids and pastes, like toothpaste. It is made of soft metal or plastic and you squeeze the tube in order to force the paste out through a hole in one end. EG *...a tube of toothpaste.*
N COUNT; N COUNT : ADJ+N; N COUNT : ALSO N PART+N UNCOUNT

2 The **tube** is an underground railway, especially the one in London. EG *When I come by tube it takes about half an hour... She lost her way on the London Tube... ...a tube train.*
N SING : *the*+N, OR *by*+N

3 A **tube** is also the same as a cathode ray tube. EG *The tube's gone on our television.*
N COUNT

4 See also **inner tube.**

tubeless /tjuːblɪ²s/. **Tubeless** tyres have no inner tube, but keep air inside them by forming a seal with the rim of the wheel. ADJ CLASSIF: USU ATTRIB

tuber /tjuːbə/, **tubers**. A **tuber** is a swollen and fleshy root of a plant such as a potato plant or a dahlia. N COUNT

tubercular /tjubɜːkjə⁴lə/ means relating to, causing, or suffering from tuberculosis. EG *...a sanatorium for tubercular patients.* ADJ CLASSIF

tuberculosis /tjubɜːkjə⁴ləʊsɪs/ is a serious infectious disease that affects someone's lungs and other parts of their body. EG *Lawrence's chronic tuberculosis is laying him low... She contracted tuberculosis.* N UNCOUNT = consumption, TB

tubing /tjuːbɪŋ/ is plastic, rubber, or another material in the shape of a tube. EG *There was a roll of thin nylon tubing lying on the desk.* N UNCOUNT

tubular /tjuːbjə⁴lə/. Something that is **tubular** is long, round, and hollow in shape, like a tube. EG *The whole thing fits into a tubular compartment for storage and carrying.* ADJ CLASSIF = cylindrical

T.U.C. The **T.U.C.** is a British association of trade unions; an abbreviation for 'Trades Union Congress'. N PROPER: *the*+N

tuck /tʌk/, **tucks, tucking, tucked. 1** If you **tuck** the loose end of a piece of clothing into a particular place or position, you push it there so that it is tidy and comfortable. EG *I sat up and tucked my shirt into my shorts... She tucked her sari round her waist.* V+O+A

2 If you **tuck** something somewhere, you put it there so that it is safe or comfortable. EG *He tucked the shell under his arm... He found the card with the name and number on it and tucked it under the phone.* V+O+A = slip

3 A **tuck** is a fold that is sewn in a piece of clothing for decoration or so that it fits you better. EG *It took me hours to make all these tucks round the waist.* N COUNT ⇑ pleat

4 Tuck is food; used mainly in British English by schoolchildren. N UNCOUNT = grub

tuck away. 1 If you **tuck away** something such as money, you store it in a safe place. EG *She had a bit of money tucked away.* PHRASAL VB: V+O+ADV = stash away

2 If you **tuck away** a lot of food, you eat it; an informal expression. EG *He managed to tuck away four bars of chocolate during the course of the afternoon.* PHRASAL VB: V+O+ADV = scoff

3 If something **is tucked away**, it is well hidden in a quiet place where very few people go. EG *The parish church is tucked away behind the cathedral.* PHRASAL VB: V+O+ADV, USU PASS

tuck in. 1 If you **tuck** someone **in**, usually a child, or if you **tuck** them **up**, you make them comfortable in bed by straightening their sheets and blankets. EG *He was asleep before I tucked him in.* PHRASAL VB: V+O+ADV

2 If you **tuck in** your shirt, you place the bottom ends of it inside your trousers or skirt. EG *I'm just tucking my shirt in.* PHRASAL VB: V+O+ADV

3 If you **tuck in**, you eat something with a lot of pleasure; an informal expression. EG *Well, there we are, tuck in... By the end of the holiday she was happily tucking into whatever dishes were put in front of her.* PHRASAL VB: V+ADV/PREP = eat up

tuck up. See **tuck in 1**.

tuck shop, tuck shops; also spelled with a hyphen. A **tuck shop** is a small shop near or in a school that sells cakes, sweets, etc. N COUNT

Tue. or **Tues.** is an abbreviation for 'Tuesday'.

Tuesday /tjuːzdi¹/, **Tuesdays**. **Tuesday** is one of the seven days of the week. It is the day after Monday and before Wednesday. EG *Our rugby team goes to Swansea on Tuesday... ...every Tuesday for the next two months...* N UNCOUNT/COUNT

tuft /tʌft/, **tufts**. A **tuft** is a bunch of hair, grass, etc that grows closely together or that is held together at the bottom. EG *...a tuft of hair... ...long, dead tufts of grass.* N COUNT: ALSO N PART+N UNCOUNT = clump

tufted /tʌftɪ²d/. Something that is **tufted** has a tuft or tufts on it. ADJ CLASSIF

tug /tʌg/, **tugs, tugging, tugged. 1** If you **tug** something or **tug** at it, you give it a quick and usually strong pull. EG *He tugged at the metal handle, and it came off in his hand... I grabbed her left ear between my thumb and forefinger, and tugged it playfully.* V+O, OR V+A (at) = yank
▸ used as a noun. EG *Tom felt a tug at his sleeve... One of them gave a tug at Clarissa's shoulder-bag.* ▸ N COUNT = yank

2 A **tug** or a **tug boat** is a small, powerful boat which pulls large ships, usually when they come into a port. EG *...an ocean-going tug... Tugs were sent to the damaged oil tankers.* N COUNT

tug-of-love is used to describe a situation in which the parents of a child are divorced and the parent who does not have custody still tries to get the child, for example by kidnapping. EG *...tug-of-love children.* ADJ CLASSIF: ATTRIB

tug-of-war. A **tug-of-war** is **1** a sport in which two teams test their strength by pulling against each other on opposite ends of a rope. EG *The tug-of-war was the last event of the afternoon.* N SING WITH DET, OR N UNCOUNT **2** a situation in which two people, or two groups of people, both want the same thing and are fairly equally matched in their struggle to get it. EG *Birmingham personality Rustie Lee is caught in a tug-of-war between Central and TV-am, who each want to sign her up.* N SING WITH DET/N UNCOUNT

tuition /tjuːɪʃə⁰n/ is **1** the teaching of a particular subject or subjects, especially to a small group or to one person. EG *Her father had decided she ought to have private tuition.* N UNCOUNT ⇑ instruction **2** the amount of money that you have to pay for tuition, especially in a university, college, private school, etc. EG *These college kids pay only £1,200 tuition each year.* N UNCOUNT ⇑ fee

tulip /tjuːlɪp/, **tulips**. A **tulip** is a brightly-coloured garden flower that is shaped like an upside-down bell and that grows from a bulb in the spring. N COUNT

tulle /tjuːl/ is a soft nylon or silk cloth that is rather like net and that is used for making evening dresses, veils, etc. N UNCOUNT

tumble /tʌmbə⁰l/, **tumbles, tumbling, tumbled. 1** If you **tumble**, you fall with a rolling, turning, or bouncing movement. EG *The dog turned over and tumbled down the slope... She pushes him and sends him tumbling downstairs.* V: USU+A ⇑ roll
▸ used as a noun. EG *He had a tumble and hurt his knee this morning.* ▸ N COUNT: USU SING

2 To **tumble** someone or something means to cause them to fall or roll over. EG *He tumbled me over backwards... ...a human body, tossed and tumbled by the water.* V+O: USU+A ⇑ push

3 If people **tumble** somewhere, they move there with a lot of quick, excited, bouncing movements, perhaps stopping frequently or often falling. EG *A wild band of children sprawl and tumble after the tiny animal... They came tumbling into the room.* V: USU+A

4 If you say that water **tumbles**, you mean that it flows quickly along over rocks and is disturbed by them so that it rolls and swirls a lot. EG *All he could hear was the water tumbling over the rocks.* V: USU+A ⇑ rush
◊ **tumbling**. EG *The water in the tumbling rivers is clear and sparkling.* ◊ ADJ CLASSIF: ATTRIB

5 If you **tumble** into a state or situation, you get into that state or situation quickly and without being able to stop yourself. EG *At any moment you may tumble to irreversible ruin... She tumbled into love.* V+A = fall

6 If prices **tumble**, they decrease suddenly by a large amount. EG *Share prices tumbled today following the Government's announcement.* V = drop, plummet ≠ rocket

7 See also **rough-and-tumble**.

tumble down. If someone or something **tumbles down**, they fall down. EG *It only needed a push and the whole building would come tumbling down.* PHRASAL VB: V+ADV ⇑ fall down

tumble over. If someone or something **tumbles over**, they fall over. EG *She tumbled over and hit her head on the concrete.* PHRASAL VB: V+ADV = fall down

tumble to. If you **tumble to** something, you suddenly understand it or realize what is happening. EG *I soon tumbled to the fact that I was wasting my time.* PHRASAL VB: V+PREP, HAS PASS = twig

tumbled /tʌmbə⁰ld/ is used to describe things or places that are untidy and in a muddled state, for example with things scattered about. EG *I marched into her tumbled room... ...tumbled beds.* ADJ CLASSIF: ATTRIB ⇑ messy ≠ tidy

tumbledown /tʌmbə⁰ldaun/. A building that is **tumbledown** is in such a bad condition that it is partly falling down or has holes in it. EG *...a deserted, tumbledown building.* ADJ QUALIT = crumbling, ramshackle

tumble dryer, tumble dryers; also spelled **tumble drier**; also spelled with a hyphen. A **tumble dryer** is an electric machine which dries washing by turning it over and over inside a drum and blowing warm air onto it. EG *Put the sheets in the tumble dryer.* N COUNT ⇑ drier

tumbler /tʌmblə/, **tumblers. 1** A **tumbler** is a drinking glass with straight sides. EG *She came up to him and handed him a large tumbler.* N COUNT
▸ also used to refer to the liquid inside a tumbler or the amount of liquid it contains. EG *He drank a tumbler of brandy.* ▸ N COUNT: ALSO N PART+N UNCOUNT

2 A **tumbler** is also an acrobat who performs on the ground rather than on a rope and who often performs with other members of a group. EG *The tumblers wore bright red costumes.* N COUNT ⇑ entertainer

tumbler dryer, tumbler dryers; also spelled **tumbler drier**. A **tumbler dryer** is the same as a tumble dryer. EG *A good tumbler drier can reduce ironing by 80 per cent.* N COUNT ⇑ drier

tumbrel /tʌmbrəl/, **tumbrels**; also spelled **tumbril**. A **tumbrel** was a cart used by farmers in former times. Tumbrels were used during the French Revolution for carrying prisoners to the guillotine. N COUNT

tumescent /tju:mesənt/. Something that is **tumescent**, especially part of a living thing, is becoming larger; a literary word. ADJ CLASSIF = swelling

tummy /tʌmi¹/, **tummies**; an informal word. Your **tummy** is 1 the part of the front of your body below your waist. EG *She tickled their tummies.* N COUNT 2 the parts inside your body where food is digested. EG *...the rumbling of empty tummies... ...tummy upsets.* N COUNT = stomach

tumour /tju:mə/, **tumours**; also spelled **tumor** in American English. A **tumour** is a mass of diseased or abnormal cells that has grown in a person's or animal's body. EG *He was suffering from a brain tumour.* N COUNT ⇑ growth

tumult /tju:mə⁹lt/, **tumults**; a formal word. A **tumult** is 1 a lot of noise caused by a crowd of people all shouting or doing noisy things at the same time. EG *A tumult of shots and yells could be heard.* N COUNT : USU SING 2 a state of confusion and excitement. EG *...the tumult of the Industrial Revolution.* N UNCOUNT = turmoil

tumultuous /tju:mʌltjuəs/. 1 A **tumultuous** period of time or state of mind is one in which many exciting and confusing events or feelings are involved. EG *...the most tumultuous decade of the century... ...the feeling of tumultuous emotion.* ADJ QUALIT : USU ATTRIB = turbulent

2 A **tumultuous** welcome or other event is very noisy, because the people involved are very happy or excited. EG *When the war was over, there was a tumultuous parade in London.* ADJ CLASSIF : USU ATTRIB = uproarious

tun /tʌn/, **tuns**. A **tun** is a large barrel. N COUNT

tuna /tju:nə/. **Tuna** is both the singular and the plural form. **Tuna** or **tuna fish** are large fish that live in warm seas and are caught for food. EG *...tins of tuna fish.* N UNCOUNT/COUNT

tundra /tʌndrə/, **tundras**. **Tundra** is one of the large flat areas of land in the north of Europe, Asia, and America. The ground below the top layer of soil is always frozen and no trees grow there. EG *...the vast tundra of Canada's Northwest Territories.* N UNCOUNT/COUNT ⇑ plain

tune /tju:n/, **tunes, tuning, tuned**. 1 A **tune** is a series of musical notes that form the main part of a piece of music, especially one that is pleasant or memorable. EG *The orchestra was playing a selection of tunes from The Merry Widow.* N COUNT = melody

2 When someone **tunes** a musical instrument, they adjust it so that it produces the right notes. EG *Always tune your violin before you start playing.* V+O

3 When someone **tunes** an engine or machine, they adjust it so that it will work as well as possible. EG *I told her the car needed tuning.* V+O ⇑ regulate

4 If someone or their radio or television **is tuned** to a particular broadcasting station or if they **tune** to that station, that station is received on their radio or television. EG *In the room were three television sets, each tuned to a different station... Stay tuned to Radio Desland for a further announcement.* V+O, V+O+A *(to)*, OR V+A *(to)* = tune in

5 If you **tune** something, you make sure that it matches or fits in with something else. EG *I have managed to tune my style to the style of the journal I am now writing for... The charge has got to be very finely tuned indeed to the amount of rent a student can afford.* V+O : IF+PREP THEN *to* ⇑ adapt

6 **in tune, out of tune**. 6.1 If a musical instrument is **in tune**, it is adjusted so that it produces the right notes. If it is **out of tune**, it does not produce the right notes. PHR : USED AS AN A 6.2 If someone who is playing an instrument or singing plays or sings **in tune**, they play or sing the right notes. If they play or sing **out of tune**, they play or sing the wrong notes. EG *She has never learnt to sing in tune.* PHR : USED AS AN A 6.3 If someone or something is **in tune** with a group of people or with things that are happening, they are in agreement or sympathy with them. If they are **out of tune**, they are not in agreement or sympathy with them. EG *His ideas are in tune with the spirit of his age... When you're completely out of tune with a class, teaching is almost impossible.* PHR : USED AS AN A

7 The word **tune** is also used in the following fairly informal expressions. 7.1 If you say that a particular person is the one who **calls the tune**, you mean that this person has authority and says what is to be done. EG *She calls the tune in their house.* PHR : VB INFLECTS 7.2 If someone **changes** their **tune** or **sings a different tune**, they say or do something different from what they previously said or did, because their opinion has changed. EG *He soon changed his tune and started working as hard as the others.* PHR : VB INFLECTS ⇑ reconsider 7.3 If you **dance to** someone else's **tune**, you do what they tell you to do; used showing disapproval. PHR : VB INFLECTS 7.4 **To the tune of** a particular amount means to the extent of that amount; usually used when emphasizing the size of an amount. EG *The university subsidises its students to the tune of £100,000 a year... The prison, which was built for about 1000, is overpopulated to the tune of 1600.* PHR ⇑ by

tune in. If you **tune in** to a particular station or programme, you set the controls of your radio, or perhaps television, so that you can listen to it. EG *Tune in next week to hear how English is taught in China.* PHRASAL VB : V+ADV

tune up. When a group of musicians **tune up**, they adjust their instruments so that they produce the right notes. EG *The orchestra was tuning up for its regular Sunday afternoon broadcast.* PHRASAL VB : V+ADV

tuned in. If someone is **tuned in** to something, they are aware of it, or ready and able to be aware of it. EG *Possibly predatory fish are tuned in to surface disturbance indicating a shoal of small fish... ...as people become more tuned in to what computers can do.* ADJ QUALIT : PRED+*to* ⇑ receptive = awake

tuneful /tju:nfυl/. A piece of music that is **tuneful** has a pleasant tune. EG *The emphasis is now on well-constructed, tuneful songs.* ADJ QUALIT = melodious

tuneless /tju:nlı²s/. A piece of music that is **tuneless** has the notes arranged in a random way or sounds unpleasant. EG *Harvey did a little dance and sang a tuneless, improvised song.* ADJ QUALIT = unmusical ≠ tuneful ◊ **tunelessly**. EG *Errol began to whistle tunelessly.* ◊ ADV WITH VB

tuner /tju:nə/, **tuners**. 1 A piano **tuner** is a person whose job consists of tuning pianos. N COUNT : MOD+N

2 The **tuner** in a radio or television set is the part which receives the radio signals or television signals. N COUNT

tungsten /tʌŋgstən/ is a greyish-white metal. N UNCOUNT

tunic /tju:nık/, **tunics**. A **tunic** is a piece of clothing which covers the top part of your body and reaches to your hips, thighs, or knees. N COUNT ⇑ garment

tuning fork, tuning forks. A **tuning fork** is a small steel instrument which produces a note of fixed musical pitch when it is struck against something. It is used to help tune musical instruments. N COUNT

Tunisian /tju⁴nıziən/, **Tunisians**. 1 A **Tunisian** person or thing comes from or relates to Tunisia or to its people. ADJ CLASSIF

2 A **Tunisian** is a person who comes from Tunisia. N COUNT

tunnel /tʌnə⁰l/, **tunnels, tunnelling, tunnelled**; also spelled **tunneling** and **tunneled** in American English. 1 A **tunnel** is a long passage which has been made under the ground, usually through a hill or under the sea. EG *Suddenly the train roared into a tunnel and everything was black... They hid it in the tunnel under our house.* ● **light at the end of the tunnel**: see **light**. N COUNT

2 If someone or something **tunnels** somewhere, they make a tunnel. EG *One person suggested tunnelling under the walls... ...an underground stream which has tunnelled a course through a flaw in the rocks.* V+A, OR V+O+A ⇑ dig

tunnel vision. 1 **Tunnel vision** is the inability to see things that are not straight in front of you. N UNCOUNT ⇑ blindness

2 If you say that someone has **tunnel vision**, you mean that they are concentrating on only one aspect of a subject, rather than considering every aspect of it; used showing disapproval. N UNCOUNT ⇑ narrow-mindedness

tuppence /tʌpəns/ means two old pence; an informal word. EG *Give them tuppence reward each.* N UNCOUNT ● If you **don't care tuppence** about something, you do not care about it at all; an informal, rather old-fashioned expression. EG *Dad didn't care tuppence what I looked like.* ● PHR : VB INFLECTS

tuppenny /tʌpə⁰ni¹/. A **tuppenny** item cost two old pence. ADJ CLASSIF : ATTRIB

turban /tɜ:bə⁰n/, **turbans**. A **turban** is a head-covering worn by a Muslim, Hindu, or Sikh man, which consists of a long piece of cloth wound round and round his head. N COUNT

turbaned /tɜ:bənd/. A **turbaned** man is wearing a turban. ADJ CLASSIF

turbid /tɜːbɪd/. **Turbid** water or air is full of mud or dirt, and is usually swirling about; a literary word. EG *He gazed down at the turbid waters of the Thames.* ADJ QUALIT = murky, cloudy

turbine /tɜːbɪ⁵n/, **turbines**. A **turbine** is a machine or engine in which power is produced when a stream of air, gas, water, or steam pushes the blades of a wheel and makes it turn round. N COUNT

turbo /tɜːbəʊ/, **turbos**. A **turbo** is a fan in a car engine that improves its performance. It is driven by the exhaust gases and helps to blow the fuel vapour into the engine. N COUNT ⇑ device

turbocharged /tɜːbəʊtʃɑːdʒd/. A **turbocharged** engine or vehicle is fitted with a turbo in order to improve its performance. ADJ CLASSIF ⇑ improved

turbot /tɜːbət/. **Turbot** is both the singular and the plural form. A **turbot** is a flat fish that lives in European seas and is caught for food. N UNCOUNT/COUNT

turbulence /tɜːbjə⁴ləns/ is 1 a state of confusion and constant, disorganized change. EG *...periods of social turbulence.* N UNCOUNT = unrest 2 violent and uneven movement within a particular area of air or water. EG *The turbulence caused the plane to turn over.* N SING : USU *the* +N

turbulent /tɜːbjə⁴lənt/. 1 A **turbulent** period of time or state of mind is one in which there are a lot of sudden changes and conflicting elements. EG *...in the turbulent days that followed... ...a period of fierce and turbulent struggle... She tried to calm her turbulent thoughts.* ADJ QUALIT ⇑ changeable = tumultuous

2 **Turbulent** people cause trouble and often quarrel or fight. EG *...a harsh land inhabited by a score of turbulent tribes.* ADJ QUALIT = unruly

3 **Turbulent** water or air contains currents which suddenly change direction or make violent circular movements. EG *...in the midst of turbulent seas and clashing rocks.* ADJ QUALIT ⇑ rough = choppy

turd /tɜːd/, **turds**. 1 A **turd** is a lump of faeces; a very rude informal use. N COUNT

2 If you describe someone as a **turd**, you mean that you think they are very unpleasant; a very rude, informal use. N COUNT OR VOC

tureen /tərɪːn/, **tureens**. A **tureen** is a large bowl with a lid from which you can serve soup or vegetables. N COUNT ⇑ dish

turf /tɜːf/, **turves, turfs, turfing, turfed**. The plural of the noun can be either **turves** or **turfs**. **Turfs** is also the third person singular, present tense of the verb. 1 **Turf** is short, thick, even grass. EG *They strode over the springy turf... He was busy digging and levelling the ground and laying turf.* N UNCOUNT

2 A **turf** is a small rectangular piece of good quality grass, with the roots and some soil still attached, that you lay on the ground in order to make a lawn. EG *...digging top quality meadow turves.* N COUNT

3 When someone **turfs** an area of ground, they cover it with turves. EG *She laid the bouquet on the newly-turfed grave.* V+O

turf out. If you **turf** someone **out**, you force them to leave a particular place; an informal expression. EG *Settlers are aware that the chief can turf them out if he takes a dislike to them.* PHRASAL VB : V+O+ADV = kick out

turf accountant, turf accountants. A **turf accountant** is the same as a bookmaker; a formal expression. N COUNT

turgid /tɜːdʒɪd/; a literary word. 1 A **turgid** mass, especially of water or mud, is thick and rather unpleasant to look at. EG *The pool was full to the brim with some very brown, turgid water.* ADJ QUALIT = oily

2 A **turgid** piece of writing, play, film, etc is difficult to understand and rather boring. EG *...turgid religious verse.* ADJ QUALIT = ponderous

Turk /tɜːk/, **Turks**. A **Turk** is a person who comes from Turkey. N COUNT

turkey /tɜːki¹/, **turkeys**. 1 A **turkey** is a large bird that is kept on a farm for its meat. Turkeys are eaten especially on special occasions, for example on Christmas Day. ▸ used of the meat of a turkey which is cooked and eaten. EG *People often drink white wine with turkey.* N COUNT ▸ N UNCOUNT

2 If you refer to someone as a **turkey**, you mean that they are stupid or silly; an informal use in American English. N COUNT : ALSO VOC = twit

3 When you **talk turkey**, you talk seriously and honestly, especially about business; an informal expression, used mainly in American English. PHR : VB INFLECTS ⇑ discuss

4 See also **cold turkey**.

Turkish /tɜːkɪʃ/. 1 A **Turkish** person or thing comes from or relates to Turkey, or to its people or language. ADJ CLASSIF

2 **Turkish** is the language that is spoken by the people who live in Turkey. N UNCOUNT

Turkish bath, Turkish baths. A **Turkish bath** is 1 a type of bath in which you sit in a very hot steamy room, then wash, have a massage, and finally swim or shower in very cold water. N COUNT 2 a place where you can have a Turkish bath. N COUNT

Turkish coffee is very strong black coffee that is usually drunk in very small cups or glasses. N MASS

Turkish delight is a jelly-like sweet that is covered with powdered sugar or chocolate. N MASS

turmeric /tɜːmərɪk/ is a spice used to flavour food, especially curries, which gives a brownish-yellow colour to the food. N UNCOUNT

turmoil /tɜːmɔɪl/ is a state of confusion, disorder, uncertainty, or great anxiety. EG *His soul, like his stomach, was in turmoil... ...his emotional turmoil... The city was in a turmoil.* N UNCOUNT OR N SING WITH DET

turn /tɜːn/, **turns, turning, turned**. 1 When you **turn** or when you **turn** your head, you move your body or your head so that you are facing in a different direction. EG *He turned to Jan and began to explain... She turned and walked away... They kept turning round to smile at friends... 'You're crying.'–'Nonsense,' Etta said, turning her head away.* ▸ used as a noun. EG *He made a smart military turn, clicking his heels.* V OR V+O : USU+A ▸ N COUNT

2 When you **turn** something or when it **turns**, it moves round, or rolls or flips over, so that the front part or top part faces in a different direction or so that the direction it faces in keeps changing. EG *I have turned the TV to the wall... The cog wheels started to turn... I turned the saucer over to look at the markings underneath... She idly turned the pages of a magazine... He turned the book upside down... She turned over, face against the sand.* ▸ used as a noun. EG *...with an agile turn of the wrist.* V-ERG : USU+A ▸ N COUNT ⇑ movement

3 When you **turn** a knob, key, switch, etc, you hold it and twist your hand, for example so that something opens, is locked, or starts working. EG *He turned the handle and pushed open the door... The key turned easily in the lock... Turn the gas as low as possible.* ▸ used as a noun. EG *The engine started second turn.* V-ERG ⇑ move ▸ N COUNT

4 If you **turn** something, for example a gun, on a person or thing, you aim or point it in their direction. EG *They turned their guns on the crowd... She turned green eyes on him.* V+O+A

5 When you **turn** in a particular direction or **turn** a corner, you change the direction in which you are moving or travelling. EG *You come over a bridge and turn sharply to the right... Turn left here... He turns down a side street... Howard turns the van towards the exit... The van turned into the Bristol Road.* ▸ used as a noun. EG *There was a long line of cars waiting to make the turn into the campus.* V OR V-ERG, OR V+O ▸ N COUNT ⇑ move

6 Where a road, path, river, etc **turns**, it has a bend or curve in it. EG *The road finally widened and turned into a courtyard.* ▸ used as a noun. EG *...a turn in the road.* V : USU+A ▸ N COUNT

7 If you **turn** part of a piece of cloth or paper in a particular direction, you fold it. EG *They undress together. They turn down the duvet... Her dress was all crumpled and turned up at the back.* V+O+A

8 If you **turn** to a particular page in a book, magazine, etc, you find that page. EG *Turn to page 349.* V+A *(to)* = go

9 If you **turn** your attention or thoughts to a particular person or thing or if you **turn** to them, you start thinking about them or discussing them. EG *I wonder if we can turn our attention to something you mentioned earlier... His thoughts turned to Calcutta... Turning to your new job, you start in August, is that right?* V-ERG+A

10 If you **turn** to someone, you ask for their help or advice. EG *She'd turned to him for help... What could I do? Where could I turn?* V+A ⇑ go

11 If you **turn** from one thing to another, you stop using or being involved in the first one and start using or being involved in the second one. EG *He served as a civil servant for a while before turning to political life... Most farmers had turned from crops to cattle... The magistrates have turned to other measures.* V+A ⇑ change

12 When something **turns** into something else or V-ERG+A

when you **turn** it into something else, it becomes something different. EG *If you apply more heat, of course the water turns into steam... Soon her glee turned to fear... ...a dramatist turned scriptwriter.*

13 If something **turns** white, sour, cold, etc or if something else **turns** it white, sour, etc, it becomes different by acquiring the quality mentioned. EG *My black hair has turned completely grey... It will turn the water blue... Things were turning nasty.* V-ERG+C

14 When someone **turns** a particular age, they pass that age. When it **has turned** a particular time, it is past that time. EG *Those who had turned fifteen could leave if they wanted to... 'What time is it?'-'Just turned three.'* V+O (NUM)

15 When the tide **turns**, it starts coming in or going out. V

16 If milk **turns** or **is turned**, it becomes sour. V-ERG

17 If you **turn** your ankle, you injure it by twisting it accidentally into an unnatural position. V+O = sprain, twist

18 When someone **turns** a cartwheel or a somersault, they do one. V+O

19 When someone **turns** a wooden or metal object that they are making, they shape it using a lathe. V+O

20 If it is your **turn** to do something, you now have the right, chance, or duty to do it, and this is fair because other people have done it before you or will do it after you. EG *It is his turn to take the children to school... He stood in the queue waiting his turn.* N COUNT : USU POSS+N = go

21 When you refer to the **turn** of the century, decade, year, etc, you are referring to the period of time covering the end of the century, decade, or year you are referring to and the beginning of the next one. EG *These issues have preoccupied sociology since the turn of the century.* N SING : *the*+N+*of*

22 A **turn** is also **22.1** a road which leads away from the side of another road, or a junction. EG *I think we missed our turn back there.* N COUNT = turning **22.2** a change in something that is happening or being done. EG *In that year things took a sharp turn for the worse... ...every twist and turn in government economic policy... Employers, needless to say, are not too happy about this turn of events.* N COUNT+SUPP **22.3** a slight attack of illness; an informal use. EG *Mrs Reilly is having one of her turns.* N COUNT = fit **22.4** a short, amusing entertainment, usually done as part of a larger performance. EG *...a comedy turn.* N COUNT **22.5** a short, gentle walk; a rather old-fashioned use. EG *She's taking a turn in the garden.* N COUNT = stroll

23 If you do someone **a good turn**, you do something that helps or benefits them. If you do someone **a bad turn**, you do something that causes problems for them. PHR : USED AS O/C/S

24 If you experience a particular thing **at every turn**, you experience it every time you try to do something. EG *We were thwarted at every turn.* PHR : USED AS AN A

25 If someone is **by turns** happy and sad, charming and irritating, etc, they have the two emotions or qualities indicated one after the other. EG *She was by turns ecstatic and terrified.* PHR+C : USED AS AN A

26 If something that is being cooked is **done to a turn**, it has been cooked just long enough; an informal expression. PHR : USED AS C ↑ perfect

27 If something **gives** you **a turn**, it gives you a shock or a great surprise. EG *This news gave me quite a turn.* PHR : VB INFLECTS

28 You use **in turn** **28.1** to refer to people, things, or actions that are in a sequence one after the other. EG *She went round the ward, talking to each woman in turn... Two men were working, hitting the anvil in turn... It became in turn a stable, a chapel, and a movie theatre.* PHR : USED AS AN A **28.2** to introduce a consequence or cause of something that you have just mentioned, or to give the next one in a series of linked events or facts. EG *This means that the turbines cannot be run efficiently which in turn means that you only get about half as much electricity... We got the idea from a hospital in Edinburgh; they in turn got it from a hospital in Leeds.* PHR : USED AS ADV SEN

29 If the tide is **on the turn**, it is just about to start coming in or going out. PHR : USED AS AN A

30 out of turn. 30.1 If you do something **out of turn**, you do it at a time when you do not have the right to do it, because someone else should have done it before you. PHR : USED AS AN A ↑ out of order **30.2** If you mention or do something **out of turn**, you mention or do it although you have no right or authority to do so. EG *He shouldn't have told you: he's spoken out of turn.* PHR : USED AS AN A

31 If two or more people **take turns** to do something or **take it in turns** to do something, they do it one after the other, especially because this is fair. EG *You can take turns paying for evening functions... The protesters are taking it in turns to chain themselves to the perimeter fence... They took turns at the same typewriter.* PHR : VB INFLECTS

32 If two or more people do something **turn and turn about**, they do it one after the other for a period of time. EG *They shared the watch, three hours each, turn and turn about.* PHR : USED AS AN A

33 If you **turn** something such as a dress or bag **inside out**, you put one end of it all the way through the inside, so that the inside then faces outwards. PHR : VB INFLECTS

34 If you **turn** a room, cupboard, etc **upside down** or **inside out**, you make it very untidy when you are looking very thoroughly for something. PHR : VB INFLECTS

35 If something such as a system or way of life **is turned upside down** or **inside out**, it is changed completely, causing great confusion. EG *All the old theories about child rearing were suddenly turned upside down... Industrial life has been turned inside out by the computer.* PHR : VB INFLECTS, USU PASS

36 If someone is of a particular **turn of mind**, they have that kind of mind or character. EG *I am of an essentially domestic turn of mind.* PHR+SUPP : USED AS O

37 A **turn of speed** is the ability to move fast or an occasion of moving fast. EG *My Jaguar's got a tremendous turn of speed.* PHR : USED AS O

38 See also **turning**.

39 The word **turn** is also used in the following expressions, which are explained at other places in this dictionary. • to **turn** your **back on** something: see **back**. • to **turn a blind eye**: see **blind**. • to **turn** your **hand to** something: see **hand**. • to **turn the tables on** someone: see **table**. • to **turn tail**: see **tail**.

• See also **about-turn**.

turn against. If someone **turns against** you or **is turned against** you, they start to dislike or distrust you, or become your enemy. EG *They might at any time turn against their masters... Public opinion turned against Hearst... You turn everyone against me.* PHRASAL VB : V-ERG+PREP

turn around. To **turn around** or to **turn** something **around** means the same as to turn round or to turn it round. PHRASAL VB : V+ADV, OR V+O+ADV

turn away. If you **turn** someone **away**, you reject them or send them away. EG *The college has been forced to turn away 300 prospective students.* PHRASAL VB : V+O+ADV

turn back. **1** If you **turn back** when travelling somewhere, you start returning to where you started from. EG *The snow started to fall, so we turned back.* PHRASAL VB : V+ADV

2 If you **turn** someone **back**, you prevent them from travelling any further and make them return in the direction they came from. EG *A lot of the convoys had been turned back at the border.* PHRASAL VB : V+O+ADV ↑ stop

3 If you cannot **turn back**, you cannot change your plans and decide not to do something, because of the action that you have already taken. EG *She had made her decision and from that point there could be no turning back.* PHRASAL VB : V+ADV, USU WITH BROAD NEG

turn down. **1** If you **turn down** someone or their request or offer, you refuse their request or offer. EG *I was invited to be foreman but I turned it down... Their claim has been turned down... I couldn't very well turn him down.* PHRASAL VB : V+O+ADV

2 When you **turn down** something such as a radio or a heater, you reduce the amount of sound or heat being produced, by adjusting the controls. EG *Turn the sound down... Could you turn the radio down a bit?... If you are very hot you can turn the heating down.* PHRASAL VB : V+O+ADV ≠ turn up

turn in; an informal expression. **1** When you **turn in**, you go to bed. EG *Before turning in for the night he asked for an early morning call.* PHRASAL VB : V+ADV = retire

2 If you **turn in** someone who is suspected of a crime, you take them to the police. EG *He's going to turn you in... You'll have to turn yourself in some time.* PHRASAL VB : V+O+ADV

3 When you **turn in** a completed piece of work, especially written work, you give it to the person who asked you to do it. EG *The work you've been turning in lately hasn't been up to scratch.* PHRASAL VB : V+O+ADV = hand in

turn off. **1** If you **turn off** the road or path you are going along or **turn off**, you start going along a different road or path which leads away from it. EG *They turned off the main road... You don't even turn off, you just go straight ahead.* PHRASAL VB : V+ADV/PREP

2 When you **turn off** something, for example a radio, light, heater, or water supply, you move the switch, knob, etc that controls it so that it stops working. EG *He must have turned off the radio... The switch was sticking and we couldn't turn the heat off... She turned off the tap.* PHRASAL VB : V+O+ADV = switch off ≠ switch on

3 If something **turns** you **off** or if you **turn off**, you suddenly stop being emotionally or sexually excited or interested; an informal use. PHRASAL VB : V-ERG+ADV = switch off

4 See also **turn-off**.

turn on. 1 When you **turn on** something, for example a radio, light, heater, or water supply, you move the switch, knob, etc that controls it so that it starts working. EG *Shall I turn the fire on low?... She turned on the shower.* PHRASAL VB : V+O+ADV = switch on ≠ switch off

2 If someone or something **turns** you **on**, they attract you and make you feel sexually excited; an informal use. EG *I don't really turn you on, do I?* PHRASAL VB : V+O+ADV ≠ turn off

3 If you **turn on** a particular way of behaving, you suddenly start behaving in that way; an informal use. EG *He can really turn on the charm when he wants to.* PHRASAL VB : ORDER V+ADV+O = switch on

4 If a person or animal **turns on** you, they attack you or speak angrily to you. EG *She turned on the men. 'How can you treat your daughters like this!'... The dog turned on her and bit her.* PHRASAL VB : V+PREP, HAS PASS = go for

5 If something **turns on** a particular thing, its success or truth depends on that thing. EG *His own future will turn on whether or not he can convince enough voters... The whole issue turns on the question of retaliation.* PHRASAL VB : V+PREP, HAS PASS = hinge on

6 See also **turn-on**.

turn out. 1 If something **turns out** a particular way, it happens in that way or has the result or degree of success indicated. EG *Nothing ever turned out right... ...even if the transaction turned out badly for them... It turned out to be a fairly sensational evening... As it turned out I needn't have worried.* PHRASAL VB : V+ADV+ADV/*to*-INF = work out

2 If something **turns out** to be a particular thing, it is discovered to be that thing. EG *The Marvins' house turned out to be an old converted barn... It turned out that the message sent to him had been intercepted.* PHRASAL VB : V+ADV+*to*-INF/REPORT-CL

3 When you **turn out** something such as a light or a gas, you move the switch, knob, etc that controls it so that it stops giving out light or heat. EG *She didn't bother to turn out the light when she went out of the room.* PHRASAL VB : V+O+ADV ≠ turn on

4 If a business or other organization **turns out** something, it produces it after making it or treating it in some way. EG *Salford was the type of institution turning out the type of graduate they wanted.* PHRASAL VB : ORDER V+ADV+O = churn out

5 If you **turn** someone **out** or **turn** them **out of** a particular place, especially the place where they have been living, you force them to leave that place. PHRASAL VB : V+O+ADV, IF+PREP THEN *of* ⇑ get rid of

6 If you **turn out** a container or **turn** its contents **out**, you empty it of its contents. EG *Come on, turn out your pockets!* PHRASAL VB : V+O+ADV

7 If people **turn out** for a particular event or activity, they go and take part in it or watch it. EG *Voters turned out in extraordinary numbers for the election.* PHRASAL VB : V+ADV

8 See also **turned out, turnout**.

turn over. 1 If you **turn** something **over** in your mind, you think carefully about it. EG *Going home that night, Dr Renshaw turned over the facts of the case.* PHRASAL VB : V+O+ADV = consider

2 If you **turn** something **over** to someone, you give it to them when they ask for it, because they have a right to it. EG *He had refused to turn over funds that belonged to Potter.* PHRASAL VB : V+O+ADV = hand over

3 If you **turn** something **over** to a different function or use, you change its function or use. EG *I'm planning to turn over a hundred of the hives to pollen production.* PHRASAL VB : V+O+ADV : USU+*to*

4 When you talk about the rate that people or things **turn over** in a particular place, you are talking about how long they stay there before moving or being sent somewhere else. EG *In a grocery store, milk turns over more rapidly than, say, canned asparagus.* PHRASAL VB : V+ADV

5 If someone **turns over** a place, they steal a lot of things from it in an organized way. EG *Half the school is on probation for turning over a supermarket.* PHRASAL VB : V+O+ADV = do over

6 See also **turnover**.

turn round. 1 If you **turn** something **round**, 1.1 you change the way in which it is expressed. EG *So by putting it in the third person I can turn it round a bit and make it funny.* PHRASAL VB : V+O+ADV 1.2 you change its nature or progress so that it becomes successful. EG *It's a cruel deception to pretend that you could turn round the economy in a week.* PHRASAL VB : V+O+ADV

2 If you say that someone **turns round** and says something, you mean that they criticize someone or defend themselves, especially unexpectedly or unfairly; a fairly informal use. EG *Won't the child turn round and blame the school?* PHRASAL VB : V+ADV+*and*

turn up 1 If someone or something **turns up**, they arrive somewhere or appear, often unexpectedly; a fairly informal use. EG *He turned up at rehearsal the next day looking awful.* PHRASAL VB : V+ADV = show up

2 If something **turns up** or **is turned up**, it is found, discovered, or noticed; a fairly informal use. EG *The missing book turned up three weeks later in the stationery cupboard... You must be willing to take a job as soon as one turns up... If I turn up anything, you'll be the first to know.* PHRASAL VB : V-ERG+ADV

3 When you **turn up** something such as a radio or heater, you increase the amount of sound or heat being produced, by adjusting the controls. EG *Turn the volume control up... Could you turn the fire up?* PHRASAL VB : V+O+ADV ≠ turn down

4 When someone **turns up** a dress, skirt, pair of trousers, etc, they fold up the bottom and stitch it in place to shorten it or make a hem. PHRASAL VB : V+O+ADV ⇑ alter ≠ let down

turnabout /tɜːnəbaʊt/, **turnabouts**. A **turnabout** is a complete change in opinion or attitude. EG *I was eager to know what had caused the turnabout.* N COUNT

turnaround /tɜːnəraʊnd/, **turnarounds**. 1 The **turnaround** or the **turnaround** time of a task, for example the unloading of an aircraft or ship, is the amount of time that it takes. EG *How long was the turnaround on that last job?* N SING WITH DET

2 A **turnaround** is also 2.1 a complete change in opinion or attitude. N COUNT 2.2 a sudden improvement, especially in the success of a business or a country's economy. N COUNT : USU SING

turncoat /tɜːnkəʊt/, **turncoats**. A **turncoat** is a person who leaves one political party or group and joins an opposing one; used showing disapproval. N COUNT ⇑ deserter

turned out. A person or animal that is well **turned out**, smartly **turned out**, etc is dressed or groomed well, smartly, etc. EG *...attractive-looking girls, well turned out and smart... ...tiny tots turned out as if for a wedding.* ADJ CLASSIF+SUPP = presented

turning /tɜːnɪŋ/, **turnings**. A **turning** is a road which leads away from the side of another road, or a junction. EG *Take the third turning on the left... We must have missed the turning.* N COUNT = turn

turning point, turning points; also spelled with a hyphen. A **turning point** is a time at which an important change takes place which affects the future of a person or thing. EG *The turning point for the business came in 1974 when I bought the computer... It proved to be a turning point in his life.* N COUNT, USU SING

turnip /tɜːnɪp/, **turnips**. A **turnip** is a round vegetable which has a white, yellow, or reddish skin and grows underneath the ground; also used of the plant which produces it. N COUNT

turn-off, turn-offs; also spelled as one word. 1 A **turn-off** is a road which leads away from the side of another road, usually a major road. N COUNT = turning

2 Something that is a **turn-off** causes you to lose interest or enthusiasm; an informal use. N COUNT : USU SING

turn-on, turn-ons. Something or someone that is a **turn-on** makes you feel sexually excited; an informal word. N COUNT : USU SING

turnout /tɜːnaʊt/, **turnouts**; also spelled with a hyphen. 1 The **turnout** at an event is the number of people who go to it or take part in it. EG *Despite hopes of a larger turnout they were well pleased with the rally... It was a good turn-out.* N COUNT : USU SING

2 Someone's **turnout** is the way that they are dressed and how neat they are. EG *Claude approved of Daniel's turnout, with the exception of his tie.* N COUNT : USU POSS+SING ⇑ appearance = get up

3 If you have a **turnout**, you sort through the things in a room, cupboard, etc and throw away the unwanted things. N COUNT : USU SING = clearout

turnover /tɜːnəʊvə/, **turnovers**. 1 The **turnover** of people in a particular organization or group is the rate at which people leave it and are replaced by others. EG *The group has an extremely high turnover of members.* N UNCOUNT

2 The **turnover** of a company is the value of the goods or services that it has sold during a particular period of time. EG *Annual turnover is about £9,000* N UNCOUNT

million... We've got a turnover here of about seven million pounds a year.

3 A **turnover** is a small piece of pastry that has been filled with fruit or jam, folded over, and baked. EG *...an apple turnover.* N COUNT : USU MOD+N ⇑ tart

turnpike /tɜːnpaɪk/, **turnpikes**. A **turnpike** is a motorway, usually one which you have to pay to drive on; used in American English. N COUNT = toll road

turnround /tɜːnraʊnd/, **turnrounds**; also spelled with a hyphen. A **turnround** is the same as a turnaround. EG *There was a remarkable turn-round from an $828,000 loss to a $175,000 surplus.* N COUNT : USU SING

turnstile /tɜːnstaɪl/, **turnstiles**. A **turnstile** is a mechanical barrier at the entrance to a zoo, football ground, etc, which has metal arms that you push round as you enter the area or building. N COUNT ⇑ gate

turntable /tɜːnteɪbəᵒl/, **turntables**. A **turntable** is 1 the flat, round part of a record player on which a record is put when it is played. N COUNT 2 a large, flat, metal area at ground level on which a train engine can be driven and then turned round. N COUNT

turn-up, turn-ups; also spelled as one word. 1 The **turn-ups** of someone's trousers are the ends of the trouser legs, which are folded upwards. N COUNT, USU PL

2 If you describe an event as **a turn-up for the book** or **a turn-up for the books**, you mean that it is very surprising or unexpected; an informal expression. PHR : USED AS C

turpentine /tɜːpəntaɪn/ is a strong-smelling, colourless liquid which is used for cleaning and for making paint thinner. N UNCOUNT = white spirit

turpitude /tɜːpɪtjuːd/ is wicked and unacceptable behaviour; a formal word. EG *She accused him of gross moral turpitude.* N UNCOUNT = degeneracy

turps /tɜːps/ is turpentine; an informal word. N UNCOUNT

turquoise /tɜːkwɔɪz, -kwɑːz/, **turquoises**. 1 Something that is **turquoise** or **turquoise blue** is of a bright blue colour that is fairly light and often greenish. EG *...the warm turquoise sea.* ADJ COLOUR ▸ used as a noun. ▸ N UNCOUNT

2 **Turquoise** or a **turquoise** is a bright blue stone that is quite valuable and is often used in jewellery. EG *...a brooch set with tiny rubies and turquoises... ...a silver and turquoise bracelet.* N COUNT/UNCOUNT ⇑ gem

turret /tʌrɪt/, **turrets**. 1 A **turret** is a small narrow tower on top of a building or a larger tower. EG *...the turrets of the White Tower.* N COUNT

2 The **turret** on a tank or warship is the part where the guns are fixed, which can be turned in any direction. N COUNT

turtle /tɜːtəᵒl/, **turtles**. 1 A **turtle** is 1.1 a large reptile that has a thick shell around its body and lives in the sea most of the time. N COUNT 1.2 in American English, any reptile that has a thick shell around its body, for example a tortoise or a terrapin. N COUNT

2 If a boat **turns turtle**, it turns upside down; an informal expression. PHR : VB INFLECTS

turtledove /tɜːtəᵒldʌv/, **turtledoves**; also spelled with a hyphen. A **turtledove** is a light-brown wild bird that makes a soft cooing sound. N COUNT ⇑ dove

turtleneck /tɜːtəᵒlnɛk/, **turtlenecks**. A **turtleneck** or a **turtleneck** sweater or jersey is a sweater with a short, round collar that fits closely around your neck. N COUNT : USU BEFORE N

tusk /tʌsk/, **tusks**. The **tusks** of an elephant, wild boar, walrus, etc are the pair of very long, pointed teeth that it has, which are often curved. N COUNT ⇑ tooth

tussle /tʌsəᵒl/, **tussles, tussling, tussled**. A **tussle** is an energetic fight, struggle, or argument between two people, especially about something that they both want. EG *He was still smarting from the tussle over the bottle... The conflict became a tussle of national wills.* N COUNT = battle ▸ used as a verb. EG *I tussled with him for a few minutes and managed to wrench the book from his grasp.* ▸ V OR V+A (with) : RECIP = scuffle

tussock /tʌsək/, **tussocks**. A **tussock** is a small clump of grass which is much longer and thicker than the grass around it. EG *...tussocks of grass.* N COUNT = tuft

tut is used in written English to represent a sound that you make by putting your tongue behind your teeth and sucking in air. You say **tut** when you are annoyed or frustrated, or to indicate that you do not approve of something. EXCLAM

tutelage /tjuːtɪlɪdʒ/. If one person, group, or country is under the **tutelage** of another one, the second one has authority over the first one, and looks after or protects the first one; a formal word. EG *He gained valuable experience and training under his father's tutelage... They began to aspire to throw off monarchical tutelage.* N UNCOUNT ⇑ guardianship

tutor /tjuːtə/, **tutors, tutoring, tutored**. 1 A **tutor** is 1.1 a member of staff at a British university or college who teaches small groups of students or gives individual students general help and advice. EG *When the students are making their choices, their tutor may well guide them.* N COUNT ⇑ teacher 1.2 a private teacher who teaches one pupil or a very small group of pupils, usually at the pupil's home. N COUNT = coach

2 If someone, especially a private teacher, **tutors** a person or a subject, they teach that person or subject. EG *The great majority were tutored by parents and priests... Next year I want to tutor A-level maths... I've got to tutor for two hours this morning.* V OR V+O = coach

tutorial /tjuːtɔːrɪəl/, **tutorials**. 1 A **tutorial** is a regular meeting in which a tutor and a small group of students discuss a subject as part of the students' course. N COUNT ⇑ class

2 **Tutorial** means belonging or relating to a tutor, especially one at a university or college. EG *First year students take two pairs of courses, chosen under tutorial guidance... All undergraduates reading English attend a tutorial group each week.* ADJ CLASSIF : ATTRIB ⇑ teaching

tutti frutti /tuːti[1] fruːti[1]/. **Tutti frutti** or **tutti frutti ice-cream** is ice cream containing little bits of different kinds of preserved fruit. N UNCOUNT

tut-tut, tut-tuts, tut-tutting, tut-tutted. 1 The word **tut-tut** is used to represent a sound you make by putting your tongue behind your teeth and sucking in air twice. You say **tut-tut** to indicate that you do not approve of something or that you sympathize with someone. CONVENTION = cluck

2 If you **tut-tut** about something, you express your disapproval or sympathy, especially by saying 'tut-tut'. EG *...a solicitous porter who tut-tutted over his plastered foot... They spent the whole evening tut-tutting about the lack of discipline in young people.* V : USU+A ⇑ complain

tutu /tuːtuː/, **tutus**. A **tutu** is a costume worn by female ballet dancers which has a very short stiff skirt that sticks out from the waist and is made from many layers of material. N COUNT

tu-whit tu-whoo /tə wɪt tə wuː/ is an expression used to represent the sound that an owl makes.

tuxedo /tʌksiːdəʊ/, **tuxedos**. A **tuxedo** is a black, or sometimes white, jacket that men wear with a bow tie at formal social events; used mainly in American English. N COUNT

TV, TVs. **TV** is television and a **TV** is a television set. EG *I've just been watching a film on TV about an earthquake... Paul scuttled back to his chair and turned on the TV... ...a TV set.* N UNCOUNT/COUNT

twaddle /twɒdəᵒl/. If you describe something that someone says as **twaddle**, you mean that it is silly, untrue, or unimportant; an informal word. EG *Beata was talking a load of twaddle.* N UNCOUNT = drivel

twain /tweɪn/. The expression **and never the twain shall meet** is used to suggest that two people or groups of people are completely different and that they will never agree with each other or understand each other. EG *My son has his views and I have mine and never the twain shall meet.* PHR

twang /twæŋ/, **twangs, twanging, twanged**. 1 A **twang** is a sound like the one that is made by pulling and then releasing a tight wire. EG *...the twang of tennis balls bouncing off tightly-strung tennis rackets.* N COUNT = thwack

2 If you **twang** something such as a tight wire or string, or if it **twangs**, it moves and makes a 'twang' sound, especially because it has been pulled and then released. EG *He was sitting twanging a guitar... The springs on the bed twanged.* V-ERG

3 A **twang** is also a nasal quality in someone's way of speaking. EG *...her nasal Oklahoma twang.* N COUNT : MOD+N

tweak /twiːk/, **tweaks, tweaking, tweaked**. If you **tweak** something, especially part of a person's or animal's body, you hold it between your finger and thumb and twist it or pull it. EG *He used to tweak the cat's tail.* V+O, OR V+A (at) = yank, tug ▸ used as a noun. EG *I'll just give the veil a tweak. That's better.* ▸ N COUNT = tug

twee /twiː/. If you say that something is **twee**, you mean that, although it is pretty, it seems to you sentimental or in bad taste. ADJ QUALIT : USU PRED = precious

tweed /twiːd/, **tweeds**. 1 **Tweed** is a thick, woollen cloth, often woven from different coloured threads. EG *He wore a tweed jacket.* N UNCOUNT ⇑ fabric

2 Someone who is wearing **tweeds** is wearing a tweed suit. EG *...a stout rosy man in tweeds.* N PLURAL ⇑ clothing

tweedy /twiːdi¹/. A **tweedy** person is wearing tweeds and perhaps looks as if they are upper-class and live in the country. ADJ QUALIT

tweet /twiːt/, **tweets, tweeting, tweeted.** When a small bird **tweets,** it makes a short, high-pitched sound, or a series of these sounds. EG *...a flock of tweeting avocets.* ▸ used as a noun and an exclamation. EG *It gave a melancholy tweet... 'Tweet, tweet!' went the little robin.* V = chirp ▸ N COUNT/ EXCLAM

tweezers /twiːzəz/ are a small tool consisting of two narrow strips of metal joined at one end. You use tweezers for tasks such as pulling out hairs and picking up small objects. EG *...a pair of tweezers... She took the glass out of the back of Farnbach's head with tweezers.* N PLURAL : ALSO *a pair of*+N ⇑ instrument

twelfth /twelfᶿθ/, **twelfths. 1** The **twelfth** item in a series is the one that you count as number twelve: see □ at NUMBER, AGE, and DATE. EG *...by the end of the twelfth century.* ORDINAL

2 A **twelfth** is one of twelve equal parts of something. N COUNT : USU+ *of*

twelve /twelv/, **twelves. Twelve** is the number 12: see □ at NUMBER, AGE, DATE, MEASUREMENT, MONEY, and TIME. EG *They have been married now for twelve years.* NUM

twelve-month, twelve-months. A **twelve-month** is a year; an old-fashioned word. EG *I've been here just over a twelve-month.* N COUNT

twentieth /twentiˈɪθ/, **twentieths. 1** The **twentieth** item in a series is the one that you count as number twenty: see □ at NUMBER, AGE, and DATE. EG *...in the latter half of the twentieth century.* ORDINAL

2 A **twentieth** is one of twenty equal parts of something. EG *He agreed to pay her something less than a twentieth of their value.* N COUNT : USU+ *of* ⇑ fraction

twenty /twenti¹/, **twenties. Twenty** is the number 20: see □ at NUMBER, AGE, DATE, MEASUREMENT, MONEY, and TIME. EG *Twenty minutes later he sighted two helicopters.* NUM

twenty-first, twenty-firsts. Someone's **twenty-first** is the birthday on which they reach the age of twenty-one, or a special party that they have to celebrate that birthday. Formerly, in Britain, people legally became adults when they were twenty-one. N COUNT : USU SING

twerp /twɜːp/, **twerps;** also spelled **twirp.** You call someone a **twerp** when you think that they are silly or stupid; an informal, fairly rude word. N COUNT : ALSO VOC = twit

twice /twaɪs/. **1** Something that happens **twice** or is done **twice** happens or is done two times. EG *I knocked on the door twice... The committee meets twice a year... We played tennis twice daily.* ADV

2 If one thing is **twice** as big, old, good, etc as another thing, or is **twice** the size, age, etc of another thing, it is two times as big, old, etc as that other thing. EG *This is twice as common in France as in England... They use twice as much electricity as compressor machines... The jet can fly at twice the speed of sound... He's twice my size... In my opinion, it's worth more than twice that figure.* PREDET, OR ADV *+as*+ADJ/ADV

3 If you say that someone is **twice the man he was** or **twice the woman she was,** you mean that they are now much fitter or more energetic than they used to be. PHR : USED AS C ⇑ improved

4 If you say that someone is **twice the man** or **woman** that a particular person is, you mean that they are much better or more admirable than that person is. EG *'She's twice the woman you are,' he said.* PHR : USED AS C ⇑ superior

● **once or twice**: see **once.** ● **twice over**: see **over.** ● to **think twice**: see **think.**

twiddle /twɪdəᵒl/, **twiddles, twiddling, twiddled. 1** If you **twiddle** something or **twiddle with** it, you move it, twist it, or turn it quickly using small movements of your fingers. EG *She twiddled the volume control till it fell off... Frank twiddled with the knobs of the radio... Ella sat twiddling her long, dark hair.* ▸ used as a noun. EG *I just gave the dial a twiddle and it fell off!* V+O, OR V+A *(with)* = fiddle with ▸ N COUNT

2 If something **twiddles** round, it spins round. EG *The youngest monkey loved dangling by one arm from a branch, twiddling round and round.* V+A = twirl

3 When you **twiddle** your **thumbs,** you move your thumbs around each other while your fingers are linked together, usually because you are bored or impatient. PHR : VB INFLECTS

twig /twɪg/, **twigs, twigging, twigged. 1** A **twig** is a very small, thin branch that grows out from a main branch of a tree or bush. EG *He was busy making a little fire from twigs and bits of log... She heard a twig snap.* N COUNT = stick

2 If you **twig,** you realize or understand something; an informal use in British English. EG *I kept dropping hints but he still didn't twig.* V, OR V+O/ REPORT-CL = catch on

twilight /twaɪlaɪt/. **1 Twilight** is **1.1** the dim light that there is outside just after sunset or perhaps just before dawn. EG *John peered forward through the twilight.* **1.2** the time after sunset when it is getting dark outside. EG *You'll most likely see these animals at twilight, when they begin the night's hunt.* N UNCOUNT, OR N SING : *the*+N; N UNCOUNT = dusk

2 The **twilight** of something is the final stages of it, when it is becoming less strong or important; a literary use. EG *...in the twilight of the campaign... Her grandfather had spent most of his twilight years working on a history of France.* N SING : *the*+N+ *of* ⇑ ending

3 You can refer to a state in which someone or something is between two other states, or in which someone is only just awake or aware of things, as a kind of **twilight**; a literary use. EG *For three days he lay in a twilight of pain and fever... ...the twilight world of adolescence.* N SING WITH DET *+of,* OR N BEFORE N

twilit /twaɪlɪt/. **1** A **twilit** place or thing is seen by the dim light that there is just after sunset or perhaps just before dawn. EG *Huge clouds were growing, blotting out the twilit sky.* ADJ CLASSIF : ATTRIB = murky

2 A **twilit** state is one in which someone or something is between two other states, or in which someone is only just awake or aware of things. EG *...as she battled in a thorny twilit region of anguish and delirium.* ADJ CLASSIF : ATTRIB = shadowy

twill /twɪl/ is cloth that is woven in a way which produces diagonal lines across it. EG *...twill trousers.* N UNCOUNT ⇑ fabric

twin /twɪn/, **twins, twinned. 1** If two people are **twins,** they have the same mother and were born on the same day. EG *The twins were very surprised to see Ralph... Dorothea was the elder twin of the two... She went to Malaya to stay with her twin sister.* ● See also **identical twin.** N COUNT ⇑ sibling

2 Twin is **2.1** used of a pair of things that look very similar and are close together; usually a fairly literary use. EG *...the twin turrets of Tower Bridge... ...a small twin-engine plane.* **2.2** used of two things or ideas that are similar or connected in some way; a fairly literary use. EG *...hoping to achieve the twin goals of saving his invention and avoiding capture.* N BEFORE N = double; N BEFORE N = dual

3 A town that **is twinned** with another town in a different country is linked in an official relationship with it. EG *Manchester is twinned with Leningrad.* V+O, OR V+O+A *(with)* : RECIP, ONLY PASS

twin bed, twin beds. Twin beds are two single beds in one bedroom. N COUNT : USU PL

twin-bedded. A **twin-bedded** room, for example in a hotel, has twin beds. ADJ CLASSIF : ATTRIB

twine /twaɪn/, **twines, twining, twined. 1 Twine** is strong, smooth string. EG *...a ball of twine.* N UNCOUNT

2 When you **twine** something round something else or when it **twines** round something else, it is twisted around it or winds around it. EG *She would twine her fingers in locks of his hair... Bindweed had started to twine around the stems of the shrubs.* V-ERG+A = weave

twinge /twɪndʒ/, **twinges.** A **twinge** is **1** a sudden sharp feeling of an emotion, usually an unpleasant one. EG *Hugh felt a twinge of fear when he saw the officer approaching him... ...a twinge of guilt.* **2** a sudden sharp pain or feeling of being ill. EG *I feel a twinge in my back now and again... It's just a twinge of appendicitis.* N COUNT+SUPP = pang, stab; N COUNT = spasm, stab

twinkle /twɪŋkəᵒl/, **twinkles, twinkling, twinkled. 1** If a star or a light **twinkles,** it shines with an unsteady light which is rapidly and constantly changing from bright to faint. EG *He stared up at the stars twinkling in the sky above him.* V = wink, glimmer

2 If your eyes **twinkle** or if you **twinkle** at someone, the way in which you look at them expresses humour, excitement, or mischief. EG *The Englishman's eyes twinkled and he grinned... He twinkled at Etta.* ▸ used as a noun. EG *He was looking at Etta with a merry twinkle... She had noticed a definite twinkle in his eye at the suggestion.* V : IF+PREP THEN *at* ▸ N SING WITH DET = sparkle

twinkling /twɪŋklɪŋ/. If you do something **in the twinkling of an eye,** you do it very quickly. EG *The table was laid and the food set out ready in the twinkling of an eye.* PHR : USED AS AN A = in a flash

twin-set, twin-sets. A **twin-set** is a matching cardigan and sweater of the same colour; used in British English. EG *Her mother was wearing a pale blue twin-set and a tweed skirt.* N COUNT

twin tub, twin tubs. A **twin tub** is a washing machine that has two separate sections, one of which is for washing clothes and the other for spinning them in order to remove most of the water. N COUNT

twirl /twɜːl/, **twirls, twirling, twirled**. 1 When you **twirl** something or when it **twirls**, you make it spin round and round. EG *In a bored way she twirled her parasol... His glass twirled in his hand.* V-ERG = pivot

2 If you **twirl**, you spin round and round rapidly, for example when you are dancing. EG *We saw a fat man dancing all by himself, twirling round and round.* V = whirl

3 If you **twirl** something long such as your hair, you twist it around another object. EG *She stared out of the window, twirling her hair absent-mindedly... Three hours later he was elegantly twirling spaghetti in a place called Pastaria.* V+O

4 If you do a **twirl**, you make a quick movement in which you spin round once or twice, often in order to show other people the clothes you are wearing. EG *I did a fashion-show twirl.-'Yes, very pretty.'* N COUNT = pirouette

twirp /twɜːp/. See **twerp**.

twist /twɪst/, **twists, twisting, twisted**. 1 When you **twist** something or when it **twists**, you turn one end of it in one direction while holding the other end still or turning it in the opposite direction. EG *Never twist or wring woollen garments... 'I like your hair,' he said, twisting a wisp of it back from her forehead... Her fingers twisted the handle of her bag.* V-ERG
▸ used as a noun. EG *He gave one short vicious twist to the chicken's neck.* ▸ N COUNT = wrench

2 If you **twist** part of your body such as your head or your shoulders, you turn that part while keeping the rest of your body still. EG *Swing your shoulders so that you twist from side to side... She twists round on the couch to watch him... She twisted herself free.* V OR V+O

3 If you **twist** part of your body such as your ankle or wrist, you injure it by turning it too sharply, too far, or in an unusual direction. EG *I twisted my ankle doing a Mexican hat dance.* V+O = sprain, wrench

4 If you **twist** someone's **arm**, you persuade them to do something; an informal expression. EG *I'm sure she'll do it for you if you twist her arm.* PHR : VB INFLECTS ⇑ pressurize

5 When something **twists** or when you **twist** it, it moves, bends, or turns into a strange, uncomfortable, or distorted shape or position, especially as a result of force, pain, or damage. EG *Her features twisted into a stare of disgusted incredulity.* V-ERG = screw up, contort
◊ **twisted**. EG *Hundreds of people were trapped under the twisted steel girders... ...a twisted smile.* ◊ ADJ CLASSIF = contorted

6 If you **twist** something, you turn it so that it moves or spins around in a circular direction. EG *You have to twist the dial on the thermostat clockwise... Brody grabbed the bottle and twisted off the cap.* V+O = screw

7 If you **twist** something around an object, you wind it around the object. EG *She twisted the long scarf round her head... The long floating weeds twisted around his legs.* V+O+A = twine

8 If you say that you can **twist** someone **round** your **little finger**, you mean that they will do anything that you want them to do; an informal expression. PHR : VB INFLECTS

9 If something such as a road **twists**, it follows a winding route that is constantly changing direction. EG *The road began to twist up past the lower slopes of a pine forest... ...one of the many tributary canals that came twisting inland from the Gambia river.* V : USU+A = weave, snake

10 If you **twist** something that a person has said, you change the meaning slightly in order to turn the situation to your own advantage or to harm the person in some way. EG *You're twisting my words: you know I didn't mean it that way... This was yet another twisted bit of masculine logic.* V+O = distort

11 A **twist** is 11.1 the shape that something has when it has been twisted. EG *...eighteen inches of shell with a slight spiral twist... There's a twist in the hose... ...a twist of blue smoke.* N COUNT = coil **11.2** a movement in which you turn something so that it spins in a circular direction, especially using your fingers. EG *She gave a lazy little twist to her parasol.* N COUNT = twirl

12 The **twists and turns** in something such as a road or river are the bends and sharp corners that it has. PHR : USED AS S/O = convolution

13 A **twist** in the aims, attitudes, or nature of something is a significant or important change in it. EG *...every twist and turn in government economic policy... The micro chip has added a new twist to the Las Vegas gambling scene.* N COUNT = variation, convolution

14 A **twist** in a story, play, or film is an unexpected and usually rather clever development or event, especially at the end. EG *There was an odd twist to the plot... The story has a humorous twist to it.* N COUNT

15 If you say that someone is **round the twist**, you mean that they are slightly mad and so are likely to do foolish things; an informal expression used in British English. EG *She must be round the twist! What on earth made her accept an offer like that?* PHR : USED AS C = bonkers, barmy, round the bend

16 The **twist** is a dance that was popular in the 1960's, in which you twist your hips, arms, and shoulders vigorously from side to side. N SING : *the*+N ▸ used as a verb. EG *We twisted the night away.* ▸ V OR V+O+A

twisted /twɪstɪ²d/. If someone's mind or the way that they behave is **twisted**, it is unpleasantly abnormal and they are likely to do or say things that are cruel or perverted. ADJ QUALIT = warped

twister /twɪstə/, **twisters**. 1 If you say that someone is a **twister**, you mean that they are dishonest and deliberately deceive people; used showing disapproval. EG *...a wretched little twister like Harrington.* N COUNT = trickster

2 A **twister** is **2.1** a difficult puzzle or problem; an informal use. EG *That's a real twister you've set.* N COUNT **2.2** a tornado; used especially in American English. N COUNT

3 See also **tongue-twister**.

twisty /twɪsti¹/. A road or river that is **twisty** has a lot of sharp bends and corners. EG *We had to steer the car down a twisty track.* ADJ QUALIT = winding

twit /twɪt/, **twits**. If you say that someone is a **twit**, you mean that they do silly or thoughtless things which annoy or irritate you. EG *Don't be a twit!... ...some cowardly twit.* N COUNT : ALSO VOC = dope, ninny

twitch /twɪtʃ/, **twitches, twitching, twitched**.
1 If you **twitch** or if parts of your body **twitch**, you make little jerky movements which you cannot completely control. EG *Ralph felt his lips twitch.* V ⇑ move

2 If you **twitch** something, you give it a little jerk in order to move it. EG *She twitched the curtain into place.* V-ERG = tweak

3 A **twitch** is a little jerky movement. N COUNT

twitchy /twɪtʃi¹/. If you are **twitchy**, you are anxious or uneasy about something and so are behaving in a rather nervous way; an informal word. EG *They are getting distinctly twitchy.* ADJ QUALIT = jumpy

twitter /twɪtə/, **twitters, twittering, twittered**. 1 When birds **twitter**, they make a lot of short, high-pitched sounds. EG *The birds were hopping about on their perches and twittering.* V = chirrup

2 If someone **twitters**, they speak very fast in a high-pitched voice about things that are not important, usually because they are nervous. EG *They talked all the time in high, twittering voices.* V = prattle

two /tuː/, **twos**. 1 **Two** is the number 2: see ☐ at NUMBER, AGE, DATE, MEASUREMENT, MONEY, and TIME. EG *I have been away from London for two weeks... The two boys glared at each other... For a moment or two Simon was happy.* NUM

2 If you **put two and two together**, you work out for yourself the real meaning of something from the things that you see and hear, especially when other people don't want you to find out. EG *I began to think. I began, as they say, to put two and two together.* PHR : VB INFLECTS ⇑ deduce
● **two's company, three's a crowd**: see **company**.
● to **kill two birds with one stone**: see **bird**. ● **two a penny**: see **penny**.

two-dimensional. 1 Something that is **two-dimensional** is flat and in two dimensions only; a technical term. EG *...the map of a two-dimensional world on the retina.* ADJ CLASSIF

2 Ideas, philosophies, and characters that are **two-dimensional** are very simple and not realistic or complicated enough. EG *But this is what rationalism, with its two-dimensional scheme of things, tries to do.* ADJ QUALIT ⇑ superficial

two-edged. 1 Knives, saws, etc that are **two-edged** have two edges that cut. ADJ CLASSIF

2 Things that are **two-edged** have two parts, meanings, etc that are opposite to each other but that happen at the same time. EG *Their relationship is thus a two-edged one, at once intimate and distant.* ADJ QUALIT = double-edged

two-faced. Someone who is **two-faced** is not sincere or honest in the way that they behave towards other people; used showing disapproval. EG *He could be briefly and accurately described as a two-faced liar and opportunist... How could she be so two-faced?* ADJ QUALIT = hypocritical

twofold /tuːfəuld/. If you say that something is **twofold**, you mean that it has two equally important parts or reasons, which you probably then talk about. EG *Their targets were twofold: inflation and unemployment... The value of this procedure is twofold. In the first place... The strategy of the nationalist movements involved a twofold operation.* ADJ CLASSIF ⇑ dual

two-handed. 1 If something such as a tool is **two-handed**, you hold it or use it with both your hands. ADJ CLASSIF
2 If something such as a job or a play is **two-handed**, it is done or acted by two people. ADJ CLASSIF

two-piece, two-pieces. A **two-piece** is a woman's set of clothing that is in two parts, for example a suit or a swimming costume. EG *Mrs Hochstadt was dressed in her usual two-piece... She wore a grey two-piece suit and a white straw hat.* N COUNT

two-ply. Material that is **two-ply** has two layers or strands. EG *...two-ply wool... ...two-ply tissues.* ADJ CLASSIF

twosome /tuːsəm/, **twosomes**. A **twosome** is a group of two people or things. N COUNT

two-way. 1 **Two-way** means moving in two opposite directions, or allowing something such as traffic or communications to move in two opposite directions. EG *...a two-way channel of communication... ...a two way street... ...two-way traffic.* ADJ CLASSIF : ATTRIB
2 **Two-way** radios and transmitters can both send and receive signals; a technical term. ADJ CLASSIF : ATTRIB
3 If there is **two-way** co-operation, learning, etc, two people or groups are co-operating and working together. EG *Creative, two-way learning between teacher and pupil can take place.* ADJ CLASSIF : ATTRIB ⇑ exchanged

tycoon /taɪkuːn/, **tycoons**. A **tycoon** is a person who is successful in business and so has become rich and powerful. EG *...a newspaper tycoon.* N COUNT = magnate

tyke /taɪk/, **tykes**. If you refer to a child as a **tyke**, you mean that he or she is mischievous; an informal word, often used showing affection. EG *Look what she's done, the little tyke!* N COUNT : ALSO VOC = monkey

type /taɪp/, **types, typing, typed**. 1 A **type** of something is a class of it that has particular features in common and that belongs to a larger group of related things. EG *What type of salt do you prefer?... There are several different types of accounts... They test your blood type during pregnancy.* N COUNT+SUPP = sort
2 If you refer to a particular thing or person as a **type**, you are thinking of them in relation to other things and people that have similar natures or qualities. EG *But how much longer can you do this type of work?... ...other simple problems of this type.* N COUNT+SUPP = kind, sort
3 You use **type** when you are describing something to say that it is like or in the style of the thing or person that is mentioned; an informal use. EG *...western-type socialism and Communism... ...an explanation of the Yuri Geller type of phenomenon.* N COUNT+SUPP = kind
4 A **type** is also 4.1 someone whose appearance, qualities, habits, etc cause you to think of them in a fixed way, instead of as an individual. EG *He was good-looking, if you like the strong, dark type... ...an eccentric painter type.* N COUNT+SUPP = sort 4.2 someone or something that has all the characteristics that are typical of a particular group of people or things, and that is therefore considered as a good example of that group. EG *...the old-fashioned type of nanny... ...a perfect type of its kind, this classic Statue of Sorrow.* N COUNT+SUPP = epitome, specimen
5 If you say that someone is **not** your **type**, you mean that they are not the sort of person who you find interesting; an informal expression. PHR : USED AS C
6 If you **type** or if you **type** something, you use a typewriter or word processor to write it. EG *Judy had finished typing... I typed the reply... She put the neatly typed papers in the drawer of her desk.* V OR V+O
7 If you **type** something into a computer or word processor, you put information or text into it by pressing keys on the keyboard. EG *You should type in the letter D... The letter was typed into a word processor.* V+O : USU+A ⇑ enter = key
8 **Type** is the particular size or style of printing that is used in a book, newspaper, etc. EG *The declaration was proclaimed in type four inches deep on the front page... The title should be in bold type.* N UNCOUNT = print
9 See also **typing**.

type away. If you **type away**, you type either quickly and busily or for a long time. PHRASAL VB : V+ADV

type up. If you **type** something **up**, you produce a typed and complete form of something that previously existed just as ideas, notes, or handwritten text. EG *After thinking about it, she typed it up, then we both read it.* PHRASAL VB : V+O+ADV

typecast /taɪpkɑːst/, **typecasts, typecasting**; also spelled with a hyphen. The form **typecast** is used in the present tense and is also the past tense and past participle. If actors or actresses **are typecast**, they play the same type of character in every play or film that they are in. V+O : USU PASS = stereotyped

typeface /taɪpfeɪs/ is the size or style of printing that is used in a book, newspaper, etc; a technical term in printing. N UNCOUNT = type

typescript /taɪpskrɪpt/, **typescripts**. A **typescript** is a typed copy of an essay, article, or literary work. EG *...the typescript of his book... ...twenty-seven pages of typescript.* N COUNT/UNCOUNT ⇑ draft

typewriter /taɪpraɪtə/, **typewriters**. A **typewriter** is a machine that you use in order to write things in print. It has a series of keys that you press in order to write a particular letter, number, or other character on the paper. EG *She inserted a new sheet of paper into her typewriter.* N COUNT

typewritten /taɪprɪtə⁰n/. Something that is **typewritten** has been typed on a typewriter or a word processor. EG *She took up some sheets of typewritten paper... His notes were typewritten.* ADJ CLASSIF

typhoid /taɪfɔɪd/ is an infectious disease that produces fever and diarrhoea and can cause death. It is spread by dirty water or food. N UNCOUNT

typhoon /taɪfuːn/, **typhoons**. A **typhoon** is a very fierce storm in the western Pacific. EG *A typhoon in 1954 sank a ferry, drowning 1,218 people.* N COUNT : ALSO IN NAMES BEFORE N = hurricane

typical /tɪpɪkə⁰l/. 1 Something that is **typical** shows the most usual characteristics of a particular type of person or thing, and is therefore a good example of that type. EG *It was typical tropical weather... Louisa is typical of many young women who attempt suicide.* ADJ QUALIT : IF+PREP THEN *of* ⇑ representative
2 Behaviour or events that are **typical** are done or happen in the way that is most usual or characteristic for them. EG *He crushed the beetle deliberately, which is very typical of him.* ADJ QUALIT : IF+PREP THEN *of*
3 If you say that something is **typical** of a person, situation, or thing, you are criticizing or complaining about them, expressing the fact that they are just as disappointing or bad as you expected them to be. EG *It was typical of our luck that it happened to be raining... How typical!* ADJ QUALIT : IF+PREP THEN *of* ⇑ predictable

typically /tɪpɪkə⁰li¹/. You use **typically** 1 to say that something usually happens in the way that you are describing. EG *She typically handles less than a dozen accounts at a time.* ADV WITH VB, OR ADV SEN = normally 2 to say that something shows all the most usual characteristics of a particular type of person or thing. EG *...this group of typically American students.* ADV+ADJ/ADV = characteristically 3 to indicate that someone has behaved in the way that you expected them to. EG *Sheila was upset too, and said, typically, that she was going away.* ADV WITH VB, OR ADV SEN = predictably

typify /tɪpɪfaɪ/, **typifies, typifying, typified**. 1 If something **typifies** a situation or a thing, it is characteristic of that situation or thing, and shows what it is like. EG *Their lack of a view on a subject as important as this typified the dilemma of such an organization.* V+O = sum up, epitomize
2 If someone **typifies** a particular type of person or attitude, they show all the most usual characteristics of that person or attitude. EG *He typified the old Liberalism of Samuel Smiles.* V+O = exemplify

typing /taɪpɪŋ/ is 1 the work or activity of typing something by means of a typewriter or word processor: see **type 6**. EG *I had to do some typing for him.* N UNCOUNT 2 the skill of using a typewriter quickly and accurately. EG *She insisted that I learned shorthand and typing... ...typing skills.* N UNCOUNT

typist /taɪpɪst/, **typists**. A **typist** is someone who works in an office and spends a lot of their time typing letters, reports, etc: see **type 6**. EG *She was a typist at the head office of Credit Lyonnais.* N COUNT ⇑ employee

typographical /taɪpəgræfɪkə⁰l/ relates to the way in which written material is presented in its published form. EG *...typographical layout... ...a few limited editions filled with typographical errors.* ADJ CLASSIF : ATTRIB

typography /taɪpɒgrəfi¹/, **typographies**. **Typography** is the way in which written material is arranged and prepared for printing. EG *The typography of dictionaries has deteriorated recently.* N UNCOUNT/COUNT ⇑ arrangement

tyrannical /tɪrænɪkə⁰l/. 1 Someone who is **tyrannical** is severe or unjust towards the people who they ADJ QUALIT = overbearing have authority over; used showing disapproval. EG *...Isabel, tyrannical and coquettish in her old age.*

2 A government or organization that is **tyrannical** acts without considering the wishes of its people and treats them unjustly; used showing disapproval. EG *...a tyrannical government.* ADJ CLASSIF = despotic

tyrannize /tɪrənaɪz/, **tyrannizes, tyrannizing, tyrannized**; also spelled **tyrannise**. If someone **tyrannizes** you, often someone you know well, they behave in a severe or unjust way towards you; used showing disapproval. EG *He used to tyrannize his younger brother.* V+O, OR V+A (over) = browbeat

tyranny /tɪrəni¹/, **tyrannies**. 1 **Tyranny** is a condition in which you are forced to live or work in a way that is very unpleasant and harsh. EG *Women should not have to submit to the tyranny of the assembly line.* N UNCOUNT ⇑ oppression

2 A **tyranny** is cruel and unjust rule by a person or small group of people who have absolute power over everyone else in their country or state. EG *They came to America to escape political tyranny... ...the prospect of a one-party tyranny.* N UNCOUNT/COUNT = dictatorship

tyrant /taɪrənt/, **tyrants**. A **tyrant** is 1 a ruler who has absolute power over other people, and who uses this power cruelly and unjustly; used showing disapproval. EG *...cruel and brutal totalitarian tyrants.* N COUNT = despot **2** someone who is severe or unjust towards people who they have authority over; used showing disapproval. EG *In the sixth grade we had a tyrant of a teacher.* N COUNT = bully

tyre /taɪə/, **tyres**; also spelled **tire** in American English. A **tyre** is a thick piece of rubber which is either solid or filled with a lot of air so that it is very hard. Tyres are fitted onto the wheels of vehicles such as cars, buses, and bicycles. EG *When he braked a tyre burst and the car swung off the road.* ● See also **spare tyre**. N COUNT

tyro /taɪrəʊ/, **tyros**; also spelled **tiro**. A **tyro** is a person who is just beginning to learn something or who has very little experience of something; a formal word. EG *Six eight-year old tyros arrived for their lesson, their new rackets neatly held in their hands.* N COUNT = beginner, novice ≠ veteran

tzar /zɑː/. See **tsar**.

tzarina /zɑːriːnə/. See **tsarina**.

tzarist /zɑːrɪst/. See **tsarist**.

tzetze fly /tsetsi¹ flaɪ/. See **tsetse fly**.

Uu

U, u /juː/, **U's, u's**. 1 **U** is the twenty-first letter of the English alphabet. N COUNT

2 **U** is used to describe the language, customs, and behaviour of the British upper classes; used in informal British English. ADJ QUALIT ≠ non-U

3 **U** or **u** is also an abbreviation for various words beginning with 'u', such as 'unit', 'united', or 'University'.

UAE /juː eɪ iː/ is an abbreviation for 'United Arab Emirates'.

ubiquitous /juːbɪkwɪtəs/. Something that is **ubiquitous** is everywhere or seems to be everywhere at the same time. EG *...the admirable and ubiquitous intelligence service.* ADJ QUALIT

ubiquity /juːbɪkwɪti¹/ is the quality of being everywhere at the same time. N UNCOUNT

UCCA /ʌkə/ is an abbreviation for 'Universities Central Council on Admissions'; a British organization which deals with applications from everyone leaving school who wants to go to a university. EG *Other overseas candidates should apply direct to UCCA.* N PROPER

udder /ʌdə/, **udders**. The **udder** on a cow or other female animal is the large organ, shaped like a bag, which hangs between her legs and produces milk. N COUNT

UFO /juː ɛf əʊ, juːfəʊ/, **UFOs**. **UFO** is an abbreviation for 'unidentified flying object'. A UFO is an object seen in the sky or landing on earth which cannot be identified and which is often believed to be a vehicle from another planet. EG *Many millions of people have allegedly seen UFOs in the United States and other countries.* N COUNT = flying saucer

Ugandan /juːgændən/, **Ugandans**. 1 **Ugandan** means belonging to or concerned with Uganda. EG *This restaurant claims to serve genuine Ugandan food.* ADJ CLASSIF

2 A **Ugandan** is someone who comes from Uganda. EG *Over 120,000 Ugandans have made this journey.* N COUNT

ugh is used in writing to represent the sound that people make if they think something is unpleasant, horrible, or disgusting. EG *Ugh–I wouldn't like to eat a snail or a frog... Your clothes are filthy and your hair too–ugh, you're awful.* EXCLAM

ugly /ʌgli¹/, **uglier, ugliest**. 1 Something or someone that is **ugly** is very unattractive and unpleasant to look at. EG *She really was frightfully ugly... This is certainly the ugliest dress I've ever worn.* ◊ **ugliness**. EG *...the architectural ugliness of the place.* ADJ QUALIT = hideous ◊ N UNCOUNT

2 An **ugly** situation is one that is very unpleasant, usually because it involves violence or aggression. EG *A couple of ugly incidents occurred, and one man was killed.* ADJ QUALIT = nasty

UHF /juː eɪtʃ ɛf/ is an abbreviation for 'ultra-high frequency'; used of a range of radio waves which allows a radio receiver to produce a good quality of sound. EG *You'll need a special UHF radio.* N UNCOUNT

uh huh, uh-huh, and **uhhuh** are used in written English to represent a sound that people make when they are agreeing with you, when they want to show that they understand what you are saying, or when they are answering 'yes' to a question; used in informal English. EG *'Did you know he was rich?'–'Uh-huh. It said so in the paper.'* CONVENTION

UHT /juː eɪtʃ tiː/ is an abbreviation for 'ultra-heat treated'; used to describe milk which has been treated at a very high temperature so that it will keep for a long time if the container is not opened. ADJ CLASSIF : USU ATTRIB

UK /juː keɪ/ is an abbreviation for 'United Kingdom'; used to refer to Great Britain and Northern Ireland. N PROPER : the+N

ukelele /juːkəleɪli¹/, **ukeleles**; also spelled **ukulele**. A **ukelele** is a small guitar with four strings. N COUNT

ulcer /ʌlsə/, **ulcers**. An **ulcer** is a sore area on your skin which is very painful and may bleed, or which may produce an unpleasant poisonous substance. Ulcers can be outside your body or inside, for example in your mouth or stomach. EG *She had an ulcer in her mouth... ...stomach ulcers.* N COUNT

ulcerated /ʌlsəreɪtɪd/. If a part of your body is **ulcerated**, ulcers have developed on it. EG *He was admitted to hospital with an ulcerated leg.* ADJ CLASSIF

ulterior /ʌltɪərɪə/. If someone has **ulterior** motives or reasons for doing something, they do not show their motives or reasons openly but hide them, usually because they are rather selfish or dishonest. EG *I assure you there was no ulterior motive in my suggestion... This game must serve some ulterior purpose.* ADJ CLASSIF : ATTRIB = hidden

ultimate /ʌltɪmə¹t/. 1 **Ultimate** describes **1.1** the final result of a long and often complicated series of events. EG *He knew this action was necessary for the ultimate success of the revolution... The book describes the Dodo's decline and ultimate disappearance.* ADJ CLASSIF : ATTRIB = eventual **1.2** the greatest power and authority in a particular system. EG *Parliament retains the ultimate authority to dismiss the government.* ADJ CLASSIF : ATTRIB **1.3** the real cause, aim, or nature of something. EG *The ultimate purpose of life is to keep alive... He firmly believed in the ultimate goodness of man.* ADJ CLASSIF : ATTRIB = fundamental **1.4** the most extreme and unpleasant example of a particular thing. EG *I now felt the calm of ultimate despair... It is the ultimate abuse of human rights.* ADJ CLASSIF : ATTRIB = supreme **1.5** the best possible example of a particular thing. EG *My idea of the ultimate perk is a car.* ADJ CLASSIF : ATTRIB = supreme

2 If you something is described as **the ultimate in** luxury, **the ultimate in** computer technology, etc, it PHR+N UNCOUNT/N IN

is considered to be the best and most modern that there is as far as luxury, computer technology, etc is concerned. EG *This car is the ultimate in luxury.* PL : USED AS C

ultimately /ʌltɪmə¹tli¹/. 1 **Ultimately** means finally, after a long and often complicated series of events. EG *Elections might ultimately produce a Communist victory... The rebels hoped to create bad feeling and ultimately war between Spain and the United States.* ADV WITH VB = eventually

2 You use **ultimately** to emphasize that what you are saying is the most important point in a particular discussion or argument. EG *Ultimately, the problems are not scientific but moral... It is ultimately the fault of the universities.* ADV SEN = basically

ultimatum /ʌltɪmeɪtəm/, **ultimatums**. An **ultimatum** is a warning that you give to someone which states that they must accept certain conditions or act in a particular way, otherwise you will take action against them. EG *He gave me an ultimatum: either Mary had to leave, or me... On 3 August Belgium rejected the ultimatum and war was declared.* N COUNT

ultra- is added to the beginning of adjectives in order to say that a particular quality is very extreme. EG *...a small band of ultra-revolutionary students... ...ultra-sophisticated equipment... ...an ultra-modern building.* PREFIX

ultramarine /ʌltrəməriːn/. Something that is **ultramarine** is of a very bright blue colour; a formal word. EG *They don their resplendent vermilion, ultramarine, and gold robes.* ADJ COLOUR

ultrasonic /ʌltrəsɒnɪk/ describes sounds which have very high frequencies, which human beings cannot hear. ADJ CLASSIF

ultraviolet /ʌltrəvaɪələ²t/; also spelled with a hyphen. **ultraviolet** light or radiation is what causes your skin to become darker in colour after you have been in sunlight. In large amounts ultraviolet light is harmful. EG *...the deadly ultraviolet rays of the sun... ...ultra-violet light.* ADJ CLASSIF : USU ATTRIB

ululate /juːljə⁴leɪt/, **ululates, ululating, ululated**. To **ululate** means to howl or wail loudly; a formal word. EG *The savage, whoever he was, ululated twice.* ◊ **ululation** /juːljə⁴leɪʃə⁰n/, **ululations**. EG *He heard far off the ululation of his pursuers.* V ⇑ cry ◊ N UNCOUNT/COUNT

um /əm, ʌm/ is used to represent a sound that people make when they are hesitating, usually while deciding what they want to say next. EG *I think that, um–the definition is not out out of date, but... What can be done about it? Well, um, the first thing you can do is colour it.* = er

umber /ʌmbə/. Something that is **umber** is of a yellowish or reddish brown colour; a formal word. EG *...the mellow umber bricks of Jo's house.* ADJ COLOUR

umbilical cord /ʌmbɪlikə⁰l kɔːd/, **umbilical cords**. An **umbilical cord** is the tube which connects a baby to its mother before it is born and through which the baby receives oxygen and nutrients. EG *The placenta is connected by the umbilical cord to the foetus.* N COUNT

umbrage /ʌmbrɪdʒ/. If you **take umbrage**, you feel upset or hurt by something that someone says or does to you; a formal expression. EG *It was clear that the Pope himself had taken great umbrage at the book.* PHR : VB INFLECTS = take offence

umbrella /ʌmbrɛlə/, **umbrellas**. 1 An **umbrella** is 1.1 a device which consists of a long stick with a cloth-covered, folding frame at one end, and which you carry to protect yourself from the rain. EG *Put your umbrella up. It's going to rain.* N COUNT 1.2 a large umbrella-like device that provides shade from the hot sun, and which people sit or lie under, for example on the beach. EG *Other hotel guests sat under similarly striped umbrellas.* N COUNT ⇑ sunshade

2 **Umbrella** describes a single organization, idea, etc that contains or covers a lot of different organizations, ideas, etc. EG *...an umbrella organisation... Corn is an umbrella word for wheat, barley and oats.* ADJ CLASSIF : ATTRIB

umlaut /ʊmlaʊt/, **umlauts**. An **umlaut** is a mark consisting of two dots which is placed over vowels in German and some other languages and which indicates that the pronunciation of the vowel is changed. The umlaut is over the 'u' in 'über'. N COUNT ⇑ sign

umpire /ʌmpaɪə/, **umpires, umpiring, umpired**. 1 An **umpire** is a person whose job is to make sure that a sports match or contest is played fairly and that the rules are not broken. EG *He was fined for arguing with the umpire.* N COUNT ⇑ judge

2 To **umpire** means to be the umpire in a sports match or contest. EG *Some of the players complained about the standard of umpiring.* V OR V+O ⇑ officiate

umpteen /ʌmp⁰tiːn/ means a great many; an informal word. EG *They recounted umpteen tales of unfair treatment.* NUM = countless

umpteenth /ʌmp⁰tiːnθ/ describes something which has happened many times before; an informal word. EG *So I went to the pictures and saw 'Hello Dolly' for the umpteenth time.* ORDINAL

UN /juː ɛn/ The **UN** is an organization to which most countries in the world belong, and which tries to encourage international peace, cooperation, and friendship; an abbreviation for 'United Nations'. EG *...the UN General Assembly... He went to New York as Uganda's deputy representative at the UN.* N PROPER : *the*+N

un- is added 1 to the beginning of adjectives, adverbs, and nouns, in order to form words that have the opposite meaning. EG *...conscious→unconscious... ...willingly→unwillingly... ...happiness→unhappiness.* PREFIX

2 to the beginning of a verb that describes a process, in order to form another verb that describes the reverse of that process. EG *...tie→untie... ...bind→unbind... ...lock→unlock.* PREFIX 3 to the beginning of the past participle of a verb, in order to form an adjective that means that the process described by the verb has not happened. EG *...sold→unsold... ...convicted→unconvicted... ...bound→unbound.* PREFIX

unabashed /ʌnəbæʃt/. If you are **unabashed**, you are not ashamed, embarrassed, or discouraged by something that has just been done or said, especially when other people think that you ought to be. EG *The little old lady seemed unabashed.* ADJ CLASSIF = undismayed

unabated /ʌnəbeɪtɪ²d/. If something continues **unabated**, it continues without any reduction in intensity or amount. EG *The war at sea continued unabated.* ▸ used as an adjective. EG *The demonstration continued outside with unabated enthusiasm.* ADV WITH VB ⇑ unchanged ▸ ADJ CLASSIF : USU ATTRIB

unable /ʌneɪbə⁰l/. If you are **unable** to do something, it is impossible for you to do it, for example because you do not have the necessary skill or knowledge, or because you do not have enough time or money. EG *I dread being old and unable to work... Many people were unable to read or write... He was unable to sleep at night because of his anxiety... We were unable to afford the entrance fee... They feel unable to agree to this.* ADJ CLASSIF : PRED+*to*-INF ≠ able

unabridged /ʌnəbrɪdʒd/. An **unabridged** piece of writing, for example a book or article, is complete and not shortened in any way. EG *This volume contains three unabridged novels.* ADJ CLASSIF ⇑ whole = full-length

unacceptable /ʌnə³ksɛptəbə⁰l/. If you describe something as **unacceptable**, you mean that you strongly disapprove of or object to it and feel that you cannot allow it to continue. EG *It is entirely unacceptable that I should have no voice in the politics of my country... ...an unacceptable violation of personal freedom.* ◊ **unacceptably**. EG *Their standard of performance has been unacceptably poor on several recent occasions.* ADJ QUALIT = intolerable ◊ ADV

unaccompanied /ʌnəkʌmpənɪd/. 1 Someone who is **unaccompanied** is alone. EG *...an unaccompanied woman.* ADJ CLASSIF = lone

2 If music, voices, or instruments are **unaccompanied**, the music or instruments are played alone or the voices sing alone, with no other instruments playing at the same time. EG *Don't you think those lovely carols would sound much better unaccompanied?* ADJ CLASSIF = solo

unaccountable /ʌnəkaʊntəbə⁰l/. 1 Something that is **unaccountable** does not seem to have any sensible explanation. EG *For some unaccountable reason, I put the letter in the wrong envelope... I was overcome by a quite unaccountable sense of menace.* ◊ **unaccountably**. EG *Elaine felt unaccountably shy for once.* ADJ QUALIT ⇑ unknown = inexplicable ◊ ADV OR ADV SEN

2 If you are **unaccountable**, you are not responsible to anyone for your actions and do not have to explain to anyone why you behave in the way you do; a formal use. EG *Many of our important decision-makers are unaccountable to the public.* ADJ CLASSIF : PRED, USU+*to* ≠ answerable

unaccounted /ʌnəkaʊntɪ²d/. If an amount of something, especially money, is **unaccounted for**, you do not know where it is or what has happened to it. EG *The remaining 30 per cent were unaccounted for.* PHR : USED AS C ⇑ missing

unaccustomed /ʌnəkʌstəmd/; a fairly formal word. 1 If you are **unaccustomed** to something, you are not used to it. EG *They were obviously unaccustomed to wearing suits and ties.* ADJ CLASSIF: PRED+*to* = unused ≠ familiar

2 **Unaccustomed** describes **2.1** something that seems strange because you are not used to it or because it does not normally happen to you. EG *...his unaccustomed and unwelcome leisure.* **2.2** someone's behaviour when it is very different from the way that they normally behave in a particular situation. EG *Judy cried with unaccustomed vehemence, 'Yes, I know!'* ADJ CLASSIF: ATTRIB = unfamiliar; ADJ CLASSIF: ATTRIB = uncharacteristic

unacknowledged /ʌnəknɒlɪdʒd/. 1 If a fact or situation is **unacknowledged**, it is ignored by people or not accepted as being true or existing. EG *...a terrible unacknowledged fear.* ADJ CLASSIF ⇑ disregarded

2 If a person, their qualities, or their achievements are **unacknowledged**, they are not officially recognized as being important. EG *Poets are the unacknowledged legislators of the world... ...unacknowledged genius... He died in 1555 with his discovery still unacknowledged.* ADJ CLASSIF

3 If you are **unacknowledged** when you enter a room, the people who are already there do not show by their behaviour that they have seen and recognized you. EG *Unacknowledged, Ginny sat down on the sofa in silence.* ADJ CLASSIF: PRED ⇑ ignored

unacquainted /ʌnəkweɪntɪ²d/. If you are **unacquainted** with something, you do not know about it or have not had much experience of it. EG *We believed that the judges were unacquainted with the black community... ...people who are unacquainted with feminist ideas.* ADJ CLASSIF: PRED, USU+ *with* = ignorant of

unadopted /ʌnədɒptɪ²d/ is used to describe a road that the local residents are responsible for maintaining, rather than the local authority; used in British English. ADJ CLASSIF

unadorned /ʌnədɔːnd/. Something that is **unadorned** has no decoration on it at all. EG *...an unadorned human body.* ADJ CLASSIF ⇑ plain

unadulterated /ʌnədʌltəreɪtɪ²d/. 1 Something that is **unadulterated** is completely pure and has had nothing added to it. EG *...fresh, clean, unadulterated spring water.* ADJ CLASSIF = virgin

2 You can also use **unadulterated** to emphasize a particular quality, often a bad quality. EG *It was going to be unadulterated misery from now on.* ADJ CLASSIF: ATTRIB = sheer

unaffected /ʌnə³fektɪ²d/. 1 Something that is **unaffected** by a particular thing is not changed in any way by that thing. EG *Jobs have been largely unaffected by automation.* ADJ CLASSIF: PRED = untouched

2 Someone who is **unaffected** is natural and genuine in their behaviour, and not snobbish or pretentious; used showing approval. EG *He was simple and unaffected and obviously sincere.* ADJ QUALIT = unpretentious

unafraid /ʌnəfreɪd/. Someone who is **unafraid** is confident and does not feel frightened or nervous at all. EG *Joseph lay there quite unafraid... She was unafraid of defeat or adverse opinion.* ADJ CLASSIF: PRED ≠ afraid

unaided /ʌneɪdɪ²d/ means without help from anyone or anything else. EG *He could not possibly have got through the window unaided. ...samples quite invisible to the unaided eye.* ADV AFTER VB, OR ADJ CLASSIF ≠ assisted

unalloyed /ʌnə³lɔɪd/. Something that is **unalloyed** is not spoiled by being mixed with something else; a rather literary word. EG *...unalloyed bliss... The report was received with almost unalloyed enthusiasm.* ADJ CLASSIF ⇑ pure

unalterable /ʌnɒltə⁰rəbə⁰l/. Something that is **unalterable** cannot be changed. EG *She had reached an unalterable decision to marry him.* ◊ **unalterably**. EG *She judged him to be unalterably wicked.* ADJ CLASSIF = fixed; ◊ ADV

unaltered /ʌnɒltəd, ʌnɔːl-/. Something that is **unaltered** has not been changed and is therefore still in its original form. EG *My dream-like state remained unaltered... The Great Hall survives relatively unaltered.* ADJ CLASSIF = unchanged

unambiguous /ʌnæmbɪgju⁴əs/. If something spoken or written is **unambiguous**, it can only be interpreted in one way. EG *The rules are quite unambiguous... ...unambiguous statements.* ◊ **unambiguously**. EG *He said unambiguously that Britain should withdraw its support.* ADJ QUALIT ⇑ clear; ◊ ADV ⇑ clearly

unambitious /ʌnæmbɪʃəs/. **Unambitious** people do not want to alter their way of life or to get a better job. EG *Guy's doctor was a pleasant unambitious GP.* ADJ QUALIT ≠ ambitious

unanimity /juːnə³nɪmɪti¹/. When there is **unanimity** among a group of people, they all agree about something. EG *About this there is unanimity among the sociologists... These discussions have led to a remarkable unanimity.* N UNCOUNT ⇑ harmony = accord

unanimous /juːnænɪməs/. When a group of people are **unanimous**, they all agree about something or all vote for the same thing. EG *The critics have been almost unanimous in their dislike of this film.* ▸ used of agreements and votes. EG *We reached unanimous agreement... The children abolished school uniform by an almost unanimous vote.* ◊ **unanimously**. EG *The union voted unanimously to boycott foreign imports.* ADJ CLASSIF = at one, united ≠ divided; ◊ ADV WITH VB

unannounced /ʌnənaʊnst/. If an action or event is **unannounced**, it happens unexpectedly and without anyone having being told about it beforehand. EG *I ask your forgiveness for this unannounced intrusion.* ▸ used as an adverb. EG *Churchill arrived unannounced at Beaverbrook's London suite.* ADJ CLASSIF ⇑ sudden = unheralded; ▸ ADV AFTER VB ⇑ suddenly

unanswerable /ʌnɑːnsə⁰rəbə⁰l/. 1 An **unanswerable** question cannot be answered, because it has no possible answer. EG *This topic is full of unanswerable questions.* ADJ CLASSIF ⇑ impossible

2 An **unanswerable** argument is so obviously correct that you cannot disagree with it. EG *...a brilliant argument which seems to be unanswerable.* ADJ CLASSIF = irrefutable

unanswered /ʌnɑːnsəd/. Something that is **unanswered** has not been answered. EG *Many questions were left unanswered... ...a pile of unanswered letters.* ADJ CLASSIF

unappealing /ʌnəpiːlɪŋ/. You describe people, places, or things as **unappealing** when you find them unpleasant. EG *He was forced to talk to his singularly unappealing hostess... They have made the place as unappealing as possible.* ADJ QUALIT = off-putting

unappetizing /ʌnæpɪ²taɪzɪŋ/; also spelled **unappetising**. You describe food as **unappetizing** when it is unpleasant to eat, or when you think that it will be unpleasant to eat because of its appearance. EG *If it is overcooked, the flesh becomes rubbery and unappetizing... ...an unappetizing hunk of dry cheese.* ADJ QUALIT = unpalatable

unapproachable /ʌnəprəʊtʃəbə⁰l/. An **unapproachable** person is difficult to talk to and not very friendly. EG *He was becoming as unapproachable and autocratic as his father.* ADJ QUALIT = aloof

unarguable /ʌnɑːgjuəbə⁰l/. If something is **unarguable**, you cannot disagree with it, because it is obviously true or correct. EG *He said something fairly unarguable... ...an unarguable computer prediction.* ◊ **unarguably**. EG *This was unarguably true... Games like chess are unarguably intellectual pursuits.* ADJ CLASSIF = indisputable; ◊ ADV + ADJ/ADV, OR ADV SEN

unarmed /ʌnɑːmd/. 1 If you are **unarmed**, you are not carrying any weapons. EG *They were shooting unarmed peasants.* ▸ used as an adverb. EG *He walked alone and unarmed into the hills.* ADJ CLASSIF ≠ armed; ▸ ADV WITH VB

2 An **unarmed** vehicle is not fitted with weapons. EG *...an unarmed salvage tug.* ADJ CLASSIF: ATTRIB

unarmed combat is a skilful way of fighting, in which you do not use any weapons except your hands and feet. EG *Girls were practising unarmed combat together.* N UNCOUNT

unashamed /ʌnəʃeɪmd/. You describe someone's behaviour as **unashamed** when they are not afraid to do things that other people might find shocking or rude. EG *He looked at her with unashamed curiosity... ...the unashamed pursuit of money.* ◊ **unashamedly** /ʌnəʃeɪmɪdli¹/. EG *She laughed unashamedly.* ADJ CLASSIF: ATTRIB = unabashed, blatant; ◊ ADV WITH VB = brazenly

unasked /ʌnɑːskt/. 1 An **unasked** question has not been asked, although it may be answered by someone as if it had been asked. EG *'She's all right,' said Stein in reply to Pitman's unasked question... ...one of the great unasked questions of our time.* ADJ CLASSIF

2 If you do something **unasked**, you do it without being asked to do it. EG *...their readiness to proffer small services, unasked, without wanting money.* ADV WITH VB = voluntarily

unassailable /ʌnəseɪləbə⁰l/. If something is **unassailable**, nothing can alter it or destroy it; a rather formal word. EG *This argument is logically unassailable... Their right to establish an independent state is unassailable... ...a man of unassailable natural dignity.* ADJ CLASSIF ⇑ firm

unassisted /ʌnəsɪstɪ²d/. If you do something **unassisted**, you do it without anyone helping you. EG *He had to drag the cart there unassisted... They were able to climb down unassisted from the roof.* ADV AFTER VB, OR ADJ CLASSIF = unaided

unassuming /ʌnəsj⁰uːmɪŋ/. An **unassuming** person is modest and quiet and shows no wish to be noticed by other people; used showing approval. EG *He was genuinely shy and unassuming... ...a pleasant, unas-* ADJ QUALIT = self-effacing *suming man.* ▸ used of behaviour. EG *...that quiet, unassuming way of his.*

unattached /ʌnətætʃt/. 1 If something is **unattached** to something else, it is not formally connected with it. EG *The centre is unattached to any hospital or clinic.* ADJ CLASSIF : USU +*to*

2 An **unattached** person is not married and is not having a steady relationship. EG *A lot of unattached women seem to be very happy.* ADJ CLASSIF = single

unattainable /ʌnəteɪnəbəºl/. If something is **unattainable**, it cannot be achieved. EG *100 per cent home-ownership is a quite unattainable goal... One of her main aims was now unattainable.* ADJ CLASSIF ⇑ impossible

unattended /ʌnətendɪ²d/. When people or things are **unattended**, they are not being watched or looked after. EG *Most of the casualties were lying unattended... She dashed through the door, leaving the bar unattended.* ADJ CLASSIF ⇑

unattractive /ʌnətræktɪv/. 1 **Unattractive** people and things are unpleasant in their appearance or behaviour and are therefore not liked or wanted. EG *He assured me that I was physically unattractive... ...queer unattractive little objects.* ADJ QUALIT = ugly ≠ pretty

2 You say that something such as a proposal is **unattractive** when people do not like it and do not want to be involved with it. EG *Being unemployed is a most unattractive prospect.* ADJ QUALIT = unappealing

unauthorized /ʌnɔːθəraɪzd/; also spelled **unauthorised**. If something is **unauthorized**, it has been made or is being done without official permission. EG *He called for the removal of unauthorized structures... She made several unauthorized visits to the laboratory.* ADJ CLASSIF

unavailable /ʌnəveɪləbəºl/. When things or people are **unavailable**, you cannot obtain them or meet them. EG *Margarine and butter were unavailable... Her father had made himself unavailable for comment.* ADJ CLASSIF ≠ available

unavailing /ʌnəveɪlɪŋ/. If an attempt to do something is **unavailing**, it does not succeed. EG *Attempts to persuade him to come down were unavailing.* ADJ CLASSIF = unsuccessful

unavoidable /ʌnəvɔɪdəbəºl/. If something is **unavoidable**, it cannot be avoided or prevented. EG *This delay was unavoidable... Such inequalities are the unavoidable result of liberty itself.* ◇ **unavoidably**. EG *Their return journey was unavoidably delayed.* ADJ CLASSIF = inevitable ◇ ADV WITH VB

unaware /ʌnəweə/. 1 If you are **unaware** of something such as a fact or a difficulty, you do not know about it. EG *I was unaware that he had any complaints.* ◇ **unawareness**. EG *...unawareness of the opportunities available.* ADJ CLASSIF : PRED, USU+*of*/REPORT-CL ≠ aware ◇ N UNCOUNT : USU+*of*

2 If you are **unaware** of something that is happening near to you, you do not know about it because you have not noticed it. EG *She seemed quite unaware of the other people sitting around her.* ADJ CLASSIF : PRED, USU+*of*/REPORT-CL = oblivious

unawares /ʌnəweəz/. If something **catches** you **unawares**, **takes** you **unawares**, etc, it happens when you are not expecting it and are not prepared for it. EG *It's a change like this that catches you unawares... Arriving on foot, he could be sure of taking his men unawares... She came unawares on a struggling circle of people.* PHR : VB INFLECTS ⇑ surprise

unbalance /ʌm¹bæləns/, **unbalances, unbalancing, unbalanced**. If something **unbalances** a system, it disturbs or upsets it so that it can no longer work properly. EG *A half-century of western intrusion had seriously unbalanced the traditional rural order... Too much sugar would unbalance any diet.* V+O = disrupt

unbalanced /ʌm¹bælənst/. 1 You say that someone is **unbalanced** or that their mind is **unbalanced** when they are disturbed or upset and talk or behave in a strange way, as if they were mad. EG *The strain of the past few days has made you mentally unbalanced... She seemed positively unbalanced... ...the product of an unbalanced mind.* ADJ QUALIT = deranged

2 You say that something is **unbalanced** when you think that it is unfair or inaccurate because it emphasizes some things and ignores others. EG *...unbalanced economic development in different parts of the world... She complained that the magazine had published an 'unbalanced' report.* ADJ QUALIT = one-sided

unbearable /ʌm¹beərəbəºl/. You say that something is **unbearable** when it is so unpleasant, painful, or upsetting that you feel unable to accept it or deal with it. EG *The heat was unbearable... ...the unbearable, agonizing boredom of it.* ◇ **unbearably**. EG *It was unbearably painful.* ADJ QUALIT = unendurable, excruciating ◇ ADV+ADJ/ADV

unbeatable /ʌm¹biːtəbəºl/. If you say that something is **unbeatable**, you mean that it is the best thing of its kind; used showing approval. EG *The food here is absolutely unbeatable... Book now! Unbeatable value for money!* ADJ CLASSIF ⇑ excellent

unbecoming /ʌm¹bi¹kʌmɪŋ/; a rather old-fashioned word, used showing disapproval. 1 **Unbecoming** clothes or colours make you look unattractive. EG *...ill-fitting, unbecoming garments... ...that dreadfully unbecoming shade of apricot they wore.* ADJ QUALIT = unflattering

2 If you say that a person's remarks or behaviour are **unbecoming**, you mean that they are rather shocking and especially unsuitable for that person. EG *Maria, such thoughts are unbecoming to you... ...conduct unbecoming to an officer.* ADJ CLASSIF : IF+PREP THEN *to/in* = discreditable

unbeknown /ʌm¹bi¹nəʊn/. If something is **unbeknown** or **unbeknownst** to you, you do not know about it; an old-fashioned word. EG *Meanwhile, unbeknown to Julie, Frank was coming down the hill... Unbeknownst to Peter, Mr Hopkins sent out invitations.* ADJ CLASSIF : PRED, USU+*to* = unknown

unbelief /ʌm¹bi¹liːf/ is the attitude of not believing that something is true. EG *'You don't know?' Luciana exclaimed in a voice of unbelief.* N UNCOUNT = disbelief

unbelievable /ʌm¹bi¹liːvəbəºl/. 1 You say that something is **unbelievable** 1.1 when it is extraordinarily large or extraordinarily great in number or degree. EG *They work with unbelievable speed... It was achieved in the face of unbelievable difficulties.* ADJ QUALIT = incredible, extraordinary 1.2 when you are extremely impressed by it and think that it is very good. EG *I went to her house in Henley: it was unbelievable... ...a sense of unbelievable luck.* ADJ CLASSIF ⇑ wonderful 1.3 when you think it is very bad or very shocking. EG *It's unbelievable they should build dual carriageways through the centre of a town.* ADJ CLASSIF = preposterous

2 You describe an idea or theory as **unbelievable** when you think that it is so unlikely or so illogical that it cannot possibly be true or correct; used showing disapproval. EG *There are so many doubtful and unbelievable aspects to this theory.* ADJ CLASSIF = implausible

unbelievably /ʌm¹bi¹liːvəbli¹/. 1 You use **unbelievably** when you are commenting on something that you are describing, in order to say that it is very surprising. EG *Unbelievably, as in a fiction, the door in the wall opened... Now this, unbelievably, was precisely the phrase used by the government's spokesman.* ADV SEN = astonishingly

2 You also use **unbelievably** 2.1 to say that you are extremely impressed by the quality of something. EG *...unbelievably beautiful scenery.* ADV+ADJ/ADV 2.2 to say that you find something, for example someone's attitude or behaviour, very shocking. EG *...a local brewer with an unbelievably arrogant manner.* ADV+ADJ/ADV 2.3 to say that something is very large or very noticeable. EG *...an unbelievably high stockpile of nuclear weapons.* ADV+ADJ/ADV

unbeliever /ʌm¹bi¹liːvə/, **unbelievers**. People are referred to as **unbelievers** when they do not believe in a particular religion. EG *Pope John's appeal had been overwhelmingly to unbelievers.* N COUNT = atheist

unbelieving /ʌm¹bi¹liːvɪŋ/. You describe people as **unbelieving** when they do not believe something that they have been told. EG *'But why?' she asked, puzzled and unbelieving... He looked unbelieving.* ADJ CLASSIF = incredulous

unbend /ʌm¹bend/, **unbends, unbending, unbent**. If someone **unbends**, their attitude becomes less strict than it was. EG *Taxi-drivers unbent so far as to take people part of the way home free.* V ⇑ relax

unbending /ʌm¹bendɪŋ/. When someone is **unbending**, they have very strict beliefs and attitudes, which they are unwilling to change. EG *The Minister was proving unbending on key issues.* ▸ used of attitudes or beliefs. EG *...his unbending attitude toward what was right and wrong... ...strict, unbending theology.* ADJ QUALIT = inflexible, immovable

unbiased /ʌm¹baɪəst/; also spelled **unbiassed**. If something is **unbiased**, it is done or produced fairly and without showing prejudice or favouritism; used showing approval. EG *...a neutral, unbiased view... ...a very fair and unbiased account.* ▸ used of people. EG *... unbiased observers.* ADJ QUALIT ⇑ neutral = impartial ▸ = impartial

unbidden /ʌm¹bɪdəºn/. If something happens **unbidden**, it happens without you expecting or wanting it to happen; a literary word. EG *The sound of his voice came again, unbidden, into her mind... The words flowed unbidden from my pen.* ADV AFTER VB

unbind /ʌm¹baɪnd/, **unbinds, unbinding, unbound**. If you **unbind** someone or something, you untie a piece of string, rope, etc that has been tied round them. EG *Unbind him, let him go free... The youth unbound his sarong.* — V+O ⇑ unfasten

unblemished /ʌm¹blɛmɪʃt/. Something that is **unblemished** has not been harmed or spoiled. EG *Her face was unblemished and unscarred... She held the flowers and looked at their white unblemished petals.* — ADJ CLASSIF

unblinking /ʌm¹blɪŋkɪŋ/. If someone is **unblinking** or if their eyes are **unblinking**, they are looking at something without blinking. EG *The cat stared at him, malevolent and unblinking... His unblinking eyes retained their sharpness... Sheila glared at 'The Angelus' with unblinking gaze.* — ADJ CLASSIF = unwavering ◊ **unblinkingly**. EG *The child stared at Hilary unblinkingly.* — ◊ ADV WITH VB = impassively

unborn /ʌm¹bɔːn/. An **unborn** child or animal has not yet been born and is still inside its mother's womb. EG *The doctor tried desperately to save her and her unborn child.* — ADJ CLASSIF

unbound /ʌm¹baʊnd/. 1 **Unbound** is the past tense and past participle of **unbind**.

2 Something that is **unbound** is not tied or has just been untied. EG *...her unbound hair... ...armfuls of unbound wheat.* — ADJ CLASSIF ⇑ LOOSE

unbounded /ʌm¹baʊndɪ²d/. Something that is **unbounded** has, or seems to have, no limits. EG *Literacy brings to the young unbounded freedom... He has an almost unbounded admiration for his wife... My relief was unbounded.* — ADJ CLASSIF ⇑ limitless

unbreakable /ʌm¹breɪkəbə⁰l/. Something that is **unbreakable** has been made so strongly that it cannot be broken. EG *...unbreakable kitchenware... The net is almost unbreakable.* — ADJ CLASSIF = indestructible

unbridled /ʌm¹braɪdəld/. You describe behaviour or feelings as **unbridled** when they are not controlled or limited in any way; used showing disapproval. EG *...unbridled gluttony.* — ADJ CLASSIF = unrestrained

unbroken /ʌm¹brəʊkə⁰n/. If something is **unbroken**, it is continuous or complete and has not been interrupted or broken. EG *The silence continued, unbroken... All night long the few unbroken windows rattled from the airstrikes.* — ADJ CLASSIF ≠ broken

unbuckle /ʌm¹bʌkə⁰l/, **unbuckles, unbuckling, unbuckled**. If you **unbuckle** something such as a belt or a shoe, you unfasten it by releasing the buckle on it. EG *She started to unbuckle her sandal.* — V+O ⇑ undo

unburden /ʌm¹bɜːdə⁰n/, **unburdens, unburdening, unburdened**. If you **unburden** yourself to someone, you tell them about something which you have been secretly worrying about. EG *Scylla unburdened herself to her guardian.* — V+O (REFL) : IF +PREP THEN *to*

unbutton /ʌm¹bʌtə⁰n/, **unbuttons, unbuttoning, unbuttoned**. If you **unbutton** something that you are wearing, you unfasten the buttons on it. EG *He unbuttoned his coat.* — V+O ⇑ undo ◊ **unbuttoned**. EG *Her tunic was unbuttoned... ...his unbuttoned mackintosh.* — ◊ ADJ CLASSIF ⇑ undone

uncalled-for; also spelled without a hyphen. You describe a remark or criticism as **uncalled-for** when you think that it should not have been made, because it was unkind or unfair. EG *That last remark was uncalled for... He cursed Penny for her uncalled-for outburst.* — ADJ QUALIT ⇑ unnecessary = unwarranted

uncanny /ʌŋ¹kæni¹/, **uncannier, uncanniest**. You describe something as **uncanny** 1 when it is strange and hard to explain. EG *It was slightly uncanny how our careers seemed to run on parallel lines... The long-eared owl strikes at its prey with uncanny accuracy.* — ADJ QUALIT = odd ◊ **uncannily**. EG *The voice sounded uncannily familiar... Their assessment of character was uncannily accurate.* — ◊ ADV+ADJ/ADV 2 when it is rather frightening for no obvious reason. EG *The silence was uncanny.* — ADJ QUALIT = eerie

uncared-for. **Uncared-for** people or animals have not been looked after properly and as a result are hungry, dirty, or ill. EG *Thousands of children were left uncared-for... ...uncared-for cats.* — ADJ CLASSIF = neglected

uncaring /ʌŋ¹kɛərɪŋ/. You describe people as **uncaring** when they do not care about other people's suffering and hardship; used showing disapproval. EG *We now know how uncaring and selfish the landlords were... ...an uncaring society.* — ADJ QUALIT = unfeeling

unceasing /ʌnsiːsɪŋ/. You describe something as **unceasing** when it continues without stopping. EG *...a profound, unceasing misery... ...an unceasing search for lower costs.* — ADJ CLASSIF = unremitting, continual ◊ **unceasingly**. EG *The stream of traffic now flowed unceasingly.* — ◊ ADV WITH VB = continuously

unceremonious /ʌnsɛrɪməʊnɪəs/. **Unceremonious** actions are 1 performed without formality or ceremony. EG *She treated him with unceremonious friendliness.* — ADJ CLASSIF = informal ◊ **unceremoniously**. EG *He walked off unceremoniously, giving her a friendly smile.* — ◊ ADV WITH VB 2 sudden and rude. EG *The answer was an unceremonious 'No'.* — ADJ QUALIT ◊ **unceremoniously**. EG *The chief can turf them out unceremoniously if he takes a dislike to them.* — ◊ ADV WITH VB ⇑ suddenly

uncertain /ʌnsɜːtən/. 1 If you are **uncertain** about something, you do not know what to do. EG *She hesitated, uncertain whether to continue... He paused, a bit uncertain how to begin.* — ADJ QUALIT = unsure ≠ certain ◊ **uncertainly**. EG *They looked at each other uncertainly.* — ◊ ADV WITH VB = hesitantly

2 If something in the future is **uncertain**, nobody knows what form it will take. EG *His future was unclear and uncertain... The outcome of his case was uncertain.* — ADJ QUALIT ≠ predictable

3 If the cause of something is **uncertain**, nobody knows what the cause is. EG *The cause of death remains uncertain.* — ADJ CLASSIF ⇑ unknown

4 You describe something such as the weather or a person's temper as **uncertain** when it is likely to change suddenly. EG *My husband was a man of uncertain temper... ...uncertain weather.* — ADJ QUALIT = changeable ≠ steady

5 **in no uncertain terms**: see **term**.

uncertainty /ʌnsɜːtənti¹/, **uncertainties**. 1 **Uncertainty** is a state of doubt about the future or about what is the right thing to do. EG *...the continued uncertainty about the future of the aircraft industry... The shyness and uncertainty of a few minutes back had gone.* — N UNCOUNT ⇑ confusion

2 **Uncertainties** are things which no one is certain about in the future. EG *The industry is still plagued by economic uncertainties.* — N COUNT : USU PL

unchain /ʌntʃeɪn/, **unchains, unchaining, unchained**. If you **unchain** animals or objects, you remove the chain by which they are fastened to something. EG *I unchained Daisy and set off down the road.* — V+O ⇑ release

unchallenged /ʌntʃæləndʒd/. 1 When something is **unchallenged** or goes **unchallenged**, people accept it without asking questions about whether it is right or wrong. EG *She found that her decisions on these matters went unchallenged... His authority was secure and unchallenged.* — ADJ CLASSIF, OR ADV WITH VB = unquestioned

2 If you do something **unchallenged**, nobody stops you and asks you questions, for example about who you are or why you are doing it. EG *Charles got up and walked, unchallenged, past a stewardess.* — ADV WITH VB = unchecked

unchangeable /ʌntʃeɪndʒəbə⁰l/. Something that is **unchangeable** cannot be changed. EG *...one of the great unchangeable facts of life.* — ADJ CLASSIF = unalterable

unchanged /ʌntʃeɪndʒd/. Something that is **unchanged** has stayed the same during a particular period of time. EG *The process remains unchanged... My orders are unchanged.* — ADJ CLASSIF : USU PRED = unaltered

unchanging /ʌntʃeɪndʒɪŋ/. Something that is **unchanging** always stays the same. EG *...a stable and relatively unchanging society.* — ADJ QUALIT = constant

uncharacteristic /ʌŋ¹kærə³ktərɪstɪk/. Something that is **uncharacteristic** of someone is not typical of them. EG *He jumped out of the car with uncharacteristic agility... She felt uncharacteristic self-pity.* — ADJ QUALIT ⇑ unusual ◊ **uncharacteristically**. EG *She was uncharacteristically silent.* — ◊ ADV ⇑ unusually

uncharitable /ʌntʃærɪtəbə⁰l/. **Uncharitable** remarks, thoughts, or behaviour are unkind or unfair to someone. EG *I hope I'm not being too uncharitable, but he really is very boring.* — ADJ QUALIT = ungenerous ◊ **uncharitably**. EG *He must have been very angry about it, thought Scylla uncharitably.* — ◊ ADV WITH VB

uncharted /ʌntʃɑːtɪ²d/. 1 If an area of land or sea is **uncharted**, no maps have been made of it. EG *...an uncharted ocean.* — ADJ CLASSIF ⇑ unknown

2 Unfamiliar situations are sometimes referred to as **uncharted** seas, **uncharted** waters, etc. EG *Each side had stepped further into the uncharted sea of confrontation... Many executives are finding themselves in deep and uncharted waters.* — ADJ CLASSIF = alien

unchecked /ʌntʃɛkt/. If something is **unchecked**, nothing prevents it from continuing or growing; used showing disapproval. EG *...the danger of unchecked military expansion... ...unchecked population growth.* — ADJ CLASSIF ▸ used as an adverb. EG *Consumer spending grew* — ▸ ADV AFTER VB *unchecked... Injustice was being allowed to go unchecked.*

uncivil /ʌnsɪvəºl/. **Uncivil** behaviour is rude and impolite. EG *He was uncivil to other members of the household.* ◊ **uncivilly**. EG *'How long are you staying?' I asked him uncivilly.* — ADJ QUALIT; ◊ ADV WITH VB

uncivilized /ʌnsɪvɪlaɪzd/; also spelled **uncivilised**. 1 **Uncivilized** people are people who are thought of as backward by members of other nations. EG *The colonists looked upon the people as uncivilized heathens.* — ADJ QUALIT = primitive ≠ civilized, cultured

2 Something such as a way of behaving that is **uncivilized** is thought to be unacceptable among civilized people, for example because it is very cruel or very rude. EG *They are kept in conditions that are, quite simply, uncivilized and inhumane.* — ADJ QUALIT = barbaric

3 An **uncivilized** hour is one that is very early in the morning; an informal use. EG *Sorry to wake you at this uncivilized hour.* — ADJ CLASSIF

unclaimed /ʌŋ¹kleɪmd/. If something is **unclaimed**, nobody has claimed it or said that it belongs to them. EG *After 14 years the reward remained unclaimed.* — ADJ CLASSIF

unclasp /ʌŋ¹klɑːsp/, **unclasps, unclasping, unclasped**. If you **unclasp** your hands, you separate them after they have been held together. EG *He was clasping and unclasping his large freckled hands.* — V+O

unclassified /ʌŋ¹klæsɪfaɪd/. If something is **unclassified**, it has not been included in any of the classes into which a set of things has been divided. EG *They were simply labelled 'unclassified'... ...unclassified waste.* — ADJ CLASSIF

uncle /ʌŋ¹kəºl/, **uncles**. Your **uncle** is the brother of your mother or father, or the husband of your aunt. EG *An uncle of mine is coming over from the States... Uncle Harold was a nuisance.* — N COUNT: ALSO IN NAMES ⇑ relative

unclean /ʌŋ¹kliːn/. 1 Something that is **unclean** is dirty and likely to cause disease. EG *A devastating cause of illness in the Third World is unclean water and poor sanitation.* — ADJ QUALIT = dirty

2 If you say that someone or something is **unclean**, you consider that they are spiritually or morally bad; used mainly in a religious context. EG *...unclean spirits... Do not make yourselves unclean by doing any of these things.* — ADJ CLASSIF = taboo, impure

unclear /ʌŋklɪə/. 1 If something is **unclear**, 1.1 it is not obvious to people. EG *The reasons for this remained unclear... It was unclear to Mrs Babcock why she had to get up so early.* 1.2 it has been badly explained or written in a confusing way, so that you cannot understand it properly. EG *The instruction books are badly written, unclear, and boring.* 1.3 it is difficult to hear or see because it is not distinct. EG *His answer was mumbled and unclear.* — ADJ QUALIT: PRED ≠ evident; ADJ QUALIT = unintelligible; ADJ QUALIT = indistinct

2 If you are **unclear** about something, you do not understand it properly. EG *I'm still very unclear about what he has actually done...* — ADJ QUALIT: IF+PREP THEN *about* ≠ clear

Uncle Sam is the USA, often shown in pictures as a man wearing a top hat with stars on it, a tail-coat, and striped trousers. — N PROPER

Uncle Tom, Uncle Toms. An **Uncle Tom** is a black person who wants to please white people and is eager to serve them; used showing disapproval. — N COUNT

unclothed /ʌŋ¹kləʊðd/. If you are **unclothed**, you are not wearing any clothes; a rather formal word. EG *...a large statue of an unclothed man.* — ADJ CLASSIF = naked

uncluttered /ʌŋ¹klʌtəd/. If a place is **uncluttered**, it is not full of unnecessary objects; used showing approval. EG *The interior was clean, bright, uncluttered, and tidy... ...a clear, uncluttered view across the prairie.* — ADJ CLASSIF ≠ cluttered

uncoil /ʌŋ¹kɔɪl/, **uncoils, uncoiling, uncoiled**. If something **uncoils** or if you **uncoil** it, it becomes straight when it has been in a coil. EG *The second rope uncoiled and tumbled overboard... An enormous cobra had uncoiled itself at the foot of the rock... He uncoiled two wires connected to the battery.* — V-ERG ⇑ unwind

uncoloured /ʌŋ¹kʌləd/. If something is **uncoloured**, no colour has been added to it. EG *Her uncoloured lips seemed sensual and soft... I thought the uncoloured prints terribly dull.* — ADJ CLASSIF

uncombed /ʌŋ¹kəʊmd/. **Uncombed** hair is untidy because it has not been tidied with a comb. EG *Harris scratched his uncombed hair.* — ADJ CLASSIF = dishevelled

uncomfortable /ʌŋ¹kʌmftəbəºl/. 1 If you are **uncomfortable**, 1.1 you are not physically content and relaxed, and feel slight pain or discomfort. EG *I was cramped and uncomfortable in the back seat... They were sprawled in uncomfortable positions amid bundles and baskets.* ◊ **uncomfortably**. EG *Some babies' stomachs become uncomfortably full before they're half-way through a feed.* 1.2 you are slightly worried or embarrassed and not relaxed and confident. EG *At first I felt uncomfortable and camera-shy... Her presence made him uncomfortable.* ◊ **uncomfortably**. EG *She smiled across the room at him uncomfortably.* — ADJ QUALIT; ◊ ADV; ADJ QUALIT = awkward; ◊ ADV = awkwardly

2 You describe a room or a piece of furniture as **uncomfortable** when it is not comfortable to be in or to use. EG *They were sitting on uncomfortable chairs... The room was uncomfortable and smelly.* — ADJ QUALIT ≠ comfortable

3 You describe a situation or way of life as **uncomfortable** when it is difficult and causes problems and worries. EG *This kind of life may prove disruptive and uncomfortable.* — ADJ QUALIT

4 You describe facts as **uncomfortable** when you do not want to believe them, because they cause difficulties or make you upset. EG *...the uncomfortable truth... They were reluctant to believe anything so uncomfortable.* — ADJ QUALIT = painful, disagreeable

uncommitted /ʌŋ¹kəmɪtɪ²d/. **Uncommitted** people are unwilling to show support for a particular group or belief. EG *Maxwell was uncommitted to the Co-operative as such... ...their uncommitted position in the Cold War.* — ADJ CLASSIF ⇑ neutral

uncommon /ʌŋ¹kɒmən/. You say that something is **uncommon** 1 when it does not happen often or when it is not often seen. EG *Shoot-outs are now uncommon... ...uncommon birds... Frost and snow are not uncommon during these months.* 2 when it is unusually great in degree or amount; used showing approval. EG *...a general of uncommon intelligence and subtlety.* ◊ **uncommonly**. EG *Marcus was uncommonly gifted.* — ADJ QUALIT: USU PRED = rare, unusual; ADJ CLASSIF: ATTRIB = exceptional; ◊ ADV+ADJ/ADV

uncommunicative /ʌŋ¹kəmjuːnɪkətɪv/. An **uncommunicative** person does not talk to other people very much and is unwilling to express opinions or give information. EG *...a diffident, uncommunicative man... Roger, uncommunicative by nature, said nothing.* — ADJ QUALIT = reserved, taciturn

uncomplaining /ʌŋ¹kə⁷mpleɪnɪŋ/. **Uncomplaining** people do difficult or unpleasant things and do not complain about them; used showing approval. EG *They remained kind, generous, warm and uncomplaining... ...these courteous, uncomplaining young men.* ◊ **uncomplainingly**. EG *She was prepared to put up uncomplainingly with his wild temper.* — ADJ CLASSIF; ◊ ADV WITH VB = meekly

uncomplicated /ʌŋ¹kɒmplɪkeɪtɪ²d/. **Uncomplicated** things are simple and straightforward. EG *The play had an uncomplicated plot... The Minister envied them for the uncomplicated simplicity of their lives.* — ADJ CLASSIF ≠ complex

uncomprehending /ʌŋ¹kɒmprɪhendɪŋ/. You describe someone as **uncomprehending** when they do not understand what is happening or what someone has said. EG *I stared at her, feverish and uncomprehending... Bonasera turned to his uncomprehending wife and explained.* ◊ **uncomprehendingly**. EG *She looked at me uncomprehendingly.* — ADJ CLASSIF = baffled; ◊ ADV WITH VB

uncompromising /ʌŋ¹kɒmprəmaɪzɪŋ/. When people are **uncompromising**, they are determined not to change their opinions or objectives in any way. EG *They were uncompromising Party men... He was an uncompromising opponent of the Great War.* ▸ used of behaviour and attitudes. EG *...an uncompromising commitment to the equality of all races... He hated to see her taking this hard, uncompromising attitude.* ◊ **uncompromisingly**. EG *They were uncompromisingly loyal to certain fundamental values.* — ADJ QUALIT ⇑ firm = steadfast; ▸ = rigid; ◊ ADV ⇑ firmly

unconcealed /ʌŋ¹kə⁷nsiːld/. If something such as an emotion is **unconcealed**, you make no attempt to hide it. EG *She had taken an unconcealed dislike to me... Mary gazed around her with unconcealed curiosity.* — ADJ CLASSIF = open

unconcern /ʌŋ¹kənsɜːn/. **Unconcern** about something, especially something that would normally worry people, is a lack of interest in it or willingness to worry about it; used showing disapproval. EG *He went his own way with unconcern for consequences that sometimes stunned others.* — N UNCOUNT ⇑ indifference

unconcerned /ʌŋ¹kənsɜːnd/. Someone who is **unconcerned** is 1 not interested in something and does not want to be involved in it. EG *We have suddenly* — ADJ QUALIT ⇑ indifferent

become an insular people, unconcerned with the underdeveloped countries. **2** not worried or troubled about anything, especially when there is something which you might expect them to be worried or troubled about. EG *They give the impression of being detached and unconcerned.* ◊ **unconcernedly** /ʌŋ¹kənsɜːnɪ²dli¹/. EG *When they demanded his pass book, he handed it over quite unconcernedly.*
ADJ QUALIT ↑ collected
◊ ADV WITH VB

unconditional /ʌŋ¹kəndɪʃə⁰nəl, -ʃənə⁰l/. Something that is **unconditional** is complete, and has no conditions or limitations attached to it. EG *...unconditional surrender... ...absolute allegiance and unconditional obedience.* ◊ **unconditionally.** EG *The laws and decrees of the State had to be obeyed unconditionally.*
ADJ CLASSIF ↑ total = unreserved
◊ ADV WITH VB

unconfirmed /ʌŋ¹kə⁷nfɜːmd/. If something such as a report or a rumour is **unconfirmed**, there is not yet any definite proof as to whether it is true or not. EG *There are rumours–so far unconfirmed–that all university teachers may have to do more teaching.*
ADJ CLASSIF

uncongenial /ʌŋ¹kə⁷ndʒiːnɪəl/. If you find a place or an event **uncongenial**, you think that it is unfriendly and unpleasant. EG *...these uncongenial surroundings.*
ADJ QUALIT ↑ inhospitable

unconnected /ʌŋ¹kə⁷nektɪ²d/. If something is **unconnected** with something else, or if two things are **unconnected,** the two things are not related to each other in any way. EG *Independence was a goal so distant that it seemed unconnected with the problems they were facing... The two incidents were unconnected.*
ADJ CLASSIF : IF+ PREP THEN *with*

unconscionable /ʌn¹kɒnʃə⁰nəbə⁰l/. If something is **unconscionable**, the person responsible for it ought to be ashamed of it; a literary word. EG *She was taking an unconscionable time over spreading her marmalade.* ◊ **unconscionably.** EG *...an unconscionably cheerful station officer.*
ADJ CLASSIF
◊ ADV+ADJ/ ADV

unconscious /ʌŋ¹kɒnʃəs/. **1** Someone who is **unconscious** is unable to notice or react to things, often because they are in a coma which has been caused by an accident or injury. EG *The blow knocked him unconscious... She lay unconscious on the table... He knelt down beside the unconscious girl.* ◊ **unconsciousness.** EG *Something in him refused to yield to unconsciousness.*
ADJ CLASSIF ↑ unaware
◊ N UNCOUNT ↑ sleep

2 If you are **unconscious** of something that you have said or done, you are not aware of it or of the way in which it affects other people. EG *The Board had been quite unconscious of the fact that they were breaking the law... Dekker seemed totally unconscious of the insult.* ◊ **unconsciously.** EG *Aunt Elizabeth unconsciously moved back a pace or two.*
ADJ QUALIT : IF+ PREP THEN *of* ↑ unaware = oblivious
◊ ADV WITH VB

3 If something is **unconscious,** it is not deliberate or planned. EG *We all indulge in unconscious role-playing... ...a kind of unconscious and therefore unquestioned bias.* ◊ **unconsciously.** EG *They can't help resenting the baby unconsciously.*
ADJ CLASSIF = unintentional
◊ ADV

4 Your **unconscious** is the part of your mind that contains feelings and ideas that you do not know about or cannot control. EG *...Freud's description of the unconscious... ...images retrieved from the unconscious.*
N SING : *the/POSS* +N

unconsidered /ʌŋ¹kə⁷nsɪdəd/. Thoughts and actions that are **unconsidered** have not been carefully thought-out and so are often hasty or careless. EG *...his unconsidered comments to the newspapers.*
ADJ CLASSIF = thoughtless

unconstitutional /ʌŋ¹kɒnstɪtjuːʃə⁰nəl, -ʃənə⁰l/. If something is **unconstitutional,** it is against the rules of an organization or political system. EG *...the General Council's proposals for dealing with unconstitutional strikes... They denied that a referendum would be unconstitutional.*
ADJ CLASSIF

uncontrollable /ʌŋ¹kə⁷ntrəʊləbə⁰l/. **1** If something such as an emotion is **uncontrollable**, you can do nothing to prevent it or control it. EG *...an uncontrollable bout of laughter... ...the sudden uncontrollable note of fear in her voice.* ◊ **uncontrollably.** EG *He found himself giggling quite uncontrollably.*
ADJ CLASSIF : USU ATTRIB ↑ helpless
◊ ADV WITH VB = helplessly

2 If you describe a person as **uncontrollable**, you mean that their behaviour is bad and you can not make them behave better or more sensibly. EG *He became violent and uncontrollable.*
ADJ CLASSIF ↑ unmanageable

uncontrolled /ʌŋ¹kə⁷ntrəʊld/. **1** If something such as a person's behaviour is **uncontrolled**, they can do nothing to prevent or change it. EG *He was letting out loud uncontrolled shrieks... ...the uncontrolled savagery of modern war.*
ADJ CLASSIF : USU ATTRIB = unbridled

2 If a situation or event is **uncontrolled**, there is nobody who is in charge and who can prevent it from getting worse. EG *...the uncontrolled acceleration of scientific experiments on animals... ...the uncontrolled use of pesticides in Britain.*
ADJ CLASSIF

unconventional /ʌŋ¹kə⁷nvenʃə⁰nəl, -ʃənə⁰l/. If someone is **unconventional**, they do not behave in the same way as most other people in their society. EG *...an intellectual and somewhat unconventional clergyman.* ▸ used also of people's attitudes, beliefs, and behaviour. EG *...Ellen's unconventional approach to life... ...her unconventional dress, hair style, and acquaintances.*
ADJ QUALIT = nonconformist

unconvinced /ʌŋ¹kənvɪnst/. If you are **unconvinced** about something, you are not at all certain that it is true or right. EG *I remained unconvinced by what she had said.*
ADJ CLASSIF : PRED = doubtful, hesitant

unconvincing /ʌŋ¹kənvɪnsɪŋ/. Arguments, reasons, etc that are **unconvincing** are not able to persuade you of the truth or correctness of what they are saying. EG *I find this argument unconvincing... ...glib promises and unconvincing excuses.* ◊ **unconvincingly.** EG *He argued unconvincingly that if he did this for them, they would leave him alone.*
ADJ QUALIT ↑ weak = dubious
◊ ADV WITH VB = feebly

uncooked /ʌŋ¹kʊkt/. Meat and other food that is **uncooked** has not yet been cooked. EG *There were three uncooked chops on the kitchen table.*
ADJ CLASSIF = raw

uncooperative /ʌŋ¹kəʊɒpə⁰rətɪv/; also spelled **unco-operative**. If someone is **uncooperative**, they make no effort at all to help other people in what they are doing. EG *Some of them plainly thought I was being uncooperative... The mining unions are probably the most uncooperative of all.*
ADJ QUALIT : USU PRED ↑ unhelpful

uncoordinated /ʌŋ¹kəʊɔːdɪneɪtɪ²d/; also spelled **unco-ordinated.** **1** If someone is **uncoordinated,** their movements are jerky and they are not in proper control of them. EG *He's careless, clumsy, and uncoordinated.*
ADJ QUALIT : USU PRED ↑ clumsy

2 Efforts or other things that are **uncoordinated** do not properly join together to form a whole. EG *The band swung into an uncoordinated rendition of 'Great Balls of Fire'.*
ADJ QUALIT

uncork /ʌŋ¹kɔːk/, **uncorks, uncorking, uncorked**. When you **uncork** a bottle, you pull the cork out of it. EG *He took a bottle of white wine out of the refrigerator and uncorked it.*
V+O ↑ undo = open

uncount noun, uncount nouns. In grammar, an **uncount noun** is a noun which cannot be treated as countable, and so has only one form. It is usually used without a determiner in front of it. In this dictionary uncount nouns are described as N UNCOUNT in the grammar notes beside entries. See ☐ at N UNCOUNT.
N COUNT

uncouth /ʌŋ¹kuːθ/. Someone who is **uncouth** behaves in a bad-mannered, unacceptable, and unpleasant way; a rather old-fashioned word. EG *To a Japanese, spilling anything is uncouth and rude... ...an uncouth soldier, a real tough guy.*
ADJ QUALIT ↑ rough = rude

uncover /ʌŋ¹kʌvə/, **uncovers, uncovering, uncovered**. **1** If you **uncover** something, especially something that has been kept secret, you discover or find out about it. EG *Another plot to assassinate General de Gaulle was uncovered... These reasons can usually be uncovered with a little inquiry.*
V+O = expose

2 If you **uncover** something, you remove the thing that covers it. EG *She sat quite still with her face covered. When she uncovered it, there was no trace of laughter... The sheet on the body next to me blew back, uncovering the face.*
V+O ↑ reveal = expose

3 In archaeology, if you **uncover** something, you find a thing or a place that has been under the ground for a long time. EG *Mr Olivier's team has uncovered a section of the Roman road network... ...their controversial dig in Jerusalem to uncover King David's city.*
V+O = discover, exhume

uncovered /ʌŋ¹kʌvəd/. Something that is **uncovered** is not covered; used especially of something which you expect to be covered. EG *The stands are uncovered, so take a raincoat if it's wet... Don't leave food uncovered.*
ADJ CLASSIF ↑ bare = exposed

uncritical /ʌŋ¹krɪtɪkə⁰l/. If you are **uncritical**, you are unable or unwilling to judge whether someone or something is good or bad or right or wrong; often used showing disapproval. EG *The uncritical reader might think that this showed that all was well.* ▸ used also of attitudes and emotions. EG *...their uncritical love of their children... ...his uncritical attitude toward the working class.* ◊ **uncritically.** EG *I accepted*
ADJ CLASSIF ↑ subjective
▸ = unquestioning
◊ ADV WITH VB

a complex theory somewhat uncritically... The results of animal experimentation have been too readily and too uncritically applied to the problems of human diseases.

uncrowned /ʌŋ'kraʊnd/. 1 If a king or queen is **uncrowned**, he or she has not yet been crowned. ADJ CLASSIF

2 You can also used **uncrowned** to describe leaders, presidents, etc, who have the power of a king or queen but who are not members of a royal family. ADJ CLASSIF : USU ATTRIB

unctuous /ʌŋktjʊᵊəs/. Someone who is **unctuous** pretends to be full of praise, kindness, or interest, but is obviously insincere; a formal word. ▸ used also of someone's behaviour. EG *...his unctuous flirtatiousness.* ADJ QUALIT = oily ▸ = fulsome

uncultivated /ʌŋ'kʌltɪveɪtɪ²d/. If land is **uncultivated**, there are no crops growing on it. EG *They have campaigned for the right of access to uncultivated land.* ADJ CLASSIF ⇑ wild

uncultured /ʌŋ'kʌltʃəd/. If you describe someone as **uncultured**, you mean that they do not know much about art, literature, and other cultural topics; used showing disapproval. EG *He had a fear of being thought uncultured.* ADJ QUALIT = ill-bred

uncut /ʌŋ'kʌt/. 1 If grass, flowers, etc are **uncut**, they have not been cut and so are still growing. EG *...the narrow garden with its few uncut flowers.* ADJ CLASSIF

2 If a book, play, or film is **uncut**, it has not been shortened or censored. EG *...the death scene, which ends the first half of the uncut 'Peer Gynt'.* ADJ CLASSIF = unabridged

3 If precious stones are **uncut**, their surfaces have not been cut in order to make them sparkle more. ADJ CLASSIF = rough

undamaged /ʌndæmɪdʒd/. Something that is **undamaged** has not been damaged or spoilt in any way. EG *The fire chief went up to inspect the undamaged part of the building.* ADJ CLASSIF ⇑ intact

undated /ʌndeɪtɪ²d/. Something that is **undated** does not have a date written on it. EG *The letter was undated but had been sent from Geneva.* ADJ CLASSIF

undaunted /ʌndɔːntɪ²d/. Someone who is **undaunted** is not discouraged or put off by disappointing things that have happened to them or bad things that other people have said. EG *Undaunted by his first setbacks he decided to try once more to swim the Channel... Undaunted, he is calling for even greater efforts.* ADJ CLASSIF

undecided /ʌndɪsaɪdɪ²d/. If you are **undecided** about something, you can not make up your mind about it. EG *She was still undecided whether she would or would not insist that he returned home... Undecided voters are seen as increasingly necessary to persuade.* ADJ CLASSIF = irresolute

undemanding /ʌndɪmɑːndɪŋ/. 1 Something such as a job that is **undemanding** does not require you to work very hard or to think a great deal about it. EG *The pay was adequate, the job undemanding... ...the television tuned to some undemanding programme.* ADJ QUALIT

2 Someone who is **undemanding** is easy to be with and does not ask other people to do a great deal for them. EG *...a serene and undemanding husband... Not everyone in the family was so agreeable, so undemanding.* ADJ QUALIT

undemocratic /ʌndɛməkrætɪk/. An **undemocratic** system, regime, or action is one in which decisions are made by a few people in power, rather than by all the people who are affected. EG *The union broke with its past undemocratic procedures.* ADJ QUALIT

undemonstrative /ʌndɪmɒnstrətɪv/. Someone who is **undemonstrative** does not allow their feelings to show. ADJ QUALIT

undeniable /ʌndɪnaɪəbəᵊl/. Something that is **undeniable** 1 can not be doubted or denied; used especially to emphasize a particular quality of something that you are describing. EG *Both of these statements are undeniable facts... The evidence is undeniable.* ADJ CLASSIF ⇑ certain = irrefutable
◇ **undeniably**. EG *The statement was undeniably true. ...Their intentions had been so undeniably commercial.* ◇ ADV+ADJ/ADV
2 is so obviously true that you have to admit that it is true even if you do not want to. EG *...the undeniable pleasure of laying down the law.* ADJ CLASSIF ⇑ certain
◇ **undeniably**. EG *He was a tall, dark, and undeniably handsome man... His original decision to support Rolls Royce was undeniably open to criticism.* ◇ ADV+ADJ/ADV

under /ʌndə/. 1 If something is **under** something else, it is 1.1 directly below it but some distance away from it. EG *Try to avoid having a fitted carpet under the dining table... There was a cask of beer under the bench... She was reading her phrase book under a parasol.* PREP = beneath **1.2** directly below it and touching it or close to it. EG *...the cupboard under the sink... The lounge is under my office... He had never slept under a sheet in his life.* PREP = underneath **1.3** at a lower level and slightly to one side of it. EG *...a smouldering rubbish heap under the high wall... He sat down on the grassy bank under the hedge.* PREP = below, beneath **1.4** behind it or covered by it. EG *Jack's face was white under the freckles... The metal is perfect under the paint.* PREP

2 You say that something is **under** a part of your body when it is below that part and near to it. EG *Under her chin was a colossal brooch... She has rings under her eyes... He glared at me from under bushy white eyebrows.* PREP

3 If you are holding something **under** your arm, it is between the upper part of your arm and your body. EG *She tucked the envelope under her arm and hurried home.* PREP

4 If something is **under** the earth or **under** the ground, it is below the surface of the ground. EG *It'll carry electricity deeper under the earth than anyone's ever done.* PREP, OR ADV AFTER VB ⇑ in

5 If something is **under** the sea, it is below the surface of the sea. EG *The agreement bans all nuclear tests in the atmosphere, under the sea and in outer space.* PREP, OR ADV AFTER VB ⇑ in

6 If you go **under** something, you go from one side of it to the other side and it is above you while you do this. EG *We squeezed under the wire and into the garden.* PREP, OR ADV AFTER VB ≠ over

7 If you put something **under** a tap, you place it below the tap while water is coming out of the tap. EG *If you hold a glass under the hot tap it may crack.* PREP

8 If you are wearing or carrying something **under** a piece of clothing, it is nearer to your body than the piece of clothing and is covered by it. EG *He had no shirt on under his thin jumper... McFee took a sheaf of papers from under his coat.* PREP = underneath

9 If something happens **under** particular circumstances or conditions, it happens **9.1** when they exist. EG *He travelled under difficult circumstances... She disappeared under mysterious circumstances.* PREP = in **9.2** in spite of them. EG *They worked reliably under battle conditions... They praised his gallantry under gunfire.* PREP **9.3** as a result of them. EG *He reeled under the bursting pain... The empire started to crack under its own pressures... This plastic loses its strength under heat.* PREP

10 If a person or thing does something **under** a heavy weight, they do it as a result of supporting the weight. EG *The whole sideboard groaned under his weight... She was struggling under many kilos of family shopping.* PREP

11 If something happens **under** a particular person or government, it happens when that person or government is in charge and is responsible for what is happening. EG *China under Chairman Mao had already provided the groundwork for economic recovery... Tonight's concert is given by the London Philharmonic Orchestra, under Klaus Tennstedt... ...the local authority budgets drawn up under the Labour government.* PREP : USU PREP +N PROPER

12 If something happens **under** a particular system, it happens when that system is operating. EG *Under capitalism, people are isolated from each other.* PREP

13 If something happens **under** a law, agreement, or system, it happens because that law, agreement, or system says that it shall happen. EG *Equal pay for men and women is guaranteed under English law... The maximum fine under the Food and Drugs Act is a hundred pounds... Under Thursday's agreement, the minimum benefit paid to the unemployed will be increased... He was the Chairman of his Department for three years under the University's rotating system.* PREP

14 If something is **under** construction, **under** discussion, etc, it is in the process of being constructed, being discussed, etc. EG *A pond is under construction... There is a new film project under discussion... Only 15% of the land is under cultivation.* PREP

15 If you are **under** guard, **under** attack, etc, someone is guarding you, attacking you, etc. EG *Williams was put under surveillance... I knew I was under suspicion... You should remain under heavy guard until the job is done... They were taken to court under heavy police escort.* PREP

16 If you are **under** someone's influence, **under** their PREP

spell, etc, they have a strong effect on the way that you behave. EG *Calcutta came heavily under European influence... The people on the stage were completely under his spell.*

17 If you are **under** something such as an impression or a delusion, you have that impression or delusion. EG *She was evidently under the impression that Morris was the doctor... She had joined under the assumption that she was to be promoted.* PREP

18 If you are **under** something such as pressure or stress, you are experiencing it. EG *The company is under enormous pressure to act quickly... The organization aims to help families under stress... The 24 acres are under no immediate threat of development.* PREP

19 If you are **under** a particular kind of medical treatment, you are receiving that treatment. EG *The patients under local anaesthesia were fully conscious during the operation... Except when under sedation he talked incessantly... I'm under treatment for an ulcer.* PREP

20 If someone is **under**, they have been made unconscious by means of a drug or anaesthetic; an informal use. EG *...a drug powerful enough to keep him under.* ADJ CLASSIF: PRED

21 If you write a book, article, etc **under** a name that is not your real name, that name appears on the book, article, etc as the name of the author. EG *He wrote an anti-war novel under an assumed name... He never wrote under his real name.* PREP

22 If you study or work **under** a particular person, you are taught by that person, for example at college or university, or are lower in rank than them at work. EG *He studied under Thomas Hart Benton... I've got two clerks under me in my section.* PREP: USU+NAME

23 **Under** is also used to say where you can find something in a list, book, or system of classification. EG *They are listed in the telephone directory under A... You'll find it under O for Orwell... The library actually classified books under Light Romance.* PREP

24 You say that a piece of land is **under** a particular type of plant or tree when plants or trees of that type are growing there; a technical use. EG *The amount of land under cash crops is dwindling... The area still lay under virgin forest.* PREP

25 You say that something is **under** a particular amount, number, or age when it is less than that amount, number or age. EG *Expenditure this year should be just under 15 billion pounds... She was well under compulsory retirement age... Tickets cost 2 pounds for adults and 50p for children under 16... Treatment will be free for everyone 17 and under.* PREP ≠ over

under- is added 1 to the beginning of words, especially nouns, in order to form other words that refer to something as being under the thing mentioned or as being used underneath something else. EG *...floor→underfloor... ...blanket→under-blanket.* PREFIX 2 to the beginning of nouns that refer to a job or rank in order to form other nouns that refer to a more junior job or rank. EG *...gardener→under-gardener... ...Secretary→Under-Secretary.* PREFIX ⇑ assistant 3 to the beginning of words, especially participles, in order to form other words which describe something as being done or having happened to an insufficient extent; used showing disapproval. EG *...exercised→under-exercised... ...spending→underspending... ...achievers→underachievers.* PREFIX

underarm /ʌndərɑːm/. You use **underarm** 1 to refer to your armpits. EG *...underarm antiperspirant.* ADJ CLASSIF 2 to describe actions that you do, such as throwing a ball, in which you do not stretch your arm over your shoulder. EG *She would throw underarm... ...underarm shots.* ADV AFTER VB, OR ADJ CLASSIF

underbelly /ʌndəbeli¹/, **underbellies**. The **underbelly** of something is the part of it that can most easily be attacked or criticized. EG *You have to go for the soft liberal underbelly... ...the underbelly of show business.* N COUNT+SUPP: USU the+N IN SING

underbrush /ʌndəbrʌʃ/ is the same as undergrowth; an American word. EG *They made their way cautiously through the underbrush.* N UNCOUNT, OR N SING: the+N

undercarriage /ʌndəkærɪdʒ/, **undercarriages**. The **undercarriage** of an aeroplane is the part, including the wheels, which supports the aeroplane when it is on the ground and when it is landing or taking off. EG *All the aeroplanes had retractable undercarriages.* N COUNT

underclothes /ʌndəkləʊðz/. Your **underclothes** are the clothes such as a vest, bra, or pants, that you wear next to your skin under your other clothes. EG *Renata's underclothes were all over the floor... Janet bought two complete sets of satin underclothes.* N PLURAL: PL FORM WHEN MOD = underwear ● If you are **in** your **underclothes**, you are wearing only your underclothes. EG *A man in his underclothes was reading his paper by the window.* ● PHR: USED AS AN A

underclothing /ʌndəkləʊðɪŋ/ is the same as underclothes; a formal word. EG *...ladies' underclothing.* N UNCOUNT = underwear

undercover /ʌndəkʌvə/. People who take part in **undercover** work or use **undercover** methods act secretly in order to obtain information for their government or for the police. EG *A federal judge upheld the undercover methods used in the case... ...police on undercover duty.* ▸ used of people doing this work. EG *...undercover agents.* ▸ used as an adverb. EG *He began working undercover for the Castro party.* ADJ CLASSIF: ATTRIB ▸ ADV AFTER VB

undercurrent /ʌndəkʌrənt/, **undercurrents**. An **undercurrent** is a feeling or opinion that you do not express and that you are hardly aware of but that influences the way that you think and behave. EG *There was a certain undercurrent of disharmony between them... He was aware of an increasing undercurrent of unease in his mind.* N COUNT: USU+of

undercut /ʌndəkʌt/, **undercuts, undercutting, undercut**. The form **undercut** is used in the present tense and is also the past tense and past participle. 1 If you **undercut** someone or **undercut** their prices, you sell a product more cheaply than they do, so that people buy the product from you rather than from them. EG *The large-scale producer can usually undercut smaller competitors... He persistently undercut their prices.* V+O

2 If something **undercuts** someone's attempts to achieve something, it makes those attempts ineffective, often by producing the opposite effect to the one intended. EG *The delay would surely undercut efforts to force modernization... His image was undercut by the fact that he reeked of manure.* V+O ⇑ weaken = undermine

underdeveloped /ʌndədɪ²veləpt/; also spelled with a hyphen. An **underdeveloped** country or region does not have modern industries or proper social organization and usually has a low standard of living. EG *We should try to help underdeveloped countries... ...the problem of underdeveloped rural areas.* ADJ CLASSIF ⇑ poor = developing

underdog /ʌndədɒg/. **underdogs**. You use **underdog** to refer to the less successful or less privileged people in a society, or the weaker of two people or teams taking part in a competition or contest. EG *...a desire for fair play, and help for the underdog... She took up the cause of the underdog.* N COUNT: the+N

underdone /ʌndədʌn/. You say that food is **underdone** when it has not been cooked for long enough; used showing disapproval. EG *The pastry crust was always underdone... ...an underdone lump of pork.* ADJ QUALIT ⇑ raw

underemployed /ʌndərɪmplɔɪd/; also spelled with a hyphen. If someone is **underemployed**, they have not got enough work to do, or they have work to do that does not make full use of their skills or abilities. EG *Migrants are much more likely to be poor and under-employed... Able people are kept underemployed.* ADJ CLASSIF

underemployment /ʌndərɪ²mplɔɪmə²nt/; also spelled with a hyphen. When there is **underemployment**, people are not provided with enough work, or are provided with work that does not make full use of their skills or abilities. EG *There is a great deal of disguised unemployment or underemployment... Underemployment is much more widespread than you might think.* N UNCOUNT

underestimate /ʌndərestɪmeɪt/, **underestimates, underestimating, underestimated**; also spelled with a hyphen. 1 If you **underestimate** something, you do not realize how large or great it is or will be. EG *Frequently we underestimate children's resilience... The Americans underestimated the power of the explosion.* V+O, OR V+WH ◇ **underestimation** /ʌndərestɪmeɪʃə⁰n/, **underestimations**. EG *...an underestimation of the amount of time the job will take.* ◇ N UNCOUNT/COUNT

2 If you **underestimate** someone, you do not realize what they are capable of doing. EG *He had underestimated Muller... I told you not to underestimate him.* V+O ⇑ misjudge

underfed /ʌndəfed/. People who are **underfed** are unhealthy because they do not get enough food to ADJ CLASSIF ⇑ deprived eat. EG *...underfed children... He really looks underfed.*

under-financed. An organization or institution that is **under-financed** does not have enough money spent on it, so that it cannot function properly. EG *The hospitals were seriously under-financed... ...a small, under-financed school.* ADJ CLASSIF

underfoot /ʌndəfʊt/. 1 You describe something as **underfoot** when it is under your feet, because you are walking on it. EG *The grass underfoot was short and springy... There was the usual litter of rubble and fallen stones underfoot... The ground was hardening underfoot.* ADJ AFTER N, OR ADV AFTER VB

2 If you trample or crush something **underfoot**, you spoil or destroy it by treading on it. EG *The banner was accidentally trampled underfoot by successive ranks of marchers.* ADV AFTER VB

3 To trample or crush something or someone **underfoot** means to treat them without any respect because you think that they are unimportant. EG *He was in no mood to be trampled underfoot by the Nationalist Government.* ADV AFTER VB

undergarment /ʌndəgɑːməˀnt/, **undergarments**. An **undergarment** is a piece of clothing that you wear next to your skin and under your other clothes; a formal word. EG *...ladies' undergarments.* N COUNT ⇑ garment = underwear

undergo /ʌndəgəʊ/, **undergoes, undergoing, underwent, undergone**. If you **undergo** something necessary or unpleasant, it happens to you or is done to you, and you endure it even though it might cause you problems, pain, or unhappiness. EG *The United States will have to undergo radical changes... China had been undergoing political and armed revolution... Her mother was about to undergo a major operation... He had to undergo three months of military training.* V+O ⇑ experience = be subjected to

undergraduate /ʌndəgrædjʊəˈt/, **undergraduates**. An **undergraduate** is a student at a university or college who has not yet taken his or her first degree. EG *He was a Cambridge undergraduate.* N COUNT
▸ used as an adjective. EG *...an undergraduate degree in Social Administration.* ▸ ADJ CLASSIF : ATTRIB

underground. The word **underground** is pronounced /ʌndəgraʊnd/ when it is an adverb, and /ʌndəgraʊnd/ when it is a noun or adjective. 1 Something that is **underground** is below the surface of the ground. EG *...an underground car park... The larvae hatch and make their way underground.* ADJ CLASSIF, OR ADV AFTER VB

2 **Underground** activities are done secretly because they are unofficial and illegal and often opposed to or aimed against the government in power. EG *...the underground activities of the banned opposition parties... ...an underground newspaper... They have continued to oppose the government, combining both legal and underground methods.* ADJ CLASSIF : ATTRIB

3 The **underground** in a country is an organized group of people who are engaged in illegal activities, often against the government in power. EG *We were fighting with the underground against the military regime... The authorities and the underground had known perfectly well what was going to happen.* N SING : *the*+N

4 If you go **underground**, you hide from the authorities or the police because your political ideas or activities are illegal. EG *The day would come when many of us would have to go underground... Among those forced underground was James Jackson.* ADV AFTER VB

5 In British English, the **Underground** in a city or town is a railway system in which electric trains travel mainly below the ground in tunnels; used especially to refer to the system in London. EG *The Underground begins at 5.20 a.m.... We went by Underground to Trafalgar Square... She walked towards the Underground station.* N SING WITH DET, OR *by*+N = tube, subway

undergrowth /ʌndəgrəʊθ/ is bushes and plants growing together under the trees in a forest or jungle. EG *She went crashing through the undergrowth... The undergrowth had been neatly cleared away.* N UNCOUNT, OR N SING : *the*+N = underbrush

underhand /ʌndəhænd/. If an action is **underhand** or is done in an **underhand** way, it is done secretly and dishonestly; used showing disapproval. EG *Did they ever do anything which you regarded as underhand?... I wondered which underhand dodges she would attempt this time.* ▸ used of people. EG *They found him ambivalent and underhand.* ADJ QUALIT ≠ open

underlay /ʌndəleɪ/, **underlays**. 1 **Underlay** is a thick material that you place between a carpet and the floor for extra warmth and in order to protect the carpet. EG *Don't use rubber underlay for this type of carpet.* N MASS

2 **Underlay** is also the past tense of **underlie**.

underlie /ʌndəlaɪ/, **underlies, underlying, underlay, underlain**. You say that something **underlies** something else when it is the cause or basis of it. EG *This thought underlies their objections... The social problems underlying these crises are unsolved.* • See also **underlying**. V+O

underline /ʌndəlaɪn/, **underlines, underlining, underlined**. 1 If something, for example an action or an event, **underlines** something such as a feeling or a problem, it emphasizes it. EG *My own experience heavily underlines the dangers inherent in this sort of work... An article in the Lancet underlined the same problem.* V+O = stress

2 If you **underline** something such as a word or a sentence, you draw a line underneath it in order to make people notice it or to give it extra importance. EG *He underlined his signature with a little flourish.* V+O ⇑ mark = underscore

underling /ʌndəlɪŋ/, **underlings**. An **underling** is a person who is inferior in rank or status to someone else and takes orders from them; used showing disapproval. EG *He expected his underlings to stand respectfully when he entered the room.* N COUNT

underlip /ʌndəlɪp/, **underlips**. Your **underlip** is your lower lip. EG *She removed a fragment of cigarette paper from her underlip.* N COUNT : USU POSS+N IN SING ⇑ lip

underlying /ʌndəlaɪɪŋ/. 1 The **underlying** features of an object, event, or situation are not obvious, and effort may be needed in order to discover or reveal them, even though they are often important or essential for an understanding of the object, event, or situation. EG *There are underlying similarities between all human beings... ...the underlying truth of the situation... The underlying theme of the novel is very serious.* ADJ CLASSIF : ATTRIB

2 You also describe something as **underlying** when it is situated below something else; a formal use. EG *...the underlying soil... ...the firm base of the underlying gravel.* ADJ CLASSIF : ATTRIB

undermanned /ʌndəmænd/. If an organization is **undermanned**, it does not have enough employees to function properly. EG *The industry is sadly undermanned.* ADJ QUALIT = understaffed

undermine /ʌndəmaɪn/, **undermines, undermining, undermined**. 1 If you **undermine** something such as an idea, a feeling, or a system, you make it less strong, less secure, or less likely to succeed than it was before, often by a gradual process or by repeated efforts. EG *There are other theories that undermine this widely accepted idea... Public confidence in the government had now been completely undermined... This trend undermines the conventional division of labour.* V+O ⇑ weaken = sabotage, shake

2 If you **undermine** a person or **undermine** their position or authority, you make their authority less secure, often by indirect methods. EG *It took a long time to undermine him... Many of them sought to undermine his position... The landowners resented government measures which undermined their authority.* V+O ⇑ weaken

3 If something **undermines** a cliff, river bank, building, etc, it gradually weakens or destroys the bottom part of it and makes it likely to collapse. EG *Tidal streams and massive erosion undermine those coastal hills... The foundations of the house have been undermined by groundwater.* V+O ⇑ weaken

underneath /ʌndəniːθ/. 1 If someone or something is **underneath** someone or something else, they are 1.1 directly below them or at a lower level than them. EG *The tortoise was underneath the table... There was a portrait with an inscription underneath... Did you find very much growing underneath the snow?... He was standing just underneath the notice.* PREP, OR ADV AFTER VB/NG = beneath, under 1.2 behind them or covered by them. EG *You haven't seen what it looks like underneath all that paint.* PREP, OR ADV AFTER VB/NG = under

2 The **underneath** part of something is the part which normally touches or faces the ground. EG *The underneath part felt damp... I lifted the dog's foot and checked the soft pad underneath... In the corner was a sofa with springs sticking out underneath.* ADJ CLASSIF : ATTRIB, OR ADV AFTER VB/NG
▸ used as a noun. EG *The underneath of the car was covered with rust.* ▸ N SING : *the*/POSS+N

3 If you are wearing or carrying something **under-** PREP, OR ADV

neath a piece of clothing, it is nearer to your body than the clothing and is covered by it. EG *What have you got underneath your shirt?... She unfastened her cloak, revealing her nightdress underneath.* AFTER VB/NG = under

4 When you feel something **underneath**, you feel it without showing it in your behaviour. EG *They kept getting angrier underneath, without knowing what to do about it... Underneath, most of us are shy... I know I seem confident, but underneath it all I'm terribly nervous.* ADV OR PREP = inside, deep down

undernourished /ʌndənʌrɪʃt/ people are unhealthy because they have not been eating enough food or because they have been eating the wrong kind of food. EG *He was badly undernourished... ...undernourished children.* ADJ QUALIT = underfed, malnourished

undernourishment /ʌndənʌrɪʃmə²nt/ is poor health caused by someone not eating enough food or eating the wrong kind of food. EG *...a body made weak through undernourishment and overwork.* N UNCOUNT = malnutrition

underpaid /ʌndəpeɪd/. People who are **underpaid** are not paid enough money for the job that they do. EG *He considered himself underpaid... ...a great mass of underpaid workers.* ADJ QUALIT

underpants /ʌndəpænts/ are a piece of clothing worn, especially by men and boys, under other clothes. Underpants have two holes to put your legs through and elastic around the waist to keep them up. EG *He put on a fresh pair of underpants.* N PLURAL: ALSO *a pair of*+N ⇑ underwear = pants

● If someone is **in** their **underpants**, they are wearing nothing else on their body except their underpants. EG *Morris took the call standing in the hall in his underpants.* ● PHR: USED AS AN A

underpass /ʌndəpɑːs/, **underpasses**. An **underpass** is a road or footpath that goes underneath something, for example under another road or a railway. EG *...the Knightsbridge Underpass.* N COUNT: ALSO IN NAMES AFTER N ⇑ subway

underpin /ʌndəpɪn/, **underpins, underpinning, underpinned**. If something **underpins** something else, it helps it to continue by supporting and strengthening it. EG *...the informal relationships that underpin any community.* V+O

◊ **underpinning, underpinnings**. EG *...the philosophic underpinning of science... We watched the imperial and commercial underpinnings of our society collapse.* ◊ N UNCOUNT/COUNT

underplay /ʌndəpleɪ/, **underplays, underplaying, underplayed**. If you **underplay** something, you make it seem less important than it really is. EG *She underplays the fact that she's got the Corporation behind her... All attitudes and expressions of emotions are to be underplayed.* V+O = play down, minimize ≠ exaggerate

underpopulated /ʌndəpɒpjə⁴leɪtɪ²d/. You describe a country or region as **underpopulated** when it could support a much larger population than it has. EG *...the richly endowed but underpopulated Ivory Coast... ...an underpopulated area of a rural state.* ADJ QUALIT

underprivileged /ʌndəprɪvɪ⁰lɪdʒd/; also spelled with a hyphen. **Underprivileged** people do not have the money, possessions, and opportunities that other people in their society have. EG *...a school for underprivileged children... ...an underprivileged family.* ADJ QUALIT ⇑ lacking = deprived, disadvantaged

▸ The **underprivileged** is used to refer to people who are underprivileged. EG *...a compassionate concern for the underprivileged.* ▸ N PLURAL: *the*+N

underrate /ʌndəreɪt/, **underrates, underrating, underrated**; also spelled with a hyphen. If you **underrate** someone or something, you do not recognize how clever, important, or significant they are. EG *He soon discovered that he had underrated Luciana... He's a subtle man. Don't underrate him... Frank had underrated Sir James's knowledge of Africa.* V+O ⇑ regard = underestimate

◊ **underrated**. EG *...an underrated poet... The role of women in European history has always been underrated.* ◊ ADJ QUALIT ≠ overrated

underscore /ʌndəskɔː/, **underscores, underscoring, underscored**. 1 If something, for example an action or an event, **underscores** something else, it draws attention to it and emphasizes its importance. EG *The urgency of doing something was underscored by a wave of horror stories about rape and muggings... This very difference underscores our break with past traditions.* V+O = underline

2 If you **underscore** something such as a word or a sentence, you draw a line underneath it in order to make people notice it or to give it extra importance. EG *The words were heavily underscored by a ballpoint pen.* V+O = underline

undersea /ʌndəsiː/ means existing or happening below the surface of the sea. EG *...undersea currents... ...undersea expeditions.* ADJ CLASSIF: ATTRIB = submarine

under-secretary, under-secretaries. An **under-secretary** is a senior official with an important post in a government department. EG *Channon was made an under-secretary at the Department of the Environment... ...the Permanent Under-Secretary of State at the Foreign Office.* N COUNT: ALSO IN TITLES

undershirt /ʌndəʃɜːt/, **undershirts**. An **undershirt** is a garment worn for warmth on the top part of your body next to your skin; used in American English. N COUNT

underside /ʌndəsaɪd/, **undersides**. The **underside** of something is the part of it which normally faces towards the ground. EG *He turned the rifle over and examined the underside... She was staring at the underside of the car roof.* N COUNT: USU WITH POSS = underneath

undersized /ʌndəsaɪzd/; also spelled with a hyphen. **Undersized** or **undersize** people or things are smaller than usual, or smaller than they should be. EG *...rows of undersized babies... ...her undersize stature... ...several bales of under-sized blankets.* ADJ CLASSIF ⇑ size

understaffed /ʌndəstɑːft/; also spelled with a hyphen. An **understaffed** organization does not have enough employees to do its work properly. EG *The Department was under-staffed and over-worked... ...babies who live in understaffed orphanages.* ADJ QUALIT = undermanned

understand /ʌndəstænd/, **understands, understanding, understood**. 1 If you **understand** someone or **understand** what they are telling you, you know what they mean when they are telling you something. EG *She understood him perfectly... Did I understand you correctly?... I don't understand what you mean.* V+O, V+WH, OR V: NO CONT = comprehend, get

2 You can also say that you **understand** someone when you know why they behave in the way that they do. EG *I'm sure you can help me understand her... His wife doesn't understand him... They understand each other well.* V+O, OR V: NO CONT

3 If you **understand** what is happening or why it is happening, you know what is happening or why it is happening. EG *I'm not sure I understand what's going on... I don't understand why the engine isn't working... How it happened has never been fully understood... It was easy to understand why he left the country.* V+WH: NO CONT

4 If you **understand** that something is the case, 4.1 you believe that is the case, because you have been told so. EG *I understand she has several aunts... You and Celia, I understand, are close friends... What he has done, as I understand it, is to try to arrange a meeting.* V+REPORT-CL: NO CONT

4.2 you become aware that it is the case. EG *Only today have I begun to understand that I do not love him.* V+REPORT-CL: NO CONT = realize

5 If you **understand** something such as a theory or a work of art, you know why its parts relate to each other in the way that they do and why it is important. EG *He didn't understand genetics... I don't understand modern pictures.* V+O

6 If you **understand** a language, you know what someone is saying when they are speaking that language. EG *I don't understand English.* V+O: NO CONT

7 The word **understand** is also used in the following expressions. 7.1 If you **make** yourself **understood**, you get someone to understand what you are telling them, although they do not speak your language. EG *They were all speaking at once in primitive dialects, trying to make themselves understood.* PHR: *make* INFLECTS

7.2 If you **give** someone **to understand** that something is the case, you make it clear to them without telling them directly; a formal expression. EG *The men gave their wives to understand that they should trust no one... I've been given to understand that I'm no longer needed.* PHR: *give* INFLECTS, USU+REPORT-CL ⇑ tell

7.3 **If it is understood** that a particular rule, condition, or system applies in a situation, everyone taking part has agreed that the rule, condition, or system will operate or be valid as long as that situation lasts. PHR: AUX INFLECTS, USU+REPORT-CL

7.4 People say **'understand?'**, **'you understand?'**, or **'is that understood?'** after they have said something to you, especially after giving you an order or instruction, to make sure that you have understood what they have said and will obey them. EG *Leave that alone, understand?... Don't give my baby another drop of that horrid jelly, you understand?*

understandable /ʌndəstændəbəᵊl/. 1 You say that someone's behaviour is **understandable** when you think that they have reacted to a situation in a natural or normal way or in the way you would expect them to. EG *His reaction was perfectly understandable... This measure provoked understandable hostility on the part of industry.* ◊ **understandably**. EG *The police were understandably displeased at his driving... Understandably he was frightened... Heissman, understandably enough, never discussed the past.* — ADJ QUALIT; ◊ ADV SEN ⇑ naturally

2 If something such as a statement or theory is **understandable**, people can understand it. EG *He could not understand the theory, and he had doubts whether it was understandable... ...the storage of information in a form which is readily understandable.* — ADJ CLASSIF = comprehensible

understanding /ʌndəstændɪŋ/, **understandings**. 1 If you have an **understanding** of something, you have some knowledge of it, know how it works, or know what it means. EG *I doubt whether he had any real understanding of Shakespeare... The job requires an understanding of Spanish.* — N UNCOUNT : USU +*of* = grasp

2 If you are **understanding** towards someone, you are kind and forgiving. EG *You were understanding and helpful... I have always thought you were an understanding person.* ▸ used as a noun. EG *She showed great love and understanding.* — ADJ QUALIT = sympathetic; ▸ N UNCOUNT = sympathy

3 If there is **understanding** between people, they are friendly towards each other and trust each other. EG *What is needed is greater understanding between management and workers.* — N UNCOUNT = cooperation

4 An **understanding** is an informal agreement about something, for example between two countries. EG *Tacit understandings had been reached.* — N COUNT

5 If you agree to do something **on the understanding that** something else will be done, you do it because you have been told that the other thing will be done. EG *I signed the contract on the understanding that delivery would be this week.* — CONJ SUBORD

understate /ʌndəsteɪt/, **understates, understating, understated**. If you **understate** something, you describe it in a way that suggests that it is smaller or less important than it really is. EG *Some landlords understate their production figures to avoid tax... This understates the magnitude of the problem.* ◊ **understated**. EG *...one of the most understated atrocities of the last few decades.* — V+O; ◊ ADJ QUALIT

understatement /ʌndəsteɪtməᵊnt/, **understatements**. 1 An **understatement** is a statement which suggests that something has much less of a particular quality than it really has. EG *To say it's been good is quite an understatement... That, I thought, could be the understatement of the year.* — N COUNT

2 **Understatement** is the practice of suggesting that things have much less of a particular quality than they really have. EG *That sounds like typical British understatement... They had been speaking with the deliberate understatement of professional people.* — N UNCOUNT

understood /ʌndəstʊd/ is the past tense and past participle of **understand**.

understudy /ʌndəstʌdi¹/, **understudies, understudying, understudied**. An actor's **understudy** is a person who has learned the actor's part in a play and can act the part if the actor is ill. EG *He was Bobby's understudy... I went to watch my understudy in action.* ▸ used as a verb. EG *I was understudying Claude Rains.* — N COUNT = second, substitute; ▸ V+O

undertake /ʌndəteɪk/, **undertakes, undertaking, undertook, undertaken**. 1 When you **undertake** a task or job, you start doing it and accept responsibility for it. EG *They are determined to succeed, whatever job they undertake... Only the state was able to undertake the required research... Reluctantly, he undertook the mission.* — V+O ⇑ do = take on

2 If you **undertake** to do something, you promise that you will do it. EG *I undertake to preserve a strictly neutral position... Most shareholders have undertaken to accept the offer.* — V+*to*-INF ⇑ state = agree

undertaker /ʌndəteɪkə/, **undertakers**. An **undertaker** is a person whose job is to look after the bodies of people who have died and to arrange their funerals. EG *The undertakers came from Tolmere to collect the body.* — N COUNT ⇑ worker = mortician

undertaking /ʌndəteɪkɪŋ/, **undertakings**. 1 An **undertaking** is a task or job that you start doing and that you accept responsibility for. EG *Every new undertaking involves effort... ...a complex and expensive undertaking.* — N COUNT

2 If you give an **undertaking** to do something, you formally promise to do it. EG *Abernethy gave an undertaking not to stand again for election... We will stand by all our pledges and undertakings.* — N COUNT ⇑ agreement

underthings /ʌndəθɪŋz/ are underclothes; an informal word. EG *Her filmy underthings were laid out on the bed... Here you all are in your underthings.* — N PLURAL ⇑ clothes = underwear

undertone /ʌndətəʊn/, **undertones**. 1 If you say something in an **undertone**, you say it very quietly. EG *Marcus said in an undertone, 'It doesn't matter, Lucas.'* — N COUNT

2 If something has **undertones** of a particular kind, it suggests ideas or attitudes of this kind without expressing them directly. EG *The custom had religious undertones... The word itself has taken on slightly comic undertones.* — N COUNT+SUPP : USU PL = overtones

undertook /ʌndətʊk/ is the past tense of **undertake**.

undertow /ʌndətəʊ/, **undertows**. An **undertow** is a strong current of water that is moving below the surface current and in a different direction to it. EG *The sea was still, with no undertow.* — N COUNT/UNCOUNT = undercurrent

underused /ʌndəjuːzd/; also spelled with a hyphen. You say that something is **underused** when it is not used as much for people's benefit as it could be. EG *A lot of the arable land was underused and poorly tended... ...under-used facilities.* — ADJ QUALIT = under-utilized

under-utilized; also spelled **under-utilised**. **Under-utilized** means the same as underused; a rather formal word. EG *There is still a great deal of under-utilized land in Third World countries... Existing capacity was commonly under-utilised.* — ADJ QUALIT

undervalue /ʌndəvæljuː/, **undervalues, undervaluing, undervalued**. If you **undervalue** something or someone, you think that they are less valuable or important than they really are. EG *We tend to overvalue money and undervalue art... Surely you realise I don't undervalue you.* — V+O = underrate

underwater /ʌndəwɔːtə/. 1 Something that exists or happens **underwater** exists or happens below the surface of the sea, a river, or a lake. EG *Dragonflies spend a year underwater before emerging as adults... ...underwater experimental stations... 17 cannon were found and measured underwater.* — ADJ CLASSIF : ATTRIB, OR ADV WITH VB

2 **Underwater** devices are specially made so that they can work underwater. EG *It was filmed with an underwater camera... ...underwater torches.* — ADJ CLASSIF : ATTRIB

underway /ʌndəweɪ/; also written **under way**. If an activity or plan is **underway**, it has begun and is now taking place. EG *Preparations for the trial were underway.* — ADJ CLASSIF : PRED

underwear /ʌndəweə/. Your **underwear** is the clothing such as a vest, bra, or pants, that you wear next to your skin under your other clothes. EG *...two changes of underwear... She had removed her underwear.* — N UNCOUNT = underclothes

underwent /ʌndəwent/ is the past tense of **undergo**.

underworld /ʌndəwɜːld/. 1 The **underworld** in a city is the organized crime there and the people who are involved in it. EG *...professional thugs from the underworld... ...the Glasgow underworld.* ▸ used as an adjective. EG *...underworld interests in the United States.* — N SING : *the*+N = gangland; ▸ N BEFORE N

2 The **underworld** is also, according to many ancient religions, myths, and legends, a world under the Earth's surface where people go after they die. EG *...the god of the underworld.* — N SING : *the*+N

underwrite /ʌndəraɪt/, **underwrites, underwriting, underwrote, underwritten**. If you **underwrite** an activity or **underwrite** the cost of it, you agree to provide any money that is needed to cover losses or to buy special equipment; a technical term. EG *2 million pounds was made available to underwrite the production of machine-tools... Madrid will extend a £290 million export credit to underwrite some of the cost.* — V+O

undeserved /ʌndi¹zɜːvd/. If you get something that is **undeserved**, you have not earned it and should not really have it. EG *He thought all the rough treatment that I underwent appeared undeserved... Their bitterness at Conway's undeserved promotion was obvious... He wallows in the undeserved praise of his colleagues.* — ADJ CLASSIF

undesirable /ʌndi[1]zaɪərəbə[0]l/, **undesirables.** 1 If you describe someone or something as **undesirable**, you disapprove of them or dislike them because of their bad effect or influence. EG *These cuts in education are very undesirable... They sent their daughters on world trips to get them away from undesirable lovers... Many parents are worried by what they think is undesirable reading matter.* — ADJ QUALIT = objectionable

2 An **undesirable** person is one whom a particular government considers to be dangerous or a threat to society and therefore wants to get rid of. EG *He was listed everywhere as an undesirable immigrant... ...an undesirable alien.* ▸ used as a noun. EG *He was charged with harbouring undesirables.* — ADJ CLASSIF : ATTRIB; ▸ N COUNT

undetected /ʌndi[1]tektɪ[2]d/. If someone or something is **undetected**, they have been kept secret and have not been found out. EG *It was important to my safety that I should remain undetected.* — ADJ CLASSIF ⇑ unnoticed

undeveloped /ʌndi[1]veləpt/. 1 **Undeveloped** countries are countries that are not industrialized and where modern methods of large-scale farming are not used. — ADJ CLASSIF = underdeveloped

2 Someone who is **undeveloped** is not yet mature or adult. EG *A child should not be considered simply as an undeveloped adult.* — ADJ CLASSIF = immature

undid /ʌndɪd/ is the past tense of **undo**.

undignified /ʌndɪgnɪfaɪd/. Someone who is **undignified** is foolish or embarrassing in their behaviour or appearance. EG *...an undignified pose... They had a somewhat undignified argument.* — ADJ QUALIT = ungainly

undiluted /ʌndaɪlu:tɪ[2]d/. 1 An **undiluted** feeling or quality is very strong and not mixed with any other feeling or quality. EG *...undying and undiluted love... ...his undiluted Scottishness.* — ADJ CLASSIF = pure, unadulterated

2 A liquid that is **undiluted** is concentrated and not diluted with water. EG *...undiluted orange squash.* — ADJ CLASSIF

undisciplined /ʌndɪsɪplɪnd/. Someone who is **undisciplined** behaves badly, with a lack of self-control. EG *People often complain that British children are undisciplined.* — ADJ QUALIT = unruly

undiscovered /ʌndɪskʌvəd/. Something that is **undiscovered** has not been discovered or found out about. EG *Old people who are ill sometimes lie undiscovered in their homes for days... ...an undiscovered country.* — ADJ CLASSIF ⇑ undetected

undisguised /ʌndɪsgaɪzd/. An **undisguised** quality, feeling, etc is one that you show openly and do not make any attempt to hide. EG *'What's going on?' Christine asked with undisguised curiosity... He looked at her with undisguised admiration and respect.* — ADJ CLASSIF = open

undismayed /ʌndɪsmeɪd/. Someone who is **undismayed** by something unpleasant or unexpected does not feel any fear, worry, or sadness about it; a fairly literary word. EG *She appeared quite undismayed and unrepentant over Amelia's reproaches.* — ADJ QUALIT : PRED ⇑ unaffected = undaunted

undisputed /ʌndɪspju:tɪ[2]d/. 1 Something which is **undisputed** is definitely true or definitely exists and cannot be questioned or doubted. EG *The facts are undisputed... ...answers which have the weight of undisputed authority... There was one undisputed cause for celebration.* — ADJ CLASSIF ⇑ unquestioned

2 If you describe someone as the **undisputed** leader, champion, etc, you mean that they have proved that nobody else has more power or ability than them. EG *Mao became undisputed leader in China.* — ADJ CLASSIF

undistinguished /ʌndɪstɪŋgwɪʃt/. Someone or something that is **undistinguished** has no specially good or bad qualities or features; used showing disapproval. EG *The new station is of undistinguished modern design... His political career had been undistinguished.* — ADJ QUALIT = mediocre

undisturbed /ʌndɪstɜ:bd/. 1 A place that is **undisturbed** is peaceful and not disturbed by noise, people, etc. EG *The village is changing but it is still very undisturbed.* — ADJ QUALIT ⇑ quiet

2 If you are **undisturbed** in something that you are doing, you are able to continue doing it and are not forced to stop or change because of something that is happening. EG *The children pursued their studies undisturbed by the many visitors... I was able to get through the usual weekend jobs undisturbed... These people remained largely unaware and undisturbed by the war.* — ADJ QUALIT : PRED ⇑ unaffected = uninterrupted

3 Something that remains **undisturbed** is not touched, moved, or used by anyone. EG *The ship's remains lay undisturbed until 1975... No matter how long you leave your money undisturbed you're bound to lose out eventually.* — ADJ CLASSIF : USU PRED

undivided /ʌndɪvaɪdɪ[2]d/. 1 If you give something your **undivided** attention, you concentrate on it fully and do not think about anything else. EG *I was listening with undivided attention... Her obvious distress had my complete and undivided concern.* — ADJ CLASSIF : ATTRIB ⇑ full = wholehearted

2 Something such as an organization that is **undivided** is not separated into different parts or groups. EG *The society is undifferentiated and undivided.* — ADJ CLASSIF

undo /ʌndu:/, **undoes, undoing, undid, undone.** 1 If you **undo** something that is tied together, you unfasten it or untie it. EG *...undoing a newspaper parcel tied with string... He undid the clasp of his belt... He bent down and undid the laces of his shoes.* — V+O ⇑ open

2 If someone **undoes** something that has been done, they destroy the effect of what has been done. EG *He appeared to be undoing all their patient work... ...practices which tend to undo land reform or prevent it from happening... Sins cannot be undone, only forgiven.* — V+O

undoing /ʌndu:ɪŋ/. If something is someone's **undoing**, it is the cause of their failure; a fairly formal word. EG *This uncompromising attitude may have led to his undoing... Stress can be the undoing of so many fine players.* — N UNCOUNT : WITH POSS = downfall

undone /ʌndʌn/. 1 Something that is **undone** is no longer held or tied by a fastening such as string, buttons, etc. EG *His bow-tie had come undone... ...barefoot and dirty, her hair all undone... I picked the knots undone.* — ADJ CLASSIF : PRED = unfastened

2 Work that is **undone** has not yet been done. EG *Some of the jobs I intended doing have been left undone.* — ADJ CLASSIF : USU PRED

3 Someone who is **undone** has failed completely in something and is therefore in trouble; a literary use. EG *The people who have no confidence are undone.* — ADJ CLASSIF : PRED = ruined

undoubted /ʌndaʊtɪ[2]d/ is used to describe something that you believe certainly exists or is certainly true. EG *...her undoubted acting ability... ...his undoubted criminal record... The play was an undoubted success.* ◊ **undoubtedly.** EG *Undoubtedly, many families are victims of bad housing... A personal chauffeur is undoubtedly a status symbol.* — ADJ CLASSIF : USU ATTRIB = obvious; ◊ ADV SEN = indisputably

undreamed of; also spelled with a hyphen. Something that is **undreamed of** is much better, worse, or more unusual than you ever imagined or thought was possible. EG *People now have achieved a physical mobility previously undreamed of... Cloning could create undreamed-of complications for the race.* — ADJ CLASSIF

undress /ʌndres/, **undresses, undressing, undressed.** 1 If you **undress**, you take off your clothes. EG *Tom undressed in the dark.* — V

2 If you **undress** someone, you take off their clothes. EG *I helped to undress the children for bed.* — V+O

3 Someone is **in a state of undress** if they do not have all their clothes on, for example if they are only wearing their underwear; a rather old-fashioned expression, often used humorously. — PHR : USED AS AN A

undressed /ʌndrest/. Someone who is **undressed** is wearing no clothes or very few clothes. EG *They had all seen each other undressed.* ● If you **get undressed**, you take off your clothes. EG *He took ages getting undressed and climbing into the sleeping bag.* — ADJ CLASSIF : PRED; ● PHR : VB INFLECTS

undue /ʌndju:/ is used to describe something that is greater or more extreme than is wanted, expected, or thought to be reasonable. EG *I had to time my enquiries carefully so as not to attract undue attention... She was reprimanded for putting undue pressure in her clients... Had either of them ever caused undue trouble to anyone?* — ADJ CLASSIF : ATTRIB = excessive

undulate /ʌndjə[4]leɪt/, **undulates, undulating, undulated.** Something that **undulates** has gentle curves or slopes, or moves gently and slowly up and down. EG *There are no mountains or ravines, the countryside undulates undramatically.* ◊ **undulating.** EG *The herd started to move towards me in a slow, undulating wave.* ◊ **undulation** /ʌndjə[4]leɪʃə[0]n/, **undulations.** EG *...the gentle undulations of the foothills.* — V; ◊ ADJ CLASSIF = sinuous; ◊ N COUNT/UNCOUNT

unduly /ʌndju:li[1]/ is used to indicate that something happens to an excessive or unnecessary extent. EG *None of the women seemed unduly worried... This attitude seemed to me unduly fussy... This would not have surprised Morris unduly.* — ADV : USU WITH BROAD NEG = excessively

undying /ʌndaɪɪŋ/ is used to describe a feeling or belief that seems as if it will last for ever; a literary word. EG *...Daniel's undying love for his wife... They showed undying defiance and militance.* ADJ CLASSIF: USU ATTRIB ⇑ lasting = eternal

unearned income /ʌnɜːnd ɪnkʌm/ is money that you gain from property, investment, etc rather than money that you earn from a job. EG *...a tax on unearned income.* N UNCOUNT

unearth /ʌnɜːθ/, **unearths, unearthing, unearthed.** 1 If you **unearth** something that is buried under the ground, you find it by digging in the ground. EG *These ruins had been unearthed six feet below the surface.* V+O

2 If you **unearth** something that was being kept secret or was being lied about, you find it or find out the truth about it. EG *This dossier was unearthed along with many others.* V+O

unearthly /ʌnɜːθli¹/. 1 Something that is **unearthly** has a strange and unnatural sound, appearance, or other quality. EG *The light was unearthly... ...an apparition of unearthly beauty... The wail rose, remote and unearthly.* ADJ CLASSIF = eerie

2 You use **unearthly** in fairly informal English 2.1 to describe a time of day that you consider to be very unreasonable because it is too early or too late. EG *I wondered when he had last risen at that unearthly hour.* ADJ CLASSIF: ATTRIB = ungodly 2.2 to describe a noise that you find very loud and unpleasant. EG *What's that unearthly squalling sound in the other room?* ADJ CLASSIF: USU ATTRIB ⇑ awful

unease /ʌniːz/. 1 If you have a feeling of **unease**, you feel rather anxious that things are not right. EG *'He'll be alright,' I said to myself, trying to quell a growing unease.* N UNCOUNT ⇑ nervousness

2 If a state of **unease** exists in a situation, many people are dissatisfied or becoming angry, but have not yet decided to take any action. EG *The letter described the growing unease between the American colonies and England.* N UNCOUNT = tension

uneasy /ʌniːzi¹/, **uneasier, uneasiest.** 1 If you are **uneasy**, you feel anxious that something may be wrong or that there may be some danger. EG *She looked uneasy but promised to follow his advice... She had an uneasy feeling that they were still following her.* ADJ QUALIT ⇑ worried ▸ used to describe a situation in which the people involved are uneasy. EG *...an uneasy alliance between the two parties... ...an uneasy peace.* ▸ ADJ QUALIT: ATTRIB ◊ **uneasily.** EG *The hunters were looking uneasily at the sky... Philip blushed and laughed uneasily.* ◊ ADV WITH VB ◊ **uneasiness.** EG *If a baby doesn't feed well, this increases the mother's uneasiness.* ◊ N UNCOUNT

2 If you are **uneasy** about doing something, you are not sure that it is correct or wise. EG *I felt increasingly uneasy about my answer... Many managements are uneasy about promoting women to higher jobs.* ADJ QUALIT: USU PRED+*about* = unsure

uneatable /ʌniːtəbə⁰l/. Food that is **uneatable** 1 is so bad or tastes so unpleasant that you do not want to eat it. EG *She used to make that uneatable gingerbread.* ADJ QUALIT 2 cannot be eaten by people. EG *Everybody knows that uncooked rice is quite uneatable.* ADJ CLASSIF = inedible

uneconomic /ʌniːkənɒmɪk, ʌnɛkə-/. An industry, business, etc that is **uneconomic** does not produce enough profit. EG *...uneconomic coal mines... Featherbedding is an increasingly uneconomic industry.* ADJ QUALIT

uneconomical /ʌniːkənɒmɪkə⁰l, ʌnɛkə-/. Something that is **uneconomical** wastes your time, energy, or money, or requires more of them than you have got or can afford to use. EG *...an uneconomical use of resources... ...groups for whom homeownership is uneconomical.* ADJ QUALIT

uneducated /ʌnɛdʒə⁴keɪtɪ²d/. Someone who is **uneducated** has not received any education, usually because they have not been to school. EG *...uneducated rural poor people.* ADJ QUALIT ⇑ ignorant

unemotional /ʌnɪməʊʃə⁰nəl, -ʃənə⁰l/. Someone who is **unemotional** does not show any feelings; often used showing disapproval. EG *He was cold and unemotional... The voice was quiet, unemotional, courteous.* ADJ QUALIT = cold ◊ **unemotionally.** EG *She received this news unemotionally.* ◊ ADV WITH VB

unemployable /ʌnɪ²mplɔɪəbə⁰l/. Someone who is **unemployable** is unemployed and unlikely to get a job, for example because of a particular handicap or way of behaving that they have. EG *Trade union activists are often considered unemployable in industry.* ADJ CLASSIF ⇑ incapable

unemployed /ʌnɪ²mplɔɪd/. Someone who is **unemployed** does not have a job, although they want one. EG *The government ought to create more job vacancies for unemployed young people... Women are currently becoming unemployed almost twice as fast as men.* ADJ CLASSIF ▸ The **unemployed** is used to refer to people who are unemployed. EG *There are now almost 11 million unemployed in all the EEC countries... They were discussing the problem of the unemployed.* ▸ N PLURAL: USU the+N

unemployment /ʌnɪ²mplɔɪmə²nt/ refers to 1 the number of people in a country or area who do not have jobs although they want one. EG *The government is concerned about the level of unemployment in Scotland... He drew attention to the rising unemployment among dockers... Youth unemployment is over 50%.* N UNCOUNT 2 the situation of someone not having a job when they want one. EG *Unemployment affects families in a lot of ways... ...the miseries of unemployment.* N UNCOUNT

unemployment benefit is money that someone receives from the state when they are unemployed; used mainly in British English. EG *If you are unemployed you may be able to get unemployment benefit.* N UNCOUNT ⇑ benefit = dole

unending /ʌnɛndɪŋ/. Something that is **unending** seems to continue without stopping for a very long time. EG *...Britain's unending economic hardships... ...the unending debate about tobacco... ...this seemingly unending horror.* ADJ CLASSIF ⇑ continual

unendurable /ʌnɪ²ndjʊərəbə⁰l/. Something that is **unendurable** is so unpleasant that you cannot bear it; a formal word. EG *He found the noises and the pushing unendurable.* ADJ CLASSIF = unbearable

unenviable /ʌnɛnvɪəbə⁰l/ is used to describe something that you do not want to have or do because it is very difficult, dangerous, or unpleasant. EG *...the unenviable task of ringing the parents of the dead child... Today's miner still works hard, and in unenviable conditions underground.* ADJ QUALIT: ATTRIB

unequal /ʌniːkwəl/. 1 A conditon, situation, etc that is **unequal** treats different people or groups in different ways, for example giving one person or group more money, status, or privileges than another; often used showing disapproval. EG *...the unequal distribution of wealth... That's certainly the main reason given by men for unequal pay... ...unequal marriages... The western powers forced China to accept unequal trade treaties, with very low tariffs.* ADJ QUALIT = discriminatory ◊ **unequally.** EG *Their relationship seems very unequally balanced.* ◊ ADV WITH VB = unevenly

2 Two things that are **unequal** are different in size, strength, ability, etc. EG *Her feet are of unequal sizes... The seed is being acted upon by unequal forces.* ADJ QUALIT ⇑ unbalanced

3 If you feel **unequal** to doing something, you feel incapable of doing it; a formal use. EG *I felt quite unequal to the challenge of responding to this alarming speech.* ADJ CLASSIF: PRED+*to*

unequalled /ʌniːkwəld/. Something that is **unequalled** is greater, better, or more extreme than anything else of the same kind. EG *His experience of organising warfare was unequalled... This was when architecture reached a point of extravagance unequalled in history.* ADJ CLASSIF: USU PRED = unparalleled

unequivocal /ʌnɪkwɪvək⁰əl/; a fairly formal word. 1 Something that is **unequivocal** is completely clear in meaning. EG *The reply next day was unequivocal.* ADJ CLASSIF ◊ **unequivocally.** EG *They have stated uneqivocally what they stand for.* ◊ ADV ⇑ clearly

2 An **unequivocal** action is done without making any conditions or demands and without any hesitation or reluctance. EG *...an unequivocal offer.* ADJ CLASSIF = categorical, unqualified ◊ **unequivocally.** EG *They do not wish yet to commit themselves totally or unequivocally in an open run for power.* ◊ ADV = unreservedly

unerring /ʌnɜːrɪŋ/ is used to describe someone's judgement or ability when it is always correct and never mistaken. EG *Sita's unerring sense of direction helped them... ...our commander's unerring ability to find a cabin for the night.* ADJ CLASSIF

unescorted /ʌnɪ²skɔːtɪ²d/. A woman who is **unescorted** does not have a man accompanying her. EG *Groups of girls came unescorted and waited to be asked to dance.* ADJ CLASSIF

unethical /ʌnɛθɪkə⁰l/. Behaviour that is **unethical** is wrong and unacceptable when considered in relation to a particular system of beliefs about right and wrong. EG *He was accused of serious and gross unethical conduct.* ADJ QUALIT = immoral

uneven /ʌniːvəⁿn/. 1 Something that is **uneven** 1.1 does not have a flat, straight, smooth, or regular surface. EG *...the uneven surface of the gravel road... ...a mouthful of white, uneven teeth.* ◊ **unevenly**. EG *The edges were unevenly finished.* 1.2 is not consistent in quality or extent; used showing disapproval. EG *It was an uneven but inspired performance.* — ADJ QUALIT ↑ crooked; ◊ ADV WITH VB; ADJ QUALIT = patchy, flawed

2 A situation that is **uneven** is unfairly arranged or organized; used showing disapproval. EG *...differences reinforced by highly uneven economic and social development... ...the uneven race between the life sciences and the physical sciences.* ◊ **unevenly**. EG *The benefits of growth are so unevenly spread.* — ADJ QUALIT ↑ unjust = inequitable; ◊ ADV WITH VB

uneventful /ʌnɪventfʊl/. If you describe an occasion or period of time as **uneventful**, you mean that nothing interesting, exciting, or important happened during the time. EG *The day was quiet and uneventful.* ◊ **uneventfully**. EG *The rest of the journey passed uneventfully.* — ADJ QUALIT ↑ peaceful = quiet; ◊ ADV WITH VB

unexceptionable /ʌnɪ²ksɛpʃənəbəⁿl/. Something that is **unexceptionable** is not likely to be criticized, objected to, or disagreed with; a formal word. EG *Their conduct is rarely unexceptionable... His explanation, although unexceptionable, is scarcely illuminating.* — ADJ CLASSIF ↑ acceptable

unexceptional /ʌnɪ²ksɛpʃəⁿnəl, -ʃənəⁿl/. Something that is **unexceptional** is only of an average quality, and not at all remarkable. EG *...an unexceptional ivory chess set.* — ADJ QUALIT ↑ ordinary = unremarkable

unexciting /ʌnɪ²ksaɪtɪŋ/. Something that is **unexciting** is slightly boring, and not likely to shock or surprise you in any way. EG *...wholesome but unexciting bread-and-butter pudding.* — ADJ QUALIT

unexpected /ʌnɪ²kspektɪ²d/. Something that is **unexpected** surprises you because you were not expecting it to happen at all or to happen in a particular way, or because it is very different from what you had planned or imagined. EG *My hostess greeted me with unexpected warmth and cordiality... This created an unexpected vacancy in the Department... His death was hardly unexpected.* ◊ **unexpectedly**. EG *He made an unexpectedly kind-hearted gesture... Some industrial materials have turned out, unexpectedly, to be serious health hazards.* — ADJ QUALIT ↑ surprising = unforeseen; ◊ ADV

unexplained /ʌnɪ²ksplеɪnd/. Something that is **unexplained** is strange or unclear because the reason for it is not known. EG *I was pondering on this unexplained mystery... An unexplained electrical failure prevented the showing of the film.* — ADJ CLASSIF

unfailing /ʌnfeɪlɪŋ/ is used to describe a quality that stays the same and does not get worse or weaker as time passes; a formal word, often used showing approval. EG *I could never have carried on without the unfailing support of the teaching staff... Their discipline and good behaviour was unfailing.* ◊ **unfailingly**. EG *He was unfailingly attentive.* — ADJ CLASSIF : USU ATTRIB ↑ continual; ◊ ADV

unfair /ʌnfeə/. 1 If you think that something is **unfair**, you think that it is unreasonable and unjustifiable according to your ideas about what is right and just. EG *It's unfair to expect such qualities in most children today... A few bad characters were gaining an unfair advantage.* ▸ used of people who behave in an unjust manner. EG *You were very unfair to them.* ◊ **unfairly**. EG *Workers who have been unfairly dismissed may claim compensation.* — ADJ QUALIT ↑ wrong; ◊ ADV WITH VB ↑ wrongly

2 An **unfair** comment is unjust and rather unkind, usually because it is exaggerated or not quite true. EG *This is, strictly speaking, unfair to Bowles.* ◊ **unfairly**. EG *It was even suggested, possibly unfairly, that he might no longer be fit for the job.* — ADJ QUALIT; ◊ ADV WITH VB

3 A situation, system, etc that is **unfair** does not give equal treatment or the same chances to everyone involved; used showing disapproval. EG *The whole academic system is unfair... We have to compete with them on unfair terms.* ◊ **unfairly**. EG *What if the defendant feels he has been unfairly judged?* ◊ **unfairness**. EG *I do see that there is a serious unfairness in the system.* — ADJ QUALIT ↑ unequal = biased; ◊ ADV WITH VB; ◊ N UNCOUNT

unfaithful /ʌnfeɪθfʊl/. If someone is **unfaithful** to their lover or to the person they are married to, they have a sexual relationship with someone else. EG *I swear I've never been unfaithful to you... ...worried girls spying on their unfaithful lovers.* — ADJ CLASSIF : IF + PREP THEN USU *to*

unfamiliar /ʌnfəmɪlɪə/. 1 If something is **unfamiliar**, it is not known to you. EG *At night, especially in unfamiliar surroundings, be alert at all times... This name may be unfamiliar to most of you.* — ADJ QUALIT ↑ unknown

2 If you are **unfamiliar** with something, you have not seen or heard it before. EG *...a person unfamiliar with French speech.* ◊ **unfamiliarity** /ʌnfəmɪlɪærɪti¹/. EG *...his unfamiliarity with the idioms of city English.* — ADJ QUALIT : PRED + *with*; ◊ N UNCOUNT

unfashionable /ʌnfæʃəⁿnəbəⁿl/. If something is **unfashionable**, it is not fashionable or popular at a particular time. EG *...the unfashionable side of Victoria Station... His ideas were unfashionable and unpopular among his colleagues.* — ADJ QUALIT

unfasten /ʌnfɑːsəⁿn/, **unfastens, unfastening, unfastened**. If you **unfasten** a piece of clothing, belt, etc, you undo the buttons, hooks, straps, etc on it. EG *You may now unfasten your seat belts... He unfastened the buttons of his shirt.* — V+O

unfathomable /ʌnfæðəməbəⁿl/. If something is **unfathomable**, it is so strange or complicated that it cannot be understood or explained; a formal word. EG *...an unfathomable mystery.* — ADJ CLASSIF = baffling

unfavourable /ʌnfeɪvəⁿrəbəⁿl/; also spelled **unfavorable** in American English. 1 Something that is **unfavourable** makes things difficult for you and means that you are unlikely to have a good result. EG *The present crisis has largely been caused by an unfavourable economic climate... ...unfavourable weather conditions.* — ADJ QUALIT = adverse

2 If you have an **unfavourable** opinion of something, you do not like it or approve of it and you criticize it. EG *He had formed an unfavourable opinion of my work... This might perhaps create an unfavourable impression.* ◊ **unfavourably**. EG *He reviewed one of your books very unfavourably... Congress looked unfavourably on the offer.* — ADJ QUALIT ↑ critical = adverse; ◊ ADV WITH VB

3 An **unfavourable** comparison is one that makes one of the things appear very poor or inferior. EG *She had been drawing unfavourable comparisons between standards here and abroad.* ◊ **unfavourably**. EG *The management was compared unfavourably with the pre-war landowners.* — ADJ CLASSIF : ATTRIB; ◊ ADV WITH VB

unfeeling /ʌnfiːlɪŋ/. Someone who is **unfeeling** is cruel and not sympathetic to other people. EG *He's a corrupt, unfeeling little creep.* — ADJ QUALIT

unfettered /ʌnfetəd/. Something that is **unfettered** is completely free and not controlled or limited by anyone or anything. EG *...the right of free speech, unfettered by the party system... They want to replace one form of unfettered power with another.* — ADJ CLASSIF : IF + PREP THEN *by* = unrestrained

unfinished /ʌnfɪnɪʃt/. If something is **unfinished**, it has not been completed. EG *People shouldn't leave jobs unfinished... There's a lot of unfinished business to get through.* — ADJ CLASSIF = incomplete

unfit /ʌnfɪt/, **unfits, unfitting, unfitted**. 1 If you are **unfit**, you have not been taking regular exercise, so that, for example, you get tired quickly when you run. EG *If you are fat and very unfit, don't choose jogging to start with.* — ADJ QUALIT

2 If someone or something is **unfit** for a particular purpose, they are not of a good enough quality or are not suitable. EG *This meat is unfit for human consumption... Adams is clearly unfit to hold an administrative post.* — ADJ CLASSIF : PRED, USU *for*/*to*-INF

3 If something **unfits** you for a task or role, it makes you unable or unwilling to do the task or fulfil the role. EG *They introduced western styles of education which unfitted people for a constructive role in society.* — V+O+A *(for)*

unflagging /ʌnflægɪŋ/. Something that is **unflagging** is maintained without any reduction in effort, intensity, or enthusiasm. EG *She felt encouraged by his unflagging attention... ...a lifetime of unflagging scrutiny.* — ADJ CLASSIF = tireless

unflappable /ʌnflæpəbəl/. Someone who is **unflappable** is always calm and never panics or gets upset or angry; a rather informal word. — ADJ QUALIT = phlegmatic

unflattering /ʌnflætəⁿrɪŋ/. Something that is **unflattering** makes someone or something seem less attractive than they really are. EG *...an unflattering picture of his mother... ...an unflattering haircut... ...an unflattering description of the city.* — ADJ QUALIT

unfocused /ʌnfəʊkəst/; also spelled **unfocussed**. 1 If someone's eyes are **unfocused**, they are open, but not looking at anything. EG *...his unfocused gaze resting on each peak in turn.* — ADJ CLASSIF

2 If someone's desires, aims, or intentions are **unfocused**, they have not got a particular purpose in mind. EG *...unfocused raw energy.* — ADJ CLASSIF

unfold /ʌnfəʊld/, **unfolds, unfolding, unfolded.** 1 If a situation **unfolds**, it develops and becomes known or understood. EG *My reaction to his story as it unfolded was one of amazement... The great invasion plan was beginning to unfold.* V

2 If you **unfold** your plans, intentions, etc, you tell someone what they are. EG *She had soon unfolded all her plans to him... Taking a deep breath, I unfolded my proposals.* V+O

3 If you **unfold** something which has been folded, you open it so that it becomes flat. EG *She thrust a small piece of paper at me. I unfolded it.* V-ERG

unforeseen /ʌnfəsiːn/. If something is **unforeseen**, it happens unexpectedly. EG *This was an unforeseen complication.* ADJ CLASSIF

unforgettable /ʌnfəgetəbəˀl/. Something that is **unforgettable** is so good, bad, impressive, etc that it can never be forgotten. EG *It was an unforgettable experience... ...the unforgettable sound of air-raid sirens.* ◊ **unforgettably.** EG *...an unforgettably beautiful sight.* ADJ QUALIT; ◊ ADV

unforgivable /ʌnfəgɪvəbəˀl/. If something you do is **unforgivable**, it is so bad or cruel that it can never be excused. EG *...an unforgivable error in judgement... It is unforgivable to wound an animal instead of killing it.* ADJ QUALIT ⇑ unpardonable

unforgiving /ʌnfəgɪvɪŋ/. Someone who is **unforgiving** is unwilling to forgive other people for their bad or mistaken actions. EG *He is unforgiving to his enemies.* ADJ CLASSIF: IF+PREP THEN *to*

unformed /ʌnfɔːmd/. Something that is **unformed** is in an early stage of development and not fully formed. EG *...unformed ideas.* ADJ CLASSIF

unfortunate /ʌnfɔːtʃəˀnəˡt/, **unfortunates.** 1 If someone is **unfortunate**, they are unlucky and do not deserve or expect something unpleasant that happens to them. EG *He's been very unfortunate.* ▸ used of something that happens. EG *It was a very unfortunate accident... It is unfortunate that this sort of thing should happen.* ADJ QUALIT ill-fated

2 **Unfortunate** is used to describe someone who is in a very difficult or unpleasant situation and who you feel sorry for. EG *We will do our utmost to help these unfortunate people.* ADJ CLASSIF: ATTRIB = hapless

3 An **unfortunate** is someone who you feel sorry for. EG *Some of the boys taunted those unfortunates still working in the fields.* N COUNT ⇑ person

4 If you describe something as **unfortunate**, you mean that you regret it, especially because it is inappropriate or embarrassing. EG *It is rather unfortunate that the Prime Minister should have said this... It's sad about that young boy. It was an unfortunate business... ...one of those unfortunate lulls in the conversation.* ADJ QUALIT

unfortunately /ʌnfɔːtʃəˀnəˡtliˡ/. You use **unfortunately** when you are talking about an event or situation that you think is sad or disappointing, or causes regret. EG *He couldn't wait to tell Judy. Unfortunately she had already left for work... Unfortunately for you, your letter never arrived... 'Will you be here in the morning?'–'No, unfortunately I won't.'* ADV SEN

unfounded /ʌnfaʊndɪ²d/. Something that is **unfounded** is not based on facts or evidence. EG *Mr King called the allegations 'untrue and unfounded'... Our worst fears have proved unfounded.* ADJ CLASSIF = groundless

unfrequented /ʌnfriˡkwentɪ²d/. An **unfrequented** place is one where very few people go. ADJ CLASSIF ⇑ deserted

unfriendly /ʌnfrendliˡ/, **unfriendlier, unfriendliest.** Someone who is **unfriendly** is not at all friendly. EG *He looked unfriendly... Why have you now come to see me, when you were so unfriendly to me before.* ▸ used of someone's behaviour or appearance. EG *...a cold, unfriendly stare.* ADJ QUALIT ⇑ hostile

unfrocked /ʌnfrɒkt/. An **unfrocked** priest has been forbidden by the Church to perform the duties of a priest, as a punishment for his bad behaviour. ADJ CLASSIF: USU ATTRIB

unfruitful /ʌnfruːtful/. Something that is **unfruitful** does not produce results or success. EG *...twelve years of unfruitful experience... This line of questioning proved unfruitful.* ADJ QUALIT = fruitless

unfulfilled /ʌnfulfɪld/. 1 If something is **unfulfilled**, it has not produced the expected results or had the success that was thought possible. EG *He has a sense of unfulfilled destiny... ...a country with unfulfilled potential for tourism.* ADJ CLASSIF: USU ATTRIB

2 If someone is **unfulfilled**, they feel dissatisfied with what they have achieved in life. ADJ QUALIT

unfurl /ʌnfɜːl/, **unfurls, unfurling, unfurled.** If you **unfurl** an umbrella, sail, flag, etc, or if it **unfurls**, you unroll or unfold it so that it is flat or spread out, and can be used or seen. EG *He began to unfurl a large scale map... The sails unfurled and filled in the breeze.* V-ERG

unfurnished /ʌnfɜːnɪʃt/. An **unfurnished** flat, house, etc has no furniture in it; used especially to describe a place that is available for sale or rent. ADJ CLASSIF

ungainly /ʌngeɪnliˡ/. **Ungainly** people are awkward or clumsy in the way they move. EG *I thought him terribly ungainly when he danced.* ADJ QUALIT

ungenerous /ʌndʒenəˀrəs/; a fairly formal word. 1 Someone who is **ungenerous** is selfish or is unwilling to give much money to other people. EG *You won't find me ungenerous.* ▸ used of an action, amount of money, etc. EG *...an irregular but not ungenerous allowance.* ADJ QUALIT ⇑ mean = stingy

2 If you or your remarks, thoughts, etc are **ungenerous**, you are judging or treating them unfairly or harshly. EG *I felt as we talked that I had been ungenerous to George... I should not be ungenerous in my thoughts.* ADJ QUALIT = uncharitable

ungodly /ʌngɒdliˡ/. 1 **Ungodly** is used to describe something that seems unreasonable to you and is therefore annoying; an informal use. EG *I had to get up at an ungodly hour... That thing made an ungodly racket.* ADJ CLASSIF: ATTRIB = unholy

2 **Ungodly** behaviour, language, etc is sinful or blasphemous. ADJ CLASSIF

ungovernable /ʌngʌvəˀnəbəˀl/. 1 An **ungovernable** country, state, region, etc is not able to be controlled or governed effectively by the government or other authority. EG *We'll make the province ungovernable.* ADJ CLASSIF ⇑ uncontrollable

2 **Ungovernable** feelings cannot be controlled. EG *Josie's worst problem was her ungovernable temper.* ADJ CLASSIF

ungracious /ʌngreɪʃəs/. If you are **ungracious**, you are not polite or friendly in your speech or behaviour, especially when someone is apologizing to you or thanking you. EG *Don't be so ungracious... ...an ungracious reply.* ADJ QUALIT ⇑ rude

ungrateful /ʌngreɪtful/. If someone is **ungrateful**, they do not show that they are thankful for something that someone has kindly or generously given them or done for them. EG *I don't want to sound ungrateful... It was ungrateful of me.* ◊ **ungratefully.** ADJ QUALIT; ◊ ADV

unguarded /ʌngɑːdɪ²d/. 1 If something is left **unguarded**, it is left without anyone to protect or look after it. EG *I couldn't go without leaving my suitcase unguarded.* ADJ CLASSIF

2 An **unguarded** moment is one when you are careless in what you say or do, with the result that someone discovers something you did not want them to know. EG *I told him, in an unguarded moment, what I planned to do.* ADJ CLASSIF: USU ATTRIB

3 If someone or what they say is **unguarded**, they show their true feelings in a wholehearted way and without worrying about the consequences; used showing approval. EG *His comment drew unguarded support from the others.* ◊ **unguardedly.** EG *There was a good chance he might talk unguardedly.* ADJ QUALIT ⇑ open = frank; ◊ ADV WITH VB ⇑ carelessly

unhampered /ʌnhæmpəd/. If you are **unhampered** by a particular problem or difficulty, you are free from it. EG *This would give black people the opportunity to live unhampered by racism... The new stock market is unhampered by tradition.* ADJ CLASSIF: PRED+*by*

unhappily /ʌnhæpɪliˡ/. 1 If you do something **unhappily**, you are not happy or contented while you do it. EG *He trudged unhappily along the crunchy gravel towards the house... The first week of school had passed unhappily.* ADV WITH VB ⇑ sadly

2 You use **unhappily** to say that you regret a particular situation or event and that you wish that it was different. EG *Unhappily, George Devine had died by the time Ralph got to America... Unhappily, due to the present local difficulties we are unable to supply you with these goods... But it is also unhappily clear that these demands are unreasonable.* ADV SEN = regrettably

unhappy /ʌnhæpiˡ/, **unhappier, unhappiest.** 1 If you are **unhappy**, you are very sad and depressed, especially because you have had a painful or unpleasant experience. EG *I'd rarely seen a man look so unhappy... He lapsed into an unhappy silence... I had an unhappy time at school.* ◊ **unhappiness.** EG *The whole episode caused her intense unhappiness and anguish... She wanted to save her sister from unhappiness.* ADJ QUALIT; ◊ N UNCOUNT

2 If you are **unhappy** about something, you are rather worried and not pleased about it. EG *The residents of the area are unhappy about the crowds and the noise... He was unhappy with the returns on his investments.... I'd be rather unhappy to see that happen.* ADJ QUALIT: PRED+A/to-INF

3 An **unhappy** situation, choice, remark, etc is one which is considered to be undesirable or inappropriate because it may cause problems or embarrassment. EG *This unhappy state of affairs would not exist if all Ministers acted in a responsible way... He referred in his speech to an unhappy accident that had taken place only a few months earlier... ...an unhappy phrase.* ADJ QUALIT: ATTRIB ⇑ unfortunate

4 **Unhappy** can also be used to describe someone who is in a very difficult or unpleasant situation and who you feel sorry for. EG *Five seconds later, the unhappy young man was face to face with his managing director.* ADJ QUALIT: ATTRIB ⇑ sad

unharmed /ʌnhɑːmd/. If someone or something is **unharmed**, they are not hurt or damaged in any way. EG *The four men managed to escape unharmed... The plane was diverted to allow a flight of wild geese to go on their way, unharmed, to the South.* ADJ CLASSIF

unhealthy /ʌnhɛlθi¹/, **unhealthier, unhealthiest.** 1 Something that is **unhealthy** is likely to cause illness or poor health. EG *This is probably the most unhealthy place in the world... Damp clothes are unhealthy.* ADJ QUALIT ⇑ harmful

2 If you are **unhealthy**, you are not very fit or well. ADJ QUALIT

3 **Unhealthy** skin, hair, etc shows that someone is ill or in poor health. EG *He had gray-white unhealthy skin.* ADJ QUALIT

4 **Unhealthy** is used to describe behaviour or attitudes that seem extreme and unnatural, and are considered to be psychologically harmful. EG *...an unhealthy interest in sex.* ADJ QUALIT = unwholesome

unheard /ʌnhɜːd/. If something goes **unheard**, it is not listened to or taken into consideration. EG *The wishes of the minority go unheard... He wrote me off, unheard, long before my trial.* ADJ CLASSIF: USU PRED ⇑ unheeded

unheard of; spelled with a hyphen when used before a noun. 1 If an event or situation is **unheard of**, it has never happened before and so is very surprising. EG *Contracts and written agreements are quite unheard of.* ADJ CLASSIF ⇑ unknown

2 Behaviour or events which are **unheard of** are shocking and offensive. EG *This is an unheard-of outrage.* ADJ CLASSIF

3 Someone who is **unheard of** is not famous or well-known. EG *...an unheard-of author.* ADJ CLASSIF = unknown

unheeded /ʌnhiːdɪ²d/. If something goes **unheeded**, it has been noticed but is not dealt with or taken seriously. EG *His cries would have gone unheeded... Our petitions were unheeded.* ADJ CLASSIF: USU PRED

unhelpful /ʌnhɛlpfʊl/. If someone is **unhelpful**, they make no effort to improve a situation and may even make it worse. EG *He didn't want to seem unhelpful.* ▸ used of information, advice, etc. EG *His mother gave him plenty of unhelpful advice.* ADJ QUALIT
◇ **unhelpfulness.** ◇ N UNCOUNT

unheralded /ʌnhɛrəldɪ²d/. If something is **unheralded**, there is no indication beforehand that it is going to happen. EG *...Tim's unheralded arrival at the party... The Prince arrived unheralded in India.* ADJ CLASSIF ⇑ unannounced

unhesitating /ʌnhɛzɪteɪtɪŋ/. If something you do, believe, or say is **unhesitating**, it is confident and immediate and not stopped or weakened by feelings of fear, embarrassment, etc. EG *His reply was unhesitating and to the point... ...spontaneous, unhesitating faith.* ADJ QUALIT ◇ **unhesitatingly.** EG *McCalden replied unhesitatingly.* ◇ ADV WITH VB

unhinge /ʌnhɪnd⁰ʒ/, **unhinges, unhinging, unhinged.** If an experience **unhinges** someone, it affects them so deeply that they become mentally ill. EG *Pregnancy had unhinged her.* V+O ⇑ disturb

unhinged /ʌnhɪnd⁰ʒd⁰/. If someone is **unhinged**, they have become mentally ill because of an experience that has affected them deeply. EG *According to Morris, Gordon Masters is quite unhinged.* ADJ QUALIT ⇑ insane = crazy

unholy /ʌnhəʊli¹/. 1 Something that is **unholy** is wicked or sinful. EG *...an unholy union of dark and ancient superstitions... I discovered the unholy pleasures of gossip and malice.* ADJ QUALIT ⇑ evil

2 **Unholy** is used to emphasize how unreasonable or unpleasant you think something is. EG *What's your business at this unholy hour of two in the morning?... Your bed is in an unholy mess.* ADJ CLASSIF: ATTRIB

3 An **unholy** alliance, union, etc, is one in which two or more people, groups, or forces come together for a common purpose, although it is unusual and often worrying or undesirable that they should come together in this way. EG *...an unholy alliance between Conservative and Labour MPs during the debate... ...the unholy marriage of political and economic power.* ADJ CLASSIF: ATTRIB

unhook /ʌnhʊk/, **unhooks, unhooking, unhooked.** 1 If you unhook a piece of clothing such as a bra, you unfasten the hooks on it. V+O ⇑ undo

2 If you **unhook** something, you remove it from a hook. EG *She followed him into the hall, where he unhooked his hat and coat.* V+O

unhurried /ʌnhʌrɪd/. Something that is **unhurried** is relaxed and slow and is not rushed or anxious. EG *Her voice was calm and unhurried... There were a lot of people strolling about in an unhurried sort of way.* ◇ **unhurriedly.** EG *She walked unhurriedly out of the building.* ADJ CLASSIF: USU PRED ⇑ leisurely ◇ ADV WITH VB ⇑ leisurely

unhurt /ʌnhɜːt/. If someone is **unhurt**, they are not injured after they have been attacked, been in an accident, etc. EG *The pilot was unhurt and climbed out with a cheerful grin... Two men crawled out unhurt.* ADJ CLASSIF: PRED

unhygienic /ʌnhaɪdʒiːnɪk/. Something that is **unhygienic** is dirty and likely to cause infection or disease. EG *...tiny unhygienic cages.* ADJ QUALIT

unicorn /juːnɪkɔːn/, **unicorns.** A **unicorn** is an imaginary animal that looks like a white horse and has a horn growing from its forehead. N COUNT

unidentifiable /ʌnaɪdɛntɪfaɪəbə⁰l/. If something is **unidentifiable**, you are not able to say exactly what it is. EG *He paused at a small unidentifiable sound from outside the room.* ADJ CLASSIF

unidentified /ʌnaɪdɛntɪfaɪd/. You use **unidentified** 1 to describe people, groups, and organizations when you or they do not want to give their names. EG *...the house of an unidentified Scottish merchant... The newspaper quoted unidentified sources in London.* 2 to describe things, people, and places that you cannot recognize or whose actual identity is unknown to you. EG *Many people had been convinced that they had seen unidentified flying objects... There was also an unidentified division just the other side of the airfield.* ADJ CLASSIF: USU ATTRIB = anonymous, unnamed ADJ CLASSIF: USU ATTRIB = unfamiliar

unification /juːnɪfɪkeɪʃə⁰n/ is the act of unifying something, or the result of doing this. EG *A process of economic unification is taking place... ...the unification of Italy.* N UNCOUNT: USU +SUPP ⇑ consolidation

uniform /juːnɪfɔːm/, **uniforms.** 1 A **uniform** is 1.1 a special set of clothes which some people, for example soldiers or the police, wear to work in and which some children wear at school. EG *...a man in the uniform of a captain in the Air Force... She wasn't in uniform.* 1.2 a particular style of clothing which a group of people wear to show they belong to a group or a movement. EG *The movement's uniform consisted of jeans and jerseys.* N COUNT/UNCOUNT N COUNT/UNCOUNT

2 If something is **uniform**, it does not vary, but is even and regular throughout. EG *...a structure of uniform width... ...a uniform distribution of load.* ◇ **uniformly.** EG *The weather throughout the region was uniformly good.* ADJ CLASSIF ◇ ADV

3 If you describe a number of things as **uniform**, you mean that they all look or are exactly the same. EG *The street consisted of uniform tall, white buildings.* ◇ **uniformly.** EG *The ceilings were uniformly low.* ADJ CLASSIF ⇑ identical ◇ ADV

uniformed /juːnɪfɔːmd/ people are wearing a uniform. EG *...uniformed policemen.* ADJ CLASSIF: USU ATTRIB

uniformity /juːnɪfɔːmɪti¹/ is a state in which everyone or everything behaves or looks the same as everyone or everything else. EG *The dreary uniformity of the housing estate appalls me... Is there a move towards uniformity between the countries in the EEC?* N UNCOUNT = sameness

unify /juːnɪfaɪ/, **unifies, unifying, unified.** 1 If you **unify** a number of things or people, you join or bring them together, for example so that they become a whole, or so that they agree to work together for a particular purpose. EG *Smaller tribes are unified into larger societies... ...a unified labour movement.* ◇ **unifying.** EG *...the importance of Hinduism as a unifying cultural force.* V+O ⇑ organize ◇ ADJ CLASSIF: USU ATTRIB

2 If you **unify** a number of things that had previously V+O

been different, you change them so that they become all the same. EG *Gauges had been unified, equipment standardized... We need to agree on a unified basic price.*

unilateral /juːnɪlætəᵒrəl/. A **unilateral** decision, declaration, etc is made by only one of the groups, organizations, or countries that are involved in a particular situation. EG *We will take unilateral action.* ◊ **unilaterally**. — ADJ CLASSIF : USU ATTRIB ⇑ one-sided; ◊ ADV

unilateral disarmament is the process or policy by which a country gets rid of its own nuclear weapons without waiting for other countries to agree to do the same. — N UNCOUNT ⇑ renunciation

unilateralism /juːnɪlætəᵒrəlɪzəᵒm/ is belief in unilateral disarmament. EG *The party had reversed its support of unilateralism in 1961.* ◊ **unilateralist, unilateralists.** EG *I am personally not a unilateralist.* — N UNCOUNT; ◊ N COUNT

unimaginable /ʌnɪmædʒɪnəbəᵒl/. Something that is **unimaginable** is difficult to imagine or understand properly, because it is not part of people's normal experience. EG *...the unimaginable vastness of space... Experiments were carried out under almost unimaginable conditions.* — ADJ CLASSIF = inconceivable

unimaginative /ʌnɪmædʒɪnətɪv/. 1 Someone who is **unimaginative** does not use their imagination enough in what they do and therefore fail to arouse other people's interest or enthusiasm. EG *...unimaginative teachers.* — ADJ QUALIT ≠ creative

2 Something that is **unimaginative** is dull and unattractive because very little imagination or effort has been used on it. EG *...plain, unimaginative clothes.* — ADJ QUALIT = boring

unimpaired /ʌnɪmpeəd/. If something is **unimpaired**, it is not damaged or made worse by a bad or unpleasant experience. EG *Her style and technique were quite unimpaired by her long absence from the theatre.* — ADJ CLASSIF

unimpeachable /ʌnɪmpiːtʃəbəᵒl/. If you describe someone as **unimpeachable**, you mean that they are completely honest and reliable and should not be doubted. EG *The woman was of unimpeachable character... She had been told by the most unimpeachable source: his mother.* — ADJ CLASSIF = impeccable

unimpeded /ʌnɪmpiːdɪ²d/. Something that is **unimpeded** goes on happening without being stopped or interrupted by anything. EG *...an unimpeded flow of information... ...making it impossible for her to walk asay unimpeded.* — ADJ CLASSIF, OR ADV

unimportant /ʌnɪmpɔːtənt/. If something is **unimportant**, it has very little significance or importance. EG *...a relatively unimportant feature of the system... The whole question seemed unimportant.* — ADJ QUALIT = minor, trivial

unimpressed /ʌnɪmprest/. If you are **unimpressed** by someone or something, you do not think they are very good, unusual, or worth your attention. EG *'I am Andre Casson', he added. Kowalski seemed unimpressed... Thus far, Wall Street has been notably unimpressed.* — ADJ QUALIT : PRED ⇑ unaffected = unmoved

unimpressive /ʌnɪmpresɪv/. If someone or something is **unimpressive**, they do not immediately make you think they are very good, unusual, or worth your attention. EG *On the whole the results of this system are unimpressive... Barney's wife was an unimpressive little woman.* — ADJ QUALIT = insignificant

uninformed /ʌnɪnfɔːmd/. Someone who is **uninformed** does not have very much knowledge or information about a particular subject. EG *This must have seemed quite plausible to the uninformed reader.* — ADJ CLASSIF ⇑ ignorant

uninhabitable /ʌnɪnhæbɪtəbəᵒl/. An **uninhabitable** place is one where it is impossible for people to live. EG *Worldwide pollution threatens to make the planet uninhabitable.* — ADJ CLASSIF

uninhabited /ʌnɪnhæbɪtɪ²d/. An **uninhabited** place or house is one where nobody lives. EG *...an uninhabited island.* — ADJ CLASSIF ⇑ empty = unoccupied

uninhibited /ʌnɪnhɪbɪtɪ²d/. If you are **uninhibited** in your behaviour, you behave freely and naturally and show your real feelings, without worrying at all about what you say or do, or what other people think about you; often used showing approval. EG *The table talk was easy and uninhibited... ...a sound of uninhibited laughter.* — ADJ QUALIT

uninitiated /ʌnɪnɪʃieɪtɪ²d/. 1 Someone who is **uninitiated** has no knowledge or experience of something. EG *This must seem a bizarre ceremony to uninitiated western eyes.* — ADJ CLASSIF = unaccustomed

2 The **uninitiated** are the people who have no knowledge or experience of something. EG *For the uninitiated, may I say that golf is one game that demands patience and concentration... ...branches of science which, to the uninitiated, may seem quite irrelevant to cancer.* — N PLURAL : *the*+ N

uninspired /ʌnɪnspaɪəd/. Someone or something that is **uninspired** is dull and not lively or exciting, and fails to arouse interest or enthusiasm in other people. EG *The production was professional but uninspired.* — ADJ QUALIT

uninspiring /ʌnɪnspaɪərɪŋ/. Someone or something that is **uninspiring** is dull and not likely to cause interest or excitement. EG *...a villa of uninspiring design.* — ADJ QUALIT = unexciting

unintelligent /ʌnɪntelɪdʒəᵒnt/. Someone who is **unintelligent** is stupid. EG *They were lazy and unintelligent.* — ADJ QUALIT

unintelligible /ʌnɪntelɪdʒəˈbəᵒl/. Something that is **unintelligible** is impossible to understand, for example because you cannot read it or hear it properly, or because it is very muddled or confusing. EG *The script was unintelligible... He answered in words unintelligible to her.* ◊ **unintelligibly**. EG *She continued muttering unintelligibly.* — ADJ QUALIT = incomprehensible; ◊ ADV WITH VB

unintended /ʌnɪntendɪ²d/ is used to describe something that happens but that was not planned to happen or intended to have a particular effect. EG *...the unintended consequences of advertising on television.* — ADJ CLASSIF = accidental

unintentional /ʌnɪntenʃəᵒnəl, -ʃənəᵒl/. Something that is **unintentional** is not done deliberately, but happens by accident. EG *...an unintentional pun.* ◊ **unintentionally.** EG *It seems I unintentionally made a rude gesture.* — ADJ CLASSIF; ◊ ADV WITH VB

uninterested /ʌnɪntəᵒrɪstɪ²d/. If you are **uninterested** in someone or something, you have no interest in them, opinions about them, or feelings towards them. EG *Etta appeared totally uninterested... Lionel was uninterested in the house.* — ADJ QUALIT : USU +*in*

uninteresting /ʌnɪntəᵒrɪ²stɪŋ/. Someone or something that is **uninteresting** is boring or dull. EG *He found her uninteresting as a person... 'They are always talking about science.'-'Oh, how uninteresting.'* — ADJ QUALIT

uninterrupted /ʌnɪntərʌptɪ²d/. If something is **uninterrupted**, it is continuous and has no breaks or interruptions in it. EG *Lynn did some uninterrupted reading... ...a long uninterrupted facade.* — ADJ CLASSIF

uninvited /ʌnɪnvaɪtɪ²d/. Someone who is **uninvited** does something or goes somewhere without being asked, often when their action or presence is not wanted. EG *...uninvited guests... Henry sat down uninvited on the side of the bed.* — ADJ CLASSIF

union /juːnjən/, **unions**. 1 A **union** is an organization formed by workers which represents their rights and has the aim of improving such things as the working conditions, pay, and benefits of its members. EG *...Mr. Ray Buckton, leader of the train drivers' union, ASLEF... In some industries you are compelled to join a union as a condition of getting a job.* — N COUNT : ALSO IN NAMES = trade union

2 **Union** is used 2.1 in the name of some clubs and societies. EG *The Students' Union has written to complain... ...the Mother's Union.* 2.2 in the name of some countries, when a group of countries or states have been joined into one for political reasons. EG *...the Soviet Union... ...the Union of South Africa.* — N IN NAMES ⇑ association; N IN NAMES

3 **Union** is the act of joining two or more things so that they become one; also the state of being joined in this way. EG *We are working for the union of the two countries.* — N UNCOUNT

4 The marriage of two people is sometimes referred to as a **union**; a formal use. EG *God will bless this union.* — N COUNT : USU SING

unionise /juːnjənaɪz/. See **unionize**.

unionism /juːnjənɪzəᵒm/. **Unionism** is 1 the same as trade unionism. 2 any set of political principles based on the idea that two political units should be joined, for example the political belief that Northern Ireland should remain part of the United Kingdom. — N UNCOUNT; N UNCOUNT

unionist /juːnjənɪst/, **unionists**. A **unionist** is 1 a member of a trade union or a supporter of a trade-union movement. 2 a believer in a political union, for example the political union between Northern Ireland and the rest of th United Kingdom. — N COUNT; N COUNT

unionize /juːnjənaɪz/, **unionizes, unionizing, unionized**; also spelled **unionise**. When a group of — V-ERG : IF V+O THEN USU PASS workers **unionize** or **are unionized**, they join or form a trade union in their place of work. EG *Clothing workers went on strike over the right to unionize... ...Belgium, where 71 per cent of employees are unionised.* ◊ **unionization** /ju:njənaɪzeɪʃə⁰n/. EG *...unionization of women office workers.* ◊ N UNCOUNT ⇑ organization

Union Jack, Union Jacks. The **Union Jack** is the national flag of Great Britain and Northern Ireland. N SING : *the*+N, OR N COUNT

unique /ju:ni:k/. **1** Something that is **unique** is **1.1** the only one of its kind. EG *..that unique human ability–speech.* ADJ CLASSIF = singular ◊ **uniqueness.** EG *...the uniqueness of the individual.* ◊ N UNCOUNT **1.2** very unusual and special; used especially of something you admire. EG *It was a unique and exquisite performance... He had a unique knowledge of the mentality of the Emperor.* ADJ CLASSIF ⇑ extraordinary = exceptional ◊ **uniquely.** EG *He had a fine singing voice, uniquely gentle and deep.* ◊ ADV+ADJ/ ADV

2 If something is **unique** to one thing, person, or group, it concerns or belongs to this thing, person, or group only. EG *These problems are not unique to nuclear power.* ADJ CLASSIF : PRED+*to* ⇑ peculiar ◊ **uniquely.** EG *His sources should be confined uniquely to those in a position to give valuable information.* ◊ ADV WITH VB

unisex /ju:nɪsɛks/ is used to describe things, usually clothes or hairdressing salons, which are designed for use by both men and women rather than by only one sex. EG *The women were dressed in nondescript, unisex clothes.* ADJ CLASSIF

unison /ju:nɪsən, -zən/. **1** If a group of people do something such as speak **in unison**, they all do it together at the same time. EG *'All of us,' they said in unison... They all fired in unison.* PHR : USED AS AN A = simultaneously

2 If a group of people sing **in unison**, they all sing the same notes together at the same time. PHR : USED AS AN A

3 If two people are **in unison** with each other, they completely agree with each other. EG *Despite our differences, we have acted in unison in our outside dealings.* PHR : USED AS AN A ⇑ in agreement

unit /ju:nɪt/, **units. 1** A **unit** refers to something that is considered as a single, complete thing, often a group of people or things being considered together for a particular reason. EG *It is not realistic to treat the world as a unit, because resources are very unevenly distributed... The Gold Coast came into being as a single unit in 1901... ...the decline of the family as a self-sufficient unit.* N COUNT ⇑ whole

2 A **unit** is also **2.1** a group of people who work together at a specific job, often in a particular place. EG *Hospital staff are fighting to keep the heart unit... An American documentary unit happened to be working on a programme... He was shot in a skirmish with a loyalist army unit.* ▸ also used to refer to the equipment and buildings that these people use. EG *...an outside broadcast unit.* N COUNT : ALSO IN NAMES ⇑ team **2.2** a small machine which has a particular function, often part of a larger machine. EG *If the cooling unit gets clogged up with ice it can't do its job properly... ...a power supply unit... ...a waste-disposal unit.* N COUNT : USU MOD+N **2.3** a piece of furniture or other equipment for a building, which can be put together with other pieces to fit into the space available. EG *...kitchen units... ...factory units... ...hi-fi units.* N COUNT : USU AFTER N **2.4** a fixed, standard quantity, length, weight, etc that is used for measuring things. EG *...a unit of electricity... The second is a unit of time... Their basic unit of currency is the franc.* N COUNT/PART

3 In arithmetic, a **unit** is **3.1** a whole number which is less than 10. EG *This column is for the tens and this one is for the units.* N COUNT **3.2** the number one, considered as a quantity rather than as a number; a technical use. EG *The number three can be thought of as three units.* N COUNT

unite /ju:naɪt/, **unites, uniting, united. 1** If a group of people or things **unite** or if you **unite** them, they join together and act as a group, for example because they share the same belief or aim. EG *When hunting, the animals unite to form a large team... Councils must be built in every area to unite all working class organizations in the struggle... I think some unseen bond unites us.* V-ERG ⇑ combine

2 If you **unite** things that are separate, or if they **unite**, you join them together so that they become one whole thing or area. EG *This measure would unite all the provinces and form a single state... The two types unite in a new amalgamated cell.* V-ERG = amalgamate

3 If you **unite** one quality with another, you possess both qualities at the same time. EG *He manages to unite charm with an ability to organise people.* V+O : USU+A (*with*) = combine

united /ju:naɪtɪ²d/. **1** If a group of people are **united** about something, they agree with each other about it and act together. EG *The workers are united in their aims... They were united in their dislike of authority... Members of the group are presenting a united front to the world.* ADJ CLASSIF ⇑ agreed

2 If different areas, groups, etc are **united**, they have been joined together to form a single country or organization. EG *Some people want a united Ireland... ...the United States... ...the United Nations.* ADJ CLASSIF : ALSO IN NAMES

United Kingdom. The **United Kingdom** is the official name for Great Britain and Northern Ireland. N PROPER : *the*+N

United Nations. The **United Nations** is an organization formed after World War II which many countries belong to. It tries to encourage international peace, cooperation, and friendship. EG *The United Nations has passed two resolutions calling for fresh talks.* N PROPER : *the*+N

unit trust, unit trusts. A **unit trust** is an organization which invests money in many different types of business and which offers units for sale to the public as an investment; used in British English. N COUNT

unity /ju:nɪti¹/ is **1** the state of people being in agreement and acting together for a particular purpose. EG *There is a need for greater unity in the party... They have no real cultural or political unity... There is little unity of purpose among the members.* N UNCOUNT ⇑ solidarity = harmony

2 the state of different areas or groups being joined together to form a single complete country, organization, etc. EG *The spokesman personally favoured unity with the Arab nation... They are discussing church unity.* N UNCOUNT = union

Univ. is a written abbreviation for 'University'. EG *...Maths Dept, Univ. of Keele.*

universal /ju:nɪvɜ:sə⁰l/, **universals. 1** Something that is **universal 1.1** relates to everyone in the world or everyone in a particular group or society; used for example of something that is common to everyone, that is available for everyone, or that affects everyone. EG *They touched on various topics of universal interest... ...the almost universal refusal on the part of the leaders... Western Nigeria introduced universal primary education in '56 or so... Every new fact discovered by science adds to the universal store of human knowledge.* ADJ CLASSIF : USU ATTRIB ⇑ widespread ◊ **universality** /ju:nɪvɜ:sælɪti¹/. EG *...its pretensions to universality, its claim to include the whole of mankind... ...the universality of art.* ◊ N UNCOUNT ⇑ ubiquity **1.2** affects or relates to every part of the world or the universe. EG *The threat of universal extinction hangs over all the world... The laws that govern the behaviour of light are universal.* ADJ CLASSIF **1.3** is true or relevant at all times and in all situations. EG *Perhaps it is a mistake to seek a single universal explanation... ...a universal truth.* ADJ CLASSIF : USU ATTRIB ⇑ absolute

2 A **universal** is something that seems to be the same or equally true at all times and in all situations. EG *...universals such as beauty and justice... We must begin from universals of experience.* N COUNT ⇑ absolute

universally /ju:nɪvɜ:səli¹/. **1** If something is **universally** believed, it is believed by everyone with no disagreement. EG *This explanation is not yet universally accepted... He was universally respected for his steadiness of character... The universally held opinion is that she is mad.* ADV WITH VB ⇑ generally

2 If something is **universally** the case, it is the case everywhere in the world or in all situations. EG *One thing was universally true... Tips are now almost universally included in hotel bills.* ADV ⇑ generally

universe /ju:nɪvɜ:s/, **universes.** The **universe** is **1** the whole of space and all the stars, planets, and other forms of matter and energy in it. EG *...trying to understand how the universe has evolved... They thought the earth was the centre of the universe.* N COUNT : USU *the*+N IN SING **2** the world, or the part of it that we live in and have experience of. EG *It is the most wicked place in the universe... Each person is the centre of his own universe.* N COUNT : USU *the*+N IN SING

university /ju:nɪvɜ:sɪti¹/, **universities.** A **university** is an institution where students study for degrees and where academic research is done. EG *She is a student at Norwich University... Her one aim in life is to go to university... The university has cut admissions by 20 per cent this year.* N COUNT, OR *at*+N : ALSO IN NAMES

unjust /ʌndʒʌst/. Someone or something that is **unjust** is not fair, reasonable, or just; used showing disapproval. EG *...regulations that are felt to be* ADJ QUALIT ⇑ wrong = inequitable *unjust... ...a thoroughly unjust society.* ◊ **unjustly.** EG *...schoolmates who had unjustly accused him of bullying.* ◊ ADV = unfairly

unjustifiable /ʌndʒʌstɪfaɪəbəˡl/. An action that is **unjustifiable** is wrong, unfair, or unacceptable, and so cannot be explained or excused; used showing disapproval. EG *...an unjustifiable and unpopular increase in licence fees... The development would be an unjustifiable extravagance.* ◊ **unjustifiably.** EG *The petition had been unjustifiably denied.* ADJ QUALIT = inexcusable ◊ ADV WITH VB = inexcusably

unjustified /ʌndʒʌstɪfaɪd/. A belief, action, etc that is **unjustified** is wrong or unnecessary and cannot be explained or excused. EG *His pessimism was unjustified... It was an unjustified attack.* ADJ QUALIT = unfounded, unreasonable

unkempt /ʌŋˡkempt/. Something that is **unkempt** is untidy and not looked after carefully or kept neat. EG *He had a shaggy, unkempt beard... The already derelict garden grew increasingly unkempt.* ADJ QUALIT ⇑ neglected

unkind /ʌŋˡkaɪnd/, **unkinder, unkindest.** Someone who is **unkind** to you behaves towards you in a rather cruel and unpleasant way. EG *Don't be so unkind–give her some.* ▸ used of actions and behaviour. EG *...a silly and unkind remark.* ◊ **unkindly.** EG *'Do it yourself,' said Arthur unkindly.* ◊ **unkindness.** EG *He wished to make amends for his former unkindness to her.* ADJ QUALIT ◊ ADV WITH VB ◊ N UNCOUNT

unknowable /ʌnnəʊəbəˡl/. If you describe something as **unknowable**, you mean that it is impossible for human beings to know anything about it. EG *The future is unknowable... For him, God was wholly transcendent, unknowable.* ADJ CLASSIF

unknowing /ʌnnəʊɪŋ/ is used to describe someone who is not aware of a particular fact, situation, or thing that is happening or that they are doing. EG *...an unknowing fool... ...an unknowing victim.* ◊ **unknowingly.** EG *William was unknowingly strengthening my trap.* ADJ CLASSIF : ATTRIB ⇑ ignorant = unwitting ◊ ADV WITH VB

unknown /ʌnnəʊn/, **unknowns. 1** A fact that is **unknown** to you is one that you do not know about. EG *The identity of the bombers remained unknown... ...this man Boris, whose real name is unknown to me... It is suspected that there are unknown effects on the body and brain.* ▸ used as a noun. EG *We are at our most insecure in the morning, with all the unknowns of the day ahead of us.* ▸ The **unknown** refers generally to things or places that people do not know about or understand. EG *...fear of the unknown... ...a journey into the unknown.* ● If you say that something is happening **unknown to** a particular person, you mean that it is happening without the person mentioned knowing. EG *Unknown to them, he is nearby.* ADJ CLASSIF = unidentified ▸ N COUNT ▸ N SING : the+N ⇑ mysterious ● PHR+NG : USED AS AN A

2 An **unknown** person is **2.1** someone whose name you do not know or whose character you do not know very well. EG *Some unknown person coughed lightly... She wouldn't be alone with an unknown male visitor.* **2.2** not famous or publicly recognized. EG *In Britain he is almost unknown.* ▸ used as a noun. EG *I wanted it played by a cast of unknowns.* ADJ CLASSIF : USU ATTRIB = stranger ADJ QUALIT ▸ N COUNT

unlawful /ʌnlɔːfʊl/. Something that is **unlawful** is not legal. EG *This Act was declared unlawful by the Supreme Court... ...unlawful business activities.* ADJ CLASSIF = illegal

unlearn /ʌnlɜːn/, **unlearns, unlearning, unlearned, unlearnt.** The forms **unlearned** and **unlearnt** are both used for the past tense and past participle of the verb. If you **unlearn** something that you have learned, you try to forget it or ignore it, often because it is wrong or it is having a bad influence on you. EG *It is learned behaviour and, as such, can be unlearned... A lot of things had to be unlearned before you could learn anything at all.* V+O

unleash /ʌnliːʃ/, **unleashes, unleashing, unleashed.** If someone or something **unleashes** a powerful or violent force, feeling, etc, they release it so that it has a sudden strong impact. EG *How could they have justified all the violence unleashed on the prisoners?... The destructive forces unleashed cannot be brought under control... Tremendous heat was unleashed... Strong feelings had been unleashed in me by the news of the bomb.* V+O

unleavened /ʌnlevənd/ bread or dough is made without any yeast. EG *...dry unleavened bread.* ADJ CLASSIF : USU ATTRIB

unless /ʌnles/. You use **unless** to introduce the only circumstances in which an event you are mentioning will not take place or in which a statement you are making is not true. EG *One major advertiser phoned me to say that unless the paper stopped my editorials he would withdraw his advertisements... I couldn't get a grant unless I had five years' teaching experience... Unless I was very much mistaken, there was something wrong with Louise... She said nothing unless spoken to... There might be a problem finding a house, unless you can somehow build your own.* CONJ SUBORD

unlike /ʌnlaɪk/. **1** If one thing is **unlike** another thing, the two things have different qualities or characteristics from each other. EG *Their own tongue, Tamazight, is totally unlike Arabic... Rodin was unlike his predecessor in every way... It was quite unlike any flu I had experienced before... ...a child with fair, frizzy hair not unlike Rose's own.* ▸ used as an adjective. EG *The sisters were completely unlike in every way.* PREP = dissimilar to ▸ ADJ CLASSIF : PRED

2 You can use **unlike** to contrast two people, things, or situations, and show how they are different. EG *Mrs Hochstadt, unlike Etta, was a careful shopper... Well, I'm prepared, unlike you, to admit it... Unlike most businessmen, they are good company.* PREP

3 If you describe something that a particular person has done as being **unlike** them, you mean that you are surprised by it because it is not typical of their character or normal behaviour. EG *'How unlike Rose to be so late,' said Diana, uneasily... It was unlike her to mention such a thing.* PREP = uncharacteristic of

unlikely /ʌnlaɪkliˡ/. **1** If you say that something is **unlikely** to happen or **unlikely** to be true, you mean that you think it will probably not happen or that it is probably not true. EG *The dispute is unlikely to be settled for a long time to come... Legislation on the peerage question seemed unlikely until 1964... It is unlikely that you will get an office to yourself... They are unlikely to have relatives living nearby... In the unlikely event that they give you any trouble, write to us.* ADJ QUALIT : USU PRED+to-INF/REPORT-CL

2 You use **unlikely** to describe a situation, event, or person's behaviour that seems strange, unexpected, and sometimes slightly amusing. EG *Brody was startled by the unlikely sight of Hendricks in a bathing suit... The gathering was an unlikely conglomeration of Marxist theoreticians... He always carried an umbrella, on even the most unlikely days.* ADJ QUALIT : ATTRIB = improbable

unlimited /ʌnlɪmɪtɪˡd/. Something that is **unlimited** **1** has no limit or end, for example something that has no fixed maximum amount. EG *...a ticket that allows unlimited travel on red buses... ...if one had unlimited funds of money... They were given unlimited amounts of food.* **2** is extremely large in size or amount. EG *Its main asset was unlimited space.* ADJ CLASSIF = indefinite, infinite ADJ CLASSIF ⇑ great

unlit /ʌnlɪt/. **1** An **unlit** fire, cigarette, etc has not been lit and is therefore not burning. ADJ CLASSIF

2 An **unlit** street, building, etc is dark because it does not have any lights switched on to make it bright. ADJ CLASSIF

unload /ʌnləʊd/, **unloads, unloading, unloaded. 1** If you **unload** goods from a container or a vehicle, you remove them, usually after they have been transported from one place to another in the container or vehicle. EG *We began to unload the bricks from Philip's car... Great barges moor to unload rice from Thailand... Their business is to load and unload aircraft.* V OR V+O

2 If you **unload** a problem that you have onto someone, you tell them about it because you need advice or sympathy. EG *He wanted to unload some of the anguish onto someone else... They looked forward to a chance of unloading some of their worries.* V+O : IF+PREP THEN *onto/on* = unburden

unlock /ʌnlɒk/, **unlocks, unlocking, unlocked.** If you **unlock** something such as a door or a container that has a lock, you open it by means of a key. EG *He unlocked the door from a key on his ring... ...a large trunk which he unlocked with his own key... ...one of these chains that never unlock.* V-ERG

unlooked-for is used to describe something which you did not expect or want to happen. EG *...an unlooked-for change in the weather... Once the play has reached dress-rehearsal unlooked-for problems suddenly emerge.* ADJ CLASSIF : USU ATTRIB = unexpected

unlovable /ʌnlʌvəbəˡl/. **Unlovable** people are not likely to be loved by anyone, because they do not have any attractive qualities. ADJ QUALIT

unloved /ʌnlʌvd/. Someone who is **unloved** is not loved by anyone. EG *She was feeling unloved and unwanted.* ADJ CLASSIF = loveless

unlovely /ʌnlʌvli¹/. Something that is **unlovely** is unattractive to look at. EG *The village hall was an unlovely corrugated iron building.* — ADJ QUALIT = ugly

unloving /ʌnlʌvɪŋ/ is used to describe someone who does not love the people they ought to love. EG *...unloving parents.* — ADJ QUALIT

unluckily /ʌnlʌkɪli¹/. You use **unluckily** when mentioning something bad or unpleasant that happens to someone, when you sympathize with them. EG *...if you unluckily brush against a jellyfish when swimming... Unluckily for Henry, they were waiting for him outside.* — ADV SEN = unfortunately

unlucky /ʌnlʌki¹/. **1** Someone who is **unlucky** has bad luck. EG *It should arrive within two or three days, but if you're unlucky you may have to wait weeks... I was unlucky enough to miss the final episode... She had been unlucky in love.* ▸ used of something that happens to you. EG *...unlucky experiences.* — ADJ QUALIT = unfortunate ≠ lucky
2 Unlucky is used to describe something that is thought to cause bad luck. EG *13 is a very unlucky number.* — ADJ QUALIT ⇑ ≠ lucky

unmade /ʌm¹meɪd/. An **unmade** bed is one that has not had its sheets and blankets neatly arranged after it has been slept in. — ADJ CLASSIF

unman /ʌm¹mæn/, **unmans, unmanning, unmanned.** **1** If something **unmans** you, it makes you lose courage or determination, or makes you unable to conceal your sadness; a literary word. EG *Their kindness quite unmanned Fanny, and she broke down and wept.* — V+O
2 See also **unmanned**.

unmanageable /ʌm¹mænɪdʒəbə⁰l/. Something that is **unmanageable** is difficult to use, deal with, or control, usually because it is too big. EG *The complete encyclopaedia is quite unmanageable in its thirteen-volume glory... We have administrative problems which are becoming increasingly unmanageable.* — ADJ QUALIT ⇑ uncontrollable

unmanly /ʌm¹mænli¹/. **Unmanly** behaviour is thought to be inappropriate for a man. EG *...the attitude that it is unmanly to be domesticated.* — ADJ QUALIT = sissy

unmanned /ʌm¹mænd/. **Unmanned** aircraft, spacecraft, etc do not carry people in them. — ADJ CLASSIF

unmarked /ʌm¹mɑːkt/. Something that is **unmarked 1** has no mark on it. EG *His face was unmarked.* **2** has no marking on it which identifies what it is. EG *...unmarked police cars... ...an unmarked container.* — ADJ CLASSIF; ADJ CLASSIF

unmarried /ʌm¹mærɪd/. Someone who is **unmarried** is not married. EG *She was still unmarried... ...an unmarried mother... ...unmarried couples.* — ADJ CLASSIF

unmask /ʌm¹mɑːsk/, **unmasks, unmasking, unmasked. 1** If you **unmask** someone or something bad, you show or make known their true nature or character, when they had previously been thought to be good. EG *He liked to unmask his guests' disreputable pasts... My ineptitude had finally been unmasked.* — V+O = expose, reveal
2 If someone **unmasks** or if you **unmask** them, the mask they are wearing is removed. — V OR V+O ⇑ uncover

unmatched /ʌm¹mætʃt/. Something that is **unmatched** is is better or greater than all other things of the same kind. EG *Their products acquired a definite, personal identity, unmatched by any other brand... Mobility in the United States is probably unmatched anywhere in the world.* — ADJ CLASSIF : USU PRED = unequalled, unrivalled

unmentionable /ʌm¹menʃənəb⁰ə⁰l/. Something that is **unmentionable** is too embarrassing or unpleasant to talk about. EG *He's been through all kinds of unmentionable operations... Sex need no longer be regarded as shameful or unmentionable.* — ADJ CLASSIF = shocking

unmercifully /ʌm¹mɜːsɪfə⁰li¹/. If you do something **unmercifully**, you do it a lot, showing no mercy or pity. EG *Pointing at Rick, we teased him unmercifully... A total stranger had been bullied unmercifully into driving her home.* — ADV WITH VB = mercilessly

unmistakable /ʌm¹mɪsteɪkəbə⁰l/; also spelled **unmistakeable**. Something that is **unmistakable** is so obvious that it cannot be mistaken for anything else. EG *...the unmistakable stench of rotting eggs... Gareth's urgency was unmistakable.* ◇ **unmistakably**. EG *He was unmistakably of Italian descent.* — ADJ CLASSIF = manifest, patent; ◇ ADV OR ADV SEN

unmitigated /ʌm¹mɪtɪgeɪtɪ²d/. **Unmitigated** means total and complete; used usually of something bad, for example a disaster or failure. EG *This government's policy on higher education is an unmitigated disaster.* — ADJ CLASSIF : ATTRIB = utter, absolute

unmolested /ʌm¹məlestɪ²d/. If someone does something **unmolested**, they do it without being stopped or interfered with. EG *The tanks were allowed through unmolested... Indeed, he could pursue his studies unmolested.* — ADV, OR ADJ CLASSIF

unmoved /ʌm¹muːvd/. If someone is **unmoved** by something, they are not emotionally affected by it, even though it would make most people feel sympathetic, sad, etc. EG *The ship had capsized off the Belgian coast in a foggy swell. Mother, unmoved, dished up Sunday breakfast... No one can remain unmoved by this music.* — ADJ QUALIT : PRED ⇑ unaffected

unmusical /ʌm¹mjuːzɪkə⁰l/. **1 Unmusical** people cannot play or appreciate music. EG *We're a very unmusical family.* — ADJ CLASSIF
2 Unmusical sounds are unpleasant to listen to. EG *...a rough, unmusical voice.* — ADJ QUALIT ≠ sweet

unnamed /ʌnneɪmd/. If someone or something is **unnamed**, **1** their name is not mentioned or known. EG *...an unnamed ministry spokesman.* **2** they have not been given a name. EG *...unnamed fears.* — ADJ CLASSIF; ADJ CLASSIF

unnatural /ʌnnætʃə⁰rəl/. **1** If you describe something as **unnatural**, you mean that **1.1** it is not at all what you would expect to find or to happen in the particular circumstances mentioned. EG *They can't help feeling that it is unnatural to be so happy... ...the house's unnatural silence... It is not unnatural, perhaps, that you should feel anxious.* ◇ **unnaturally**. EG *To hide his despondency, Castle became unnaturally elated... His voice suddenly became unnaturally loud.* — ADJ QUALIT = peculiar, unusual; ◇ ADV
1.2 it seems to be different from what nature intended to happen. EG *The divorce of art from technology is completely unnatural... ...children who have an unnatural interest in death.* — ADJ QUALIT = abnormal ≠ normal
2 If your behaviour is **unnatural**, it is different from normal, so that you do not look or sound genuine or spontaneous. EG *He lectures with a prolonged, unrelenting stare, which gives an unnatural feel to his delivery... She will have to teach herself to smile so that it doesn't seem unnatural and forced.* — ADJ QUALIT = contrived, stilted

unnaturally /ʌnætʃə⁰rəli¹/. **1** You use **not unnaturally** to indicate that the situation you are referring to is exactly what you would expect in the circumstances. EG *His behaviour had not unnaturally flustered her... Belinda not unnaturally concluded that he was drunk.* — PHR : USED AS ADV SEN = naturally
2 See also **unnatural**.

unnecessary /ʌnnesɪsə⁰ri¹/. Something that is **unnecessary** is not necessary. EG *The reason behind this is to avoid unnecessary expenses... They made a lot of unnecessary fuss... It is all quite unnecessary.* ◇ **unnecessarily**. EG *Some parents worry unnecessarily about their children.* — ADJ QUALIT = needless ≠ needed; ◇ ADV = needlessly

unnerve /ʌnnɜːv/, **unnerves, unnerving, unnerved.** If something **unnerves** you, it bothers, frightens, or startles you. EG *His touch unnerved her.* — V+O = rattle

unnerving /ʌnnɜːvɪŋ/. Something that is **unnerving** is rather frightening and startling. EG *This kind of experience can be quite unnerving... It's an unnerving book, I thought.* ◇ **unnervingly**. EG *His grip was unnervingly strong.* — ADJ QUALIT = upsetting; ◇ ADV

unnoticed /ʌnnəʊtɪst/. If something happens, passes, goes, etc **unnoticed**, it is not seen or noticed by people. EG *We tried to get into the room unnoticed... He hoped his departure had passed unnoticed.* — ADJ CLASSIF : PRED = unremarked

unnumbered /ʌnnʌmbəd/. **1** Something that is **unnumbered** does not have a number. EG *She moved six spaces and landed on an unnumbered square.* — ADJ CLASSIF
2 If you describe things as **unnumbered**, you mean that there are too many of them to be counted; a formal use. — ADJ CLASSIF = countless

unobserved /ʌnə⁷bzɜːvd/. If you do something **unobserved**, you do it without being seen by other people. EG *She was able to slip past the guard unobserved... He imagined that he was unobserved.* — ADJ CLASSIF = unremarked, unseen

unobtainable /ʌnə⁷bteɪnəbə⁰l/. If something is **unobtainable**, you cannot get it. EG *Timber is virtually unobtainable in the islands.* — ADJ CLASSIF = unavailable

unobtrusive /ʌnə⁷btruːsɪv/. Something that is **unobtrusive** is not easily noticed or does not draw attention to itself. EG *We'll try to be as unobtrusive as possible... The four-cylinder, 88-horsepower engine is smooth and unobtrusive.* ◇ **unobtrusively**. EG *Unobtrusively, Ginny tried to close the drawer.* — ADJ QUALIT = inconspicuous, quiet; ◇ ADV WITH VB

unoccupied /ʌnɒkjə⁴paɪd/. If a place is **unoccupied**, there is nobody in it. EG *The house was left unoccupied for fifteen years.* — ADJ CLASSIF = empty

unofficial /ʌnəfɪʃəᵒl/. 1 An action which is **unofficial** is not authorized, approved, or organized by the relevant organization, authority, or person. EG *...an unofficial strike... My participation is unofficial.* ◊ **unofficially**. EG *I have already consulted him unofficially.* — ADJ CLASSIF ≠ official; ◊ ADV WITH VB

2 If something that is said or written is **unofficial**, it is not yet formally confirmed, or is not a formal statement. EG *You will normally be sent unofficial notification of the results... This is strictly unofficial, but I think the Minister is about to resign.* ◊ **unofficially**. EG *I told you that unofficially... Officially, I'm in favour of it; unofficially, I have my doubts.* — ADJ CLASSIF ≠ formal, official; ◊ ADV SEN, OR ADV WITH VB ⇑ privately

unopened /ʌnəʊpəᵒnd/. If something is **unopened**, it has not been opened yet. EG *...an unopened bottle of whisky... I started sending the letters back unopened.* — ADJ CLASSIF

unorthodox /ʌnɔːθədɒks/. 1 **Unorthodox** behaviour, beliefs, customs, etc are unusual and not generally accepted. EG *I am afraid your English is somewhat unorthodox... Many doctors don't approve of unorthodox medicine.* — ADJ QUALIT = unconventional

2 Someone who is **unorthodox** has unusual and not generally accepted opinions, beliefs, etc. EG *She was described as 'brilliantly unorthodox.'* — ADJ QUALIT = unconventional

unpack /ʌm¹pæk/, **unpacks, unpacking, unpacked**. When you **unpack**, you take everything out of a suitcase, bag, or box. EG *He began to unpack his briefcase... I'll leave you now so that you can unpack... I try to get unpacked as fast as possible... We'd better unpack the dishes.* — V OR V+O

unpaid /ʌm¹peɪd/. 1 If you are **unpaid**, you do not receive any money or wages for doing a particular job. EG *Carol was Pat's unpaid teacher.* — ADJ CLASSIF ≠ paid, salaried

2 **Unpaid** work, leave, etc is work, leave, etc that you do not get paid for. EG *...unpaid overtime.* — ADJ CLASSIF

3 If something such as rent or a bill is **unpaid**, it has not yet been paid. — ADJ CLASSIF

unpalatable /ʌm¹pælə¹təbəᵒl/. 1 **Unpalatable** food is unpleasant to taste. EG *...an unpalatable breakfast.* — ADJ QUALIT

2 An **unpalatable** idea, conclusion, truth, etc is one that you find unpleasant and difficult to accept. EG *What I have to say may be unpalatable to some of you... The truth, the unpalatable truth, stared him in the face.* — ADJ QUALIT = distasteful

unparalleled /ʌm¹pærələld/. Something that is **unparalleled** is bigger or better than anything else of the same kind. EG *Our specialist library is unparalleled... Speech is an unparalleled medium for exchanging complex information... ...a world economic crisis unparalleled since the 1930s.* — ADJ CLASSIF = unequalled

unpardonable /ʌm¹pɑːdəᵒnəbəᵒl/. **Unpardonable** behaviour is very wrong or rude, and completely unacceptable; used showing disapproval. EG *...an unpardonable affront... Such attacks were utterly unpardonable.* — ADJ CLASSIF = unforgivable

unparliamentary /ʌm¹pɑːlə¹mentəᵒri¹/. **Unparliamentary** language or behaviour is not suitable for Parliament, usually because it is too rude or abusive. — ADJ CLASSIF : USU ATTRIB ⇑ unsuitable

unpick /ʌm¹pɪk/, **unpicks, unpicking, unpicked**. If you **unpick** a piece of sewing, you remove the stitches from it. EG *You'll have to unpick that seam.* — V+O = undo

unplayable /ʌm¹pleɪəbəᵒl/. In sport, if a ball is **unplayable**, it is impossible to hit properly, either because of the skill or speed with which it was thrown or hit, or because of its position. — ADJ CLASSIF ⇑ impossible

unpleasant /ʌm¹plezənt/. 1 Something that is **unpleasant** is rather nasty and not at all enjoyable. EG *The only work available is dirty, unpleasant and dangerous... The smell was unpleasant... ...an unpleasant surprise... It's pretty unpleasant having a tube forced down your throat.* ◊ **unpleasantly**. EG *An unpleasantly chilly wind still blew.* — ADJ QUALIT = disagreeable ≠ nice; ◊ ADV

2 Someone who is **unpleasant** is very unfriendly or quarrelsome. EG *Their son is even more ill-tempered, difficult, and unpleasant... ...a most unpleasant memo.* ◊ **unpleasantly**. EG *He laughed unpleasantly.* ◊ **unpleasantness**. EG *I have exposed the unpleasantness of a rude young man.* — ADJ QUALIT ⇑ nasty = disagreeable; ◊ ADV WITH VB; ◊ N UNCOUNT

unpleasantness /ʌm¹plezəntnɪs/. 1 **Unpleasantness** is trouble or quarrelling. EG *Once people realized what was happening, there would be public unpleasantness... I hate unpleasantness.* — N UNCOUNT

2 See also **unpleasant**.

unplug /ʌm¹plʌg/, **unplugs, unplugging, unplugged**. If you **unplug** a piece of electrical equipment, you take the plug out of the electric socket. EG *Will you unplug the iron?* — V+O

unpolluted /ʌm¹pəluːtɪ²d/. **Unpolluted** air and water is completely pure and clean and free from pollution. — ADJ CLASSIF

unpopular /ʌm¹pɒpjə⁴lə/. Something or someone that is **unpopular** is not at all popular but is disliked and disapproved of. EG *The war was both costly and unpopular... Certain personality traits had made her unpopular... ...unpopular increases in television licence fees.* ◊ **unpopularity** /ʌm¹pɒpjə⁴lærɪti¹/. EG *...the President's fear of unpopularity.* — ADJ QUALIT = unwelcome ≠ popular; ◊ N UNCOUNT = disfavour

unprecedented /ʌm¹presɪdentɪ²d/. Something that is **unprecedented** has never happened before; often used to emphasize the great degree or extent of something. EG *The frankness of the interview was unprecedented... ...a period of unprecedented wealth and prosperity... ...examples of cruelty and mass slaughter on an unprecedented scale.* — ADJ CLASSIF = unheard-of, unparalleled ≠ usual

unpredictable /ʌm¹prɪdɪktəbəᵒl/. If someone or something is **unpredictable**, their behaviour, nature, or effect cannot be predicted and therefore you never know what they are going to do. EG *She was totally unpredictable... There are enormous and unpredictable risks... Poisons are notoriously unpredictable.* ◊ **unpredictably**. EG *Terrorism strikes unpredictably.* ◊ **unpredictability** /ʌm¹prɪdɪktəbɪlɪti¹/. EG *...the unpredictability of the climate.* — ADJ QUALIT ≠ foreseeable, expected; ◊ ADV WITH VB; ◊ N UNCOUNT

unprepared /ʌm¹prɪpeəd/. If you are **unprepared** for something, you are not ready for it, and you are therefore surprised or at a disadvantage when it happens. EG *Students from tropical countries are often unprepared for the British climate... ...untrained and unprepared civilians... We were pushed into battle unprepared.* — ADJ CLASSIF : USU PRED, IF+PREP THEN *for* ⇑ unready ≠ prepared

unprepossessing /ʌm¹priːpəsesɪŋ/. Someone or something that is **unprepossessing** is not very attractive or appealing in appearance. EG *He was externally very unprepossessing.* — ADJ QUALIT = unattractive

unpretentious /ʌm¹pri¹tenʃəs/. Something that is **unpretentious** does not have an appearance or nature that suggests too much importance or wealth. EG *...a large but unpretentious building.* — ADJ QUALIT = modest, unassuming

unprincipled /ʌm¹prɪnsɪpəᵒld/. Someone who is **unprincipled** has no moral principles and does things which are wrong. EG *...a ruthless and unprincipled man.* — ADJ QUALIT = unscrupulous

unprintable /ʌm¹prɪntəbᵒəl/. If you describe something that someone said or did as **unprintable**, you mean that it is so rude or shocking that you do not want to say exactly what it was. EG *We continued yelling at each other, and she said unprintable things.* — ADJ CLASSIF ⇑ shocking

unproductive /ʌm¹prədʌktɪv/. Something that is **unproductive** does not produce any good results. EG *...an unproductive use of assets... ...unproductive conversations... Their land is unproductive.* — ADJ QUALIT = unprofitable

unprofessional /ʌm¹prəfeʃəᵒnəl, -ʃənəᵒl/. If someone is **unprofessional**, they do not behave according to the standards that are expected of a person in their profession. EG *...indiscreet and unprofessional conduct.* — ADJ QUALIT = unethical, improper

unprofitable /ʌm¹prɒfɪtəbəᵒl/. 1 An **unprofitable** company, product, etc does not make any profit or does not make enough profit. — ADJ QUALIT ≠ profitable

2 An **unprofitable** conversation, inquiry, etc does not produce any useful or helpful results. EG *...an unprofitable line of thinking... There was little point in continuing so unprofitable a dialogue.* — ADJ QUALIT ⇑ useless ≠ constructive

unpronounceable /ʌm¹prənaʊnsəbəᵒl/. An **unpronounceable** word or name is too difficult to say. — ADJ CLASSIF

unprotected /ʌm¹prətektɪ²d/. 1 If you are **unprotected**, you are not looked after or defended, so that you may be attacked or hurt. EG *They feel quite naked and unprotected.* — ADJ CLASSIF = defenceless

2 Something that is **unprotected** is not covered or protected by anything. EG *The explosion would puncture tyres, fuel tanks, and radiators of unprotected vehicles... Beware of the sun beating on unprotected fair skin.* — ADJ QUALIT = uncovered ≠ shielded

unprovoked /ʌm¹prəvəʊkt/. If something such as an attack or an unpleasant remark is **unprovoked**, it happens without being caused by anything that someone else has said or done. — ADJ CLASSIF = uncalled-for ≠ justified

unpublished /ʌm¹pʌblɪʃd/. **Unpublished** books, manuscripts, letters, etc have not been published. — ADJ CLASSIF

unpunished /ʌmˈpʌnɪʃt/. If a person or crime goes **unpunished**, the person is not punished. EG *On this occasion the guilty should go unpunished... Would he then forget the crime and let it go unpunished?* ADJ CLASSIF: PRED

unputdownable /ʌmˈpʊtdaʊnəbəl/. If you say that a book is **unputdownable**, you mean that it is so exciting or interesting that you cannot stop reading it; an informal word. ADJ QUALIT

unqualified /ʌnkwɒlɪfaɪd/. **1** If you are **unqualified**, you do not have any qualifications, or do not have the qualifications that are needed for a particular job. EG *...an unqualified child-minder... He is unqualified to undertake this enquiry.* ADJ CLASSIF ≠ qualified

2 Something that is **unqualified** has no restrictions or limitations. EG *The Government does not have unqualified control over the economy... You have my unqualified approval... I asked for a prompt and unqualified denial.* ADJ CLASSIF ↑ unlimited = unconditional

3 Unqualified also means total and complete. EG *The party was an unqualified disaster... ...an unqualified success.* ADJ CLASSIF: ATTRIB

unquestionable /ʌnkwestʃənəbəl/. Something that is **unquestionable** is so obviously true or real that nobody can doubt it. EG *His courage and commitment are unquestionable... These are unquestionable facts.* ◇ **unquestionably**. EG *This is a serious business, unquestionably... The visit to Greenland was unquestionably the highlight of the voyage.* ADJ CLASSIF = indisputable ≠ doubtful; ◇ ADV SEN, OR ADV = undeniably

unquestioned /ʌnkwestʃənd/. **1** Something that is **unquestioned** is accepted by everyone, without anyone doubting or disagreeing. EG *A system in which obedience and fortitude were unquestioned virtues.* ADJ CLASSIF = received

2 You use **unquestioned** to emphasize that something is so obvious, real, or great that nobody can doubt it or disagree with it. EG *This put the Alliance in a position of unquestioned security.* ADJ CLASSIF = indisputable

unquestioning /ʌnkwestʃənɪŋ/. You use **unquestioning** to describe a belief or attitude that someone has which they do not think about or doubt to be right. EG *You were chosen for this operation on the basis of your unquestioning obedience.* ◇ **unquestioningly**. EG *I accept my place in society unquestioningly.* ADJ CLASSIF; ◇ ADV WITH VB ↑ obediently

unquote /ʌnkwəʊt/. You use **unquote** to mark the end of a quotation which you have introduced with the word 'quote'. EG *Then he referred to the, quote, 'inequality of our circumstances', unquote.* ADV SEN: AFTER QUOTE

unravel /ʌnrævəl/, **unravels, unravelling, unravelled**; also spelled **unraveling, unraveled** in American English. **1** If you **unravel** something that is knotted, twisted, woven, knitted, etc, or it **unravels**, it becomes undone. EG *Her knitting was starting to unravel.* V-ERG ↑ undo

2 If you **unravel** a mystery or puzzle, you explain it or work out the answer to it. EG *He felt he must unravel the mystery.* V+O = solve

unread /ʌnred/. If you describe a book or other piece of writing as **unread**, you mean that it has not been read. EG *I returned the book unread... ...a pile of unread magazines.* ADJ CLASSIF

unreadable /ʌnriːdəbəl/. **1** An **unreadable** book or other piece of writing is very difficult or unpleasant to read, especially because it is dull or complicated. EG *I found the book virtually unreadable.* ADJ QUALIT ↑ bad

2 Something that is **unreadable** is impossible to read because the letters are so unclear, especially because it has been damaged in some way. EG *The labels were blurred and unreadable.* ADJ QUALIT = illegible

unreal /ʌnrɪəl/. If you describe something as **unreal**, you mean that it is **1** so strange that it seems to exist only in your mind or as part of a dream. EG *I felt unreal, in a bad dream, still not properly awake... This conversation is getting more and more unreal.* ◇ **unreality** /ʊnrɪælɪti/. EG *I had a deep feeling of unreality, of struggling in a dream.* **2** false or artificial. EG *There were flowers that looked unreal... They all have an unreal politeness and phony manners.* ADJ QUALIT ↑ odd; ◇ N UNCOUNT; ADJ QUALIT = fake

unrealistic /ʌnrɪəlɪstɪk/. Someone who is **unrealistic** or has **unrealistic** ideas does not take account of the truth and facts about a situation, and is not prepared to accept it or to deal with it in a practical way. EG *This demand proved unrealistic and unworkable... It is unrealistic to expect better conditions in the near future... You have unrealistic expectations.* ◇ **unrealistically**. EG *This policy has kept Boston's tax assessments unrealistically low.* ADJ QUALIT = blinkered, impractical; ◇ ADV = unnaturally

unreasonable /ʌnriːznəbəl/. **1** People who are **unreasonable** behave in a way that is unfair and not sensible. EG *She was a thoroughly unreasonable person... We think he is being unreasonable.* ◇ **unreasonably**. EG *He is behaving unreasonably and irrationally.* ADJ QUALIT = unjust ≠ reasonable; ◇ ADV WITH VB = unfairly

2 Something such as a decision, demand, or judgement that is **unreasonable** is unfair and difficult to justify. EG *The request didn't seem unreasonable... The demands being placed on the system were not unreasonable... It was unreasonable to expect more.* ◇ **unreasonably**. EG *Consent had been unreasonably withheld.* ADJ QUALIT; ◇ ADV WITH VB

3 If you describe something such as an amount, degree, or cost as **unreasonable**, you mean that it is too great or too much. ADJ QUALIT = excessive

unreasoning /ʌnriːzənɪŋ/. **Unreasoning** feelings or beliefs are not logical, sensible, or controlled. EG *His fear turned into unreasoning panic.* ADJ CLASSIF: ATTRIB = irrational

unrecognizable /ʌnrekəgnaɪzəbəl/; also spelled **unrecognisable**. Something that is **unrecognizable** is impossible to recognize or identify because it has changed or been damaged so much. EG *His voice was very low and hoarse and almost unrecognizable.* ADJ CLASSIF ↑ unknown ≠ recognizable

unrecognized /ʌnrekəgnaɪzd/; also spelled **unrecognised**. **1** If something is **unrecognized**, its nature or existence is not fully realized. EG *There was another consequence, at that time almost unrecognised.* ADJ CLASSIF

2 If someone remains **unrecognized** on a particular occasion, they are seen or heard by a person who would normally recognize them but the person does not realize who they are. EG *Unrecognized by any of the women, he heard them talking about him.* ADJ CLASSIF: PRED ↑ unknown

3 If you or your achievements or qualities are **unrecognized**, you have not been properly appreciated or acknowledged by other people for what you have done. EG *It is a disgrace that such talent should go unrecognised... ...largely unrecognized research.* ADJ CLASSIF = unacknowledged

unrecorded /ʌnrɪˈkɔːdɪd/. You use **unrecorded** to describe an event or statement that has not been written down or recorded, especially when it should have been. EG *The incident had gone unrecorded.* ADJ CLASSIF

unrefined /ʌnrɪˈfaɪnd/. **1** An **unrefined** food or other substance is in its natural state and has not been processed. EG *...a variety of wholesome, unrefined foods... ...unrefined sugar... ...unrefined oil.* ADJ CLASSIF: USU ATTRIB ↑ crude

2 Unrefined people have poor manners; used showing disapproval. EG *Refined girls are often drawn to unrefined men.* ADJ CLASSIF ↑ coarse = vulgar

unrehearsed /ʌnrɪˈhɜːst/. If something is **unrehearsed**, it has not been prepared, planned, or practised beforehand. EG *The highlight of the afternoon was an unrehearsed incident.* ADJ CLASSIF ↑ unprepared = improvised

unrelated /ʌnrɪˈleɪtɪd/. Things which are **unrelated** have no connection with each other. EG *...a series of unrelated incidents... New issues may arise, unrelated to the original ones.* ADJ CLASSIF: IF+PREP THEN *to*

unrelenting /ʌnrɪˈlentɪŋ/. If someone's behaviour is **unrelenting**, they continue to do something in a very determined way, often without caring whether they hurt or embarrass other people. EG *They kept up a sustained, unrelenting barrage of questions... ...the unrelenting pursuit of growth and industrial expansion.* ADJ CLASSIF ↑ continuous = relentless

unreliable /ʌnrɪˈlaɪəbəl/. If people, machines, or methods are **unreliable**, you cannot trust them or rely on them. EG *Godwin was a thoroughly unreliable man... In the early 1950s computers were expensive and unreliable.* ◇ **unreliability** /ʊnrɪbaɪəbɪlɪti/. EG *Too much originality in dress suggests unreliability.* ADJ QUALIT ↑ untrustworthy; ◇ N UNCOUNT

unrelieved /ʌnrɪˈliːvd/. is used of something unpleasant that is complete and is never replaced by anything better, even for a short time. EG *...a prospect of almost unrelieved gloom... ...a life of unrelieved misery.* ADJ CLASSIF: USU ATTRIB, IF PRED THEN+*by* ↑ total = unmitigated

unremarkable /ʌnrɪˈmɑːkəbəl/. You say that something is **unremarkable** when it is not beautiful, interesting, or exciting. EG *The view is unremarkable... ...an unremarkable garden... This may seem an unremarkable conclusion.* ADJ CLASSIF ↑ ordinary

unremarked /ʌnrɪˈmɑːkt/. **1** If something goes or remains **unremarked**, nobody notices it. EG *His absence had gone unremarked... These qualities remained unremarked.* ADJ CLASSIF = unnoticed

2 If you do something **unremarked**, nobody notices ADJ CLASSIF:

you doing it. EG *He was able to pass through the countryside unremarked.* PRED = unnoticed

unremitting /ʌnri¹mɪtɪŋ/. You describe something as **unremitting** when it continues without stopping or becoming less intense; a formal word. EG *...their unremitting efforts... ...the unremitting demands of hunger and thirst.* ◊ **unremittingly**. EG *This experience made me unremittingly hostile towards the police.* ADJ CLASSIF ⇑ continuing = sustained ◊ ADV+ADJ/ADV

unrepentant /ʌnri¹pɛntənt/. If you are **unrepentant**, you are not ashamed of your beliefs or of something that you have done. EG *He believes that all Labour MPs are unrepentant Marxists... I am an unrepentant believer in free enterprise.* ADJ QUALIT = unabashed

unrepresentative /ʌnrɛprɪ²zɛntətɪv/. If you describe a group of people as **unrepresentative**, you mean that their views are not typical of the community or society to which they belong; used showing disapproval. EG *They see the community activists as unrepresentative minority groups... ...an unrepresentative elite.* ADJ CLASSIF ⇑ atypical

unrepresented /ʌnrɛprɪ²zɛntɪ²d/. If you are **unrepresented** at a meeting or in a law court, parliament, etc, there is nobody there speaking or acting for you. EG *Some of the accused were technically unrepresented during a part of the hearing... ...the constitutional rights of the unrepresented colonies.* ADJ CLASSIF

unrequited /ʌnri¹kwaɪtɪ²d/. If your love for someone is **unrequited**, they do not love you; a literary word. EG *...the miseries of unrequited love.* ADJ CLASSIF

unreserved /ʌnri¹zɜːvd/. If something has your **unreserved** support, **unreserved** admiration, etc, you support it, admire it, etc completely and without any doubts. EG *The government did not have the unreserved support of any national newspaper.* ◊ **unreservedly**. EG *I accept your word unreservedly.* ADJ CLASSIF : USU ATTRIB = total, wholehearted ◊ ADV WITH VB

unresolved /ʌnri¹zɒlvd/. If a problem or difficulty is **unresolved**, no satisfactory solution has been found to it; a formal word. EG *Several major problems remain unresolved... ...unresolved issues of individual responsibility.* ADJ CLASSIF

unresponsive /ʌnri¹spɒnsɪv/. If you are **unresponsive** to a situation or to something that is happening, you do not let it affect your behaviour; used showing disapproval. EG *...a government unresponsive to their needs... The audience was unresponsive.* ADJ QUALIT : IF+ PREP THEN *to* ⇑ unaffected

unrest /ʌnrɛst/. When there is **unrest** somewhere, people there are angry and dissatisfied because they think something is wrong and should be changed. EG *...the causes of industrial unrest... People are predicting civil unrest in the area.* N UNCOUNT ⇑ trouble = dissatisfaction

unrestrained /ʌnri¹streɪnd/. You describe something as **unrestrained** when it is not controlled or limited in any way. EG *...the unrestrained use of state power... ...the dangers of unrestrained growth.* ◊ **unrestrainedly**. EG *For some time she wept unrestrainedly.* ADJ CLASSIF ⇑ unlimited = uncontrolled ◊ ADV WITH VB

unrestricted /ʌnri¹strɪktɪ²d/. When something is **unrestricted**, it is not limited by any laws or rules. EG *...the unrestricted dumping of waste.* ADJ CLASSIF ⇑ unlimited

unrewarded /ʌnri¹wɔːdɪ²d/. You say that someone is **unrewarded** or that their activities are **unrewarded** when they do not achieve what they are trying to achieve. EG *...an unrewarded band of anglers... His search was unrewarded.* ADJ CLASSIF ⇑ unsuccessful

unrewarding /ʌnri¹wɔːdɪŋ/. You describe an activity as **unrewarding** when it does not give you any feelings of achievement or pleasure. EG *Learning a language often seems unrewarding at the time... This proved a decidedly unrewarding task.* ADJ QUALIT

unripe /ʌnraɪp/. **Unripe** fruit is not yet ripe. EG *...unripe blackberries.* ADJ CLASSIF

unrivalled /ʌnraɪvəld/. If you describe something as **unrivalled**, you mean that it is better than anything else of the same kind. EG *The gallery has an unrivalled collection of modern art.* ADJ CLASSIF ⇑ excellent = unmatched, unsurpassed

unroll /ʌnrəʊl/, **unrolls, unrolling, unrolled**. **1** If you **unroll** something such as a sheet of paper or cloth or if it **unrolls**, it opens up and becomes flat when it was previously rolled in a cylindrical shape. EG *Someone unrolled a map of America... They set off across the prairie with long streamers of cloth unrolling behind them.* V-ERG

2 When you experience or remember a series of events, you say that these events **unroll** before your eyes, **unroll** in your memory, etc; a literary use. EG *...her own children, whose whole lives had unrolled before her eyes... The remembered scenes unrolled in his mind.* ▸ used also of periods of time. EG *The months have unrolled rapidly until now it is April.* V+A ⇑ happen = unfold

unruffled /ʌnrʌfəld/. **1** You describe someone as **unruffled** when they are calm and do not seem to be affected by surprising or frightening events. EG *She remained singularly unruffled when confronted with my discovery.* ADJ CLASSIF = placid, tranquil

2 You describe something such as the surface of a pond as **unruffled** when it is smooth and undisturbed. EG *...the unruffled surface of the pool... He picked up her limp hand from where it lay on the unruffled sheet.* ADJ CLASSIF

unruly /ʌnruːli¹/. **1** **Unruly** people are difficult to control or organize. EG *...unruly children... Day by day his men became bolder and more unruly.* ADJ QUALIT = wayward

2 **Unruly** hair is difficult to keep tidy. EG *He smoothed his unruly hair.* ADJ QUALIT ⇑ untidy

unsaddle /ʌnsædə⁰l/, **unsaddles, unsaddling, unsaddled**. When someone **unsaddles** a horse, pony, etc, they take the saddle off its back. V+O

unsafe /ʌnseɪf/. **1** If a building, machine, activity, etc is **unsafe**, it is dangerous. EG *It was unsafe to wander there... The house was declared unsafe for habitation.* ADJ QUALIT : USU PRED ⇑ harmful

2 If you are **unsafe**, you are in danger of being harmed. EG *I feel very unsafe.* ADJ QUALIT : PRED

unsaid /ʌnsɛd/. If something is left **unsaid** or goes **unsaid** in a particular situation, it is not said, although it might have been said. EG *He left the rest unsaid... There was a lot that went unsaid.* ADJ CLASSIF : PRED = unspoken

unsaleable /ʌnseɪləbə⁰l/; also spelled **unsalable** in American English. If something is **unsaleable**, it cannot be sold, because nobody wants to buy it. EG *...unsaleable items... Their calves make poor beef and are practically unsaleable.* ADJ CLASSIF

unsanitary /ʌnsænɪtə⁰ri¹/. Something that is **unsanitary** is dirty and unhealthy, so that you may catch a disease from it. EG *They lived eight to a room in some unsanitary quarter.* ADJ QUALIT

unsatisfactory /ʌnsætɪsfæktə⁰ri¹/. Something that is **unsatisfactory** is not good enough to be considered acceptable. EG *Shops are often reluctant to take back unsatisfactory goods... The middle class is finding life increasingly unsatisfactory... I had an unsatisfactory discussion with him about the future.* ADJ QUALIT ⇑ inadequate

unsatisfied /ʌnsætɪsfaɪd/. If you are **unsatisfied**, you are disappointed because you have not got what you hoped to get. EG *...an unsatisfied husband... He asked a lot of questions, and was unsatisfied with the answers.* ADJ QUALIT : IF+ PREP THEN *with* = dissatisfied

unsatisfying /ʌnsætɪsfaɪɪŋ/. If you find something **unsatisfying**, you do not get any satisfaction from it. EG *...the unsatisfying pursuit of economic growth... She plunged into a few unsatisfying affairs.* ADJ QUALIT = unrewarding

unsavoury /ʌnseɪvə⁰ri¹/; also spelled **unsavory** in American English. You describe people, places, and things as **unsavoury** when you find them unpleasant or morally unacceptable. EG *He looks so unsavoury... Parts of Birmingham are pretty unsavoury... ...their unsavoury habits.* ADJ QUALIT = distasteful

unscathed /ʌnskeɪðd/. If you are **unscathed** after a dangerous experience, you have not been injured or harmed by it. EG *The shell went by him and left him unscathed... We all escaped unscathed... The guerrillas emerged unscathed.* ADJ CLASSIF : PRED ⇑ safe = unharmed

unscheduled /ʌnʃɛdjuːld, ʌnskɛd-/. An **unscheduled** event was not planned to happen, but happens unexpectedly or because someone changes their plans at a late stage. EG *Grimes was about to make an unscheduled announcement... The plane made an unscheduled landing at Smoky Hill.* ADJ CLASSIF

unscientific /ʌnsaɪəntɪfɪk/. If you say that something is **unscientific**, you mean that it is not based on facts or is not objective; used showing disapproval. EG *They argue that psychotherapy is unscientific.* ADJ QUALIT ⇑ irrational

unscrew /ʌnskruː/, **unscrews, unscrewing, unscrewed**. **1** If you **unscrew** something such as a lid, you keep turning it until you can remove it. EG *He unscrewed the top and put the bottle to his mouth.* V+O ⇑ undo

2 If you **unscrew** a sign, mirror, etc, you remove it by taking out the screws by which it is fastened to something. EG *She carefully unscrewed the bottom plate... The mirrors had been unscrewed and removed.* V+O ⇑ unfasten

unscripted /ʌnskrɪptɪ²d/. An **unscripted** talk, speech, etc is spoken without a previously prepared ADJ CLASSIF = improvised script. EG *The President inserted one unscripted item in his speech.*

unscrupulous /ʌnskruːpjə⁴ləs/. **Unscrupulous** people are prepared to act dishonestly or in an immoral way in order to get what they want; used showing disapproval. EG *He was cruel, treacherous and unscrupulous... ...unscrupulous property salesmen.* ▸ used of behaviour. EG *...his unscrupulous manipulation of people... ...unscrupulous methods.* — ADJ QUALIT ⇑ immoral = unprincipled

unseasonable /ʌnsiːzə⁰nəbə⁰l/. **Unseasonable** weather, clothing, or food is unusual or inappropriate for the time of year. EG *...an unseasonable heatwave... He was sweating mightily in his unseasonable suit.* ◊ **unseasonably**. EG *...an unseasonably cold and foggy night.* — ADJ CLASSIF; ◊ ADV + ADJ/ADV

unseat /ʌnsiːt/, **unseats, unseating, unseated**. 1 When a person in an important post **is unseated**, they are removed from that post. EG *An attempt was made by the right wing to unseat Mr Hobbs.* — V+O = depose

2 To **unseat** someone also means to remove them from the place where they are sitting. EG *The donkey jibbed suddenly, almost unseating her.* — V+O

unseeing /ʌnsiːɪŋ/. You describe a person as **unseeing** or say that their eyes are **unseeing** when they are not looking at anything, or not noticing something, although their eyes are open; a literary word. EG *She stared ahead, unseeing... She was gazing with unseeing eyes at the harbour.* ◊ **unseeingly**. EG *Thomas was staring unseeingly at the shuttered window.* — ADJ CLASSIF; ◊ ADV WITH VB

unseemly /ʌnsiːmli¹/. You say that someone's behaviour is **unseemly** when it is not polite or not suitable for a particular situation or occasion; used showing disapproval. EG *...an unseemly public squabble... It is unseemly to gesticulate.* — ADJ QUALIT = improper, undignified

unseen /ʌnsiːn/. 1 **Unseen** is used to describe something 1.1 when people cannot see it, for example because it is dark. EG *A large unseen orchestra was playing jazzy rhythms.* 1.2 when it is something that cannot be seen because it is not a solid object, often something mysterious. EG *...unseen forces... It was as if some unseen hand held him back.* — ADJ CLASSIF = invisible; ADJ CLASSIF : ATTRIB

2 If you do something **unseen**, nobody sees you do it. EG *The Englishman had departed unseen.* — ADV WITH VB ⇑ unnoticed

unselfish /ʌnselfɪʃ/. **Unselfish** people regard other people's wishes and interests as more important than their own; used showing approval. EG *Haldane was a brave and unselfish man.* ▸ used of behaviour. EG *...an unselfish act.* ◊ **unselfishly**. EG *They unselfishly left their farms in order to help their neighbours.* ◊ **unselfishness**. EG *They show more loyalty and unselfishness than sophisticated people.* — ADJ QUALIT ⇑ generous = selfless; ◊ ADV WITH VB = selflessly; ◊ N UNCOUNT = selflessness

unsentimental /ʌnsentɪmentə⁰l/. **Unsentimental** people do not allow gentle or affectionate feelings to interfere with their work or decisions. EG *He is astute, unsentimental and realistic... Antique dealers are an unsentimental lot.* — ADJ QUALIT

unsettle /ʌnsetə⁰l/, **unsettles, unsettling, unsettled**. If something **unsettles** you, it causes you to feel restless, dissatisfied, or rather worried. EG *Her behaviour was beginning to unsettle the other kids... It unsettled him not to know where he was.* ◊ **unsettling**. EG *Swift change is extremely uncomfortable and unsettling.* — V+O ⇑ upset = disturb; ◊ ADJ QUALIT = disturbing

unsettled /ʌnsetə⁰ld/. 1 In an **unsettled** situation, there is a lot of uncertainty about what will happen. EG *...in the days of 1968, when everything was unsettled... ...the unsettled conditions that now prevail.* — ADJ CLASSIF = unstable, unpredictable

2 If you are **unsettled**, you are unable to concentrate on anything, because you are worried or excited about something. EG *I felt pretty unsettled all that week.* — ADJ QUALIT : PRED = restless

3 You also describe people as **unsettled** when they never live in one place for long. EG *...the unsettled, rootless, frustrated cosmopolitans.* — ADJ QUALIT = itinerant

4 **Unsettled** places are places where no people have yet lived. EG *...previously unsettled areas.* — ADJ CLASSIF

5 An **unsettled** argument or dispute has not yet been resolved; a formal use. EG *This argument remained unsettled until January 1975.* — ADJ CLASSIF ⇑ unfinished

unshaded /ʌnʃeɪdɪ²d/. An **unshaded** light or light bulb has no shade fitted to it. EG *A single unshaded light hung from a roof-beam.* — ADJ CLASSIF : ATTRIB = naked

unshakable /ʌnʃeɪkəbə⁰l/; also spelled **unshakeable**. **Unshakable** beliefs, decisions, etc are so strong that they cannot be destroyed or altered. EG *...his unshakable conviction that in the end socialism must win... ...her unshakable faith in progress.* ◊ **unshakably**; also spelled **unshakeably**. EG *He was unshakeably convinced of the correctness of his actions.* — ADJ CLASSIF = total, unwavering; ◊ ADV WITH VB = totally

unshaken /ʌnʃeɪkə⁰n/. If your beliefs are **unshaken** or if you are **unshaken** in your beliefs, you still have these beliefs, although they have been attacked or challenged. EG *He emerged with his faith in the capitalist system unshaken... He was unshaken in his belief that history would prove him right.* — ADJ CLASSIF ⇑ unchanged

unshaven /ʌnʃeɪvə⁰n/. If a man is **unshaven** or if his face or chin are **unshaven**, he has not shaved recently and there are short hairs on his face or chin. EG *Franklin was unwashed and unshaven... I can't bear a man's unshaven face across the table.* — ADJ CLASSIF ⇑ hairy

unshockable /ʌnʃɒkəbə⁰l/. **Unshockable** people are never shocked by anything that they hear, read, or see. EG *He was warm-hearted, sensible and unshockable.* — ADJ CLASSIF ⇑ broadminded

unsightly /ʌnsaɪtli¹/. You describe something as **unsightly** when it is unattractive to look at; used showing disapproval. EG *His skin was covered with unsightly blotches... ...an unsightly Dutch barn.* — ADJ QUALIT ⇑ hideous

unsigned /ʌnsaɪnd/. An **unsigned** document does not have anybody's signature on it. EG *The message, typewritten and unsigned, simply read: 'Your wife is having an affair.'* — ADJ CLASSIF

unskilled /ʌnskɪld/. **Unskilled** workers do work that does not require any special training. EG *Their fathers were unskilled manual workers... ...unskilled labourers.* ▸ used of the work that these people do. EG *Thirty-eight per cent of the women do unskilled work... They are all in low-paid, unskilled jobs.* — ADJ CLASSIF ⇑ untrained

unsmiling /ʌnsmaɪlɪŋ/. An **unsmiling** person is not smiling, and looks serious or unfriendly. EG *...an unsmiling blonde secretary... Lebel had remained silent and unsmiling throughout the interchange.* ◊ **unsmilingly**. EG *He nodded, unsmilingly but kindly.* — ADJ CLASSIF = dour; ◊ ADV

unsociable /ʌnsəʊʃəbə⁰l/. **Unsociable** people do not like talking to other people and try to avoid meeting them; used showing disapproval. EG *She was an awkward and unsociable girl... I went along, not wishing to appear unsociable.* — ADJ QUALIT ⇑ unfriendly

unsold /ʌnsəʊld/. **Unsold** goods have been available for people to buy but nobody has bought them. EG *The wheat remained unsold... ...unsold food.* — ADJ CLASSIF

unsolicited /ʌnsəlɪsɪtɪ²d/. **Unsolicited** pieces of advice, goods, etc are given or sent without being asked for. EG *She was given much unsolicited advice from her companions... He received several unsolicited letters from publishers.* — ADJ CLASSIF = unwarranted

unsolved /ʌnsɒlvd/. An **unsolved** problem or mystery has never been solved. EG *This is the major unsolved problem in evolution theory... The mystery will probably remain forever unsolved.* — ADJ CLASSIF = unresolved

unsophisticated /ʌnsəfɪstɪkeɪtɪ²d/. 1 You describe people as **unsophisticated** when they do not have a wide range of experience or knowledge and their tastes are simple, common, or rather childish. EG *It is easy to write because the readers are relatively unsophisticated... ...unsophisticated peasants.* — ADJ QUALIT = natural, simple

2 An **unsophisticated** method, device, etc is simple, often too simple to deal properly and effectively with something. EG *...a relatively unsophisticated means of discouraging attack... These forecasts are based on rather unsophisticated economic analyses.* — ADJ QUALIT = crude

unsound /ʌnsaʊnd/. 1 You describe a conclusion, method, or system as **unsound** when it is based on faulty ideas or reasoning. EG *Her intuition was not unsound... The basic design research seems unsound.* — ADJ QUALIT ⇑ weak = shaky

2 If someone is **unsound** or **of unsound mind**, they are mentally ill. EG *Gareth was psychologically unsound... They said that he was of unsound mind when he wrote this document.* — ADJ QUALIT, OR PHR : USED AS A

3 **An unsound** building or other structure is in poor condition and is likely to collapse. EG *...a building with unsound foundations.* — ADJ QUALIT ⇑ weak = shaky

unspeakable /ʌnspiːkəbə⁰l/. You describe something as **unspeakable** when it is extremely unpleasant. EG *All I really remember is the pain, the unspeakable pain... Their treatment of women is unspeakable.* ◊ **unspeakably**. EG *They sounded unspeakably horrible... ...an unspeakably vile response.* — ADJ QUALIT = awful, terrible; ◊ ADV + ADJ/ADV

unspecified /ʌnspesɪfaɪd/. You say that something is **unspecified** when you are not told exactly what it is, for example in a statement or a report. EG *They called for the pull-out of all foreign troops at an* — ADJ CLASSIF : U ATTRIB ⇑ unnamed *unspecified date... ...a terse statement threatening unspecified reprisals... James had been called away on urgent business (unspecified).*

unspectacular /ʌnspɛktækjəˈlə/. You describe something as **unspectacular** when it is not remarkable in any way. EG *The newspaper's growth has been unspectacular... He sat down to an unspectacular meal.* — ADJ CLASSIF ⇑ ordinary

unspoiled /ʌnspɔɪld/; also spelled **unspoilt**. 1 You say that something is **unspoiled** when it has not been damaged or harmed. EG *The wine's flavour was unspoiled... ...healthy, free children whose lives are unspoiled by fear and hate.* — ADJ CLASSIF ⇑ unaffected

2 You describe a place as **unspoiled** when it has not changed for a long time; used showing approval. EG *...an unspoiled village... ...areas of unspoiled countryside.* — ADJ CLASSIF

3 An **unspoiled** child has not been spoiled by its parents; used showing approval. — ADJ CLASSIF ⇑ pleasant

unspoken /ʌnspəʊkəⁿn/. 1 You say that someone's thoughts, wishes, or feelings are **unspoken** when they do not tell anyone about them. EG *His unspoken thought is: I am happy here... ...the unspoken wishes of the masses... I was full of unspoken fears.* — ADJ CLASSIF

2 When there is **unspoken** agreement between people, their behaviour shows that they agree about something, although they have never discussed it. EG *By unspoken agreement they all increased their pace... ...a bond between them, privately acknowledged but unspoken.* — ADJ CLASSIF = tacit

unsporting /ʌnspɔːtɪŋ/. If you are **unsporting** during a game, you behave in a selfish way that is unfair to your opponent; used showing disapproval. EG *Do not spend too long looking for your lost ball: this is unsporting.* — ADJ QUALIT

unstable /ʌnsteɪbəˈl/. 1 If something is **unstable**, **1.1** it is likely to change suddenly and to create difficulty or danger. EG *...unstable world wheat prices... ...unstable governments... The atmosphere is too unstable for life.* — ADJ QUALIT ⇑ uncertain = unpredictable **1.2** it is not firm or not fixed properly, and is likely to move or fall because of this. EG *...the unstable guttering on the houses opposite.* — ADJ QUALIT ⇑ unsteady

2 If people are **unstable**, their emotions and behaviour keep changing because their minds are disturbed or upset. EG *Alec's C.O. was a neurotic and unstable major.* — ADJ QUALIT = unbalanced

unstated /ʌnsteɪtɪˀd/. You say that something is **unstated** when it has not been expressed in words. EG *Stephanie preferred things unstated and undiscussed... ...a judgement based on unstated assumptions.* — ADJ CLASSIF ⇑ unsaid

unsteady /ʌnstɛdiˈ/. 1 If you are **unsteady**, you have difficulty standing or walking because you cannot completely control your legs or your body. EG *She was pregnant and somewhat unsteady... She seemed unsteady on her feet... Louis made his unsteady way to the top.* ◊ **unsteadily**. EG *Halliday was lurching unsteadily in my direction.* — ADJ QUALIT ⇑ uneven = shaky; ◊ ADV WITH VB = shakily

2 If your hands are **unsteady**, you have difficulty controlling them. EG *Stephen poured two brandies with an unsteady hand.* — ADJ QUALIT = shaking

3 **Unsteady** objects are not held, fixed, or balanced securely. EG *The foundations became unsteady... She was balancing three boxes in an unsteady pile against her cardigan.* — ADJ QUALIT ⇑ uneven

unstick /ʌnstɪk/, **unsticks, unsticking, unstuck**. If you **unstick** something or if it **unsticks**, it becomes separated from something that it was stuck to. EG *He unstuck his fingers... The damp gradually unstuck the wallpaper.* ● See also **unstuck**. — V-ERG ⇑ detach

unstinting /ʌnstɪntɪŋ/. **Unstinting** help, care, praise, etc is great in amount or degree and is given generously. EG *This incident did show the unstinting care that this firm takes of its clients... I cannot speak too highly of the unstinting help I received.* — ADJ CLASSIF ⇑ generous

unstoppable /ʌnstɒpəbəˈl/. Something that is **unstoppable** cannot be prevented from continuing or developing. EG *This waste of resources is neither inevitable nor unstoppable... The advance of science is unstoppable.* — ADJ CLASSIF

unstrap /ʌnstræp/, **unstraps, unstrapping, unstrapped**. If you **unstrap** something, you release it by removing the straps by which it is fastened to something else. EG *He unstrapped his saddle bags... The seatbelt sign winked off and Betty unstrapped herself.* — V+O (NG/REFL)

unstructured /ʌnstrʌktʃəd/. If an activity is **unstructured**, it is not organized in a complete or detailed way. EG *...an unstructured but effective method of education... We dance in completely unstructured groupings.* — ADJ QUALIT

unstuck /ʌnstʌk/. 1 If something **comes unstuck**, it becomes separated from something else that it was stuck to. EG *Some of the posters regularly came unstuck.* — PHR : VB INFLECTS

2 If a plan or system **comes unstuck**, it fails; an informal use. EG *The system is not so likely to come unstuck in a small organization.* — PHR : VB INFLECTS

3 If someone **comes unstuck**, they fail badly in something that they are trying to achieve; an informal use. EG *I always knew he'd come unstuck somewhere.* — PHR : VB INFLECTS

unsubstantiated /ʌnsəbstænʃɪeɪtɪˀd/. A statement or story that is **unsubstantiated** has not been proved to be true. EG *There have been many unsubstantiated reports of gas used in war zones... It is a dangerous, absurd, and totally unsubstantiated accusation.* — ADJ CLASSIF = unconfirmed

unsuccessful /ʌnsʌksɛsful/. 1 If you are **unsuccessful** in an attempt to do something, you do not succeed in doing it. EG *One of Tom's colleagues tried to hypnotize me but he was unsuccessful... If you are unsuccessful in the June examinations you can retake them in November.* ▸ used of people's actions. EG *Each unsuccessful attempt to win fame brought me nearer to despair.* ◊ **unsuccessfully**. EG *Several times I had tried unsuccessfully to talk to him.* — ADJ QUALIT ≠ successful; ▸ = abortive; ◊ ADV WITH VB

2 Someone who is **unsuccessful** has not managed to achieve the things that they wanted, especially in their career. EG *It is not known how Henry, an unsuccessful farmer, raised the money... ...an unsuccessful and impecunious son.* — ADJ QUALIT ≠ successful

unsuitable /ʌnsuːtəbəˈl/. Someone or something that is **unsuitable** has qualities that are not right or appropriate for a particular purpose or occasion. EG *...areas that are entirely unsuitable for agriculture... ...a high-rise block of flats, surely the most unsuitable environment in the world for small children... The parents blame their son's problems on a succession of unsuitable nannies.* ◊ **unsuitably**. EG *She was most unsuitably dressed.* — ADJ QUALIT : IF + PREP THEN *for/as* ⇑ wrong ≠ suitable; ◊ ADV

unsuited /ʌnsuːtɪˀd/. 1 Someone or something that is **unsuited** to a particular situation, place, task, etc has qualities that are not right or appropriate for that situation, place, task, etc. EG *...vehicles that are clearly unsuited for use in the desert... I think he is unsuited to be leader of a great party... Mills was a likeable man unsuited to politics.* — ADJ CLASSIF : USU PRED + *to/for* ⇑ wrong ≠ suited

2 If two people, especially a man and a woman, are **unsuited** to each other, they have different personalities, interests, etc, and so are unlikely to have a successful relationship. EG *It's only in the last year that I've realized how totally unsuited they are to each other.* — ADJ QUALIT : IF + PREP THEN *to* ≠ suited

unsullied /ʌnsʌlɪd/. Something that is **unsullied** has not been spoiled or made less pure by the addition of something unpleasant or unacceptable; a fairly literary word. EG *...an unsullied reputation... She possessed an innocence unsullied by contact with the world.* — ADJ CLASSIF : IF + PREP THEN *by* = unblemished

unsung /ʌnsʌŋ/ is used to describe someone who is not appreciated or praised although you think they deserve to be. EG *I have great respect for that unsung army of men and women who trudged to work every day... He has been an unsung hero of New Zealand's recent improvement.* — ADJ CLASSIF : USU ATTRIB

unsupported /ʌnsəpɔːtɪˀd/. 1 Someone who is **unsupported** does not have anyone such as a husband or wife to provide them with money and the things they need. EG *The problems are most intense for unsupported mothers.* — ADJ CLASSIF = single

2 Someone or something that is **unsupported** is not being physically supported or held up by anything. EG *They could not stand for long unsupported.* — ADJ CLASSIF ⇑ unaided

3 A statement or theory that is **unsupported** is not supported by any evidence which proves that it is true or correct. EG *They should not make unsupported accusations.* — ADJ CLASSIF = unsubstantiated

unsure /ʌnʃʊə/. 1 If you are **unsure** or **unsure** of yourself, you are lacking in confidence. EG *His demands made the boy nervous and unsure of himself... She was unprepared, stammering and unsure in her classes.* — ADJ QUALIT : USU PRED + *of* = uncertain ≠ confident

2 If you are **unsure** about something, you feel — ADJ QUALIT : USU

uncertain about it or about what to do. EG *She took a step back, unsure of his reaction... This issue is one that many tutors feel unsure about... The various people in the department are unsure which of them is actually supposed to deal with it.* PRED+*about/of/* REPORT-CL ≠ sure, decided

unsurpassed /ʌnsəpɑːst/. Something that is **unsurpassed** is better or greater than anything else of its kind. EG *...great literature which is unsurpassed... ...an economic analyst of unsurpassed genius... ...a variety of trees, unsurpassed anywhere in the world.* ADJ CLASSIF = unparalleled, unrivalled

unsurprising /ʌnsəpraɪzɪŋ/. If something is **unsurprising**, you are not surprised by it because you would expect it to happen or be like it is. EG *Their hostility was unsurprising.* ◊ **unsurprisingly**. EG *The nets were, unsurprisingly, still far too wet for use today... This brief address was received, not unsurprisingly, in total silence.* ADJ CLASSIF = predictable; ◊ ADV WITH VB, OR ADV SEN = predictably

unsuspected /ʌnsəspɛktɪ²d/. 1 Something that is **unsuspected** was not expected or realized. EG *He discovered in himself an unsuspected, long repressed appetite for pleasure... As the project developed, unsuspected difficulties came to the fore.* ADJ CLASSIF ⇑ hidden ≠ foreseen

2 Someone who is **unsuspected** is not noticed or not suspected of doing something wrong. EG *He was able to get in the building unspotted and unsuspected.* ADJ CLASSIF

unsuspecting /ʌnsəspɛktɪŋ/. Someone who is **unsuspecting** is not at all aware of something that is happening or going to happen. EG *He could take off his dog-collar and be taken by some unsuspecting stranger for the gardener... He will sit and wait until the news breaks on an unsuspecting world... Just then she came in, all unsuspecting, from the garden.* ADJ CLASSIF ⇑ unaware ≠ suspicious

unsweetened /ʌnswiːtə⁰nd/. Food or drink that is **unsweetened** does not have any sugar or other sweet substance added to it. EG *...unsweetened cooked fruit.* ADJ CLASSIF ≠ sweetened

unswerving /ʌnswɜːvɪŋ/. An **unswerving** attitude, feeling, or way of behaving is strong and firm and does not weaken or change. EG *...the consistent, unswerving loyalty of his supporters... ...her unswerving devotion to Miss Crabbe... They all have the same unswerving aim.* ADJ CLASSIF ⇑ constant = unflagging

unsympathetic /ʌnsɪmpəθɛtɪk/. 1 Someone who is **unsympathetic** is unwilling to be friendly or helpful to a person who needs help or sympathy. EG *Posy had been utterly unsympathetic when she heard about it.* ADJ QUALIT = unfeeling, heartless

2 An **unsympathetic** person is unpleasant and difficult to like. EG *...this highly unsympathetic character, a self-righteous prig.* ADJ QUALIT = disagreeable

3 If you are **unsympathetic** to a particular idea or aim, you are not willing to support it. EG *They had no qualms about killing people unsympathetic to the revolution.* ADJ QUALIT : USU PRED+*to* ⇑ hostile

untamed /ʌnteɪmd/. 1 An **untamed** place or area of land is wild or unmanageable because it has not been greatly changed and people do not often go there. EG *...a distant hill, scarred but still untamed.* ADJ CLASSIF ≠ cultivated

2 Someone who is **untamed** is independent and not at all controlled or influenced by other people. EG *...spinsters, untamed by marriage.* ADJ QUALIT ⇑ free ≠ subjugated

3 An **untamed** wild animal has not been trained to accept humans and be obedient to them. ADJ CLASSIF ≠ domesticated

untangle /ʌntæŋgə⁰l/, **untangles, untangling, untangled**. 1 If you **untangle** something such as string that is twisted together in a messy way, you undo the knots in it or free the twisted parts. EG *He untangled the cable carefully and stepped out of the loop... She untangled her hair from the branch.* V+O = disentangle, extricate

2 If you **untangle** something complicated or confusing, you work out what it means. EG *It seems important to try to untangle them, in my own mind at least.* V+O ⇑ sort out

untapped /ʌntæpt/. An **untapped** supply or source of something has not yet been used. EG *Britain's long-term strength lay in its vast untapped reserves of coal... ...a hitherto untapped source of food... ...the biggest untapped market in the world.* ADJ CLASSIF ⇑ unused

untenable /ʌntɛnəbə⁰l/. An argument, theory, position, etc that is **untenable** cannot be defended successfully against criticism or attack. EG *I would regard his theory as untenable if it should fail in certain tests... His position is morally untenable.* ADJ CLASSIF = indefensible, unsound

untested /ʌntɛstɪ²d/. Something that is **untested** has not yet been tested, so that you do not know what it is really like or what will happen. EG *Our potential as a new party was untested in national politics... Marriage is very much like a flight in an untested airplane.* ADJ CLASSIF = untried

unthinkable /ʌnθɪŋkəbə⁰l/. 1 If you describe something as **unthinkable**, you mean that it is so shocking or awful that you cannot imagine it happening or being true. EG *It would be unthinkable for the West to turn its back on this crisis... Five years ago, interest rates in excess of 20 per cent would have been unthinkable... It was an unthinkable intrusion.* ADJ CLASSIF : USU PRED ⇑ impossible = inconceivable

2 You could refer to a situation or event that is very shocking or unexpected as **the unthinkable**. EG *Thompson plainly cannot bear to think about the unthinkable... In late 1975 the unthinkable occurred: the company went bankrupt.* N SING : *the*+N

unthinking /ʌnθɪŋkɪŋ/. Someone who is **unthinking** does not think carefully about the effects of their behaviour and therefore does foolish things. EG *The ships were ordered out of the bay by some unthinking landlubbers at headquarters... Our society seems to be rushing ahead, unthinking, into ever greater mechanisation.* ▸ used of people's behaviour and actions. EG *...the automatic, unthinking use of these words.* ◊ **unthinkingly**. EG *We see others doing it and unthinkingly do likewise.* ADJ QUALIT = heedless, thoughtless; ▸ = careless; ◊ ADV WITH VB

untidy /ʌntaɪdi¹/, **untidier, untidiest**. 1 Something that is **untidy** is messy and disordered and not neat or well arranged. EG *It's a neglected, untidy park... The living-room was untidier than usual, with papers scattered about.* ◊ **untidily**. EG *She wore her hair untidily pinned up.* ◊ **untidiness**. EG *She can't stand untidiness.* ADJ QUALIT = unkempt, disorderly; ◊ ADV WITH VB; ◊ N UNCOUNT = mess

2 Someone who is **untidy** does not care about whether things are neat and well arranged, for example in their house. EG *She is so careless and untidy.* ADJ QUALIT = messy

untie /ʌntaɪ/, **unties, untying, untied**. If you **untie** someone or something, you remove string, rope, etc that has been tied round them by undoing the knots in it. EG *He quickly untied the captives... She tried to break the chain and untie the knot... He began untying the parcel.* V+O = undo, unbind

untied /ʌntaɪd/. Something such as a tie, shoelace, or ribbon that is **untied** has its ends loose rather than tied together in a bow or knot. EG *He has a lace untied.* ADJ CLASSIF ⇑ undone

until /ʌntɪl/. 1 You use **until** to say that an activity, situation, or event stops at the time or point mentioned. EG *We went on duty at six in the evening and worked until 2 a.m... You can get free prescriptions until you are 16... They were here until quite recently... She waited until he had gone... We've been given until the end of next year to come up with a solution... Until next week then, goodnight.* PREP, OR CONJ SUBORD = till ● The expression **up until** can usually be used to mean the same as **until**. EG *I've been thinking that up until last night I've never even raised a finger to help... Up until now my best decisions were always my negative ones.* ● PREP = till

2 You also use **until** to say that something does not happen before the time or point mentioned but that it does happen then. EG *I have nothing to say until I see my lawyer... They didn't find her until the next day... Women did not gain the vote until after the First World War... Don't turn the gas on again until the gasman tells you it's safe to do so.* PREP, OR CONJ SUBORD : WITH BROAD NEG = till

untimely /ʌntaɪmli¹/. 1 An **untimely** event happens too soon or sooner than expected. EG *His illness led to his untimely death.* ADJ CLASSIF : USU ATTRIB = premature

2 **Untimely** is used to describe something which is not suitable for a particular time. EG *But that is now an untimely subject.* ADJ CLASSIF : USU ATTRIB ⇑ inappropriate

untiring /ʌntaɪərɪŋ/. Someone who is **untiring** continues what they are doing without slowing down or stopping; often used showing approval. EG *His energy and enthusiasm were untiring... The girl was still talking in the same untiring voice.* ◊ **untiringly**. EG *They worked untiringly.* ADJ CLASSIF = indefatigable, unflagging; ◊ ADV WITH VB

unto /ʌntuː/; a very old-fashioned, literary word. **Unto** is used 1 to indicate that something is done or given to someone. EG *Do unto others as you would have them do unto you... ...a burnt offering unto the Lord.* 2 to indicate that something continues until a particular time. EG *...someone who might be a true friend and confidant unto death.* PREP; PREP = till

untold /ʌntəʊld/; a fairly literary word. **Untold** is used 1 to emphasize how great in degree or extent something is, usually something unpleasant. EG *A* ADJ CLASSIF : ATTRIB *spiteful parental tongue can do untold damage to a child... The war brought untold suffering upon the population.* 2 to emphasize how great an amount or quantity is. EG *There are untold millions of dollars for everyone to make... ...the war, with its untold number of human victims.* ADJ CLASSIF: ATTRIB = countless, innumerable

untouchable /ʌntʌtʃəbə⁰l/, **untouchables**. 1 An **untouchable** is a person who belongs to the lowest caste in Indian society. EG *...low-grade workers–a position not unlike the untouchables of India... They are landless labourers from Bihar, of the untouchable caste.* N COUNT

2 Someone who is **untouchable** cannot be affected or punished in any way. EG *Their names are known but they are untouchable because they have never committed any known crime... I felt invincible, untouchable.* ADJ CLASSIF

untouched /ʌntʌtʃt/. 1 Something that is **untouched** 1.1 has not been changed, moved, or affected in any way. EG *The old façade of the station remains untouched... The discovery lay untouched for another century... ...areas of the business world so far virtually untouched by the women's movement.* ADJ CLASSIF 1.2 is not damaged in any way, although it has been in a situation where it could easily have been damaged. EG *It's undamaged. In fact, it's completely untouched... The security car clung to its tail, untouched by any bullets at all.* ADJ CLASSIF = unscathed

2 If food that has been prepared is **untouched**, none of it has been eaten. EG *The coffee was still lukewarm but untouched... She sent back her breakfast tray untouched.* ADJ CLASSIF

untoward /ʌntə⁰wɔːd/ is used to describe something that happens which is unexpected and which causes difficulties; a formal word. EG *Nothing untoward had happened... Should any untoward side-effects occur, consult a doctor.* ADJ CLASSIF = unforeseen, adverse

untrained /ʌntreɪnd/. 1 Someone who is **untrained** has had no education in the skills that they need for a particular job, activity, or situation. EG *...untrained assistants... We do not expect untrained people to accept risky occupations.* ADJ CLASSIF = unskilled, unqualified

2 An **untrained** voice, mind, sense, etc has not been developed through formal education or training. EG *Even to an untrained eye it was obvious that something peculiar was there... He had a deep, untrained voice.* ADJ CLASSIF: USU ATTRIB ≠ trained

3 An **untrained** animal has not been trained to obey its owner's commands. EG *Her small, brown, untrained terrier has bitten the ankle of a new arrival.* ADJ CLASSIF ≠ trained

untrammelled /ʌntræmə⁰ld/; also spelled **untrammeled** in American English. Someone who is **untrammelled** is able to act freely, in the way they want to, rather than being restricted by rules, conventions, etc; a literary word. EG *I felt free and untrammelled and I wanted to stay that way... ...its fight for the untrammelled self-expression of the individual.* ADJ CLASSIF ⇑ free ≠ impeded, restrained

untreated /ʌntriːtɪ²d/. 1 If a person or an injury or illness that they have is **untreated**, they are not given medical treatment. EG *...a period of time during which a brain tumour remained untreated.* ADJ CLASSIF ≠ treated

2 Harmful materials or chemicals that are **untreated** have not been treated and made safe. EG *Our rivers have been poisoned by industrial waste and untreated effluent.* ADJ CLASSIF

3 Something that is **untreated** is in its natural or original state before being prepared for use or used in a particular process. ADJ CLASSIF ≠ refined, processed

untried /ʌntraɪd/. 1 An **untried** prisoner has not had a trial in a court of law. EG *He ordered the shooting of five unarmed, untried prisoners.* ADJ CLASSIF

2 Something that is **untried** has not yet been used, done, or tested. EG *It is still an untried policy... The piece exploits varieties of touch untried by Debussy.* ADJ CLASSIF ⇑ new

untroubled /ʌntrʌbə⁰ld/. 1 If you are **untroubled** by something, you are not affected or worried by it. EG *He appeared untroubled by doubts of any kind... ...nations that were untroubled by the presence of terrorists on their streets.* ADJ CLASSIF: PRED+*by* = undisturbed

2 Someone who appears **untroubled** appears calm and relaxed. EG *She had a kind untroubled face and a gentle manner.* ADJ CLASSIF = serene

untrue /ʌntruː/. 1 Something such as a statement or idea that is **untrue** is false and not based on facts. EG *The story was probably untrue... The belief that all cancer is incurable is obviously untrue.* ADJ CLASSIF ≠ true

2 If someone is **untrue** to you, they are unfaithful to you or lie to you; a literary use. EG *He never felt guilty about being untrue to them.* ADJ CLASSIF: PRED+*to* = disloyal

untrustworthy /ʌntrʌstwɜːðɪ¹/. Someone who is **untrustworthy** is unreliable and cannot be trusted. EG *He has proved himself completely untrustworthy.* ADJ QUALIT

untruth /ʌntruːθ/, **untruths** /ʌntruːðz/. An **untruth** is a statement that is not true; often used euphemistically. EG *His statement was an extraordinary stream of misrepresentation, untruths, and inaccuracies.* N COUNT = fiction, lie

untruthful /ʌntruːθfʊl/. Someone who is **untruthful** is dishonest and says things that are not true. EG *He was being untruthful when he claimed that he had never seen her before.* ▸ used of things that people say. EG *He told them such unkind, untruthful things.* ADJ QUALIT ≠ truthful ▸ = untrue

◊ **untruthfully**. EG *'I don't know,' said Ruth untruthfully.* ◊ ADV WITH VB ≠ truthfully

untutored /ʌntjuːtəd/. Someone who is **untutored** in a particular area of knowledge has not learnt about it; a formal word. EG *He was apparently untutored in the arts of polite social behaviour... The temple looks, to the untutored eye, bogus.* ADJ CLASSIF = uneducated

unusable /ʌnjuːzəbə⁰l/. Something that is **unusable** is not in a good enough state or condition to be used. EG *The living room was unusable with paper hanging down in shreds.* ADJ CLASSIF ⇑ useless

unused. The word **unused** is pronounced /ʌnjuːzd/ in paragraph 1 and /ʌnjuːst/ in paragraph 2. 1 Something that is **unused** has not been used. EG *Five out of every six hectares of estate land were unused... A pile of unused fuel lay ready.* ADJ CLASSIF = untouched ≠ in use

2 If you are **unused** to something, you have not often done it or experienced it before, so it feels unusual and unfamiliar to you. EG *They were unused to going without water... She was unused to hardship.* ADJ QUALIT: PRED+*to* = unaccustomed

unusual /ʌnjuːʒʊ⁰əl/. 1 Something that is **unusual** 1.1 is rather surprising because it is different from what is normal and does not occur very often. EG *He had an unusual name... It was not unusual for me to come home at two or three in the morning... In Britain, dual career families are still unusual... ...grumbling at the unusual length of the Cabinet's deliberations.* ADJ QUALIT = uncommon ≠ ordinary 1.2 is interesting or attractive because it is different from other things of the same kind; used showing approval. EG *...the unusual and most elegant communion rails... Madeira is very nice, I think. Unusual.* ADJ QUALIT ≠ dull, pedestrian

2 Someone or something that is **unusual** has strange and extraordinary qualities and is not as you would normally expect people or things of that kind to be. EG *You were an unusual child.* ADJ QUALIT = remarkable ≠ typical

unusually /ʌnjuːʒʊ⁰əlɪ¹/. You use **unusually** 1 to emphasize that someone or something has more of a particular quality than normal or than you would expect. EG *I noticed he looked unusually sombre... ...a clump of weed that seemed unusually large... ...unusually high speeds.* ADV+ADJ/ADV ⇑ very = exceptionally 2 to suggest that something is not normal or common and is therefore unexpected. EG *The service charge, unusually, is 10 per cent.* ADV SEN = surprisingly

unutterable /ʌnʌtərəbə⁰l/ is used to describe something that is very great in degree or intensity, especially a bad quality; a literary word. EG *...expression of unutterable misery on the father's face... I tried to think how I could relieve my unutterable boredom.* ADJ CLASSIF: ATTRIB ⇑ extreme = overwhelming ◊ **unutterably**. EG *It tasted unutterably foul... I was busy and unutterably tired.* ◊ ADV+ADJ/ADV

unvarying /ʌnvɛərɪɪŋ/ is used to describe something that stays the same and never changes. EG *A label is useful only if it has an unvarying meaning... This familiarity is provided by the unvarying breakfast menu.* ADJ CLASSIF: USU ATTRIB ⇑ unchanging

unveil /ʌnveɪl/, **unveils, unveiling, unveiled**. 1 If someone formally **unveils** something such as a new plaque, painting, etc, they draw back a curtain which is covering it, for example to open a new building, or to present a new work of art officially. EG *...a statue of Winston Churchill, unveiled late in 1973.* V+O ⇑ uncover

◊ **unveiling**. EG *...the official unveiling of a memorial to the martyrs.* ◊ N UNCOUNT

2 If you **unveil** something that you have been keeping secret, you make it known to the public. EG *He recently unveiled his plans for a new musical.* V+O ⇑ reveal

unwaged /ʌnweɪdʒd/. People who are **unwaged** do not have a paid job. ADJ CLASSIF

unwanted /ʌnwɒntɪ²d/. If something is **unwanted**, you do not want it and want to get rid of it. EG *...the* ADJ CLASSIF = unwelcome *appalling suffering caused by unwanted pregnancies... She was starting to feel unwanted... ...herbicides used to keep down any unwanted plants.*

unwarranted /ʌnwɒrəntɪ²d/. Something that is **unwarranted** is unnecessary and unjustified. EG *The concern proved unwarranted... I think it was a totally unwarranted waste of public money... ...this unwarranted punishment.*
ADJ CLASSIF ≠ deserved, justifiable

unwary /ʌnweəri¹/. Someone who is **unwary** is not cautious or experienced and is therefore likely to be harmed or deceived. EG *The unwary reader might be led to regard it as the primary target... ...the shrieks of unwary animals taken by surprise.*
ADJ QUALIT = unguarded, incautious

unwavering /ʌnweɪvə⁰rɪŋ/. An **unwavering** feeling or attitude is strong and firm and does not weaken. EG *...the government's unwavering support for this policy... This was a desperate attempt to convince them of her unwavering faith.*
ADJ CLASSIF ⇑ firm = unswerving ≠ tentative

unwelcome /ʌnwelkə⁰m/. 1 Someone who is **unwelcome** is not welcome because you do not like them or do not want to see them. EG *...an unwelcome guest... ...an unwelcome intruder.*
ADJ QUALIT = unwanted

2 An **unwelcome** situation is one which you do not want and which therefore makes you feel embarrassed, upset, etc. EG *...the suppression of unwelcome facts... I feared that my arrival might draw the unwelcome attention of officials... ...unwelcome publicity.*
ADJ QUALIT = embarrassing, inconvenient

unwelcoming /ʌnwelkəmɪŋ/. 1 Someone who is **unwelcoming** towards you is unfriendly or hostile when you visit or approach them. EG *He fixed her with an unwelcoming stare.*
ADJ QUALIT = cool

2 A place that looks **unwelcoming** looks unattractive or difficult to live in. EG *...the island with its unwelcoming coastline.*
ADJ QUALIT = unfriendly

unwell /ʌnwel/. If you are **unwell**, you are ill and not completely healthy or fit. EG *I informed her that I was unwell and could not come.*
ADJ QUALIT : PRED = sick, poorly

unwholesome /ʌnhəʊlsə⁰m/. 1 Food or drink that is **unwholesome** is not healthy or good for you.
ADJ QUALIT = unhealthy

2 If you describe someone's behaviour as **unwholesome**, you mean that you find it unpleasant or unnatural. EG *She disapproves of my unwholesome living.*
ADJ QUALIT = insalubrious

unwieldy /ʌnwiːldi¹/. 1 An **unwieldy** object is difficult to move or carry because it is so big or heavy. EG *We set about the task of towing the unwieldy structure into the shelter.*
ADJ QUALIT = cumbersome, ungainly

2 A system that is **unwieldy** does not work very well because it is too large or badly organized. EG *...the country's unwieldy banking system.*
ADJ QUALIT ⇑ inefficient

unwilling /ʌnwɪlɪŋ/. 1 If you are **unwilling** to do something, you do not want to do it and will not agree to do it. EG *He's unwilling to accept advice.* ◊ **unwillingness**. EG *...their fundamental unwillingness to discuss common problems.*
ADJ QUALIT : USU PRED + *to*-INF = disinclined, reluctant
◊ N UNCOUNT = reluctance

2 **Unwilling** is used to describe someone who does something unenthusiastically and often hesitantly because they do not really want to do it. EG *The Clyde shipyards had from the first been unwilling partners.* ▸ used of people's actions. EG *They had the unwilling but inevitable assistance of the local authority.* ◊ **unwillingly**. EG *He submitted unwillingly to his mother.*
ADJ QUALIT : ATTRIB = reluctant, grudging
◊ ADV WITH VB = reluctantly

unwind /ʌnwaɪnd/, **unwinds, unwinding, unwound**. 1 When you **unwind** after you have done something tiring or something that makes you tense, you relax. EG *Reading is a good way to unwind, better than television... They began to unwind and talk to us.*
V

2 If you **unwind** something that is wrapped round something else or wound in a ball, you undo it or straighten it out. EG *She slowly unwound her sarong... Francis was unwinding his bandage.*
V+O

unwise /ʌnwaɪz/. Something that is **unwise** is foolish and likely to lead to a bad result. EG *Since Guppy was set on it, she saw how very unwise it would be to refuse... It would be very unwise for the boy to marry her.* ◊ **unwisely**. EG *In 1963, he unwisely left the country.*
ADJ QUALIT : USU PRED = ill-advised, imprudent ≠ sensible
◊ ADV WITH VB

unwitting /ʌnwɪtɪŋ/. If something that you do is **unwitting**, you do it without realizing it or without intending to do it. EG *I became the unwitting instrument of that unscrupulous man.* ◊ **unwittingly**. EG *Sometimes we ourselves unwittingly invite interruption... I had to be grateful to her for having, however unwittingly, saved my life.*
ADJ CLASSIF : USU ATTRIB ⇑ unintentional
◊ ADV WITH VB = unintentionally

unwonted /ʌnwəʊntɪ²d/. Something that is **unwonted** is unusual or has not often been experienced before; a formal word. EG *...things which were common and everyday to him, but unwonted luxuries to them... ...an unwonted sensation of buoyancy and freedom.*
ADJ CLASSIF : USU ATTRIB ≠ customary, everyday

unworkable /ʌnwɜːkəbə⁰l/. If an idea, plan, etc is **unworkable**, it is certain to be unsuccessful. EG *His proposals for reform of the Trades Unions are unworkable and ill-judged... She turned down all his suggestions as unworkable without giving them a try.*
ADJ CLASSIF = impossible ≠ feasible

unworldly /ʌnwɜːldli¹/. Someone who is **unworldly** is not interested in having a lot of money or possessions. EG *It says something for America that so unworldly a man not only survived but was appreciated by everyone.*
ADJ QUALIT ≠ worldly

unworthy /ʌnwɜːði¹/. 1 If someone or something is **unworthy** of something such as honour, love, or attention, they do not deserve it. EG *I am unworthy of the honour you propose... ...occupations so trifling as to be unworthy of his full attention... He felt himself quite unworthy of her... How unworthy I felt!*
ADJ QUALIT : IF + PREP THEN *of*

2 If you describe an action or remark as **unworthy**, you mean that you think it is unacceptable and not what someone good would do. EG *...an odd and unworthy piece of folly... Oh that's unworthy of you! You wicked girl!*
ADJ QUALIT ≠ noble

unwrap /ʌnræp/, **unwraps, unwrapping, unwrapped**. When you **unwrap** something, you take off the paper or other covering that is around it. EG *I started to unwrap my sandwiches... Ellen carefully unwrapped the parcel.*
V+O ≠ wrap

unwritten /ʌnrɪtə⁰n/. 1 Something that is **unwritten** is not printed or written down. EG *Thoughts of my unwritten novel nagged me.*
ADJ CLASSIF

2 Something such as a rule or a law that is **unwritten** is known about, accepted, or understood by everyone without being officially laid down. EG *...the influence of unwritten social rules... I hope there's no unwritten law about what type of wine you should drink with this.*
ADJ CLASSIF : USU ATTRIB = tacit, unofficial ≠ official

unzip /ʌnzɪp/, **unzips, unzipping, unzipped**. When you **unzip** something which is fastened by a zip or when it **unzips**, you unfasten it. EG *He unzipped his anorak.*
V-ERG ⇑ undo

up /ʌp/, **ups, upping, upped**. 1 **Up** is used in phrasal verbs, for example 'get up' and 'let up', and after some other verbs such as 'add', 'ice', and 'cover'. See individual verb and phrasal verb entries for such items, which are not treated here.

2 **Up** is used referring to movement or position in the following ways: **2.1** to say that someone looks or goes towards a higher place or that something is moved to a higher place. EG *Mrs Haul looked up at her in surprise... I carried my suitcase up the stairs behind her... Bill put up his hand.* **2.2** to say that someone moves into an upright or standing position. EG *He straightened up and combed his hair... She helped Henry up from the bench... She scrambled up from the floor.* **2.3** to say that something is raised into a position where it is closed. EG *Why doesn't she put the hood up?... This zip won't stay up... He was sitting in his car with the windows up.* **2.4** to say that something is facing towards the sky or the ceiling. EG *He was lying face up on the grass, watching the clouds.* **2.5** to say that something moves to a higher floor in a building or that it is on a higher floor. EG *The coffee was sent up by the caterer from the kitchens below... 'I'll be right up,' called the voice of Albert Morris... He is up in his own bedroom.* **2.6** to say that someone moves northwards or that they are further north than someone else. EG *She went up north... Why did you come up to Edinburgh?... We're having this brilliant sunshine up here.* **2.7** to say that something is situated in a high place. EG *...comfortable houses up in the hills.* **2.8** to say that something is situated further along a road, street, etc in the direction that you are going. EG *There's a cafe just a hundred yards further up... ...a motorcycle cop up ahead.* **2.9** to say that someone goes somewhere or that they are looking in a particular direction. EG *She is walking up to see her auntie in the village... Come back up now into the main body of the church... He stared up the garden.* **2.10** to say that someone goes along a river in the direction of its source. EG *...a voyage up the Nile... I went up the tributary instead of sticking to the river.* **2.11** to say that something is
2.1 ADV AFTER VB, OR PREP = upwards ≠ down
2.2 ADV AFTER VB
2.3 ADJ AFTER VB, OR ADJ CLASSIF : PRED ≠ down
2.4 ADV AFTER N = upwards ≠ downwards
2.5 ADV AFTER VB, OR ADJ CLASSIF : PRED = upstairs ≠ downstairs
2.6 ADV + ADV/*to* ≠ down
2.7 ADV + ADV/*in* ≠ down
2.8 ADV WITH ADV ⇑ ahead
2.9 PREP, OR ADV + *to/into* ⇑ along
2.10 PREP, OR ADV + *to/towards* ≠ down
2.11 ADV + ADV/PREP

close to something else and is touching it or nearly touching it. EG *Up close, he was a man with inquisitive twinkling eyes... It's only when you get right up to them that you realise what they are... Women in ball-gowns were crushed up against their partners.*
3 If you go **up** to someone or something, you move to the place where they are, and stop there. EG *Ferdinard ran up to his father-in-law... Etta came up behind her... A bus drew up... Up came a tough bouncy little man.* ADV WITH VB : USU+PREP
4 If you move or look **up and down**, **4.1** you move or look repeatedly upwards and then downwards. EG *I was so happy I jumped up and down... She looked me up and down.* PHR : USED AS AN A **4.2** you move or look repeatedly in one direction and then in the opposite direction. EG *He started pacing up and down the office... He looked up and down the long table.* PHR : USED AS AN A
5 If you have **ups and downs**, you experience a mixture of good things and bad things. EG *We have had our ups and downs... Talks ended after a day of ups and downs at the bargaining table.* PHR : USED AS O
6 If you put something **up** somewhere or if you pin it **up**, write it **up**, etc, you put it on a vertical surface such as a wall where people can see it. EG *Write it up on the board... I might stick up a picture of Steve Ovett or Mohammed Ali... I saw a notice up about it.* ADV AFTER VB
7 If you are **up**, you are no longer in bed. EG *They were up early doing things... He has been up half the night talking to himself.* ADJ CLASSIF : PRED ● If you are **up and about** or **up and around**, you are well again and out of bed after being ill. EG *He's much better. He'll be up and around this afternoon.* ● PHR : USED AS AN A
8 You also say that you are **up** when you are feeling cheerful and happy and not depressed; an informal use. ADJ CLASSIF : PRED ≠ down
9 If you are **up** before someone in authority, you are in their presence and they can decide whether you have done something wrong or not. EG *They had the mother up because the child hadn't been going to school... If you did drop out you had to go up before the medical officer.* ADV AFTER VB, OR ADJ CLASSIF : PRED
10 If people or things are **up** for examination, **up** for election, etc, they are about to be evaluated or judged in some way. EG *Everything was up for examination... A third of my colleagues will come up for election next week.* ADV AFTER VB, OR ADJ CLASSIF : PRED
11 If a period of time is **up**, it has come to an end. EG *When the six weeks were up, everybody was sad that she had to leave... There came a loud announcement that time was up.* ADJ CLASSIF : PRED = over
12 If a woman's hair is **up**, it is arranged in a style in which it is pinned on the top or back of her head. EG *Barbara came hurrying down the stairs, her hair up in a bun.* ADJ CLASSIF : PRED, OR ADV AFTER VB ≠ loose, down
13 You say that a road is **up** when it is being repaired and cannot be used. EG *They had the road up right down to the lakeside.* ADJ CLASSIF : PRED
14 You say that a building is **up** when it has been erected. EG *None of these buildings were up in those days.* ADJ CLASSIF : PRED
15 If you say that the wind is **up** or that a person's bad temper is **up**, you mean that it has become strong or violent. ADJ CLASSIF : PRED
16 You tell people that food or drink is **up** when it is ready to be eaten or drunk; an informal use. EG *'Tea's up!' shouted his mother-in-law.* ADJ CLASSIF : PRED
17 If a sports team is a particular number of points or goals **up**, they are in a winning position by that number of points or goals. EG *They were two goals up at half time.* ADJ AFTER NUM = ahead ≠ down
18 If a number or an amount goes **up**, it goes towards a higher point or level on a scale. EG *Interest rates go up and it affects the Building Societies... At this time of year the numbers go up and up... The temperature was up in the nineties.* ADV AFTER VB, OR ADJ CLASSIF : PRED+*in* ≠ down
19 up to. 19.1 Up to is used to say how large something is, or how large it can be, by indicating that it can be any size or amount, provided that it is not above a particular level. EG *They might be up to about a metre wide... Savings up to 65% are obtainable... We've got them all ages–right up to ninety-two.* PREP = as much as **19.2 Up to** is used to say that something has risen until it has reached a particular level, position, or point on a scale. EG *Our total energy consumption is now up to about 40% and still rising... There would be crisis in central Europe, up to and including full scale warfare... Losses in the air were well up to the levels that peacetime analysis had predicted.* PREP = as high as ≠ as low as **19.3** If something is **up to** a particular standard, it is of a good enough quality to reach that standard. EG *The work isn't up to the standard I require... ...a studio which is up to broadcasting standard.* PREP **19.4** If you are **up to** doing something or feel **up to** doing it, you are well enough or not too tired to do it. EG *Are you up to doing some work?... I'm not going to Hazel's party–I don't think I feel up to it... McFee's feet were no longer up to walking.* PREP, OR PREP+-ING **19.5** If you say that someone is **up to** something, you mean that they are doing something secretly that they should not be doing; used showing disapproval. EG *Let's go and see what he's up to... The neighbours will think the Hochstadts are up to something... A lot was written about what they got up to in their private lives... You can't fool me–I see what you are up to.* PREP **19.6** If you say that it is **up to** someone to do something, you mean that it is their responsibility to do it. EG *It will be up to her to tell you what she has in mind... It is up to the teacher not to accept shoddy work... It's up to you, isn't it?* PREP **19.7** If something happens **up to** or **up until** a particular time, it happens until that time. EG *They were using charcoal right up to my day... Up until the early sixties there was no shortage... Up to now they've had very little say.* PREP
20 If you **up** something connected with money, you increase it; an informal use. EG *I upped the mortgage... The milk barons upped the cost to the public.* V+O = raise ≠ decrease, lower
21 If you say that someone **upped** and did something, you mean that they did it suddenly or unexpectedly; an informal use. EG *He just upped and went one day.* V+*and*+VB
22 The word **up** is also used in the following expressions. **22.1** If you are **up against** something, you have to deal with a very difficult situation or problem. EG *...when you really find yourself up against something... They seem to come up against a lot of problems... They are up against the intractable nature of the system.* PREP **22.2** If you say that it is **all up with** someone, you mean that something has come to an end for them, and there is no hope left. EG *All was up with herself and Christopher.* PHR+NG : USED AS C **22.3** If you say that something is **not up to much**, you mean that it is of poor quality and therefore not enjoyable; an informal expression. EG *The dances weren't up to much... Actually their football is not up to much.* PHR : USED AS C **22.4** If something is **on the up and up**, it is getting better and better; an informal expression. EG *The business is on the up and up this year.* PHR : USED AS AN A ≠ going downhill **22.5** If you say to someone **'What's up?'**, you are asking them what is wrong or what is worrying them; an informal expression. EG *What's up, Myra? You look sad.* CONVENTION = what's the matter? **22.6** If you say that **something is up**, you mean that something is wrong or that something worrying is happening; an informal expression. EG *I know something's up... I could see that something was up.* PHR **22.7** People sometimes say **'Up yours!'** when you have said something annoying or insulting to them. They do it in order to suggest that they do not care at all about you or about what you have said; a very rude expression. EXCLAM
23 You also use **up** to indicate that you strongly support something, especially a group of people who you want to win a contest. EG *Tom yelled 'Up the rebels!'... Up the Rangers!... Up with the revolution!* ADV+NG : USED AS CONVENTION ≠ down with

up-and-coming. Something that is **up-and-coming** is likely to be very successful in the future. EG *...up-and-coming Third World Exporters.* ADJ CLASSIF ≠ declining

upbraid /ʌpbreɪd/, **upbraids, upbraiding, upbraided**. If you **upbraid** someone, you tell them that they have done something wrong and criticize them for doing it; a formal word. EG *You mustn't upbraid Brian for comparing them.* V+O = reproach ≠ praise

upbringing /ʌpbrɪŋɪŋ/. Your **upbringing** is the way your parents treat you and the things that they teach you to care about and believe in. EG *Tony never rebelled against his upbringing... ...a strict upbringing... Fathers and mothers should share the upbringing of small babies.* N UNCOUNT : USU WITH POSS/SUPP

upcountry /ʌpkʌntri[1]/; also spelled with a hyphen. If you describe parts of large countries or land masses as **upcountry**, you mean that they are farther north, farther inland, or more remote than other places that you have been mentioning. EG *She was moved by train to a detention camp up-country.* ADV WITH VB, OR ADJ CLASSIF : PRED

update /ʌpdeɪt/, **updates, updating, updated**. If you **update** something, you make it more modern, V+O ⇑ modernize usually by adding newer parts to it. EG *...the fighter-bombers that India has selected to update its air force... The information will need updating from time to time... ...regularly updated criminal records.*

upend /ʌpend/, **upends, upending, upended**; also spelled with a hyphen. If something **is upended**, it is turned upside down so that the surface that should be at the top is at the bottom. EG *The car stood, upended in the grass... ...an up-ended motorbike.* — V+O : USU PASS = overturn ≠ right

up-front; an informal word, also spelled as two words. **1** If you do something that is up-front, you act openly or publicly so that people know what you are doing or what you believe. EG *We all get programmed anyhow–we may as well be up front about it.* — ADJ QUALIT = direct, frank

2 If a payment is **up front**, it is made openly, so that the person being paid can see that the money is there. EG *All right, I'll do it but I want £5 up front... The owners like to pay a portion of their wages up front, and the remainder under the table in cash which is not declared.* — ADV WITH VB, OR ADJ CLASSIF : USU PRED

upgrade /ʌpgreɪd/, **upgrades, upgrading, upgraded**. If you **upgrade** something such as a person's job or status, you change it, so that the person becomes more important or receives more money. EG *We need to upgrade the pay and status of doctors... They promised to upgrade foreign aid and cut down on arms sales.* — V+O = improve

upheaval /ʌphiːvəˡl/, **upheavals**. **Upheaval** or an **upheaval** is a big change in society or in family life which causes a lot of trouble, confusion, and worry in people's lives. EG *They have brought social upheaval and violent conflict into the country... At the time great upheavals were taking place in the States... It was a terrible upheaval when Dad died.* — N UNCOUNT/COUNT = disturbance

upheld /ʌphɛld/ is the past tense and past participle of **uphold**.

uphill /ʌphɪl/. **1** If you go **uphill**, you go up a slope. If you move something **uphill**, you move it up a slope. EG *She ran furiously uphill... ...the effort of pushing the cart uphill.* ▸ used as an adjective. EG *I resumed my uphill pushing.* — ADV WITH VB ⇑ upwards; ▸ ADJ CLASSIF : ATTRIB

2 You describe someone's attempts to achieve something as **uphill** when they require a great deal of effort and determination. EG *This is hard, uphill work... ...the magazine's uphill battle.* — ADJ CLASSIF : USU ATTRIB ⇑ difficult = gruelling

uphold /ʌphəʊld/, **upholds, upholding, upheld**; a formal word. **1** If you **uphold** something such as a law, a principle, or a system, you support and maintain it. EG *He had sworn to uphold the law... We will loyally uphold the principles of the United Nations... ...the need to uphold our system of parliamentary government.* — V+O ≠ abandon

2 If a court of law **upholds** a legal decision that has already been made, it decides that it was the correct decision. EG *His conviction was upheld on appeal.* — V+O ≠ reverse, change

upholder /ʌphəʊldə/, **upholders**. If you are an **upholder** of a principle or system, you support and maintain it, because you believe that it is right; a formal word. EG *This presents difficulties for the upholders of the present order.* — N COUNT+*of* ⇑ supporter

upholstered /ʌphɒlstəd/. **Upholstered** chairs, sofas, etc have a soft covering that makes them comfortable to sit on. EG *...huge upholstered armchairs.* — ADJ CLASSIF : IF+ PREP THEN *in* ⇑ padded

upholstery /ʌphʊlstəˡriˡ/ is soft covering on chairs, sofas, etc that makes them more comfortable to sit on. EG *It was black with real leather upholstery... He sank into the supple upholstery.* — N UNCOUNT ⇑ padding

upkeep /ʌpkiːp/. The **upkeep** of a building is the continual process of keeping it in good condition. EG *We have to pay for the upkeep of the chapel.* — N UNCOUNT : USU +*of* ⇑ maintenance

upland /ʌpləˡnd/, **uplands**. **1 Upland** places are situated on high hills, plateaus, or mountains. EG *Single-stem trees can be grown in less fertile upland areas... They move with their flocks to upland pastures.* ▸ used of people, activities, and things connected with upland places. EG *...upland farmers... ...upland forestry.* — ADJ CLASSIF : ATTRIB

2 Uplands are areas of land on high hills, plateaus, or mountains. EG *...the chalk uplands of Wiltshire... ...food production in the uplands.* — N PLURAL ≠ lowlands

uplift, uplifts, uplifting, uplifted. The word **uplift** is pronounced /ʌplɪft/ when it is a verb and /ʌplɪft/ when it is a noun. If something **uplifts** people, it helps them to have a better life, for example by improving their social conditions; a fairly formal word. EG *I want to see the poor uplifted.* ▸ used as a noun. EG *He devoted his life to their uplift... ...a new scheme for the uplift of the nation.* — V+O : USU PASS ⇑ raise; ▸ N UNCOUNT

uplifted /ʌplɪftɪˡd/. If people's faces, arms, etc are **uplifted**, they are pointing them upwards or holding them in a high position. EG *They stood in silence, their uplifted faces expressing their joy... We could just see him, a tiny silhouette with uplifted arms.* — ADJ CLASSIF = raised

uplifting /ʌplɪftɪŋ/. You describe something as **uplifting** when it improves your life in some way. EG *My experience of love has hardly been uplifting... She regarded the Book of Common Prayer as uplifting literature.* — ADJ QUALIT = edifying, enriching

upmarket /ʌpmɑːkɪt/; also spelled with a hyphen. **Upmarket** places and goods are visited or bought by people who have sophisticated and expensive tastes; a rather informal word. EG *Paleo is an upmarket resort... ...upmarket shops.* — ADJ QUALIT = exclusive, posh

upon /əpɒn/. **1 Upon** is used in phrasal verbs, for example 'come upon' and 'look upon', and after some other verbs such as 'decide' and 'depend'. See individual verb and phrasal verb entries for such items, which are not treated here. — PREP = on

2 In rather formal English, you use **upon** in place of 'on' in the following ways: **2.1** to refer to the position of an object or person. EG *She was sitting in a rocking-chair with a mangy cat upon her knee... He lay down upon the grass.* — PREP **2.2** to refer to a place where something is or where something is happening. EG *...pictures of a man walking upon the moon... Kingston-upon-Hull.* — PREP = on **2.3** to say that someone's face shows a particular expression. EG *He had a furtive look upon his face.* — PREP = on **2.4** to say that something happens immediately after you have done something or at the same time as you do it. EG *Upon entering the cabin, she sat down.* — PREP = on **2.5** to specify the person or thing that is affected, used, or involved in a particular situation or action. EG *He recalled the attacks upon him... All eyes were upon him... They laid particular emphasis upon the duty of pilgrimage.* — PREP = on

3 You also use **upon** between two occurrences of the same noun in order to say that there are very large numbers of the thing referred to. EG *We drove through mile upon mile of brick villas and terraces... There were thousands upon thousands of people arriving... Margaret submitted request upon request to the administration.* — PREP

4 You also use **upon** in some expressions of time to indicate that a certain event is about to happen. EG *Christmas is almost upon us again.* — PREP

upper /ʌpə/, **uppers**. **1 Upper** describes **1.1** something that is above something else, usually the top one of a pair of things. EG *I pulled down a book from an upper shelf... Four of his front upper teeth were missing.* — ADJ CLASSIF : ATTRIB ⇑ higher **1.2** the first or more important one of two organizations, groups, or systems that work together, for example in law or government. In Britain, the House of Commons is sometimes called the Lower House, and the House of Lords is sometimes called the Upper House. EG *He hoped some peer would put a question in the Upper House.* — ADJ CLASSIF : ATTRIB ≠ lower **1.3** the top or higher part of something. EG *Dark glasses masked the upper half of his face... ...the upper atmosphere.* — ADJ CLASSIF : ATTRIB **1.4** a place that is further inland or further north than somewhere else. EG *The upper valley of the Tiber.* — ADJ CLASSIF : ATTRIB

2 You also use **upper** to describe people or things that have more importance than other people or things, or that are near the top of a particular scale. EG *...an upper servant... ...the upper strata of society.* — ADJ CLASSIF : ATTRIB

3 If you have **the upper hand**, you have more power than someone else and can make decisions about what happens. EG *The farmers had got the upper hand now... Neither of them is concerned with gaining the upper hand.* — PHR : USED AS O ⇑ control

4 The **upper** of a shoe is the top part of it, which is attached to the sole and the heel. EG *A lot of shoes now have nylon uppers, rather than the old-fashioned leather.* — N COUNT

upper case. **Upper case** letters are capital letters. EG *An upper case M.* — N UNCOUNT, OR ADJ CLASSIF

upper class, upper classes. The **upper class** or **upper classes** are the people who belong to the social class above the middle class. EG *The upper classes still send their children to Eton or Harrow.* ▸ used as an adjective, usually spelled with a hyphen. EG *...upper-class families.* — N COUNT : USU SING=PL = aristocracy; ▸ ADJ CLASSIF

upper crust; also spelled with a hyphen. **Upper crust** means the same as upper class; an informal expression. EG *...an upper crust eccentric... ...her upper-crust admirers.*
ADJ CLASSIF = highborn

upper lip, upper lips. 1 Your **upper lip** is 1.1 the part of your face between your mouth and your nose. EG *His chin and upper lip were clean shaven... The cleft of his upper lip filled with perspiration.*
N COUNT : USU SING
1.2 the higher of your two lips. EG *He licked his upper lip.*
N COUNT : USU SING
2 • **a stiff upper lip**: see **lip**.

uppermost /ʌpəməʊst/. 1 You say that something is **uppermost** when it is higher than the rest of something or when it is the highest one of a group of things. EG *Turn it upside down so that the shell markings are uppermost... He was pointing with the whole of his hand, thumb uppermost... He gently examined the uppermost leaves.*
ADJ CLASSIF, OR ADV AFTER VB/NG ⇑ top
2 If something is **uppermost** in a particular situation, it is the most important and obvious thing in that situation. EG *Where political motives were uppermost, private enterprise still worked... Social role rather than social status was uppermost... The really good side of him was uppermost.*
ADJ CLASSIF : PRED = prominent
3 If something is **uppermost in** your **mind** in a particular situation, it is the main thing that you are thinking about in that situation. EG *None of this is uppermost in your mind when you first meet her... There were two thoughts uppermost in my mind.*
PHR : USED AS C

uppish /ʌpɪʃ/. If you say that someone is **uppish**, you mean that they are behaving as if they were very important and you do not think that they are; an old-fashioned expression, used showing disapproval. EG *They were being frightfully uppish and rude.*
ADJ QUALIT ⇑ superior = uppity

uppity /ʌpɪti[1]/ means the same as uppish; used mainly in American English. EG *My boss felt I was getting slightly uppity... These uppity kids are all the same.*
ADJ QUALIT = arrogant

upraised /ʌpreɪzd/. If your hand or arm is **upraised**, you are holding it up in the air. EG *The man just stood there with his arm upraised... ...her upraised hand.* ▸ used also of things that you hold in your hand. EG *With her upraised flag, she marched valiantly forward.*
ADJ CLASSIF ⇑ raised

upright /ʌpraɪt/, **uprights.** 1 If you are **upright**, you are sitting or standing with your back straight, rather than bending or lying down. EG *I cannot stand upright any more... He sat bolt upright.*
ADJ CLASSIF, OR ADV AFTER VB ⇑ erect
2 An **upright** vacuum cleaner, freezer, etc stands vertically and is taller than it is wide. EG *...a small upright model light enough to carry upstairs.*
ADJ CLASSIF : ATTRIB
3 An **upright** chair has a straight back and no arms.
ADJ CLASSIF
4 An **upright** is one of the tall vertical parts of something, for example a bookcase or shelving unit, which horizontal parts are attached to; a technical use.
N COUNT
5 You also describe people as **upright** when they are careful to follow rules of behaviour and behave in a moral way. EG *...the upright and respectable Charles Smithson.* ◊ **uprightness.** EG *He was a paragon of honesty and uprightness.*
ADJ QUALIT ⇑ good = virtuous
◊ N UNCOUNT = virtue

uprising /ʌpraɪzɪŋ/, **uprisings.** When an **uprising** happens, a group of people start fighting against those in power because, for example, they want to bring about a political change in a country. EG *...the Sepoy uprising of 1857... He refused to man the barricades during the uprising.*
N COUNT = rebellion, revolt

up-river; also spelled as one word. 1 If something moves **up-river**, it moves along a river towards its source. EG *We paddled some 60 miles up-river to Bordeaux... He had advised that torpedo boats be brought upriver.*
ADV AFTER VB = upstream ≠ downstream
2 If something is **up-river** from a place, it is on the same river but further towards the river's source. EG *...the village of Juffure, four days up-river.*
ADJ CLASSIF : PRED = upstream ≠ downstream

uproar /ʌprɔː/. **Uproar** or an **uproar** is 1 a lot of noise and shouting made by people who are very angry or shocked about something. EG *Soon all was uproar... She could hear the uproar in the prisoners' coaches.*
N UNCOUNT, OR N SING WITH DET = commotion, pandemonium
2 public criticism and debate about something that has made people angry. EG *The Parisian intellectuals were in an uproar... There is an increasing uproar over who the Arts Council chooses to support.*
N UNCOUNT, OR N SING WITH DET ⇑ protest = outcry

uproarious /ʌprɔːrɪəs/. When people are **uproarious**, they laugh in a noisy way. EG *The Colonel was the centre of an uproarious group of men... ...an uproarious burst of laughter.* ▸ used of things that make you laugh like this. EG *The play came to its uproarious conclusion.* ◊ **uproariously.** EG *He laughed uproariously... This comment was received uproariously.*
ADJ CLASSIF = rowdy, rollicking
▸ = hilarious
◊ ADV WITH VB = hilariously

uproot /ʌpruːt/, **uproots, uprooting, uprooted.** 1 If you **uproot** yourself or if you **are uprooted**, you leave, or are made to leave, a place where you have lived for a long time. EG *The wife had to uproot herself from family and friends... People were uprooted and rehoused.*
V+O (NG) : USU PASS, OR V+O (REFL) ⇑ move
2 If someone **uproots** a tree or if the wind **uproots** it, it is pulled out of the ground. EG *Windows were smashed and 3ft wide trees uprooted.* ◊ **uprooted.** EG *...uprooted hedges and levelled fields.*
V+O
◊ ADJ CLASSIF : ATTRIB

upset, upsets, upsetting, upset. The form **upset** is used in the present tense and is the past tense and past participle of the verb. **Upset** is pronounced /ʌpset/ when it is an adjective in predicative position or a verb, and /ʌpset/ when it is an adjective in attributive position or a noun. 1 If you are **upset**, you are unhappy or disappointed because something unpleasant has happened to you. EG *I'm dreadfully upset about it all... They were upset by the poverty they saw in Dublin... I was very upset that the production had to come off.*
ADJ QUALIT : USU PRED = distressed
2 If something **upsets** you, it makes you feel worried or unhappy. EG *Something has upset him... I didn't mean to upset you.* ◊ **upsetting.** EG *It was a very upsetting experience.*
V+O = distress
◊ ADJ QUALIT ⇑ disturbing
3 If you **upset** something such as a procedure or a state of affairs, you cause it to go wrong. EG *Davis's death has upset the routine... This may upset a solution to Turkey's disputes... They wouldn't fit in. They would upset the whole atmosphere.* ▸ used as a noun. EG *Can we dispose of radioactive material without ecological upset?*
V+O = mess up, disturb
▸ N UNCOUNT = disruption
4 To **upset** something also means to turn it over accidentally. EG *He almost upset the canoe... I've upset a tin of paint on the carpet.*
V+O ⇑ overturn
5 If your stomach is **upset**, it is not working properly, so that you feel uncomfortable or ill.
ADJ QUALIT ⇑ disordered
6 A stomach **upset** or tummy **upset** is a slight illness in your stomach caused by an infection or by something that you have eaten. EG *Everyone gets stomach upsets from time to time.*
N COUNT ⇑ disorder

upshot /ʌpʃɒt/. The **upshot** of a series of events or discussions is the final result of them. EG *The upshot was that the agreement had to be re-negotiated... The upshot of this episode was that we had to make a hasty retreat.*
N SING WITH DET : IF+PREP THEN *of* = outcome

upside down; also spelled with a hyphen. 1 If something is **upside down**, it has been turned round so that the part that is usually lowest is above the part that is usually highest. EG *They were hanging upside down... He turned his wallet upside down.*
ADJ CLASSIF : PRED, OR ADV AFTER VB
2 If you turn something such as a system **upside down**, you change it completely, so that its most important features are replaced by others. EG *They want to turn society upside down... He had offered to turn her life upside down.*
ADV AFTER VB
3 If you turn a place **upside down**, you create disorder or untidiness, for example because you change the positions of things carelessly or hurriedly. EG *I turned the place upside down looking for his watch.*
ADV AFTER VB

upstage /ʌpsteɪdʒ/, **upstages, upstaging, upstaged.** 1 If you **upstage** someone, you take people's attention away from them by making them watch or listen to you instead. EG *He seems to be attempting to upstage the Prime Minister... They were anxious not to be upstaged.*
V+O = outshine
2 When an actor goes **upstage**, he or she moves to the back part of the stage from another part of it; a technical use. EG *He was stalking upstage as the curtain fell... At the end they march triumphantly upstage.*
ADV AFTER VB, OR ADJ CLASSIF : PRED

upstairs /ʌpsteəz/. 1 If you go **upstairs** in a building, you go up towards a higher floor, usually by a staircase. EG *He went upstairs and pulled down the blind... I ran back upstairs.*
ADV AFTER VB ≠ downstairs
2 If something or somebody is **upstairs** in a building, they are on an upper floor or on a higher floor than you. EG *Upstairs, there were three little bedrooms... From upstairs came the sound of running water.*
ADV = above ≠ downstairs
3 The **upstairs** of a building is its upper floor or floors; a rather informal use. EG *They had to rent out the upstairs to make the mortgage payments.*
N SING WITH DET/N UNCOUNT ≠ downstairs

4 An **upstairs** room or object is one which is situated on an upper floor of a building. EG *Neighbours watched from their upstairs windows... ...the upstairs drawing room.* — ADJ CLASSIF: ATTRIB ≠ downstairs

5 When you refer to a person **upstairs**, you are referring to someone who lives in a flat or room on an upper floor or on the floor above you. EG *...the people upstairs.* — ADJ AFTER N

upstanding /ʌpstæ̲ndɪŋ/. **Upstanding** people behave in a morally respectable way; a rather formal word, sometimes used humorously. EG *You're a decent upstanding young man.* — ADJ QUALIT: USU ATTRIB = upright

upstart /ʌ̲pstɑːt/, **upstarts**. You refer to someone as an **upstart** when they behave as if they are important, but you think that they are too new in a place or job to be treated as important; used showing disapproval. EG *He regarded me as a young upstart... We have to put this upstart in his place.* ▸ used as an adjective. EG *...this upstart interloper.* — N COUNT; ▸ ADJ CLASSIF: ATTRIB

upstream /ʌpstri̲ːm/. 1 If something moves **upstream**, it moves along a river towards its source. EG *He was making his way upstream.* — ADV AFTER VB = up-river

2 If something is **upstream** from a place, it is on the same river but further towards the river's source. EG *...the chemical plant upstream.* — ADJ CLASSIF: PRED = up-river

upsurge /ʌ̲psɜːdʒ/. An **upsurge** is a sudden and serious increase in something. EG *...a massive upsurge of social unrest... ...an upsurge in industrial production... ...the inflationary upsurge.* — N SING WITH DET: USU+SUPP ⇑ rise = swell

upswing /ʌ̲pswɪŋ/, **upswings**. An **upswing** is a sudden improvement in something that had previously been declining. EG *The second half of the 1960s brought an upswing in sales... Their fortunes took an upswing.* — N COUNT ⇑ recovery

uptake /ʌ̲pteɪk/. 1 You say that someone is **quick on the uptake** when they understand things quickly. You say that someone is **slow on the uptake** when they have difficulty understanding simple or obvious things; an informal expression. EG *Colin was as quick on the uptake as he was brave and good-looking... The officer on duty had been slow on the uptake.* — PHR: USED AS C

2 A person's or machine's **uptake** of something is the amount of it that they use; a technical term. EG *An athlete has a maximum oxygen uptake of four litres per minute... He increased the water uptake.* — N SING WITH DET +SUPP = intake

uptight /ʌptaɪ̲t/. You say that someone is **uptight** when they are nervous or annoyed about something but are not saying so directly; an informal word. EG *He seemed very uptight about my being there... You get so uptight whenever I raise the subject.* — ADJ QUALIT ⇑ anxious = edgy

up-to-date; also spelled without hyphens. 1 If something is **up-to-date**, it is the newest thing of its kind that you can get. EG *...a housewife with every up-to-date convenience... ...a fleet of up-to-date lorries.* — ADJ QUALIT ⇑ modern

2 If you are **up-to-date** about something, you have the latest information about it. EG *Tony was more up-to-date than I... I was doing my best to keep up-to-date.* — ADJ QUALIT ≠ out-of-date

up-to-the-minute information is the latest information that you can obtain about something. EG *...up-to-the-minute news flashes... ...up-to-the-minute lists.* — ADJ CLASSIF: ATTRIB ⇑ current

uptown /ʌ̲ptaʊn/. In American English, if you go **uptown**, you go away from the centre of a town or city towards one of its outer parts. If you are **uptown**, you are in one of these outer parts. EG *He walked uptown... The cab swept uptown... She always met him at his apartment uptown.* — ADV AFTER VB, OR ADJ CLASSIF

upturn /ʌ̲ptɜːn/, **upturns**. If there is an **upturn** in something such as a country's economy, it starts to improve. EG *The economy is experiencing an upturn... ...an upturn in demand.* — N COUNT: USU SING ⇑ improvement

upturned /ʌptɜ̲ːnd/. Something that is **upturned** 1 points upwards. EG *She had a small upturned nose... Mr Turner grinned down at the upturned face.* 2 is upside down. EG *She sat on an upturned bucket.* — ADJ CLASSIF; ADJ CLASSIF

upwards /ʌ̲pwədz/; also **upward**. 1 If something moves, looks, etc **upwards** or **upward**, it moves or looks up towards a higher place. EG *He had happened to look upwards.* — ADV AFTER VB = up

2 An **upward** movement or look is directed towards a higher place. EG *He would steal upward glances at the clock.* — ADJ CLASSIF: USU ATTRIB

3 **Upwards** or **upward** is used to say that something rises to a higher level or point on a scale. EG *The world urban population is rocketing upward at a rate of 6.5 per cent per year.* ▸ **Upward** can be used as an adjective. EG *...the inflationary upward spiral.* — ADV AFTER VB = up; ▸ ADJ CLASSIF: USU ATTRIB

4 **Upwards of** or **upward of** a particular number of people or things means more than that number. You use this expression when you are uncertain of the exact number of people or things. EG *The cyclone killed upwards of 200,000 people... All we know is that upward of 2,000 boats made the journey.* — PREP+NUM = over

upwind /ʌpwɪ̲nd/. If something is **upwind**, it is in a place, position, or direction that the wind is blowing away from. EG *The fallout stretched roughly 20 miles upwind of the island.* — ADJ CLASSIF, OR ADV WITH VB ≠ downwind

uranium /jʊreɪ̲nɪəm/ is a radioactive metal that is used to produce nuclear energy and nuclear weapons. — N UNCOUNT

urban /ɜ̲ːbən/ means belonging to or relating to a town or city. EG *More and more people are moving to urban areas... ...urban unemployment.* — ADJ CLASSIF: ATTRIB ≠ rural

urbane /ɜːbeɪ̲n/. Someone who is **urbane** is well-mannered, relaxed, and appears comfortable in social situations. EG *David was the most urbane of correspondents.* ◇ **urbanely**. EG *...the College over which he urbanely presided for many years.* ◇ **urbanity** /ɜːbæ̲nɪti[1]/. EG *John Crow was surprised at the urbanity and good-temper of Mr Owen Evans.* — ADJ QUALIT = sophisticated ≠ awkward; ◇ ADV WITH VB; ◇ N UNCOUNT

urbanize /ɜ̲ːbənaɪz/, **urbanizes, urbanizing, urbanized**; also spelled **urbanise**. If a country area **is urbanized**, it is made more like a town, with more buildings, industry, business, etc. EG *...highly urbanized and industrialized areas.* ◇ **urbanization** /ɜ̲ːbənaɪzeɪ̲ʃəⁿn/. EG *Each year, the urbanization of farmland eats further into the countryside.* — V+O: USU PASS; ◇ N UNCOUNT

urchin /ɜ̲ːtʃɪn/, **urchins**. 1 An **urchin** is a young child who is very poor, has no home or family, and lives in a town or a city; a rather old-fashioned use. — N COUNT = waif

2 You refer to a child as an **urchin** when you like the child, but he or she is behaving badly or looks untidy. EG *I'll be glad to see the little urchin again.* — N COUNT: USU ADJ+N = ragamuffin

3 See also **sea urchin**.

Urdu /ʊ̲ədu:, ɜ̲:-/ is one of the languages that is spoken by people who live in Pakistan, and by some people in India. — N UNCOUNT

urge /ɜ̲ːdʒ/, **urges, urging, urged**. 1 An **urge** is a strong desire to do or have something, especially a desire which you cannot control or explain. EG *They have a strong urge to communicate... Telephone a friend when you get the urge to spend... ...our insane urge for greater and greater material wealth.* — N COUNT: USU+ to-INF

2 If you **urge** someone to do something, you ask or advise them very strongly to do it. EG *I urged him to take a year off to study drawing... 'At least stay for Christmas,' Pam urged... She urged that I should support the girls in their endeavour... Workers in other industries should be urged into action.* — V+O+to-INF/A, OR V+QUOTE/ REPORT-CL = press

3 If you **urge** a particular course of action, you suggest or advise very strongly that it should be taken; a rather formal use. EG *US officials urged restraint... The report urged a more positive role for local government... He accepted the wording urged upon him by his colleagues.* — V+O: IF+PREP THEN *on/upon* ⇑ request

4 If you **urge** an animal or person, you make them go somewhere or move faster by touching them or talking to them. EG *Allen took her arm and urged her gently towards the door... She urged her pony into an energetic trot.* — V+O+A

urge on. If you **urge** someone **on**, you encourage them to do something. EG *The President, reportedly urged on by his vice-president, has decided to attend the talks... I am trying to urge him on to 'try things out for himself'.* — PHRASAL VB: V+O+ADV ≠ discourage

urgency /ɜ̲ːdʒənsi[1]/ is the need for something to be done without delay, because it is important. EG *The city needs, as a matter of urgency, £45m for schools... ...moving in a very deliberate manner, without any sense of urgency... There was a note of urgency in his voice.* — N UNCOUNT

urgent /ɜ̲ːdʒənt/. 1 Something that is **urgent** needs to be dealt with at once and before other things. EG *Most of the motorway network is in urgent need of repair... ...urgent messages.* ◇ **urgently**. EG *Improved health and education are urgently needed.* — ADJ QUALIT = pressing; ◇ ADV WITH VB

2 If something you say is **urgent**, it is said in a way that shows other people that you badly want them to notice something or do something. EG *The shouts became louder and more urgent... He went over to Smithy and spoke to him in a low and urgent voice.* ◇ **urgently**. EG *'Do you see it?' he demanded urgently.* — ADJ QUALIT = desperate; ◇ ADV WITH VB

urinal /jʊraɪnəºl, jʊərɪnəºl/, **urinals**. A **urinal** is a bowl or trough which is fixed to the wall of men's public lavatories for men to urinate in. N COUNT

urinary /jʊərɪnəºriˡ/ means belonging to or related to the parts of a person's body through which urine flows. EG ...*a minor urinary complaint.* ADJ CLASSIF: ATTRIB

urinate /jʊərɪneɪt/, **urinates, urinating, urinated**. When you **urinate**, you get rid of urine from your body. V

urine /jʊərɪn/ is the yellow liquid that you get rid of from your body when you go to the toilet. N UNCOUNT

urn /ɜːn/, **urns**. An **urn** is 1 a decorated container with handles and a lid that is used to hold the ashes of a person who has been cremated. N COUNT 2 a container used for making a large quantity of tea or coffee and for keeping it warm. Urns have a tap on them. N COUNT: USU MOD+N

us /ʌs, əs/ is used as the object of a verb or preposition. 1 A speaker or writer uses **us** to refer both to himself or herself and to one or more other people as a group. See **we**. EG *Why didn't you tell us?... There wasn't room for us all... Most of us went about three times a week.* PRON: PL, USED AS O

2 A speaker sometimes says **us** instead of 'me' in informal spoken English. EG *Give us a chance. I've hardly started.* PRON: USED AS O

US /juː ɛs/is an abbreviation for 'United States'. EG *The US was in a better position than most countries... ...the US Army.* N PROPER: *the*+N

USA /juː ɛs eɪ/is an abbreviation for 'United States of America'. EG ...*the President of the USA.* N PROPER: *the*+N

usable /juːzəbəºl/. If something is **usable**, it is in a state or condition which makes it possible to use it. EG *He told me which wells were usable along the road... The information is not in a usable form.* ADJ CLASSIF ≠ unusable, useless

USAF /juː ɛs eɪ ɛf/is an abbreviation for 'United States Air Force'. N PROPER: *the*+N

usage /juːsɪdʒ, -zɪdʒ/, **usages**. 1 **Usage** is the way in which words are actually used in particular contexts, especially with regard to their meanings. EG ...*a guide to English usage... Today the word has virtually dropped out of usage... It is interesting that in common usage, 'jerk' is an epithet applied to men only.* N UNCOUNT = use

2 A **usage** is a particular meaning that a word has or a particular way in which it can be used. EG *It's a curious usage, isn't it?... This is not the familiar usage of the phrase, but depends on your understanding its French origins.* N COUNT = use

3 **Usage** is also the degree to which something is used or the way in which it is used. EG ...*the environmental effects of energy usage.* N UNCOUNT = use

use, uses, using, used. The word **use** is pronounced /juːz/ when it is a verb, and /juːs/ when it is a noun. 1 If you **use** something such as a tool, service, or a course of action, you do something with it in order to do a job, achieve something, or solve a problem. EG *Using a knife, peal off the outer plastic cover... He wants to use the phone... He walked over to a closet that he used for hanging up his clothes... No violence was used... Can you actually use computers to diagnose illnesses?... The scissors are specially shaped for women's small hands and easy to use.* V+O

2 If you have a limited supply of something and you **use** it, you consume it and so reduce the supply of it. EG *Who's used all my shampoo?... In 1900 we used a negligible amount of oil... I had used my allotted tickets for Phil and Jenny.* V+O

3 If you **use** something such as a skill, quality, or advantage, you deliberately and sensibly do something with it, so that you get the greatest possible benefit from it. EG *We have to use our initiative... He'd got brains but wouldn't use them... Efforts are being made to use these assets... I could use the time to look round the city... A woman should be able to use her looks to her advantage.* V+O, OR V+O+*to*-INF ⇑ exploit

4 If you **use** a particular kind or brand of product, you buy or choose it regularly. EG *It was the perfume my first wife had used... What kind of shampoo do you use?* V+O

5 If you **use** a particular word or expression, you say or write it, because it has the meaning that you want to express. EG *Both Dick and Roger use the word 'open' about themselves... It's a phrase I once heard him use in a sermon... I hardly ever use any adjectives when I'm talking.* V+O

6 If you **use** a particular name, you call yourself by that name, although it is not your real name. EG *The name she used was Elizabeth Gregory... Doesn't he use the name Aspiazu?* V+O

7 If you **use** a situation in a particular way, you take advantage of it. EG *The United States might use Britain's behaviour as an excuse to put pressure on other European countries.* V+O: USU+*as*/*to*-INF = exploit

8 If you **use** people, you make them do things for you because you want to benefit or gain some advantage from it, and not because you care about them. EG *For the first time he felt used... She just uses people.* V+O ⇑ exploit

9 If you **make use of** something, you do something with it in order to do a job, achieve something, or solve a problem. EG *There's a great deal here that you can make use of... Industry is making increasing use of robots... They do not make the maximum use of new ideas.* PHR: VB INFLECTS

10 If something has a **use** or if you have a **use** for it, there is a purpose for which it can be used. EG *He might later have a use for it... It was built as a sanatorium for which apparently no use has arisen.* N COUNT

11 If something **has** its **uses**, it can sometimes be useful in some way. EG *Fathers have their uses.* PHR: VB INFLECTS

12 If something is intended **for use as** a particular thing or **for** a particular **use**, it is intended to be used for a particular purpose or in a particular situation. EG *It should be feasible to develop the gun for battlefield use... Biologists will be growing micro-organisms for use as animal feed... ...a pamphlet for use in schools.* PREP, OR PHR: USED AS AN A

13 If something is **for the use of** a particular person or group of people, it is available for that person or group to use. EG *Food is provided for the use of you and your household... This car park is for the use of staff and customers only.* PHR+NG: USED AS AN A

14 If a device, machine, technique, etc is **in use**, it is used by people, especially regularly. If it has gone **out of use**, it is no longer used regularly by people. EG *Within the next decade industrial robots will be in widespread use... No major British weapon system in use in 1978 offered plausible protection against a nuclear attack... There may be occasions when they can be called into use for some particular issue.* PHR: USED AS AN A

15 The **use** of something is the act or fact of using it. EG *More prosperity means a greater use of fuel... ...the dangers of the large-scale use of fertilisers and insecticides.* N UNCOUNT: USU WITH POSS

16 If you have the **use** of something, you have the ability or the permission to use it. EG *He lost the use of his legs... I've got the use of the car this evening.* N UNCOUNT: USU WITH POSS

17 If something is **of use**, it is useful. EG *She kept in touch with friends who would be of use in later life... Many kinds of evidence are not of much use in court... You will be more use as an ally than an enemy... I don't know whether any of these things will be any use to you.* PHR: USED AS AN A

18 You say **it is no use** or **there is no use** doing or saying something when you mean that an action is pointless and will not achieve anything. EG *It's no use being much more accurate than that... It is no use arguing with you... The owners knew there really was no use... It's no use your worrying about me.* PHR: VB INFLECTS

19 If you say **it is no use**, you mean that you have failed to do something and realize that it is useless to continue trying because it is impossible. EG *It's no use. I can't get the door open... I tried giving up drinking but it was no use–I was an alcoholic.* PHR: VB INFLECTS

20 You say **what is the use** or **what use is there** to emphasize that an action is pointless and will achieve nothing. EG *What is the use of sitting and waiting for success to come?... What possible use is there in keeping my brain alive?... Oh, what's the use?* CONVENTION

21 A **use** of a word is a particular meaning that it has or a particular way in which it can be used. EG *This is an old-fashioned use.* N COUNT+SUPP

22 See also **used**.

use up. If you **use up** a supply of something, you finish it so that none of it is left. EG *She did use up a tremendous amount of energy... He used up all the coins he had.* PHRASAL VB: V+O+ADV

used. The word **used** is pronounced /juːst/ in paragraphs 1, 2, and 3, and /juːzd/ in paragraphs 4 and 5.

1 If something **used** to be done or be true, it was done regularly in the past or was true in the past, but is not done or is not true now. EG *I used to live in this street... I used to be very mean... What an agreeable town this used to be... The two children used to send* SEMI-MODAL+*to*-INF

me a card at Christmas time... It's not true so much these days, but you did used to see whole classes of children sitting in silence.

2 If you **are used to** something or **are used to** doing something, you are familiar with it because you have done or seen it often or because you know someone quite well. EG *San Diego was not used to such demonstrations... We're particularly wasteful, really, having been used to such cheap energy... He was not used to English actors... We are used to working together.* — PHR : AUX INFLECTS ≠ be unused to

3 If you **get used to** something or someone, you become familiar with it, or get to know someone, so that you no longer feel that the thing or person is unusual or surprising. EG *She had got used to Robin and liked him... Once you get used to the idea, there's no attraction in it... You get used to the kind of mistakes that people make.* — PHR : *get* INFLECTS

4 A **used** handkerchief, glass, etc is dirty as a result of being used and needs to be washed. EG *There was a bottle of whisky and a used glass on the coffee table... ...a used napkin.* — ADJ CLASSIF : USU ATTRIB ≠ clean

5 A **used** car is no longer new but has already had an owner. — ADJ CLASSIF = second-hand

> **USED** □ In this dictionary **used** is described as a SEMI-MODAL in paragraph 1 of the entry for **used** because it behaves like the modals in some ways but not in all. See □ at MODAL. **Used** behaves in the following ways. **1** It is always followed by the word *to*, usually as a *to*-infinitive. EG *I **used** to feel guilty about this.* **2** It does not inflect. **3** It can be used followed by *to* to refer back to a previous verbal group. EG *She still went dancing, but not as often as she **used to**.* **4** In fairly formal English, it can be used before a negative. EG *It **used** not to be there.* **5** In formal English, it can be used before the subject of a verb to form questions. EG ***Used** you to live in London?*

useful /juːsfʊl/. **1** If something is **useful**, you can use it in order to do something or to help you in some way. EG *Our useful booklet on this subject will be sent on request... It will be useful to discuss each of these in turn... She gave us some useful information... They feel they should be doing something useful with their time.* ◊ **usefully**. EG *His time could be more usefully spent... A man might usefully make a lifetime study of the impact of the motor car.* ◊ **usefulness**. EG *The usefulness of the computer extends way beyond its ability to add and subtract... ...the great usefulness of play.* — ADJ QUALIT = handy; ◊ ADV WITH VB = profitably; ◊ N UNCOUNT = utility

2 If someone is **useful**, they do things that are important or that help other people. EG *Make yourself useful and fry up some bacon... Gretchen felt motherly and useful.* — ADJ CLASSIF : USU PRED

3 If an object or skill **comes in useful**, you are pleased that you have it or can do it because it can sometimes help you in some way. EG *I bought the bike because I thought it might come in useful if the car broke down.* — PHR : VB INFLECTS

useless /juːslɪ²s/. **1** If something is **useless**, you cannot use it. EG *Land is useless without labour... My left arm was asleep, wholly numb and almost useless... It's useless from a practical point of view.* — ADJ CLASSIF

2 If it is **useless** to do something or if something is **useless**, it does not achieve anything helpful or beneficial. EG *I realized it was useless to pursue the subject... She underwent some twenty entirely useless and unnecessary operations.* ◊ **uselessly**. EG *Animals were being uselessly slaughtered in hundreds of thousands.* — ADJ CLASSIF = vain; ◊ ADV WITH VB = needlessly

3 If someone is **useless**, they do not or cannot do anything that is important or that helps other people. EG *No longer should we be made to feel guilty and useless because we are housewives.* ◊ **uselessness**. EG *She'd been made gloomy by her uselessness.* — ADJ QUALIT; ◊ N UNCOUNT

4 If you describe someone or something as **useless**, you mean that they are no good at all. EG *I was always useless at maths... The school was useless.* — ADJ QUALIT ⇑ bad = hopeless

user /juːzə/, **users**. A **user** is a person or thing that uses a product, machine, facility, place, etc. EG *...vehicle users... ...electricity users... The early computer user had to learn to speak the language of the computer... I'm a great user of roadside facilities.* — N COUNT+SUPP ⇑ consumer

usher /ʌʃə/, **ushers, ushering, ushered**. **1** If you **usher** someone somewhere, you show them where they should go or should sit, often politely letting them go in front of you. EG *The hostess ushered me into the room... He ushered me to a chair.* — V+O+A ⇑ lead

2 An **usher** is **2.1** a person who shows people where to sit, for example at a wedding or at a concert. EG *The usher came down the aisle towards them.* **2.2** a person who organises people attending a law court. — N COUNT ⇑ official; N COUNT ⇑ official

usher in. If one thing **ushers in** something else, it comes before it or it causes something to happen, usually a great and important change in society; a formal expression. EG *The French Revolution ushered in a new age.* — PHRASAL VB : V+O+ADV ⇑ precede = herald

usherette /ʌʃərɛt/, **usherettes**. An **usherette** is a woman who shows people where to sit in a cinema or theatre and who sells refreshments or programmes. — N COUNT ⇑ employee

USSR /juː ɛs ɛs ɑː/ is an abbreviation for 'The Union of Soviet Socialist Republics'. EG *...the southern regions of the USSR.* — N PROPER : *the*+N

usu. is an abbreviation for 'usual' or 'usually'.

> **USU** □ In this dictionary USU is used in the grammar notes beside entries to mean 'usually' and indicates that the word is very often found in the way given after USU. For example, N COUNT: USU SING means that the noun is usually used in the singular. An example is **tackle 3.1**, described as N UNCOUNT: USU MOD+N. This means that the noun usually has an adjective or noun in front of it. EG *...fishing **tackle**... ...swimming **tackle**.* Another example is **take 2.7**, described as V+O, USU *can, could* +V. This means that the verb usually has *can* or *could* in front of it. EG *I **can't take** any more.*

usual /juːʒʊ⁰əl/. **1** If you describe something as **usual** you mean that it is the thing that occurs or is used, shown, done, etc most often in a particular situation or by a particular person. EG *He asked the usual questions... He sat in his usual chair... She got up earlier than usual.* ▸ used as a noun. EG *'Let me get you a drink.'–'Okay,' he said. 'The usual.'* — ADJ CLASSIF ⇑ normal = customary; ▸ N SING : *the*/POSS+N

2 If something happens **as usual**, **2.1** it is not surprising because that particular situation or event happens often. EG *Lady Sackville, as usual, took command... The telephone box on the corner is broken, as usual... As usual at the weekend, the club was almost empty.* **2.2** it happens or is done in the way that it normally happens or is done, especially when other things have changed. EG *She had to try and carry on as usual... ...business as usual... For her it's just life as usual, only lonelier.* — PHR : USED AS AN A; PHR : USED AS AN A = as always

usually /juːʒʊ⁰əli¹/. **1** If something **usually** happens, it is the thing that most often happens or is the case in a particular situation. EG *She usually found it easy to go to sleep at night... He realized he was talking more freely than he usually did with strangers.* — ADV WITH VB, OR ADV SEN = generally, normally

2 If someone is **more than usually** happy, sad, etc, they are happier, sadder, etc than they normally are. EG *They had shown themselves to be more than usually slow.* — PHR+ADJ/ADV = unusually

usurer /juːʒərə/, **usurers**. If you say that someone is a **usurer**, you mean that they lend other people money and charge more interest on it than they should; an old-fashioned word. EG *The tractor owners were often acting the role of usurers as well.* — N COUNT = loan shark

usurp /juːzɜːp/, **usurps, usurping, usurped**. If you **usurp** a job, role, title, or position, you take it from someone, especially when you have no right to do this; a fairly formal word. EG *...the position of control that enables them to usurp power and privilege... Parents are anxious about usurping the role of the teacher.* — V+O = seize

usury /juːʒəri¹/ is the practice of lending money at interest rates that are much higher than they should be; a formal and old-fashioned word. — N UNCOUNT

utensil /juːtɛnsə⁰l/, **utensils**. A **utensil** is a tool or object that you use in order to help you to cook or to do other tasks in your home. EG *...cooking utensils.* — N COUNT = implement

uterus /juːtərəs/, **uteruses**. The **uterus** of a woman or female mammal is her womb; a medical term. EG *The placenta allows the young to remain within the uterus for a very long time.* — N COUNT ⇑ organ

utilise /juːtɪlaɪz/. See **utilize**.

utilitarian /juːtɪlɪtɛərɪən/. Something that is **utilitarian** is **1** intended to produce the greatest benefit for the greatest number of people; a technical term in philosophy. EG *He had not entered science for ambitious or utilitarian purposes.* **2** designed to be useful rather than beautiful. EG *We toured a number of clean, utilitarian flats.* — ADJ CLASSIF; ADJ QUALIT = functional

utility /juːtɪlɪti¹/, **utilities**. 1 The **utility** of something is how useful and practical it is. EG *...the utility and potential of computers.* N UNCOUNT ⇑ function = usefulness

2 A **utility** is an important service such as water, electricity, or gas that is provided for everyone, and that everyone pays for. EG *...the development of roads and utilities... He wanted municipal ownership instead of public utility companies.* N COUNT

utilize /juːtɪlaɪz/, **utilizes, utilizing, utilized**; also spelled **utilise**. If you **utilize** something, you use it in a way that is practical or effective; a formal word. EG *The carbohydrate from the potatoes helps the body to utilize all the protein from the fish.* V+O
◇ **utilization** /juːtɪlaɪzeɪʃəⁿn/. EG *...the utilization of things like wind energy and wave-power.* ◇ N UNCOUNT = exploitation

utmost /ʌtməʊst/. 1 If something is of the **utmost** importance, seriousness, etc, it is extremely important or serious. EG *Learning is of the utmost importance... I write this sadly, with the utmost respect for what he has achieved.* ADJ CLASSIF : USU the+ADJ+N UNCOUNT ⇑ greatest = uttermost

2 If something is done to the **utmost**, it is done to the greatest extent, amount, or degree possible. EG *Its facilities were stretched to the utmost... We will do our utmost to help these unfortunate people... Children need the utmost in love and security.* N SING : the/DETPOSS+N = uttermost

utopia /juːtəʊpɪə/, **utopias**. If you say that a situation is a **utopia**, you mean that it is one in which society is perfect and everyone is happy. EG *...a thing in the mind, a Utopia we secretly retreat to... Ideas of rural utopias have always fascinated the radicals of New England.* N COUNT/UNCOUNT

utopian /juːtəʊpɪən/; **utopians**. You use **utopian** 1 to refer to political or religious ideas which believe that the existing order can be changed, and a completely new society built in which everyone will be happy. EG *...a land where they could build utopian communities in accordance with their beliefs.* ADJ CLASSIF = idealist ▸ used also of people or groups who believe in such ideas. EG *The totalitarian is a utopian who is intoxicated by some scheme for perfection.* ▸ N COUNT 2 to refer to ideas that are foolish or impractical because the person holding them believes that a situation can be changed or improved much more than anyone else thinks it can; used showing disapproval. EG *Some will say it is dreamy, escapist, or utopian.* ADJ CLASSIF = idealistic ▸ used also of someone who believes such foolish ideas. EG *He claimed they were text-book utopians who saw a workers' paradise emerging.* ▸ N COUNT = idealist

utter /ʌtə/, **utters, uttering, uttered**. 1 When you **utter** sounds or words, you say them in order to communicate ideas and feelings. EG *Sam opened his mouth, then quickly shut it again without uttering a sound... She had never been known to utter an unkind word to anyone... He seldom uttered, but when he did everyone listened.* V OR V+O

2 You use **utter** to give emphasis to the noun which follows it by indicating that the quality or emotion mentioned is total and without any limits. EG *To my utter amazement I was made managing director... Most of my friends believe that Judith is a complete and utter fool... Only now can I say with utter conviction that I do believe in God... He laboured in the service of his country with utter disregard of his own well-being.* ADJ CLASSIF : ATTRIB = absolute

utterance /ʌtəⁿrəns/, **utterances**; a fairly formal word. 1 An **utterance** is something which is expressed in speech or in writing, such as a word, a sentence, or a number of sentences. EG *The children watched and copied every act and utterance of the older men... May I suggest that in your public utterances you should emphasize the things the Government has achieved.* N COUNT ⇑ expression

2 **Utterance** is the expression in words of ideas, thoughts, and feelings. EG *He was now ready to give utterance to his intentions... The mere utterance of the word 'Rogers' seemed to frighten my aunt.* N UNCOUNT

utterly /ʌtəli¹/. You use **utterly** to give emphasis to the adjective or verb with which it is being used, in order to indicate that the quality mentioned is complete and total. EG *I am utterly convinced of your loyalty to your colleagues... On the other side of the island, the view was utterly different... My thirteen-year-old niece was standing at the door trying to look like a young lady but failing utterly.* ADV = absolutely, totally, completely

uttermost /ʌtəməʊst/ means the same as utmost; a rather literary word.

U-turn, U-turns. A **U-turn** is 1 a movement in which you drive or cycle in a half circle so that you are then going in the opposite direction. EG *You can't do a U-turn here.* N COUNT ⇑ turn 2 a complete change in policy, plans, action, or beliefs. EG *Is this decision in the nature of a U-turn, or merely a modification of policy?* N COUNT

Vv

V, v /viː/, **Vs, v's**. 1 **V** is the twenty-second letter of the English alphabet. N COUNT

2 **v.** is an abbreviation for verse, usually in references to verses in the Bible. EG *John ch. 3 v. 16.*

3 **V** or **v** is an abbreviation for various words beginning with V or v, such as 'very', 'verb', 'volume', 'volt', and 'versus'.

4 **V** or **v** is the Roman numeral for 5.

> **V** □ In this dictionary v is used in the grammar notes beside entries to mean 'verb'. Where v is used alone or is followed by a colon, the verb is intransitive and does not have an object. Examples of v are **die** and **rise**. EG *All his friends **had died**... Prices will inevitably **rise**.* For explanations of different kinds of verb see □ at RECIP, PHRASAL VB, V+A, V+C, V-ERG, V+O, V+O+A, V+O+C, V+O+O, which can be found in alphabetical order. See also □ at VB.

> **V+A** □ In this dictionary V+A is used in the grammar notes beside entries to indicate that the verb is intransitive and that it requires an adjunct. The adjunct can be an adverbial group or a prepositional group. An example is **behave**. EG *He **behaved** in a very strange way... They **behaved** disgracefully.*

vac /væk/, **vacs**; an informal word used in British English. A **vac** is 1 a vacation. EG *I can work all my vac... ...the Easter vac.* N COUNT 2 a vacuum cleaner. EG *I'll just get the vac out.* N COUNT : USU SING

vacancy /veɪkənsi¹/, **vacancies**. A **vacancy** is 1 a job or position which is not being done or held by anyone and which people can apply for. EG *...an unexpected vacancy in the Department... ...parliamentary vacancies to be filled at by-elections.* N COUNT 2 a room in a hotel or guest house which is not being occupied by anyone and so is available for people to stay in. EG *At the moment there are a lot more vacancies on the 8th than the 15th... ...'No Vacancies'.* N COUNT

vacant /veɪkənt/. 1 If something such as a room, chair, or toilet is **vacant**, it is not being used or occupied by anyone at the moment. EG *I sat down in a vacant chair... I couldn't even find a hotel with a vacant room.* ADJ CLASSIF ⇑ unused = empty

2 A job or position that is **vacant** is one which is not being done or held by anyone and which people can apply for. EG *There are usually 8 or 9 vacant places to be filled by election at the Annual General Meeting... ...'situations vacant' advertisements.* ADJ CLASSIF ⇑ available

3 A **vacant** look or expression is one that suggests that someone does not understand something or that they are not very intelligent. EG *She looked round her with a rather vacant expression... ...a vacant look.* ADJ QUALIT ⇑ stupid = blank
◇ **vacantly**. EG *The boy looked vacantly at his father.* ◇ ADV WITH VB

4 A **vacant** mind or piece of work has no worthwhile ideas or thoughts in it. EG *It was a vacant film for vacant minds.* ADJ CLASSIF ⇑ worthless = superficial

5 A period of time that is **vacant** is time in which you have not yet arranged to do anything. EG *That left plenty of hours vacant.* ADJ CLASSIF = free, spare

vacate /vəkeɪt/, **vacates, vacating, vacated.** 1 If you **vacate** a job or position, you make it available for other people by leaving it or giving it up. EG *I got the job Allister was vacating because I had editorial experience... The title vacated by Ali's retirement would be fiercely contested.* — V+O ⇑ liberate

2 If you **vacate** a room, seat, or space, you leave it and so cause it to be available for someone else to use. EG *He drove neatly into the vacated space.* — V+O

vacation /vəkeɪʃəⁿn/, **vacations, vacationing, vacationed.** A **vacation** is 1 a period of the year when universities, colleges or law courts are officially closed. EG *I've a lot of reading to do over the vacation... ...the summer vacation... ...a vacation job.* — N COUNT = holiday

2 a holiday; an American use. EG *Harold used to take a vacation at that time... She plans to go on vacation for most of August.* ▸ used as a verb. EG *...city tourists vacationing in the mountains.* — N COUNT, OR *on*+N; ▸ V : USU CONT+A

vaccinate /væksɪneɪt/, **vaccinates, vaccinating, vaccinated.** If you **vaccinate** someone, you give them a vaccine, usually by injecting it into their body, in order to protect them from a disease. EG *When were people first vaccinated against measles?.* ◊ **vaccination** /væksɪneɪʃəⁿn/, **vaccinations.** EG *...vaccination against smallpox.* — V+O : IF+PREP THEN *against* ⇑ immunize = inoculate; ◊ N UNCOUNT/COUNT

vaccine /væksiːn/, **vaccines.** A **vaccine** is a substance made from the germs that cause a particular disease which have been treated so that they are no longer harmful. A vaccine is given to people, usually by injection, to protect them from the disease that the germs would normally cause. EG *...polio vaccine.* — N COUNT/UNCOUNT

vacillate /væsɪleɪt/, **vacillates, vacillating, vacillated.** If you **are vacillating**, you are unable to make up your mind between one feeling or opinion and another; a fairly formal word. EG *I tend to vacillate between admiration and pity for him.* ◊ **vacillating.** EG *...the vacillating behaviour of the Parliamentary party.* ◊ **vacillation** /væsɪleɪʃəⁿn/. EG *There was a good deal of vacillation among her opponents.* — V : IF+PREP THEN *between* ⇑ fluctuate; ◊ ADJ CLASSIF; ◊ N UNCOUNT

vacuity /vəˈkjuːɪti¹/. The **vacuity** of something is its lack of intelligent thought or ideas; a formal word. EG *...the shabby ideology and vacuity of his painting.* — N UNCOUNT : WITH POSS ⇑ emptiness = banality

vacuous /vækjʊəs/; a formal word. 1 Something that is **vacuous** does not express any intelligent ideas; used showing disapproval. EG *Much abstract sculpture is more vacuous than its realistic counterpart.* — ADJ QUALIT ⇑ empty = mindless

2 A **vacuous** expression or look is one that shows no sign of intelligence or understanding. EG *He has vacuous eyes.* — ADJ QUALIT ⇑ stupid = vacant

vacuum /vækjʊᵘəm/, **vacuums, vacuuming, vacuumed.** 1 A **vacuum** is 1.1 a space which contains no air or other gas, especially an enclosed space from which the air has been completely or partly removed. EG *Nature is said to abhor a vacuum... We could not pull apart two plates which enclosed a vacuum.* — N COUNT : USU SING **1.2** a temporary situation which occurs when a person, organization, idea, etc no longer fits a particular role adequately and therefore the need is created for someone or something else to fill the same role. EG *Rival groups would seek to fill the power vacuum that the departing British would leave... He saw a dangerous political vacuum which had to be filled.* — N COUNT : USU SING+SUPP ⇑ gap = void

2 If something is **in a vacuum**, it is isolated from all the other things which you would normally expect to have an influence on it. EG *You don't use language in a vacuum... I am not speaking in a moral vacuum.* — PHR : USED AS AN A ⇑ isolation

3 If you **vacuum** something, you clean it using a vacuum cleaner. EG *I'm going to vacuum the car... I moved the chairs back so that I could start vacuuming.* ▸ used as a noun. EG *Can you give the living room a quick vacuum?* — V OR V+O; ▸ N SING : a+N

4 A **vacuum** is also a vacuum cleaner. EG *I'll just turn off the vacuum.* — N COUNT

vacuum cleaner, vacuum cleaners; also spelled with a hyphen. A **vacuum cleaner** is an electric machine which removes dirt from carpets, furniture, etc by sucking it into the machine. — N COUNT

vacuum flask, vacuum flasks; also spelled with a hyphen. A **vacuum flask** is a container which is used to keep hot drinks hot and cold drinks cold. A vacuum flask has two thin silvery glass walls with a vacuum between them. — N COUNT

vacuum-packed. Food that is **vacuum-packed** is packed in a container or packet from which most of the air has been removed, in order to keep the food fresh. — ADJ CLASSIF ⇑ packaged

vagabond /vægəbɒnd/, **vagabonds.** A **vagabond** is someone who goes about from place to place and has no real home or job; an old-fashioned word. — N COUNT = hobo, vagrant

vagary /veɪgəri¹, vəgeəri¹/, **vagaries. Vagaries** are unexpected and unpredictable changes in a situation or in someone's behaviour which you have no control over; a fairly formal word. EG *The final will take place on Sunday, subject to the vagaries of the weather... ...the vagaries of politics.* — N COUNT : USU PL +*of* = whim, quirk

vagina /vədʒaɪnə/, **vaginas.** A woman's **vagina** is the passage that connects her outer sex organs to her womb. — N COUNT

vaginal /vədʒaɪnəⁿl/ means concerned with the vagina. EG *...a vaginal examination.* — ADJ CLASSIF : ATTRIB

vagrancy /veɪgrənsi¹/ is a way of life in which someone goes aimlessly from place to place, has no real home, job, or money, and has to beg or steal in order to live. EG *I don't want you to be arrested for vagrancy.* — N UNCOUNT ⇑ lifestyle

vagrant /veɪgrənt/, **vagrants.** A **vagrant** is someone who goes aimlessly from place to place and does not have a home or a job, and who often begs or steals in order to get food. EG *The country is full of beggars and vagrants.* ▸ used as an adjective. EG *...a vagrant hippy.* — N COUNT = vagabond; ▸ ADJ CLASSIF : USU ATTRIB

vague /veɪg/, **vaguer, vaguest.** 1 **Vague** is used to describe things that people say or write that are not clearly explained or expressed, so that they can be understood in different ways. EG *Robertson made a few vague replies... The terms of the agreement were left deliberately vague... ...vague instructions.* ◊ **vaguely.** EG *...some film job he had been vaguely promised... 'What happened?'-'Oh, a lot of things,' she said vaguely.* ◊ **vagueness.** EG *The vagueness of the statement enabled both sides to claim a moral victory.* — ADJ QUALIT ⇑ obscure = ambiguous; ◊ ADV; ◊ N UNCOUNT = ambiguity

2 If you are **vague** about something, you deliberately do not tell people much about it. EG *Uncle Harold had pried, but Thomas had been vague and merely said that he was doing badly... They were vague and evasive about their backgrounds.* — ADJ QUALIT : PRED, USU+*about* ⇑ obscure

3 You use **vague** to describe the way people look and behave when they are not thinking in a clear or precise way. EG *Jones looked very vague and wondered aloud how it could have happened... He was a small man with vague watery eyes.* ◊ **vaguely.** EG *He looked up vaguely from the paper... She looked vaguely around her and said: 'I think I'm lost.'... They blinked vaguely in the bright sunshine.* — ADJ QUALIT ⇑ imprecise; ◊ ADV WITH VB

4 If you describe gestures or signals as **vague**, you mean that their meaning is unclear or uncertain. EG *She indicated where I should go with a vague gesture toward a door at the far end of the room.* ◊ **vaguely.** EG *She waved a hand vaguely in the air.* — ADJ QUALIT = careless; ◊ ADV WITH VB = carelessly

5 **Vague** thoughts, memories, plans, etc are not definite or clear in your mind. EG *It would only be a vague possibility... I've got a vague recollection of going there once as a child... She had a vague idea of finding Sam and explaining it all to him.* ◊ **vaguely.** EG *What this could mean I could not even guess: I vaguely suspected that it wasn't anything good... We plan vaguely to get married at the end of the year.* — ADJ QUALIT = dim; ◊ ADV WITH VB

6 **Vague** feelings or sensations are ones that you experience to only a slight degree or amount. EG *...my vague misery and sense of defeat... I couldn't sleep for vague pains all over... I realized with a vague feeling of surprise that he had gone.* ◊ **vaguely.** EG *They were vaguely amused... He's got a desk that looks vaguely like yours... ...a sweetish smell, vaguely reminiscent of coffee.* — ADJ QUALIT ⇑ faint; ◊ ADV

7 If the shape or outline of something is **vague**, it is not clear and so the thing is not easy to see. EG *The coffin lay undisturbed, a vague blur of insubstantial whiteness in the gathering dusk... The final letter is very vague; possibly an R or a K.* — ADJ QUALIT ⇑ obscure = faint

vain /veɪn/, **vainer, vainest.** 1 If something is done or happens **in vain**, it happens **1.1** without success, so that it fails to achieve what was intended. EG *We tried in vain to discover what orders would be given... They knew that all their efforts might be in vain.* — PHR : USED AS A **1.2** for no good reason or purpose. EG *Your son didn't die in vain.* — PHR : USED AS A

2 If you **take** someone's **name in vain**, you say that someone has a particular opinion or belief when they are not there to confirm or deny it. — PHR : VB INFLECTS

3 A **vain** attempt or action is one that fails to achieve what was intended. EG *He criticized his mechanics in a vain attempt to make them perform better... ...the teacher's vain plea for silence.* ◇ **vainly**. EG *They often live on inadequate pensions, trying vainly to catch up with the soaring cost of living.* — ADJ CLASSIF : ATTRIB ⇑ useless = fruitless; ◇ ADV WITH VB = in vain

4 Someone who is **vain** is extremely proud of their own beauty, intelligence, or other good qualities; used showing disapproval. EG *...a highly-strung, vain young aristocrat.* — ADJ QUALIT = conceited

vainglorious /veɪnglɔːrɪəs/. **Vainglorious** behaviour is very boastful or proud, so that other people find it ridiculous; a literary word. — ADJ CLASSIF : ATTRIB

valance /væləns/, **valances**; also spelled **valence**. A **valance** is a decorative cover for the bottom part of a bed with a frill which hangs around the edge of the bed touching the floor. — N COUNT

vale /veɪl/, **vales**. A **vale** is a valley; a literary word. EG *...a rich, lush vale of meadows and blossoms... ...the Vale of Evesham.* — N COUNT : ALSO IN NAMES

valediction /vælɪdɪkʃəⁿn/, **valedictions**. A **valediction** is a formal speech made in order to say goodbye to someone, especially as part of a farewell ceremony; a formal word. — N COUNT

valedictory /vælɪdɪktəⁿri¹/. A **valedictory** speech, letter, etc is one that is intended as a way of saying goodbye to someone, especially as part of a farewell ceremony; a formal word. — ADJ CLASSIF : ATTRIB

valence /veɪləns/, **valences**. **1 Valence** is the ability of atoms and chemical groups to form compounds; a technical term in chemistry. — N UNCOUNT

2 In American English, **valence** is the same as valency. — N UNCOUNT

3 See also **valance**.

valency /veɪlənsi¹/, **valencies**. The **valency** of an atom or chemical group is the number of atoms of hydrogen that it is able to combine with in forming compounds; a technical term in chemistry, used especially in British English. — N COUNT

valentine /væləntaɪn/, **valentines**. **1** Your **valentine** is someone you love or are attracted to, who you send a card or a present to on St Valentine's Day, February 14th. — N SING : USU POSS +N = sweetheart

2 A **valentine** or a **valentine card** is a greetings card with a special message in it, which you send to someone you love or are attracted to, usually without signing your name, on St Valentine's Day, February 14th. — N COUNT

valet /vælɪt, væleɪ/, **valets**. A **valet** is a male servant who looks after his employer by doing things such as caring for his clothes and cooking for him. — N COUNT = manservant

valiant /væljənt/. Behaviour that is **valiant** is very brave, especially when the situation you are in is dangerous or difficult. EG *He made a valiant attempt to rescue the struggling victim.* ▸ used of people and groups. EG *...a small, valiant community.* ◇ **valiantly**. EG *Joe valiantly accepted the challenge.* — ADJ QUALIT = courageous; ◇ ADV WITH VB ⇑ bravely

valid /vælɪd/. **1** Something that is **valid** is **1.1** based on sound reasoning. EG *This is a valid, if selfish, argument against economic growth... This was the real reason, and it was a valid reason.* ◇ **validity** /vəlɪdɪti¹/. EG *We should question the validity of those figures.* **1.2** important or serious enough to make it worth saying or doing. EG *It was probably a more valid protest than picketing missile bases... Do you find his interpretation of Chopin entirely valid?* ◇ **validity**. EG *...the validity of modern art.* — ADJ QUALIT ⇑ reasonable; ◇ N UNCOUNT; ADJ QUALIT = meaningful; ◇ N UNCOUNT

2 If a ticket or other document is **valid** for a particular period of time, it officially allows you to do something, such as travel, during the stated period of time. EG *It's valid for six months from the date of issue... The fare by air from London is £71 return, valid for up to three months... This pass is no longer valid.* — ADJ CLASSIF

validate /vælɪdeɪt/, **validates, validating, validated**. To **validate** a statement or claim means to prove or confirm that it is true or correct; a fairly formal word. EG *Their remarkable achievement seems to validate Bomberg's claim.* — V+O = corroborate

valise /vəliːz/, **valises**. A **valise** is a small suitcase; an old-fashioned word. — N COUNT

Valium /vælɪəm/. **Valium** is both the singular and the plural form. **Valium** is a trademark for a drug which is given to people to calm their nerves when they are worried or upset. — N UNCOUNT/ COUNT ⇑ tranquillizer

valley /væli¹/, **valleys**. A **valley** is a low stretch of land between hills, especially one that has a river flowing through it. EG *...a wooded valley with a winding river... ...the valley floor.* — N COUNT : ALSO IN NAMES

valour /vælə/; also spelled **valor** in American English. **1 Valour** is great bravery, especially in battle; a literary word. EG *...an act of epic valour.* — N UNCOUNT ⇑ courage

2 Discretion is the better part of valour is an expression that people use when they want to say that avoiding a dangerous or unpleasant situation is sometimes the most sensible thing to do. — PHR

valuable /væljuᵒəbəᵒl/, **valuables**. **1** Something such as help or advice that is **valuable** is very useful and can help someone a great deal. EG *They could also give valuable help and practical advice... This was one of the most valuable lessons I learned.* — ADJ QUALIT ⇑ beneficial = precious

2 Something such as jewellery or a work of art that is **valuable** is worth a lot of money. EG *...very small valuable items, such as miniature paintings... It's rather attractive, but not valuable.* — ADJ QUALIT

3 Valuables are things that you own that are worth a lot of money, especially small objects such as jewellery. EG *...good silver or other valuables... They were robbed of money and valuables at gunpoint.* — N PLURAL ⇑ possessions

valuation /væljueɪʃəⁿn/, **valuations**. A **valuation** is **1** a judgement that someone makes about how much money something is worth. EG *She asked for a valuation on her house.* **2** a judgement that someone makes about how good or bad something is. EG *...his rather low valuation of the novel.* — N COUNT/ UNCOUNT; N COUNT/ UNCOUNT

value /væljuː/, **values, valuing, valued**. **1** The **value** of a quality, attitude, method, etc is its importance or usefulness, which makes people appreciate it or want to possess it themselves. EG *Everyone realizes the value of sincerity... Books and lectures may have value in answering specific questions and doubts.* — N UNCOUNT = worth

2 The **value** of a house, painting, piece of jewellery, etc is the amount of money that it is worth, for example the amount that you would be given for it if you sold it. EG *What will happen to the value of my property?... They paid 28% above market value for it... The dollar has depreciated in value.* — N UNCOUNT/ COUNT

3 If something is or gives **good value** or is **value for money**, it is worth the money that it costs. EG *The set lunch is good value at £5.95... It no longer provides value for money.* — PHR : USED AS C/O

4 Something that is **of value** or is **of** a particular **value** is useful or important or has the particular degree of usefulness or importance that is stated. EG *People have to work at it if they are to succeed in building something of value in their marriage... It might have been of great value if a couple of women had been present... As soon as the information is of no more value I forget it.* — PHR : USED AS AN A, OR AFTER N = worth

5 If you put or place **a high value** on something, you think that it is very important. EG *They tend to place a high value on permanence.* — PHR : USU USED AS O ⇑ appreciate = prize

6 The **values** of a person or group are the moral principles and beliefs that they think are important in life and that they tend to live their lives by. EG *...the traditional values of civility, moderation, and family... ...the need for a system of moral values... ...the fundamental revolution in human values.* — N PLURAL ⇑ code

7 If you **take** a remark, compliment, etc **at face value**, you accept it without thinking about it very much and without considering what its real meaning or purpose might be. EG *She took the praise at face value.* — PHR : VB INFLECTS

8 Value is used after another noun when mentioning an important or noticeable feature about something. EG *It has novelty value... It was the tourists who were the nuisance value.* — N UNCOUNT AFTER N

9 If you **value** something, **9.1** you think that it is important and appreciate it or want to possess it yourself. EG *By the time they get to that age they value their independence... Which do you value most–wealth or health?* ◇ **valued**. EG *...a highly valued and powerful member of the hierarchy... ...one of our valued customers.* **9.2** you decide how much it is worth, by comparing it with the amount of money that similar things are being sold for at the time. EG *...a display of table silver, valued at £20,000... They had gone to have their jewels valued.* — V+O = treasure, prize; ◇ ADJ QUALIT = prized; V+O : USU PASS ⇑ assess = price

10 A **value** is a particular number or quantity that can replace a general expression such as x or y in a particular case; a technical term in maths and logic. EG *What is the value for x when y is 5?... The highest value this expression can have is 0.3.* — N COUNT

value added tax. See **VAT**.

value judgement, value judgements. A **value judgement** is an opinion about something that is based on the values of the person expressing the opinion and not on facts which can be checked or proved; often used showing disapproval. EG *It is difficult to answer that question without making a value judgement... ...an argument based on value judgements.* N COUNT : USU PL

valueless /væljuːlɪ²s/. Something that is **valueless** is not effective or useful. EG *A campaign, however inspired, is valueless without the backing of an organization.* ADJ CLASSIF = worthless

valuer /væljuːə/, **valuers**. A **valuer** is someone whose job is to decide how much property is worth, for example jewellery, land, property, etc. N COUNT

valve /vælv/, **valves**. A **valve** is 1 a part attached to a pipe or a tube which controls the flow of air or liquid. When the valve is open it lets the air or liquid pass through. When the valve is closed it stops the air or liquid passing through. EG *This tap has a valve in the middle... The exhaust valve on my car has burnt out three times.* ● See also **safety-valve**. N COUNT ⇑ device 2 a small flap in your heart or in a vein which controls the flow of blood and keeps it flowing in one direction only. N COUNT

vamoose /vəmuːs/. If you say **'Vamoose!'** to someone, you are telling them to go away quickly; a rather old-fashioned informal word. CONVENTION ⇑ leave = scram

vamp /væmp/, **vamps, vamping, vamped**. 1 A **vamp** is a woman who is sexually attractive and who uses her attractiveness to get what she wants from men; a rather old-fashioned word, used showing disapproval. N COUNT

2 If a woman **vamps**, she uses her sexual attractiveness to get what she wants from men; used showing disapproval. V

vamp up. If you **vamp** something **up**, for example a story or some music, you make it seem as if it is new and exciting by adding extra parts which you have invented; an informal use. PHRASAL VB : V+O+ADV ⇑ renovate = embellish

vampire /væmpaɪə/, **vampires**. 1 A **vampire** is 1.1 a creature in horror stories. Vampires are believed to come out of graves at night and to suck the blood of living people. EG *...the purplish spot on her naked neck where a vampire had feasted.* N COUNT 1.2 an unpleasant person who tries to get money or other things from other people; an informal use, showing disapproval. EG *Honestly, that brother of yours is a vampire!* N COUNT

2 A **vampire** or a **vampire bat** is a bat from South America, which feeds by sucking the blood of other animals. N COUNT

van /væn/, **vans**. A **van** is 1 a road vehicle which has a roof and no side windows, and is used to carry goods. EG *We bought a van and travelled through Belgium, France, and Germany... The police van was waiting in the courtyard.* N COUNT 2 a railway carriage with a roof and sides, often without windows, which is used to carry luggage, goods, or mail; used in British English. EG *A heap of luggage had been flung from the guard's van.* N COUNT AFTER N

vandal /vændə⁰l/, **vandals**. A **vandal** is someone who damages something useful or beautiful on purpose and for no good reason. EG *The phone box is attacked by vandals from time to time.* N COUNT

vandalise /vændəlaɪz/. See **vandalize**.

vandalism /vændəlɪzə⁰m/ is the deliberate destruction of something useful or beautiful, especially public property. EG *These housing estates suffer from widespread vandalism.* N UNCOUNT

vandalize /vændəlaɪz/, **vandalizes, vandalizing, vandalized**; also spelled **vandalise**. If someone **vandalizes** something, they damage it on purpose, for no good reason. EG *All our telephones were vandalized.* V+O : USU PASS = wreck

vane /veɪn/, **vanes**. A **vane** is a flat blade, for example on a propeller, which is part of the mechanism for using the energy of wind or water to drive a machine. ● See also **weather-vane**. N COUNT

vanguard /væŋgɑːd/. 1 The **vanguard** of an army is the front part of it. EG *...the vanguard of this great army.* N SING WITH DET : USU+SUPP

2 If someone is in the **vanguard** of scientific research, a revolution, a movement, etc, they are involved in the most modern or advanced work, or are responsible for the most important changes that are being made. EG *They are in the vanguard of technological advance... She was in the vanguard of the struggle against sex discrimination.* N SING WITH DET : USU+SUPP ⇑ lead = forefront

vanilla /vənɪlə/ is a flavouring put into ice cream and other sweet food. It is made from the pods of the vanilla plant, which grows in tropical countries. EG *...vanilla ice-cream... He used to love cold milk flavoured with vanilla.* N UNCOUNT : USU BEFORE N

vanish /vænɪʃ/, **vanishes, vanishing, vanished**. To **vanish** means 1 to disappear suddenly or in a way which cannot be explained. EG *The car had vanished from sight... On Easter Sunday, Madeleine vanished without trace... Her smile vanished.* V ⇑ go away = disappear 2 to cease to exist. EG *These old preoccupations lose importance or vanish altogether... ...laws to protect vanishing American species.* V ⇑ end = die, disappear

vanishing point, vanishing points. The **vanishing point** is the point in the distance where parallel lines seem to meet. N COUNT : USU SING

vanity /vænɪtɪ¹/, **vanities**. **Vanity** is 1 a very great feeling of pride about your appearance, cleverness, etc; used showing disapproval. EG *He refused to wear glasses. It was sheer vanity... We should use the chairman's vanity for our own ends... All of us have our vanities and frailties.* N UNCOUNT/COUNT = conceit 2 the small value or worth that something has when it is compared with things that have real importance. EG *...the vanity of worldly goods.* N UNCOUNT : IF+PREP THEN *of*

vanquish /væŋkwɪʃ/, **vanquishes, vanquishing, vanquished**. To **vanquish** someone means to defeat them completely in a battle or a competition; a fairly literary word. V+O = conquer, overcome

vantage point /vɑːntɪdʒ pɔɪnt/, **vantage points**; also spelled with a hyphen. A **vantage point** is 1 a good position from which you can see a lot of things. EG *From the vantage point on the hill, Port Philip shimmered beneath them.* N COUNT 2 a point of view or opinion that you hold which gives you an advantage in understanding a situation. EG *We can see the reasons for the revolutions from our 20th century vantage point.* N COUNT : USU POSS+N IN SING ⇑ perspective = viewpoint

vapid /væpɪd/. Something that is **vapid** is dull and uninteresting because it contains nothing stimulating or challenging. EG *Their publications were vapid and amateurish... I'm not willing to waste two days arguing with a bunch of vapid schoolgirls.* ◊ **vapidity** /və³pɪdɪtɪ¹/. EG *Her eyes rose to meet mine with a kind of adoring vapidity.* ADJ QUALIT = insipid ◊ N UNCOUNT

vapor /veɪpə/. See **vapour**.

vaporize /veɪpəraɪz/, **vaporizes, vaporizing, vaporized**; also spelled **vaporise**. If a liquid or solid **vaporizes** or you **vaporize** it, it changes into vapour or gas. EG *...a fluid that vaporises at a much lower temperature than water.* ◊ **vaporization** /veɪpəraɪzeɪʃə⁰n/. EG *Vaporisation occurs at body temperature.* V-ERG ◊ N UNCOUNT

vaporous /veɪpərəs/. Something that is **vaporous** is full of vapour or mist; a literary word. EG *The air was vaporous and steamy.* ADJ QUALIT = hazy

vapour /veɪpə/, **vapours**; also spelled **vapor** in American English. 1 **Vapour** is a mass of tiny drops of water or other liquids in the air, which appear as smoke, clouds, mist, or fumes. EG *...water vapour... ...chlorine gas vapour... ...a little cloud of exhaust vapour.* N UNCOUNT

2 The **vapours** is a feeling of faintness, dizziness, and depression; an old-fashioned expression. EG *They have hysterics, they weep, they have the vapours.* N PLURAL : *the*+N

vapour trail, vapour trails; also spelled with a hyphen. A **vapour trail** is a white trail of water vapour left in the sky by a high-flying aeroplane. N COUNT = jet stream

variability /veəri¹əbɪlɪtɪ¹/. The **variability** of something is the range of different forms that it can take. EG *...the enormous variability you get in speech sounds.* N UNCOUNT = range, difference

variable /veəri¹əbəl/, **variables**. 1 Something that is **variable** is 1.1 likely to change at any time, so that you cannot expect it to remain the same. EG *In the tropics, rainfall is notoriously variable and unreliable.* ADJ QUALIT ⇑ changeable = unstable 1.2 able to be changed deliberately or when you want to change it. EG *Speech is very much more variable than printed text.* ADJ QUALIT ⇑ adaptable

2 A **variable** is 2.1 a factor, which can change in quality, quantity, or size, which you have to take into account when looking at a situation as a whole. EG *How long your shoes will last depends on a lot of variables, such as how much you weigh, how far you* N COUNT

walk, and so on. **2.2** a quantity belonging to a particular mathematical or logical set that can have a number of different values; a technical term. EG *T becomes the dependent variable.* — N COUNT

variance /vɛəri¹əns/. If two things or people are **at variance** with each other, they disagree and cannot be made to agree; a fairly formal expression. EG *He is a writer who expresses views totally at variance with the contemporary climate... On education, his ideas and mine have been at variance for many years.* — PHR : USED AS AN A, USU + *with* = at odds, in conflict

variant /vɛəri¹ənt/, **variants**. A **variant** of something has a different form from the normal or usual one. Two spellings of the same word or two versions of the same story would be variants. EG *There are several variants of beckoning or 'come hither' signals... The shrew group of rodents has produced a variant that seeks its prey entirely underground.* — N COUNT : USU + *of*
▸ used as an adjective. EG *'Judgment' is a variant spelling of 'judgement'.* — ▸ ADJ CLASSIF : ATTRIB

variation /vɛəri¹eɪʃəⁿn/, **variations**. **1** A **variation** is **1.1** a member of a group or set which is different in some way from what is normal or usual or most common. EG *It is always the same story whatever the cultural variations... ... the same programme with only nightly variations... His books are all variations on a basic theme.* — N COUNT : USU + *on/of/in* **1.2** a change in a level, amount or quantity. EG *The Electricity Boards have learned how to cope with a large variation in demand for electricity at various time... ...the constantly altering variation in the depth of the engine note... ...variation in blood pressure.* — N COUNT/UNCOUNT : USU + *in/of* = fluctuation
2 In music, a **variation** is the repetition of a simple melody or tune with the addition of new harmonies, a change in the rhythm, etc. EG *...a record of Art Tatum playing his variations on 'Tea for Two'.* — N COUNT : USU PL

varicose veins /værɪkəˢs veɪnz/ are veins in your legs which are very swollen and painful and which sometimes need to be operated on. — N PLURAL

varied /vɛərɪd/. **1 Varied** is the past tense and past participle of **vary.**
2 Something that is **varied** consists of things that are of different types, sizes, or qualities. EG *Many varied motives prompt individuals to join a political party... ...the immigrants' varied ethnic and religious traditions... The work of a JP is very interesting and varied.* — ADJ QUALIT = wide-ranging

variegated /vɛərɪgeɪtɪ²d/. **1** Something such as a plant or leaf that is **variegated** has different coloured markings on it. EG *...'Golden Queen', a fine yellow variegated holly... ...variegated scraps of paper.* — ADJ CLASSIF = mottled
2 If something such as a system or a company's output is **variegated**, it consists of a lot of very different types of thing; a formal use. EG *A new rich, variegated and highly sophisticated culture sprang up... ...variegated family systems.* — ADJ QUALIT

variety /vəraɪɪti¹/, **varieties**. **1** If a group of things has **variety**, the things are different from each other instead of all being exactly the same, so that the group is interesting or offers people a wide choice; often used showing approval. EG *Reptiles survived and increased in numbers and variety... Those are the holiday brochures that give you the most variety.* — N UNCOUNT ⇑ difference = diversity
2 A **variety** of something is **2.1** a type which is different from others in the same general group. EG *The north country produced a different variety of populist movement... ...a wine glass of a rather ornate variety... I was incapable of making a choice from three varieties of whisky.* — N COUNT : USU + *of* = kind, sort **2.2** a group of different kinds or examples of the same thing. EG *Dolphins produce a great variety of noises... The college library had a wide variety of books... I want to leave for a whole variety of reasons.* — N PART : SING = assortment **2.3** a type of plant in a species of plants which is produced by special breeding. EG *There is an excellent variety named 'Decorus'... All varieties are evergreen and all are good growers.* — N COUNT = strain
3 Variety is a type of theatre or television entertainment which brings together in one show many different kinds of act, for example singing, dancing, and comedy. EG *She's worked too long in variety... ...a variety show... ...a famous variety actor.* — N UNCOUNT : USU BEFORE N ⇑ show = vaudeville

various /vɛərɪəs/. **1 Various** means that there are several different things of the type mentioned. **Various** usually occurs immediately after any determiner that there is in a noun group. EG *There were various questions he wanted to ask... ...drugs of various kinds... ...trying to piece together the various bits of information... ...various areas of visual perception.* — ADJ CLASSIF : ATTRIB + N IN PL
2 If a number of things are described as **various**, they are very different from one another. EG *His excuses are many and various... Their body colours are vivid and various.* — ADJ CLASSIF : USU PRED, WITH N IN PL = varied

variously /vɛərɪəsli¹/ is used to introduce a number of different opinions, descriptions, names, etc that people have or use about something. EG *The street dwellers are variously estimated to number anything from 40,000 to 65,000... He married a Japanese lady who was variously described as a painter and a film maker.* — ADV

varnish /vɑːnɪʃ/, **varnishes, varnishing, varnished**. **1 Varnish** is **1.1** a liquid made from oil and other substances which is painted onto wood or other material to give it a hard, clear, shiny surface. EG *...tins of varnish... ...a special varnish which he had invented himself.* ● See also **nail varnish**. — N MASS **1.2** the hard, clear, shiny surface of an object when it has been painted with varnish. EG *The varnish was slightly chipped.* — N SING : *the/POSS* + N
2 If you **varnish** something, you paint it with varnish. EG *She sanded the shelf and varnished it.* — V + O
◇ **varnished.** EG *...varnished wood.* — ◇ ADJ CLASSIF

varnish over. If you **varnish over** a situation or an event, you hide unpleasant aspects of it or pretend that they do not exist. EG *Conflict is varnished over with polite words.* — PHRASAL VB : V + O + ADV ⇑ cover up = gloss over

vary /vɛəri¹/, **varies, varying, varied**. **1** Things that **vary** are different in size, amount, intensity, etc at different times or in different cases. EG *The fees vary a lot... The screens will vary in size depending upon what one wants... The sums they receive vary from individual to individual... Estimates vary considerably... The picture varied in detail from place to place.* — V = differ ◇ **varying**. EG *Its members have widely varying views on foreign policy... Democracy soon gave way to varying degrees of dictatorship.* — ◇ ADJ QUALIT : ATTRIB = differing
2 If something **varies with** something else, it changes when the other thing changes. EG *Our style will vary with our changes in mood... The colour of the fruit varies with age.* — PHRASAL VB : V + PREP = alter
3 If you **vary** your behaviour or the things you do, you deliberately make changes in them. EG *He took special care to vary his daily routine... ...encouraging firms to vary the working pattern.* — V + O = alter

vascular /væskjə⁴ə/ is used to describe the channels, veins, etc through which fluids pass in the bodies of animals and plants; a technical term in biology and anatomy. EG *...a stem with separate vascular bundles.* — ADJ CLASSIF : ATTRIB

vase /vɑːz/, **vases**. A **vase** is a jar, usually made of glass or pottery, used for holding cut flowers or as an ornament. EG *...two huge flower vases.* — N COUNT ⇑ container

vasectomy /vɛ³sɛktəmi¹/, **vasectomies**. A **vasectomy** is a surgical operation that is done in order to sterilize a man, by cutting the tube that carries the sperm to his penis. — N COUNT/UNCOUNT ⇑ sterilization

Vaseline /væsɪli¹n/ is a trademark for a soft, clear jelly made from petroleum, which is used as an ointment or as grease. — N UNCOUNT

vassal /væsəⁿl/, **vassals**. A **vassal**, in feudal society, was a man who was protected by a lord, to whom he gave military service and from whom he received lands to live on. ▸ also used to refer to a nation that is dominated by another. EG *...vassal states.* — N COUNT ⇑ servant

vast /vɑːst/, **vaster, vastest**. Something that is **vast** is extremely large and includes a great number of things or covers a wide area. EG *He was responsible for running a vast organization... ...the vast majority of people... ...the roads that they're building at vast expense.* — ADJ QUALIT : USU ATTRIB = huge, immense ◇ **vastness**. EG *...the unimaginable vastness of space.* — ◇ N UNCOUNT

vastly /vɑːstli¹/ means very greatly or to a great degree or extent, and is used to emphasize the word that follows. EG *Management of the factory could be vastly improved... ...a vastly overrated player... ...vastly inferior equipment.* — ADV + ADJ/ADV = immensely

vat /væt/, **vats**. A **vat** is a large barrel or tank in which liquids can be stored. — N COUNT/PART

VAT /viː eɪ tiː, væt/; used in British English. **VAT** is an abbreviation for 'value added tax'; a tax on the — N UNCOUNT difference between the cost of an item and its selling price.

Vatican /vætıkən/. The **Vatican** is the group of buildings in Rome in which the Pope lives and where the central administration of the Roman Catholic Church has its offices. ▸ used to refer to the authority, beliefs, and pronouncements of the Pope and the Roman Catholic Church. EG *The Press as a whole paid small attention to the Vatican's offer of mediation.* — N PROPER : *the*+N

vatman /vætmə³n/. If you refer to the **vatman**, you mean the government department which advises and checks the accounts of people who have to pay VAT; an informal word in British English. — N SING : *the*+N

vaudeville /vəʊdəvıl, vɔː-/ is a type of theatre or television entertainment in which the shows have many different kinds of acts in them, for example singing, dancing, and comedy. EG *He ended up there a year or so after his vaudeville flop.* — N UNCOUNT = variety

vault /vɔːlt/, **vaults, vaulting, vaulted.** 1 A **vault** is 1.1 a room with thick walls, a strong door, and strong locks where money, important documents, and jewels can be kept safely. EG *...far more secure than any bank vault... It was deposited in the vaults of a firm of solicitors.* 1.2 a room underneath a church or in a cemetery where people are buried, usually the members of a single family. 1.3 a roof or a ceiling, for example in a church, that is made of several arches joined together at the top. — N COUNT; N COUNT = tomb, crypt; N COUNT

2 If you **vault** something or **vault** over it, you jump quickly onto or over it, especially by putting a hand on top of it to help you balance while you jump. EG *The boy vaulted onto the platform.* — V+O, OR V+A = leap, spring

vaunt /vɔːnt/, **vaunts, vaunting, vaunted.** If you **vaunt** something, you describe, praise, or display your success, possessions, etc in a boastful and pompous way; a formal word. EG *They vaunt their approach to life as if it were something unique.* — V+O ⇑ boast = parade
◇ **vaunted.** EG *...a new and much vaunted national cinema.* — ◇ ADJ CLASSIF : ATTRIB

vb is a written abbreviation for 'verb'.

> **VB** □ In this dictionary VB is used in the grammar notes beside entries to mean 'verb', without indicating what type of verb it is, as in, for example ADV AFTER VB.

VC, VCs. **VC** is an abbreviation for 1 'Victoria Cross'; a medal awarded to soldiers, sailors, and airmen in Britain and the Commonwealth for acts of special bravery in battle. ▸ also used to refer to someone who has been awarded a Victoria Cross. 2 'vice-chancellor'. — N COUNT

> **V+C** □ In this dictionary V+C is used in the grammar notes beside entries to indicate that the verb is followed by a complement which refers to the subject of the verb. The complement is usually an adjectival group but it can also be a noun group, especially after the verb *be*. Examples are **look** and **seem**. EG *You **look** very pale... He **seems** quite happy to come... She **seems** a likely candidate.*

VCR, VCRs. **VCR** is an abbreviation for 'video cassette recorder'; a machine that can be used to record television programmes, films, etc onto video tapes, so that people can play them back and watch them later on a television set. — N COUNT

VD is an abbreviation for 'venereal disease'.

VDU /viː diː juː/, **VDUs.** A **VDU** is a machine which looks rather like a television set and which shows information from a computer on its screen; an abbreviation for 'visual display unit'. — N COUNT = terminal

veal /viːl/ is meat from a calf. EG *...best Dutch veal... ...veal escalope.* — N UNCOUNT

vector /vɛktə/, **vectors.** A **vector** is 1 a variable quantity, such as force, that has magnitude and direction; a technical term in maths and science. 2 the course or compass direction that an aeroplane is following. — N COUNT; N COUNT

veer /vıə/, **veers, veering, veered.** 1 If you **veer** in a certain direction, 1.1 you suddenly change direction. EG *He veered away from a tree... The plane seemed to veer off to one side.* 1.2 you change from one opinion, belief, attitude, or position to another, usually suddenly and unexpectedly. EG *She was anxious not to hurt Harold, for whom her feelings veered from tenderness to sudden spurts of genuine love.* — V+A = swerve; V+A = swing

2 When the wind **veers**, it changes direction, moving clockwise in the northern hemisphere, and anti-clockwise in the southern hemisphere. EG *I assumed that the wind was still veering in a northerly direction.* — V+A

veg /vɛdʒ/. In informal English, you sometimes call vegetables **veg.** EG *He sells fruit and veg... Every night there was meat and two veg.* — N PLURAL

vegan /viːgə⁰n/, **vegans.** A **vegan** is a vegetarian who does not eat any animal products such as cheese, butter, or milk. ▸ used as an adjective. EG *A vegan diet can be very healthy.* — N COUNT; ▸ ADJ CLASSIF

vegetable /vɛdʒı⁰təbə⁰l/, **vegetables.** 1 A **vegetable** is 1.1 a plant, such as a cabbage, potato, or onion, which is eaten either raw or cooked. EG *...only the best and freshest fruit and vegetables... ...digging up potatoes in the vegetable garden.* 1.2 someone whose brain has been damaged and who is in a coma or unable to move and think; an informal use. EG *He will be a vegetable for the rest of his life.* — N COUNT : USU PL; N COUNT : USU USED AS C = cabbage

2 **Vegetable** is also used to refer to plants in general or to plant life. EG *Pollution affects everything on the planet, animal, vegetable, and mineral... ...a pile of vegetable matter.* — N UNCOUNT : USU BEFORE N

vegetable marrow, vegetable marrows. A **vegetable marrow** is the same as a marrow. — N COUNT

vegetarian /vɛdʒıtɛərıən/, **vegetarians.** A **vegetarian** is someone who does not eat meat or fish. EG *She was a strict vegetarian.* ▸ used as an adjective. EG *...a largely vegetarian diet.* — N COUNT; ▸ ADJ CLASSIF

vegetarianism /vɛdʒıtɛərıənızə⁰m/. If you practise **vegetarianism**, you do not eat meat or fish. EG *My friends were talking about vegetarianism.* — N UNCOUNT ⇑ diet

vegetate /vɛdʒıteıt/, **vegetates, vegetating, vegetated.** If you **vegetate**, you have a very boring life, during which you stay in one place, do nothing, and have no mental stimulation. EG *Many elderly folk vegetate and die in loneliness.* — V ⇑ exist = stagnate

vegetated /vɛdʒıteıtı²d/. An area of land that is **vegetated** has plants growing on it. EG *The area was only sparsely vegetated.* — ADJ QUALIT

vegetation /vɛdʒıteıʃə⁰n/ is plant life in general, especially plants of a particular place or type. EG *The forest floor is not rich in vegetation... ...a musty odour of rotten vegetation.* — N UNCOUNT

vehemence /viːə¹məns/ is very intense and violent emotion, especially anger. EG *Judy cried with unaccustomed vehemence, 'Yes, I know!'... ...the hate and vehemence in Hubert's eyes.* — N UNCOUNT = passion, ferocity

vehement /viːə¹mənt/. 1 Someone who is **vehement** has very strong feelings or opinions and expresses them forcefully. EG *She was very vehement and very sure... They are most vehement in their praises of the new system.* ◇ **vehemently.** EG *They were arguing vehemently.* — ADJ QUALIT = passionate; ◇ ADV WITH VB

2 A **vehement** action or movement is one done with great force or energy. EG *With a vehement gesture he flung away his chicken leg.* ◇ **vehemently.** EG *Bob shook his head vehemently.* — ADJ QUALIT = violent; ◇ ADV WITH VB

vehicle /viːıkə⁰l/, **vehicles.** A **vehicle** is 1 a machine such as a bus, car, or truck, that carries people or things from place to place. EG *...amphibious vehicles... ...the motor vehicle industry.* 2 something that you use in order to achieve a particular purpose or in order to express your thoughts and feelings. EG *People should not look upon the Institute as a vehicle for introducing Western technology... They saw the English language as a vehicle of liberation.* — N COUNT ⇑ conveyance; N COUNT : USU SING+*for/of* ⇑ medium = means

vehicular /vi¹h⁰ıkjə⁴lə/ is used to describe something which relates to vehicles and traffic; a formal word. EG *Most of the roads were still impassable to vehicular movement.* — ADJ CLASSIF : ATTRIB

veil /veıl/, **veils, veiling, veiled.** 1 A **veil** is a piece of thin soft material, traditionally worn by Western women over their heads on formal occasions such as weddings and funerals, or attached to a woman's hat. EG *...a black hat with a veil... The bride's face was covered in a white veil.* — N COUNT ⇑ covering

2 If a woman **takes the veil**, she becomes a nun. EG *She took the veil when she was twenty.* — PHR : VB INFLECTS

3 A **veil** is also 3.1 something which seems to cover an object but which you can partly see through, for example mist or light. EG *Everything was wrapped in a veil of pearl-grey evening light.* 3.2 something which hides or partly hides a real situation, so that you do not know what is actually happening. EG *The* — N COUNT : USU SING+*of* = haze, film; N COUNT : USU SING+*of* ⇑ disguise

research centre shrouded its communications with every possible veil of secrecy.

4 If you **draw a veil over** something, you stop talking about it because it is too unpleasant to talk about; a fairly formal expression. EG *Let us draw a veil over the rest of the episode.* PHR : VB INFLECTS = skip

5 If you **veil** a situation, you hide or disguise it so that it is not obvious what is really happening. EG *The book veils its critique of authoritarian politics in a fairy tale setting.* V+O = mask, cloak

veiled /veɪld/. 1 A **veiled** comment or remark is presented in a disguised form, so that the speaker or writer does not actually say what he or she really means. EG *...a thinly veiled criticism... ...veiled hints and uneasy silences.* ADJ CLASSIF : ATTRIB ↑ indirect

2 If someone has a **veiled** expression on their face, the expression shows that they are hiding their real feelings or thoughts; a fairly literary use. EG *There was a veiled inward expression about her eyes.* ADJ CLASSIF : ATTRIB ↑ hidden = guarded

3 A woman or girl who is **veiled** is wearing a veil. EG *...her noble head veiled in a white silk scarf.* ADJ CLASSIF ↑ covered

vein /veɪn/, **veins.** 1 A **vein** is 1.1 a tube in the body of a person or animal, which carries blood to the heart. EG *The blood is drained away by two large veins... Just over each temple there were little blue veins.* • See also **varicose veins.** N COUNT ↑ blood vessel **1.2** any blood vessel in the body of a person or animal. EG *The blood curdles in my veins as I think of the atrocity.* N COUNT **1.3** one of the thin branching lines on a leaf or on the wings of some insects. N COUNT **1.4** a thin line of a particular colour in marble, some kinds of wood, and some kinds of cheese. N COUNT = streak

2 A **vein** of a particular metal or mineral is a layer of this metal or mineral lying in rock. EG *The mine tapped the world's richest vein of copper... ...veins of pink granite.* N COUNT+*of* ↑ deposit = seam

3 Something that is written or spoken in a particular **vein** is written or spoken in this style or mood. EG *John Gielgud can also be heard in much lighter vein on Radio Four... The letter continued in this vein for several pages.* N UNCOUNT+ SUPP, USU *in*+N

4 A **vein** of a particular quality is evidence of that quality which someone often shows in their behaviour or work. EG *Throughout her writing, there's this lovely vein of subtlety... ...a deep vein of malice.* N SING+*of* = streak, strand

veined /veɪnd/. **Veined** skin has a lot of veins showing on it. EG *...his veined nervous hand.* ▸ used also to describe veins on rock, cheese, etc. EG *The black rock was cool, veined with little cracks... ...pink-veined marble.* ADJ CLASSIF ▸ ADJ CLASSIF : USU PRED+*with*

veldt /fɛlt, vɛlt/; also spelled **veld.** The **veldt** is an area of flat, high grassland with very few trees, in southern Africa. EG *...nights on the African veldt hunting lions.* N SING : *the*+N

vellum /vɛlə^{0}m/ is 1 fine parchment made from the skin of calves, lambs, or kids, which is used for binding books, lampshades, etc, and was formerly used for writing on. N UNCOUNT 2 strong, good quality paper for writing on. N UNCOUNT

velocity /vɪ^{1}lɒsɪti^{1}/, **velocities.** The **velocity** of something is the speed at which it moves in a particular direction. EG *...the velocity of light... ...high-velocity bullets.* N UNCOUNT/ COUNT

velour /və^{2}lʊə/ is a silk or cotton cloth similar to velvet. EG *...the plush velour interior of his new car.* N UNCOUNT : USU BEFORE N

velvet /vɛlvɪt/. 1 **Velvet** is soft material made from cotton, silk, or nylon, which has a thick layer of short, cut threads on one side. EG *...a long black velvet ballgown... ...velvet curtains.* N UNCOUNT : USU BEFORE N

2 If you describe someone as having **an iron fist in a velvet glove,** you mean that they hide a firm and determined personality behind a gentle and quiet manner. PHR : USED AS O

velvety /vɛlvɪti^{1}/. 1 Something that is **velvety** is soft to touch and has the appearance or quality of velvet. EG *The black widow spider has a velvety black body... ...some sort of velvety material.* ADJ QUALIT ↑ smooth

2 A **velvety** sound is soft and without sharpness; used showing approval. EG *I heard the maid's velvety voice calling me softly from the stairs.* ADJ QUALIT ↑ gentle = mellow

venal /viːn^{0}əl/. Someone who is **venal** is prepared to accept bribes in return for acting dishonestly or unfairly. EG *Authoritarian rulers are typically venal and capricious.* ADJ QUALIT ↑ corrupt = crooked

vend /vɛnd/, **vends, vending, vended.** If you **vend** something, you sell it; used in formal or legal English. V+O

vendetta /vɛndɛtə/, **vendettas.** A **vendetta** is 1 a long-lasting and bitter quarrel in which people attempt to harm or destroy other people or organizations. EG *He conducted a vendetta against Haldane behind the scenes... As part of the Council's vendetta, funds to the college were being cut.* N COUNT ↑ feud 2 a private feud between families in which the members of one family believe it is their duty to kill members of the other family in revenge for previous murders. N COUNT = blood feud

vending machine, vending machines. A **vending machine** is a machine from which you can get cigarettes, chocolate, coffee, etc by putting in money and pressing a button. N COUNT = automat

vendor /vɛndə^{8}/, **vendors.** A **vendor** is 1 someone who sells magazines, cigarettes, hamburgers, etc from a small stall or cart. EG *...cigarette vendors... The streets were crowded with vendors and buyers.* N COUNT : USU MOD+N = seller

2 someone who is selling land, a house, or other property; a technical term in law. N COUNT = seller

veneer /vɪ^{2}nɪə/. 1 If you refer to the way that someone behaves as a **veneer,** you mean that they are behaving in a way which hides their real character or feelings. EG *He hides his values beneath a veneer of scientific objectivity... Modern social attitudes have assumed a moralistic veneer.* N SING WITH DET : USU+SUPP ↑ appearance = mask, facade

2 **Veneer** is a thin layer of wood, plastic, etc which is glued onto the outside of something made of cheaper material, in order to improve its appearance. EG *...a dining-room table whose veneer had come loose.* N UNCOUNT ↑ covering

venerable /vɛnə^{0}rəbə^{0}l/. 1 Someone who is **venerable** is entitled to respect because they are old and wise. EG *The only person my father ever visited socially was a venerable elder for whom he had enormous respect.* ADJ QUALIT : USU ATTRIB ↑ revered = esteemed

2 Something that is **venerable** is impressive because it is old or important historically; often used humorously. EG *There are plans to renovate Blair House, Washington's venerable residence for distinguished visitors... ...her venerable old bicycle.* ADJ QUALIT : USU ATTRIB = distinguished

3 **Venerable** is also a title used in the Roman Catholic Church for someone who is going to be declared a saint, and in the Anglican Church for a priest who is an Archdeacon. ADJ IN TITLES

venerate /vɛnəreɪt/, **venerates, venerating, venerated.** If you **venerate** someone, you feel great respect for them; a fairly formal word. EG *Most Italians venerate the name of Dante.* ◇ **veneration** /vɛnəreɪʃə^{0}n/. EG *This statue is an object of religious veneration.* V+O = revere ◇ N UNCOUNT

venereal disease /və^{1}nɪərɪəl dɪziːz/, **venereal diseases.** **Venereal disease** is a disease that results from or is passed on by sexual intercourse. There are several different venereal diseases, for example syphilis. N UNCOUNT/ COUNT = VD

Venetian blind /vəniːʃə^{0}n blaɪnd/, **Venetian blinds.** A **Venetian blind** is a window blind made of thin horizontal strips of wood, plastic, or metal. The strips can be raised, lowered, or turned to a different angle in order to let in more or less light. N COUNT ↑ screen

vengeance /vɛndʒəns/ 1 is the act of killing, hurting, or harming someone in return for something harmful that they have done. EG *I want vengeance for the deaths of my parents and sisters... I will never seek vengeance.* N UNCOUNT = revenge

2 If something is done or happens **with a vengeance,** it is done or happens to a much greater extent than was expected or than was thought possible. EG *He now broke the rules with a vengeance.* PHR : USED AS AN A

vengeful /vɛndʒfʊl/. If you are **vengeful,** you feel a great desire for revenge; a fairly literary word. EG *...a wicked, vengeful sort of person... The whole episode made me vengeful.* ▸ used of people's behaviour. EG *...a kind of vengeful pleasure.* ADJ QUALIT = vindictive

venial /viːnɪəl/ is used to describe sin, wrongdoing, etc that is not very serious and is therefore easily forgiven or excused; a formal or religious word. ADJ CLASSIF = pardonable

venison /vɛnɪ^{0}zən, -sən/ is the meat of a deer. N UNCOUNT

venom /vɛnəm/ is 1 the poison that some snakes, scorpions, and spiders produce and which they use when biting or stinging their enemy or prey. EG *Their venom dissolves the walls of blood vessels.* N UNCOUNT 2 a feeling of great bitterness, shown in the way you say something, when you want to hurt other people or when you really hate or despise them. EG *'Bastards!' He murmured the word quietly and with great venom.* N UNCOUNT = malice

venomous /vɛnəməs/. **1** A **venomous** snake, scorpion, or spider has a gland that produces poison which it uses to attack its enemy or prey. ADJ CLASSIF ⇑ poisonous

2 Venomous is also used to describe people, expressions, or behaviour that show great bitterness and ill-will towards other people. EG *The beautiful green eyes were venomous.* ◊ **venomously**. EG *'You filthy spoiled brat,' he said venomously.* ADJ QUALIT ⇑ bitter = malevolent ◊ ADV = spitefully

venous /viːnəs/ is used to describe something which is related to veins; a technical term in medicine and biology. EG *...the venous channels that drain the blood from the brain.* ADJ CLASSIF : ATTRIB

vent /vɛnt/, **vents, venting, vented. 1** A **vent** is **1.1** a hole in something, such as the wall of a room, through which air can come in and smoke, gas, or smells can go out. EG *Water heaters are safe unless you block up vents and close windows and doors... ...the air vents of the bunkers.* N COUNT ⇑ duct **1.2** a hole in the earth's surface through which molten lava, hot water, or gases come out. EG *Around the vents, the water is a cloudy blue... The gas pours out, caking the mouths of the vents with yellow sulphur.* N COUNT

2 If you **give vent to** your feelings, you express strong feelings that you have by acting or behaving in a particular way; a fairly formal expression. EG *They formed Residents Associations and gave vent to their feelings in drawing up petitions and writing letters of complaint.* PHR : VB INFLECTS = air

3 If you **give vent** to a noise, you make a particular type of noise, especially suddenly or as a reaction to something; a formal expression. EG *John gave vent to a strange animal sound.* PHR : VB INFLECTS = emit

4 If you **vent** your feelings on something or someone, you express what you feel by acting or behaving in a particular way. EG *...an innocent man who had done nothing more than vent his anger on a garbage can.* V+O : USU+A (on) = release

ventilate /vɛntɪleɪt/, **ventilates, ventilating, ventilated. 1** To **ventilate** a room or building means to allow fresh air to get into it, for example by means of windows. ◊ **ventilated**. EG *...badly ventilated houses.* ◊ **ventilation** /vɛntɪleɪʃən/. EG *The only ventilation was through a small door at the back.* V+O ◊ ADJ QUALIT ◊ N UNCOUNT

2 If you **ventilate** your ideas or feelings, you talk about them or express them freely in front of other people; a formal use. EG *...police violence, a subject seldom ventilated in the press before that time.* V+O = air

ventilator /vɛntɪleɪtə/, **ventilators**. A **ventilator** is something such as a fan or airbrick which lets fresh air into a room or building and lets stale air out. N COUNT

ventricle /vɛntrɪkəl/, **ventricles**. A **ventricle** is **1** a chamber of the heart that pumps blood to the arteries; a technical term in anatomy. N COUNT **2** one of the four main cavities of the brain; a technical term in anatomy. N COUNT

ventriloquism /vɛntrɪləkwɪzəm/ is the ability to speak without moving your lips so that what you say seems to come from another person or from another part of the room. N UNCOUNT

ventriloquist /vɛntrɪləkwɪst/, **ventriloquists**. A **ventriloquist** is a person who practises ventriloquism, usually in order to entertain people. EG *...a ventriloquist's dummy.* N COUNT ⇑ entertainer

venture /vɛntʃə/, **ventures, venturing, ventured. 1** A **venture** is **1.1** something you do that is new and might be difficult and so involves the risk of failure. EG *...an interesting scientific venture... The artistic success of the venture was assured.* N COUNT ⇑ undertaking = enterprise, project **1.2** a business operation that involves spending money in the hope of getting more money back. EG *The number of successful new business ventures is dwindling.* N COUNT = endeavour **1.3** a journey which might be dangerous and is therefore very exciting. EG *He was the moving spirit behind this venture to the Arctic.* N COUNT ⇑ expedition

2 If you **venture** into something, you do something that involves the risk of failure because it is new and different. EG *I might actually venture into advertising if I had enough money.* V+A ⇑ tackle

3 If you **venture** something such as an opinion, you say it in a cautious, hesitant manner because you are afraid it might be stupid or wrong. EG *'Anyway,' Marsha ventured, 'If we want to know what's going on, we'll have to do our own research.'... If I may be allowed to venture an opinion, I think we should leave right away... No one has ventured to suggest why this should be.* V+O/QUOTE/REPORT-CL, OR V +to-INF = volunteer, hazard

4 If you **venture** somewhere, you go somewhere that might be dangerous. EG *It was a long time before Hughes ventured into our district again... He wouldn't venture far from his mother's door.* V+A

venturesome /vɛntʃəsəm/. Someone who is **venturesome** is willing to take risks and try out new things; a fairly literary word. EG *There is a new venturesome spirit among today's young people.* ADJ QUALIT ⇑ daring = adventurous

venue /vɛnjuː/, **venues**. A **venue** is a place where an action or event has been arranged to happen. EG *Where is the venue for the conference?... The band will tour most of the leading venues... I'm afraid there's a change of venue.* N COUNT

veracious /vɛ²reɪʃəs/. Someone who is **veracious** always tells the truth; a formal word. ADJ CLASSIF = truthful

veracity /vɛ²ræsɪti¹/ is the quality or habit of telling the truth; a formal word. EG *There is no reason to doubt the veracity of the evidence... He'll have a hard time proving his veracity before the jury.* N UNCOUNT = truthfulness

veranda /vərændə/, **verandas**; also spelled **verandah**. A **veranda** is an area along one of the outside walls of a house, with a floor that is slightly higher than the ground outside, and with a roof supported by pillars. EG *She sat on the veranda, sipping tea.* N COUNT : USU the+N IN SING ⇑ terrace = porch

verb /vɜːb/, **verbs**. In grammar, a **verb** is a word which is concerned with what people and things do, and what happens to them. N COUNT

verbal /vɜːbəl/ means **1** connected with words and the use of words. EG *It was a contest in verbal skills... You might take a verbal reasoning test.* ADJ CLASSIF : USU ATTRIB **2** spoken rather than written. EG *...a succession of verbal attacks on the chairman... ...a series of tough written papers followed by verbal questioning by a panel of three judges.* ◊ **verbally**. EG *I will communicate your views verbally to the members of the committee... ...verbally aggressive men.* ADJ CLASSIF : USU ATTRIB ◊ ADV **3** consisting of or relating to verbs. EG *...the structure of verbal groups in English.* ADJ CLASSIF

verbalize /vɜːbəlaɪz/, **verbalizes, verbalizing, verbalized**; also spelled **verbalise**. If you **verbalize** or **verbalize** something, you use words to express your ideas, feelings, etc. EG *She cannot verbalize her emotions... Children of his age group don't usually verbalize at this stage.* V OR V+O : USU WITH MODAL/BROAD NEG

verbatim /vɜːbeɪtɪm/. If you repeat something **verbatim** or remember it **verbatim**, you repeat or remember it using exactly the same words that the original speaker or writer used. EG *What I remember of the letter I remember verbatim... He repeated it verbatim.* ▸ used as an adjective. EG *It was almost a verbatim quotation of the article.* ADV AFTER VB ▸ ADJ CLASSIF : ATTRIB

verbiage /vɜːbi¹ɪdʒ/ is the use of too many unnecessary words, which make something difficult to understand; a fairly formal word, used showing disapproval. EG *...a lot of meaningless verbiage.* N UNCOUNT

verbose /vɜːbəʊs/. A person or a piece of writing that is **verbose** uses more words than are necessary, and so makes you feel bored or annoyed. EG *Who was your verbose companion?* ◊ **verbosity** /və⁵bɒsɪti¹/. EG *...empty rhetoric and verbosity.* ADJ QUALIT ⇑ wordy = long-winded ◊ N UNCOUNT

verdant /vɜːdənt/. A place that is **verdant** is covered with green grass, trees, and plants; a rather literary word. EG *...the verdant slopes of Plotinus.* ADJ QUALIT = lush

verdict /vɜːdɪkt/, **verdicts**. A **verdict** is **1** the decision at the end of a trial in a law court as to whether the prisoner is guilty or whether the plaintiff or the defendant was right. EG *Everybody was agreed that the jury gave the right verdict... ...a verdict of not guilty.* N COUNT : USU SING ⇑ finding **2** a statement of an opinion reached after a certain amount of thought on a particular subject. EG *Okay, then, what's your verdict on the new uniform?... The critics may have hated the film, but the public verdict was favourable.* N COUNT : USU SING+SUPP

verdigris /vɜːdɪgrɪs/ is a greenish-blue poisonous substance that forms on copper, brass, or bronze after it has been left in wet or damp conditions; a technical word. N UNCOUNT ⇑ deposit

verdure /vɜːdʒə/ is used to refer to green plants, trees, grass, etc, when they are growing in great quantities; a literary word. N UNCOUNT OR N SING : the+N ⇑ greenery

V-ERG ☐ In this dictionary V-ERG is used in the grammar notes beside entries to describe verbs which are both transitive (V+O) and intransitive (V) in the same meaning. They are described as V-ERG because there is a restriction on the type of subject which can be used with the intransitive verb. With V-ERGS, the object of the transitive verb can be used as the subject of the intransitive verb.

For example *peas* is the object of the transitive verb *freeze* in *You can freeze peas* and it is the subject of the intransitive verb in *Peas freeze well.* Other examples are **open** and **boil**. EG *We couldn't* ***open*** *the window... The window* ***opened*** *easily... He had* ***boiled*** *the kettle... The kettle* ***boiled.*** Some verbs are described as V OR V-ERG. Verbs described in this way have a transitive and intransitive use in the same way as the examples shown above and, in addition, they have an intransitive use with a subject which is different from the object of the transitive verb. An example is **sail**. EG *He* ***sailed*** *the boat towards Dover... The boat* ***sailed*** *towards Dover... He* ***sailed*** *towards Dover.*

verge /vɜːdʒ/, **verges, verging, verged. 1** If you are **on the verge of** something, you are going to do it very soon or it is likely to happen or begin very soon. EG *...people living on the verge of starvation... West Germany's unions appear on the verge of settling their latest pay dispute.* PREP ⇑ near = close to

2 The **verge** of a road is a narrow piece of ground by the side of a road, which is usually covered with grass or flowers. EG *The two of us began walking together along the grass verge.* N COUNT ⇑ border = roadside

verge on. If a particular quality **verges on** or **verges upon** another, it is almost the same as it. EG *I had a feeling of distrust verging on panic... It was the kind of smile that verged on laughter.* PHRASAL VB : V+PREP = border on

verger /vɜːdʒə/, **vergers.** In the Anglican church, a **verger** is someone whose job is to look after the building and contents of a church. N COUNT

verifiable /verɪfaɪəbə⁰l/. Something that is **verifiable** can be proved to be true. EG *...verifiable evidence.* ADJ CLASSIF = provable

verify /verɪfaɪ/, **verifies, verifying, verified.** If you **verify** something, **1** you check that it is true by careful investigation. EG *...evidence that could be tested and verified... I remember one story, which I have never verified, but which rings true.* V+O = substantiate ◊ **verification** /verɪfɪkeɪʃə⁰n/. EG *Any hypothesis must depend for its verification on observable evidence.* ◊ N UNCOUNT **2** you state or confirm that it is true. EG *She was asked to verify his statement.* V+O ◊ **verification.** EG *He looked at his daughter for verification.* ◊ N UNCOUNT

verily /verɪli¹/ means really or truly; an old-fashioned word. ADV SEN

verisimilitude /verɪsɪmɪlɪtjuːd/ is the quality of seeming to be true or real; a fairly formal word. EG *...the American theatre's obsession with social verisimilitude.* N UNCOUNT = authenticity

veritable /verɪtəbə⁰l/ is used to emphasize a description of something and to suggest that, although the description might seem exaggerated, it is really accurate. EG *The water descended like a veritable Niagara... I'm sure the audience has a veritable host of questions... ...a veritable passion for the cinema.* ADJ CLASSIF : ATTRIB ⇑ real = positive, absolute

verity /verɪti¹/, **verities.** The **verities** of something are all the things that are believed to be true about it; a formal word. EG *...scientific verities.* N COUNT : USU PL

vermicelli /vɜːmɪseli¹/ is very thin spaghetti. N UNCOUNT

vermilion /və⁵mɪljən/. Something that is **vermilion** is bright red in colour. EG *They don their resplendent vermilion robes.* ADJ COLOUR

vermin /vɜːmɪn/ are **1** small animals such as rats and mice, which carry disease and damage crops or food. EG *In Scotland, wild cats are treated as vermin, and so poisoned.* N PLURAL = pests **2** people who are regarded as harmful to others or dangerous to society. EG *He says that football hooligans are vermin.* N PLURAL

verminous /vɜːmɪnəs/. Something that is **verminous** is covered with or full of insects such as lice and fleas. ADJ CLASSIF ⇑ infested

vermouth /vɜːməθ/, **vermouths. Vermouth** is an alcoholic drink made from red or white wine flavoured with herbs. N MASS

vernacular /vənækjə⁴lə/, **vernaculars.** The **vernacular** of a country or region is the language that is most widely spoken there. EG *Wherever we go for our holidays, he never seems to have any problem with the local vernacular.* N COUNT : USU the+N IN SING ▸ used as an adjective. EG *...the vernacular programmes for new citizens of the UK.* ▸ ADJ CLASSIF : ATTRIB

2 A **vernacular** is a style of architecture in which ordinary people's houses are built, for example using local building materials and having low ceilings, rather than copying the grand architecture of palaces and churches; a technical term. EG *Architects are consciously trying to re-create a true English vernacular.* N COUNT : USU SING, OR N UNCOUNT ▸ used as an adjective. EG *...the vernacular architecture of Britain.* ▸ ADJ CLASSIF : ATTRIB

verruca /və²ruːkə/, **verrucas.** A **verruca** is a small, hard, infectious growth on the skin rather like a wart, which most commonly occurs on the sole of the foot. N COUNT

versatile /vɜːsətaɪl/. **1** Someone who is **versatile** has many different skills and is able to change quickly from using one to using another; used showing approval. EG *He's the most versatile of actors.* ADJ QUALIT ⇑ talented = adaptable ◊ **versatility** /vɜːsətɪlɪti¹/. EG *He had impressed us with his versatility as a journalist.* ◊ N UNCOUNT = skill

2 Something such as a tool, machine, or material that is **versatile** can be used for many different purposes. EG *...this extremely versatile new kitchen machine... ...silicon, a highly versatile substance.* ADJ QUALIT ⇑ useful ◊ **versatility.** EG *...the versatility of plastics and other new materials.* ◊ N UNCOUNT

verse /vɜːs/, **verses. 1 Verse** is writing which is arranged in lines which have a pattern of beats and which often rhyme at the end of the lines. EG *He has published an anthology of verse... She used to write plays in verse.* ● See also **blank verse.** N UNCOUNT = poetry

2 A **verse** is **2.1** one of the parts into which a poem or song is divided. Usually, each verse of a song has the same metre and rhyme structure. EG *He sang a verse of 'Lili Marlene'.* N COUNT ⇑ section = stanza **2.2** one of the short sections into which chapters of books of the Bible are divided. EG *...the Second Book of Kings, Chapter 6, verse 25.* N COUNT

versed /vɜːst/. If you are **versed in** something, you know a lot about it. EG *She is well versed in French history.* PHR+NG : USED AS C

version /vɜːʃə⁰n, -ʒə⁰n/, **versions.** A **version** of something is **1** a form of it in which certain details are different or have been changed from previous forms. EG *There are two versions of this statue... She asked a different version of the question... ...from the first draft to the final printed version.* N COUNT+SUPP : USU+*of* **2** a play, film, or other production based on a story or other work that had been previously written in another form, for example as a novel. EG *...the 1939 film version of 'Wuthering Heights'... ...a concert version of Telemann's opera.* N COUNT+SUPP : USU+*of* = adaptation **3** a description of an event or idea by a particular person, especially when this disagrees with another person's description of the same event or idea. EG *Each of the women would have a different version of what actually happened that day... The committee accepted Carleson's version of the incident.* N COUNT+SUPP : USU+*of* ⇑ account

versus /vɜːsəs/. You use **versus** to say **1** that two ideas or things are opposed, especially when a choice has to be made between them. EG *...the problem of determinism versus freedom... We argued about pipes versus cigarettes.* PREP : NG+PREP+NG = against **2** that two people, groups of people, or teams are competing against each other, for example in a sporting event or a case in law. EG *The big match tonight is England versus Spain.* PREP : NG+PREP+NG

vertebra /vɜːtɪbrə/, **vertebrae. Vertebrae** are the small circular bones that form the backbone of an animal or human being. EG *...a painful stiffness in the upper vertebrae.* N COUNT : USU PL

vertebrate /vɜːtɪbrɪ³t/ **vertebrates.** A **vertebrate** is a creature which has a backbone. Mammals, birds, reptiles, amphibians, and most fishes are all vertebrates; a technical term. EG *The insects colonised the land before the vertebrates.* N COUNT ▸ used as an adjective. EG *...the bones of those first vertebrate inhabitants of the land, the amphibians.* ▸ ADJ CLASSIF : ATTRIB

vertical /vɜːtɪkə⁰l/. **1** Something that is **vertical** stands or points straight up from a flat surface, or goes straight up from the bottom to the top. EG *The monument consists of a horizontal slab supported by two vertical pillars... A vertical line divides the page into two halves.* ADJ CLASSIF ⇑ upright ≠ horizontal ◊ **vertically.** EG *The human brain is divided vertically down the middle into two hemispheres.* ◊ ADV WITH VB

2 Vertical is used to describe a cliff or drop which is so steep that it goes straight up or straight down without sloping at all. EG *The cliff plunged in a vertical drop to the bottom... ...a bay surrounded on three sides by vertical cliffs.* ADJ CLASSIF = sheer ◊ **vertically.** EG *The slope drops off almost vertically.* ◊ ADV

3 The **vertical** is the direction that points straight up, at an angle of 90 degrees to a flat surface. EG *The sun had swung over the vertical and the afternoon heat was closing in.* N SING : the+N = perpendicular

4 If an organization has a **vertical** power structure, those at the top of it have more power than those at the bottom. EG *The local party is trying to replace vertical domination from above... ...a vertical chain of command.* ◊ **vertically**. EG *Most societies are divided vertically.* ADJ CLASSIF: ATTRIB = hierarchical ◊ ADV

vertiginous /vɜːtɪdʒɪnəs/. Something that is **vertiginous** makes you feel dizzy and sick, as if you were looking down from a high place; a formal word. EG *...a vertiginous window.* ADJ CLASSIF : USU ATTRIB

vertigo /vɜːtɪgəʊ/ is a feeling of dizziness and sickness caused by looking down from a high place. EG *Looking out of the window still gives him vertigo.* N UNCOUNT

verve /vɜːv/ is lively and forceful enthusiasm. EG *Rosa wrote with great verve.* N UNCOUNT = gusto

very /veri[1]/. 1 **Very** is used to give emphasis to an adjective or adverb. **Very** cannot be used with comparative adjectives. EG *...a very small child... That's very nice of you... It's a very good idea... I'm very, very sorry... Think very carefully... He very rarely drank... I know very little about this... 'Is it urgent?'-'Very.'... I liked it very much... I began to feel very much better... She seemed very much changed by this experience.* ADV+ADJ/ADV/ QUANTIF ⇑ extremely

2 **Not very** is used to say that something is not at all true, or that it is true only to a small degree. EG *I'm not very sure... He's not there very often... 'Is the work difficult?'-'Not very, but it's boring.'... 'That was kind of you.'-'Not very.'* PHR+ADJ/ADV = really

3 You also use **very** 3.1 to give emphasis to an adjective which you would not normally expect to vary in degree. EG *...a very pregnant woman... She seemed very English to him... That is very true.* 3.2 to give emphasis to a superlative adjective. EG *It's one of Shaw's very best plays... ...the very latest techniques... It must be a matter of joy, or relief at the very least.* 3.3 with certain nouns in order to specify exactly a position or extreme point in space or time. EG *I walked up to the very top... ...the very back of the auditorium... We were in on their discussions from the very beginning... ...the very middle of the front row.* 3.4 with nouns to emphasize that something is exactly the right one or the same. EG *Ah, there you are. The very man I've been looking for!... Those are the very words he used... We met in this very room.* 3.5 with nouns to emphasize the importance or seriousness of what you are saying. EG *The commercial theatre is fighting for its very life... Respect for the law is the very foundation of civilised living... I shall make this boy vanish before your very eyes... The role of the peacemaker is, by its very nature, a thankless one.* ADV+ADJ CLASSIF = really ADV+ADJ QUALIT: SUPERL ADJ CLASSIF: ATTRIB = absolute ADJ CLASSIF: ATTRIB = exact ADJ CLASSIF: ATTRIB

4 The expression **very much so** is an emphatic way of saying 'yes'. EG *'Did your father resist this ambition?'-'Very much so.'* CONVENTION

5 Something **of** your **very own** is something that belongs to you and that you do not have to share with anyone else; a slightly childish expression. EG *They love children and want some of their very own... The town has its very own bus service.* PHR WITH NG

6 **Very good** is used to tell someone in authority that you agree to carry out a suggestion or order; a slightly formal expression. EG *'Bring the men in, Sergeant.'-'Very good, sir.'... 'That will be all, nurse.'-'Very good, doctor.'* CONVENTION = certainly, right

7 **Very well** is used to say that you agree to do something, even though you might not really want to do it. EG *'Will you do it?'-'Very well, then.'... Very well, if that's the way you want it... 'Mr Brown wants to see you.'-'Very well. I'll be along in a moment.'* CONVENTION = okay, all right

8 If you say that you **cannot very well** do something, you mean that it would not be the right thing to do. EG *I can't very well drag him out of the meeting, can I?* PHR: USU+INF = really

very high frequency. See **VHF**.

vespers /vespəz/ is an evening service in some Christian churches. N UNCOUNT = evensong

vessel /vesə[0]l/, **vessels**. A **vessel** is 1 a ship or large boat; a fairly formal word. EG *...fishing vessels... ...anti-submarine vessels... We had sighted the vessel and were following it.* 2 a bowl or other container in which liquid is kept; a fairly literary word. EG *He began putting the sacred vessels away... ...wooden vessels.* 3 a thin tube in the body of an animal or plant, along which liquid moves. EG *...the sap vessels of the elm.* ● See also **blood vessel**. N COUNT N COUNT N COUNT

vest /vest/, **vests**. A **vest** is 1 a piece of clothing which you wear on the top half of your body underneath a shirt, blouse, dress, etc in order to keep warm; used in British English. N COUNT

2 a waistcoat; used in American English. N COUNT

vested /vestɪ[2]d/. Something that is **vested** in someone is given to them as a right or a responsibility. EG *...the authority vested in him by the Commonwealth of Massachusetts.* ADJ CLASSIF: PRED+*in* = entrusted

vested interest, vested interests. A **vested interest** is a very strong reason that someone has for acting in a particular way, for example to protect their own money, power, or reputation. EG *Each of the major political parties has a vested interest in promoting various myths about itself... People are simply protecting their vested interests.* N COUNT/ UNCOUNT: SING=PL

vestibule /vestɪbjuːl/, **vestibules**. A **vestibule** is an enclosed area between the outside door of a building and the doors to the rooms; a formal word. N COUNT = entrance hall

vestige /vestɪdʒ/, **vestiges**. A **vestige** of something is a very small part that still remains of something that was once much larger or more important; a fairly formal word. EG *They are trying to break down the last vestige of resistance... ...a country without any vestige of political freedom.* N COUNT: USU+ *of*, SING=PL ⇑ remnant = trace

vestigial /və[2]stɪdʒɪəl/ is used to describe the small amounts of something that still remain of a larger or more important thing; a formal word. EG *In Lorraine's mind there lurked some vestigial traces of conscience.* ADJ CLASSIF: USU ATTRIB ⇑ remaining

vestments /vestmə[2]nts/ are the special clothes worn by priests during church ceremonies. N PLURAL = robes

vestry /vestri[1]/, **vestries**. A **vestry** is a room in a church which a priest or minister uses as an office or to change into his official clothes for taking a church service. N COUNT

vet /vet/, **vets, vetting, vetted**; used mainly in British English. 1 A **vet** is someone who is specially trained to look after the health of animals. EG *Get your kitten checked by the vet.* N COUNT = veterinary surgeon

2 If you **vet** something, you check it carefully, to make sure that it is acceptable to people in authority. EG *His speeches were vetted for content and tone... Weaponry purchased by police forces is vetted by a committee.* V+O: USU PASS = appraise

3 If you **vet** someone, you make sure that they are suitable for a particular role, position, or job, especially when the position or job involves dealing with military or political secrets. EG *She says she vets her girls very carefully... He was very thoroughly vetted.* ◊ **vetting**. EG *He had introduced a bill to tighten the security vetting of civil servants.* ● See also **positive vetting**. V+O: USU PASS ⇑ check = screen ◊ N UNCOUNT = screening

4 **vets**, in American English, are veterans. ● See **veteran 1**.

vetch /vetʃ/, **vetches**. EG *Vetch is a climbing or creeping plant found in temperate climates. Some kinds of vetch produce beans which are used to feed cattle.* N MASS

veteran /vetə[0]rən/, **veterans**. A **veteran** is 1 someone who has served in the armed forces of their country, especially during a war. EG *...the veterans of two wars... ...a World War Two veteran. ...veterans day.* 2 someone who has been involved in a particular activity for a long time. EG *...a veteran of the civil rights movement in Mississippi... ...a much-loved veteran of stage and screen... She's a veteran blood donor.* N COUNT = ex-serviceman N COUNT, OR N BEFORE N = old hand ≠ novice

veterinarian /vetə[0]rɪneərɪən/, **veterinarians**. A **veterinarian** is someone who is specially trained to look after the health of animals; used in American English. N COUNT

veterinary /vetə[0]rɪnə[0]ri[1]/ is used to describe the work of a vet and the medical treatment of animals. EG *They managed a veterinary practice in Perth.* ADJ CLASSIF: ATTRIB

veterinary surgeon, veterinary surgeons. A **veterinary surgeon** is the same as a vet; used in British English. EG *She is the secretary to a veterinary surgeon.* N COUNT

veto /viːtəʊ/, **vetoes, vetoing, vetoed**. 1 If someone in authority **vetoes** something, they forbid it to happen or to be put into action. EG *White could still veto the plan... The government vetoed this proposal... ...the vetoing by Britain, France, and the United States of four UN resolutions.* ▸ used as a noun. EG *The rest of the committee could not accept the veto.* V+O ⇑ stop = block ▸ N COUNT

2 **Veto** is the right that a person or organization has N UNCOUNT

to decide officially that a scheme or plan must not be put into action and the power to prevent it being put into action. EG *...the Sovereign's effective power of veto.*

vex /veks/, **vexes, vexing, vexed**. If something **vexes** you, it makes you feel annoyed and puzzled; a fairly formal word. EG *It vexed her to be ignored like this.* ◇ **vexing**. EG *...the vexing subject of summer colds.* ● See also **vexed**. — V+O: USU PASS ⇑ annoy = irritate; ◇ ADJ QUALIT

vexation /vekseɪʃəⁿn/, **vexations**. A **vexation** is something which makes you feel annoyed and puzzled; a fairly formal word. EG *It will be nothing but an annoyance and a vexation.* ▸ used as an uncount noun. EG *She was crying with vexation and shock.* — N COUNT ⇑ annoyance = trial; ▸ N UNCOUNT

vexed /vekst/. 1 If you are **vexed**, you feel annoyed and puzzled. EG *We knew she was really a bit vexed... ...a vexed frown.* — ADJ QUALIT

2 A **vexed** problems or question is one that causes people a lot of trouble, especially so that they spend a lot of time discussing the problems. EG *We live in vexed and troubled times... This leads to the vexed issue of priorities.* — ADJ QUALIT: USU ATTRIB ⇑ troublesome = difficult

v.g. is a written abbreviation for 'very good'; written especially by a teacher at the end of an essay or other piece of work.

VHF is a radio frequency band between 300 and 30 megahertz; an abbreviation for 'very high frequency'. — N UNCOUNT

via. **Via** can be pronounced either /vaɪə/ or /viːə/. You use **via** to say 1 that someone or something goes through a particular place on the way to somewhere else. EG *He booked a ticket to Washington via Frankfurt and New York.* 2 that you do or achieve something by making use of the person or thing mentioned. EG *The swift transmission of television pictures, via satellite, all over the globe... It was so kind of you to send that message via Toby... He hopes to get a job in television via journalism.* — PREP = by way of; PREP = by means of

viable /vaɪəbəⁿl/. 1 Something that is **viable** is capable of doing what it is intended to do, without needing any extra help or financial support. EG *We should be doing everything in our power to develop viable alternatives to petrol... When are tidal electricity generators likely to become viable?* ◇ **viability** /vaɪəbɪlɪti¹/. EG *...the commercial viability of the new product.* — ADJ QUALIT = feasible ≠ unworkable; ◇ N UNCOUNT = feasibility

2 Things such as foetuses, seeds, and eggs are described as **viable** if they are capable of developing into a living being without outside help; a technical term in biology. EG *Bacteria can grow at up to 65°C and stay viable right up to just below the boiling point of water.* — ADJ CLASSIF

viaduct /vaɪədʌkt/, **viaducts**. A **viaduct** is a long, high bridge that carries a road or a railway across a valley. EG *I live near where the viaduct straddles the river Wye.* — N COUNT: ALSO IN NAMES

vial /vaɪəⁿl/, **vials**. A **vial** is a very small bottle containing something such as perfume or medicine; a fairly formal word. EG *She took out a vial of perfume from her bag.* — N PART+N UNCOUNT = phial

viands /viːəndz/ are items of food; an old-fashioned word. — N PLURAL

vibes /vaɪbz/. 1 **Vibes** are the good or bad emotional reactions which you feel that a person has towards you or the good or bad atmosphere that you sense in a place; an informal use. EG *There are bad vibes between us... The city held such hostile vibes that you felt you were being watched continually.* — N PLURAL ⇑ feelings

2 If you play **vibes**, you play the vibraphone; an informal word used by jazz musicians. EG *The band got talking about a woman that played vibes and was getting a lot of work.* — N PLURAL

vibrancy /vaɪbrənsi¹/ is a strong feeling of energy and enthusiasm. EG *...the tremendous vibrancy of the young people who were gathering there.* — N UNCOUNT = vitality

vibrant /vaɪbrənt/. 1 Something that is **vibrant** is full of life, energy, and enthusiasm. EG *His vibrant talk fascinated and excited me... ...Ice Age art with its vibrant and dynamic images of animals.* — ADJ QUALIT: IF+PREP THEN *with* ⇑ lively

2 A **vibrant** voice or sound is full of emotion and is very exciting. EG *...the vibrant tones of Richard Burton... ...a voice vibrant with scorn and hatred.* — ADJ QUALIT: USU ATTRIB = resonant

3 **Vibrant** light and colours are very bright and clear. EG *...a splash of vibrant, living colour.* — ADJ QUALIT = brilliant

vibraphone /vaɪbrəfəʊn/, **vibraphones**. A **vibraphone** is an electronic musical instrument which consists of a set of metal bars in a frame. When you hit the bars, they produce vibrating notes that do not fade away immediately. — N COUNT = vibes

vibrate /vaɪbreɪt/, **vibrates, vibrating, vibrated**. If something **vibrates** or if you **vibrate** it, it shakes with a very slight, very quick movement, which can often be felt rather than seen. EG *He heard a strange sound that seemed to vibrate through the ceiling over his head... The foundation of the city began to rumble and vibrate... The air seemed to vibrate with heat... These birds vibrate the whole thorax.* ◇ **vibration** /vaɪbreɪʃəⁿn/, **vibrations**. EG *Your finger will probably feel the vibration on the violin string. ...vibrations such as those produced by a footstep.* — V-ERG = quiver; ◇ N COUNT/UNCOUNT

vibrato /vɪbrɑːtəʊ/, **vibratos**. A **vibrato** is a rapidly repeated slight variation in the pitch of a musical note, produced by a tiny shaking movement of the finger on a violin string or by a slight unsteadiness of the voice, in order to add expressiveness to the music. — N COUNT/UNCOUNT

vibrator /vaɪbreɪtə/, **vibrators**. A **vibrator** is a device which causes vibrations, especially one which is used in massage to give relief from pain or one used for giving sexual pleasure. — N COUNT

vicar /vɪkə/, **vicars**. A **vicar** is a priest in the Church of England who is in charge of a church and who looks after the spiritual needs of people in his parish. — N COUNT: ALSO VOC ⇑ clergyman

vicarage /vɪkərɪdʒ/, **vicarages**. A **vicarage** is a house in which a vicar lives. — N COUNT

vicarious /vɪkeərɪəs, vaɪ-/ describes something that is experienced by watching, listening to, or reading about other people doing it or living through it, rather than by doing it or living through it yourself. EG *...a vicarious sense of power and adventure.* ◇ **vicariously**. EG *...the frustration I felt at being forced to experience it all vicariously.* — ADJ CLASSIF: ATTRIB; ◇ ADV WITH VB = by proxy

vice /vaɪs/, **vices**; also spelled **vise** for the meaning in paragraph 3, in American English. 1 A **vice** is 1.1 a serious moral fault in someone's character. EG *...human vices such as greed and envy.* 1.2 a habit which is regarded as a weakness in someone's character, but not usually as a serious fault. EG *Her one small vice was smoking.* — N COUNT ≠ virtue; N COUNT = failing

2 **Vice** is criminal behaviour that is regarded as immoral, usually because it involves pornography, prostitution, drugs, or gambling. EG *...a campaign against local vice and violence... ...vice laws.* — N UNCOUNT

3 A **vice** is also a tool with a pair of jaws which you tighten with a screw. Vices are used to hold an object tightly while work is done on it. EG *I once caught my tie in the vice... His fingers tightened like a vice around his rifle.* — N COUNT = clamp

vice- is used before a rank or title to indicate that the person who holds that rank or title is next in importance to the person who holds the full rank or title. EG *...the vice-chairman of the Welsh Arts Council... ...the vice-presidency.* — PREFIX = deputy

vice-chancellor, vice-chancellors. The **vice-chancellor** of a British University is the person who is in charge of its academic and administrative policies and activities. — N COUNT: USU *the*+N, ALSO VOC

vice squad, vice squads. The **vice squad** is the section of a police force that deals with crime relating to pornography, prostitution, drugs, and gambling. — N PROPER: *the*+N, OR N COUNT

vice versa /vaɪsə vɜːsə/ is used to indicate that the reverse of what you have said is also true. For example 'women may bring their husbands with them, and vice versa' means that men may also bring their wives with them. EG *Progress was industrialization and vice versa... He believed that a man should have as many wives as he wants, but not vice-versa.* — ADV

vicinity /vɪsɪnɪti¹/. The **vicinity** of a place is the area immediately around it. EG *The hotels in the vicinity of the campus were cheap and shabby.* — N SING WITH DET: USU *in*+*the*+N

vicious /vɪʃəs/. 1 Someone or something that is **vicious** is very cruel and violent in hurting other people. EG *...a vicious killer... He gave one short vicious twist to the neck... ...the most vicious totalitarian system in history.* ◇ **viciously**. EG *...viciously lashing whips.* ◇ **viciousness**. EG *It was a campaign of singular viciousness.* — ADJ QUALIT = brutal ≠ gentle; ◇ ADV WITH VB; ◇ N UNCOUNT = brutality

2 Language that is **vicious** is cruel and intended to hurt or upset people. EG *I got the most vicious letters from all over Britain... Men can be unbelievably* — ADJ QUALIT = savage ≠ kind

vicious about each other. ◇ **viciously**. EG *The words came from Jack viciously, as if they were a curse.* ◇ ADV WITH VB
◇ **viciousness**. EG *Gareth spoke with unconcealed viciousness.* ◇ N UNCOUNT

vicious circle, vicious circles. A **vicious circle** is a problem or difficult situation that has an effect which creates new problems which in turn re-create the original problems. EG *We were chained to a vicious circle of violence.* N COUNT

vicissitudes /vɪsɪsɪtju:dz/ are the changes in circumstances at different times in the life of someone or in the development of something; a formal word. EG *...the vicissitudes of life.* N PLURAL = ups and downs

victim /vɪktɪm/, **victims**. 1 A **victim** is 1.1 someone who has been hurt or killed by someone or something. EG *Most of the victims were shot in the back while trying to run away... ...a rape victim.* N COUNT 1.2 someone who has suffered as a result of someone else's actions or of unpleasant circumstances. EG *After about two weeks, the victim's hair starts to fall out... She was not the victim of circumstance that she made herself out to be.* N COUNT

2 If you **fall victim to** something, you suffer as a result of it. EG *He fell victim to a wasting disease.* PHR : VB INFLECTS

victimize /vɪktɪmaɪz/, **victimizes, victimizing, victimized**; also spelled **victimise**. If you **victimize** someone, you deliberately treat them unfairly, especially because you do not like their beliefs. EG *Management insisted that she was not being victimized.* V+O : USU PASS = persecute ◇ **victimization** /vɪktɪmaɪzeɪʃə⁰n/. EG *There must be no victimization of workers or shop stewards.* ◇ N UNCOUNT = persecution

victor /vɪktə/, **victors**. A **victor** is someone who has defeated an enemy or opponent, especially in war; a rather old-fashioned word. N COUNT ⇑ winner ≠ loser

Victorian /vɪktɔ:rɪən/, **Victorians**. 1 **Victorian** describes 1.1 things that happened or were made in England in the 19th century, when Victoria was the Queen of England. EG *...forbidding Victorian architecture and statues... Many Victorian households did without a bathroom.* ADJ CLASSIF 1.2 people who have old-fashioned qualities which are thought to have been common in the time of Queen Victoria, especially an attitude of strict discipline and morals. EG *They were both very Victorian and very domineering...* ADJ QUALIT

2 A **Victorian** was someone who was alive when Victoria was the Queen of England. EG *...an earnest, upright, morally striving Victorian.* N COUNT

Victoriana /vɪktɔ:rɪɑ:nə/. Objects which were made in the time of Queen Victoria (1837-1901) are referred to as **Victoriana**. N UNCOUNT ⇑ antiques

victorious /vɪktɔ:rɪəs/. Someone who is **victorious** has won a victory, especially in war. EG *...riding at the head of his victorious troops... The army came home victorious.* ADJ CLASSIF ⇑ successful = triumphant

victory /vɪktə⁰ri¹/, **victories**. A **victory** is a situation in which you gain complete success, for example in defeating an opponent in a war or in any other hard struggle. EG *In A.D. 636, an Arab army won a famous victory over a much larger Persian force... In 1960, the Party won a convincing victory at the polls... The final agreement was a victory for common sense... This was the first step on the road to victory.* N COUNT/ UNCOUNT

victuals /vɪtəlz/ are food and drink; an old-fashioned word. N PLURAL

video /vɪdɪəʊ/, **videos, videoing, videoed**. 1 **Video** is the recording and showing of television programmes, films, or actual events for entertainment or educational purposes, using a television set, video tapes, and a video recorder. EG *I know that you use video for teaching these students... The film's on video... ...a video film we have made with language students.* N UNCOUNT

2 A **video** is 2.1 a machine which can be used to play video tapes on a television set and to record television programmes onto video tape. EG *Turn off the video... Four years ago I got this video, but I quickly got bored with it.* N COUNT 2.2 a film or television programme recorded on video tape for people to watch on a television set. EG *I've seen this video before.* N COUNT ⇑ recording

3 If you **video** something, you record it on magnetic tape, either by using a television camera and recording the actual events, or by using a video to record a television programme as it is being transmitted, in order to watch it later. V+O

video cassette, video cassettes. A **video cassette** is a cassette containing a video tape. N COUNT

video recorder, video recorders. A **video recorder** or a **video cassette recorder** is a machine that can be used to record television programmes, films, etc onto video tapes, so that people can play them back and watch them later on a television set. EG *He pointed out that the video recorder was, in fact, a key factor in restoring family life.* N COUNT

video tape, video tapes; also spelled with a hyphen and as one word. **Video tape** is magnetic tape that is used to record the frequencies in an electric signal which are then converted into pictures on television. EG *The information can be printed, or put on video tape.* ▸ used as a count noun. EG *They saw the videotapes of Mr Frost's interviews.* N UNCOUNT ▸ N COUNT

vie /vaɪ/, **vies, vying, vied**. If you **vie** with someone for something, you try hard to get it or do it before they do, or to do it better than they do; a fairly formal word. EG *While other artists vied for the prime sites, he chose a dead corner... ...vying with each other to express their disgust.* V OR V+A (with) : RECIP, USU+for/to-INF = compete

view /vju:/, **views, viewing, viewed**. 1 A **view** is 1.1 a belief or opinion that you have on a particular topic. EG *He was sent to jail for his political views... Barbara seemed dismayed at my views on race... I have strong views about politics and the Church... The scientific view cannot be questioned on its own ground.* N COUNT : USU WITH SUPP 1.2 the way that someone understands and thinks about the things that are happening around them. EG *She has a view of life which is in fact deeply corrupt... He tends to take a wider, more overall view of things than most people... With every word you utter, you state your world view.* N SING WITH DET +SUPP ⇑ attitude = outlook

2 If you **view** something in a particular way, you think of it in that way. EG *He viewed the future with gloom... It seemed probable that he would view Julie's request with favour... Their missiles are viewed as a defensive and deterrent force.* V+O+A ⇑ consider = regard

3 The **view** from a window or high place is everything which can be seen from that place, especially when it is considered to be beautiful. EG *The windows of her flat looked out on to a superb view of London.* N COUNT : USU SING ⇑ scene = vista

4 If you have a **view** of something, you can see it. EG *The police driver blocked his view... I looked over my shoulder for one last view of the gorge... They pushed forward for a better view.* N SING WITH DET +SUPP ⇑ sight = glimpse

5 To **view** something means to look at it carefully or with great interest; a fairly formal use. EG *A drop from a pond, viewed through a microscope, swarms with tiny organisms... The soldier twisted round to view the damage... Viewed from the air or on a map, the parks of London are seen to be extensive.* V+O = examine

6 If you **view** a house or a flat, you go and see it in order to decide whether you want to buy it. V+O ⇑ inspect

7 If you **view** a television programme, video, or film, you watch it; a formal use. EG *I spent hours taping things that could be viewed and immediately erased... 80 per cent of the viewing audience will be watching the Olympics.* V OR V+O

8 The word **view** is also used in the following expressions: 8.1 You use **in my view** when you want to emphasize that you are stating a personal opinion, which other people might not agree with. EG *All I can say is that, in my view, it's a long way to a United States of Europe.* PHR : USED AS ADV SEN 8.2 If you **take the view that** something is true, your opinion is that it is true. EG *The civil servants generally took the view that experts know best.* PHR : VB INFLECTS ⇑ believe = feel 8.3 If you **take a dim view of** something or **a poor view of** it, you disapprove of it. EG *He is a Democrat and an economist, who takes a generally dim view of Mr Nixon.* PHR : VB INFLECTS = disapprove 8.4 If you **take the long view**, you consider what is likely to happen in the future over a long period, rather than thinking only about the immediate effects of something. EG *Parliament should be prepared to take the long view.* PHR : VB INFLECTS 8.5 You use **in view of** something when you are taking into consideration facts that have just been mentioned or are just about to be mentioned. EG *The folder was marked 'Very Secret', not surprisingly, in view of the contents... In view of the fact that all the other members of the group are going, I think you should go too.* PREP = considering 8.6 If you do something **with a view to** something else, you do it in order to achieve a particular result. EG *We have exchanged letters with a view to meeting to discuss these problems...* PREP

They entered into talks with a view to amalgamation. ● See also **point of view**.

9 In view. 9.1 If something is **in view**, you can see it from where you are. EG *We crept back around the cage to keep the monkey in view.* PHR : USED AS AN A **9.2** If an event is **in view**, it is likely to happen in the near future. EG *Is there anything else in view for the cinema?* PHR : USED AS AN A **9.3** If you have something **in view**, you are aware of it and your actions are aimed towards it. EG *I don't teach with the exams in view... What end has he in view?* PHR : USED AS AN A = in mind **9.4** If something is **in full view**, it can be seen easily by everyone who is there. EG *Dame Marie turned her back on her rival in full view of the audience... There in full view was a large bed rumpled and unmade.* PHR : USED AS AN A ↑ visible

10 If something **comes into view,** you become able to see it, either because it has moved or because you have moved. EG *The bridge suddenly came into view... A dark figure on the roof came into view.* PHR : VB INFLECTS ↑ appear = materialize

11 Something that is **on view** is exhibited in public for people to see and examine. EG *The Turner exhibition is on view at the Tate Gallery until August.* PHR : USED AS AN A = on show

viewer /vjuːə/, **viewers**. **1** A **viewer** is **1.1** someone who watches television. EG *Many of these programmes are an insult to the viewer's intelligence.* N COUNT **1.2** someone who is looking carefully at a picture, antique, or other interesting object. EG *Picasso's forms and colours draw out certain emotions in the viewer... At the Montreal World's Fair, viewers in pavilion after pavilion were confronted with traditional crafts.* N COUNT

2 A **viewer** is also a box-like object with a magnifying lens. You use a viewer for looking at transparent colour photographs. N COUNT ↑ device

viewfinder /vjuːfaɪndə/, **viewfinders**. A **viewfinder** is a small square of glass in a camera that you look through so that you can see what you are about to photograph. N COUNT ↑ device

viewpoint /vjuːpɔɪnt/, **viewpoints**. **1** Someone's **viewpoint** is the way that they think about things in general or about one thing in particular. EG *...a large group working hard to press the consumer viewpoint... I try to make sense of what's happening from my particular viewpoint as a Christian minister.* N COUNT+SUPP ↑ attitude = standpoint

2 A **viewpoint** is also a place from which you can get a good view of something that is happening. N COUNT

vigil /vɪdʒɪl/, **vigils**. A **vigil** is a period of time, especially at night, when you remain quiet and watchful in one place. You do this, for example, because you are looking after a sick person, praying, or making a political protest. EG *Last weekend a nun on a hunger strike held a vigil at the United Nations... I just had to sit there and keep a sleepless vigil until the morning came.* N COUNT ↑ watch

vigilance /vɪdʒɪləns/ is very careful attention that you give to a situation, so that you notice any danger or trouble that there might be. EG *Constant vigilance is required from all of us.* N UNCOUNT = watchfulness

vigilant /vɪdʒɪlənt/. Someone who is **vigilant** gives careful attention to a particular problem or situation and concentrates on noticing any danger or trouble that there might be. EG *This evening, I had to be especially vigilant... He has to learn how to remain vigilant through these long nights.* ADJ QUALIT = watchful

vigilante /vɪdʒɪlænti¹/, **vigilantes**. A **vigilante** is a member of a group of people who join together to catch and punish anyone who they think is doing wrong or breaking the law. Vigilantes organize themselves when they think the police are not keeping order properly. EG *...a mob of hysterical vigilantes... ...the growth of vigilante societies around the country.* N COUNT : USU PL

vignette /vɪnjet/, **vignettes**. A **vignette** is a short description or piece of acting, which expresses very clearly and neatly the typical characteristics of the thing that it represents. EG *...a fascinating vignette of family life.* N COUNT ↑ picture = peep

vigorous /vɪgərəs/. **1** A physical action that is **vigorous** is done with a lot of energy; used especially of short and repeated actions. EG *Mary gave her skirt a vigorous shake.* ADJ QUALIT ↑ energetic = hearty ◊ **vigorously**. EG *Lolita stretched out her hand, nodding vigorously... We shook hands vigorously and he went off.* ◊ ADV WITH VB = heartily

2 An activity or campaign that is **vigorous** involves energetic and enthusiastic actions, often in support of a particular cause. EG *Their old home has only been saved by a vigorous campaign... The League remained in overt and vigorous opposition to the war.* ADJ QUALIT ↑ active = spirited ◊ **vigorously**. EG *Chomsky defended very vigorously what was an older view.* ◊ ADV WITH VB = hotly

3 Someone who is **vigorous 3.1** is strong and healthy and full of energy. EG *...an elderly but vigorous man with a white moustache.* ADJ QUALIT = robust **3.2** shows great energy and enthusiasm in stating opinions and in doing things. EG *He was one of the most vigorous advocates of workers' control.* ADJ QUALIT ↑ energetic = keen

vigour /vɪgə/; also spelled **vigor** in American English. **Vigour** is physical or mental energy and enthusiasm. EG *These problems were discussed with great vigour... Benn admired the vigour of American democracy.* N UNCOUNT : USU +SUPP

Viking /vaɪkɪŋ/, **Vikings**. The **Vikings** were groups of seamen from Scandinavia who attacked villages, especially coastal villages, in most parts of north-western Europe from the 8th to the 11th centuries. N COUNT : USU PL, OR N BEFORE N ↑ pirate

vile /vaɪl/, **viler, vilest**. If you say that someone or something is **vile**, **1** you are emphasizing how unpleasant they are and how much you dislike them. EG *...England's vile weather.* ADJ QUALIT = ghastly **2** you are saying that they are so disgusting that people are likely to be shocked or horrified by them. EG *'You're vile!' she shouted... ...her vile language.* ADJ QUALIT ↑ immoral = shameful ◊ **vilely**. EG *Her situation was vilely exploited by the other two.* ◊ ADV WITH VB = shamefully

vilify /vɪlɪfaɪ/, **vilifies, vilifying, vilified**. If you **vilify** someone, you say or write very unpleasant things about them, so that people will be influenced against them; a formal word. EG *He was vilified for making those broadcasts.* V+O ↑ revile = malign ◊ **vilification** /vɪlɪfɪkeɪʃəⁿn/. EG *...the vilification of the Spanish government.* ◊ N UNCOUNT : USU+of ↑ attack = maligning

villa /vɪlə/, **villas**. A **villa** is **1** a big pleasant house with its own large gardens. N COUNT **2** a house which people can rent for their holidays. EG *They had rented a villa not far from Pisa.* N COUNT **3** in Britain, a house built as one of a row of similar houses along a street; used especially as part of an address. EG *10, Edith Villas, London W14.* N COUNT : ALSO IN NAMES

village /vɪlɪdʒ/, **villages**. A **village** is a small group of houses and other buildings, such as a few shops, a pub, a church, and a school, all grouped together in a country area. EG *They entered the village of Northwold... ...an obscure Austrian mountain village... The very next day we held a jumble sale in the village hall.* ▸ used to refer to the people who live in a village. EG *The village was entertaining important visitors.* N COUNT

villager /vɪlɪdʒə/, **villagers**. A **villager** is someone who lives in a village, especially someone who has lived there for most or all of their life. EG *The villagers were suspicious of anything new.* N COUNT : USU PL ↑ inhabitant

villain /vɪlən/, **villains**. **1** A **villain** is **1.1** someone who deliberately harms other people or breaks the law in order to get what he or she wants. EG *He was financially involved with an out-and-out villain.* N COUNT ↑ person = scoundrel **1.2** the main bad character in a play, film, or novel. EG *He was cast as the villain in the forthcoming production.* N COUNT

2 The villain of the piece is someone who is seen as being the cause of all the trouble in a situation; an old-fashioned or humorous expression. EG *Mayor White was increasingly cast as the villain of the piece.* PHR : USED AS C

villainous /vɪlənəs/. Someone who is **villainous** is very bad and willing to harm other people or break the law in order to get what he or she wants. EG *...a villainous archbishop.* ▸ used of people's actions and behaviour. EG *They were enmeshed in villainous machinations.* ADJ CLASSIF = wicked

villainy /vɪləni¹/ is very bad or criminal behaviour. EG *...the villainy of her landlord.* N UNCOUNT, OR N COUNT : USU PL

vinaigrette /vɪnəgret/ is a sauce made by mixing oil, vinegar, salt, pepper, and herbs, which is put on cold food, especially salads. EG *Use mayonnaise, not vinaigrette, for chicken salads.* N UNCOUNT ↑ dressing

vindicate /vɪndɪkeɪt/, **vindicates, vindicating, vindicated**. To **vindicate** somebody or something means to show or prove that their actions or ideas were correct, after people have said that they were wrong; a formal word. EG *Benn was decisively vindicated at the polls, receiving 23,275 votes to 10,231... His gloomy forecasts have been increasingly vindicated.* V+O = justify ◊ **vindication** /vɪndɪkeɪʃəⁿn/, **vindications**. EG ◊ N COUNT/

These changes to the law were widely regarded as a vindication of his long campaign. UNCOUNT

vindictive /vɪndɪktɪv/. Someone who is **vindictive** tries deliberately and cold-bloodedly to hurt someone who they think has done them harm. EG *He was just being vindictive.* ▸ used of people's actions. EG *...vindictive measures.* ◊ **vindictively**. EG *Joan had made her wait–not vindictively, but to save her from getting wet.* ◊ **vindictiveness**. EG *...spells of sulking, withdrawal, and vindictiveness...*

ADJ QUALIT ⇑ malicious = spiteful; ◊ ADV WITH VB ⇑ maliciously; ◊ N UNCOUNT = spite

vine /vaɪn/, **vines**. A **vine** is **1** a climbing plant which produces grapes as its fruit. EG *...a big greenhouse with a vine which came from Hampton Court.* N COUNT = grapevine

2 a climbing or trailing plant with long twisting stems. Several different types of plants are called vines, especially ones which grow in hot countries. EG *...a jungle woven with creepers and vines.* N COUNT

vinegar /vɪnɪgə/ is a sharp-tasting liquid, usually made from sour wine or malt, which is used in making things such as chutney or salad dressing. EG *...oil and vinegar dressing... Use half a lemon dipped in salt and vinegar.* N UNCOUNT

vinegary /vɪnɪgə[0]ri[1]/. **1** Something that is **vinegary** tastes or smells of vinegar. EG *...the vinegary smell of the cabbage.* ADJ QUALIT ⇑ sour

2 If you describe someone as **vinegary**, you mean that they are bad tempered and quick to say nasty things. EG *...a vinegary and ill-tempered old woman.* ADJ QUALIT : USU ATTRIB ⇑ disagreeable = peevish

vineyard /vɪnjəd/, **vineyards**. A **vineyard** is an area of land where grape vines are grown in order to produce wine. N COUNT

vintage /vɪntɪdʒ/, **vintages**. **1 Vintage** wine is wine of good quality that was made in a particular year and that has been stored for several years in order to improve its quality still further. EG *...grouse washed down with claret and vintage port.* ADJ CLASSIF : ATTRIB = choice

2 Vintage describes something which is the best or most typical of its kind, especially because it was produced at a time when the thing was at its best. EG *...vintage Chandler dialogue.* ADJ CLASSIF : ATTRIB = classic

3 A **vintage** is a very good wine which was made in a particular year. EG *...the last bottle of a rare vintage.* ▸ used to refer to the year in which a particular wine was made. EG *...1978 vintage.* N COUNT

4 A **vintage** car is a car made between 1919 and 1930. ADJ CLASSIF

vintner /vɪntnə/, **vintners**. A **vintner** is someone whose job is to buy and sell wines. N COUNT

vinyl /vaɪnə[0]l/ is a strong plastic used for making furniture, floor coverings, etc. EG *...white vinyl chairs... ...leather and vinyl upholstery.* N UNCOUNT : USU BEFORE N

viola /vi[1]əʊlə/ **violas**. **1** A **viola** is a musical instrument played with a bow. It is like a violin, but is slightly larger and produces a slightly deeper sound when played. N COUNT

2 A **viola** is also a small garden flower rather like a pansy. N COUNT

violate /vaɪəleɪt/, **violates, violating, violated**. **1** If you **violate** an agreement, law, or promise, you break it. EG *This did not violate international agreements... Ancient property laws are openly violated.* ◊ **violation** /vaɪəleɪʃə[0]n/, **violations**. EG *They blockaded the Suez Canal in violation of international agreement... ...violations of the Constitution.*

V+O ⇑ break = infringe; ◊ N UNCOUNT/COUNT : USU+*of* = infringement

2 If you **violate** someone's privacy or peace, you disturb it. EG *She did not return. Neither did anyone else violate his privacy.* V+O = interrupt

3 If someone **violates** a place, especially a tomb, they treat it with no respect, for example by breaking into it and removing its treasures. EG *There's a curse laid on those who violated the tomb of the king.* ◊ **violation, violations**. EG *...the violation of our homes.*

V+O ⇑ dishonour = desecrate; ◊ N UNCOUNT/COUNT : USU+*of*

4 If a man **violates** a woman, he rapes her; a formal use. EG *She said I had attempted to violate her several times.* V+O

violence /vaɪələns/ is **1** behaviour which is meant to hurt or kill people, for example by hitting or kicking or using guns or bombs. EG *...threats of terrorist violence... ...acts of violence... ...robbery with violence.* N UNCOUNT **2** a great deal of energy that you use in saying something or doing something, often because you are angry. EG *He flung open the door with unnecessary violence.* N UNCOUNT = force **3** words, actions, or other forms of expression which are critical or destructive. EG *They are exerting ever greater violence against the environment.* N UNCOUNT ⇑ damage

violent /vaɪələnt/. **1** If you are **violent**, you behave in a way that is intended to hurt or kill people, for example by hitting or kicking or using guns or bombs. EG *People in this society are prepared to be violent.* ▸ used of events. EG *...violent clashes with the police... We live in a uniquely violent age.* ◊ **violently**. EG *They have come into conflict, sometimes violently.*

ADJ QUALIT ⇑ aggressive; ◊ ADV WITH VB ⇑ aggressively

2 A **violent** death is painful and unexpected, usually because the person who dies has been murdered. EG *...the constant threat of violent death.* ◊ **violently**. EG *...a poison that can kill violently and quickly.*

ADJ CLASSIF : USU ATTRIB; ◊ ADV WITH VB

3 Violent describes something that is said or argued with a lot of force and energy and so is almost frightening. EG *At other times the argument grew violent... Burt's work came under violent attack.* ◊ **violently**. EG *They violently disagreed with their Commander-in-Chief. 'Stinking bitch,' she would say, violently.*

ADJ QUALIT ⇑ intense = vehement; ◊ ADV WITH VB ⇑ intensely

4 Violent also describes something which happens suddenly and with a lot of force. EG *...a violent explosion... ...violent acceleration.* ◊ **violently**. EG *The train braked violently. She seized him by the collar and shook him violently.*

ADJ QUALIT : USU ATTRIB; ◊ ADV WITH VB

5 Violent emotions or sensations are ones that you feel or experience very strongly indeed. EG *...extreme fright, grief, aggression, or some other violent emotion... ...violent indigestion.* ◊ **violently**. EG *This drug can make some people violently ill.*

ADJ QUALIT : USU ATTRIB ⇑ intense; ◊ ADV ⇑ intensely

6 Violent is also used to describe changes which are very extreme, from one state to another. EG *We have been going through violent changes the past couple of years.* ◊ **violently**. EG *Her emotions swung violently.*

ADJ QUALIT = dramatic; ◊ ADV WITH VB

7 Violent colours are extremely bright; used showing disapproval. EG *His shirt was a violent red.* ADJ QUALIT+COLOUR : ATTRIB

8 Violent weather is extremely stormy and windy. EG *...the violent storms of summer.* ADJ QUALIT ⇑ forceful

violet /vaɪəlɪ[2]t/, **violets**. **1** A **violet** is a small wild or garden plant which has sweet-smelling purple or white flowers and blooms in the spring. N COUNT ⇑ flower

2 If you say that a person, especially a woman, is a **shrinking violet**, you mean that he or she is a shy, timid person; often used humorously. EG *She's no shrinking violet.* PHR : USED AS C

3 Something that is **violet** is a bluish purple colour. EG *A spotlight threw a pool of violet light on the stage.* ▸ used as a noun. ADJ COLOUR; ▸ N UNCOUNT

violin /vaɪəlɪn/, **violins**. A **violin** is a musical instrument consisting of a shaped and polished hollow wooden box, with four strings stretched over it. You hold a violin under your chin and play it with a bow. EG *Do you play the violin, by any chance, Rudolph?... The sonatas are all written for piano and violin.* N COUNT, OR *for* +N

violinist /vaɪəlɪnɪst/, **violinists**. A **violinist** is someone who plays the violin, especially as their job. N COUNT ⇑ musician

VIP, VIPs. **VIP** is an abbreviation for 'very important person'; someone who is given better treatment than ordinary people because they are famous, influential, or important. EG *The room was full of VIPs... She gave us the full VIP treatment.* N COUNT

viper /vaɪpə/, **vipers**. **1** A **viper** is a small poisonous snake found mainly in Britain and Europe. There are several kinds of viper, most of which have a zigzag pattern down their backs. N COUNT = adder

2 If you refer to someone as a **viper**, you mean that you cannot trust them or that they have betrayed you; a formal or literary use. EG *...the landlady downstairs, who raged against the viper she had taken to her bosom.* N COUNT ⇑ traitor

virago /vɪrɑːgəʊ/, **viragos**. A **virago** is a bad-tempered woman who is always shouting at people and criticizing their behaviour; an old-fashioned word. N COUNT = tartar

virgin /vɜːdʒɪn/, **virgins**. **1** A **virgin** is someone who has never had sex; used especially of a woman or a girl. EG *Men in this part of the world still demand that the girls they marry should be virgins.* ▸ used as an adjective. EG *...a spinster or a virgin lady.* ◊ **virginity** /və[5]dʒɪnɪti[1]/. EG *His sister had lost her virginity many years before.*

N COUNT; ▸ ADJ CLASSIF : ATTRIB; ◊ N UNCOUNT : USU POSS+N

2 Something that is **virgin** is **2.1** fresh and clean, and its appearance shows that it has never been used before. EG *There were piles and piles of books, all virgin, all untouched... Her sweater was of virgin wool.* ADJ CLASSIF : USU ATTRIB ⇑ new **2.2** not yet explored, cultivated, or spoiled by ADJ CLASSIF :

human beings. EG ...*virgin territory... ...virgin rain forest.* ATTRIB ⇑ unspoiled = uncharted

virginal /vɜːdʒɪnəl/, **virginals**. 1 Someone who is **virginal** looks young and innocent, and has had no experience of sex; used when you consider this to be a virtue. EG *The menfolk have decreed that their women must be pure, virginal, innocent.* ADJ QUALIT ⇑ chaste

2 Something that is **virginal** is fresh and clean, and looks as if it has never been used. EG *My notebooks were virginal white.* ADJ CLASSIF : ATTRIB ⇑ new = pristine

3 The **virginal** is a musical instrument that used to be played in former times. It has a keyboard and is similar to a harpsichord but without legs. N COUNT : ALSO SING=PL

virile /vɪraɪl/. 1 A man who is **virile** has the qualities that a man is traditionally expected to have, such as physical strength, forcefulness, and strong sexuality; used showing approval. EG *If you have got lots of wives you have to keep healthy and virile.* ◊ **virility** /vɪrɪlɪti[1]/. EG *Tim strode in, positively radiating virility.* ADJ QUALIT ⇑ manly; ◊ N UNCOUNT

2 Something that is **virile** is forceful and energetic. EG ...*a new and virile leadership.* ADJ QUALIT = masterful

virtual /vɜːtʃʊ(ə)əl/ is used to suggest that something is in effect what you say it is, although it is not formally recognized as such. EG *The seamen's strike led to the virtual closure of the whole vast dock area... The once elegant temple lay in virtual ruins... The workers remain in a perpetual state of virtual slavery.* ADJ CLASSIF : ATTRIB

virtually /vɜːtʃʊ(ə)əli[1]/ is used to suggest that in effect what you say is true and that any exceptions or differences are small and unimportant. EG *This opinion was held by virtually all the experts... Virtually nothing has been said about the incident... It was virtually impossible to decide.* ADV

virtue /vɜːtjuː, -tʃuː/, **virtues**. 1 **Virtue** is thinking and doing what is right and avoiding what is wrong. EG *We accept certain principles of religion and traditional virtue.* N UNCOUNT ⇑ moral = goodness

2 A **virtue** is 2.1 a good quality, for example one that a religion or society teaches you to respect, or one that you find in a particular person. EG *Charity is the greatest of Christian virtues... He had one virtue, I suppose: he read other people's moods fairly accurately.* N COUNT ≠ vice 2.2 an advantage or benefit; often used in comparing two things with each other or in comparing the advantages and disadvantages of the same thing. EG *He was extolling the virtues of female independence... The school had its drawbacks and it had its virtues.* N COUNT/N UNCOUNT

3 You use **by virtue of** to say that something happens or becomes necessary because of the circumstances surrounding it; a fairly formal expression. EG *The President, by virtue of his office, cannot rudely ignore any head of state... He was an object of interest simply by virtue of being British.* PREP

4 If you **make a virtue of** something, you pretend that you did it out of goodness, although in fact you did it because you had no choice. EG ...*making a virtue of necessity.* PHR : VB INFLECTS

virtuoso /vɜːtjʊəʊzəʊ, -səʊ/, **virtuosos, virtuosi** /vɜːtjʊəʊzi[1]/. The plural can be either **virtuosos** or **virtuosi**. A **virtuoso** is someone who is exceptionally good at something, especially at playing a musical instrument. EG *He was a virtuoso of the jazz guitar... This is an immensely strong, virtuoso performance.* ◊ **virtuosity** /vɜːtjʊɒsɪti[1]/. EG ...*an astonishing feat of virtuosity.* N COUNT ⇑ expert = master; ◊ N UNCOUNT

virtuous /vɜːtʃʊəs, -tjʊəs/. 1 Someone who is **virtuous** 1.1 behaves correctly and strictly according to the moral code of a particular religion or society. EG *People who lead virtuous lives in this world are assured of paradise in the next.* ◊ **virtuously**. EG *I feel virtuously patriotic.* ADJ QUALIT ⇑ good = pious; ◊ ADV 1.2 is pleased with their own good behaviour or satisfied that no one can blame them for their misfortunes, especially when they express this attitude by complaining or by criticizing other people; used showing disapproval. EG *They had such an air of virtuous poverty... His voice lifted into the whine of virtuous recrimination.* ◊ **virtuously**. EG *Guppy protested and quoted virtuously: 'A promise is a promise.'* ADJ CLASSIF : ATTRIB = righteous; ◊ ADV

2 A **virtuous** woman is one who is careful to behave in a morally correct way, especially in not having sex before marriage and having sex only with her husband; an old-fashioned use. EG ...*Nicholas and his very virtuous sister, Kate.* ADJ QUALIT ⇑ chaste = moral

virulence /vɪrʊləns/. 1 **Virulence** is 1.1 strong and bitter hatred that is directed against someone, usually in the form of an unpleasant verbal attack on them; a formal use. EG *The Left has approached student politics with its customary virulence.* N UNCOUNT ⇑ quality = hostility 1.2 the ability that something such as a belief, political movement, etc has to survive and to do harm. EG *The heresy flourished there with peculiar virulence.* N UNCOUNT ⇑ strength

2 The **virulence** of a disease or poison is its ability to harm or kill people or animals. N UNCOUNT ⇑ strength

virulent /vɪrʊlənt/. 1 Feelings, actions, or speeches that are **virulent** are full of hatred and extremely bitter and hostile. EG *Nehru and Nasser were the objects of special hatred and virulent attack... He has a positively virulent loathing of academics.* ◊ **virulently**. EG *Fighting broke out again much more virulently, and there was a real bloodbath.* ADJ QUALIT = vicious; ◊ ADV ⇑ bitterly

2 A **virulent** disease or poison is extremely powerful and dangerous. EG ...*a peculiarly virulent form of leprosy... Its poison is as virulent as that of the cobra.* ADJ QUALIT ⇑ deadly = pernicious

3 A **virulent** colour is extremely harsh, strong, and unpleasant to look at. EG *his trousers were a virulent green.* ADJ QUALIT + COLOUR : USU ATTRIB

virus /vaɪrəs/, **viruses**. 1 A **virus** is a kind of germ, smaller than bacteria, that can cause disease in people, animals, or plants. EG *The doctor assured me it was a virus infection... He went down with a virus last week.* N COUNT

2 A **virus** is also an idea, influence, or belief that is thought to be evil or corrupting; used showing disapproval. EG *The free trade virus killed off developing industries.* N COUNT+SUPP : USU SING

visa /viːzə/, **visas**. A **visa** is an official stamp which is put in your passport by the embassy or consulate of a country you want to visit, and which allows you to enter or leave that country, or to travel through it. EG *I obtained a visa to visit East Germany.* N COUNT = permit

visage /vɪzɪdʒ/, **visages**. Someone's **visage** is their face; a formal old-fashioned word. EG *A maudlin smile played across her normally grim visage.* N COUNT : USU POSS+N = countenance

vis-à-vis /viːz æ viː/. You use **vis-à-vis** when you are considering one thing or quantity in comparison with another. EG *One solution would be for us to lower our exchange rate vis-à-vis other countries... ...the position of workers vis-à-vis management.* PREP

viscera /vɪsərə/ are the large organs inside the body, such as the heart, liver, and stomach; a medical word. N PLURAL : the/POSS+N

visceral /vɪsərəl/ is used to refer to feelings and emotions that are deep and instinctive rather than rational and carefully thought out; a literary word. EG *She felt this excitement on the most visceral level.* ADJ QUALIT : ATTRIB ⇑ emotional, gut

viscosity /vɪskɒsɪti[1]/ is the quality that some fluids have of being sticky and therefore not flowing easily; a fairly technical word. EG ...*the viscosity of motor engine oils.* N UNCOUNT ⇑ stickiness

viscount /vaɪkaʊnt/, **viscounts**. In Britain, a **viscount** is a nobleman who is below an earl and above a baron in rank. N COUNT : ALSO IN TITLES

viscountess /vaɪkaʊntɪ[2]s/, **viscountesses**. A **viscountess** is 1 the wife of a viscount. EG ... *and she become a viscountess.* N COUNT : ALSO IN TITLES 2 a woman who holds the rank of viscount in her own right. N COUNT : ALSO IN TITLES

viscous /vɪskəs/. Something that is **viscous** is thick and sticky, and therefore does not flow easily; a fairly technical word. EG *We spent all day wading through viscous mud and water up to our necks.* ADJ QUALIT = glutinous

vise /vaɪs/. See **vice**.

visibility /vɪzɪbɪlɪti[1]/. You use **visibility** to refer to 1 how clearly you can see in particular conditions of weather. EG *Visibility, for the most part, was excellent... ...a nightmare of near-zero visibility.* N UNCOUNT ⇑ clarity 2 the condition of being able to be seen clearly by other people. N UNCOUNT

visible /vɪzɪbə(ə)l/. 1 Something that is **visible** is large enough to be seen and is in a position where it can be seen. EG *The moon was fully visible... These tiny creatures are hardly visible to the naked eye.* ADJ QUALIT ⇑ detectable

2 You also use the word **visible** to describe an effect that can be seen and recognized by other people. EG *The results are visible in the growth of the Conservative vote... ...a period of little visible advance.* ◊ **visibly**. EG *She was visibly nervous... The reply visibly hurt his feelings... It was a city visibly scarred by war.* ADJ QUALIT ⇑ obvious = apparent; ◊ ADV = clearly

vision /vɪʒə(ə)n/. 1 A **vision** is 1.1 a mental picture of a possible situation or state of affairs, in which you N COUNT : USU+ of imagine how things might be different from the way they are now. EG *...fighting for the vision of the new China... I had nightmarish visions of what could go wrong.* **1.2** a mental picture which you have as a result of divine inspiration, madness, or taking drugs. EG *...the visions God granted to me.* N COUNT : USU PL = hallucination

2 Vision is **2.1** the ability to see clearly with your eyes. EG *One eye is completely shut, and he has very little vision in the other.* N UNCOUNT = sight **2.2** everything that you can see from a particular place or position. EG *The President's car flashed past the bus-stop and into vision.* N UNCOUNT = view **2.3** the picture that is shown by a television set. EG *We apologize for the temporary loss of vision.* N UNCOUNT

visionary /vɪʒənə^{0}ri^1/, **visionaries.** **1** A **visionary** is someone who has visions, especially about how things might be different in the future. EG *...left-wing visionaries.* N COUNT ⇑ person = seer ▸ used as an adjective. EG *...the greatest visionary king in Ethiopian history.* ▸ ADJ QUALIT ⇑ imaginative

2 Something that is **visionary** seems to have been imagined by or to exist in the mind of an unusually imaginative person. EG *...a place of such mystic and visionary loveliness.* ADJ QUALIT ⇑ unreal = dreamlike

visit /vɪzɪt/, **visits, visiting, visited.** **1** If you **visit** someone or are **visiting**, you go and see them and spend time with them, usually in order to be friendly and sociable. EG *She visited some of her relatives for a few days... My friends never come to visit me... The grownups and families did a lot of visiting.* V+O, OR V ▸ used as a noun. EG *It would be nice if you paid me a visit.* ▸ N COUNT

2 If you **visit** a professional person such as a doctor or solicitor, you go and see them in order to get professional advice. EG *You might need to visit a solicitor before thinking seriously about divorce.* V+O = consult

3 If a professional person, such as a doctor or solicitor, **visits** a patient or client, they go and see them in order to give them professional advice. EG *The doctor has been visiting patients all afternoon.* V+O ▸ used as a noun. EG *When they were sick the doctor made home visits.* ▸ N COUNT

4 If you **visit** a place, you go and see it for interest, to inspect it, or to learn more about it. EG *This is the best museum we've visited... More than a million foreigners visit the United States every year... 'Do you live here?' 'No, we're just visiting.'... Members of the board visit the prison once a week.* V+O, OR V ⇑ view ▸ used as a noun. EG *He wrote to me after a brief visit to the U.S.* ▸ N COUNT = trip

5 If you **are visited** by something, you are affected by it in an unpleasant or frightening way; used in old-fashioned English. EG *He was visited by a terrible dream.* V+O : ONLY PASS ⇑ suffer

6 If something **is visited** upon you, something very unpleasant happens to you; used in old-fashioned English. EG *The sins of the fathers shall be visited upon the children... What new horror had been visited upon them?* V+O+A : ONLY PASS ⇑ inflict

visit with. If you **visit with** someone, you go and see them and spend time with them; an American expression. EG *He had not visited with the rascal since 1946.* PHRASAL VB : V+PREP

visitation /vɪzɪteɪʃə^{0}n/, **visitations.** A **visitation** is **1** an event which is thought to be a message from God, an angel, or some other divine force. EG *She thought her dream was a visitation from God.* N COUNT **2** an official visit; often used humorously. EG *...the visitation of the Council for National Academic Awards.* N COUNT

visiting hours are the times during which visitors can go to see someone in a hospital or other institution. N PLURAL

visitor /vɪzɪtə/, **visitors.** A **visitor** is someone who is visiting a person or place. EG *Marsha was a frequent visitor to our house... ...the testimony of recent foreign visitors to China.* N COUNT ⇑ guest = caller

visor /vaɪzə/, **visors.** A **visor** is **1** a movable part of a helmet, for example one worn by a motorcyclist, which can be pulled down to protect a person's eyes or face. N COUNT ⇑ screen **2** a piece of plastic or other material fixed above the windscreen inside a car, which can be turned down to protect the driver's eyes from bright sunshine. EG *...peering through the windscreen, the visor down, a map on his knee.* N COUNT ⇑ flap

vista /vɪstə/, **vistas.** A **vista** is **1** the view that you get when you look from a particular place, especially a beautiful view from a high place; a literary word. EG *...a rolling vista of heather-covered hills.* N COUNT+SUPP = panorama **2** a range of exciting or worrying new ideas and possibilities. EG *This turn of events opened a whole new vista of troubles for me.* N PART

visual /vɪʒʊəl, -zjʊ-/ means relating to sight. EG *...visual jokes... Not all situations can be examined in terms of visual images... ...a centre which provides exhibitions in the visual arts.* ADJ CLASSIF ◊ **visually.** EG *Visually, it is a very exciting film... ...a feeling of shock when one sees it presented visually.* ◊ ADV SEN, OR ADV

visual aid, visual aids. A **visual aid** is something that you can look at, such as a film, model, map, or slides, in order to help you understand, learn, or remember information of some kind. N COUNT : USU PL

visualize /vɪʒʊ^{0}əlaɪz/, **visualizes, visualizing, visualized;** also spelled **visualise.** If you **visualize** something, you imagine what it is like by forming a mental picture of it. EG *He found he could visualise her face quite clearly... Much of his mind was taken up with visualizing the champagne buffet waiting for them.* V+O = picture ◊ **visualization** /vɪʒʊ^{0}əlaɪzeɪʃə^{0}n/. EG *You've got problems here, I think, in visualization.* ◊ N UNCOUNT

vital /vaɪtə^{0}l/. **1** Something or someone that is **vital** is extremely important and necessary in order that something else can take place, succeed, etc. EG *It is vital to keep an accurate record of every transaction... He is of vital importance if you want to get something urgently.* ADJ QUALIT = crucial ◊ **vitally.** EG *The way we choose to bring up children is vitally important.* ◊ ADV+ADJ ⇑ crucially

2 A person or organization that is **vital** is one that is energetic, exciting, and full of life; used showing approval. EG *The Chinese I knew were trusting, open, and vital... We want this country to have a modern vital parliament.* ADJ QUALIT ⇑ alive = dynamic

vitality /vaɪtælɪti^1/ is the quality of great energy and liveliness of a person or organization; used showing approval. *...the vitality and eagerness of a normal toddler.* N UNCOUNT

vital statistics. 1 Vital statistics are statistics concerning the size of a population and the number of births, deaths, marriages, etc, which take place in it; a technical term. N PLURAL ⇑ data

2 A woman's **vital statistics** are the measurements of her bust, waist, and hips. These are often used to indicate how attractive and shapely a woman's figure is. N PLURAL : POSS +N

vitamin, vitamins. The word **vitamin** is pronounced /vɪtəmɪn/ in British English and /vaɪtəmɪn/ in American English. A **vitamin** is an organic substance which people need in order to remain healthy. Vitamins occur naturally in many kinds of food and are also sold in the form of pills. EG *She needs extra vitamins and protein... ...vitamin deficiencies... One tiny berry contained more vitamin C than an orange.* N COUNT : IF *vitamin+A/B/C/D/E*, THEN N UNCOUNT

vitiate /vɪʃieɪt/, **vitiates, vitiating, vitiated.** If something **is vitiated**, its effectiveness is spoiled or weakened; a formal word. V+O : USU PASS ⇑ debase

vitreous /vɪtrɪəs/. Something that is **vitreous** is made of or resembles glass. ADJ CLASSIF

vitriol /vɪtrɪə^{7}l/ is speech or writing that is full of hatred and bitterness and that is deliberately intended to cause distress or pain. EG *Much later, after the divorce and the vitriol, I agreed to see him again.* N UNCOUNT ⇑ abuse = acrimony

vitriolic /vɪtrɪɒlɪk/. Language or behaviour that is **vitriolic** is full of bitterness and hate, and so causes a lot of distress and pain. EG *He was subjected to the most vitriolic personal abuse.* ADJ QUALIT : USU ATTRIB ⇑ bitter = virulent, abusive

vituperation /vɪtjuːpəreɪʃə^{0}n/ is spiteful, bitter, and abusive language expressed with great fluency; a formal word. N UNCOUNT ⇑ abuse

vituperative /vɪtjuːpərətɪv/ means full of spiteful and bitter verbal abuse; a formal word. EG *...vituperative monologues.* ADJ QUALIT ⇑ abusive = vitriolic

viva, vivas. The word **viva** is pronounced /vaɪvə/ in paragraph 1 and /viːvə/ in paragraph 2. **1** A **viva** is an oral examination, especially one taken in a university. N COUNT

2 Viva is used as a way of showing that you approve of someone or something. EG *Viva Diana!* PHR+NAME : CONVENTION

vivacious /vɪveɪʃəs/. Someone who is **vivacious** is lively, exciting, and attractive. EG *She was not as young or as vivacious as she once had been.* ADJ QUALIT = bubbly ◊ **vivaciously.** EG *She held out her hand, smiling vivaciously. 'How are you? What a great pleasure.'* ◊ ADV WITH VB = animatedly

vivacity /vɪvæsɪti^1/ is the quality of being lively in an attractive and exciting way. EG *He stood aside, registering the vivacity of the street life.* N UNCOUNT ⇑ liveliness = animation

vivid /vɪvɪd/. 1 Something that is **vivid** is very bright in colour. EG *She was walking slowly across a vivid green lawn.* ◊ **vividly**. EG *They are the most vividly coloured birds in Australia.* ◊ **vividness**. EG *...an attempt to recapture the vividness of their colours.* ADJ QUALIT = dazzling ◊ ADV ◊ N UNCOUNT ⇑ brightness

2 Memories, descriptions, etc that are **vivid** are very clear and detailed, so that they remain firmly fixed in your mind. EG *I do have a vivid memory of an excursion with my grandmother... Her own bedtime stories were far more vivid.* ◊ **vividly**. EG *'You remember Captain Van Donck?'–'Oh, yes. Vividly.'* ◊ **vividness**. EG *The letter brought back to them with incredible vividness the image of their grandfather.* ADJ QUALIT ◊ ADV ⇑ clearly ◊ N UNCOUNT ⇑ clarity

vivisection /vɪvɪsekʃəⁿn/ is the practice of cutting open living animals in order to perform scientific or medical experiments on them. EG *She aims to educate the public to the horrors of vivisection.* N UNCOUNT

vivisectionist /vɪvɪsekʃənɪst/, **vivisectionists**. A **vivisectionist** is 1 someone who believes that experiments on living animals should be allowed because they are useful to science and medicine. 2 a scientist who cuts open living animals for experiments. N COUNT N COUNT

vixen /vɪksəⁿn/, **vixens**. A **vixen** is 1 a female fox. 2 an unpleasant, bad-tempered woman; an old-fashioned word. N COUNT

viz. is used in written English to introduce a list of specific items or examples. EG *These insects appear in warm wet weather, viz. early summer and early autumn.* CONJ SUBORD = namely, i.e.

V-neck, V-necks. A **V-neck** is a neck on a pullover, dress, etc in the shape of the letter V. N COUNT

V-necked. A **V-necked** pullover or dress is one that has a neck in the shape of the letter V. ADJ CLASSIF

V+O □ In this dictionary V+O is used in the grammar notes beside entries to indicate that the verb is transitive and needs an object. The object can be a noun group or a reflexive pronoun (*myself, herself*, etc). Verbs of this type can be used in the passive, unless the grammar note tells you that they cannot. Examples are **greet** and **kick**. EG *They waited to **greet** a crowd of friends... I **was greeted** at the door by my mother... He kept **kicking** me in the stomach... They **were kicked** to death.*

V+O+A □ In this dictionary V+O+A is used in the grammar notes beside entries to indicate that the verb needs both an object and an adjunct. The object is a noun group. The adjunct can be a prepositional group or an adverbial group. Verbs of this type can be used in the passive unless the grammar note tells you that they cannot. An example is **put**. EG *Dolly **put** the stamp on her letter... He **put** the fork into his mouth... The book **had been put** back on the shelf.* You do not say 'Dolly put the stamp' (no adjunct) and you do not say 'She put on her letter' (no object). Where the prepositional group begins with 'to' or 'for' it may be related to V+O+O. See □ at V+O+O.

VOC □ In this dictionary VOC is used in the grammar notes beside entries to show that an important use of the word is in addressing someone. Examples are **honey 2** and **sir 1**. EG *Hello, **honey**!... Mr Hink to see you, **sir**.*

V+O+C □ In this dictionary V+O+C is used in the grammar notes beside entries to indicate that the verb needs both an object and a complement. The complement refers back to the object of the verb. The object is usually a noun group and the complement can be either an adjectival group or a noun group. Verbs of this type can be used in the passive unless the grammar note tells you they cannot. An example is **consider**. EG *You may **consider** this sort of information unimportant... Some British generals **considered** the attack a mistake... In theory a nuclear war **had** always **been considered** a possibility.*

vocabulary /vəᵏkæbjə⁴ləri¹/, **vocabularies**. 1 Someone's **vocabulary** is the total number of words in a language that he or she knows. EG *By the age of five, the child has a working vocabulary of more than 2,000 words... He searched his vocabulary for the exact word.* N COUNT/UNCOUNT

2 The **vocabulary** of a language is the total number of words in it. EG *New words are coming into use and then dropping out of the vocabulary at heightened speeds.* N SING WITH DET ⇑ lexicon

3 The **vocabulary** of a subject is the group of words that are typically used when discussing it. EG *'Struggle' is a key word in the Marxist-Leninist vocabulary... ...the vocabulary of deceit.* N COUNT/UNCOUNT+SUPP

vocal /vəʊkəⁿl/, **vocals**. 1 Someone who is **vocal** expresses their opinion clearly and strongly in spoken language. EG *The members had been quite vocal on issues of academic freedom... Today the young are much more vocal.* ◊ **vocally**. EG *He could be vocally very vicious towards people he considered stupid.* ADJ QUALIT ◊ ADV

2 **Vocal** means involving the use of the human voice, especially in singing. EG *She riveted her audiences with her superb authority and vocal power.* ◊ **vocally**. EG *She was technically vocally perfect in the role of Tosca.* ADJ CLASSIF: ATTRIB ◊ ADV WITH VB

3 When you refer to the **vocals** in a pop song, you are referring to the singing. EG *Lead vocals: Boy George. Backing vocals: Helen Terry..* N PLURAL

vocal cords; also spelled **vocal chords**. Your **vocal cords** are the part of your larynx which can be made to vibrate when you breathe out, making the sounds which you use for speaking. EG *It was possible that their vocal cords were paralysed.* N PLURAL

vocalist /vəʊkəlɪst/, **vocalists**. A **vocalist** is a singer who sings with a pop group. N COUNT

vocation /vəʊkeɪʃəⁿn/, **vocations**. A **vocation** is 1 a strong feeling that you are especially suitable to do a particular job or to fulfil a particular role in life, especially one which involves serving other people. EG *I believe that one must have a vocation for teaching... By vocation I'm not a politician.* 2 a profession or career which you feel that you are especially suitable to do. EG *Medicine is my vocation.* N COUNT/UNCOUNT = calling N COUNT/UNCOUNT

vocational /vəʊkeɪʃəⁿnəl, -ʃənəⁿl/ is used to describe the skills needed for a particular job or profession. EG *...a college that does technical and vocational training.* ◊ **vocationally**. EG *...vocationally relevant subjects.* ADJ CLASSIF: USU ATTRIB ⇑ work ◊ ADV+ADJ

vocative /vɒkətɪv/. 1 In some languages, for example Latin, the **vocative** or the **vocative** case is the form of a word, especially a name, that is used when you are speaking directly to someone or writing to them. N COUNT, OR ADJ CLASSIF

2 In grammar, **vocative** refers to words that you use when you are speaking directly to someone or writing to them, for example 'darling', 'vicar', etc. In this dictionary, when words are frequently used in this way, they are described as VOC in the grammar notes beside the entry. See □ at VOC. N COUNT, OR N SING: *the*+N

vociferous /vəˢsɪfərəs/. Someone who is **vociferous** is very loud and noisy when they speak, because they are determined to make sure what they are saying is heard by other people. EG *They were supported by a vociferous group in the actors' union...* ▸ used to refer to the things that are said. EG *...vociferous protests against the new motorway.* ◊ **vociferously**. EG *...those who had vociferously declared that the pill had no harmful effects.* ADJ QUALIT = strident ▸ = vehement ◊ ADV WITH VB = vehemently

vodka /vɒdkə/, **vodkas**, is a strong, clear alcoholic drink which is made from rye or other vegetable products. Vodka was first made in Russia and Poland. N MASS ⇑ liquor

vogue /vəʊg/. 1 If something is the **vogue**, it is very popular and fashionable. You can also say that something has a **vogue** or that there is a **vogue** for it. EG *The current vogue is for decentralization... Flowery carpets became the vogue... Brightly coloured raincoats had a brief vogue in the previous decade... ...a vogue for real or imitation Oriental silks... ...vogue words.* N SING WITH DET ⇑ trend = fad

2 Something that is **in vogue** is very popular and fashionable. EG *Agriculture is back in vogue these days... At that time aftershave was not in vogue in France.* PHR: USED AS AN A = in

voice /vɔɪs/, **voices, voicing, voiced**. 1 When someone speaks, you hear their **voice**. EG *She heard a voice calling her name... There was the sound of voices outside... He recognized me by my voice... 'I suppose we'd better go,' said John in a low voice.* N COUNT ⇑ sound

2 Someone's **voice** is 2.1 their physical ability to produce speech sounds. EG *She lost her voice... He had shouted so hard and for so long that he had no voice left.* 2.2 the particular musical quality of a singer's voice. EG *Jessye Norman has perhaps the most deeply spiritual and moving voice in the world.* N SING WITH DETPOSS, OR N UNCOUNT N COUNT

3 You use **voice** to refer to 3.1 someone's opinion on a particular topic and what they say about it. EG *The only dissenting voice was Mr Foot's... Numerous* N COUNT

voices were raised against the idea. **3.3** the expression of the opinions of a nation, institution, or other group of people. EG *...the powerful voice of the BBC... Resources must be found to make the voice of the Black community more articulate.* N SING : *the*+N+*of*

4 If you have a **voice** in something, you have the right to express an opinion on a topic. EG *It's only right that the students should have a voice in determining the way in which universities should develop.* N SING : *a*+N = say

5 If you refer to the **voice** of a particular attitude or quality, you are referring to what people with that attitude or quality say. EG *His lawyers called upon the voice of reason... ...the voice of American pragmatism.* N SING : *the*+N+*of*

6 If you **voice** something such as an opinion or an emotion, you say what you think or feel, especially in a forceful way. EG *The African delegates voiced their anger... Some fierce public criticism of it had been voiced... She voiced a comment which had particular relevance.* V+O ⇑ express = vent

7 A **voice** is also a sound that resembles or reminds you of a human voice; a fairly literary word. EG *The kettle started to add its slow voice... ...the various voices of the sea.* N COUNT : USU+SUPP

8 In grammar, the **active voice** and the **passive voice** refer to the relation between a verb and its subject. N SING : *the*+N

9 The word **voice** is also used in the following expressions. **9.1** If you **raise** your **voice** when you are speaking, you speak more loudly than usual, often because you are angry or upset. If you **lower** your **voice**, you speak more quietly, usually because you do not want everyone to hear what you are saying. EG *Gregory began to raise his voice in protest... She lowered her voice to a discreet whisper.* PHR : VB INFLECTS **9.2** If you **raise** your **voice** in public, you express an opinion. EG *The United Nations has not yet raised a voice to condemn the oppression of the Kurds.* PHR : VB INFLECTS **9.3** If someone tells you to **keep** your **voice down**, they are asking you to to speak more quietly. EG *'Can't you keep your voice down?' Brody said in a hoarse whisper.* PHR : VB INFLECTS, USU IMPER **9.4** If you **find** your **voice**, you manage to speak in spite of fear, nervousness, or other difficulties. EG *Somehow Bill found his voice... The shock had helped her find her voice.* PHR : VB INFLECTS **9.5** If you **give voice** to something such as an opinion, you express it aloud. EG *She gave voice to her misgivings.* PHR : VB INFLECTS **9.6** If you say something **at the top of** your **voice**, you say it as loudly as possible. EG *'I am drenched,' she declared at the top of her voice.* PHR : USED AS AN A **9.7** If a number of people say something **with one voice**, they all agree about it; a formal expression. EG *The Council felt that they should speak on the matter with one voice.* PHR : USED AS AN A = unanimously

voiced /vɔɪst/. A **voiced** speech sound is one that is produced with vibration of the vocal cords; a technical term in phonetics. EG *Vowels, and some consonants such as /v/ and /z/,* are voiced sounds. ADJ CLASSIF

voiceless /vɔɪslɪ²s/. A **voiceless** speech sound is one that is produced without vibration of the vocal cords; a technical term in phonetics. EG */f/ and /s/ are voiceless consonants.* ADJ CLASSIF

voice-over, voice-overs. A **voice-over** is a commentary or explanation which is heard as part of a film or television programme but which is spoken by someone who is not actually seen. EG *The narrative, the voice-over that accompanies much of the film, is all in the third person.* N COUNT

void /vɔɪd/, **voids**. **1** A **void** is **1.1** a situation or state of affairs which seems empty because it has no interest, excitement, or value. EG *...the need to fill the void of materialism with humane and spiritual values... ...French academics, seeking to fill an intellectual void left by the fading of existentialism.* N COUNT : USU SING ⇑ emptiness = vacuum **1.2** a feeling of emptiness which is caused in you by sadness or loneliness, for example because someone has gone away or died. EG *...an aching void in his heart.* N COUNT : USU SING = vacuum **1.3** a big hole or space, especially one which is frightening, for example because it is deep or because you see it suddenly and unexpectedly. EG *He looked down into the gaping void at his feet.* N COUNT = abyss, chasm

2 Something that is **void** or that is **null and void** has no official value or authority; a technical term used in law to describe an agreement or contract in which the conditions have not been fulfilled or have been broken. ADJ CLASSIF : PRED ⇑ invalid

3 **Void** means empty; a literary or formal use. EG *...the armchair, now void of all live content.* ADJ CLASSIF : PRED

voile /vɔɪl/ is thin material which is used for making women's dresses, blouses, scarves, etc. N UNCOUNT ⇑ fabric

vol. is an abbreviation for 'volume'.

volatile /vɒlətaɪl/. **1** A situation that is **volatile** is liable to change suddenly and unexpectedly, and to do so repeatedly. EG *They described the situation in Lebanon as 'tense, dangerous and volatile'... With the markets being so volatile, investments are at great risk.* ADJ QUALIT ⇑ changeable = unstable ◇ **volatility** /vɒlətɪlɪti¹/. EG *...the volatility of modern exchange rates.* ◇ N UNCOUNT = instability

2 Someone who is **volatile** is liable to change their mood or behaviour suddenly, unexpectedly, and regularly. EG *He was a very clever, volatile actor... It was the same Judy, wild-eyed, dreamy, volatile as ever.* ADJ QUALIT ⇑ changeable = mercurial, unpredictable ◇ **volatility**. ◇ N UNCOUNT

3 A **volatile** liquid or substance is one that will quickly change into a gas; a technical term in chemistry. ADJ QUALIT ⇑ unstable ◇ **volatility**. ◇ N UNCOUNT

vol-au-vent /vɒl ə⁶ vɒŋ/, **vol-au-vents**. A **vol-au-vent** is a small, light pastry case that is usually eaten when filled with a sauce made with chicken, ham, mushrooms, etc. N COUNT

volcanic /vɒlkænɪk/. **1** A place or region that is **volcanic** has a lot of volcanoes or was created by volcanoes. EG *The islands are volcanic and were formed comparatively recently.* ADJ CLASSIF

2 Something such as an explosion that is **volcanic** happens or is likely to happen suddenly and violently, with a great deal of force. EG *...the volcanic eruption of gunfire on a modern battlefield.* ADJ CLASSIF

volcano /vɒlkeɪnəʊ/, **volcanoes**. A **volcano** is a mountain out of which hot melted rock, gas, steam, and ash sometimes burst through a hole called a crater, coming up from inside the earth. EG *Six other volcanoes were still erupting. ...Mount Erebus, an active volcano.* N COUNT

vole /vəʊl/, **voles**. A **vole** is a small animal that looks like a mouse but has very small ears and a short tail. Voles usually live in fields or near rivers. N COUNT ⇑ rodent

volition /və⁶lɪʃə⁰n/ is the power to decide something for yourself; a formal word. N UNCOUNT ● If you do something **of** your **own volition**, you do it because you have decided for yourself that you will do it and not because somebody else has told you to. EG *She didn't go down there of her own volition.* ● PHR : USED AS AN A = by choice

volley /vɒli¹/, **volleys, volleying, volleyed**. **1** A **volley** of shots or gunfire is a lot of shots that are fired from guns very fast, so that they seem to be fired almost at the same time. EG *...a volley of automatic rifle fire... They fired in disciplined volleys.* N COUNT ⇑ discharge = salvo

2 A **volley** of objects is a lot of objects being thrown at someone or something very fast and at the same time. EG *He had been chased from the room by a volley of darts.* N PART = barrage

3 A **volley** of words, questions, etc is a lot of words, questions, etc which someone says very quickly and in an aggressive way, without giving anyone else a chance to reply. EG *The visitor is hit with a volley of facts and figures... ...the volley of four-letter words that were his only answer.* N PART = barrage

4 In tennis, a **volley** is a stroke or shot in which the player hits the ball while it is moving and before it bounces on the ground. EG *Her volley was quite impossible to return.* N COUNT ▸ used as a verb. EG *She volleys better than anyone else I know.* ▸ V OR V+O

volleyball /vɒli¹bɔːl/ is a game in which two teams hit a large ball with their hands, backwards and forwards over a high net. The ball is not allowed to bounce on the ground. N UNCOUNT

volt /vəʊlt/, **volts**. A **volt** is a unit used to measure the force of an electrical current. N COUNT : USU NUM+N = V

voltage /vəʊltɪdʒ/, **voltages**. A voltage is an electrical force measured in volts. EG *We shall vary the output voltage... ...steady voltages or currents.* N UNCOUNT/COUNT

volte-face /vɒlt fɑːs/. A **volte-face** is a complete change in someone's opinions about something, so that their opinion or their decision is the opposite of what it was before; a fairly literary word. EG *His colleagues demanded an explanation of his extraordinary volte-face.* N SING WITH DET = reversal

voluble /vɒljəbə⁰l/. Someone who is **voluble** talks a lot with great energy and enthusiasm. EG *He became very voluble and told her everything... ...her voluble but disjointed account of the day's events.* ADJ QUALIT ⇑ talkative ◇ **volubly**. EG *He talked volubly about the problems of the* ◇ ADV WITH VB *ghetto.* ◇ **volubility** /vɒljəˈbɪlɪti/. EG *Words poured out of her with a volubility I had never suspected.* ◇ N UNCOUNT

volume /vɒljuːm/, **volumes**. 1 A **volume** is 1.1 a book; a formal use. EG *She took from the shelf a large green volume containing all of Chopin's works... James Mitchell edited a volume of essays under the title 'The God I Want'... The Society has already published its own scholarly volume on Stonehenge.* N COUNT : IF + PREP THEN *of/on*
1.2 a book which forms part of a larger literary work, especially one of a series of books on a particular subject. EG *It's in three volumes... ...Volume One of 'Clarissa Harlow'.* N COUNT, OR N + NUM **1.3** a collection of several issues of a magazine or journal, for example all the issues for one year. EG *...three bound volumes of 'The Family Circle'.* N COUNT + SUPP
2 The **volume** of an object is the amount of space that it contains or occupies. EG *...a gas expanded to nine times its original volume... 1300 Earths could fit within Jupiter's volume.* N SING : USU WITH POSS
3 The **volume** of public opinion, protest, support, etc is the amount or degree of it connected with a particular subject. EG *Among Roman Catholics, however, the volume of disagreement and disaffection was no less... ...a substantial volume of opinion in the Conservative Party was in favour of capital punishment.* N SING : USU + *of* ⇑ level = extent, weight
4 The **volume** of trade, imports, etc is the amount or total of it, especially when it is a large amount or total. EG *It carries the largest volume of traffic in the world... ...the growing volume of business with EEC countries.* N SING : USU + *of*
5 The **volume** of a radio, TV, or record player is the amount of sound produced by it. EG *She turned up the volume on the radio. ... They kept the radio playing at full volume... He cursed as he fiddled with the volume control.* ▸ also used to mean the switch which turns the sound up or down. N UNCOUNT ▸ N SING WITH *the*
6 If you say that something **speaks volumes,** you mean that it gives you a great deal of information about its background, history, and the people associated with it. EG *That one photograph speaks volumes.* PHR : VB INFLECTS ⇑ informs

voluminous /vəluːmɪnəs/ describes 1 clothes that are or seem to be too large for the person who is wearing them. EG *...a voluminous white apron... ...a voluminous skirt of blue Indian cotton.* ADJ QUALIT = huge, billowing **2** written information which is very great in amount and is full of detail. EG *I took voluminous notes and the other women listened... ...voluminous correspondence... ...a special case, on which voluminous documentation is available.* ADJ QUALIT ⇑ wordy = copious

voluntary /vɒləntəʳriˡ/, **voluntaries**. 1 **Voluntary** describes actions that you do freely, because you choose to do them and not because you have been forced to do them. EG *...25,000 pounds raised by voluntary subscription... Attendance at the parade was voluntary.* ◇ **voluntarily**. EG *They were said to have left their land voluntarily.* ADJ CLASSIF ⇑ chosen ◇ ADV WITH VB = by choice
2 **Voluntary** work is done by people who are not paid for it, but who do it because they want to. EG *A large amount of voluntary work is done by people in the neighbourhood... We run the meals-on-wheels service on a voluntary basis.* ADJ CLASSIF : USU ATTRIB
3 A **voluntary** worker is someone who does work, especially social work, without being paid for it, because they want to do it and feel that it needs to be done. EG *All the helpers for this organization are voluntary... Voluntary workers can claim travel expenses, but nothing else.* ADJ CLASSIF : USU ATTRIB ⇑ unpaid
4 A **voluntary** organization is controlled and organized by the people who have chosen to work for it, often without being paid, rather than receiving help or money from the government. EG *They received no fees for the work they did in the voluntary hospital.* ◇ **voluntarily**. EG *The hostel is voluntarily run, with local authority support.* ADJ CLASSIF : ATTRIB ⇑ private ◇ ADV WITH VB ⇑ privately
5 A **voluntary** is a piece of music, usually for the organ, which is frequently played at the beginning or end of a church service. N COUNT : ALSO IN NAMES AFTER N

volunteer /vɒləntɪə/, **volunteers, volunteering, volunteered**. 1 A **volunteer** is 1.1 someone who does work, especially socially useful work, for which they are not paid but which they have chosen to do because they feel that the work needs doing. EG *Teaching literacy to adults using volunteers began in 1963... ...volunteer work at the hospital.* N COUNT ⇑ worker **1.2** someone who chooses to join the army, navy, or air force, especially in wartime, as opposed to one who is forced by law to join. EG *Many Australians fought as volunteers on the Allied side... ...units from the regular and volunteer armies.* N COUNT
2 If you **volunteer** to do something, you offer to do it without being forced to do it and without expecting any reward. EG *He volunteered to do whatever he could for them... ...an extra payment to those who volunteer for redundancy before the end of the month.* V, V+O, OR V + *to*-INF/*for*
3 If you **volunteer** for the army, navy, or air force, you offer to join it when you do not have to join by law. EG *When World War Two broke out, he volunteered for the Marine Corps.* V : IF + PREP THEN *for* ⇑ enlist
4 If you **volunteer** information or an explanation, you tell someone something without being asked. EG *I volunteered no explanation for our visit... 'Lovely fishing up in the mountains,' he volunteered.* V + O, OR V + QUOTE/REPORT-CL ⇑ suggest

voluptuous /vəlʌptjuəs/. 1 A **voluptuous** woman has large breasts and hips and is considered by some men to be sexually exciting and desirable. EG *She stood as majestically as ever, a voluptuous creature with blonde hair.* ▸ used of women's behaviour and appearance. EG *...voluptuous curves.* ◇ **voluptuousness**. ADJ QUALIT ⇑ plump = buxom ◇ N UNCOUNT
2 Something that is **voluptuous** gives you a great deal of pleasure because of the rich way it is experienced through your senses. EG *...voluptuous echoing violin strings... Inside the cowsheds it was warm and voluptuous, smelling sweetly of milk.* ◇ **voluptuously**. EG *Her voice was low, a voluptuously soft contralto... He inhaled voluptuously.* ◇ **voluptuousness**. EG *He was conscious of a delicious sense of voluptuousness.* ADJ QUALIT ⇑ pleasing = sensuous ◇ ADV ⇑ pleasantly ◇ N UNCOUNT ⇑ sensuality

vomit /vɒmɪt/, **vomits, vomiting, vomited**. 1 If you **vomit**, you bring food and drink back up from your stomach and out through your mouth, usually because you are ill or because you have eaten something that you cannot digest. EG *She was stricken by pain and began to vomit.* ◇ **vomiting**. EG *It begins with nausea and vomiting.* V OR V + O ⇑ expel = be sick N UNCOUNT = sickness
2 **Vomit** is partly digested food and drink that someone has brought back through their mouth from their stomach. EG *The stink of vomit reached Brody almost instantly.* N UNCOUNT ⇑ substance = sick

> **V+O+O** □ In this dictionary V+O+O is used in the grammar notes beside verb entries to indicate that the verb requires two objects. Verbs of this kind are sometimes called ditransitive verbs. Each object of a V+O+O is a noun group. Examples are **make**, **give**, and **fix**. EG *She **made** her mother a dress... **Give** me that book... He **fixed** himself a stiff drink.* Instead of the first object, it is possible to have a prepositional group after the other object introduced by *to* or *for*. EG *She **made** a dress for her mother... **Give** that book to me... He **fixed** a stiff drink for himself.* See □ at V+O+A. Note that verbs do not always have both forms. For example, you can say *I **gave** her a kiss* but you do not normally say 'I gave a kiss to her'.

voodoo /vuːduː/ is a form of magic practised by Black people in the West Indies, especially in Haiti. N UNCOUNT

voracious /vəˈreɪʃəs/. If you say that someone is **voracious** or that they have a **voracious** appetite, you mean that they get through a lot of something, especially food, and that they always want more; a literary word. EG *The Duke's voracious capacity for food was abnormal... Nearly all of them were voracious readers of detective stories... ...the nation's voracious appetite for imports.* ◇ **voraciously**. EG *He follows history and politics, he reads voraciously.* ADJ CLASSIF ◇ ADV WITH VB = insatiably

vortex /vɔːtɛks/, **vortexes, vortices** /vɔːtəsiːz/. The plural can be either **vortexes** or **vortices**. A **vortex** is 1 a mass of wind, water, etc that spins round so fast that it pulls objects down into its empty centre; a formal or literary word. EG *They went galloping down the valley into a vortex of dust.* N COUNT **2** a situation, especially one involving a lot of people, activity, or emotion, which you feel you are being pulled into without being able to prevent it. EG *The Social Democrats found themselves sucked into the revolutionary vortex.* N COUNT + SUPP : USU SING ⇑ whirl = maelstrom

vote /vəʊt/, **votes, voting, voted**. 1 A **vote** is 1.1 a choice made by a particular person or group in a meeting or an election. EG *...when it comes to casting my vote on any issue... ...a marked increase in the votes for the Conservative Party... He's the one who gets my vote... The motion was defeated by 221 votes to 152.* N COUNT **1.2** a method of making a decision in which each person involved indicates their own choice, and N COUNT ⇑ process the choice which most people support is accepted. EG *Let's have a vote... We took a vote.*

2 The **vote** is the total number of votes cast or the total number of people who have indicated their choice in an election, or the number or percentage of votes received by a particular group. EG *They captured 13 per cent of the vote... Labour increased its total vote by a million... An MP ought to be elected by a majority vote.* N SING WITH DET

3 If you have the **vote**, you have the legal right to indicate in a political election who you would like to be elected to represent you. EG *Women have had the vote for over fifty years.* N SING : *the*+N

4 When you **vote**, you make your choice or state your opinion, especially officially at a meeting or in an election, for example by raising your hand or writing on a piece of paper. EG *381 delegates voted for unilateral disarmament... They voted against their own party... We'll vote on it, and you'll have to accept their decision... The students voted to continue the sit-in.* V : USU+A

5 If someone says that they **vote** that a particular thing should happen, they are suggesting that this is what should happen. EG *I vote we try again later.* V+REPORT-CL/*to*-INF = propose

6 If you **vote** Liberal, Conservative, yes, no, etc, you make that choice with a vote that you have. EG *We've always voted Conservative... The citizens voted yes in a referendum to cut property tax.* V+O/REPORT-CL/*to*-INF : NO PASS ⇑ choose

7 If an organization such as a government, trade union, etc **votes** a sum of money to or for something, they decide to spend that money for the stated purpose. EG *The government has just voted another nine million pounds to the defence budget... The union voted itself larger welfare benefits.* V+O+O, OR V+O+A ⇑ allocate = allot

8 If you **are voted** a particular title or **are voted** to a particular position, you are chosen for that title or position by the people who voted. EG *She was voted Most Promising New Actress by the London theatre critics... All of the 13 men were voted on to the Executive Committee.* V+O, OR V+A : USU PASS = elected

9 If you **vote with** your **feet**, you show that you do not support something by leaving the place where it is happening or by leaving the organization that is supporting it. EG *Teachers are voting with their feet in large numbers at the moment.* PHR : VB INFLECTS

10 One man one vote is a system of voting in which every person in a group or country has the right to cast their vote, and in which each individual's vote is counted and has equal value. PHR

vote down. If something or someone **is voted down**, it is rejected, especially as a result of a formal vote. EG *My proposal was voted down... This particular group got voted down.* PHRASAL VB : V+O+ADV : USU PASS = throw out

vote in. To **vote in** a person, political party, or other group means to give that person or political party enough votes in an official election for them to hold a position of power. EG *There are already enough pensioners to vote a government in or out.* PHRASAL VB : V+O+ADV ⇑ elect

vote out. To **vote out** a person, political party, or other group means to give that person or political party so few votes in an official election that they no longer hold a position of power. PHRASAL VB : V+O+ADV ⇑ reject

vote of confidence, votes of confidence. A **vote of confidence** is **1** a vote which is taken in which members of a group are asked to indicate by a vote that they still support the person or group in power, usually the government. EG *The government lost a vote of confidence and a general election was called.* N COUNT **2** something that you say or do which shows that you approve of or support a person or a group such as a political party. N COUNT ⇑ gesture

vote of no confidence, votes of no confidence. A **vote of no confidence** is a vote which is taken in which members of a group are asked to indicate by a vote that they no longer support the person or group in power, usually the government. EG *The government survived two votes of no confidence last night.* N COUNT ⇑ rejection

vote of thanks, votes of thanks. A **vote of thanks** is an official speech, usually at a meeting or formal dinner, in which the speaker formally thanks a person or an organization for doing something such as giving a speech, making a donation, etc. EG *The chairman will be proposing the vote of thanks.* N COUNT

voter /vəʊtə/, **voters.** A **voter** is someone who has the legal right to vote in an election, especially a political election. EG *Many of Britain's voters are looking for new answers.* N COUNT

vouch /vaʊtʃ/, **vouches, vouching, vouched. 1** If you say that you can or will **vouch for** someone or their behaviour, you are saying that you are sure that they will behave correctly, and that you take responsibility for their good behaviour. EG *All he said was simply that he could vouch for your discretion... He said you'd vouch for him.* PHRASAL VB : V+PREP, HAS PASS ⇑ guarantee = speak for

2 If you say that you can **vouch for** something, you mean that you have evidence from your own personal experience or knowledge that it is true or correct. EG *I can vouch for the accuracy of my information.* PHRASAL VB : V+PREP, HAS PASS ⇑ prove

voucher /vaʊtʃə/, **vouchers.** A **voucher** is **1** a ticket or piece of paper that can be used instead of money for a particular purchase; used in British English. EG *I got a ten pound gift voucher for my birthday... ...meal vouchers worth up to 15p a day.* N COUNT : USU MOD+N **2** an official written record of a transaction, especially a receipt for money that has been paid. EG *The Army issued a warning against losing pay vouchers and currency exchange slips.* N COUNT

vouchsafe /vaʊtʃseɪf/, **vouchsafes, vouchsafing, vouchsafed**; a fairly formal old-fashioned word. If you **vouchsafe** something to someone, **1** you give or offer it to them and trust them with it. EG *I have at least been vouchsafed a glimpse of what love might be... ...facts which are vouchsafed to him.* V+O, V+O+O, OR V+O+A *(to)* ⇑ entrust = accord **2** you offer an assurance that something is settled and safe. EG *...to achieve economic arrangements that vouchsafe peace and permanence.* V+O ⇑ assure = guarantee

vow /vaʊ/, **vows, vowing, vowed. 1** If you **vow** to do something, you make a solemn promise or decision that you will do it. EG *The group had vowed to disrupt the elections... He had vowed never to let it happen again... My father vowed quite solemnly that if I did marry Christopher, he would disown me.* V+*to*-INF, OR V+REPORT-CL

2 A **vow** is a solemn decision or promise to do a particular thing, or to stop doing a particular thing. EG *She made a vow to give up smoking... I told him to remember his vow about not competing...* N COUNT = resolution

3 Vows are a set of solemn promises and decisions, such as the promises two people make when they are getting married or the promises that people make when they become priests, monks, or nuns. EG *Jenny and I recited the marriage vows... Nuns still take vows of poverty and celibacy and obedience.* N PLURAL

vowel /vaʊəl/, **vowels.** A **vowel** is **1** a sound made by the human voice in which your vocal cords vibrate, your mouth is open, and your tongue does not touch your teeth or the roof of your mouth. This means that the air can flow freely and the sound can continue for some time. EG *He spoke very carefully, sharply enunciating each vowel and consonant and baring his teeth in the process.* N COUNT **2** a letter or symbol that is used to represent a vowel sound in writing. The letters A, E, I, O, and U are English vowels. N COUNT

voyage /vɔɪɪdʒ/, **voyages, voyaging, voyaged.**

1 A **voyage** is a long journey on a ship or in a spacecraft. EG *...an arduous voyage of many weeks or months... ...the long sea voyage from London to Bombay.* N COUNT

2 If you **voyage** to a place, you travel there; a slightly old-fashioned use. EG *I will voyage into that dark interior.* V+A = journey

voyager /vɔɪɪ⁰dʒə/, **voyagers.** A **voyager** is someone who goes on a voyage, especially a difficult or dangerous one. EG *...our first voyagers to the stars.* N COUNT ⇑ traveller

voyeur /vwaɪɜː/, **voyeurs.** A **voyeur** is someone who gets sexual pleasure from secretly watching other people having sex or from watching them undress. N COUNT

vs. is an abbreviation for 'versus'.

V-sign, V-signs. A **V-sign** is **1** in Britain, a rude gesture which is made by moving your hand quickly upwards with your first finger and your middle finger pointing up and spread out like a V, and your thumb and other two fingers folded and facing you. EG *If you try and stop them, all you get is V-signs and a load of filthy language... I just gave him a V-sign and ran.* N COUNT **2** a similar gesture made with your hand facing the other way, meaning that you have won something or that you are confident of winning it. EG *If a defeated politician performs the victory V-sign, it may reflect his fighting spirit.* N COUNT

VSO is an abbreviation for 'Voluntary Service Overseas'; a British organization that sends young volun- N PROPER/N UNCOUNT teers to developing countries to work on projects that help the local community.

vulgar /vʌlgə/. 1 Something that is **vulgar** is regarded as being of poor artistic quality and taste; used showing disapproval. EG *He wore vulgar, commercialized spectacles... What is now admired as Art Deco was then scorned as vulgar extravagance.* ◇ **vulgarity** /vʌlgærɪti¹/. EG *The vulgarity of the decor made me wince.* — ADJ QUALIT ⇑ tasteless; ◇ N UNCOUNT

2 Pictures, gestures, remarks, etc that are **vulgar** are rude because they refer to sex and other bodily functions in an offensive way. EG *The boys had scrawled some outrageously vulgar graffiti about him in the loo... It was quite a vulgar play.* ◇ **vulgarity**. EG *...the vulgarity and brutality of his speech.* — ADJ QUALIT = crude; ◇ N UNCOUNT = coarseness

3 Someone who is **vulgar** lacks taste and behaves in a socially unacceptable way; used showing disapproval. EG *They will consider you a vulgar, irritating, and objectionable person.* ▸ used of things that people say and do. EG *She did not like him to play on the streets, it was vulgar.* ◇ **vulgarity**. EG *He hated that world of money and vulgarity.* — ADJ QUALIT ⇑ unrefined = uncouth; ▸ = common; ◇ N UNCOUNT

vulnerable /vʌlnə⁰rəbə⁰l/. 1 Someone who is **vulnerable** is 1.1 weak and without protection, with the result that they are easily hurt physically or emotionally. EG *Elderly people, living alone, are especially vulnerable... Lack of employment outside the home tends to make women more vulnerable to depression.* ▸ used of weaknesses that lead to physical illness. EG *It was no place to raise a child with lungs so vulnerable to infection.* ◇ **vulnerability** /vʌlnə⁰rəbɪlɪti¹/. EG *...our vulnerability to life's events.* — ADJ QUALIT : IF+ PREP THEN *to*; ◇ N UNCOUNT : USU+TO

1.2 easily influenced in a morally bad way, because they are weak, innocent, or in a difficult position. EG *Children go through a very vulnerable age... Their participation in government has made them much more vulnerable to the corruption of power.* ◇ **vulnerability**. 1.3 unable to defend themselves against people who are questioning or criticizing them, especially because they are ill-informed about something or are guilty of behaving immorally. EG *These are the points on which Giscard is vulnerable.* ◇ **vulnerability**. EG *...their vulnerability to any criticism.* — ADJ QUALIT : IF+ PREP THEN *to*; ADJ QUALIT : IF+ PREP THEN *to*; ◇ N UNCOUNT ⇑ weakness

2 Something such as a country or a company that is **vulnerable** is 2.1 weak, especially economically or financially, and therefore likely to fail. EG *This is a double threat to the incomes of the most vulnerable groups... Any country acting in isolation would be vulnerable to competition in world markets.* 2.2 easy to attack and to damage or destroy. EG *Khrushchev was shocked to see how vulnerable the tank had become to guided missiles... A land frontier seemed a good deal more vulnerable than several thousand miles of ocean.* ◇ **vulnerability**. EG *...the awakening of public opinion to Britain's extreme vulnerability to attack.* — ADJ QUALIT : IF+ PREP THEN *to*; ADJ QUALIT : IF+ PREP THEN *to*; ◇ N UNCOUNT : USU+*to*

vulture /vʌltʃə/, **vultures**. A **vulture** is a large bird which eats the flesh of dead animals. Vultures live in the hot parts of the world. They usually have no feathers on their head or neck. — N COUNT

2 If you refer to a person as a **vulture**, you mean that he or she is eager to gain something or to make a profit out of someone else's misfortune, distress, or weakness, and shows no sympathy or mercy. EG *The death of the tycoon disappointed the vultures round his bedside.* — N COUNT ⇑ person = scavenger

vulva /vʌlvə/, **vulvas**. The **vulva** is the outer part of a woman's sexual organ; a technical term. — N COUNT : USU SING ⇑ genitals

vying /vaɪɪŋ/ is the present participle of **vie**.

Ww

W, w /dʌbəlju:/, **Ws, w's**. 1 **W** is the twenty-third letter of the English alphabet. — N COUNT

2 **W** or **w** is an abbreviation for words beginning with 'w', such as 'west', 'watt', or 'Welsh'.

wacky /wæki¹/, **wackier, wackiest**; also spelled **whacky**. Something that is **wacky** is eccentric, funny, and exciting; an informal and rather old-fashioned word. EG *...a wacky new comedy.* — ADJ QUALIT = zany

wad /wɒd/, **wads**. A **wad** of paper, cloth, bank notes, etc is a tight bundle or ball of paper, cloth, bank notes, etc. EG *She handed over a wad of forms and leaflets... ...a wad of tobacco.* — N COUNT : ALSO N PART+N UNCOUNT/N IN PL = wodge

wadding /wɒdɪŋ/ is soft material which is put around things to protect them, for example in packing. — N UNCOUNT ⇑ padding

waddle /wɒdə⁰l/, **waddles, waddling, waddled**. To **waddle** means to walk with short, quick steps, swaying slightly from side to side. A person or animal that waddles usually has short legs and a fat body. EG *A family of ducks waddled past... A little squat man waddled out of the bathroom.* — V : USU+A

wade /weɪd/, **wades, wading, waded**. If you **wade** through water, you walk slowly through it with an effort, usually with your legs or the lower part of your body in the water. EG *The children waded out into the lake... We saw one of them trying to wade across a creek.* — V : USU+A = paddle

wade in. If you **wade in** or **wade into** something, you start doing something difficult in a determined and energetic way. EG *If you've got a great idea for a film, you should wade into it.* — PHRASAL VB : V+ ADV/PREP = go for

wade through. If you **wade through** a difficult book, report, etc, you spend a lot of time and effort reading it. EG *Each evening, he would wade through columns of Parliamentary reports.* — PHRASAL VB : V+ PREP = plough through

wader /weɪdə/, **waders**. 1 A **wader** is a bird with long legs and a long neck, which lives near water and feeds on fish. There are several different kinds of waders. — N COUNT

2 **Waders** are long rubber boots which cover all of the legs and are worn by fishermen when they are standing in water. — N PLURAL : ALSO *a pair of*+N

wadge /wɒdʒ/. See **wodge**.

wadi /wɒdi¹/, **wadis**. A **wadi** is a river in North Africa and Arabia which is dry except in the rainy season; a technical term in geography. — N COUNT

wading bird. A **wading bird** is a bird with long legs and a long neck, which lives near water and feeds on fish. There are several different kinds of wading birds. — N COUNT = wader

wafer /weɪfə/, **wafers**. A **wafer** is 1 a thin crisp biscuit which is usually eaten with icecream. 2 a circular, thin piece of special bread which the priest gives people to eat in the Christian service of Holy Communion. EG *She opened her mouth to receive the papery-thin wafer.* — N COUNT; N COUNT

wafer-thin means extremely thin and flat. EG *...wafer-thin slices of bread.* — ADJ CLASSIF

waffle /wɒfə⁰l/, **waffles, waffling, waffled**. 1 When someone **waffles**, they talk or write a lot without actually saying very much that is clear or important. EG *He's still waffling away about economic recovery.* ▸ used as a noun. EG *I don't want waffle, I want the real figures.* — V = rabbit; ▸ N UNCOUNT = hot air

2 A **waffle** is a thick crisp pancake with squares marked on it. Waffles are usually eaten with syrup poured over them. — N COUNT

waft /wɑ:ft, wɒft/, **wafts, wafting, wafted**. If a sound, scent, etc **wafts** or **is wafted** through the air, it moves gently through the air as if being carried by a light wind. EG *A scent of lemon and eucalyptus wafted up from the hotel gardens below... ...the sounds of drunken battle wafting over from the camp... Delicious odours were wafted towards the girl from the neighbouring cottages.* ▸ used as a noun. EG *...a waft of delicious perfume.* — V-ERG+A : IF V+ O THEN USU PASS = drift, float; ▸ N COUNT+*of* = breath

wag /wæg/, **wags, wagging, wagged**. 1 If you **wag** your finger, head, etc or if it **wags**, you shake it repeatedly from side to side, using very small quick movements. EG *She started to wag her finger in front of my face while she spoke.* — V-ERG = waggle

2 When a dog **wags** its tail or when its tail **wags**, the dog repeatedly waves its tail from side to side because it is happy. EG *The dog waited, making happy little barks and wagging his tail.* V-ERG = waggle

3 If **tongues wag** about something, people are gossiping about other people and their behaviour; an informal expression. EG *He dared not give her a scarf as a gift, because tongues might wag.* PHR : VB INFLECTS

4 A **wag** is someone who makes jokes; an old-fashioned use. EG *Some wag said that even cats and dogs voted in New York elections.* N COUNT = wit, clown

wage /weɪdʒ/, **wages, waging, waged.** 1 A **wage** is the amount of money that is regularly paid to someone or to a group of people for a particular type of work, especially manual or unskilled work. EG *...the problems of families bringing up children on a low wage... They're campaigning for a legal minimum wage for each industry... They stopped work to press for better wages and conditions... Tomorrow union leaders meet the company for wage talks.* N COUNT ⇑ pay

2 Someone's **wages** are the money that they are paid each week for the work that they do, especially when they have a manual or unskilled job. EG *My wages had not increased for two full years.* N PLURAL ⇑ income

3 If a person, group, or country **wages** a campaign, war, etc, they start it and carry it on over a period of time. EG *He believes that they are plotting to wage a limited nuclear war in Europe... Together with the Conservative Party, industry waged a full-scale anti-nationalisation campaign.* V+O ⇑ conduct = engage in

wage-packet, wage-packets. Someone's **wage-packet** is the envelope containing their wages that they are given at the end of every week. EG *When I opened my wage-packet, I found that I had more money than usual.* N COUNT

wager /weɪdʒə/, **wagers, wagering, wagered**; a rather literary and old-fashioned word. 1 A **wager** is an agreement you make with someone in which you decide on an amount of money, and depending on the result of a particular event or activity, one of you loses and has to pay that amount of money to the other. EG *For a wager, he drove a coach and four across the river.* N COUNT = bet

2 If you **wager** something, you agree with someone on something, for example a sum of money, that you will win or lose, depending on the result of an event or activity. EG *I'll wager my reputation on the outcome of the case.* V+O ⇑ gamble = stake

waggish /wægɪʃ/. Someone who is **waggish** makes amusing jokes; an old-fashioned word. ◊ **waggishly.** EG *Miss Wells laughed at him waggishly.* ADJ QUALIT ◊ ADV WITH VB

waggle /wægəᵒl/, **waggles, waggling, waggled.** If you **waggle** something or it **waggles**, it moves up and down or from side to side with short quick movements. EG *He waggled his eyebrows.* V-ERG = wiggle

wagon /wægəᵒn/, **wagons**; also spelled **waggon** in rather old-fashioned English. A **wagon** is 1 a strong vehicle with four wheels, usually pulled by horses or oxen and used for carrying heavy loads. EG *Behind them was a covered wagon being pulled by two horses.* 2 a large container on wheels which is pulled by a train; used mainly in British English. EG *The cattle go by rail in wagons.* • See also **bandwagon**. N COUNT = cart; N COUNT = truck

wagtail /wægteɪl/, **wagtails.** A **wagtail** is a small bird which moves its tail quickly up and down as it walks. There are several different kinds of wagtail. N COUNT

waif /weɪf/, **waifs.** A **waif** is a young, thin person, especially a child, who looks as if he or she has nowhere to live and not enough to eat. EG *There she sat, huddled up, like a waif.* N COUNT = orphan

wail /weɪl/, **wails, wailing, wailed.** 1 If someone **wails**, they make long, loud, high-pitched cries which express sorrow or pain. EG *One of the small children began to wail with terror.* ▸ used as a noun. EG *I could hear the wail of a baby in the house next door.* ◊ **wailing.** EG *He could hear in his mind the wailing of the women.* V ⇑ cry = howl; ▸ N COUNT; ◊ N UNCOUNT = weeping

2 If you **wail** something, you say it in a loud, high-pitched voice that shows that you are unhappy or in pain. EG *He raised a red, wet face and wailed, 'I didn't start the fight, she did.'... He sat in the middle of his Christmas presents wailing that the one thing he really wanted was a puppy.* ▸ used as a noun. EG *There was a plaintive wail from the sofa: 'What about me?'* V+O/REPORT-CL/QUOTE = howl, moan; ▸ N COUNT = cry

wainscot /weɪnzkəᵗt/, **wainscots.** A **wainscot** is a wooden covering on the lower half of the wall of a room, especially in old houses. N COUNT = skirting board

waist /weɪst/, **waists.** 1 Your **waist** is the middle part of your body where it narrows slightly above your hips. EG *She tied an apron around her waist... He was naked from the waist up.* N COUNT : USU POSS+N

2 The **waist** of a dress, coat, etc is the part of it which covers the middle part of your body. EG *She tucked the folded bills down into the waist of her skirt.* N COUNT

waistband /weɪstᵒbænd/, **waistbands.** A **waistband** is a narrow piece of material which is sewn on to a pair of trousers, a skirt, or other item of clothing at the waist in order to strengthen it. EG *...the waistband of his trousers.* N COUNT ⇑ strip

waistcoat /weɪstᵒkəʊt/, **waistcoats.** A **waistcoat** is a sleeveless piece of clothing with buttons which you wear on the top part of your body. Men often wear waistcoats over their shirts and under their jackets. EG *...a black corduroy waistcoat... He put the ticket into his waistcoat pocket.* N COUNT ⇑ garment = vest

waisted /weɪstɪᶻd/ describes pieces of clothing that are narrower at the point where they cover a person's waist. EG *...a waisted denim jacket.* ADJ CLASSIF ⇑ fitted

-waisted combines with adjectives 1 to indicate the size or shape of someone's waist. EG *...slim-waisted women.* 2 to describe the waistline of a piece of clothing. EG *...high-waisted... ...narrow-waisted.* COMB : FORMS ADJ QUALITS; COMB : FORMS ADJ QUALITS

waistline /weɪstᵒlaɪn/, **waistlines.** 1 Your **waistline** is an imaginary line around your waist which you use as a way of measuring how slim or fat you are. EG *...a 40-year-old lady with a generous waistline.* N COUNT

2 The **waistline** of a piece of clothing is the place where the upper and lower parts of it are sewn together. EG *The low waistline is back in fashion this year.* N COUNT ⇑ line

wait /weɪt/, **waits, waiting, waited.** 1 If you **wait**, you spend some time, usually doing very little, before something happens or before you can do something or see someone. EG *He waited patiently for her... She had been waiting in the queue to buy some stamps... I've been waiting to see you, you know... Wait until we sit down... You'll have to wait till tomorrow... He will have to wait two years before he can have a car of his own.* ◊ **waiting.** EG *There was a waiting period of one month.* • **ready and waiting**: see **ready**. • **to wait in the wings**: see **wing**. V, V+*to*-INF, OR V+A = hang around; ◊ ADJ CLASSIF : ATTRIB

2 A **wait** is a period of time in which you do very little, before something happens or before you can do something or see someone. EG *There was a long wait... The tourists were always complaining about the wait... Has it been worth the wait, do you think?* N COUNT : USU SING = delay

3 If you **can't wait** to do something or **can hardly wait** to do something, you are very excited about it and eager to do it. EG *He couldn't wait to tell Judy... Oh Cyril, I can hardly wait! Isn't it exciting?... The boys could hardly wait to begin their duties.* PHR : VB INFLECTS = be bursting

4 If you say **wait until** something happens, **just wait**, etc, 4.1 you are showing how excited, amused, or annoyed you are about something and that you expect it to excite, amuse, or annoy the person you are talking to.' EG *Just wait till you hear what's happened!.. 'Oh, wait until I tell Tony!' John continued... Have you been on a drilling yet? No? Just you wait!* 4.2 you are threatening someone. EG *You wait, Mr Crow! You wait! You'll find Robinson isn't a fellow to tangle with.* PHR, OR CONVENTION; PHR, OR CONVENTION

5 If you say to someone **'What are you waiting for?'**, you are telling them to hurry up and do something that you have already told them to do. CONVENTION = get cracking

6 You use the expression **wait for it** 6.1 to stop someone from doing something too soon because you have not yet given them the command to do it. EG *Ready, steady–wait for it–go!* 6.2 to tell someone that what you are about to say is very predictable and therefore rather amusing. EG *They were out of stock in our local shop, so I tried to buy some in a shop in Birmingham and the girl there said–wait for it–'We're out of stock at the moment but I'm sure we'll have some in by next week.'* CONVENTION; PHR : USED AS ADV SEN = guess what

7 You use the expression **wait and see** to tell someone that they must be patient or that they must not worry about what is going to happen in the future. EG *We shall just have to wait and see... All you can do is wait and see... I prefer to wait and see how things go.* PHR : NO INFLECTION

8 You use the expressions **wait a minute, wait a second, wait a moment**, etc, 8.1 to interrupt someone when they are speaking, for example because you want to say something, because you object to what they are saying, or because you want them to repeat something. EG *Wait a minute, are you proposing to rewrite the entire play?... 'I guess we'll just go our separate ways.'–'Wait a minute, what are you talking about?'* [CONVENTION OR PHR : USED AS ADV SEN = hold on] 8.2 to interrupt yourself when you are speaking, for example because you are trying to remember something, because you want to correct what you have just said, or because you have noticed or remembered something surprising. EG *Wait a minute. What did I do with the other one?... The Ravenscrofts? Now wait a minute. That was that very sad tragedy, wasn't it?... Wait a second. It might have been further down the street.* [PHR : USED AS ADV SEN = hang on]

9 If something **is waiting** for you, it is ready for you to use or do. EG *His bicycle waited for him at the station... I have a lot of work waiting.* [V] ◊ **waiting**. EG *He took her down the steps to the waiting taxi.* [◊ ADJ CLASSIF : ATTRIB]

10 If you say that something can **wait**, you mean that it is not important or urgent and so you will do or deal with it later. EG *The dishes can wait.* [V : USU WITH MODAL]

11 If you **wait** on people in a restaurant or **wait** at table, you serve people food as part of your job. EG *The women were very eager to wait on his table.* [V+A] ● See also **wait on**.

12 If you **wait on** someone **hand and foot**, you provide everything that they need and do everything for them; used showing disapproval. EG *She came home from the hospital where she had been waited on hand and foot.* [PHR : VB INFLECTS ↑ pamper]

wait about. 1 If you **wait about** or **wait around**, you spend a lot of time, usually doing very little, before something happens or before you can do something or see someone. EG *Don't keep him waiting about in the hotel... She had waited around for nearly a whole year.* [PHRASAL VB : V+ADV = hang around]

wait behind. If you **wait behind**, you stay in a place after everyone else has left, for example because you want to talk to someone alone. EG *He waited behind to have a word with her in private.* [PHRASAL VB : V+ADV ↑ remain = hang back]

wait in. If you **wait in**, you deliberately stay at home and do not go out, for example because someone is coming to see you. EG *I waited in all the afternoon.* [PHRASAL VB : V+ADV = stay in]

wait on. If you **wait on** something, you wait for that thing to happen before you do anything else or make any important decisions; a rather old-fashioned expression. EG *The company is prepared to bide its time and wait on events.* [PHRASAL VB : V+PREP = await]

wait up. If you **wait up**, you deliberately do not go to bed, especially because you are expecting a member of your family or a friend to return home late at night. EG *She said that you shouldn't bother to wait up for her.* [PHRASAL VB : V+ADV = stay up]

waiter /weɪtə/, **waiters**. A **waiter** is a man who works in a restaurant, serving people with food and drink. EG *The waiter came to take their order... The head waiter poured the wine into her glass.* ● See also **dumb waiter**. [N COUNT ↑ server]

waiting game, waiting games. If you play a **waiting game** in a situation, you deal with the situation by deliberately not doing anything, because you gain an advantage by waiting and acting later. EG *The waiting game has gone on long enough.* [N COUNT : USU SING ↑ strategy]

waiting list, waiting lists. A **waiting list** is a list of people who have asked for something which cannot be given to them immediately, for example medical treatment or a job, and who must therefore wait until it is available. EG *Doctors are the first to deplore long hospital waiting lists... ...a long waiting list of applicants... He's on the waiting list for a new company car.* [N COUNT]

waiting-room, waiting-rooms. A **waiting-room** is a room in a place such as a railway station or a doctor's surgery, where people can sit and wait until it is time for their train, until the doctor is ready to see them, etc. [N COUNT]

waitress /weɪtrɪ²s/, **waitresses**. A **waitress** is a woman who works in a restaurant, serving people with food and drink. EG *The waitress brought the drinks and left two menus... ...the restaurant where she worked as a waitress.* [N COUNT ↑ server]

waive /weɪv/, **waives, waiving, waived**. If you **waive** something such as a rule which should be enforced or a right that you have, you decide not to enforce it or claim it; a fairly formal word. EG *We would waive formal entry requirements for strongly motivated applicants... Rules about proper dress may be waived... They will waive the penalty if you give two months' notice.* [V+O]

wake /weɪk/, **wakes, waking, woken**. American English also uses the form **waked** for the past tense and past participle. 1 When you **wake** or when someone **wakes** you, you become conscious again after being asleep. EG *I sometimes wake at four in the morning... He woke me early.* [V-ERG ↑ rouse = awaken] ● Your **waking hours** are the times when you are awake rather than asleep. EG *I spend most of my waking hours in the library.* [● PHR : USED AS S/O, POSS+N]

2 The **wake** of a boat or other object moving in water is the track of waves which it makes behind it as it moves through the water. EG *He found her staring at the wake of the boat.* [N COUNT : USU *the*+N = backwash]

3 If you leave something **in** your **wake**, you leave it behind you as you go. EG *They left trails of sweet papers in their wake.* [PHR : USED AS AN A]

4 If a second thing follows **in the wake of** a first thing, it follows after the first thing is over, often as a result of it. EG *Famine came in the wake of disastrous floods... Many expressionist movements sprang up in the wake of the Second World War.* [PREP ↑ following]

5 A **wake** is a gathering of people, especially in Ireland, who mourn together and watch over the body of a dead person on the night before the burial. [N COUNT ↑ vigil]

wake up. 1 When you wake up or someone **wakes** you **up**, you become conscious again after being asleep. EG *Ralph, wake up!... I woke up to discover that he had gone... They went back to sleep but I woke them up again.* [PHRASAL VB : V-ERG+ADV]

2 If something such as an activity **wakes** you **up**, it makes you more alert and ready to do things after you have been lazy or inactive. EG *The art course stimulated me, woke me up... Those exercises woke Donald up, I can tell you.* [PHRASAL VB : ORDER V+O+ADV ↑ rouse]

3 If you **wake up** to something such as a dangerous situation, you become aware of it. EG *People are waking up at last to this threat... The west began to wake up to the danger it faced.* [PHRASAL VB : V+ADV+A *(to)* = wise up]

wakeful /weɪkful/. Someone who is **wakeful** 1 is constantly waking up and not sleeping very much. EG *Some babies are hungry and wakeful from birth.* [ADJ QUALIT = sleepless] 2 is awake and alert; a formal use. EG *This alarmed her and made her more wakeful.* [ADJ QUALIT = vigilant] ◊ **wakefulness**. EG *The music shook me into wakefulness.* [◊ N UNCOUNT = attention]

waken /weɪkə⁰n/, **wakens, wakening, wakened**. When you **waken** or when someone **wakens** you, you wake; a literary word. EG *It is frightening to most children to waken and find a stranger... Once she was sleeping nothing wakened her.* [V-ERG = awaken]

walk /wɔːk/, **walks, walking, walked**. 1 When you **walk**, you move along fairly slowly by putting one foot in front of the other on the ground. EG *Most children learn to walk when they are about one... I shan't take the bus, I'm going to walk... We walked along in silence for a bit... Just open the door and walk in... 'Hello,' she said, walking up to Brody.* [V : USU+A]

2 If you **walk** a particular distance or a particular road, you travel this distance or along this road by walking. EG *They used to walk ten miles to school each day... Walk three steps to your left... We saw barefoot doctors walking country roads.* [V+O]

3 A **walk** is 3.1 the action of walking rather than running. EG *He ran, and then slowed down to a walk.* [N SING : *a*+N ↑ movement] 3.2 a short journey which you make by walking, usually for pleasure. EG *He went out for a long walk... Has the dog had its walk yet?... Felicity will take the children for a walk on the beach.* [N COUNT = stroll] 3.3 a path which is designed or used for people to walk along. EG *The north walk of the garden proceeds through grass and trees.* [N COUNT ↑ footpath] 3.4 a route suitable for walking along for pleasure. EG *There are some beautiful walks along the coast.* [N COUNT ↑ way]

4 Someone's **walk** is the way that they walk. EG *I can always recognise her by her walk.* [N SING : POSS+N = gait]

5 A **walk** of a particular distance is this distance which a person has to walk to get somewhere. EG *The station is a three minute walk from the park... It's a long walk from Mowbray.* [N SING+SUPP : *a*+N]

6 If you **walk** someone somewhere, you walk there with them as a way of being polite or to protect [V+O+A : NO PASS = escort, see]

them. EG *He walked her home... I walked him to his car.*

7 If you **walk** your dog, you take it for a walk in order to keep it healthy. EG *Have you walked the dog yet?* [V+O; ⇑ exercise]

8 If someone **walks** you **off** your **feet**, they make you walk so far or so fast that you feel exhausted; a fairly informal expression. [PHR : VB INFLECTS; ⇑ tire]

9 If you tell someone to **take a walk**, you tell them to go away because you are annoyed with them; a very informal expression, used mainly in American English. [CONVENTION; = get lost]

10 • **walking on air**: see **air**. • to **walk tall**: see **tall**. • to **walk the plank**: see **plank**. • to **walk the streets**: see **street**. • See also **walking**.

walk away from. If someone **walks away from** a situation that they find unpleasant, they leave it without trying to make it better before they leave; used showing disapproval. EG *Are you just going to walk away from your marriage?* [PHRASAL VB : V+ADV+PREP; = abandon]

walk away with. If you **walk away with** something such as a prize, you win it or achieve it very easily. EG *She walked away with the title.* [PHRASAL VB : V+ADV+PREP]

walk in on. If you **walk in on** someone, you go into a place and interrupt them unintentionally because you are not expecting them to be there. EG *He walked in on me while I was having a bath.* [PHRASAL VB : V+ADV+PREP; ⇑ disturb]

walk into. 1 If you **walk into** an unpleasant situation, you become involved in it without expecting to, sometimes because you are careless. EG *She's always walking into trouble.* [PHRASAL VB : V+PREP; ⇑ meet]

2 If you **walk into** a job, you manage to get it very easily; a fairly informal use. EG *He just walked into the job without any problem.* [PHRASAL VB : V+PREP; ⇑ obtain]

walk off. If you try to **walk off** an unpleasant feeling of illness, sadness, etc, you go for a walk in order to stop having the feeling. EG *He managed to walk off his headache... She tried to walk off her depressed mood.* [PHRASAL VB : V+O+ADV]

walk off with. 1 If someone **walks off with** something, they take it without asking the person to whom it belongs; an informal use. EG *Who's walked off with my pen?* [PHRASAL VB : V+ADV+PREP; = go off with]

2 If you **walk off with** something such as a prize, you win it or achieve it very easily. EG *She'll walk off with a first class degree.* [PHRASAL VB : V+ADV+PREP]

walk out. 1 If you **walk out** of a meeting, a performance, or an unpleasant situation, you leave it suddenly without explaining why, usually as a way of showing that you do not like it or that you are angry. EG *Most of the audience walked out after the first half hour... He walked out of his job.* [PHRASAL VB : V+ADV]

2 If workers **walk out**, they go on strike. EG *All the workers in the factory walked out last week.* [PHRASAL VB : V+ADV]

walk out on. If you **walk out on** someone with whom you have a close relationship, you leave them suddenly. EG *She walked out on her boyfriend.* [PHRASAL VB : V+ADV+PREP; = desert]

walk over. If someone **walks over** you, they treat you very badly, for example by telling you what to do all the time; an informal expression. EG *I've had enough of him walking all over me.* [PHRASAL VB : V+PREP, HAS PASS; ⇑ oppress]

walkabout /wɔ:kəbaʊt/, **walkabouts**. 1 If you **go walkabout**, you go on a journey walking through the countryside; used especially to refer to Australian Aborigines walking in the bush alone. EG *Put on some stout shoes and go walkabout in the countryside.* [PHR : VB INFLECTS; ⇑ travel]

2 When a king, queen, or other important person **goes walkabout** or **does a walkabout**, he or she walks through crowds in a public place in order to meet people in an informal way. EG *The Pope suddenly went walkabout.* [PHR : VB INFLECTS]

walker /wɔ:kə/, **walkers**. A **walker** is a person who walks, especially in the countryside for pleasure or in order to keep healthy. EG *Walkers and cyclists flowed down the long hills.* [N COUNT; = hiker]

walkie-talkie /wɔ:ki[1] tɔ:ki[1]/, **walkie-talkies**. A **walkie-talkie** is a small portable radio which you can talk into and hear messages through so that you can communicate with someone far away. EG *There were hundreds of policemen around with walkie-talkies.* [N COUNT]

walking /wɔ:kɪŋ/. 1 **Walking** is the activity or sport of going for long walks in the country. EG *Walking and mountaineering are now very popular... ...a walking holiday... I put on my walking shoes.* [N UNCOUNT; = hiking]

2 You can also use **walking** to describe a person in terms of an object, in order to emphasize a particular quality that the person has; a humorous usage. EG *She's a walking history book.* [ADJ CLASSIF : ATTRIB]

walking stick, walking sticks; also spelled with a hyphen. A **walking stick** is a long wooden stick which a person uses, especially an old person, to lean on while they are walking. [N COUNT]

Walkman /wɔ:kmə[3]n/, **Walkmans**. A **Walkman** is a trademark for a small cassette player with very light headphones which people carry around so that they can listen to music while they are walking, cycling, sitting on the bus, etc. EG *...Walkmans, the latest craze for city dwellers.* [N COUNT; ⇑ machine]

walk of life, walks of life. The **walk of life** that you come from is the position that you have in society in terms of the kind of job you have. EG *Members of this club come from many different walks of life.* [N COUNT : USU+SUPP; = milieu]

walk-on. A **walk-on** part in a play is a very small part which usually does not involve any speaking. EG *All the others had walk-on parts.* [ADJ CLASSIF : ATTRIB; = bit]

walkout /wɔ:kaʊt/, **walkouts**. A **walkout** is a strike. EG *The pay deal ended the 43-day-old walkout.* [N COUNT]

walkover /wɔ:kəʊvə/, **walkovers**. If a competition or contest is a **walkover** for you, you win it very easily indeed. EG *It was a walkover for the Tories.* [N COUNT : USU USED AS C; = pushover]

walk-up, walk-ups. A **walk-up** is a tall block of flats which has no lift or a flat in such a block; used in American English. EG *I couldn't even afford the rent in my fifth-floor walk-up.* [N COUNT; ⇑ building]

walkway /wɔ:kweɪ/, **walkways**. A **walkway** is a passage or pathway between two buildings for pedestrians to use; used especially in American English. [N COUNT]

wall /wɔ:l/, **walls, walling, walled**. 1 A **wall** is 1.1 one of the vertical sides of a building or room. EG *There was a picture on the wall... The snake got into the hut through a hole in the wall... A sideboard stood against the wall... ...a library with glass walls... ...a wall light.* [N COUNT] **1.2** a long narrow vertical structure made of stone or brick that encloses or divides an area of land. EG *...the old stone walls of the garden... There was enough material to build a wall nine feet high and one foot thick... We crouched behind the wall and waited.* [N COUNT; ⇑ barrier]

2 If an area of land **is walled**, it is surrounded or enclosed by a wall. EG *On your right is Threadneedle Street and walling its north side a great grey wall.* [V+O : USU PASS; = encircle] ◊ **walled**. EG *...a convent set in walled gardens... ...the old walled city of Jerusalem.* [◊ ADJ CLASSIF]

3 The **wall** of something hollow is the side of it. EG *...cellulose, the material from which the cell walls of plants are built... Occasionally its tail would flick sharply against the wall of the box.* [N COUNT+SUPP]

4 A **wall** of things or people is a large amount of them forming a vertical barrier. EG *The ship was struck by a great wall of water... ...a wall of fire... ...a wall of Secret Service men.* [N COUNT+*of*+N UNCOUNT/N IN PL]

5 You refer to a **wall** of a particular quality or attitude to indicate that this quality or attitude forms a kind of barrier which prevents people from communicating or working with each other, or which protects someone or something. EG *A door has been opened in an ancient wall of mutual suspicion... Their enthusiasm is stifled when they are met with this stone wall of apathy... He needed someone who could penetrate the wall of security now built up round him.* [N COUNT+*of*+N UNCOUNT]

6 The word **wall** is also used in the following expressions. **6.1** If you **are banging** your **head against a brick wall**, you are not making any progress in something that you are trying hard to achieve because something such as a person or an organization is preventing you. EG *It's no good–we're just banging our heads against a brick wall.* [PHR : VB INFLECTS; = get nowhere] **6.2** If you **come up against a brick wall**, you are unable to progress any further or get what you want because someone or something is preventing you. EG *I keep coming up against a brick wall... The latest talks about Northern Ireland have come up against a brick wall.* [PHR : VB INFLECTS] **6.3** If someone or something **drives** you **up the wall, sends** you **up the wall**, or makes you **go up the wall**, they make you very irritated or annoyed; an informal expression. EG *This drove him up the wall... I'll go up the wall if I stay here much longer.* [PHR : VB INFLECTS] **6.4** If someone **drives** you **to the wall** or **pushes** you **to the wall**, they force you into a very difficult situation. [PHR : VB INFLECTS] **6.5** If a person or a business **goes to the wall**, they are defeated in a struggle for [PHR : VB INFLECTS]

survival or success, often so that they are ruined financially. EG *It's a jungle in which the weakest go to the wall... Agriculture and fishing are going to the wall.* **6.6** If someone **has** their **back to the wall**, they are in a very difficult situation and can see no way out; an informal expression. PHR : VB INFLECTS **6.7** The expressions **the writing is on the wall** and **the writing on the wall** are used to indicate that there are signs that something such as a business is unlikely to be able to exist much longer. EG *The writing is on the wall for industries like these... They've seen the writing on the wall.* PHR : VB INFLECTS, OR PHR : USED AS O

wall in. If someone or something **is walled in**, they are completely enclosed in a room or place. EG *Once in it you are enclosed, walled in by tombs of kings.* PHRASAL VB : V+O+ADV, USU PASS

wall off. If one area **is walled off** from another, it is separated from it by a wall, usually inside a building. EG *It had an end walled off to form a gas chamber.* PHRASAL VB : V+O+ADV, USU PASS

wall up. If someone or something **is walled up**, they are completely enclosed in a room or covered by a wall built around them. EG *...a girl walled up in her cell.* PHRASAL VB : V+O+ADV, USU PASS

wallaby /wɒləbi¹/, **wallabies**. A **wallaby** is an animal rather like a small kangaroo. Wallabies live in Australia and New Guinea. N COUNT

-walled combines with adjectives and nouns to describe buildings or containers that have walls of a particular kind. EG *...a mud-walled hut... ...a thin-walled vessel.* COMB : FORMS ADJS

wallet /wɒlɪt/, **wallets**. A **wallet** is a small flat folded case made of leather or plastic, which is used for keeping paper money in and other small things such as credit cards. EG *He took a wallet from the inside pocket of his jacket and extracted a five pound note.* N COUNT

wallflower /wɔːlflauə/, **wallflowers**. **1** A **wallflower** is a plant that is grown in gardens and has lots of yellow, red, orange, or purple flowers. N COUNT

2 If someone is a **wallflower** at a party or a dance, they are shy or have no one to dance with and therefore stand or sit doing nothing. EG *I'm fed up with being a wallflower.* N COUNT : USU USED AS C

wallop /wɒləp/, **wallops, walloping, walloped**. If you **wallop** someone or something, you hit them very hard; an informal word. EG *His mother would have walloped him if she'd known what he was up to... Hold it in your hand and wallop it with a hammer.* ▸ used as a noun. EG *Lally called out something about giving me a good wallop.* V+O = belt, clout ▸ N COUNT : USU SING

walloping /wɒləpɪŋ/, **wallopings**. If someone gives a child a **walloping**, they beat him or her severely, usually as a punishment. EG *I got a terrific walloping from our father.* N COUNT : USU SING = hiding

wallow /wɒləʊ/, **wallows, wallowing, wallowed**. **1** If you **wallow** in a particular situation or emotion, you think about the situation or remain in the emotional state longer than is normal or reasonable, because you are enjoying it or only thinking about yourself. EG *At first I only wanted to wallow in their misery... Her mother was living in deep retirement, wallowing in widowhood... It isn't just a nostalgic wallowing in things of the past.* V+A *(in)* = luxuriate, revel

2 If a person or animal **wallows** in mud or water, they lie or roll about in it slowly for pleasure. EG *...creatures who wallowed like hippopotami in mud.* ▸ used as a noun. EG *He would like to have a bath, a proper wallow with soap.* V : USU+A *(in)* ⇑ bathe = loll ▸ N SING : a+N = soak

3 If a ship **wallows** in a rough sea, it rolls violently from side to side. EG *Waves smashed over one end of the wallowing craft.* V : USU+A *(in)* ⇑ struggle = flounder

wallpaper /wɔːlpeɪpə/, **wallpapers, wallpapering, wallpapered**. **1 Wallpaper** is thick coloured or patterned paper that is used for covering and decorating the walls of rooms. EG *Floral wallpaper adorned the walls of the guest room.* N MASS

2 If someone **wallpapers** a room, they cover the walls with wallpaper. EG *The rooms had been emptied ready for wallpapering.* V OR V+O = paper

Wall Street is a street in New York where the Stock Exchange and important banks are. It is considered to be the place where the most important financial business goes on; often used to refer to this financial business and to the people who work there. EG *He started gambling on Wall Street... Wall Street welcomed this move as a sign of determination.* N PROPER

wall-to-wall. A **wall-to-wall** carpet or rug covers the floor of a room completely. ADJ CLASSIF

wally /wɒli¹/, **wallies**. If you refer to someone as a **wally**, you mean that they are stupid or foolish; a very informal word, used in British English. N COUNT = twerp

walnut /wɔːlnʌt/, **walnuts**. **1** A **walnut** is an edible nut which has a wrinkled shape and a very hard round shell that is light brown in colour. EG *...a big walnut tree... ...coffee and walnut cake.* N COUNT

2 Walnut is the wood from a walnut tree, which is light brown in colour and is often used for making expensive furniture. EG *He took his seat at the polished walnut table.* N UNCOUNT

walrus /wɔːlrəs, wɒl-/, **walruses**. A **walrus** is an animal which lives in the sea and looks like a large seal with coarse whiskers and two long teeth pointing down. Walruses are found mainly in the Arctic region. N COUNT

waltz /wɔːls/, **waltzes, waltzing, waltzed**. **1** A **waltz** is **1.1** a piece of music with a rhythm of three beats in each bar, which people can dance to. EG *They could hear the band playing waltzes.* N COUNT **1.2** a dance in which two people hold each other and move around the floor with special steps in time to waltz music. N COUNT

2 If you **waltz** with someone, you dance a waltz with them. EG *I dreamt of going to Hollywood to waltz with Ginger Rogers.* V OR V+A *(with)* : RECIP

3 If you **waltz** somewhere, you walk there in a very relaxed and confident way, especially in a way which makes other people notice you; an informal use. EG *She waltzed into an off-licence and asked for a bottle of champagne... She waltzed across to Helen and sat down beside her.* V+A = breeze

wan /wɒn/. Someone who is **wan** looks pale and tired, often because they are ill or unhappy; a literary word. EG *He looked suddenly so wan and defeated when I said this... She was beginning to look wan and fragile.* ▸ used of people's expressions. EG *She gave me a wan smile, at once tremulous and brave.* ◊ **wanly**. EG *He smiled wanly.* ADJ QUALIT = waxen, washed out ▸ = weak ◊ ADV AFTER VB

wand /wɒnd/, **wands**. A **wand** is a long thin rod that magicians and fairies wave when they are performing tricks and magic. EG *She seemed to expect him to wave a magic wand and make the problem disappear.* N COUNT ⇑ stick

wander /wɒndə/, **wanders, wandering, wandered**. **1** If you **wander** in a place, you walk around there in a casual way, often without intending to go in any particular direction. EG *We wandered round the little harbour town... A man was found wandering in the hills near Eskdale... He lost interest in the book and wandered off... The children wandered the streets after school.* ▸ used as a noun. EG *I think I'll take a wander in the garden.* V+A, OR V+O = roam, ramble ▸ N SING : a+N = stroll

2 If a person or animal **wanders** from a place where they are supposed to stay, they move away from the place without going in a particular direction. EG *Tie him to a tree with a bit of string, then he won't wander... He used the dogs to reassemble his goats which had begun to wander.* V : NO IMPER = stray

3 If your mind **wanders** or your thoughts **wander**, you stop concentrating on something and start thinking about other things. EG *When she was alone, she would let her mind wander... He noticed my attention wandering... My thoughts kept wandering back to that night... This discussion has wandered off the point.* V : NO IMPER = stray

wanderer /wɒndəʳrə/, **wanderers**. A **wanderer** is a person who travels around rather than settling in one place. N COUNT = drifter

wandering /wɒndəʳrɪŋ/, **wanderings**. **1 Wandering** is used to describe people who travel around rather than staying in one place for a long time. EG *...travelling with a wandering troupe of actors.* ADJ CLASSIF : ATTRIB = itinerant

2 Someone's **wanderings** are journeys that they make from place to place without staying in one place for a long time. EG *I was tired of all our wanderings and never having a home for longer than a month.* N PLURAL

wanderlust /wɒndəlʌst/. Someone who has **wanderlust** has a strong desire to travel. EG *Her wanderlust took her all round the world.* N UNCOUNT ⇑ restlessness

wane /weɪn/, **wanes, waning, waned**. **1** If a condition, attitude, emotion, etc **wanes**, it becomes weaker or smaller, often disappearing completely in the end. EG *Her enthusiasm for Harold was beginning* V = lessen, fade *to wane... The influence of this group waned considerably... The bond of friendship has not waned but has survived the passage of time.*

2 If a condition, attitude, emotion, etc is **on the wane,** it is becoming weaker or smaller. EG *Their mutual enjoyment was on the wane... They could claim that pollution for the first time was on the wane.* PHR : USED AS AN A = diminishing

3 When the moon **wanes**, it shows a smaller area of brightness each day as it changes from a full moon to a new moon. EG *...by the light of a waning moon.* V = dwindle

● to **wax and wane**: see **wax.**

wangle /wæŋgəˡl/, **wangles, wangling, wangled.** If you **wangle** something that you want, you manage to get it by being crafty or very persuasive; an informal word. EG *He always managed to wangle the easy jobs... He fancied going on the African expedition and wangled his way onto it... With a bit of wangling, they will insure our freight free.* V+O ⇑ arrange

wank /wæŋk/, **wanks, wanking, wanked.** If someone **wanks**, they masturbate; a very informal word, used in British English. ▸ used as a noun. V ▸ N SING : a+N

wanker /wæŋkə/, **wankers**; an offensive word. Someone might refer to a person, usually a man, as a **wanker 1** when they think that he is very stupid or useless. **2** to say that he masturbates. N COUNT N COUNT

want /wɒnt/, **wants, wanting, wanted. 1** If you **want** something, you feel a desire to have it or you feel a need for it. EG *Do you want a cup of coffee?... Smaller babies may want less milk than the books say... All they want is a holiday... Money had brought everything he had wanted so far.* V+O : NO IMPER ⇑ require

2 If you **want** to do something or **want** something to happen, you have a desire to do it or for it to happen. EG *I want to be an actress... He doesn't want to get up... You can borrow that pen if you want to... What do you want me to do?... I didn't want him to go.* V+to-INF, OR V+O+to-INF : NO IMPER = wish

3 Your **wants** are the things that you want. EG *They developed new wants: for bicycles, shirts, and bottles of whisky.* N PLURAL : USU POSS+N = demands

4 If something **wants** doing, there is a need for it to be done. EG *We've got a couple of jobs that want doing in the garden... Mr Gerran wants his head examined.* V+-ING, OR V+O+-ING/PAST PART : NO IMPER ⇑ require

5 If you tell someone that they **want** to do a particular thing, you are advising them about what they should do. EG *You want to book a holiday as soon as the brochures come out... You want to be more careful: you may not be so lucky next time.* V+to-INF : NO IMPER = ought

6 If someone **is wanted**, the police are searching for them because they are thought to have committed a crime. EG *He is wanted for the crimes of murder and kidnapping... ...a 'wanted' poster of the suspected rapist.* V+O : USU PASS, NO IMPER

7 If you **want** someone, you have a great desire to have sex with them. EG *I want you so badly... He had never wanted anything the way he wanted Eileen.* V+O : NO IMPER

8 A **want** of something is a lack of it; a formal use. EG *They had to confess their complete want of foresight.* N SING WITH DET : N+of = absence

9 If you do something **for want of** something else, you do it because the other thing is not available or not possible. EG *For want of anything better to do, he continued to read... We'll call them rocks, for want of a better name.* PHR

10 If you are **in want of** something, you need it; an old-fashioned expression. EG *Many of the children there are in want of shoes.* PHR+NG : USED AS AN A = lack

11 If you **want for nothing**, you have everything you could possibly desire or need; a literary expression. PHR : VB INFLECTS

want out. If you **want out**, you no longer want to be involved in a plan, project, etc that you are part of; an informal expression. EG *I was afraid, and I told him I wanted out.* PHRASAL VB : V+ADV

wanting /wɒntɪŋ/. If you find something **wanting** or if it proves **wanting**, it is not of as high a standard as you think it should be. EG *He judged the nation and found it wanting... He is put to the test and he is quickly found wanting... The forms all in the end proved wanting.* ADJ CLASSIF : PRED = deficient, inadequate

wanton /wɒntən/. **1** A **wanton** action deliberately causes harm, damage, or waste without having any reason to. EG *...senseless and wanton cruelty... ...wanton aggression.* ▸ used of people. EG *...the wanton destroyers of the national heritage.* ◊ **wantonly.** EG *Someone wantonly knocked his crutch away and pushed him over.* ADJ CLASSIF : USU ATTRIB = malicious ▸ = wilful ◊ ADV = spitefully

2 Someone who is **wanton** is playful and slightly strange in behaviour; a literary use. EG *Under the hedge, the old man in some wanton mood had planted hyacinths.* ADJ QUALIT

3 A **wanton** woman is not shy or modest in her behaviour towards men and shows them if she is attracted towards them; an old-fashioned use, used showing disapproval. ADJ QUALIT ⇑ provocative

war /wɔː/, **wars, warring, warred. 1** A **war** is a period of fighting between countries or states when weapons are used and lots of people get killed. EG *They fought in the war against Britain... They did not want to lose another war... I did a lot of heavy work in the war years.* ▸ used as an uncount noun to refer to fighting in general. EG *Peace isn't just the absence of war... There are no winners in nuclear war... England and Germany used to be at war... The president was broadcasting within hours of the outbreak of war.* ● If a country **goes to war**, it starts fighting a war with another country. EG *Under the terms of the treaty, we are obliged to go to war.* N COUNT ⇑ conflict = battle ▸ N UNCOUNT ⇑ conflict ● PHR : VB INFLECTS, RECIP (with)

2 If two countries, states, or groups **war** with each other, they fight a war with each other. EG *India and Pakistan warred in 1965 over Kashmir.* ◊ **warring.** EG *Reason appeared powerless to reconcile the warring tribes.* V OR V+A (with) : RECIP ◊ ADJ CLASSIF : ATTRIB = battling

3 A **war** is also competition between groups of people or a campaign against a particular thing. EG *...a trade war... ...a newspaper circulation war in New York... The administration is planning a new war on drugs... She was at peace with her surroundings, not at war.* N COUNT/UNCOUNT ⇑ conflict

4 If you **have been in the wars**, you have been involved in a fight or some other situation where you have been hurt or injured; an informal expression. EG *You look as though you've been in the wars.* ● See also **civil war, cold war.** PHR : VB INFLECTS

warble /wɔːbəˡl/, **warbles, warbling, warbled. 1** If a bird **warbles**, it sings pleasantly with high notes and many variations. EG *Birds were warbling in the trees as they built their nests.* V OR V+O = chirrup

2 If a person, usually a woman, **warbles** a song, she sings it in a high-pitched voice, often with trills like a bird. EG *...a woman warbling arias.* V OR V+O

warbler /wɔːblə/, **warblers.** A **warbler** is a small bird which sings pleasantly. There are several kinds of warbler. N COUNT

ward /wɔːd/, **wards, warding, warded. 1** A **ward** is **1.1** a room or section of a hospital which has beds for several people who have similar illnesses or injuries or who need similar kinds of care. EG *The doctor insisted on my staying another five days in the ante-natal ward for observation... She had worked in nurseries and on hospital wards.* **1.2** a district, especially in a town or city, which forms part of a political constituency or local council; used in British English. EG *We had at our ward meetings a wide range of active Labour members... We shall analyse the votes ward by ward.* N COUNT ⇑ unit; N COUNT ⇑ area

2 A **ward** or a **ward of court** is a person, especially a child, who is officially put in the care of an older person or a court of law. A child may be made a ward for their protection or because their parents are dead. EG *She was made a ward-of-court and Christopher was forbidden to see her.* N COUNT

ward off. If you **ward off** something such as a danger or an illness, you do something to prevent it from affecting you or harming you. EG *He wears a copper bracelet to ward off rheumatism... He placed charms at the head of his bed to ward off evil spirits.* PHRASAL VB : V+O+ADV = keep away

-ward. The form **-wards** is also used. **-ward** is added to nouns that refer to places and directions, or to the adverbs 'in', 'out', 'up', or 'down', to form adverbs or adjectives that indicate the direction in which something is moving or facing, the direction in which someone is looking, etc. EG *The blast wave travelled outwards... He was gazing skyward... ...the homeward trail... ...the seaward edge of the platform.* SUFFIX : FORMS ADVS OR ADJ CLASSIFS

warden /wɔːdəⁿn/, **wardens. 1** A **warden** of a particular type is an official who makes sure that certain laws are being obeyed. EG *...traffic wardens... ...game wardens.* N COUNT : USU MOD+N

2 A **warden** in a building is a person who is in charge of the building and the people in it, for example in a youth hostel or an old people's home. N COUNT ⇑ caretaker

3 The **warden** of a prison is the person who is in charge of the prison. EG *They went directly to Acre jail where they were taken to the warden's office.* N COUNT = governor

warder /wɔːdə/, **warders**. A **warder** is a person who works in a prison in charge of prisoners. EG *The day-to-day security is the responsibility of the warder.* N COUNT ⇑ guard

wardress /wɔːdrɪ²s/, **wardresses**. A **wardress** is a woman who works in a prison in charge of prisoners. N COUNT ⇑ guard

wardrobe /wɔːdrəub/, **wardrobes**. 1 A **wardrobe** is a tall cupboard in which you can hang your clothes. EG *The red dress hung in her wardrobe.* N COUNT

2 Someone's **wardrobe** is the total collection of clothes that they have. EG *We throw away all our clothes each year and buy a whole new wardrobe... If she went away she'd have taken half her wardrobe.* N COUNT ⇑ clothing

3 The **wardrobe** in a theatre company is the part of the company which is concerned with making and storing the actors' and actresses' costumes. EG *He had always done wardrobe for school plays... She had to go directly to wardrobe for a fitting.* N UNCOUNT ⇑ department

wardrobe mistress, wardrobe mistresses. A **wardrobe mistress** is a woman who is in charge of the wardrobe in a theatre company. N COUNT ⇑ manageress

-wards. See **-ward**.

ware /wɛə/, **wares**. 1 **Ware** of a particular kind refers to objects of this kind, for example objects which are made of the same material such as glass or china, or which are made to be used for the same purpose. EG *...kitchen ware... ...glass ware.* N UNCOUNT : USU MOD+N

2 Someone's **wares** are the things that they sell, usually in the street or in a market. EG *The stallholders began to sell their wares at half-price.* N PLURAL = merchandise

warehouse /wɛəhaus/, **warehouses**. A **warehouse** is a large building where large quantities of raw materials or manufactured goods are stored until they are exported to other countries or distributed to shops to be sold. EG *The boxes are sealed with metal clamps and stacked in a warehouse.* N COUNT ⇑ store

warfare /wɔːfɛə/ is 1 the activity of fighting a war. EG *They are anxious to prevent this conflict from erupting into open warfare... ...tactical nuclear warfare.* N UNCOUNT 2 a violent struggle or conflict. EG *...gangs engaged in open warfare.* N UNCOUNT

warhead /wɔːhɛd/, **warheads**. A **warhead** is the front part of a bomb or missile where the explosives are carried. EG *...medium range missiles with nuclear warheads.* N COUNT

war horse, war horses; also spelled with a hyphen. 1 A **war horse** was a large horse used to carry a knight in battle in former times. N COUNT = charger

2 An old soldier or politician who is still active and aggressive might be referred to as an old **war horse**. N COUNT ⇑ veteran

warlike /wɔːlaɪk/. 1 **Warlike** equipment is equipment that is intended for use in a war. EG *...warlike equipment appropriate for hot climate operations.* ADJ CLASSIF : ATTRIB ⇑ military

2 People who are **warlike** seem aggressive and eager to start a war. EG *...a warlike, imperialistic leader... ...a warlike nation.* ADJ QUALIT = bloodthirsty

warm /wɔːm/, **warmer, warmest; warms, warming, warmed**. 1 Something that is **warm** has some heat but not enough to be hot. EG *There was no way of keeping the shop warm... ...a bowl of warm water... They won't grow until the warmer weather comes.* ◇ **warmly**. EG *The sun began shining more warmly upon the group on the terrace... The museum was very warmly heated.* ADJ QUALIT ≠ cold, hot ◇ ADV WITH VB = strongly

2 If you **warm** part of your body, you put it near something hot so that it stops feeling cold. EG *I warmed my hand on the radiator... Come and warm yourself in front of the fire... ...the strong sunshine, warming their bodies through all their clothes.* V+O ⇑ heat

3 Clothes and blankets that are **warm** are made of a material such as wool which protects you from the cold and reduces the amount of heat which is lost from your body. EG *...a pair of nice warm socks... Dress the children in their warmest clothing.* ◇ **warmly**. EG *I'll see that Chris dresses warmly.* ADJ QUALIT = thick, heavy ◇ ADV WITH VB

4 **Warm** colours, sounds, etc are pleasant and make you feel comfortable and relaxed. EG *...warm reds, browns and blacks... ...a record with a warm, mellow sound.* ADJ QUALIT = rich, mellow

5 A **warm** person is friendly and shows a lot of affection or enthusiasm in their behaviour. EG *She had a warm, generous heart... ...critics ranging from the warmest to the most hostile.* ▸ used of people's behaviour and actions. EG *He was given a warm welcome.* ◇ **warmly**. EG *Monty greeted his visitor warmly... He shook Tony warmly by the hand.* ADJ QUALIT = kindly ▸ = hospitable ◇ ADV WITH VB = heartily

6 If you say that someone is **warm** when they are trying to guess the answer to something or find the place where something is hidden, you mean that they are close to getting the answer or finding the place; an informal use. EG *You're not even warm. I'll give you a hint.* ADJ QUALIT : PRED = near

7 If you **warm** to a person or an idea, you become fonder of the person or more interested in the idea. EG *This makes you warm to Meadows... He had warmed to his theme of the joys of being a bachelor.* V+A *(to)*

8 to **warm the cockles of** your **heart**: see **cockle**.

warm up. 1 If you **warm** something **up** or if it **warms up**, it gets hotter. EG *Start warming up the soup now... Gradually the sun warms us up... We're not leaving here until the weather warms up.* PHRASAL VB : V-ERG+ADV

2 If you **warm up** for an event or activity such as a race, you prepare yourself physically or mentally for it by doing some gentle exercise or practising the activity in a less intense way. EG *Finish with the same stretches that you warmed up with... She is warming up, preparing for a full onslaught... I always spend ten minutes warming up before a race.* ● See also **warm-up**. PHRASAL VB : V+ADV = limber up

3 When a machine or engine **warms up**, it starts working or becomes ready for use by being switched on or started and then left for a short period of time. EG *I turned on the radio. It warmed up and a radio announcer's voice came out.* PHRASAL VB : V+ADV

warm-blooded. An animal such as a bird or mammal that is **warm-blooded** has a relatively high body temperature which remains constant and does not change according to the surrounding temperature. ADJ CLASSIF

warm front, warm fronts. A **warm front** is the weather condition that occurs when the front part of a mass of warm air pushes into a mass of cold air; a technical term in meteorology. N COUNT

warm-hearted. Someone who is **warm-hearted** is friendly and affectionate towards other people. ADJ QUALIT = kindly

warmonger /wɔːmʌŋgə/, **warmongers**. A **warmonger** is a person, for example a politician or a newspaper editor, who encourages people to expect war or who tries to get a war started. N COUNT

warmongering /wɔːmʌŋgə⁰rɪŋ/ is the activity of encouraging people to expect war or trying to get a war started. N UNCOUNT

warmth /wɔːmθ/. 1 **Warmth** is a moderate amount of heat that something has, for example enough heat to make you feel comfortable. EG *...the warmth of the sun... All we did was huddle together for warmth.* N UNCOUNT ≠ cold

2 The **warmth** of clothes or blankets is the ability that they have to protect you from the cold and reduce the amount of heat which is lost from your body. EG *...blankets which have little warmth.* N UNCOUNT

3 Someone who has **warmth** is friendly and enthusiastic in their behaviour towards other people. EG *...my uncle's warmth and affection... She basked in the warmth of public approval... 'How do you do, sir?' she said, without warmth.* N UNCOUNT = enthusiasm

warm-up, warm-ups. A **warm-up** is preparation which you do for a short time before an event or activity, for example gentle physical exercises before a sports event. EG *During the warm-up exercises, I was still shaking.* N COUNT : USU SING = limbering up

warn /wɔːn/, **warns, warning, warned**. 1 If you **warn** someone about something such as a possible danger or problem, you tell them about it so that they are aware of it. EG *The least I can do is warn them that there is a danger... I did warn you of possible failure... I warn you it's going to be expensive... 'Be careful with that,' he warned... I feel my duty is to warn people against these books.* V+O+REPORT-CL/A/QUOTE, OR V+O/QUOTE ⇑ inform = caution

2 If you **warn** someone to do something, you advise them to do it in order to avoid possible danger or punishment. EG *Warn them to be on the lookout... I warned him not to lose his temper with her... I'm warning you, if you do that again there'll be trouble.* V+O : USU+to-INF

warn off. If you **warn** someone **off** or **warn** them **away** from something, you tell them to go away or to stop doing something because of possible danger or punishment. EG *Intruders are warned off by the sound of her rattle... He crossed the line but he knew that he was being warned away... He realized that his doctor was warning him off drink.* PHRASAL VB : V+O+ADV/PREP

warning /wɔːnɪŋ/, **warnings**. 1 A **warning** is 1.1 something which is said or written to tell people of N COUNT

possible danger or problems. EG *A warning of the danger of smoking is printed on every pack of cigarettes... The hospital issued special warnings about drugs to be avoided... There had been fog warnings on the radio all day.* **1.2** advice which is given to someone not to do something. EG *Dad gave a final warning to them not to look directly at the sun.*
N COUNT = caution

1.3 advance notice of something that will happen, often something unpleasant or dangerous. EG *No advance warning of the President's departure was given... Mary left her husband without any warning.*
N COUNT/UNCOUNT ⇑ notification

2 Warning is used to describe actions or signs that give a warning or are intended to serve as a warning. EG *His wife made warning faces at him not to irritate their guest... Watch out for the warning signs of depression like insomnia.* ◊ **warningly**. EG *'It had better be good,' she said warningly.*
ADJ CLASSIF: ATTRIB
◊ ADV WITH VB

war of nerves. A **war of nerves** is a conflict in which the opposing sides use psychological means to weaken each other, for example by making each other frightened or telling lies about each other. EG *It was a kind of war of nerves with the publishers.*
N SING WITH DET = cold war

warp /wɔːp/, **warps, warping, warped**. **1** If something **warps** or **is warped**, it changes shape and becomes damaged by bending or curving; used especially of wooden things which have been affected by water or heat. EG *The cabinet doors began to warp soon after they were installed.* ◊ **warped**. EG *The wooden balconies were warped and weatherbeaten... ...a warped tree.*
V-ERG: IF V+O THEN USU PASS ⇑ bend
◊ ADJ QUALIT = twisted

2 A **warp** in something is a fault that it has, for example a bump or an irregular surface, which makes it lose its proper shape. EG *There's a warp in this record.*
N COUNT ⇑ defect

3 If something **warps** someone's character, it influences them and makes them abnormal or bad. EG *...a man whose whole character was warped by being bullied... A moralistic training warps the thinking process.* ◊ **warped**. EG *...his warped, perverted mind.*
V+O ⇑ alter = corrupt, distort
◊ ADJ QUALIT

4 A **warp** in someone's character is a fault or abnormality that they have. EG *The same warp in my nature made me do it again.*
N COUNT = kink, quirk

5 A **warp** in time or space is an imaginary break or sudden change in the normal experience of time or space. EG *There's a kind of time warp in his education.*
N COUNT ⇑ dislocation

6 The **warp** in a piece of weaving is the threads which are held along a loom while other threads are passed across them in the weaving of cloth. EG *...going over one and under the next thread of the warp.*
N SING: *the*+N

war-paint is **1** paint which some people use to decorate their bodies before fighting a battle. **2** a woman's make-up; a humorous use. EG *I went into the nearest public lavatory and put on my war-paint.*
N UNCOUNT
N UNCOUNT ⇑ cosmetics

warpath /wɔːpɑːθ/. If someone is **on the warpath**, they are angry and getting ready for a fight or conflict; an informal expression. EG *He scares me to death when he's on the warpath.*
PHR: USED AS AN A = in a rage

warrant /wɒrənt/, **warrants, warranting, warranted**. **1** If something **warrants** a particular action, it makes the action seem necessary or proper for the circumstances. EG *The situation is serious enough to warrant a special effort... The girl had suffered more than her behaviour had warranted... A reading below 100 should warrant further investigation.* ◊ **warranted**. EG *He earned far more warranted glory on the deck of HMS Victory.*
V+O ⇑ require = call for, merit
◊ ADJ QUALIT = deserved

2 A **warrant** is an official written order, usually signed by a judge or magistrate, which gives the police special permission to do something such as search someone's house, take away their property for investigation, or arrest them. EG *A warrant was issued for his arrest.* ● See also **death warrant**.
N COUNT

3 You say **I'll warrant** when you want to indicate that you are fairly sure of the truth of what you are saying; an old-fashioned expression. EG *Not many people know that, I'll warrant.*
PHR: USED AS ADV SEN

warrant officer, warrant officers. A **warrant officer** is a person in the army, the air force, or the marines, whose rank is above the rank of sergeant and below the rank of lieutenant.
N COUNT

warranty /wɒrənti¹/, **warranties**. A **warranty** is the same as a guarantee. EG *The car was still under warranty.*
N UNCOUNT/COUNT

warren /wɒrən/, **warrens**. A **warren** is **1** a group of holes in the ground which are connected by tunnels and which rabbits live in as a community. EG *...the rabbit warren.* **2** a building or an area of a city in which many people live in crowded conditions and there are many passages, corridors, or narrow streets. EG *Large dormitories had been divided into a warren of little cubicles... ...a small restaurant in the warrens of Old Delhi.*
N COUNT ⇑ habitation
N COUNT = maze

warrior /wɒrɪə/, **warriors**. A **warrior** is a fighting man or soldier, especially one in former times who was very brave and experienced in fighting. EG *...stories of ancient kings, warriors and great battles... ...the knights and warriors who valued glory and honour above life.*
N COUNT ⇑ fighter = combatant

warship /wɔːʃɪp/, **warships**. A **warship** is a ship with guns and other equipment needed for fighting in wars.
N COUNT

wart /wɔːt/, **warts**. **1** A **wart** is a small hard piece of skin which can grow and stick out on part of your body, usually your face or hands. EG *...a large woman with a wart on her nose.*
N COUNT ⇑ growth

2 If someone is described **warts and all**, the description is complete, containing all the details about them including the faults. EG *You have to reveal yourself, warts and all.*
PHR: USED AS AN A

warthog /wɔːthɒg/, **warthogs**. A **warthog** is a wild pig with two small tusks and several bumps on its face that look like warts. Warthogs live in Africa.
N COUNT

wartime /wɔːtaɪm/; also spelled with a hyphen. **Wartime** is a period of time when there is a war going on. EG *...the disruption of the environment in wartime.* ▸ used as an adjective. EG *...wartime memories... ...a novel about a wartime romance.*
N UNCOUNT
▸ N BEFORE N

war widow, war widows. A **war widow** is a woman whose husband was in the armed forces and was killed in a war.
N COUNT

wary /weəri¹/, **warier, wariest**. If you are **wary** about something, you are cautious because you are not sure about it, for example because it is a new experience or there may be dangers or problems. EG *People are understandably wary of the new government... The banks may be wary of allowing this practice... ...keeping a wary eye on the grazing goats... I'm very wary about believing these stories.* ◊ **warily**. EG *Cal eyed his sister warily.*
ADJ QUALIT = chary
◊ ADV WITH VB

was /wəʔz/ is the first and third person singular of the past tense of **be**.

wash /wɒʃ/, **washes, washing, washed**. **1** If you **wash** something, you clean it because it is dirty, using water and soap or detergent. EG *Wash brushes in warm water with detergent... ...the clatter of dishes being washed and put away... She washes and irons his clothes.* ▸ used as a noun. EG *Give it a good wash and we'll see... The dye comes out with the first wash... An average wash and rinse uses 6 gallons.*
V+O
▸ N COUNT: USU SING ⇑ cleaning

2 The **wash** is all the clothes, sheets, etc that are washed together on one occasion, for example once a week. EG *...the average weekly wash... She got up to take in the wash.* ● If a piece of clothing is **in the wash**, it is in the collection of clothes that are to be washed together soon. EG *Your red shirt is in the wash.*
N SING: *the*+N = laundry
● PHR: USED AS AN A

3 If you **wash** or if you **wash** part of your body, you clean part of your body using soap and water, especially your hands and face. EG *First wash your hands with soap and water... I went to the bathroom to wash my face... The children were encouraged to wash and dress themselves.* ▸ used as a noun. EG *He was having a wash in his bathroom.... There's a towel behind the bathroom door for you if you want a wash.*
V OR V+O
▸ N COUNT: USU SING = scrub

4 If a liquid or something carried by a liquid **washes** or **is washed** in a particular direction, it flows there gently; used especially of things such as sand or soil which are carried by rivers or by the sea. EG *The gentle surf washed over her ankles... Soil from the mountains washes down in the rivers... The body was washed ashore in Norway.*
V-ERG+A: IF V+O THEN USU PASS

5 The **wash** in a sea or river is water which has a lot of waves and froth, for example because a boat has just passed by. EG *...the wash of a passing boat.*
N SING: *the*+N = wake

6 A **wash** is a thin layer of something such as a liquid or a colour. EG *...covered by a wash of fine sand by the next tide... On his dark skin there was a wash of pallid green.*
N COUNT+*of*+N UNCOUNT

7 If you say that you **wash** your **hands of** something, you say that you refuse to be involved with it any longer and refuse to accept responsibility for any
PHR: VB INFLECTS ⇑ abandon

action that has already been taken. EG *...a building that the authorities had put up and then washed their hands of... He washed his hands of the Family Welfare aspects of the case... It was hypocritical of the committee to wash its hands of the deed afterwards.*

8 If you say that someone's actions or ideas **won't wash**, you mean that they cannot be accepted or believed; an informal expression. EG *I told him it wouldn't wash.* PHR : VB INFLECTS

9 If you say that something will **come out in the wash**, you mean that it will be found out in the end; an informal expression. PHR : VB INFLECTS

10 • See also **washing**. • to **wash** your **dirty linen in public**: see **linen**.

wash away. If rains, floods, etc **wash away** something such as a building, they destroy it and carry it away by the force of the water. EG *The dam collapsed, washing away twenty-five villages... The flood washed the old bridge away... The topsoil has been almost completely washed away.* PHRASAL VB : V+O+ADV ⇑ remove

wash down. **1** If you **wash down** some food, you drink something after you have eaten it or while you are eating it. EG *We had smoked salmon and grouse, washed down with claret and vintage port.* PHRASAL VB : V+O+ADV

2 If you **wash** an object **down**, you wash it all, from top to bottom. PHRASAL VB : V+O+ADV

wash out. **1** If you **wash** a stain or colour **out** of something, or if it **washes out** or **washes off**, you manage to remove the stain or colour by using water and sometimes soap or detergent. EG *Leave it for an hour, then wash out with detergent and warm water... I bathed my face and washed off the blood... It'll just wash off in the rain.* PHRASAL VB : V-ERG+ADV = clean

2 If you **wash out** a container, you wash the inside of it. EG *I'll go and wash the cups out.* PHRASAL VB : V+O+ADV

3 See also **washed-out**, **washout**.

wash up. **1** If you **wash up**, **1.1** you wash the plates, cups, knives, forks, etc which have been used in cooking and eating a meal. EG *He insisted on helping me wash up.* PHRASAL VB : V+ADV, OR V+O+ADV ⇑ clean **1.2** you clean part of your body with soap and water, especially your hands and face; used in American English. EG *I washed up as best I could in the adjacent bathroom.* PHRASAL VB : V+ADV = wash

2 If something **is washed up** on a piece of land, it is carried by a river or sea and left there. EG *Old bones are often washed up on the seashore... His body was washed up under the bridge at Dakao.* PHRASAL VB : V+O+ADV, USU PASS +A

3 See also **washed-up**, **washing-up**.

washable /wɒʃəbəºl/. Clothes or materials that are **washable** can be washed in water without being damaged and do not need to be dry-cleaned. EG *Acrylic blankets and shawls are both warm and washable.* ADJ CLASSIF

washbasin /wɒʃbeɪsəºn/, **washbasins**; also spelled with a hyphen. A **washbasin** is a large basin for washing your hands and face. Washbasins are usually fixed to a wall and have taps for hot and cold water. N COUNT = sink

washbowl /wɒʃbəʊl/, **washbowls**. A **washbowl** is a washbasin; used especially in American English. N COUNT = sink

washcloth /wɒʃklɒθ/, **washcloths**. A **washcloth** is a flannel; used in American English. EG *I put my face against the damp washcloth.* N COUNT ⇑ cloth

washday /wɒʃdeɪ/, **washdays**. A **washday** is a day on which you wash your clothes, often the same day every week. N COUNT

washed-out; also spelled without a hyphen. **1** Something that is **washed-out** is pale in colour and dull, not shining. EG *...eyes of washed-out grey... ...a canopy of washed-out blue.* ADJ QUALIT = lifeless, dreary

2 If someone looks **washed-out**, they look very tired and lacking in energy. EG *He had hordes of children and a washed-out wife.* ADJ QUALIT = exhausted

washed up; also spelled with a hyphen. Someone who is **washed up** is at the end of their career and no longer of any use; an informal expression used especially in American English. EG *I was not going to be all washed up, an ex-sportsman with nothing to do at 30.* ADJ QUALIT ⇑ finished = burnt out

washer /wɒʃə/, **washers**. A **washer** is **1** a thin flat ring of metal, plastic or some other substance, which is placed over a bolt before the nut is screwed on or between two pipes when they are being screwed onto each other, in order to make a tighter connection. EG *Unscrew the nut, remove and replace the washer and reassemble the tap... Check whether it needs a new tap washer.* N COUNT = gasket, seal **2** a washing machine; an informal use. EG *...an automatic washer and drier.* N COUNT **3** a person who washes things, especially as a paid job. N COUNT

washing /wɒʃɪŋ/ is a collection of clothes, sheets, etc which need to be washed or are in the process of being washed or dried. EG *Her husband comes home bringing his washing with him... Do you have a very large amount of washing each week?... There was nowhere to hang washing.* N UNCOUNT = laundry

washing machine, washing machines; also spelled with a hyphen. A **washing machine** is a machine which you can wash clothes in. EG *...a fully automatic washing machine.* N COUNT

washing powder, washing powders. **Washing powder** is powdered detergent that you use to wash clothes, sheets, etc in a washing machine or by hand. N MASS

washing soda is a chemical in the form of crystals which are added to water and used to clean things, especially very dirty things such as sinks or drains in a house. N UNCOUNT

washing-up. If you do the **washing-up**, you wash the plates, cups, knives, forks, etc which have been used in cooking and eating a meal. EG *We share the cooking and the washing-up... ...a washing-up bowl.* N UNCOUNT : ⇑ cleaning ▸ used to refer to the plates, cups, knives, forks, etc which you wash. EG *There's stacks of washing-up.* ▸ ⇑ dishes

washing-up liquid, washing-up liquids. **Washing-up liquid** is a thick soapy liquid which you add to hot water to clean dirty dishes after a meal, and which is usually sold in a plastic bottle from which you can squeeze small amounts. N MASS ⇑ detergent

washout /wɒʃaʊt/, **washouts**. If an event, project, etc is a **washout**, it is a total failure; an informal word. EG *Thanks to you, today's been an appalling washout.* N COUNT : USU USED AS C = flop, disaster

washroom /wɒʃru⁴m/, **washrooms**. A **washroom** is a room with toilets and washing facilities, situated in a large building such as an office block or a hostel. N COUNT = cloakroom, lavatory

washstand /wɒʃstænd/, **washstands**. A **washstand** is a piece of furniture designed to hold a washbasin and facilities for washing your face and hands, especially one that was kept in bedrooms in former times. EG *...a washstand with a jug and basin on it.* N COUNT

wasn't /wɒzəºnt/ is the usual contracted form of 'was not'. It is also used in tag questions: see **be**. EG *I wasn't ready for it... He was first, wasn't he?*

wasp /wɒsp/, **wasps**. A **wasp** is an insect with wings and yellow and black stripes across its body, which can sting like a bee but does not produce honey. EG *There was a wasp buzzing about her ear.* N COUNT

waspish /wɒspɪʃ/. Someone who is **waspish** speaks or behaves in a sharp and bad-tempered way. EG *Macleod was being very waspish.* ADJ QUALIT = petulant ◊ **waspishness**. EG *Despite his reputation for waspishness, he was positively angelic this time.* ◊ N UNCOUNT = irritability

wastage /weɪstɪdʒ/. **1 Wastage** of something is a waste of it. EG *The Government is to blame for this very serious wastage of talent among the young.* N UNCOUNT : USU +SUPP ⇑ loss ▸ used to refer to the amount of something which is wasted. EG *I could not afford either the wastage of materials or the loss of time... ...the tremendous wastage from inefficient energy use.* ▸ N UNCOUNT = loss

2 Wastage also refers to a number of people who leave a job or an educational establishment or who are rejected for a job or an educational course. EG *They take the most able students and usually lose a few of them by wastage... There was a large wastage rate: 60 per cent of the candidates failed.* N UNCOUNT ⇑ elimination = failure

waste /weɪst/, **wastes, wasting, wasted**. **1** If you **waste** something such as time, money, or energy, you use too much of it on something that is not important, valuable, or likely to be successful. EG *You're wasting your time... There was no need to waste any energy thinking about it... ...fear of wasting money on a new idea.* V+O ⇑ misuse = squander

2 If you **waste** an opportunity for something, you do not take advantage of it when it is available. V+O ⇑ miss

3 If you say that something **is wasted** on someone, you mean that it is too good, clever, or sophisticated for them. EG *Fine clothes are wasted on her–she's a tomboy... Your jokes are wasted on him.* V+O+A *(on)* : USU PASS

4 If you say that an action or activity is a **waste** of something such as time, money, or energy, you mean that it involves using too much of it and it is not important, valuable, or likely to be successful. EG *It's probably a waste of time... It's a bit of a waste of* N SING : a+N+*of*

money hiring skis... It seemed a waste of money to buy anything but the best... A jury would be a waste of time.

5 Waste is **5.1** the use of too much money or other type of resources on things that do not need it. EG *They thought that cutting out waste was going to solve all their problems... A committee was set up to avoid future waste of public money... The local paper declared such waste inexcusable.* **5.2** material which has been used and is no longer wanted, for example because the valuable or useful part of it has been taken out. EG *...the problem of the safe disposal of radioactive waste from the power stations... The river was thick with industrial waste... A new textile factory was now pumping its waste upstream.* ▸ used as an adjective. EG *...waste material from the oil industry... ...waste products... ...a scrap of waste paper.*

N UNCOUNT ⇑ inefficiency = abuse, misuse

N UNCOUNT ⇑ by-product = detritus

▸ ADJ CLASSIF : ATTRIB ⇑ unwanted

6 Waste land is land, especially near a city, which is not used or looked after by anyone, and so is covered by wild plants, rubbish, etc. EG *The car was found abandoned on waste ground near Leeds... Avoid lonely places such as commons, churchyards, and waste land.* ▸ used as a noun to refer to this kind of land. EG *Much of the farm was all waste and ruin then.*

ADJ CLASSIF : USU ATTRIB = derelict

▸ N UNCOUNT

7 Wastes are a large area of land, for example a desert, in which there are very few people, plants, or animals. EG *...the endless wastes of the Simpson Desert... ...the polar wastes.*

N PLURAL

8 The word **waste** is also used in the following expressions. **8.1** If something **goes to waste**, it remains unused, goes bad, or is thrown away. EG *It's a shame to let that food go to waste–I'll finish it off!* **8.2** If you **waste no time** in doing something, you are quick and efficient and take the opportunity to do it at once. EG *The new Swedish Company wasted no time in going to India.* **8.3** If you **are wasting** your **breath**, you are talking to someone without having any effect or influence on them; an informal expression. EG *I can see that I'm wasting my breath.* **8.4** If a group of people such as an army **lays** something **waste** or **lays waste to** it, it completely destroys it; a literary expression. EG *They did not expect the invaders to lay waste to their civilization... The nation was in mourning for a whole generation laid waste.* **8.5 Waste not, want not** is a saying which means that if you do not use too much of something now you will have some left later when you need it.

PHR : VB INFLECTS

PHR : VB INFLECTS

PHR : AUX INFLECTS

PHR : VB INFLECTS = annihilate

PHR

9 See also **wasted**.

waste away. If someone **wastes away**, they become extremely thin or weak because they are ill or worried and they are not eating properly. EG *I don't want you to waste away.*

PHRASAL VB : V+ADV

wastebasket /weɪstbɑːskɪt/, **wastebaskets**. A **wastebasket** is the same as a wastepaper basket; used especially in American English. EG *Tear it up and throw it in the wastebasket.*

N COUNT ⇑ bin

wasted /weɪstɪ²d/. **1** A **wasted** action is one that is unnecessary. EG *It was a wasted journey.*

ADJ CLASSIF

2 Someone who is **wasted** is very tired and weak, often because of an illness. EG *You look absolutely wasted.*

ADJ QUALIT = emaciated

wasteful /weɪstfʊl/. Action that is **wasteful** causes waste, especially because of carelessness. EG *...the wasteful use of scarce resources... ...progress towards being less wasteful in energy.* ◇ **wastefully**. EG *We must not spend money wastefully.*

ADJ QUALIT = wanton

◇ ADV WITH VB = wantonly

wasteland /weɪstlænd/, **wastelands**. A **wasteland** is **1** land which is of no use, for example because it is infertile or because it has been misused by people. EG *The highways cross endless wastelands of charred stumps... ...vast tracks of wasteland... ...the wastelands of old industry.* **2** a physical or mental situation in which there is very little hope of improvement or development; a literary use. EG *They try to erect an edifice of philosophy on a wasteland of sterile dogma... ...the spiritual wasteland... ...trapped in this wasteland inhabited by the sick, the drugged, and their indifferent keepers.*

N COUNT/UNCOUNT

N COUNT : USU+SUPP

wastepaper basket, wastepaper baskets. A **wastepaper basket** or **wastepaper bin** is a container for rubbish, especially for waste paper, which is usually placed on the floor in the corner of a room or next to a desk. EG *He crumpled the note and tossed it into the wastepaper basket.*

N COUNT = wastebasket

waster /weɪstə/, **wasters**. If you refer to someone as a **waster**, you mean that they are lazy and spend their time and money on foolish things; an informal word.

N COUNT ⇑ person

wasting /weɪstɪŋ/. A **wasting** disease is one which makes you gradually become thinner and weaker.

ADJ CLASSIF : ATTRIB

watch /wɒtʃ/, **watches, watching, watched**. **1** A **watch** is a small clock which you wear on a strap on your wrist or on a chain. EG *He looked at his watch... My watch has stopped.*

N COUNT

2 If you **watch** something, you look at it, usually for a period of time, and pay attention to what is happening. EG *A policeman stood watching... I leant over the side to watch the fish... I watched the sun rise... I used to sit and watch the boats moving down the river... Watch me, Grandma.*

V OR V+O = observe

3 If you **watch** a sports event or something on television, you spend time looking at it, especially when you see it from the beginning to the end. EG *I'm just watching television... She went home to watch 'Alien'... I think I'll watch the news for a while... When did you last watch a football match?*

V+O

4 If you **watch** people, especially children or animals, you are responsible for them, and make sure that they do not need anything and are not in danger. EG *Let me watch the baby for a few hours while you go out.*

V+O = look after

5 If you **watch** someone, you follow them secretly or spy on them, so that you know everything they do and everyone they meet. EG *Liebermann's going to be watched from now on... ...a feeling of being watched... A neighbour had seen someone watching the house the night before.*

V+O

6 If you **watch** a situation or event, you pay attention to it or you are aware of it. EG *The federation never ceases to watch events and fight injustices... She sits back and just watches a situation develop... Many companies have watched helplessly as their stock prices fell.*

V+O, OR V+A

7 If you **keep watch** on events or a situation, you pay attention to what is happening, so that you can take action at the right moment. EG *The closest watch should be kept on any signs of industrial unrest.*

PHR : VB INFLECTS

8 If you are **on the watch** for something, you are expecting it to happen and you therefore pay attention to events so that you will be prepared when it does happen. EG *Bureaucrats will be on the watch, charting your every move.*

PHR : USED AS AN A = on the lookout

9 If someone **keeps watch** or **is on watch**, they look around all the time, usually when other people are asleep, so that they can warn the others of danger or an attack. EG *A woman kept watch at the gate... One should have been asleep and one on watch.*

PHR : VB INFLECTS

10 A **watch** also consists of the guards or soldiers who have the job of carefully looking around so that they can warn others of danger or an attack from the enemy. EG *The day watch had been on duty for a couple of hours... They change watches at eleven.*

N COUNT : IF SING, VB CAN BE SING OR PL

11 If someone is **under watch**, they are being guarded or observed all the time. EG *He was secure under close and continuous watch.*

PHR : USED AS AN A

12 If you **watch** someone or something, you take care that they do not get out of control or do something unpleasant; sometimes used as a warning. EG *You ought to watch Barbara... Unless I watch myself closely my emotions will be overflowing... I'm watching my weight... Hey–watch where you're going!*

V+O = keep an eye on

13 You say **'watch it'** in order to warn someone to be careful. EG *'Do it yourself'–'Watch it.'... You've got to watch it with these people–they're crooks.*

PHR : ONLY IMPER/INF

14 If you tell someone to **watch** their **step**, you are warning them to be careful what they say and do. EG *I'm cleverer than you are, so watch your step.*

PHR : VB INFLECTS

15 You say to someone **'you watch'** when you are predicting that something will happen. EG *There's going to be an enormous row about this, you watch.*

PHR : ONLY IMPER = you wait

watch for. If you **watch for** something which is likely to happen in the future, or you **watch out for** it, you are alert and careful about it, either because you do not want to miss it or because it will be unpleasant or harmful and you need to avoid it. EG *You have to watch for the union problem... During the long car journey Mom had told me to watch out for the white lions near East London... When you buy a quilt, watch out for inferior or inadequate fillings.*

PHRASAL VB : V+PREP, OR V+ADV+PREP,

watch out. If you **watch out**, you are very careful

PHRASAL VB : V+

because something unpleasant might happen to you. *EG If you don't watch out, he might stick a knife into you... You behave yourself or you'd better watch out.* ADV, ONLY INF, ALSO IMPER = look out

watch over. If you **watch over** someone or something, you care for them, especially because it is your responsibility or because it interests you. *EG The wives took turns to watch over the children... God watches over us.* PHRASAL VB : V+PREP, HAS PASS

watchband /wɒtʃbænd/, **watchbands**. A **watchband** is the same as a watchstrap; used in American English. N COUNT

watch-chain, watch-chains; also spelled without a hyphen. A **watch-chain** is a small chain with a watch attached to it at one end, which can be fastened to a person's jacket at the other end. N COUNT

watchdog /wɒtʃdɒg/, **watchdogs**. A **watchdog** is a person or committee whose job is to make sure that companies do not act illegally or irresponsibly. *EG They established the Atomic Energy Commission to act as a watchdog... ...a permanent watchdog service.* N COUNT

watcher /wɒtʃə/, **watchers**. A **watcher** is a person who looks at something, usually for a period of time, and who pays attention to what is happening. *EG Many of them were as baffled by the proceedings as the watchers in the public gallery.* N COUNT = observer

-watcher, -watchers. **-watcher** combines with nouns to form other nouns which refer to people who are interested in a group of people or animals, and who study them closely. *EG Even the most expert Kremlin-watchers on the Western side were taken by surprise... There are over 2 million serious bird-watchers in the United States.* COMB : FORMS N COUNTS

watchful /wɒtʃful/. Someone who is **watchful** is careful to notice everything that is happening. *EG It is important that health organizations and governments remain watchful... ...an air of watchful intelligence.* ▸ often used of a person's eyes. *EG He spent his days under the watchful eyes of several old grandmothers.* ◇ **watchfully**. *EG Conrad was standing watchfully by the door.* ◇ **watchfulness**. *EG The need for watchfulness in this area is immense.* ADJ QUALIT = alert, vigilant ◇ ADV WITH VB ◇ N UNCOUNT

-watching combines with nouns to form other nouns which refer to the activity of looking at a group of people or animals and studying them because they interest you. *EG My main interest is bird-watching.* COMB : FORMS N UNCOUNTS

watchman /wɒtʃməⁿ/, **watchmen**. A **watchman** is a person whose job is to guard a building, a ship, or property. ● See also **nightwatchman**. N COUNT

watchstrap /wɒtʃstræp/, **watchstraps**. A **watchstrap** is a piece of leather or plastic, or a metal chain, which is attached to a watch so that you can wear it round your wrist. N COUNT = watchband

watchtower /wɒtʃtauə/, **watchtowers**; also spelled with a hyphen. A **watchtower** is a high building where you have a good view around a place which you want to guard. From the watchtower you can see anyone coming towards it when they are still a long way away. N COUNT

watchword /wɒtʃwɜːd/, **watchwords**. A **watchword** is a word or phrase that sums up the way that a particular group of people should think or behave. *EG Discretion is the watchword... Today the watchword is 'Learn through playing'.* N COUNT = slogan, catch-phrase

water /wɔːtə/, **waters, watering, watered**. **1 Water** is **1.1** a clear, thin liquid that all animals and people need to drink in order to live, and which has no colour or taste when it is pure. It falls from clouds as rain and enters rivers and seas. *EG ...a drink of water... ...a bowl of hot water... ...the sound of the water pouring down on the metal roof.* ● See also **freshwater**. N UNCOUNT **1.2** a supply of clean water which flows through pipes to houses and factories where it comes out of taps. *EG You don't have to turn the water off at the mains... ...the Welsh Water Authority.* N SING : the+N, ALSO IN NAMES **1.3** a large amount or area of water, for example a lake or the sea. *EG The children played at the water's edge... ...men, money and supplies on this side of the water... I walked the last six miles in water up to my thighs... ...the black waters of the Thames.* N COUNT/UNCOUNT **1.4** the surface of an area of water. *EG They swim below water... A snorkel helps you to breathe under water... They held his head under the water.* N UNCOUNT

2 A country's **waters** consist of the area of sea which is near to it and which is regarded as belonging to that country. *EG The ship was in European waters... ...the coastal waters of neutral powers... ...violating territorial waters.* N PLURAL+SUPP

3 Water which comes out of the ground as a spring and which contains minerals is sometimes referred to as the **waters**. People drink it because they think it will improve their health. *EG He came to take the waters... He had lost three pounds, drinking the waters... We go to Cheltenham for the waters.* N PLURAL : the+N

4 You sometimes use **waters** to refer to a situation which is very complex or difficult. *EG We will succeed, however rough the economic waters... He felt he was now in deep and uncharted waters.* N PLURAL : ADJ+N

5 If you **water** plants, you pour water over them in order to help them to grow. *EG I've been watering the garden.* V+O

6 If you **water** a horse or other animal, you provide water for it to drink. *EG ...a good place for watering cattle.* V+O

7 If your eyes **water**, you have tears in them because they are hurting and not because you are sad. *EG The onions made his eyes water... She kept fanning the smoke away from her watering eyes.* V

8 If your mouth **waters**, it fills with water, usually because you can smell or see some appetizing food. *EG This should make your mouth water.* V

9 Just before a woman gives birth to a baby her **waters break**, which means that the liquid which surrounds the baby in the womb passes out of her body, showing that the baby is ready to be born. *EG We'd better get her to hospital before her waters break.* PHR : VB INFLECTS

10 When you **make** or **pass water**, you urinate. *EG Do you have difficulty passing water?* PHR : VB INFLECTS = pee

11 The word **water** is also used in the following expressions. **11.1 Water on the brain** and **water on the knee** are medical conditions which cause liquid to collect on the brain or knee. PHR : USED AS S/O **11.2** If you say that an event or incident is **water under the bridge**, you mean that it has happened and cannot now be changed, so there is no point in worrying about it any more. PHR : USED AS C **11.3** If you **pour** or **throw cold water on** an idea or suggestion, you show that you have a low opinion of it. PHR : VB INFLECTS **11.4** If you are **in deep water**, you are in a difficult situation which you cannot get out of. PHR : USED AS AN A **11.5** If you refer to something **of the first water**, you mean that it is one of the best examples of that thing. *EG She's a fool of the first water.* PHR AFTER N **11.6** If you **keep** your **head above water**, you avoid getting into difficulties, especially in business. PHR : VB INFLECTS **11.7** If a theory or argument **holds water**, it appears reasonable and agrees with the facts. *EG The theory no longer holds water.* PHR : VB INFLECTS **11.8** If you get **into hot water**, you get into trouble; an informal expression. *EG We don't want to get them into hot water... She's likely to land in hot water unless restrained by wiser counsel.* PHR : USED AS AN A **11.9** If you spend money **like water**, you spend a great amount of it, without worrying if you can afford it or not. PHR : USED AS AN A **11.10** If you **pour oil on troubled waters**, you end a quarrel by talking to people and calming them down. PHR : VB INFLECTS **11.11** If you say **still waters run deep** or sometimes just **still waters**, you mean that a person who does not say much may actually have strong feelings or good ideas. PHR **11.12** If you **test the water** or **test the waters**, you try to find out what views and opinions people have, before you ask them something or try to sell something to them. PHR : VB INFLECTS

12 ● **water off a duck's back**: see **duck**. ● **like a duck to water**: see **duck**. ● **fish out of water**: see **fish**.

water down. **1** If you **water down** food or drink, you add water to it to make it weaker. PHRASAL VB : V+O+ADV

2 If something, especially a speech or written statement, **is watered down**, it is made much weaker and less forceful or controversial. *EG The whole article had been watered down.* ◇ **watered-down**. *EG He eventually sent a watered-down version of the letter... The Equal Pay Act is so watered down as to be useless.* PHRASAL VB : V+O+ADV, USU PASS = dilute ◇ ADJ QUALIT = diluted

waterbed /wɔːtəbɛd/, **waterbeds**. A **waterbed** is a waterproof mattress filled with water. N COUNT ⇑ bed

water bird, water birds; also spelled as one word. A **water bird** is a bird that swims or wades in water, especially freshwater. There are many kinds of water bird. N COUNT

water biscuit, water biscuits. A **water biscuit** is a thin, crisp biscuit which is not sweet and which is usually eaten with butter or cheese. N COUNT = cracker

water blister, water blisters. A **water blister** is a blister on a person's skin which contains a clear liquid and no blood. N COUNT

water-borne; also spelled as one word. Something that is **water-borne** is carried or passed on by water. EG *...water-borne diseases.* ADJ CLASSIF

water bottle, water bottles; also spelled with a hyphen. A **water bottle** is 1 a small container for carrying water to drink on a long journey. N COUNT 2 the same as a hot water bottle. N COUNT

water buffalo, water buffaloes. **Water buffalo** can also be used as the plural form. A **water buffalo** is an animal from Asia which is like a large black cow and has long horns which curve backwards. They are often kept to pull ploughs or for their milk. N COUNT

water butt, water butts; also spelled with a hyphen. A **water butt** is a large barrel for collecting rain as it flows off the roof. N COUNT

water cannon, water cannons. **Water cannon** can also be used as the plural form. A **water cannon** is a large machine which shoots out a powerful jet of water. It is used to break up crowds of people. N COUNT ↑ weapon

water chestnut, water chestnuts. A **water chestnut** is the thick bottom part of the stem of a plant which grows in China. Water chestnuts have a mild taste and are used in Chinese cooking. N COUNT

water-closet, water-closets. A **water-closet** is a toilet; an old-fashioned expression. N COUNT = lavatory

watercolour /wɒtəkʌlə/, **watercolours**; also spelled **watercolor** in American English. 1 **Watercolours** are coloured paints, used for painting pictures, which you put on the paper with a wet brush or dissolve in water first. N PLURAL

2 A **watercolour** is a picture which has been painted with watercolours. EG *...a Turner watercolour containing gondolas, canals, and St Mark's Cathdral... ...an exhibition of watercolours.* N COUNT

watercourse /wɔ:təkɔ:s/, **watercourses**. A **watercourse** is the channel that a river or stream flows along; often used when there is little water in it. N COUNT = bed

watercress /wɔ:təkrɛs/ is a small plant with white flowers which grows in streams and pools. Its leaves taste hot and are eaten raw in salads or with meat or fish as a garnish. N UNCOUNT

waterfall /wɔ:təfɔ:l/, **waterfalls**. A **waterfall** is water that flows over the edge of a steep cliff in hills or mountains, and falls to the ground below. EG *The creek came pouring down in a waterfall off the hill.* N COUNT

waterfowl /wɔ:təfaʊl/. **Waterfowl** is both the singular and the plural form. **Waterfowl** are birds that swim in water, especially ducks, geese, and swans. N COUNT

waterfront /wɔ:təfrʌnt/, **waterfronts**. A **waterfront** is a street or piece of land which is next to an area of water, for example a harbour or the sea. EG *...a warehouse on the waterfront... ...a waterfront saloon.* N COUNT : USU SING = waterside

waterhole /wɔ:təhəʊl/, **waterholes**; also spelled with a hyphen. A **waterhole** is a pond or pool in a desert or other dry area where animals can find water to drink. EG *Even the forest's waterholes dried up... We camped that evening by a water-hole.* N COUNT

water-ice, water-ices. A **water-ice** is a type of ice cream made of frozen fruit juice, sugar and water. N MASS ↑ dessert = sorbet

watering can, watering cans; also spelled with a hyphen. A **watering can** is a container shaped like a bucket with a long spout on one side and a handle on the other side, which you use to water plants. N COUNT

watering hole, watering holes. A **watering hole** is a place, especially a café or pub, where people go to drink and meet; often used humorously. EG *The restaurant was once a cosmopolitan watering hole for actors and writers.* N COUNT

water jump, water jumps. A **water jump** is a fence with a pool of water on the far side of it, which people or horses jump over as part of a race or competition. N COUNT

waterless /wɔ:təlɪ[2]s/. A **waterless** area of land has no water for people or animals to drink. EG *The smaller islands are largely waterless.* ADJ CLASSIF ↑ arid = dry

waterlily /wɔ:təlɪli[1]/, **waterlilies**; also spelled with a hyphen. A **waterlily** is a plant with large flat leaves and colourful flowers which floats on the surface of lakes and rivers. N COUNT

waterline /wɔ:təlaɪn/, **waterlines**. 1 The **waterline** is the highest level on the bank which the water in a river normally reaches. N SING : *the*+N = water mark

2 A ship's **waterline** is a line painted on the side of the ship which shows how high the water reaches when the ship is at sea. N COUNT : USU SING

waterlogged /wɔ:təlɒgd/. 1 An area of land that is **waterlogged** is so wet that the soil cannot contain any more water, so that a layer of water remains on the surface of the ground. EG *The pitch was completely waterlogged.* ADJ QUALIT = saturated

2 A **waterlogged** boat or other floating object is so full of water that it may soon sink. ADJ QUALIT

water main, water mains. A **water main** is a very large underground pipe used for supplying water to houses and factories. EG *A water main had broken and water was gushing.* N COUNT

watermark /wɔ:təmɑ:k/, **watermarks**. A **watermark** is 1 a design which is put onto paper by the people who make it, and which you can only see if you hold the paper up to the light. Bank-notes often have a watermark. N COUNT ↑ pattern 2 a mark which shows the highest or the lowest level reached by a river or the sea. EG *The tide is almost at the high watermark.* N COUNT

water-meadow, water-meadows; also spelled without a hyphen. A **water-meadow** is a wet field of grass near a river. It is often flooded and is usually very fertile. EG *Cowslips were waving in the water meadows.* N COUNT

watermelon /wɔ:təmɛlən/, **watermelons**; also spelled with a hyphen. A **watermelon** is a large round fruit which has a green skin on the outside and is pink and juicy inside with a lot of black seeds. N COUNT ↑ melon

watermill /wɔ:təmɪl/, **watermills**; also spelled with a hyphen. A **watermill** is a mill with a large wheel which is turned by moving water, for example a stream. N COUNT

water pistol, water pistols; also spelled with a hyphen. A **water pistol** is a small toy gun which shoots out water. N COUNT

water-polo; also spelled without a hyphen. **Water-polo** is a game played in a swimming pool in which two teams of swimmers try to score goals with a ball. N UNCOUNT ↑ sport

water power is the power obtained from flowing water which is used to drive machines or to make electricity. N UNCOUNT

waterproof /wɔ:təpru:f/, **waterproofs, waterproofing, waterproofed**. 1 Something which is **waterproof** does not let water pass through it. EG *...a pair of waterproof trousers.* ADJ CLASSIF ↑ impermeable

2 A **waterproof** is a coat or other piece of clothing which does not let water in. EG *Remember to put your waterproofs on.* N COUNT : USU PL

3 If you **waterproof** something, you make it waterproof. EG *...a system for waterproofing damp walls.* V+O ↑ seal

water rat, water rats; also spelled with a hyphen. A **water rat** is the same as a water vole. N COUNT ↑ rodent

water rate, water rates. A **water rate** is the charge made for the use of water from the public water supply; used in British English. N COUNT : SING=PL

water-resistant. Something that is **water-resistant** does not allow water to pass through easily, but does not keep it out completely. EG *...a water-resistant lotion.* ADJ QUALIT ↑ repellent

watershed /wɔ:təʃɛd/, **watersheds**. A **watershed** is 1 an event or period which is important because it marks the beginning of a new way of life, a new stage in a person's career, etc. EG *The Vietnam war was one of the great watersheds of modern history... 1968 marked a watershed for him... Our own marriage was however at a watershed.* N SING WITH DET = turning point 2 an area of high ground which divides two or more river systems, so that all streams on one side flow into one river and those on the other side flow into a different river; a technical use. N COUNT

waterside /wɔ:təsaɪd/. The **waterside** is a street or shore beside an area of water such as a river or lake. EG *I drove down to the waterside... ...waterside footpaths.* N SING : *the*+N = waterfront

water-ski, water-skis, water-skiing, water-skied; also spelled without a hyphen. If you **water-ski**, you ski on water while you are pulled along by a boat. EG *I'd prefer to go water-skiing.* V ◇ **water-skiing**. EG *...excellent facilities for sailing, water-skiing, and skin-diving.* ◇ N UNCOUNT ↑ sport

water softener, water softeners; also spelled with a hyphen. A **water softener** is a device or substance which you can add to water in order to remove minerals, for example calcium, so that soap mixes more easily and makes a lather. N COUNT

water-soluble. Something that is **water-soluble** is able to dissolve in water. EG *Felt pen ink is water-soluble.* ADJ CLASSIF

waterspout /wɔːtəspaut/, **waterspouts**. A **waterspout** is a whirlwind over the sea, which causes a tall column of water to be formed. N COUNT

water supply, water supplies. The **water supply** in an area is the water which is collected and passed through pipes to buildings for people to use. EG *...the purification of the water supply.* N COUNT : USU SING

water table, water tables. The **water table** is the level below the surface of the ground where water can be found. EG *It was necessary to bore deep wells through to the water table.* N COUNT : the+N

watertight /wɔːtətaɪt/. 1 Something that is **watertight** does not allow water to pass through it, for example because it is so tightly sealed. EG *...watertight doors... The reptiles have watertight skins and eggs.* ADJ CLASSIF = waterproof

2 A **watertight** agreement, case, argument, etc is one that has been so carefully put together that nobody should be able to find a fault in it. EG *Our case is not all that watertight... It sounded a good watertight story.* ADJ CLASSIF ⇑ perfect

water tower, water towers; also spelled with a hyphen. A **water tower** is a large tank of water which is placed on a high metal structure so that water can be supplied at a steady pressure to surrounding buildings. N COUNT

water vole, water voles; also spelled with a hyphen. A **water vole** is a small rat-like animal that can swim. Water voles live in holes in the banks of rivers. N COUNT ⇑ rodent = water rat

waterway /wɔːtəweɪ/, **waterways**. A **waterway** is a canal, river, or narrow channel of sea which ships or boats can sail along. EG *...the inland waterway system.* N COUNT ⇑ route

waterwheel /wɔːtəwiːl/, **waterwheels**. A **waterwheel** is a large wheel which is turned by water flowing through it. Water wheels are used to provide power to drive machinery. N COUNT

water-wings are air-filled rings which you can put round your arms in order to help you to learn to swim. N PLURAL = armbands

waterworks /wɔːtəwɜːks/. In paragraph 1 **waterworks** is both the singular and the plural form. 1 A **waterworks** is the factory, system of pipes, etc where a public supply of water is stored, cleaned, and distributed from. EG *They've made forty redundant down at the waterworks.* N COUNT

2 Your **waterworks** are the parts inside your body, for example your bladder, which remove urine from your body; an informal use, sometimes used by doctors when talking to patients. EG *How are the waterworks?* N PLURAL = urinary system

3 If someone **turns on the waterworks**, they start crying, especially in order to get attention; an informal expression, especially used by adults to children. EG *You needn't turn on the waterworks for me, my girl.* PHR : VB INFLECTS = cry, weep

watery /wɔːtəʳri¹/. 1 Something that is **watery** is weak or pale. EG *...a watery smile... ...a watery April sun.* ADJ QUALIT = feeble

2 Food and drink that is **watery** contains a lot of water or is thin like water. EG *...watery cabbage... ...watery milk.* ADJ QUALIT

3 **Watery** is also used to describe something which is related to water in some way. EG *...a watery world of deep-cut streams... ...a succession of gurgling, watery noises.* ADJ QUALIT

watt /wɒt/, **watts**. A **watt** is a unit of measurement of electrical power. EG *...a 60 watt bulb.* N COUNT : NUM+N

wattage /wɒtɪdʒ/, **wattages**. The **wattage** of something, especially a piece of electrical equipment, is the amount of electrical power, expressed in watts, which it uses or generates. N COUNT/UNCOUNT ⇑ quantity = rating

wattle /wɒtəᵊl/, **wattles**. 1 **Wattle** is a frame made by weaving thin sticks and twigs over thick sticks, used for making fences and walls. EG *...wattle walls.* N UNCOUNT

2 A **wattle** is the piece of red flesh that hangs down from the head or throat of some birds, for example turkeys. N COUNT

wattle and daub; also spelled with a hyphen. **Wattle and daub** is a building material made from a mixture of wattle and clay. EG *...houses of wattle-and-daub.* N UNCOUNT

wave /weɪv/, **waves, waving, waved**. 1 If you **wave** or **wave** your hand, you move your hand from side to side in the air, especially in order to say hello or goodbye to someone or to tell them to do something. EG *His mother waved to him... We waved at them from the train... Peter waved his hand towards the house... Ralph waved again for silence.* ▸ used as a noun. EG *With a wave of the hand, she turned away... Jack gave his usual cheery wave.* V OR V+O : USU+A ⇑ gesture ▸ N COUNT ⇑ gesture = salutation

2 If you **wave** someone away, **wave** them on, etc, you tell them to move in a particular direction by making a movement with your hand. EG *She lapsed into silence and waved me away... He waves on the traffic... At the border the guard waved me through.* V+O+A ⇑ motion

3 If you **wave** something, you hold it up and move it rapidly from side to side, for example in order to attract someone's attention or to frighten them. EG *All along the route, people applauded and waved flags at them... One of the men dashed towards them waving his spear... Dad likes to wave his hands about while speaking.* V+O ⇑ agitate = brandish

4 If something **waves**, it moves gently up and down or from side to side; used especially to describe things that are being blown by the wind. EG *Flags were waving... The grass was waving in the wind.* V

5 A **wave** is also 5.1 a raised line of water on the surface of water, especially the sea, which is caused by the wind or by tides making the surface of the water rise and fall. EG *She could see the line of white foam where the waves broke on the beach.* ▸ The sea is sometimes referred to as the **waves**. EG *'Rule Britannia, Britannia rules the waves.'* ● See also **tidal wave**. N COUNT = billow, ripple ▸ N PLURAL

5.2 part of the hair on someone's head that forms a gentle curving shape. EG *I like the waves in your hair.* N COUNT

5.3 the sudden increase in heat or energy that spreads out from an earthquake, eruption, or explosion. EG *The boat rocked as the blast wave from the explosion swept past... ...the shock wave from a one megaton bomb.* N COUNT+SUPP ⇑ movement = ripple

5.4 the form in which some types of energy, for example light, sound, or radio signals are thought to travel. EG *Radar employs radio waves whereas sonar uses sound waves.* ● See also **long wave, medium wave** and **short wave**. N COUNT+SUPP : USU PL

6 A **wave** of sympathy, alarm, panic, etc is a steady increase in that feeling which spreads through you or which spreads through a place or group of people. EG *A mounting wave of dislike and anger rose within me... In the general wave of panic, nobody thought of phoning for an ambulance.* N COUNT+SUPP : USU SING = surge, tide

7 A **wave** is also 7.1 a sudden increase in a particular activity or type of behaviour. EG *In Paris in May 1968 there was a massive wave of student riots... ...the recent wave of bombings... ...a crime wave.* ● See also **heatwave, new wave**. N COUNT+SUPP : USU SING = boom, spate

7.2 a sudden increase in the number of people moving somewhere. EG *...the last great wave of migrants.* N COUNT+SUPP : USU SING

7.3 a group of soldiers, tanks, aircraft, etc that move forward and attack the enemy together. Sometimes an attack or invasion consists of a number of waves. EG *We attack from the north-east in two waves.* N COUNT = batch

8 If things come or appear in **waves**, they come or appear in groups and at regular intervals. EG *The questions came in waves... Wave after wave of images hit the audience... ...the first wave of a new range of products.* N COUNT

wave aside. If you **wave aside** something such as an idea or reason, you decide that it is not important enough to be used. EG *The Chief waved his objection aside.* PHRASAL VB : V+O+ADV ⇑ dismiss = brush aside

wave down. If someone **waves down** a vehicle, they wave their hand as a signal to the driver to stop the vehicle. EG *I was driving along quite happily when a policeman waved me down.* PHRASAL VB : V+O+ADV = flag down

wave off. If you **wave** someone **off**, you wave to them as they leave. EG *They go to wave their boys off on the troop trains.* PHRASAL VB : V+O+ADV = see off

waveband /weɪvbænd/, **wavebands**. A **waveband** is a group of radio waves of similar length which are used for particular types of radio transmission. N COUNT ⇑ band

wavelength /weɪvleŋkθ/, **wavelengths**. 1 A **wavelength** is 1.1 the distance between the same point on two waves of energy, for example light or N COUNT ⇑ size sound, that are next to one another. EG *What you see in a microscope is limited by the wavelength of light.*

1.2 the size of radio wave which a particular radio station uses to broadcast its programmes. EG *The authorities were able to jam this wavelength.* N COUNT ⇑ frequency

2 If two people are **on the same wavelength**, they share the same interests and attitudes and understand each other very well. PHR : USED AS AN A = agree, click

waver /weɪvə/, **wavers, wavering, wavered.**

1 If you **waver** or your confidence, faith, etc **wavers**, you are no longer firm or confident in your opinions, attitudes, or beliefs. EG *Her love for him never wavered... Meehan has never wavered in his assertions of innocence.* V ⇑ weaken = falter

2 If someone **wavers**, they hesitate before making a decision. EG *After some wavering I accepted this view.* ◇ **wavering**. EG *We must get those wavering MPs on our side.* V = dither ◇ ADJ CLASSIF : ATTRIB = undecided

3 If something **wavers**, 3.1 it shakes or moves unsteadily. EG *I looked into his eyes. They didn't waver... The landscape seemed to waver before our eyes.* ◇ **wavering**. EG *I took three wavering steps in the direction of my seat... ...a wavering voice.* 3.2 it does not stay the same but keeps changing, first one way then the other. EG *The temperature wavered between freezing and thawing... His fate still wavered in the balance.* V = falter ◇ ADJ QUALIT V : USU+A = fluctuate

wavy /weɪvi^{1}/, **wavier, waviest**. 1 **Wavy** hair grows in waves or is combed into waves. EG *She had wavy grey hair pulled back in a bun.* ADJ QUALIT ⇑ undulating

2 A **wavy** line has a series of regular curves along it. EG *The wavy lines are meant to represent water.* ADJ QUALIT ⇑ undulating

wax /wæks/, **waxes, waxing, waxed**. 1 **Wax** is 1.1 a solid, slightly shiny substance made of fat or oil and used, for example, to make candles and polish. Wax goes soft and melts when it is heated. EG *...wax candles... The packet was then sealed with wax.* • See also **paraffin wax** and **sealing wax**. 1.2 the same as beeswax. 1.3 the sticky yellow substance found in your ears. N UNCOUNT N UNCOUNT N UNCOUNT ⇑ secretion

2 If you **wax** a surface, you put a thin layer of wax onto it, especially in order to polish it. EG *Get the car really clean and dry before you wax it... I started waxing the floor.* V+O

3 When the moon **waxes**, it grows larger; a formal or literary use. V ⇑ increase

4 If something **waxes and wanes**, it first increases and then decreases over a period of time. EG *My feelings for John wax and wane... The popularity of the film stars waxed and waned.* PHR : VBS INFLECT

5 If you **wax** eloquent, romantic, etc, you start to show that quality in the way you talk; a formal use. EG *I can just imagine David waxing lyrical about Ireland.* V+ADJ ⇑ become = grow

waxen /wæks^{ə}n/. A **waxen** face is very pale and unhealthy looking. EG *She had pink-rimmed eyes and a waxen complexion.* ADJ CLASSIF = pasty

wax paper. **Wax paper** or **waxed paper** is paper that has a layer of wax on it to make it waterproof. N UNCOUNT

waxwork /wækswɜːk/, **waxworks**. In paragraph 2 **waxworks** is both the singular and the plural form.

1 A **waxwork** is a model of a person, especially a famous person, made out of wax. N COUNT

2 A **waxworks** is a place where waxworks are displayed for the public to look at. N COUNT ⇑ museum

waxy /wæksi^{1}/, **waxier, waxiest**. Something that is **waxy** looks or feels like wax. EG *The skin was fleshy and slightly waxy to the touch.* ADJ QUALIT

way /weɪ/, **ways**. 1 If you refer to a **way** of doing something or a **way** to do it, you are referring to how you do it, for example the series of things that you do in order to achieve it, or the course of action that you take. EG *...different ways of cooking fish... A pushchair is a handy way to take a young child shopping... You can qualify for a pension in two ways... ...ways in which the present service could be improved... In what way can I help you?... She had decided on this course as the only way out of a hopeless situation.* N COUNT, OR N COUNT+*to*-INF/A = means, method

2 Your **way** of doing something is the manner or method of doing it which you use or think is suitable or correct. EG *She is convinced her way is the only way... I'm going to handle this my way.* N SING : USU POSS +N = approach

3 You say that someone behaves or something is done in a particular **way** when you describe the quality that they show, for example in their behaviour or actions. EG *He smiles in a superior way... He had a strange fierce way of grinning that showed his teeth... I never like the way doctors speak to you... ...the beautiful way in which the drawer slid open.* N COUNT : USU SING+SUPP = manner

4 The **ways** of a particular society or group are the customs which are characteristic of it. EG *We will not impose our ways on them... He was brought up in the old ways.* N PLURAL+SUPP

5 Someone's **ways** are their habits and characteristic behaviour. EG *...her dancing black eyes and winning little ways... ...the difficulty of changing one's ways.* N PLURAL : USU POSS+N

6 You refer to someone's **way** in relation to their characteristic behaviour or manner with other people. EG *She's not as cross as she sounds. It's just her way... ...his blunt East Anglian way.* N SING : USU WITH POSS/SUPP

7 If you have a **way** with something or someone, you are very skilful at doing it, using it, dealing with them, etc. EG *Peter certainly has a way with children.* N SING WITH DET +*with* = facility

8 You use **way** when mentioning 8.1 a point of view that makes you have a particular attitude about something or that leads you to a particular interpretation. EG *Well, there are two ways to look at this... Try to see it my way... If you're a Democrat, you look at things one way, and if you're a Republican, another way.* 8.2 one of the number of choices or alternatives that there are, for example in a judgement or election. EG *The union is today deciding which way to cast its huge vote in Brighton... The vote would have gone the other way.* 8.3 a fact, feature, or effect which demonstrates the truth of the statement that you are making. EG *Breast feeding is valuable in a number of ways... The job was changing me in a way that I had not in the least expected.* N COUNT N COUNT N COUNT = respect

9 You say that you feel or think a particular **way** when you refer to an opinion or attitude that you have. EG *I'm just wondering why you feel this way... Do you still feel the same way?* N SING : *the/this/that*+N

10 You mention the **way** that something happens or the **way** it is when you are describing what happens or what it is like, often when you expect other people to know about it or remember it. EG *Do you remember the way the boat leaked?... It is disgusting the way taxes keep going up... Things won't ever again be the way they used to be.* N SING : *the*+N+ SUPP ⇑ how

11 You also use **way** in expressions such as 'push your way', 'work your way', or 'eat your way' in order to suggest an idea of movement, progress, or force as well as the action described by the verb. EG *You can't force your way into somebody's house... He started to work his way through the back copies of 'The Times'... She glumly forked her way through the risotto.* N SING : POSS+N +A

12 The **way** to a particular place is the route that you take in order to get there. EG *Do you know the way?... A man asked me the way to St Paul's.* N SING : *the*+N, USU+A

13 If you go or look a particular **way**, you go or look in that direction EG *Will you come this way, please?... Which way did she go?... I drove the wrong way round a roundabout... The average walk for water is five miles each way.* • If you go or look **the other way**, you go or look in the opposite direction. EG *She started to cry. I looked the other way.* N SING WITH DET : USU+SUPP • PHR : USED AS AN A = away

14 If someone is going your **way**, they are travelling in the same direction as you. N SING : POSS+N

15 You talk about people going different **ways** in order to say that their lives develop differently and they have less to do with each other. EG *They went their separate ways... I was at school with her. After that our ways led apart... You go your way, and I'll go mine.* N COUNT : USU POSS+PL = path

16 If something or someone is in the **way**, they prevent you from moving freely, moving forward, seeing clearly, etc. If they move or are moved out of the **way**, they are no longer blocking you. EG *A large tree was in the way... Judy barred Jim's way... Get out of the way.* N SING : *the*/POSS +N

17 If you clear or prepare the **way** for something, you create an opportunity for it to happen. If you block the **way** for it, you prevent it happening. EG *The way is now clear for us to take over the company... By killing them you prepare the way for the fulfilment of the destiny.* N SING : *the*+N+ *for*

18 A **way** is also a road; used especially in names. EG *...the Grande Rue, now a pedestrian way... ...54 Kingfisher Way.* N COUNT+SUPP, OR N IN NAMES = street

19 You also use **way** 19.1 to refer to a door in a N COUNT+SUPP :

building which is used as an entrance or exit. 'Way' is often written on signs. EG *I went out the back way... Which is the way in?... Way Out.* USU SING **19.2** when you refer to the area near where someone lives or near a specified place; an informal use. EG *If you're ever down our way again, do drop in... ...a farmer from Thornbury way.* N SING : MOD/ POSS+N ⇑ locality **19.3** in expressions like 'the right way up' and 'the other way round' to refer to one of two or more possible positions or arrangements that something can have. EG *Have I got this the right way up?... You've got this the wrong way round.* N SING WITH DET +SUPP

20 You also use **way** in front of an adjunct that describes distance or extent in order to emphasize it; a fairly informal use. EG *You're way below the standard required... I'm way over thirty... They're way ahead of us... ...way back in the eighteenth century.* ADV+PREP/ADV = considerably, far

21 If you divide something two, three, etc **ways**, you divide it into two or three parts or shares. EG *The money was divided three ways.* N PLURAL : NUM/ QUANTIF+N

22 Way is used with words such as 'long' and 'little' in the following expressions. **22.1** You use **a long way, quite a way, a little way**, etc to say how far away something is or how far you have travelled. EG *You could see them from a long way off... I can swim quite a way now... Judy sat on the grass a little way off.* PHR : USED AS AN A = a distance **22.2** You use **a long way, quite a way, a little way**, etc to say how far away in time something is. EG *The spring's a long way off... One has to go back such a long way.* PHR : USED AS AN A = a time **22.3** If something is **a long way** or **a considerable way from** being the case, it is definitely not the case. EG *That is a long way from the truth... They were still a long way from trusting him.* PREP = far from **22.4** If you say that something **goes a long way** towards doing a particular thing, you mean that it is an important factor in achieving that thing. EG *The account of his good character had gone a long way to mitigating his sentence... Goodwill and cooperation can go a long way towards smoothing your way to the top.* PHR : +A *(to/ towards)*, VB INFLECTS ⇑ contribute **22.5** If you say that someone **has come a long way**, you mean that they have achieved a lot of success. PHR : AUX INFLECTS **22.6** You use **by a long way** to say that one person or thing is much better, more successful, etc than all the others. EG *This is my favourite painting by a long way... He was by a very long way the most popular politician in Northern Ireland.* PHR : USED AS AN A = easily

23 Expressions such as **all the way, most of the way**, and **half the way** are used **23.1** to refer to a particular amount of a journey or distance. EG *They drove all the way back without a word... A thunderstorm accompanied me most of the way back to Grimm Road... I was a third of the way through my trip.* PHR : USED AS AN A **23.2** to refer to the extent to which an action has been completed. EG *Don't fill the glass all the way... She played it all the way through.* PHR : USED AS AN A

24 You also use **all the way** to emphasize that a particular state of affairs lasts for the whole of the period you are talking about. EG *It was downhill all the way after that... He had had the worst of it all the way along.* PHR : USED AS AN A

25 You say **by the way 25.1** when you add something to what you are saying, especially a question or piece of information that you have just thought of. EG *By the way, this visit of Muller's is strictly secret... My father's dead, by the way.* PHR : USED AS ADV SEN = incidentally **25.2** to indicate that a comment or remark is not directly relevant to the main topic of the discussion. EG *That point is quite by the way.* PHR : USED AS AN A = incidental

26 by way of. 26.1 You use **by way of** when you are explaining the purpose of something that you have said or are about to say, for example whether it is intended as an introduction, example, apology, etc. EG *I'm going to sketch in a bit of the background by way of introduction.* PREP **26.2** If you go somewhere **by way of** a particular place, you go through that place on your journey. EG *I came by way of Madrid and Athens... We drove back to Central Park West, by way of Briceland.* PREP = via

27 You use **either way 27.1** in order to introduce a statement which is true whichever of the two possible outcomes or explanations just mentioned is right. EG *If I win I get a prize. If she wins she's got to pay me the money she owes me. Either way I can't lose.* PHR **27.2** when you have estimated a measurement, amount, or period of time, in order to say that it does not matter if the actual value or period is slightly more or less than the one mentioned. PHR

28 Way is used with 'have' in the following expressions. **28.1** If you say that someone or something **has a way** of doing a particular thing, you mean that they commonly do it. EG *Ex-wives have a way of reappearing.* PHR : VB INFLECTS **28.2** If you **get** or **have** your **way**, nobody stops you from doing what you want. EG *If Baker has his way the money will be forthcoming.* PHR : VB INFLECTS **28.3** If you **have it all** your **own way** or **have everything** your **own way**, everything happens exactly as you want it to. EG *You've had it all your own way for too long.* PHR : VB INFLECTS **28.4** If you say to someone **'Have it your way'**, you mean that you agree with or accept their suggestion but that you are rather reluctant about it. CONVENTION **28.5** You say to someone **'You can't have it both ways'** to remind them that they have to choose between two things and cannot do or have them both. EG *Do you want a party or a holiday? You can't have it both ways.* CONVENTION **28.6** If a man **has** his **evil** or **wicked way with** a woman, he seduces her and has sex with her; a rather old-fashioned informal expression. PHR : VB INFLECTS

29 Way is used after 'in' in the following expressions. **29.1** You use expressions such as **in some ways, in many ways**, or **in every way** to indicate the degree or extent to which a statement is true. EG *She is rather bad-tempered in some ways... It seemed the best year of my life, and in many ways it still does... They are excellent girls in every way.* PHR : USED AS ADV SEN **29.2** You use **in the same way** to say that the same or similar conditions apply to the situation you are talking about as to the situation you have just described. EG *Every baby's face is different from every other's. In the same way, every baby's pattern of development is different from every other's.* PHR : USED AS ADV SEN = likewise **29.3** You use expressions such as **in the way that** or **in a way** when you make a comparison between two situations. EG *The death of Martin Luther King intruded on the war in a way that no other outside event had ever done.* CONJ SUBORD = like **29.4** You use **in no way** or **not in any way** to emphasize that a statement is not at all true. EG *In no way am I a politically effective person... This in no way alters the fact that you have behaved very foolishly... I was not put off in any way.* PHR : USED AS ADV SEN **29.5** You say **in more ways than one** to indicate that what you have said is intended to have more than one meaning. EG *He was hurt in more ways than one.* PHR : USED AS AN A **29.6** You use **in a way** to indicate that although a statement is not completely true, it is true to a limited extent or in certain respects. EG *In a way, these officers were prisoners themselves... I'd like to marry Mr Barter–in a way.* PHR : USED AS ADV SEN **29.7** You say that something is the case **in its way** in order to weaken a description, or to imply that something is not as good as other people think. EG *It's quite pretty in its way... Fred, in his own way, was an actor... This was, in its small way, a crisis.* PHR : USED AS AN A **29.8** You use **in the way of** in order to specify exactly what you are talking or asking about. EG *He received very little in the way of wages... What else have you got today in the way of problems?* PREP = as regards **29.9** You use **in a big way, in a small way**, etc to suggest the scale or importance of an activity. EG *They are going into the arms business in a big way... She started business in a small way.* PHR : USED AS AN A **29.10** If someone is **in a bad** or **good way**, they are in a good or poor state of health; an informal expression. EG *Amy's in a bad way... His liver was in a bad way... He's not in too good a way.* PHR : USED AS AN A **29.11** If someone **gets in the way**, they are a nuisance and disturb you when you are trying to do something. EG *The children were getting in the way.* PHR : VB INFLECTS **29.12** If something **gets in the way** of a particular thing, it makes it difficult for it to happen, continue, or be appreciated properly. EG *She was getting in the way of my ambitions.* PHR : VB INFLECTS = block, impede

30 Way is used after 'make' in the following expressions. **30.1** When you **make** your **way** somewhere, you walk or travel there; a slightly formal use. EG *I made my way back to my seat... Will passengers for Manchester please make their way to platform 6?* PHR : VB INFLECTS+A = go **30.2** To **make way** means to move away or be removed so that some other person or thing is able to stand there or take place there. EG *Slums have been cleared to make way for new, hygienic, high-rise apartments... He refused to make way for anyone.* PHR : VB INFLECTS, USU+ *for*

31 Way is used after 'no' in the following expressions. **31.1** You say **there's no way** or **there isn't any way** when you mean that a particular course of action is PHR : VB INFLECTS+

impossible. EG *There's no way that the department can check every case... There's no way I can tell him.* REPORT-CL **31.2** You say **no way** as an emphatic way of saying no; an informal expression. EG *'Will you come?'–'No way.'* CONVENTION **31.3** If you say that there are **no two ways about it**, you mean that there is no doubt at all about the situation or an interpretation of it. EG *'He's not on board,' said Brody. 'No two ways about it.'* CONVENTION

32 Way is used after 'on' and 'along' in the following expressions. **32.1 On the way, on** your **way**, or **along the way** means in the course of the journey that you are making somewhere. EG *Lynn was on her way home... They had exchanged only two sentences on the way back from the house... They stopped overnight at various towns along the way.* PHR : USED AS AN A **32.2** If you **are on** your **way**, you have started your journey somewhere. EG *At last we were on our way.* PHR : VB INFLECTS **32.3** If you **go on** your **way**, you continue with your journey. EG *He waved to us and went on his way.* PHR : VB INFLECTS **32.4** If something happens **on** or **along the way**, it happens during the course of a particular event or process. EG *There were, of course, a few problems along the way.* PHR : USED AS AN A **32.5** If you are **on** or **well on** your **way** to something, you have made so much progress that you are almost certain to achieve that thing. EG *She is well on her way to being one of the best directors we've ever had... He's well on the way to success.* PHR : USED AS AN A, USU + *to*-INF/*to* ⇑ close **32.6** If something is **on the way** or **on its way**, it is due to appear in the near future. EG *A third book is on its way.* PHR : USED AS AN A **32.7** If a woman has a baby **on the way**, she is pregnant. EG *She's got a baby and another on the way.* PHR : USED AS AN A **32.8** If someone or something is **on the way out**, they are likely to disappear or to be replaced very soon. EG *The chairman is on the way out.* PHR : USED AS AN A

33 You use **one way or another** or **one way or the other 33.1** to say that something will definitely happen or be achieved although you are not sure exactly how. EG *One way or another, I was going to leave Birmingham... Every year since that first trip, I have managed, one way or another, to get back to the tropics.* PHR : USED AS ADV SEN = somehow **33.2** to say that neither of two possible conclusions has been reached or no preference has been expressed. EG *It didn't matter to them one way or the other... I didn't think she'd care one way or another.* PHR : USED AS AN A, WITH BROAD NEG **33.3** when you have estimated a measurement, amount, or period of time, in order to say that it does not matter if the actual value or period is slightly more or less than the one mentioned. EG *I've been given six months to do the job. A week one way or the other will make no real difference.* PHR : USED AS AN A

34 Way is used after 'out' in the following expressions. **34.1** If a place is **out of** your **way**, it is not in the direction that you are going in. EG *'Would you like a lift?'–'Please, if it's not out of your way.'* PHR : USED AS AN A **34.2** If you **go out of** your **way** to do something, you make a special effort to do it, for example to help someone. EG *He didn't really go out of his way to help me.* PHR : VB INFLECTS, USU + *to*-INF **34.3** If you **keep out of** someone's **way**, you avoid them. EG *He had kept out of her way.* PHR : VB INFLECTS **34.4** When something **is out of the way** or when you **have got** it **out of the way**, it is over or you have dealt with it, for example so that it is no longer a problem or needs no more time spent on it. EG *We'll be all right once this meeting is out of the way.* PHR : VB INFLECTS

35 You use **that way** and **this way 35.1** to refer to a statement or comment that has just been mentioned. EG *'Are you going to stay out there all night?'–'It looks that way, Harry.'... Anne usually arrived just in time for lunch. She was clever that way.* PHR : USED AS AN A ⇑ so **35.2** to refer to a possible course of action that you have just mentioned, when you go on to mention the likely consequence or effect of it. EG *He could do it on Sundays. That way, it wouldn't interfere with his work at all... You should refuse to believe in either ghosts or the laws of science. That way you're safe.* PHR

36 The word **way** is also used in the following expressions. **36.1 Across** or **over the way** means nearby, especially on the opposite side of a road or area; a fairly informal expression. EG *...the derelict houses across the way... We just live over the way.* PHR : USED AS AN A **36.2** If something **comes** your **way**, you find, obtain, or experience it by chance. EG *...the opportunities that have come my way.* PHR : VB INFLECTS **36.3** If you **see** or **realize the error of** your **ways**, you realize and admit that you have made a mistake or behaved badly. PHR : VB INFLECTS **36.4** If you **go** your **own way**, you do what you want rather than what everyone else does or expects. EG *We believe in going our own way.* PHR : VB INFLECTS **36.5** You use expressions such as **that is the way** or **as is the way** to say that a particular situation or example of behaviour is typical and you would not expect it to be different. EG *He was totally unprepared, as is the way with American he-men, for anything that could not be settled with a fist or a gun... 'As soon as I put the washing on the line it started to rain.'–'Isn't that always the way?'* PHR : VB INFLECTS **36.6** If you **know** or **have learned** your **way about** or **around**, you know all the procedures and facts about a particular job or situation. EG *There was little time to learn my way about.* PHR : VB INFLECTS **36.7** If you **lose** your **way**, you become unsure about the correct course of action to take. EG *The Church has lost its way.* PHR : VB INFLECTS = go astray **36.8** You use **the other way round** or **around** to refer to the opposite of what you have just said. EG *It was you who invited him along, not the other way around.* PHR : USED AS AN A = vice versa **36.9** If you can **see** your **way clear** to doing something, you are able to do it; an informal expression. EG *Can you see your way clear to lending me a fiver?* PHR : VB INFLECTS **36.10** If you **take the easy way out**, you do what is easy rather than what really needs to be done. PHR : VB INFLECTS **36.11** You say **that's the way** in order to indicate your pleasure at something, for example at a particular situation. EG *'How are you?'–'Fine, thanks.'–'That's the way.'* CONVENTION = jolly good **36.12** You add **to my way of thinking** to a statement in order to indicate that you are giving your opinion. EG *They are faced with issues which to my way of thinking are some of the fundamental human issues.* PHR : USED AS ADV SEN **36.13** If an activity or plan is **under way**, it has begun and is now taking place. EG *Formal negotiations are under way... The plan was smothered almost before it had got under way.* PHR : USED AS AN A = in progress **36.14** The word **way** is also used in other expressions, which are explained at other places in this dictionary.

-way combines with numbers in order to form adjectives that describe **1** a means of communication that functions or takes place between the stated number of people. EG *...a two-way radio... ...a three-way conversation.* COMB : FORMS ADJ CLASSIFS **2** a division of something into the stated number of parts. EG *...a four-way split.* COMB : FORMS ADJ CLASSIFS

wayfarer /weɪfɛərə/, **wayfarers**. A **wayfarer** is a traveller who walks from place to place; an old-fashioned word. N COUNT

waylay /weɪleɪ/, **waylays, waylaying, waylaid**. If you **waylay** someone, you stop them when they are going, for example in order to talk to them, to steal something from them, or to attack them; a fairly old-fashioned word. EG *She lingered out on the street to waylay him after the show.* V+O = catch

way of life, ways of life. 1 A **way of life** is the behaviour and habits that are typical of a particular person or group, or that are chosen by them. EG *I've had a rather curious way of life for the last few years... ...the British way of life.* N COUNT : USU SING = lifestyle

2 If you describe a particular activity as a **way of life**, you mean that it is the most important thing in your life, rather than just a hobby or interest. EG *'Teaching at a university,' she said, 'is not a job, it's a way of life.'* N SING : a+N, USU USED AS C

way-out. Someone or something that is **way-out** is unusual or different from other things or people, especially by being very modern or fashionable; an old-fashioned word. EG *It was written about ten years ago as a piece of way-out black comedy.* ADJ QUALIT ⇑ odd = eccentric

wayside /weɪsaɪd/, **waysides**; an old-fashioned word. **1** The **wayside** is the side of the road. EG *The number of wayside emergency telephones was distressingly inadequate.* N COUNT : USU *the* +N IN SING = roadside

2 If someone **falls by the wayside**, they fail in an attempt to do something, or they stop trying to do it, especially because they do not have the strength or ability to carry on. EG *We must care for the weak who would otherwise fall by the wayside.* PHR : VB INFLECTS = give up

wayward /weɪwəd/. If a person or their behaviour is **wayward**, they are likely to change suddenly, are often selfish or stubborn, and are therefore difficult to control. EG *She could be wayward, petulant, and disagreeable... ...children who've got this wayward, curious, imaginative quality.* ADJ QUALIT = wilful, unruly

wc, wc's; also written **WC**. A **wc** is a toilet; an abbreviation for 'water closet', used especially on signs or in advertisements for houses or flats. N COUNT = lavatory

we /wiː/ is used as the subject of a verb. **1** A speaker or writer uses **we** to refer both to himself or herself PRON : PL, USED AS S and to one or more other people as a group. EG *We both sat down... We could hear the birds singing... We all get cross with our children... Go home. We don't want you. We are in fact a multicultural society... We may never know the truth.*

2 In fairly formal English, a speaker or writer may use **we** instead of 'I' in order to refer to the listeners or readers as well as to himself or herself. EG *We saw in chapter 1 how the most powerful government in western Europe had to yield in a conflict with a comparatively weak trade union... We are on the dangerous ground of amateur psychiatry.* PRON : PL, USED AS S

weak /wiːk/, **weaker, weakest**. **1** People or animals that are **weak** do not have very much physical strength or energy, for example because they are small in size, old, ill, starving, or exhausted. EG *George was crawling along a fence, too weak to walk... He was weak from hunger... James felt frozen and weak with fear... He found his legs were weak and his tongue gave him pain.* ◊ **weakly**. EG *He struggled weakly to his knees.* ◊ **weakness**. EG *...his worsening pain and physical weakness, his struggle for breath.* ADJ QUALIT = frail, sickly ◊ ADV WITH VB ◊ N UNCOUNT = infirmity

2 Something such as a part of your body that is **weak** is not able to work properly or for long periods of time. EG *Some livers are weaker than others.* ◊ **weakness**. EG *...minor cardiac weakness.* ADJ QUALIT = defective ◊ N UNCOUNT

3 If an object or part of an object is **weak**, it is made of material that breaks easily and is likely to collapse or be worn away. EG *A fuse is a deliberately weak link in an electrical system... Don't stand on that chair–it's got a weak leg!... ...valleys cut into weak materials.* ADJ QUALIT = delicate, soft

4 If individuals or groups are **weak**, they are not very important and do not have very much influence. EG *Internationally the movement has appeared weak and isolated.* ◊ **weakness**. EG *Despite its weakness, the group has always been very active.* ADJ QUALIT = powerless ◊ N UNCOUNT = impotence

5 A country or military force that is **weak** has a smaller defence force or less military equipment than other countries. EG *In Northern Germany, Allied forces were weaker.* ◊ **weakly**. EG *...a weakly defended bridge.* ◊ **weakness, weaknesses**. EG *The defender must study the weaknesses of the city he defends... This would exploit a known weakness on the enemy's Eastern Front.* ADJ QUALIT ◊ ADV ◊ N UNCOUNT/COUNT

6 A **weak** system or method is not very good at achieving its purpose. EG *Incomes policy is a weak instrument for reducing inflation... The state machinery is weak.* ◊ **weakness**. EG *...a weakness in Robertson's critical method... ...the strengths and weaknesses of international economic co-operation.* ADJ QUALIT ⇑ ineffective = poor ◊ N UNCOUNT/COUNT

7 Industries, economies, currencies, etc that are **weak** are not successful financially, and are often in danger of collapsing. EG *The small farmer is economically weak by himself... A substantial migration of weak firms from the private sector to the public.* ◊ **weakness**. EG *...the pound's recent weakness against the dollar.* ADJ QUALIT = impotent, poor ◊ N UNCOUNT

8 If you describe someone as **weak**, you mean that they are easily influenced by other people because they are not strong enough to insist on their own opinion or belief; often used showing disapproval. EG *She was so shockingly weak and trusting... I have been weak and I have permitted your father to accompany you... It's just that they're weak willed... ...incompetent and weak leadership.* ◊ **weakness**. EG *...the childish weakness of his character... ...his apparent weakness under pressure.* ADJ QUALIT = gullible, feeble ◊ N UNCOUNT

9 If you describe someone's facial features as **weak**, you mean that they are not very distinct, especially when you want to imply that the person does not have a strong character. ADJ QUALIT

10 If something such as an argument or reason is **weak**, it does not convince you that it is right or logical. EG *That was an incredibly weak answer... The film had a weak plot and the acting was awful... 'Important' is too weak a word to describe it.* ◊ **weakly**. EG *...a weakly worded communiqué.* ◊ **weakness**. EG *The weakness of Henry's case was that he could not show us any of the letters.* ADJ QUALIT = flimsy, feeble ◊ ADV WITH VB ◊ N UNCOUNT/COUNT

11 Sounds, light, etc that are **weak** are very faint and difficult to distinguish clearly. EG *She asked in a weak voice for water... A weak sun shines on the promenade... In the weak light of the headlamp, I wrote down the number.* ◊ **weakly**. EG *Otto spoke in a weakly querulous voice... We drove through the weakly lighted streets.* ◊ **weakness**. EG *The weakness of the signal made it impossible to decode.* ADJ QUALIT = feeble ◊ ADV = feebly ◊ N UNCOUNT = faintness

12 If your senses are **weak**, you are not able to see, hear, smell, or taste things very well. EG *Our poor human ears are too weak... ...weak eyesight.* ADJ QUALIT = inadequate, poor

13 Drinks such as tea or coffee that are **weak** are made using a lot of water and therefore do not have a strong taste. EG *He sat sipping weak tea from a chipped mug... I'll have mine a tiny bit weaker, I think.* ADJ QUALIT = watery, mild

14 A **weak** reaction or response to something is done without enthusiasm or emphasis. EG *I ended it with as weak an assent as I could politely deliver... He managed a weak smile.* ◊ **weakly**. EG *'It's a beautiful place,' I say weakly.* ADJ QUALIT ⇑ faint = feeble ◊ ADV WITH VB = lamely

15 If someone or something is **weak** on a particular subject or field, they do not have as much ability, skill, information, etc as they would like. EG *Our orchestra is weak on string players... The book was weak on fact and documentation... The course was very weak on traditional grammar.* ◊ **weakness**. EG *...the strengths and weaknesses of international co-operation.* ADJ QUALIT : USU PRED+*on/in/at* ⇑ deficient = poor, shaky ◊ N UNCOUNT/COUNT

16 The **weak** are people who have weak bodies, very little money, or very little power in society, and who therefore cannot protect themselves against misfortune or against strong, rich, or powerful people. EG *Some, the old and the weak and the sick, began to die... The state took over responsibility for the poor, the weak and the unfortunate... The triumph of the strong over the weak.* N PLURAL : *the*+N = needy, vulnerable

17 If you say that someone is **weak in the head**, you mean that they are slightly stupid; an informal expression. EG *She's a bit weak in the head, if you ask me.* PHR : USED AS C = soft

weaken /wiːkəⁿn/, **weakens, weakening, weakened**. **1** If someone **weakens** something such as a political group, a social institution, or a military force, they make it less important, powerful, or effective. EG *Economic pressures tend to weaken and even destroy the family... It was a Bill to strengthen not weaken the Lords... Her armed forces had been weakened by the restriction on equipment supplies.* V OR V+O ⇑ diminish = undermine

2 When a currency **weakens** or when something **weakens** it, it becomes lower in value. EG *It looks as if the dollar could weaken further.* V-ERG ⇑ decrease = drop, fall

3 If someone **weakens** or if you **weaken** them, they become less certain about something that they had previously decided. EG *Well, perhaps Cynthia's weakening–after all, she is making your bed... ...the government's weakening resolve.* V OR V+O = soften

4 If something **weakens** you, it causes you to lose some of your physical strength. EG *I was weakened by my exertions, and fell and broke my arm.* V OR V+O = sap

5 If you **weaken** an object, you do something to it which causes it to become less firm and more likely to break. EG *Her repeated pushing may even weaken the catch and damage it.* V+O

6 If you **weaken** someone's argument or standpoint, you make it less effective by showing that it is not right or logical. EG *They clearly tried to weaken the legal position of the unions.* V+O = undermine

weak-kneed. Someone who is **weak-kneed** is not able or willing to make their own decisions or to stand up for their rights; an informal word. EG *I feared she'd think me very weak-kneed for giving in to him.* ADJ QUALIT ⇑ irresolute

weakling /wiːklɪŋ/, **weaklings**. A **weakling** is **1** a person or animal that is physically weak; used showing disapproval. EG *'Weakling,' she taunted, 'to leave me there and run off.'* **2** a person who is weak in character or in a particular skill. EG *A picture emerges of a moral weakling with an IQ of about 70.* N COUNT ◊ N COUNT : USU+SUPP

weakness /wiːknɪ²s/, **weaknesses**. If you have a **weakness** for something, you like it so much that you want it or want to do it whenever you can, even though you know that it might have unpleasant results. EG *She had a weakness for garlic... Food was his weakness.* ● See also **weak**. N COUNT : IF+PREP THEN *for* = penchant

weal /wiːl/, **weals**. A **weal** is a mark made on someone's skin by a blow, especially from something sharp or thin such as a sword or whip. EG *...the great multi-coloured and blood-encrusted weal on my neck.* N COUNT ⇑ scar = welt

wealth /welθ/. **1 Wealth** is the possession of a large amount of money, property, or other valuable things. EG *...a woman of considerable wealth... It was a* N UNCOUNT = opulence *period of wealth and prosperity... ...the juxtaposition of extreme wealth and poverty.* ▸ also used to refer to the money, property, etc that someone owns. EG *...redistributing wealth among profits, wages, and investment.* ▸ = riches

2 If someone or something has a **wealth** of qualities, attributes, etc, they have a very large number or amount of them. EG *His air of confidence and his wealth of knowledge made him seem ageless.* N PART : SING ⇑ lot = abundance

wealthy /welθiˡ/, **wealthier, wealthiest.** 1 Someone who is **wealthy** has a large amount of money, property, or valuable possessions. EG *...a wealthy man... Her parents were very wealthy.* ADJ QUALIT ⇑ rich = affluent
▸ The **wealthy** is used to refer to people who are wealthy. EG *The wealthy sent their children to Switzerland to be educated.* ▸ N PLURAL : *the* +N = rich

2 If a place is **wealthy** in something, it has a lot of that thing, especially when it is something that is valuable or useful. EG *...a continent exceptionally wealthy in minerals.* ADJ QUALIT : PRED+*in* ⇑ rich

wean /wiːn/, **weans, weaning, weaned.** 1 When you **wean** a baby or animal, you stop feeding it milk from its mother's breast and start giving it other food, especially solid food. EG *Traditionally piglets were weaned at eight weeks... The earlier a child is weaned, the greater risk he runs of serious illness.* V OR V+O : USU+ *from/off/to* ⇑ change
◇ **weaning.** EG *Early weaning is becoming more common.* ◇ N UNCOUNT

2 If you **wean** someone from something, you gradually make them stop doing it, especially when it is something that they do regularly and that you think is bad for them; a fairly formal use. EG *...trying to wean people from cigarettes by gradually reducing the nicotine content.* V+O+A *(from/off)* ⇑ dissuade = discourage

weapon /wepən/, **weapons.** A **weapon** is 1 an object such as a gun, a knife, or a missile, which is used to kill or hurt people in a fight or a war. EG *I wasn't carrying a weapon... ...nuclear weapons... ...special weapon stores.* N COUNT ⇑ instrument 2 something such as knowledge about a particular subject, which you can use to protect yourself or to get what you want in a difficult situation. EG *Complete anonymity is the best weapon I have.* N COUNT ⇑ defence

weaponry /wepənriˡ/. **Weaponry** is all the weapons that a country has or that are available to it. EG *They are improving and perfecting existing weaponry.* N UNCOUNT

wear /weə/, **wears, wearing, wore, worn.** 1 When you **wear** something such as clothes, shoes, or jewellery, you have them on your body or on part of your body. EG *She was wearing a smart French T-shirt and jeans... ...a girl called Ella, who wore spectacles... I don't like to wear things around my neck.* V+O

2 If you **wear** your hair or beard in a particular way, you have it cut in that style or shape. EG *his face was framed by his curly hair which he wore too long.* V+O+A

3 If you **wear** a particular expression, your face shows the emotions that you are feeling; a fairly literary use. EG *Their faces wore a look that said they were no longer afraid.* V+O

4 Evening **wear**, summer **wear**, etc are clothes that are suitable to wear in the evening, in the summer, etc. EG *It was suitable for evening wear... ...the dinner tie he affected for dinner wear.* N UNCOUNT : MOD +N

5 **Wear** is the amount of use your clothes have over a period of time. EG *You've had about as much wear out of those shoes as they'll take.* N UNCOUNT

6 If something **wears**, it becomes thinner or weaker because it is constantly being used over a long period of time. EG *Move the carpet up or down as it starts to wear.* V ⇑ deteriorate

7 If you say that something **wears** well, you mean that it can be used for a long time without becoming weak or thin. If you say that it **wears** badly, you mean that it is not very strong and will not last for a long time. EG *Rayon blankets are less warm and don't wear as well as woollen ones.* V+ADV

8 If you **wear** a situation that you do not really approve of, you agree to tolerate it and to not become angry or oppose it; an informal use. EG *She's gone too far this time. I wouldn't wear it if I were you.* V+O : USU WITH BROAD NEG

9 **Wear** is also 9.1 the damage or change that is caused by something being used a lot or for a long time. EG *These sheets are showing signs of wear but they're not too thin... ...microprocessors which monitor tyre wear.* N UNCOUNT ⇑ deterioration 9.2 the amount or type of use that something has. EG *Allow about two years for heavy wear (as in a kitchen).* N UNCOUNT : MOD +N

10 If you say that something **is wearing thin**, you mean that it is becoming less useful or interesting or more annoying because it has been used too much. EG *His excuses are wearing a bit thin.* PHR : VB INFLECTS

11 If you say that someone or something is **the worse for wear**, you mean that they are in a poor condition or tired because they have been very active or have been used a lot; an informal expression. EG *Most of them were looking rather the worse for wear.* PHR : USED AS C

wear away. If you **wear** something **away** or if it **wears away**, it becomes thin and eventually disappears because it is used a lot or rubbed a lot. EG *The grass was still worn away where the children used to play.* PHRASAL VB : V-ERG+ADV = erode

wear down. 1 If you **wear** something **down** or if it **wears down**, it becomes shorter as a result of constantly rubbing against something else. EG *As the teeth wear down, new ones start growing.* PHRASAL VB : V-ERG+ADV

2 If you **wear** people **down** you weaken them or their position by being more persistent than they are. EG *They tried to wear down the management's resistance by holding a series of strikes.* PHRASAL VB : V+O+ADV

wear off. If something such as pain **wears off**, it disappears slowly until it no longer exists or has any effect. EG *By the next afternoon the shock had worn off.* PHRASAL VB : V+ADV = pass off

wear on. If time **wears on**, it seems to pass very slowly. EG *So the day wore on and still they sat, drinking, smoking, talking.* PHRASAL VB : V+ADV

wear out. 1 When something **wears out** or when you **wear** it **out**, it is used so much that it becomes thin or weak and unable to be used any more. EG *His shoes keep wearing out.* ● See also **worn-out**. PHRASAL VB : V-ERG+ADV

2 If you **wear** someone **out**, you make them feel extremely tired; an informal use. EG *They wore us out with their constant screaming and crying.* PHRASAL VB : V+O+ADV = exhaust

wear through. If something such as a piece of clothing **wears through**, it develops a hole where the material has become weak and thin. PHRASAL VB : V+ADV

wearable /weərəbəˡl/. Clothes or shoes that are **wearable** are in a suitable condition to be worn. EG *In any case, it was hardly wearable by now.* ADJ CLASSIF

wear and tear is the damage or change that happens to something in the course of normal use. EG *The carpet should be made from good quality materials so that it stands up to the wear and tear of continual use.* N UNCOUNT

wearing /weərɪŋ/. 1 A **wearing** activity is one which requires a lot of energy and makes you feel very tired. EG *It is a very wearing and demanding job.* ADJ QUALIT ⇑ tiring = exhausting

2 If an object is **wearing**, it has the effect of making something thinner or weaker or smaller, for example by rubbing against it a lot. EG *This type of grass aids the sheep's digestion, but it is very wearing on the teeth.* ADJ QUALIT : PRED, IF+PREP THEN*on*

wearisome /wɪərɪsəm/. Something that is **wearisome** is very tiring and boring or frustrating; a formal word. EG *...a wearisome meeting... This ruled out any wearisome opposition from within.* ADJ QUALIT

weary /wɪəriˡ/, **wearier, weariest; wearies, wearying, wearied.** 1 If you are **weary**, you are very tired, for example because you have been working hard or because you have lost your enthusiasm for something. EG *...a weary young woman, struggling through the door... ...my father, weary of it all.* ADJ QUALIT = exhausted ▸ used of people's behaviour and appearance. EG *...the eyes weary under drooping lids... Both of them grunted at Daintry with weary politeness.* ▸ = jaded ◇ **wearily.** EG *'Leave her alone,' Etta said wearily. 'She doesn't know what you're talking about.'... The farmers trudged wearily to the nearest stream.* ◇ ADV WITH VB ◇ **weariness.** EG *Utter weariness overtook me an hour later... He didn't want to give in to his weariness.* ◇ N UNCOUNT = exhaustion

2 If you describe an experience as **weary**, you mean that it makes you tired or bored; a formal use. EG *He had already spent many, many weary years there... Most politicians tread a weary path from constituency to constituency.* ADJ QUALIT : ATTRIB = fatiguing

3 If you **weary** of something, you become very tired and lose your enthusiasm for it; a formal use. EG *He is beginning to weary of sitting still.* V : USU+A *(of)*, OR V+O ◇ **wearied.** EG *Wearied by these constant demands, the Master told them to ask later.* ◇ ADJ CLASSIF = fatigued

weasel /wiːzəˡl/, **weasels.** A **weasel** is a small wild animal with a long thin body, a tail, four short legs, N COUNT ⇑ mammal and reddish-brown fur which may turn white in winter. Weasels can move very fast and kill rats, mice, and birds for food.

weather /wɛðə/, **weathers, weathering, weathered.** 1 The **weather** is the condition of the atmosphere, for example whether it is raining, sunny, hot, windy, etc in one area at a particular time. EG *The weather was good for the time of year.... They wore boots and galoshes in wet weather... It was terribly cold weather–a blizzard in fact... ...bad weather conditions.* — N UNCOUNT, OR N SING : *the*+N ⇑ climate

2 If you say that someone does something **in all weathers**, you mean that they do it regularly whether or not the weather is good or bad. EG *They walked more than fifteen miles to do a job, and in all weathers.* — PHR : USED AS AN A

3 If you keep **a weather eye on** something, you stay alert so that you will notice if anything unpleasant happens. EG *Lynn kept a weather eye on her windows when the boys were playing cricket.* — PHR : USED AS O

4 If you say that someone **is making heavy weather** of a task, you mean that they are doing it very inefficiently and are making it more difficult than it needs to be. — PHR : VB INFLECTS

5 If you say that you are **under the weather**, you mean that you feel slightly ill. EG *You look a bit under the weather.* — PHR : USED AS AN A = low, unwell

6 If something such as rock or wood **weathers**, it changes colour or shape as a result of the wind, sun, rain, or other weather conditions. EG *The rocks weathered and turned to clay and mud.* ◊ **weathered.** EG *...a huge wooden warehouse, its red paint weathered and fading.* — V-ERG ⇑ erode; ◊ ADJ QUALIT ⇑ worn

7 If you **weather** a problem or difficulty, you survive throughout it and are able to continue normally after it has passed or been solved. EG *There are plenty of marriages that can weather bad patches... Anyone who weathers the first four years seems to be all right.* — V+O = withstand

weatherbeaten /wɛðəbiːtəⁿn/; also spelled with a hyphen. 1 If your face or skin is **weatherbeaten**, it is brown and rough with deep lines because you have spent a lot of time outside in bad weather. EG *...his weather-beaten face.* — ADJ QUALIT = weathered

2 Something that is **weatherbeaten** has become roughened and slightly damaged after being out in the weather for a long time. EG *The wooden balconies were warped and weatherbeaten.* — ADJ QUALIT ⇑ worn

weathercock /wɛðəkɒk/, **weathercocks.** A **weathercock** is a metal object in the shape of a cock which is fixed to the roof of a building. It turns round in the wind to show which way the wind is blowing. — N COUNT ⇑ weather vane

weather forecast, weather forecasts. A **weather forecast** is a statement that is broadcast on television or radio, or printed in a newspaper, saying what the weather will be like the next day or for the next few days. — N COUNT ⇑ prediction

weather forecaster, weather forecasters. A **weather forecaster** is a person whose job is to study weather conditions and make reports predicting what the weather will be like in the next few days. — N COUNT ⇑ meteorologist

weatherman /wɛðəmæ³n/, **weathermen.** A **weatherman** is a person who makes weather forecasts at regular times on television or radio as part of their job; an informal word. EG *The day proved to be as bright as the weatherman had predicted.* — N COUNT ⇑ meteorologist

weatherproof /wɛðəpruːf/. Something that is **weatherproof** is made of material which protects it from the weather or keeps out wind and rain. EG *Miraculously, the new skylight seems weatherproof.* — ADJ CLASSIF ⇑ resistant

weather station, weather stations. A **weather station** is a building used for studying and recording facts about the weather, so that weather forecasts can be made. — N COUNT

weather-vane, weather-vanes; also spelled without a hyphen. A **weather-vane** is a metal object on the roof of a building, which turns round as the wind blows in order to show the direction of the wind. — N COUNT = weathercock

weave /wiːv/, **weaves, weaving, wove, woven.** The form **weaved** is sometimes used as the past tense and past participle for the meaning in paragraph 5. 1 If you **weave** cloth, you make it by crossing the threads over and under each other using a machine called a loom. EG *He had a tapestry loom in his bedroom so that he could weave early in the morning... Let's weave a rug.* ◊ **woven** /wəʊvəⁿn/. EG *...woven fabrics.* ◊ **weaving.** EG *...painting, weaving and other types of craft work.* — V OR V+O; ◊ ADJ CLASSIF; ◊ N UNCOUNT ⇑ craft

2 The **weave** of a cloth is the way in which the threads are arranged and the pattern that they form. EG *...a tight, firm weave... Avoid loose weaves.* — N COUNT+SUPP

3 If you **weave** something such as a fence or a basket, you make it by twisting twigs, branches, or pieces of cane together and pushing them in and out and across each other. EG *Hanging upside down, the bird deftly weaves the twigs into a hollow ball.* — V+O+A

4 If you **weave** something into a speech or piece of writing, you carefully include it in such a way that it appears to be a logical part of the speech or text. EG *The loophole of divorce is woven into the marriage contract.* — V+O+A ⇑ introduce = interweave

5 If you **weave** a complicated story or plan, you piece it together carefully in order to make sure that it appears complete. EG *He was a diabolical man, weaving lifetime plots.* — V+O ⇑ create

6 If you **weave** your way somewhere, you go there by moving through and around things and changing direction often in order to avoid hitting them. EG *...weaving expertly among the rush-hour traffic... He holds a tray aloft as he weaves his way through the crowd.* — V+O+A, OR V+A = wend

7 If you say to someone **'get weaving'**, you mean that you want them to hurry up and start what they are supposed to be doing; an informal expression. EG *Come on, get weaving, we've got to be there by ten!* — PHR : ONLY IMPER = shift

weaver /wiːvə/, **weavers.** A **weaver** is a person who weaves cloth. — N COUNT

web /wɛb/, **webs.** A **web** is 1 a fine net made by a spider from a sticky substance which it produces in its body. Insects stick to the web as they fly past and are eaten by the spider. EG *...a spider's web... ...a female hanging, large and menacing, on her web.* 2 a complicated pattern or structure, with many different connections and relationships, sometimes considered as an obstacle or a danger. EG *They are a way of fitting ourselves into the web of social life... ...the complex web of reasons.* 3 a piece of skin which connects the toes on the feet of water birds such as ducks, and which helps them swim well. EG *The web of skin that unites their toes has become greatly enlarged.* — N COUNT = cobweb; N COUNT+SUPP : USU SING = network, tangle; N COUNT = flap

webbed /wɛbd/. **Webbed** feet or toes have a piece of skin between the toes. Water birds such as ducks have webbed feet. EG *The otter has webbed feet and spends much of its time swimming.* — ADJ CLASSIF

webbing /wɛbɪŋ/ is strong material which is woven in strips and used to make belts or straps, or used in seats to support the springs. EG *...a belt of green webbing... ...canvas webbing.* — N UNCOUNT ⇑ fabric

wed /wɛd/, **weds, wedding, wedded**; the form **wed** is used in the present tense and is also the past participle. If you **wed** someone or if you **wed**, you get married; a very old-fashioned word. EG *A year later they got wed... We were both nineteen when we wed... She received the blessing of her parents to wed Oliver.* • See also **newlyweds.** — V OR V+O : RECIP, OR V ⇑ unite = marry

Wed. is an abbreviation for 'Wednesday'.

we'd /wiːd/ is 1 the usual spoken form of 'we had', especially when 'had' is an auxiliary verb. EG *We'd done a good job... ...the worst thing we'd ever seen... We'd better go and see.* 2 the usual spoken form of 'we would'. EG *We'd have managed somehow... We'd have given them five if they'd asked... ...the questions we'd all like to ask.*

wedded /wɛdɪ²d/; a formal word. 1 If you are **wedded** to something such as an idea, you support it so strongly that you are unable to give it up. EG *...a party genuinely wedded to unrestricted free enterprise... My thoughts became thoroughly wedded to philosophical things.* — ADJ QUALIT : PRED+*to* = committed

2 If two or more things are **wedded** to each other, they are so closely connected that they cannot be considered separately. EG *Authority remains firmly wedded to doctrinal orthodoxies which many rejected a generation ago.* — ADJ QUALIT : PRED+*to* ⇑ attached

wedding /wɛdɪŋ/, **weddings.** A **wedding** is a marriage ceremony held in a church or registry office, and the party or special meal that often takes place after the ceremony. EG *I'm going to a wedding this weekend... ...a wedding cake... ...a wedding dress... ...wedding presents.* — N COUNT

wedding ring, wedding rings; also spelled with a hyphen. A **wedding ring** is a plain ring that you — N COUNT wear to show that you are married. In Britain, people wear wedding rings on the third finger of the left hand.

wedge /wed3/, **wedges, wedging, wedged.** 1 If you **wedge** something, you force it to remain in a particular position by holding it there tightly or by fixing something next to it to prevent it from moving. EG *Open the door wide and wedge it with a wad of newspaper... Captain Imrie wedged himself more deeply into his chair... For a moment the pigeon remained where it was, wedged in the fork of a branch, then it fell... She sat in a chair wedged between table and bunk.* V+O: USU+A ⇑ fix = jam

2 A **wedge** is 2.1 a piece of wood, rubber, metal, or plastic which has one pointed edge and one thick edge. The pointed edge can be pushed into a gap, for example the gap between a door and the floor, and the thick edge then prevents any movement by either object. N COUNT = stop 2.2 a piece of metal with a pointed edge which is used for splitting stone, wood, slate, etc by being hammered into a crack in the material. N COUNT ⇑ chisel 2.3 a piece of something that has a thick triangular shape, for example a slice of cheese or pie. EG ...*a huge wedge of cherry pie.* N COUNT: ALSO N +*of*+N UNCOUNT

3 If someone **drives a wedge** between people or groups, they cause bad feelings between them in order to weaken their relationship. EG *They are trying to drive a wedge between us and the Arabs... The Government aim was to drive wedges between the main groups.* PHR: VB INFLECTS ⇑ separate = divide

4 If you describe something as **the thin end of the wedge**, you mean that it appears to be unimportant at the moment, but that you think it is the beginning of a harmful development. EG *'Immigration control,' he declaimed, 'is the thin end of the wedge.'* PHR: USED AS C ⇑ sign

wedlock /wedlɒk/; an old-fashioned word. 1 **Wedlock** is the state of being married. N UNCOUNT = marriage

2 If someone is **born in wedlock**, they are born while their parents are married. If they are **born out of wedlock**, they are born at a time when their parents are not married. PHR: USED AS C

Wednesday /wenzdi[3]/, **Wednesdays. Wednesday** is one of the seven days of the week. It is the day after Tuesday and before Thursday. EG *Do they know you're coming next Wednesday?... There are two performances on Wednesdays.* N UNCOUNT/COUNT

Weds. is an abbreviation for Wednesday.

wee /wi:/, **wees, weeing, weed.** 1 Something that is **wee** is small in size, amount, or extent; used mainly in spoken English, especially in Scotland. EG ...*Kinlochbervie, which is a wee fishing place... I got a wee bit worried... It's a nice wee thing.* ADJ CLASSIF: ATTRIB = little

2 When someone **wees**, they urinate; an informal use which some people consider rude and avoid using. EG *The dog stopped to wee at every lamp-post.* ▸ used as a noun. EG *I want a wee.* V ▸ N SING: *a*+N

3 In very informal English, **wee** is the same as urine. EG *A puddle of wee on the kitchen floor.* N UNCOUNT

weed /wi:d/, **weeds, weeding, weeded.** 1 A **weed** is 1.1 a wild plant that grows in gardens or fields of crops and prevents the cultivated plants from growing properly. EG ...*pulling out the weeds from among the tall, green rows of rice.* N COUNT 1.2 a flowerless plant that grows in water and usually forms a thick floating mass. There are many different kinds of weed. EG ...*strange growths of coral, polyp, and weed... ...green pond weeds.* ● See also **seaweed.** N UNCOUNT/COUNT

2 If you **weed**, you remove the weeds from a place or from among the cultivated plants in a place. EG *They were weeding in the fields... I had weeded the garden... I need someone to help me plant potatoes and weed the onions.* ◇ **weeding.** EG *There's weeding to be done in the vegetable garden.* V OR V+O ⇑ tidy ◇ N UNCOUNT

3 If you call someone a **weed**, you mean that they are thin and physically weak and that they seem to have a weak character; used showing disapproval in informal English. EG *He's such a weed.* N COUNT: ALSO VOC = wimp

4 In informal English, people sometimes refer to tobacco or marijuana as **weed.** N UNCOUNT

weed out. If you **weed out** things that are useless or unwanted in a group, you get rid of them. EG *Natural selection had weeded out the weakest... Lightning strikes were excellent for weeding out the pacifists.* PHRASAL VB: V+O+ADV ⇑ remove

weedy /wi:di[1]/, **weedier, weediest.** 1 A place that is **weedy** is full of weeds. EG ...*the long weedy path... The pond was quite large, and very weedy.* ADJ QUALIT ⇑ untidy = overgrown

2 If you describe someone as **weedy**, you mean that they are thin and physically weak, and that they seem weak in character; used showing disapproval in informal English. EG ...*an ugly weedy pimply little brute.* ADJ QUALIT = scrawny

week /wi:k/, **weeks.** 1 A **week** is 1.1 a period of seven days, beginning on a Sunday and ending on a Saturday. Some people say that a week starts on Monday and ends on Sunday. EG *That was a terrible air crash last week... She won't be back till next week... ...once a week, on Tuesdays... He worked seven days a week... I've been wanting to ring you all week.* N COUNT 1.2 a period of about seven days. EG *Death usually occurs within a week... ...a few weeks ago... Nothing has happened in the past week or two.* N COUNT 1.3 the number of hours that you normally spend at work during a week. EG *They went on strike for more pay and a shorter working week... A thirty-five hour week.* N COUNT: USU SING ⇑ period 1.4 the part of the week that does not include Saturday and Sunday; used mainly in spoken English. EG *I can never be bothered to cook much during the week... In the week, we get up at seven.* N SING: *the*+N ≠ weekend

2 The word **weeks** can mean quite a long time. EG *He was seriously ill, and it was weeks before he fully recovered... For weeks and weeks I studied... It's the first time I've seen her in weeks.* N PLURAL ⇑ ages

3 The word **week** is also used in the following expressions. 3.1 **Week after week** means regularly every week; used mainly in spoken English. EG *He sits for hour after hour, week after week and year after year, watching television.* PHR: USED AS AN A ⇑ continually 3.2 **Week by week** means each week; used especially in relation to things that change or develop at the same rate or that happen in the same way each week. EG *The nervous tension had been growing week by week.* PHR: USED AS AN A

3.3 When you are describing or comparing changes that happen rapidly over a fairly short period of time, you can say that they change **from week to week.** EG *How much do babies' weights change from week to week?... Prices change from week to week.* PHR: USED AS AN A

3.4 If something happens **week in, week out,** it happens all the time, with the situation never seeming to change or improve. EG *It got on their nerves, this drip-drip-drip, week in, week out.* PHR: USED AS AN A ⇑ continuously 3.5 **For weeks on end** means for a long time. EG *Temperatures drop to forty degrees below freezing and remain there for weeks on end... I never get lonely even if I don't see anyone for weeks on end.* PHR: USED AS AN A = for ages

4 **Week** is also used 4.1 in expressions like 'a week on Monday', 'a week next Tuesday', 'tomorrow week', etc, to mean exactly one week after the day that you mention. EG *She said, 'when is it to open?' and he replied 'Monday week.'... The party's three weeks on Saturday... It's due a week tomorrow.* 4.2 in expressions like 'a week last Monday', 'a week ago this Tuesday', 'a week ago yesterday', etc, to mean exactly one week before the day that you mention. EG *She died a week last Thursday... A week ago today.*

weekday /wi:kdeɪ/, **weekdays.** A **weekday** is any of the days of the week except Saturday and Sunday; however, sometimes Saturday is considered to be a weekday. EG ...*an ordinary, working weekday... The Tower is open 9.30 to 6.0 on weekdays, 2.0 to 6.0 on Sundays.* N COUNT

weekend /wi:kend/, **weekends**; also spelled with a hyphen. A **weekend** is Saturday and Sunday. Sometimes Friday evening is also considered to be part of the weekend. The weekend is the time when many people in the West do not go to work or school. EG *I spent the weekend at home with my friends... The tower is often open to the public at week-ends... We might be able to go skiing this weekend.* ▸ used to refer to a holiday or visit that lasts over a weekend. EG *I know exactly what I need. A weekend in London.* ● **dirty weekend**: see **dirty.** N COUNT

weekly /wi:kli[1]/, **weeklies.** 1 **Weekly** is used 1.1 to describe something that happens, appears, or is done once a week or every week. EG ...*a weekly newspaper... ...a weekly payment of seven shillings.* ▸ used as an adverb. EG *We played chess two or three times weekly... Several groups meet weekly.* ADJ CLASSIF: USU ATTRIB ⇑ periodical ▸ ADV WITH VB ⇑ periodically 1.2 to describe an amount of something relating to a period of one week. EG *What are your weekly earnings?* ADJ CLASSIF: USU ATTRIB

▸ used as an adverb. EG *The magazine was selling only 125,000 copies weekly.* ▸ ADV WITH VB

2 A **weekly** is a newspaper or magazine that is published once a week. EG *He had been a jazz critic on the university weekly... He controlled two daily newspapers and four local weeklies.* N COUNT ⇑ periodical

weeny /wi:ni¹/, **weenier, weeniest.** **Weeny** is used to describe something that is very small; an informal word. EG *Take just a weeny bit more.* ADJ CLASSIF: ATTRIB = tiny

weep /wi:p/, **weeps, weeping, wept.** 1 If someone **weeps**, they cry; a literary use. EG *The girl was weeping as she kissed him goodbye... She was weeping real tears... James wept when he heard the news... She was weeping with joy at the ceremony.* V OR V+O

▸ used as a noun. EG *They had a little weep together.* ▸ N SING: a+N

2 If a wound **is weeping**, it is bleeding or giving out some other liquid because it is not healing properly. EG *That gash is weeping badly.* V: USU CONT = oozing

weeping willow, weeping willows. A **weeping willow** is a willow tree with long, thin branches that hang down to the ground. N COUNT

weepy /wi:pi¹/, **weepies.** 1 Someone who is **weepy** is sad and likely to cry easily. EG *She came in very weepy. 'Dad's leaving home.'* ADJ QUALIT ⇑ tearful

2 A **weepy** is a film or a story which is sentimental and makes you cry; an informal use. N COUNT

weevil /wi:vɪl/, **weevils.** A **weevil** is a small beetle which feeds on grain and seeds and destroys crops. N COUNT

wee-wee. Small children sometimes use the word **wee-wee** to mean urine. N UNCOUNT

weft /weft/. The **weft** of a piece of woven material is the threads which are passed sideways in and out of the threads held in the loom; a technical word. N SING: the+N ⇑ yarn = woof

weigh /weɪ/, **weighs, weighing, weighed.** 1 If something **weighs** a particular amount, this amount is how heavy it is. EG *It's made of steel and weighs ten tons... The old lady was five feet high and weighed about eighty-two pounds... It looks just like a calculator and weighs about the same.* V+C ⇑ measure

2 If you **weigh** something, you measure how heavy it is, using scales of some sort. EG *The doctor will want to weigh the baby... He weighed all our papers wrong... She was weighing a parcel.* V+O

3 If you **weigh** the facts about a situation, you consider them very carefully before you make a decision, especially by comparing the various facts involved. EG *We have to weigh the evidence and make a decision... These factors have to be weighed against the dangers and anxiety of pregnancy... She had weighed the risks and decided it wasn't worth it.* V+O

● If you **weigh** your **words**, you think very carefully before you speak. EG *'I like Tom very much,' she said, scrupulously weighing her words.* ● PHR: VB INFLECTS

4 Something that **weighs** on a situation has a strong influence or important effect on it. EG *Political events weighed heavily against having children... It has two characteristics which weigh heavily with comparative anatomists.* V+A, OR V+ADV +A

5 to **weigh anchor**: see **anchor**.

weigh down. 1 If a heavy load **weighs** you **down**, it stops you moving easily by making you heavier. EG *He tried to run, but the bags weighed him down too much... He seemed weighed down with weapons and equipment.* PHRASAL VB: V+O+ADV ⇑ burden

2 If you **are weighed down** by a difficulty, it is making you extremely worried. EG *So you're weighed down with problems... Maybe he was weighed down by the burden of state secrets.* PHRASAL VB: V+O+ADV, USU PASS ⇑ oppress

weigh in. 1 If you **weigh in** on a discussion or a conversation, you join in the discussion or conversation by saying something significant or important. EG *The Treasury Secretary weighed in with an opinion.* PHRASAL VB: V+ADV, USU+A ⇑ speak = chip in

2 When the competitors in a boxing match or a horse race **weigh in**, they are weighed to check their weight shortly before the event starts. EG *He weighed in this morning at 185 pounds.* ● See also **weigh-in.** PHRASAL VB: V+ADV, USU+at ⇑ verify

weigh on. If a problem **weighs on** you or **weighs upon** you, it makes you worry. EG *I could still sleep at night, however serious the problems weighing on me were... Her absence began to weigh upon me.* PHRASAL VB: V+PREP, HAS PASS ⇑ oppress

weigh out. If you **weigh** something **out**, you measure a certain weight of it in order to make sure that you have the correct amount. EG *He weighed out a pound of tomatoes.* PHRASAL VB: V+O+ADV = measure out

weigh up. 1 If you **weigh** things **up**, you consider their importance in relation to each other in order to help you make a decision. EG *I weighed up the pros and cons... You have to weigh up in your mind whether to pursue the matter or not.* PHRASAL VB: V+O+ADV = balance

2 If you **weigh** someone **up**, you try and find out what they are like and form an opinion of them by talking to them, watching them, and listening to them. EG *We fenced like this for a while, weighing each other up.* PHRASAL VB: V+O+ADV ⇑ assess = size up

weigh-in, weigh-ins. When there is a **weigh-in** on the day of a boxing match or a horse race, each competitor is weighed to check their weight shortly before the event. EG *Angry words were exchanged at the weigh-in this morning.* N COUNT: USU SING ⇑ verification

weight /weɪt/, **weights, weighting, weighted.** 1 The **weight** of something is its heaviness which can be measured in units such as kilos, pounds, tons, etc. EG *The weight of the load is too great... It was 25 metres long and 30 tons in weight... He became conscious of the weight of his clothes... The whole sideboard groaned under his weight.* N SING WITH DET ⇑ measure

2 A **weight** is 2.1 a metal object which has a certain known heaviness. Weights are used with sets of scales to weigh things by balancing the thing that you are weighing against one or more weights. EG *...big brass scales with all the weights sparkling in a row... The smallest one there is the one ounce weight.* N COUNT ⇑ standard 2.2 an object that is heavy or that seems to be heavy. EG *I'm not allowed to do heavy work, nor can I carry heavy weights any more.* N COUNT ⇑ load

3 If you **weight** something or **weight** it **down**, you make it heavier, often so that it cannot move easily. EG *His gun weighted him to one side... ...men heavily weighted with equipment... ...a plastic sheet weighted down with straw bales... The rope was weighted at the bottom with a two-pound weight.* V+O, OR PHRASAL VB: V+O+ADV

4 The **weight** of something is its large amount or its great power, which means that it is difficult to contradict it or fight against it. EG *The weight of the evidence convinces me that he was wrongly imprisoned... They had the weight of European official support behind them... The sheer numerical weight of demonstrators produced a bitter confrontation.* N SING WITH DET +of

5 If you give **weight** to something that you say or do, you emphasize its importance by using the influence or authority that you have. EG *The fact that he is captain of the hockey team does not give his voice added weight in a General School Meeting.* N UNCOUNT

6 If you feel a **weight** of some kind on you, you have a problem or a responsibility that is difficult for you to manage and that you are very worried about. EG *This was a great weight lifted off my back... Without a producer, the weight of responsibility fell upon me... The fathers of many daughters groan under the weight of paying large sums for marriage ceremonies.* N SING WITH DET = burden

7 The word **weight** is also used in the following expressions. 7.1 If you **put on weight** or **gain weight**, the amount that your body weighs increases. If you **lose weight**, the amount that your body weighs becomes less. EG *I was twelve, and starting to put on weight and grow taller... He seemed happy, except that he had gained a lot of weight... I think she might have lost a bit of weight.* PHR: VB INFLECTS 7.2 If you **pull** your **weight**, you work as hard as everyone else who is involved in the same task or activity as you are. EG *They'll refuse to fund anyone who is not pulling their weight.* PHR: VB INFLECTS 7.3 If you **take the weight off** your **feet**, you sit down to have a rest; an informal expression. EG *Take the weight off your feet for an hour.* PHR: VB INFLECTS 7.4 If you **throw** your **weight about**, you act aggressively and use your authority over other people more than you need to. EG *But here he was back again and throwing his weight about.* PHR: VB INFLECTS ⇑ bully 7.5 If you **throw** your **weight behind** someone, you use all your influence and do everything you can to support them. EG *They countered by throwing their weight behind a rejuvenated Northern People's Congress.* PHR: VB INFLECTS = back 7.6 ● to **carry weight**: see **carry**. ● **worth** your **weight in gold**: see **gold**. ● a **weight off** your **mind**: see **mind**. ● See also **dead weight.**

weighted /weɪtɪ²d/. A system that is **weighted** in favour of a particular person or group is organized in such a way that this person or group will have an advantage. EG *The law is weighted in favour of landlords.* ADJ QUALIT: PRED+A ⇑ biased = prejudiced

weighting /weɪtɪŋ/ is an advantage that a particular group of people receives in a system, especially an extra sum of money that people receive if they work in a city such as London where the cost of N UNCOUNT: USU +SUPP ⇑ allowance = bonus living is very high. EG *Salary range: £26,172-£28,497 plus £1,419 London weighting allowance.*

weightless /weɪtlɪ²s/. 1 Something that is **weightless** seems to have very little weight or no weight at all. EG *These creatures may have been virtually weightless in water... ...a little sporty runabout with a miraculously weightless engine.* ADJ CLASSIF

2 A person or object is **weightless** when they are in space and the earth's gravity does not affect them, so that they float around. EG *Hot drinks are obviously quite dangerous in weightless conditions.* ADJ CLASSIF ≠ heavy

◇ **weightlessness**. EG *...experiencing the weightlessness of space travel.* ◇ N UNCOUNT

weightlifter /weɪtlɪftə/, **weightlifters**. A **weightlifter** is a person who does weightlifting. EG *...muscles that looked as if they should belong to a weightlifter.* N COUNT

weightlifting /weɪtlɪftɪŋ/ is a sport in which competitors try to lift very heavy weights. The winner is the person who lifts the heaviest weight. N UNCOUNT ⇑ activity

weighty /weɪti¹/, **weightier, weightiest**. You use **weighty 1** to describe something that seems serious or important. EG *Let us turn to less weighty matters... This was a subject most of the people thought weighty and dull.* ADJ QUALIT **2** to describe something that is heavy or heavier than you would expect; a formal use. EG *...the problems involved in carrying weighty and noisy infants.* ADJ QUALIT

weir /wɪə/, **weirs**. A **weir** is **1** a low dam which is built across a river in order to control the flow of water or to change its direction. N COUNT **2** a wooden fence which is built across a stream in order to create a pool for catching fish. N COUNT

weird /wɪəd/, **weirder, weirdest**. 1 Something that is **weird** seems strange and peculiar, usually because you have not seen or experienced it before. EG *The markets sell all sorts of weird vegetables... The time I spent with him had had a weird effect on me... Peculiar things have happened before, but this is even weirder.* ADJ QUALIT = bizarre ◇ **weirdly**. EG *...weirdly shaped baobab trees.* ◇ ADV ◇ **weirdness**. EG *There was a futuristic weirdness about the place.* ◇ N UNCOUNT ⇑ strangeness

2 If you describe someone as **weird**, you mean that they behave in an unusual way which most people find difficult to understand or to accept as normal; used in informal British English. EG *He wasn't mad but he was certainly weird.* ADJ QUALIT ⇑ strange = odd

weirdo /wɪədəʊ/, **weirdos**. A **weirdo** is someone who behaves in an unusual way which most people find difficult to understand or to accept as normal; an informal word, used mainly in spoken English. EG *When we started up, the locals thought we were weirdos.* N COUNT

welcome /welkəm/, **welcomes, welcoming, welcomed**. 1 If you **welcome** someone, you greet them in a friendly way when they arrive at the place where you are. EG *He moved eagerly towards the door to welcome his visitor... Vernon welcomed me back with a smile and a handshake.* V+O = receive ▸ You also say **'welcome'** in expressions when you are greeting someone in this way. EG *Welcome to Peking... Welcome home, Marsha... 'Welcome back,' said Howard, kissing Barbara on the cheek.* ▸ CONVENTION : USU+A ▸ used as a noun. EG *I was given a warm welcome by the President of Harvard himself... The tumultuous welcome home he received there was token enough of his popularity.* ▸ N COUNT : USU SING ⇑ greeting

2 If you say that you **welcome** certain people, actions, etc, you are inviting and encouraging people to do something, for example to come to a particular place. EG *We always welcome people from outside the university in the extra-mural department... Nominations from organizations are welcomed.* V+O

3 If you say that someone is **welcome** in a particular place, you encourage them that they will be accepted there gladly. EG *You'll be welcome on the staff of the Dispatch, son... All members of the public are welcome... It was clear some members were more welcome than others... Because I was neutral in the conflict I was a welcome visitor in both camps.* ADJ QUALIT : USU PRED ● If you **make** someone **welcome**, you make them feel happy and accepted in a new place. EG *The women made her welcome... Our children seem to be made most welcome.* ● PHR : VB INFLECTS

4 If you tell someone that they are **welcome** to do something, you encourage them to do it by assuring them that they are allowed to do it. EG *You know you will always be welcome to come back... You're welcome to use my bicycle at any time.* ADJ QUALIT : PRED+to-INF

5 If you say that someone is **welcome** to something, you mean that you do not want it yourself and you are very willing for them to have it. EG *That dog's more trouble than it's worth-they're welcome to it.* ADJ QUALIT : PRED+to

6 If you **welcome** an action, you approve of it and support it. EG *I warmly welcomed his proposal... First of all I think we must welcome the Report... This legislation is particularly welcomed.* V+O ● If you **welcome** someone or something **with open arms**, you accept them very enthusiastically. EG *Our teaching degree is welcomed with open arms over there.* ● PHR : VB INFLECTS

7 If someone **welcomes** a situation or event, they are pleased about it; a fairly literary use. EG *Victoria's marriage was not welcomed by the family... He welcomed the long days of hard work, for they kept him from thinking too much.* V+O ⇑ accept

8 You use **welcome** to describe something that someone does or gives you which you want and greatly appreciate. EG *These awards are a welcome tribute to Radio... ...a most welcome trend... ...a welcome cup of cocoa... A little drop of Scotch would be very welcome.* ADJ QUALIT ⇑ pleasant

9 If you say **'You're welcome'** to someone who has thanked you for something, you acknowledge their thanks in a polite way; used especially in American English. EG *'Thank you for the beautiful charm.'-'You're welcome. I'm glad you like it.'* CONVENTION

welcoming /welkəmɪŋ/. Someone who is **welcoming** is friendly to you when you arrive in a place so that you feel happy and accepted. EG *Should she be cool and withdrawn, or warm and welcoming?* ADJ QUALIT ⇑ cordial ▸ used of people's actions and behaviour. EG *She gave him a warm welcoming smile.*

weld /weld/, **welds, welding, welded**. 1 If you **weld** two pieces of metal together, you join them, usually by heating the edges and fixing them so that they cool and harden solidly together. EG *It takes speed and skill to weld steel at this heat... Put this on top of the shaft and weld it on.* V+O : USU+A/ADV *(together)*

2 A **weld** is a join where two pieces of metal have been welded together. EG *There are faults in every piece of weld.* N COUNT

3 If you **weld** people into a group, you join them together to form a united organization; a formal use. EG *His task was to take the vast and disorderly assemblies of soldiers and weld them into a smoothly operating whole.* V+O+A ⇑ unite

welder /weldə/, **welders**. A **welder** is a person whose job is welding metal. N COUNT ⇑ worker

welfare /welfeə/. 1 The **welfare** of a person, group, or organization is their general state of well-being, for example the good health and comfort of the person or group, or the stability and prosperity of the organization. EG *...a society in which all cooperate and work for the welfare of all its members... I would devote all my life to the child's welfare... Our old people's welfare committee was started here in 1952.* N UNCOUNT : WITH POSS = benefit

2 **Welfare** is used to describe the activities of an organization, especially the government, which are concerned with the health, education, living conditions, and financial problems of the people in society. EG *...cut-backs in health and welfare services... ...welfare workers.* N BEFORE N ⇑ help = social

3 **Welfare** is money which is paid by the government to people who are unemployed, have poorly paid jobs, or cannot work because of illness or disability; used in American English. EG *They were living off welfare.* N UNCOUNT = supplementary benefit

welfare state. The **welfare state** is a system in which the government provides free social services such as health and education and gives money to people when they are old, unemployed, or sick. N SING : *the*+N

well /wel/, **wells, welling, welled**. The comparative and superlative of **well** when it is used as an adverb are **better** and **best**: see separate entries for these words. **1** You use **'Well'**, mainly in spoken English, **1.1** to indicate that you are about to say something. EG *'Is that right?'-'Well, I think so.'... 'You talk as though he were already condemned.'-'Well, John, I'm quite convinced he's our man.'* **1.2** to indicate that you intend or want to carry on speaking. EG *You know I wanted to go swimming? Well, it turned out much better... Well, let me finish.* **1.3** to indicate that you are changing the topic, and are either going back to something that was being = anyway, so discussed earlier or are going on to something new. EG *And of course I'd always loved London. Well then, after the war I'd got a job and settled there... Right, well. We've got to cover several basic things.* **1.4** to indicate that you have reached the end of a conversation. EG *Well thank you Jim for talking to us about your work... Well thank you very much for having us.* = anyway

1.5 to make a suggestion, criticism or correction seem less definite or strong. EG *Well, let's play the tape back... Well then, you just need to let go of the steering wheel... Well, obviously you have to take it carefully... It was, well, it was a little bit tactless I think.* **1.6** when you are explaining or justifying something that you have just said. EG *It's cheap there, well a litre of whisky was two pounds.* **1.7** just before or after you pause, especially to give yourself time to think about what you are going to say, or because you want to rephrase something that you have just said. EG *I've told her that you are, well, helping me in this matter.* **1.8** when you are modifying or correcting something that you have just said. EG *We walked along in silence for a bit; well, not really silence because she was humming... It took me years, well months at least, to realise that he'd actually lied to me.* **1.9** to express your doubt about something that someone has said. EG *'He also has a great love for his father.'–'Well. Do you really think so?'* **1.10** to express your surprise or anger at something that someone has just said or done. EG *Well, really! What cheek!* **1.11** in the expression 'oh well' to indicate that you accept that the situation cannot be changed, although you are not happy about it. EG *Oh well, you wouldn't understand.* **1.12** to indicate amused acknowledgement of something that someone has said, and often to introduce a comment on it. EG *'Well, well,' said Flora, 'now we know why she came to see me.'... Twenty years since you've been home, eh? Well, well, well, what do you think of America?* = you know

● **very well**: see **very**.

2 If you do something **well**, **2.1** you do it to a high standard or to a great extent. EG *She speaks French well... The strategy has worked very well in the past... You say you don't know this man very well?... I get on really well with all his family... He handled it well.* **2.2** you do it thoroughly and completely. EG *They grew their hair long and oiled it well... Make sure that you cook that pork well.* ADV AFTER VB / ADV AFTER VB

3 Well is used in front of past participles to indicate that something is done to a high standard or to a great extent. Combinations like this are often written with a hyphen or spelled as one word. Many of the commonest combinations are treated as separate headwords in this dictionary. The comparative and superlative forms of all these combinations are formed with 'better-' and 'best-'. EG *The roots of democracy are very well established there... He came from a well-educated family... He was well satisfied with the success of the aircraft... The hotels are new and well-equipped.* ADV+PAST PART ⇑ very

4 You also use **well** **4.1** in questions or statements about the extent or standard of something. EG *How well do you think they've worn? Are they still as good as they were?... I could see almost as well at night as I could in sunlight.* **4.2** in front of a prepositional phrase to provide emphasis, for example in order to say that something happens a long time before or after a particular point, or is a long way from a place, or is much greater or less than the extent mentioned. EG *I woke well before dawn... We always had to book the same room well in advance... We did not know how the votes were cast until well after the conference... They were well out of range of the rocket launcher... They stood well back from the heat... ...marvellous colour illustrations, and well over one hundred of them.* **4.3** in front of certain adjectives to give emphasis to them. EG *I was very well aware that my little boat was far too frail to cope with the crossing... The interior of the building is well worth a look... The film is well worth seeing.* **4.4** after adverbs such as 'perfectly', 'jolly', or 'damn' in order to emphasize an opinion or the truth of what you are saying. EG *We managed perfectly well without you... They each suspected only too well what the other might be up to... They must jolly well settle it themselves... 'What is it?'–'You know damn well what it is.'* ● **pretty well**: see **pretty**. ADV: how+ADV, OR as/so+ADV+as / ADV+PREP / ADV+ADJ = definitely, certainly / ADV AFTER ADV: WITH VB

5 You use **well** when you are saying what you think is likely to happen. EG *Coal and gas supplies may well last one or two hundred years... As a matter of fact, your eyesight may well improve... He could equally well be using the story as a cloak for something slightly illegal.* ADV AFTER MODAL ⇑ possibly

6 If you are **well**, you are healthy and not ill. EG *She answered, 'I am very well.'... On examination she looked well... I'm not a well man.* ADJ QUALIT: USU PRED = fit

7 The word **well** is also used in the following expressions. **7.1** If you say that things are **going well**, that **all is well**, etc, you mean that the situation is satisfactory or as you would like it to be. EG *Things went well for John until the First World War... The courses he was working out were going well, amassing a considerable following... Is it going well?... All well at the office I hope?* **7.2** If you say that you like something, know someone, etc **well enough**, you mean that you quite like it, know them fairly well, etc; used especially when you find a situation reasonably adequate or acceptable. EG *That would suit Godley well enough... I like it well enough but I'm thinking of the future.* **7.3** If you **speak well** or **think well** of someone or something, you say or think favourable things about them. EG *I've heard him speak well of 'The Way we Live Now.'* **7.4** If you say that you **are well in with** someone, you mean that you are very friendly with them and have a close relationship with them; an informal expression. EG *She's well in with the people next door.* **7.5** If you say that you **are well out of** a situation, you mean that you are no longer involved in it, usually when you are pleased about this. EG *I'm glad to be well out of it.* **7.6** You say **well and good** to indicate that you find a particular situation acceptable or satisfactory. EG *If the worker can do it in less time, well and good... If you want to stay here all on your own, well and good.* **7.7** You use the expression **well and truly** to emphasize that something is completely finished or gone, or that it is thoroughly done. EG *I think that school of theology is well and truly dead... It's well and truly over... Make sure your tyres are well and truly wet.* **7.8** ● **all very well**: see **all**. ● **do well to** do something: see **do**. PHR: VB INFLECTS = OK, satisfactorily / PHR: USED AS AN A / PHR: VB INFLECTS+of / PHR: VB INFLECTS / PHR: VB INFLECTS / PHR: USED AS ADV SEN / PHR+ADJ/ADV

8 as well. **8.1** You use **as well** when mentioning something which happens in the same way as something else already mentioned, or which should be considered at the same time as something else already mentioned. EG *You've already been late for breakfast, and if you don't eat fast, you'll be late for school as well... It brought him a good deal of local fame–money as well, obviously... Now she stretched out the other leg as well... He needs to develop his reading further, and his writing as well.* **8.2** If you refer to a second thing **as well as** a first thing, you refer to the second thing in addition to the first. EG *Women, as well as men, have a fundamental right to work... It has symbolic as well as economic significance.* **8.3** If you say, after stating something that has happened, **'as well it might'** or **'as well it may'**, you mean that it is right, fair, or appropriate for this to have happened in the way it did. EG *Mr Baldwin looked astounded, as well he might.* **8.4** If you say that you **may as well** do something, or that you **might as well** do it, you mean that you will do it although you do not have a strong desire to do it and may even feel slightly reluctant about it. EG *I may as well admit that I knew the answer all along... I thought I might as well go, you can't keep saying no to people.* **8.5** If you say that something that has happened **is just as well**, you mean that it is fortunate that it happened in the way it did. EG *He didn't have to speak very often, which was just as well as he was a man who liked to keep words to himself.* PHR: USED AS ADV SEN = also, too / PREP / PHR / PHR / PHR: VB INFLECTS

9 A **well** is **9.1** a hole in the ground from which a supply of water is extracted. EG *Everyone digs his own well, but in the dry season these dry up... No other well has such sweet water.* **9.2** an oil well. N COUNT ⇑ shaft / N COUNT

10 If liquids **well** or **well up** somewhere, especially if tears **well up** in someone's eyes, they come to the surface and form a pool. EG *Tears welled in my eyes... Tears welled up in his eyes and he brushed them aside... ...where water has welled up from the ocean beneath.* ▸ used of emotions; a literary use. EG *Happiness welled up inside me.* V+A, OR PHRASAL VB: V+ADV+A ⇑ appear / ▸ = surged

we'll /wiːl/ is the usual spoken form of 'we shall' or 'we will'. EG *We'll all meet in a few hours... Come on, then, we'll have to hurry.*

well-advised; also spelled without a hyphen. If someone says that you would be **well-advised** to do a particular thing, they are advising you to do it. EG *Tom would have been well advised to tear himself away from Newmarket before he lost any more money.* — ADJ QUALIT: PRED, USU+to-INF ⇑ sensible = wise

well-appointed; also spelled without a hyphen. A **well-appointed** room or building is equipped or furnished to a very high standard. EG *...an exceptionally well-appointed kitchen.* — ADJ QUALIT

well-balanced; also spelled without a hyphen. If someone is **well-balanced**, they are sensible and do not have many emotional problems. EG *His children are sufficiently mature and well balanced to be able to live on equal terms with their step-mother.* — ADJ QUALIT = stable

well-behaved; also spelled without a hyphen. If someone, especially a child, is **well-behaved**, they behave in a way that adults generally like and think is correct. EG *She's a very well behaved little girl.* — ADJ QUALIT ⇑ good

well-being; also spelled as one word. If you refer to someone's **well-being**, you are referring to whether they are healthy, happy, etc, so that life is enjoyable and worth living. EG *Such concern for our wellbeing was pleasing... ...the belief that every technological advance contributes to the wellbeing of mankind.* — N UNCOUNT: USU WITH SUPP = welfare

well-born; also spelled without a hyphen. Someone who is **well-born** belongs to an upper-class family. — ADJ CLASSIF

well-bred; also spelled without a hyphen. Someone who is **well-bred** is very polite and has good manners. EG *She looked tired, but she was too well bred to ask her visitors to leave.* — ADJ QUALIT = well-mannered

well-brought-up; also spelled without hyphens. People, especially children, who are **well-brought-up** are very polite because they have been taught good manners. EG *They're very well-brought-up children.* — ADJ QUALIT

well-built; also spelled without a hyphen. Someone, especially a man, who is **well-built** is strong and muscular; used showing approval. EG *Johnny was well built, with fair hair and a natural belligerence.* — ADJ QUALIT

well-connected; also spelled without a hyphen. Someone who is **well-connected** has important or influential relatives or friends. — ADJ QUALIT

well-defined; also spelled without a hyphen. Something that is **well-defined** is easy to recognize or understand because it is clear or precise. EG *...a set of well-defined values.* — ADJ QUALIT

well-disposed; also spelled without a hyphen. If you are **well-disposed** to a person, plan, or activity, you are likely to be sympathetic or friendly towards that person or willing to take part in that plan or activity. EG *Our kids are very well disposed to what we're doing.* — ADJ QUALIT: USU +to

well done. 1 You say **well done** when you want to indicate how pleased you are that someone has got something right or has done something properly, successfully, etc. EG *'Which sea is this?'–'The Atlantic Ocean.'–'Atlantic Ocean. Well done.'... That's right. Well done.* — CONVENTION ⇑ good

2 If something has been **well done**, it has been performed, accomplished, or carried out successfully or properly. EG *The adaptation of the play from TV to theatre was exceptionally well done... ...a good job well done.* — ADJ QUALIT: PRED

3 If something such as meat or vegetables is **well done**, it has been cooked thoroughly so that it is slightly over-cooked rather than still slightly raw. EG *Pork has to be very well done, or you can't eat it.* — ADJ QUALIT

well-dressed; also spelled without a hyphen. Someone who is **well-dressed** wears smart or elegant clothes. EG *...two dainty welldressed women... They like to see their children well dressed.* — ADJ QUALIT

well-earned; also spelled without a hyphen. If you describe something as **well-earned**, you mean that it is deserved, usually because you have been working very hard. EG *Let us take a well-earned rest.* — ADJ QUALIT

well-established; also spelled without a hyphen. Something that is **well-established** has been in existence for quite a long time and is successful. EG *Senegal already has a well-established film industry.* — ADJ QUALIT

well-fed; also spelled without a hyphen. Someone who is **well-fed** gets good food regularly. EG *The people there are wellfed.* — ADJ QUALIT

well-founded; also spelled without a hyphen. If an idea, opinion, or feeling is **well-founded**, it is based on facts and can therefore be justified. EG *Once again, these warnings proved well-founded... ...a wellfounded complaint.* — ADJ CLASSIF = justifiable

well-groomed; also spelled without a hyphen. Someone who is **well-groomed** is very neat and tidy, so that they look as if they have taken care over their appearance. EG *...a stout and wellgroomed man in his mid-fifties.* — ADJ QUALIT

well-grounded means the same as well-founded. EG *They put on 'Guys and Dolls' on the assumption (which is well-grounded) that musicals always do well.* — ADJ CLASSIF

well-heeled; also spelled without a hyphen. Someone who is **well-heeled** is wealthy; an informal word. — ADJ CLASSIF = rich

well-informed; also spelled without a hyphen. Someone who is **well-informed** knows a lot, usually about many different subjects but sometimes about one subject in particular. EG *They become as well-informed as possible on the issues involved... She explained it in terms which any intelligent and reasonably well-informed layman can understand.* — ADJ QUALIT ⇑ knowledgeable

wellington /we̱lɪŋtən/, **wellingtons**. **Wellingtons** or **wellington boots** are long rubber boots which you wear to keep your feet dry. — N COUNT: ALSO a *pair of*+N = gumboot

well-intentioned; also spelled without a hyphen. Something that is **well-intentioned** is meant to be helpful, useful, or kind, but is unsuccessful or has unfortunate results. EG *...a well-intentioned effort to obtain evidence failed abysmally.* ▸ used of people. EG *He was well-intentioned, but faint-hearted.* — ADJ QUALIT

well-kept; also spelled without a hyphen. A **well-kept** building, room, place, etc is looked after carefully, so that it is always neat and tidy. EG *...a quiet, wellkept street... ...a curious-looking mansion with a well-kept lawn.* — ADJ QUALIT

well-known; also spelled without a hyphen. Something or someone that is **well-known** is known by a lot of people and is therefore famous or familiar. EG *...his two well-known books on modern art... She was a friend of Edward VII and well known to the German Emperor... It's well known that separating children from their mothers can lead to problems in later life.* — ADJ QUALIT

well-mannered; also spelled without a hyphen. Someone who is **well-mannered** is polite and has good manners. — ADJ QUALIT

well-meaning; also spelled without a hyphen. Someone who is **well-meaning** acts kindly and from the best of motives, but often with unfortunate results. EG *Well-meaning friends said: 'You cannot afford to do it.'* ▸ used of their actions. EG *Their sympathy was well-meaning but ineffective.* — ADJ QUALIT

well-meant; also spelled without a hyphen. Something that is **well-meant** is intended to be helpful, useful, or kind, but is unsuccessful or has unfortunate results. EG *I don't want anyone else's opinion, however well-meant.* — ADJ CLASSIF

well-nigh; also spelled without a hyphen. You use **well-nigh** to say that something almost has the particular quality or identity mentioned. EG *It's extremely difficult, well nigh impossible to choose between them... The otter is well-nigh extinct in most of Britain.* — ADV+ADJ = nearly

well-off; also spelled without a hyphen; an informal word. 1 Someone who is **well-off** is rich enough to be able to do and buy most of the things that they want. EG *She's quite well-off, isn't she?* ▸ The **well-off** is used to refer to people who are rich. EG *These buyers tend to be the relatively well-off.* — ADJ QUALIT: USU PRED; ▸ N PLURAL: *the*+N

2 Someone who is **well-off** for something has as much of it as they want or need. EG *You're well off for coal, I hope?* — ADJ QUALIT: PRED+*for*

3 If you say to someone that they **don't know when** they **are well off**, you are criticizing them for not appreciating how fortunate they are. — PHR: AUX INFLECTS

well-paid; also spelled without a hyphen. Someone who is **well-paid** receives a good salary or payment for the job that they do. EG *Secretaries are quite well paid these days.* ▸ used of jobs. EG *...an important-sounding and wellpaid job.* — ADJ QUALIT

well-preserved; also spelled without a hyphen. If you say that someone or something old is **well-preserved**, you mean that they do not show many signs of their age. EG *...a well-preserved man in his late fifties.* — ADJ QUALIT

well-read; also spelled without a hyphen. Someone who is **well-read** has read a lot of books and has learnt a lot from them. EG *Her brother was immensely companionable, active, intelligent, very well-read... She was very well read in the literary classics.* ADJ QUALIT ⇑ learned

well-spoken; also spelled without a hyphen. Someone who is **well-spoken** speaks in a polite, correct way and with an accent which is considered socially acceptable. EG *She was well-spoken and had a pleasant manner.* ADJ QUALIT

well-thought-of; also spelled without hyphens. Someone or something that is **well-thought-of** is admired, respected, and has a good reputation. EG *She's very well-thought-of as a solicitor.* ADJ QUALIT

well-thought-out; also spelled without hyphens. Something that is **well-thought-out** is very carefully planned, so that all the details have been thought about and all the necessary decisions have been taken. EG *...a well written, entertaining, and outstandingly well thought-out first novel.* ADJ QUALIT

well-thumbed; also spelled without a hyphen. A book or magazine that is **well-thumbed** is creased and marked because it has been read so often. ADJ QUALIT

well-timed; also spelled without a hyphen. An action or remark that is **well-timed** is said or done at the most appropriate or suitable time. EG *...well-timed purchases of stock.* ADJ QUALIT = timely

well-to-do. Someone who is **well-to-do** is rich enough to be able to do and buy most of the things that they want. EG *He came from a well-to-do family.* ADJ QUALIT ⇑ wealthy
▸ The **well-to-do** is used to refer to people who are rich. EG *...the children of the well-to-do.* ▸ N PLURAL : *the*+N

well-tried; also spelled without a hyphen. Something that is **well-tried** has been used or done many times before and so is known to work well or to be successful. EG *...a well-tried technique.* ADJ QUALIT

well-turned; a rather old-fashioned word. **1** A **well-turned** remark is expressed in a careful and pleasing way. ADJ QUALIT : ATTRIB
2 A **well-turned** limb or object has an attractive shape. EG *...a glimpse of a well-turned ankle.* ADJ QUALIT = shapely

well-versed; also spelled without a hyphen. Someone who is **well-versed** in a particular subject knows a lot about it. EG *They were relatively well versed in the rhetoric of Black liberation.* ADJ QUALIT : USU PRED+*in* = knowledgeable

wellwisher /wɛlwɪʃə/, **wellwishers**; also spelled with a hyphen. A **wellwisher** is someone who hopes that a particular person or thing will be successful and who does something to show their feelings. EG *Hundreds of telegrams arrived from wellwishers.* N COUNT ⇑ supporter

well-worn; also spelled without a hyphen. **1** A **well-worn** word, remark, etc, has been used so often that it no longer seems to have much meaning or to be interesting. EG *...a well-worn joke.* ADJ QUALIT = hackneyed
2 A **well-worn** object, piece of clothing, etc has been worn or used so frequently that it looks rather old and untidy. ADJ QUALIT

welly /wɛli[1]/, **wellies**. A **welly** is a wellington; an informal word used in British English. N COUNT : ALSO *a pair of*+N

Welsh /wɛlʃ/. **1 Welsh** means belonging or relating to Wales. EG *...a Welsh border town... ...Welsh farmers.* ADJ CLASSIF ⇑ Celtic
2 Welsh is the language that is spoken in some parts of Wales. EG *The amount of literature in Welsh is quite small.* N UNCOUNT
3 The **Welsh** are the people who live in or come from Wales. N PLURAL : *the*+N

Welshman /wɛlʃmə[3]m/, **Welshmen**. A **Welshman** is a man who comes from Wales. N COUNT

Welsh rarebit or **Welsh rabbit** is a savoury food which you make by putting cheese, sometimes mixed with other things such as milk, flour, and spices, onto bread, and heating it so that the cheese melts. N UNCOUNT

Welshwoman /wɛlʃwʊ[1]mə[0]n/, **Welshwomen**. A **Welshwoman** is a woman who comes from Wales. N COUNT

welt /wɛlt/, **welts**. A **welt** is a mark which is made on someone's skin, usually by a blow from something such as a whip or sword. EG *...a fresh pink welt on his throat.* N COUNT ⇑ wound = weal

welter /wɛltə/. A **welter** of something is a large quantity of it which occurs in a confusing or sudden mixture; a formal or literary word. EG *Soldiers fought and died in a welter of blood and bullets... ...the daily welter of details and little problems.* N PART : SING = jumble, confusion

wench /wɛntʃ/, **wenches**. A **wench** is a girl or young woman, especially a servant or prostitute; an old-fashioned word. EG *...serving wenches.* N COUNT

wend /wɛnd/, **wends, wending, wended**. If you **wend** your **way** in a particular direction, you walk, especially slowly, casually, or carefully, in that direction; a formal or literary word. EG *We watched them wend their leisurely way up and down the street.* PHR : VB INFLECTS+A ⇑ go = amble, saunter

wendy house, wendy houses. A **wendy house** is a small toy house for a child to play in. N COUNT = play house

went /wɛnt/ is the past tense of **go**.

wept /wɛpt/ is the past tense and past participle of **weep**.

were /wə, wɜː/ is **1** the plural and the second person singular of the past tense of **be**. EG *His eyes were blue... Were you in any danger?... We weren't there for long, were we?* **2** sometimes used in formal English instead of 'was' in conditional clauses or when you are wishing for something. EG *He treated me as if I were crazy... He wished he were taking a bath... She felt as though she were stumbling up a mountain.* ● **as it were**: see **as**.

we're /wɪə/ is the usual spoken form of 'we are'. EG *We're all here... It's too dark to see what we're doing... What we're trying to do is much more difficult.*

weren't /wɜːnt/ is the usual spoken form of 'were not'. EG *We weren't asleep... Why weren't you listening?... They were staying with you, weren't they?*

werewolf /wɛəwʊlf/, **werewolves**. A **werewolf** is an imaginary person, especially in horror films and stories, who changes his or her appearance and behaviour and starts to look and behave like a wolf. N COUNT

west /wɛst/. The word **west** is often spelled with a capital letter, especially for paragraph 5. **1** The **west** is **1.1** the direction which you look towards in the evening in order to see the sun set. EG *The next settlement is two hundred miles to the west... The bare hills behind Agadir in the west are built of blue limestones... He stares across the river at the clouded west.* N SING : *the*+N **1.2** the part of a place, country, or region which is towards the west. EG *...in remote rural areas of the west of Ireland... He belonged to one of the peoples living in China's far west.* ● See also **Middle West, Wild West**. N SING : WITH *the*/POSS
2 West means towards the west or to the west of a place or thing. EG *She was apparently intent on what lay further west... I was accompanied by an English friend who had never been West.* ADV AFTER VB = westward
3 The **west** part of a place, country, or region is the part which is towards the west. EG *I got off the plane and into the muggy, perfumed air of West Africa... ...the Labour MP for Oldham West.* ADJ CLASSIF : ALSO IN NAMES
4 A **west** wind blows from the west. ADJ CLASSIF
5 The **West** is also used to refer to the United States, Canada, and the countries of Western and Southern Europe. EG *...the capitalist West... ...China's strengthening links with the West... The West exported capital and manufactures to the third world.* N SING : *the*+N

westbound /wɛstbaʊnd/. **Westbound** roads, cars, trains, etc lead or are travelling towards the west. EG *...the westbound passenger express.* ADJ CLASSIF ≠ eastbound

westerly /wɛstəli[1]/. **1** A **westerly** point, area, or direction is to the west or towards the west. EG *We were standing on the most westerly point of England.* ADJ QUALIT = western
2 A **westerly** wind blows from the west. EG *The ship was driven by the incessant westerly gales.* ADJ CLASSIF ≠ easterly

western /wɛstə[5]n/, **westerns**. The word **western** is often spelled with a capital letter. **1 Western** means **1.1** in or from the west of a region or country. EG *The sun began to turn crimson on the western horizon... I've just had four years in Western Nigeria.* ADJ CLASSIF : ATTRIB ≠ eastern
1.2 coming from or associated with the people of Europe and North America, and the way in which they live, especially their attitudes, technology, or political and economic systems. EG *...the end of smallpox as a scourge in the western world... ...the impact of western technology... ...western-style housing.* ADJ CLASSIF ⇑ modern
2 A **western** is a book or film about life in the west of America in the nineteenth century. The story usually involves a lot of fighting and shooting. N COUNT

westerner /wɛstənə/, **westerners**. A **westerner** is **1** a person who was born in or lives in the West, especially in Europe or North America. EG *We found ourselves in a swirl of Westerners and Chinese.* N COUNT **2** a N COUNT person who was born in or who lives in the west of a place or country.

westernize /wɛ̲stənaɪz/, **westernizes, westernizing, westernized**; also spelled **westernise**. To **westernize** a society, place, system, etc means to introduce into it ideas and behaviour which are common in Europe and North America, so that people who originally had different traditions change their habits or attitudes. EG *From 1867, the Meiji rulers westernized Japan with astonishing speed... Westernized tastes spread and traditions weaken.* ◇ **westernization** /wɛ̲stənaɪzeɪ̲ʃəⁿn/. EG *...the first wave of westernization in West Africa.* — V+O; ◇ N UNCOUNT

westernmost /wɛ̲stəˢnməʊst/. The **westernmost** part of an area or the **westernmost** thing in a line is the one that is farther towards the west than any other. EG *...the westernmost stretches of the desert.* — ADJ CLASSIF : ATTRIB

West German, West Germans. 1 West German means belonging or relating to the Federal Republic of Germany. EG *The West German leaders are still divided among themselves... It was built by a West German firm.* — ADJ CLASSIF

2 A **West German** is someone who comes from the Federal Republic of Germany. — N COUNT

West Indian, West Indians. 1 West Indian means belonging or relating to the West Indies. EG *...the West Indian community in Paddington.* — ADJ CLASSIF

2 A **West Indian** is a person who comes from the West Indies. — N COUNT

westward /wɛ̲stwəd/, **westwards. Westward** or **westwards** means towards the west. EG *She suggested we just continue westward... The reef stretches westwards from the tip of Florida.* ▸ **Westward** is also used as an adjective. EG *Its desirability as building land for the westward expansion of the city had long been recognised.* — ADV AFTER VB ≠ eastward; ▸ ADJ CLASSIF

wet /wɛ̲t/, **wetter, wettest; wets, wetting, wetted**. The forms **wet** and **wetted** are both used as the past participle and past tense of the verb. **1** If something is **wet**, it is covered in water, rain, sweat, or another liquid. EG *I don't want to get my feet wet... The grass is wet... I'm soaking wet... His long face was wet with perspiration.* ◇ **wetly**. EG *She stood there, glistening wetly.* ◇ **wetness**. EG *...the sticky wetness of blood.* — ADJ QUALIT = damp, soaked; ◇ ADV WITH VB; ◇ N UNCOUNT

2 If the weather is **wet**, it is raining. EG *Take a raincoat if it's wet... It was a wet day, pouring wet... The American winter was cold, wet and windy... ...wet weather.* ▸ The **wet** is used to mean wet weather or rain. EG *...all night long in the dark and wet... There was the caravan, glistening in the wet.* ◇ **wetness**. EG *...the coldness and wetness of the British climate.* — ADJ QUALIT = rainy; ▸ N SING : the+N = rain; ◇ N UNCOUNT

3 If something such as paint, ink, or cement is **wet**, it is not yet dry or solid. EG *While the colours were still wet, he drew a crude pair of eyes... ...a fan-shaped pattern in the wet plaster... ...wet paint.* — ADJ CLASSIF = damp, tacky

4 If people's faces, cheeks, or eyes are **wet**, they are full of or covered in tears. EG *She raised a red, wet face to me and wailed... I realized that my eyes were wet and I was breathing hard.* — ADJ QUALIT = moist, tearful

5 If a child is **wet**, its nappies or clothes are soaked in urine. EG *He was wet so I changed him.* ▸ used of clothes or bedding. EG *...a wet nappy.* — ADJ CLASSIF

6 Wet fish on sale in a shop or market is fish that is fresh and uncooked, and not frozen or dried. EG *Is there a wet fish stall in the market?* — ADJ CLASSIF : ATTRIB ⇑ raw

7 If you say that someone is **wet**, you mean that they are weak and lacking in enthusiasm, energy, or confidence; an informal word showing disapproval. EG *'I don't see what I can do.'–'Judy! Don't be so wet.'* ▸ used of their behaviour, actions, or achievements. EG *I think it's wet, utterly wet... It's a wet, weak piece of work.* ◇ **wetly**. — ADJ QUALIT = feeble; ◇ ADV WITH VB

8 If you say that someone is **wet behind the ears**, you mean that they do not have much experience of things and are unaware of difficulties and dangers; an informal expression. — PHR : USED AS C ⇑ innocent = naive

9 A **wet** is someone, especially a Conservative politician, who supports moderate political policies and opposes extreme ones; used in informal British English. EG *...the Tory Wets.* — N COUNT

10 To **wet** something means to get water or some other liquid over it. EG *Uncle Ted wet his lips... A column of spray wetted them... He walked carefully so as not to wet his shoes.* ● **to wet your whistle**: see **whistle**. — V+O = moisten, drench

11 If people, especially children, **wet** their beds or clothes or **wet** themselves, they urinate in their beds or clothes because they cannot control their bladder. EG *Martin's wet his pyjama trousers... He's wet himself again.* — V+O (NG/REFL)

wet blanket, wet blankets. If you say that someone is a **wet blanket**, you mean that they refuse to join other people in a particular activity or that they speak or behave in such a way that they stop other people enjoying themselves; an informal word showing disapproval. — N COUNT : USU USED AS C ⇑ person = bore

wet-nurse, wet-nurses; also spelled without a hyphen. A **wet-nurse** is a woman, especially in former times, who was paid to feed another woman's baby with her breast milk. — N COUNT

wet suit, wet suits; also spelled with a hyphen. A **wet suit** is a close-fitting rubber suit which is worn by a diver, underwater swimmer, etc in order to keep his or her body warm. — N COUNT

we've /wi̲ːv/ is the usual spoken form of 'we have', especially when 'have' is an auxiliary verb. EG *We've been waiting to hear from you... We've got to keep on struggling... We've had a very interesting discussion.*

> **WH** □ In this dictionary WH is used in the grammar notes beside entries for the words 'who', 'whom', 'whose', 'what', 'which', 'when', 'where', 'why', 'how', and also these words when they are combined with 'ever', as in 'whoever'. WH words are used in the following ways. **1** They are used to begin information questions. EG ***What** are the dangers?... **When** did the pains start?... **Where** are you going?* **2** They are used to begin report clauses which are related to information questions. EG *Do we know **where** he went?... I can't see **why** they are interested... He saw them **whenever** he wanted to.* **3** All the WH words except 'what' are used to introduce relative clauses. EG *...a place **where** they could go swimming... There are a number of reasons **why** this is important... ...my sister, **who** lives in London.*

whack /wæ̲k/, **whacks, whacking, whacked**.

1 If you **whack** someone or something, you hit them hard. EG *His father might whack him if he found out... She walked in and whacked the walls with a ruler.* ▸ used as a noun. EG *He gave the ball an almighty whack.* — V+O = beat, clout; ▸ N COUNT : USU SING

2 If someone has their **whack** or gets their **whack**, they receive the share of something that they expect to receive; an informal use. EG *Whatever happens, I've got to have my whack. That was in the agreement.* — N COUNT : USU DETPOSS+SING = cut, slice

whacked /wæ̲kt/. If you are **whacked**, you are extremely tired; an informal word. EG *By 9 p.m. I was whacked. By 9.30 I was asleep in bed.* — ADJ QUALIT : PRED = exhausted

whacking /wæ̲kɪŋ/, **whackings. 1** A **whacking** is a severe beating, especially one given to a child by a parent as a punishment; an old-fashioned use. EG *He waited until his father had gone, to avoid another whacking.* — N COUNT : USU SING

2 If you use **whacking** to describe something, you mean that it is very large. EG *They greeted me from work by plonking down a whacking great tea in front of the fire... We had a whacking phone bill this month.* — ADJ QUALIT : ATTRIB, OR ADV + ADJ/ADV

whacky /wæ̲ki¹/. See **wacky**.

whale /weɪ̲l/, **whales. 1** A **whale** is a very large animal that lives in the sea and looks like a huge fish. Whales are killed for their meat and their oil. EG *...a killer whale... ...whale oil.* — N COUNT

2 If you say that you **had a whale of a time**, you mean that you enjoyed yourself very much; an informal expression. EG *I gather they've all been having a whale of a time these last few days.* — PHR : VB INFLECTS

whalebone /weɪ̲lbəʊn/ is a hard material which is taken from the mouth of a whale. It was used, especially in former times, to put between two layers of cloth to make the cloth stiffer, for example in corsets. — N UNCOUNT

whaler /weɪ̲lə/, **whalers**. A **whaler** is **1** a ship which is used in hunting whales. **2** someone who works on a ship which is used in hunting whales. — N COUNT; N COUNT ⇑ sailor

whaling /weɪ̲lɪŋ/ is the activity of hunting and killing whales, especially as a part of the fishing industry. EG *...the whaling industry.* — N UNCOUNT

wham /wæ̲m/. You use **wham** to indicate that a punch, kick, idea, etc happens suddenly or forcefully; used in informal English. EG *'Wham!' said Charlie, and hit him. ...tears on both sides, packing up a* — EXCLAM ⇑ bang = wallop *suitcase–and wham! You're alone for the first time in years.*

wharf /wɔːf/, **wharves**. A **wharf** is a platform built of stone or wood along the side of a river or the sea, often stretching out into the water, so that ships can be tied up there while goods are loaded or unloaded or while people get on or off. EG *We walked her to the wharf and put her aboard the steamer.* N COUNT = jetty, quay

what /wɒt/. 1 You use **what** 1.1 in questions when you ask for specific information about something that you do not know. EG *What is your name?... 'What did he die of?'–'Pneumonia.'... What are you doing here?... What's that machine for?... What's five times 260?* WH : USED AS PRON ▸ used as a determiner. EG *What time is it?... What books can I read on the subject?... In what sense is George Eliot moralistic?* ▸ WH : USED AS DET 1.2 in indirect questions and other structures when you refer to information about something that is not known. EG *Do you know what a pendulum is?... I find it quite difficult to understand what people are saying... I don't know what to do... Tell me what's wrong.* WH : USED AS PRON ▸ used as a determiner. EG *We didn't know what bus to get.* ▸ WH : USED AS DET

2 You also use **what** at the beginning of a clause 2.1 to focus attention on the thing that you mention at the end. EG *What he really needs is a nice cup of tea... What you have to do is to choose five of them.* WH : USED AS PRON 2.2 to refer in a general way to something with a particular quality or nature. EG *He mixes what is real with what is unreal... A computer can only do what you have programmed it to do... What once took a century now took only ten months.* WH : USED AS DET/PRON = that which 2.3 to indicate that you are talking about the whole of an amount that is available to you. EG *I've spent what money I had... The house consumed what little there was of my spare time... It took what I could give.* WH : USED AS DET/PRON = whatever

3 You say **'What'** 3.1 to tell someone who has indicated that they want to speak to you that you have heard them and are inviting them to continue. EG *'Dad?'–'What?'–'Can I have the car tonight?'* WH : USED AS CONVENTION 3.2 when you ask someone to repeat the thing that they have just said because you did not hear it properly or are surprised by it. 'What' is not as polite as 'pardon'. EG *'Do you want another coffee?'–'What?'–'Do you want another coffee?'... 'We're going to have to slow down.'–'What?'–'I don't think we should go over fifty.'* WH : USED AS CONVENTION 3.3 to express surprise or disbelief. EG *What, another book about the Pre-Raphaelites?... 'Could I see you?'–'What, now?'* WH : USED AS CONVENTION 3.4 to emphasize an opinion or reaction, especially in exclamations. EG *What a beautiful girl!... What a good question!... What a pity... What rubbish!* WH : USED AS PREDET/DET 3.5 to indicate that you are making a guess about something such as an amount or value. EG *I've been an academic for, what, something like 18 years... 'Well she's, what, 13?'–'13, yes.'*

4 You say **what about** at the beginning of a question 4.1 when you make a suggestion or offer. EG *What about a spot of lunch, Colonel?... What about a Wednesday then?* PHR = how about 4.2 when you introduce a new topic or a point which seems relevant to something that someone has just said or which is an argument against it. EG *'I never trust anyone over thirty.'–'What about men under thirty?'... And your other promise? What about that?* PHR = how about

5 You say **what about** or **what of** a particular person or thing when you ask someone to explain why they have asked you about that person or thing. EG *'Do you remember Mary Stuart?'–'What of her?'* PHR

6 You say **what if** at the beginning of a question when you ask about the consequences of something happening, especially something undesirable. EG *What if there's no one at home?... What if you break a leg?... What if I miss the train?* PHR = supposing

7 You use expressions such as **'what is it?'** and **'what's the matter?'** when you ask someone to explain why they want to speak to you or why they are excited or upset. EG *'Mummy!'–'What is it this time?'... What's the matter?... 'You must help me.'–'What's wrong?'* CONVENTION

8 You use **what** in structures such as 'what is called' and 'what amounts to' in order to name or describe something; a fairly formal use. EG *We're here during what amounts to our holidays... This leads us fairly naturally into what careers advisers call the milk-round... I share your concern about what is rapidly becoming a desperate situation.* WH : USED AS PRON

9 You say **what with** in order to introduce the reasons for a particular situation, especially an undesirable one. EG *What with paying for lunch and all the eating and drinking we've done tonight, I'm very short of cash... What with one thing and another I suppose I got quite drunk... What with all the Marathon fever about, you didn't expect me to sit at home, did you?* CONJ SUBORD = because of

10 **What's what** means the important things that need to be known about a situation, such as the facts about it or how people should behave; an informal expression. EG *This is a meeting to find out what's what... Tell them what's what.* PHR : USED AS O

11 The word **what** is also used in the following informal or spoken expressions. 11.1 If you say **'and I don't know what'**, **'and God knows what'**, etc, you mean that there are other things like those which you have mentioned but that you do not know them or cannot be bothered to mention them. EG *He said I was stupid and thoughtless and I don't know what... The chickens are injected with antibiotics and God knows what.* PHR 11.2 You say **'guess what'**, **'do you know what'**, etc to introduce a piece of information which is surprising, which is not generally known, or which you want to emphasize. EG *Guess what, she's turned up at last... You know what, I think I need a holiday.* PHR 11.3 You say **'I tell you what'**, **'I know what'**, etc to introduce a suggestion or offer. EG *Tell you what–let's go for a walk.* PHR 11.4 You say **'or what?'** after you have asked a question in order to make it sound more challenging, usually because you think there is only one possible answer to your question. EG *Is this a marathon or what?... Do you want to be accepted or what?* PHR 11.5 You say **'so what?'**, **'what of it?'**, etc to indicate that the remark or statement which has just been made seems unimportant, uninteresting, or irrelevant to you. EG *'Someone will see.'–'So what?'... 'Your parents are coming tomorrow.' – 'What of it?'* CONVENTION 11.6 You say **what have you** at the end of a list in order to refer generally to other things of the same kind. EG *...the needs, cultural, recreational, what have you, of the members of this community... ...mythological violence, that is Grimm's Fairy Tales and what have you.* PHR = etc 11.7 You say **what's his name, what's her name**, etc instead of a person's name when you cannot remember it. EG *Where's what's her name?... It was Mr–what's his name, you know, the new people.* PHR : USED AS S/O 11.8 People say **'you what?'** to indicate that they do not believe or accept the remark or statement that someone has just made, or that they have not heard or understood it properly. EG *'I'm going to be an actor.'–'You what? You must be joking!'* CONVENTION 11.9 • to **give** someone **what for**: see **give**. • **what's more**: see **more**.

whatever /wə'tevə/. 1 You use **whatever** 1.1 to refer to anything or everything of a particular type when you are not able to say precisely what you are referring to. EG *I went to the library and read whatever I could find about Robert Owens... He volunteered to do whatever he could.* WH : USED AS PRON ▸ used as a determiner. EG *She had to rely on whatever books were lying around... Davis had given up whatever hopes he may have had.* ▸ WH : USED AS DET = any 1.2 when you want to say that something is the case in all possible circumstances, even in circumstances that might seem unsuitable or unfavourable. EG *He wore antique clothes and, whatever the weather, galoshes... It is always the same story, whatever the cultural variations... Sam is English by birth whatever anyone may say... Whatever you do don't take a trip to the Arctic... I have to bring my family back whatever happens.* WH : USED AS CONJ SUBORD = regardless of 1.3 after a noun group in order to emphasize a negative statement or a statement which includes the word 'any'. EG *There is no scientific evidence whatever to support such a view... He knew nothing whatever about it... You can ask me questions on any topic whatever... This scheme had no chance whatever of success.* WH : USED AS ADV AFTER N, USU WITH BROAD NEG = at all 1.4 to ask in an emphatic way about something which you are very surprised about. EG *Whatever is the matter?... Whatever do you want to go up there for?... 'You don't think a great deal of us, do you?'–'Whatever gave you that impression?'* WH : USED AS PRON = what 1.5 at the beginning of a clause in which you indicate that you do not know the precise identity, meaning, or value of something that you have just mentioned or are about to mention. EG *She said she was going to serve up a bowl of chilli, whatever that is... I suppose that I would like to become 'myself', whatever that may mean... Couldn't* WH : USED AS PRON/DET *we 'heave to' or whatever it is you do?... Whatever the reason, Rudolph was glad that she had come back.*

2 You say **or whatever** to refer generally to something else of the same kind as the thing or things that you have just mentioned; an informal expression. EG *You plug it into some sort of microcomputer or whatever and it does the typing for you... And then you add the numbers or subtract them or whatever... I don't really want to be a poet or study English or whatever.* PHR

3 You say **'whatever you say', 'whatever you think'**, etc to indicate that you accept what someone has told you or that you will do what they have suggested, even though you do not really believe them or do not think it is a good idea. EG *'What's the matter?'–'Nothing.'–'Whatever you say.'... 'I want to speak to the manager.'–'Whatever you say, sir.'* CONVENTION

whatnot /wɒtnɒt/. You can add **and whatnot** or **or whatnot** to a list, in order to refer to other things like those that you have just mentioned but which you are not going to specify; an informal expression. EG *I had breakfast, hot cakes, eggs and whatnot.* PHR = such, the like

what's /wɒts/ is the usual spoken form of 'what is' or 'what has', especially when 'has' is an auxiliary verb.

whatsoever /wɒtsəʊevə/. You use **whatsoever** after a noun group in order to strongly emphasize a negative statement or a statement which includes the word 'any'. EG *'You don't think he has any chance of winning?'–'None whatsoever.'... I had no social life whatsoever... I don't think there's any evidence of that whatsoever.* ADV AFTER VB: USU WITH BROAD NEG = at all

wheat /wiːt/, **wheats**. **Wheat** is 1 a grain which people usually grind into flour and use to make bread. N MASS = corn 2 a plant which people grow in order to use its grain for food. EG *The rabbit stops, spurts, and finally runs back into the wheat.* N MASS ↑ grass

wheatgerm /wiːtdʒɜːm/ is the middle part of a grain of wheat which is rich in vitamins and is often added to other food. N UNCOUNT

wheatmeal /wiːtmiːl/ is a flour which is made from wheat grains but from which some part has been removed or to which something has been added. N UNCOUNT

wheedle /wiːdəl/, **wheedles, wheedling, wheedled**. If you **wheedle**, you try to persuade someone to do or give you something, for example by saying nice things to them which you do not mean. EG *She wheedled money out of him... They tried to wheedle her into leaving the house.* V OR V+O: IF+ PREP THEN *into/out of* = cajole

◊ **wheedling**. EG *...myriads of threatening, wheedling beggars.* ◊ ADJ CLASSIF = cajoling

wheel /wiːl/, **wheels, wheeling, wheeled**. 1 A **wheel** is 1.1 a circular object which turns round on a rod attached to its centre. Wheels are fixed underneath cars, bicycles, trains, etc so that they can move along. EG *The train started, its wheels squealing against the metal tracks... ...bicycle wheels.* N COUNT 1.2 a circular object which forms part of a machine, for example to make other parts move round. EG *...the wheels of a Swiss watch.* N COUNT 1.3 a large, circular, wooden object used to steer a ship, especially in former times. N COUNT: USU SING 1.4 the same as a steering wheel. N COUNT

2 **Wheels** is sometimes used to refer to a car or van; used in informal English. EG *I don't have wheels, so I'll need a lift.* N PLURAL ↑ vehicle = motor

3 **Wheel** is also used to refer to a natural series of changes and stages that something goes through, repeated again and again over a period of time; a fairly literary use. EG *...the rapid spin of the wheel of fashion.* N COUNT+SUPP: USU SING ↑ cycle

4 If you **wheel** something that has wheels, for example a bicycle or cart, you move it by pushing it along. EG *My father appeared wheeling his bicycle up the hill.* V+O ↑ push = propel

5 If you **wheel** someone or something in a particular direction, they are in a wheelchair, pushchair, cart, or other object with wheels and you move them by pushing it along. EG *Wheel me into that store over there... The equipment was so bulky that it had to be wheeled around on a large trolley.* V+O: USU+A ↑ push

6 If something **wheels**, for example if a vehicle or group of people, animals, or birds **wheels**, it moves in a direction in which it follows the shape of a circle or part of a circle. EG *The sky becomes filled with birds wheeling back and forth... The plane banked and wheeled.* V: USU+A

7 If you **wheel** round, you turn round suddenly on the place where you are standing, for example because of surprise, shock, or anger. EG *I wheeled around and shook off the hand she had placed on my shoulder.* V: USU+A *(round/around)* = spin round

8 The word **wheel** is also used in the following expressions. 8.1 If someone is **at** or **behind the wheel** of a car or other vehicle, they are driving it or are ready to drive. EG *After many hours at the wheel, I was ready for a stop... ...the old man behind the wheel of the taxi.* PHR: USED AS AN A 8.2 If something is **on wheels**, it has wheels attached to the bottom, so that it can be moved easily. EG *...a shopping basket on wheels.* PHR: USED AS AN A 8.3 If someone **takes** or **grabs the wheel** of a car or other vehicle, they start to drive it, instead of someone else. EG *He had to remain sober to take the wheel.* PHR: VB INFLECTS 8.4 If you say that there are **wheels within wheels** when you are talking about a situation, you mean that there are a number of different influences, reasons, and actions which together make it complicated and difficult to understand. PHR: USED AS C 8.5 • to **oil the wheels**: see **oil**. • to **put** your **shoulder to the wheel**: see **shoulder**. • See also **catherine wheel, meals-on-wheels, potter's wheel, spinning wheel, waterwheel.**

wheelbarrow /wiːlbærəʊ/, **wheelbarrows**. A **wheelbarrow** is a small cart that is used in the garden for carrying things such as plants, soil, or bricks. Wheelbarrows are usually shaped like open boxes, with one wheel at the front, two legs at the back, and two handles to lift and push it with. N COUNT ↑ barrow

wheelbase /wiːlbeɪs/, **wheelbases**. The **wheelbase** of a car or other vehicle is the distance between its front and back wheels. N COUNT

wheelchair /wiːltʃeə/, **wheelchairs**. A **wheelchair** is a chair with wheels on the bottom that is used by people who cannot walk properly, so that they can move about. EG *We want easier access to buildings for those disabled or using a wheelchair.* N COUNT

wheeler-dealer, wheeler-dealers. A **wheeler-dealer** is someone who does a lot of wheeling and dealing; used showing disapproval. N COUNT

wheelhouse /wiːlhaʊs/, **wheelhouses**. A **wheelhouse** is a small room or shelter on a boat or old-fashioned ship, where the wheel used for steering the boat is situated. N COUNT

wheeling and dealing is the process of trying to get something, especially in business, or to create a situation which will be of advantage to you, often by means of deception or unfair methods; used showing disapproval. EG *...complex business deals and financial wheeling and dealing.* N UNCOUNT ▸ used as a verb in continuous tenses only. EG *Margaret was wheeling and dealing in high places.* ▸ V: ONLY CONT

wheelwright /wiːlraɪt/, **wheelwrights**. A **wheelwright** is someone who makes and repairs wooden wheels and other wooden things such as carts, carriages, and gates. N COUNT

wheeze /wiːz/, **wheezes, wheezing, wheezed**.
1 If you **wheeze**, you breathe with difficulty, making a hissing or whistling sound, for example because you are very old or have an illness such as asthma. EG *Coughing and wheezing, he climbed up the last few steps.* V = pant ▸ used as a noun. EG *All this was said very slowly, between wheezes.* ▸ N COUNT

2 A **wheeze** is a clever idea, often a joke or a trick; used in old-fashioned, informal British English. N COUNT = prank

wheezy /wiːzi¹/, **wheezier, wheeziest**. **Wheezy** coughs or other sounds are made by people who have difficulty in breathing and so are hissing or whistling. ADJ QUALIT ↑ noisy

whelk /welk/, **whelks**. A **whelk** is a creature like a snail that is found in the sea near the shore. Whelks have hard shells and very soft bodies which can be eaten. N COUNT ↑ shellfish

whelp /welp/, **whelps, whelping, whelped**. When a female dog, wolf, or other animal **whelps**, she gives birth; a rather old-fashioned word. V

when /wen/. 1 You use **when** in questions in which you ask about the time things happened or will happen. EG *'I have to go to Germany.' – 'When?' – 'Now.'... When did you arrive?... When was the last time you cleaned the garage?... When are you getting married?* WH: USED AS ADV = how soon

2 You also use **when** at the beginning of a clause that refers to time in the following ways: 2.1 to link clauses in which you talk about the time at which something happens. EG *He didn't know when he was coming back... I can't remember when I last wrote...* WH: USED AS CONJ SUBORD = how soon

'She's been working in a pub.'–'Since when?'–'About a month ago.'... The only disagreement was on when to eliminate the benefit... There are rather detailed rules of when you can and can't appeal. **2.2** to introduce a clause in which you mention the specific time or period at which something happens or is the case. EG *He left school when he was eleven... When the weather was warm, all the children played in the park... When he had finished reading, he looked up... She was fatter than when he had last seen her... When completed in 1982 it will employ about 200 people.... When I have free time, I always spend it fishing.* WH : USED AS CONJ SUBORD **2.3** to introduce a relative clause in which you specify the particular time you mean. EG *Do you remember that time when Adrian phoned up from Tunbridge Wells?... There were times when I didn't know what to do... This is one of those occasions when I really do regret not being able to drive.* WH : USED AS PRON REL = that **2.4** to introduce a clause in which you add more information or a further comment about a time that you mentioned in the previous clause. EG *Join us next week, when we shall be talking about solar energy... I'd prefer general issues to wait to the end, when the argument is clear... Twenty years ago, when I was a student, I worshipped Conrad's novels.* WH : USED AS CONJ SUBORD

3 You also use **when** at the beginning of a clause, especially in spoken English, **3.1** to say that something happened which stopped you from doing what you had planned or intended to do. You usually use 'just' or 'about to' in the previous clause. EG *I was just going out when there was a knock at the door... I was about to go to bed when I heard cars purr in the distance... We hadn't gone ten miles when Sam decided he wanted to go home.* WH : USED AS CONJ SUBORD **3.2** to indicate why you have just given a particular opinion, made a particular comment, or asked a particular question. EG *You know nothing about your history. It's ridiculous, when it's all around you... How can I ever get a job in America when I can't even remember any English?... How silly we are to sit around inside when outside it is so lovely.* WH : USED AS CONJ SUBORD = since, given that **3.3** instead of 'although' in order to introduce a fact or comment which makes the other part of the sentence rather surprising or unlikely. EG *You describe this policy as rigid and inflexible, when in fact it has been extremely flexible... I stop for cigarettes when I already have two packs in the glove compartment.* WH : USED AS CONJ SUBORD

whence /wɛns/ means from where; a formal or old-fashioned word. EG *He returned hastily to the United States, whence there presently came an announcement that some of the harsher rules of the order were to be relaxed.* ADV WITH VB, OR CONJ SUBORD

whenever /wɛnɛvə/. **1** You use **whenever** **1.1** to say that something happens or is true no matter what time you are talking about. EG *Come to see me whenever you feel you have to talk... I avoided physical conflict whenever possible... Whenever I recollect her face it is smiling or laughing.* WH : USED AS CONJ SUBORD = when **1.2** to refer to an unknown time; a fairly informal use. EG *It was right back in whenever it was–sixty-three or somewhere then... At 5 p.m. or whenever they had done their eight hours, they would just get up and go home.* WH : USED AS ADV WITH VB

2 You say **or whenever** to refer generally to a time at which something happened, especially when you cannot remember the exact date or want to be deliberately vague; an informal expression. EG *I started work in March or whenever.* PHR

where /wɛə/. **1** You use **where** when you refer to places, directions, and positions in the following ways: **1.1** in questions. EG *Where's Jane?... Where are you going?... Where does all this energy come from?... Where do you want to fly to?... 'Why don't we just go?'–'Go where?'* WH : USED AS ADV **1.2** to link clauses. EG *I think I know where we are... I asked someone where the cheapest accommodation was... How did you know where to find me?... He used to own a restaurant. I forget where... I want information on where graduates are employed.* WH : USED AS CONJ SUBORD **1.3** at the beginning of a clause in which you refer to a specific place or in which you specify the particular place you mean. EG *She walked over to where Madeleine stood... ...over the road, where the Union Club is... Keep your tool box where you can get at it... The place where they landed was relatively green... It was a hideous hotel, the kind where they hold conventions.* WH : USED AS CONJ SUBORD OR PRON REL **1.4** at the beginning of a clause in which you add more information or a further comment about a place that you mentioned in the previous clause. EG *Quincy, where I was born, is an industrial suburb of Boston... Later he went to New Zealand, where I understand he did all sorts of jobs... My next visit was to the Standard Bank, where I asked to see the manager.* WH : USED AS CONJ SUBORD OR PRON REL

2 You also use **where** when you refer to abstract things like situations, points, or cases in the following ways: **2.1** in questions, for example when you are asking about the particular situation, point, stage, etc that has been reached. EG *Now then. Where had you got to? Got an answer yet?... The question is, Paul, where are you going to draw the line?... If a man is to be judged by what he was ten years ago, where would we all be?* WH : USED AS ADV **2.2** to link clauses in which you talk about the particular situation, point, stage, etc that has been reached. EG *Bryan wouldn't know where to start... I'd like to know where they stand on this issue... He just wants to get into the question of where things went wrong.* WH : USED AS CONJ SUBORD **2.3** at the beginning of a clause in which you specify the particular situation, case, instance, or aspect of something that you are talking about. EG *Where a husband and wife both work they often feel it is better not to rely on the wife's pay in case she has children... A coroner only issues an order where there's a suspicion of foul play... I wished, where possible, to avoid any mention of my family... I think where the book succeeds very well is its portrait of London... This is where I profoundly disagree with you.* WH : USED AS CONJ SUBORD **2.4** at the beginning of a relative clause in which you specify the particular situation, point, stage, etc that you mean. Another way of introducing clauses like these is to use 'in which' or 'at which' instead of 'where'. EG *...a situation where unemployment is three million and rising fast... We had one or two cases today where people returned goods... I'm at the stage now where I'm ready to have a go... They got themselves into a position where there was simply no way out.* WH : USED AS PRON REL

3 You also use **where** at the beginning of a clause when you mention something in the clause that contrasts with what you mention in the other part of the sentence. EG *Where others saw a doomed couple, I saw the irresistible unfolding of a rare love affair... Sometimes a teacher will be listened to, where a parent might not.* WH : USED AS CONJ SUBORD = whereas

whereabouts /wɛərəbaʊts/. **1** If you refer to the **whereabouts** of a particular person or thing, you mean the place where that person or thing may be found. EG *I will not give anyone my whereabouts... We have succeeded in obtaining the whereabouts of one of the main ringleaders.* N PLURAL : WITH POSS = location

2 You use **whereabouts** in questions when you want to know roughly where something is. EG *'I have a flat there.' – 'Oh yes. Whereabouts?' – 'Barclay Street.'... Whereabouts are you going in Yugoslavia?* ADV WITH VB ⇑ where

whereas /wɛəræz/. You use **whereas** at the beginning of a clause in which you mention something that contrasts with what you mention in the other part of the sentence, especially when the two things are similar in some way; a fairly formal word. EG *Radar employs radio waves whereas sonar uses sound waves... Humans are capable of error whereas the computer is not... I used to think that money was incredibly important. Whereas I look at it now in quite a different way.* CONJ SUBORD ⇑ but = while

whereby /wɛəbaɪ/. A system or process **whereby** something is possible or is the case is a system or process which provides the means by which that thing is possible or is the case; a formal word. EG *I had worked out a rotating arrangement whereby each person would have a different roommate each term... You have to devise a means whereby you can settle the issue... ...a system whereby we work more overtime than any other country.* PRON REL

wherefores /wɛəfɔːz/. **The whys and wherefores** of something are the reasons for it; a formal expression. EG *Martin wanted to know all the whys and wherefores.* PHR : USED AS O

wherein /wɛərɪn/; a formal or old-fashioned word. **Wherein** means **1** in which place. EG *...the pink workbox wherein she kept her wools... ...the left wing of the Labour Party, wherein is seen a potential leadership.* PRON REL **2** in which part or respect. EG *Wherein lay her greatness?... She knew wherein her gross defects lay.* ADV, OR CONJ SUBORD

whereof /wɛərɒv/ means of which; a very formal or old-fashioned word. EG *...sixteen children, ten whereof had been baptized.* PRON REL

whereupon /wɛərəpɒn/. You use **whereupon** to say that something happens immediately after, and usually as a result of, the thing that you have just described; a formal word. EG *His department was shut down, whereupon he returned to Calcutta... His or her name will be tapped into the terminal, whereupon a complete record will immediately appear on the screen.* CONJ SUBORD = at which

wherever /wɛərɛvə/. **1** You use **wherever** at the beginning of a clause **1.1** when you say that something is true or happens not just in one place or situation but in any place or situation. EG *In Bali wherever you go you come across ceremonies... Wherever he was, he was happy most of the time... They have tried to restore the house wherever possible to its original state... We'd drive to the theater or amusement park or wherever I wanted to go.* WH : USED AS CONJ SUBORD **1.2** when you indicate that you do not know where a place is which you have just mentioned. EG *'Where does she live?'–'Altadena Drive, wherever that is.'* WH : USED AS CONJ SUBORD

2 You also use **wherever** in questions as an emphatic form of 'where', usually when you are surprised about something. EG *Wherever have you been?... 'Let's go away.'–'Wherever to?'* WH : USED AS ADV

3 You use **or wherever** to say that something might happen in a place other than the place you have mentioned, but that you are not able to specify where; an informal use. EG *Once in a while the boss rings to explain that he is stuck in Milan or wherever and will everyone please carry on as best they can... ...a terraced house in Islington or wherever.* PHR

wherewithal /wɛəwɪðɔːl/. The **wherewithal** is the money that you need for a particular purpose. EG *Where did they get the wherewithal to finance all those concerts?* N SING : *the*+N = finance

whet /wɛt/, **whets, whetting, whetted. 1** To **whet** someone's **appetite** for something means to increase their desire for it. EG *The tutor at the night-classes had whetted her appetite for more work... Appetites had been whetted for further advances.* PHR : VB INFLECTS, IF + PREP THEN *for*

2 If you **whet** a knife, chisel, or other tool, you sharpen it; an old-fashioned use. V+O

whether /wɛðə/. You use **whether** at the beginning of a clause **1** when talking about a choice or doubt between two or more alternatives. EG *I can't tell whether she loves me or she hates me... I wasn't sure whether I liked him or not... The barman didn't ask whether or not they were over eighteen... I asked Fred whether he agreed... Everybody was talking at once, so it wasn't clear whether the meeting had begun.* CONJ SUBORD = if **2** to say that something is true in any of the circumstances that you mention. EG *He's going to buy a house whether he gets married or not... A fresh pepper, whether red or green, lasts about three weeks... ...a long history of repression, whether by official policy or unofficial practice.* CONJ SUBORD

whetstone /wɛtstəʊn/, **whetstones**. A **whetstone** is a stone which is used for sharpening knives, chisels, or other tools; a technical term. N COUNT

whew /hwjuː/ is used in writing to represent a sound that you make, for example when you are very surprised, or when a difficult task is finished, or when you have just avoided an accident. EG *Whew! It's nice to have that over with.* EXCLAM

whey /weɪ/ is the watery liquid that is separated from the curds in sour milk, for example when you are making cheese. N UNCOUNT

which /wɪtʃ/. **1** You use **which 1.1** in questions when you ask for specific information about something and when there is a choice between a definite number of possible answers or alternatives. EG *When you get your daily paper which page do you read first?... Which department do you want?... 'You could look in the English Tourist Board Brochure.'–'Which one's that?'–'That one there.'* WH : USED AS DET ▸ used as a pronoun EG *Which is mine?* ▸ WH : USED AS PRON **1.2** in indirect questions and other structures when you refer to a choice between a definite number of possible answers or alternatives. EG *Do you know which country he played for?... He didn't know which one it was, Ethel or Edna.* WH : USED AS DET ▸ used as a pronoun. EG *I tried to decide which I wanted most: the meal or sleep... The book says one thing and you say another. I don't know which to believe.* ▸ WH : USED AS PRON

2 You also use **which** at the beginning of a relative clause **2.1** where you specify the thing that you are talking about. EG *A flywheel is basically a heavy disc which can rotate at a high speed... Last week we heard about the awful conditions which exist in British prisons... I will tell you the first thing which I can remember... There's one last question which I'd like to put to you... Astronomy is a subject in which truth may well be stranger than fiction.* WH : USED AS PRON REL **2.2** where you give more information about something that you mentioned in the previous clause. EG *I'm teaching at Selly Oak Centre, which is just over the road... ...schools of study, which bring together groups of subjects... ...the cogs (each of which has ten teeth)... The whole room was blue except for the carpet which was pale green.* WH : USED AS PRON REL

3 You also use **which** when you refer back to what has previously been mentioned or suggested, especially when you want to give your opinion about it. EG *It takes me an hour from door to door which is not bad... It's all a question of priorities. Which brings me back to my main point.* WH : USED AS PRON REL ▸ used as a determiner. EG *I really enjoy these dinners, unless I have to make a speech, in which case I'm in a state of dreadful anxiety throughout the meal.* ▸ WH : USED AS DET

whichever /wɪtʃɛvə/. You use **whichever 1** in order to indicate that it does not matter which of the possible alternatives is done or chosen. EG *I'm sure he would do full justice to whichever role he might be called... He came into our lives, or we came into his, whichever way you care to look at it.* WH : USED AS DET = whatever ▸ used as a pronoun. EG *Then they have their lunch, have a chat, have a sleep, whichever they like, up in the lounge.* ▸ WH : USED AS PRON **2** when you specify which of a number of possibilities is the right one or the one you mean. EG *Use whichever water softener is recommended by the manufacturer.* WH : USED AS DET ▸ used as a pronoun. EG *Use whichever of the other three dyes is appropriate.* ▸ WH : USED AS PRON

whiff /wɪf/. **1** If there is a **whiff** of a particular smell, you smell it faintly or for only a brief period of time, for example as you walk past someone or something. EG *Now and again, he caught a whiff of a peculiar smell... ...a little whiff of perfume.* N COUNT+*of*: USU SING = trace

2 A **whiff** of something such as a particular type of behaviour is a slight sign of it, or a sign which makes you think of a past or future situation. EG *...a whiff of rebellion... Even your best friends will betray you at the first whiff of political danger.* N COUNT+*of*: USU SING = hint, trace

Whig /wɪg/, **Whigs**. A **Whig** was a member of an English political grouping which in the 19th century represented people who were eager for political and social reforms. N COUNT ⇑ politician

while /waɪl/, **whiles, whiling, whiled. 1** You use **while** at the beginning of a clause that refers to time. If something happens **while** something else is happening, **1.1** the two things are happening at the same time. EG *He stayed with Mom and me while Dad sat with Dr Leon in the living-room... While I was overseas she was in Maritzburg studying... They decided to seek a less expensive place to stay while in Paris... Poirot had been wondering, while eating his dinner, what it was that was driving Mrs Oliver to visit him.* CONJ SUBORD = whilst **1.2** the first thing happens at some point during the time that the second thing is happening. EG *While he was turning the key in the lock, someone opened a door on the other side of the corridor... The car got three severe bumps while parked in the street in London... He had taken out his handkerchief several times while talking to her and blown his nose.* CONJ SUBORD ⇑ when = whilst ● **while you're about it, while I'm about it**, etc: see **about**.

2 You also use **while** at the beginning of a clause **2.1** when you mention something in the clause that contrasts with what you mention in the other part of the sentence. EG *One group of children was fairly stable, while the second group was severely disturbed... Fred gambled his money away while Julia spent hers all on dresses and bric-a-brac.* CONJ SUBORD ⇑ but = whereas **2.2** when you admit in the clause that something is the case but say that it does not affect the truth of the other part of the sentence, although the two statements partly conflict. EG *So while I have sympathy for these fellows who reacted against the formality of their predecessors, I think they went too far... Your missive, while complete in other regards, skirted the subject of cost.* CONJ SUBORD = though, whilst

3 A short, little, long, etc **while** is a short, little, or N SING WITH long period of time. EG *They talked for a short while and then went home together... ...a book that I read a little while ago... He is allowed to sleep a while longer... It took quite a while to sort out all our luggage.* ● You use expressions such as **all the while** or **the whole while** in order to say that something happens continually or that it happens throughout the time when something else is happening. EG *This target's getting lower all the while... I hugged him, fussed over him, and all the while I felt sick and tired and beaten.* ● to **make it worth** your **while**: see **worth.** ● **once in a while**: see **once**. DET : USU ADJ+N ● PHR : USED AS AN A

while away. If you **while away** the time in a particular way, you spend time in that way, often just talking, because you are waiting for something, or because you have nothing else to do. EG *How about whiling away the time by telling me a fairy story?... Shapiro had been whiling away the time with this flow of reminiscences.* PHRASAL VB : V+ADV+O ⇑ pass

whilst /waɪlst/ means the same as while when it is used as a conjunction; a fairly formal word. EG *I wouldn't want to stay at home whilst I was at university... Remembrance Day is held in particular veneration, whilst Good Friday is barely observed at all... Whilst these bulky vehicles are reasonably economical at a steady 56 mph, they perform very badly in stop-start conditions.* CONJ SUBORD

whim /wɪm/, **whims**. A **whim** is a wish to do or have something, which is not the result of any strong reason or purpose and often occurs suddenly. EG *She might go, or might not, as the whim took her... They are completely subject to the whims and moods of a single superior... ...his tendency to change his mind at whim.* N COUNT/UNCOUNT = fancy, caprice

whimper /wɪmpə/, **whimpers, whimpering, whimpered**. 1 If people, especially children, or animals **whimper**, they make little, low, unhappy sounds. EG *You don't have to feed the baby the minute she whimpers... She picked up the whimpering dog and carried it home.* ▸ used as a noun. EG *I was listening for a cry or a whimper from upstairs.* V ⇑ cry ▸ N COUNT

2 If someone **whimpers** something, they say it in an unhappy or frightened way, sounding as if they are about to start crying. EG *'I want to go home,' she whimpered.* V+QUOTE

whimsical /wɪmzɪkəl/. Something that is **whimsical** is unusual and often slightly playful, and is done without any strong reason or purpose. EG *...players who know each other's whimsical ways... ...a whimsical smile.* ▸ used of people who behave in a whimsical way. EG *He was a whimsical man, much concerned with the curious.* ADJ QUALIT = quirky ▸ = peculiar

whimsy /wɪmzi[1]/, **whimsies**; also spelled **whimsey. Whimsy** is behaviour which is unusual and often slightly playful, and which has no strong reason or purpose. EG *They have through whimsy put these drums to use as stools... ...a spasm of whimsy and malice.* N UNCOUNT/COUNT = foible

whine /waɪn/, **whines, whining, whined**. 1 To **whine** means to make a long, high-pitched noise, especially one which sounds sad or unpleasant. EG *Nearby was his dog, whining in pain from its broken leg... I pressed the button and the clattering and whining elevator began to move.* ▸ used as a noun. EG *...the whine of the motor-cycle sirens.* V ▸ N COUNT : USU SING

2 If someone **whines** about something, especially something unimportant, they complain about it in a way that annoys you. EG *My father was a brave man who never whined or complained about his illness.* ◇ **whining**. EG *He was annoying Sarah with his non-stop whining.* V, V+A *(about)*, OR V+QUOTE ◇ N UNCOUNT

whinge /wɪndʒ/, **whinges, whinging, whinged**. The spelling **whingeing** is also used. If someone **whinges** about something, they complain about it in a way that annoys you; an informal word. EG *Oh, stop whinging!* V : IF+PREP THEN *about*

whinny /wɪni[1]/, **whinnies, whinnying, whinnied**. When a horse **whinnies**, it neighs softly. V

whip /wɪp/, **whips, whipping, whipped**. 1 A **whip** is a piece of leather, rope, etc fastened to a stiff handle. It is used for hitting people or animals. EG *Again he was lashed with whips.* N COUNT

2 If someone **whips** a person or animal, they beat them or hit them with a whip. EG *I saw him whipping his team of mules... The whipped child, like the whipped puppy, grows into an obedient, inferior creature.* ◇ **whipping, whippings**. EG *He could not possibly have endured a whipping without a moan or a whimper.* V+O ◇ N COUNT

3 If something, especially the wind, **whips** something, it strikes it sharply. EG *The wind whipped my face.* V+O

4 If something flexible **whips** in the wind or **whips** back, it moves sharply backwards and forwards, or moves sharply back, when it is affected by some force. EG *All that could be seen of the ship were her flags whipping in the wind.* V+A

5 If someone **whips** something out, off, etc, they take it out or off very quickly and suddenly. EG *I whipped out a hundred-dollar bill... Glenn whipped off the mask to reveal his identity... He took hold of the cheque and whipped it away.* V+O+A

6 If someone or something **whips** somewhere, they go there quickly and suddenly. EG *I whipped in, got my coat, whipped out, and got back in the car... ...the sound of the ball whipping past my nose... He heard the wind whipping through the trees.* V+A

7 When someone **whips** cream or egg white, they stir it very fast until it is thick and frothy or fairly stiff. ◇ **whipped**. EG *...fruit flan with whipped cream.* V+O = whisk ◇ ADJ CLASSIF

8 Strawberry **whip**, raspberry **whip**, etc is a kind of pudding made from egg white or cream stirred until it is fairly stiff. N MASS : MOD+N

9 If you **whip** people into a state of hatred, excitement, etc, you deliberately make them feel that emotion. EG *His men were not a particularly brave lot, but they could be whipped into a frenzy.* V+A *(into)* ⇑ rouse

10 If someone **whips** something, they steal it; an informal, rather old-fashioned use. EG *There's ten tins in the back I whipped from the stores at Amirya.* V+O : USU+A

11 A **whip** is also 11.1 a member of a particular party in parliament, who is responsible for making sure that party members are present to vote on important issues. EG *The party whips had to give group lessons on how to vote.* 11.2 a notice sent out by a party whip which tells the members of parliament belonging to that party how important it is for them to vote in a particular way on a particular issue. N COUNT N COUNT

12 If you **have** or **get the whip hand** over someone, you have power over them and can control what they do. PHR : VB INFLECTS

13 If someone or perhaps something is **a whipping boy**, they get all the blame for a particular situation. EG *The South's been the whipping boy long enough.* PHR : USED AS C = scapegoat

14 **a fair crack of the whip**: see **crack**.

whip up. 1 If you **whip up** hatred, excitement, etc or if you **whip** people **up** into a state of hatred, excitement, etc, you deliberately make people feel that emotion. EG *He did not succeed in any considerable measure in whipping up hatred for the British... The interview whipped up half the American people into a frenzy of rage.* PHRASAL VB : V+O+ADV, IF+PREP THEN *into* ⇑ arouse

2 If the wind **whips up** dust, water, etc, it makes it rise up. EG *A cool breeze whipped up a swirl of dust... ...large waves whipped up by unexpected storms.* PHRASAL VB : V+O+ADV

3 When someone **whips up** cream or egg, they stir it very fast. PHRASAL VB : V+O+ADV

4 If you **whip up** something, especially a meal, you make it quickly; an informal use. PHRASAL VB : V+O+ADV

whiplash /wɪplæʃ/, **whiplashes**. A **whiplash** is the long piece of leather or rope that is part of a whip. N COUNT

whiplash injury, whiplash injuries. A **whiplash injury** is a neck injury caused by your head suddenly jerking forwards and then back again, for example in a car accident. N COUNT

whippersnapper /wɪpəsnæpə/, **whippersnappers**. If you refer to a young person as a **whippersnapper**, you mean that they are behaving more confidently and boldly than you think they should; an informal, rather old-fashioned word. EG *Impatient young whippersnapper!* N COUNT : USU SING, ALSO VOC

whippet /wɪpɪt/, **whippets**. A **whippet** is a small thin dog which looks like a greyhound. Some whippets take part in races. N COUNT

whipping cream is cream that becomes stiff when it is stirred very fast. N UNCOUNT

whippy /wɪpi[1]/. A stick, pole, etc that is **whippy** bends quite easily. ADJ QUALIT = flexible

whip-round, whip-rounds; also spelled without a hyphen. When a group of people, for example people who work in the same place, have a **whip-round**, money is collected from each person, especially so N COUNT : USU SING ⇑ collection that it can be used to buy something for all of them or for someone they all know; an informal word.

whir /wɜː/. See **whirr**.

whirl /wɜːl/, **whirls, whirling, whirled**. 1 When something or someone **whirls** or when you **whirl** it round, it moves round or turns round very fast. EG *Whirl me round like you always do... ...the whirling, leaping, writhing people... ...the whirling blades of a helicopter... He rushed out of the house into a whirling snowstorm.* ▸ used as a noun. EG *...a whirl of dust.* V-ERG : USU+A ⇑ rotate ▸ N COUNT : USU SING

2 You can refer to a lot of intense activity as a **whirl** of activity, pleasure, parties, etc. EG *We flung ourselves into the mad whirl of pleasure... The next three days passed in a whirl of activity.* N COUNT+SUPP : USU SING = round

3 If you say that someone's head or mind **is whirling**, you mean that they are very confused or excited by what they have seen or heard; a fairly literary use. EG *My head's whirling with impressions.* V : USU CONT = reel

4 If someone or their mind is **in a whirl**, they are very confused or excited; a fairly literary expression. PHR : USED AS AN A

5 If you say that you will **give it a whirl**, you mean that you will try doing something new or allow something new to happen for a while; an informal expression. PHR : VB INFLECTS

whirlpool /wɜːlpuːl/, **whirlpools**. 1 A **whirlpool** is a small area in a river or the sea where the water is moving quickly round and round, so that objects floating near it are pulled into its centre. N COUNT ⇑ current = eddy

2 You can describe a situation in which there is a lot of activity and which you feel you cannot escape from as a **whirlpool** of some kind. EG *We seemed to be caught in a whirlpool of violence and blood.* N COUNT+SUPP = maelstrom, vortex

whirlwind /wɜːlwɪnd/, **whirlwinds**. 1 A **whirlwind** is a tall column of air which spins round and round very fast and moves across the land or sea. N COUNT ⇑ wind

2 A **whirlwind** action or event happens or is done much more quickly than normal. EG *...a whirlwind courtship... ...a whirlwind tour.* ADJ CLASSIF : ATTRIB ⇑ speedy

whirr /wɜː/, **whirrs, whirring, whirred**; also spelled **whir**. When something **whirrs**, it continuously makes a series of low sounds so fast that they seem like one continuous sound; used especially of a machine, or of insects or birds moving their wings very fast. EG *Fans whirred on the ceiling... ...large populations of insects, whirring and buzzing through the air.* ▸ used as a noun. EG *...the far-off whirr of an electric motor.* V ⇑ buzz = hum ▸ N COUNT : USU SING

whisk /wɪsk/, **whisks, whisking, whisked**. 1 If you **whisk** someone or something away or to a particular place or if they **whisk** away, they are moved there quickly and in an efficient way. EG *I was whisked into hospital with fierce abdominal pains... She was whisked off by her parents to a nice school... The curtain whisked back.* V-ERG+A

2 When an animal **whisks** its tail, it makes one or more quick, sweeping movements with its tail. ▸ used as a noun. EG *With a whisk of its tail, it was gone.* V+O ▸ N COUNT : USU SING

3 When someone **whisks** eggs, cream, etc, they stir air into it very fast. EG *Whisk the egg whites until stiff.* V+O ⇑ beat = whip

4 A **whisk** is a kitchen tool used for stirring air into eggs, cream, etc very fast. N COUNT ⇑ utensil

whisker /wɪskə/, **whiskers**. 1 The **whiskers** of an animal such as a cat or a mouse are the long, stiff hairs that grow near its mouth. EG *The animal's whiskers began to twitch.* N COUNT : USU PL

2 You can refer to the hair on a man's face, especially on the sides of his face, as his **whiskers**. EG *He tugged at his side whiskers.* N PLURAL

3 **By a whisker** means by a very small amount; an informal expression. EG *Most journalists believe that Mr Brown will be elected, by a whisker.* PHR : USED AS AN A ⇑ just

whiskered /wɪskəd/. A **whiskered** animal or man has whiskers. ADJ CLASSIF ⇑ hairy

whiskery /wɪskəri[1]/ means the same as whiskered. EG *...his whiskery face.* ▸ used of a smile, kiss, etc. EG *He gave her a whiskery kiss.* ADJ QUALIT ⇑ hairy

whiskey /wɪski[1]/, **whiskeys**. **Whiskey** is whisky that is made in Ireland or the United States. ▸ also used to refer to a glass of whiskey. N MASS ▸ N COUNT

whisky /wɪski[1]/, **whiskies**. **Whisky** is a strong alcoholic drink made from grain such as barley or rye, especially in Scotland. EG *He had drunk too much whisky... ...the Scotch whisky trade.* ▸ also used to refer to a glass of whisky. EG *...a large whisky and soda... Castle finished his whisky and poured himself another small one.* N MASS ⇑ spirits ▸ N COUNT

whisper /wɪspə/, **whispers, whispering, whispered**. 1 When you **whisper** something or **whisper**, you say something to someone very quietly, using only your breath rather than using your throat, so that other people cannot hear what you are saying. EG *'Follow me,' Claude whispered. 'And keep quiet.'... She whispered in my ear that she wanted to go to the toilet... When we were washing I whispered the news to my sister... What are you two whispering about in there?* ◇ **whispered**. EG *She had had a long whispered conversation with the maid.* V, V+O/REPORT-CL/QUOTE, OR V+A (about) ◇ ADJ CLASSIF : ATTRIB

2 If something **whispers**, it makes a low, quiet sound which can only just be heard; a literary use. EG *A green car whispered to a halt in front of her.* V

3 A **whisper** is 3.1 a very quiet voice in which you use your breath not your throat. EG *Hooper lowered his voice to a whisper... We spoke in whispers.* N COUNT **3.2** something which is said very quietly in a whisper, especially a rumour. EG *There was the sound of steps and then there were whispers outside his door... There were whispers about the Colonel's strangeness.* N COUNT ⇑ utterance **3.3** a low, quiet sound which can only just be heard. EG *...the whisper of wind through the branches of the trees.* N COUNT : USU SING

whist /wɪst/ is a card game in which one pair of players tries to win more tricks than another pair. N UNCOUNT

whist drive, whist drives. A **whist drive** is a social event at which people play whist. N COUNT

whistle /wɪsə[0]l/, **whistles, whistling, whistled**. 1 When you **whistle** or when you **whistle** a tune, you make a loud, high sound or a series of such sounds by forcing your breath out between your lips, or perhaps between your teeth or two fingers in your mouth. EG *He came home for dinner whistling cheerfully... Mary was singing and I was whistling little bits of it... 'It'll cost five million.' Hagen whistled softly to show that he was impressed.* V OR V+O

2 If something **whistles**, it makes a loud, high sound as it moves quickly through the air or quickly along. EG *The wind whistling in across the lake blew my papers away... ...the bullets that whistled past his head.* V : USU+A

3 When something such as a steam train or a kettle **whistles**, a loud, high sound is produced as steam is forced through a small opening. EG *The train whistled as it approached the tunnel.* V

4 When a bird **whistles**, it makes a loud, high sound. V

5 A **whistle** is 5.1 a sound which you make when you whistle. EG *Sally let out a low whistle of surprise.* N COUNT **5.2** a loud sound produced by something moving quickly through the air or by air or steam being forced through a small opening. EG *I lay listening to the whistle of the wind in the clock-tower... The whistle from the kettle told me that breakfast was nearly ready.* N COUNT

6 A **whistle** is also 6.1 a small metal tube which you blow in order to produce a loud sound and attract someone's attention. EG *By shrill blasts on his whistle the policeman stopped all the traffic... The guard blew his whistle and waved his green flag.* N COUNT ⇑ device **6.2** a tube-shaped musical instrument which produces different sounds when you blow through it and cover different holes with your fingers. N COUNT **6.3** a device on a steam train through which steam can be forced to produce a loud sound. EG *The train whistle blows; the train pulls out.* N COUNT

7 To **whistle** also means to make a loud sound by blowing a whistle. EG *The referee whistled for the end of the match.* V

8 The word **whistle** is also used in the following informal expressions. **8.1** If you **blow the whistle** on someone or on something secret or illegal that they are doing, you tell someone else, especially someone in authority, what they are doing. PHR : VB INFLECTS, IF+PREP THEN *on* = inform on **8.2** If you say that someone **can whistle for** a particular thing, you mean that you are not willing or able to give it to them. EG *'He wants that report today.'–'Well, he can whistle for it.'* PHR **8.3** To **wet your whistle** means to have a drink. PHR : VB INFLECTS **8.4** See also **wolf whistle**.

whistle-stop. A **whistle-stop** tour is one in which you stop for a short time in a lot of different places, often as part of a political campaign. EG *The leader of the Liberal Party is making a whistle-stop tour of Scotland.* ADJ CLASSIF : ATTRIB

whit /wɪt/. The word **whit** is always spelled with a

capital letter for paragraph 2. 1 You say **not a whit** or **no whit** to emphasize that something is not the case at all; a rather old-fashioned, formal use. EG *Some of these places haven't changed a whit... He was no whit less friendly for all that.* PHR : USED AS AN A

2 **Whit** means the same as Whitsun; an informal use. EG *...the difficulty of getting anything done at Whit weekend when everyone is away.* N UNCOUNT

white /waɪt/, **whiter, whitest; whites.** 1 Something that is **white** is of the lightest colour that there is, the colour of snow or milk. EG *The air was warm and there were little white clouds high in the blue sky... She smiled, showing all her strong white teeth.* ADJ COLOUR
▸ used as a noun. EG *A woman dressed in white came up to me.* ▸ N MASS ◊ **whiteness.** EG *She loved the whiteness of his arms.* ◊ N UNCOUNT ● to **bleed** something **white**: see **bleed.**

2 Someone who is **white** belongs to a race with pale skins and of European origin. EG *They had never seen a white person before.* ADJ CLASSIF ▸ used as a noun. EG *The earlier race riots had been caused by whites attacking blacks.* ▸ N COUNT

3 **White** is used of things relating to white people. EG *They chose to go to live in a white area.* ADJ CLASSIF

4 If someone goes **white, 4.1** their hair becomes white in colour because of ageing. EG *My grandfather went white at the age of thirty.* ADJ COLOUR **4.2** they become very pale, for example because of fear, shock, anger, or illness. EG *My sister went white with rage.* ADJ QUALIT : USU PRED ● If someone looks **as white as a sheet,** they look very frightened, shocked, or ill. ● PHR : USED AS C

5 **White** coffee contains milk or cream. EG *Two white coffees, please.* ADJ CLASSIF = milky

6 **White** wine is pale yellowish in colour. EG *...a dry white wine.* ADJ CLASSIF ▸ used as a noun. EG *I prefer to drink white at lunch-time.* ▸ N MASS

7 **White** blood cells are the cells in your blood which you use to fight infection. ADJ CLASSIF : ATTRIB

8 The **white** of an egg, especially a hen's egg, is the transparent liquid that surrounds the yolk. N COUNT = albumen

9 The **white** of someone's eye is the white part of their eyeball. N COUNT

10 **Whites** are white-coloured clothes that you wear for playing some sports, for example tennis or cricket. N PLURAL ⇑ kit

whitebait /waɪtbeɪt/ are very small, young herrings or sprats that are fried and eaten as food. N PLURAL/ UNCOUNT

whitecaps /waɪtkæps/ are waves in the sea or on a lake which are blown by the wind, so that their tops appear white. N PLURAL = white horses

white Christmas, white Christmases. A **white Christmas** is a Christmas when it snows. N COUNT

white-collar. A **white-collar** worker is someone who works in an office as opposed to someone who works with their hands. ADJ CLASSIF : USU ATTRIB ▸ used of jobs. EG *...white-collar work.*

whited sepulchre, whited sepulchres. If you refer to someone as a **whited sepulchre,** you mean that they appear to be morally good but are in reality evil or bad; a literary word. N COUNT ⇑ hypocrite

white elephant, white elephants. If you refer to something as a **white elephant,** you mean that it is expensive but completely useless. EG *The new naval base has proved to be a white elephant.* N COUNT : USU USED AS C

white ensign, white ensigns. The **white ensign** is a flag that is flown by ships of the British Royal Navy. N COUNT

white goods. People in business sometimes refer to fridges, washing machines, and other large pieces of electrical household equipment as **white goods.** N PLURAL

white-haired. Someone who is **white-haired** has white hair, usually because they are old. ADJ CLASSIF

Whitehall /waɪthɔːl/ is the name of a street in London near which there are many government offices. N PROPER ▸ **Whitehall** is also used to mean the British Government itself. EG *Whitehall does not seem to care about this problem at all.*

white horses are the same as whitecaps. N PLURAL

white-hot /waɪt hɒt/. If something is **white-hot,** it is extremely hot. EG *...the white-hot centre of the bonfire.* ADJ CLASSIF

White House. The **White House** is the official home of the American President in Washington DC. N PROPER : *the*+ N ▸ The **White House** is also used to mean the President or the people who work with the President on government business. EG *The White House immediately denied the story*

white lie, white lies. If someone tells a **white lie,** they say something untruthful in order to avoid hurting someone else's feelings, and not for an evil purpose. N COUNT

white meat is meat such as chicken and pork, which is pale in colour after it has been cooked. N UNCOUNT

whiten /waɪtəᵒn/, **whitens, whitening, whitened.** When something **whitens** or when you **whiten** it, it becomes whiter or paler in colour. EG *Use very mild bleach to whiten white nylon.* V-ERG+A ⇑ lighten = blanch, bleach

whiteness /waɪtnɪ²s/. A **whiteness** is something that is paler than its surroundings, but that you cannot see clearly. EG *He could see a whiteness ahead of him in the dark tunnel.* ● See also **white.** N UNCOUNT/N SING WITH DET ⇑ blur

whitening /waɪtəᵒnɪŋ/ is a white substance that is used to make things white in colour, for example a liquid used to make tennis shoes whiter. N UNCOUNT = whiting

whiteout /waɪtaʊt/, **whiteouts.** If there is a **whiteout,** it is snowing or has snowed so heavily that everything seems white and it is very difficult to see. N COUNT ⇑ weather condition

White Paper, White Papers. A **White Paper** is, in Britain, Australia, Canada, and some other countries, an official report which gives the policy of the Government on a particular subject. N COUNT ⇑ document

white pepper is pepper which has been made from the dried insides of the fruits of the pepper plant. N UNCOUNT

white sauce is a thick, white-coloured sauce that is usually made from milk, flour, and butter. N MASS

white spirit is a colourless liquid that is made from petrol and is used, for example, to make paint thinner or to clean surfaces; used in British English. N UNCOUNT

whitewash /waɪtwɒʃ/, **whitewashes, whitewashing, whitewashed.** 1 **Whitewash** is a mixture of lime or chalk and water that is used for painting walls white. N UNCOUNT

2 If a wall or building has been **whitewashed,** it has been painted white with whitewash. V+O

3 If you **whitewash** something or someone you hide the unpleasant facts or truth about them in order to make them acceptable. EG *The government lost no time in whitewashing themselves and their part in this affair.* V+O (NG/REFL) ⇑ conceal

4 **Whitewash** is also an attempt to hide the unpleasant facts or truth about someone or something. EG *...the refusal to accept official whitewash in police enquiries.* N UNCOUNT/N SING WITH DET ⇑ concealment

white wedding, white weddings. A **white wedding** is a wedding where the bride wears white and the ceremony takes place in a church. N COUNT

whither /wɪðə/ means to where; a formal or old-fashioned word. EG *...Traitor's Gate, whither so many came by water to their death.* ADV WITH VB, OR CONJ SUBORD

whiting /waɪtɪŋ/. **Whiting** is both the singular and the plural form. 1 A **whiting** is a black and silver fish that lives in the sea and is cooked and eaten as food. N COUNT

2 **Whiting** is the same as whitening. N UNCOUNT

whitish /waɪtɪʃ/ means very pale and almost white in colour. EG *The sky was a pale whitish blue.* ADJ COLOUR

Whitsun /wɪtsəᵒn/ is the seventh Sunday after Easter, and the week which follows that Sunday. EG *...the annual Whitsun festival.* N UNCOUNT

whittle /wɪtəᵒl/, **whittles, whittling, whittled.** If you **whittle** something from a piece of wood, you carve it by cutting or shaving parts off the wood with a penknife or other small tool. EG *I showed her how to whittle pegs from white-wood.* V OR V+O

whittle away. To **whittle** something **away** or to **whittle away** at something means to make it smaller or less effective. EG *This may whittle away our liberties.* PHRASAL VB : V+O+ADV OR V+ADV+A *(at)* ⇑ reduce

whittle down. To **whittle** something **down** means to make it smaller over a period of time. EG *Profits are whittled down by the ever-rising cost of energy.* PHRASAL VB : V+O+ADV ⇑ reduce = pare down

whizz /wɪz/, **whizzes, whizzing, whizzed;** also spelled **whiz;** an informal word. 1 To **whizz** means to move very fast. EG *We just stood there with the cars whizzing by... The potter's wheel whizzed round.* V+A = shoot, zap

2 If you are a **whizz** at something, you are very good at it. EG *She's a whiz at electronics.* N COUNT : IF+ PREP THEN *at*

whizz-kid /wɪz kɪd/, **whizz-kids;** also spelled **whiz-kid,** and as two words. A **whizz-kid** is someone who is very good at their job and achieves success quickly because of their clever ideas; an informal word. EG *...a multi-millionaire insurance whizz-kid.* N COUNT

who /huː/. You can use **who** as the subject or object of a verb: see also **whom, whose.** 1 You use **who 1.1** WH : USED AS

in questions when you ask about the name or identity of someone. EG *Who are you?... Who are you going to invite?... 'I got a letter from Sian today.' – 'Sian who?'* [PRON] **1.2** in indirect questions and other structures in which you refer to someone whose name or identity is unknown. EG *She didn't know who I was... I told her who I was... Have you found out who Hegel is yet?... Posy had not specified who was coming.* [WH : USED AS PRON]

2 You also use **who** at the beginning of a relative clause **2.1** in which you specify the particular person you are talking about. EG *You are the only person in the world who knows anything about me... If you can't do it, we'll find someone who can... Those who joined the congregation were frequently new to church life... It is the 'living in' nannies who are in really short supply.* [WH : USED AS PRON REL = that] **2.2** in which you give more information about someone you mentioned in the previous clause. EG *Professor Marvin, who was always early, was there already... He handed the basket to Boylan, who slung it over his shoulder... I went to the cinema with Mary, who I think you once met.* [WH : USED AS PRON REL]

WHO /dʌbə⁰lju: eɪtʃ əʊ/ is an abbreviation for 'World Health Organization'; an international agency which is part of the United Nations and which is concerned with improving health standards and services throughout the world. [N PROPER : *the*+N ⇑ organization]

whoa /wəʊ/ is a command that you give to a horse to slow down or stop. ▸ You can also say **whoa** to someone who is talking to you, if you think they are going too fast or making assumptions; an informal use. [EXCLAM]

who'd /hu:d/ is **1** the usual spoken form of 'who had', especially when 'had' is an auxiliary verb. EG *I gave my ski sticks to a girl who'd lost hers in the snow... It was the little girl who'd come to play with her that afternoon.* **2** a spoken form of 'who would'. EG *I don't think he's the sort of young man who'd be thinking of marriage.*

whodunit /hu:dʌnɪt/, **whodunits**; also spelled **whodunnit**. A **whodunit** is a novel, film, or other story which is about a murder and in which the identity of the murderer is kept a mystery until the end; an informal word. [N COUNT]

whoever /hu:ɛvə/. **1** You use **whoever 1.1** to refer to someone who you are unable to identify precisely. EG *If death occurs at home, whoever discovers the body should contact the family doctor... Whoever answered the telephone was a very charming woman... Come out, whoever you are... I think it was all fixed up by lawyers or whoever arranges adoptions.* [WH : USED AS PRON]

1.2 to say that something is the case in any circumstances or for anyone. EG *Whoever wins this civil war, there will be little peace... I hope, whoever you vote for in the next election, that at least you know why you are voting.* [WH : USED AS PRON] **1.3** at the beginning of a clause in which you indicate that you do not know the precise identity of someone who you have just mentioned or are about to mention. EG *...Trevor Cowper (whoever he may be)... Whoever they are, they've called our bluff.* [WH : USED AS PRON] **1.4** in questions as an emphatic way of saying 'who', usually when you are surprised about something. EG *Whoever could that be?... Whoever saw a placard saying 'Sign SALT now'?* [WH : USED AS PRON]

2 You say **or whoever** to refer vaguely to someone, especially when you are not sure if you are talking about the right person; an informal expression. EG *Then I give the report to the director or accounts manager or whoever.* [PHR]

whole /həʊl/, **wholes. 1** If you refer to the **whole** of something, you mean all of it, including every part of it. EG *...the whole of Europe... ...the whole of July... The whole of the eyeball was visible.* [N SING : *the*+N+*of*] ▸ used as an adjective. EG *Get back to the others and we'll forget the whole thing... They're the best in the whole world... I've never told this to anyone else in my whole life.* [▸ ADJ CLASSIF : ATTRIB] ● If you refer to something **as a whole**, you are referring to it generally and as a single unit. EG *Is this true just in India, or in the world as a whole?* [● PHR AFTER N]

2 A **whole** is something which is made of parts but which you are considering as a single thing. EG *...a fragment of a greater whole... How big is that by comparison with the whole?... The earth's weather system is an integrated whole.* [N COUNT : USU SING = totality]

3 You use **whole** to say that an action is done to something as a unit or single thing, without dividing it up. For example, if you eat or swallow something **whole**, you do not bite or chew it. EG *The snake can swallow a small rat whole.* [ADV AFTER VB]

4 If something is **whole**, it is not broken or damaged; a slightly formal use. EG *Fortunately, the plates were still whole.* [ADJ CLASSIF : PRED = intact]

5 You also use **whole** to emphasize how different, large, varied, etc something is; an informal use. EG *...a whole new way of life... Charles was a whole lot younger, nicer and better-looking than I had expected... 'What's in the marinade?'–'Ginger, soy sauce, a whole bunch of things.'* [ADV+ADJ/ADV, OR ADJ CLASSIF : ATTRIB]

6 You say **on the whole** to indicate that what you are saying is only true in general and may not be true in every case, or that you are only giving a general opinion or summary of something. EG *One or two were all right but on the whole I used to hate going to lectures... On the whole criticism was muted... On the whole he is a very difficult character.* [PHR : USED AS ADV SEN]

wholefood /həʊlfu:d/, **wholefoods. Wholefoods** are foods which have not been refined very much or processed and which do not contain additives or artificial ingredients. EG *Low-fat wholefoods and fresh vegetables and fruits should be included regularly in your diet.* [N PLURAL/N UNCOUNT] ▸ used as an adjective. EG *...wholefood diets.* [▸ N BEFORE N]

wholehearted /həʊlhɑ:tɪ²d/; also spelled with a hyphen. If you support or agree to something in a **wholehearted** way, you support or agree to it enthusiastically and completely. EG *He had the wholehearted backing of the younger members.* [ADJ QUALIT ⇑ full = total] ◊ **wholeheartedly.** EG *I agreed wholeheartedly to her suggestions.* [◊ ADV WITH VB ⇑ fully]

wholemeal /həʊlmi:l/. **Wholemeal** flour is made from the complete grain of the wheat plant, including the husk. ▸ used of bread and other things that are made from wholemeal flour. EG *...the brown wholemeal bread on her plate.* [ADJ CLASSIF : ATTRIB = wholewheat]

wholeness /həʊlnɪ²s/ is the quality of being complete or a single unit and not broken or divided into parts; a formal or literary word. EG *The peace, the wholeness, all that India promised, seemed fulfilled.* [N UNCOUNT = unity]

whole note, whole notes. A **whole note** is a semibreve; used in American English. [N COUNT]

whole number, whole numbers. A **whole number** is an exact number such as 1, 7, 24, etc as opposed to a number with fractions or decimals. [N COUNT = integer]

wholesale /həʊlseɪl/. **1** You use **wholesale** to refer to the activity of buying and selling goods in large quantities and therefore at cheaper prices, especially the activity of selling goods to shopkeepers who then sell them to the public. EG *...wholesale and retail distribution... ...a sharp rise in wholesale prices... Stein got the machine for me wholesale.* [ADJ CLASSIF : ATTRIB, OR ADV AFTER VB ≠ retail]

2 You also use **wholesale** to describe something that is done to an excessive extent, for example because it has not been thought about carefully enough; used showing disapproval. EG *Wholesale slaughter was carried out in the name of progress... ...a wholesale belief in the professional's competence.* [ADJ CLASSIF : ATTRIB, OR ADV AFTER VB ⇑ complete = outright]

wholesaler /həʊlseɪlə/, **wholesalers.** A **wholesaler** is a person whose business is buying large quantities of goods and selling them in smaller amounts, for example to shops. [N COUNT ⇑ trader = distributor]

wholesome /həʊlsə⁰m/. **1** Something that is **wholesome** is good and likely to improve your life, behaviour, or mental state; used showing approval. EG *Young people enter marriage nowadays with a much more wholesome attitude... This has had a wholesome effect on babies and parents.* [ADJ QUALIT = healthy]

2 Wholesome food is good for your health; used showing approval. EG *...wholesome but unexciting bread-and-butter pudding.* [ADJ QUALIT = healthy, nourishing]

wholewheat /həʊlwi:t/ means the same as wholemeal; used in American English. EG *...wholewheat spaghetti.* [ADJ CLASSIF : ATTRIB]

who'll /hu:l/ is a spoken form of 'who will' or 'who shall'. EG *Who'll believe him?... You'll occasionally meet men who'll say, 'Thank God–those days have gone!'*

wholly /həʊlli¹/ means completely and not partly or slightly. EG *The idea was not a wholly new one... ...people whom we could not wholly trust... They had wholly ceased to be in control of it.* [ADV = absolutely]

whom /hu:m/. The word **whom** is used in formal or written English instead of 'who' when it is the object of a verb or preposition. 1 You use **whom** in questions, indirect questions, and other structures in which you refer to someone whose name or identity is unknown. EG *'I'm a reporter.'–'Oh yes? For whom?'... Whom do you suggest I should ask?... I know who you are and whom you represent.* WH : USED AS PRON

2 You also use **whom** at or near the beginning of a relative clause 2.1 in which you specify the particular person you are talking about. EG *She was a girl whom it was difficult to know well... He is a man for whom I have immense respect.* 2.2 in which you give more information about someone you mentioned in the previous clause. EG *She was engaged to a sailor named Raikes, whom she had met at Dartmouth... The paper is by Firth, of whom you will already have heard... We have a large number of customers most of whom have slightly different requirements.* WH : USED AS PRON REL / WH : USED AS PRON REL

whoop, whoops, whooping, whooped; pronounced /wu:p/ for paragraph 1 and /wʊps/ for paragraph 2. 1 If you **whoop**, you shout loudly in a very happy or excited way; a fairly literary word. EG *Eddie whooped with delight.* ▸ used as a noun. EG *There were whoops of approval by the bar customers.* V / ▸ N COUNT

2 People say **whoops** 2.1 when they have a slight accident or see someone else having one. EG *Whoops. You nearly dropped it again.* 2.2 when they have just said something which they should not have said, for example something which was secret or which may have sounded rude. EG *He's not in this afternoon. Whoops, that was a bit of a give-away.* EXCLAM = oh dear / EXCLAM = oh dear

whoopee /wʊpi:/; an old-fashioned informal word. 1 People sometimes shout **whoopee** when they are very happy or excited. EG *'Whoopee!' he shouted. 'We've hit the jackpot.'* EXCLAM = hooray

2 **Whoopee** also means a noisy or happy celebration. EG *...a time for rejoicing and whoopee.* N UNCOUNT

whooping cough /hu:pɪŋ kɒf/; also spelled with a hyphen. **Whooping cough** is an illness which mainly children get and which makes them cough and make a loud noise when they breathe in. N UNCOUNT

whoosh /wʊʃ/, **whooshes, whooshing, whooshed**; an informal word. 1 People sometimes say **whoosh** when they want to describe something that appears suddenly or moves very fast. EG *Then suddenly, whoosh, out it came.* EXCLAM

2 If something **whooshes** somewhere, it moves very fast or suddenly in that direction. EG *Thousands of flashing rockets whooshed over our heads.* V+A ⇑ rush

3 A **whoosh** of air, water, etc is a sudden rush of it. EG *The train came in with a whoosh of country dust.* N SING WITH DET : IF+PREP THEN *of*

whopper /wɒpə/, **whoppers**; a rather old-fashioned informal word. A **whopper** is 1 a very big lie. EG *They swallow any whopper which they hear.* 2 an unusually large example of something; used showing approval. EG *What a whopper! That must be the biggest one we've seen this year.* N COUNT / N COUNT ⇑ specimen = giant

whopping /wɒpɪŋ/ means much larger than usual or much larger than you expected; a rather old-fashioned informal word. EG *Real growth was at a whopping six and a half per cent.* ADJ CLASSIF : ATTRIB, OR ADV+ ADJ/ADV ⇑ huge

whore /hɔ:/, **whores**. A **whore** is a prostitute or a women who is considered to behave like a prostitute; an offensive word. N COUNT

who're /hu:ə/ is a spoken form of 'who are'. EG *...married couples who're waiting to be housed.*

whorehouse /hɔ:haus/, **whorehouses**. A **whorehouse** is a brothel; an informal word. N COUNT

whorl /wɜ:l/, **whorls**. A **whorl** is a spiral shape, for example the pattern on the tips of your fingers; a rather literary word. EG *The smoke dispersed into threads and clouds and whorls.* N COUNT

who's /hu:z/ is the usual spoken form of 'who is' or 'who has', especially when 'has' is an auxiliary verb. EG *'Edward drove me up.'–'Who's Edward?'... Paul Theroux is an American author who's settled in London.*

whose /hu:z/. Although you usually use **whose** to refer to something which belongs to or is associated with a person, you can also use it to refer to something which belongs to or is associated with a thing; however, many people dislike this use. 1 You use **whose** at the beginning of a relative clause 1.1 in which you specify something that belongs to or is associated with a person or thing that you mentioned in the previous clause. EG *...a woman whose husband deserted her... There are three witnesses whose testimony I know about... I would like to pay tribute to my constituents without whose loyalty I would not be in this House today... ...an old suit whose jacket had gone through at the elbows.* 1.2 in which you give more information about a person or thing that you mentioned in the previous clause. EG *He used to read aloud to his wife, whose eyesight was failing... ...the poacher, whose name was Dave... ...small houses, whose doors open directly onto the street.* WH : USED AS PRON REL / WH : USED AS PRON REL

2 You also use **whose** in questions, indirect questions, and other structures in which you ask about or refer to the person that something belongs to or is associated with. EG *Whose little boy are you?... Do you know whose fault it is?... It's morally her responsibility–no matter whose it is in law.* WH : USED AS DETPOSS/ PRONPOSS

whosoever /hu:səʊɛvə/ means the same as whoever; a formal or old-fashioned word. EG *Whosoever sins, sins only against himself.* WH : USED AS PRON

who've /hu:v/ is the usual spoken form of 'who have,' especially when 'have' is an auxiliary verb. EG *There are many examples of local authorities who've taken special measures... ...people who've gone to universities.*

why /waɪ/, **whys**. 1 You use **why** in questions when you ask about the reasons for something. EG *'I had to say no.'–'Why?'... Why did you do it, Martin?... 'Come here.'–'Why should I?'... 'It's very hard to find.'–'Why is that?'... Why the sudden invitation?... 'He hates you too, Ralph'–'Me? Why me?'* WH : USED AS ADV

2 You also use **why** at the beginning of a clause 2.1 to link clauses in which you talk about the reasons for something. EG *He wondered why she had come... The room was cold, but that wasn't why he was trembling... I did not know why, but I knew I was afraid... He likes you–I can't imagine why.* 2.2 to introduce a relative clause after the word 'reason'. EG *...the reasons why the government fell... There are seven good reasons why I have a freezer.* WH : USED AS CONJ SUBORD / WH : USED AS PRON REL

3 You use **why** with 'not' in order to introduce a suggestion that is in the form of a question. EG *Why don't we all go?... 'I'll ring her up when I go out to lunch.' – 'Why not do it now?'* WH : USED AS ADV +*not*

4 You say **why not** as a response to what someone has just said or suggested in order to confirm it or to express your agreement. EG *'Can I come too?' – 'I don't see why not.'* PHR

5 People also say **'why!'** to indicate their surprise, shock, indignation, etc. They also say **'why!'** to indicate that they have just realized something or that they are going to contradict what has just been said; used especially in American English and in novels. EG *Why, Dr Kirk, I do believe you are serious... What could possibly happen in King's Road? Why, there's a police station two hundred yards away.*

6 A **why** is a question about the reason for something. EG *So many whys, Smithy, so many whys.* ● **the whys and wherefores**: see **wherefores**. N COUNT : USU PL

WI /dʌbəᵒlju: aɪ/. The **WI** is an organization for women in England and Wales. It holds meetings in many towns and villages where women can meet socially and take part in various classes and activities; an abbreviation for 'Women's Institute'. EG *She was a lifelong member of the W.I.* N PROPER : *the*+ N

wick /wɪk/, **wicks**. 1 The **wick** of a candle is the piece of string in it which burns when it is lit. N COUNT ⇑ thread

2 The **wick** of a paraffin lamp or cigarette lighter is the part which supplies the fuel to the flame when it is lit. EG *It's very hard to turn the wick up and down.* N COUNT

3 If you say that someone **gets on your wick**, you mean that they irritate you; used in informal British English. PHR : VB INFLECTS

wicked /wɪkɪ²d/. 1 Something or someone that is **wicked** is 1.1 very bad in a way that is deliberately immoral or harmful to other people. EG *It was very clear to him that he had done something wicked.* ◇ **wickedness**. EG *...appalled by the wickedness of his crime.* 1.2 very dangerous and may cause physical harm. EG *The bull had gored them with its wicked horns.* ◇ **wickedly**. EG *The knife glinted wickedly.* ADJ QUALIT = evil, sinful / ◇ N UNCOUNT / ADJ QUALIT ⇑ harmful / ◇ ADV WITH VB

2 If you describe someone or something as **wicked**, you mean that they are rather mischievous or seem slightly immoral, but that you find them attractive or enjoyable. EG *He had a wicked grin... ...the wicked wit* ADJ QUALIT : USU ATTRIB = roguish

of the cartoonist. ◊ **wickedly**. EG *She smiled wickedly... ...a wickedly exciting, musky smell.* ◊ ADV

3 If you describe something such as a situation as **wicked**, you mean that it is unpleasant and upsetting; an informal use. EG *It was wicked when we got demobbed because you couldn't get any kind of work... The prices there are wicked.* ADJ QUALIT : USU PRED ⇑ awful

wicker /wɪkə/. A **wicker** basket, chair, mat, etc is made of wickerwork. EG *He dumped the spoons in a wicker basket.* N UNCOUNT : USU BEFORE N

wickerwork /wɪkəwɜːk/ is made by weaving twigs, canes, or reeds together. It is usually used to make baskets or furniture. EG *...lots of wickerwork armchairs with feathery cushions.* N UNCOUNT : USU BEFORE N ⇑ basketwork = wicker

wicket /wɪkɪt/, **wickets**; a technical term in cricket. A **wicket** is 1 a set of three upright sticks called stumps, with two small sticks called bails on top of them, at which the ball is bowled in cricket. There are two wickets on a cricket pitch. N COUNT 2 the area of grass in between the two wickets. N COUNT = pitch, strip

wicket-keeper, wicket-keepers; also spelled without a hyphen. A **wicket-keeper** is the player in a cricket team who stands behind the wicket in order to stop balls that the batsman misses or to catch balls that the batsman hits. N COUNT

wide /waɪd/, **wider, widest; wides**. 1 Something that is **wide** measures a large distance from one side to the other, especially in comparison to its length or height. EG *...a wide bed... She looked across the wide, flat meadow... He was a tall man with wide shoulders... ...a wide grin.* ADJ QUALIT = broad ◊ **widely**. EG *'That's all right,' she said, smiling widely... He yawned widely.* ◊ ADV WITH VB ⇑ broadly

2 If you open or spread something **wide**, you open or spread it as far as possible or to the fullest extent. EG *Rudolph always opened the window wide at night... He left his office door wide open... I spread my arms wide... She leaned forward, hands resting wide apart on the bar.* ADV WITH VB, OR ADV BEFORE ADV

3 If your eyes are **wide** or **wide** open, they are open more than usual because you are surprised or frightened. EG *Lamin watched with wide eyes... She sat there looking up at me, her eyes wide with pleasure... She opened her eyes wide and stared.* ADJ CLASSIF

4 You use **wide** when you are talking about how much something measures from one side or edge to the other. EG *The bay is about thirty miles long and five to six miles wide... ...a narrow ledge of rock a few yards wide... The meteorite left a 3-mile-wide crater... How wide is the doorway?* ADJ CLASSIF : USU PRED, USU AFTER NUM/QUANTIF/ *how*

5 A **wide** variety, range, selection, etc is one that includes a lot of different things or qualities. EG *The college library had a wide variety of books... ...a wide range of interests.* ADJ QUALIT ⇑ large = broad ◊ **widely**. EG *Conversation does not range widely... Over the next twelve years, he travelled widely.* ◊ ADV WITH VB = broadly

6 You also use **wide** when describing something which is found, believed, known, supported, etc by many people or throughout a large area. EG *The movement developed a wide following among the middle classes... The inauguration received wide publicity in the press.* ADJ QUALIT = general, popular ◊ **widely**. EG *Your views on education are already widely known... The publications are widely available... Her books sell widely.* ◊ ADV = generally

7 A **wide** difference or gap between two things, ideas, or qualities is a large difference or gap. EG *The gap between the poor and the rich is very wide indeed... Wide class differences still remain.* ADJ QUALIT ⇑ great = broad ◊ **widely**. EG *Policies vary widely from one project to another.* ◊ ADV WITH VB ⇑ greatly

8 **Wide** is used to describe something which relates to the most important or general parts of a situation, rather than to the smaller parts or to details. EG *Your campaign must not be allowed to obscure the wider political issues... ...the wider context of world events.* ADJ QUALIT : USU COMPAR = broad

9 If something such as a shot or punch is **wide**, it does not hit its target. EG *The first shot went wide, the second hit the engine room.* ADJ CLASSIF : USU PRED, OR ADV AFTER VB ⇑ out

10 In cricket, a **wide** is a ball that is bowled too far away from the batsman for him to hit it, and for which the batsman's team scores a run. N COUNT

11 ● **far and wide**: see **far**. ● **wide of the mark**: see **mark**.

-wide combines with nouns to form adjectives or adverbs which indicate that something exists or happens throughout the place or area that the noun refers to. EG *...nation→nationwide... ...state→statewide... ...ocean→oceanwide... ...world→worldwide.* COMB : FORMS ADJ CLASSIFS OR ADVS

wide-angle lens, wide-angle lenses. A **wide-angle lens** is a lens which allows you to photograph a wider view than a normal lens. N COUNT

wide-awake; also spelled without a hyphen. If you are **wide-awake**, you are completely awake. EG *By 6 she was wide awake... Jimmie felt wide-awake again.* ADJ CLASSIF : PRED

wide-eyed. If you describe someone as **wide-eyed**, you mean that 1 they seem inexperienced, and perhaps lack common sense. EG *I didn't know I had to do that, I said, all wide-eyed... Part of me was still a wide-eyed American.* ADJ CLASSIF : USU PRED ⇑ innocent = naive 2 their eyes are more open than usual, especially because they are surprised or frightened. EG *She gave me tea and sat wide-eyed while I drank it.* ADJ CLASSIF : USU PRED

widen /waɪdə⁰n/, **widens, widening, widened**. 1 If something **widens** or if you **widen** it, 1.1 it becomes greater in measurement from one side or edge to the other. EG *The original single-file trail had already been widened by many feet... Below Wapping, the river widens... The road finally widened and turned into a courtyard.* V-ERG = broaden 1.2 it becomes greater in range or variety or includes or affects a larger number of people or things. EG *Labour had to widen its appeal if it was to win the election... We would like to see the scheme widened... They could widen their experience by going on a course.* V-ERG ⇑ increase = broaden

2 If your eyes **widen**, they open more. EG *Sandy stared at me, his eyes widening.* ▸ used of someone's smile. EG *Mary's smile widened.* V

3 If a difference or gap **widens**, it becomes more extreme. EG *The gap between the rich and poor regions widened... Society continues to widen the gulf between specialists and non-specialists.* V-ERG ⇑ increase

wide-ranging. 1 If something is **wide-ranging**, it deals with or includes a great variety of different things. EG *...a wide-ranging interview.* ADJ QUALIT

2 **Wide-ranging** effects, implications, etc spread or reach a long way. EG *This attack carried wide-ranging implications for the government.* ADJ QUALIT ⇑ serious = far-reaching

widespread /waɪdspred/. If something is **widespread**, it exists or happens over a large area, or to a great extent. EG *Housing estates suffer from widespread vandalism and neglect... Industrial robots will be in widespread use... There was a widespread belief that the newspapers had not told the truth.* ADJ QUALIT ⇑ general

widow /wɪdəʊ/, **widows**. A **widow** is a woman whose husband has died and who has not married again. EG *My mother is a widow... His savings had been left to his widow.* N COUNT

widowed /wɪdəʊd/. If someone is **widowed**, their husband or wife has died and they have not married again; used especially of women. EG *...his widowed mother... I have been widowed for ten years.* ADJ CLASSIF ⇑ bereaved

widower /wɪdəʊə/, **widowers**. A **widower** is a man whose wife has died and who has not married again. EG *Mr Starke, a widower, owned the practice.* N COUNT

widowhood /wɪdəʊhʊd/ is the state of being a widow; also used to refer to the period of time during which a woman is a widow. EG *The shock of widowhood weakens resistance to illness... She continued to worship his memory throughout her long widowhood.* N UNCOUNT

width /wɪdθ/, **widths**. 1 The **width** of something is the distance it measures from one side or edge to the other. EG *The area was just over a thousand yards in width... ...the width of a man's hand... The carpet is the full width of the stairs.* N UNCOUNT = breadth

2 **Width** is the quality of being wide. EG *He might make a boxer, with his width and heaviness... I was beginning to get used to the width of American streets.* N UNCOUNT ⇑ size

3 A **width** is the distance from one side of a swimming pool to the other. EG *I can nearly swim a width.* N COUNT ≠ length

widthways /wɪdθweɪz/. If something is measured, folded, etc **widthways**, it is measured, folded, etc along its width rather than along its length. ADV AFTER VB = sideways

wield /wiːld/, **wields, wielding, wielded**. 1 If you **wield** a weapon, tool, or piece of equipment, you carry and use it. EG *They surrounded the Embassy, hurling stones and wielding sticks... They came back onto the deck, wielding their paint brushes.* V+O = brandish

2 If someone **wields** power, they have it and are able to use it. EG *It is still the rich nations which wield the power... They were able to wield enormous political power.* V+O = exert

wife /waɪf/, **wives** /waɪvz/. A man's **wife** is the woman that he is married to. EG *His wife looked at the clock... She is the wife of an army colonel.* • See also **old wives' tale**. N COUNT : USU WITH POSS = spouse

wifely /waɪfli[1]/. **Wifely** is used to describe behaviour which is supposed to be typical of a good wife, for example obedience and loyalty. EG *Where's your wifely loyalty?... ...wifely duty.* ADJ CLASSIF : ATTRIB ⇑ womanly

wig /wɪg/, **wigs**. 1 A **wig** is 1.1 a mass of false hair which you wear on your head, because you are bald or because you want to cover up your own hair. EG *She used to wear a wig... ...a blonde wig.* N COUNT 1.2 a mass of white, curly, false hair which judges and other officials wear on formal occasions as a sign of authority. N COUNT

2 • See also **bigwig**.

wigged /wɪgd/. Someone who is **wigged** is wearing a wig. EG *...wigged judges.* ADJ CLASSIF : ATTRIB

wiggle /wɪgə[0]l/, **wiggles, wiggling, wiggled**. 1 If you **wiggle** something, you move it up and down or from side to side in small quick movements. EG *They wiggle their hips to the sound of pop music... Can you wiggle your ears?* V-ERG = wriggle

2 A **wiggle** is 2.1 a small quick movement in which something moves up and down or from side to side. EG *...the wiggle of her hips.* N COUNT : USU SING 2.2 a line that has a lot of little bumps in it. EG *He drew the sea as a series of wiggles.* N COUNT : USU PL = wave

wigwam /wɪgwæm/, **wigwams**. A **wigwam** is a tent made by North American Indians from animal skins. N COUNT ⇑ tepee

wild /waɪld/, **wilder, wildest; wilds**. 1 **Wild** animals and birds live in natural surroundings such as forests, mountains, or grasslands, and are not kept by people as pets or farm animals. EG *They hunted wild animals for food... As they passed, wild pigs would go rushing into the bush.* ADJ CLASSIF : ATTRIB

2 **Wild** plants, flowers, trees, etc grow naturally and are not specially grown by people as crops. EG *He lived on berries and wild herbs.* ADJ CLASSIF : ATTRIB

3 Animals in **the wild** are living in their natural, free state in their natural surroundings, in contrast to being kept in a cage, in a zoo, or as farm animals or pets. EG *...a rare creature that few people have seen in the wild... They couldn't survive long in the wild.* N SING : the+N = natural habitat

4 **Wild** land is natural and not cultivated at all. It is usually not suitable for people to live on or for farming. EG *The country was spread out around us, wild and harsh and primitive... ...the wilder parts of Scotland.* ◊ **wildness**. ADJ QUALIT ⇑ rough = uninhabited ◊ N UNCOUNT

5 The **wilds** are remote areas, far away from towns or cities, where there are not many people living. EG *We live out in the wilds... ...the wilds of Australia... We went further north up into the wilds.* N PLURAL : the+N

6 **Wild** is used to describe the weather or the sea when it is very stormy and rough. EG *...wild November nights.* ADJ QUALIT = tempestuous

7 **Wild** hair is long and very untidy in appearance. ADJ QUALIT

8 If you have **wild** eyes or a **wild** look, your eyes are wide open and staring, often looking around very quickly in different directions, because you are frightened, angry, or mad. EG *His eyes were wild and his voice shook... She had a wild haunted look... They crowded the wild-eyed animals into a truck.* ADJ QUALIT ⇑ excited = frantic

9 If people are **wild**, they indicate in their behaviour that they are very excited, for example by shouting or cheering a lot. EG *The audience went wild... The men were wild with excitement... The announcement met with wild cheers in the Commons.* ◊ **wildly**. EG *The audience applauded wildly.* ADJ QUALIT = frenzied ◊ ADV WITH VB

10 If you **are not wild about** something, you do not like it very much; an informal expression. EG *I'm not wild about the wallpaper.* PHR : VB INFLECTS

11 If someone is **wild**, they are very angry; an informal use. EG *Dad just went wild... She was having a wild argument with Joe.* ADJ QUALIT = furious

12 **Wild** is used to describe 12.1 emotions which are very strong and out of control. EG *He felt a wild ecstatic happiness... He struck at me in wild fury.* ADJ CLASSIF : ATTRIB ⇑ extreme = absolute 12.2 behaviour which lacks any discipline or control, especially behaviour that involves sex or violence. EG *...wild parties... The film portrays the wilder excesses of the Roman Empire.* ADJ QUALIT ⇑ outrageous

13 If something **runs wild**, it grows or behaves in a natural or free way, without being controlled or looked after. EG *...an old house with ivy running wild all over it... Early in the morning, dogs run wild in the park.* PHR : VB INFLECTS = run amok

14 A **wild** idea, scheme, etc is very unusual and original, and perhaps rather silly. EG *You have wild fantasies... Their schemes began to sound wilder and wilder.* ◊ **wildness**. EG *...her wildness of imagination.* ADJ QUALIT ⇑ imaginative = vivid ◊ N UNCOUNT

15 When some people say that something is **wild**, they mean that it is very good or interesting, and perhaps very unusual; an informal use. EG *Wow, this trip has been really wild.* ADJ QUALIT = wonderful

16 If something is **beyond** your **wildest dreams**, it is more than you had ever hoped for or believed possible. EG *He's paying them a salary beyond their wildest dreams... In all their wildest dreams the boys could never have anticipated a room so full of chocolate.* PHR : USED AS AN A ⇑ unexpected

17 **Wild** is used to describe a movement, blow, attack, etc which is extremely forceful or energetic, but not controlled at all. EG *He made a wild dash for the door... This enraged him and made his attacks wilder.* ◊ **wildly**. EG *The shark kept thrashing wildly against the boat.* ADJ QUALIT ⇑ impulsive = desperate ◊ ADV WITH VB = violently

18 A **wild** guess is one which is very unlikely and made without much thought. ◊ **wildly**. EG *I was guessing wildly.* ADJ QUALIT ◊ ADV WITH VB ⇑ madly

19 If someone **sows** their **wild oats**, they behave in an uncontrolled way, especially involving sexual activity, when they are young and before they settle down to a career or to family life. PHR : VB INFLECTS

wild boar, wild boars. **Wild boar** can also be used as the plural form. A **wild boar** is a large fierce pig which has tusks and a lot of hair and which lives in forests. In former times, wild boars were often hunted. N COUNT

wildcat /waɪldkæt/, **wildcats**. 1 A **wildcat** is a cat which looks like a large pet cat but is very fierce and lives especially in mountains and forests. N COUNT

2 A **wildcat** strike happens suddenly, as a result of a decision by a group of workers, and is not officially approved by a trade union. ADJ CLASSIF : ATTRIB ⇑ unofficial

3 A **wildcat** scheme, project, business, etc is risky and likely to fail, usually because there has not been enough planning. ADJ CLASSIF : ATTRIB

wildebeest /wɪldɪbi:st, vɪl-/. **Wildebeest** is both the singular and the plural form. A **wildebeest** is a large African antelope which has a hairy tail, short curved horns, and hair under its neck that looks like a beard. Wildebeest usually live in large herds. N COUNT = gnu

wilderness /wɪldənɪ[2]s/, **wildernesses**. 1 A **wilderness** is 1.1 a desert or other area of land which has very few plants or animals and which has not yet been used by people. EG *The surrounding country was a black wilderness... ...the arctic wilderness.* N COUNT : USU SING = wasteland 1.2 an area where grass or plants are growing very thickly and without any control. EG *The garden's turned into a wilderness... His yard is a wilderness of weeds and heaps of coal.* N COUNT : USU SING = jungle

2 If a politician spends time **in the wilderness**, he or she is for a time no longer in an important or influential position in politics, and is not heard about very much. EG *He is enjoying a revival after four years in the wilderness... Will she follow her predecessor into the backbench wilderness?* PHR : USED AS AN A

wildfire /waɪldfaɪə/. If something, especially news or a rumour, **spreads like wildfire**, it spreads very quickly. EG *The news spread like wildfire round the world... The infection spread like wildfire.* PHR : VB INFLECTS

wild flower, wild flowers. **Wild flowers** are plants and their flowers which grow naturally, for example in the countryside, rather than being grown by people in gardens or nurseries. N COUNT

wildfowl /waɪldfaʊl/ are birds such as ducks, pheasants, and quails which are hunted and shot by some people. N PLURAL = game bird

wild-goose chase, wild-goose chases. If you are on a **wild-goose chase**, you waste a lot of time searching for something that you have little chance of finding, because you have been given misleading information. EG *I'm afraid I'm on a wild-goose chase... He sent us on a wild-goose chase.* N COUNT ⇑ search

wildlife /waɪldlaɪf/ is used to refer to animals and other living things that live in the wild. EG *These chemicals would destroy crops and all wildlife... ...a wildlife photographer.* N UNCOUNT = fauna, flora

wildly /waɪldli[1]/. You use **wildly** to emphasize that a quality is very great indeed; an informal word. EG ADV+ADJ = grossly

...wildly erratic behaviour... ...a wildly romantic book... ...wildly inefficient. ● See also **wild**.

Wild West. The **Wild West** is used to refer to the western part of the United States during the time when Europeans were first settling there. Films and stories about this period are mainly about cowboys, gun-fights, American Indians, etc. N SING : *the*+N ⇑ west

wiles /waɪlz/ are clever tricks that people use to persuade other people to do something. EG *I was tired of her wiles and cunning... You seem familiar with the wiles of children.* N PLURAL ⇑ ruse = play

wilful /wɪlfʊl/. 1 Something that is **wilful** is done or said deliberately, especially with the intention of hurting someone; used showing disapproval. EG *She described the speech as wilful nonsense... All the disagreements of their marriage had sprung from her wilful determination to disinherit herself.* ADJ CLASSIF : ATTRIB
◊ **wilfully**. EG *She had deliberately and wilfully betrayed him to his father.* ◊ ADV WITH VB
2 Someone who is **wilful** is determined to have their own way. EG *She was a wilful child.* ◊ **wilfulness**. ADJ QUALIT ◊ N UNCOUNT

will /wɪl/, **wills, willing, willed**. 1 You use **will** 1.1 to refer to something that is going to happen in the future. EG *The gardens will be opened to the public later this month... Inflation is rising and will continue to rise... Perhaps this time it won't rain... That will be best for all of us, won't it?... Next week we will be reporting on the state of the Health Service... 'It'll be good to see the mountains again.'–'Yes, it will.'* MODAL 1.2 with 'I' and 'we' when you are saying that you intend to do something. EG *I will see you tomorrow... I will never betray you... I'll be back in a half-hour... 'You still haven't told me anything.'–'I will.'* MODAL : WITH *I/we*
2 You use **will** in questions 2.1 to ask someone about what is going to happen in the future. EG *Will I get paid?... Will I hate school?... What will I do if he doesn't come?... Shall I speak to Mr Wolfe or will you?* MODAL 2.2 to ask someone what they intend to do. EG *Where will you live?... Will you be coming in later?* MODAL
2.3 as an informal way of inviting someone to do something or of offering someone something. EG *Will you stay for lunch?... Will you have a whisky, Doctor?* MODAL 2.4 to ask or tell someone to do something. EG *Will you do me a favour?... Please keep an eye on him, will you?... Will you shut up!... You won't forget the canary, will you?... Won't you change your mind?* MODAL = would, could
3 You can use **will** to give an order to someone; a fairly formal use. EG *You will forget this conversation immediately... You will please go into the other room.* MODAL
4 You also use **will** 4.1 to say that someone is willing to do something. EG *Any bank will do it for you... I will not be buried in Westminster... We won't accept that... 'Have another whisky.'–'Thank you. I will.'... Yes, I will admit it was a silly thing to do.* MODAL 4.2 to say that someone or something is able to do something. EG *I doubt if you will actually see the comet... A hot water dye which will dye up to 2lb dry weight... The car won't go.* MODAL ⇑ can 4.3 to say that an action usually happens in the particular way mentioned. EG *The bonus will usually be paid automatically... A second hand car dealer will always look at the bodywork rather than the engine... Never mind, these things will happen.* MODAL 4.4 in the second part of some 'if' sentences. EG *If you are getting supplementary benefit, you will get help with your rent and rates as well.* MODAL : AFTER *if* 4.5 to say that you are assuming or guessing that something is true, because you have good reasons for thinking it. EG *You will probably already be a member of a union... Those of you who are familiar with the game will know this... That'll be young Christopher there... They'll be retired now, won't they?* MODAL 4.6 to say that someone insists on behaving or doing something in a particular way and you cannot change them. You emphasize the word **will** when you use it in this way. EG *He will leave his socks lying around all over the place and it drives me mad.* MODAL
5 **will have**. You use **will have** 5.1 when you are saying that something will be true by a particular time in the future. EG *Soon, nearly a third of a century will have passed since the Second World War... Perhaps when I am fifty I will have forgotten... By the time you hear this, he will probably have won ten more races.* MODAL 5.2 when you are assuming or guessing that something has happened. EG *You will already have gathered that I don't like her... I suspect you will have seen them.* MODAL
6 **Will** is 6.1 the determination to do something and to fight or make an effort if someone or something tries to stop you. EG *He lacked will and ambition... She lost her will to live... She has a very strong will... Their marriage became a fierce battle of wills.* N UNCOUNT/COUNT 6.2 the power to control your mind. EG *She was able to stop herself by an effort of will.* ● See also **free will**. N UNCOUNT = will-power
7 If something is someone's **will**, it is something that they want or wish for, especially when they have great power or authority. EG *I must abide by the will of the people... It is the will of Allah... We never have had the courage to defy his expressed will.* N SING : WITH POSS = wishes
8 The word **will** is also used in the following expressions. 8.1 If something is done **against** your **will**, it is done even though you do not want it to be done. EG *Do you always make people drink against their will?* PHR : USED AS AN A
8.2 If you can do something **at will**, you can do it when you want and as much as you want. EG *Chang told us that we could wander around at will... He can change his personality at will.* PHR : USED AS AN A 8.3 When you say **'where there's a will, there's a way'**, you mean that if you are determined enough to do something, you will find a way of doing it. PHR 8.4 If you do something **with a will**, you do it with a lot of enthusiasm and energy. EG *She attacked the garden with a will.* PHR : USED AS AN A
9 If you **will** something to happen, you make it happen or try to make it happen by using mental effort rather than physical means. EG *I willed my trembling legs to walk straight... I willed my feet to grow... These things are willed to happen.* V+O+*to*-INF
10 If you **will** something, you want it to happen; a formal or old-fashioned use. EG *He never willed this outcome... I must do whatever God wills.* V+O = wish
11 A **will** is a document in which you declare what you want to happen to your money and property when you die. EG *Has Desmond made a will?... There's nothing for me in Grandfather's will.* N COUNT
12 If you **will** something to someone, you leave it to them in your will when you die. EG *He willed everything he had to Vietnamese charities.* V+O+A *(to)*
13 ● See also **willing**.

willie /wɪli[1]/, **willies**. See **willy**.

willing /wɪlɪŋ/. 1 If someone is **willing** to do something, they do not mind doing it or have no objection to doing it. EG *I was still willing to marry her... Some babies are willing and able to go four hours without a feed.* ADJ QUALIT : PRED, USU+*to*-INF = prepared ≠ unwilling ◊ **willingness**. EG *Your willingness to experiment does you credit.* ◊ N UNCOUNT = readiness ● **God willing**: see **god**.
2 **Willing** is used of someone who does something fairly enthusiastically and because they want to do it rather than because they are forced to do it. EG *He was a willing participant in my plays... ...a class of willing students.* ADJ QUALIT : USU ATTRIB = eager ◊ **willingness**. EG *They complied with his request with the greatest willingness and interest.* ◊ N UNCOUNT = good will ◊ **willingly**. EG *Many established liberties were given up quite willingly during the war.* ◊ ADV WITH VB = readily

will-o'-the-wisp /wɪl ə ðə wɪsp/, **will-o'-the-wisps**. You can refer to something that keeps disappearing or that is impossible to catch or reach as a **will-o'-the-wisp**. N COUNT : USU SING

willow /wɪləʊ/, **willows**. A **willow** or a **willow tree** is a tree with long branches and long narrow leaves that grows near water. EG *...the willows along the river bank.* N COUNT

willowy /wɪləʊi[1]/. A person who is **willowy** is tall, thin, and graceful; used showing approval. ADJ QUALIT = slender

will-power; also spelled without a hyphen. **Will-power** is a very strong determination to do something. EG *She stayed calm by sheer will-power.* N UNCOUNT ⇑ resolve

willy /wɪli[1]/, **willies**; also spelled **willie**. 1 A boy's or man's **willy** is his penis; an informal word used mainly by children. N COUNT
2 If someone or something **gives** you **the willies**, they make you feel nervous or frightened; an informal expression. PHR : VB INFLECTS ⇑ frighten

willy-nilly /wɪli[1] nɪli[1]/; also spelled without a hyphen. If you experience something **willy-nilly** or do something **willy-nilly**, you experience it or do it without being asked whether you want it to happen or not, or without being able to prevent it happening. EG *I was sent, willy nilly, to a very expensive tutor for a year.* ADV WITH VB ⇑ forcibly

wilt /wɪlt/, **wilts, wilting, wilted**. 1 If a plant **wilts**, it gradually bends downwards and becomes weak rather than being firm or upright, because it V ⇑ droop needs more water or is dying. EG *Some graves had little jam jars with a few wilting daisies in them... ...wilted flowers.*

2 If someone **wilts**, they become weak or tired, or lose confidence. EG *Man and beast wilted under the merciless sun... She stared at us so fiercely that even Gareth wilted.* V ⇑ weaken

3 If something stiff **wilts**, it becomes limp or floppy. EG *She took off her wilting straw hat.* V = droop

wily /waɪli¹/, **wilier, wiliest**. Someone who is **wily** is clever at thinking of ways to achieve what they want to achieve, especially ways that involve deceiving people. EG *...a wily diplomat.* ▸ used of plans and actions. EG *...wily tricks.* ADJ QUALIT = cunning ▸ = crafty

wimp /wɪmp/, **wimps**. A **wimp** is someone who lacks confidence and is rather timid, and is perhaps thin and weak as well; an informal word. N COUNT = wet, weed

wimpish /wɪmpɪʃ/. You say that someone is **wimpish** when they lack confidence and are rather timid, and are perhaps thin and weak as well; an informal word. ADJ QUALIT = wet, weedy

wimple /wɪmpəºl/, **wimples**. A **wimple** is a piece of cloth that is wrapped around a woman's head so that you can only see her face. Wimples were worn by women in medieval times and are worn now by some nuns. N COUNT

win /wɪn/, **wins, winning, won**. **1** If you **win** a competition, battle, argument, bet, etc, you defeat the person or people competing with you or fighting you, or do better than everyone else involved. EG *Their side was winning... Aren't you boys interested in who's winning the war?... The Party won a convincing victory at the polls... He has not won a major championship since 1974.* ▸ used as a noun. EG *They had a run of wins in December... ...another win for our side.* V OR V+O ⇑ succeed ≠ lose ▸ N COUNT = victory

2 If something **wins** you a competition, battle, etc, it causes you to defeat the person or people competing with you or fighting you, or to do better than anyone else involved. EG *I'm convinced that it was her loyalty and support that won me the championship.* V+O+O

3 If you **win** something, for example a prize or a medal, you get it because you have defeated everyone else in a competition, battle, etc or have done very well in it. EG *Mum has just won a microwave cooker in a competition... She won second prize in a baby show... The party failed to win any seats.* V+O ⇑ receive

4 If you **win** something that you want, for example someone's approval or support or your own freedom, you succeed in getting it. EG *...the party's failure to win mass support among the working class... They are winning honour and glory... We must win the hearts of the new generation... In this way they can win converts to their cause.* V+O ⇑ gain = secure

5 If something **wins** you a prize or **wins** you something else that you want, it causes you to get it. EG *This speech may have won him the Democratic nomination... His cynical and often savage vision of life and love has won him considerable critical acclaim.* V+O+O = earn, gain

6 If you say that someone **can't win** in a particular situation, you mean that they are certain to fail or to suffer in some way whatever they do; an informal expression. EG *Either you give in or you lose your job. You can't win... She's up against the Establishment. She can't win.* PHR

7 The word **win** is also used in the following expressions. **7.1** If you **win hands down**, you win a competition, battle, etc very easily or by a great amount; a fairly informal expression. EG *If it came to a fight, he would win hands down.* PHR : VB INFLECTS **7.2** You say **'you win'** when you have been having a slight argument with someone to indicate that you agree to do what they want you to do or that you accept their suggestion, even though you do not really want to. EG *'Very well,' said the Englishman, 'you win. I can have a thousand pounds here by noon tomorrow.'* CONVENTION **7.3** ● **to win the day**: see **day**. ● See also **winning**.

win back. If you **win back** something that you have lost, for example someone's approval or support, you get it back through your own efforts. EG *The party badly needs to find a way to win back straying voters.* PHRASAL VB : V+O+ADV ⇑ regain

win out. If something or someone **wins out** or **wins through**, they defeat others or become most powerful, after a struggle. EG *When the forces for change win out, these people's power will be destroyed... If the idea is really good enough it will win through in the end.* PHRASAL VB : V+ADV = triumph

win over. If you **win** someone **over** or **win** them **round**, you persuade them to support you or agree with you. EG *We began to win over a sizeable number of faculty members to our cause.* PHRASAL VB : V+O+ADV = convert

wince /wɪns/, **winces, wincing, winced**. If you **wince**, the muscles of your face tighten suddenly because you have felt a pain or because you have just seen, heard, or remembered something unpleasant. EG *He winces at the memory of that experience... ...a sound that made her wince.* ▸ used as a noun. EG *His smile became a wince as pain stabbed through him.* V = flinch, cringe ▸ N COUNT

winch /wɪntʃ/, **winches, winching, winched**. **1** A **winch** is a machine which is used to lift heavy objects or people who need to be rescued. It consists of a drum around which a rope or chain is wound. N COUNT = hoist

2 If you **winch** an object or person somewhere, you lift or lower them using a winch. EG *The two boys were winched to safety.* V+O+A = hoist

wind, winds, winding, winded, wound. The word **wind** is pronounced /wɪnd/ for paragraphs 1-10 and /waɪnd/ for paragraphs 11-13 and the phrasal verbs. **Winded** is the past tense and past participle of the verbs in paragraphs 4 and 6, and **wound** is the past tense and past participle of the verbs in paragraphs 11-13 and the phrasal verbs. **1** A **wind** is a current of air that is moving across the earth's surface. EG *The wind had dropped considerably... ...poppies fluttering in the wind... There was a fierce wind blowing... ...a gust of wind.* N COUNT/UNCOUNT

2 You can refer in a literary way to something that influences events as a **wind** of some kind. EG *...the wind of change... The nation was left to the cold winds of budgetary control.* N PART

3 Your **wind** is your ability to breathe easily. You can lose your wind when you do something physically energetic. EG *I had to stop and regain my wind before I could carry on.* ● See also **second wind**. N SING WITH DETPOSS = breath

4 If you **are winded** by something such as a blow, the air is suddenly knocked out of your lungs so that you have difficulty breathing for a short time. EG *I was winded by the force of his punch.* V+O : USU PASS

5 **Wind** is the air that you sometimes swallow with food or drink, or gas that is produced in your intestines, which causes an uncomfortable feeling; a fairly informal use. EG *She said she suffered from wind.* N UNCOUNT ⇑ flatulence

6 If you **wind** a baby, you pat its back in order to help it to release air from its stomach; a fairly informal use. V+O = burp

7 The **wind** section of an orchestra or band is the group of people who produce musical sounds by blowing into their instruments. N BEFORE N

8 If you refer to what someone says as **wind**, you mean that it is foolish or meaningless; an informal use. EG *That's all a lot of wind.* N UNCOUNT = hot air

9 When someone **breaks wind**, they release air from their intestines through their anus; a rather formal expression. PHR : VB INFLECTS

10 The word **wind** is also used in the following expressions. **10.1** If someone who is intending to do something **gets the wind up**, they become very afraid, usually with the result that they decide not to do it after all; an informal expression. PHR : VB INFLECTS = take fright **10.2** If you **get wind of** something, you hear about it, especially when someone else did not want you to know about it; a fairly informal expression. EG *The British Ambassador got wind of it, and La Fayette was arrested.* PHR : VB INFLECTS

10.3 If a particular event is **in the wind**, it is likely to happen; a fairly informal expression. EG *A trip to India may be in the wind.* PHR : USED AS AN A **10.4** If you **put the wind up** someone, you make them feel afraid; an informal expression. PHR : VB INFLECTS = scare **10.5** If you **sail close to the wind**, you take a risk by doing or saying something that is only just legal or acceptable. PHR : VB INFLECTS **10.6** If something **takes the wind out of** your **sails**, it suddenly makes you much less confident in what you are doing or saying. EG *His statement took a great deal of the wind out of her sails.* PHR : VB INFLECTS ⇑ deflate **10.7** If you **throw caution to the wind**, you stop worrying about the risks or danger involved in a particular action, and you do it. EG *Throwing caution to the wind, I barged into the director's office.* PHR : VB INFLECTS **10.8** If you want to find out **which way the wind is blowing**, you want to find out what is likely to happen, for PHR : USED AS O example whether a particular plan is likely to be accepted.

11 If a road, river, line of people, etc **winds** in a particular direction, it goes in that direction with a lot of bends or twists in it. EG *The river winds through the town... ...a dark hall with a big staircase winding up from it... The procession wound its way through the sunlit streets.* ◇ **winding**. EG *...the winding road leading to the Castle.* V+A, OR V+O (DETPOSS+ *way*) +A = zigzag, snake ◇ ADJ CLASSIF

12 When you **wind** something flexible round something else, you wrap it round it several times. EG *Wind the wire round the screws until it is taut... I wet the cloths and wound them around my head.* V+O+A *(round/around)* = twist, coil

13 When you **wind** a mechanical device, for example a watch or a clock, you turn a knob, key, or handle on it round and round in order to make it operate. V+O

14 See also **winded.**

wind back. When you **wind back** the tape in a tape recorder or the film in a camera, you make it move back towards its starting position. PHRASAL VB : V+O+ADV

wind down. 1 When you **wind down** something such as the window of a car, you make it move downwards by turning a handle. PHRASAL VB : V+O+ADV = roll down

2 If a mechanical device such as a clock **winds down**, it gradually works more slowly before stopping completely. PHRASAL VB : V+ADV

3 If you **wind down**, you relax after doing something that has made you feel tired or tense; a fairly informal use. EG *We went to the local pub to wind down.* PHRASAL VB : V+ADV = unwind

4 If someone **winds down** a business, they gradually reduce the amount of work that it does or reduce the number of people employed, before closing it down completely. PHRASAL VB : V-ERG+ADV

wind forward. When you **wind forward** the tape in a tape recorder, you make it move forward to a new position. PHRASAL VB : V+O+ADV

wind up. 1 When you **wind up** an activity, you finish it or stop doing it. EG *Eventually I signalled that it was time to wind up the game... Let's wind up now.* PHRASAL VB : V+ADV, OR V-ERG+ADV

2 When someone **winds up** a business or other organization, they stop running it and close it down completely. EG *Four years later the company was wound up.* PHRASAL VB : V+ADV, OR V-ERG+ADV = liquidate

3 If you **wind up** in a particular place or situation, you are in that place or situation at the end of a series of travels or events so that it is the last place or event in the series. EG *We wound up at the Szanghi restaurant... It wouldn't surprise me if he winds up in jail... If I stay here long enough, I'll wind up marrying him.* PHRASAL VB : V+ADV+A = finish up

4 When you **wind up** a mechanical device, for example a watch or clock, you turn a knob, key, or handle on it round and round in order to make it operate. PHRASAL VB : V+O+ADV

5 When you **wind up** something such as the window of a car, you make it move upwards by turning a handle. PHRASAL VB : V+O+ADV = roll up

6 If you **wind** someone **up**, 6.1 you deliberately say things which annoy them; an informal use. EG *He's always winding his teachers up.* **6.2** you say untrue things in order to trick them; an informal use. EG *Are you winding me up?* PHRASAL VB : V+O+ADV; PHRASAL VB : V+O+ADV = kid

7 See also **wind-up, wound up.**

windbag /wɪndbæg/, **windbags**. If you describe someone as a **windbag**, you mean that they talk a great deal in a boring way; an informal word. N COUNT = gasbag

wind-blown. **Wind-blown** things are 1 carried by the wind to a different place. EG *...a wind-blown pollen grain.* 2 blown about by the wind. EG *Their faces were all but obscured by wind-blown hair.* ADJ CLASSIF : ATTRIB; ADJ QUALIT = windswept

windbreak /wɪndbreɪk/, **windbreaks**. A **windbreak** is a line of trees, fence, etc which gives protection against the wind. EG *The orchard provides a natural windbreak.* N COUNT ⇑ barrier

winded /wɪndɪ²d/. If you are **winded**, you are out of breath, either because you have been doing hard exercise such as running fast, or because you have been hit in the stomach. EG *If you go too fast you get winded... I fell with a crash, winded but not hurt.* ADJ QUALIT : USU PRED ⇑ breathless

windfall /wɪndfɔːl/, **windfalls**. A **windfall** is 1 a sum of money that you receive unexpectedly or by luck, for example if you win a lottery. EG *He had a windfall from the football pools.* 2 a fruit, especially an apple, that has fallen from a tree. EG *The grass of the orchard was littered with windfalls... She was giving baskets of windfall apples to the neighbours.* N COUNT; N COUNT

wind instrument, wind instruments. A **wind instrument** is a musical instrument that you blow into in order to produce sounds, for example a trumpet or a clarinet. N COUNT

windlass /wɪndləs/, **windlasses**. A **windlass** is a mechanical device for lifting heavy objects, which uses a motor to pull a rope or chain around a cylinder. EG *...a bucket hauled up with a windlass.* N COUNT = winch

windless /wɪndlɪ²s/. If the air is **windless** or if it is a **windless** day, it is very calm and still; a literary word. EG *...one of those warm windless September mornings... Outside, the flags slumped in the windless air.* ADJ CLASSIF ≠ windy

windmill /wɪnd⁰mɪl/, **windmills**. A **windmill** is a building with large sails on the outside which turn round as the wind blows. This provides energy for a machine which crushes corn or wheat or is used for other purposes. EG *We will build another windmill... The water system was powered by a windmill.* N COUNT

window /wɪndəʊ/, **windows**. 1 A **window** is a space in a wall or roof or in the side of a vehicle, which has glass in it so that light can come in and you can see out. Many windows can be opened. EG *Sunlight streamed through the window... The kitchen windows were wide open... I stood at the window and watched her... Hooper stuck his hand out of the car window and waved.* N COUNT ⇑ opening

2 A **window** is also **2.1** a large glass window along the front of a shop, where some of the goods that the shop sells are displayed. EG *...a jeweller's window... How much is that suite in the window?... ...a window display.* **2.2** a glass-covered opening above a counter, for example in a bank or post office or at a railway station, which the person serving you sits behind. EG *She went up to the ticket window.* **2.3** a transparent panel or an opening in a cover or case which allows you to see what is behind or beneath it. EG *On the very earliest computers, numbers appeared in a window.* N COUNT; N COUNT; N COUNT ⇑ hole

3 If you say that something has flown, gone, or disappeared **out of the window**, you mean that it has disappeared completely. EG *Kate's confidence now flew out of the window.* PHR : USED AS AN A

window-box, window-boxes; also spelled without a hyphen. A **window-box** is a long, narrow container on a window-sill outside a house, in which plants are grown. N COUNT

window-dresser, window-dressers; also spelled without a hyphen. A **window-dresser** is a person whose job is arranging goods attractively in a shop window. N COUNT ⇑ employee

window-dressing; also spelled without a hyphen. 1 **Window-dressing** is the skill of arranging goods attractively in a shop window, or the way in which they are arranged. EG *...the principles of window-dressing.* N UNCOUNT ⇑ display

2 **Window-dressing** is also used to refer to things that are done in order to create a good impression and to prevent people from realizing the real or more unpleasant nature of someone's activities; used showing disapproval. N UNCOUNT = facade

window-frame, window-frames; also spelled without a hyphen. A **window-frame** is a frame round the edges of a window, into which the glass is fixed. N COUNT

window-pane, window-panes; also spelled without a hyphen. A **window-pane** is a piece of glass in the window of a building. EG *...the occasional clatter of rain against the window-pane.* N COUNT

window seat, window seats; also spelled with a hyphen. A **window seat** is 1 a seat which is fixed to the wall underneath a window in a room. EG *I sat on the window seat in the hall.* 2 a seat next to a window in a train, bus, or aeroplane. EG *I'd like a window seat, please.* N COUNT; N COUNT

window-shop, window-shops, window-shopping, window-shopped. If you **window-shop**, you spend time looking at the goods in the windows of shops without intending to buy anything. EG *We window-shopped along Madison Avenue... ...an afternoon window-shopping with Grandma.* V

window-sill, window-sills; also spelled without a hyphen. A **window-sill** is a ledge along the bottom of a window, either inside or outside a building. EG *Pots of herbs stood on the window-sill.* N COUNT

windpipe /wɪndpaɪp/, **windpipes**. Your **windpipe** is the tube in your body that carries air into your N COUNT = trachea lungs when you breathe. EG *Nuts are easily breathed into the windpipe and can cause choking.*

windscreen /wɪndskriːn/, **windscreens**. The **windscreen** of a car or other vehicle is the glass window at the front through which the driver looks; used in British English. EG *It is dangerous to drive with a dirty windscreen.*
N COUNT = windshield

windscreen wiper, windscreen wipers. A **windscreen wiper** is a long thin piece of metal with a rubber edge which is electrically operated and which wipes rain from the windscreen of a vehicle; used in British English.
N COUNT : USU PL

windshield /wɪndʃiːld/, **windshields**. A **windshield** is 1 a windscreen; used in American English.
N COUNT
2 any glass or plastic screen that is used to provide protection from the wind, for example on the front of a motorbike.
N COUNT

windsurfer /wɪndsɜːfə/, **windsurfers**. A **windsurfer** is 1 a long narrow board with a sail attached, which you stand on in the sea or in a lake and move along as the wind blows you.
N COUNT
2 a person who moves along the surface of the sea or a lake on a windsurfer.
N COUNT

windsurfing /wɪndsɜːfɪŋ/. **Windsurfing** is the activity of moving along the surface of the sea or a lake on a windsurfer. EG *Would you call windsurfing a sport?*
N UNCOUNT
● If you **go windsurfing**, you take part in the activity of windsurfing. EG *On the beach you can go windsurfing or sailing.*
● PHR : VB INFLECTS

windswept /wɪndswept/. 1 A **windswept** place is open and not protected against strong winds. EG *...a beautiful windswept hillside... ...a windswept plain.*
ADJ CLASSIF ↑ exposed ≠ sheltered
2 Someone who looks **windswept** has untidy hair because they have been out in the wind. EG *His hair was windswept and his face streaked with dirt.*
ADJ QUALIT = wind-blown

wind-up is used to describe a device which has a mechanism that is operated by clockwork. EG *...a wind-up racing car... ...a wind-up gramophone.*
ADJ CLASSIF : ATTRIB

windward /wɪndwəd/ is used to refer to the side of something which is facing the wind. EG *Light a small fire in the hole on the windward side.*
ADJ CLASSIF : ATTRIB, OR ADV AFTER VB = weather

windy /wɪndi[1]/, **windier, windiest**. 1 If it is **windy**, the wind is blowing a lot. EG *It was a windy early spring day, although not very cold... ...trucks roaring through the wet and windy night... The American winter was cold, wet and windy.*
ADJ QUALIT = blustery ≠ calm
2 **Windy** speech or writing contains long and important sounding words chosen to impress people rather than to express things clearly; used informally showing disapproval. EG *The chairman was finally through with his windy introduction... He took my letter and added a number of his own windy phrases.*
ADJ QUALIT = pompous
3 If you say that a person is **windy** or gets **windy**, you mean that they are afraid or worried; an old-fashioned informal use. EG *Pretty soon she'd get windy left up there on her own... I was a bit windy about my ability to navigate.*
ADJ QUALIT : PRED = nervous

wine /waɪn/, **wines, wining, wined**. 1 **Wine** is 1.1 an alcoholic drink which is made from grapes and is usually either red or white. To make wine, grapes are fermented with water and sugar. EG *I was drinking white wine... ...two bottles of red wine... He poured her a glass of wine.*
N MASS
1.2 an alcoholic drink which you can make from any fruit or vegetable by fermenting it with water and sugar. EG *Have you tried his turnip wine?... ...home-made rhubarb wine.*
N MASS : MOD+N
2 **Wine** or **wine red** is used to describe the colour of something that is very dark red like the colour of red wine. EG *His face became an angry wine red... ...a girl wearing a wine-coloured costume.*
ADJ+ADJ
3 **wine and dine**. 3.1 If someone **wines and dines** you, they give you a very good meal, usually at an expensive restaurant. EG *He was being wined and dined by one of his clients.*
PHR : VBS INFLECT ↑ entertain
3.2 If you go out **wining and dining**, you go out and eat and drink in an expensive restaurant. EG *...a lively evening with wining, dining and dancing till the small hours.*
PHR : VBS INFLECT

wine bar, wine bars; also spelled with a hyphen. A **wine bar** is a place where people can buy and drink wine, and sometimes eat food as well.
N COUNT : ALSO IN NAMES

wine glass, wine glasses; also spelled with a hyphen. A **wine glass** is a glass which you use for drinking wine. Most wine glasses are round with a narrow stem and a flat round base.
N COUNT

wing /wɪŋ/, **wings, winging, winged**. 1 The **wings** of a bird or insect are the two limbs on its body that it uses for flying. A bird's wings have feathers on them and an insect's wings are usually thin and transparent. EG *A bird changes direction by dipping one wing and lifting the other... ...butterflies' wings... The female beats her wings as fast as 500 times a second.*
N COUNT
2 The **wings** of an aeroplane are the long flat parts sticking out of its side which support it while it is flying.
N COUNT : USU PL
3 The **wing** of a building is a part of it which sticks out from the main part or which has been built later than the main part. EG *...the west wing of the museum... She had been planning to build a wing on to the house.*
N COUNT : USU+SUPP = extension
4 A **wing** of an organization, especially a political organization, is a group within the organization which has a particular function or particular political beliefs. EG *...Provisional Sinn Fein, the political wing of the IRA.* ● See **left-wing, right-wing**.
N COUNT+SUPP = branch, section
5 The **wings** on a stage in a theatre are the sides of the stage which the audience cannot see because of curtains or scenery. EG *I watched them from the wings... A doctor was waiting in the wings.*
N PLURAL : *the*+N
6 **Wings** refer to a badge in the shape of wings which a pilot wears to show that he or she is qualified to fly aeroplanes. EG *He had medals and wings on his green jacket.*
N PLURAL
7 The **wings** of a car are the parts of the body which are around the wheels; used in British English. EG *The car hit the truck with its nearside wing... Look in your wing mirror.*
N COUNT ↑ side
8 In football or hockey, a **wing** or **winger** is a player who plays on the far left or the far right of the field. EG *We need a right wing for Saturday's match.*
N COUNT : USU+SUPP
▸ also used to refer to the far left or the far right of the field. EG *Get the ball out to the wing.*
▸ N COUNT ↑ side
9 The word **wing** is also used in the following expressions. 9.1 If you say that you are waiting **in the wings**, you mean that you are ready to take action when necessary. EG *I was standing there in the wings, just waiting until I was needed.*
PHR : USED AS AN A
9.2 A bird that is **on the wing** is flying, usually over a long distance; a literary use. EG *They spend at least nine months of the year continuously on the wing.*
PHR : USED AS AN A
9.3 If you **spread** your **wings**, you do something new and rather difficult or move to a new place, because you feel more confident in your abilities than you used to and you want to gain wider experience. EG *It's time to spread my wings.*
PHR : VB INFLECTS = branch out
9.4 If a bird **takes wing**, it starts flying away; a literary use. EG *Suddenly, the crows took wing.*
PHR : VB INFLECTS
9.5 If you **take** someone **under** your **wing**, you look after them and protect them.
PHR : VB INFLECTS

wing commander, wing commanders. A **wing commander** is a senior officer in the air force. EG *...Wing Commander Warburton.*
N COUNT : ALSO IN TITLES

winged /wɪŋd/ is used to describe an animal that has wings or an object that looks as if it has wings. EG *...winged insects... ...Eros, that winged statue in Piccadilly Circus.*
ADJ CLASSIF : ATTRIB

winger /wɪŋə/, **wingers**. A **winger** is a football or hockey player who plays on the far left or the far right of the field.
N COUNT = wing

wingspan /wɪŋspæn/, **wingspans**. The **wingspan** of a bird, insect, or aeroplane is the distance from the end of one wing to the end of the other wing. EG *...dragonflies with a wingspan of 70 centimetres.*
N COUNT : USU+SUPP ↑ width

wink /wɪŋk/, **winks, winking, winked**. 1 When you **wink**, you close one eye very briefly, often as a signal to someone that something is a joke or a secret, or as an informal greeting or invitation. EG *Uncle John winked at me across the table... At the other side of the room Amelia was winking and raising a cautionary finger.*
V : IF+PREP THEN *at*
▸ used as a noun. EG *'What a hostess!' said Clarissa with a big wink at George.*
▸ N COUNT : USU SING
2 If a light **winks**, it shines or reflects light in short flashes; a rather literary use. EG *...lights winking from behind makeshift curtains... ...the sea, sparkling and winking in the sun.*
V = twinkle
3 The word **wink** is also used in the following expressions. 3.1 If you have **forty winks**, you sleep for a short while; an old-fashioned informal expression.
PHR : USED AS O
3.2 If you **don't sleep a wink, don't get a wink of sleep**, etc, you stay awake and don't sleep at all. EG *I never slept a wink that night.*
PHR : VB INFLECTS
3.3 If you say **'A nod is as good as a wink'**, you mean that something that someone has said or implied has been understood, and that there is therefore no need to say any more
PHR = say no more

about it. **3.4** to **tip** someone **the wink**: see **tip**.

winkle /wɪŋkəˀl/, **winkles, winkling, winkled.** A **winkle** is a small sea-snail with a hard shell and a soft body which you can eat. EG *...freshly boiled winkles.* — N COUNT = periwinkle

winkle out. 1 If you **winkle** information **out** of someone, you get it from them when they do not want to give it to you, often by tricking them; a fairly informal expression. EG *They usually manage to winkle out of people what they want to know.* — PHRASAL VB : V+O+ADV = worm out

2 If you **winkle** someone **out** of a place where they are hiding or which they do not want to leave, you make them come out of the place; an informal use. EG *The officers sometimes have to winkle idlers out of cupboards and toilets.* — PHRASAL VB : V+O+ADV = flush out

winner /wɪnə/, **winners. 1** The **winner** of a prize, race, or competition is the person, thing, or animal that wins it. EG *The winner received a silver cup and £10,000... All prize-winners will be notified by post.* — N COUNT

2 If you refer to something as a **winner**, you mean that it is popular and successful, or that it is likely to be popular and successful; a fairly informal use. EG *Her new film is a real winner.* — N COUNT : USU SING, USU USED AS C ⇑ success = hit

winning /wɪnɪŋ/, **winnings. 1** The **winning** competitor, team, entry in a competition, etc is the one that has won. EG *Here are some extracts from the five winning entries.* — ADJ CLASSIF : ATTRIB ⇑ successful

2 Winning is used to describe actions or qualities that please other people and make them feel friendly towards you. EG *His chief asset is his winning smile.* — ADJ CLASSIF : ATTRIB = engaging

3 The money that someone wins in a competition or by gambling is referred to as their **winnings**. EG *Mark laughed and went to collect his winnings.* — N PLURAL

winnow /wɪnəʊ/, **winnows, winnowing, winnowed.** When people **winnow** grain, they separate the chaff from it by blowing a stream of air across it. EG *The fan produces an artificial wind to winnow the grain.* — V+O

winsome /wɪnsəˀm/. Someone who is **winsome** is attractive and charming; a literary word. EG *She looked winsome and alluring.* ▸ used of a person's expression. EG *She gave him her most winsome smile.* — ADJ QUALIT = fetching

winter /wɪntə/, **winters, wintering, wintered. 1 Winter** is the season between autumn and spring. In the winter the weather is usually colder than during the other seasons, and many trees and plants have lost their leaves. EG *It was a terrible winter... In the winter when the lakes are frozen over he goes skating... I was walking one winter day in Hyde Park... ...a dark winter's night... We often get very wet cold winters here.* — N UNCOUNT/COUNT

2 If you **winter** somewhere, you spend the winter there; a formal use. EG *In the 18th century the gentry wintered in Ludlow... This quiet seaside town is their favoured wintering spot.* — V+A ⇑ stay

winter sports are sports that take place on ice or snow, for example skating, skiing or bobsleigh racing. — N PLURAL : PL FORM WHEN MOD

wintertime /wɪntətaɪm/ is the period of time during which winter lasts. — N UNCOUNT

wintry /wɪntri¹/. **1** Something that is **wintry** has features that are typical of winter. EG *...one wintry day early in March... ...the pale wintry light.* — ADJ QUALIT

2 If you describe a person's expression or behaviour as **wintry**, you mean that they seem very unfriendly. EG *...a wintry smile.* — ADJ QUALIT = cold

wipe /waɪp/, **wipes, wiping, wiped. 1** If you **wipe** something, you rub its surface lightly, for example with a cloth or your hand, in order to remove dirt or liquid from it. EG *Steel knives should be wiped clean after use... He wiped his mouth with the back of his hand... Ida wiped her hands on her apron.* ▸ used as a noun. EG *He gave the table one last wipe.* — V+O : USU+A; ▸ N COUNT : USU SING

2 If you **wipe** dirt or liquid from something, you remove it, for example by using a cloth or your hand. EG *She wiped the tears from her eyes... ...wiping the sweat from his brow.* — V+O+A

3 If you **wipe** the dishes, you dry plates, knives, forks, etc with a cloth when they have been washed after a meal. EG *I'll wipe the dishes... Shall I wash or wipe?* — V OR V+O

4 If you **wipe** the sounds or pictures recorded on a magnetic tape, you remove them, for example by recording different sounds or pictures on the tape; a technical use. EG *Have you wiped that tape?* — V+O

5 If you say that something **wipes the grin, smile,** etc **off** someone's **face**, you mean that it suddenly spoils or stops their enjoyment or amusement and that you are pleased about it; an informal expression. EG *That'll wipe the grin off his face... I told her where we were going and that wiped the smile off her stupid face.* — PHR : VB AND NOUNS INFLECT

6 to **wipe the floor with** someone: see **¹floor**.

wipe at. To **wipe at** something is the same as to wipe it. EG *He went on talking, occasionally wiping at his face with a towel.* — PHRASAL VB : V+PREP = dab at

wipe away. If you **wipe away** or **wipe off** dirt or liquid from something, you remove it, for example by using a cloth or your hand. EG *She wiped away their childish tears... ...wiping away the chalk marks... I need a handkerchief to wipe off the sand.* — PHRASAL VB : V+O+ADV

wipe down. If you **wipe down** something, you wash or dry its surface completely. EG *The walls will have to be wiped down.* — PHRASAL VB : V+O+ADV ⇑ clean

wipe out. To **wipe out** places, groups of people, etc means to destroy them completely, especially suddenly or violently; an informal expression. EG *...a substance guaranteed to wipe out a city in a night... Epidemics wiped out the local population.* — PHRASAL VB : ORDER V+ADV+O = eradicate, obliterate

wipe up. If you **wipe up** dirt or liquid from something, you remove it using a cloth. EG *He begins to wipe up the mess.* — PHRASAL VB : V+O+ADV ⇑ clean up

wiper /waɪpə/, **wipers.** A **wiper** is the same as a windscreen wiper. — N COUNT : USU PL

wire /waɪə/, **wires, wiring, wired. 1** A **wire** is a long thin piece of metal that is used to fasten things or to make fences, cages, baskets, etc. EG *You can mend it with pliers and a length of wire... ...overhead lights suspended from wires... ...an eight-foot high wire fence.* ● See also **barbed wire, high wire, trip-wire.** — N COUNT/UNCOUNT

2 A **wire** is also **2.1** a wire that carries electricity or electrical signals. EG *He touched a wire and was immediately electrocuted... ...a powerful electric current running through the wires... ...a telephone wire.* ● See also **fuse wire, live wire. 2.2** a telegram; used mainly in American English. EG *I decided to send a wire ordering a room with twin beds.* — N COUNT ⇑ conductor; N COUNT

3 If you **wire** one thing to another, you fasten them together using wire. EG *She was still in the hospital with her broken jaw wired together... He wired one end of the chain to the hook.* — V+O+A *(to)*

4 If you **wire** something or **wire** it **up**, you connect it to something else with electrical wires so that electricity or electrical signals can pass between them. EG *Wire one end of the cable to the plug... ...the wiring of forty-eight homes to the police station... ...electrical fittings wired up to the mains.* — V+O+A *(to)*, OR PHRASAL VB : V+O+ADV

5 If you **wire** a person, you send them a telegram; used mainly in American English. EG *I wired Renata yesterday and asked her to marry me.* — V+O, OR V+O+REPORT-CL

6 If you **wire** an amount of money to a person or place, you instruct a bank to send it to the person or place by a telegram message; used mainly in American English. EG *He wired Betty money to fly home... The money's being wired to the bank in Century City.* — V+O, V+O+O, OR V+O+A

wired /waɪəd/. **1** Clothing or material that is **wired** has wires sewn into it in order to keep it stiff. EG *...padded and wired bras... ...the little wired cap.* — ADJ CLASSIF : USU ATTRIB

2 If a place is **wired, 2.1** it is connected by electrical wires to an alarm system, in order to discourage burglars from entering it. EG *All the windows were wired.* **2.2** it has hidden microphones placed in it, so that conversations taking place in it can be listened to by someone outside. EG *Their letters would be censored, their hotel rooms wired.* — ADJ CLASSIF : USU PRED; ADJ CLASSIF : USU PRED = bugged

wireless /waɪəlɪ²s/, **wirelesses**; an old-fashioned word. **1 Wireless** is the system by which sounds are sent over a distance by radio signals. EG *...wireless waves... ...messages sent by cable or wireless... ...wireless operators on ships.* — N UNCOUNT

2 A **wireless** or **wireless set** is **2.1** a piece of equipment for listening to radio programmes broadcast to the public. EG *Turn the wireless on... There was an old wireless in my room... They always announce the results on the wireless... The Smiths had bought themselves a wireless set.* **2.2** a piece of equipment for sending and receiving radio messages. EG *The spy had a secret wireless hidden on the roof.* — N COUNT = radio, radio set; N COUNT = radio

wire-tap, wire-taps, wire-tapping, wire-tapped; also spelled as one word. If someone **wire-taps** you or **wire-taps** your telephone, they make a secret connection to a telephone line so that they can listen to your telephone conversations without you knowing about it; used mainly in American English. EG *He sent men out to wire-tap the opposition party... He wire-tapped conversations of Democratic Party officials... ...the possibility of wire-tapping in our rooms.*
V OR V+O

wire wool consists of very thin pieces of wire twisted together, often in the form of small pads. These are used to clean metal objects, especially saucepans and other kitchen equipment.
N UNCOUNT ⇑ scourer

wiring /waɪərɪŋ/. The **wiring** in a building is the system of wires that supply electricity to the rooms in it. EG *Will the cottage need new wiring or plumbing?... ...damp walls and dangerous electric wiring.*
N UNCOUNT

wiry /waɪəri¹/. 1 Someone who is **wiry** is rather thin but has strong muscles. EG *...a short, wiry man.*
ADJ CLASSIF

2 Something that is **wiry** is stiff and rough to touch. EG *...a few clumps of wiry grass... ...her wiry, black hair.*
ADJ CLASSIF = coarse

wisdom /wɪzdəᵊm/, **wisdoms**. 1 **Wisdom** is 1.1 a person's ability to use their experience and knowledge in order to make sensible and reasonable decisions or judgements. EG *She spoke with authority as well as wisdom... At least she had the wisdom to marry a lawyer... They overestimate their parents' wisdom and power.*
N UNCOUNT = judgement, integrity

1.2 the store of knowledge that a society or culture has collected over a long period of time. EG *...this gem of folk wisdom... ...the wisdom and the accumulated experience of generations.* ▸ used as a count noun. EG *...ancient wisdoms and ancient powers... This text contains much of the old wisdoms.*
N UNCOUNT
▸ N COUNT

2 If you discuss the **wisdom** of a particular action or decision, you are discussing how sensible it is in a particular situation. EG *Events were to show the wisdom of maintaining these reserve forces... Doubts were expressed about the wisdom of the visit.*
N SING : *the*+N+*of* ⇑ sense

3 The **wisdom** of a group of people on a particular subject is their opinion about it. EG *He voiced the conventional wisdom about the need to conserve energy... The prevailing Wall Street wisdom is that this performance cannot be sustained.*
N SING : *the*+N+SUPP

wisdom tooth, wisdom teeth. Your **wisdom teeth** are the four teeth at the back of your mouth which usually grow much later than your other teeth and sometimes cause pain.
N COUNT = third molar

wise /waɪz/, **wiser, wisest; wises, wising, wised**. 1 Someone who is **wise** is able to use their experience and knowledge in order to make sensible and reasonable decisions or judgements. EG *He's a very wise man... She was ten years older and wiser than me.* ▸ used of actions, decisions, and remarks. EG *It would be wiser to wait for the best moment... Hugh made the wisest decision of all... ...a wise and perceptive comment.* ◇ **wisely**. EG *You have chosen wisely.*
ADJ QUALIT = prudent
◇ ADV WITH VB = prudently

2 The word **wise** is also used in the following expressions. 2.1 If you say that a person **would be wise** to do something, you are advising them to do it or suggesting that they should do it, because it is the most sensible and reasonable action or decision in a particular situation. EG *It would be wise to give up now and try again later... I think you'd be very wise to accept it... She would be wise to move before the police arrive.*
PHR : VB INFLECTS+*to*-INF = prudent

2.2 If you **get wise to** something, you find out about it, especially when someone has been trying to keep it secret; an informal expression in American English. EG *They tried to burn the evidence before the cops got wise.*
PHR : VB INFLECTS

2.3 If you say that nobody is **any the wiser** after an event or an explanation, or that someone is **none the wiser** or **no wiser** after it, you mean that they know or understand no more about it than they did before the event took place or before the explanation was given. EG *Nobody in the village will be any the wiser... Whatever they say, you'll be none the wiser... I read the article, but I'm no wiser.*
PHR : USED AS C

2.4 If you say that something is **in no wise** true or correct, you mean that it is not true or correct at all; a rather old-fashioned expression. EG *We were assured that the people in no wise want to reform these institutions.*
PHR : USED AS AN A

wise up. If someone **wises up**, they understand or realise something, often something unpleasant that they did not want to accept or know about; an informal expression in American English. EG *Christopher wised up to the fact that she wasn't coming back... They were too young to be wised up to that kind of thing... Wise up, Barrett!*
PHRASAL VB : V+ADV, USU+*to* ⇑ learn

-wise is added to nouns to form adverbs indicating 1 that someone behaves in the same way as the person or thing that is mentioned. EG *I edged my way crabwise along the row to my seat... Don't hide your head in the sand, ostrich-wise.*
COMB : FORMS ADVS = -like

2 that something is true or is the case when considering the particular thing mentioned, but not necessarily when considering other things. EG *You're at a disadvantage status-wise... We are mostly Socialists vote-wise.*
COMB : FORMS ADV SENS

wisecrack /waɪzkræk/, **wisecracks, wisecracking, wisecracked**. A **wisecrack** is a clever remark that is intended to be amusing, but is often rather unkind. EG *I fought down the temptation to make a wisecrack about his clothes.* ▸ used as a verb. EG *She went on wisecracking.*
N COUNT ⇑ joke = quip
▸ V = quip

wish /wɪʃ/, **wishes, wishing, wished**. 1 A **wish** is 1.1 a longing or desire for something, often something that is difficult to obtain or achieve. EG *She told me of her wish to leave the convent... I have an insane wish to see Geoffrey again... ...an all-powerful king whose every wish was obeyed... We have no wish to repeat their mistakes.* ● See also **death wish**.
N COUNT

1.2 the particular thing that someone wants. EG *The government should reflect the wishes of the majority in the country... My last wish is for you to leave this house and never return.*
N COUNT : USU PL, USU WITH POSS

1.3 the expression of a hope that someone will be happy or successful in the future; a rather formal use. EG *My parents send their best wishes... Please accept this gift with my sincere good wishes for the future.*
N COUNT : USU PL

2 If you **wish** to do something or to have it done for you, you want to do it or have it done; a formal use. EG *They are in love and wish to marry... He could, if he wished, do most of his work at home... 'I want him brought here immediately.'–'Just as you wish.'*
V OR V+*to*-INF/*for*

3 If you **wish** that something were the case, you would like it to be the case, even though you know that it is impossible or unlikely. EG *I often wish that I were really wealthy... My sister occasionally wished she were a boy.*
V+REPORT-CL, OR V+*to*-INF

4 If you **wish** for something, you express the desire silently to yourself, often as part of a traditional ritual. In fairy stories, when someone wishes for something, it often happens by magic. EG *She blew out the candles on her birthday cake and wished for a new doll.* ▸ used as a noun. EG *Have you made your wish yet?... The genie then granted Sinbad three wishes.*
V : IF+PREP THEN *for*
▸ N COUNT

5 If you **wish** someone good luck, happy birthday, etc, you express the hope that they will have good luck, enjoy their birthday, etc. EG *Before their exam they wished each other luck... It's Mary's birthday today. Don't forget to wish her many happy returns.*
V+O+O

6 People sometimes say **'I don't wish to be rude'**, **'I don't wish to** interrupt', etc as a way of apologising or of warning you before they say something which they think might upset, worry, or annoy you. EG *I don't wish to be melodramatic but I'm sure I can hear someone downstairs.*
PHR+-INF, OR PHR+-INF+C

7 If you say that you **would not wish** something **on** a particular person, you mean that the thing is so unpleasant that you would not want the person to be forced to experience or deal with it. EG *...an illness I would not wish on my worst enemy... They would not wish so gloomy a creature upon their friend Julie.*
PHR : VB INFLECTS

wishbone /wɪʃbəʊn/, **wishbones**. A **wishbone** is a V-shaped bone in chickens, turkeys, and other birds. When the meat has been eaten, two people pull the ends of the bone until it breaks. The person with the longer piece of bone is allowed to make a wish.
N COUNT

wishful thinking is used to refer to a hope or wish that has failed to come true or that is very unlikely to come true. EG *She hoped he might come with her to America, but it was pure wishful thinking... It is wishful thinking to assume that the generals will agree to elections.*
N UNCOUNT

wishy-washy /wɪʃi¹ wɒʃi¹/. Someone who is **wishy-washy** is not very clear in their ideas or beliefs and not very firm or enthusiastic in expressing their opinions or their support for other people; an informal expression used showing disapproval. EG *He's just a wishy-washy liberal... In a sort of wishy-washy way they are supporting it.*
ADJ QUALIT ⇑ vague = half-hearted

wisp /wɪsp/, **wisps**. 1 A **wisp** of grass, hair, etc, is a small, thin, untidy bunch of it. EG *A wisp of grey hair stuck out from under her hat... ...birds carrying wisps of hay in their beaks.* [N COUNT/PART]

2 A **wisp** of smoke, fog, etc, is a long thin amount of it. EG *...wisps of smoke from a small fire... ...the remaining wisps of fog... ...sky streaked by wisps of cloud.* [N PART ⇑ strand]

3 A **wisp** of something is also a very small trace of it that you can see, hear, or notice only with difficulty; a literary use. EG *...picking up a wisp of a clue here... Wisps of noise reached her... ...wisps of memory.* [N PART]

wispy /wɪspi¹/. Hair that is **wispy** is thin and growing in small, untidy bunches. EG *...wispy grey hair... ...wispy beards.* [ADJ QUALIT = straggly]

wisteria /wɪstɪəriə/ is a climbing plant with mauve or white flowers. [N UNCOUNT ⇑ creeper]

wistful /wɪstful/. Someone who is **wistful** is rather sad because they want something and know that they cannot have it. EG *She had a last wistful look round the flat... ...a little wistful smile.* [ADJ QUALIT] ◊ **wistfully**. EG *'Ah, dear Eva,' said Dr Board, wistfully.* [◊ ADV WITH VB] ◊ **wistfulness**. EG *...a nostalgic wistfulness.* [◊ N UNCOUNT]

wit /wɪt/, **wits**. 1 **Wit** in speech or writing is the ability to use words or ideas in an amusing, clever, and imaginative way. EG *The girl laughed at his wit... ...the wit of the American cartoonist... ...his quick wit and chirpy humour.* [N UNCOUNT ⇑ humour] ▸ used of a person who has this ability. EG *He acquired a reputation as a wit.* [▸ N COUNT ⇑ humorist]

2 If someone has **the wit** to do something, they have the intelligence and understanding to make the right decision or take the right action in a particular situation. EG *No one had had the wit to bring a bottle-opener... It needed the wit of a woman to think of such a simple thing.* [N SING : *the*+N+*to*-INF]

3 Your **wits** are your ability to think quickly and cleverly in a difficult situation. EG *Her only chance was to use her wits to bluff and outsmart the enemy... Terror was depriving Tim of his wits.* [N PLURAL : USU DETPOSS+N]

4 **Wits** is also used in the following expressions. **4.1** If you **have** or **keep** your **wits about** you, you are alert and ready to act in a difficult situation. EG *In this part of the city you have to keep your wits about you all the time.* [PHR : VB INFLECTS] **4.2** If something **sharpens** your **wits**, it makes you more able to think quickly and clearly in difficult situations. EG *Living in continual poverty had sharpened their wits... The intrigues of court had sharpened her wits.* [PHR : VB INFLECTS] **4.3** If you **collect** or **gather** your **wits**, you make an effort to control your thoughts and feelings, for example after a frightening or shocking experience. EG *By the time I had collected my wits, he was dead... Before I had gathered my wits, she had disappeared.* [PHR : VB INFLECTS] **4.4** If you **scare** or **terrify** someone **out of their wits**, **frighten the wits out of** someone, etc, you make them so afraid that they can no longer think clearly. EG *He had a loud horn to frighten the wits out of people who were being slow... We were frightened out of our wits by a banging at the door.* [PHR : VB INFLECTS] **4.5** If someone is **at** their **wits' end**, they are so worried and exhausted by problems or difficulties that they do not know what to do next. EG *The authorities are at their wits' end about juvenile delinquency... I am at my wits' end to know what to do with my son.* [PHR : USED AS AN A] **4.6** If someone **lives by** or **on** their **wits**, they manage to live by using clever but sometimes dishonest methods, rather than by having a regular job. EG *I knew a fellow who lived for years on his wits.* [PHR : VB INFLECTS] **4.7** ● **battle of wits**: see **battle**. ● **to pit your wits**: see **pit**.

5 **To wit** is used to indicate that you are about to state or describe something more precisely; a rather formal old-fashioned expression. EG *We speak in a language they don't know: to wit, English... There could be only one conclusion, to wit, that the evidence they sought existed.* [PHR : USED AS ADV SEN = i.e., namely]

witch /wɪtʃ/, **witches**. 1 A **witch** was a woman in former times who was thought to have evil magic powers. In Britain, other parts of Europe, and North America, witches are traditionally supposed to have worn long black clothes and tall black pointed hats and to have been able to fly through the air on broomsticks. [N COUNT]

2 A **witch** is a man or woman in modern times who claims to have magic powers and to be able to use them for good or bad purposes. [N COUNT]

witchcraft /wɪtʃkrɑːft/ is the skill of using magic powers, especially evil ones. [N UNCOUNT ⇑ sorcery]

witch doctor, witch doctors; also spelled with a hyphen. A **witch doctor** is a person in some societies, for example in Africa, who heals people or has religious functions and who is thought to have magic powers. [N COUNT]

witch-hazel; also spelled without a hyphen. **Witch-hazel** is a liquid that you put on your skin when it is sore or bruised, in order to heal it. [N UNCOUNT ⇑ medicine]

witch-hunt, witch-hunts; also spelled without a hyphen. 1 A **witch-hunt**, in former times, was a search for witches, which was carried out by church and government officials in order to kill the witches. [N COUNT]

2 In modern times, a **witch-hunt** is an attempt to find and punish people who are thought to be responsible for things that have gone wrong. The victims of a witch-hunt are often people who have independent opinions, even if they have not actually done any harm; used showing disapproval. EG *Hearst's campaign developed into a witch-hunt that terrorized the campuses.* [N COUNT ⇑ persecution]

witch-hunting is the activity of identifying and punishing people because of their opinions, especially when those opinions are thought to be harmful to society; used showing disapproval. EG *The organization is notorious for witch-hunting and stupidity.* [N UNCOUNT]

with /wɪð, wɪθ/. 1 You use **with** to indicate a relationship or connection between people or things in the following ways. **1.1** You use **with** to indicate that two or more people are together or are doing something together. EG *I stayed with her until dusk... 'Isn't Mr Boon with you?' was his hostess's first question... He didn't want to walk home with any of the others.* [PREP] **1.2** You use **with** to indicate that two or more people or groups have an agreement, arrangement, or relationship, or that they are having a meeting, discussion, etc. EG *Britain has a treaty with America that the two countries share the results of scientific research... ...a series of meetings with Jewish leaders... I discussed the idea with my publishers... He pleaded with Desiree to give their marriage another chance.* [PREP] **1.3** You use **with** to indicate that two or more people are fighting, arguing, competing against each other, etc. EG *...a naval war with France... ...a row with my brother.* [PREP] **1.4** You use **with** to indicate that something is placed next to something else, or that it is accompanied by it or included in it. EG *The X-ray showed enlargement of the heart with slight expansion of the aorta... Put the knives with the other cutlery... ...meat with potatoes and gravy.* [PREP] **1.5** You use **with** to indicate that there is a close link between two things. EG *We tend to forget that there are risks associated with ordinary fuels... People's moods are often tied up with how well they feel.* [PREP]

2 If you do something **with** a particular object, tool, or other thing, you do it using that object, tool, or thing. EG *Leather needs polishing with furniture cream... Remove hair spray from mirrors with a mop soaked in surgical spirit... He brushed back his hair with his hand.* [PREP]

3 You use **with** when you mention a physical feature, characteristic, possession, etc that someone or something has. EG *...an old man with a beard... ...a worried looking young man with a bad complexion and thick glasses... ...an old house with steep stairs and dark corridors... It was hard to find anyone with any previous experience... ...a fair with street bands, folk music, displays and tombola.* [PREP]

4 You use **with** when you mention the objects or things that fill or cover something or that have been provided for a particular person or place. EG *The floor was littered with ashtrays, plates, cups, glasses, and magazines... Madeleine's eyes filled with tears... The room was furnished with low tables, mattresses and cushions... They will provide you with a written statement to this effect... The building is decorated with bright banners.* [PREP]

5 If you do something **with** a smile, sigh, groan, etc, you smile, sigh, groan, etc while you do it or just before you do it. EG *She greeted him with a smile... 'Then there is a blanket missing,' said Matron with a sigh... With a wave of her hand she was gone... With these words he handed me the letter... With a cheery 'See you later, then,' he strolled off.* [PREP]

6 You use **with** to introduce the words that someone speaks, especially when they interrupt someone else. [PREP+QUOTE ⇑ saying]

EG *She broke in with, 'How dare you suggest such a thing!'*

7 If you do something **with** speed, care, etc, you do it quickly, carefully, etc. EG *These files can be inspected by the computer at any time with great accuracy and speed... The newspaper was produced with great professionalism by the students... This new law will restrict the power of business to operate with its traditional freedom.* PREP

8 If you do something **with** a particular feeling, you do it expressing or showing that feeling. EG *Jordache looked over at his son with genuine surprise... She gazed on me with a sudden fear and mistrust.* PREP = in

9 You use **with** to indicate the reason why someone or something is behaving in a particular way. EG *I am crazy with love... The children were screaming with laughter... This experience leaves him quaking with fear... She was turning blue with cold... Metals expand with heat and contract with cold and damp.* PREP ⇑ because of

10 You also use **with** 10.1 when you mention the subject or activity to which a remark or fact relates. EG *Don't be inflexible with shopping... There was a particular problem with claims for maternity allowance... Is anybody familiar with it?... I believe this is what happened with Mr Nixon... Gretchen was not concerned with Boylan's profits and losses.* PREP = concerning, regarding **10.2** when you mention the thing that you are asking someone to think about or consider. EG *She always comes to me with her problems... I won't bother you with pages of tedious reasoning.* PREP

11 **With** is the preposition that you use after some verbs, adjectives, and nouns. **11.1** You use **with** after words that mean 'agree' or 'disagree', and also after words such as 'comply'. EG *I agree with a good deal of that... I disagree with the decisions taken by conference... Schools which do not comply with basic educational requirements should be closed.* PREP **11.2** You use **with** after words such as 'break', 'split', or 'part' to indicate a separation between two people or between a person and a thing. EG *I took it, thanked her, and told her I would never part with it... The group's break with the TUC could be serious... I've split up with him.* PREP ⇑ from **11.3** You use **with** after words that describe feelings when you mention the thing or person that the feeling is directed towards. EG *I've just got fed up with washing up... Oh Cicely, you wouldn't be pleased with us at all... They became dissatisfied with pastries from local bakeries... All three ladies are in love with Lawrence.* PREP **11.4** You use **with** after words that mean 'help'. EG *Madeleine spent the rest of the day assisting Matron with her inventory... We ought to be encouraging him to help with the cooking.* PREP

12 You use **with** to say that something happens at the same time that something else happens. EG *She walked back to the bus stop, with him following her... He didn't have the courage to put his hat on with Perkins watching him.* PREP

13 You use **with** to introduce something which seems relevant to what you are saying or discussing. EG *With unemployment in the county growing, numbers staying on at school are increasing... I'm sure that Anne, with her special knowledge of French politics, would be better at answering this question than me.* PREP

14 If something moves **with** a wind or current, it moves in the same direction as the wind or current. EG *...sailing with the wind... The boat drifted with the tide.* PREP ≠ against

15 A film, television programme, etc **with** a particular performer or item is one in which that performer or item appears. EG *'The Bells of Hell', with Gregory Peck... The Academy of St Martin-in-the-Fields will be playing Vivaldi's 'Four Seasons', with Iona Brown as soloist... We shall be back in the Autumn with more news and views to share with you.* PREP = featuring

16 Someone **with** a particular illness is suffering from that illness. EG *I was taken to hospital with fierce abdominal pains... He's in bed with flu.* PREP

17 **With** a particular length of time or distance remaining means that there is that length of time or distance remaining before something happens or is done. EG *With only two weeks to go before the birth of my baby, I was involved in an accident... We stopped for a break, with another five miles to cover before night.* PREP

18 To increase, decrease, improve etc **with** something means to increase, decrease, or improve as a result of it and in relation to it. EG *This wine always improves with keeping... Such a pension scheme provides a degree of security increasing with age and length of service.* PREP

19 You can say that you are **with** someone **19.1** when you understand what they are talking about; an informal use. EG *Are you still with me?... Sorry, I'm not quite with you.* PREP+PRON **19.2** when you support or approve of what they are doing. EG *I'm with the government in this.* PREP = behind

20 **with it. 20.1** If you say that someone or something is **with it**, you mean that they are fashionable and up-to-date; a rather old-fashioned informal expression. PHR : USED AS C = trendy **20.2** To **get with it** means to become aware of all the latest events, developments, ideas, etc; an informal expression. PHR : VB INFLECTS

21 • **in with**: see **in**. • **what with**: see **what**. • **to start with**: see **start**.

withdraw /wɪðdrɔ:/, **withdraws, withdrawing, withdrew, withdrawn**; a fairly formal word. **1** If you **withdraw** something from a place, you remove it or take it away from the place. EG *She withdrew the key from the door... Tony grinned, withdrawing his hand from his pocket.* V+O : IF+PREP THEN *from*

2 If you **withdraw** money from a bank account or savings account, you take it out of the account in order to spend it or use it. EG *You must present your cheque card when you withdraw any money.* V+O

3 If you **withdraw** to another place, you leave the place where you are and go to the other place, for example because it is quieter or more private. EG *He breathed a sigh of relief and withdrew to his office to count the money... We withdrew into the library.* V : USU+A

4 When troops **withdraw** or **are withdrawn**, they leave the place where they are fighting or where they are based. EG *Resolutions were passed calling for the Republic to withdraw from the Eastern Provinces... The garrison was immediately withdrawn.* V-ERG : IF+PREP THEN *from* = retreat

5 If you **withdraw** from an activity, you decide that you will no longer take part in it. EG *Marsha withdrew from the argument.* V OR V+O : IF+ PREP THEN *from*

6 If you **withdraw** a remark or statement, you say formally that you wish to change or deny it. EG *I want to withdraw a statement I made earlier on.* V+O = retract

withdrawal /wɪðdrɔ:əl/, **withdrawals**; a fairly formal word. **1** The **withdrawal** of something is the activity or process of withdrawing or removing it. EG *...major matters like the withdrawal of public services.* N UNCOUNT : USU +*of* ⇑ removal

2 The **withdrawal** of troops, weapons, etc is the activity or process of removing them from the place where they are fighting or where they are based. EG *They are trying to negotiate the withdrawal of 20,000 troops... Last weekend saw the first withdrawals of foreign soldiers from the region.* N UNCOUNT/ COUNT : IF+ PREP THEN *from/of* ⇑ removal

3 The **withdrawal** of a remark or statement is the act of saying formally that you wish to change or deny it. EG *...the withdrawal of what he had said.* N UNCOUNT : USU +*of* = retraction

4 **Withdrawal** is also **4.1** a decision to stop taking part in an activity or to stop belonging to a particular organization. EG *...withdrawal from the Common Market.* N UNCOUNT **4.2** behaviour in which someone, especially a child, prefers to be alone and does not want to communicate with other people. EG *...intermittent spells of sulking, withdrawal and vindictiveness.* N UNCOUNT **4.3** the period during which someone feels ill after they have stopped taking a drug to which they were addicted. EG *...the intense physical discomfort of withdrawal.* N UNCOUNT

5 A **withdrawal** is an amount of money that you take from your bank account or savings account. EG *It is not the bank's policy to deduct interest on withdrawals.* N COUNT ▸ used also of the taking out of the money. EG *...the withdrawal of all his savings.* ▸ N UNCOUNT

withdrawal symptoms. If you experience **withdrawal symptoms**, you have unpleasant feelings because you have stopped taking a drug to which you were addicted. N PLURAL

withdrawn /wɪðdrɔ:n/. **1 Withdrawn** is the past participle of **withdraw**.

2 Someone who is **withdrawn** is extremely shy or quiet, and finds it difficult to talk to other people. EG *The isolated life made them withdrawn.* ADJ QUALIT = introvert

withdrew /wɪðdru:/ is the past tense of **withdraw**.

wither /wɪðə/, **withers, withering, withered**.

1 When something **withers** or **withers away**, it V, OR PHRASAL

becomes weaker, often until it no longer exists. EG *Links with the outside community withered... His eagerness to fight back could not be permitted to wither away.* VB: V+ADV ⇑ decline = wane

2 If a plant **withers** or if heat or drought **withers** it, it shrinks and dries up, and dies, usually because it does not get enough water. EG *The leaves had withered and fallen.* V-ERG ⇑ die = droop, wilt

3 The highest part of a horse's back, behind its neck, is referred to as its **withers**. N PLURAL

withered /wɪðəd/. 1 A **withered** plant is shrunken, dried up, and dead. EG *...a pot of withered roses.* ADJ CLASSIF

2 If you describe a person or a part of their body as **withered**, you mean that their skin is very wrinkled and dry, and looks old. EG *...a withered old lady... A tear trickled down the thin, withered cheek.* ADJ QUALIT: USU ATTRIB ⇑ shrunken = wizened

3 If someone has a **withered** arm, hand, or leg, their arm, hand, or leg is thin and weak because of disease or paralysis. ADJ CLASSIF: ATTRIB ⇑ deformed = diseased

withering /wɪðəʳrɪŋ/. A **withering** look or remark makes the person it is directed at feel very stupid, ashamed, or inferior. EG *Clarissa gave her a withering look... ...a withering reproof.* ADJ CLASSIF ⇑ condemnatory = contemptuous

withhold /wɪðhəʊld/, **withholds, withholding, withheld** /wɪðhɛld/. If you **withhold** something that someone wants or should have, you do not let them have it; a formal word. EG *I decided to withhold the information till later... Families withheld rent and were evicted.* V+O ⇑ refuse

within /wɪðɪn/; a fairly formal word. 1 If something is **within** a place, area, object, etc, it is inside it or surrounded by it. EG *The central shrine was a huge copper dome within a railing... The prisoners also demanded the freedom to congregate within the prison... The fish's body has a high proportion of water within it.* PREP ⇑ in ▸ used as an adverb, especially when referring to a building or room. EG *'Who is it, Mel?' said a voice from within... She cut open the fruit and began to suck out the soft flesh within.* ▸ ADV

2 You also use **within** 2.1 when you are referring to something that exists or happens inside a society, organization, system, group, etc, or to something that is a part of it. EG *It ensured a balance of forces within society... He was in no position to influence affairs within Russia... We were told to work within the system... ...the dominant role of women within the family.* PREP ⇑ in ▸ used as an adverb. EG *Membership is by nomination from within.* ▸ ADV 2.2 when you are referring to something that belongs to a particular type or area of work, thought, art, etc. EG *...drawings within that English tradition of Victorian Art... They were basically operating within a European framework of thought.* PREP ⇑ in 2.3 when you are referring to a very strong emotion which a person feels but does not express. EG *A mounting wave of dislike and anger rose within me.* PREP ▸ used as an adverb. EG *...the hatred he felt within.* ▸ ADV

3 If something is **within** particular limits or restrictions, it does not go beyond those limits or is not more than what is possible or allowed. EG *Within these limitations there were a number of options open to me... We must ask the schools to keep within their budget... It may not be within their power to help in practical matters.* PREP

4 If you are **within** a particular distance of a place, you are less than that distance from the place. EG *They were within fifty miles of Chicago... The property is within a short distance of the shops.* PREP

5 If something is **within** sight, **within** earshot, **within** reach, etc, it is nearer than the farthest distance that you can see, hear, or reach. EG *They finally came within sight of the bamboo gates... ...a somewhat undignified argument to which everyone within earshot tried to listen... Matches should not be left within reach of small children.* PREP ≠ out of

6 **Within** a particular length of time means 6.1 before that length of time has passed. EG *Within minutes I was called to his office... I knew that within a fortnight I should feel restless again... The old lady died within the hour.* PREP ⇑ in 6.2 during that length of time. EG *Sixteen houses were vandalized within a few weeks.* PREP ⇑ in

7 You can refer to something that is a part of something else and that is also a smaller thing of the same kind as a community **within** a community, a prison **within** a prison, etc. EG *The University can be seen as a community within a community... ...a play within a play.* PREP: NG+PREP +NG

without /wɪðaʊt/. 1 You use **without** 1.1 to indicate that someone or something does not have or use the thing mentioned, especially when you would normally expect them to have it or use it. EG *The chairs were of black teak, without cushions... ...city slums without light, roads or water... How much better he looked without his glasses, Judy thought... She was without an ambition in the world... ...a city without a history... He left school at seventeen without being able to read... She walked without a stick.* PREP 1.2 to indicate that someone does not have something that is considered to be a basic necessity. EG *We don't want another night without fire... Phil had been there three days without food... Thousands are without work.* PREP

2 You use **without** 2.1 to indicate that someone does not do a particular thing or have a particular type of feeling or behaviour when they do something. EG *'No,' she said, without explanation... They greeted him without enthusiasm... I turned round without haste... This agreement I call, without originality, the social contract... 'Goodbye, dear,' Miss Saunders said, without looking up... They drove into town without talking to each other.* PREP, OR CONJ SUBORD+-ING 2.2 to indicate that a particular thing does not happen when something else happens. EG *The rest of the press conference passed without incident... I knocked twice, without reply.* PREP, OR CONJ SUBORD+-ING 2.3 to indicate that something that is normally considered necessary or important is not done or does not happen. EG *The Count had joined the meeting without invitation... ...putting people in jail without trial... She had threatened to marry without her parents' consent.* PREP, OR CONJ SUBORD+-ING

3 If you say that something unpleasant would happen **without** a particular thing or person, you mean that the thing or person prevents it from happening. EG *Thousands of families would have died without his leadership... Sarah was certain that without their protection he would be murdered... Without the people the party is powerless.* PREP, OR CONJ SUBORD+-ING

4 **Without** someone means not in their company or not living or working with them. EG *You can go without me... Her husband felt he couldn't face life without her.* PREP

5 **Without** also means outside; an old-fashioned or formal use. EG *The door itself opened from without.* ADV

6 **Without so much as** means the same as 'without'. You use this expression when you are emphasizing that someone or something does not have or do a particular thing. EG *John strolled by without so much as a glance of recognition.* PREP

7 • to **do without**: see **do**. • to **go without**: see **go**.

withstand /wɪðstænd/, **withstands, withstanding, withstood** /wɪðstʊd/. When something or someone **withstands** a force or action, they survive it or do not give in to it; a fairly formal word. EG *They have to make the walls strong enough to withstand high winds... Nicola bravely withstood their taunts.* V+O ⇑ resist

witless /wɪtlɪ²s/. Someone who is **witless** is silly; a rather formal word. EG *I felt an unreasonable hatred for that witless woman.* ADJ CLASSIF • If you say that something **scares** you **witless**, you mean that it scares you very much indeed. • PHR: VB INFLECTS

witness /wɪtnɪ²s/, **witnesses, witnessing, witnessed**. 1 A **witness** is 1.1 a person who sees an event such as an accident and is able to tell other people what happened. EG *They listened avidly as witnesses to the murder told what they had seen... She accused him of corruption, in front of witnesses.* N COUNT = bystander, onlooker 1.2 a person who appears in a court of law to tell what he or she knows about a crime or other event. EG *Other witnesses were called, and gave similar evidence... ...an expert witness.* N COUNT ⇑ observer 1.3 a person who writes his or her name on a document to confirm that the person who was meant to sign the document has actually signed it. N COUNT

2 Something that is **witness** to something else or is a **witness** to it shows that it exists or happened; a formal use. EG *His smile is a witness to his new found happiness... The statue was put up in 1912, witness to the popularity of a remarkable man.* N COUNT/ UNCOUNT+*to* ⇑ sign = testimony • If something or someone **bears witness to** something else, they show or say that it exists or happened; a formal expression. EG *This lack of action bears witness to a* • PHR: VB INFLECTS

complacency which has survived two World Wars... They attempt through their art to bear witness to the truth as they see it.

3 If you **witness** something, you see it happen; a fairly formal use. EG *At least fifteen persons witnessed the attack on Morris... He scored the most fantastic goal I have ever witnessed.* — V+O ⇑ observe

4 If you **are witness to** something, you see it happen; a fairly formal use. EG *This was the first time I was witness to one of his rages.* — PHR : VB INFLECTS

5 If you say that a place or period of time **witnessed** a particular event or change, you mean that it happened in that place or during that period of time. You can also say that a person **witnessed** an event or change, meaning that it happened during that person's lifetime. EG *The park witnessed a number of duels... The period 1930-50 had witnessed important changes in juvenile behaviour... We are witnessing not the triumph but the breakdown of bureaucracy.* — V+O = see

6 If you **witness** someone's signature on a document, you sign your name on it to confirm that he or she was the person who actually signed it. — V+O

7 If you **witness** to something, you confirm that it exists or happened; a formal use. EG *He had called several members of his family to witness to his wife's obstinacy.* — V+A *(to)* = testify

8 You say **witness** when you are mentioning something as an example of what you have just been talking about; a fairly formal use. EG *Furthermore, diagnoses can be wrong: witness the number of people wrongly sent to mental hospitals.* — V+O : ONLY IMPER

witness-box, witness-boxes; also spelled without a hyphen. The **witness-box** or **witness-stand** in a court of law is the place where people stand or sit when they are giving evidence. — N COUNT : USU SING

witter /wɪtə/, **witters, wittering, wittered.** If you say that someone **is wittering** about something, you mean that they are saying a lot of silly and boring things; an informal word. EG *...a lot of twits in open sandals wittering on about The Middle Way.* — V : USU+A

witticism /wɪtɪsɪzəm/, **witticisms.** A **witticism** is a witty remark or joke; a formal word. EG *How much he appreciates his own witticisms!* — N COUNT = quip

wittingly /wɪtɪŋli¹/. If you do something **wittingly**, you are fully aware of what you are doing and what its consequences will be; a formal word. EG *Wittingly or not, he had ruined the plan.* — ADV WITH VB = intentionally

witty /wɪti¹/, **wittier, wittiest.** A remark or a piece of writing that is **witty** is amusing in a clever way. EG *It's a neat and witty play... ...one of my wittier observations.* ▸ used of people who are speaking or writing. EG *Deborah was as clever and witty as she was beautiful.* ◇ **wittily.** EG *He found her wittily describing a weekend spent with her in-laws.* — ADJ QUALIT ⇑ funny = humorous; ◇ ADV WITH VB

wives /waɪvz/ is the plural of **wife.**

wizard /wɪzəd/, **wizards. 1** A **wizard** is a man, usually in a fairy story, who has magic powers. — N COUNT = magician

2 You can describe someone who is very good at doing a particular thing as an economic **wizard**, a **wizard** with machines, etc. EG *...a financial wizard... My new friend was a wizard with camels.* — N COUNT+SUPP ⇑ person = expert

wizardry /wɪzədri¹/. You can refer to a very clever achievement or piece of work as **wizardry** of some kind, especially when you do not understand how it is done. EG *...a sophisticated piece of computing wizardry... ...her reputation for financial wizardry.* — N UNCOUNT+SUPP

wizened /wɪzənd/. A **wizened** person, fruit, or vegetable is old and shrunken, with wrinkled skin. EG *Mr Solomon was a wizened little man with frizzy gray hair. ...a wizened pumpkin.* — ADJ QUALIT = shrivelled

wk, wks. wk is a written abbreviation for 'week'. EG *...3 wks holiday.* — N COUNT : NUM+N

woad /wəʊd/ was a blue dye used by the ancient Britons to paint their bodies. — N UNCOUNT

wobble /wɒbəl/, **wobbles, wobbling, wobbled. 1** If something **wobbles** or **wobbles about,** it makes small movements from side to side, because it is loose or unsteady. EG *She glared at me, her three chins wobbling aggressively... I hit her, and she wobbled and fell into a ditch... My legs were wobbling under me.* — V, OR PHRASAL VB : V+ADV = shake, rock

2 If someone or something **wobbles** in a particular direction, they move in that direction, wobbling from side to side as they do so. EG *I got on my bicycle and wobbled off down the road.* — V+A = judder, shake

wobbly /wɒbli¹/. **1** Something that is **wobbly** moves unsteadily from side to side. EG *...a wobbly bed.* — ADJ QUALIT = unstable

2 If you feel **wobbly** or if your legs feel **wobbly**, you feel weak and shaky because you are afraid, ill, or exhausted, or because you have had a shock. EG *She said she must sit down somewhere, she felt wobbly... My legs still feel weak and wobbly.* — ADJ QUALIT ⇑ unsteady

3 If a person's voice is **wobbly**, it sounds weak and keeps varying in pitch, because the person is very unhappy or afraid. — ADJ QUALIT

4 A **wobbly** line has little irregular bends and curves in it. — ADJ QUALIT

wodge /wɒdʒ/, **wodges.** A **wodge** of something is a large amount of it or a large piece of it; an informal word in British English. EG *...computers churning out great wodges of information... He helped himself to a wodge of chocolate cake.* — N COUNT/PART

woe /wəʊ/, **woes**; a formal or literary word. **1 Woe** is very great unhappiness or sorrow. EG *...a bird cry like an exclamation of woe.* — N UNCOUNT

2 You can refer to someone's problems or misfortunes as **woes** or **woe.** EG *We don't want to add to your woes... They would invite him back and listen sympathetically to his woes... His distraught wife poured out her tale of woe.* — N PLURAL/N UNCOUNT

3 Woe is an exclamation expressing grief or warning in a literary or humorous way. EG *Voices cry: 'Woe, woe, the great city.'... Oh woe! Woe! Listen to this from the 'Guardian'.* — EXCLAM

4 If you say **woe betide** someone who does a particular thing or **woe to** them, you mean that something unpleasant will happen to them if they do it. EG *Woe betide the youngster who is less than respectful... Woe to the man who asked him as a guest to his golf club.* — PHR

woebegone /wəʊbɪgɒn/. Someone who looks or feels **woebegone** looks or feels very sad; a formal or humorous word. EG *Poor Claude, he looked so woebegone.* ▸ used of people's expressions. EG *...a little woebegone face.* — ADJ QUALIT = sorrowful

woeful /wəʊfʊl/; a formal word. **1** Someone or something that is **woeful** is very sad. EG *...the teenage girl whose woeful face floods with excitement when the phone rings... ...the bearer of woeful tidings.* ◇ **woefully.** EG *One day, she came home and announced woefully, 'I've lost my job.'* — ADJ QUALIT; ◇ ADV WITH VB

2 You also say that something is **woeful** when it is very bad or undesirable. EG *His work displays a woeful lack of imagination... This ignorance has led to some woeful choices.* ◇ **woefully.** EG *Supervision of students on teaching practice is woefully inadequate.* — ADJ QUALIT : USU ATTRIB; ◇ ADV+ADJ/ADV

wog /wɒg/, **wogs. Wog** is an extremely offensive word for anyone whose skin is not white. — N COUNT

wok /wɒk/, **woks.** A **wok** is a large bowl-shaped pan which is used especially for Chinese-style cooking. — N COUNT

woke /wəʊk/ is the past tense of **wake.**

woken /wəʊkən/ is the past participle of **wake.**

wolf /wʊlf/, **wolves; wolfs, wolfing, wolfed. Wolves** is the plural of the noun. **Wolfs** is the 3rd person singular, present tense, of the verb. **1** A **wolf** is a wild animal that looks like a large dog and that kills and eats other animals. Wolves live in groups, usually in forests. — N COUNT ⇑ carnivore

2 When people or animals **wolf** food or **wolf** it **down,** they eat it all very quickly and greedily. EG *They wolfed the meal as if they were starving... He wolfed the food down, bones and all.* — V+O, OR PHRASAL VB : V+O+ADV = gobble

3 The word **wolf** is also used in the following expressions. **3.1** If someone **cries wolf,** they ask for help so many times when they do not need it that people no longer believe them when they say that they are in danger or trouble, even when they really are. EG *She had cried wolf so often that her claims for attention were ignored.* — PHR : VB INFLECTS ⇑ bluff **3.2** If you **keep the wolf from the door,** you succeed in providing food and other necessary things for yourself or your family; an informal expression. — PHR : VB INFLECTS **3.3** If you describe someone as a **lone wolf,** you mean that they like to do things alone, rather than in the company of other people. — PHR : USU USED AS C

3.4 If you **throw** someone **to the wolves,** you allow them to be criticized severely or treated roughly, and do not try to protect them. — PHR : VB INFLECTS **3.5** If you describe someone as a **wolf in sheep's clothing,** you mean that they seem to be, or pretend to be, nice and harmless but are in fact rather dangerous. — PHR : USU USED AS C

wolfhound /wʊlfhaʊnd/, **wolfhounds.** A **wolfhound** is a very large dog. — N COUNT

wolf-whistle, wolf-whistles, wolf-whistling, wolf-whistled. A **wolf-whistle** is a whistle which has a short rising note and a longer falling note. Some men make this sound to show that they think a woman is attractive, especially a woman who is passing in the street. EG *I'm always getting wolf-whistles.* ▸ used as a verb. EG *They stared after her, laughing and wolf-whistling.*
N COUNT
▸ V, OR V+A *(at)*

wolves /wʊlvz/ is the plural of **wolf**.

woman /wʊmən/, **women.** 1 A **woman** is an adult female human being. EG *...a tall, dark-eyed woman in a simple brown dress... There were men and women working in the fields... Fifty women and children picketed the office.* ▸ **Woman** and **women** are also used before other nouns. EG *We had one woman teacher... ...women drivers... ...a woman friend.*
N COUNT
= lady
▸ N BEFORE N

2 People sometimes refer to a woman as **the woman** instead of 'she' or 'her', especially when they do not like her; an informal use. EG *Drat the woman, she really gets on my nerves!... I've never even met the woman.*
N SING : *the*+N
⇑ person

3 Women sometimes say **a woman** when they want to make a general statement that applies especially to themselves; a fairly informal use. EG *A woman can only stand so much.*
N SING : *a*+N
⇑ one

4 A gardening **woman**, a dog **woman**, etc is a woman who likes gardening, dogs, etc; an informal use. EG *No, really, I'm not a drinking woman... I'm a small car woman, myself.*
N COUNT : MOD+N, USU SING
⇑ person
= fan

5 A man's **woman** is his lover or his wife; an informal use.
N COUNT : POSS+N

6 You can refer to women in general as **woman.** EG *...man's inhumanity to woman.*
N UNCOUNT

7 A **woman** is also 7.1 a woman who works for or represents a particular company or organization. EG *The publicity woman had planned to take me there and show me around.* 7.2 a female worker. EG *You may be able to employ a woman to do the washing for you.*
N COUNT+SUPP
⇑ representative
= lady
N COUNT

8 People sometimes address a woman as **woman** when they are ordering her to do something or when they are angry or impatient with her; an offensive use. EG *Oh, for God's sake, woman, sit down!*
N VOC
⇑ you

9 If a group of women do something **as one woman,** they do it at exactly the same time. EG *They turned on him as one woman.*
PHR : USED AS AN A

10 People used to address a woman as **my good woman** when they considered her to be socially inferior to themselves. EG *Thank you, my good woman, that will be all.*
PHR : ONLY VOC

11 If you say that a woman **is** her **own woman,** you mean that she is able to make her own decisions and plans without having to obey other people.
PHR : VB INFLECTS
⇑ be independent

12 If a group of women think something, believe something, etc **to a woman,** every one of them thinks or believes it. EG *They believe to a woman that they will win.*
PHR : USED AS AN A
⇑ all

13 If two women talk to each other **woman to woman,** they talk honestly and openly, treating each other as equals. EG *I want to chat to her, woman to woman, on her own level.* ▸ used as an adjective. EG *You should approach her in a friendly woman to woman way.*
PHR : USED AS AN A
⇑ frankly
▸ ADJ CLASSIF : ATTRIB
⇑ frank

-woman, -women. 1 **-woman** is added to some adjectives and nouns in order to form nouns referring to a woman who comes from a particular country or county. EG *...English→Englishwoman... ...Yorkshire→Yorkshirewoman.*
SUFFIX : FORMS N COUNTS

2 **-woman** also combines with numbers to indicate that something involves the number of women mentioned. EG *She plays in a four-woman band.*
COMB : FORMS ADJ CLASSIFS

womanhood /wʊmənhʊd/. 1 **Womanhood** is the state of being a woman rather than a girl or a man. EG *...when a girl is on the threshold of womanhood.*
N UNCOUNT

2 You can refer to women in general or the women of a particular country or community as **womanhood.** EG *Who will hear the cry of suffering womanhood?... ...a perfect specimen of English womanhood.*
N UNCOUNT

womanish /wʊmənɪʃ/. A man who is **womanish** behaves in a way that is considered typical of women, for example in a weak or emotional way, or looks rather like a woman in some way; used showing disapproval.
ADJ QUALIT
= effeminate

womanizer /wʊmənaɪzə/, **womanizers;** also spelled **womaniser.** A **womanizer** is a man who likes to spend a lot of his time in the company of women, usually in order to have short sexual relationships with them; used showing disapproval.
N COUNT

womanizing /wʊmənaɪzɪŋ/; also spelled **womanising.** When a man spends a lot of his time in the company of women, usually in order to have short sexual relationships with them, this practice is known as **womanizing;** used showing disapproval. EG *Scott had made formal complaints about Gibson's womanizing.*
N UNCOUNT

womankind /wʊmənkaɪnd/. You can refer to all women as **womankind** when considering them as a group; a formal word.
N UNCOUNT

womanly /wʊmənli¹/. People describe a woman's behaviour, character, or appearance as **womanly** when they think that it is typical of, or suitable for, a woman rather than a man or girl; used showing approval. EG *She never stood for parliament, thinking it more womanly to manipulate from the rear... Her figure had become more womanly... ...the womanly virtues of gentleness and compassion.*
ADJ QUALIT
⇑ feminine

womb /wuːm/, **wombs.** A woman's **womb** is the part inside her body where a baby grows before it is born. Some female animals also have wombs. EG *...a tiny little baby in its mother's womb.*
N COUNT : USU *the/POSS*+N
= uterus

wombat /wɒmbæt/, **wombats.** A **wombat** is a furry Australian animal which has very short legs and eats plants.
N COUNT
⇑ marsupial

women /wɪmɪn/ is the plural of **woman.**

womenfolk /wɪmɪnfəʊk/. The **womenfolk** of a particular community are its women. This word is used especially when the community is ruled or organized by men. EG *They emigrated to the towns with their womenfolk.*
N PLURAL : USU *the/POSS*+N

women's group, women's groups. A **women's group** is a group of women who meet regularly, usually in order to organize campaigns.
N COUNT

Women's Lib is the same as Women's Liberation; an informal expression.
N UNCOUNT
⇑ feminism

Women's Libber, Women's Libbers. A **Women's Libber** is a woman who is active in the Women's Liberation movement; an informal expression.
N COUNT
⇑ feminist

Women's Liberation is the ideal that women should have the same social and economic rights and privileges as men. EG *We discussed women's liberation with the local women... I was in the first women's liberation group that was ever started.*
N UNCOUNT
⇑ feminism

women's movement. The **women's movement** is a social and political movement which aims to achieve women's liberation by organizing groups and campaigns and by causing individual women and men to change their attitudes.
N SING : *the*+N

won /wʌn/ is the past tense and past participle of **win.**

wonder /wʌndə/, **wonders, wondering, wondered.** 1 If you **wonder** about something, 1.1 you think about it with curiosity and wish you knew more about it. EG *I wonder what she'll look like... The questions were good because they made you wonder about real things... 'Where do they all come from?'–'I often wonder that myself.'* 1.2 you think about it because you are uncertain or worried about it. EG *I wondered if she'd been expecting me to sit down... I keep wondering and worrying about what you said... I am beginning to wonder why we ever invited them... I wondered whether I too would become one of its victims.*
V+REPORT-CL/ QUOTE, OR V+A *(about)*
V+REPORT-CL/ QUOTE, OR V+A *(about)*
= ask oneself

2 You can introduce a request or enquiry by saying 'I **wonder** if' or 'I **wonder** whether' when you are being very polite. EG *I wonder if you'd mind closing the window... I wonder whether by any chance you would care to join me?*
V+REPORT-CL *(if/whether)*

3 If you **wonder** at something, you are surprised and amazed about it. EG *I used to wonder at their slowness... I don't wonder that she didn't come.–You didn't invite her.*
V+REPORT-CL *(that),* OR V+A *(at)*

4 If you say that it is a **wonder** that something happened or is happening, you mean that it is very surprising and unexpected. EG *It was a wonder that she managed to come at all–she's so busy nowadays.*
N SING : USED AS C+*that*
= miracle

5 **Wonder** is the feeling of astonishment and disbelief that you have, for example when you see something that you had thought was impossible or something unusually beautiful. EG *I shall never forget the look of wonder on her face the first time it snowed.*
N UNCOUNT
= awe

6 A **wonder** is something or someone that causes people to feel astonishment or great admiration. EG
N COUNT : USU+*of*

...the wonders of modern technology... ...the seven wonders of the world.

7 If you refer to someone or something as a **wonder** boy, a **wonder** drug, etc, you mean that they are greatly admired or praised because of their skills or qualities. EG *...the wonder boy of American racing.* N BEFORE N ⇑ super

8 **Wonder** is also used in the following expressions.

8.1 If you say **wonders will never cease**, you mean that you are surprised because something unexpected and pleasant has happened; an informal expression. CONVENTION 8.2 If you say that someone or something is a **nine days' wonder**, you mean that they are popular and interesting for only a short time; used showing disapproval. PHR : USED AS C = fad 8.3 If you say **no wonder, little wonder, small wonder**, etc, you mean that you are not surprised by something that happens. EG *Little wonder that today we are in such a mess... 'Anyway, he didn't win.'–'No wonder.'... In this atmosphere it is small wonder that people feel afraid.* PHR : USED AS C, USU + *that* 8.4 If you say that something **works wonders** or **does wonders**, you mean that it has a very good effect on something. EG *A whisky and soda at the end of the day will sometimes work wonders... ...an aerosol powder which works wonders on greasy marks... The nurse tells me the doctors have done wonders for your leg.* PHR : VB INFLECTS, USU + A

wonderful /wʌndəful/. If you describe something as **wonderful**, 1 you mean that it makes you feel very happy and pleased. EG *'Guess what? I've got a job at last.'–'Wonderful!'... It was wonderful to be able to walk again.* ADJ QUALIT = delightful 2 you mean that it is of very high quality. EG *You've got such a wonderful memory.* ADJ QUALIT 3 you mean that it is very impressive or successful. EG *The human body is a wonderful thing when you think about it... Isn't it wonderful how they built the airport so quickly?* ADJ QUALIT = astonishing

wonderfully /wʌndəfuli¹/. You use **wonderfully** 1 to emphasize that something is much better than usual or much better than you expected. EG *Both plays are wonderfully funny... She was always wonderfully kind to me... Dr Landy says you are doing wonderfully well.* ADV + ADJ/ADV ⇑ very = tremendously 2 to say that something happens or is done extremely well. EG *I had slept wonderfully.* ADV WITH VB = splendidly

wonderland /wʌndəlænd/, **wonderlands**. 1 **Wonderland** is an imaginary world that exists in fairy tales. N UNCOUNT = fairyland

2 You can refer to a place as **wonderland** or a **wonderland** when it seems very strange or unusually beautiful. EG *He went into the old lady's house and found himself in wonderland... She drew back the curtain and gazed at the winter wonderland before her.* N COUNT : USU SING

wonderment /wʌndəmə²nt/ is a feeling of pleasant amazement. EG *'Two hundred,' I said, shaking my head in wonderment.* N UNCOUNT = astonishment

wondrous /wʌndrəs/ means amazing and impressive; an old-fashioned and literary word. EG *...the wondrous inventions of the twentieth century.* ADJ QUALIT : USU ATTRIB = wonderful

wonky /wɒŋki¹/. Something that is **wonky** is likely to shake or not work properly because it is not steady and not firmly in place. EG *Don't put it on there! That table's wonky... I had to keep to the paths because I've got a wonky knee.* ADJ QUALIT ⇑ unsteady = wobbly

wont /wəʊnt/; a very old-fashioned word. 1 If someone is **wont** to do something, they do it regularly as a habit. EG *They were wont to take long walks in the evening.* ADJ CLASSIF : PRED + *to*-INF = inclined

2 If you say that someone does something **as is their wont**, you mean that it is something that they do regularly as a habit. EG *They were all talking, as is their wont, about cars.* PHR : USED AS AN A

won't /wəʊnt/ is the usual spoken form of 'will not'.

woo /wu:/, **woos, wooing, wooed**. 1 If you **woo** people, you try to encourage them to help you, support you, or vote for you, for example by promising them things which they would like. EG *She was considered to be the most suitable candidate to woo the working-class voters of Warrington.* V+O = attract

2 When a man **woos** a woman, he tries to make himself seem attractive to her, for example because he wants to marry her; an old-fashioned use. EG *He was trying to woo the daughter of a Missouri aristocrat.* V+O = court

wood /wud/, **woods**. 1 **Wood** is the material which forms the trunks of trees. It can be used to make things such as furniture, or it can be burned to provide heating or to cook food. EG *If the timber is replaced, iron and steel is used, not wood... ...a piece of wood... The screws are very fine and won't split the wood... We filled the back of the car with wood for the fire.* N MASS

2 If beer or wine is kept in **wood**, it is kept in barrels until it is ready to be drunk; a technical use. EG *The wine had had forty years in wood before bottling... ...beer from the wood.* N UNCOUNT = barrel, cask

3 A **wood** is a large area of trees growing near each other. You can use **the woods** to refer to one very large wood. EG *...the big wood where the pheasants lived... I lost my new sweater in the woods... They walked through the woods towards the main house.* N COUNT : USU SING = PL = copse

4 **Wood** is also used in the following expressions. 4.1 If you say that someone **can't see the wood for the trees**, you mean that they are so involved in the details of something that they forget or do not realise the general purpose or importance of the thing as a whole. PHR : VB INFLECTS 4.2 If you say that someone is **not out of the woods** yet, you mean that they are still involved in a difficult or dangerous situation; an informal expression. EG *Things are looking up, but we're still not out of the woods yet.* PHR : USED AS C 4.3 • **touch wood**: see **touch**.

wood-carving, wood-carvings. A **wood-carving** is a decorative piece of wood or panelling that has been carved in an artistic way. EG *You said you wanted to look at the wood-carving in the chapel... ...some of the finest wood-carving in Europe.* N COUNT/UNCOUNT

woodcock /wudkɒk/. **Woodcock** is both the singular and the plural form. A **woodcock** is a small brown bird with a long beak. Woodcock are sometimes shot for sport or food. N COUNT ⇑ game bird

woodcutter /wudkʌtə/, **woodcutters**. A **woodcutter** is someone who cuts down trees or who chops wood as a job; an old-fashioned word. N COUNT

wooded /wudɪ²d/. An area that is **wooded** is covered in trees. EG *...a deep, narrow wooded valley in the Ardennes.* ADJ QUALIT

wooden /wudə⁰n/. 1 An object that is **wooden** is made of wood. EG *...a wooden box with instructions on the lid... They were all sitting at a long wooden table drinking out of little glasses.* ADJ CLASSIF

2 If you say that someone such as an actor is **wooden**, you mean that they act without any liveliness, especially showing no sign of emotion in their face or movements; used showing disapproval. EG *Performances might become wooden and under-expressive.* ADJ QUALIT ⇑ dull = leaden ◇ **woodenly**. EG *'Thanks,' she said woodenly. 'You've done your good deed for the day.'* ◇ ADV WITH VB = stiffly

wooden-headed. If you describe someone as **wooden-headed**, you mean that they are stupid; an informal word. EG *...their wooden-headed supporters.* ADJ QUALIT = dumb

wooden spoon, wooden spoons. 1 A **wooden spoon** is a spoon made of wood that you can use when you are cooking. N COUNT

2 You say that the person or team that comes last in a race or competition gets the **wooden spoon**; an informal expression. N SING : *the*+N

woodland /wudlə²nd/, **woodlands**. **Woodland** is land which is mostly covered with trees. EG *...a patch of woodland in Malaysia... ...the temperate woodlands of Tasmania.* N UNCOUNT/COUNT = forest

woodlouse /wudlaus/, **woodlice**. A **woodlouse** is a very small grey creature that looks rather like an insect. It has fourteen legs and lives in damp places. N COUNT

woodpecker /wudpɛkə/, **woodpeckers**. A **woodpecker** is a bird with a long sharp beak that makes holes in tree trunks in order to eat the insects which live there. N COUNT

woodpile /wudpaɪl/, **woodpiles**. A **woodpile** is a pile of firewood. N COUNT : USU SING

wood pulp is wood that has been cut up into small pieces and crushed. Wood pulp is used to make paper. EG *The Company guaranteed supplies of the wood pulp needed for the newsprint.* N UNCOUNT

woodshed /wudʃɛd/, **woodsheds**. A **woodshed** is a small building which is used for storing firewood. EG *I fixed a small leak in the roof of the woodshed.* N COUNT ⇑ shed

woodwind /wudwɪnd/, **woodwinds**. A **woodwind** instrument or a **woodwind** is a musical instrument such as a clarinet or oboe. You play a woodwind instrument by blowing into it. ADJ CLASSIF : ATTRIB, OR N COUNT ▸ The **woodwind** is used to refer to all the woodwind instruments in an orchestra, which are thought of as a distinct section. ▸ N SING : *the*+N = wind

woodwork /wudwɜ:k/. 1 The woodwork in a house or room consists of the parts that are made of wood such as the doors, window-frames, and skirting N UNCOUNT ⇑ wood boards. EG *The paint was peeling from the woodwork on their doors and windows... ...panelled oak woodwork.*

2 If you say that someone or something **is crawling out of the woodwork**, you mean that they are beginning to be active after an unfavourable situation has improved, because they now feel safe; used showing disapproval. PHR : VB INFLECTS ⇑ emerge

3 Woodwork is the activity of making things out of wood, especially when this is done skilfully or artistically. EG *...leisurely pastimes like gardening, woodwork, music and toy-making.* N UNCOUNT ⇑ work = carpentry

woodworm /wʊdwɜːm/, **woodworms**. **Woodworm** is the usual plural form. **1 Woodworm** are the larvae of a type of beetle. They make holes in wood by feeding on it. They look like very small worms. N COUNT

2 Woodworm is damage caused to wood, especially to the wooden parts of a house or to furniture, by woodworm making holes in the wood. EG *If your house timber has woodworm, get expert treatment.* N UNCOUNT

woody /wʊdi[1]/, **woodier, woodiest**. **1** Plants that are **woody** have very hard stems. EG *The roots of woody plants grow deep.* ADJ QUALIT

2 An area that is **woody** has a lot of trees in it. EG *The picnic in the woody valley became a monthly affair.* ADJ QUALIT = wooded

wooer /wuːə/, **wooers**. A woman's **wooer** is a man who is trying to make himself seem attractive to her, usually because he wants to marry her; a very old-fashioned word. N COUNT = suitor

woof /wʊf/, **woofs, woofing, woofed**. A **woof** is the sound that a dog makes when it barks; an informal word, especially used by children. EG *The dog gave a loud woof.* ▸ used as a verb. EG *Whenever I used to go into the garden, she used to woof.* N COUNT = bow-wow ▸ V

wool /wʊl/, **wools**. **1 Wool** is **1.1** the hair that grows on sheep and on some other animals. N MASS **1.2** material that is made from wool and that is used to make clothes, blankets, carpets, etc. EG *...a little bobble hat made from wool... He was dressed in a good wool suit.* N MASS ⇑ fabric **1.3** long thick threads of wool or artificial fibre that are used for knitting clothes. EG *She jabbed her knitting needles into a ball of wool.* N MASS ⇑ yarn

2 If you **pull the wool over** someone's **eyes**, you deliberately tell them something that is not true in order to have an advantage over them; an informal expression. PHR : VB INFLECTS ⇑ deceive

3 See also **cotton wool, dyed-in-the-wool, steel wool, wire wool.**

woolen. See **woollen**.

wool-gathering. If someone **is wool-gathering**, they are thinking vaguely about something and not paying attention to what other people are saying or doing; an informal expression. PHR : AUX INFLECTS ⇑ daydreaming

woollen /wʊlən/; also spelled **woolen** in American English. **1 Woollen** clothes or materials are made from wool or from a mixture of wool and artificial fibres. EG *...woollen rugs... ...a woollen scarf... ...long woollen socks.* ADJ CLASSIF : USU ATTRIB ⇑ fabric

2 Woollens are clothes that are made of wool. EG *...a good fabric softener for woollens.* N PLURAL

woolly /wʊli[2]/, **woollies; woollier, woolliest**; also spelled **wooly** in American English. **1** Something that is **woolly** is made of wool or looks like wool. EG *...a woolly cap.* ADJ CLASSIF

2 A **woolly** is a woollen garment, especially a pullover; an informal use. EG *She wore a long droopy woolly... They sat round the fire muffled in their woollies.* N COUNT = jumper, sweater

3 Ideas that are **woolly** are very unclear and not presented carefully or in detail; used showing disapproval. ▸ used of people. EG *They cannot afford to be vague and woolly with their messages; they must be crisp and sharp.* ADJ QUALIT = vague

woolly-minded. If you describe someone as **woolly-minded**, you mean that they are confused or vague in their ideas; used showing disapproval. ADJ QUALIT = wishy-washy

wooly. See **woolly**.

woozy /wuːzi[1]/, **woozier, wooziest**. If you feel **woozy**, you feel rather weak and unsteady and cannot think clearly; an informal word. EG *I smiled uncertainly, feeling woozy from the whisky.* ADJ QUALIT

wop /wɒp/, **wops**. A **wop** is an Italian; a very offensive word. N COUNT

word /wɜːd/, **words, wording, worded**. **1** A **word** is **1.1** a single unit of language that can be represented in writing or speech. In English, a word has a space on either side of it when it is written. A word can usually have one or more meanings. EG *...a short passage of about seventy words... His eye had been caught by the word 'scandal' in the headline... He spoke slowly, placing emphasis on each word... None of the children knew what the word meant... He's morose–that's the word.* N COUNT **1.2** a short conversation with someone, usually about something specific; a fairly informal use. EG *May I have a word with you please?... I want to have a little word with you about last night... 'Have you come to get your book back?'–'No, no. I just wanted a word before the seminar.'* N SING : a+N **1.3** a short statement, especially one that gives advice, information, or a warning. EG *A word to fathers: don't frighten away your daughter's friends... One word of warning: you may need planning permission.* N SING : a+N, USU +A

2 Word can be used to refer to everything that someone says or writes at a particular time, especially when you want to emphasize that it has not been heard or understood. EG *I realized that I did not understand one word of what she'd said... Marsha, have you heard a word I've said?... She didn't believe it anyway, not a word.* N SING : a+N, USU WITH BROAD NEG

3 If someone does not say a **word** or if they do something without a **word**, they do not say anything. EG *They went without a word... He ate his carefully prepared dinner without a word of thanks.* N SING : a+N, USU WITH BROAD NEG

4 Someone's **words** are what they say or write at a particular time. EG *His father's words rang in his head... ...shaking his head as if unable to believe his own words... He was, in the words of his doctor, going downhill fast.* N PLURAL : WITH POSS

5 Word or the **word** can mean a story or message which is passed from one person to another, but which might not be true. EG *The young man brought them word of her visit... The word got out that he would, after all, go ahead with the project... The word was that Nichols was writing a new play.* N UNCOUNT, OR N SING : *the*+N

6 Your **word** is a sincere promise that you make to someone. EG *I promised her: I must keep my word... I give you my word I won't ask him... I apologized for having doubted his word.* N SING : POSS+N

7 If someone gives the **word** to do something, they give an order to do it. EG *The light was growing as he gave the word to move... We waited for the word to start shooting.* N SING : *the*+N

8 In Christianity, the **Word** is the message and teachings that are contained in the Bible. EG *...the divine Word... ...the Word of God.* N SING : *the*+N

9 Words are **9.1** language considered as a means of communicating feelings and ideas. EG *Visual images have a fluidity that words can never achieve... Between people like us there is no need for words... How could he put his profound feeling into words?... There are no words to describe the loss they have suffered.* N PLURAL **9.2** discussion and talk about something as opposed to action; used showing disapproval. EG *They have a right to expect results, not words... 'Words, words,' he accused. 'When is something going to be done about it?'* N PLURAL

10 The **words** of a song are the text, as opposed to the musical notes. EG *I can't sing that–I don't know the words... She was trying to get the proper words to this famous tune.* N PLURAL : USU *the*+N = lyrics

11 When you **word** something in a particular way, you carefully choose the words that you use in order to express your ideas in an accurate or acceptable way. EG *How would one word such an announcement?* V+O ◊ **worded**. EG *...one of the most sharply worded attacks on EEC ministers... ...strongly worded editorials.* ◊ ADJ CLASSIF : ADV+ADJ+N

12 word for word. **12.1** If you repeat something **word for word**, you repeat it exactly as it was originally said or written. EG *That's word for word what the man said... We had a long chat and he printed it more or less word for word.* PHR : USED AS AN A, OR BEFORE N = verbatim **12.2** A **word for word** translation has been done by translating each individual word separately rather than by representing the general meaning of a group of words. PHR : USED AS AN A, OR BEFORE N

13 Word is also used in the following expressions.

13.1 If you say that someone has to **eat** their **words**, you mean that they have to admit that they were wrong about something they had said in the past. EG *They said he'd never win another tournament, but a year later he forced them to eat their words as he won the US Open.* PHR : VB INFLECTS **13.2** You can say **'words fail me'** in order to emphasize that you feel very shocked, PHR : VB INFLECTS surprised, or angry. EG *Looking at them, words failed him... Words fail me!–I just don't believe it!* 13.3 If you **have a few words** with someone or **exchange a few words** with them, you have a brief conversation with them. EG *I wanted an excuse to exchange a few more words with her... I met her at a luncheon recently and had a few words with her.* 13.4 A **man of few words** or a **woman of few words** is someone who says very little, especially someone who rarely expresses their opinions or feelings. 13.5 If you say that someone was **as good as** their **word**, you mean that they did what they promised they would do. 13.6 If you **never have a good word to say for** someone or something, you never say anything favourable about them, but always criticize them. 13.7 If you **have words with** someone, you have a serious discussion or argument with them, often because you want to complain about their behaviour. EG *I can see I'll have to have words with him about this... They've been having words again.* 13.8 If you say that someone **doesn't know the meaning of the word**, you are criticizing them and saying that they do not have a particular quality that you mention, often after they have just been talking about that quality. EG *Honesty? She doesn't know the meaning of the word!* 13.9 **The last word** is the statement or comment that finishes a discussion or an argument. Often the person who has the last word is thought to have won the argument. EG *The last word was Philip's: 'Think over that offer of mine, won't you?'... Doctors always have the last word... The last word belonged to Councillor Joe Servis.* 13.10 If you say that something is **the last word in** comfort, luxury, etc, you mean that it is the most comfortable or luxurious thing of its kind. EG *The car's designers claim that this latest model is the last word in comfort.* 13.11 You say to someone **'mark my words'** in order to emphasize that you are sure of what you are saying, especially when you are giving them a warning of something unpleasant that might happen; an old-fashioned informal expression. EG *You mark my words, you're going to have a lot of trouble with that child.* 13.12 If news or information passes **by word of mouth** or **through word of mouth**, people tell it to each other rather than write it down. EG *People hear about it through word of mouth.* 13.13 You say **in other words** in order to introduce a simpler explanation or interpretation of something that has just been said. EG *Is there a cheaper solution? In other words, can you make a cheaper device?... 'They seem to have problems with directionality.' In other words they get lost.* 13.14 If you say something **in your own words**, you express it in your own way, without copying or repeating someone else's description. EG *He was asked to tell the story in his own words.* 13.15 If you tell someone to **pass the word**, you are telling them to give other people a message that has been given to you. EG *She told him to pass the word, just in case... Pass the word that we are attacking an enemy submarine.* 13.16 If you **put in a word** for someone or **put in a good word** for them, you speak favourably about them to a person who has influence and who may be able to help them. EG *I'll put in a good word at the meeting if I get the chance... Later, the king put in a word for her and she was forgiven.* 13.17 If someone suggests that you meant one thing when you really meant something different, you can say that they **are putting words into** your **mouth**. EG *'So you refuse to explain?' she asked sharply.–'Now don't go putting words into my mouth, please,' Jean retorted getting cross.* 13.18 If you say that someone **took the words out of** your **mouth**, you mean that they have just said what you were about to say. EG *'Wasn't that a magnificent performance?'–'You took the words right out of my mouth!'* 13.19 If someone **says the word**, they give their approval as a sign that something should start to happen. EG *I only have to say the word and the plan will be put into action.* 13.20 If you say that someone said something **in so many words**, you mean that they said it clearly and in a way that was plain and understandable. If you say that they said it **not in so many words**, you mean that they expressed it in an indirect way. EG *For a member to say in so many words that another has lied is not acceptable in Parliament... This is what he is claiming, only he does not state it in so many words... 'They said they want to?'–'No, not in so many words.'* 13.21 If you **take** someone **at** their **word**, you accept what they say as literally true or as literally what they want, although they may have actually meant something different. EG *We just took her at her word and left straight away.* 13.22 If you say to someone **'take my word for it'**, you mean that they should believe you because you are telling the truth. EG *You can take my word for it, she's not there.* 13.23 If you want to emphasize that someone or something is very stupid, stubborn, etc, you can say that they are **too silly for words, too stubborn for words,** etc. EG *'This case is too silly for words,' exclaimed his solicitor... I'm too angry for words!* 13.24 If you want to emphasize that a word that you are using is the right one, even though it seems surprising or unbelievable, you can say **there is no other word for it** or **that's the only word for it**. EG *I was happy, there is simply no other word for it.* 13.25 You say **in a word** to indicate that you are summarizing what you have just been saying. EG *The house is roomy, cool in summer and winter, and in a word comfortable... In a word, we are in the midst of the super-industrial revolution.* 13.26 If you say that someone is **a man of his word** or **a woman of her word**, you mean that he or she can be relied upon to do something that they have promised to do; used showing approval. 13.27 You say **'my word!'** or **'upon my word!'** as an expression of surprise or amazement at something unusual; an old-fashioned expression.

PHR : VB INFLECTS, RECIP (with) ↑ converse
PHR : USED AS C
PHR : USED AS C
PHR : VB INFLECTS
PHR : VB INFLECTS ↑ tell off = row
PHR : VB INFLECTS
PHR : USED AS O/S/C
PHR + N UNCOUNT : USED AS C ↑ superior
PHR : USED AS ADV SEN
PHR : USED AS AN A = orally
PHR : USED AS ADV SEN
PHR : USED AS AN A
PHR : VB INFLECTS
PHR : VB INFLECTS
PHR : VB INFLECTS
PHR : VB INFLECTS
PHR : VB INFLECTS
PHR : USED AS AN A
PHR : VB INFLECTS ↑ act
PHR
PHR : USED AS C
PHR
PHR : USED AS ADV SEN = in short
PHR : USED AS C
EXCLAM = goodness me

14 See also **wording, code word, four-letter word.** ● **bandy words** with someone: see **bandy.** ● **get a word in edgeways**: see **edgeways.** ● **not mince** your **words**: see **mince.** ● **the operative word**: see **operative.** ● **the printed word**: see **print.** ● **send word**: see **send.**

word-blind. Someone who is **word-blind** has difficulty with reading because of a slight disorder of their brain. ADJ CLASSIF = dyslexic

word-blindness is difficulty with reading caused by a slight disorder of the brain. N UNCOUNT = dyslexia

word class, word classes. A **word class** is a particular grammatical class of word, such as noun, adjective, or verb. N COUNT

wording /wɜ:dɪŋ/. The **wording** of a piece of writing or a speech is the way it is written when you consider the exact words which are used and the way that they are meant to be understood. EG *For a full hour he argued over the wording of the editorial... Another child's card had similar wording.* N UNCOUNT

wordless /wɜ:dlɪ²s/; a fairly literary word. 1 You say that someone is **wordless** when they do not say anything, especially at a time when they are expected to say something. EG *Her mother sat there, wordless, staring at the wall.* ADJ CLASSIF : USU PRED ↑ silent

2 When people utter **wordless** sounds, they utter sounds that do not seem to contain any words. EG *The chant was audible but at that distance still wordless.* ADJ CLASSIF

word-perfect. If you are **word-perfect**, you are able to repeat from memory the exact words of a text that you have learned. EG *Noel was word-perfect at the first rehearsal.* ADJ CLASSIF ↑ accurate

wordplay /wɜ:dpleɪ/. **Wordplay** involves making jokes by using the meanings of words in an unusual, amusing, or clever way. N UNCOUNT ↑ joking = punning

word processing; also spelled with a hyphen. **Word processing** is the work of producing printed material using a word processor. N UNCOUNT ↑ activity

word processor, word processors; also spelled with a hyphen. A **word processor** is an electronic machine which has a keyboard and a screen like a computer terminal, but which is used as a typewriter to produce documents, letters, and other printed material. N COUNT

wordy /wɜ:di¹/, **wordier, wordiest.** Someone or something that is **wordy** uses too many words, especially words which are very long, formal, or literary in style; used showing disapproval. EG *The professor is a rather wordy man... ...this very wordy book on biology.* ADJ QUALIT ↑ lengthy = verbose

wore /wɔ:/ is the past tense of **wear.**

work /wɜ:k/, **works, working, worked.** 1 People who **work** have a job which they are paid to do. EG *He was working in a bank... Large numbers of them now work as labourers... Some of my salesmen formerly worked for a rival concern.* V OR V+A = be employed

2 People who have **work** or who are in **work** have a N UNCOUNT

job which they are paid to do. EG *It's increasingly difficult to get back into work after raising a family... ...the numbers out of work... The local peasants may be lucky enough to find eight months work a year.*

3 When you **work**, **3.1** you do tasks or duties which are your job and which you are being paid to do. EG *I used to work a ten-hour day, Monday to Friday... On the evenings when he was not working, Jo liked to visit the bars in town.* — V: USU+A, OR V +O

3.2 you spend time and effort on a task or activity, especially something which is useful or necessary. EG *All through the winter term, the Kirks worked on their terrace house... She had gone down into the cellar where her father was working.* — V: USU+A

3.3 you study by learning from books or by writing essays or doing exercises. EG *You haven't worked but you'll pass your exams.* — V: USU+A

4 Work is **4.1** the tasks and duties which are your job and which you are paid to do. EG *I must go, I've got loads of work to do... He has to get up early and do a day's work... I finish work at 3... The work of a doctor is very interesting and varied.* — N UNCOUNT = responsibilities

4.2 the place where you do your job. EG *I can't leave work till 5.* — N UNCOUNT

4.3 making an effort and doing things which are useful or necessary rather than relaxing or doing things which you enjoy. EG *Hard work is good for you.* — N UNCOUNT

4.4 an activity or set of tasks on which you spend time and effort and which you do for a particular purpose. EG *A housewife's work can take ten or twelve hours a day... That work on the cycle has given me an appetite.* — N UNCOUNT

4.5 time and effort which has to be spent on a particular task or activity. EG *I asked him to write down points needing extra work.* — N UNCOUNT

4.6 something which you produce as a result of an activity or as a result of doing your job. EG *It is standard practice to put remarks on their work... That's an absolutely fascinating piece of work.* — N UNCOUNT

4.7 study or research on a particular subject. EG *There has been considerable work done in America on this subject.* — N UNCOUNT

4.8 time and effort which is spent in trying to help a person or group of people in some way. EG *The organization, through its work among immigrant groups, has gained an excellent reputation... Work with handicapped children can be especially rewarding.* — N UNCOUNT: USU +SUPP

4.9 movement caused by force being applied to something, so that energy is transferred; a technical term in physics. EG *Its energy content is used to perform work.* — N UNCOUNT

5 If you **work** a particular area, you travel around that area as part of your job, especially in order to sell a product. EG *He had worked the London area for several publishers... They work the streets round Paddington.* — V+O = cover, do

6 If you **work** someone, you make them spend time and effort doing a particular activity or job. EG *I was worked mercilessly.* — V+O+A = drive

7 If you **work** metal, leather, stone, etc, you cut, sew, or shape it in order to make something or to create a design. EG *We marvelled at the fantastic accuracy with which they worked the stone.* — V+O = fashion

8 If you **work** with a particular substance or material or in that substance or material, you use it in order to make something or to create a design. EG *People who have never worked with steel have trouble understanding this... He always works in oil paints.* — V+A *(with/in)*

9 If you **work** the land, you cultivate it and do all the various tasks involved in growing and harvesting crops. EG *He'd visited a commune and watched the peasants and intellectuals working the land together... The farmers are now able to work a much larger area with a smaller workforce.* — V+O

10 If people **work** a mine or well, they remove a substance such as coal or oil from it. EG *There had been as many as 180 Norwegians working the coal mines at Tunheim... For the men who work the wells it will be a tough life.* — V+O

11 If you **work** a machine or piece of equipment, you use or control it. EG *From inside the garage there came the sound of Coyne working a lathe... I ran off to help the boy who worked the milking machine.* — V+O = operate

12 If a machine or piece of equipment **works**, it operates efficiently and performs a particular function. EG *I thought your bell worked... The traffic lights weren't working properly.* — V

13 If something such as an idea or system **works**, it is successful. EG *In terms of theatrical effect, it seems to me to work amazingly well... That kind of democracy will never work... Frankness works best.* — V = succeed

14 If a drug or medicine **works**, it produces a particular physical effect. EG *How long does a sleeping pill take to work?* — V

15 If something **works** in a particular way, it functions or operates in that way. EG *There is a special wire cutter which works off a battery... He assiduously applied himself to learning how Parliament worked.* — V+A

16 If something **works** in your favour, it helps you in some way. If something **works** against you, it causes problems for you in some way. EG *He can count on this factor working in his favour... All these factors work against the young entrant to the labour market... The restraining influence seemed to be working on both sides.* — V+A = operate

17 If your mind or brain **is working**, you are thinking about something or trying to solve a problem. EG *His brain is working furiously to cope with the complexities.* — V

18 If you **work** for something or **work** to achieve something, you spend time and effort trying to achieve it. EG *They work also for international peace... We worked hard to persuade them that we were genuinely interested.* — V+*for/to*-INF

19 If you **work** with a person or a group of people, you spend time and effort trying to help them in some way. EG *I had the opportunity to work with a great many foster children... I worked with the masses on land reform.* — V+A *(with)*

20 If you **work** on something or at something, **20.1** you spend time and effort trying to improve it. EG *He has been working all season on his game... She works hard at keeping herself fit.* — V+A *(at/on)*

20.2 you try to move it or open it by using your physical strength. EG *Someone must have worked at it with a crowbar... He worked on the lock with a nail file and finally managed to get the door to open.* — V+A *(at/on)*

21 If you **work** on an assumption or idea, you rely on it being true or correct and use it in order to develop your own ideas. EG *Mr Reagan said he was working on the assumption that formal negotiations would shortly take place... Evolution theory works on the idea that the fittest survive and produce fit offspring.* — V+A *(on)* = operate

22 If you **work** something into a particular shape or form, you change it so that it is in that shape or form. EG *As soon as an idea tentatively appears, it is quickly worked into a form suitable for an experimental programme.* — V+O+A *(into)*

23 If something **works** into a particular state or condition, it gradually moves so that it is in that state or condition. EG *The ropes had worked loose... The thin frock worked up as she bent over.* — V+A/C

24 If you **work** someone into a state of being very upset or angry, you make them become very upset or angry. EG *She was working herself into a rage about his attitude.* — V+O (NG/REFL) +A *(into)* = get

25 If you **work** it so that something happens, you arrange for that thing to happen by acting in a clever or skilful way. EG *She worked it so that he never had a chance to be at home on his own.* — V+O+REPORT-CL = contrive, fix

26 If something or someone **works** magic or **works** their charms on someone, they have a magical or influential effect on them. EG *The flood of warm golden stage lighting was working its magic on the audience.* — V+O = create

27 If you **work** your way somewhere, you move or progress there slowly and with a lot of effort. EG *I worked my way slowly out of the marsh... Gridgeley left school at 14, and worked his way up to the position of Head of Supplies... I worked my way through his writings.* — V+O+A

28 If you **work** a part of your body, or if it **works**, you move it. EG *The men huddled down in the trench worked their lips to ease the dryness... His face worked expressively before the words came out.* — V-ERG

29 If you **work** the answer to a mathematical problem, you calculate it; used in American English. EG *You work a percentage in a table.* — V+O = work out

30 A **work** is something such as a painting, book, or piece of music, produced by an artist, writer, or composer. EG *The juxtaposition of colours was the most striking thing about the work... He pulled out a large green volume containing all of Chopin's works.* — N COUNT+SUPP

31 A **works** is a place where something is made or where an industrial process is carried out. EG *...the brick works... ...a printing works... He was the works foreman.* — N COUNT: IF SING, VB CAN BE SING OR PL = factory

32 Works are activities such as digging the ground or building on a large scale, especially in order to install systems of pipes or wires, or to construct roads, bridges, or buildings. EG *He was in charge of planning the great plumbing and civic engineering works of the city... The land is sparsely peopled and would need extensive irrigation works if they were to grow crops all the year.*

N PLURAL : USU+SUPP ⇑ operations = installations

33 If you refer to the **works**, you mean everything in a particular group or everything which you associate with a particular situation; an informal use. EG *If I watched that I'd have the most awful nightmares. You know, the works. Bad fights, guys dying, me dying... 'Sausages? Tea or coffee?' Percival said. 'The works, coffee, bacon, eggs and sausages, if that's all right.'*

N SING : *the*+N = the lot

34 at work. 34.1 If someone is **at work**, they are doing their job or are busy doing a particular activity. EG *You saw the saddlers at work in the lamplight... He had been at work on a book... I'll be at work tomorrow... Computers will be hard at work on these problems.*

PHR : USED AS AN A = working

34.2 If a situation or process is **at work**, it is having a particular influence or effect. EG *The same disastrous processes are at work in the whole of this area... My face was hollowed out by the infection that by then was at work on me... There were other elements at work as well.*

PHR : USED AS AN A = operating

35 The word **work** is also used in the following expressions. **35.1** If you say that something was **nice work** or **quick work**, you mean that someone has done something well or quickly; a fairly informal expression. EG *Nice work, Jack... 'Thank you,' he said, 'that was quick work.'*

N UNCOUNT : MOD+N ⇑ action

35.2 If you say that a task is **all in a day's work**, you mean that you do not mind doing it although it is difficult or causes problems for you. EG *It is all in a day's work, and I do not feel any strain.*

PHR : USED AS C

35.3 If you **make short work of** something or **make light work of** it, you do it quickly and without much effort or difficulty. EG *He made short work of the ironing.*

PHR : VB INFLECTS

35.4 If you say that you will **have your work cut out** to do something, you mean that it will be very difficult for you to do it. EG *We'll have our work cut out to finish on time.*

PHR : VB INFLECTS, USU+*to*-INF/A

35.5 If you **put** or **set** someone to **work**, you give them a job or task to do. EG *The people were put to work on huge farms.*

PHR : VB INFLECTS

35.6 If you **go**, **set**, or **get to work**, you start doing a particular task or activity. EG *Smithy set to work on the painting... They sat there for half an hour and then he said, 'Get to work'... He found the corkscrew and went to work on the two bottles of wine.*

PHR : VB INFLECTS = get going

35.7 If someone or something **gums up the works** or **bungs up the works**, they prevent an event from happening in the way that was intended. EG *You all go along and gum up the works.*

PHR : VB INFLECTS

35.8 If people **work to rule**, they follow all the established rules of work for their job but they do no extra work, with the result that things are done more slowly and less is achieved. People work to rule as a way of protesting. • See also **work-to-rule.**

PHR : VB INFLECTS

36 See also **donkey work, paperwork, piecework, road works, social work.** • to **work** your **fingers to the bone**: see **bone.** • to **throw a spanner in the works**: see **spanner.** • to **work like a Trojan**: see **Trojan.**

37 See also **working.**

work in. 1 If you **work** a substance **in**, or if you **work** it **into** another substance, you add it to the other substance and mix the two together thoroughly. EG *To get the necessary lightness it should be worked into the soil with sand or ashes... We worked the fat in with our fingers.*

PHRASAL VB : V+O+ADV/PREP

2 If you **work** something **in**, you make an opportunity to do or say it in addition to everything else you intended to do or say. EG *He managed to work in several sly remarks about the Prime Minister... I'll try and work it in some time during the day.*

PHRASAL VB : V+O+ADV ⇑ include = fit in

3 See also **work-in.**

work off. If you **work off** a feeling such as anger or embarrassment, you gradually overcome it, especially by being unpleasant or violent towards other people. EG *He worked off his embarrassment by harassing us with questions.*

PHRASAL VB : V+O+ADV

work on. If you **work on** someone, you spend time trying to influence them or persuade them to do something. EG *The good priest worked on me with the finest tenderness and understanding.*

PHRASAL VB : V+PREP, HAS PASS

work out. 1 If you **work out** a solution to a problem, you find a solution to it. EG *We are always hoping that a more peaceful solution can be worked out... Economists have tried to work out an alternative economic system.*

PHRASAL VB : V+O+ADV, OR V+ADV+REPORT-CL = formulate, produce

2 If you **work out** the answer to a mathematical problem, you calculate it. EG *I've worked it out, it's 3,171.875 tons... The weekly rate is worked out by dividing by 52.*

PHRASAL VB : V+O+ADV, OR ORDER V+ADV+REPORT-CL

3 If you **work** something **out**, you think about it and manage to understand it. EG *He couldn't at first work out why the room was at once so strange and so familiar... I haven't really worked it out in my own mind yet... It is fascinating to work out who is who in the company.*

PHRASAL VB : V+O+ADV, OR ORDER V+ADV+REPORT-CL = sort out

4 If you say that you cannot **work** someone **out**, you mean that you cannot understand them; an informal expression. EG *I just can't work you out, you never seem to enjoy anything.*

PHRASAL VB : ORDER V+O+ADV = read, suss out

5 If you **have** something **all worked out**, you have thought about it carefully and know exactly what you must say or do in order to achieve the results that you want. EG *She had it all worked out.*

PHR : VB INFLECTS

6 If something **works out** at a particular amount, it is calculated to be that amount after all the facts and figures have been considered. EG *It worked out about a hundred pounds in the end... Petrol prices here are among the cheapest in Europe, working out at around £1.15 a gallon.*

PHRASAL VB : V+ADV, USU+A = come to

7 If a situation **works out** in a particular way, it happens or progresses in that way. EG *I asked him how he was, and how his job was working out... It's funny how life worked out.*

PHRASAL VB : V+ADV, USU+A

8 If a process **works** itself **out**, it reaches a conclusion or satisfactory end; a formal use. EG *Popular theories depend on the great historical purpose working itself out.*

PHRASAL VB : V+O (REFL)+ADV = resolve

9 If you **work out** your service or your notice, you continue to work at your job until you have completed a necessary specified period of time. EG *This was including 30,000 conscripts still working out their reserve service.*

PHRASAL VB : V+O+ADV ⇑ finish = complete

10 If a mine **is worked out**, all the coal or metal is removed from it. EG *More and more seams were worked out.*

PHRASAL VB : V+O+ADV, USU PASS = exhaust

11 If you **work out**, you do physical exercises in order to make your body fit and strong. EG *She worked out in a ballet class three hours a week.*

PHRASAL VB : V+ADV

12 If something **works** a feeling **out** of you, it causes it to become less intense and to disappear. EG *That will work the wickedness out of them.*

PHRASAL VB : V+O+ADV, USU+*of* ⇑ remove = knock out

13 See also **workout.**

work over. If you **work** someone **over**, you beat and kick them very violently; an informal expression. EG *Dave got one of his mates to work John over.*

PHRASAL VB : V+O+ADV ⇑ assault = do over

work up. 1 If you **work** yourself **up** or **work** someone else **up**, you make yourself or another person very upset or angry about something. EG *She's remembered now what she's heard and she's worked herself up about them... He worked himself up into a frenzy and wouldn't listen to any of us.* ◇ **worked up.** EG *Why are you so worked up over that editorial?... Claude was all worked up.*

PHRASAL VB : ORDER V+O (NG/REFL)+ADV

◇ ADJ QUALIT : PRED = het up

2 If you **work up** enthusiasm or an appetite, you start to have it or feel it. EG *I couldn't work up much enthusiasm for his plan... He had worked up a healthy appetite and finished a large plate of spaghetti very quickly.*

PHRASAL VB : V+O+ADV = develop

3 If something or someone **works up** to a point of excitement or interest, they gradually develop or progress towards that point. EG *The action was working up to a climax... She gradually worked up to the main point of her speech.*

PHRASAL VB : V+ADV+A *(to)* = build up

4 If you **work up** something such as a piece of writing or a particular skill, you spend time and effort on it in order to improve it. EG *You'll have to work up your languages, of course, if you want that sort of job.*

PHRASAL VB : V+O+ADV

-work is added to nouns to form other nouns referring to things made with the substance or material mentioned. EG *His elbows rested heavily upon Nell's wicker-work garden table... There were cracks in the cement-work.*

COMB : FORMS N UNCOUNTS

workable /wɜːkəbəᵊl/. Something that is **workable** can operate efficiently or can be used for a particular purpose. EG *This doesn't seem to me to be a workable system... We will examine the test and see how workable it is.*

ADJ QUALIT = practicable

workaday /wɜːkədeɪ/ means ordinary and not especially interesting or unusual. EG *...a quiet workaday man... Gloucester is now a sprawling, even ugly, workaday city.* ADJ CLASSIF: ATTRIB = prosaic

workaholic /wɜːkəhɒlɪk/, **workaholics**. A **workaholic** is a person who finds it difficult to stop working in order to do other things. N COUNT

work basket, work baskets. A **work basket** is a small box or container in which people keep needles, cotton, etc for sewing. N COUNT

workbench /wɜːkbɛntʃ/, **workbenches**. A **workbench** is a heavy wooden table on which people use tools such as a hammer and nails to make or repair things. EG *On one side ran a long wooden workbench with shelves above cluttered with boxes.* N COUNT

workbook /wɜːkbʊk/, **workbooks**. A **workbook** is an exercise book or textbook that is used for study, especially a textbook which has questions in it and spaces for you to fill in the answers. N COUNT

workday /wɜːkdeɪ/, **workdays**. A **workday** is 1 the amount of time during a day which you spend doing your job. EG *Regan could hold to a 9-to-5 workday, with occasional Friday afternoons off.* N COUNT: USU SING 2 a day on which people go to work. EG *Tomorrow's a workday.* N COUNT = working day

worker /wɜːkə/, **workers**. 1 A **worker** is a person who is employed by another person or organization in a particular type of industry or business and who has no responsibility for managing the industry or business. EG *The dispute affected relations between management and workers... We went to the home of a woman factory worker named Liang.* N COUNT = employee

2 If someone is a good **worker**, a hard **worker**, etc, they work well, hard, etc. EG *He had been an efficient and painstaking worker... My husband was a hard worker given the opportunity.* N COUNT: ADJ+N ⇑ person

3 A **worker** is also someone who does a particular kind of job. EG *A series of experiments by American research workers have provided some of the answers... Rescue workers are hoping to reach the trapped man by midnight.* ● See also **social worker**. N COUNT: USU+SUPP

4 A **worker** is also a female of some kinds of insects, such as bees and ants. Workers cannot produce any young and they search for food for other bees or ants. EG *The workers have little pollen baskets on their legs... ...a worker bee.* N COUNT

workforce /wɜːkfɔːs/, **workforces**. The **workforce** is 1 the total number of people in a country or region who are physically able to do a job and are available for work. EG *Asia's workforce will expand by 60 per cent.* N COUNT+SUPP: USU SING 2 the total number of people who are employed by a particular company. EG *We are now able to work a much larger area with a smaller workforce... They had since 1969 agreed to reduce the workforce by 3500.* N COUNT+SUPP: USU SING ⇑ group = staff

workhorse /wɜːkhɔːs/, **workhorses**. A **workhorse** is 1 a horse which is used to do a job, for example to pull a plough. EG *I milked the cows and led the workhorses to the watering trough.* N COUNT 2 a person who does a large amount of work, especially work which is dull or routine. EG *Jerry's always a willing workhorse.* N COUNT = slave

workhouse /wɜːkhaʊs/, **workhouses**. A **workhouse** was a place where, in the seventeenth to nineteenth centuries in Britain, very poor people who had no money and nowhere to live did very unpleasant jobs in return for food and shelter. EG *They tramped from workhouse to workhouse... The ultimate dread was the workhouse.* N COUNT

work-in, work-ins. A **work-in** is a form of protest in which workers in a factory or other business that is going to be closed down occupy the buildings and run the factory or business. N COUNT: USU SING

working /wɜːkɪŋ/, **workings**. 1 **Working** people 1.1 have jobs which they are paid to do. EG *...children with working mothers.* ADJ CLASSIF 1.2 have jobs in industry or agriculture which involve using physical strength rather than intellectual skills. EG *Is the Labour Party the great champion of the working man?... He has never found the right language for addressing working people.* ADJ CLASSIF: ATTRIB = working class

2 A **working** day or week is the number of hours that you work during a day or a week. EG *They are asking for a cut in the working week to an average of thirty hours... The unions will be demanding a reduction in working hours.* ADJ CLASSIF: ATTRIB

3 A **working** day is also a day on which people normally have to do their job. EG *It was an ordinary working day for them... People are now losing their jobs each and every working day.* ADJ CLASSIF: ATTRIB = workday

4 Your **working** life is the period of your life in which you have a job or are of a suitable age to have a job. EG *60 per cent of these people spend their entire working lives at General Motors... Over the next few years there will be more people of working age in our society.* ADJ CLASSIF: ATTRIB

5 The **working** population of an area is all the people in that area who have a job or who are of a suitable age to have a job. EG *She's a part of the working population of this country just the same as you.* ADJ CLASSIF: ATTRIB

6 **Working** conditions or practices are ones which you have in your job. EG *The organization is seeking to achieve better pay, training and working conditions for all women citizens... Changes in working patterns had to be examined.* ADJ CLASSIF: ATTRIB

7 **Working** clothes are designed for doing work in and so are not intended to be attractive. EG *I didn't bring anything down with me but working clothes.* ADJ CLASSIF: ATTRIB

8 A **working** relationship is a good relationship that you have with someone you work with. EG *All this is detrimental to peaceful working relations... ...a close working relationship.* ADJ CLASSIF: ATTRIB

9 A **working** farm or business is being managed in order to make a profit and not just for the owner's interest or pleasure. EG *The kitchen on any working farm is the centre of things.* ADJ CLASSIF: ATTRIB

10 The **working** parts of a machine are the parts which move and operate the machine, in contrast to the outer case or container in which they are enclosed. EG *Minute computers with minute working components are invaluable in this kind of work.* ADJ CLASSIF: ATTRIB ⇑ moving

11 A **working** model is one that has parts that actually move. ADJ CLASSIF: ATTRIB

12 If something is **in working order**, it is functioning properly and is not broken. PHR: USED AS AN A

13 If you have a **working** knowledge of something such as a foreign language, you do not know it very well but you know it well enough to be able to use it. EG *In the first week I picked up a tolerable working knowledge.* ADJ CLASSIF: ATTRIB

14 A **working** majority is not very large but is large enough to be useful. EG *...a precarious working majority of four.* ADJ CLASSIF: ATTRIB

15 A **working** theory or definition is one which you use as the basis for a particular job or piece of research, but which you are likely to change or improve. EG *This is a good general purpose working definition.* ADJ CLASSIF: ATTRIB

16 The **workings** of a piece of equipment, an organization, or a system are the ways in which it operates and the processes which are involved in it. EG *The general workings of a Wall Street bank are discussed in the programme... It's as incomprehensible to ordinary people as the workings of a breeder reactor.* N PLURAL+SUPP = mechanics

17 A **working** is a mine or quarry which has been dug in the ground in order to remove metals or stone. EG *The company has always been associated with iron workings... They now had a monopoly of the big workings.* N COUNT: USU PL ⇑ excavation

working capital is money which is available for use immediately, especially for business purposes, and not money which is invested in land or equipment and which becomes available only after the land or equipment has been sold. EG *Grants and loans had gone to finance the Company's working capital requirements.* N UNCOUNT

working class, working classes. The **working class** or **working classes** are the group of people in a society who do not own much property and who do jobs which involve using physical skills rather than intellectual skills. EG *...the urban working class... They were ordinary people drawn from working, managerial and professional classes.* N COUNT: *the*+N, SING=PL = proletariat ▸ used as an adjective, usually spelled with a hyphen. EG *The group cannot muster sufficient working-class support... Eleven members of a Cabinet of twenty were of working-class origins.* ▸ ADJ CLASSIF = proletarian

working group, working groups. A **working group** is the same as a working party. EG *He's head of the current Working Group on Terrorism.* N COUNT: IF SING, VB CAN BE SING OR PL ⇑ committee

working party, working parties. A **working party** is a committee which is established to investigate a particular situation or problem and to pro- N COUNT: IF SING, VB CAN BE SING OR PL duce a report containing its opinions and recommendations about what should be done. EG *...the 1957 working party on African land tenure... The working party's report was hardly controversial.*

workload /wɜːkləʊd/, **workloads**; also spelled with a hyphen and as two words. The **workload** of a particular person or machine is the amount of work which has to be done by that person or machine. EG *Often union positions entail a workload that is quite impossible to combine with doing a job... The critics will shut up once profits improve and their own workload increases.* — N COUNT+SUPP

workman /wɜːkmən/, **workmen**. A **workman** is a man whose job involves him doing work with his hands, for example building houses or plumbing. EG *On the very first day of school, workmen arrived and put up a fence.* — N COUNT ⇑ person

workmanlike /wɜːkmənlaɪk/. A piece of work that is **workmanlike** has been done well and skilfully. — ADJ QUALIT = efficient

workmanship /wɜːkmənʃɪp/ is the skill with which something is made and which affects the appearance of the finished object. EG *It was made of very cheap materials without any very beautiful workmanship... ...good materials and sound workmanship.* — N UNCOUNT : USU ADJ+N

workmate /wɜːkmeɪt/, **workmates**. A **workmate** is a friend who you do your job with; an informal word. EG *This happened in front of his friends, neighbours and workmates.* — N COUNT = chum, pal

work of art, works of art. A **work of art** is 1 a painting or piece of sculpture which is of high quality. EG *Whether buying stocks or works of art he adopted the same technique.* 2 something which is very complex or which has been skilfully made or produced. EG *His own papers were works of art on which he laboured with loving care.* — N COUNT = masterpiece; N COUNT

workout /wɜːkaʊt/, **workouts**; also spelled with a hyphen. A **workout** is a period of physical exercise or training. EG *He felt relaxed because of the light workout he had just done.* — N COUNT : USU SING

workpeople /wɜːkpiːpəl/ are people who are employed in a company or business and who have no responsibility for managing the company. EG *They are seeking to achieve the permanent and active involvement of workpeople in the organisations for which they work.* — N PLURAL = staff, workers

workshop /wɜːkʃɒp/, **workshops**. A **workshop** is 1 a room or building which contains tools or machinery for making or repairing things, especially using wood or metal. EG *A workshop was built on Babbage's estate, skilled workmen hired and construction got underway... ...a small engineering workshop.* 2 a period of discussion or practical work on a particular subject in which a group of people learn about the subject by sharing their knowledge or experience; also used to refer to the group of people. EG *I watched Franklin as he chaired a workshop on the subject of Black Politics and Economics... She runs a theatre workshop.* — N COUNT; N COUNT = study group

work-shy. If you say that someone is **work-shy**, you mean that they do not want to have a job or do not want to put any effort into their job. EG *What does the party have to gain by saying that the unemployed are work-shy?* — ADJ QUALIT : USU PRED = lazy

work surface, work surfaces. A **work surface** is the same as a worktop. — N COUNT

worktop /wɜːktɒp/, **worktops**; also spelled with a hyphen. A **worktop** is a flat surface on top of a fridge or low cupboard which is easily cleaned and on which you can prepare food. EG *The kitchen has a tiled floor and worktop units.* — N COUNT

work-to-rule. A **work-to-rule** is a way of protesting in your job, in which you follow all the established rules of the job but you do no extra work, with the result that you work more slowly and achieve a lot less. EG *The bus drivers were planning a work-to-rule.* — N SING WITH DET

world /wɜːld/, **worlds**. 1 The **world** is the planet that we live on. EG *He attempted to sail round the world... ...in many parts of the world... ...one of the most famous artists in the world.* ▸ also used to refer to the people who live on this planet. EG *The famine in Ethiopia has shocked the world.* ▸ used before a noun. EG *...the growth in world population... ...the World Snooker Championships... ...war on a world scale... ...world peace.* — N SING : *the*+N, OR N+SUPP = Earth; ▸ ⇑ everyone; ▸ N BEFORE N ⇑ international = global

2 The **world** also refers to all the societies, institutions, and ways of life of people living on this planet. EG *They are content for the world to stay as it is, poverty, pain, and everything... We are now moving forward into a world which will be more and more dominated by energy crises.* — N SING : *the*+N, OR N+SUPP

3 **World** is used to describe someone or something that is one of the best or most important of its kind in the world. EG *She became a world figure... He argued that Britain was still a world power... ...one of the few English books that's an absolute world classic.* — N BEFORE N ⇑ major

4 You can refer to a particular group of countries or a particular period in history as the Western **World**, the Arab **World**, the Ancient **World**, etc. ● See also **Third World**. — N COUNT : *the*+MOD+N

5 Someone's **world** is the life they lead, the people they have contact with, and the things they experience, especially considered as separate from other people's lives. EG *They were letting me into their world... Look, Howard, we're in different worlds now, you and I... He was big enough to be a link with the adult world.* — N COUNT+SUPP

6 The **world** is also 6.1 places, events, and ways of life that someone who has experienced only a limited range of things has had little contact with. EG *They don't want to go out into the outside world and fend for themselves... ...the world beyond the village.* — N SING WITH DET

6.2 the way of life that most people have. EG *She decided to give up the world and enter a convent.* — N SING : *the*+N

7 A particular **world** is 7.1 a particular field of activity, and the people involved in it. EG *They are well-known names in the film world... We have a high reputation in the world of science for the quality of our research work.* 7.2 a particular place or way of life, in which something that you mention is so great a part of it or so strong a characteristic of it that you notice hardly anything else. EG *I found myself entering a world of hypothesis and speculation... ...a semi-magical world of rich colours and patterns.* — N COUNT+SUPP : USU *the*+SING = circles; N COUNT+SUPP = realm, sphere

8 You can refer to the state of being alive as this **world** and to a state of existence after death as the next **world**, the **world** to come, etc. EG *He is heading for the next world, the way he drinks.* — N SING WITH DET : USU+SUPP ⇑ plane

9 You can refer to a particular group of living things as the animal **world**, the plant **world**, the insect **world**, etc. — N COUNT+SUPP : USU *the*+SING ⇑ class = kingdom

10 A **world** is another planet or a moon, and anything living on it. EG *Two small spacecraft find a bizarre world.* — N COUNT

11 If you say that someone **is all the world to** you or **means the world to** you, you mean that they are dearer and more important to you than anyone else. EG *You may not think much of him but he's all the world to Mary.* — PHR : VB INFLECTS

12 If you say that someone has or wants **the best of both worlds**, you mean that they have or want all the benefits from two different situations, without the disadvantages. — PHR : USED AS O

13 If a woman or a doctor **brings** a child **into the world**, the woman gives birth to it or the doctor delivers it; a formal, literary expression. — PHR : VB INFLECTS = have

14 When a child **comes into the world**, it is born; a formal, literary expression. — PHR : VB INFLECTS

15 If you say that something **has done** or **will do** someone **the world of good**, you mean that it has made them or will make them feel much better; a fairly informal expression. EG *A bit of fresh air will do you the world of good.* — PHR : VB INFLECTS

16 If you say that someone does something **for all the world as if** a particular thing was the case, you mean that they do it exactly as if that thing was the case, and you find this surprising; a fairly informal expression. EG *She took out a paperback and began to read, for all the world as if she was at home in bed.* — CONJ SUBORD

17 If you say that someone **wouldn't** do a particular thing **for the world**, you mean that they definitely do not want to do it and would not change their mind under any circumstances; a fairly informal expression. EG *I wouldn't change it for the world.* — PHR ⇑ never

18 If you say that someone is or lives **in a world of their own**, you mean that they seem not to notice other people or the things going on around them. — PHR : USED AS AN A ⇑ apart

19 You use **in the world** 19.1 to emphasize a statement that you are making. EG *Nothing in the world can save him now... She didn't have a care in the world... To them housework was the most important activity in the world.* 19.2 after words such as 'what', — PHR : USED AS AN A = on earth; PHR : USED AS AN

'where', and 'who' to emphasize a question or exclamation, especially when expressing surprise, anger, or despair. EG *What in the world are you doing all the way up here?... Who in the world can afford that kind of treatment?* **19.3** in expressions such as 'all the time in the world' and 'all the apologies in the world' to emphasize or exaggerate what you are saying. EG *We've got all the time in the world... All the motions in the world will not bring about equality for women.* A, WH+PHR = the hell; PHR : USED AS AN A

20 If someone **has gone** or **come up in the world**, they are much richer than they used to be and have a higher social status. If someone **has gone** or **come down in the world**, they are much less rich than they used to be and have a lower social status. PHR : VB INFLECTS

21 If you say that someone is **a man of the world** or **a woman of the world**, you mean that they know about the things that people do, including immoral or dishonest things, and are not easily shocked. PHR : USED AS C

22 You can refer to people of a particular type as **the** Kurts **of this world, the** Marlowes **of this world**, etc when making a general statement about the person whose name you mention. EG *The Kurts of this world would always win.* PHR : USED AS S/O

23 If you feel **on top of the world**, you feel extremely happy; an informal expression. PHR : USED AS AN A

24 If you say that something is **out of this world**, you mean that it is extremely good or impressive; an informal expression. EG *The view from the top is out of this world... His cooking is out of this world.* PHR : USED AS AN A ⇑ wonderful

25 If someone **sets the world on fire**, they are very successful; an informal expression. EG *Let's face it, he'll never set the world on fire.* PHR : VB INFLECTS ⇑ succeed

26 If you **think the world of** someone or something, you like them, and admire them or care about them very much. PHR : VB INFLECTS

27 If you say that two people or things are **worlds apart**, you mean that they are very different from each other. EG *They're good friends, but they're worlds apart politically.* PHR : USED AS C

28 If you say that **there is a world of difference** between one thing and another, you mean that they are very different from each other. EG *There's a world of difference between the English civil servant and the continental.* PHR

29 **The world over** means everywhere, throughout the world. EG *Journalists the world over speculated on the assassination attempt... The bourgeoisie are the same the world over.* ● **dead to the world**: see **dead.** ● **the world is your oyster**: see **oyster**. PHR : USED AS AN A

world-class. Someone, especially a sports player, who is **world-class** is one of the best in the world at what they do. EG *...a world-class cricketer.* ADJ CLASSIF : USU ATTRIB

world-famous. Someone or something that is **world-famous** is known about by people all over the world. EG *...a world-famous physicist.* ADJ CLASSIF ⇑ famous

worldly /wɜ:ldli¹/. **1 Worldly** is used to describe **1.1** things relating to this life and ordinary activities, rather than to spiritual or eternal things. EG *Their worldly business occupies them to the exclusion of all else... Coleridge had experienced a conversion and put aside worldly things.* **1.2** things relating to success, wealth, and possessions. EG *I certainly could not call Barney a failure in worldly terms.* ADJ CLASSIF : USU ATTRIB = earthly; ADJ CLASSIF : ATTRIB ⇑ material

2 You can refer to someone's possessions as their **worldly** goods, possessions, etc, especially when referring to everything they possess; a formal or literary use. EG *He made a will leaving all his worldly goods to his daughter.* ADJ CLASSIF : ATTRIB

3 Someone who is **worldly** is experienced, practical, and knowledgeable about life, and practical rather than very moral. EG *She was surprised at their outspokenness, their educated, even worldly manner.* ◇ **worldliness.** EG *He has acquired a worldliness that his juniors cannot muster.* ADJ QUALIT = sophisticated; ◇ N UNCOUNT

worldly-wise; also spelled without a hyphen. Someone who is **worldly-wise** is experienced and knowledgeable about life, and is not often shocked or impressed by anything. EG *He had a friend called Clive who was younger but far more worldly-wise.* ADJ QUALIT = sophisticated

world war, world wars. A **world war** is a war that involves countries all over the world. EG *...men who risked their lives in two world wars for their king and country... ...during World War II... ...the First World War.* N COUNT/ UNCOUNT : ALSO IN NAMES

world-weary. A **world-weary** person no longer feels excited or enthusiastic about anything. ADJ QUALIT = jaded

worldwide /wɜ:ldwaɪd/; also spelled with a hyphen. **Worldwide** is used to describe something that exists or happens throughout the world. EG *...in 1930, during the world-wide economic depression.* ▸ used as an adverb. EG *This move made headlines worldwide last year.* ADJ CLASSIF : USU ATTRIB ⇑ universal; ▸ ADV WITH VB ⇑ everywhere

worm /wɜ:m/, **worms, worming, wormed. 1** A **worm** is **1.1** a small animal with a long thin body, no bones, and no legs, which lives in the soil. EG *The lawns were crawling with worms... ...eating insects, worms, frogs.* **1.2** an insect such as a beetle or moth when it is at a very early stage of its life and looks like a very small worm. These worms often cause damage by eating things. EG *The carpet would be full of worms... All the apples had worms in them.* N COUNT; N COUNT ⇑ larva = grub, maggot

2 If animals or people have **worms**, they are ill because they have worms living as parasites in their intestines. These worms enter their body for example when they eat food that is not clean, and often cause disease. EG *He wiggled about like a dog with worms.* N PLURAL ⇑ illness

3 If you **worm** an animal, usually a cat or dog, you give it medicine in order to kill the worms that are living in its intestines. EG *Consult the vet about worming your puppy.* V+O ⇑ treat

4 If you refer to someone or something as the **worm in the bud** or the **worm in the apple**, you mean that they are spoiling a good situation and gradually destroying it; a literary expression. EG *Inequality is the worm in the bud of love... Try to see the best in everything and to ignore the worm in the apple.* PHR : USED AS S/O/C

5 If you talk about the **worm** of an unpleasant or worrying feeling, you mean that the feeling starts in a mild and unimportant way, but is likely to become stronger and not go away. EG *Rod felt a worm of unease... This brings with it the worm of envy.* N SING WITH DET +*of*

6 If you call a person a **worm**, you mean that they have a very weak or nasty character and that you have no respect for them. EG *You're no worm, you're a man; so get up, lad, and fight... The worm! Maybe he thought he was doing me a favour.* N SING WITH DET, ALSO VOC = louse, weed

7 If you say that **the worm will turn**, you mean that even someone who is usually quiet and obedient will become forceful in an extreme situation. PHR : VB INFLECTS

8 worm your **way. 8.1** If you **worm** your **way** somewhere, you move there slowly and carefully or with difficulty, usually because of danger or obstacles. EG *He wormed his way forward... Sheila wormed her way back through the crowd.* **8.2** If you **worm** your **way** into the confidence or affection of someone, you gradually make them trust you or like you, often in order to deceive them or gain some advantage; used showing disapproval. EG *It hadn't occurred to him that Kathy might worm her way so deep into his life... These aliens could worm their way into French society.* PHR : VB INFLECTS+A; PHR : VB INFLECTS+A

worm out. If you **worm** information **out** of someone, you gradually find it out from them when they were trying to keep it secret, often by tricking them or by constantly asking them about it. EG *He might worm the story out of her by emotional pressure... The truth had been wormed out of him by his lawyers.* PHRASAL VB : V+O+ADV, USU+*of* ⇑ learn = coax

worm cast, worm casts. A **worm cast** is a small coil of earth or sand produced by a worm and left on the surface of the ground. EG *...evidence of worm casts on the mud.* N COUNT

worm-eaten. Something that is **worm-eaten** has been damaged by insects such as beetles or moths which have made holes in it during a very early stage of their life. EG *...an old, worm-eaten piece of furniture.* ADJ QUALIT ⇑ rotten

wormwood /wɜ:mwʊd/. **1 Wormwood** is a plant that has a very bitter taste and is used in making medicines and alcoholic drinks. N UNCOUNT

2 Wormwood is used to refer to an experience which causes extreme bitterness, resentment, or regret. EG *The performances at the National must be wormwood to disappointed members... All his posturing before his friends was wormwood now.* N UNCOUNT

wormy /wɜ:mi¹/, **wormier, wormiest**. Something that is **wormy** is covered with worms or full of worms, for example because of neglect or decay. EG *...the wormy floor of the shack... It's a big apple, but probably wormy.* ADJ QUALIT

worn /wɔ:n/. **1 Worn** is the past participle of **wear**.

2 Something that is **worn** is damaged or thin because ADJ QUALIT it is old and has been used a great deal. EG *...the worn carpet beneath the rug... ...leather shoes, extremely worn... ...worn engine bearings.*

3 Someone who is **worn** looks old and tired, for example because of hard work, illness, or a difficult or unpleasant experience. EG *He lay on his bed, looking pinched and worn... ...the worn face of Viv.* — ADJ QUALIT

worn-out. 1 Something that is **worn-out** is so old, damaged, or thin from use that it cannot be used any more. EG *...a worn-out sofa... ...to replace worn-out diesel trains.* — ADJ CLASSIF

2 Someone who is **worn-out** is extremely tired after hard work or a difficult or unpleasant experience. EG *She was as worn-out as the horse... You look worn-out.* — ADJ QUALIT : USU PRED = exhausted

worried /wʌrɪd/. 1 Someone who is **worried** is unhappy because they keep thinking about problems that they have or about unpleasant things that might happen in the future. EG *People are becoming increasingly worried about pollution... I was worried that she'd say no... ...a worried frown.* ◇ **worriedly**. EG *'I wonder what to do?' she said worriedly.* — ADJ QUALIT ⇑ fearful = anxious; ◇ ADV WITH VB = anxiously

2 If you say that someone **had** you **worried**, you mean that they made you feel confused or anxious, often because you misunderstood what they were saying or because they were teasing you; an informal expression. EG *Oh good, you had me worried for a moment.* — PHR : VB INFLECTS

3 If someone says they are **not worried**, they mean that they have no strong feelings about a choice or a situation and will not be upset whatever they receive or whatever happens; an informal expression. EG *'Do you want it now or later?'-'I'm not worried-either.'* — PHR : USED AS C

worrier /wʌrɪə/, **worriers**. Someone who is a **worrier** spends a lot of time thinking about problems that they have or unpleasant things that might happen. EG *Your mother's a worrier... He was a worrier by nature.* — N COUNT

worrisome /wʌrɪsəm/. Something that is **worrisome** makes people worry; an old-fashioned word. EG *Mrs Ford's health had been worrisome... The destruction of your radio is a serious and worrisome affair.* — ADJ QUALIT = worrying

worry /wʌri[1]/, **worries, worrying, worried**. 1 If you **worry**, you keep thinking about problems that you have or about unpleasant things that might happen. EG *Don't worry, Andrew, you can do it... I worried that when I got back he wouldn't be there... People worry about the safety of nuclear energy... 'I'm fine,' he said. 'Don't worry about me.'* — V, V+O (REFL), OR V+REPORT-CL/A *(about)* = be anxious, fret

2 If someone or something **worries** you, **2.1** they cause you to worry. EG *Terry was worried by the challenge... I'm sorry if I worried you... It worried him to think that Sylvie was alone... ...a speech which worried many people.* — V+O ⇑ alarm = bother **2.2** they annoy you. EG *His bossiness didn't worry her unduly... Would it worry you if I turned the TV on?* — V+O ⇑ upset = bother

3 If you **worry** someone with a problem, you tell them about it in order to get their help or advice, sometimes causing them trouble or irritation by doing so. EG *Why worry her when it's all over?... Why should she come worrying Mrs Oliver here?* — V+O ⇑ disturb = bother

4 If a dog **worries** sheep or other farm animals, it frightens them and sometimes harms them by chasing them, barking at them, and trying to bite them. — V+O

5 **Worry** is the state or feeling of anxiety and unhappiness caused by the problems that you have or by thinking about unpleasant things that might happen. EG *She would be free from all financial worry... Bad housing is their main source of worry... Meditation may help to reduce stress, worry and nervous tension.* — N UNCOUNT

6 A **worry** is a problem that you keep thinking about and that makes you unhappy. EG *The cost of fuel is a major worry for old people... My only worry was that my aunt would be upset... I don't have any worries... ...if you have any worries concerning the safety of your gas supply.* — N COUNT = concern

7 If you say that something is a particular person's **worry**, you mean that it is part of that person's job or what that person has agreed to do. EG *The tutor's worry is to continue to make the course enjoyable... Let that be my worry.* — N UNCOUNT : POSS +N ⇑ responsibility = problem

8 If you tell someone that there is **nothing to worry about** or that something is **nothing to worry about**, you are trying to reassure them that a situation or problem is not serious. — PHR : USED AS C

9 If you say that someone **has enough to worry about**, you mean that they already have problems and should not be asked or expected to deal with any more. EG *He's got quite enough to worry about without that.* — PHR : VB INFLECTS

10 You say **'Not to worry'** to someone to indicate that you are not upset or angry when something has gone wrong; an informal expression. EG *Not to worry. We'll find something.* — CONVENTION

worry at. 1 If you **worry at** a problem, you think about it carefully and continually because you want to find a way of solving it. — PHRASAL VB : V+ PREP

2 When a dog or other animal **worries at** something such as a bone, they continually bite it, move it about, and shake it. — PHRASAL VB : V+ PREP ⇑ gnaw

worrying /wʌri[1]ɪŋ/. Something that is **worrying** causes you a lot of worry. EG *...a very worrying situation... He's had a worrying time at the office.* — ADJ QUALIT ⇑ upsetting

worse /wɜːs/. **Worse** is the comparative of **bad** and **badly**. 1 If something is **worse**, it is **1.1** more unpleasant, harmful, or difficult than it was before or than something else. EG *I have even worse news for you... His bag was heavy, and what was worse, one of his heels had got blistered... If things get any worse you'll just have to come home... Far from helping, he made things worse... Which punishment did she consider the worse?... Worse was to come.* — ADJ QUALIT : COMPAR ≠ better **1.2** more severe and serious than before. EG *The noise is getting worse... Sam's desperation grew worse and worse as they approached the church door.* — ADJ QUALIT : COMPAR ≠ better ▸ used as an adverb. EG *His feet bled worse but he walked faster.* — ▸ ADV COMPAR : WITH VB **1.3** of a lower standard or quality, or less successful than before or than others. EG *Her marks are getting worse and worse... The worse Dudley's game got the more his stomach ached.* — ADJ QUALIT : COMPAR ≠ better ▸ used as an adverb. EG *Some people ski worse than others.* — ▸ ADV COMPAR : WITH VB

2 If someone who is ill gets **worse**, they get more ill than before. EG *You'll get worse instead of better unless you get back into bed.* — ADJ QUALIT : COMPAR ≠ better

3 If someone or something is **none the worse** for something, they have not been harmed or made less acceptable by it. EG *The children had been on their own for a week but they were none the worse for it... We do have harsh conditions, I know, but we're none the worse for that.* — PHR+NG : USED AS C

4 If you say that someone **might do worse than** something, you mean that you think it is a good idea for them to do it. EG *The rest of you might do worse than read a few books on the subject.* — PHR

5 If something happens **for the worse**, the situation becomes more unpleasant or difficult as a result of it. EG *There were constant changes, usually for the worse.* — PHR : USED AS AN A

6 The word **worse** is also used in the following expressions, which are explained at other places in this dictionary. • to **go from bad to worse**: see **bad**. • someone's **bark is worse than** their **bite**: see **bark**. • **for better or worse**: see **better**. • **worse luck**: see **luck**. • to **make matters worse**: see **matter**. • **the worse for wear**: see **wear**.

worsen /wɜːsən/, **worsens, worsening, worsened**. If a situation **worsens** or if someone or something **worsens** it, it becomes more difficult, unpleasant, unacceptable, or severe. EG *Economic sanctions would only worsen the situation... The weather steadily worsened... ...Ray's worsening pain.* ◇ **worsening**. EG *...a continued worsening of raw material prices.* — V-ERG ⇑ change ≠ improve; ◇ N UNCOUNT

worse off. 1 Someone who is **worse off** has less money than before or than someone else. EG *This budget would leave taxpayers far worse off... He'd be two pounds a week worse off.* — ADJ QUALIT : COMPAR, PRED = poorer

2 Someone or something that is **worse off** is in a more unfavourable or unpleasant situation than before or than someone else. EG *You believe the world to be worse off because of Kennedy's death.* — ADJ QUALIT : COMPAR, PRED = poorer

worship /wɜːʃɪp/, **worships, worshipping, worshipped**; also spelled **worshiping, worshiped** in American English. 1 **Worship** is **1.1** the feeling of respect, admiration, and love for God or a god, or the demonstration of this feeling, for example by praying, singing hymns, etc. EG *...an act of worship... ...places of worship... ...the basic right of freedom of worship.* — N UNCOUNT **1.2** strong feelings of love or admiration for someone or something, often making you unable to see faults or weaknesses in them. EG *She became an* — N UNCOUNT = veneration *object of worship... ...the worship of the strong and the spectacular.*

2 You use **Worship** when referring to or addressing a magistrate or mayor in a formal situation; used mainly in British English. EG *...His Worship the Mayor... But, Your Worships, suppose clouds cover the stars?* N IN TITLES, ALSO VOC : DETPOSS+N

3 If you **worship** God, you show respect, admiration, and love for Him, for example by praying, singing hymns, etc. EG *I knelt down and worshipped the Lord... ...the church where Harry had worshipped for years.* V OR V+O

4 If you **worship** someone or something, you love them or admire them very much, often with the result that you cannot see faults or weaknesses in them. EG *Vita worshipped her father... ...a society that worships television and motor cars.* V+O = adore, venerate

worshipful /wɜːʃɪpfʊl/ means feeling or showing respect, admiration, or love. EG *Worshipful regard was a duty owed by the living to the dead.* ADJ CLASSIF : ATTRIB ⇑ respectful

worshipper /wɜːʃɪpə/, **worshippers**; also spelled **worshiper** in American English. **1** A **worshipper** is someone who believes in and worships God or a god. EG *Is she a regular worshipper?... ...shoes left there by worshippers who had gone into the mosque.* N COUNT

2 If you are a **worshipper** of someone or something, you love or admire them very much and are often unable to see faults or weaknesses in them. EG *...a worshipper of the past... ...worshippers of the dollar.* N COUNT+SUPP

worst /wɜːst/, **worsts, worsting, worsted.** **Worst** is the superlative of **bad** and **badly** in paragraphs 1 to 3. **1** The **worst** event, situation, or aspect of a situation is the most unpleasant, harmful, or difficult one. EG *...the worst thing which ever happened to me... The worst is over... He's been out looking for work all day, but I fear the worst... Worst of all, the barmen were threatening to strike.* ADJ QUALIT : SUPERL ≠ best

2 The **worst** person, thing, or area in an unpleasant situation is the one that is most severely or seriously affected by it. EG *The old are the worst victims of inflation... The situation is at its worst in urban centres.* ▸ used as an adverb. EG *...the worst affected areas... This University was the worst hit by Government spending cuts.* ADJ QUALIT : SUPERL ▸ ADV SUPERL : WITH VB

3 The **worst** person or thing when you are comparing standards, quality, or success is the one that is of the lowest standard or quality, or is the least successful. EG *Am I the worst cricketer ever to play in first class cricket?... In the 1870's the farms were at their worst.* ADJ QUALIT : SUPERL = poorest

4 If you say that something is true or possible **at worst** or **at the worst**, you mean that it is true or possible when you consider a situation in the most unfavourable or most pessimistic way. EG *At best her ideas are misguided and at worst they reveal a refusal to confront reality... At the worst, they can only say no.* PHR : USED AS AN A

5 If you say that an action may be done **if the worst comes to the worst**, you mean that it may be done if the situation develops in the most unfavourable way. EG *The situation may improve but if the worst comes to the worst I'll have to sell the house... If the worst came to the worst, a vessel could always take another route.* PHR : USED AS ADV SEN, VB INFLECTS

6 If you **worst** someone in a fight or competition, you defeat them; a very old-fashioned use. EG *Nelly had worsted her persecutor with a blow to the stomach.* V+O

worsted /wʊstɪ²d/ is a kind of woollen cloth which is used to make jackets, trousers, and skirts. EG *...a beret of green worsted... ...his favourite dark blue worsted suit.* N UNCOUNT ⇑ fabric

worth /wɜːθ/. **1** If something is **worth** a particular amount of money, it can be sold for that amount or is considered to have that value in terms of money. EG *...a two-bedroom house worth 50,000 pounds... ...sales of aircraft worth 200m pounds a year... The new penny would be worth 2.4 old pennies... It was worth eight times as much now.* PREP : USU+ NUM/QUANTIF+ N

2 If you talk about a particular amount of money's **worth** of something, you mean the quantity of it that you can buy for that amount of money or that is equal in value to that amount. EG *...fifty thousand dollars' worth of equipment... There was about $400 worth of damage.* N UNCOUNT : USU NUM/POSS+N+*of*

3 If you talk about an hour's **worth** of work, a week's **worth** of food, etc, you mean an amount of work that usually takes an hour to do, an amount of food that is usually enough for a week, etc. EG *...selling a week's worth of stock in a single day.* N UNCOUNT : USU NUM/POSS+N+*of*

4 If you say that something is **worth** a particular activity, amount of effort, time, money, etc, you mean that anyone who does the activity, puts in the effort, spends the time or money, etc is likely to benefit or feel satisfied afterwards. EG *The building is well worth a visit... He felt it wasn't worth the effort... The risk is worth taking... To Mr Hazel it was worth every penny.* PREP

5 If you say that something is **worth** doing, you mean that it is enjoyable, beneficial, or useful. EG *This film's really worth seeing... It is worth pausing to consider his words... I doubt that it was worth working so hard.* PREP+-ING

6 If you say that someone or something is **worth it**, you mean that you are likely to benefit or feel satisfied with the effort, time or money that you have spent on them. EG *They're expensive, but they're worth it... I'm not coming. It's not worth it... She was worth it.* PHR : USED AS C

7 for all it is worth. **7.1** If someone does something **for all it is worth**, they do it as much as possible and for as long as they can get benefit from it. EG *They'll exploit it for all it's worth.* PHR : USED AS AN A **7.2** If you add **for all it is worth** or **for what it's worth** to a statement, you mean that you do not really think that something you are talking about will have any useful results. EG *You may ask her, for all it's worth, if it's true or not... I've brought my notes, for what it's worth.* PHR : USED AS AN A

8 If an action or activity is **worth** someone's **while**, it will be of benefit to them if they do it. EG *It will be well worth your while to track down these treasures.* PHR : USED AS C, USU+*to*-INF = worthwhile

9 If you say that you will **make it worth** someone's **while** if they do something for you, you mean that you will pay them well or reward them well in some other way for doing it. PHR : VB INFLECTS

10 A person's **worth** is the value, usefulness, or importance that they are considered to have, especially by other people in society; a formal or literary use. EG *I judge people by their worth... This job has robbed me of all worth... The elderly should enjoy the sense of worth which is their right.* ▸ used as an adjective. EG *No man can say what another man is worth.* N UNCOUNT ▸ ADJ CLASSIF : PRED

11 The word **worth** is also used in the following expressions, which are explained at other places in this dictionary. ● **the game is not worth the candle**: see **candle**. ● **worth** your **weight in gold**: see **gold**. ● **to make life worth living**: see **life**. ● to **get** your **money's worth**: see **money**. ● **not worth the paper it's written on**: see **paper**.

worthless /wɜːθlɪ²s/. **1** Something that is **worthless** is of no real value or use. EG *The goods are often worthless by the time they arrive... It's worthless desert in the south... This made the treaty worthless.* ADJ CLASSIF = useless

2 Someone who is **worthless** is considered to lack the qualities or skills that they should have. EG *They made you feel that you were a worthless human being... He was worthless as a painter... His brother is a worthless fool.* ◇ **worthlessness.** EG *...their feelings of worthlessness.* ADJ CLASSIF ◇ N UNCOUNT

worthwhile /wɜːθwaɪl/. If something is **worthwhile**, it is enjoyable, beneficial, or useful, and worth the time, money, or effort that is spent on it. EG *A visit to London will always be worthwhile... It would not prove worthwhile to instigate an attack... ...a really worthwhile qualification.* ADJ QUALIT

worthy /wɜːðiˡ/, **worthier, worthiest; worthies.** **1** If someone or something is **worthy** of something, they deserve it because they have the qualities or abilities required; used showing approval. EG *Their cause is worthy of our continued support... ...convincing us that they're worthy to do the job... He was a worthy winner of the Nobel Prize.* ◇ **worthily.** EG *The Navy lived up worthily to its high traditions.* ◇ **worthiness.** EG *...parents with too little confidence in their own worthiness.* ADJ QUALIT : IF+ PREP THEN *of* ◇ ADV ◇ N UNCOUNT

2 A **worthy** person or thing deserves people's respect or admiration; used showing approval, sometimes in a humorous way. EG *Tilly had really upset the worthy man... ...our worthy commanding officer.* ADJ QUALIT

3 A **worthy** is an important person; often used in a humorous way. EG *...a century ago, when those old Scottish worthies Morris and Park were playing... The local worthies were staring at him.* N COUNT

wot /wɒt/ is sometimes used in written English to represent a very informal way of saying 'what'. EG *Wot do you think?*

would /wə^{4}d/. **1** You use **would** when you are saying what someone said or thought was going to happen, or when you are referring to an event or situation that was in the future at the time that you are talking about. EG *I felt confident that everything would be all right... He had been aware that they would be checking up on him... He made me promise that I would never break the law... In a few hours it would be time for dinner, and he would get out... This was to be the last book I would ever sell.* MODAL

2 You use **would** when you are referring to the result or effect of a possible situation or a situation which you are considering as if it were possible. EG *If you can manage to help me I would be very grateful... A picnic wouldn't be any fun without you... Wouldn't it be simpler to chop it down?* MODAL

3 You use **would** or **would** not when you are referring to someone's willingness or unwillingness to do something. EG *After visiting a children's burns ward I wouldn't have an open bar electric fire in the house... Some men would do more for a dog than they would for a wife.* MODAL

4 If you say that a particular person or thing **would** not do something, you mean that the person refused to do it or that it was impossible for the thing to do it. EG *Though we were as rude as possible, she wouldn't go... He tried to fire Judy into joining his applause, but she wouldn't... He thought I was a freak because I wouldn't carry a weapon... It just wouldn't bolt on.* MODAL : WITH BROAD NEG

5 You use **would** to say that someone wants to do or have something or wants something to happen. EG *Posy said she'd love to stay... I would like to brush up my zoology... I wouldn't like to rule that out... I wouldn't mind one of these student bed sitters... They'd much sooner go to the pictures.* • **would rather**: see **rather**. MODAL

6 You use **would** in questions **6.1** when you are politely offering someone something or inviting someone to do something. EG *Would you like a drink?... Would you like to come and read Proust with me?* **6.2** when you are politely asking someone to do something. EG *Would you tell her that Adrian phoned?... Put the light on, Bryan, would you?* MODAL : USED AS WH; MODAL : USED AS WH = could, will

7 You use **would** when mentioning something that someone has done which does not surprise you because it seems typical of them, especially when you are criticizing them. You emphasize the word **would** when using it in this way. EG *'Of course you would say that,' says Miss Callendar... 'He's backed out of it.'–'He would.'* MODAL

8 You use **would** or sometimes **would have** when you are expressing your opinion about something or seeing if people agree with you, especially when you are not certain that what you are saying is correct. EG *I would think that possibly in our climate we might have a few problems... Comedy, I would submit, is just as true as tragedy... I wouldn't agree with you... I would have thought that his chief asset was his enthusiasm... You'd expect it to blow up, wouldn't you?... The strike, I think you'd agree, was not a normal industrial strike.* MODAL

9 You use **would** when you are saying something that you are assuming or guessing is true. EG *We had an intricate discussion on jazz, but you wouldn't remember that... That would be his third wife.* MODAL = will

10 You use **I would** when you are giving someone advice in an informal way. EG *I would have a word with him about it... I wouldn't worry too much, if I were you.* PHR : USED AS MODAL = I should

11 You use **you would** in negative sentences with verbs such as 'guess' and 'know' when you want to say that something is not obvious, especially something surprising. EG *You wouldn't guess that from the text... You'd never know she wasn't a native speaker.* PHR : USED AS MODAL, WITH BROAD NEG = could

12 If you say that someone or something **would** do something or **would** be in a particular state, you mean that they often used to do that thing or used to be in that state. EG *I used to meet her and she would say 'Can't stop. I must get home.'... She would often hear him grumbling to himself... Sometimes they'd wave at us.* MODAL

13 You use **would have** when you are saying what someone said or thought was going to have happened by a particular time in the future, or when you are referring to an event or situation that was going to have happened by a particular time in the future. EG *Like as not, Tuesday would be hot and she would have burnt half the coal up Monday night... She planned to do it on Friday. By then she would have finished her other work.* MODAL

14 You use **would have** when you are referring to the result or effect of something that might have happened, or to circumstances that might have existed in the past but in fact did not. EG *If the bosses had known that he voted Liberal years ago, he would have got the sack... The chances are he wouldn't have approved of my vice... Denial would have been useless... I would've remembered sooner or later.* MODAL

15 If you say that someone **would have** liked or preferred something, you mean that they wanted to do it or have it but they did not, often because it was not possible. EG *I would have liked a year more... I would've preferred to stay at home.* MODAL

16 When you say what someone **would have** expected or hoped to happen or be true, you are referring to what they in fact expected or hoped to happen or what it was reasonable to expect, especially when it did not happen or was not true. EG *There were more than one would have expected... He found less time than he would have hoped to follow up his private hobbies... I wouldn't have thought it possible.* MODAL

17 You use **would have** when you are mentioning something that you are assuming or guessing happened or was true. EG *They'd had a hundred the previous year. That would've been in '62... She wouldn't have noticed. She was too far away.* MODAL = will have

18 If you say **'would that** something were the case', you are saying that you wish it were the case; a formal expression. EG *They're not much better off now than they were two years ago. Would that they were.* PHR

would-be. You can describe someone who wants to do a particular thing, often as a career, as a **would-be** writer, a **would-be** MP, a **would-be** murderer, etc. EG *I met him first when I was a very young would-be writer... ...a would-be stowaway.* ADJ CLASSIF : ATTRIB

wouldn't /wʊdə^{0}nt/ is the usual spoken form of 'would not'.

would've /wʊdəv/ is a spoken form of 'would have', when 'have' is an auxiliary verb.

wound, wounds, wounding, wounded. The word **wound** is pronounced /wu:nd/ except when it is the past tense and past participle of the verb **wind**, when it is pronounced /waʊnd/. **1** A **wound** is damage to part of your body, especially a cut or a hole in your flesh, which is caused by a gun, knife, or other weapon. EG *The wound was healing, the doctor said... He died from his wounds nine days after the shooting.* N COUNT = injury

2 If someone **wounds** you, they damage your body using a gun, knife, or other weapon. EG *The gunmen opened fire, wounding many and killing one... He had been badly wounded in the fighting... He was wounded in the leg.* ◇ **wounded**. EG *...a truck full of wounded men.* ▸ The **wounded** are people who are wounded. EG *The living, the wounded, and the dead flew together in crowded helicopters... It would take hours for the Marines to get their wounded out.* V+O : USU PASS = injure; ◇ ADJ CLASSIF; ▸ N PLURAL : the +N = injured

3 A **wound** is also great unhappiness or damage to a person's mind which is caused by a very upsetting experience; a literary use. EG *She needed something to ease the wound of Mr Marvin's desertion... The war has left deep psychological wounds.* N COUNT = hurt

4 If you **are wounded** by what someone says or does, your feelings are deeply hurt. EG *She had been grievously wounded by his words.* ◇ **wounded**. EG *He felt wounded and betrayed.* ◇ **wounding**. EG *...wounding and false charges of disloyalty.* V+O : USU PASS = pain; ◇ ADJ QUALIT; ◇ ADJ QUALIT = hurtful

5 Something that **opens old wounds** reminds someone all about an upsetting experience in the past which they would prefer to forget; a literary expression. EG *The trial was a painful experience–the opening of old wounds.* • **to lick your wounds**: see **lick**. • **to rub salt in the wound**: see **salt**. PHR : VB INFLECTS

6 Wound is also the past tense and past participle of **wind**.

wound up /waʊnd ʌp/. If someone is **wound up**, they are very tense and nervous. ADJ QUALIT = uptight

wove /wəʊv/ is the past tense of **weave**.

woven /wəʊvə^{0}n/ is the past participle of **weave**.

wow /waʊ/. You say **'wow'** when you are very impressed by something or very pleased about something; an informal word. EG *'Wow,' said the woman. 'You sure mix a strong drink.'* — EXCLAM

WPC, WPCs. WPC is an abbreviation for 'woman police constable'; used especially as a title. EG *WPC Bird accompanied me.* — N COUNT: ALSO IN TITLES ⇑ policewoman

wpm is a written abbreviation for 'words per minute'; used after a number to indicate the speed at which a person can type or take shorthand. EG *A typing speed of 40 wpm is required for both posts.*

wrack /ræk/. See **rack**.

wraith /reɪθ/, **wraiths**. A **wraith** is a ghost; a literary word. EG *She moved through the soft light like a wraith.* — N COUNT ⇑ apparition = spectre

wrangle /ræŋgəl/, **wrangles, wrangling, wrangled**. If you **wrangle** with someone, you argue with them angrily for quite a long time, often about something unimportant or about small details. EG *They wrangled over whose turn it was to do the washing up.* ▸ used as a noun. EG *This debate is a dry, procedural wrangle.* ◊ **wrangling**. EG *There was a certain amount of wrangling before agreement was reached.* — V OR V+A (with): RECIP = squabble; ▸ N COUNT; ◊ N UNCOUNT = squabbling

wrap /ræp/, **wraps, wrapping, wrapped. 1** When you **wrap** something, you fold a piece of paper, cloth, plastic, etc tightly round it so that it is completely covered, for example in order to protect it or so that you can give it to someone as a present. EG *The book was wrapped in brown paper... The food must be wrapped so that all air is excluded.* — V+O: USU+A (in) ⇑ cover

2 When you **wrap** a piece of paper, cloth, etc round something, you put it round it. EG *They wrote the news on a piece of paper, wrapped it round a stone, and threw it into the next door garden... A handkerchief was wrapped around his left hand.* — V+O+A (round/around) ⇑ fold

3 Someone or something that **is wrapped** in cloth, paper, etc has a piece of cloth, paper, etc put round them or it. EG *We were all sleeping in ditches wrapped in our great coats... Hit it with your fist wrapped in a towel.* — V+O: USU PASS+ in

4 If a person or animal **wraps** their arms, fingers, legs, or tail round something, they put their arms, fingers, etc round that thing fairly tightly. EG *He wrapped his arms around me.* — V+O+A (round/around)

5 A **wrap** is a piece of clothing which you wear round your shoulders; a rather old-fashioned use. — N COUNT

6 If you **keep** something **under wraps**, you keep it secret. EG *She was very good at keeping her emotions under wraps.* — PHR: VB INFLECTS ⇑ conceal

7 When **the wraps come off**, something that has been kept secret is revealed. EG *When the war ended the security wraps came off.* — PHR: VB INFLECTS

8 See also **wrapping**.

wrap up. 1 When you **wrap** something **up**, you fold a piece of paper, cloth, plastic, etc tightly round it so that it is completely covered. EG *He had bought a teapot and was waiting for them to wrap it up... ...a little box wrapped up in white paper.* — PHRASAL VB: V+O+ADV = wrap, do up

2 Someone or something that **is wrapped up** in cloth, paper, etc, has a piece of cloth, paper, etc put round them or it. EG *Our mother sat in front wrapped up in a furry rug... Let me wrap you up before you go out in the cold.* — PHRASAL VB: V+O+ADV, USU PASS ⇑ envelop = wrap

3 If you **wrap up** or **wrap up** warmly or well, you put warm clothes on. EG *Wrap up well. It's pretty cold tonight.* — PHRASAL VB: V+ADV, OR V+O (REFL)+ADV

4 If you **wrap up** something such as a job or an agreement, you complete it, especially in a satisfactory way; an informal use. EG *The whole deal was wrapped up within a few days... That about wraps it up for this week.* — PHRASAL VB: V+O+ADV

5 If you **wrap up** what you are saying, you say it in an indirect or complicated way, or using a lot of unnecessary words. EG *He had learnt how to wrap up bad news.* — PHRASAL VB: V+O+ADV

6 If you tell someone to **wrap up**, you are telling them in a rather rude, informal way to stop talking. — PHRASAL VB: V+ADV, USU IMPER ⇑ be quiet

7 See also **wrapped up**.

wrap-around. A **wrap-around** skirt is one that you put on by tying it round your body rather than by stepping into it. — ADJ CLASSIF: ATTRIB

wrapped up. If someone is **wrapped up** in a particular person, thing, or activity, they spend most of their time thinking about the person or thing or doing the activity. EG *They are completely wrapped up in the baby... All his life he had been wrapped up in his work.* — ADJ QUALIT: PRED+in ⇑ involved = engrossed

wrapper /ræpə/, **wrappers**. A **wrapper** is a piece of paper, plastic, or foil which covers and protects something that you buy. EG *...the rustle of chocolate wrappers... The bottle was still in its tissue-paper wrapper.* — N COUNT ⇑ covering = wrapping

wrapping /ræpɪŋ/, **wrappings**. A **wrapping** is a piece of paper, plastic, etc which is used to cover and protect something. EG *He picked up the bottle and tore off its paper wrapping... Take the polythene wrappings off mattresses and pillows you are going to store away.* — N COUNT/UNCOUNT ⇑ covering

wrapping paper is special pretty paper which is used for wrapping presents. — N UNCOUNT

wrath /rɒθ/ means the same as anger; a formal or old-fashioned word. EG *I wanted someone to protect me from the wrath of Miss Templeman... The Liberals incurred his wrath for 'committing suicide'... ...the manifestations of God's wrath.* — N UNCOUNT ⇑ displeasure = ire

wreak /riːk/, **wreaks, wreaking, wreaked**; a fairly formal word. **1** Something or someone that **wreaks** havoc or damage causes a great amount of disorder or damage. EG *Traces of these chemicals can wreak havoc on sensitive crops... ...the terrible damage wreaked by heavy bombardment.* — V+O: USU+A

2 If you **wreak** revenge or vengeance on someone, you do something that will harm them very much, because you feel very angry about the harm that they have done to you. EG *He wanted to wreak revenge on his colleagues.* — V+O: USU+A

wreath /riːθ/, **wreaths**. A **wreath** is **1** an arrangement of flowers and leaves, usually in the shape of a circle, which is put onto a grave or by a statue as a sign of remembrance for the dead. EG *They all went to lay wreaths in front of the statue... ...a funeral wreath.* — N COUNT **2** a circle of leaves or flowers which someone wears round their head or neck. EG *He was dressed in a kilt and laurel wreath.* — N COUNT

wreathe /riːð/, **wreathes, wreathing, wreathed**; a literary word. **1** If something **is wreathed** in something else, especially mist or smoke, it is surrounded by it. EG *The dawn sky was pale, the sun was wreathed in mist... The woman was sitting wreathed in smoke... Smoke wreathed the Colonel's head like a halo.* — V+O: USU PASS+ in/with = shrouded

2 If something **is wreathed** in flowers or leaves, it has a circle or chain of flowers or leaves put round it. EG *...hats wreathed in artificial flowers... ...a cross wreathed with roses.* — V+O: USU PASS+ in/with ⇑ decorated

3 If you say that someone is **wreathed in smiles**, you mean that they are smiling a lot and look very happy. — PHR: USED AS C

wreck /rɛk/, **wrecks, wrecking, wrecked. 1** If someone or something **wrecks** something, **1.1** they break it or destroy it completely. EG *I wrecked a good stereo by not following the instructions properly... ...acres of wasteland, covered with wrecked cars and rubbish.* — V+O **1.2** they spoil it completely. EG *I'm sorry if I wrecked your weekend... He wrecked my only serious relationship.* — V+O = ruin

2 If a ship **is wrecked**, it is sunk or is damaged so much that it can no longer sail, for example when it hits rocks. EG *Many Spanish vessels were wrecked off the North American coast.* — V+O: USU PASS

3 A **wreck** is **3.1** a plane, car, or other vehicle which has been involved in an accident and has been very badly damaged. EG *All around were the wrecks of previous crashes.* — N COUNT **3.2** a ship which has sunk or been destroyed at sea. EG *The seabed where the wreck lies is level and rocky.* — N COUNT

4 If you say that someone is a **wreck**, you mean that they are very unhealthy or weak, or are unable to cope with life; an informal use. ● See also **nervous wreck**. — N COUNT: USU SING, USED AS C

wreckage /rɛkɪdʒ/. **1** You refer to what remains of a plane, car, building, etc that has been very badly damaged as **wreckage**. EG *Experts arrived to examine the wreckage of a cargo plane... They hauled Peter clear of the wreckage.* — N UNCOUNT ⇑ debris

2 You can refer to what remains after something such as a plan has failed or been spoilt completely as the **wreckage** of it. EG *He believed that it was now time to consider how much could be saved from the wreckage of Government policies... ...contemplating the wreckage of my attempted careers in law and politics.* — N SING: the+N, IF+PREP THEN of = remnants

wrecker /rekə/, **wreckers**. A **wrecker** is 1 someone who destroys or spoils something. EG *These people are the relationship wreckers and the misery producers.* 2 in American English, a truck which can remove broken down vehicles or vehicles that are stuck somewhere.
N COUNT : USU MOD+N ↑ destroyer; N COUNT ↑ vehicle = breakdown truck

wren /ren/, **wrens**. A **wren** is a very small brown bird. N COUNT

wrench /rentʃ/, **wrenches, wrenching, wrenched**. 1 If you **wrench** something away or into a particular position, you pull or twist it suddenly or violently, especially in order to move it from a fixed or firm position. EG *So I set about trying to wrench my button off... He tried desperately to wrench away the club... I wrenched the door open.* V+O+A ↑ release
▸ used as a noun. EG *With a wrench, Eileen gained possession of the crayon again.* ▸ N COUNT : USU SING

2 If someone who is held by a person or thing **wrenches** free or away, they move away from the person or thing with a great physical effort, especially by twisting the part of their body that is held. EG *Travers grabbed his arm. David wrenched free and went on furiously: 'You don't understand!'... She wrenched herself away from him.* V+A, OR V+O (REFL)+A

3 If you **wrench** your arm or leg, or one of your joints, you twist it and injure it. EG *She wrenched her arm badly.* V+O

4 If you **wrench** your eyes or mind away from something, you make a great effort to stop looking at it or thinking about it. EG *I tried to wrench my gaze away from the appalling sight... Finally he would wrench his mind away to something else.* V+O+A

5 A **wrench** is also a metal tool with parts which can be moved in order to fit round a nut so that the nut can be loosened or tightened. N COUNT = spanner

6 If you describe the experience of leaving someone or something as a **wrench**, you mean that the person who is leaving feels very sad about it. EG *It was a great wrench to leave the home where I had been so happy.* N SING : *a*+N

wrest /rest/, **wrests, wresting, wrested**; a formal or literary word. 1 If you **wrest** something away from someone who is holding it, you take it from them by pulling or twisting it violently. EG *He wrested the knife from her... He barely tasted the small piece he managed to wrest away for himself.* V+O+A = grab, snatch

2 If you **wrest** something from someone else, you take it from them with an effort or unlawfully. EG *...the near-impossibility of wresting the seat from the United Party... His nephew wrested away control of the company.* V+O+A = usurp

wrestle /resəºl/, **wrestles, wrestling, wrestled**. 1 If you **wrestle** with someone, you fight them by forcing them into painful positions or throwing them to the ground, rather than by hitting them. Some people wrestle as a sport. EG *He taught his little brother how to wrestle... John wrestled with the intruder... The men grabbed him again, wrestling him to the ground.* ● See also **wrestling**. V, V+A *(with)* OR V+O : RECIP, OR V = grapple, struggle

2 When you **wrestle** with a problem or a difficult situation, you try to deal with it or to work out how to deal with it. EG *For decades, mathematicians have wrestled with this problem... Viktor Kowalski was wrestling with the intricacies of international telephone enquiries.* V+A *(with)* ↑ organize = tussle

3 If you **are wrestling** with something large, heavy, or complicated, you are having difficulty holding it or controlling it. EG *She wondered if she should go and help the man wrestle with the map.* V+A *(with)* = struggle

wrestler /reslə/, **wrestlers**. A **wrestler** is someone who wrestles as a sport, usually for money. EG *He was built like a wrestler.* N COUNT ↑ fighter

wrestling /reslɪŋ/ is a sport in which two people wrestle and try to throw each other to the ground. EG *...a wrestling match.* N UNCOUNT ↑ fighting

wretch /retʃ/, **wretches**; a slightly old-fashioned word. You can refer to someone as a **wretch** 1 when you think that they are wicked. EG *...the terrible deed of the wretch who shot down the President.* 2 when you feel sorry for them because they are unhappy or unfortunate. EG *And the poor wretch put his head down on the table and groaned.*
N COUNT : ALSO VOC; N COUNT : ADJ+N, ALSO VOC

wretched /retʃɪ²d/. 1 You describe someone as **wretched** when you feel sorry for them because they are in an unpleasant situation or have suffered unpleasant experiences. EG *That wretched woman, what she went through God knows.* ◇ **wretchedly**. EG *A million others live wretchedly as refugees... ...wretchedly poor farm workers.* ◇ **wretchedness**. EG *...the poverty and wretchedness I saw around me.*
ADJ CLASSIF ↑ unfortunate = pitiable; ◇ ADV; ◇ N UNCOUNT ↑ misery

2 Someone who feels **wretched** feels very unhappy or ill. EG *She spent most of the day in her room lying down and feeling wretched... I was wretched afterwards, thinking what I'd done to you.* ◇ **wretchedly**. EG *He looked wretchedly ill... ...the toddler howling wretchedly for its mother.* ◇ **wretchedness**. EG *...a feeling of wretchedness.*
ADJ QUALIT : PRED = awful; ◇ ADV; ◇ N UNCOUNT

3 Something that is **wretched** is very bad or of very poor quality. EG *The dressing rooms were wretched... Her own poverty meant her child had a wretched diet.* ADJ QUALIT = atrocious

4 You use **wretched** to emphasize a noun when you feel angry or dislike the thing or person you are referring to; an informal use. EG *He insisted on telling his wretched story... I had to remount the wretched animal.* ADJ CLASSIF : ATTRIB ↑ unfavourable = stupid

wriggle /rɪgəºl/, **wriggles, wriggling, wriggled**. 1 When a person or animal **wriggles** or when they **wriggle** part of their body, they twist and turn their body with quick movements. EG *The children were wriggling in anticipation... She wriggled her toes... My father started wriggling about in his chair.* V OR V+O ↑ shift = wiggle
▸ used as a noun. EG *'Are we nearly there?' she said with an impatient wriggle.* ▸ N COUNT : USU SING

2 When a person or animal **wriggles** somewhere, especially through a small gap, or **wriggles** their way somewhere, they move there by twisting and turning their body. EG *We had to wriggle under the fence... When the tadpoles hatch, they immediately wriggle to the male and climb on his back.* V+A, OR V+O+A = crawl, slither

wriggle out of. If you **wriggle out of** doing something which you do not want to do, you manage to avoid doing it, although someone else wants or expects you to do it. EG *I can't manage to wriggle out of accompanying my parents to Europe.* PHRASAL VB : V+ADV+PREP = get out of

wring /rɪŋ/, **wrings, wringing, wrung**. 1 If you **wring** something you want such as money, information, or pleasure from a person, situation, or thing, you manage to get it from them or it with a lot of effort. EG *...trying to wring the utmost from the social occasion... To prosper, ranchers must wring more dollars out of their land.* V+O+A *(from/out of)* ↑ extract

2 When you **wring** a wet cloth or a wet piece of clothing or **wring it out**, you squeeze the water out of it by twisting it strongly. V+O, OR PHRASAL VB : V+O+ADV

3 When someone **wrings** their hands, they hold them together and twist and turn them, usually because they are very worried or upset about something. EG *He looked dazed and wrung his hands.* ▸ also used to say that someone is expressing sorrow in words. EG *We could have prevented losses over which we today can merely wring our hands.* V+O

4 If you **wring** someone's hand, you shake it while squeezing it tightly; a rather old-fashioned use. V+O

5 If someone **wrings** a bird's neck, they kill the bird by twisting its neck. ● If you say that you will **wring** someone's **neck** or that you would like to **wring** their **neck**, you mean that you are very angry with them. EG *Shut up or I'll wring your bloody neck... I'd gladly wring his neck.* V+O; ● PHR

6 If someone or something **wrings** your heart, soul, etc, they make you feel very sad or very sorry for them. EG *David was wringing my heart with his pitiful little efforts to help.* V+O

wringer /rɪŋə/. If you say that someone **is put through the wringer**, you mean that they are forced to undergo a very difficult, stressful experience; an informal expression. PHR : VB INFLECTS

wringing wet. If a person or something made of cloth is **wringing wet**, the person's clothing or the thing is extremely wet; a fairly informal expression. ADJ CLASSIF : USU PRED = drenched

wrinkle /rɪŋkəºl/, **wrinkles, wrinkling, wrinkled**. 1 A **wrinkle** is 1.1 a line in someone's skin, especially on their face, that forms as they grow old. EG *His small eyes were surrounded by many wrinkles.* 1.2 a raised fold in something such as a piece of cloth or thin paper, usually one made unintentionally. EG *She brushed out the wrinkles in her dress nervously... The prime minister's toe fidgeted with a wrinkle in the carpet.*
N COUNT : USU PL ↑ crease; N COUNT = crease

2 If something **wrinkles** or if someone or something **wrinkles** it, it gets folds or lines in it. EG *Make sure you clean the surface well otherwise the new paint* V-ERG ↑ crease

might wrinkle and peel... He's always telling me that the sun will wrinkle my skin.

3 When you **wrinkle** your nose, forehead, or eyes, you tighten the muscles in it or around it so that the skin folds into several lines. EG *He wrinkled his nose, as if detecting a foul smell... Jordache wrinkled his forehead, as though he was trying to remember something.*
V+O = crumple, screw up

wrinkled /rɪŋkəld/. 1 A person or a person's skin that is **wrinkled** has wrinkles as a result of old age. EG *...a very old woman with a wrinkled face.*
ADJ QUALIT

2 If something is **wrinkled**, it has raised folds or lines in it. EG *She looked over her shoulder to make sure her dress wasn't wrinkled at the back... The flowers have wrinkled brown petals.*
ADJ QUALIT

wrist /rɪst/, **wrists**. Your **wrist** is the part of your body between your hand and your arm which bends when you move your hand. EG *She grabbed her husband firmly by the wrist and dragged him away... Her body seemed shrunken and her wrists and ankles pitifully thin.*
N COUNT ⇑ joint

wristwatch /rɪstwɒtʃ/, **wristwatches**. A **wristwatch** is a watch with a strap or band which you wear round your wrist.
N COUNT ⇑ timepiece

writ /rɪt/, **writs**. 1 A **writ** is a legal document that orders a particular person to do a particular thing or not to do it, or that gives permission for something to happen at a stated time. EG *He reacted instead by issuing a writ for libel against the magazine.*
N COUNT

2 **writ large**; a formal expression. **2.1** If something is **writ large**, it is very obvious. EG *The effect of these fifteen years of irregular life could be seen writ large on his gaunt features.*
PHR : USED AS C

2.2 If one thing is another thing **writ large**, the first thing is a larger or exaggerated version of the second thing. EG *What we were getting was the old conservatism writ large.*
PHR : USED AS AN A

3 See also **Holy Writ**.

write /raɪt/, **writes, writing, wrote, written**.
1 When you **write** something on a surface, usually a piece of paper, you use something such as a pen or pencil to produce words, letters, or numbers on the surface. EG *I'm learning to read and write... Write the word 'torque' here... Write the appropriate letter on the label... There's something written here in French.*
V OR V+O ⇑ represent

2 When someone **writes** something such as a book, poem, article, essay, or piece of music, they create it and record it on paper or perhaps on a computer. EG *I have been asked to write a biography of Dylan Thomas... I decided to write a program for a microprocessor... He asked the girl to write him an essay... I have no particular qualifications to write about love... The story was quite well written.*
V+O, V+O+O, OR V+O+A *(for)* ⇑ produce

3 Someone who **writes** creates books, stories, or articles, usually for publication. EG *I always felt that I wanted to write... She was looking for a masculine name to write under... He writes on anthropology.*
V : NO CONT

4 When you **write** to someone or **write** them a letter, you give them information, ask them something, or express your feelings in a letter or note. EG *Why didn't you write and tell me?... She wrote me a letter from Singapore... She wrote asking him if he had ever loved her... I've written to thank them... The address to write to is in the Radio Times.*
V, V+A *(to)*, V+O+O, OR V+O+A *(to)* ⇑ communicate

▸ In American English, you can also **write** someone. EG *If there is anything you want, write me.* ● **nothing to write home about**: see **home**.
▸ V+O

5 If someone **writes** that something is the case, they say it in a letter, book, or article. EG *'All the research on learning,' writes Dr Lostock of Yale, 'seems to confirm this suggestion.'... He wrote that he was never depressed by anything.*
V+REPORT-CL/ QUOTE

6 When someone **writes** something such as a cheque, receipt, or prescription, they put the necessary information on it and usually sign it. EG *I wrote a cheque for £100... I'll write you a prescription.*
V+O, V+O+O, OR V+O+A *(for)* ⇑ complete

7 See also **writing, written**.

write away. If you **write away** to a company or organization, you send them a letter, usually asking them to send you one of their products or information about their products.
PHRASAL VB : V+ADV, USU+A = send off

write back. If you **write back** to someone or **write** them **back** a letter, you reply to a letter that they sent you. EG *He wrote back accepting our offer.*
PHRASAL VB : V+ADV, OR V+O+ADV+O ⇑ respond

write down. When you **write** something **down**, you record it on a piece of paper using a pen, pencil, etc. EG *The magistrate had to write all the evidence down in longhand... Write down any four digit number.*
PHRASAL VB : V+O+ADV

write in. 1 If you **write in** to an organization, you send them a letter. EG *Hundreds of people have written in asking for details.*
PHRASAL VB : V+ADV

2 If someone who is voting in an American election **writes in** a person whose name is not on the list of candidates, they write that person's name on the voting paper and vote for him or her.
PHRASAL VB : V+O+ADV

write into. If a particular rule or detail **is written into** a contract or agreement, it is included in it when the contract or agreement is made. EG *The new arrangements have been written into the agreement.*
PHRASAL VB : V+O+PREP, USU PASS

write off. 1 If you **write off** to a company or organization, you send them a letter, usually asking them to send you one of their products or information about their products. EG *I've written off for a set of special pens I saw advertised in the paper... He sat down and wrote off letters in answer to the advertisements.*
PHRASAL VB : V+ADV, OR V+O+ADV

2 If someone **writes off** a debt or an amount of money that has been spent on a project, they accept that they are never going to get the money back. EG *Unless the debts can be re-scheduled or written off, the world will soon face a financial crisis... He urged the government to write off the corporation's losses.*
PHRASAL VB : V+O+ADV ⇑ forget

3 If you **write off** a plan or project, you accept that it is not going to be successful and do not continue with it.
PHRASAL VB : V+O+ADV = ditch

4 If you **write** someone **off**, you decide that they are unimportant or useless and that they are not worth further serious attention. EG *Do not sound harassed, or you will be written off as a hysterical woman.*
PHRASAL VB : V+O+ADV ⇑ reject = dismiss

5 If someone **writes off** a vehicle, they have a crash in it and it is so badly damaged that it is not worth repairing.
PHRASAL VB : V+O+ADV

6 See also **write-off**.

write out. 1 When you **write out** something fairly long such as a report or a list, you write it on paper. EG *She wrote out her report and sent it off to be typed.*
PHRASAL VB : V+O+ADV

2 When someone **writes out** something such as a cheque, receipt, or prescription, they put the necessary information on it and usually sign it. EG *I went directly to my cabin to write out the death certificate.*
PHRASAL VB : V+O+ADV

3 If a character in a drama series on television or radio **is written out**, he or she is taken out of the series.
PHRASAL VB : V+O+ADV

write up. 1 When you **write up** something that has been done or said, you record it on paper in a neat and complete form, usually using notes that you have made. EG *These findings were then written up into a report... These are the notes that you are going to write up afterwards?*
PHRASAL VB : V+O+ADV

2 See also **write-up**.

write-off, write-offs. If a vehicle is a **write-off** after an accident, it is so badly damaged that it is not worth repairing.
N COUNT : USU SING, USED AS C

writer /raɪtə/, **writers**. 1 A **writer** is a person who writes books, stories, or articles as a job. EG *I did not yet take the idea of becoming a writer seriously... ...the writer and critic, Hilary Spurling.*
N COUNT = author

2 The **writer** of a particular article, report, story, etc is the person who wrote it. EG *What sources did the original writers have on which to base their account?*
N COUNT ⇑ author

writer's cramp is a feeling of uncomfortable stiffness in your hand which you can get as a result of writing continuously for a long time.
N UNCOUNT

write-up, write-ups. A **write-up** is an article in a newspaper or magazine, in which someone describes a play, a new product, a hotel, etc and says how good or bad they think it is. EG *Somebody told me you got a terrific write-up in the 'Guardian'.*
N COUNT

writhe /raɪð/, **writhes, writhing, writhed**. If you **writhe** or your body **writhes**, your body twists and turns violently backwards and forwards, usually because you are in great pain or discomfort. EG *His body writhed, his face contorted, his eyes rolled wildly... He writhed in agony.*
V

writing /raɪtɪŋ/, **writings**. 1 **Writing** is **1.1** something that has been written or printed. EG *Put the papers face down on each desk so that the writing cannot be seen... She saw that there was writing on the other side... You must get the offer in writing.*
N UNCOUNT

1.2
N UNCOUNT

a piece of written work, especially considered from the point of view of the style of language used and how well the ideas, emotions, etc are expressed. EG *The book contains some brilliant and very witty writing... Do you distinguish between serious writing and popular writing?* **1.3** the activity of writing, especially of writing books for money. EG *Writing has made me a millionaire... ...a course in novel writing.* N UNCOUNT

2 Your **writing** is the way that you write with a pen or pencil, which can usually be recognized as belonging to you. EG *...the small, neat, forward sloping writing that she knew so well... I can't read your writing.* N UNCOUNT : USU POSS+N = handwriting

3 Writings are all the things that a particular author has written, or pieces of writing by different people on a particular subject. EG *The idea crops up with increasing frequency in the writings of scientists and technologists... His political writings remind me of those of Sartre.* • **the writing on the wall**: see **wall**. N PLURAL : USU+SUPP = works

writing desk, writing desks; also spelled with a hyphen. A **writing desk** is a piece of furniture with drawers and an area for keeping paper, pens, ink, etc and a surface on which you can rest your paper while writing. N COUNT = bureau

writing materials are pens, pencils, ink, paper and other things which you use for writing. N PLURAL

writing paper, writing papers; also spelled with a hyphen. **Writing paper** is paper for writing letters on. It is usually of good, smooth quality. N MASS = notepaper

written /rɪtəᵊn/. **1 Written** is the past participle of **write**.

2 A **written** test, exam, piece of work, etc is one where the student has to write something, rather than do something or answer verbally. EG *There are two exams. One is practical and the other is written.* ADJ CLASSIF ≠ practical, oral

3 A **written** agreement, guarantee, rule, law, etc, is recorded or expressed in writing rather than verbally. EG *...countries that don't have a written Bill of Rights... I will send written confirmation.* ADJ CLASSIF : ATTRIB ≠ verbal

4 If a feeling is **written all over** your **face** or is **written on** your **face**, it is very obvious to other people from your expression. EG *He gazed at it with pleasure written all over his face... My worries must have been clearly written on my face, for he hastily assured me that everything was alright.* PHR : USED AS C ⇑ visible

written word. You use **the written word** to refer to language expressed in written form, considered especially from the point of view of the skill required to express your thoughts and ideas well in writing. EG *When nobler examples of the written word were not to hand he read comics... ...the power of the written word.* N SING : *the*+N

wrong /rɒŋ/, **wrongs, wronging, wronged**. **1** You use **wrong** in expressions like 'something is wrong' and 'what's wrong?' **1.1** when you are referring to a difficulty or problem that you have or that someone else has. EG *The front door was unlocked–something was wrong... I knew something was dreadfully wrong... I sat with her on the bus one day and asked what was wrong... 'What's wrong?' Castle asked... 'Is anything wrong?'–'Sam's got measles.'* **1.2** when something is not working properly or someone is ill or behaving badly. EG *What's wrong with the electrical system?... Something is wrong with this calculator... There was nothing wrong with his eyesight... You've got no sense of human dignity, that's what's wrong with you.* ADJ QUALIT : PRED = amiss, the matter / ADJ QUALIT : PRED, USU+*with* = the matter

2 If something such as a choice, action, or decision is the **wrong** one, it is not the one that was intended or the most appropriate one out of a number of possibilities. EG *I'm afraid I'll make the wrong decision... He could not afford to make the wrong choice... They have come to the wrong place... They are the wrong people for the job... He was deliberately driving on the wrong side of the road.* ADJ CLASSIF : ATTRIB ≠ correct, right

3 If something that you do or something that happens is **wrong**, it is not acceptable or suitable in the circumstances. EG *I think the timing was wrong... It seemed wrong to him that she should have to go out to work.* ▸ used as an adverb. EG *We have brought you up all wrong.* ◊ **wrongly**. EG *These children are likely to be wrongly placed in school.* ADJ QUALIT : PRED ≠ right / ▸ ADV AFTER VB / ◊ ADV WITH VB

4 Something that is **wrong** is not correct, because it is not in accordance with the facts. EG *The report in the papers was wrong... He had been given some wrong information... ...a clock which showed the wrong time.* ▸ used as an adverb. EG *Her name was spelt wrong... 'His name's Clough.'–'Oh, then I heard it wrong.'* ◊ **wrongly**. EG *She supposed, wrongly, that the other two agreed with her.* ADJ CLASSIF = incorrect ≠ correct, right / ▸ ADV AFTER VB / ◊ ADV WITH VB

5 If you are **wrong** about something, you are inaccurate or incorrect in your statements, judgement, or opinions. EG *If they are right, then I am wrong... We had to admit the possibility that we might be wrong... He has yet to be proved wrong.* ADJ CLASSIF : PRED ≠ right

6 If you are **wrong** to do something, it is considered bad or immoral in the circumstances. EG *You were wrong to speak to the newspapers first.* ADJ QUALIT : PRED+*to*-INF ≠ right

7 If something that you do is **wrong**, it is generally considered to be bad or immoral by most people in society. EG *She never did anything wrong... It's wrong for one group of people to take land from another.* ◊ **wrongly**. EG *...the number of people wrongly incarcerated in psychiatric institutions.* ADJ QUALIT ≠ right / ◊ ADV WITH VB

8 If you are **in the wrong**, you are behaving in a way that is not morally or legally justifiable. EG *I'm sorry, I realise I'm in the wrong... Mary's generous apology put Ralph in the wrong.* PHR : USED AS AN A ≠ in the right

9 You use **wrong** to describe something which is not thought to be socially acceptable or desirable. EG *They went to the wrong school... He had the wrong accent.* ◊ **wrongly**. EG *Her sense of being the wrong age, wrongly dressed, wrongly made-up, made her hostile.* ADJ CLASSIF : ATTRIB ≠ right / ◊ ADV WITH VB

10 The **wrong** side of a piece of cloth, knitting, etc, is the side which is intended to face inwards and not be seen. EG *The point of ironing on the wrong side is that ironing makes the materials shiny.* ADJ CLASSIF : ATTRIB ≠ right

11 If you **get** something **wrong**, you make a mistake about what someone has said or done, usually because you did not hear it or understand it properly. EG *I think she got his name wrong... Don't you see it was just in fun. You got it all wrong.* PHR : VB INFLECTS = misunderstand

12 You say **'Don't get me wrong'** when you want to make sure that someone does not misunderstand you. EG *Now don't get me wrong: we liked him.* PHR : USED AS ADV SEN

13 go wrong. **13.1** If you **go wrong**, you make a mistake in what you are doing. EG *Where did I go wrong? I'm sure I added it up right... You can see where you're going wrong.* **13.2** If something **goes wrong**, it stops progressing in the way that you expected or intended, and changes for the worse. EG *Their relationship went wrong after the birth of their child... Nothing much seems to go wrong with budgerigars... They took turns staying awake in case anything went wrong.* **13.3** If a machine or piece of equipment **goes wrong**, it stops working properly. EG *My clock keeps going wrong.* PHR : VB INFLECTS / PHR : VB INFLECTS / PHR : VB INFLECTS

14 Wrong is used to refer to standards or behaviour that are considered to be bad or immoral by most people in society. EG *Any good parent feels strongly about right and wrong... In my heart I know I did no wrong.* N UNCOUNT ≠ right

15 A **wrong** is an immoral or unjust action or situation, especially one which causes pain or distress to people. EG *In a democracy wrongs should be righted by the vote and not by violence... He remembered the wrong done to him many years previously by his brother.* • If you say **'two wrongs don't make a right'**, you mean that people shouldn't do harm to a person who has done harm to them, even if the person deserves it. N COUNT = injustice / • PHR

16 If you **are wronged** by someone, you are treated in an unfair or unjust way by them. EG *He was obsessed with hitting back at those who had wronged him... Many people experience real anxiety if they feel they've been wronged.* V+O : USU PASS ⇑ injure

17 If you **wrong** someone, you judge them unfairly, especially by saying or thinking unpleasant things about them. EG *I knew I had wronged her terribly when I accused her of being unfaithful.* V+O = malign

18 The word **wrong** is also used in the following expressions. **18.1** If you **have** or **get the wrong number**, you have not telephoned the person you meant to telephone, but someone else by mistake. EG *I think you've got the wrong number.* **18.2** If you say that someone is **the wrong side of** a particular age, you mean that they are older than that. EG *She must be on the wrong side of thirty-five.* **18.3** If you **say the wrong thing**, you say something which upsets or embarrasses someone. EG *I've said the wrong thing, haven't I?* • to **be barking up the wrong tree**: see **bark**. • to **start off on the wrong foot**: see **foot**. • to **get hold of the wrong end of the stick**: see **stick**. PHR : VB INFLECTS / PHR+NUM : USED AS C = over / PHR : VB INFLECTS

wrongdoer /rɒŋduːə/, **wrongdoers**. A **wrongdoer** is a person who does things that are immoral or illegal. N COUNT

wrongdoing /rɒŋduːɪŋ/, **wrongdoings**. **Wrongdoing** is behaviour that is illegal or immoral. EG *Maurice still felt the unease of wrongdoing... He was warned that he would be punished for his wrongdoings.* N UNCOUNT/ COUNT

wrong-foot, wrong-foots, wrong-footing, wrong-footed; also spelled without a hyphen. **1** If you **wrong-foot** your opponent in a sports game, you cause your opponent to be off-balance by playing your shot in an unexpected way. EG *He was wrong-footed by a beautiful passing backhand.* V+O ⇑ trick

2 If you **wrong-foot** someone, you surprise and upset them by putting them into an embarrassing situation, often by asking a question that they cannot answer. EG *I tried to wrong-foot them with another question.* V+O

wrongful /rɒŋfʊl/. A **wrongful** act is one that is thought to be illegal, immoral, or unjust. EG *He couldn't sue for wrongful arrest... ...the wrongful imprisonment of Napoleon.* ◇ **wrongfully**. EG *He had 1 million dollars in a safe in New York that he had wrongfully concealed there.* ADJ CLASSIF: ATTRIB ◇ ADV WITH VB

wrong-headed. Someone who is **wrong-headed** is constantly making wrong judgements, often in a very determined way. ADJ QUALIT = clear-headed

wrote /rəʊt/ is the past tense of **write**.

wrought /rɔːt/. **1** If something has **wrought** a change or a particular state, it has made it happen; a formal or literary use. EG *...the change that time has wrought... That moment had wrought a profound change in him... The disease wrought havoc on livestock.* V+O: ONLY PAST TENSE ⇑ work

2 Wrought metal has been made into a particular shape, often in a decorative way. EG *...wrought silver.* ADJ CLASSIF: ATTRIB

wrought iron; spelled with a hyphen when used before another noun. **Wrought iron** is a pure type of iron that is formed into decorative shapes and is used for making gates, railings, etc. EG *...a wrought-iron gate.* N UNCOUNT

wrung /rʌŋ/ is the past tense of **wring**.

wry /raɪ/. **1** A **wry** expression is **1.1** one which shows that you find a situation slightly amusing because you know more about it than other people or you can see how ironic it is. EG *He came out with a wry smile on his face... She said this with a wry glance at me.* ◇ **wryly**. EG *My friend smiled wryly when she saw my embarrassment.* **1.2** one which is rather strange or twisted, usually showing that you dislike something. EG *Over the beer she made a wry face and said 'Nasty!'* ADJ QUALIT: USU ATTRIB ◇ ADV WITH VB ADJ QUALIT: USU ATTRIB

2 Wry humour is humour in which you find a situation slightly amusing because you know more about it than other people, or you can see how ironic it is. EG *I felt a certain wry amusement at finding myself in Jenny's role now... ...a wry, bitter-sweet picture of the harsh realities of the human condition.* ◇ **wryly**. EG *My fellow editors began commenting wryly on his readiness to see me.* ADJ QUALIT ◇ ADV WITH VB

wt is a written abbreviation for 'weight'.

Xx Yy Zz

X, x /ɛks/, **Xs, x's**. **1 X** is the twenty-fourth letter of the English alphabet. N COUNT

2 X or **x** can be used to represent the name of a person or place when you do not know their real name, or when you are trying to keep their real name a secret. EG *I was born in x, a town somewhere in the south.* N UNCOUNT

3 If you say that there are **x** number of things, you mean there are a certain number, but that the exact number is not important to what you are saying. EG *...a house that will cost less than x number of pounds.*

4 In algebra, **x** is used as a symbol to represent a number whose value or quantity is not known. EG $y=x_2$

5 People sometimes write **X** on a map to mark a precise position that they want to refer to. EG *X marks the spot.*

6 x is used to represent a kiss at the end of a letter or written message. EG *Hope to see you soon, all my love, Jenny, xxx.*

7 X or **x** is the Roman numeral for 10.

X chromosome, X chromosomes; a technical term in biology. An **X chromosome** is one of an identical pair of chromosomes found in a woman's cells, or one of a non-identical pair found in a man's cells. X chromosomes are associated with female characteristics: compare **Y chromosome**. N COUNT

xenophobia /zɛnəfəʊbɪə/ is a fear or extremely strong dislike of people from other countries; a formal word. EG *They are nationalist to the point of xenophobia.* N UNCOUNT

xenophobic /zɛnəfəʊbɪk/. Someone who is **xenophobic** shows a fear or extremely strong dislike of people from other countries; a formal word. EG *He adopted a curiously xenophobic attitude for an educated man.* ADJ CLASSIF ⇑ afraid

Xerox /zɪərɒks/, **Xeroxes, Xeroxing, Xeroxed**. **Xerox** is a trademark. **1** A **Xerox** is a **1.1** a machine that makes photographic copies of pieces of paper which have writing or printing on them. EG *...a small Xerox copier... Who's got the key to the Xerox room?* **1.2** a copy of what is written or printed on a piece of paper, made by using a Xerox copier. EG *I enclose a Xerox of the letter.* N COUNT: USU BEFORE N ⇑ photocopier N COUNT ⇑ photocopy

2 If you **Xerox** a document or page of writing, you make a copy of it using a Xerox copier. EG *That morning, Bernstein had Xeroxed copies of notes from reporters at the scene.* V+O

Xmas /ɛksməs, krɪsməs/ is the same as Christmas. 'Xmas' is used especially on Christmas cards. EG *Merry Xmas!* N UNCOUNT

X-ray, X-rays, X-raying, X-rayed. **1** An **X-ray** is **1.1** a stream of radiation that can pass through some solid materials. X-rays are used by doctors to examine the bones or organs inside your body and are sometimes used at airports to see inside people's luggage. EG *...the X-rays that are produced by the electron beam... ...X-ray photography... Her baggage was put into a brand-new X-ray machine.* **1.2** a picture made by sending X-rays through your body onto a photographic plate or film in order to help a doctor see if there is anything wrong with you. EG *Your X-rays have just come back from the lab... The chest X-ray showed moderate enlargement of the heart.* **1.3** a medical examination in which a doctor uses X-rays to look at the inside of your body; a fairly informal use. EG *After an injury an X-ray is often desirable... I have to go and have an X-ray tomorrow.* N COUNT: USU PL OR BEFORE N N COUNT ⇑ photograph = radiograph N COUNT

2 If someone **X-rays** you, they take a picture of the inside of your body by using a machine which sends X-rays through you. EG *He had been X-rayed, weighed, and measured.* V+O ⇑ examine

xylophone /zaɪləfəʊn/, **xylophones**. A **xylophone** is a musical instrument made of wooden bars of different lengths which are arranged in a row. The longest bar is at one end and the shortest bar is at the other end. You play a xylophone by hitting the bars with special hammers. N COUNT ⇑ percussion instrument

Y, y /waɪ/, **Ys, y's**. **1 Y** is the twenty-fifth letter of the English alphabet. N COUNT

2 In algebra, **y** is used as a symbol to represent a number whose value or quantity is not known, usually in equations with 'x' representing another unknown number. EG *If we say y = 8x, then we get a line like this.*

-y, -ier, -iest; -ies. **-y** is **1** added to nouns in order to form adjectives that describe something or someone as having the characteristics of what the noun refers to or as being full of it, or covered in it. EG SUFFIX: FORMS ADJS

...*fleece→fleecy... ...juice→juicy... ...cloud→cloudy... ...smoke→smoky.* **2** added to colours in order to form adjectives that describe something as being roughly that colour or having some of that colour in it. EG *...yellow→yellowy... ...plum→plummy.* SUFFIX : FORMS ADJ COLOURS **3** added to nouns or names in order to form other nouns or names that are used by children or to express affection. EG *...dog→doggy... ...kid→kiddy... ...dad→daddy... ...Fred→Freddy.* SUFFIX : FORMS NOUNS/NAMES

yacht /jɒt/, **yachts**. A **yacht** is a large boat with sails or a motor, used for racing or pleasure trips. EG *...the white sails of the yachts... ...the California Yacht Club.* N COUNT

yachting /jɒtɪŋ/ is the sport or activity of sailing a yacht. EG *...yachting holidays.* N UNCOUNT

yachtsman /jɒtsmə³n/, **yachtsmen**. A **yachtsman** is a man who sails a yacht. N COUNT ⇑ sailor

yachtswoman /jɒtswʊ¹mə⁰n/, **yachtswomen**. A **yachtswoman** is a woman who sails a yacht. N COUNT ⇑ sailor

yak /jæk/, **yaks**. A **yak** is a type of ox that has long horns and long hair. Yaks live mainly in the Himalaya mountains and in Tibet, and are used to provide meat and milk. N COUNT ⇑ animal

yam /jæm/, **yams**. A **yam** is a root vegetable which grows in tropical regions and is fairly similar to a potato in appearance and texture; also used of the climbing plant from which the vegetable comes. N COUNT

yammer /jæmə/, **yammers, yammering, yammered**. **1** If someone **yammers**, they complain in an annoying way; an informal use. EG *Stop that yammering, I don't want to listen to you.* V = whine

2 If a dog **yammers**, it howls or wails loudly. EG *A dog yammered excitedly.* V = yowl

yank /jæŋk/, **yanks, yanking, yanked**. **1** A **Yank** is a person from the United States of America; a slightly offensive word used mainly in British English. N COUNT = American

2 If you **yank** someone or something in a particular direction, you pull them there suddenly and with a lot of force. EG *Glenn yanked out the sore tooth... He was yanking the cork out of a bottle... He yanked me to my feet in a moment.* V+O : USU+A

Yankee /jæŋki¹/, **Yankees**. A **Yankee** is **1** the same as a Yank. **2** a person from the northern United States. N COUNT

yap /jæp/, **yaps, yapping, yapped**. **1** If a dog **yaps**, it barks a lot with a high sound. EG *There was a dog running along the streets, yapping and barking.* V = yelp

2 If someone **yaps**, they talk continuously in an annoying way; an informal use. EG *I hate people on trains who keep yapping at you.* V = nag

yard /jɑːd/, **yards**. **1** A **yard** is an imperial unit for measuring length, equal to three feet or thirty-six inches, or approximately 91.4 centimetres. EG *Jack was standing under a tree about ten yards away... He parked about a hundred yards from the gates... ...a narrow ledge of rock a few yards wide.* N COUNT/PART : USU NUM/QUANTIF+N ⇑ measurement

2 A **yard** is also **2.1** a flat area of concrete or stone that is usually next to a building and often has a wall around it. EG *...a tiny cramped house without even a back yard... I walked out into the yard and through the gate.* N COUNT **2.2** a large area or place of work where a particular type of work is done, or where vehicles deliver and collect things. EG *Mitsubishi opened a ship repair yard and trained the work force... The road was lined with builders' yards and garages.* N COUNT : USU WITH SUPP

yardstick /jɑːdstɪk/, **yardsticks**. A **yardstick** is someone or something that you compare other people or things with when judging how good, valuable, or important these other people or things are. EG *She was a yardstick against which I could measure what I had achieved... ...an educational situation where the yardstick for success is exam achievement.* N COUNT ⇑ standard = criterion

yarn /jɑːn/, **yarns**. **1** **Yarn** is thread, made for example from wool or cotton, which is used for knitting or making cloth. EG *...a process to turn wool straight from the sheep into yarn ready for weaving.* N MASS

2 A **yarn** is a story that someone tells and often makes more exciting by adding invented details. EG *We swapped yarns for a while, always the same stories.* N COUNT = tale ● If someone **spins** you **a yarn**, they tell you a story which is not true, often as an excuse for something. EG *He spun me some yarn this morning about having to have the day off on Friday... They joked and spun tall yarns all night long.* ● PHR : VB AND N INFLECT ⇑ lie

yashmak /jæʃmæk/, **yashmaks**. A **yashmak** is a veil that some Muslim women wear in order to cover their faces when they are in public. N COUNT

yaw /jɔː/, **yaws, yawing, yawed**. If an aircraft or a ship **yaws**, it turns to one side so that it changes the direction in which it is moving; a technical term. EG *The planes yaw and tilt as they enter the cloud.* V = pitch

yawn /jɔːn/, **yawns, yawning, yawned**. **1** If you **yawn**, you open your mouth very wide and breathe in more air than usual, often when you are tired or when you are not interested in something. EG *He sat up and stretched and yawned... I yawned all through the first part of the concert.* V ▸ used as a noun. EG *'I'm tired,' he said, and gave a big yawn... She stifled a yawn.* ▸ N COUNT

2 If you describe something such as a book or a film as a **yawn**, you mean that you think it is very boring; an informal use. EG *The play was a big yawn from start to finish.* N SING : a+N, USED AS C = bore

3 A gap or opening that **yawns** is large and wide, sometimes so wide that it is rather frightening. EG *A great gap yawned between the rocks... The yawning craters stretched back towards the mainland.* V : USU+A ⇑ open = gape

Y chromosome, Y chromosomes; a technical term in biology. A **Y chromosome** is the single chromosome in a man's cells which will produce a male baby if it joins with an X chromosome during the reproductive process: compare **X chromosome**. N COUNT

yd, yds. **yd** is a written abbreviation for 'yard'; used after a number to indicate a measurement of length. EG *The reel holds 400 yds of line.*

ye /jiː, jə/ is **1** an old-fashioned, poetic, or religious word for 'you' when you are talking to more than one person. EG *Abandon all hope, ye who enter here.* PRON : PL

2 a very old-fashioned written form for 'the'. EG *...Ye Olde Coffee Shoppe.* DET

yea /jeɪ/. **1** You use **yea** to indicate that you are accepting, confirming, or agreeing with something; a formal use. EG *They are taught to say yea to all that is negative in life.* CONVENTION = yes ● You use the expression **yea or nay** in referring to or asking about someone's answer to an offer or suggestion. EG *I'll send you an estimate and you can answer yea or nay.* ● PHR : USED AS O = yes or no

2 **Yea** is a very old-fashioned or biblical form for 'yes', used especially to emphasize or to introduce what you are saying. EG *Yea, unto lost sheep will I liken them.* ADV SEN

yeah /jɛə/ is the usual written form of a casual pronunciation of 'yes': see **yes** for examples. CONVENTION

year /jɪə/, **years**. **1** A **year** is **1.1** a period of twelve months or 365 or 366 days, beginning on the first of January and ending on the thirty-first of December. EG *...during the summer holidays last year... ...at the end of next year... ...in the year 2000.* N COUNT : ALSO the+N+NUM **1.2** a period of about twelve months. EG *...a hundred million years ago... For seven years I was a designer... ...a year or two after I had left... He was due to retire in a few years' time.* N COUNT

2 A school **year** or a university **year** is the period of time in each twelve months when the school or university is open and people are studying or being taught there. In Britain, the school year usually lasts from September to July, and the university year from October to June. EG *...at the end of the last school year... We start to look forward to the next academic year.* N COUNT : USU MOD+N ▸ used to refer to one of these periods of time during which a student is attending a school or taking a course at a university. EG *He took Greek in his first year at University... I'm in my final year at Birmingham now.* ▸ N COUNT : ORDINAL+N ▸ also used to refer to a student who is in the particular year mentioned at school or university. EG *...a first year medical student... I hated teaching 4th and 5th years.* ▸ N COUNT : ORDINAL+N

3 A **year** is also a period of twelve months, beginning on a particular day of the year, which is used by businesses or institutions as a basis for recording or organizing their finances and accounts. EG *...the final account at the end of each trading year.* N COUNT+SUPP

4 You can use **years** to emphasize that you are referring to a very long time but without stating the exact number of years. EG *I haven't seen him for years... It took her years to realize this... They've known each other for years and years.* N PLURAL = ages

5 If you refer to your **years** in a particular place or doing a particular activity, you are referring to the period of time during which you have been in the place or during which you have been doing the N PLURAL : POSS+N activity. EG *In all my years of motoring I've never had an accident... There were never any detectable profits in my two years there.*

6 The word **year** is also used in the following expressions. **6.1** If you do something **all year round** or **all the year round**, you do it continually throughout the year. EG *They grow crops all the year round... All year round we get new members of staff coming in.* PHR : USED AS AN A **6.2** If you do something **year after year**, you do it regularly every year. EG *Tens of thousands of men, year after year, have travelled southwards to find work.* PHR : USED AS AN A ⇑ continually **6.3** If something changes **year by year**, it changes each year; used especially in relation to things which change at the same rate or which happen in the same way each year. EG *Prices tended to rise year by year... The university gets bigger, year by year.* PHR : USED AS AN A **6.4** If something happens **year in, year out**, it happens every year without changing, and is often boring. EG *It got on their nerves, this drip-drip-drip, week in, week out, year in, year out.* PHR : USED AS AN A ⇑ continuously

7 The word **year** is used in expressions referring to the age of a person or thing. **7.1** If, for example, someone or something is ten **years old** or ten **years of age**, they have lived or existed for ten years but not yet eleven. EG *These rocks are thought to be about 650 million years old... ...a woman of about fifty years of age.* PHR : NUM+PHR, USED AS C **7.2** If, for example, someone is in their tenth **year**, they are nine years old and not yet ten; a fairly formal use. EG *He died in 1951 in his eighty-ninth year.* N COUNT : ORDINAL+N, USU SING **7.3** You use the expression **a man of his years** or **a woman of her years** when you mention something about a man or woman in relation to their age. EG *He's very agile for a man of his years.* PHR : USED AS S/O **7.4** If you say that something such as an experience or a way of dressing **has put years on** someone, you mean that it has made them look or feel much older; an informal expression. If you say that something such as an experience or a way of dressing **has taken years off** someone, you mean that it has made them look or feel much younger; an informal expression. EG *His work has put years on him... That hair-do takes years off you.* PHR : VB INFLECTS ⇑ change

8 • **donkey's years**: see **donkey**. • See also **financial year**, **fiscal year**, **leap year**, **New Year**, **tax year**.

yearbook /jɪəbʊk/, **yearbooks**. A **yearbook** is a book that is published once a year and contains information about events and achievements of the previous year, usually concerning a particular place or organization. EG *...the yearbook for the class of 1953 at her school.* N COUNT : ALSO IN NAMES AFTER N ⇑ report

year-long is used to describe something that lasts for a year. EG *...attending year-long courses to help them with reading.* ADJ CLASSIF : ATTRIB

yearly /jɪəli¹/. You use **yearly 1** to describe something that happens or is done once a year or every year. EG *...a yearly meeting... The interest is normally paid twice yearly.* ADJ CLASSIF : ATTRIB, OR ADV WITH VB **2** to describe something such as an amount that relates to a period of one year. EG *...the yearly cash income of the workers... ...infections that afflicted tens of thousands of babies yearly.* ADJ CLASSIF : ATTRIB, OR ADV WITH VB

yearn /jɜːn/, **yearns, yearning, yearned**. If you **yearn** for something, often something that you are unlikely to get, you want it very much. EG *We yearn for beauty, truth and meaning in our lives... She yearned to go back to the south.* V+*for/to*-INF = long, crave

yearning /jɜːnɪŋ/, **yearnings**. A **yearning** is a very strong desire for something, especially something that you are unlikely to get. EG *She had developed a great yearning to set eyes on her grandchildren... He makes no secret of his yearning for power.* N COUNT/ UNCOUNT = longing

-year-old, -year-olds. **-year-old** combines with numbers to refer to people or things of a particular age mentioned. EG *...a class of 4-year-olds... ...a fifteen-year-old boy... ...awaiting a court verdict on five-year-old charges.* COMB : FORMS NOUNS OR ADJ CLASSIFS

year-round is used to describe something that happens, exists, or is done throughout the year. EG *Nothing dries easily in Guangdon's year-round steamy heat... The strain of year-round cricket is telling on many of the world's top cricketers.* ADJ CLASSIF : ATTRIB ⇑ continuous

yeast /jiːst/, **yeasts**. **Yeast** is a kind of fungus which is used for making alcoholic drinks such as beer, or to make bread rise. You can use yeast fresh or as a dry powder. N MASS

yeasty /jiːsti¹/. Something that is **yeasty** tastes or smells strongly of yeast. EG *...warm yeasty bread... There was a strong yeasty smell.* ADJ QUALIT

yell /jɛl/, **yells, yelling, yelled**. **1** If you **yell** or **yell out**, you shout loudly, for example because you are excited, angry, or in pain. EG *'Speed up!' he yelled to the driver... I yelled out, 'Come down!'... I yelled at Richard to hang on... He turned to yell for Helen... I yelled out in pain.* V, V+QUOTE/A/ REPORT-CL, OR PHRASAL VB : V+ ADV = cry out

2 If you **yell** something or if you **yell** it **out**, you shout it loudly at someone, often when you are angry with them. EG *She came in and started yelling abuse at the cops... You've got to yell the destination you want... The older boys yelled out insults.* V+O, OR PHRASAL VB : V+ O+ADV = call out

3 If a child or baby **yells**, it cries loudly because it is miserable or hurt. EG *Not all babies yell when they are being fed too little... He was picked up by his playmates, stunned and yelling.* V = bawl, howl

4 A **yell** is a loud and sudden shout given by someone who is afraid or in pain. EG *Ian said he heard a yell inside... ...a little high-pitched yell.* N COUNT = cry, scream

yellow /jɛləʊ/, **yellower, yellowest; yellows, yellowing, yellowed**. **1** Something that is **yellow** is the colour of lemons or egg yolks. EG *He became aware of a yellow light far across the fields.* ADJ COLOUR ▸ used as a noun. EG *...the vivid greens and yellows of the sun filtering through the trees.* ▸ N MASS

2 When something **yellows** or **is yellowed**, it becomes yellow in colour, often because it is old. EG *The sun was shining on the snow, yellowing it and making it glow.* V-ERG : IF V+O, THEN USU PASS ◇ **yellowing**. EG *...old yellowing newspapers.* ◇ ADJ CLASSIF ◇ **yellowed**. EG *...a photograph of her, yellowed with age.* ◇ ADJ QUALIT

3 People who belong to a race with pale yellow skins, for example the Chinese or Japanese, are sometimes described as **yellow**. EG *All races, whether black, brown, white, or yellow, mix freely here.* ADJ CLASSIF

4 If you describe someone as **yellow**, you mean that they are cowardly or afraid; an informal use showing disapproval. EG *I always knew you were yellow!* ADJ QUALIT = lily-livered

yellow fever is a very infectious and serious disease that people can catch in tropical countries. It causes the skin to turn yellow. N UNCOUNT ⇑ illness

yellowish /jɛləʊɪʃ/. Something that is **yellowish** is slightly yellow in colour. EG *Each leaf had several lighter yellowish patches on it.* ADJ COLOUR = yellowy

yellow pages. The **yellow pages** are a telephone directory or part of a directory in which companies and people are listed under the headings of the kind of business or service that they provide. EG *Look in your yellow pages for your nearest frozen food supplier.* N PLURAL : *the*+N

yellowy /jɛləʊi¹/. Something that is **yellowy** is slightly yellow in colour. EG *On one branch there was a bunch of yellowy-green mistletoe growing.* ADJ COLOUR = yellowish

yelp /jɛlp/, **yelps, yelping, yelped**. If people or animals **yelp**, they give a sudden short cry, often when they are frightened or in pain. EG *He yelped in pain... The puppy tucked its tail between its legs and ran indoors yelping.* V = squeal ▸ used as a noun. EG *I gave a little yelp and fled upstairs.* ▸ N COUNT

Yemeni /jɛmɪni¹/, **Yemenis**. **1** Something that is **Yemeni** belongs or relates to the Yemen or to its people. ADJ CLASSIF

2 A **Yemeni** is a person who comes from the Yemen. N COUNT

yen /jɛn/. **Yen** is both the singular and the plural form. **1** A **yen** is the unit of money that is used in Japan. EG *Yu Soong Kwong earned 15 yen a month.* N COUNT ⇑ currency

2 If you have a **yen** to do something, you have a strong desire to do it; an informal use. EG *Nicholas has a yen to hike through Canada... My cat had a particular yen for sweetbreads.* N SING : *a*+N, USU +*to*-INF/*for* = craving

yeoman /jəʊməˀn/, **yeomen**. A **yeoman** was a man in former times who was free and not a servant, and who cultivated his own land. N COUNT ⇑ farmer

yes /jɛs/, **yeses**; **yeah** is an informal form. **Yes** and **yeah** are used in speech to express different sorts of responses and reactions, and this entry shows the commonest ones. **1** You use **yes**, mainly in spoken English, **1.1** to answer a question to which the answer could be 'yes' or 'no'. EG *'Did you enjoy it?'–'Yes.'... 'You'll be away next Friday, won't you?'–'Yeah.'... I wanted to say yes... I nodded yes.* CONVENTION ⇑ affirmative ≠ no **1.2** to accept an offer. EG *'Do you want some coffee?'–'Yes please.'... 'Do you want a cushion?'–'Oh yes. Thank you.'* CONVENTION ≠ no **1.3** to say that you are willing to do or allow what someone has asked you. EG *'Will you* CONVENTION ≠ no *let us know about it?'–'Yes I will.'* **1.4** to tell someone that they have answered a question correctly. EG *'What state is it in?'–'Louisiana.'–'Yes, it's in Louisiana.'... 'Thirty kilohertz.'–'Yeah that's right.'* **1.5** to show that you are ready or willing to speak to the person who wants to speak to you, for example when you are answering a telephone or doorbell. EG *'Sir.'–'Yes?'–'Can I have my book now?'... 'Hello? 435-1916?'–'Yes?'* CONVENTION = correct; CONVENTION

2 You say **yes and no** in reply to a question when you cannot give a definite answer because there are several different possible answers which are all partly true. EG *'Do they actually use computers to diagnose illnesses?'–'Yes and no.'* CONVENTION = sort of

3 A **yes** is a person who has answered 'yes' to a question or who has voted in favour of something; also used to refer to their answer or vote. EG *There were seventeen yeses and only two don't knows.* N COUNT = aye

4 You also use **yes** in a conversation **4.1** to indicate your involvement in the conversation and to say that you agree with, accept, or understand what the previous speaker has said. EG *'Really, one should ignore people like that.'–'Oh agreed, yeah.'... 'You'll have to fill in a form when you come.'–'Oh yes, that'll be no problem.'... 'It was a beautiful day.'–'It was nice, yes.'* **4.2** to encourage someone to continue speaking. EG *'I miss the country very much.'–'Yes?'–'And yet, you see, it would be mad to give everything up and go and live there.'* **4.3** as a polite way of introducing an objection to what the previous speaker has just said. EG *'It's a waste of time.'–'Yes but there's still some point in going.'... 'Nobody can understand Joyce.'–'Ah yes, but that's the beauty of him you know.'* **4.4** to say that a negative statement or question that the previous speaker has made is wrong or untrue. EG *'Nowadays you don't learn any basic principles in maths.'–'Oh, yes you do.'... 'Don't you know Latin?'–'Yes, of course he does.'* **4.5** to suggest that you do not believe what the previous speaker has said, especially when you are feeling annoyed or scornful. EG *'This is a musical cat.'–'Oh, yes?'* **4.6** to introduce an opinion, statement, or remark. EG *'What do you think, Jack?'–'Yes, well I agree too.'... The answer to that is, yes I think that's what is happening.* **4.7** to introduce something that you had forgotten to say and have just remembered. EG *I had a vital question in my mind–oh, yeah. How difficult is it to get there?... What was I going to mention? Ah yes, accidents.* **4.8** to emphasize and confirm a statement that you are making. EG *You see, I was a coward, yes a real coward... 'Do you know he crashed the car?'–'No.'–'Oh yeah.'* CONVENTION = certainly; CONVENTION = and; CONVENTION ⇑ however; CONVENTION; CONVENTION = really; CONVENTION; CONVENTION; CONVENTION

yes-man, yes-men. A **yes-man** is someone who always agrees with their employer in order to gain favour; used showing disapproval. EG *The boss is surrounded by yes-men fearful for their jobs.* N COUNT ⇑ sycophant

yesterday /jestədɪ[3]/ means **1** the day before today. EG *It was terribly hot yesterday... Yesterday morning there were more than 500 boats on the lake... 'When did you go?'–'The day before yesterday.'* ▸ also used like a noun. EG *...an interview published in yesterday's New York Times... Yesterday was to have been the start of the soccer season.* **2** the past, especially the recent past. EG *The worker of today is different from the worker of yesterday.* ▸ also used like a noun. EG *We must exchange yesterday's products for today's.* ADV; ADV

yesteryear /jestəjɪə/ means the past; an old-fashioned word, used especially to refer to a past era or a way of life that has disappeared. EG *He often mentioned the scandals of yesteryear.* N UNCOUNT = bygone days

yet /jet/. **1** You use **yet** in negative statements when you are saying that up to the present time something has not happened. Sometimes you are suggesting that this is surprising, and sometimes you are just making the point that it is going to happen later. EG *It isn't dark yet... I haven't yet met Davis... His uncles weren't married even yet... By good fortune the leak has done no damage–yet... There was blood, not yet congealed, on his mouth.* ▸ used in questions to ask if something has happened up to the present time. EG *Have you had your lunch yet?* ADV WITH VB : WITH BROAD NEG = as yet ≠ already; ▸ ADV WITH VB

2 If you say that an event is **not yet**, you mean that it is not going to happen at the present time although it will happen at some time in the future. EG *I hope the end is not yet... The time for fairness is not yet... 'Are you coming?'–'Not just yet.'* PHR/ CONVENTION

3 You use **as yet** with negative statements to describe a situation that has existed up until the present time; a fairly formal use. EG *As yet the king had taken no wife... No one, as yet, is suspicious... We have as yet no name... This extract is taken from an as yet unpublished novel.* PHR : USED AS AN A, WITH BROAD NEG = so far

4 You also use **yet 4.1** after a superlative to refer to something that has been the case up to the present time. EG *This is the most lethal of all poisons yet identified... She's the best yet.* **4.2** to say that, although something has not already happened, it is possible or probable that it will happen at some time in the future. EG *There is hope for me yet... The figures may yet be revised again... We'll make a footballer of you yet... There were revelations yet to come.* **4.3** after an expression which refers to a period of time, when you want to emphasize how long a situation is likely to last or how long it will be before something happens in the future. EG *Quiz shows are going to be around for a long while yet... It will not be dark for half an hour yet... It'll be ages yet before I get my driving licence.* ADV : SUPERL + ADV = so far; ADV WITH VB = still; ADV AFTER NG

5 If you say that you have **yet** to do something, or that something is **yet** to happen, you mean that you have not done it or that it has not happened, often suggesting that it is surprising or bad that this is so. EG *I have yet to meet a man I can trust... A just, ordered society without a bureaucracy has yet to be established.* ADV + *to*-INF = still

6 You also use **yet** to introduce a comment or statement which is rather surprising after the previous statement you have just made. EG *Everything around him was blown to pieces, yet the minister escaped without a scratch... They attack the state, yet draw money from it... ...a firm yet gentle hand... He was a jealous, slightly bitter man and yet very funny.* CONJ COORD = but

7 Yet is used to give emphasis **7.1** with comparatives and superlatives to show that the degree of something is even greater than what has just been mentioned. EG *The dole queues are likely to grow longer yet... Yet louder shouts rose when the police car arrived... To this list, worst yet, he might have added political conflict.* **7.2** before words like 'another', 'more', and 'again' to emphasize the quantity or frequency of something. EG *Ovett was celebrating yet another 1500 metres victory... I am sorry to bring up the subject of money yet again... This week it's been work, work and yet more work.* ADV : COMPAR/ SUPERL + ADV = still; ADV

yeti /jetiˡ/, **yetis**. A **yeti** is a large animal like a very hairy ape which is supposed to live in the Himalayas but which many people do not believe exists. N COUNT

yew /juː/, **yews**. A **yew** or a **yew tree** is a tree that has dark green, thin, sharp leaves on its branches all year round and red berries. ▸ also used to refer to the wood from this tree. N COUNT; ▸ N UNCOUNT

YHA /waɪ eɪtʃ eɪ/ is an abbreviation for 'Youth Hostels Association'; an organization which owns many large houses throughout the world where young people can stay cheaply when they are travelling around on holiday. N PROPER : *the* + N

Yiddish /jɪdɪʃ/ is a language mainly derived from German, which many Jewish people of European origin speak. N UNCOUNT

yield /jiːld/, **yields, yielding, yielded**. **1** If you **yield** to a person or thing that is putting pressure of some kind on you, you stop resisting the person or thing. EG *The Chancellor yielded to his critics and halved the March Budget... He was yielding to public pressure... I decided to yield to my cowardice.* V : USU + A(*to*) = give in ≠ resist

2 If you **yield** something that you have control of or responsibility for, you unwillingly stop having control of it or responsibility for it, and allow someone else to take control or have responsibility for it. EG *He will not yield even a limited measure of editorial control... They were obliged to yield fifteen to twenty kilometres.* V+O = give up, surrender ≠ retain

3 If one thing **yields** to another thing, it is replaced by this other thing; a formal use. EG *The wilderness of ugly warehouses is to yield to complete redevelopment... Radio has long been under pressure to yield to television.* V + A(*to*) = give way

4 If something **yields**, it breaks or moves position as a result of a lot of force or pressure being put on it. EG *The flesh and bone yielded under his weight... Any lock will yield to a bit of brute force.* V = give way ≠ hold

5 If an investigation, discussion, etc **yields** something, it produces a result, answer, or piece of information. EG *Talks between the two sides yielded no results... Human IQ tests yield a score between 0 and about 200.* V+O = provide

6 If an area of land or a number of animals **yields** a particular amount of food, plants, etc, this amount of food or plants is produced by the land or animals. EG *0.23 acres would yield only 200 pounds of rice... They could recoup these costs from the extra harvest yielded.* ▸ used as a noun to refer to the amount of food produced. EG *They have a far better yield than any farm round here for miles... Wheat yields doubled in India between 1964 and 1972.* V+O ⇑ produce; ▸ N COUNT = harvest

7 If a tax or investment **yields** an amount of money or profit, often expressed as a percentage, this money or profit is obtained from it as a result. EG *The rent control board yields them an extra 7% a year... Congress will spend every penny that is yielded by taxes.* ▸ used as a noun to refer to the amount of money or profit produced. EG *The yield after only 12 months is 9%.* V+O ⇑ produce = bring in, earn; ▸ N COUNT = return

yield up. If you **yield up** a secret, you reveal it; a formal use. EG *...methods of making the brain yield up its secrets.* PHRASAL VB: V+O+ADV = disclose

yielding /jiːldɪŋ/. A material that is **yielding** is quite soft and will move or bend rather than stay stiff if you put pressure on it. ADJ QUALIT = spongy, flexible

yippee /jɪpiː/. If you shout **'Yippee!'**, you are showing that you are very happy and excited about something; used especially by children. EXCLAM = hooray

YMCA /waɪ ɛm siː eɪ/, **YMCAs**. The **YMCA** is an organization which encourages young men to have Christian moral values; an abbreviation for 'Young Men's Christian Association'. ▸ often used to refer to one of the hostels run by the organization where men can stay. EG *The group meets in the local YMCA.* N PROPER: *the*+N; ▸ N COUNT: USU*the*+N IN SING

yob /jɒb/, **yobs**. A **yob** is a boy or young man who behaves in a noisy and bad-mannered way in public places, usually with a group of other similar people; an informal word used in British English showing disapproval. EG *They looked a real bunch of yobs.* N COUNT = hooligan, thug

yobbo /jɒbəʊ/, **yobbos**. A **yobbo** is the same as a yob. N COUNT

yodel /jəʊdəᵊl/, **yodels, yodelling, yodelled**; also spelled **yodeling, yodeled** in American English. When someone **yodels**, they sing normal notes with very high quick falsetto notes in between. This style of singing comes traditionally from Switzerland. EG *...a Swiss yodelling song.* ▸ used as a noun to refer to this style of singing. EG *I tried to do a yodel at the end.* V; ▸ N COUNT

yoga /jəʊgə/ is **1** a type of exercise in which you move your body into various positions, which helps you to become fitter, improve the way you breathe, and relax your mind. EG *I do two hours yoga every day.* **2** a philosophy which first developed in India, in which physical exercises and meditation are supposed to help people to become calmer and gradually united in spirit with a Supreme Being. EG *They were deeply interested in meditation, the East, and yoga.* N UNCOUNT; N UNCOUNT

yoghurt /jɒgət/, **yoghurts**; also spelled **yoghourt** or **yogurt**. **Yoghurt** is a slightly sour, thick liquid which is made from milk that has had bacteria added to it. You can eat it with fruit, or with meat or vegetables. EG *...a spoonful of yoghurt... ...a diet of nuts and natural yoghurt.* N MASS

yogi /jəʊgiⁱ/, **yogis**. A **yogi** is a person who has spent many years practising yoga and has reached a high level of awareness of the Supreme Being. EG *A yogi in India can consciously lower his blood pressure.* N COUNT ⇑ philosopher

yogurt /jɒgət/. See **yoghurt**.

yoke /jəʊk/, **yokes, yoking, yoked. 1** If people are suffering under a **yoke** of a particular kind, they are suffering a difficult or unhappy condition, for example having to work extremely hard or being governed by a severe leader; a literary use. EG *...those few nations who escaped the colonial yoke... ...a war against the yoke of tyranny.* N SING WITH DET +SUPP ⇑ burden

2 A **yoke** is a long piece of wood attached to two collars, which is laid across the necks of two animals such as oxen, in order to make them walk close together when they are pulling a plough. N COUNT ⇑ frame

3 If you **yoke** two animals such as oxen together, you fasten them together by laying a yoke across their necks, in order to make them walk close together when they are pulling a plough. EG *...two oxen yoked to a hay-cart... Huge, roofed carts lumber along, pulled by yoked bullocks.* V+O: USU+A(*together/to*) ⇑ join = harness

4 If two or more people or ideas **are yoked** together, they are closely linked because they will be more successful together than separately; a formal use. EG *The personal qualities of the leader must be yoked to a social policy.* V+O: USU PASS+A(*together/to*)

5 The **yoke** of a dress or skirt is a part of it, usually just below the collar or the waist, onto which a fuller part with a lot of material is pleated or gathered. N COUNT

yokel /jəʊkəᵊl/, **yokels**. A **yokel** is a person who lives in the countryside, especially one who does not seem to be very intelligent or interested in any form of culture; used especially by people who live in towns, showing disapproval. EG *...country yokels.* N COUNT = bumpkin

yolk /jəʊk/, **yolks**. A **yolk** is the yellow part in the middle of an egg, which provides food for the embryo as it develops in the egg. EG *The food a reptile mother provides for its baby is the yolk in its egg... Egg yolk is a particularly good source of iron... Stuart dipped a piece of toast into the soft yolk of his egg and ate in silence.* N COUNT/UNCOUNT

Yom Kippur /jɒm kɪpʊə/ is an annual Jewish holiday which is a day of fasting and prayers of repentance. N UNCOUNT

yon /jɒn/ is a very old-fashioned word for 'that' or 'those'. EG *What's yon place in America, Coney Island?* DET

yonder /jɒndə/ means 'over there'; a very old-fashioned word. EG *They came galloping over that hill yonder.* ADV OR DET

yonks /jɒŋks/. If you say that you have not done something for **yonks**, you mean that you have not done it for a very long time; an informal word. EG *I kept spotting people I hadn't seen for yonks.* N UNCOUNT

yore /jɔː/. The expression **of yore** is used to refer to something that was a long time ago; a very old-fashioned literary expression. EG *In days of yore I had shared with him all my secrets.* PHR AFTER N ⇑ past

Yorkshire pudding /jɔːkʃə pʊdɪŋ/, **Yorkshire puddings**. **Yorkshire pudding** is a food which is made by baking a thick liquid mixture of flour, milk, and eggs, and which is often eaten in Britain with roast beef. N UNCOUNT/COUNT

you /juː/ is used as the subject of a verb or as the object of a verb or preposition. It can refer to one or more people. A speaker or writer uses **you 1** to refer to the person or group of people that he or she is speaking to or writing for. EG *Have you got any money?... What do you think?... Would you like to have a drink with me?... The same rule applies to you... You people don't smoke, do you?... You all know why we're here.* **2** to refer to people in general rather than a particular person, for example in statements about what usually happens in a particular situation; used mainly in informal spoken English. EG *Of course, you get differences in organization... It's awful when you can't remember someone's name.* PRON; PRON

you'd /juːd/ is **1** the usual spoken form of 'you had', especially when 'had' is an auxiliary verb. EG *If you'd asked me that ten years ago, I'd have said yes.* **2** the usual spoken form of 'you would'. EG *You'd be surprised how easy it is, when you try.*

you'll /juːl/ is the usual spoken form of 'you will'. EG *I think you'll find it comes out to be shorter that way... You'll have to get a job.*

young /jʌŋ/, **younger, youngest. 1** A **young** person, animal, or plant has not lived or existed for a long time; often used of a living thing that is still developing and has not yet reached maturity. EG *Julia has two young boys... The young couple met a week before they got married... Have a word with young Colin... The young seedlings grow very rapidly... She is 2 years younger than me... Aunt Mabel was the youngest of my mother's three sisters.* ▸ The **young** is used to refer to people who are young. EG *This area teems with the young, especially with art students.* ADJ QUALIT ≠ adult, mature, old; ▸ N PLURAL: *the*+N = youth ≠ the aged

2 Someone who is **young** in appearance or behaviour looks or behaves as if they are young, for example because they are lively and energetic. EG *She's very young in her movements.* ADJ QUALIT = youthful

3 You also use **young 3.1** to describe a time when a ADJ QUALIT: ATTRIB person or thing was young. EG *No one was more fond of dancing than I was in my younger days.* **3.2** to describe things relating to young people. EG *This boutique deals mainly with young fashion.* **3.3** to describe a group representing the younger members of a larger organization, usually a political party. EG *...students in the Young Liberals.* ADJ CLASSIF : ATTRIB; ADJ CLASSIF : ATTRIB

4 The **young** of an animal are its babies. EG *The tie between the young and their mothers is very close... When the young first hatch, they are naked.* N PLURAL = offspring

youngish /jʌŋᵍɪʃ/. Someone or something that is **youngish** is fairly young in appearance, behaviour, or age. EG *...a youngish man with long, blond hair.* ADJ CLASSIF

young lady, young ladies. A man's **young lady** is his girlfriend; a rather old-fashioned expression. N COUNT : POSS+N

young man, young men. A girl's **young man** is her boyfriend; a rather old-fashioned expression. EG *Is your young man coming for tea?* N COUNT : POSS+N

youngster /jʌŋkᵒstə/, **youngsters**. A **youngster** is a young person, especially a child; a fairly informal word. EG *I don't know what the youngsters of today would think.* N COUNT

your /jɔː, jʊə/. **1** A speaker or writer uses **your** to indicate that something belongs or relates to the person or group of people that he or she is speaking to or writing for. See **you**. EG *Where's your father?... If you begin to feel dizzy again, put your head in your hands... What's your name?... You saw it with your own eyes.* DET POSS

2 A speaker or writer also uses **your** in informal, mainly spoken English, **2.1** to indicate that something belongs or relates to people in general rather than a particular person. See **you**. EG *You can't use your own name in a novel... The whole system is geared to taking your O levels when you're sixteen.* DET POSS = one's

2.2 to indicate that he or she is naming something as an example of a particular group of things with similar qualities. EG *...your Hamburgs and Kiels and big trading ports... On the subject of world-class footballers, where are your Bobby Charltons these days?* DET POSS

3 A speaker or writer also uses **your** in some titles when he or she addresses a person or people with that title. EG *...Your Majesty... I have told your Lordship all there is bearing on the matter.* DET POSS : USED IN TITLES

you're /jɔː, jʊə/ is the usual spoken form of 'you are'. EG *You're quite right... You're not an expert... If you're going to stop you're supposed to signal.*

yours /jɔːz, jʊəz/. **1** A speaker or writer uses **yours** to indicate that something belongs or relates to the person or group of people that he or she is speaking to or writing for. See **you**. EG *Our swimming pool isn't as deep as yours... The future is yours, don't let them take it from you... A student of yours has just been to see me.* PRON POSS

2 People write **yours** at the end of a letter before they sign their names, often with another word such as 'truly' or 'sincerely' afterwards when it is a formal letter. EG *Yours sincerely, Richard Thomas... Yours faithfully, R.H. Thomas, Editorial Director... Let me know what happens. Yours, Richard.*

3 Yours truly is sometimes used instead of 'I' or 'me' by a speaker in order to refer to himself or herself; an informal expression. EG *If it goes wrong, don't blame yours truly.* PRON : SING

yourself /jəˢself/, **yourselves**. **1** A speaker or writer uses **yourself 1.1** as the object of a verb or preposition in a clause where 'you' is the subject or a previous object. See **you**. EG *Don't strain yourself... Would you call yourself a Marxist?... Help yourselves to sandwiches... You might be making a fool of yourself... Tell me about yourself.* ▸ **Yourself** is also used to emphasize the subject or object of a clause. It is usually used in addition to a subject or object, although it is sometimes used instead of 'you' as an object. EG *You yourself said it's only a routine check.* PRON REFL : USED AS O, HAS PL; ▸ PRON REFL : HAS PL

1.2 instead of 'you', especially after a preposition, when the subject of the clause is not 'you'; used to express politeness or emphasis. EG *There is always someone worse off than yourself... 'What about yourself?' retorted Charles... Aren't people like yourselves being a little bit presumptuous?* PRON REFL : USED AS O, HAS PL

2 If you do something **yourself**, you do it without any help or interference from anyone else. EG *Did you make them yourself?* PRON REFL : HAS PL ⇑ alone

youth /juːθ/, **youths** /juːðz/. **1** Someone's **youth** is the period of their life during which they are a child and before they are a fully mature adult, especially when they are an adolescent. EG *We change and learn from youth to old age... He had visited Calcutta in his youth... The dream of his youth had come true... Youth has always been the time for rebellion.* N UNCOUNT ≠ adulthood

2 Youth is the quality or state of being young, and sometimes also immature and inexperienced. EG *She had everything, beauty, intelligence, youth and, above all, money... She was full of the idealism of youth.* N UNCOUNT = youthfulness

3 A **youth** is a boy or a young man, especially a teenager. EG *The road was occupied by a long line of youths and girls carrying black flags.* N COUNT = adolescent

4 The **youth** are young people considered as a group. EG *There's high unemployment among the youth of this country.* N PLURAL : the+N

youth club, youth clubs. A **youth club** is a club where young people can go to meet each other and take part in various leisure activities, usually run by a church or local authority. EG *There's a disco at the youth club tonight.* N COUNT : ALSO IN NAMES

youthful /juːθfʊl/. Someone who is **youthful 1** is young, lively, and full of energy, but sometimes also immature in their behaviour and attitudes. EG *...youthful dancers.* ▸ used of people's attitudes and behaviour. EG *He was full of youthful curiosity and idealism.* ◊ **youthfulness**. EG *...the total lack of youthfulness in the young man.* **2** has qualities or characteristics that are thought to be typical of young people. EG *Despite her age she still had a youthful body... There's a high value placed on youthful attractiveness today.* ◊ **youthfully**. EG *She dressed youthfully.* ADJ QUALIT; ▸ ADJ QUALIT : ATTRIB; ◊ N UNCOUNT; ADJ QUALIT ≠ aged; ◊ ADV WITH VB

youth hostel, youth hostels. A **youth hostel** is a large house where young people can stay cheaply when they are travelling around on holiday, especially when hiking or on bicycle tours. EG *They travelled through France and Germany, always staying in youth hostels.* N COUNT : ALSO IN NAMES ⇑ lodging

you've /juːv/ is the usual spoken form of 'you have', especially when 'have' is an auxiliary verb. EG *You've got two conflicting principles here... You've been very lucky.*

yowl /jaʊl/, **yowls, yowling, yowled**. If a person or an animal **yowls**, they make a loud wailing noise. EG *Mountain lions yowled like tom-cats.* ▸ used as a noun. EG *...the incessant screech and yowl of emergency sirens.* ◊ **yowling**. EG *...the high-pitched yowling of a rock singer.* V = howl; ▸ N COUNT/UNCOUNT; ◊ N UNCOUNT

yo-yo /jəʊ jəʊ/, **yo-yos**. A **yo-yo** is a toy which is made of two connected round pieces of wood or plastic attached to a piece of string. You play with the yo-yo by letting it rise and fall on the string. N COUNT

yr, yrs. yr is a written abbreviation for 'year'. EG *...a 29 yr old woman.*

yuan /juːæn/. **Yuan** is both the singular and the plural form. A **yuan** is the unit of money that is used in the People's Republic of China. N COUNT ⇑ currency

Yugoslav /juːgəˢslɑːv/, **Yugoslavs**. **1** Something that is **Yugoslav** belongs or relates to Yugoslavia or to its people. EG *...the Yugoslav embassy.* ADJ CLASSIF = Yugoslavian

2 A **Yugoslav** is a person who comes from Yugoslavia. N COUNT

Yugoslavian /juːgəˢslɑːvɪən/. Something that is **Yugoslavian** belongs or relates to Yugoslavia or to its people. EG *...Yugoslavian socialism.* ADJ CLASSIF = Yugoslav

yuk /yək, jʌk/. You say **yuk** to indicate that you think something is very unpleasant or disgusting; a very informal word. EG *Cornflakes, yuk!* EXCLAM = ugh

Yule /juːl/ means Christmas; an old-fashioned word. N UNCOUNT

Yuletide /juːltaɪd/ means the time of year at or around Christmas; an old-fashioned word. EG *...Yuletide festivities.* N UNCOUNT

yummy /jʌmi¹/. If you say that some food is **yummy**, you mean that you think it is delicious; a very informal word, used mainly in spoken English. EG *Can I have some more of that yummy yoghurt?* ADJ QUALIT = scrumptious

YWCA /waɪ dʌbəᵒljuː siː eɪ/, **YWCAs**. The **YWCA** is an organization which encourages young women to have Christian moral values; an abbreviation for 'Young Women's Christian Association'. ▸ often used to refer to one of the hostels run by the organization where women can stay. EG *She had a new address. She had moved from the YWCA.* N PROPER : the+N; ▸ N COUNT : USU the+N IN SING

Z, z, Zs, z's. The letter Z is pronounced /zed/ in British English and /ziː/ in American English. Z or z N COUNT

is the twenty sixth letter of the English alphabet.
• **from A to Z**: see **A**.

zany /zeɪni¹/, **zanier, zaniest**. Something or someone that is **zany** is strange or eccentric in a comical way; an informal word. EG *20,000 of these zany gadgets are sold each month... His brother's the zaniest person I've ever met.* — ADJ QUALIT = crazy, wacky

zap /zæp/, **zaps, zapping, zapped**; an informal word. 1 If someone **zaps** someone else, they kill them, usually by shooting them. EG *That guy got zapped later on the same day.* — V+O = bump off

2 If you **zap** somewhere or **zap** through something, you go there very quickly or you do it very quickly. EG *I'll just zap into town... He zapped through the work.* — V+A

zeal /ziːl/ is great enthusiasm, especially in connection with work, religion, or politics. EG *We have to beware that missionary zeal doesn't blind us to reality... Hate and revolutionary zeal raged... They worked with great zeal to finish the project.* — N UNCOUNT = fanaticism

zealot /zelət/, **zealots**. A **zealot** is a person who acts with extreme or fanatical enthusiasm, especially in following a political or religious ideal. EG *Meadows was a zealot against the use of narcotics... There were threats by religious zealots to prevent the excavations.* — N COUNT = fanatic

zealous /zeləs/. Someone who is **zealous** spends a lot of time or energy in supporting something, especially a political or religious ideal, that they believe in very strongly. EG *He was a zealous anti-smoker... Politically she was very zealous.* ◊ **zealously**. EG *The landowners zealously kept people off their grouse moors.* — ADJ QUALIT ⇑ enthusiastic = fanatical; ◊ ADV WITH VB ⇑ enthusiastically

zebra /zebrə, ziː-/, **zebras**. A **zebra** is an African wild animal which looks rather like a horse with black and white stripes on its body. — N COUNT

zebra crossing, zebra crossings. In Britain, a **zebra crossing** is a special place where people can cross the road in safety. The road is marked with black and white stripes and cars and other vehicles must stop to allow people to cross. — N COUNT

Zen /zen/ or **Zen Buddhism** is a form of Buddhism that concentrates more on learning through meditation than on learning through religious writings. — N UNCOUNT ⇑ religion

zenith /zenɪθ/; a literary word. 1 The **zenith** of a country, an idea, or a person's career is the time when it is most successful or most powerful. EG *...Greek civilization at its zenith... He was forty-eight years old and at the zenith of his career.* — N SING WITH DET = peak, height ≠ nadir

2 The **zenith** is also the point at which the sun or moon seems to be at its highest. EG *The sun reached its zenith.* — N SING WITH DET

zephyr /zefə/, zephyrs. A **zephyr** is a gentle wind; a literary word. EG *Leaves turned to shimmering silver as zephyrs played through them.* — N COUNT = breeze

zero /zɪərəʊ/, **zeros, zeroes, zeroing, zeroed**. The plural form of the number and the third person singular of the verb can be spelled either **zeros** or **zeroes**. 1 **Zero** is the number 0: see ☐ at NUMBER and MEASUREMENT. EG *This scale goes from zero to forty.* — NUM = nought

2 **Zero** is also freezing point, or 0°C. EG *It had been fourteen below zero when they woke up.* — NUM

3 You also use **zero** to say that there is none at all of the particular thing mentioned. EG *There is zero resistance... We drove on in zero visibility... Its running costs were zero.* — ADJ CLASSIF = nil

zero in on. 1 To **zero in on** a target means to aim at it or move towards it. EG *The missile then zeros in on the target.* — PHRASAL VB : V+ADV+PREP = home in on

2 If you **zero in on** a problem or subject, you give your attention to it. — PHRASAL VB : V+ADV+PREP

zero hour is the time at which something such as a military operation is planned to begin. — N UNCOUNT

zest /zest/. 1 **Zest** is 1.1 a feeling of pleasure, excitement, and interest in what you are doing. EG *The children were full of life and zest... She had traced our route with immense zest... I think there's a kind of zest for life in those plays.* — N UNCOUNT : IF+PREP THEN *for* = enthusiasm. 1.2 the quality in a particular activity or in your life which you find exciting, interesting, and enjoyable. EG *He felt that some of the zest had gone out of his life.* — N UNCOUNT ⇑ excitement

2 **Zest** is also the skin of an orange or lemon when it is used to give flavour to something such as a cake or a drink. — N UNCOUNT = peel

zigzag /zɪgzæg/, **zigzags, zigzagging, zigzagged**; also spelled with a hyphen. 1 A **zigzag** is a line which has a series of angles in it like a continuous series of 'W's. EG *Suddenly there was a flash and a zigzag of forked lightning.* — N COUNT

2 If something moves in a **zigzag** way, it moves by going at an angle first to the right and then to the left. EG *We hurried in a zigzag way along the path... You have to catch a little train from Cuzco that shunts zigzag fashion up the steep slopes.* — ADJ CLASSIF : ATTRIB

3 To **zigzag** means to move forward by going at an angle first to the right and then to the left. EG *We zigzagged up the hill.* — V+A

zinc /zɪŋk/ is a bluish-white metal which is used to make other metals such as brass or to cover other metals such as iron to stop them rusting. EG *Zaire is rich in diamonds, copper, oil, and zinc.* — N UNCOUNT

zing /zɪŋ/ is a quality in something that makes it lively or interesting; an informal word. EG *Small enterprises may lose their zing... Add a little white wine to give an extra zing to a recipe.* — N UNCOUNT = oomph

Zionism /zaɪənɪzəᵒm/ is a movement which was originally concerned with establishing a political and religious state in Palestine for Jewish people and is now concerned with the development of Israel. EG *...the democratic and humanistic principles of early Zionism.* ◊ **Zionist, Zionists**. EG *...a Zionist millionaire in New York.* — N UNCOUNT; ◊ N COUNT, OR ADJ CLASSIF

zip /zɪp/, **zips, zipping, zipped**. 1 A **zip** or a **zip fastener** is a fastener used on clothes, bags, and other things. Zips consist of two rows of metal or plastic teeth that are pulled together in order to fasten a skirt, pair of trousers, etc; used mainly in British English. EG *If your zip sticks, it might be because a thread has caught.* — N COUNT = zipper

2 When you **zip** something, you fasten it using a zip. EG *The two sleeping bags can be zipped to each other to make a double sleeping bag.* — V+O : USU+A ⇑ attach

zip up. 1 When you **zip up** something such as a piece of clothing, you fasten it using a zip. EG *She zipped up the dress with difficulty... He zipped his jeans up.* — PHRASAL VB : V+O+ADV

2 If you **zip** someone **up**, you fasten the zip on their clothes for them. EG *Zip me up at the back, please.* — PHRASAL VB : V+O+ADV ⇑ do up

zip code, zip codes. In America, a **zip code** is a combination of letters and numbers that are part of an address and that help the post office to sort the mail. — N COUNT = post code

zipper /zɪpə/, **zippers**. A **zipper** is a zip; used mainly in American English. EG *The young man tugged at the zipper of his blue and white airline bag.* — N COUNT ⇑ fastener

zither /zɪðə/, **zithers**. A **zither** is a musical instrument which consists of a number of strings stretched over a box. You play a zither by plucking the strings. — N COUNT

zodiac /zəʊdiæk/. The **zodiac** is a diagram used by astrologers to represent the circular movement of the planets and stars and their positions in space at particular times. It is divided into 12 sections, each of which has a special name and sign. The zodiac is used by astrologers to help calculate the influence of the planets on people's lives. — N SING : *the*+N ⇑ system

zombie /zɒmbi¹/, **zombies**. If you refer to someone as a **zombie** or if you say that they are like a **zombie**, you mean that they seem completely unaware of what is happening around them and seem to act without thinking about what they are doing; used showing disapproval. EG *Some of the men had begun to act as if they were zombies... I'd have to be a zombie not to have noticed all that was going on.* — N COUNT ⇑ person = automaton

2 In certain religions, a **zombie** is also a dead person who has been brought back to life by magic. — N COUNT

zone /zəʊn/, **zones**. A **zone** is an area of land or sea that is considered to be different from the areas around it, for example because it has particular geographic features, particular military status, or a particular political system. EG *...50,000 refugees from the war zone... I'd like to see Europe as a nuclear-free zone... ...looking across the border zone over the hills towards East Germany... ...the more scattered inhabitants of infertile zones.* — N COUNT+SUPP ⇑ district

zonked /zɒŋkt/. If you are **zonked** or you feel **zonked**, you are completely exhausted; an informal word. — ADJ QUALIT : PRED ⇑ tired

zoo /zuː/, **zoos**. A **zoo** is a park where live animals are kept so that people can look at them or study them. EG *He went to the zoo... I spent the summer visiting zoos, parks, and beaches.* — N COUNT : ALSO IN NAMES AFTER N

zoology /zəʊɒlədʒi¹, zuː-/ is the study of animals in general, and of their structure, lives, habits, and classification in particular. EG *If you want to do* — N UNCOUNT ⇑ science